Hospital, Address, Telephone, Administrator, Approval, Facility, and Physician Codes, Health Care System, Network	Classi-fication Codes		Utilization Data					Expense (thousands) of dollars		
	Control	Service	Staffed Beds	Admissions	Census	Outpatient Visits	Births	Total	Payroll	Personnel

★ American Hospital Association (AHA) membership
☐ Joint Commission on Accreditation of Healthcare Organizations (JCAHO) accreditation
+ American Osteopathic Healthcare Association (AOHA) membership
○ American Osteopathic Association (AOA) accreditation
△ Commission on Accreditation of Rehabilitation Facilities (CARF) accreditation
Control codes 61, 63, 64, 71, 72 and 73 indicate hospitals listed by AOHA, but not registered by AHA. For definition of numerical codes, see page A4

| ANYTOWN—Universal County
★ COMMUNITY HOSPITAL, First Street and Main Avenue Zip 62835; tel 204/391–2345; Jane Doe, Administrator **A**1 2 3 4 6 9 10 **F**1 2 3 4 5 6 8 9 10 23 24 34; **P**1 2 3 4; **S** Acme HCS **N** ABC | 23 | 10 | 346 | 10778 | 248 | 75953 | 1693 | 20695 | 9973 | 796 |

> 1   2   3

1 Approval Codes

Reported by the approving bodies specified, as of the dates noted.

1 Accreditation under the hospital program of the Joint Commission on Accreditation of Healthcare Organizations (April 1998).
2 Cancer program approved by American College of Surgeons (January 1998).
3 Approval to participate in residency training, by the Accreditation Council for Graduate Medical Education (January 1998). As of June 30, 1975, internship (formerly code 4) was included under residency, code 3.
5 Medical school affiliation, reported to the American Medical Association (January 1998).

6 Hospital–controlled professional nursing school, reported by National League for Nursing.
7 Accreditation by Commission on Accreditation of Rehabilitation Facilities (January 1998).
8 Member of Council of Teaching Hospitals of the Association of American Medical Colleges (January 1998).
9 Hospitals contracting or participating in Blue Cross Plan, reported by the Blue Cross and Blue Shield Association (April 1998).
10 Certified for participation in the Health Insurance for the Aged (Medicare) Program

by the U.S. Department of Health and Human Services (January 1998).
11 Accreditation by American Osteopathic Association (January 1998).
12 Internship approved by American Osteopathic Association (January 1998).
13 Residency approved by American Osteopathic Association (January 1998).

Nonreporting indicates that the hospital was registered **after** the mailing of the 1997 Annual Survey, or, that the 1997 Annual Survey questionnaire for the hospital had not been received prior to publication.

2 Facility Codes

Provided directly by the hospital, its health care system, or network, or through a formal arrangement with another provider; for definitions, see page A6.

(Alphabetical/Numerical Order)
1 Adult day care program
2 Alcoholism–drug abuse or dependency inpatient unit
3 Alcoholism–drug abuse or dependency outpatient services
4 Angioplasty
5 Arthritis treatment center
6 Assisted living
7 Birthing room–LDR room–LDRP room
8 Breast cancer screening/mammograms
9 Burn care services
10 Cardiac catheterization laboratory
11 Cardiac intensive care services
12 Case management
13 Children wellness program
14 Community health reporting
15 Community health status assessment
16 Community health status based service planning
17 Community outreach
18 Crisis prevention
19 CT scanner
20 Dental services
21 Diagnostic radioisotope facility

22 Emergency department
23 Extracorporeal shock wave lithotripter (ESWL)
24 Fitness center
25 Freestanding outpatient care center
26 Geriatric services
27 Health facility transportation (to/from)
28 Health fair
29 Health information center
30 Health screenings
31 HIV–AIDS services
32 Home health services
33 Hospice
34 Hospital–based outpatient care center–services
35 Magnetic resonance imaging (MRI)
36 Meals on wheels
37 Medical surgical intensive care services
38 Neonatal intensive care services
39 Nutrition programs
40 Obstetrics services
41 Occupational health services
42 Oncology services
43 Open heart surgery
44 Outpatient surgery
45 Patient education center
46 Patient representative services
47 Pediatric intensive care services
48 Physical rehabilitation inpatient services
49 Physical rehabilitation outpatient services

50 Positron emission tomography scanner (PET)
51 Primary care department
52 Psychiatric acute inpatient services
53 Psychiatric child adolescent services
54 Psychiatric consultation–liaison services
55 Psychiatric education services
56 Psychiatric emergency services
57 Psychiatric geriatric services
58 Psychiatric outpatient services
59 Psychiatric partial hospitalization program
60 Radiation therapy
61 Reproductive health services
62 Retirement housing
63 Single photon emission computerized tomography (SPECT)
64 Skilled nursing or other long–term care services
65 Social work services
66 Sports medicine
67 Support groups
68 Teen outreach services
69 Transplant services
70 Trauma center (certified)
71 Ultrasound
72 Urgent care center
73 Volunteer services department
74 Women's health center/services

3 Physician Codes

Actually available within, and reported by the institution; for definitions, see page A9.

(Alphabetical/Numerical Order)
1 Closed physician–hospital organization (PHO)

2 Equity model
3 Foundation
4 Group practice without walls
5 Independent practice association (IPA)

6 Integrated salary model
7 Management service organization (MSO)
8 Open physician–hospital organization (PHO)

Hospital, Address, Telephone, Administrator, Approval, Facility, and Physician Codes, Health Care System, Network	Classi-fication Codes		Utilization Data						Expense (thousands) of dollars		
★ American Hospital Association (AHA) membership □ Joint Commission on Accreditation of Healthcare Organizations (JCAHO) accreditation + American Osteopathic Healthcare Association (AOHA) membership ○ American Osteopathic Association (AOA) accreditation △ Commission on Accreditation of Rehabilitation Facilities (CARF) accreditation Control codes 61, 63, 64, 71, 72 and 73 indicate hospitals listed by AOHA, but not registered by AHA. For definition of numerical codes, see page A4	Control	Service	Staffed Beds	Admissions	Census	Outpatient Visits	Births	Total	Payroll	Personnel
ANYTOWN—Universal County ★ COMMUNITY HOSPITAL, First Street and Main Avenue Zip 62835; tel 204/391–2345; Jane Doe, Administrator **A**1 2 3 4 6 9 10 **F**1 2 3 4 5 6 8 9 10 23 24 34; **P**1 2 3 4; **S** Acme HCS **N** ABC	23	10	346	10778	248	75953	1693	20695	9973	796

    4   5   6   7

4 Health Care System Code and Name

A code number has been assigned to each health care system headquarters. The inclusion *of one of these codes (1) indicates that the hospital belongs to a health care system and* *(2) identifies the specific system to which the hospital belongs.*

5 Network Name

The presence of the letter "N" indicates that the hospital belongs to one or more networks. The *name(s) following the "N" identifies the specific network(s) to which the hospital belongs.*

6 Classification Codes

Control

Government, nonfederal
12 State
13 County
14 City
15 City–county
16 Hospital district or authority

Nongovernment not–for–profit
21 Church operated
23 Other

Investor–owned (for–profit)
31 Individual
32 Partnership
33 Corporation

Government, federal
41 Air Force
42 Army
43 Navy

44 Public Health Service other than 47
45 Veterans Affairs
46 Federal other than 41–45, 47–48
47 Public Health Service Indian Service
48 Department of Justice

Osteopathic
61 Church operated
63 Other not–for–profit
64 Other
71 Individual for–profit
72 Partnership for–profit
73 Corporation for–profit

Service
10 General medical and surgical
11 Hospital unit of an institution (prison hospital, college infirmary, etc.)
12 Hospital unit within an institution for the mentally retarded
22 Psychiatric

33 Tuberculosis and other respiratory diseases
44 Obstetrics and gynecology
45 Eye, ear, nose, and throat
46 Rehabilitation
47 Orthopedic
48 Chronic disease
49 Other specialty
50 Children's general
51 Children's hospital unit of an institution
52 Children's psychiatric
53 Children's tuberculosis and other respiratory diseases
55 Children's eye, ear, nose, and throat
56 Children's rehabilitation
57 Children's orthopedic
58 Children's chronic disease
59 Children's other specialty
62 Institution for mental retardation
82 Alcoholism and other chemical dependency

* Control codes 61, 63, 64, 71, 72 and 73 indicate hospitals listed by the AOHA but not registered by AHA.

When a hospital restricts its service to a specialty not defined by a specific code, it is coded 49 (59 if a children's hospital) and the specialty is indicated in parentheses following the name of the hospital.

7 Headings

Definitions are based on the American Hospital Association's Hospital Administration Terminology. Where a 12–month period is specified, hospitals were requested to report on the Annual Survey of Hospitals for the 12 months ending September 30, 1997. Hospitals reporting for less than a 12–month period are so designated.

Utilization Data:

Beds–Number of beds, cribs, and pediatric bassinets regularly maintained (set up and staffed for use) for inpatients as of the close of the reporting period.

Admissions–Number of patients accepted for inpatient service during a 12–month period; does not include newborn.

Census–Average number of inpatients receiving care each day during the 12–month reporting period; does not include newborn.

Outpatient Visits–A visit by a patient who is not lodged in the hospital while receiving medical, dental, or other services. Each appearance of an outpatient in each unit constitutes one visit regardless of the number of diagnostic and/or therapeutic treatments that a patient receives.

Births–Number of infants born in the hospital and accepted for service in a newborn infant bassinet during a 12–month period; excludes stillbirths.

Expense: Expense for a 12–month period; both total expense and payroll components are

shown. Payroll expenses include all salaries and wages.

Personnel: Includes persons on payroll on September 30, 1997; includes full–time equivalents of part–time personnel. Full–time equivalents were calculated on the basis that two part–time persons equal one full–time person.

AHA Guide™ to the Health Care Field

1998–99 Edition

Healthcare InfoSource, Inc., a subsidiary
of the American Hospital Association
One North Franklin
Chicago, Illinois 60606-3401

AHA Institutional Members $140
Nonmembers $280
AHA catalog NUMBER C–010098
Telephone ORDERS 1–800–AHA–2626

ISSN 0094–8969
ISBN 0–87258–733–9

Copyright 1998 by
Healthcare InfoSource, Inc., a subsidiary
of the American Hospital Association
One North Franklin
Chicago, Illinois 60606-3401

Contents

† List supplied by the Joint Commission on
Accreditation of Healthcare Organizations

Acknowledgements and Advisements

Acknowledgements

The AHA Guide™ to the Health Care Field is published annually by Healthcare InfoSource, Inc., a subsidiary of the American Hospital Association. Contributions made by Computer Application Services, Member Relations, Office of the President, Office of the Secretary, Printing Services Group and Resource Center.

Healthcare InfoSource, Inc. acknowledges the cooperation given by many professional groups and government agencies in the health care field, particularly the following: American College of Surgeons; American Medical Association; American Osteopathic Healthcare Association; Blue Cross and Blue Shield Association; Council of Teaching Hospitals of the Association of American Medical Colleges; Joint Commission on Accreditation of Healthcare Organizations; Commission on Accreditation of Rehabilitation Facilities; American Osteopathic Association; Health Care Financing Administration; and various offices within the U.S. Department of Health and Human Services.

Advisements

The data published here should be used with the following advisements: The data are based on replies to an annual survey that seeks a variety of information, not all of which is published in this book. The information gathered by the survey includes specific services, but not all of each hospital's services. Therefore, the data do not reflect an exhaustive list of all services offered by all hospitals. For information on the availability of additional data, please contact Healthcare InfoSource, Inc. 312/422–2100.

Healthcare InfoSource, Inc. does not assume responsibility for the accuracy of information voluntarily reported by the individual institutions surveyed. The purpose of this publication is to provide basic data reflecting the delivery of health care in the United States and associated areas, and is not to serve as an official and all inclusive list of services offered by individual hospitals. **The information reflected is based on data collected as of April 17, 1998**.

Introduction

Each of the three major sections of the AHA Guide begins with its own table of contents and pertinent definitions or explanatory information. Sections B, C and indices have bleed bar tabs for easy identification. The three major sections are:
- Hospitals
- Networks, Health Care Systems and Alliances
- Health Organizations, Agencies and other Health Care Providers

Please note that many area codes may have changed, check before you call.

Hospitals

This section lists:
- AHA–registered and osteopathic hospitals in the U.S. and associated areas, by state within city.
- U.S. government hospitals outside the United States.
- Index of hospitals alphabetically.
- Index of health care professionals.
- AHA Associate members.

AHA member hospitals are identified by a star (★). Hospitals accredited under one of the programs of the Joint Commission on Accreditation of Healthcare Organizations are identified by a hollow box (☐). Preceding the list of hospitals is a statement of the formal requirements for registration by the AHA.

The lists provide a variety of information about each hospital, including the administrator's name; various approvals; selected facilities and services; relationship to a network and/or health care system; classification by control, service; physician arrangement relationships, and other selected statistical data from the 1997 AHA Annual Survey.

Also the *AHA Guide* includes state population data from the U.S. Bureau of the Census, *Statistical Abstract of the United States: 1997 (117th edition.) Washington, DC, 1997. They include the following:*
- Total resident population (in thousands)
- Percent of resident population in metro areas
- Birth rate per 1,000 population
- Percent of population 65 years and over
- Percent of persons without health insurance

Some of this information is coded. These include approval, facility and classification codes.

Approval codes refer to approvals held by a hospital; they represent information supplied by various national approving and reporting bodies. For example, code A–1 indicates accreditation under one of the programs of the Joint Commission on Accreditation of Healthcare Organizations – formal evidence that a hospital meets established standards for quality of patient care.

Physician codes refer to the different types of physician arrangements in which the hospital participates.

Health Care system names reference specific health care system headquarters. The presence of the system name indicates the hospital belongs to a health care system. Absence of a system name indicates that the hospital does not belong to a health care system.

Network names reference specific network headquarters. The presence of the network name indicates the hospital belongs to a network. Absence of a network name indicates that the hospital does not belong to a network.

Classification codes indicate the type of organization that controls or operates the hospital and type of service. Code numbers in the 10s denote nonfederal (states and local) government hospitals; in the 20s, nongovernment not–for–profit hospitals; in the 40s, federal government hospitals; and in the 60s and 70s, nonregistered osteopathic hospitals.

Among **service codes,** the most common code is 10, indicating a general hospital. Other numbers designate various special services. For example, code 22 indicates psychiatric hospitals and codes in the 50s indicate different types of children's hospitals.

Facility codes refer to facilities and services provided directly by the hospital, its health care system or network or through a formal arrangement with another provider.

(For easy reference, there is an alphabetical/numerical list for all of the codes on page A4).

Names of osteopathic hospitals, supplied by the American Osteopathic Healthcare Association are provided in the list of hospitals. Codes and symbols identifying these institutions are explained on page A4 and in the headnote at the top of each page of the list of hospitals. Also included in this section is an **index of hospitals** in alphabetical order by hospital name, followed by the city and state and the page reference to the hospital's listing in Section A. This section is designated by tabs along the side of the pages. Immediately following this section is an **index of health care professionals** in alphabetical order by name, followed by the hospital and/or health care system, the city and state and the page reference to the health care professional's listing in section A or B. This section is also designated by tabs along the side of the pages.

This section also lists **other AHA institutional members** not listed elsewhere in the AHA Guide and **AHA associate members.** The list of AHA institutional members includes Canadian hospitals, associated university programs in health administration, hospital schools of nursing, and nonhospital preacute and postacute care facilities. The list of associate members includes ambulatory centers and home care agencies, Blue Cross plans, health maintenance organizations/health care corporations, health system agencies, other inpatient care institutions, shared services organizations and other associate members.

Networks, Health Care Systems and Alliances

Networks
The *AHA Guide* lists the names and addresses of networks including network partners by state, alphabetically by name. **Please see page B2 for more information**.

Health Care Systems
This is an alphabetical listing of health care systems and their hospitals. Data on bed size for each hospital in the system is provided along with an indication of whether the hospital is owned, leased, sponsored, or contract–managed.

Following this listing is an index for health care system headquarters listed geographically by state. **Please see page B2 for more information**.

Alliances
Alliances provide information on multistate alliances and their members. Alliances are listed alphabetically by name. Members are listed alphabetically by state, city and then by name. **Please see page B2 for more information**.

Health Organizations, Agencies and Other Health Care Providers

There are four major categories in this section.

First is an alphabetical listing of national, international, and regional organizations. Many voluntary organizations that are interested in, or of interest to, the health care field are included. Also included is the Healthfinder listing.

The second category lists United States government agencies.

The third category presents a list of state and local organizations and government agencies. The list for states and provinces include Blue Cross and Blue Shield plans, health systems agencies, hospital associations and councils, hospital licensure agencies, medical and nursing licensure agencies, peer review organizations, state health planning and development agencies, and state and provincial government agencies.

The fourth category consists of lists of various health care providers including JCAHO accredited freestanding long–term care organizations, JCAHO accredited freestanding substance abuse organizations, and JCAHO accredited freestanding mental health care organizations, freestanding hospices, freestanding ambulatory surgery centers and health maintenance organizations (HMOs). **Please see page B2 for more information**.

We hope you find the *AHA Guide* a valuable resource. If you have any questions or comments, please call Healthcare InfoSource, Inc., at 312/ 422–2100.

AHA Offices, Officers, and Historical Data

Chicago: One North Franklin, Chicago, IL 60606–3401; tel. 312/422–3000

Washington: 325 Seventh Street, N.W., Suite 700, Washington, DC 20004; tel. 202/638–1100

Speaker of the House of Delegates: Reginald M. Ballantyne III, PMH Health Resources, Inc., 1201 S. Seventh Avenue, Box 21207, Phoenix, AZ 85036
Chairman of the Board of Trustees: John G. King, Legacy Health System, 1919 N.W. Lovejoy, Portland, OR 97209

Chairman–Elect of the Board of Trustees: Fred L. Brown, BJC Health System, 4444 Forest Park Avenue, St. Louis, MO 63108
President: Richard J. Davidson, 325 Seventh Street, N.W., Suite 700, Washington, DC 20004; tel. 202/638–1100

Senior Vice President and Secretary: Michael P. Guerin, One North Franklin, Chicago, IL 60606–3401
Treasurer: Dallas Carroll, One North Franklin, Chicago, IL 60606–3401

Past Presidents/Chairmen†

1899	★James S. Knowles	1931	★Lewis A. Sexton, M.D.	1964	Stanley A. Ferguson
1900	★James S. Knowles	1932	★Paul H. Fesler	1965	Clarence E. Wonnacott
1901	★Charles S. Howell	1933	★George F. Stephens, M.D.	1966	Philip D. Bonnet, M.D.
1902	★J. T. Duryea	1934	★Nathaniel W. Faxon, M.D.	1967	George E. Cartmill
1903	★John Fehrenbatch	1935	★Robert Jolly	1968	★David B. Wilson, M.D.
1904	★Daniel D. Test	1936	★Robin C. Buerki, M.D.	1969	George William Graham, M.D.
1905	★George H. M. Rowe, M.D.	1937	★Claude W. Munger, M.D.	1970	★Mark Berke
1906	★George P. Ludlam	1938	★Robert E. Neff	1971	★Jack A. L. Hahn
1907	★Renwick R. Ross, M.D.	1939	★G. Harvey Agnew, M.D.	1972	Stephen M. Morris
1908	★Sigismund S. Goldwater, M.D.	1940	★Fred G. Carter, M.D.	1973	John W. Kauffman
1909	★John M. Peters, M.D.	1941	★B. W. Black, M.D.	1974	★Horace M. Cardwell
1910	★H. B. Howard, M.D.	1942	★Basil C. MacLean, M.D.	1975	Wade Mountz
1911	★W. L. Babcock, M.D.	1943	★James A. Hamilton	1976	H. Robert Cathcart
1912	★Henry M. Hurd, M.D.	1944	★Frank J. Walter	1977	John M. Stagl
1913	★F. A. Washburn, M.D.	1945	★Donald C. Smelzer, M.D.	1978	★Samuel J. Tibbitts
1914	★Thomas Howell, M.D.	1946	★Peter D. Ward, M.D.	1979	W. Daniel Barker
1915	★William O. Mann, M.D.	1947	★John H. Hayes	1980	Sister Irene Kraus
1916	★Winford H. Smith, M.D.	1948	★Graham L. Davis	1981	Bernard J. Lachner
1917	★Robert J. Wilson, M.D.	1949	★Joseph G. Norby	1982	Stanley R. Nelson
1918	★A. B. Ancker, M.D.	1950	★John H. Hatfield	1983	Elbert E. Gilbertson
1919	★A. R. Warner, M.D.	1951	★Charles F. Wilinsky, M.D.	1984	Thomas R. Matherlee
1920	★Joseph B. Howland, M.D.	1952	★Anthony J. J. Rourke, M.D.	1985	Jack A. Skarupa
1921	★Louis B. Baldwin, M.D.	1953	★Edwin L. Crosby, M.D.	1986	Scott S. Parker
1922	★George O'Hanlon, M.D.	1954	★Ritz E. Heerman	1987	Donald C. Wegmiller
1923	★Asa S. Bacon	1955	★Frank R. Bradley	1988	Eugene W. Arnett
1924	★Malcolm T. MacEachern, M.D.	1956	★Ray E. Brown	1989	Edward J. Connors
1925	★E. S. Gilmore	1957	★Albert W. Snoke, M.D.	1990	David A. Reed
1926	★Arthur C. Bachmeyer, M.D.	1958	★Tol Terrell	1991	C. Thomas Smith
1927	★R. G. Brodrick, M.D.	1959	★Ray Amberg	1992	D. Kirk Oglesby, Jr.
1928	★Joseph C. Doane, M.D.	1960	Russell A. Nelson, M.D.	1993	Larry L. Mathis
1929	★Louis H. Burlingham, M.D.	1961	★Frank S. Groner	1994	Carolyn C. Roberts
1930	★Christopher G. Parnall, M.D.	1962	★Jack Masur, M.D.	1995	Gail L. Warden
		1963	T. Stewart Hamilton, M.D.	1996	Gordon M. Sprenger
				1997	Reginald M. Ballantyne III

Chief Executive Officers

1917–18	★William H. Walsh, M.D.	1943–54	★George Bugbee	1986–91	Carol M. McCarthy, Ph.D., J.D.
1919–24	★Andrew Robert Warner, M.D.	1954–72	★Edwin L. Crosby, M.D.	1991	Jack W. Owen (acting)
1925–27	★William H. Walsh, M.D.	1972	Madison B. Brown, M.D. (acting)	1991	Richard J. Davidson (current)
1928–42	★Bert W. Caldwell, M.D.	1972–86	J. Alexander McMahon		

Distinguished Service Award

1934	★Matthew O. Foley	1958	★John N. Hatfield	1980	Donald W. Cordes
1939	★Malcolm T. MacEachern, M.D.	1959	★Edwin L. Crosby, M.D.	1981	★Sister Mary Brigh Cassidy
1940	★Sigismund S. Goldwater, M.D.	1960	★Oliver G. Pratt	1982	R. Zach Thomas, Jr.
1941	★Frederic A. Washburn, M.D.	1961	★E. M. Bluestone, M.D.	1983	H. Robert Cathcart
1942	★Winford H. Smith, M.D.	1962	Mother Loretto Bernard, S.C., R.N.	1984	Matthew F. McNulty, Jr., Sc.D.
1943	★Arthur C. Bachmeyer, M.D.	1963	★Ray E. Brown	1985	J. Alexander McMahon
1944	★Rt. Rev. Msgr. Maurice F. Griffin, LL.D.	1964	Russell A. Nelson, M.D.	1986	Sister Irene Kraus
1945	★Asa S. Bacon	1965	★Albert W. Snoke, M.D.	1987	W. Daniel Barker
1946	★George F. Stephens, M.D.	1966	★Frank S. Groner	1988	Elbert E. Gilbertson
1947	★Robin C. Buerki, M.D.	1967	★Rev. John J. Flanagan, S.J.	1989	Donald G. Shropshire
1948	★James A. Hamilton	1968	Stanley W. Martin	1990	John W. Colloton
1949	★Claude W. Munger, M.D.	1969	T. Stewart Hamilton, M.D.	1991	Carol M. McCarthy, Ph.D., J.D.
1950	★Nathaniel W. Faxon, M.D.	1970	★Charles Patteson Cladwell, Jr.	1992	David H. Hitt
1951	★Bert W. Caldwell, M.D.	1971	★Mark Berke	1993	Edward J. Connors
1952	★Fred G. Carter, M.D.	1972	Stanley A. Ferguson		Jack W. Owen
1953	★asil C. MacLean, M.D.	1973	★Jack A. L. Hahn	1994	George Adams
1954	★George Bugbee	1974	George William Graham, M.D.	1995	Scott S. Parker
1955	★Joseph G. Norby	1975	George E. Cartmill	1996	John A. Russell
1956	★Charles F. Wilinsky, M.D.	1976	D. O. McClusky, Jr.	1997	D. Kirk Oglesby, Jr.
1957	★John H. Hayes	1977	★Boone Powell	1998	Henry B. Betts, M.D.
		1978	★Richard J. Stull		
		1979	★Horace M. Cardwell		

★Deceased

†On June 3, 1972, the House of Delegates changed the title of the chief elected officer to chairman of the Board of Trustees, and the title of president was conferred on the chief executive officer of the Association.

A

**Hospitals,
Institutional and
Associate Members**

*AHA–registered hospitals in the United States and associated areas are approved for registration by the Executive Committee of the Board of Trustees of the American Hospital Association. This list of registered hospitals is complete as of April 1998. The list of osteopathic hospitals, integrated in this section is supplied by the American Osteopathic Healthcare Association.

Registration Requirements for Hospitals

This directory includes hospitals registered by the American Hospital Association and osteopathic hospitals listed by the American Osteopathic Association. Identification codes for both types of hospitals are explained fully on pages A4–5. For the reader's convenience, the codes for osteopathic hospitals are also summarized in the notes at the top of each page of this section. Beginning in November 1970, osteopathic hospitals became eligible to apply for registration with the American Hospital Association. Registered osteopathic hospitals carry the same codes as all other hospitals registered by the American Hospital Association.

The following requirements were approved by the Executive Committee of the Board of Trustees, May 13, 1986.

AHA–Registered Hospitals

Any institution that can be classified as a hospital according to the requirements may be registered if it so desires. Membership in the American Hospital Association is not a prerequisite.

The American Hospital Association may, at the sole discretion of the Executive Committee of the Board of Trustees, grant, deny, or withdraw the registration of an institution.

An institution may be registered by the American Hospital Association as a hospital if it is accredited as a hospital by the Joint Commission on Accreditation of Healthcare Organizations or is certified as a provider of acute services under Title 18 of the Social Security Act and has provided the Association with documents verifying the accreditation or certification.

In lieu of the preceding accreditation or certification, an institution licensed as a hospital by the appropriate state agency may be registered by AHA as a hospital by meeting the following alternative requirements:

Function: The primary function of the institution is to provide patient services, diagnostic and therapeutic, for particular or general medical conditions.

1. The institution shall maintain at least six inpatient beds, which shall be continuously available for the care of patients who are nonrelated and who stay on the average in excess of 24 hours per admission.
2. The institution shall be constructed, equipped, and maintained to ensure the health and safety of patients and to provide uncrowded, sanitary facilities for the treatment of patients.
3. There shall be an identifiable governing authority legally and morally responsible for the conduct of the hospital.
4. There shall be a chief executive to whom the governing authority delegates the continuous responsibility for the operation of the hospital in accordance with established policy.
5. There shall be an organized medical staff of fully licensed physicians* that may include other licensed individuals permitted by law and by the hospital to provide patient care services independently in the hospital. The medical staff shall be accountable to the governing authority for maintaining proper standards of medical care, and it shall be governed by bylaws adopted by said staff and approved by the governing authority.
6. Each patient shall be admitted on the authority of a member of the medical staff who has been granted the privilege to admit patients to inpatient services in accordance with state law and criteria for standards of medical care established by the individual medical staff. Each patient's general medical condition is the responsibility of a qualified physician member of the medical staff. When nonphysician members of the medical staff are granted privileges to admit patients, provision is made for prompt medical evaluation of these patients by a qualified physician. Any graduate of a foreign medical school who is permitted to assume responsibilities for patient care shall possess a valid license to practice medicine, or shall be certified by the Educational Commission for Foreign Medical Graduates, or shall have qualified for and have successfully completed an academic year of supervised clinical training under the direction of a medical school approved by the Liaison Committee onGAT Medical Education.
7. Registered nurse supervision and other nursing services are continuous.
8. A current and complete+ medical record shall be maintained by the institution for each patient and shall be available for reference.
9. Pharmacy service shall be maintained in the institution and shall be supervised by a registered pharmacist.
10. The institution shall provide patients with food service that meets their nutritional and therapeutic requirements; special diets shall also be available.

*Physician—Term used to describe an individual with an M.D. or D.O. degree who is fully licensed to practice medicine in all its phases.

‡The completed records in general shall contain at least the following: the patient's identifying data and consent forms, medical history, record of physical examination, physicians' progress notes, operative notes, nurses' notes, routine x–ray and laboratory reports, doctors' orders, and final diagnosis.

Types of Hospitals

In addition to meeting these 10 general registration requirements, hospitals are registered as one of four types of hospitals: general, special, rehabilitation and chronic disease, or psychiatric. The following definitions of function by type of hospital and special requirements for registration are employed:

General

The primary function of the institution is to provide patient services, diagnostic and therapeutic, for a variety of medical conditions. A general hospital also shall provide:
- diagnostic x–ray services with facilities and staff for a variety of procedures
- clinical laboratory service with facilities and staff for a variety of procedures and with anatomical pathology services regularly and conveniently available
- operating room service with facilities and staff.

Special

The primary function of the institution is to provide diagnostic and treatment services for patients who have specified medical conditions, both surgical and nonsurgical. A special hospital also shall provide:
- such diagnostic and treatment services as may be determined by the Executive Committee of the Board of Trustees of the American Hospital Association to be appropriate for the specified medical conditions for which medical services

are provided shall be maintained in the institution with suitable facilities and staff. If such conditions do not normally require diagnostic x–ray service, laboratory service, or operating room service, and if any such services are therefore not maintained in the institution, there shall be written arrangements to make them available to patients requiring them.
- clinical laboratory services capable of providing tissue diagnosis when offering pregancy termination services.

Rehabilitation and Chronic Disease

The primary function of the institution is to provide diagnostic and treatment services to handicapped or disabled individuals requiring restorative and adjustive services. A rehabilitation and chronic disease hospital also shall provide:
- arrangements for diagnostic x–ray services, as required, on a regular and conveniently available basis
- arrangements for clinical laboratory service, as required on a regular and conveniently available basis
- arrangements for operating room service, as required, on a regular and conveniently available basis
- a physical therapy service with suitable facilities and staff in the institution
- an occupational therapy service with suitable facilities and staff in the institution
- arrangements for psychological and social work services on a regular and conveniently available basis
- arrangements for educational and vocational services on a regular and conveniently available basis

- written arrangements with a general hospital for the transfer of patients who require medical, obstetrical, or surgical services not available in the institution.

Psychiatric

The primary function of the institution is to provide diagnostic and treatment services for patients who have psychiatric–related illnesses. A psychiatric hospital also shall provide:
- arrangements for clinical laboratory service, as required, on a regular and conveniently available basis
- arrangements for diagnostic x–ray services, as required on a regular and conveniently available basis
- psychiatric, psychological, and social work service with facilities and staff in the institution
- arrangements for electroencephalograph services, as required, on a regular and conveniently available basis.
- written arrangements with a general hospital for the transfer of patients who require medical, obstetrical, or surgical services not available in the institution.

The American Hospital Association may, at the sole discretion of the Executive Committee of the Board of Trustees, grant, deny, or withdraw the registration of an institution.

AOHA–Listed Hospitals

The list of osteopathic hospitals includes both members and nonmembers of the American Osteopathic Healthcare Association.

---

*Physician–Term used to describe an individual with an M.D. or D.O. degree who is fully licensed to practice medicine in all its phases.

‡The completed records in general shall contain at least the following: the patient's identifying data and consent forms, medical history, record of physical examination, physicians' progress notes, operative notes, nurses' notes, routine x–ray and laboratory reports, doctors' orders, and final diagnosis.

Explanation
of Hospital Listings

Hospital, Address, Telephone, Administrator, Approval, Facility, and Physician Codes, Health Care System, Network	Classi-fication Codes		Utilization Data						Expense (thousands) of dollars		
★ American Hospital Association (AHA) membership □ Joint Commission on Accreditation of Healthcare Organizations (JCAHO) accreditation + American Osteopathic Healthcare Association (AOHA) membership ○ American Osteopathic Association (AOA) accreditation △ Commission on Accreditation of Rehabilitation Facilities (CARF) accreditation Control codes 61, 63, 64, 71, 72 and 73 indicate hospitals listed by AOHA, but not registered by AHA. For definition of numerical codes, see page A4	Control	Service	Staffed Beds	Admissions	Census	Outpatient Visits	Births	Total	Payroll	Personnel
ANYTOWN—Universal County											
★ COMMUNITY HOSPITAL, First Street and Main Avenue Zip 62835; tel 204/391–2345; Jane Doe, Administrator **A**1 2 3 4 6 9 10 **F**1 2 3 4 5 6 8 9 10 23 24 34; **P**1 2 3 4; **S** Acme HCS **N** ABC	23	10	346	10778	248	75953	1693	20695	9973	796

        1   **2**   **3**

1 Approval Codes

Reported by the approving bodies specified, as of the dates noted.

1 Accreditation under the hospital program of the Joint Commission on Accreditation of Healthcare Organizations (April 1998).

2 Cancer program approved by American College of Surgeons (January 1998).

3 Approval to participate in residency training, by the Accreditation Council for Graduate Medical Education (January 1998). As of June 30, 1975, internship (formerly code 4) was included under residency, code 3.

5 Medical school affiliation, reported to the American Medical Association (January 1998).

6 Hospital–controlled professional nursing school, reported by National League for Nursing.

7 Accreditation by Commission on Accreditation of Rehabilitation Facilities (January 1998).

8 Member of Council of Teaching Hospitals of the Association of American Medical Colleges (January 1998).

9 Hospitals contracting or participating in Blue Cross Plan, reported by the Blue Cross and Blue Shield Association (April 1998).

10 Certified for participation in the Health Insurance for the Aged (Medicare) Program

by the U.S. Department of Health and Human Services (January 1998).

11 Accreditation by American Osteopathic Association (January 1998).

12 Internship approved by American Osteopathic Association (January 1998).

13 Residency approved by American Osteopathic Association (January 1998).

Nonreporting indicates that the hospital was registered **after** the mailing of the 1997 Annual Survey, or, that the 1997 Annual Survey questionnaire for the hospital had not been received prior to publication.

2 Facility Codes

Provided directly by the hospital, its health care system, or network, or through a formal arrangement with another provider; for definitions, see page A6.

(Alphabetical/Numerical Order)

1 Adult day care program
2 Alcoholism–drug abuse or dependency inpatient unit
3 Alcoholism–drug abuse or dependency outpatient services
4 Angioplasty
5 Arthritis treatment center
6 Assisted living
7 Birthing room–LDR room–LDRP room
8 Breast cancer screening/mammograms
9 Burn care services
10 Cardiac catheterization laboratory
11 Cardiac intensive care services
12 Case management
13 Children wellness program
14 Community health reporting
15 Community health status assessment
16 Community health status based service planning
17 Community outreach
18 Crisis prevention
19 CT scanner
20 Dental services
21 Diagnostic radioisotope facility

22 Emergency department
23 Extracorporeal shock wave lithotripter (ESWL)
24 Fitness center
25 Freestanding outpatient care center
26 Geriatric services
27 Health facility transportation (to/from)
28 Health fair
29 Health information center
30 Health screenings
31 HIV–AIDS services
32 Home health services
33 Hospice
34 Hospital–based outpatient care center–services
35 Magnetic resonance imaging (MRI)
36 Meals on wheels
37 Medical surgical intensive care services
38 Neonatal intensive care services
39 Nutrition programs
40 Obstetrics services
41 Occupational health services
42 Oncology services
43 Open heart surgery
44 Outpatient surgery
45 Patient education center
46 Patient representative services
47 Pediatric intensive care services
48 Physical rehabilitation inpatient services
49 Physical rehabilitation outpatient services

50 Positron emission tomography scanner (PET)
51 Primary care department
52 Psychiatric acute inpatient services
53 Psychiatric child adolescent services
54 Psychiatric consultation–liaison services
55 Psychiatric education services
56 Psychiatric emergency services
57 Psychiatric geriatric services
58 Psychiatric outpatient services
59 Psychiatric partial hospitalization program
60 Radiation therapy
61 Reproductive health services
62 Retirement housing
63 Single photon emission computerized tomography (SPECT)
64 Skilled nursing or other long–term care services
65 Social work services
66 Sports medicine
67 Support groups
68 Teen outreach services
69 Transplant services
70 Trauma center (certified)
71 Ultrasound
72 Urgent care center
73 Volunteer services department
74 Women's health center/services

3 Physician Codes

Actually available within, and reported by the institution; for definitions, see page A9.

(Alphabetical/Numerical Order)

1 Closed physician–hospital organization (PHO)

2 Equity model
3 Foundation
4 Group practice without walls
5 Independent practice association (IPA)

6 Integrated salary model
7 Management service organization (MSO)
8 Open physician–hospital organization (PHO)

Hospital, Address, Telephone, Administrator, Approval, Facility, and Physician Codes, Health Care System, Network	Classi-fication Codes		Utilization Data						Expense (thousands) of dollars		
	Control	Service	Staffed Beds	Admissions	Census	Outpatient Visits	Births	Total	Payroll	Personnel

★ American Hospital Association (AHA) membership
☐ Joint Commission on Accreditation of Healthcare Organizations (JCAHO) accreditation
+ American Osteopathic Healthcare Association (AOHA) membership
○ American Osteopathic Association (AOA) accreditation
△ Commission on Accreditation of Rehabilitation Facilities (CARF) accreditation
Control codes 61, 63, 64, 71, 72 and 73 indicate hospitals listed by AOHA, but not registered by AHA. For definition of numerical codes, see page A4

ANYTOWN—Universal County
★ COMMUNITY HOSPITAL, First Street and Main Avenue Zip 62835; tel 204/391–2345; Jane Doe, Administrator **A**1 2 3 4 6 9 10 **F**1 2 3 4 5 6 8 9 10 23 24 34; **P**1 2 3 4; **S** Acme HCS **N** ABC

| 23 | 10 | 346 | 10778 | 248 | 75953 | 1693 | 20695 | 9973 | 796 |

4 5 6 7

4 Health Care System Code and Name

A code number has been assigned to each health care system headquarters. The inclusion of one of these codes (1) indicates that the hospital belongs to a health care system and (2) identifies the specific system to which the hospital belongs.

5 Network Name

The presence of the letter "N" indicates that the hospital belongs to one or more networks. The name(s) following the "N" identifies the specific network(s) to which the hospital belongs.

6 Classification Codes

Control

Government, nonfederal
12 State
13 County
14 City
15 City–county
16 Hospital district or authority

Nongovernment not–for–profit
21 Church operated
23 Other

Investor–owned (for–profit)
31 Individual
32 Partnership
33 Corporation

Government, federal
41 Air Force
42 Army
43 Navy

44 Public Health Service other than 47
45 Veterans Affairs
46 Federal other than 41–45, 47–48
47 Public Health Service Indian Service
48 Department of Justice

Osteopathic
61 Church operated
63 Other not–for–profit
64 Other
71 Individual for–profit
72 Partnership for–profit
73 Corporation for–profit

Service
10 General medical and surgical
11 Hospital unit of an institution (prison hospital, college infirmary, etc.)
12 Hospital unit within an institution for the mentally retarded
22 Psychiatric

33 Tuberculosis and other respiratory diseases
44 Obstetrics and gynecology
45 Eye, ear, nose, and throat
46 Rehabilitation
47 Orthopedic
48 Chronic disease
49 Other specialty
50 Children's general
51 Children's hospital unit of an institution
52 Children's psychiatric
53 Children's tuberculosis and other respiratory diseases
55 Children's eye, ear, nose, and throat
56 Children's rehabilitation
57 Children's orthopedic
58 Children's chronic disease
59 Children's other specialty
62 Institution for mental retardation
82 Alcoholism and other chemical dependency

* Control codes 61, 63, 64, 71, 72 and 73 indicate hospitals listed by the AOHA but not registered by AHA.

When a hospital restricts its service to a specialty not defined by a specific code, it is coded 49 (59 if a children's hospital) and the specialty is indicated in parentheses following the name of the hospital.

7 Headings

Definitions are based on the American Hospital Association's Hospital Administration Terminology. Where a 12–month period is specified, hospitals were requested to report on the Annual Survey of Hospitals for the 12 months ending September 30, 1997. Hospitals reporting for less than a 12–month period are so designated.

Utilization Data:

Beds–Number of beds, cribs, and pediatric bassinets regularly maintained (set up and staffed for use) for inpatients as of the close of the reporting period.

Admissions–Number of patients accepted for inpatient service during a 12–month period; does not include newborn.

Census–Average number of inpatients receiving care each day during the 12–month reporting period; does not include newborn.

Outpatient Visits–A visit by a patient who is not lodged in the hospital while receiving medical, dental, or other services. Each appearance of an outpatient in each unit constitutes one visit regardless of the number of diagnostic and/or therapeutic treatments that a patient receives.

Births–Number of infants born in the hospital and accepted for service in a newborn infant bassinet during a 12–month period; excludes stillbirths.

Expense: Expense for a 12–month period; both total expense and payroll components are shown. Payroll expenses include all salaries and wages.

Personnel: Includes persons on payroll on September 30, 1997; includes full–time equivalents of part–time personnel. Full–time equivalents were calculated on the basis that two part–time persons equal one full–time person.

Each year, an annual survey of hospitals is conducted by Healthcare InfoSource, Inc., a subsidiary of the American Hospital Association (AHA).

The facilities and services found below are either provided by the hospital, its health care system, or network or through a formal arrangement with another provider.

The AHA Guide to the Health Care Field does not include all data collected from the 1997 Annual Survey. Requests for purchasing other Annual Survey data should be directed to Healthcare InfoSource, Inc., One North Franklin, Chicago, IL 60606–3401, 312/422–2100.

Definitions of Facility Codes

1. **Adult day care program** Program providing supervision, medical and psychological care, and social activities for older adults who live at home or in another family setting, but cannot be alone or prefer to be with others during the day. May include intake assessment, health monitoring, occupational therapy, personal care, noon meal, and transportation services.

2. **Alcoholism–drug abuse or dependency inpatient services** Provides, diagnosis and therapeutic services to patients with alcoholism or other drug dependencies. Includes care for inpatient/residential treatment for patients whose course of treatment involves more intensive care than provided in an outpatient setting or where patient requires supervised withdrawal.

3. **Alcoholism–drug abuse or dependency outpatient services** Organized hospital services that provide medical care and/or rehabilitative treatment services to outpatients for whom the primary diagnosis is alcoholism or other chemical dependency.

4. **Angioplasty** The reconstruction or restructuring of a blood vessel by operative means or by nonsurgical techniques such as balloon dilation or laser.

5. **Arthritis treatment center** Specifically equipped and staffed center for the diagnosis and treatment of arthritis and other joint disorders.

6. **Assisted living** A special combination of housing, supportive services, personalized assistance and health care designed to respond to the individual needs of those who need help in activities of daily living and instrumental activities of daily living. Supportive services are available, 24 hours a day, to meet scheduled and unscheduled needs, in a way that promotes maximum independence and dignity for each resident and encourages the involvement of a resident's family, neighbor and friends.

7. **Birthing room–LDR room–LDRP room** A single room–type of maternity care with a more homelike setting for families than the traditional three–room unit (labor/delivery/recovery) with a separate postpartum area. A birthing room combines labor and delivery in one room. An LDR room accommodates three stages in the birthing process—labor, delivery, and recovery. An LDRP room accommodates all four stages of the birth process—labor, delivery, recovery and postpartum.

8. **Breast cancer screening/mammograms** Mammography screening–the use of breast x–ray to detect unsuspected breast cancer in asymptomatic women. Diagnostic mammography–the x–ray imaging of breast tissue in symptomatic women who are considered to have a substantial likelihood of having breast cancer already.

9. **Burn care services** Provides care to severely burned patients. Severely burned patients are those with any of the following: 1. Second–degree burns of more than 25% total body surface area for adults or 20% total body surface area for children; 2. Third–degree burns of more than 10% total body surface area; 3. Any severe burns of the hands, face, eyes, ears or feet or; 4. All inhalation injuries, electrical burns, complicated burn injuries involving fractures and other major traumas, and all other poor risk factors.

10. **Cardiac catheterization laboratory** Facilities offering special diagnostic procedures for cardiac patients. Available procedures must include, but need not be limited to, introduction of a catheter into the interior of the heart by way of a vein or artery or by direct needle puncture. Procedures must be performed in a laboratory or a special procedure room.

11. **Cardiac intensive care services** Provides patient care of a more specialized nature than the usual medical and surgical care, on the basis of physicians' orders and approved nursing care plans. The unit is staffed with specially trained nursing personnel and contains monitoring and specialized support or treatment equipment for patients who, because of heart seizure, open–heart surgery, or other life–threatening conditions, require intensified, comprehensive observation and care. May include myocardial infarction, pulmonary care, and heart transplant units.

12. **Case management** A system of assessment, treatment planning, referral and follow–up that ensures the provision of comprehensive and continuous services and the coordination of payment and reimbursement for care.

13. **Children wellness program** A program that encourages improved health status and a healthful lifestyle of children through health education, exercise, nutrition and health promotion.

14. **Community health reporting** Does your hospital either by itself or in conjunction with others disseminate reports to the community on the quality and costs of health care services?

15. **Community health status assessment** Does your hospital work with other providers, public agencies, or community representatives to conduct a health status assessment of the community?

16. **Community health status based service planning** Does your hospital use health status indicators (such as

rates of health problems or surveys of self–reported health) for defined populations to design new services or modify existing services?

17. Community outreach A program that systematically interacts with the community to identify those in need of services, alerting persons and their families to the availability of services, locating needed services, and enabling persons to enter the service delivery system.

18. Crisis prevention Services provided in order to promote physical and mental well being and the early identification of disease and ill health prior to the onset and recognition of symptoms so as to permit early treatment.

19. CT scanner Computed tomographic scanner for head or whole body scans.

20. Dental services An organized dental service, not necessarily involving special facilities, that provides dental or oral services to inpatients or outpatients.

21. Diagnostic radioisotope facility The use of radioactive isotopes (Radiopharmaceutical) as tracers or indicators to detect an abnormal condition or disease.

22. Emergency department Hospital facilities for the provision of unscheduled outpatient services to patients whose conditions require immediate care. Must be staffed 24 hours a day.

23. Extracorporeal shock wave lithotripter (ESWL) A medical device used for treating stones in the kidney or ureter. The device disintegrates kidney stones noninvasively through the transmission of acoustic shock waves directed at the stones.

24. Fitness center Provides exercise, testing, or evaluation programs and fitness activities to the community and hospital employees.

25. Freestanding outpatient care center A facility owned and operated by the hospital, but physically separate from the hospital, that provides various medical treatments on an outpatient basis only. In addition to treating minor illnesses or injuries, the center will stabilize seriously ill or injured patients before transporting them to a hospital. Laboratory and radiology services are usually available.

26. Geriatric services The branch of medicine dealing with the physiology of aging and the diagnosis and treatment of disease affecting the aged. Services could include: Adult day care program; Alzheimer's diagnostic–assessment services; Comprehensive geriatric assessment; Emergency response system; Geriatric acute care unit; and/or Geriatric clinics.

27. Health facility transportation (to/from) A long–term care support service designed to assist the mobility of the elderly. Some programs offer improved financial access by offering reduced rates and barrier–free buses or vans with ramps and lifts to assist the elderly or handicapped; others offer subsidies for public transport systems or operate mini–bus services exclusively for use by senior citizens.

28. Health fair Community health education events that focus on the prevention of disease and promotion of health through such activities as audiovisual exhibits and free diagnostic services.

29. Health information center Education which is directed at increasing the information of individuals and populations. It is intended to increase the ability to make informed personal, family and community health decisions by providing consumers with informed choices about health matters with the objective of improving health status.

30. Health screenings A preliminary procedure, such as a test or examination to detect the most characteristic sign or signs of a disorder that may require further investigation.

31. HIV–AIDS services Services may include one or more of the following: HIV–AIDS unit (special unit or team designated and equipped specifically for diagnosis, treatment, continuing care planning, and counseling services for HIV–AIDS patients and their families.) General inpatient care for HIV–AIDS (inpatient diagnosis and treatment for human immunodeficiency virus and acquired immunodeficiency syndrome patients, but dedicated unit is not available.) Specialized outpatient program for HIV–AIDS (special outpatient program providing diagnostic, treatment, continuing care planning, and counseling for HIV–AIDS patients and their families.)

32. Home health services Service providing nursing, therapy, and health–related homemaker or social services in the patient's home.

33. Hospice A program providing palliative care, chiefly medical relief of pain and supportive services, addressing the emotional, social, financial, and legal needs of terminally ill patients and their families. Care can be provided in a variety of settings, both inpatient and at home.

34. Hospital–based outpatient care center–services Organized hospital health care services offered by appointment on an ambulatory basis. Services may include outpatient surgery, examination, diagnosis, and treatment of a variety of medical conditions on a nonemergency basis, and laboratory and other diagnostic testing as ordered by staff or outside physician referral.

35. Magnetic resonance imaging (MRI) The use of a uniform magnetic field and radio frequencies to study tissue and structure of the body. This procedure enables the visualization of biochemical activity of the cell in vivo without the use of ionizing radiation, radioisotopic substances, or high–frequency sound.

36. Meals on wheels A hospital sponsored program which delivers meals to people, usually the elderly, who are unable to prepare their own meals. Low cost, nutritional meals are delivered to individuals' homes on a regular basis.

37. Medical surgical intensive care services Provides patient care of a more intensive nature than the usual medical and surgical care, on the basis of physicians' orders and approved nursing care plans. These units are staffed with specially trained nursing personnel and contain monitoring and specialized support equipment of patients who, because of shock, trauma, or other life–threatening conditions, require intensified, comprehensive observation and care. Includes mixed intensive care units.

38. Neonatal intensive care services A unit that must be separate from the newborn nursery providing intensive care to all sick infants including those with the very lowest birth weights (less that 1500 grams). NICU has potential for providing mechanical ventilation, neonatal surgery, and special care for the sickest infants born in the hospital or transferred from another institution.

A full–time neonatologist serves as director of the NICU.

39. **Nutrition programs** Those services within a health care facility which are designed to provide inexpensive, nutritionally sound meals to patients.

40. **Obstetrics services** Levels should be designated: (1) unit provides services for uncomplicated maternity and newborn cases; (2) unit provides services for uncomplicated cases, the majority of complicated problems, and special neonatal services; and (3) unit provides services for all serious illnesses and abnormalities and is supervised by a full–time maternal/fetal specialist.

41. **Occupational health services** Includes services designed to protect the safety of employees from hazards in the work environment.

42. **Oncology services** An organized program for the treatment of cancer by the use of drugs or chemicals.

43. **Open heart surgery** Heart surgery where the chest has been opened and the blood recirculated and oxygenated with the proper equipment and the necessary staff to perform the surgery.

44. **Outpatient surgery** Scheduled surgical services provided to patients who do not remain in the hospital overnight. The surgery may be performed in operating suites also used for inpatient surgery, specially designated surgical suites for outpatient surgery, or procedure rooms within an outpatient care facility.

45. **Patient education center** Written goals and objectives for the patient and/or family related to therapeutic regimens, medical procedures, and self care.

46. **Patient representative services** Organized hospital services providing personnel through whom patients and staff can seek solutions to institutional problems affecting the delivery of high–quality care and services.

47. **Pediatric intensive care services** Provides care to pediatric patients that is of a more intensive nature than that usually provided to pediatric patients. The unit is staffed with specially trained personnel and contains monitoring and specialized support equipment for treatment of patients who, because of shock, trauma, or other life–threatening conditions, require intensified, comprehensive observation and care.

48. **Physical rehabilitation inpatient services** Provides care encompassing a comprehensive array of restoration services for the disabled and all support services necessary to help patients attain their maximum functional capacity.

49. **Physical rehabilitation outpatient services** Outpatient program providing medical, health–related, therapy, social, and/or vocational services to help disabled persons attain or retain their maximum functional capacity.

50. **Positron emission tomography scanner (PET)** is a nuclear medicine imaging technology which uses radioactive (positron emitting) isotopes created in a cyclotron or generator and computers to produce composite pictures of the brain and heart at work. PET scanning produces sectional images depicting metabolic activity or blood flow rather than anatomy.

51. **Primary care department** A unit of clinic within the hospital that provides primary care services (e.g. general pediatric care, general internal medicine, family practice and gynecology) through hospital–salaried medical and or nursing staff, focusing on evaluating and diagnosing medical problems and providing medical treatment on an outpatient basis.

52. **Psychiatric acute inpatient services** Provides acute or long–term care to emotionally disturbed patients, including patients admitted for diagnosis and those admitted for treatment of psychiatric problems, on the basis of physicians' orders and approved nursing care plans. Long–term care may include intensive supervision to the chronically mentally ill, mentally disordered, or other mentally incompetent persons.

53. **Psychiatric child adolescent services** Provides care to emotionally disturbed children and adolescents, including those admitted for diagnosis and those admitted for treatment.

54. **Psychiatric consultation–liaison services** Provides organized psychiatric consultation/liaison services to nonpsychiatric hospital staff and/or department on psychological aspects of medical care that may be generic or specific to individual patients.

55. **Psychiatric education services** Provides psychiatric educational services to community agencies and workers such as schools, police, courts, public health nurses, welfare agencies, clergy and so forth. The purpose is to expand the mental health knowledge and competence of personnel not working in the mental health field and to promote good mental health through improved understanding, attitudes, and behavioral patterns.

56. **Psychiatric emergency services** Services or facilities available on a 24–hour basis to provide immediate unscheduled outpatient care, diagnosis, evaluation, crisis intervention, and assistance to persons suffering acute emotional or mental distress.

57. **Psychiatric geriatric services** Provides care to emotionally disturbed elderly patients, including those admitted for diagnosis and those admitted for treatment.

58. **Psychiatric outpatient services** Provides medical care, including diagnosis and treatment of psychiatric outpatients.

59. **Psychiatric partial hospitalization program** Organized hospital services of intensive day/evening outpatient services of three hours or more duration, distinguished from other outpatient visits of one hour.

60. **Radiation therapy** The branch of medicine concerned with radioactive substances and using various techniques of visualization, with the diagnosis and treatment of disease using any of the various sources of radiant energy. Services could include: megavoltage radiation therapy; radioactive implants; stereotactic radiosurgery; therapeutic radioisotope facility; X–ray radiation therapy.

61. **Reproductive health services** Services that include any or all of the following:

Fertility counseling A service that counsels and educates on infertility problems and includes laboratory and surgical workup and management for individuals having problems conceiving children.

In vitro fertilization Program providing for the induction of fertilization of a surgically removed ovum by donated sperm in a culture medium followed by a short incubation period. The embryo is then reimplanted in the womb.

62. **Retirement housing** A facility which provides social activities to senior citizens, usually retired persons, who do not require health care but some short–term skilled nursing care may be provided. A retirement center may furnish housing and may also have acute hospital and long–term care facilities, or it may arrange for acute and long term care through affiliated institutions.

63. **Single photon emission computerized tomography (SPECT)** is a nuclear medicine imaging technology that combines existing technology of gamma camera imaging with computed tomographic imaging technology to provide a more precise and clear image.

64. **Skilled nursing or other long–term care services** Provides non–acute medical and skilled nursing care services, therapy, and social services under the supervision of a licensed registered nurse on a 24–hour basis.

65. **Social work services** Services may include one or more of the following: Organized social work services (services that are properly directed and sufficiently staffed by qualified individuals who provide assistance and counseling to patients and their families in dealing with social, emotional, and environmental problems associated with illness or disability, often in the context of financial or discharge planning coordination.) Outpatient social work services (social work services provided in ambulatory care areas.) Emergency department social work services (social work services provided to emergency department patients by social workers dedicated to the emergency department or on call.)

66. **Sports medicine** Provision of diagnostic screening and assessment and clinical and rehabilitation services for the prevention and treatment of sports–related injuries.

67. **Support groups** A hospital sponsored program which allows a group of individuals with the same or similar problems who meet periodically to share experiences, problems, and solutions, in order to support each other.

68. **Teen outreach services** A program focusing on the teenager which encourages an improved health status and a healthful lifestyle including physical, emotional, mental, social, spiritual and economic through health education, exercise, nutrition and health promotion.

69. **Transplant services** The branch of medicine that transfers an organ or tissue from one person to another or from one body part to another to replace a diseased structure or to restore function or to change appearance. Services could includes: Bone marrow transplant program; kidney transplant; organ transplant (other than kidney); tissue transplant.

70. **Trauma center (certified)** A facility certified to provide emergency and specialized intensive care to critically ill and injured patients.

71. **Ultrasound** The use of acoustic waves above the range of 20,000 cycles per second to visualize internal body structures.

72. **Urgent care center** A facility that provides care and treatment for problems that are not life–threatening but require attention over the short term. These units function like emergency rooms but are separate from hospitals with which they may have backup affiliation arrangements.

73. **Volunteer services department** An organized hospital department responsible for coordinating the services of volunteers working within the institution.

74. **Women's health center/services** An area set aside for coordinated education and treatment services specifically for and promoted by women as provided by this special unit. Services may or may not include obstetrics but include a range of services other than OB.

Definitions of Physician Codes

1. **Closed physician–hospital organization (PHO)** A PHO that restricts physician membership to those practitioners who meet criteria for cost effectiveness and/or high quality.

2. **Equity model** Allows established practitioners to become shareholders in a professional corporation in exchange for tangible and intangible assets of their existing practices.

3. **Foundation** A corporation, organized either as a hospital affiliate or subsidiary, which purchases both the tangible and intangible assets of one or more medical group practices. Physicians remain in a separate corporate entity but sign a professional services agreement with the foundation.

4. **Group practice without walls** Hospital sponsors the formation of, or provides capital to physicians to establish, a 'quasi' group to share administrative expenses while remaining independent practitioners.

5. **Independent practice association (IPA)** An IPA is a legal entity that hold managed care contracts. The IPA then contracts with physicians, usually in solo practice, to provide care either on a fee–for–services or capitated basis. The purpose of an IPA is to assist solo physicians in obtaining managed care contracts.

6. **Integrated salary model** Physicians are salaried by the hospital or another entity of a health system to provide medical services for primary care and specialty care.

7. **Management services organization (MSO)** A corporation, owned by the hospital or a physician/hospital joint venture, that provides management services to one or more medical group practices. The MSO purchases the tangible assets of the practices and leases them back as part of a full–service management agreement, under which the MSO employs all non–physician staff and provides all supplies/administrative systems for a fee.

8. **Open physician–hospital organization (PHO)** A joint venture between the hospital and all members of the medical staff who wish to participate. The PHO can act as a unified agent in managed care contracting, own a managed care plan, own and operate ambulatory care centers or ancillary services projects, or provide administrative services to physician members.

Hospitals in the United States, by State

ALABAMA

Resident population 4,319 (in thousands)
Resident population in metro areas 67.5%
Birth rate per 1,000 population 14.4
65 years and over 13.0%
Percent of persons without health insurance 12.9%

Hospital, Address, Telephone, Administrator, Approval, Facility, and Physician Codes, Health Care System, Network	Classi-fication Codes		Utilization Data					Expense (thousands) of dollars		
★ American Hospital Association (AHA) membership □ Joint Commission on Accreditation of Healthcare Organizations (JCAHO) accreditation + American Osteopathic Healthcare Association (AOHA) membership ○ American Osteopathic Association (AOA) accreditation △ Commission on Accreditation of Rehabilitation Facilities (CARF) accreditation Control codes 61, 63, 64, 71, 72 and 73 indicate hospitals listed by AOHA, but not registered by AHA. For definition of numerical codes, see page A4	Control	Service	Staffed Beds	Admissions	Census	Outpatient Visits	Births	Total	Payroll	Personnel

ALABASTER—Shelby County
☒ SHELBY BAPTIST MEDICAL CENTER, 1000 First Street North, Zip 35007–0488, Mailing Address: Box 488, Zip 35007–0488; tel. 205/620–8100; Charles C. Colvert, President (Total facility includes 18 beds in nursing home–type unit) (Nonreporting) **A**1 2 9 10 **S** Baptist Health System, Birmingham, AL **N** Baptist Health System, Birmingham, AL — 13 10 228 — — — — — — —

ALEXANDER CITY—Tallapoosa County
☒ RUSSELL HOSPITAL, U.S. 280 By–Pass, Zip 35010, Mailing Address: P.O. Box 38, Zip 35011–0939; tel. 205/329–7100; Frank W. Harris, President and Chief Executive Officer **A**1 9 10 **F**8 14 15 16 19 21 22 28 29 30 32 33 34 36 37 38 39 40 42 44 45 46 49 51 56 58 63 65 67 70 71 73 74 **P**7 — 23 10 81 3774 35 61104 354 24908 11149 412

ANDALUSIA—Covington County
☒ COLUMBIA ANDALUSIA HOSPITAL, 849 South Three Notch Street, Zip 36420–5325, Mailing Address: P.O. Box 760, Zip 36420–0760; tel. 334/222–8466; James L. Sample, Chief Executive Officer **A**1 9 10 **F**7 8 12 14 15 16 19 21 22 32 33 34 35 36 37 40 44 51 65 71 73 **S** Columbia/HCA Healthcare Corporation, Nashville, TN — 33 10 87 3384 31 33011 408 17712 7964 328

ANNISTON—Calhoun County
☒ NORTHEAST ALABAMA REGIONAL MEDICAL CENTER, 400 East Tenth Street, Zip 36207–4716, Mailing Address: P.O. Box 2208, Zip 36202–2208; tel. 256/235–5121; Allen P. Fletcher, President (Nonreporting) **A**1 2 9 10 — 16 10 259 — — — — — — —

□ STRINGFELLOW MEMORIAL HOSPITAL, 301 East 18th Street, Zip 36207–3999; tel. 205/235–8900; Vincent T. Cherry, Jr., Administrator **A**1 9 10 **F**8 12 15 16 19 21 22 28 30 32 34 35 36 37 39 41 42 44 49 65 71 73 **S** Health Management Associates, Naples, FL — 33 10 72 2642 30 27174 — 17643 6816 247

ASHLAND—Clay County
CLAY COUNTY HOSPITAL, 544 East First Avenue, Zip 36251, Mailing Address: P.O. Box 1270, Zip 36251–1277; tel. 205/354–2131; Linda U. Jordan, Administrator (Total facility includes 73 beds in nursing home–type unit) **A**9 10 **F**11 16 19 20 22 32 33 35 44 64 65 67 71 73 — 15 10 119 2841 86 15139 124 9746 5584 297

ATHENS—Limestone County
☒ ATHENS–LIMESTONE HOSPITAL, 700 West Market Street, Zip 35611–2457, Mailing Address: P.O. Box 999, Zip 35612–0999; tel. 205/233–9292; Philip E. Dotson, Administrator and Chief Executive Officer **A**1 9 10 **F**7 8 12 14 15 16 19 21 22 28 30 32 37 39 40 44 45 49 65 71 74 **P**6 **N** HealthGroup of Alabama, L.L.C., Madison, AL — 16 10 101 4765 53 49597 410 35170 15286 512

ATMORE—Escambia County
□ ATMORE COMMUNITY HOSPITAL, 401 Medical Park Drive, Zip 36502–3091; tel. 334/368–2500; Robert E. Gowing, Interim Administrator (Nonreporting) **A**1 9 10 **S** Escambia County Health Care Authority, Brewton, AL **N** Baptist Health Care, Inc., Pensacola, FL — 13 10 51 — — — — — — —

BAY MINETTE—Baldwin County
☒ NORTH BALDWIN HOSPITAL, 1815 Hand Avenue, Zip 36507–4110, Mailing Address: P.O. Box 1409, Zip 36507–1409; tel. 334/937–5521; John Shankle, Interim Chief Executive Officer (Nonreporting) **A**1 9 10 — 13 10 55 — — — — — — —

BESSEMER—Jefferson County
☒ BESSEMER CARRAWAY MEDICAL CENTER, 995 Ninth Avenue S.W., Zip 35023, Mailing Address: P.O. Box 847, Zip 35021–0847; tel. 205/481–7000; Dan M. Eagar, Jr., Administrator **A**1 2 9 10 **F**2 3 7 8 10 11 12 14 19 21 27 28 33 37 39 41 42 44 48 49 52 54 55 56 57 65 67 70 71 73 74 **P**4 — 23 10 210 7113 107 86982 312 56831 22061 792

BIRMINGHAM—Jefferson County
☒ BIRMINGHAM BAPTIST MEDICAL CENTER–MONTCLAIR CAMPUS, 800 Montclair Road, Zip 35213–1984; tel. 205/592–1000; Dana S. Hensley, President (Total facility includes 112 beds in nursing home–type unit) (Nonreporting) **A**1 2 3 5 8 9 10 **S** Baptist Health System, Birmingham, AL **N** Baptist Health System, Birmingham, AL — 21 10 1023 — — — — — — —

☒ BIRMINGHAM BAPTIST MEDICAL CENTER–PRINCETON, 701 Princeton Avenue S.W., Zip 35211–1305; tel. 205/783–3000; Dana S. Hensley, President and Chief Executive Officer (Nonreporting) **A**1 2 3 5 8 9 10 **S** Baptist Health System, Birmingham, AL **N** Baptist Health System, Birmingham, AL — 21 10 1033 — — — — — — —

BRADFORD HEALTH SERVICES AT BIRMINGHAM, 1221 Alton Drive, Zip 35210–4308, Mailing Address: P.O. Box 129, Warrior, Zip 35180–0129; tel. 205/833–4000; W. Clay Simmons, Executive Director (Nonreporting) **A**9 — 33 82 90 — — — — — — —

☒ BROOKWOOD MEDICAL CENTER, 2010 Brookwood Medical Center Drive, Zip 35209; tel. 205/877–1000; Gregory H. Burfitt, President and Chief Executive Officer **A**1 2 9 10 **F**1 2 4 5 7 8 10 11 12 14 16 17 18 19 21 22 23 24 25 26 28 29 30 31 32 33 34 35 37 38 39 40 41 42 43 44 45 48 49 51 52 53 56 57 58 59 60 61 64 65 67 71 73 74 **P**6 **S** TENET Healthcare Corporation, Santa Barbara, CA **N** Alabama Health Services, Birmingham, AL — 33 10 501 20643 284 101411 3610 — 51352 —

Hospitals **A11**

Hospital, Address, Telephone, Administrator, Approval, Facility, and Physician Codes, Health Care System, Network	Classi-fication Codes		Utilization Data					Expense (thousands) of dollars		
	Control	Service	Staffed Beds	Admissions	Census	Outpatient Visits	Births	Total	Payroll	Personnel

★ American Hospital Association (AHA) membership
□ Joint Commission on Accreditation of Healthcare Organizations (JCAHO) accreditation
+ American Osteopathic Healthcare Association (AOHA) membership
○ American Osteopathic Association (AOA) accreditation
△ Commission on Accreditation of Rehabilitation Facilities (CARF) accreditation
Control codes 61, 63, 64, 71, 72 and 73 indicate hospitals listed by AOHA, but not registered by AHA. For definition of numerical codes, see page A4.

Hospital	Control	Service	Staffed Beds	Admissions	Census	Outpatient Visits	Births	Total	Payroll	Personnel
✸ △ CARRAWAY METHODIST MEDICAL CENTER, 1600 Carraway Boulevard, Zip 35234–1990; tel. 205/502–6000; Cindy Williams, FACHE, Administrator **A**1 2 3 5 7 8 9 10 **F**2 4 7 8 10 11 12 14 15 16 17 19 20 21 22 23 24 25 26 28 30 31 32 33 34 35 37 39 40 41 42 43 44 45 46 48 49 51 52 53 54 55 56 57 58 60 65 67 70 71 73 **P**6 8 **S** Carraway Methodist Health System, Birmingham, AL	23	10	383	15043	233	33400	520	145876	56477	1534
✸ CHILDREN'S HOSPITAL OF ALABAMA, 1600 Seventh Avenue South, Zip 35233–1785; tel. 205/939–9100; Jim Dearth, M.D., Chief Executive Officer **A**1 3 5 9 10 **F**9 11 13 14 15 16 17 19 20 21 22 25 29 30 31 32 34 35 38 39 41 42 44 45 46 47 49 51 52 53 54 55 56 58 65 66 67 70 71 72 73 **P**5 7 8	23	50	195	11472	156	381799	—	120529	67589	1863
□ COOPER GREEN HOSPITAL, 1515 Sixth Avenue South, Zip 35233–1688; tel. 205/930–3600; Max Michael, M.D., Chief Executive Officer and Medical Director **A**1 3 5 9 10 **F**4 7 8 10 12 14 15 16 17 19 21 22 23 30 31 32 34 35 37 38 39 40 41 42 43 44 47 48 49 51 52 53 54 56 60 65 71 73 74 **P**6	13	10	131	5764	73	105827	1373	57918	24675	682
✸ EYE FOUNDATION HOSPITAL, 1720 University Boulevard, Zip 35233–1816; tel. 205/325–8100; Steve Schultz, President (Nonreporting) **A**1 3 5 9 10	23	45	23							
□ △ HEALTHSOUTH LAKESHORE REHABILITATION HOSPITAL, 3800 Ridgeway Drive, Zip 35209–5599; tel. 205/868–2000; Terry Brown, Administrator and Chief Executive Officer (Nonreporting) **A**1 7 9 10 **S** HEALTHSOUTH Corporation, Birmingham, AL	33	46	100							
✸ HEALTHSOUTH MEDICAL CENTER, 1201 11th Avenue South, Zip 35205–5299; tel. 205/930–7000; Frank R. Gannon, Administrator and Regional Vice President **A**1 9 10 **F**1 8 10 12 14 19 21 22 27 34 35 37 44 48 49 63 64 65 66 71 73 **S** HEALTHSOUTH Corporation, Birmingham, AL	33	10	201	6647	84	38398	—	71684	23952	647
□ HILL CREST BEHAVIORAL HEALTH SERVICES, 6869 Fifth Avenue South, Zip 35212–1866; tel. 205/833–9000; Steve McCabe, Chief Executive Officer (Nonreporting) **A**1 9 10 **S** Ramsay Health Care, Inc., Coral Gables, FL	32	22	100							
✸ △ MEDICAL CENTER EAST, 50 Medical Park East Drive, Zip 35235–9987; tel. 205/838–3000; David E. Crawford, FACHE, Executive Vice President and Chief Operating Officer **A**1 2 3 5 7 9 10 **F**1 2 3 4 6 7 8 9 10 11 12 14 15 16 17 19 21 22 23 24 25 27 28 29 30 31 32 33 34 35 37 38 39 40 41 42 43 44 45 46 47 48 49 51 52 53 54 55 56 57 58 59 60 61 62 64 65 67 69 70 71 72 73 74 **P**5 6 7 **S** Eastern Health System, Inc., Birmingham, AL **N** Alabama Health Services, Birmingham, AL	23	10	282	12297	139	105723	915	90352	32129	1125
✸ ST. VINCENT'S HOSPITAL, 810 St. Vincent's Drive, Zip 35205–1695, Mailing Address: P.O. Box 12407, Zip 35202–2407; tel. 205/939–7000; Vincent C. Caponi, President and Chief Executive Officer **A**1 2 3 5 9 10 **F**4 5 7 8 10 11 12 15 16 17 18 19 21 22 24 25 26 27 28 29 30 31 32 33 34 35 36 37 38 39 40 41 42 43 44 45 46 49 51 52 54 55 56 57 60 63 65 67 71 73 **P**5 8 **S** Daughters of Charity National Health System, Saint Louis, MO	23	11	338	15173	206	114070	2461	120524	51726	1710
✸ UNIVERSITY OF ALABAMA HOSPITAL, 619 South 19th Street, Zip 35233–6505; tel. 205/934–4011; Martin Nowak, Interim Executive Director (Total facility includes 39 beds in nursing home–type unit) **A**1 2 3 5 8 9 10 12 **F**3 4 5 7 8 9 10 11 12 14 15 16 17 19 20 21 22 23 24 25 26 28 30 31 32 33 34 35 37 38 40 41 42 43 44 46 48 49 51 52 53 54 55 57 60 61 64 65 66 67 69 70 71 74 **P**3 **N** University of Alabama Hospital/UAB Health System, Birmingham, AL	12	10	851	38665	617	—	3134	435508	165294	4578
✸ VETERANS AFFAIRS MEDICAL CENTER, 700 South 19th Street, Zip 35233–1927; tel. 205/933–8101; Y. C. Parris, Director **A**1 2 3 5 8 9 **F**1 2 3 5 8 10 11 12 14 15 16 17 19 20 21 22 25 26 27 28 29 30 31 32 33 34 35 37 39 41 42 43 44 45 46 48 49 50 51 52 54 56 58 60 63 64 65 67 69 71 72 73 74 **P**1 6 **S** Department of Veterans Affairs, Washington, DC	45	10	156	4792	118	190688	—	123244	57933	1556
BOAZ—Marshall County										
✸ MARSHALL MEDICAL CENTER SOUTH, (Formerly Boaz–Albertville Medical Center), U.S. Highway 431 North, Zip 35957–0999, Mailing Address: P.O. Box 758, Zip 35957–0758; tel. 256/593–8310; Marlin Hanson, Administrator **A**1 9 10 **F**7 8 14 15 16 17 19 21 22 24 28 30 34 35 37 40 41 42 44 49 54 60 63 65 66 71 73 74 **S** Marshall County Health Care Authority, Guntersville, AL	12	10	102	4844	63	98543	534	39589	17482	580
BREWTON—Escambia County										
✸ D. W. MCMILLAN MEMORIAL HOSPITAL, 1301 Belleville Avenue, Zip 36426–1306, Mailing Address: P.O. Box 908, Zip 36427–0908; tel. 334/867–8061; Phillip L. Parker, Administrator **A**1 9 10 **F**7 14 15 16 19 21 22 28 29 32 34 35 37 40 42 44 49 65 70 71 73 **S** Escambia County Health Care Authority, Brewton, AL **N** Baptist Health Care, Inc., Pensacola, FL	23	10	60	3013	30	32594	295	12633	6614	264
BRIDGEPORT—Jackson County										
□ NORTH JACKSON HOSPITAL, Mailing Address: 47005 U.S. Highway 72, Zip 35740; tel. 205/437–2101; Tom O. Lackey, Administrator (Total facility includes 60 beds in nursing home–type unit) (Nonreporting) **A**1 9 10	16	10	109	—	—	—	—	—	—	—
CAMDEN—Wilcox County										
J. PAUL JONES HOSPITAL, 317 McWilliams Avenue, Zip 36726–1610; tel. 205/682–4131; Arden Chesnut, Administrator (Nonreporting) **A**9 10	15	10	20	—	—	—	—	—	—	—
CARROLLTON—Pickens County										
□ PICKENS COUNTY MEDICAL CENTER, Route 2, Zip 35447, Mailing Address: P.O. Box 478, Zip 35447–0478; tel. 205/367–8111; Tunisia Lavender, R.N., Chief Operating Officer **A**1 9 10 **F**7 8 14 15 16 19 22 24 28 32 34 35 37 40 44 49 65 71 73 **P**6	23	10	47	2234	31	28294	242	—	—	260

Hospital, Address, Telephone, Administrator, Approval, Facility, and Physician Codes, Health Care System, Network	Classi-fication Codes		Utilization Data					Expense (thousands) of dollars		
★ American Hospital Association (AHA) membership □ Joint Commission on Accreditation of Healthcare Organizations (JCAHO) accreditation + American Osteopathic Healthcare Association (AOHA) membership ○ American Osteopathic Association (AOA) accreditation △ Commission on Accreditation of Rehabilitation Facilities (CARF) accreditation Control codes 61, 63, 64, 71, 72 and 73 indicate hospitals listed by AOHA, but not registered by AHA. For definition of numerical codes, see page A4	Control	Service	Staffed Beds	Admissions	Census	Outpatient Visits	Births	Total	Payroll	Personnel

CENTRE—Cherokee County

✚ CHEROKEE BAPTIST MEDICAL CENTER, 400 Northwood Drive, Zip 35960–1023; tel. 205/927–5531; Barry S. Cochran, President **A**1 9 10 **F**8 11 12 14 15 16 17 19 21 22 24 27 28 30 32 33 44 45 51 66 71 73 74 **S** Baptist Health System, Birmingham, AL **N** The Medical Resource Network, L.L.C., Atlanta, GA; Baptist Health System, Birmingham, AL	23	10	45	1319	13	71699	—	10616	4164	156

CENTREVILLE—Bibb County

BIBB MEDICAL CENTER, 164 Pierson Avenue, Zip 35042–1199; tel. 205/926–4881; Terry J. Smith, Administrator (Total facility includes 113 beds in nursing home–type unit) (Nonreporting) **A**9 10	13	10	138	—	—	—	—	—	—	—

CHATOM—Washington County

WASHINGTON COUNTY INFIRMARY AND NURSING HOME, St. Stephens Avenue, Zip 36518, Mailing Address: P.O. Box 597, Zip 36518–0597; tel. 334/847–2223; Howard C. Holcomb, Administrator (Total facility includes 73 beds in nursing home–type unit) (Nonreporting) **A**9 10 **S** Infirmary Health System, Inc., Mobile, AL	13	10	88	—	—	—	—	—	—	—

CLANTON—Chilton County

□ VAUGHAN CHILTON MEDICAL CENTER, 1010 Lay Dam Road, Zip 35045; tel. 205/755–2500; Donald J. Jones, Administrator (Nonreporting) **A**1 9 10 **S** Healthcorp of Tennessee, Inc., Chattanooga, TN	33	10	45	—	—	—	—	—	—	—

CULLMAN—Cullman County

✚ CULLMAN REGIONAL MEDICAL CENTER, 1912 Alabama Highway 157, Zip 35055, Mailing Address: P.O. Box 1108, Zip 35056–1108; tel. 205/737–2000; Jesse O. Weatherly, President **A**1 2 9 10 **F**4 7 8 10 12 14 15 16 17 19 21 22 24 28 30 32 33 35 37 40 41 42 44 46 49 60 65 66 67 71 73 74 **S** Baptist Health System, Birmingham, AL **N** Baptist Health System, Birmingham, AL	23	10	115	6471	66	183322	576	43284	16784	647
✚ WOODLAND MEDICAL CENTER, (Formerly Woodland Community Hospital), 1910 Cherokee Avenue S.E., Zip 35055–5599; tel. 205/739–3500; Lowell Benton, Executive Director **A**1 9 10 **F**7 8 11 12 14 15 16 17 19 21 28 30 32 34 39 40 42 44 45 46 49 52 54 56 57 60 63 65 67 71 73 **P**8 **S** Community Health Systems, Inc., Brentwood, TN	33	10	100	2488	27	26911	158	17075	6287	243

DADEVILLE—Tallapoosa County

★ LAKESHORE COMMUNITY HOSPITAL, 201 Mariarden Road, Zip 36853, Mailing Address: P.O. Box 248, Zip 36853–0248; tel. 205/825–7821; Mavis B. Halko, Administrator **A**9 10 **F**19 22 32 44 71 **S** Healthcorp of Tennessee, Inc., Chattanooga, TN	23	10	28	1380	10	13116	0	9433	4041	158

DAPHNE—Baldwin County

✚ MERCY MEDICAL, 101 Villa Drive, Zip 36526–4653, Mailing Address: P.O. Box 1090, Zip 36526–1090; tel. 334/626–2694; Sister Mary Eileen Wilhelm, President and Chief Executive Officer (Total facility includes 132 beds in nursing home–type unit) **A**1 **F**6 12 15 16 17 20 26 31 32 33 34 36 39 42 49 62 64 65 67 73 **S** Catholic Health East, Radnor, PA	21	46	157	1499	135	—	—	28560	14941	650

DECATUR—Morgan County

✚ DECATUR GENERAL HOSPITAL, 1201 Seventh Street S.E., Zip 35601, Mailing Address: P.O. Box 2239, Zip 35609–2239; tel. 205/341–2000; Robert L. Smith, President and Chief Executive Officer **A**1 2 9 10 **F**7 8 10 11 15 16 19 21 22 28 29 30 32 34 35 37 39 40 41 42 44 45 46 49 52 53 54 55 56 57 58 60 65 67 71 73 74 **N** HealthGroup of Alabama, L.L.C., Madison, AL	16	10	256	9379	127	99475	1838	67551	28488	950
DECATUR GENERAL HOSPITAL–WEST, 2205 Beltline Road S.W., Zip 35601–3687, Mailing Address: P.O. Box 2240, Zip 35609–2240; tel. 205/350–1450; Dennis Griffith, Vice President (Nonreporting) **A**9 **N** HealthGroup of Alabama, L.L.C., Madison, AL	33	22	64	—	—	—	—	—	—	—
□ NORTH ALABAMA REGIONAL HOSPITAL, Highway 31 South, Zip 35609, Mailing Address: P.O. Box 2221, Zip 35609–2221; tel. 205/353–9433; Kay Greenwood, R.N., MS, Facility Director **A**1 10 **F**15 16 22 45 52 65 **P**6	12	22	74	446	87	0	—	—	4291	153
✚ PARKWAY MEDICAL CENTER HOSPITAL, 1874 Beltline Road S.W., Zip 35601–5509, Mailing Address: P.O. Box 2211, Zip 35609–2211; tel. 205/350–2211; Philip J. Mazzuca, Executive Director (Nonreporting) **A**1 9 10 **S** Community Health Systems, Inc., Brentwood, TN	33	10	94	—	—	—	—	—	—	—

DEMOPOLIS—Marengo County

✚ BRYAN W. WHITFIELD MEMORIAL HOSPITAL, Highway 80 West, Zip 36732, Mailing Address: P.O. Box 890, Zip 36732–0890; tel. 334/289–4000; Charles E. Nabors, Chief Executive Officer and Administrator **A**1 9 10 **F**1 8 12 14 15 16 17 19 21 22 24 28 30 32 34 37 39 40 42 44 45 63 65 71 73 **P**5 **N** Provider of Rural Health Network, Montgomery, AL	14	10	99	3662	46	21247	480	18401	8596	344

DOTHAN—Houston County

✚ FLOWERS HOSPITAL, 4370 West Main Street, Zip 36305, Mailing Address: P.O. Box 6907, Zip 36302–6907; tel. 334/793–5000; Keith Granger, President and Chief Executive Officer (Nonreporting) **A**1 2 9 10 **S** Quorum Health Group/Quorum Health Resources, Inc., Brentwood, TN	33	10	215	—	—	—	—	—	—	—
□ SOUTHEAST ALABAMA MEDICAL CENTER, 1108 Ross Clark Circle, Zip 36301–3024, Mailing Address: P.O. Box 6987, Zip 36302–6987; tel. 334/793–8111; Ronald S. Owen, Chief Executive Officer **A**1 2 9 10 **F**4 7 8 10 11 12 14 19 21 22 26 28 29 30 31 32 34 35 37 39 40 41 42 43 44 45 46 49 51 52 54 55 56 57 60 61 63 65 66 67 69 70 71 73 **N** Principal Health Care of Georgia, Atlanta, GA	16	10	347	16065	198	149222	1077	127223	55799	1762

Hospital, Address, Telephone, Administrator, Approval, Facility, and Physician Codes, Health Care System, Network	Classi-fication Codes		Utilization Data					Expense (thousands) of dollars		
★ American Hospital Association (AHA) membership □ Joint Commission on Accreditation of Healthcare Organizations (JCAHO) accreditation + American Osteopathic Healthcare Association (AOHA) membership ○ American Osteopathic Association (AOA) accreditation △ Commission on Accreditation of Rehabilitation Facilities (CARF) accreditation Control codes 61, 63, 64, 71, 72 and 73 indicate hospitals listed by AOHA, but not registered by AHA. For definition of numerical codes, see page A4	Control	Service	Staffed Beds	Admissions	Census	Outpatient Visits	Births	Total	Payroll	Personnel

ELBA—Coffee County

| ELBA GENERAL HOSPITAL, 987 Drayton Street, Zip 36323–1494; tel. 334/897–2257; Ellen Briley, Administrator and Chief Executive Officer (Total facility includes 101 beds in nursing home–type unit) **A**9 10 **F**19 22 34 50 64 71 | 16 | 10 | 121 | 1272 | 106 | 7359 | — | — | — | 175 |

ENTERPRISE—Coffee County

| ✠ MEDICAL CENTER ENTERPRISE, 400 North Edwards Street, Zip 36330–9981; tel. 334/347–0584; Earl S. Whiteley, CHE, Chief Executive Officer (Total facility includes 195 beds in nursing home–type unit) **A**1 9 10 **F**1 3 14 15 16 17 18 19 20 22 26 27 28 29 30 31 32 35 37 39 41 42 46 48 49 51 52 54 55 56 57 58 59 64 65 67 71 73 74 **S** Quorum Health Group/Quorum Health Resources, Inc., Brentwood, TN | 45 | 22 | 437 | 2469 | 399 | 103566 | — | — | — | 919 |

EUFAULA—Barbour County

| □ LAKEVIEW COMMUNITY HOSPITAL, 820 West Washington Street, Zip 36027–1899; tel. 205/687–5761; Carl D. Brown, Administrator (Nonreporting) **A**1 9 10 **S** Healthcorp of Tennessee, Inc., Chattanooga, TN | 33 | 10 | 74 | | | | | | | |

EUTAW—Greene County

| GREENE COUNTY HOSPITAL, 509 Wilson Avenue, Zip 35462–1099; tel. 205/372–3388; Robert J. Coker, Jr., Administrator (Nonreporting) **A**9 10 | 13 | 10 | 72 | — | — | — | — | — | — | — |

FAIRFIELD—Jefferson County

| ✠ LLOYD NOLAND HOSPITAL AND HEALTH SYSTEM, 701 Lloyd Noland Parkway, Zip 35064–2699; tel. 205/783–5106; Gary M. Glasscock, Administrator (Nonreporting) **A**1 2 3 5 9 10 **S** TENET Healthcare Corporation, Santa Barbara, CA **N** Alabama Health Services, Birmingham, AL | 33 | 10 | 222 | | | | | | | |

FAIRHOPE—Baldwin County

| ✠ THOMAS HOSPITAL, 750 Morphy Avenue, Zip 36532–1812, Mailing Address: Drawer 929, Zip 36533–0929; tel. 334/928–2375; Owen Bailey, Administrator (Nonreporting) **A**1 9 10 | 16 | 10 | 108 | | | | | | | |

FAYETTE—Fayette County

| ✠ FAYETTE MEDICAL CENTER, 1653 Temple Avenue North, Zip 35555–1314, Mailing Address: P.O. Drawer 878, Zip 35555–0878; tel. 205/932–5966; Harold Reed, Administrator (Total facility includes 122 beds in nursing home–type unit) **A**1 9 10 **F**4 8 19 21 22 28 30 32 33 34 35 37 39 42 44 45 49 63 64 65 67 71 73 **S** DCH Health System, Tuscaloosa, AL | 13 | 10 | 183 | 1723 | 172 | 42227 | — | 18484 | 7275 | 302 |

FLORALA—Covington County

| FLORALA MEMORIAL HOSPITAL, 515 East Fifth Avenue, Zip 36442–0189, Mailing Address: P.O. Box 189, Zip 36442–0189; tel. 334/858–3287; Blair W. Henson, Administrator (Nonreporting) **A**9 10 **S** United Hospital Corporation, Memphis, TN | 33 | 10 | 23 | | | | | | | |

FLORENCE—Lauderdale County

| ✠ ELIZA COFFEE MEMORIAL HOSPITAL, (Includes Mitchell–Hollingsworth Annex), 205 Marengo Street, Zip 35630–6033, Mailing Address: P.O. Box 818, Zip 35631–0818; tel. 256/768–9191; Richard H. Peck, Administrator (Total facility includes 214 beds in nursing home–type unit) **A**1 9 10 **F**4 7 8 10 11 15 19 21 22 28 34 37 40 42 43 44 45 46 49 52 53 54 55 56 57 64 65 67 71 73 **N** HealthGroup of Alabama, L.L.C., Madison, AL | 16 | 10 | 458 | 11043 | 376 | 57087 | 1180 | 84246 | 34695 | 1549 |
| ✠ FLORENCE HOSPITAL, (Formerly Columbia Florence Hospital), 2111 Cloyd Boulevard, Zip 35630–1595, Mailing Address: P.O. Box 2010, Zip 35631–2010; tel. 205/767–8700; Doug Dailey, Chief Executive Officer (Nonreporting) **A**1 9 10 **S** Columbia/HCA Healthcare Corporation, Nashville, TN | 33 | 10 | 155 | | | | | | | |

FOLEY—Baldwin County

| ✠ SOUTH BALDWIN REGIONAL MEDICAL CENTER, (Formerly South Baldwin Hospital), 1613 North McKenzie Street, Zip 36535–2299; tel. 334/952–3400; Robert F. Jernigan, Jr., Administrator **A**1 9 10 **F**7 8 12 15 16 17 19 21 22 26 28 32 34 35 37 39 40 41 44 45 46 49 50 65 67 71 73 74 | 16 | 10 | 74 | 4457 | 49 | 37466 | 381 | 23730 | 10733 | 380 |

FORT PAYNE—DeKalb County

| ✠ DEKALB BAPTIST MEDICAL CENTER, 200 Medical Center Drive, Zip 35967, Mailing Address: P.O. Box 680778, Zip 35968–0778; tel. 205/845–3150; Barry S. Cochran, President **A**1 9 10 **F**7 8 12 14 15 16 19 21 22 24 26 27 28 30 31 32 33 35 37 40 41 44 46 62 66 68 70 71 73 74 **P**3 5 7 **S** Baptist Health System, Birmingham, AL **N** Baptist Health System, Birmingham, AL | 21 | 10 | 91 | 3775 | 40 | — | 616 | 28113 | 10351 | — |

FORT RUCKER—Coffee County

| ✠ LYSTER U. S. ARMY COMMUNITY HOSPITAL, U.S. Army Aeromedical Center, Zip 36362–5333; tel. 334/255–7360; Lieutenant Colonel Melvin Leggett, Jr., Deputy Commander, Administration **A**1 **F**1 3 4 5 6 7 8 10 12 13 14 15 16 17 18 19 20 21 22 23 24 25 26 27 28 29 30 31 32 33 34 35 36 39 41 42 43 44 45 46 49 50 51 53 54 55 56 57 58 59 60 61 63 65 66 67 69 70 71 72 73 74 **S** Department of the Army, Office of the Surgeon General, Falls Church, VA | 42 | 10 | 42 | 1430 | 8 | 162427 | — | — | 19012 | — |

GADSDEN—Etowah County

✠ GADSDEN REGIONAL MEDICAL CENTER, 1007 Goodyear Avenue, Zip 35999–1100; tel. 205/494–4000; William Russell Spray, Chief Executive Officer **A**1 2 9 10 **F**4 7 8 10 11 12 14 16 19 21 22 23 30 32 33 35 37 40 42 43 44 46 49 52 56 57 60 65 70 71 74 **P**5 **S** Quorum Health Group/Quorum Health Resources, Inc., Brentwood, TN	33	10	257	11698	156	84227	1174	79594	30126	1113
□ MOUNTAIN VIEW HOSPITAL, 3001 Scenic Highway, Zip 35901–9956, Mailing Address: P.O. Box 8406, Zip 35902–8406; tel. 205/546–9265; Jon Orr, Administrator (Nonreporting) **A**1 9 10	33	22	68	—	—	—	—	—	—	—
□ RIVERVIEW REGIONAL MEDICAL CENTER, 600 South Third Street, Zip 35901–5399, Mailing Address: P.O. Box 268, Zip 35999–0268; tel. 205/543–5200; J. David McCormack, Executive Director **A**1 9 10 **F**4 7 8 10 11 12 15 16 17 19 21 22 26 28 29 30 32 34 35 36 37 39 40 41 42 43 44 45 46 49 60 65 66 70 71 72 73 74 **P**5 **S** Health Management Associates, Naples, FL	33	10	281	7960	116	58822	155	—	—	720

Hospital, Address, Telephone, Administrator, Approval, Facility, and Physician Codes, Health Care System, Network	Classi-fication Codes		Utilization Data					Expense (thousands) of dollars		
★ American Hospital Association (AHA) membership □ Joint Commission on Accreditation of Healthcare Organizations (JCAHO) accreditation + American Osteopathic Healthcare Association (AOHA) membership ○ American Osteopathic Association (AOA) accreditation △ Commission on Accreditation of Rehabilitation Facilities (CARF) accreditation Control codes 61, 63, 64, 71, 72 and 73 indicate hospitals listed by AOHA, but not registered by AHA. For definition of numerical codes, see page A4	Control	Service	Staffed Beds	Admissions	Census	Outpatient Visits	Births	Total	Payroll	Personnel

GENEVA—Geneva County

★ WIREGRASS HOSPITAL, 1200 West Maple Avenue, Zip 36340–1694; tel. 334/684–3655; Mark LeNeave, Chief Executive Officer (Total facility includes 86 beds in nursing home–type unit) **A**9 10 **F**8 19 22 28 34 37 44 49 64 65 71 **S** Quorum Health Group/Quorum Health Resources, Inc., Brentwood, TN
| | | 13 | 10 | 151 | 2382 | 110 | 21829 | 0 | 12566 | 5876 | 202 |

GEORGIANA—Butler County

GEORGIANA DOCTORS HOSPITAL, 515 Miranda Street, Zip 36033, Mailing Address: P.O. Box 548, Zip 36033–0548; tel. 334/376–2205; Sheridan Hanks, Administrator (Nonreporting) **A**9 10
| | | 33 | 10 | 22 | — | — | — | — | — | — | — |

GREENSBORO—Hale County

HALE COUNTY HOSPITAL, 508 Green Street, Zip 36744–2316; tel. 334/624–3024; Richard M. McGill, Administrator (Nonreporting) **A**9 10
| | | 13 | 10 | 30 | — | — | — | — | — | — | — |

GREENVILLE—Butler County

★ L. V. STABLER MEMORIAL HOSPITAL, Highway 10 West, Zip 36037–0915, Mailing Address: Box 1000, Zip 36037–0915; tel. 334/382–2676; Dwayne Moss, Administrator **A**9 10 **F**7 8 11 12 14 15 16 17 19 20 21 22 24 26 28 30 32 34 35 41 44 45 46 49 52 57 63 71 73 **S** Community Health Systems, Inc., Brentwood, TN
| | | 33 | 10 | 74 | 1730 | 25 | 18109 | — | 12274 | — | 178 |

GROVE HILL—Clarke County

GROVE HILL MEMORIAL HOSPITAL, 295 South Jackson Street, Zip 36451, Mailing Address: P.O. Box 935, Zip 36451; tel. 334/275–3191; Floyd N. Price, Administrator (Nonreporting) **A**9 10 **S** Infirmary Health System, Inc., Mobile, AL
| | | 14 | 10 | 46 | — | — | — | — | — | — | — |

GUNTERSVILLE—Marshall County

⊠ MARSHALL MEDICAL CENTER NORTH, (Formerly Guntersville–Arab Medical Center), 8000 Alabama Highway 69, Zip 35976; tel. 205/753–8000; Gary R. Gore, Administrator **A**1 9 10 **F**7 8 11 12 14 15 16 17 19 21 22 24 27 28 30 32 39 40 41 44 46 49 55 56 57 63 65 66 71 73 **S** Marshall County Health Care Authority, Guntersville, AL
| | | 16 | 10 | 90 | 4497 | 51 | — | 615 | 28745 | 9932 | 396 |

HALEYVILLE—Winston County

⊠ CARRAWAY BURDICK WEST MEDICAL CENTER, Highway 195 East, Zip 35565–9536, Mailing Address: P.O. Box 780, Zip 35565–0780; tel. 205/486–5213; Ronald L. Sparkman, Administrator **A**1 9 10 **F**8 10 15 17 19 20 22 25 26 29 32 35 37 41 42 44 48 49 59 60 65 71 **P**5 8 **S** Carraway Methodist Health System, Birmingham, AL
| | | 23 | 10 | 36 | 2227 | 24 | — | — | — | — | — |

HAMILTON—Marion County

⊠ MARION BAPTIST MEDICAL CENTER, 1256 Military Street South, Zip 35570–5001; tel. 205/921–6200; Evan S. Dillard, President (Total facility includes 69 beds in nursing home–type unit) **A**1 9 10 **F**8 12 14 15 16 19 21 24 26 28 30 32 34 35 37 42 44 46 49 51 63 64 65 66 71 73 74 **P**4 **S** Baptist Health System, Birmingham, AL **N** Baptist Health System, Birmingham, AL
| | | 33 | 10 | 112 | 1421 | 84 | 21088 | — | 12678 | 5745 | 154 |

HARTSELLE—Morgan County

⊠ HARTSELLE MEDICAL CENTER, 201 Pine Street N.W., Zip 35640–2309, Mailing Address: P.O. Box 969, Zip 35640–0969; tel. 205/773–6511; Mike H. McNair, Chief Executive Officer (Nonreporting) **A**1 9 10 **S** Community Health Systems, Inc., Brentwood, TN
| | | 33 | 10 | 150 | — | — | — | — | — | — | — |

HUNTSVILLE—Madison County

⊠ COLUMBIA MEDICAL CENTER OF HUNTSVILLE, One Hospital Drive, Zip 35801–3403; tel. 256/882–3100; Thomas M. Weiss, Chief Executive Officer (Nonreporting) **A**1 9 10 **S** Columbia/HCA Healthcare Corporation, Nashville, TN
| | | 33 | 10 | 120 | — | — | — | — | — | — | — |

□ △ HEALTHSOUTH REHABILITATION HOSPITAL OF NORTH ALABAMA, 107 Governors Drive S.W., Zip 35801–4329; tel. 205/535–2300; Rod Moss, Chief Executive Officer (Nonreporting) **A**1 7 9 10 **S** HEALTHSOUTH Corporation, Birmingham, AL
| | | 33 | 46 | 50 | — | — | — | — | — | — | — |

⊠ HUNTSVILLE HOSPITAL, (Includes Huntsville Hospital East, 911 Big Cove Road S.E., Zip 35801–3784; tel. 205/517–8020), 101 Sivley Road, Zip 35801–4470; tel. 256/517–8020; Edward D. Boston, Chief Executive Officer **A**1 2 3 5 9 10 **F**4 7 8 10 11 12 14 15 16 17 19 21 22 23 24 25 27 28 29 30 32 34 35 37 38 39 40 41 42 43 44 45 46 47 49 52 55 56 57 58 59 60 65 71 72 73 74 **P**6 7 **N** HealthGroup of Alabama, L.L.C., Madison, AL
| | | 16 | 10 | 706 | 34442 | 412 | 239267 | 4571 | 233163 | 115618 | 3380 |

JACKSON—Clarke County

VAUGHN JACKSON MEDICAL CENTER, 220 Hospital Drive, Zip 36545–2459, Mailing Address: P.O. Box 428, Zip 36545–0428; tel. 205/246–9021; Teresa F. Grimes, Administrator (Nonreporting) **A**9 10
| | | 33 | 10 | 35 | — | — | — | — | — | — | — |

JACKSONVILLE—Calhoun County

⊠ JACKSONVILLE HOSPITAL, 1701 Pelham Road South, Zip 36265–3399, Mailing Address: P.O. Box 999, Zip 36265–0999; tel. 205/435–4970; Charles Mitchener, Jr., Chief Executive Officer **A**1 9 10 **F**7 8 12 13 14 17 19 21 25 26 28 29 30 31 36 37 40 41 44 61 71 73 **S** Quorum Health Group/Quorum Health Resources, Inc., Brentwood, TN
| | | 33 | 10 | 56 | 1888 | 16 | 31053 | 219 | 15790 | 5346 | 172 |

JASPER—Walker County

⊠ WALKER BAPTIST MEDICAL CENTER, 3400 Highway 78 East, Zip 35501–8956, Mailing Address: P.O. Box 3547, Zip 35502–3547; tel. 205/387–4000; Jeff Brewer, President (Nonreporting) **A**1 9 10 **S** Baptist Health System, Birmingham, AL **N** Baptist Health System, Birmingham, AL
| | | 21 | 10 | 267 | — | — | — | — | — | — | — |

LUVERNE—Crenshaw County

CRENSHAW BAPTIST HOSPITAL, 1625 South Forrest Avenue, Zip 36049; tel. 334/335–3374; L. Wayne Sasser, Vice President and Administrator (Nonreporting) **A**9 10
| | | 23 | 10 | 52 | — | — | — | — | — | — | — |

Hospital, Address, Telephone, Administrator, Approval, Facility, and Physician Codes, Health Care System, Network	Classi-fication Codes		Utilization Data					Expense (thousands) of dollars		
★ American Hospital Association (AHA) membership □ Joint Commission on Accreditation of Healthcare Organizations (JCAHO) accreditation + American Osteopathic Healthcare Association (AOHA) membership ○ American Osteopathic Association (AOA) accreditation △ Commission on Accreditation of Rehabilitation Facilities (CARF) accreditation Control codes 61, 63, 64, 71, 72 and 73 indicate hospitals listed by AOHA, but not registered by AHA. For definition of numerical codes, see page A4	Control	Service	Staffed Beds	Admissions	Census	Outpatient Visits	Births	Total	Payroll	Personnel

MADISON—Madison County

BRADFORD HEALTH SERVICES AT HUNTSVILLE, 1600 Browns Ferry Road, Zip 35758–9769, Mailing Address: P.O. Box 176, Zip 35758–0176; tel. 205/461–7272; Bob Hinds, Executive Director (Nonreporting) **A**9 **S** Bradford Health Services, Birmingham, AL — 33 82 84 — — — — — —

MARION—Perry County

VAUGHAN PERRY HOSPITAL, 505 East Lafayette Street, Zip 36756–0149, Mailing Address: P.O. Box 149, Zip 36756–0149; tel. 334/683–9696; Hugh Nichols, Administrator (Total facility includes 61 beds in nursing home–type unit) (Nonreporting) **A**10 — 23 10 76 — — — — — —

MOBILE—Mobile County

□ CHARTER BEHAVIORAL HEALTH SYSTEM, 5800 Southland Drive, Zip 36693–3396, Mailing Address: P.O. Box 991800, Zip 36691–1800; tel. 334/661–3001; Keith Cox, CHE, Chief Executive Officer (Nonreporting) **A**1 5 9 10 **F**2 3 15 17 52 53 54 55 56 57 58 59 **S** Magellan Health Services, Atlanta, GA — 33 22 70 1472 36 — — — — 96

✠ MOBILE INFIRMARY MEDICAL CENTER, (Includes Rotary Rehabilitation Hospital), 5 Mobile Infirmary Drive North, Zip 36601, Mailing Address: P.O. Box 2144, Zip 36652–2144; tel. 334/431–2400; E. Chandler Bramlett, Jr., President and Chief Executive Officer **A**1 2 9 10 **F**4 5 6 7 8 10 11 12 13 14 15 17 19 21 22 24 25 26 27 28 29 31 32 33 34 35 37 39 40 41 42 43 44 45 46 47 48 49 51 52 53 54 55 57 58 60 61 62 63 64 65 66 67 71 72 73 74 **S** Infirmary Health System, Inc., Mobile, AL — 23 10 511 23028 356 222565 1027 157093 61326 2310

✠ PROVIDENCE HOSPITAL, 6801 Airport Boulevard, Zip 36608–3785, Mailing Address: P.O. Box 850429, Zip 36685–0429; tel. 334/633–1000; John R. Roeder, President **A**1 2 9 10 **F**4 7 8 10 11 12 15 16 17 19 21 22 23 24 25 30 31 32 33 34 35 37 40 42 43 44 45 46 49 60 65 66 67 71 73 **P**5 6 7 **S** Daughters of Charity National Health System, Saint Louis, MO — 21 10 349 16983 231 177908 1115 114814 46943 1589

ROTARY REHABILITATION HOSPITAL See Mobile Infirmary Medical Center

□ SPRINGHILL MEMORIAL HOSPITAL, 3719 Dauphin Street, Zip 36608–1798, Mailing Address: P.O. Box 8246, Zip 36608–8246; tel. 334/344–9630; Bill A. Mason, President **A**1 9 10 — 31 10 218 9095 113 60292 1375 — — 1061

□ UNIVERSITY OF SOUTH ALABAMA KNOLLWOOD PARK HOSPITAL, 5600 Girby Road, Zip 36693–3398; tel. 334/660–5120; Thomas J. Gibson, Administrator (Nonreporting) **A**1 3 5 9 10 **S** University of South Alabama Hospitals, Mobile, AL — 12 10 150 — — — — — —

□ UNIVERSITY OF SOUTH ALABAMA MEDICAL CENTER, 2451 Fillingim Street, Zip 36617–2293; tel. 334/471–7000; Stephen H. Simmons, Administrator (Nonreporting) **A**1 2 3 5 8 9 10 **S** University of South Alabama Hospitals, Mobile, AL — 12 10 316 — — — — — —

□ USA CHILDREN'S AND WOMEN'S HOSPITAL, (Formerly USA Doctors Hospital), 1700 Center Street, Zip 36604–3391; tel. 334/415–1000; Stanley K. Hammack, Administrator (Nonreporting) **A**1 3 5 9 10 **S** University of South Alabama Hospitals, Mobile, AL — 12 10 131 — — — — — —

MONROEVILLE—Monroe County

✠ MONROE COUNTY HOSPITAL, 1901 South Alabama Avenue, Zip 36460, Mailing Address: P.O. Box 886, Zip 36461–0886; tel. 334/575–3111; Joe Zager, Chief Executive Officer (Nonreporting) **A**1 9 10 **S** Quorum Health Group/Quorum Health Resources, Inc., Brentwood, TN — 13 10 59 — — — — — —

MONTGOMERY—Montgomery County

✠ BAPTIST MEDICAL CENTER, 2105 East South Boulevard, Zip 36116–2498, Mailing Address: Box 11010, Zip 36111–0010; tel. 334/288–2100; Michael D. DeBoer, President and Chief Executive Officer **A**1 3 5 9 10 **F**2 3 4 7 8 10 11 12 13 14 15 16 17 19 21 22 23 24 25 28 30 31 32 33 35 37 38 40 41 42 43 44 46 49 51 52 55 56 58 59 62 65 71 72 73 — 23 10 331 17661 213 91412 2534 120203 45100 1962

✠ CENTRAL ALABAMA VETERAN AFFAIRS HEALTH CARE SYSTEM, (Includes Montgomery Division, 215 Perry Hill Road, tel. 334/272–4670; Tuskegee Division, 2400 Hospital Road, Tuskegee, Zip 36083–5001; tel. 334/727–0550), 215 Perry Hill Road, Zip 36109–3798; tel. 334/272–4670; James L. Clay, Director (Total facility includes 160 beds in nursing home–type unit) **A**1 3 5 **F**1 3 12 15 17 18 19 20 21 22 25 26 27 28 29 30 33 34 35 37 39 41 44 45 46 48 49 51 52 55 56 57 58 59 65 67 71 72 73 74 **S** Department of Veterans Affairs, Washington, DC — 45 10 499 4211 — 160374 — — 67990

✠ COLUMBIA EAST MONTGOMERY MEDICAL CENTER, 400 Taylor Road, Zip 36117–3512, Mailing Address: P.O. Box 241267, Zip 36124–1267; tel. 334/277–8330; John W. Melton, Chief Executive Officer (Nonreporting) **A**1 9 10 **S** Columbia/HCA Healthcare Corporation, Nashville, TN — 33 10 150 — — — — — —

✠ COLUMBIA REGIONAL MEDICAL CENTER, 301 South Ripley Street, Zip 36104–4495; tel. 334/269–8000; Wayne S. Heatherly, Chief Executive Officer **A**1 9 10 **F**1 3 4 7 8 10 11 12 15 16 19 21 22 30 32 35 37 38 40 43 44 46 48 49 50 51 52 58 59 63 71 73 **S** Columbia/HCA Healthcare Corporation, Nashville, TN — 33 10 165 6287 79 39195 1166 56871 20823 498

□ HEALTHSOUTH REHABILITATION HOSPITAL OF MONTGOMERY, 4465 Narrow Lane Road, Zip 36116–2900; tel. 334/284–7700; Arnold F. McRae, Administrator and Chief Executive Officer (Nonreporting) **A**1 9 10 **S** HEALTHSOUTH Corporation, Birmingham, AL — 33 46 80 — — — — — —

✠ JACKSON HOSPITAL AND CLINIC, 1725 Pine Street, Zip 36106; tel. 334/293–8000; Donald M. Ball, President **A**1 2 9 10 **F**7 8 10 11 14 15 19 21 22 23 28 29 30 33 34 35 37 39 40 41 42 44 45 46 49 51 52 54 56 58 60 65 66 71 73 74 **P**6 — 23 10 264 11775 158 66477 1022 59704 34244 1188

Hospital, Address, Telephone, Administrator, Approval, Facility, and Physician Codes, Health Care System, Network	Classi-fication Codes		Utilization Data					Expense (thousands) of dollars		
★ American Hospital Association (AHA) membership □ Joint Commission on Accreditation of Healthcare Organizations (JCAHO) accreditation + American Osteopathic Healthcare Association (AOHA) membership ○ American Osteopathic Association (AOA) accreditation △ Commission on Accreditation of Rehabilitation Facilities (CARF) accreditation Control codes 61, 63, 64, 71, 72 and 73 indicate hospitals listed by AOHA, but not registered by AHA. For definition of numerical codes, see page A4	Control	Service	Staffed Beds	Admissions	Census	Outpatient Visits	Births	Total	Payroll	Personnel

	Control	Service	Staffed Beds	Admissions	Census	Outpatient Visits	Births	Total	Payroll	Personnel
⊠ MAXWELL HOSPITAL, 330 Kirkpatrick Avenue East, Zip 36112–6219; tel. 334/953–7801; Colonel Herman R. Greenberg, Administrator (Nonreporting) **A**1 **S** Department of the Air Force, Bowling AFB, DC	41	10	30	—	—	—	—	—	—	—
MOULTON—Lawrence County										
⊠ LAWRENCE BAPTIST MEDICAL CENTER, 202 Hospital Street, Zip 35650–0039; Mailing Address: P.O. Box 39, Zip 35650–0039; tel. 205/974–2200; Cheryl Hays, Administrator (Nonreporting) **A**1 9 10 **S** Baptist Health System, Birmingham, AL **N** Baptist Health System, Birmingham, AL	13	10	30	—	—	—	—	—	—	—
MOUNT VERNON—Mobile County										
□ SEARCY HOSPITAL, Mailing Address: P.O. Box 1001, Zip 36560–1001; tel. 334/829–9411; John T. Bartlett, Director (Nonreporting) **A**1 3 5 10	12	52	530	—	—	—	—	—	—	—
MUSCLE SHOALS—Colbert County										
⊠ MEDICAL CENTER SHOALS, 201 Avalon Avenue, Zip 35661–2805, Mailing Address: P.O. Box 3359, Zip 35662–3359; tel. 205/386–1600; Connie Hawthorne, Chief Executive Officer (Nonreporting) **A**1 9 10 **S** Columbia/HCA Healthcare Corporation, Nashville, TN	33	10	128	—	—	—	—	—	—	—
NORTHPORT—Tuscaloosa County										
⊠ NORTHPORT HOSPITAL–DCH, 2700 Hospital Drive, Zip 35476–3380; tel. 205/333–4500; Charles L. Stewart, Administrator **A**1 9 10 **F**2 4 7 8 10 11 12 14 15 16 17 18 19 21 22 23 24 25 26 28 29 30 31 32 34 35 37 38 39 40 41 42 43 44 45 46 47 48 49 52 54 55 56 57 60 65 66 67 70 71 73 74 **P**7 8 **S** DCH Health System, Tuscaloosa, AL	16	10	132	5270	98	61348	695	35705	16928	520
ONEONTA—Blount County										
★ BLOUNT MEMORIAL HOSPITAL, 1000 Lincoln Avenue, Zip 35121–2534, Mailing Address: P.O. Box 1000, Zip 35121–1000; tel. 205/625–3511; George McGowan, FACHE, Chief Executive Officer **A**9 10 **F**8 13 14 15 16 19 21 22 28 29 30 32 33 34 37 39 42 44 46 49 65 71 73 **S** Eastern Health System, Inc., Birmingham, AL **N** Alabama Health Services, Birmingham, AL	23	10	57	1815	22	34177	—	11591	5058	—
OPELIKA—Lee County										
⊠ EAST ALABAMA MEDICAL CENTER, 2000 Pepperell Parkway, Zip 36802–3201; tel. 334/749–3411; Terry W. Andrus, President (Total facility includes 28 beds in nursing home–type unit) **A**1 2 9 10 **F**1 2 3 4 7 8 10 11 12 14 16 19 21 22 26 29 30 31 32 33 34 35 37 39 40 42 43 44 45 49 52 53 56 57 58 60 64 65 71 73 **P**8	16	10	279	13890	195	77412	1554	92130	40517	1392
OPP—Covington County										
★ MIZELL MEMORIAL HOSPITAL, 702 Main Street, Zip 36467–1626, Mailing Address: P.O. Box 1010, Zip 36467–1010; tel. 334/493–3541; Allen Foster, Administrator **A**9 10 **F**7 8 11 12 15 16 17 19 21 28 31 32 35 40 41 44 45 49 65 66 70 71 73 74 **S** Baptist Health Care Corporation, Pensacola, FL **N** Baptist Health Care, Inc., Pensacola, FL	23	10	57	1967	22	20745	142	7052	4071	180
OZARK—Dale County										
□ DALE MEDICAL CENTER, 100 Hospital Avenue, Zip 36360–2080; tel. 334/774–2601; Robert F. Bigley, Administrator (Nonreporting) **A**1 9 10	15	10	85	—	—	—	—	—	—	—
PELHAM—Shelby County										
BRADFORD HEALTH SERVICES AT OAK MOUNTAIN, 2280 Highway 35, Zip 35124–6120; tel. 205/664–3460; Jerry Caltrider, Administrator (Nonreporting) **A**9 **S** Bradford Health Services, Birmingham, AL	33	52	84	—	—	—	—	—	—	—
PELL CITY—St. Clair County										
★ ST. CLAIR REGIONAL HOSPITAL, 2805 Hospital Drive, Zip 35125–1499; tel. 205/338–3301; Douglas H. Beverly, CHE, Chief Operating Officer (Nonreporting) **A**9 10 **S** Eastern Health System, Inc., Birmingham, AL **N** Alabama Health Services, Birmingham, AL	13	10	51	—	—	—	—	—	—	—
PHENIX CITY—Russell County										
⊠ PHENIX REGIONAL HOSPITAL, 1707 21st Avenue, Zip 36867–3753, Mailing Address: P.O. Box 190, Zip 36868–0190; tel. 334/291–8502; Lance B. Duke, FACHE, President and Chief Executive Officer **A**1 9 10 **F**2 3 7 8 10 12 14 15 16 17 18 19 21 22 26 28 29 30 31 32 34 35 37 38 40 41 42 44 45 46 47 48 49 51 52 54 55 56 60 63 64 65 68 69 70 71 72 73 74 **P**6 7 8 **N** Columbus Regional HealthCare System, Inc., Columbus, GA; Principal Health Care of Georgia, Atlanta, GA; The Medical Resource Network, L.L.C., Atlanta, GA	23	10	114	3652	50	36283	500	20169	8594	315
PRATTVILLE—Autauga County										
⊠ NORTHRIDGE MEDICAL CENTER, (Formerly Columbia Northridge Medical Center), 124 South Memorial Drive, Zip 36067–3619, Mailing Address: P.O. Box 681630, Zip 36067–1638; tel. 334/365–0651; Duane Brookhart, Ph.D., President and Chief Executive Officer (Nonreporting) **A**1 9 10 **S** Columbia/HCA Healthcare Corporation, Nashville, TN	33	10	50	—	—	—	—	—	—	—
RED BAY—Franklin County										
RED BAY HOSPITAL, 211 Hospital Road, Zip 35582, Mailing Address: Box 490, Zip 35582; tel. 205/356–9532; Ralph J. Wilson, Administrator **A**9 10 **F**8 14 19 32 44 71 **P**5	13	10	33	976	11	22022	—	4510	2235	108
REDSTONE ARSENAL—Madison County										
⊠ FOX ARMY HEALTH CENTER, (Formerly Fox Army Community Hospital), Zip 35809–7000; tel. 205/876–4147; Major Mark A. Miller, Deputy Commander **A**1 **F**2 3 4 5 6 7 8 9 10 11 12 13 14 15 16 17 18 19 20 21 22 23 24 25 26 27 28 29 30 31 32 33 34 35 36 37 38 39 40 41 42 43 44 45 46 47 48 49 50 51 52 53 54 55 56 57 58 59 60 61 62 63 64 65 66 67 68 69 70 71 72 73 74 **P**1 **S** Department of the Army, Office of the Surgeon General, Falls Church, VA	42	10	22	183	1	92533	0	7426	5570	313

Hospital, Address, Telephone, Administrator, Approval, Facility, and Physician Codes, Health Care System, Network	Classi-fication Codes		Utilization Data					Expense (thousands) of dollars		
	Control	Service	Staffed Beds	Admissions	Census	Outpatient Visits	Births	Total	Payroll	Personnel

★ American Hospital Association (AHA) membership
□ Joint Commission on Accreditation of Healthcare Organizations (JCAHO) accreditation
+ American Osteopathic Healthcare Association (AOHA) membership
○ American Osteopathic Association (AOA) accreditation
△ Commission on Accreditation of Rehabilitation Facilities (CARF) accreditation
Control codes 61, 63, 64, 71, 72 and 73 indicate hospitals listed by AOHA, but not registered by AHA. For definition of numerical codes, see page A4

ROANOKE—Randolph County

★ RANDOLPH COUNTY HOSPITAL, 59928 Highway 22, Zip 36274, Mailing Address: P.O. Box 670, Zip 36274–0670; tel. 334/863–4111; Moultrie D. Plowden, CHE, President **A**9 10 **F**2 15 19 22 32 34 35 37 40 44 49 59 65 71 73 **S** Baptist Health System, Birmingham, AL — 13 10 66 1699 18 7269 131 10308 4696 215

RUSSELLVILLE—Franklin County

✚ NORTHWEST MEDICAL CENTER, Highway 43 By-Pass, Zip 35653, Mailing Address: P.O. Box 1089, Zip 35653–1089; tel. 205/332–1611; Christine R. Stewart, President and Chief Executive Officer (Nonreporting) **A**1 9 10 **S** Columbia/HCA Healthcare Corporation, Nashville, TN — 33 10 100 — — — — — — —

SCOTTSBORO—Jackson County

□ JACKSON COUNTY HOSPITAL, 380 Woods Cove Road, Zip 35768–2428, Mailing Address: P.O. Box 1050, Zip 35768–1050; tel. 205/259–4444; James Armour, Administrator (Total facility includes 50 beds in nursing home–type unit) **A**1 9 10 **F**7 11 14 15 16 19 22 32 35 40 44 64 71 73 — 13 10 142 4338 100 36710 355 24462 10503 328

SELMA—Dallas County

✚ COLUMBIA FOUR RIVERS MEDICAL CENTER, 1015 Medical Center Parkway, Zip 36701–6352; tel. 334/872–8461; John Anderson, Chief Executive Officer (Nonreporting) **A**1 2 3 5 9 10 **S** Columbia/HCA Healthcare Corporation, Nashville, TN — 33 10 150 — — — — — — —

✚ VAUGHAN REGIONAL MEDICAL CENTER, 1050 West Dallas Avenue, Zip 36701–6515, Mailing Address: P.O. Box 328, Zip 36702–0328; tel. 334/418–6000; Jerome H. Horn, President and Chief Executive Officer **A**1 3 5 9 10 **F**6 7 8 12 16 17 19 21 22 24 28 29 30 32 35 40 44 46 63 65 71 73 **P**3 7 — 23 10 106 5225 60 38369 748 27032 11712 420

SHEFFIELD—Colbert County

✚ HELEN KELLER HOSPITAL, 1300 South Montgomery Avenue, Zip 35660–6334, Mailing Address: P.O. Box 610, Zip 35660–0610; tel. 205/386–4556; Ralph Clark, Jr., President **A**1 9 10 **F**2 3 7 8 10 11 12 15 16 17 19 21 22 24 27 28 29 30 34 35 37 40 41 42 44 46 49 52 57 58 59 60 63 65 66 71 73 74 — 16 10 152 6272 87 73211 781 39369 15882 695

SYLACAUGA—Talladega County

✚ COOSA VALLEY BAPTIST MEDICAL CENTER, 315 West Hickory Street, Zip 35150–2996; tel. 205/249–5000; Steven M. Johnson, President (Total facility includes 75 beds in nursing home–type unit) (Nonreporting) **A**1 9 10 **S** Baptist Health System, Birmingham, AL **N** Baptist Health System, Birmingham, AL — 21 10 176 — — — — — — —

TALLADEGA—Talladega County

✚ CITIZENS BAPTIST MEDICAL CENTER, 604 Stone Avenue, Zip 35160–2217, Mailing Address: P.O. Box 978, Zip 35161–0978; tel. 205/362–8111; Steven M. Johnson, President (Nonreporting) **A**1 9 10 **S** Baptist Health System, Birmingham, AL **N** Baptist Health System, Birmingham, AL — 23 10 97 — — — — — — —

TALLASSEE—Elmore County

★ COMMUNITY HOSPITAL, 805 Friendship Road, Zip 36078–1234, Mailing Address: P.O. Box 707, Zip 36078–0707; tel. 334/283–6541; Jennie Rhinehart, Administrator (Nonreporting) **A**9 10 — 23 10 69 — — — — — — —

THOMASVILLE—Clarke County

THOMASVILLE INFIRMARY, (Formerly Vaughn Thomasville Medical Center), 1440 Highway 43 North, Zip 36784–3302; tel. 334/636–4431; Albert Ban, Jr., Administrator **A**9 10 **F**8 14 16 19 22 26 32 33 44 49 65 71 — 23 10 24 859 9 14566 — 4774 2263 87

TROY—Pike County

✚ EDGE REGIONAL MEDICAL CENTER, 1330 Highway 231 South, Zip 36081–1224; tel. 334/670–5000; David E. Loving, Chief Executive Officer **A**1 9 10 **F**7 8 11 12 19 21 32 35 37 40 44 49 66 71 73 **P**6 **S** Community Health Systems, Inc., Brentwood, TN — 33 10 97 2896 27 — 325 — — 201

TUSCALOOSA—Tuscaloosa County

□ BRYCE HOSPITAL, 200 University Boulevard, Zip 35401–1294; tel. 205/759–0750; James F. Reddoch, Jr., Director (Total facility includes 354 beds in nursing home–type unit) **A**1 10 **F**8 15 16 19 20 21 31 35 37 41 44 49 52 53 54 55 56 57 58 59 64 65 67 71 73 **P**6 — 12 22 838 660 817 — — 52264 29646 —

✚ DCH REGIONAL MEDICAL CENTER, 809 University Boulevard East, Zip 35401–9961; tel. 205/759–7111; Bryan N. Kindred, President and Chief Executive Officer **A**1 2 3 5 9 10 **F**4 7 8 10 11 12 14 16 17 18 19 21 22 23 24 25 28 30 31 32 33 34 35 37 38 39 40 41 42 43 44 45 46 47 48 49 52 54 55 56 57 60 63 64 65 66 67 70 71 73 74 **P**3 7 **S** DCH Health System, Tuscaloosa, AL — 23 10 457 23678 382 239088 2073 166077 75213 2422

✚ VETERANS AFFAIRS MEDICAL CENTER, 3701 Loop Road, Zip 35404–5015; tel. 205/554–2000; W. Kenneth Ruyle, Director (Total facility includes 195 beds in nursing home–type unit) (Nonreporting) **A**1 **S** Department of Veterans Affairs, Washington, DC — 45 22 307 — — — — — — —

TUSKEGEE—Macon County

TUSKEGEE DIVISION See Central Alabama Veteran Affairs Health Care System, Montgomery

UNION SPRINGS—Bullock County

BULLOCK COUNTY HOSPITAL, 102 West Conecuh Avenue, Zip 36089–1303; tel. 334/738–2140; Diane S. Hall, Administrator (Nonreporting) **A**9 10 — 33 10 30 — — — — — — —

VALLEY—Chambers County

□ GEORGE H. LANIER MEMORIAL HOSPITAL AND HEALTH SERVICES, 4800 48th Street, Zip 36854–3666; tel. 334/756–3111; Robert J. Humphrey, Administrator (Total facility includes 93 beds in nursing home–type unit) **A**1 9 10 **F**8 10 14 16 19 22 23 32 34 35 37 40 42 44 46 49 63 64 65 71 73 — 23 10 179 4144 140 42992 326 26563 9102 338

Hospital, Address, Telephone, Administrator, Approval, Facility, and Physician Codes, Health Care System, Network	Classi-fication Codes		Utilization Data					Expense (thousands) of dollars		
	Control	Service	Staffed Beds	Admissions	Census	Outpatient Visits	Births	Total	Payroll	Personnel

WEDOWEE—Randolph County

★ WEDOWEE HOSPITAL, 290 North Main Street, Zip 36278–5138, Mailing Address: P.O. Box 307, Zip 36278–0307; tel. 205/357–2111; Karlene Mitchell, President (Nonreporting) **A**9 10 **S** Baptist Health System, Birmingham, AL — 23 10 34 — — — — — — — —

WETUMPKA—Elmore County

★ ELMORE COMMUNITY HOSPITAL, 500 Hospital Drive, Zip 36092–1625, Mailing Address: P.O. Box 120, Zip 36092–0120; tel. 334/567–4311; Marshall L. Nero, Chief Executive Officer (Nonreporting) **A**9 10 — 15 10 46 — — — — — — — —

WINFIELD—Marion County

✠ CARRAWAY NORTHWEST MEDICAL CENTER, Highway 78 West, Zip 35594, Mailing Address: P.O. Box 130, Zip 35594–0130; tel. 205/487–4234; Robert E. Henger, Administrator **A**1 9 10 **F**7 8 12 14 15 16 17 19 21 22 28 29 30 32 34 37 39 40 41 42 44 45 46 49 51 59 61 63 65 66 71 73 74 **P**1 5 **S** Carraway Methodist Health System, Birmingham, AL — 21 10 63 2297 28 25425 300 14702 6128 272

ALASKA

Resident population 604 (in thousands)
Resident population in metro areas 41.8%
Birth rate per 1,000 population 17.6
65 years and over 5.2%
Percent of persons without health insurance 13.5%

★ American Hospital Association (AHA) membership
☐ Joint Commission on Accreditation of Healthcare Organizations (JCAHO) accreditation
+ American Osteopathic Healthcare Association (AOHA) membership
○ American Osteopathic Association (AOA) accreditation
△ Commission on Accreditation of Rehabilitation Facilities (CARF) accreditation
Control codes 61, 63, 64, 71, 72 and 73 indicate hospitals listed by AOHA, but not registered by AHA. For definition of numerical codes, see page A4

Hospital, Address, Telephone, Administrator, Approval, Facility, and Physician Codes, Health Care System, Network	Control	Service	Staffed Beds	Admissions	Census	Outpatient Visits	Births	Total	Payroll	Personnel
ANCHORAGE—2nd Judicial Division										
☐ ALASKA PSYCHIATRIC HOSPITAL, 2900 Providence Drive, Zip 99508–4677; tel. 907/269–7100; Randall P. Burns, Director and Chief Executive Officer (Nonreporting) **A**1 10	12	22	79	—	—	—	—	—	—	—
☒ ALASKA REGIONAL HOSPITAL, (Formerly Columbia Alaska Regional Hospital), 2801 Debarr Road, Zip 99508, Mailing Address: P.O. Box 143889, Zip 99514–3889; tel. 907/276–1131; Ernie Meier, President and Chief Executive Officer (Nonreporting) **A**1 9 10 **S** Columbia/HCA Healthcare Corporation, Nashville, TN	33	10	189	—	—	—	—	—	—	—
☐ CHARTER NORTH STAR BEHAVIORAL HEALTH SYSTEM, 2530 DeBarr Road, Zip 99508; tel. 907/258–7575; Kathleen Cronen, Chief Executive Officer (Nonreporting) **A**1 10 **S** Magellan Health Services, Atlanta, GA	33	22	80	—	—	—	—	—	—	—
☐ CHARTER NORTH STAR HOSPITAL AND COUNSELING CENTER, (Formerly North Star Hospital), 1650 South Bragaw, Zip 99508–3467; tel. 907/274–7313; Bob Marshall, Administrator (Nonreporting) **A**1 10 **S** Magellan Health Services, Atlanta, GA **N**	33	22	34	—	—	—	—	—	—	—
COLUMBIA ALASKA REGIONAL HOSPITAL See Alaska Regional Hospital										
NORTH STAR HOSPITAL See Charter North Star Hospital and Counseling Center										
☒ PROVIDENCE ALASKA MEDICAL CENTER, 3200 Providence Drive, Zip 99508, Mailing Address: P.O. Box 196604, Zip 99519–6604; tel. 907/562–2211; Gene L. O'Hara, Administrator (Nonreporting) **A**1 3 5 9 10 **S** Sisters of Providence Health System, Seattle, WA	21	10	222	—	—	—	—	—	—	—
☒ U. S. PUBLIC HEALTH SERVICE ALASKA NATIVE MEDICAL CENTER, 4315 Diplomacy Drive, Zip 99508; tel. 907/563–2662; Richard Mandsager, M.D., Director **A**1 10 **F**3 4 7 8 9 10 12 13 14 15 16 19 20 22 27 28 29 30 31 32 33 34 35 36 37 38 40 42 43 44 45 46 47 48 49 51 53 54 55 56 57 58 60 61 65 68 70 71 72 73 74 **S** U. S. Public Health Service Indian Health Service, Rockville, MD	47	10	150	4499	88	214487	948	—	—	—
BARROW—4th Judicial Division										
☒ SAMUEL SIMMONDS MEMORIAL HOSPITAL, (Formerly U. S. Public Health Service Alaska Native Hospital), 1296 Agvik Street, Zip 99723, Mailing Address: P.O. Box 29, Zip 99723; tel. 907/852–4611; Michael S. Herring, Administrator (Nonreporting) **A**1 10 **S** U. S. Public Health Service Indian Health Service, Rockville, MD	47	10	15	—	—	—	—	—	—	—
BETHEL—1st Judicial Division										
☒ YUKON–KUSKOKWIM DELTA REGIONAL HOSPITAL, Mailing Address: P.O. Box 528, Zip 99559–3000; tel. 907/543–6300; Edwin L. Hansen, Vice President (Nonreporting) **A**1 10 **S** U. S. Public Health Service Indian Health Service, Rockville, MD	47	10	50	—	—	—	—	—	—	—
CORDOVA—2nd Judicial Division										
★ CORDOVA COMMUNITY MEDICAL CENTER, 602 Chase Avenue, Zip 99574, Mailing Address: Box 160, Zip 99574; tel. 907/424–8000; Greg Porter, Administrator and Chief Executive Officer (Total facility includes 13 beds in nursing home–type unit) (Nonreporting) **A**10	14	10	23	—	—	—	—	—	—	—
DILLINGHAM—1st Judicial Division										
☒ KANAKANAK HOSPITAL, Mailing Address: P.O. Box 130, Zip 99576; tel. 907/842–5201; Darrel C. Richardson, Chief Operating Officer (Nonreporting) **A**1 10 **S** U. S. Public Health Service Indian Health Service, Rockville, MD	47	10	16	—	—	—	—	—	—	—
ELMENDORF AFB—2nd Judicial Division										
☒ U. S. AIR FORCE REGIONAL HOSPITAL, 24800 Hospital Drive, Zip 99506–3700; tel. 907/552–4033; Colonel Larry J. Sutterer, MSC, USAF, Administrator **A**1 **F**2 3 7 8 12 14 15 16 18 19 21 22 28 29 30 31 34 35 37 38 39 40 41 44 46 51 53 54 56 58 59 61 65 67 71 73 **S** Department of the Air Force, Bowling AFB, DC	41	10	50	2934	22	250129	688	—	—	—
FAIRBANKS—1st Judicial Division										
☒ FAIRBANKS MEMORIAL HOSPITAL, 1650 Cowles Street, Zip 99701; tel. 907/452–8181; Michael K. Powers, Administrator (Total facility includes 92 beds in nursing home–type unit) **A**1 2 9 10 **F**3 4 7 8 9 12 14 15 16 19 21 22 30 32 34 35 37 38 39 40 41 42 44 49 52 56 63 64 65 67 71 73 74 **S** Lutheran Health Systems, Fargo, ND	23	10	200	5727	83	187510	973	80587	33849	812
FORT WAINWRIGHT—1st Judicial Division										
☒ BASSETT ARMY COMMUNITY HOSPITAL, Fort Wainwright, Zip 99703–7400; tel. 907/353–5108; Lieutenant Colonel Gordon Lewis, Deputy Commander for Administration **A**1 **F**3 7 8 12 14 15 16 19 20 22 27 30 31 39 40 44 46 49 51 53 54 55 56 58 59 65 71 73 74 **P**1 **S** Department of the Army, Office of the Surgeon General, Falls Church, VA	42	10	55	2148	13	119292	596	—	—	—
HOMER—3rd Judicial Division										
★ SOUTH PENINSULA HOSPITAL, 4300 Bartlett Street, Zip 99603; tel. 907/235–8101; Charles C. Franz, Chief Executive Officer (Total facility includes 20 beds in nursing home–type unit) **A**10 **F**7 8 11 12 15 19 21 22 28 32 37 40 44 49 64 65 71	16	10	40	905	9	13350	168	13730	6368	181

Hospital, Address, Telephone, Administrator, Approval, Facility, and Physician Codes, Health Care System, Network	Classi-fication Codes		Utilization Data					Expense (thousands) of dollars		
★ American Hospital Association (AHA) membership □ Joint Commission on Accreditation of Healthcare Organizations (JCAHO) accreditation + American Osteopathic Healthcare Association (AOHA) membership ○ American Osteopathic Association (AOA) accreditation △ Commission on Accreditation of Rehabilitation Facilities (CARF) accreditation Control codes 61, 63, 64, 71, 72 and 73 indicate hospitals listed by AOHA, but not registered by AHA. For definition of numerical codes, see page A4	Control	Service	Staffed Beds	Admissions	Census	Outpatient Visits	Births	Total	Payroll	Personnel

JUNEAU—3rd Judicial Division

☒ BARTLETT REGIONAL HOSPITAL, 3260 Hospital Drive, Zip 99801; tel. 907/586–2611; Robert F. Valliant, Administrator (Nonreporting) **A**1 10 **S** Quorum Health Group/Quorum Health Resources, Inc., Brentwood, TN

| | 15 | 10 | 64 | — | — | — | — | — | — | — |

KETCHIKAN—3rd Judicial Division

☒ KETCHIKAN GENERAL HOSPITAL, 3100 Tongass Avenue, Zip 99901–5746; tel. 907/225–5171; Edward F. Mahn, Chief Executive Officer (Total facility includes 28 beds in nursing home–type unit) **A**1 9 10 **F**3 7 8 11 14 15 16 17 19 21 22 28 32 33 37 40 41 42 44 49 54 56 58 61 64 65 66 71 73 74 **P**6 **S** PeaceHealth, Bellevue, WA **N** PeaceHealth, Bellevue, WA

| | 23 | 10 | 65 | 1927 | 36 | 63534 | 315 | 25966 | 13269 | 268 |

KODIAK—2nd Judicial Division

★ PROVIDENCE KODIAK ISLAND MEDICAL CENTER, (Formerly Providence Kodiak Island Hospital and Medical Center), 1915 East Rezanof Drive, Zip 99615; tel. 907/486–3281; Phillip E. Cline, Administrator (Total facility includes 19 beds in nursing home–type unit) **A**9 10 **F**7 8 15 19 22 28 30 31 32 37 39 40 41 44 48 52 64 65 71 73 **S** Sisters of Providence Health System, Seattle, WA

| | 21 | 10 | 44 | 661 | 20 | 7454 | 162 | 8125 | 4178 | 184 |

KOTZEBUE—2nd Judicial Division

☒ MANIILAQ HEALTH CENTER, Zip 99752–0043; tel. 907/442–3321; Clinton Gray, Jr., Administrator (Nonreporting) **A**1 10 **S** U. S. Public Health Service Indian Health Service, Rockville, MD

| | 47 | 10 | 17 | — | — | — | — | — | — | — |

NOME—2nd Judicial Division

☒ NORTON SOUND REGIONAL HOSPITAL, Bering Straits, Zip 99762, Mailing Address: P.O. Box 966, Zip 99762–0966; tel. 907/443–3311; Charles Fagerstrom, Vice President (Total facility includes 15 beds in nursing home–type unit) (Nonreporting) **A**1 10 **S** U. S. Public Health Service Indian Health Service, Rockville, MD **N** Ketchikan General Hospital, Ketchikan, AK

| | 23 | 10 | 34 | — | — | — | — | — | — | — |

PALMER—2nd Judicial Division

☒ VALLEY HOSPITAL, 515 East Dahlia Street, Zip 99645, Mailing Address: P.O. Box 1687, Zip 99645; tel. 907/352–2860; Cliff Orme, Executive Director **A**1 10 **F**7 8 12 14 15 16 17 19 21 22 25 28 30 32 33 34 35 37 39 40 44 45 46 49 65 71 72

| | 23 | 10 | 36 | 2183 | 20 | 52513 | 383 | 29687 | 13801 | 382 |

PETERSBURG—3rd Judicial Division

PETERSBURG MEDICAL CENTER, 103 Fram Street, Zip 99833, Mailing Address: Box 589, Zip 99833–0589; tel. 907/772–4291; John F. Bringhurst, Administrator (Total facility includes 14 beds in nursing home–type unit) **A**10 **F**7 8 11 14 15 21 22 32 37 40 44 51 52 56 64 66 71

| | 14 | 10 | 25 | 136 | 14 | 18375 | 13 | 4187 | 2230 | 40 |

SEWARD—2nd Judicial Division

★ PROVIDENCE SEWARD MEDICAL CENTER, 417 First Avenue, Zip 99664, Mailing Address: P.O. Box 365, Zip 99664–0365; tel. 907/224–5205; Gary Hughes, Administrator (Nonreporting) **A**9 10 **S** Sisters of Providence Health System, Seattle, WA

| | 14 | 10 | 20 | — | — | — | — | — | — | — |

SITKA—3rd Judicial Division

☒ SEARHC MT. EDGECUMBE HOSPITAL, 222 Tongass Drive, Zip 99835–9416; tel. 907/966–2411; Arthur C. Willman, Vice President Operations **A**1 10 **F**7 8 12 15 16 19 20 22 24 27 28 34 39 40 44 52 53 54 56 57 58 65 67 68 71 74 **S** U. S. Public Health Service Indian Health Service, Rockville, MD

| | 23 | 10 | 62 | 1814 | 24 | 35272 | 86 | — | — | 283 |

★ SITKA COMMUNITY HOSPITAL, 209 Moller Avenue, Zip 99835–7145; tel. 907/747–3241; Grant Asay, Chief Executive Officer (Total facility includes 5 beds in nursing home–type unit) (Nonreporting) **A**10

| | 15 | 10 | 22 | — | — | — | — | — | — | — |

SOLDOTNA—3rd Judicial Division

☒ CENTRAL PENINSULA GENERAL HOSPITAL, 250 Hospital Place, Zip 99669; tel. 907/262–4404; Rulon J. Barlow, Administrator **A**1 9 10 **F**7 8 12 14 15 16 17 19 22 26 28 31 37 40 41 42 44 49 56 65 70 71 73 **P**5

| | 23 | 10 | 46 | 2282 | 17 | 32666 | 405 | 20598 | 9447 | 222 |

VALDEZ—3rd Judicial Division

★ VALDEZ COMMUNITY HOSPITAL, 911 Meals Avenue, Zip 99686–0550, Mailing Address: P.O. Box 550, Zip 99686–0550; tel. 907/835–2249; James R. Culley, Administrator **A**9 10 **F**3 7 8 14 15 18 22 28 32 40 44 64 67 71 **P**4

| | 14 | 10 | 13 | 120 | 2 | 5096 | 39 | 2767 | 1266 | 32 |

WRANGELL—3rd Judicial Division

★ WRANGELL GENERAL HOSPITAL AND LONG TERM CARE FACILITY, First Avenue & Bennett Street, Zip 99929, Mailing Address: P.O. Box 1081, Zip 99929; tel. 907/874–7000; Brian D. Gilbert, Administrator (Total facility includes 14 beds in nursing home–type unit) (Nonreporting) **A**10

| | 14 | 10 | 21 | — | — | — | — | — | — | — |

ARIZONA

Resident population 4,555 (in thousands)
Resident population in metro areas 87.3%
Birth rate per 1,000 population 17.4
65 years and over 13.2%
Percent of persons without health insurance 24.1%

Hospital, Address, Telephone, Administrator, Approval, Facility, and Physician Codes, Health Care System, Network	Classi-fication Codes		Utilization Data					Expense (thousands) of dollars		
	Control	Service	Staffed Beds	Admissions	Census	Outpatient Visits	Births	Total	Payroll	Personnel

★ American Hospital Association (AHA) membership
□ Joint Commission on Accreditation of Healthcare Organizations (JCAHO) accreditation
+ American Osteopathic Healthcare Association (AOHA) membership
○ American Osteopathic Association (AOA) accreditation
△ Commission on Accreditation of Rehabilitation Facilities (CARF) accreditation
Control codes 61, 63, 64, 71, 72 and 73 indicate hospitals listed by AOHA, but not registered by AHA. For definition of numerical codes, see page A4

Hospital	Control	Service	Staffed Beds	Admissions	Census	Outpatient Visits	Births	Total	Payroll	Personnel
BENSON—Cochise County										
□ BENSON HOSPITAL, 450 South Ocotillo Street, Zip 85602, Mailing Address: P.O. Box 2290, Zip 85602; tel. 520/586–2261; Ronald A. McKinnon, Administrator (Nonreporting) **A**1 9 10	16	10	22	—						
BISBEE—Cochise County										
□ COPPER QUEEN COMMUNITY HOSPITAL, 101 Cole Avenue, Zip 85603–1399; tel. 520/432–5383; Jim Tavary, Chief Executive Officer and Administrator (Total facility includes 21 beds in nursing home–type unit) (Nonreporting) **A**1 9 10	23	10	49	—						
BULLHEAD CITY—Mohave County										
BULLHEAD COMMUNITY HOSPITAL See Western Arizona Regional Medical Center										
★ MOHAVE VALLEY HOSPITAL AND MEDICAL CENTER, 1225 East Hancock Road, Zip 86442–5941; tel. 520/758–3931; John L. Hoopes, Administrator **A**9 10 **F**12 14 15 16 19 22 26 30 31 34 35 42 44 50 51 60 63 71 72 73 **P**1	33	10	12	606	5	24236	—	6392	2491	—
⊞ WESTERN ARIZONA REGIONAL MEDICAL CENTER, (Formerly Bullhead Community Hospital), 2735 Silver Creek Road, Zip 86442–8303; tel. 520/763–2273; Rita A. Campbell, Executive Vice President and Chief Executive Officer (Total facility includes 120 beds in nursing home–type unit) (Nonreporting) **A**1 9 10 **S** Baptist Hospitals and Health Systems, Inc., Phoenix, AZ **N** Baptist Hospitals and Health Systems, Phoenix, AZ	23	10	182	—						
CASA GRANDE—Pinal County										
⊞ CASA GRANDE REGIONAL MEDICAL CENTER, 1800 East Florence Boulevard, Zip 85222–5399; tel. 520/426–6300; Claudia N. Griffiths, President (Total facility includes 128 beds in nursing home–type unit) (Nonreporting) **A**1 9 10 **N** Arizona Voluntary Hospital Federation, Tempe, AZ	23	10	244	—						
CHANDLER—Maricopa County										
⊞ CHANDLER REGIONAL HOSPITAL, 475 South Dobson Road, Zip 85224–4230; tel. 602/963–4561; Kaylor E. Shemberger, President and Chief Executive Officer **A**1 9 10 **F**7 8 12 14 15 16 17 19 21 22 25 28 30 31 32 34 35 37 39 40 41 42 44 46 49 54 60 65 67 70 71 72 73 74 **P**1 5 **N** Arizona Voluntary Hospital Federation, Tempe, AZ	23	10	120	10114	88	43349	3117	70382	27284	690
□ CHARTER BEHAVIORAL HEALTH SYSTEM–EAST VALLEY, 2190 North Grace Boulevard, Zip 85224–7903; tel. 602/899–8989; Michael D. Todd, Chief Executive Officer (Nonreporting) **A**1 9 10 **S** Magellan Health Services, Atlanta, GA	33	22	80	—						
CHINLE—Apache County										
⊞ CHINLE COMPREHENSIVE HEALTH CARE FACILITY, Highway 191, Zip 86503, Mailing Address: P.O. Drawer PH, Zip 86503; tel. 520/674–7011; Ronald Tso, Chief Executive Officer (Nonreporting) **A**1 10 **S** U. S. Public Health Service Indian Health Service, Rockville, MD	47	10	60	—						
CLAYPOOL—Gila County										
⊞ COBRE VALLEY COMMUNITY HOSPITAL, One Hospital Drive, Zip 85532, Mailing Address: P.O. Box 3261, Zip 85532–3261; tel. 520/425–3261; Charles E. Bill, CHE, Chief Executive Officer **A**1 9 10 **F**7 8 11 12 14 15 16 17 19 21 22 26 28 30 34 35 37 39 40 41 42 44 45 46 48 49 63 64 65 67 68 71 73 **S** Brim, Inc., Portland, OR	23	10	41	1845	36	—	390	15818	5648	201
COTTONWOOD—Yavapai County										
⊞ MARCUS J. LAWRENCE MEDICAL CENTER, 202 South Willard Street, Zip 86326–4170; tel. 520/634–2251; Craig A. Owens, President and Chief Executive Officer (Nonreporting) **A**1 9 10 **N** Northern Arizona Healthcare, Flagstaff, AZ	23	10	64	—						
DAVIS–MONTHAN AFB—Pima County										
⊞ U. S. AIR FORCE HOSPITAL, 4175 South Alamo Avenue, Zip 85707–4405; tel. 520/228–2930; Colonel Robert E. Edwards, Administrator and Deputy Commander **A**1 **F**3 4 8 10 12 13 14 15 16 17 18 19 20 21 24 25 28 29 30 31 34 35 39 41 42 43 44 45 46 49 50 51 53 54 55 56 58 59 60 61 69 71 72 73 **S** Department of the Air Force, Bowling AFB, DC	41	10	20	1037	5	169136	—	—	28900	—
DOUGLAS—Cochise County										
SOUTHEAST ARIZONA MEDICAL CENTER, Route 1, Box 30, Zip 85607; tel. 520/364–7931; Thomas L. Haywood, Chief Executive Officer (Total facility includes 43 beds in nursing home–type unit) (Nonreporting) **A**9 10	23	10	75	—						
FLAGSTAFF—Coconino County										
⊞ BHC ASPEN HILL HOSPITAL, 305 West Forest Avenue, Zip 86001–1464; tel. 520/773–1060; Alan G. Chapman, Administrator and Chief Executive Officer (Nonreporting) **A**1 9 10 **S** Behavioral Healthcare Corporation, Nashville, TN	33	22	26	—						
⊞ △ FLAGSTAFF MEDICAL CENTER, 1200 North Beaver Street, Zip 86001–3198; tel. 520/779–3366; Stephen G. Carlson, President and Chief Operating Officer (Total facility includes 28 beds in nursing home–type unit) **A**1 7 9 10 **F**7 10 12 14 15 16 17 19 21 22 23 32 33 34 35 37 39 40 41 42 44 48 49 60 64 65 67 70 71 72 73 **P**8 **N** Northern Arizona Healthcare, Flagstaff, AZ; Arizona Voluntary Hospital Federation, Tempe, AZ	23	10	150	9117	102	46833	1263	69296	31957	936

Hospital, Address, Telephone, Administrator, Approval, Facility, and Physician Codes, Health Care System, Network	Classi-fication Codes		Utilization Data					Expense (thousands) of dollars		
★ American Hospital Association (AHA) membership ☐ Joint Commission on Accreditation of Healthcare Organizations (JCAHO) accreditation + American Osteopathic Healthcare Association (AOHA) membership ○ American Osteopathic Association (AOA) accreditation △ Commission on Accreditation of Rehabilitation Facilities (CARF) accreditation Control codes 61, 63, 64, 71, 72 and 73 indicate hospitals listed by AOHA, but not registered by AHA. For definition of numerical codes, see page A4	Control	Service	Staffed Beds	Admissions	Census	Outpatient Visits	Births	Total	Payroll	Personnel

FLORENCE—Pinal County

☐ CENTRAL ARIZONA MEDICAL CENTER, Adamsville Road, Zip 85232, Mailing Address: P.O. Box 2080, Zip 85232–2080; tel. 520/868–2003; Darrold Bertsch, Administrator (Total facility includes 27 beds in nursing home–type unit) (Nonreporting) **A**1 9 10

| | 23 | 10 | 77 | — | — | — | — | — | — | — |

FORT DEFIANCE—Apache County

✠ FORT DEFIANCE INDIAN HEALTH SERVICE HOSPITAL, (Formerly U.S. Public Health Service Fort Defiance Indian Health Service Hospital), Mailing Address: P.O. Box 649, Zip 86504–0649; tel. 520/729–3223; Franklin Freeland, Ed.D., Chief Executive Officer (Nonreporting) **A**1 10 **S** U. S. Public Health Service Indian Health Service, Rockville, MD

| | 47 | 10 | 49 | — | — | — | — | — | — | — |

GANADO—Apache County

☐ SAGE MEMORIAL HOSPITAL, Highway 264, Zip 86505, Mailing Address: P.O. Box 457, Zip 86505–0457; tel. 520/755–3411; Elizabeth Johnson, Chief Executive Officer (Nonreporting) **A**1 9 10

| | 23 | 33 | 25 | — | — | — | — | — | — | — |

GLENDALE—Maricopa County

✠ ARROWHEAD COMMUNITY HOSPITAL AND MEDICAL CENTER, 18701 North 67th Avenue, Zip 85308–5722; tel. 602/561–1000; Richard S. Alley, Regional Vice President and Administrator **A**1 9 10 **F**1 3 4 6 7 8 10 11 12 16 17 19 21 22 25 26 28 29 30 32 33 34 35 37 40 42 43 44 49 60 62 64 65 67 70 71 73 74 **S** Baptist Hospitals and Health Systems, Inc., Phoenix, AZ **N** Baptist Hospitals and Health Systems, Phoenix, AZ

| | 23 | 10 | 104 | 6091 | 54 | 51040 | 1856 | 44906 | 14416 | — |

☐ CHARTER BEHAVIORAL HEALTH SYSTEM–GLENDALE, 6015 West Peoria Avenue, Zip 85302–1201; tel. 602/878–7878; Kim Hall, Chief Executive Officer (Nonreporting) **A**1 9 10 **S** Magellan Health Services, Atlanta, GA

| | 33 | 22 | 90 | — | — | — | — | — | — | — |

☐ △ HEALTHSOUTH VALLEY OF THE SUN REHABILITATION HOSPITAL, 13460 North 67th Avenue, Zip 85304–1042; tel. 602/878–8800; Michael S. Wallace, Director (Total facility includes 18 beds in nursing home–type unit) (Nonreporting) **A**1 7 10 **S** HEALTHSOUTH Corporation, Birmingham, AL
SAMARITAN BEHAVIORAL HEALTH CENTER–THUNDERBIRD SAMARITAN CAMPUS See Thunderbird Samaritan Medical Center

| | 33 | 46 | 42 | — | — | — | — | — | — | — |

✠ THUNDERBIRD SAMARITAN MEDICAL CENTER, (Includes Samaritan Behavioral Health Center–Thunderbird Samaritan Campus), 5555 West Thunderbird Road, Zip 85306–4696; tel. 602/588–5555; Robert H. Curry, Senior Vice President and Chief Executive Officer **A**1 9 10 **F**1 3 4 7 8 10 12 14 15 16 17 18 19 21 22 23 25 26 27 28 30 31 32 33 34 35 39 40 41 42 43 44 46 49 50 51 52 53 54 55 56 57 58 59 60 61 63 65 67 68 69 71 72 73 74 **P**3 5 7 **S** Samaritan Health System, Phoenix, AZ **N** Samaritan Health Services, Phoenix, AZ

| | 23 | 10 | 220 | 15563 | 159 | 88721 | 3810 | 93257 | 33920 | 1077 |

✠ U. S. AIR FORCE HOSPITAL LUKE, Luke AFB, 7219 Litchfield Road, Zip 85309–1525; tel. 602/856–7501; Colonel Talbot N. Vivian, MSC, USAF, Administrator (Nonreporting) **A**1 **S** Department of the Air Force, Bowling AFB, DC

| | 41 | 10 | 23 | — | — | — | — | — | — | — |

KEAMS CANYON—Navajo County

✠ U. S. PUBLIC HEALTH SERVICES INDIAN HOSPITAL, Mailing Address: P.O. Box 98, Zip 86034–0098; tel. 520/738–2211; Taylor Satala, Service Unit Director (Nonreporting) **A**1 10 **S** U. S. Public Health Service Indian Health Service, Rockville, MD

| | 47 | 10 | 17 | — | — | — | — | — | — | — |

KINGMAN—Mohave County

✠ KINGMAN REGIONAL MEDICAL CENTER, 3269 Stockton Hill Road, Zip 86401–3691; tel. 520/757–0602; Brian Turney, Chief Executive Officer (Total facility includes 14 beds in nursing home–type unit) **A**1 9 10 **F**7 8 10 14 19 21 22 32 35 37 39 40 41 42 44 45 46 49 63 64 65 70 71 73 **P**2 5 8 **N** Arizona Voluntary Hospital Federation, Tempe, AZ

| | 23 | 10 | 124 | 5963 | 77 | 52660 | 548 | 34110 | 13948 | 498 |

LAKE HAVASU CITY—Mohave County

✠ HAVASU SAMARITAN REGIONAL HOSPITAL, 101 Civic Center Lane, Zip 86403–5683; tel. 520/855–8185; Kevin P. Poorten, Vice President and Chief Executive Officer (Total facility includes 20 beds in nursing home–type unit) **A**1 9 10 **F**7 8 12 15 16 19 22 31 32 34 37 40 41 42 44 46 49 54 56 58 64 65 71 73 **P**3 5 7 **N** Samaritan Health Services, Phoenix, AZ

| | 23 | 10 | 118 | 5440 | 66 | 40914 | 580 | 41688 | 13555 | 494 |

MESA—Maricopa County

✠ DESERT SAMARITAN MEDICAL CENTER, (Includes Samaritan Behavioral Health Center–Desert Samaritan Medical Center, 2225 West Southern Avenue, Zip 85202; tel. 602/464–4000), 1400 South Dobson Road, Zip 85202–9879; tel. 602/835–3000; Bruce E. Pearson, Vice President and Chief Executive Officer (Total facility includes 166 beds in nursing home–type unit) **A**1 2 9 10 **F**3 4 7 8 10 11 12 14 15 16 18 19 21 22 27 28 29 30 31 32 33 34 35 37 39 40 41 42 43 44 46 47 48 49 50 52 53 54 55 56 58 59 60 61 63 64 65 66 67 69 70 71 72 73 74 **P**3 5 7 **S** Samaritan Health System, Phoenix, AZ **N** Samaritan Health Services, Phoenix, AZ

| | 23 | 10 | 511 | 23886 | 387 | 81811 | 6156 | 156052 | 55129 | 1834 |

☐ DESERT VISTA BEHAVIORAL HEALTH SERVICES, 570 West Brown Road, Zip 85201–3227; tel. 602/962–3900; Allen S. Nohre, Chief Executive Officer **A**1 9 10 **F**1 2 3 12 16 17 18 26 29 30 41 45 52 53 54 55 56 57 58 59 64 65 67 **P**6 **S** Ramsay Health Care, Inc., Coral Gables, FL

| | 33 | 22 | 119 | 1302 | 61 | 5459 | — | 7942 | 3854 | 169 |

✠ ○ MESA GENERAL HOSPITAL MEDICAL CENTER, 515 North Mesa Drive, Zip 85201–5989; tel. 602/969–9111; J. O. Lewis, Chief Executive Officer (Total facility includes 13 beds in nursing home–type unit) (Nonreporting) **A**1 9 10 11 12 13 **S** TENET Healthcare Corporation, Santa Barbara, CA

| | 33 | 10 | 125 | — | — | — | — | — | — | — |

Hospital, Address, Telephone, Administrator, Approval, Facility, and Physician Codes, Health Care System, Network	Classi-fication Codes		Utilization Data					Expense (thousands) of dollars		
	Control	Service	Staffed Beds	Admissions	Census	Outpatient Visits	Births	Total	Payroll	Personnel

★ American Hospital Association (AHA) membership
□ Joint Commission on Accreditation of Healthcare Organizations (JCAHO) accreditation
+ American Osteopathic Healthcare Association (AOHA) membership
○ American Osteopathic Association (AOA) accreditation
△ Commission on Accreditation of Rehabilitation Facilities (CARF) accreditation
Control codes 61, 63, 64, 71, 72 and 73 indicate hospitals listed by AOHA, but not registered by AHA. For definition of numerical codes, see page A4

Hospital	Control	Service	Staffed Beds	Admissions	Census	Outpatient Visits	Births	Total	Payroll	Personnel
★ △ MESA LUTHERAN HOSPITAL, 525 West Brown Road, Zip 85201–3299; tel. 602/834–1211; Robert A. Rundio, Executive Director of Hospital Operations (Total facility includes 60 beds in nursing home–type unit) **A**1 2 7 9 10 **F**4 7 8 10 12 14 15 16 17 18 19 20 21 22 23 25 26 27 28 29 30 32 33 34 35 36 37 39 40 41 42 43 44 45 46 48 49 51 52 57 59 64 65 67 70 71 72 73 74 **P**1 3 5 **S** Lutheran Health Systems, Fargo, ND **N** Lutheran Healthcare Network, Mesa, AZ	23	10	278	11809	165	57170	2153	95762	39566	1141
★ VALLEY LUTHERAN HOSPITAL, 6644 Baywood Avenue, Zip 85206–1797; tel. 602/981–2000; Robert A. Rundio, Executive Director of Hospital Operations **A**1 9 10 **F**4 7 8 10 12 14 15 16 17 18 19 20 21 22 23 25 26 27 28 29 30 32 33 34 35 36 37 39 40 41 42 43 44 45 46 49 57 60 65 67 70 71 73 74 **P**1 3 5 **S** Lutheran Health Systems, Fargo, ND **N** Lutheran Healthcare Network, Mesa, AZ	23	10	231	11305	141	84641	829	76392	32581	—
NOGALES—Santa Cruz County										
★ CARONDELET HOLY CROSS HOSPITAL, 1171 Target Range Road, Zip 85621–2496; tel. 520/287–2771; Carol Field, Senior Corporate Director and Administrator (Total facility includes 49 beds in nursing home–type unit) (Nonreporting) **A**1 9 10 **S** Carondelet Health System, Saint Louis, MO **N** Carondelet Health Network, Inc., Tucson, AZ	21	10	80	—	—	—	—	—	—	—
PAGE—Coconino County										
★ PAGE HOSPITAL, 501 North Navajo Drive, Zip 86040, Mailing Address: P.O. Box 1447, Zip 86040–1447; tel. 520/645–2424; Richard Polheber, Chief Executive Officer **A**1 9 10 **F**1 7 8 12 15 16 19 22 28 30 31 32 34 35 40 41 42 44 46 48 49 65 71 73 **P**3 5 7 **S** Samaritan Health System, Phoenix, AZ	23	10	25	503	4	15318	187	6582	3062	73
PARKER—La Paz County										
★ ○ LA PAZ REGIONAL HOSPITAL, (Formerly Parker Community Hospital), 1200 Mohave Road, Zip 85344–6349, Mailing Address: P.O. Box 1149, Zip 85344–1149; tel. 520/669–9201; William G. Coe, Executive Vice President and Chief Executive Officer (Nonreporting) **A**9 10 11 **S** Baptist Hospitals and Health Systems, Inc., Phoenix, AZ	23	10	39	—	—	—	—	—	—	—
★ U. S. PUBLIC HEALTH SERVICE INDIAN HOSPITAL, Mailing Address: Route 1, Box 12, Zip 85344; tel. 520/669–2137; Gary Davis, Service Unit Director (Nonreporting) **A**1 10 **S** U. S. Public Health Service Indian Health Service, Rockville, MD	47	10	18	—	—	—	—	—	—	—
PAYSON—Gila County										
★ PAYSON REGIONAL MEDICAL CENTER, 807 South Ponderosa Street, Zip 85541–5599; tel. 520/474–3222; Duane H. Anderson, Chief Executive Officer **A**1 9 10 **F**7 8 11 12 19 22 26 28 29 30 32 34 35 40 41 42 44 46 49 60 65 66 67 68 70 71 73 **S** Community Health Systems, Inc., Brentwood, TN **N** Arizona Voluntary Hospital Federation, Tempe, AZ	33	10	49	1842	18	24083	151	15407	6943	188
PHOENIX—Maricopa County										
□ ARIZONA STATE HOSPITAL, 2500 East Van Buren Street, Zip 85008–6079; tel. 602/244–1331; Jack B. Silver, M.P.H., Chief Executive Officer **A**1 **F**1 2 3 4 5 6 7 8 9 10 11 12 14 15 16 17 18 19 20 21 22 23 26 27 28 29 30 31 32 33 34 35 37 39 40 41 42 43 44 45 46 49 50 51 52 53 54 55 56 57 58 59 60 61 63 64 65 67 68 69 70 71 72 73 74 **P**6	12	22	315	335	315	—	—	34437	13335	484
★ CARL T. HAYDEN VETERANS AFFAIRS MEDICAL CENTER, 650 East Indian School Road, Zip 85012–1894; tel. 602/277–5551; John R. Fears, Director (Total facility includes 120 beds in nursing home–type unit) **A**1 2 3 5 **F**1 2 3 4 8 9 10 11 12 14 16 17 18 19 20 21 22 23 24 25 26 27 28 29 30 31 32 33 34 35 37 39 40 41 42 43 44 45 46 48 49 50 51 52 54 56 57 58 60 63 64 65 67 69 71 72 73 74 **P**6 **S** Department of Veterans Affairs, Washington, DC	45	10	365	9604	254	315055	—	136647	62857	1700
★ COLUMBIA MEDICAL CENTER PHOENIX, 1947 East Thomas Road, Zip 85016–7795; tel. 602/650–7600; Denny W. Powell, Chief Executive Officer (Total facility includes 13 beds in nursing home–type unit) **A**1 9 10 **F**4 8 10 11 12 15 16 17 19 21 22 26 28 29 30 32 34 35 37 39 41 42 43 44 48 49 54 57 63 65 67 69 70 71 73 **S** Columbia/HCA Healthcare Corporation, Nashville, TN **N**	32	10	290	7654	108	25038	0	67845	24371	660
COLUMBIA PARADISE VALLEY HOSPITAL See Paradise Valley Hospital										
★ ○ COMMUNITY HOSPITAL MEDICAL CENTER, 6501 North 19th Avenue, Zip 85015–1690; tel. 602/249–3434; Patrick Walz, Chief Executive Officer (Nonreporting) **A**1 10 11 12 13 **S** TENET Healthcare Corporation, Santa Barbara, CA	33	10	59	—	—	—	—	—	—	—
★ △ GOOD SAMARITAN REGIONAL MEDICAL CENTER, 1111 East McDowell Road, Zip 85006–2666, Mailing Address: P.O. Box 2989, Zip 85062–2989; tel. 602/239–2000; Steven L. Seiler, Senior Vice President and Chief Executive Officer (Total facility includes 158 beds in nursing home–type unit) **A**1 2 3 5 7 8 9 10 **F**3 4 5 7 8 10 14 15 16 19 21 22 23 26 29 31 32 35 37 39 40 41 42 43 44 48 49 50 52 53 54 55 57 58 59 60 61 63 64 65 69 70 71 72 73 74 **P**3 5 7 **S** Samaritan Health System, Phoenix, AZ **N** Samaritan Health Services, Phoenix, AZ	23	10	714	27299	463	193064	6949	273081	97958	3315
★ ○ JOHN C LINCOLN HOSPITAL–DEER VALLEY, (Formerly John C Lincoln Health Network), 19829 North 27th Avenue, Zip 85027–4002; tel. 602/879–6100; Tim Tracy, Senior Vice President and Chief Operating Officer (Total facility includes 23 beds in nursing home–type unit) (Nonreporting) **A**9 10 11 13	23	10	97	—	—	—	—	—	—	—
★ JOHN C. LINCOLN HEALTH NETWORK, (Formerly John C Lincoln Hospital and Health Center), 250 East Dunlap Avenue, Zip 85020–2446; tel. 602/943–2381; Dan C. Coleman, President and Chief Executive Officer (Total facility includes 22 beds in nursing home–type unit) (Nonreporting) **A**1 9 10	23	10	223	—	—	—	—	—	—	—

Hospital, Address, Telephone, Administrator, Approval, Facility, and Physician Codes, Health Care System, Network	Classi-fication Codes		Utilization Data					Expense (thousands) of dollars		
★ American Hospital Association (AHA) membership □ Joint Commission on Accreditation of Healthcare Organizations (JCAHO) accreditation + American Osteopathic Healthcare Association (AOHA) membership ○ American Osteopathic Association (AOA) accreditation △ Commission on Accreditation of Rehabilitation Facilities (CARF) accreditation Control codes 61, 63, 64, 71, 72 and 73 indicate hospitals listed by AOHA, but not registered by AHA. For definition of numerical codes, see page A4	Control	Service	Staffed Beds	Admissions	Census	Outpatient Visits	Births	Total	Payroll	Personnel
✚ MARICOPA MEDICAL CENTER, 2601 East Roosevelt Street, Zip 85008–4956, Mailing Address: P.O. Box 5099, Zip 85010–5099; tel. 602/267–5111; Frank D. Alvarez, Chief Executive Officer **A**1 2 3 5 8 9 10 12 **F**4 7 8 9 11 12 13 14 15 16 17 18 19 20 21 22 23 25 26 27 28 29 30 31 32 33 34 35 37 38 39 40 42 43 44 45 46 47 49 51 52 53 54 55 56 57 58 60 61 63 65 69 70 71 72 73 74 **P**1 **S** Quorum Health Group/Quorum Health Resources, Inc., Brentwood, TN **N** Maricopa Integrated Health System, Phoenix, AZ	13	10	491	18836	291	394650	2633	193764	78749	3782
✚ MARYVALE SAMARITAN MEDICAL CENTER, 5102 West Campbell Avenue, Zip 85031–1799; tel. 602/848–5000; Connie Beldon, Senior Administrator (Total facility includes 26 beds in nursing home–type unit) **A**1 2 9 10 **F**1 3 4 7 8 10 14 15 16 19 21 22 31 32 33 34 35 40 42 44 45 46 49 50 60 63 64 65 69 70 73 **P**3 5 7 **N** Samaritan Health Services, Phoenix, AZ	23	10	209	12288	116	71538	2748	63062	24357	708
✚ PARADISE VALLEY HOSPITAL, (Formerly Columbia Paradise Valley Hospital), 3929 East Bell Road, Zip 85032–2196; tel. 602/867–1881; Rebecca C. Kuhn, R.N., President and Chief Executive Officer (Total facility includes 15 beds in nursing home–type unit) **A**1 2 9 10 **F**7 8 10 11 12 19 22 23 26 30 32 33 35 37 39 40 42 44 48 49 57 59 60 64 65 67 71 73 74 **S** Columbia/HCA Healthcare Corporation, Nashville, TN	33	10	125	5923	55	45588	1162	33190	14729	392
✚ PHOENIX BAPTIST HOSPITAL AND MEDICAL CENTER, 2000 West Bethany Home Road, Zip 85015–2110; tel. 602/249–0212; Richard S. Alley, Chief Executive Officer **A**1 2 3 5 9 10 **F**1 4 6 7 8 10 11 12 16 17 19 21 22 25 26 28 29 30 32 33 34 35 37 40 42 43 44 49 62 63 64 65 67 70 71 73 74 **S** Baptist Hospitals and Health Systems, Inc., Phoenix, AZ **N** Baptist Hospitals and Health Systems, Phoenix, AZ	23	10	201	8678	106	108626	1495	81201	31668	—
✚ PHOENIX CHILDREN'S HOSPITAL, (Pediatric Tertiary Care), 1111 East McDowell Road, Zip 85006–2666, Mailing Address: 1300 North 12th Street, Suite 404, Zip 85006–2896; tel. 602/239–5960; Terrence Slaven, Interim President and Chief Executive Officer **A**1 3 5 9 **F**10 12 13 15 16 17 19 20 21 22 25 27 28 29 30 31 32 34 35 38 39 41 42 43 44 45 46 47 49 50 52 53 54 55 56 58 59 63 65 67 69 70 71 72 73	23	59	127	9476	160	40262	—	89721	33372	775
✚ PMH HEALTH SERVICES NETWORK, 1201 South Seventh Avenue, Zip 85007–3995; tel. 602/258–5111; Jeffrey K. Norman, Chief Executive Officer (Total facility includes 28 beds in nursing home–type unit) **A**1 2 9 10 **F**1 4 5 7 8 10 11 12 13 14 15 16 17 19 20 21 22 25 26 28 29 30 32 34 35 37 39 40 41 42 43 44 45 46 49 51 60 61 63 64 65 66 67 68 70 71 72 73 74 **S** PMH Health Resources, Inc., Phoenix, AZ **N** Arizona Voluntary Hospital Federation, Tempe, AZ	23	10	183	13644	126	200916	2098	117673	35538	920
✚ SAMARITAN–WENDY PAINE O'BRIEN TREATMENT CENTER, 5055 North 34th Street, Zip 85018–1498; tel. 602/955–6200; Robert F. Meyer, M.D., Chief Executive Officer (Nonreporting) **A**1 9 10 **S** Samaritan Health System, Phoenix, AZ **N** Samaritan Health Services, Phoenix, AZ	23	52	88	—	—	—	—	—	—	—
✚ △ ST. JOSEPH'S HOSPITAL AND MEDICAL CENTER, 350 West Thomas Road, Zip 85013–4496, Mailing Address: P.O. Box 2071, Zip 85001–2071; tel. 602/406–3100; Mary G. Yarbrough, President and Chief Executive Officer **A**1 2 3 5 7 8 9 10 **F**1 4 7 8 10 11 12 13 15 16 17 18 19 20 21 22 23 24 25 26 27 28 29 30 31 32 33 34 35 37 38 39 40 41 42 43 44 45 46 47 49 50 51 53 54 60 61 63 65 66 67 68 70 71 73 74 **P**1 6 **S** Catholic Healthcare West, San Francisco, CA **N** Catholic HealthCare West (CHW), San Francisco, CA	21	10	426	23764	322	391661	4416	263078	104705	3239
□ ST. LUKE'S BEHAVIORAL HEALTH CENTER, 1800 East Van Buren, Zip 85006–3742; tel. 602/251–8484; Patrick D. Waugh, Chief Executive Officer **A**1 9 10 **F**2 3 12 15 18 22 52 53 55 56 57 58 59 **S** TENET Healthcare Corporation, Santa Barbara, CA **N** Saint Lukes Health System, Phoenix, AZ	33	22	70	2016	35	3583	0	—	—	137
✚ ST. LUKE'S MEDICAL CENTER, 1800 East Van Buren Street, Zip 85006–3742; tel. 602/251–8100; William W. Webster, Chief Executive Officer (Total facility includes 55 beds in nursing home–type unit) (Nonreporting) **A**1 9 10 **S** TENET Healthcare Corporation, Santa Barbara, CA **N** Saint Lukes Health System, Phoenix, AZ	33	10	296	—	—	—	—	—	—	—
✚ U. S. PUBLIC HEALTH SERVICE PHOENIX INDIAN MEDICAL CENTER, 4212 North 16th Street, Zip 85016–5389; tel. 602/263–1200; Anna Albert, Chief Executive Officer **A**1 10 **F**4 7 8 10 11 12 13 14 15 16 17 19 20 21 22 23 25 26 27 28 29 30 31 32 34 35 37 39 40 42 43 44 45 46 49 51 53 54 56 58 60 61 65 67 68 69 71 73 74 **P**6 **S** U. S. Public Health Service Indian Health Service, Rockville, MD	47	10	137	5347	65	188885	735	45458	26919	742
□ VENCOR HOSPITAL–PHOENIX, 40 East Indianola Avenue, Zip 85012–2059; tel. 602/280–7000; John L. Harrington, Jr., FACHE, Administrator **A**1 **F**4 6 10 12 14 19 20 21 22 27 31 32 33 35 37 39 41 42 44 45 46 49 50 54 60 63 65 67 71 **S** Vencor, Incorporated, Louisville, KY	33	10	58	453	41	0	—	11341	5291	146
WESTBRIDGE TREATMENT CENTER, 1830 East Roosevelt Street, Zip 85006–3641; tel. 602/254–0884; Mike Perry, Chief Executive Officer (Nonreporting) **A**9 **S** Century Healthcare Corporation, Tulsa, OK	33	52	78	—	—	—	—	—	—	—
PRESCOTT—Yavapai County										
✚ VETERANS AFFAIRS MEDICAL CENTER, 500 Highway 89 North, Zip 86313–5000; tel. 520/445–4860; Patricia A. McKlem, Medical Center Director (Total facility includes 90 beds in nursing home–type unit) **A**1 **F**1 2 3 6 8 15 16 17 18 19 20 21 22 26 28 30 31 32 33 35 37 39 41 42 44 45 46 48 49 51 52 54 56 57 58 60 64 65 67 70 71 73 74 **P**6 **S** Department of Veterans Affairs, Washington, DC	45	10	235	2413	240	115627	—	40581	26564	564

Hospital, Address, Telephone, Administrator, Approval, Facility, and Physician Codes, Health Care System, Network	Classi-fication Codes		Utilization Data					Expense (thousands) of dollars		
	Control	Service	Staffed Beds	Admissions	Census	Outpatient Visits	Births	Total	Payroll	Personnel

Approval / membership key:

★ American Hospital Association (AHA) membership
□ Joint Commission on Accreditation of Healthcare Organizations (JCAHO) accreditation
+ American Osteopathic Healthcare Association (AOHA) membership
○ American Osteopathic Association (AOA) accreditation
△ Commission on Accreditation of Rehabilitation Facilities (CARF) accreditation
Control codes 61, 63, 64, 71, 72 and 73 indicate hospitals listed by AOHA, but not registered by AHA. For definition of numerical codes, see page A4

Hospital	Control	Service	Staffed Beds	Admissions	Census	Outpatient Visits	Births	Total	Payroll	Personnel
✠ YAVAPAI REGIONAL MEDICAL CENTER, 1003 Willow Creek Road, Zip 86301–1668; tel. 520/445–2700; Timothy Barnett, Chief Executive Officer (Nonreporting) **A**1 9 10 **N** Arizona Voluntary Hospital Federation, Tempe, AZ	23	10	84	—	—	—	—	—	—	—
SACATON—Pinal County										
✠ HUHUKAM MEMORIAL HOSPITAL, Seed Farm & Skill Center Road, Zip 85247–0038, Mailing Address: P.O. Box 38, Zip 85247–0038; tel. 602/562–3321; Viola L. Johnson, Chief Executive Officer (Nonreporting) **A**1 9 10 **S** U. S. Public Health Service Indian Health Service, Rockville, MD	47	10	10	—	—	—	—	—	—	—
SAFFORD—Graham County										
✠ MOUNT GRAHAM COMMUNITY HOSPITAL, 1600 20th Avenue, Zip 85546–4097; tel. 520/348–4000; Karl E. Johnson, Chief Executive Officer **A**1 9 10 **F**7 8 11 14 15 16 19 21 22 24 28 30 32 33 34 35 37 40 41 42 44 46 49 65 68 71 73 **P**8	16	10	44	2921	21	52448	589	15933	6513	240
SAN CARLOS—Gila County										
✠ U. S. PUBLIC HEALTH SERVICE INDIAN HOSPITAL, Mailing Address: P.O. Box 208, Zip 85550–0208; tel. 520/475–2371; Nella Ben, Chief Executive Officer (Nonreporting) **A**1 10 **S** U. S. Public Health Service Indian Health Service, Rockville, MD	47	10	28	—	—	—	—	—	—	—
SCOTTSDALE—Maricopa County										
□ △ HEALTHSOUTH MERIDIAN POINT REHABILITATION HOSPITAL, 11250 North 92nd Street, Zip 85260–6148; tel. 602/860–0671; Michael S. Wallace, Chief Executive Officer **A**1 7 10 **F**1 5 12 14 15 16 20 26 27 34 42 46 48 49 53 54 55 57 58 67 73 **P**5 **S** HEALTHSOUTH Corporation, Birmingham, AL	33	46	43	606	25	5442	0	6206	3123	—
★ SAMARITAN BEHAVIORAL HEALTH CENTER–SCOTTSDALE, 7575 East Earll Drive, Zip 85251–6998; tel. 602/941–7500; Robert F. Meyer, M.D., Chief Executive Officer (Nonreporting) **A**9 10 **S** Samaritan Health System, Phoenix, AZ **N** Samaritan Health Services, Phoenix, AZ	23	22	60	—	—	—	—	—	—	—
✠ △ SCOTTSDALE HEALTHCARE–OSBORN, (Formerly Scottsdale Memorial Hospital), 7400 East Osborn Road, Zip 85251–6403; tel. 602/675–4000; David R. Carpenter, FACHE, Senior Vice President and Administrator (Total facility includes 60 beds in nursing home–type unit) **A**1 2 3 5 7 9 10 **F**1 4 7 8 10 11 12 13 14 15 16 17 19 21 22 24 25 26 27 28 29 30 32 33 34 35 36 37 39 40 41 42 43 44 45 46 48 49 51 54 56 60 61 63 64 65 67 70 71 72 73 **P**1 3 **S** Scottsdale Healthcare, Scottsdale, AZ	23	10	328	14038	184	65678	1243	145447	60590	2313
✠ SCOTTSDALE HEALTHCARE–SHEA, (Formerly Scottsdale Memorial Hospital–North), 9003 East Shea Boulevard, Zip 85260–6771; tel. 602/860–3000; Thomas J. Sadvary, FACHE, Senior Vice President and Administrator **A**1 2 3 5 9 10 **F**1 2 3 4 5 6 7 8 9 10 11 12 13 14 15 16 17 18 19 20 21 22 23 24 25 26 27 28 29 30 31 32 33 34 35 36 37 38 39 40 41 42 43 44 45 46 47 48 49 51 52 56 60 61 63 64 65 67 68 69 70 71 72 73 74 **P**1 3 7 **S** Scottsdale Healthcare, Scottsdale, AZ	23	10	250	16246	178	68595	2405		—	1181
SELLS—Pima County										
✠ U. S. PUBLIC HEALTH SERVICE INDIAN HOSPITAL, Mailing Address: P.O. Box 548, Zip 85634–0548; tel. 520/383–7251; Darrell Rumley, Service Unit Director and Chief Executive Officer (Nonreporting) **A**1 10 **S** U. S. Public Health Service Indian Health Service, Rockville, MD	47	10	34	—	—	—	—	—	—	—
SHOW LOW—Navajo County										
✠ NAVAPACHE REGIONAL MEDICAL CENTER, 2200 Show Low Lake Road, Zip 85901–7800; tel. 520/537–4375; Leigh Cox, Administrator **A**1 9 10 **F**7 8 12 14 15 16 17 19 22 24 29 30 32 35 37 40 41 44 49 63 65 71 73 **S** Brim, Inc., Portland, OR	23	10	52	3752	29	40304	702	21892	10571	365
SIERRA VISTA—Cochise County										
✠ SIERRA VISTA COMMUNITY HOSPITAL, 300 El Camino Real, Zip 85635–2899; tel. 520/458–4641; Dale A. Decker, Chief Executive Officer **A**1 9 10 **F**7 8 15 17 19 21 22 28 29 32 33 34 35 37 39 40 44 48 49 65 71 73 **P**4 5	23	10	60	3955	30	136554	1086	27755	12922	407
SPRINGERVILLE—Apache County										
✠ WHITE MOUNTAIN REGIONAL MEDICAL CENTER, (Formerly White Mountain Community Hospital), 118 South Mountain Avenue, Zip 85938, Mailing Address: P.O. Box 880, Zip 85938–0880; tel. 520/333–4368; David J. Ross, Chief Executive Officer (Total facility includes 64 beds in nursing home–type unit) (Nonreporting) **A**1 9 10 **N** Samaritan Health Services, Phoenix, AZ	23	10	89	—	—	—	—	—	—	—
SUN CITY—Maricopa County										
✠ WALTER O. BOSWELL MEMORIAL HOSPITAL, 10401 West Thunderbird Boulevard, Zip 85351–3092, Mailing Address: P.O. Box 1690, Zip 85372–1690; tel. 602/876–5356; George Perez, Executive Vice President and Chief Operating Officer (Total facility includes 45 beds in nursing home–type unit) **A**1 2 9 10 **F**4 8 10 11 12 17 19 21 22 24 26 27 28 29 30 32 33 34 35 36 37 41 42 43 44 45 48 49 54 55 56 57 58 59 60 64 65 67 71 73 **P**1 6 7 **S** Sun Health Corporation, Sun City, AZ **N** Sun Health Corporation, Sun City, AZ	23	10	268	14103	206	70292	—	105477	39006	1075
SUN CITY WEST—Maricopa County										
✠ DEL E. WEBB MEMORIAL HOSPITAL, 14502 West Meeker Boulevard, Zip 85375–5299, Mailing Address: P.O. Box 5169, Sun City, Zip 85375–5169; tel. 602/214–4000; Thomas C. Dickson, Executive Vice President and Chief Operating Officer (Total facility includes 40 beds in nursing home–type unit) **A**1 9 10 **F**1 3 4 8 10 11 12 15 16 17 19 21 22 26 27 28 29 30 31 32 33 34 35 36 39 41 42 43 44 45 46 48 49 52 54 55 56 57 58 59 60 64 65 67 70 71 73 **P**1 5 **S** Sun Health Corporation, Sun City, AZ **N** Sun Health Corporation, Sun City, AZ	23	10	177	5885	100	48501	0	40361	16181	449

Hospital, Address, Telephone, Administrator, Approval, Facility, and Physician Codes, Health Care System, Network	Classi-fication Codes		Utilization Data					Expense (thousands) of dollars		
	Control	Service	Staffed Beds	Admissions	Census	Outpatient Visits	Births	Total	Payroll	Personnel

★ American Hospital Association (AHA) membership
□ Joint Commission on Accreditation of Healthcare Organizations (JCAHO) accreditation
+ American Osteopathic Healthcare Association (AOHA) membership
○ American Osteopathic Association (AOA) accreditation
△ Commission on Accreditation of Rehabilitation Facilities (CARF) accreditation
  Control codes 61, 63, 64, 71, 72 and 73 indicate hospitals listed by AOHA, but not registered by AHA. For definition of numerical codes, see page A4

TEMPE—Maricopa County

☒ TEMPE ST. LUKE'S HOSPITAL, 1500 South Mill Avenue, Zip 85281–6699; tel. 602/784–5510; Mary Jo Gregory, Chief Executive Officer (Nonreporting) **A**1 9 10 12 13 **S** TENET Healthcare Corporation, Santa Barbara, CA **N** Saint Lukes Health System, Phoenix, AZ — *33 10 110*

| | 33 | 10 | 110 | — | — | — | — | — | — | — |

TUBA CITY—Coconino County

☒ TUBA CITY INDIAN MEDICAL CENTER, Main Street, Zip 86045–6211, Mailing Address: P.O. Box 600, Zip 86045–6211; tel. 520/283–2827; Susie John, M.D., Chief Executive Officer **A**1 10 **F**3 7 14 15 16 17 19 20 22 27 30 34 37 40 44 45 46 49 51 53 54 55 56 58 61 65 71 **S** U. S. Public Health Service Indian Health Service, Rockville, MD

| | 47 | 10 | 69 | 4065 | 37 | 129508 | 643 | 24527 | 14003 | 463 |

TUCSON—Pima County

☒ △ CARONDELET ST. JOSEPH'S HOSPITAL, 350 North Wilmot Road, Zip 85711–2678; tel. 520/296–3211; Sister St. Joan Willert, President and Chief Executive Officer **A**1 7 9 10 **F**3 4 7 8 9 10 11 12 14 15 16 17 18 19 21 22 25 28 29 30 31 32 33 34 35 37 39 40 41 42 43 44 46 48 49 53 54 55 56 57 58 59 63 64 65 67 68 71 72 73 74 **P**1 2 6 7 **S** Carondelet Health System, Saint Louis, MO **N** Carondelet Health Network, Inc., Tucson, AZ

| | 21 | 10 | 300 | 13112 | 160 | 105563 | 2007 | 91827 | 42586 | 1242 |

☒ △ CARONDELET ST. MARY'S HOSPITAL, 1601 West St. Mary's Road, Zip 85745–2682; tel. 520/622–5833; Sister St. Joan Willert, President and Chief Executive Officer **A**1 7 9 10 **F**4 7 8 9 10 11 12 14 15 16 17 19 21 22 26 28 29 30 31 32 33 34 35 36 37 39 40 41 42 43 44 46 48 49 52 53 54 55 56 57 58 59 63 65 67 68 71 72 73 74 **P**1 2 6 7 **S** Carondelet Health System, Saint Louis, MO **N** Carondelet Health Network, Inc., Tucson, AZ

| | 21 | 10 | 354 | 16991 | 220 | 128545 | 721 | 133916 | 62998 | 1780 |

COLUMBIA EL DORADO HOSPITAL See El Dorado Hospital

DESERT HILLS CENTER FOR YOUTH AND FAMILIES, 2797 North Introspect Drive, Zip 85745–9491; tel. 520/622–5437; Richard R. Hardin, Chief Executive Officer (Nonreporting) **A**3

| | 33 | 52 | 140 | — | — | — | — | — | — | — |

☒ △ EL DORADO HOSPITAL, (Formerly Columbia El Dorado Hospital), 1400 North Wilmot Road, Zip 85712–4498, Mailing Address: P.O. Box 13070, Zip 85732–3070; tel. 520/886–6361; Rhonda Dean, Chief Executive Officer **A**1 7 9 10 **F**4 8 10 11 12 15 16 19 22 26 28 32 34 35 36 37 39 41 43 44 48 49 52 57 64 65 71 73 **P**5 6 7 **S** Columbia/HCA Healthcare Corporation, Nashville, TN

| | 33 | 10 | 166 | 4277 | 68 | 21460 | — | 30109 | 13339 | — |

□ △ HEALTHSOUTH REHABILITATION INSTITUTE OF TUCSON, 2650 North Wyatt Drive, Zip 85712–6108; tel. 520/325–1300; Jay Underwood, Chief Executive Officer (Nonreporting) **A**1 7 10 **S** HEALTHSOUTH Corporation, Birmingham, AL

| | 33 | 46 | 80 | — | — | — | — | — | — | — |

□ KINO COMMUNITY HOSPITAL, 2800 East Ajo Way, Zip 85713–6289; tel. 520/294–4471; Richard Carmona, M.D., Chief Executive Officer (Total facility includes 20 beds in nursing home–type unit) (Nonreporting) **A**1 3 5 9 10

| | 13 | 10 | 114 | — | — | — | — | — | — | — |

☒ NORTHWEST MEDICAL CENTER, (Formerly Northwest Hospital), 6200 North La Cholla Boulevard, Zip 85741–3599; tel. 520/742–9000; W. Jefferson Comer, FACHE, Chief Executive Officer (Total facility includes 16 beds in nursing home–type unit) (Nonreporting) **A**1 2 9 10 **S** Columbia/HCA Healthcare Corporation, Nashville, TN

| | 33 | 10 | 152 | — | — | — | — | — | — | — |

PALO VERDE MENTAL HEALTH SERVICES See Tucson Medical Center

SIERRA TUCSON, 16500 North Lago Del Oro Parkway, Zip 85739–9631; tel. 520/624–4000; Terry A. Stephens, Executive Director (Nonreporting)

| | 33 | 49 | 70 | — | — | — | — | — | — | — |

☒ ○ TUCSON GENERAL HOSPITAL, 3838 North Campbell Avenue, Zip 85719–1497; tel. 520/318–6300; Allan Harrington, Jr., Chief Executive Officer (Nonreporting) **A**1 9 10 11 12 13 **S** TENET Healthcare Corporation, Santa Barbara, CA

| | 33 | 10 | 80 | — | — | — | — | — | — | — |

☒ TUCSON MEDICAL CENTER, (Includes Palo Verde Mental Health Services, 2695 North Craycroft, Zip 85712–2244; tel. 520/324–5438), 5301 East Grant Road, Zip 85712–2874; tel. 520/324–5438; Darrell P. Thorpe, M.D., President and Chief Executive Officer (Nonreporting) **A**1 2 3 5 9 10

| | 23 | 10 | 523 | — | — | — | — | — | — | — |

☒ UNIVERSITY MEDICAL CENTER, 1501 North Campbell Avenue, Zip 85724–0002; tel. 520/694–0111; Gregory A. Pivirotto, President and Chief Executive Officer (Nonreporting) **A**1 3 5 8 9 10 **N** Arizona Voluntary Hospital Federation, Tempe, AZ

| | 23 | 10 | 322 | — | — | — | — | — | — | — |

□ VENCOR HOSPITAL – TUCSON, 355 North Wilmot Road, Zip 85711–2635; tel. 520/747–8200; Kevin Christiansen, Chief Executive Officer (Nonreporting) **A**1 **S** Vencor, Incorporated, Louisville, KY

| | 33 | 49 | 51 | — | — | — | — | — | — | — |

☒ VETERANS AFFAIRS MEDICAL CENTER, 3601 South 6th Avenue, Zip 85723–0002; tel. 520/792–1450; Jonathan H. Gardner, Chief Executive Officer (Total facility includes 66 beds in nursing home–type unit) **A**1 3 5 8 9 **F**2 3 4 5 6 8 10 11 17 19 20 21 22 23 25 26 27 28 29 30 31 32 33 34 35 37 39 41 42 43 44 45 46 48 49 51 52 54 55 56 57 58 60 63 64 65 66 67 71 72 73 74 **P**6 **S** Department of Veterans Affairs, Washington, DC

| | 45 | 10 | 306 | 5793 | 137 | 235560 | — | 111784 | 51579 | 1544 |

WHITERIVER—Navajo County

☒ U. S. PUBLIC HEALTH SERVICE INDIAN HOSPITAL, State Route 73, Box 860, Zip 85941–0860; tel. 520/338–4911; Carla Alchesay–Nachu, Service Unit Director (Nonreporting) **A**1 **S** U. S. Public Health Service Indian Health Service, Rockville, MD

| | 47 | 10 | 45 | — | — | — | — | — | — | — |

WICKENBURG—Maricopa County

☒ WICKENBURG REGIONAL HOSPITAL, 520 Rose Lane, Zip 85390–1447; tel. 520/684–5421; Carol Schmoyer, Administrator (Total facility includes 57 beds in nursing home–type unit) **A**1 9 10 **F**8 17 19 22 28 29 34 37 39 44 48 49 64 65 71 73 **S** Lutheran Health Systems, Fargo, ND

| | 23 | 10 | 80 | 636 | 48 | 10209 | 1 | 6151 | 2768 | 131 |

Hospital, Address, Telephone, Administrator, Approval, Facility, and Physician Codes, Health Care System, Network	Classi-fication Codes		Utilization Data					Expense (thousands) of dollars		
★ American Hospital Association (AHA) membership □ Joint Commission on Accreditation of Healthcare Organizations (JCAHO) accreditation + American Osteopathic Healthcare Association (AOHA) membership ○ American Osteopathic Association (AOA) accreditation △ Commission on Accreditation of Rehabilitation Facilities (CARF) accreditation Control codes 61, 63, 64, 71, 72 and 73 indicate hospitals listed by AOHA, but not registered by AHA. For definition of numerical codes, see page A4	Control	Service	Staffed Beds	Admissions	Census	Outpatient Visits	Births	Total	Payroll	Personnel

WILLCOX—Cochise County

✠ NORTHERN COCHISE COMMUNITY HOSPITAL, 901 West Rex Allen Drive, Zip 85643–1009; tel. 520/384–3541; Chris Cronberg, Chief Executive Officer (Total facility includes 24 beds in nursing home–type unit) **A**1 9 10 **F**7 8 12 14 15 16 19 22 26 28 29 34 39 44 46 49 51 64 65 71 73 **S** Brim, Inc., Portland, OR	16	10	48	591	28	—	53	5931	2969	95

WINSLOW—Navajo County

★ WINSLOW MEMORIAL HOSPITAL, 1501 Williamson Avenue, Zip 86047–2797; tel. 520/289–4691; Michael King, Administrator (Nonreporting) **A**9 10	33	10	34	—	—	—	—	—	—	—

YUMA—Imperial County

U. S. PUBLIC HEALTH SERVICE INDIAN HOSPITAL See Winterhaven, CA										
✠ YUMA REGIONAL MEDICAL CENTER, 2400 South Avenue A., Zip 85364–7170; tel. 520/344–2000; Robert T. Olsen, CHE, President and Chief Executive Officer (Total facility includes 20 beds in nursing home–type unit) **A**1 9 10 **F**4 7 8 10 11 12 15 16 17 19 20 21 22 23 24 26 28 30 31 32 34 35 37 39 40 41 42 44 56 60 64 65 67 70 71 73 **P**5 8 **N** Arizona Voluntary Hospital Federation, Tempe, AZ	23	10	258	13888	157	—	2949	82588	35617	1095

ARKANSAS

Resident population 2,553 (in thousands)
Resident population in metro areas 45.0%
Birth rate per 1,000 population 14.2
65 years and over 14.4%
Percent of persons without health insurance 21.7%

Hospital, Address, Telephone, Administrator, Approval, Facility, and Physician Codes, Health Care System, Network	Classi-fication Codes		Utilization Data					Expense (thousands) of dollars		
★ American Hospital Association (AHA) membership ☐ Joint Commission on Accreditation of Healthcare Organizations (JCAHO) accreditation + American Osteopathic Healthcare Association (AOHA) membership ○ American Osteopathic Association (AOA) accreditation △ Commission on Accreditation of Rehabilitation Facilities (CARF) accreditation Control codes 61, 63, 64, 71, 72 and 73 indicate hospitals listed by AOHA, but not registered by AHA. For definition of numerical codes, see page A4	Control	Service	Staffed Beds	Admissions	Census	Outpatient Visits	Births	Total	Payroll	Personnel

ARKADELPHIA—Clark County

✠ BAPTIST MEDICAL CENTER ARKADELPHIA, 3050 Twin Rivers Drive, Zip 71923–4299; tel. 870/245–1100; Dan Gathright, Senior Vice President and Administrator **A**1 9 10 **F**7 8 12 15 16 19 21 22 27 30 31 32 33 35 36 37 40 41 42 44 49 65 71 73 **P**1 3 5 6 7 **S** Baptist Health, Little Rock, AR **N** Arkansas' FirstSource, Little Rock, AR; Baptist Health, Little Rock, AR	23	10	57	1622	19	19910	225	13745	5146	235

ASHDOWN—Little River County

LITTLE RIVER MEMORIAL HOSPITAL, Fifth and Locke Streets, Zip 71822–0577, Mailing Address: P.O. Box 577, Zip 71822–0577; tel. 870/898–5011; Judy Adams, Administrator and Chief Executive Officer **A**10 **F**8 11 15 16 19 22 32 41 44 49 63 71 **P**5 **N** Arkansas' FirstSource, Little Rock, AR	13	10	33	985	12	6203	—	4881	2339	116

BATESVILLE—Independence County

✠ WHITE RIVER MEDICAL CENTER, 1710 Harrison Street, Zip 72501–2197, Mailing Address: P.O. Box 2197, Zip 72503–2197; tel. 870/793–1200; Gary Bebow, Administrator and Chief Executive Officer **A**1 9 10 **F**7 8 10 11 12 14 15 16 19 21 22 28 30 31 32 34 35 37 40 41 42 44 46 49 50 57 63 64 65 66 71 73 **P**3 8 **N** Arkansas' FirstSource, Little Rock, AR	23	10	146	8032	105	59904	420	—	18183	665

BENTON—Saline County

☐ RIVENDELL BEHAVIORAL HEALTH SERVICES, 100 Rivendell Drive, Zip 72015–9100; tel. 501/316–1255; Mark E. Schneider, Chief Executive Officer (Nonreporting) **A**1 9 10 **S** Children's Comprehensive Services, Inc., Nashville, TN	33	52	77	—	—	—	—	—	—	—
✠ SALINE MEMORIAL HOSPITAL, 1 Medical Park Drive, Zip 72015–3354; tel. 501/776–6000; Roger D. Feldt, FACHE, President and Chief Executive Officer (Total facility includes 12 beds in nursing home–type unit) **A**1 9 10 **F**7 8 12 19 21 22 32 33 34 35 37 40 44 52 57 64 65 71 73 **P**8 **S** Quorum Health Group/Quorum Health Resources, Inc., Brentwood, TN **N** Arkansas' FirstSource, Little Rock, AR; Arkansas Network, North Little Rock, AR	23	10	141	4488	61	39127	365	28799	11943	490

BENTONVILLE—Benton County

BATES MEDICAL CENTER See Northwest Medical Center, Springdale

BERRYVILLE—Carroll County

★ CARROLL REGIONAL MEDICAL CENTER, 214 Carter Street, Zip 72616–4303; tel. 870/423–3355; J. Rudy Darling, President and Chief Executive Officer **A**9 10 **F**8 12 15 16 19 20 22 28 29 30 31 32 33 37 39 40 41 44 45 46 49 51 57 64 65 67 71 73 74 **P**1 **S** Sisters of Mercy Health System–St. Louis, Saint Louis, MO **N** Arkansas' FirstSource, Little Rock, AR	23	10	38	1724	15	14391	231	10135	4879	—

BLYTHEVILLE—Mississippi County

✠ BAPTIST MEMORIAL HOSPITAL–BLYTHEVILLE, 1520 North Division Street, Zip 72315, Mailing Address: P.O. Box 108, Zip 72316–0108; tel. 870/838–7300; Al Sypniewski, Administrator (Total facility includes 70 beds in nursing home–type unit) **A**1 9 10 **F**3 8 11 12 13 14 15 16 17 19 21 22 23 24 27 28 29 30 31 32 33 35 37 39 40 41 42 44 45 46 49 52 53 57 58 59 60 65 67 71 73 **P**3 7 8 **S** Baptist Memorial Health Care Corporation, Memphis, TN **N** Arkansas' FirstSource, Little Rock, AR	21	10	210	3318	106	30573	726	17474	6418	297

BOONEVILLE—Logan County

★ BOONEVILLE COMMUNITY HOSPITAL, 880 West Main Street, Zip 72927–3420, Mailing Address: P.O. Box 290, Zip 72927–0290; tel. 501/675–2800; Robert R. Bash, Administrator **A**9 10 **F**8 19 22 30 32 34 44 49 65 71 73 **P**1 **N** Arkansas' FirstSource, Little Rock, AR	23	10	26	554	8	19647	—	2777	1637	80

CALICO ROCK—Izard County

MEDICAL CENTER OF CALICO ROCK, 103 Grasse Street, Zip 72519, Mailing Address: P.O. Box 438, Zip 72519–0438; tel. 870/297–3726; Terry L. Amstutz, CHE, Chief Executive Officer and Administrator (Nonreporting) **A**10 **N** Arkansas' FirstSource, Little Rock, AR	23	10	26	—	—	—	—	—	—	—

CAMDEN—Ouachita County

✠ OUACHITA MEDICAL CENTER, 638 California Street, Zip 71701–4699, Mailing Address: P.O. Box 797, Zip 71701–0797; tel. 870/836–1000; C. C. McAllister, President and Chief Executive Officer **A**1 9 10 **F**1 2 3 7 8 12 14 15 16 17 19 21 22 26 27 28 30 32 33 34 36 37 40 42 44 45 46 49 51 52 57 63 65 67 71 73 **P**1 **N** Arkansas' FirstSource, Little Rock, AR; Arkansas Network, North Little Rock, AR	23	10	118	3511	47	23258	354	18951	9956	515

CHEROKEE VILLAGE—Sharp County

✠ EASTERN OZARKS REGIONAL HEALTH SYSTEM, 122 South Allegheny Drive, Zip 72529–7300; tel. 870/257–4101; Cindy Hall, Administrator (Nonreporting) **A**1 9 10 **N** Arkansas' FirstSource, Little Rock, AR	33	10	40	—	—	—	—	—	—	—

CLARKSVILLE—Johnson County

JOHNSON REGIONAL MEDICAL CENTER, 1100 East Poplar Street, Zip 72830–4419, Mailing Address: P.O. Box 738, Zip 72830–0738; tel. 501/754–5454; Kenneth R. Wood, Administrator (Nonreporting) **A**9 10 **N** Arkansas' FirstSource, Little Rock, AR	23	10	58	—	—	—	—	—	—	—

Hospital, Address, Telephone, Administrator, Approval, Facility, and Physician Codes, Health Care System, Network	Classi-fication Codes		Utilization Data					Expense (thousands) of dollars		
★ American Hospital Association (AHA) membership ☐ Joint Commission on Accreditation of Healthcare Organizations (JCAHO) accreditation + American Osteopathic Healthcare Association (AOHA) membership ○ American Osteopathic Association (AOA) accreditation △ Commission on Accreditation of Rehabilitation Facilities (CARF) accreditation Control codes 61, 63, 64, 71, 72 and 73 indicate hospitals listed by AOHA, but not registered by AHA. For definition of numerical codes, see page A4	Control	Service	Staffed Beds	Admissions	Census	Outpatient Visits	Births	Total	Payroll	Personnel

CLINTON—Van Buren County

VAN BUREN COUNTY MEMORIAL HOSPITAL, Highway 65 South, Zip 72031, Mailing Address: P.O. Box 206, Zip 72031–0206; tel. 501/745–2401; Barry Brady, Administrator (Total facility includes 120 beds in nursing home–type unit) **A**9 10 **F**8 12 15 16 22 26 27 28 29 30 34 44 45 49 64 65 71 **P**8 **S** United Hospital Corporation, Memphis, TN **N** Arkansas' FirstSource, Little Rock, AR — 23 10 | 144 | 525 | 5 | 10990 | 2 | 2941 | 1757 | 160

CONWAY—Faulkner County

✠ CONWAY REGIONAL MEDICAL CENTER, 2302 College Avenue, Zip 72032–6297; tel. 501/329–3831; James A. Summersett, III, FACHE, President and Chief Executive Officer **A**1 9 10 **F**7 8 10 11 12 14 15 16 19 20 21 22 24 28 32 34 35 37 40 41 44 46 49 52 57 60 64 65 66 71 73 **P**3 8 **N** Arkansas' FirstSource, Little Rock, AR — 23 10 | 116 | 5980 | 60 | 51614 | 1138 | 51220 | 21270 | 785

CROSSETT—Ashley County

★ ASHLEY COUNTY MEDICAL CENTER, (Formerly Ashley Memorial Hospital), 1015 Unity Road, Zip 71635–2930, Mailing Address: P.O. Box 400, Zip 71635–0400; tel. 870/364–4111; Ernie Helin, Chief Executive Officer **A**9 10 **F**8 15 16 19 21 22 24 26 32 34 35 37 42 44 51 52 57 58 62 65 67 71 73 **P**5 — 23 10 | 44 | 1459 | 12 | 25599 | 4 | 8677 | 4070 | 158

DANVILLE—Yell County

CHAMBERS MEMORIAL HOSPITAL, Highway 10 at Detroit, Zip 72833, Mailing Address: P.O. Box 639, Zip 72833–0639; tel. 501/495–2241; Scott Peek, Administrator **A**10 **F**19 22 32 40 44 49 65 71 **N** Arkansas' FirstSource, Little Rock, AR — 13 10 | 41 | 918 | 9 | 43222 | 56 | — | 2378 | 99

DARDANELLE—Yell County

DARDANELLE HOSPITAL, 200 North Third Street, Zip 72834–3802, Mailing Address: P.O. Box 578, Zip 72834–0578; tel. 501/229–4677; Shawn Cathey, Administrator **A**9 10 **F**8 14 16 19 21 22 23 26 28 29 30 32 44 46 57 64 66 71 — 13 10 | 44 | 1220 | 16 | 12328 | 0 | 3421 | 1979 | 84

DE QUEEN—Sevier County

★ COLUMBIA DE QUEEN REGIONAL MEDICAL CENTER, 1306 Collin Raye Drive, Zip 71832–2198; tel. 501/584–4111; Charles H. Long, Chief Executive Officer **A**9 10 **F**7 8 11 12 16 19 20 21 22 23 25 28 29 30 32 33 34 35 37 39 40 44 48 49 65 69 71 73 74 **P**1 7 **S** Columbia/HCA Healthcare Corporation, Nashville, TN **N** Arkansas' FirstSource, Little Rock, AR — 33 10 | 75 | 1907 | 20 | 11093 | 186 | 11074 | 3865 | 180

DE WITT—Arkansas County

DEWITT CITY HOSPITAL, Highway 1 and Madison Street, Zip 72042, Mailing Address: P.O. Box 32, Zip 72042–0032; tel. 870/946–3571; Joe E. Smith, Administrator and Chief Executive Officer (Total facility includes 54 beds in nursing home–type unit) (Nonreporting) **A**9 10 **N** Arkansas' FirstSource, Little Rock, AR — 14 10 | 88

DUMAS—Desha County

★ DELTA MEMORIAL HOSPITAL, 300 East Pickens Street, Zip 71639–2710, Mailing Address: P.O. Box 887, Zip 71639–0887; tel. 870/382–4303; Rodney McPherson, Administrator **A**9 10 **F**1 8 12 15 17 19 21 22 26 27 28 30 32 34 41 44 46 49 51 52 57 59 63 65 71 73 **P**8 **S** Quorum Health Group/Quorum Health Resources, Inc., Brentwood, TN **N** Arkansas' FirstSource, Little Rock, AR; Arkansas Network, North Little Rock, AR — 23 10 | 35 | 1028 | 9 | 49686 | 119 | 7535 | 3419 | —

EL DORADO—Union County

✠ MEDICAL CENTER OF SOUTH ARKANSAS, (Includes Union Medical Center, 700 West Grove Street, Zip 71730; Warner Brown Hospital, 460 West Oak Street, Zip 71730; tel. 501/863–2000), 700 West Grove Street, Zip 71730–4416, Mailing Address: P.O. Box 1998, Zip 71731–1998; tel. 870/864–3200; Luther J. Lewis, Chief Executive Officer **A**1 3 5 9 10 **F**7 8 10 12 14 15 16 17 19 21 22 23 26 28 29 30 31 32 33 34 35 37 38 39 40 41 42 44 45 46 48 49 56 60 63 64 65 66 67 68 71 73 74 **P**3 8 **S** Columbia/HCA Healthcare Corporation, Nashville, TN **N** Arkansas' FirstSource, Little Rock, AR — 32 10 | 195 | 6048 | 87 | 35834 | 815 | 39318 | 16078 | 645

EUREKA SPRINGS—Carroll County

★ EUREKA SPRINGS HOSPITAL, 24 Norris Street, Zip 72632–3541; tel. 501/253–7400; Joe Hammond, Administrator (Nonreporting) **A**9 10 **N** Arkansas' FirstSource, Little Rock, AR — 23 10 | 16 | — | — | — | — | — | — | —

FAYETTEVILLE—Washington County

☐ CHARTER BEHAVIORAL HEALTH SYSTEM OF NORTHWEST ARKANSAS, 4253 North Crossover Road, Zip 72703–4596; tel. 501/521–5731; Lucinda DeBruce, Administrator **A**1 9 10 **F**14 15 16 52 53 58 59 **S** Magellan Health Services, Atlanta, GA — 33 22 | 49 | 942 | 36 | — | — | — | — | 99

☐ △ HEALTHSOUTH REHABILITATION HOSPITAL, (Formerly Northwest Arkansas Rehabilitation Hospital), 153 East Monte Painter Drive, Zip 72703–4002; tel. 501/444–2200; Dennis R. Shelby, Chief Executive Officer (Nonreporting) **A**1 7 9 10 **S** HEALTHSOUTH Corporation, Birmingham, AL — 33 46 | 60

NORTHWEST ARKANSAS REHABILITATION HOSPITAL See HEALTHSOUTH Rehabilitation Hospital

✠ VETERANS AFFAIRS MEDICAL CENTER, 1100 North College Avenue, Zip 72703–6995; tel. 501/443–4301; Richard F. Robinson, Director **A**1 5 9 **F**3 12 15 16 19 20 26 27 28 29 30 32 34 37 42 44 45 46 49 51 52 56 58 60 64 65 67 71 72 73 74 **S** Department of Veterans Affairs, Washington, DC — 45 10 | 51 | 2890 | 51 | 105371 | 0 | 37011 | 20435 | 501

✠ WASHINGTON REGIONAL MEDICAL CENTER, 1125 North College Avenue, Zip 72703–1994; tel. 501/442–1000; Patrick D. Flynn, President and Chief Executive Officer (Total facility includes 22 beds in nursing home–type unit) **A**1 2 3 5 9 10 **F**4 6 7 8 10 11 12 13 14 15 16 17 19 20 21 22 23 24 26 27 28 29 30 31 32 33 35 37 39 40 41 42 43 44 45 46 49 52 57 63 64 65 67 71 73 74 **P**8 **N** Arkansas' FirstSource, Little Rock, AR — 23 10 | 193 | 10551 | 129 | 120246 | 1962 | 82650 | 34762 | 1265

Hospital, Address, Telephone, Administrator, Approval, Facility, and Physician Codes, Health Care System, Network	Classi-fication Codes		Utilization Data					Expense (thousands) of dollars		
★ American Hospital Association (AHA) membership □ Joint Commission on Accreditation of Healthcare Organizations (JCAHO) accreditation + American Osteopathic Healthcare Association (AOHA) membership ○ American Osteopathic Association (AOA) accreditation △ Commission on Accreditation of Rehabilitation Facilities (CARF) accreditation Control codes 61, 63, 64, 71, 72 and 73 indicate hospitals listed by AOHA, but not registered by AHA. For definition of numerical codes, see page A4	Control	Service	Staffed Beds	Admissions	Census	Outpatient Visits	Births	Total	Payroll	Personnel

FORDYCE—Dallas County

DALLAS COUNTY HOSPITAL, 201 Clifton Street, Zip 71742–3099; tel. 501/352–3155; Greg R. McNeil, Administrator **A**9 10 **F**8 19 22 27 32 49 52 57 65 71 **S** Healthcorp of Tennessee, Inc., Chattanooga, TN	33	10	31	902	12	126021	—	11058	5569	209

FORREST CITY—St. Francis County

✠ BAPTIST MEMORIAL HOSPITAL–FORREST CITY, 1601 Newcastle Road, Zip 72335, Mailing Address: P.O. Box 667, Zip 72336–0667; tel. 870/633–2020; Charles R. Daugherty, Administrator (Nonreporting) **A**1 9 10 **S** Baptist Memorial Health Care Corporation, Memphis, TN **N** Arkansas' FirstSource, Little Rock, AR	23	10	86	—	—	—	—	—	—	—

FORT SMITH—Sebastian County

HARBOR VIEW MERCY HOSPITAL, 10301 Mayo Road, Zip 72903–1631, Mailing Address: P.O. Box 17000, Zip 72917–7000; tel. 501/484–5550; Ron Summerhill, Administrator **A**9 10 **F**1 2 15 16 19 22 26 32 34 35 52 53 54 55 56 57 58 59 65 67 71 73 **P**1 **S** Sisters of Mercy Health System–St. Louis, Saint Louis, MO **N** Saint Edward Mercy Medical Center, Fort Smith, AR; Arkansas' FirstSource, Little Rock, AR	21	22	80	1074	37	31104	0	—	4288	110
HEALTHSOUTH REHABILITATION HOSPITAL OF FORT SMITH, 1401 South J. Street, Zip 72901–5155; tel. 501/785–3300; Claudia A. Eisenmann, Director Operations (Total facility includes 9 beds in nursing home–type unit) **A**9 10 **F**12 15 16 32 41 48 49 64 66 67 **S** HEALTHSOUTH Corporation, Birmingham, AL	33	46	80	987	58	26616	—	—	5730	189
✠ SPARKS REGIONAL MEDICAL CENTER, 1311 South I. Street, Zip 72901–4995, Mailing Address: P.O. Box 17006, Zip 72917–7006; tel. 501/441–4000; Michael D. Helm, President **A**1 2 3 5 9 10 **F**3 4 7 8 10 11 12 13 16 17 19 21 22 23 24 25 26 27 28 29 30 31 32 34 35 37 38 39 40 42 43 44 45 47 49 52 53 55 56 57 58 63 64 65 67 71 73 **P**1	23	10	440	15954	253	77343	1733	98992	40956	1594
✠ ST. EDWARD MERCY MEDICAL CENTER, 7301 Rogers Avenue, Zip 72903–4189, Mailing Address: P.O. Box 17000, Zip 72917–7000; tel. 501/484–6000; Michael L. Morgan, President and Chief Executive Officer **A**1 2 5 9 10 **F**2 3 4 7 8 9 10 14 15 16 19 21 22 24 25 28 30 32 33 34 35 37 38 39 40 41 42 43 44 50 52 53 54 55 56 57 58 59 60 62 64 65 66 67 69 71 73 74 **P**1 **S** Sisters of Mercy Health System–St. Louis, Saint Louis, MO **N** Saint Edward Mercy Medical Center, Fort Smith, AR; Arkansas' FirstSource, Little Rock, AR	21	10	357	13967	198	96599	1778	86038	34207	1109

GRAVETTE—Benton County

GRAVETTE MEDICAL CENTER HOSPITAL, 1101 Jackson Street S.W., Zip 72736–0470, Mailing Address: P.O. Box 470, Zip 72736–0470; tel. 501/787–5291; John F. Phillips, Administrator **A**9 10 **F**8 11 14 17 19 22 28 30 34 40 41 44 46 49 64 65 71 73 **N** Arkansas' FirstSource, Little Rock, AR	23	10	58	2075	22	—	410	6857	4006	190

HARRISON—Boone County

★ NORTH ARKANSAS REGIONAL MEDICAL CENTER, 620 North Willow Street, Zip 72601–2994; tel. 870/365–2000; Timothy E. Hill, Chief Executive Officer (Total facility includes 14 beds in nursing home–type unit) **A**9 10 **F**7 8 10 12 14 15 16 17 19 21 22 23 28 30 32 33 34 35 41 42 44 45 46 49 60 64 65 67 71 73 74 **N** Arkansas' FirstSource, Little Rock, AR	23	10	125	4623	49	258427	454	31277	14459	615

HEBER SPRINGS—Cleburne County

✠ BAPTIST MEDICAL CENTER HEBER SPRINGS, 2319 Highway 110 West, Zip 72543; tel. 501/206–3000; Dan Gathright, Vice President and Administrator **A**1 9 10 **F**8 14 15 16 19 22 28 30 32 34 44 71 **P**3 7 **S** Baptist Health, Little Rock, AR **N** Arkansas' FirstSource, Little Rock, AR	23	10	24	370	4	13516	0	5041	2276	97

HELENA—Phillips County

✠ HELENA REGIONAL MEDICAL CENTER, 1801 Martin Luther king Drive, Zip 72342, Mailing Address: P.O. Box 788, Zip 72342–0788; tel. 870/338–5800; Steve Reeder, Chief Executive Officer **A**1 9 10 **F**7 19 21 22 27 28 32 37 40 41 44 48 49 52 54 57 65 67 71 73 **P**1 **S** Quorum Health Group/Quorum Health Resources, Inc., Brentwood, TN **N** Arkansas' FirstSource, Little Rock, AR	23	10	115	3199	35	—	521	17890	7934	311

HOPE—Hempstead County

✠ COLUMBIA MEDICAL PARK HOSPITAL, (Formerly Medical Park Hospital), 2001 South Main Street, Zip 71801–8194; tel. 870/777–2323; Jimmy Leopard, Chief Executive Officer (Nonreporting) **A**1 9 10 **S** Columbia/HCA Healthcare Corporation, Nashville, TN **N** Arkansas' FirstSource, Little Rock, AR	33	10	75	—	—	—	—	—	—	—

HOT SPRINGS—Garland County

✠ NATIONAL PARK MEDICAL CENTER, 1910 Malvern Avenue, Zip 71901–7799; tel. 501/321–1000; Jerry D. Mabry, Executive Director (Total facility includes 10 beds in nursing home–type unit) **A**1 9 10 **F**4 7 8 10 12 16 19 21 22 23 27 28 29 32 34 35 37 39 40 41 42 43 44 45 46 48 49 52 55 56 57 63 64 65 67 71 73 74 **P**1 4 5 7 8 **S** TENET Healthcare Corporation, Santa Barbara, CA	33	10	166	6592	123	46037	573	51283	18584	1120
✠ ST. JOSEPH'S REGIONAL HEALTH CENTER, 300 Werner Street, Zip 71913–6448; tel. 501/622–1000; Randall J. Fale, FACHE, President and Chief Executive Officer **A**1 2 9 10 **F**4 7 8 10 11 12 14 15 16 17 19 21 22 23 26 27 28 29 30 32 34 35 36 37 39 40 42 43 44 46 48 49 51 60 63 64 65 66 67 70 71 73 74 **P**7 **S** Sisters of Mercy Health System–St. Louis, Saint Louis, MO **N** Arkansas' FirstSource, Little Rock, AR	21	10	278	10969	191	216472	871	81590	35165	1366

HOT SPRINGS NATIONAL PARK—Garland County

✠ LEVI HOSPITAL, 300 Prospect Avenue, Zip 71901–4097; tel. 501/624–1281; Patrick McCabe, Jr., Executive Director **A**1 9 10 **F**5 15 16 19 21 26 27 28 29 32 33 34 35 52 53 54 56 57 58 59 65 66 67 71	23	22	20	293	7	286	0	5737	3771	177

Hospital, Address, Telephone, Administrator, Approval, Facility, and Physician Codes, Health Care System, Network	Classification Codes		Utilization Data					Expense (thousands) of dollars		
★ American Hospital Association (AHA) membership □ Joint Commission on Accreditation of Healthcare Organizations (JCAHO) accreditation + American Osteopathic Healthcare Association (AOHA) membership ○ American Osteopathic Association (AOA) accreditation △ Commission on Accreditation of Rehabilitation Facilities (CARF) accreditation Control codes 61, 63, 64, 71, 72 and 73 indicate hospitals listed by AOHA, but not registered by AHA. For definition of numerical codes, see page A4	Control	Service	Staffed Beds	Admissions	Census	Outpatient Visits	Births	Total	Payroll	Personnel

JACKSONVILLE—Pulaski County

⊞ REBSAMEN REGIONAL MEDICAL CENTER, 1400 West Braden Street, Zip 72076–3788; tel. 501/985–7000; Thomas R. Siemers, Chief Executive Officer **A**1 7 9 10 **F**7 8 10 11 12 17 19 21 22 25 26 28 30 32 34 35 37 39 40 41 42 44 45 46 48 49 51 52 57 63 65 66 67 71 73 74 **P**3 7 8 **S** Quorum Health Group/Quorum Health Resources, Inc., Brentwood, TN **N** Arkansas' FirstSource, Little Rock, AR; Arkansas Network, North Little Rock, AR — 23 | 10 | 113 | 3630 | 56 | 51642 | 399 | 28856 | 12144 | 497

⊞ U. S. AIR FORCE HOSPITAL LITTLE ROCK, Little Rock AFB, Zip 72099–5057; tel. 501/987–7411; Colonel Norman L. Sims, MSC, USAF, Commander (Nonreporting) **A**1 9 **S** Department of the Air Force, Bowling AFB, DC — 41 | 10 | 12

JONESBORO—Craighead County

⊞ △ HEALTHSOUTH REHABILITATION HOSPITAL OF JONESBORO, (Formerly Northeast Arkansas Rehabilitation Hospital), 1201 Fleming Avenue, Zip 72401–4311, Mailing Address: P.O. Box 1680, Zip 72403–1680; tel. 870/932–0440; Brenda Antwine, Administrator (Nonreporting) **A**1 7 9 10 **S** HEALTHSOUTH Corporation, Birmingham, AL **N** Arkansas' FirstSource, Little Rock, AR — 33 | 46 | 60

⊞ METHODIST HOSPITAL OF JONESBORO, 3024 Stadium Boulevard, Zip 72401–7493; tel. 870/972–7000; Philip H. Walkley, Jr., Chief Executive Officer **A**1 5 9 10 **F**2 4 7 8 10 11 12 17 19 20 21 22 26 28 29 30 31 32 33 34 35 37 38 39 40 41 42 43 44 45 46 47 48 49 53 54 56 58 59 63 65 66 67 69 71 73 74 **P**8 **S** TENET Healthcare Corporation, Santa Barbara, CA — 33 | 10 | 104 | 4271 | 51 | 115561 | 931 | 19336 | 10472 | 379

NORTHEAST ARKANSAS REHABILITATION HOSPITAL See HEALTHSOUTH Rehabilitation Hospital of Jonesboro

□ ST. BERNARD'S BEHAVIORAL HEALTH, (Formerly Greenleaf Center), 2712 East Johnson Avenue, Zip 72401–1874; tel. 870/932–2800; Andrew DeYoung, Administrator **A**1 10 **F**2 3 4 6 7 8 10 11 12 14 15 16 17 18 19 20 21 23 24 26 27 28 29 30 32 33 34 35 37 39 40 41 42 43 44 45 46 48 49 52 53 54 55 56 57 58 59 60 61 62 64 65 66 67 70 71 73 74 **P**3 8 **N** Arkansas' FirstSource, Little Rock, AR — 33 | 22 | 60 | 976 | 34 | — | — | 6554 | 3271 | 130

⊞ ST. BERNARDS REGIONAL MEDICAL CENTER, 224 East Matthews Street, Zip 72401–3156, Mailing Address: P.O. Box 9320, Zip 72403–9320; tel. 870/972–4100; Ben E. Owens, President (Total facility includes 27 beds in nursing home–type unit) **A**1 2 3 5 9 10 **F**2 3 4 6 7 8 10 11 12 14 15 16 17 18 19 20 21 23 24 26 27 28 29 30 32 33 34 35 37 39 40 41 42 43 44 45 49 52 53 54 55 56 57 58 60 61 62 64 65 66 67 70 71 73 74 **P**3 8 **N** Arkansas' FirstSource, Little Rock, AR — 21 | 10 | 325 | 16491 | 221 | 47706 | 1418 | — | — | 1341

LAKE VILLAGE—Chicot County

★ CHICOT MEMORIAL HOSPITAL, 2729 Highway 65 and 82 South, Zip 71653, Mailing Address: P.O. Box 512, Zip 71653–0512; tel. 870/265–5351; Robert R. Reddish, Administrator and Chief Executive Officer (Nonreporting) **A**9 10 **S** Quorum Health Group/Quorum Health Resources, Inc., Brentwood, TN **N** Arkansas' FirstSource, Little Rock, AR; Arkansas Network, North Little Rock, AR — 13 | 10 | 35

LITTLE ROCK—Pulaski County

⊞ △ ARKANSAS CHILDREN'S HOSPITAL, 800 Marshall Street, Zip 72202–3591; tel. 501/320–1100; Jonathan R. Bates, M.D., President and Chief Executive Officer **A**1 3 5 7 8 9 10 **F**3 4 5 9 10 11 12 13 16 17 19 20 21 22 27 28 30 31 34 35 38 39 42 43 44 46 47 48 49 51 52 53 54 56 58 60 63 65 66 67 69 71 73 **P**8 **N** Arkansas' FirstSource, Little Rock, AR — 23 | 50 | 258 | 8237 | 181 | 258357 | — | 145118 | 65579 | 2307

⊞ ARKANSAS STATE HOSPITAL, 4313 West Markham Street, Zip 72205–4096; tel. 501/686–9000; Glenn R. Sago, Administrator **A**1 3 5 9 10 — 12 | 22 | 206

⊞ BAPTIST MEDICAL CENTER, 9601 Interstate 630, Exit 7, Zip 72205–7299; tel. 501/202–2000; Steven Douglas Weeks, Senior Vice President and Administrator **A**1 3 5 6 9 10 **F**2 3 4 6 7 8 10 11 12 13 15 16 17 18 19 20 21 22 23 24 25 26 27 28 29 30 31 32 33 34 35 37 38 39 40 41 42 43 44 45 46 48 49 52 53 54 55 56 57 59 60 61 62 63 64 65 66 67 68 69 70 71 72 73 74 **P**1 3 5 6 7 **S** Baptist Health, Little Rock, AR **N** Arkansas' FirstSource, Little Rock, AR; Baptist Health, Little Rock, AR — 23 | 10 | 621 | 27514 | 442 | 184735 | 2125 | 223157 | 87762 | 2873

⊞ △ BAPTIST REHABILITATION INSTITUTE, 9601 Interstate 630, Exit 7, Zip 72205–7249; tel. 501/202–7000; Steven Douglas Weeks, Senior Vice President and Administrator **A**1 3 5 7 9 10 **F**2 3 4 6 7 8 10 11 12 13 15 16 17 18 19 20 21 22 23 24 25 26 27 28 29 30 31 32 33 34 35 36 37 38 39 40 41 42 43 44 45 46 48 49 51 52 53 54 55 56 57 58 59 60 62 63 64 65 66 67 68 69 70 71 72 73 74 **P**1 3 5 6 7 **S** Baptist Health, Little Rock, AR **N** Arkansas' FirstSource, Little Rock, AR; Baptist Health, Little Rock, AR — 23 | 46 | 100 | 1551 | 62 | 92323 | — | 17247 | 8141 | 245

□ BHC PINNACLE POINTE HOSPITAL, 11501 Financial Center Parkway, Zip 72211–3715; tel. 501/223–3322; Joseph Fischer, Chief Executive Officer (Nonreporting) **A**1 9 10 **S** Behavioral Healthcare Corporation, Nashville, TN — 33 | 22 | 98

⊞ COLUMBIA DOCTORS HOSPITAL, 6101 West Capitol, Zip 72205–5331; tel. 501/661–4000; Maura Walsh, President and Chief Executive Officer (Nonreporting) **A**1 9 10 **S** Columbia/HCA Healthcare Corporation, Nashville, TN — 33 | 10 | 308

□ SOUTHWEST HOSPITAL, 11401 Interstate 30, Zip 72209–7056; tel. 501/455–7100; R. Mark Cain, Executive Director (Nonreporting) **A**1 9 10 — 23 | 10 | 125

⊞ ST. VINCENT INFIRMARY MEDICAL CENTER, Two St. Vincent Circle, Zip 72205–5499; tel. 501/660–3000; Diana T. Hueter, President and Chief Executive Officer (Total facility includes 52 beds in nursing home–type unit) **A**1 2 3 5 9 10 **F**4 5 6 7 8 10 11 12 14 15 16 17 18 19 20 21 22 23 24 25 27 29 30 32 33 34 35 36 37 38 39 40 41 42 43 44 46 47 49 50 51 52 53 54 55 57 58 59 60 63 64 65 66 71 73 74 **P**2 7 8 **S** Catholic Health Initiatives, Denver, CO **N** Arkansas Network, North Little Rock, AR — 21 | 10 | 537 | 18692 | 309 | 324220 | 744 | 179143 | 75713 | 2584

Hospital, Address, Telephone, Administrator, Approval, Facility, and Physician Codes, Health Care System, Network	Classi-fication Codes		Utilization Data					Expense (thousands) of dollars		
★ American Hospital Association (AHA) membership □ Joint Commission on Accreditation of Healthcare Organizations (JCAHO) accreditation + American Osteopathic Healthcare Association (AOHA) membership ○ American Osteopathic Association (AOA) accreditation △ Commission on Accreditation of Rehabilitation Facilities (CARF) accreditation Control codes 61, 63, 64, 71, 72 and 73 indicate hospitals listed by AOHA, but not registered by AHA. For definition of numerical codes, see page A4	Control	Service	Staffed Beds	Admissions	Census	Outpatient Visits	Births	Total	Payroll	Personnel

Hospital	Control	Service	Staffed Beds	Admissions	Census	Outpatient Visits	Births	Total	Payroll	Personnel
⊠ UNIVERSITY HOSPITAL OF ARKANSAS, 4301 West Markham Street, Zip 72205–7102; tel. 501/686–7000; Richard Pierson, Executive Director, Clinical Programs **A**1 2 3 5 8 9 10 **F**5 7 8 10 11 12 14 15 16 19 21 22 26 28 30 31 32 34 35 37 38 39 40 41 42 43 44 45 46 49 51 54 55 56 57 58 60 61 63 65 66 67 69 70 71 72 73 74 **P**4	12	10	291	12810	220	271634	1952	178546	71993	—
⊠ VETERANS AFFAIRS MEDICAL CENTER, (Includes North Little Rock Division, North Little Rock), 4300 West Seventh Street, Zip 72205–5484; tel. 501/661–1202; George H. Gray, Jr., Director (Total facility includes 152 beds in nursing home–type unit) **A**1 2 3 5 8 9 **F**1 3 4 5 8 10 11 12 17 18 19 20 21 22 24 26 28 30 31 32 34 35 37 39 41 42 44 45 46 48 49 51 52 54 55 56 57 58 59 62 63 64 66 71 73 74 **P**6 **S** Department of Veterans Affairs, Washington, DC	45	10	456	10228	374	352376	—	209585	110549	2935
MAGNOLIA—Columbia County										
⊠ MAGNOLIA HOSPITAL, 101 Hospital Drive, Zip 71753–2416, Mailing Address: Box 629, Zip 71753–0629; tel. 870/235–3000; Kirk Reamey, Administrator **A**1 9 10 **F**7 8 14 19 21 22 32 37 39 40 44 45 49 65 71 73 **S** Sisters of Charity of the Incarnate Word Healthcare System, Houston, TX **N** Arkansas' FirstSource, Little Rock, AR	14	10	58	2125	31	31681	197	13015	6247	299
MALVERN—Hot Spring County										
★ H.S.C. MEDICAL CENTER, 1001 Schneider Drive, Zip 72104–4828; tel. 501/337–4911; Jeff Curtis, President and Chief Executive Officer **A**9 10 **F**7 8 11 14 15 16 17 19 21 22 24 27 28 29 30 32 35 37 39 40 41 44 45 46 49 51 52 54 55 56 57 58 59 67 71 73 **P**8 **S** Sisters of Mercy Health System–St. Louis, Saint Louis, MO **N** Arkansas' FirstSource, Little Rock, AR	23	10	74	2798	39	23459	88	15534	7769	359
MAUMELLE—Pulaski County										
□ CHARTER BEHAVIORAL HEALTH SYSTEM OF LITTLE ROCK, 1601 Murphy Drive, Zip 72113; tel. 501/851–8700; Lucinda DeBruce, Chief Executive Officer (Nonreporting) **A**1 9 10 **S** Magellan Health Services, Atlanta, GA	33	22	60	—	—	—	—	—	—	—
MCGEHEE—Desha County										
MCGEHEE–DESHA COUNTY HOSPITAL, 900 South Third, Zip 71654–0351, Mailing Address: Box 351, Zip 71654–0351; tel. 501/222–5600; Edward L. Lacy, Administrator **A**9 10 **F**14 16 22 32 40 44 52 58 **N** Arkansas' FirstSource, Little Rock, AR	13	10	34	1214	11	11537	173	6802	3980	—
MENA—Polk County										
MENA MEDICAL CENTER, 311 North Morrow Street, Zip 71953–2516; tel. 501/394–6100; Albert Pilkington, III, Administrator and Chief Executive Officer **A**9 10 **F**7 8 12 19 21 22 23 24 26 32 33 34 35 37 40 41 44 46 49 51 52 57 66 71 **P**8 **S** Quorum Health Group/Quorum Health Resources, Inc., Brentwood, TN **N** Arkansas' FirstSource, Little Rock, AR; Arkansas Network, North Little Rock, AR	14	10	48	1827	21	33977	257	11569	5664	233
MONTICELLO—Drew County										
★ DREW MEMORIAL HOSPITAL, 778 Scogin Drive, Zip 71655–5728; tel. 870/367–2411; Darren Caldwell, Chief Executive Officer **A**9 10 **F**8 12 15 16 19 21 22 28 30 32 33 34 35 37 39 40 41 44 46 65 71 **P**1 **N** Arkansas' FirstSource, Little Rock, AR	13	10	50	2632	28	17488	328	10316	4474	—
MORRILTON—Conway County										
★ ST. ANTHONY'S HEALTHCARE CENTER, 4 Hospital Drive, Zip 72110–4510; tel. 501/354–3512; Johnson L. Smith, Chief Executive Officer and Administrator **A**9 10 **F**1 7 8 11 12 16 17 19 21 22 26 27 32 33 35 37 40 41 44 46 49 52 56 57 64 65 66 67 71 73 **P**8 **N** Arkansas' FirstSource, Little Rock, AR	21	10	73	1629	26	19037	92	10669	5122	255
MOUNTAIN HOME—Baxter County										
⊠ BAXTER COUNTY REGIONAL HOSPITAL, 624 Hospital Drive, Zip 72653–2954; tel. 870/424–1000; H. William Anderson, Administrator **A**1 9 10 **F**7 8 10 11 12 15 16 19 20 21 22 23 24 27 28 30 32 33 34 35 37 38 39 40 41 42 44 45 46 48 49 60 64 65 66 67 71 73 74 **P**8 **N** Arkansas' FirstSource, Little Rock, AR	23	10	191	9988	134	66318	650	57920	27168	1003
MOUNTAIN VIEW—Stone County										
STONE COUNTY MEDICAL CENTER, Highway 14 East, Zip 72560, Mailing Address: P.O. Box 510, Zip 72560–0510; tel. 870/269–4361; Stanley Townsend, Administrator (Nonreporting) **A**9 10 **N** Arkansas' FirstSource, Little Rock, AR	33	10	48	—	—	—	—	—	—	—
MURFREESBORO—Pike County										
PIKE COUNTY MEMORIAL HOSPITAL, 315 East 13th Street, Zip 71958–9541; tel. 870/285–3182; Rosemary Fritts, Administrator (Total facility includes 5 beds in nursing home–type unit) **A**9 10 **F**19 22 32 34 64 71 **P**5 **N** Arkansas' FirstSource, Little Rock, AR	13	10	32	544	5	5978	—	1695	921	57
NASHVILLE—Howard County										
★ HOWARD MEMORIAL HOSPITAL, 800 West Leslie Street, Zip 71852–0381, Mailing Address: Box 381, Zip 71852–0381; tel. 870/845–4400; Lynn Crowell, Chief Executive Officer **A**10 **F**8 14 15 16 19 21 22 26 28 29 30 32 37 44 46 49 52 57 64 67 71 **P**3 8 **S** Quorum Health Group/Quorum Health Resources, Inc., Brentwood, TN **N** Arkansas' FirstSource, Little Rock, AR; Arkansas Network, North Little Rock, AR	23	10	50	1051	16	41135	—	8957	3924	174
NEWPORT—Jackson County										
⊠ HARRIS HOSPITAL, 1205 McLain Street, Zip 72112–3533; tel. 870/523–8911; Robin E. Lake, Chief Executive Officer **A**1 9 10 **F**7 8 10 11 12 14 15 16 17 18 19 20 21 22 26 28 29 30 32 34 35 39 40 41 44 45 46 49 51 52 54 55 56 57 58 61 64 65 67 68 70 71 73 74 **P**8 **S** Community Health Systems, Inc., Brentwood, TN **N** Arkansas' FirstSource, Little Rock, AR	33	10	88	3370	46	17392	351	12559	5562	229

Hospital, Address, Telephone, Administrator, Approval, Facility, and Physician Codes, Health Care System, Network	Classi-fication Codes		Utilization Data					Expense (thousands) of dollars		
★ American Hospital Association (AHA) membership □ Joint Commission on Accreditation of Healthcare Organizations (JCAHO) accreditation + American Osteopathic Healthcare Association (AOHA) membership ○ American Osteopathic Association (AOA) accreditation △ Commission on Accreditation of Rehabilitation Facilities (CARF) accreditation Control codes 61, 63, 64, 71, 72 and 73 indicate hospitals listed by AOHA, but not registered by AHA. For definition of numerical codes, see page A4	Control	Service	Staffed Beds	Admissions	Census	Outpatient Visits	Births	Total	Payroll	Personnel

	Control	Service	Staffed Beds	Admissions	Census	Outpatient Visits	Births	Total	Payroll	Personnel
★ NEWPORT HOSPITAL AND CLINIC, 2000 McLain Street, Zip 72112–3697; tel. 870/523–6721; Eugene Zuber, Administrator **A**9 10 **F**8 10 11 17 19 21 22 28 30 31 32 34 40 42 44 71 73 **N** Arkansas' FirstSource, Little Rock, AR	33	10	86	2905	38	16818	119	10403	4364	207
NORTH LITTLE ROCK—Pulaski County										
⊞ BAPTIST MEMORIAL MEDICAL CENTER, One Pershing Circle, Zip 72114–1899; tel. 501/202–3000; Harrison M. Dean, Senior Vice President and Administrator **A**1 9 10 **F**3 4 6 7 8 10 11 12 13 14 16 17 19 21 22 23 24 26 27 28 29 30 31 32 33 34 35 37 39 40 41 42 43 44 45 46 48 49 51 52 53 54 55 56 57 58 59 62 63 64 65 67 68 69 71 73 74 **P**1 3 5 7 **S** Baptist Health, Little Rock, AR **N** Arkansas' FirstSource, Little Rock, AR; Baptist Health, Little Rock, AR	23	10	200	7512	92	33697	546	57101	23478	841
□ BRIDGEWAY, 21 Bridgeway Road, Zip 72113; tel. 501/771–1500; Barry Pipkin, Chief Executive Officer and Managing Director **A**1 9 10 **F**2 3 15 16 20 22 27 35 39 41 42 53 54 55 56 57 58 59 64 65 67 **S** Universal Health Services, Inc., King of Prussia, PA	33	22	70	1299	47	3314	—	7713	3365	103
NORTH LITTLE ROCK DIVISION See Veterans Affairs Medical Center, Little Rock										
OSCEOLA—Mississippi County										
⊞ BAPTIST MEMORIAL HOSPITAL–OSCEOLA, 611 West Lee Avenue, Zip 72370–3001, Mailing Address: P.O. Box 607, Zip 72370–0607; tel. 870/563–7000; Joel E. North, Administrator (Nonreporting) **A**1 9 10 **S** Baptist Memorial Health Care Corporation, Memphis, TN **N** Arkansas' FirstSource, Little Rock, AR	21	10	59	—	—	—	—	—	—	—
OZARK—Franklin County										
★ MERCY HOSPITAL–TURNER MEMORIAL, 801 West River Street, Zip 72949–3000; tel. 501/667–4138; John C. Neal, Administrator **A**9 10 **F**2 3 4 7 8 9 10 11 14 15 16 19 21 22 24 25 28 30 31 32 33 34 35 37 38 39 40 41 42 44 47 48 50 52 53 54 55 56 57 58 59 60 62 65 66 67 71 73 **P**1 6 **S** Sisters of Mercy Health System–St. Louis, Saint Louis, MO **N** Saint Edward Mercy Medical Center, Fort Smith, AR; Arkansas' FirstSource, Little Rock, AR	21	10	39	429	5	7616	—	2544	1537	61
PARAGOULD—Greene County										
⊞ ARKANSAS METHODIST HOSPITAL, 900 West Kingshighway, Zip 72450–5942, Mailing Address: P.O. Box 339, Zip 72451–0339; tel. 870/239–7000; Ronald K. Rooney, President **A**1 9 10 **F**7 8 10 11 12 14 15 16 19 22 23 28 30 32 33 35 39 40 44 46 48 49 65 71 73 **P**8 **N** Arkansas' FirstSource, Little Rock, AR	23	10	129	4483	60	62142	340	22491	9085	404
PARIS—Logan County										
★ NORTH LOGAN MERCY HOSPITAL, 500 East Academy, Zip 72855–4099; tel. 501/963–6101; Jim L. Maddox, Chief Administrative Officer **A**9 10 **F**2 3 4 7 8 9 10 11 14 15 16 19 20 21 22 24 25 27 28 30 31 32 33 34 35 37 38 39 40 41 42 43 44 47 50 52 53 54 55 56 57 58 59 60 62 64 66 67 68 71 73 **P**1 **S** Sisters of Mercy Health System–St. Louis, Saint Louis, MO **N** Saint Edward Mercy Medical Center, Fort Smith, AR; Arkansas' FirstSource, Little Rock, AR	21	10	16	247	4	8592	0	2624	1250	45
PIGGOTT—Clay County										
★ PIGGOTT COMMUNITY HOSPITAL, 1206 Gordon Duckworth Drive, Zip 72454–1911; tel. 870/598–3881; James L. Magee, Executive Director **A**9 10 **F**8 17 19 22 27 28 32 44 49 64 65 71 **N** Arkansas' FirstSource, Little Rock, AR	14	10	35	889	12	23584	0	4873	3145	121
PINE BLUFF—Jefferson County										
⊞ JEFFERSON REGIONAL MEDICAL CENTER, 1515 West 42nd Avenue, Zip 71603–7089; tel. 870/541–7100; Robert P. Atkinson, President and Chief Executive Officer (Total facility includes 114 beds in nursing home–type unit) **A**1 2 3 5 6 9 10 **F**3 4 7 8 10 11 12 14 15 16 18 19 21 22 23 24 25 27 28 29 30 31 32 33 34 35 37 39 40 41 42 43 44 45 46 48 49 51 52 54 55 56 57 58 59 60 63 64 65 66 67 68 70 71 72 73 74 **N** Arkansas' FirstSource, Little Rock, AR	23	10	489	13110	221	74459	1578	103808	41031	1599
POCAHONTAS—Randolph County										
★ RANDOLPH COUNTY MEDICAL CENTER, 2801 Medical Center Drive, Zip 72455–9497; tel. 870/892–4511; Kenneth Breaux, Chief Executive Officer (Nonreporting) **A**9 10 **S** Community Health Systems, Inc., Brentwood, TN **N** Arkansas' FirstSource, Little Rock, AR	33	10	50	—	—	—	—	—	—	—
ROGERS—Benton County										
⊞ ST. MARY–ROGERS MEMORIAL HOSPITAL, 1200 West Walnut Street, Zip 72756–3599; tel. 501/636–0200; Michael J. Packnett, President and Chief Executive Officer **A**1 2 9 10 **F**1 7 8 10 11 12 14 15 16 19 21 22 24 28 32 33 34 35 38 39 40 41 42 44 49 63 64 65 66 67 71 73 **P**3 5 **S** Sisters of Mercy Health System–St. Louis, Saint Louis, MO **N** Arkansas' FirstSource, Little Rock, AR	21	10	102	5957	59	44118	1221	36344	17774	621
RUSSELLVILLE—Pope County										
⊞ △ SAINT MARY'S REGIONAL MEDICAL CENTER, 1808 West Main Street, Zip 72801–2724; tel. 501/968–2841; Mike McCoy, Chief Executive Officer **A**1 7 9 10 **F**7 8 10 11 12 15 16 17 19 21 22 23 24 25 26 28 29 30 32 34 35 37 40 41 42 44 45 46 48 49 57 59 60 63 64 65 66 67 71 73 74 **P**7 8 **S** TENET Healthcare Corporation, Santa Barbara, CA **N** Arkansas' FirstSource, Little Rock, AR	33	10	151	5787	79	39241	1055	34594	10999	683
SALEM—Fulton County										
FULTON COUNTY HOSPITAL, Highway 9, Zip 72576, Mailing Address: P.O. Box 517, Zip 72576–0517; tel. 501/895–2691; Franklin E. Wise, Administrator **A**9 10 **F**19 20 32 34 40 44 71 **N** Arkansas' FirstSource, Little Rock, AR	13	10	30	813	9	19781	30	3682	1942	108
SEARCY—White County										
⊞ △ CENTRAL ARKANSAS HOSPITAL, 1200 South Main Street, Zip 72143–7397; tel. 501/278–3131; David C. Laffoon, CHE, Chief Executive Officer **A**1 2 7 9 10 **F**7 10 11 14 15 16 19 21 22 24 27 32 34 35 37 38 40 42 44 48 52 54 56 65 67 71 73 74 **P**8 **S** TENET Healthcare Corporation, Santa Barbara, CA	33	10	173	5719	89	78584	739	24992	12620	—

Hospital, Address, Telephone, Administrator, Approval, Facility, and Physician Codes, Health Care System, Network	Classi-fication Codes		Utilization Data					Expense (thousands) of dollars		
★ American Hospital Association (AHA) membership □ Joint Commission on Accreditation of Healthcare Organizations (JCAHO) accreditation + American Osteopathic Healthcare Association (AOHA) membership ○ American Osteopathic Association (AOA) accreditation △ Commission on Accreditation of Rehabilitation Facilities (CARF) accreditation Control codes 61, 63, 64, 71, 72 and 73 indicate hospitals listed by AOHA, but not registered by AHA. For definition of numerical codes, see page A4	Control	Service	Staffed Beds	Admissions	Census	Outpatient Visits	Births	Total	Payroll	Personnel

⊠ WHITE COUNTY MEDICAL CENTER, 3214 East Race, Zip 72143–4847; tel. 501/268–6121; Raymond W. Montgomery, II, President and Chief Executive Officer **A**1 2 9 10 **F**7 10 11 12 13 15 16 19 20 21 22 25 28 30 31 32 34 35 37 38 39 40 41 42 44 45 46 49 62 65 66 68 71 73 74 **N** Arkansas' FirstSource, Little Rock, AR	23	10	104	5710	62	31475	439	25081	11023	487
SHERWOOD—Pulaski County										
□ △ ST. VINCENT–NORTH REHABILITATION HOSPITAL, 2201 Wildwood Avenue, Zip 72120–5074, Mailing Address: P.O. Box 6930, Zip 72124–6930; tel. 501/834–1800; Douglas W. Parker, Chief Executive Officer (Total facility includes 10 beds in nursing home–type unit) (Nonreporting) **A**1 7 9 10 **S** HEALTHSOUTH Corporation, Birmingham, AL	32	46	60	—	—	—	—	—	—	—
SILOAM SPRINGS—Benton County										
★ SILOAM SPRING MEMORIAL HOSPITAL, 205 East Jefferson Street, Zip 72761–3697; tel. 501/524–4141; Donald E. Patterson, Administrator **A**9 10 **F**7 8 12 16 19 21 22 28 30 32 34 37 39 40 44 46 64 65 67 71 73 **S** Quorum Health Group/Quorum Health Resources, Inc., Brentwood, TN **N** Arkansas' FirstSource, Little Rock, AR; Arkansas Network, North Little Rock, AR	14	10	52	1336	14	16521	182	11398	5657	235
SPRINGDALE—Washington County										
⊠ NORTHWEST MEDICAL CENTER, (Includes Bates Medical Center, 602 North Walton Boulevard, Bentonville, Zip 72712; tel. 501/273–2481; Thomas P. O'Neal, Executive Vice President and Chief Operating Officer), 609 West Maple Avenue, Zip 72764–5394, Mailing Address: P.O. Box 47, Zip 72765–0047; tel. 501/751–5711; Greg K. Stock, Chief Executive Officer (Total facility includes 22 beds in nursing home–type unit) (Nonreporting) **A**1 2 9 10 **S** Quorum Health Group/Quorum Health Resources, Inc., Brentwood, TN **N** Arkansas Network, North Little Rock, AR	23	10	222	—	—	—	—	—	—	—
STUTTGART—Arkansas County										
★ STUTTGART REGIONAL MEDICAL CENTER, North Buerkle Road, Zip 72160, Mailing Address: P.O. Box 1905, Zip 72160–1905; tel. 870/673–3511; Jim E. Bushmaier, Administrator and Chief Executive Officer (Nonreporting) **A**9 10 **N** Arkansas' FirstSource, Little Rock, AR	23	10	89	—	—	—	—	—	—	—
VAN BUREN—Crawford County										
□ CRAWFORD MEMORIAL HOSPITAL, East Main & South 20th Streets, Zip 72956, Mailing Address: P.O. Box 409, Zip 72956–0409; tel. 501/474–3401; Richard Boone, Executive Director **A**1 9 10 **F**8 11 12 15 16 17 19 21 22 23 24 26 27 28 29 30 32 34 35 37 39 41 44 46 49 65 67 71 73 74 **P**6 **S** Health Management Associates, Naples, FL **N** Arkansas' FirstSource, Little Rock, AR	33	10	103	3287	40	23770	0	17624	7476	315
WALDRON—Scott County										
★ MERCY HOSPITAL OF SCOTT COUNTY, Highways 71 and 80, Zip 72958–9984, Mailing Address: Box 2230, Zip 72958–2230; tel. 501/637–4135; Sister Mary Alvera Simon, Administrator (Total facility includes 105 beds in nursing home–type unit) (Nonreporting) **A**9 10 **S** Sisters of Mercy Health System–St. Louis, Saint Louis, MO **N** Saint Edward Mercy Medical Center, Fort Smith, AR; Arkansas' FirstSource, Little Rock, AR	21	10	127	—	—	—	—	—	—	—
WALNUT RIDGE—Lawrence County										
LAWRENCE MEMORIAL HOSPITAL, (Includes Lawrence Hall Nursing Home), 1309 West Main, Zip 72476–1430, Mailing Address: P.O. Box 839, Zip 72476–0839; tel. 501/886–1200; Lee Gentry, President (Total facility includes 189 beds in nursing home–type unit) **A**9 10 **F**8 15 19 21 22 25 26 28 30 32 34 36 39 41 44 49 50 51 64 65 67 71 73 **P**6 **N** Arkansas' FirstSource, Little Rock, AR	13	10	206	603	6	7849	0	—	2463	138
WARREN—Bradley County										
★ BRADLEY COUNTY MEDICAL CENTER, (Formerly Bradley County Memorial Hospital), 404 South Bradley Street, Zip 71671; tel. 870/226–3731; Edward L. Nilles, President and Chief Executive Officer **A**9 10 **F**1 6 7 8 11 12 13 16 17 18 19 20 21 22 26 27 28 29 30 31 32 33 34 36 39 41 44 46 49 51 53 54 55 56 57 58 59 63 65 67 68 71 73 **P**1 3 **N** Arkansas' FirstSource, Little Rock, AR	13	10	56	1617	27	17925	169	11356	5084	241
WEST MEMPHIS—Crittenden County										
□ △ CRITTENDEN MEMORIAL HOSPITAL, 200 Tyler Avenue, Zip 72301–4223, Mailing Address: P.O. Box 2248, Zip 72303–2248; tel. 501/735–1500; Ross Hooper, Chief Executive Officer (Nonreporting) **A**1 7 9 10 **N** Arkansas' FirstSource, Little Rock, AR	23	10	95	—	—	—	—	—	—	—
WYNNE—Cross County										
★ CROSS COUNTY HOSPITAL, 310 South Falls Boulevard, Zip 72396–3013, Mailing Address: P.O. Box 590, Zip 72396–0590; tel. 870/238–3300; Harry M. Baker, Chief Executive Officer **A**9 10 **F**11 15 19 22 32 35 40 44 65 71 **N** Arkansas' FirstSource, Little Rock, AR	13	10	53	1345	17	13114	111	6214	2995	147

CALIFORNIA

Resident population 32,268 (in thousands)
Resident population in metro areas 96.7%
Birth rate per 1,000 population 18.1
65 years and over 11.0%
Percent of persons without health insurance 20.1%

Hospital, Address, Telephone, Administrator, Approval, Facility, and Physician Codes, Health Care System, Network	Classi-fication Codes		Utilization Data					Expense (thousands) of dollars		
★ American Hospital Association (AHA) membership ☐ Joint Commission on Accreditation of Healthcare Organizations (JCAHO) accreditation + American Osteopathic Healthcare Association (AOHA) membership ○ American Osteopathic Association (AOA) accreditation △ Commission on Accreditation of Rehabilitation Facilities (CARF) accreditation Control codes 61, 63, 64, 71, 72 and 73 indicate hospitals listed by AOHA, but not registered by AHA. For definition of numerical codes, see page A4	Control	Service	Staffed Beds	Admissions	Census	Outpatient Visits	Births	Total	Payroll	Personnel

ALAMEDA—Alameda County

⊠ ALAMEDA HOSPITAL, 2070 Clinton Avenue, Zip 94501; tel. 510/522–3700; William J. Dal Cielo, Chief Executive Officer (Total facility includes 23 beds in nursing home–type unit) **A**1 9 10 **F**7 8 11 15 16 19 21 22 26 28 29 32 33 34 37 39 40 41 42 44 45 49 52 57 63 64 71 73 **P**1 4 5 6 7 **N** East Bay Medical Network, Emeryville, CA
| | 23 | 10 | 135 | 4184 | 58 | 35243 | 485 | 35644 | 20906 | 366 |

ALHAMBRA—Los Angeles County

☐ ALHAMBRA HOSPITAL, 100 South Raymond Avenue, Zip 91801, Mailing Address: Box 510, Zip 91802–0510; tel. 626/570–1606; Timothy McGlew, Chief Executive Officer (Total facility includes 42 beds in nursing home–type unit) (Nonreporting) **A**1 2 9 10
| | 32 | 10 | 144 | — | — | — | — | — | — | — |

ALTURAS—Modoc County

MODOC MEDICAL CENTER, 228 McDowell Street, Zip 96101; tel. 916/233–5131; Woody J. Laughnan, Chief Executive Officer (Total facility includes 71 beds in nursing home–type unit) **A**9 10 **F**7 8 15 16 17 20 22 27 28 32 34 40 44 45 49 64 71 73 **N** InterMountain Rural Health Network, Alturas, CA
| | 13 | 10 | 87 | 251 | 47 | — | 44 | 7490 | 3383 | 144 |

ANAHEIM—Orange County

☐ ANAHEIM GENERAL HOSPITAL, 3350 West Ball Road, Zip 92804–9998; tel. 714/827–6700; Reynold R. Welch, Chief Executive Officer **A**1 10 **F**1 8 12 15 19 21 22 27 28 29 31 32 35 37 40 41 42 43 44 49 52 57 59 61 64 65 71 73 74 **P**5 **S** Pacific Health Corporation, Long Beach, CA
| | 32 | 10 | 88 | 4235 | 46 | 17306 | 974 | 33588 | 12864 | 522 |

⊠ ANAHEIM MEMORIAL MEDICAL CENTER, 1111 West La Palma Avenue, Zip 92801; tel. 714/774–1450; Michael C. Carter, Chief Executive Officer (Nonreporting) **A**1 2 9 10 **S** Memorial Health Services, Long Beach, CA
| | 23 | 10 | 192 | — | — | — | — | — | — | — |

COLUMBIA WEST ANAHEIM MEDICAL CENTER See West Anaheim Medical Center

⊠ KAISER FOUNDATION HOSPITAL, 441 North Lakeview Avenue, Zip 92807; tel. 714/279–4100; Gerald A. McCall, Administrator **A**1 2 3 10 **F**2 3 4 7 8 10 11 12 13 14 15 16 17 18 19 20 21 22 23 28 29 30 31 32 33 35 37 38 39 40 41 42 43 44 45 46 47 48 49 51 52 53 54 55 57 58 59 60 61 63 64 65 66 67 68 69 71 72 73 **P**4 **S** Kaiser Foundation Hospitals, Oakland, CA
| | 23 | 10 | 150 | 9163 | 90 | 57270 | 3133 | — | — | 884 |

⊠ MARTIN LUTHER HOSPITAL, (Formerly Martin Luther Hospital–Anaheim), 1830 West Romneya Drive, Zip 92801–1854; tel. 714/491–5200; Stephen E. Dixon, President and Chief Executive Officer (Total facility includes 22 beds in nursing home–type unit) **A**1 2 9 10 **F**1 3 4 7 8 9 10 11 12 13 14 15 16 17 19 20 21 22 23 27 28 29 30 32 33 35 37 38 39 40 41 43 44 45 46 49 51 53 54 55 56 57 58 59 60 61 64 65 66 67 68 69 70 71 72 73 74 **P**3 5 7 **S** UniHealth, Burbank, CA **N** UniHealth, Burbank, CA
| | 23 | 10 | 205 | 6452 | 80 | 51562 | 1912 | 51228 | 20023 | 504 |

⊠ WEST ANAHEIM MEDICAL CENTER, (Formerly Columbia West Anaheim Medical Center), 3033 West Orange Avenue, Zip 92804–3184; tel. 714/827–3000; David Culberson, Chief Executive Officer (Total facility includes 22 beds in nursing home–type unit) (Nonreporting) **A**1 2 9 10 **S** Columbia/HCA Healthcare Corporation, Nashville, TN
| | 33 | 10 | 219 | — | — | — | — | — | — | — |

⊠ WESTERN MEDICAL CENTER HOSPITAL ANAHEIM, 1025 South Anaheim Boulevard, Zip 92805; tel. 714/533–6220; Doug Norris, Chief Operating Officer (Nonreporting) **A**1 9 10 **S** TENET Healthcare Corporation, Santa Barbara, CA
| | 33 | 10 | 171 | — | — | — | — | — | — | — |

ANTIOCH—Contra Costa County

⊠ SUTTER DELTA MEDICAL CENTER, 3901 Lone Tree Way, Zip 94509; tel. 925/779–7200; Linda Horn, Administrator **A**1 9 10 **F**2 3 4 7 8 9 10 11 12 14 15 16 17 18 19 20 21 22 23 28 29 30 31 32 33 34 35 37 38 40 41 42 43 44 45 46 47 48 49 50 51 52 53 54 55 56 57 58 59 60 63 64 65 67 69 70 71 72 73 74 **P**3 5 7 **S** Sutter Health, Sacramento, CA **N** East Bay Medical Network, Emeryville, CA; Sutter\CHS, Sacramento, CA
| | 23 | 10 | 80 | 5760 | 59 | 61584 | 1104 | 48255 | 17867 | 505 |

APPLE VALLEY—San Bernardino County

⊠ ST. MARY REGIONAL MEDICAL CENTER, 18300 Highway 18, Zip 92307–0725, Mailing Address: Box 7025, Zip 92307–0725; tel. 760/242–2311; Catherine M. Pelley, President and Chief Executive Officer (Nonreporting) **A**1 2 9 10 **S** St. Joseph Health System, Orange, CA **N** Saint Joseph Health System, Orange, CA
| | 21 | 10 | 137 | — | — | — | — | — | — | — |

ARCADIA—Los Angeles County

⊠ METHODIST HOSPITAL OF SOUTHERN CALIFORNIA, 300 West Huntington Drive, Zip 91007, Mailing Address: P.O. Box 60016, Zip 91066–6016; tel. 626/445–4441; Dennis M. Lee, President (Total facility includes 26 beds in nursing home–type unit) (Nonreporting) **A**1 2 9 10 **S** Southern California Healthcare Systems, Pasadena, CA **N** Southern California Healthcare Systems, Pasadena, CA
| | 23 | 10 | 304 | — | — | — | — | — | — | — |

ARCATA—Humboldt County

MAD RIVER COMMUNITY HOSPITAL, 3800 Janes Road, Zip 95521, Mailing Address: P.O. Box 1115, Zip 95521–1115; tel. 707/822–3621; Doug Shaw, Administrator (Nonreporting) **A**9 10
| | 33 | 10 | 78 | — | — | — | — | — | — | — |

ARROYO GRANDE—San Luis Obispo County

☐ ARROYO GRANDE COMMUNITY HOSPITAL, 345 South Halcyon Road, Zip 93420; tel. 805/489–4261; Richard N. Woolslayer, Chief Executive Officer **A**1 9 10 **F**4 8 15 16 19 21 22 23 26 28 31 32 34 35 37 41 42 44 49 66 71 72
| | 23 | 10 | 32 | 2188 | 24 | 65651 | — | 17366 | 6514 | 213 |

Hospital, Address, Telephone, Administrator, Approval, Facility, and Physician Codes, Health Care System, Network	Classi-fication Codes		Utilization Data					Expense (thousands) of dollars		
★ American Hospital Association (AHA) membership □ Joint Commission on Accreditation of Healthcare Organizations (JCAHO) accreditation + American Osteopathic Healthcare Association (AOHA) membership ○ American Osteopathic Association (AOA) accreditation △ Commission on Accreditation of Rehabilitation Facilities (CARF) accreditation Control codes 61, 63, 64, 71, 72 and 73 indicate hospitals listed by AOHA, but not registered by AHA. For definition of numerical codes, see page A4	Control	Service	Staffed Beds	Admissions	Census	Outpatient Visits	Births	Total	Payroll	Personnel

ARTESIA—Los Angeles County

PIONEER HOSPITAL, 17831 South Pioneer Boulevard, Zip 90701; tel. 310/865–6291; Sharon L. Jose, MS, R.N., Vice President, Hospital Operations (Nonreporting) **A**9	33	10	99	—	—	—	—	—	—	—

ATASCADERO—San Luis Obispo County

□ ATASCADERO STATE HOSPITAL, 10333 El Camino Real, Zip 93422–7001, Mailing Address: P.O. Box 7001, Zip 93423–7001; tel. 805/461–2000; Jon Demorales, Executive Director **A**1 3 5 **F**14 15 16 45 46 52 62 **P**6	12	22	1040	1226	983	—	0	—	—	—

AUBURN—Placer County

✠ SUTTER AUBURN FAITH COMMUNITY HOSPITAL, 11815 Education Street, Zip 95604, Mailing Address: Box 8992, Zip 95604–8992; tel. 530/888–4518; Joel E. Grey, Administrator (Total facility includes 12 beds in nursing home–type unit) (Nonreporting) **A**1 9 10 **S** Sutter Health, Sacramento, CA **N** Sutter\CHS, Sacramento, CA	23	10	105	—	—	—	—	—	—	—

AVALON—Los Angeles County

AVALON MUNICIPAL HOSPITAL AND CLINIC, 100 Falls Canyon Road, Zip 90704, Mailing Address: Box 1563, Zip 90704–1563; tel. 310/510–0700; Kiki Nocella, Administrator (Total facility includes 4 beds in nursing home–type unit) (Nonreporting) **A**9 10	23	10	12	—	—	—	—	—	—	—

BAKERSFIELD—Kern County

✠ BAKERSFIELD MEMORIAL HOSPITAL, (Includes Memorial Center, 5201 White Lane, Zip 93309; tel. 805/398–1800), 420 34th Street, Zip 93301, Mailing Address: P.O. Box 1888, Zip 93303–1888; tel. 805/327–1792; C. Larry Carr, President (Nonreporting) **A**1 2 9 10 **S** Catholic Healthcare West, San Francisco, CA	23	10	293	—	—	—	—	—	—	—
COLUMBIA GOOD SAMARITAN HOSPITAL See Good Samaritan Hospital										
✠ GOOD SAMARITAN HOSPITAL, (Formerly Columbia Good Samaritan Hospital), 901 Olive Drive, Zip 93308–4137; tel. 805/399–4461; Victor F. Brewer, Administrator (Nonreporting) **A**1 9 10 **S** Columbia/HCA Healthcare Corporation, Nashville, TN	33	10	64	—	—	—	—	—	—	—
□ HEALTHSOUTH BAKERSFIELD REHABILITATION HOSPITAL, 5001 Commerce Drive, Zip 93309; tel. 805/323–5500; Thomas J. Meagher, Chief Operating Officer (Nonreporting) **A**1 9 10 **S** HEALTHSOUTH Corporation, Birmingham, AL	33	46	60	—	—	—	—	—	—	—
□ KERN MEDICAL CENTER, 1830 Flower Street, Zip 93305–4197; tel. 805/326–2000; Gerald A. Starr, Chief Executive Officer (Nonreporting) **A**1 2 3 5 8 9 10	13	10	198	—	—	—	—	—	—	—
MEMORIAL CENTER See Bakersfield Memorial Hospital										
✠ MERCY HEALTHCARE–BAKERSFIELD, (Includes Mercy Southwest Hospital, 400 Old River Road, Zip 93311; tel. 805/663–6000), 2215 Truxtun Avenue, Zip 93301, Mailing Address: Box 119, Zip 93302; tel. 805/632–5000; Bernard J. Herman, President and Chief Executive Officer (Total facility includes 50 beds in nursing home–type unit) **A**1 2 9 10 **F**7 8 10 15 16 17 19 22 23 30 32 34 35 37 38 39 40 42 44 45 46 49 60 64 65 67 71 72 73 74 **P**5 7 **S** Catholic Healthcare West, San Francisco, CA **N** Catholic HealthCare West (CHW), San Francisco, CA	21	10	261	11563	167	148143	1995	92611	38227	1245
✠ SAN JOAQUIN COMMUNITY HOSPITAL, 2615 Eye Street, Zip 93301, Mailing Address: Box 2615, Zip 93303–2615; tel. 805/395–3000; Fred Manchur, President (Nonreporting) **A**1 9 10 **S** Adventist Health, Roseville, CA	23	10	178	—	—	—	—	—	—	—

BANNING—Riverside County

✠ SAN GORGONIO MEMORIAL HOSPITAL, 600 North Highland Springs Avenue, Zip 92220; tel. 909/845–1121; Donald N. Larkin, Chief Executive Officer **A**1 9 10 **F**8 13 14 15 17 18 19 21 22 26 27 28 29 30 32 33 34 37 39 40 41 42 44 45 46 49 51 54 58 59 65 67 68 71 73 **S** Brim, Inc., Portland, OR	23	10	68	2749	26	31143	315	15024	7134	194

BARSTOW—San Bernardino County

✠ BARSTOW COMMUNITY HOSPITAL, 555 South Seventh Street, Zip 92311; tel. 760/256–1761; Russell V. Judd, Chief Executive Officer **A**1 2 9 10 **F**7 8 11 12 14 15 16 19 21 22 28 35 37 40 41 44 71 73 **P**7 **S** Community Health Systems, Inc., Brentwood, TN	33	10	46	2954	30	27170	430	15200	7085	203

BEALE AFB—Yuba County

✠ U. S. AIR FORCE HOSPITAL, 15301 Warren Shingle Road, Zip 95903–1907; tel. 530/634–4838; Lieutenant Colonel Robert G. Quinn, MSC, USAF, FACHE, Administrator (Nonreporting) **A**1 **S** Department of the Air Force, Bowling AFB, DC	41	10	6	—	—	—	—	—	—	—

BELLFLOWER—Los Angeles County

□ BELLFLOWER MEDICAL CENTER, 9542 East Artesia Boulevard, Zip 90706; tel. 310/925–8355; Stanley Otake, Chief Executive Officer (Nonreporting) **A**1 9 10 **S** Pacific Health Corporation, Long Beach, CA	33	10	145	—	—	—	—	—	—	—
□ BELLWOOD GENERAL HOSPITAL, 10250 East Artesia Boulevard, Zip 90706; tel. 562/866–9028; Michael Kerr, Administrator (Nonreporting) **A**1 9 **S** Paracelsus Healthcare Corporation, Houston, TX	33	10	65	—	—	—	—	—	—	—
✠ KAISER FOUNDATION HOSPITAL–BELLFLOWER, 9400 East Rosecrans Avenue, Zip 90706–2246; tel. 562/461–3000; Timothy A. Reed, Administrator **A**1 2 3 10 **F**2 3 4 7 8 9 10 12 13 14 15 16 17 18 19 21 22 23 25 26 28 29 30 31 32 33 34 35 37 38 39 40 41 42 43 44 45 46 47 48 49 50 51 52 53 54 55 56 57 58 59 60 61 63 64 65 67 68 69 71 72 73 74 **P**6 **S** Kaiser Foundation Hospitals, Oakland, CA	23	10	272	17889	152	1380183	5226	—	—	1511

Hospital, Address, Telephone, Administrator, Approval, Facility, and Physician Codes, Health Care System, Network	Classi-fication Codes		Utilization Data					Expense (thousands) of dollars		
★ American Hospital Association (AHA) membership □ Joint Commission on Accreditation of Healthcare Organizations (JCAHO) accreditation + American Osteopathic Healthcare Association (AOHA) membership ○ American Osteopathic Association (AOA) accreditation △ Commission on Accreditation of Rehabilitation Facilities (CARF) accreditation Control codes 61, 63, 64, 71, 72 and 73 indicate hospitals listed by AOHA, but not registered by AHA. For definition of numerical codes, see page A4	Control	Service	Staffed Beds	Admissions	Census	Outpatient Visits	Births	Total	Payroll	Personnel

BELMONT—San Mateo County

□ BHC BELMONT HILLS HOSPITAL, 1301 Ralston Avenue, Zip 94002;
tel. 415/593–2143; Harold G. Marohn, Acting Chief Executive Officer
(Nonreporting) **A**1 9 10
| | 33 | 22 | 53 | — | — | — | — | — | — | — |

BERKELEY—Alameda County

☒ △ ALTA BATES MEDICAL CENTER–ASHBY CAMPUS, (Includes Alta Bates
Medical Center–Herrick Campus, 2001 Dwight Way, Zip 94704;
tel. 510/204–4444), 2450 Ashby Avenue, Zip 94705; tel. 510/204–4444;
George P. Caralis, President and Chief Executive Officer (Total facility includes 81
beds in nursing home–type unit) **A**1 2 7 9 10 **F**4 7 8 9 10 11 12 14 15 16 17
19 21 22 23 25 26 27 28 29 30 31 32 33 34 35 37 38 40 41 42 43 44 45
46 48 49 52 53 54 55 56 57 58 59 60 61 63 64 65 66 67 69 71 73 74 **P**5 7
S Sutter Health, Sacramento, CA **N** East Bay Medical Network, Emeryville, CA;
Sutter\CHS, Sacramento, CA
| | 23 | 10 | 555 | 15493 | 368 | 130485 | 4891 | 266695 | 106451 | |

BIG BEAR LAKE—San Bernardino County

☒ BEAR VALLEY COMMUNITY HOSPITAL, 41870 Garstin Road, Zip 92315, Mailing
Address: P.O. Box 1649, Zip 92315–1649; tel. 909/866–6501; James Sato,
Chief Executive Officer (Total facility includes 17 beds in nursing home–type unit)
A1 9 10 **F**15 16 19 21 22 28 32 36 44 46 49 60 64 71 73 **P**5 **S** Brim, Inc.,
Portland, OR
| | 16 | 10 | 30 | 549 | 19 | 17045 | — | 6440 | 3259 | |

BISHOP—Inyo County

☒ NORTHERN INYO HOSPITAL, 150 Pioneer Lane, Zip 93514–2599;
tel. 760/873–5811; Herman J. Spencer, Administrator **A**1 9 10 **F**7 15 19 22 33
34 37 40 44 49 65 71
| | 16 | 10 | 30 | 1369 | 11 | 22788 | 336 | 18281 | 9173 | 238 |

BLYTHE—Riverside County

★ PALO VERDE HOSPITAL, 250 North First Street, Zip 92225, Mailing Address: P.O.
Drawer Z., Zip 92226; tel. 760/922–4115; M. Victoria Clark, Administrator **A**9
10 **F**7 8 12 14 15 17 19 20 22 26 28 29 30 32 34 35 36 37 39 40 41 44 45
46 49 62 64 65 71 73
| | 33 | 10 | 36 | 1884 | 14 | 14097 | 366 | 9321 | 3670 | 120 |

BRAWLEY—Imperial County

☒ PIONEERS MEMORIAL HEALTHCARE DISTRICT, 207 West Legion Road,
Zip 92227–9699; tel. 760/351–3333; William W. Daniel, Chief Executive Officer
(Nonreporting) **A**1 9 10 **S** Brim, Inc., Portland, OR
| | 16 | 10 | 80 | — | — | — | — | — | — | — |

BREA—Orange County

□ BREA COMMUNITY HOSPITAL, 380 West Central Avenue, Zip 92821;
tel. 714/529–0211; Gaetano Zanfini, Chief Executive Officer (Nonreporting) **A**1 9
10
| | 33 | 10 | 60 | — | — | — | — | — | — | — |

□ VENCOR HOSPITAL–BREA, (Formerly THC – Orange County), 875 Brea Boulevard,
Zip 92821; tel. 714/529–6842; Mindy S. Moore, Administrator (Nonreporting) **A**1
10 **S** Vencor, Incorporated, Louisville, KY
| | 33 | 10 | 48 | — | — | — | — | — | — | — |

BUENA PARK—Orange County

BUENA PARK MEDICAL CENTER, 5742 Beach Boulevard, Zip 90621;
tel. 714/521–4770; Timothy L. Carda, Administrator and Chief Executive Officer
(Nonreporting) **S** Pacific Health Corporation, Long Beach, CA
| | 33 | 10 | 58 | — | — | — | — | — | — | — |

ORANGE COUNTY COMMUNITY HOSPITAL OF BUENA PARK, 6850 Lincoln Avenue,
Zip 90620–5703; tel. 562/827–1161; Joseph Sharp, Acting Administrator
(Nonreporting) **A**10 **S** Paracelsus Healthcare Corporation, Houston, TX
| | 33 | 22 | 55 | — | — | — | — | — | — | — |

BURBANK—Los Angeles County

☒ PROVIDENCE SAINT JOSEPH MEDICAL CENTER, 501 South Buena Vista Street,
Zip 91505–4866; tel. 818/843–5111; Michael J. Madden, Chief Executive Los
Angeles Service Area (Total facility includes 121 beds in nursing home–type unit)
A1 2 9 10 **F**4 7 8 10 11 12 13 14 15 16 17 19 20 21 22 23 24 26 27 28 29
30 31 32 33 34 35 37 38 39 40 41 42 43 44 45 46 48 49 60 64 65 67 68
71 72 73 74 **P**5 **S** Sisters of Providence Health System, Seattle, WA
N Providence Health System in California, Burbank, CA
| | 21 | 10 | 423 | 20000 | 318 | 321686 | 2581 | 171340 | 76494 | 1971 |

THOMPSON MEMORIAL MEDICAL CENTER, 466 East Olive Avenue, Zip 91501;
tel. 818/953–6500; Jerry Gillman, President and Chief Executive Officer
(Nonreporting)
| | 33 | 10 | 56 | — | — | — | — | — | — | — |

BURLINGAME—San Mateo County

☒ △ MILLS–PENINSULA HEALTH SERVICES, (Includes Mills Hospital, 100 South
San Mateo Drive, San Mateo, Zip 94401; tel. 415/696–4400; Peninsula Hospital,
1783 El Camino Real, tel. 415/696–5400), 1783 El Camino Real,
Zip 94010–3205; tel. 650/696–5400; Robert W. Merwin, Chief Executive Officer
(Total facility includes 55 beds in nursing home–type unit) (Nonreporting) **A**1 2 7 9
10 **S** Sutter Health, Sacramento, CA **N** Sutter\CHS, Sacramento, CA
| | 23 | 10 | 414 | — | — | — | — | — | — | — |

CAMARILLO—Ventura County

☒ ST. JOHN'S PLEASANT VALLEY HOSPITAL, 2309 Antonio Avenue,
Zip 93010–1459; tel. 805/389–5800; William J. Clearwater, Vice President and
Administrator **A**1 9 10 **F**7 8 11 15 16 17 19 21 22 23 28 29 30 32 35 37 40
44 45 46 49 63 64 65 67 71 73 **P**3 4 5 7 **S** Catholic Healthcare West, San
Francisco, CA **N** Catholic HealthCare West (CHW), San Francisco, CA
| | 23 | 10 | 110 | 3967 | 110 | 36448 | 622 | 29984 | 12714 | 440 |

CAMP PENDLETON—San Diego County

☒ NAVAL HOSPITAL, Mailing Address: Box 555191, Zip 92055–5191;
tel. 760/725–1288; Captain Thomas Burkhard, Commanding Officer
(Nonreporting) **A**1 3 5 **S** Department of Navy, Washington, DC
| | 43 | 10 | 209 | — | — | — | — | — | — | — |

CANOGA PARK—Los Angeles County, See Los Angeles

Hospital, Address, Telephone, Administrator, Approval, Facility, and Physician Codes, Health Care System, Network	Classi-fication Codes		Utilization Data					Expense (thousands) of dollars		
★ American Hospital Association (AHA) membership □ Joint Commission on Accreditation of Healthcare Organizations (JCAHO) accreditation + American Osteopathic Healthcare Association (AOHA) membership ○ American Osteopathic Association (AOA) accreditation △ Commission on Accreditation of Rehabilitation Facilities (CARF) accreditation Control codes 61, 63, 64, 71, 72 and 73 indicate hospitals listed by AOHA, but not registered by AHA. For definition of numerical codes, see page A4	Control	Service	Staffed Beds	Admissions	Census	Outpatient Visits	Births	Total	Payroll	Personnel

CARMICHAEL—Sacramento County

☒ MERCY AMERICAN RIVER/MERCY SAN JUAN HOSPITAL, (Includes Mercy American River Hospital, ; Mercy San Juan Hospital), 6501 Coyle Avenue, Zip 95608, Mailing Address: P.O. Box 479, Zip 95608; tel. 916/537–5000; Sister Bridget McCarthy, President (Nonreporting) **A**1 2 9 10 **S** Catholic Healthcare West, San Francisco, CA **N** Catholic HealthCare West (CHW), San Francisco, CA — 21 10 352 — — — — — — — —

CASTRO VALLEY—Alameda County

☒ EDEN MEDICAL CENTER, (Formerly Eden Hospital Medical Center), 20103 Lake Chabot Road, Zip 94546; tel. 510/537–1234; George Bischalaney, Interim President and Chief Executive Officer (Total facility includes 67 beds in nursing home–type unit) (Nonreporting) **A**1 2 9 10 **S** Sutter Health, Sacramento, CA **N** Sutter\CHS, Sacramento, CA — 16 10 258 — — — — — — — —

CATHEDRAL CITY—Riverside County

□ CHARTER BEHAVIORAL HEALTH SYSTEM–PALM SPRINGS, 69–696 Ramon Road, Zip 92234; tel. 619/321–2000; Robert Deney, Chief Executive Officer (Nonreporting) **A**1 9 10 **S** Magellan Health Services, Atlanta, GA — 33 22 80 — — — — — — — —

CEDARVILLE—Modoc County

SURPRISE VALLEY COMMUNITY HOSPITAL, Main and Washington Streets, Zip 96104, Mailing Address: P.O. Box 246, Zip 96104–0246; tel. 530/279–6111; Joyce Gysin, Administrator (Total facility includes 4 beds in nursing home–type unit) **A**9 10 **F**14 15 20 22 26 28 30 32 34 36 39 52 71 73 **P**6 **N** InterMountain Rural Health Network, Alturas, CA — 16 10 26 127 21 2219 8 2343 1606 64

CERRITOS—Los Angeles County

□ COLLEGE HOSPITAL, 10802 College Place, Zip 90703–1579; tel. 562/924–9581; Stephen Witt, Chief Executive Officer (Nonreporting) **A**1 3 9 10 **S** College Health Enterprises, Cerritos, CA — 33 22 125 — — — — — — — —

CHESTER—Plumas County

SENECA DISTRICT HOSPITAL, 130 Brentwood Drive, Zip 96020, Mailing Address: Box 737, Zip 96020; tel. 530/258–2151; Bernard G. Hietpas, Administrator (Total facility includes 16 beds in nursing home–type unit) **A**9 10 **F**7 8 14 22 28 33 34 40 44 64 65 71 72 73 — 16 10 26 398 19 22848 32 7170 3348 98

CHICO—Butte County

□ CHICO COMMUNITY HOSPITAL, 560 Cohasset Road, Zip 95926; tel. 916/896–5000; John E. Fidler, FACHE, Chief Executive Officer (Total facility includes 22 beds in nursing home–type unit) **A**1 9 10 **F**10 12 14 15 16 19 21 22 23 27 29 35 37 41 44 49 52 56 57 63 64 65 67 71 73 **P**5 **S** Paracelsus Healthcare Corporation, Houston, TX — 33 10 109 2805 43 30263 0 20848 9709 325

☒ N. T. ENLOE MEMORIAL HOSPITAL, 1531 Esplanade, Zip 95926–3386; tel. 530/891–7300; Philip R. Wolfe, Chief Executive Officer **A**1 2 9 10 **F**4 7 8 10 11 12 13 14 15 17 19 21 22 25 28 30 31 32 33 34 35 36 37 38 39 40 41 42 43 44 45 51 60 65 67 70 71 72 73 **P**7 — 23 10 208 10670 128 — 1613 112610 51515 1412

CHINO—San Bernardino County

□ BHC CANYON RIDGE HOSPITAL, 5353 G. Street, Zip 91710; tel. 909/590–3700; Diana L. Goulet, Chief Executive Officer (Nonreporting) **A**1 10 **S** Behavioral Healthcare Corporation, Nashville, TN — 33 22 59 — — — — — — — —

☒ CHINO VALLEY MEDICAL CENTER, (Formerly Columbia Chino Valley Medical Center), 5451 Walnut Avenue, Zip 91710; tel. 909/464–8600; David Chu, Interim Chief Executive Officer (Total facility includes 14 beds in nursing home–type unit) (Nonreporting) **A**1 9 10 **S** Columbia/HCA Healthcare Corporation, Nashville, TN — 33 10 104 — — — — — — — —

COLUMBIA CHINO VALLEY MEDICAL CENTER See Chino Valley Medical Center

HOSPITAL OF THE CALIFORNIA INSTITUTION FOR MEN, 14901 Central Avenue, Zip 91710, Mailing Address: Box 128, Zip 91710; tel. 909/597–1821; Pat Garleb, Administrator **F**1 2 3 4 5 6 9 10 11 12 18 19 20 21 22 25 27 29 30 31 33 34 35 37 39 41 42 43 44 45 46 48 49 50 51 52 54 55 56 57 58 59 60 63 64 65 67 69 70 71 72 — 12 11 80 1375 59 194115 — — — 277

CHOWCHILLA—Madera County

CHOWCHILLA DISTRICT MEMORIAL HOSPITAL, 1104 Ventura Avenue, Zip 93610, Mailing Address: Box 1027, Zip 93610; tel. 209/665–3781; Paul F. Dyer, President (Nonreporting) **A**9 10 — 16 10 23 — — — — — — — —

CHULA VISTA—San Diego County

□ BAYVIEW HOSPITAL AND MENTAL HEALTH SYSTEM, 330 Moss Street, Zip 91911–2005; tel. 619/426–6310; Roy Rodriguez, M.D., Chief Executive Officer (Nonreporting) **A**1 10 — 33 22 64 — — — — — — — —

☒ SCRIPPS HOSPITAL–CHULA VISTA, 435 H. Street, Zip 91912–1537, Mailing Address: P.O. Box 1537, Zip 91910–1537; tel. 619/691–7000; Thomas A. Gammiere, Vice President and Administrator **A**1 9 10 **F**1 2 3 4 6 7 8 10 11 12 14 15 16 17 19 21 22 23 24 25 26 27 28 29 30 31 32 33 34 35 36 37 39 40 41 42 43 44 45 46 48 50 51 52 53 54 55 56 57 58 59 60 63 64 65 67 68 69 70 71 72 73 74 **P**3 4 5 7 **S** Scripps Health, San Diego, CA **N** ScrippsHealth, San Diego, CA — 23 10 159 7879 96 56119 1680 55963 23911 414

☒ SHARP CHULA VISTA MEDICAL CENTER, 751 Medical Center Court, Zip 91911, Mailing Address: Box 1297, Zip 91912; tel. 619/482–5800; Britt Berrett, Chief Executive Officer (Total facility includes 133 beds in nursing home–type unit) **A**1 2 3 9 10 **F**3 4 7 8 10 11 12 13 14 15 16 17 18 19 21 22 23 24 25 26 27 28 29 30 31 32 33 34 35 36 37 38 39 40 41 42 43 44 45 46 49 51 53 54 55 56 57 58 59 60 61 64 65 66 67 68 69 71 72 73 74 **P**4 5 7 **S** Sharp Healthcare, San Diego, CA **N** Sharp Healthcare, San Diego, CA — 23 10 306 9871 233 43128 2049 62778 28958 676

Hospital, Address, Telephone, Administrator, Approval, Facility, and Physician Codes, Health Care System, Network	Classi-fication Codes		Utilization Data					Expense (thousands) of dollars		
★ American Hospital Association (AHA) membership □ Joint Commission on Accreditation of Healthcare Organizations (JCAHO) accreditation + American Osteopathic Healthcare Association (AOHA) membership ○ American Osteopathic Association (AOA) accreditation △ Commission on Accreditation of Rehabilitation Facilities (CARF) accreditation Control codes 61, 63, 64, 71, 72 and 73 indicate hospitals listed by AOHA, but not registered by AHA. For definition of numerical codes, see page A4	Control	Service	Staffed Beds	Admissions	Census	Outpatient Visits	Births	Total	Payroll	Personnel

CLEARLAKE—Lake County

★ REDBUD COMMUNITY HOSPITAL, 18th Avenue and Highway 53, Zip 95422, Mailing Address: Box 6720, Zip 95422; tel. 707/994–6486; Michael Schultz, President (Nonreporting) **A**9 10 **S** Adventist Health, Roseville, CA	16	10	34	—	—	—	—	—	—	—

CLOVIS—Fresno County

□ CLOVIS COMMUNITY MEDICAL CENTER, (Formerly Clovis Community Hospital), 2755 Herndon Avenue, Zip 93611; tel. 209/323–4060; Mike Barber, Facility Service Integrator (Nonreporting) **A**1 9 10 **S** Community Hospitals of Central California, Fresno, CA	23	10	143	—	—	—	—	—	—	—

COALINGA—Fresno County

COALINGA REGIONAL MEDICAL CENTER, 1191 Phelps Avenue, Zip 93210; tel. 209/935–6562; James J. Dickson, Administrator and Chief Executive Officer (Total facility includes 54 beds in nursing home–type unit) (Nonreporting) **A**9 10	16	10	78	—	—	—	—	—	—	—

COLUSA—Colusa County

□ COLUSA COMMUNITY HOSPITAL, 199 East Webster Street, Zip 95932, Mailing Address: P.O. Box 331, Zip 95932–0331; tel. 530/458–5821; Edward C. Bland, Chief Executive Officer (Nonreporting) **A**1 9 10	23	10	36	—	—	—	—	—	—	—

CONCORD—Contra Costa County

⊞ MOUNT DIABLO MEDICAL CENTER, 2540 East Street, Zip 94520, Mailing Address: P.O. Box 4110, Zip 94524–4110; tel. 925/682–8200; J. Kendall Anderson, President and Chief Executive Officer (Nonreporting) **A**1 2 9 10 **N** East Bay Medical Network, Emeryville, CA	16	10	209	—	—	—	—	—	—	—

CORCORAN—Kings County

CORCORAN DISTRICT HOSPITAL, 1310 Hanna Avenue, Zip 93212, Mailing Address: Box 758, Zip 93212; tel. 209/992–5051; Jimmy M. Knight, Administrator and Chief Executive Officer **A**9 10 **F**8 12 14 19 22 28 44 64 71 73 **P**4	16	10	32	1156	14	73350	1	10087	2320	108

CORONA—Riverside County

□ CHARTER BEHAVIORAL HEALTH SYSTEM OF SOUTHERN CALIFORNIA–CORONA, 2055 Kellogg Avenue, Zip 91719; tel. 909/735–2910; Diana C. Hanyak, Chief Executive Officer **A**1 9 10 **F**3 12 26 52 53 54 55 56 57 58 **S** Magellan Health Services, Atlanta, GA	33	22	92	2081	35	8747	0	6499	2698	92
□ CORONA REGIONAL MEDICAL CENTER, (Includes Corona Regional Medical Center–Rehabilitation, 730 Magnolia Avenue, Zip 91719; tel. 909/736–7200), 800 South Main Street, Zip 91720; tel. 909/737–4343; John Calderone, Ph.D., Chief Executive Officer **A**1 2 9 10 **F**7 8 12 14 15 16 17 19 20 21 22 26 27 28 29 30 32 33 35 37 39 40 41 42 44 45 46 48 49 54 57 58 59 61 64 65 67 71 73 74	23	10	225	8944	135	27927	1723	65933	22158	573

CORONADO—San Diego County

⊞ SHARP CORONADO HOSPITAL, 250 Prospect Place, Zip 92118; tel. 619/522–3600; Marcia K. Hall, Chief Executive Officer (Total facility includes 149 beds in nursing home–type unit) (Nonreporting) **A**1 9 10 **S** Sharp Healthcare, San Diego, CA	23	10	195	—	—	—	—	—	—	—

COSTA MESA—Orange County

□ COLLEGE HOSPITAL COSTA MESA, 301 Victoria Street, Zip 92627; tel. 714/642–2607; Susan Burden, Acting Chief Executive Officer **A**1 9 10 **F**1 12 15 17 18 19 25 26 28 34 35 37 44 52 53 54 55 56 57 58 59 65 67 68 69 71 73 **S** College Health Enterprises, Cerritos, CA	33	22	122	4451	82	15780	0	23114	9634	327

COVINA—Los Angeles County

⊞ CHARTER BEHAVIORAL HEALTH SYSTEM OF SOUTHERN CALIFORNIA–CHARTER OAK, 1161 East Covina Boulevard, Zip 91724–1161; tel. 626/966–1632; Todd A. Smith, Chief Executive Officer (Nonreporting) **A**1 10 **S** Magellan Health Services, Atlanta, GA	33	22	95	—	—	—	—	—	—	—
□ CITRUS VALLEY MEDICAL CENTER INTER–COMMUNITY CAMPUS, 210 West San Bernardino Road, Zip 91723–1901; tel. 626/331–7331; Warren J. Kirk, Administrator **A**1 2 9 10 **F**4 7 8 10 11 12 13 14 15 16 17 19 21 22 23 28 29 30 31 32 33 34 35 36 37 38 39 40 41 42 43 44 45 46 48 49 52 60 63 64 65 67 68 71 72 73 74 **P**1 5 7 **S** Citrus Valley Health Partners, Covina, CA	23	10	508	29682	362	164359	4477	162855	64267	2063

CRESCENT CITY—Del Norte County

⊞ SUTTER COAST HOSPITAL, 800 East Washington Boulevard, Zip 95531; tel. 707/464–8511; John E. Menaugh, Chief Executive Officer **A**1 9 10 **F**7 8 13 16 17 19 22 23 28 29 30 31 32 33 34 35 37 40 41 44 45 49 65 71 72 73 74 **P**3 5 7 **S** Sutter Health, Sacramento, CA **N** Sutter\CHS, Sacramento, CA	23	10	47	2573	32	98206	316	—	—	352

CULVER CITY—Los Angeles County

⊞ BROTMAN MEDICAL CENTER, 3828 Delmas Terrace, Zip 90231–2459, Mailing Address: Box 2459, Zip 90231–2459; tel. 310/836–7000; John V. Fenton, Chief Executive Officer (Total facility includes 21 beds in nursing home–type unit) (Nonreporting) **A**1 9 10 **S** TENET Healthcare Corporation, Santa Barbara, CA	33	10	240	—	—	—	—	—	—	—
□ WASHINGTON MEDICAL CENTER, 12101 West Washington Boulevard, Zip 90231, Mailing Address: Box 2787, Zip 90231; tel. 310/391–0601; Harry F. Adams, Administrator (Total facility includes 18 beds in nursing home–type unit) **A**1 9 10 **F**1 2 3 8 11 19 21 22 35 37 44 64 65 71	33	10	99	2017	49	13394	—	17206	6777	—

DALY CITY—San Mateo County

⊞ SETON MEDICAL CENTER, 1900 Sullivan Avenue, Zip 94015; tel. 650/992–4000; Bernadette Smith, Chief Operating Officer **A**1 2 3 5 9 10 **F**4 7 8 9 10 11 12 13 14 15 16 17 18 22 23 24 25 26 28 29 30 31 32 33 34 37 39 40 41 42 43 44 46 48 49 51 52 54 55 56 57 58 59 60 63 64 65 67 73 74 **P**3 5 **S** Catholic Healthcare West, San Francisco, CA **N** Catholic HealthCare West (CHW), San Francisco, CA	21	10	273	11266	208	284124	1031	127711	54752	1026

Hospital, Address, Telephone, Administrator, Approval, Facility, and Physician Codes, Health Care System, Network	Classi-fication Codes		Utilization Data					Expense (thousands) of dollars		
★ American Hospital Association (AHA) membership □ Joint Commission on Accreditation of Healthcare Organizations (JCAHO) accreditation + American Osteopathic Healthcare Association (AOHA) membership ○ American Osteopathic Association (AOA) accreditation △ Commission on Accreditation of Rehabilitation Facilities (CARF) accreditation Control codes 61, 63, 64, 71, 72 and 73 indicate hospitals listed by AOHA, but not registered by AHA. For definition of numerical codes, see page A4	Control	Service	Staffed Beds	Admissions	Census	Outpatient Visits	Births	Total	Payroll	Personnel

DANA POINT—Orange County

□ CAPISTRANO BY THE SEA HOSPITAL, 34000 Capistrano by the Sea Drive, Zip 92629–2104, Mailing Address: Box 398, Zip 92629–2104; tel. 714/496–5702; Barbara Messer, R.N., Administrator **A**1 9 10 **F**1 2 3 15 17 18 52 53 54 55 56 59 67 **P**8 — 33 22 68 711 21 — 0 — — 100

DAVIS—Yolo County

✚ SUTTER DAVIS HOSPITAL, 2000 Sutter Place, Zip 95616, Mailing Address: P.O. Box 1617, Zip 95617; tel. 530/756–6440; Lawrence A. Maas, Administrator **A**1 3 9 10 **F**7 12 13 15 16 17 19 20 23 28 32 35 37 40 41 42 44 65 68 71 73 **P**3 **S** Sutter Health, Sacramento, CA **N** Sutter\CHS, Sacramento, CA — 23 10 48 3161 20 70722 1029 29140 10588 —

DEER PARK—Napa County

✚ ST. HELENA HOSPITAL, 650 Sanitarium Road, Zip 94576, Mailing Address: P.O. Box 250, Zip 94576; tel. 707/963–3611; JoAline Olson, R.N., President (Total facility includes 23 beds in nursing home–type unit) (Nonreporting) **A**1 9 10 **S** Adventist Health, Roseville, CA **N** Adventist Health–Northern California, Deer Park, CA — 21 10 168 — — — — — — —

DELANO—Kern County

□ DELANO REGIONAL MEDICAL CENTER, 1401 Garces Highway, Zip 93215, Mailing Address: Box 460, Zip 93216; tel. 805/725–4800; Gerald A. Starr, Chief Executive Officer (Total facility includes 45 beds in nursing home–type unit) **A**1 9 10 **F**7 8 10 12 14 15 16 17 19 20 21 22 27 28 30 31 32 35 37 39 40 41 44 45 46 49 59 64 65 71 73 **P**5 — 23 10 156 3857 75 34256 1305 29341 10002 497

DINUBA—Tulare County

ALTA DISTRICT HOSPITAL, 500 Adelaide Way, Zip 93618–1698; tel. 209/591–4171; Joseph A. DeStefano, Chief Executive Officer (Total facility includes 18 beds in nursing home–type unit) **A**9 10 **F**15 19 22 34 35 36 44 64 65 71 73 — 16 10 39 1368 17 22243 — 8863 3480 126

DOS PALOS—Merced County

DOS PALOS MEMORIAL HOSPITAL, 2118 Marguerite Street, Zip 93620; tel. 209/392–6106; Darryl E. Henley, Administrator (Nonreporting) **A**9 10 — 23 10 15 — — — — — — —

DOWNEY—Los Angeles County

□ DOWNEY COMMUNITY HOSPITAL FOUNDATION, (Includes Downey Community Hospital, 11500 Brookshire Avenue, ; Rio Hondo Memorial Hospital, 8300 East Telegraph Road, Zip 90240; tel. 310/806–1821), 11500 Brookshire Avenue, Zip 90241–4990; tel. 310/904–5000; Allen R. Korneff, President and Chief Executive Officer (Total facility includes 20 beds in nursing home–type unit) **A**1 9 10 12 13 **F**4 7 8 10 11 12 19 21 22 26 27 28 30 32 35 36 37 38 40 41 42 43 44 45 49 63 64 65 67 71 73 **P**7 — 23 10 174 8696 94 148434 1257 93646 35688 924

✚ △ LAC–RANCHO LOS AMIGOS MEDICAL CENTER, 7601 East Imperial Highway, Zip 90242; tel. 562/401–7022; Consuelo C. Diaz, Chief Executive Officer **A**1 3 5 7 9 10 **F**1 4 5 6 7 8 10 12 13 14 15 17 19 20 21 22 23 25 26 27 28 29 30 31 32 33 34 35 37 39 41 42 43 44 45 46 48 49 50 51 53 54 55 56 57 58 59 60 61 63 65 66 68 69 70 71 72 73 74 **P**3 5 6 **S** Los Angeles County–Department of Health Services, Los Angeles, CA — 13 46 207 3023 192 62126 — 186628 58195 1379

RIO HONDO MEMORIAL HOSPITAL See Downey Community Hospital Foundation

DUARTE—Los Angeles County

✚ CITY OF HOPE NATIONAL MEDICAL CENTER, 1500 East Duarte Road, Zip 91010–3000; tel. 626/359–8111; Charles M. Balch, M.D., President and Chief Executive Officer **A**1 2 3 5 9 10 **F**8 12 14 15 16 17 19 20 21 30 32 34 35 37 39 41 42 44 45 46 49 50 60 65 69 71 73 **P**7 — 23 10 145 3956 102 107208 — 180561 75058 1644

□ SANTA TERESITA HOSPITAL, 819 Buena Vista Street, Zip 91010–1703; tel. 626/359–3243; Michael J. Costello, Jr., Chief Executive Officer (Total facility includes 133 beds in nursing home–type unit) (Nonreporting) **A**1 2 10 — 21 10 283 — — — — — — —

EDWARDS AFB—Kern County

✚ U. S. AIR FORCE HOSPITAL, 30 Hospital Road, Building 5500, Zip 93524–1730; tel. 805/277–2010; Lieutenant Colonel Greg Allen, MSC, USAF, Administrator **A**1 **F**2 3 4 5 6 7 8 10 11 12 13 14 15 16 17 18 19 20 21 22 23 24 25 26 27 28 29 30 31 32 33 34 35 36 37 38 39 40 41 42 43 44 45 46 47 48 49 50 51 52 53 54 56 57 58 59 60 61 62 63 64 65 66 67 68 69 71 72 73 74 **S** Department of the Air Force, Bowling AFB, DC — 41 10 7 756 2 96000 211 20300 12300 347

EL CAJON—San Diego County

KAISER FOUNDATION HOSPITAL See Kaiser Foundation Hospital, San Diego

✚ SCRIPPS HOSPITAL–EAST COUNTY, 1688 East Main Street, Zip 92021; tel. 619/593–5600; Deborah Dunne, Administrator (Total facility includes 35 beds in nursing home–type unit) **A**1 9 10 **F**4 7 8 10 11 12 13 17 19 22 27 28 31 32 34 35 36 37 40 41 42 43 44 45 46 48 49 52 56 57 59 64 65 69 70 71 73 74 **P**1 3 5 7 8 **S** Scripps Health, San Diego, CA **N** ScrippsHealth, San Diego, CA — 23 10 105 4026 54 29321 — 34724 12911 277

EL CENTRO—Imperial County

✚ EL CENTRO REGIONAL MEDICAL CENTER, 1415 Ross Avenue, Zip 92243; tel. 760/339–7100; Ted Fox, Administrator and Chief Executive Officer (Nonreporting) **A**1 9 10 — 14 10 107 — — — — — — —

ELDRIDGE—Sonoma County

SONOMA DEVELOPMENTAL CENTER, (INSTITUTION FOR DEV DISABLED), 15000 Arnold Drive, Zip 95431; tel. 707/938–6000; Timothy L. Meeker, Executive Director **A**9 10 **F**1 12 15 16 17 24 26 28 30 33 39 46 51 53 54 55 57 64 65 73 — 12 49 959 14 988 — — 106035 61413 1797

Hospital, Address, Telephone, Administrator, Approval, Facility, and Physician Codes, Health Care System, Network	Classi-fication Codes		Utilization Data					Expense (thousands) of dollars		
	Control	Service	Staffed Beds	Admissions	Census	Outpatient Visits	Births	Total	Payroll	Personnel

★ American Hospital Association (AHA) membership
□ Joint Commission on Accreditation of Healthcare Organizations (JCAHO) accreditation
+ American Osteopathic Healthcare Association (AOHA) membership
○ American Osteopathic Association (AOA) accreditation
△ Commission on Accreditation of Rehabilitation Facilities (CARF) accreditation
  Control codes 61, 63, 64, 71, 72 and 73 indicate hospitals listed by AOHA, but not registered by AHA. For definition of numerical codes, see page A4

ENCINITAS—San Diego County

□ BHC SAN LUIS REY HOSPITAL, 335 Saxony Road, Zip 92024–2723; tel. 619/753–1245; William T. Sparrow, Chief Executive Officer (Nonreporting) **A**1 9 10 **S** Behavioral Healthcare Corporation, Nashville, TN	33	22	122	—	—	—	—	—	—	—
✶ △ SCRIPPS MEMORIAL HOSPITAL–ENCINITAS, 354 Santa Fe Drive, Zip 92024, Mailing Address: P.O. Box 230817, Zip 92023; tel. 760/753–6501; Gerald E. Bracht, Vice President and Administrator (Nonreporting) **A**1 2 7 9 10 **S** Scripps Health, San Diego, CA **N** ScrippsHealth, San Diego, CA	23	10	145	—	—	—	—	—	—	—

ENCINO—Los Angeles County, See Los Angeles

ESCONDIDO—San Diego County

✶ PALOMAR MEDICAL CENTER, 555 East Valley Parkway, Zip 92025–3084; tel. 760/739–3000; Victoria M. Penland, Administrator and Chief Operating Officer (Total facility includes 96 beds in nursing home–type unit) **A**1 2 9 10 **F**3 4 7 8 10 17 19 21 22 23 25 27 28 29 30 31 32 33 34 35 36 37 38 39 40 41 42 43 44 45 46 49 51 52 54 55 56 57 58 59 60 61 63 64 65 66 70 71 73 **P**6 7 **S** Palomar Pomerado Health System, San Diego, CA **N** Health First Network, San Diego, CA	16	10	395	15321	242	196690	3044	132561	51266	1449

EUREKA—Humboldt County

★ △ GENERAL HOSPITAL, 2200 Harrison Avenue, Zip 95501; tel. 707/445–5111; David S. Wanger, Chief Executive Officer (Nonreporting) **A**7 9 10 **S** Province Healthcare Corporation, Brentwood, TN	33	10	65	—	—	—	—	—	—	—
✶ SAINT JOSEPH HOSPITAL, 2700 Dolbeer Street, Zip 95501; tel. 707/269–4223; Neil Martin, President and Chief Executive Officer **A**1 2 9 10 **F**2 3 4 7 8 10 11 14 15 16 17 19 20 21 22 27 28 29 30 31 32 33 34 35 37 40 41 42 43 44 45 46 48 49 51 60 65 67 71 73 74 **P**2 5 6 **S** St. Joseph Health System, Orange, CA **N** Saint Joseph Health System, Orange, CA	21	10	102	3733	48	169161	28	44272	14584	570

EXETER—Tulare County

□ MEMORIAL HOSPITAL AT EXETER, 215 Crespi Avenue, Zip 93221–1399; tel. 209/592–2151; Sally Brewer, Chief Executive Officer (Total facility includes 62 beds in nursing home–type unit) (Nonreporting) **A**1 9 10	23	10	80	—	—	—	—	—	—	—

FAIRFIELD—Solano County

✶ NORTHBAY MEDICAL CENTER, 1200 B. Gale Wilson Boulevard, Zip 94533–3587; tel. 707/429–3600; Deborah Sugiyama, President (Total facility includes 11 beds in nursing home–type unit) **A**1 2 9 10 **F**7 8 10 12 13 14 15 16 17 19 21 22 23 28 30 32 33 35 36 39 40 41 42 44 49 60 65 67 71 73 **P**3 **S** NorthBay Healthcare System, Fairfield, CA **N** NorthBay Healthcare System, Fairfield, CA	23	10	121	5185	53	73614	1462	54442	22559	354

FALL RIVER MILLS—Shasta County

MAYERS MEMORIAL HOSPITAL DISTRICT, Highway 299 East, Zip 96028, Mailing Address: Box 459, Zip 96028; tel. 530/336–5511; Judi Beck, Administrator (Total facility includes 50 beds in nursing home–type unit) (Nonreporting) **A**9 10 **N** InterMountain Rural Health Network, Alturas, CA	16	10	72	—	—	—	—	—	—	—

FALLBROOK—San Diego County

✶ FALLBROOK HOSPITAL DISTRICT, 624 East Elder Street, Zip 92028; tel. 760/728–1191; Corey A. Seale, Chief Executive Officer (Total facility includes 95 beds in nursing home–type unit) (Nonreporting) **A**1 9 10	16	10	142	—	—	—	—	—	—	—

FOLSOM—Sacramento County

✶ MERCY HOSPITAL OF FOLSOM, 1650 Creekside Drive, Zip 95630–3405; tel. 916/983–7400; Donald C. Hudson, Vice President and Chief Operating Officer **A**1 9 10 **F**4 7 8 10 12 14 17 19 22 25 26 28 30 31 32 33 35 37 40 41 42 43 44 46 49 50 62 65 67 71 72 73 74 **P**3 5 **S** Catholic Healthcare West, San Francisco, CA **N** Catholic HealthCare West (CHW), San Francisco, CA	21	10	66	3141	27	30656	660	21605	9545	—
□ VENCOR HOSPITAL–SACRAMENTO, 223 Fargo Way, Zip 95630; tel. 916/351–9151; Meredith Taylor, Administrator (Nonreporting) **A**1 9 10 **S** Vencor, Incorporated, Louisville, KY	33	10	32	—	—	—	—	—	—	—

FONTANA—San Bernardino County

✶ KAISER FOUNDATION HOSPITAL, 9961 Sierra Avenue, Zip 92335–6794; tel. 909/427–5000; Patricia Siegel, Senior Vice President and Area Manager **A**1 2 3 5 10 **F**3 7 8 9 10 11 12 14 15 16 19 21 22 23 25 28 29 30 32 33 35 37 38 40 41 42 43 44 45 46 47 48 49 51 52 53 54 55 56 58 59 60 61 63 64 65 66 67 68 69 71 73 **S** Kaiser Foundation Hospitals, Oakland, CA	23	10	241	19966	199	—	3823	—	—	—

FORT BRAGG—Mendocino County

□ MENDOCINO COAST DISTRICT HOSPITAL, 700 River Drive, Zip 95437; tel. 707/961–1234; Elizabeth MacGard, Chief Executive Officer **A**1 9 10 **F**7 8 11 12 14 15 16 17 19 21 22 26 28 29 30 31 32 33 34 35 36 37 39 40 41 42 44 45 46 49 60 63 64 65 67 68 71 73 **P**3	16	10	51	1777	22	55613	178	20050	9256	222

FORT IRWIN—San Bernardino County

✶ WEED ARMY COMMUNITY HOSPITAL, Zip 92310–5065; tel. 760/380–3108; Colonel James Beson, Commander (Nonreporting) **A**1 **S** Department of the Army, Office of the Surgeon General, Falls Church, VA	42	10	27	—	—	—	—	—	—	—

FORTUNA—Humboldt County

✶ REDWOOD MEMORIAL HOSPITAL, 3300 Renner Drive, Zip 95540; tel. 707/725–3361; Neil Martin, President and Chief Executive Officer **A**1 2 9 10 **F**7 8 15 16 19 21 22 27 28 29 32 33 37 40 44 45 64 67 73 **S** St. Joseph Health System, Orange, CA **N** Saint Joseph Health System, Orange, CA	21	10	35	2014	21	31421	377	15187	5599	180

FOUNTAIN VALLEY—Orange County

✶ FOUNTAIN VALLEY REGIONAL HOSPITAL AND MEDICAL CENTER, 17100 Euclid at Warner, Zip 92708; tel. 714/966–7200; Timothy Smith, President and Chief Executive Officer **A**1 2 5 9 10 **F**1 4 7 8 10 11 12 14 15 16 17 19 21 22 23 27 28 29 30 31 32 33 34 35 37 38 39 40 42 43 44 45 46 47 49 52 57 59 60 61 63 64 65 66 67 71 73 74 **P**5 **S** TENET Healthcare Corporation, Santa Barbara, CA	33	10	396	15659	191	82153	4402	101884	43166	1187

Hospital, Address, Telephone, Administrator, Approval, Facility, and Physician Codes, Health Care System, Network	Classi-fication Codes		Utilization Data					Expense (thousands) of dollars		
★ American Hospital Association (AHA) membership □ Joint Commission on Accreditation of Healthcare Organizations (JCAHO) accreditation + American Osteopathic Healthcare Association (AOHA) membership ○ American Osteopathic Association (AOA) accreditation △ Commission on Accreditation of Rehabilitation Facilities (CARF) accreditation Control codes 61, 63, 64, 71, 72 and 73 indicate hospitals listed by AOHA, but not registered by AHA. For definition of numerical codes, see page A4	Control	Service	Staffed Beds	Admissions	Census	Outpatient Visits	Births	Total	Payroll	Personnel

□ ORANGE COAST MEMORIAL MEDICAL CENTER, 9920 Talbert Avenue, Zip 92708; tel. 714/378–7000; Barry Arbuckle, Ph.D., Chief Executive Officer **A**1 3 9 10 **F**2 3 4 7 8 9 10 12 13 14 16 17 19 21 22 23 25 26 28 29 30 32 33 34 35 36 37 38 39 40 41 42 43 44 45 46 47 48 49 50 51 52 53 54 55 56 57 58 59 60 61 63 64 65 66 67 69 70 71 72 73 74 **P**2 3 5 6 7 **S** Memorial Health Services, Long Beach, CA	23	10	230	6335	67	33468	607	71857	19912	539
FREMONT—Alameda County										
□ BHC FREMONT HOSPITAL, 39001 Sundale Drive, Zip 94538; tel. 510/796–1100; Ed Owen, Chief Executive Officer **A**1 9 10 **F**2 3 12 15 16 22 52 53 55 56 57 59 65 67 **S** Behavioral Healthcare Corporation, Nashville, TN	33	22	78	1171	36	6778	—	—	—	66
★ WASHINGTON TOWNSHIP HEALTH CARE DISTRICT, 2000 Mowry Avenue, Zip 94538–1716; tel. 510/797–1111; Nancy D. Farber, Chief Executive Officer **A**1 2 9 10 **F**4 7 8 10 11 12 13 14 15 16 17 18 19 21 22 28 29 30 32 33 34 35 37 39 40 41 42 43 44 46 49 52 54 56 57 59 60 63 64 65 67 71 72 73 **P**5 7 **N** East Bay Medical Network, Emeryville, CA	16	10	252	13031	152	125339	2425	117821	56283	945
FRENCH CAMP—San Joaquin County										
□ △ SAN JOAQUIN GENERAL HOSPITAL, 500 West Hospital Road, Zip 95231, Mailing Address: P.O. Box 1020, Stockton, Zip 95201; tel. 209/468–6600; Michael N. Smith, Director Healthcare Services (Nonreporting) **A**1 3 5 7 9 10	13	10	195	—	—	—	—	—	—	—
FRESNO—Fresno County										
□ BHC CEDAR VISTA HOSPITAL, 7171 North Cedar Avenue, Zip 93720; tel. 209/449–8000; Richard Adams, Ph.D., Administrator **A**1 9 10 **F**2 3 12 14 15 26 52 53 54 56 57 58 59 65 **S** Behavioral Healthcare Corporation, Nashville, TN	32	22	61	1156	22	—	0	3715	—	149
★ △ FRESNO COMMUNITY HOSPITAL AND MEDICAL CENTER, Fresno and R. Streets, Zip 93721, Mailing Address: Box 1232, Zip 93715; tel. 209/442–6000; J. Philip Hinton, M.D., President and Chief Executive Officer (Nonreporting) **A**1 2 7 9 10 **S** Community Hospitals of Central California, Fresno, CA	23	10	375	—	—	—	—	—	—	—
FRESNO SURGERY CENTER–THE HOSPITAL FOR SURGERY, 6125 North Fresno Street, Zip 93710; tel. 209/431–8000; Alan H. Pierrot, M.D., Chief Executive Officer (Nonreporting) **A**10	32	49	20	—	—	—	—	—	—	—
★ KAISER FOUNDATION HOSPITAL, 7300 North Fresno Street, Zip 93720; tel. 209/448–4555; Edward S. Glavis, Administrator **A**1 10 **F**2 3 4 7 8 9 10 11 12 13 14 15 16 17 18 19 21 22 23 25 26 27 28 29 30 31 32 33 34 35 37 38 39 40 41 42 43 44 45 46 47 48 49 50 51 52 53 54 55 56 57 58 59 60 61 63 64 65 66 67 68 69 70 71 72 73 74 **P**6 **S** Kaiser Foundation Hospitals, Oakland, CA	23	10	116	5219	51	597323	1328	—	—	482
★ SAINT AGNES MEDICAL CENTER, 1303 East Herndon Avenue, Zip 93720–3397; tel. 209/449–3000; Sister Ruth Marie Nickerson, President and Chief Executive Officer **A**1 2 9 10 **F**1 3 4 7 8 10 11 12 13 14 15 16 17 18 19 20 21 22 23 25 26 27 29 30 31 32 33 34 35 37 39 40 41 42 43 44 45 46 49 53 54 55 56 58 59 60 65 67 68 69 71 72 73 74 **P**5 7 **S** Holy Cross Health System Corporation, South Bend, IN	21	10	326	20765	218	264883	2771	177152	69635	1841
□ △ SAN JOAQUIN VALLEY REHABILITATION HOSPITAL, 7173 North Sharon Avenue, Zip 93720; tel. 209/436–3600; W. David Smiley, Chief Executive Officer (Nonreporting) **A**1 7 9 10	33	46	62	—	—	—	—	—	—	—
□ UNIVERSITY MEDICAL CENTER, (Formerly Valley Medical Center of Fresno), 445 South Cedar Avenue, Zip 93702–2907; tel. 209/453–4000; Terry Henry, Interim Administrator (Nonreporting) **A**1 8 10 **S** Community Hospitals of Central California, Fresno, CA	13	10	334	—	—	—	—	—	—	—
□ △ VALLEY CHILDREN'S HOSPITAL, 3151 North Millbrook, Zip 93703; tel. 209/225–3000; Rex Riley, President and Chief Executive Officer **A**1 3 5 7 9 10 **F**10 13 14 15 16 17 19 21 22 25 28 30 32 34 35 38 41 42 43 44 45 46 47 48 49 51 58 60 65 67 71 72 73 **P**1 5	23	50	201	8788	149	135743	—	128079	57828	1784
VALLEY MEDICAL CENTER OF FRESNO See University Medical Center										
★ VETERANS AFFAIRS MEDICAL CENTER, 2615 East Clinton Avenue, Zip 93703; tel. 209/225–6100; Ada Neale, Acting Director (Total facility includes 50 beds in nursing home–type unit) **A**1 2 3 5 **F**2 3 4 10 14 15 16 19 20 21 22 26 27 28 29 30 31 32 33 34 37 39 41 42 44 45 46 49 51 52 54 56 57 58 65 67 71 73 74 **S** Department of Veterans Affairs, Washington, DC	45	10	135	3825	79	148207	—	66972	33924	776
FULLERTON—Orange County										
★ △ ST. JUDE MEDICAL CENTER, 101 East Valencia Mesa Drive, Zip 92635; tel. 714/992–3000; Robert J. Fraschetti, President and Chief Executive Officer (Nonreporting) **A**1 2 7 9 10 **S** St. Joseph Health System, Orange, CA **N** Friendly Hills HealthCare Network, LaHabra, CA; Saint Joseph Health System, Orange, CA	21	10	347	—	—	—	—	—	—	—
GARBERVILLE—Humboldt County										
SOUTHERN HUMBOLDT COMMUNITY HEALTHCARE DISTRICT, 733 Cedar Street, Zip 95542–3292; tel. 707/923–3921; Steven G. Cherry, Administrator and Chief Executive Officer (Total facility includes 8 beds in nursing home–type unit) **A**9 10 **F**7 8 13 15 16 17 22 29 30 31 32 34 36 38 39 40 41 52 56 61 64 66 71 74 **P**5	16	10	16	342	11	7217	16	3836	2015	79
GARDEN GROVE—Orange County										
★ GARDEN GROVE HOSPITAL AND MEDICAL CENTER, 12601 Garden Grove Boulevard, Zip 92843–1959; tel. 714/741–2700; Timothy Smith, President and Chief Executive Officer (Total facility includes 12 beds in nursing home–type unit) **A**1 9 10 **F**7 13 16 19 21 22 26 27 28 30 31 32 34 35 37 38 40 41 42 44 49 63 64 65 71 73 **P**5 7 **S** TENET Healthcare Corporation, Santa Barbara, CA **N** Tenet Healthcare Corporation, Santa Barbara, CA	33	10	167	8426	84	66073	2648	41417	20633	505

Hospital, Address, Telephone, Administrator, Approval, Facility, and Physician Codes, Health Care System, Network	Classi-fication Codes		Utilization Data					Expense (thousands) of dollars		
	Control	Service	Staffed Beds	Admissions	Census	Outpatient Visits	Births	Total	Payroll	Personnel

★ American Hospital Association (AHA) membership
☐ Joint Commission on Accreditation of Healthcare Organizations (JCAHO) accreditation
+ American Osteopathic Healthcare Association (AOHA) membership
○ American Osteopathic Association (AOA) accreditation
△ Commission on Accreditation of Rehabilitation Facilities (CARF) accreditation
   Control codes 61, 63, 64, 71, 72 and 73 indicate hospitals listed by AOHA, but not registered by AHA. For definition of numerical codes, see page A4

GARDENA—Los Angeles County

☐ COMMUNITY HOSPITAL OF GARDENA, 1246 West 155th Street, Zip 90247–4062; tel. 310/323–5330; Raymond N. Smith, Chief Executive Officer (Total facility includes 20 beds in nursing home–type unit) (Nonreporting) **A**1 10	33	10	58	—	—	—	—	—	—	—
☐ MEMORIAL HOSPITAL OF GARDENA, 1145 West Redondo Beach Boulevard, Zip 90247; tel. 310/532–4200; Frank Katsuda, Administrator (Nonreporting) **A**1 10	33	10	107	—	—	—	—	—	—	—

GILROY—Santa Clara County

✠ COLUMBIA SOUTH VALLEY HOSPITAL, 9400 No Name Uno, Zip 95020–2368; tel. 408/848–2000; Beverly Gilmore, Chief Executive Officer (Total facility includes 21 beds in nursing home–type unit) (Nonreporting) **A**1 9 10 **S** Columbia/HCA Healthcare Corporation, Nashville, TN	33	10	93	—	—	—	—	—	—	—

GLENDALE—Los Angeles County

✠ △ GLENDALE ADVENTIST MEDICAL CENTER, 1509 Wilson Terrace, Zip 91206–4007; tel. 818/409–8000; Robert G. Carmen, President and Chief Executive Officer **A**1 2 3 5 7 9 10 **F**3 4 5 6 7 8 10 12 15 16 17 18 19 21 22 23 24 27 28 29 30 32 34 35 41 42 43 44 49 53 54 55 56 57 58 59 60 65 67 68 69 71 72 73 74 **P**3 5 **S** Adventist Health, Roseville, CA **N** Adventist Health–Southern California, Glendale, CA	21	10	396	13866	227	236182	2846	122223	53441	1558
✠ GLENDALE MEMORIAL HOSPITAL AND HEALTH CENTER, 1420 South Central Avenue, Zip 91204–2594; tel. 818/502–1900; Arnold R. Schaffer, President and Chief Executive Officer **A**1 2 9 10 **F**2 3 4 7 8 10 11 12 13 14 15 16 17 18 19 20 21 22 26 27 28 29 30 31 32 33 34 35 37 38 39 40 41 42 43 44 48 49 52 54 55 56 57 58 59 60 63 65 67 68 71 72 73 74 **P**5 7 **S** UniHealth, Burbank, CA **N** UniHealth, Burbank, CA	23	10	275	13176	180	116119	1712	96148	46114	1033
✠ VERDUGO HILLS HOSPITAL, 1812 Verdugo Boulevard, Zip 91208; tel. 818/790–7100; Bernard Glossy, President **A**1 2 9 10 **F**7 8 11 12 13 14 15 16 19 20 21 22 24 26 28 29 30 32 35 37 40 42 44 45 49 52 57 59 63 64 65 66 67 71 73 **P**5 6 **S** Southern California Healthcare Systems, Pasadena, CA **N** Southern California Healthcare Systems, Pasadena, CA	23	10	112	5612	65	34641	1070	36909	18739	370

GLENDORA—Los Angeles County

✠ FOOTHILL PRESBYTERIAN HOSPITAL–MORRIS L. JOHNSTON MEMORIAL, 250 South Grand Avenue, Zip 91741; tel. 626/963–8411; Bryan R. Rogers, President and Chief Executive Officer **A**1 2 9 10 **F**4 7 8 10 11 12 14 15 16 17 19 21 22 28 29 30 32 33 34 35 36 37 39 40 41 42 43 44 45 46 49 60 63 65 66 67 71 73 74 **P**1 3 5 7 **S** Citrus Valley Health Partners, Covina, CA	23	10	106	5370	52	69330	1392	33718	14015	—
✠ HUNTINGTON EAST VALLEY HOSPITAL, 150 West Alosta Avenue, Zip 91740–4398; tel. 626/335–0231; James W. Maki, Chief Executive Officer (Nonreporting) **A**1 9 10 **S** Southern California Healthcare Systems, Pasadena, CA **N** Southern California Healthcare Systems, Pasadena, CA	23	10	128	—	—	—	—	—	—	—

GRANADA HILLS—Los Angeles County, See Los Angeles
GRASS VALLEY—Nevada County

✠ SIERRA NEVADA MEMORIAL HOSPITAL, 155 Glasson Way, Zip 95945–5792, Mailing Address: P.O. Box 1029, Zip 95945–5792; tel. 530/274–6000; C. Thomas Collier, President and Chief Executive Officer **A**1 9 10 **F**7 8 11 12 14 15 16 19 22 32 34 35 37 40 42 44 45 49 60 64 71 72 **P**3 5 **S** Catholic Healthcare West, San Francisco, CA **N** Catholic HealthCare West (CHW), San Francisco, CA	23	10	111	6020	65	111353	531	52557	22346	513

GREENBRAE—Marin County

✠ MARIN GENERAL HOSPITAL, 250 Bon Air Road, Zip 94904, Mailing Address: Box 8010, San Rafael, Zip 94912–8010; tel. 415/925–7000; Henry J. Buhrmann, President and Chief Executive Officer **A**1 2 9 10 **F**4 7 8 10 11 12 14 15 16 19 21 22 23 24 27 28 29 30 31 32 34 35 37 38 40 41 42 43 44 45 46 49 52 53 54 55 56 57 58 59 60 64 65 67 71 73 74 **P**1 3 7 **S** Sutter Health, Sacramento, CA **N** Sutter\CHS, Sacramento, CA	23	10	110	10112	101	83152	1573	101006	40791	1042

GREENVILLE—Plumas County

INDIAN VALLEY HOSPITAL DISTRICT, 184 Hot Springs Road, Zip 95947; tel. 530/284–7191; Lynn Seaberg, Administrator and Chief Executive Officer (Total facility includes 19 beds in nursing home–type unit) **A**9 10 **F**14 15 16 20 21 22 26 28 30 32 33 34 36 44 49 64 71 **P**6 **N** InterMountain Rural Health Network, Alturas, CA	16	10	26	244	23	11859	2	3909	1912	83

GRIDLEY—Butte County

BIGGS–GRIDLEY MEMORIAL HOSPITAL, 240 Spruce Street, Zip 95948, Mailing Address: Box 97, Zip 95948; tel. 916/846–5671; Charles R. Norton, Administrator (Nonreporting) **A**9 10	23	10	55	—	—	—	—	—	—	—

HANFORD—Kings County

☐ CENTRAL VALLEY GENERAL HOSPITAL, 1025 North Douty Street, Zip 93230, Mailing Address: Box 480, Zip 93232; tel. 209/583–2100; Gary K. Wiggins, Chief Executive Officer (Nonreporting) **A**1 9 10	33	10	40	—	—	—	—	—	—	—
✠ HANFORD COMMUNITY MEDICAL CENTER, 450 Greenfield Avenue, Zip 93230–0240, Mailing Address: Box 240, Zip 93232–0240; tel. 209/582–9000; Darwin R. Remboldt, President and Chief Executive Officer **A**1 9 10 **F**7 8 10 12 14 15 16 19 22 23 25 28 30 32 33 34 35 37 39 40 41 42 44 45 46 51 60 70 71 72 73 **P**3 **S** Adventist Health, Roseville, CA	21	10	59	4988	46	232005	1098	48094	18009	681

HARBOR CITY—Los Angeles County, See Los Angeles
HAWTHORNE—Los Angeles County

HAWTHORNE HOSPITAL See Los Angeles Metropolitan Medical Center, Los Angeles

Hospital, Address, Telephone, Administrator, Approval, Facility, and Physician Codes, Health Care System, Network	Classi-fication Codes		Utilization Data					Expense (thousands) of dollars		
★ American Hospital Association (AHA) membership ☐ Joint Commission on Accreditation of Healthcare Organizations (JCAHO) accreditation + American Osteopathic Healthcare Association (AOHA) membership ○ American Osteopathic Association (AOA) accreditation △ Commission on Accreditation of Rehabilitation Facilities (CARF) accreditation Control codes 61, 63, 64, 71, 72 and 73 indicate hospitals listed by AOHA, but not registered by AHA. For definition of numerical codes, see page A4	Control	Service	Staffed Beds	Admissions	Census	Outpatient Visits	Births	Total	Payroll	Personnel
☒ ROBERT F. KENNEDY MEDICAL CENTER, 4500 West 116th Street, Zip 90250; tel. 310/973–1711; Peter P. Aprato, Administrator and Chief Operating Officer (Total facility includes 34 beds in nursing home–type unit) **A**1 9 10 **F**1 3 4 7 8 10 11 12 13 14 15 16 17 18 19 20 21 22 27 28 29 30 31 32 33 35 36 37 39 41 42 43 44 45 46 49 52 53 54 55 56 57 59 60 61 63 64 65 67 69 71 73 **P**5 **S** Catholic Healthcare West, San Francisco, CA **N** Catholic HealthCare West (CHW), San Francisco, CA; Essential HealthCare Network, Monterey Park, CA	21	10	195	5475	111	34477	—	49962	23053	514
HAYWARD—Alameda County										
☒ KAISER FOUNDATION HOSPITAL, 27400 Hesperian Boulevard, Zip 94545–4297; tel. 510/784–4313; Bernard J. Tyson, Administrator (Nonreporting) **A**1 10 **S** Kaiser Foundation Hospitals, Oakland, CA **N** Kaiser Foundation Health Plan of Northern California, Oakland, CA	23	10	190	—	—	—	—	—	—	—
☐ ST. ROSE HOSPITAL, 27200 Calaroga Avenue, Zip 94545–4383; tel. 510/264–4000; Michael P. Mahoney, President and Chief Executive Officer (Total facility includes 46 beds in nursing home–type unit) (Nonreporting) **A**1 2 9 10 **S** Marian Health System, Tulsa, OK	21	10	175	—	—	—	—	—	—	—
HEALDSBURG—Sonoma County										
★ HEALDSBURG GENERAL HOSPITAL, 1375 University Avenue, Zip 95448; tel. 707/431–6500; Mary Schwind, R.N., MS, Chief Executive Officer (Nonreporting) **A**9 10 **S** Columbia/HCA Healthcare Corporation, Nashville, TN	33	10	49	—	—	—	—	—	—	—
HEMET—Riverside County										
☒ HEMET VALLEY MEDICAL CENTER, 1117 East Devonshire Avenue, Zip 92543; tel. 909/652–2811; John Ruffner, Administrator (Nonreporting) **A**1 9 10 **S** Valley Health System, Hemet, CA	16	10	285	—	—	—	—	—	—	—
HOLLISTER—San Benito County										
HAZEL HAWKINS MEMORIAL HOSPITAL, (Includes Hazel Hawkins Convalescent Hospital–Southside, 3110 Southside Road, Zip 95023; tel. 408/637–5711), 911 Sunset Drive, Zip 95023–5695; tel. 408/637–5711; Keith Mesmer, Interim Administrator (Total facility includes 52 beds in nursing home–type unit) (Nonreporting) **A**9 10 **S** Brim, Inc., Portland, OR	16	10	86	—	—	—	—	—	—	—
HOLLYWOOD—Los Angeles County, See Los Angeles										
HUNTINGTON BEACH—Orange County										
☒ COLUMBIA HUNTINGTON BEACH HOSPITAL AND MEDICAL CENTER, 17772 Beach Boulevard, Zip 92647–9932; tel. 714/842–1473; Carol B. Freeman, Chief Executive Officer **A**1 9 10 **F**4 8 11 12 15 16 17 18 19 21 22 27 32 35 37 39 41 42 44 49 52 55 59 64 65 71 73 **P**5 **S** Columbia/HCA Healthcare Corporation, Nashville, TN	33	10	135	3873	54	—	—	33790	14087	312
☐ PACIFICA HOSPITAL, 18800 Delaware Street, Zip 92648; tel. 714/596–8000; Michael H. Sussman, President and Chief Executive Officer (Nonreporting) **A**1 10	33	10	83	—	—	—	—	—	—	—
HUNTINGTON PARK—Los Angeles County										
☒ COMMUNITY HOSPITAL OF HUNTINGTON PARK, (Includes Mission Hospital of Huntington Park, 3111 East Florence Avenue, tel. 213/582–8261), 2623 East Slauson Avenue, Zip 90255; tel. 213/583–1931; Charles Martinez, Ph.D., Chief Executive Officer (Nonreporting) **A**1 9 10 **S** TENET Healthcare Corporation, Santa Barbara, CA **N** Essential HealthCare Network, Monterey Park, CA	33	10	226	—	—	—	—	—	—	—
INDIO—Riverside County										
☒ JOHN F. KENNEDY MEMORIAL HOSPITAL, 47–111 Monroe Street, Zip 92201, Mailing Address: P.O. Drawer LLLL, Zip 92202–2558; tel. 760/347–6191; Michael A. Rembis, FACHE, Chief Executive Officer **A**1 9 10 **F**4 7 8 10 11 12 16 17 19 21 22 23 24 25 27 28 29 30 31 32 34 35 37 38 39 40 41 42 43 44 45 46 48 49 52 53 54 55 56 57 58 59 60 64 65 67 70 71 72 73 **P**5 **S** TENET Healthcare Corporation, Santa Barbara, CA **N** Tenet Healthcare Corporation, Santa Barbara, CA	33	10	130	7752	74	50453	2015	37045	17768	—
INGLEWOOD—Los Angeles County										
☒ △ CENTINELA HOSPITAL MEDICAL CENTER, 555 East Hardy Street, Zip 90301–4073, Mailing Address: Box 720, Zip 90307–0720; tel. 310/673–4660; John Smithhisler, CHE, Chief Executive Officer (Total facility includes 24 beds in nursing home–type unit) (Nonreporting) **A**1 2 3 7 9 10 **S** TENET Healthcare Corporation, Santa Barbara, CA	33	10	375	—	—	—	—	—	—	—
☒ △ DANIEL FREEMAN MEMORIAL HOSPITAL, 333 North Prairie Avenue, Zip 90301–4514; tel. 310/674–7050; Joseph W. Dunn, Ph.D., Chief Executive Officer (Total facility includes 29 beds in nursing home–type unit) (Nonreporting) **A**1 2 5 7 9 10 **S** Carondelet Health System, Saint Louis, MO	21	10	365	—	—	—	—	—	—	—
IRVINE—Orange County										
☒ IRVINE MEDICAL CENTER, 16200 Sand Canyon Avenue, Zip 92618–3714; tel. 714/753–2000; Richard H. Robinson, Chief Executive Officer (Total facility includes 20 beds in nursing home–type unit) **A**1 9 10 **F**7 8 10 12 14 15 16 19 22 28 29 30 32 34 35 37 38 40 41 42 44 46 49 60 64 65 71 73 74 **P**5 7 **S** TENET Healthcare Corporation, Santa Barbara, CA **N** Tenet Healthcare Corporation, Santa Barbara, CA	33	10	153	6029	83	80818	1611	67884	19762	525
JACKSON—Amador County										
☒ SUTTER AMADOR HOSPITAL, 810 Court Street, Zip 95642–2379; tel. 209/223–7500; Scott Stenberg, Chief Executive Officer (Total facility includes 44 beds in nursing home–type unit) (Nonreporting) **A**1 9 10 **S** Sutter Health, Sacramento, CA **N** Sutter\CHS, Sacramento, CA	23	10	85	—	—	—	—	—	—	—
JOSHUA TREE—San Bernardino County										
☒ HI–DESERT MEDICAL CENTER, 6601 White Feather Road, Zip 92252–6601; tel. 760/366–3711; James R. Larson, President and Chief Executive Officer (Total facility includes 81 beds in nursing home–type unit) **A**1 9 10 **F**8 15 16 17 19 20 21 22 25 26 27 28 30 31 32 33 34 35 37 39 41 44 45 46 49 59 64 65 67 71 73 **P**1	16	10	110	2989	110	52616	—	30787	11372	458

Hospital, Address, Telephone, Administrator, Approval, Facility, and Physician Codes, Health Care System, Network	Classi-fication Codes		Utilization Data					Expense (thousands) of dollars		
★ American Hospital Association (AHA) membership □ Joint Commission on Accreditation of Healthcare Organizations (JCAHO) accreditation + American Osteopathic Healthcare Association (AOHA) membership ○ American Osteopathic Association (AOA) accreditation △ Commission on Accreditation of Rehabilitation Facilities (CARF) accreditation Control codes 61, 63, 64, 71, 72 and 73 indicate hospitals listed by AOHA, but not registered by AHA. For definition of numerical codes, see page A4	Control	Service	Staffed Beds	Admissions	Census	Outpatient Visits	Births	Total	Payroll	Personnel

KENTFIELD—Marin County

□ BHC ROSS HOSPITAL, 1111 Sir Francis Drake Boulevard, Zip 94904; tel. 415/258–6900; Judy G. House, Chief Executive Officer (Nonreporting) **A**1 10 **S** Behavioral Healthcare Corporation, Nashville, TN	33	22	56	—	—	—	—	—	—	—
□ KENTFIELD REHABILITATION HOSPITAL, 1125 Sir Francis Drake Boulevard, Zip 94904, Mailing Address: P.O. Box 338, Zip 94914–0338; tel. 415/456–9680; John Behrmann, Administrator and Chief Executive Officer (Total facility includes 12 beds in nursing home–type unit) (Nonreporting) **A**1 9 10 **S** Continental Medical Systems, Inc., Mechanicsburg, PA	33	46	60	—	—	—	—	—	—	—

KING CITY—Monterey County

□ GEORGE L. MEE MEMORIAL HOSPITAL, 300 Canal Street, Zip 93930–3410; tel. 408/385–6000; Walter Beck, Chief Executive Officer (Total facility includes 16 beds in nursing home–type unit) **A**1 9 10 **F**7 8 11 15 19 21 22 25 26 28 32 34 35 36 37 39 40 41 44 49 60 64 65 71 73 74	23	10	39	1058	22	13750	414	—	—	—

KINGSBURG—Fresno County

KINGSBURG DISTRICT HOSPITAL, 1200 Smith Street, Zip 93631; tel. 209/897–5841; William J. Casey, Administrator (Total facility includes 20 beds in nursing home–type unit) (Nonreporting) **A**9 10	16	10	35	—	—	—	—	—	—	—

LA HABRA—Orange County

✚ FRIENDLY HILLS REGIONAL MEDICAL CENTER, 1251 West Lambert Road, Zip 90631; tel. 562/694–3838; Kathleen Smith, Executive Director (Nonreporting) **A**1 2 9 10 **N** Friendly Hills HealthCare Network, LaHabra, CA	33	10	140	—	—	—	—	—	—	—

LA JOLLA—San Diego County

✚ GREEN HOSPITAL OF SCRIPPS CLINIC, 10666 North Torrey Pines Road, Zip 92037–1093; tel. 619/455–9100; Linda L. Hodges, R.N., Associate Administrator **A**1 2 3 5 8 9 10 **F**1 2 3 4 7 8 10 11 12 14 15 16 17 19 20 21 22 24 25 26 27 28 29 30 31 32 34 35 36 37 39 40 41 42 43 44 45 48 51 52 53 54 55 56 57 58 59 60 61 63 64 65 66 67 68 69 70 71 72 73 74 **P**3 5 7 **S** Scripps Health, San Diego, CA **N** ScrippsHealth, San Diego, CA	23	10	149	8170	88	112306	—	86239	27882	616
✚ △ SCRIPPS MEMORIAL HOSPITAL–LA JOLLA, 9888 Genesee Avenue, Zip 92037–1276, Mailing Address: P.O. Box 28, Zip 92038–0028; tel. 619/626–4123; Thomas C. Gagen, Administrator **A**1 2 3 7 9 10 **F**1 2 3 4 7 8 10 11 12 14 15 16 19 20 21 22 23 24 25 26 27 32 33 35 36 37 38 40 41 42 43 44 45 46 49 50 53 54 55 56 57 58 59 60 61 63 65 66 67 69 70 71 72 73 74 **P**5 7 **S** Scripps Health, San Diego, CA **N** ScrippsHealth, San Diego, CA	23	10	424	13611	193	—	2716	128052	49659	1444

LA MESA—San Diego County

✚ △ GROSSMONT HOSPITAL, 5555 Grossmont Center Drive, Zip 91942, Mailing Address: Box 158, Zip 91944–0158; tel. 619/465–0711; Michele T. Tarbet, R.N., Chief Executive Officer (Total facility includes 27 beds in nursing home–type unit) **A**1 2 3 7 9 10 12 **F**4 7 8 10 11 12 15 16 17 19 20 21 23 25 26 27 30 31 32 33 34 35 36 37 38 39 40 41 42 43 44 46 48 49 51 52 54 55 56 57 58 59 60 61 63 64 65 66 67 69 71 72 73 74 **P**5 7 **S** Sharp Healthcare, San Diego, CA **N** Sharp Healthcare, San Diego, CA	23	10	444	18258	219	170223	2450	144966	61667	1543

LA PALMA—Orange County

✚ △ LA PALMA INTERCOMMUNITY HOSPITAL, 7901 Walker Street, Zip 90623–5850, Mailing Address: P.O. Box 5850, Buena Park, Zip 90622; tel. 714/670–7400; Stephen E. Dixon, President and Chief Executive Officer **A**1 2 7 9 10 **F**3 7 12 14 15 16 17 19 22 27 28 31 35 37 39 40 41 44 48 49 52 57 58 59 65 71 73 74 **P**5 7 **S** UniHealth, Burbank, CA **N** UniHealth, Burbank, CA	23	10	139	4029	53	29718	859	38143	13947	360

LAGUNA HILLS—Orange County

□ △ SADDLEBACK MEMORIAL MEDICAL CENTER, 24451 Health Center Drive, Zip 92653; tel. 714/837–4500; Barry Arbuckle, Ph.D., Chief Executive Officer (Total facility includes 18 beds in nursing home–type unit) (Nonreporting) **A**1 2 7 9 10 **S** Memorial Health Services, Long Beach, CA	23	10	220	—	—	—	—	—	—	—

LAKE ARROWHEAD—San Bernardino County

□ SAN BERNARDINO MOUNTAINS COMMUNITY HOSPITAL DISTRICT, 29101 Hospital Road, Zip 92352, Mailing Address: Box 70, Zip 92352; tel. 909/336–3651; John J. McCormick, Chief Executive Officer (Total facility includes 18 beds in nursing home–type unit) (Nonreporting) **A**1 9 10	16	10	36	—	—	—	—	—	—	—

LAKE ISABELLA—Kern County

□ KERN VALLEY HOSPITAL DISTRICT, 6412 Laurel Avenue, Zip 93240, Mailing Address: P.O. Box 1628, Zip 93240; tel. 760/379–2681; Robert Knight, Chief Executive Officer (Total facility includes 74 beds in nursing home–type unit) (Nonreporting) **A**1 9 10	16	10	101	—	—	—	—	—	—	—

LAKEPORT—Lake County

✚ SUTTER LAKESIDE HOSPITAL, 5176 Hill Road East, Zip 95453–6111; tel. 707/262–5001; Paul J. Hensler, Chief Executive Officer (Nonreporting) **A**1 9 10 **S** Sutter Health, Sacramento, CA **N** Sutter\CHS, Sacramento, CA	23	10	54	—	—	—	—	—	—	—

LAKEWOOD—Los Angeles County

✚ LAKEWOOD REGIONAL MEDICAL CENTER, (Includes Doctors Hospital of Lakewood, 3700 East South Street, ; New Beginnings Doctors Hospital of Lakewood–Clark, 5300 Clark Avenue, tel. 213/866–9711), 3700 East South Street, Zip 90712; tel. 562/531–2550; Gustavo A. Valdespino, Chief Executive Officer **A**1 2 3 9 10 **F**3 4 7 8 10 11 12 15 16 19 21 22 26 27 28 30 33 34 35 37 39 40 41 42 43 44 46 48 49 52 57 58 59 60 65 67 71 73 74 **P**5 7 **S** TENET Healthcare Corporation, Santa Barbara, CA **N** Tenet Healthcare Corporation, Santa Barbara, CA	33	10	148	6758	91	58651	733	48349	19745	524

Hospital, Address, Telephone, Administrator, Approval, Facility, and Physician Codes, Health Care System, Network	Classi-fication Codes		Utilization Data					Expense (thousands) of dollars		
★ American Hospital Association (AHA) membership ☐ Joint Commission on Accreditation of Healthcare Organizations (JCAHO) accreditation + American Osteopathic Healthcare Association (AOHA) membership ○ American Osteopathic Association (AOA) accreditation △ Commission on Accreditation of Rehabilitation Facilities (CARF) accreditation Control codes 61, 63, 64, 71, 72 and 73 indicate hospitals listed by AOHA, but not registered by AHA. For definition of numerical codes, see page A4	Control	Service	Staffed Beds	Admissions	Census	Outpatient Visits	Births	Total	Payroll	Personnel

LANCASTER—Los Angeles County

☒ ANTELOPE VALLEY HOSPITAL, 1600 West Avenue J., Zip 93534–2894; tel. 805/949–5000; Robert J. Harenski, Chief Executive Officer (Total facility includes 32 beds in nursing home–type unit) (Nonreporting) **A**1 9 10	16	10	281	—	—	—	—	—	—	—
☒ LAC–HIGH DESERT HOSPITAL, 44900 North 60th Street West, Zip 93536; tel. 805/945–8461; Mel Grussing, Administrator (Total facility includes 50 beds in nursing home–type unit) **A**1 10 **F**4 8 12 13 17 19 20 28 31 32 34 35 37 42 43 44 46 49 51 53 54 55 56 57 58 59 60 64 65 71 73 **P**6 **S** Los Angeles County–Department of Health Services, Los Angeles, CA	13	10	76	1313	78	59169	—	71823	19079	500
☐ LANCASTER COMMUNITY HOSPITAL, 43830 North Tenth Street West, Zip 93534; tel. 805/948–4781; Steve Schmidt, Administrator and Chief Executive Officer (Total facility includes 22 beds in nursing home–type unit) (Nonreporting) **A**1 9 10 **S** Paracelsus Healthcare Corporation, Houston, TX	33	10	123	—	—	—	—	—	—	—

LEMOORE—Kings County

☒ NAVAL HOSPITAL, 930 Franklin Avenue, Zip 93246–5000; tel. 209/998–4201; Captain Steven Hart, Commanding Officer **A**1 **F**2 3 4 7 8 10 11 12 13 16 17 19 21 22 25 28 29 30 32 33 35 37 39 40 41 42 43 44 48 49 51 52 53 54 56 58 59 64 71 **S** Department of Navy, Washington, DC	43	10	21	743	4	112327	328	—	—	—

LINDSAY—Tulare County

★ LINDSAY DISTRICT HOSPITAL, 740 North Sequoia Avenue, Zip 93247, Mailing Address: Box 40, Zip 93247; tel. 209/562–4955; Edwin L. Ermshar, President and Chief Executive Officer (Total facility includes 53 beds in nursing home–type unit) (Nonreporting) **A**9 10 **N** UniHealth, Burbank, CA	16	10	106	—	—	—	—	—	—	—

LIVERMORE—Alameda County

LIVERMORE DIVISION See Veterans Affairs Palo Alto Health Care System, Palo Alto VALLEY MEMORIAL HOSPITAL, 1111 East Stanley Boulevard, Zip 94550; tel. 510/447–7000; Marcelina Feit, President and Chief Executive Officer (Total facility includes 14 beds in nursing home–type unit) (Nonreporting) **A**2 9 10 **S** ValleyCare Health System, Pleasanton, CA	23	10	110	—	—	—	—	—	—	—

LODI—San Joaquin County

☒ △ LODI MEMORIAL HOSPITAL, (Includes Lodi Memorial Hospital West, 800 South Lower Sacramento Road, Zip 95242; tel. 209/333–0211), 975 South Fairmont Avenue, Zip 95240–5179, Mailing Address: P.O. Box 3004, Zip 95241–1908; tel. 209/334–3411; Joseph P. Harrington, Chief Executive Officer **A**1 7 9 10 **F**1 2 3 4 5 7 8 9 10 11 12 13 14 15 16 17 19 20 21 22 23 24 25 27 28 29 30 32 34 35 37 38 39 40 41 42 43 44 45 46 47 48 49 51 52 53 54 55 56 57 58 59 60 61 63 64 65 66 67 69 71 72 73 **P**5 7	23	10	181	6440	95	135949	1208	—	27957	—

LOMA LINDA—San Bernardino County

☒ JERRY L. PETTIS MEMORIAL VETERANS MEDICAL CENTER, 11201 Benton Street, Zip 92357; tel. 909/825–7084; Dean R. Stordahl, Director (Total facility includes 106 beds in nursing home–type unit) **A**1 3 5 8 **F**3 4 5 8 10 11 12 14 18 19 20 21 22 23 26 27 28 30 31 32 33 34 35 37 39 41 42 43 44 45 46 49 51 52 54 55 56 57 58 59 60 61 63 64 65 67 69 71 72 73 74 **P**1 **S** Department of Veterans Affairs, Washington, DC	45	10	231	5154	105	252848	—	—	—	1263
☒ △ LOMA LINDA UNIVERSITY MEDICAL CENTER, (Includes Loma Linda University Community Medical Center, 25333 Barton Road, Zip 92354–3053; tel. 909/796–0167), 11234 Anderson Street, Zip 92354–2870, Mailing Address: P.O. Box 2000, Zip 92354–0200; tel. 909/824–0800; J. David Moorhead, M.D., President (Nonreporting) **A**1 2 3 5 7 8 9 10 **S** Loma Linda University Health Sciences Center, Loma Linda, CA **N** Adventist Health System–Loma Linda, Loma Linda, CA	21	10	653	—	—	—	—	—	—	—

LOMPOC—Santa Barbara County

☐ LOMPOC DISTRICT HOSPITAL, 508 East Hickory Street, Zip 93436, Mailing Address: Box 1058, Zip 93438; tel. 805/737–3300; Scott Rhine, Administrator and Chief Executive Officer (Total facility includes 110 beds in nursing home–type unit) (Nonreporting) **A**1 9 10 **S** Quorum Health Group/Quorum Health Resources, Inc., Brentwood, TN	16	10	170	—	—	—	—	—	—	—

LONE PINE—Inyo County

SOUTHERN INYO COUNTY LOCAL HEALTH CARE DISTRICT, (Formerly Southern Inyo Healthcare District), 501 East Locust Street, Zip 93545, Mailing Address: Box 1009, Zip 93545; tel. 760/876–5501; Keith D. Brady, Chief Executive Officer and Administrator (Nonreporting) **A**9 10	16	10	37	—	—	—	—	—	—	—

LONG BEACH—Los Angeles County

☒ LONG BEACH COMMUNITY MEDICAL CENTER, 1720 Termino Avenue, Zip 90804; tel. 562/498–1000; Makoto Nakayama, President and Chief Executive Officer **A**1 2 9 10 **F**1 4 7 8 10 11 12 14 15 16 17 19 21 22 26 27 28 29 30 31 33 34 35 37 38 39 40 41 42 43 44 45 46 47 49 51 52 54 55 56 57 58 59 60 63 64 65 67 68 71 72 73 74 **S** UniHealth, Burbank, CA **N** UniHealth, Burbank, CA	23	10	278	10417	124	47095	2607	90245	32835	760
☐ LONG BEACH DOCTORS HOSPITAL, 1725 Pacific Avenue, Zip 90813–1798; tel. 310/599–3551; Manuel Anel, M.D., Administrator and Chief Executive Officer (Nonreporting) **A**1 10	32	10	43	—	—	—	—	—	—	—
☐ △ LONG BEACH MEMORIAL MEDICAL CENTER, 2801 Atlantic Avenue, Zip 90806, Mailing Address: Box 1428, Zip 90801–1428; tel. 562/933–2000; Chris D. Van Gorder, Chief Executive Officer (Total facility includes 69 beds in nursing home–type unit) **A**1 2 3 5 7 8 9 10 **F**4 5 6 7 8 10 12 14 15 16 17 19 20 21 22 23 25 26 28 29 30 31 32 33 34 35 37 38 39 40 41 42 43 44 45 46 47 48 49 50 51 60 61 63 64 65 66 67 70 71 72 73 74 **P**5 7 **S** Memorial Health Services, Long Beach, CA	23	10	726	28810	421	—	4892	300834	125740	—

Hospital, Address, Telephone, Administrator, Approval, Facility, and Physician Codes, Health Care System, Network	Classi-fication Codes		Utilization Data					Expense (thousands) of dollars		

★ American Hospital Association (AHA) membership
□ Joint Commission on Accreditation of Healthcare Organizations (JCAHO) accreditation
+ American Osteopathic Healthcare Association (AOHA) membership
○ American Osteopathic Association (AOA) accreditation
△ Commission on Accreditation of Rehabilitation Facilities (CARF) accreditation
Control codes 61, 63, 64, 71, 72 and 73 indicate hospitals listed by AOHA, but not registered by AHA. For definition of numerical codes, see page A4

	Control	Service	Staffed Beds	Admissions	Census	Outpatient Visits	Births	Total	Payroll	Personnel
□ ○ PACIFIC HOSPITAL OF LONG BEACH, 2776 Pacific Avenue, Zip 90806–2699, Mailing Address: P.O. Box 1268, Zip 90801; tel. 562/595–1911; Michael D. Drobot, President and Chief Executive Officer **A**1 5 9 10 11 12 13 **F**8 11 12 15 16 17 19 20 21 22 26 27 28 30 31 32 33 34 35 37 40 41 42 44 49 51 52 56 57 58 59 61 64 65 71 73 **P**5	23	10	179	3640	79	33316	1270	26306	11426	395
REDGATE MEMORIAL HOSPITAL, 1775 Chestnut Avenue, Zip 90813; tel. 310/599–8444; Robert Worrell, Chief Executive Officer (Nonreporting)	23	82	63	—	—	—	—	—	—	—
⊠ SAINT MARY MEDICAL CENTER, 1050 Linden Avenue, Zip 90801, Mailing Address: P.O. Box 887, Zip 90801; tel. 562/491–9000; Tammie McMann Brailsford, Administrator (Total facility includes 80 beds in nursing home–type unit) (Nonreporting) **A**1 2 3 5 10 **S** Catholic Healthcare West, San Francisco, CA **N** Catholic HealthCare West (CHW), San Francisco, CA	23	10	479							
⊠ VETERANS AFFAIRS MEDICAL CENTER, 5901 East Seventh Street, Zip 90822–5201; tel. 562/494–5400; Lawrence C. Stewart, Director (Total facility includes 110 beds in nursing home–type unit) **A**1 2 3 5 8 **F**1 3 4 5 8 9 10 11 12 16 17 18 19 20 21 22 23 24 25 26 27 28 29 30 31 32 33 34 35 37 39 40 41 42 43 44 45 46 48 49 50 51 52 54 55 56 57 58 59 60 64 65 66 67 69 70 71 72 73 74 **P**6 **S** Department of Veterans Affairs, Washington, DC	45	10	353	8083	261	412354	0	—	—	—
LOS ALAMITOS—Orange County										
⊠ LOS ALAMITOS MEDICAL CENTER, 3751 Katella Avenue, Zip 90720; tel. 562/598–1311; Gustavo A. Valdespino, Chief Executive Officer (Total facility includes 20 beds in nursing home–type unit) (Nonreporting) **A**1 2 9 10 **S** TENET Healthcare Corporation, Santa Barbara, CA **N** Tenet Healthcare Corporation, Santa Barbara, CA	33	10	173	—	—	—	—	—	—	—
LOS ANGELES—Los Angeles County **(Mailing Addresses - Canoga Park, Encino, Granada Hills, Harbor City, Hollywood, Mission Hills, North Hollywood, Northridge, Panorama City, San Pedro, Sepulveda, Sherman Oaks, Sun Valley, Sylmar, Tarzana, Van Nuys, West Hills, West Los Angeles, Woodland Hills)**										
⊠ BARLOW RESPIRATORY HOSPITAL, 2000 Stadium Way, Zip 90026–2696; tel. 213/250–4200; Margaret W. Crane, Chief Executive Officer (Nonreporting) **A**1 3 5 10	23	33	49	—	—	—	—	—	—	—
⊠ BAY HARBOR HOSPITAL, 1437 West Lomita Boulevard, Harbor City, Zip 90710–2097; tel. 310/325–1221; John M. Wilson, President (Total facility includes 212 beds in nursing home–type unit) (Nonreporting) **A**1 2 9 10	23	10	346	—	—	—	—	—	—	—
⊠ CALIFORNIA HOSPITAL MEDICAL CENTER, 1401 South Grand Avenue, Zip 90015–3063; tel. 213/748–2411; Melinda D. Beswick, President and Chief Executive Officer (Total facility includes 19 beds in nursing home–type unit) (Nonreporting) **A**1 2 3 5 9 10 **S** UniHealth, Burbank, CA **N** UniHealth, Burbank, CA	23	10	309	—	—	—	—	—	—	—
⊠ CEDARS–SINAI MEDICAL CENTER, 8700 Beverly Boulevard, Zip 90048–1865, Mailing Address: Box 48750, Zip 90048–0750; tel. 310/855–5000; Thomas M. Priselac, President and Chief Executive Officer **A**1 2 3 5 8 9 10 **F**3 4 5 7 8 10 11 12 13 14 15 16 17 18 19 20 21 22 23 26 27 28 29 30 31 32 33 34 35 36 37 38 39 40 41 42 43 44 45 46 47 48 49 50 51 52 53 54 55 56 57 58 59 60 61 63 64 65 66 67 68 69 70 71 72 73 74 **P**3 5 8 **N** Cedars–Sinai Health System, Los Angeles, CA	23	10	762	38908	586	—	6575	605592	241363	5368
⊠ CENTURY CITY HOSPITAL, 2070 Century Park East, Zip 90067; tel. 310/553–6211; John R. Nickens, III, Chief Executive Officer (Nonreporting) **A**1 9 10 **S** TENET Healthcare Corporation, Santa Barbara, CA **N** Tenet Healthcare Corporation, Santa Barbara, CA	33	10	156	—	—	—	—	—	—	—
⊠ CHILDRENS HOSPITAL OF LOS ANGELES, 4650 Sunset Boulevard, Zip 90027–6089, Mailing Address: Box 54700, Zip 90054–0700; tel. 213/660–2450; Walter W. Noce, Jr., President and Chief Executive Officer **A**1 2 3 5 9 10 **F**4 10 11 12 13 15 16 17 19 20 21 22 27 28 31 32 35 38 42 43 44 45 46 47 50 51 60 63 65 66 67 68 69 70 71 72 73 **P**7	23	50	216	11113	216	188436	—	215084	112237	2247
⊠ COLUMBIA WEST HILLS MEDICAL CENTER, 7300 Medical Center Drive, Canoga Park, Zip 91307–9937, Mailing Address: P.O. Box 7937, West Hills, Zip 91309–7937; tel. 818/676–4000; Mark Meyers, President and Chief Executive Officer **A**1 9 10 **F**4 7 8 10 11 12 15 16 19 20 21 22 24 26 28 30 31 32 34 35 37 38 39 40 41 42 43 44 45 46 49 51 54 60 64 65 66 67 71 73 74 **P**4 5 7 **S** Columbia/HCA Healthcare Corporation, Nashville, TN	33	10	236	8280	112	31022	1465	67997	31285	755
□ EAST LOS ANGELES DOCTORS HOSPITAL, 4060 Whittier Boulevard, Zip 90023–2596; tel. 213/268–5514; Frank Kutsuda, Administrator and Chief Executive Officer (Total facility includes 25 beds in nursing home–type unit) **A**1 9 10 **F**1 2 3 4 5 6 7 8 9 10 11 12 13 14 15 16 17 18 19 20 21 22 23 24 25 26 27 28 29 30 31 32 33 34 35 36 37 38 39 40 41 42 43 44 45 46 47 48 49 50 51 52 53 54 61 62 63 64 65 66 67 68 69 70 71 72 73 74	33	10	127	2105	43	13860	623	21261	6004	285
□ EDGEMONT HOSPITAL, 4841 Hollywood Boulevard, Zip 90027–5388; tel. 213/913–9000; Cynthia L. Kern, Administrator (Nonreporting) **A**1 9 10	33	22	61	—	—	—	—	—	—	—
⊠ ENCINO–TARZANA REGIONAL MEDICAL CENTER ENCINO CAMPUS, 16237 Ventura Boulevard, Encino, Zip 91436–2201; tel. 818/995–5000 (Total facility includes 14 beds in nursing home–type unit) (Nonreporting) **A**1 3 9 10 **S** TENET Healthcare Corporation, Santa Barbara, CA	33	10	165	—	—	—	—	—	—	—
□ GATEWAYS HOSPITAL AND MENTAL HEALTH CENTER, 1891 Effie Street, Zip 90026–1711; tel. 213/644–2000; Saul Goldfarb, Chief Executive Officer **A**1 10 **F**52 53 57 58 59	23	22	35	596	30	5371	—	6491	4615	106

Hospital, Address, Telephone, Administrator, Approval, Facility, and Physician Codes, Health Care System, Network	Classi-fication Codes		Utilization Data					Expense (thousands) of dollars		
★ American Hospital Association (AHA) membership □ Joint Commission on Accreditation of Healthcare Organizations (JCAHO) accreditation + American Osteopathic Healthcare Association (AOHA) membership ○ American Osteopathic Association (AOA) accreditation △ Commission on Accreditation of Rehabilitation Facilities (CARF) accreditation Control codes 61, 63, 64, 71, 72 and 73 indicate hospitals listed by AOHA, but not registered by AHA. For definition of numerical codes, see page A4	Control	Service	Staffed Beds	Admissions	Census	Outpatient Visits	Births	Total	Payroll	Personnel

Hospital	Control	Service	Staffed Beds	Admissions	Census	Outpatient Visits	Births	Total	Payroll	Personnel
□ △ GOOD SAMARITAN HOSPITAL, (Formerly Hospital of the Good Samaritan), 1225 Wilshire Boulevard, Zip 90017–2395; tel. 213/977–2121; Andrew B. Leeka, President and Chief Executive Officer (Nonreporting) **A**1 2 7 9 10	23	10	318	—	—	—	—	—	—	—
⊠ GRANADA HILLS COMMUNITY HOSPITAL, 10445 Balboa Boulevard, Granada Hills, Zip 91394–9400; tel. 818/360–1021; Dennis E. Coleman, President and Chief Executive Officer (Total facility includes 23 beds in nursing home–type unit) **A**1 9 10 **F**4 8 10 11 12 15 16 17 19 20 21 22 24 26 27 28 29 30 34 35 39 40 41 42 43 44 49 56 61 63 64 65 67 71 72 73 74 **P**5 7	23	10	146	4303	47	20970	1133	37110	14188	369
□ HOLLYWOOD COMMUNITY HOSPITAL OF HOLLYWOOD, (Includes Hollywood Community Hospital of Van Nuys, 14433 Emelita Street, Zip 91401; tel. 818/787–1511), 6245 De Longpre Avenue, Zip 90028–9001; tel. 213/462–2271; Steven Courtier, Chief Executive Officer (Nonreporting) **A**1 10 **S** Paracelsus Healthcare Corporation, Houston, TX	33	10	160	—	—	—	—	—	—	—
HOLLYWOOD COMMUNITY HOSPITAL OF VAN NUYS See Hollywood Community Hospital of Hollywood										
HOSPITAL OF THE GOOD SAMARITAN See Good Samaritan Hospital										
⊠ KAISER FOUNDATION HOSPITAL, (Includes Kaiser Foundation Mental Health Center, 765 West College Street, Zip 90012; tel. 213/580–7200), 4747 Sunset Boulevard, Zip 90027–6072; tel. 213/783–4011; Joseph W. Hummel, Administrator **A**1 2 3 5 10 **F**3 4 7 8 9 10 11 13 14 15 16 19 21 22 23 24 26 28 29 30 31 32 33 34 35 37 38 39 40 41 42 43 44 45 46 47 48 49 50 51 52 53 54 55 56 57 58 59 60 63 64 65 67 69 71 72 73 **S** Kaiser Foundation Hospitals, Oakland, CA	23	10	384	18640	218	21713	3130	—	—	—
⊠ KAISER FOUNDATION HOSPITAL, 25825 South Vermont Avenue, Harbor City, Zip 90710; tel. 310/325–5111; Mary Ann Barnes, Administrator **A**1 2 10 **F**3 4 7 8 10 11 12 17 18 19 21 22 23 25 26 28 29 30 31 32 33 34 35 39 40 41 42 43 44 45 46 49 51 53 54 55 56 57 58 59 60 61 65 66 67 68 69 71 72 73 **S** Kaiser Foundation Hospitals, Oakland, CA	23	10	164	8788	86	85368	1838	—	—	915
⊠ KAISER FOUNDATION HOSPITAL, 13652 Cantara Street, Panorama City, Zip 91402; tel. 818/375–2000; Dev Mahadevan, Administrator **A**1 2 5 10 **F**3 4 7 8 10 12 13 14 15 16 17 18 19 21 22 26 27 28 29 30 31 32 33 34 35 37 38 40 41 42 43 44 45 46 49 50 51 53 54 55 56 57 58 59 60 61 63 65 66 67 68 69 71 72 73 **P**4 **S** Kaiser Foundation Hospitals, Oakland, CA	23	10	266	11021	97	—	2167	—	—	628
⊠ KAISER FOUNDATION HOSPITAL, 5601 DeSoto Avenue, Woodland Hills, Zip 91365–4084; tel. 818/719–2000; James L. Breeden, Administrator **A**1 3 5 10 **F**2 3 4 7 8 11 12 13 14 15 16 17 18 19 21 22 26 28 29 30 31 32 33 35 37 38 39 40 41 42 43 44 45 48 49 50 51 52 53 54 55 56 58 59 60 61 63 64 65 66 67 68 69 71 72 74 **S** Kaiser Foundation Hospitals, Oakland, CA	23	10	139	9471	95	1012225	2042	—	—	868
⊠ KAISER FOUNDATION HOSPITAL–WEST LOS ANGELES, 6041 Cadillac Avenue, Zip 90034; tel. 213/857–2201; Joseph W. Hummel, Administrator **A**1 2 3 5 10 **F**2 3 4 7 8 9 10 13 19 20 22 23 25 26 28 29 30 31 32 33 34 35 37 38 39 40 41 42 43 44 45 46 47 48 49 50 51 52 53 54 55 56 57 58 60 63 64 65 67 69 71 72 73 **S** Kaiser Foundation Hospitals, Oakland, CA	23	10	161	10871	101	—	1772	—	—	622
KAISER FOUNDATION MENTAL HEALTH CENTER See Kaiser Foundation Hospital										
⊠ LAC–KING–DREW MEDICAL CENTER, 12021 South Wilmington Avenue, Zip 90059; tel. 310/668–4321; Randall S. Foster, Administrator and Chief Executive Officer **A**1 2 3 5 8 9 10 **F**1 4 7 8 10 11 12 13 15 16 17 18 19 20 21 22 23 25 26 27 28 30 31 32 34 35 37 38 40 41 42 44 45 47 48 49 50 51 52 53 54 55 56 57 58 59 60 61 63 65 69 70 71 72 73 74 **P**3 5 **S** Los Angeles County–Department of Health Services, Los Angeles, CA	13	10	240	16004	242	279274	2423	357724	143671	3127
⊠ LAC–UNIVERSITY OF SOUTHERN CALIFORNIA MEDICAL CENTER, (Includes General Hospital, 1200 North State Street, Zip 90033; Women's and Children's Hospital, 1240 North Mission Road, Zip 90033), 1200 North State Street, Zip 90033–1084; tel. 323/226–2622; Douglas D. Bagley, Executive Director **A**1 2 3 5 8 9 10 **F**1 3 4 5 6 7 8 9 10 11 12 13 14 15 16 17 18 19 20 21 22 23 25 26 27 28 29 30 31 32 34 35 37 38 39 40 41 42 43 44 45 46 47 49 51 52 53 54 55 56 57 58 59 60 61 63 65 66 67 68 69 70 71 72 73 74 **P**1 3 6 8 **S** Los Angeles County–Department of Health Services, Los Angeles, CA	13	10	1330	45979	843	744933	4190	1003302	290527	—
□ LINCOLN HOSPITAL MEDICAL CENTER, 443 South Soto Street, Zip 90033–4398; tel. 213/261–1181; Tim Kollars, Administrator and Chief Executive Officer (Nonreporting) **A**1 10	33	10	61	—	—	—	—	—	—	—
□ LOS ANGELES COMMUNITY HOSPITAL, (Includes Los Angeles Community Hospital of Norwalk, 13222 Bloomfield Avenue, Zip 90650; tel. 310/863–4763), 4081 East Olympic Boulevard, Zip 90023–3300; tel. 213/267–0477; Ted R. Estrada, Chief Executive Officer (Nonreporting) **A**1 9 10 **S** Paracelsus Healthcare Corporation, Houston, TX	33	10	186	—	—	—	—	—	—	—
LOS ANGELES COUNTY CENTRAL JAIL HOSPITAL, 441 Bauchet Street, Zip 90012–2994; tel. 213/974–5045; Tom Flaherty, Assistant Administrator (Nonreporting)	13	11	190	—	—	—	—	—	—	—
□ LOS ANGELES METROPOLITAN MEDICAL CENTER, (Includes Hawthorne Hospital, 13300 South Hawthorne Boulevard, Zip 90250; tel. 310/679–3321; Marvin Herschberg, Chief Executive Officer), 2231 South Western Avenue, Zip 90018–1399; tel. 213/730–7342; Marc A. Furstman, Chief Executive Officer **A**1 10 **F**8 26 27 34 35 37 40 41 44 49 52 54 57 64 65 71 **P**5 **S** Pacific Health Corporation, Long Beach, CA	33	10	163	11806	77	6845	791	26376	11012	344
⊠ MIDWAY HOSPITAL MEDICAL CENTER, 5925 San Vicente Boulevard, Zip 90019–6696; tel. 213/938–3161; John V. Fenton, Chief Executive Officer (Total facility includes 21 beds in nursing home–type unit) **A**1 9 10 **F**2 3 4 10 11 12 14 15 16 18 19 21 22 23 25 27 28 31 32 33 34 35 37 38 40 41 42 43 44 46 47 48 49 52 53 54 56 57 58 60 63 64 65 66 67 70 71 72 73 **P**5 **S** TENET Healthcare Corporation, Santa Barbara, CA	33	10	141	6112	89	36971	—	49655	20785	550

Hospital, Address, Telephone, Administrator, Approval, Facility, and Physician Codes, Health Care System, Network	Classi-fication Codes		Utilization Data					Expense (thousands) of dollars		
★ American Hospital Association (AHA) membership □ Joint Commission on Accreditation of Healthcare Organizations (JCAHO) accreditation + American Osteopathic Healthcare Association (AOHA) membership ○ American Osteopathic Association (AOA) accreditation △ Commission on Accreditation of Rehabilitation Facilities (CARF) accreditation Control codes 61, 63, 64, 71, 72 and 73 indicate hospitals listed by AOHA, but not registered by AHA. For definition of numerical codes, see page A4	Control	Service	Staffed Beds	Admissions	Census	Outpatient Visits	Births	Total	Payroll	Personnel

	Control	Service	Staffed Beds	Admissions	Census	Outpatient Visits	Births	Total	Payroll	Personnel
MISSION COMMUNITY HOSPITAL–PANORAMA CITY CAMPUS See Mission Community Hospital–San Fernando Campus, San Fernando										
★ MOTION PICTURE AND TELEVISION FUND HOSPITAL AND RESIDENTIAL SERVICES, 23388 Mulholland Drive, Woodland Hills, Zip 91364–2792; tel. 818/876–1888; William F. Haug, FACHE, President and Chief Executive Officer (Total facility includes 165 beds in nursing home–type unit) (Nonreporting) **A**1 10	23	10	218	—	—	—	—	—	—	—
★ NORTH HOLLYWOOD MEDICAL CENTER, 12629 Riverside Drive, North Hollywood, Zip 91607–3495; tel. 818/980–9200; Sonja Hagel, Chief Executive Officer **A**1 9 10 **F**1 4 5 7 8 10 11 12 13 16 17 19 21 22 26 28 29 30 31 32 34 35 37 38 40 41 42 43 44 45 46 47 48 49 52 56 57 58 59 61 63 64 65 71 73 74 **P**2 5 6 7 **S** TENET Healthcare Corporation, Santa Barbara, CA **N** Tenet Healthcare Corporation, Santa Barbara, CA	33	10	150	4582	103	23342	1275	30798	13116	—
★ NORTHRIDGE HOSPITAL AND MEDICAL CENTER, SHERMAN WAY CAMPUS, 14500 Sherman Circle, Van Nuys, Zip 91405; tel. 818/997–0101; Richard D. Lyons, President and Chief Executive Officer (Total facility includes 38 beds in nursing home–type unit) **A**1 9 10 **F**1 2 3 4 7 8 9 10 11 12 15 16 17 18 19 21 22 23 24 26 27 28 30 31 32 33 34 35 37 38 39 40 41 42 43 44 45 46 47 48 49 51 52 53 54 55 56 57 58 59 60 61 63 64 65 66 67 68 69 71 73 74 **P**5 7 **S** UniHealth, Burbank, CA **N** UniHealth, Burbank, CA	23	10	211	6594	93	51056	1491	39009	16773	454
★ △ NORTHRIDGE HOSPITAL MEDICAL CENTER–ROSCOE BOULEVARD CAMPUS, 18300 Roscoe Boulevard, Northridge, Zip 91328; tel. 818/885–8500; Roger E. Seaver, President and Chief Executive Officer (Total facility includes 31 beds in nursing home–type unit) **A**1 2 5 7 9 10 **F**1 3 4 7 8 10 11 12 15 16 17 18 19 21 22 24 26 30 31 32 33 34 35 37 38 39 40 41 42 43 44 45 46 47 48 49 51 52 53 54 55 56 57 58 59 60 63 64 65 67 68 70 71 72 73 74 **P**3 5 7 **S** UniHealth, Burbank, CA **N** UniHealth, Burbank, CA	23	10	404	16071	271	126326	2643	158717	59444	1477
★ OLIVE VIEW–UCLA MEDICAL CENTER, 14445 Olive View Drive, Sylmar, Zip 91342–1495; tel. 818/364–1555; Melinda Anderson, Administrator **A**1 3 5 10 **F**3 4 7 8 10 11 12 13 17 19 20 21 22 25 26 27 28 29 30 31 32 33 34 35 37 38 39 40 41 42 43 44 45 46 49 50 51 52 53 54 56 57 58 59 60 61 63 65 67 68 69 70 71 72 73 74 **P**6 **S** Los Angeles County–Department of Health Services, Los Angeles, CA	13	10	219	13563	200	170014	2432	257592	73080	1575
□ ORTHOPAEDIC HOSPITAL, 2400 South Flower Street, Zip 90007–2697, Mailing Address: Box 60132, Terminal Annex, Zip 90060; tel. 213/742–1000; James V. Luck, Jr., M.D., Chief Executive Officer and Medical Director **A**1 2 3 5 9 10 **F**12 15 16 17 19 22 24 25 30 34 35 37 42 44 49 60 65 66 68 71 73 **P**5 7	23	47	73	1630	18	51727	—	29810	9305	238
□ PACIFIC ALLIANCE MEDICAL CENTER, 531 West College Street, Zip 90012–2385; tel. 213/624–8411; John R. Edwards, Chief Executive Officer (Nonreporting) **A**1 9 10 **N** Essential HealthCare Network, Monterey Park, CA	32	10	89							
□ PACIFICA HOSPITAL OF THE VALLEY, 9449 San Fernando Road, Sun Valley, Zip 91352; tel. 818/252–2380; Trude Williams, R.N., Administrator **A**1 9 10 **F**4 8 10 11 12 14 15 16 17 19 20 22 29 34 35 37 38 40 41 42 43 44 45 47 49 52 54 56 59 64 65 71 73 **P**5	33	10	195	5451	38	35658	672	44918	18085	459
★ △ PROVIDENCE HOLY CROSS MEDICAL CENTER, 15031 Rinaldi Street, Mission Hills, Zip 91345–1285; tel. 818/365–8051; Michael J. Madden, Chief Executive Los Angeles Service Area (Total facility includes 48 beds in nursing home–type unit) **A**1 2 7 9 10 **F**4 7 8 10 11 12 14 15 16 17 19 21 22 25 28 29 30 32 33 34 35 37 40 41 42 43 44 45 46 48 49 60 64 65 67 70 71 73 74 **P**3 5 **S** Sisters of Providence Health System, Seattle, WA **N** Providence Health System in California, Burbank, CA	21	10	257	9891	162	85190	1365	82194	37019	892
□ QUEEN OF ANGELS–HOLLYWOOD PRESBYTERIAN MEDICAL CENTER, 1300 North Vermont Avenue, Zip 90027–0069; tel. 213/413–3000; Sylvester Graff, President and Chief Executive Officer (Total facility includes 89 beds in nursing home–type unit) **A**1 2 9 10 **F**4 7 8 10 11 15 16 17 19 21 22 27 28 30 31 32 33 34 35 37 38 40 41 42 43 44 45 46 48 49 51 60 64 65 71 72 73 74 **P**5 7 **N** Essential HealthCare Network, Monterey Park, CA	23	10	409	18330	262	—	5849	107757	46308	1308
□ △ SAN PEDRO PENINSULA HOSPITAL, 1300 West Seventh Street, San Pedro, Zip 90732; tel. 310/832–3311; John M. Wilson, President (Total facility includes 128 beds in nursing home–type unit) (Nonreporting) **A**1 2 7 9 10 **N** Little Company of Mary Health Services, Torrance, CA	23	10	309							
□ SAN VICENTE HOSPITAL, 6000 San Vicente Boulevard, Zip 90036; tel. 213/937–2504; R. Wayne Ives, Administrator (Nonreporting) **A**1 9 10	33	44	17	—	—	—	—	—	—	—
★ SANTA MARTA HOSPITAL, 319 North Humphreys Avenue, Zip 90022–1499; tel. 213/266–6500; Harry E. Whitney, Interim President and Chief Executive Officer **A**1 9 10 **F**8 11 15 16 17 19 22 27 35 37 38 40 44 45 46 47 65 71 72 73 74 **P**5 8 **S** Carondelet Health System, Saint Louis, MO **N** Essential HealthCare Network, Monterey Park, CA	21	10	110	3722	49	16599	1018	31412	11352	359
□ SHERMAN OAKS HOSPITAL AND HEALTH CENTER, 4929 Van Nuys Boulevard, Sherman Oaks, Zip 91403; tel. 818/981–7111; David Levinsonn, Chief Executive Officer **A**1 9 10 **F**8 9 11 12 15 17 19 21 22 26 27 28 30 31 32 34 35 37 39 41 42 44 45 46 49 52 54 57 59 63 64 65 66 67 71 73 **P**3 5 7 8	23	10	153	3233	53	—	—	41060	16041	416
★ SHRINERS HOSPITALS FOR CHILDREN, LOS ANGELES, 3160 Geneva Street, Zip 90020–1199; tel. 213/388–3151; Frank LaBonte, FACHE, Administrator **A**1 3 5 **F**15 17 19 21 22 27 34 35 41 47 48 51 56 65 70 71 73 **P**6 **S** Shriners Hospitals for Children, Tampa, FL	23	57	60	1612	35	10678	0	—	—	241

Hospital, Address, Telephone, Administrator, Approval, Facility, and Physician Codes, Health Care System, Network	Classi-fication Codes		Utilization Data					Expense (thousands) of dollars		
★ American Hospital Association (AHA) membership □ Joint Commission on Accreditation of Healthcare Organizations (JCAHO) accreditation + American Osteopathic Healthcare Association (AOHA) membership ○ American Osteopathic Association (AOA) accreditation △ Commission on Accreditation of Rehabilitation Facilities (CARF) accreditation Control codes 61, 63, 64, 71, 72 and 73 indicate hospitals listed by AOHA, but not registered by AHA. For definition of numerical codes, see page A4	Control	Service	Staffed Beds	Admissions	Census	Outpatient Visits	Births	Total	Payroll	Personnel

✠ ST. VINCENT MEDICAL CENTER, 2131 West Third Street, Zip 90057–0992, Mailing Address: P.O. Box 57992, Zip 90057; tel. 213/484–7111; Myda Magarian–Morse, Administrator and Chief Operating Officer (Total facility includes 27 beds in nursing home–type unit) (Nonreporting) **A**1 3 5 9 10 **S** Catholic Healthcare West, San Francisco, CA **N** Catholic HealthCare West (CHW), San Francisco, CA	21	10	350	—	—	—	—	—	—	—
□ TEMPLE COMMUNITY HOSPITAL, 235 North Hoover Street, Zip 90004–3672; tel. 213/382–7252; Herbert G. Needman, Administrator and Chief Executive Officer (Total facility includes 11 beds in nursing home–type unit) **A**1 10 **F**8 11 14 19 20 21 31 35 37 44 45 52 60 63 71 73 **P**5	33	10	130	3514	69	—	—	27894	9346	288
✠ UNIVERSITY OF CALIFORNIA LOS ANGELES MEDICAL CENTER, 10833 Le Conte Avenue, Zip 90095–1730; tel. 310/825–9111; Michael Karpf, M.D., Vice Provost Hospital System and Director Medical Center **A**1 2 3 5 8 9 10 **F**4 5 7 8 10 11 12 13 17 19 20 21 22 23 25 26 27 28 29 30 31 32 34 35 37 38 40 41 42 43 44 45 46 47 48 49 50 51 60 65 67 69 70 72 73 74 **P**6 **S** University of California–Systemwide Administration, Oakland, CA	23	10	610	24378	407	553653	1426	486917	207185	5998
✠ UNIVERSITY OF CALIFORNIA LOS ANGELES NEUROPSYCHIATRIC HOSPITAL, 760 Westwood Plaza, Zip 90095; tel. 310/825–0511; Fawzy I. Fawzy, M.D., Medical Director (Nonreporting) **A**1 3 5 9 10 **S** University of California–Systemwide Administration, Oakland, CA	12	22	117	—	—	—	—	—	—	—
✠ UNIVERSITY OF SOUTHERN CALIFORNIA–KENNETH NORRIS JR. CANCER HOSPITAL, (ACUTE CANCER CARE), 1441 Eastlake Avenue, Zip 90033–1085, Mailing Address: P.O. Box 33804, Zip 90033–3804; tel. 323/764–3000; Adrianne Black Bass, Administrator **A**1 2 3 5 9 10 **F**8 12 14 15 16 19 20 21 28 29 31 32 33 34 35 37 39 41 42 44 45 46 49 50 54 60 64 65 67 69 71 73 **P**5 6 **S** TENET Healthcare Corporation, Santa Barbara, CA	23	49	60	1965	35	43187	0	51464	13372	359
✠ USC UNIVERSITY HOSPITAL, 1500 San Pablo Street, Zip 90033–4585; tel. 213/342–8482; Lee Domanico, Chief Executive Officer **A**1 5 9 10 **F**1 4 5 8 10 11 12 16 19 23 25 26 27 28 30 31 32 34 35 37 39 41 42 43 44 46 48 49 50 52 54 57 58 59 60 61 63 64 65 66 67 69 71 72 73 **P**4 5 6 7 **S** TENET Healthcare Corporation, Santa Barbara, CA	33	10	247	5449	124	44425	0	123175	41899	959
✠ VALLEY PRESBYTERIAN HOSPITAL, 15107 Vanowen Street, Van Nuys, Zip 91405; tel. 818/782–6600; Robert C. Bills, President and Vice Chairman (Total facility includes 32 beds in nursing home–type unit) (Nonreporting) **A**1 2 9 10	23	10	347	—	—	—	—	—	—	—
□ VALUEMARK PINE GROVE BEHAVIORAL HEALTHCARE SYSTEM, 7011 Shoup Avenue, Canoga Park, Zip 91307; tel. 818/348–0500; Diane Sharpe, Chief Executive Officer (Nonreporting) **A**1 10 **S** ValueMark Healthcare Systems, Inc., Atlanta, GA	33	22	62	—	—	—	—	—	—	—
□ VAN NUYS HOSPITAL, 15220 Vanowen Street, Van Nuys, Zip 91405; tel. 818/787–0123; Brent Lamb, Administrator (Nonreporting) **A**1 9 10	33	22	41	—	—	—	—	—	—	—
□ VENCOR HOSPITAL–LOS ANGELES, 5525 West Slauson Avenue, Zip 90056; tel. 310/642–0325; Michael F. Hunn, Chief Executive Officer (Nonreporting) **A**1 9 10 **S** Vencor, Incorporated, Louisville, KY	33	49	81	—	—	—	—	—	—	—
✠ VETERANS AFFAIRS MEDICAL CENTER–WEST LOS ANGELES, 11301 Wilshire Boulevard, Zip 90073–0275; tel. 310/268–3132; Kenneth J. Clark, Executive Director and Chief Executive Officer (Total facility includes 240 beds in nursing home–type unit) (Nonreporting) **A**1 3 5 8 9 **S** Department of Veterans Affairs, Washington, DC	45	10	1327	—	—	—	—	—	—	—
✠ △ WHITE MEMORIAL MEDICAL CENTER, 1720 Cesar E. Chavez Avenue, Zip 90033–2481; tel. 213/268–5000; Beth D. Zachary, Chief Operating Officer (Total facility includes 41 beds in nursing home–type unit) (Nonreporting) **A**1 3 5 7 9 10 **S** Adventist Health, Roseville, CA **N** Adventist Health–Southern California, Glendale, CA	21	10	354	—	—	—	—	—	—	—
LOS GATOS—Santa Clara County										
✠ △ COMMUNITY HOSPITAL OF LOS GATOS, 815 Pollard Road, Zip 95030; tel. 408/378–6131; Truman L. Gates, Chief Executive Officer (Nonreporting) **A**1 2 7 9 10 **S** TENET Healthcare Corporation, Santa Barbara, CA **N** Tenet Healthcare Corporation, Santa Barbara, CA	33	10	153	—	—	—	—	—	—	—
LOYALTON—Sierra County										
SIERRA VALLEY DISTRICT HOSPITAL, 700 Third Street, Zip 96118, Mailing Address: Box 178, Zip 96118; tel. 530/993–1225; Chase Mearian, Administrator (Total facility includes 34 beds in nursing home–type unit) (Nonreporting) **A**9 10 **N** Northern Sierra Rural Health Network, Downieville, CA	16	10	40	—	—	—	—	—	—	—
LYNWOOD—Los Angeles County										
✠ ST. FRANCIS MEDICAL CENTER, 3630 East Imperial Highway, Zip 90262; tel. 310/603–6000; Gerald T. Kozai, Administrator and Chief Operating Officer (Total facility includes 30 beds in nursing home–type unit) (Nonreporting) **A**1 6 9 10 **S** Catholic Healthcare West, San Francisco, CA **N** Catholic HealthCare West (CHW), San Francisco, CA; Essential HealthCare Network, Monterey Park, CA	21	10	414	—	—	—	—	—	—	—
MADERA—Madera County										
□ MADERA COMMUNITY HOSPITAL, 1250 East Almond Avenue, Zip 93637–5606, Mailing Address: Box 1328, Zip 93639–1328; tel. 209/675–5501; Robert C. Kelley, President and Chief Executive Officer **A**1 9 10 **F**7 8 11 15 19 21 22 23 25 30 32 35 37 39 40 41 42 44 46 47 49 65 71 73 **P**8	23	10	100	4880	50	98093	1449	27632	13071	491
MAMMOTH LAKES—Mono County										
□ MAMMOTH HOSPITAL, 85 Sierra Park Road, Zip 93546, Mailing Address: P.O. Box 660, Zip 93546; tel. 619/934–3311; Gary Myers, Administrator (Nonreporting) **A**1 9 10	23	10	15	—	—	—	—	—	—	—

Hospital, Address, Telephone, Administrator, Approval, Facility, and Physician Codes, Health Care System, Network	Classi-fication Codes		Utilization Data					Expense (thousands) of dollars		
★ American Hospital Association (AHA) membership □ Joint Commission on Accreditation of Healthcare Organizations (JCAHO) accreditation + American Osteopathic Healthcare Association (AOHA) membership ○ American Osteopathic Association (AOA) accreditation △ Commission on Accreditation of Rehabilitation Facilities (CARF) accreditation Control codes 61, 63, 64, 71, 72 and 73 indicate hospitals listed by AOHA, but not registered by AHA. For definition of numerical codes, see page A4	Control	Service	Staffed Beds	Admissions	Census	Outpatient Visits	Births	Total	Payroll	Personnel

MANTECA—San Joaquin County

⊞ DOCTORS HOSPITAL OF MANTECA, 1205 East North Street, Zip 95336, Mailing Address: Box 191, Zip 95336; tel. 209/823–3111; Patrick W. Rafferty, Administrator (Nonreporting) **A**1 9 10 **S** TENET Healthcare Corporation, Santa Barbara, CA **N** Tenet Healthcare Corporation, Santa Barbara, CA	33	10	73	—	—	—	—	—	—	—
★ ST. DOMINIC'S HOSPITAL, 1777 West Yosemite Avenue, Zip 95337; tel. 209/825–3500; Richard Aldred, Chief Administrative Officer **A**9 10 **F**3 4 6 7 8 10 11 12 13 14 15 16 17 19 21 22 28 29 30 32 33 35 37 38 40 41 42 43 44 45 46 49 51 54 55 56 57 58 59 60 62 63 64 65 67 71 72 73 74 **P**7 **S** Catholic Healthcare West, San Francisco, CA **N** Catholic HealthCare West (CHW), San Francisco, CA	21	10	63	1828	35	21629	423	17227	6314	221

MARIPOSA—Mariposa County

JOHN C. FREMONT HEALTHCARE DISTRICT, 5189 Hospital Road, Zip 95338, Mailing Address: Box 216, Zip 95338; tel. 209/966–3631; Claire Kuczkowski, Administrator (Total facility includes 10 beds in nursing home–type unit) (Nonreporting) **A**9 10	16	10	34	—	—	—	—	—	—	—

MARTINEZ—Contra Costa County

□ CONTRA COSTA REGIONAL MEDICAL CENTER, (Formerly Merrithew Memorial Hospital), 2500 Alhambra Avenue, Zip 94553; tel. 925/370–5000; Frank J. Puglisi, Jr., Executive Director **A**1 2 3 5 10 **F**1 3 8 10 12 13 15 16 17 18 19 20 21 22 23 26 27 28 29 30 31 32 33 34 35 36 37 38 39 40 41 42 43 44 45 46 49 51 52 53 54 55 56 57 58 59 60 61 65 67 68 69 70 71 72 73 74 **P**6	13	10	109	7388	152	312019	1201	139936	73234	1018

KAISER FOUNDATION HOSPITAL See Kaiser Foundation Hospital, Walnut Creek

MARYSVILLE—Yuba County

RIDEOUT MEMORIAL HOSPITAL, 726 Fourth Street, Zip 95901–2128, Mailing Address: Box 2128, Zip 95901–2128; tel. 916/749–4300; Thomas P. Hayes, Chief Executive Officer (Total facility includes 11 beds in nursing home–type unit) (Nonreporting) **A**9 10 **S** Fremont–Rideout Health Group, Yuba City, CA **N** Fremont–Rideout Health Group, Yuba City, CA	23	10	97	—	—	—	—	—	—	—

MENLO PARK—San Mateo County

□ RECOVERY INN OF MENLO PARK, 570 Willow Road, Zip 94025; tel. 415/324–8500; Ann Klein, Executive Director (Nonreporting) **A**1 9 10	33	10	16	—	—	—	—	—	—	—

MERCED—Merced County

⊞ MERCY HOSPITAL AND HEALTH SERVICES, 2740 M. Street, Zip 95340–2880; tel. 209/384–6444; John Headding, Chief Administrative Officer **A**1 9 10 **F**8 11 12 14 15 16 17 19 22 23 25 26 29 32 34 35 39 40 41 42 44 46 49 65 67 71 73 **S** Catholic Healthcare West, San Francisco, CA **N** Catholic HealthCare West (CHW), San Francisco, CA	21	10	101	5150	61	39306	933	34548	15783	496
⊞ SUTTER MERCED MEDICAL CENTER, 301 East 13th Street, Zip 95340–6211; tel. 209/385–7000; Brian S. Bentley, Administrator **A**1 3 5 9 10 **F**7 8 10 11 12 13 14 15 16 17 19 21 22 23 25 28 30 32 34 35 37 38 39 40 41 44 46 49 51 63 65 66 67 71 73 **P**5 **S** Sutter Health, Sacramento, CA **N** Sutter\CHS, Sacramento, CA	23	10	180	5604	61	80915	1617	43671	18561	551

MISSION HILLS—Los Angeles County, See Los Angeles

MISSION VIEJO—Orange County

□ CHARTER BEHAVIORAL HEALTH SYSTEM OF SOUTHERN CALIFORNIA/MISSION VIEJO, 23228 Madero, Zip 92691; tel. 714/830–4800; Timothy Allen, Chief Executive Officer (Nonreporting) **A**1 9 10 **S** Magellan Health Services, Atlanta, GA	33	22	80	—	—	—	—	—	—	—
⊞ △ MISSION HOSPITAL REGIONAL MEDICAL CENTER, 27700 Medical Center Road, Zip 92691; tel. 714/364–1400; Peter F. Bastone, President and Chief Executive Officer **A**1 2 5 7 9 10 **F**4 7 8 10 11 12 13 14 15 16 17 19 21 22 23 24 25 26 27 28 29 30 32 33 34 35 37 38 39 40 41 42 43 44 45 46 47 48 49 60 63 65 66 67 68 70 71 73 74 **P**3 5 7 **S** St. Joseph Health System, Orange, CA	21	10	234	13304	149	101965	2887	111092	38143	1182

MODESTO—Stanislaus County

⊞ △ DOCTORS MEDICAL CENTER, 1441 Florida Avenue, Zip 95350–4418, Mailing Address: P.O. Box 4138, Zip 95352–4138; tel. 209/578–1211; Chris DiCicco, Chief Executive Officer **A**1 2 3 5 7 9 10 **F**1 4 7 10 11 12 14 15 16 17 19 21 22 23 25 26 27 28 30 32 34 35 37 38 39 40 41 42 43 44 45 46 48 49 51 63 64 65 67 68 71 72 73 **P**5 **S** TENET Healthcare Corporation, Santa Barbara, CA **N** Tenet Healthcare Corporation, Santa Barbara, CA	33	10	368	15926	212	67624	3931	121967	55358	1548
⊞ MEMORIAL HOSPITALS ASSOCIATION, (Includes Memorial Hospital Los Banos, 520 West I. Street, Los Banos, Zip 93635; tel. 209/826–0591; Memorial Medical Center, 1700 Coffee Road, Zip 95355), Mailing Address: P.O. Box 942, Zip 95353; tel. 209/526–4500; David P. Benn, President and Chief Executive Officer (Total facility includes 48 beds in nursing home–type unit) (Nonreporting) **A**1 2 9 10 **S** Sutter Health, Sacramento, CA **N** Sutter\CHS, Sacramento, CA	23	10	373	—	—	—	—	—	—	—
MEMORIAL MEDICAL CENTER See Memorial Hospitals Association										
STANISLAUS BEHAVIORAL HEALTH CENTER, 1501 Claus Road, Zip 95355; tel. 209/524–4888; Larry B. Poaster, Ph.D., Director (Nonreporting)	13	22	46	—	—	—	—	—	—	—

MONROVIA—Los Angeles County

□ MONROVIA COMMUNITY HOSPITAL, 323 South Heliotrope Avenue, Zip 91016, Mailing Address: Box 707, Zip 91017–0707; tel. 626/359–8341; Sheila M. Jordan, R.N., Administrator **A**1 10 **F**19 21 22 26 32 34 35 36 37 44 49 65 71 **S** Paracelsus Healthcare Corporation, Houston, TX	32	10	49	2125	29	3575	—	10925	4415	132

Hospital, Address, Telephone, Administrator, Approval, Facility, and Physician Codes, Health Care System, Network	Classi-fication Codes		Utilization Data					Expense (thousands) of dollars		
★ American Hospital Association (AHA) membership □ Joint Commission on Accreditation of Healthcare Organizations (JCAHO) accreditation + American Osteopathic Healthcare Association (AOHA) membership ○ American Osteopathic Association (AOA) accreditation △ Commission on Accreditation of Rehabilitation Facilities (CARF) accreditation Control codes 61, 63, 64, 71, 72 and 73 indicate hospitals listed by AOHA, but not registered by AHA. For definition of numerical codes, see page A4	Control	Service	Staffed Beds	Admissions	Census	Outpatient Visits	Births	Total	Payroll	Personnel

MONTCLAIR—San Bernardino County

□ U.S. FAMILYCARE MEDICAL CENTER, 5000 San Bernardino Street, Zip 91763; tel. 909/625–5411; Ronald W. Porter, Chief Executive Officer (Nonreporting) **A**1 9 10 12 13	33	10	102	—	—	—	—	—	—	—

MONTEBELLO—Los Angeles County

✠ BEVERLY HOSPITAL, 309 West Beverly Boulevard, Zip 90640; tel. 213/726–1222; Matthew S. Gerlach, Chief Executive Officer and President **A**1 2 9 10 **F**4 7 8 10 11 15 16 19 20 21 22 27 28 30 32 35 37 38 40 43 44 45 49 60 63 65 67 71 73 **P**3 4 5 7 **S** Southern California Healthcare Systems, Pasadena, CA **N** Southern California Healthcare Systems, Pasadena, CA	23	10	142	10605	115	62063	2530	64061	27261	567

MONTEREY—Monterey County

✠ COMMUNITY HOSPITAL OF THE MONTEREY PENINSULA, 23625 Holman Highway, Zip 93940, Mailing Address: Box 'HH', Zip 93942–1085; tel. 408/624–5311; Jay Hudson, President and Chief Executive Officer **A**1 2 9 10 **F**1 3 7 8 12 14 15 16 17 19 21 22 23 25 28 30 31 32 33 34 35 37 40 41 42 44 46 49 52 53 54 55 56 57 58 59 60 63 64 65 67 71 73 **P**5 7	23	10	197	10740	120	224744	1759	138680	59103	1254

MONTEREY PARK—Los Angeles County

✠ △ GARFIELD MEDICAL CENTER, 525 North Garfield Avenue, Zip 91754; tel. 626/573–2222; Philip A. Cohen, Chief Executive Officer (Nonreporting) **A**1 2 7 9 10 **S** TENET Healthcare Corporation, Santa Barbara, CA **N** Tenet Healthcare Corporation, Santa Barbara, CA; Essential HealthCare Network, Monterey Park, CA	33	10	207	—	—	—	—	—	—	—
✠ MONTEREY PARK HOSPITAL, 900 South Atlantic Boulevard, Zip 91754; tel. 626/570–9000; Dan F. Ausman, Chief Executive Officer **A**1 2 9 10 **F**5 8 12 17 19 22 27 28 30 32 34 35 37 38 40 44 46 48 65 71 73 **P**5 7 **S** TENET Healthcare Corporation, Santa Barbara, CA	33	10	93	5247	50	29551	1993	28318	12589	325

MORENO VALLEY—Riverside County

✠ MORENO VALLEY COMMUNITY HOSPITAL, 27300 Iris Avenue, Zip 92555; tel. 909/243–0811; Janice Ziomek, Administrator **A**1 9 10 **F**2 3 4 6 7 8 9 10 11 12 13 14 15 16 17 18 19 20 21 22 23 24 25 27 28 29 30 32 33 34 35 36 37 38 39 40 41 42 43 44 45 46 47 48 49 52 53 54 56 58 60 63 64 65 67 68 69 70 71 72 73 **P**5 7 **S** Valley Health System, Hemet, CA	16	10	73	4944	45	24492	1346	25537	8610	262
□ RIVERSIDE COUNTY REGIONAL MEDICAL CENTER, (Formerly Riverside General Hospital–University Medical Center), 26520 Cactus Avenue, Zip 92555; tel. 909/486–4000; Kenneth B. Cohen, Director **A**1 3 5 10 **F**4 7 8 10 12 14 15 16 17 18 19 20 21 22 27 28 29 30 31 32 34 35 37 38 39 40 41 42 43 44 45 46 47 49 51 53 54 55 56 58 60 61 65 67 70 71 72 73 74 **P**5	13	10	239	9876	126	163544	1391	118045	44973	1089

MORGAN HILL—Santa Clara County

✠ SAINT LOUISE HOSPITAL, 18500 Saint Louise Drive, Zip 95037; tel. 408/779–1500; Joan A. Bero, Regional Vice President and Chief Operating Officer (Total facility includes 19 beds in nursing home–type unit) **A**1 9 10 **F**3 4 7 8 10 12 13 14 15 16 17 19 21 22 28 30 32 33 34 35 37 40 41 42 43 44 45 46 49 50 57 60 64 65 67 68 71 73 **P**2 3 5 6 7 **S** Catholic Healthcare West, San Francisco, CA **N** Catholic HealthCare West (CHW), San Francisco, CA	21	10	55	2049	29	—	359	19667	7758	139

MOSS BEACH—San Mateo County

✠ SETON MEDICAL CENTER COASTSIDE, 600 Marine Boulevard, Zip 94038; tel. 650/728–5521; Bernadette Smith, Chief Operating Officer (Total facility includes 116 beds in nursing home–type unit) (Nonreporting) **A**1 9 10 **S** Catholic Healthcare West, San Francisco, CA **N** Catholic HealthCare West (CHW), San Francisco, CA	21	49	121	—	—	—	—	—	—	—

MOUNT SHASTA—Siskiyou County

✠ MERCY MEDICAL CENTER MOUNT SHASTA, 914 Pine Street, Zip 96067, Mailing Address: P.O. Box 239, Zip 96067–0239; tel. 530/926–6111; Rick J. Barnett, Executive Vice President and Chief Operating Officer (Total facility includes 47 beds in nursing home–type unit) **A**1 9 10 **F**7 8 15 17 19 22 24 25 26 28 31 32 33 35 37 39 40 41 44 56 64 65 66 70 71 73 **P**5 **S** Catholic Healthcare West, San Francisco, CA **N** Catholic HealthCare West (CHW), San Francisco, CA	23	10	80	1717	52	37292	170	18338	8166	260

MOUNTAIN VIEW—Santa Clara County

✠ CAMINO HEALTHCARE, 2500 Grant Road, Zip 94040, Mailing Address: P.O. Box 7025, Zip 94039; tel. 650/940–7000; Richard A. Warren, Chief Executive Officer (Nonreporting) **A**1 9 10	16	10	290	—	—	—	—	—	—	—

MURRIETA—Riverside County

SHARP HEALTHCARE MURRIETA, 25500 Medical Center Drive, Zip 92562–5966; tel. 909/696–6000; Juanice Lovett, Chief Executive Officer (Total facility includes 42 beds in nursing home–type unit) (Nonreporting) **A**2 9 10 **S** Sharp Healthcare, San Diego, CA **N** Sharp Healthcare, San Diego, CA	23	10	91	—	—	—	—	—	—	—

NAPA—Napa County

□ NAPA STATE HOSPITAL, 2100 Napa–Vallejo Highway, Zip 94558; tel. 707/253–5454; Frank Turley, Ph.D., Executive Director **A**1 3 10 **F**1 19 20 22 26 29 31 35 37 41 45 52 53 57 58 59 64 65 71 73	12	22	970	485	828	—	0	109013	65501	1651
✠ QUEEN OF THE VALLEY HOSPITAL, 1000 Trancas Street, Zip 94558, Mailing Address: Box 2340, Zip 94558; tel. 707/252–4411; Dennis Sisto, Acting President and Chief Executive Officer (Total facility includes 24 beds in nursing home–type unit) (Nonreporting) **A**1 2 9 10 **S** St. Joseph Health System, Orange, CA **N** Saint Joseph Health System, Orange, CA	21	10	176	—	—	—	—	—	—	—

NATIONAL CITY—San Diego County

✠ △ PARADISE VALLEY HOSPITAL, 2400 East Fourth Street, Zip 91950; tel. 619/470–4321; Eric Martinsen, President (Total facility includes 12 beds in nursing home–type unit) (Nonreporting) **A**1 7 9 10 **S** Adventist Health, Roseville, CA	21	10	130	—	—	—	—	—	—	—

Hospital, Address, Telephone, Administrator, Approval, Facility, and Physician Codes, Health Care System, Network	Classi-fication Codes		Utilization Data					Expense (thousands) of dollars		
	Control	Service	Staffed Beds	Admissions	Census	Outpatient Visits	Births	Total	Payroll	Personnel

★ American Hospital Association (AHA) membership
□ Joint Commission on Accreditation of Healthcare Organizations (JCAHO) accreditation
+ American Osteopathic Healthcare Association (AOHA) membership
○ American Osteopathic Association (AOA) accreditation
△ Commission on Accreditation of Rehabilitation Facilities (CARF) accreditation
Control codes 61, 63, 64, 71, 72 and 73 indicate hospitals listed by AOHA, but not registered by AHA. For definition of numerical codes, see page A4

NEEDLES—San Bernardino County

☒ COLORADO RIVER MEDICAL CENTER, (Formerly Needles–Desert Communities Hospital), 1401 Bailey Avenue, Zip 92363; tel. 760/326–4531; Harley Smith, Chief Executive Officer (Nonreporting) **A**1 10 **S** Province Healthcare Corporation, Brentwood, TN **N** Samaritan Health Services, Phoenix, AZ — 14 10 39 — — — — — — — —

NEWHALL—Los Angeles County

NEWHALL COMMUNITY HOSPITAL, 22607 6th Street, Zip 91322–1328, Mailing Address: Box 221328, Zip 91321–1328; tel. 805/259–4555; Bienvenido Tan, M.D., Chief Executive Officer (Nonreporting) — 12 10 13 — — — — — — — —

NEWPORT BEACH—Orange County

☒ HOAG MEMORIAL HOSPITAL PRESBYTERIAN, One Hoag Drive, Zip 92663–4120, Mailing Address: Box 6100, Zip 92658–6100; tel. 949/645–8600; Michael D. Stephens, President and Chief Executive Officer **A**1 2 5 9 10 **F**2 3 4 7 8 10 12 15 16 17 19 21 22 23 25 28 30 32 34 35 36 37 38 39 40 41 42 43 44 46 49 60 61 63 64 65 67 69 71 72 73 74 **P**5 — 23 10 356 20553 228 174457 4254 233878 73273 2336

NORTH HOLLYWOOD—Los Angeles County, See Los Angeles
NORTHRIDGE—Los Angeles County, See Los Angeles
NORWALK—Los Angeles County

□ COAST PLAZA DOCTORS HOSPITAL, 13100 Studebaker Road, Zip 90650; tel. 562/868–3751; Gerald J. Garner, Chairman of the Board **A**1 10 **F**8 11 19 21 22 27 28 35 37 44 45 46 58 59 64 65 66 71 73 **P**5 — 32 10 83 5029 38 9887 2 17169 7710 256

LOS ANGELES COMMUNITY HOSPITAL OF NORWALK See Los Angeles Community Hospital, Los Angeles

□ METROPOLITAN STATE HOSPITAL, 11400 Norwalk Boulevard, Zip 90650; tel. 562/863–7011; William G. Silva, Executive Director **A**1 5 10 **F**19 20 22 24 26 30 31 35 41 45 46 52 53 55 57 59 64 65 67 71 73 — 12 22 1000 1093 768 — — — — 1657

NOVATO—Marin County

☒ NOVATO COMMUNITY HOSPITAL, 1625 Hill Road, Zip 94947, Mailing Address: P.O. Box 1108, Zip 94948; tel. 415/897–3111; Anne Hosfeld, Chief Administrative Officer (Total facility includes 8 beds in nursing home–type unit) **A**1 9 10 **F**4 7 8 10 11 12 14 15 16 19 21 22 23 24 27 28 29 30 31 32 34 35 37 38 40 41 42 43 44 45 46 49 52 53 54 55 56 57 58 59 60 64 65 71 73 74 **P**1 3 4 7 **S** Sutter Health, Sacramento, CA **N** Sutter\CHS, Sacramento, CA — 23 10 28 2313 30 38073 229 22830 10276 251

OAKDALE—Stanislaus County

☒ OAK VALLEY DISTRICT HOSPITAL, 350 South Oak Street, Zip 95361; tel. 209/847–3011; Norman J. Andrews, Chief Executive Officer (Total facility includes 108 beds in nursing home–type unit) (Nonreporting) **A**1 9 10 **N** Sutter\CHS, Sacramento, CA — 16 10 141 — — — — — — —

OAKLAND—Alameda County

□ ALAMEDA COUNTY MEDICAL CENTER–HIGHLAND CAMPUS, 1411 East 31st Street, Zip 94602; tel. 510/437–5081; Michael Smart, Chief Executive Officer (Nonreporting) **A**1 3 5 10 12 **S** Alameda County Health Care Services Agency, San Leandro, CA — 13 10 247 — — — — — — —

□ CHILDREN'S HOSPITAL OAKLAND, 747 52nd Street, Zip 94609; tel. 510/428–3000; Antonie H. Paap, President and Chief Executive Officer **A**1 3 5 9 10 **F**4 9 10 12 13 14 15 16 17 19 20 21 22 25 28 29 30 31 32 33 34 35 38 39 42 43 44 45 47 48 49 51 53 54 55 56 58 65 66 67 68 70 71 72 73 **P**5 8 — 23 50 205 9820 146 158146 — 154084 73085 1419

☒ KAISER FOUNDATION HOSPITAL, 280 West MacArthur Boulevard, Zip 94611; tel. 510/987–1000; Bernard J. Tyson, Administrator (Nonreporting) **A**1 3 5 10 **S** Kaiser Foundation Hospitals, Oakland, CA **N** Kaiser Foundation Health Plan of Northern California, Oakland, CA — 23 10 264 — — — — — — —

□ SUMMIT MEDICAL CENTER, 350 Hawthorne Avenue, Zip 94609; tel. 510/655–4000; Irwin C. Hansen, President and Chief Executive Officer (Total facility includes 48 beds in nursing home–type unit) (Nonreporting) **A**1 2 9 10 — 23 10 420 — — — — — — —

OCEANSIDE—San Diego County

☒ TRI–CITY MEDICAL CENTER, 4002 Vista Way, Zip 92056–4593; tel. 760/724–8411; John P. Lauri, President and Chief Executive Officer **A**1 2 9 10 **F**1 4 5 7 8 10 11 12 14 15 16 17 18 19 20 21 22 23 26 28 29 30 32 33 34 35 37 38 39 40 41 42 43 44 45 46 49 50 52 53 54 55 56 57 58 59 60 63 64 65 70 71 72 73 74 **P**7 8 — 16 10 397 16230 182 201135 3681 127878 49096 1538

OJAI—Ventura County

★ OJAI VALLEY COMMUNITY HOSPITAL, 1306 Maricopa Highway, Zip 93023–3180; tel. 805/646–1401; Mark Turner, Chief Executive Officer (Total facility includes 45 beds in nursing home–type unit) (Nonreporting) **A**9 10 **S** Province Healthcare Corporation, Brentwood, TN — 33 10 116 — — — — — — —

ONTARIO—San Bernardino County

□ VENCOR HOSPITAL–ONTARIO, 550 North Monterey, Zip 91764; tel. 909/391–0333; Virgis Narbutas, Administrator (Nonreporting) **A**1 5 10 **S** Vencor, Incorporated, Louisville, KY — 33 10 100 — — — — — — —

ORANGE—Orange County

☒ CHAPMAN MEDICAL CENTER, 2601 East Chapman Avenue, Zip 92869; tel. 714/633–0011; Maxine T. Cooper, Chief Executive Officer **A**1 9 10 **F**1 2 3 4 7 8 10 11 16 17 18 19 21 22 25 26 27 28 29 30 31 32 34 35 37 38 39 40 41 42 43 44 45 46 47 48 49 52 57 60 63 64 65 66 67 68 69 70 71 72 73 74 **P**5 7 **S** TENET Healthcare Corporation, Santa Barbara, CA — 33 10 40 2774 31 18667 578 — — 265

Hospital, Address, Telephone, Administrator, Approval, Facility, and Physician Codes, Health Care System, Network	Classi-fication Codes		Utilization Data					Expense (thousands) of dollars		
★ American Hospital Association (AHA) membership □ Joint Commission on Accreditation of Healthcare Organizations (JCAHO) accreditation + American Osteopathic Healthcare Association (AOHA) membership ○ American Osteopathic Association (AOA) accreditation △ Commission on Accreditation of Rehabilitation Facilities (CARF) accreditation Control codes 61, 63, 64, 71, 72 and 73 indicate hospitals listed by AOHA, but not registered by AHA. For definition of numerical codes, see page A4	Control	Service	Staffed Beds	Admissions	Census	Outpatient Visits	Births	Total	Payroll	Personnel
□ CHILDREN'S HOSPITAL OF ORANGE COUNTY, 455 South Main Street, Zip 92868–3874; tel. 714/997–3000; Kimberly C. Cripe, Chief Executive Officer (Nonreporting) **A**1 2 3 5 9 10	23	50	192	—	—	—	—	—	—	—
✚ ST. JOSEPH HOSPITAL, 1100 West Stewart Drive, Zip 92668, Mailing Address: P.O. Box 5600, Zip 92613–5600; tel. 714/633–9111; Larry K. Ainsworth, President and Chief Executive Officer (Total facility includes 34 beds in nursing home–type unit) **A**1 2 3 5 9 10 **F**2 3 4 7 8 10 11 12 14 15 16 17 18 19 20 21 22 23 24 25 26 28 30 32 33 34 35 36 37 38 39 40 41 42 43 44 46 47 49 52 56 58 59 60 64 65 67 69 71 73 74 **P**2 3 4 5 7 **S** St. Joseph Health System, Orange, CA **N** Saint Joseph Health System, Orange, CA	21	10	367	19520	240	194333	5330	205988	76699	1963
✚ UNIVERSITY OF CALIFORNIA, IRVINE MEDICAL CENTER, 101 The City Drive, Zip 92668–3298; tel. 714/456–7890; Mark R. Laret, Executive Director **A**1 2 3 5 8 9 10 **F**4 5 8 9 10 11 12 13 15 16 17 18 19 21 22 25 26 28 29 30 31 34 35 37 38 39 40 41 42 43 44 45 46 47 48 49 51 52 53 54 55 56 57 58 59 60 65 66 67 68 69 70 71 72 73 74 **P**6 **S** University of California–Systemwide Administration, Oakland, CA	23	10	383	13273	223	399200	1781	191885	81538	2088
OROVILLE—Butte County										
□ OROVILLE HOSPITAL, 2767 Olive Highway, Zip 95966–6185; tel. 916/533–8500; Robert J. Wentz, President and Chief Executive Officer (Total facility includes 20 beds in nursing home–type unit) **A**1 9 10 **F**7 8 12 13 15 16 17 19 20 21 22 25 26 28 29 30 31 32 34 35 37 39 40 41 42 44 45 46 49 51 61 63 64 65 67 70 71 72 73 74 **P**8	23	10	120	5657	72	208800	577	52661	24081	746
OXNARD—Ventura County										
✚ △ ST. JOHN'S REGIONAL MEDICAL CENTER, 1600 North Rose Avenue, Zip 93030; tel. 805/988–2500; James R. Hoss, President and Chief Operating Officer **A**1 7 9 10 **F**4 7 8 10 11 14 15 16 17 19 21 22 23 28 29 30 32 34 35 37 38 40 41 42 43 44 45 46 48 49 52 60 63 71 **P**3 4 5 7 **S** Catholic Healthcare West, San Francisco, CA **N** Catholic HealthCare West (CHW), San Francisco, CA	23	10	236	11301	142	90178	2275	88080	32191	954
PALM SPRINGS—Riverside County										
✚ DESERT REGIONAL MEDICAL CENTER, (Formerly Desert Hospital), 1150 North Indian Canyon Drive, Zip 92262, Mailing Address: Box 2739, Zip 92263; tel. 760/323–6511; Robert A. Minkin, CHE, President and Chief Executive Officer (Nonreporting) **A**1 2 9 10 **S** TENET Healthcare Corporation, Santa Barbara, CA	33	10	348	—	—	—	—	—	—	—
PALO ALTO—Santa Clara County										
□ LUCILE SALTER PACKARD CHILDREN'S HOSPITAL AT STANFORD, 725 Welch Road, Zip 94304; tel. 415/497–8000; Christopher G. Dawes, President (Nonreporting) **A**1 3 5 9 10	23	50	162	—	—	—	—	—	—	—
✚ △ VETERANS AFFAIRS PALO ALTO HEALTH CARE SYSTEM, (Includes Livermore Division, 4951 Arroyo Road, Livermore, Zip 94550; tel. 510/447–2560; Clarence H. Nixon, Director; Palo Alto Division, 3801 Miranda Avenue, tel. 415/493–5000), 3801 Miranda Avenue, Zip 94304–1207; tel. 650/493–5000; James A. Goff, FACHE, Director (Total facility includes 379 beds in nursing home–type unit) **A**1 2 3 5 7 8 **F**1 2 3 4 5 6 8 10 11 12 14 15 16 17 18 19 20 21 22 23 24 25 26 27 28 29 30 31 32 33 34 35 37 39 41 42 43 44 45 46 48 49 50 51 52 54 55 56 57 58 59 60 61 63 64 65 67 69 71 72 73 74 **S** Department of Veterans Affairs, Washington, DC	45	10	1009	10156	774	456909	—	315946	196463	3399
PANORAMA CITY—Los Angeles County, See Los Angeles										
PARADISE—Butte County										
✚ FEATHER RIVER HOSPITAL, 5974 Pentz Road, Zip 95969–5593; tel. 530/877–9361; George Pifer, President **A**1 9 10 **F**7 8 10 11 12 14 15 16 17 19 22 25 27 28 29 30 31 32 33 34 35 36 37 40 41 44 46 49 64 65 67 71 73 74 **P**3 4 5 **S** Adventist Health, Roseville, CA **N** Adventist Health–Northern California, Deer Park, CA	21	10	122	3949	53	71916	478	37985	18074	578
PARAMOUNT—Los Angeles County										
✚ SUBURBAN MEDICAL CENTER, 16453 South Colorado Avenue, Zip 90723; tel. 562/531–3110; Gustavo Valdespino, Chief Executive Officer (Nonreporting) **A**1 9 10 **S** TENET Healthcare Corporation, Santa Barbara, CA **N** Essential HealthCare Network, Monterey Park, CA	33	10	130	—	—	—	—	—	—	—
PASADENA—Los Angeles County										
✚ HUNTINGTON MEMORIAL HOSPITAL, 100 West California Boulevard, Zip 91105, Mailing Address: P.O. Box 7013, Zip 91109–7013; tel. 626/397–5000; Stephen A. Ralph, President and Chief Executive Officer (Total facility includes 75 beds in nursing home–type unit) **A**1 2 3 5 8 9 10 **F**4 7 8 10 11 12 14 15 16 17 18 19 21 22 23 25 26 27 28 29 30 31 32 33 34 35 37 38 39 40 41 42 43 44 45 46 47 48 49 51 52 54 55 56 57 58 59 60 61 64 65 67 70 71 72 73 74 **P**1 5 7 **S** Southern California Healthcare Systems, Pasadena, CA **N** Southern California Healthcare Systems, Pasadena, CA	23	10	520	23000	323	196000	4100	199600	90600	2150
IMPACT DRUG AND ALCOHOL TREATMENT CENTER, 1680 North Fair Oaks Avenue, Zip 91103; tel. 818/681–2575; James M. Stillwell, Director (Nonreporting)	23	82	130	—	—	—	—	—	—	—
✚ LAS ENCINAS HOSPITAL, (Formerly Columbia Las Encinas Hospital), 2900 East Del Mar Boulevard, Zip 91107–4375; tel. 626/795–9901; Roland Metivier, Chief Executive Officer **A**1 9 10 **F**1 2 3 4 5 6 7 8 9 10 11 12 13 15 16 17 18 19 20 21 22 23 24 25 26 27 28 29 30 31 32 33 34 35 36 37 38 39 40 41 42 43 44 45 46 47 48 49 50 51 52 53 54 55 56 57 58 59 60 61 62 63 64 65 66 67 68 69 70 71 72 73 74 **P**7 **S** Columbia/HCA Healthcare Corporation, Nashville, TN	33	22	138	1984	61	7430	—	14127	8165	259

Hospital, Address, Telephone, Administrator, Approval, Facility, and Physician Codes, Health Care System, Network	Classi-fication Codes			Utilization Data					Expense (thousands) of dollars		
	Control	Service	Staffed Beds	Admissions	Census	Outpatient Visits	Births	Total	Payroll	Personnel

★ American Hospital Association (AHA) membership
□ Joint Commission on Accreditation of Healthcare Organizations (JCAHO) accreditation
+ American Osteopathic Healthcare Association (AOHA) membership
○ American Osteopathic Association (AOA) accreditation
△ Commission on Accreditation of Rehabilitation Facilities (CARF) accreditation
Control codes 61, 63, 64, 71, 72 and 73 indicate hospitals listed by AOHA, but not registered by AHA. For definition of numerical codes, see page A4

Hospital	Control	Service	Staffed Beds	Admissions	Census	Outpatient Visits	Births	Total	Payroll	Personnel
✚ ST. LUKE MEDICAL CENTER, 2632 East Washington Boulevard, Zip 91107–1994; tel. 626/797–1141; Mark H. Uffer, Chief Executive Officer (Total facility includes 18 beds in nursing home–type unit) (Nonreporting) **A**1 2 9 10 **S** TENET Healthcare Corporation, Santa Barbara, CA	33	10	120	—	—	—	—	—	—	—
PATTON—San Bernardino County										
□ PATTON STATE HOSPITAL, 3102 East Highland Avenue, Zip 92369; tel. 909/425–7000; William L. Summers, Executive Director (Nonreporting) **A**1 **N** East Bay Medical Network, Emeryville, CA	12	22	1133	—	—	—	—	—	—	—
PETALUMA—Sonoma County										
✚ PETALUMA VALLEY HOSPITAL, 400 North McDowell Boulevard, Zip 94954–2339; tel. 707/778–1111; Alanna Brogan, Chief Operating Officer (Total facility includes 14 beds in nursing home–type unit) (Nonreporting) **A**1 2 9 10 **S** St. Joseph Health System, Orange, CA	16	10	84	—	—	—	—	—	—	—
PINOLE—Contra Costa County										
✚ DOCTORS MEDICAL CENTER–PINOLE CAMPUS, (Formerly Doctors Hospital of Pinole), 2151 Appian Way, Zip 94564; tel. 510/724–5000; Gary Sloan, Chief Executive Officer (Total facility includes 40 beds in nursing home–type unit) (Nonreporting) **A**1 9 10 **S** TENET Healthcare Corporation, Santa Barbara, CA **N** Tenet Healthcare Corporation, Santa Barbara, CA	33	10	137	—	—	—	—	—	—	—
PLACENTIA—Orange County										
✚ PLACENTIA–LINDA HOSPITAL, 1301 Rose Drive, Zip 92870; tel. 714/993–2000; Maxine T. Cooper, Chief Executive Officer **A**1 9 10 **F**7 8 11 14 15 16 17 18 19 21 22 27 28 29 30 31 32 34 35 36 37 39 40 41 42 44 46 49 54 56 61 63 65 66 67 71 73 **P**5 7 8 **S** TENET Healthcare Corporation, Santa Barbara, CA **N** Tenet Healthcare Corporation, Santa Barbara, CA	33	10	114	2191	20	18635	457	20165	7296	229
PLACERVILLE—El Dorado County										
✚ MARSHALL HOSPITAL, Marshall Way, Zip 95667; tel. 530/622–1441; Frank Nachtman, Administrator (Nonreporting) **A**1 9 10	23	10	107	—	—	—	—	—	—	—
PLEASANTON—Alameda County										
VALLEYCARE MEDICAL CENTER, 5555 West Los Positas Boulevard, Zip 94588; tel. 510/847–3000; Marcy Feit, Chief Executive Officer (Nonreporting) **A**9 **S** ValleyCare Health System, Pleasanton, CA	23	10	68	—	—	—	—	—	—	—
POMONA—Los Angeles County										
✚ △ CASA COLINA HOSPITAL FOR REHABILITATIVE MEDICINE, 255 East Bonita Avenue, Zip 91767–9966, Mailing Address: P.O. Box 6001, Zip 91769–6001; tel. 909/593–7521; Dale E. Eazell, Ph.D., President and Chief Executive Officer (Total facility includes 11 beds in nursing home–type unit) (Nonreporting) **A**1 7 9 10	23	46	38	—	—	—	—	—	—	—
LANTERMAN DEVELOPMENTAL CENTER, 3530 Pomona Boulevard, Zip 91768, Mailing Address: P.O. Box 100, Zip 91769; tel. 909/595–1221; Ruth Maples, Executive Director (Nonreporting) **A**10	12	62	771	—	—	—	—	—	—	—
✚ POMONA VALLEY HOSPITAL MEDICAL CENTER, 1798 North Garey Avenue, Zip 91767–2918; tel. 909/865–9500; Richard E. Yochum, President (Total facility includes 38 beds in nursing home–type unit) **A**1 2 3 9 10 **F**4 7 8 10 11 12 14 15 16 17 19 20 21 22 23 24 25 28 29 30 31 34 35 36 37 38 39 40 41 42 43 44 45 46 47 60 64 65 66 67 71 72 73 74 **P**5	23	10	381	18935	237	421057	4777	179702	80941	1792
PORT HUENEME—Ventura County										
□ ANACAPA HOSPITAL, 307 East Clara Street, Zip 93041; tel. 805/488–3661; John J. Megara, Chief Executive Officer (Nonreporting) **A**1 9 10	33	22	40	—	—	—	—	—	—	—
PORTERVILLE—Tulare County										
PORTERVILLE DEVELOPMENTAL CENTER, 26501 Avenue 140, Zip 93257–9430, Mailing Address: Box 2000, Zip 93258–2000; tel. 209/782–2222; Harold Pitchford, Executive Director **A**10 **F**6 12 16 17 18 19 20 21 24 26 28 29 30 31 32 35 41 44 46 50 53 54 57 60 64 65 67 73 **P**6	12	62	829	193	763	0	0	—	—	1428
SIERRA VIEW DISTRICT HOSPITAL, 465 West Putnam Avenue, Zip 93257–3320; tel. 209/784–1110; Edwin L. Ermshar, President and Chief Executive Officer **A**9 10 **F**7 8 13 14 15 16 19 21 22 24 28 29 30 32 35 39 40 42 44 45 46 60 65 67 68 71 73 74 **P**5 8	16	10	165	5575	58	38404	1135	47600	16192	491
PORTOLA—Plumas County										
EASTERN PLUMAS DISTRICT HOSPITAL, 500 First Avenue, Zip 96122; tel. 530/832–4277; Charles Guenther, Administrator (Total facility includes 14 beds in nursing home–type unit) (Nonreporting) **A**9 10	16	10	24	—	—	—	—	—	—	—
POWAY—San Diego County										
✚ POMERADO HOSPITAL, 15615 Pomerado Road, Zip 92064; tel. 619/485–4600; Marvin W. Levenson, M.D., Administrator and Chief Operating Officer (Total facility includes 149 beds in nursing home–type unit) **A**1 2 9 10 **F**3 4 7 8 10 11 12 14 15 16 17 19 22 23 27 29 30 31 32 33 34 35 36 37 38 39 40 41 42 43 44 45 46 49 52 54 55 56 57 58 59 60 61 64 65 67 68 70 71 72 73 74 **P**7 **S** Palomar Pomerado Health System, San Diego, CA **N** Health First Network, San Diego, CA	16	10	258	6084	188	91803	1322	50451	20527	409
QUINCY—Plumas County										
□ PLUMAS DISTRICT HOSPITAL, 1065 Bucks Lake Road, Zip 95971–9599; tel. 530/283–2121; R. Michael Barry, Administrator (Nonreporting) **A**1 9 10	16	10	32	—	—	—	—	—	—	—

Hospital, Address, Telephone, Administrator, Approval, Facility, and Physician Codes, Health Care System, Network	Classi-fication Codes		Utilization Data					Expense (thousands) of dollars		

★ American Hospital Association (AHA) membership
□ Joint Commission on Accreditation of Healthcare Organizations (JCAHO) accreditation
+ American Osteopathic Healthcare Association (AOHA) membership
○ American Osteopathic Association (AOA) accreditation
△ Commission on Accreditation of Rehabilitation Facilities (CARF) accreditation
Control codes 61, 63, 64, 71, 72 and 73 indicate hospitals listed by AOHA, but not registered by AHA. For definition of numerical codes, see page A4

	Control	Service	Staffed Beds	Admissions	Census	Outpatient Visits	Births	Total	Payroll	Personnel
RANCHO MIRAGE—Riverside County										
★ EISENHOWER MEMORIAL HOSPITAL AND BETTY FORD CENTER AT EISENHOWER, 39000 Bob Hope Drive, Zip 92270; tel. 760/773–1228; Andrew W. Deems, President and Chief Executive Officer **A**1 2 5 9 10 **F**1 4 5 7 8 10 11 12 15 16 19 21 22 23 24 25 29 30 32 33 34 35 37 38 39 40 41 42 43 44 45 46 49 60 65 66 67 71 72 73 74 **P**5	23	10	261	13344	152	241644	1547	138467	46535	1166
RED BLUFF—Tehama County										
★ ST. ELIZABETH COMMUNITY HOSPITAL, 2550 Sister Mary Columba Drive, Zip 96080–4397; tel. 530/529–8005; Thomas F. Grimes, III, Executive Vice President and Chief Operating Officer **A**1 9 10 **F**7 11 12 17 19 22 28 32 33 34 35 40 44 49 65 68 71 73 **P**3 **S** Catholic Healthcare West, San Francisco, CA **N** Catholic HealthCare West (CHW), San Francisco, CA	21	10	53	3351	35	40734	611	30196	12193	372
REDDING—Shasta County										
★ MERCY MEDICAL CENTER, 2175 Rosaline Avenue, Zip 96001, Mailing Address: Box 496009, Zip 96049–6009; tel. 916/225–6000; George A. Govier, President and Chief Executive Officer (Total facility includes 17 beds in nursing home–type unit) **A**1 2 3 5 9 10 **F**1 4 7 8 10 11 12 15 16 19 21 22 23 24 25 27 29 30 31 32 33 34 35 36 37 38 39 40 41 42 43 44 49 60 63 64 65 67 69 70 71 72 73 74 **P**3 5 **S** Catholic Healthcare West, San Francisco, CA **N** Catholic HealthCare West (CHW), San Francisco, CA	21	10	220	9466	111	172146	1494	107313	38668	1091
★ REDDING MEDICAL CENTER, 1100 Butte Street, Zip 96001–0853, Mailing Address: Box 496072, Zip 96049–6072; tel. 530/244–5454; Steve Schmidt, Chief Executive Officer (Nonreporting) **A**1 9 10 **S** TENET Healthcare Corporation, Santa Barbara, CA **N** Tenet Healthcare Corporation, Santa Barbara, CA; Kaiser Foundation Health Plan of Northern California, Oakland, CA	33	10	162	—	—	—	—	—	—	—
REDLANDS—San Bernardino County										
□ LOMA LINDA UNIVERSITY BEHAVIORAL MEDICINE CENTER, 1710 Barton Road, Zip 92373; tel. 909/793–9333; Alan Soderblom, Administrator (Nonreporting) **A**1 5 9 10 **S** Loma Linda University Health Sciences Center, Loma Linda, CA **N** Adventist Health System–Loma Linda, Loma Linda, CA	21	22	89	—	—	—	—	—	—	—
□ REDLANDS COMMUNITY HOSPITAL, 350 Terracina Boulevard, Zip 92373, Mailing Address: Box 3391, Zip 92373–0742; tel. 909/335–5500; James R. Holmes, President (Nonreporting) **A**1 9 10	23	10	194	—	—	—	—	—	—	—
REDWOOD CITY—San Mateo County										
★ KAISER FOUNDATION HOSPITAL, 1150 Veterans Boulevard, Zip 94063–2087; tel. 650/299–2000; Helen Wilmot, Administrator (Nonreporting) **A**1 3 5 10 **S** Kaiser Foundation Hospitals, Oakland, CA **N** Kaiser Foundation Health Plan of Northern California, Oakland, CA	23	10	144	—	—	—	—	—	—	—
★ SEQUOIA HOSPITAL, 170 Alameda De Las Pulgas, Zip 94062–2799; tel. 650/369–5811; Glenna L. Vaskelis, Administrator (Total facility includes 60 beds in nursing home–type unit) **A**1 9 10 **F**4 8 10 11 12 15 16 17 19 21 22 28 29 30 34 35 37 40 41 42 43 44 48 49 52 59 60 63 64 65 67 71 73 74 **P**4 5 6 7 **S** Catholic Healthcare West, San Francisco, CA **N** Catholic HealthCare West (CHW), San Francisco, CA	16	10	228	10444	140	95649	1313	116486	49017	671
REEDLEY—Fresno County										
★ SIERRA–KINGS DISTRICT HOSPITAL, 372 West Cypress Avenue, Zip 93654; tel. 209/638–8155; Daniel DeSantis, Administrator (Total facility includes 9 beds in nursing home–type unit) **A**1 9 10 **F**7 8 12 14 15 16 17 19 22 24 28 30 34 39 40 44 45 49 64 65 71 73 74	16	10	27	1423	8	29108	747	10089	4206	175
RICHMOND—Contra Costa County										
EAST BAY HOSPITAL, 820 23rd Street, Zip 94804–1397; tel. 510/234–2525; Lois K. Patsey, Administrator and Chief Executive Officer (Nonreporting)	33	10	87	—	—	—	—	—	—	—
RIDGECREST—Kern County										
★ RIDGECREST REGIONAL HOSPITAL, (Formerly Ridgecrest Community Hospital), 1081 North China Lake Boulevard, Zip 93555; tel. 760/446–3551; David A. Mechtenberg, Chief Executive Officer **A**1 9 10 **F**7 11 15 16 19 22 28 32 33 35 36 37 40 41 44 45 46 49 65 71 73	23	10	80	2360	23	47821	461	21548	8700	274
RIVERSIDE—Riverside County										
★ KAISER FOUNDATION HOSPITAL–RIVERSIDE, 10800 Magnolia Avenue, Zip 92505–3000; tel. 909/353–4600; Robert S. Lund, Administrator **A**1 2 3 10 **F**3 4 7 8 10 12 14 15 16 21 22 31 32 33 35 37 38 40 41 42 43 44 45 46 53 54 55 56 58 63 65 69 71 72 73 74 **S** Kaiser Foundation Hospitals, Oakland, CA	23	10	118	9620	87	53514	2645	—	—	—
□ PARKVIEW COMMUNITY HOSPITAL MEDICAL CENTER, 3865 Jackson Street, Zip 92503; tel. 909/688–2211; Norm Martin, President and Chief Executive Officer (Nonreporting) **A**1 2 9 10	23	10	193	—	—	—	—	—	—	—
□ RIVERSIDE COMMUNITY HOSPITAL, 4445 Magnolia Avenue, Zip 92501–1669, Mailing Address: Box 1669, Zip 92502–1669; tel. 909/788–3000; Jeffrey P. Winter, Chief Executive Officer **A**1 9 10 **F**4 7 8 10 11 12 13 14 15 17 19 21 22 23 25 31 32 33 35 36 37 38 39 40 41 42 43 44 48 49 60 63 64 65 69 70 71 72 73 74 **P**5	32	10	276	11481	140	64985	1458	87239	32818	763

Hospital, Address, Telephone, Administrator, Approval, Facility, and Physician Codes, Health Care System, Network	Classi-fication Codes		Utilization Data					Expense (thousands) of dollars		
★ American Hospital Association (AHA) membership □ Joint Commission on Accreditation of Healthcare Organizations (JCAHO) accreditation + American Osteopathic Healthcare Association (AOHA) membership ○ American Osteopathic Association (AOA) accreditation △ Commission on Accreditation of Rehabilitation Facilities (CARF) accreditation Control codes 61, 63, 64, 71, 72 and 73 indicate hospitals listed by AOHA, but not registered by AHA. For definition of numerical codes, see page A4	Control	Service	Staffed Beds	Admissions	Census	Outpatient Visits	Births	Total	Payroll	Personnel

ROSEMEAD—Los Angeles County

□ BHC ALHAMBRA HOSPITAL, 4619 North Rosemead Boulevard, Zip 91770–1498, Mailing Address: P.O. Box 369, Zip 91770; tel. 626/286–1191; Peggy Minnick, Administrator (Nonreporting) **A**1 9 10 **S** Behavioral Healthcare Corporation, Nashville, TN	33	22	98	—	—	—	—	—	—	—

ROSEVILLE—Placer County

✠ SUTTER ROSEVILLE MEDICAL CENTER, One Medical Plaza, Zip 95661–3477; tel. 916/781–1000; Joel E. Grey, Chief Executive Officer (Total facility includes 14 beds in nursing home–type unit) (Nonreporting) **A**1 2 9 10 **S** Sutter Health, Sacramento, CA **N** Sutter\CHS, Sacramento, CA	23	10	183	—	—	—	—	—	—	—

SACRAMENTO—Sacramento County

✠ BHC HERITAGE OAKS HOSPITAL, 4250 Auburn Boulevard, Zip 95841; tel. 916/489–3336; Ingrid L. Whipple, Chief Executive Officer (Nonreporting) **A**1 9 10 **S** Behavioral Healthcare Corporation, Nashville, TN	33	22	76	—	—	—	—	—	—	—
□ BHC SIERRA VISTA HOSPITAL, 8001 Bruceville Road, Zip 95823; tel. 916/423–2000; Kenneth A. Meibert, Chief Executive Officer (Nonreporting) **A**1 9 10 **S** Behavioral Healthcare Corporation, Nashville, TN	33	22	72	—	—	—	—	—	—	—
✠ KAISER FOUNDATION HOSPITAL, 2025 Morse Avenue, Zip 95825–2115; tel. 916/973–5000; Sarah Krevans, Administrator (Nonreporting) **A**1 3 5 10 **S** Kaiser Foundation Hospitals, Oakland, CA	23	10	304	—	—	—	—	—	—	—
✠ KAISER FOUNDATION HOSPITAL, 6600 Bruceville Road, Zip 95823; tel. 916/688–2430; Sarah Krevans, Administrator (Nonreporting) **A**1 3 10 **S** Kaiser Foundation Hospitals, Oakland, CA **N** Kaiser Foundation Health Plan of Northern California, Oakland, CA	23	10	221	—	—	—	—	—	—	—
✠ MERCY GENERAL HOSPITAL, 4001 J. Street, Zip 95819; tel. 916/453–4950; Thomas A. Petersen, Vice President and Chief Operating Officer (Total facility includes 117 beds in nursing home–type unit) (Nonreporting) **A**1 2 9 10 **S** Catholic Healthcare West, San Francisco, CA **N** Catholic HealthCare West (CHW), San Francisco, CA	21	10	405	—	—	—	—	—	—	—
✠ METHODIST HOSPITAL, 7500 Hospital Drive, Zip 95823–5477; tel. 916/423–3000; Stanley C. Oppegard, Vice President and Chief Operating Officer (Total facility includes 142 beds in nursing home–type unit) (Nonreporting) **A**1 3 9 10 **S** Catholic Healthcare West, San Francisco, CA **N** Catholic HealthCare West (CHW), San Francisco, CA	23	10	303	—	—	—	—	—	—	—
✠ SHRINERS HOSPITALS FOR CHILDREN, NORTHERN CALIFORNIA, 2425 Stockton Boulevard, Zip 95817–2215; tel. 916/453–2000; Margaret Bryan–Williams, Administrator **A**1 3 5 **F**9 12 15 16 19 21 28 34 35 39 41 44 45 46 48 49 54 65 67 71 73 **P**6 **S** Shriners Hospitals for Children, Tampa, FL	23	57	50	853	24	12297	—	—	—	307
★ SUTTER CENTER FOR PSYCHIATRY, 7700 Folsom Boulevard, Zip 95826–2608; tel. 916/386–3000; Diane Gail Stewart, Administrator **A**9 10 **F**3 4 7 8 9 10 11 12 13 14 15 16 17 18 19 20 21 22 26 28 29 30 31 32 33 34 35 37 38 39 40 41 42 43 44 45 46 47 48 49 50 51 53 54 55 56 57 58 59 60 61 62 63 64 65 66 67 68 69 71 72 73 74 **P**3 5 **S** Sutter Health, Sacramento, CA **N** Sutter\CHS, Sacramento, CA	23	22	69	1729	35	19107	—	8344	4565	199
✠ SUTTER COMMUNITY HOSPITALS, (Includes Sutter General Hospital, 2801 L. Street, Zip 95816; tel. 916/454–2222; Sutter Memorial Hospital, 5151 F. Street), 5151 F. Street, Zip 95819–3295; tel. 916/454–3333; Lou Lazatin, Chief Executive Officer (Total facility includes 198 beds in nursing home–type unit) **A**1 2 3 5 9 10 **F**1 3 4 6 7 8 10 11 12 14 15 16 17 18 19 20 21 22 23 25 26 27 28 29 30 31 32 33 34 35 36 37 38 40 41 42 43 44 45 46 47 49 50 53 54 55 56 57 58 59 60 61 62 63 64 65 67 68 69 70 71 72 73 74 **P**3 5 **S** Sutter Health, Sacramento, CA **N** Sutter\CHS, Sacramento, CA SUTTER GENERAL HOSPITAL See Sutter Community Hospitals SUTTER MEMORIAL HOSPITAL See Sutter Community Hospitals	23	10	497	27716	318	256283	4871	240531	104872	2979
✠ UNIVERSITY OF CALIFORNIA, DAVIS MEDICAL CENTER, 2315 Stockton Boulevard, Zip 95817–2282; tel. 916/734–2011; Frank J. Loge, Director **A**1 2 3 5 8 9 10 **F**4 5 7 8 9 10 11 12 13 14 15 16 17 18 19 20 21 23 24 25 26 27 28 29 30 31 32 33 34 35 37 38 39 40 41 42 43 44 45 46 47 49 50 51 56 60 63 65 66 67 69 71 72 73 74 **P**6 **S** University of California–Systemwide Administration, Oakland, CA	12	10	446	24896	344	676102	1273	—	174422	—

SALINAS—Monterey County

✠ NATIVIDAD MEDICAL CENTER, 1330 Natividad Road, Zip 93906, Mailing Address: Box 81611, Zip 93912–1611; tel. 408/755–4111; Howard H. Classen, Chief Executive Officer (Total facility includes 52 beds in nursing home–type unit) **A**1 3 5 9 10 **F**7 8 11 12 14 15 16 17 18 19 22 25 26 31 34 35 37 38 39 40 41 44 49 51 56 61 64 65 66 71 73 74 **P**3 5	13	10	181	6431	103	187200	1440	66664	26806	536
✠ SALINAS VALLEY MEMORIAL HOSPITAL, 450 East Romie Lane, Zip 93901–4098; tel. 408/757–4333; Samuel W. Downing, Chief Executive Officer (Total facility includes 21 beds in nursing home–type unit) **A**1 2 9 10 **F**4 6 7 8 10 11 12 13 14 15 16 17 19 20 21 22 24 25 26 27 28 29 30 31 32 33 35 36 37 39 40 41 42 43 44 45 46 48 49 60 62 63 64 65 67 71 72 73 74 **P**5 8	16	10	174	11929	131	86610	2629	153395	67404	1149

SAN ANDREAS—Calaveras County

✠ MARK TWAIN ST. JOSEPH'S HOSPITAL, 768 Mountain Ranch Road, Zip 95249–9710; tel. 209/754–2515; Michael P. Lawson, Administrator (Nonreporting) **A**1 9 10 **S** Catholic Healthcare West, San Francisco, CA **N** Catholic HealthCare West (CHW), San Francisco, CA	23	10	33	—	—	—	—	—	—	—

Hospital, Address, Telephone, Administrator, Approval, Facility, and Physician Codes, Health Care System, Network	Classification Codes		Utilization Data					Expense (thousands) of dollars		
	Control	Service	Staffed Beds	Admissions	Census	Outpatient Visits	Births	Total	Payroll	Personnel

★ American Hospital Association (AHA) membership
□ Joint Commission on Accreditation of Healthcare Organizations (JCAHO) accreditation
+ American Osteopathic Healthcare Association (AOHA) membership
○ American Osteopathic Association (AOA) accreditation
△ Commission on Accreditation of Rehabilitation Facilities (CARF) accreditation
Control codes 61, 63, 64, 71, 72 and 73 indicate hospitals listed by AOHA, but not registered by AHA. For definition of numerical codes, see page A4.

SAN BERNARDINO—San Bernardino County

□ COMMMUNITY HOSPITAL OF SAN BERNARDINO, 1805 Medical Center Drive, Zip 92411; tel. 909/887–6333; Bruce G. Satzger, Administrator and Chief Executive Officer (Total facility includes 99 beds in nursing home–type unit) **A**1 10 **F**1 7 8 10 12 13 15 16 18 19 20 21 22 27 28 29 30 31 32 33 35 36 37 38 39 40 41 42 44 45 46 48 49 52 53 54 56 57 58 61 64 65 67 71 72 73 74 **P**5 7
— Control 23, Service 10, Staffed Beds 380, Admissions 10425, Census 221, Outpatient Visits 123985, Births 2348, Total 73234, Payroll 34987, Personnel 1069

🖈 ○ SAN BERNARDINO COUNTY MEDICAL CENTER, 780 East Gilbert Street, Zip 92415–0935; tel. 909/387–8188; Charles R. Jervis, Director **A**1 2 3 5 10 11 12 13 **F**3 4 7 9 10 11 12 14 15 16 17 18 19 20 21 22 25 26 27 28 29 30 31 32 34 35 37 38 40 41 42 44 45 46 51 52 53 55 56 57 58 59 60 61 63 65 67 69 70 71 72 73 **P**5
— Control 13, Service 10, Staffed Beds 293, Admissions 14635, Census 197, Outpatient Visits 210436, Births 1567, Total 151666, Payroll 66271, Personnel 1659

🖈 ST. BERNARDINE MEDICAL CENTER, 2101 North Waterman Avenue, Zip 92404; tel. 909/883–8711; Margo Walter, Administrator and Chief Operating Officer **A**1 2 9 10 **F**3 4 7 8 10 11 12 15 16 19 21 22 23 24 28 32 33 34 35 37 40 41 42 43 44 46 49 53 54 58 59 60 64 68 69 71 72 73 **P**5 7 **S** Catholic Healthcare West, San Francisco, CA **N** Catholic HealthCare West (CHW), San Francisco, CA
— Control 23, Service 10, Staffed Beds 323, Admissions 12331, Census 171, Outpatient Visits 75407, Births 1898, Total 100125, Payroll 37882, Personnel 997

SAN CLEMENTE—Orange County

🖈 SAN CLEMENTE HOSPITAL AND MEDICAL CENTER, (Formerly Columbia San Clemente Hospital and Medical Center), 654 Camino De Los Mares, Zip 92673; tel. 714/496–1122; Karen Poole, Interim Chief Executive Officer **A**1 9 10 **F**7 8 12 16 17 19 20 21 22 23 28 30 32 34 35 36 37 39 40 41 44 45 49 64 65 71 73 **P**5 **S** NetCare Health Systems, Inc., Nashville, TN **N** Samaritan Health Services, Phoenix, AZ
— Control 33, Service 10, Staffed Beds 83, Admissions 2648, Census 28, Outpatient Visits 15507, Births 451, Total 20625, Payroll 3009, Personnel 300

SAN DIEGO—San Diego County

🖈 ALVARADO HOSPITAL MEDICAL CENTER, 6655 Alvarado Road, Zip 92120–5298; tel. 619/287–3270; Barry G. Weinbaum, Chief Executive Officer (Nonreporting) **A**1 2 3 9 10 **S** TENET Healthcare Corporation, Santa Barbara, CA **N** Tenet Healthcare Corporation, Santa Barbara, CA
— Control 33, Service 10, Staffed Beds 144

□ CHARTER BEHAVIORAL HEALTH SYSTEM OF SAN DIEGO, 11878 Avenue of Industry, Zip 92128; tel. 619/487–3200; Lorraine Watson, Ph.D., Chief Executive Officer (Nonreporting) **A**1 9 10 **S** Magellan Health Services, Atlanta, GA
— Control 33, Service 22, Staffed Beds 80

□ △ CHILDREN'S HOSPITAL AND HEALTH CENTER, 3020 Children's Way, Zip 92123–4282; tel. 619/576–1700; Blair L. Sadler, President (Total facility includes 59 beds in nursing home–type unit) **A**1 2 3 5 7 9 10 **F**5 10 13 15 16 17 19 20 21 22 28 31 32 33 34 35 38 41 42 43 44 46 47 49 53 54 58 64 65 69 70 71 72 73 **P**5
— Control 23, Service 50, Staffed Beds 274, Admissions 10335, Census 183, Outpatient Visits 207022, Births —, Total 155982, Payroll 64857, Personnel 1491

🖈 KAISER FOUNDATION HOSPITAL, (Includes Kaiser Foundation Hospital, 203 Travelodge Drive, El Cajon, Zip 92020; tel. 619/528–5000), 4647 Zion Avenue, Zip 92120; tel. 619/528–5000; Kenneth F. Colling, Senior Vice President and Area Manager (Nonreporting) **A**1 2 3 5 10 **S** Kaiser Foundation Hospitals, Oakland, CA
— Control 23, Service 10, Staffed Beds 277

🖈 MISSION BAY HOSPITAL, (Formerly Columbia Mission Bay Hospital), 3030 Bunker Hill Street, Zip 92109–5780; tel. 619/274–7721; Deborah Brehe, Chief Executive Officer (Total facility includes 26 beds in nursing home–type unit) **A**1 9 10 **F**8 11 12 14 16 17 19 22 26 27 28 30 32 35 37 44 46 52 57 64 65 71 73 **P**7 **S** Columbia/HCA Healthcare Corporation, Nashville, TN
— Control 33, Service 10, Staffed Beds 108, Admissions 2471, Census 36, Outpatient Visits 30828, Births —, Total 26044, Payroll 10875, Personnel 255

🖈 NAVAL MEDICAL CENTER, 34800 Bob Wilson Drive, Zip 92134–5000; tel. 619/532–6400; Rear Admiral R. A. Nelson, MC, USN, Commander **A**1 2 3 5 **F**3 4 5 7 8 10 11 12 13 16 18 19 20 21 22 23 24 25 28 29 30 31 35 37 38 39 40 41 42 43 44 45 46 47 49 51 52 53 54 56 58 60 61 63 65 66 67 69 71 73 **S** Department of Navy, Washington, DC
— Control 43, Service 10, Staffed Beds 342, Admissions 19146, Census 185, Outpatient Visits 1102576, Births 3742, Total 180515, Payroll 39750, Personnel —

□ SAN DIEGO COUNTY PSYCHIATRIC HOSPITAL, 3851 Rosecrans Street, Zip 92110, Mailing Address: P.O. Box 85524, Zip 92138–5524; tel. 619/692–8211; Karen C. Hogan, Administrator and Chief Executive Officer (Nonreporting) **A**1 10
— Control 13, Service 22, Staffed Beds 109

★ SAN DIEGO HOSPICE, 4311 Third Avenue, Zip 92103; tel. 619/688–1600; Janet E. Cetti, President and Chief Executive Officer (Nonreporting) **A**10
— Control 23, Service 49, Staffed Beds 24

🖈 SCRIPPS MERCY HOSPITAL, 4077 Fifth Avenue, Zip 92103–2180; tel. 619/260–7101; Nancy Wilson, Senior Vice President and Regional Administrator (Nonreporting) **A**1 2 3 5 9 10 **S** Scripps Health, San Diego, CA **N** ScrippsHealth, San Diego, CA
— Control 21, Service 10, Staffed Beds 417

★ SHARP CABRILLO HOSPITAL, 3475 Kenyon Street, Zip 92110–5067; tel. 619/221–3400; Randi Larsson, Chief Operating Officer and Administrator (Total facility includes 79 beds in nursing home–type unit) (Nonreporting) **A**9 10 **S** Sharp Healthcare, San Diego, CA **N** Sharp Healthcare, San Diego, CA
— Control 23, Service 10, Staffed Beds 227

🖈 △ SHARP MEMORIAL HOSPITAL, 7901 Frost Street, Zip 92123–2788; tel. 619/541–3400; Dan Gross, Chief Executive Officer (Nonreporting) **A**1 2 3 7 9 10 **S** Sharp Healthcare, San Diego, CA **N** Sharp Healthcare, San Diego, CA
— Control 23, Service 10, Staffed Beds 488

🖈 UNIVERSITY OF CALIFORNIA SAN DIEGO MEDICAL CENTER, 200 West Arbor Drive, Zip 92103–8970; tel. 619/543–6222; Sumiyo E. Kastelic, Director **A**1 2 3 5 8 9 10 **F**4 7 8 9 10 11 12 15 19 21 22 23 25 26 28 29 30 31 32 34 35 37 38 39 40 41 42 43 44 45 46 47 49 51 52 53 54 56 57 58 60 61 65 69 70 71 72 73 74 **P**1 **S** University of California–Systemwide Administration, Oakland, CA
— Control 12, Service 10, Staffed Beds 413, Admissions 18032, Census 253, Outpatient Visits 475508, Births 1811, Total 263124, Payroll 95988, Personnel —

Hospital, Address, Telephone, Administrator, Approval, Facility, and Physician Codes, Health Care System, Network	Classi-fication Codes		Utilization Data					Expense (thousands) of dollars		
	Control	Service	Staffed Beds	Admissions	Census	Outpatient Visits	Births	Total	Payroll	Personnel

★ American Hospital Association (AHA) membership
☐ Joint Commission on Accreditation of Healthcare Organizations (JCAHO) accreditation
+ American Osteopathic Healthcare Association (AOHA) membership
○ American Osteopathic Association (AOA) accreditation
△ Commission on Accreditation of Rehabilitation Facilities (CARF) accreditation
Control codes 61, 63, 64, 71, 72 and 73 indicate hospitals listed by AOHA, but not registered by AHA. For definition of numerical codes, see page A4

☐ VENCOR HOSPITAL–SAN DIEGO, 1940 El Cajon Boulevard, Zip 92104; tel. 619/543–4500; Michael D. Cress, Administrator (Nonreporting) **A**1 10 **S** Vencor, Incorporated, Louisville, KY	33	10	70	—	—	—	—	—	—	—
✠ VETERANS AFFAIRS MEDICAL CENTER, 3350 LaJolla Village Drive, Zip 92161; tel. 619/552–8585; Gary J. Rossio, Acting Director (Total facility includes 44 beds in nursing home–type unit) **A**1 2 3 5 8 9 **F**1 2 3 4 5 6 8 10 11 12 14 15 16 17 18 19 20 21 22 23 24 25 26 27 28 29 30 31 32 33 34 35 37 39 41 42 43 44 45 46 48 49 51 52 54 55 56 57 58 59 60 64 65 67 69 71 72 73 74 **P**6 **S** Department of Veterans Affairs, Washington, DC	45	10	238	5833	163	301125	—	156590	88947	1890
☐ VILLAVIEW COMMUNITY HOSPITAL, 5550 University Avenue, Zip 92105, Mailing Address: P.O. Box 5587, Zip 92105; tel. 619/582–3516; Reggie Panis, President (Nonreporting) **A**1 10	23	10	100	—	—	—	—	—	—	—
SAN DIMAS—Los Angeles County										
✠ SAN DIMAS COMMUNITY HOSPITAL, 1350 West Covina Boulevard, Zip 91773–0308; tel. 909/599–6811; Patrick A. Petre, Chief Executive Officer (Nonreporting) **A**1 2 9 10 **S** TENET Healthcare Corporation, Santa Barbara, CA **N** Tenet Healthcare Corporation, Santa Barbara, CA	33	10	93	—	—	—	—	—	—	—
SAN FERNANDO—Los Angeles County										
MISSION COMMUNITY HOSPITAL–SAN FERNANDO CAMPUS, (Includes Mission Community Hospital–Panorama City Campus, 14850 Roscoe Boulevard, Panorama City, Zip 91402–4618; tel. 818/787–2222), 700 Chatsworth Drive, Zip 91340–4299; tel. 818/361–7331; Cathy Fickes, R.N., Chief Executive Officer (Nonreporting) **A**9	23	10	152	—	—	—	—	—	—	—
SAN FRANCISCO—San Francisco County										
✠ △ CALIFORNIA PACIFIC MEDICAL CENTER, 2333 Buchanan Street, Zip 94115, Mailing Address: P.O. Box 7999, Zip 94120; tel. 415/563–4321; Martin Brotman, M.D., President and Chief Executive Officer (Total facility includes 95 beds in nursing home–type unit) (Nonreporting) **A**1 2 3 5 7 8 9 10 **S** Sutter Health, Sacramento, CA **N** Sutter\CHS, Sacramento, CA	23	10	520	—	—	—	—	—	—	—
✠ CHINESE HOSPITAL, 845 Jackson Street, Zip 94133–4899; tel. 415/982–2400; Thomas M. Harlan, Chief Executive Officer **A**1 9 10 **F**4 7 8 9 10 12 14 15 16 17 19 21 22 25 28 29 30 32 33 35 37 38 40 41 42 43 44 45 46 47 48 50 52 60 63 64 65 67 69 71 73 **P**5 7	23	10	47	2221	34	39422	185	27856	7600	230
✠ DAVIES MEDICAL CENTER, Castro and Duboce Streets, Zip 94114; tel. 415/565–6000; Greg Monardo, President and Chief Executive Officer (Total facility includes 51 beds in nursing home–type unit) **A**1 3 5 9 10 **F**8 11 12 14 15 16 17 19 20 21 22 26 28 31 32 33 34 35 39 41 42 44 46 48 49 51 52 54 55 56 57 60 64 65 66 67 71 72 73 74 **P**5	23	10	205	3310	87	77627	—	65136	27766	665
✠ KAISER FOUNDATION HOSPITAL, 2425 Geary Boulevard, Zip 94115; tel. 415/202–2000; Richard R. Pettingill, Administrator (Nonreporting) **A**1 3 5 10 **S** Kaiser Foundation Hospitals, Oakland, CA **N** Kaiser Foundation Health Plan of Northern California, Oakland, CA	23	10	210	—	—	—	—	—	—	—
★ LAGUNA HONDA HOSPITAL AND REHABILITATION CENTER, 375 Laguna Honda Boulevard, Zip 94116–1499; tel. 415/664–1580; Lawrence J. Funk, Executive Administrator (Total facility includes 1214 beds in nursing home–type unit) **A**10 **F**1 2 3 4 7 8 9 10 11 12 13 15 17 18 19 20 21 22 25 26 27 28 29 30 31 32 33 34 35 37 38 39 40 41 42 43 44 45 46 48 49 51 52 53 54 55 56 57 58 59 60 61 64 65 67 68 69 70 71 72 73 74 **P**6	15	48	1249	1315	1186	0	0	111719	75786	1615
☐ PACIFIC COAST HOSPITAL, 1210 Scott Street, Zip 94115–4000; tel. 415/292–0554; Robert D. Roberts, Interim President and Chief Executive Officer (Nonreporting) **A**1 9 10	23	49	28	—	—	—	—	—	—	—
✠ SAINT FRANCIS MEMORIAL HOSPITAL, 900 Hyde Street, Zip 94109, Mailing Address: Box 7726, Zip 94120–7726; tel. 415/353–6000; Cheryl A. Fama, Administrator, Vice President and Chief Operating Officer (Total facility includes 34 beds in nursing home–type unit) (Nonreporting) **A**1 2 3 9 10 **S** Catholic Healthcare West, San Francisco, CA **N** Catholic HealthCare West (CHW), San Francisco, CA	23	10	190	—	—	—	—	—	—	—
☐ SAN FRANCISCO GENERAL HOSPITAL MEDICAL CENTER, 1001 Potrero Avenue, Zip 94110; tel. 415/206–8000; Richard Cordova, Executive Director **A**1 2 3 5 8 10 **F**3 4 7 8 10 11 12 15 16 17 18 19 20 22 29 31 34 35 37 38 39 40 41 42 44 45 46 49 51 52 54 56 61 63 64 65 66 67 70 71 73 74 **P**1	15	10	375	18348	278	349886	2038	306823	138382	3335
☐ ST. LUKE'S HOSPITAL, 3555 Cesar Chavez Street, Zip 94110; tel. 415/647–8600; Jack Fries, President (Total facility includes 33 beds in nursing home–type unit) (Nonreporting) **A**1 9 10	23	10	254	—	—	—	—	—	—	—
✠ ST. MARY'S MEDICAL CENTER, 450 Stanyan Street, Zip 94117–1079; tel. 415/668–1000; John G. Williams, President (Total facility includes 48 beds in nursing home–type unit) (Nonreporting) **A**1 2 3 5 8 9 10 **S** Catholic Healthcare West, San Francisco, CA **N** Catholic HealthCare West (CHW), San Francisco, CA	21	10	256	—	—	—	—	—	—	—
✠ UNIVERSITY OF CALIFORNIA SAN FRANCISCO MEDICAL CENTER, (Includes University of California–San Francisco Mount Zion Medical Center, 1600 Divisadero Street, Zip 94143–1601; tel. 415/567–6600), 500 Parnassus, Zip 94143–0296; tel. 415/476–1000; Bruce Schroffel, Chief Operating Officer (Total facility includes 31 beds in nursing home–type unit) (Nonreporting) **A**1 2 3 5 8 9 10 **S** University of California–Systemwide Administration, Oakland, CA UNIVERSITY OF CALIFORNIA–SAN FRANCISCO MOUNT ZION MEDICAL CENTER See University of California San Francisco Medical Center	23	10	663	—	—	—	—	—	—	—

Hospital, Address, Telephone, Administrator, Approval, Facility, and Physician Codes, Health Care System, Network	Classi-fication Codes		Utilization Data					Expense (thousands) of dollars		
★ American Hospital Association (AHA) membership □ Joint Commission on Accreditation of Healthcare Organizations (JCAHO) accreditation + American Osteopathic Healthcare Association (AOHA) membership ○ American Osteopathic Association (AOA) accreditation △ Commission on Accreditation of Rehabilitation Facilities (CARF) accreditation Control codes 61, 63, 64, 71, 72 and 73 indicate hospitals listed by AOHA, but not registered by AHA. For definition of numerical codes, see page A4	Control	Service	Staffed Beds	Admissions	Census	Outpatient Visits	Births	Total	Payroll	Personnel

✠ VETERANS AFFAIRS MEDICAL CENTER, 4150 Clement Street, Zip 94121–1598; tel. 415/750–2041; Sheila M. Cullen, Acting Director (Total facility includes 120 beds in nursing home–type unit) (Nonreporting) **A**1 2 3 5 8 9 **S** Department of Veterans Affairs, Washington, DC	45	10	372	—	—	—	—	—	—	—

SAN GABRIEL—Los Angeles County

✠ SAN GABRIEL VALLEY MEDICAL CENTER, 438 West Las Tunas Drive, Zip 91776, Mailing Address: P.O. Box 1507, Zip 91778–1507; tel. 626/289–5454; Thomas D. Mone, President and Chief Executive Officer (Total facility includes 46 beds in nursing home–type unit) **A**1 9 10 **F**7 8 10 12 19 21 22 27 28 32 35 37 38 40 42 44 46 48 52 55 56 57 59 60 64 65 67 68 71 73 **P**5 7 **S** UniHealth, Burbank, CA **N** UniHealth, Burbank, CA	23	10	273	9249	154	51102	1689	67519	28066	753

SAN JOSE—Santa Clara County

□ ALEXIAN BROTHERS HOSPITAL, 225 North Jackson Avenue, Zip 95116–1691; tel. 408/259–5000; Steven R. Barron, President and Chief Executive Officer (Nonreporting) **A**1 9 10 **S** Alexian Brothers Health System, Inc., Elk Grove Village, IL	21	10	192	—	—	—	—	—	—	—
COLUMBIA GOOD SAMARITAN HOSPITAL See Good Samaritan Hospital										
COLUMBIA SAN JOSE MEDICAL CENTER See San Jose Medical Center										
✠ GOOD SAMARITAN HOSPITAL, (Formerly Columbia Good Samaritan Hospital), 2425 Samaritan Drive, Zip 95124, Mailing Address: P.O. Box 240002, Zip 95154–2402; tel. 408/559–2011; William K. Piche, Chief Executive Officer (Nonreporting) **A**1 9 10 **S** Columbia/HCA Healthcare Corporation, Nashville, TN	33	10	388	—	—	—	—	—	—	—
✠ O'CONNOR HOSPITAL, 2105 Forest Avenue, Zip 95128–1471; tel. 408/947–2500; John G. Williams, President and Chief Executive Officer (Total facility includes 24 beds in nursing home–type unit) **A**1 2 9 10 **F**3 4 7 8 10 11 12 13 14 15 16 17 19 21 22 24 28 30 32 33 34 35 37 38 40 41 42 43 44 45 46 49 52 57 60 63 64 65 67 68 71 73 **P**2 3 5 6 7 **S** Catholic Healthcare West, San Francisco, CA **N** Catholic HealthCare West (CHW), San Francisco, CA	21	10	257	11350	125	—	2628	102517	37736	883
✠ SAN JOSE MEDICAL CENTER, (Formerly Columbia San Jose Medical Center), 675 East Santa Clara Street, Zip 95112, Mailing Address: P.O. Box 240003, Zip 95154–2403; tel. 408/998–3212; William L. Gilbert, Chief Executive Officer (Total facility includes 26 beds in nursing home–type unit) (Nonreporting) **A**1 2 3 5 9 10 **S** Columbia/HCA Healthcare Corporation, Nashville, TN	33	10	327	—	—	—	—	—	—	—
□ △ SANTA CLARA VALLEY MEDICAL CENTER, 751 South Bascom Avenue, Zip 95128; tel. 408/885–5000; Robert Sillen, Executive Director (Nonreporting) **A**1 2 3 5 7 10	13	10	377	—	—	—	—	—	—	—
✠ SANTA TERESA COMMUNITY HOSPITAL, 250 Hospital Parkway, Zip 95119; tel. 408/972–7000; Neil Humphrey, Administrator (Nonreporting) **A**1 3 10 **S** Kaiser Foundation Hospitals, Oakland, CA	23	10	178	—	—	—	—	—	—	—

SAN LEANDRO—Alameda County

ALAMEDA COUNTY MEDICAL CENTER, 15400 Foothill Boulevard, Zip 94578–1091; tel. 510/667–7920; Michael G. Smart, Administrator (Total facility includes 119 beds in nursing home–type unit) (Nonreporting) **S** Alameda County Health Care Services Agency, San Leandro, CA	13	49	193	—	—	—	—	—	—	—
COLUMBIA SAN LEANDRO HOSPITAL See San Leandro Hospital										
✠ SAN LEANDRO HOSPITAL, (Formerly Columbia San Leandro Hospital), 13855 East 14th Street, Zip 94578–0398; tel. 510/667–4510; Kelly Mather, Chief Executive Officer (Nonreporting) **A**1 9 10 **S** Columbia/HCA Healthcare Corporation, Nashville, TN **N** East Bay Medical Network, Emeryville, CA	33	10	136	—	—	—	—	—	—	—
□ VENCOR HOSPITAL–SAN LEANDRO, 2800 Benedict Drive, Zip 94577; tel. 510/357–8300; Wayne M. Lingenfelter, Ed.D., Administrator and Chief Executive Officer (Nonreporting) **A**1 9 10 **S** Vencor, Incorporated, Louisville, KY	33	10	42	—	—	—	—	—	—	—

SAN LUIS OBISPO—San Luis Obispo County

CALIFORNIA MENS COLONY HOSPITAL, Highway 1, Zip 93409–8101, Mailing Address: P.O. Box 8101, Zip 93409–8101; tel. 805/547–7913; Galen Kirn, Administrator (Nonreporting)	12	11	39	—	—	—	—	—	—	—
□ FRENCH HOSPITAL MEDICAL CENTER, 1911 Johnson Avenue, Zip 93401; tel. 805/543–5353; James H. Youree, Chief Executive Officer (Nonreporting) **A**1 9 10	33	10	124	—	—	—	—	—	—	—
□ SAN LUIS OBISPO GENERAL HOSPITAL, 2180 Johnson Avenue, Zip 93401, Mailing Address: Box 8113, Zip 93403–8113; tel. 805/781–4800; Susan G. Zepeda, Ph.D., Chief Executive Officer **A**1 9 10 **F**7 14 15 16 19 22 25 26 27 31 34 35 36 37 40 44 45 46 49 51 71 72 73 **P**6	13	10	46	1531	14	49703	639	25434	10891	279
✠ △ SIERRA VISTA REGIONAL MEDICAL CENTER, 1010 Murray Street, Zip 93405, Mailing Address: Box 1367, Zip 93406–1367; tel. 805/546–7600; Harold E. Chilton, Chief Executive Officer (Nonreporting) **A**1 7 9 10 **S** TENET Healthcare Corporation, Santa Barbara, CA **N** Tenet Healthcare Corporation, Santa Barbara, CA	33	10	117	—	—	—	—	—	—	—

SAN MATEO—San Mateo County

MILLS HOSPITAL See Mills–Peninsula Health Services, Burlingame										
□ SAN MATEO COUNTY GENERAL HOSPITAL, 222 West 39th Avenue, Zip 94403–4398; tel. 415/573–2222; Timothy B. McMurdo, Chief Executive Officer (Total facility includes 124 beds in nursing home–type unit) **A**1 3 5 10 **F**4 6 8 10 11 12 14 15 16 17 19 20 22 23 25 26 27 28 29 30 31 32 33 34 35 36 37 38 39 41 42 43 44 45 46 47 49 51 52 54 56 57 60 61 64 65 69 71 73 74 **P**4 6	13	10	240	3992	192	146248	2	88391	35200	—

Hospital, Address, Telephone, Administrator, Approval, Facility, and Physician Codes, Health Care System, Network	Classi-fication Codes		Utilization Data					Expense (thousands) of dollars		
★ American Hospital Association (AHA) membership ☐ Joint Commission on Accreditation of Healthcare Organizations (JCAHO) accreditation + American Osteopathic Healthcare Association (AOHA) membership ○ American Osteopathic Association (AOA) accreditation △ Commission on Accreditation of Rehabilitation Facilities (CARF) accreditation Control codes 61, 63, 64, 71, 72 and 73 indicate hospitals listed by AOHA, but not registered by AHA. For definition of numerical codes, see page A4	Control	Service	Staffed Beds	Admissions	Census	Outpatient Visits	Births	Total	Payroll	Personnel

SAN PABLO—Contra Costa County

⊠ DOCTORS MEDICAL CENTER–SAN PABLO CAMPUS, (Formerly Brookside Hospital), 2000 Vale Road, Zip 94806; tel. 510/235–7000; Gary Sloan, Chief Executive Officer (Total facility includes 106 beds in nursing home–type unit) (Nonreporting) **A**1 2 9 10 **S** TENET Healthcare Corporation, Santa Barbara, CA	33	10	286	—	—	—	—	—	—	—

SAN PEDRO—Los Angeles County, See Los Angeles

SAN RAFAEL—Marin County

⊠ KAISER FOUNDATION HOSPITAL, 99 Montecillo Road, Zip 94903–3397; tel. 415/444–2000; Richard R. Pettingill, Administrator **A**1 10 **F**4 8 9 10 14 19 21 22 23 29 31 32 33 34 35 37 38 39 40 41 42 43 44 45 46 47 48 49 52 53 54 63 64 65 69 70 71 73 **S** Kaiser Foundation Hospitals, Oakland, CA **N** Kaiser Foundation Health Plan of Northern California, Oakland, CA	23	10	119	3991	48	380452	—	—	—	310

SAN RAMON—Contra Costa County

⊠ △ SAN RAMON REGIONAL MEDICAL CENTER, 6001 Norris Canyon Road, Zip 94583; tel. 925/275–9200; Philip P. Gustafson, Administrator **A**1 7 9 10 **F**1 2 3 4 7 8 10 11 12 15 16 17 19 21 22 26 27 28 30 31 34 35 37 38 39 40 41 42 44 46 49 60 61 65 66 67 68 71 73 74 **P**4 5 **S** TENET Healthcare Corporation, Santa Barbara, CA **N** Tenet Healthcare Corporation, Santa Barbara, CA	33	10	95	4018	40	42591	929	32853	15323	273

SANGER—Fresno County

☐ SANGER GENERAL HOSPITAL, 2558 Jensen Avenue, Zip 93657–2296; tel. 209/875–6571; William J. Casey, Chief Executive Officer (Nonreporting) **A**1 9 10	32	10	25	—	—	—	—	—	—	—

SANTA ANA—Orange County

⊠ COASTAL COMMUNITIES HOSPITAL, 2701 South Bristol Street, Zip 92704–9911, Mailing Address: P.O. Box 5240, Zip 92704–0240; tel. 714/754–5454; Kent G. Clayton, Chief Executive Officer (Total facility includes 46 beds in nursing home–type unit) **A**1 9 10 **F**8 12 15 16 19 20 21 22 34 35 39 40 41 44 46 51 52 57 60 63 64 65 71 73 74 **P**5 7 **S** TENET Healthcare Corporation, Santa Barbara, CA	32	10	177	4178	61	23715	1696	—	—	314
★ SANTA ANA HOSPITAL MEDICAL CENTER, 1901 North Fairview Street, Zip 92706; tel. 714/554–1653; Kent G. Clayton, Chief Executive Officer (Nonreporting) **A**9 10 **S** TENET Healthcare Corporation, Santa Barbara, CA	33	10	69	—	—	—	—	—	—	—
SPECIALTY HOSP OF SANTA ANA, (Formerly Doctors Hospital of Santa Ana), 1901 North College Avenue, Zip 92706; tel. 714/564–7800 (Nonreporting)	33	10	54	—	—	—	—	—	—	—
⊠ WESTERN MEDICAL CENTER–SANTA ANA, 1001 North Tustin Avenue, Zip 92705–3502; tel. 714/835–3555; Richard E. Butler, Chief Executive Officer (Nonreporting) **A**1 2 3 5 9 10 **S** TENET Healthcare Corporation, Santa Barbara, CA	33	10	288	—	—	—	—	—	—	—

SANTA BARBARA—Santa Barbara County

☐ GOLETA VALLEY COTTAGE HOSPITAL, 351 South Patterson Avenue, Zip 93111, Mailing Address: Box 6306, Zip 93160; tel. 805/967–3411; Diane Wisby, President and Chief Executive Officer (Nonreporting) **A**1 9 10 **S** Cottage Health System, Santa Barbara, CA	23	10	79	—	—	—	—	—	—	—
☐ △ REHABILITATION INSTITUTE AT SANTA BARBARA, 427 Camino Del Remedio, Zip 93110; tel. 805/683–3788; Rusty Pollock, President and Chief Executive Officer (Nonreporting) **A**1 7 9 10	23	46	40	—	—	—	—	—	—	—
☐ SANTA BARBARA COTTAGE HOSPITAL, (Includes Santa Barbara Cottage Care Center), Pueblo at Bath Streets, Zip 93105, Mailing Address: Box 689, Zip 93102; tel. 805/682–7111; James L. Ash, President and Chief Executive Officer (Nonreporting) **A**1 2 3 5 9 10 **S** Cottage Health System, Santa Barbara, CA	23	10	307	—	—	—	—	—	—	—
⊠ ST. FRANCIS MEDICAL CENTER OF SANTA BARBARA, 601 East Micheltorena Street, Zip 93103; tel. 805/568–5705; Ron Biscaro, Administrator (Total facility includes 34 beds in nursing home–type unit) (Nonreporting) **A**1 9 10 **S** Catholic Healthcare West, San Francisco, CA	21	10	96	—	—	—	—	—	—	—

SANTA CLARA—Santa Clara County

⊠ KAISER FOUNDATION HOSPITAL, 900 Kiely Boulevard, Zip 95051–5386; tel. 408/236–6400; Helen Wilmot, Administrator (Nonreporting) **A**1 3 5 10 **S** Kaiser Foundation Hospitals, Oakland, CA **N** Kaiser Foundation Health Plan of Northern California, Oakland, CA	23	10	249	—	—	—	—	—	—	—

SANTA CRUZ—Santa Cruz County

⊠ DOMINICAN SANTA CRUZ HOSPITAL, 1555 Soquel Drive, Zip 95065–1794; tel. 408/462–7700; Sister Julie Hyer, President and Chief Executive Officer (Total facility includes 36 beds in nursing home–type unit) **A**1 9 10 **F**4 6 7 8 10 12 13 14 15 16 17 19 22 25 30 34 35 37 40 41 42 43 44 45 46 48 49 52 54 56 59 62 64 65 66 67 71 72 73 74 **P**3 5 7 **S** Catholic Healthcare West, San Francisco, CA **N** Catholic HealthCare West (CHW), San Francisco, CA	21	10	270	11681	169	115173	1362	109462	48217	975
★ SUTTER MATERNITY AND SURGERY CENTER OF SANTA CRUZ, 2900 Chanticleer Avenue, Zip 95065–1816; tel. 408/477–2200; Iris C. Frank, Administrator (Nonreporting) **A**10 **S** Sutter Health, Sacramento, CA	23	10	30	—	—	—	—	—	—	—

SANTA MARIA—Santa Barbara County

⊠ MARIAN MEDICAL CENTER, 1400 East Church Street, Zip 93454, Mailing Address: Box 1238, Zip 93456; tel. 805/739–3000; Charles J. Cova, Executive Vice President (Total facility includes 95 beds in nursing home–type unit) **A**1 2 9 10 **F**4 7 8 10 11 12 14 15 16 17 19 20 21 22 26 27 28 29 30 31 32 33 35 36 39 40 41 42 43 44 45 46 53 55 56 57 60 64 65 67 68 70 71 73 74 **P**7 **S** Catholic Healthcare West, San Francisco, CA	21	10	225	7763	150	91654	1583	60080	21944	607

Hospital, Address, Telephone, Administrator, Approval, Facility, and Physician Codes, Health Care System, Network	Classification Codes		Utilization Data					Expense (thousands) of dollars		
	Control	Service	Staffed Beds	Admissions	Census	Outpatient Visits	Births	Total	Payroll	Personnel

American Hospital Association (AHA) membership
Joint Commission on Accreditation of Healthcare Organizations (JCAHO) accreditation
American Osteopathic Healthcare Association (AOHA) membership
American Osteopathic Association (AOA) accreditation
Commission on Accreditation of Rehabilitation Facilities (CARF) accreditation
Control codes 61, 63, 64, 71, 72 and 73 indicate hospitals listed by AOHA, but not registered by AHA. For definition of numerical codes, see page A4.

Hospital	Control	Service	Beds	Adm	Cen	OPV	Births	Total	Payroll	Pers
✠ VALLEY COMMUNITY HOSPITAL, 505 East Plaza Drive, Zip 93454–9943; tel. 805/925–0935; William C. Rasmussen, Administrator (Nonreporting) A1 9 10 S TENET Healthcare Corporation, Santa Barbara, CA	33	10	70	—	—	—	—	—	—	—
SANTA MONICA—Los Angeles County										
✠ SAINT JOHN'S HOSPITAL AND HEALTH CENTER, 1328 22nd Street, Zip 90404–2032; tel. 310/829–5511; Bruce Lamoureux, Chief Executive Officer (Total facility includes 22 beds in nursing home–type unit) A1 2 9 10 F2 3 4 7 8 10 11 12 14 15 16 17 19 21 22 28 29 30 32 33 34 35 36 37 38 39 40 41 42 43 44 45 49 50 52 54 55 56 57 58 59 60 64 65 71 73 74 P1 5 7 S Sisters of Charity of Leavenworth Health Services Corporation, Leavenworth, KS	21	10	271	12918	191	196424	1273	132452	58921	1207
✠ SANTA MONICA–UCLA MEDICAL CENTER, 1250 16th Street, Zip 90404–1200; tel. 310/319–4000; William D. Parente, Director and Chief Executive Officer (Nonreporting) A1 2 3 5 9 10 S University of California–Systemwide Administration, Oakland, CA N UniHealth, Burbank, CA	12	10	221	—	—	—	—	—	—	—
SANTA PAULA—Ventura County										
☐ SANTA PAULA MEMORIAL HOSPITAL, 825 North Tenth Street, Zip 93060–0270, Mailing Address: P.O. Box 270, Zip 93060–0270; tel. 805/525–7171; William M. Greene, FACHE, President A1 9 10 F7 8 14 15 16 17 19 21 22 25 30 34 35 37 39 40 42 44 48 49 65 71 73 P5 S Quorum Health Group/Quorum Health Resources, Inc., Brentwood, TN	23	10	54	1889	18	35095	335	12826	5397	210
SANTA ROSA—Sonoma County										
COMMUNITY HOSPITAL See Sutter Medical Center, Santa Rosa										
✠ KAISER FOUNDATION HOSPITAL, 401 Bicentennial Way, Zip 95403; tel. 707/571–4000; Dorcas Walton, Administrator (Nonreporting) A1 10 S Kaiser Foundation Hospitals, Oakland, CA	23	10	117	—	—	—	—	—	—	—
☐ NORTH COAST HEALTH CARE CENTERS, 1287 Fulton Road, Zip 95401; tel. 707/543–2400; Pamela J. McFadden, President and Chief Executive Officer (Nonreporting) A1 9 10	33	10	119	—	—	—	—	—	—	—
✠ SANTA ROSA MEMORIAL HOSPITAL, 1165 Montgomery Drive, Zip 95405, Mailing Address: Box 522, Zip 95402; tel. 707/546–3210; Robert H. Fish, President and Chief Executive Officer (Nonreporting) A1 2 9 10 S St. Joseph Health System, Orange, CA N Saint Joseph Health System, Orange, CA	21	10	225	—	—	—	—	—	—	—
✠ SUTTER MEDICAL CENTER, SANTA ROSA, (Formerly Community Hospital), 3325 Chanate Road, Zip 95404; tel. 707/576–4000; Cliff Coates, Chief Executive Officer (Total facility includes 16 beds in nursing home–type unit) (Nonreporting) A1 3 5 10 S Sutter Health, Sacramento, CA N Sutter\CHS, Sacramento, CA	23	10	128	—	—	—	—	—	—	—
☐ WARRACK MEDICAL CENTER HOSPITAL, 2449 Summerfield Road, Zip 95405; tel. 707/542–9030; Dale E. Iversen, President and Chief Executive Officer (Nonreporting) A1 10	33	10	79	—	—	—	—	—	—	—
SEBASTOPOL—Sonoma County										
✠ COLUMBIA PALM DRIVE HOSPITAL, 501 Petaluma Avenue, Zip 95472; tel. 707/823–8511; Jeff Frandsen, Chief Executive Officer (Total facility includes 10 beds in nursing home–type unit) (Nonreporting) A1 9 10 S Columbia/HCA Healthcare Corporation, Nashville, TN	33	10	48	—	—	—	—	—	—	—
SELMA—Fresno County										
☐ SELMA DISTRICT HOSPITAL, 1141 Rose Avenue, Zip 93662–3293; tel. 209/891–2201; Terrence A. Curley, Executive Director (Total facility includes 14 beds in nursing home–type unit) (Nonreporting) A1 9 10 S Adventist Health, Roseville, CA	16	10	57	—	—	—	—	—	—	—
SEPULVEDA—Los Angeles County, See Los Angeles										
SHERMAN OAKS—Los Angeles County, See Los Angeles										
SIMI VALLEY—Ventura County										
✠ SIMI VALLEY HOSPITAL AND HEALTH CARE SERVICES, (Includes Simi Valley Hospital and Health Care Services–South Campus, 1850 Heywood Street, Zip 93065; tel. 805/582–5050), 2975 North Sycamore Drive, Zip 93065–1277; tel. 805/527–2462; Alan J. Rice, President (Total facility includes 74 beds in nursing home–type unit) (Nonreporting) A1 2 9 10 S Adventist Health, Roseville, CA N Adventist Health–Southern California, Glendale, CA	21	10	225	—	—	—	—	—	—	—
SOLVANG—Santa Barbara County										
☐ SANTA YNEZ VALLEY COTTAGE HOSPITAL, 700 Alamo Pintado Road, Zip 93463; tel. 805/688–6431; James L. Ash, Chief Executive Officer (Nonreporting) A1 9 10 S Cottage Health System, Santa Barbara, CA	23	10	20	—	—	—	—	—	—	—
SONOMA—Sonoma County										
☐ SONOMA VALLEY HOSPITAL, 347 Andrieux Street, Zip 95476–6811, Mailing Address: Box 600, Zip 95476–0600; tel. 707/935–5000; Dennis R. Burns, Administrator and Chief Executive Officer (Nonreporting) A1 9 10	16	10	86	—	—	—	—	—	—	—
SONORA—Tuolumne County										
★ SONORA COMMUNITY HOSPITAL, 1 South Forest Road, Zip 95370; tel. 209/532–3161; Lary Davis, President (Total facility includes 63 beds in nursing home–type unit) A9 10 F7 8 11 12 15 16 17 19 22 25 26 28 30 32 34 35 37 39 40 41 42 44 46 49 51 64 65 66 67 71 72 73 S Adventist Health, Roseville, CA	21	10	113	3534	95	148477	501	43990	18007	603
☐ TUOLUMNE GENERAL HOSPITAL, 101 Hospital Road, Zip 95370; tel. 209/533–7100; Joseph K. Mitchell, Administrator (Total facility includes 32 beds in nursing home–type unit) (Nonreporting) A1 9 10	13	10	77	—	—	—	—	—	—	—

Hospital, Address, Telephone, Administrator, Approval, Facility, and Physician Codes, Health Care System, Network	Classi-fication Codes		Utilization Data					Expense (thousands) of dollars		
★ American Hospital Association (AHA) membership □ Joint Commission on Accreditation of Healthcare Organizations (JCAHO) accreditation + American Osteopathic Healthcare Association (AOHA) membership ○ American Osteopathic Association (AOA) accreditation △ Commission on Accreditation of Rehabilitation Facilities (CARF) accreditation Control codes 61, 63, 64, 71, 72 and 73 indicate hospitals listed by AOHA, but not registered by AHA. For definition of numerical codes, see page A4	Control	Service	Staffed Beds	Admissions	Census	Outpatient Visits	Births	Total	Payroll	Personnel

SOUTH EL MONTE—Los Angeles County

★ GREATER EL MONTE COMMUNITY HOSPITAL, 1701 South Santa Anita Avenue, Zip 91733–9918; tel. 626/579–7777; Elizabeth A. Primeaux, Chief Executive Officer (Total facility includes 13 beds in nursing home–type unit) **A**1 9 10 **F**7 12 14 15 16 17 19 21 22 28 29 34 37 40 41 44 45 46 49 51 64 65 71 72 73 74 **P**5 **S** TENET Healthcare Corporation, Santa Barbara, CA **N** Essential HealthCare Network, Monterey Park, CA

| 16 | 10 | 113 | 4281 | 48 | 24649 | 1406 | 21487 | 11777 | 247 |

SOUTH LAGUNA—Orange County

★ SOUTH COAST MEDICAL CENTER, 31872 Coast Highway, Zip 92677; tel. 714/499–1311; T. Michael Murray, President (Total facility includes 29 beds in nursing home–type unit) **A**1 9 10 **F**2 3 7 8 11 12 15 16 17 19 21 22 25 27 28 29 30 31 32 34 35 36 37 39 40 41 42 44 45 46 49 52 56 57 58 59 60 64 65 67 71 73 74 **P**5 7 **S** Adventist Health, Roseville, CA

| 23 | 10 | 155 | 4743 | 66 | 43014 | 499 | 41125 | 17826 | 478 |

SOUTH LAKE TAHOE—El Dorado County

□ BARTON MEMORIAL HOSPITAL, 2170 South Avenue, Zip 96158, Mailing Address: Box 9578, Zip 96158; tel. 916/541–3420; William G. Gordon, Chief Executive Officer (Nonreporting) **A**1 9 10

| 23 | 10 | 81 | — | — | — | — | — | — | — |

SOUTH SAN FRANCISCO—San Mateo County

★ KAISER FOUNDATION HOSPITAL, 1200 El Camino Real, Zip 94080–3299; tel. 650/742–2547; Richard R. Pettingill, Administrator (Nonreporting) **A**1 10 **S** Kaiser Foundation Hospitals, Oakland, CA **N** Kaiser Foundation Health Plan of Northern California, Oakland, CA

| 23 | 10 | 79 | — | — | — | — | — | — | — |

STANFORD—Santa Clara County

★ STANFORD UNIVERSITY HOSPITAL, 300 Pasteur Drive, Zip 94305–5584; tel. 650/723–4000; Peter Van Etten, President and Chief Executive Officer (Total facility includes 22 beds in nursing home–type unit) (Nonreporting) **A**1 3 5 8 9 10

| 23 | 10 | 479 | — | — | — | — | — | — | — |

STOCKTON—San Joaquin County

□ DAMERON HOSPITAL, 525 West Acacia Street, Zip 95203; tel. 209/944–5550; Luis Arismendi, M.D., Administrator (Nonreporting) **A**1 9 10 **N** Sutter\CHS, Sacramento, CA

| 23 | 10 | 211 | — | — | — | — | — | — | — |

★ ST. JOSEPH'S BEHAVIORAL HEALTH CENTER, 2510 North California Street, Zip 95204–5568; tel. 209/948–2100; James Sondecker, Administrator **A**1 9 10 **F**1 3 4 5 6 7 8 9 10 11 12 13 14 15 16 17 18 19 20 21 22 23 24 25 26 27 28 29 30 31 32 33 34 35 36 37 38 39 40 41 42 43 44 45 46 47 48 49 51 52 53 54 55 56 57 58 59 60 61 62 64 65 66 67 68 69 70 71 72 73 74 **P**1 4 5 7 **S** Catholic Healthcare West, San Francisco, CA **N** Catholic HealthCare West (CHW), San Francisco, CA

| 23 | 22 | 35 | 1282 | 25 | 4970 | — | 4690 | 2326 | — |

★ ST. JOSEPH'S MEDICAL CENTER, 1800 North California Street, Zip 95204–6088, Mailing Address: P.O. Box 213008, Zip 95213–9008; tel. 209/943–2000; Edward G. Schroeder, President and Chief Executive Officer (Total facility includes 43 beds in nursing home–type unit) **A**1 2 9 10 **F**3 4 6 7 8 10 11 12 13 14 15 16 17 18 19 20 21 22 23 25 26 27 28 29 30 31 32 33 35 37 38 40 44 45 46 49 53 54 55 56 57 58 59 60 62 64 65 66 67 68 69 71 72 73 74 **P**5 7 **S** Catholic Healthcare West, San Francisco, CA **N** Catholic HealthCare West (CHW), San Francisco, CA

| 21 | 10 | 294 | 15610 | 198 | 338625 | 1938 | 139556 | 62519 | 2169 |

SUN CITY—Riverside County

★ MENIFEE VALLEY MEDICAL CENTER, 28400 McCall Boulevard, Zip 92585–9537; tel. 909/679–8888; Susan Ballard, Administrator (Nonreporting) **A**1 9 10 **S** Valley Health System, Hemet, CA

| 16 | 10 | 84 | — | — | — | — | — | — | — |

SUN VALLEY—Los Angeles County, See Los Angeles

SUSANVILLE—Lassen County

□ LASSEN COMMUNITY HOSPITAL, 560 Hospital Lane, Zip 96130–4809; tel. 530/257–5325; David S. Anderson, FACHE, Administrator (Total facility includes 31 beds in nursing home–type unit) **A**1 9 10 **F**7 8 12 15 16 20 22 26 28 30 32 33 35 40 44 51 64 65 71 73 **S** Lutheran Health Systems, Fargo, ND **N** Saint Mary's Health Network, Reno, NV; Northern Sierra Rural Health Network, Downieville, CA

| 21 | 10 | 59 | 1095 | 31 | 22658 | 302 | 10607 | 4746 | 172 |

SYLMAR—Los Angeles County, See Los Angeles

TAFT—Kern County

WEST SIDE DISTRICT HOSPITAL, 110 East North Street, Zip 93268; tel. 805/763–4211; Margo Arnold, Administrator (Total facility includes 63 beds in nursing home–type unit) (Nonreporting) **A**9 10

| 12 | 10 | 73 | — | — | — | — | — | — | — |

TARZANA—Los Angeles County, See Los Angeles

TEHACHAPI—Kern County

TEHACHAPI HOSPITAL, 115 West E. Street, Zip 93561, Mailing Address: P.O. Box 1900, Zip 93581; tel. 805/822–3241; David P. Jacobsen, Administrator **A**9 10 **F**8 22 28 34 44 49 73

| 16 | 10 | 21 | 131 | 17 | 29398 | 2 | 6046 | 2540 | 95 |

TEMPLETON—San Luis Obispo County

★ TWIN CITIES COMMUNITY HOSPITAL, 1100 Las Tablas Road, Zip 93465; tel. 805/434–3500; Harold E. Chilton, Chief Executive Officer (Nonreporting) **A**1 9 10 **S** TENET Healthcare Corporation, Santa Barbara, CA **N** Tenet Healthcare Corporation, Santa Barbara, CA

| 33 | 10 | 84 | — | — | — | — | — | — | — |

THOUSAND OAKS—Los Angeles County

★ COLUMBIA LOS ROBLES HOSPITAL AND MEDICAL CENTER, 215 West Janss Road, Zip 91360–1899; tel. 805/497–2727; Robert C. Shaw, Administrator and Chief Executive Officer (Total facility includes 42 beds in nursing home–type unit) **A**1 2 9 10 **F**4 7 10 11 14 15 16 17 19 21 22 26 29 30 31 32 34 35 36 37 38 39 40 41 42 43 44 45 46 48 49 52 54 57 60 63 64 65 67 71 73 74 **S** Columbia/HCA Healthcare Corporation, Nashville, TN

| 33 | 10 | 236 | 10688 | 144 | 68482 | 2017 | 94401 | 38757 | 929 |

Hospital, Address, Telephone, Administrator, Approval, Facility, and Physician Codes, Health Care System, Network	Classi-fication Codes		Utilization Data					Expense (thousands) of dollars		
★ American Hospital Association (AHA) membership □ Joint Commission on Accreditation of Healthcare Organizations (JCAHO) accreditation + American Osteopathic Healthcare Association (AOHA) membership ○ American Osteopathic Association (AOA) accreditation △ Commission on Accreditation of Rehabilitation Facilities (CARF) accreditation Control codes 61, 63, 64, 71, 72 and 73 indicate hospitals listed by AOHA, but not registered by AHA. For definition of numerical codes, see page A4	Control	Service	Staffed Beds	Admissions	Census	Outpatient Visits	Births	Total	Payroll	Personnel

TORRANCE—Los Angeles County

□ DEL AMO HOSPITAL, 23700 Camino Del Sol, Zip 90505; tel. 310/530–1151; E. Daniel Thomas, Administrator and Chief Executive Officer (Nonreporting) **A**1 10 **S** Universal Health Services, Inc., King of Prussia, PA

| | 33 | 22 | 166 | — | — | — | — | — | — | — |

✚ LAC–HARBOR–UNIVERSITY OF CALIFORNIA AT LOS ANGELES MEDICAL CENTER, 1000 West Carson Street, Zip 90509; tel. 310/222–2101; Tecla A. Mickoseff, Administrator **A**1 2 3 5 9 10 **F**4 8 10 11 16 19 21 22 23 29 31 34 35 37 38 40 41 42 43 44 45 47 52 54 56 58 60 61 63 65 66 69 70 71 72 73 74 **P**6 **S** Los Angeles County–Department of Health Services, Los Angeles, CA

| | 13 | 10 | 336 | 22783 | 335 | 323223 | 1889 | 403330 | 129327 | — |

□ LITTLE COMPANY OF MARY HOSPITAL, 4101 Torrance Boulevard, Zip 90503–4698; tel. 310/540–7676; Mark Costa, President (Total facility includes 121 beds in nursing home–type unit) **A**1 2 9 10 **F**3 4 5 7 8 10 12 17 19 21 22 23 25 27 29 32 33 34 37 38 40 41 42 43 44 46 49 51 60 63 64 65 67 71 73 74 **P**3 5 7 **S** Little Company of Mary Sisters Healthcare System, Evergreen Park, IL **N** Little Company of Mary Health Services, Torrance, CA

| | 23 | 10 | 354 | 13594 | 242 | 131885 | 2489 | 100649 | 41681 | 1131 |

✚ TORRANCE MEMORIAL MEDICAL CENTER, 3330 Lomita Boulevard, Zip 90505–5073; tel. 310/325–9110; George W. Graham, President **A**1 2 9 10 **F**3 4 7 8 9 10 17 19 21 22 23 25 26 27 28 29 30 31 32 33 34 35 37 38 40 41 42 43 44 45 46 49 51 54 55 56 57 58 59 60 64 65 67 71 72 73 74 **P**5

| | 23 | 10 | 360 | 21669 | 242 | 128717 | 4536 | 144631 | 59272 | 1532 |

TRACY—San Joaquin County

✚ SUTTER TRACY COMMUNITY HOSPITAL, (Formerly Tracy Community Memorial Hospital), 1420 North Tracy Boulevard, Zip 95376–3497; tel. 209/835–1500; Gary D. Rapaport, Chief Executive Officer (Total facility includes 15 beds in nursing home–type unit) **A**1 9 10 **F**7 8 11 15 16 17 19 21 22 28 29 30 32 33 34 35 37 39 40 41 42 44 49 64 65 66 67 71 72 73 **P**3 5 **S** Sutter Health, Sacramento, CA **N** Sutter\CHS, Sacramento, CA

| | 23 | 10 | 80 | 2831 | 29 | — | 492 | 22601 | 8755 | 305 |

TRAVIS AFB—Solano County

✚ DAVID GRANT MEDICAL CENTER, 101 Bodin Circle, Zip 94535–1800; tel. 707/423–7300; Lieutenant Colonel John Hill, MSC, USAF, FACHE, Administrator (Nonreporting) **A**1 2 3 5 **S** Department of the Air Force, Bowling AFB, DC

| | 41 | 10 | 185 | — | — | — | — | — | — | — |

TRUCKEE—Nevada County

□ TAHOE FOREST HOSPITAL DISTRICT, 10121 Pine Avenue, Zip 96161, Mailing Address: Box 759, Zip 96160; tel. 530/587–6011; Lawrence C. Long, Chief Executive Officer (Total facility includes 36 beds in nursing home–type unit) **A**1 9 10 **F**3 7 8 12 15 16 17 19 22 23 28 29 30 32 33 34 35 37 40 41 42 44 46 49 64 65 66 67 71 72 73 **P**5 7 8

| | 16 | 10 | 72 | 2051 | 50 | 65306 | 364 | 31186 | 11769 | 366 |

TULARE—Tulare County

✚ TULARE DISTRICT HOSPITAL, 869 Cherry Street, Zip 93274–2287; tel. 209/688–0821; Robert M. Montion, Chief Executive Officer **A**1 9 10 **F**7 8 12 14 15 16 17 19 22 30 32 34 35 37 40 42 44 46 65 71 73 **P**5

| | 16 | 10 | 88 | 4175 | 45 | 93510 | 920 | 34380 | 12505 | 397 |

TURLOCK—Stanislaus County

✚ EMANUEL MEDICAL CENTER, 825 Delbon Avenue, Zip 95382, Mailing Address: P.O. Box 819005, Zip 95381–9005; tel. 209/667–4200; Robert A. Moen, President and Chief Executive Officer (Total facility includes 145 beds in nursing home–type unit) **A**1 9 10 **F**6 7 8 12 15 17 19 21 22 25 26 28 29 30 32 33 34 35 36 37 38 40 41 42 44 45 46 49 64 65 67 71 72 73 74 **P**1

| | 21 | 10 | 307 | 7627 | 245 | 39918 | 1606 | 52853 | 21516 | 761 |

TUSTIN—Orange County

□ TUSTIN HOSPITAL, 14662 Newport Avenue, Zip 92680; tel. 714/838–9600; Timothy L. Carda, Chief Executive Officer (Total facility includes 24 beds in nursing home–type unit) **A**1

| | 33 | 10 | 117 | — | — | — | — | — | — | — |

□ △ TUSTIN REHABILITATION HOSPITAL, 14851 Yorba Street, Zip 92680; tel. 714/832–9200; Beverly Quaye, Administrator (Nonreporting) **A**1 7 9 10

| | 33 | 46 | 117 | — | — | — | — | — | — | — |

TWENTYNINE PALMS—San Bernardino County

✚ NAVAL HOSPITAL, Mailing Address: Box 788250, MCAGCC, Zip 92278–8250; tel. 760/830–2492; Captain R. S. Kayler, MSC, USN, Commanding Officer **A**1 **F**3 7 8 19 20 22 24 25 28 30 34 35 39 40 41 44 46 49 51 54 56 58 64 71 73 **P**2 **S** Department of Navy, Washington, DC

| | 43 | 10 | 29 | 1000 | 10 | 140995 | 502 | — | — | 531 |

UKIAH—Mendocino County

✚ UKIAH VALLEY MEDICAL CENTER, (Includes Ukiah Valley Medical Center–Dora Street, 1120 South Dora Street, ; Ukiah Valley Medical Center–Hospital Drive), 275 Hospital Drive, Zip 95482; tel. 707/462–3111; ValGene Devitt, President and Chief Executive Officer (Nonreporting) **A**1 9 10 **S** Adventist Health, Roseville, CA **N** Adventist Health–Northern California, Deer Park, CA

| | 21 | 10 | 101 | — | — | — | — | — | — | — |

UPLAND—San Bernardino County

✚ SAN ANTONIO COMMUNITY HOSPITAL, 999 San Bernardino Road, Zip 91786–4920, Mailing Address: Box 5001, Zip 91785; tel. 909/985–2811; George A. Kuykendall, President and Chief Executive Officer **A**1 2 9 10 **F**3 4 7 8 10 11 12 14 15 19 21 22 25 28 29 30 32 34 35 37 38 40 41 43 44 46 49 52 58 59 60 61 63 65 67 71 72 73

| | 23 | 10 | 308 | 17522 | 177 | 250494 | 3833 | 132790 | 56209 | 1508 |

VACAVILLE—Solano County

CALIFORNIA MEDICAL FACILITY, 1600 California Drive, Zip 95696–2000; tel. 707/448–6841; Shelby Farrow, Administrator (Nonreporting)

| | 12 | 11 | 215 | — | — | — | — | — | — | — |

★ VACAVALLEY HOSPITAL, 1000 Nut Tree Road, Zip 95687; tel. 707/429–7717; Deborah Sugiyama, President **A**9 10 **F**7 8 10 12 13 14 15 16 17 19 21 22 23 28 30 32 33 35 36 37 39 41 42 44 49 60 65 67 71 73 **P**3 **S** NorthBay Healthcare System, Fairfield, CA **N** NorthBay Healthcare System, Fairfield, CA

| | 23 | 10 | 43 | 1803 | 16 | 20844 | 0 | 21894 | 7867 | 101 |

Hospital, Address, Telephone, Administrator, Approval, Facility, and Physician Codes, Health Care System, Network	Classi-fication Codes		Utilization Data					Expense (thousands) of dollars		
★ American Hospital Association (AHA) membership □ Joint Commission on Accreditation of Healthcare Organizations (JCAHO) accreditation + American Osteopathic Healthcare Association (AOHA) membership ○ American Osteopathic Association (AOA) accreditation △ Commission on Accreditation of Rehabilitation Facilities (CARF) accreditation Control codes 61, 63, 64, 71, 72 and 73 indicate hospitals listed by AOHA, but not registered by AHA. For definition of numerical codes, see page A4	Control	Service	Staffed Beds	Admissions	Census	Outpatient Visits	Births	Total	Payroll	Personnel

VALENCIA—Los Angeles County

□ △ HENRY MAYO NEWHALL MEMORIAL HOSPITAL, 23845 McBean Parkway, Zip 91355; tel. 805/253–8000; Duffy Watson, President and Chief Executive Officer (Total facility includes 62 beds in nursing home–type unit) **A**1 2 7 9 10 **F**1 7 8 11 12 14 15 16 17 18 19 20 21 22 25 26 27 28 29 30 31 32 33 35 37 40 41 42 44 45 46 48 49 52 56 57 58 59 63 64 65 67 70 71 73 — 23 10 227 8577 138 125069 1414 73641 25663 847

VALLEJO—Solano County

□ FIRST HOSPITAL VALLEJO, 525 Oregon Street, Zip 94590; tel. 707/648–2200; Joe H. McWaters, Jr., Administrator and Chief Executive Officer (Nonreporting) **A**1 9 10 — 33 22 61 — — — — — — — —

☒ KAISER FOUNDATION HOSPITAL AND REHABILITATION CENTER, 975 Sereno Drive, Zip 94589; tel. 707/651–1000; Sandra Small, Administrator (Nonreporting) **A**1 10 **S** Kaiser Foundation Hospitals, Oakland, CA **N** Kaiser Foundation Health Plan of Northern California, Oakland, CA — 23 10 219 — — — — — — — —

☒ SUTTER SOLANO MEDICAL CENTER, 300 Hospital Drive, Zip 94589–2517, Mailing Address: P.O. Box 3189, Zip 94589; tel. 707/554–4444; Patrick R. Brady, Administrator (Total facility includes 8 beds in nursing home–type unit) **A**1 9 10 **F**7 8 10 11 12 14 15 16 19 21 22 28 30 32 34 35 36 39 40 41 42 44 49 63 64 65 71 73 74 **S** Sutter Health, Sacramento, CA **N** Sutter\CHS, Sacramento, CA — 23 10 55 4591 49 54314 803 39889 18096 448

VAN NUYS—Los Angeles County, See Los Angeles

VANDENBERG AFB—Santa Barbara County

☒ U. S. AIR FORCE HOSPITAL, 338 South Dakota, Zip 93437–6307; tel. 805/734–8232; Colonel Donald T. Davis, Commander (Nonreporting) **A**1 **S** Department of the Air Force, Bowling AFB, DC — 41 10 8 — — — — — — — —

VENICE—Los Angeles County

☒ △ DANIEL FREEMAN MARINA HOSPITAL, 4650 Lincoln Boulevard, Zip 90291–6360; tel. 310/823–8911; Joseph W. Dunn, Ph.D., Chief Executive Officer **A**1 7 9 10 **F**2 3 4 8 10 12 15 16 17 18 19 21 22 23 24 26 27 28 30 31 32 34 35 36 37 39 41 42 43 44 45 46 49 52 53 54 55 56 57 58 59 60 63 64 65 66 67 68 71 72 73 **P**5 7 **S** Carondelet Health System, Saint Louis, MO — 21 10 138 4346 85 — — 39992 17795 322

VENTURA—Ventura County

□ BHC VISTA DEL MAR HOSPITAL, 801 Seneca Street, Zip 93001; tel. 805/653–6434; Jerry Conway, Chief Executive Officer (Nonreporting) **A**1 9 10 **S** Behavioral Healthcare Corporation, Nashville, TN — 33 22 87 — — — — — — — —

☒ COMMUNITY MEMORIAL HOSPITAL OF SAN BUENAVENTURA, 147 North Brent Street, Zip 93003–2854; tel. 805/652–5011; Michael D. Bakst, Ph.D., Executive Director (Nonreporting) **A**1 9 10 — 23 10 217 — — — — — — — —

□ VENTURA COUNTY MEDICAL CENTER, 3291 Loma Vista Road, Zip 93003; tel. 805/652–6058; Samuel Edwards, Administrator (Nonreporting) **A**1 3 5 9 10 — 13 10 162 — — — — — — — —

VICTORVILLE—San Bernardino County

☒ DESERT VALLEY HOSPITAL, 16850 Bear Valley Road, Zip 92392; tel. 760/241–8000; Sidney Ono, Administrator (Nonreporting) **A**1 9 10 — 31 10 83 — — — — — — — —

□ VICTOR VALLEY COMMUNITY HOSPITAL, 15248 11th Street, Zip 92392; tel. 619/245–8691; Ralph L. Parks, Administrator and Chief Executive Officer (Nonreporting) **A**1 2 9 10 — 23 10 119 — — — — — — — —

VISALIA—Tulare County

☒ KAWEAH DELTA HEALTHCARE DISTRICT, (Includes Community Health Center, 1633 South Court Street, Zip 93277, Mailing Address: Box 911, Zip 93277; tel. 209/625–7221; Lindsay K. Mann, Senior Vice President), 400 West Mineral King Avenue, Zip 93291; tel. 209/625–2211; Thomas M. Johnson, Chief Executive Officer (Total facility includes 63 beds in nursing home–type unit) **A**1 2 9 10 **F**3 4 7 8 10 12 14 15 16 17 19 21 22 23 24 26 28 29 30 32 34 35 37 40 41 42 43 44 45 46 48 49 52 57 60 64 65 67 71 72 73 — 16 10 372 15493 217 247226 3600 126678 56969 1809

WALNUT CREEK—Contra Costa County

□ BHC WALNUT CREEK HOSPITAL, 175 La Casa Via, Zip 94598; tel. 925/933–7990; Jay R. Kellison, Chief Executive Officer (Nonreporting) **A**1 9 10 **S** Behavioral Healthcare Corporation, Nashville, TN — 33 22 108 — — — — — — — —

☒ JOHN MUIR MEDICAL CENTER, 1601 Ygnacio Valley Road, Zip 94598–3194; tel. 510/939–3000; Michael L. Wall, President and Chief Executive Officer (Total facility includes 20 beds in nursing home–type unit) (Nonreporting) **A**1 2 9 10 — 23 10 256 — — — — — — — —

☒ KAISER FOUNDATION HOSPITAL, (Includes Kaiser Foundation Hospital, 200 Muir Road, Martinez, Zip 94553–4696; tel. 510/372–1000), 1425 South Main Street, Zip 94596; tel. 510/295–4000; Sandra Small, Administrator **A**1 10 **F**2 3 4 7 8 9 10 11 12 13 14 15 16 17 19 21 22 23 25 26 28 29 30 31 32 33 34 35 37 38 40 41 42 43 44 45 46 47 48 49 50 51 52 53 54 55 56 57 58 59 60 61 63 64 65 67 68 69 71 72 73 74 **P**1 **S** Kaiser Foundation Hospitals, Oakland, CA **N** Kaiser Foundation Health Plan of Northern California, Oakland, CA — 23 10 210 17509 160 99586 3562 — — 653

WATSONVILLE—Santa Cruz County

□ WATSONVILLE COMMUNITY HOSPITAL, 298 Green Valley Road, Zip 95076; tel. 408/724–4741; John P. Friel, President and Chief Executive Officer (Total facility includes 13 beds in nursing home–type unit) **A**1 9 10 **F**2 3 7 8 10 11 15 16 17 19 21 22 25 28 30 31 32 34 35 37 38 39 40 41 42 44 46 49 64 65 67 68 71 72 73 **P**4 5 — 23 10 117 5029 47 139508 1642 — 26783 528

WEAVERVILLE—Trinity County

TRINITY HOSPITAL, 410 North Taylor Street, Zip 96093, Mailing Address: P.O. Box 1229, Zip 96093–1229; tel. 916/623–5541; Kathy Yarbrough, Interim Administrator (Total facility includes 42 beds in nursing home–type unit) (Nonreporting) **A**9 10 — 13 10 65 — — — — — — — —

Hospital, Address, Telephone, Administrator, Approval, Facility, and Physician Codes, Health Care System, Network	Classi-fication Codes		Utilization Data					Expense (thousands) of dollars		
★ American Hospital Association (AHA) membership □ Joint Commission on Accreditation of Healthcare Organizations (JCAHO) accreditation + American Osteopathic Healthcare Association (AOHA) membership ○ American Osteopathic Association (AOA) accreditation △ Commission on Accreditation of Rehabilitation Facilities (CARF) accreditation Control codes 61, 63, 64, 71, 72 and 73 indicate hospitals listed by AOHA, but not registered by AHA. For definition of numerical codes, see page A4	Control	Service	Staffed Beds	Admissions	Census	Outpatient Visits	Births	Total	Payroll	Personnel

WEST COVINA—Los Angeles County

□ CITRUS VALLEY MEDICAL CENTER–QUEEN OF THE VALLEY CAMPUS, 1115 South Sunset Avenue, Zip 91790, Mailing Address: Box 1980, Zip 91793; tel. 818/962–4011; Warren J. Kirk, Administrator and Chief Operating Officer (Nonreporting) **A**1 9 10 **S** Citrus Valley Health Partners, Covina, CA | 23 | 10 | 263 | — | — | — | — | — | — | — |

COVINA VALLEY COMMUNITY HOSPITAL, 845 North Lark Ellen Avenue, Zip 91791; tel. 818/339–5451; John Hogue, Administrator (Nonreporting) **A**9 10 | 32 | 10 | 76 | — | — | — | — | — | — | — |

□ DOCTORS HOSPITAL OF WEST COVINA, 725 South Orange Avenue, Zip 91790–2614; tel. 626/338–8481; Gerald H. Wallman, Administrator (Total facility includes 24 beds in nursing home–type unit) (Nonreporting) **A**1 10 | 33 | 10 | 51 | — | — | — | — | — | — | — |

WEST HILLS—Los Angeles County, See Los Angeles

WEST LOS ANGELES—Los Angeles County, See Los Angeles

WHITTIER—Los Angeles County

□ PRESBYTERIAN INTERCOMMUNITY HOSPITAL, 12401 Washington Boulevard, Zip 90602–1099; tel. 562/698–0811; Daniel F. Adams, President and Chief Executive Officer (Nonreporting) **A**1 2 3 5 9 10 | 23 | 10 | 312 | — | — | — | — | — | — | — |

✠ WHITTIER HOSPITAL MEDICAL CENTER, 9080 Colima Road, Zip 90605; tel. 562/907–1541; Sandra M. Chester, Chief Executive Officer (Total facility includes 39 beds in nursing home–type unit) (Nonreporting) **A**1 9 10 **S** TENET Healthcare Corporation, Santa Barbara, CA | 33 | 10 | 172 | — | — | — | — | — | — | — |

WILDOMAR—Riverside County

□ INLAND VALLEY REGIONAL MEDICAL CENTER, 36485 Inland Valley Drive, Zip 92595; tel. 909/677–1111; Christopher L. Boyd, Chief Executive Officer and Managing Director **A**1 9 10 **F**7 8 10 12 14 15 16 19 21 22 27 28 29 30 32 37 39 40 41 44 46 49 67 70 71 73 74 **S** Universal Health Services, Inc., King of Prussia, PA | 33 | 10 | 80 | 6671 | 42 | 35221 | 995 | 26094 | 13464 | 354 |

WILLITS—Mendocino County

✠ FRANK R. HOWARD MEMORIAL HOSPITAL, 1 Madrone Street, Zip 95490; tel. 707/459–6801; Kevin R. Erich, Administrator **A**1 9 10 **F**8 12 15 16 17 19 22 28 32 33 35 37 39 41 44 45 49 71 72 73 **P**3 **S** Adventist Health, Roseville, CA **N** Adventist Health–Northern California, Deer Park, CA | 23 | 10 | 28 | 933 | 10 | 23506 | — | 10086 | 4050 | 119 |

WILLOWS—Glenn County

GLENN MEDICAL CENTER, 1133 West Sycamore Street, Zip 95988; tel. 916/934–1800; Bernard G. Hietpas, Chief Executive Officer (Nonreporting) **A**9 10 | 23 | 10 | 27 | — | — | — | — | — | — | — |

WINTERHAVEN—Imperial County

✠ U. S. PUBLIC HEALTH SERVICE INDIAN HOSPITAL, Mailing Address: P.O. Box 1368, Yuma, AZ, Zip 85366–1368; tel. 760/572–0217; Hortense Miguel, R.N., Service Unit Director (Nonreporting) **A**1 10 **S** U. S. Public Health Service Indian Health Service, Rockville, MD | 47 | 10 | 34 | — | — | — | — | — | — | — |

WOODLAND—Yolo County

✠ WOODLAND MEMORIAL HOSPITAL, 1325 Cottonwood Street, Zip 95695–5199; tel. 530/662–3961; William Hunt, Chief Operating Officer (Nonreporting) **A**1 9 10 **S** Catholic Healthcare West, San Francisco, CA **N** Catholic HealthCare West (CHW), San Francisco, CA | 23 | 10 | 103 | — | — | — | — | — | — | — |

WOODLAND HILLS—Los Angeles County, See Los Angeles

YOUNTVILLE—Napa County

VETERANS HOME OF CALIFORNIA, 100 California Drive, Zip 94599–1413; tel. 707/944–4500; James D. Helzer, Administrator (Total facility includes 514 beds in nursing home–type unit) (Nonreporting) **A**10 | 12 | 10 | 540 | — | — | — | — | — | — | — |

YREKA—Siskiyou County

□ FAIRCHILD MEDICAL CENTER, (Formerly Siskiyou General Hospital), 444 Bruce Street, Zip 96097; tel. 530/842–4121; Dwayne Jones, Chief Executive Officer (Nonreporting) **A**1 9 10 | 23 | 10 | 48 | — | — | — | — | — | — | — |

YUBA CITY—Sutter County

□ FREMONT MEDICAL CENTER, 970 Plumas Street, Zip 95991; tel. 530/751–4000; Thomas P. Hayes, Chief Executive Officer **A**1 9 10 **F**7 8 10 14 15 16 17 19 22 25 26 28 30 32 33 34 35 37 38 39 40 44 45 49 60 71 **S** Fremont–Rideout Health Group, Yuba City, CA **N** Fremont–Rideout Health Group, Yuba City, CA | 23 | 10 | 78 | 7761 | 77 | 37370 | 2045 | 38825 | 15951 | 408 |

Resident population 3,893 (in thousands)
Resident population in metro areas 84.4%
Birth rate per 1,000 population 14.8
65 years and over 10.1%
Percent of persons without health insurance 16.6%

Hospital, Address, Telephone, Administrator, Approval, Facility, and Physician Codes, Health Care System, Network	Classi-fication Codes		Utilization Data					Expense (thousands) of dollars		
★ American Hospital Association (AHA) membership ☐ Joint Commission on Accreditation of Healthcare Organizations (JCAHO) accreditation + American Osteopathic Healthcare Association (AOHA) membership ○ American Osteopathic Association (AOA) accreditation △ Commission on Accreditation of Rehabilitation Facilities (CARF) accreditation Control codes 61, 63, 64, 71, 72 and 73 indicate hospitals listed by AOHA, but not registered by AHA. For definition of numerical codes, see page A4	Control	Service	Staffed Beds	Admissions	Census	Outpatient Visits	Births	Total	Payroll	Personnel

ALAMOSA—Alamosa County

★ SAN LUIS VALLEY REGIONAL MEDICAL CENTER, 106 Blanca Avenue, Zip 81101–2393; tel. 719/589–2511; Paul Herman, Chief Executive Officer **A**1 9 10 **F**6 7 8 12 14 15 16 17 18 19 20 21 22 23 25 26 27 28 29 30 31 32 33 34 35 37 39 40 41 42 44 45 46 49 51 53 54 55 56 57 58 59 65 66 67 68 69 70 71 72 73 74 **P**3

| | 21 | 10 | 85 | 3292 | 27 | 25399 | 575 | 14034 | 6313 | 247 |

ASPEN—Pitkin County

★ ASPEN VALLEY HOSPITAL DISTRICT, 401 Castle Creek Road, Zip 81611–1159; tel. 970/925–1120; Randy Middlebrook, Chief Executive Officer and Administrator (Nonreporting) **A**1 9 10

| | 16 | 10 | 41 | — | — | — | — | — | — | — |

AURORA—Adams County

★ COLUMBIA MEDICAL CENTER OF AURORA, (Includes Columbia Regional Medical Center–South Campus, 1501 South Potomac, Zip 80012; North Campus and Columbia Aurora Presbyterian Transitional Care Center, 700 Potomac Street, Zip 80011–6792; tel. 303/363–7200), 1501 South Potomac Street, Zip 80012–5499; tel. 303/695–2600; Louis O. Garcia, President and Chief Executive Officer (Nonreporting) **A**1 2 9 10 **S** Columbia/HCA Healthcare Corporation, Nashville, TN **N** Columbia – Health One, Englewood, CO

| | 33 | 10 | 334 | | | | | | | |

★ △ SPALDING REHABILITATION HOSPITAL, 900 Potomac Street, Zip 80011–6716; tel. 303/367–1166; Lynn Dawson, Chief Executive Officer (Nonreporting) **A**1 5 7 10 **S** Columbia/HCA Healthcare Corporation, Nashville, TN **N** Exempla, Denver, CO

| | 33 | 46 | 176 | | | | | | | |

BOULDER—Boulder County

★ △ BOULDER COMMUNITY HOSPITAL, 1100 Balsam, Zip 80304–3496, Mailing Address: P.O. Box 9019, Zip 80301–9019; tel. 303/440–2273; David P. Gehant, President and Chief Executive Officer **A**1 2 7 9 10 **F**2 3 4 5 7 8 10 11 12 14 15 19 21 22 24 25 26 29 30 31 32 33 34 35 37 40 41 42 43 44 45 46 48 49 51 52 53 54 55 56 57 58 59 60 63 65 66 67 68 71 72 73 74 **P**6 7

| | 23 | 10 | 197 | 9553 | 119 | 153994 | 1686 | 105672 | 46710 | 1251 |

BRIGHTON—Adams County

★ PLATTE VALLEY MEDICAL CENTER, 1850 Egbert Street, Zip 80601–2404, Mailing Address: P.O. Box 98, Zip 80601–0098; tel. 303/659–1531; John R. Hicks, President and Chief Executive Officer **A**1 9 10 **F**7 8 11 13 14 15 16 17 19 21 22 24 27 28 30 32 33 34 35 36 37 39 40 41 42 44 46 49 51 65 66 67 69 71 73 **P**4 8

| | 21 | 10 | 40 | 1821 | 17 | 24671 | 642 | 17070 | 7856 | 240 |

BRUSH—Morgan County

★ EAST MORGAN COUNTY HOSPITAL, 2400 West Edison Street, Zip 80723–1640; tel. 970/842–5151; Anne Platt, Administrator (Nonreporting) **A**1 9 10 **S** Lutheran Health Systems, Fargo, ND **N** High Plains Rural Health Network, Fort Morgan, CO

| | 23 | 10 | 29 | — | — | — | — | — | — | — |

BURLINGTON—Kit Carson County

KIT CARSON COUNTY MEMORIAL HOSPITAL, 286 16th Street, Zip 80807–1697; tel. 719/346–5311; DeAnn K. Cure, Chief Executive Officer (Nonreporting) **A**9 10 **N** High Plains Rural Health Network, Fort Morgan, CO

| | 13 | 10 | 24 | — | — | — | — | — | — | — |

CANON CITY—Fremont County

★ ST. THOMAS MORE HOSPITAL AND PROGRESSIVE CARE CENTER, 1338 Phay Avenue, Zip 81212–2221; tel. 719/269–2000; C. Ray Honaker, Administrator (Total facility includes 163 beds in nursing home–type unit) (Nonreporting) **A**1 9 10 **S** Catholic Health Initiatives, Denver, CO

| | 21 | 10 | 218 | — | — | — | — | — | — | — |

CHEYENNE WELLS—Cheyenne County

★ KEEFE MEMORIAL HOSPITAL, 602 North Sixth Street West, Zip 80810, Mailing Address: P.O. Box 578, Zip 80810–0578; tel. 719/767–5661; Curtis Hawkinson, Chief Executive Officer **A**1 9 10 **F**8 13 14 15 16 19 20 22 26 28 30 32 35 36 39 42 44 45 46 49 65 71 73 74 **N** High Plains Rural Health Network, Fort Morgan, CO

| | 13 | 10 | 12 | 126 | 2 | 8489 | 0 | 2621 | 1112 | 56 |

COLORADO SPRINGS—El Paso County

☐ CEDAR SPRINGS PSYCHIATRIC HOSPITAL, 2135 Southgate Road, Zip 80906–2693; tel. 719/633–4114; Connie Mull, Chief Executive Officer **A**1 9 10 **F**1 2 3 12 15 18 26 46 52 53 54 55 56 57 58 59 65 67 **S** Healthcare America, Inc., Austin, TX

| | 33 | 22 | 100 | 812 | 67 | 8991 | — | — | — | 115 |

★ MEMORIAL HOSPITAL, 1400 East Boulder Street, Zip 80909–5599, Mailing Address: Box 1326, Zip 80901–1326; tel. 719/365–5000; J. Robert Peters, Executive Director **A**1 2 9 10 **F**4 7 8 10 11 12 14 15 16 17 19 21 22 26 28 29 30 31 32 34 35 37 38 39 40 41 42 43 44 45 46 47 49 51 60 63 65 67 70 71 73 74 **P**5 **N** Health & Medical Network of Colorado, Colorado Springs, CO

| | 14 | 10 | 340 | 16225 | 218 | 196663 | 2507 | 168072 | 81407 | 2414 |

PENROSE COMMUNITY HOSPITAL See Penrose–St. Francis Health Services

Hospital, Address, Telephone, Administrator, Approval, Facility, and Physician Codes, Health Care System, Network	Classi-fication Codes		Utilization Data					Expense (thousands) of dollars		
★ American Hospital Association (AHA) membership □ Joint Commission on Accreditation of Healthcare Organizations (JCAHO) accreditation + American Osteopathic Healthcare Association (AOHA) membership ○ American Osteopathic Association (AOA) accreditation △ Commission on Accreditation of Rehabilitation Facilities (CARF) accreditation Control codes 61, 63, 64, 71, 72 and 73 indicate hospitals listed by AOHA, but not registered by AHA. For definition of numerical codes, see page A4	Control	Service	Staffed Beds	Admissions	Census	Outpatient Visits	Births	Total	Payroll	Personnel

PENROSE HOSPITAL See Penrose–St. Francis Health Services

⊞ △ PENROSE–ST. FRANCIS HEALTH SERVICES, (Includes Penrose Community Hospital, 3205 North Academy Boulevard, Zip 80917; tel. 719/776–3000; Penrose Hospital, 2215 North Cascade Avenue, Zip 80907; tel. 719/776–5000; St Francis Health Center, 825 East Pikes Peak Avenue, Zip 80903; tel. 719/776–8800), Donna L. Bertram, R.N., Administrator **A**1 2 3 5 7 9 10 **F**1 3 4 5 6 7 8 10 11 12 13 14 15 16 17 18 19 20 21 22 23 24 26 27 28 29 30 31 32 33 34 35 37 38 39 40 41 42 43 44 45 46 48 49 51 52 53 54 55 56 57 58 59 60 61 62 63 64 65 66 67 69 70 71 72 73 74 **P**3 7 **S** Catholic Health Initiatives, Denver, CO **N** Centura Penrose–St Francis Health Services, Colorado Springs, CO	21	10	424	20666	272	189082	3638	154969	72890	2837

ST FRANCIS HEALTH CENTER See Penrose–St. Francis Health Services

CORTEZ—Montezuma County

⊞ SOUTHWEST MEMORIAL HOSPITAL, 1311 North Mildred Road, Zip 81321–2299; tel. 970/565–6666; Stephen R. Selzer, President and Chief Executive Officer **A**1 9 10 **F**7 8 12 14 15 16 17 19 20 22 27 30 31 33 35 36 37 39 40 41 44 45 46 49 65 67 71 73 **P**3 7 8 **S** Quorum Health Group/Quorum Health Resources, Inc., Brentwood, TN	23	10	61	2458	20	23528	224	18831	7767	237

CRAIG—Moffat County

⊞ MEMORIAL HOSPITAL, 785 Russell Street, Zip 81625–9906; tel. 970/824–9411; M. Randell Phelps, Administrator **A**1 9 10 **F**7 8 15 17 19 21 22 28 30 35 37 39 40 41 42 44 49 56 64 65 67 70 71 73 **P**5 8 **S** Quorum Health Group/Quorum Health Resources, Inc., Brentwood, TN	13	10	29	965	8	13211	136	9301	3686	101

DELTA—Delta County

⊞ DELTA COUNTY MEMORIAL HOSPITAL, 100 Stafford Lane, Zip 81416–2297, Mailing Address: P.O. Box 10100, Zip 81416–5003; tel. 970/874–7681; Jerry Cantwell, Administrator **A**1 9 10 **F**8 14 19 21 22 28 32 35 37 40 41 44 49 65 71 73 **P**5 **S** Presbyterian Healthcare Services, Albuquerque, NM	16	10	44	2225	21	30650	237	14069	6695	252

DENVER—Denver, Adams and Arapahoe Counties

□ CENTURA SPECIAL CARE HOSPITAL, 1601 North Lowell Boulevard, Zip 80204–1597; tel. 303/899–5170; Silas M. Weir, Chief Executive Officer (Nonreporting) **A**1 9	23	10	24	—	—	—	—	—	—	—
⊞ CHILDREN'S HOSPITAL, 1056 East 19th Avenue, Zip 80218–1088; tel. 303/861–8888; Doris J. Biester, Jr., Chief Executive Officer **A**1 3 5 9 10 **F**4 5 9 10 12 13 14 15 16 17 18 19 20 21 22 25 28 29 31 32 34 35 38 39 41 42 43 44 45 46 47 49 51 52 53 54 55 56 58 59 60 65 67 68 69 70 71 72 73 **P**4 7 **N** KidSmart Health Partners, Denver, CO	23	50	198	7887	134	239655	0	151955	69172	1872
□ COLORADO MENTAL HEALTH INSTITUTE AT FORT LOGAN, 3520 West Oxford Avenue, Zip 80236–3197; tel. 303/761–0220; Allan Brock Willett, M.D., Director **A**1 9 10 **F**1 3 4 5 6 7 8 9 10 11 12 13 14 15 16 17 18 19 20 21 22 23 24 25 26 27 28 29 30 31 32 33 34 35 36 37 38 39 40 41 42 43 44 45 46 47 48 49 50 51 52 53 54 55 56 57 58 59 60 61 62 63 64 65 66 67 68 69 70 71 72 73 74 **P**4 6	12	22	315	909	287	2200	0	30113	18953	447
⊞ COLUMBIA PRESBYTERIAN–ST. LUKE'S MEDICAL CENTER, (Includes Presbyterian–Denver Hospital, 1719 East 19th Avenue, Zip 80218–1124; tel. 303/839–6565), 1719 East 19th Avenue, Zip 80218–1281; tel. 303/839–6000; Kevin Gross, Chief Executive Officer **A**1 2 3 5 9 10 12 13 **F**2 3 4 6 7 8 10 12 13 14 15 16 17 18 19 20 21 22 24 25 26 27 28 29 30 32 33 34 35 36 37 38 39 40 41 42 43 44 45 46 47 49 51 52 54 55 58 59 60 63 64 65 68 69 70 71 72 73 74 **P**5 6 7 **S** Columbia/HCA Healthcare Corporation, Nashville, TN **N** Columbia – Health One, Englewood, CO	32	10	461	14343	237	—	1562	156513	58540	1942

COLUMBIA ROSE MEDICAL CENTER See Rose Medical Center

□ DENVER HEALTH MEDICAL CENTER, 777 Bannock Street, Zip 80204–4507; tel. 303/436–6000; Patricia A. Gabow, M.D., Chief Executive Officer and Medical Director **A**1 3 5 9 10 **F**2 3 4 7 8 9 10 11 12 13 14 15 16 17 19 20 21 22 25 26 27 28 29 30 31 32 33 34 35 37 38 39 40 41 42 43 44 46 47 48 49 51 52 53 54 56 58 59 60 61 63 65 66 67 68 69 70 71 72 73 74 **P**6	16	10	303	15983	204	539409	2584	218415	106674	3084
⊞ EXEMPLA SAINT JOSEPH HOSPITAL, (Formerly Saint Joseph Hospital), 1835 Franklin Street, Zip 80218–1191; tel. 303/837–7111; David Hamm, Interim Chief Executive Officer (Nonreporting) **A**1 2 3 9 10 **S** Exempla Healthcare, Inc., Denver, CO **N** Exempla, Denver, CO	21	10	394	—	—	—	—	—	—	—
⊞ NATIONAL JEWISH MEDICAL AND RESEARCH CENTER, 1400 Jackson Street, Zip 80206–2762; tel. 303/388–4461; Lynn M. Taussig, M.D., President and Chief Executive Officer (Nonreporting) **A**1 3 5 9 10	23	49	58	—	—	—	—	—	—	—
⊞ PORTER ADVENTIST HOSPITAL, (Formerly Porter Care Hospital), 2525 South Downing Street, Zip 80210–5876; tel. 303/778–1955; Ruthita J. Fike, Administrator **A**1 2 9 10 **F**3 4 6 7 8 10 12 14 15 16 17 19 21 24 25 26 28 29 30 31 32 33 34 35 39 41 42 43 44 45 46 49 51 54 55 56 57 58 59 60 61 62 63 65 66 67 68 69 71 72 73 74 **P**5 6	21	10	339	12624	179	100948	897	116466	48105	—
★ PRECEDENT HEALTH CENTER, 1650 Fillmore Street, Zip 80206; tel. 303/226–2000; Jeffrey Mishell, M.D., Chief Executive Officer (Nonreporting)	32	10	57	—	—	—	—	—	—	—

PRESBYTERIAN–DENVER HOSPITAL See Columbia Presbyterian–St. Luke's Medical Center

⊞ ROSE MEDICAL CENTER, (Formerly Columbia Rose Medical Center), 4567 East Ninth Avenue, Zip 80220–3941; tel. 303/320–2121; Kenneth H. Feiler, President and Chief Executive Officer (Nonreporting) **A**1 2 3 5 9 10 **S** Columbia/HCA Healthcare Corporation, Nashville, TN **N** Columbia – Health One, Englewood, CO	33	10	250	—	—	—	—	—	—	—

Hospital, Address, Telephone, Administrator, Approval, Facility, and Physician Codes, Health Care System, Network	Classi-fication Codes		Utilization Data					Expense (thousands) of dollars		
★ American Hospital Association (AHA) membership □ Joint Commission on Accreditation of Healthcare Organizations (JCAHO) accreditation + American Osteopathic Healthcare Association (AOHA) membership ○ American Osteopathic Association (AOA) accreditation △ Commission on Accreditation of Rehabilitation Facilities (CARF) accreditation Control codes 61, 63, 64, 71, 72 and 73 indicate hospitals listed by AOHA, but not registered by AHA. For definition of numerical codes, see page A4	Control	Service	Staffed Beds	Admissions	Census	Outpatient Visits	Births	Total	Payroll	Personnel

✠ ST. ANTHONY CENTRAL HOSPITAL, (Formerly St. Anthony Hospital Central), 4231 West 16th Avenue, Zip 80204–4098; tel. 303/629–3511; Michael H. Erne, Senior Vice President and Administrator (Nonreporting) **A**1 2 3 5 9 10 **S** Catholic Health Initiatives, Denver, CO	21	10	238	—	—	—	—	—	—	—
✠ UNIVERSITY OF COLORADO HOSPITAL, 4200 East Ninth Avenue, Zip 80262; tel. 303/372–0000; Dennis C. Brimhall, President **A**1 2 5 8 9 10 **F**4 5 7 8 9 10 12 14 15 16 17 18 19 20 21 22 24 25 26 28 29 30 31 34 35 37 38 39 40 41 42 43 44 45 46 48 49 51 53 54 55 56 57 58 59 60 61 63 65 66 67 68 69 70 71 72 73 74 **P**4	16	10	349	14271	197	309251	1921	223348	76809	2082
✠ △ VETERANS AFFAIRS MEDICAL CENTER, 1055 Clermont Street, Zip 80220–3877; tel. 303/399–8020; Edgar Thorsland, Director **A**1 2 3 5 7 8 **F**3 16 37 48 52 64 **S** Department of Veterans Affairs, Washington, DC	45	10	212	6303	165	254424	0	131980	60091	1699
DURANGO—La Plata County										
✠ MERCY MEDICAL CENTER, 375 East Park Avenue, Zip 81301; tel. 970/247–4311; Renato V. Baciarelli, Administrator **A**1 2 9 10 **F**3 4 7 8 10 11 12 14 15 17 19 20 21 22 23 24 25 26 28 29 30 31 32 33 34 35 36 37 38 39 40 41 42 44 46 47 48 49 51 52 53 56 58 60 65 66 67 70 71 72 73 74 **P**1 4 5 6 7 8 **S** Catholic Health Initiatives, Denver, CO	21	10	83	4110	—	193155	675	—	27835	—
EADS—Kiowa County										
★ WEISBROD MEMORIAL HOSPITAL, 1208 Luther Street, Zip 81036, Mailing Address: P.O. Box 817, Zip 81036–0817; tel. 719/438–5401; Marvin O. Bishop, Administrator (Total facility includes 34 beds in nursing home–type unit) (Nonreporting) **A**9 10	16	10	42	—	—	—	—	—	—	—
ENGLEWOOD—Arapahoe County										
✠ △ CRAIG HOSPITAL, 3425 South Clarkson Street, Zip 80110–2899; tel. 303/789–8000; Dennis O'Malley, President **A**1 7 9 10 **F**12 14 15 16 17 19 20 21 22 23 24 32 34 35 39 41 44 45 46 48 49 50 60 63 65 67 70 71 73	23	46	75	467	68	5435	—	30879	13367	401
✠ SWEDISH MEDICAL CENTER, (Formerly Columbia Swedish Medical Center), 501 East Hampden Avenue, Zip 80110–0101; tel. 303/788–5000; Mary M. White, President and Chief Executive Officer **A**1 2 3 5 9 10 **F**1 2 3 4 5 6 7 8 9 10 12 13 14 15 16 17 18 19 20 21 22 23 24 25 26 27 28 29 30 31 32 33 34 35 37 38 39 40 41 42 43 44 45 46 47 48 49 52 53 54 55 56 57 58 59 60 61 62 63 64 65 66 67 68 69 70 71 72 73 74 **P**6 8 **S** Columbia/HCA Healthcare Corporation, Nashville, TN **N** Columbia – Health One, Englewood, CO	32	10	335	15900	215	122245	2391	156753	50633	1542
ESTES PARK—Larimer County										
★ ESTES PARK MEDICAL CENTER, 555 Prospect Avenue, Zip 80517, Mailing Address: P.O. Box 2740, Zip 80517; tel. 970/586–2317; Andrew Wills, Chief Executive Officer (Total facility includes 60 beds in nursing home–type unit) (Nonreporting) **A**9 10 **N** High Plains Rural Health Network, Fort Morgan, CO	16	10	74	—	—	—	—	—	—	—
FORT CARSON—El Paso County										
✠ EVANS U. S. ARMY COMMUNITY HOSPITAL, Zip 80913–5101; tel. 719/526–7200; Colonel Kenneth W. Leisher, Deputy Commander, Administration (Nonreporting) **A**1 2 **S** Department of the Army, Office of the Surgeon General, Falls Church, VA	42	10	103	—	—	—	—	—	—	—
FORT COLLINS—Larimer County										
□ MOUNTAIN CREST HOSPITAL, 4601 Corbett Drive, Zip 80525; tel. 970/225–9191; Kathleen Mechler, Chief Executive Officer (Nonreporting) **A**1 9 10	33	22	44	—	—	—	—	—	—	—
✠ POUDRE VALLEY HOSPITAL, 1024 Lemay Avenue, Zip 80524–3998; tel. 970/495–7000; Rulon F. Stacey, President and Chief Executive Officer **A**1 2 3 9 10 **F**4 7 8 10 11 12 13 14 15 17 19 20 21 22 24 29 30 32 34 35 36 37 39 40 41 42 43 44 45 46 47 48 49 50 51 52 53 54 55 56 57 58 59 63 65 67 70 71 73 **P**1 3	23	10	225	13590	149	312987	2105	128552	—	—
FORT LYON—Bent County										
✠ VETERANS AFFAIRS MEDICAL CENTER, Zip 81038; tel. 719/456–1260; W. David Smith, Director (Total facility includes 209 beds in nursing home–type unit) (Nonreporting) **A**1 **S** Department of Veterans Affairs, Washington, DC	45	22	299	—	—	—	—	—	—	—
FORT MORGAN—Morgan County										
✠ COLORADO PLAINS MEDICAL CENTER, 1000 Lincoln Street, Zip 80701–3298; tel. 970/867–3391; Thomas Thomson, Administrator and Chief Executive Officer (Nonreporting) **A**1 9 10 **S** Province Healthcare Corporation, Brentwood, TN **N** High Plains Rural Health Network, Fort Morgan, CO	33	10	40	—	—	—	—	—	—	—
FRUITA—Mesa County										
FAMILY HEALTH WEST, 228 North Cherry Street, Zip 81521–2101, Mailing Address: P.O. Box 130, Zip 81521–0130; tel. 303/858–9871; Dennis E. Ficklin, Chief Executive Officer (Total facility includes 352 beds in nursing home–type unit) (Nonreporting) **A**9 10	23	10	358	—	—	—	—	—	—	—
GLENWOOD SPRINGS—Garfield County										
✠ VALLEY VIEW HOSPITAL, 1906 Blake Avenue, Zip 81601–4259, Mailing Address: P.O. Box 1970, Zip 81602–1970; tel. 970/945–6535; Gary L. Brewer, Chief Executive Officer **A**1 9 10 **F**2 7 8 15 16 19 21 22 32 33 34 35 36 37 38 39 40 41 42 44 46 49 63 65 66 70 71 73 **P**5 **S** Quorum Health Group/Quorum Health Resources, Inc., Brentwood, TN	23	10	60	2730	27	16060	503	29444	12583	386
GRAND JUNCTION—Mesa County										
□ + ○ COMMUNITY HOSPITAL, 2021 North 12th Street, Zip 81501–2999; tel. 970/242–0920; Roger C. Zumwalt, Executive Director **A**1 9 10 11 **F**7 8 12 14 15 16 19 20 22 24 26 29 30 32 33 34 35 37 39 40 41 44 45 46 49 65 66 67 71 73 **P**8 **N** Community Health Providers Organization, Grand Junction, CO	23	10	51	2040	23	44709	239	20716	9518	338

Hospital, Address, Telephone, Administrator, Approval, Facility, and Physician Codes, Health Care System, Network	Classi-fication Codes		Utilization Data					Expense (thousands) of dollars		
★ American Hospital Association (AHA) membership □ Joint Commission on Accreditation of Healthcare Organizations (JCAHO) accreditation + American Osteopathic Healthcare Association (AOHA) membership ○ American Osteopathic Association (AOA) accreditation △ Commission on Accreditation of Rehabilitation Facilities (CARF) accreditation Control codes 61, 63, 64, 71, 72 and 73 indicate hospitals listed by AOHA, but not registered by AHA. For definition of numerical codes, see page A4	Control	Service	Staffed Beds	Admissions	Census	Outpatient Visits	Births	Total	Payroll	Personnel
☒ ST. MARY'S HOSPITAL AND MEDICAL CENTER, 2635 North 7th Street, Zip 81501–8204, Mailing Address: P.O. Box 1628, Zip 81502–1628; tel. 970/244–2273; Sister Lynn Casey, President and Chief Executive Officer **A**1 2 3 9 10 **F**1 2 3 4 5 6 7 8 10 11 12 13 14 15 16 17 18 19 21 22 23 24 26 27 28 29 30 31 32 33 34 35 36 37 38 39 40 41 42 43 44 45 46 48 49 51 52 53 54 55 56 57 58 59 60 61 63 64 65 66 67 68 70 71 72 73 74 **P**3 5 6 7 **S** Sisters of Charity of Leavenworth Health Services Corporation, Leavenworth, KS	23	10	250	13789	183	135168	1247	127049	57098	1952
☒ VETERANS AFFAIRS MEDICAL CENTER, 2121 North Avenue, Zip 81501–6499; tel. 970/242–0731; Kurt W. Schlegelmilch, M.D., Director (Total facility includes 30 beds in nursing home–type unit) **A**1 **F**2 3 4 8 10 14 15 16 17 19 20 21 22 26 28 30 31 32 33 34 35 37 39 41 42 44 45 46 49 51 52 54 56 57 58 59 60 64 65 67 71 73 74 **P**6 **S** Department of Veterans Affairs, Washington, DC	45	10	73	1504	66	54577	—	24468	12920	321
GREELEY—Weld County										
☒ NORTH COLORADO MEDICAL CENTER, 1801 16th Street, Zip 80631–5199; tel. 970/350–6000; Karl B. Gills, Administrator **A**1 2 3 9 10 **F**2 3 4 7 8 9 10 12 14 15 16 17 19 21 22 23 25 27 28 29 30 31 32 33 34 35 37 39 40 41 42 43 44 45 46 48 49 51 52 53 54 55 56 57 58 59 60 63 64 65 66 67 70 71 73 74 **P**5 7 8 **S** Lutheran Health Systems, Fargo, ND **N** High Plains Rural Health Network, Fort Morgan, CO	23	10	262	12753	154	246830	1846	126082	52557	1461
GUNNISON—Gunnison County										
GUNNISON VALLEY HOSPITAL, 214 East Denver Avenue, Zip 81230–2296; tel. 970/641–1456; Robert S. Austin, President **A**9 10 **F**7 8 11 12 14 17 19 20 22 28 29 32 34 35 37 40 41 44 46 47 49 65 66 71 73	13	10	24	561	5	23899	109	5363	2695	74
HAXTUN—Phillips County										
★ HAXTUN HOSPITAL DISTRICT, 235 West Fletcher Street, Zip 80731–0308, Mailing Address: Box 308, Zip 80731–0308; tel. 970/774–6123; James E. Brundige, Administrator (Total facility includes 32 beds in nursing home–type unit) (Nonreporting) **A**9 10 **N** High Plains Rural Health Network, Fort Morgan, CO	16	10	48	—	—	—	—	—	—	—
HOLYOKE—Phillips County										
★ MELISSA MEMORIAL HOSPITAL, 505 South Baxter Avenue, Zip 80734–1496; tel. 970/854–2241; George V. Larson, II, Chief Executive Officer **A**9 10 **F**7 8 14 15 17 19 20 22 24 27 28 30 32 34 40 41 44 45 49 51 71 **P**3 6 **N** High Plains Rural Health Network, Fort Morgan, CO	16	10	18	261	4	9932	34	3164	1579	—
HUGO—Lincoln County										
★ LINCOLN COMMUNITY HOSPITAL AND NURSING HOME, 111 Sixth Street, Zip 80821, Mailing Address: P.O. Box 248, Zip 80821–0248; tel. 719/743–2421; Mary L. Thompson, Administrator (Total facility includes 31 beds in nursing home–type unit) **A**9 10 **F**7 19 32 34 35 44 49 64 70 71 **N** High Plains Rural Health Network, Fort Morgan, CO	13	10	56	466	30	11933	46	4166	1972	91
JULESBURG—Sedgwick County										
SEDGWICK COUNTY HEALTH CENTER, (Formerly Sedgwick County Memorial Hospital), 900 Cedar Street, Zip 80737–1199; tel. 970/474–3323; Bill Patten, Administrator (Total facility includes 32 beds in nursing home–type unit) **A**9 10 **F**1 7 8 11 14 15 16 19 20 22 24 27 28 29 30 32 33 34 35 37 39 40 41 42 44 45 46 49 51 64 65 66 71 **P**1	13	10	58	214	34	6515	22	3113	1501	49
KREMMLING—Grand County										
KREMMLING MEMORIAL HOSPITAL, Fourth and Grand Avenue, Zip 80459, Mailing Address: P.O. Box 399, Zip 80459–0399; tel. 970/724–3442; Thomas Andron, Chief Executive Officer **A**9 10 **F**8 14 15 16 17 22 24 28 34 39 42 44 49 51 71 73 **P**6	16	10	19	205	11	13278	—	3137	1320	65
LA JARA—Conejos County										
□ CONEJOS COUNTY HOSPITAL, Mailing Address: P.O. Box 639, Zip 81140–0639; tel. 719/274–5121; Monica Morris, Chief Executive Officer (Total facility includes 34 beds in nursing home–type unit) (Nonreporting) **A**1 9 10	16	10	49	—	—	—	—	—	—	—
LA JUNTA—Otero County										
☒ ARKANSAS VALLEY REGIONAL MEDICAL CENTER, 1100 Carson Avenue, Zip 81050–2799; tel. 719/383–6000; Dale D. Stoll, Chief Executive Officer (Total facility includes 119 beds in nursing home–type unit) **A**1 9 10 **F**7 8 10 15 17 19 22 23 28 30 32 33 34 35 37 40 42 44 46 49 64 65 67 71	21	10	187	2720	152	52469	312	20369	9124	432
LAMAR—Prowers County										
☒ PROWERS MEDICAL CENTER, 401 Kendall Drive, Zip 81052–3993; tel. 719/336–4343; Earl J. Steinhoff, Chief Executive Officer **A**1 9 10 **F**1 2 3 4 5 7 8 9 10 11 14 15 16 17 19 20 21 22 23 25 26 27 28 29 30 32 33 34 35 36 37 38 39 40 41 42 43 44 45 46 47 48 49 50 51 52 53 54 55 56 57 58 59 60 61 63 64 65 66 67 69 70 71 73 74 **S** Quorum Health Group/Quorum Health Resources, Inc., Brentwood, TN **N** High Plains Rural Health Network, Fort Morgan, CO	16	10	40	1578	13	25489	240	12532	5889	182
LEADVILLE—Lake County										
ST. VINCENT GENERAL HOSPITAL, 822 West Fourth Street, Zip 80461–3897; tel. 719/486–0230; Phillip Lowe, Chief Executive Officer (Nonreporting) **A**9 10	16	10	31	—	—	—	—	—	—	—
LITTLETON—Arapahoe County										
☒ LITTLETON ADVENTIST HOSPITAL, (Formerly Porter Care Hospital–Littleton), 7700 South Broadway Street, Zip 80122–2628; tel. 303/730–8900; Ruthita J. Fike, Administrator (Nonreporting) **A**1 9	21	10	106	—	—	—	—	—	—	—

Hospital, Address, Telephone, Administrator, Approval, Facility, and Physician Codes, Health Care System, Network	Classi-fication Codes		Utilization Data					Expense (thousands) of dollars		
★ American Hospital Association (AHA) membership □ Joint Commission on Accreditation of Healthcare Organizations (JCAHO) accreditation + American Osteopathic Healthcare Association (AOHA) membership ○ American Osteopathic Association (AOA) accreditation △ Commission on Accreditation of Rehabilitation Facilities (CARF) accreditation Control codes 61, 63, 64, 71, 72 and 73 indicate hospitals listed by AOHA, but not registered by AHA. For definition of numerical codes, see page A4	Control	Service	Staffed Beds	Admissions	Census	Outpatient Visits	Births	Total	Payroll	Personnel

LONGMONT—Boulder County

⊞ LONGMONT UNITED HOSPITAL, 1950 West Mountain View Avenue, Zip 80501–3162, Mailing Address: Box 1659, Zip 80502–1659; tel. 303/651–5024; Kenneth R. Huey, President and Chief Executive Officer (Total facility includes 15 beds in nursing home–type unit) **A**1 2 9 10 **F**1 3 7 8 10 12 14 15 16 17 19 20 21 22 24 25 26 27 28 29 30 31 32 33 34 35 37 39 40 41 42 44 45 46 48 49 52 53 54 55 56 57 58 59 60 64 65 66 67 68 69 70 71 73 **P**8	23	10	122	5548	67	194132	832	48883	21891	712

LOUISVILLE—Boulder County

⊞ AVISTA ADVENTIST HOSPITAL, (Formerly PorterCare Hospital – Avista), 100 Health Park Drive, Zip 80027–9583; tel. 303/673–1000; John Sackett, Administrator (Nonreporting) **A**1 3 9 10	21	10	58	—	—	—	—	—	—	—
□ CHARTER CENTENNIAL PEAKS BEHAVIORAL HEALTH SYSTEM, 2255 South 88th Street, Zip 80027–9716; tel. 303/673–9990; Sharon Worsham, Administrator (Nonreporting) **A**1 9 10 **S** Magellan Health Services, Atlanta, GA	33	22	72	—	—	—	—	—	—	—

LOVELAND—Larimer County

⊞ MCKEE MEDICAL CENTER, 2000 Boise Avenue, Zip 80538–4281; tel. 970/669–4640; Charles F. Harms, Administrator (Total facility includes 11 beds in nursing home–type unit) **A**1 9 10 **F**1 7 8 12 14 15 16 17 18 19 21 22 23 28 30 31 32 33 34 35 39 41 44 45 46 49 55 60 63 64 65 70 71 73 **P**7 8 **S** Lutheran Health Systems, Fargo, ND	23	10	109	4956	52	50522	677	39736	18433	630

MEEKER—Rio Blanco County

★ PIONEERS HOSPITAL OF RIO BLANCO COUNTY, (Includes Walbridge Memorial Convalescent Wing), 345 Cleveland Street, Zip 81641–0000; tel. 970/878–5047; Thomas E. Lake, Chief Executive Officer (Total facility includes 29 beds in nursing home–type unit) **A**9 10 **F**1 8 13 14 15 20 22 24 25 26 27 28 29 32 36 39 41 44 49 51 64 71 72 73 74 **P**1 **S** Quorum Health Group/Quorum Health Resources, Inc., Brentwood, TN **N** Quorum Health Network of Colorado, Boulder, CO	13	10	46	325	29	8040	—	4581	2125	94

MONTROSE—Montrose County

⊞ MONTROSE MEMORIAL HOSPITAL, 800 South Third Street, Zip 81401–4291; tel. 970/249–2211; Tyler Erickson, Administrator **A**1 9 10 **F**2 3 7 8 11 12 14 15 16 17 19 20 21 22 23 24 26 28 29 30 34 35 37 39 40 41 42 44 45 46 47 48 49 52 53 54 55 56 57 58 63 65 66 67 68 71 72 73 74 **P**5 8 **S** Quorum Health Group/Quorum Health Resources, Inc., Brentwood, TN	13	10	63	2662	29	61537	400	24871	11075	356

PUEBLO—Pueblo County

□ COLORADO MENTAL HEALTH INSTITUTE AT PUEBLO, 1600 West 24th Street, Zip 81003–1499; tel. 719/546–4000; Robert L. Hawkins, Superintendent (Nonreporting) **A**1 9 10	12	22	605	—	—	—	—	—	—	—
⊞ PARKVIEW MEDICAL CENTER, (Formerly Parkview Episcopal Medical Center), 400 West 16th Street, Zip 81003–2781; tel. 719/584–4000; C. W. Smith, President and Chief Executive Officer (Total facility includes 9 beds in nursing home–type unit) **A**1 9 10 **F**1 2 3 4 7 8 10 12 14 15 16 17 18 19 22 23 26 28 30 31 32 35 37 39 40 41 42 43 44 45 46 48 49 52 53 54 55 56 57 58 59 64 65 66 70 71 73 **P**7 8 **S** Quorum Health Group/Quorum Health Resources, Inc., Brentwood, TN	23	10	260	9921	143	62254	956	81171	36438	1168
⊞ ST. MARY–CORWIN MEDICAL CENTER, (Formerly St. Mary–Corwin Regional Medical Center), 1008 Minnequa Avenue, Zip 81004–3798; tel. 719/560–4000; Walter Sackett, Senior Vice President and Administrator (Total facility includes 16 beds in nursing home–type unit) (Nonreporting) **A**1 2 3 9 10 12 **S** Catholic Health Initiatives, Denver, CO	21	10	261	—	—	—	—	—	—	—

RANGELY—Rio Blanco County

★ RANGELY DISTRICT HOSPITAL, 511 South White Avenue, Zip 81648–2104; tel. 970/675–5011; Merrill A. Frank, Chief Executive Officer **A**9 10 **F**8 13 15 22 28 30 32 34 36 44 46 49 51 70 71 **P**6	16	10	25	72	13	15882	1	3391	1848	62

RIFLE—Garfield County

★ GRAND RIVER HOSPITAL DISTRICT, 701 East Fifth Street, Zip 81650–2970, Mailing Address: P.O. Box 912, Zip 81650–0912; tel. 970/625–1510; Edwin A. Gast, Administrator (Total facility includes 57 beds in nursing home–type unit) (Nonreporting) **A**9 10 **S** Quorum Health Group/Quorum Health Resources, Inc., Brentwood, TN **N** Quorum Health Network of Colorado, Boulder, CO	16	10	75	—	—	—	—	—	—	—

SALIDA—Chaffee County

★ HEART OF THE ROCKIES REGIONAL MEDICAL CENTER, 448 East First Street, Zip 81201–0429, Mailing Address: P.O. Box 429, Zip 81201–0429; tel. 719/539–6661; Howard D. Turner, Chief Executive Officer **A**9 10 **F**7 8 11 12 17 19 21 22 28 32 33 35 36 37 40 41 42 44 49 70 71 73 **P**5 **S** Quorum Health Group/Quorum Health Resources, Inc., Brentwood, TN	16	10	33	1423	13	25200	111	10127	4605	175

SPRINGFIELD—Baca County

★ SOUTHEAST COLORADO HOSPITAL AND LONG TERM CARE, 373 East Tenth Avenue, Zip 81073–1699; tel. 719/523–4501; Annie L. Dukes, JD, Chief Executive Officer and Administrator (Total facility includes 56 beds in nursing home–type unit) (Nonreporting) **A**9 10	23	10	81	—	—	—	—	—	—	—

STEAMBOAT SPRINGS—Routt County

⊞ ROUTT MEMORIAL HOSPITAL, 80 Park Avenue, Zip 80487–5010; tel. 970/879–1322; Margaret D. Sabin, Chief Executive Officer (Total facility includes 50 beds in nursing home–type unit) (Nonreporting) **A**1 9 10	23	10	74	—	—	—	—	—	—	—

Hospital, Address, Telephone, Administrator, Approval, Facility, and Physician Codes, Health Care System, Network	Classi-fication Codes		Utilization Data						Expense (thousands) of dollars			
★ American Hospital Association (AHA) membership □ Joint Commission on Accreditation of Healthcare Organizations (JCAHO) accreditation + American Osteopathic Healthcare Association (AOHA) membership ○ American Osteopathic Association (AOA) accreditation △ Commission on Accreditation of Rehabilitation Facilities (CARF) accreditation Control codes 61, 63, 64, 71, 72 and 73 indicate hospitals listed by AOHA, but not registered by AHA. For definition of numerical codes, see page A4	Control	Service	Staffed Beds	Admissions	Census	Outpatient Visits	Births	Total	Payroll	Personnel

	Control	Service	Staffed Beds	Admissions	Census	Outpatient Visits	Births	Total	Payroll	Personnel
STERLING—Logan County										
⊞ STERLING REGIONAL MEDCENTER, 615 Fairhurst Street, Zip 80751–4523, Mailing Address: P.O. Box 3500, Zip 80751–3500; tel. 970/522–0122; James O. Pernau, Administrator (Nonreporting) **A**1 9 10 **S** Lutheran Health Systems, Fargo, ND **N** High Plains Rural Health Network, Fort Morgan, CO	23	10	36	—	—	—	—	—	—	—
THORNTON—Adams County										
⊞ COLUMBIA NORTH SUBURBAN MEDICAL CENTER, (Formerly North Suburban Medical Center), 9191 Grant Street, Zip 80229–4341; tel. 303/451–7800; Margaret C. Cain, Chief Executive Officer (Total facility includes 15 beds in nursing home–type unit) (Nonreporting) **A**1 9 10 **S** Columbia/HCA Healthcare Corporation, Nashville, TN **N** Columbia – Health One, Englewood, CO	33	10	125	—	—	—	—	—	—	—
□ MEDIPLEX REHABILITATION–DENVER, 8451 Pearl Street, Zip 80229–4804; tel. 303/288–3000; Harvey Ross, Executive Director and Chief Executive Officer (Total facility includes 50 beds in nursing home–type unit) (Nonreporting) **A**1 5 9 10	33	46	117	—	—	—	—	—	—	—
TRINIDAD—Las Animas County										
⊞ MOUNT SAN RAFAEL HOSPITAL, 410 Benedicta Avenue, Zip 81082–2093; tel. 719/846–9213; James P. D'Agostino, Executive Director **A**1 9 10 **F**7 19 21 22 32 35 37 40 44 46 51 71 **P**8 **S** Quorum Health Group/Quorum Health Resources, Inc., Brentwood, TN	23	10	31	1112	15	36735	126	8496	3918	144
USAF ACADEMY—El Paso County										
⊞ U. S. AIR FORCE ACADEMY HOSPITAL, 4102 Pinion Drive, Zip 80840–4000; tel. 719/333–5102; Colonel David L. Hammer, USAF, MC, Commander **A**1 **F**7 8 9 12 14 15 16 19 20 21 22 24 25 28 29 30 34 35 37 38 39 40 41 44 45 46 47 48 49 51 53 54 55 56 57 58 61 65 66 67 71 73 74 **S** Department of the Air Force, Bowling AFB, DC	41	10	48	2548	17	232269	610	—	—	—
VAIL—Eagle County										
⊞ VAIL VALLEY MEDICAL CENTER, 181 West Meadow Drive, Zip 81657–5059; tel. 970/476–2451; Clifford M. Eldredge, President and Chief Executive Officer **A**1 3 9 10 **F**1 7 8 10 12 13 14 15 16 17 19 20 21 22 24 26 27 28 29 30 31 32 33 34 35 37 39 40 41 42 44 45 46 49 65 66 67 68 70 71 72 73 74	23	10	49	2148	16	37761	514	40601	13767	450
WALSENBURG—Huerfano County										
★ HUERFANO MEDICAL CENTER, 23500 U.S. Highway 160, Zip 81089–9524; tel. 719/738–5100; Vonnie Maier, President and Chief Executive Officer **A**9 10 **F**3 5 8 15 16 17 19 20 22 26 27 28 29 30 31 32 33 34 35 39 41 44 45 46 49 64 65 66 71 73 74	16	10	24	841	16	23266	—	6154	2308	183
WESTMINSTER—Jefferson County										
⊞ CLEO WALLACE CENTERS HOSPITAL, 8405 Church Ranch Boulevard, Zip 80021; tel. 303/639–1700; James M. Cole, President and Chief Executive Officer **A**1 10 **F**2 3 12 16 22 39 44 45 46 52 53 54 55 56 59 65 **P**8	23	52	231	3894	299	—	—	23640	13903	542
★ ST. ANTHONY NORTH HOSPITAL, (Formerly St. Anthony Hospital North), 2551 West 84th Avenue, Zip 80030–3887; tel. 303/426–2151; Michael H. Erne, Chief Executive Officer (Nonreporting) **A**9 10 **S** Catholic Health Initiatives, Denver, CO	21	10	110	—	—	—	—	—	—	—
WHEAT RIDGE—Jefferson County										
⊞ △ EXEMPLA LUTHERAN MEDICAL CENTER, (Formerly Lutheran Medical Center), (Includes Exempla West Pines, 3400 Lutheran Parkway, Zip 80033; tel. 303/467–4000), 8300 West 38th Avenue, Zip 80033–6005; tel. 303/425–4500; Jeffrey D. Selberg, President and Chief Executive Officer (Total facility includes 138 beds in nursing home–type unit) **A**1 2 7 9 10 **F**2 3 4 6 7 8 9 10 11 12 14 15 16 17 19 21 22 23 24 25 26 28 29 30 32 33 34 35 37 38 39 40 41 42 43 44 45 46 47 48 49 51 52 53 54 55 56 57 58 59 60 61 62 64 65 66 67 70 71 72 73 74 **P**5 7 **S** Exempla Healthcare, Inc., Denver, CO **N** Exempla, Denver, CO	23	10	472	15203	178	153441	2277	146247	74953	1990
WRAY—Yuma County										
★ WRAY COMMUNITY DISTRICT HOSPITAL, 1017 West 7th Street, Zip 80758–1420; tel. 970/332–4811; Daniel Dennis, Administrator (Nonreporting) **A**3 9 10 **N** High Plains Rural Health Network, Fort Morgan, CO	16	10	25	—	—	—	—	—	—	—
YUMA—Yuma County										
★ YUMA DISTRICT HOSPITAL, 910 South Main Street, Zip 80759–3098, Mailing Address: P.O. Box 306, Zip 80759–0306; tel. 970/848–5405; Timothy F. Reardon, FACHE, Chief Executive Officer (Nonreporting) **A**9 10 **N** High Plains Rural Health Network, Fort Morgan, CO	16	10	11	—	—	—	—	—	—	—

CONNECTICUT

Resident population 3,270 (in thousands)
Resident population in metro areas 95.7%
Birth rate per 1,000 population 13.9
65 years and over 14.3%
Percent of persons without health insurance 11.0%

Hospital, Address, Telephone, Administrator, Approval, Facility, and Physician Codes, Health Care System, Network	Classi-fication Codes		Utilization Data					Expense (thousands) of dollars		
★ American Hospital Association (AHA) membership □ Joint Commission on Accreditation of Healthcare Organizations (JCAHO) accreditation + American Osteopathic Healthcare Association (AOHA) membership ○ American Osteopathic Association (AOA) accreditation △ Commission on Accreditation of Rehabilitation Facilities (CARF) accreditation Control codes 61, 63, 64, 71, 72 and 73 indicate hospitals listed by AOHA, but not registered by AHA. For definition of numerical codes, see page A4	Control	Service	Staffed Beds	Admissions	Census	Outpatient Visits	Births	Total	Payroll	Personnel

BETHLEHEM—Litchfield County

★ WELLSPRING FOUNDATION, 21 Arch Bridge Road, Zip 06751–0370, Mailing Address: P.O. Box 370, Zip 06751–0370; tel. 203/266–7235; Herbert L. Hall, Chief Executive Officer **F**1 3 52 53 54 55 58 59	23	22	36	65	20	331	0	3139	2119	67

BRANFORD—New Haven County

□ THE CONNECTICUT HOSPICE, 61 Burban Drive, Zip 06405–4003; tel. 203/481–6231; Rosemary Johnson Hurzeler, President and Chief Executive Officer (Nonreporting) **A**1 10	33	49	52	—	—	—	—	—	—	—

BRIDGEPORT—Fairfield County

✚ BRIDGEPORT HOSPITAL, 267 Grant Street, Zip 06610–2875, Mailing Address: P.O. Box 5000, Zip 06610–0120; tel. 203/384–3000; Robert J. Trefry, President and Chief Executive Officer **A**1 2 3 5 6 8 9 10 **F**2 3 4 7 8 9 10 11 12 13 14 15 16 17 18 19 20 21 22 25 27 28 29 30 31 32 33 34 35 36 37 38 39 40 41 42 43 44 45 46 47 48 49 51 52 53 54 55 56 57 58 59 60 61 65 66 67 68 69 70 71 72 73 74 **P**1 7	23	10	358	16824	242	131857	2471	179375	73396	2172
GREATER BRIDGEPORT COMMUNITY MENTAL HEALTH CENTER, 1635 Central Avenue, Zip 06610–2700, Mailing Address: P.O. Box 5117, Zip 06610–5117; tel. 203/579–6646; James M. Lehane, III, Director (Nonreporting) **A**10 **S** Connecticut State Department of Mental Health, Hartford, CT	12	22	62	—	—	—	—	—	—	—
✚ ST. VINCENT'S MEDICAL CENTER, 2800 Main Street, Zip 06606–4292; tel. 203/576–6000; William J. Riordan, President and Chief Executive Officer **A**1 2 3 5 8 9 10 **F**1 3 4 7 8 10 11 12 14 15 16 17 19 21 22 25 26 27 28 29 30 31 34 35 37 39 40 41 42 43 44 46 49 51 52 53 54 55 56 57 58 59 60 65 67 68 70 71 72 73 74 **P**1 2 7 **S** Daughters of Charity National Health System, Saint Louis, MO	21	10	289	14805	235	113973	1844	134321	66423	1378

BRISTOL—Hartford County

✚ BRISTOL HOSPITAL, P.O. Box 977, Brewster Road, Zip 06011–0977; tel. 860/585–3000; Thomas D. Kennedy, III, President and Chief Executive Officer (Nonreporting) **A**1 2 9 10	23	10	160	—	—	—	—	—	—	—

DANBURY—Fairfield County

✚ DANBURY HOSPITAL, 24 Hospital Avenue, Zip 06813–6099; tel. 203/797–7000; Frank J. Kelly, President and Chief Executive Officer (Nonreporting) **A**1 2 3 5 8 9 10	23	10	250	—	—	—	—	—	—	—

DERBY—New Haven County

✚ GRIFFIN HOSPITAL, 130 Division Street, Zip 06418–1377; tel. 203/735–7421; Patrick Charmel, Interim President and Chief Executive Officer **A**1 2 3 5 9 10 **F**1 3 7 8 14 15 16 19 20 21 22 28 29 30 35 37 38 41 42 44 45 46 49 51 52 53 56 58 59 61 71 72 73 74 **P**5	23	10	160	5278	78	95606	569	64050	29081	592

FARMINGTON—Hartford County

✚ UNIVERSITY OF CONNECTICUT HEALTH CENTER, JOHN DEMPSEY HOSPITAL, 263 Farmington Avenue, Zip 06030–1956; tel. 860/679–2000; Andria Martin, R.N., MS, Director and Vice President Operations **A**1 2 3 5 8 9 10 **F**2 3 4 5 7 8 10 12 14 15 16 17 19 21 22 23 26 28 30 34 35 36 37 38 39 40 41 42 43 44 45 46 49 51 52 54 55 56 58 59 60 61 65 66 67 71 72 73 74 **P**6	12	10	138	6505	124	452564	518	119666	46716	1022

GREENWICH—Fairfield County

✚ GREENWICH HOSPITAL, 5 Perryridge Road, Zip 06830–4697; tel. 203/863–3901; Frank A. Corvino, President and Chief Executive Officer **A**1 2 3 5 9 10 **F**2 3 7 8 10 11 12 13 14 15 16 17 18 19 20 21 22 24 26 28 29 30 31 32 33 34 35 37 38 39 40 41 42 44 45 46 49 51 53 54 55 56 57 58 60 61 63 64 65 66 67 68 71 73 74 **P**5	23	10	160	7171	109	274895	1420	102408	49460	1119

HARTFORD—Hartford County

✚ CONNECTICUT CHILDREN'S MEDICAL CENTER, 282 Washington Street, Zip 06106–3316; tel. 860/545–8551; Larry M. Gold, President and Chief Executive Officer **A**1 9 10 **F**10 14 15 16 17 19 20 21 22 32 35 38 39 41 42 43 44 47 49 51 54 56 65 67 69 71 73	23	50	123	4696	77	1040128	—	70237	26463	889
✚ △ HARTFORD HOSPITAL, (Includes Institute of Living, 400 Washington Street, Zip 06106–3392; tel. 860/545–7000), 80 Seymour Street, Zip 06102–5037, Mailing Address: P.O. Box 5037, Zip 06102–5037; tel. 860/545–5000; John J. Meehan, President and Chief Executive Officer (Total facility includes 104 beds in nursing home–type unit) **A**1 2 3 5 7 8 9 10 **F**1 3 4 7 8 10 11 14 15 16 19 20 21 22 26 30 31 32 33 34 35 36 37 38 40 41 42 43 44 45 46 47 48 49 50 51 52 53 54 55 56 57 58 59 60 61 64 65 66 67 69 70 71 72 73 74 **P**4 5 8	23	10	923	32521	603	168963	4451	359131	199720	5262
✚ SAINT FRANCIS HOSPITAL AND MEDICAL CENTER, 114 Woodland Street, Zip 06105–1299; tel. 860/714–4000; David D'Eramo, President and Chief Executive Officer **A**1 2 3 5 6 8 9 10 **F**3 4 7 8 10 11 12 13 14 15 16 17 19 20 21 22 24 25 26 28 29 30 31 32 33 34 35 37 38 40 41 42 43 44 45 46 48 49 51 52 53 54 55 56 57 58 59 60 61 63 65 66 67 68 70 71 72 73 74 **P**4 7 8 **N** Saint Francis Physician Hospital Organization, Hartford, CT; Saint Mary's Hospital, Waterbury, CT	21	10	528	25667	386	299456	3201	316056	140866	3376

Hospital, Address, Telephone, Administrator, Approval, Facility, and Physician Codes, Health Care System, Network	Classi-fication Codes		Utilization Data					Expense (thousands) of dollars		
	Control	Service	Staffed Beds	Admissions	Census	Outpatient Visits	Births	Total	Payroll	Personnel

★ American Hospital Association (AHA) membership
□ Joint Commission on Accreditation of Healthcare Organizations (JCAHO) accreditation
+ American Osteopathic Healthcare Association (AOHA) membership
○ American Osteopathic Association (AOA) accreditation
△ Commission on Accreditation of Rehabilitation Facilities (CARF) accreditation
Control codes 61, 63, 64, 71, 72 and 73 indicate hospitals listed by AOHA, but not registered by AHA. For definition of numerical codes, see page A4

MANCHESTER—Hartford County

✦ MANCHESTER MEMORIAL HOSPITAL, 71 Haynes Street, Zip 06040–4188; tel. 860/646–1222; David Stahelski, Senior Vice President Hospital Operations (Nonreporting) **A**1 9 10 **N** Eastern Connecticut Health Network, Manchester, CT — Control 23, Service 10, Staffed Beds 178

MANSFIELD CENTER—Tolland County

□ NATCHAUG HOSPITAL, 189 Storrs Road, Zip 06250–1638; tel. 860/456–1311; Stephen W. Larcen, Ph.D., Chief Executive Officer **A**1 9 10 **F**2 3 15 16 52 53 54 55 56 57 58 59 **P**1 6 — Control 23, Service 22, Staffed Beds 58, Admissions 1632, Census 39, Outpatient Visits 28284, Births 0, Total 12948, Payroll 7121, Personnel 175

MERIDEN—New Haven County

✦ VETERANS MEMORIAL MEDICAL CENTER, (Includes East Campus, 883 Paddock Avenue, Zip 06450–7094; tel. 203/238–8200), One King Place, Zip 06450–1009, Mailing Address: P.O. Box 1009, Zip 06450–1009; tel. 203/238–8200; Theodore H. Horwitz, FACHE, President **A**1 2 9 10 **F**3 7 8 12 15 16 17 18 19 21 22 24 26 28 30 31 32 33 34 35 37 40 41 42 44 46 49 52 53 54 55 56 57 58 59 60 63 65 67 68 71 72 73 **P**1 5 8 — Control 23, Service 10, Staffed Beds 103, Admissions 7245, Census 87, Outpatient Visits 109954, Births 1056, Total 92656, Payroll 46891, Personnel 1130

MIDDLETOWN—Middlesex County

□ CONNECTICUT VALLEY HOSPITAL, (Includes Whiting Forensic Division of Connecticut Valley Hospital, O'Brien Drive, Zip 06457, Mailing Address: Box 70, Zip 06457–3942; tel. 203/344–2541), Eastern Drive, Zip 06457–7023, Mailing Address: P.O. Box 351, Zip 06457–7023; Garrell S. Mullaney, Superintendent (Nonreporting) **A**1 3 5 9 10 **S** Connecticut State Department of Mental Health, Hartford, CT — Control 12, Service 22, Staffed Beds 418

✦ MIDDLESEX HOSPITAL, 28 Crescent Street, Zip 06457–3650; tel. 860/344–6000; Robert Gerard Kiely, President and Chief Executive Officer **A**1 2 3 5 9 10 **F**7 8 11 12 13 14 15 16 17 18 19 20 21 22 25 26 27 28 29 30 31 32 33 34 35 37 39 40 41 42 44 45 49 51 52 53 54 55 56 57 58 59 60 61 63 64 65 66 67 68 71 72 73 **P**3 5 — Control 23, Service 10, Staffed Beds 120, Admissions 9556, Census 103, Outpatient Visits 697661, Births 1250, Total 121294, Payroll 61963, Personnel 1269

RIVERVIEW HOSPITAL FOR CHILDREN, River Road, Zip 06457–3918, Mailing Address: P.O. Box 621, Zip 06457–0621; tel. 203/344–2700; Richard J. Wiseman, Ph.D., Superintendent (Nonreporting) **A**3 — Control 12, Service 52, Staffed Beds 55

WHITING FORENSIC DIVISION OF CONNECTICUT VALLEY HOSPITAL See Connecticut Valley Hospital

MILFORD—New Haven County

✦ MILFORD HOSPITAL, 300 Seaside Avenue, Zip 06460–4603; tel. 203/876–4000; Paul E. Moss, President **A**1 2 9 10 **F**7 8 12 14 17 19 21 22 28 30 32 34 35 36 37 39 40 42 44 46 63 65 67 68 71 73 **P**5 — Control 23, Service 10, Staffed Beds 72, Admissions 3799, Census 50, Outpatient Visits 47425, Births 450, Total 33433, Payroll 18724, Personnel 396

NEW BRITAIN—Hartford County

✦ △ HOSPITAL FOR SPECIAL CARE, (CHRONIC DISEASE AND REHAB), 2150 Corbin Avenue, Zip 06053–2263; tel. 860/827–4258; David Crandall, President and Chief Executive Officer **A**1 7 9 10 **F**12 20 24 26 34 39 41 48 49 54 65 66 67 73 **P**6 — Control 23, Service 49, Staffed Beds 199, Admissions 478, Census 174, Outpatient Visits 16270, Births —, Total 52799, Payroll 29349, Personnel 700

✦ NEW BRITAIN GENERAL HOSPITAL, 100 Grand Street, Zip 06052–2000, Mailing Address: P.O. Box 100, Zip 06050–0100; tel. 860/224–5011; Laurence A. Tanner, President and Chief Executive Officer **A**1 2 3 5 8 9 10 **F**1 2 3 4 6 7 8 10 11 12 14 15 16 17 18 19 21 22 23 24 25 26 27 29 30 31 32 33 34 35 36 37 38 39 40 41 42 43 44 45 46 48 49 51 52 53 54 55 56 57 58 59 60 61 63 65 66 67 69 71 73 74 **P**5 8 — Control 23, Service 10, Staffed Beds 264, Admissions 13395, Census 179, Outpatient Visits 267091, Births 2026, Total 153844, Payroll 86780, Personnel 2047

NEW CANAAN—Fairfield County

✦ SILVER HILL HOSPITAL, 208 Valley Road, Zip 06840–3899; tel. 203/966–3561; Richard J. Frances, M.D., President and Medical Director (Nonreporting) **A**1 9 10 — Control 23, Service 22, Staffed Beds 61

NEW HAVEN—New Haven County

□ CONNECTICUT MENTAL HEALTH CENTER, 34 Park Street, Zip 06519–1187, Mailing Address: P.O. Box 1842, Zip 06508–1842; tel. 203/789–7290; Selby Jacobs, M.D., M.P.H., Director **A**1 3 5 9 10 **F**3 12 17 18 19 20 21 22 35 39 46 52 53 55 56 58 59 65 67 71 **S** Connecticut State Department of Mental Health, Hartford, CT — Control 12, Service 22, Staffed Beds 44, Admissions 721, Census 34, Outpatient Visits 9397, Births —, Total —, Payroll —, Personnel 518

✦ HOSPITAL OF SAINT RAPHAEL, 1450 Chapel Street, Zip 06511–1450; tel. 203/789–3000; James J. Cullen, President (Total facility includes 125 beds in nursing home–type unit) **A**1 2 3 5 8 9 10 **F**3 4 7 8 10 11 12 13 14 15 16 17 18 19 20 21 22 26 27 28 29 30 31 32 34 35 37 39 40 41 42 43 44 45 46 48 49 51 52 53 54 55 56 57 58 59 60 61 63 64 65 67 68 70 71 72 73 74 **P**2 5 8 **N** Connecticut Health System, Inc., Hartford, CT — Control 21, Service 10, Staffed Beds 471, Admissions 21121, Census 344, Outpatient Visits 181598, Births 1151, Total 241759, Payroll 110528, Personnel 2641

□ YALE PSYCHIATRIC INSTITUTE, 184 Liberty Street, Zip 06520, Mailing Address: P.O. Box 208038, Zip 06520; tel. 203/785–7200; Thomas H. McGlashan, M.D., Director (Nonreporting) **A**1 3 5 9 10 — Control 23, Service 22, Staffed Beds 55

✦ YALE–NEW HAVEN HOSPITAL, 20 York Street, Zip 06504–3202; tel. 203/688–4242; Joseph A. Zaccagnino, President and Chief Executive Officer **A**1 2 3 5 8 9 10 **F**3 4 7 8 10 11 12 14 15 16 17 18 19 20 21 22 23 25 26 27 28 30 31 34 35 37 38 39 40 42 43 44 45 46 47 48 49 50 51 52 53 54 55 56 57 58 59 60 61 63 65 66 67 68 69 70 71 72 73 74 **P**4 5 7 8 — Control 23, Service 10, Staffed Beds 757, Admissions 35970, Census 525, Outpatient Visits 363614, Births 4933, Total 432785, Payroll 204431, Personnel 4885

NEW LONDON—New London County

✦ LAWRENCE AND MEMORIAL HOSPITAL, 365 Montauk Avenue, Zip 06320–4769; tel. 860/442–0711; William T. Christopher, President and Chief Executive Officer **A**1 9 10 **F**3 7 8 10 11 12 13 14 15 16 19 21 22 25 30 31 34 35 37 38 39 40 41 42 44 45 46 48 49 52 53 54 55 56 58 59 60 61 65 71 72 73 74 **P**4 5 6 — Control 23, Service 10, Staffed Beds 228, Admissions 13967, Census 174, Outpatient Visits 95839, Births 1951, Total 126866, Payroll 62646, Personnel —

Hospital, Address, Telephone, Administrator, Approval, Facility, and Physician Codes, Health Care System, Network	Classi-fication Codes		Utilization Data					Expense (thousands) of dollars		
★ American Hospital Association (AHA) membership □ Joint Commission on Accreditation of Healthcare Organizations (JCAHO) accreditation + American Osteopathic Healthcare Association (AOHA) membership ○ American Osteopathic Association (AOA) accreditation △ Commission on Accreditation of Rehabilitation Facilities (CARF) accreditation Control codes 61, 63, 64, 71, 72 and 73 indicate hospitals listed by AOHA, but not registered by AHA. For definition of numerical codes, see page A4	Control	Service	Staffed Beds	Admissions	Census	Outpatient Visits	Births	Total	Payroll	Personnel

NEW MILFORD—Litchfield County

✚ NEW MILFORD HOSPITAL, 21 Elm Street, Zip 06776–2993; tel. 860/355–2611; Richard E. Pugh, President and Chief Executive Officer (Nonreporting) **A**1 9 10 **N** Columbia Presbyterian Regional Network, New York, NY	23	10	63	—	—	—	—	—	—	—

NEWINGTON—Hartford County

□ CEDARCREST HOSPITAL, (Formerly Cedarcrest Regional Hospital), 525 Russell Road, Zip 06111–1595; tel. 860/666–4613; Andrew J. Phillips, Ed.D., Superintendent (Nonreporting) **A**1 9 10 **S** Connecticut State Department of Mental Health, Hartford, CT NEWINGTON CAMPUS See Veterans Affairs Connecticut Healthcare System–West Haven Division, West Haven	12	22	146	—	—	—	—	—	—	—

NORWALK—Fairfield County

✚ △ NORWALK HOSPITAL, 34 Maple Street, Zip 06856–5050; tel. 203/852–2000; David W. Osborne, President and Chief Executive Officer **A**1 2 3 5 7 9 10 **F**2 3 7 8 10 11 12 13 15 16 17 18 19 20 21 22 24 25 28 29 30 31 32 33 34 35 37 38 39 40 41 42 44 45 46 48 49 51 52 53 54 55 56 57 58 59 60 61 65 67 68 71 73 74 **P**5 7	23	10	279	12456	190	133476	2013	151189	78771	1630

NORWICH—New London County

✚ WILLIAM W. BACKUS HOSPITAL, 326 Washington Street, Zip 06360–2742; tel. 860/889–8331; Thomas P. Pipicelli, President and Chief Executive Officer **A**1 3 9 10 **F**7 8 10 12 14 15 16 19 21 22 25 28 29 30 31 32 33 34 35 37 38 39 40 41 42 44 45 49 52 54 56 58 59 60 65 67 68 70 71 72 73	23	10	176	9675	119	694865	1146	89110	41413	991

PORTLAND—Middlesex County

□ ELMCREST PSYCHIATRIC INSTITUTE, 25 Marlborough Street, Zip 06480–1829; tel. 860/342–0480; Anthony A. Ferrante, M.D., President and Chief Executive Officer (Nonreporting) **A**1 9 10 **S** Magellan Health Services, Atlanta, GA	32	22	92	—	—	—	—	—	—	—

PUTNAM—Windham County

✚ DAY KIMBALL HOSPITAL, 320 Pomfret Street, Zip 06260–1869, Mailing Address: P.O. Box 6001, Zip 06260–6001; tel. 860/928–6541; Charles F. Schneider, President **A**1 9 10 **F**3 7 8 12 13 15 16 17 18 19 21 22 25 26 27 28 29 30 32 33 34 35 37 39 40 41 42 44 45 46 49 52 54 55 56 57 58 59 61 63 65 66 67 68 71 72 73 74	23	10	101	4412	50	206674	541	48066	23015	535

ROCKY HILL—Hartford County

□ VETERANS HOME AND HOSPITAL, 287 West Street, Zip 06067–3501; tel. 860/529–2571; Sharon R. Wood, Administrator (Nonreporting) **A**1 10	12	48	296	—	—	—	—	—	—	—

SHARON—Litchfield County

✚ SHARON HOSPITAL, 50 Hospital Hill Road, Zip 06069–0789, Mailing Address: P.O. Box 789, Zip 06069–0789; tel. 860/364–4141; Michael R. Gallagher, Interim President and Chief Executive Officer **A**1 2 9 10 **F**7 8 14 15 16 19 21 22 29 30 33 34 35 37 39 40 41 42 44 46 49 63 65 67 70 71 72 73 **P**5 7	23	10	78	2847	37	17643	311	30757	12904	379

SOMERS—Tolland County

CONNECTICUT DEPARTMENT OF CORRECTION'S HOSPITAL, 100 Bilton Road, Zip 06071, Mailing Address: P.O. Box 100, Zip 06071–0100; tel. 860/749–8391; Edward A. Blanchette, M.D., Director (Nonreporting)	12	11	29	—	—	—	—	—	—	—

SOUTHINGTON—Hartford County

✚ BRADLEY MEMORIAL HOSPITAL AND HEALTH CENTER, 81 Meriden Avenue, Zip 06489–3297; tel. 860/276–5000; Clarence J. Silvia, President **A**1 9 10 **F**8 11 12 15 17 19 21 23 26 28 29 30 33 34 35 37 39 41 42 44 45 49 55 56 63 65 67 71 73 74	16	10	74	2420	37	60740	—	24910	12526	273

STAFFORD SPRINGS—Tolland County

□ JOHNSON MEMORIAL HOSPITAL, 201 Chestnut Hill Road, Zip 06076–0860, Mailing Address: P.O. Box 860, Zip 06076–0860; tel. 860/684–4251; Alfred A. Lerz, President and Chief Executive Officer **A**1 9 10 **F**3 7 8 12 13 14 15 16 17 18 19 21 22 24 25 26 28 29 30 31 32 33 34 35 37 39 40 41 42 44 45 46 49 51 52 53 54 55 56 57 58 59 63 65 67 68 71 73 74 **P**5	23	10	89	3874	50	62073	287	35435	18575	405

STAMFORD—Fairfield County

✚ ST. JOSEPH MEDICAL CENTER, 128 Strawberry Hill Avenue, Zip 06904–1222, Mailing Address: P.O. Box 1222, Zip 06904–1222; tel. 203/353–2000; Philip D. Cusano, President and Chief Executive Officer **A**1 3 5 9 10 **F**7 8 10 12 15 16 17 18 19 21 22 26 28 29 30 31 32 33 34 35 37 39 40 41 42 44 45 46 48 49 54 56 57 58 59 60 63 64 65 67 68 71 72 73 74 **P**6 7	23	10	134	3755	64	71837	430	51999	24045	530
✚ STAMFORD HOSPITAL, Shelburne Road and West Broad Street, Zip 06902–3696, Mailing Address: P.O. Box 9317, Zip 06904–9317; tel. 203/325–7000; Philip D. Cusano, President and Chief Executive Officer **A**1 2 3 5 8 9 10 **F**1 3 6 7 8 10 12 14 15 16 17 19 20 21 22 24 25 26 27 28 29 30 31 32 33 34 35 37 38 39 40 41 42 44 45 46 48 49 51 52 53 54 55 56 57 58 59 60 61 63 64 65 67 69 70 71 72 73 74 **P**5 7 8 **N** Westchester Health Services Network, Mt Kisco, NY	23	10	241	11176	157	137470	2157	112320	54644	1006

TORRINGTON—Litchfield County

□ CHARLOTTE HUNGERFORD HOSPITAL, 540 Litchfield Street, Zip 06790, Mailing Address: P.O. Box 988, Zip 06790–0988; tel. 860/496–6666; Rosanne U. Griswold, Chief Executive Officer **A**1 2 9 10 **F**7 8 11 12 13 14 15 16 17 18 19 20 21 22 25 28 29 30 31 32 33 34 35 37 39 40 41 42 44 45 46 49 52 53 54 56 58 59 60 63 65 66 67 70 71 72 73 74 **P**6 8	23	10	85	5394	74	181127	546	61283	29735	716

VERNON ROCKVILLE—Hartford County

✚ ROCKVILLE GENERAL HOSPITAL, 31 Union Street, Zip 06066–3160; tel. 860/872–0501; David Stahelski, Senior Vice President Hospital Operations (Nonreporting) **A**1 9 10 **N** Eastern Connecticut Health Network, Manchester, CT	23	10	95	—	—	—	—	—	—	—

Hospital, Address, Telephone, Administrator, Approval, Facility, and Physician Codes, Health Care System, Network	Classi-fication Codes		Utilization Data					Expense (thousands) of dollars		
	Control	Service	Staffed Beds	Admissions	Census	Outpatient Visits	Births	Total	Payroll	Personnel

★ American Hospital Association (AHA) membership
□ Joint Commission on Accreditation of Healthcare Organizations (JCAHO) accreditation
+ American Osteopathic Healthcare Association (AOHA) membership
○ American Osteopathic Association (AOA) accreditation
△ Commission on Accreditation of Rehabilitation Facilities (CARF) accreditation
   Control codes 61, 63, 64, 71, 72 and 73 indicate hospitals listed by AOHA, but not registered by AHA. For definition of numerical codes, see page A4

WALLINGFORD—New Haven County

☒ △ GAYLORD HOSPITAL, Gaylord Farm Road, Zip 06492, Mailing Address: P.O. Box 400, Zip 06492; tel. 203/284–2800; Paul H. Johnson, President and Chief Executive Officer **A**1 5 7 9 10 **F**12 14 16 25 26 28 34 41 45 46 48 49 54 65 66 67 71 73 **P**6 **N** Connecticut Health System, Inc., Hartford, CT	23	46	88	1112	76	48947	—	31907	18488	545
☒ MASONIC GERIATRIC HEALTHCARE CENTER, 22 Masonic Avenue, Zip 06492–3048, Mailing Address: P.O. Box 70, Zip 06492–7002; tel. 203/284–3900; Barry M. Spero, President (Total facility includes 468 beds in nursing home–type unit) **A**1 10 **F**1 8 12 15 16 17 20 26 27 28 30 32 33 34 39 41 42 49 51 52 54 57 58 62 64 65 67 71 73 **P**4	23	10	503	1051	471	12129	0	39117	21176	573

WATERBURY—New Haven County

☒ ST. MARY'S HOSPITAL, 56 Franklin Street, Zip 06706–1200; tel. 203/574–6000; Sister Marguerite Waite, President and Chief Executive Officer **A**1 2 3 5 9 10 **F**3 5 7 8 10 11 12 13 14 15 16 17 18 19 20 21 22 25 26 28 29 30 31 33 34 35 36 37 39 40 41 42 44 45 46 49 51 52 54 55 56 58 59 60 63 65 67 70 71 72 73 **P**7 8 **N** Saint Mary's Hospital, Waterbury, CT	21	10	206	9809	123	164511	1227	112951	56047	1337
☒ WATERBURY HOSPITAL, 64 Robbins Street, Zip 06721, Mailing Address: P.O. Box 1589, Zip 06721–1589; tel. 203/573–6000; John H. Tobin, President **A**1 2 3 5 9 10 **F**3 5 7 8 10 11 12 14 15 16 17 18 19 20 21 22 24 27 28 29 30 31 32 33 34 35 37 38 39 40 41 42 44 45 46 49 51 52 53 54 55 56 57 58 59 60 65 66 67 69 70 71 72 73 74 **P**1 7	23	10	246	12264	175	140152	1412	128312	63615	1343

WEST HARTFORD—Hartford County

★ HEBREW HOME AND HOSPITAL (COMPREHENSIVE GERIATRIC), 1 Abrahms Boulevard, Zip 06117–1525; tel. 860/523–3800; Irving Kronenberg, President and Executive Director (Total facility includes 293 beds in nursing home–type unit) (Nonreporting) **A**10	23	49	334	—	—	—	—	—	—	—

WEST HAVEN—New Haven County

☒ VETERANS AFFAIRS CONNECTICUT HEALTHCARE SYSTEM–WEST HAVEN DIVISION, (Includes Newington Campus, 555 Willard Avenue, Newington, Zip 06111–2600; tel. 860/666–6951; West Haven Division, 950 Campbell Avenue, Zip 06516–2700; tel. 203/932–5711), 950 Campbell Avenue, Zip 06516; tel. 203/932–5711; Vincent Ng, Director (Total facility includes 34 beds in nursing home–type unit) **A**1 2 3 5 8 9 **F**1 2 3 4 8 10 11 12 15 16 17 19 20 21 22 23 25 26 27 29 30 31 32 33 34 35 37 39 42 43 44 45 46 48 49 50 51 52 54 55 56 57 58 59 60 61 63 64 65 67 69 71 72 73 74 **P**6 **S** Department of Veterans Affairs, Washington, DC	45	10	208	5336	16	359170	—	178145	112917	1638

WESTPORT—Fairfield County

☒ HALL–BROOKE HOSPITAL, A DIVISION OF HALL–BROOKE FOUNDATION, 47 Long Lots Road, Zip 06880–3800; tel. 203/227–1251; Seth Berman, Executive Director **A**1 9 10 **F**1 2 3 14 15 16 26 34 52 53 54 56 57 58 59 **P**1	23	22	52	838	40	21904	—	10878	6315	183

WILLIMANTIC—Windham County

□ WINDHAM COMMUNITY MEMORIAL HOSPITAL, 112 Mansfield Avenue, Zip 06226–2082; tel. 860/456–9116; Duane A. Carlberg, President and Chief Executive Officer **A**1 9 10 **F**3 7 8 12 13 16 17 18 19 21 22 25 28 30 31 33 34 35 36 37 39 40 41 42 44 45 49 53 54 56 58 59 63 65 67 68 71 73 **P**5 8	23	10	94	4244	51	96126	497	47004	—	405

DELAWARE

Resident population 732 (in thousands)
Resident population in metro areas 82.7%
Birth rate per 1,000 population 14.7
65 years and over 12.8%
Percent of persons without health insurance 13.4%

Hospital, Address, Telephone, Administrator, Approval, Facility, and Physician Codes, Health Care System, Network	Classi-fication Codes		Utilization Data					Expense (thousands) of dollars		
★ American Hospital Association (AHA) membership □ Joint Commission on Accreditation of Healthcare Organizations (JCAHO) accreditation + American Osteopathic Healthcare Association (AOHA) membership ○ American Osteopathic Association (AOA) accreditation △ Commission on Accreditation of Rehabilitation Facilities (CARF) accreditation Control codes 61, 63, 64, 71, 72 and 73 indicate hospitals listed by AOHA, but not registered by AHA. For definition of numerical codes, see page A4	Control	Service	Staffed Beds	Admissions	Census	Outpatient Visits	Births	Total	Payroll	Personnel

DOVER—Kent County

☒ BAYHEALTH MEDICAL CENTER, (Formerly Kent General Hospital), 640 South State Street, Zip 19901–3597; tel. 302/674–4700; Dennis E. Klima, President and Chief Executive Officer **A**1 2 9 10 **F**1 3 7 8 11 12 13 17 19 21 22 23 24 25 27 28 29 30 31 32 34 35 37 38 39 40 41 42 44 45 46 48 49 51 52 53 54 55 56 57 59 60 61 63 64 65 66 67 70 71 72 73 74 **P**6 8 **S** Bayhealth Medical Center, Dover, DE

	23	10	324	15092	214	262500	1596	121105	57124	1665

☒ U. S. AIR FORCE HOSPITAL DOVER, 260 Chad Street, Zip 19902–7260; tel. 302/677–2525; Major David M. Allen, MSC, Administrator (Nonreporting) **A**1 **S** Department of the Air Force, Bowling AFB, DC

| | 41 | 10 | 16 | — | — | — | — | — | — | — |

LEWES—Sussex County

☒ BEEBE MEDICAL CENTER, 424 Savannah Road, Zip 19958–0226; tel. 302/645–3300; Jeffrey M. Fried, FACHE, President and Chief Executive Officer (Total facility includes 89 beds in nursing home–type unit) **A**1 2 6 9 10 **F**1 3 4 7 8 12 14 15 16 17 19 21 22 23 25 27 30 31 32 34 35 37 39 40 41 42 44 49 51 52 53 54 55 56 57 58 59 60 63 64 65 67 71 72 73 74 **P**6 8

| | 23 | 10 | 214 | 6995 | 161 | 131415 | 613 | 62710 | 27675 | 881 |

MILFORD—Sussex County

☒ △ BAYHEALTH MEDICAL CENTER, MILFORD MEMORIAL CAMPUS, 21 West Clarke Avenue, Zip 19963–1840, Mailing Address: P.O. Box 199, Zip 19963–0199; tel. 302/424–5613; Joseph K. Whiting, Executive Vice President and Chief Operating Officer (Nonreporting) **A**1 2 7 9 10 **S** Bayhealth Medical Center, Dover, DE

| | 23 | 10 | 130 | — | — | — | — | — | — | — |

NEW CASTLE—New Castle County

□ DELAWARE PSYCHIATRIC CENTER, Dupont Highway, Zip 19720–1199; tel. 302/577–4381; Jiro R. Shimono, Director (Total facility includes 59 beds in nursing home–type unit) **A**1 3 9 10 **F**12 14 17 18 19 20 21 22 26 29 35 36 39 41 45 46 49 50 52 56 57 58 63 65 67 71 73 **P**6

| | 12 | 22 | 334 | 856 | 308 | — | — | 32837 | 18649 | — |

□ MEADOW WOOD BEHAVIORAL HEALTH SYSTEM, 575 South Dupont Highway, Zip 19720–4600; tel. 302/328–3330; Joseph Pyle, Administrator (Nonreporting) **A**1 9 10 **S** Hospital Group of America, Wayne, PA

| | 33 | 52 | 50 | — | — | — | — | — | — | — |

NEWARK—New Castle County

☒ CHRISTIANA HOSPITAL, (Formerly Medical Center of Delaware), 4755 Ogletown–Stanton Road, Zip 19718; tel. 302/733–1000; Charles M. Smith, M.D., President and Chief Executive Officer **A**1 3 5 8 9 10 **F**7 11 15 16 17 19 20 21 22 23 24 25 29 30 31 32 34 37 38 39 40 41 42 44 45 46 47 48 49 51 52 54 56 58 59 61 63 64 65 67 68 69 70 71 73 74 **P**8 **S** Christiana Care Corporation, Wilmington, DE **N** Medical Center of Delaware Foundation, Wilmington, DE

| | 23 | 10 | 737 | 37223 | 588 | 476203 | 6204 | 496228 | 228710 | 5607 |

☒ ROCKFORD CENTER, 100 Rockford Drive, Zip 19713–2121; tel. 302/996–5480; Walter J. Yokobosky, Jr., Chief Executive Officer (Nonreporting) **A**1 9 10 **S** Columbia/HCA Healthcare Corporation, Nashville, TN

| | 33 | 22 | 70 | — | — | — | — | — | — | — |

SEAFORD—Sussex County

☒ NANTICOKE MEMORIAL HOSPITAL, 801 Middleford Road, Zip 19973–3698; tel. 302/629–6611; Edward H. Hancock, President (Total facility includes 90 beds in nursing home–type unit) **A**1 9 10 **F**3 4 7 8 10 12 14 15 16 17 19 22 24 28 30 32 35 37 39 40 41 42 44 45 46 49 52 56 57 58 59 64 65 66 67 71 73 74 **P**1 5 6 **N** Nanticoke Health Services, Seaford, DE

| | 23 | 10 | 201 | 5612 | 147 | 45765 | 769 | 47432 | 20597 | 697 |

WILMINGTON—New Castle County

☒ △ ALFRED I.DUPONT HOSPITAL FOR CHILDREN, (Formerly duPont Hospital for Children), 1600 Rockland Road, Zip 19803–3616, Mailing Address: Box 269, Zip 19899–0269; tel. 302/651–4000; Thomas P. Ferry, Administrator and Chief Executive (Nonreporting) **A**1 3 5 7 9 10 **N** Jefferson Health System, Radnor, PA

| | 23 | 52 | 128 | — | — | — | — | — | — | — |

☒ ST. FRANCIS HOSPITAL, Seventh and Clayton Streets, Zip 19805–0500, Mailing Address: P.O. Box 2500, Zip 19805–0500; tel. 302/421–4100; Daniel J. Sinnott, President and Chief Executive Officer **A**1 2 3 5 9 10 **F**2 4 5 7 8 10 12 13 14 15 16 17 18 19 20 21 22 23 25 26 28 29 30 31 32 33 34 35 37 38 39 40 41 42 44 45 46 47 48 49 51 52 54 55 56 57 58 59 63 64 65 66 67 68 71 72 73 74 **P**6 **S** Catholic Health Initiatives, Denver, CO

| | 21 | 10 | 283 | 10415 | 164 | 214838 | 1117 | 104184 | 47590 | 1271 |

☒ VETERANS AFFAIRS MEDICAL CENTER, 1601 Kirkwood Highway, Zip 19805–4989; tel. 302/633–5201; Dexter D. Dix, Director (Total facility includes 60 beds in nursing home–type unit) **A**1 2 3 5 8 9 **F**2 3 4 5 6 8 10 12 14 15 16 17 19 20 21 22 23 24 25 26 28 29 30 31 32 33 34 35 37 39 41 42 43 44 46 49 51 52 54 56 57 58 59 60 63 64 65 67 69 71 73 74 **P**6 **S** Department of Veterans Affairs, Washington, DC

| | 45 | 10 | 160 | 1891 | 126 | 113887 | — | 48257 | 27190 | 596 |

★ △ WILMINGTON HOSPITAL, 501 West 14th Street, Zip 19801, Mailing Address: Box 1668, Zip 19899; tel. 302/428–2570; Charles M. Smith, M.D., President and Chief Executive Officer (Nonreporting) **A**2 7 **S** Christiana Care Corporation, Wilmington, DE

| | 23 | 10 | 291 | — | — | — | — | — | — | — |

DISTRICT OF COLUMBIA

Resident population 529 (in thousands)
Resident population in metro areas 100%
Birth rate per 1,000 population 17.4
65 years and over 13.9%
Percent of persons without health insurance 14.8%

Hospital, Address, Telephone, Administrator, Approval, Facility, and Physician Codes, Health Care System, Network

- ★ American Hospital Association (AHA) membership
- □ Joint Commission on Accreditation of Healthcare Organizations (JCAHO) accreditation
- \+ American Osteopathic Healthcare Association (AOHA) membership
- ○ American Osteopathic Association (AOA) accreditation
- △ Commission on Accreditation of Rehabilitation Facilities (CARF) accreditation

Control codes 61, 63, 64, 71, 72 and 73 indicate hospitals listed by AOHA, but not registered by AHA. For definition of numerical codes, see page A4

Hospital, Address, Telephone, Administrator, Approval, Facility, and Physician Codes, Health Care System, Network	Classification Codes		Utilization Data					Expense (thousands) of dollars		
	Control	Service	Staffed Beds	Admissions	Census	Outpatient Visits	Births	Total	Payroll	Personnel
WASHINGTON—District of Columbia County										
[★] CHILDREN'S NATIONAL MEDICAL CENTER, 111 Michigan Avenue N.W., Zip 20010–2970; tel. 202/884–5000; Edwin K. Zechman, Jr., President and Chief Executive Officer **A**1 3 5 8 9 10 **F**4 5 10 12 14 15 16 17 19 20 21 22 25 27 28 29 30 31 32 33 34 35 38 39 41 42 43 44 45 46 47 49 51 52 53 54 55 56 58 59 63 65 67 68 69 70 71 73 **P**6	23	50	157	9632	169	195664	—	177961	83025	2074
[★] COLUMBIA HOSPITAL FOR WOMEN MEDICAL CENTER, 2425 L. Street N.W., Zip 20037–1433; tel. 202/293–6500; Gerald Beaulieu, Acting President and Chief Executive Officer (Nonreporting) **A**1 9 10	23	44	75	—	—	—	—	—	—	—
[★] DISTRICT OF COLUMBIA GENERAL HOSPITAL, 19th Street and Massachusetts Avenue S.E., Zip 20003; tel. 202/675–5000; John A. Fairman, Executive Director (Nonreporting) **A**1 3 5 9 10	14	10	250	—	—	—	—	—	—	—
[★] GEORGE WASHINGTON UNIVERSITY HOSPITAL, 901 23rd Street N.W., Zip 20037–2377; tel. 202/994–1000; Phillip S. Schaengold, JD, Chief Executive Officer (Nonreporting) **A**1 2 3 5 8 9 10 **S** Universal Health Services, Inc., King of Prussia, PA	33	10	295	—	—	—	—	—	—	—
[★] GEORGETOWN UNIVERSITY HOSPITAL, 3800 Reservoir Road N.W., Zip 20007–2197; tel. 202/784–3000; Sharon Flynn Hollander, Chief Executive Officer **A**1 2 3 5 8 9 10 **F**3 4 5 7 8 10 11 12 13 14 17 18 19 21 22 23 25 26 28 29 30 31 32 33 34 35 37 38 39 40 41 42 43 44 45 46 47 49 51 52 53 54 55 56 57 58 59 60 61 63 65 66 67 68 69 70 71 72 73 74 **P**6	23	10	335	14603	264	175322	1298	217210	90631	2135
[★] △ GREATER SOUTHEAST COMMUNITY HOSPITAL, 1310 Southern Avenue S.E., Zip 20032–4699; tel. 202/574–6000; Robert C. Winfrey, President and Chief Operating Officer (Total facility includes 24 beds in nursing home–type unit) (Nonreporting) **A**1 2 3 5 7 9 10 **S** Greater Southeast Healthcare System, Washington, DC	23	10	305	—	—	—	—	—	—	—
□ HADLEY MEMORIAL HOSPITAL, 4601 Martin Luther King Jr. Avenue S.W., Zip 20032–1199; tel. 202/574–5700; Ana Raley, Administrator (Total facility includes 77 beds in nursing home–type unit) **A**1 9 10 **F**8 15 19 21 22 25 28 30 37 39 41 44 49 64 65 71 73 **P**5 7	33	10	148	2044	111	13649	0	—	10455	379
[★] △ HOSPITAL FOR SICK CHILDREN, 1731 Bunker Hill Road N.E., Zip 20017–3096; tel. 202/832–4400; Thomas W. Chapman, President and Chief Executive Officer (Nonreporting) **A**1 7 9	23	56	114	—	—	—	—	—	—	—
[★] HOWARD UNIVERSITY HOSPITAL, 2041 Georgia Avenue N.W., Zip 20060–0002; tel. 202/865–6100; Sherman P. McCoy, Executive Director and Chief Executive Officer **A**1 2 3 5 8 9 10 **F**7 8 10 11 12 14 15 16 17 19 20 21 22 25 28 29 30 31 34 35 37 38 40 41 42 44 45 46 49 50 52 53 54 56 57 58 60 61 63 64 65 66 69 70 71 73 74 **P**8	23	10	340	10622	207	108174	668	166438	85228	—
[★] △ NATIONAL REHABILITATION HOSPITAL, 102 Irving Street N.W., Zip 20010–2949; tel. 202/877–1000; Edward A. Eckenhoff, President and Chief Executive Officer **A**1 3 5 7 9 10 **F**3 4 5 8 10 12 13 14 16 17 19 20 21 22 25 26 27 28 29 30 31 32 33 34 35 36 39 41 42 43 44 45 46 48 49 50 51 53 54 55 56 57 58 59 60 61 64 65 66 67 70 71 72 73 74 **P**3 6 8 **S** Medlantic Healthcare Group, Washington, DC **N** Medlantic Healthcare Group, Washington, DC	23	46	160	1746	109	82458	—	53512	28609	682
[★] PROVIDENCE HOSPITAL, 1150 Varnum Street N.E., Zip 20017–2180; tel. 202/269–7000; Sister Carol Keehan, President (Total facility includes 240 beds in nursing home–type unit) **A**1 2 3 5 9 10 **F**3 7 8 10 11 14 15 16 17 18 19 22 24 25 26 27 28 29 30 31 33 34 35 36 37 38 39 40 41 42 44 45 49 51 52 54 55 56 57 58 59 61 64 65 67 71 72 73 74 **S** Daughters of Charity National Health System, Saint Louis, MO	21	10	556	12811	461	68330	1517	122809	63516	1723
□ PSYCHIATRIC INSTITUTE OF WASHINGTON, 4228 Wisconsin Avenue N.W., Zip 20016–2138; tel. 202/965–8550; Kenneth F. Courage, Jr., Chief Executive Officer (Nonreporting) **A**1 5 9 10	33	22	99	—	—	—	—	—	—	—
[★] SIBLEY MEMORIAL HOSPITAL, 5255 Loughboro Road N.W., Zip 20016–2695; tel. 202/537–4000; Robert L. Sloan, Chief Executive Officer (Total facility includes 17 beds in nursing home–type unit) **A**1 2 3 5 9 10 **F**7 8 10 11 12 16 17 19 21 22 26 30 31 34 35 37 39 40 41 44 45 46 49 52 53 55 56 57 58 60 61 64 65 66 67 71 73 74 **P**8	23	10	245	11231	170	80040	1140	98959	47450	1107
[★] ST. ELIZABETHS HOSPITAL, 2700 Martin Luther King Jr. Avenue S.E., Zip 20032–2698; tel. 202/373–7166; Sam Fantasia, Director, Division of Administration and Financial Services (Nonreporting) **A**1 10	14	22	817	—	—	—	—	—	—	—
[★] VETERANS AFFAIRS MEDICAL CENTER, 50 Irving Street N.W., Zip 20422–0002; tel. 202/745–8100; Sanford M. Garfunkel, Medical Center Director (Total facility includes 120 beds in nursing home–type unit) **A**1 2 3 5 8 9 **F**1 3 4 6 8 10 11 12 14 15 16 17 18 19 20 21 22 23 26 28 29 30 31 32 33 35 37 39 41 42 43 44 45 46 48 49 51 52 54 55 56 57 58 59 60 64 65 67 71 73 74 **S** Department of Veterans Affairs, Washington, DC	45	10	197	6649	157	322457	—	178103	110494	1799
[★] WALTER REED ARMY MEDICAL CENTER, (Formerly Walter Reed Health Care System), 6825 16th Street N.W., Zip 20307–5001; tel. 202/782–6393; Colonel Robert James Heckert, Jr., MSC, Chief of Staff (Nonreporting) **A**1 2 3 5 **S** Department of the Army, Office of the Surgeon General, Falls Church, VA	42	10	474	—	—	—	—	—	—	—

Hospital, Address, Telephone, Administrator, Approval, Facility, and Physician Codes, Health Care System, Network	Classi-fication Codes		Utilization Data					Expense (thousands) of dollars		
★ American Hospital Association (AHA) membership □ Joint Commission on Accreditation of Healthcare Organizations (JCAHO) accreditation + American Osteopathic Healthcare Association (AOHA) membership ○ American Osteopathic Association (AOA) accreditation △ Commission on Accreditation of Rehabilitation Facilities (CARF) accreditation Control codes 61, 63, 64, 71, 72 and 73 indicate hospitals listed by AOHA, but not registered by AHA. For definition of numerical codes, see page A4	Control	Service	Staffed Beds	Admissions	Census	Outpatient Visits	Births	Total	Payroll	Personnel
✶ WASHINGTON HOSPITAL CENTER, 110 Irving Street N.W., Zip 20010–2975; tel. 202/877–7000; Kenneth A. Samet, President **A**1 2 3 5 8 9 10 **F**3 4 5 7 8 9 10 11 12 15 16 17 19 20 21 22 26 27 28 29 30 31 32 33 35 37 38 39 40 41 42 43 44 45 46 48 49 51 52 54 56 57 58 60 61 63 64 65 66 67 68 69 70 71 73 **P**1 6 **S** Medlantic Healthcare Group, Washington, DC **N** Medlantic Healthcare Group, Washington, DC	23	10	773	33090	561	248203	2963	455744	216100	4332

FLORIDA

Resident population 14,654 (in thousands)
Resident population in metro areas 93.0%
Birth rate per 1,000 population 13.7
65 years and over 18.5%
Percent of persons without health insurance 18.9%

Hospital, Address, Telephone, Administrator, Approval, Facility, and Physician Codes, Health Care System, Network	Control	Service	Staffed Beds	Admissions	Census	Outpatient Visits	Births	Total	Payroll	Personnel

★ American Hospital Association (AHA) membership
□ Joint Commission on Accreditation of Healthcare Organizations (JCAHO) accreditation
+ American Osteopathic Healthcare Association (AOHA) membership
○ American Osteopathic Association (AOA) accreditation
△ Commission on Accreditation of Rehabilitation Facilities (CARF) accreditation
Control codes 61, 63, 64, 71, 72 and 73 indicate hospitals listed by AOHA, but not registered by AHA. For definition of numerical codes, see page A4

ALTAMONTE SPRINGS—Seminole County
FLORIDA HOSPITAL–ALTAMONTE See Florida Hospital, Orlando

APALACHICOLA—Franklin County
GEORGE E. WEEMS MEMORIAL HOSPITAL, (Formerly Emerald Coast Hospital), 135 Avenue G., Zip 32320, Mailing Address: P.O. Box 580, Zip 32329–0580; tel. 850/653–8853; David Paris, Administrator (Nonreporting) **A**9 10 — *Control 33, Service 10, Staffed Beds 29*

APOPKA—Orange County
FLORIDA HOSPITAL–APOPKA See Florida Hospital, Orlando

ARCADIA—De Soto County
✦ DESOTO MEMORIAL HOSPITAL, 900 North Robert Avenue, Zip 34266–8765, Mailing Address: P.O. Box 2180, Zip 34265–2180; tel. 941/494–3535; Gary M. Moore, President and Chief Executive Officer (Nonreporting) **A**1 9 10 **S** Quorum Health Group/Quorum Health Resources, Inc., Brentwood, TN — *Control 23, Service 10, Staffed Beds 62*

G. PIERCE WOOD MEMORIAL HOSPITAL, 5847 S.E. Highway 31, Zip 34266–9627; tel. 941/494–3323; Myers R. Kurtz, Administrator (Nonreporting) **A**5 10 — *Control 12, Service 22, Staffed Beds 450*

ATLANTIS—Palm Beach County
✦ J. F. K. MEDICAL CENTER, (Formerly Columbia JFK Medical Center), 5301 South Congress Avenue, Zip 33462–1197; tel. 561/965–7300; Phillip D. Robinson, Chief Executive Officer (Total facility includes 20 beds in nursing home–type unit) (Nonreporting) **A**1 2 9 10 **S** Columbia/HCA Healthcare Corporation, Nashville, TN **N** Lake Okeechobee Rural Health Network, Belle Glade, FL — *Control 33, Service 10, Staffed Beds 363*

AVON PARK—Highlands County
FLORIDA CENTER FOR ADDICTIONS AND DUAL DISORDERS, 100 West College Drive, Zip 33825–9341; tel. 941/452–3858; Arthur J. Cox, Sr., Director (Nonreporting) — *Control 23, Service 82, Staffed Beds 50*

BARTOW—Polk County
✦ BARTOW MEMORIAL HOSPITAL, (Formerly Columbia Bartow Memorial Hospital), 1239 East Main Street, Zip 33830–5005, Mailing Address: Box 1050, Zip 33830–1050; tel. 941/533–8111; Thomas C. Mathews, Administrator **A**1 9 10 **F**1 3 4 7 8 10 12 16 17 19 20 21 22 23 24 26 27 28 29 30 31 32 33 34 35 36 39 40 41 42 43 44 45 46 49 50 51 53 54 55 56 57 58 59 60 61 63 65 69 70 71 72 73 **P**5 **S** Columbia/HCA Healthcare Corporation, Nashville, TN **N** Columbia/HCA West Florida Division, Tampa, FL — *Control 32, Service 10, Staffed Beds 56, Admissions 2620, Census 23, Outpatient Visits 33815, Births 489, Total 15753, Payroll 5924, Personnel 234*

BAY PINES—Pinellas County
✦ △ VETERANS AFFAIRS MEDICAL CENTER, Bay Pines & 100 Way, Zip 33744, Mailing Address: P.O. Box 5005, Zip 33744–5005; tel. 813/398–6661; Thomas H. Weaver, FACHE, Director (Total facility includes 218 beds in nursing home–type unit) **A**1 2 3 5 7 9 **F**2 3 8 11 14 15 16 17 19 20 21 22 25 26 30 31 32 33 34 35 37 39 41 42 44 45 46 48 49 51 52 54 55 56 57 58 59 63 64 65 67 71 73 74 **P**6 **S** Department of Veterans Affairs, Washington, DC — *Control 45, Service 10, Staffed Beds 628, Admissions 9114, Census 505, Outpatient Visits 316178, Personnel 2212*

BELLE GLADE—Palm Beach County
✦ GLADES GENERAL HOSPITAL, 1201 South Main Street, Zip 33430–4911; tel. 561/996–6571; Gene Faile, Chief Executive Officer **A**1 9 10 **F**7 8 12 15 17 19 21 22 24 26 28 29 30 31 33 34 35 37 40 44 45 48 49 63 65 68 71 73 74 **S** Quorum Health Group/Quorum Health Resources, Inc., Brentwood, TN **N** Lake Okeechobee Rural Health Network, Belle Glade, FL — *Control 16, Service 10, Staffed Beds 47, Admissions 2333, Census 22, Outpatient Visits 22731, Births 408, Total 15284, Payroll 6576*

BLOUNTSTOWN—Calhoun County
★ CALHOUN–LIBERTY HOSPITAL, 424 Burns Avenue, Zip 32424–1097; tel. 850/674–5411; Josh Plummer, Administrator (Nonreporting) **A**9 10 **N** Panhandle Area Health Network, Marianna, FL — *Control 23, Service 10, Staffed Beds 30*

BOCA RATON—Palm Beach County
✦ BOCA RATON COMMUNITY HOSPITAL, 800 Meadows Road, Zip 33486–2368; tel. 561/393–4002; Randolph J. Pierce, President and Chief Executive Officer **A**1 2 9 10 **F**7 8 10 11 14 15 16 17 18 19 21 22 24 28 29 30 32 35 37 39 40 41 42 44 45 46 49 60 61 63 65 66 67 71 72 73 74 **N** Florida Health Choice, Del Ray Beach, FL — *Control 23, Service 10, Staffed Beds 345, Admissions 16384, Census 224, Outpatient Visits 162159, Births 1422, Total 140329, Payroll 55739, Personnel 1609*

✦ WEST BOCA MEDICAL CENTER, 21644 State Road 7, Zip 33428–1899; tel. 561/488–8000; Richard Gold, Chief Executive Officer (Nonreporting) **A**1 9 10 **S** TENET Healthcare Corporation, Santa Barbara, CA **N** Tenet South Florida Health System Network, Fort Lauderdale, FL — *Control 33, Service 10, Staffed Beds 150*

BONIFAY—Holmes County
✦ DOCTORS MEMORIAL HOSPITAL, 401 East Byrd Avenue, Zip 32425–3007, Mailing Address: P.O. Box 188, Zip 32425–0188; tel. 850/547–1120; Dale Larson, Chief Executive Officer (Nonreporting) **A**1 9 10 **S** Community Health Systems, Inc., Brentwood, TN **N** Panhandle Area Health Network, Marianna, FL — *Control 33, Service 10, Staffed Beds 34*

BOYNTON BEACH—Palm Beach County
✦ BETHESDA MEMORIAL HOSPITAL, 2815 South Seacrest Boulevard, Zip 33435–7995; tel. 561/737–7733; Robert B. Hill, President (Nonreporting) **A**1 2 9 10 **N** Florida Health Choice, Del Ray Beach, FL — *Control 23, Service 10, Staffed Beds 362*

Hospital, Address, Telephone, Administrator, Approval, Facility, and Physician Codes, Health Care System, Network	Classi-fication Codes		Utilization Data					Expense (thousands) of dollars		
★ American Hospital Association (AHA) membership □ Joint Commission on Accreditation of Healthcare Organizations (JCAHO) accreditation + American Osteopathic Healthcare Association (AOHA) membership ○ American Osteopathic Association (AOA) accreditation △ Commission on Accreditation of Rehabilitation Facilities (CARF) accreditation Control codes 61, 63, 64, 71, 72 and 73 indicate hospitals listed by AOHA, but not registered by AHA. For definition of numerical codes, see page A4	Control	Service	Staffed Beds	Admissions	Census	Outpatient Visits	Births	Total	Payroll	Personnel

BRADENTON—Manatee County

✠ △ BLAKE MEDICAL CENTER, (Formerly Columbia Blake Medical Center), 2020 59th Street West, Zip 34209–4669, Mailing Address: P.O. Box 25004, Zip 34206–5004; tel. 941/792–6611; Lindell W. Orr, Chief Executive Officer (Total facility includes 28 beds in nursing home–type unit) **A**1 2 7 9 10 **F**4 7 10 11 12 13 14 15 16 17 19 21 22 23 24 25 26 28 30 32 33 34 35 37 39 40 41 42 43 44 45 46 48 49 60 64 65 67 71 72 73 74 **S** Columbia/HCA Healthcare Corporation, Nashville, TN **N** Columbia/HCA West Florida Division, Tampa, FL; The Health Advantage Network, Winter Park, FL	33	10	284	12237	182	108202	433	71747	33602	803
□ MANATEE MEMORIAL HOSPITAL, 206 Second Street East, Zip 34208–1000; tel. 941/746–5111; Michael Marquez, Chief Executive Officer (Total facility includes 10 beds in nursing home–type unit) **A**1 2 9 10 **F**2 3 4 7 8 10 11 12 14 15 16 17 19 21 22 24 25 28 30 32 34 37 38 40 41 42 43 44 45 46 52 53 58 59 64 65 67 71 72 73 74 **P**8 **S** Universal Health Services, Inc., King of Prussia, PA **N** BayCare Health Network, Inc., Clearwater, FL	33	10	512	14437	193	93302	1820	95659	38821	—

BRANDON—Hillsborough County

✠ BRANDON REGIONAL MEDICAL CENTER, (Formerly Columbia Brandon Regional Medical Center), 119 Oakfield Drive, Zip 33511–5799; tel. 813/681–5551; Michael M. Fencel, Chief Executive Officer **A**1 9 10 **F**7 8 10 11 12 14 16 19 21 22 27 28 30 32 35 37 38 40 44 45 47 49 59 63 64 65 67 71 73 **P**5 **S** Columbia/HCA Healthcare Corporation, Nashville, TN **N** Columbia/HCA West Florida Division, Tampa, FL; The Health Advantage Network, Winter Park, FL	33	10	225	14288	159	94034	2955	—	—	—

BROOKSVILLE—Hernando County

✠ BROOKSVILLE REGIONAL HOSPITAL, 55 Ponce De Leon Boulevard, Zip 34601–0037, Mailing Address: P.O. Box 37, Zip 34605–0037; tel. 352/796–5111; Robert Foreman, Associate Administrator **A**1 9 10 **F**8 10 12 17 19 21 22 25 26 28 30 34 35 37 41 42 44 45 46 49 65 71 72 73 **S** Quorum Health Group/Quorum Health Resources, Inc., Brentwood, TN **N** BayCare Health Network, Inc., Clearwater, FL	23	10	91	3733	58	47324	0	28876	8551	272
□ GREENBRIER HOSPITAL, 7007 Grove Road, Zip 34609–8610; tel. 352/596–4306; James E. O'Shea, Administrator **A**1 9 10 **F**2 3 12 14 15 16 17 19 20 21 27 32 35 48 50 52 54 55 56 57 58 59 63 65 71 **P**8	33	22	36	1265	28	0	0	—	1993	96

BUNNELL—Flagler County

★ MEMORIAL HOSPITAL–FLAGLER, Moody Boulevard, Zip 32110, Mailing Address: HCR1, Box 2, Zip 32110; tel. 904/437–2211; Clark P. Christianson, Senior Vice President and Administrator (Total facility includes 8 beds in nursing home–type unit) **A**9 10 **F**8 12 14 15 16 17 19 20 21 22 25 26 28 29 30 31 32 33 34 37 39 41 42 44 45 46 49 64 65 66 67 71 73 74 **P**1 2 6 8 **S** Memorial Health Systems, Ormond Beach, FL	23	10	81	2017	26	—	—	17500	7910	—

CAPE CORAL—Lee County

□ CAPE CORAL HOSPITAL, 636 Del Prado Boulevard, Zip 33990–2695; tel. 941/574–2323; Earl Tamar, Chief Operating Officer, Acute Care Services (Nonreporting) **A**1 2 9 10	23	10	201	—	—	—	—	—	—	—

CHATTAHOOCHEE—Gadsden County

FLORIDA STATE HOSPITAL, U.S. Highway 90 East, Zip 32324–1000, Mailing Address: P.O. Box 1000, Zip 32324–1000; tel. 904/663–7536; Robert B. Williams, Administrator (Total facility includes 20 beds in nursing home–type unit) **A**10 **F**4 8 10 11 12 17 19 20 21 22 23 26 28 29 30 31 35 37 39 40 41 42 43 45 46 50 52 54 55 57 60 63 64 65 67 70 71 73 74 **P**6	12	22	997	658	938	—	—	91689	53322	2320

CHIPLEY—Washington County

✠ NORTHWEST FLORIDA COMMUNITY HOSPITAL, 1360 Brickyard Road, Zip 32428–6303, Mailing Address: P.O. Box 889, Zip 32428–0889; tel. 850/638–1610; Stephen D. Mason, Administrator (Nonreporting) **A**1 9 10 **N** Panhandle Area Health Network, Marianna, FL	13	10	45	—	—	—	—	—	—	—

CLEARWATER—Pinellas County

✠ CLEARWATER COMMUNITY HOSPITAL, (Formerly Columbia Clearwater Community Hospital), 1521 Druid Road East, Zip 34616–6193, Mailing Address: P.O. Box 9068, Zip 34618–9068; tel. 813/447–4571; Betsy Bomar, Chief Executive Officer (Total facility includes 20 beds in nursing home–type unit) (Nonreporting) **A**1 9 10 **S** Columbia/HCA Healthcare Corporation, Nashville, TN **N** Columbia/HCA West Florida Division, Tampa, FL; The Health Advantage Network, Winter Park, FL	32	10	133	—	—	—	—	—	—	—
MORTON PLANT HOSPITAL, 323 Jeffords Street, Zip 34616–3892, Mailing Address: Box 210, Zip 34617–0210; tel. 813/462–7000; Frank V. Murphy, III, President and Chief Executive Officer (Total facility includes 126 beds in nursing home–type unit) (Nonreporting) **A**2 5 10 **S** Morton Plant Mease Health Care, Dunedin, FL **N** Morton Plant Mease Health Care, Dunedin, FL; BayCare Health Network, Inc., Clearwater, FL	23	10	742	—	—	—	—	—	—	—
□ WINDMOOR HEALTHCARE OF CLEARWATER, (Formerly Psychiatric Hospital of Florida), 11300 U.S. 19 North, Zip 33764; tel. 813/541–2646; C. William Brett, Ph.D., President and Chief Executive Officer **A**1 10 **F**2 12 15 45 46 52 55 56 57 58 65	33	22	56	860	32	5778	0	7079	3202	96

CLERMONT—Lake County

✠ SOUTH LAKE HOSPITAL, 847 Eighth Street, Zip 34711–2196; tel. 352/394–4071; Leslie Longacre, Executive Director and Chief Executive Officer **A**1 9 10 **F**8 12 14 15 16 19 21 22 24 29 30 32 34 35 37 41 44 45 49 62 63 64 73 **S** Orlando Regional Healthcare System, Orlando, FL **N** Orlando Regional Healthcare System, Orlando, FL	16	10	68	2177	28	23181	—	15907	7217	193

Hospital, Address, Telephone, Administrator, Approval, Facility, and Physician Codes, Health Care System, Network	Classification Codes		Utilization Data					Expense (thousands) of dollars		
★ American Hospital Association (AHA) membership □ Joint Commission on Accreditation of Healthcare Organizations (JCAHO) accreditation + American Osteopathic Healthcare Association (AOHA) membership ○ American Osteopathic Association (AOA) accreditation △ Commission on Accreditation of Rehabilitation Facilities (CARF) accreditation Control codes 61, 63, 64, 71, 72 and 73 indicate hospitals listed by AOHA, but not registered by AHA. For definition of numerical codes, see page A4	Control	Service	Staffed Beds	Admissions	Census	Outpatient Visits	Births	Total	Payroll	Personnel

CLEWISTON—Hendry County

⊞ HENDRY REGIONAL MEDICAL CENTER, 500 West Sugarland Highway, Zip 33440–3094; tel. 941/983–9121; J. Rudy Reinhardt, Administrator **A**1 9 10 **F**3 8 12 13 15 16 17 18 19 20 21 22 25 26 28 29 30 31 32 33 34 35 37 39 41 42 44 45 49 51 53 54 55 56 57 58 63 65 69 71 73 **P**6 **S** Quorum Health Group/Quorum Health Resources, Inc., Brentwood, TN **N** Lake Okeechobee Rural Health Network, Belle Glade, FL	16	10	45	1038	14	24757	—	12212	5173	184

COCOA BEACH—Brevard County

⊞ HEALTH FIRST/CAPE CANAVERAL HOSPITAL, 701 West Cocoa Beach Causeway, Zip 32931–5595, Mailing Address: P.O. Box 320069, Zip 32932–0069; tel. 407/799–7111; Christopher S. Kennedy, President and Chief Operating Officer (Nonreporting) **A**1 9 10	23	10	128	—	—	—	—	—	—	—

CORAL GABLES—Dade County

⊞ CORAL GABLES HOSPITAL, 3100 Douglas Road, Zip 33134–6990; tel. 305/445–8461; Martha Garcia, Chief Executive Officer (Nonreporting) **A**1 9 10 **S** TENET Healthcare Corporation, Santa Barbara, CA **N** Tenet South Florida Health System Network, Fort Lauderdale, FL	33	10	205	—	—	—	—	—	—	—
□ HEALTHSOUTH DOCTORS' HOSPITAL, 5000 University Drive, Zip 33146–2094; tel. 305/666–2111; Lincoln S. Mendez, Chief Executive Officer (Total facility includes 29 beds in nursing home–type unit) **A**1 3 9 10 **F**5 7 8 10 12 14 15 16 19 21 22 24 27 30 31 32 34 35 37 40 41 42 44 45 46 49 64 65 66 67 71 73 74 **S** HEALTHSOUTH Corporation, Birmingham, AL	33	10	157	6053	79	70038	1053	61646	23667	692
□ VENCOR HOSPITAL–CORAL GABLES, 5190 S.W. Eighth Street, Zip 33134–2495; tel. 305/445–1364; Theodore Welding, Chief Executive Officer (Nonreporting) **A**1 10 **S** Vencor, Incorporated, Louisville, KY	33	10	53	—	—	—	—	—	—	—

CORAL SPRINGS—Broward County

⊞ CORAL SPRINGS MEDICAL CENTER, 3000 Coral Hills Drive, Zip 33065; tel. 954/344–3000; A. Gary Muller, FACHE, Administrator and Regional Vice President (Nonreporting) **A**1 3 5 9 10 12 **S** North Broward Hospital District, Fort Lauderdale, FL	16	10	167	—	—	—	—	—	—	—

CRESTVIEW—Okaloosa County

⊞ NORTH OKALOOSA MEDICAL CENTER, 151 Redstone Avenue S.E., Zip 32539–6026; tel. 850/689–8100; Roger L. Hall, Chief Executive Officer (Total facility includes 10 beds in nursing home–type unit) **A**1 9 10 **F**7 8 10 12 14 15 16 17 19 22 28 29 30 32 34 35 37 40 44 45 46 49 51 63 64 65 67 71 72 73 74 **P**7 **S** Community Health Systems, Inc., Brentwood, TN **N** The Health Advantage Network, Winter Park, FL	33	10	93	3858	42	53192	539	26054	10970	421

CRYSTAL RIVER—Citrus County

⊞ SEVEN RIVERS COMMUNITY HOSPITAL, 6201 North Suncoast Boulevard, Zip 34428–6712; tel. 352/795–6560; Michael L. Collins, Chief Executive Officer **A**1 9 10 **F**7 8 10 11 12 14 16 17 19 21 22 23 24 25 28 29 30 34 35 37 39 40 41 42 44 45 49 52 54 55 56 57 59 60 63 65 67 71 73 74 **S** TENET Healthcare Corporation, Santa Barbara, CA	33	10	128	5777	72	50337	74	—	—	429

DADE CITY—Pasco County

⊞ PASCO COMMUNITY HOSPITAL, (Formerly Columbia Dade City Hospital), 13100 Fort King Road, Zip 33525–5294; tel. 352/521–1100; Robert Meade, Chief Executive Officer (Nonreporting) **A**1 9 10 **S** Columbia/HCA Healthcare Corporation, Nashville, TN **N** The Health Advantage Network, Winter Park, FL	33	10	120	—	—	—	—	—	—	—

DAVENPORT—Polk County

□ HEART OF FLORIDA REGIONAL MEDICAL CENTER, 1615 U.S. Highway 27N, Zip 33837, Mailing Address: P.O. Box 67, Haines City, Zip 33844–0067; tel. 941/422–4971; Robert Mahaffey, Administrator (Nonreporting) **A**1 10 **S** Health Management Associates, Naples, FL	33	10	51	—	—	—	—	—	—	—

DAYTONA BEACH—Volusia County

⊞ ATLANTIC MEDICAL CENTER–DAYTONA, (Formerly Columbia Medical Center–Daytona), 400 North Clyde Morris Boulevard, Zip 32114–2770, Mailing Address: P.O. Box 9000, Zip 32120–9000; tel. 904/239–5000; Thomas R. Pentz, Chief Executive Officer **A**1 9 10 **F**3 8 10 12 14 15 16 17 18 19 22 26 27 28 29 30 31 32 34 35 37 41 44 45 46 48 49 51 52 55 56 57 58 59 63 65 67 71 73 74 **P**7 **S** Columbia/HCA Healthcare Corporation, Nashville, TN **N** The Health Advantage Network, Winter Park, FL	33	10	214	3843	48	64613	—	35779	13072	352
⊞ HALIFAX COMMUNITY HEALTH SYSTEM, (Includes Halifax Behavioral Services, 841 Jimmy Ann Drive, Zip 32117–4599; tel. 904/274–5333), 303 North Clyde Morris Boulevard, Zip 32114–2700; tel. 904/322–4785; Ron R. Rees, President and Chief Executive Officer **A**1 2 3 5 9 10 **F**1 7 8 10 12 13 14 15 16 17 18 19 21 22 23 24 25 26 27 28 29 30 31 32 33 34 35 37 38 39 40 41 42 44 45 46 49 51 52 53 54 55 56 57 58 59 60 61 63 64 65 66 67 68 69 70 71 72 73 74 **P**5 6	16	10	492	20423	270	301794	2339	190065	66761	2193

DE FUNIAK SPRINGS—Walton County

WALTON REGIONAL HOSPITAL, 336 College Avenue, Zip 32433; tel. 904/892–5171; Jon Hufstedler, Administrator (Nonreporting) **A**9 10	33	10	34	—	—	—	—	—	—	—

DE LAND—Union County

⊞ MEMORIAL HOSPITAL–WEST VOLUSIA, 701 West Plymouth Avenue, Zip 32720–3291, Mailing Address: P.O. Box 940, DeLand, Zip 32721–0509; tel. 904/734–3320; Johnette L. Vodenicker, Administrator **A**1 9 10 **F**2 3 4 7 8 9 10 11 12 14 15 16 17 19 21 22 23 27 28 29 30 32 33 34 35 37 38 39 40 42 43 44 45 46 47 48 49 52 56 57 60 63 64 65 66 67 71 72 73 74 **P**8 **S** Memorial Health Systems, Ormond Beach, FL	23	10	156	6596	87	76109	928	48982	17677	505

Hospital, Address, Telephone, Administrator, Approval, Facility, and Physician Codes, Health Care System, Network	Classi-fication Codes		Utilization Data					Expense (thousands) of dollars		
	Control	Service	Staffed Beds	Admissions	Census	Outpatient Visits	Births	Total	Payroll	Personnel

★ American Hospital Association (AHA) membership
☐ Joint Commission on Accreditation of Healthcare Organizations (JCAHO) accreditation
+ American Osteopathic Healthcare Association (AOHA) membership
○ American Osteopathic Association (AOA) accreditation
△ Commission on Accreditation of Rehabilitation Facilities (CARF) accreditation
Control codes 61, 63, 64, 71, 72 and 73 indicate hospitals listed by AOHA, but not registered by AHA. For definition of numerical codes, see page A4

DELRAY BEACH—Palm Beach County

Hospital	Control	Service	Staffed Beds	Admissions	Census	Outpatient Visits	Births	Total	Payroll	Personnel
✠ DELRAY MEDICAL CENTER, (Formerly Delray Community Hospital), 5352 Linton Boulevard, Zip 33484–6580; tel. 561/498–4440; Mitchell S. Feldman, Chief Executive Officer **A**1 9 10 **F**4 8 10 11 12 14 15 16 17 19 22 25 28 29 30 31 32 34 35 37 39 41 42 43 44 46 47 48 49 53 54 55 56 57 58 59 60 64 65 70 71 73 74 **P**1 5 7 **S** TENET Healthcare Corporation, Santa Barbara, CA **N** Tenet South Florida Health System Network, Fort Lauderdale, FL	33	10	224	12503	195	97673	—	—	—	856
☐ FAIR OAKS HOSPITAL, 5440 Linton Boulevard, Zip 33484–6578; tel. 561/495–1000; Bill Russell, Chief Operating Officer and Administrator (Nonreporting) **A**1 10 **S** TENET Healthcare Corporation, Santa Barbara, CA **N** Tenet South Florida Health System Network, Fort Lauderdale, FL	33	22	102							
☐ △ PINECREST REHABILITATION HOSPITAL , 5360 Linton Boulevard, Zip 33484–6538; tel. 561/495–0400; Paul D. Echelard, Administrator (Nonreporting) **A**1 7 10 **S** TENET Healthcare Corporation, Santa Barbara, CA	33	46	90							

DUNEDIN—Pinellas County

Hospital	Control	Service	Staffed Beds	Admissions	Census	Outpatient Visits	Births	Total	Payroll	Personnel
MEASE HOSPITAL DUNEDIN, 601 Main Street, Zip 34698–5891, Mailing Address: P.O. Box 760, Zip 34697–0760; tel. 813/733–1111; James A. Pfeiffer, Vice President and Chief Operating Officer (Total facility includes 20 beds in nursing home–type unit) (Nonreporting) **A**9 10 **S** Morton Plant Mease Health Care, Dunedin, FL **N** Morton Plant Mease Health Care, Dunedin, FL; BayCare Health Network, Inc., Clearwater, FL	23	10	258							

EGLIN AFB—Okaloosa County

Hospital	Control	Service	Staffed Beds	Admissions	Census	Outpatient Visits	Births	Total	Payroll	Personnel
✠ U. S. AIR FORCE REGIONAL HOSPITAL, 307 Boatner Road, Suite 114, Zip 32542–1282; tel. 850/883–8221; Colonel William C. Head, MSC, USAF, Administrator **A**1 3 5 **F**3 7 8 11 12 13 14 15 16 17 18 19 20 21 22 24 26 28 29 30 37 39 40 41 42 44 46 49 51 52 54 55 56 58 61 63 65 67 71 73 **P**6 **S** Department of the Air Force, Bowling AFB, DC	41	10	90	4439	50	392080	1036	—	6191	—

ENGLEWOOD—Sarasota County

Hospital	Control	Service	Staffed Beds	Admissions	Census	Outpatient Visits	Births	Total	Payroll	Personnel
✠ ENGLEWOOD COMMUNITY HOSPITAL, 700 Medical Boulevard, Zip 34223–3978; tel. 941/475–6571; Terry L. Moore, Chief Executive Officer (Nonreporting) **A**1 9 10 **S** Columbia/HCA Healthcare Corporation, Nashville, TN **N** Columbia/HCA West Florida Division, Tampa, FL; The Health Advantage Network, Winter Park, FL	33	10	100							

EUSTIS—Lake County

Hospital	Control	Service	Staffed Beds	Admissions	Census	Outpatient Visits	Births	Total	Payroll	Personnel
✠ FLORIDA HOSPITAL WATERMAN, 201 North Eustis Street, Zip 32726–3488, Mailing Address: P.O. Box B., Zip 32727–0377; tel. 352/589–3333; Kenneth R. Mattison, President and Chief Executive Officer (Total facility includes 29 beds in nursing home–type unit) (Nonreporting) **A**1 2 9 10 **S** Adventist Health System Sunbelt Health Care Corporation, Winter Park, FL **N** Adventist Health System, Winter Park, FL; Florida Hospital Health Network, Orlando, FL	21	10	182							

FERNANDINA BEACH—Nassau County

Hospital	Control	Service	Staffed Beds	Admissions	Census	Outpatient Visits	Births	Total	Payroll	Personnel
✠ BAPTIST MEDICAL CENTER–NASSAU, 1250 South 18th Street, Zip 32034–3098; tel. 904/321–3501; Jim L. Mayo, Administrator **A**1 9 10 **F**7 8 11 17 19 21 22 30 32 34 35 37 40 44 48 49 65 66 71 73 **P**6 8 **S** Daughters of Charity National Health System, Saint Louis, MO **N** Baptist/St. Vincent's Health System, Jacksonville, FL	23	10	24	1661	17	33653	382	15671	6474	228

FORT LAUDERDALE—Broward County

Hospital	Control	Service	Staffed Beds	Admissions	Census	Outpatient Visits	Births	Total	Payroll	Personnel
☐ ATLANTIC SHORES HOSPITAL, (Formerly Coral Ridge Psychiatric Hospital), 4545 North Federal Highway, Zip 33308–5274; tel. 954/771–2711; Sophia Perialas–Grady, Chief Executive Officer (Nonreporting) **A**1 10	31	22	86	—	—	—	—	—	—	—
☐ BHC FORT LAUDERDALE HOSPITAL, 1601 East Las Olas Boulevard, Zip 33301–2393; tel. 954/463–4321; Andrew Fuhrman, Chief Executive Officer (Nonreporting) **A**1 9 10 **S** Behavioral Healthcare Corporation, Nashville, TN	33	22	100	—	—	—	—	—	—	—
✠ BROWARD GENERAL MEDICAL CENTER, 1600 South Andrews Avenue, Zip 33316–2510; tel. 954/355–4400; Ruth A. Eldridge, R.N., Regional Vice President, Administration (Total facility includes 20 beds in nursing home–type unit) (Nonreporting) **A**1 2 3 9 10 12 **S** North Broward Hospital District, Fort Lauderdale, FL	16	10	548	—	—	—	—	—	—	—
☐ CLEVELAND CLINIC HOSPITAL, 2835 North Ocean Boulevard, Zip 33308–7599; tel. 954/568–1000; Margaret S. McRae, Site Administrator **A**1 3 9 10 **F**8 10 12 14 15 16 17 19 21 22 24 26 27 29 30 31 32 33 34 37 39 41 42 43 44 45 46 49 50 51 60 63 65 66 67 73 74 **P**3 5	23	10	120	5502	74	36461	0	50823	20346	529
CORAL RIDGE PSYCHIATRIC HOSPITAL See Atlantic Shores Hospital										
✠ FLORIDA MEDICAL CENTER HOSPITAL, 5000 West Oakland Park Boulevard, Zip 33313–1585; tel. 954/735–6000; Denny De Narvaez, Chief Executive Officer (Nonreporting) **A**1 10 **S** TENET Healthcare Corporation, Santa Barbara, CA **N** Tenet South Florida Health System Network, Fort Lauderdale, FL; Med Connect, Ft Lauderdale, FL	32	10	459	—	—	—	—	—	—	—
☐ HEALTHSOUTH SUNRISE REHABILITATION HOSPITAL, 4399 Nob Hill Road, Zip 33351–5899; tel. 954/749–0300; Kevin R. Conn, Administrator **A**1 10 **F**1 3 5 12 14 15 16 17 19 25 26 27 28 34 35 39 41 42 46 48 49 65 66 67 71 73 **S** HEALTHSOUTH Corporation, Birmingham, AL	33	46	108	2076	105	34580	—	22804	11956	336
☐ △ HOLY CROSS HOSPITAL, 4725 North Federal Highway, Zip 33308–4668, Mailing Address: P.O. Box 23460, Zip 33307–3460; tel. 954/771–8000; John C. Johnson, Chief Executive Officer (Nonreporting) **A**1 2 7 9 10 **S** Catholic Health East, Radnor, PA **N** Holy Cross Health Ministries, Ft Lauderdale, FL; Florida Health Choice, Del Ray Beach, FL	21	10	437	—	—	—	—	—	—	—

Hospital, Address, Telephone, Administrator, Approval, Facility, and Physician Codes, Health Care System, Network	Classi-fication Codes		Utilization Data					Expense (thousands) of dollars		
	Control	Service	Staffed Beds	Admissions	Census	Outpatient Visits	Births	Total	Payroll	Personnel

Approval/membership symbols:

★ American Hospital Association (AHA) membership
☐ Joint Commission on Accreditation of Healthcare Organizations (JCAHO) accreditation
+ American Osteopathic Healthcare Association (AOHA) membership
○ American Osteopathic Association (AOA) accreditation
△ Commission on Accreditation of Rehabilitation Facilities (CARF) accreditation
  Control codes 61, 63, 64, 71, 72 and 73 indicate hospitals listed by AOHA, but not registered by AHA. For definition of numerical codes, see page A4

Hospital	Control	Service	Staffed Beds	Admissions	Census	Outpatient Visits	Births	Total	Payroll	Personnel
⊠ IMPERIAL POINT MEDICAL CENTER, 6401 North Federal Highway, Zip 33308–1495; tel. 954/776–8500; Dorothy J. Mancini, R.N., Regional Vice President Administration **A**1 9 10 **F**4 5 7 8 10 12 14 15 16 17 19 22 23 24 26 28 30 31 32 33 34 35 37 39 41 42 43 44 49 51 52 56 57 58 59 60 65 66 70 71 73 **P**6 7 **S** North Broward Hospital District, Fort Lauderdale, FL	16	10	154	5049	97	56616	—	46548	18969	528
⊠ NORTH RIDGE MEDICAL CENTER, 5757 North Dixie Highway, Zip 33334–4182, Mailing Address: P.O. Box 23160, Zip 33307; tel. 954/776–6000; Emil P. Miller, Chief Executive Officer (Nonreporting) **A**1 9 10 **S** TENET Healthcare Corporation, Santa Barbara, CA **N** Tenet South Florida Health System Network, Fort Lauderdale, FL; Med Connect, Ft Lauderdale, FL	33	10	391	—	—	—	—	—	—	—
☐ VENCOR HOSPITAL–FORT LAUDERDALE, 1516 East Las Olas Boulevard, Zip 33301–2399; tel. 954/764–8900; Lewis A. Ransdell, Administrator **A**1 10 **F**12 14 15 16 20 22 26 27 28 32 37 41 45 46 65 67 71 73 **S** Vencor, Incorporated, Louisville, KY	33	10	64	409	56	0	—	—	—	285

FORT MYERS—Lee County

Hospital	Control	Service	Staffed Beds	Admissions	Census	Outpatient Visits	Births	Total	Payroll	Personnel
☐ CHARTER GLADE BEHAVIORAL HEALTH SYSTEM, 3550 Colonial Boulevard, Zip 33912–1065, Mailing Address: P.O. Box 60120, Zip 33906–0120; tel. 941/939–0403; Martin Schappell, Chief Executive Officer (Nonreporting) **A**1 9 10 **S** Magellan Health Services, Atlanta, GA	33	22	104	—	—	—	—	—	—	—
COLUMBIA GULF COAST HOSPITAL See Gulf Coast Hospital										
COLUMBIA REGIONAL MEDICAL CENTER See Southwest Florida Regional Medical Center										
⊠ ○ GULF COAST HOSPITAL, (Formerly Columbia Gulf Coast Hospital), 13681 Doctors Way, Zip 33912–4309; tel. 941/768–5000; Valerie A. Jackson, Chief Executive Officer (Nonreporting) **A**1 9 10 11 **S** Columbia/HCA Healthcare Corporation, Nashville, TN **N** Columbia/HCA West Florida Division, Tampa, FL; The Health Advantage Network, Winter Park, FL	33	10	120	—	—	—	—	—	—	—
⊠ △ LEE MEMORIAL HEALTH SYSTEM, 2776 Cleveland Avenue, Zip 33901–5855, Mailing Address: P.O. Box 2218, Zip 33902–2218; tel. 941/332–1111; William D. Johnson, President (Total facility includes 90 beds in nursing home–type unit) **A**1 2 7 9 10 **F**4 7 8 10 11 12 14 15 17 19 21 22 24 26 29 30 31 32 34 35 37 38 39 40 41 42 43 44 45 47 48 49 60 61 63 64 65 66 67 69 70 71 73 **P**6 8	16	10	949	33344	527	217178	3797	311488	140199	3950
⊠ SOUTHWEST FLORIDA REGIONAL MEDICAL CENTER, (Formerly Columbia Regional Medical Center), 2727 Winkler Avenue, Zip 33901–9396; tel. 941/939–1147; Larry Pieretti, President and Chief Executive Officer (Total facility includes 20 beds in nursing home–type unit) **A**1 2 10 **F**4 8 10 11 12 14 15 19 21 22 25 26 27 30 31 32 34 35 37 39 41 42 43 44 45 46 49 50 51 59 61 63 64 65 67 69 71 72 73 **P**8 **S** Columbia/HCA Healthcare Corporation, Nashville, TN **N** The Health Advantage Network, Winter Park, FL	33	10	330	13137	166	—	—	157095	64457	1415

FORT PIERCE—St. Lucie County

Hospital	Control	Service	Staffed Beds	Admissions	Census	Outpatient Visits	Births	Total	Payroll	Personnel
⊠ LAWNWOOD REGIONAL MEDICAL CENTER, (Formerly Columbia Lawnwood Regional Medical Center), (Includes Lawnwood Pavilion, 1860 North Lawnwood Circle, Zip 34950; tel. 407/466–1500), 1700 South 23rd Street, Zip 34950–0188; tel. 561/461–4000; Gary Cantrell, President and Chief Executive Officer (Total facility includes 33 beds in nursing home–type unit) **A**1 9 10 **F**3 4 7 8 10 11 12 13 14 15 16 17 19 20 22 23 24 25 28 29 30 31 32 33 34 35 36 37 38 39 40 41 42 44 45 46 49 52 53 55 58 59 60 64 65 66 70 71 73 74 **S** Columbia/HCA Healthcare Corporation, Nashville, TN **N** Columbia/HCA East Florida Division, Winter Park, FL; The Health Advantage Network, Winter Park, FL	33	10	363	12975	229	72157	1322	—	—	—

FORT WALTON BEACH—Okaloosa County

Hospital	Control	Service	Staffed Beds	Admissions	Census	Outpatient Visits	Births	Total	Payroll	Personnel
⊠ FORT WALTON BEACH MEDICAL CENTER, (Formerly Columbia Fort Walton Beach Medical Center), 1000 Mar–Walt Drive, Zip 32547–6795; tel. 850/862–1111; Wayne Campbell, Chief Executive Officer **A**1 9 10 **F**7 8 10 11 12 14 15 16 17 19 20 21 22 23 25 26 28 29 31 33 35 36 37 39 40 41 44 45 46 48 49 52 56 63 64 70 71 73 74 **S** Columbia/HCA Healthcare Corporation, Nashville, TN **N** Columbia/HCA North Florida Division, Tallahassee, FL; The Health Advantage Network, Winter Park, FL	33	10	247	9895	146	33064	931	50534	21484	707
GULF COAST TREATMENT CENTER, 1015 Mar–Walt Drive, Zip 32547–6612; tel. 850/863–4160; Raul D. Ruelas, M.D., Administrator (Nonreporting) **A**10 **S** Ramsay Health Care, Inc., Coral Gables, FL	33	52	79	—	—	—	—	—	—	—

GAINESVILLE—Alachua County

Hospital	Control	Service	Staffed Beds	Admissions	Census	Outpatient Visits	Births	Total	Payroll	Personnel
⊠ NORTH FLORIDA REGIONAL MEDICAL CENTER, (Formerly Columbia North Florida Regional Medical Center), 6500 Newberry Road, Zip 32605–4392, Mailing Address: P.O. Box 147006, Zip 32614–7006; tel. 352/333–4000; Brian C. Robinson, Chief Executive Officer (Total facility includes 24 beds in nursing home–type unit) (Nonreporting) **A**1 2 9 10 **S** Columbia/HCA Healthcare Corporation, Nashville, TN **N** Columbia/HCA North Florida Division, Tallahassee, FL; The Health Advantage Network, Winter Park, FL	33	10	278	—	—	—	—	—	—	—
⊠ SHANDS AT AGH, (Includes Shands at Vista, 8900 N.E. 39th Avenue, Zip 32606; tel. 904/338–0097), 801 S.W. Second Avenue, Zip 32601–6289; tel. 352/372–4321; Robert B. Williams, Administrator (Total facility includes 30 beds in nursing home–type unit) **A**1 2 3 5 9 10 **F**1 2 3 4 7 8 10 11 12 14 15 16 17 18 19 20 21 22 23 25 26 28 29 30 31 32 34 35 36 37 38 39 40 41 42 43 44 45 46 48 49 51 52 53 54 55 56 57 58 59 60 63 64 65 66 67 71 73 74 **P**6 **S** Shands HealthCare, Gainesville, FL	23	10	267	10476	150	259307	1020	82032	32291	931

Hospital, Address, Telephone, Administrator, Approval, Facility, and Physician Codes, Health Care System, Network	Classi-fication Codes		Utilization Data					Expense (thousands) of dollars		
	Control	Service	Staffed Beds	Admissions	Census	Outpatient Visits	Births	Total	Payroll	Personnel

★ American Hospital Association (AHA) membership
□ Joint Commission on Accreditation of Healthcare Organizations (JCAHO) accreditation
+ American Osteopathic Healthcare Association (AOHA) membership
○ American Osteopathic Association (AOA) accreditation
△ Commission on Accreditation of Rehabilitation Facilities (CARF) accreditation
Control codes 61, 63, 64, 71, 72 and 73 indicate hospitals listed by AOHA, but not registered by AHA. For definition of numerical codes, see page A4

★ SHANDS AT THE UNIVERSITY OF FLORIDA, 1600 S.W. Archer Road, Zip 32610–0326, Mailing Address: P.O. Box 100326, Zip 32610–0326; tel. 352/395–0111; Jodi J. Mansfield, Senior Vice President and Chief Operating Officer **A**1 2 3 5 8 9 10 **F**2 3 4 7 8 9 10 11 12 14 15 16 17 18 19 20 21 22 23 25 26 28 29 30 31 32 34 35 36 37 38 39 40 41 42 43 44 45 46 47 48 49 50 51 52 53 54 55 56 57 58 59 60 61 63 64 65 66 67 69 71 73 74 **P**6 **S** Shands HealthCare, Gainesville, FL	23	10	564	24469	402	302678	2511	333139	118701	3862
★ SHANDS REHAB HOSPITAL, 8900 N.W. 39th Avenue, Zip 32606–5625; tel. 352/338–0091; Cynthia M. Toth, Administrator **A**1 7 10 **F**2 3 4 7 8 9 10 11 12 14 15 16 17 18 19 21 22 23 25 28 29 30 31 32 34 35 36 37 38 39 40 41 42 43 44 45 46 47 48 49 50 52 53 54 55 56 57 58 59 60 63 64 65 66 67 69 71 73 74 **P**6 **S** Shands HealthCare, Gainesville, FL	23	46	40	548	22	6137	—	5629	2636	73
★ VETERANS AFFAIRS MEDICAL CENTER, 1601 S.W. Archer Road, Zip 32608–1197; tel. 352/376–1611; Malcom Randall, Director (Total facility includes 60 beds in nursing home–type unit) **A**1 3 5 8 9 **F**1 2 3 4 8 10 15 16 17 18 19 20 21 25 26 27 28 29 30 31 32 34 35 37 39 41 42 43 44 46 49 51 52 54 55 56 57 58 59 63 64 65 67 71 73 74 **P**1 **S** Department of Veterans Affairs, Washington, DC	45	10	268	6494	149	340311	—	145143	67674	1651
GRACEVILLE—Jackson County										
CAMPBELLTON GRACEVILLE HOSPITAL, 5429 College Drive, Zip 32440; tel. 850/263–4431; Neil Whipkey, Administrator **A**9 10 **F**14 15 19 22 28 30 32 33 49 56 64 65 71 **P**5 **N** Panhandle Area Health Network, Marianna, FL	16	10	37	563	7	5225	—	3479	1783	69
GREEN COVE SPRINGS—Clay County										
□ VENCOR–NORTH FLORIDA, 801 Oak Street, Zip 32043–4317; tel. 904/284–9230; Tim Simpson, Administrator (Nonreporting) **A**1 10 **S** Vencor, Incorporated, Louisville, KY	33	49	48	—						
GULF BREEZE—Santa Rosa County										
GULF BREEZE HOSPITAL, 1110 Gulf Breeze Parkway, Zip 32561, Mailing Address: P.O. Box 159, Zip 32562; tel. 850/934–2000; Richard C. Fulford, Administrator **A**9 10 **F**2 3 4 7 8 9 10 11 12 13 14 15 16 19 21 22 23 26 27 28 29 31 32 33 35 37 39 40 41 42 43 44 45 46 48 49 51 52 53 54 55 56 57 58 59 60 61 62 63 64 65 66 67 70 71 72 73 74 **P**4 5 7 **S** Baptist Health Care Corporation, Pensacola, FL **N** Baptist Health Care, Inc., Pensacola, FL	23	10	45	2076	25	37565	2	17014	5723	181
THE FRIARY OF BAPTIST HEALTH CENTER, 4400 Hickory Shores Boulevard, Zip 32561–9113; tel. 904/932–9375; Leo J. Donnelly, Executive Director (Nonreporting) **A**9	23	82	30							
HIALEAH—Dade County										
★ HIALEAH HOSPITAL, 651 East 25th Street, Zip 33013–3878; tel. 305/693–6100; Clifford J. Bauer, Chief Executive Officer **A**1 9 10 **F**7 8 12 14 15 16 17 19 21 22 25 27 28 29 30 31 32 33 35 41 42 44 45 46 49 51 54 55 56 57 58 59 65 67 71 73 **P**5 8 **S** TENET Healthcare Corporation, Santa Barbara, CA **N** Tenet South Florida Health System Network, Fort Lauderdale, FL	33	10	256	11050	156	61500	1568	55466	24072	—
□ PALM SPRINGS GENERAL HOSPITAL, 1475 West 49th Street, Zip 33012–3275, Mailing Address: Box 2804, Zip 33012–2804; tel. 305/558–2500; Carlos Milanes, Executive Vice President and Administrator **A**1 9 10 **F**19 22 26 30 34 35 37 44 45 46 49 65 67 71 73 **P**5	33	10	190	8207	134	24932	—	—	—	—
★ PALMETTO GENERAL HOSPITAL, 2001 West 68th Street, Zip 33016–1898; tel. 305/823–5000; Ron Stern, Chief Executive Officer (Nonreporting) **A**1 9 10 12 13 **S** TENET Healthcare Corporation, Santa Barbara, CA **N** Tenet South Florida Health System Network, Fort Lauderdale, FL	33	10	360	—						
□ ○ SOUTHERN WINDS HOSPITAL, 4225 West 20th Street, Zip 33012–5835; tel. 305/558–9700; Gilda Baldwin, Chief Executive Officer (Nonreporting) **A**1 10 11 13	33	22	60	—						
HOLLYWOOD—Broward County										
★ △ HOLLYWOOD MEDICAL CENTER, 3600 Washington Street, Zip 33021–8216; tel. 954/966–4500; Holly Lerner, Chief Executive Officer (Nonreporting) **A**1 7 9 10 **S** TENET Healthcare Corporation, Santa Barbara, CA **N** Tenet South Florida Health System Network, Fort Lauderdale, FL	33	10	238	—						
□ HOLLYWOOD PAVILION, 1201 North 37th Avenue, Zip 33021–5498; tel. 954/962–1355; Karen Kallen–Zury, Chief Executive Officer (Nonreporting) **A**1 10	33	22	46	—						
★ △ MEMORIAL REGIONAL HOSPITAL, 3501 Johnson Street, Zip 33021–5421; tel. 954/987–2000; C. Kennon Hetlage, Administrator (Total facility includes 20 beds in nursing home–type unit) **A**1 2 3 7 9 10 **F**1 2 3 4 7 8 10 11 12 14 15 16 17 18 19 20 21 22 23 24 25 26 27 28 30 31 32 33 34 35 37 38 39 40 41 42 43 44 45 46 47 48 49 51 52 56 57 58 59 60 64 65 66 67 68 69 70 71 72 73 74 **P**2 5 7 8 **S** Memorial Healthcare System, Hollywood, FL **N** Memorial Healthcare System, Hollywood, FL; Florida Health Choice, Del Ray Beach, FL	16	10	674	26547	414	294682	2719	367706	165344	3694
HOMESTEAD—Dade County										
★ HOMESTEAD HOSPITAL, 160 N.W. 13th Street, Zip 33030–4299; tel. 305/248–3232; Bo Boulenger, Chief Executive Officer **A**1 9 10 **F**2 3 4 6 7 8 9 10 11 12 13 15 16 17 19 20 22 23 25 26 28 29 30 31 32 33 34 35 36 37 38 39 40 41 42 43 44 45 46 47 48 49 51 52 58 60 61 64 65 66 67 68 69 70 71 72 73 74 **P**5 6 **S** Baptist Health System of South Florida, Miami, FL **N** Dimensions Health/Baptist Health Systems, Miami, FL	23	10	105	5690	70	—	861	34295	13557	390

Hospital, Address, Telephone, Administrator, Approval, Facility, and Physician Codes, Health Care System, Network	Classi-fication Codes		Utilization Data					Expense (thousands) of dollars		
★ American Hospital Association (AHA) membership □ Joint Commission on Accreditation of Healthcare Organizations (JCAHO) accreditation + American Osteopathic Healthcare Association (AOHA) membership ○ American Osteopathic Association (AOA) accreditation △ Commission on Accreditation of Rehabilitation Facilities (CARF) accreditation Control codes 61, 63, 64, 71, 72 and 73 indicate hospitals listed by AOHA, but not registered by AHA. For definition of numerical codes, see page A4	Control	Service	Staffed Beds	Admissions	Census	Outpatient Visits	Births	Total	Payroll	Personnel

HUDSON—Pasco County

| ✠ REGIONAL MEDICAL CENTER–BAYONET POINT, (Formerly Columbia Regional Medical Center), 14000 Fivay Road, Zip 34667-7199; tel. 813/863-2411; Don Griffin, Ph.D., President and Chief Executive Officer (Nonreporting) **A**1 9 10 **S** Columbia/HCA Healthcare Corporation, Nashville, TN **N** Columbia/HCA West Florida Division, Tampa, FL; The Health Advantage Network, Winter Park, FL | 33 | 10 | 256 | — | — | — | — | — | — | — |

INVERNESS—Citrus County

| ✠ CITRUS MEMORIAL HOSPITAL, 502 Highland Boulevard, Zip 34452-4754; tel. 352/344-6582; Charles A. Blasband, Chief Executive Officer **A**1 9 10 **F**7 8 10 12 14 15 19 21 22 25 28 30 32 34 35 36 37 39 40 44 49 51 65 67 71 72 73 | 23 | 10 | 171 | 10924 | 120 | 163523 | 504 | 64313 | 22610 | 788 |

JACKSONVILLE—Duval County

✠ BAPTIST MEDICAL CENTER, 800 Prudential Drive, Zip 32207-8203; tel. 904/202-2000; A. Hugh Greene, Executive Vice President and Chief Operating Officer (Nonreporting) **A**1 2 3 5 9 10 **S** Daughters of Charity National Health System, Saint Louis, MO **N** Baptist/St. Vincent's Health System, Jacksonville, FL	23	10	501	—	—	—	—	—	—	—
□ BHC ST. JOHNS RIVER HOSPITAL, 6300 Beach Boulevard, Zip 32216-2782; tel. 904/724-9202; Patricia Vandergrift, Administrator (Nonreporting) **A**1 9 10 **S** Behavioral Healthcare Corporation, Nashville, TN COLUMBIA MEMORIAL HOSPITAL OF JACKSONVILLE See Memorial Hospital of Jacksonville	33	22	60	—	—	—	—	—	—	—
✠ △ GENESIS REHABILITATION HOSPITAL, 3599 University Boulevard South, Zip 32216-4211, Mailing Address: P.O. Box 16406, Zip 32245-6406; tel. 904/858-7600; Stephen K. Wilson, President and Chief Executive Officer **A**1 7 10 **F**12 14 15 16 17 19 20 21 22 24 25 27 28 30 32 34 35 41 45 46 48 49 50 53 54 63 65 66 67 71 73 **N** Genesis Health, Inc., Jacksonville, FL	23	46	110	1248	104	—	0	24152	12940	338
✠ MEMORIAL HOSPITAL OF JACKSONVILLE, (Formerly Columbia Memorial Hospital of Jacksonville), 3625 University Boulevard South, Zip 32216-4240, Mailing Address: P.O. Box 16325, Zip 32216-6325; tel. 904/399-6111; H. Rex Etheredge, President and Chief Executive Officer (Nonreporting) **A**1 2 9 10 **S** Columbia/HCA Healthcare Corporation, Nashville, TN **N** Columbia/HCA North Florida Division, Tallahassee, FL; The Health Advantage Network, Winter Park, FL	33	10	310	—	—	—	—	—	—	—
□ METHODIST MEDICAL CENTER, 580 West Eighth Street, Zip 32209-6553; tel. 904/798-8000; Marcus E. Drewa, President and Chief Executive Officer (Total facility includes 24 beds in nursing home-type unit) **A**1 5 9 **F**2 3 4 7 8 9 10 11 12 14 15 16 17 19 21 22 27 28 29 30 31 32 33 34 35 37 38 39 40 41 42 43 44 45 46 47 48 49 51 52 53 54 55 56 57 58 59 60 64 65 67 69 70 71 73 74 **P**7 **S** Methodist Health System, Jacksonville, FL **N** Methodist Health Systems, Jacksonville, FL	23	10	204	7326	127	46418	0	70520	24222	806
✠ NAVAL HOSPITAL, 2080 Child Street, Zip 32214-5000; tel. 904/777-7300; Captain M. J. Benson, MSC, USN, Commanding Officer **A**1 3 5 **F**3 7 8 12 13 14 15 16 17 19 20 21 22 24 27 28 29 30 34 35 37 39 41 44 45 46 49 51 52 55 56 58 59 60 61 65 67 71 72 73 74 **S** Department of Navy, Washington, DC	43	10	70	4895	35	432468	1249	63842	16935	550
✠ SPECIALTY HOSPITAL JACKSONVILLE, (Formerly Columbia Specialty Hospital Jacksonville), (LONG TERM ACUTE CARE), 4901 Richard Street, Zip 32207; tel. 904/737-3120; W. Raymond C. Ford, Chief Executive Officer **A**1 9 10 **F**3 4 7 8 9 10 11 12 14 16 17 19 21 22 23 24 25 26 28 29 30 33 34 35 37 39 40 41 42 43 44 45 46 48 49 50 51 54 55 56 57 58 59 60 61 65 66 67 71 73 74 **P**7 8 **S** Columbia/HCA Healthcare Corporation, Nashville, TN **N** Columbia/HCA North Florida Division, Tallahassee, FL; The Health Advantage Network, Winter Park, FL	33	49	61	622	48	—	—	17466	7521	195
✠ ST. LUKE'S HOSPITAL, 4201 Belfort Road, Zip 32216-5898; tel. 904/296-3700; J. Larry Read, President (Total facility includes 17 beds in nursing home-type unit) **A**1 2 3 5 8 9 10 **F**4 7 8 10 12 19 21 22 23 25 28 30 32 34 35 37 39 40 41 42 43 44 49 51 60 63 64 65 66 67 69 71 73 **P**3 6 **S** Mayo Foundation, Rochester, MN	23	10	230	9031	140	31149	395	109869	40499	1405
✠ ST. VINCENT'S MEDICAL CENTER, 1800 Barrs Street, Zip 32204-2982, Mailing Address: P.O. Box 2982, Zip 32203-2982; tel. 904/308-7300; John W. Logue, Executive Vice President and Chief Operating Officer (Total facility includes 240 beds in nursing home-type unit) **A**1 2 3 5 9 10 **F**2 3 4 7 8 10 11 12 14 15 16 17 18 19 21 22 23 25 26 27 28 29 30 31 32 33 34 35 36 37 38 39 40 41 42 43 44 45 47 49 51 52 53 54 55 56 57 58 59 60 61 63 64 65 66 67 68 71 73 74 **P**1 **S** Daughters of Charity National Health System, Saint Louis, MO **N** Baptist/St. Vincent's Health System, Jacksonville, FL	21	10	768	21401	506	265020	1979	196649	73078	2405
□ UNIVERSITY MEDICAL CENTER, 655 West Eighth Street, Zip 32209-6595; tel. 904/549-5000; W. A. McGriff, III, President and Chief Executive Officer **A**1 2 3 5 8 9 10 **F**4 7 8 10 11 12 14 15 16 17 18 19 20 21 22 26 27 28 30 31 34 37 38 40 41 42 43 44 45 46 47 49 50 51 52 53 54 55 56 57 58 59 60 61 62 65 66 67 68 69 70 71 72 73 74	23	10	438	20546	261	304583	3215	163597	61477	2432

JACKSONVILLE BEACH—Duval County

| ✠ BAPTIST MEDICAL CENTER–BEACHES, 1350 13th Avenue South, Zip 32250-3205; tel. 904/247-2900; Joseph Mitrick, Administrator **A**1 9 10 **F**4 7 8 9 10 11 12 14 15 16 17 19 21 22 24 28 29 30 32 34 35 37 38 39 40 41 42 43 44 45 46 47 49 52 53 54 56 59 60 63 65 67 71 73 74 **P**1 **S** Daughters of Charity National Health System, Saint Louis, MO **N** Baptist/St. Vincent's Health System, Jacksonville, FL | 23 | 10 | 80 | 3368 | 42 | 69910 | 53 | 29185 | 11439 | 574 |

Hospital, Address, Telephone, Administrator, Approval, Facility, and Physician Codes, Health Care System, Network	Classi-fication Codes		Utilization Data					Expense (thousands) of dollars		
	Control	Service	Staffed Beds	Admissions	Census	Outpatient Visits	Births	Total	Payroll	Personnel

★ American Hospital Association (AHA) membership
□ Joint Commission on Accreditation of Healthcare Organizations (JCAHO) accreditation
+ American Osteopathic Healthcare Association (AOHA) membership
○ American Osteopathic Association (AOA) accreditation
△ Commission on Accreditation of Rehabilitation Facilities (CARF) accreditation
Control codes 61, 63, 64, 71, 72 and 73 indicate hospitals listed by AOHA, but not registered by AHA. For definition of numerical codes, see page A4

JASPER—Hamilton County

★ HAMILTON MEDICAL CENTER, (Formerly Columbia Hamilton Medical Center), 506 N.W. Fourth Street, Zip 32052; tel. 904/792–7200; Amelia Tuten, R.N., Administrator **A**9 10 **F**19 22 32 44 71 **S** Columbia/HCA Healthcare Corporation, Nashville, TN **N** The Health Advantage Network, Winter Park, FL
— Control 33, Service 10, Staffed Beds 20, Admissions 548, Census 5, Outpatient Visits 9378, Births —, Total 5270, Payroll 2687, Personnel 63

JAY—Santa Rosa County

JAY HOSPITAL, 221 South Alabama Street, Zip 32565–1070, Mailing Address: P.O. Box 397, Zip 32565–0397; tel. 850/675–8000; Robert E. Gowing, Administrator (Nonreporting) **A**9 10 **S** Baptist Health Care Corporation, Pensacola, FL **N** Baptist Health Care, Inc., Pensacola, FL
— Control 23, Service 10, Staffed Beds 47

JUPITER—Palm Beach County

⊞ JUPITER MEDICAL CENTER, 1210 South Old Dixie Highway, Zip 33458–7299; tel. 561/747–2234; Hart Ransdell, Chief Executive Officer **A**1 2 9 10 **F**8 11 12 19 22 24 28 30 32 34 35 37 41 42 44 49 60 65 67 71 73 74 **S** Quorum Health Group/Quorum Health Resources, Inc., Brentwood, TN
— Control 23, Service 10, Staffed Beds 156, Admissions 6792, Census 88, Outpatient Visits 70984, Births —, Total 62799, Payroll 22779, Personnel 880

KEY WEST—Monroe County

⊞ LOWER FLORIDA KEYS HEALTH SYSTEM, (Includes De Poo Hospital, 1200 Kennedy Drive, Zip 33041; tel. 305/294–4692; Florida Keys Memorial Hospital, 5900 College Road, Zip 33040; tel. 305/294–5531), 5900 College Road, Zip 33040–4396, Mailing Address: P.O. Box 9107, Zip 33041–9107; tel. 305/294–5531; Roberto Sanchez, Administrator **A**1 9 10 **F**1 2 3 4 5 6 7 8 10 11 12 13 14 15 16 17 19 20 21 22 23 24 25 26 27 28 29 30 31 32 33 34 35 36 38 39 40 41 42 43 44 45 46 49 51 52 53 54 55 56 57 59 60 61 62 63 64 65 66 67 68 69 70 71 72 73 74 **P**8
— Control 16, Service 10, Staffed Beds 169, Admissions 4307, Census 69, Outpatient Visits 41155, Births 1229, Total 37411, Payroll 14821, Personnel 508

KISSIMMEE—Osceola County

□ CHARTER BEHAVIORAL HEALTH SYSTEM–ORLANDO, (Formerly Charter Hospital Orlando South), 206 Park Place Drive, Zip 34741–2356; tel. 407/846–0444; Daniel Kearney, Chief Executive Officer **A**1 9 10 **F**2 3 14 22 26 29 34 45 52 53 54 55 56 57 58 59 65 67 **P**6 **S** Magellan Health Services, Atlanta, GA
— Control 33, Service 22, Staffed Beds 60, Admissions 1333, Census 33, Outpatient Visits 2704, Births 0, Total 8149, Payroll 2476, Personnel 73

COLUMBIA MEDICAL CENTER–OSCEOLA See Osceola Medical Center

FLORIDA HOSPITAL KISSIMMEE See Florida Hospital, Orlando

⊞ OSCEOLA MEDICAL CENTER, (Formerly Columbia Medical Center–Osceola), 700 West Oak Street, Zip 34741–4996, Mailing Address: P.O. Box 422589, Zip 34742–2589; tel. 407/846–2266; E. Tim Cook, Chief Executive Officer (Nonreporting) **A**1 9 10 **S** Columbia/HCA Healthcare Corporation, Nashville, TN **N** Columbia/HCA East Florida Division, Winter Park, FL; The Health Advantage Network, Winter Park, FL
— Control 33, Service 10, Staffed Beds 156

LAKE BUTLER—Union County

NORTH FLORIDA RECEPTION CENTER HOSPITAL, State Road 231 South, Zip 32054, Mailing Address: P.O. Box 628, Zip 32054–0628; tel. 904/496–6111; Bob Torrescano, Administrator (Nonreporting)
— Control 12, Service 11, Staffed Beds 153

LAKE CITY—Columbia County

⊞ LAKE CITY MEDICAL CENTER, (Formerly Columbia Lake City Medical Center), 1701 West U.S. Highway 90, Zip 32055–3718; tel. 904/752–2922; Todd Gallati, Chief Executive Officer (Total facility includes 5 beds in nursing home–type unit) **A**1 9 10 **F**8 12 14 15 16 17 19 21 22 23 26 28 31 32 33 34 35 37 39 41 44 45 49 52 54 55 56 57 58 59 63 64 65 66 71 73 **P**7 **S** Columbia/HCA Healthcare Corporation, Nashville, TN **N** The Health Advantage Network, Winter Park, FL
— Control 33, Service 10, Staffed Beds 75, Admissions 3632, Census 45, Outpatient Visits 42472, Births —, Total 18898, Payroll 8713, Personnel 320

⊞ SHANDS AT LAKE SHORE, 560 East Franklin Street, Zip 32055–3047, Mailing Address: P.O. Box 1989, Zip 32056–1989; tel. 904/754–8000; Linda A. McKnew, R.N., Administrator **A**1 9 10 **F**1 2 3 4 5 7 8 9 10 11 12 14 15 16 17 18 19 20 21 22 23 24 26 28 29 30 31 32 34 35 36 37 38 39 40 41 42 43 44 45 46 47 48 49 51 52 53 56 57 59 60 61 64 65 66 67 69 71 73 **S** Shands HealthCare, Gainesville, FL
— Control 23, Service 10, Staffed Beds 128, Admissions 3867, Census 46, Outpatient Visits 78728, Births 363, Total 20957, Payroll 8688, Personnel 327

⊞ VETERANS AFFAIRS MEDICAL CENTER, 801 South Marion Street, Zip 32025–5898; tel. 904/755–3016; Marlis Meyer, Interim Director (Total facility includes 210 beds in nursing home–type unit) **A**1 3 5 9 **F**3 15 16 19 20 21 22 25 26 28 32 33 37 39 41 44 45 46 49 51 52 54 55 56 57 58 64 65 67 71 73 74 **S** Department of Veterans Affairs, Washington, DC
— Control 45, Service 10, Staffed Beds 350, Admissions 3322, Census 275, Outpatient Visits 94419, Births —, Total 73868, Payroll 46112, Personnel 1253

LAKE WALES—Polk County

⊞ LAKE WALES MEDICAL CENTERS, 410 South 11th Street, Zip 33853–4256, Mailing Address: P.O. Box 3460, Zip 33859–3460; tel. 941/676–1433; Joe M. Connell, Chief Executive Officer (Total facility includes 177 beds in nursing home–type unit) (Nonreporting) **A**1 9 **N** Mid–Florida Medical Services, Inc., Winter Haven, FL
— Control 23, Service 10, Staffed Beds 264

LAKELAND—Polk County

□ HEART OF FLORIDA BEHAVIORAL CENTER, (Formerly Palmview Hospital), 2510 North Florida Avenue, Zip 33805–2298; tel. 941/682–6105; David M. Polunas, Administrator and Chief Executive Officer (Nonreporting) **A**1 **S** Health Management Associates, Naples, FL
— Control 33, Service 22, Staffed Beds 40

⊞ LAKELAND REGIONAL MEDICAL CENTER, 1324 Lakeland Hills Boulevard, Zip 33805–4543, Mailing Address: P.O. Box 95448, Zip 33804–5448; tel. 941/687–1100; Jack T. Stephens, Jr., President and Chief Executive Officer **A**1 2 5 9 10 **F**2 3 4 7 10 11 14 15 16 17 19 21 22 23 26 27 28 29 30 34 37 38 39 40 42 43 44 47 52 53 54 55 56 57 58 59 60 65 67 70 71 72 73 74
— Control 23, Service 10, Staffed Beds 649, Admissions 27818, Census 353, Outpatient Visits 127026, Births 2729, Total 218768, Payroll 91209, Personnel 2318

PALMVIEW HOSPITAL See Heart of Florida Behavioral Center

Hospital, Address, Telephone, Administrator, Approval, Facility, and Physician Codes, Health Care System, Network	Classi-fication Codes		Utilization Data					Expense (thousands) of dollars		
★ American Hospital Association (AHA) membership □ Joint Commission on Accreditation of Healthcare Organizations (JCAHO) accreditation + American Osteopathic Healthcare Association (AOHA) membership ○ American Osteopathic Association (AOA) accreditation △ Commission on Accreditation of Rehabilitation Facilities (CARF) accreditation Control codes 61, 63, 64, 71, 72 and 73 indicate hospitals listed by AOHA, but not registered by AHA. For definition of numerical codes, see page A4	Control	Service	Staffed Beds	Admissions	Census	Outpatient Visits	Births	Total	Payroll	Personnel

LANTANA—Palm Beach County

| A. G. HOLLEY STATE HOSPITAL, 1199 West Lantana Road, Zip 33462–1514, Mailing Address: P.O. Box 3084, Zip 33465–3084; tel. 561/582–5666; David Ashkin, M.D., Medical Executive Director (Nonreporting) **A**10 | 12 | 33 | 50 | — | | | | | | |

LARGO—Pinellas County

□ CHARTER BEHAVIORAL HEALTH SYSTEM OF TAMPA BAY AT LARGO, 12891 Seminole Boulevard, Zip 33778; tel. 813/587–6000; Jim Hill, Chief Executive Officer (Nonreporting) **A**1 9 **S** Magellan Health Services, Atlanta, GA	33	22	64	—						
□ △ HEALTHSOUTH REHABILITATION HOSPITAL, 901 North Clearwater–Largo Road, Zip 34640–1955; tel. 813/586–2999; Vincent O. Nico, Regional Vice President (Nonreporting) **A**1 7 10 **S** HEALTHSOUTH Corporation, Birmingham, AL	33	46	60	—						
✚ LARGO MEDICAL CENTER, (Formerly Columbia Largo Medical Center), 201 14th Street S.W., Zip 33770–3133, Mailing Address: P.O. Box 2905, Zip 33779–2905; tel. 813/588–5200; Thomas L. Herron, FACHE, President and Chief Executive Officer (Total facility includes 13 beds in nursing home–type unit) **A**1 2 9 10 **F**4 7 8 10 11 12 15 16 18 19 21 22 23 24 26 28 29 30 31 32 33 34 35 37 38 39 40 41 42 43 44 45 49 60 61 64 65 71 73 74 **P**7 8 **S** Columbia/HCA Healthcare Corporation, Nashville, TN **N** Columbia/HCA West Florida Division, Tampa, FL; The Health Advantage Network, Winter Park, FL	33	10	243	10850	127	53290	610	—	—	730
□ + ○ SUN COAST HOSPITAL, 2025 Indian Rocks Road, Zip 34644, Mailing Address: P.O. Box 2025, Zip 34649–2025; tel. 813/581–9474; Jeffrey A. Collins, Chief Executive Officer (Total facility includes 14 beds in nursing home–type unit) (Nonreporting) **A**1 9 10 11 12 13 **S** Quorum Health Group/Quorum Health Resources, Inc., Brentwood, TN	23	10	241	—						

LECANTO—Citrus County

| □ HERITAGE BEVERLY HILLS HOSPITAL, 2804 West Marc Knighton Court, Zip 34461–8334; tel. 352/746–9000; Charles Visalli, Administrator (Nonreporting) **A**1 9 10 | 33 | 22 | 88 | — | | | | | | |

LEESBURG—Lake County

| ✚ △ LEESBURG REGIONAL MEDICAL CENTER, 600 East Dixie Avenue, Zip 34748–5999; tel. 352/323–5000; Richard L. Wooten, President and Chief Executive Officer (Total facility includes 120 beds in nursing home–type unit) **A**1 7 9 10 **F**7 8 10 15 16 19 21 22 23 24 26 28 29 30 31 32 33 34 35 37 39 40 41 42 44 45 46 48 49 60 64 65 71 72 73 | 23 | 10 | 414 | 12260 | 253 | 81885 | 1074 | 85696 | 34117 | 1042 |

LEHIGH ACRES—Lee County

| ✚ EAST POINTE HOSPITAL, (Formerly Columbia East Pointe Hospital), 1500 Lee Boulevard, Zip 33936–4897; tel. 941/369–2101; Valerie A. Jackson, Chief Executive Officer (Total facility includes 13 beds in nursing home–type unit) **A**1 9 10 **F**4 7 8 10 12 13 14 15 16 17 18 19 20 21 22 23 24 26 27 28 29 30 31 32 34 35 36 37 39 40 41 42 43 44 45 46 49 52 55 57 59 61 63 64 65 66 67 69 71 72 73 74 **P**8 **S** Columbia/HCA Healthcare Corporation, Nashville, TN **N** Columbia/HCA West Florida Division, Tampa, FL; The Health Advantage Network, Winter Park, FL | 33 | 10 | 88 | 2405 | 31 | 32568 | 207 | 23612 | 9669 | 243 |

LIVE OAK—Suwannee County

| ✚ SHANDS AT LIVE OAK, 1100 S.W. 11th Street, Zip 32060–3608, Mailing Address: P.O. Drawer X., Zip 32060; tel. 904/362–1413; Rhonda Sherrod, Administrator **A**1 9 10 **F**8 12 16 19 22 26 28 30 34 39 44 51 65 71 73 **P**6 **S** Shands HealthCare, Gainesville, FL | 23 | 10 | 20 | 405 | 4 | 62465 | — | 6506 | 2724 | 93 |

LONGWOOD—Seminole County

| ✚ SOUTH SEMINOLE HOSPITAL, 555 West State Road 434, Zip 32750–4999; tel. 407/767–1200; Sue Whelan–Williams, Site Administrator (Nonreporting) **A**1 9 10 **S** Orlando Regional Healthcare System, Orlando, FL **N** Orlando Regional Healthcare System, Orlando, FL; The Health Advantage Network, Winter Park, FL | 32 | 10 | 206 | — | | | | | | |

LOXAHATCHEE—Palm Beach County

| ✚ PALMS WEST HOSPITAL, (Formerly Columbia Palms West Hospital), 13001 Southern Boulevard, Zip 33470–1150; tel. 561/798–3300; Alex M. Marceline, Chief Executive Officer (Nonreporting) **A**1 9 10 **S** Columbia/HCA Healthcare Corporation, Nashville, TN **N** Med Connect, Ft Lauderdale, FL; Columbia/HCA East Florida Division, Winter Park, FL; The Health Advantage Network, Winter Park, FL | 33 | 10 | 117 | — | | | | | | |

LUTZ—Hillsborough County

| □ CHARTER HOSPITAL OF PASCO, 21808 State Road 54, Zip 33549–6938; tel. 813/948–2441; Miriam K. Williams, Administrator **A**1 10 **F**3 15 52 54 55 56 57 58 59 65 67 **S** Magellan Health Services, Atlanta, GA | 33 | 22 | 72 | 1321 | 36 | 0 | — | — | — | 65 |

MACCLENNY—Baker County

| ED FRASER MEMORIAL HOSPITAL, 159 North Third Street, Zip 32063–0484; tel. 904/259–3151; Dennis R. Markos, Chief Executive Officer (Total facility includes 62 beds in nursing home–type unit) (Nonreporting) **A**9 10 | 23 | 10 | 68 | — | | | | | | |

MACDILL AFB—Hillsborough County

| ✚ U. S. AIR FORCE HOSPITAL, 8415 Bayshore Boulevard, Zip 33621–1607; tel. 813/828–3258; Colonel Roger H. Bower, MC, USAF, Commander (Nonreporting) **A**1 **S** Department of the Air Force, Bowling AFB, DC | 41 | 10 | 50 | — | | | | | | |

MADISON—Madison County

| MADISON COUNTY MEMORIAL HOSPITAL, 201 East Marion Street, Zip 32340–2561; tel. 850/973–2271; Jeffrey S. Howell, Administrator (Nonreporting) **A**9 10 | 23 | 10 | 26 | — | | | | | | |

MARATHON—Monroe County

| □ FISHERMEN'S HOSPITAL, 3301 Overseas Highway, Zip 33050–0068; tel. 305/743–5533; Patrice L. Tavernier, Administrator (Nonreporting) **A**1 9 10 **S** Health Management Associates, Naples, FL | 33 | 10 | 58 | — | | | | | | |

Hospital, Address, Telephone, Administrator, Approval, Facility, and Physician Codes, Health Care System, Network	Classi-fication Codes		Utilization Data					Expense (thousands) of dollars		
★ American Hospital Association (AHA) membership ☐ Joint Commission on Accreditation of Healthcare Organizations (JCAHO) accreditation + American Osteopathic Healthcare Association (AOHA) membership ○ American Osteopathic Association (AOA) accreditation △ Commission on Accreditation of Rehabilitation Facilities (CARF) accreditation Control codes 61, 63, 64, 71, 72 and 73 indicate hospitals listed by AOHA, but not registered by AHA. For definition of numerical codes, see page A4	Control	Service	Staffed Beds	Admissions	Census	Outpatient Visits	Births	Total	Payroll	Personnel

MARIANNA—Jackson County

⊞ JACKSON HOSPITAL, 4250 Hospital Drive, Zip 32446–1939, Mailing Address: P.O. Box 1608, Zip 32447–1608; tel. 850/526–2200; Randy Smith, Interim Administrator (Nonreporting) **A**1 9 10 **S** Quorum Health Group/Quorum Health Resources, Inc., Brentwood, TN **N** Panhandle Area Health Network, Marianna, FL
| | 16 | 10 | 84 | — | — | — | — | — | — | — |

MELBOURNE—Brevard County

☐ CIRCLES OF CARE, 400 East Sheridan Road, Zip 32901–3184; tel. 407/722–5200; James B. Whitaker, President (Nonreporting) **A**1 9 10
| | 23 | 22 | 72 | — | — | — | — | — | — | — |

DEVEREUX HOSPITAL AND CHILDREN'S CENTER OF FLORIDA, 8000 Devereux Drive, Zip 32940–7907; tel. 407/242–9100; James E. Colvin, Executive Director (Nonreporting) **S** Devereux Foundation, Villanova, PA
| | 23 | 52 | 100 | — | — | — | — | — | — | — |

☐ △ HEALTHSOUTH SEA PINES REHABILITATION HOSPITAL, 101 East Florida Avenue, Zip 32901–9966; tel. 407/984–4600; Henry J. Cranston, Chief Executive Officer (Nonreporting) **A**1 7 10 **S** HEALTHSOUTH Corporation, Birmingham, AL
| | 33 | 46 | 80 | — | — | — | — | — | — | — |

⊞ HOLMES REGIONAL MEDICAL CENTER, 1350 South Hickory Street, Zip 32901–3276; tel. 407/727–7000; Stephen P. Bunker, President and Chief Operating Officer (Total facility includes 30 beds in nursing home–type unit) (Nonreporting) **A**1 2 9 10
| | 23 | 10 | 528 | — | — | — | — | — | — | — |

MIAMI—Dade County

⊞ AVENTURA HOSPITAL AND MEDICAL CENTER, (Formerly Columbia Aventura Hospital and Medical Center), 20900 Biscayne Boulevard, Zip 33180–1407; tel. 305/682–7100; Davide M. Carbone, Chief Executive Officer **A**1 9 10 **F**1 2 3 4 5 7 8 10 11 12 13 14 15 16 17 18 19 20 21 22 23 25 26 27 28 29 30 31 32 33 34 35 37 38 39 40 42 43 44 45 46 47 49 51 52 53 54 55 56 57 58 59 60 61 63 64 65 67 71 72 73 74 **P**5 7 **S** Columbia/HCA Healthcare Corporation, Nashville, TN **N** Columbia/HCA East Florida Division, Winter Park, FL; The Health Advantage Network, Winter Park, FL
| | 33 | 10 | 407 | 12995 | 176 | 59945 | 760 | 78885 | 28909 | 871 |

⊞ △ BAPTIST HOSPITAL OF MIAMI, 8900 North Kendall Drive, Zip 33176–2197; tel. 305/596–6503; Fred M. Messing, Chief Executive Officer **A**1 2 3 7 9 10 **F**2 3 4 5 7 8 10 12 14 15 16 17 19 21 22 24 25 26 27 28 29 30 31 32 33 34 35 37 38 40 41 42 43 44 45 46 47 48 49 50 60 61 63 64 65 66 67 71 72 73 74 **P**1 5 6 7 **S** Baptist Health System of South Florida, Miami, FL **N** Dimensions Health/Baptist Health Systems, Miami, FL
| | 23 | 10 | 457 | 25241 | 366 | 200540 | 3436 | 238604 | 95690 | 2739 |

⊞ BASCOM PALMER EYE INSTITUTE–ANNE BATES LEACH EYE HOSPITAL, 900 N.W. 17th Street, Zip 33136–1199, Mailing Address: Box 016880, Zip 33101–6880; tel. 305/326–6000; John Rossfeld, Administrator (Nonreporting) **A**1 3 5 9 10 **S** Quorum Health Group/Quorum Health Resources, Inc., Brentwood, TN
| | 23 | 45 | 35 | — | — | — | — | — | — | — |

⊞ CEDARS MEDICAL CENTER, (Formerly Columbia Cedars Medical Center), 1400 N.W. 12th Avenue, Zip 33136–1003; tel. 305/325–5511; Ralph A. Aleman, Chief Executive Officer (Nonreporting) **A**1 2 3 5 9 10 **S** Columbia/HCA Healthcare Corporation, Nashville, TN **N** Columbia/HCA East Florida Division, Winter Park, FL; The Health Advantage Network, Winter Park, FL
| | 33 | 10 | 500 | — | — | — | — | — | — | — |

COLUMBIA AVENTURA HOSPITAL AND MEDICAL CENTER See Aventura Hospital and Medical Center

⊞ COLUMBIA BEHAVIORAL HEALTH CENTER, 11100 N.W. 27th Street, Zip 33172–5000; tel. 305/591–3230; Cheryl Siegwald–Mays, Administrator (Nonreporting) **A**1 9 10 **S** Columbia/HCA Healthcare Corporation, Nashville, TN
| | 33 | 22 | 88 | — | — | — | — | — | — | — |

COLUMBIA CEDARS MEDICAL CENTER See Cedars Medical Center
COLUMBIA DEERING HOSPITAL See Deering Hospital
COLUMBIA KENDALL MEDICAL CENTER See Kendall Medical Center

⊞ DEERING HOSPITAL, (Formerly Columbia Deering Hospital), 9333 S.W. 152nd Street, Zip 33157–1780; tel. 305/256–5100; Jude Torchia, Chief Executive Officer (Nonreporting) **A**1 9 10 **S** Columbia/HCA Healthcare Corporation, Nashville, TN **N** Columbia/HCA East Florida Division, Winter Park, FL; The Health Advantage Network, Winter Park, FL
| | 33 | 10 | 233 | — | — | — | — | — | — | — |

HARBOR VIEW See Windmoor Healthcare of Miami

☐ △ HEALTHSOUTH REHABILITATION HOSPITAL, 20601 Old Cutler Road, Zip 33189–2400; tel. 305/251–3800; Nelson Lazo, Chief Executive Officer (Nonreporting) **A**1 7 10 **S** HEALTHSOUTH Corporation, Birmingham, AL
| | 33 | 46 | 45 | — | — | — | — | — | — | — |

HIGHLAND PARK HOSPITAL See Jackson Memorial Hospital

⊞ △ JACKSON MEMORIAL HOSPITAL, (Includes Highland Park Hospital, 1660 N.W. Seventh Court, Zip 33136; tel. 305/324–8111; Stuart Podolnick, Administrator), 1611 N.W. 12th Avenue, Zip 33136–1094; tel. 305/585–6754; Ira C. Clark, President (Nonreporting) **A**1 2 3 5 6 7 8 9 10
| | 13 | 10 | 1376 | — | — | — | — | — | — | — |

⊞ KENDALL MEDICAL CENTER, (Formerly Columbia Kendall Medical Center), 11750 Bird Road, Zip 33175–3530; tel. 305/223–3000; Victor Maya, Chief Executive Officer (Nonreporting) **A**1 9 10 **S** Columbia/HCA Healthcare Corporation, Nashville, TN **N** Columbia/HCA East Florida Division, Winter Park, FL; The Health Advantage Network, Winter Park, FL
| | 33 | 10 | 235 | — | — | — | — | — | — | — |

⊞ △ MERCY HOSPITAL, 3663 South Miami Avenue, Zip 33133–4237; tel. 305/854–4400; Edward J. Rosasco, Jr., President **A**1 2 6 7 9 10 **F**4 8 10 11 12 14 15 16 17 19 21 22 23 25 27 28 31 32 33 34 35 37 39 40 41 42 43 44 45 46 49 51 55 57 58 59 60 65 71 73 **P**4 5 8
| | 21 | 10 | 368 | 15729 | 263 | 117246 | 1657 | 143207 | 64077 | 2125 |

⊞ MIAMI CHILDREN'S HOSPITAL, 3100 S.W. 62nd Avenue, Zip 33155–3009; tel. 305/666–6511; William A. McDonald, President and Chief Executive Officer **A**1 3 5 9 10 **F**2 4 5 10 11 12 13 14 17 18 19 20 21 22 24 25 27 28 29 30 31 32 33 34 35 38 39 41 42 43 44 45 46 49 51 52 53 54 55 56 58 59 64 65 67 68 69 70 71 72 73 **P**5
| | 23 | 50 | 268 | 7993 | 132 | 175778 | — | 178066 | 83619 | 1949 |

Hospital, Address, Telephone, Administrator, Approval, Facility, and Physician Codes, Health Care System, Network	Classi-fication Codes		Utilization Data					Expense (thousands) of dollars		

★ American Hospital Association (AHA) membership
□ Joint Commission on Accreditation of Healthcare Organizations (JCAHO) accreditation
+ American Osteopathic Healthcare Association (AOHA) membership
○ American Osteopathic Association (AOA) accreditation
△ Commission on Accreditation of Rehabilitation Facilities (CARF) accreditation
Control codes 61, 63, 64, 71, 72 and 73 indicate hospitals listed by AOHA, but not registered by AHA. For definition of numerical codes, see page A4

	Control	Service	Staffed Beds	Admissions	Census	Outpatient Visits	Births	Total	Payroll	Personnel
⊞ MIAMI HEART INSTITUTE AND MEDICAL CENTER, (Includes North Campus, 4701 Meridian Avenue, Zip 33140; tel. 305/672–1111; South Campus, 250 63rd Street, Zip 33141; tel. 305/672–1111), 4701 Meridian Avenue, Zip 33140–2910; tel. 305/674–3114; Tim Parker, Chief Executive Officer (Total facility includes 10 beds in nursing home–type unit) (Nonreporting) **A**1 9 10 12 **S** Columbia/HCA Healthcare Corporation, Nashville, TN **N** Columbia/HCA East Florida Division, Winter Park, FL; The Health Advantage Network, Winter Park, FL	32	10	278	—	—	—	—	—	—	—
★ MIAMI JEWISH HOME AND HOSPITAL FOR AGED, (GERIATRIC CARE CENTER), 5200 N.E. Second Avenue, Zip 33137–2706; tel. 305/751–8626; Terry Goodman, Executive Director (Total facility includes 462 beds in nursing home–type unit) **A**3 10 **F**1 3 5 6 12 14 15 16 17 18 20 24 25 26 27 28 29 30 32 33 34 39 41 42 45 46 49 51 54 55 56 57 58 59 62 64 65 67 73	23	49	494	1089	449	14000	0	31854	16326	—
⊞ NORTH SHORE MEDICAL CENTER, 1100 N.W. 95th Street, Zip 33150–2098; tel. 305/835–6000; Steven M. Klein, President and Chief Executive Officer **A**1 2 9 10 **F**3 4 5 8 10 11 12 13 14 15 16 17 18 19 20 21 22 23 24 25 26 27 28 29 30 31 32 33 34 35 37 38 39 40 41 42 43 44 45 46 49 50 51 52 53 54 55 56 57 58 59 61 63 65 66 67 68 69 71 72 73 74 **P**1 **S** TENET Healthcare Corporation, Santa Barbara, CA	33	10	320	4147	180	47636	1421	29699	12391	1071
⊞ PAN AMERICAN HOSPITAL, 5959 N.W. Seventh Street, Zip 33126–3198; tel. 305/264–1000; Carolina Calderin, Chief Executive Officer (Nonreporting) **A**1 9 10	23	10	144	—	—	—	—	—	—	—
□ SOUTH FLORIDA EVALUATION AND TREATMENT CENTER, 2200 N.W. 7th Avenue, Zip 33127–4291; tel. 305/637–2500; Cheryl Y. Brantley, Administrator (Nonreporting) **A**1	12	22	200	—	—	—	—	—	—	—
⊞ △ SOUTH MIAMI HOSPITAL, 6200 S.W. 73rd Street, Zip 33143–9990; tel. 305/661–4611; D. Wayne Brackin, Chief Executive Officer **A**1 2 7 9 10 **F**2 3 4 7 8 10 11 14 17 18 19 21 22 24 25 26 27 28 29 30 31 32 34 35 37 38 40 41 42 43 44 45 46 48 49 50 60 61 63 64 65 66 67 69 71 72 73 74 **P**1 5 6 7 **S** Baptist Health System of South Florida, Miami, FL **N** Dimensions Health/Baptist Health Systems, Miami, FL	23	10	334	14438	215	268096	3704	149230	58023	1281
⊞ UNIVERSITY OF MIAMI HOSPITAL AND CLINICS, 1475 N.W. 12th Avenue, Zip 33136–1002; tel. 305/243–6418; John Rossfeld, Administrator **A**1 2 3 5 9 10 **F**8 12 14 15 16 17 19 20 21 22 27 29 30 31 34 35 42 44 45 46 51 54 58 60 63 65 67 71 73 **P**1 **S** Quorum Health Group/Quorum Health Resources, Inc., Brentwood, TN	23	10	40	925	17	141418	—	51672	14077	427
⊞ VETERANS AFFAIRS MEDICAL CENTER, 1201 N.W. 16th Street, Zip 33125–1624; tel. 305/324–4455; Thomas C. Doherty, Medical Center Director (Total facility includes 240 beds in nursing home–type unit) (Nonreporting) **A**1 3 5 8 9 **S** Department of Veterans Affairs, Washington, DC	45	10	669	—	—	—	—	—	—	—
+ ○ WESTCHESTER GENERAL HOSPITAL, 2500 S.W. 75th Avenue, Zip 33155–9947; tel. 305/264–5252; Gilda Baldwin, Chief Executive Officer (Nonreporting) **A**5 9 10 11 12 13	33	10	110	—	—	—	—	—	—	—
□ WINDMOOR HEALTHCARE OF MIAMI, (Formerly Harbor View), 1861 N.W. South River Drive, Zip 33125–2787; tel. 305/642–3555; Lee Ghezzi, Administrator (Nonreporting) **A**1 10	33	22	94	—	—	—	—	—	—	—
MIAMI BEACH—Dade County										
□ △ MOUNT SINAI MEDICAL CENTER, 4300 Alton Road, Zip 33140–2800; tel. 305/674–2121; Fred D. Hirt, President and Chief Executive Officer (Total facility includes 150 beds in nursing home–type unit) **A**1 2 3 5 7 8 9 10 **F**2 3 4 7 8 10 12 13 14 15 16 17 18 19 20 21 22 23 25 26 27 28 29 30 31 32 33 34 35 37 38 40 41 42 43 44 45 46 48 49 51 52 54 57 58 59 60 63 64 65 67 71 72 73 74 **P**1 6 7	23	10	553	20397	381	174500	1641	220371	109890	3616
⊞ △ SOUTH SHORE HOSPITAL AND MEDICAL CENTER, 630 Alton Road, Zip 33139–5502; tel. 305/672–2100; William Zubkoff, Ph.D., Chief Executive Officer (Nonreporting) **A**1 7 9 10	23	49	178	—	—	—	—	—	—	—
MILTON—Santa Rosa County										
⊞ SANTA ROSA MEDICAL CENTER, 1450 Berryhill Road, Zip 32570–4028, Mailing Address: P.O. Box 648, Zip 32572–0648; tel. 850/626–7762; Renate Darby, Interim Chief Executive Officer (Total facility includes 10 beds in nursing home–type unit) **A**1 9 10 **F**1 3 4 7 8 10 11 12 14 15 16 17 19 21 22 26 28 29 30 33 35 36 39 40 41 42 44 45 49 51 54 56 64 65 67 71 73 74 **P**7 8 **S** Paracelsus Healthcare Corporation, Houston, TX **N** The Health Advantage Network, Winter Park, FL	33	10	78	3305	34	50405	424	21181	9246	343
NAPLES—Collier County										
⊞ △ NAPLES COMMUNITY HOSPITAL, 350 Seventh Street North, Zip 34102–4746, Mailing Address: P.O. Box 413029, Zip 34101–3029; tel. 941/436–5000; William G. Crone, President and Chief Executive Officer (Total facility includes 24 beds in nursing home–type unit) **A**1 2 7 9 10 **F**2 3 4 7 8 9 10 11 12 13 14 15 16 17 19 21 22 23 24 25 26 27 28 29 30 31 32 33 34 35 37 38 39 40 41 42 43 44 45 46 47 48 49 51 52 56 57 59 60 64 65 66 67 71 72 73 74 **P**7 8	23	10	458	23113	292	158138	2243	173956	71053	2102
WILLOUGH AT NAPLES, 9001 Tamiami Trail East, Zip 34113–3316; tel. 941/775–4500; Patricia Perfetto, MSN, Executive Director (Nonreporting) **A**10	33	22	64	—	—	—	—	—	—	—
NEW PORT RICHEY—Pasco County										
COLUMBIA NEW PORT RICHEY HOSPITAL See Community Hospital of New Port Richey										

Hospital, Address, Telephone, Administrator, Approval, Facility, and Physician Codes, Health Care System, Network	Classification Codes		Utilization Data					Expense (thousands) of dollars		
★ American Hospital Association (AHA) membership □ Joint Commission on Accreditation of Healthcare Organizations (JCAHO) accreditation + American Osteopathic Healthcare Association (AOHA) membership ○ American Osteopathic Association (AOA) accreditation △ Commission on Accreditation of Rehabilitation Facilities (CARF) accreditation Control codes 61, 63, 64, 71, 72 and 73 indicate hospitals listed by AOHA, but not registered by AHA. For definition of numerical codes, see page A4	Control	Service	Staffed Beds	Admissions	Census	Outpatient Visits	Births	Total	Payroll	Personnel
★□ COMMUNITY HOSPITAL OF NEW PORT RICHEY, (Formerly Columbia New Port Richey Hospital), 5637 Marine Parkway, Zip 34652–4331, Mailing Address: P.O. Box 996, Zip 34656–0996; tel. 813/848–1733; Andrew Oravec, Jr., Administrator (Nonreporting) **A**1 9 10 **S** Columbia/HCA Healthcare Corporation, Nashville, TN **N** Columbia/HCA West Florida Division, Tampa, FL; The Health Advantage Network, Winter Park, FL	33	10	414	—	—	—	—	—	—	—
★□ △ NORTH BAY MEDICAL CENTER, 6600 Madison Street, Zip 34652–1900; tel. 813/842–8468; Dennis A. Taylor, Administrator (Nonreporting) **A**1 7 9 10 **S** TENET Healthcare Corporation, Santa Barbara, CA **N** BayCare Health Network, Inc., Clearwater, FL	33	10	122	—	—	—	—	—	—	—
NEW SMYRNA BEACH—Volusia County										
★□ BERT FISH MEDICAL CENTER, 401 Palmetto Street, Zip 32168–7399; tel. 904/424–5000; Kathy Leonard, Vice President and Administrator **A**1 9 10 **F**8 14 15 16 19 21 22 26 28 29 30 32 33 34 35 37 39 42 44 45 46 49 51 60 65 67 71 **P**1 6 **S** Quorum Health Group/Quorum Health Resources, Inc., Brentwood, TN	16	10	85	3461	51	152301	—	39880	13744	470
NICEVILLE—Okaloosa County										
★□ TWIN CITIES HOSPITAL, (Formerly Columbia Twin Cities Hospital), 2190 Highway 85 North, Zip 32578–1045; tel. 850/678–4131; David L. Blair, President **A**1 9 10 **F**8 12 14 15 16 17 19 21 22 25 28 29 30 32 33 37 44 45 49 51 63 64 71 **S** Columbia/HCA Healthcare Corporation, Nashville, TN **N** Columbia/HCA North Florida Division, Tallahassee, FL; The Health Advantage Network, Winter Park, FL	33	10	60	2330	28	14709	0	15568	6808	221
NORTH MIAMI—Dade County										
□ △ VILLA MARIA HOSPITAL, 1050 N.E. 125th Street, Zip 33161–5881; tel. 305/891–8850; Jack Rutenberg, Administrator (Total facility includes 212 beds in nursing home–type unit) (Nonreporting) **A**1 7 10	21	46	272	—	—	—	—	—	—	—
NORTH MIAMI BEACH—Dade County										
★□ △ PARKWAY REGIONAL MEDICAL CENTER, 160 N.W. 170th Street, Zip 33169–5576; tel. 305/654–5050; Stephen M. Patz, Chief Executive Officer (Nonreporting) **A**1 7 9 **S** TENET Healthcare Corporation, Santa Barbara, CA **N** Tenet South Florida Health System Network, Fort Lauderdale, FL	33	10	392	—	—	—	—	—	—	—
OCALA—Marion County										
□ CHARTER SPRINGS HOSPITAL, 3130 S.W. 27th Avenue, Zip 34474–4485, Mailing Address: P.O. Box 3338, Zip 34478–3338; tel. 352/237–7293; David C. Nissen, Chief Executive Officer (Nonreporting) **A**1 9 10 **S** Magellan Health Services, Atlanta, GA	33	22	92	—	—	—	—	—	—	—
★□ MUNROE REGIONAL MEDICAL CENTER, 131 S.W. 15th Street, Zip 34474–4059, Mailing Address: P.O. Box 6000, Zip 34478–6000; tel. 352/351–7200; Dyer T. Michell, President **A**1 5 9 10 **F**4 7 8 10 11 12 13 14 15 16 19 21 22 23 24 26 28 29 30 31 32 34 35 37 39 40 41 43 44 45 46 49 51 65 66 71 72 73 74 **P**6 7 8	23	10	313	15963	210	87898	1228	122421	47177	1574
★□ OCALA REGIONAL MEDICAL CENTER, (Formerly Columbia Ocala Regional Medical Center), 1431 S.W. First Avenue, Zip 34474–4058, Mailing Address: P.O. Box 2200, Zip 34478–2200; tel. 352/401–1000; Stephen Mahan, Chief Executive Officer (Nonreporting) **A**1 2 9 10 **S** Columbia/HCA Healthcare Corporation, Nashville, TN **N** Columbia/HCA North Florida Division, Tallahassee, FL; The Health Advantage Network, Winter Park, FL	33	10	216	—	—	—	—	—	—	—
OCOEE—Orange County										
★□ HEALTH CENTRAL, 10000 West Colonial Drive, Zip 34761–3499; tel. 407/296–1000; Richard M. Irwin, Jr., President and Chief Executive Officer (Total facility includes 228 beds in nursing home–type unit) **A**1 9 10 **F**1 4 7 8 10 11 12 14 15 17 19 20 21 22 23 27 28 30 31 32 33 34 35 37 39 40 41 42 44 45 46 49 64 65 66 67 69 70 71 72 73 74 **P**3	16	10	338	4831	266	49392	628	45088	16506	530
OKEECHOBEE—Okeechobee County										
★□ RAULERSON HOSPITAL, (Formerly Columbia Raulerson Hospital), 1796 Highway 441 North, Zip 34972, Mailing Address: P.O. Box 1307, Zip 34973–1307; tel. 941/763–2151; Frank Irby, Chief Executive Officer **A**1 9 10 **F**8 11 12 16 19 22 23 25 28 30 32 35 37 39 42 44 46 60 64 71 73 **S** Columbia/HCA Healthcare Corporation, Nashville, TN **N** Columbia/HCA East Florida Division, Winter Park, FL; The Health Advantage Network, Winter Park, FL	33	10	101	4321	64	45398	5	25015	10570	328
ORANGE PARK—Clay County										
★□ ORANGE PARK MEDICAL CENTER, (Formerly Columbia Orange Park Medical Center), 2001 Kingsley Avenue, Zip 32073–5156; tel. 904/276–8500; Robert M. Krieger, Chief Executive Officer (Nonreporting) **A**1 9 10 **S** Columbia/HCA Healthcare Corporation, Nashville, TN **N** Columbia/HCA North Florida Division, Tallahassee, FL; The Health Advantage Network, Winter Park, FL	33	10	196	—	—	—	—	—	—	—
ORLANDO—Orange County										
COLUMBIA PARK MEDICAL CENTER See Lucerne Medical Center										
★□ ○ △ FLORIDA HOSPITAL, (Includes Florida Hospital East Orlando, 7727 Lake Underhill Drive, Zip 32822; tel. 407/277–8110; Florida Hospital Kissimmee, 200 Hilda Street, Kissimmee, Zip 34741–2301; tel. 407/846–4343; Florida Hospital–Altamonte, 601 East Altamonte Drive, Altamonte Springs, Zip 32701; tel. 407/830–4321; Florida Hospital–Apopka, 201 North Park Avenue, Apopka, Zip 32703; tel. 407/889–2566), 601 East Rollins Street, Zip 32803–1489; tel. 407/896–6611; Thomas L. Werner, President (Total facility includes 50 beds in nursing home–type unit) **A**1 2 3 5 7 9 10 11 12 13 **F**3 4 6 7 8 10 11 12 14 15 16 17 18 19 20 21 22 23 24 25 26 28 29 30 31 32 34 35 37 38 39 40 41 42 43 44 45 46 47 48 49 51 52 53 54 55 56 57 58 59 60 61 63 64 65 66 67 69 71 72 73 74 **P**8 **S** Adventist Health System Sunbelt Health Care Corporation, Winter Park, FL **N** Adventist Health System, Winter Park, FL; Florida Hospital Health Network, Orlando, FL	23	10	1354	60260	869	456759	7622	611123	252050	8898

Hospital, Address, Telephone, Administrator, Approval, Facility, and Physician Codes, Health Care System, Network	Classi-fication Codes		Utilization Data					Expense (thousands) of dollars		
★ American Hospital Association (AHA) membership □ Joint Commission on Accreditation of Healthcare Organizations (JCAHO) accreditation + American Osteopathic Healthcare Association (AOHA) membership ○ American Osteopathic Association (AOA) accreditation △ Commission on Accreditation of Rehabilitation Facilities (CARF) accreditation Control codes 61, 63, 64, 71, 72 and 73 indicate hospitals listed by AOHA, but not registered by AHA. For definition of numerical codes, see page A4	Control	Service	Staffed Beds	Admissions	Census	Outpatient Visits	Births	Total	Payroll	Personnel
✶ △ LUCERNE MEDICAL CENTER, (Formerly Columbia Park Medical Center), 818 Main Lane, Zip 32801; tel. 407/649–6111; Rick O'Connell, Chief Executive Officer (Total facility includes 20 beds in nursing home–type unit) **A**1 7 9 10 **F**1 3 4 7 8 10 11 12 15 16 17 19 20 21 22 23 24 25 26 27 28 29 30 31 32 33 34 35 36 37 39 40 41 42 43 44 45 46 48 49 51 53 54 55 56 57 58 59 60 61 63 64 65 66 67 71 72 73 74 **P**1 **S** Columbia/HCA Healthcare Corporation, Nashville, TN **N** Columbia/HCA East Florida Division, Winter Park, FL; The Health Advantage Network, Winter Park, FL	33	10	267	9332	133	43100	868	77115	28949	632
✶ △ ORLANDO REGIONAL MEDICAL CENTER, (Includes Arnold Palmer Hospital for Children and Women; M. D. Anderson Cancer Center–Orlando; Sand Lake Hospital; St. Cloud Hospital; South Seminole Hospital; South Lake Hospital and Leesburg Regional Medical Center), 1414 Kuhl Avenue, Zip 32806–2093; tel. 407/841–5111; Abe Lopman, Executive Director **A**1 2 3 5 7 8 9 10 **F**2 3 4 7 8 9 10 11 12 13 14 15 16 17 18 19 20 21 22 23 24 25 26 27 28 29 30 31 32 34 35 37 38 39 40 41 42 43 44 45 46 47 48 49 51 52 53 54 55 56 57 58 59 60 61 63 64 65 66 67 70 71 72 73 74 **P**5 7 **S** Orlando Regional Healthcare System, Orlando, FL **N** Orlando Regional Healthcare System, Orlando, FL	23	10	904	44031	596	452930	5716	439859	214383	6513
□ PRINCETON HOSPITAL, 1800 Mercy Drive, Zip 32808–5694; tel. 407/295–5151; Randall Phillips, President and Chief Executive Officer (Nonreporting) **A**1 9 10	23	10	150	—	—	—	—	—	—	—
□ UNIVERSITY BEHAVIORAL CENTER, 2500 Discovery Drive, Zip 32826–3711; tel. 407/281–7000; David L. Beardsley, Administrator **A**1 10 **F**3 17 26 27 28 39 52 53 54 55 56 57 58 59 65 **S** Health Management Associates, Naples, FL	33	22	47	828	34	15995	—	6779	3133	97
□ VALUEMARK BEHAVIORAL HEALTHCARE SYSTEM OF FLORIDA, (Formerly ValueMark–Laurel Oaks Health), 6601 Central Florida Parkway, Zip 32821–8091; tel. 407/345–5000; Robert Berteau, Chief Executive Officer **A**1 **F**1 14 15 16 52 53 56 58 59 **P**6 **S** ValueMark Healthcare Systems, Inc., Atlanta, GA	33	52	48	93	119	18083	0	3764	2335	86
ORMOND BEACH—Volusia County										
✶ ○ ATLANTIC MEDICAL CENTER–ORMOND, (Formerly Columbia Medical Center), 264 South Atlantic Avenue, Zip 32176–8192; tel. 904/672–4161; Thomas R. Pentz, Chief Executive Officer (Nonreporting) **A**1 9 10 11 12 13 **S** Columbia/HCA Healthcare Corporation, Nashville, TN	33	10	119	—	—	—	—	—	—	—
✶ △ MEMORIAL HOSPITAL–ORMOND BEACH, 875 Sterthaus Avenue, Zip 32174–5197; tel. 904/676–6000; Clark P. Christianson, Senior Vice President and Administrator (Total facility includes 17 beds in nursing home–type unit) **A**1 7 9 10 **F**4 7 8 10 11 12 14 15 16 17 19 20 21 22 23 24 25 26 28 29 30 31 32 33 34 35 37 39 40 41 42 43 44 45 46 49 60 61 64 65 66 67 71 73 74 **P**1 6 8 **S** Memorial Health Systems, Ormond Beach, FL	23	10	205	8521	128	48730	516	75604	28076	—
PAHOKEE—Palm Beach County										
□ EVERGLADES REGIONAL MEDICAL CENTER, 200 South Barfield Highway, Zip 33476–1897; tel. 407/924–5200; Donald A. Anderson, President and Chief Executive Officer (Nonreporting) **A**1 9 10 **N** Lake Okeechobee Rural Health Network, Belle Glade, FL	23	10	63	—	—	—	—	—	—	—
PALATKA—Putnam County										
✶ PUTNAM COMMUNITY MEDICAL CENTER, (Formerly Columbia Putnam Medical Center), Highway 20 West, Zip 32177, Mailing Address: P.O. Box 778, Zip 32178–0778; tel. 904/328–5711; David Whalen, President and Chief Executive Officer **A**1 9 10 **F**7 8 12 14 15 16 17 19 21 22 26 27 28 29 30 31 32 33 34 35 37 39 40 41 42 44 45 46 49 51 52 54 55 56 57 59 60 63 64 65 66 67 71 72 73 74 **P**4 5 7 8 **S** Columbia/HCA Healthcare Corporation, Nashville, TN **N** Columbia/HCA North Florida Division, Tallahassee, FL; The Health Advantage Network, Winter Park, FL	33	10	161	6677	93	82764	453	—	—	482
PALM BEACH GARDENS—Palm Beach County										
✶ PALM BEACH GARDENS MEDICAL CENTER, 3360 Burns Road, Zip 33410–4304; tel. 561/622–1411; Clint Matthews, Chief Executive Officer (Nonreporting) **A**1 9 10 **S** TENET Healthcare Corporation, Santa Barbara, CA **N** Tenet South Florida Health System Network, Fort Lauderdale, FL; Med Connect, Ft Lauderdale, FL	33	10	204	—	—	—	—	—	—	—
PANAMA CITY—Bay County										
✶ BAY MEDICAL CENTER, 615 North Bonita Avenue, Zip 32401–3600, Mailing Address: P.O. Box 2515, Zip 32402–2515; tel. 850/769–1511; Ronald V. Wolff, President and Chief Executive Officer **A**1 2 9 10 **F**4 7 8 10 11 12 14 15 16 17 19 21 22 24 25 27 28 30 31 32 33 34 35 37 39 40 41 42 43 44 46 48 49 52 59 60 63 65 71 72 73 74 **P**5	16	10	315	12804	184	92458	762	108848	43575	1525
✶ GULF COAST MEDICAL CENTER, (Formerly Columbia Gulf Coast Hospital), 449 West 23rd Street, Zip 32405–4593, Mailing Address: P.O. Box 15309, Zip 32406–5309; tel. 850/769–8341; Donald E. Butts, Chief Executive Officer (Nonreporting) **A**1 2 9 10 **S** Columbia/HCA Healthcare Corporation, Nashville, TN **N** Columbia/HCA North Florida Division, Tallahassee, FL; The Health Advantage Network, Winter Park, FL	33	10	176	—	—	—	—	—	—	—
✶ U. S. AIR FORCE HOSPITAL, Tyndall AFB, Zip 32403–5300; tel. 850/283–7515; Colonel Harvey R. Crowder, Commander (Nonreporting) **A**1 **S** Department of the Air Force, Bowling AFB, DC	41	10	25	—	—	—	—	—	—	—
PATRICK AFB—Brevard County										
★ U. S. AIR FORCE HOSPITAL, 1381 South Patrick Drive, Zip 32925–3606; tel. 407/494–8102; Colonel William Swindling, Commanding Officer (Nonreporting) **S** Department of the Air Force, Bowling AFB, DC	41	10	15	—	—	—	—	—	—	—

Hospital, Address, Telephone, Administrator, Approval, Facility, and Physician Codes, Health Care System, Network	Classi-fication Codes		Utilization Data					Expense (thousands) of dollars		
	Control	Service	Staffed Beds	Admissions	Census	Outpatient Visits	Births	Total	Payroll	Personnel

★ American Hospital Association (AHA) membership
□ Joint Commission on Accreditation of Healthcare Organizations (JCAHO) accreditation
+ American Osteopathic Healthcare Association (AOHA) membership
○ American Osteopathic Association (AOA) accreditation
△ Commission on Accreditation of Rehabilitation Facilities (CARF) accreditation
Control codes 61, 63, 64, 71, 72 and 73 indicate hospitals listed by AOHA, but not registered by AHA. For definition of numerical codes, see page A4

PEMBROKE PINES—Broward County

✠ MEMORIAL HOSPITAL PEMBROKE, 2301 University Drive, Zip 33024; tel. 954/962–9650; J. E. Piriz, Administrator **A**1 9 10 **F**1 2 3 4 5 6 7 8 9 10 11 12 13 14 15 16 17 18 19 20 21 22 23 24 25 26 27 28 29 30 31 32 33 34 35 36 37 38 39 41 42 43 44 45 46 47 48 49 50 51 52 53 54 55 56 57 58 59 60 61 62 63 64 65 66 67 68 69 70 71 72 73 74 **P**5 8 **S** Memorial Healthcare System, Hollywood, FL **N** Memorial Healthcare System, Hollywood, FL; Columbia/HCA East Florida Division, Winter Park, FL; The Health Advantage Network, Winter Park, FL	16	10	190	4215	62	47683	0	37158	2254	347
✠ MEMORIAL HOSPITAL WEST, 703 North Flamingo Road, Zip 33028; tel. 954/436–5000; Zeff Ross, Administrator **A**1 9 10 **F**1 2 3 4 7 8 10 11 12 13 14 15 16 17 18 19 20 21 22 23 24 25 26 27 28 29 30 31 32 33 34 35 37 38 39 40 41 42 43 44 46 47 48 49 51 52 53 54 55 56 57 58 59 60 61 63 64 65 66 67 68 70 71 72 73 74 **P**1 3 5 7 **S** Memorial Healthcare System, Hollywood, FL **N** Memorial Healthcare System, Hollywood, FL	16	10	110	9771	101	135320	3069	62131	28605	602
SOUTH FLORIDA STATE HOSPITAL, 1000 S.W. 84th Avenue, Zip 33025; tel. 954/967–7000; Thomas S. Gramley, Administrator (Nonreporting) **A**10	12	22	355	—	—	—	—	—	—	—

PENSACOLA—Escambia County

✠ BAPTIST HOSPITAL, 1000 West Moreno, Zip 32501–2393, Mailing Address: P.O. Box 17500, Zip 32522–7500; tel. 850/469–2313; Quinton Studer, President (Total facility includes 57 beds in nursing home–type unit) **A**1 2 9 10 **F**2 3 4 6 7 8 10 11 12 14 15 16 17 18 19 21 22 23 24 25 26 27 28 29 30 31 32 34 35 37 40 41 42 43 44 45 46 49 51 52 53 54 55 56 57 58 59 60 61 62 63 64 65 66 67 68 69 70 71 72 73 74 **P**4 5 7 **S** Baptist Health Care Corporation, Pensacola, FL **N** Baptist Health Care, Inc., Pensacola, FL	23	10	492	13050	242	129936	961	105766	39797	1627
✠ NAVAL HOSPITAL, 6000 West Highway 98, Zip 32512–0003; tel. 850/505–6413; Commander H. M. Chinnery, Director, Administration (Nonreporting) **A**1 3 5 **S** Department of Navy, Washington, DC	43	10	113	—	—	—	—	—	—	—
REHABILITATION INSTITUTE OF WEST FLORIDA See West Florida Regional Medical Center										
✠ SACRED HEART HOSPITAL OF PENSACOLA, 5151 North Ninth Avenue, Zip 32504–8795, Mailing Address: P.O. Box 2700, Zip 32513–2700; tel. 850/416–7000; Patrick J. Madden, President and Chief Executive Officer (Total facility includes 89 beds in nursing home–type unit) **A**1 2 3 5 9 10 **F**4 7 8 10 11 12 13 14 15 16 17 19 20 21 22 23 24 25 28 30 31 32 33 34 35 37 38 39 40 41 42 43 44 45 47 49 56 60 63 64 65 66 67 68 70 71 72 73 74 **P**6 **S** Daughters of Charity National Health System, Saint Louis, MO	21	10	520	19077	339	271499	2875	148653	59956	2318
THE PAVILION See West Florida Regional Medical Center										
△ WEST FLORIDA REGIONAL MEDICAL CENTER, (Formerly Columbia West Florida Regional Medical Center), (Includes Rehabilitation Institute of West Florida, tel. 850/494–6000; The Pavilion, tel. 904/494–5000), 8383 North Davis Highway, Zip 32514–6088, Mailing Address: P.O. Box 18900, Zip 32523–8900; tel. 850/494–4000; Stephen Brandt, President and Chief Executive Officer **A**1 2 7 9 10 **F**3 4 7 8 10 11 12 14 15 16 17 19 21 23 24 26 27 28 29 30 32 35 36 37 39 40 41 42 43 44 45 48 49 52 53 54 56 57 58 59 60 63 64 65 66 67 70 71 73 74 **S** Columbia/HCA Healthcare Corporation, Nashville, TN **N** Columbia/HCA North Florida Division, Tallahassee, FL; Columbia/HCA West Florida Division, Tampa, FL; The Health Advantage Network, Winter Park, FL	33	10	531	13998	235	129282	741	96228	41960	1520

PERRY—Taylor County

DOCTOR'S MEMORIAL HOSPITAL, 407 East Ash Street, Zip 32347–2104, Mailing Address: P.O. Box 1847, Zip 32348–1847; tel. 904/584–0800; H. D. Cannington, Chief Executive Officer **A**9 10 **F**3 8 15 16 19 20 22 28 30 32 33 34 35 44 49 51 64 65 71 73	23	10	15	987	12	22730	3	11072	5338	191

PLANT CITY—Hillsborough County

✠ SOUTH FLORIDA BAPTIST HOSPITAL, 301 North Alexander Street, Zip 33566–9058, Mailing Address: Drawer H., Zip 33564–9058; tel. 813/757–1200; William H. Anderson, Administrator and Chief Executive Officer (Total facility includes 15 beds in nursing home–type unit) (Nonreporting) **A**1 9 10 **N** BayCare Health Network, Inc., Clearwater, FL	23	10	100	—	—	—	—	—	—	—

PLANTATION—Broward County

COLUMBIA PLANTATION GENERAL HOSPITAL See Plantation General Hospital										
✠ PLANTATION GENERAL HOSPITAL, (Formerly Columbia Plantation General Hospital), 401 N.W. 42nd Avenue, Zip 33317–2882; tel. 954/587–5010; Anthony M. Degina, Jr., Chief Executive Officer (Nonreporting) **A**1 9 10 **S** Columbia/HCA Healthcare Corporation, Nashville, TN **N** Med Connect, Ft Lauderdale, FL; Columbia/HCA East Florida Division, Winter Park, FL; The Health Advantage Network, Winter Park, FL	33	10	264	—	—	—	—	—	—	—
✠ WESTSIDE REGIONAL MEDICAL CENTER, (Formerly Columbia Westside Regional Medical Center), 8201 West Broward Boulevard, Zip 33324–9937; tel. 954/473–6600; Michael G. Joseph, Chief Executive Officer (Nonreporting) **A**1 9 10 **S** Columbia/HCA Healthcare Corporation, Nashville, TN **N** Columbia/HCA East Florida Division, Winter Park, FL; The Health Advantage Network, Winter Park, FL	33	10	204	—	—	—	—	—	—	—

POMPANO BEACH—Broward County

✠ COLUMBIA NORTHWEST MEDICAL CENTER, 2801 North State Road 7, Zip 33063–5727, Mailing Address: P.O. Box 639002, Margate, Zip 33063–9002; tel. 954/978–4000; Gina Melby, Chief Executive Officer **A**1 9 10 **F**1 2 3 4 5 6 7 8 9 10 11 12 13 14 15 16 17 18 19 20 21 22 23 24 25 26 27 28 29 30 31 32 33 34 35 36 37 39 40 41 42 43 44 45 46 47 48 49 50 51 52 53 54 55 56 57 58 59 60 61 62 63 64 65 66 67 68 69 70 71 72 73 74 **S** Columbia/HCA Healthcare Corporation, Nashville, TN **N** Columbia/HCA East Florida Division, Winter Park, FL; The Health Advantage Network, Winter Park, FL	33	10	150	7291	87	50283	1035	44167	18828	—

Hospital, Address, Telephone, Administrator, Approval, Facility, and Physician Codes, Health Care System, Network	Classi-fication Codes		Utilization Data					Expense (thousands) of dollars		
★ American Hospital Association (AHA) membership □ Joint Commission on Accreditation of Healthcare Organizations (JCAHO) accreditation + American Osteopathic Healthcare Association (AOHA) membership ○ American Osteopathic Association (AOA) accreditation △ Commission on Accreditation of Rehabilitation Facilities (CARF) accreditation Control codes 61, 63, 64, 71, 72 and 73 indicate hospitals listed by AOHA, but not registered by AHA. For definition of numerical codes, see page A4	Control	Service	Staffed Beds	Admissions	Census	Outpatient Visits	Births	Total	Payroll	Personnel
✠ △ NORTH BROWARD MEDICAL CENTER, 201 Sample Road, Zip 33064–3502; tel. 954/941–8300; James R. Chromik, Regional Vice President, Administration (Total facility includes 18 beds in nursing home–type unit) **A**1 2 7 9 10 **F**2 3 4 7 8 10 11 12 13 14 15 16 17 18 19 21 22 23 24 26 27 28 29 30 31 32 33 34 35 37 38 39 40 41 42 43 44 45 46 47 48 49 50 51 52 53 54 55 56 57 58 59 60 61 63 64 65 66 67 68 69 70 71 72 73 **P**3 7 **S** North Broward Hospital District, Fort Lauderdale, FL	16	10	334	13046	202	122808	—	96085	39617	—
PORT CHARLOTTE—Charlotte County										
✠ BON SECOURS–ST. JOSEPH HOSPITAL, 2500 Harbor Boulevard, Zip 33952–5396; tel. 941/766–4122; Michael L. Harrington, Executive Vice President and Administrator (Total facility includes 104 beds in nursing home–type unit) **A**1 5 9 10 **F**1 8 10 12 14 15 16 17 18 19 22 24 25 26 27 28 29 30 32 33 34 35 37 39 40 41 42 44 45 46 49 60 61 64 65 66 67 71 72 73 74 **P**5 8 **S** Bon Secours Health System, Inc., Marriottsville, MD	21	10	316	8012	196	54809	920	59580	21559	1074
✠ △ FAWCETT MEMORIAL HOSPITAL, 21298 Olean Boulevard, Zip 33952–6765, Mailing Address: P.O. Box 4028, Punta Gorda, Zip 33949–4028; tel. 941/629–1181; Steve Dobbs, Chief Executive Officer (Total facility includes 15 beds in nursing home–type unit) (Nonreporting) **A**1 7 9 10 **S** Columbia/HCA Healthcare Corporation, Nashville, TN **N** Columbia/HCA West Florida Division, Tampa, FL; The Health Advantage Network, Winter Park, FL	33	10	249	—	—	—	—	—	—	—
PORT SAINT JOE—Gulf County										
GULF PINES HOSPITAL, 102 20th Street, Zip 32456–2356, Mailing Address: P.O. Box 70, Zip 32456–0070; tel. 850/227–1121; Kenneth E. Dykes, Sr., Administrator and Chief Executive Officer (Nonreporting) **A**9 10	33	10	45	—	—	—	—	—	—	—
PORT ST. LUCIE—St. Lucie County										
✠ COLUMBIA MEDICAL CENTER–PORT ST. LUCIE, 1800 S.E. Tiffany Avenue, Zip 34952–7580; tel. 561/335–4000; Michael P. Joyce, President and Chief Executive Officer **A**1 9 10 **F**2 3 4 7 8 10 11 12 14 16 17 19 21 22 23 24 25 26 28 29 30 32 34 35 37 38 39 40 42 44 45 46 48 49 50 51 52 53 54 55 56 57 58 59 60 64 65 66 67 71 72 73 74 **P**7 **S** Columbia/HCA Healthcare Corporation, Nashville, TN **N** Columbia/HCA East Florida Division, Winter Park, FL; The Health Advantage Network, Winter Park, FL	33	10	150	8284	110	67523	761	45339	18686	759
□ SAVANNAS HOSPITAL, 2550 S.E. Walton Road, Zip 34952–7197; tel. 561/335–0400; Patricia W. Brown, Executive Director (Nonreporting) **A**1 10	33	22	70	—	—	—	—	—	—	—
PUNTA GORDA—Charlotte County										
□ CHARLOTTE REGIONAL MEDICAL CENTER, 809 East Marion Avenue, Zip 33950–3898, Mailing Address: P.O. Box 51–1328, Zip 33951–1328; tel. 941/639–3131; John D. Harryman, Executive Director (Nonreporting) **A**1 9 10 **S** Health Management Associates, Naples, FL	33	10	148	—	—	—	—	—	—	—
QUINCY—Gadsden County										
GADSDEN COMMUNITY HOSPITAL, U.S. Highway 90 East, Zip 32353, Mailing Address: P.O. Box 1979, Zip 32353–1979; tel. 850/875–1100; Alex Hicks, Acting Chief Executive Officer (Nonreporting) **A**9 10	23	10	51	—	—	—	—	—	—	—
ROCKLEDGE—Brevard County										
□ WUESTHOFF HOSPITAL, 110 Longwood Avenue, Zip 32955–2887, Mailing Address: P.O. Box 565002, Mail Stop 1, Zip 32956–5002; tel. 407/636–2211; Robert O. Carman, President **A**1 2 9 10 **F**3 4 6 7 8 10 11 12 13 14 15 19 20 21 22 23 25 26 28 29 30 31 32 33 34 35 37 38 39 40 41 42 43 44 45 46 49 52 53 54 55 57 58 59 63 65 66 67 71 72 73 74 **P**7	23	10	239	11053	138	149276	957	86287	36658	1654
SAFETY HARBOR—Pinellas County										
MEASE COUNTRYSIDE HOSPITAL, 3231 McMullen–Booth Road, Zip 34695–1098, Mailing Address: P.O. 1098, Zip 34695–1098; tel. 813/725–6111; James A. Pfeiffer, Chief Administrative Officer (Nonreporting) **A**9 10 **S** Morton Plant Mease Health Care, Dunedin, FL **N** Morton Plant Mease Health Care, Dunedin, FL; BayCare Health Network, Inc., Clearwater, FL	23	10	100	—	—	—	—	—	—	—
SAINT AUGUSTINE—St. Johns County										
✠ FLAGLER HOSPITAL, (Includes Flagler Hospital Psychiatric Center, 200 River Haven Way, Zip 32086; tel. 904/824–9800; Brian Trella, Program Director; Flagler Hospital–West, 1955 U.S. 1 South, Zip 32086; tel. 904/826–4700), 400 Health Park Boulevard, Zip 32086–5779; tel. 904/829–5155; James D. Conzemius, President **A**1 9 10 **F**4 7 8 10 15 16 19 21 22 24 28 32 34 35 37 40 41 44 49 52 64 65 67 71 73 74	23	10	260	8991	143	95932	838	66698	26829	794
SAINT CLOUD—Lowndes County										
★ ST. CLOUD HOSPITAL, A DIVISION OF ORLANDO REGIONAL HEALTHCARE SYSTEM, 2906 17th Street, Zip 34769–6099; tel. 407/892–2135; Jim Norris, Executive Director (Nonreporting) **A**9 **S** Orlando Regional Healthcare System, Orlando, FL **N** Orlando Regional Healthcare System, Orlando, FL	23	10	68	—	—	—	—	—	—	—
SAINT PETERSBURG—Pinellas County										
□ ALL CHILDREN'S HOSPITAL, (PEDIATRIC SPECIALTY), 801 Sixth Street South, Zip 33701–4899; tel. 813/898–7451; J. Dennis Sexton, President **A**1 3 5 8 9 10 **F**4 10 12 13 14 17 19 20 21 22 24 25 27 28 29 30 31 32 34 35 37 38 39 41 42 43 44 45 49 51 53 65 66 67 68 69 71 73 **P**1 5 **N** BayCare Health Network, Inc., Clearwater, FL	23	59	216	6868	131	86642	—	133986	60616	1587
✠ BAYFRONT MEDICAL CENTER, 701 Sixth Street South, Zip 33701–4891; tel. 813/823–1234; Sue G. Brody, President and Chief Executive Officer (Total facility includes 13 beds in nursing home–type unit) **A**1 2 3 5 7 9 10 **F**4 7 8 10 11 12 13 14 15 16 17 19 21 24 25 26 27 28 29 30 31 32 34 35 37 38 39 40 41 42 43 44 45 46 48 49 51 60 61 63 64 65 66 67 70 71 72 73 74 **P**1 **N** BayCare Health Network, Inc., Clearwater, FL COLUMBIA ST. PETERSBURG MEDICAL CENTER See St. Petersburg Medical Center	23	10	344	16539	243	185313	3194	141031	56421	1983

Hospital, Address, Telephone, Administrator, Approval, Facility, and Physician Codes, Health Care System, Network	Classi-fication Codes		Utilization Data					Expense (thousands) of dollars		
★ American Hospital Association (AHA) membership □ Joint Commission on Accreditation of Healthcare Organizations (JCAHO) accreditation + American Osteopathic Healthcare Association (AOHA) membership ○ American Osteopathic Association (AOA) accreditation △ Commission on Accreditation of Rehabilitation Facilities (CARF) accreditation Control codes 61, 63, 64, 71, 72 and 73 indicate hospitals listed by AOHA, but not registered by AHA. For definition of numerical codes, see page A4	Control	Service	Staffed Beds	Admissions	Census	Outpatient Visits	Births	Total	Payroll	Personnel
✖ EDWARD WHITE HOSPITAL, (Formerly Columbia Edward White Hospital), 2323 Ninth Avenue North, Zip 33713–6898, Mailing Address: P.O. Box 12018, Zip 33733–2018; tel. 813/323–1111; Barry S. Stokes, President and Chief Executive Officer (Total facility includes 10 beds in nursing home–type unit) **A**1 9 10 **F**4 7 8 10 12 14 17 19 20 21 22 23 24 25 26 28 29 30 31 32 33 34 35 37 41 42 43 44 46 49 51 59 63 64 65 66 67 71 73 74 **P**1 7 **S** Columbia/HCA Healthcare Corporation, Nashville, TN **N** Columbia/HCA West Florida Division, Tampa, FL; The Health Advantage Network, Winter Park, FL	33	10	135	3177	50	41772	—	31606	13442	274
✖ NORTHSIDE HOSPITAL AND HEART INSTITUTE, (Formerly Columbia Northside Medical Center), 6000 49th Street North, Zip 33709–2145; tel. 813/521–4411; Bradley K. Grover, Sr., FACHE, Chief Executive Officer **A**1 9 10 12 13 **F**3 4 7 8 10 11 12 13 15 16 19 20 21 22 23 24 25 26 27 28 29 30 32 33 34 35 37 39 40 41 42 43 44 45 46 49 53 54 55 56 57 58 59 61 64 65 66 67 71 73 74 **P**1 2 7 **S** Columbia/HCA Healthcare Corporation, Nashville, TN **N** Columbia/HCA West Florida Division, Tampa, FL; The Health Advantage Network, Winter Park, FL	33	10	301	8237	119	48770	—		—	633
✖ PALMS OF PASADENA HOSPITAL, 1501 Pasadena Avenue South, Zip 33707–3798; tel. 813/381–1000; John D. Bartlett, Chief Executive Officer (Total facility includes 13 beds in nursing home–type unit) **A**1 2 9 10 **F**8 10 11 12 15 19 22 25 27 32 34 35 37 42 44 46 60 64 65 66 71 73 **P**5 7 **S** TENET Healthcare Corporation, Santa Barbara, CA **N** Tenet South Florida Health System Network, Fort Lauderdale, FL	33	10	267	6666	107	113718	—	59027	20268	615
✖ ST. ANTHONY'S HOSPITAL, 1200 Seventh Avenue North, Zip 33705–1388, Mailing Address: P.O. Box 12588, Zip 33733–2588; tel. 813/825–1100; Sue G. Brody, President and Chief Executive Officer (Total facility includes 30 beds in nursing home–type unit) **A**1 2 9 10 **F**1 2 4 7 8 10 11 12 15 16 17 19 21 24 25 26 27 28 29 30 31 32 33 34 35 37 39 40 41 42 43 44 45 46 48 49 52 54 55 56 57 58 59 60 61 64 65 66 67 71 73 74 **P**7 8 **S** Catholic Health East, Radnor, PA **N** BayCare Health Network, Inc., Clearwater, FL; Allegany Health System, Tampa, FL	23	10	329	11688	198	163699	432	84043	32031	1174
✖ ST. PETERSBURG MEDICAL CENTER, (Formerly Columbia St. Petersburg Medical Center), 6500 38th Avenue North, Zip 33710–1629; tel. 813/384–1414; Bradley K. Grover, Sr., FACHE, President and Chief Executive Officer (Total facility includes 20 beds in nursing home–type unit) (Nonreporting) **A**1 9 10 **S** Columbia/HCA Healthcare Corporation, Nashville, TN **N** Columbia/HCA West Florida Division, Tampa, FL; The Health Advantage Network, Winter Park, FL	33	10	199	—	—	—	—	—	—	—
VENCOR HOSPITAL–ST PETERSBURG, 3030 Sixth Street South, Zip 33705–3720; tel. 813/894–8719; Pamela M. Riter, R.N., Administrator (Nonreporting) **S** Vencor, Incorporated, Louisville, KY	33	49	60	—	—	—	—	—	—	—
SANFORD—Seminole County										
✖ CENTRAL FLORIDA REGIONAL HOSPITAL, (Formerly Columbia Medical Center Sanford), 1401 West Seminole Boulevard, Zip 32771–6764; tel. 407/321–4500; Doug Sills, President and Chief Executive Officer (Nonreporting) **A**1 9 10 **S** Columbia/HCA Healthcare Corporation, Nashville, TN **N** Columbia/HCA East Florida Division, Winter Park, FL; The Health Advantage Network, Winter Park, FL	33	10	226	—	—	—	—	—	—	—
SARASOTA—Sarasota County										
COLUMBIA DOCTORS HOSPITAL See Doctors Hospital of Sarasota										
✖ DOCTORS HOSPITAL OF SARASOTA, (Formerly Columbia Doctors Hospital), 5731 Bee Ridge Road, Zip 34233–5056; tel. 941/342–1100; William C. Lievense, President and Chief Executive Officer (Nonreporting) **A**1 2 9 10 **S** Columbia/HCA Healthcare Corporation, Nashville, TN **N** Columbia/HCA West Florida Division, Tampa, FL; The Health Advantage Network, Winter Park, FL	12	10	147	—	—	—	—	—	—	—
□ △ HEALTHSOUTH REHABILITATION HOSPITAL OF SARASOTA, 3251 Proctor Road, Zip 34231–8538; tel. 941/921–8600; Jeff Garber, Administrator and Chief Executive Officer (Nonreporting) **A**1 7 10 **S** HEALTHSOUTH Corporation, Birmingham, AL	33	46	60	—	—	—	—	—	—	—
✖ △ SARASOTA MEMORIAL HOSPITAL, 1700 South Tamiami Trail, Zip 34239–3555; tel. 941/917–9000; Michael H. Covert, FACHE, President and Chief Executive Officer **A**1 2 5 7 9 10 **F**2 3 4 7 8 10 11 12 14 15 16 17 19 21 22 23 25 26 28 29 30 32 34 35 37 38 39 40 42 43 44 45 46 48 49 50 51 52 53 54 55 56 58 59 60 63 64 65 66 67 71 72 73 74 **P**4 7 8	16	10	607	25453	383	313657	2315	253603	91958	2455
SEBASTIAN—Indian River County										
□ SEBASTIAN RIVER MEDICAL CENTER, 13695 North U.S. Highway 1, Zip 32958–3230, Mailing Address: Box 780838, Zip 32978–0838; tel. 561/589–3186; Stephen L. Midkiff, Executive Director (Nonreporting) **A**1 9 10 **S** Health Management Associates, Naples, FL	33	10	133	—	—	—	—	—	—	—
SEBRING—Highlands County										
✖ FLORIDA HOSPITAL HEARTLAND DIVISION, (Formerly Florida Hospital–Walker), 4200 Sun'n Lake Boulevard, Zip 33872, Mailing Address: P.O. Box 9400, Zip 33872; tel. 941/314–4466; John R. Harding, President and Chief Executive Officer **A**1 9 10 **F**7 8 11 12 13 14 15 16 17 18 19 20 21 22 24 28 29 30 32 35 37 39 40 41 44 45 46 48 49 52 54 55 56 57 58 63 64 65 66 67 71 73 74 **P**6 7 8 **S** Adventist Health System Sunbelt Health Care Corporation, Winter Park, FL **N** Adventist Health System, Winter Park, FL	21	10	195	6970	99	82919	448	64092	23843	827
□ HIGHLANDS REGIONAL MEDICAL CENTER, 3600 South Highlands Avenue, Zip 33870–5495, Mailing Address: Drawer 2066, Zip 33871–2066; tel. 941/385–6101; Micheal Terry, Executive Director (Nonreporting) **A**1 9 10 **S** Health Management Associates, Naples, FL	33	10	126	—	—	—	—	—	—	—

Hospital, Address, Telephone, Administrator, Approval, Facility, and Physician Codes, Health Care System, Network	Classi-fication Codes		Utilization Data					Expense (thousands) of dollars		
★ American Hospital Association (AHA) membership □ Joint Commission on Accreditation of Healthcare Organizations (JCAHO) accreditation + American Osteopathic Healthcare Association (AOHA) membership ○ American Osteopathic Association (AOA) accreditation △ Commission on Accreditation of Rehabilitation Facilities (CARF) accreditation Control codes 61, 63, 64, 71, 72 and 73 indicate hospitals listed by AOHA, but not registered by AHA. For definition of numerical codes, see page A4	Control	Service	Staffed Beds	Admissions	Census	Outpatient Visits	Births	Total	Payroll	Personnel

SOUTH MIAMI—Dade County

□ LARKIN COMMUNITY HOSPITAL, 7031 S.W. 62nd Avenue, Zip 33143–4781; tel. 305/284–7500; Mel D. Deutsch, Administrator (Nonreporting) **A**1 9 10	33	10	112	—	—	—	—	—	—	—

SPRING HILL—Hernando County

✚ OAK HILL HOSPITAL, (Formerly Columbia Regional Medical Center), 11375 Cortez Boulevard, Zip 34611, Mailing Address: P.O. Box 5300, Zip 34611–5300; tel. 352/596–6632; Jay Finnegan, Chief Executive Officer **A**1 2 9 10 **F**7 8 10 11 12 14 15 16 17 19 20 21 22 25 28 29 30 32 34 37 39 40 41 42 44 46 49 63 65 71 73 **P**1 **S** Columbia/HCA Healthcare Corporation, Nashville, TN **N** Columbia/HCA West Florida Division, Tampa, FL; The Health Advantage Network, Winter Park, FL	33	10	204	9832	124	64171	542	—	—	824
✚ SPRING HILL REGIONAL HOSPITAL, 10461 Quality Drive, Zip 34609; tel. 352/688–8200; Sonia I. Gonzalez, R.N., Chief Operating Officer (Nonreporting) **A**1 9 10 **S** Quorum Health Group/Quorum Health Resources, Inc., Brentwood, TN **N** BayCare Health Network, Inc., Clearwater, FL	23	10	75	—	—	—	—	—	—	—

STARKE—Bradford County

✚ SHANDS AT STARKE, 922 East Call Street, Zip 32091–3699; tel. 904/964–6000; Jeannie Baker, Administrator **A**1 9 10 **F**1 19 22 28 30 44 48 49 51 71 73 **S** Shands HealthCare, Gainesville, FL	23	10	23	682	8	58628	—	8457	3469	114

STUART—Martin County

✚ MARTIN MEMORIAL HEALTH SYSTEMS, (Includes Martin Memorial Hospital South, 2100 S.E. Salerno Road, Zip 34997; tel. 407/223–2300), 300 S.E. Hospital Drive, Zip 34994, Mailing Address: P.O. Box 9010, Zip 34995–9010; tel. 561/223–5945; Richmond M. Harman, President and Chief Executive Officer **A**1 2 9 10 **F**5 7 8 10 12 14 15 16 17 19 21 22 23 24 25 26 27 28 29 30 31 32 33 34 35 36 37 39 40 41 42 44 45 46 49 51 54 57 58 59 60 63 65 66 67 71 72 73 74 **P**6 **N** Lake Okeechobee Rural Health Network, Belle Glade, FL; Florida Health Choice, Del Ray Beach, FL	23	10	252	14417	187	192992	1178	127837	56213	1655

SUN CITY CENTER—Hillsborough County

✚ SOUTH BAY HOSPITAL, (Formerly Columbia South Bay Hospital), 4016 State Road 674, Zip 33573–5298; tel. 813/634–3301; Hal Muetzel, Chief Executive Officer **A**1 9 10 **F**8 12 14 16 17 19 21 22 26 28 29 30 32 33 35 36 37 39 41 42 44 45 46 49 59 64 65 67 71 73 **P**7 **S** Columbia/HCA Healthcare Corporation, Nashville, TN **N** Columbia/HCA West Florida Division, Tampa, FL; The Health Advantage Network, Winter Park, FL	33	10	112	4172	66	47517	0	26003	11635	312

SUNRISE—Broward County

□ THE RETREAT, 555 S.W. 148th Avenue, Zip 33325–3072; tel. 954/370–0200; Nancy J. Ansley, Executive Director and Chief Financial Officer (Nonreporting) **A**1 10	33	22	100	—	—	—	—	—	—	—

TALLAHASSEE—Leon County

COLUMBIA TALLAHASSEE COMMUNITY HOSPITAL See Tallahassee Community Hospital

□ △ HEALTHSOUTH REHABILITATION HOSPITAL OF TALLAHASSEE, 1675 Riggins Road, Zip 32308–5315; tel. 850/656–4800; Mike Marshall, Chief Executive Officer (Nonreporting) **A**1 7 10 **S** HEALTHSOUTH Corporation, Birmingham, AL	33	46	70	—	—	—	—	—	—	—
✚ TALLAHASSEE COMMUNITY HOSPITAL, (Formerly Columbia Tallahassee Community Hospital), 2626 Capital Medical Boulevard, Zip 32308–4499; tel. 850/656–5000; Thomas Paul Pemberton, Chief Executive Officer (Nonreporting) **A**1 9 10 **S** Columbia/HCA Healthcare Corporation, Nashville, TN **N** Columbia/HCA North Florida Division, Tallahassee, FL; The Health Advantage Network, Winter Park, FL	33	10	180	—	—	—	—	—	—	—
✚ TALLAHASSEE MEMORIAL REGIONAL MEDICAL CENTER, 1300 Miccosukee Road, Zip 32308–5093; tel. 850/681–1155; Duncan Moore, President and Chief Executive Officer (Total facility includes 110 beds in nursing home–type unit) **A**1 2 3 5 9 10 **F**3 4 7 8 10 11 14 15 16 17 19 21 22 23 24 25 26 27 28 29 30 31 32 34 35 37 38 39 40 41 42 43 44 45 46 47 49 51 52 53 54 55 56 57 58 59 60 61 63 64 65 66 67 69 71 73 74 **P**6	23	10	574	23631	421	260522	3666	196487	91468	2825

TAMARAC—Broward County

✚ UNIVERSITY HOSPITAL AND MEDICAL CENTER, (Formerly Columbia University Hospital), (Includes University Pavilion, 7425 North University Drive, Zip 33328; tel. 305/722–9933), 7201 North University Drive, Zip 33321–2996; tel. 954/721–2200; James A. Cruickshank, Chief Executive Officer (Nonreporting) **A**1 9 10 **S** Columbia/HCA Healthcare Corporation, Nashville, TN **N** Columbia/HCA East Florida Division, Winter Park, FL; The Health Advantage Network, Winter Park, FL	33	10	211	—	—	—	—	—	—	—

TAMPA—Hillsborough County

□ CHARTER BEHAVIORAL HEALTH SYSTEM OF TAMPA BAY, 4004 North Riverside Drive, Zip 33603–3212; tel. 813/238–8671; James C. Hill, Chief Executive Officer (Nonreporting) **A**1 **S** Magellan Health Services, Atlanta, GA	33	22	146	—	—	—	—	—	—	—
✚ H. LEE MOFFITT CANCER CENTER AND RESEARCH INSTITUTE, (CANCER), 12902 Magnolia Drive, Zip 33612–9497; tel. 813/972–4673; John C. Ruckdeschel, M.D., Director and Chief Executive Officer **A**1 2 3 5 8 9 10 **F**8 14 16 17 19 20 21 26 30 31 33 34 37 39 42 44 45 46 49 54 55 58 60 65 67 69 71 73 74	23	49	115	4245	77	89477	—	94739	35034	1109
✚ △ JAMES A. HALEY VETERANS HOSPITAL, 13000 Bruce B. Downs Boulevard, Zip 33612–4798; tel. 813/972–2000; Richard A. Silver, Director (Total facility includes 209 beds in nursing home–type unit) (Nonreporting) **A**1 3 5 7 8 9 **S** Department of Veterans Affairs, Washington, DC	45	10	640	—	—	—	—	—	—	—

Hospital, Address, Telephone, Administrator, Approval, Facility, and Physician Codes, Health Care System, Network	Classi-fication Codes		Utilization Data					Expense (thousands) of dollars		
	Control	Service	Staffed Beds	Admissions	Census	Outpatient Visits	Births	Total	Payroll	Personnel

Approval/membership symbols legend:
★ American Hospital Association (AHA) membership
□ Joint Commission on Accreditation of Healthcare Organizations (JCAHO) accreditation
+ American Osteopathic Healthcare Association (AOHA) membership
○ American Osteopathic Association (AOA) accreditation
△ Commission on Accreditation of Rehabilitation Facilities (CARF) accreditation
Control codes 61, 63, 64, 71, 72 and 73 indicate hospitals listed by AOHA, but not registered by AHA. For definition of numerical codes, see page A4

Hospital	Control	Service	Staffed Beds	Admissions	Census	Outpatient Visits	Births	Total	Payroll	Personnel
✸ MEMORIAL HOSPITAL OF TAMPA, 2901 Swann Avenue, Zip 33609–4057; tel. 813/873–6400; Charles F. Scott, President and Chief Executive Officer **A**1 5 9 10 **F**1 3 4 8 10 11 12 16 17 18 19 21 22 24 26 28 29 30 31 32 33 35 37 38 39 41 42 44 45 47 48 49 51 52 53 56 57 58 59 63 64 65 66 71 73 74 **P**7 8 **S** TENET Healthcare Corporation, Santa Barbara, CA	33	10	138	4402	68	29996	—	27065	11438	463
✸ SHRINERS HOSPITALS FOR CHILDREN, TAMPA, 12502 North Pine Drive, Zip 33612–9499; tel. 813/972–2250; John Holtz, Administrator **A**1 3 5 **F**14 15 17 19 21 27 30 34 35 44 49 63 64 65 71 73 **S** Shriners Hospitals for Children, Tampa, FL	23	57	60	1113	34	10380	0	—	—	272
✸ ST. JOSEPH'S HOSPITAL, (Includes Tampa Children's Hospital at St. Joseph's, St. Joseph's Women's Hospital – Tampa, 3030 West Dr. Martin L. King Boulevard, Zip 33607–6394; tel. 813/879–4730), 3001 West Martin Luther King Boulevard, Zip 33607–6387, Mailing Address: P.O. Box 4227, Zip 33677–4227; tel. 813/870–4000; Isaac Mallah, President and Chief Executive Officer (Total facility includes 19 beds in nursing home–type unit) **A**1 2 5 9 10 **F**4 7 8 10 11 15 16 17 19 21 22 24 26 29 30 31 32 34 35 37 38 40 41 42 43 44 46 47 49 52 54 55 56 58 59 60 63 64 65 67 70 71 73 74 **P**7 8 **S** Catholic Health East, Radnor, PA **N** BayCare Health Network, Inc., Clearwater, FL; Allegany Health System, Tampa, FL	21	10	883	33541	496	—	5827	282266	96619	3911
✸ △ TAMPA GENERAL HEALTHCARE, Davis Islands, Zip 33606, Mailing Address: P.O. Box 1289, Zip 33601–1289; tel. 813/251–7000; Bruce Siegel, M.D., M.P.H., President and Chief Executive Officer (Total facility includes 24 beds in nursing home–type unit) **A**1 3 5 7 8 9 10 **F**3 4 5 7 8 9 10 11 12 13 14 15 16 17 18 19 21 22 23 24 25 26 28 29 30 31 32 34 35 37 38 40 41 42 43 44 45 46 47 48 49 51 52 53 54 55 56 57 58 59 60 61 64 65 66 67 68 69 70 71 72 73 74 **P**4 7	16	10	811	22996	430	315074	3260	289019	—	2607
✸ TOWN AND COUNTRY HOSPITAL, 6001 Webb Road, Zip 33615–3291; tel. 813/885–6666; Charles F. Scott, President (Nonreporting) **A**1 5 9 10 **S** TENET Healthcare Corporation, Santa Barbara, CA **N** Tenet South Florida Health System Network, Fort Lauderdale, FL	32	10	148	—	—	—	—	—	—	—
TRANSITIONAL HOSPITAL OF TAMPA See Vencor Hospital – Central Tampa										
□ UNIVERSITY COMMUNITY HOSPITAL, 3100 East Fletcher Avenue, Zip 33613–4688; tel. 813/971–6000; Norman V. Stein, President (Total facility includes 20 beds in nursing home–type unit) **A**1 2 9 10 **F**4 7 8 10 11 12 14 15 16 17 19 20 21 22 23 24 26 27 28 29 30 31 32 34 35 37 38 39 40 41 42 43 44 45 46 47 48 49 60 61 63 64 65 67 71 72 73 74 **N** BayCare Health Network, Inc., Clearwater, FL	23	10	424	17373	241	—	2226	145138	64623	2049
○ UNIVERSITY COMMUNITY HOSPITAL–CARROLLWOOD, 7171 North Dale Mabry Highway, Zip 33614–2699; tel. 813/558–8001; Larry J. Archbell, Vice President Operations **A**9 10 11 12 13 **F**4 7 8 10 11 12 14 15 16 17 19 20 21 22 23 24 26 27 28 29 30 31 32 34 35 37 38 39 40 41 42 43 44 45 46 47 48 49 60 61 63 64 65 67 71 72 73 74 **N** BayCare Health Network, Inc., Clearwater, FL	23	10	120	3516	43	28160	—	23229	11315	373
□ VENCOR HOSPITAL – CENTRAL TAMPA, (Formerly Transitional Hospital of Tampa), 4801 North Howard Avenue, Zip 33603–1484; tel. 813/874–7575; Ken Stone, Administrator (Nonreporting) **A**1 5 10 **S** Transitional Hospitals Corporation, Las Vegas, NV	33	49	102	—	—	—	—	—	—	—
□ VENCOR HOSPITAL–TAMPA, 4555 South Manhattan Avenue, Zip 33611–2397; tel. 813/839–6341; Theresa Hunkins, Administrator (Nonreporting) **A**1 3 5 10 **S** Vencor, Incorporated, Louisville, KY	33	49	73	—	—	—	—	—	—	—
TARPON SPRINGS—Pinellas County										
✸ HELEN ELLIS MEMORIAL HOSPITAL, 1395 South Pinellas Avenue, Zip 34689–3721, Mailing Address: P.O. Box 1487, Zip 34688–1487; tel. 813/942–5000; Joseph N. Kiefer, Administrator (Total facility includes 18 beds in nursing home–type unit) **A**1 9 10 **F**7 8 10 11 12 16 17 19 21 22 25 26 28 29 30 32 34 35 37 39 40 41 42 44 45 46 49 64 65 67 71 72 73 **P**8	23	10	168	7566	115	66309	496	56207	22128	670
TAVERNIER—Monroe County										
✸ MARINERS HOSPITAL, 50 High Point Road, Zip 33070–2031; tel. 305/852–4418; Robert H. Luse, Chief Executive Officer **A**1 9 10 **F**8 15 16 17 19 21 22 28 29 30 32 33 34 35 37 44 49 63 65 71 73 **P**1 **S** Baptist Health System of South Florida, Miami, FL **N** Dimensions Health/Baptist Health Systems, Miami, FL	23	10	31	1111	13	15310	1	11805	4761	160
TEQUESTA—Martin County										
□ SANDYPINES, 11301 S.E. Tequesta Terrace, Zip 33469–8146; tel. 561/744–0211; David L. Beardsley, Administrator (Nonreporting) **A**1 9 **S** Health Management Associates, Naples, FL	33	52	60	—	—	—	—	—	—	—
TITUSVILLE—Brevard County										
□ PARRISH MEDICAL CENTER, 951 North Washington Avenue, Zip 32796–2194; tel. 407/268–6111; Rod L. Baker, President and Chief Executive Officer **A**1 2 9 10 **F**1 3 4 7 8 10 12 14 15 16 17 19 20 21 22 24 25 27 28 29 30 31 32 33 34 35 37 39 40 42 44 45 46 49 56 60 63 65 66 67 69 71 72 73 74 **P**4 8	16	10	210	8174	102	87988	582	54178	24615	731
VENICE—Sarasota County										
✸ BON SECOURS–VENICE HOSPITAL, 540 The Rialto, Zip 34285–2900; tel. 941/485–7711; Roy E. Hess, Executive Vice President and Administrator (Total facility includes 36 beds in nursing home–type unit) **A**1 2 9 10 **F**8 10 12 15 16 17 19 21 22 23 25 26 27 28 29 30 31 32 34 35 37 41 42 44 46 49 52 56 57 64 65 67 71 72 73 **P**8 **S** Bon Secours Health System, Inc., Marriottsville, MD	21	10	209	9202	122	147268	—	69986	25923	1013

Hospital, Address, Telephone, Administrator, Approval, Facility, and Physician Codes, Health Care System, Network	Classi-fication Codes		Utilization Data					Expense (thousands) of dollars		
★ American Hospital Association (AHA) membership □ Joint Commission on Accreditation of Healthcare Organizations (JCAHO) accreditation + American Osteopathic Healthcare Association (AOHA) membership ○ American Osteopathic Association (AOA) accreditation △ Commission on Accreditation of Rehabilitation Facilities (CARF) accreditation Control codes 61, 63, 64, 71, 72 and 73 indicate hospitals listed by AOHA, but not registered by AHA. For definition of numerical codes, see page A4	Control	Service	Staffed Beds	Admissions	Census	Outpatient Visits	Births	Total	Payroll	Personnel

VERO BEACH—Indian River County

□ △ HEALTHSOUTH TREASURE COAST REHABILITATION HOSPITAL, 1600 37th Street, Zip 32960–6549; tel. 561/778–2100; Denise B. McGrath, Chief Executive Officer (Nonreporting) **A**1 7 10 **S** HEALTHSOUTH Corporation, Birmingham, AL	33	46	70	—	—	—	—	—	—	—
✸ INDIAN RIVER MEMORIAL HOSPITAL, 1000 36th Street, Zip 32960–6592; tel. 561/567–4311; Michael J. O'Grady, Jr., President and Chief Executive Officer (Total facility includes 20 beds in nursing home–type unit) **A**1 2 9 10 **F**3 7 8 10 11 12 14 15 16 17 19 21 22 23 28 29 30 31 32 33 34 35 37 39 40 41 42 44 45 46 49 51 52 53 54 55 56 57 58 59 60 63 64 65 66 67 71 73 74 **P**8 **N** Community Health Network of Indian River County, Vero Beach, FL	23	10	247	10227	154	65927	837	90408	36826	1070

WEST PALM BEACH—Palm Beach County

45TH STREET MENTAL HEALTH CENTER, 1041 45th Street, Zip 33407–2494; tel. 561/844–9741; Terry H. Allen, Executive Director (Nonreporting) **A**10	23	22	44							
✸ ○ COLUMBIA HOSPITAL, 2201 45th Street, Zip 33407–2069; tel. 561/842–6141; Sharon L. Roush, Chief Executive Officer **A**1 9 10 11 12 **F**3 4 5 7 8 10 11 12 13 14 16 17 19 20 21 22 23 25 26 27 28 29 30 31 32 34 35 37 39 40 41 42 43 44 45 46 47 49 52 53 54 55 56 57 58 59 60 61 64 65 66 67 68 69 71 72 73 74 **P**7 **S** Columbia/HCA Healthcare Corporation, Nashville, TN	33	10	250	7067	119	45211	350	—	—	666
✸ GOOD SAMARITAN MEDICAL CENTER, Flagler Drive at Palm Beach Lakes Boulevard, Zip 33401–3499; tel. 561/655–5511; Phillip C. Dutcher, Interim President (Nonreporting) **A**1 2 9 10 **S** Catholic Health East, Radnor, PA **N** Med Connect, Ft Lauderdale, FL; Florida Health Choice, Del Ray Beach, FL	23	10	341	—	—	—	—	—	—	—
HOSPICE OF PALM BEACH COUNTY, 5300 East Avenue, Zip 33407–2352; tel. 561/848–5200; Deborah S. Dailey, President and Chief Executive Officer (Nonreporting)	23	49	24							
✸ △ ST. MARY'S HOSPITAL, 901 45th Street, Zip 33407–2495, Mailing Address: P.O. Box 24620, Zip 33416–4620; tel. 561/844–6300; Phillip C. Dutcher, President and Chief Executive Officer (Nonreporting) **A**1 7 9 10 **S** Catholic Health East, Radnor, PA **N** The Mount Sinai Health System, New York, NY; Lake Okeechobee Rural Health Network, Belle Glade, FL; Med Connect, Ft Lauderdale, FL; Allegany Health System, Tampa, FL; Florida Health Choice, Del Ray Beach, FL	23	10	433	—	—	—	—	—	—	—
✸ VETERANS AFFAIRS MEDICAL CENTER, 7305 North Military Trail, Zip 33410–6400; tel. 561/882–8262; Lucille W. Swanson, Ph.D., Acting Director (Total facility includes 98 beds in nursing home–type unit) **A**1 9 **F**1 2 3 4 8 10 11 12 14 15 16 17 18 19 20 21 22 23 25 26 27 28 29 30 31 32 33 34 35 37 39 42 43 44 45 46 48 49 50 51 52 54 55 56 57 58 59 60 61 64 65 67 69 71 72 73 74 **S** Department of Veterans Affairs, Washington, DC	45	10	233	4097	172	269621	0	115527	74250	1509
□ ○ WELLINGTON REGIONAL MEDICAL CENTER, 10101 Forest Hill Boulevard, Zip 33414–6199; tel. 561/798–8500; Gregory E. Boyer, Chief Executive Officer (Nonreporting) **A**1 2 9 10 11 12 13 **S** Universal Health Services, Inc., King of Prussia, PA	33	10	93	—	—	—	—	—	—	—

WILLISTON—Levy County

□ NATURE COAST REGIONAL HEALTH NETWORK, 125 S.W. Seventh Street, Zip 32696, Mailing Address: P.O. Drawer 550, Zip 32696–0550; tel. 352/528–2801; Chris Wearmouth, Administrator **A**1 9 10 **F**8 12 14 17 19 21 22 26 27 28 30 32 33 34 37 41 44 46 48 49 57 59 64 65 71 72 73 **P**4	33	10	40	835	10	21322	—	—	—	—

WINTER GARDEN—Orange County
HEALTH CENTRAL See Ocoee

WINTER HAVEN—Polk County

✸ △ WINTER HAVEN HOSPITAL, 200 Avenue F. N.E., Zip 33881–4193; tel. 941/297–1899; Lance W. Anastasio, President (Total facility includes 47 beds in nursing home–type unit) (Nonreporting) **A**1 7 9 10 **N** Mid–Florida Medical Services, Inc., Winter Haven, FL	23	10	435	—	—	—	—	—	—	—

WINTER PARK—Orange County

✸ WINTER PARK MEMORIAL HOSPITAL, (Includes Winter Park Psychiatric Care Center, 1600 Dodd Road, Zip 32792; tel. 407/677–6842), 200 North Lakemont Avenue, Zip 32792–3273; tel. 407/646–7000; Douglas P. DeGraaf, Chief Executive Officer (Nonreporting) **A**1 2 9 10 **S** Columbia/HCA Healthcare Corporation, Nashville, TN **N** Columbia/HCA East Florida Division, Winter Park, FL; The Health Advantage Network, Winter Park, FL	33	10	339	—	—	—	—	—	—	—

ZEPHYRHILLS—Pasco County

✸ EAST PASCO MEDICAL CENTER, 7050 Gall Boulevard, Zip 33541–1399; tel. 813/788–0411; Paul Michael Norman, President (Total facility includes 11 beds in nursing home–type unit) (Nonreporting) **A**1 9 10 **S** Adventist Health System Sunbelt Health Care Corporation, Winter Park, FL **N** BayCare Health Network, Inc., Clearwater, FL; Adventist Health System, Winter Park, FL	21	10	120	—	—	—	—	—	—	—

GEORGIA

Resident population 7,486 (in thousands)
Resident population in metro areas 68.1%
Birth rate per 1,000 population 15.7
65 years and over 9.9%
Percent of persons without health insurance 17.8%

Hospital, Address, Telephone, Administrator, Approval, Facility, and Physician Codes, Health Care System, Network	Classi-fication Codes		Utilization Data					Expense (thousands) of dollars		
★ American Hospital Association (AHA) membership ☐ Joint Commission on Accreditation of Healthcare Organizations (JCAHO) accreditation + American Osteopathic Healthcare Association (AOHA) membership ○ American Osteopathic Association (AOA) accreditation △ Commission on Accreditation of Rehabilitation Facilities (CARF) accreditation Control codes 61, 63, 64, 71, 72 and 73 indicate hospitals listed by AOHA, but not registered by AHA. For definition of numerical codes, see page A4	Control	Service	Staffed Beds	Admissions	Census	Outpatient Visits	Births	Total	Payroll	Personnel

ADEL—Cook County

☐ MEMORIAL HOSPITAL OF ADEL, 706 North Parrish Avenue, Zip 31620–0677, Mailing Address: Box 677, Zip 31620–0677; tel. 912/896–2251; Wade E. Keck, Chief Executive Officer (Total facility includes 95 beds in nursing home–type unit) **A**1 9 10 **F**7 14 15 16 17 19 22 32 37 40 44 46 49 64 71 73 **S** Memorial Health Services, Adel, GA	33	10	155	2331	116	9611	169	10719	4714	274

ALBANY—Dougherty County

⊠ PALMYRA MEDICAL CENTERS, (Formerly Columbia Palmyra Medical Centers), 2000 Palmyra Road, Zip 31701–1528, Mailing Address: P.O. Box 1908, Zip 31702–1908; tel. 912/434–2000; Allen Golson, Chief Executive Officer **A**1 9 10 **F**10 13 14 18 19 21 22 23 24 26 28 30 31 34 35 37 39 41 42 44 45 46 48 49 66 67 70 71 73 **P**5 **S** Columbia/HCA Healthcare Corporation, Nashville, TN **N** Principal Health Care of Georgia, Atlanta, GA; Georgia 1st, Inc., Decatur, GA	33	10	216	4472	83	25449	0	—	14079	465
⊠ PHOEBE PUTNEY MEMORIAL HOSPITAL, 417 Third Avenue, Zip 31701–1828, Mailing Address: P.O. Box 1828, Zip 31703–1828; tel. 912/883–1800; Joel Wernick, President and Chief Executive Officer (Nonreporting) **A**1 2 3 5 9 10 **N** The Medical Resource Network, L.L.C., Atlanta, GA	23	10	418	—	—	—	—	—	—	—

ALMA—Bacon County

☐ BACON COUNTY HOSPITAL, 302 South Wayne Street, Zip 31510–2997, Mailing Address: P.O. Drawer 1987, Zip 31510–1987; tel. 912/632–8961; Patsy Busbin, Acting Chief Executive Officer (Total facility includes 88 beds in nursing home–type unit) (Nonreporting) **A**1 9 10	16	10	126	—	—	—	—	—	—	—

AMERICUS—Sumter County

⊠ SUMTER REGIONAL HOSPITAL, 100 Wheatley Drive, Zip 31709–3799; tel. 912/924–6011; Jerry W. Adams, President (Total facility includes 100 beds in nursing home–type unit) **A**1 9 10 **F**4 7 8 10 11 14 15 16 19 21 22 23 27 28 29 30 32 33 34 35 37 39 40 42 43 44 45 46 48 49 51 52 56 57 64 65 69 70 71 72 73 **P**8 **N** Principal Health Care of Georgia, Atlanta, GA; Georgia 1st, Inc., Decatur, GA	15	10	221	5186	158	41534	901	35657	15133	633

ARLINGTON—Calhoun County

CALHOUN MEMORIAL HOSPITAL, 209 Academy & Carswell Streets, Zip 31713, Mailing Address: Drawer R., Zip 31713; tel. 912/725–4272; Peggy Pierce, Administrator (Nonreporting) **A**9 10 **N** The Medical Resource Network, L.L.C., Atlanta, GA	16	10	24	—	—	—	—	—	—	—

ATHENS—Clarke County

⊠ ATHENS REGIONAL MEDICAL CENTER, 1199 Prince Avenue, Zip 30606–2793; tel. 706/549–9977; John A. Drew, President and Chief Executive Officer **A**1 9 10 **F**3 4 7 8 10 11 12 15 16 17 19 21 22 23 25 30 31 34 35 37 38 40 41 42 43 44 46 49 52 57 59 60 61 65 66 71 73 **N** Georgia 1st, Inc., Decatur, GA; The Medical Resource Network, L.L.C., Atlanta, GA	16	10	315	15853	215	93373	1442	131297	52366	1653
☐ CHARTER WINDS HOSPITAL, 240 Mitchell Bridge Road, Zip 30606–2043; tel. 706/546–7277; Susan Lister, Chief Executive Officer (Nonreporting) **A**1 10 **S** Magellan Health Services, Atlanta, GA	33	22	80	—	—	—	—	—	—	—
⊠ ST. MARY'S HOSPITAL, 1230 Baxter Street, Zip 30606–3791; tel. 706/548–7581; Edward J. Fechtel, Jr., President and Chief Executive Officer (Total facility includes 120 beds in nursing home–type unit) (Nonreporting) **A**1 9 10 **N** Principal Health Care of Georgia, Atlanta, GA	23	10	290	—	—	—	—	—	—	—

ATLANTA—Fulton and De Kalb Counties County

★ CHARTER ANCHOR HOSPITAL, (Formerly Anchor Hospital), 5454 Yorktowne Drive, Zip 30349–5305; tel. 770/991–6044; Matthew Crouch, Chief Executive Officer **A**9 10 **F**2 3 14 15 16 17 27 34 45 46 52 53 54 55 56 57 58 59 65 67 73 **P**6 **S** Magellan Health Services, Atlanta, GA	33	82	84	2380	37	8975	0	5166	2289	151
☐ CHARTER BEHAVIORAL HEALTH SYSTEM OF ATLANTA, 811 Juniper Street N.E., Zip 30308–1398; tel. 404/881–5800; Dennis Workman, M.D., Medical Director (Nonreporting) **A**1 9 10 **S** Magellan Health Services, Atlanta, GA	33	22	40	—	—	—	—	—	—	—
☐ CHARTER BEHAVIORAL HEALTH SYSTEM OF ATLANTA AT PEACHFORD, 2151 Peachford Road, Zip 30338–6599; tel. 770/455–3200; Aleen S. Davis, Chief Executive Officer (Nonreporting) **A**1 9 10 **S** Magellan Health Services, Atlanta, GA	33	22	224	—	—	—	—	—	—	—
COLUMBIA DUNWOODY MEDICAL CENTER See Dunwoody Medical Center										
⊠ COLUMBIA METROPOLITAN HOSPITAL, 3223 Howell Mill Road N.W., Zip 30327–4135; tel. 404/351–0500; Neil Heatherly, Chief Executive Officer (Nonreporting) **A**1 10 **S** Columbia/HCA Healthcare Corporation, Nashville, TN	33	49	64	—	—	—	—	—	—	—
COLUMBIA NORTHLAKE REGIONAL MEDICAL CENTER See Northlake Regional Medical Center										
COLUMBIA WEST PACES MEDICAL CENTER See West Paces Medical Center										
⊠ CRAWFORD LONG HOSPITAL OF EMORY UNIVERSITY, 550 Peachtree Street N.E., Zip 30365–2225; tel. 404/686–4411; John Dunklin Henry, Sr., FACHE, Chief Executive Officer **A**1 2 3 5 8 9 10 **F**1 2 3 4 7 8 10 11 12 13 14 17 19 21 22 23 24 25 26 30 31 32 33 34 35 37 38 39 40 41 42 43 44 46 47 48 49 50 51 52 53 54 55 56 57 58 59 60 61 63 64 65 66 67 69 71 74 **N** Georgia 1st, Inc., Decatur, GA	23	10	433	18741	313	84311	1930	191232	73342	1525

Hospital, Address, Telephone, Administrator, Approval, Facility, and Physician Codes, Health Care System, Network	Classi-fication Codes		Utilization Data					Expense (thousands) of dollars		
	Control	Service	Staffed Beds	Admissions	Census	Outpatient Visits	Births	Total	Payroll	Personnel

★ American Hospital Association (AHA) membership
□ Joint Commission on Accreditation of Healthcare Organizations (JCAHO) accreditation
+ American Osteopathic Healthcare Association (AOHA) membership
○ American Osteopathic Association (AOA) accreditation
△ Commission on Accreditation of Rehabilitation Facilities (CARF) accreditation
Control codes 61, 63, 64, 71, 72 and 73 indicate hospitals listed by AOHA, but not registered by AHA. For definition of numerical codes, see page A4

Hospital	Control	Service	Staffed Beds	Admissions	Census	Outpatient Visits	Births	Total	Payroll	Personnel
✚ DUNWOODY MEDICAL CENTER, (Formerly Columbia Dunwoody Medical Center), 4575 North Shallowford Road, Zip 30338–6499; tel. 770/454–2000; Thomas D. Gilbert, President and Chief Executive Officer (Nonreporting) **A**1 10 **S** Columbia/HCA Healthcare Corporation, Nashville, TN	33	10	122	—	—	—	—	—	—	—
✚ △ EGLESTON CHILDREN'S HOSPITAL AT EMORY UNIVERSITY, 1405 Clifton Road N.E., Zip 30322–1101; tel. 404/325–6000; James E. Tally, Ph.D., President and Chief Executive Officer **A**1 3 5 7 8 9 10 **F**4 10 11 12 13 15 16 17 19 20 21 22 25 27 28 29 30 31 32 34 35 38 39 42 43 44 45 46 47 48 49 51 53 54 63 65 66 68 69 70 71 72 73 **P**1 7 **N** Principal Health Care of Georgia, Atlanta, GA; Georgia 1st, Inc., Decatur, GA; The Medical Resource Network, L.L.C., Atlanta, GA	23	50	190	8308	147	178662	—	171626	66868	1585
✚ △ EMORY UNIVERSITY HOSPITAL, 1364 Clifton Road N.E., Zip 30322–1102; tel. 404/727–7021; John Dunklin Henry, Sr., FACHE, Chief Executive Officer **A**1 2 3 5 7 8 9 10 **F**2 3 4 7 8 10 11 12 14 16 17 19 21 22 23 25 26 28 29 30 31 34 35 37 39 41 42 43 44 45 46 48 49 50 51 52 54 55 56 57 58 59 60 61 63 65 66 67 69 71 72 73 74 **P**1 3 **N** Candler Health System, Savannah, GA; Georgia 1st, Inc., Decatur, GA	23	10	513	20336	376	72898	—	290196	100644	2110
✚ △ GEORGIA BAPTIST MEDICAL CENTER, (Formerly Georgia Baptist Health Care System), 303 Parkway Drive N.E., Zip 30312–1239; tel. 404/265–4000; James E. Lathren, President and Chief Executive Officer (Total facility includes 72 beds in nursing home–type unit) (Nonreporting) **A**1 2 3 5 7 8 10 **S** TENET Healthcare Corporation, Santa Barbara, CA	33	10	450	—	—	—	—	—	—	—
GEORGIA MENTAL HEALTH INSTITUTE, 1256 Briarcliff Road N.E., Zip 30306–2694; tel. 404/894–5911; B. C. Robbins, Superintendent (Nonreporting) **A**3 5 10	12	22	222	—	—	—	—	—	—	—
✚ GRADY MEMORIAL HOSPITAL, 80 Butler Street S.E., Zip 30335–3801, Mailing Address: P.O. Box 26189, Zip 30335–3801; tel. 404/616–4252; Edward J. Renford, President and Chief Executive Officer (Total facility includes 354 beds in nursing home–type unit) (Nonreporting) **A**1 2 3 5 8 10 **N** Grady Health System, Atlanta, GA	16	10	1200	—	—	—	—	—	—	—
★ △ HILLSIDE HOSPITAL, 690 Courtney Drive N.E., Zip 30306–0206, Mailing Address: P.O. Box 8247, Zip 31106–0247; tel. 404/875–4551; Teresa Stoker, Executive Director **A**7 **F**12 14 15 16 39 45 52 53 55 59 65	23	52	61	28	61			7892	3939	147
✚ NORTHLAKE REGIONAL MEDICAL CENTER, (Formerly Columbia Northlake Regional Medical Center), 1455 Montreal Road, Zip 30084; tel. 770/270–3000; Michael R. Burroughs, President and Chief Executive Officer **A**1 2 10 **F**7 8 12 14 17 19 21 22 28 32 35 37 38 39 40 41 42 44 48 49 65 71 73 **P**5 **S** Columbia/HCA Healthcare Corporation, Nashville, TN	33	10	120	2899	41	27467	392		—	308
✚ NORTHSIDE HOSPITAL, 1000 Johnson Ferry Road N.E., Zip 30342–1611; tel. 404/851–8000; Sidney Kirschner, President and Chief Executive Officer **A**1 2 9 10 **F**3 7 8 10 11 12 14 15 16 17 18 19 21 22 23 24 25 28 29 30 31 32 33 34 35 37 38 39 40 41 42 44 45 46 49 51 52 54 55 56 58 59 60 61 63 64 65 67 69 71 72 73 74 **N** Principal Health Care of Georgia, Atlanta, GA; Georgia 1st, Inc., Decatur, GA; The Medical Resource Network, L.L.C., Atlanta, GA	23	10	392	32011	26	149387	12660	256660	99988	3050
✚ PIEDMONT HOSPITAL, 1968 Peachtree Road N.W., Zip 30309–1231; tel. 404/605–5000; Richard B. Hubbard, III, President and Chief Executive Officer (Total facility includes 37 beds in nursing home–type unit) (Nonreporting) **A**1 2 3 5 9 10 **N** Promina Health System, Inc., Atlanta, GA; Principal Health Care of Georgia, Atlanta, GA; The Medical Resource Network, L.L.C., Atlanta, GA	23	10	444	—	—	—	—	—	—	—
✚ SAINT JOSEPH'S HOSPITAL OF ATLANTA, 5665 Peachtree Dunwoody Road N.E., Zip 30342–1764; tel. 404/851–7001; Brue Chandler, President and Chief Executive Officer **A**1 2 9 10 **F**4 8 10 11 12 14 15 16 17 19 21 22 23 24 27 28 29 30 31 34 35 37 39 41 42 43 44 45 46 49 50 51 54 60 63 64 65 67 69 71 73 74 **P**4 8 **S** Catholic Health East, Radnor, PA **N** Saint Joseph's Hospital of Atlanta, Atlanta, GA	23	10	346	18234	253	116836	0	199388	78607	2311
□ △ SCOTTISH RITE CHILDREN'S MEDICAL CENTER, 1001 Johnson Ferry Road N.E., Zip 30342–1600; tel. 404/256–5252; James E. Tally, Ph.D., President and Chief Executive Officer **A**1 3 5 7 9 **F**12 13 15 16 17 19 20 21 22 28 29 30 34 35 38 39 41 42 44 45 46 47 48 49 51 54 65 66 67 70 71 72 73 **P**1 **N** Principal Health Care of Georgia, Atlanta, GA	23	59	165	12996	113	148340	0	137071	59247	1482
✚ △ SHEPHERD CENTER, 2020 Peachtree Road N.W., Zip 30309–1465; tel. 404/352–2020; Gary R. Ulicny, Ph.D., President and Chief Executive Officer **A**1 7 9 10 **F**12 14 15 17 20 22 24 34 37 39 45 46 48 49 53 54 58 61 65 67 70 73 **P**6 **N** Principal Health Care of Georgia, Atlanta, GA; The Medical Resource Network, L.L.C., Atlanta, GA	23	46	100	833	72	15060	—	43310	21196	608
□ SOUTHWEST HOSPITAL AND MEDICAL CENTER, 501 Fairburn Road S.W., Zip 30331–2099; tel. 404/699–1111; Marie Cameron, FACHE, President and Chief Executive Officer (Nonreporting) **A**1 3 5 9 10	23	10	80	—	—	—	—	—	—	—
□ VENCOR HOSPITAL–ATLANTA, 705 Juniper Street N.E., Zip 30365–2500; tel. 404/873–2871; Skip Wright, Administrator (Nonreporting) **A**1 10 **S** Vencor, Incorporated, Louisville, KY	33	49	66	—	—	—	—	—	—	—
✚ WESLEY WOODS GERIATRIC HOSPITAL, 1821 Clifton Road N.E., Zip 30329–5102; tel. 404/728–6200; William L. Minnix, Jr., President and Chief Executive Officer **A**1 3 5 10 **F**3 4 6 8 10 11 12 17 19 20 21 22 25 26 27 28 29 30 32 34 35 37 39 41 42 43 44 45 46 48 49 50 51 52 54 55 56 57 58 59 60 62 63 65 67 69 70 71 73 74 **P**6 **N**	23	22	91	1867	60	31416	—	25272	10344	346

Hospital, Address, Telephone, Administrator, Approval, Facility, and Physician Codes, Health Care System, Network	Classi-fication Codes		Utilization Data					Expense (thousands) of dollars		
★ American Hospital Association (AHA) membership □ Joint Commission on Accreditation of Healthcare Organizations (JCAHO) accreditation + American Osteopathic Healthcare Association (AOHA) membership ○ American Osteopathic Association (AOA) accreditation △ Commission on Accreditation of Rehabilitation Facilities (CARF) accreditation Control codes 61, 63, 64, 71, 72 and 73 indicate hospitals listed by AOHA, but not registered by AHA. For definition of numerical codes, see page A4	Control	Service	Staffed Beds	Admissions	Census	Outpatient Visits	Births	Total	Payroll	Personnel

⊠ WEST PACES MEDICAL CENTER, (Formerly Columbia West Paces Medical Center), 3200 Howell Mill Road N.W., Zip 30327–4101; tel. 404/351–0351; Charles H. Keaton, President and Chief Executive Officer **A**1 2 3 10 **F**3 7 8 10 14 15 18 19 21 22 23 25 26 28 29 30 31 32 34 35 37 38 39 40 42 44 48 49 52 53 54 56 58 59 60 64 65 66 67 68 71 72 73 74 **P**7 **S** Columbia/HCA Healthcare Corporation, Nashville, TN	33	10	150	4417	66	24014	597	49255	17928	414
AUGUSTA—Richmond County										
⊠ COLUMBIA AUGUSTA MEDICAL CENTER, 3651 Wheeler Road, Zip 30909–6426; tel. 706/651–3232; Michael K. Kerner, President and Chief Executive Officer **A**1 9 10 **F**3 7 8 9 10 12 16 19 21 22 25 28 29 30 33 34 35 37 40 41 42 44 46 48 49 51 52 53 58 59 60 65 66 71 73 **P**1 6 **S** Columbia/HCA Healthcare Corporation, Nashville, TN	33	10	245	8733	124	78773	1107	63442	28088	793
□ GEORGIA REGIONAL HOSPITAL AT AUGUSTA, 3405 Mike Padgett Highway, Zip 30906–3897; tel. 706/792–7019; Benjamin H. Walker, Acting Superintendent **A**1 3 10 **F**1 3 4 5 6 7 8 9 10 11 12 13 14 17 18 19 20 21 22 23 24 25 26 27 28 29 30 31 32 33 34 35 36 37 38 39 40 41 42 43 44 45 46 47 48 49 50 51 52 53 54 55 56 57 58 59 60 61 62 63 64 65 66 67 68 69 70 71 72 73 74 **P**3 6	12	22	210	2537	171	0	0	20127	13544	422
⊠ MEDICAL COLLEGE OF GEORGIA HOSPITAL AND CLINICS, 1120 15th Street, Zip 30912–5000; tel. 706/721–0211; Patricia Sodomka, FACHE, Executive Director **A**1 2 3 5 8 9 10 12 **F**4 7 8 9 10 11 12 13 15 16 17 19 20 21 22 23 26 27 28 29 30 31 34 35 37 38 39 40 41 42 43 44 46 47 49 51 52 53 54 55 56 57 58 59 60 61 63 65 66 67 69 70 71 73 74 **P**6 **N** Georgia 1st, Inc., Decatur, GA	12	10	496	15025	282	442368	1612	407986	116043	—
⊠ ST. JOSEPH HOSPITAL, 2260 Wrightsboro Road, Zip 30904–4726; tel. 706/481–7000; J. William Paugh, President and Chief Executive Officer **A**1 9 10 **F**7 8 10 12 14 15 16 17 19 22 23 25 26 28 29 30 32 33 34 35 37 38 39 40 42 44 45 49 51 62 65 67 71 73 74 **P**8 **S** Carondelet Health System, Saint Louis, MO	21	10	143	5698	88	21164	1249	73556	32845	964
⊠ UNIVERSITY HOSPITAL, 1350 Walton Way, Zip 30901–2629; tel. 706/722–9011; Donald C. Bray, President and Chief Executive Officer **A**1 2 3 5 9 10 **F**1 2 3 4 6 7 8 10 11 12 14 15 16 17 18 20 21 22 23 24 25 28 29 30 31 32 34 35 37 38 39 40 41 42 43 44 45 46 47 48 49 51 52 54 55 56 57 58 59 61 63 64 65 66 67 68 71 72 73 74 **P**1 5 7 **N** Principal Health Care of Georgia, Atlanta, GA; The Medical Resource Network, L.L.C., Atlanta, GA; University Health, Inc., Augusta, GA	23	10	528	20700	312	238154	2567	220854	84997	3492
⊠ VETERANS AFFAIRS MEDICAL CENTER, 1 Freedom Way, Zip 30904–6285; tel. 706/733–0188; Ralph R. Angelo, Acting Director (Total facility includes 60 beds in nursing home–type unit) **A**1 2 3 5 8 **F**1 3 4 8 10 11 12 14 15 16 17 19 20 21 22 24 26 27 31 32 33 34 35 37 39 41 42 43 44 45 46 48 49 51 52 54 56 57 58 59 60 63 64 65 67 71 73 74 **S** Department of Veterans Affairs, Washington, DC	45	10	526	7277	372	244103	—	157595	79696	2154
⊠ △ WALTON REHABILITATION HOSPITAL, 1355 Independence Drive, Zip 30901–1037; tel. 706/724–7746; Dennis B. Skelley, President and Chief Executive Officer **A**1 7 10 **F**1 2 3 4 5 6 7 8 9 10 11 12 13 14 15 16 17 18 19 20 21 22 23 24 25 26 27 28 29 30 31 32 33 34 35 36 37 38 39 40 41 42 43 44 45 46 47 48 49 50 51 52 53 54 55 56 57 58 59 60 61 62 63 64 65 66 67 68 69 70 71 72 73 74 **P**6 7 **N** Principal Health Care of Georgia, Atlanta, GA	23	46	58	265	41	21355	0	4538	2262	241
AUSTELL—Cobb County										
⊠ △ WELLSTAR COBB HOSPITAL, (Formerly Promina Cobb Hospital), 3950 Austell Road, Zip 30106–1121; tel. 770/732–4000; Thomas E. Hill, Chief Executive Officer **A**1 2 7 9 10 **F**2 3 4 6 7 8 10 11 12 13 14 15 16 17 18 19 20 21 22 24 25 26 28 29 30 31 32 33 34 35 37 38 39 40 41 42 43 44 45 46 48 49 50 51 52 53 54 55 56 57 58 59 60 61 62 64 65 66 67 69 70 71 72 73 74 **P**1 3 7 **S** WellStar Health System, Austell, GA **N** Promina Health System, Inc., Atlanta, GA; Principal Health Care of Georgia, Atlanta, GA; The Medical Resource Network, L.L.C., Atlanta, GA	23	10	311	15196	189	115155	2989	109394	47744	841
BAINBRIDGE—Decatur County										
★ MEMORIAL HOSPITAL AND MANOR, 1500 East Shotwell Street, Zip 31717–4294; tel. 912/246–3500; James G. Peak, Director (Total facility includes 107 beds in nursing home–type unit) (Nonreporting) **A**9 10 **N** Principal Health Care of Georgia, Atlanta, GA	16	10	187	—	—	—	—	—	—	—
BAXLEY—Appling County										
□ APPLING HEALTHCARE SYSTEM, 301 East Tollison Street, Zip 31513–2898; tel. 912/367–9841; Luther E. Reeves, Chief Executive Officer (Total facility includes 101 beds in nursing home–type unit) **A**1 10 **F**7 8 19 22 27 28 30 33 34 37 40 44 48 49 64 71 **P**6 **N** Candler Health System, Savannah, GA; Principal Health Care of Georgia, Atlanta, GA; Georgia 1st, Inc., Decatur, GA; The Medical Resource Network, L.L.C., Atlanta, GA	16	10	137	973	104	18160	58	8678	4253	261
BLAIRSVILLE—Union County										
★ UNION GENERAL HOSPITAL, 214 Hospital Drive, Zip 30512–6538; tel. 706/745–2111; Rebecca T. Dyer, Administrator (Total facility includes 147 beds in nursing home–type unit) **A**9 10 **F**7 8 15 16 19 20 21 22 27 28 30 34 42 44 65 71 73	13	10	147	2023	143	29216	248	9975	6250	190
BLAKELY—Early County										
EARLY MEMORIAL HOSPITAL, 630 Columbia Street, Zip 31723–1798; tel. 912/723–4241; Rodney C. Watford, Administrator (Total facility includes 127 beds in nursing home–type unit) (Nonreporting) **A**10 **S** Archbold Medical Center, Thomasville, GA **N** Georgia 1st, Inc., Decatur, GA; The Medical Resource Network, L.L.C., Atlanta, GA	16	10	176	—	—	—	—	—	—	—

Hospital, Address, Telephone, Administrator, Approval, Facility, and Physician Codes, Health Care System, Network	Classi-fication Codes		Utilization Data					Expense (thousands) of dollars		
★ American Hospital Association (AHA) membership □ Joint Commission on Accreditation of Healthcare Organizations (JCAHO) accreditation + American Osteopathic Healthcare Association (AOHA) membership ○ American Osteopathic Association (AOA) accreditation △ Commission on Accreditation of Rehabilitation Facilities (CARF) accreditation Control codes 61, 63, 64, 71, 72 and 73 indicate hospitals listed by AOHA, but not registered by AHA. For definition of numerical codes, see page A4	Control	Service	Staffed Beds	Admissions	Census	Outpatient Visits	Births	Total	Payroll	Personnel

BLUE RIDGE—Fannin County

⊞ FANNIN REGIONAL HOSPITAL, Highway 5 North, Zip 30513, Mailing Address: P.O. Box 1549, Zip 30513–1549; tel. 706/632–3711; Kent W. McMackin, Chief Executive Officer (Nonreporting) **A**1 9 10 **S** Community Health Systems, Inc., Brentwood, TN	33	10	46	—	—	—	—	—	—	—

BOWDON—Carroll County

BOWDON AREA HOSPITAL, 501 Mitchell Avenue, Zip 30108–1499; tel. 770/258–7207; Yvonne Willis, Administrator **A**9 10 **F**8 22 28 30 33 39 41 44 48 49 65 71 73 **S** Bowdon Corporate Offices, Atlanta, GA	33	10	41	613	12	4508	0	4496	1559	66

BREMEN—Haralson County

⊞ HIGGINS GENERAL HOSPITAL, 200 Allen Memorial Drive, Zip 30110–2012, Mailing Address: P.O. Box 655, Zip 30110–0655; tel. 770/537–5851; Robbie Smith, Administrator **A**1 9 10 **F**8 11 15 19 22 28 29 30 44 46 49 71 **N** Principal Health Care of Georgia, Atlanta, GA; Georgia 1st, Inc., Decatur, GA; The Medical Resource Network, L.L.C., Atlanta, GA	15	10	39	848	13	17792	0	8307	3617	130

BRUNSWICK—Glynn County

⊞ SOUTHEAST GEORGIA REGIONAL MEDICAL CENTER, 3100 Kemble Avenue, Zip 31520–4252, Mailing Address: P.O. Box 1518, Zip 31521–1518; tel. 912/264–7000; E. Berton Whitaker, President and Chief Executive Officer **A**1 2 10 **F**7 8 10 11 14 15 16 19 21 22 23 27 28 29 30 31 33 34 35 37 40 41 42 44 45 46 49 52 56 58 59 60 65 67 71 73 **P**1 3 **S** Quorum Health Group/Quorum Health Resources, Inc., Brentwood, TN **N** Principal Health Care of Georgia, Atlanta, GA; Georgia 1st, Inc., Decatur, GA	16	10	341	12752	177	101946	1191	103107	42869	1289

CAIRO—Grady County

□ GRADY GENERAL HOSPITAL, 1155 Fifth Street S.E., Zip 31728–3142, Mailing Address: P.O. Box 360, Zip 31728–0360; tel. 912/377–1150; Glen C. Davis, Administrator (Nonreporting) **A**1 9 10 **S** Archbold Medical Center, Thomasville, GA **N** Georgia 1st, Inc., Decatur, GA; The Medical Resource Network, L.L.C., Atlanta, GA	23	10	45	—	—	—	—	—	—	—

CALHOUN—Gordon County

⊞ GORDON HOSPITAL, 1035 Red Bud Road, Zip 30701–2082, Mailing Address: P.O. Box 12938, Zip 30703–7013; tel. 706/629–2895; Dennis Kiley, President **A**1 9 10 **F**8 10 12 15 17 19 21 22 23 26 28 30 32 34 35 37 40 44 45 49 50 57 63 65 67 71 72 74 **P**1 **S** Adventist Health System Sunbelt Health Care Corporation, Winter Park, FL **N** Principal Health Care of Georgia, Atlanta, GA; The Medical Resource Network, L.L.C., Atlanta, GA	21	10	54	2193	24	98859	454	23893	10154	308

CAMILLA—Mitchell County

□ MITCHELL COUNTY HOSPITAL, 90 Stephens Street, Zip 31730–1899, Mailing Address: P.O. Box 639, Zip 31730–0639; tel. 912/336–5284; Ronald M. Gilliard, FACHE, Administrator (Total facility includes 156 beds in nursing home–type unit) (Nonreporting) **A**1 10 **S** Archbold Medical Center, Thomasville, GA **N** Georgia 1st, Inc., Decatur, GA; The Medical Resource Network, L.L.C., Atlanta, GA	23	10	182	—	—	—	—	—	—	—

CANTON—Cherokee County

⊞ NORTHSIDE HOSPITAL – CHEROKEE, (Formerly R. T. Jones Hospital), 201 Hospital Road, Zip 30114–2408, Mailing Address: P.O. Box 906, Zip 30114–0906; tel. 770/720–5100; Douglas M. Parker, Chief Executive Officer **A**1 9 10 **F**7 8 15 16 19 21 22 28 29 31 35 39 42 44 45 49 65 67 70 71 73 **N** Principal Health Care of Georgia, Atlanta, GA	16	10	55	2595	31	30991	288	21116	8609	276

CARROLLTON—Carroll County

⊞ TANNER MEDICAL CENTER, 705 Dixie Street, Zip 30117–3818; tel. 770/836–9666; Loy M. Howard, Chief Executive Officer **A**1 9 10 **F**7 8 10 12 15 16 17 19 21 22 23 26 28 29 32 33 34 35 36 37 39 40 41 42 44 46 49 52 58 59 60 62 63 64 65 67 68 69 71 73 74 **P**7 8 **S** Quorum Health Group/Quorum Health Resources, Inc., Brentwood, TN **N** Principal Health Care of Georgia, Atlanta, GA; Georgia 1st, Inc., Decatur, GA	23	10	162	7993	103	—	1119	55351	23693	914

CARTERSVILLE—Bartow County

⊞ COLUMBIA CARTERSVILLE MEDICAL CENTER, 960 Joe Frank Harris Parkway, Zip 30120, Mailing Address: P.O. Box 200008, Zip 30120–9001; tel. 770/382–1530; Keith Sandlin, Chief Executive Officer (Nonreporting) **A**1 9 10 **S** Columbia/HCA Healthcare Corporation, Nashville, TN **N** Principal Health Care of Georgia, Atlanta, GA	33	10	80	—	—	—	—	—	—	—

CEDARTOWN—Polk County

⊞ COLUMBIA POLK GENERAL HOSPITAL, 424 North Main Street, Zip 30125–2698; tel. 770/748–2500; Mark Nichols, Chief Executive Officer **A**1 9 10 **F**8 15 16 19 22 30 32 34 44 65 71 **P**6	33	10	35	739	7	20927	0	—	—	87

CHATSWORTH—Murray County

⊞ MURRAY MEDICAL CENTER, (Formerly Columbia Murray Medical Center), 707 Old Ellijay Road, Zip 30705–2060, Mailing Address: P.O. Box 1406, Zip 30705–1406; tel. 706/517–2031; Mickey Rabuka, Administrator (Nonreporting) **A**1 9 10 **S** Columbia/HCA Healthcare Corporation, Nashville, TN **N**	33	10	42	—	—	—	—	—	—	—

CLAXTON—Evans County

□ EVANS MEMORIAL HOSPITAL, 200 North River Street, Zip 30417–1659, Mailing Address: P.O. Box 518, Zip 30417–0518; tel. 912/739–5000; Eston Price, Jr., Administrator (Nonreporting) **A**1 9 10	16	10	32	—	—	—	—	—	—	—

CLAYTON—Rabun County

★ RABUN COUNTY MEMORIAL HOSPITAL, South Main Street, Zip 30525, Mailing Address: P.O. Box 705, Zip 30525–0705; tel. 706/782–4233; Richard B. Wallace, Chief Executive Officer (Nonreporting) **A**10	16	10	26	—	—	—	—	—	—	—

Hospital, Address, Telephone, Administrator, Approval, Facility, and Physician Codes, Health Care System, Network	Classi-fication Codes		Utilization Data					Expense (thousands) of dollars		
★ American Hospital Association (AHA) membership □ Joint Commission on Accreditation of Healthcare Organizations (JCAHO) accreditation + American Osteopathic Healthcare Association (AOHA) membership ○ American Osteopathic Association (AOA) accreditation △ Commission on Accreditation of Rehabilitation Facilities (CARF) accreditation Control codes 61, 63, 64, 71, 72 and 73 indicate hospitals listed by AOHA, but not registered by AHA. For definition of numerical codes, see page A4	Control	Service	Staffed Beds	Admissions	Census	Outpatient Visits	Births	Total	Payroll	Personnel
⊞ RIDGECREST HOSPITAL, 393 Ridgecrest Circle, Zip 30525; tel. 706/782–4297; Maryann J. Greenwell, Chief Executive Officer (Nonreporting) **A**1 9 10 **S** Quorum Health Group/Quorum Health Resources, Inc., Brentwood, TN **N** Principal Health Care of Georgia, Atlanta, GA	23	10	45	—	—	—	—	—	—	—
★ WOODRIDGE HOSPITAL, 394 Ridgecrest Circle, Zip 30525; tel. 706/782–3100; Maryann J. Greenwell, Chief Executive Officer (Nonreporting) **A**9 10 **S** Quorum Health Group/Quorum Health Resources, Inc., Brentwood, TN	23	22	32	—	—	—	—	—	—	—
COCHRAN—Bleckley County										
BLECKLEY MEMORIAL HOSPITAL, 408 Peacock Street, Zip 31014–1559, Mailing Address: Box 536, Zip 31014–0536; tel. 912/934–6211; Henry T. Gibbs, Administrator **A**10 **F**15 16 19 20 22 28 32 34 37 44 46 49 65 67 71 73 **P**5 **S** Memorial Health Services, Adel, GA	16	10	45	775	7	4989	0	3752	1848	88
COLQUITT—Miller County										
MILLER COUNTY HOSPITAL, 209 North Cuthbert Street, Zip 31737–1015, Mailing Address: P.O. Box 7, Zip 31737–0007; tel. 912/758–3385; Colleen B. Houston, Administrator (Total facility includes 97 beds in nursing home–type unit) (Nonreporting) **A**10	16	10	135	—	—	—	—	—	—	—
COLUMBUS—Muscogee County										
BRADLEY CENTER OF ST. FRANCIS See St. Francis Hospital										
⊞ COLUMBIA DOCTORS HOSPITAL, 616 19th Street, Zip 31901–1528, Mailing Address: P.O. Box 2188, Zip 31902–2188; tel. 706/571–4262; Hugh D. Wilson, Chief Executive Officer **A**1 2 9 10 **F**2 3 4 7 8 10 11 12 15 16 17 19 21 22 26 28 30 34 35 37 40 42 43 44 45 46 48 49 52 60 65 66 71 73 74 **P**3 4 5 **S** Columbia/HCA Healthcare Corporation, Nashville, TN **N** Principal Health Care of Georgia, Atlanta, GA	33	47	100	3653	39	7536	0	26973	8052	334
⊞ HUGHSTON SPORTS MEDICINE HOSPITAL, (Formerly Columbia Hughston Sports Medicine Hospital), 100 Frist Court, Zip 31908–7188, Mailing Address: P.O. Box 7188, Zip 31908–7188; tel. 706/576–2100; Hugh D. Wilson, Chief Executive Officer (Nonreporting) **A**1 3 5 10 **S** Columbia/HCA Healthcare Corporation, Nashville, TN	33	47	100	—	—	—	—	—	—	—
⊞ ST. FRANCIS HOSPITAL, (Includes Bradley Center of St. Francis, 2000 16th Avenue, Zip 31906–0308; tel. 706/320–3700), 2122 Manchester Expressway, Zip 31904–6878, Mailing Address: P.O. Box 7000, Zip 31908–7000; tel. 706/596–4000; Michael E. Garrigan, President and Chief Executive Officer (Nonreporting) **A**1 9 10	23	10	281	—	—	—	—	—	—	—
⊞ THE MEDICAL CENTER, 710 Center Street, Zip 31902, Mailing Address: P.O. Box 951, Zip 31902–0951; tel. 706/571–1000; Lance B. Duke, FACHE, President and Chief Executive Officer (Total facility includes 128 beds in nursing home–type unit) **A**1 2 3 5 9 10 **F**2 3 7 8 10 12 15 16 17 18 19 21 22 23 24 26 27 28 29 30 31 32 34 35 37 38 40 41 42 44 45 46 47 48 49 51 52 54 55 56 58 60 63 64 65 67 68 70 71 72 73 74 **P**2 6 7 8 **N** Community Healthcare Network, Columbus, GA; Columbus Regional HealthCare System, Inc., Columbus, GA; Principal Health Care of Georgia, Atlanta, GA; Georgia 1st, Inc., Decatur, GA; The Medical Resource Network, L.L.C., Atlanta, GA	23	10	565	12640	183	107584	2842	—	41048	1434
COMMERCE—Jackson County										
⊞ BJC MEDICAL CENTER, 70 Medical Center Drive, Zip 30529–9989; tel. 706/335–1000; J. David Lawrence, Jr., Chief Executive Officer (Total facility includes 167 beds in nursing home–type unit) **A**1 9 10 **F**8 11 15 16 19 21 22 28 30 34 39 40 42 44 46 49 64 65 67 71 73	16	10	233	1466	181	18659	113	9840	5593	316
CONYERS—Rockdale County										
⊞ ROCKDALE HOSPITAL, 1412 Milstead Avenue N.E., Zip 30207–9990; tel. 770/918–3000; Nelson Toebbe, Chief Executive Officer **A**1 2 9 10 **F**7 8 11 12 14 15 16 17 19 21 22 23 24 25 28 29 30 31 32 34 35 37 39 40 42 44 45 46 49 65 67 71 73 74 **P**5 **N** Principal Health Care of Georgia, Atlanta, GA	23	10	107	6246	62	86720	1738	48001	19740	554
CORDELE—Crisp County										
⊞ CRISP REGIONAL HOSPITAL, 902 North Seventh Street, Zip 31015–5007; tel. 912/276–3100; D. Wayne Martin, President and Chief Executive Officer (Total facility includes 143 beds in nursing home–type unit) **A**1 9 10 **F**6 7 8 11 13 14 16 17 19 21 22 23 25 27 28 29 30 32 33 34 35 37 39 40 41 42 44 46 49 50 51 62 64 65 67 71 73 **P**8 **N** Georgia 1st, Inc., Decatur, GA; The Medical Resource Network, L.L.C., Atlanta, GA	16	10	208	5089	170	78699	363	28612	10368	514
COVINGTON—Newton County										
⊞ NEWTON GENERAL HOSPITAL, 5126 Hospital Drive, Zip 30209; tel. 770/786–7053; James F. Weadick, Administrator and Chief Executive Officer **A**1 9 10 **F**7 8 15 17 19 22 23 28 29 30 32 33 34 35 37 40 41 44 45 56 63 65 67 69 71 73 **P**8 **N** Principal Health Care of Georgia, Atlanta, GA; Georgia 1st, Inc., Decatur, GA	23	10	90	3548	36	85259	281	25190	13671	408
CUMMING—Forsyth County										
⊞ BAPTIST NORTH HOSPITAL, 133 Samaritan Drive, Zip 30130, Mailing Address: P.O. Box 768, Zip 30130–0768; tel. 770/887–2355; John M. Herron, Administrator (Nonreporting) **A**1 10 **S** Georgia Baptist Health Care System, Atlanta, GA	21	10	30	—	—	—	—	—	—	—
CUTHBERT—Randolph County										
★ SOUTHWEST GEORGIA REGIONAL MEDICAL CENTER, 109 Randolph Street, Zip 31740–1338; tel. 912/732–2181; David J. Carney, Chief Executive Officer (Total facility includes 80 beds in nursing home–type unit) **A**9 10 **F**8 19 22 34 40 44 46 49 51 71 73 **N** Community Healthcare Network, Columbus, GA; The Medical Resource Network, L.L.C., Atlanta, GA	16	10	120	692	90	8851	113	5949	3501	180

Hospital, Address, Telephone, Administrator, Approval, Facility, and Physician Codes, Health Care System, Network	Classi-fication Codes		Utilization Data					Expense (thousands) of dollars		
★ American Hospital Association (AHA) membership □ Joint Commission on Accreditation of Healthcare Organizations (JCAHO) accreditation + American Osteopathic Healthcare Association (AOHA) membership ○ American Osteopathic Association (AOA) accreditation △ Commission on Accreditation of Rehabilitation Facilities (CARF) accreditation Control codes 61, 63, 64, 71, 72 and 73 indicate hospitals listed by AOHA, but not registered by AHA. For definition of numerical codes, see page A4	Control	Service	Staffed Beds	Admissions	Census	Outpatient Visits	Births	Total	Payroll	Personnel

DAHLONEGA—Lumpkin County

Hospital	Control	Service	Staffed Beds	Admissions	Census	Outpatient Visits	Births	Total	Payroll	Personnel
□ CHESTATEE REGIONAL HOSPITAL, 1111 Mountain Drive, Zip 30533; tel. 706/864–6136; Stephen G. Widener, President and Chief Executive Officer (Nonreporting) **A**1 10 **S** NetCare Health Systems, Inc., Nashville, TN	33	10	52	—	—	—	—	—	—	—

DALLAS—Paulding County

Hospital	Control	Service	Staffed Beds	Admissions	Census	Outpatient Visits	Births	Total	Payroll	Personnel
★ WELLSTAR PAULDING HOSPITAL, (Formerly Promina Paulding Memorial Medical Center), 600 West Memorial Drive, Zip 30132–1335; tel. 770/445–4411; Thomas E. Hill, Chief Executive Officer (Total facility includes 169 beds in nursing home–type unit) **A**1 9 10 **F**2 3 4 6 7 8 10 11 12 13 14 15 16 17 18 19 20 21 22 24 25 26 28 29 30 31 32 33 34 35 37 38 39 40 41 42 43 44 45 46 48 49 50 51 52 53 54 55 56 57 58 59 60 61 62 64 65 66 67 69 70 71 72 73 74 **P**1 3 7 **S** WellStar Health System, Austell, GA **N** Promina Health System, Inc., Atlanta, GA; Principal Health Care of Georgia, Atlanta, GA; The Medical Resource Network, L.L.C., Atlanta, GA	23	10	212	1017	173	29631	—	13342	5242	245

DALTON—Whitfield County

Hospital	Control	Service	Staffed Beds	Admissions	Census	Outpatient Visits	Births	Total	Payroll	Personnel
★ HAMILTON MEDICAL CENTER, 1200 Memorial Drive, Zip 30720–2529, Mailing Address: P.O. Box 1168, Zip 30722–1168; tel. 706/272–6000; Ned B. Wilford, President and Chief Executive Officer **A**1 2 10 **F**1 3 6 7 8 10 15 16 17 18 19 21 22 23 24 25 27 28 30 31 32 33 34 35 37 39 40 41 42 44 45 46 49 52 53 54 55 56 57 58 59 60 62 65 66 67 70 71 72 73 74 **P**8 **N** The Medical Resource Network, L.L.C., Atlanta, GA	23	10	282	11001	124	191290	2242	88245	36074	1143

DECATUR—De Kalb County

Hospital	Control	Service	Staffed Beds	Admissions	Census	Outpatient Visits	Births	Total	Payroll	Personnel
□ DECATUR HOSPITAL, 450 North Candler Street, Zip 30030–2671, Mailing Address: P.O. Box 40, Zip 30031–0040; tel. 404/377–0221; Richard T. Schmidt, Executive Director (Nonreporting) **A**1 9 10 **N** Promina Health System, Inc., Atlanta, GA; Principal Health Care of Georgia, Atlanta, GA; The Medical Resource Network, L.L.C., Atlanta, GA	23	10	120	—	—	—	—	—	—	—
★ △ DEKALB MEDICAL CENTER, 2701 North Decatur Road, Zip 30033–5995; tel. 404/501–1000; John R. Gerlach, Chief Executive Officer/Administrator (Total facility includes 48 beds in nursing home–type unit) (Nonreporting) **A**1 2 7 9 10 **N** Promina Health System, Inc., Atlanta, GA; Principal Health Care of Georgia, Atlanta, GA; The Medical Resource Network, L.L.C., Atlanta, GA	23	10	397	—	—	—	—	—	—	—
□ GEORGIA REGIONAL HOSPITAL AT ATLANTA, 3073 Panthersville Road, Zip 30034–3828; tel. 404/243–2100; Ronald C. Hogan, Superintendent (Total facility includes 43 beds in nursing home–type unit) **A**1 3 5 10 **F**1 3 4 5 6 7 8 10 12 13 14 15 17 18 19 20 21 22 23 24 25 26 27 28 29 30 31 32 33 34 35 36 39 41 42 43 44 45 46 49 50 51 52 53 54 55 56 57 58 59 60 61 63 64 65 66 67 68 69 70 71 72 73 74 **P**6	12	22	238	4825	180	0	0	30243	17937	—
★ VETERANS AFFAIRS MEDICAL CENTER, 1670 Clairmont Road, Zip 30033–4004; tel. 404/321–6111; Robert A. Perreault, Director (Total facility includes 110 beds in nursing home–type unit) **A**1 3 5 8 **F**3 4 8 10 11 12 19 20 21 22 23 26 27 28 29 30 31 32 33 35 36 37 39 41 42 43 44 45 46 48 49 51 52 54 55 56 57 58 59 60 63 64 65 67 71 72 73 74 **S** Department of Veterans Affairs, Washington, DC	45	10	378	5879	181	289318	0	148336	61056	1667

DEMOREST—Habersham County

Hospital	Control	Service	Staffed Beds	Admissions	Census	Outpatient Visits	Births	Total	Payroll	Personnel
★ HABERSHAM COUNTY MEDICAL CENTER, Highway 441, Zip 30535, Mailing Address: P.O. Box 37, Zip 30535–0037; tel. 706/754–2161; C. Richard Dwozan, President (Total facility includes 85 beds in nursing home–type unit) **A**1 9 10 **F**6 7 8 12 13 15 16 17 19 21 22 24 27 28 30 32 34 35 37 39 40 44 45 46 48 49 64 65 66 67 68 71 73 **P**1 3 7 **S** Quorum Health Group/Quorum Health Resources, Inc., Brentwood, TN **N** Georgia 1st, Inc., Decatur, GA	16	10	138	2675	135	42063	377	22551	8479	383

DONALSONVILLE—Seminole County

Hospital	Control	Service	Staffed Beds	Admissions	Census	Outpatient Visits	Births	Total	Payroll	Personnel
□ DONALSONVILLE HOSPITAL, Hospital Circle, Zip 31745, Mailing Address: P.O. Box 677, Zip 31745–0677; tel. 912/524–5217; Charles H. Orrick, Administrator (Total facility includes 75 beds in nursing home–type unit) **A**1 10 **F**8 14 15 16 19 21 22 34 44 49 64 71 **N** The Medical Resource Network, L.L.C., Atlanta, GA	23	10	140	2273	87	18385	1	10999	4235	214

DOUGLAS—Coffee County

Hospital	Control	Service	Staffed Beds	Admissions	Census	Outpatient Visits	Births	Total	Payroll	Personnel
★ COFFEE REGIONAL MEDICAL CENTER, 1101 Ocilla Road, Zip 31533–3617, Mailing Address: P.O. Box 1248, Zip 31534–1248; tel. 912/384–1900; George L. Heck, III, President and Chief Executive Officer (Nonreporting) **A**1 10	16	10	108	—	—	—	—	—	—	—

DOUGLASVILLE—Douglas County

Hospital	Control	Service	Staffed Beds	Admissions	Census	Outpatient Visits	Births	Total	Payroll	Personnel
INNER HARBOUR HOSPITALS, 4685 Dorsett Shoals Road, Zip 30135–4999; tel. 770/942–2391; Susan Hallman, Administrator **F**15 16 22 39 46 52 53 54 55 59 65 67 73 **P**6	23	52	165	358	151	—	—	13419	8229	318
★ WELLSTAR DOUGLAS HOSPITAL, (Formerly Promina Douglas Hospital), 8954 Hospital Drive, Zip 30134–2282; tel. 770/949–1500; Thomas E. Hill, Chief Executive Officer **A**1 9 10 **F**2 3 6 7 8 10 11 12 13 14 15 16 17 18 19 20 21 22 24 25 26 28 29 30 31 32 33 34 35 37 38 39 40 41 42 43 44 45 46 48 49 50 51 52 53 54 55 56 57 58 59 60 61 62 64 65 66 67 69 70 71 72 73 74 **P**1 3 7 **S** WellStar Health System, Austell, GA **N** Promina Health System, Inc., Atlanta, GA; Principal Health Care of Georgia, Atlanta, GA; The Medical Resource Network, L.L.C., Atlanta, GA	23	10	79	3127	32	49116	201	23392	10321	278

DUBLIN—Laurens County

Hospital	Control	Service	Staffed Beds	Admissions	Census	Outpatient Visits	Births	Total	Payroll	Personnel
★ COLUMBIA FAIRVIEW PARK HOSPITAL, 200 Industrial Boulevard, Zip 31021–2997, Mailing Address: P.O. Box 1408, Zip 31040–1408; tel. 912/275–2000; Richard P. Cook, Chief Executive Officer **A**1 2 9 10 **F**7 8 11 12 14 15 16 17 19 21 22 23 24 28 35 37 40 44 45 48 49 63 65 66 71 73 **S** Columbia/HCA Healthcare Corporation, Nashville, TN **N** Principal Health Care of Georgia, Atlanta, GA; Georgia 1st, Inc., Decatur, GA	33	10	190	7924	95	64419	1015	—	—	620

Hospital, Address, Telephone, Administrator, Approval, Facility, and Physician Codes, Health Care System, Network	Classi-fication Codes		Utilization Data					Expense (thousands) of dollars		
★ American Hospital Association (AHA) membership □ Joint Commission on Accreditation of Healthcare Organizations (JCAHO) accreditation + American Osteopathic Healthcare Association (AOHA) membership ○ American Osteopathic Association (AOA) accreditation △ Commission on Accreditation of Rehabilitation Facilities (CARF) accreditation Control codes 61, 63, 64, 71, 72 and 73 indicate hospitals listed by AOHA, but not registered by AHA. For definition of numerical codes, see page A4	Control	Service	Staffed Beds	Admissions	Census	Outpatient Visits	Births	Total	Payroll	Personnel
⊠ VETERANS AFFAIRS MEDICAL CENTER, 1826 Veterans Boulevard, Zip 31021–3620; tel. 912/277–2701; James F. Trusley, III, Director (Total facility includes 112 beds in nursing home–type unit) (Nonreporting) **A**1 **S** Department of Veterans Affairs, Washington, DC	45	10	253	—	—	—	—	—	—	—
DULUTH—Gwinnett County										
JOAN GLANCY MEMORIAL HOSPITAL See Promina Gwinnett Hospital System, Lawrenceville										
EAST POINT—Fulton County										
⊠ SOUTH FULTON MEDICAL CENTER, 1170 Cleveland Avenue, Zip 30344; tel. 404/305–3500; H. Neil Copelan, President and Chief Executive Officer (Total facility includes 36 beds in nursing home–type unit) **A**1 2 9 10 **F**6 7 8 10 11 12 15 16 17 19 21 22 26 28 29 30 34 35 37 38 39 40 41 42 44 46 48 49 50 60 63 64 65 67 68 72 73 74 **P**1 6 **N** Principal Health Care of Georgia, Atlanta, GA; The Medical Resource Network, L.L.C., Atlanta, GA	23	10	369	10994	155	72039	1961	76426	43572	949
EASTMAN—Dodge County										
□ DODGE COUNTY HOSPITAL, 715 Griffin Street S.W., Zip 31023–2223, Mailing Address: P.O. Box 4309, Zip 31023–4309; tel. 912/374–4000; Meredith H. Smith, Administrator **A**1 9 10 **F**8 15 17 19 21 22 30 36 37 40 44 45 46 49 52 57 67 71 73 **N** Principal Health Care of Georgia, Atlanta, GA; The Medical Resource Network, L.L.C., Atlanta, GA	16	10	87	3044	45	22500	133	15840	7793	297
EATONTON—Putnam County										
□ PUTNAM GENERAL HOSPITAL, Lake Oconee Parkway, Zip 31024–4330, Mailing Address: Box 4330, Zip 31024–4330; tel. 706/485–2711; Darrell M. Oglesby, Administrator (Nonreporting) **A**1 10 **N** Principal Health Care of Georgia, Atlanta, GA; The Medical Resource Network, L.L.C., Atlanta, GA	16	10	50	—	—	—	—	—	—	—
ELBERTON—Elbert County										
⊠ ELBERT MEMORIAL HOSPITAL, 4 Medical Drive, Zip 30635–1897; tel. 706/283–3151; Ronald J. Vigus, Interim Chief Executive Officer **A**1 9 10 **F**7 8 14 15 16 19 21 22 23 24 28 30 34 35 37 40 44 45 46 49 65 66 67 71 73 **P**5 **S** Quorum Health Group/Quorum Health Resources, Inc., Brentwood, TN **N** Georgia 1st, Inc., Decatur, GA	16	10	52	2222	25	8884	145	11973	5572	210
ELLIJAY—Gilmer County										
□ NORTH GEORGIA MEDICAL CENTER, 1362 South Main Street, Zip 30540–0346, Mailing Address: P.O. Box 2239, Zip 30540–0346; tel. 706/276–4741; Steve Grimm, Chief Executive Officer (Total facility includes 100 beds in nursing home–type unit) (Nonreporting) **A**1 9 10 **S** NetCare Health Systems, Inc., Nashville, TN **N** Principal Health Care of Georgia, Atlanta, GA	33	10	150	—	—	—	—	—	—	—
FITZGERALD—Ben Hill County										
□ DORMINY MEDICAL CENTER, Perry House Road, Zip 31750, Mailing Address: Drawer 1447, Zip 31750–1447; tel. 912/424–7100; Steve Barber, Administrator **A**1 9 10 **F**7 8 14 19 21 22 28 33 34 35 37 40 44 49 50 63 65 71 73 **P**7	16	10	60	2164	29	22507	232	13805	6477	288
FOLKSTON—Charlton County										
□ CHARLTON MEMORIAL HOSPITAL, 1203 North Third Street, Zip 31537–1303, Mailing Address: P.O. Box 188, Zip 31537–0188; tel. 912/496–2531; James L. Leis, Jr., Administrator and Chief Executive Officer **A**1 9 10 **F**14 15 19 22 26 27 29 34 37 44 45 46 49 51 71 73 **P**6	16	10	46	812	9	11519	0	4417	2455	93
FORSYTH—Monroe County										
□ MONROE COUNTY HOSPITAL, 88 Martin Luther King Jr. Drive, Zip 31029–1682, Mailing Address: P.O. Box 1068, Zip 31029–1068; tel. 912/994–2521; Gale V. Tanner, Administrator **A**1 9 10 **F**8 19 22 31 34 35 42 44 48 59 65 71 73 **N** The Medical Resource Network, L.L.C., Atlanta, GA	16	10	37	1084	12	14746	—	6505	2607	105
FORT BENNING—Muscogee County										
⊠ MARTIN ARMY COMMUNITY HOSPITAL, Mailing Address: P.O. Box 56100, Building 9200, Zip 31905–6100; tel. 706/544–2516; Colonel Joe W. Butler, Deputy Commander Administration (Nonreporting) **A**1 2 3 **S** Department of the Army, Office of the Surgeon General, Falls Church, VA	42	10	126	—	—	—	—	—	—	—
FORT GORDON—Richmond County										
⊠ DWIGHT DAVID EISENHOWER ARMY MEDICAL CENTER, Hospital Drive, Building 300, Zip 30905–5650; tel. 706/787–3253; Lieutenant Colonel David A. Rubenstein, Chief Operating Officer **A**1 2 3 5 **F**3 4 8 10 11 12 14 15 16 17 19 20 21 22 28 30 31 34 35 37 39 40 41 42 43 44 46 50 51 52 53 54 56 58 60 64 65 71 73 **P**6 **S** Department of the Army, Office of the Surgeon General, Falls Church, VA	42	10	150	6864	113	567407	0	—	—	1947
FORT OGLETHORPE—Catoosa County										
□ GREENLEAF CENTER, 500 Greenleaf Circle, Zip 30742–3886; tel. 706/861–4357; R. Lindsay Shuff, Administrator (Nonreporting) **A**1 9 10 **S** Greenleaf Health Systems, Inc., Chattanooga, TN	33	22	90	—	—	—	—	—	—	—
⊠ HUTCHESON MEDICAL CENTER, 100 Gross Crescent Circle, Zip 30742–3669; tel. 706/858–2000; Robert T. Jones, M.D., President and Chief Executive Officer (Total facility includes 109 beds in nursing home–type unit) **A**1 9 10 **F**1 3 7 8 10 11 12 14 15 16 19 21 22 28 29 30 32 33 35 37 38 40 44 49 53 54 55 56 57 58 64 65 66 70 71 73 74 **N** Principal Health Care of Georgia, Atlanta, GA	16	10	300	7960	205	72838	1092	76133	32316	1175
FORT VALLEY—Peach County										
□ PEACH REGIONAL MEDICAL CENTER, 601 North Camellia Boulevard, Zip 31030–4599; tel. 912/825–8691; Nancy Peed, Administrator **A**1 9 10 **F**8 11 14 15 16 19 22 28 30 37 41 44 45 46 48 49 51 65 71 **N** The Medical Resource Network, L.L.C., Atlanta, GA	16	10	36	722	7	22627	—	5023	2919	115

Hospital, Address, Telephone, Administrator, Approval, Facility, and Physician Codes, Health Care System, Network	Classi-fication Codes		Utilization Data					Expense (thousands) of dollars		
★ American Hospital Association (AHA) membership □ Joint Commission on Accreditation of Healthcare Organizations (JCAHO) accreditation + American Osteopathic Healthcare Association (AOHA) membership ○ American Osteopathic Association (AOA) accreditation △ Commission on Accreditation of Rehabilitation Facilities (CARF) accreditation Control codes 61, 63, 64, 71, 72 and 73 indicate hospitals listed by AOHA, but not registered by AHA. For definition of numerical codes, see page A4	Control	Service	Staffed Beds	Admissions	Census	Outpatient Visits	Births	Total	Payroll	Personnel

GAINESVILLE—Hall County

✚ LANIER PARK HOSPITAL, (Formerly Columbia Lanier Park Hospital), 675 White Sulphur Road, Zip 30505, Mailing Address: P.O. Box 1354, Zip 30503–1354; tel. 770/503–3000; Jerry Fulks, Chief Executive Officer (Total facility includes 10 beds in nursing home–type unit) **A**1 10 **F**8 10 12 14 15 16 17 19 21 22 23 28 29 30 32 34 35 37 39 41 42 44 45 46 49 51 60 64 65 66 67 71 73 74 **P**8 **S** Columbia/HCA Healthcare Corporation, Nashville, TN **N** Chattahoochee Health Network, Gainesville, GA	33	10	119	3660	46	14878	—	28498	11493	353
✚ △ NORTHEAST GEORGIA MEDICAL CENTER, 743 Spring Street N.E., Zip 30501–3899; tel. 770/535–3553; Henry Rigdon, Executive Vice President (Total facility includes 15 beds in nursing home–type unit) (Nonreporting) **A**1 2 7 9 10 **N** Principal Health Care of Georgia, Atlanta, GA; Georgia 1st, Inc., Decatur, GA; The Medical Resource Network, L.L.C., Atlanta, GA	23	10	338	—	—	—	—	—	—	—

GLENWOOD—Wheeler County

WHEELER COUNTY HOSPITAL, Third Street, Zip 30428, Mailing Address: P.O. Box 398, Zip 30428–0398; tel. 912/523–5113; James L. Jarrett, Administrator (Nonreporting) **A**10 **S** Accord Health Care Corporation, Clearwater, FL	33	10	30	—	—	—	—	—	—	—

GRACEWOOD—Richmond County

GRACEWOOD STATE SCHOOL AND HOSPITAL, 100 Myrtle Boulevard, Zip 30812–1500; tel. 706/790–2030; Joanne P. Miklas, Ph.D., Superintendent (Total facility includes 637 beds in nursing home–type unit) **A**10 **F**18 20 27 29 30 39 41 44 45 46 64 65 73 **P**6	12	12	652	385	616	0	0	52165	32035	382

GREENSBORO—Greene County

✚ MINNIE G. BOSWELL MEMORIAL HOSPITAL, 1201 Siloam Highway, Zip 30642–2811, Mailing Address: P.O. Box 329, Zip 30642–0329; tel. 706/453–7331; Earnest E. Benton, Chief Executive Officer (Total facility includes 29 beds in nursing home–type unit) (Nonreporting) **A**1 9 10 **N** The Medical Resource Network, L.L.C., Atlanta, GA; University Health, Inc., Augusta, GA	16	10	58	—	—	—	—	—	—	—

GRIFFIN—Spalding County

✚ SPALDING REGIONAL HOSPITAL, 601 South Eighth Street, Zip 30224–4294, Mailing Address: P.O. Drawer V., Zip 30224–1168; tel. 770/228–2721; Phil Shaw, Executive Director **A**1 2 9 10 **F**3 4 6 7 8 9 10 12 14 15 16 19 20 21 22 23 27 28 30 32 33 34 35 36 37 38 39 40 41 42 43 44 47 48 49 52 53 54 55 56 57 58 59 60 64 65 67 71 73 **P**8 **S** TENET Healthcare Corporation, Santa Barbara, CA **N** Principal Health Care of Georgia, Atlanta, GA; Georgia 1st, Inc., Decatur, GA	33	10	160	6977	82	68719	843	35986	15182	654

HAHIRA—Lowndes County

SMITH HOSPITAL, 117 East Main Street, Zip 31632–1156, Mailing Address: P.O. Box 337, Zip 31632–0337; tel. 912/794–2502; Amanda M. Hall, Administrator (Nonreporting) **A**9 10 **S** Memorial Health Services, Adel, GA	33	10	71	—	—	—	—	—	—	—

HARTWELL—Hart County

✚ HART COUNTY HOSPITAL, Gibson and Cade Streets, Zip 30643–0280, Mailing Address: P.O. Box 280, Zip 30643–0280; tel. 706/856–6100; Matt McRee, Administrator **A**1 9 10 **F**7 8 12 15 16 17 19 22 28 37 40 41 48 64 66 71 73 **N** Principal Health Care of Georgia, Atlanta, GA	23	10	82	1215	15	23040	—	—	—	182

HAWKINSVILLE—Pulaski County

✚ TAYLOR REGIONAL HOSPITAL, Macon Highway, Zip 31036, Mailing Address: P.O. Box 1297, Zip 31036–1297; tel. 912/783–0200; Dan S. Maddock, President **A**1 9 10 **F**7 8 10 12 14 15 16 19 21 22 27 28 30 31 32 34 35 36 37 41 44 46 49 51 63 65 66 70 71 73 74 **P**6 **N** Principal Health Care of Georgia, Atlanta, GA; The Medical Resource Network, L.L.C., Atlanta, GA	23	10	55	2068	17	24084	387	20356	7672	364

HAZLEHURST—Jeff Davis County

□ JEFF DAVIS HOSPITAL, 1215 South Tallahassee Street, Zip 31539–2921, Mailing Address: P.O. Box 1200, Zip 31539–1200; tel. 912/375–7781; Oreta Williams, Administrator (Nonreporting) **A**1 10	16	10	50	—	—	—	—	—	—	—

HIAWASSEE—Towns County

□ CHATUGE REGIONAL HOSPITAL AND NURSING HOME, 110 Main Street, Zip 30546, Mailing Address: P.O. Box 509, Zip 30546–0509; tel. 706/896–2222; Thomas I. Edwards, President and Chief Executive Officer **A**1 9 10 **F**16 19 22 27 28 30 33 34 35 37 41 44 46 49 64 65 67 71 73 **P**8 **S** NetCare Health Systems, Inc., Nashville, TN	33	10	39	969	13	13090	0	6525	2518	—

HINESVILLE—Liberty County

□ LIBERTY REGIONAL MEDICAL CENTER, 112 East Oglethorpe Boulevard, Zip 31313–3600, Mailing Address: P.O. Box 919, Zip 31313–0919; tel. 912/369–9400; H. Scott Kroell, Jr., Chief Executive Officer **A**1 9 10 **F**7 8 14 15 16 19 22 35 40 44 45 49 66 71 73 **N** Candler Health System, Savannah, GA; Principal Health Care of Georgia, Atlanta, GA; Georgia 1st, Inc., Decatur, GA; The Medical Resource Network, L.L.C., Atlanta, GA	16	10	41	1465	11	27615	266	5804	4385	192
✚ WINN ARMY COMMUNITY HOSPITAL, 1061 Harmon Avenue, Zip 31314–5611; tel. 912/370–6001; Colonel Donald J. Kasperik, Commander (Nonreporting) **A**1 **S** Department of the Army, Office of the Surgeon General, Falls Church, VA	42	10	100	—	—	—	—	—	—	—

HOMERVILLE—Clinch County

★ CLINCH MEMORIAL HOSPITAL, 524 North Carswell Street, Zip 31634–1507, Mailing Address: P.O. Box 516, Zip 31634–0516; tel. 912/487–5211; Michael Alexander, Administrator (Nonreporting) **A**10	13	10	36	—	—	—	—	—	—	—

Hospital, Address, Telephone, Administrator, Approval, Facility, and Physician Codes, Health Care System, Network	Classi-fication Codes		Utilization Data					Expense (thousands) of dollars		
	Control	Service	Staffed Beds	Admissions	Census	Outpatient Visits	Births	Total	Payroll	Personnel

★ American Hospital Association (AHA) membership
☐ Joint Commission on Accreditation of Healthcare Organizations (JCAHO) accreditation
+ American Osteopathic Healthcare Association (AOHA) membership
○ American Osteopathic Association (AOA) accreditation
△ Commission on Accreditation of Rehabilitation Facilities (CARF) accreditation
Control codes 61, 63, 64, 71, 72 and 73 indicate hospitals listed by AOHA, but not registered by AHA. For definition of numerical codes, see page A4

JACKSON—Butts County

★ SYLVAN GROVE HOSPITAL, 1050 McDonough Road, Zip 30233–1599; tel. 770/775–7861; Mike Patterson, Administrator **A**9 10 **F**19 22 28 29 30 34 44 45 49 51 71 **S** TENET Healthcare Corporation, Santa Barbara, CA

| | 33 | 10 | 28 | 260 | 3 | 12647 | — | 4117 | 1698 | 73 |

JESUP—Wayne County

✠ WAYNE MEMORIAL HOSPITAL, 865 South First Street, Zip 31598, Mailing Address: P.O. Box 408, Zip 31598–0408; tel. 912/427–6811; Charles R. Morgan, Administrator **A**1 9 10 **F**7 8 12 15 19 22 28 29 30 34 35 37 39 40 41 44 45 46 49 65 71 73 **S** Quorum Health Group/Quorum Health Resources, Inc., Brentwood, TN **N** Principal Health Care of Georgia, Atlanta, GA

| | 16 | 10 | 110 | 3707 | 51 | 36023 | 295 | 24053 | 10739 | 403 |

KENNESAW—Cobb County

DEVEREUX GEORGIA TREATMENT NETWORK, (Formerly Devereux Center–Georgia), 1291 Stanley Road N.W., Zip 30152–4359; tel. 770/427–0147; Elizabeth M. Chadwick, JD, Executive Director **F**14 15 16 22 52 53 55 **P**6 **S** Devereux Foundation, Villanova, PA

| | 23 | 52 | 115 | 73 | 110 | — | — | 12843 | 7490 | 261 |

LA GRANGE—Troup County

✠ WEST GEORGIA HEALTH SYSTEM, 1514 Vernon Road, Zip 30240–4199; tel. 706/882–1411; Charles L. Foster, Jr., FACHE, President and Chief Executive Officer (Total facility includes 150 beds in nursing home–type unit) **A**1 2 9 10 **F**2 3 4 7 8 10 11 12 13 14 15 16 17 18 19 21 22 26 27 28 29 30 32 33 34 37 39 40 41 42 44 45 46 49 50 51 52 53 54 55 57 58 59 60 63 64 65 67 68 70 71 73 74 **P**7 **N** Community Healthcare Network, Columbus, GA; Georgia 1st, Inc., Decatur, GA

| | 15 | 10 | 346 | 8952 | 258 | 378412 | 1057 | 74652 | 33116 | 1494 |

LAKELAND—Lanier County

✠ LOUIS SMITH MEMORIAL HOSPITAL, 852 West Thigpen Avenue, Zip 31635–1099; tel. 912/482–3110; Randy Sauls, Administrator (Total facility includes 62 beds in nursing home–type unit) **A**1 10 **F**7 8 14 15 16 19 22 26 31 33 34 35 40 41 44 46 49 64 65 69 71 73 **P**3 **N** Principal Health Care of Georgia, Atlanta, GA; Georgia 1st, Inc., Decatur, GA

| | 23 | 10 | 102 | 737 | 71 | 10508 | 42 | 5099 | 2397 | 169 |

LAWRENCEVILLE—Gwinnett County

✠ PROMINA GWINNETT HOSPITAL SYSTEM, (Includes Gwinnett Medical Center, 1000 Medical Center Boulevard, Zip 30245; Joan Glancy Memorial Hospital, McClure Bridge Road, Duluth, Zip 30136; tel. 770/497–4800), Mailing Address: P.O. Box 348, Zip 30246–0348; tel. 770/995–4321; Franklin M. Rinker, President and Chief Executive Officer (Nonreporting) **A**1 2 9 10 **N** Promina Health System, Inc., Atlanta, GA; Principal Health Care of Georgia, Atlanta, GA

| | 16 | 10 | 390 | — | | | | | | |

LITHIA SPRINGS—Douglas County

✠ △ COLUMBIA PARKWAY MEDICAL CENTER, 1000 Thornton Road, Zip 30057, Mailing Address: P.O. Box 570, Zip 30057–0570; tel. 770/732–7777; Deborah S. Guthrie, Chief Executive Officer (Nonreporting) **A**1 2 7 10 **S** Columbia/HCA Healthcare Corporation, Nashville, TN

| | 33 | 10 | 233 | — | | | | | | |

LOUISVILLE—Jefferson County

☐ JEFFERSON HOSPITAL, 1067 Peachtree Street, Zip 30434–1599; tel. 912/625–7000; Rita Culvern, Administrator **A**1 9 10 **F**8 14 15 16 19 22 24 28 30 44 65 71 73 **N** Principal Health Care of Georgia, Atlanta, GA; The Medical Resource Network, L.L.C., Atlanta, GA; University Health, Inc., Augusta, GA

| | 16 | 10 | 37 | 932 | 10 | 50737 | 2 | 6684 | 3247 | 107 |

MACON—Bibb County

☐ CHARTER BEHAVIORAL HEALTH SYSTEM/CENTRAL GEORGIA, 3500 Riverside Drive, Zip 31210–2509; tel. 912/474–6200; Blair R. Johanson, Administrator (Nonreporting) **A**1 10 **S** Magellan Health Services, Atlanta, GA

| | 33 | 22 | 118 | — | | | | | | |

✠ COLISEUM MEDICAL CENTERS, (Formerly Columbia Coliseum Medical Centers), 350 Hospital Drive, Zip 31213; tel. 912/765–7000; Michael S. Boggs, Chief Executive Officer (Nonreporting) **A**1 9 10 **S** Columbia/HCA Healthcare Corporation, Nashville, TN **N** Principal Health Care of Georgia, Atlanta, GA

| | 33 | 10 | 188 | — | | | | | | |

✠ COLUMBIA COLISEUM PSYCHIATRIC HOSPITAL, 340 Hospital Drive, Zip 31201–8002; tel. 912/741–1355; Edward W. Ruffin, Administrator (Nonreporting) **A**1 9 10 **S** Columbia/HCA Healthcare Corporation, Nashville, TN

| | 33 | 22 | 92 | — | | | | | | |

☐ HEALTHSOUTH CENTRAL GEORGIA REHABILITATION HOSPITAL, 3351 Northside Drive, Zip 31210–2591; tel. 912/471–3536; Elbert T. McQueen, Chief Executive Officer (Nonreporting) **A**1 9 10 **S** HEALTHSOUTH Corporation, Birmingham, AL **N** The Medical Resource Network, L.L.C., Atlanta, GA

| | 33 | 46 | 50 | — | | | | | | |

✠ MACON NORTHSIDE HOSPITAL, 400 Charter Boulevard, Zip 31210–4853, Mailing Address: P.O. Box 4627, Zip 31208–4627; tel. 912/757–8200; Richard Gaston, Administrator **A**1 9 10 **F**2 3 4 7 8 10 11 12 16 18 19 20 21 22 23 24 25 26 28 29 30 31 32 33 34 35 36 37 38 39 40 41 42 43 44 46 47 48 49 51 52 53 54 55 56 57 58 59 60 61 62 63 64 65 66 67 68 69 70 71 72 73 74 **S** Quorum Health Group/Quorum Health Resources, Inc., Brentwood, TN

| | 33 | 10 | 103 | 2312 | 28 | 30661 | 0 | 31628 | 10847 | 373 |

✠ MEDICAL CENTER OF CENTRAL GEORGIA, 777 Hemlock Street, Zip 31201–2155, Mailing Address: P.O. Box 6000, Zip 31208–6000; tel. 912/633–1000; A. Donald Faulk, FACHE, President **A**1 2 3 5 8 9 10 **F**4 7 8 10 11 12 13 14 15 16 17 19 20 21 22 24 25 26 27 28 29 30 31 32 34 35 37 38 39 40 41 42 43 44 45 46 47 49 51 52 53 54 56 57 60 61 65 67 68 71 72 73 74 **P**1 7 **N** Georgia 1st, Inc., Decatur, GA; The Medical Resource Network, L.L.C., Atlanta, GA

| | 23 | 10 | 495 | 24408 | 330 | 297570 | 3067 | 235956 | 109996 | 3417 |

✠ MIDDLE GEORGIA HOSPITAL, 888 Pine Street, Zip 31201–2186, Mailing Address: P.O. Box 6278, Zip 31208–6278; tel. 912/751–1111; Richard L. McConahy, Chief Executive Officer (Nonreporting) **A**1 10 **S** Quorum Health Group/Quorum Health Resources, Inc., Brentwood, TN

| | 33 | 10 | 119 | — | | — | — | — | — | — |

Hospital, Address, Telephone, Administrator, Approval, Facility, and Physician Codes, Health Care System, Network	Classi-fication Codes		Utilization Data					Expense (thousands) of dollars		
★ American Hospital Association (AHA) membership □ Joint Commission on Accreditation of Healthcare Organizations (JCAHO) accreditation + American Osteopathic Healthcare Association (AOHA) membership ○ American Osteopathic Association (AOA) accreditation △ Commission on Accreditation of Rehabilitation Facilities (CARF) accreditation Control codes 61, 63, 64, 71, 72 and 73 indicate hospitals listed by AOHA, but not registered by AHA. For definition of numerical codes, see page A4	Control	Service	Staffed Beds	Admissions	Census	Outpatient Visits	Births	Total	Payroll	Personnel

MADISON—Morgan County

MORGAN MEMORIAL HOSPITAL, Canterbury Park, Zip 30650, Mailing Address: P.O. Box 860, Zip 30650–0860; tel. 706/342–1667; Patrick Green, Administrator **A**9 10 **F**12 14 15 17 22 28 44 45

| | 16 | 10 | 26 | 395 | 4 | 8380 | 0 | 2248 | 1267 | 64 |

MARIETTA—Cobb County

✠ △ WELLSTAR KENNESTONE HOSPITAL, (Formerly Promina–Kennestone Hospital), 677 Church Street, Zip 30060–1148; tel. 770/793–5000; Thomas E. Hill, Chief Executive Officer **A**1 2 7 9 10 **F**2 3 4 6 7 8 10 11 12 13 14 15 16 17 18 19 20 21 22 24 25 26 28 29 30 31 32 33 34 35 37 38 39 40 41 42 43 44 45 46 48 49 50 51 52 53 54 55 56 57 58 59 60 61 62 63 64 65 66 67 69 70 71 72 73 74 **P**1 3 7 **S** WellStar Health System, Austell, GA **N** Promina Health System, Inc., Atlanta, GA; The Medical Resource Network, L.L.C., Atlanta, GA

| | 23 | 10 | 415 | 23807 | 293 | 250778 | 4647 | 179134 | 78708 | 1993 |

✠ △ WELLSTAR WINDY HILL HOSPITAL, (Formerly Promina Windy Hill Hospital), 2540 Windy Hill Road, Zip 30067–8632; tel. 770/644–1000; Thomas E. Hill, Chief Executive Officer **A**1 7 9 10 **F**2 3 4 6 7 8 10 11 12 13 14 15 16 17 18 19 20 21 22 24 25 26 28 29 30 31 32 33 34 35 37 38 39 40 41 42 43 44 45 46 48 49 50 51 52 53 54 55 56 57 58 59 60 61 62 64 65 66 67 69 70 71 72 73 74 **P**1 3 7 **S** WellStar Health System, Austell, GA **N** Promina Health System, Inc., Atlanta, GA; Principal Health Care of Georgia, Atlanta, GA; The Medical Resource Network, L.L.C., Atlanta, GA

| | 23 | 10 | 60 | 148 | 3 | 6320 | — | 18115 | 6636 | 115 |

MCRAE—Telfair County

TELFAIR COUNTY HOSPITAL, U.S. 341 South, Zip 31055, Mailing Address: P.O. Box 150, Zip 31055–0150; tel. 912/868–5621; Gail B. Norris, Administrator (Nonreporting) **A**9 10 **S** Memorial Health Services, Adel, GA

| | 33 | 10 | 52 | — | — | — | — | — | — | — |

METTER—Candler County

★ CANDLER COUNTY HOSPITAL, Cedar Road, Zip 30439, Mailing Address: P.O. Box 597, Zip 30439–0597; tel. 912/685–5741; Charles Balkcom, President (Nonreporting) **A**9 10 **N** Candler Health System, Savannah, GA; Principal Health Care of Georgia, Atlanta, GA; Georgia 1st, Inc., Decatur, GA; The Medical Resource Network, L.L.C., Atlanta, GA

| | 16 | 10 | 47 | — | — | — | — | — | — | — |

MILLEDGEVILLE—Baldwin County

□ CENTRAL STATE HOSPITAL, Broad Street, Zip 31062; tel. 912/445–4128; Joseph T. Hodge, Jr., Facility Administrator (Total facility includes 923 beds in nursing home–type unit) **A**1 3 10 **F**1 2 3 6 8 12 17 18 19 20 21 22 26 28 30 34 35 37 39 41 42 44 45 46 49 51 52 53 54 55 56 57 58 59 60 64 65 67 68 71 73 **P**6

| | 12 | 49 | 1302 | 2821 | 1241 | 36206 | 0 | 126354 | 74988 | 2801 |

✠ OCONEE REGIONAL MEDICAL CENTER, 821 North Cobb Street, Zip 31061–2351, Mailing Address: P.O. Box 690, Zip 31061–0690; tel. 912/454–3500; Brian L. Riddle, Chief Executive Officer (Nonreporting) **A**1 9 10 **S** Quorum Health Group/Quorum Health Resources, Inc., Brentwood, TN **N** Principal Health Care of Georgia, Atlanta, GA; Georgia 1st, Inc., Decatur, GA; The Medical Resource Network, L.L.C., Atlanta, GA

| | 16 | 10 | 145 | — | — | — | — | — | — | — |

MILLEN—Jenkins County

★ JENKINS COUNTY HOSPITAL, 515 East Winthrope Avenue, Zip 30442–1600; tel. 912/982–4221; Watson W. Rocker, President and Chief Executive Officer (Nonreporting) **A**9 10

| | 16 | 10 | 35 | — | — | — | — | — | — | — |

MONROE—Walton County

✠ WALTON MEDICAL CENTER, 330 Alcovy Street, Zip 30655–2140, Mailing Address: P.O. Box 1346, Zip 30655–1346; tel. 770/267–8461; Edgar L. Belcher, Administrator (Total facility includes 58 beds in nursing home–type unit) **A**1 9 10 **F**7 8 16 19 20 21 22 23 24 28 30 34 35 37 40 42 44 49 64 65 67 70 71 73 74 **S** Quorum Health Group/Quorum Health Resources, Inc., Brentwood, TN **N** Georgia 1st, Inc., Decatur, GA

| | 16 | 10 | 115 | 2164 | 78 | 45977 | 188 | 19941 | 8807 | 274 |

MONTEZUMA—Macon County

★ FLINT RIVER COMMUNITY HOSPITAL, 509 Sumter Street, Zip 31063–0770, Mailing Address: P.O. Box 770, Zip 31063–0770; tel. 912/472–3100; James D. Tesar, Chief Executive Officer (Nonreporting) **A**9 10 **S** Paracelsus Healthcare Corporation, Houston, TX

| | 33 | 10 | 50 | — | — | — | — | — | — | — |

MONTICELLO—Jasper County

JASPER MEMORIAL HOSPITAL, 898 College Street, Zip 31064–1298; tel. 706/468–6411; Donna Holman, Administrator (Total facility includes 44 beds in nursing home–type unit) (Nonreporting) **A**9 10

| | 16 | 10 | 72 | — | — | — | — | — | — | — |

MOODY AFB—Lowndes County

★ U. S. AIR FORCE HOSPITAL MOODY, 3278 Mitchell Boulevard, Zip 31699–1500; tel. 912/257–3772; Colonel Stephan A. Giesecke, USAF, MSC, Commander (Nonreporting) **S** Department of the Air Force, Bowling AFB, DC

| | 41 | 10 | 16 | — | — | — | — | — | — | — |

MOULTRIE—Colquitt County

✠ COLQUITT REGIONAL MEDICAL CENTER, 3131 South Main Street, Zip 31768–6701, Mailing Address: P.O. Box 40, Zip 31776–0040; tel. 912/985–3420; James R. Lowry, FACHE, Chief Executive Officer (Nonreporting) **A**1 10

| | 16 | 10 | 155 | — | — | — | — | — | — | — |

TURNING POINT HOSPITAL, 319 East By-Pass, Zip 31776, Mailing Address: P.O. Box 1177, Zip 31768–1177; tel. 912/985–4815; Ben Marion, Chief Executive Officer (Nonreporting) **A**10 **S** Universal Health Services, Inc., King of Prussia, PA

| | 33 | 82 | 59 | — | — | — | — | — | — | — |

Hospital, Address, Telephone, Administrator, Approval, Facility, and Physician Codes, Health Care System, Network	Classi-fication Codes		Utilization Data					Expense (thousands) of dollars		
★ American Hospital Association (AHA) membership □ Joint Commission on Accreditation of Healthcare Organizations (JCAHO) accreditation + American Osteopathic Healthcare Association (AOHA) membership ○ American Osteopathic Association (AOA) accreditation △ Commission on Accreditation of Rehabilitation Facilities (CARF) accreditation Control codes 61, 63, 64, 71, 72 and 73 indicate hospitals listed by AOHA, but not registered by AHA. For definition of numerical codes, see page A4	Control	Service	Staffed Beds	Admissions	Census	Outpatient Visits	Births	Total	Payroll	Personnel

NASHVILLE—Berrien County

☒ BERRIEN COUNTY HOSPITAL, 1221 East McPherson Street, Zip 31639–2326, Mailing Address: P.O. Box 665, Zip 31639–0665; tel. 912/686–7471; James P. Seward, Jr., Chief Executive Officer (Total facility includes 108 beds in nursing home–type unit) **A**1 10 **F**8 12 15 19 21 22 26 28 30 32 35 44 46 49 58 59 64 65 71 **S** Community Health Systems, Inc., Brentwood, TN **N** Principal Health Care of Georgia, Atlanta, GA; The Medical Resource Network, L.L.C., Atlanta, GA

| | 33 | 10 | 154 | 1109 | 116 | 19403 | — | 11968 | 5816 | 272 |

NEWNAN—Coweta County

☒ COLUMBIA PEACHTREE REGIONAL HOSPITAL, 60 Hospital Road, Zip 30264, Mailing Address: P.O. Box 2228, Zip 30264–2228; tel. 770/253–1912; Linda Jubinsky, Chief Executive Officer **A**1 10 **F**7 8 10 12 15 16 17 18 19 20 21 22 23 24 28 29 30 32 34 35 36 37 40 41 42 44 49 65 71 73 74 **S** Columbia/HCA Healthcare Corporation, Nashville, TN **N** Principal Health Care of Georgia, Atlanta, GA

| | 33 | 10 | 96 | 3550 | 37 | 18343 | 757 | 23353 | 10457 | 329 |

☒ NEWNAN HOSPITAL, 80 Jackson Street, Zip 30263–1941, Mailing Address: Box 997, Zip 30264–0997; tel. 770/253–2330; Glenn M. Flake, Executive Director (Total facility includes 153 beds in nursing home–type unit) **A**1 9 10 **F**8 10 12 14 19 21 22 23 24 30 35 37 41 42 44 46 64 65 67 71 73

| | 23 | 10 | 253 | 3978 | 195 | 46456 | — | 39816 | 16486 | 588 |

OCILLA—Irwin County

IRWIN COUNTY HOSPITAL, 710 North Irwin Avenue, Zip 31774–1098; tel. 912/468–3845; Sue Spivey, Administrator (Total facility includes 30 beds in nursing home–type unit) **A**10 **F**7 17 19 22 32 40 44 46 51 64 71 73 **P**6

| | 16 | 10 | 64 | 865 | 38 | 4198 | 67 | 6520 | 2429 | 166 |

PERRY—Houston County

☒ PERRY HOSPITAL, 1120 Morningside Drive, Zip 31069–2906, Mailing Address: Drawer 1004, Zip 31069–1004; tel. 912/987–3600; Nadine L. Weems, Administrator (Nonreporting) **A**1 9 10 **N** The Medical Resource Network, L.L.C., Atlanta, GA

| | 16 | 10 | 45 | — | — | — | — | — | — | — |

QUITMAN—Brooks County

□ BROOKS COUNTY HOSPITAL, 903 North Court Street, Zip 31643–1315, Mailing Address: P.O. Box 5000, Zip 31643–5000; tel. 912/263–4171; Andrew J. Finnegan, CHE, Administrator (Nonreporting) **A**1 9 10 **S** Archbold Medical Center, Thomasville, GA **N** Georgia 1st, Inc., Decatur, GA; The Medical Resource Network, L.L.C., Atlanta, GA

| | 23 | 10 | 35 | — | — | — | — | — | — | — |

REIDSVILLE—Tattnall County

TATTNALL MEMORIAL HOSPITAL, Highway 121 South, Zip 30453, Mailing Address: Route 1, Box 261, Zip 30453; tel. 912/557–4731; Ken Ford, Administrator **A**10 **F**7 8 15 16 19 22 35 40 44 49 71 73

| | 16 | 10 | 40 | 796 | 7 | 15466 | 61 | 4445 | 1825 | 83 |

RICHLAND—Stewart County

STEWART–WEBSTER HOSPITAL, 300 Alston Street, Zip 31825–1406, Mailing Address: P.O. Box 190, Zip 31825–0190; tel. 912/887–3366; Jerry R. Wise, Administrator (Nonreporting) **A**9 10 **S** Accord Health Care Corporation, Clearwater, FL

| | 33 | 10 | 25 | — | — | — | — | — | — | — |

RIVERDALE—Clayton County

☒ SOUTHERN REGIONAL MEDICAL CENTER, 11 Upper Riverdale Road S.W., Zip 30274–2600; tel. 770/991–8000; Eugene A. Leblond, FACHE, President and Chief Executive Officer (Nonreporting) **A**1 2 9 10 **N** Promina Health System, Inc., Atlanta, GA; Principal Health Care of Georgia, Atlanta, GA; Georgia 1st, Inc., Decatur, GA

| | 23 | 10 | 324 | — | — | — | — | — | — | — |

ROBINS AFB—Houston County

★ U. S. AIR FORCE HOSPITAL ROBINS, 655 Seventh Street, Zip 31098–2227; tel. 912/327–7996; Lieutenant Colonel Carl M. Alley, USAF, MSC, Deputy Commander and Administrator (Nonreporting) **S** Department of the Air Force, Bowling AFB, DC

| | 41 | 10 | 32 | — | — | — | — | — | — | — |

ROME—Floyd County

COLUMBIA REDMOND REGIONAL MEDICAL CENTER See Redmond Regional Medical Center

☒ △ FLOYD MEDICAL CENTER, 304 Turner McCall Boulevard, Zip 30165–2734, Mailing Address: P.O. Box 233, Zip 30162–0233; tel. 706/802–2000; Kurt Stuenkel, FACHE, President and Chief Executive Officer **A**1 2 3 5 7 9 10 **F**2 3 7 8 10 11 12 14 16 18 19 21 22 23 26 27 28 29 30 32 33 34 35 37 38 40 41 42 44 45 46 48 49 51 52 54 55 56 57 58 59 60 61 63 64 65 66 67 70 71 72 73 **P**8 **N** Principal Health Care of Georgia, Atlanta, GA; Georgia 1st, Inc., Decatur, GA; The Medical Resource Network, L.L.C., Atlanta, GA

| | 16 | 10 | 284 | 10846 | 131 | 164479 | 2145 | 88394 | 34690 | 1529 |

□ NORTHWEST GEORGIA REGIONAL HOSPITAL, 1305 Redmond Circle, Zip 30165–1393; tel. 706/295–6246; Thomas W. Muller, M.D., Superintendent (Total facility includes 97 beds in nursing home–type unit) **A**1 10 **F**14 15 16 20 52 53 55 56 57 64 65 73

| | 12 | 22 | 265 | 2791 | 232 | — | — | — | 17055 | 668 |

☒ REDMOND REGIONAL MEDICAL CENTER, (Formerly Columbia Redmond Regional Medical Center), 501 Redmond Road, Zip 30165–7001, Mailing Address: Box 107001, Zip 30164–7001; tel. 706/291–0291; James R. Thomas, Chief Executive Officer **A**1 2 9 10 **F**4 8 10 11 12 19 21 22 23 25 28 30 32 34 35 37 41 42 43 44 45 46 49 50 63 65 67 71 72 73 74 **P**4 **S** Columbia/HCA Healthcare Corporation, Nashville, TN

| | 33 | 10 | 199 | 9518 | 119 | — | 0 | 76186 | 22887 | 750 |

ROSWELL—Fulton County

☒ NORTH FULTON REGIONAL HOSPITAL, 3000 Hospital Boulevard, Zip 30076–9930; tel. 770/751–2500; Frederick R. Bailey, Chief Executive Officer **A**1 9 10 **F**7 11 19 21 22 23 25 28 34 35 36 37 38 39 40 41 42 44 46 48 49 50 51 65 66 67 70 71 73 74 **P**1 **S** TENET Healthcare Corporation, Santa Barbara, CA **N** Georgia 1st, Inc., Decatur, GA

| | 33 | 10 | 167 | 6390 | 81 | 52009 | 637 | — | — | 565 |

Hospital, Address, Telephone, Administrator, Approval, Facility, and Physician Codes, Health Care System, Network	Classi-fication Codes		Utilization Data					Expense (thousands) of dollars		
★ American Hospital Association (AHA) membership □ Joint Commission on Accreditation of Healthcare Organizations (JCAHO) accreditation + American Osteopathic Healthcare Association (AOHA) membership ○ American Osteopathic Association (AOA) accreditation △ Commission on Accreditation of Rehabilitation Facilities (CARF) accreditation Control codes 61, 63, 64, 71, 72 and 73 indicate hospitals listed by AOHA, but not registered by AHA. For definition of numerical codes, see page A4	Control	Service	Staffed Beds	Admissions	Census	Outpatient Visits	Births	Total	Payroll	Personnel

ROYSTON—Franklin County

☒ COBB MEMORIAL HOSPITAL, (Includes Brown Memorial Convalescent Center, Cobb Health Care Center and Cobb Terrace Personal Care Center), 577 Franklin Springs Street, Zip 30662–3909, Mailing Address: P.O. Box 589, Zip 30662–0589; tel. 706/245–5034; H. Thomas Brown, Administrator (Total facility includes 260 beds in nursing home–type unit) **A**1 9 10 **F**6 7 12 13 14 15 16 17 19 21 22 28 32 33 36 37 39 40 41 44 46 49 62 64 65 71 73 **N** Principal Health Care of Georgia, Atlanta, GA ... 23 10 | 331 | 2305 | 288 | 35600 | 173 | 20848 | 10389 | 263

SAINT MARYS—Camden County

☒ CAMDEN MEDICAL CENTER, 2000 Dan Proctor Drive, Zip 31558, Mailing Address: 2000 Dan Proctor Dirve, Zip 31558; tel. 912/576–4200; Warren Manley, Administrator (Nonreporting) **A**1 9 10 **S** Quorum Health Group/Quorum Health Resources, Inc., Brentwood, TN **N** Georgia 1st, Inc., Decatur, GA ... 23 10 | 40 | — | — | — | — | — | — | —

SAINT SIMONS ISLAND—Glynn County

□ CHARTER BY–THE–SEA BEHAVIORAL HEALTH SYSTEM, 2927 Demere Road, Zip 31522–1620; tel. 912/638–1999; Wes Robbins, Chief Executive Officer (Nonreporting) **A**1 9 10 **S** Magellan Health Services, Atlanta, GA ... 33 22 | 101 | — | — | — | — | — | — | —

SANDERSVILLE—Washington County

☒ WASHINGTON COUNTY REGIONAL HOSPITAL, 610 Sparta Highway, Zip 31082–1362, Mailing Address: P.O. Box 636, Zip 31082–0636; tel. 912/552–3901; Shirley R. Roberts, Administrator (Total facility includes 60 beds in nursing home–type unit) (Nonreporting) **A**1 9 10 **N** Principal Health Care of Georgia, Atlanta, GA ... 16 10 | 116 | — | — | — | — | — | — | —

SAVANNAH—Chatham County

☒ CANDLER HOSPITAL, 5353 Reynolds Street, Zip 31405–6013, Mailing Address: P.O. Box 9787, Zip 31412–9787; tel. 912/692–6000; Paul P. Hinchey, President and Chief Executive Officer (Nonreporting) **A**1 9 10 **N** Candler Health System, Savannah, GA; Principal Health Care of Georgia, Atlanta, GA; Georgia 1st, Inc., Decatur, GA; The Medical Resource Network, L.L.C., Atlanta, GA ... 23 10 | 335 | — | — | — | — | — | — | —

□ CHARTER SAVANNAH BEHAVIORAL HEALTH SYSTEM, 1150 Cornell Avenue, Zip 31406–2797; tel. 912/354–3911; Thomas L. Ryba, Chief Executive Officer (Nonreporting) **A**1 9 10 **S** Magellan Health Services, Atlanta, GA ... 33 22 | 112 | — | — | — | — | — | — | —

□ GEORGIA REGIONAL HOSPITAL AT SAVANNAH, Eisenhower Drive at Varnedoe, Zip 31406, Mailing Address: P.O. Box 13607, Zip 31416–0607; tel. 912/356–2011; Doug Osborne, Facility Administrator (Nonreporting) **A**1 10 ... 12 22 | 232 | — | — | — | — | — | — | —

☒ △ MEMORIAL HEALTH SYSTEM, 4700 Waters Avenue, Zip 31404–6283, Mailing Address: P.O. Box 23089, Zip 31403–3089; tel. 912/350–8000; Robert A. Colvin, President and Chief Executive Officer (Nonreporting) **A**1 2 3 5 7 8 10 **S** Quorum Health Group/Quorum Health Resources, Inc., Brentwood, TN **N** Principal Health Care of Georgia, Atlanta, GA ... 16 10 | 373 | — | — | — | — | — | — | —

□ △ ST. JOSEPH'S HOSPITAL, 11705 Mercy Boulevard, Zip 31419–1791; tel. 912/927–5404; Paul P. Hinchey, President and Chief Executive Officer (Nonreporting) **A**1 2 7 9 10 **S** Sisters of Mercy of the Americas–Regional Community of Baltimore, Baltimore, MD **N** Premier Health Systems, Inc., Columbia, SC ... 21 10 | 305 | — | — | — | — | — | — | —

SMYRNA—Cobb County

☒ EMORY–ADVENTIST HOSPITAL, 3949 South Cobb Drive S.E., Zip 30080–6300; tel. 770/434–0710; Terry Owen, Chief Executive Officer (Total facility includes 12 beds in nursing home–type unit) (Nonreporting) **A**1 10 **S** Adventist Health System Sunbelt Health Care Corporation, Winter Park, FL **N** Georgia 1st, Inc., Decatur, GA ... 23 10 | 54 | — | — | — | — | — | — | —

☒ RIDGEVIEW INSTITUTE, 3995 South Cobb Drive S.E., Zip 30080–6397; tel. 770/434–4567; John E. Gronewald, Chief Operating Officer **A**1 3 5 9 10 **F**3 12 14 15 52 53 54 55 56 57 58 59 65 74 ... 23 22 | 70 | 2252 | 38 | 23304 | 0 | 15094 | 7221 | 236

□ VALUEMARK–BRAWNER BEHAVIORAL HEALTHACARE SYSTEM–NORTH, 3180 Atlanta Street S.E., Zip 30080–8256; tel. 404/436–0081; Edward J. Osborne, Chief Executive Officer (Nonreporting) **A**1 3 10 **S** ValueMark Healthcare Systems, Inc., Atlanta, GA ... 33 22 | 108 | — | — | — | — | — | — | —

SNELLVILLE—Gwinnett County

☒ COLUMBIA EASTSIDE MEDICAL CENTER, 1700 Medical Way, Zip 30078, Mailing Address: P.O. Box 587, Zip 30078–0587; tel. 770/979–0200; Les Beard, Chief Executive Officer (Nonreporting) **A**1 9 10 **S** Columbia/HCA Healthcare Corporation, Nashville, TN **N** Georgia 1st, Inc., Decatur, GA ... 33 10 | 114 | — | — | — | — | — | — | —

SPARTA—Hancock County

★ HANCOCK MEMORIAL HOSPITAL, 453 Boland Street, Zip 31087–1105, Mailing Address: P.O. Box 490, Zip 31087–0490; tel. 706/444–7006; Daniel D. Holtz, FACHE, Administrator and Chief Executive Officer **A**9 10 **F**8 14 19 22 28 44 48 71 **S** Quorum Health Group/Quorum Health Resources, Inc., Brentwood, TN **N** ... 23 10 | 35 | 1287 | 14 | 6593 | 4 | 8103 | 3765 | 108

SPRINGFIELD—Effingham County

☒ EFFINGHAM HOSPITAL, 459 Highway 119 South, Zip 31329–3021, Mailing Address: P.O. Box 386, Zip 31329–0386; tel. 912/754–6451; W. Scott Burnette, Chief Executive Officer (Total facility includes 105 beds in nursing home–type unit) **A**1 10 **F**8 12 17 19 22 24 26 28 30 33 34 41 44 45 49 64 71 72 73 **P**4 **N** Candler Health System, Savannah, GA; Principal Health Care of Georgia, Atlanta, GA; Georgia 1st, Inc., Decatur, GA; The Medical Resource Network, L.L.C., Atlanta, GA ... 16 10 | 150 | 360 | 106 | 17029 | 0 | 9385 | 4317 | 204

Hospital, Address, Telephone, Administrator, Approval, Facility, and Physician Codes, Health Care System, Network	Classi-fication Codes		Utilization Data					Expense (thousands) of dollars		
★ American Hospital Association (AHA) membership □ Joint Commission on Healthcare Organizations (JCAHO) accreditation + American Osteopathic Healthcare Association (AOHA) membership ○ American Osteopathic Association (AOA) accreditation △ Commission on Accreditation of Rehabilitation Facilities (CARF) accreditation Control codes 61, 63, 64, 71, 72 and 73 indicate hospitals listed by AOHA, but not registered by AHA. For definition of numerical codes, see page A4	Control	Service	Staffed Beds	Admissions	Census	Outpatient Visits	Births	Total	Payroll	Personnel

STATESBORO—Bulloch County

□ BULLOCH MEMORIAL HOSPITAL, 500 East Grady Street, Zip 30458–5105, Mailing Address: P.O. Box 1048, Zip 30459–1048; tel. 912/486–1000; C. Scott Campbell, Executive Director **A**1 2 9 10 **F**7 8 11 12 17 19 20 21 22 23 26 28 29 30 32 33 34 35 37 39 40 44 45 49 63 65 66 67 70 71 73 **S** Health Management Associates, Naples, FL **N** Principal Health Care of Georgia, Atlanta, GA	33	10	158	5853	68	72478	1134	31902	14335	464
WILLINGWAY HOSPITAL, 311 Jones Mill Road, Zip 30458–4765; tel. 912/764–6236; Jimmy Mooney, Chief Executive Officer **F**3 **N** Premier Health Systems, Inc., Columbia, SC; Candler Health System, Savannah, GA; The Medical Resource Network, L.L.C., Atlanta, GA	33	82	40	496	24	6107	—	4209	2457	104

STOCKBRIDGE—Henry County

✚ HENRY MEDICAL CENTER, 1133 Eagle's Landing Parkway, Zip 30281–5099; tel. 770/389–2200; Joseph G. Brum, President and Chief Executive Officer (Nonreporting) **A**1 9 10	16	10	118	—	—	—	—	—	—	—

SWAINSBORO—Emanuel County

★ EMANUEL COUNTY HOSPITAL, 117 Kite Road, Zip 30401–3231, Mailing Address: P.O. Box 879, Zip 30401–0879; tel. 912/237–9911; Richard W. Clarke, Chief Executive Officer (Total facility includes 49 beds in nursing home–type unit) (Nonreporting) **A**10 **N** Principal Health Care of Georgia, Atlanta, GA; The Medical Resource Network, L.L.C., Atlanta, GA; University Health, Inc., Augusta, GA	16	10	119	—	—	—	—	—	—	—

SYLVANIA—Screven County

★ SCREVEN COUNTY HOSPITAL, 215 Mims Road, Zip 30467–2097; tel. 912/564–7426; Don E. Tomberlin, Interim Chief Executive Officer **A**9 10 **F**8 19 22 34 41 44 49 64 65 71 73	16	10	40	732	11	12251	0	4474	1839	71

SYLVESTER—Worth County

✚ BAPTIST HOSPITAL, WORTH COUNTY, (Formerly Worth County Hospital), 807 South Isabella Street, Zip 31791–0545, Mailing Address: Box 545, Zip 31791–0545; tel. 912/776–6961; Billy Hayes, Administrator **A**1 9 10 **F**15 17 19 22 25 30 40 44 46 71 73 **S** Georgia Baptist Health Care System, Atlanta, GA	33	10	50	996	10	15997	48	6094	2116	91

THOMASTON—Upson County

✚ UPSON REGIONAL MEDICAL CENTER, 801 West Gordon Street, Zip 30286–2831, Mailing Address: P.O. Box 1059, Zip 30286–1059; tel. 706/647–8111; Samuel S. Gregory, Administrator **A**1 9 10 **F**7 8 14 15 16 19 21 22 23 28 33 35 37 40 44 49 65 71 72 73 **S** Quorum Health Group/Quorum Health Resources, Inc., Brentwood, TN **N** Principal Health Care of Georgia, Atlanta, GA; Georgia 1st, Inc., Decatur, GA; The Medical Resource Network, L.L.C., Atlanta, GA	23	10	115	5423	62	66579	733	—	—	530

THOMASVILLE—Thomas County

✚ JOHN D. ARCHBOLD MEMORIAL HOSPITAL, Gordon Avenue at Mimosa Drive, Zip 31792–6113, Mailing Address: P.O. Box 1018, Zip 31799–1018; tel. 912/228–2000; Jason H. Moore, President and Chief Executive Officer (Total facility includes 64 beds in nursing home–type unit) **A**1 2 9 10 **F**1 3 4 7 8 10 11 12 14 15 16 17 18 19 20 21 22 23 25 26 27 28 29 30 31 32 33 34 35 37 39 40 41 42 44 45 46 48 49 50 51 52 53 54 55 56 57 58 59 60 61 63 64 65 66 67 69 70 71 72 73 **P**8 **S** Archbold Medical Center, Thomasville, GA **N** Georgia 1st, Inc., Decatur, GA; The Medical Resource Network, L.L.C., Atlanta, GA	23	10	328	10524	157	159419	944	80895	36756	1354

THOMSON—McDuffie County

✚ MCDUFFIE COUNTY HOSPITAL, 521 Hill Street S.W., Zip 30824–2199; tel. 706/595–1411; Douglas C. Keir, Chief Executive Officer **A**1 9 10 **F**8 11 12 16 17 19 20 22 24 28 29 30 32 33 34 37 41 44 45 46 47 48 49 65 66 71 73 **S** Quorum Health Group/Quorum Health Resources, Inc., Brentwood, TN **N** Principal Health Care of Georgia, Atlanta, GA; The Medical Resource Network, L.L.C., Atlanta, GA; University Health, Inc., Augusta, GA	16	10	47	1566	17	26328	—	10513	4942	203

TIFTON—Tift County

✚ TIFT GENERAL HOSPITAL, 901 East 18th Street, Zip 31794–3648, Mailing Address: Drawer 747, Zip 31793–0747; tel. 912/382–7120; William T. Richardson, President and Chief Executive Officer **A**1 10 **F**7 8 10 12 14 15 16 17 19 21 22 23 28 33 35 37 39 40 41 42 44 45 46 48 49 61 65 71 72 73 74 **P**7 8 **N** Georgia 1st, Inc., Decatur, GA	16	10	181	7877	92	42400	1193	55119	19181	—

TOCCOA—Stephens County

✚ STEPHENS COUNTY HOSPITAL, 2003 Falls Road, Zip 30577–9700; tel. 706/886–6841; Edward C. Gambrell, Jr., Administrator (Total facility includes 82 beds in nursing home–type unit) **A**1 9 10 **F**6 7 8 14 15 16 17 19 22 23 30 35 37 40 41 44 45 49 62 63 64 65 69 71 73 **N** Principal Health Care of Georgia, Atlanta, GA	16	10	178	3778	108	32887	322	25180	11863	453

VALDOSTA—Lowndes County

GREENLEAF CENTER, 2209 Pineview Drive, Zip 31602–7316; tel. 912/247–4357; Michael Lane, Administrator and Chief Executive Officer (Nonreporting) **A**9 10 **S** Greenleaf Health Systems, Inc., Chattanooga, TN	33	22	70	—	—	—	—	—	—	—
✚ SOUTH GEORGIA MEDICAL CENTER, 2501 North Patterson Street, Zip 31602–1735, Mailing Address: P.O. Box 1727, Zip 31603–1727; tel. 912/333–1000; John S. Bowling, President and Chief Executive Officer **A**1 2 10 **F**1 4 6 7 8 10 11 12 13 15 16 17 19 20 21 22 23 25 26 27 28 29 30 32 33 34 35 37 38 39 40 41 42 44 45 46 49 51 53 54 55 56 57 60 62 63 65 66 67 70 71 72 73 74 **P**8 **N** Principal Health Care of Georgia, Atlanta, GA; Georgia 1st, Inc., Decatur, GA; The Medical Resource Network, L.L.C., Atlanta, GA	16	10	288	13382	175	—	1743	103547	37820	1585

Hospital, Address, Telephone, Administrator, Approval, Facility, and Physician Codes, Health Care System, Network	Classi-fication Codes		Utilization Data					Expense (thousands) of dollars		
★ American Hospital Association (AHA) membership □ Joint Commission on Accreditation of Healthcare Organizations (JCAHO) accreditation + American Osteopathic Healthcare Association (AOHA) membership ○ American Osteopathic Association (AOA) accreditation △ Commission on Accreditation of Rehabilitation Facilities (CARF) accreditation Control codes 61, 63, 64, 71, 72 and 73 indicate hospitals listed by AOHA, but not registered by AHA. For definition of numerical codes, see page A4	Control	Service	Staffed Beds	Admissions	Census	Outpatient Visits	Births	Total	Payroll	Personnel

VIDALIA—Toombs County

□ MEADOWS REGIONAL MEDICAL CENTER, 1703 Meadows Lane, Zip 30474–8915, Mailing Address: P.O. Box 1048, Zip 30474–1048; tel. 912/537–8921; Barry Michael, Chief Executive Officer (Total facility includes 35 beds in nursing home–type unit) (Nonreporting) **A**1 10 **N** Candler Health System, Savannah, GA; Principal Health Care of Georgia, Atlanta, GA

| | 16 | 10 | 122 | — | — | — | — | — | — | — |

VIENNA—Dooly County

✖ DOOLY MEDICAL CENTER, 1300 Union Street, Zip 31092–7541, Mailing Address: P.O. Box 278, Zip 31092–0278; tel. 912/268–4141; Kevin Paul, Administrator (Nonreporting) **A**1 9 10 **S** Georgia Baptist Health Care System, Atlanta, GA **N** Principal Health Care of Georgia, Atlanta, GA; The Medical Resource Network, L.L.C., Atlanta, GA

| | 16 | 10 | 38 | — | — | — | — | — | — | — |

VILLA RICA—Carroll County

✖ TANNER MEDICAL CENTER–VILLA RICA, 601 Dallas Road, Zip 30180–1202, Mailing Address: P.O. Box 638, Zip 30180–0638; tel. 770/459–7100; Larry N. Steed, Administrator (Nonreporting) **A**1 9 10 **S** Quorum Health Group/Quorum Health Resources, Inc., Brentwood, TN **N** Principal Health Care of Georgia, Atlanta, GA; Georgia 1st, Inc., Decatur, GA

| | 16 | 10 | 45 | — | — | — | — | — | — | — |

WARM SPRINGS—Meriwether County

★ BAPTIST MERIWETHER HOSPITAL, (Formerly Meriwether Regional Hospital), 5995 Spring Street, Zip 31830, Mailing Address: P.O. Box 8, Zip 31830–0008; tel. 706/655–3331; William E. Daniel, Administrator (Total facility includes 79 beds in nursing home–type unit) (Nonreporting) **A**10 **S** Georgia Baptist Health Care System, Atlanta, GA **N** Community Healthcare Network, Columbus, GA
MERIWETHER REGIONAL HOSPITAL See Baptist Meriwether Hospital

| | 21 | 10 | 105 | — | — | — | — | — | — | — |

□ ROOSEVELT WARM SPRINGS INSTITUTE FOR REHABILITATION, Highway 27, Zip 31830, Mailing Address: P.O. Box 1000, Zip 31830–0268; tel. 706/655–5001; Frank C. Ruzycki, Executive Director **A**1 10 **F**48

| | 12 | 46 | 78 | 680 | 46 | 6173 | 0 | 17195 | 5818 | 439 |

WARNER ROBINS—Houston County

✖ HOUSTON MEDICAL CENTER, 1601 Watson Boulevard, Zip 31093–3431, Mailing Address: Box 2886, Zip 31099–2886; tel. 912/922–4281; Arthur P. Christie, Administrator **A**1 9 10 **F**7 8 10 11 12 14 15 16 17 19 20 22 23 25 28 29 30 34 35 37 39 40 42 44 45 46 48 49 52 54 55 56 57 58 59 65 66 67 71 72 73 74 **P**7 **N** Georgia 1st, Inc., Decatur, GA; The Medical Resource Network, L.L.C., Atlanta, GA

| | 16 | 10 | 186 | 10541 | 108 | 76176 | 1064 | 56185 | 24373 | 943 |

WASHINGTON—Wilkes County

★ WILLS MEMORIAL HOSPITAL, 120 Gordon Street, Zip 30673–1602, Mailing Address: P.O. Box 370, Zip 30673–0370; tel. 706/678–2151; Vincent DiFranco, Chief Executive Officer **A**9 10 **F**7 8 16 19 21 22 28 30 33 37 40 44 49 71 73 **S** Quorum Health Group/Quorum Health Resources, Inc., Brentwood, TN **N** University Health, Inc., Augusta, GA

| | 16 | 10 | 50 | 1556 | 22 | 19009 | 66 | 8994 | 3820 | 145 |

WAYCROSS—Ware County

✖ SATILLA REGIONAL MEDICAL CENTER, 410 Darling Avenue, Zip 31501–5246, Mailing Address: P.O. Box 139, Zip 31502–0139; tel. 912/283–3030; Eugene Johnson, President and Chief Executive Officer (Nonreporting) **A**1 9 10 **N** Principal Health Care of Georgia, Atlanta, GA

| | 23 | 10 | 116 | — | — | — | — | — | — | — |

WAYNESBORO—Burke County

□ BURKE COUNTY HOSPITAL, 351 Liberty Street, Zip 30830–9686; tel. 706/554–4435; Gloria Cochran, Administrator **A**1 9 10 **F**7 8 14 15 16 19 22 28 30 37 40 44 45 46 49 65 67 71 73 **N** Principal Health Care of Georgia, Atlanta, GA; The Medical Resource Network, L.L.C., Atlanta, GA; University Health, Inc., Augusta, GA

| | 13 | 10 | 40 | 1545 | 16 | 18016 | 186 | 7964 | 2543 | 124 |

WILDWOOD—Dade County

WILDWOOD LIFESTYLE CENTER AND HOSPITAL, Lifestyle Lane, Zip 30757; tel. 706/820–1493; Larry E. Clements, Administrator (Nonreporting)

| | 23 | 10 | 13 | — | — | — | — | — | — | — |

WINDER—Barrow County

✖ BARROW MEDICAL CENTER, (Formerly Columbia Barrow Medical Center), 316 North Broad Street, Zip 30680–2150, Mailing Address: P.O. Box 768, Zip 30680–0768; tel. 770/867–3400; Joe T. Hutchins, Chief Executive Officer **A**1 9 10 **F**7 8 12 15 16 17 19 21 22 28 29 30 34 35 37 39 40 44 45 49 60 64 65 67 70 71 73 74 **S** Columbia/HCA Healthcare Corporation, Nashville, TN

| | 33 | 10 | 56 | 1650 | 17 | 22706 | 320 | — | — | 0 |

Resident population 1,187 (in thousands)
Resident population in metro areas 74.2%
Birth rate per 1,000 population 16.6
65 years and over 12.9%
Percent of persons without health insurance 8.6%

Hospital, Address, Telephone, Administrator, Approval, Facility, and Physician Codes, Health Care System, Network	Classi-fication Codes		Utilization Data					Expense (thousands) of dollars		
★ American Hospital Association (AHA) membership □ Joint Commission on Accreditation of Healthcare Organizations (JCAHO) accreditation + American Osteopathic Healthcare Association (AOHA) membership ○ American Osteopathic Association (AOA) accreditation △ Commission on Accreditation of Rehabilitation Facilities (CARF) accreditation Control codes 61, 63, 64, 71, 72 and 73 indicate hospitals listed by AOHA, but not registered by AHA. For definition of numerical codes, see page A4	Control	Service	Staffed Beds	Admissions	Census	Outpatient Visits	Births	Total	Payroll	Personnel

EWA BEACH—Honolulu County

✴ KAHI MOHALA, 91–2301 Fort Weaver Road, Zip 96706; tel. 808/671–8511; Margi Drue, Administrator **A**1 3 9 10 **F**3 12 25 27 34 52 53 56 58 59 65 **P**6 **S** Sutter Health, Sacramento, CA	23	22	88	1105	66	18497	0	14722	8379	258
✴ ST. FRANCIS MEDICAL CENTER–WEST, 91–2141 Fort Weaver Road, Zip 96706; tel. 808/678–7000; Sister Gretchen Gilroy, President and Chief Executive Officer **A**1 10 **F**4 7 8 10 11 12 15 16 17 19 20 21 22 23 26 28 29 30 31 32 33 34 35 37 39 40 41 42 43 44 45 46 49 60 65 68 69 71 73 **P**3 **S** Sisters of the 3rd Franciscan Order, Syracuse, NY	21	10	100	3514	74	82854	465	41820	16557	387

HILO—Hawaii County

✴ HILO MEDICAL CENTER, 1190 Waianuenue Avenue, Zip 96720–2095; tel. 808/974–4743; Robert Morris, M.D., Administrator (Total facility includes 108 beds in nursing home–type unit) **A**1 5 9 10 **F**7 8 14 15 16 19 20 21 22 25 26 29 31 32 33 35 40 41 42 44 45 49 52 54 55 56 57 59 60 64 65 71 73 **P**5 **S** State of Hawaii, Department of Health, Honolulu, HI	12	10	274	7498	219	33938	1110	47842	26105	717

HONOKAA—Hawaii County

★ HONOKAA HOSPITAL, Mailing Address: P.O. Box 237, Zip 96727–0237; tel. 808/775–7211; Romel Dela Cruz, Administrator **A**9 10 **F**14 15 16 65 73 **S** State of Hawaii, Department of Health, Honolulu, HI	12	10	50	131	44	1266	0	5193	2346	82

HONOLULU—Honolulu County

✴ KAISER FOUNDATION HOSPITAL, 3288 Moanalua Road, Zip 96819; tel. 808/834–5333; Bruce Behnke, Administrator (Total facility includes 55 beds in nursing home–type unit) **A**1 2 3 5 9 10 **F**4 7 8 10 12 13 14 16 17 19 20 21 22 24 26 28 30 31 32 33 34 35 37 38 40 41 42 43 44 45 46 49 51 53 54 55 57 58 59 61 63 64 65 67 68 69 70 71 72 73 74 **P**3 **S** Kaiser Foundation Hospitals, Oakland, CA	23	10	188	10689	159	1210711	1981	—	—	941
✴ KAPIOLANI MEDICAL CENTER FOR WOMEN AND CHILDREN, 1319 Punahou Street, Zip 96826–1032; tel. 808/983–6000; Frances A. Hallonquist, Chief Executive Officer **A**1 3 5 9 10 **F**4 7 8 10 12 13 17 18 19 21 22 25 27 28 29 30 31 32 34 37 38 39 40 41 42 43 44 45 46 47 49 51 53 54 55 56 58 60 61 65 66 67 68 70 71 72 73 74	23	10	172	11625	142	132859	5308	118681	44647	1224
✴ KUAKINI MEDICAL CENTER, 347 North Kuakini Street, Zip 96817–2381; tel. 808/536–2236; Gary K. Kajiwara, President and Chief Executive Officer **A**1 2 3 5 9 10 **F**1 4 8 10 11 12 14 15 16 19 21 22 23 25 26 28 29 30 32 33 34 35 37 39 41 42 43 44 45 46 49 60 63 64 65 66 67 71 73 **P**8 **N** Pacific Health Care, Honolulu, HI	23	10	158	6013	125	36909	—	87532	43589	1116
★ LEAHI HOSPITAL, 3675 Kilauea Avenue, Zip 96816; tel. 808/733–8000; Jerry Walker, Administrator (Total facility includes 179 beds in nursing home–type unit) (Nonreporting) **A**3 5 9 10 **S** State of Hawaii, Department of Health, Honolulu, HI	12	33	192	—	—	—	—	—	—	—
✴ QUEEN'S MEDICAL CENTER, 1301 Punchbowl Street, Zip 96813; tel. 808/538–9011; Arthur A. Ushijima, President and Chief Executive Officer (Total facility includes 29 beds in nursing home–type unit) **A**1 2 3 5 8 9 10 **F**3 4 7 8 10 11 12 13 14 15 16 18 19 20 21 22 23 25 26 28 29 30 31 32 33 34 35 36 37 39 40 41 42 43 44 45 46 49 51 52 54 55 56 57 58 59 60 63 64 65 67 69 71 72 73 **P**5 **S** Queen's Health Systems, Honolulu, HI **N** Queens Health Systems, Honolulu, HI	23	10	457	18698	419	200353	1808	308903	135701	2913
✴ △ REHABILITATION HOSPITAL OF THE PACIFIC, 226 North Kuakini Street, Zip 96817–9881; tel. 808/531–3511; William D. O'Connor, President and Chief Executive Officer (Nonreporting) **A**1 7 9 10	23	46	86	—	—	—	—	—	—	—
✴ SHRINERS HOSPITALS FOR CHILDREN, HONOLULU, 1310 Punahou Street, Zip 96826–1099; tel. 808/941–4466; James B. Brasel, Administrator **A**1 3 5 **F**5 15 20 34 47 48 49 65 71 **S** Shriners Hospitals for Children, Tampa, FL	23	57	40	363	31	4457	0	—	—	133
□ ST. FRANCIS MEDICAL CENTER, 2230 Liliha Street, Zip 96817–9979, Mailing Address: P.O. Box 30100, Zip 96820–0100; tel. 808/547–6011; Cynthia Okinaka, Administrator (Total facility includes 46 beds in nursing home–type unit) (Nonreporting) **A**1 2 3 5 9 10 **S** Sisters of the 3rd Franciscan Order, Syracuse, NY **N** Pacific Health Care, Honolulu, HI	21	10	221	—	—	—	—	—	—	—
□ STRAUB CLINIC AND HOSPITAL, 888 South King Street, Zip 96813; tel. 808/522–4000; Blake E. Waterhouse, M.D., Chief Executive Officer **A**1 2 3 5 9 10 **F**5 15 20 34 47 48 49 65 71	33	10	139	363	31	4457	0	—	—	133
✴ TRIPLER ARMY MEDICAL CENTER, Zip 96859–5000; tel. 808/433–6661; Brigadier General Nancy R. Adams, Commander **A**1 2 3 5 9 **F**3 4 7 8 10 11 12 13 14 15 16 17 18 19 20 21 22 23 24 25 26 28 29 30 31 34 35 37 38 39 40 41 42 43 44 45 46 47 49 51 52 53 54 55 56 57 58 59 60 61 63 65 66 67 68 69 70 71 72 73 74 **P**5 6 **S** Department of the Army, Office of the Surgeon General, Falls Church, VA	42	10	298	12709	222	566019	2893	184973	39685	2961

KAHUKU—Honolulu County

✴ KAHUKU HOSPITAL, 56–117 Puala Lea Street, Zip 96731–2052; tel. 808/293–9221; Keith R. Ridley, Chief Executive Officer (Nonreporting) **A**1 9 10	23	10	24	—	—	—	—	—	—	—

Hospital, Address, Telephone, Administrator, Approval, Facility, and Physician Codes, Health Care System, Network	Classi-fication Codes		Utilization Data					Expense (thousands) of dollars		
★ American Hospital Association (AHA) membership □ Joint Commission on Accreditation of Healthcare Organizations (JCAHO) accreditation + American Osteopathic Healthcare Association (AOHA) membership ○ American Osteopathic Association (AOA) accreditation △ Commission on Accreditation of Rehabilitation Facilities (CARF) accreditation Control codes 61, 63, 64, 71, 72 and 73 indicate hospitals listed by AOHA, but not registered by AHA. For definition of numerical codes, see page A4	Control	Service	Staffed Beds	Admissions	Census	Outpatient Visits	Births	Total	Payroll	Personnel

KAILUA—Honolulu County
☒ CASTLE MEDICAL CENTER, 640 Ulukahiki Street, Zip 96734–4498; tel. 808/263–5500; Robert J. Walker, President (Total facility includes 10 beds in nursing home–type unit) **A**1 9 10 **F**2 3 7 8 10 14 15 16 17 19 21 22 28 29 30 32 37 40 41 42 44 46 49 52 53 58 59 64 65 67 71 73 74 **P**5 8 **S** Adventist Health, Roseville, CA

| | 21 | 10 | 150 | 6088 | 100 | 120435 | 466 | 60954 | 28184 | 842 |

KANEOHE—Honolulu County
□ HAWAII STATE HOSPITAL, 45–710 Keaahala Road, Zip 96744–3597; tel. 808/236–8237; Marvin O. St. Clair, Administrator (Nonreporting) **A**1 3 5

| | 12 | 22 | 167 | — | — | — | — | — | — | — |

KAPAA—Kauai County
★ SAMUEL MAHELONA MEMORIAL HOSPITAL, 4800 Kawaihau Road, Zip 96746–1998; tel. 808/822–4961; Neva M. Olson, Chief Executive Officer (Total facility includes 61 beds in nursing home–type unit) (Nonreporting) **A**9 10 **S** State of Hawaii, Department of Health, Honolulu, HI

| | 12 | 49 | 82 | — | — | — | — | — | — | — |

KAUNAKAKAI—Maui County
☒ MOLOKAI GENERAL HOSPITAL, Mailing Address: P.O. Box 408, Zip 96748–0408; tel. 808/553–5331; Phillip W. Reyes, M.D., Co–Medical Executive Director (Total facility includes 16 beds in nursing home–type unit) **A**1 9 10 **F**3 4 7 8 10 11 14 15 16 17 19 20 21 22 23 28 29 30 31 32 33 35 37 38 39 40 42 43 44 45 47 49 50 60 61 64 65 67 70 71 72 74 **P**4 5 7 8 **S** Queen's Health Systems, Honolulu, HI **N** Queens Health Systems, Honolulu, HI

| | 23 | 10 | 29 | 223 | 19 | 6394 | 43 | 6046 | 2835 | 87 |

KEALAKEKUA—Hawaii County
☒ KONA COMMUNITY HOSPITAL, Mailing Address: P.O. Box 69, Zip 96750–0069; tel. 808/322–4429; Joseph C. Wall, Chief Executive Officer (Total facility includes 22 beds in nursing home–type unit) **A**1 9 10 **F**1 7 14 15 16 19 20 22 37 40 41 44 49 56 59 64 65 71 73 **S** State of Hawaii, Department of Health, Honolulu, HI

| | 12 | 10 | 75 | 3009 | 51 | — | 487 | 25064 | 11420 | 340 |

KOHALA—Hawaii County
★ KOHALA HOSPITAL, (GENERAL HOSPITAL ACUTE LTC ER), Mailing Address: P.O. Box 10, Kapaau, Zip 96755–0010; tel. 808/889–6211; Herbert K. Yim, Administrator **A**9 10 **F**22 34 49 64 **S** State of Hawaii, Department of Health, Honolulu, HI

| | 12 | 49 | 26 | 40 | 23 | 1875 | — | 2347 | 1368 | 43 |

KULA—Maui County
★ KULA HOSPITAL, 204 Kula Highway, Zip 96790–9499; tel. 808/878–1221; Alan G. Lee, Administrator (Total facility includes 103 beds in nursing home–type unit) (Nonreporting) **A**9 10 **S** State of Hawaii, Department of Health, Honolulu, HI

| | 12 | 49 | 105 | — | — | — | — | — | — | — |

LANAI CITY—Maui County
★ LANAI COMMUNITY HOSPITAL, 628 Seventh Street, Zip 96763–0797, Mailing Address: P.O. Box 797, Zip 96763–0797; tel. 808/565–6411; John Schaumburg, Administrator (Nonreporting) **A**9 10 **S** State of Hawaii, Department of Health, Honolulu, HI

| | 12 | 10 | 14 | — | — | — | — | — | — | — |

LIHUE—Kauai County
☒ WILCOX MEMORIAL HOSPITAL, 3420 Kuhio Highway, Zip 96766; tel. 808/245–1100; Larry K. Mangold, Interim President and Chief Executive Officer **A**1 2 9 10 **F**1 3 7 8 12 15 16 17 19 20 21 22 25 26 27 28 29 30 31 32 33 34 37 39 40 41 44 45 49 51 52 61 63 64 65 67 68 70 71 72 73 **P**5 6

| | 23 | 10 | 177 | 4469 | 154 | 57104 | 759 | 43406 | 21388 | 605 |

PAHALA—Hawaii County
★ KAU HOSPITAL, Mailing Address: P.O. Box 40, Zip 96777–0040; tel. 808/928–8331; Dawn S. Pung, Administrator (Total facility includes 19 beds in nursing home–type unit) (Nonreporting) **A**9 10 **S** State of Hawaii, Department of Health, Honolulu, HI

| | 12 | 10 | 21 | — | — | — | — | — | — | — |

WAHIAWA—Honolulu County
☒ WAHIAWA GENERAL HOSPITAL, 128 Lehua Street, Zip 96786, Mailing Address: P.O. Box 580, Zip 96786–0580; tel. 808/621–8411; David L. Hill, President and Chief Executive Officer (Total facility includes 93 beds in nursing home–type unit) **A**1 3 5 9 10 **F**4 7 8 10 13 15 16 17 18 19 21 22 23 24 25 26 27 28 29 30 31 32 33 34 35 36 37 39 40 41 42 44 49 50 51 53 54 56 57 58 63 64 65 66 67 68 69 71 73 74 **P**6

| | 23 | 10 | 162 | 2216 | 125 | 29842 | 346 | 34462 | 13804 | 411 |

WAILUKU—Maui County
☒ MAUI MEMORIAL HOSPITAL, 221 Mahalani Street, Zip 96793–2581; tel. 808/244–9056; David W. Patton, Chief Executive Officer (Nonreporting) **A**1 2 9 10 **S** State of Hawaii, Department of Health, Honolulu, HI

| | 12 | 10 | 203 | — | — | — | — | — | — | — |

WAIMEA—Kauai County
☒ KAUAI VETERANS MEMORIAL HOSPITAL, Waimea Canyon Road, Zip 96796, Mailing Address: P.O. Box 337, Zip 96796–0337; tel. 808/338–9431; Orianna A. Skomoroch, Chief Executive Officer (Total facility includes 20 beds in nursing home–type unit) (Nonreporting) **A**1 9 10 **S** State of Hawaii, Department of Health, Honolulu, HI

| | 12 | 10 | 49 | — | — | — | — | — | — | — |

Resident population 1,210 (in thousands)
Resident population in metro areas 30.7%
Birth rate per 1,000 population 15.5
65 years and over 11.4%
Percent of persons without health insurance 16.5%

Hospital, Address, Telephone, Administrator, Approval, Facility, and Physician Codes, Health Care System, Network	Classi-fication Codes		Utilization Data					Expense (thousands) of dollars		
★ American Hospital Association (AHA) membership ☐ Joint Commission on Accreditation of Healthcare Organizations (JCAHO) accreditation + American Osteopathic Healthcare Association (AOHA) membership ○ American Osteopathic Association (AOA) accreditation △ Commission on Accreditation of Rehabilitation Facilities (CARF) accreditation Control codes 61, 63, 64, 71, 72 and 73 indicate hospitals listed by AOHA, but not registered by AHA. For definition of numerical codes, see page A4	Control	Service	Staffed Beds	Admissions	Census	Outpatient Visits	Births	Total	Payroll	Personnel
AMERICAN FALLS—Power County										
★ HARMS MEMORIAL HOSPITAL DISTRICT, 510 Roosevelt Road, Zip 83211–0420, Mailing Address: P.O. Box 420, Zip 83211–0420; tel. 208/226–3200; Dale E. Polla, Administrator (Total facility includes 31 beds in nursing home–type unit) **A**9 10 **F**1 3 7 15 17 20 21 32 41 46 49 51 64 65 71 73 **P**5	16	10	41	198	33	11211	5	—	1512	86
ARCO—Butte County										
★ LOST RIVERS DISTRICT HOSPITAL, 551 Highland Drive, Zip 83213–9771, Mailing Address: P.O. Box 145, Zip 83213–0145; tel. 208/527–8206; Cindy Charyulu, Chief Executive Officer (Total facility includes 33 beds in nursing home–type unit) (Nonreporting) **A**9 10	16	10	41	—	—	—	—	—	—	—
BLACKFOOT—Bingham County										
⊞ BINGHAM MEMORIAL HOSPITAL, 98 Poplar Street, Zip 83221–1799; tel. 208/785–4100; Robert M. Peterson, Administrator (Total facility includes 70 beds in nursing home–type unit) **A**1 9 10 **F**7 11 14 15 16 19 21 22 28 29 30 35 37 39 40 41 44 45 46 49 64 65 67 71 73 **P**8 **S** Quorum Health Group/Quorum Health Resources, Inc., Brentwood, TN	13	10	110	1400	74	61435	345	13304	5439	216
STATE HOSPITAL SOUTH, 700 East Alice Street, Zip 83221–0400, Mailing Address: Box 400, Zip 83221–0400; tel. 208/785–1200; Ray Laible, Administrative Director (Total facility includes 30 beds in nursing home–type unit) **A**9 10 **F**52 53 54 55 56 57 64 **P**6	12	22	136	375	106	—	—	16426	8561	284
BOISE—Ada County										
☐ BHC INTERMOUNTAIN HOSPITAL, 303 North Allumbaugh Street, Zip 83704–9266; tel. 208/377–8400; Vernon G. Garrett, Chief Executive Officer (Nonreporting) **A**1 9 10 **S** Behavioral Healthcare Corporation, Nashville, TN	33	22	75							
★ △ IDAHO ELKS REHABILITATION HOSPITAL, 204 Fort Place, Zip 83702–4597, Mailing Address: Box 1100, Zip 83701–1100; tel. 208/343–2583; Joseph P. Caroselli, Administrator **A**7 9 10 **F**12 16 24 28 41 48 49 53 64 65 66 73	23	46	64	1202	39	18016	0	12330	7161	271
⊞ △ SAINT ALPHONSUS REGIONAL MEDICAL CENTER, 1055 North Curtis Road, Zip 83706–1370; tel. 208/378–2121; Sandra B. Bruce, President and Chief Executive Officer (Total facility includes 11 beds in nursing home–type unit) **A**1 2 3 5 7 9 10 **F**3 4 8 10 11 12 14 15 16 17 18 19 21 22 25 26 27 28 29 30 31 32 33 34 35 37 39 41 42 43 44 45 46 48 49 51 52 53 54 55 56 57 58 60 64 65 67 69 70 71 72 73 **P**5 6 7 8 **S** Holy Cross Health System Corporation, South Bend, IN	21	10	280	12629	181	282395	0	132028	49056	1815
⊞ ST. LUKE'S REGIONAL MEDICAL CENTER, 190 East Bannock Street, Zip 83712–6298; tel. 208/381–2222; Edwin E. Dahlberg, President **A**1 2 3 5 9 10 **F**4 7 8 10 11 12 13 14 15 16 17 19 20 21 22 23 24 25 26 28 29 30 31 32 33 34 35 37 38 39 40 41 42 43 44 45 46 47 49 51 53 54 56 57 58 60 61 63 64 65 67 68 69 71 72 73 74 **P**6	23	10	303	17145	182	408398	4387	176094	72540	2167
⊞ VETERANS AFFAIRS MEDICAL CENTER, 500 West Fort Street, Zip 83702–4598; tel. 208/422–1100; Wayne C. Tippets, Director (Total facility includes 40 beds in nursing home–type unit) (Nonreporting) **A**1 3 5 9 **S** Department of Veterans Affairs, Washington, DC	45	10	176	—	—	—	—	—	—	—
BONNERS FERRY—Boundary County										
★ BOUNDARY COMMUNITY HOSPITAL, (Includes Boundary County Nursing Home), 6640 Kaniksu Street, Zip 83805–7532, Mailing Address: HCR 61, Box 61A, Zip 83805–9500; tel. 208/267–3141; William T. McClintock, FACHE, Chief Executive Officer (Total facility includes 52 beds in nursing home–type unit) **A**9 10 **F**1 8 12 14 15 17 22 26 27 28 30 32 33 34 39 41 44 49 51 56 57 64 65 67 72 73 74 **P**8 **N** North Idaho Rural Health Network, Coeur d'Alene, ID	13	10	62	396	48	10546	—	5077	2923	139
BURLEY—Cassia County										
⊞ CASSIA REGIONAL MEDICAL CENTER, 1501 Hiland Avenue, Zip 83318–2675; tel. 208/678–4444; Richard Packer, Administrator **A**1 2 9 10 **F**7 8 12 14 15 16 17 19 21 22 27 28 30 32 33 34 35 37 39 40 41 44 45 46 49 65 66 71 73 74 **P**6 **S** Intermountain Health Care, Inc., Salt Lake City, UT **N** Intermountain HealthCare/Amerinet, Salt Lake City, UT	23	10	38	2571	20	65568	583	19800	7483	236
CALDWELL—Canyon County										
⊞ WEST VALLEY MEDICAL CENTER, (Formerly Columbia West Valley Medical Center), 1717 Arlington, Zip 83605–4864; tel. 208/459–4641; Mark Adams, Chief Executive Officer **A**1 9 10 **F**7 8 10 11 12 15 18 19 20 21 22 23 26 28 30 32 33 34 35 36 40 41 44 46 49 52 53 54 55 56 57 58 64 65 66 67 71 73 **P**5 **S** Columbia/HCA Healthcare Corporation, Nashville, TN	33	10	122	4237	45	27719	620	30011	12826	489
CASCADE—Valley County										
★ CASCADE MEDICAL CENTER, 402 Old State Highway, Zip 83611, Mailing Address: P.O. Box 151, Zip 83611–0151; tel. 208/382–4242; Richard Holm, Administrator (Nonreporting) **A**9 10 **S** Holy Cross Health System Corporation, South Bend, IN	13	10	10	—	—	—	—	—	—	—

Hospital, Address, Telephone, Administrator, Approval, Facility, and Physician Codes, Health Care System, Network	Classi-fication Codes		Utilization Data					Expense (thousands) of dollars		
★ American Hospital Association (AHA) membership □ Joint Commission on Accreditation of Healthcare Organizations (JCAHO) accreditation + American Osteopathic Healthcare Association (AOHA) membership ○ American Osteopathic Association (AOA) accreditation △ Commission on Accreditation of Rehabilitation Facilities (CARF) accreditation Control codes 61, 63, 64, 71, 72 and 73 indicate hospitals listed by AOHA, but not registered by AHA. For definition of numerical codes, see page A4	Control	Service	Staffed Beds	Admissions	Census	Outpatient Visits	Births	Total	Payroll	Personnel

COEUR D'ALENE—Kootenai County

✠ KOOTENAI MEDICAL CENTER, (Includes North Idaho Behavioral Health, Division of Kootenai Medical Center, 2301 North Ironwood Place, Zip 83814-2650; tel. 208/765-4800; Albert J. Gale, Chief Operating Officer), 2003 Lincoln Way, Zip 83814-2677; tel. 208/666-2000; Joe Morris, Chief Executive Officer (Total facility includes 25 beds in nursing home–type unit) **A**1 2 9 10 **F**1 4 7 8 10 11 15 16 17 18 19 21 22 23 25 27 28 29 30 31 32 34 35 37 39 40 41 42 44 45 46 48 49 52 54 55 56 57 58 59 60 64 65 66 67 70 71 72 73 **P**8 **N** North Idaho Rural Health Network, Coeur d'Alene, ID	16	10	212	9973	95	82055	1216	57598	28226	786

NORTH IDAHO BEHAVIORAL HEALTH, DIVISION OF KOOTENAI MEDICAL CENTER See Kootenai Medical Center

COTTONWOOD—Idaho County

★ ST. MARY'S HOSPITAL, Lewiston and North Streets, Zip 83522, Mailing Address: P.O. Box 137, Zip 83522-0137; tel. 208/962-3251; Casey Uhling, Administrator (Total facility includes 10 beds in nursing home–type unit) (Nonreporting) **A**9 10 **S** Benedictine Health System, Duluth, MN	21	10	28	—	—	—	—	—	—	—

COUNCIL—Adams County

COUNCIL COMMUNITY HOSPITAL AND NURSING HOME, 205 North Berkley Street, Zip 83612; tel. 208/253-4242; Sandy Niehm, Administrator (Total facility includes 20 beds in nursing home–type unit) (Nonreporting) **A**9 10	13	10	26	—	—	—	—	—	—	—

DRIGGS—Teton County

★ TETON VALLEY HOSPITAL, 283 North First East, Zip 83422-0728, Mailing Address: P.O. Box 728, Zip 83422-0728; tel. 208/354-2383; Susan Kunz, Administrator **A**9 10 **F**3 7 8 14 15 16 17 20 22 28 29 31 32 33 34 36 40 41 44 46 49 51 65 67 68 71 73	13	10	13	390	3	11903	52	3660	1797	59

EMMETT—Gem County

WALTER KNOX MEMORIAL HOSPITAL, 1202 East Locust Street, Zip 83617-2715; tel. 208/365-3561; Max Long, Chief Executive Officer **A**9 10 **F**7 8 17 19 22 28 32 34 40 44 49 65 71 **P**6	13	10	24	556	4	14212	83	3557	1780	61

GOODING—Gooding County

GOODING COUNTY MEMORIAL HOSPITAL, 1120 Montana Street, Zip 83330-1858; tel. 208/934-4433; Kenneth W. Archer, Administrator (Total facility includes 13 beds in nursing home–type unit) (Nonreporting) **A**9 10 **N** South Central Health Network, Twin Falls, ID	16	10	27	—	—	—	—	—	—	—

GRANGEVILLE—Idaho County

SYRINGA GENERAL HOSPITAL, 607 West Main Street, Zip 83530-1396; tel. 208/983-1700; Jess Hawley, Administrator (Nonreporting) **A**9 10	16	10	16	—	—	—	—	—	—	—

HAILEY—Blaine County

BLAINE COUNTY MEDICAL CENTER See Wood River Medical Center, Sun Valley

IDAHO FALLS—Bonneville County

✠ COLUMBIA EASTERN IDAHO REGIONAL MEDICAL CENTER, 3100 Channing Way, Zip 83404-7533, Mailing Address: P.O. Box 2077, Zip 83403-2077; tel. 208/529-6111; Ronald G. Butler, Chief Executive Officer **A**1 2 9 10 **F**4 5 7 8 10 12 14 15 16 17 18 19 21 22 24 25 28 30 32 35 37 38 39 40 41 42 43 44 45 48 49 52 53 54 56 58 63 64 65 66 67 70 71 72 73 74 **P**8 **S** Columbia/HCA Healthcare Corporation, Nashville, TN	33	10	286	11142	165	173393	1751	75810	32620	1165
★ IDAHO FALLS RECOVERY CENTER, 1957 East 17th Street, Zip 83404-6429; tel. 208/529-5285; Jackie Street, President (Nonreporting) **A**9 10	23	10	10	—	—	—	—	—	—	—

JEROME—Jerome County

★ ST. BENEDICTS FAMILY MEDICAL CENTER, 709 North Lincoln Avenue, Zip 83338-1851, Mailing Address: P.O. Box 586, Zip 83338-0586; tel. 208/324-4301; Michael C. Wiltermood, Administrator (Total facility includes 40 beds in nursing home–type unit) (Nonreporting) **A**9 10 **S** Holy Cross Health System Corporation, South Bend, IN **N** South Central Health Network, Twin Falls, ID	21	10	65	—	—	—	—	—	—	—

KELLOGG—Shoshone County

✠ SHOSHONE MEDICAL CENTER, 3 Jacobs Gulch, Zip 83837-2096; tel. 208/784-1221; Robert A. Morasko, Chief Executive Officer (Total facility includes 14 beds in nursing home–type unit) **A**1 9 10 **F**2 3 7 8 11 19 22 24 25 27 28 32 34 37 38 39 40 41 42 44 47 49 64 65 66 67 71 72 73 **P**6 8 **N** North Idaho Rural Health Network, Coeur d'Alene, ID	23	10	46	746	18	21784	80	7220	3358	138

LEWISTON—Nez Perce County

✠ ST. JOSEPH REGIONAL MEDICAL CENTER, 415 Sixth Street, Zip 83501-0816; tel. 208/743-2511; Howard A. Hayes, President and Chief Executive Officer (Total facility includes 16 beds in nursing home–type unit) (Nonreporting) **A**1 2 9 10 **S** Carondelet Health System, Saint Louis, MO	21	10	156	—	—	—	—	—	—	—

MALAD CITY—Oneida County

ONEIDA COUNTY HOSPITAL, 150 North 200 West, Zip 83252-0126, Mailing Address: Box 126, Zip 83252-0126; tel. 208/766-2231; Garda Cuthbert, Administrator (Total facility includes 41 beds in nursing home–type unit) (Nonreporting) **A**9 10	13	10	52	—	—	—	—	—	—	—

MCCALL—Valley County

★ MCCALL MEMORIAL HOSPITAL, 1000 State Street, Zip 83638, Mailing Address: P.O. Box 906, Mc Call, Zip 83638-0906; tel. 208/634-2221; Karen J. Kellie, President **A**9 10 **F**7 8 14 15 19 22 28 32 37 39 40 41 44 45 49 65 71 73 **S** Holy Cross Health System Corporation, South Bend, IN	16	10	15	551	4	13826	100	5013	2035	62

Hospital, Address, Telephone, Administrator, Approval, Facility, and Physician Codes, Health Care System, Network	Classi-fication Codes		Utilization Data					Expense (thousands) of dollars		
	Control	Service	Staffed Beds	Admissions	Census	Outpatient Visits	Births	Total	Payroll	Personnel

★ American Hospital Association (AHA) membership
□ Joint Commission on Accreditation of Healthcare Organizations (JCAHO) accreditation
+ American Osteopathic Healthcare Association (AOHA) membership
○ American Osteopathic Association (AOA) accreditation
△ Commission on Accreditation of Rehabilitation Facilities (CARF) accreditation
Control codes 61, 63, 64, 71, 72 and 73 indicate hospitals listed by AOHA, but not registered by AHA. For definition of numerical codes, see page A4

MONTPELIER—Bear Lake County

★ BEAR LAKE MEMORIAL HOSPITAL, 164 South Fifth Street, Zip 83254–1597; tel. 208/847–1630; Rod Jacobson, Administrator (Total facility includes 37 beds in nursing home–type unit) **A**9 10 **F**12 14 15 16 19 22 28 30 32 34 37 39 44 46 49 64 65 71 73	13	10	58	452	40	—	77	5012	2699	128

MOSCOW—Latah County

⊡ GRITMAN MEDICAL CENTER, 700 South Washington Street, Zip 83843–3047; tel. 208/882–4511; Daniel R. Smigelski, Chief Executive Officer **A**1 9 10 **F**7 8 12 15 16 17 19 21 22 27 28 29 30 32 33 34 35 37 39 40 41 42 44 45 46 49 65 67 70 71 72 73 74 **P**5 8 **S** Quorum Health Group/Quorum Health Resources, Inc., Brentwood, TN	23	10	35	1982	18	44978	449	17010	7812	246

MOUNTAIN HOME—Elmore County

★ ELMORE MEDICAL CENTER, 895 North Sixth East Street, Zip 83647–2207, Mailing Address: P.O. Box 1270, Zip 83647–1270; tel. 208/587–8401; Gregory L. Maurer, Administrator (Total facility includes 55 beds in nursing home–type unit) **A**9 10 **F**7 8 14 15 19 22 28 40 44 49 64 71 **S** Holy Cross Health System Corporation, South Bend, IN	16	10	78	1213	55	20678	74	7856	3669	159

MOUNTAIN HOME AFB—Elmore County

⊡ U. S. AIR FORCE HOSPITAL MOUNTAIN HOME, 90 Hope Drive, Zip 83648–5300; tel. 208/828–7600; Lieutenant Colonel Randall E. Fellman, MC, USAF, Commanding Officer **A**1 **F**3 7 8 20 22 24 28 29 34 39 40 41 44 51 58 65 71 73 **S** Department of the Air Force, Bowling AFB, DC	41	10	29	1209	8	88141	330	—	—	—

NAMPA—Canyon County

⊡ MERCY MEDICAL CENTER, 1512 12th Avenue Road, Zip 83686–6008; tel. 208/467–1171; Joseph Messmer, President and Chief Executive Officer **A**1 9 10 **F**2 3 4 7 8 10 14 15 16 19 22 27 32 33 35 36 37 40 41 44 49 64 65 66 71 73 **S** Catholic Health Initiatives, Denver, CO	21	10	149	5994	76	111901	1317	40014	17450	596

OROFINO—Clearwater County

★ CLEARWATER VALLEY HOSPITAL, 301 Cedar, Zip 83544–9029; tel. 208/476–4555; Richard L. Wheat, Chief Financial Officer (Nonreporting) **A**9 10 **S** Brim, Inc., Portland, OR	13	10	23	—	—	—	—	—	—	—
STATE HOSPITAL NORTH, 300 Hospital Drive, Zip 83544–9034; tel. 208/476–4511; Barbara Hancock, Interim Administrator (Nonreporting)	12	22	60	—	—	—	—	—	—	—

POCATELLO—Bannock County

⊡ BANNOCK REGIONAL MEDICAL CENTER, 651 Memorial Drive, Zip 83201–4004; tel. 208/239–1000; Fred R. Eaton, Administrator (Total facility includes 118 beds in nursing home–type unit) **A**1 2 3 9 10 **F**7 8 12 13 14 15 16 17 19 21 22 23 25 26 28 29 30 31 32 33 35 37 38 39 40 41 42 44 45 46 47 49 60 63 64 65 66 67 69 70 71 72 73 74	13	10	243	5517	156	141099	1315	49176	19068	635
★ △ POCATELLO REGIONAL MEDICAL CENTER, 777 Hospital Way, Zip 83201–2797; tel. 208/234–0777; Earl L. Christison, Administrator **A**3 7 9 10 **F**7 8 10 11 12 14 15 16 17 19 21 22 23 28 29 30 32 34 35 39 40 41 44 46 48 49 63 64 65 67 71 73 74 **P**8 **S** Intermountain Health Care, Inc., Salt Lake City, UT **N** Intermountain HealthCare/Amerinet, Salt Lake City, UT	23	10	87	2534	33	74947	333	27948	12783	428

PRESTON—Franklin County

★ FRANKLIN COUNTY MEDICAL CENTER, 44 North First East Street, Zip 83263–1399; tel. 208/852–0137; Michael G. Andrus, Administrator and Chief Executive Officer (Total facility includes 45 beds in nursing home–type unit) (Nonreporting) **A**9 10	13	10	65	—	—	—	—	—	—	—

REXBURG—Madison County

★ MADISON MEMORIAL HOSPITAL, 450 East Main Street, Zip 83440–2048, Mailing Address: P.O. Box 310, Zip 83440–0310; tel. 208/356–3691; Keith M. Steiner, Administrator **A**9 10 **F**8 11 15 17 18 19 20 21 22 28 29 31 32 35 37 39 40 41 44 45 46 49 58 65 66 71 73 **P**8	13	10	46	2704	18	30422	861	12284	5983	250

RUPERT—Minidoka County

★ MINIDOKA MEMORIAL HOSPITAL AND EXTENDED CARE FACILITY, 1224 Eighth Street, Zip 83350–1599; tel. 208/436–0481; Carl Henson, Administrator (Total facility includes 78 beds in nursing home–type unit) **A**9 10 **F**8 15 16 19 21 22 26 28 30 31 32 34 35 37 40 41 44 46 51 64 65 71 73 **N** South Central Health Network, Twin Falls, ID	13	10	101	1292	74	19981	173	10819	5088	120

SAINT MARIES—Benewah County

★ BENEWAH COMMUNITY HOSPITAL, 229 South Seventh Street, Zip 83861–1894; tel. 208/245–5551; Camille Scott, Administrator **A**9 10 **F**7 8 12 14 15 16 17 19 22 27 28 30 32 33 37 39 40 41 44 49 51 65 71 72 74 **P**8 **N** North Idaho Rural Health Network, Coeur d'Alene, ID	13	10	25	614	5	11660	73	6615	2876	—

SALMON—Lemhi County

★ STEELE MEMORIAL HOSPITAL, Main and Daisy Streets, Zip 83467, Mailing Address: P.O. Box 700, Zip 83467–0700; tel. 208/756–4291; Kay H. Springer, Administrator **A**9 10 **F**7 8 22 34 37 40 44 46 56 71	13	10	28	590	5	11501	82	3172	1660	58

SANDPOINT—Bonner County

⊡ BONNER GENERAL HOSPITAL, 520 North Third Avenue, Zip 83864–0877, Mailing Address: Box 1448, Zip 83864–0877; tel. 208/263–1441; Gene Tomt, FACHE, Chief Executive Officer **A**1 9 10 **F**7 8 11 17 19 22 28 30 31 32 33 34 39 40 41 44 46 48 49 56 65 71 73 **P**3 8 **N** North Idaho Rural Health Network, Coeur d'Alene, ID	23	10	62	2183	16	26398	413	13480	7070	210

SODA SPRINGS—Caribou County

★ CARIBOU MEMORIAL HOSPITAL AND NURSING HOME, 300 South Third West Street, Zip 83276–1598; tel. 208/547–3341; Arthur J. Phillips, Administrator (Total facility includes 43 beds in nursing home–type unit) (Nonreporting) **A**9 10	13	10	65	—	—	—	—	—	—	—

Hospital, Address, Telephone, Administrator, Approval, Facility, and Physician Codes, Health Care System, Network	Classi-fication Codes		Utilization Data					Expense (thousands) of dollars		
★ American Hospital Association (AHA) membership □ Joint Commission on Accreditation of Healthcare Organizations (JCAHO) accreditation + American Osteopathic Healthcare Association (AOHA) membership ○ American Osteopathic Association (AOA) accreditation △ Commission on Accreditation of Rehabilitation Facilities (CARF) accreditation Control codes 61, 63, 64, 71, 72 and 73 indicate hospitals listed by AOHA, but not registered by AHA. For definition of numerical codes, see page A4	Control	Service	Staffed Beds	Admissions	Census	Outpatient Visits	Births	Total	Payroll	Personnel

SUN VALLEY—Blaine County

★ WOOD RIVER MEDICAL CENTER, (Includes Blaine County Medical Center, 706 South Main Street, Hailey, Zip 83333, Mailing Address: Box 927, Zip 83333; tel. 208/788–2222; Moritz Community Hospital, Mailing Address: P.O. Box 86, Zip 83353; tel. 208/622–3333; Sun Valley Road, Zip 83353, Mailing Address: P.O. Box 86, Zip 83353–0086; tel. 208/622–3333; Jon Moses, Administrator (Total facility includes 25 beds in nursing home–type unit) (Nonreporting) **A**9 10 **N** South Central Health Network, Twin Falls, ID

| | 15 | 10 | 64 | — | — | — | — | — | — | — |

TWIN FALLS—Twin Falls County

⊞ MAGIC VALLEY REGIONAL MEDICAL CENTER, 650 Addison Avenue West, Zip 83301–5444, Mailing Address: P.O. Box 409, Zip 83303–0409; tel. 208/737–2000; John Bingham, Administrator (Total facility includes 20 beds in nursing home–type unit) **A**1 2 9 10 **F**3 4 7 8 10 15 16 19 21 22 26 28 30 32 33 35 37 38 39 40 41 42 44 45 46 47 49 52 53 54 56 57 58 60 64 65 67 70 71 73 **P**5 **N** South Central Health Network, Twin Falls, ID

| | 13 | 10 | 178 | 5028 | 54 | 89620 | 1147 | 50409 | 19221 | 695 |

TWIN FALLS CLINIC HOSPITAL, 666 Shoshone Street East, Zip 83301–6168, Mailing Address: P.O. Box 1233, Zip 83301–1233; tel. 208/733–3700; Marley D. Jackman, Administrator (Nonreporting) **A**9 10 **N** South Central Health Network, Twin Falls, ID

| | 33 | 10 | 40 | — | — | — | — | — | — | — |

WEISER—Washington County

★ MEMORIAL HOSPITAL, 645 East Fifth Street, Zip 83672–2202, Mailing Address: P.O. Box 550, Zip 83672–0550; tel. 208/549–0370; Susan McGough, Administrator (Nonreporting) **A**9 10

| | 16 | 10 | 18 | — | — | — | — | — | — | — |

Resident population 11,896 (in thousands)
Resident population in metro areas 84.1%
Birth rate per 1,000 population 16.1
65 years and over 12.5%
Percent of persons without health insurance 11.3%

Hospital, Address, Telephone, Administrator, Approval, Facility, and Physician Codes, Health Care System, Network	Classi-fication Codes		Utilization Data					Expense (thousands) of dollars		
	Control	Service	Staffed Beds	Admissions	Census	Outpatient Visits	Births	Total	Payroll	Personnel

★ American Hospital Association (AHA) membership
□ Joint Commission on Accreditation of Healthcare Organizations (JCAHO) accreditation
+ American Osteopathic Healthcare Association (AOHA) membership
○ American Osteopathic Association (AOA) accreditation
△ Commission on Accreditation of Rehabilitation Facilities (CARF) accreditation
Control codes 61, 63, 64, 71, 72 and 73 indicate hospitals listed by AOHA, but not registered by AHA. For definition of numerical codes, see page A4

ALEDO—Mercer County

★ MERCER COUNTY HOSPITAL, 409 N.W. Ninth Avenue, Zip 61231–1296; tel. 309/582–5301; Bruce D. Peterson, Administrator (Total facility includes 18 beds in nursing home–type unit) **A**9 10 **F**8 15 19 22 27 30 31 32 33 34 36 37 40 44 51 64 65 71 73 **N** Mercer County Community Care Network, Aledo, IL	13	10	45	806	24	26610	46	8444	4255	217

ALTON—Madison County

✠ ALTON MEMORIAL HOSPITAL, One Memorial Drive, Zip 62002–6722; tel. 618/463–7311; Ronald B. McMullen, President (Total facility includes 64 beds in nursing home–type unit) **A**1 2 9 10 **F**7 8 10 12 15 16 17 19 21 22 28 30 31 32 33 34 35 36 37 40 41 42 44 46 49 60 63 64 65 67 71 73 **P**1 5 6 7 **S** BJC Health System, Saint Louis, MO **N** BJC Health System, St. Louis, MO	23	10	224	5592	135	71134	568	50814	22486	728
□ ALTON MENTAL HEALTH CENTER, 4500 College Avenue, Zip 62002–5099; tel. 618/465–5593; Karl Kruckeberg, Director (Nonreporting) **A**1 10	12	22	194	—	—	—	—	—	—	—
✠ SAINT ANTHONY'S HEALTH CENTER, (Includes Saint Clare's Hospital, 915 East Fifth Street, Zip 62002–6434; tel. 618/463–5151), 1 Saint Anthony's Way, Zip 62002–4579, Mailing Address: P.O. Box 340, Zip 62002–0340; tel. 618/465–2571; William E. Kessler, President (Total facility includes 38 beds in nursing home–type unit) **A**1 2 9 10 **F**1 3 4 7 8 10 12 13 14 15 16 17 18 19 20 21 22 23 26 28 29 30 31 32 33 34 35 36 37 39 40 41 42 44 45 48 49 51 52 54 55 56 57 58 59 60 61 63 64 65 67 71 72 73 74	23	10	292	6795	98	141895	747	63513	25922	805
SAINT CLARE'S HOSPITAL See Saint Anthony's Health Center										

ANNA—Union County

□ CHOATE MENTAL HEALTH AND DEVELOPMENTAL CENTER, 1000 North Main Street, Zip 62906–1699; tel. 618/833–5161; Tom Richards, Facility Director **A**1 **F**1 2 3 14 15 18 19 20 21 31 35 50 52 53 54 55 56 57 58 59 63 71	12	22	488	508	295	0	0	26298	21070	568
✠ UNION COUNTY HOSPITAL DISTRICT, 517 North Main Street, Zip 62906–1696; tel. 618/833–4511; Carol L. Goodman, Administrator and Chief Executive Officer (Total facility includes 22 beds in nursing home–type unit) **A**1 9 10 **F**8 14 15 16 17 19 21 22 32 33 34 44 45 46 49 51 64 65 70 71 72 73 **P**8	16	10	58	1028	17	27507	0	9492	5361	227

ARLINGTON HEIGHTS—Cook County

✠ NORTHWEST COMMUNITY HEALTHCARE, (Formerly Northwest Community Hospital), 800 West Central Road, Zip 60005–2392; tel. 847/618–1000; Bruce K. Crowther, President and Chief Executive Officer **A**1 2 9 10 **F**1 4 7 8 10 11 12 14 15 16 17 19 21 22 23 24 26 27 28 29 30 32 33 34 35 37 39 40 41 42 43 44 45 46 49 52 53 54 55 56 57 58 59 60 63 64 65 66 67 70 71 72 73 74 **P**8 **N** Northwestern HealthCare Network, Chicago, IL	23	10	401	18609	212	362520	2442	167532	76495	2040

AURORA—Du Page and Kane Counties County

✠ PROVENA MERCY CENTER, (Formerly Mercy Center for Health Care Services), 1325 North Highland Avenue, Zip 60506; tel. 630/859–2222; John K. Barto, Jr., President and Chief Executive Officer **A**1 2 9 10 **F**1 2 3 4 6 7 8 10 12 13 14 15 16 17 18 19 20 21 22 23 24 25 26 27 28 29 30 31 32 33 34 35 36 37 39 40 41 42 43 44 45 46 49 50 51 52 53 54 55 56 57 58 59 60 61 62 63 64 65 66 67 68 69 70 71 72 73 74 **P**5 **S** Provena Health, Frankfort, IL	21	10	245	8999	119	130260	1093	62496	27844	829
✠ △ RUSH–COPLEY MEMORIAL HOSPITAL, (Formerly Copley Memorial Hospital), 2000 Ogden Avenue, Zip 60504–4206; tel. 630/978–6200; Martin Losoff, President and Chief Operating Officer **A**1 2 3 5 7 9 10 **F**1 3 4 5 6 7 8 10 12 13 14 15 16 17 18 19 20 21 22 23 24 25 26 27 28 29 30 31 32 33 34 35 36 37 38 39 40 41 42 43 44 45 46 48 49 50 51 53 54 55 56 57 58 59 60 61 62 63 64 65 66 67 68 69 70 71 72 73 74 **P**3 5 6 7 8 **S** Rush–Presbyterian–St. Luke's Medical Center, Chicago, IL **N** Rush System for Health, Chicago, IL	23	10	142	7419	90	84552	1723	65427	25666	572

BARRINGTON—Lake County

✠ GOOD SHEPHERD HOSPITAL, 450 West Highway 22, Zip 60010–1901; tel. 847/381–9600; Russell E. Feurer, Chief Executive **A**1 2 9 10 **F**7 8 12 15 16 17 18 19 21 22 23 27 28 30 32 34 35 36 37 41 42 44 46 49 52 53 54 55 56 57 58 63 65 66 67 70 71 73 **P**5 7 8 **S** Advocate Health Care, Oak Brook, IL **N** Advocate Health Care, Oak Brook, IL; MEDACOM Tri–State, Oakbrook, IL	21	10	154	7734	79	85254	2047	67223	26321	—

BELLEVILLE—St. Clair County

✠ MEMORIAL HOSPITAL, 4500 Memorial Drive, Zip 62226–5399; tel. 618/233–7750; Harry R. Maier, President (Total facility includes 108 beds in nursing home–type unit) **A**1 2 9 10 **F**3 4 7 8 10 16 19 21 22 23 24 28 30 32 33 34 35 37 40 41 42 43 44 45 46 49 52 56 58 60 63 64 65 66 67 71 73 **P**8	23	10	449	15205	281	199503	1409	108638	47278	1671
✠ △ ST. ELIZABETH'S HOSPITAL, 211 South Third Street, Zip 62222–0694; tel. 618/234–2120; Gerald M. Harman, Executive Vice President **A**1 2 3 7 9 10 **F**1 2 3 4 5 7 8 9 10 12 13 14 15 16 17 18 19 20 21 22 23 24 25 26 28 29 30 31 32 33 34 35 36 37 38 39 40 41 42 43 44 45 46 47 48 49 52 54 55 56 57 58 59 60 64 65 66 67 68 71 72 73 **P**8 **S** Hospital Sisters Health System, Springfield, IL	21	10	289	12573	213	111938	545	100618	37776	1283

BELVIDERE—Boone County

□ HIGHLAND COMMUNITY HOSPITAL, 1625 South State Street, Zip 61008–5900; tel. 815/547–5441; Ronald J. Dedic, President and Chief Executive Officer (Nonreporting) **A**1 9 10	23	10	69	—	—	—	—	—	—	—

Hospital, Address, Telephone, Administrator, Approval, Facility, and Physician Codes, Health Care System, Network	Classification Codes		Utilization Data					Expense (thousands) of dollars		
	Control	Service	Staffed Beds	Admissions	Census	Outpatient Visits	Births	Total	Payroll	Personnel

★ American Hospital Association (AHA) membership
□ Joint Commission on Accreditation of Healthcare Organizations (JCAHO) accreditation
+ American Osteopathic Healthcare Association (AOHA) membership
○ American Osteopathic Association (AOA) accreditation
△ Commission on Accreditation of Rehabilitation Facilities (CARF) accreditation
Control codes 61, 63, 64, 71, 72 and 73 indicate hospitals listed by AOHA, but not registered by AHA. For definition of numerical codes, see page A4

Hospital	Control	Service	Staffed Beds	Admissions	Census	Outpatient Visits	Births	Total	Payroll	Personnel
✠ SAINT JOSEPH HOSPITAL, 1005 Julien Street, Zip 61008–9932; tel. 815/544–3411; David A. Schertz, Administrator (Total facility includes 34 beds in nursing home–type unit) (Nonreporting) **A**1 9 10 **S** OSF Healthcare System, Peoria, IL	21	10	58	—	—	—	—	—	—	—
BENTON—Franklin County										
★ FRANKLIN HOSPITAL AND SKILLED NURSING CARE UNIT, 201 Bailey Lane, Zip 62812–1999; tel. 618/439–3161; Virgil Hannig, Senior Vice President and Administrator (Total facility includes 83 beds in nursing home–type unit) (Nonreporting) **A**9 10 **S** Southern Illinois Hospital Services, Carbondale, IL	16	10	117	—	—	—	—	—	—	—
BERWYN—Cook County										
✠ MACNEAL HOSPITAL, 3249 South Oak Park Avenue, Zip 60402–0715; tel. 708/795–9100; Brian J. Lemon, President (Total facility includes 40 beds in nursing home–type unit) **A**1 2 3 5 8 9 10 **F**2 3 4 7 8 10 12 14 15 16 17 18 19 20 21 22 25 26 27 28 29 30 31 32 33 34 35 36 37 39 40 41 42 44 45 46 49 51 52 53 54 55 56 57 58 59 60 61 63 64 65 66 67 68 70 71 73 74 **P**6 7 8	23	10	342	17064	222	69190	2174	144319	64101	2189
BLOOMINGTON—McLean County										
BROMENN LIFECARE CENTER See BroMenn Healthcare, Normal										
✠ ST. JOSEPH MEDICAL CENTER, 2200 East Washington Street, Zip 61701–4323; tel. 309/662–3311; Kenneth J. Natzke, Administrator (Total facility includes 13 beds in nursing home–type unit) **A**1 2 9 10 **F**4 7 8 10 12 14 15 16 19 21 22 23 25 28 29 30 31 32 33 34 35 37 39 40 41 42 43 44 45 46 49 51 60 63 64 65 66 67 70 71 72 73 74 **P**6 7 **S** OSF Healthcare System, Peoria, IL	21	10	154	5576	67	66772	830	63506	26126	758
BLUE ISLAND—Cook County										
✠ SAINT FRANCIS HOSPITAL AND HEALTH CENTER, 12935 South Gregory Street, Zip 60406–2470; tel. 708/597–2000; Jay E. Kreuzer, FACHE, President **A**1 2 9 10 **F**4 7 8 10 12 14 16 17 18 19 21 22 24 25 28 29 30 31 32 33 34 35 36 37 39 40 41 42 43 44 49 54 60 63 65 67 71 72 73 74 **P**6 8 **S** SSM Health Care System, Saint Louis, MO **N** MEDACOM Tri-State, Oakbrook, IL	21	10	254	12249	151	82207	1107	108991	49640	1221
BREESE—Clinton County										
✠ ST. JOSEPH'S HOSPITAL, 9515 Holy Cross Lane, Zip 62230–0099; tel. 618/526–4511; Jacolyn M. Schlautman, Executive Vice President **A**1 9 10 **F**7 8 14 15 16 19 21 22 28 30 32 33 34 35 37 40 44 49 65 71 73 **S** Hospital Sisters Health System, Springfield, IL	21	10	57	2039	20	39237	459	14556	6321	220
CANTON—Fulton County										
✠ GRAHAM HOSPITAL, 210 West Walnut Street, Zip 61520–2497; tel. 309/647–5240; D. Ray Slaubaugh, President (Total facility includes 54 beds in nursing home–type unit) **A**1 6 9 10 **F**7 8 12 14 15 16 17 19 21 22 28 30 32 33 35 37 40 42 44 46 64 65 67 71 73	23	10	124	3033	77	46441	295	26095	11844	462
CARBONDALE—Jackson County										
✠ MEMORIAL HOSPITAL OF CARBONDALE, 405 West Jackson Street, Zip 62901–1467, Mailing Address: P.O. Box 10000, Zip 62902–9000; tel. 618/549–0721; George Maroney, Administrator **A**1 2 3 5 9 10 **F**7 8 10 15 16 17 19 21 22 23 28 30 32 33 35 37 38 40 42 44 45 49 60 63 65 66 67 71 73 **P**8 **S** Southern Illinois Hospital Services, Carbondale, IL	23	10	132	6915	72	110182	1986	51006	21707	746
CARLINVILLE—Macoupin County										
✠ CARLINVILLE AREA HOSPITAL, 1001 East Morgan Street, Zip 62626–1499; tel. 217/854–3141; Robert W. Porteus, President and Chief Executive Officer (Nonreporting) **A**1 9 10	23	10	31	—	—	—	—	—	—	—
CARMI—White County										
★ WHITE COUNTY MEDICAL CENTER, (Formerly Carmi Township Hospital), 400 Plum Street, Zip 62821–1799; tel. 618/382–4171; Joe E. Gamble, Chief Executive Officer (Total facility includes 98 beds in nursing home–type unit) **A**9 10 **F**8 12 19 21 22 30 32 33 34 39 41 44 49 64 65 71	16	10	112	268	89	26262	—	6850	3022	220
CARROLLTON—Greene County										
★ THOMAS H. BOYD MEMORIAL HOSPITAL, (Includes Reisch Memorial Nursing Home), 800 School Street, Zip 62016–1498; tel. 217/942–6946; Deborah Campbell, Administrator (Total facility includes 38 beds in nursing home–type unit) (Nonreporting) **A**9 10 **S** Quorum Health Group/Quorum Health Resources, Inc., Brentwood, TN	23	10	60	—	—	—	—	—	—	—
CARTHAGE—Hancock County										
✠ MEMORIAL HOSPITAL, South Adams Street, Zip 62321, Mailing Address: P.O. Box 160, Zip 62321–0160; tel. 217/357–3131; Keith E. Heuser, Chief Executive Officer **A**1 9 10 **F**7 8 12 15 19 21 22 28 29 34 35 36 40 41 44 49 65 67 71 73 74 **S** Quorum Health Group/Quorum Health Resources, Inc., Brentwood, TN	23	10	59	1068	10	14678	67	8575	3870	144
CENTRALIA—Marion County										
✠ ST. MARY'S HOSPITAL, 400 North Pleasant Avenue, Zip 62801–3091; tel. 618/532–6731; James W. McDowell, President and Chief Executive Officer **A**1 2 9 10 **F**1 2 3 7 8 12 14 15 16 17 18 19 20 21 22 26 27 30 31 32 33 34 35 37 39 40 41 42 44 45 46 49 51 52 53 54 55 56 57 58 59 60 63 65 66 67 69 71 73 74 **P**6 **S** SSM Health Care System, Saint Louis, MO **N** Felician Health Care, Inc., Chicago, IL	21	10	276	8379	121	144288	596	59680	22255	902
CENTREVILLE—St. Clair County										
✠ TOUCHETTE REGIONAL HOSPITAL, 5900 Bond Avenue, Zip 62207; tel. 618/332–3060; Robert Klutts, Chief Executive Officer (Nonreporting) **A**1 10	23	10	104	—	—	—	—	—	—	—
CHAMPAIGN—Champaign County										
BURNHAM HOSPITAL See Provena Covenant Medical Center, Urbana										

Hospital, Address, Telephone, Administrator, Approval, Facility, and Physician Codes, Health Care System, Network	Classi-fication Codes		Utilization Data					Expense (thousands) of dollars		
★ American Hospital Association (AHA) membership □ Joint Commission on Accreditation of Healthcare Organizations (JCAHO) accreditation + American Osteopathic Healthcare Association (AOHA) membership ○ American Osteopathic Association (AOA) accreditation △ Commission on Accreditation of Rehabilitation Facilities (CARF) accreditation Control codes 61, 63, 64, 71, 72 and 73 indicate hospitals listed by AOHA, but not registered by AHA. For definition of numerical codes, see page A4	Control	Service	Staffed Beds	Admissions	Census	Outpatient Visits	Births	Total	Payroll	Personnel
□ THE PAVILION, 809 West Church Street, Zip 61820; tel. 217/373–1700; Nina W. Eisner, Chief Executive Officer (Nonreporting) A1 9 10 S Universal Health Services, Inc., King of Prussia, PA N The Carle Foundation, Urbana, IL	33	22	46	—	—	—	—	—	—	—
CHESTER—Randolph County										
□ CHESTER MENTAL HEALTH CENTER, Chester Road, Zip 62233–0031, Mailing Address: Box 31, Zip 62233–0031; tel. 618/826–4571; Stephen L. Hardy, Ph.D., Facility Director (Nonreporting) A1	12	22	314							
□ MEMORIAL HOSPITAL, 1900 State Street, Zip 62233–0609, Mailing Address: P.O. Box 609, Zip 62233–0609; tel. 618/826–4581; Eric Freeburg, Administrator A1 9 10 F3 7 8 11 15 16 17 18 19 21 22 23 27 28 30 33 35 36 39 40 42 44 49 58 65 66 67 71 72 73 S Quorum Health Group/Quorum Health Resources, Inc., Brentwood, TN	16	10	47	1153	16	51288	112	10549	4682	189
CHICAGO—Cook County										
BERNARD MITCHELL HOSPITAL See University of Chicago Hospitals										
★ BETHANY HOSPITAL, 3435 West Van Buren Street, Zip 60624–3399; tel. 773/265–7700; Lena L. Shields, Chief Executive A1 9 10 F7 8 12 13 14 15 16 17 18 19 21 22 25 26 27 28 29 30 32 33 34 35 37 39 40 41 42 44 49 51 52 54 59 60 61 71 73 P6 8 S Advocate Health Care, Oak Brook, IL N Advocate Health Care, Oak Brook, IL; MEDACOM Tri-State, Oakbrook, IL	23	10	102	5811	65	62807	1077	40903	17334	366
★ CHICAGO LAKESHORE HOSPITAL, (Formerly Columbia Chicago Lakeshore Hospital), 4840 North Marine Drive, Zip 60640–4296; tel. 773/878–9700; Marcia S. Shapiro, Chief Executive Officer (Nonreporting) A1 3 5 10 S Columbia/HCA Healthcare Corporation, Nashville, TN	33	22	102	—	—	—	—	—	—	—
CHICAGO LYING–IN HOSPITAL See University of Chicago Hospitals										
□ CHICAGO-READ MENTAL HEALTH CENTER, 4200 North Oak Park Avenue, Zip 60634–1457; tel. 773/794–4000; Thomas Simpatico, M.D., Facility Director and Network System Manager A1 10 F1 3 11 12 14 15 16 20 26 37 52 53 56 57 58 64 65 73	12	22	210	1842	208	—	—	31651	25653	567
CHILDREN'S HOSPITAL See University of Chicago Hospitals										
★ CHILDREN'S MEMORIAL HOSPITAL, 2300 Children's Plaza, Zip 60614–3394; tel. 773/880–4000; Patrick M. Magoon, President and Chief Executive Officer A1 2 3 5 8 9 10 F4 5 10 12 13 15 16 17 18 19 20 21 22 25 28 29 30 31 32 34 35 38 39 42 43 44 45 46 47 49 51 52 53 54 55 56 58 59 60 63 65 67 69 70 71 72 73 P7 8 N Northwestern HealthCare Network, Chicago, IL	23	50	218	9070	148	240592	—	200767	84787	2104
★ △ COLUMBIA GRANT HOSPITAL, 550 Webster Avenue, Zip 60614–9980; tel. 773/883–2000; Nancy R. Hellyer, R.N., Chief Executive Officer (Total facility includes 33 beds in nursing home–type unit) A1 3 7 9 10 F3 4 8 10 12 14 16 17 19 20 21 22 26 28 29 30 31 32 34 35 37 39 42 43 44 48 49 51 52 54 55 56 57 58 59 64 65 67 71 73 P2 5 7 S Columbia/HCA Healthcare Corporation, Nashville, TN	33	10	242	5682	101	37461	0	57236	21461	507
★ △ COLUMBIA MICHAEL REESE HOSPITAL AND MEDICAL CENTER, 2929 South Ellis Avenue, Zip 60616–3376; tel. 312/791–2000; F. Scott Winslow, President and Chief Executive Officer (Nonreporting) A1 2 3 5 7 8 9 10 S Columbia/HCA Healthcare Corporation, Nashville, TN	33	10	523							
★ COLUMBUS HOSPITAL, 2520 North Lakeview Avenue, Zip 60614–1895; tel. 773/388–7300; Sister Theresa Peck, President and Chief Executive Officer A1 2 3 5 9 10 F2 3 4 5 6 7 8 10 11 12 13 16 17 19 21 22 25 26 27 28 29 30 31 32 33 34 35 37 38 39 41 42 43 44 45 46 48 49 51 52 54 55 56 57 58 59 60 61 62 63 64 65 66 67 68 71 72 73 74 P6 8 S Catholic Health Partners, Chicago, IL N Catholic Health Partners, Chicago, IL	21	10	239	8647	142	67444	1180	105582	43510	980
★ COOK COUNTY HOSPITAL, 1835 West Harrison Street, Zip 60612–3785; tel. 312/633–6000; Ruth M. Rothstein, Hospital Director (Nonreporting) A1 2 3 5 8 9 10 12 S Cook County Bureau of Health Services, Chicago, IL	13	10	770							
□ DOCTORS HOSPITAL OF HYDE PARK, 5800 South Stony Island Avenue, Zip 60637–2099; tel. 773/643–9200; Stephen M. Weinstein, Chief Executive Officer (Nonreporting) A1 9 10 N Family Health Network, Inc., Chicago, IL	31	10	200							
★ EDGEWATER MEDICAL CENTER, 5700 North Ashland Avenue, Zip 60660–4086; tel. 773/878–6000; Joann A. Skvarek, Executive Vice President A1 2 3 9 10 F4 8 10 14 15 17 19 21 22 26 27 28 30 31 32 33 34 37 42 43 44 49 54 56 60 65 71 P5	23	10	213	7692	130	27830	0	59080	23019	674
□ HARTGROVE HOSPITAL, 520 North Ridgeway Avenue, Zip 60624–1299; tel. 773/722–3113; Karen E. Johnson, Administrator (Nonreporting) A1 9 10 S Hospital Group of America, Wayne, PA	33	22	119							
★ △ HOLY CROSS HOSPITAL, 2701 West 68th Street, Zip 60629–1882; tel. 773/471–8000; Mark C. Clement, President and Chief Executive Officer (Total facility includes 37 beds in nursing home–type unit) A1 2 7 9 10 F4 7 8 10 11 12 14 15 16 17 19 21 22 25 27 28 29 30 32 33 34 35 37 40 42 44 46 48 49 51 60 63 64 65 67 71 72 73 74 P6 8	21	10	299	13077	208	137885	1099	102668	57023	1398
★ ILLINOIS MASONIC MEDICAL CENTER, 836 West Wellington Avenue, Zip 60657–5193; tel. 773/975–1600; Bruce C. Campbell, President and Chief Executive Officer (Total facility includes 200 beds in nursing home–type unit) A1 2 3 5 8 9 10 12 F1 3 4 7 8 10 11 12 13 14 15 16 17 18 19 20 21 22 25 26 27 28 29 30 31 32 33 34 35 37 38 39 40 41 42 43 44 45 46 47 49 51 52 53 54 55 56 57 58 59 60 61 63 64 65 66 67 69 70 71 73 74 P5 6 8 N Family Health Network, Inc., Chicago, IL; Rush System for Health, Chicago, IL	23	10	566	18765	431	352987	3887	246229	124986	3129
□ JACKSON PARK HOSPITAL AND MEDICAL CENTER, (Formerly Jackson Park Hospital), 7531 Stony Island Avenue, Zip 60649–3993; tel. 773/947–7500; Peter E. Friedell, M.D., President A1 2 3 9 10 F2 3 5 8 12 14 15 16 17 18 19 20 21 22 26 28 29 30 31 33 37 40 41 42 44 45 46 49 51 52 54 56 57 58 60 65 66 71 72 73	23	10	236	13632	166	40559	501	—	—	663

Hospital, Address, Telephone, Administrator, Approval, Facility, and Physician Codes, Health Care System, Network	Classi-fication Codes		Utilization Data						Expense (thousands) of dollars		
	Control	Service	Staffed Beds	Admissions	Census	Outpatient Visits	Births	Total	Payroll	Personnel

★ American Hospital Association (AHA) membership
□ Joint Commission on Accreditation of Healthcare Organizations (JCAHO) accreditation
+ American Osteopathic Healthcare Association (AOHA) membership
○ American Osteopathic Association (AOA) accreditation
△ Commission on Accreditation of Rehabilitation Facilities (CARF) accreditation
Control codes 61, 63, 64, 71, 72 and 73 indicate hospitals listed by AOHA, but not registered by AHA. For definition of numerical codes, see page A4

JOHNSTON R. BOWMAN HEALTH CENTER See Rush–Presbyterian–St. Luke's Medical Center

☒ LARABIDA CHILDREN'S HOSPITAL AND RESEARCH CENTER, East 65th Street at Lake Michigan, Zip 60649–1395; tel. 773/363–6700; Paula Kienberger Jaudes, M.D., President and Chief Executive Officer **A**1 5 9 10 **F**12 19 20 22 34 35 45 49 53 54 65 67 71 72 73 **P**6 — 23 58 62 1414 36 27157 — 24621 12132 358

□ LORETTO HOSPITAL, 645 South Central Avenue, Zip 60644–9987; tel. 773/626–4300; Steven C. Drucker, President **A**1 10 **F**2 3 8 14 15 16 18 19 21 22 28 30 34 37 39 41 44 49 51 52 56 58 65 67 71 **P**5 — 23 10 223 5412 125 33100 — 29859 14342 406

☒ LOUIS A. WEISS MEMORIAL HOSPITAL, 4646 North Marine Drive, Zip 60640–1501; tel. 773/878–8700; Gregory A. Cierlik, President and Chief Executive Officer (Nonreporting) **A**1 2 3 5 9 10 **S** University of Chicago Health System, Chicago, IL **N** University of Chicago Hospitals & Health System, Chicago, IL — 23 10 200 — — — — — — —

☒ MERCY HOSPITAL AND MEDICAL CENTER, 2525 South Michigan Avenue, Zip 60616–2477; tel. 312/567–2000; Charles B. Van Vorst, President and Chief Executive Officer (Total facility includes 28 beds in nursing home–type unit) **A**1 2 3 5 8 9 10 **F**2 3 4 5 7 8 10 11 12 13 16 17 18 19 20 21 22 24 25 26 27 28 29 30 31 32 33 34 35 37 38 39 40 41 42 43 44 45 46 47 48 49 51 52 53 54 55 56 57 58 59 60 61 63 64 65 66 67 68 71 72 73 **P**5 6 **N** Family Health Network, Inc., Chicago, IL — 21 10 444 16793 238 319549 2771 169269 83112 1921

□ METHODIST HOSPITAL OF CHICAGO, 5025 North Paulina Street, Zip 60640–2797; tel. 773/271–9040; Steven H. Friedman, Ph.D., Executive Vice President (Total facility includes 17 beds in nursing home–type unit) (Nonreporting) **A**1 2 10 — 23 10 189 — — — — — — —

□ METROPOLITAN CHILDREN AND ADOLESCENT INSTITUTE, 1601 Taylor Street, Zip 60612–4397; tel. 312/433–8300; James T. Barter, M.D., Director (Nonreporting) **A**1 — 12 22 83 — — — — — — —

☒ MOUNT SINAI HOSPITAL MEDICAL CENTER OF CHICAGO, California Avenue and 15th Street, Zip 60608–1610; tel. 773/542–2000; Benn Greenspan, President and Chief Executive Officer (Nonreporting) **A**1 2 3 5 8 9 10 **N** Family Health Network, Inc., Chicago, IL — 23 10 315 — — — — — — —

NORMAN AND IDA STONE INSTITUTE OF PSYCHIATRY See Northwestern Memorial Hospital

☒ NORTHWESTERN MEMORIAL HOSPITAL, (Includes Norman and Ida Stone Institute of Psychiatry, 320 East Huron Street, Zip 60611; Passavant Pavilion, 303 East Superior Street, Zip 60611; Prentice Women's Hospital, 333 East Superior Street, Zip 60611; Wesley Pavilion, 250 East Superior Street, Zip 60611), Superior Street and Fairbanks Court, Zip 60611–2950; tel. 312/908–2000; Gary A. Mecklenburg, President and Chief Executive Officer **A**1 2 3 5 8 9 10 **F**3 4 5 7 8 10 12 13 14 15 16 17 18 19 20 21 22 23 24 26 27 28 29 30 31 32 33 34 35 37 38 39 40 41 42 43 44 45 46 47 49 51 52 53 54 55 56 57 58 59 60 61 63 64 65 66 67 68 69 70 71 73 74 **P**3 5 6 8 **N** Northwestern HealthCare Network, Chicago, IL — 23 10 683 36451 429 224098 5962 379959 157414 4352

□ NORWEGIAN–AMERICAN HOSPITAL, 1044 North Francisco Avenue, Zip 60622–2794; tel. 773/292–8200; Clarence A. Nagelvoort, President and Chief Executive Officer (Nonreporting) **A**1 9 10 **N** Family Health Network, Inc., Chicago, IL — 23 10 230 — — — — — — —

☒ OUR LADY OF THE RESURRECTION MEDICAL CENTER, 5645 West Addison Street, Zip 60634–4455; tel. 773/282–7000; Ronald E. Struxness, Executive Vice President and Chief Executive Officer (Total facility includes 56 beds in nursing home–type unit) **A**1 9 10 **F**2 3 4 6 7 8 9 10 11 12 15 16 17 18 19 20 21 22 24 25 26 27 28 29 30 31 32 33 34 35 36 37 38 39 40 41 42 43 44 45 46 47 48 49 51 52 54 56 58 60 61 62 63 64 65 67 69 70 71 73 74 **P**5 6 7 **N** Unified Health Care Network, Maywood, IL — 21 10 293 11308 208 111820 0 79139 32926 1020

PASSAVANT PAVILION See Northwestern Memorial Hospital
PRENTICE WOMEN'S HOSPITAL See Northwestern Memorial Hospital

☒ PROVIDENT HOSPITAL OF COOK COUNTY, 500 East 51st Street, Zip 60615–2494; tel. 312/572–2000; Stephanie Wright–Griggs, Chief Operating Officer **A**1 3 10 **F**2 3 4 5 7 8 9 10 11 12 13 14 15 16 17 18 19 20 21 22 23 25 26 28 29 30 31 34 35 37 38 39 40 41 42 43 44 45 49 52 63 64 65 66 67 68 69 70 71 72 73 74 **P**6 **S** Cook County Bureau of Health Services, Chicago, IL — 13 10 110 5210 70 98833 843 70899 33132 748

☒ △ RAVENSWOOD HOSPITAL MEDICAL CENTER, 4550 North Winchester Avenue, Zip 60640–5205; tel. 773/878–4300; John E. Blair, President and Chief Executive Officer **A**1 2 3 5 6 7 9 10 **F**3 4 5 7 8 10 11 12 13 14 15 16 17 18 19 21 22 24 25 26 27 29 30 31 32 33 34 37 39 40 41 42 43 44 46 48 49 51 52 53 54 55 56 57 58 59 61 63 64 65 67 68 71 72 73 74 **P**1 **S** Advocate Health Care, Oak Brook, IL **N** Advocate Health Care, Oak Brook, IL — 23 10 306 11913 179 222282 1787 107217 46147 1642

☒ △ REHABILITATION INSTITUTE OF CHICAGO, 345 East Superior Street, Zip 60611–4496; tel. 312/908–6017; Wayne M. Lerner, Dr.PH, President and Chief Executive Officer (Total facility includes 40 beds in nursing home–type unit) **A**1 3 5 7 8 9 10 **F**12 24 25 27 34 48 49 65 66 67 73 74 **P**6 — 23 46 155 2051 117 — — 67707 36248 1031

☒ △ RESURRECTION MEDICAL CENTER, 7435 West Talcott Avenue, Zip 60631–3746; tel. 773/774–8000; Sister Donna Marie, Executive Vice President and Chief Executive Officer (Total facility includes 298 beds in nursing home–type unit) **A**1 2 3 5 7 9 10 **F**3 4 7 8 10 15 16 17 19 21 22 24 29 31 32 34 35 37 38 40 41 42 43 44 45 48 49 53 54 55 56 57 58 59 60 64 65 66 67 71 73 74 **P**1 5 6 7 **N** Unified Health Care Network, Maywood, IL — 21 10 667 16867 512 163986 1254 176529 71909 2868

Hospital, Address, Telephone, Administrator, Approval, Facility, and Physician Codes, Health Care System, Network	Classi-fication Codes		Utilization Data					Expense (thousands) of dollars		
	Control	Service	Staffed Beds	Admissions	Census	Outpatient Visits	Births	Total	Payroll	Personnel

★ American Hospital Association (AHA) membership
□ Joint Commission on Accreditation of Healthcare Organizations (JCAHO) accreditation
+ American Osteopathic Healthcare Association (AOHA) membership
○ American Osteopathic Association (AOA) accreditation
△ Commission on Accreditation of Rehabilitation Facilities (CARF) accreditation
Control codes 61, 63, 64, 71, 72 and 73 indicate hospitals listed by AOHA, but not registered by AHA. For definition of numerical codes, see page A4

Hospital	Control	Service	Staffed Beds	Admissions	Census	Outpatient Visits	Births	Total	Payroll	Personnel
☒ ROSELAND COMMUNITY HOSPITAL, 45 West 111th Street, Zip 60628–4294; tel. 773/995–3000; Oliver D. Krage, President and Chief Executive Officer **A**1 9 10 **F**11 12 14 16 17 19 21 22 25 26 27 28 30 31 33 34 39 40 42 43 44 46 49 51 56 65 67 71 72 73 **P**8 **N** Family Health Network, Inc., Chicago, IL	23	10	128	5511	69	37898	714	30063	14717	479
☒ △ RUSH–PRESBYTERIAN–ST. LUKE'S MEDICAL CENTER, (Includes Johnston R. Bowman Health Center, 700 South Paulina, Zip 60612; tel. 312/942–7000; James T. Frankenbach, President), 1653 West Congress Parkway, Zip 60612–3833; tel. 312/942–5000; Leo M. Henikoff, M.D., President and Chief Executive Officer (Total facility includes 44 beds in nursing home–type unit) (Nonreporting) **A**1 2 3 5 7 8 9 10 **S** Rush–Presbyterian–St. Luke's Medical Center, Chicago, IL **N** Family Health Network, Inc., Chicago, IL; Rush System for Health, Chicago, IL	23	10	783	—	—	—	—	—	—	—
□ SACRED HEART HOSPITAL, 3240 West Franklin Boulevard, Zip 60624–1599; tel. 773/722–3020; Edward Novak, President and Chief Executive Officer (Nonreporting) **A**1 10	33	10	96	—	—	—	—	—	—	—
☒ SAINT ANTHONY HOSPITAL, 2875 West 19th Street, Zip 60623–3596; tel. 773/521–1710; Sister Theresa Peck, President and Chief Executive Officer **A**1 3 9 10 **F**2 3 4 5 6 7 8 10 11 12 13 16 17 19 21 22 25 26 27 28 29 30 31 32 33 34 35 37 38 39 40 41 42 43 44 45 46 48 49 51 52 54 55 56 57 58 59 60 61 62 63 64 65 66 67 68 69 71 72 73 74 **P**6 8 **S** Catholic Health Partners, Chicago, IL **N** Catholic Health Partners, Chicago, IL	21	10	165	8398	118	49791	2144	54834	25393	667
□ SAINT BERNARD HOSPITAL AND HEALTH CARE CENTER, 326 west 64th Street, Zip 60621; tel. 773/962–3900; Sister Elizabeth Van Straten, President and Chief Executive Officer (Nonreporting) **A**1 9 10 **N** Family Health Network, Inc., Chicago, IL; Unified Health Care Network, Maywood, IL	21	10	194	—	—	—	—	—	—	—
☒ SAINT MARY OF NAZARETH HOSPITAL CENTER, 2233 West Division Street, Zip 60622–3086; tel. 312/770–2000; Sister Stella Louise, President and Chief Executive Officer (Total facility includes 20 beds in nursing home–type unit) **A**1 2 3 9 10 **F**4 8 10 11 14 15 16 17 19 21 22 26 27 28 30 31 32 33 34 35 37 39 40 41 42 43 44 45 48 49 52 53 54 55 56 57 58 59 60 61 64 65 67 71 72 73 74 **P**5 8 **S** Sisters of the Holy Family of Nazareth–Sacred Heart Province, Des Plaines, IL **N** Family Health Network, Inc., Chicago, IL; Unified Health Care Network, Maywood, IL	21	10	325	13058	218	171288	—	109116	53642	1422
☒ △ SCHWAB REHABILITATION HOSPITAL AND CARE NETWORK, 1401 South California Boulevard, Zip 60608–1612; tel. 773/522–2010; Kathleen C. Yosko, President and Chief Executive Officer (Nonreporting) **A**1 3 7 9 10 **N** Family Health Network, Inc., Chicago, IL	23	46	85	—	—	—	—	—	—	—
☒ SHRINERS HOSPITALS FOR CHILDREN–CHICAGO, 2211 North Oak Park Avenue, Zip 60707; tel. 773/622–5400; A. James Spang, Administrator (Nonreporting) **A**1 3 5 **S** Shriners Hospitals for Children, Tampa, FL	23	57	60	—	—	—	—	—	—	—
☒ SOUTH SHORE HOSPITAL, 8012 South Crandon Avenue, Zip 60617–1199; tel. 773/768–0810; John D. Harper, President **A**1 9 10 **F**8 12 15 16 17 19 20 21 22 26 28 29 33 34 37 42 44 46 49 51 55 65 71 73 **P**5 8	23	10	125	3499	59	24999	—	26491	14130	425
☒ ST. ELIZABETH'S HOSPITAL, 1431 North Claremont Avenue, Zip 60622–1791; tel. 773/278–2000; JoAnn Birdzell, President and Chief Executive Officer (Total facility includes 27 beds in nursing home–type unit) **A**1 2 3 9 10 **F**3 4 5 7 8 10 13 14 15 16 17 18 19 22 23 25 26 27 28 29 30 31 32 33 34 35 36 37 39 42 43 44 45 46 49 51 52 53 54 55 56 57 58 59 62 64 65 67 71 73 **P**3 5 6 7 8 **S** Ancilla Systems Inc., Hobart, IN **N** Ancilla Systems, Inc., Hobart, IN; Midwest Health Net, LLC., Fort Wayne, IN	21	10	240	10110	168	145239	0	68536	31768	934
☒ ST. JOSEPH HOSPITAL, 2900 North Lake Shore Drive, Zip 60657–6274; tel. 773/665–3000; Sister Theresa Peck, President and Chief Executive Officer **A**1 2 3 5 9 10 **F**2 3 4 5 6 7 8 10 11 12 13 16 17 19 21 22 25 26 27 28 29 30 31 32 33 34 35 37 38 39 40 41 42 43 44 45 46 48 49 51 52 54 55 56 57 58 59 60 61 62 63 64 65 66 67 68 71 72 73 74 **P**6 8 **S** Catholic Health Partners, Chicago, IL **N** Catholic Health Partners, Chicago, IL	21	10	335	11185	210	69341	1716	105494	46362	1260
☒ SWEDISH COVENANT HOSPITAL, 5145 North California Avenue, Zip 60625–3688; tel. 773/878–8200; Edward A. Cucci, President and Chief Executive Officer **A**1 3 5 9 10 **F**4 7 8 10 12 13 14 15 16 17 18 19 20 21 22 23 24 26 27 28 29 30 31 32 33 34 35 36 37 38 39 40 41 42 43 44 45 46 47 48 49 51 52 55 56 57 58 60 62 63 64 65 66 67 69 70 71 72 73 74 **P**1 5 6 7 **N** Northwestern HealthCare Network, Chicago, IL	21	10	279	7304	135	95693	828	65479	31982	449
☒ THOREK HOSPITAL AND MEDICAL CENTER, 850 West Irving Park Road, Zip 60613–3099; tel. 773/525–6780; Frank A. Solare, President and Chief Executive Officer **A**1 9 10 **F**8 14 15 17 19 21 22 23 27 28 30 31 33 35 36 37 39 41 42 44 46 49 51 60 65 67 71 73 **P**4	23	10	142	4854	86	132176	—	47859	20338	518
TRANSITIONAL HOSPITAL OF CHICAGO See Vencor Hospital–Chicago Central										
☒ TRINITY HOSPITAL, 2320 East 93rd Street, Zip 60617–3982; tel. 773/978–2000; John N. Schwartz, Chief Executive Officer (Nonreporting) **A**1 9 10 **S** Advocate Health Care, Oak Brook, IL **N** Advocate Health Care, Oak Brook, IL; MEDACOM Tri-State, Oakbrook, IL	21	10	218	—	—	—	—	—	—	—
☒ UNIVERSITY OF CHICAGO HOSPITALS, (Includes Bernard Mitchell Hospital, ; Chicago Lying–in Hospital, ; Children's Hospital), 5841 South Maryland Avenue, Zip 60637–1470; tel. 773/702–1000; Steven Lipstein, President and Chief Operating Officer **A**1 2 3 5 8 9 10 **F**4 5 7 8 9 10 11 12 13 15 16 17 19 20 21 22 23 27 30 31 32 33 34 35 36 37 38 39 40 42 43 44 45 46 47 49 50 51 52 53 54 55 56 57 58 59 60 61 63 65 66 67 69 70 71 73 74 **P**4 5 6 8 **S** University of Chicago Health System, Chicago, IL **N** University of Chicago Hospitals & Health System, Chicago, IL	23	10	514	23470	408	428396	2903	448694	194239	1593

Hospital, Address, Telephone, Administrator, Approval, Facility, and Physician Codes, Health Care System, Network	Classi- fication Codes		Utilization Data					Expense (thousands) of dollars		
★ American Hospital Association (AHA) membership □ Joint Commission on Accreditation of Healthcare Organizations (JCAHO) accreditation + American Osteopathic Healthcare Association (AOHA) membership ○ American Osteopathic Association (AOA) accreditation △ Commission on Accreditation of Rehabilitation Facilities (CARF) accreditation Control codes 61, 63, 64, 71, 72 and 73 indicate hospitals listed by AOHA, but not registered by AHA. For definition of numerical codes, see page A4	Control	Service	Staffed Beds	Admissions	Census	Outpatient Visits	Births	Total	Payroll	Personnel

Hospital	Control	Service	Staffed Beds	Admissions	Census	Outpatient Visits	Births	Total	Payroll	Personnel
⊠ △ UNIVERSITY OF ILLINOIS AT CHICAGO MEDICAL CENTER, 1740 West Taylor Street, Zip 60612–7236; tel. 312/996–7000; Sidney E. Mitchell, Executive Director (Nonreporting) **A**1 2 3 5 7 8 9 10	12	10	430	—	—	—	—	—	—	—
□ VENCOR HOSPITAL–CHICAGO CENTRAL, (Formerly Transitional Hospital of Chicago), 4058 West Melrose Street, Zip 60641–4797; tel. 773/736–7000; Richard Cerceo, Administrator (Nonreporting) **A**1 10 **S** Transitional Hospitals Corporation, Las Vegas, NV	33	10	81	—	—	—	—	—	—	—
VENCOR HOSPITAL–CHICAGO NORTH, 2544 West Montrose Avenue, Zip 60618–1589; tel. 773/267–2622; Steven A. Matarelli, Administrator (Nonreporting) **S** Vencor, Incorporated, Louisville, KY	33	49	111	—	—	—	—	—	—	—
⊠ VETERANS AFFAIRS CHICAGO HEALTH CARE SYSTEM–LAKESIDE DIVISION, 333 East Huron Street, Zip 60611–3004; tel. 312/640–2100; Joseph L. Moore, Director **A**1 3 5 8 **F**2 3 4 5 8 10 11 12 14 15 16 17 18 19 20 21 22 23 25 26 28 29 30 31 32 33 34 35 37 39 41 42 43 44 45 46 48 49 50 51 52 54 55 56 57 58 60 63 65 67 69 71 72 73 74 **S** Department of Veterans Affairs, Washington, DC	45	10	442	13529	343	495300	—	212725	141232	2315
⊠ VETERANS AFFAIRS CHICAGO HEALTH CARE SYSTEM–WEST SIDE DIVISION, 820 South Damen Avenue, Zip 60612–3776, Mailing Address: P.O. Box 8195, Zip 60680–8195; tel. 312/666–6500; Joseph L. Moore, Director (Nonreporting) **A**1 2 3 5 8 **S** Department of Veterans Affairs, Washington, DC	45	10	323	—	—	—	—	—	—	—
WESLEY PAVILION See Northwestern Memorial Hospital										
CHICAGO HEIGHTS—Cook County										
⊠ ST. JAMES HOSPITAL AND HEALTH CENTERS, 1423 Chicago Road, Zip 60411–3483; tel. 708/756–1000; Peter J. Murphy, President and Chief Executive Officer (Total facility includes 101 beds in nursing home–type unit) (Nonreporting) **A**1 2 9 10 **S** Sisters of St. Francis Health Services, Inc., Mishawaka, IN **N** MEDACOM Tri–State, Oakbrook, IL	21	10	332	—	—	—	—	—	—	—
CLIFTON—Iroquois County										
⊠ CENTRAL COMMUNITY HOSPITAL, 335 East Fifth Avenue, Zip 60927, Mailing Address: P.O. Box 68, Zip 60927–0068; tel. 815/694–2392; Steven S. Wilder, President and Chief Executive Officer (Nonreporting) **A**1 9 **N** Servantcor, Clifton, IL	23	10	33	—	—	—	—	—	—	—
CLINTON—Dewitt County										
★ DR. JOHN WARNER HOSPITAL, 422 West White Street, Zip 61727–2199; tel. 217/935–9571; Hervey Davis, Administrator (Total facility includes 9 beds in nursing home–type unit) (Nonreporting) **A**9 10	14	10	37	—	—	—	—	—	—	—
DANVILLE—Vermilion County										
⊠ PROVENA UNITED SAMARITANS MEDICAL CENTER, (Formerly United Samaritans Medical Center), (Includes United Samaritans Medical Center, 600 Sager Avenue, Zip 61832; tel. 217/442–6300), 812 North Logan, Zip 61832–3788; tel. 217/442–6300; Dennis J. Doran, President and Chief Executive Officer (Total facility includes 49 beds in nursing home–type unit) **A**1 2 9 10 **F**3 7 8 12 15 16 19 23 26 28 29 30 32 33 34 35 36 37 39 40 41 42 43 44 45 46 49 52 55 57 58 59 64 65 67 70 71 73 **P**6 8 **S** Provena Health, Frankfort, IL **N** MEDACOM Tri–State, Oakbrook, IL	21	10	282	10546	161	237138	969	85701	35894	1426
⊠ VETERANS AFFAIRS MEDICAL CENTER, 1900 East Main Street, Zip 61832–5198; tel. 217/442–8000; James S. Jones, Director (Total facility includes 175 beds in nursing home–type unit) **A**1 3 5 **F**1 3 6 8 12 14 15 16 17 18 19 20 21 22 25 26 27 28 29 30 31 32 34 37 39 41 44 45 46 48 49 51 52 54 55 57 58 59 63 64 65 67 71 73 74 **P**6 **S** Department of Veterans Affairs, Washington, DC	45	10	490	4342	445	165369	—	77448	46153	1225
DE KALB—De Kalb County										
⊠ KISHWAUKEE COMMUNITY HOSPITAL, 626 Bethany Road, Zip 60115–4939, Mailing Address: P.O. Box 707, Zip 60115–0707; tel. 815/756–1521; Robert S. Thebeau, President **A**1 2 9 10 **F**3 7 8 14 15 16 19 21 22 26 28 29 30 31 35 37 40 41 44 46 49 52 53 54 55 56 57 58 59 60 61 65 66 67 71 73 74 **P**3 5	23	10	114	4480	41	138212	811	34414	13619	467
DECATUR—Macon County										
⊠ DECATUR MEMORIAL HOSPITAL, 2300 North Edward Street, Zip 62526–4192; tel. 217/876–8121; Kenneth L. Smithmier, President and Chief Executive Officer (Total facility includes 59 beds in nursing home–type unit) (Nonreporting) **A**1 2 3 5 9 10	23	10	247	—	—	—	—	—	—	—
⊠ ST. MARY'S HOSPITAL, 1800 East Lake Shore Drive, Zip 62521–3883; tel. 217/464–2966; Keith L. Callahan, Executive Vice President and Administrator (Total facility includes 45 beds in nursing home–type unit) **A**1 2 3 5 9 10 **F**1 3 7 8 14 15 16 17 18 19 21 22 23 26 27 28 29 30 32 33 34 35 36 37 39 40 41 42 44 45 47 49 52 53 54 55 56 57 58 59 60 64 65 67 71 73 **P**6 7 **S** Hospital Sisters Health System, Springfield, IL	21	10	192	7340	86	186501	853	61051	26210	937
DES PLAINES—Cook County										
□ FOREST HOSPITAL, 555 Wilson Lane, Zip 60016–4794; tel. 847/635–4100; Richard Michael Ackley, Administrator and Chief Executive Officer (Nonreporting) **A**1 10	31	22	80	—	—	—	—	—	—	—
□ HOLY FAMILY MEDICAL CENTER, 100 North River Road, Zip 60016–1255; tel. 847/297–1800; Sister Patricia Ann Koschalke, President and Chief Executive Officer (Nonreporting) **A**1 2 9 10 **S** Sisters of the Holy Family of Nazareth–Sacred Heart Province, Des Plaines, IL **N** Rush System for Health, Chicago, IL	23	10	183	—	—	—	—	—	—	—
DIXON—Lee County										
★ KATHERINE SHAW BETHEA HOSPITAL, 403 East First Street, Zip 61021–3187; tel. 815/288–5531; Darryl L. Vandervort, President and Chief Executive Officer (Total facility includes 15 beds in nursing home–type unit) **A**9 10 **F**1 3 7 8 11 12 14 15 16 17 19 20 21 22 24 26 27 28 29 30 32 33 34 35 36 37 39 40 41 42 44 45 46 49 51 52 53 54 55 56 57 58 59 60 63 64 65 66 67 71 73 **P**4	23	10	100	3690	45	77211	355	37679	15204	511

Hospital, Address, Telephone, Administrator, Approval, Facility, and Physician Codes, Health Care System, Network	Classi-fication Codes		Utilization Data					Expense (thousands) of dollars		
	Control	Service	Staffed Beds	Admissions	Census	Outpatient Visits	Births	Total	Payroll	Personnel

★ American Hospital Association (AHA) membership
□ Joint Commission on Accreditation of Healthcare Organizations (JCAHO) accreditation
+ American Osteopathic Healthcare Association (AOHA) membership
○ American Osteopathic Association (AOA) accreditation
△ Commission on Accreditation of Rehabilitation Facilities (CARF) accreditation
Control codes 61, 63, 64, 71, 72 and 73 indicate hospitals listed by AOHA, but not registered by AHA. For definition of numerical codes, see page A4

DOWNERS GROVE—Du Page County

✶ GOOD SAMARITAN HOSPITAL, 3815 Highland Avenue, Zip 60515–1590; tel. 630/275–5900; David M. McConkey, Chief Executive (Total facility includes 20 beds in nursing home–type unit) **A**1 2 9 10 **F**1 4 7 8 10 11 12 13 15 16 17 19 21 22 23 24 25 26 27 28 29 30 31 32 33 34 35 37 38 39 40 41 42 43 44 45 49 51 52 53 54 55 56 57 58 59 61 62 63 64 65 66 67 70 71 72 73 74 **P**1 2 3 4 5 6 7 **S** Advocate Health Care, Oak Brook, IL **N** Advocate Health Care, Oak Brook, IL; MEDACOM Tri–State, Oakbrook, IL	21	10	255	13780	185	146454	2243	143118	56630	1456

DU QUOIN—Perry County

✶ MARSHALL BROWNING HOSPITAL, 900 North Washington Street, Zip 62832–1230, Mailing Address: P.O. Box 192, Zip 62832–0192; tel. 618/542–2146; William J. Huff, Chief Executive Officer **A**1 9 10 **F**6 7 8 15 16 19 21 22 32 33 34 35 36 40 41 44 49 63 65 71	23	10	33	925	12	24679	99	7947	3388	136

EAST ST. LOUIS—St. Clair County

✶ ST. MARY'S HOSPITAL, 129 North Eighth Street, Zip 62201–2999; tel. 618/274–1900; Richard J. Mark, President and Chief Executive Officer **A**1 9 10 **F**8 14 15 16 17 18 19 22 27 28 29 30 32 34 37 44 45 46 49 51 52 56 58 59 65 66 67 70 71 72 73 74 **P**4 **S** Ancilla Systems Inc., Hobart, IN **N** Ancilla Systems, Inc., Hobart, IN; Midwest Health Net, LLC., Fort Wayne, IN; SSM Health Care – Saint Louis, St. Louis, MO	21	10	135	3606	59	111582	0	30510	15084	581

EFFINGHAM—Effingham County

✶ ST. ANTHONY'S MEMORIAL HOSPITAL, 503 North Maple Street, Zip 62401–2099; tel. 217/347–1495; Anthony D. Pfitzer, Administrator (Total facility includes 13 beds in nursing home–type unit) **A**1 2 9 10 **F**7 8 14 15 16 19 21 22 23 32 33 34 35 36 37 39 40 42 44 49 60 63 64 65 67 71 73 **S** Hospital Sisters Health System, Springfield, IL	21	10	146	6159	72	158029	748	41103	15547	502

ELDORADO—Saline County

★ FERRELL HOSPITAL, 1201 Pine Street, Zip 62930–1634; tel. 618/273–3361; E. T. Seely, Administrator (Nonreporting) **A**9 10 **S** Southern Illinois Hospital Services, Carbondale, IL	33	10	51	—	—	—	—	—	—	—

ELGIN—Kane County

□ ELGIN MENTAL HEALTH CENTER, 750 South State Street, Zip 60123–7692; tel. 847/742–1040; Nancy Staples, MS, Administrator (Nonreporting) **A**1	12	22	708	—	—	—	—	—	—	—
✶ PROVENA SAINT JOSEPH HOSPITAL, (Formerly Saint Joseph Hospital), 77 North Airlite Street, Zip 60123–4912; tel. 847/695–3200; Larry Narum, President **A**1 2 9 10 **F**3 7 8 10 12 15 16 17 18 19 21 22 25 26 27 28 29 30 31 32 33 34 35 36 37 39 40 41 42 44 45 46 48 49 52 53 54 55 56 57 58 59 60 64 65 66 67 70 71 72 73 74 **P**3 5 8 **S** Provena Health, Frankfort, IL **N** MEDACOM Tri–State, Oakbrook, IL	23	10	202	6187	93	233639	764	67321	29185	—
✶ SHERMAN HOSPITAL, 934 Center Street, Zip 60120–2198; tel. 847/742–9800; John A. Graham, President and Chief Executive Officer **A**1 2 9 10 **F**3 4 7 8 10 11 12 13 15 16 17 19 20 21 22 25 26 27 28 29 30 31 32 33 34 35 36 37 39 40 41 42 43 44 45 49 55 56 63 65 67 68 70 71 72 73 74 **P**5 8	23	10	353	11173	130	107216	2233	109097	41691	1702

ELK GROVE VILLAGE—Cook County

✶ △ ALEXIAN BROTHERS MEDICAL CENTER, 800 Biesterfield Road, Zip 60007–3397; tel. 847/437–5500; Michael J. Schwartz, President (Total facility includes 28 beds in nursing home–type unit) **A**1 2 7 9 10 **F**3 4 7 8 9 10 11 12 13 15 16 17 18 19 20 21 22 26 27 28 29 30 31 32 33 34 35 36 37 38 39 40 41 42 43 44 45 46 48 49 51 52 53 54 55 56 57 58 59 60 61 63 64 65 66 67 70 71 72 73 74 **P**3 5 **S** Alexian Brothers Health System, Inc., Elk Grove Village, IL **N**	21	10	393	17188	252	95724	3211	—	70187	2176

ELMHURST—Du Page County

✶ ELMHURST MEMORIAL HOSPITAL, 200 Berteau Avenue, Zip 60126–2989; tel. 630/833–1400; Leo F. Fronza, Jr., President and Chief Executive Officer (Total facility includes 28 beds in nursing home–type unit) **A**1 2 9 10 **F**3 4 14 15 16 19 21 22 23 24 26 28 29 30 31 32 33 34 35 37 38 39 40 41 42 43 44 45 46 49 52 54 55 56 57 58 59 60 61 63 64 65 67 69 70 71 73 74 **P**1 4 5 6 7 8	23	10	330	16247	217	138701	2038	146748	67301	2100

EUREKA—Woodford County

EUREKA COMMUNITY HOSPITAL See BroMenn Healthcare, Normal

EVANSTON—Cook County

✶ △ EVANSTON HOSPITAL, (Includes Glenbrook Hospital, 2100 Pfingsten Road, Glenview, Zip 60025; tel. 847/657–5800), 2650 Ridge Avenue, Zip 60201–1797; tel. 847/570–2000; Mark R. Neaman, President and Chief Executive Officer **A**1 2 3 5 7 8 9 10 **F**1 2 3 4 5 8 9 10 11 12 14 15 16 17 18 19 20 21 22 23 24 25 26 27 28 29 30 31 32 33 34 35 36 37 38 39 40 41 42 43 44 45 46 48 49 51 52 53 54 55 56 57 58 59 60 61 63 64 65 66 67 68 69 70 71 73 74 **P**1 5 6 7 **N** Northwestern HealthCare Network, Chicago, IL	23	10	481	28390	378	796525	3966	270244	113093	3486
✶ ST. FRANCIS HOSPITAL, 355 Ridge Avenue, Zip 60202–3399; tel. 847/316–4000; John Sullivan, Chief Executive Officer (Total facility includes 105 beds in nursing home–type unit) (Nonreporting) **A**1 2 3 5 9 10 **N**	21	10	440	—	—	—	—	—	—	—

EVERGREEN PARK—Cook County

□ LITTLE COMPANY OF MARY HOSPITAL AND HEALTH CARE CENTERS, 2800 West 95th Street, Zip 60805–2795; tel. 708/422–6200; Sister Kathleen McIntyre, President **A**1 2 9 10 **F**1 2 3 7 8 10 11 12 15 16 17 18 19 21 22 25 26 28 29 30 31 32 33 34 35 37 38 39 40 41 42 44 45 46 47 49 51 52 53 54 55 56 57 58 59 60 63 65 67 71 72 73 74 **P**1 7 **S** Little Company of Mary Sisters Healthcare System, Evergreen Park, IL	21	10	326	16604	207	169631	2045	149568	56368	1559

Hospital, Address, Telephone, Administrator, Approval, Facility, and Physician Codes, Health Care System, Network	Classi-fication Codes		Utilization Data					Expense (thousands) of dollars		
★ American Hospital Association (AHA) membership □ Joint Commission on Accreditation of Healthcare Organizations (JCAHO) accreditation + American Osteopathic Healthcare Association (AOHA) membership ○ American Osteopathic Association (AOA) accreditation △ Commission on Accreditation of Rehabilitation Facilities (CARF) accreditation Control codes 61, 63, 64, 71, 72 and 73 indicate hospitals listed by AOHA, but not registered by AHA. For definition of numerical codes, see page A4	Control	Service	Staffed Beds	Admissions	Census	Outpatient Visits	Births	Total	Payroll	Personnel

FAIRFIELD—Wayne County

☒ FAIRFIELD MEMORIAL HOSPITAL, 303 N.W. 11th Street, Zip 62837–1203; tel. 618/842–2611; Jay Purvis, Acting Chief Executive Officer (Total facility includes 104 beds in nursing home–type unit) **A**1 9 10 **F**7 8 15 16 19 22 26 28 32 34 35 36 37 40 42 44 49 64 65 71 73 **S** Alliant Health System, Louisville, KY

| | 23 | 10 | 185 | 1302 | 123 | 17436 | 132 | 10580 | 4601 | 242 |

FLORA—Clay County

☒ CLAY COUNTY HOSPITAL, 700 North Mill Street, Zip 62839–1823, Mailing Address: P.O. Box 280, Zip 62839–0280; tel. 618/662–2131; John E. Monnahan, President and Senior Executive Officer **A**1 9 10 **F**7 8 15 16 17 19 22 28 30 33 34 36 39 40 44 49 65 73 **S** BJC Health System, Saint Louis, MO **N** BJC Health System, St. Louis, MO

| | 13 | 10 | 31 | 1019 | 11 | 22943 | 82 | 6307 | 2629 | 128 |

FOREST PARK—Cook County

☒ RIVEREDGE HOSPITAL, (Formerly Columbia Riveredge Hospital), 8311 West Roosevelt Road, Zip 60130–2500; tel. 708/771–7000; Thomas J. Dattalo, Chief Executive Officer **A**1 9 10 **F**2 3 15 16 52 53 55 56 57 58 59 65 67 **S** Columbia/HCA Healthcare Corporation, Nashville, TN

| | 33 | 22 | 100 | 1137 | 63 | 6821 | — | 13965 | 6036 | 129 |

FREEPORT—Stephenson County

☒ FREEPORT MEMORIAL HOSPITAL, 1045 West Stephenson Street, Zip 61032–4899; tel. 815/235–4131; Joseph E. Bonnett, Executive Vice President and Chief Executive Officer (Total facility includes 43 beds in nursing home–type unit) **A**1 2 9 10 **F**1 3 7 8 10 11 12 14 15 16 17 19 21 22 23 24 28 30 32 33 35 36 37 40 41 42 44 45 49 60 64 65 66 70 71 **P**3 5 6 8 **N** Freeport Regional Health Plan, Freeport, IL

| | 23 | 10 | 174 | 6008 | 93 | 138969 | 633 | 43277 | 16508 | 656 |

GALENA—Jo Daviess County

★ GALENA–STAUSS HOSPITAL, 215 Summit Street, Zip 61036–1697; tel. 815/777–1340; Roger D. Hervey, Administrator (Total facility includes 60 beds in nursing home–type unit) **A**9 10 **F**1 15 19 22 24 44 49 64 65 71

| | 16 | 10 | 85 | 479 | 63 | 20104 | 3 | 4453 | 2035 | 106 |

GALESBURG—Knox County

☒ GALESBURG COTTAGE HOSPITAL, 695 North Kellogg Street, Zip 61401–2885; tel. 309/343–8131; Dennis J. Renander, President and Chief Executive Officer (Total facility includes 18 beds in nursing home–type unit) **A**1 10 **F**2 3 7 8 15 19 21 22 30 32 33 35 36 37 39 40 42 44 49 52 54 55 56 58 63 64 65 70 71 73 **P**8

| | 23 | 10 | 168 | 5272 | 78 | 54619 | 477 | 39746 | 16992 | 568 |

☒ ST. MARY MEDICAL CENTER, (Formerly OSF Saint Mary Medical Center), 3333 North Seminary Street, Zip 61401–1299; tel. 309/344–3161; Richard S. Kowalski, Administrator and Chief Executive Officer (Total facility includes 14 beds in nursing home–type unit) **A**1 2 9 10 **F**7 8 11 12 14 15 16 17 19 21 22 23 28 30 32 33 34 35 37 40 41 42 44 46 49 51 60 64 65 67 70 71 73 74 **P**6 **S** OSF Healthcare System, Peoria, IL

| | 21 | 10 | 141 | 4336 | 54 | 46761 | 433 | 35222 | 15953 | 406 |

GENESEO—Henry County

☒ HAMMOND–HENRY HOSPITAL, 210 West Elk Street, Zip 61254–1099; tel. 309/944–6431; Nathan C. Olson, President and Chief Executive Officer (Total facility includes 57 beds in nursing home–type unit) (Nonreporting) **A**1 9 10 **S** Brim, Inc., Portland, OR

| | 16 | 10 | 105 | — | — | — | — | — | — | — |

GENEVA—Kane County

☒ DELNOR–COMMUNITY HOSPITAL, 300 Randall Road, Zip 60134–4200; tel. 630/208–3000; Craig A. Livermore, President and Chief Executive Officer **A**1 2 9 10 **F**7 8 10 12 14 15 16 17 19 20 21 22 24 26 28 29 30 32 33 35 37 39 40 41 42 44 45 46 49 53 63 65 66 67 70 71 73 74 **P**5 7 **N** MEDACOM Tri–State, Oakbrook, IL

| | 23 | 10 | 118 | 6822 | 67 | 78051 | 1519 | 54536 | 22597 | 677 |

GIBSON CITY—Ford County

★ GIBSON COMMUNITY HOSPITAL, (Includes Gibson Community Hospital Nursing Home), 1120 North Melvin Street, Zip 60936–1066, Mailing Address: P.O. Box 429, Zip 60936–0429; tel. 217/784–4251; Craig A. Jesiolowski, Chief Executive Officer (Total facility includes 42 beds in nursing home–type unit) **A**9 10 **F**7 8 15 16 17 19 20 22 24 26 30 32 33 34 35 36 37 39 40 41 42 44 49 63 64 65 69 71 73 **S** Quorum Health Group/Quorum Health Resources, Inc., Brentwood, TN

| | 23 | 10 | 82 | 1109 | 49 | 24934 | 82 | 11175 | 4728 | 209 |

GLENDALE HEIGHTS—Du Page County

☒ GLENOAKS HOSPITAL, (Formerly GlenOaks Hospital and Medical Center), 701 Winthrop Avenue, Zip 60139–1403; tel. 630/545–8000; Jorge A. Heyde, CHE, Administrator **A**1 9 10 **F**1 2 3 4 7 8 10 11 12 15 16 17 18 19 21 22 25 27 28 29 30 31 32 33 34 35 37 39 40 41 42 43 44 46 47 48 49 52 53 54 55 56 58 59 60 61 63 65 66 67 68 69 70 71 73 **P**5 7 8 **S** Adventist Health System Sunbelt Health Care Corporation, Winter Park, FL

| | 21 | 10 | 116 | 3370 | 43 | 47756 | 622 | 36305 | 13190 | 401 |

GLENVIEW—Cook County

GLENBROOK HOSPITAL See Evanston Hospital, Evanston

GRANITE CITY—Madison County

☒ ST. ELIZABETH MEDICAL CENTER, 2100 Madison Avenue, Zip 62040–4799; tel. 618/798–3000; Ted Eilerman, President **A**1 2 3 9 10 **F**3 7 8 10 12 13 14 15 16 17 18 19 21 22 24 28 29 30 32 33 34 35 36 37 39 40 41 42 44 45 46 49 51 52 53 54 55 56 57 58 59 63 64 65 66 67 68 71 73 74 **P**3

| | 21 | 10 | 185 | 6126 | 86 | 145442 | 367 | 63716 | 25417 | 994 |

GREAT LAKES—Lake County

☒ NAVAL HOSPITAL, 3001A Sixth Street, Zip 60088–5230; tel. 847/688–4560; Captain R. William Holden, MC, USN, Commanding Officer **A**1 2 **F**3 8 12 13 14 15 16 17 18 19 20 21 22 24 25 27 28 29 30 34 35 37 39 41 44 45 46 49 51 52 55 56 58 63 65 66 67 68 71 73 74 **P**1 **S** Department of Navy, Washington, DC

| | 43 | 10 | 89 | 1932 | 39 | 554960 | 0 | 106582 | 58391 | — |

Hospital, Address, Telephone, Administrator, Approval, Facility, and Physician Codes, Health Care System, Network	Classi-fication Codes		Utilization Data					Expense (thousands) of dollars		
	Control	Service	Staffed Beds	Admissions	Census	Outpatient Visits	Births	Total	Payroll	Personnel

★ American Hospital Association (AHA) membership
□ Joint Commission on Accreditation of Healthcare Organizations (JCAHO) accreditation
+ American Osteopathic Healthcare Association (AOHA) membership
○ American Osteopathic Association (AOA) accreditation
△ Commission on Accreditation of Rehabilitation Facilities (CARF) accreditation
   Control codes 61, 63, 64, 71, 72 and 73 indicate hospitals listed by AOHA, but not registered by AHA. For definition of numerical codes, see page A4.

GREENVILLE—Bond County

✠ EDWARD A. UTLAUT MEMORIAL HOSPITAL, (Includes Fair Oaks), 200 Health Care Drive, Zip 62246–1156; tel. 618/664–1230; Charles Bouis, President and Chief Executive Officer (Total facility includes 139 beds in nursing home–type unit) **A**1 9 10 **F**1 7 8 19 22 28 29 34 35 40 41 44 45 49 64 65 67 71 73	23	10	192	1532	133	30680	158	11486	5149	165

HARRISBURG—Saline County

✠ HARRISBURG MEDICAL CENTER, 100 Hospital Drive, Zip 62946–0017, Mailing Address: P.O. Box 428, Zip 62946–0428; tel. 618/253–7671; Claude Chatterton, Administrator and Chief Executive Officer **A**1 9 10 **F**8 14 15 17 19 21 22 26 30 31 32 34 35 37 39 41 42 44 45 48 49 52 54 56 57 58 59 60 63 65 66 67 71 73	23	10	78	2691	38	33735	0	15725	6638	302

HARVARD—McHenry County

✠ HARVARD MEMORIAL HOSPITAL, 901 Grant Street, Zip 60033–1898, Mailing Address: P.O. Box 850, Zip 60033–0850; tel. 815/943–5431; Dan Colby, President and Chief Executive Officer (Total facility includes 45 beds in nursing home–type unit) (Nonreporting) **A**1 9 10	16	10	81	—	—	—	—	—	—	—

HARVEY—Cook County

✠ △ INGALLS HOSPITAL, (Formerly Ingalls Memorial Hospital), One Ingalls Drive, Zip 60426–3591; tel. 708/333–2300; Robert L. Harris, President and Chief Executive Officer (Total facility includes 39 beds in nursing home–type unit) **A**1 2 7 9 10 **F**2 3 4 7 8 10 11 15 16 17 18 19 20 21 22 24 25 26 27 28 29 30 31 32 33 34 35 37 39 40 41 42 43 44 45 46 48 49 51 52 55 56 57 58 59 60 61 64 65 66 67 71 72 73 74 **N** Northwestern HealthCare Network, Chicago, IL	23	10	410	18372	267	262146	2199	148184	67252	1803

HAVANA—Mason County

✠ MASON DISTRICT HOSPITAL, 520 East Franklin Street, Zip 62644–0530, Mailing Address: Box 530, Zip 62644–0530; tel. 309/543–4431; Harry Wolin, Administrator and Chief Executive Officer **A**1 9 10 **F**8 14 16 19 22 28 32 35 36 37 41 44 49 64 65 71 72 73	16	10	36	651	8	36487	0	7912	3645	153

HAZEL CREST—Cook County

✠ SOUTH SUBURBAN HOSPITAL, 17800 South Kedzie Avenue, Zip 60429–0989; tel. 708/799–8000; Robert Rutkowski, Chief Executive (Total facility includes 41 beds in nursing home–type unit) **A**1 2 9 10 **F**7 8 10 12 14 15 16 17 19 21 22 25 27 28 30 32 33 34 35 37 40 41 42 44 49 63 64 67 71 73 **P**1 7 **S** Advocate Health Care, Oak Brook, IL **N** Advocate Health Care, Oak Brook, IL; MEDACOM Tri–State, Oakbrook, IL	23	10	191	9899	114	85986	1308	83223	38537	885

HERRIN—Williamson County

✠ HERRIN HOSPITAL, 201 South 14th Street, Zip 62948–3631; tel. 618/942–2171; Virgil Hannig, Administrator (Total facility includes 13 beds in nursing home–type unit) **A**1 9 10 **F**7 8 10 11 15 16 17 19 21 22 23 24 27 28 29 30 31 32 33 34 35 37 38 40 41 42 44 45 46 47 49 61 64 65 66 67 71 73 74 **P**8 **S** Southern Illinois Hospital Services, Carbondale, IL	23	10	80	2703	36	63849	0	26639	12378	351

HIGHLAND—Madison County

✠ ST. JOSEPH'S HOSPITAL, 1515 Main Street, Zip 62249–1656; tel. 618/654–7421; Anthony G. Mastrangelo, Executive Vice President and Chief Executive Officer (Total facility includes 30 beds in nursing home–type unit) **A**1 9 10 **F**8 17 19 21 22 27 28 29 30 31 32 33 34 35 36 37 39 41 42 44 46 49 51 54 63 64 65 66 67 71 73 **P**1 **S** Hospital Sisters Health System, Springfield, IL **N** Unity Health System, St. Louis, MO	21	10	76	1282	36	36817	—	12656	5586	209

HIGHLAND PARK—Lake County

✠ HIGHLAND PARK HOSPITAL, 718 Glenview Avenue, Zip 60035–2497; tel. 847/480–3905; Ronald G. Spaeth, President and Chief Executive Officer (Total facility includes 28 beds in nursing home–type unit) (Nonreporting) **A**1 2 9 10 **N** Northwestern HealthCare Network, Chicago, IL	23	10	219	—	—	—	—	—	—	—

HILLSBORO—Montgomery County

□ HILLSBORO AREA HOSPITAL, 1200 East Tremont Street, Zip 62049–1900; tel. 217/532–6111; Rex H. Brown, President (Total facility includes 40 beds in nursing home–type unit) **A**1 9 10 **F**7 8 12 14 15 16 17 19 20 21 22 26 27 28 30 32 33 34 35 37 39 40 42 44 45 49 64 65 66 67 70 71 73 **S** Brim, Inc., Portland, OR	23	10	95	1604	39	29917	101	9826	4390	188

HINES—Cook County

□ JOHN J. MADDEN MENTAL HEALTH CENTER, 1200 South First Avenue, Zip 60141; tel. 708/338–7202; Ugo Formigoni, Metro–West Network Manager (Nonreporting) **A**1 10	12	22	185	—	—	—	—	—	—	—
✠ △ VETERANS AFFAIRS EDWARD HINES, JR. HOSPITAL, Fifth Avenue & Roosevelt Road, Zip 60141–5000, Mailing Address: P.O. Box 5000, Zip 60141–5000; tel. 708/343–7200; John J. DeNardo, Director (Total facility includes 240 beds in nursing home–type unit) (Nonreporting) **A**1 3 5 7 8 **S** Department of Veterans Affairs, Washington, DC	45	10	957	—	—	—	—	—	—	—

HINSDALE—Du Page County

✠ △ HINSDALE HOSPITAL, 120 North Oak Street, Zip 60521–3890; tel. 630/856–9000; Ernie W. Sadau, President and Chief Executive Officer **A**1 2 3 5 7 9 10 **F**1 3 4 7 8 10 11 12 13 14 17 18 19 20 21 22 23 24 25 26 27 28 29 30 31 32 33 34 35 36 37 38 39 40 41 42 43 44 45 46 47 48 49 51 52 53 54 55 56 57 58 59 60 61 63 64 65 66 67 68 69 70 71 72 73 74 **P**3 5 7 **S** Adventist Health System Sunbelt Health Care Corporation, Winter Park, FL	21	10	344	14051	163	267654	2774	164184	65131	2141
□ R. M. SPECIALTY HOSPITAL, (Formerly Suburban Hospital), 5601 South County Line Road, Zip 60521–8900; tel. 708/783–5800; James Richard Prister, President (Nonreporting) **A**1 9 10	16	10	81	—	—	—	—	—	—	—

Hospital, Address, Telephone, Administrator, Approval, Facility, and Physician Codes, Health Care System, Network	Classi-fication Codes		Utilization Data					Expense (thousands) of dollars		
	Control	Service	Staffed Beds	Admissions	Census	Outpatient Visits	Births	Total	Payroll	Personnel

★ American Hospital Association (AHA) membership
□ Joint Commission on Accreditation of Healthcare Organizations (JCAHO) accreditation
+ American Osteopathic Healthcare Association (AOHA) membership
○ American Osteopathic Association (AOA) accreditation
△ Commission on Accreditation of Rehabilitation Facilities (CARF) accreditation
   Control codes 61, 63, 64, 71, 72 and 73 indicate hospitals listed by AOHA, but not registered by AHA. For definition of numerical codes, see page A4

HOFFMAN ESTATES—Cook County

COLUMBIA HOFFMAN ESTATES MEDICALCENTER See Hoffman Estates Medical Center

✠ COLUMBIA WOODLAND HOSPITAL, 1650 Moon Lake Boulevard, Zip 60194–5000; tel. 847/882–1600; Carmen I. Fontanez, Chief Executive Officer (Nonreporting) **A**1 10 **S** Columbia/HCA Healthcare Corporation, Nashville, TN	33	22	94	—	—	—	—	—	—	—
✠ HOFFMAN ESTATES MEDICAL CENTER, (Formerly Columbia Hoffman Estates MedicalCenter), 1555 North Barrington Road, Zip 60194; tel. 847/843–2000; Edward M. Goldberg, President and Chief Executive Officer (Total facility includes 23 beds in nursing home–type unit) **A**1 2 9 10 **F**1 2 3 4 7 8 10 11 12 14 15 16 17 19 21 22 27 30 32 34 35 37 39 40 41 42 44 45 46 49 51 52 53 54 55 56 57 61 63 64 65 67 70 71 73 74 **P**1 2 5 7 8 **S** Columbia/HCA Healthcare Corporation, Nashville, TN	33	10	195	11508	123	60367	2509	—	—	981

HOOPESTON—Vermilion County

✠ HOOPESTON COMMUNITY MEMORIAL HOSPITAL, 701 East Orange Street, Zip 60942–1871; tel. 217/283–5531; Darryl Wahler, Chief Executive Officer (Total facility includes 75 beds in nursing home–type unit) **A**1 9 10 **F**6 8 17 19 21 22 33 34 44 46 49 62 64 65 67 71 72	23	10	97	409	79	9492	—	6639	3245	136

HOPEDALE—Tazewell County

HOPEDALE MEDICAL COMPLEX, 107 Tremont Street, Zip 61747; tel. 309/449–3321; L. J. Rossi, M.D., Chief Executive Officer (Total facility includes 95 beds in nursing home–type unit) (Nonreporting) **A**9 10	23	10	119	—	—	—	—	—	—	—

JACKSONVILLE—Morgan County

✠ PASSAVANT AREA HOSPITAL, 1600 West Walnut Street, Zip 62650–1136; tel. 217/245–9541; Chester A. Wynn, President and Chief Executive Officer **A**1 2 9 10 **F**4 7 8 15 16 17 19 20 21 22 28 29 30 31 33 35 36 37 39 40 42 44 45 46 49 51 53 57 59 63 65 66 67 70 71 72 73 **P**8	23	10	130	4011	49	34050	428	39000	16696	431

JERSEYVILLE—Jersey County

□ JERSEY COMMUNITY HOSPITAL, 400 Maple Summit Road, Zip 62052–2028, Mailing Address: P.O. Box 426, Zip 62052–0426; tel. 618/498–6402; Lawrence P. Bear, Administrator **A**1 9 10 **F**3 7 8 10 14 15 16 17 19 21 22 27 28 30 31 33 35 36 37 39 40 41 42 43 44 45 46 49 53 54 58 60 65 66 67 71 73	16	10	67	1687	15	31517	258	13127	5094	177

JOLIET—Will County

✠ △ PROVENA SAINT JOSEPH MEDICAL CENTER, (Formerly Saint Joseph Medical Center), 333 North Madison Street, Zip 60435–6595; tel. 815/725–7133; David W. Benfer, President and Chief Executive Officer **A**1 2 7 9 10 **F**3 4 7 8 10 11 12 13 14 15 16 17 18 19 20 21 22 24 25 26 27 28 29 30 31 32 33 34 35 37 39 40 41 42 43 44 45 46 47 48 49 51 52 53 54 55 56 57 58 59 60 63 64 65 66 67 68 70 71 73 74 **P**1 5 6 7 **S** Provena Health, Frankfort, IL **N** MEDACOM Tri-State, Oakbrook, IL	21	10	409	16901	261	386889	1887	155723	69760	1870
✠ SILVER CROSS HOSPITAL, 1200 Maple Road, Zip 60432–1497; tel. 815/740–1100; Paul Pawlak, President and Chief Executive Officer **A**1 2 9 10 **F**1 2 3 4 5 6 7 8 9 10 11 12 13 14 15 16 17 18 19 20 21 22 23 24 25 26 27 28 29 30 32 33 34 35 36 38 39 40 41 42 43 44 45 46 47 48 49 50 53 54 55 56 57 58 59 60 61 62 64 65 66 67 68 69 70 71 73 **P**5 6 7 8 **N** Northwestern HealthCare Network, Chicago, IL	23	10	228	9874	117	115519	1355	96286	39550	809

KANKAKEE—Kankakee County

✠ PROVENA ST. MARY'S HOSPITAL, (Formerly St. Mary's Hospital), 500 West Court Street, Zip 60901–3661; tel. 815/937–2400; Allan C. Sonduck, President and Chief Executive Officer (Total facility includes 24 beds in nursing home–type unit) (Nonreporting) **A**1 2 10 **S** Provena Health, Frankfort, IL **N** Servantcor, Clifton, IL	21	10	209	—	—	—	—	—	—	—
✠ △ RIVERSIDE MEDICAL CENTER, (Formerly Riverside Healthcare), 350 North Wall Street, Zip 60901–0749; tel. 815/933–1671; Dennis C. Millirons, President and Chief Executive Officer (Total facility includes 100 beds in nursing home–type unit) **A**1 2 7 9 10 **F**3 6 7 8 10 11 12 13 14 15 16 17 18 19 20 21 23 26 27 28 29 30 31 32 33 34 35 36 37 39 40 41 42 44 45 46 48 49 50 52 53 54 55 56 57 58 59 60 61 62 63 64 65 66 67 68 70 71 73 74 **P**5 6 8 **N** Rush System for Health, Chicago, IL	23	10	378	8513	139	254502	1017	94363	39724	1296

KEWANEE—Henry County

✠ KEWANEE HOSPITAL, 719 Elliott Street, Zip 61443–2711, Mailing Address: P.O. Box 747, Zip 61443–0747; tel. 309/853–3361; Roger L. Holloway, Chief Executive Officer (Total facility includes 14 beds in nursing home–type unit) **A**1 9 10 **F**7 8 11 12 15 16 19 22 24 27 30 32 33 34 35 36 37 39 40 42 44 46 49 64 65 66 67 71 73 74 **P**6 8	23	10	63	2316	29	48398	159	24475	11351	370

LA GRANGE—Cook County

✠ LA GRANGE MEMORIAL HOSPITAL, (Formerly Columbia La Grange Memorial Hospital), 5101 South Willow Spring Road, Zip 60525–2680; tel. 708/352–1200; Cathleen D. Biga, President and Chief Executive Officer (Total facility includes 51 beds in nursing home–type unit) **A**1 2 3 5 9 10 **F**3 4 5 7 8 10 11 12 13 15 16 17 18 19 20 21 22 26 27 28 29 30 31 32 33 34 35 36 37 39 40 41 42 43 44 45 46 49 51 53 54 55 56 57 58 59 60 61 63 64 65 66 67 70 71 73 74 **P**1 **S** Columbia/HCA Healthcare Corporation, Nashville, TN **N** MEDACOM Tri-State, Oakbrook, IL	33	10	175	8648	97	111025	1000	83568	38047	—

LAKE FOREST—Lake County

✠ △ LAKE FOREST HOSPITAL, 660 North Westmoreland Road, Zip 60045–1696; tel. 847/234–5600; William G. Ries, President (Total facility includes 88 beds in nursing home–type unit) **A**1 2 7 9 10 **F**1 3 5 7 8 12 14 15 17 19 21 22 24 25 26 28 30 31 32 33 34 35 36 37 39 40 41 42 44 45 46 49 51 54 56 58 60 61 63 64 65 66 67 70 71 73 74 **P**1 6 7 **N** Rush System for Health, Chicago, IL	23	10	200	6749	146	193330	2141	94276	43382	996

Hospital, Address, Telephone, Administrator, Approval, Facility, and Physician Codes, Health Care System, Network	Classification Codes		Utilization Data					Expense (thousands) of dollars		
★ American Hospital Association (AHA) membership □ Joint Commission on Accreditation of Healthcare Organizations (JCAHO) accreditation + American Osteopathic Healthcare Association (AOHA) membership ○ American Osteopathic Association (AOA) accreditation △ Commission on Accreditation of Rehabilitation Facilities (CARF) accreditation Control codes 61, 63, 64, 71, 72 and 73 indicate hospitals listed by AOHA, but not registered by AHA. For definition of numerical codes, see page A4	Control	Service	Staffed Beds	Admissions	Census	Outpatient Visits	Births	Total	Payroll	Personnel

LAWRENCEVILLE—Lawrence County

★ LAWRENCE COUNTY MEMORIAL HOSPITAL, 2200 West State Street, Zip 62439–1853; tel. 618/943–1000; Gerald E. Waldroup, Administrator **A**9 10 **F**8 11 14 15 17 18 19 22 28 29 30 33 34 35 37 39 40 44 46 49 52 53 54 55 56 57 59 63 65 67 71 73 | 13 | 10 | 59 | 1408 | 20 | 27851 | 61 | 7763 | 3248 | 144

LEMONT—Cook County

□ ROCK CREEK CENTER, 40 Timberline Drive, Zip 60439; tel. 630/257–3636; Wendy Mamoon, Chief Executive Officer **A**1 10 **F**14 16 52 53 54 55 56 57 58 59 65 | 32 | 22 | 60 | 1247 | 49 | 35955 | 0 | 20151 | 8139 | 243

LIBERTYVILLE—Lake County

⊞ CONDELL MEDICAL CENTER, 801 South Milwaukee Avenue on Condell Drive, Zip 60048–3199; tel. 847/362–2900; Eugene Pritchard, President **A**1 2 9 10 **F**1 3 7 8 10 12 13 15 16 17 18 19 20 21 22 24 25 28 29 32 33 34 35 37 39 40 41 42 44 45 46 49 52 54 55 56 57 59 65 66 67 70 71 72 73 74 **P**1 5 | 23 | 10 | 175 | 9873 | 95 | 250368 | 1488 | 36898 | 32441 | 1060

LINCOLN—Logan County

⊞ ABRAHAM LINCOLN MEMORIAL HOSPITAL, 315 8th Street, Zip 62656–2698; tel. 217/732–2161; Forrest G. Hester, President and Chief Executive Officer **A**1 9 10 **F**1 2 3 8 12 15 16 18 19 21 22 27 33 34 35 37 39 40 42 44 46 49 52 56 58 65 71 72 73 **P**3 5 **S** Memorial Health System, Springfield, IL | 23 | 10 | 45 | 2057 | 22 | 41251 | 241 | 16715 | 7711 | 282

LINCOLN DEVELOPMENTAL CENTER, 861 South State Street, Zip 62656–2599; tel. 217/735–2361; Martin Downs, Facility Director (Nonreporting) | 12 | 62 | 450 | — | — | — | — | — | — | —

LITCHFIELD—Montgomery County

⊞ ST. FRANCIS HOSPITAL, 1215 Franciscan Drive, Zip 62056, Mailing Address: P.O. Box 1215, Zip 62056–1215; tel. 217/324–2191; Michael Sipkoski, Executive Vice President and Chief Executive Officer (Total facility includes 35 beds in nursing home–type unit) **A**1 9 10 **F**7 8 11 14 15 16 19 22 30 32 33 35 37 39 40 41 44 45 63 64 65 67 71 **S** Hospital Sisters Health System, Springfield, IL | 21 | 10 | 97 | 2933 | 42 | 56145 | — | 18446 | 8020 | 282

MACOMB—McDonough County

⊞ MCDONOUGH DISTRICT HOSPITAL, 525 East Grant Street, Zip 61455–3318; tel. 309/833–4101; Stephen R. Hopper, President and Chief Executive Officer (Total facility includes 16 beds in nursing home–type unit) **A**1 2 9 10 **F**1 3 7 8 14 15 16 19 21 22 23 24 26 28 29 30 32 33 37 39 40 41 42 44 45 46 53 56 57 58 64 65 67 71 73 74 **P**6 7 8 | 16 | 10 | 144 | 4156 | 58 | 41664 | 356 | 31691 | 15065 | 517

MARION—Williamson County

⊞ MARION MEMORIAL HOSPITAL, 917 West Main Street, Zip 62959–1836; tel. 618/997–5341; Ronald Seal, President and Chief Executive Officer (Nonreporting) **A**1 9 10 **S** Community Health Systems, Inc., Brentwood, TN | 33 | 10 | 84 | — | — | — | — | — | — | —

⊞ VETERANS AFFAIRS MEDICAL CENTER, 2401 West Main Street, Zip 62959–1194; tel. 618/997–5311; Marilyn Small, Acting Site Executive Officer (Total facility includes 58 beds in nursing home–type unit) **A**1 9 **F**3 8 16 19 20 21 22 25 26 28 30 31 32 33 34 35 37 41 42 44 46 49 51 54 58 64 65 67 71 72 73 **S** Department of Veterans Affairs, Washington, DC | 45 | 10 | 97 | 2092 | 97 | 157138 | — | 45931 | 28740 | 597

MARYVILLE—Madison County

⊞ ANDERSON HOSPITAL, 6800 State Route 162, Zip 62062–8500, Mailing Address: P.O. Box 1000, Zip 62062–1000; tel. 618/288–5711; R. Coert Shepard, President **A**1 9 10 **F**4 7 8 10 12 14 15 16 17 19 21 22 26 28 30 31 32 33 34 35 36 37 39 40 44 45 46 49 56 63 65 66 67 71 73 74 | 23 | 10 | 110 | 4852 | 46 | 63887 | 880 | 33092 | 14914 | 462

MATTOON—Coles County

⊞ SARAH BUSH LINCOLN HEALTH SYSTEM, 1000 Health Center Drive, Zip 61938–0372, Mailing Address: P.O. Box 372, Zip 61938–0372; tel. 217/258–2525; LeRoy D. Fahle, Interim President and Chief Executive Officer (Total facility includes 23 beds in nursing home–type unit) **A**1 2 9 10 **F**7 8 11 12 14 15 16 19 20 21 22 23 24 26 28 30 31 32 35 37 39 40 41 42 44 45 46 49 52 53 54 55 56 57 58 59 60 63 64 65 66 67 71 73 74 **P**4 5 6 7 | 23 | 10 | 174 | 6581 | 71 | 191264 | 903 | 68893 | 31402 | 776

MAYWOOD—Cook County

□ LOYOLA UNIVERSITY MEDICAL CENTER, 2160 South First Avenue, Zip 60153–5585; tel. 708/216–9000; Anthony L. Barbato, M.D., President and Chief Executive Officer **A**1 2 5 8 9 10 **F**3 4 5 7 8 9 10 11 12 13 16 17 18 19 20 21 22 24 25 26 27 28 29 30 31 32 33 34 35 37 38 39 40 41 42 43 44 45 46 47 49 51 52 53 54 55 56 57 58 59 60 61 63 64 65 66 67 68 69 70 71 72 73 74 **P**3 7 8 **N** Unified Health Care Network, Maywood, IL; MEDACOM Tri–State, Oakbrook, IL | 23 | 10 | 545 | 18406 | 323 | 320489 | 1348 | 354286 | 154052 | 3975

MCHENRY—McHenry County

□ △ NORTHERN ILLINOIS MEDICAL CENTER, 4201 Medical Center Drive, Zip 60050–9506; tel. 815/759–8110; Paul E. Laudick, President and Chief Executive Officer (Total facility includes 12 beds in nursing home–type unit) **A**1 2 7 9 10 **F**2 3 4 7 8 10 12 14 15 16 17 19 20 22 23 24 25 26 27 28 29 30 32 33 34 35 36 37 39 40 41 42 44 45 46 48 49 52 53 54 55 56 57 58 59 60 64 65 67 70 71 73 74 **P**7 **N** Centegra Health System, McHenry, IL | 23 | 10 | 160 | 7296 | 87 | 157615 | 965 | 77330 | 32139 | 886

MCLEANSBORO—Hamilton County

⊞ HAMILTON MEMORIAL HOSPITAL DISTRICT, 611 South Marshall Avenue, Zip 62859–1297; tel. 618/643–2361; James M. Hayes, Administrator (Total facility includes 60 beds in nursing home–type unit) **A**1 9 10 **F**15 16 19 21 22 28 30 32 34 35 44 45 46 49 64 65 71 **P**6 | 16 | 10 | 91 | 1189 | 72 | 16934 | — | 7097 | 3776 | 170

MELROSE PARK—Cook County

⊞ GOTTLIEB MEMORIAL HOSPITAL, 701 West North Avenue, Zip 60160–1692; tel. 708/681–3200; John Morgan, President (Total facility includes 32 beds in nursing home–type unit) **A**1 5 9 10 **F**4 5 7 8 10 11 12 15 16 17 18 19 21 22 26 27 28 29 30 31 32 33 34 35 37 39 40 41 42 43 44 45 49 63 64 65 66 67 70 71 73 74 **P**8 | 23 | 10 | 212 | 9482 | 119 | 136419 | 1140 | 82834 | 38807 | 1077

Hospital, Address, Telephone, Administrator, Approval, Facility, and Physician Codes, Health Care System, Network	Classi- fication Codes		Utilization Data					Expense (thousands) of dollars		
	Control	Service	Staffed Beds	Admissions	Census	Outpatient Visits	Births	Total	Payroll	Personnel

★ American Hospital Association (AHA) membership
□ Joint Commission on Accreditation of Healthcare Organizations (JCAHO) accreditation
+ American Osteopathic Healthcare Association (AOHA) membership
○ American Osteopathic Association (AOA) accreditation
△ Commission on Accreditation of Rehabilitation Facilities (CARF) accreditation
Control codes 61, 63, 64, 71, 72 and 73 indicate hospitals listed by AOHA, but not registered by AHA. For definition of numerical codes, see page A4

MENDOTA—La Salle County

✠ MENDOTA COMMUNITY HOSPITAL, 1315 Memorial Drive, Zip 61342–1496; tel. 815/539–7461; Susan Urso, Administrator **A**1 9 10 **F**3 7 8 12 15 16 17 19 21 22 28 29 30 32 33 36 37 39 40 41 42 44 45 46 49 65 67 71 73	23	10	68	1597	17	51419	90	11709	6094	184

METROPOLIS—Massac County

✠ MASSAC MEMORIAL HOSPITAL, 28 Chick Street, Zip 62960–2481, Mailing Address: P.O. Box 850, Zip 62960–0850; tel. 618/524–2176; Mark Edwards, Chief Executive Officer **A**1 9 10 **F**19 21 22 32 37 44 71 **S** Alliant Health System, Louisville, KY	16	10	35	1369	13	22680	—	8493	3717	168

MOLINE—Rock Island County

TRINITY MEDICAL CENTER–SEVENTH STREET CAMPUS See Trinity Medical Center–West Campus, Rock Island

MONMOUTH—Warren County

COMMUNITY MEMORIAL HOSPITAL, 1000 West Harlem Avenue, Zip 61462–1099; tel. 309/734–3141; Donald G. Brown, Chief Executive Officer (Total facility includes 34 beds in nursing home–type unit) **A**9 10 **F**8 11 14 15 16 17 18 19 20 21 22 26 28 30 32 37 39 41 44 45 49 51 63 64 65 67 70 71 73	14	10	67	1227	38	18714	0	7316	3382	135

MONTICELLO—Piatt County

✠ JOHN AND MARY KIRBY HOSPITAL, 1111 North State Street, Zip 61856–1116; tel. 217/762–2115; Thomas D. Dixon, Administrator **A**1 9 10 **F**2 8 9 14 15 16 22 28 30 32 33 41 44 45 46 52 53 54 55 56 57 58 59 60 64 65 67 69 71 73	23	10	16	479	6	21890	—	4799	1934	85

MORRIS—Grundy County

✠ MORRIS HOSPITAL, 150 West High Street, Zip 60450–1497; tel. 815/942–2932; Clifford L. Corbett, President and Chief Executive Officer **A**1 2 9 10 **F**8 15 16 19 21 22 26 28 29 30 33 34 35 36 37 39 40 41 42 44 46 49 54 56 58 65 70 71 73 **P**5	23	10	82	3151	33	—	273	37079	17142	387

MORRISON—Whiteside County

★ MORRISON COMMUNITY HOSPITAL, 303 North Jackson Street, Zip 61270–3042; tel. 815/772–4003; Mark F. Fedyk, Administrator (Total facility includes 38 beds in nursing home–type unit) (Nonreporting) **A**9 10 **S** Mercy Health Services, Farmington Hills, MI	16	10	60	—	—	—	—	—	—	—

MOUNT CARMEL—Wabash County

✠ WABASH GENERAL HOSPITAL DISTRICT, 1418 College Drive, Zip 62863–2638; tel. 618/262–8621; James R. Farris, CHE, Chief Executive Officer **A**1 9 10 **F**8 12 15 16 19 22 28 30 32 33 35 37 39 41 42 44 46 49 65 71 73 **S** Alliant Health System, Louisville, KY	16	10	56	1100	13	19580	—	9595	3898	153

MOUNT VERNON—Jefferson County

★ CROSSROADS COMMUNITY HOSPITAL, 8 Doctors Park Road, Zip 62864–6224; tel. 618/244–5500; Donald J. Frederic, Chief Executive Officer (Nonreporting) **A**9 10 **S** Community Health Systems, Inc., Brentwood, TN	33	10	37	—	—	—	—	—	—	—
✠ GOOD SAMARITAN REGIONAL HEALTH CENTER, 605 North 12th Street, Zip 62864–2899; tel. 618/242–4600; Leo F. Childers, Jr., FACHE, President (Total facility includes 14 beds in nursing home–type unit) **A**1 2 9 10 **F**4 7 8 10 12 14 15 16 17 18 19 20 21 22 23 24 25 28 29 30 31 32 33 34 35 37 39 40 42 44 45 46 48 49 51 57 58 60 64 65 67 71 73 74 **P**2 3 4 5 6 7 8 **S** SSM Health Care System, Saint Louis, MO **N** MEDACOM Tri-State, Oakbrook, IL	21	10	127	5211	70	78016	607	56664	25329	832

MURPHYSBORO—Jackson County

✠ ST. JOSEPH MEMORIAL HOSPITAL, 2 South Hospital Drive, Zip 62966–3333; tel. 618/684–3156; Betty Gaffney, Administrator **A**1 9 10 **F**7 8 15 16 17 19 22 26 29 31 32 33 34 40 44 45 46 49 56 65 67 68 71 73 74 **P**8 **S** Southern Illinois Hospital Services, Carbondale, IL	23	10	59	2063	23	20751	253	11971	5222	227

NAPERVILLE—Du Page County

✠ EDWARD HOSPITAL, 801 South Washington Street, Zip 60566–7060; tel. 630/355–0450; Pamela Meyer Davis, President and Chief Executive Officer (Total facility includes 14 beds in nursing home–type unit) **A**1 2 9 10 **F**3 4 7 8 10 12 13 14 15 16 17 18 19 22 24 25 28 29 30 32 34 35 37 39 40 41 42 43 44 45 46 49 51 53 54 55 56 57 58 59 61 65 67 70 71 72 73 74 **P**1 5 6	21	10	155	9893	106	192386	2514	105523	40048	1001

NASHVILLE—Washington County

✠ WASHINGTON COUNTY HOSPITAL, 705 South Grand Street, Zip 62263; tel. 618/327–8236; Michael P. Ellermann, Administrator (Total facility includes 27 beds in nursing home–type unit) **A**1 9 10 **F**3 4 5 7 8 9 10 11 12 13 14 17 18 19 21 22 25 28 29 30 31 32 33 34 35 37 38 39 40 41 42 43 44 45 47 48 49 51 52 53 54 55 56 57 58 59 60 61 63 64 65 66 69 70 71 72 73 74 **P**1 6 7 **S** SSM Health Care System, Saint Louis, MO	16	10	53	699	29	28778	50	6302	2754	121

NORMAL—McLean County

✠ BROMENN HEALTHCARE, (Includes Bromenn Lifecare Center, 807 North Main Street, Bloomington, Zip 61701; tel. 309/454–1400; Bromenn Regional Medical Center, tel. 309/454–1400; Eureka Community Hospital, 101 South Major Street, Eureka, Zip 61530, Mailing Address: P.O. Box 203, Zip 61530; tel. 309/467–2371), Virginia and Franklin Streets, Zip 61761, Mailing Address: P.O. Box 2850, Bloomington, Zip 61702–2850; tel. 309/454–0700; Dale S. Strassheim, President (Total facility includes 146 beds in nursing home–type unit) **A**1 2 9 10 **F**1 2 3 7 8 10 12 13 15 16 17 18 19 21 22 24 25 26 27 28 29 30 31 32 33 34 35 37 38 39 40 41 42 44 45 46 48 49 51 53 54 55 56 57 58 59 61 64 65 67 68 69 70 71 72 73 **P**1 6 7	21	10	324	8303	223	95003	1323	102057	45291	1309

BROMENN REGIONAL MEDICAL CENTER See BroMenn Healthcare

Hospital, Address, Telephone, Administrator, Approval, Facility, and Physician Codes, Health Care System, Network	Classi-fication Codes		Utilization Data					Expense (thousands) of dollars		
★ American Hospital Association (AHA) membership □ Joint Commission on Accreditation of Healthcare Organizations (JCAHO) accreditation + American Osteopathic Healthcare Association (AOHA) membership ○ American Osteopathic Association (AOA) accreditation △ Commission on Accreditation of Rehabilitation Facilities (CARF) accreditation Control codes 61, 63, 64, 71, 72 and 73 indicate hospitals listed by AOHA, but not registered by AHA. For definition of numerical codes, see page A4	Control	Service	Staffed Beds	Admissions	Census	Outpatient Visits	Births	Total	Payroll	Personnel

NORTH CHICAGO—Lake County

★ VETERANS AFFAIRS MEDICAL CENTER, 3001 Green Bay Road, Zip 60064–3049; tel. 847/688–1900; Alfred S. Pate, Director (Total facility includes 373 beds in nursing home–type unit) (Nonreporting) **A**1 3 5 **S** Department of Veterans Affairs, Washington, DC

| | 45 | 49 | 836 | — | — | — | — | — | — | — |

OAK FOREST—Cook County

★ △ OAK FOREST HOSPITAL OF COOK COUNTY, (LONG TERM ACUTE CARE HOSPITAL), 15900 South Cicero Avenue, Zip 60452; tel. 708/687–7200; Cynthia T. Henderson, M.D., M.P.H., Hospital Director and Chief Operating Officer (Total facility includes 488 beds in nursing home–type unit) **A**1 3 5 7 10 **F**3 8 10 12 13 14 15 16 17 20 22 25 26 27 28 29 30 31 33 34 36 37 39 41 42 44 45 46 48 49 51 54 57 58 64 65 67 71 73 **P**6 **S** Cook County Bureau of Health Services, Chicago, IL

| | 15 | 49 | 633 | 2861 | 239 | 65492 | 0 | 104205 | 63703 | 1663 |

OAK LAWN—Cook County

★ △ CHRIST HOSPITAL AND MEDICAL CENTER, 4440 West 95th Street, Zip 60453–2699; tel. 708/425–8000; Carol Schneider, Chief Executive **A**1 2 3 5 7 9 10 **F**1 2 3 4 7 8 10 11 12 13 15 16 17 18 19 21 22 24 25 26 27 28 30 31 32 33 34 35 36 37 38 39 40 41 42 43 44 46 47 48 49 51 52 53 54 55 57 58 59 60 61 62 64 65 66 67 68 70 71 73 74 **P**1 **S** Advocate Health Care, Oak Brook, IL **N** Advocate Health Care, Oak Brook, IL; MEDACOM Tri–State, Oakbrook, IL

| | 21 | 10 | 626 | 31452 | 460 | 236900 | 3714 | 323725 | 143991 | 3301 |

OAK PARK—Cook County

★ △ OAK PARK HOSPITAL, 520 South Maple Avenue, Zip 60304–1097; tel. 708/383–9300; Bruce M. Elegant, President and Chief Executive Officer (Total facility includes 47 beds in nursing home–type unit) **A**1 2 5 7 9 10 **F**1 5 8 10 11 12 15 16 19 21 22 26 27 28 29 30 33 34 35 37 39 41 42 44 45 46 48 49 50 51 60 63 64 65 66 67 71 73 74 **P**4 5 7 **S** Wheaton Franciscan Services, Inc., Wheaton, IL **N** Rush System for Health, Chicago, IL; Synergon Health System, Oak Park, IL

| | 21 | 10 | 176 | 3819 | 81 | 12784 | 1 | 41624 | 19887 | 478 |

□ WEST SUBURBAN HOSPITAL MEDICAL CENTER, Erie at Austin Boulevard, Zip 60302–2599; tel. 708/383–6200; David M. Cecero, President and Chief Executive Officer (Total facility includes 47 beds in nursing home–type unit) **A**1 2 3 5 9 10 **F**4 5 7 8 9 10 11 12 13 14 16 17 18 19 20 21 22 24 25 26 27 28 29 30 31 32 33 34 35 37 38 39 40 41 42 43 44 45 46 47 49 51 52 53 54 56 57 58 60 61 63 64 65 66 69 70 71 72 73 74 **P**8

| | 23 | 10 | 255 | 11869 | 159 | 119624 | 1957 | 138888 | 51752 | 1809 |

OLNEY—Richland County

★ RICHLAND MEMORIAL HOSPITAL, 800 East Locust Street, Zip 62450–2598; tel. 618/395–2131; Harvey H. Pettry, President and Chief Executive Officer (Total facility includes 28 beds in nursing home–type unit) **A**1 2 9 10 **F**7 8 12 14 15 16 19 20 21 22 27 28 29 30 31 32 33 34 35 36 37 39 40 41 42 44 45 46 49 51 52 54 56 63 64 65 66 67 71 73

| | 23 | 10 | 77 | 3002 | 53 | 68407 | 274 | 20590 | 9135 | 364 |

OLYMPIA FIELDS—Cook County

★ ○ COLUMBIA OLYMPIA FIELDS OSTEOPATHIC HOSPITAL AND MEDICAL CENTER, 20201 South Crawford Avenue, Zip 60461–1080; tel. 708/747–4000; Solon Boggus, Jr., Interim Chief Executive Officer **A**9 11 12 13 **F**4 5 7 8 10 11 12 13 14 16 17 19 21 22 25 26 28 29 30 32 34 35 37 38 39 40 41 42 43 44 45 46 48 49 51 52 54 55 56 57 60 61 64 65 66 67 70 71 72 73 74 **P**5 7 **S** Columbia/HCA Healthcare Corporation, Nashville, TN

| | 33 | 10 | 174 | 6294 | 83 | 131574 | 536 | 67875 | 24521 | 631 |

OTTAWA—La Salle County

★ COMMUNITY HOSPITAL OF OTTAWA, 1100 East Norris Drive, Zip 61350–1687; tel. 815/433–3100; Robert Schmelter, President **A**1 9 10 **F**1 2 3 4 6 7 8 11 15 19 20 21 22 26 27 28 29 30 32 33 36 39 40 41 42 44 45 46 49 52 53 54 56 57 58 59 65 67 70 71 73 **P**8

| | 23 | 10 | 124 | 3798 | 43 | 55730 | 383 | 29170 | 13255 | 429 |

PALOS HEIGHTS—Cook County

★ PALOS COMMUNITY HOSPITAL, 12251 South 80th Avenue, Zip 60463–0930; tel. 708/923–4000; Sister Margaret Wright, President **A**1 2 9 10 **F**3 7 8 10 11 16 19 21 22 25 31 32 33 34 35 36 37 39 40 41 42 44 45 49 52 53 54 56 57 58 59 63 65 66 67 71 72 73

| | 23 | 10 | 337 | 17610 | 218 | 181565 | 2242 | 159187 | 81274 | 1760 |

PANA—Christian County

★ PANA COMMUNITY HOSPITAL, 101 East Ninth Street, Zip 62557–1785; tel. 217/562–2131; Michael J. Laird, Administrator and Chief Executive Officer (Nonreporting) **A**1 9 10

| | 23 | 10 | 44 | — | — | — | — | — | — | — |

PARIS—Edgar County

★ PARIS COMMUNITY HOSPITAL, 721 East Court Street, Zip 61944–2420; tel. 217/465–4141; John M. Dillon, Chief Executive Officer **A**9 10 **F**8 15 17 19 21 22 28 30 33 34 36 37 41 42 44 48 49 64 65 67 71 73 **P**6 **S** Alliant Health System, Louisville, KY

| | 23 | 10 | 49 | 963 | 18 | 16391 | 0 | 8501 | 3806 | 252 |

PARK RIDGE—Cook County

★ △ LUTHERAN GENERAL HOSPITAL, 1775 Dempster Street, Zip 60068–1174; tel. 847/723–2210; Kenneth J. Rojek, Chief Executive **A**1 2 3 5 7 8 9 10 **F**1 3 4 5 6 7 8 10 11 12 14 15 16 17 19 21 22 23 24 26 27 28 29 30 31 32 33 34 35 36 37 38 39 40 41 42 43 44 45 46 47 48 49 50 51 52 53 54 55 56 57 58 59 60 61 62 65 66 67 68 69 70 71 72 73 74 **P**1 2 3 4 5 6 7 8 **S** Advocate Health Care, Oak Brook, IL **N** Advocate Health Care, Oak Brook, IL

| | 21 | 10 | 545 | 25707 | 369 | 198777 | 4369 | 321820 | 118662 | 3456 |

PEKIN—Tazewell County

★ PEKIN HOSPITAL, 600 South 13th Street, Zip 61554–5098; tel. 309/347–1151; Robert J. Moore, CHE, Chief Executive Officer (Total facility includes 20 beds in nursing home–type unit) **A**1 9 10 **F**2 3 4 7 8 10 12 14 15 16 17 18 19 20 21 22 23 24 26 28 29 30 31 32 34 35 36 37 38 39 40 41 42 43 44 45 46 47 49 51 52 53 54 55 56 57 58 59 60 61 63 64 65 66 67 68 70 71 72 73 74 **P**1

| | 23 | 10 | 125 | 4521 | 66 | 67632 | 459 | 35985 | 14635 | 586 |

Hospital, Address, Telephone, Administrator, Approval, Facility, and Physician Codes, Health Care System, Network	Classi-fication Codes		Utilization Data					Expense (thousands) of dollars		
★ American Hospital Association (AHA) membership □ Joint Commission on Accreditation of Healthcare Organizations (JCAHO) accreditation + American Osteopathic Healthcare Association (AOHA) membership ○ American Osteopathic Association (AOA) accreditation △ Commission on Accreditation of Rehabilitation Facilities (CARF) accreditation Control codes 61, 63, 64, 71, 72 and 73 indicate hospitals listed by AOHA, but not registered by AHA. For definition of numerical codes, see page A4	Control	Service	Staffed Beds	Admissions	Census	Outpatient Visits	Births	Total	Payroll	Personnel

PEORIA—Peoria County

□ GEORGE A. ZELLER MENTAL HEALTH CENTER, 5407 North University Street, Zip 61614–4785; tel. 309/693–5228; Robert W. Vyverberg, Ed.D., Director (Nonreporting) **A**1 10

	12	22	154	—	—	—	—	—	—	—

⊠ △ METHODIST MEDICAL CENTER OF ILLINOIS, 221 N.E. Glen Oak Avenue, Zip 61636–4310; tel. 309/672–5522; James K. Knoble, President (Total facility includes 37 beds in nursing home–type unit) **A**1 2 3 5 6 7 10 **F**2 4 5 7 8 10 11 12 14 15 16 17 18 19 21 22 24 25 26 27 28 29 30 31 32 33 34 35 37 39 40 41 42 43 44 45 46 48 49 50 51 52 53 54 55 56 57 58 59 60 61 63 64 65 67 69 70 71 72 73 74 **P**1 2 4 7

	23	10	298	13297	203	274038	1703	157797	78282	1900

⊠ PROCTOR HOSPITAL, 5409 North Knoxville Avenue, Zip 61614–5094; tel. 309/691–1000; Norman H. LaConte, President and Chief Executive Officer (Total facility includes 40 beds in nursing home–type unit) **A**1 9 10 **F**2 3 4 7 8 10 12 13 14 15 16 19 21 22 24 25 28 29 30 32 34 35 36 37 39 40 41 43 44 45 46 49 51 63 64 65 70 71 72 73 **P**1 3

	23	10	185	5857	108	154476	535	57823	22630	877

⊠ △ SAINT FRANCIS MEDICAL CENTER, (Formerly OSF Saint Francis Medical Center), 530 N.E. Glen Oak Avenue, Zip 61637; tel. 309/655–2000; Sister M. Canisia, Administrator **A**1 2 3 5 7 9 10 **F**4 5 7 8 10 11 12 13 14 15 16 17 19 20 21 22 23 24 25 26 28 29 30 31 32 33 34 35 36 37 38 39 40 41 42 43 44 45 46 47 48 49 51 52 53 54 55 56 57 58 59 60 63 64 65 66 67 68 69 70 71 72 73 74 **S** OSF Healthcare System, Peoria, IL **N** Unified Health Care Network, Maywood, IL

	21	10	552	21757	361	504564	2381	278623	130032	3737

PERU—La Salle County

⊠ ILLINOIS VALLEY COMMUNITY HOSPITAL, 925 West Street, Zip 61354–2799; tel. 815/223–3300; Ralph B. Berkley, Administrator (Total facility includes 12 beds in nursing home–type unit) **A**1 9 10 **F**1 7 8 10 15 16 19 21 22 23 26 28 29 30 31 32 33 35 36 37 39 40 41 42 44 45 46 49 52 53 54 55 56 57 58 59 64 65 66 67 71 73 74 **P**8

	23	10	104	3592	52	77633	393	31392	12522	450

PINCKNEYVILLE—Perry County

★ PINCKNEYVILLE COMMUNITY HOSPITAL, 101 North Walnut Street, Zip 62274–1099; tel. 618/357–2187; John D. Schubert, Administrator and Chief Executive Officer (Total facility includes 58 beds in nursing home–type unit) **A**9 10 **F**15 16 19 22 24 32 33 34 35 36 44 49 64 65 66 **P**6

	23	10	92	778	127	17374	—	9259	4507	176

PITTSFIELD—Pike County

⊠ ILLINI COMMUNITY HOSPITAL, 640 West Washington Street, Zip 62363–1397; tel. 217/285–2113; Jete Edmisson, President and Chief Executive Officer **A**1 9 10 **F**8 11 15 16 19 20 22 24 26 28 29 30 32 33 36 37 39 40 41 44 46 49 51 65 71 73 **P**6 **S** Quorum Health Group/Quorum Health Resources, Inc., Brentwood, TN

	23	10	45	1347	14	11689	88	9956	4538	175

PONTIAC—Livingston County

⊠ SAINT JAMES HOSPITAL, (Formerly OSF Saint James Hospital), 610 East Water Street, Zip 61764–2194; tel. 815/842–2828; David Ochs, Administrator (Total facility includes 16 beds in nursing home–type unit) **A**1 9 10 **F**7 8 12 14 15 16 17 19 21 22 24 28 29 30 32 33 35 36 37 39 40 41 42 44 45 49 64 65 66 67 71 74 **P**4 6 7 **S** OSF Healthcare System, Peoria, IL **N** Unified Health Care Network, Maywood, IL

	21	10	81	2257	26	62718	324	23337	10508	289

PRINCETON—Bureau County

⊠ PERRY MEMORIAL HOSPITAL, 530 Park Avenue East, Zip 61356–2598; tel. 815/875–2811; William H. Spitler, III, President (Total facility includes 15 beds in nursing home–type unit) **A**1 9 10 **F**7 8 15 16 17 19 21 22 28 29 30 34 35 41 44 49 65 67 71 **P**3 8

	14	10	87	2384	23	40819	180	18933	8404	277

QUINCY—Adams County

⊠ BLESSING HOSPITAL, (Includes Blessing Hospital, Broadway & 14th Street, Mailing Address: P.O. Box 7005, Zip 62305–7005; tel. 217/223–1200), Broadway at 11th Street, Zip 62301, Mailing Address: P.O. Box 7005, Zip 62305–7005; tel. 217/223–5811; Lawrence L. Swearingen, President and Chief Executive Officer (Total facility includes 44 beds in nursing home–type unit) **A**1 2 3 5 9 10 **F**1 2 7 8 10 12 13 14 15 16 17 19 20 21 22 23 24 26 28 29 30 31 32 33 34 35 36 37 39 40 41 42 44 45 46 49 52 53 56 60 63 64 65 67 70 71 72 73 74 **P**1 6

	23	10	323	11303	193	253046	1170	87405	39764	1346

RED BUD—Randolph County

⊠ ST. CLEMENT HEALTH SERVICES, One St. Clement Boulevard, Zip 62278–1194; tel. 618/282–3831; Michael Thomas McManus, President (Total facility includes 40 beds in nursing home–type unit) **A**1 9 10 **F**7 8 14 15 16 17 19 21 22 24 28 29 30 32 33 34 35 37 40 42 44 49 63 64 65 66 67 71 **S** Sisters of Mercy Health System–St. Louis, Saint Louis, MO **N** Unity Health System, St. Louis, MO

	21	10	105	1456	43	47152	126	15701	7478	337

ROBINSON—Crawford County

⊠ CRAWFORD MEMORIAL HOSPITAL, 1000 North Allen Street, Zip 62454–1114, Mailing Address: P.O. Box 151, Zip 62454–0151; tel. 618/544–3131; Leslie P. Luke, Chief Executive Officer (Total facility includes 48 beds in nursing home–type unit) **A**1 9 10 **F**7 8 13 14 15 16 18 19 22 26 27 28 30 32 33 34 35 36 37 39 40 41 42 44 46 49 51 64 65 67 71 **P**8 **S** Quorum Health Group/Quorum Health Resources, Inc., Brentwood, TN

	16	10	102	1854	50	29717	280	15836	6592	253

ROCHELLE—Ogle County

⊠ ROCHELLE COMMUNITY HOSPITAL, 900 North Second Street, Zip 61068–0330; tel. 815/562–2181; Thomas R. Lemon, Administrator **A**1 9 10 **F**7 8 12 15 16 19 21 22 30 31 32 37 40 41 44 46 49 51 65 66 67 71 72 73 **P**5 8

	23	10	42	1083	13	84311	78	9425	4448	143

Hospital, Address, Telephone, Administrator, Approval, Facility, and Physician Codes, Health Care System, Network	Classi-fication Codes		Utilization Data					Expense (thousands) of dollars		
★ American Hospital Association (AHA) membership □ Joint Commission on Accreditation of Healthcare Organizations (JCAHO) accreditation + American Osteopathic Healthcare Association (AOHA) membership ○ American Osteopathic Association (AOA) accreditation △ Commission on Accreditation of Rehabilitation Facilities (CARF) accreditation Control codes 61, 63, 64, 71, 72 and 73 indicate hospitals listed by AOHA, but not registered by AHA. For definition of numerical codes, see page A4	Control	Service	Staffed Beds	Admissions	Census	Outpatient Visits	Births	Total	Payroll	Personnel

ROCK ISLAND—Rock Island County

☒ △ TRINITY MEDICAL CENTER–WEST CAMPUS, (Includes Trinity Medical Center–Seventh Street Campus, 500 John Deere Road, Moline, Zip 61265; tel. 309/757–3131), 2701 17th Street, Zip 61201–5393; tel. 309/779–5000; Eric Crowell, President and Chief Executive Officer (Total facility includes 29 beds in nursing home–type unit) **A**1 2 7 9 10 **F**3 4 7 8 10 11 12 14 15 16 17 19 21 22 23 24 25 26 27 28 29 30 31 32 33 34 35 37 38 39 40 41 42 43 44 45 46 48 49 51 52 53 54 55 56 57 58 59 60 61 64 65 66 67 68 70 71 72 73 74 **P**1 **N** Advocate Health Care, Oak Brook, IL

| | 23 | 10 | 369 | 14406 | 203 | 270318 | 1596 | 113517 | 52345 | 1482 |

ROCKFORD—Winnebago County

□ H. DOUGLAS SINGER MENTAL HEALTH AND DEVELOPMENTAL CENTER, 4402 North Main Street, Zip 61103 1278; tel. 815/987 7096; Gail Tennant, Director **A**1 10 **F**1 2 3 4 7 8 9 10 11 12 13 14 15 17 18 19 20 21 22 25 26 27 31 32 35 37 38 39 40 41 42 43 44 45 46 47 48 49 50 51 52 53 54 55 56 57 58 59 60 61 63 65 67 70 71 73 74

| | 12 | 22 | 144 | 636 | 135 | — | 0 | 13587 | 10174 | — |

☒ △ ROCKFORD MEMORIAL HOSPITAL, 2400 North Rockton Avenue, Zip 61103–3692; tel. 815/971–5000; Thomas David DeFauw, President and Chief Executive Officer **A**1 2 5 7 9 10 **F**2 3 4 5 7 8 10 11 12 14 15 16 17 19 21 22 26 27 28 29 30 31 32 34 35 36 38 39 40 41 42 43 44 45 46 47 48 49 51 52 53 54 55 56 57 58 59 60 61 65 66 67 70 71 72 73 74

| | 23 | 10 | 363 | 16785 | 249 | 276728 | 2175 | 163332 | 65245 | 1205 |

☒ SAINT ANTHONY MEDICAL CENTER, (Formerly OSF Saint Anthony Medical Center), 5666 East State Street, Zip 61108–2472; tel. 815/226–2000; David A. Schertz, Administrator **A**1 2 3 5 9 10 **F**4 7 8 9 10 11 12 14 15 16 17 19 21 22 23 24 26 27 28 29 30 31 32 34 35 36 37 39 40 41 42 43 44 46 48 49 51 60 63 65 66 67 70 71 72 73 **P**6 **S** OSF Healthcare System, Peoria, IL

| | 21 | 10 | 210 | 8750 | 115 | 110780 | 847 | 113715 | 46701 | 1278 |

☒ SWEDISHAMERICAN HEALTH SYSTEM, (Formerly SwedishAmerican Hospital), 1313 East State Street, Zip 61104; tel. 815/968–4400; Robert B. Klint, M.D., President and Chief Executive Officer **A**1 2 3 5 9 10 **F**2 3 4 7 8 10 11 12 14 16 17 18 19 21 22 26 28 29 30 31 32 33 34 35 37 38 39 40 41 42 43 44 45 46 47 48 49 51 52 53 54 55 56 57 58 59 60 63 64 65 67 70 71 72 73 74 **P**6 7 **N** SwedishAmerican Health System, Rockford, IL; MEDACOM Tri–State, Oakbrook, IL

| | 23 | 10 | 291 | 10818 | 134 | — | 1792 | 104646 | 45555 | 1361 |

ROSICLARE—Hardin County

☒ HARDIN COUNTY GENERAL HOSPITAL, Ferrell Road, Zip 62982; tel. 618/285–6634; Roby D. Williams, Administrator (Nonreporting) **A**1 9 10

| | 23 | 10 | 48 | — | — | — | — | — | — | — |

RUSHVILLE—Schuyler County

★ SARAH D. CULBERTSON MEMORIAL HOSPITAL, 238 South Congress Street, Zip 62681–1472, Mailing Address: P.O. Box 440, Zip 62681–0440; tel. 217/322–4321; Michael C. O'Brien, Administrator (Total facility includes 30 beds in nursing home–type unit) **A**9 10 **F**8 14 19 22 28 30 34 36 40 44 49 64 71 72 73 **P**6

| | 16 | 10 | 57 | 771 | 36 | 18907 | 122 | 5995 | 2160 | 106 |

SALEM—Marion County

☒ PUBLIC HOSPITAL OF THE TOWN OF SALEM, 1201 Ricker Drive, Zip 62881–6250, Mailing Address: P.O. Box 1250, Zip 62881–1250; tel. 618/548–3194; Clarence E. Lay, Chief Executive Officer **A**1 9 10 **F**8 14 15 16 17 19 20 22 25 28 30 32 33 34 37 39 41 44 45 54 56 65 66 69 70 71 73 **N** BJC Health System, St. Louis, MO

| | 14 | 10 | 32 | 1550 | 19 | 36338 | — | 12026 | 5258 | 205 |

SANDWICH—De Kalb County

★ SANDWICH COMMUNITY HOSPITAL, 11 East Pleasant Avenue, Zip 60548–0901; tel. 815/786–8484; Roland R. Carlson, Chief Executive Officer **A**9 10 **F**19 21 22 28 30 34 35 37 39 40 41 44 45 49 65 71 73

| | 23 | 10 | 35 | 1131 | 11 | 12653 | 100 | 9830 | 3887 | 120 |

SCOTT AFB—St. Clair County

☒ SCOTT MEDICAL CENTER, 310 West Losey Street, Zip 62225–5252; tel. 618/256–7012; Colonel Stephen J. Pribyl, MSC, USAF, Administrator **A**1 2 3 5 **F**3 7 8 12 13 15 16 18 19 20 22 24 25 27 28 29 30 34 35 37 38 39 40 41 42 44 45 46 49 51 54 55 56 58 61 65 67 68 71 73 74 **S** Department of the Air Force, Bowling AFB, DC

| | 41 | 10 | 59 | 4706 | 29 | 292105 | 556 | 33014 | 6272 | 1193 |

SHELBYVILLE—Shelby County

☒ SHELBY MEMORIAL HOSPITAL, 200 South Cedar Street, Zip 62565–1899; tel. 217/774–3961; John Bennett, President and Chief Executive Officer (Total facility includes 15 beds in nursing home–type unit) **A**1 9 10 **F**8 11 14 15 16 19 21 22 31 32 35 37 41 42 44 49 62 63 64 65 66 71

| | 23 | 10 | 60 | 1926 | 34 | 33017 | 0 | 8819 | 3722 | 154 |

SILVIS—Rock Island County

☒ ILLINI HOSPITAL, 801 Hospital Road, Zip 61282–1893; tel. 309/792–9363; Gary E. Larson, Chief Executive Officer **A**1 9 10 **F**6 7 8 19 21 22 24 25 26 28 29 30 32 35 37 40 41 44 45 62 63 65 70 71 72 73 **P**6 7 8 **N** Genesis Health System, Davenport, IA

| | 23 | 10 | 133 | 4623 | 44 | 74797 | 583 | 33000 | 14301 | 453 |

SKOKIE—Cook County

☒ RUSH NORTH SHORE MEDICAL CENTER, 9600 Gross Point Road, Zip 60076–1257; tel. 847/677–9600; John S. Frigo, President **A**1 2 3 5 9 10 **F**4 7 8 10 14 15 17 19 21 22 27 28 29 30 35 36 37 39 40 41 42 43 44 46 49 52 54 55 56 57 58 59 60 61 63 65 67 70 71 73 74 **P**8 **S** Rush–Presbyterian–St. Luke's Medical Center, Chicago, IL **N** Rush System for Health, Chicago, IL

| | 23 | 10 | 231 | 9846 | 155 | 199715 | 668 | 94522 | 41663 | 1234 |

SPARTA—Randolph County

★ SPARTA COMMUNITY HOSPITAL, 818 East Broadway Street, Zip 62286–0297, Mailing Address: P.O. Box 297, Zip 62286–0297; tel. 618/443–2177; Joann Emge, Chief Executive Officer **A**9 10 **F**7 8 12 14 15 19 21 22 27 28 30 32 33 35 40 41 42 44 46 49 65 66 67 71 73 **P**5 **S** Brim, Inc., Portland, OR

| | 16 | 10 | 39 | 937 | 9 | 30297 | 150 | 9501 | 3833 | 134 |

Hospital, Address, Telephone, Administrator, Approval, Facility, and Physician Codes, Health Care System, Network	Classi-fication Codes		Utilization Data					Expense (thousands) of dollars		
★ American Hospital Association (AHA) membership □ Joint Commission on Accreditation of Healthcare Organizations (JCAHO) accreditation + American Osteopathic Healthcare Association (AOHA) membership ○ American Osteopathic Association (AOA) accreditation △ Commission on Accreditation of Rehabilitation Facilities (CARF) accreditation Control codes 61, 63, 64, 71, 72 and 73 indicate hospitals listed by AOHA, but not registered by AHA. For definition of numerical codes, see page A4	Control	Service	Staffed Beds	Admissions	Census	Outpatient Visits	Births	Total	Payroll	Personnel

SPRING VALLEY—Bureau County

⊞ ST. MARGARET'S HOSPITAL, 600 East First Street, Zip 61362–2034; tel. 815/664–5311; Timothy Muntz, President (Total facility includes 33 beds in nursing home–type unit) **A**1 2 9 10 **F**1 7 8 10 14 15 16 19 21 22 23 24 27 30 31 32 35 37 39 40 41 42 44 48 49 60 62 64 65 66 67 71 73 74 **P**6 **S** Sisters of Mary of the Presentation Health Corporation, Fargo, ND | 21 | 10 | 127 | 3313 | 57 | 102344 | 335 | 29716 | 12544 | 404

SPRINGFIELD—Sangamon County

□ ANDREW MCFARLAND MENTAL HEALTH CENTER, 901 Southwind Road, Zip 62703–5195; tel. 217/786–6994; Nieves Tan–Lachica, M.D., Superintendent (Nonreporting) **A**1 | 12 | 22 | 146 | — | — | — | — | — | — | —

□ DOCTORS HOSPITAL, 5230 South Sixth Street, Zip 62703–5194, Mailing Address: P.O. Box 19254, Zip 62794–9254; tel. 217/529–7151; Jim Bohl, President and Chief Executive Officer (Nonreporting) **A**1 9 10 | 33 | 10 | 150 | — | — | — | — | — | — | —

⊞ △ MEMORIAL MEDICAL CENTER, 800 North Rutledge Street, Zip 62781–0001; tel. 217/788–3000; Robert T. Clarke, President and Chief Executive Officer **A**1 2 3 5 7 8 9 10 **F**3 4 5 7 8 9 10 11 12 14 15 16 17 18 19 20 21 22 23 25 26 27 28 29 30 31 32 33 34 35 36 37 39 40 41 42 43 44 46 48 49 51 52 53 54 55 56 57 58 59 60 61 65 66 67 68 69 70 71 72 73 **P**3 5 7 **S** Memorial Health System, Springfield, IL | 23 | 10 | 457 | 18645 | 317 | 387390 | 1963 | 210405 | 86222 | 2586

⊞ ST. JOHN'S HOSPITAL, 800 East Carpenter Street, Zip 62769–0002; tel. 217/544–6464; Allison C. Laabs, Executive Vice President and Administrator (Total facility includes 53 beds in nursing home–type unit) **A**1 2 3 5 8 9 10 **F**1 3 4 8 10 12 15 16 19 21 22 26 28 30 32 33 35 37 38 39 40 42 43 44 46 47 49 52 57 58 59 60 64 65 69 70 71 73 74 **P**7 **S** Hospital Sisters Health System, Springfield, IL **N** | 21 | 10 | 579 | 22488 | 363 | 183762 | 1616 | 222238 | 87568 | 2977

STAUNTON—Macoupin County

★ COMMUNITY MEMORIAL HOSPITAL, 400 Caldwell Street, Zip 62088–1499; tel. 618/635–2200; Patrick B. Heise, Chief Executive Officer **A**9 10 **F**8 19 22 32 44 65 71 73 **P**3 **S** Quorum Health Group/Quorum Health Resources, Inc., Brentwood, TN **N** Unity Health System, St. Louis, MO | 23 | 10 | 57 | 863 | 10 | 16965 | — | 8638 | 3847 | 154

STERLING—Whiteside County

⊞ CGH MEDICAL CENTER, 100 East LeFevre Road, Zip 61081–1279; tel. 815/625–0400; Edward Andersen, President and Chief Executive Officer **A**1 2 9 10 **F**7 8 12 14 15 16 17 19 20 22 23 27 28 29 32 33 35 36 37 39 40 42 44 46 49 60 63 64 65 67 71 73 **P**1 | 14 | 10 | 143 | 5834 | 62 | 64070 | 776 | 42872 | 18772 | 629

STREAMWOOD—Cook County

□ BHC STREAMWOOD HOSPITAL, 1400 East Irving Park Road, Zip 60107–3203; tel. 630/837–9000; Jeff Bergren, Chief Executive Officer and Administrator (Nonreporting) **A**1 10 **S** Behavioral Healthcare Corporation, Nashville, TN | 33 | 52 | 100 | — | — | — | — | — | — | —

STREATOR—La Salle County

⊞ ST. MARY'S HOSPITAL, 111 East Spring Street, Zip 61364–3399; tel. 815/673–2311; James F. Dover, Administrator and Executive Vice President (Total facility includes 30 beds in nursing home–type unit) **A**1 2 9 10 **F**1 3 7 8 14 15 16 17 19 20 21 22 24 26 27 28 29 30 31 32 33 34 35 37 39 40 41 42 44 45 49 60 63 64 65 67 69 71 73 **S** Hospital Sisters Health System, Springfield, IL | 21 | 10 | 170 | 4170 | 70 | 36017 | 271 | 26002 | 12507 | 406

SYCAMORE—De Kalb County

□ VENCOR HOSPITAL–SYCAMORE, 225 Edward Street, Zip 60178–2197; tel. 815/895–2144; Betty Walker, Administrator (Nonreporting) **A**1 9 10 **S** Vencor, Incorporated, Louisville, KY | 33 | 10 | 50 | — | — | — | — | — | — | —

TAYLORVILLE—Christian County

★ ST. VINCENT MEMORIAL HOSPITAL, 201 East Pleasant Street, Zip 62568–1597; tel. 217/824–3331; Daniel J. Raab, President and Chief Executive Officer (Total facility includes 50 beds in nursing home–type unit) **A**9 10 **F**7 8 13 14 15 16 17 19 21 22 26 28 29 31 32 33 34 35 36 37 39 40 41 42 44 45 49 50 51 63 64 65 67 71 73 74 **P**5 **S** Memorial Health System, Springfield, IL | 21 | 10 | 151 | 2325 | 68 | 25374 | 185 | 16895 | 8439 | 360

TINLEY PARK—Cook County

□ TINLEY PARK MENTAL HEALTH CENTER, 7400 West 183rd Street, Zip 60477–3695; tel. 708/614–4000; Delores Newman, MS, Network Manager, Metro South Network (Nonreporting) **A**1 5 10 | 12 | 22 | 280 | — | — | — | — | — | — | —

URBANA—Champaign County

⊞ △ CARLE FOUNDATION HOSPITAL, 611 West Park Street, Zip 61801–2595; tel. 217/383–3311; Michael H. Fritz, President (Total facility includes 240 beds in nursing home–type unit) **A**1 2 3 5 7 9 10 **F**2 4 6 7 8 10 12 13 14 15 16 17 19 22 23 25 26 27 28 29 30 31 32 33 34 35 37 38 39 40 41 42 43 44 45 46 48 49 52 62 65 66 67 70 71 72 73 74 **P**5 **N** The Carle Foundation, Urbana, IL | 23 | 10 | 504 | 12304 | 321 | 39291 | 1692 | 114253 | 43520 | 1605

COVENANT MEDICAL CENTER See Provena Covenant Medical Center

MERCY HOSPITAL See Provena Covenant Medical Center

⊞ △ PROVENA COVENANT MEDICAL CENTER, (Formerly Covenant Medical Center), (Includes Burnham Hospital, 407 South Fourth Street, Champaign, Zip 61820; tel. 217/337–2500; Mercy Hospital, 1400 West Park Street, Zip 61801), 1400 West Park Street, Zip 61801–2396; tel. 217/337–2000; Diane Friedman, R.N., President and Chief Executive Officer **A**1 2 3 5 7 9 10 **F**4 7 10 12 16 17 21 22 26 30 32 33 34 37 38 39 40 42 43 44 45 46 48 49 52 53 54 55 57 58 59 63 64 65 67 71 73 **S** Provena Health, Frankfort, IL **N** Servantcor, Clifton, IL | 21 | 10 | 258 | 9950 | 125 | 121004 | 1327 | 88222 | 35949 | 1161

Hospital, Address, Telephone, Administrator, Approval, Facility, and Physician Codes, Health Care System, Network	Classi-fication Codes		Utilization Data					Expense (thousands) of dollars		
★ American Hospital Association (AHA) membership □ Joint Commission on Accreditation of Healthcare Organizations (JCAHO) accreditation + American Osteopathic Healthcare Association (AOHA) membership ○ American Osteopathic Association (AOA) accreditation △ Commission on Accreditation of Rehabilitation Facilities (CARF) accreditation Control codes 61, 63, 64, 71, 72 and 73 indicate hospitals listed by AOHA, but not registered by AHA. For definition of numerical codes, see page A4	Control	Service	Staffed Beds	Admissions	Census	Outpatient Visits	Births	Total	Payroll	Personnel

VANDALIA—Fayette County

⊞ FAYETTE COUNTY HOSPITAL AND LONG TERM CARE, Seventh and Taylor Streets, Zip 62471–1296; tel. 618/283–1231; Daniel L. Gantz, President (Total facility includes 101 beds in nursing home–type unit) **A**1 9 10 **F**8 14 15 16 17 19 20 21 22 28 30 32 33 35 36 41 42 44 45 46 49 50 57 58 64 65 71 72 73 **P**7 **S** BJC Health System, Saint Louis, MO **N** BJC Health System, St. Louis, MO	16	10	142	1429	97	27876	—	10963	5095	227

WATSEKA—Iroquois County

⊞ IROQUOIS MEMORIAL HOSPITAL AND RESIDENT HOME, 200 Fairman Avenue, Zip 60970–1644; tel. 815/432–5841; Rex D. Conger, President and Chief Executive Officer (Total facility includes 46 beds in nursing home–type unit) (Nonreporting) **A**1 9 10	23	10	112	—	—	—	—	—	—	—

WAUKEGAN—Lake County

⊞ △ PROVENA SAINT THERESE MEDICAL CENTER, (Formerly Saint Therese Medical Center), 2615 Washington Street, Zip 60085–4988; tel. 847/249–3900; Timothy P. Selz, President and Chief Executive Officer (Total facility includes 25 beds in nursing home–type unit) **A**1 2 7 9 10 **F**7 8 10 11 12 14 15 16 17 18 19 20 22 27 28 29 30 32 33 35 39 40 41 42 44 48 49 52 53 56 58 59 64 65 70 71 72 73 **P**5 7 **S** Provena Health, Frankfort, IL **N** MEDACOM Tri–State, Oakbrook, IL	21	10	254	8083	107	216325	1178	65910	28676	793
⊞ VICTORY MEMORIAL HOSPITAL, 1324 North Sheridan Road, Zip 60085–2181; tel. 847/360–3000; Timothy Harrington, President **A**1 2 9 10 **F**1 3 4 7 8 10 12 14 15 16 18 19 21 22 24 25 26 28 29 30 32 33 34 37 39 40 42 44 45 46 49 52 54 55 56 57 58 59 60 63 64 65 67 71 73 **P**1 7	23	10	171	7181	85	82244	1268	62266	27048	768

WEST FRANKFORT—Franklin County

★ UNITED MINE WORKERS OF AMERICA UNION HOSPITAL, 507 West St. Louis Street, Zip 62896–1999; tel. 618/932–2155; Virgil Hannig, Senior Vice President and Administrator **A**9 10 **F**19 22 32 44 71 73 **S** Southern Illinois Hospital Services, Carbondale, IL	23	10	32	338	4	5427	—	4598	2087	—

WHEATON—Du Page County

⊞ △ MARIANJOY REHABILITATION HOSPITAL AND CLINICS, 26 West 171 Roosevelt Road, Zip 60187–0795, Mailing Address: P.O. Box 795, Zip 60189–0795; tel. 630/462–4000; Bruce A. Schurman, President **A**1 3 5 7 9 10 **F**5 17 19 21 22 25 27 29 34 35 41 45 46 48 49 50 53 62 63 65 66 67 71 73 **P**1 **S** Wheaton Franciscan Services, Inc., Wheaton, IL	21	46	107	1518	88	0	0	40838	18582	497

WINFIELD—Du Page County

ALCOHOLISM TREATMENT CENTER See Behavioral Health Center										
BEHAVIORAL HEALTH CENTER, (Formerly Alcoholism Treatment Center), 27 West 350 High Lake Road, Zip 60190; tel. 630/653–4000; David S. Fox, President (Nonreporting)	23	82	52	—	—	—	—	—	—	—
⊞ CENTRAL DUPAGE HOSPITAL, 25 North Winfield Road, Zip 60190; tel. 630/682–1600; David S. Fox, President **A**1 2 9 10 **F**2 3 4 7 8 10 11 12 14 15 16 17 19 20 21 22 23 24 25 28 29 30 32 33 34 35 37 38 40 41 42 43 44 45 46 47 49 51 52 53 54 56 57 58 59 62 64 65 67 70 71 72 73 **P**6	23	10	326	13518	146	223863	3185	144988	56189	1354

WOOD RIVER—Madison County

⊞ WOOD RIVER TOWNSHIP HOSPITAL, 101 East Edwardsville Road, Zip 62095–1332; tel. 618/251–7103; Max L. Ludeke, FACHE, President and Chief Executive Officer **A**1 9 10 **F**2 3 7 8 10 12 13 14 15 16 17 18 19 21 22 26 27 28 29 33 34 35 37 39 40 41 44 48 49 51 52 54 55 56 58 65 67 68 71 73 **S** Brim, Inc., Portland, OR	16	10	113	1325	25	18073	195	18205	7364	193

WOODSTOCK—McHenry County

⊞ MEMORIAL MEDICAL CENTER, Highway 14 and Doty Road, Zip 60098–3797, Mailing Address: P.O. Box 1990, Zip 60098–1990; tel. 815/338–2500; Paul E. Laudick, President and Chief Executive Officer (Total facility includes 20 beds in nursing home–type unit) **A**1 2 9 10 **F**2 3 7 8 10 12 14 15 16 17 18 19 20 22 23 24 26 27 28 29 30 32 33 34 35 36 37 39 40 41 42 44 45 46 49 52 53 54 55 56 57 58 59 60 65 66 67 70 71 73 74 **P**5 7 **N** Centegra Health System, McHenry, IL	23	10	108	4791	56	55952	570	49244	20083	563

ZION—Lake County

□ MIDWESTERN REGIONAL MEDICAL CENTER, (ONCOLOGY), 2520 Elisha Avenue, Zip 60099–2587; tel. 847/872–4561; Roger C. Cary, President and Chief Executive Officer **A**1 2 10 **F**8 12 14 15 16 17 19 20 21 27 28 29 30 31 32 33 34 35 37 39 41 42 44 45 46 49 51 60 65 66 68 69 71 73 **S** Cancer Treatment Centers of America, Arlington Heights, IL	33	49	70	2138	30	20588	0	42945	13494	365

INDIANA

Resident population 5,864 (in thousands)
Resident population in metro areas 71.7%
Birth rate per 1,000 population 14.4
65 years and over 12.6%
Percent of persons without health insurance 10.6%

Hospital, Address, Telephone, Administrator, Approval, Facility, and Physician Codes, Health Care System, Network	Classi-fication Codes		Utilization Data					Expense (thousands) of dollars		
★ American Hospital Association (AHA) membership □ Joint Commission on Accreditation of Healthcare Organizations (JCAHO) accreditation + American Osteopathic Healthcare Association (AOHA) membership ○ American Osteopathic Association (AOA) accreditation △ Commission on Accreditation of Rehabilitation Facilities (CARF) accreditation Control codes 61, 63, 64, 71, 72 and 73 indicate hospitals listed by AOHA, but not registered by AHA. For definition of numerical codes, see page A4	Control	Service	Staffed Beds	Admissions	Census	Outpatient Visits	Births	Total	Payroll	Personnel

ANDERSON—Madison County

COMMUNITY HOSPITAL OF ANDERSON AND MADISON COUNTY See Community Hospitals Indianapolis, Indianapolis

✠ SAINT JOHN'S HEALTH SYSTEM, 2015 Jackson Street, Zip 46016–4339; tel. 765/649–2511; Jerry D. Brumitt, President and Chief Executive Officer (Total facility includes 27 beds in nursing home–type unit) **A**1 2 9 10 **F**2 3 7 8 10 12 14 15 16 17 18 19 20 21 22 23 25 26 27 28 29 30 31 32 33 34 35 37 39 40 41 42 44 45 48 49 52 53 54 55 56 57 58 59 60 63 64 65 66 67 68 71 72 73 74 **P**7 8 **S** Holy Cross Health System Corporation, South Bend, IN **N** Sagamore Health Network, Inc., Carmel, IN; Holy Cross Health System, South Bend, IN ... 21 10 261 8079 130 298768 566 91978 37335 1268

ANGOLA—Steuben County

★ CAMERON MEMORIAL COMMUNITY HOSPITAL, 416 East Maumee Street, Zip 46703–2015; tel. 219/665–2141; Dennis L. Knapp, President (Nonreporting) **A**9 10 **N** LutheranPreferred Network, Fort Wayne, IN; Midwest Health Net, LLC., Fort Wayne, IN; Sagamore Health Network, Inc., Carmel, IN ... 23 10 30 — — — — — — —

AUBURN—De Kalb County

✠ DEKALB MEMORIAL HOSPITAL, 1316 East Seventh Street, Zip 46706–2515, Mailing Address: P.O. Box 542, Zip 46706–0542; tel. 219/925–4600; Jack M. Corey, President **A**1 9 10 **F**7 8 11 12 14 15 16 17 19 21 22 24 26 28 29 30 32 33 34 35 37 39 40 41 42 44 45 46 49 51 63 65 66 67 71 72 73 **P**4 6 7 8 **N** LutheranPreferred Network, Fort Wayne, IN; Midwest Health Net, LLC., Fort Wayne, IN ... 23 10 47 1940 17 45057 415 22274 11191 322

BATESVILLE—Franklin County

✠ MARGARET MARY COMMUNITY HOSPITAL, 321 Mitchell Avenue, Zip 47006–8953, Mailing Address: P.O. Box 226, Zip 47006–0226; tel. 812/934–6624; James L. Amos, President (Total facility includes 35 beds in nursing home–type unit) **A**1 9 10 **F**7 8 14 15 19 20 21 22 26 28 30 32 33 34 35 36 37 39 40 44 49 63 64 65 66 67 71 73 ... 23 10 94 1999 49 90459 373 18427 8791 264

BEDFORD—Lawrence County

✠ BEDFORD REGIONAL MEDICAL CENTER, 2900 West 16th Street, Zip 47421–3583; tel. 812/275–1200; John R. Birdzell, FACHE, Chief Executive Officer **A**1 2 9 10 **F**7 8 14 15 16 17 19 20 21 22 27 28 30 32 33 34 35 37 39 40 41 42 44 45 46 49 51 63 65 67 71 72 73 **P**4 6 7 **N** Midwest Health Net, LLC., Fort Wayne, IN ... 23 10 60 2771 25 168377 349 30410 13776 408

✠ DUNN MEMORIAL HOSPITAL, 1600 23rd Street, Zip 47421–4704; tel. 812/275–3331; William W. Wissman, Interim Executive Director **A**1 9 10 **F**1 7 8 10 11 14 17 19 21 22 23 27 28 29 30 31 32 33 34 37 39 40 41 42 44 45 46 49 51 65 71 72 73 74 **N** Sagamore Health Network, Inc., Carmel, IN ... 13 10 104 2825 28 52852 277 26182 12970 436

BEECH GROVE—Marion County

✠ ST. FRANCIS HOSPITAL AND HEALTH CENTERS, 1600 Albany Street, Zip 46107–1593; tel. 317/787–3311; Robert J. Brody, President and Chief Executive Officer **A**1 2 3 5 9 10 **F**3 4 7 8 10 11 12 14 15 16 17 18 19 21 22 26 28 29 30 32 33 34 35 37 38 39 40 41 42 43 44 46 48 49 52 53 54 55 56 57 58 59 60 63 64 65 66 67 68 71 72 73 74 **P**3 7 8 **S** Sisters of St. Francis Health Services, Inc., Mishawaka, IN **N** Sagamore Health Network, Inc., Carmel, IN ... 21 10 417 18394 251 619339 2378 193287 91223 2915

BLOOMINGTON—Monroe County

✠ BLOOMINGTON HOSPITAL, 601 West Second Street, Zip 47403–2317, Mailing Address: Box 1149, Zip 47402–1149; tel. 812/336–6821; Nancy S. Carlstedt, President (Total facility includes 594 beds in nursing home–type unit) **A**1 9 10 **F**1 3 4 6 7 8 10 11 12 14 15 16 17 18 19 21 22 23 25 26 27 28 29 30 31 32 33 34 35 36 37 39 40 41 42 43 44 45 46 49 52 53 54 55 56 57 58 59 60 64 65 66 67 70 71 73 74 **P**8 ... 23 10 837 14842 610 416404 1814 142168 66408 1939

BLUFFTON—Wells County

✠ CAYLOR–NICKEL MEDICAL CENTER, One Caylor–Nickel Square, Zip 46714–2529; tel. 219/824–3500; William F. Brockmann, President and Chief Executive Officer (Total facility includes 19 beds in nursing home–type unit) **A**1 2 9 10 **F**3 5 7 8 10 11 12 14 15 16 17 19 20 21 22 24 25 26 30 32 33 34 35 37 39 40 41 42 44 45 46 49 51 52 53 54 56 57 58 60 64 65 67 71 73 **P**8 **N** LutheranPreferred Network, Fort Wayne, IN; Caylor–Nickel Health Network, Bluffton, IN; Midwest Health Net, LLC., Fort Wayne, IN ... 23 10 99 3294 41 79851 301 27648 11821 465

✠ WELLS COMMUNITY HOSPITAL, 1100 South Main Street, Zip 46714–3697; tel. 219/824–3210; Dianne Surfus, Interim Chief Executive Officer **A**1 9 10 **F**7 8 10 14 15 16 19 22 24 26 28 29 30 32 33 35 37 39 40 44 45 46 49 51 56 61 65 67 71 73 74 **N** LutheranPreferred Network, Fort Wayne, IN; Midwest Health Net, LLC., Fort Wayne, IN; Sagamore Health Network, Inc., Carmel, IN ... 13 10 22 1241 10 31833 216 10900 5542 185

BOONVILLE—Warrick County

✠ ST. MARY'S HOSPITAL WARRICK, 1116 Millis Avenue, Zip 47601–0629, Mailing Address: Box 629, Zip 47601–0629; tel. 812/897–4800; John D. O'Neil, Executive Vice President and Administrator **A**1 9 10 **F**8 14 15 16 17 19 20 22 28 31 32 37 41 44 48 49 65 71 73 **S** Daughters of Charity National Health System, Saint Louis, MO **N** Sagamore Health Network, Inc., Carmel, IN ... 23 10 30 1069 13 19076 — 10249 5452 198

Hospital, Address, Telephone, Administrator, Approval, Facility, and Physician Codes, Health Care System, Network	Control	Service	Staffed Beds	Admissions	Census	Outpatient Visits	Births	Total	Payroll	Personnel

★ American Hospital Association (AHA) membership
☐ Joint Commission on Accreditation of Healthcare Organizations (JCAHO) accreditation
+ American Osteopathic Healthcare Association (AOHA) membership
○ American Osteopathic Association (AOA) accreditation
△ Commission on Accreditation of Rehabilitation Facilities (CARF) accreditation
Control codes 61, 63, 64, 71, 72 and 73 indicate hospitals listed by AOHA, but not registered by AHA. For definition of numerical codes, see page A4

BRAZIL—Clay County

✠ CLAY COUNTY HOSPITAL, 1206 East National Avenue, Zip 47834–2797; tel. 812/448–2675; Jay P. Jolly, Administrator and Chief Executive Officer **A**1 9 10 **F**7 8 19 20 21 22 30 34 35 37 40 42 44 45 51 64 65 71 73 **N** Sagamore Health Network, Inc., Carmel, IN — 13 10 58 1082 11 30191 70 — 3726 146

BREMEN—Marshall County

★ COMMUNITY HOSPITAL OF BREMEN, 411 South Whitlock Street, Zip 46506–1699; tel. 219/546–2211; Scott R. Graybill, Chief Executive Officer and Administrator **A**9 10 **F**8 12 15 17 19 22 26 27 32 33 34 41 44 45 49 51 53 54 55 56 57 58 59 65 66 71 73 **P**1 **S** Ancilla Systems Inc., Hobart, IN **N** Sagamore Health Network, Inc., Carmel, IN — 23 10 28 420 3 31752 86 5904 2376 99

CARMEL—Hamilton County

ST. VINCENT CARMEL HOSPITAL See St. Vincent Hospitals and Health Services, Indianapolis

CHARLESTOWN—Clark County

☐ MEDICAL CENTER OF SOUTHERN INDIANA, 2200 Market Street, Zip 47111–0069, Mailing Address: P.O. Box 69, Zip 47111–0069; tel. 812/256–3301; Kevin J. Miller, Chief Executive Officer **A**1 9 10 **F**8 14 15 16 19 20 22 26 28 30 32 34 35 37 41 42 44 46 48 49 51 52 55 57 58 59 63 64 65 66 71 73 **P**5 7 **N** Sagamore Health Network, Inc., Carmel, IN — 23 10 77 2086 43 17324 0 18223 8707 313

CLINTON—Vermillion County

☐ WEST CENTRAL COMMUNITY HOSPITAL, 801 South Main Street, Zip 47842–0349; tel. 765/832–2451; Marilyn J. Custer–Mitchell, Administrator **A**1 9 10 **F**7 8 11 14 15 19 21 22 24 25 28 30 34 39 40 42 44 46 49 65 67 71 73 **P**8 — 23 10 27 1395 16 33722 76 5768 4725 168

COLUMBIA CITY—Whitley County

☐ WHITLEY MEMORIAL HOSPITAL, 353 North Oak Street, Zip 46725–1623; tel. 219/244–6191; John M. Hatcher, President (Total facility includes 81 beds in nursing home–type unit) **A**1 9 10 **F**7 8 11 14 15 16 19 22 24 28 30 32 33 35 36 37 39 40 41 44 48 49 51 67 71 73 **P**8 **N** Parkview Health System, Fort Wayne, IN; Midwest Health Net, LLC., Fort Wayne, IN; Sagamore Health Network, Inc., Carmel, IN — 33 10 131 1763 93 35641 337 20011 8892 329

COLUMBUS—Bartholomew County

☐ BEHAVIORAL HEALTHCARE–COLUMBUS, (Formerly Koala Behavioral Health–Columbus Campus), 2223 Poshard Drive, Zip 47203–1844; tel. 812/376–1711; Darla Derks, Administrator (Nonreporting) **A**1 9 10 **S** Behavioral Healthcare Corporation, Nashville, TN — 33 22 60 — — — — — — —

✠ COLUMBUS REGIONAL HOSPITAL, 2400 East 17th Street, Zip 47201–5360; tel. 812/379–4441; Douglas J. Leonard, Chief Executive Officer (Total facility includes 21 beds in nursing home–type unit) **A**1 2 9 10 **F**14 15 16 19 21 22 23 28 29 30 32 33 35 36 37 39 40 41 42 44 45 46 48 52 54 55 56 58 59 60 63 64 65 66 67 70 71 72 73 **P**3 4 5 8 — 13 10 230 9929 124 116444 1278 95131 39794 1367

CONNERSVILLE—Fayette County

✠ FAYETTE MEMORIAL HOSPITAL, 1941 Virginia Avenue, Zip 47331–9990; tel. 765/825–5131; David Brandon, Chief Executive Officer (Nonreporting) **A**1 9 10 — 23 10 111 — — — — — — —

CORYDON—Harrison County

✠ HARRISON COUNTY HOSPITAL, 245 Atwood Street, Zip 47112–1774; tel. 812/738–4251; Steven L. Taylor, Chief Executive Officer **A**1 9 10 **F**7 8 11 14 15 17 19 21 22 30 32 34 35 40 41 42 44 45 46 49 63 65 66 67 71 **P**2 7 **S** Alliant Health System, Louisville, KY — 13 10 50 1359 15 32070 113 — 6156 256

CRAWFORDSVILLE—Montgomery County

✠ CULVER UNION HOSPITAL, 1710 Lafayette Road, Zip 47933–1099; tel. 765/362–2800; Gregory D. Starnes, Chief Executive Officer (Total facility includes 17 beds in nursing home–type unit) (Nonreporting) **A**1 9 10 **S** TENET Healthcare Corporation, Santa Barbara, CA — 33 10 98 — — — — — — —

CROWN POINT—Lake County

✠ ST. ANTHONY MEDICAL CENTER, 1201 South Main Street, Zip 46307–8483; tel. 219/738–2100; Stephen O. Leurck, President and Chief Executive Officer **A**1 2 6 9 10 **F**1 4 6 7 8 10 11 12 13 14 15 16 17 18 19 21 22 24 25 26 28 29 30 32 33 34 35 39 40 41 42 43 44 45 46 48 49 50 51 60 63 64 65 66 67 71 72 73 **P**6 7 8 **N** Sagamore Health Network, Inc., Carmel, IN — 21 10 248 8274 108 78503 965 87158 36740 782

DANVILLE—Hendricks County

✠ HENDRICKS COMMUNITY HOSPITAL, 1000 East Main Street, Zip 46122–0409, Mailing Address: P.O. Box 409, Zip 46122–0409; tel. 317/745–4451; Dennis W. Dawes, President **A**1 9 10 **F**2 7 8 12 14 15 16 19 20 21 22 24 28 29 30 31 32 34 35 36 37 39 40 41 42 44 45 49 51 52 54 55 56 57 60 65 66 67 71 72 73 74 **P**1 6 7 **N** Sagamore Health Network, Inc., Carmel, IN; Suburban Health Organization, Indianapolis, IN — 13 10 127 5488 61 176446 918 47537 21826 630

DECATUR—Adams County

★ ADAMS COUNTY MEMORIAL HOSPITAL, 805 High Street, Zip 46733–2311, Mailing Address: P.O. Box 151, Zip 46733–0151; tel. 219/724–2145; Marvin L. Baird, Executive Director (Total facility includes 22 beds in nursing home–type unit) **A**9 10 **F**1 11 14 16 19 21 22 26 27 28 30 32 35 40 41 42 44 49 52 53 54 55 56 57 58 59 64 65 66 71 72 73 74 **N** LutheranPreferred Network, Fort Wayne, IN; Sagamore Health Network, Inc., Carmel, IN — 13 10 87 2332 41 52677 223 19521 7524 333

Hospital, Address, Telephone, Administrator, Approval, Facility, and Physician Codes, Health Care System, Network	Classi- fication Codes		Utilization Data					Expense (thousands) of dollars		
★ American Hospital Association (AHA) membership □ Joint Commission on Accreditation of Healthcare Organizations (JCAHO) accreditation + American Osteopathic Healthcare Association (AOHA) membership ○ American Osteopathic Association (AOA) accreditation △ Commission on Accreditation of Rehabilitation Facilities (CARF) accreditation Control codes 61, 63, 64, 71, 72 and 73 indicate hospitals listed by AOHA, but not registered by AHA. For definition of numerical codes, see page A4	Control	Service	Staffed Beds	Admissions	Census	Outpatient Visits	Births	Total	Payroll	Personnel

DYER—Lake County

SAINT MARGARET MERCY HEALTHCARE CENTERS–SOUTH CAMPUS See Saint Margaret Mercy Healthcare Centers, Hammond

EAST CHICAGO—Lake County

✚ ST. CATHERINE HOSPITAL, 4321 Fir Street, Zip 46312–3097; tel. 219/392–7000; JoAnn Birdzell, President and Chief Executive Officer **A**1 9 10 **F**4 7 8 10 12 14 15 16 17 19 21 22 23 24 25 28 29 30 31 32 33 34 35 39 40 41 42 43 44 45 46 49 50 52 54 55 56 63 64 65 71 73 74 **P**8 **S** Ancilla Systems Inc., Hobart, IN **N** Ancilla Systems, Inc., Hobart, IN; Midwest Health Net, LLC., Fort Wayne, IN; Sagamore Health Network, Inc., Carmel, IN	21	10	190	7810	122	45375	560	65850	25052	689

ELKHART—Elkhart County

✚ △ ELKHART GENERAL HOSPITAL, 600 East Boulevard, Zip 46514–2499, Mailing Address: P.O. Box 1329, Zip 46515–1329; tel. 219/294–2621; Gregory W. Lintjer, President (Total facility includes 42 beds in nursing home–type unit) **A**1 7 9 10 **F**3 4 7 8 10 11 12 15 16 17 19 21 22 23 29 30 31 32 35 37 38 39 40 41 42 43 44 48 49 52 53 54 55 56 58 59 60 64 65 67 71 73 **P**5 8 **N** Community Health Alliance, South Bend, IN	23	10	322	12175	165	104811	1700	104439	43776	1369

ELWOOD—Madison County

✚ ST. VINCENT MERCY HOSPITAL, 1331 South A. Street, Zip 46036–1942; tel. 765/552–4600; Ann C. Parsons, Interim Administrator (Nonreporting) **A**1 9 10 **S** Daughters of Charity National Health System, Saint Louis, MO **N** Sagamore Health Network, Inc., Carmel, IN; Saint Vincent Hospitals and Health Services, Inc., Indianapolis, IN	21	10	40	—	—	—	—	—	—	—

EVANSVILLE—Vanderburgh County

✚ DEACONESS HOSPITAL, 600 Mary Street, Zip 47747–0001; tel. 812/426–3000; Thomas H. Kramer, President **A**1 2 3 5 9 10 **F**4 7 8 10 11 12 14 15 16 17 19 21 22 23 24 26 27 28 29 30 31 32 33 34 35 36 37 39 40 41 42 43 44 46 47 49 51 54 56 60 61 62 63 64 65 67 70 71 73 74 **P**1 6 7 8	23	10	333	16291	238	143946	1314	141233	63157	1870
□ EVANSVILLE STATE HOSPITAL, 3400 Lincoln Avenue, Zip 47714–0146; tel. 812/473–2100; Ralph Nichols, Superintendent **A**1 **F**14 20 49 52 57 64 65 73	12	22	292	102	256	—	—	26586	12117	523
□ △ HEALTHSOUTH TRI–STATE REHABILITATION HOSPITAL, 4100 Covert Avenue, Zip 47714–5567, Mailing Address: P.O. Box 5349, Zip 47716–5349; tel. 812/476–9983; Gerald F. Vozel, Administrator and Chief Executive Officer **A**1 7 9 10 **F**12 15 16 34 48 49 65 67 73 **S** HEALTHSOUTH Corporation, Birmingham, AL	23	10	80	906	54	6706	0	6799	6007	182
✚ ST. MARY'S MEDICAL CENTER OF EVANSVILLE, 3700 Washington Avenue, Zip 47750; tel. 812/485–4000; Richard C. Breon, President and Chief Executive Officer (Total facility includes 128 beds in nursing home–type unit) **A**1 2 3 5 9 10 **F**3 4 6 7 8 10 11 12 14 15 16 17 19 21 22 23 24 25 26 28 30 32 33 34 35 37 38 40 41 42 43 44 47 49 51 52 54 55 56 57 58 59 60 61 64 65 66 67 68 71 72 73 74 **P**6 7 **S** Daughters of Charity National Health System, Saint Louis, MO **N** Ancilla Systems, Inc., Hobart, IN; Sagamore Health Network, Inc., Carmel, IN	21	10	488	13733	311	214969	1965	122587	55116	1918
✚ △ WELBORN MEMORIAL BAPTIST HOSPITAL, 401 Southeast Sixth Street, Zip 47713–1299; tel. 812/426–8000; Marjorie Z. Soyugenc, President and Chief Executive Officer (Total facility includes 19 beds in nursing home–type unit) **A**1 2 7 9 10 **F**2 3 4 7 8 10 11 12 14 15 16 19 21 22 23 24 26 28 29 30 31 32 33 35 36 37 38 39 40 41 42 43 44 45 46 48 49 51 52 53 54 55 56 58 59 60 61 63 64 65 67 69 71 73 **P**5 6	23	10	274	9978	145	49377	773	86397	42625	1283

FORT WAYNE—Allen County

□ CHARTER BEACON, 1720 Beacon Street, Zip 46805–4700; tel. 219/423–3651; Robert Hails, Chief Executive Officer (Nonreporting) **A**1 10 **S** Magellan Health Services, Atlanta, GA	33	22	97	—	—	—	—	—	—	—
✚ LUTHERAN HOSPITAL OF INDIANA, 7950 West Jefferson Boulevard, Zip 46804–1677; tel. 219/435–7001; Thomas D. Miller, Chief Executive Officer **A**1 3 5 9 10 **F**2 3 4 7 8 10 11 12 14 15 16 17 19 21 22 23 25 26 27 28 29 30 31 34 35 36 37 38 39 40 41 42 43 44 46 47 48 49 52 54 56 57 58 59 60 64 65 67 69 71 72 73 74 **P**7 **S** Quorum Health Group/Quorum Health Resources, Inc., Brentwood, TN **N** LutheranPreferred Network, Fort Wayne, IN; Community Health Alliance, South Bend, IN	33	10	341	15357	211	153923	1759	—	—	—
✚ △ PARKVIEW HOSPITAL, (Formerly Parkview Memorial Hospital), 2200 Randallia Drive, Zip 46805–4699; tel. 219/484–6636; Frank D. Byrne, M.D., President (Total facility includes 28 beds in nursing home–type unit) **A**1 3 5 7 9 10 **F**1 2 4 7 8 10 11 12 14 15 16 17 19 21 22 24 25 27 28 30 32 33 34 36 37 38 39 40 41 42 43 44 45 46 47 48 49 51 52 53 54 55 56 57 58 59 60 64 65 67 68 71 72 73 74 **P**6 7 8 **N** Parkview Health System, Fort Wayne, IN; Midwest Health Net, LLC., Fort Wayne, IN; Sagamore Health Network, Inc., Carmel, IN	23	10	509	23607	319	140006	4062	—	106228	2782
✚ △ ST. JOSEPH MEDICAL CENTER OF FORT WAYNE, 700 Broadway, Zip 46802–1493; tel. 219/425–3000; John T. Farrell, Sr., President and Chief Executive Officer **A**1 3 5 7 9 10 **F**4 7 8 9 10 11 12 13 14 15 16 17 19 20 21 22 24 26 27 28 30 31 32 34 35 36 37 39 40 41 43 44 46 48 49 64 65 71 72 73 **P**3 6 7 8 **S** Ancilla Systems Inc., Hobart, IN **N** Ancilla Systems, Inc., Hobart, IN; Midwest Health Net, LLC., Fort Wayne, IN; Sagamore Health Network, Inc., Carmel, IN	21	10	175	6505	97	119409	611	67952	25176	748
✚ VETERANS AFFAIRS NORTHERN INDIANA HEALTH CARE SYSTEM, (Includes Veterans Affairs Northern Indiana Health Care System–Marion Campus, 1700 East 38th Street, Marion, Zip 46953–4589; tel. 765/674–3321), 2121 Lake Avenue, Zip 46805–5347; tel. 219/460–1310; Michael W. Murphy, Ph.D., Director (Total facility includes 122 beds in nursing home–type unit) (Nonreporting) **A**1 **S** Department of Veterans Affairs, Washington, DC	45	10	731	—	—	—	—	—	—	—

Hospital, Address, Telephone, Administrator, Approval, Facility, and Physician Codes, Health Care System, Network	Classi-fication Codes		Utilization Data					Expense (thousands) of dollars		
★ American Hospital Association (AHA) membership □ Joint Commission on Accreditation of Healthcare Organizations (JCAHO) accreditation + American Osteopathic Healthcare Association (AOHA) membership ○ American Osteopathic Association (AOA) accreditation △ Commission on Accreditation of Rehabilitation Facilities (CARF) accreditation Control codes 61, 63, 64, 71, 72 and 73 indicate hospitals listed by AOHA, but not registered by AHA. For definition of numerical codes, see page A4	Control	Service	Staffed Beds	Admissions	Census	Outpatient Visits	Births	Total	Payroll	Personnel

FRANKFORT—Clinton County

⊞ CLINTON COUNTY HOSPITAL, 1300 South Jackson Street, Zip 46041–3394, Mailing Address: P.O. Box 669, Zip 46041–0669; tel. 765/659–4731; Brian R. Zeh, Executive Director **A**1 9 10 **F**7 8 14 19 20 21 22 24 26 27 28 29 30 31 32 34 35 37 39 40 41 42 44 45 46 49 54 63 65 66 71 73 74 **P**1 6 **S** Quorum Health Group/Quorum Health Resources, Inc., Brentwood, TN **N** Midwest Health Net, LLC., Fort Wayne, IN; Sagamore Health Network, Inc., Carmel, IN; Suburban Health Organization, Indianapolis, IN

| | 33 | 10 | 53 | 1475 | 14 | 43357 | 339 | 14830 | 6624 | 205 |

FRANKLIN—Johnson County

★ JOHNSON MEMORIAL HOSPITAL, 1125 West Jefferson Street, Zip 46131–2140, Mailing Address: P.O. Box 549, Zip 46131–0549; tel. 317/736–3300; Gregg A. Bechtold, President and Chief Executive Officer (Total facility includes 87 beds in nursing home–type unit) (Nonreporting) **A**9 10 **N** Midwest Health Net, LLC., Fort Wayne, IN; Sagamore Health Network, Inc., Carmel, IN; Suburban Health Organization, Indianapolis, IN

| | 13 | 10 | 160 | — | — | — | — | — | — | — |

GARY—Lake County

⊞ △ METHODIST HOSPITALS, (Includes Northlake Campus, ; Southlake Campus, 8701 Broadway, Merrillville, Zip 46410; tel. 219/738–5500), 600 Grant Street, Zip 46402–6099; tel. 219/886–4000; John H. Betjemann, President **A**1 2 3 5 7 9 10 **F**1 2 3 4 5 7 8 10 14 15 16 19 21 22 23 26 28 29 30 34 35 37 38 39 40 41 42 43 44 46 48 49 51 52 53 54 56 57 58 60 63 64 65 67 71 72 73 74 **P**5

| | 23 | 10 | 601 | 22833 | 366 | 241346 | 2273 | 205803 | 91526 | 2533 |

GOSHEN—Elkhart County

⊞ GOSHEN GENERAL HOSPITAL, 200 High Park Avenue, Zip 46526–4899, Mailing Address: P.O. Box 139, Zip 46527–0139; tel. 219/533–2141; James O. Dague, President (Nonreporting) **A**1 9 10

| | 23 | 10 | 90 | — | — | — | — | — | — | — |

□ OAKLAWN PSYCHIATRIC CENTER, INC., 330 Lakeview Drive, Zip 46526–9365, Mailing Address: P.O. Box 809, Zip 46527–0809; tel. 219/533–1234; Harold C. Loewen, President (Nonreporting) **A**1 9 10 **N** Sagamore Health Network, Inc., Carmel, IN

| | 23 | 22 | 40 | — | — | — | — | — | — | — |

GREENCASTLE—Putnam County

⊞ PUTNAM COUNTY HOSPITAL, 1542 Bloomington Street, Zip 46135–2297; tel. 765/653–5121; John D. Fajt, Executive Director **A**1 2 9 10 **F**7 8 14 15 16 17 19 20 21 22 26 28 30 32 35 37 39 40 41 42 44 46 49 56 63 65 67 71 **P**8 **N** Sagamore Health Network, Inc., Carmel, IN

| | 13 | 10 | 85 | 1871 | 25 | 45919 | 256 | 13496 | 6150 | 243 |

GREENFIELD—Hancock County

⊞ HANCOCK MEMORIAL HOSPITAL AND HEALTH SERVICES, 801 North State Street, Zip 46140–1270, Mailing Address: P.O. Box 827, Zip 46140–0827; tel. 317/462–5544; Robert C. Keen, Ph.D., CHE, President and Chief Executive Officer (Total facility includes 21 beds in nursing home–type unit) **A**1 9 10 **F**1 3 7 8 10 12 14 15 16 17 19 21 22 24 26 28 30 31 32 33 34 35 36 39 40 41 42 44 45 46 49 52 57 60 61 64 65 66 67 68 71 72 73 74 **P**1 7 **N** Midwest Health Net, LLC., Fort Wayne, IN; Sagamore Health Network, Inc., Carmel, IN; Suburban Health Organization, Indianapolis, IN

| | 13 | 10 | 102 | 3725 | 53 | 117482 | 553 | 39193 | 18314 | 548 |

GREENSBURG—Decatur County

⊞ DECATUR COUNTY MEMORIAL HOSPITAL, 720 North Lincoln Street, Zip 47240–1398; tel. 812/663–4331; Charles Duffy, President **A**1 9 10 **F**1 7 8 11 15 16 19 21 22 23 26 27 28 30 32 33 35 36 37 39 40 41 42 44 49 60 63 65 67 71 73 **S** Alliant Health System, Louisville, KY **N** Midwest Health Net, LLC., Fort Wayne, IN

| | 13 | 10 | 70 | 1889 | 32 | 64456 | 347 | 22438 | 7729 | 251 |

GREENWOOD—Johnson County

□ BHC VALLE VISTA HOSPITAL, 898 East Main Street, Zip 46143–1400; tel. 317/887–1348; Sheila Mishler, Chief Executive Officer (Nonreporting) **A**1 9 10 **S** Behavioral Healthcare Corporation, Nashville, TN

| | 33 | 22 | 96 | — | — | — | — | — | — | — |

HAMMOND—Lake County

⊞ SAINT MARGARET MERCY HEALTHCARE CENTERS, (Includes Saint Margaret Mercy Healthcare Centers–North Campus, 5454 Hohman Avenue, Zip 46320; tel. 219/932–2300; Saint Margaret Mercy Healthcare Centers–South Campus, 24 Joliet Street, Dyer, Zip 46311–1799; tel. 219/865–2141), 5454 Hohman Avenue, Zip 46320–1999; tel. 219/933–2074; Eugene C. Diamond, President and Chief Executive Officer (Total facility includes 67 beds in nursing home–type unit) **A**1 2 9 10 **F**1 2 3 4 7 8 10 11 12 13 14 15 16 17 18 19 21 22 24 25 27 28 29 30 32 34 35 36 37 38 39 40 41 42 43 44 45 46 47 48 49 51 52 53 54 55 56 57 58 59 60 64 65 66 67 68 71 73 74 **P**7 8 **S** Sisters of St. Francis Health Services, Inc., Mishawaka, IN **N** Sagamore Health Network, Inc., Carmel, IN

| | 21 | 10 | 624 | 20752 | 328 | 122577 | 1651 | 175453 | 75678 | 2283 |

HARTFORD CITY—Blackford County

⊞ BLACKFORD COUNTY HOSPITAL, 503 East Van Cleve Street, Zip 47348–1897; tel. 765/348–0300; David Masterson, Chief Executive Officer **A**1 9 10 **F**7 8 12 15 16 17 19 22 28 30 32 35 40 44 45 49 51 66 67 71 72 73 74 **S** Alliant Health System, Louisville, KY **N** LutheranPreferred Network, Fort Wayne, IN

| | 13 | 10 | 36 | 862 | 11 | 18667 | 54 | 6914 | 2841 | 123 |

HOBART—Lake County

□ CHARTER BEHAVIORAL HEALTH SYSTEM OF NORTHWEST INDIANA, 101 West 61st Avenue and State Road 51, Zip 46342–6489; tel. 219/947–4464; Michael J. Perry, Chief Executive Officer (Nonreporting) **A**1 9 10 **S** Magellan Health Services, Atlanta, GA

| | 33 | 22 | 60 | — | — | — | — | — | — | — |

⊞ ST. MARY MEDICAL CENTER, 1500 South Lake Park Avenue, Zip 46342–6699; tel. 219/942–0551; Milton Triana, President and Chief Executive Officer (Nonreporting) **A**1 9 10 **S** Ancilla Systems Inc., Hobart, IN **N** Midwest Health Net, LLC., Fort Wayne, IN; Sagamore Health Network, Inc., Carmel, IN

| | 21 | 10 | 102 | — | — | — | — | — | — | — |

Hospital, Address, Telephone, Administrator, Approval, Facility, and Physician Codes, Health Care System, Network	Classi-fication Codes		Utilization Data					Expense (thousands) of dollars		
★ American Hospital Association (AHA) membership ☐ Joint Commission on Accreditation of Healthcare Organizations (JCAHO) accreditation + American Osteopathic Healthcare Association (AOHA) membership ○ American Osteopathic Association (AOA) accreditation △ Commission on Accreditation of Rehabilitation Facilities (CARF) accreditation Control codes 61, 63, 64, 71, 72 and 73 indicate hospitals listed by AOHA, but not registered by AHA. For definition of numerical codes, see page A4	Control	Service	Staffed Beds	Admissions	Census	Outpatient Visits	Births	Total	Payroll	Personnel

HUNTINGBURG—Dubois County

☐ ST. JOSEPH'S HOSPITAL, 1900 Medical Arts Drive, Zip 47542–9521; tel. 812/683–2121; John T. Graves, President and Chief Executive Officer (Nonreporting) **A**1 10 — 23, 10, 76

	23	10	76	—	—	—	—	—	—	—

HUNTINGTON—Huntington County

✠ HUNTINGTON MEMORIAL HOSPITAL, 1215 Etna Avenue, Zip 46750–3696; tel. 219/356–3000; L. Kent McCoy, President **A**1 9 10 **F**3 7 8 14 15 16 17 19 22 24 29 32 33 34 35 36 39 40 41 42 44 48 49 51 71 73 **P**4 **N** Parkview Health System, Fort Wayne, IN; LutheranPreferred Network, Fort Wayne, IN; Midwest Health Net, LLC., Fort Wayne, IN; Sagamore Health Network, Inc., Carmel, IN

	23	10	37	1121	14	40048	227	16258	988	291

INDIANAPOLIS—Marion County

☐ CHARTER INDIANAPOLIS BEHAVIORAL HEALTH SYSTEM, 5602 Caito Drive, Zip 46226–1356; tel. 317/545–2111; Marina Cecchini, Chief Executive Officer **A**1 9 10 **F**2 3 14 15 52 53 54 55 56 57 58 59 **P**8 **S** Magellan Health Services, Atlanta, GA

	33	22	80	1600	49	1556	—	—	—	84

✠ CLARIAN HEALTH PARTNERS, (Includes Indiana University Medical Center, 550 North University Boulevard, Zip 46202–5262; tel. 317/274–5000; Methodist Hospital of Indiana, 1701 North Senate Boulevard, Zip 46202, Mailing Address: I. 65 at 21st Street, P.O. Box 1367, Zip 46206–1367; tel. 317/929–2000; Riley Hospital for Childrern), 702 Barnhill Drive, Zip 46202–5250; tel. 317/274–5000; William J. Loveday, President and Chief Executive Officer (Total facility includes 45 beds in nursing home–type unit) **A**1 2 3 5 8 9 10 **F**2 3 4 5 7 8 9 10 11 12 13 14 15 16 17 18 19 20 21 22 23 25 26 28 29 30 31 32 33 34 35 36 37 38 39 40 41 42 43 44 45 46 47 48 49 50 51 52 53 54 55 56 57 58 59 60 61 63 64 65 66 67 68 69 70 71 72 73 74 **P**6 7

	23	10	1263	62372	951	917301	5025	737024	317235	8984

✠ COLUMBIA WOMEN'S HOSPITAL–INDIANAPOLIS, 8111 Township Line Road, Zip 46260–8043; tel. 317/875–5994; Steven B. Reed, President and Chief Executive Officer (Nonreporting) **A**1 9 10 **S** Columbia/HCA Healthcare Corporation, Nashville, TN

	33	10	132	—	—	—	—	—	—	—

☐ △ COMMUNITY HOSPITALS INDIANAPOLIS, (Includes Community Hospital East, 1500 North Ritter Avenue, tel. 317/355–1411; Community Hospital North, 7150 Clearvista Drive, Zip 46256; tel. 317/849–6262; Community Hospital South, 1402 East County Line Road South, Zip 46227; tel. 317/887–7000; Community Hospital of Anderson and Madison County, 1515 North Madison Avenue, Anderson, Zip 46011–3453; tel. 765/642–8011), 1500 North Ritter Avenue, Zip 46219–3095; tel. 317/355–1411; William E. Corley, President (Total facility includes 30 beds in nursing home–type unit) (Nonreporting) **A**1 2 3 5 7 9 10

	23	10	999	—	—	—	—	—	—	—

FAIRBANKS HOSPITAL, 8102 Clearvista Parkway, Zip 46256–4698; tel. 317/849–8222; Timothy J. Kelly, M.D., President (Nonreporting) **A**9 10 **N** Sagamore Health Network, Inc., Carmel, IN

	23	82	96	—	—	—	—	—	—	—

INDIANA UNIVERSITY MEDICAL CENTER See Clarian Health Partners

☐ LARUE D. CARTER MEMORIAL HOSPITAL, 2601 Cold Spring Road, Zip 46222–2273; tel. 317/941–4000; Diana Haugh, MS, Superintendent (Nonreporting) **A**1 3 5 10

	12	22	146	—	—	—	—	—	—	—

METHODIST HOSPITAL OF INDIANA See Clarian Health Partners

☐ △ REHABILITATION HOSPITAL OF INDIANA, 4141 Shore Drive, Zip 46254–2607; tel. 317/329–2000; Kim D. Eicher, President and Chief Executive Officer (Nonreporting) **A**1 7 9 10 **N** Sagamore Health Network, Inc., Carmel, IN; Methodist Hospital of Indiana, Indianapolis, IN

	23	46	80	—	—	—	—	—	—	—

✠ RICHARD L. ROUDEBUSH VETERANS AFFAIRS MEDICAL CENTER, 1481 West Tenth Street, Zip 46202–2884; tel. 317/554–0000; Alice Wood, Director (Total facility includes 20 beds in nursing home–type unit) **A**1 2 3 5 8 **F**1 3 4 8 10 11 12 14 15 16 17 18 19 20 21 22 23 24 26 28 29 30 31 32 34 35 37 39 41 42 43 44 45 46 48 49 50 51 52 54 55 56 57 58 59 60 64 65 67 69 71 73 74 **P**6 **S** Department of Veterans Affairs, Washington, DC

	45	10	176	5697	120	300329	—	144924	65490	1565

RILEY HOSPITAL FOR CHILDRERN See Clarian Health Partners

✠ ST. VINCENT HOSPITALS AND HEALTH SERVICES, (Includes St. Vincent Carmel Hospital, 13500 North Meridian Street, Carmel, Zip 46032; tel. 317/582–7000; St. Vincent Stress Center, 8401 Harcourt Road, Zip 46260, Mailing Address: P.O. Box 80160, Zip 46280; tel. 317/338–4600; Paul Lefkovitz, Ph.D., Administrator), 2001 West 86th Street, Zip 46260–1991, Mailing Address: P.O. Box 40970, Zip 46240–0970; tel. 317/338–2345; Douglas D. French, President and Chief Executive Officer **A**1 2 3 5 9 10 **F**3 4 6 7 8 9 10 12 13 14 15 16 17 18 19 20 21 22 23 24 25 26 27 28 29 30 31 32 33 34 35 39 41 42 43 44 45 46 47 48 49 51 53 54 55 56 57 58 59 60 63 64 65 66 67 68 69 70 71 72 73 74 **P**6 7 8 **S** Daughters of Charity National Health System, Saint Louis, MO **N** Sagamore Health Network, Inc., Carmel, IN

	21	10	621	31849	466	894028	3695	407812	175316	4467

ST. VINCENT STRESS CENTER See St. Vincent Hospitals and Health Services

+ ○ WESTVIEW HOSPITAL, 3630 Guion Road, Zip 46222–1699; tel. 317/924–6661; David C. Dyar, President and Administrator (Total facility includes 18 beds in nursing home–type unit) (Nonreporting) **A**9 10 11 12 13 **N** Midwest Health Net, LLC., Fort Wayne, IN; Sagamore Health Network, Inc., Carmel, IN; Suburban Health Organization, Indianapolis, IN

	23	10	67	—	—	—	—	—	—	—

✠ WINONA MEMORIAL HOSPITAL, 3232 North Meridian Street, Zip 46208–4693; tel. 317/924–3392; Keith R. King, Chief Executive Officer (Total facility includes 28 beds in nursing home–type unit) (Nonreporting) **A**1 9 10 **S** TENET Healthcare Corporation, Santa Barbara, CA

	33	10	159	—	—	—	—	—	—	—

Hospital, Address, Telephone, Administrator, Approval, Facility, and Physician Codes, Health Care System, Network	Classi-fication Codes		Utilization Data					Expense (thousands) of dollars		
★ American Hospital Association (AHA) membership ☐ Joint Commission on Accreditation of Healthcare Organizations (JCAHO) accreditation + American Osteopathic Healthcare Association (AOHA) membership ○ American Osteopathic Association (AOA) accreditation △ Commission on Accreditation of Rehabilitation Facilities (CARF) accreditation Control codes 61, 63, 64, 71, 72 and 73 indicate hospitals listed by AOHA, but not registered by AHA. For definition of numerical codes, see page A4	Control	Service	Staffed Beds	Admissions	Census	Outpatient Visits	Births	Total	Payroll	Personnel

✠ WISHARD HEALTH SERVICES, 1001 West 10th Street, Zip 46202–2879; tel. 317/630–7356; John F. Williams, Jr., M.D., Director (Total facility includes 240 beds in nursing home–type unit) (Nonreporting) **A**1 3 5 8 9 10	16	10	531	—	—	—	—	—	—	—
JASPER—Dubois County										
✠ MEMORIAL HOSPITAL AND HEALTH CARE CENTER, 800 West Ninth Street, Zip 47546–2516; tel. 812/482–2345; Sister M. Adrian Davis, Ph.D., President and Chief Executive Officer (Total facility includes 24 beds in nursing home–type unit) **A**1 2 9 10 **F**7 8 10 14 15 16 18 19 21 22 26 28 29 30 32 33 34 35 37 39 40 41 42 44 45 49 52 53 54 55 56 57 58 63 64 65 66 67 71 73 **S** Little Company of Mary Sisters Healthcare System, Evergreen Park, IL	21	10	124	4674	70	93013	575	41578	20670	601
JEFFERSONVILLE—Clark County										
☐ CHARTER BEHAVIORAL HEALTH SYSTEM OF INDIANA AT JEFFERSON, 2700 River City Park Road, Zip 47130–5943; tel. 812/284–3400; James E. Ledbetter, Ph.D., Chief Executive Officer (Nonreporting) **A**1 9 10 **S** Magellan Health Services, Atlanta, GA	33	22	100	—	—	—	—	—	—	—
✠ CLARK MEMORIAL HOSPITAL, 1220 Missouri Avenue, Zip 47130–3743, Mailing Address: Box 69, Zip 47131–0069; tel. 812/282–6631; Merle E. Stepp, President and Chief Executive Officer (Total facility includes 66 beds in nursing home–type unit) **A**1 9 10 **F**3 7 8 10 11 14 15 16 17 19 21 22 23 28 29 30 31 32 33 34 35 39 40 41 42 44 45 46 49 51 52 53 54 55 56 57 59 60 63 64 65 71 73 74 **S** Jewish Hospital HealthCare Services, Louisville, KY **N** Jewish Hospital Healthcare Services, Louisville, KY	13	10	244	9731	173	103595	1217	71691	33804	1224
KENDALLVILLE—Noble County										
✠ MCCRAY MEMORIAL HOSPITAL, 951 East Hospital Drive, Zip 46755–2293, Mailing Address: P.O. Box 249, Zip 46755–0249; tel. 219/347–1100; John Berhow, President **A**1 9 10 **F**3 7 8 15 16 17 19 20 21 22 25 27 28 30 32 33 34 35 37 40 41 42 44 46 49 52 54 55 56 57 58 63 65 71 73 **P**5 **S** Continuum, Kendallville, IN **N** LutheranPreferred Network, Fort Wayne, IN; Midwest Health Net, LLC., Fort Wayne, IN; Sagamore Health Network, Inc., Carmel, IN	15	10	43	1581	22	76303	209	19114	6222	166
KNOX—Starke County										
✠ STARKE MEMORIAL HOSPITAL, 102 East Culver Road, Zip 46534–2299; tel. 219/772–6231; Kathryn J. Norem, Executive Director (Nonreporting) **A**1 9 10 **S** Province Healthcare Corporation, Brentwood, TN **N** Sagamore Health Network, Inc., Carmel, IN	13	10	35	—	—	—	—	—	—	—
KOKOMO—Howard County										
✠ HOWARD COMMUNITY HOSPITAL, 3500 South La Fountain Street, Zip 46904–9011; tel. 765/453–0702; James C. Bigogno, FACHE, President and Chief Executive Officer (Total facility includes 18 beds in nursing home–type unit) **A**1 2 9 10 **F**3 7 8 10 12 13 14 15 16 19 21 22 23 24 26 29 30 32 34 35 37 39 40 42 44 45 46 49 53 54 55 56 57 58 59 60 61 65 67 68 71 73 74 **P**2 8 **N** Midwest Health Net, LLC., Fort Wayne, IN	13	10	115	5166	71	85979	361	47305	22499	789
☐ △ KOKOMO REHABILITATION HOSPITAL, 829 North Dixon Road, Zip 46901–7709; tel. 765/452–6700; David Bailey, Chief Executive Officer (Nonreporting) **A**1 7 9 10 **S** HEALTHSOUTH Corporation, Birmingham, AL	33	46	60	—	—	—	—	—	—	—
✠ SAINT JOSEPH HOSPITAL & HEALTH CENTER, 1907 West Sycamore Street, Zip 46904–9010, Mailing Address: P.O. Box 9010, Zip 46904–9010; tel. 765/452–5611; Kathleen M. Korbelak, President and Chief Executive Officer **A**1 9 10 **F**2 3 7 8 10 12 14 15 16 17 19 21 22 23 25 26 27 28 30 31 32 33 34 35 36 37 39 40 41 42 43 44 46 49 52 53 54 55 56 58 59 60 63 64 65 66 67 68 69 71 72 73 74 **P**8 **S** Daughters of Charity National Health System, Saint Louis, MO **N** Saint Vincent Hospitals and Health Services, Inc., Indianapolis, IN	21	10	157	6389	86	295219	1149	54230	23667	804
LA PORTE—La Porte County										
✠ LA PORTE HOSPITAL AND HEALTH SERVICES, 1007 Lincolnway, Zip 46352–0250, Mailing Address: P.O. Box 250, Zip 46350–0250; tel. 219/326–1234; Leigh E. Morris, President (Total facility includes 55 beds in nursing home–type unit) **A**1 2 9 10 **F**3 6 7 8 10 11 12 14 15 16 17 18 19 20 21 22 23 24 25 28 29 30 31 32 33 34 35 36 37 39 40 41 42 44 49 51 52 53 54 55 56 57 58 61 63 64 65 66 67 71 72 73 **P**7 **N** Sagamore Health Network, Inc., Carmel, IN; Community Health Alliance, South Bend, IN	23	10	227	6034	114	64125	716	57009	25386	806
LAFAYETTE—Tippecanoe County										
☐ CHARTER BEHAVIORAL HEALTH SYSTEMS, 3700 Rome Drive, Zip 47905–4465, Mailing Address: P.O. Box 5969, Zip 47903–5969; tel. 765/448–6999; Mark Dooley, Chief Executive Officer (Nonreporting) **A**1 9 10 **S** Magellan Health Services, Atlanta, GA	33	22	64	—	—	—	—	—	—	—
✠ △ LAFAYETTE HOME HOSPITAL, 2400 South Street, Zip 47904–3052, Mailing Address: P.O. Box 7518, Zip 47903–7518; tel. 765/447–6811; John R. Walling, President and Chief Executive Officer **A**1 7 9 10 **F**5 6 7 8 10 12 14 15 16 17 19 20 21 22 23 24 26 28 30 31 32 33 34 35 36 37 38 39 40 41 44 45 46 48 49 51 52 53 54 55 56 57 58 60 61 62 63 65 66 67 69 71 72 73 74 **P**6	23	10	280	9903	140	88346	2369	80415	35270	1159
✠ ST. ELIZABETH MEDICAL CENTER, 1501 Hartford Street, Zip 47904–2126, Mailing Address: Box 7501, Zip 47903–7501; tel. 765/423–6011; Douglas W. Eberle, President and Chief Executive Officer (Total facility includes 43 beds in nursing home–type unit) **A**1 2 6 9 10 **F**4 7 8 10 11 14 15 16 17 19 21 22 23 25 26 28 30 31 32 33 34 35 37 39 40 41 42 43 44 45 49 56 60 63 64 65 66 67 71 72 73 74 **S** Sisters of St. Francis Health Services, Inc., Mishawaka, IN	21	10	205	6752	111	140698	423	78434	32478	1012

Hospital, Address, Telephone, Administrator, Approval, Facility, and Physician Codes, Health Care System, Network	Classification Codes		Utilization Data					Expense (thousands) of dollars		
★ American Hospital Association (AHA) membership ☐ Joint Commission on Accreditation of Healthcare Organizations (JCAHO) accreditation + American Osteopathic Healthcare Association (AOHA) membership ○ American Osteopathic Association (AOA) accreditation △ Commission on Accreditation of Rehabilitation Facilities (CARF) accreditation Control codes 61, 63, 64, 71, 72 and 73 indicate hospitals listed by AOHA, but not registered by AHA. For definition of numerical codes, see page A4	Control	Service	Staffed Beds	Admissions	Census	Outpatient Visits	Births	Total	Payroll	Personnel

LAGRANGE—LaGrange County

☐ VENCOR HOSPITAL–LAGRANGE, 207 North Townline Road, Zip 46761–1325; tel. 219/463–2143; Joe Murrell, Administrator (Nonreporting) **A**1 9 10 **S** Vencor, Incorporated, Louisville, KY — 33 10 57 — — — — — — —

LAGRANGE—LaGrange County										
☐ VENCOR HOSPITAL–LAGRANGE	33	10	57	—	—	—	—	—	—	—
LAWRENCEBURG—Dearborn County										
⊞ DEARBORN COUNTY HOSPITAL	13	10	87	2976	30	100011	399	31067	13291	443
LEBANON—Boone County										
☐ WITHAM MEMORIAL HOSPITAL	13	10	60	—	—	—	—	—	—	—
LINTON—Greene County										
⊞ GREENE COUNTY GENERAL HOSPITAL	13	10	56	1380	17	—	65	13033	4980	230
LOGANSPORT—Cass County										
☐ LOGANSPORT STATE HOSPITAL	12	22	396	208	375	0	0	—	18451	764
⊞ MEMORIAL HOSPITAL	13	10	104	2863	29	47296	544	25482	11458	403
MADISON—Jefferson County										
⊞ KING'S DAUGHTERS' HOSPITAL	23	10	115	4915	72	52038	420	43347	20930	714
☐ MADISON STATE HOSPITAL	12	22	332	241	303	0	—	22524	13111	526
MARION—Grant County										
⊞ MARION GENERAL HOSPITAL	23	10	212	8419	107	212619	779	68428	32405	1104
MARTINSVILLE—Morgan County										
★ MORGAN COUNTY MEMORIAL HOSPITAL	13	10	86	2202	29	79751	254	21558	9153	280
MICHIGAN CITY—La Porte County										
⊞ MEMORIAL HOSPITAL OF MICHIGAN CITY	23	10	120	—	—	—	—	—	—	—
⊞ △ SAINT ANTHONY MEMORIAL HEALTH CENTERS	21	10	162	7391	105	188491	616	55614	22342	935
MISHAWAKA—St. Joseph County										
⊞ + ○ △ ST. JOSEPH COMMUNITY HOSPITAL	21	10	100	4235	—	67304	1135	—	20612	—
MONTICELLO—White County										
☐ WHITE COUNTY MEMORIAL HOSPITAL	13	10	59	1488	13	42327	128	12160	5085	185

LAGRANGE—LaGrange County

☐ VENCOR HOSPITAL–LAGRANGE, 207 North Townline Road, Zip 46761–1325; tel. 219/463–2143; Joe Murrell, Administrator (Nonreporting) **A**1 9 10 **S** Vencor, Incorporated, Louisville, KY

LAWRENCEBURG—Dearborn County

⊞ DEARBORN COUNTY HOSPITAL, 600 Wilson Creek Road, Zip 47025–1199; tel. 812/537–1010; Peter V. Resnick, Executive Director (Total facility includes 13 beds in nursing home–type unit) **A**1 9 10 **F**7 8 10 15 16 19 21 22 23 28 30 32 33 35 37 40 41 42 44 49 60 63 64 65 66 67 71 73 **P**3

LEBANON—Boone County

☐ WITHAM MEMORIAL HOSPITAL, 1124 North Lebanon Street, Zip 46052–1776, Mailing Address: P.O. Box 1200, Zip 46052–3005; tel. 765/482–2700; Ray Ingham, President and Chief Executive Officer (Nonreporting) **A**1 9 10 **N** Midwest Health Net, LLC., Fort Wayne, IN; Sagamore Health Network, Inc., Carmel, IN; Suburban Health Organization, Indianapolis, IN

LINTON—Greene County

⊞ GREENE COUNTY GENERAL HOSPITAL, Rural Route 1, Box 1000, Zip 47441–9457; tel. 812/847–2281; Jonas S. Uland, Executive Director **A**1 9 10 **F**8 14 15 16 19 20 22 28 29 30 32 34 37 40 42 44 49 54 56 71 73 **N** Midwest Health Net, LLC., Fort Wayne, IN; Sagamore Health Network, Inc., Carmel, IN

LOGANSPORT—Cass County

☐ LOGANSPORT STATE HOSPITAL, 1098 South State Road 25, Zip 46947–9699; tel. 219/722–4141; Jeffrey H. Smith, Ph.D., Superintendent **A**1 **F**20 26 45 52 65 73

⊞ MEMORIAL HOSPITAL, 1101 Michigan Avenue, Zip 46947–7013, Mailing Address: P.O. Box 7013, Zip 46947–7013; tel. 219/753–7541; George W. Poor, President and Chief Executive Officer **A**1 9 10 **F**7 8 14 15 16 19 21 22 23 28 30 32 33 35 36 37 39 40 42 44 46 49 63 65 67 71 73 **P**8 **N** Sagamore Health Network, Inc., Carmel, IN

MADISON—Jefferson County

⊞ KING'S DAUGHTERS' HOSPITAL, One King's Daughters' Drive, Zip 47250–3357, Mailing Address: P.O. Box 447, Zip 47250–0447; tel. 812/265–5211; Roger J. Allman, Chief Executive Officer (Total facility includes 29 beds in nursing home–type unit) **A**1 2 9 10 **F**7 8 10 11 14 15 16 17 19 21 22 23 25 27 28 30 32 33 34 35 39 40 41 42 44 49 60 64 65 66 67 71 73 **P**6

☐ MADISON STATE HOSPITAL, 711 Green Road, Zip 47250–2199; tel. 812/265–2611; Steven Covington, Superintendent **A**1 10 **F**2 15 16 20 52 53 57 65 73 **P**6

MARION—Grant County

⊞ MARION GENERAL HOSPITAL, 441 North Wabash Avenue, Zip 46952–2690; tel. 765/662–1441; Albert C. Knauss, President and Chief Executive Officer (Total facility includes 21 beds in nursing home–type unit) **A**1 9 10 **F**7 8 10 11 14 15 16 19 21 22 28 30 32 33 34 35 36 37 39 40 41 42 44 46 49 63 64 65 66 67 68 71 73 74 **P**6

VETERANS AFFAIRS NORTHERN INDIANA HEALTH CARE SYSTEM–MARION CAMPUS See Veterans Affairs Northern Indiana Health Care System, Fort Wayne

MARTINSVILLE—Morgan County

★ MORGAN COUNTY MEMORIAL HOSPITAL, 2209 John R. Wooden Drive, Zip 46151–1840, Mailing Address: P.O. Box 1717, Zip 46151–1717; tel. 765/342–8441; S. Dean Melton, President and Chief Executive Officer **A**9 10 **F**7 8 12 14 15 16 19 21 22 28 29 30 32 34 35 36 37 39 40 41 42 44 45 49 51 64 65 71 73 **P**8 **N** Midwest Health Net, LLC., Fort Wayne, IN; Sagamore Health Network, Inc., Carmel, IN; Suburban Health Organization, Indianapolis, IN

MERRILLVILLE—Lake County

SOUTHLAKE CAMPUS See Methodist Hospitals, Gary

MICHIGAN CITY—La Porte County

⊞ MEMORIAL HOSPITAL OF MICHIGAN CITY, 515 Pine Street, Zip 46360–3370; tel. 219/879–0202; Norman D. Steider, President (Nonreporting) **A**1 9 10

⊞ △ SAINT ANTHONY MEMORIAL HEALTH CENTERS, 301 West Homer Street, Zip 46360–4358; tel. 219/879–8511; Bruce E. Rampage, President and Chief Executive Officer **A**1 7 9 10 **F**2 4 7 8 10 11 12 17 19 21 22 23 28 29 30 32 33 35 36 37 39 40 41 42 44 46 48 49 51 52 53 55 56 57 59 60 63 64 65 66 67 71 73 74 **S** Sisters of St. Francis Health Services, Inc., Mishawaka, IN **N** Sagamore Health Network, Inc., Carmel, IN

MISHAWAKA—St. Joseph County

⊞ + ○ △ ST. JOSEPH COMMUNITY HOSPITAL, 215 West Fourth Street, Zip 46544–1999; tel. 219/259–2431; Stephen L. Crain, President and Chief Executive Officer **A**1 7 9 10 11 12 13 **F**3 4 7 8 10 12 13 14 15 16 17 18 19 21 22 23 25 26 28 30 32 34 35 37 39 40 41 42 44 45 46 49 51 53 63 65 66 67 71 72 73 **P**3 4 6 7 8 **S** Ancilla Systems Inc., Hobart, IN

MONTICELLO—White County

☐ WHITE COUNTY MEMORIAL HOSPITAL, 1101 O'Connor Boulevard, Zip 47960–1698; tel. 219/583–7111; John M. Avers, Chief Executive Officer **A**1 9 10 **F**8 14 15 16 17 19 20 21 22 24 26 27 29 30 32 34 35 36 37 39 40 41 42 44 45 46 48 49 51 63 65 66 67 68 71 72 73 **P**6 **N** Midwest Health Net, LLC., Fort Wayne, IN; Sagamore Health Network, Inc., Carmel, IN

Hospital, Address, Telephone, Administrator, Approval, Facility, and Physician Codes, Health Care System, Network	Classification Codes		Utilization Data					Expense (thousands) of dollars		
★ American Hospital Association (AHA) membership □ Joint Commission on Accreditation of Healthcare Organizations (JCAHO) accreditation + American Osteopathic Healthcare Association (AOHA) membership ○ American Osteopathic Association (AOA) accreditation △ Commission on Accreditation of Rehabilitation Facilities (CARF) accreditation Control codes 61, 63, 64, 71, 72 and 73 indicate hospitals listed by AOHA, but not registered by AHA. For definition of numerical codes, see page A4	Control	Service	Staffed Beds	Admissions	Census	Outpatient Visits	Births	Total	Payroll	Personnel

MOORESVILLE—Morgan County

| □ KENDRICK MEMORIAL HOSPITAL, 1201 Hadley Road N.W., Zip 46158–1789; tel. 317/831–1160; Charles D. Swisher, Executive Director (Nonreporting) **A**1 2 9 10 **N** Sagamore Health Network, Inc., Carmel, IN | 23 | 10 | 60 | — | — | — | — | — | — | — |

MUNCIE—Delaware County

| ★△ BALL MEMORIAL HOSPITAL, 2401 University Avenue, Zip 47303–3499; tel. 765/747–3111; Mitchell C. Carson, President (Total facility includes 31 beds in nursing home–type unit) **A**1 3 5 7 9 10 **F**2 3 4 7 8 10 11 14 15 16 17 19 20 21 22 23 24 25 26 28 29 30 31 32 33 34 35 36 37 38 39 40 41 42 43 44 45 46 48 49 51 52 54 55 56 57 60 61 63 64 65 66 67 71 72 73 74 **P**6 8 | 23 | 10 | 431 | 17374 | 267 | — | 1771 | 157533 | 65621 | 1814 |

MUNSTER—Lake County

| □ COMMUNITY HOSPITAL, 901 MacArthur Boulevard, Zip 46321–2959; tel. 219/836–1600; Edward P. Robinson, Administrator (Nonreporting) **A**1 2 9 10 | 23 | 10 | 292 | — | — | — | — | — | — | — |

NEW ALBANY—Floyd County

| ★ FLOYD MEMORIAL HOSPITAL AND HEALTH SERVICES, 1850 State Street, Zip 47150–4997; tel. 812/949–5500; Bryant R. Hanson, President and Chief Executive Officer **A**1 2 9 10 **F**7 8 10 11 12 14 15 16 19 21 22 23 32 35 37 40 41 42 44 46 49 60 63 67 70 71 72 73 74 **P**1 6 **N** Sagamore Health Network, Inc., Carmel, IN | 13 | 10 | 178 | 8638 | 102 | 157692 | 787 | 70679 | 31523 | 887 |
| ★△ SOUTHERN INDIANA REHABILITATION HOSPITAL, 3104 Blackiston Boulevard, Zip 47150–9579; tel. 812/941–8300; Randy L. Napier, President and Chief Executive Officer **A**1 7 10 **F**3 4 5 7 8 10 11 12 13 14 15 17 19 21 22 23 25 26 27 28 29 30 32 34 35 37 38 39 40 41 42 43 44 45 46 47 48 49 51 52 53 54 55 56 57 58 59 60 64 65 66 67 68 69 70 71 72 73 74 **S** Jewish Hospital HealthCare Services, Louisville, KY | 23 | 46 | 60 | 665 | 48 | 7969 | 0 | 10706 | 4370 | 180 |

NEW CASTLE—Henry County

| ★ HENRY COUNTY MEMORIAL HOSPITAL, 1000 North 16th Street, Zip 47362–4319, Mailing Address: P.O. Box 490, Zip 47362–0490; tel. 765/521–0890; Jack Basler, President **A**1 9 10 **F**7 8 14 15 16 17 19 21 22 32 34 35 37 40 42 44 46 65 66 67 71 73 74 **P**8 **N** Midwest Health Net, LLC., Fort Wayne, IN; Sagamore Health Network, Inc., Carmel, IN; Suburban Health Organization, Indianapolis, IN | 13 | 10 | 107 | 3195 | 34 | 47556 | 457 | 28769 | 12861 | 539 |

NOBLESVILLE—Hamilton County

| ★ RIVERVIEW HOSPITAL, 395 Westfield Road, Zip 46060–1425, Mailing Address: P.O. Box 220, Zip 46061–0220; tel. 317/773–0760; Seward Horner, President **A**1 9 10 **F**4 7 8 10 14 15 16 19 22 28 30 32 35 36 37 40 41 42 44 46 48 49 60 63 65 66 67 71 72 73 74 **P**6 7 8 **N** Midwest Health Net, LLC., Fort Wayne, IN; Sagamore Health Network, Inc., Carmel, IN; Suburban Health Organization, Indianapolis, IN | 13 | 10 | 111 | 3909 | 45 | 144771 | 670 | 50700 | 23300 | 720 |

NORTH VERNON—Jennings County

| ★ JENNINGS COMMUNITY HOSPITAL, 301 Henry Street, Zip 47265–1097; tel. 812/346–6200; Dalton L. Smart, Administrator (Nonreporting) **A**9 10 **N** Saint Vincent Hospitals and Health Services, Inc., Indianapolis, IN | 23 | 10 | 34 | — | — | — | — | — | — | — |

OAKLAND CITY—Gibson County

| ★ WIRTH REGIONAL HOSPITAL, Highway 64 West, Zip 47660–9379, Mailing Address: Rural Route 3, Box 14A, Zip 47660–9379; tel. 812/749–6111; Frank G. Fougerouse, President and Chief Executive Officer **A**9 10 **F**16 17 22 26 34 41 44 49 52 54 55 56 71 **S** Brim, Inc., Portland, OR | 23 | 10 | 21 | 618 | 5 | 13777 | 11 | 3401 | 1615 | 60 |

PAOLI—Orange County

| ★ ORANGE COUNTY HOSPITAL, 642 West Hospital Road, Zip 47454–0499, Mailing Address: P.O. Box 499, Zip 47454–0499; tel. 812/723–2811; James W. Pope, Chief Executive Officer **A**1 9 10 **F**7 8 11 12 15 17 19 22 28 29 30 32 33 34 35 37 40 41 42 44 49 57 64 67 71 72 73 **P**6 **N** Sagamore Health Network, Inc., Carmel, IN | 13 | 10 | 37 | 1007 | 11 | 28568 | 144 | 11201 | 5744 | 192 |

PERU—Miami County

| ★ DUKES MEMORIAL HOSPITAL, 275 West 12th Street, Zip 46970–1698; tel. 765/473–6621; R. Joe Johnston, President and Chief Executive Officer (Total facility includes 35 beds in nursing home–type unit) (Nonreporting) **A**1 9 10 **N** LutheranPreferred Network, Fort Wayne, IN; Midwest Health Net, LLC., Fort Wayne, IN; Sagamore Health Network, Inc., Carmel, IN | 15 | 10 | 140 | — | — | — | — | — | — | — |

PLYMOUTH—Marshall County

| □ BEHAVIORAL HEALTHCARE OF NORTHERN INDIANA, (Formerly Koala Hospital and Counseling Center), 1800 North Oak Road, Zip 46563–3492; tel. 219/936–3784; Wayne T. Miller, Administrator (Nonreporting) **A**1 10 **S** Behavioral Healthcare Corporation, Nashville, TN | 33 | 22 | 80 | — | — | — | — | — | — | — |
| ★ SAINT JOSEPH'S HOSPITAL OF MARSHALL COUNTY, 1915 Lake Avenue, Zip 46563–9905, Mailing Address: P.O. Box 670, Zip 46563–9905; tel. 219/936–3181; Brian E. Dietz, FACHE, Executive Vice President **A**1 9 10 **F**1 4 6 7 8 10 12 14 15 16 19 21 22 23 24 26 27 28 31 33 35 36 37 40 41 42 43 44 47 48 49 60 64 65 70 71 73 74 **P**7 8 **S** Holy Cross Health System Corporation, South Bend, IN **N** Sagamore Health Network, Inc., Carmel, IN; Holy Cross Health System, South Bend, IN | 21 | 10 | 36 | 2057 | 21 | 47260 | 312 | 17061 | 6176 | 207 |

PORTLAND—Jay County

| ★ JAY COUNTY HOSPITAL, 500 West Votaw Street, Zip 47371–1322; tel. 219/726–7131; Sheri Frankenfield, Chief Executive Officer (Nonreporting) **A**9 10 **N** LutheranPreferred Network, Fort Wayne, IN; Caylor–Nickel Health Network, Bluffton, IN | 13 | 10 | 55 | — | — | — | — | — | — | — |

Hospital, Address, Telephone, Administrator, Approval, Facility, and Physician Codes, Health Care System, Network	Classification Codes		Utilization Data					Expense (thousands) of dollars		
★ American Hospital Association (AHA) membership □ Joint Commission on Accreditation of Healthcare Organizations (JCAHO) accreditation + American Osteopathic Healthcare Association (AOHA) membership ○ American Osteopathic Association (AOA) accreditation △ Commission on Accreditation of Rehabilitation Facilities (CARF) accreditation Control codes 61, 63, 64, 71, 72 and 73 indicate hospitals listed by AOHA, but not registered by AHA. For definition of numerical codes, see page A4	Control	Service	Staffed Beds	Admissions	Census	Outpatient Visits	Births	Total	Payroll	Personnel

PRINCETON—Gibson County

⊞ GIBSON GENERAL HOSPITAL, 1808 Sherman Drive, Zip 47670–1043; tel. 812/385–3401; Michael J. Budnick, Administrator and Chief Executive Officer (Total facility includes 45 beds in nursing home–type unit) **A**1 9 10 **F**3 6 7 8 12 14 15 16 17 18 19 20 22 26 28 29 30 32 34 35 37 39 40 41 42 44 49 52 53 54 55 56 57 58 64 65 66 71 73 74 **S** Alliant Health System, Louisville, KY **N** Sagamore Health Network, Inc., Carmel, IN	23	10	109	1476	59	21859	119	12865	6167	266

RENSSELAER—Jasper County

★ JASPER COUNTY HOSPITAL, 1104 East Grace Street, Zip 47978–3296; tel. 219/866–5141; Timothy M. Schreeg, President and Chief Executive Officer (Total facility includes 21 beds in nursing home–type unit) **A**9 10 **F**7 8 11 14 17 19 20 21 22 23 24 26 27 28 29 30 31 32 33 34 35 36 37 39 40 41 42 44 45 46 49 53 54 55 56 57 58 59 64 65 66 67 71 73 **P**6	13	10	69	1546	36	42291	162	15378	7924	288

RICHMOND—Wayne County

⊞ REID HOSPITAL AND HEALTH CARE SERVICES, 1401 Chester Boulevard, Zip 47374–1986; tel. 765/983–3000; Barry S. MacDowell, President (Total facility includes 17 beds in nursing home–type unit) **A**1 2 9 10 **F**3 7 8 10 11 14 15 16 17 19 21 22 23 28 29 35 37 40 41 42 44 46 49 50 52 54 56 60 63 64 65 67 71 73 **P**8	23	10	212	12029	—	114767	866	79679	35922	1056
□ RICHMOND STATE HOSPITAL, 498 N.W. 18th Street, Zip 47374–2898; tel. 765/966–0511; James McCormick, Superintendent (Nonreporting) **A**1 10	12	22	339	—	—	—	—	—	—	—

ROCHESTER—Fulton County

WOODLAWN HOSPITAL, 1400 East Ninth Street, Zip 46975–8937; tel. 219/224–1173; Michael L. Gordon, President and Chief Executive Officer **A**9 10 **F**6 7 8 11 12 17 19 21 22 26 28 30 31 32 34 35 36 37 40 41 42 44 49 67 71 73 **P**6	13	10	35	1576	15	22877	223	19819	1644	273

RUSHVILLE—Rush County

★ RUSH MEMORIAL HOSPITAL, 1300 North Main Street, Zip 46173–1198; tel. 765/932–4111; H. William Hartley, Chief Executive Officer **A**9 10 **F**8 15 16 17 19 22 26 29 30 32 34 35 37 39 42 44 45 46 49 51 65 66 71 73 **P**6 **S** Alliant Health System, Louisville, KY **N** Sagamore Health Network, Inc., Carmel, IN	13	10	52	891	21	87118	—	9471	4361	191

SALEM—Washington County

⊞ WASHINGTON COUNTY MEMORIAL HOSPITAL, 911 North Shelby Street, Zip 47167; tel. 812/883–5881; Rodney M. Coats, President and Chief Executive Officer **A**1 9 10 **F**2 3 7 8 11 14 15 16 17 19 22 26 28 30 32 34 35 37 40 41 42 44 49 52 58 59 64 65 66 71 73 **S** Jewish Hospital HealthCare Services, Louisville, KY **N** Jewish Hospital Healthcare Services, Louisville, KY	13	10	50	1376	19	30898	110	12863	5226	198

SCOTTSBURG—Scott County

⊞ SCOTT MEMORIAL HOSPITAL, 1415 North Gardner Street, Zip 47170–0456, Mailing Address: Box 430, Zip 47170–0430; tel. 812/752–8500; Clifford D. Nay, Executive Director **A**1 9 10 **F**7 8 11 12 14 15 16 17 19 22 28 30 32 34 35 39 40 41 42 44 46 49 65 67 71 73 **S** Jewish Hospital HealthCare Services, Louisville, KY **N** Jewish Hospital Healthcare Services, Louisville, KY	13	10	45	1194	11	—	172	9145	4710	—

SEYMOUR—Jackson County

⊞ MEMORIAL HOSPITAL, 411 West Tipton Street, Zip 47274–5000, Mailing Address: P.O. Box 2349, Zip 47274–2349; tel. 812/522–2349; George H. James, Jr., President and Chief Executive Officer **A**1 2 9 10 **F**7 8 12 14 15 16 17 19 21 22 23 26 28 30 32 33 34 35 36 37 39 40 41 42 44 45 46 49 51 63 65 67 71 73 74	13	10	107	4561	42	107360	712	32650	14515	467

SHELBYVILLE—Shelby County

⊞ MAJOR HOSPITAL, 150 West Washington Street, Zip 46176–1236; tel. 317/392–3211; Anthony B. Lennen, President and Chief Executive Officer **A**1 9 10 **F**7 8 12 14 15 16 17 19 21 22 28 29 30 32 34 35 36 37 39 40 41 42 44 45 46 49 51 54 56 58 63 65 66 67 71 73 74 **P**7 8	15	10	49	2294	24	94668	248	21659	9881	313

SOUTH BEND—St. Joseph County

⊞ △ MEMORIAL HOSPITAL OF SOUTH BEND, 615 North Michigan Street, Zip 46601–9986; tel. 219/234–9041; Philip A. Newbold, President and Chief Executive Officer **A**1 2 3 5 7 9 10 **F**2 3 4 7 8 10 11 13 14 15 16 17 18 19 20 21 22 23 24 25 26 27 28 29 30 31 32 34 35 37 38 39 40 41 42 43 44 46 47 48 49 50 51 52 53 54 55 56 57 58 59 60 61 63 64 65 66 67 70 71 72 73 74 **P**1 6	23	10	352	14974	207	110754	2641	155097	61771	1704
ST MARY COMMUNITY HOSPITAL See St Mary Medical Plaza										
○ ST MARY MEDICAL PLAZA, (Formerly St Mary Community Hospital), 2515 East Jefferson Boulevard, Zip 46615–2691; tel. 219/288–8311; Stephen L. Crain, President (Nonreporting) **A**9 10 11 **N** Midwest Health Net, LLC., Fort Wayne, IN; Sagamore Health Network, Inc., Carmel, IN	23	10	70	—	—	—	—	—	—	—
⊞ △ ST. JOSEPH'S MEDICAL CENTER, 801 East LaSalle, Zip 46617–2800, Mailing Address: P.O. Box 1935, Zip 46634–1935; tel. 219/237–7111; Robert L. Beyer, President and Chief Executive Officer (Nonreporting) **A**1 2 3 5 7 9 10 **S** Holy Cross Health System Corporation, South Bend, IN **N** Select Health Network, South Bend, IN; Sagamore Health Network, Inc., Carmel, IN; Holy Cross Health System, South Bend, IN	21	10	289	—	—	—	—	—	—	—

SULLIVAN—Sullivan County

⊞ MARY SHERMAN HOSPITAL, 320 North Section Street, Zip 47882–1239, Mailing Address: P.O. Box 10, Zip 47882–0010; tel. 812/268–4311; Thomas J. Hudgins, Administrator **A**1 9 10 **F**7 8 12 13 14 15 16 17 19 20 22 26 28 29 30 31 32 37 39 40 41 42 44 45 49 53 54 55 56 57 58 63 65 66 67 68 71 73 74 **S** Quorum Health Group/Quorum Health Resources, Inc., Brentwood, TN **N** Sagamore Health Network, Inc., Carmel, IN	13	10	53	1597	22	42287	140	10397	4444	190

Hospital, Address, Telephone, Administrator, Approval, Facility, and Physician Codes, Health Care System, Network	Classi-fication Codes		Utilization Data					Expense (thousands) of dollars		
	Control	Service	Staffed Beds	Admissions	Census	Outpatient Visits	Births	Total	Payroll	Personnel

★ American Hospital Association (AHA) membership
□ Joint Commission on Accreditation of Healthcare Organizations (JCAHO) accreditation
+ American Osteopathic Healthcare Association (AOHA) membership
○ American Osteopathic Association (AOA) accreditation
△ Commission on Accreditation of Rehabilitation Facilities (CARF) accreditation
Control codes 61, 63, 64, 71, 72 and 73 indicate hospitals listed by AOHA, but not registered by AHA. For definition of numerical codes, see page A4

TELL CITY—Perry County

⊞ PERRY COUNTY MEMORIAL HOSPITAL, 1 Hospital Road, Zip 47586–0362; tel. 812/547–7011; Bradford W. Dykes, Chief Executive Officer **A**1 9 10 **F**1 7 8 12 15 16 17 19 20 21 22 26 28 29 30 32 33 34 35 37 39 40 41 42 45 46 49 51 55 56 58 63 64 65 67 71 73 **S** Alliant Health System, Louisville, KY — 13 10 38 1114 11 52123 78 10688 4349 163

TERRE HAUTE—Vigo County

HAMILTON CENTER, 620 Eighth Avenue, Zip 47804–0323; tel. 812/231–8323; Galen Goode, Chief Executive Officer (Nonreporting) **A**9 10 — 23 22 45 — — — — — — — —

⊞ TERRE HAUTE REGIONAL HOSPITAL, (Formerly Columbia Terre Haute Regional Hospital), 3901 South Seventh Street, Zip 47802–4299; tel. 812/232–0021; Jerry Dooley, Chief Executive Officer (Total facility includes 25 beds in nursing home–type unit) **A**1 9 10 **F**3 4 7 8 10 11 12 14 16 17 19 21 22 26 28 30 32 34 36 37 39 40 41 42 43 44 46 50 52 54 55 56 57 58 59 60 61 64 65 66 67 71 72 73 74 **P**5 8 **S** Columbia/HCA Healthcare Corporation, Nashville, TN — 33 10 236 7756 111 108480 751 — 17945 830

⊞ △ UNION HOSPITAL, 1606 North Seventh Street, Zip 47804–2780; tel. 812/238–7000; Frank Shelton, President **A**1 2 3 5 7 9 10 **F**3 4 5 7 8 10 11 12 14 15 16 17 19 20 21 22 23 24 25 28 29 30 31 32 34 35 37 38 39 40 41 42 43 44 45 46 47 48 49 51 52 53 56 58 59 60 61 64 65 66 67 71 72 73 74 **P**1 5 6 **N** Sagamore Health Network, Inc., Carmel, IN — 23 10 295 12925 197 348356 1600 141771 59188 1929

TIPTON—Tipton County

⊞ TIPTON COUNTY MEMORIAL HOSPITAL, 1000 South Main Street, Zip 46072–9799; tel. 765/675–8500; Alfonso W. Gatmaitan, Chief Executive Officer (Total facility includes 50 beds in nursing home–type unit) **A**1 2 9 10 **F**6 7 8 12 17 19 21 22 28 29 30 32 35 36 37 39 40 41 42 44 45 46 49 50 63 64 65 66 68 71 73 74 **P**6 8 **N** Midwest Health Net, LLC., Fort Wayne, IN; Sagamore Health Network, Inc., Carmel, IN; Suburban Health Organization, Indianapolis, IN — 13 10 100 1829 55 46198 111 18082 8509 314

VALPARAISO—Porter County

⊞ △ PORTER MEMORIAL HOSPITAL, 814 La Porte Avenue, Zip 46383–5898; tel. 219/465–4600; Wiley N. Carr, President and Chief Executive Officer **A**1 7 9 10 **F**3 4 7 8 10 14 15 16 17 18 19 21 22 23 25 27 28 30 32 33 34 35 36 37 38 39 40 41 42 43 44 45 48 49 52 53 54 55 56 57 58 59 60 61 63 64 65 66 68 70 71 72 73 74 **P**3 7 8 — 13 10 303 12989 197 302956 1315 113480 46318 1425

VINCENNES—Knox County

⊞ GOOD SAMARITAN HOSPITAL, 520 South Seventh Street, Zip 47591–1098; tel. 812/882–5220; A. John Hidde, President and Chief Executive Officer (Total facility includes 26 beds in nursing home–type unit) **A**1 2 9 10 **F**3 4 7 8 10 11 12 13 14 15 16 19 20 21 22 23 24 28 29 30 32 33 34 35 37 39 40 41 42 43 44 45 46 49 52 53 54 55 56 57 58 59 60 63 64 65 67 71 72 73 74 **P**8 — 13 10 263 10397 159 226285 498 88562 39858 1427

WABASH—Wabash County

⊞ WABASH COUNTY HOSPITAL, 710 North East Street, Zip 46992–1924, Mailing Address: P.O. Box 548, Zip 46992–0548; tel. 219/563–3131; David C. Hunter, Chief Executive Officer (Total facility includes 25 beds in nursing home–type unit) **A**1 2 9 10 **F**7 8 12 13 14 16 17 19 21 22 24 28 29 30 32 33 34 35 36 39 41 42 44 45 46 49 64 65 66 67 71 73 **N** LutheranPreferred Network, Fort Wayne, IN; Midwest Health Net, LLC., Fort Wayne, IN; Sagamore Health Network, Inc., Carmel, IN — 13 10 75 1660 31 64805 249 17189 8533 —

WARSAW—Kosciusko County

⊞ KOSCIUSKO COMMUNITY HOSPITAL, 2101 East Dubois Drive, Zip 46580–3288; tel. 219/267–3200; Wayne Hendrix, President (Total facility includes 89 beds in nursing home–type unit) (Nonreporting) **A**1 9 10 **N** LutheranPreferred Network, Fort Wayne, IN; Midwest Health Net, LLC., Fort Wayne, IN; Sagamore Health Network, Inc., Carmel, IN — 23 10 161 — — — — — — —

WASHINGTON—Daviess County

⊞ DAVIESS COUNTY HOSPITAL, 1314 Grand Avenue, Zip 47501–2198, Mailing Address: P.O. Box 760, Zip 47501–0760; tel. 812/254–2760; Marc Chircop, Chief Executive Officer (Total facility includes 29 beds in nursing home–type unit) **A**1 9 10 **F**7 8 11 15 16 17 19 21 22 32 33 34 35 36 37 39 40 41 42 44 45 49 53 55 56 58 59 63 64 65 66 67 71 73 **P**3 7 8 **S** Quorum Health Group/Quorum Health Resources, Inc., Brentwood, TN — 13 10 85 2520 44 69156 348 19232 8852 329

WEST LAFAYETTE—Tippecanoe County

WABASH VALLEY HOSPITAL, 2900 North River Road, Zip 47906–3766; tel. 765/463–2555; R. Craig Lysinger, Administrator (Nonreporting) **A**9 10 — 23 22 70 — — — — — — —

WILLIAMSPORT—Warren County

★ ST. VINCENT WILLIAMSPORT HOSPITAL, 412 North Monroe Street, Zip 47993–0215; tel. 765/762–2496; Jane Craigin, Chief Executive Officer (Nonreporting) **A**9 10 **S** Daughters of Charity National Health System, Saint Louis, MO **N** Saint Vincent Hospitals and Health Services, Inc., Indianapolis, IN — 23 10 22 — — — — — — —

WINAMAC—Pulaski County

⊞ PULASKI MEMORIAL HOSPITAL, 616 East 13th Street, Zip 46996–1117; tel. 219/946–6131; Richard H. Mynark, Administrator **A**1 9 10 **F**7 8 15 16 17 19 20 21 22 27 28 29 30 32 33 34 35 37 39 40 41 42 44 45 46 49 54 55 58 61 65 67 71 73 74 **N** Sagamore Health Network, Inc., Carmel, IN — 13 10 19 1036 10 42252 101 9622 5083 159

WINCHESTER—Randolph County

★ RANDOLPH COUNTY HOSPITAL AND HEALTH SERVICES, 325 South Oak Street, Zip 47394–2235, Mailing Address: P.O. Box 407, Zip 47394–0407; tel. 765/584–9001; James M. Full, Chief Executive Officer **A**9 10 **F**7 8 13 14 15 16 17 19 22 23 25 28 30 32 33 34 35 40 41 42 44 49 51 61 65 66 68 71 73 74 **P**7 **S** Alliant Health System, Louisville, KY **N** Caylor–Nickel Health Network, Bluffton, IN; Midwest Health Net, LLC., Fort Wayne, IN; Sagamore Health Network, Inc., Carmel, IN — 13 10 27 841 7 — 118 10766 4471 209

IOWA

Resident population 5,864 (in thousands)
Resident population in metro areas 71.7%
Birth rate per 1,000 population 14.4
65 years and over 12.6%
Percent of persons without health insurance 10.6%

Hospital, Address, Telephone, Administrator, Approval, Facility, and Physician Codes, Health Care System, Network	Classi-fication Codes		Utilization Data					Expense (thousands) of dollars		
★ American Hospital Association (AHA) membership ☐ Joint Commission on Accreditation of Healthcare Organizations (JCAHO) accreditation + American Osteopathic Healthcare Association (AOHA) membership ○ American Osteopathic Association (AOA) accreditation △ Commission on Accreditation of Rehabilitation Facilities (CARF) accreditation Control codes 61, 63, 64, 71, 72 and 73 indicate hospitals listed by AOHA, but not registered by AHA. For definition of numerical codes, see page A4	Control	Service	Staffed Beds	Admissions	Census	Outpatient Visits	Births	Total	Payroll	Personnel

ALBIA—Monroe County

MONROE COUNTY HOSPITAL, RR 3, Box 311–11, Zip 52531; tel. 515/932–2134; Gregory A. Paris, Administrator (Total facility includes 20 beds in nursing home–type unit) **A**9 10 **F**11 12 14 15 16 17 19 28 30 32 33 35 36 44 48 49 64 71 **P**5 **N** Mercy Network of Health Services, Des Moines, IA — 13 10 38 530 23 24162 — 4985 1900 116

ALGONA—Kossuth County

★ KOSSUTH REGIONAL HEALTH CENTER, 1515 South Phillips Street, Zip 50511–3649; tel. 515/295–2451; James G. Fitzpatrick, Administrator **A**9 10 **F**7 8 12 13 14 15 16 17 19 22 26 27 28 30 31 32 33 34 35 36 37 39 40 41 42 44 45 49 58 65 66 67 71 73 **P**1 **S** Mercy Health Services, Farmington Hills, MI **N** North Iowa Mercy Health Network, Mason City, IA — 13 10 29 689 8 15775 74 7402 2455 112

AMES—Story County

✚ MARY GREELEY MEDICAL CENTER, 1111 Duff Avenue, Zip 50010–5792; tel. 515/239–2011; Kimberly A. Russel, President and Chief Executive Officer (Total facility includes 20 beds in nursing home–type unit) **A**1 2 9 10 **F**7 8 10 14 15 16 17 18 19 21 22 26 28 29 30 31 32 33 34 35 36 37 38 39 40 41 42 44 45 48 49 52 53 54 55 56 57 58 59 60 61 63 64 65 66 67 71 73 — 14 10 195 9413 118 119242 1163 64101 28648 988

ANAMOSA—Jones County

✚ ANAMOSA COMMUNITY HOSPITAL, 104 Broadway Place, Zip 52205–1100; tel. 319/462–6131; Margaret Robinson, Administrator **A**1 9 10 **F**1 7 8 12 13 15 16 17 19 22 26 30 32 33 34 39 41 44 45 46 49 65 71 73 **P**4 **S** Iowa Health System, Des Moines, IA — 23 10 17 409 6 14730 8 4023 1604 99

ATLANTIC—Cass County

★ CASS COUNTY MEMORIAL HOSPITAL, 1501 East Tenth Street, Zip 50022–1997; tel. 712/243–3250; Patricia Markham, Administrator **A**9 10 **F**1 7 8 15 16 19 21 22 28 30 32 33 34 35 36 37 39 40 41 42 44 49 52 53 55 56 57 58 59 63 65 67 71 **P**8 — 13 10 72 1896 29 35252 184 14691 7366 312

AUDUBON—Audubon County

AUDUBON COUNTY MEMORIAL HOSPITAL, 515 Pacific Street, Zip 50025–1099; tel. 712/563–2611; David G. Couser, FAAMA, FACHE, Administrator **A**9 10 **F**8 14 15 19 22 30 33 34 35 40 42 44 49 63 71 **P**1 3 **N** Mercy Network of Health Services, Des Moines, IA — 13 10 29 511 5 15011 45 3603 1575 59

BELMOND—Wright County

★ BELMOND COMMUNITY HOSPITAL, 403 First Street S.E., Zip 50421–1201, Mailing Address: P.O. Box 326, Zip 50421–0326; tel. 515/444–3223; Allan Atkinson, Administrator **A**9 10 **F**3 8 14 15 16 17 19 22 26 27 28 30 31 32 33 34 36 39 44 49 53 54 55 58 71 73 **P**1 2 3 4 5 6 7 8 **S** Mercy Health Services, Farmington Hills, MI **N** North Iowa Mercy Health Network, Mason City, IA — 14 10 22 304 7 6428 — 2539 1201 57

BLOOMFIELD—Davis County

★ DAVIS COUNTY HOSPITAL, 507 North Madison Street, Zip 52537–1299; tel. 515/664–2145; Randy Simmons, Administrator (Total facility includes 32 beds in nursing home–type unit) **A**9 10 **F**7 8 13 14 15 16 19 20 22 24 28 30 31 32 34 35 36 37 39 40 42 44 45 49 64 71 73 **N** Mercy Network of Health Services, Des Moines, IA — 13 10 80 929 44 13841 59 8266 3826 172

BOONE—Boone County

✚ BOONE COUNTY HOSPITAL, 1015 Union Street, Zip 50036–4898; tel. 515/432–3140; Joseph S. Smith, Chief Executive Officer **A**1 9 10 **F**7 8 15 19 22 24 28 30 32 34 35 36 37 39 40 41 44 49 71 73 **S** Quorum Health Group/Quorum Health Resources, Inc., Brentwood, TN — 13 10 57 1594 23 46102 107 13308 5717 201

BRITT—Hancock County

★ HANCOCK COUNTY MEMORIAL HOSPITAL, 531 First Street N.W., Zip 50423–0068, Mailing Address: P.O. Box 68, Zip 50423–0068; tel. 515/843–3801; Harriet Thompson, Administrator **A**9 10 **F**1 7 8 14 15 17 19 22 27 30 33 34 36 40 41 44 46 65 67 71 **P**1 **S** Mercy Health Services, Farmington Hills, MI **N** North Iowa Mercy Health Network, Mason City, IA — 13 10 26 734 14 12612 5 3869 1503 57

BURLINGTON—Des Moines County

✚ BURLINGTON MEDICAL CENTER, (Includes Burlington Medical Center Klein Unit, 2910 Madison Road, Zip 52601; tel. 319/753–3500), 602 North Third Street, Zip 52601–5088; tel. 319/753–3011; Mark D. Richardson, President and Chief Executive Officer (Total facility includes 167 beds in nursing home–type unit) **A**1 9 10 **F**3 4 8 10 12 13 14 15 16 17 18 19 21 22 23 24 28 29 30 32 34 35 36 37 38 39 40 41 42 44 45 46 48 49 52 53 54 55 56 57 58 60 63 64 65 66 67 70 71 73 — 23 10 366 7284 223 181430 790 55926 24520 815

CARROLL—Carroll County

✚ ST. ANTHONY REGIONAL HOSPITAL, South Clark Street, Zip 51401; tel. 712/792–8231; Gary P. Riedmann, President and Chief Executive Officer (Total facility includes 79 beds in nursing home–type unit) **A**1 9 10 **F**1 7 8 12 14 15 16 17 19 20 21 22 26 28 29 30 31 32 33 34 35 36 39 40 41 42 43 44 45 46 49 51 52 53 54 55 56 57 58 59 62 63 64 65 66 67 68 71 73 **P**6 **N** Mercy Network of Health Services, Des Moines, IA — 21 10 142 2417 107 58126 216 18781 8149 321

Hospital, Address, Telephone, Administrator, Approval, Facility, and Physician Codes, Health Care System, Network	Classi-fication Codes		Utilization Data					Expense (thousands) of dollars		
★ American Hospital Association (AHA) membership □ Joint Commission on Accreditation of Healthcare Organizations (JCAHO) accreditation + American Osteopathic Healthcare Association (AOHA) membership ○ American Osteopathic Association (AOA) accreditation △ Commission on Accreditation of Rehabilitation Facilities (CARF) accreditation Control codes 61, 63, 64, 71, 72 and 73 indicate hospitals listed by AOHA, but not registered by AHA. For definition of numerical codes, see page A4	Control	Service	Staffed Beds	Admissions	Census	Outpatient Visits	Births	Total	Payroll	Personnel

CEDAR FALLS—Black Hawk County

☒ SARTORI MEMORIAL HOSPITAL, 515 College Street, Zip 50613–2599; tel. 319/266–3584; Daniel J. Woods, Chief Executive Officer (Total facility includes 18 beds in nursing home–type unit) **A**1 9 10 **F**3 8 12 17 19 20 22 24 30 32 33 34 35 36 37 39 41 44 49 51 64 65 66 67 71 73 — 21 10 | 101 | 1672 | 21 | 59458 | — | 18088 | 8071 | 258

CEDAR RAPIDS—Linn County

☒ MERCY MEDICAL CENTER, 701 Tenth Street S.E., Zip 52403–1292; tel. 319/398–6011; A. James Tinker, President and Chief Executive Officer (Total facility includes 87 beds in nursing home–type unit) **A**1 2 3 9 10 **F**2 3 4 7 8 10 12 14 15 16 19 21 22 24 26 28 29 30 31 32 33 34 35 37 38 40 41 42 44 45 46 47 49 52 54 55 56 57 58 59 60 63 64 65 67 69 71 73 74 **P**1 5 — 21 10 | 377 | 9958 | 196 | 111835 | 1167 | 89721 | 39827 | 1345

☒ △ ST. LUKE'S HOSPITAL, 1026 A. Avenue N.E., Zip 52402–3026, Mailing Address: P.O. Box 3026, Zip 52406–3026; tel. 319/369–7211; Stephen E. Vanourny, M.D., President and Chief Executive Officer (Total facility includes 28 beds in nursing home–type unit) **A**1 3 7 9 10 **F**3 4 7 8 10 11 12 14 15 16 17 19 20 21 22 24 25 26 27 28 29 30 31 32 33 34 35 36 37 38 39 40 41 42 43 44 45 46 47 48 49 51 52 53 54 55 56 57 58 59 61 63 64 65 66 67 68 70 71 72 73 74 **P**3 5 7 8 **S** Iowa Health System, Des Moines, IA — 23 10 | 391 | 13400 | 206 | 233246 | 2099 | 126625 | 53054 | 1686

CENTERVILLE—Appanoose County

☒ ST. JOSEPH'S MERCY HOSPITAL, 1 St. Joseph's Drive, Zip 52544; tel. 515/437–3411; William C. Assell, President and Chief Executive Officer (Total facility includes 24 beds in nursing home–type unit) **A**1 9 10 **F**7 8 14 15 16 19 22 24 26 28 29 30 32 33 34 35 36 37 39 40 44 45 49 53 58 64 65 67 71 73 **S** Catholic Health Initiatives, Denver, CO **N** Mercy Network of Health Services, Des Moines, IA — 21 10 | 58 | 1124 | 45 | 47245 | 57 | 8574 | 4055 | 185

CHARITON—Lucas County

★ LUCAS COUNTY HEALTH CENTER, 1200 North Seventh Street, Zip 50049–1258; tel. 515/774–3000; Robert J. Trautman, Chief Executive Officer **A**9 10 **F**1 3 6 7 8 11 12 14 15 16 17 18 19 23 27 28 30 32 33 34 35 37 40 41 42 44 46 49 53 54 55 56 57 58 59 64 67 68 70 71 73 **P**7 — 13 10 | 22 | 836 | 7 | 13140 | 80 | 9258 | 3582 | 164

CHARLES CITY—Floyd County

FLOYD COUNTY MEMORIAL HOSPITAL, 800 Eleventh Street, Zip 50616–3499; tel. 515/228–6830; Bill D. Faust, Administrator **A**9 10 **F**7 8 11 12 14 15 16 19 21 22 28 29 30 32 33 34 35 36 37 39 40 41 42 44 49 51 53 57 58 65 66 67 71 73 **S** Mayo Foundation, Rochester, MN — 13 10 | 29 | 1354 | 15 | 41064 | 113 | 9411 | 3879 | 149

CHEROKEE—Cherokee County

□ MENTAL HEALTH INSTITUTE, 1200 West Cedar Street, Zip 51012–1599; tel. 712/225–2594; Tom Deiker, Ph.D., Superintendent **A**1 10 **F**1 12 14 16 45 52 53 54 55 56 58 59 65 — 12 22 | 110 | 878 | 72 | 1612 | — | 13942 | 9366 | 260

★ SIOUX VALLEY MEMORIAL HOSPITAL, 300 Sioux Valley Drive, Zip 51012–1205; tel. 712/225–5101; John M. Comstock, Chief Executive Officer **A**9 10 **F**7 8 11 12 14 15 16 17 19 22 24 26 28 29 30 31 32 33 34 35 36 39 40 42 44 45 46 51 53 54 55 56 57 58 65 66 67 71 73 **P**4 6 — 23 10 | 40 | 1279 | 17 | 21546 | 125 | 9062 | 4553 | 169

CLARINDA—Page County

★ CLARINDA REGIONAL HEALTH CENTER, 17th and Wells Streets, Zip 51632, Mailing Address: P.O. Box 217, Zip 51632–0217; tel. 712/542–2176; Rudy Snedigar, Chief Executive Officer **A**9 10 **F**8 14 15 16 17 19 22 24 26 27 28 30 32 33 34 35 36 39 40 41 42 44 46 49 58 65 66 67 71 73 — 14 10 | 26 | 598 | 10 | 32313 | 74 | 6062 | 2753 | 147

MENTAL HEALTH INSTITUTE, Mailing Address: P.O. Box 338, Zip 51632–0338; tel. 712/542–2161; Mark Lund, Superintendent (Total facility includes 63 beds in nursing home–type unit) **F**14 15 16 19 20 21 25 26 35 39 41 44 50 52 54 55 56 57 58 60 63 64 65 71 73 — 12 22 | 83 | 192 | 71 | 0 | 0 | — | — | 119

CLARION—Wright County

★ COMMUNITY MEMORIAL HOSPITAL, 1316 South Main Street, Zip 50525–0429; tel. 515/532–2811; Steve J. Simonin, Chief Executive Officer **A**9 10 **F**7 8 14 19 20 22 24 30 32 33 34 35 36 37 39 40 41 42 44 49 62 65 71 73 — 14 10 | 33 | 729 | 15 | 20600 | 101 | 5979 | 1958 | 91

CLINTON—Clinton County

☒ SAMARITAN HEALTH SYSTEM, (Includes Samaritan Services for Aging, 600 14th Avenue North, Zip 52732; tel. 319/244–3888), 1410 North Fourth Street, Zip 52732–2999, Mailing Address: P.O. Box 2960, Zip 52733–2960; tel. 319/244–5555; Thomas J. Hesselmann, President and Chief Executive Officer (Total facility includes 189 beds in nursing home–type unit) **A**1 9 10 **F**1 3 7 8 10 11 12 15 16 17 18 19 20 21 22 23 26 27 28 29 30 32 33 34 35 36 40 41 42 44 46 49 52 53 54 55 56 57 58 59 60 62 63 64 65 67 71 73 74 **P**8 **S** Mercy Health Services, Farmington Hills, MI — 21 10 | 360 | 6302 | 246 | 47341 | 535 | 41454 | 17668 | 829

CORNING—Adams County

☒ ALEGENT HEALTH MERCY HOSPITAL, Rosary Drive, Zip 50841, Mailing Address: P.O. Box 368, Zip 50841–0368; tel. 515/322–3121; James C. Ruppert, Regional Administrator **A**1 9 10 **F**8 12 14 15 16 19 22 28 29 30 32 33 34 35 36 39 40 41 42 44 49 58 63 65 67 71 73 **P**6 **S** Catholic Health Initiatives, Denver, CO **N** Alegent Health, Omaha, NE — 21 10 | 24 | 457 | 7 | 41802 | 42 | 4585 | 2223 | 110

CORYDON—Wayne County

★ WAYNE COUNTY HOSPITAL, 417 South East Street, Zip 50060–1860, Mailing Address: P.O. Box 305, Zip 50060–0305; tel. 515/872–2260; Bill D. Wilson, Administrator **A**9 10 **F**7 8 12 13 14 15 17 19 20 22 28 30 32 33 34 36 37 39 40 42 44 45 49 51 64 65 70 71 73 **P**8 **N** Mercy Network of Health Services, Des Moines, IA — 13 10 | 20 | 901 | 11 | 10860 | 72 | 4624 | 2131 | 63

Hospital, Address, Telephone, Administrator, Approval, Facility, and Physician Codes, Health Care System, Network	Classi-fication Codes		Utilization Data					Expense (thousands) of dollars		
★ American Hospital Association (AHA) membership □ Joint Commission on Accreditation of Healthcare Organizations (JCAHO) accreditation + American Osteopathic Healthcare Association (AOHA) membership ○ American Osteopathic Association (AOA) accreditation △ Commission on Accreditation of Rehabilitation Facilities (CARF) accreditation Control codes 61, 63, 64, 71, 72 and 73 indicate hospitals listed by AOHA, but not registered by AHA. For definition of numerical codes, see page A4	Control	Service	Staffed Beds	Admissions	Census	Outpatient Visits	Births	Total	Payroll	Personnel

COUNCIL BLUFFS—Pottawattamie County

⊞ ALEGENT HEALTH MERCY HOSPITAL, 800 Mercy Drive, Zip 51503–3128, Mailing Address: P.O. Box 1C, Zip 51502–3001; tel. 712/328–5000; Richard A. Hachten, II, Chief Executive Officer (Total facility includes 24 beds in nursing home–type unit) **A**1 9 10 **F**1 2 3 4 7 8 10 11 12 15 16 17 18 19 20 21 22 24 25 26 27 28 29 30 31 32 33 34 35 36 37 38 39 40 41 42 43 44 45 46 48 49 50 51 52 53 54 55 56 57 58 59 60 61 62 63 64 65 66 67 68 71 72 73 74 **P**7 8 **S** Catholic Health Initiatives, Denver, CO **N** Alegent Health, Omaha, NE	21	10	194	5356	82	48413	520	42104	17721	712
⊞ JENNIE EDMUNDSON MEMORIAL HOSPITAL, 933 East Pierce Street, Zip 51503–4652, Mailing Address: P.O. Box 2C, Zip 51502–3002; tel. 712/328–6000; David M. Holcomb, President and Chief Executive Officer (Total facility includes 16 beds in nursing home–type unit) **A**1 2 5 6 9 10 **F**4 8 10 12 13 15 18 19 21 22 23 27 28 29 30 31 32 33 35 36 37 39 40 41 42 44 46 49 52 53 54 55 56 57 58 59 60 63 64 65 66 67 71 72 73 **P**6 8	23	10	103	5841	95	66913	613	46899	23524	649

CRESCO—Howard County

★ REGIONAL HEALTH SERVICES OF HOWARD COUNTY, (Formerly Howard County Hospital), 235 Eighth Avenue West, Zip 52136–1098; tel. 319/547–2101; Elizabeth A. Doty, Administrator **A**9 10 **F**7 8 15 19 22 30 33 35 39 40 44 49 65 71 73 **P**3 4 5 8 **S** Mercy Health Services, Farmington Hills, MI **N** North Iowa Mercy Health Network, Mason City, IA	13	10	32	411	5	14684	65	4093	1757	80

CRESTON—Union County

★ GREATER COMMUNITY HOSPITAL, 1700 West Townline, Zip 50801–1099; tel. 515/782–7091; Marlys Scherlin, Chief Executive Officer **A**9 10 **F**7 8 12 14 15 16 19 20 22 24 29 30 31 32 33 34 35 36 37 39 40 41 42 44 49 50 54 58 59 60 63 65 67 69 71 72 **P**6	13	10	49	1501	19	29140	185	11248	5142	195

DAVENPORT—Scott County

⊞ ○ DAVENPORT MEDICAL CENTER, 1111 West Kimberly Road, Zip 52806–5913; tel. 319/391–2020; James Fraser, Interim Chief Executive Officer **A**1 9 10 11 12 13 **F**7 8 12 14 15 16 19 20 22 26 30 32 34 35 37 39 40 41 42 44 45 46 61 63 65 67 71 72 73 74 **P**1 2 5	33	10	100	1545	20	48803	237	20681	7423	231
⊞ △ GENESIS MEDICAL CENTER, (Includes Genesis Medical Center–East Campus, 1227 East Rusholme Street, Zip 52803; tel. 319/421–1000; Genesis Medical Center–West Campus, 1401 West Central Park, Zip 52804–1769; tel. 319/421–1000), 1227 East Rusholme Street, Zip 52803–2498; tel. 319/421–1000; Leo A. Bressanelli, President and Chief Executive Officer **A**1 2 3 5 7 9 10 **F**2 3 4 8 10 11 12 15 16 17 18 19 20 21 22 23 25 27 29 30 31 32 33 34 35 36 37 38 39 40 41 42 43 44 46 48 49 51 52 53 54 56 57 60 63 64 65 67 71 72 73 **P**6 7 8 **N** MEDACOM Tri–State, Oakbrook, IL; Genesis Health System, Davenport, IA	23	10	448	19600	324	172546	2217	175987	67777	3218

DE WITT—Clinton County

⊞ DEWITT COMMUNITY HOSPITAL, 1118 11th Street, Zip 52742–1296; tel. 319/659–4200; Robert G. Senneff, Chief Executive Officer (Total facility includes 77 beds in nursing home–type unit) **A**1 9 10 **F**8 9 12 14 15 16 17 19 20 22 26 27 28 29 30 33 36 38 39 44 45 46 49 51 65 66 67 71 72 73 **P**5 **N** Genesis Health System, Davenport, IA	33	10	101	508	82	22597	—	6057	2572	130

DECORAH—Winneshiek County

⊞ WINNESHIEK COUNTY MEMORIAL HOSPITAL, 901 Montgomery Street, Zip 52101–2325; tel. 319/382–2911; Paul J. Anderson, Administrator **A**1 9 10 **F**7 8 11 12 14 15 17 19 21 22 27 28 30 31 32 33 34 35 36 37 39 40 41 42 44 45 46 49 64 65 66 67 71 73	13	10	83	989	8	38159	234	9155	4748	181

DENISON—Crawford County

CRAWFORD COUNTY MEMORIAL HOSPITAL, 2020 First Avenue South, Zip 51442–2299; tel. 712/263–5021; Gary L. Petersen, Administrator **A**9 10 **F**3 7 8 14 15 16 17 18 19 20 21 22 24 26 27 28 29 30 31 32 33 34 35 37 39 40 41 42 44 45 46 49 51 53 54 55 56 57 58 59 62 65 66 67 68 71 72 73 74	13	10	72	867	11	22457	159	4762	3422	118

DES MOINES—Polk County

⊞ BROADLAWNS MEDICAL CENTER, 1801 Hickman Road, Zip 50314–1597; tel. 515/282–2200; Willis F. Fry, Executive Director **A**1 3 5 9 10 **F**1 3 7 8 12 14 15 16 17 18 19 20 21 22 26 27 31 33 35 36 37 38 39 40 41 44 46 49 51 52 53 54 55 56 58 59 65 67 71 72 73 **P**6	13	10	107	5043	59	199183	533	59724	28480	855
DES MOINES DIVISION See Veterans Affairs Central Iowa Health Care System										
⊞ + ○ DES MOINES GENERAL HOSPITAL, 603 East 12th Street, Zip 50309–5515; tel. 515/263–4200; Roy W. Wright, President and Chief Executive Officer (Total facility includes 15 beds in nursing home–type unit) **A**1 9 10 11 12 13 **F**2 3 7 10 12 15 17 19 22 23 25 26 28 29 30 34 35 37 40 41 43 44 45 46 49 52 57 58 59 63 64 71 73 **P**8 **S** Quorum Health Group/Quorum Health Resources, Inc., Brentwood, TN	23	10	174	4085	74	27560	219	44196	17032	623
⊞ IOWA LUTHERAN HOSPITAL, 700 East University Avenue, Zip 50316–2392; tel. 515/263–5612; James H. Skogsbergh, President (Total facility includes 16 beds in nursing home–type unit) **A**1 3 5 9 10 **F**1 2 3 4 7 8 9 10 11 12 13 14 15 16 17 18 19 20 21 22 23 24 25 26 27 28 29 30 31 32 33 34 35 37 38 39 40 41 42 43 44 45 46 47 48 49 51 52 53 54 55 56 57 58 59 60 61 63 64 65 66 67 68 69 70 71 73 74 **P**1 2 3 6 7 **S** Iowa Health System, Des Moines, IA	23	10	770	28956	453	553553	3026	315099	128442	4307

Hospital, Address, Telephone, Administrator, Approval, Facility, and Physician Codes, Health Care System, Network	Classi-fication Codes		Utilization Data					Expense (thousands) of dollars		
★ American Hospital Association (AHA) membership □ Joint Commission on Accreditation of Healthcare Organizations (JCAHO) accreditation + American Osteopathic Healthcare Association (AOHA) membership ○ American Osteopathic Association (AOA) accreditation △ Commission on Accreditation of Rehabilitation Facilities (CARF) accreditation Control codes 61, 63, 64, 71, 72 and 73 indicate hospitals listed by AOHA, but not registered by AHA. For definition of numerical codes, see page A4	Control	Service	Staffed Beds	Admissions	Census	Outpatient Visits	Births	Total	Payroll	Personnel

Hospital	Control	Service	Staffed Beds	Admissions	Census	Outpatient Visits	Births	Total	Payroll	Personnel
★ IOWA METHODIST MEDICAL CENTER, (Includes Powell Convalescent Center, ; Raymond Blank Memorial Hospital for Children, ; Younker Memorial Rehabilitation Center), 1200 Pleasant Street, Zip 50309–9976; tel. 515/241–6212; James H. Skogsbergh, President (Total facility includes 16 beds in nursing home–type unit) A1 2 3 5 6 9 10 F1 3 4 7 8 9 10 11 12 13 14 15 16 17 18 19 20 21 22 23 24 25 26 27 28 29 30 31 32 33 34 35 37 38 39 40 41 42 43 44 45 46 47 48 49 51 53 54 55 56 57 58 59 60 61 63 65 66 67 68 69 70 71 73 74 P1 3 7 S Iowa Health System, Des Moines, IA N St Lukes/Iowa Health System, Des Moines, IA	23	10	770	28956	453	553553	3026	315099	128442	4307
★ MERCY HOSPITAL MEDICAL CENTER, (Includes Mercy Franklin Center, 1818 48th Street, Zip 50310; tel. 515/271–6000), 400 University Avenue, Zip 50314–3190; tel. 515/247–4278; Thomas A. Reitinger, President and Chief Executive Officer (Total facility includes 35 beds in nursing home–type unit) A1 2 3 6 9 10 F1 3 4 5 6 7 8 10 11 12 14 15 16 17 18 19 20 21 22 23 24 25 26 28 29 30 31 32 33 34 35 37 38 39 40 41 42 43 44 47 49 51 52 53 54 55 56 57 58 59 60 62 64 65 66 67 69 70 71 72 73 74 P1 S Catholic Health Initiatives, Denver, CO N Mercy Network of Health Services, Des Moines, IA	21	10	555	25881	361	188068	3680	288991	110399	3462
★ VETERANS AFFAIRS CENTRAL IOWA HEALTH CARE SYSTEM, (Includes Des Moines Division, 3600 30th Street, tel. 515/699–5999; Knoxville Division, 1515 West Pleasant, Knoxville, Zip 50138–3399; tel. 515/842–3101), 3600 30th Street, Zip 50310–5774; tel. 515/699–5999; Ellen DeGeorge-Smith, Director (Total facility includes 223 beds in nursing home–type unit) A1 2 3 5 F1 2 3 4 5 8 10 11 12 17 18 19 20 21 22 23 24 25 26 27 28 29 30 31 32 33 34 35 37 41 42 43 44 45 46 48 49 50 51 52 54 55 56 57 58 60 63 64 65 67 69 70 71 73 74 S Department of Veterans Affairs, Washington, DC	45	22	523	4789	482	166007	0	—	—	1386
DUBUQUE—Dubuque County										
★ FINLEY HOSPITAL, 350 North Grandview Avenue, Zip 52001–6392; tel. 319/582–1881; Kevin L. Rogols, President and Chief Executive Officer (Total facility includes 17 beds in nursing home–type unit) A1 2 9 10 F4 7 8 12 14 15 16 17 19 20 21 22 23 24 26 27 28 29 30 31 32 33 34 35 36 37 39 40 41 42 44 45 46 49 60 61 63 64 65 66 67 70 71 72 73 74 P1 5 7 S Iowa Health System, Des Moines, IA	23	10	138	5139	63	80756	562	45917	20639	681
★ △ MERCY HEALTH CENTER, (Includes Mercy Health Center–St. Mary's Unit, 1111 Third Street S.W., Dyersville, Zip 52040; tel. 319/875–7101), 250 Mercy Drive, Zip 52001–7360; tel. 319/589–8000; Russell M. Knight, President and Chief Executive Officer (Total facility includes 69 beds in nursing home–type unit) A1 7 9 10 F1 2 3 4 7 8 10 12 13 15 16 17 19 20 21 22 23 24 26 27 28 29 30 31 32 34 35 37 38 39 40 41 42 43 44 45 48 49 52 53 54 55 56 57 58 59 60 63 64 65 66 67 68 69 70 71 72 73 74 P8 S Mercy Health Services, Farmington Hills, MI	21	10	385	9241	113	45728	1143	73255	31653	1305
DYERSVILLE—Dubuque County										
MERCY HEALTH CENTER–ST. MARY'S UNIT See Mercy Health Center, Dubuque										
ELDORA—Hardin County										
★ ELDORA REGIONAL MEDICAL CENTER, 2413 Edgington Avenue, Zip 50627–1541; tel. 515/858–5416; Richard C. Hamilton, Administrator A9 10 F8 12 15 16 17 19 21 22 26 28 30 32 33 34 39 41 42 44 45 49 51 56 58 63 64 65 66 71 72 73 P6 S Mercy Health Services, Farmington Hills, MI N North Iowa Mercy Health Network, Mason City, IA	14	10	18	281	4	9454	0	3056	1565	51
ELKADER—Clayton County										
★ CENTRAL COMMUNITY HOSPITAL, 901 Davidson Street, Zip 52043–9799; tel. 319/245–2250; Lisa Manson, Administrator A9 10 F8 11 12 13 15 16 17 19 20 22 24 26 27 28 29 30 32 33 34 36 37 39 40 41 42 44 45 46 49 51 64 65 67 71 74	23	10	29	304	4	8540	15	2792	1171	58
EMMETSBURG—Palo Alto County										
★ PALO ALTO COUNTY HOSPITAL, 3201 West First Street, Zip 50536–2599; tel. 712/852–2434; Darrell E. Vondrak, Administrator (Total facility includes 22 beds in nursing home–type unit) A9 10 F7 8 12 14 15 16 19 21 22 26 27 29 30 32 33 34 36 37 39 40 41 42 44 49 64 65 67 71 P7 S Mercy Health Services, Farmington Hills, MI	13	10	54	1044	33	19216	74	5778	2791	131
ESTHERVILLE—Emmet County										
★ HOLY FAMILY HEALTH SERVICES, 826 North Eighth Street, Zip 51334–1598; tel. 712/362–2631; Thomas Nordwick, President and Chief Executive Officer A1 9 10 F1 3 7 8 12 13 15 17 18 19 22 26 27 30 31 32 33 34 35 36 37 39 40 41 42 44 49 65 67 71 S Avera Health, Yankton, SD	21	10	36	1108	14	32296	89	8448	3944	180
FAIRFIELD—Jefferson County										
★ JEFFERSON COUNTY HOSPITAL, 400 Highland Avenue, Zip 52556–3713, Mailing Address: P.O. Box 588, Zip 52556–0588; tel. 515/472–4111; Walter W. Brownlee, President (Total facility includes 36 beds in nursing home–type unit) A9 10 F3 7 8 11 14 15 16 19 22 30 32 34 35 37 39 40 41 42 44 49 52 53 54 56 58 59 64 65 67 71	13	10	83	1786	52	27981	102	11160	4678	191
FORT DODGE—Webster County										
★ TRINITY REGIONAL HOSPITAL, 802 Kenyon Road, Zip 50501–5795; tel. 515/573–3101; Tom Tibbitts, President (Total facility includes 12 beds in nursing home–type unit) A1 9 10 F2 3 7 8 12 14 15 16 17 19 21 22 23 27 29 30 31 32 33 34 35 37 39 40 41 44 46 48 49 52 53 54 55 56 57 58 59 61 63 64 65 66 67 68 71 73 P7	23	10	174	6224	81	107155	488	48740	21123	686

Hospital, Address, Telephone, Administrator, Approval, Facility, and Physician Codes, Health Care System, Network	Classi-fication Codes		Utilization Data					Expense (thousands) of dollars		
★ American Hospital Association (AHA) membership □ Joint Commission on Accreditation of Healthcare Organizations (JCAHO) accreditation + American Osteopathic Healthcare Association (AOHA) membership ○ American Osteopathic Association (AOA) accreditation △ Commission on Accreditation of Rehabilitation Facilities (CARF) accreditation Control codes 61, 63, 64, 71, 72 and 73 indicate hospitals listed by AOHA, but not registered by AHA. For definition of numerical codes, see page A4	Control	Service	Staffed Beds	Admissions	Census	Outpatient Visits	Births	Total	Payroll	Personnel

FORT MADISON—Lee County
☒ FORT MADISON COMMUNITY HOSPITAL, Highway 61 West, Zip 52627–0174, Mailing Address: 5445 Avenue O, Box 174, Zip 52627–0174; tel. 319/372–6530; C. James Platt, Administrator **A**1 9 10 **F**8 12 14 15 16 19 22 24 27 28 30 32 34 35 37 40 41 42 44 45 46 49 59 60 65 71 74 **S** Quorum Health Group/Quorum Health Resources, Inc., Brentwood, TN — 23 10 | 50 | 2242 | 26 | 32996 | 179 | 16449 | 6859 | 214

GLENWOOD—Mills County
GLENWOOD STATE HOSPITAL SCHOOL, 711 South Vine, Zip 51534–1927; tel. 712/527–4811; William E. Campbell, Ph.D., Superintendent (Nonreporting) — 12 62 | 437 | — | — | — | — | — | — | —

GREENFIELD—Adair County
ADAIR COUNTY MEMORIAL HOSPITAL, 609 S.E. Kent Street, Zip 50849–9454; tel. 515/743–2123; Myrna Erb, Administrator **A**9 10 **F**7 8 14 15 21 22 26 30 32 34 36 39 42 44 49 60 63 **N** Mercy Network of Health Services, Des Moines, IA — 13 10 | 22 | 464 | 6 | 6712 | 23 | 3680 | 1725 | 82

GRINNELL—Poweshiek County
☒ GRINNELL REGIONAL MEDICAL CENTER, 210 Fourth Avenue, Zip 50112–1833; tel. 515/236–7511; Todd C. Linden, President and Chief Executive Officer **A**1 9 10 **F**1 8 12 13 14 15 16 17 19 22 24 27 28 29 30 31 32 33 35 37 39 40 41 42 44 45 46 49 51 58 63 65 67 70 71 73 **P**7 — 23 10 | 46 | 2143 | 24 | 38761 | 196 | 19990 | 9304 | 345

GRUNDY CENTER—Grundy County
GRUNDY COUNTY MEMORIAL HOSPITAL, 201 East J. Avenue, Zip 50638–2096; tel. 319/824–5421; James A. Faulwell, Administrator (Total facility includes 55 beds in nursing home–type unit) **A**9 10 **F**15 16 17 19 22 26 28 30 33 39 41 44 46 49 64 65 67 71 72 73 **P**3 **S** Iowa Health System, Des Moines, IA — 13 10 | 71 | 353 | 62 | 38185 | — | 3595 | 1758 | 87

GUTHRIE CENTER—Guthrie County
★ GUTHRIE COUNTY HOSPITAL, 710 North 12th Street, Zip 50115–1544; tel. 515/747–2201; Todd Hudspeth, Administrator **A**9 10 **F**8 11 12 15 17 19 20 21 22 30 32 33 34 35 36 39 41 42 44 49 51 58 65 70 71 73 — 13 10 | 26 | 463 | 5 | 7553 | 8 | 3170 | 1253 | 55

GUTTENBERG—Clayton County
★ GUTTENBERG MUNICIPAL HOSPITAL, Second and Main Street, Zip 52052–0550, Mailing Address: Box 550, Zip 52052–0550; tel. 319/252–1121; Roland D. Gee, Chief Executive Officer **A**9 10 **F**7 8 16 19 21 22 28 30 32 33 34 36 37 39 40 42 44 71 **S** Brim, Inc., Portland, OR — 14 10 | 21 | 495 | 5 | 13282 | 47 | 3777 | 1469 | 77

HAMBURG—Fremont County
GRAPE COMMUNITY HOSPITAL, Highway 275 North, Zip 51640, Mailing Address: P.O. Box 246, Zip 51640–0246; tel. 712/382–1515; Carolyn K. Hess, Administrator **A**9 10 **F**7 8 15 19 22 32 33 35 36 39 40 41 42 44 45 49 71 73 — 23 10 | 49 | 644 | 17 | 18907 | 27 | 4951 | 2451 | 73

HAMPTON—Franklin County
★ FRANKLIN GENERAL HOSPITAL, 1720 Central Avenue East, Zip 50441–1859; tel. 515/456–5000; Scott Wells, Interim Chief Executive Officer (Total facility includes 52 beds in nursing home–type unit) **A**9 10 **F**3 4 5 7 8 10 11 12 14 15 16 18 19 20 22 26 27 29 30 31 32 33 34 35 37 39 40 41 42 43 44 45 49 56 58 60 62 64 65 66 67 71 72 73 74 **P**2 6 8 **S** Mercy Health Services, Farmington Hills, MI **N** North Iowa Mercy Health Network, Mason City, IA — 13 10 | 82 | 495 | 62 | 12272 | — | 4800 | 2346 | 121

HARLAN—Shelby County
★ SHELBY COUNTY MYRTUE MEMORIAL HOSPITAL, 1213 Garfield Avenue, Zip 51537–2057; tel. 712/755–5161; Stephen L. Goeser, Administrator **A**9 10 **F**7 8 12 13 15 16 17 18 19 21 22 24 28 30 32 33 34 35 36 37 40 41 42 44 49 51 53 54 56 58 66 67 68 71 73 **P**6 8 — 13 10 | 52 | 1901 | 34 | 21358 | 81 | 9406 | 3851 | 169

HAWARDEN—Sioux County
HAWARDEN COMMUNITY HOSPITAL, 1111 11th Street, Zip 51023–1999; tel. 712/552–3100; Stuart A. Katz, FACHE, Administrator **A**9 10 **F**12 15 17 19 22 26 27 28 29 30 32 34 41 44 67 71 73 **S** Mercy Health Services, Farmington Hills, MI — 14 10 | 17 | 224 | 5 | 13220 | 5 | 1844 | 807 | 44

HUMBOLDT—Humboldt County
HUMBOLDT COUNTY MEMORIAL HOSPITAL, 1000 North 15th Street, Zip 50548–1008; tel. 515/332–4200; Kari L. Engholm, Administrator **A**9 10 **F**7 8 15 17 19 22 30 32 33 34 35 36 39 40 42 44 49 64 65 71 — 13 10 | 49 | 449 | 4 | 34985 | 71 | 5494 | 2915 | 129

IDA GROVE—Ida County
★ HORN MEMORIAL HOSPITAL, 701 East Second Street, Zip 51445–1699; tel. 712/364–3311; Dan Ellis, Administrator **A**9 10 **F**14 15 16 19 22 32 33 34 35 36 40 41 42 44 51 54 71 73 — 23 10 | 36 | 729 | 10 | 22461 | 87 | 4308 | 2138 | 75

INDEPENDENCE—Buchanan County
□ MENTAL HEALTH INSTITUTE, 2277 Iowa Avenue, Zip 50644–9106, Mailing Address: P.O. Box 111, Zip 50644–0111; tel. 319/334–2583; Bashker J. Dave, M.D., Superintendent **A**1 10 **F**14 15 16 20 22 27 45 46 51 52 53 54 55 56 65 67 73 **P**6 — 12 22 | 181 | 986 | 139 | 17 | — | 17432 | 12858 | 353
★ PEOPLE'S MEMORIAL HOSPITAL OF BUCHANAN COUNTY, 1600 First Street East, Zip 50644–3155; tel. 319/334–6071; Robert J. Richard, Administrator (Total facility includes 59 beds in nursing home–type unit) **A**9 10 **F**7 8 12 14 15 16 17 19 26 28 30 31 32 33 36 40 44 49 64 65 71 **P**4 — 13 10 | 109 | 458 | 64 | 26770 | 35 | 6428 | 3280 | 156

IOWA CITY—Johnson County
☒ MERCY HOSPITAL, 500 East Market Street, Zip 52245–2689; tel. 319/339–0300; Ronald R. Reed, President and Chief Executive Officer (Total facility includes 12 beds in nursing home–type unit) **A**1 2 3 5 9 10 **F**3 4 7 8 10 12 14 15 16 17 19 21 22 23 28 29 30 32 33 34 35 37 38 39 40 41 42 43 44 45 49 52 53 54 55 56 57 58 59 60 61 64 65 66 67 70 71 72 73 74 **P**1 — 21 10 | 240 | 9012 | 127 | 214713 | 1260 | 66241 | 29268 | 843
STATE PSYCHIATRIC HOSPITAL See University of Iowa Hospitals and Clinics

Hospital, Address, Telephone, Administrator, Approval, Facility, and Physician Codes, Health Care System, Network	Classification Codes		Utilization Data					Expense (thousands) of dollars		
★ American Hospital Association (AHA) membership □ Joint Commission on Accreditation of Healthcare Organizations (JCAHO) accreditation + American Osteopathic Healthcare Association (AOHA) membership ○ American Osteopathic Association (AOA) accreditation △ Commission on Accreditation of Rehabilitation Facilities (CARF) accreditation Control codes 61, 63, 64, 71, 72 and 73 indicate hospitals listed by AOHA, but not registered by AHA. For definition of numerical codes, see page A4	Control	Service	Staffed Beds	Admissions	Census	Outpatient Visits	Births	Total	Payroll	Personnel
✠ UNIVERSITY OF IOWA HOSPITALS AND CLINICS, (Includes Chemical Dependency Center, tel. 319/384–8765; State Psychiatric Hospital, tel. 319/356–4658; University Hospital School, tel. 319/353–6456), 200 Hawkins Drive, Zip 52242–1009; tel. 319/356–1616; R. Edward Howell, Director and Chief Executive Officer **A**1 2 3 5 8 9 10 **F**2 3 4 5 7 8 9 10 11 12 13 14 15 16 17 19 20 21 22 23 24 25 26 27 28 29 30 31 32 33 34 35 37 38 39 40 41 42 43 44 45 46 47 48 49 50 51 52 53 54 55 56 57 58 59 60 61 63 65 66 67 69 70 71 72 73 74 **P**1 7	12	10	858	40420	605	687984	1398	406227	166958	5253
✠ VETERANS AFFAIRS MEDICAL CENTER, Highway 6 West, Zip 52246–2208; tel. 319/338–0581; Gary L. Wilkinson, Director **A**1 3 5 8 9 **F**1 3 4 8 10 12 16 19 20 21 22 23 25 26 27 28 30 31 32 33 35 37 39 41 42 43 44 45 46 49 50 51 52 54 56 58 60 63 65 67 69 71 72 73 74 **S** Department of Veterans Affairs, Washington, DC	45	10	113	3988	83	136461	—	70231	40864	999
IOWA FALLS—Hardin County										
✠ ELLSWORTH MUNICIPAL HOSPITAL, 110 Rocksylvania Avenue, Zip 50126–2431; tel. 515/648–4631; John O'Brien, Administrator **A**1 2 9 10 **F**1 3 7 8 15 17 18 19 21 22 24 27 28 29 30 31 34 35 36 37 38 39 40 41 42 43 44 45 46 47 49 52 53 54 55 56 57 58 59 60 61 63 65 67 71 73 **P**8 **S** Mercy Health Services, Farmington Hills, MI	14	10	40	1402	18	20629	146	8223	4281	157
JEFFERSON—Greene County										
★ GREENE COUNTY MEDICAL CENTER, 1000 West Lincolnway, Zip 50129–1697; tel. 515/386–2114; Karen L. Bossard, Administrator (Total facility includes 62 beds in nursing home–type unit) **A**9 10 **F**7 8 11 12 13 14 15 16 17 18 19 21 22 26 28 29 30 31 32 33 34 35 39 40 41 42 44 45 49 62 64 65 67 68 71 73 **P**5	13	10	121	1046	93	24136	100	9727	5059	217
KEOKUK—Lee County										
✠ KEOKUK AREA HOSPITAL, 1600 Morgan Street, Zip 52632–3456; tel. 319/524–7150; Allan Zastrow, FACHE, Chief Executive Officer (Total facility includes 20 beds in nursing home–type unit) **A**1 9 10 **F**3 7 8 11 14 15 16 17 19 21 22 23 28 29 30 32 33 34 35 40 44 45 46 49 52 53 54 55 56 61 64 65 66 67 71 73 **P**7	23	10	113	4404	63	44092	293	21670	10176	413
KEOSAUQUA—Van Buren County										
★ VAN BUREN COUNTY HOSPITAL, Highway 1 North, Zip 52565, Mailing Address: P.O. Box 70, Zip 52565–0070; tel. 319/293–3171; Lisa Wagner Schnedler, Administrator **A**9 10 **F**1 7 8 12 16 17 19 22 28 30 32 34 35 41 42 44 49 58 65 70 71 73 **P**6 **S** Sisters of Mary of the Presentation Health Corporation, Fargo, ND	13	10	40	658	18	8879	30	5290	2660	127
KNOXVILLE—Marion County										
✠ KNOXVILLE AREA COMMUNITY HOSPITAL, 1002 South Lincoln Street, Zip 50138–3121; tel. 515/842–2151; Jim Murphy, Chief Executive Officer **A**1 9 10 **F**7 8 11 15 16 19 21 22 28 30 33 34 35 37 40 41 44 45 49 56 63 64 65 66 67 71 73 **P**8 **S** Quorum Health Group/Quorum Health Resources, Inc., Brentwood, TN KNOXVILLE DIVISION See Veterans Affairs Central Iowa Health Care System, Des Moines	23	10	52	1379	27	15578	99	8069	3121	149
LAKE CITY—Calhoun County										
★ STEWART MEMORIAL COMMUNITY HOSPITAL, 1301 West Main, Zip 51449–1585; tel. 712/464–3171; Kris Baumgart, Chief Executive Officer (Nonreporting) **A**9 10	23	10	49	—	—	—	—	—	—	—
LE MARS—Plymouth County										
FLOYD VALLEY HOSPITAL, Highway 3 East, Zip 51031, Mailing Address: P.O. Box 10, Zip 51031–0010; tel. 712/546–7871; Michael Donlin, Chief Executive Officer **A**9 10 **F**3 7 8 11 13 15 16 17 18 19 22 24 28 29 30 32 33 34 35 36 39 40 41 42 44 45 46 48 49 56 65 66 67 71 73 **P**5 **S** Avera Health, Yankton, SD	14	10	22	1388	20	33422	131	8875	3365	125
LEON—Decatur County										
✠ DECATUR COUNTY HOSPITAL, 1405 N.W. Church Street, Zip 50144–1299; tel. 515/446–4871; Susan Dutrey, Administrator (Nonreporting) **A**1 9 10	13	10	49	—	—	—	—	—	—	—
MANCHESTER—Delaware County										
DELAWARE COUNTY MEMORIAL HOSPITAL, 709 West Main Street, Zip 52057–0359; tel. 319/927–3232; Lon D. Butikofer, R.N., Ph.D., Administrator and Chief Executive Officer **A**9 10 **F**7 8 12 13 14 15 16 17 18 19 22 24 26 27 28 29 30 31 32 33 34 37 39 40 41 44 45 46 49 51 53 54 55 56 58 65 66 67 71 73 **P**3 5	13	10	35	813	9	50407	163	9709	5084	162
MANNING—Carroll County										
MANNING REGIONAL HEALTHCARE CENTER, (Formerly Manning General Hospital), 410 Main Street, Zip 51455–1093; tel. 712/653–2072; Michael S. Ketcham, Administrator (Total facility includes 12 beds in nursing home–type unit) **A**9 10 **F**1 2 3 7 8 14 18 19 21 22 26 29 30 31 32 34 35 40 41 44 45 46 51 54 56 64 65 67 71 73 **N** Mercy Network of Health Services, Des Moines, IA	23	10	41	424	12	8976	29	3042	1421	75
MAQUOKETA—Jackson County										
★ JACKSON COUNTY PUBLIC HOSPITAL, 700 West Grove Street, Zip 52060–0910; tel. 319/652–2474; Harold S. Geller, Administrator (Total facility includes 18 beds in nursing home–type unit) **A**9 10 **F**7 8 15 19 21 22 24 30 32 34 36 37 39 40 44 45 46 49 63 64 65 71 73	13	10	61	1134	28	14020	129	8669	4063	168
MARENGO—Iowa County										
MARENGO MEMORIAL HOSPITAL, 300 West May Street, Zip 52301–1261, Mailing Address: P.O. Box 228, Zip 52301–0228; tel. 319/642–5543; James H. Ragland, Administrator **A**9 10 **F**16 19 22 27 28 30 36 39 44 49 65 71 73 **P**6 **N** St Lukes/Iowa Health System, Des Moines, IA	14	10	44	374	33	11450	0	3985	2013	106

Hospital, Address, Telephone, Administrator, Approval, Facility, and Physician Codes, Health Care System, Network	Classi-fication Codes		Utilization Data					Expense (thousands) of dollars		
★ American Hospital Association (AHA) membership □ Joint Commission on Accreditation of Healthcare Organizations (JCAHO) accreditation + American Osteopathic Healthcare Association (AOHA) membership ○ American Osteopathic Association (AOA) accreditation △ Commission on Accreditation of Rehabilitation Facilities (CARF) accreditation Control codes 61, 63, 64, 71, 72 and 73 indicate hospitals listed by AOHA, but not registered by AHA. For definition of numerical codes, see page A4	Control	Service	Staffed Beds	Admissions	Census	Outpatient Visits	Births	Total	Payroll	Personnel

MARSHALLTOWN—Marshall County

☒ MARSHALLTOWN MEDICAL AND SURGICAL CENTER, 3 South Fourth Avenue, Zip 50158–2998; tel. 515/754–5151; Robert Cooper, Chief Executive Officer (Total facility includes 26 beds in nursing home–type unit) **A**1 9 10 **F**7 8 12 13 14 15 16 17 19 21 22 25 26 27 28 29 30 32 33 34 35 36 37 39 40 41 42 44 45 46 49 51 64 65 66 67 70 71 73 74 **P**7

23 10 | 111 | 3647 | 47 | 141159 | 390 | 33359 | 16033 | 505

MASON CITY—Cerro Gordo County

☒ NORTH IOWA MERCY HEALTH CENTER, 1000 Fourth Street S.W., Zip 50401–2800; tel. 515/422–7000; David H. Vellinga, President and Chief Executive Officer (Total facility includes 30 beds in nursing home–type unit) **A**1 2 3 5 9 10 **F**1 3 4 7 8 10 12 13 14 15 16 17 18 19 20 21 22 23 26 27 28 29 30 31 32 33 34 35 36 37 38 39 40 41 42 43 44 45 46 49 51 52 53 54 55 56 57 58 59 60 62 64 65 66 67 68 71 73 74 **P**1 6 **S** Mercy Health Services, Farmington Hills, MI **N** North Iowa Mercy Health Network, Mason City, IA

21 10 | 285 | 11624 | 139 | 599315 | 1168 | 127796 | 56476 | 1769

MISSOURI VALLEY—Harrison County

☒ ALEGENT HEALTH COMMUNITY MEMORIAL HOSPITAL, 631 North Eighth Street, Zip 51555–1199; tel. 712/642–2784; James A. Seymour, Regional Administrator **A**1 9 10 **F**8 12 15 16 19 22 28 29 30 32 33 34 39 41 42 44 49 53 54 56 58 65 66 67 71 **P**8 **N** Alegent Health, Omaha, NE

23 10 | 35 | 581 | 7 | 14926 | — | 4955 | 2368 | 92

MOUNT AYR—Ringgold County

RINGGOLD COUNTY HOSPITAL, 211 Shellway Drive, Zip 50854–1299; tel. 515/464–3226; Gordon W. Winkler, Administrator **A**9 10 **F**2 3 8 19 22 27 30 40 42 44 71 **P**6 **N** Mercy Network of Health Services, Des Moines, IA

13 10 | 36 | 560 | 9 | 15459 | — | 4333 | 1949 | 89

MOUNT PLEASANT—Henry County

★ HENRY COUNTY HEALTH CENTER, 407 South White Street, Zip 52641–2299; tel. 319/385–3141; Robert Miller, Chief Executive Officer (Total facility includes 49 beds in nursing home–type unit) **A**9 10 **F**8 13 15 16 17 19 21 22 26 28 29 30 32 34 35 37 40 41 42 44 45 49 51 64 65 66 67 71 73 **P**7 8

13 10 | 71 | 1400 | 65 | — | 142 | 13601 | 6072 | 250

MENTAL HEALTH INSTITUTE, 1200 East Washington Street, Zip 52641–1898; tel. 319/385–7231; David J. Scurr, Superintendent **A**10 **F**2 20 45 52 65 73

12 82 | 80 | 952 | 66 | 18 | — | 4850 | 3252 | 75

MUSCATINE—Muscatine County

□ MUSCATINE GENERAL HOSPITAL, 1518 Mulberry Avenue, Zip 52761–3499; tel. 319/264–9100; Karmon Bejlla, System Chief Executive Officer (Total facility includes 8 beds in nursing home–type unit) **A**1 9 10 **F**3 7 8 14 16 17 19 21 22 26 30 35 36 37 39 40 42 44 49 64 65 71

13 10 | 66 | 2584 | 28 | 33585 | 410 | 19983 | 8623 | 322

NEVADA—Story County

★ STORY COUNTY HOSPITAL AND LONG TERM CARE FACILITY, 630 Sixth Street, Zip 50201–2266; tel. 515/382–2111; Todd Willert, Administrator (Total facility includes 80 beds in nursing home–type unit) **A**9 10 **F**19 20 22 24 26 27 30 32 33 34 36 37 39 41 42 44 48 49 59 64 65 66 67 71 73 **P**3 6 7 **N** Mercy Network of Health Services, Des Moines, IA

13 10 | 122 | 304 | 86 | 16806 | — | 6155 | 2519 | 132

NEW HAMPTON—Chickasaw County

☒ SAINT JOSEPH COMMUNITY HOSPITAL, 308 North Maple Avenue, Zip 50659–1142; tel. 515/394–4121; Carolyn Martin–Shaw, President (Total facility includes 35 beds in nursing home–type unit) **A**1 9 10 **F**7 8 12 15 16 17 19 20 22 26 30 32 33 34 37 39 40 44 49 64 65 67 71 73 74 **S** Mercy Health Services, Farmington Hills, MI

21 10 | 55 | 749 | 39 | 18537 | 61 | 6079 | 2766 | 118

NEWTON—Jasper County

☒ SKIFF MEDICAL CENTER, 204 North Fourth Avenue East, Zip 50208–3100; tel. 515/792–1273; Eric L. Lothe, President and Chief Executive Officer **A**1 9 10 **F**7 8 13 15 16 19 22 32 33 34 35 37 39 40 41 44 49 52 53 54 55 56 57 59 63 67 71

14 10 | 68 | 2144 | 23 | 54200 | 166 | 16399 | 8131 | 279

OAKDALE—Johnson County

IOWA MEDICAL AND CLASSIFICATION CENTER, Mailing Address: IMCC, Box A., Zip 52319; tel. 319/626–2391; Russell E. Rogerson, Warden **F**2 3 4 5 6 7 8 9 10 11 12 19 20 21 22 23 25 26 29 30 31 35 37 39 40 41 42 43 44 45 46 48 49 50 51 52 54 55 56 57 58 60 61 63 64 65 66 67 69 70 71 72 73 74

12 22 | 23 | 152 | 18 | 0 | 0 | — | — | 26

OELWEIN—Fayette County

☒ MERCY HOSPITAL OF FRANCISCAN SISTERS, 201 Eighth Avenue S.E., Zip 50662–2447; tel. 319/283–6000; Richard Schrupp, President and Chief Executive Officer (Total facility includes 39 beds in nursing home–type unit) **A**1 9 10 **F**3 7 8 15 19 21 22 26 27 28 29 30 32 33 34 35 36 37 39 40 41 44 45 46 51 63 64 65 66 67 71 **P**6 **S** Wheaton Franciscan Services, Inc., Wheaton, IL

21 10 | 64 | 955 | 48 | 52659 | 72 | 8884 | 4037 | 134

ONAWA—Monona County

☒ BURGESS MEMORIAL HOSPITAL, 1600 Diamond Street, Zip 51040–1548; tel. 712/423–9206; Francis Tramp, President **A**1 9 10 **F**7 8 14 15 16 17 19 21 22 24 28 30 32 33 34 40 41 42 44 49 58 65 67 71 73 74

23 10 | 17 | 1529 | 18 | 31625 | 93 | 9487 | 4314 | 160

ORANGE CITY—Sioux County

★ ORANGE CITY MUNICIPAL HOSPITAL, 400 Central Avenue N.W., Zip 51041–1398; tel. 712/737–4984; Martin W. Guthmiller, Administrator (Total facility includes 83 beds in nursing home–type unit) **A**9 10 **F**7 8 13 14 15 16 17 18 19 20 21 22 29 30 32 33 35 36 37 39 40 41 42 44 45 46 58 64 65 66 67 71 73 74 **P**6 **S** Sioux Valley Hospitals and Health System, Sioux Falls, SD

14 10 | 113 | 1155 | 97 | 42053 | 173 | 11243 | 5293 | 228

OSAGE—Mitchell County

★ MITCHELL COUNTY REGIONAL HEALTH CENTER, 616 North Eighth Street, Zip 50461–1498; tel. 515/732–3781; Kimberly J. Miller, Administrator **A**9 10 **F**7 8 15 16 19 22 37 39 40 41 42 44 49 65 71 **P**1 **S** Mercy Health Services, Farmington Hills, MI **N** North Iowa Mercy Health Network, Mason City, IA

13 10 | 40 | 874 | 9 | 53222 | 79 | 7699 | 2268 | 111

Hospital, Address, Telephone, Administrator, Approval, Facility, and Physician Codes, Health Care System, Network	Classi-fication Codes		Utilization Data					Expense (thousands) of dollars		
★ American Hospital Association (AHA) membership □ Joint Commission on Accreditation of Healthcare Organizations (JCAHO) accreditation + American Osteopathic Healthcare Association (AOHA) membership ○ American Osteopathic Association (AOA) accreditation △ Commission on Accreditation of Rehabilitation Facilities (CARF) accreditation Control codes 61, 63, 64, 71, 72 and 73 indicate hospitals listed by AOHA, but not registered by AHA. For definition of numerical codes, see page A4	Control	Service	Staffed Beds	Admissions	Census	Outpatient Visits	Births	Total	Payroll	Personnel

OSCEOLA—Clarke County
★ CLARKE COUNTY HOSPITAL, 800 South Fillmore Street, Zip 50213; tel. 515/342–2184; David Stark, Interim Administrator **A**9 10 **F**8 14 15 16 19 21 22 23 30 33 36 37 42 44 49 71 **S** Iowa Health System, Des Moines, IA

	13	10	48	653	35	13195	—	4304	1812	98

OSKALOOSA—Mahaska County
✠ MAHASKA COUNTY HOSPITAL, 1229 C. Avenue East, Zip 52577–4298; tel. 515/672–3100; David E. Rutter, Administrator **A**1 9 10 **F**3 7 8 11 12 13 14 15 16 17 18 19 20 21 22 25 26 27 28 29 30 31 32 33 34 35 36 39 40 41 42 44 45 46 49 51 53 54 55 56 57 58 59 65 66 67 68 71 72 73 74 **P**1

	13	10	53	1585	14	61694	181	11099	5838	203

OTTUMWA—Wapello County
✠ OTTUMWA REGIONAL HEALTH CENTER, 1001 Pennsylvania Avenue, Zip 52501–2186; tel. 515/684–2300; Clarence Cory, President (Total facility includes 13 beds in nursing home–type unit) (Nonreporting) **A**1 2 9 10

	23	10	90	—	—	—	—	—	—	—

PELLA—Marion County
✠ PELLA REGIONAL HEALTH CENTER, 404 Jefferson Street, Zip 50219–1257; tel. 515/628–3150; Robert D. Kroese, Chief Executive Officer (Total facility includes 109 beds in nursing home–type unit) **A**1 9 10 **F**1 7 8 11 14 15 16 17 19 22 28 29 30 32 33 34 35 40 41 42 43 44 45 46 49 64 65 67 71 73 **P**1 5 6

	23	10	156	1585	138	71233	224	16734	7549	409

PERRY—Dallas County
★ DALLAS COUNTY HOSPITAL, 610 10th Street, Zip 50220–2221, Mailing Address: P.O. Box 608, Zip 50220–0608; tel. 515/465–3547; Vernette Riley, Administrator and Chief Executive Officer **A**9 10 **F**1 17 19 26 30 33 34 39 41 42 44 49 67 70 71 72 73 **P**4 **S** Iowa Health System, Des Moines, IA

	13	10	49	678	7	7925	—	7130	2621	104

POCAHONTAS—Pocahontas County
★ POCAHONTAS COMMUNITY HOSPITAL, 606 N.W. Seventh, Zip 50574–1099; tel. 712/335–3501; Jay Christensen, Administrator **A**9 10 **F**8 15 19 22 28 30 32 33 34 37 42 44 49 64 65 67 71 **P**6

	14	10	25	364	4	21339	—	2963	1336	64

PRIMGHAR—Obrien County
★ BAUM HARMON MEMORIAL HOSPITAL, 255 North Welch Avenue, Zip 51245–1034, Mailing Address: P.O. Box 528, Zip 51245–0528; tel. 712/757–3905; Ronald Bender, Administrator **A**9 10 **F**7 8 12 15 19 22 24 28 30 32 33 34 35 36 37 40 41 42 44 49 65 66 67 71 **P**6 8 **S** Mercy Health Services, Farmington Hills, MI

	14	10	17	178	2	8855	1	2397	837	44

RED OAK—Montgomery County
★ MONTGOMERY COUNTY MEMORIAL HOSPITAL, 2301 Eastern Avenue, Zip 51566–1300; tel. 712/623–7000; Allen E. Pohren, Administrator **A**9 10 **F**7 8 12 14 15 16 17 19 22 23 30 32 33 34 35 36 37 39 40 41 42 44 49 58 63 64 65 67 71 73

	13	10	40	1853	29	40716	1	12740	5361	209

ROCK RAPIDS—Lyon County
★ MERRILL PIONEER COMMUNITY HOSPITAL, 801 South Greene Street, Zip 51246–1998; tel. 712/472–2591; Gordon Smith, Administrator **A**9 10 **F**7 8 14 15 19 22 28 30 33 35 40 44 49 71 **P**6 **S** Sioux Valley Hospitals and Health System, Sioux Falls, SD **N** Sioux Valley Health System, Sioux Falls, SD

	23	10	16	513	7	6864	41	2416	1111	52

ROCK VALLEY—Sioux County
★ HEGG MEMORIAL HEALTH CENTER, 1202 21st Avenue, Zip 51247–1497; tel. 712/476–5305; Chris Thomas, Administrator and Chief Executive Officer (Total facility includes 95 beds in nursing home–type unit) **A**9 10 **F**7 8 15 16 17 19 22 24 28 29 30 32 33 34 35 36 37 39 40 41 42 44 45 49 52 59 62 64 65 66 67 71 73 **P**5 **S** Avera Health, Yankton, SD

	23	10	123	293	84	9441	28	4604	2592	148

SAC CITY—Sac County
★ LORING HOSPITAL, Highland Avenue, Zip 50583–0217; tel. 712/662–7105; Greg Miner, Administrator (Total facility includes 21 beds in nursing home–type unit) **A**9 10 **F**3 4 5 7 8 10 11 13 14 15 16 17 19 22 23 26 28 29 30 31 32 33 34 35 39 40 42 43 44 45 46 49 51 53 54 55 56 57 58 59 60 64 65 67 69 71 73

	23	10	54	866	26	8256	23	—	2287	102

SHELDON—Obrien County
★ NORTHWEST IOWA HEALTH CENTER, 118 North Seventh Avenue, Zip 51201–1235; tel. 712/324–5041; Charles R. Miller, Chief Executive Officer (Total facility includes 70 beds in nursing home–type unit) **A**9 10 **F**1 3 8 14 15 16 17 18 19 20 22 26 28 30 32 33 34 35 36 39 40 41 42 44 45 46 49 53 54 55 56 57 58 59 64 65 66 67 71 73 **P**6 **S** Sioux Valley Hospitals and Health System, Sioux Falls, SD **N** Sioux Valley Health System, Sioux Falls, SD

	23	10	95	967	79	22410	105	6727	3081	173

SHENANDOAH—Page County
★ SHENANDOAH MEMORIAL HOSPITAL, 300 Pershing Avenue, Zip 51601–2397; tel. 712/246–1230; Charles L. Millburg, CHE, Chief Executive Officer (Total facility includes 62 beds in nursing home–type unit) **A**9 10 **F**7 8 12 14 15 16 19 21 22 24 27 28 32 34 35 36 37 39 41 42 44 46 60 63 64 65 71 73 **P**1 7

	23	10	106	1087	71	20967	88	10312	4553	219

SIBLEY—Osceola County
★ OSCEOLA COMMUNITY HOSPITAL, Ninth Avenue North, Zip 51249–0258, Mailing Address: P.O. Box 258, Zip 51249–0258; tel. 712/754–2574; Janet Dykstra, Chief Executive Officer **A**9 10 **F**2 7 8 11 13 14 15 16 17 19 20 22 26 27 28 29 30 31 32 33 34 35 36 39 40 41 42 44 45 46 49 51 53 54 55 56 57 58 60 62 64 65 66 67 68 69 71 73 74 **P**5

	23	10	32	452	6	15720	70	3691	—	80

SIGOURNEY—Keokuk County
KEOKUK COUNTY HEALTH CENTER, 1312 South Stuart Street, Zip 52591–0286, Mailing Address: P.O. Box 286, Zip 52591–0286; tel. 515/622–2720; Douglas A. Sheetz, Chief Executive Officer **A**9 10 **F**14 19 22 39 44 45 46 49 51 53 56 58 63 65 69 71

	13	10	26	165	14	7999	—	2087	1067	51

Hospital, Address, Telephone, Administrator, Approval, Facility, and Physician Codes, Health Care System, Network	Classi-fication Codes		Utilization Data					Expense (thousands) of dollars		
	Control	Service	Staffed Beds	Admissions	Census	Outpatient Visits	Births	Total	Payroll	Personnel

★ American Hospital Association (AHA) membership
□ Joint Commission on Accreditation of Healthcare Organizations (JCAHO) accreditation
+ American Osteopathic Healthcare Association (AOHA) membership
○ American Osteopathic Association (AOA) accreditation
△ Commission on Accreditation of Rehabilitation Facilities (CARF) accreditation
Control codes 61, 63, 64, 71, 72 and 73 indicate hospitals listed by AOHA, but not registered by AHA. For definition of numerical codes, see page A4

SIOUX CENTER—Sioux County

SIOUX CENTER COMMUNITY HOSPITAL AND HEALTH CENTER, 605 South Main Avenue, Zip 51250–1398; tel. 712/722–1271; Marla Toering, Administrator (Total facility includes 69 beds in nursing home–type unit) **A**9 10 **F**7 8 15 16 19 21 22 28 30 32 33 34 35 39 41 44 49 64 65 66 67 71 74 **S** Avera Health, Yankton, SD | 23 | 10 | 90 | 578 | 77 | 29540 | 226 | 7849 | 3506 | 163

SIOUX CITY—Woodbury County

⊞ △ MARIAN HEALTH CENTER, (Includes Marian Behavioral Health Center, 4301 Sergeant Road, Zip 51106; tel. 712/279–2446; 801 Fifth Street, Zip 51102, Mailing Address: P.O. Box 3168, Zip 51102–3168; tel. 712/279–2010; Deborah VandenBroek, President and Chief Executive Officer (Total facility includes 20 beds in nursing home–type unit) **A**1 2 3 5 7 9 10 **F**1 3 4 7 8 10 11 12 13 14 15 16 17 19 21 22 25 26 27 28 29 30 31 32 33 35 36 37 39 40 41 42 43 44 45 46 48 49 51 52 53 54 55 56 57 58 59 60 64 65 67 70 71 73 **P**5 6 7 8 **S** Mercy Health Services, Farmington Hills, MI | 21 | 10 | 284 | 10906 | 167 | 303616 | 961 | 125339 | 51423 | 317

⊞ ST. LUKE'S REGIONAL MEDICAL CENTER, 2720 Stone Park Boulevard, Zip 51104–2000; tel. 712/279–3500; John D. Daniels, President and Chief Executive Officer **A**1 2 3 5 6 9 10 **F**1 4 6 7 8 9 10 11 12 15 16 17 18 19 21 22 23 25 26 27 29 30 32 33 34 35 36 37 38 39 40 41 42 44 45 46 47 49 52 54 56 59 60 62 64 65 67 71 72 73 74 **P**5 6 **S** Iowa Health System, Des Moines, IA | 23 | 10 | 187 | 10418 | 128 | 100801 | 1611 | 78566 | 32248 | 1346

SPENCER—Clay County

★ SPENCER MUNICIPAL HOSPITAL, 1200 First Avenue East, Zip 51301–4321; tel. 712/264–6198; Jerry Poehling, Interim Administrator (Total facility includes 14 beds in nursing home–type unit) **A**9 10 **F**3 7 8 12 14 15 16 17 19 20 21 22 23 26 27 28 30 32 33 34 35 36 37 39 40 41 42 44 45 46 49 52 54 55 56 57 58 59 60 63 64 65 66 67 71 73 **S** Sioux Valley Hospitals and Health System, Sioux Falls, SD | 14 | 10 | 86 | 2892 | 34 | 34166 | 259 | 20911 | 9805 | 363

SPIRIT LAKE—Dickinson County

□ DICKINSON COUNTY MEMORIAL HOSPITAL, Highway 71 South, Zip 51360, Mailing Address: Box AB, Zip 51360; tel. 712/336–1230; Richard C. Kielman, President and Chief Executive Officer **A**1 9 10 **F**7 8 14 15 16 19 22 27 28 30 32 35 36 37 40 42 44 65 66 67 71 73 | 13 | 10 | 47 | 1640 | 19 | 31199 | 160 | 12320 | 5241 | 202

STORM LAKE—Buena Vista County

⊞ BUENA VISTA COUNTY HOSPITAL, 1525 West Fifth Street, Zip 50588–0309; tel. 712/732–4030; James O. Nelson, Administrator **A**1 9 10 **F**1 3 7 8 11 12 14 15 16 19 22 24 30 32 33 34 35 36 39 40 41 42 44 49 64 67 71 73 **P**3 5 | 13 | 10 | 30 | 1755 | 15 | 65715 | 259 | 12586 | 5863 | 248

SUMNER—Bremer County

COMMUNITY MEMORIAL HOSPITAL, 909 West First Street, Zip 50674–1203, Mailing Address: P.O. Box 148, Zip 50674–0148; tel. 319/578–3275 **A**9 10 **F**3 7 8 14 19 22 30 32 33 34 35 36 39 41 44 49 65 71 73 | 23 | 10 | 29 | 389 | 4 | 13510 | 21 | 3397 | 1566 | 59

VINTON—Benton County

★ VIRGINIA GAY HOSPITAL, 502 North Ninth Avenue, Zip 52349–2299; tel. 319/472–6200; Michael J. Riege, Chief Executive Officer (Total facility includes 68 beds in nursing home–type unit) **A**9 10 **F**14 15 16 19 22 27 30 32 34 39 41 44 45 49 51 62 64 65 66 71 **P**6 **N** St Lukes/Iowa Health System, Des Moines, IA | 23 | 10 | 97 | 272 | 62 | — | — | 5612 | 2637 | 120

WASHINGTON—Washington County

★ WASHINGTON COUNTY HOSPITAL, 400 East Polk Street, Zip 52353, Mailing Address: P.O. Box 909, Zip 52353; tel. 319/653–5481; Ronald D. Davis, Chief Executive Officer (Total facility includes 43 beds in nursing home–type unit) **A**9 10 **F**7 8 11 15 19 22 28 30 32 36 40 44 45 49 64 65 71 73 **S** Quorum Health Group/Quorum Health Resources, Inc., Brentwood, TN | 13 | 10 | 83 | 1415 | 57 | 41673 | 126 | 9649 | 4259 | 174

WATERLOO—Black Hawk County

⊞ ALLEN MEMORIAL HOSPITAL, 1825 Logan Avenue, Zip 50703–1916; tel. 319/235–3987; Richard A. Seidler, FACHE, Chief Executive Officer (Total facility includes 20 beds in nursing home–type unit) **A**1 3 5 6 9 10 **F**3 4 7 8 10 12 14 15 16 17 19 20 21 22 23 24 25 28 29 30 31 32 33 34 35 37 39 40 41 42 43 44 45 46 49 51 52 53 54 55 56 57 58 59 60 64 65 67 68 71 73 74 **P**3 6 7 8 **S** Iowa Health System, Des Moines, IA | 23 | 10 | 175 | 8080 | 109 | 200048 | 793 | 65083 | 28006 | 875

⊞ △ COVENANT MEDICAL CENTER, (Includes Kimball–Ridge Center, 2101 Kimball Avenue, Zip 50702), 3421 West Ninth Street, Zip 50702–5499; tel. 319/272–8000; Raymond F. Burfeind, President (Total facility includes 44 beds in nursing home–type unit) **A**1 2 3 5 7 9 10 **F**2 3 4 6 7 8 12 15 16 17 18 19 20 21 22 23 24 27 28 29 30 31 32 33 34 35 37 39 40 41 42 44 45 48 49 51 52 53 54 55 56 57 58 59 60 63 64 65 66 67 68 70 71 73 74 **P**6 **S** Wheaton Franciscan Services, Inc., Wheaton, IL | 21 | 10 | 293 | 11136 | 161 | 431500 | 1428 | 106340 | 51132 | 1616

KIMBALL–RIDGE CENTER See Covenant Medical Center

WAUKON—Allamakee County

VETERANS MEMORIAL HOSPITAL, 40 First Street S.E., Zip 52172–2099; tel. 319/568–3411 **A**9 10 **F**3 7 8 14 15 16 17 19 22 24 28 29 30 32 33 34 39 40 42 44 49 58 65 66 67 68 71 72 | 14 | 10 | 25 | 682 | 7 | 39501 | 49 | 4654 | 2115 | 151

WAVERLY—Bremer County

★ WAVERLY MUNICIPAL HOSPITAL, 312 Ninth Street S.W., Zip 50677–2999; tel. 319/352–4120; Arnold Flessner, Administrator **A**9 10 **F**7 8 14 15 16 19 22 24 26 27 28 29 30 32 33 34 35 37 39 40 41 44 45 46 47 49 64 65 66 67 71 73 | 14 | 10 | 38 | 1036 | 11 | 18800 | 112 | 7735 | 3358 | 134

Hospital, Address, Telephone, Administrator, Approval, Facility, and Physician Codes, Health Care System, Network	Classi-fication Codes		Utilization Data					Expense (thousands) of dollars		
	Control	Service	Staffed Beds	Admissions	Census	Outpatient Visits	Births	Total	Payroll	Personnel

★ American Hospital Association (AHA) membership
☐ Joint Commission on Accreditation of Healthcare Organizations (JCAHO) accreditation
+ American Osteopathic Healthcare Association (AOHA) membership
○ American Osteopathic Association (AOA) accreditation
△ Commission on Accreditation of Rehabilitation Facilities (CARF) accreditation
Control codes 61, 63, 64, 71, 72 and 73 indicate hospitals listed by AOHA, but not registered by AHA. For definition of numerical codes, see page A4

WEBSTER CITY—Hamilton County

☐ HAMILTON COUNTY PUBLIC HOSPITAL, 800 Ohio Street, Zip 50595–2824, Mailing Address: P.O. Box 430, Zip 50595–0430; tel. 515/832–9400; Roger W. Lenz, Administrator **A**1 9 10 **F**7 8 15 16 19 22 28 30 32 35 36 39 40 41 44 49 63 65 67 71 73 **P**8 **N** Mercy Network of Health Services, Des Moines, IA	13	10	40	2134	23	15425	178	10951	5293	213

WEST UNION—Fayette County

★ PALMER LUTHERAN HEALTH CENTER, 112 Jefferson Street, Zip 52175–1022; tel. 319/422–3811; Debrah Chensvold, President **A**9 10 **F**7 8 15 16 19 22 26 29 30 31 32 33 34 35 41 42 44 49 52 57 58 64 65 66 67 71 73	23	10	30	817	11	47950	123	8223	3650	143

WINTERSET—Madison County

MADISON COUNTY MEMORIAL HOSPITAL, 300 Hutchings Street, Zip 50273–2199; tel. 515/462–2373; Jill Kordick, Administrator **A**9 10 **F**3 8 12 17 19 22 26 30 31 32 33 34 35 37 39 41 42 44 45 49 51 53 54 55 56 57 58 59 64 65 66 67 68 71 73	13	10	31	680	12	36480	—	7062	2509	109

WOODWARD—Boone County

WOODWARD STATE HOSPITAL–SCHOOL, Zip 50276–9999; tel. 515/438–2600; Michael J. Davis, Ph.D., Superintendent **F**4 5 8 9 10 11 19 20 21 22 23 27 31 35 37 42 43 44 47 50 52 53 54 55 56 57 58 60 63 64 65 70 71 73	12	62	291	32	279	—	—	28978	19907	—

KANSAS

Resident population 2,852 (in thousands)
Resident population in metro areas 44.0%
Birth rate per 1,000 population 13.1
65 years and over 15.2%
Percent of persons without health insurance 11.6%

Hospital, Address, Telephone, Administrator, Approval, Facility, and Physician Codes, Health Care System, Network	Classi-fication Codes		Utilization Data					Expense (thousands) of dollars		
★ American Hospital Association (AHA) membership □ Joint Commission on Accreditation of Healthcare Organizations (JCAHO) accreditation + American Osteopathic Healthcare Association (AOHA) membership ○ American Osteopathic Association (AOA) accreditation △ Commission on Accreditation of Rehabilitation Facilities (CARF) accreditation Control codes 61, 63, 64, 71, 72 and 73 indicate hospitals listed by AOHA, but not registered by AHA. For definition of numerical codes, see page A4	Control	Service	Staffed Beds	Admissions	Census	Outpatient Visits	Births	Total	Payroll	Personnel

ABILENE—Dickinson County
★ MEMORIAL HOSPITAL, 511 N.E. Tenth Street, Zip 67410–2100, Mailing Address: P.O. Box 219, Zip 67410–0219; tel. 913/263–2100; Leon J. Boor, Chief Executive Officer **A**9 10 **F**7 8 15 19 22 24 30 32 33 34 36 39 40 42 44 49 52 57 64 65 67 71 73 **P**8 **N** Sunflower Health Network, Inc., Salina, KS — 16 10 | 31 | 923 | 14 | 10957 | 74 | 6527 | 3288 | 138

ANTHONY—Harper County
HOSPITAL DISTRICT NUMBER SIX OF HARPER COUNTY, 1101 East Spring Street, Zip 67003–2199; tel. 316/842–5111; Cindy M. McCray, Administrator and Director Nursing **A**9 10 **F**8 15 19 22 42 44 51 61 64 65 71 **P**6 — 16 10 | 30 | 265 | 21 | 18054 | — | 3512 | 1766 | 68

ARKANSAS CITY—Cowley County
⌖ SOUTH CENTRAL KANSAS REGIONAL MEDICAL CENTER, 216 West Birch Avenue, Zip 67005–1598, Mailing Address: P.O. Box 1107, Zip 67005–1107; tel. 316/442–2500; Webster T. Russell, Chief Executive Officer (Total facility includes 10 beds in nursing home–type unit) **A**1 9 10 **F**7 8 11 12 14 15 16 17 19 22 29 30 32 33 34 35 36 39 40 42 44 46 49 51 63 64 65 71 72 73 **P**8 — 14 10 | 75 | 1110 | 11 | 77322 | 167 | 8763 | 3682 | 153

ASHLAND—Clark County
★ ASHLAND HEALTH CENTER, 709 Oak Street, Zip 67831, Mailing Address: P.O. Box 188, Zip 67831; tel. 316/635–2241; Bryan Stacey, Administrator (Total facility includes 36 beds in nursing home–type unit) **A**9 10 **F**1 8 20 24 27 29 30 32 33 34 41 44 46 49 54 56 58 64 65 71 **S** Great Plains Health Alliance, Inc., Phillipsburg, KS **N** Great Plains Health Alliance, Phillipsburg, KS — 16 10 | 48 | 46 | 31 | 5145 | — | 2187 | 1242 | 58

ATCHISON—Atchison County
⌖ ATCHISON HOSPITAL, 1301 North Second Street, Zip 66002–1297; tel. 913/367–2131; W. David Drew, President and Chief Executive Officer (Total facility includes 38 beds in nursing home–type unit) **A**1 9 10 **F**7 8 14 15 17 19 21 22 23 27 28 30 32 33 34 35 37 40 44 48 49 51 52 54 57 64 65 66 67 71 73 **P**4 — 23 10 | 121 | 2504 | 58 | 28558 | 235 | 15738 | 8026 | 263

ATWOOD—Rawlins County
RAWLINS COUNTY HEALTH CENTER, (Formerly Rawlins County Hospital), 707 Grant Street, Zip 67730–4700, Mailing Address: Box 47, Zip 67730–4700; tel. 785/626–3211; Donald J. Kessen, Administrator and Chief Executive Officer **A**9 10 **F**3 7 8 14 15 16 17 19 20 22 26 27 30 31 32 34 35 39 42 44 49 62 63 64 65 71 73 **S** Great Plains Health Alliance, Inc., Phillipsburg, KS **N** Great Plains Health Alliance, Phillipsburg, KS; Hays Medical Center, Hays, KS; High Plains Rural Health Network, Fort Morgan, CO — 13 10 | 24 | 150 | 1 | 6524 | 8 | 2392 | 1314 | 48

AUGUSTA—Butler County
AUGUSTA MEDICAL COMPLEX, 2101 Dearborn Street, Zip 67010–0430, Mailing Address: Box 430, Zip 67010–0430; tel. 316/775–5421; Larry D. Wilkerson, Chief Executive Officer (Total facility includes 107 beds in nursing home–type unit) (Nonreporting) **A**9 10 — 23 10 | 147 | — | — | — | — | — | — | —

BELLEVILLE—Republic County
★ REPUBLIC COUNTY HOSPITAL, 2420 G. Street, Zip 66935–2499; tel. 785/527–2255; Charles A. Westin, FACHE, Administrator (Total facility includes 38 beds in nursing home–type unit) **A**9 10 **F**7 8 12 14 15 17 19 20 21 22 26 28 33 34 39 41 42 44 45 46 49 64 65 66 71 **P**8 **S** Great Plains Health Alliance, Inc., Phillipsburg, KS **N** Sunflower Health Network, Inc., Salina, KS; Great Plains Health Alliance, Phillipsburg, KS — 23 10 | 86 | 1220 | 51 | 6648 | 66 | 6110 | 2819 | 136

BELOIT—Mitchell County
★ MITCHELL COUNTY HOSPITAL, 400 West Eighth, Zip 67420–1605, Mailing Address: P.O. Box 399, Zip 67420–0399; tel. 785/738–2266; John M. Osse, Administrator (Total facility includes 40 beds in nursing home–type unit) **A**9 10 **F**7 8 12 17 19 20 22 26 32 33 34 35 36 41 42 44 45 49 64 65 67 71 **S** Great Plains Health Alliance, Inc., Phillipsburg, KS **N** Sunflower Health Network, Inc., Salina, KS; Great Plains Health Alliance, Phillipsburg, KS — 23 10 | 89 | 1593 | 60 | 12921 | 95 | 9386 | 4508 | 181

BURLINGTON—Coffey County
COFFEY COUNTY HOSPITAL, 801 North Fourth Street, Zip 66839–2602, Mailing Address: P.O. Box 189, Zip 66839–0189; tel. 316/364–2121; Dennis L. George, Chief Executive Officer (Total facility includes 40 beds in nursing home–type unit) **A**9 10 **F**7 8 11 15 19 22 25 28 32 34 37 40 41 44 49 62 64 65 71 73 **P**6 — 13 10 | 60 | 868 | 38 | 10787 | 67 | 9841 | 4582 | 181

CALDWELL—Sumner County
SUMNER COUNTY HOSPITAL DISTRICT ONE, 601 South Osage Street, Zip 67022–1698; tel. 316/845–6492; Virgil Watson, Administrator **A**9 10 **F**15 28 32 33 39 42 44 49 51 64 73 **P**5 — 16 10 | 22 | 423 | 10 | — | 0 | — | 961 | —

CEDAR VALE—Chautauqua County
CEDAR VALE COMMUNITY HOSPITAL, 501 Cedar Street, Zip 67024, Mailing Address: P.O. Box 398, Zip 67024–0398; tel. 316/758–2266; William A. Lybarger, Administrator **A**9 10 **F**15 21 27 28 32 51 64 71 **P**5 — 23 10 | 16 | 238 | 15 | — | — | 935 | 887 | 39

CHANUTE—Neosho County
⌖ NEOSHO MEMORIAL REGIONAL MEDICAL CENTER, 629 South Plummer, Zip 66720–1928; tel. 316/431–4000; Murray L. Brown, Administrator **A**1 9 10 **F**7 8 12 15 19 20 22 23 27 28 32 33 35 37 40 41 44 49 64 65 71 73 **P**8 **S** Quorum Health Group/Quorum Health Resources, Inc., Brentwood, TN **N** — 13 10 | 60 | 2190 | 23 | 15010 | 287 | — | 5781 | 229

Hospital, Address, Telephone, Administrator, Approval, Facility, and Physician Codes, Health Care System, Network	Classi-fication Codes		Utilization Data					Expense (thousands) of dollars		
★ American Hospital Association (AHA) membership □ Joint Commission on Accreditation of Healthcare Organizations (JCAHO) accreditation + American Osteopathic Healthcare Association (AOHA) membership ○ American Osteopathic Association (AOA) accreditation △ Commission on Accreditation of Rehabilitation Facilities (CARF) accreditation Control codes 61, 63, 64, 71, 72 and 73 indicate hospitals listed by AOHA, but not registered by AHA. For definition of numerical codes, see page A4	Control	Service	Staffed Beds	Admissions	Census	Outpatient Visits	Births	Total	Payroll	Personnel

CLAY CENTER—Clay County

	Control	Service	Staffed Beds	Admissions	Census	Outpatient Visits	Births	Total	Payroll	Personnel
★ CLAY COUNTY HOSPITAL, 617 Liberty Street, Zip 67432–1599; tel. 913/632–2144; John F. Wiebe, Chief Executive Officer **A**9 10 **F**7 8 15 19 22 28 32 36 44 45 49 65 67 71 **P**8 **N** Sunflower Health Network, Inc., Salina, KS	13	10	35	740	9	12202	53	5906	2542	118

COFFEYVILLE—Montgomery County

	Control	Service	Staffed Beds	Admissions	Census	Outpatient Visits	Births	Total	Payroll	Personnel
⊞ COFFEYVILLE REGIONAL MEDICAL CENTER, 1400 West Fourth, Zip 67337–3306; tel. 316/251–1200; Gerald Joseph Marquette, Jr., Administrator (Total facility includes 33 beds in nursing home–type unit) **A**1 2 9 10 **F**7 8 14 15 16 19 21 22 27 28 30 31 32 33 37 40 42 44 49 52 53 57 58 60 64 65 66 71 73 74 **P**8 **S** Quorum Health Group/Quorum Health Resources, Inc., Brentwood, TN **N**	14	10	123	3779	68	18212	222	19688	9140	—

COLBY—Thomas County

	Control	Service	Staffed Beds	Admissions	Census	Outpatient Visits	Births	Total	Payroll	Personnel
CITIZENS MEDICAL CENTER, 100 East College Drive, Zip 67701–3799; tel. 785/462–7511; Richard B. Gamel, Chief Executive Officer **A**9 10 **F**7 8 15 19 21 22 29 32 34 35 36 37 40 42 44 45 46 49 51 64 65 67 71 73 **N** MED–OP, Oakley, KS	23	10	40	1173	13	9926	152	6782	2684	113

COLDWATER—Comanche County

	Control	Service	Staffed Beds	Admissions	Census	Outpatient Visits	Births	Total	Payroll	Personnel
COMANCHE COUNTY HOSPITAL, Second and Frisco Streets, Zip 67029, Mailing Address: HC 65, Box 8A, Zip 67029; tel. 316/582–2144; Nancy Zimmerman, Administrator **A**9 10 **F**8 15 19 20 24 30 31 32 33 36 39 41 42 44 49 56 64 66 71 **P**6 **S** Great Plains Health Alliance, Inc., Phillipsburg, KS	13	10	14	191	2	—	0	2131	1051	38

COLUMBUS—Cherokee County

	Control	Service	Staffed Beds	Admissions	Census	Outpatient Visits	Births	Total	Payroll	Personnel
MAUDE NORTON MEMORIAL CITY HOSPITAL, 220 North Pennsylvania Street, Zip 66725–1197; tel. 316/429–2545; Cindy Neely, Administrator and Chief Executive Officer **A**9 **F**8 15 16 19 22 28 29 30 32 36 41 44 49 64 71 73 **N**	14	10	30	68	0	7963	0	1746	913	42

CONCORDIA—Cloud County

	Control	Service	Staffed Beds	Admissions	Census	Outpatient Visits	Births	Total	Payroll	Personnel
★ CLOUD COUNTY HEALTH CENTER, 1100 Highland Drive, Zip 66901–3997; tel. 785/243–1234; Daniel R. Bartz, Chief Executive Officer **A**9 10 **F**8 15 16 17 19 20 21 22 26 27 28 30 33 34 35 36 37 39 41 44 45 46 49 50 51 53 54 55 56 57 58 59 64 65 67 70 71 73 **P**7 8 **N** Sunflower Health Network, Inc., Salina, KS	23	10	40	1163	17	56146	0	7061	3468	153

COUNCIL GROVE—Morris County

	Control	Service	Staffed Beds	Admissions	Census	Outpatient Visits	Births	Total	Payroll	Personnel
MORRIS COUNTY HOSPITAL, 600 North Washington Street, Zip 66846–1499, Mailing Address: P.O. Box 275, Zip 66846–0275; tel. 316/767–6811; Jim Reagan, M.D., Administrator **A**9 10 **F**7 8 14 15 16 17 19 22 25 28 30 32 33 34 37 39 40 41 42 44 46 49 65 67 71 73 **P**3 **N** Community Health Alliance, Winchester, KS	13	10	28	850	11	11595	79	4055	1867	84

DIGHTON—Lane County

	Control	Service	Staffed Beds	Admissions	Census	Outpatient Visits	Births	Total	Payroll	Personnel
★ LANE COUNTY HOSPITAL, 243 South Second, Zip 67839, Mailing Address: P.O. Box 969, Zip 67839–0969; tel. 316/397–5321; Donna McGowan, R.N., Administrator (Total facility includes 21 beds in nursing home–type unit) **A**9 10 **F**8 19 22 26 28 32 34 35 46 49 64 65 66 71 **S** Great Plains Health Alliance, Inc., Phillipsburg, KS **N** Great Plains Health Alliance, Phillipsburg, KS	13	10	31	235	24	5362	0	2236	1192	51

DODGE CITY—Ford County

	Control	Service	Staffed Beds	Admissions	Census	Outpatient Visits	Births	Total	Payroll	Personnel
⊞ WESTERN PLAINS REGIONAL HOSPITAL, (Formerly Columbia Western Plains Hospital), 3001 Avenue A., Zip 67801–6508, Mailing Address: P.O. Box 1478, Zip 67801–1478; tel. 316/225–8401; Ken Hutchenrider, President and Chief Executive Officer (Total facility includes 9 beds in nursing home–type unit) **A**1 9 10 **F**7 8 11 12 14 15 16 17 19 20 21 22 23 28 29 30 32 33 35 37 39 41 44 45 46 48 49 60 63 64 65 66 67 71 73 74 **S** Columbia/HCA Healthcare Corporation, Nashville, TN	33	10	88	3757	44	26874	726	—	—	293

EL DORADO—Butler County

	Control	Service	Staffed Beds	Admissions	Census	Outpatient Visits	Births	Total	Payroll	Personnel
⊞ SUSAN B. ALLEN MEMORIAL HOSPITAL, 720 West Central Avenue, Zip 67042–2144; tel. 316/321–3300; Jim Wilson, President and Chief Executive Officer (Total facility includes 21 beds in nursing home–type unit) **A**1 9 10 **F**7 19 21 22 24 26 28 32 35 36 37 39 40 44 52 57 64 65 71 73 **P**8	23	10	82	1921	29	46984	167	16860	8363	266

ELKHART—Morton County

	Control	Service	Staffed Beds	Admissions	Census	Outpatient Visits	Births	Total	Payroll	Personnel
★ MORTON COUNTY HEALTH SYSTEM, 445 Hilltop Street, Zip 67950–0937, Mailing Address: Box 937, Zip 67950–0937; tel. 316/697–2141; Bruce K. Birchell, Chief Executive Officer (Total facility includes 60 beds in nursing home–type unit) **A**9 10 **F**7 8 15 19 20 22 26 28 29 30 32 33 37 39 40 41 44 45 46 48 49 51 52 53 54 55 56 57 58 64 65 66 67 71 73 74 **P**5 6	13	10	100	1223	76	9904	54	9504	6105	212

ELLINWOOD—Barton County

	Control	Service	Staffed Beds	Admissions	Census	Outpatient Visits	Births	Total	Payroll	Personnel
★ ELLINWOOD DISTRICT HOSPITAL, 605 North Main Street, Zip 67526–1440; tel. 316/564–2548; Marge Conell, R.N., Administrator **A**9 **F**8 19 20 22 34 35 36 49 64 65 69 71 **S** Great Plains Health Alliance, Inc., Phillipsburg, KS **N** Great Plains Health Alliance, Phillipsburg, KS	23	10	12	198	4	3716	0	1524	678	31

ELLSWORTH—Ellsworth County

	Control	Service	Staffed Beds	Admissions	Census	Outpatient Visits	Births	Total	Payroll	Personnel
ELLSWORTH COUNTY HOSPITAL, 300 Kingsley Street, Zip 67439–0087, Mailing Address: P.O. Drawer 87, Zip 67439–0087; tel. 785/472–3111; Roger W. Pearson, Administrator **A**9 10 **F**19 21 28 41 45 49 64 65 71 **P**8 **N** Sunflower Health Network, Inc., Salina, KS	13	10	25	575	5	7108	0	3063	1290	60

EMPORIA—Lyon County

	Control	Service	Staffed Beds	Admissions	Census	Outpatient Visits	Births	Total	Payroll	Personnel
⊞ NEWMAN MEMORIAL COUNTY HOSPITAL, 1201 West 12th Avenue, Zip 66801–2597; tel. 316/343–6800; Terry R. Lambert, Chief Executive Officer (Total facility includes 18 beds in nursing home–type unit) **A**1 9 10 **F**3 7 8 15 16 19 21 22 23 28 30 31 32 33 34 35 37 40 41 42 44 45 49 64 65 67 71 **S** Quorum Health Group/Quorum Health Resources, Inc., Brentwood, TN	13	10	110	3447	42	28647	547	27722	12093	406

Hospital, Address, Telephone, Administrator, Approval, Facility, and Physician Codes, Health Care System, Network	Classi-fication Codes		Utilization Data					Expense (thousands) of dollars		
★ American Hospital Association (AHA) membership □ Joint Commission on Accreditation of Healthcare Organizations (JCAHO) accreditation + American Osteopathic Healthcare Association (AOHA) membership ○ American Osteopathic Association (AOA) accreditation △ Commission on Accreditation of Rehabilitation Facilities (CARF) accreditation Control codes 61, 63, 64, 71, 72 and 73 indicate hospitals listed by AOHA, but not registered by AHA. For definition of numerical codes, see page A4	Control	Service	Staffed Beds	Admissions	Census	Outpatient Visits	Births	Total	Payroll	Personnel

EUREKA—Greenwood County

★ GREENWOOD COUNTY HOSPITAL, 100 West 16th Street, Zip 67045–1096; tel. 316/583–7451; Emmett Schuster, Administrator and Chief Executive Officer **A**9 10 **F**3 7 8 12 15 16 17 19 20 21 22 28 30 31 32 33 34 39 44 46 49 53 54 55 65 71 73 74 **P**8 **S** Quorum Health Group/Quorum Health Resources, Inc., Brentwood, TN

| 13 | 10 | 46 | 993 | 17 | 7293 | 3 | 5706 | 2727 | 120 |

FORT LEAVENWORTH—Leavenworth County

★ MUNSON ARMY HEALTH CENTER, (Formerly Munson Army Community Hospital), 550 Pope Avenue, Zip 66027–2332; tel. 913/684–6420; Colonel Cloyd B. Gatrell, Commander **F**3 4 5 6 7 8 9 10 11 12 14 15 16 18 19 20 21 22 24 25 26 27 28 29 30 31 32 33 34 35 36 37 38 39 40 41 42 43 44 45 46 47 48 49 50 51 52 53 60 61 62 63 64 65 66 67 68 69 70 71 72 73 74 **P**6 **S** Department of the Army, Office of the Surgeon General, Falls Church, VA

| 42 | 10 | 20 | 295 | 2 | 149791 | — | 23785 | 12493 | 171 |

FORT RILEY—Geary County

✠ IRWIN ARMY COMMUNITY HOSPITAL, Building 600, Zip 66442; tel. 913/239–7000; Colonel J. Thomas Hardy, Commanding Officer (Nonreporting) **A**1 2 **S** Department of the Army, Office of the Surgeon General, Falls Church, VA

| 42 | 10 | 56 | — | — | — | — | — | — | — |

FORT SCOTT—Bourbon County

✠ MERCY HEALTH SYSTEM OF KANSAS, 821 Burke Street, Zip 66701–2497; tel. 316/223–2200; Susan Barrett, President and Chief Executive Officer (Total facility includes 23 beds in nursing home–type unit) **A**1 9 10 **F**7 8 12 14 15 16 17 19 21 22 23 24 27 28 30 32 33 35 37 38 39 40 41 44 48 49 51 63 64 65 66 67 71 73 **P**6 **S** Sisters of Mercy Health System–St. Louis, Saint Louis, MO **N**

| 21 | 10 | 105 | 3859 | 53 | 53784 | 285 | 21453 | 10698 | 414 |

FREDONIA—Wilson County

★ FREDONIA REGIONAL HOSPITAL, 1527 Madison Street, Zip 66736–1751, Mailing Address: P.O. Box 579, Zip 66736–0579; tel. 316/378–2121; Terry Deschaine, Chief Executive Officer **A**9 10 **F**8 14 15 19 22 32 44 49 58 62 64 65 71 **S** Great Plains Health Alliance, Inc., Phillipsburg, KS **N** Great Plains Health Alliance, Phillipsburg, KS

| 14 | 10 | 42 | 618 | 9 | 14366 | — | 3857 | 1727 | 70 |

GARDEN CITY—Finney County

✠ ST. CATHERINE HOSPITAL, 410 East Walnut, Zip 67846–5672; tel. 316/272–2222; Gary L. Rowe, President and Chief Executive Officer **A**1 9 10 **F**7 8 14 15 16 17 19 20 21 22 23 26 28 30 31 32 33 35 36 37 38 39 40 41 42 44 46 49 52 54 55 56 57 58 60 65 69 71 73 **S** Catholic Health Initiatives, Denver, CO

| 21 | 10 | 100 | 5167 | 61 | 70074 | 1103 | 37329 | 15276 | 509 |

GARDNER—Johnson County

△ MEADOWBROOK HOSPITAL, 427 West Main Street, Zip 66030–1197; tel. 913/884–8711; Anita Macke, Administrator (Total facility includes 21 beds in nursing home–type unit) **A**7 9 10 **F**12 15 48 49 64 73

| 33 | 46 | 63 | 334 | 22 | — | 0 | — | | 86 |

GARNETT—Anderson County

ANDERSON COUNTY HOSPITAL, 421 South Maple, Zip 66032–1334, Mailing Address: P.O. Box 309, Zip 66032–0309; tel. 913/448–3131; James K. Johnson, Senior Executive Officer (Total facility includes 32 beds in nursing home–type unit) **A**9 10 **F**8 15 19 26 28 32 33 34 35 44 52 57 58 64 65 71 **P**8 **S** Saint Luke's Shawnee Mission Health System, Kansas City, MO **N** Jayhawk Health Alliance, Olathe, KS

| 23 | 10 | 66 | 568 | 40 | 22124 | 0 | 5059 | 2390 | 126 |

GIRARD—Crawford County

★ CRAWFORD COUNTY HOSPITAL DISTRICT ONE, 302 North Hospital Drive, Zip 66743–2000; tel. 316/724–8291; Jerry Hanson, Administrator and Chief Executive Officer **A**9 10 **F**3 6 7 8 11 15 19 20 21 22 32 33 35 36 37 39 40 42 44 45 54 56 58 63 64 71 73

| 16 | 10 | 38 | 1272 | 16 | 24583 | 108 | 8802 | 3776 | 151 |

GOODLAND—Sherman County

GOODLAND REGIONAL MEDICAL CENTER, 220 West Second Street, Zip 67735–1602; tel. 785/899–3625; Jim Chaddic, Administrator and Chief Executive Officer **A**9 10 **F**3 8 10 11 14 15 16 19 20 21 22 26 28 31 33 34 36 37 39 40 42 44 45 46 48 49 58 63 64 65 67 70 71 73 **N** MED–OP, Oakley, KS

| 13 | 10 | 49 | 1043 | 15 | 32194 | 80 | 6746 | 2870 | 129 |

GREAT BEND—Barton County

✠ CENTRAL KANSAS MEDICAL CENTER, (Includes Central Kansas Medical Center–St. Joseph Campus, 923 Carroll Avenue, Larned, Zip 67550; tel. 316/285–3161), 3515 Broadway Street, Zip 67530–3691; tel. 316/792–2511; Gary L. Barnett, President and Chief Executive Officer (Total facility includes 79 beds in nursing home–type unit) **A**1 9 10 **F**3 7 8 15 19 21 22 23 28 30 32 33 34 35 36 37 39 40 41 44 45 49 51 60 64 65 66 67 71 73 **P**8 **S** Catholic Health Initiatives, Denver, CO

| 21 | 10 | 175 | 3211 | 74 | 171776 | 400 | 32407 | 15369 | 583 |

GREENSBURG—Kiowa County

KIOWA COUNTY MEMORIAL HOSPITAL, 501 South Walnut Street, Zip 67054–1951; tel. 316/723–3341; Ronald J. Baker, Administrator **A**9 10 **F**8 15 22 24 28 30 32 34 36 39 44 49 64 65 71 **P**6 **S** Great Plains Health Alliance, Inc., Phillipsburg, KS **N** Great Plains Health Alliance, Phillipsburg, KS

| 13 | 10 | 38 | 328 | 10 | 8457 | 1 | 3620 | 2069 | 67 |

HALSTEAD—Harvey County

✠ HALSTEAD HOSPITAL, (Formerly Columbia Halstead Hospital), 328 Poplar Street, Zip 67056–2099; tel. 316/835–2651; David Nevill, President and Chief Executive Officer (Total facility includes 17 beds in nursing home–type unit) **A**1 9 10 **F**3 4 7 8 10 11 13 14 15 16 19 20 21 22 23 24 26 27 28 29 30 32 33 34 35 36 37 39 41 42 43 44 45 46 49 52 53 54 55 56 57 58 60 61 63 64 65 67 71 72 73 **P**7 **S** Columbia/HCA Healthcare Corporation, Nashville, TN

| 33 | 10 | 140 | 2876 | 52 | 3192 | 0 | 22324 | 9346 | 308 |

Hospital, Address, Telephone, Administrator, Approval, Facility, and Physician Codes, Health Care System, Network	Classi-fication Codes		Utilization Data					Expense (thousands) of dollars		
	Control	Service	Staffed Beds	Admissions	Census	Outpatient Visits	Births	Total	Payroll	Personnel

★ American Hospital Association (AHA) membership
☐ Joint Commission on Accreditation of Healthcare Organizations (JCAHO) accreditation
+ American Osteopathic Healthcare Association (AOHA) membership
○ American Osteopathic Association (AOA) accreditation
△ Commission on Accreditation of Rehabilitation Facilities (CARF) accreditation
Control codes 61, 63, 64, 71, 72 and 73 indicate hospitals listed by AOHA, but not registered by AHA. For definition of numerical codes, see page A4

HANOVER—Washington County

HANOVER HOSPITAL, 205 South Hanover, Zip 66945–8857, Mailing Address: P.O. Box 38, Zip 66945–0038; tel. 913/337–2214; Roger D. Warren, M.D., Administrator (Total facility includes 27 beds in nursing home–type unit) **A**9 10 **F**1 11 15 16 26 32 34 36 37 40 44 48 49 64 65 71 73 **P**5

| | 16 | 10 | 45 | 464 | 25 | 946 | 17 | 2194 | 1221 | 63 |

HARPER—Harper County

★ HOSPITAL DISTRICT NUMBER FIVE OF HARPER COUNTY, 1204 Maple, Zip 67058–1438; tel. 316/896–7324; Vernon Minnis, Chief Executive Officer **A**9 10 **F**1 8 12 14 19 22 24 28 30 32 33 34 35 36 41 44 49 51 64 65 69 71 73 **P**6

| | 16 | 10 | 38 | 557 | 5 | 4451 | 1 | 3491 | 1897 | 97 |

HAYS—Ellis County

⊞ △ HAYS MEDICAL CENTER, (Includes Hadley Campus, 201 East Seventh Street, Zip 67601–4198; St. Anthony Campus, 2220 Canterbury Drive, Mailing Address: P.O. Box 8100, Zip 67601), 2220 Canterbury Road, Zip 67601–2342, Mailing Address: P.O. Box 8100, Zip 67601–8100; tel. 785/623–5113; John H. Jeter, M.D., President and Chief Executive Officer **A**1 2 3 5 7 9 10 **F**4 7 8 10 11 12 13 15 16 17 18 19 21 22 23 26 27 28 29 30 32 33 34 35 36 37 38 39 40 41 42 44 45 48 49 51 52 54 55 56 57 58 60 63 64 65 67 71 73 74 **P**6 7 **N** MED–OP, Oakley, KS; High Plains Rural Health Network, Fort Morgan, CO

| | 23 | 10 | 161 | 5789 | 92 | 142861 | 475 | 61671 | 26646 | 834 |

HERINGTON—Dickinson County

HERINGTON MUNICIPAL HOSPITAL, 100 East Helen Street, Zip 67449–1697; tel. 913/258–2207; William D. Peterson, Administrator (Total facility includes 18 beds in nursing home–type unit) **A**9 **F**7 8 11 14 15 16 19 20 22 26 28 33 35 40 41 44 64 71 **N** Sunflower Health Network, Inc., Salina, KS

| | 14 | 10 | 38 | 538 | 16 | 17006 | 26 | 3418 | 1568 | 85 |

HIAWATHA—Brown County

⊞ HIAWATHA COMMUNITY HOSPITAL, 300 Utah Street, Zip 66434–2399; tel. 913/742–2131; John Moore, Administrator **A**1 9 10 **F**7 11 19 21 22 28 32 33 35 36 37 40 44 49 64 65 71 73 **P**6

| | 23 | 10 | 29 | 902 | 13 | 23797 | 52 | 6234 | 2635 | 101 |

HILL CITY—Graham County

★ GRAHAM COUNTY HOSPITAL, 304 West Prout Street, Zip 67642–1435, Mailing Address: P.O. Box 339, Zip 67642–0339; tel. 785/421–2121; Fred J. Meis, Administrator and Chief Executive Officer **A**9 10 **F**1 7 8 12 15 16 19 22 28 32 33 34 36 39 44 71 **N** MED–OP, Oakley, KS

| | 13 | 10 | 26 | 729 | 9 | 12938 | 16 | 4585 | 2083 | 84 |

HILLSBORO—Marion County

SALEM HOSPITAL, 701 South Main Street, Zip 67063–9981; tel. 316/947–3114; J. H. Seitz, Administrator (Total facility includes 52 beds in nursing home–type unit) **A**9 10 **F**1 7 8 12 14 15 16 17 19 22 26 28 30 32 33 34 35 44 49 52 57 62 64 65 67 71 **P**5 **S** Great Plains Health Alliance, Inc., Phillipsburg, KS **N** Great Plains Health Alliance, Phillipsburg, KS

| | 21 | 10 | 90 | 441 | 51 | 6814 | 29 | 4363 | 2397 | 117 |

HOISINGTON—Barton County

CLARA BARTON HOSPTIAL, 250 West Ninth Street, Zip 67544–1799; tel. 316/653–2114; James Turnbull, Administrator and Chief Executive Officer (Total facility includes 12 beds in nursing home–type unit) **A**9 10 **F**3 7 8 15 19 20 22 24 34 35 36 37 40 44 49 64 71 72

| | 23 | 10 | 48 | 453 | 10 | 15366 | 60 | 3909 | 2044 | 93 |

HOLTON—Jackson County

HOLTON COMMUNITY HOSPITAL, 510 Kansas Avenue, Zip 66436–1545; tel. 913/364–2116; Diane S. Gross, Administrator **A**9 10 **F**1 7 8 12 15 16 17 19 22 27 29 30 32 33 34 36 39 40 41 44 45 46 49 64 65 67 68 71 73 74 **P**8 **N** Community Health Alliance, Winchester, KS

| | 14 | 10 | 13 | 377 | 5 | 25214 | 21 | 2893 | 1540 | 74 |

HORTON—Brown County

HORTON HEALTH FOUNDATION, 240 West 18th Street, Zip 66439–1245; tel. 785/486–2642; Dale A. White, Chief Executive Officer **A**9 10 **F**3 8 12 15 16 19 28 30 32 35 36 39 41 42 44 64 65 71 **P**8 **N** Community Health Alliance, Winchester, KS

| | 23 | 10 | 35 | 521 | 7 | 1605 | — | 4572 | 2273 | — |

HOXIE—Sheridan County

SHERIDAN COUNTY HOSPITAL, 826 18th Street, Zip 67740–0167, Mailing Address: P.O. Box 167, Zip 67740–0167; tel. 785/675–3281; Brian Kirk, Chief Executive Officer (Total facility includes 48 beds in nursing home–type unit) **A**9 10 **F**1 6 8 14 15 16 19 22 28 32 33 36 40 44 58 63 64 65 71 **N** MED–OP, Oakley, KS

| | 13 | 10 | 74 | 301 | 48 | 6947 | 3 | 3803 | 1850 | 111 |

HUGOTON—Stevens County

STEVENS COUNTY HOSPITAL, 1006 South Jackson Street, Zip 67951–2842, Mailing Address: P.O. Box 10, Zip 67951–0010; tel. 316/544–8511; Ted Strote, Administrator **A**9 10 **F**8 12 15 19 24 28 30 32 34 41 44 45 49 64 65 67 71 73 **N** Allina Health System, Minnetonka, MN

| | 13 | 10 | 17 | 279 | 4 | 9735 | 0 | 4241 | 2341 | 95 |

HUTCHINSON—Reno County

★ HUTCHINSON HOSPITAL CORPORATION, 1701 East 23rd Street, Zip 67502–1191; tel. 316/665–2000; Gene E. Schmidt, President (Total facility includes 19 beds in nursing home–type unit) **A**9 10 **F**3 4 6 7 10 15 16 18 19 21 22 23 32 33 34 37 40 41 42 43 44 46 48 49 51 52 53 54 55 56 57 58 59 60 62 64 65 67 68 71 73

| | 23 | 10 | 157 | 6961 | 113 | 86319 | 663 | 45159 | 19417 | 744 |

INDEPENDENCE—Montgomery County

⊞ MERCY HOSPITALS OF KANSAS, 800 West Myrtle Street, Zip 67301–3240, Mailing Address: P.O. Box 388, Zip 67301–0388; tel. 316/331–2200; Susan Barrett, President and Chief Executive Officer (Total facility includes 18 beds in nursing home–type unit) **A**1 9 10 **F**7 8 12 13 15 16 17 18 19 21 22 24 26 27 28 30 32 34 35 37 40 41 44 49 51 64 65 71 73 **P**6 **S** Sisters of Mercy Health System–St. Louis, Saint Louis, MO

| | 21 | 10 | 58 | 1868 | 23 | 56851 | 158 | 13710 | 6033 | 228 |

Hospital, Address, Telephone, Administrator, Approval, Facility, and Physician Codes, Health Care System, Network	Classi- fication Codes		Utilization Data					Expense (thousands) of dollars		
★ American Hospital Association (AHA) membership □ Joint Commission on Accreditation of Healthcare Organizations (JCAHO) accreditation + American Osteopathic Healthcare Association (AOHA) membership ○ American Osteopathic Association (AOA) accreditation △ Commission on Accreditation of Rehabilitation Facilities (CARF) accreditation Control codes 61, 63, 64, 71, 72 and 73 indicate hospitals listed by AOHA, but not registered by AHA. For definition of numerical codes, see page A4	Control	Service	Staffed Beds	Admissions	Census	Outpatient Visits	Births	Total	Payroll	Personnel

IOLA—Allen County

★ ALLEN COUNTY HOSPITAL, 101 South First Street, Zip 66749–3505, Mailing Address: P.O. Box 540, Zip 66749–0540; tel. 316/365–3131; Bill May, Chief Executive Officer **A**9 10 **F**7 19 21 22 23 28 30 31 32 33 35 37 40 42 44 48 49 64 65 67 71 72 73 **S** Health Midwest, Kansas City, MO **N** Health Midwest, Kansas City, MO

23	10	41	1503	19	20202	101	9162	3729	142

JETMORE—Hodgeman County

★ HODGEMAN COUNTY HEALTH CENTER, 809 Bramley Street, Zip 67854–9320, Mailing Address: P.O. Box 367, Zip 67854–0367; tel. 316/357–8361; Roger Salisbury, Administrator (Total facility includes 36 beds in nursing home–type unit) **A**9 10 **F**7 8 12 14 15 19 27 28 33 35 44 45 49 51 64 65 71

13	10	52	323	32	4400	10	3158	1101	74

JOHNSON—Stanton County

★ STANTON COUNTY HEALTH CARE FACILITY, 404 North Chestnut Street, Zip 67855–0779, Mailing Address: Box 779, Zip 67855–0779; tel. 316/492–6250; Larry V. Gales, Administrator (Total facility includes 25 beds in nursing home–type unit) **A**9 10 **F**7 8 14 15 16 22 29 30 32 34 39 40 49 64 71 73

15	10	37	164	21	2546	55	2239	655	53

JUNCTION CITY—Geary County

⊠ GEARY COMMUNITY HOSPITAL, Ash and St. Mary's Road, Zip 66441, Mailing Address: P.O. Box 490, Zip 66441–0490; tel. 785/238–4131; David K. Bradley, Chief Executive Officer **A**1 3 9 10 **F**3 8 12 15 16 19 20 21 22 23 31 32 33 34 35 37 39 40 42 44 45 46 49 51 65 67 71 **N** Community Health Alliance, Winchester, KS

13	10	49	1512	18	120643	119	13296	7061	258

KANSAS CITY—Wyandotte County

⊠ △ BETHANY MEDICAL CENTER, 51 North 12th Street, Zip 66102–9990; tel. 913/281–8400; Paul F. Herzog, President and Chief Executive Officer (Total facility includes 47 beds in nursing home–type unit) **A**1 2 3 5 7 9 10 **F**3 4 7 8 10 15 16 19 21 22 23 26 27 30 32 35 37 38 39 40 41 42 43 44 46 48 49 52 53 54 55 56 59 60 64 65 71 73 **P**1 **S** Columbia/HCA Healthcare Corporation, Nashville, TN

23	10	240	8210	139	63667	634	64852	25847	876

⊠ PROVIDENCE MEDICAL CENTER, 8929 Parallel Parkway, Zip 66112–1636; tel. 913/596–4000; Francis V. Creeden, Jr., President and Chief Executive Officer **A**1 2 9 10 **F**4 7 8 10 12 15 16 17 18 19 20 21 22 26 27 28 29 30 31 32 33 34 35 37 39 40 41 42 43 44 45 46 49 52 53 54 55 56 57 58 59 60 63 64 65 66 67 71 73 74 **P**5 6 7 8 **S** Sisters of Charity of Leavenworth Health Services Corporation, Leavenworth, KS **N** Jayhawk Health Alliance, Olathe, KS

21	10	219	8553	133	45882	1009	63357	26838	847

⊠ △ UNIVERSITY OF KANSAS MEDICAL CENTER, 3901 Rainbow Boulevard, Zip 66160–7200; tel. 913/588–5000; Irene M. Cumming, Chief Executive Officer **A**1 2 3 5 7 8 9 10 **F**3 4 5 7 8 9 10 11 12 15 16 17 18 19 21 22 23 24 26 28 29 30 31 34 35 37 38 39 40 41 42 43 44 45 46 47 48 49 51 52 53 54 55 56 57 58 59 60 61 63 65 66 67 69 71 73 74 **P**5 **N** Jayhawk Health Alliance, Olathe, KS

12	10	409	12312	226	380591	968	161831	61650	1990

KINGMAN—Kingman County

★ KINGMAN COMMUNITY HOSPITAL, 750 Avenue D. West, Zip 67068; tel. 316/532–3147; Gary L. Tiller, Chief Executive Officer **A**9 10 **F**7 8 14 15 16 17 19 22 28 29 30 32 34 35 36 37 40 41 42 44 46 48 49 58 64 65 67 71 73 **P**3 6 7

23	10	40	665	9	15167	45	5373	2670	108

KIOWA—Barber County

★ KIOWA DISTRICT HOSPITAL, 810 Drumm Street, Zip 67070–1699; tel. 316/825–4131; Buck McKinney, Jr., Chief Executive Officer **A**9 10 **F**7 10 14 15 16 19 22 28 33 44 51 64 65 71

16	10	24	361	4	3512	0	1553	779	37

LA CROSSE—Rush County

★ RUSH COUNTY HEALTHCARE CENTER, (Formerly Rush County Memorial Hospital), 801 Locust Street, Zip 67548–9673, Mailing Address: P.O. Box 520, Zip 67548–0520; tel. 785/222–2545; Donna L. Myers, Administrator and Chief Executive Officer (Total facility includes 26 beds in nursing home–type unit) **A**9 10 **F**16 22 28 32 34 40 44 64 **N** MED–OP, Oakley, KS

13	10	50	404	34	13468	14	2547	1235	70

LAKIN—Kearny County

KEARNY COUNTY HOSPITAL, 500 North Thorpe Street, Zip 67860–9604; tel. 316/355–7111; Steven S. Reiner, Administrator **A**9 10 **F**1 7 14 15 16 21 22 28 36 37 40 44 48 49 51 62 64 65 67 **P**6

13	10	20	192	5	7809	0	2665	1315	54

LARNED—Pawnee County

□ LARNED STATE HOSPITAL, Mailing Address: Rural Route 3, P.O. Box 89, Zip 67550–9365; tel. 316/285–2131; Mani Lee, Ph.D., Superintendent **A**1 10 **F**2 7 8 11 19 20 21 23 31 35 37 39 40 41 42 44 45 46 47 52 53 56 57 60 65 67 71 72 73 **P**6

12	22	342	1259	298	0	0	28246	18783	790

LAWRENCE—Douglas County

□ LAWRENCE MEMORIAL HOSPITAL, 325 Maine, Zip 66044–1393; tel. 785/749–6100; Eugene W. Meyer, President and Chief Executive Officer (Total facility includes 21 beds in nursing home–type unit) **A**1 5 9 10 **F**7 8 10 14 15 16 19 20 21 22 28 31 32 33 35 36 37 39 40 41 42 44 46 49 52 64 65 71 73 **P**6 **N** Jayhawk Health Alliance, Olathe, KS

14	10	98	6183	86	76352	841	46343	20964	727

LEAVENWORTH—Leavenworth County

□ CUSHING MEMORIAL HOSPITAL, 711 Marshall Street, Zip 66048–3235; tel. 913/684–1100; Charles L. Rogers, President (Nonreporting) **A**1 9 10

23	10	77	—	—	—	—	—	—	—

⊠ DWIGHT D. EISENHOWER VETERANS AFFAIRS MEDICAL CENTER, 4101 South Fourth Street Trafficway, Zip 66048–5055; tel. 913/682–2000; Edgar L. Tucker, Director **A**1 3 5 **F**1 3 4 6 8 10 15 16 19 20 21 22 23 26 27 29 30 31 32 33 34 35 37 41 42 43 44 45 46 48 49 50 51 52 54 56 57 58 60 63 65 67 69 70 71 73 74 **S** Department of Veterans Affairs, Washington, DC **N** Hays Medical Center, Hays, KS

45	10	63	1996	55	113856	—	59870	34357	832

Hospital, Address, Telephone, Administrator, Approval, Facility, and Physician Codes, Health Care System, Network	Classi-fication Codes		Utilization Data					Expense (thousands) of dollars		
	Control	Service	Staffed Beds	Admissions	Census	Outpatient Visits	Births	Total	Payroll	Personnel

★ American Hospital Association (AHA) membership
□ Joint Commission on Accreditation of Healthcare Organizations (JCAHO) accreditation
+ American Osteopathic Healthcare Association (AOHA) membership
○ American Osteopathic Association (AOA) accreditation
△ Commission on Accreditation of Rehabilitation Facilities (CARF) accreditation
Control codes 61, 63, 64, 71, 72 and 73 indicate hospitals listed by AOHA, but not registered by AHA. For definition of numerical codes, see page A4

	Control	Service	Staffed Beds	Admissions	Census	Outpatient Visits	Births	Total	Payroll	Personnel
⊠ SAINT JOHN HOSPITAL, 3500 South Fourth Street, Zip 66048–5092; tel. 913/680–6000; Francis V. Creeden, Jr., President and Chief Executive Officer **A**1 9 10 **F**7 8 15 16 17 19 22 23 26 28 30 31 32 33 34 37 40 41 42 44 49 63 64 65 67 71 73 74 **P**5 6 7 8 **S** Sisters of Charity of Leavenworth Health Services Corporation, Leavenworth, KS **N** Jayhawk Health Alliance, Olathe, KS	21	10	36	1796	20	49092	293	14270	6509	212
LENEXA—Johnson County										
□ BHC COLLEGE MEADOWS HOSPITAL, 14425 College Boulevard, Zip 66215; tel. 913/469–1100; James E. Ferguson, Chief Executive Officer (Nonreporting) **A**1 10 **S** Behavioral Healthcare Corporation, Nashville, TN	33	22	120	—	—	—	—	—	—	—
LEOTI—Wichita County										
★ WICHITA COUNTY HOSPITAL, (Includes Wichita County Hospital Long Term Care, Mailing Address: P.O. Box 968, Zip 67861), 211 East Earl, Zip 67861–0968, Mailing Address: Rural Route 2, Box 38, Zip 67861–0968; tel. 316/375–2233; Ed Finley, Administrator (Total facility includes 28 beds in nursing home–type unit) **A**1 9 10 **F**2 3 4 5 6 7 8 9 10 11 12 15 17 19 21 22 23 24 26 28 30 32 33 34 35 36 37 38 39 40 42 43 44 47 48 49 52 53 54 55 56 58 60 64 65 67 69 71 73 **P**6	13	10	41	222	20	5707	1	1675	910	56
LIBERAL—Seward County										
⊠ SOUTHWEST MEDICAL CENTER, 315 West 15th Street, Zip 67901–1340, Mailing Address: Box 1340, Zip 67905–1340; tel. 316/624–1651; Dave Kindel, President and Chief Executive Officer **A**1 9 10 **F**7 8 12 15 16 18 19 21 22 24 25 26 28 29 32 33 34 35 37 39 40 41 42 44 45 46 49 52 57 58 60 63 64 65 70 71 73 **P**5 6	13	10	87	3402	46	68400	705	26601	10592	511
LINCOLN—Lincoln County										
LINCOLN COUNTY HOSPITAL, 624 North Second Street, Zip 67455–1738, Mailing Address: P.O. Box 406, Zip 67455–0406; tel. 913/524–4403; Jolene Yager, R.N., Administrator (Total facility includes 20 beds in nursing home–type unit) **A**9 10 **F**15 19 22 32 33 34 36 41 44 49 64 65 71 **S** Great Plains Health Alliance, Inc., Phillipsburg, KS **N** Sunflower Health Network, Inc., Salina, KS; Great Plains Health Alliance, Phillipsburg, KS	13	10	34	502	21	5972	0	3102	1725	70
LINDSBORG—McPherson County										
★ LINDSBORG COMMUNITY HOSPITAL, 605 West Lincoln Street, Zip 67456–2399; tel. 785/227–3308; Greg Lundstrom, Administrator and Chief Executive Officer **A**9 10 **F**8 15 22 24 28 30 32 34 36 42 43 44 64 65 71 **P**6 **N** Sunflower Health Network, Inc., Salina, KS	23	10	12	753	8	29757	0	3294	1297	68
LYONS—Rice County										
★ RICE COUNTY HOSPITAL DISTRICT NUMBER ONE, 619 South Clark Street, Zip 67554–3003, Mailing Address: P.O. Box 828, Zip 67554–0828; tel. 316/257–5173; Robert L. Mullen, Administrator **A**9 10 **F**6 7 8 14 15 16 17 20 26 28 30 32 36 39 40 49 62 65 71 **N** Heart of America Network, Wichita, KS	16	10	44	651	21	5714	102	3631	1700	79
MANHATTAN—Riley County										
★ MERCY HEALTH CENTER OF MANHATTAN, (Includes Memorial Hospital, 1105 Sunset Avenue, Zip 66502, Mailing Address: Box 1208, Zip 66502; tel. 913/776–3300; Saint Mary Hospital, 1823 College Avenue, Zip 66502, Mailing Address: Box 1289, Zip 66502–0041), Mailing Address: 1823 College Avenue, Zip 66502–3381; E. Michael Nunamaker, President and Chief Executive Officer **A**9 10 **F**7 8 11 12 14 15 16 19 21 22 23 24 28 29 30 31 32 35 36 37 39 40 41 44 45 46 48 49 52 53 54 55 56 58 59 65 66 67 71 73 74 **S** Via Christi Health System, Wichita, KS **N** Community Health Alliance, Winchester, KS	23	10	99	5225	49	103608	1101	39975	18818	562
MANKATO—Jewell County										
JEWELL COUNTY HOSPITAL, 100 Crestvue Avenue, Zip 66956–2407, Mailing Address: P.O. Box 327, Zip 66956–0327; tel. 913/378–3137; Rodney Brockelman, Administrator (Total facility includes 45 beds in nursing home–type unit) **A**9 **F**20 22 28 32 33 34 49 62 64 **N** Sunflower Health Network, Inc., Salina, KS	13	10	57	88	41	712	0	1930	1200	68
MARION—Marion County										
★ ST. LUKE HOSPITAL, 1014 East Melvin, Zip 66861–1299; tel. 316/382–2179; Craig Hanson, Administrator (Total facility includes 32 beds in nursing home–type unit) **A**9 10 **F**7 8 11 12 14 15 17 19 20 21 22 26 29 30 32 33 34 36 37 39 40 41 42 44 45 46 49 51 64 65 71 73 74 **S** Lutheran Health Systems, Fargo, ND	23	10	54	598	38	17573	47	4736	2447	103
MARYSVILLE—Marshall County										
★ COMMUNITY MEMORIAL HOSPITAL, 708 North 18th Street, Zip 66508–1399; tel. 913/562–2311; Harley B. Appel, Chief Executive Officer (Total facility includes 60 beds in nursing home–type unit) **A**9 10 **F**1 3 7 8 12 14 15 16 19 21 22 24 26 28 32 33 34 35 36 40 41 42 44 46 52 53 54 55 56 57 58 59 63 64 65 67 71 73 **P**3 7 2 **N** Community Health Alliance, Winchester, KS	23	10	109	1312	66	2928	82	8760	3246	168
MCPHERSON—McPherson County										
★ MEMORIAL HOSPITAL, 1000 Hospital Drive, Zip 67460–2321; tel. 316/241–2250; Stan Regehr, President and Chief Executive Officer **A**9 10 **F**7 8 14 15 16 17 19 21 24 28 31 32 33 35 36 37 39 40 41 42 44 45 46 49 65 71 73 **N** Sunflower Health Network, Inc., Salina, KS	23	10	41	1542	19	70127	159	11654	5221	183
MEADE—Meade County										
MEADE DISTRICT HOSPITAL, 510 East Carthage Street, Zip 67864–0680, Mailing Address: P.O. Box 680, Zip 67864–0680; tel. 316/873–2141; Michael P. Thomas, Administrator **A**9 10 **F**7 15 16 19 22 24 26 28 32 35 40 42 44 49 64 65 71	16	10	20	457	6	14891	9	3687	1701	68

Hospital, Address, Telephone, Administrator, Approval, Facility, and Physician Codes, Health Care System, Network	Classification Codes		Utilization Data					Expense (thousands) of dollars		
★ American Hospital Association (AHA) membership □ Joint Commission on Accreditation of Healthcare Organizations (JCAHO) accreditation + American Osteopathic Healthcare Association (AOHA) membership ○ American Osteopathic Association (AOA) accreditation △ Commission on Accreditation of Rehabilitation Facilities (CARF) accreditation Control codes 61, 63, 64, 71, 72 and 73 indicate hospitals listed by AOHA, but not registered by AHA. For definition of numerical codes, see page A4	Control	Service	Staffed Beds	Admissions	Census	Outpatient Visits	Births	Total	Payroll	Personnel

MEDICINE LODGE—Barber County

★ MEDICINE LODGE MEMORIAL HOSPITAL, 710 North Walnut Street, Zip 67104–1019, Mailing Address: P.O. Drawer C., Zip 67104; tel. 316/886–3771; Kevin A. White, Administrator **A**9 10 **F**8 15 16 20 22 26 34 44 49 64 71 **S** Great Plains Health Alliance, Inc., Phillipsburg, KS **N** Great Plains Health Alliance, Phillipsburg, KS	16	10	42	683	16	6853	0	4429	2243	63

MINNEAPOLIS—Ottawa County

★ OTTAWA COUNTY HEALTH CENTER, (Formerly Ottawa County Hospital), 215 East Eighth, Zip 67467–1999, Mailing Address: P.O. Box 209, Zip 67467–0209; tel. 785/392–2122; Joy Reed, R.N., Administrator (Total facility includes 23 beds in nursing home–type unit) **A**9 10 **F**1 6 14 15 16 17 20 21 22 24 26 27 32 34 36 45 49 58 64 65 71 **S** Great Plains Health Alliance, Inc., Phillipsburg, KS **N** Sunflower Health Network, Inc., Salina, KS; Great Plains Health Alliance, Phillipsburg, KS	23	10	53	520	48	4806	0	3141	1699	89

MINNEOLA—Clark County

★ MINNEOLA DISTRICT HOSPITAL, 212 Main Street, Zip 67865–8511; tel. 316/885–4264; Blaine K. Miller, Administrator (Total facility includes 15 beds in nursing home–type unit) **A**9 10 **F**8 16 22 28 33 34 44 49 56 62 64 65 71 **S** Great Plains Health Alliance, Inc., Phillipsburg, KS **N** Great Plains Health Alliance, Phillipsburg, KS	16	10	15	585	7	5790	43	2608	939	39

MOUNDRIDGE—McPherson County

★ MERCY HOSPITAL, 218 East Pack Street, Zip 67107, Mailing Address: P.O. Box 180, Zip 67107–0180; tel. 316/345–6391; Doyle K. Johnson, Administrator (Total facility includes 4 beds in nursing home–type unit) **A**9 10 **F**15 22 26 40 44 49 64	21	10	16	358	5	5455	35	1225	634	31

NEODESHA—Wilson County

★ WILSON COUNTY HOSPITAL, 205 Mill Street, Zip 66757–1817, Mailing Address: P.O. Box 360, Zip 66757–0360; tel. 316/325–2611; Deanna Pittman, Administrator **A**9 10 **F**7 8 15 16 17 19 22 26 28 30 31 32 33 39 40 41 44 49 52 57 63 65 67 68 73 **S** Quorum Health Group/Quorum Health Resources, Inc., Brentwood, TN **N**	13	10	38	556	11	5765	54	4309	2068	87

NESS CITY—Ness County

★ NESS COUNTY HOSPITAL NUMBER TWO, 312 East Custer Street, Zip 67560–1654; tel. 913/798–2291; Clyde T. McCracken, Administrator (Total facility includes 27 beds in nursing home–type unit) **A**9 10 **F**15 17 19 26 29 35 39 44 49 64 65 66 71 **P**6 **N** MED–OP, Oakley, KS	16	10	52	361	29	4707	0	2980	1646	92

NEWTON—Harvey County

⊞ NEWTON MEDICAL CENTER, Mailing Address: P.O. Box 308, Zip 67114–0308; tel. 316/283–2700; W. Charles Waters, President (Total facility includes 11 beds in nursing home–type unit) **A**1 9 10 **F**7 14 15 19 21 22 23 26 28 29 30 31 32 33 34 35 37 40 41 44 49 56 64 65 71	23	10	66	2877	37	25964	411	20101	8624	271
□ PRAIRIE VIEW, 1901 East First Street, Zip 67114–5010, Mailing Address: P.O. Box 467, Zip 67114–0467; tel. 316/283–2400; Melvin Goering, Chief Executive Officer **A**1 9 10 **F**3 12 14 15 16 17 18 22 27 28 30 32 52 53 54 55 56 57 58 59 65 67 73 **P**6	23	22	30	969	20	—	—	13067	8319	247

NORTON—Norton County

★ NORTON COUNTY HOSPITAL, 102 East Holme, Zip 67654–0250, Mailing Address: P.O. Box 250, Zip 67654–0250; tel. 785/877–3351; Richard Miller, Administrator and Chief Executive Officer **A**9 10 **F**7 8 15 16 19 20 21 22 26 28 30 32 33 34 36 39 40 42 44 45 46 48 49 51 53 54 55 56 57 58 64 65 71 73 **P**4 **N** MED–OP, Oakley, KS	13	10	22	503	13	18882	1	4136	2251	83

OAKLEY—Logan County

LOGAN COUNTY HOSPITAL, 211 Cherry Street, Zip 67748–1201; tel. 913/672–3211; Rodney Bates, Administrator (Total facility includes 30 beds in nursing home–type unit) **A**9 10 **F**6 7 15 22 27 34 36 37 44 49 62 64 65 71 **N** MED–OP, Oakley, KS	15	10	51	423	13	10393	14	2686	1509	65

OBERLIN—Decatur County

★ DECATUR COUNTY HOSPITAL, 810 West Columbia Street, Zip 67749–2450, Mailing Address: P.O. Box 268, Zip 67749–0268; tel. 785/475–2208; Asa B. Wilson, Administrator (Total facility includes 50 beds in nursing home–type unit) **A**9 10 **F**7 8 12 14 15 16 19 22 26 32 33 34 35 36 37 42 44 49 63 64 65 71 **S** Lutheran Health Systems, Fargo, ND **N** MED–OP, Oakley, KS	23	10	74	564	52	9400	37	4171	2143	—

OLATHE—Johnson County

⊞ OLATHE MEDICAL CENTER, 20333 West 151st Street, Zip 66061–5352; tel. 913/791–4200; Frank H. Devocelle, President and Chief Executive Officer **A**1 2 9 10 **F**4 7 8 10 12 14 15 16 17 19 21 22 28 30 31 32 33 34 35 37 40 41 42 43 44 46 49 50 65 66 67 71 72 73 **P**3 8 **N** Jayhawk Health Alliance, Olathe, KS	23	10	130	7717	83	106439	1008	48985	24521	701

ONAGA—Pottawatomie County

COMMUNITY HOSPITAL ONAGA, 120 West Eighth Street, Zip 66521–0120; tel. 785/889–4272; Joseph T. Engelken, Chief Executive Officer (Total facility includes 177 beds in nursing home–type unit) **A**9 10 **F**1 3 6 7 8 11 12 13 15 17 19 20 22 24 26 27 28 29 30 31 32 33 34 35 36 37 39 40 41 42 44 45 46 48 49 51 53 54 55 56 57 58 61 62 64 65 66 67 68 70 71 72 73 74 **P**6 **N** Community Health Alliance, Winchester, KS	23	10	218	1197	120	57220	84	10724	5894	373

OSAWATOMIE—Miami County

□ OSAWATOMIE STATE HOSPITAL, 500 State Hospital Drive, Zip 66064–9757, Mailing Address: P.O. Box 500, Zip 66064–9757; tel. 913/755–3151; Randy Proctor, Superintendent **A**1 10 **F**8 19 20 21 22 26 42 44 45 46 50 51 52 57 60 65 70 73 **P**6	12	22	214	794	168	0	0	21517	13795	494

Hospital, Address, Telephone, Administrator, Approval, Facility, and Physician Codes, Health Care System, Network	Classi-fication Codes		Utilization Data					Expense (thousands) of dollars		
★ American Hospital Association (AHA) membership ☐ Joint Commission on Accreditation of Healthcare Organizations (JCAHO) accreditation + American Osteopathic Healthcare Association (AOHA) membership ○ American Osteopathic Association (AOA) accreditation △ Commission on Accreditation of Rehabilitation Facilities (CARF) accreditation Control codes 61, 63, 64, 71, 72 and 73 indicate hospitals listed by AOHA, but not registered by AHA. For definition of numerical codes, see page A4	Control	Service	Staffed Beds	Admissions	Census	Outpatient Visits	Births	Total	Payroll	Personnel

OSBORNE—Osborne County

★ OSBORNE COUNTY MEMORIAL HOSPITAL, 424 West New Hampshire Street, Zip 67473–0070, Mailing Address: P.O. Box 70, Zip 67473–0070; tel. 785/346–2121; Patricia Bernard, R.N., Administrator **A**9 10 **F**7 8 19 20 22 33 34 36 44 64 71 **S** Great Plains Health Alliance, Inc., Phillipsburg, KS **N** Sunflower Health Network, Inc., Salina, KS; Great Plains Health Alliance, Phillipsburg, KS

| | 13 | 10 | 29 | 343 | 4 | 6111 | 19 | 2474 | 1185 | 66 |

OTTAWA—Franklin County

⊞ RANSOM MEMORIAL HOSPITAL, 1301 South Main Street, Zip 66067–3598; tel. 785/229–8200; Robert E. Bregant, Jr., Administrator **A**1 9 10 **F**7 8 15 17 19 21 22 26 27 28 30 32 33 34 35 37 39 40 41 42 44 45 46 56 63 64 65 66 67 68 71 73

| | 13 | 10 | 45 | 2019 | 27 | 38570 | 170 | 13441 | 6359 | 238 |

OVERLAND PARK—Johnson County

COLUMBIA OVERLAND PARK REGIONAL CENTER See Overland Park Regional Medical Center

⊞ MENORAH MEDICAL CENTER, 5721 West 119th Street, Zip 66209; tel. 913/498–6000; Steven D. Wilkinson, President and Chief Executive Officer **A**1 2 9 10 **F**1 2 3 4 5 7 8 10 11 12 14 15 16 17 18 19 21 22 23 24 25 26 27 28 29 30 31 32 33 34 35 36 37 38 39 40 41 42 43 44 45 46 48 49 51 52 53 54 55 56 57 58 59 60 61 63 64 65 66 67 68 69 70 71 72 73 74 **P**1 5 6 **S** Health Midwest, Kansas City, MO

| | 23 | 10 | 109 | 4827 | 61 | 45387 | 927 | 60686 | 23809 | 613 |

⊞ △ MID–AMERICA REHABILITATION HOSPITAL, 5701 West 110th Street, Zip 66211; tel. 913/491–2400; Richard L. Allen, Chief Executive Officer (Total facility includes 10 beds in nursing home–type unit) **A**1 7 9 10 **F**12 14 15 16 17 19 20 21 25 27 34 35 41 42 46 48 49 60 64 65 66 67 71 73 **P**5 7 **S** HEALTHSOUTH Corporation, Birmingham, AL

| | 33 | 46 | 75 | 882 | 55 | 18561 | — | 17132 | 6974 | 162 |

⊞ OVERLAND PARK REGIONAL MEDICAL CENTER, (Formerly Columbia Overland Park Regional Center), 10500 Quivira Road, Zip 66215–2373, Mailing Address: P.O. Box 15959, Shawnee Mission, Zip 66215–5959; tel. 913/541–5000; Kevin J. Hicks, Chief Executive Officer (Total facility includes 17 beds in nursing home–type unit) **A**1 9 10 **F**2 3 4 7 8 9 10 11 12 13 14 15 16 17 18 19 20 21 22 24 25 26 27 28 29 30 32 33 34 35 36 37 38 39 40 41 42 43 44 45 46 48 49 51 52 53 54 55 56 57 58 59 60 61 63 64 65 66 67 70 71 72 73 74 **P**3 6 7 **S** Columbia/HCA Healthcare Corporation, Nashville, TN

| | 33 | 10 | 262 | 9238 | 127 | 104982 | 1957 | 71669 | 29901 | 1021 |

PAOLA—Miami County

★ MIAMI COUNTY MEDICAL CENTER, 2100 Baptiste, Zip 66071–0365, Mailing Address: P.O. Box 365, Zip 66071–0365; tel. 913/294–2327; Gerald Wiesner, Vice President and Chief Operating Officer **A**9 10 **F**8 13 16 19 21 22 28 30 31 32 34 39 41 42 44 46 49 56 65 66 71 73 **P**8 **N** Jayhawk Health Alliance, Olathe, KS

| | 23 | 10 | 20 | 616 | 7 | 24761 | 0 | 8424 | 3225 | 128 |

PARSONS—Labette County

⊞ LABETTE COUNTY MEDICAL CENTER, 1902 South U.S. Highway 59, Zip 67357–7404, Mailing Address: P.O. Box 956, Zip 67357–0956; tel. 316/421–4880; Robert E. Mac Devitt, Chief Executive Officer **A**1 9 10 **F**7 8 10 12 14 15 16 19 20 21 22 23 26 32 34 35 36 37 39 40 41 42 44 45 46 49 63 64 65 66 71 73 **P**4 **N**

| | 13 | 10 | 76 | 3062 | 40 | 39261 | 301 | 27765 | 11245 | 393 |

PARSONS STATE HOSPITAL AND TRAINING CENTER, 2601 Gabriel Street, Zip 67357–0738, Mailing Address: Box 738, Zip 67357–0738; tel. 316/421–6550; Gary J. Daniels, Ph.D., Superintendent **F**8 17 19 20 21 22 28 35 37 42 44 52 64 65 71 73

| | 12 | 62 | 240 | 22 | 207 | 0 | 0 | 19122 | 12377 | 255 |

PHILLIPSBURG—Phillips County

★ PHILLIPS COUNTY HOSPITAL, 1150 State Street, Zip 67661–1799, Mailing Address: P.O. Box 607, Zip 67661–0607; tel. 913/543–5226; James L. Giedd, Administrator (Total facility includes 33 beds in nursing home–type unit) **A**9 10 **F**1 7 8 14 15 19 20 22 28 34 35 42 44 46 49 64 65 71 73 **S** Great Plains Health Alliance, Inc., Phillipsburg, KS **N** Great Plains Health Alliance, Phillipsburg, KS; Hays Medical Center, Hays, KS

| | 23 | 10 | 62 | 898 | 43 | 10522 | 24 | 5812 | 2575 | 114 |

PITTSBURG—Crawford County

⊞ MOUNT CARMEL MEDICAL CENTER, 1102 East Centennial, Zip 66762–6686; tel. 316/231–6100; John Daniel Lingor, President and Chief Executive Officer **A**1 2 9 10 **F**1 7 8 12 15 16 19 21 22 23 27 28 29 30 32 33 34 35 36 37 39 40 41 42 44 45 46 49 52 54 55 56 58 59 60 63 64 65 66 67 71 73 **P**1 2 3 4 5 6 7 8 **S** Marian Health System, Tulsa, OK **N**

| | 21 | 10 | 119 | 4412 | 61 | 52322 | 307 | 32608 | 15104 | 563 |

PLAINVILLE—Rooks County

PLAINVILLE RURAL HOSPITAL DISTRICT NUMBER ONE, 304 South Colorado Avenue, Zip 67663–2505; tel. 785/434–4553; Leonard Hernandez, Administrator and Chief Executive Officer **A**9 10 **F**8 14 15 16 19 21 27 28 30 32 36 39 44 45 71 73 **N** MED–OP, Oakley, KS

| | 15 | 10 | 27 | 316 | 5 | 1074 | 4 | 2600 | 1222 | 64 |

PRATT—Pratt County

★ PRATT REGIONAL MEDICAL CENTER, 200 Commodore Street, Zip 67124–3099; tel. 316/672–7451; Susan M. Page, President and Chief Executive Officer (Total facility includes 70 beds in nursing home–type unit) **A**9 10 **F**7 8 15 16 19 21 22 23 24 25 26 28 29 30 31 32 33 34 35 36 37 39 40 42 44 45 46 49 61 64 65 66 67 71 73 **P**6 7

| | 23 | 10 | 84 | 1807 | 51 | 31270 | 166 | 16866 | 7631 | 337 |

QUINTER—Gove County

GOVE COUNTY MEDICAL CENTER, 520 West Fifth Street, Zip 67752, Mailing Address: P.O. Box 129, Zip 67752; tel. 785/754–3341; Paul Davis, Administrator (Total facility includes 59 beds in nursing home–type unit) **A**9 10 **F**6 7 8 19 22 28 32 33 34 44 49 64 65 71 **P**5 **N** MED–OP, Oakley, KS

| | 13 | 10 | 80 | 762 | 12 | 7507 | 68 | 3083 | 1970 | 131 |

Hospital, Address, Telephone, Administrator, Approval, Facility, and Physician Codes, Health Care System, Network	Classification Codes		Utilization Data					Expense (thousands) of dollars		
	Control	Service	Staffed Beds	Admissions	Census	Outpatient Visits	Births	Total	Payroll	Personnel

RANSOM—Ness County
★ GRISELL MEMORIAL HOSPITAL DISTRICT ONE, 210 South Vermont, Zip 67572–0268, Mailing Address: P.O. Box 268, Zip 67572–0268; tel. 785/731–2231; Kristine Ochs, R.N., Administrator (Total facility includes 34 beds in nursing home–type unit) **A**9 10 **F**7 8 14 19 20 22 26 32 33 36 41 44 49 51 56 64 65 71 **S** Great Plains Health Alliance, Inc., Phillipsburg, KS **N** Great Plains Health Alliance, Phillipsburg, KS; Hays Medical Center, Hays, KS | 16 | 10 | 46 | 151 | 34 | 7576 | 1 | 2571 | 1401 | 71

RUSSELL—Russell County
✠ RUSSELL REGIONAL HOSPITAL, 200 South Main Street, Zip 67665–2997; tel. 913/483–3131; Talton L. Francis, FACHE, Administrator (Total facility includes 25 beds in nursing home–type unit) **A**1 9 10 **F**7 14 15 16 19 21 22 27 28 29 30 34 36 37 40 44 45 49 51 64 65 67 71 73 **N** Sunflower Health Network, Inc., Salina, KS | 23 | 10 | 57 | 916 | 30 | 14372 | 20 | 6262 | 3417 | 148

SABETHA—Nemaha County
★ SABETHA COMMUNITY HOSPITAL, 14th and Oregon Streets, Zip 66534, Mailing Address: P.O. Box 229, Zip 66534; tel. 785/284–2121; Rita K. Buurman, Chief Executive Officer **A**9 10 **F**1 7 8 15 16 17 19 20 21 22 26 28 30 32 34 35 41 42 44 45 49 54 56 58 64 65 71 **P**5 6 **S** Great Plains Health Alliance, Inc., Phillipsburg, KS **N** Great Plains Health Alliance, Phillipsburg, KS | 23 | 10 | 27 | 474 | 8 | 16731 | 59 | 4365 | 2286 | 74

SAINT FRANCIS—Cheyenne County
★ CHEYENNE COUNTY HOSPITAL, 210 West First Street, Zip 67756, Mailing Address: P.O. Box 547, Zip 67756–0547; tel. 785/332–2104; Leslie Lacy, Administrator **A**9 10 **F**7 8 15 16 19 22 42 44 49 51 64 65 71 **S** Great Plains Health Alliance, Inc., Phillipsburg, KS **N** Great Plains Health Alliance, Phillipsburg, KS; Hays Medical Center, Hays, KS; High Plains Rural Health Network, Fort Morgan, CO | 23 | 10 | 16 | 216 | 2 | 11264 | 0 | 2851 | 1101 | 47

SALINA—Saline County
✠ △ SALINA REGIONAL HEALTH CENTER, (Includes Salina Regional Health Center–Penn Campus, 139 North Penn Street, Zip 67401; Salina Regional Health Center–Santa Fe Campus, 400 South Santa Fe Avenue, Zip 67401), 400 South Santa Fe Avenue, Zip 67401–4198, Mailing Address: P.O. Box 5080, Zip 67401–5080; tel. 785/452–7000; Randy Peterson, President and Chief Executive Officer (Total facility includes 32 beds in nursing home–type unit) **A**1 2 3 7 9 10 **F**7 8 10 12 15 16 17 19 20 21 22 23 24 26 27 28 29 30 31 32 33 34 35 36 37 38 39 40 41 42 44 45 46 48 49 52 54 55 56 57 58 59 60 63 64 65 66 67 68 71 73 74 **P**8 **N** Sunflower Health Network, Inc., Salina, KS | 23 | 10 | 209 | 9417 | 148 | 122168 | 1082 | 74885 | 32016 | 1072
★ ST. FRANCIS AT SALINA, 5097 West Cloud Street, Zip 67401–2348; tel. 785/825–0541; Father Phillip J. Rapp, President and Chief Executive Officer (Nonreporting) **A**9 | 23 | 22 | 26 | — | — | — | — | — | — | —

SATANTA—Haskell County
★ SATANTA DISTRICT HOSPITAL, 401 South Cheyenne Street, Zip 67870, Mailing Address: P.O. Box 159, Zip 67870–0159; tel. 316/649–2761; T. G. Lee, Administrator (Total facility includes 29 beds in nursing home–type unit) **A**9 10 **F**7 8 15 17 19 22 32 34 35 39 41 44 45 49 64 65 71 **P**4 **S** Great Plains Health Alliance, Inc., Phillipsburg, KS **N** Pioneer Network, Santana, KS; Great Plains Health Alliance, Phillipsburg, KS; Hays Medical Center, Hays, KS | 16 | 10 | 42 | 255 | 29 | 5272 | 1 | 4153 | 1898 | 90

SCOTT CITY—Scott County
★ SCOTT COUNTY HOSPITAL, 310 East Third Street, Zip 67871–1299; tel. 316/872–5811; Greg Unruh, Chief Executive Officer **A**9 10 **F**7 8 10 14 15 16 17 19 20 22 28 30 34 35 36 39 40 42 44 49 64 71 73 74 **N** MED–OP, Oakley, KS | 13 | 10 | 27 | 718 | 9 | 8099 | 71 | 3860 | 1872 | 100

SEDAN—Chautauqua County
SEDAN CITY HOSPITAL, 300 West North Street, Zip 67361–1051, Mailing Address: P.O. Box C., Zip 67361–1051; tel. 316/725–3115; Janice Shippy, R.N., Administrator (Nonreporting) **A**9 10 | 14 | 10 | 30 | — | — | — | — | — | — | —

SENECA—Nemaha County
NEMAHA VALLEY COMMUNITY HOSPITAL, 1600 Community Drive, Zip 66538–9758; tel. 785/336–6181; Michael J. Ryan, Administrator **A**9 10 **F**7 8 15 16 19 22 26 28 30 32 34 35 39 40 41 44 49 65 66 70 71 **N** Community Health Alliance, Winchester, KS | 23 | 10 | 24 | 477 | 6 | 10228 | 51 | 3703 | 1540 | 72

SHAWNEE MISSION—Johnson County
MENORAH MEDICAL CENTER See Overland Park
✠ SHAWNEE MISSION MEDICAL CENTER, 9100 West 74th Street, Zip 66204–4019, Mailing Address: Box 2923, Zip 66201–1323; tel. 913/676–2000; William G. Robertson, Senior Executive Officer **A**1 2 9 10 **F**3 4 7 8 10 11 12 13 15 16 17 19 21 22 23 24 25 29 30 31 32 34 35 37 38 39 40 41 42 43 44 45 46 49 52 53 54 55 56 57 58 59 61 64 65 66 67 71 72 73 74 **P**4 5 6 8 **S** Saint Luke's Shawnee Mission Health System, Kansas City, MO | 21 | 10 | 333 | 16832 | 195 | 236772 | 3042 | 136843 | 61069 | 1731

SMITH CENTER—Smith County
★ SMITH COUNTY MEMORIAL HOSPITAL, 614 South Main Street, Zip 66967–0349, Mailing Address: P.O. Box 349, Zip 66967–0349; tel. 785/282–6845; John Terrill, Administrator (Total facility includes 28 beds in nursing home–type unit) **A**9 10 **F**1 7 8 19 22 34 35 44 49 64 65 71 **S** Great Plains Health Alliance, Inc., Phillipsburg, KS **N** Sunflower Health Network, Inc., Salina, KS; Great Plains Health Alliance, Phillipsburg, KS | 23 | 10 | 54 | 648 | 34 | 9689 | 39 | 3568 | 1731 | 91

Hospital, Address, Telephone, Administrator, Approval, Facility, and Physician Codes, Health Care System, Network	Classi-fication Codes		Utilization Data					Expense (thousands) of dollars		
★ American Hospital Association (AHA) membership □ Joint Commission on Accreditation of Healthcare Organizations (JCAHO) accreditation + American Osteopathic Healthcare Association (AOHA) membership ○ American Osteopathic Association (AOA) accreditation △ Commission on Accreditation of Rehabilitation Facilities (CARF) accreditation Control codes 61, 63, 64, 71, 72 and 73 indicate hospitals listed by AOHA, but not registered by AHA. For definition of numerical codes, see page A4	Control	Service	Staffed Beds	Admissions	Census	Outpatient Visits	Births	Total	Payroll	Personnel

STAFFORD—Stafford County

STAFFORD DISTRICT HOSPITAL, 502 South Buckeye Street, Zip 67578–2035, Mailing Address: P.O. Box 190, Zip 67578–0190; tel. 316/234–5221; Douglas Newman, Administrator **A**9 10 **F**8 11 12 13 15 16 17 19 20 21 22 25 26 28 29 30 31 32 33 34 35 42 44 45 46 49 51 53 54 56 58 64 65 66 71 73 74 **P**6 — 16 | 10 | 25 | 324 | 6 | 3853 | 0 | 2081 | 895 | 45

SYRACUSE—Hamilton County

HAMILTON COUNTY HOSPITAL, East Avenue G. and Huser Street, Zip 67878–0909, Mailing Address: Box 909, Zip 67878–0909; tel. 316/384–7461; Cynthia O. Akers, R.N., Administrator (Total facility includes 48 beds in nursing home–type unit) **A**9 10 **F**19 22 40 44 64 71 **P**4 5 — 13 | 10 | 74 | 234 | 0 | 8114 | 4 | 4074 | 1960 | 88

TOPEKA—Shawnee County

☒ C. F. MENNINGER MEMORIAL HOSPITAL, (Includes Child and Adolescent Services of the Menninger Clinic), 5800 West Sixth Avenue, Zip 66606–9699, Mailing Address: P.O. Box 829, Zip 66601–0829; tel. 913/350–5000; Ephram Bleiberg, M.D., President and Chief of Staff (Nonreporting) **A**1 3 9 10 — 23 | 22 | 143 | — | — | — | — | — | — | —

CHILD AND ADOLESCENT SERVICES OF THE MENNINGER CLINIC See C. F. Menninger Memorial Hospital

☒ COLMERY–O'NEIL VETERANS AFFAIRS MEDICAL CENTER, 2200 Gage Boulevard, Zip 66622–0002; tel. 785/350–3111; Edgar Tucker, Director (Total facility includes 96 beds in nursing home–type unit) **A**1 3 9 **F**1 3 6 8 10 12 14 15 16 17 18 19 20 21 22 24 26 27 28 29 30 31 32 34 35 37 39 41 42 44 45 46 48 49 51 52 54 55 56 57 58 59 63 64 65 67 71 72 73 74 **S** Department of Veterans Affairs, Washington, DC — 45 | 22 | 218 | 3161 | 205 | 174325 | 0 | 75205 | 42090 | 1125

KANSAS NEUROLOGICAL INSTITUTE, 3107 West 21st Street, Zip 66604–3298; tel. 913/296–5301; Robert Day, Ph.D., Superintendent **F**20 64 **P**1 — 12 | 62 | 225 | 8 | 227 | 0 | 0 | 24117 | 16016 | 678

□ △ KANSAS REHABILITATION HOSPITAL, 1504 S.W. Eighth, Zip 66606–2714; tel. 785/235–6600; Julie De Jean, Administrator and Chief Executive Officer (Total facility includes 17 beds in nursing home–type unit) **A**1 7 10 **F**12 16 24 34 41 46 48 49 64 65 67 73 74 — 33 | 46 | 62 | 676 | 40 | 16126 | — | 10389 | 4360 | 151

□ PARKVIEW HOSPITAL OF TOPEKA, 3707 S.W. Sixth Street, Zip 66606–2085; tel. 913/295–3000; Thomas G. Smith, Chief Executive Officer **A**1 9 10 **F**3 12 14 15 16 18 19 21 27 35 52 53 56 57 58 59 65 67 71 73 **S** Health Management Associates, Naples, FL — 33 | 22 | 80 | 746 | 21 | 10074 | 0 | 4861 | 2591 | 111

☒ △ ST. FRANCIS HOSPITAL AND MEDICAL CENTER, 1700 West Seventh Street, Zip 66606–1690; tel. 913/295–8000; Sister Loretto Marie Colwell, President **A**1 2 3 5 7 9 10 **F**3 4 7 8 10 11 12 14 15 16 19 20 21 22 24 27 28 30 31 32 34 37 40 41 42 43 44 45 46 48 49 51 56 60 63 65 67 71 72 73 **P**8 **S** Sisters of Charity of Leavenworth Health Services Corporation, Leavenworth, KS **N** Community Health Alliance, Winchester, KS; Heart of America Network, Wichita, KS — 21 | 10 | 291 | 10004 | 138 | 232890 | 1052 | 97613 | 45921 | 1093

☒ STORMONT–VAIL HEALTHCARE, 1500 S.W. Tenth Street, Zip 66604–1353; tel. 785/354–6000; Maynard F. Oliverius, President and Chief Executive Officer **A**1 3 5 9 10 **F**4 7 8 10 11 12 14 15 16 17 19 21 22 23 24 26 27 28 29 30 31 32 33 34 35 36 37 38 39 40 41 42 43 44 45 46 47 49 52 53 55 56 57 58 60 65 67 71 73 74 **P**6 **S** Stormont–Vail HealthCare, Topeka, KS — 23 | 10 | 313 | 10814 | 159 | 87666 | 2095 | 161720 | 82532 | 2193

TRIBUNE—Greeley County

★ GREELEY COUNTY HOSPITAL, 506 Third Street, Zip 67879, Mailing Address: P.O. Box 338, Zip 67879–0338; tel. 316/376–4221; Cynthia K. Schneider, Administrator (Total facility includes 32 beds in nursing home–type unit) **A**9 10 **F**7 8 15 16 19 20 22 27 32 33 36 39 44 46 49 56 57 64 65 66 67 71 **S** Great Plains Health Alliance, Inc., Phillipsburg, KS **N** Great Plains Health Alliance, Phillipsburg, KS — 23 | 10 | 50 | 424 | 32 | 6058 | 62 | 3333 | 1602 | 82

ULYSSES—Grant County

★ BOB WILSON MEMORIAL GRANT COUNTY HOSPITAL, 415 North Main Street, Zip 67880–2196; tel. 316/356–1266; Steven G. Daniel, Administrator **A**9 10 **F**7 19 22 28 32 35 37 40 44 46 49 51 52 57 65 71 73 **S** Quorum Health Group/Quorum Health Resources, Inc., Brentwood, TN — 13 | 10 | 42 | 920 | 15 | 36699 | 107 | 8898 | 3659 | 141

WAKEENEY—Trego County

★ TREGO COUNTY–LEMKE MEMORIAL HOSPITAL, 320 North 13th Street, Zip 67672–2099; tel. 785/743–2182; James Wahlmeier, Administrator (Total facility includes 45 beds in nursing home–type unit) **A**9 10 **F**3 7 8 15 16 17 19 20 22 32 33 34 44 45 49 64 65 71 **S** Great Plains Health Alliance, Inc., Phillipsburg, KS **N** Great Plains Health Alliance, Phillipsburg, KS; Hays Medical Center, Hays, KS — 13 | 10 | 73 | 630 | 50 | 7157 | 1 | 4560 | 2110 | 105

WAMEGO—Pottawatomie County

WAMEGO CITY HOSPITAL, 711 Genn Drive, Zip 66547–1199; tel. 913/456–2295; Lisa J. Freeborn, R.N., Administrator **A**9 10 **F**15 16 19 22 28 32 35 44 49 64 65 71 **S** Stormont–Vail HealthCare, Topeka, KS — 14 | 10 | 26 | 605 | 7 | 13576 | 0 | 4495 | 2500 | 90

WASHINGTON—Washington County

WASHINGTON COUNTY HOSPITAL, 304 East Third Street, Zip 66968–2098; tel. 913/325–2211; Everett Lutjemeier, Administrator **A**9 10 **F**1 7 8 9 14 15 22 24 28 30 33 36 37 40 41 44 49 51 64 65 71 **P**5 — 13 | 10 | 27 | 272 | 8 | 3698 | 14 | 1601 | 749 | 35

WELLINGTON—Sumner County

★ SUMNER REGIONAL MEDICAL CENTER, 1323 North A. Street, Zip 67152–1323; tel. 316/326–7453; Raymond Williams, III, President and Chief Executive Officer (Total facility includes 11 beds in nursing home–type unit) **A**9 10 **F**7 8 14 15 16 19 21 22 30 32 34 36 40 42 44 46 49 52 57 64 71 **P**8 — 14 | 10 | 49 | 1118 | 16 | 28872 | 139 | 6785 | 3194 | —

Hospital, Address, Telephone, Administrator, Approval, Facility, and Physician Codes, Health Care System, Network	Classi-fication Codes		Utilization Data						Expense (thousands) of dollars		
★ American Hospital Association (AHA) membership □ Joint Commission on Accreditation of Healthcare Organizations (JCAHO) accreditation + American Osteopathic Healthcare Association (AOHA) membership ○ American Osteopathic Association (AOA) accreditation △ Commission on Accreditation of Rehabilitation Facilities (CARF) accreditation Control codes 61, 63, 64, 71, 72 and 73 indicate hospitals listed by AOHA, but not registered by AHA. For definition of numerical codes, see page A4	Control	Service	Staffed Beds	Admissions	Census	Outpatient Visits	Births	Total	Payroll	Personnel

WESTMORELAND—Pottawatomie County

DECHAIRO HOSPITAL, First and North Streets, Zip 66549; tel. 913/457–3311; Paula Lauer, Operations Manager **A**9 10 **F**8 15 16 21 22 32 34 41 44 65 **S** Stormont–Vail HealthCare, Topeka, KS	33	10	13	207	3	4225	—	1098	586	27

WICHITA—Sedgwick County

COLUMBIA WESLEY MEDICAL CENTER See Wesley Medical Center

+ ○ RIVERSIDE HEALTH SYSTEM, 2622 West Central Street, Zip 67203–4999; tel. 316/946–5000; Robert Dixon, President and Chief Executive Officer **A**9 10 11 12 13 **F**7 8 11 12 13 14 15 16 17 19 20 21 22 26 28 29 30 35 37 39 40 41 42 44 45 46 49 54 56 57 63 64 65 66 67 71 73 **P**3 6	23	10	103	3323	46	28979	209	35689	17814	588

ST. JOSEPH CAMPUS See Via Christi Regional Medical Center

⊞ VETERANS AFFAIRS MEDICAL AND REGIONAL OFFICE CENTER, 5500 East Kellogg, Zip 67218; tel. 316/685–2221; Kent D. Hill, Director (Nonreporting) **A**1 3 5 9 **S** Department of Veterans Affairs, Washington, DC	45	10	83	—		—	—	—	—	—
⊞ △ VIA CHRISTI REGIONAL MEDICAL CENTER, (Includes St. Francis Campus, 929 North St. Francis Street, tel. 316/268–5000; St. Joseph Campus, 3600 East Harry Street, Zip 67218–3713; tel. 316/685–1111), 929 North St. Francis Street, Zip 67214–3882; tel. 316/268–5000; Randall G. Nyp, President and Chief Executive Officer **A**1 3 5 7 10 **F**1 4 5 6 7 8 9 10 11 12 13 14 15 17 18 19 21 22 23 24 25 26 27 28 29 30 31 32 34 35 37 38 39 40 41 42 43 44 46 47 49 50 51 52 53 54 55 56 57 58 59 60 61 63 64 65 66 67 68 69 70 71 72 73 74 **P**3 6 7 **S** Marian Health System, Tulsa, OK **N** Heart of America Network, Wichita, KS; Via Christi, Wichita, KS	21	10	1009	37068	582	375844	3572	434816	181541	5253
□ VIA CHRISTI REHABILITATION CENTER, 1151 North Rock Road, Zip 67206–1262; tel. 316/634–3400; Laurie Labarca, Chief Operating Officer (Total facility includes 19 beds in nursing home–type unit) **A**1 10 **F**1 2 3 4 5 6 7 8 9 10 11 12 13 14 15 16 17 18 19 20 21 22 23 24 25 26 27 28 29 30 31 32 33 34 35 37 38 39 40 41 42 43 44 45 46 47 48 49 50 51 52 53 54 55 56 57 58 59 60 62 63 64 65 66 67 68 69 70 71 72 73 74	21	46	42	393	18	5160	—	8907	4473	166
⊞ WESLEY MEDICAL CENTER, (Formerly Columbia Wesley Medical Center), 550 North Hillside Avenue, Zip 67214–4976; tel. 316/688–2000; Carl W. Fitch, Sr., President and Chief Executive Officer **A**1 2 3 5 9 10 **F**4 7 8 10 11 12 15 16 18 19 20 21 22 23 24 26 27 28 29 30 32 34 35 37 38 39 40 41 42 43 44 46 47 49 51 54 57 60 61 64 65 66 67 69 70 71 73 74 **P**6 **S** Columbia/HCA Healthcare Corporation, Nashville, TN	33	10	510	23772	333	220994	4708	257932	90029	2405
□ △ WESLEY REHABILITATION HOSPITAL, 8338 West 13th Street North, Zip 67212–2984; tel. 316/729–9999; Lisa James, Administrator **A**1 7 9 10 **F**12 17 27 34 46 48 49 65 66 67 73 **P**5 **S** HEALTHSOUTH Corporation, Birmingham, AL	33	46	65	613	34	13057	0	10553	5529	122

WINCHESTER—Jefferson County

JEFFERSON COUNTY MEMORIAL HOSPITAL, 408 Delaware Street, Zip 66097–4002, Mailing Address: Rural Route 1, Box 1, Zip 66097–0001; tel. 913/774–4340; W. David Drew, Interim Administrator (Total facility includes 85 beds in nursing home–type unit) **A**9 **F**8 15 16 19 21 22 26 27 30 33 34 35 36 39 49 64 65 71 73 **N** Community Health Alliance, Winchester, KS	23	10	113	99	63	4045	2	2919	1918	103

WINFIELD—Cowley County

⊞ WILLIAM NEWTON MEMORIAL HOSPITAL, 1300 East Fifth Street, Zip 67156–2495; tel. 316/221–2300; Richard H. Vaught, Administrator (Total facility includes 14 beds in nursing home–type unit) **A**1 9 10 **F**7 8 13 16 17 19 21 22 27 28 30 32 36 37 39 40 41 42 44 45 46 49 52 58 64 65 66 67 71 73	14	10	41	1418	15	40347	266	13148	7286	292
WINFIELD STATE HOSPITAL AND TRAINING CENTER, 1320 North McCabe, Zip 67156–9701; tel. 316/221–1200; William P. Brooks, Superintendent (Nonreporting)	12	62	222	—	—	—	—	—	—	—

Resident population 3,908 (in thousands)
Resident population in metro areas 48.3%
Birth rate per 1,000 population 13.8
65 years and over 12.6%
Percent of persons without health insurance 15.4%

Hospital, Address, Telephone, Administrator, Approval, Facility, and Physician Codes, Health Care System, Network	Classi-fication Codes		Utilization Data					Expense (thousands) of dollars		
★ American Hospital Association (AHA) membership □ Joint Commission on Accreditation of Healthcare Organizations (JCAHO) accreditation + American Osteopathic Healthcare Association (AOHA) membership ○ American Osteopathic Association (AOA) accreditation △ Commission on Accreditation of Rehabilitation Facilities (CARF) accreditation Control codes 61, 63, 64, 71, 72 and 73 indicate hospitals listed by AOHA, but not registered by AHA. For definition of numerical codes, see page A4	Control	Service	Staffed Beds	Admissions	Census	Outpatient Visits	Births	Total	Payroll	Personnel

ALBANY—Clinton County

CLINTON COUNTY HOSPITAL, 723 Burkesville Road, Zip 42602–1654; tel. 606/387–6421; Randel Flowers, Ph.D., Administrator **A**9 10 **F**11 19 22 71 **N** Center Care, Bowling Green, KY

| 23 | 10 | 42 | 2229 | 26 | 14280 | — | 6444 | 3019 | 132 |

ASHLAND—Boyd County

✠ △ KING'S DAUGHTERS' MEDICAL CENTER, 2201 Lexington Avenue, Zip 41101–2874, Mailing Address: P.O. Box 151, Zip 41105–0151; tel. 606/327–4000; Fred L. Jackson, Chief Executive Officer (Total facility includes 10 beds in nursing home–type unit) **A**1 2 7 9 10 **F**1 4 7 8 10 12 15 16 17 19 21 22 25 27 28 30 31 32 33 34 35 36 37 38 39 40 41 42 43 44 45 46 48 49 52 53 54 55 56 57 58 60 63 64 65 66 67 71 72 73 74 **P**8

| 23 | 10 | 341 | 16499 | 247 | 132803 | 1020 | 129045 | 50175 | 1423 |

✠ OUR LADY OF BELLEFONTE HOSPITAL, St. Christopher Drive, Zip 41101, Mailing Address: P.O. Box 789, Zip 41105–0789; tel. 606/833–3333; Robert J. Maher, President (Nonreporting) **A**1 9 10 **S** Franciscan Sisters of the Poor Health System, Inc., Latham, NY **N** CHA Provider Network, Inc., Lexington, KY

| 21 | 10 | 194 | — | — | — | — | — | — | — |

BARBOURVILLE—Knox County

✠ KNOX COUNTY HOSPITAL, (Formerly Knox County General Hospital), 321 High Street, Zip 40906–1317, Mailing Address: P.O. Box 160, Zip 40906–0160; tel. 606/546–4175; Craig Morgan, Administrator (Total facility includes 16 beds in nursing home–type unit) **A**1 9 10 **F**7 19 21 22 37 40 44 64 65 71 73 **N** CHA Provider Network, Inc., Lexington, KY; Blue Grass Family Health Plan, Lexington, KY

| 13 | 10 | 58 | 1664 | 36 | 25469 | 28 | 7721 | 4202 | 182 |

BARDSTOWN—Nelson County

✠ FLAGET MEMORIAL HOSPITAL, 201 Cathedral Manor, Zip 40004–1299; tel. 502/348–3923; Suzanne Reasbeck, President and Chief Executive Officer (Nonreporting) **A**1 9 10 **S** Catholic Health Initiatives, Denver, CO **N** Community Health Delivery System, Inc., Louisville, KY

| 21 | 10 | 36 | — | — | — | — | — | — | — |

BENTON—Marshall County

✠ MARSHALL COUNTY HOSPITAL, 503 George McClain Drive, Zip 42025–1399, Mailing Address: P.O. Box 630, Zip 42025–0630; tel. 502/527–4800; David G. Fuqua, R.N., Chief Executive Officer (Total facility includes 34 beds in nursing home–type unit) **A**1 9 10 **F**8 15 16 19 21 22 26 33 35 37 41 42 44 49 57 64 65 71 **P**8 **S** Quorum Health Group/Quorum Health Resources, Inc., Brentwood, TN

| 16 | 10 | 80 | 823 | 47 | 10409 | 0 | 8086 | 3623 | 244 |

BEREA—Madison County

✠ BEREA HOSPITAL, 305 Estill Street, Zip 40403–1909; tel. 606/986–3151; David E. Burgio, FACHE, President and Chief Executive Officer (Total facility includes 65 beds in nursing home–type unit) **A**1 9 10 **F**8 12 14 15 16 17 19 20 21 22 26 27 28 30 31 34 37 39 41 44 46 49 64 65 67 71 72 73 74 **P**2 8 **N** CHA Provider Network, Inc., Lexington, KY; Blue Grass Family Health Plan, Lexington, KY

| 23 | 10 | 113 | 1768 | 80 | 40818 | — | 17372 | 7233 | 300 |

BOWLING GREEN—Warren County

✠ GREENVIEW REGIONAL HOSPITAL, (Formerly Columbia Greenview Hospital), 1801 Ashley Circle, Zip 42104–3384, Mailing Address: P.O. Box 90024, Zip 42102–9024; tel. 502/793–1000; Philip A. Clendenin, Chief Executive Officer **A**1 9 10 **F**4 7 8 10 11 12 14 15 16 17 19 20 21 22 23 28 29 30 32 33 34 37 40 41 42 44 45 49 58 60 64 65 66 67 71 73 74 **P**5 7 **S** Columbia/HCA Healthcare Corporation, Nashville, TN

| 33 | 10 | 211 | 5724 | 84 | 50735 | 885 | — | — | 535 |

□ △ MEDIPLEX REHABILITATION HOSPITAL, 1300 Campbell Lane, Zip 42104–4162; tel. 502/782–6900; Jeffrey L. Durham, Chief Executive Officer (Total facility includes 10 beds in nursing home–type unit) **A**1 7 10 **F**12 48 64 65 67

| 33 | 46 | 55 | 921 | 54 | 0 | 0 | 16055 | 4729 | 173 |

✠ THE MEDICAL CENTER AT BOWLING GREEN, 250 Park Street, Zip 42101–1795, Mailing Address: P.O. Box 90010, Zip 42102–9010; tel. 502/745–1000; Connie Smith, Chief Executive Officer (Nonreporting) **A**1 9 10 **N** Center Care, Bowling Green, KY

| 23 | 10 | 298 | — | — | — | — | — | — | — |

BURKESVILLE—Cumberland County

★ CUMBERLAND COUNTY HOSPITAL, Highway 90 West, Zip 42717–0280, Mailing Address: P.O. Box 280, Zip 42717–0280; tel. 502/864–2511; Mark E. Thompson, Chief Executive Officer **A**9 10 **F**7 8 12 15 19 22 27 34 44 46 49 65 71 **S** Quorum Health Group/Quorum Health Resources, Inc., Brentwood, TN **N** Center Care, Bowling Green, KY

| 23 | 10 | 31 | 1568 | 18 | 18682 | — | 5170 | 2154 | 94 |

CADIZ—Trigg County

★ TRIGG COUNTY HOSPITAL, Highway 68 East, Zip 42211, Mailing Address: P.O. Box 312, Zip 42211–0312; tel. 502/522–3215; Richard Chapman, Administrator **A**9 10 **F**8 19 22 27 32 34 41 44 46 48 49 65 71 73 **N** Community Health Delivery System, Inc., Louisville, KY

| 15 | 10 | 35 | 477 | 5 | 9489 | — | 3813 | 1754 | — |

CALHOUN—McLean County

MCLEAN COUNTY HEALTH CENTER, 200 Highway 81 North, Zip 42327–2104; tel. 502/273–5252; Brenda Wright, Acting Administrator (Nonreporting) **A**9 10

| 13 | 10 | 26 | — | — | — | — | — | — | — |

Hospital, Address, Telephone, Administrator, Approval, Facility, and Physician Codes, Health Care System, Network	Classi-fication Codes		Utilization Data					Expense (thousands) of dollars		
★ American Hospital Association (AHA) membership □ Joint Commission on Accreditation of Healthcare Organizations (JCAHO) accreditation + American Osteopathic Healthcare Association (AOHA) membership ○ American Osteopathic Association (AOA) accreditation △ Commission on Accreditation of Rehabilitation Facilities (CARF) accreditation Control codes 61, 63, 64, 71, 72 and 73 indicate hospitals listed by AOHA, but not registered by AHA. For definition of numerical codes, see page A4	Control	Service	Staffed Beds	Admissions	Census	Outpatient Visits	Births	Total	Payroll	Personnel

CAMPBELLSVILLE—Taylor County

☒ TAYLOR COUNTY HOSPITAL, 1700 Old Lebanon Road, Zip 42718–9600; tel. 502/465–3561; David R. Hayes, President **A**1 2 9 10 **F**7 8 10 14 15 19 21 22 23 24 27 28 29 30 32 33 35 37 39 40 42 44 45 46 49 50 63 70 71 73 **S** Jewish Hospital HealthCare Services, Louisville, KY **N** Jewish Hospital Healthcare Services, Louisville, KY; Center Care, Bowling Green, KY 16 10 90 3203 41 40613 364 25637 9335 409

CARLISLE—Nicholas County

☒ NICHOLAS COUNTY HOSPITAL, (Includes Johnson–Mathers Nursing Home), 2323 Concrete Road, Zip 40311–9721, Mailing Address: P.O. Box 232, Zip 40311–0232; tel. 606/289–7181; Doris Ecton, Administrator and Chief Executive Officer (Total facility includes 67 beds in nursing home–type unit) **A**1 9 10 **F**1 8 14 15 16 19 22 26 28 34 41 44 49 64 65 67 71 73 **N** CHA Provider Network, Inc., Lexington, KY .... 23 10 85 655 73 15571 — 5492 2831 135

CARROLLTON—Carroll County

★ CARROLL COUNTY HOSPITAL, (Formerly Carroll County Memorial Hospital), 309 11th Street, Zip 41008–1400; tel. 502/732–4321; Roger Williams, Chief Executive Officer (Nonreporting) **A**9 10 **S** Alliant Health System, Louisville, KY **N** Community Health Delivery System, Inc., Louisville, KY .... 13 10 39 — — — — — — —

COLUMBIA—Adair County

□ WESTLAKE REGIONAL HOSPITAL, Westlake Drive, Zip 42728–1149, Mailing Address: P.O. Box 468, Zip 42728–0468; tel. 502/384–4753; Rex A. Tungate, Administrator (Nonreporting) **A**1 9 10 **N** Center Care, Bowling Green, KY .... 16 10 80 — — — — — — —

CORBIN—Whitley County

☒ BAPTIST REGIONAL MEDICAL CENTER, 1 Trillium Way, Zip 40701–8420; tel. 606/528–1212; John S. Henson, President (Total facility includes 23 beds in nursing home–type unit) **A**1 9 10 **F**2 3 7 8 10 12 16 17 18 19 21 22 24 28 30 34 35 40 41 42 44 45 46 48 49 52 53 54 55 56 57 58 59 64 65 67 71 72 73 74 **P**7 8 **S** Baptist Healthcare System, Louisville, KY **N** Blue Grass Family Health Plan, Lexington, KY; Community Health Delivery System, Inc., Louisville, KY; Center Care, Bowling Green, KY; Baptist Healthcare System, Louisville, KY .... 23 10 255 10216 155 63733 968 56151 23273 —

COVINGTON—Kenton County

□ CHILDREN'S PSYCHIATRIC HOSPITAL OF NORTHERN KENTUCKY, 502 Farrell Drive, Zip 41011–3799, Mailing Address: P.O. Box 2680, Zip 41012–2680; tel. 606/578–3200; Edward G. Muntel, Ph.D., President and Chief Executive Officer **A**1 10 **F**14 15 16 52 53 54 56 58 .... 23 52 26 333 16 195 — 2915 1308 64

□ HEALTHSOUTH NORTHERN KENTUCKY REHABILITATION HOSPITAL, 201 Medical Village Drive, Zip 41017–3407; tel. 606/341–2044; Ronald L. Bierman, Chief Executive Officer (Nonreporting) **A**1 10 **S** HEALTHSOUTH Corporation, Birmingham, AL .... 33 46 40 — — — — — — —

□ ST. ELIZABETH MEDICAL CENTER–NORTH, (Includes St. Elizabeth Medical Center–South, 1 Medical Village Drive, Edgewood, Zip 41017; tel. 606/344–2000), 401 East 20th Street, Zip 41014–1585; tel. 606/292–4000; Joseph W. Gross, President and Chief Executive Officer (Total facility includes 66 beds in nursing home–type unit) (Nonreporting) **A**1 2 10 **S** Catholic Healthcare Partners, Cincinnati, OH **N** Community Health Delivery System, Inc., Louisville, KY; Center Care, Bowling Green, KY; Saint Elizabeth Medical Center, Covington, KY .... 21 10 466 — — — — — — —

CYNTHIANA—Harrison County

☒ HARRISON MEMORIAL HOSPITAL, Millersburg Road, Zip 41031–0250, Mailing Address: P.O. Box 250, Zip 41031–0250; tel. 606/234–2300; Darwin E. Root, Administrator (Total facility includes 38 beds in nursing home–type unit) **A**1 9 10 **F**7 8 19 21 22 24 26 28 32 33 34 37 39 40 42 44 49 64 65 67 71 73 **N** CHA Provider Network, Inc., Lexington, KY; Blue Grass Family Health Plan, Lexington, KY 23 10 99 1901 59 36151 148 14217 6071 268

DANVILLE—Boyle County

☒ EPHRAIM MCDOWELL REGIONAL MEDICAL CENTER, 217 South Third Street, Zip 40422–9983; tel. 606/239–1000; Thomas W. Smith, President and Chief Executive Officer (Total facility includes 25 beds in nursing home–type unit) **A**1 9 10 **F**1 3 7 8 10 12 14 15 16 17 19 20 22 24 25 26 28 29 30 33 34 36 37 38 39 40 41 42 44 45 46 49 52 55 56 57 60 64 65 66 67 71 73 74 **P**5 8 **N** CHA Provider Network, Inc., Lexington, KY 23 10 177 6446 99 71386 923 48746 20738 689

EDGEWOOD—Kenton County

ST. ELIZABETH MEDICAL CENTER–SOUTH See St. Elizabeth Medical Center–North, Covington

ELIZABETHTOWN—Hardin County

☒ HARDIN MEMORIAL HOSPITAL, 913 North Dixie Avenue, Zip 42701–2599; tel. 502/737–1212; David L. Gray, President (Total facility includes 15 beds in nursing home–type unit) **A**1 9 10 **F**5 7 8 10 11 12 16 17 19 21 22 27 28 30 32 34 35 37 40 42 44 46 48 49 52 56 60 63 64 65 71 72 73 74 **S** Baptist Healthcare System, Louisville, KY **N** Jewish Hospital Healthcare Services, Louisville, KY; Center Care, Bowling Green, KY; Baptist Healthcare System, Louisville, KY 13 10 291 11505 173 107715 1319 83659 35318 1112

□ △ LAKEVIEW REHABILITATION HOSPITAL, 134 Heartland Drive, Zip 42701–2778; tel. 502/769–3100; Kevin Stevenson, Chief Executive Officer **A**1 7 9 10 **F**5 12 14 15 16 17 25 26 28 30 34 41 42 45 46 48 49 65 66 67 73 74 **S** HEALTHSOUTH Corporation, Birmingham, AL **N** Center Care, Bowling Green, KY .... 32 46 40 542 28 9864 — 8084 4078 122

Hospital, Address, Telephone, Administrator, Approval, Facility, and Physician Codes, Health Care System, Network	Classi-fication Codes		Utilization Data					Expense (thousands) of dollars		
	Control	Service	Staffed Beds	Admissions	Census	Outpatient Visits	Births	Total	Payroll	Personnel

★ American Hospital Association (AHA) membership
□ Joint Commission on Accreditation of Healthcare Organizations (JCAHO) accreditation
+ American Osteopathic Healthcare Association (AOHA) membership
○ American Osteopathic Association (AOA) accreditation
△ Commission on Accreditation of Rehabilitation Facilities (CARF) accreditation
Control codes 61, 63, 64, 71, 72 and 73 indicate hospitals listed by AOHA, but not registered by AHA. For definition of numerical codes, see page A4

FLEMINGSBURG—Fleming County

✠ FLEMING COUNTY HOSPITAL, 920 Elizaville Avenue, Zip 41041, Mailing Address: P.O. Box 388, Zip 41041–0388; tel. 606/849–5000; Bobby B. Emmons, Administrator **A**1 9 10 **F**8 11 16 19 22 28 30 37 44 63 64 65 67 71 73 **S** Quorum Health Group/Quorum Health Resources, Inc., Brentwood, TN **N** CHA Provider Network, Inc., Lexington, KY	16	10	43	1508	18	18821	0	8468	3347	139

FLORENCE—Boone County

★ ST. LUKE HOSPITAL WEST, 7380 Turfway Road, Zip 41042–1337; tel. 606/525–5200; Daniel M. Vinson, CPA, Interim Administrator (Total facility includes 16 beds in nursing home–type unit) **A**9 10 **F**1 2 3 4 7 8 9 10 11 12 13 14 15 16 17 18 19 20 21 22 24 25 26 27 28 29 30 31 32 33 34 35 36 37 38 39 40 41 42 43 44 45 46 48 49 50 51 52 53 54 55 56 57 58 59 60 61 63 64 65 66 67 69 70 71 72 73 74 **P**8 **S** Health Alliance of Greater Cincinnati, Cincinnati, OH **N** The Healthcare Alliance of Greater Cincinnati, Cincinnati, OH; CHA Provider Network, Inc., Lexington, KY	23	10	160	6584	80	91769	776	45492	18955	525

FORT CAMPBELL—Christian County

✠ COLONEL FLORENCE A. BLANCHFIELD ARMY COMMUNITY HOSPITAL, 650 Joel Drive, Zip 42223–5349; tel. 502/798–8040; Colonel Lester Martinez–Lopez, Director Health Services **A**1 2 **F**3 8 12 18 19 20 22 25 29 30 34 35 37 39 40 41 44 46 49 51 52 53 54 56 58 65 71 74 **P**6 **S** Department of the Army, Office of the Surgeon General, Falls Church, VA	42	10	106	5988	232	652991	1923	—	—	—

FORT KNOX—Hardin County

✠ IRELAND ARMY COMMUNITY HOSPITAL, 851 Ireland Loop, Zip 40121–5520; tel. 502/624–9020; Lieutenant Colonel Robert T. Foster, Deputy Commander for Administration **A**1 5 **F**3 7 8 12 14 15 16 17 19 20 21 22 27 28 29 30 31 34 39 40 41 44 45 46 49 51 55 56 57 58 61 63 65 67 71 72 73 74 **S** Department of the Army, Office of the Surgeon General, Falls Church, VA	42	10	54	2119	17	337542	597	40680	13430	866

FORT THOMAS—Campbell County

✠ ST. LUKE HOSPITAL EAST, 85 North Grand Avenue, Zip 41075–1796; tel. 606/572–3100; Daniel M. Vinson, CPA, Senior Executive Officer (Total facility includes 26 beds in nursing home–type unit) **A**1 2 10 **F**1 2 3 4 7 8 9 10 11 12 13 14 15 16 17 18 19 20 21 22 24 25 26 27 28 29 30 31 32 33 34 35 36 37 38 39 40 41 42 43 44 45 46 48 49 50 51 52 53 54 55 56 57 58 59 60 61 63 64 65 66 67 69 70 71 72 73 74 **P**8 **S** Health Alliance of Greater Cincinnati, Cincinnati, OH **N** The Healthcare Alliance of Greater Cincinnati, Cincinnati, OH; CHA Provider Network, Inc., Lexington, KY	23	10	221	9388	124	82424	899	59991	23209	932

FRANKFORT—Franklin County

✠ FRANKFORT REGIONAL MEDICAL CENTER, (Formerly Columbia Hospital Frankfort), 299 King's Daughters Drive, Zip 40601–4186; tel. 502/875–5240; David P. Steitz, Chief Executive Officer **A**1 9 10 **F**3 7 8 10 11 12 14 15 16 19 20 21 22 28 29 32 33 34 35 37 39 42 44 46 49 51 54 58 59 60 63 65 67 71 73 **S** Columbia/HCA Healthcare Corporation, Nashville, TN **N** Blue Grass Family Health Plan, Lexington, KY	33	10	147	4941	59	56665	596	—	10737	447

FRANKLIN—Simpson County

★ FRANKLIN–SIMPSON MEMORIAL HOSPITAL, Brookhaven Road, Zip 42135–2929, Mailing Address: P.O. Box 2929, Zip 42135–2929; tel. 502/586–3253; William P. Macri, Chief Executive Officer (Total facility includes 6 beds in nursing home–type unit) **A**9 10 **F**8 14 15 16 19 22 28 37 44 46 51 64 71 73 **P**8 **S** Quorum Health Group/Quorum Health Resources, Inc., Brentwood, TN **N** Community Care Network, Henderson, KY; Center Care, Bowling Green, KY	13	10	34	958	12	11952	0	6485	2655	85

FULTON—Fulton County

★ PARKWAY REGIONAL HOSPITAL, 2000 Holiday Lane, Zip 42041; tel. 502/472–2522; Mary Jo Lewis, Chief Executive Officer (Nonreporting) **A**9 10 **S** Community Health Systems, Inc., Brentwood, TN	33	10	70	—	—	—	—	—	—	—

GEORGETOWN—Scott County

✠ GEORGETOWN COMMUNITY HOSPITAL, (Formerly Columbia Hospital Georgetown), 1140 Lexington Road, Zip 40324–9362; tel. 502/868–1100; Ronald T. Tyrer, Interim Chief Executive Officer (Total facility includes 10 beds in nursing home–type unit) (Nonreporting) **A**1 9 10 **S** Columbia/HCA Healthcare Corporation, Nashville, TN **N** Blue Grass Family Health Plan, Lexington, KY	33	10	61	—	—	—	—	—	—	—

GLASGOW—Barren County

✠ T. J. SAMSON COMMUNITY HOSPITAL, 1301 North Race Street, Zip 42141–3483; tel. 502/651–4444; H. Glenn Joiner, Chief Executive Officer (Total facility includes 16 beds in nursing home–type unit) (Nonreporting) **A**1 3 9 10 **N** Center Care, Bowling Green, KY	23	10	196	—	—	—	—	—	—	—

GREENSBURG—Green County

★ JANE TODD CRAWFORD HOSPITAL, (Formerly Jane Todd Crawford Memorial Hospital), 202–206 Milby Street, Zip 42743–1100, Mailing Address: P.O. Box 220, Zip 42743–0220; tel. 502/932–4211; Larry Craig, Chief Executive Officer (Total facility includes 18 beds in nursing home–type unit) **A**9 10 **F**2 8 15 16 19 22 28 34 37 42 44 52 53 56 57 64 71 **N** Community Health Delivery System, Inc., Louisville, KY	13	10	64	1375	37	20215	0	6600	2911	123

GREENVILLE—Muhlenberg County

✠ MUHLENBERG COMMUNITY HOSPITAL, 440 Hopkinsville Street, Zip 42345–1172, Mailing Address: P.O. Box 387, Zip 42345–0387; tel. 502/338–8000; Charles D. Lovell, Jr., Chief Executive Officer (Total facility includes 45 beds in nursing home–type unit) (Nonreporting) **A**1 9 10 **S** Quorum Health Group/Quorum Health Resources, Inc., Brentwood, TN **N** Community Care Network, Henderson, KY; Center Care, Bowling Green, KY	23	10	135	—	—	—	—	—	—	—

Hospital, Address, Telephone, Administrator, Approval, Facility, and Physician Codes, Health Care System, Network	Classi-fication Codes		Utilization Data					Expense (thousands) of dollars		
★ American Hospital Association (AHA) membership □ Joint Commission on Accreditation of Healthcare Organizations (JCAHO) accreditation + American Osteopathic Healthcare Association (AOHA) membership ○ American Osteopathic Association (AOA) accreditation △ Commission on Accreditation of Rehabilitation Facilities (CARF) accreditation Control codes 61, 63, 64, 71, 72 and 73 indicate hospitals listed by AOHA, but not registered by AHA. For definition of numerical codes, see page A4	Control	Service	Staffed Beds	Admissions	Census	Outpatient Visits	Births	Total	Payroll	Personnel

HARDINSBURG—Breckinridge County

★ BRECKINRIDGE MEMORIAL HOSPITAL, 1011 Old Highway 60, Zip 40143–2597; tel. 502/756–7000; George Walz, CHE, Chief Executive Officer (Total facility includes 18 beds in nursing home–type unit) **A**9 10 **F**8 14 19 20 22 32 33 34 42 44 46 64 71 73 **P**5 **S** Alliant Health System, Louisville, KY **N** Community Health Delivery System, Inc., Louisville, KY — 23 10 45 1001 24 38668 0 6371 2835 145

HARLAN—Harlan County

□ HARLAN ARH HOSPITAL, 81 Ball Park Road, Zip 40831–1792; tel. 606/573–8100; Daniel Fitzpatrick, Chief Executive Officer (Nonreporting) **A**1 9 10 **S** Appalachian Regional Healthcare, Lexington, KY **N** CHA Provider Network, Inc., Lexington, KY — 23 10 125 — — — — — — —

HARRODSBURG—Mercer County

★ THE JAMES B. HAGGIN MEMORIAL HOSPITAL, 464 Linden Avenue, Zip 40330–1862; tel. 606/734–5441; Earl James Motzer, Ph.D., FACHE, Chief Executive Officer (Total facility includes 25 beds in nursing home–type unit) **A**9 10 **F**8 11 14 15 16 17 19 22 28 29 30 32 33 34 37 39 42 44 49 58 64 65 67 68 71 **P**5 **S** Alliant Health System, Louisville, KY **N** CHA Provider Network, Inc., Lexington, KY; Blue Grass Family Health Plan, Lexington, KY; Center Care, Bowling Green, KY — 23 10 64 922 39 23840 — 7588 3367 143

HARTFORD—Ohio County

⊞ OHIO COUNTY HOSPITAL, 1211 Main Street, Zip 42347–1619; tel. 502/298–7411; Blaine Pieper, Administrator (Nonreporting) **A**1 9 10 **S** Quorum Health Group/Quorum Health Resources, Inc., Brentwood, TN **N** Center Care, Bowling Green, KY — 23 10 54 — — — — — — —

HAZARD—Perry County

□ ARH REGIONAL MEDICAL CENTER, 100 Medical Center Drive, Zip 41701–1000; tel. 606/439–6610; Steven F. Ashcraft, Interim Administrator **A**1 2 3 5 9 10 **F**7 8 10 16 19 21 22 32 33 34 35 37 40 41 42 44 49 51 52 53 54 55 58 60 65 67 71 72 73 **P**5 8 **S** Appalachian Regional Healthcare, Lexington, KY **N** CHA Provider Network, Inc., Lexington, KY — 23 10 288 8188 117 207682 530 62546 24429 904

HENDERSON—Henderson County

⊞ COMMUNITY METHODIST HOSPITAL, 1305 North Elm Street, Zip 42420–2775, Mailing Address: P.O. Box 48, Zip 42420–0048; tel. 502/827–7700; Bruce D. Begley, Executive Director **A**1 9 10 **F**3 7 8 10 12 17 19 21 22 23 24 25 28 30 32 34 35 37 39 40 41 42 44 45 46 49 51 52 53 54 56 57 58 59 63 64 66 67 68 71 73 74 **P**8 **N** Community Care Network, Henderson, KY — 21 10 197 7545 119 158796 818 45814 21945 734

HOPKINSVILLE—Christian County

□ CUMBERLAND HALL HOSPITAL, 210 West 17th Street, Zip 42240–1999; tel. 502/886–1919; William C. Heard, Administrator and Chief Executive Officer **A**1 9 10 **F**15 16 52 53 57 58 64 — 33 52 64 700 47 252 — 4760 2324 99

⊞ JENNIE STUART MEDICAL CENTER, 320 West 18th Street, Zip 42241–2400, Mailing Address: P.O. Box 2400, Zip 42241–2400; tel. 502/887–0100; Lewis T. Peeples, Chief Executive Officer **A**1 2 9 10 **F**7 8 10 11 12 15 16 19 21 22 23 28 32 35 37 40 42 44 45 46 49 60 65 67 71 73 **P**5 7 8 **S** Quorum Health Group/Quorum Health Resources, Inc., Brentwood, TN **N** Community Care Network, Henderson, KY — 23 10 139 5888 64 50452 574 46182 17093 558

□ WESTERN STATE HOSPITAL, Russellville Road, Zip 42241, Mailing Address: P.O. Box 2200, Zip 42241–2200; tel. 502/886–4431; Stephen P. Wiggins, Director (Total facility includes 144 beds in nursing home–type unit) **A**1 10 **F**14 15 16 20 41 45 52 54 55 56 57 59 65 **P**5 — 12 22 175 1214 163 — — 28410 15126 434

HORSE CAVE—Hart County

★ CAVERNA MEMORIAL HOSPITAL, 1501 South Dixie Street, Zip 42749–1477; tel. 502/786–2191; James J. Kerins, Sr., Administrator (Nonreporting) **A**9 10 **S** Alliant Health System, Louisville, KY **N** Community Health Delivery System, Inc., Louisville, KY; Center Care, Bowling Green, KY — 23 10 28 — — — — — — —

HYDEN—Leslie County

MARY BRECKINRIDGE HOSPITAL, Hospital Drive, Zip 41749–0000; tel. 606/672–2901; A. Ray Branaman, Administrator **A**9 10 **F**19 22 32 40 49 65 71 **N** CHA Provider Network, Inc., Lexington, KY — 23 10 40 1425 13 41990 140 13556 7075 275

IRVINE—Estill County

MARCUM AND WALLACE MEMORIAL HOSPITAL, 60 Mercy Court, Zip 40336–1331, Mailing Address: P.O. Box 928, Zip 40336–0928; tel. 606/723–2115; Christopher M. Goddard, Administrator (Nonreporting) **A**9 10 **S** Catholic Healthcare Partners, Cincinnati, OH **N** CHA Provider Network, Inc., Lexington, KY; Blue Grass Family Health Plan, Lexington, KY — 21 10 16 — — — — — — —

JACKSON—Breathitt County

⊞ KENTUCKY RIVER MEDICAL CENTER, 540 Jett Drive, Zip 41339–9620; tel. 606/666–6305; O. David Bevins, Chief Executive Officer **A**1 3 9 10 **F**8 11 14 15 16 19 21 22 25 26 30 34 35 37 44 46 49 51 65 66 71 73 74 **P**7 **S** Community Health Systems, Inc., Brentwood, TN — 33 10 55 3706 26 39730 — 18174 5954 143

JENKINS—Letcher County

□ JENKINS COMMUNITY HOSPITAL, Main Street, Zip 41537–9614, Mailing Address: P.O. Box 472, Zip 41537–0472; tel. 606/832–2171; Sherrie Newcomb, Administrator **A**1 9 10 **F**15 19 22 28 32 34 37 44 65 71 **S** First Health, Inc., Batesville, MS **N** CHA Provider Network, Inc., Lexington, KY — 31 10 60 1075 9 11408 — 4244 2393 132

Hospital, Address, Telephone, Administrator, Approval, Facility, and Physician Codes, Health Care System, Network	Classi-fication Codes		Utilization Data					Expense (thousands) of dollars		
★ American Hospital Association (AHA) membership □ Joint Commission on Accreditation of Healthcare Organizations (JCAHO) accreditation + American Osteopathic Healthcare Association (AOHA) membership ○ American Osteopathic Association (AOA) accreditation △ Commission on Accreditation of Rehabilitation Facilities (CARF) accreditation Control codes 61, 63, 64, 71, 72 and 73 indicate hospitals listed by AOHA, but not registered by AHA. For definition of numerical codes, see page A4	Control	Service	Staffed Beds	Admissions	Census	Outpatient Visits	Births	Total	Payroll	Personnel

LA GRANGE—Oldham County

✠ TRI COUNTY BAPTIST HOSPITAL, 1025 New Moody Lane, Zip 40031–0559; tel. 502/222–5388; Dennis B. Johnson, Administrator (Total facility includes 30 beds in nursing home–type unit) **A**1 9 10 **F**2 3 4 7 8 10 11 12 13 15 16 17 18 19 21 22 26 28 29 30 31 32 34 35 37 38 39 40 41 42 43 44 45 46 48 49 52 53 54 55 56 57 58 59 60 61 64 65 67 68 71 73 74 **S** Baptist Healthcare System, Louisville, KY **N** Community Health Delivery System, Inc., Louisville, KY; Baptist Healthcare System, Louisville, KY	23	10	95	2500	57	30953	306	19251	8839	244

LANCASTER—Garrard County

★ GARRARD COUNTY MEMORIAL HOSPITAL, 308 West Maple Avenue, Zip 40444–1098; tel. 606/792–6844; John P. Rigsby, Administrator (Total facility includes 112 beds in nursing home–type unit) **A**9 10 **F**8 19 22 27 34 35 41 44 49 64 65 71 **N** CHA Provider Network, Inc., Lexington, KY; Blue Grass Family Health Plan, Lexington, KY	13	10	131	870	112	16056	0	7747	3569	153

LEBANON—Marion County

✠ SPRING VIEW HOSPITAL, (Formerly Columbia Spring View Hospital), 320 Loretto Road, Zip 40033–0320; tel. 502/692–3161; John D. Brock, Chief Executive Officer (Total facility includes 38 beds in nursing home–type unit) (Nonreporting) **A**1 9 10 **S** Columbia/HCA Healthcare Corporation, Nashville, TN	33	10	113	—	—	—	—	—	—	—

LEITCHFIELD—Grayson County

★ TWIN LAKES REGIONAL MEDICAL CENTER, 910 Wallace Avenue, Zip 42754–1499; tel. 502/259–9400; Stephen L. Meredith, Chief Executive Officer **A**9 10 **F**8 12 14 15 16 19 22 24 32 35 37 40 44 45 46 49 62 65 66 71 73 **S** Alliant Health System, Louisville, KY **N** Community Health Delivery System, Inc., Louisville, KY; Center Care, Bowling Green, KY	23	10	75	2308	31	37276	294	15203	6513	247

LEXINGTON—Fayette County

★ △ CARDINAL HILL REHABILITATION HOSPITAL, 2050 Versailles Road, Zip 40504–1499; tel. 606/254–5701; Kerry G. Gillihan, President and Chief Executive Officer **A**3 5 7 9 10 **F**5 12 14 15 16 17 20 25 27 28 30 32 34 39 41 45 46 48 49 65 66 67 72 73 **P**6 **N** CHA Provider Network, Inc., Lexington, KY	23	46	90	1557	73	36011	—	23327	13245	449
✠ CENTRAL BAPTIST HOSPITAL, 1740 Nicholasville Road, Zip 40503; tel. 606/275–6100; William G. Sisson, President (Total facility includes 12 beds in nursing home–type unit) **A**1 2 3 5 9 10 **F**4 7 8 10 11 12 15 16 19 22 29 30 32 35 37 38 40 42 43 44 45 46 49 60 61 63 71 73 74 **P**6 7 **S** Baptist Healthcare System, Louisville, KY **N** CHA Provider Network, Inc., Lexington, KY; Blue Grass Family Health Plan, Lexington, KY; Community Health Delivery System, Inc., Louisville, KY; Center Care, Bowling Green, KY; Baptist Healthcare System, Louisville, KY	21	10	344	17541	250	129634	3197	170238	62344	1460
□ CHARTER RIDGE HOSPITAL, 3050 Rio Dosa Drive, Zip 40509–9990; tel. 606/269–2325; Ali A. Elhaj, Chief Executive Officer (Nonreporting) **A**1 3 5 9 10 **S** Magellan Health Services, Atlanta, GA **N** CHA Provider Network, Inc., Lexington, KY	33	22	110	—	—	—	—	—	—	—
COLUMBIA HOSPITAL LEXINGTON See Samaritan Hospital										
□ EASTERN STATE HOSPITAL, 627 West Fourth Street, Zip 40508–1294; tel. 606/246–7000; Daniel J. Luchtefeld, Director (Nonreporting) **A**1 5 10	12	22	197	—	—	—	—	—	—	—
□ FEDERAL MEDICAL CENTER, 3301 Leestown Road, Zip 40511–8799; tel. 606/255–6812; J. T. Holland, Warden (Nonreporting) **A**1	33	22	56	—	—	—	—	—	—	—
✠ JEWISH HOSPITAL LEXINGTON, (Formerly Lexington Hospital), 150 North Eagle Creek Drive, Zip 40509–1807; tel. 606/268–4800; Rebecca Lewis, President (Nonreporting) **A**1 5 9 10 **S** Jewish Hospital HealthCare Services, Louisville, KY **N** Jewish Hospital Healthcare Services, Louisville, KY	23	10	174	—	—	—	—	—	—	—
LEXINGTON HOSPITAL See Jewish Hospital Lexington										
✠ SAMARITAN HOSPITAL, (Formerly Columbia Hospital Lexington), 310 South Limestone Street, Zip 40508–3008; tel. 606/252–6612; Frank Beirne, Chief Executive Officer (Total facility includes 34 beds in nursing home–type unit) (Nonreporting) **A**1 2 9 10 **S** Columbia/HCA Healthcare Corporation, Nashville, TN	33	10	219	—	—	—	—	—	—	—
✠ SHRINERS HOSPITALS FOR CHILDREN–LEXINGTON UNIT, 1900 Richmond Road, Zip 40502–1298; tel. 606/266–2101; Tony Lewgood, Administrator (Nonreporting) **A**1 3 5 **S** Shriners Hospitals for Children, Tampa, FL	23	57	50	—	—	—	—	—	—	—
✠ ST. JOSEPH HOSPITAL, One St. Joseph Drive, Zip 40504–3754; tel. 606/278–3436; Thomas J. Murray, President (Total facility includes 22 beds in nursing home–type unit) **A**1 2 3 5 9 10 **F**2 3 4 8 10 11 12 13 15 16 17 19 21 22 23 25 26 29 30 31 32 33 34 35 36 37 39 41 42 43 44 45 46 49 52 56 57 58 59 64 65 67 71 73 **P**3 **S** Catholic Health Initiatives, Denver, CO **N** Blue Grass Family Health Plan, Lexington, KY; Community Health Delivery System, Inc., Louisville, KY; Center Care, Bowling Green, KY	21	10	468	13532	215	66862	—	131550	52462	1646
✠ UNIVERSITY OF KENTUCKY HOSPITAL, 800 Rose Street, Zip 40536–0084; tel. 606/323–5000; Frank Butler, Director **A**1 2 3 5 8 9 10 **F**3 4 7 8 9 10 11 12 13 14 15 16 17 18 19 20 21 22 23 24 25 26 28 29 30 31 32 33 34 35 37 38 39 40 41 42 43 44 45 46 47 48 49 51 52 53 54 55 56 57 58 60 61 63 64 65 66 67 68 69 70 71 73 74 **P**1 **N** CHA Provider Network, Inc., Lexington, KY	12	10	414	20614	344	382971	2226	242530	88399	2843
✠ VETERANS AFFAIRS MEDICAL CENTER–LEXINGTON, 2250 Leestown Pike, Zip 40511–1093; tel. 606/233–4511; Helen K. Cornish, Director (Total facility includes 198 beds in nursing home–type unit) **A**1 2 3 5 8 9 **F**3 4 8 10 11 12 16 17 19 20 21 22 24 26 27 28 29 30 31 32 33 34 35 37 39 41 42 43 44 45 46 48 49 51 52 54 56 57 58 60 63 64 65 67 71 73 74 **P**6 **S** Department of Veterans Affairs, Washington, DC	45	10	467	6122	390	179676	0	114160	69051	1618

Hospital, Address, Telephone, Administrator, Approval, Facility, and Physician Codes, Health Care System, Network	Classi-fication Codes		Utilization Data					Expense (thousands) of dollars		
★ American Hospital Association (AHA) membership ☐ Joint Commission on Accreditation of Healthcare Organizations (JCAHO) accreditation + American Osteopathic Healthcare Association (AOHA) membership ○ American Osteopathic Association (AOA) accreditation △ Commission on Accreditation of Rehabilitation Facilities (CARF) accreditation Control codes 61, 63, 64, 71, 72 and 73 indicate hospitals listed by AOHA, but not registered by AHA. For definition of numerical codes, see page A4	Control	Service	Staffed Beds	Admissions	Census	Outpatient Visits	Births	Total	Payroll	Personnel

LONDON—Laurel County

✠ MARYMOUNT MEDICAL CENTER, 310 East Ninth Street, Zip 40741–1299; tel. 606/878–6520; Lowell Jones, President (Total facility includes 24 beds in nursing home–type unit) **A**1 9 10 **F**7 10 11 12 14 15 16 19 20 21 22 28 30 32 33 39 40 42 43 44 45 46 49 64 65 67 71 72 73 74 **P**3 7 **S** Catholic Health Initiatives, Denver, CO **N** Blue Grass Family Health Plan, Lexington, KY; Community Health Delivery System, Inc., Louisville, KY	21	10	70	3975	49	43142	394	30421	13941	494

LOUISA—Lawrence County

✠ THREE RIVERS MEDICAL CENTER, Highway 644, Zip 41230, Mailing Address: P.O. Box 769, Zip 41230–0769; tel. 606/638–9451; Greg Kiser, Chief Executive Officer **A**1 9 10 **F**7 8 11 12 15 16 19 22 23 26 28 29 30 35 37 40 44 45 46 52 55 56 57 58 63 65 71 73 **S** Community Health Systems, Inc., Brentwood, TN **N** CHA Provider Network, Inc., Lexington, KY	33	10	90	2466	32	20496	92	—	—	183

LOUISVILLE—Jefferson County

✠ ALLIANT HOSPITALS, (Includes Alliant Medical Pavilion, 315 East Broadway, Zip 40202; tel. 502/629–2000; Kosair Children's Hospital, 231 East Chestnut Street, Zip 40202, Mailing Address: P.O. Box 35070, Zip 40232–5070; tel. 502/629–6000; Norton Hospital, 200 East Chestnut, Zip 40202, Mailing Address: P.O. Box 35070, Zip 40232–5070; tel. 502/629–8000), 200 East Chestnut Street, Zip 40202–1800, Mailing Address: P.O. Box 35070, Zip 40232–5070; tel. 502/629–8000; Stephen M. Tullman, Administrator (Total facility includes 17 beds in nursing home–type unit) **A**1 2 3 5 9 10 **F**3 4 5 7 8 9 10 11 12 13 14 15 16 17 19 20 21 22 23 24 26 28 29 30 31 32 34 37 38 40 41 42 43 44 45 46 47 49 52 53 54 55 56 57 58 59 61 64 65 67 69 70 71 72 73 74 **P**3 **S** Alliant Health System, Louisville, KY **N** Community Health Delivery System, Inc., Louisville, KY; Alliant Health System, Louisville, KY	23	10	709	29381	429	182817	5601	348790	127378	4199
✠ AUDUBON HOSPITAL, (Formerly Columbia Audubon Hospital), One Audubon Plaza Drive, Zip 40217–1397, Mailing Address: P.O. Box 17550, Zip 40217–0550; tel. 502/636–7111; Stephen L. Newman, M.D., President and Chief Executive Officer **A**1 2 5 9 10 **F**4 7 8 10 11 12 13 14 15 16 17 18 19 21 22 24 26 28 29 30 31 32 34 35 37 39 40 41 42 43 44 46 49 51 54 56 60 63 64 65 67 71 73 74 **P**7 **S** Columbia/HCA Healthcare Corporation, Nashville, TN	33	10	421	13143	202	98681	627	98390	39845	—
✠ △ BAPTIST HOSPITAL EAST, 4000 Kresge Way, Zip 40207–4676; tel. 502/897–8100; Susan Stout Tamme, President (Total facility includes 23 beds in nursing home–type unit) **A**1 2 7 9 10 **F**2 3 4 7 8 10 11 12 13 14 15 16 17 18 19 21 22 26 28 29 30 32 34 35 37 38 40 41 42 43 44 45 46 48 49 52 53 54 55 56 57 58 59 60 63 64 65 67 68 71 72 73 74 **S** Baptist Healthcare System, Louisville, KY **N** Community Health Delivery System, Inc., Louisville, KY; Center Care, Bowling Green, KY; Baptist Healthcare System, Louisville, KY	23	10	407	21540	322	148494	3014	157037	70036	2303
✠ CARITAS MEDICAL CENTER, 1850 Bluegrass Avenue, Zip 40215–1199; tel. 502/361–6000; Peter J. Bernard, President and Chief Executive Officer (Total facility includes 33 beds in nursing home–type unit) **A**1 9 10 **F**1 2 3 5 6 8 10 11 12 14 15 16 17 19 21 22 24 26 27 28 32 34 35 36 37 39 41 42 44 45 46 49 50 51 52 53 54 55 56 57 58 59 60 63 64 65 66 67 68 71 73 **P**7 **S** Catholic Health Initiatives, Denver, CO **N** Community Health Delivery System, Inc., Louisville, KY; Baptist Healthcare System, Louisville, KY; Caritas Health Services, Louisville, KY	21	10	213	9692	148	97471	—	79908	37847	995
✠ CARITAS PEACE CENTER, 2020 Newburg Road, Zip 40205–1879; tel. 502/451–3330; Peter J. Bernard, President and Chief Executive Officer **A**1 9 10 **F**3 14 15 16 52 53 54 55 56 57 58 59 65 67 73 **S** Catholic Health Initiatives, Denver, CO **N** Community Health Delivery System, Inc., Louisville, KY; Baptist Healthcare System, Louisville, KY; Caritas Health Services, Louisville, KY	23	22	208	2017	125	41572	—	20763	9717	342
☐ CENTRAL STATE HOSPITAL, 10510 LaGrange Road, Zip 40223–1228; tel. 502/253–7000; Paula Tamme, Chief Executive Officer (Nonreporting) **A**1 10	12	22	175	—	—	—	—	—	—	—
☐ CHARTER LOUISVILLE BEHAVIORAL HEALTH SYSTEM, 1405 Browns Lane, Zip 40207–4672; tel. 502/896–0495; Charles L. Webb, Jr., Administrator **A**1 9 10 **F**1 2 3 12 14 15 16 17 18 19 21 35 44 45 46 49 50 51 52 53 54 55 56 57 58 59 60 61 63 65 67 68 71 **S** Magellan Health Services, Atlanta, GA	33	22	66	1668	48	—	—	—	—	103
COLUMBIA AUDUBON HOSPITAL See Audubon Hospital										
COLUMBIA SOUTHWEST HOSPITAL See Southwest Hospital										
COLUMBIA SUBURBAN HOSPITAL See Suburban Hospital										
✠ △ FRAZIER REHABILITATION CENTER, 220 Abraham Flexner Way, Zip 40202–1887; tel. 502/582–7400; Jason Roeback, President **A**1 3 5 7 9 **F**1 2 3 4 5 6 7 8 9 10 11 12 13 14 15 16 17 18 19 20 21 22 23 24 25 26 27 28 29 30 31 32 33 34 35 36 37 38 39 40 41 42 43 44 45 46 47 48 49 51 52 53 54 55 56 57 58 59 60 61 62 63 64 65 66 67 68 69 70 71 72 73 74 **P**3 4 5 6 **S** Jewish Hospital HealthCare Services, Louisville, KY **N** Jewish Hospital Healthcare Services, Louisville, KY	23	46	95	1478	85	54120	0	25452	12229	344
✠ JEWISH HOSPITAL, 217 East Chestnut Street, Zip 40202–1886; tel. 502/587–4011; Douglas E. Shaw, President **A**1 2 3 5 8 9 10 **F**1 2 3 4 5 6 7 8 9 10 11 12 13 14 15 16 17 18 19 20 21 22 23 24 25 26 27 28 29 30 31 32 33 34 35 36 37 38 39 40 41 42 43 44 45 46 47 48 49 51 52 53 54 55 56 57 58 59 60 61 62 63 64 65 66 67 68 69 70 71 72 73 74 **P**3 4 5 6 **S** Jewish Hospital HealthCare Services, Louisville, KY **N** Jewish Hospital Healthcare Services, Louisville, KY; Center Care, Bowling Green, KY	23	10	433	20004	349	434880	—	248275	91570	2633
KOSAIR CHILDREN'S HOSPITAL See Alliant Hospitals										
NORTON HOSPITAL See Alliant Hospitals										

Hospital, Address, Telephone, Administrator, Approval, Facility, and Physician Codes, Health Care System, Network	Classi- fication Codes		Utilization Data					Expense (thousands) of dollars		
★ American Hospital Association (AHA) membership □ Joint Commission on Accreditation of Healthcare Organizations (JCAHO) accreditation + American Osteopathic Healthcare Association (AOHA) membership ○ American Osteopathic Association (AOA) accreditation △ Commission on Accreditation of Rehabilitation Facilities (CARF) accreditation Control codes 61, 63, 64, 71, 72 and 73 indicate hospitals listed by AOHA, but not registered by AHA. For definition of numerical codes, see page A4	Control	Service	Staffed Beds	Admissions	Census	Outpatient Visits	Births	Total	Payroll	Personnel
✠ SOUTHWEST HOSPITAL, (Formerly Columbia Southwest Hospital), 9820 Third Street Road, Zip 40272–9984; tel. 502/933–8100; Cathryn A. Hibbs, Chief Executive Officer (Total facility includes 23 beds in nursing home–type unit) (Nonreporting) **A**1 9 10 **S** Columbia/HCA Healthcare Corporation, Nashville, TN	33	10	150	—	—	—	—	—	—	—
✠ SUBURBAN HOSPITAL, (Formerly Columbia Suburban Hospital), 4001 Dutchmans Lane, Zip 40207–4799; tel. 502/893–1000; John A. Marshall, President and Chief Executive Officer (Total facility includes 37 beds in nursing home–type unit) (Nonreporting) **A**1 9 10 **S** Columbia/HCA Healthcare Corporation, Nashville, TN	33	10	380	—	—	—	—	—	—	—
□ TEN BROECK HOSPITAL, 8521 Old LaGrange Road, Zip 40242–3800; tel. 502/426–6380; Pat Hammer, Chief Executive Officer (Nonreporting) **A**1 9 10 **S** United Medical Corporation, Windermere, FL	33	22	94	—	—	—	—	—	—	—
✠ UNIVERSITY OF LOUISVILLE HOSPITAL, 530 South Jackson Street, Zip 40202–3611; tel. 502/562–3000; James H. Taylor, President and Chief Executive Officer (Nonreporting) **A**1 2 3 5 8 9 10 **S** Jewish Hospital HealthCare Services, Louisville, KY	23	10	269	—	—	—	—	—	—	—
✠ VENCOR HOSPITAL–LOUISVILLE, 1313 St. Anthony Place, Zip 40204–1765; tel. 502/627–1102; James H. Wesp, Administrator (Total facility includes 37 beds in nursing home–type unit) (Nonreporting) **A**1 9 10 **S** Vencor, Incorporated, Louisville, KY	33	10	156	—	—	—	—	—	—	—
✠ VETERANS AFFAIRS MEDICAL CENTER–LOUISVILLE, 800 Zorn Avenue, Zip 40206–1499; tel. 502/895–3401; Larry J. Sander, FACHE, Director **A**1 2 3 5 8 9 **F**3 8 10 11 16 19 20 22 25 26 28 30 31 32 33 34 35 37 39 41 42 43 44 46 49 51 52 54 58 60 64 65 71 73 74 **S** Department of Veterans Affairs, Washington, DC	45	10	168	5862	117	200385	—	124022	50332	1360
MADISONVILLE—Hopkins County										
✠ REGIONAL MEDICAL CENTER OF HOPKINS COUNTY, 900 Hospital Drive, Zip 42431–1694; tel. 502/825–5202; Bobby H. Dampier, Chief Executive Officer **A**1 2 3 5 9 10 **F**3 4 7 8 10 11 12 15 16 17 19 20 21 22 23 24 28 30 31 32 33 34 35 37 38 39 40 41 42 43 44 45 46 47 48 49 52 53 56 57 58 60 63 65 66 67 71 73 **P**6 **N** Community Care Network, Henderson, KY	23	10	410	10914	150	57815	729	80520	36215	1247
MANCHESTER—Clay County										
✠ MEMORIAL HOSPITAL, 401 Memorial Drive, Zip 40962–9156; tel. 606/598–5104; Jimm Bunch, Chief Executive Officer (Total facility includes 16 beds in nursing home–type unit) **A**1 9 10 **F**12 15 16 17 19 22 24 26 28 29 30 31 32 34 35 37 40 41 44 45 46 49 61 62 64 65 71 73 74 **P**6 **S** Adventist Health System Sunbelt Health Care Corporation, Winter Park, FL **N** CHA Provider Network, Inc., Lexington, KY	21	10	61	2801	24	54538	276	20753	9022	—
MARION—Crittenden County										
✠ CRITTENDEN COUNTY HOSPITAL, Highway 60 South, Zip 42064, Mailing Address: P.O. Box 386, Zip 42064–0386; tel. 502/965–5281; Rick Napper, Chief Executive Officer (Nonreporting) **A**1 9 10 **S** Quorum Health Group/Quorum Health Resources, Inc., Brentwood, TN **N** Community Care Network, Henderson, KY	33	22	67	—	—	—	—	—	—	—
MARTIN—Floyd County										
★ OUR LADY OF THE WAY HOSPITAL, 11022 Main Street, Zip 41649–0910; tel. 606/285–5181; Lowell Jones, Chief Executive Officer (Total facility includes 13 beds in nursing home–type unit) (Nonreporting) **A**9 10 **S** Catholic Health Initiatives, Denver, CO **N** CHA Provider Network, Inc., Lexington, KY	21	10	39	—	—	—	—	—	—	—
MAYFIELD—Graves County										
✠ PINELAKE REGIONAL HOSPITAL, 1099 Medical Center Circle, Zip 42066–1179, Mailing Address: P.O. Box 1099, Zip 42066–1099; tel. 502/251–4100; Don A. Horstkotte, Chief Executive Officer (Total facility includes 14 beds in nursing home–type unit) **A**1 9 10 **F**7 8 10 12 15 16 19 21 22 28 29 30 32 34 35 37 39 40 41 42 44 45 54 59 63 64 65 66 67 70 71 73 74 **P**1 2 3 4 5 6 7 8 **S** Columbia/HCA Healthcare Corporation, Nashville, TN **N** Center Care, Bowling Green, KY	33	10	106	3870	50	53424	451	24529	9420	472
MAYSVILLE—Mason County										
✠ MEADOVIEW REGIONAL MEDICAL CENTER, (Formerly Columbia Hospital Maysville), 989 Medical Park Drive, Zip 41056–8750; tel. 606/759–5311; Ronald T. Tyrer, Interim Chief Executive Officer (Total facility includes 10 beds in nursing home–type unit) **A**1 9 10 **F**7 8 10 11 12 14 15 16 18 19 21 22 28 30 35 37 38 40 42 44 45 46 49 60 64 65 71 73 74 **S** Columbia/HCA Healthcare Corporation, Nashville, TN **N** Blue Grass Family Health Plan, Lexington, KY; Center Care, Bowling Green, KY	33	10	87	3356	33	32172	455	21265	8162	278
MCDOWELL—Floyd County										
□ MCDOWELL ARH HOSPITAL, Route 122, Zip 41647, Mailing Address: P.O. Box 247, Mc Dowell, Zip 41647–0247; tel. 606/377–3400; Dena C. Sparkman, Administrator (Nonreporting) **A**1 9 10 **S** Appalachian Regional Healthcare, Lexington, KY **N** CHA Provider Network, Inc., Lexington, KY	23	10	74	—	—	—	—	—	—	—
MIDDLESBORO—Bell County										
□ MIDDLESBORO APPALACHIAN REGIONAL HOSPITAL, 3600 West Cumberland Avenue, Zip 40965–2614, Mailing Address: P.O. Box 340, Zip 40965–0340; tel. 606/242–1101; Paul V. Miles, Administrator (Nonreporting) **A**1 9 10 **S** Appalachian Regional Healthcare, Lexington, KY **N** CHA Provider Network, Inc., Lexington, KY	23	10	96	—	—	—	—	—	—	—
MONTICELLO—Wayne County										
□ WAYNE COUNTY HOSPITAL, 166 Hospital Street, Zip 42633–2416; tel. 606/348–9343; Eddy R. Stockton, Administrator (Nonreporting) **A**1 9 10	23	10	30							

Hospital, Address, Telephone, Administrator, Approval, Facility, and Physician Codes, Health Care System, Network	Classi-fication Codes		Utilization Data					Expense (thousands) of dollars		
★ American Hospital Association (AHA) membership □ Joint Commission on Accreditation of Healthcare Organizations (JCAHO) accreditation + American Osteopathic Healthcare Association (AOHA) membership ○ American Osteopathic Association (AOA) accreditation △ Commission on Accreditation of Rehabilitation Facilities (CARF) accreditation Control codes 61, 63, 64, 71, 72 and 73 indicate hospitals listed by AOHA, but not registered by AHA. For definition of numerical codes, see page A4	Control	Service	Staffed Beds	Admissions	Census	Outpatient Visits	Births	Total	Payroll	Personnel

MOREHEAD—Rowan County

☒ ST. CLAIRE MEDICAL CENTER, 222 Medical Circle, Zip 40351–1180; tel. 606/783–6500; Mark J. Neff, President and Chief Executive Officer **A**1 2 9 10 **F**3 4 7 8 10 14 15 16 17 18 19 20 21 22 23 25 26 28 30 31 32 33 34 35 37 40 41 42 44 46 49 51 52 53 54 55 56 57 58 60 63 65 67 70 71 73 74 **P**6 **N** CHA Provider Network, Inc., Lexington, KY — 21 10 133 5524 63 338949 485 52851 26207 918

MORGANFIELD—Union County

□ UNION COUNTY METHODIST HOSPITAL, 4604 Highway 60 West, Zip 42437–9570; tel. 502/389–3030; Patrick Donahue, Administrator (Total facility includes 16 beds in nursing home–type unit) **A**1 9 10 **F**8 10 12 15 16 19 20 22 26 28 30 32 33 35 37 39 44 49 53 56 57 58 64 65 71 73 **P**8 **N** Community Care Network, Henderson, KY — 21 10 54 566 20 16948 — 5406 2278 99

MOUNT STERLING—Montgomery County

☒ GATEWAY REGIONAL HEALTH SYSTEM, Sterling Avenue, Zip 40353–1158, Mailing Address: P.O. Box 7, Zip 40353–0007; tel. 606/497–6000; Jeffrey L. Buckley, President and Chief Executive Officer (Total facility includes 40 beds in nursing home–type unit) **A**1 9 10 **F**7 8 11 12 14 15 16 17 19 20 21 22 28 30 37 39 40 41 42 44 46 49 50 51 56 63 64 65 71 73 74 **P**6 7 — 23 10 103 2306 71 50487 689 21477 9103 354

MOUNT VERNON—Rockcastle County

★ ROCKCASTLE HOSPITAL AND RESPIRATORY CARE CENTER, 145 Newcomb Avenue, Zip 40456–2733, Mailing Address: P.O. Box 1310, Zip 40456–1310; tel. 606/256–2195; Lee D. Keene, Administrator (Total facility includes 60 beds in nursing home–type unit) (Nonreporting) **A**9 10 **N** CHA Provider Network, Inc., Lexington, KY — 23 10 86 — — — — — — —

MURRAY—Calloway County

☒ MURRAY–CALLOWAY COUNTY HOSPITAL, 803 Poplar Street, Zip 42071–2432; tel. 502/762–1100; Stuart Poston, President (Total facility includes 174 beds in nursing home–type unit) **A**1 9 10 **F**1 7 8 10 12 15 16 17 19 20 21 22 26 28 29 30 32 33 34 35 37 39 40 41 42 44 46 49 54 55 56 57 58 60 63 64 65 67 70 71 73 74 **N** Community Care Network, Henderson, KY — 15 10 302 5335 237 156632 590 45568 20302 871

OWENSBORO—Daviess County

MERCY HOSPITAL See Owensboro Mercy Health System

☒ △ OWENSBORO MERCY HEALTH SYSTEM, (Includes Mercy Hospital, 1006 Ford Avenue, Zip 42301, Mailing Address: P.O. Box 2839, Zip 42302; tel. 502/686–6100; Owensboro–Daviess County Hospital, 811 East Parrish Avenue, Zip 42304; tel. 502/688–2000), 811 East Parrish Avenue, Zip 42303–3268, Mailing Address: P.O. Box 20007, Zip 42303–0007; tel. 502/688–2000; Greg L. Carlson, President and Chief Executive Officer (Total facility includes 24 beds in nursing home–type unit) **A**1 2 7 9 10 **F**4 7 8 10 11 12 14 15 16 17 19 20 21 22 23 24 25 26 27 28 29 30 31 32 33 34 35 37 39 40 41 42 43 44 45 46 48 49 52 54 55 56 57 58 60 64 65 66 67 71 72 73 74 **P**7 **N** Community Care Network, Henderson, KY; Center Care, Bowling Green, KY — 23 10 363 17120 230 218337 1643 120006 49441 1842

OWENSBORO–DAVIESS COUNTY HOSPITAL See Owensboro Mercy Health System

RIVERVALLEY BEHAVIORAL HEALTH HOSPITAL, 1000 Industrial Drive, Zip 42301–8715; tel. 502/686–8477; Gayle DiCesare, President and Chief Officer **A**9 10 **F**15 16 52 53 54 55 56 59 **P**6 — 23 52 77 529 65 — — 9145 4619 179

OWENTON—Owen County

OWEN COUNTY MEMORIAL HOSPITAL, 330 Roland Avenue, Zip 40359–1502; tel. 502/484–3441; Richard D. McLeod, Administrator (Total facility includes 20 beds in nursing home–type unit) (Nonreporting) **A**9 10 **N** CHA Provider Network, Inc., Lexington, KY; Blue Grass Family Health Plan, Lexington, KY — 33 10 50 — — — — — — —

PADUCAH—McCracken County

□ CHARTER BEHAVIORAL HEALTH SYSTEM OF PADUCAH, 435 Berger Road, Zip 42003–4579, Mailing Address: P.O. Box 7609, Zip 42002–7609; tel. 502/444–0444; Pat Harrod, Chief Executive Officer (Nonreporting) **A**1 9 10 **S** Magellan Health Services, Atlanta, GA — 33 22 56 — — — — — — —

□ △ LOURDES HOSPITAL, 1530 Lone Oak Road, Zip 42003, Mailing Address: P.O. Box 7100, Zip 42002–7100; tel. 502/444–2444; Robert P. Goodwin, President and Chief Executive Officer (Total facility includes 30 beds in nursing home–type unit) **A**1 7 9 10 **F**1 4 7 8 10 11 12 14 15 16 17 19 20 21 22 23 24 26 28 29 30 31 32 33 34 35 36 37 39 40 41 42 43 44 45 46 48 49 52 55 56 64 65 67 71 73 **P**5 7 **S** Catholic Healthcare Partners, Cincinnati, OH — 21 10 290 10684 160 233250 432 91450 39620 1297

☒ WESTERN BAPTIST HOSPITAL, 2501 Kentucky Avenue, Zip 42003–3200; tel. 502/575–2100; Larry O. Barton, President **A**1 9 10 **F**2 3 4 7 8 10 11 12 15 17 19 21 22 24 27 28 29 30 32 34 35 37 38 39 40 41 42 43 44 48 49 51 52 53 54 55 56 57 58 59 60 64 65 67 71 72 73 74 **P**5 7 8 **S** Baptist Healthcare System, Louisville, KY **N** Community Health Delivery System, Inc., Louisville, KY; Baptist Healthcare System, Louisville, KY — 21 10 325 12780 186 96135 1164 98675 37415 1227

PAINTSVILLE—Johnson County

□ PAUL B. HALL REGIONAL MEDICAL CENTER, 625 James S. Trimble Boulevard, Zip 41240–1055, Mailing Address: P.O. Box 1487, Zip 41240–1487; tel. 606/789–3511; Deborah C. Trimble, Administrator (Nonreporting) **A**1 9 10 **S** Health Management Associates, Naples, FL — 33 10 72 — — — — — — —

PARIS—Bourbon County

☒ BURBON COMMUNITY HOSPITAL, (Formerly Bourbon General Hospital), 9 Linville Drive, Zip 40361–2196; tel. 606/987–1000; Bernie Mattingly, Chief Executive Officer **A**1 9 10 **F**12 16 19 21 22 28 30 35 37 39 44 49 52 53 55 65 71 **S** Columbia/HCA Healthcare Corporation, Nashville, TN **N** Blue Grass Family Health Plan, Lexington, KY — 33 10 58 1624 23 26409 — 10972 4527 174

Hospital, Address, Telephone, Administrator, Approval, Facility, and Physician Codes, Health Care System, Network	Classi-fication Codes		Utilization Data					Expense (thousands) of dollars		
★ American Hospital Association (AHA) membership □ Joint Commission on Accreditation of Healthcare Organizations (JCAHO) accreditation + American Osteopathic Healthcare Association (AOHA) membership ○ American Osteopathic Association (AOA) accreditation △ Commission on Accreditation of Rehabilitation Facilities (CARF) accreditation Control codes 61, 63, 64, 71, 72 and 73 indicate hospitals listed by AOHA, but not registered by AHA. For definition of numerical codes, see page A4	Control	Service	Staffed Beds	Admissions	Census	Outpatient Visits	Births	Total	Payroll	Personnel

PIKEVILLE—Pike County

☒ PIKEVILLE UNITED METHODIST HOSPITAL OF KENTUCKY, 911 South Bypass, Zip 41501–1595; tel. 606/437–3500; Martha O'Regan Chill, Administrator and Chief Executive Officer **A**1 2 9 10 **F**7 8 10 11 12 14 15 16 17 19 20 21 22 23 26 27 28 35 36 37 38 39 41 42 44 46 49 52 60 65 66 67 71 72 73 74 **N** Center Care, Bowling Green, KY

| | | 23 | 10 | 188 | 8455 | 107 | 94192 | 953 | — | — | — |

PINEVILLE—Bell County

☒ PINEVILLE COMMUNITY HOSPITAL ASSOCIATION, Riverview Avenue, Zip 40977–0850; tel. 606/337–3051; J. Milton Brooks, III, Administrator (Total facility includes 30 beds in nursing home–type unit) (Nonreporting) **A**1 9 10 **N** CHA Provider Network, Inc., Lexington, KY

| | | 23 | 10 | 150 | — | — | — | — | — | — | — |

PRESTONSBURG—Floyd County

☒ HIGHLANDS REGIONAL MEDICAL CENTER, 5000 Kentucky Route 321, Zip 41653, Mailing Address: P.O. Box 668, Zip 41653–0668; tel. 606/886–8511; Clarence Traum, President and Chief Executive Officer (Nonreporting) **A**1 2 9 10 **N** CHA Provider Network, Inc., Lexington, KY

| | | 23 | 10 | 184 | — | — | — | — | — | — | — |

PRINCETON—Caldwell County

☒ CALDWELL COUNTY HOSPITAL, 101 Hospital Drive, Zip 42445–0410, Mailing Address: Box 410, Zip 42445–0410; tel. 502/365–0300; Marsha Woodall, Interim Chief Executive Officer **A**1 9 10 **F**7 8 14 15 16 19 22 28 29 30 32 34 36 40 44 45 46 73 **P**4 **S** Alliant Health System, Louisville, KY **N** Community Care Network, Henderson, KY; Community Health Delivery System, Inc., Louisville, KY

| | | 23 | 10 | 50 | 917 | 9 | 30853 | 131 | 14010 | 4265 | 169 |

RADCLIFF—Hardin County

☒ LINCOLN TRAIL BEHAVIORAL HEALTH SYSTEM, 3909 South Wilson Road, Zip 40160–9714, Mailing Address: P.O. Box 369, Zip 40159–0369; tel. 502/351–9444; Melvin E. Modderman, Administrator **A**1 9 10 **F**2 3 15 16 17 22 34 52 53 54 55 56 57 58 59 65 73 **S** Park Healthcare Company, Nashville, TN

| | | 33 | 22 | 67 | 747 | 34 | 5596 | — | 5816 | 2863 | 96 |

RICHMOND—Madison County

☒ PATTIE A. CLAY HOSPITAL, EKU By–Pass, Zip 40475, Mailing Address: P.O. Box 1600, Zip 40476–2603; tel. 606/625–3131; Richard M. Thomas, President (Nonreporting) **A**1 9 10 **S** Jewish Hospital HealthCare Services, Louisville, KY **N** CHA Provider Network, Inc., Lexington, KY; Jewish Hospital Healthcare Services, Louisville, KY; Blue Grass Family Health Plan, Lexington, KY

| | | 23 | 10 | 96 | — | — | — | — | — | — | — |

RUSSELL SPRINGS—Russell County

RUSSELL COUNTY HOSPITAL, Dowell Road, Zip 42642, Mailing Address: P.O. Box 1610, Zip 42642–1610; tel. 502/866–4141; Richard Hacker, Interim Administrator **A**9 10 **F**8 14 15 16 19 22 27 30 37 39 44 45 46 49 63 65 67 71 73 **P**5 **S** Alliant Health System, Louisville, KY

| | | 13 | 10 | 45 | 913 | 21 | 10662 | — | 6440 | 3008 | 141 |

RUSSELLVILLE—Logan County

☒ LOGAN MEMORIAL HOSPITAL, (Formerly Columbia Logan Memorial Hospital), 1625 South Nashville Road, Zip 42276–8834, Mailing Address: P.O. Box 10, Zip 42276–0010; tel. 502/726–4011; Michael Clark, Chief Executive Officer **A**1 9 10 **F**4 7 8 11 12 15 16 17 19 20 21 22 28 30 32 34 35 40 42 44 45 48 49 64 65 66 67 69 71 73 74 **S** Columbia/HCA Healthcare Corporation, Nashville, TN **N** Center Care, Bowling Green, KY

| | | 33 | 10 | 100 | 1597 | 20 | 22409 | 133 | — | — | 189 |

SALEM—Livingston County

★ LIVINGSTON HOSPITAL AND HEALTHCARE SERVICES, 131 Hospital Drive, Zip 42078; tel. 502/988–2299; William C. Smith, Chief Executive Officer **A**9 10 **F**8 14 15 16 17 28 30 32 33 42 44 46 48 49 53 55 58 **N** Community Care Network, Henderson, KY

| | | 23 | 10 | 26 | 996 | 10 | 13924 | 0 | 8827 | 3336 | 135 |

SCOTTSVILLE—Allen County

★ MEDICAL CENTER AT SCOTTSVILLE, 456 Burnley Road, Zip 42164–6355; tel. 502/622–2800; Sarah Moore, Vice President (Total facility includes 105 beds in nursing home–type unit) **A**9 **F**1 2 3 4 7 8 10 11 12 13 14 15 16 17 19 20 21 22 28 29 30 32 33 34 35 37 38 39 40 41 42 43 44 45 46 48 52 56 57 58 59 60 64 65 67 71 72 73 74 **P**6 7 8 **N** Center Care, Bowling Green, KY

| | | 23 | 10 | 132 | 1029 | 97 | 16049 | — | 10277 | 3172 | 156 |

SHELBYVILLE—Shelby County

☒ JEWISH HOSPITAL–SHELBYVILLE, 727 Hospital Drive, Zip 40065–1699; tel. 502/647–4000; Timothy L. Jarm, President (Total facility includes 8 beds in nursing home–type unit) **A**1 9 10 **F**2 4 7 8 9 10 11 12 13 14 15 16 17 18 19 21 22 23 24 25 26 27 28 29 30 31 32 33 34 35 37 39 40 41 42 43 44 45 46 48 49 50 51 52 53 54 55 56 57 58 59 60 62 63 64 65 66 67 69 70 71 73 74 **S** Jewish Hospital HealthCare Services, Louisville, KY **N** Jewish Hospital Healthcare Services, Louisville, KY

| | | 23 | 10 | 58 | 2606 | 33 | 31919 | 213 | — | — | 282 |

SOMERSET—Pulaski County

☒ △ LAKE CUMBERLAND REGIONAL HOSPITAL, (Formerly Columbia Lake Cumberland Hospital), 305 Langdon Street, Zip 42501, Mailing Address: P.O. Box 620, Zip 42502–2750; tel. 606/679–7441; Jon C. O'Shaughnessy, President and Chief Executive Officer (Nonreporting) **A**1 7 9 10 **S** Columbia/HCA Healthcare Corporation, Nashville, TN

| | | 33 | 10 | 227 | — | — | — | — | — | — | — |

SOUTH WILLIAMSON—Pike County

□ WILLIAMSON ARH HOSPITAL, 260 Hospital Drive, Zip 41503–4072; tel. 606/237–1700; John A. Grah, Administrator (Total facility includes 50 beds in nursing home–type unit) **A**1 9 10 **F**4 7 8 12 13 15 16 17 19 22 25 28 30 32 34 35 37 39 40 42 44 49 52 54 56 57 58 60 63 64 65 73 **P**2 3 5 6 **S** Appalachian Regional Healthcare, Lexington, KY **N** Partners in Health Network, Inc., Charleston, WV; CHA Provider Network, Inc., Lexington, KY

| | | 23 | 10 | 148 | 4345 | 107 | 52882 | 118 | 26188 | 10726 | 477 |

Hospital, Address, Telephone, Administrator, Approval, Facility, and Physician Codes, Health Care System, Network	Classi-fication Codes		Utilization Data					Expense (thousands) of dollars		
	Control	Service	Staffed Beds	Admissions	Census	Outpatient Visits	Births	Total	Payroll	Personnel

★ American Hospital Association (AHA) membership
□ Joint Commission on Accreditation of Healthcare Organizations (JCAHO) accreditation
+ American Osteopathic Healthcare Association (AOHA) membership
○ American Osteopathic Association (AOA) accreditation
△ Commission on Accreditation of Rehabilitation Facilities (CARF) accreditation
Control codes 61, 63, 64, 71, 72 and 73 indicate hospitals listed by AOHA, but not registered by AHA. For definition of numerical codes, see page A4

STANFORD—Lincoln County

⊞ FORT LOGAN HOSPITAL, 124 Portman Avenue, Zip 40484–1200; tel. 606/365–2187; Terry C. Powers, Administrator (Total facility includes 30 beds in nursing home–type unit) **A**1 9 10 **F**7 8 14 15 16 19 20 22 26 30 31 32 33 34 40 41 44 46 49 64 65 71 73 **N** CHA Provider Network, Inc., Lexington, KY; Blue Grass Family Health Plan, Lexington, KY ... 23 10 73 1352 43 12636 118 7889 3502 168

TOMPKINSVILLE—Monroe County

⊞ MONROE COUNTY MEDICAL CENTER, 529 Capp Harlan Road, Zip 42167–1840; tel. 502/487–9231; Carolyn E. Riley, Chief Executive Officer **A**1 9 10 **F**8 15 16 19 22 27 32 34 39 44 45 49 65 70 71 **P**8 **S** Quorum Health Group/Quorum Health Resources, Inc., Brentwood, TN **N** Center Care, Bowling Green, KY ... 23 10 49 2672 35 25168 — 11711 5259 270

VERSAILLES—Woodford County

★ WOODFORD HOSPITAL, 360 Amsden Avenue, Zip 40383–1286; tel. 606/873–3111; Nancy Littrell, Chief Executive Officer (Total facility includes 23 beds in nursing home–type unit) **A**9 10 **F**7 11 14 15 16 19 22 24 32 44 49 63 64 65 71 73 74 **N** CHA Provider Network, Inc., Lexington, KY; Blue Grass Family Health Plan, Lexington, KY ... 23 10 56 1022 16 18340 0 9187 3978 170

WEST LIBERTY—Morgan County

□ MORGAN COUNTY APPALACHIAN REGIONAL HOSPITAL, 476 Liberty Road, Zip 41472–2049, Mailing Address: P.O. Box 579, Zip 41472–0579; tel. 606/743–3186; Dennis R. Chaney, Administrator (Total facility includes 25 beds in nursing home–type unit) **A**1 9 10 **F**8 15 16 19 22 28 29 30 32 33 34 40 64 65 71 73 **S** Appalachian Regional Healthcare, Lexington, KY **N** CHA Provider Network, Inc., Lexington, KY ... 23 10 45 965 33 39316 0 8676 4226 130

WHITESBURG—Letcher County

□ WHITESBURG APPALACHIAN REGIONAL HOSPITAL, 240 Hospital Road, Zip 41858–1254; tel. 606/633–3600; Nick Lewis, Administrator **A**1 9 10 **F**7 8 10 12 14 15 16 17 19 21 22 28 29 30 32 33 34 35 37 40 43 44 46 49 53 54 55 56 58 60 63 65 71 73 **P**6 **S** Appalachian Regional Healthcare, Lexington, KY **N** CHA Provider Network, Inc., Lexington, KY ... 23 10 76 4195 44 68621 384 18764 7957 287

WILLIAMSTOWN—Grant County

ST. ELIZABETH MEDICAL CENTER–GRANT COUNTY, 238 Barnes Road, Zip 41097–9460; tel. 606/824–2400; Chris Carle, Administrator **A**9 10 **F**2 3 4 8 10 11 12 14 15 16 19 21 22 27 32 33 35 37 39 40 42 43 44 46 48 49 52 64 65 71 73 74 **P**1 5 **S** Catholic Healthcare Partners, Cincinnati, OH **N** Community Health Delivery System, Inc., Louisville, KY; Center Care, Bowling Green, KY; Saint Elizabeth Medical Center, Covington, KY ... 21 10 20 448 4 22777 — 4343 1735 61

WINCHESTER—Clark County

⊞ CLARK REGIONAL MEDICAL CENTER, West Lexington Avenue, Zip 40391, Mailing Address: P.O. Box 630, Zip 40392–0630; tel. 606/745–3500; Robert D. Fraraccio, Administrator (Total facility includes 25 beds in nursing home–type unit) **A**1 9 10 **F**7 8 11 12 19 20 21 22 28 30 33 34 37 39 40 41 42 44 49 64 65 67 71 73 74 **N** CHA Provider Network, Inc., Lexington, KY; Blue Grass Family Health Plan, Lexington, KY ... 23 10 75 2296 29 — 276 — — 256

LOUISIANA

Resident population 4,352 (in thousands)
Resident population in metro areas 75.1%
Birth rate per 1,000 population 15.7
65 years and over 11.4%
Percent of persons without health insurance 20.9%

Hospital, Address, Telephone, Administrator, Approval, Facility, and Physician Codes, Health Care System, Network	Classi-fication Codes		Utilization Data					Expense (thousands) of dollars		
★ American Hospital Association (AHA) membership □ Joint Commission on Accreditation of Healthcare Organizations (JCAHO) accreditation + American Osteopathic Healthcare Association (AOHA) membership ○ American Osteopathic Association (AOA) accreditation △ Commission on Accreditation of Rehabilitation Facilities (CARF) accreditation Control codes 61, 63, 64, 71, 72 and 73 indicate hospitals listed by AOHA, but not registered by AHA. For definition of numerical codes, see page A4	Control	Service	Staffed Beds	Admissions	Census	Outpatient Visits	Births	Total	Payroll	Personnel

ABBEVILLE—Vermilion Parish

□ ABBEVILLE GENERAL HOSPITAL, 118 North Hospital Drive, Zip 70510–4077, Mailing Address: P.O. Box 580, Zip 70511–0580; tel. 318/893–5466; Ray A. Landry, Administrator **A**1 9 10 **F**7 8 14 15 16 19 21 22 28 32 33 34 35 37 39 40 42 44 51 52 57 58 59 64 65 71 73 **N** Franciscan Missionaries of Our Lady Health Network, Baton Rouge, LA	16	10	120	3723	55	47852	234	19007	9279	336

ALEXANDRIA—Rapides Parish

⊞ RAPIDES REGIONAL MEDICAL CENTER, 211 Fourth Street, Zip 71301–8421, Mailing Address: Box 30101, Zip 71301–8421; tel. 318/473–3000; Lynn Truelove, President and Chief Executive Officer **A**1 2 3 5 9 10 **F**1 3 4 5 6 7 8 10 12 13 14 15 17 18 19 20 21 22 23 24 25 26 27 28 29 30 31 32 33 34 35 36 37 39 40 41 42 43 44 45 46 47 49 50 51 52 53 54 55 56 57 58 59 60 61 62 63 64 65 66 67 68 69 70 71 72 73 74 **P**8 **S** Columbia/HCA Healthcare Corporation, Nashville, TN	32	10	359	13821	190	99972	1551	103462	44116	1450
⊞ △ ST. FRANCES CABRINI HOSPITAL, 3330 Masonic Drive, Zip 71301–3899; tel. 318/487–1122; Sister Olive Bordelon, Chief Executive Officer **A**1 2 7 10 **F**4 7 8 10 11 12 13 14 15 16 17 19 21 22 23 24 26 27 28 29 30 31 32 33 34 35 37 38 39 40 41 42 43 44 45 46 48 49 50 52 53 54 56 60 63 64 65 66 67 68 70 71 72 73 74 **P**3 7 8 **S** Sisters of Charity of the Incarnate Word Healthcare System, Houston, TX **N** Ochsner/Sisters of Charity Health Network, New Orleans, LA	23	10	228	9015	131	123324	—	85003	32921	1114
⊞ VETERANS AFFAIRS MEDICAL CENTER, Shreveport Highway, Zip 71306–6002; tel. 318/473–0010; Allan S. Goss, Director (Total facility includes 175 beds in nursing home–type unit) **A**1 2 3 5 9 **F**3 12 16 18 19 20 21 22 25 26 27 28 30 34 37 41 42 44 46 49 51 52 54 57 58 64 65 67 71 73 74 **P**6 **S** Department of Veterans Affairs, Washington, DC	45	10	308	2426	293	113947	—	65637	43450	892

AMITE—Tangipahoa Parish

★ HOOD MEMORIAL HOSPITAL, 301 West Walnut Street, Zip 70422–2098; tel. 504/748–9485; A. D. Richardson, Administrator (Nonreporting) **A**9 10	16	10	40	—	—	—	—	—	—	—

BASTROP—Morehouse Parish

⊞ MOREHOUSE GENERAL HOSPITAL, 323 West Walnut Street, Zip 71220–4521, Mailing Address: P.O. Box 1060, Zip 71221–1060; tel. 318/283–3600; William W. Bing, Administrator (Total facility includes 18 beds in nursing home–type unit) (Nonreporting) **A**1 9 10	16	10	100	—	—	—	—	—	—	—

BATON ROUGE—East Baton Rouge Parish

★ △ BATON ROUGE GENERAL HEALTH CENTER, 8585 Picardy Avenue, Zip 70809–3679, Mailing Address: P.O. Box 84330, Zip 70884–4330; tel. 504/763–4000; Linda Lee, Campus Administrator **A**7 10 **F**1 3 4 6 7 8 10 12 14 15 16 17 18 21 22 24 25 26 28 30 31 32 34 35 37 38 40 41 42 43 44 45 46 49 51 53 54 55 56 57 58 59 60 65 66 71 72 73 74 **P**3 4 7 **S** General Health System, Baton Rouge, LA	23	10	70	3566	36	4571	851	29688	9818	—
⊞ BATON ROUGE GENERAL MEDICAL CENTER, 3600 Florida Street, Zip 70806–3889, Mailing Address: P.O. Box 2511, Zip 70821–2511; tel. 504/387–7770; Chris W. Barnette, President and Chief Executive Officer (Total facility includes 31 beds in nursing home–type unit) **A**1 2 3 5 6 8 10 **F**1 3 4 6 7 8 9 10 11 12 14 15 16 17 18 19 21 22 24 25 26 28 30 31 32 34 35 37 38 40 41 42 43 44 45 46 47 48 49 51 52 53 54 55 56 57 58 59 60 64 65 66 71 72 73 74 **P**3 4 7 **S** General Health System, Baton Rouge, LA	23	10	355	13966	235	—	—	111137	46619	—
□ BHC MEADOW WOOD HOSPITAL, 9032 Perkins Road, Zip 70810–1507; tel. 504/766–8553; Ralph J. Waite, III, Chief Executive Officer (Nonreporting) **A**1 10 **S** Behavioral Healthcare Corporation, Nashville, TN	33	22	55	—	—	—	—	—	—	—
⊞ COLUMBIA MEDICAL CENTER, 17000 Medical Center Drive, Zip 70816–3224; tel. 504/755–4800; Joseph R. Dicapo, Chief Executive Officer (Total facility includes 24 beds in nursing home–type unit) (Nonreporting) **A**1 10 **S** Columbia/HCA Healthcare Corporation, Nashville, TN **N** Ochsner/Sisters of Charity Health Network, New Orleans, LA	33	10	183	—	—	—	—	—	—	—
□ CONCORD HOSPITAL, 2414 Bunker Hill Drive, Zip 70808–3394; tel. 504/925–1290; Dean Swindle, Chief Executive Officer (Nonreporting) **A**1 10	33	22	170	—	—	—	—	—	—	—
⊞ EARL K. LONG MEDICAL CENTER, 5825 Airline Highway, Zip 70805–2498; tel. 504/358–1000; Jonathan Roberts, Dr.PH, Chief Executive Officer **A**1 3 5 10 **F**7 19 22 31 34 37 38 40 44 47 52 54 61 65 71 73 **P**1 6 **S** LSU Medical Center Health Care Services Division, Baton Rouge, LA **N** Louisiana Health Care Authority, Baton Rouge, LA	12	10	204	9392	144	175109	1713	68771	25566	—
□ HEALTHSOUTH REHABILITATION HOSPITAL OF SOUTH LOUISIANA, 4040 North Boulevard, Zip 70806–3829; tel. 504/383–5055; Sharon S. Black, R.N., Administrator and Chief Operating Officer (Nonreporting) **A**1 10 **S** HEALTHSOUTH Corporation, Birmingham, AL	33	46	40	—	—	—	—	—	—	—

Hospital, Address, Telephone, Administrator, Approval, Facility, and Physician Codes, Health Care System, Network	Classi-fication Codes		Utilization Data					Expense (thousands) of dollars		
★ American Hospital Association (AHA) membership □ Joint Commission on Accreditation of Healthcare Organizations (JCAHO) accreditation + American Osteopathic Healthcare Association (AOHA) membership ○ American Osteopathic Association (AOA) accreditation △ Commission on Accreditation of Rehabilitation Facilities (CARF) accreditation Control codes 61, 63, 64, 71, 72 and 73 indicate hospitals listed by AOHA, but not registered by AHA. For definition of numerical codes, see page A4	Control	Service	Staffed Beds	Admissions	Census	Outpatient Visits	Births	Total	Payroll	Personnel

Hospital	Control	Service	Staffed Beds	Admissions	Census	Outpatient Visits	Births	Total	Payroll	Personnel
✠ △ OUR LADY OF THE LAKE REGIONAL MEDICAL CENTER, (Includes Our Lady of the Lake–Assumption, 135 Highway 402, Napoleonville, Zip 70390, Mailing Address: P.O. Drawer 546, Zip 70390; tel. 504/369–3600), 5000 Hennessy Boulevard, Zip 70808–4350; tel. 504/765–6565; Robert C. Davidge, President and Chief Executive Officer (Total facility includes 178 beds in nursing home–type unit) **A**1 2 7 9 10 **F**1 2 3 4 6 8 10 11 12 14 15 16 17 19 21 22 23 24 26 27 28 29 30 31 32 33 34 35 37 39 41 42 43 44 45 46 47 48 49 50 51 52 53 54 55 56 57 58 59 60 62 63 64 65 66 67 68 69 71 73 74 **P**6 7 8 **S** Franciscan Missionaries of Our Lady Health System, Inc., Baton Rouge, LA **N** Franciscan Missionaries of Our Lady Health Network, Baton Rouge, LA	21	10	660	23064	399	662721	0	—	—	2718
✠ △ REHABILITATION HOSPITAL OF BATON ROUGE, 8595 United Plaza Boulevard, Zip 70809–2251; tel. 504/927–0567; Jay Pullman, Chief Executive Officer **A**1 7 10 **F**14 15 16 34 48 49 **S** HEALTHSOUTH Corporation, Birmingham, AL	33	46	80	502	36	—	—	15834	6889	190
✠ WOMAN'S HOSPITAL, 9050 Airline Highway, Zip 70815–4192, Mailing Address: P.O. Box 95009, Zip 70895–9009; tel. 504/927–1300; Teri G. Fontenot, President and Chief Executive Officer **A**1 2 9 10 **F**7 8 12 14 15 16 17 18 19 24 25 28 29 30 32 34 37 38 40 42 44 45 46 49 61 65 67 68 71 73 74	23	44	198	11217	108	209477	6758	79025	37176	1043
BERNICE—Union Parish										
TRI–WARD GENERAL HOSPITAL, 409 First Street, Zip 71222–9709, Mailing Address: P.O. Box 697, Zip 71222–0697; tel. 318/285–9066; Charolette Thompson, Administrator (Nonreporting) **A**9 10	16	10	11							
BOGALUSA—Washington Parish										
✠ BOGALUSA COMMUNITY MEDICAL CENTER, 433 Plaza Street, Zip 70429–0940; tel. 504/732–7122; Terry G. Whittington, Chief Executive Officer and Administrator **A**1 9 10 **F**7 8 19 21 22 30 32 34 35 37 39 40 41 44 45 46 49 65 71 73 **S** Quorum Health Group/Quorum Health Resources, Inc., Brentwood, TN	23	10	99	3313	45	30814	145	16296	7925	297
✠ WASHINGTON–ST. TAMMANY REGIONAL MEDICAL CENTER, 400 Memphis Street, Zip 70427–0040, Mailing Address: Box 40, Zip 70429–0040; tel. 504/735–1322; Larry R. King, Administrator **A**1 10 **F**19 22 31 41 44 45 52 59 65 71 **P**6 **S** LSU Medical Center Health Care Services Division, Baton Rouge, LA **N** Louisiana Health Care Authority, Baton Rouge, LA	12	10	55	1929	29	53561	—	12705	6352	195
BOSSIER CITY—Bossier Parish										
✠ BOSSIER MEDICAL CENTER, 2105 Airline Drive, Zip 71111–3190; tel. 318/741–6000; Jack F. Houghton, Chief Executive Officer (Total facility includes 20 beds in nursing home–type unit) **A**1 9 10 **F**4 7 8 10 12 15 16 19 22 25 26 27 28 29 31 32 33 35 37 39 40 41 42 43 44 46 48 49 52 57 63 64 65 71 72 73 **P**5 8	14	10	131	4319	62	128942	229	43648	19855	579
□ SUMMIT HOSPITAL OF NORTHWEST LOUISIANA, 4900 Medical Drive, Zip 71112–4596; tel. 318/747–9500; Louise Wiggins, Chief Executive Officer and Administrator (Nonreporting) **A**1 10 **S** Summit Hospital Corporation, Atlanta, GA	33	22	54	—	—	—	—	—	—	—
BREAUX BRIDGE—St. Martin Parish										
GARY MEMORIAL HOSPITAL, 210 Champagne Boulevard, Zip 70517–3852, Mailing Address: Box 357, Zip 70517–0357; tel. 318/332–2178; Burton Dupuis, Administrator (Nonreporting) **A**9 10	16	10	12							
BUNKIE—Avoyelles Parish										
★ BUNKIE GENERAL HOSPITAL, Evergreen Highway, Zip 71322, Mailing Address: P.O. Box 380, Zip 71322–0380; tel. 318/346–6681; Donald L. Kannady, Administrator **A**9 10 **F**12 14 15 19 22 24 26 28 32 35 44 51 52 57 71 **P**8 **N** Ochsner/Sisters of Charity Health Network, New Orleans, LA	16	10	48	696	7	—	0	5185	2895	—
CAMERON—Cameron Parish										
SOUTH CAMERON MEMORIAL HOSPITAL, 5360 West Creole Highway, Zip 70631–5127; tel. 318/542–4111; Joseph L. Soileau, Chief Executive Officer (Nonreporting) **A**9 10	16	10	33	—	—	—	—	—	—	—
CHALMETTE—St. Bernard Parish										
□ CHALMETTE MEDICAL CENTER, (Includes Virtue Street Medical Pavilion, 801 Virtue Street, Zip 70043), 9001 Patricia Street, Zip 70043–1799; tel. 504/277–8011; Larry M. Graham, Chief Executive Officer (Nonreporting) **A**1 9 10 **S** Universal Health Services, Inc., King of Prussia, PA	33	10	196							
CHURCH POINT—Acadia Parish										
ACADIA–ST. LANDRY HOSPITAL, 810 South Broadway Street, Zip 70525–4497; tel. 318/684–5435; Alcus Trahan, Administrator (Nonreporting) **A**9 10 **N** Franciscan Missionaries of Our Lady Health Network, Baton Rouge, LA	23	10	39	—	—	—	—	—	—	—
COLUMBIA—Caldwell Parish										
CALDWELL MEMORIAL HOSPITAL, 411 Main Street, Zip 71418, Mailing Address: P.O. Box 899, Zip 71418–0899; tel. 318/649–6111; Faye Long, Administrator (Nonreporting) **A**10	33	10	31	—	—	—	—	—	—	—
COUSHATTA—Red River Parish										
L. S. HUCKABAY MD MEMORIAL HOSPITAL, 1635 Marvel Street, Zip 71019–9022, Mailing Address: P.O. Box 369, Zip 71019–0369; tel. 318/932–5784; Betty Bell, Team Administrator (Nonreporting) **A**9 10	33	10	74							
COVINGTON—St. Tammany Parish										
✠ COLUMBIA LAKEVIEW REGIONAL MEDICAL CENTER, 95 East Fairway Drive, Zip 70433–7507; tel. 504/876–3800; Scott Koenig, Chief Executive Officer **A**1 10 **F**4 7 8 10 12 14 15 16 17 19 22 25 26 27 28 32 34 35 37 39 40 41 43 44 45 46 49 51 52 57 59 64 65 66 67 71 72 73 74 **P**1 7 **S** Columbia/HCA Healthcare Corporation, Nashville, TN **N** Columbia Lakeview Regional Medical Center, Covington, LA	33	10	163	5476		—	1177	48272	17598	

Hospital, Address, Telephone, Administrator, Approval, Facility, and Physician Codes, Health Care System, Network	Classi-fication Codes		Utilization Data					Expense (thousands) of dollars		
★ American Hospital Association (AHA) membership ☐ Joint Commission on Accreditation of Healthcare Organizations (JCAHO) accreditation + American Osteopathic Healthcare Association (AOHA) membership ○ American Osteopathic Association (AOA) accreditation △ Commission on Accreditation of Rehabilitation Facilities (CARF) accreditation Control codes 61, 63, 64, 71, 72 and 73 indicate hospitals listed by AOHA, but not registered by AHA. For definition of numerical codes, see page A4	Control	Service	Staffed Beds	Admissions	Census	Outpatient Visits	Births	Total	Payroll	Personnel

☐ GREENBRIER BEHAVIORAL HEALTH SYSTEM, (Formerly Greenbrier Hospital), 201 Greenbrier Boulevard, Zip 70433–9126; tel. 504/893–2970; Cheryl M. Schleuss, Chief Executive Officer **A**1 10 **F**3 26 28 30 32 46 52 53 56 57 58 59 **S** Ramsay Health Care, Inc., Coral Gables, FL	33	22	67	871	25	61354	—	7083	4224	135
✠ ST. TAMMANY PARISH HOSPITAL, 1202 South Tyler Street, Zip 70433–2394; tel. 504/898–4000; Thomas J. Stone, Administrator **A**1 2 9 10 **F**4 7 8 10 12 14 15 19 21 22 23 25 26 30 31 32 33 34 35 36 37 38 39 40 41 42 43 44 46 49 51 61 63 64 65 71 72 73 74 **P**6	16	10	136	6610	80	91631	922	58049	26231	867
CROWLEY—Acadia Parish										
★ AMERICAN LEGION HOSPITAL, 1305 Crowley Rayne Highway, Zip 70526–9410; tel. 318/783–3222; Leonard J. Spears, Vice President and Chief Executive Officer **A**9 10 **F**2 8 15 16 19 21 22 32 37 39 40 44 46 52 57 65 71 **P**2 **N** Franciscan Missionaries of Our Lady Health Network, Baton Rouge, LA	23	10	178	3339	35	31009	485	20529	8568	367
CUT OFF—Lafourche Parish										
✠ LADY OF THE SEA GENERAL HOSPITAL, 200 West 134th Place, Zip 70345–4145; tel. 504/632–6401; Lane M. Cheramie, Chief Executive Officer **A**1 9 10 **F**1 8 12 15 16 17 19 22 23 26 28 29 30 32 34 35 37 39 42 44 45 46 51 52 57 58 59 65 67 68 71 72 73 **S** Brim, Inc., Portland, OR **N** Ochsner/Sisters of Charity Health Network, New Orleans, LA	16	10	55	1507	22	18400	—	14756	4998	210
DE RIDDER—Beauregard Parish										
✠ BEAUREGARD MEMORIAL HOSPITAL, 600 South Pine Street, Zip 70634–4998, Mailing Address: P.O. Box 730, Zip 70634–0730; tel. 318/462–7100; Theodore J. Badger, Jr., Chief Executive Officer **A**1 9 10 **F**8 10 15 16 19 20 21 22 23 24 28 30 32 33 34 37 42 44 46 63 64 65 71 73 **P**1 8 **N** Ochsner/Sisters of Charity Health Network, New Orleans, LA	16	10	93	4025	50	27004	602	19817	9412	354
DELHI—Richland Parish										
RICHLAND PARISH HOSPITAL–DELHI, 507 Cincinnati Street, Zip 71232–3009; tel. 318/878–5171; Michael W. Carroll, Administrator (Nonreporting) **A**9 10	16	10	42	—	—	—	—	—	—	—
DEQUINCY—Calcasieu Parish										
DEQUINCY MEMORIAL HOSPITAL, 110 West Fourth Street, Zip 70633–3508, Mailing Address: P.O. Box 1166, Zip 70633–1166; tel. 318/786–1200; Michael E. Daiken, Administrator (Nonreporting) **A**9 10	14	10	41	—	—	—	—	—	—	—
DONALDSONVILLE—Ascension Parish										
✠ PREVOST MEMORIAL HOSPITAL, 301 Memorial Drive, Zip 70346–4376, Mailing Address: P.O. Box 186, Zip 70346–0186; tel. 504/473–7931; Vince A. Cataldo, Administrator **A**1 9 10 **F**8 22 28 44 64 65 71 73 **P**4	16	10	35	250	4	22788	—	3264	1199	57
EUNICE—St. Landry Parish										
✠ EUNICE REGIONAL MEDICAL CENTER, (Formerly Moosa Memorial Hospital), 400 Moosa Boulevard, Zip 70535–3628, Mailing Address: P.O. Box 1026, Zip 70535–1026; tel. 318/457–5244; Mark L. Manuel, Administrator (Nonreporting) **A**1 9 10	16	10	67	—	—	—	—	—	—	—
FARMERVILLE—Union Parish										
UNION GENERAL HOSPITAL, 901 James Avenue, Zip 71241–2234, Mailing Address: P.O. Box 398, Zip 71241–0398; tel. 318/368–9751; Evalyn Ormond, Administrator **A**9 10 **F**22 32 44 52 57 65	23	10	27	651	8	26734	—	5226	2080	71
FERRIDAY—Concordia Parish										
PROFESSIONAL REHABILITATION HOSPITAL, 6818–A Highway 84, Zip 71334; tel. 318/757–7575; Bobby E. Ewell, Executive Director **A**10 **F**12 48 65	33	46	28	303	—	2793	0	—	509	—
RIVERLAND MEDICAL CENTER, 1700 North E. 'E' Wallace Boulevard, Zip 71334, Mailing Address: P.O. Box 111, Zip 71334–0111; tel. 318/757–6551; Vernon R. Stevens, Jr., Administrator **A**9 10 **F**7 11 15 16 19 22 27 28 30 32 34 37 40 42 44 48 49 51 71 73 **P**5 **N** Ochsner/Sisters of Charity Health Network, New Orleans, LA	13	10	49	1714	19	26177	243	14720	6654	209
FORT POLK—Vernon Parish										
✠ BAYNE–JONES ARMY COMMUNITY HOSPITAL, 1585 Third Street, Zip 71459–5110; tel. 318/531–3928; Colonel Joe W. Butler, Deputy Commander and Administrator (Nonreporting) **A**1 **S** Department of the Army, Office of the Surgeon General, Falls Church, VA	42	10	58	—	—	—	—	—	—	—
FRANKLIN—St. Mary Parish										
✠ FRANKLIN FOUNDATION HOSPITAL, 1501 Hospital Avenue, Zip 70538–3724, Mailing Address: P.O. Box 577, Zip 70538–0577; tel. 318/828–0760; Patricia Luker, Chief Executive Officer **A**1 9 10 **F**4 8 19 20 21 22 30 32 35 37 41 44 48 49 65 71 **P**1 6 **S** Quorum Health Group/Quorum Health Resources, Inc., Brentwood, TN	16	10	60	1361	19	19815	186	11308	4565	192
FRANKLINTON—Washington Parish										
✠ RIVERSIDE MEDICAL CENTER, 1900 Main Street, Zip 70438–3688; tel. 504/839–4431; John E. Walker, Chief Executive Officer **A**1 9 10 **F**8 12 19 21 22 28 30 32 34 35 37 41 44 48 64 65 71 73	16	10	48	1670	23	16881	—	10353	4426	178
GONZALES—Ascension Parish										
☐ ASCENSION HOSPITAL, (LONG TERM ACUTE CARE), 615 East Worthy Road, Zip 70737–4240; tel. 504/647–2891; Michael J. Nolan, Chief Executive Officer **A**1 10 **F**1 12 14 15 16 17 19 22 28 29 30 37 44 52 65 71 72 73	16	49	88	349	38	6367	0	9375	8387	184
★ COLUMBIA RIVERVIEW MEDICAL CENTER, 1125 West Louisiana Highway 30, Zip 70737; tel. 504/647–5000; Kathy Bobbs, Chief Executive Officer (Total facility includes 15 beds in nursing home–type unit) (Nonreporting) **A**9 10 **S** Columbia/HCA Healthcare Corporation, Nashville, TN	33	10	104	—	—	—	—	—	—	—

Hospital, Address, Telephone, Administrator, Approval, Facility, and Physician Codes, Health Care System, Network	Control	Service	Staffed Beds	Admissions	Census	Outpatient Visits	Births	Total	Payroll	Personnel
★ American Hospital Association (AHA) membership □ Joint Commission on Accreditation of Healthcare Organizations (JCAHO) accreditation + American Osteopathic Healthcare Association (AOHA) membership ○ American Osteopathic Association (AOA) accreditation △ Commission on Accreditation of Rehabilitation Facilities (CARF) accreditation Control codes 61, 63, 64, 71, 72 and 73 indicate hospitals listed by AOHA, but not registered by AHA. For definition of numerical codes, see page A4										

Classification Codes: Control, Service. Utilization Data: Staffed Beds, Admissions, Census, Outpatient Visits, Births. Expense (thousands) of dollars: Total, Payroll, Personnel.

GREENSBURG—St. Helena Parish

★ ST. HELENA PARISH HOSPITAL, Highway 43 North, Zip 70441, Mailing Address: P.O. Box 337, Zip 70441–0337; tel. 504/222–6111; Louis Cenac, M.D., Administrator (Total facility includes 72 beds in nursing home–type unit) (Nonreporting) **A**9 10	16	10	99	—	—	—	—	—	—	—

GREENWELL SPRINGS—East Baton Rouge Parish

GREENWELL SPRINGS HOSPITAL, 23260 Greenwell Springs Road, Zip 70739–0999, Mailing Address: P.O. Box 549, Zip 70739–0549; tel. 504/261–2730; Warren T. Price, Jr., Chief Executive Officer (Nonreporting) **S** Louisiana State Hospitals, New Orleans, LA	12	22	104	—	—	—	—	—	—	—

GRETNA—Jefferson Parish

⊞ MEADOWCREST HOSPITAL, 2500 Belle Chase Highway, Zip 70056–7196; tel. 504/392–3131; Jaime A. Wesolowski, Chief Executive Officer **A**1 3 10 **F**2 3 4 7 8 10 11 12 14 16 19 21 22 24 31 32 35 37 38 40 41 42 43 44 45 46 48 49 52 53 54 55 56 57 58 59 61 63 64 65 66 71 73 74 **P**1 5 7 **S** TENET Healthcare Corporation, Santa Barbara, CA **N** Tenet Health System, Metairie, LA	33	10	181	7529	98	35745	1626	46454	20621	622

HAMMOND—Tangipahoa Parish

⊞ NORTH OAKS MEDICAL CENTER, (Formerly North Oaks Health System), 15790 Medical Center Drive, Zip 70403–1436, Mailing Address: P.O. Box 2668, Zip 70404–2668; tel. 504/345–2700; James E. Cathey, Jr., Chief Executive Officer **A**1 9 10 **F**1 4 7 8 10 12 15 16 19 22 25 26 31 32 33 35 36 37 38 39 41 42 43 44 45 46 48 52 56 57 58 64 65 66 67 71 73 74 **S** Quorum Health Group/Quorum Health Resources, Inc., Brentwood, TN **N** Center Care, Bowling Green, KY	16	10	251	8967	115	127287	1476	86367	46050	1411

HOMER—Claiborne Parish

HOMER MEMORIAL HOSPITAL, 620 East College Street, Zip 71040–3202; tel. 318/927–2024; J. Larry Jordan, Administrator (Nonreporting) **A**3 5 9 10 **N** Ochsner/Sisters of Charity Health Network, New Orleans, LA	14	10	57	—	—	—	—	—	—	—

HOUMA—Terrebonne Parish

□ BAYOU OAKS BEHAVIORAL HEALTH SYSTEM, (Formerly Bayou Oaks Hospital), 8134 Main Street, Zip 70360–3404, Mailing Address: P.O. Box 4374, Zip 70361–4374; tel. 504/876–2020; George H. Perry, Ph.D., Chief Executive Officer **A**1 10 **F**2 3 12 14 15 18 28 30 52 53 55 56 57 58 59 65 67 **S** Ramsay Health Care, Inc., Coral Gables, FL	33	22	98	1212	33	7558	—	6170	3309	121
⊞ LEONARD J. CHABERT MEDICAL CENTER, 1978 Industrial Boulevard, Zip 70363–7094; tel. 504/873–2200; Stanley E. Hurstell, Administrator **A**1 3 10 **F**8 19 21 22 25 31 37 38 40 41 42 44 45 49 51 52 53 65 70 71 73 74 **S** LSU Medical Center Health Care Services Division, Baton Rouge, LA **N** Louisiana Health Care Authority, Baton Rouge, LA	12	10	133	6306	76	172253	1284	55663	22064	847
⊞ △ TERREBONNE GENERAL MEDICAL CENTER, 8166 Main Street, Zip 70360, Mailing Address: P.O. Box 6037, Zip 70361–6037; tel. 504/873–4664; Alex B. Smith, Ph.D., Executive Director (Total facility includes 16 beds in nursing home–type unit) **A**1 7 9 10 **F**4 7 8 10 11 12 13 14 15 16 17 18 19 21 22 26 27 28 29 30 32 33 34 35 37 39 40 41 42 43 44 45 46 48 49 51 53 54 55 56 57 58 59 60 63 64 65 67 68 71 72 73 74 **P**5 6 7	16	10	261	10895	166	80290	942	95032	43331	1328

INDEPENDENCE—Tagipahoa Parish

★ LALLIE KEMP MEDICAL CENTER, 52579 Highway 51 South, Zip 70443–2231; tel. 504/878–9421; LeVern Meades, Acting Administrator **A**10 **F**8 13 15 19 20 21 22 28 29 30 31 32 34 37 39 42 44 45 49 51 65 67 71 72 73 74 **P**6 **S** LSU Medical Center Health Care Services Division, Baton Rouge, LA **N** Louisiana Health Care Authority, Baton Rouge, LA	12	10	68	2360	35	116998	—	24797	13963	459

JACKSON—East Feliciana Parish

□ EAST LOUISIANA STATE HOSPITAL, Mailing Address: P.O. Box 498, Zip 70748–0498; tel. 504/634–0100; Warren T. Price, Jr., Chief Executive Officer (Nonreporting) **A**1 10 **S** Louisiana State Hospitals, New Orleans, LA	12	22	452	—	—	—	—	—	—	—
⊞ VILLA FELICIANA MEDICAL COMPLEX, (Formerly Villa Feliciana Chronic Disease Hospital and Rehabilitation Center), 5002 Highway 10, Zip 70748–3627, Mailing Address: P.O. Box 438, Zip 70748–0438; tel. 504/634–4000; Bob L. Wilson, Administrator (Total facility includes 264 beds in nursing home–type unit) (Nonreporting) **A**1 10	12	48	275	—	—	—	—	—	—	—

JENA—La Salle Parish

★ LA SALLE GENERAL HOSPITAL, Highway 84, Zip 71342–1388, Mailing Address: P.O. Box 1388, Zip 71342–1388; tel. 318/992–9200; Mary M. Denton, Administrator (Total facility includes 10 beds in nursing home–type unit) **A**9 10 **F**19 22 28 30 32 44 49 59 64 71	16	10	67	1553	33	10837	—	8891	4018	180

JENNINGS—Jefferson Davis Parish

⊞ JENNINGS AMERICAN LEGION HOSPITAL, 1634 Elton Road, Zip 70546–3614; tel. 318/821–4151; Terry J. Terrebonne, Administrator (Nonreporting) **A**1 9 10 **N** Franciscan Missionaries of Our Lady Health Network, Baton Rouge, LA; Ochsner/Sisters of Charity Health Network, New Orleans, LA	23	10	49	—	—	—	—	—	—	—

JONESBORO—Jackson Parish

JACKSON PARISH HOSPITAL, 165 Beech Springs Road, Zip 71251–2059; tel. 318/259–4435; Delmar J. Medill, Interim Chief Executive Officer (Nonreporting) **A**9 10	13	10	59	—	—	—	—	—	—	—

KAPLAN—Vermilion Parish

ABROM KAPLAN MEMORIAL HOSPITAL, 1310 West Seventh Street, Zip 70548–2998; tel. 318/643–8300; Lyman Trahan, Administrator (Nonreporting) **A**9 10 **N** Franciscan Missionaries of Our Lady Health Network, Baton Rouge, LA	16	10	60	—	—	—	—	—	—	—

Hospital, Address, Telephone, Administrator, Approval, Facility, and Physician Codes, Health Care System, Network	Classi-fication Codes		Utilization Data					Expense (thousands) of dollars		
★ American Hospital Association (AHA) membership □ Joint Commission on Accreditation of Healthcare Organizations (JCAHO) accreditation + American Osteopathic Healthcare Association (AOHA) membership ○ American Osteopathic Association (AOA) accreditation △ Commission on Accreditation of Rehabilitation Facilities (CARF) accreditation Control codes 61, 63, 64, 71, 72 and 73 indicate hospitals listed by AOHA, but not registered by AHA. For definition of numerical codes, see page A4	Control	Service	Staffed Beds	Admissions	Census	Outpatient Visits	Births	Total	Payroll	Personnel

KENNER—Jefferson Parish

⊞ KENNER REGIONAL MEDICAL CENTER, 180 West Esplanade Avenue, Zip 70065–6001; tel. 504/468–8600; Deborah C. Keel, Chief Executive Officer (Nonreporting) **A**1 8 10 **S** TENET Healthcare Corporation, Santa Barbara, CA **N** Tenet Health System, Metairie, LA	33	10	213	—	—	—	—	—	—	—

KINDER—Allen Parish

★ ALLEN PARISH HOSPITAL, 108 North Sixth Avenue, Zip 70648–3519, Mailing Address: P.O. Box 1670, Zip 70648–1670; tel. 318/738–2527; William C. Jeanmard, Chief Executive Officer **A**9 10 **F**13 16 19 27 32 34 41 45 52 59 64 65 71 **P**5 6	16	10	49	699	14	4555	—	4545	1642	80

LA PLACE—St. John the Baptist Parish

□ RIVER PARISHES HOSPITAL, 500 Ruc Dc Santc, Zip 70068 5418; tel. 504/652–7000; B. Ann Kuss, Chief Executive Officer and Managing Director **A**1 9 10 **F**7 8 12 14 15 16 17 19 21 22 26 27 28 30 32 35 37 40 44 49 57 58 59 63 64 65 66 71 73 **P**1 **S** Universal Health Services, Inc., King of Prussia, PA	33	10	54	2444	26	34533	450	22230	10600	255

LAFAYETTE—Lafayette Parish

□ CHARTER CYPRESS BEHAVIORAL HEALTH SYSTEM, 302 Dulles Drive, Zip 70506–3099; tel. 318/233–9024; Denise Guthrie, Chief Executive Officer (Nonreporting) **A**1 10 **S** Magellan Health Services, Atlanta, GA	33	22	70							
COLUMBIA MEDICAL CENTER OF SOUTHWEST LOUISIANA See Medical Center of Southwest Louisiana										
COLUMBIA WOMEN'S AND CHILDREN HOSPITAL See Women's and Children's Hospital										
⊞ LAFAYETTE GENERAL MEDICAL CENTER, 1214 Coolidge Avenue, Zip 70503–2696, Mailing Address: P.O. Box 52009 OCS, Zip 70505–2009; tel. 318/289–7991; John J. Burdin, Jr., President and Chief Executive Officer (Total facility includes 122 beds in nursing home–type unit) **A**1 2 6 9 10 **F**1 3 4 7 8 10 11 12 13 14 15 16 17 18 19 20 21 22 24 25 27 28 29 30 32 33 34 35 36 37 38 39 40 41 42 43 44 45 46 47 48 49 50 51 52 53 54 55 56 57 58 60 61 63 64 65 66 67 68 71 72 73 74 **P**7 8	23	10	308	12806	166	48456	1323	117241	48910	1605
⊞ MEDICAL CENTER OF SOUTHWEST LOUISIANA, (Formerly Columbia Medical Center of Southwest Louisiana), 2810 Ambassador Caffery Parkway, Zip 70506–5900; tel. 318/981–2949; Madeleine L. Roberson, Chief Executive Officer **A**1 10 **F**4 8 10 12 15 16 19 21 22 30 32 34 35 37 39 41 43 44 45 48 49 63 64 65 71 73 **P**7 8 **S** Columbia/HCA Healthcare Corporation, Nashville, TN **N** Center Care, Bowling Green, KY	33	10	107	3815	57	104873	—	34982	14185	441
⊞ OUR LADY OF LOURDES REGIONAL MEDICAL CENTER, 611 St. Landry Street, Zip 70506–4697, Mailing Address: Box 4027, Zip 70502–4027; tel. 318/289–2000; Dudley Romero, President and Chief Executive Officer (Total facility includes 25 beds in nursing home–type unit) **A**1 2 10 **F**4 7 8 10 11 12 14 15 16 17 19 21 22 23 24 25 26 29 30 31 32 33 34 35 37 39 40 41 42 43 44 45 46 48 49 60 63 64 65 66 67 71 72 73 74 **P**2 8 **S** Franciscan Missionaries of Our Lady Health System, Inc., Baton Rouge, LA **N** Franciscan Missionaries of Our Lady Health Network, Baton Rouge, LA	21	10	280	10387	153	71236	428	96712	38597	1243
⊞ UNIVERSITY MEDICAL CENTER, 2390 West Congress Street, Zip 70506–4298, Mailing Address: P.O. Box 69300, Zip 70596–9300; tel. 318/261–6004; Lawrence T. Dorsey, Administrator **A**1 2 3 5 10 **F**2 3 8 10 15 16 18 19 21 22 25 31 34 37 38 39 40 42 44 45 46 49 52 65 71 73 74 **P**1 **S** LSU Medical Center Health Care Services Division, Baton Rouge, LA **N** Louisiana Health Care Authority, Baton Rouge, LA	12	10	141	7819	105	181241	1087	54109	23429	1036
★ VERMILION HOSPITAL, 2520 North University Avenue, Zip 70507–5306, Mailing Address: P.O. Box 91526, Zip 70509–1526; tel. 318/234–5614; John P. Patout, Administrator (Nonreporting) **A**10 **S** General Health System, Baton Rouge, LA	23	22	54	—	—	—	—	—	—	—
⊞ WOMEN'S AND CHILDREN'S HOSPITAL, (Formerly Columbia Women's and Children Hospital), 4600 Ambassador Caffery Parkway, Zip 70508–6923, Mailing Address: P.O. Box 88030, Zip 70598–8030; tel. 318/981–9100; Madeleine L. Roberson, Chief Executive Officer (Nonreporting) **A**1 9 10 **S** Columbia/HCA Healthcare Corporation, Nashville, TN **N** Center Care, Bowling Green, KY	33	44	96							

LAKE CHARLES—Calcasieu Parish

□ △ LAKE CHARLES MEMORIAL HOSPITAL, 1701 Oak Park Boulevard, Zip 70601–8911, Mailing Address: P.O. Drawer M., Zip 70602; tel. 318/494–3000; Elton L. Williams, Jr., CPA, President **A**1 2 3 7 9 10 **F**1 2 3 4 7 8 10 12 13 17 18 19 20 21 22 23 24 25 26 27 28 29 30 32 33 34 35 36 37 38 39 40 41 42 43 44 46 48 49 52 53 54 55 56 57 58 60 63 64 65 66 67 68 70 71 72 73 74 **P**1 5 7	23	10	303	11386	180	82938	1207	100929	33938	1096
⊞ △ ST. PATRICK HOSPITAL OF LAKE CHARLES, 524 South Ryan Street, Zip 70601–5799, Mailing Address: P.O. Box 3401, Zip 70602–3401; tel. 318/436–2511; James E. Gardner, Jr., Chief Executive Officer (Total facility includes 23 beds in nursing home–type unit) **A**1 2 7 10 **F**2 3 4 7 8 10 11 12 13 15 16 17 19 21 22 24 28 29 30 32 33 34 35 37 40 41 42 43 44 46 48 49 51 52 57 58 59 60 64 65 67 71 73 74 **P**2 5 6 7 8 **S** Sisters of Charity of the Incarnate Word Healthcare System, Houston, TX **N** Ochsner/Sisters of Charity Health Network, New Orleans, LA	21	10	298	9552	164	78975	343	87105	33475	1275
★ WALTER OLIN MOSS REGIONAL MEDICAL CENTER, 1000 Walters Street, Zip 70605; tel. 318/475–8100; Patrick C. Robinson, M.D., Administrator (Nonreporting) **A**5 10 **S** LSU Medical Center Health Care Services Division, Baton Rouge, LA **N** Louisiana Health Care Authority, Baton Rouge, LA	12	10	66	—	—	—	—	—	—	—

Hospital, Address, Telephone, Administrator, Approval, Facility, and Physician Codes, Health Care System, Network	Classi-fication Codes		Utilization Data					Expense (thousands) of dollars		
★ American Hospital Association (AHA) membership □ Joint Commission on Accreditation of Healthcare Organizations (JCAHO) accreditation + American Osteopathic Healthcare Association (AOHA) membership ○ American Osteopathic Association (AOA) accreditation △ Commission on Accreditation of Rehabilitation Facilities (CARF) accreditation Control codes 61, 63, 64, 71, 72 and 73 indicate hospitals listed by AOHA, but not registered by AHA. For definition of numerical codes, see page A4	Control	Service	Staffed Beds	Admissions	Census	Outpatient Visits	Births	Total	Payroll	Personnel

⊞ WOMEN AND CHILDREN'S HOSPITAL–LAKE CHARLES, (Formerly Columbia Women and Children's Hospital–Lake Charles), 4200 Nelson Road, Zip 70605–4118; tel. 318/474–6370; Alan E. McMillin, Chief Executive Officer **A**1 9 10 **F**7 8 12 19 22 37 38 40 44 49 61 65 71 73 74 **P**8 **S** Columbia/HCA Healthcare Corporation, Nashville, TN	33	10	70	2106	23	14831	1134	9155	6273	240
LAKE PROVIDENCE—East Carroll Parish										
EAST CARROLL PARISH HOSPITAL, 226 North Hood Street, Zip 71254–2194; tel. 318/559–2441; Ladonna Englerth, Administrator (Nonreporting) **A**9 10	16	10	29	—	—	—	—	—	—	—
LEESVILLE—Vernon Parish										
⊞ BYRD REGIONAL HOSPITAL, 1020 West Fertitta Boulevard, Zip 71446–4697; tel. 318/239–9041; Donald Henderson, Chief Executive Officer **A**1 9 10 **F**3 8 10 12 14 15 16 19 22 26 30 32 33 35 37 39 41 44 52 57 63 71 **P**7 8 **S** Community Health Systems, Inc., Brentwood, TN **N** Ochsner/Sisters of Charity Health Network, New Orleans, LA	33	10	59	2241	28	16583	—	—	—	262
LULING—St. Charles Parish										
□ ST. CHARLES PARISH HOSPITAL, 1057 Paul Maillard Road, Zip 70070–4349, Mailing Address: P.O. Box 87, Zip 70070–0087; tel. 504/785–6242; Fred Martinez, Jr., Chief Executive Officer **A**1 9 10 **F**8 11 12 14 15 17 19 22 26 28 29 30 32 34 35 37 41 42 44 45 49 52 54 55 56 57 65 66 67 71 73 **P**8	16	10	56	2333	38	17679	—	17880	8264	317
LUTCHER—St. James Parish										
⊞ ST. JAMES PARISH HOSPITAL, 2471 Louisiana Avenue, Zip 70071–5413; tel. 504/869–5512; Joan Murray, R.N., Administrator (Total facility includes 10 beds in nursing home–type unit) **A**1 9 10 **F**8 15 16 22 26 28 32 34 36 39 41 42 44 49 52 57 63 64 65 71 **P**8 **S** Quorum Health Group/Quorum Health Resources, Inc., Brentwood, TN	16	10	26	360	6	12794	—	6014	2670	120
MAMOU—Evangeline Parish										
⊞ SAVOY MEDICAL CENTER, 801 Poinciana Avenue, Zip 70554–2298; tel. 318/468–5261; J. E. Richardson, Chief Executive Officer (Total facility includes 325 beds in nursing home–type unit) **A**1 9 10 **F**1 2 3 7 8 12 15 16 19 21 22 26 28 29 30 31 32 33 34 35 37 40 44 45 46 48 49 52 53 57 61 64 65 68 71 73 **P**1 **S** Columbia/HCA Healthcare Corporation, Nashville, TN	33	10	520	5776	354	118041	563	40093	16694	593
MANDEVILLE—St. Tammany Parish										
□ SOUTHEAST LOUISIANA HOSPITAL, Mailing Address: P.O. Box 3850, Zip 70470–3850; tel. 504/626–6300; Joseph C. Vinturella, Chief Executive Officer **A**1 10 **F**15 16 52 53 54 56 57 58 59 65 73 **S** Louisiana State Hospitals, New Orleans, LA	12	22	251	653	209	—	—	28945	18295	637
MANSFIELD—De Soto Parish										
★ DE SOTO REGIONAL HEALTH SYSTEM, 207 Jefferson Street, Zip 71052–2603, Mailing Address: P.O. Box 672, Zip 71052–0672; tel. 318/871–3101; William F. Barrow, President and Chief Executive Officer **A**9 10 **F**8 15 17 19 20 22 24 26 28 30 32 34 35 39 41 42 44 45 49 52 55 56 57 58 59 71 73 74 **P**7 **N** Ochsner/Sisters of Charity Health Network, New Orleans, LA	23	10	49	1331	22	11687	—	7976	2670	130
MANY—Sabine Parish										
⊞ SABINE MEDICAL CENTER, 240 Highland Drive, Zip 71449–3718; tel. 318/256–5691; Karen Ford, Chief Executive Officer **A**1 9 10 **F**12 16 17 19 20 21 22 28 30 32 35 44 71 73 **S** Community Health Systems, Inc., Brentwood, TN **N** Ochsner/Sisters of Charity Health Network, New Orleans, LA	33	10	48	1455	11	11866	—	7727	3718	—
MARKSVILLE—Avoyelles Parish										
⊞ AVOYELLES HOSPITAL, 4231 Highway 1192, Zip 71351, Mailing Address: P.O. Box 255, Zip 71351; tel. 318/253–8611; David M. Mitchel, Chief Executive Officer (Nonreporting) **A**1 9 10 **S** Columbia/HCA Healthcare Corporation, Nashville, TN	33	10	55	—	—	—	—	—	—	—
MARRERO—Jefferson Parish										
⊞ △ WEST JEFFERSON MEDICAL CENTER, 1101 Medical Center Boulevard, Zip 70072–3191; tel. 504/347–5511; David M. Smith, FACHE, President and Chief Executive Officer **A**1 7 9 10 **F**3 4 7 8 10 11 13 19 20 21 22 23 24 32 35 37 38 40 41 42 43 44 47 48 49 52 57 58 59 60 63 64 65 66 71 73 74 **P**5 **N** Healthcare Advantage, Inc., New Orleans, LA; Ochsner/Sisters of Charity Health Network, New Orleans, LA	16	10	340	13405	166	126000	1080	111268	49814	1436
METAIRIE—Jefferson Parish										
COLUMBIA LAKESIDE HOSPITAL See Lakeside Hospital										
⊞ DOCTORS HOSPITAL OF JEFFERSON, 4320 Houma Boulevard, Zip 70006–2973; tel. 504/456–5800; Gerald L. Parton, Chief Executive Officer **A**1 9 10 **F**1 2 3 4 5 6 7 8 9 10 12 13 14 15 16 17 18 19 20 21 22 23 24 25 26 27 28 29 30 31 32 33 34 35 36 37 38 39 40 41 42 43 44 45 46 47 48 49 51 52 53 54 55 56 57 58 59 60 61 62 63 64 65 66 67 69 70 71 72 73 74 **P**1 5 **S** TENET Healthcare Corporation, Santa Barbara, CA **N** Tenet Health System, Metairie, LA; Healthcare Advantage, Inc., New Orleans, LA	33	10	138	2764	429	17907	1	32936	10177	234
⊞ △ EAST JEFFERSON GENERAL HOSPITAL, 4200 Houma Boulevard, Zip 70006–2996; tel. 504/454–4000; Peter J. Betts, President and Chief Executive Officer (Total facility includes 71 beds in nursing home–type unit) **A**1 2 3 5 7 9 10 **F**4 7 8 10 11 12 14 17 19 20 21 22 23 25 27 28 29 30 32 33 34 35 37 38 39 40 41 42 43 44 45 46 48 49 51 52 54 55 56 57 58 60 64 65 67 71 73 74 **P**5 6 8 **N** Healthcare Advantage, Inc., New Orleans, LA	16	10	460	19205	329	152831	1727	182808	73668	2798
⊞ △ LAKESIDE HOSPITAL, (Formerly Columbia Lakeside Hospital), 4700 I–10 Service Road, Zip 70001–1269; tel. 504/885–3342; Gerald A. Fornoff, Chief Executive Officer (Nonreporting) **A**1 10 **S** Columbia/HCA Healthcare Corporation, Nashville, TN	33	44	99	—	—	—	—	—	—	—

Hospital, Address, Telephone, Administrator, Approval, Facility, and Physician Codes, Health Care System, Network	Classification Codes		Utilization Data					Expense (thousands) of dollars		
★ American Hospital Association (AHA) membership □ Joint Commission on Accreditation of Healthcare Organizations (JCAHO) accreditation + American Osteopathic Healthcare Association (AOHA) membership ○ American Osteopathic Association (AOA) accreditation △ Commission on Accreditation of Rehabilitation Facilities (CARF) accreditation Control codes 61, 63, 64, 71, 72 and 73 indicate hospitals listed by AOHA, but not registered by AHA. For definition of numerical codes, see page A4	Control	Service	Staffed Beds	Admissions	Census	Outpatient Visits	Births	Total	Payroll	Personnel

MINDEN—Webster Parish

★ MINDEN MEDICAL CENTER, 1 Medical Plaza, Zip 71055–3330; tel. 318/377–2321; George E. French, III, Chief Executive Officer **A**1 9 10 **F**7 8 12 14 15 16 17 19 22 28 29 32 35 37 40 41 42 44 46 49 52 57 65 66 71 73 74 **S** TENET Healthcare Corporation, Santa Barbara, CA **N** Tenet Health System, Metairie, LA; Ochsner/Sisters of Charity Health Network, New Orleans, LA	33	10	121	3095	31	29277	711	18711	9450	313

MONROE—Ouachita Parish

COLUMBIA NORTH MONROE HOSPITAL See North Monroe Hospital										
★ E. A. CONWAY MEDICAL CENTER, 4864 Jackson Street, Zip 71202–6497, Mailing Address: P.O. Box 1881, Zip 71210–1881; tel. 318/330–7000; Roy D. Bostick, Director **A**1 3 5 10 **F**8 15 19 22 28 31 35 37 38 39 40 42 43 44 52 56 60 65 71 73 **P**1 **S** LSU Medical Center Health Care Services Division, Baton Rouge, LA **N** Louisiana Health Care Authority, Baton Rouge, LA	12	10	187	7680	129	160374	1551	54523	23032	889
★ △ NORTH MONROE HOSPITAL, (Formerly Columbia North Monroe Hospital), 3421 Medical Park Drive, Zip 71203–2399; tel. 318/388–1946; George E. Miller, Chief Executive Officer (Total facility includes 13 beds in nursing home–type unit) (Nonreporting) **A**1 7 9 10 **S** Columbia/HCA Healthcare Corporation, Nashville, TN	33	10	210	—	—	—	—	—	—	—
★ ST. FRANCIS MEDICAL CENTER, 309 Jackson Street, Zip 71201–7498, Mailing Address: P.O. Box 1901, Zip 71210–1901; tel. 318/327–4000; H. Gerald Smith, President and Chief Executive Officer **A**1 2 9 10 **F**4 7 8 10 11 12 13 14 15 16 17 19 20 21 22 24 26 28 29 30 31 32 33 34 35 36 37 38 39 40 41 42 43 44 49 50 51 52 57 59 64 65 71 73 74 **P**6 7 8 **S** Franciscan Missionaries of Our Lady Health System, Inc., Baton Rouge, LA **N** Franciscan Missionaries of Our Lady Health Network, Baton Rouge, LA	21	10	372	13774	238	82320	1114	128851	47047	1505
□ ST. FRANCIS SPECIALTY HOSPITAL, Mailing Address: P.O. Box 71210, Zip 71210; tel. 318/327–4267; Michael G. Ryan, President and Chief Executive Officer (Nonreporting) **A**1 10	21	49	29	—	—	—	—	—	—	—

MORGAN CITY—St. Mary Parish

★ LAKEWOOD MEDICAL CENTER, 1125 Marguerite Street, Zip 70380–1855, Mailing Address: Drawer 2308, Zip 70381–2308; tel. 504/384–2200; Joyce Grove Hein, Chief Executive Officer **A**1 9 10 **F**7 8 10 11 14 15 16 17 19 22 23 26 28 30 32 34 35 37 39 40 42 44 45 46 49 52 55 56 57 59 64 65 71 73 74 **S** Quorum Health Group/Quorum Health Resources, Inc., Brentwood, TN	16	10	122	3017	31	40824	456	22268	9547	352

NAPOLEONVILLE—Assumption Parish

OUR LADY OF THE LAKE–ASSUMPTION See Our Lady of the Lake Regional Medical Center, Baton Rouge										

NATCHITOCHES—Natchitoches Parish

□ NATCHITOCHES PARISH HOSPITAL, 501 Keyser Avenue, Zip 71457–6036, Mailing Address: P.O. Box 2009, Zip 71457–2009; tel. 318/352–1200; Eugene Spillman, Executive Director (Total facility includes 112 beds in nursing home–type unit) **A**1 9 10 **F**1 7 8 14 15 16 19 20 22 26 28 30 32 36 37 40 44 46 49 52 57 59 64 65 71 73 **P**5 7 **S** Sisters of Charity of the Incarnate Word Healthcare System, Houston, TX **N** Ochsner/Sisters of Charity Health Network, New Orleans, LA	16	10	175	3065	132	16692	617	18655	7332	333

NEW IBERIA—Iberia Parish

★ DAUTERIVE HOSPITAL, (Formerly Columbia Dauterive Hospital), 600 North Lewis Street, Zip 70560, Mailing Address: P.O. Box 11210, Zip 70562–1210; tel. 318/365–7311; Kyle J. Viator, Chief Executive Officer (Nonreporting) **A**1 9 10 **S** Columbia/HCA Healthcare Corporation, Nashville, TN **N** Center Care, Bowling Green, KY	33	10	92	—	—	—	—	—	—	—
★ IBERIA GENERAL HOSPITAL AND MEDICAL CENTER, 2315 East Main Street, Zip 70560–4031, Mailing Address: P.O. Box 13338, Zip 70562–3338; tel. 318/364–0441; Robert R. Stanley, Chief Executive Officer (Total facility includes 12 beds in nursing home–type unit) **A**1 10 **F**7 8 10 12 13 14 19 20 21 22 23 26 27 28 30 32 34 35 37 40 41 42 44 49 64 65 67 71 73 **N** Franciscan Missionaries of Our Lady Health Network, Baton Rouge, LA	16	10	75	3834	52	52353	395	32054	13759	530

NEW ORLEANS—Orleans Parish

□ BHC EAST LAKE HOSPITAL, 5650 Read Boulevard, Zip 70127–3145; tel. 504/241–0888; Darlene Salvant, Chief Executive Officer **A**1 10 **F**1 2 3 12 16 18 22 25 29 52 53 54 55 56 57 58 59 65 67 **S** Behavioral Healthcare Corporation, Nashville, TN	33	22	36	650	38	4922	—	2813	1927	89
CHARITY CAMPUS See Medical Center of Louisiana at New Orleans										
□ △ CHILDREN'S HOSPITAL, 200 Henry Clay Avenue, Zip 70118–5799; tel. 504/899–9511; Steve Worley, President and Chief Executive Officer **A**1 2 3 5 7 9 10 **F**4 5 10 12 13 19 20 21 22 25 28 31 34 35 38 39 42 43 44 46 47 48 49 53 54 56 58 65 66 67 69 71 72 73 **P**8	23	50	175	6797	98	124596	0	—	—	1066
COLUMBIA LAKELAND MEDICAL CENTER See Lakeland Medical Center										
★ DEPAUL/TULANE BEHAVIORAL HEALTH CENTER, (Formerly Columbia DePaul Hospital), 1040 Calhoun Street, Zip 70118–5999; tel. 504/899–8282; David Hoidel, Chief Executive Officer (Nonreporting) **A**1 3 **S** Behavioral Healthcare Corporation, Nashville, TN	33	22	102	—	—	—	—	—	—	—
□ JO ELLEN SMITH MEDICAL CENTER, 4444 General Meyer Avenue, Zip 70131–3595; tel. 504/363–7011; Rene Goux, Chief Executive Officer (Nonreporting) **A**1 3 10 **S** TENET Healthcare Corporation, Santa Barbara, CA **N** Tenet Health System, Metairie, LA	33	10	186	—	—	—	—	—	—	—

Hospital, Address, Telephone, Administrator, Approval, Facility, and Physician Codes, Health Care System, Network	Classi-fication Codes		Utilization Data					Expense (thousands) of dollars		
	Control	Service	Staffed Beds	Admissions	Census	Outpatient Visits	Births	Total	Payroll	Personnel

★ American Hospital Association (AHA) membership
□ Joint Commission on Accreditation of Healthcare Organizations (JCAHO) accreditation
+ American Osteopathic Healthcare Association (AOHA) membership
○ American Osteopathic Association (AOA) accreditation
△ Commission on Accreditation of Rehabilitation Facilities (CARF) accreditation
Control codes 61, 63, 64, 71, 72 and 73 indicate hospitals listed by AOHA, but not registered by AHA. For definition of numerical codes, see page A4

Hospital	Control	Service	Staffed Beds	Admissions	Census	Outpatient Visits	Births	Total	Payroll	Personnel
✠ △ LAKELAND MEDICAL CENTER, (Formerly Columbia Lakeland Medical Center), 6000 Bullard Avenue, Zip 70128; tel. 504/241–6335; Trudy Land, Chief Executive Officer A1 7 9 10 F2 3 4 7 8 10 11 12 13 15 16 17 18 19 20 21 22 23 24 25 26 28 30 31 32 33 34 35 37 38 40 41 42 43 44 45 46 47 48 49 51 52 53 54 55 56 57 58 59 60 61 63 64 65 66 67 69 70 71 72 73 P7 8 S Columbia/HCA Healthcare Corporation, Nashville, TN	33	10	140	5116	76	35101	946	39670	17623	546
✠ MEDICAL CENTER OF LOUISIANA AT NEW ORLEANS, (Includes Charity Campus, 1532 Tulane Avenue, Zip 70140; tel. 504/568–3201; University Campus, 2021 Perdido Street), 2021 Perdido Street, Zip 70112–1396; tel. 504/588–3000; John S. Berault, Chief Executive Officer (Nonreporting) A1 2 3 5 8 10 S LSU Medical Center Health Care Services Division, Baton Rouge, LA N Tenet Health System, Metairie, LA; Louisiana Health Care Authority, Baton Rouge, LA	12	10	681	—	—	—	—	—	—	—
✠ MEMORIAL MEDICAL CENTER–BAPTIST CAMPUS, (Includes Eye, Ear, Nose and Throat Hospital, 2626 Napoleon Avenue, Zip 70115; tel. 504/896–1100), Randall L. Hoover, Chief Executive Officer A1 2 3 5 8 9 10 F4 7 8 10 11 12 15 16 17 19 20 21 22 24 26 27 28 29 30 31 32 33 35 37 38 39 40 41 42 43 44 45 46 48 49 51 53 54 55 56 57 58 59 60 61 63 64 65 66 67 69 71 73 74 P5 7 8 S TENET Healthcare Corporation, Santa Barbara, CA N Tenet Health System, Metairie, LA	33	10	634	17346	304	86258	1764	149439	66759	2148
✠ MEMORIAL MEDICAL CENTER–MERCY CAMPUS, 301 North Jefferson Davis Parkway, Zip 70119–5397; tel. 504/483–5000; Randall L. Hoover, Chief Executive Officer (Nonreporting) A1 9 S TENET Healthcare Corporation, Santa Barbara, CA N Tenet Health System, Metairie, LA	33	10	272	—	—	—	—	—	—	—
□ METHODIST BEHAVIORAL RESOURCES, 5610 Read Boulevard, Zip 70127–3155; tel. 504/244–5661; John A. Baker, Chief Executive Officer A1 10 F1 2 3 14 18 22 25 26 34 41 52 53 54 55 56 57 58 59 65 P5	32	22	36	1091	38	0	—	6905	3121	122
□ NEW ORLEANS ADOLESCENT HOSPITAL, 210 State Street, Zip 70118–5797; tel. 504/897–3400; Walter W. Shervington, M.D., Chief Executive Officer (Nonreporting) A1 10 S Louisiana State Hospitals, New Orleans, LA	12	52	95	—	—	—	—	—	—	—
✠ △ OCHSNER FOUNDATION HOSPITAL, 1516 Jefferson Highway, Zip 70121–2484; tel. 504/842–3000; Mary W. Brown, Executive Vice President and Director (Total facility includes 52 beds in nursing home–type unit) (Nonreporting) A1 2 3 5 7 8 9 10 N Ochsner/Sisters of Charity Health Network, New Orleans, LA	23	10	392	—	—	—	—	—	—	—
✠ PENDLETON MEMORIAL METHODIST HOSPITAL, 5620 Read Boulevard, Zip 70127–3154; tel. 504/244–5100; Frederick C. Young, Jr., President (Total facility includes 22 beds in nursing home–type unit) (Nonreporting) A1 9 10 N Healthcare Advantage, Inc., New Orleans, LA; Ochsner/Sisters of Charity Health Network, New Orleans, LA	23	10	163	—	—	—	—	—	—	—
□ RIVER OAKS HOSPITAL, 1525 River Oaks Road West, Zip 70123–2199; tel. 504/734–1740; Daryl Sue White, R.N., Managing Director A1 F2 3 25 52 53 54 55 56 57 58 59 65 S Universal Health Services, Inc., King of Prussia, PA	33	22	56	1291	40	—	—	—	—	90
✠ ST. CHARLES GENERAL HOSPITAL, 3700 St. Charles Avenue, Zip 70115–4680; tel. 504/899–7441; Lynn C. Orfgen, Chief Executive Officer A1 10 F1 3 4 7 8 10 12 15 16 17 19 21 22 23 26 28 29 30 31 32 34 35 37 41 42 43 44 46 49 52 53 56 57 58 59 60 63 64 65 69 71 73 74 P5 6 7 8 S TENET Healthcare Corporation, Santa Barbara, CA N Tenet Health System, Metairie, LA	33	10	173	3530	59	8667	—	25086	8599	255
□ ST. CLAUDE MEDICAL CENTER, 3419 St. Claude Avenue, Zip 70117–6198; tel. 504/948–8200; Joseph R. Tucker, President (Nonreporting) A1 10 S United Medical Corporation, Windermere, FL	33	10	136	—	—	—	—	—	—	—
□ TOURO INFIRMARY, 1401 Foucher Street, Zip 70115–3593; tel. 504/897–7011; Gary M. Stein, President and Chief Executive Officer A1 2 3 5 7 8 9 10 F1 4 7 8 10 11 12 15 16 17 18 19 21 22 23 24 25 26 28 29 30 32 34 35 37 38 39 40 41 42 43 44 45 46 48 49 51 52 54 55 56 57 58 59 60 61 62 63 64 65 66 67 70 71 72 73 74 P1 7	23	10	315	9813	198	116458	971	—	49282	1375
✠ TULANE UNIVERSITY HOSPITAL AND CLINIC, 1415 Tulane Avenue, Zip 70112–2632; tel. 504/588–5263; Shirley A. Stewart, President and Chief Executive Officer (Nonreporting) A1 2 3 5 8 9 10 S Columbia/HCA Healthcare Corporation, Nashville, TN	33	10	259	—	—	—	—	—	—	—
UNIVERSITY CAMPUS See Medical Center of Louisiana at New Orleans										
UNIVERSITY REHABILITATION HOSPITAL, 3125 Canal Street, Zip 70119–6285; tel. 504/822–8222; Robert A. Leonhard, Jr., Administrator (Nonreporting) A10	33	10	40	—	—	—	—	—	—	—
□ VENCOR HOSPITAL – NEW ORLEANS, (Formerly THC–New Orleans), 3601 Coliseum Street, Zip 70115–3606; tel. 504/899–1555; John R. Watkins, Chief Executive Officer (Nonreporting) A1 10 S Transitional Hospitals Corporation, Las Vegas, NV	33	10	78	—	—	—	—	—	—	—
✠ VETERANS AFFAIRS MEDICAL CENTER, 1601 Perdido Street, Zip 70146–1262; tel. 504/568–0811; John D. Church, Jr., Director (Total facility includes 60 beds in nursing home–type unit) A1 2 3 5 8 F2 3 4 5 8 10 11 12 14 15 16 17 18 19 20 21 22 25 26 27 28 29 30 31 32 33 34 35 37 39 42 43 44 45 46 49 51 52 54 55 56 57 58 59 60 63 64 65 67 69 71 72 73 74 S Department of Veterans Affairs, Washington, DC	45	10	243	5888	148	283486	—	—	—	1930

NEW ROADS—Pointe Coupee Parish

Hospital	Control	Service	Staffed Beds	Admissions	Census	Outpatient Visits	Births	Total	Payroll	Personnel
★ POINTE COUPEE GENERAL HOSPITAL, 2202 False River Drive, Zip 70760–2698; tel. 504/638–6331; Larry J. Ayres, Administrator and Chief Executive Officer (Nonreporting) A9 10	16	10	29							

Hospital, Address, Telephone, Administrator, Approval, Facility, and Physician Codes, Health Care System, Network	Classi-fication Codes		Utilization Data					Expense (thousands) of dollars		
	Control	Service	Staffed Beds	Admissions	Census	Outpatient Visits	Births	Total	Payroll	Personnel

★ American Hospital Association (AHA) membership
☐ Joint Commission on Accreditation of Healthcare Organizations (JCAHO) accreditation
+ American Osteopathic Healthcare Association (AOHA) membership
○ American Osteopathic Association (AOA) accreditation
△ Commission on Accreditation of Rehabilitation Facilities (CARF) accreditation
Control codes 61, 63, 64, 71, 72 and 73 indicate hospitals listed by AOHA, but not registered by AHA. For definition of numerical codes, see page A4

OAK GROVE—West Carroll Parish

WEST CARROLL MEMORIAL HOSPITAL, 706 Ross Street, Zip 71263, Mailing Address: P.O. Box 748, Zip 71263–0748; tel. 318/428–3237; Randall R. Morris, Administrator (Nonreporting) **A**9 10

	23	10	21	—	—	—	—	—	—	—

OAKDALE—Allen Parish

✠ OAKDALE COMMUNITY HOSPITAL, 130 North Hospital Drive, Zip 71463–4004, Mailing Address: P.O. Box 629, Zip 71463–0629; tel. 318/335–3700; LaQuita Johnson, Chief Executive Officer **A**1 9 10 **F**1 8 12 15 16 19 21 22 24 28 32 34 37 39 44 46 49 52 64 65 71 73 **P**8 **S** Columbia/HCA Healthcare Corporation, Nashville, TN

	32	10	60	2713	32	16519	—	11200	5072	161

OLLA—La Salle Parish

★ HARDTNER MEDICAL CENTER, Highway 165 South, Zip 71465, Mailing Address: P.O. Box 1218, Zip 71465–1218; tel. 318/495–3131; David Hamner, Administrator **A**9 10 **F**7 16 19 22 26 40 44 46 49 52 57 65 71 73

	16	10	31	928	15	10821	131	5148	1762	80

OPELOUSAS—St. Landry Parish

✠ COLUMBIA DOCTORS' HOSPITAL OF OPELOUSAS, 5101 Highway 167 South, Zip 70570–8975; tel. 318/948–2100; Daryl J. Doise, Administrator (Nonreporting) **A**1 9 10 **S** Columbia/HCA Healthcare Corporation, Nashville, TN **N** Center Care, Bowling Green, KY

	32	10	105	—	—	—	—	—	—	—

✠ OPELOUSAS GENERAL HOSPITAL, 520 Prudhomme Lane, Zip 70570–6454, Mailing Address: P.O. Box 1208, Zip 70571–1208; tel. 318/948–3011; Patrick Brian Carrier, Administrator (Total facility includes 13 beds in nursing home–type unit) **A**1 2 10 **F**7 10 15 16 17 19 21 22 24 28 31 32 35 37 38 40 42 44 45 46 49 51 59 60 63 64 65 71 73 74 **P**7 8 **S** Quorum Health Group/Quorum Health Resources, Inc., Brentwood, TN **N** Franciscan Missionaries of Our Lady Health Network, Baton Rouge, LA

	16	10	121	5101	65	62226	633	36833	14328	547

PINEVILLE—Rapides Parish

☐ CENTRAL LOUISIANA STATE HOSPITAL, 242 West Shamrock Avenue, Zip 71360–6439, Mailing Address: P.O. Box 5031, Zip 71361–5031; tel. 318/484–6200; Gary S. Grand, Chief Executive Officer (Nonreporting) **A**1 10 **S** Louisiana State Hospitals, New Orleans, LA

	12	22	280	—	—	—	—	—	—	—

✠ HUEY P. LONG MEDICAL CENTER, 352 Hospital Boulevard, Zip 71360, Mailing Address: P.O. Box 5352, Zip 71361–5352; tel. 318/448–0811; James E. Morgan, Director **A**1 3 5 10 **F**3 5 7 8 13 17 19 20 22 31 34 35 37 40 41 42 44 46 52 56 65 67 71 73 **S** LSU Medical Center Health Care Services Division, Baton Rouge, LA **N** Louisiana Health Care Authority, Baton Rouge, LA

	12	10	123	4038	51	115935	795	40522	15266	576

PLAQUEMINE—Iberville Parish

✠ RIVER WEST MEDICAL CENTER, 59355 River West Drive, Zip 70764–9543; tel. 504/687–9222; Mark Nosacka, Chief Executive Officer **A**1 9 10 **F**7 8 12 19 21 22 28 32 34 35 37 40 42 44 48 49 64 65 71 73 74 **S** Community Health Systems, Inc., Brentwood, TN **N** Ochsner/Sisters of Charity Health Network, New Orleans, LA

	33	10	60	2533	30	37770	503	14720	6776	197

RACELAND—Lafourche Parish

ST. ANNE GENERAL HOSPITAL, 4608 Highway 1, Zip 70394, Mailing Address: P.O. Box 440, Zip 70394–0440; tel. 504/537–6841; Milton D. Bourgeois, Jr., Administrator (Total facility includes 12 beds in nursing home–type unit) **A**9 10 **F**10 16 19 21 22 32 35 37 40 44 46 52 56 57 58 64 65 71 73 **N** Ochsner/Sisters of Charity Health Network, New Orleans, LA

	16	10	70	1609	17	9143	265	15287	6368	262

RAYVILLE—Richland Parish

RICHARDSON MEDICAL CENTER, Christian Drive at Greer Road, Zip 71269–9985, Mailing Address: P.O. Box 388, Zip 71269–9985; tel. 318/728–4181; David D. Kervin, Administrator (Nonreporting) **A**9 10

	16	10	60	—	—	—	—	—	—	—

RUSTON—Lincoln Parish

✠ LINCOLN GENERAL HOSPITAL, 401 East Vaughn Street, Zip 71270–5950, Mailing Address: P.O. Drawer 1368, Zip 71273–1368; tel. 318/254–2100; E. Allen Tuten, Administrator **A**1 9 10 **F**8 10 12 19 22 23 28 30 32 33 34 35 37 39 40 42 44 64 65 71

	23	10	149	5887	76	33028	564	32834	13881	537

☐ NORTH LOUISIANA REHABILITATION HOSPITAL, 1401 Ezell Street, Zip 71270–7221, Mailing Address: P.O. Box 490, Zip 71273–0490; tel. 318/251–5354; Alice M. Prophit, Chief Executive Officer (Nonreporting) **A**1 10 **S** HEALTHSOUTH Corporation, Birmingham, AL

	33	46	90	—	—	—	—	—	—	—

SAINT FRANCISVILLE—West Feliciana Parish

✠ WEST FELICIANA PARISH HOSPITAL, Mailing Address: Box 368, Zip 70775–0368; tel. 504/635–3811; John H. Green, Administrator **A**1 9 10 **F**8 16 22 25 28 32 56 64 65 **P**5 6 **N** Franciscan Missionaries of Our Lady Health Network, Baton Rouge, LA

	16	10	23	139	2	7508	0	3941	1817	66

SHREVEPORT—Bossier Parish

☐ BRENTWOOD BEHAVIORAL HEALTHCARE, 1006 Highland Avenue, Zip 71101–4103; tel. 318/227–2221; Scott F. Blakley, Administrator (Nonreporting) **A**1 10

	33	22	200	—	—	—	—	—	—	—

☐ CHARTER FOREST BEHAVIORAL HEALTH SYSTEM, 9320 Linwood Avenue, Zip 71106–7098, Mailing Address: P.O. Box 18130, Zip 71138–1130; tel. 318/688–3930; Randy J. Watson, Administrator (Nonreporting) **A**1 3 10 **S** Magellan Health Services, Atlanta, GA

	33	22	60	—	—	—	—	—	—	—

☐ △ DOCTORS' HOSPITAL OF SHREVEPORT, 1130 Louisiana Avenue, Zip 71101–3998, Mailing Address: P.O. Box 1526, Zip 71165–1526; tel. 318/227–1211; Charles E. Boyd, Administrator (Nonreporting) **A**1 7 9 10 **S** Universal Health Services, Inc., King of Prussia, PA

	33	10	118	—	—	—	—	—	—	—

Hospital, Address, Telephone, Administrator, Approval, Facility, and Physician Codes, Health Care System, Network	Classi-fication Codes		Utilization Data					Expense (thousands) of dollars		
	Control	Service	Staffed Beds	Admissions	Census	Outpatient Visits	Births	Total	Payroll	Personnel

Approval / code legend:

★ American Hospital Association (AHA) membership
□ Joint Commission on Accreditation of Healthcare Organizations (JCAHO) accreditation
+ American Osteopathic Healthcare Association (AOHA) membership
○ American Osteopathic Association (AOA) accreditation
△ Commission on Accreditation of Rehabilitation Facilities (CARF) accreditation
  Control codes 61, 63, 64, 71, 72 and 73 indicate hospitals listed by AOHA, but not registered by AHA. For definition of numerical codes, see page A4

Hospital	Control	Service	Staffed Beds	Admissions	Census	Outpatient Visits	Births	Total	Payroll	Personnel
⊞ HIGHLAND HOSPITAL, (Formerly Columbia Highland Hospital), 1453 East Bert Kouns Industrial Loop, Zip 71105–6050; tel. 318/798–4300; Anthony S. Sala, Jr., Chief Executive Officer **A**1 9 10 **F**4 7 8 10 11 12 14 15 16 17 19 22 23 24 28 29 30 32 34 35 37 39 40 41 42 43 44 45 46 48 50 63 64 65 66 67 71 72 73 **P**1 2 7 **S** Columbia/HCA Healthcare Corporation, Nashville, TN	33	10	158	5083	79	66303	340	43645	16605	390
⊞ LIFECARE HOSPITALS, (LONG TERM ACUTE CARE), 1128 Louisiana Avenue, Suite A., Zip 71101–3976, Mailing Address: P.O. Box 1680, Zip 71165–1680; tel. 318/222–2273; Kim B. Bird, Administrator **A**1 10 **F**14 16 **P**1	33	49	40	337	36	—	—	16465	4608	124
⊞ LSU MEDICAL CENTER–UNIVERSITY HOSPITAL, 1541 Kings Highway, Zip 71130–4299, Mailing Address: P.O. Box 33932, Zip 71130–3932; tel. 318/675–5000; Ingo Angermeier, FACHE, Administrator and Chief Executive Officer **A**1 2 3 5 8 10 **F**4 7 8 9 10 13 14 15 19 20 21 22 23 26 31 34 35 37 38 39 40 41 42 43 44 47 49 50 51 52 56 58 60 61 63 65 66 68 69 70 71 73 74 **P**1 5 **S** LSU Medical Center Health Care Services Division, Baton Rouge, LA	12	10	424	19338	302	429727	2410	184544	106189	4703
⊞ OVERTON BROOKS VETERANS AFFAIRS MEDICAL CENTER, 510 East Stoner Avenue, Zip 71101–4295; tel. 318/221–8411; Billy M. Valentine, Director **A**1 2 3 5 8 **F**3 4 8 10 15 16 17 19 20 21 22 23 25 26 27 28 30 31 32 33 34 35 37 39 41 42 43 44 46 49 50 51 52 54 56 57 58 60 63 65 67 69 71 73 74 **P**6 **S** Department of Veterans Affairs, Washington, DC	45	10	123	5299	105	180234	—	82277	41328	994
⊞ SCHUMPERT MEDICAL CENTER, One St. Mary Place, Zip 71101–4399, Mailing Address: P.O. Box 21976, Zip 71120–1076; tel. 318/681–4500; Arthur A. Gonzalez, Dr.PH, President and Chief Executive Officer (Nonreporting) **A**1 2 3 5 9 10 **S** Sisters of Charity of the Incarnate Word Healthcare System, Houston, TX **N** Ochsner/Sisters of Charity Health Network, New Orleans, LA; Regional Healthcare Alliance, Tyler, TX	21	10	486	—	—	—	—	—	—	—
⊞ SHRINERS HOSPITALS FOR CHILDREN, SHREVEPORT, 3100 Samford Avenue, Zip 71103–4289; tel. 318/222–5704; Thomas R. Schneider, Administrator **A**1 3 5 **F**5 15 16 34 39 49 65 71 73 **S** Shriners Hospitals for Children, Tampa, FL	23	57	45	768	6	9314	0	—	—	148
⊞ U. S. AIR FORCE HOSPITAL, Barksdale AFB, Zip 71110–5300; tel. 318/456–6004; Colonel Dennis Marquardt, USAF, Commander (Nonreporting) **A**1 **S** Department of the Air Force, Bowling AFB, DC	41	10	25	—	—	—	—	—	—	—
⊞ △ WILLIS–KNIGHTON MEDICAL CENTER, 2600 Greenwood Road, Zip 71103–2600, Mailing Address: P.O. Box 32600, Zip 71130–2600; tel. 318/632–4600; James K. Elrod, President **A**1 3 5 7 9 10 **F**2 3 4 5 7 8 10 11 12 14 15 16 17 19 20 22 24 26 27 28 29 30 31 32 33 34 35 37 38 39 40 41 42 43 44 45 46 48 49 50 51 52 53 54 55 56 57 58 59 60 61 64 65 66 67 69 71 74 **P**5 8 **N** Regional Healthcare Alliance, Tyler, TX	23	10	502	24637	348	146591	2050	—	—	—
SLIDELL—St. Tammany Parish										
□ NORTH SHORE PSYCHIATRIC HOSPITAL, 104 Medical Center Drive, Zip 70461–7838; tel. 504/646–5500 (Nonreporting) **A**1 9 10 **S** TENET Healthcare Corporation, Santa Barbara, CA **N** Tenet Health System, Metairie, LA	33	22	58	—	—	—	—	—	—	—
⊞ NORTHSHORE REGIONAL MEDICAL CENTER, 100 Medical Center Drive, Zip 70461–8572; tel. 504/649–7070; George J. Saucier, Chief Executive Officer (Total facility includes 13 beds in nursing home–type unit) (Nonreporting) **A**1 10 **S** TENET Healthcare Corporation, Santa Barbara, CA **N** Tenet Health System, Metairie, LA; Ochsner/Sisters of Charity Health Network, New Orleans, LA	33	10	147	—	—	—	—	—	—	—
⊞ SLIDELL MEMORIAL HOSPITAL AND MEDICAL CENTER, 1001 Gause Boulevard, Zip 70458–2987; tel. 504/643–2200; Monica P. Gates, Chief Executive Officer **A**1 2 9 10 **F**4 7 8 10 11 12 14 15 16 17 19 22 23 24 26 28 29 30 32 33 34 35 37 38 39 40 41 42 43 44 45 46 48 49 51 60 63 64 65 66 67 68 71 73 74 **P**1 7	16	10	173	8501	101	63648	735	77089	33647	914
SPRINGHILL—Webster Parish										
★ COLUMBIA SPRINGHILL MEDICAL CENTER, 2001 Doctors Drive, Zip 71075, Mailing Address: P.O. Box 920, Zip 71075–0920; tel. 318/539–1000; James W. White, Chief Executive Officer (Nonreporting) **A**9 10 **S** Columbia/HCA Healthcare Corporation, Nashville, TN	33	10	86	—	—	—	—	—	—	—
STERLINGTON—Ouachita Parish										
STERLINGTON HOSPITAL, Highway 2, Zip 71280, Mailing Address: P.O. Box 567, Zip 71280–0567; tel. 318/665–2526; Evalyn Ormond, Administrator **A**10 **F**19 21 35 50 63 64 65 71	23	10	32	834	14	1070	—	3137	1368	—
SULPHUR—Calcasieu Parish										
⊞ WEST CALCASIEU CAMERON HOSPITAL, 701 East Cypress Street, Zip 70663–5000, Mailing Address: P.O. Box 2509, Zip 70664–2509; tel. 318/527–4240; Wayne A. Swiniarski, FACHE, Chief Executive Officer (Total facility includes 11 beds in nursing home–type unit) **A**1 9 10 **F**7 8 12 15 16 17 19 21 22 24 28 29 30 32 34 35 37 39 40 41 44 46 49 63 64 65 71 72 73 74 **P**5 **N** Ochsner/Sisters of Charity Health Network, New Orleans, LA	16	10	85	4088	41	62301	509	33129	15591	565
TALLULAH—Madison Parish										
MADISON PARISH HOSPITAL, 900 Johnson Street, Zip 71282–4537, Mailing Address: P.O. Box 1559, Zip 71284–1559; tel. 318/574–2374; Elizabeth A. Bullard, Administrator (Nonreporting) **A**9 10	23	10	47	—	—	—	—	—	—	—
THIBODAUX—Lafourche Parish										
⊞ △ THIBODAUX REGIONAL MEDICAL CENTER, 602 North Acadia Road, Zip 70301–4847, Mailing Address: P.O. Box 1118, Zip 70302–1118; tel. 504/447–5500; Karen A. Fiducia, Interim Chief Executive Officer **A**1 7 9 10 **F**4 7 8 10 11 12 14 15 16 19 21 22 23 28 29 30 32 34 35 37 39 40 41 42 43 44 45 46 48 49 59 60 65 66 67 71 73 74 **P**2 8 **S** Quorum Health Group/Quorum Health Resources, Inc., Brentwood, TN	16	10	130	6786	79	79882	763	49806	19397	665

Hospital, Address, Telephone, Administrator, Approval, Facility, and Physician Codes, Health Care System, Network	Classi-fication Codes		Utilization Data					Expense (thousands) of dollars		
	Control	Service	Staffed Beds	Admissions	Census	Outpatient Visits	Births	Total	Payroll	Personnel

★ American Hospital Association (AHA) membership
□ Joint Commission on Accreditation of Healthcare Organizations (JCAHO) accreditation
+ American Osteopathic Healthcare Association (AOHA) membership
○ American Osteopathic Association (AOA) accreditation
△ Commission on Accreditation of Rehabilitation Facilities (CARF) accreditation
Control codes 61, 63, 64, 71, 72 and 73 indicate hospitals listed by AOHA, but not registered by AHA. For definition of numerical codes, see page A4

Hospital	Control	Service	Staffed Beds	Admissions	Census	Outpatient Visits	Births	Total	Payroll	Personnel
VILLE PLATTE—Evangeline Parish										
✠ VILLE PLATTE MEDICAL CENTER, 800 East Main Street, Zip 70586–4618, Mailing Address: P.O. Box 349, Zip 70586–0349; tel. 318/363–5684; Linda Deville, Chief Executive Officer **A**1 9 10 **F**12 15 16 19 22 32 34 35 37 40 42 44 49 52 57 65 71 **P**5 8 **N** Franciscan Missionaries of Our Lady Health Network, Baton Rouge, LA	23	10	80	3665	39	8668	219	15302	6710	261
VIVIAN—Caddo Parish										
★ NORTH CADDO MEDICAL CENTER, 1000 South Spruce Street, Zip 71082–3232, Mailing Address: P.O. Box 792, Zip 71082–0792; tel. 318/375–3235; Patricia S. Wilkins, Administrator (Nonreporting) **A**9 10	16	10	33	—	—	—	—	—	—	—
WELSH—Jefferson Davis Parish										
WELSH GENERAL HOSPITAL, 410 South Simmons Street, Zip 70591–5000; tel. 318/734–2555; Doug Landreneau, Administrator (Total facility includes 60 beds in nursing home–type unit) (Nonreporting) **A**10	14	10	128	—	—	—	—	—	—	—
WEST MONROE—Ouachita Parish										
✠ GLENWOOD REGIONAL MEDICAL CENTER, 503 McMillan Road, Zip 71291–5327, Mailing Address: P.O. Box 35805, Zip 71294–5805; tel. 318/329–4200; Raymond L. Ford, President and Chief Executive Officer (Total facility includes 12 beds in nursing home–type unit) (Nonreporting) **A**1 2 10	23	10	184	—	—	—	—	—	—	—
□ LAKEVIEW REGIONAL HOSPITAL, 6200 Cypress Street, Zip 71291; tel. 318/396–5900; Tom Holman, Administrator **A**1 10 **F**2 15 16 52	33	22	40	859	113	2251	0	4663	2569	94
WINNFIELD—Winn Parish										
★ WINN PARISH MEDICAL CENTER, 301 West Boundary Street, Zip 71483–3427, Mailing Address: P.O. Box 152, Zip 71483–0152; tel. 318/628–2721; Bobby Jordan, Chief Executive Officer (Nonreporting) **A**9 10 **S** Columbia/HCA Healthcare Corporation, Nashville, TN	33	10	103	—	—	—	—	—	—	—
WINNSBORO—Franklin Parish										
FRANKLIN MEDICAL CENTER, 2106 Loop Road, Zip 71295–3398; tel. 318/435–9411; Ann Netherland, Chief Executive Officer **A**9 10 **F**14 15 16 17 19 21 22 26 27 28 32 37 42 44 52 57 59 71 73	16	10	55	2515	30	31068	—	11300	3948	178
ZACHARY—East Baton Rouge Parish										
✠ LANE MEMORIAL HOSPITAL, 6300 Main Street, Zip 70791–9990; tel. 504/658–4000; David W. Fuller, Chief Executive Officer (Total facility includes 50 beds in nursing home–type unit) **A**1 9 10 **F**7 8 12 17 19 20 21 22 26 28 29 30 31 32 34 35 37 39 41 44 45 49 64 65 71 73 **P**6 7 **S** Quorum Health Group/Quorum Health Resources, Inc., Brentwood, TN **N** Ochsner/Sisters of Charity Health Network, New Orleans, LA	16	10	136	4378	93	101876	376	30349	14986	495

MAINE

Resident population 1,242 (in thousands)
Resident population in metro areas 35.9%
Birth rate per 1,000 population 11.6
65 years and over 13.9%
Percent of persons without health insurance 12.1%

Hospital, Address, Telephone, Administrator, Approval, Facility, and Physician Codes, Health Care System, Network	Classi-fication Codes		Utilization Data					Expense (thousands) of dollars		
	Control	Service	Staffed Beds	Admissions	Census	Outpatient Visits	Births	Total	Payroll	Personnel

★ American Hospital Association (AHA) membership
□ Joint Commission on Accreditation of Healthcare Organizations (JCAHO) accreditation
+ American Osteopathic Healthcare Association (AOHA) membership
○ American Osteopathic Association (AOA) accreditation
△ Commission on Accreditation of Rehabilitation Facilities (CARF) accreditation
Control codes 61, 63, 64, 71, 72 and 73 indicate hospitals listed by AOHA, but not registered by AHA. For definition of numerical codes, see page A4

AUGUSTA—Kennebec County

□ AUGUSTA MENTAL HEALTH INSTITUTE, Arsenal Street, Zip 04330, Mailing Address: P.O. Box 724, Zip 04330–0724; tel. 207/287–7200; Rodney Bouffard, Superintendent (Nonreporting) **A**1 9 10
Control 12, Service 22, Staffed Beds 133, all other columns —

KENNEBEC VALLEY MEDICAL CENTER See MaineGeneral Medical Center–Waterville Campus, Waterville

MAINEGENERAL MEDICAL CENTER–AUGUSTA CAMPUS See MaineGeneral Medical Center–Waterville Campus, Waterville

BANGOR—Penobscot County

✠ ACADIA HOSPITAL, 268 Stillwater Avenue, Zip 04401–3945, Mailing Address: P.O. Box 422, Zip 04402–0422; tel. 207/973–6100; Dennis P. King, President **A**1 9 10 **F**2 3 4 5 6 7 8 10 11 13 16 17 18 19 21 22 24 26 28 29 30 31 32 33 34 37 38 39 40 41 42 43 44 45 46 47 48 49 51 52 53 54 55 56 57 58 59 60 61 63 64 65 66 67 68 71 72 73 74 **P**5 6 **S** Eastern Maine Healthcare, Bangor, ME **N** Health Net, Inc., Bangor, ME
Control 23, Service 22, Staffed Beds 72, Admissions 1300, Census 69, Outpatient Visits 3303, Births —, Total 18158, Payroll 9451, Personnel 235

□ BANGOR MENTAL HEALTH INSTITUTE, 656 State Street, Zip 04402–0926, Mailing Address: P.O. Box 926, Zip 04402–0926; tel. 207/941–4000; N. Lawrence Ventura, Superintendent **A**1 9 10 **F**1 19 20 21 22 27 28 30 35 39 41 50 52 54 55 56 57 58 63 65 71 73 **P**6
Control 12, Service 22, Staffed Beds 160, Admissions 325, Census 141, Outpatient Visits 3993, Births —, Total 25402, Payroll 13436, Personnel 433

✠ EASTERN MAINE MEDICAL CENTER, (Includes Ross Skilled Nursing Facility), 489 State Street, Zip 04401–6674, Mailing Address: P.O. Box 404, Zip 04402–0404; tel. 207/973–7000; Norman A. Ledwin, President and Chief Executive Officer (Total facility includes 15 beds in nursing home–type unit) **A**1 2 3 5 9 10 12 **F**2 3 4 6 7 8 10 11 12 13 14 15 16 17 18 19 21 22 24 26 28 29 30 31 32 33 34 35 37 38 39 40 41 42 43 44 45 46 47 48 49 51 52 53 54 55 56 57 58 59 60 61 63 64 65 66 67 68 71 72 73 74 **P**2 4 7 8 **S** Eastern Maine Healthcare, Bangor, ME **N** Health Net, Inc., Bangor, ME
Control 23, Service 10, Staffed Beds 344, Admissions 16581, Census 250, Outpatient Visits 263870, Births 1611, Total 190180, Payroll 82377, Personnel 2270

✠ ST. JOSEPH HOSPITAL, 360 Broadway, Zip 04401–3897, Mailing Address: P.O. Box 403, Zip 04402–0403; tel. 207/262–1000; Sister Mary Norberta Malinowski, President **A**1 9 10 **F**8 12 14 15 16 17 19 21 22 23 27 28 30 31 32 33 35 37 39 41 42 44 48 49 65 66 67 71 73 74 **P**7 **N** Synernet, Portland, ME
Control 21, Service 10, Staffed Beds 66, Admissions 3290, Census 46, Outpatient Visits 110294, Births —, Total 40777, Payroll 15201, Personnel —

BAR HARBOR—Hancock County

✠ MOUNT DESERT ISLAND HOSPITAL, Wayman Lane, Zip 04609–0008, Mailing Address: P.O. Box 8, Zip 04609–0008; tel. 207/288–5081; Leslie A. Hawkins, Chief Executive Officer **A**1 9 10 **F**3 7 8 15 16 17 19 21 22 28 30 34 37 39 40 41 42 44 49 51 56 65 67 71 74 **P**6 **N** Synernet, Portland, ME; Health Net, Inc., Bangor, ME
Control 23, Service 10, Staffed Beds 37, Admissions 1650, Census 19, Outpatient Visits 22946, Births 101, Total 12040, Payroll 6125, Personnel —

BATH—Sagadahoc County

✠ MID COAST HOSPITAL, (Includes Bath Health Care Center, Mailing Address: 1356 Washington Street, Zip 04530–2897; Mid Coast Hospital, 58 Baribeau Drive, Brunswick, Zip 04011–3286; tel. 207/729–0181), 1356 Washington Street, Zip 04530–2897; tel. 207/443–5524; Herbert Paris, President (Total facility includes 16 beds in nursing home–type unit) **A**1 9 10 **F**3 6 7 8 12 15 16 17 18 19 21 22 25 26 27 28 29 30 31 32 33 34 35 37 39 40 41 42 44 45 46 49 52 53 54 55 56 57 58 59 60 62 63 64 65 67 69 71 72 73 74 **N** Synernet, Portland, ME
Control 23, Service 10, Staffed Beds 88, Admissions 4112, Census 60, Outpatient Visits 85800, Births 319, Total 29164, Payroll 13663, Personnel 401

BELFAST—Waldo County

□ WALDO COUNTY GENERAL HOSPITAL, Northport Avenue, Zip 04915, Mailing Address: P.O. Box 287, Zip 04915–0287; tel. 207/338–2500; Mark A. Biscone, Executive Director **A**1 9 10 **F**1 3 6 7 8 11 14 15 16 18 19 22 24 28 30 32 33 34 35 37 39 40 41 42 44 46 49 53 54 55 56 57 58 62 63 65 66 67 71 73 **N** Synernet, Portland, ME; Health Net, Inc., Bangor, ME
Control 23, Service 10, Staffed Beds 45, Admissions 2024, Census 26, Outpatient Visits 78534, Births 186, Total 14771, Payroll 7632, Personnel 277

BIDDEFORD—York County

✠ SOUTHERN MAINE MEDICAL CENTER, One Medical Center Drive, Zip 04005–9496, Mailing Address: P.O. Box 626, Zip 04005–0626; tel. 207/283–7000; Edward J. McGeachey, President and Chief Executive Officer **A**1 2 9 10 **F**7 8 14 15 16 19 21 22 26 28 29 30 31 32 33 34 37 39 40 41 42 44 45 49 53 54 55 57 58 59 61 65 67 71 73 74 **N** Synernet, Portland, ME
Control 23, Service 10, Staffed Beds 113, Admissions 5177, Census 70, Outpatient Visits 102797, Births 606, Total 44253, Payroll 22235, Personnel 740

BLUE HILL—Hancock County

✠ BLUE HILL MEMORIAL HOSPITAL, Water Street, Zip 04614–0823, Mailing Address: P.O. Box 823, Zip 04614–0823; tel. 207/374–2836; Bruce D. Cummings, Chief Executive Officer **A**1 9 10 **F**3 6 7 8 11 12 13 14 15 16 17 19 26 28 29 30 32 33 34 40 42 44 45 49 51 58 61 62 65 67 71 72 73 74 **P**6 **N** Synernet, Portland, ME; Health Net, Inc., Bangor, ME; Blue Hill Memorial Hospital Foundation, Blue Hill, ME
Control 23, Service 10, Staffed Beds 19, Admissions 1315, Census 14, Outpatient Visits 27113, Births 161, Total 12021, Payroll 5811, Personnel 210

BOOTHBAY HARBOR—Lincoln County

✠ ST. ANDREWS HOSPITAL AND HEALTHCARE CENTER, 3 St. Andrews Lane, Zip 04538–1732, Mailing Address: P.O. Box 417, Zip 04538–0417; tel. 207/633–2121; Margaret G. Pinkham, President and Chief Executive Officer (Total facility includes 30 beds in nursing home–type unit) **A**1 9 10 **F**1 2 3 4 7 8 9 11 12 13 14 15 16 17 18 19 22 28 30 32 33 34 37 38 39 40 41 44 47 48 49 51 52 61 64 65 66 67 71 74 **P**6
Control 23, Service 10, Staffed Beds 48, Admissions 369, Census 34, Outpatient Visits 13368, Births —, Total 6738, Payroll 3472, Personnel 142

Hospital, Address, Telephone, Administrator, Approval, Facility, and Physician Codes, Health Care System, Network	Classi-fication Codes		Utilization Data					Expense (thousands) of dollars		
★ American Hospital Association (AHA) membership □ Joint Commission on Accreditation of Healthcare Organizations (JCAHO) accreditation + American Osteopathic Healthcare Association (AOHA) membership ○ American Osteopathic Association (AOA) accreditation △ Commission on Accreditation of Rehabilitation Facilities (CARF) accreditation Control codes 61, 63, 64, 71, 72 and 73 indicate hospitals listed by AOHA, but not registered by AHA. For definition of numerical codes, see page A4	Control	Service	Staffed Beds	Admissions	Census	Outpatient Visits	Births	Total	Payroll	Personnel

BRIDGTON—Cumberland County

✠ NORTHERN CUMBERLAND MEMORIAL HOSPITAL, South High Street, Zip 04009, Mailing Address: P.O. Box 230, Zip 04009–0230; tel. 207/647–8841; Laird Covey, Interim President **A**1 9 10 **F**7 8 11 12 15 17 19 21 22 39 40 41 42 44 45 63 65 71 73 **P**4 7 8 **N** Synernet, Portland, ME; Central Maine Healthcare Corp, Lewiston, ME
| | 23 | 10 | 40 | 1647 | 16 | 32056 | 78 | 12272 | 5738 | — |

BRUNSWICK—Cumberland County

✠ PARKVIEW HOSPITAL, 329 Maine Street, Zip 04011–3398; tel. 207/373–2000; Jon W. Gepford, President and Chief Executive Officer **A**1 9 10 **F**7 8 15 16 17 19 22 26 28 29 30 31 32 33 34 37 39 40 42 44 45 46 49 54 65 67 71 73 74
| | 21 | 10 | 40 | 1841 | 17 | 53736 | 501 | 16059 | 7723 | 215 |

CALAIS—Washington County

✠ CALAIS REGIONAL HOSPITAL, 50 Franklin Street, Zip 04619–1398; tel. 207/454–7521; Ray H. Davis, Jr., Chief Executive Officer (Total facility includes 8 beds in nursing home–type unit) **A**1 9 10 **F**3 7 8 14 16 19 21 22 34 35 37 40 44 49 60 64 65 71 73 **S** Quorum Health Group/Quorum Health Resources, Inc., Brentwood, TN
| | 23 | 10 | 57 | 1287 | 15 | 25424 | 146 | 10982 | 4898 | — |

CARIBOU—Aroostook County

✠ CARY MEDICAL CENTER, 163 Van Buren Road, Suite 1, Zip 04736–2599; tel. 207/498–3111; Lee Ashjian, Chief Executive Officer (Total facility includes 9 beds in nursing home–type unit) **A**1 9 10 **F**4 7 8 10 11 12 13 15 16 17 18 19 20 21 22 24 25 26 27 28 29 30 31 32 33 34 35 36 37 39 40 41 42 44 45 46 49 51 53 54 55 56 57 58 59 60 63 65 66 67 69 70 71 72 73 74 **S** Quorum Health Group/Quorum Health Resources, Inc., Brentwood, TN
| | 14 | 10 | 64 | 2453 | 43 | 67904 | 190 | 25980 | 10793 | 404 |

DAMARISCOTTA—Lincoln County

✠ MILES MEMORIAL HOSPITAL, Bristol Road, Zip 04543, Mailing Address: Rural Route 2, Box 4500, Zip 04543–9767; tel. 207/563–1234; Judith Tarr, Chief Executive Officer **A**1 9 10 **F**1 7 8 11 12 14 15 16 17 18 19 22 24 32 33 37 39 40 44 48 49 62 64 65 68 71 72 74 **P**2 6 7 8 **N** Synernet, Portland, ME
| | 23 | 10 | 31 | 1037 | 13 | 43258 | 166 | 16128 | 6873 | 225 |

DOVER-FOXCROFT—Piscataquis County

✠ MAYO REGIONAL HOSPITAL, 75 West Main Street, Zip 04426–1099; tel. 207/564–8401; Ralph Gabarro, Chief Executive Officer **A**1 9 10 **F**1 7 8 14 15 16 17 19 22 28 30 33 37 40 41 42 44 51 65 71 73 **P**7 **S** Quorum Health Group/Quorum Health Resources, Inc., Brentwood, TN
| | 16 | 10 | 46 | 1704 | 18 | 40599 | 139 | 14320 | 5881 | 225 |

ELLSWORTH—Hancock County

✠ MAINE COAST MEMORIAL HOSPITAL, 50 Union Street, Zip 04605–1599; tel. 207/667–5311; Paul R. Barrette, Chief Executive Officer **A**1 9 10 **F**7 8 12 15 16 17 18 19 21 24 25 26 28 29 30 31 33 34 35 37 39 40 41 44 45 46 49 51 53 56 57 58 60 63 65 66 71 72 74 **P**6 7 **S** Quorum Health Group/Quorum Health Resources, Inc., Brentwood, TN
| | 23 | 10 | 48 | 2754 | 33 | 32864 | 193 | 26840 | 12490 | 466 |

FARMINGTON—Franklin County

✠ FRANKLIN MEMORIAL HOSPITAL, One Hospital Drive, Zip 04938–9990; tel. 207/778–6031; Richard A. Batt, President and Chief Executive Officer **A**1 9 10 **F**3 6 7 8 12 13 14 15 16 17 19 20 22 24 27 28 30 32 33 34 37 39 40 41 42 44 45 46 49 53 54 55 56 57 58 59 65 66 67 68 71 73 74 **P**1 6 **N** Synernet, Portland, ME
| | 23 | 10 | 70 | 2611 | 25 | 84736 | 402 | 23868 | 10183 | 366 |

FORT FAIRFIELD—Aroostook County

COMMUNITY GENERAL HOSPITAL See Aroostook Medical Center, Presque Isle

FORT KENT—Aroostook County

✠ NORTHERN MAINE MEDICAL CENTER, 143 East Main Street, Zip 04743–1497; tel. 207/834–3155; Martin B. Bernstein, Chief Executive Officer (Total facility includes 45 beds in nursing home–type unit) **A**1 9 10 **F**7 8 12 14 15 16 19 21 22 28 32 33 34 35 36 37 39 40 41 42 44 45 46 49 52 53 54 55 56 57 58 63 64 65 71 **P**6 **N** Synernet, Portland, ME; Health Net, Inc., Bangor, ME
| | 23 | 10 | 81 | 1336 | 60 | 32969 | 84 | 16653 | 5845 | 267 |

GREENVILLE—Piscataquis County

CHARLES A. DEAN MEMORIAL HOSPITAL, Pritham Avenue, Zip 04441–1395, Mailing Address: P.O. Box 1129, Zip 04441–1129; tel. 207/695–2223; Nancy Pelletier, Interim Administrator (Total facility includes 36 beds in nursing home–type unit) **A**9 10 **F**8 14 15 16 22 24 40 44 64 65 71 **N** Health Net, Inc., Bangor, ME
| | 23 | 10 | 50 | 505 | 35 | 16431 | 48 | 4343 | 2375 | 95 |

HOULTON—Aroostook County

✠ HOULTON REGIONAL HOSPITAL, 20 Hartford Street, Zip 04730–9998; tel. 207/532–9471; Thomas J. Moakler, Chief Executive Officer (Total facility includes 26 beds in nursing home–type unit) **A**1 9 10 **F**3 7 8 12 14 15 16 17 19 20 21 22 24 28 31 32 33 34 35 36 37 39 40 41 42 44 45 46 49 54 56 57 63 64 65 71 73 **P**8 **S** Quorum Health Group/Quorum Health Resources, Inc., Brentwood, TN
| | 23 | 10 | 41 | 2073 | 26 | 40549 | 162 | 17697 | 8110 | 265 |

LEWISTON—Androscoggin County

✠ CENTRAL MAINE MEDICAL CENTER, 300 Main Street, Zip 04240–0305; tel. 207/795–0111; William W. Young, Jr., President **A**1 2 3 5 9 10 12 **F**7 8 10 11 12 13 14 15 16 17 19 21 22 24 28 29 30 31 32 34 35 37 39 40 41 42 44 45 46 48 49 51 60 63 65 67 69 70 71 72 73 **P**6 8
| | 23 | 10 | 106 | 8234 | 105 | 146309 | 816 | 72756 | 30597 | 959 |

✠ ST. MARY'S REGIONAL MEDICAL CENTER, 45 Golder Street, Zip 04240–6033, Mailing Address: P.O. Box 291, Zip 04243–0291; tel. 207/777–8100; James E. Cassidy, President and Chief Executive Officer **A**1 2 9 10 **F**2 3 7 8 10 12 14 15 16 17 18 19 20 21 22 23 24 26 28 29 30 34 35 37 39 40 41 42 44 45 46 49 51 52 53 54 55 56 57 58 59 60 63 64 65 67 70 71 73 74 **P**6 **S** Covenant Health Systems, Inc., Lexington, MA **N** Synernet, Portland, ME
| | 23 | 10 | 187 | 5481 | 100 | 91763 | 333 | 47194 | 15736 | 574 |

Hospital, Address, Telephone, Administrator, Approval, Facility, and Physician Codes, Health Care System, Network	Classi-fication Codes		Utilization Data					Expense (thousands) of dollars		
★ American Hospital Association (AHA) membership □ Joint Commission on Accreditation of Healthcare Organizations (JCAHO) accreditation + American Osteopathic Healthcare Association (AOHA) membership ○ American Osteopathic Association (AOA) accreditation △ Commission on Accreditation of Rehabilitation Facilities (CARF) accreditation Control codes 61, 63, 64, 71, 72 and 73 indicate hospitals listed by AOHA, but not registered by AHA. For definition of numerical codes, see page A4	Control	Service	Staffed Beds	Admissions	Census	Outpatient Visits	Births	Total	Payroll	Personnel

LINCOLN—Penobscot County

✚ PENOBSCOT VALLEY HOSPITAL, Transalpine Road, Zip 04457–0368, Mailing Address: P.O. Box 368, Zip 04457–0368; tel. 207/794–3321; Ronald D. Victory, Administrator (Total facility includes 9 beds in nursing home–type unit) **A**1 3 9 10 **F**7 8 14 15 16 19 21 22 26 27 28 30 31 34 35 36 37 39 40 41 42 44 45 46 49 64 65 73 **P**6 **S** Quorum Health Group/Quorum Health Resources, Inc., Brentwood, TN	16	10	32	1103	16	36499	91	9588	4487	169

MACHIAS—Washington County

✚ DOWN EAST COMMUNITY HOSPITAL, Upper Court Street, Zip 04654, Mailing Address: Rural Route 1, Box 11, Zip 04654–9702; tel. 207/255–3356; Richard Hanley, Chief Executive Officer (Nonreporting) **A**1 9 10 **S** Quorum Health Group/Quorum Health Resources, Inc., Brentwood, TN	23	10	38	—	—	—	—	—	—	—

MARS HILL—Aroostook County

AROOSTOOK HEALTH CENTER See Aroostook Medical Center, Presque Isle

MILLINOCKET—Penobscot County

✚ MILLINOCKET REGIONAL HOSPITAL, 200 Somerset Street, Zip 04462–1298; tel. 207/723–5161; Craig A. Kantos, Chief Executive Officer (Nonreporting) **A**1 9 10 **S** Quorum Health Group/Quorum Health Resources, Inc., Brentwood, TN **N** Health Net, Inc., Bangor, ME	23	10	20	—	—	—	—	—	—	—

NORWAY—Oxford County

✚ STEPHENS MEMORIAL HOSPITAL, 181 Main Street, Zip 04268–1297; tel. 207/743–5933; Timothy A. Churchill, President **A**1 9 10 **F**3 6 7 8 15 16 18 19 21 22 28 29 32 33 35 37 40 41 42 44 45 49 54 56 64 65 71 73 **P**8 **N** Synernet, Portland, ME; Central Maine Healthcare Corp, Lewiston, ME	23	10	50	1789	21	91782	247	17344	8742	267

PITTSFIELD—Somerset County

★ SEBASTICOOK VALLEY HOSPITAL, 99 Grove Street, Zip 04967–1199; tel. 207/487–5141; Ann Morrison, R.N., Chief Executive Officer **A**9 10 **F**2 3 8 11 12 17 19 22 28 29 30 33 34 37 39 41 42 44 45 46 48 49 52 54 56 58 65 67 71 72 73 **N** Synernet, Portland, ME; Health Net, Inc., Bangor, ME	23	10	26	1481	13	36380	—	9534	4029	142

PORTLAND—Cumberland County

BRIGHTON CAMPUS–MAINE MEDICAL CENTER See Maine Medical Center

✚ MAINE MEDICAL CENTER, (Includes Maine Medical Center, Brighton Campus, 335 Brighton Avenue, Zip 04102–9735, Mailing Address: P.O. Box 9735, Zip 04102–9735; tel. 207/879–8000), 22 Bramhall Street, Zip 04102–3175; tel. 207/871–0111; Vincent S. Conti, President and Chief Executive Officer **A**1 2 3 5 8 9 10 **F**3 4 8 10 11 12 13 14 15 16 17 18 19 20 21 22 23 25 26 27 28 29 30 31 32 33 34 35 37 38 39 40 41 42 43 44 45 46 49 51 52 53 54 55 56 57 58 59 60 61 63 65 66 67 69 70 71 72 73 74 **P**4 6 7 8 **N**	23	10	573	26392	418	121321	2154	329667	128158	3928

MAINE MEDICAL CENTER, BRIGHTON CAMPUS See Maine Medical Center

✚ MERCY HOSPITAL PORTLAND, 144 State Street, Zip 04101–3795; tel. 207/879–3000; Howard R. Buckley, President **A**1 3 9 10 **F**2 3 7 8 13 14 15 16 17 19 21 22 25 26 27 28 30 31 32 33 34 35 37 39 40 42 44 49 51 54 58 65 67 71 72 73 74 **P**6 **S** Catholic Health East, Radnor, PA **N** Synernet, Portland, ME	21	10	159	9361	113	103515	1316	59732	27914	856
□ △ NEW ENGLAND REHABILITATION HOSPITAL OF PORTLAND, (Formerly HealthSouth Rehabilitation Hospital), 335 Brighton Avenue, Zip 04102; tel. 207/775–4000; Patricia McMurry, Chief Executive Officer (Nonreporting) **A**1 7 9 10 **S** HEALTHSOUTH Corporation, Birmingham, AL	33	46	76	—	—	—	—	—	—	—

PRESQUE ISLE—Aroostook County

✚ AROOSTOOK MEDICAL CENTER, (Includes Aroostook Health Center, 15 Highland Avenue, Mars Hill, Zip 04758, Mailing Address: P.O. Box 410, Zip 04758; tel. 207/768–4900; Arthur R. Gould Memorial Hospital, 140 Academy Street, Zip 04769, Mailing Address: P.O. Box 151, Zip 04769; tel. 207/768–4000; Community General Hospital, 3 Green Street, Fort Fairfield, Zip 04742; tel. 207/768–4700; Washburn Regional Health Center, Washburn, Mailing Address: P.O. Box 510, Zip 04786), 140 Academy Street, Zip 04769–3171, Mailing Address: P.O. Box 151, Zip 04769–0151; tel. 207/768–4000; David A. Peterson, President and Chief Executive Officer (Total facility includes 70 beds in nursing home–type unit) **A**1 9 10 **F**7 8 15 16 19 21 22 25 26 28 30 34 35 36 37 39 40 41 42 44 48 49 51 52 53 55 56 58 59 60 64 65 67 71 73 74 **P**2 6 **N** Health Net, Inc., Bangor, ME	23	10	153	2945	100	66117	284	33788	14583	532

ROCKPORT—Knox County

✚ PENOBSCOT BAY MEDICAL CENTER, 6 Glen Cove Drive, Zip 04856–4241; tel. 207/596–8000; Gary R. Daniels, President (Total facility includes 62 beds in nursing home–type unit) **A**1 2 9 10 **F**2 3 7 8 11 15 16 19 22 27 28 32 33 35 37 40 41 42 44 49 52 54 56 59 64 65 67 71 73 74 **P**6 **N** Synernet, Portland, ME	23	10	142	4235	114	79401	381	39718	21358	—

RUMFORD—Oxford County

✚ RUMFORD COMMUNITY HOSPITAL, 420 Franklin Street, Zip 04276–2145, Mailing Address: P.O. Box 619, Zip 04276–0619; tel. 207/364–4581; John H. Welsh, Chief Executive Officer **A**1 9 10 **F**3 7 8 11 12 14 16 17 19 20 21 22 24 28 30 40 44 49 65 67 71 73 **P**1 **N** Synernet, Portland, ME; Central Maine Healthcare Corp, Lewiston, ME	23	10	27	1174	15	28916	74	12567	4701	139

SANFORD—York County

✚ HENRIETTA D. GOODALL HOSPITAL, 25 June Street, Zip 04073–2645; tel. 207/324–4310; Peter G. Booth, President (Total facility includes 88 beds in nursing home–type unit) **A**1 9 10 **F**6 7 8 13 15 16 17 19 22 28 30 34 35 37 40 41 44 49 64 65 71 73 **N** Synernet, Portland, ME	23	10	137	2030	102	41341	266	24841	10659	372

Hospital, Address, Telephone, Administrator, Approval, Facility, and Physician Codes, Health Care System, Network	Classi-fication Codes		Utilization Data					Expense (thousands) of dollars		
★ American Hospital Association (AHA) membership □ Joint Commission on Accreditation of Healthcare Organizations (JCAHO) accreditation + American Osteopathic Healthcare Association (AOHA) membership ○ American Osteopathic Association (AOA) accreditation △ Commission on Accreditation of Rehabilitation Facilities (CARF) accreditation Control codes 61, 63, 64, 71, 72 and 73 indicate hospitals listed by AOHA, but not registered by AHA. For definition of numerical codes, see page A4	Control	Service	Staffed Beds	Admissions	Census	Outpatient Visits	Births	Total	Payroll	Personnel

SKOWHEGAN—Somerset County

✦ REDINGTON–FAIRVIEW GENERAL HOSPITAL, Fairview Avenue, Zip 04976, Mailing Address: P.O. Box 468, Zip 04976–0468; tel. 207/474–5121; Richard Willett, Chief Executive Officer **A**1 2 9 10 **F**7 8 11 12 15 16 17 19 21 22 28 30 32 33 35 40 41 42 44 49 54 56 58 63 65 66 67 71 73 **N** Synernet, Portland, ME	23	10	65	3033	29	60936	241	22198	9933	335

SOUTH PORTLAND—Cumberland County

□ JACKSON BROOK INSTITUTE, 175 Running Hill Road, Zip 04106; tel. 207/761–2200; Steven E. Katz, M.D., President (Nonreporting) **A**1 3 9 10 **S** Community Care Systems, Inc., Wellesley Hills, MA	33	22	106	—	—	—	—	—	—	—

TOGUS—Kennebec County

✦ VETERANS AFFAIRS MEDICAL CENTER, 1 VA Center, Zip 04330; tel. 207/623–8411; John H. Sims, Jr., Director (Total facility includes 100 beds in nursing home–type unit) **A**1 2 3 5 9 **F**1 2 3 12 17 18 19 20 21 22 25 26 27 30 31 32 33 34 37 39 41 42 44 46 49 51 52 54 56 57 58 59 63 64 65 67 71 72 73 74 **P**6 **S** Department of Veterans Affairs, Washington, DC	45	10	206	3142	169	156933	—	60288	34649	964

WASHBURN—Aroostook County

WASHBURN REGIONAL HEALTH CENTER See Aroostook Medical Center, Presque Isle

WATERVILLE—Kennebec County

★ + ○ INLAND HOSPITAL, 200 Kennedy Memorial Drive, Zip 04901–4595; tel. 207/861–3000; Wilfred J. Addison, President and Chief Executive Officer **A**9 10 11 **F**7 8 15 19 22 24 34 35 37 40 41 42 44 45 49 71 73 **S** Eastern Maine Healthcare, Bangor, ME **N** Synernet, Portland, ME; Health Net, Inc., Bangor, ME	23	10	44	1497	17	35357	295	17714	7700	198
★ MAINEGENERAL MEDICAL CENTER–WATERVILLE CAMPUS, (Formerly Mid–Maine General Medical Center), (Includes MaineGeneral Medical Center–Augusta Campus, 6 East Chestnut Street, Augusta, Zip 04330–9988; tel. 207/626–1000), 149 North Street, Zip 04901–4974; tel. 207/872–1000; Scott B. Bullock, President (Total facility includes 47 beds in nursing home–type unit) **A**2 3 5 9 10 **F**1 2 3 7 8 11 12 13 14 15 16 17 19 20 21 22 24 25 26 28 29 30 31 32 34 35 37 39 40 41 42 43 44 45 46 48 49 51 52 53 54 55 56 58 60 61 64 65 66 67 68 71 73 74 **P**1	23	10	391	13737	210	393549	1146	124640	56490	1610

WESTBROOK—Cumberland County

WESTBROOK COMMUNITY HOSPITAL, 40 Park Road, Zip 04092–3158; tel. 207/854–8464; Charlene Wallace, Interim President **A**9 10 **F**2 3 8 22 44 67 **N** Synernet, Portland, ME	23	10	22	276	6	10273	0	4820	2220	72

YORK—York County

□ YORK HOSPITAL, 15 Hospital Drive, Zip 03909–1099; tel. 207/351–2395; Jud Knox, President (Total facility includes 13 beds in nursing home–type unit) **A**1 9 10 **F**3 4 7 8 10 11 13 15 16 17 19 21 22 23 24 26 27 29 30 31 32 33 35 39 40 42 44 45 46 49 54 64 65 67 68 71 73 74 **P**8 **N** Synernet, Portland, ME	23	10	79	2793	33	43174	319	32338	13436	387

MARYLAND

Resident population 5,094 (in thousands)
Resident population in metro areas 92.7%
Birth rate per 1,000 population 14.8
65 years and over 11.4%
Percent of persons without health insurance 11.4%

Hospital, Address, Telephone, Administrator, Approval, Facility, and Physician Codes, Health Care System, Network	Classi-fication Codes		Utilization Data					Expense (thousands) of dollars		
★ American Hospital Association (AHA) membership □ Joint Commission on Accreditation of Healthcare Organizations (JCAHO) accreditation + American Osteopathic Healthcare Association (AOHA) membership ○ American Osteopathic Association (AOA) accreditation △ Commission on Accreditation of Rehabilitation Facilities (CARF) accreditation Control codes 61, 63, 64, 71, 72 and 73 indicate hospitals listed by AOHA, but not registered by AHA. For definition of numerical codes, see page A4	Control	Service	Staffed Beds	Admissions	Census	Outpatient Visits	Births	Total	Payroll	Personnel

ANDREWS AFB—Prince George's County

✠ MALCOLM GROW MEDICAL CENTER, 1050 West Perimeter, Zip 20762–6600, Mailing Address: 1050 West Perimeter, Suite A1–19, Zip 20762–6600; tel. 301/981–3002; Colonel Jeffrey L. Butler, Administrator **A**1 2 3 5 9 **F**2 3 4 5 7 8 9 10 11 12 13 14 15 16 17 18 19 20 21 22 24 26 27 28 30 31 32 33 34 35 36 37 38 39 40 41 42 43 44 45 46 47 48 49 51 52 53 54 55 56 57 58 59 60 61 65 66 67 68 69 70 71 72 73 74 **S** Department of the Air Force, Bowling AFB, DC

| | | 41 | 10 | 110 | 7866 | 73 | 434757 | 1039 | — | 84900 | — |

ANNAPOLIS—Anne Arundel County

✠ ANNE ARUNDEL MEDICAL CENTER, 64 Franklin Street, Zip 21401–2777; tel. 410/267–1000; Martin L. Doordan, President (Nonreporting) **A**1 2 9 10

| | | 23 | 10 | 291 | — | — | — | — | — | — | — |

BALTIMORE—Baltimore City County

✠ BON SECOURS BALTIMORE HEALTH SYSTEM, (Formerly Bon Secours Hospital), 2000 West Baltimore Street, Zip 21223–1597; tel. 410/362–3000; Jane Durney Crowley, President and Chief Executive Officer (Total facility includes 32 beds in nursing home–type unit) **A**1 9 10 **F**2 3 4 8 10 11 12 15 16 17 18 19 20 21 22 25 26 27 28 30 31 32 33 34 37 39 41 42 44 46 49 51 53 54 56 58 59 62 64 65 67 71 73 **P**5 6 7 **S** Bon Secours Health System, Inc., Marriottsville, MD CHILDREN'S HOSPITAL AND CENTER FOR RECONSTRUCTIVE SURGERY See The New Children's Hospital

| | | 21 | 10 | 142 | 6262 | 115 | — | — | 66891 | 25666 | 702 |

✠ CHURCH HOSPITAL CORPORATION, 100 North Broadway, Zip 21231–1593; tel. 410/522–8000; Ann C. Failing, President (Total facility includes 31 beds in nursing home–type unit) **A**1 9 10 **F**1 2 3 4 5 6 7 8 10 12 13 14 15 16 17 18 19 20 21 22 23 25 26 27 28 29 30 31 32 33 34 35 37 38 39 40 41 42 43 44 45 46 48 49 51 53 54 55 56 57 58 59 60 61 62 63 64 65 66 67 68 71 72 73 74 **P**1 5 **S** Helix Health, Lutherville Timonium, MD **N** Helix Health System, Lutherville, MD

| | | 23 | 10 | 151 | 5704 | 101 | 29758 | — | 45086 | 19745 | 682 |

✠ DEATON SPECIALTY HOSPITAL AND HOME, 611 South Charles Street, Zip 21230–3898; tel. 410/547–8500; James E. Ross, FACHE, Chief Executive Officer (Total facility includes 152 beds in nursing home–type unit) (Nonreporting) **A**1 9 10 **N** University of Maryland Medical System, Baltimore, MD

| | | 21 | 48 | 275 | — | — | — | — | — | — | — |

✠ FRANKLIN SQUARE HOSPITAL CENTER, 9000 Franklin Square Drive, Zip 21237–3998; tel. 410/682–7000; Charles D. Mross, President and Chief Executive Officer **A**1 2 3 5 8 9 10 **F**2 3 4 7 8 10 11 12 14 16 17 18 19 21 22 23 24 25 26 28 29 30 31 32 33 34 35 37 38 39 40 41 42 43 44 45 46 49 51 52 53 54 55 56 57 58 59 60 61 62 63 64 65 66 67 68 71 72 73 74 **P**2 4 5 6 7 **S** Helix Health, Lutherville Timonium, MD **N** Helix Health System, Lutherville, MD

| | | 23 | 10 | 243 | 20136 | 256 | 148148 | 2664 | 154813 | 75415 | 2276 |

✠ △ GOOD SAMARITAN HOSPITAL OF MARYLAND, 5601 Loch Raven Boulevard, Zip 21239–2995; tel. 410/532–8000; Lawrence M. Beck, President (Nonreporting) **A**1 3 5 7 9 10 **S** Helix Health, Lutherville Timonium, MD **N** Helix Health System, Lutherville, MD

| | | 23 | 10 | 274 | — | — | — | — | — | — | — |

✠ GREATER BALTIMORE MEDICAL CENTER, 6701 North Charles Street, Zip 21204–6892; tel. 410/828–2000; Robert P. Kowal, President (Nonreporting) **A**1 2 3 5 8 9 10 **N** Maryland Health Network, Columbia, MD

| | | 23 | 10 | 304 | — | — | — | — | — | — | — |

□ GUNDRY–GLASS HOSPITAL, 2 North Wickham Road, Zip 21229–3399, Mailing Address: 1777 Reisterstown Road, Pikesville, Zip 21208; tel. 410/484–2700; Sheldon D. Glass, M.D., President (Nonreporting) **A**1 9 10

| | | 33 | 22 | 84 | — | — | — | — | — | — | — |

✠ HARBOR HOSPITAL CENTER, 3001 South Hanover Street, Zip 21225–1290; tel. 410/347–3200; L. Barney Johnson, President and Chief Executive Officer (Total facility includes 26 beds in nursing home–type unit) **A**1 2 3 5 9 10 **F**1 7 8 10 12 14 15 16 17 19 21 22 24 26 27 28 30 32 34 35 37 39 40 41 42 44 45 46 49 51 53 54 56 58 60 63 64 65 67 68 71 73 74 **P**6 **S** Helix Health, Lutherville Timonium, MD

| | | 23 | 10 | 192 | 11232 | 154 | 61931 | 1602 | 97187 | — | 1300 |

✠ △ JAMES LAWRENCE KERNAN HOSPITAL, 2200 Kernan Drive, Zip 21207–6697; tel. 410/448–2500; James E. Ross, FACHE, Chief Executive Officer (Nonreporting) **A**1 3 5 7 9 10 **N** University of Maryland Medical System, Baltimore, MD

| | | 23 | 46 | 152 | — | — | — | — | — | — | — |

✠ JOHNS HOPKINS BAYVIEW MEDICAL CENTER, 4940 Eastern Avenue, Zip 21224–2780; tel. 410/550–0100; Ronald R. Peterson, President (Total facility includes 321 beds in nursing home–type unit) **A**1 3 5 8 9 10 **F**1 2 3 4 5 7 8 9 10 11 12 13 14 15 16 17 18 19 20 21 22 23 24 25 26 27 28 29 30 31 34 35 37 38 39 40 41 42 43 44 45 46 47 48 49 50 51 52 53 54 55 56 57 58 59 60 61 63 64 65 66 67 68 69 70 71 72 73 74 **P**5 6 **S** Johns Hopkins Health System, Baltimore, MD **N** Johns Hopkins Medicine, Baltimore, MD

| | | 23 | 10 | 684 | 18636 | 508 | 247373 | 1090 | 177101 | 64079 | 2335 |

✠ △ JOHNS HOPKINS HOSPITAL, 600 North Wolfe Street, Zip 21287–0002; tel. 410/955–5000; Ronald R. Peterson, President **A**1 2 3 5 7 8 9 10 **F**1 2 3 4 5 6 7 8 9 10 11 12 13 14 15 16 17 18 19 20 21 22 23 24 25 26 27 28 29 30 31 32 33 34 35 37 38 39 40 41 42 43 44 45 46 47 48 49 50 51 52 53 54 55 56 57 58 59 60 61 63 64 65 66 67 68 69 70 71 72 73 74 **P**1 2 5 6 7 8 **S** Johns Hopkins Health System, Baltimore, MD **N** Johns Hopkins Medicine, Baltimore, MD

| | | 23 | 10 | 853 | 39197 | 692 | 290079 | 1918 | 546639 | 207110 | 6061 |

Hospital, Address, Telephone, Administrator, Approval, Facility, and Physician Codes, Health Care System, Network	Classi-fication Codes		Utilization Data					Expense (thousands) of dollars		
	Control	Service	Staffed Beds	Admissions	Census	Outpatient Visits	Births	Total	Payroll	Personnel

Legend:

★ American Hospital Association (AHA) membership
□ Joint Commission on Accreditation of Healthcare Organizations (JCAHO) accreditation
+ American Osteopathic Healthcare Association (AOHA) membership
○ American Osteopathic Association (AOA) accreditation
△ Commission on Accreditation of Rehabilitation Facilities (CARF) accreditation
Control codes 61, 63, 64, 71, 72 and 73 indicate hospitals listed by AOHA, but not registered by AHA. For definition of numerical codes, see page A4

Hospital	Control	Service	Staffed Beds	Admissions	Census	Outpatient Visits	Births	Total	Payroll	Personnel
☒ △ KENNEDY KRIEGER CHILDREN'S HOSPITAL, 707 North Broadway, Zip 21205–1890; tel. 410/502–9000; Gary W. Goldstein, M.D., President (Nonreporting) **A**1 7 9 10	23	59	63	—	—	—	—	—	—	—
★ △ LEVINDALE HEBREW GERIATRIC CENTER AND HOSPITAL, 2434 West Belvedere Avenue, Zip 21215–5299; tel. 410/466–8700; David Z. Ross, Acting Chief Executive Officer (Nonreporting) **A**7 9 10	23	49	288	—	—	—	—	—	—	—
☒ LIBERTY MEDICAL CENTER, 2600 Liberty Heights Avenue, Zip 21215–7892; tel. 410/383–4000; Jane Durney Crowley, Chief Executive Officer **A**1 9 10 **F**3 4 8 10 12 14 15 16 17 18 19 20 21 22 25 26 27 28 29 30 31 32 33 34 35 37 39 42 44 46 49 50 52 53 54 55 56 57 58 59 63 64 65 67 71 73 **P**5 6 7 **S** Bon Secours Health System, Inc., Marriottsville, MD	23	10	95	5831	91	63363	—	53971	24738	604
☒ △ MARYLAND GENERAL HOSPITAL, 827 Linden Avenue, Zip 21201–4606; tel. 410/225–8000; James R. Wood, Chairman and Chief Executive Officer **A**1 2 3 5 7 9 10 **F**3 7 8 10 11 12 14 15 16 17 19 21 22 25 26 27 28 29 30 31 32 34 35 37 39 40 41 42 44 45 46 48 49 51 52 54 55 56 57 58 59 60 61 63 64 65 67 68 71 72 73 74 **P**8	23	10	225	8187	138	89248	496	84347	45164	1231
☒ MERCY MEDICAL CENTER, 301 St. Paul Place, Zip 21202–2165; tel. 410/332–9000; Sister Helen Amos, President and Chief Executive Officer **A**1 3 5 9 10 **F**2 7 8 10 11 12 13 14 15 16 17 19 20 21 22 25 26 29 32 33 35 37 38 41 42 44 46 48 49 52 58 59 60 61 64 65 67 71 72 73 74 **P**2 5 6 7 **S** Sisters of Mercy of the Americas–Regional Community of Baltimore, Baltimore, MD	21	10	218	13573	166	127646	2709	116556	46220	1652
☒ △ MT. WASHINGTON PEDIATRIC HOSPITAL, 1708 West Rogers Avenue, Zip 21209–4596; tel. 410/578–8600; Sheldon J. Stein, Chief Operating Officer (Nonreporting) **A**1 7 9 10	23	59	84	—	—	—	—	—	—	—
☒ SHEPPARD AND ENOCH PRATT HOSPITAL, 6501 North Charles Street, Zip 21285–6815, Mailing Address: P.O. Box 6815, Zip 21285–6815; tel. 410/938–3000; Steven S. Sharfstein, M.D., President, Medical Director and Chief Executive Officer **A**1 3 5 9 10 **F**1 3 6 12 14 15 16 17 18 25 26 27 28 29 30 34 45 46 52 53 54 55 57 58 59 65 67 68 72 73 **P**3 6	23	22	168	4101	127	—	—	49556	28256	972
☒ SINAI HOSPITAL OF BALTIMORE, 2401 West Belvedere Avenue, Zip 21215–5271; tel. 410/601–9000; Warren A. Green, President and Chief Executive Officer **A**1 2 3 5 7 8 9 10 **F**1 2 3 4 5 6 7 8 9 10 11 12 13 15 16 17 18 19 20 21 22 23 24 25 26 27 28 29 30 31 32 33 34 35 36 37 38 39 40 41 42 43 44 45 46 47 48 49 50 51 52 53 54 55 56 57 58 59 60 61 62 63 64 65 66 67 68 69 70 71 72 73 74 **P**5 6 7 **N**	23	10	446	20821	302	105559	2267	239879	121203	2791
□ SPRING GROVE HOSPITAL CENTER, 60 Wade Avenue, Zip 21228–4689; tel. 410/455–6000; Mark Pecevich, M.D., Superintendent (Total facility includes 70 beds in nursing home–type unit) (Nonreporting) **A**1 3 5 10	12	22	360	—	—	—	—	—	—	—
☒ ST. AGNES HEALTHCARE, 900 Caton Avenue, Zip 21229–5299; tel. 410/368–6000; Robert E. Pezzoli, President and Chief Executive Officer (Total facility includes 187 beds in nursing home–type unit) **A**1 2 3 5 9 10 **F**3 6 7 8 10 11 12 13 14 15 16 17 19 21 22 25 27 28 29 30 31 32 33 34 35 37 38 39 40 41 42 44 45 46 47 49 51 53 54 56 58 60 63 64 65 67 71 73 74 **P**6 8 **S** Daughters of Charity National Health System, Saint Louis, MO **N** Maryland Health Network, Columbia, MD	21	10	565	18495	390	232875	2318	189338	92127	2288
☒ △ THE NEW CHILDREN'S HOSPITAL, (Formerly Children's Hospital and Center for Reconstructive Surgery), 3825 Greenspring Avenue, Zip 21211–1398; tel. 410/462–6800; Robert A. Chrzan, President and Chief Executive Officer **A**1 3 5 7 9 10 **F**12 15 19 20 21 24 28 30 32 34 35 37 39 41 44 45 46 48 49 65 66 73	23	47	76	427	8	28639	—	12096	5237	197
☒ △ UNION MEMORIAL HOSPITAL, 201 East University Parkway, Zip 21218–2391; tel. 410/554–2000; Kenneth R. Buser, President and Chief Executive Officer (Total facility includes 31 beds in nursing home–type unit) (Nonreporting) **A**1 3 5 6 7 9 10 **S** Helix Health, Lutherville Timonium, MD **N** Helix Health System, Lutherville, MD	23	10	378	—	—	—	—	—	—	—
☒ UNIVERSITY OF MARYLAND MEDICAL SYSTEM, 22 South Greene Street, Zip 21201–1595; tel. 410/328–8667; Morton I. Rapoport, M.D., President and Chief Executive Officer (Nonreporting) **A**1 2 3 5 8 9 10 **N** University of Maryland Medical System, Baltimore, MD	23	10	768	—	—	—	—	—	—	—
☒ VETERANS AFFAIRS MARYLAND HEALTH CARE SYSTEM–BALTIMORE DIVISION, 10 North Greene Street, Zip 21201–1524; tel. 410/605–7001; Dennis H. Smith, Director (Total facility includes 140 beds in nursing home–type unit) (Nonreporting) **A**1 2 3 5 8 9 **S** Department of Veterans Affairs, Washington, DC	45	10	897	—	—	—	—	—	—	—

BERLIN—Worcester County

Hospital	Control	Service	Staffed Beds	Admissions	Census	Outpatient Visits	Births	Total	Payroll	Personnel
☒ ATLANTIC GENERAL HOSPITAL, 9733 Healthway Drive, Zip 21811–1151; tel. 410/641–1100; Charles Neumann, Chief Executive Officer (Total facility includes 24 beds in nursing home–type unit) **A**1 9 10 **F**8 14 15 16 17 19 21 22 28 30 35 37 39 41 44 45 51 64 71 72	23	10	62	2162	33	25629	0	—	—	284

BETHESDA—Montgomery County

Hospital	Control	Service	Staffed Beds	Admissions	Census	Outpatient Visits	Births	Total	Payroll	Personnel
☒ NATIONAL NAVAL MEDICAL CENTER, 8901 Wisconsin Avenue, Zip 20889–5600; tel. 301/295–5800; Rear Admiral Richard T. Ridenour, MC, USN, Commander (Nonreporting) **A**1 2 3 5 9 **S** Department of Navy, Washington, DC	43	10	217	—	—	—	—	—	—	—
☒ SUBURBAN HOSPITAL, 8600 Old Georgetown Road, Zip 20814–1497; tel. 301/896–3100; Brian G. Grissler, President and Chief Executive Officer (Total facility includes 31 beds in nursing home–type unit) **A**1 2 3 5 9 10 **F**2 3 4 6 8 10 12 15 16 17 18 19 22 26 28 30 32 34 35 37 39 42 44 45 49 51 52 56 57 58 59 60 61 63 64 65 67 68 70 71 73 **P**1 7 **N** Johns Hopkins Medicine, Baltimore, MD	23	10	227	11405	184	88323	—	110716	50094	1222

Hospital, Address, Telephone, Administrator, Approval, Facility, and Physician Codes, Health Care System, Network	Classi-fication Codes		Utilization Data					Expense (thousands) of dollars		
	Control	Service	Staffed Beds	Admissions	Census	Outpatient Visits	Births	Total	Payroll	Personnel

★ American Hospital Association (AHA) membership
□ Joint Commission on Accreditation of Healthcare Organizations (JCAHO) accreditation
+ American Osteopathic Healthcare Association (AOHA) membership
○ American Osteopathic Association (AOA) accreditation
△ Commission on Accreditation of Rehabilitation Facilities (CARF) accreditation
Control codes 61, 63, 64, 71, 72 and 73 indicate hospitals listed by AOHA, but not registered by AHA. For definition of numerical codes, see page A4

⊞ WARREN G. MAGNUSON CLINICAL CENTER, NATIONAL INSTITUTES OF HEALTH, (BIOMEDICAL RESEARCH), 9000 Rockville Pike, Zip 20892–1504; tel. 301/496–4114; John I. Gallin, M.D., Director **A**1 3 5 8 **F**3 4 8 10 19 20 21 24 26 27 31 34 35 37 39 41 42 43 44 46 49 50 52 53 54 55 57 58 59 60 63 65 67 71 73 **S** U. S. Public Health Service Indian Health Service, Rockville, MD	44	49	314	6664	155	73296	—	—	—	1810
CAMBRIDGE—Dorchester County										
⊞ DORCHESTER GENERAL HOSPITAL, 300 Byrn Street, Zip 21613–1908; tel. 410/228–5511; Joseph P. Ross, President and Chief Executive Officer **A**1 2 9 10 **F**3 7 8 10 12 14 15 16 17 19 21 22 23 25 28 29 30 32 34 35 37 39 40 41 42 44 49 51 52 53 54 56 57 58 59 60 63 64 65 71 72 73 **P**7	23	10	60	3532	48	30975	256	23065	10554	343
□ EASTERN SHORE HOSPITAL CENTER, Route 50, State Route 479, Zip 21613, Mailing Address: P.O. Box 800, Zip 21613–0800; tel. 410/221–2300; Mary K. Noren, Superintendent **A**1 9 10 **F**14 15 16 37 45 46 48 52 54 55 57 58 65 73 **P**6	12	22	89	175	77	—	—	12787	7975	224
CHESTERTOWN—Kent County										
⊞ KENT & QUEEN ANNE'S HOSPITAL, 100 Brown Street, Zip 21620–1499; tel. 410/778–3300; William R. Kirk, Jr., President and Chief Executive Officer **A**1 9 10 **F**7 8 11 12 14 15 16 17 19 21 22 24 28 30 35 37 39 40 42 44 45 49 56 63 64 65 67 69 71 73 **N** Johns Hopkins Medicine, Baltimore, MD	23	10	64	2536	29	39805	214	17112	8327	239
□ UPPER SHORE COMMUNITY MENTAL HEALTH CENTER, Scheeler Road, Zip 21620, Mailing Address: P.O. Box 229, Zip 21620–0229; tel. 410/778–6800; Mary K. Noren, Chief Executive Officer **A**1 10 **F**20 52 54 55 56	12	22	64	135	44	—	—	4343	3357	107
CHEVERLY—Prince George's County										
⊞ PRINCE GEORGE'S HOSPITAL CENTER, 3001 Hospital Drive, Zip 20785–1189; tel. 301/618–2000; Allan Earl Atzrott, President **A**1 3 5 9 10 **F**2 3 4 7 8 10 11 12 14 15 16 17 18 19 20 21 22 24 25 26 27 28 29 30 31 32 34 35 36 37 38 39 40 41 42 43 44 45 46 49 51 52 53 54 56 58 59 60 63 65 67 68 70 71 72 73 74 **P**1 7 **S** Dimensions Health Corporation, Largo, MD **N** Dimensions HealthCare System, Largo, MD	23	10	370	15373	240	120096	3158	137027	67495	1632
CLINTON—Prince George's County										
⊞ SOUTHERN MARYLAND HOSPITAL, 7503 Surratts Road, Zip 20735–3395; tel. 301/868–8000; Francis P. Chiaramonte, M.D., Chief Executive Officer (Total facility includes 20 beds in nursing home–type unit) (Nonreporting) **A**1 2 9 10	33	10	260	—	—	—	—	—	—	—
COLUMBIA—Howard County										
⊞ HOWARD COUNTY GENERAL HOSPITAL, 5755 Cedar Lane, Zip 21044–2999; tel. 410/740–7890; Victor A. Broccolino, President and Chief Executive Officer (Nonreporting) **A**1 2 5 9 10 **S** Johns Hopkins Health System, Baltimore, MD	23	10	182	—	—	—	—	—	—	—
CRISFIELD—Somerset County										
□ EDWARD W. MCCREADY MEMORIAL HOSPITAL, 201 Hall Highway, Zip 21817–1299; tel. 410/968–1200; J. Allan Bickling, Chief Executive Officer (Nonreporting) **A**1 9 10	23	10	45	—	—	—	—	—	—	—
CROWNSVILLE—Anne Arundel County										
□ CROWNSVILLE HOSPITAL CENTER, 1520 Crownsville Road, Zip 21032–2306; tel. 410/729–6000; James L. Collins, M.D., Clinical Director' (Nonreporting) **A**1 9 10	12	22	248	—	—	—	—	—	—	—
CUMBERLAND—Allegany County										
⊞ △ MEMORIAL HOSPITAL AND MEDICAL CENTER OF CUMBERLAND, 600 Memorial Avenue, Zip 21502–3797; tel. 301/723–4000; Thomas C. Dowdell, Executive Director **A**1 2 7 9 10 **F**1 5 7 8 10 11 12 14 15 16 17 18 19 20 21 22 24 26 27 28 29 30 31 32 33 34 35 36 37 39 40 41 42 44 45 48 49 51 52 54 55 56 57 58 59 60 64 65 66 67 70 71 72 73	23	10	222	8588	123	67743	551	66971	30678	836
⊞ SACRED HEART HOSPITAL, 900 Seton Drive, Zip 21502–1874; tel. 301/759–4200; William T. Bradel, Executive Director (Total facility includes 32 beds in nursing home–type unit) **A**1 2 9 10 **F**1 3 7 8 10 12 13 14 15 16 17 18 19 21 22 24 25 26 27 28 30 31 32 33 34 35 36 37 39 40 41 42 44 45 46 49 51 52 53 55 56 57 58 59 60 61 64 65 66 67 70 71 73 74 **S** Daughters of Charity National Health System, Saint Louis, MO	23	10	272	8988	176	80739	624	63869	30065	871
□ THOMAS B. FINAN CENTER, Country Club Road, Zip 21501, Mailing Address: P.O. Box 1722, Zip 21501–1722; tel. 301/777–2240; Archie T. Wallace, Chief Executive Officer **A**1 9 10 **F**14 15 16 52 53 54 55 57	12	22	114	365	99	—	0	—	—	240
EAST NEW MARKET—Dorchester County										
CHARTER BEHAVIORAL HEALTH SYSTEM AT WARWICK MANOR, 3680 Warwick Road, Zip 21631–1420; tel. 410/943–8108; Marie McBee, Chief Executive Officer (Nonreporting) **A**9	33	82	42	—	—	—	—	—	—	—
EASTON—Talbot County										
⊞ MEMORIAL HOSPITAL AT EASTON MARYLAND, 219 South Washington Street, Zip 21601–2996; tel. 410/822–1000; Joseph P. Ross, President and Chief Executive Officer (Total facility includes 31 beds in nursing home–type unit) **A**1 2 6 9 10 **F**3 7 8 10 12 14 15 16 17 19 20 21 22 23 25 26 27 28 29 30 31 32 33 34 35 37 39 40 41 42 44 45 49 54 56 57 58 59 60 62 63 64 65 67 70 71 72 73 74 **P**3 5 7	23	10	164	8051	88	339402	846	67215	25609	1043
ELKTON—Cecil County										
⊞ UNION HOSPITAL, 106 Bow Street, Zip 21921–5596; tel. 410/398–4000; Michael V. Sack, President and Chief Executive Officer **A**1 9 10 **F**1 7 8 12 14 15 16 17 19 21 22 25 28 29 30 31 34 35 37 40 41 44 45 49 52 54 56 65 66 71 73 **P**5 7	23	10	105	6251	64	103225	589	43323	17837	545

Hospital, Address, Telephone, Administrator, Approval, Facility, and Physician Codes, Health Care System, Network	Classi-fication Codes		Utilization Data					Expense (thousands) of dollars		
	Control	Service	Staffed Beds	Admissions	Census	Outpatient Visits	Births	Total	Payroll	Personnel

★ American Hospital Association (AHA) membership
☐ Joint Commission on Accreditation of Healthcare Organizations (JCAHO) accreditation
+ American Osteopathic Healthcare Association (AOHA) membership
○ American Osteopathic Association (AOA) accreditation
△ Commission on Accreditation of Rehabilitation Facilities (CARF) accreditation
Control codes 61, 63, 64, 71, 72 and 73 indicate hospitals listed by AOHA, but not registered by AHA. For definition of numerical codes, see page A4

ELLICOTT CITY—Howard County

☐ TAYLOR MANOR HOSPITAL, 4100 College Avenue, Zip 21043–5506, Mailing Address: P.O. Box 396, Zip 21041–0396; tel. 410/465–3322; Morris L. Scherr, Executive Vice President **A**1 9 10 **F**14 15 16 19 21 34 35 46 50 52 53 55 56 57 58 59 63 65 71 **P**6	33	22	125	1252	73	5462	—	10283	6430	204

EMMITSBURG—Frederick County

MOUNTAIN MANOR TREATMENT CENTER, Route 15, Zip 21727, Mailing Address: Box E., Zip 21727; tel. 301/447–2361; William J. Roby, Executive Vice President (Nonreporting)	33	82	140	—	—	—	—	—	—	—

FALLSTON—Harford County

✠ FALLSTON GENERAL HOSPITAL, 200 Milton Avenue, Zip 21047–2777; tel. 410/877–3700; Lyle Ernest Sheldon, Executive Vice President and Chief Operating Officer **A**1 9 10 **F**7 8 10 11 12 14 15 16 17 18 19 21 22 24 25 28 29 30 32 33 35 37 40 41 44 45 46 49 52 54 55 56 57 58 63 65 67 71 72 73 **P**3 7 **S** Upper Chesapeake Health System, Fallston, MD	23	10	115	6544	73	42125	0	40087	16625	516

FORT HOWARD—Baltimore County

✠ VA MARYLAND HEALTH CARE SYSTEM—FORT HOWARD DIVISION, 9600 North Point Road, Zip 21052–9989; tel. 410/477–1800; Dennis H. Smith, Director (Total facility includes 47 beds in nursing home–type unit) (Nonreporting) **A**1 5 9 **S** Department of Veterans Affairs, Washington, DC	45	10	245	—	—	—	—	—	—	—

FORT WASHINGTON—Prince George's County

✠ FORT WASHINGTON HOSPITAL, 11711 Livingston Road, Zip 20744–5164; tel. 301/292–7000; Theodore M. Lewis, President (Nonreporting) **A**1 9 10 **S** Greater Southeast Healthcare System, Washington, DC	23	50	35	—	—	—	—	—	—	—

FREDERICK—Frederick County

✠ FREDERICK MEMORIAL HOSPITAL, 400 West Seventh Street, Zip 21701–4593; tel. 301/698–3300; James K. Kluttz, President and Chief Executive Officer (Total facility includes 19 beds in nursing home–type unit) **A**1 2 9 10 **F**7 8 10 11 12 13 14 15 16 17 18 19 20 21 22 25 28 29 30 31 32 33 34 35 37 39 40 41 42 44 45 46 48 49 52 53 54 55 56 58 59 60 63 64 65 66 67 71 72 73 74 **P**1 5	23	10	179	13262	151	276258	—	98703	47539	1373

GLEN BURNIE—Anne Arundel County

✠ NORTH ARUNDEL HOSPITAL, 301 Hospital Drive, Zip 21061–5899; tel. 410/787–4000; James R. Walker, FACHE, President and Chief Executive Officer **A**1 9 10 **F**6 7 8 10 11 12 14 15 16 17 19 21 22 26 27 28 29 30 31 32 34 37 39 41 42 44 49 51 52 54 55 56 57 59 65 66 67 71 72 73 74 **P**2 7 8	23	10	314	14716	180	64852	0	107991	47108	1495

HAGERSTOWN—Washington County

☐ BROOK LANE PSYCHIATRIC CENTER, 13218 Brook Lane Drive, Zip 21742–1945, Mailing Address: P.O. Box 1945, Zip 21742–1945; tel. 301/733–0330; R. Lynn Rushing, Chief Executive Officer **A**1 9 10 **F**1 3 14 15 16 25 26 34 39 46 52 53 54 55 56 57 58 59 65 **P**5	23	22	65	1171	25	23002	—	7718	4797	171
✠ △ WASHINGTON COUNTY HOSPITAL ASSOCIATION, 251 East Antietam Street, Zip 21740–5771; tel. 301/790–8000; Horace W. Murphy, President and Chief Executive Officer (Total facility includes 47 beds in nursing home–type unit) **A**1 2 7 9 10 **F**3 4 7 8 10 11 14 15 16 17 18 19 21 22 23 25 26 28 29 30 31 32 33 34 35 36 37 39 40 41 42 44 45 46 48 49 51 52 54 55 56 58 59 60 61 63 64 65 66 67 70 71 73 74 **P**6 8	23	10	333	14919	213	168358	1611	115500	58155	—
☐ WESTERN MARYLAND CENTER, 1500 Pennsylvania Avenue, Zip 21742–3194; tel. 301/791–4400; Cynthia Miller Pellegrino, Director and Chief Executive Officer (Total facility includes 60 beds in nursing home–type unit) (Nonreporting) **A**1 9 10	12	48	120	—	—	—	—	—	—	—

HAVRE DE GRACE—Harford County

✠ HARFORD MEMORIAL HOSPITAL, 501 South Union Avenue, Zip 21078–3493; tel. 410/939–2400; Lyle Ernest Sheldon, President and Chief Executive Officer **A**1 9 10 **F**3 4 7 8 10 11 12 14 15 16 17 18 19 21 22 23 24 27 28 29 30 31 32 33 35 37 40 42 44 45 46 49 52 54 55 56 57 58 63 65 67 71 73 **P**3 7 **S** Upper Chesapeake Health System, Fallston, MD	23	10	168	6828	68	49370	733	39760	17515	565

HYATTSVILLE—Prince George's County

☐ GLADYS SPELLMAN SPECIALTY HOSPITAL AND NURSING CENTER, 2900 Mercy Lane, Zip 20785–1157; tel. 301/618–2010; Hattie Courtney, Administrator (Nonreporting) **A**1	33	48	30	—	—	—	—	—	—	—

JESSUP—Anne Arundel County

☐ CLIFTON T. PERKINS HOSPITAL CENTER, 8450 Dorsey Run Road, Zip 20794–9486, Mailing Address: P.O. Box 1000, Zip 20794–1000; tel. 410/724–3000; M. Richard Fragala, M.D., Superintendent (Nonreporting) **A**1 3 9	12	22	200	—	—	—	—	—	—	—

LA PLATA—Charles County

✠ CIVISTA MEDICAL CENTER, (Formerly Physicians Memorial Hospital), 701 East Charles Street, Zip 20646, Mailing Address: P.O. Box 1070, Zip 20646–1070; tel. 301/609–4000; Susan L. Hunsaker, CHE, President and Chief Executive Officer (Nonreporting) **A**1 2 9 10	23	10	110	—	—	—	—	—	—	—

LANHAM—Prince George's County

✠ DOCTORS COMMUNITY HOSPITAL, 8118 Good Luck Road, Zip 20706–3596; tel. 301/552–8085; Philip Down, President (Total facility includes 17 beds in nursing home–type unit) **A**1 9 10 **F**4 8 10 11 12 14 16 17 19 21 22 28 29 30 32 34 37 39 41 42 44 45 49 60 64 65 67 71 73	23	10	131	8427	134	72080	—	72024	28858	779

Hospital, Address, Telephone, Administrator, Approval, Facility, and Physician Codes, Health Care System, Network	Classi-fication Codes		Utilization Data					Expense (thousands) of dollars		
★ American Hospital Association (AHA) membership □ Joint Commission on Accreditation of Healthcare Organizations (JCAHO) accreditation + American Osteopathic Healthcare Association (AOHA) membership ○ American Osteopathic Association (AOA) accreditation △ Commission on Accreditation of Rehabilitation Facilities (CARF) accreditation Control codes 61, 63, 64, 71, 72 and 73 indicate hospitals listed by AOHA, but not registered by AHA. For definition of numerical codes, see page A4	Control	Service	Staffed Beds	Admissions	Census	Outpatient Visits	Births	Total	Payroll	Personnel

LAUREL—Prince George's County

★ △ LAUREL REGIONAL HOSPITAL, 7300 Van Dusen Road, Zip 20707–9266; tel. 301/725–4300; Patrick F. Mutch, President **A**1 7 9 10 **F**2 3 4 5 7 8 10 11 12 15 17 18 19 20 21 22 23 25 26 28 29 30 31 32 33 34 35 36 37 38 39 40 41 42 43 44 45 46 47 48 49 51 52 53 54 55 56 57 58 59 64 65 67 68 69 70 71 72 73 74 **P**1 6 7 **S** Dimensions Health Corporation, Largo, MD **N** Dimensions HealthCare System, Largo, MD	23	10	185	6399	100	43949	788	53991	25436	604

LEONARDTOWN—St. Marys County

★ ST. MARY'S HOSPITAL, 25500 Point Lookout Road, Zip 20650, Mailing Address: P.O. Box 527, Zip 20650; tel. 301/475–6001; Christine R. Wray, Chief Executive Officer **A**1 2 9 10 **F**7 8 12 15 16 17 18 19 22 23 26 28 29 30 31 32 34 35 37 39 40 41 42 44 45 46 49 52 53 54 55 56 57 58 59 65 67 71 73 74 **P**2	23	10	100	5462	60	148757	825	34714	16140	508

OAKLAND—Garrett County

★ GARRETT COUNTY MEMORIAL HOSPITAL, 251 North Fourth Street, Zip 21550–1334; tel. 301/334–2155; Walter P. Donalson, III, President and Chief Executive Officer **A**1 9 10 **F**7 8 14 15 16 17 18 19 20 21 22 28 30 33 34 36 37 39 40 44 45 46 49 54 57 58 63 65 67 71 73 **P**3	23	10	76	3092	31	61155	301	20135	9677	280

OLNEY—Montgomery County

★ MONTGOMERY GENERAL HOSPITAL, 18101 Prince Philip Drive, Zip 20832–1512; tel. 301/774–8882; Peter W. Monge, President and Chief Executive Officer **A**1 2 9 10 **F**1 2 3 7 8 11 12 15 17 18 19 21 22 26 27 28 29 32 35 36 37 39 40 41 42 44 49 51 52 56 57 58 59 60 63 64 65 67 68 71 73 74 **P**1 6 7 **N** Maryland Health Network, Columbia, MD	23	10	170	7882	111	30616	1119	59741	29290	988

PATUXENT RIVER—St. Marys County

★ NAVAL HOSPITAL, 47149 Buse Road, Zip 20670–5370; tel. 301/342–1460; Captain Ralph A. Puckett, M.D., USN, Commanding Officer (Nonreporting) **A**9 **S** Department of Navy, Washington, DC	43	10	5	—	—	—	—	—	—	—

PERRY POINT—Cecil County

★ VETERANS AFFAIRS MARYLAND HEALTH CARE SYSTEM–PERRY POINT DIVISION, Circle Drive, Zip 21902; tel. 410/642–2411; Dennis H. Smith, Director (Total facility includes 80 beds in nursing home–type unit) (Nonreporting) **A**1 5 9 **S** Department of Veterans Affairs, Washington, DC	45	22	526	—	—	—	—	—	—	—

PRINCE FREDERICK—Calvert County

★ CALVERT MEMORIAL HOSPITAL, 100 Hospital Road, Zip 20678–9675; tel. 410/535–4000; James J. Xinis, President and Chief Executive Officer (Total facility includes 16 beds in nursing home–type unit) **A**1 2 9 10 **F**1 8 13 14 15 16 17 18 19 22 25 28 29 30 32 33 35 36 37 39 40 41 42 44 45 46 49 52 53 54 55 59 65 66 67 71 72 73 74 **P**7 8	23	10	125	5540	60	42313	784	31658	15695	434

RANDALLSTOWN—Baltimore County

★ NORTHWEST HOSPITAL CENTER, 5401 Old Court Road, Zip 21133–5185; tel. 410/521–2200; Robert W. Fischer, President (Total facility includes 17 beds in nursing home–type unit) **A**1 2 9 10 **F**8 12 14 15 17 19 21 22 28 29 30 34 35 37 41 44 46 49 63 65 67 71 72 73 **P**1 7 **N** Maryland Health Network, Columbia, MD	23	10	177	10857	157	61588	—	87519	40749	1020

ROCKVILLE—Montgomery County

□ CHARTER BEHAVIORAL HEALTH SYSTEM OF MARYLAND AT POTOMAC RIDGE, 14901 Broschart Road, Zip 20850–3321; tel. 301/251–4500; Craig S. Juengling, Chief Executive Officer (Nonreporting) **A**1 9 10 **S** Magellan Health Services, Atlanta, GA	33	22	140	—	—	—	—	—	—	—
★ CHESTNUT LODGE HOSPITAL, 500 West Montgomery Avenue, Zip 20850–3892; tel. 301/424–8300; Steven Goldstein, Ph.D., President and Chief Executive Officer (Nonreporting) **A**1 9 10 **S** Community Psychiatric Centers	33	22	50	—	—	—	—	—	—	—
□ SHADY GROVE ADVENTIST HOSPITAL, 9901 Medical Center Drive, Zip 20850–3395; tel. 301/279–6000; Cory Chambers, President and Chief Executive Officer **A**1 9 10 **F**1 3 4 6 7 8 10 12 13 14 15 16 17 19 21 22 23 24 25 26 27 28 29 30 31 32 34 35 37 38 39 40 41 42 43 44 45 46 47 49 51 53 54 55 56 57 58 59 60 63 64 65 67 69 71 72 73	21	10	253	16116	175	116261	4388	—	44326	2988

SALISBURY—Wicomico County

□ DEER'S HEAD CENTER, (LONG TERM CARE), 351 Deer's Head Hospital Road, Zip 21802, Mailing Address: P.O. Box 2018, Zip 21802–2018; tel. 410/543–4000; Dorothy A. Bradshaw, Director (Total facility includes 68 beds in nursing home–type unit) **A**1 10 **F**4 8 10 11 14 15 16 19 20 21 22 26 28 29 30 31 33 35 37 42 44 45 46 48 49 52 53 54 55 56 57 58 60 65 67 69 71 73 74 **P**6	12	48	80	69	67	21852	—	11778	6391	273
□ △ HEALTHSOUTH CHESAPEAKE REHABILITATION HOSPITAL, 220 Tilghman Road, Zip 21804–1921; tel. 410/546–4600; William Roth, Chief Executive Officer **A**1 7 9 10 **F**14 48 49 **S** HEALTHSOUTH Corporation, Birmingham, AL	33	46	44	730	37	14954	—	9204	4551	122
★ PENINSULA REGIONAL MEDICAL CENTER, 100 East Carroll Street, Zip 21801–5422; tel. 410/546–6400; R. Alan Newberry, President and Chief Executive Officer **A**1 2 9 10 **F**4 7 8 10 11 12 13 14 15 16 17 19 20 21 22 23 24 25 26 28 29 30 31 32 34 35 37 39 40 41 42 43 44 45 51 52 54 56 57 58 60 64 65 67 70 71 72 73 **P**5 6	23	10	370	17031	223	420463	2014	131632	59131	1689

SILVER SPRING—Montgomery County

★ HOLY CROSS HOSPITAL OF SILVER SPRING, 1500 Forest Glen Road, Zip 20910–1484; tel. 301/754–7000; Cornelius McKelvey, Interim Chief Executive Officer **A**1 3 5 8 9 10 **F**1 2 4 7 8 9 10 11 12 13 15 16 17 18 19 21 22 25 28 29 30 32 33 34 35 36 37 38 39 40 42 43 44 45 46 47 51 52 53 54 55 56 57 58 59 60 63 64 65 66 67 69 71 73 74 **P**1 7 **S** Holy Cross Health System Corporation, South Bend, IN **N** Maryland Health Network, Columbia, MD	21	10	454	23536	285	203910	6563	163114	65531	1899

Hospital, Address, Telephone, Administrator, Approval, Facility, and Physician Codes, Health Care System, Network	Classi-fication Codes		Utilization Data					Expense (thousands) of dollars		
★ American Hospital Association (AHA) membership □ Joint Commission on Accreditation of Healthcare Organizations (JCAHO) accreditation + American Osteopathic Healthcare Association (AOHA) membership ○ American Osteopathic Association (AOA) accreditation △ Commission on Accreditation of Rehabilitation Facilities (CARF) accreditation Control codes 61, 63, 64, 71, 72 and 73 indicate hospitals listed by AOHA, but not registered by AHA. For definition of numerical codes, see page A4	Control	Service	Staffed Beds	Admissions	Census	Outpatient Visits	Births	Total	Payroll	Personnel
★ SAINT LUKE INSTITUTE, 8901 New Hampshire Avenue, Zip 20903–3611; tel. 301/445–7970; Father Stephen J. Rossetti, Ph.D., President and Chief Executive Officer (Nonreporting)	23	22	24	—	—	—	—	—	—	—
SYKESVILLE—Carroll County										
□ SPRINGFIELD HOSPITAL CENTER, 6655 Sykesville Road, Zip 21784–7966; tel. 410/795–2100; Paula A. Langmead, Superintendent **A**1 9 10 **F**14 16 41 45 52 55 57 65 67	12	22	328	620	318	—	—	—	—	846
TAKOMA PARK—Montgomery County										
⊞ WASHINGTON ADVENTIST HOSPITAL, 7600 Carroll Avenue, Zip 20912–6392; tel. 301/891–7600; Kiltie Leach, Chief Operating Officer (Nonreporting) **A**1 9 10	21	10	300	—	—	—	—	—	—	—
TOWSON—Baltimore County										
⊞ ST. JOSEPH MEDICAL CENTER, 7620 York Road, Zip 21204–7582; tel. 410/337–1000; Rene Kessler, Executive Vice President and Chief Operating Officer (Total facility includes 26 beds in nursing home–type unit) **A**1 9 10 **F**4 5 7 8 10 11 12 13 14 15 16 17 18 19 20 21 22 23 24 25 26 28 29 30 31 32 33 34 35 37 38 39 40 41 42 43 44 45 46 49 51 52 54 55 56 57 58 59 60 63 65 67 71 72 73 74 **P**2 5 7 **S** Catholic Health Initiatives, Denver, CO	21	10	460	20299	277	174098	2034	164495	68806	1893
WESTMINSTER—Carroll County										
⊞ CARROLL COUNTY GENERAL HOSPITAL, 200 Memorial Avenue, Zip 21157–5799; tel. 410/871–6900; John M. Sernulka, President and Chief Executive Officer **A**1 9 10 **F**7 8 10 11 12 15 16 19 22 32 33 35 37 40 44 46 52 53 54 56 59 65 67 70 71 **P**3 7	23	10	158	9220	115	83098	940	59466	27188	850

MASSACHUSETTS

Resident population 6,118 (in thousands)
Resident population in metro areas 96.1%
Birth rate per 1,000 population 13.9
65 years and over 14.1%
Percent of persons without health insurance 12.4%

Hospital, Address, Telephone, Administrator, Approval, Facility, and Physician Codes, Health Care System, Network	Classi-fication Codes		Utilization Data					Expense (thousands) of dollars		
★ American Hospital Association (AHA) membership ☐ Joint Commission on Accreditation of Healthcare Organizations (JCAHO) accreditation + American Osteopathic Healthcare Association (AOHA) membership ○ American Osteopathic Association (AOA) accreditation △ Commission on Accreditation of Rehabilitation Facilities (CARF) accreditation Control codes 61, 63, 64, 71, 72 and 73 indicate hospitals listed by AOHA, but not registered by AHA. For definition of numerical codes, see page A4	Control	Service	Staffed Beds	Admissions	Census	Outpatient Visits	Births	Total	Payroll	Personnel

AMHERST—Hampshire County

☐ UNIVERSITY HEALTH SERVICES, University of Massachusetts, Zip 01003–4310; tel. 413/577–5000; Bernette A. Melby, Executive Director (Nonreporting) **A**3 10 | 12 | 11 | 6 | — | — | — | — | — | — | —

ANDOVER—Essex County

ISHAM HEALTH CENTER, Phillips Academy, Zip 01810–4161; tel. 978/749–4455; Nneka Anaebonam, Administrator (Nonreporting) | 23 | 59 | 20 | — | — | — | — | — | — | —

ARLINGTON—Middlesex County

☐ SYMMES HOSPITAL AND MEDICAL CENTER, (Formerly Medical Center at Symmes), Hospital Road, Zip 02174–2199; tel. 781/646–1500; Peter D. Goldbach, M.D., Chief Executive Officer (Nonreporting) **A**1 9 10 | 23 | 10 | 88 | — | — | — | — | — | — | —

ATHOL—Worcester County

☐ ATHOL MEMORIAL HOSPITAL, 2033 Main Street, Zip 01331–3598; tel. 978/249–3511; William DiFederico, President **A**1 9 10 **F**8 15 16 17 19 20 22 29 30 31 32 33 34 37 39 41 42 44 45 46 49 53 54 58 65 67 71 73 **P**5 8 **N** Fallon Healthcare System, Worcester, MA | 23 | 10 | 46 | 1488 | 19 | 36978 | — | 14537 | 7509 |

ATTLEBORO—Bristol County

✠ STURDY MEMORIAL HOSPITAL, 211 Park Street, Zip 02703–3137, Mailing Address: P.O. Box 2963, Zip 02703–2963; tel. 508/222–5200; Linda Shyavitz, President and Chief Executive Officer **A**1 2 9 10 **F**7 8 12 13 15 16 17 18 19 20 21 22 23 25 26 28 29 30 31 33 34 35 37 39 40 41 42 44 45 46 49 51 54 61 63 65 67 68 71 72 73 74 **P**5 | 23 | 10 | 100 | 5335 | 62 | 172105 | 806 | 53578 | 28592 | 663

AYER—Middlesex County

✠ DEACONESS–NASHOBA HOSPITAL, 200 Groton Road, Zip 01432–3300; tel. 978/784–9000; Jeffrey R. Kelly, President and Chief Executive Officer **A**1 9 10 **F**1 2 3 4 5 7 8 10 11 12 13 14 15 16 17 18 19 20 21 22 23 24 25 26 27 28 29 30 31 32 33 34 35 36 37 38 39 40 41 42 43 44 45 46 47 49 51 52 53 54 55 56 57 58 59 60 61 63 64 65 66 67 68 69 70 71 72 73 74 **P**5 **S** CareGroup, Boston, MA **N** CareGroup, Boston, MA; Fallon Healthcare System, Worcester, MA | 23 | 10 | 49 | 1911 | 21 | 83102 | — | 22059 | 10595 | 300

BEDFORD—Middlesex County

✠ EDITH NOURSE ROGERS MEMORIAL VETERANS HOSPITAL, (PSHCGUATRIC AND LONG TERM CARE), 200 Springs Road, Zip 01730–1198; tel. 781/687–2000; William A. Conte, Director (Total facility includes 225 beds in nursing home–type unit) **A**1 3 5 9 **F**1 2 3 4 8 9 10 11 12 17 19 20 21 22 23 26 27 28 30 31 32 33 35 37 39 40 41 42 43 44 45 46 48 49 50 51 52 54 55 56 57 58 59 60 63 64 65 67 69 71 73 74 **P**6 **S** Department of Veterans Affairs, Washington, DC | 45 | 49 | 608 | 2173 | 563 | 177524 | — | — | — | 1093

BELMONT—Middlesex County

✠ MCLEAN HOSPITAL, 115 Mill Street, Zip 02178–9106; tel. 617/855–2000; Bruce M. Cohen, M.D., President and Psychiatrist–in–Chief (Nonreporting) **A**1 3 5 9 10 **S** Partners HealthCare System, Inc., Boston, MA | 23 | 22 | 161 | — | — | — | — | — | — | —

BEVERLY—Essex County

✠ BEVERLY HOSPITAL, (Includes Addison Gilbert Hospital, 298 Washington Street, Gloucester, Zip 01930–4887; tel. 978/283–4000; Robert L. Shafner, President), 85 Herrrick Street, Zip 01915–1777; tel. 978/922–3000; Robert R. Fanning, Jr., Chief Executive Officer **A**1 2 3 9 10 **F**1 2 3 5 6 7 8 10 11 12 14 15 16 17 18 19 22 23 26 28 29 30 31 32 33 34 35 36 37 39 40 41 42 44 45 46 48 49 51 52 53 54 55 56 57 58 59 60 61 62 64 65 66 67 68 69 71 73 74 **P**1 6 **N** Northeast Health Systems, Beverly, MA | 23 | 10 | 364 | 14286 | 217 | — | 2781 | 126222 | 51378 | 1626

BOSTON—Suffolk County

☐ ARBOUR HOSPITAL, 49 Robinwood Avenue, Zip 02130–2156, Mailing Address: P.O. Box 9, Zip 02130; tel. 617/522–4400; Roy A. Ettlinger, Chief Executive Officer (Nonreporting) **A**1 9 10 **S** Universal Health Services, Inc., King of Prussia, PA | 33 | 22 | 118 | — | — | — | — | — | — | —

✠ BETH ISRAEL DEACONESS MEDICAL CENTER, 330 Brookline Avenue, Zip 02215–5491; tel. 617/667–2000; David Dolins, President (Total facility includes 48 beds in nursing home–type unit) **A**1 2 3 5 8 9 10 **F**1 2 3 4 5 7 8 10 11 12 13 14 15 16 17 18 19 20 21 22 23 24 25 26 27 28 29 30 31 32 33 34 35 36 37 38 39 40 41 42 43 44 45 46 47 49 51 52 53 54 55 56 57 58 59 60 61 63 64 65 66 67 68 69 70 71 72 73 74 **P**2 3 4 5 6 7 8 **S** CareGroup, Boston, MA **N** CareGroup, Boston, MA; Fallon Healthcare System, Worcester, MA | 23 | 10 | 656 | 55352 | 505 | 309322 | 5047 | 683158 | 223358 | 7615

✠ BOSTON MEDICAL CENTER, One Boston Medical Center Place, Zip 02118–2393; tel. 617/638–8000; Elaine S. Ullian, President and Chief Executive Officer (Total facility includes 17 beds in nursing home–type unit) **A**1 2 3 5 8 9 10 **F**1 3 4 5 6 7 8 10 11 12 13 14 15 16 17 18 19 20 21 22 23 24 25 26 27 28 29 30 31 32 33 34 35 36 37 38 39 40 41 42 43 44 45 46 47 48 49 51 52 53 54 55 56 57 58 59 60 61 62 63 64 65 67 68 69 70 71 72 73 74 **P**3 4 5 6 8 **N** New England Health Partnership, Waltham, MA | 23 | 10 | 362 | 19661 | 337 | 510133 | 1567 | 506319 | 152761 | 3911

Hospital, Address, Telephone, Administrator, Approval, Facility, and Physician Codes, Health Care System, Network	Classi-fication Codes		Utilization Data					Expense (thousands) of dollars		
	Control	Service	Staffed Beds	Admissions	Census	Outpatient Visits	Births	Total	Payroll	Personnel

★ American Hospital Association (AHA) membership
□ Joint Commission on Accreditation of Healthcare Organizations (JCAHO) accreditation
+ American Osteopathic Healthcare Association (AOHA) membership
○ American Osteopathic Association (AOA) accreditation
△ Commission on Accreditation of Rehabilitation Facilities (CARF) accreditation
Control codes 61, 63, 64, 71, 72 and 73 indicate hospitals listed by AOHA, but not registered by AHA. For definition of numerical codes, see page A4

Hospital, Address, Telephone, Administrator, Approval, Facility, and Physician Codes, Health Care System, Network	Control	Service	Staffed Beds	Admissions	Census	Outpatient Visits	Births	Total	Payroll	Personnel
✠ BRIGHAM AND WOMEN'S HOSPITAL, 75 Francis Street, Zip 02115–6195; tel. 617/732–5500; Jeffrey Otten, President **A**1 2 3 5 8 9 10 **F**2 3 4 5 7 8 9 10 11 12 13 14 15 16 17 18 19 20 21 22 23 24 25 26 27 28 29 30 31 32 33 34 35 37 38 39 40 41 42 43 44 45 46 47 48 49 50 51 52 53 54 55 56 57 58 59 60 61 63 64 65 66 67 68 69 70 71 72 73 74 **P**1 3 5 6 7 8 **S** Partners HealthCare System, Inc., Boston, MA **N** Fallon Healthcare System, Worcester, MA; Partners HealthCare System, Boston, MA	23	10	617	39167	524	698483	8680	687142	257138	7418
✠ CARNEY HOSPITAL, 2100 Dorchester Avenue, Zip 02124–5666; tel. 617/296–4000; Joyce A. Murphy, President (Total facility includes 27 beds in nursing home–type unit) **A**1 2 3 5 9 10 **F**3 8 14 15 16 17 18 19 22 24 25 26 28 29 30 31 34 37 39 41 42 44 46 49 51 52 54 55 56 58 59 64 65 68 71 72 73 74 **P**4 5 6 **S** Caritas Christi Health Care, Boston, MA	21	10	216	8327	150	100747	—	89477	50672	1304
✠ CHILDREN'S HOSPITAL, 300 Longwood Avenue, Zip 02115–5737; tel. 617/355–6000; David Stephen Weiner, President **A**1 3 5 8 9 10 **F**10 11 12 13 15 16 17 19 21 23 29 30 34 35 38 39 41 42 43 44 45 46 47 49 50 51 52 53 54 55 56 58 60 61 63 65 66 67 68 69 70 71 72 73 **P**5 7 **N** Fallon Healthcare System, Worcester, MA; Children's Hospital, Boston, MA	23	50	325	18712	236	285441	—	363215	125300	3941
✠ DANA–FARBER CANCER INSTITUTE, (COMPREHENSIVE CANCER CENTER), 44 Binney Street, Zip 02115–6084; tel. 617/632–3000; David G. Nathan, M.D., President **A**1 3 9 10 **F**12 15 16 17 19 21 25 28 29 31 34 39 41 42 45 63 65 67 69 71 73 74 **N** Fallon Healthcare System, Worcester, MA	23	49	34	1003	24	70779	—	179363	69701	1354
✠ FAULKNER HOSPITAL, Mailing Address: 1153 Centre Sreet, Zip 02130–3400; tel. 617/983–7000; David J. Trull, President and Chief Executive Officer **A**1 2 3 5 8 9 10 **F**1 3 4 8 10 11 12 14 15 16 17 18 19 21 22 25 30 31 34 35 37 39 41 42 44 45 46 49 51 52 54 55 56 57 58 59 61 65 67 68 71 72 73 74 **P**5	23	10	130	5940	88	160645	—	65332	32236	791
□ FRANCISCAN CHILDREN'S HOSPITAL AND REHABILITATION CENTER, Mailing Address: 30 Warren Street, Zip 02135–3680; tel. 617/254–3800; Paul J. Dellarocco, President and Chief Executive Officer **A**1 5 10 **F**12 13 14 15 16 17 19 20 21 32 33 34 35 39 41 44 49 51 52 53 58 59 65 72 **P**5 6	23	58	100	413	39	15612	0	26418	14460	—
★ HEBREW REHABILITATION CENTER FOR AGED, (LTC, GERIATRIC), Mailing Address: 1200 Centre Street, Zip 02131–1097; tel. 617/325–8000; Maurice I. May, President (Nonreporting) **A**10	23	49	725	—	—	—	—	—	—	—
✠ JEWISH MEMORIAL HOSPITAL AND REHABILITATION CENTER, (CHRONIC DISEASE REHAB AND PSYC), 59 Townsend Street, Zip 02119–9918; tel. 617/442–8760; Donald E. Schwarz, President and Chief Executive Officer **A**1 3 5 9 10 **F**1 12 15 16 19 20 21 22 26 30 31 32 33 35 36 39 42 45 48 49 52 54 57 65 67 71 73 **P**6 8	23	49	110	985	100	9900	—	26236	13690	314
✠ LEMUEL SHATTUCK HOSPITAL, 170 Morton Street, Jamaica Plain, Zip 02130–3787; tel. 617/522–8110; Robert D. Wakefield, Jr., Executive Director (Nonreporting) **A**1 3 5 6 10 **S** Massachusetts Department of Mental Health, Boston, MA	12	10	230	—	—	—	—	—	—	—
□ MASSACHUSETTS EYE AND EAR INFIRMARY, 243 Charles Street, Zip 02114–3096; tel. 617/523–7900; F. Curtis Smith, President **A**1 3 5 9 10 **F**14 19 22 35 46 65 70 73 **P**8	23	45	63	1866	18	189449	—	77004	22873	1022
✠ MASSACHUSETTS GENERAL HOSPITAL, 55 Fruit Street, Zip 02114–2696; tel. 617/726–2000; James J. Mongan, M.D., President **A**1 2 3 5 8 9 10 **F**3 4 5 6 7 9 10 11 12 14 15 16 17 19 20 21 22 23 25 26 27 28 29 30 31 32 33 34 35 37 38 39 40 41 42 43 44 45 46 47 49 50 51 52 53 54 55 56 57 58 59 60 61 62 63 65 66 67 68 69 70 71 72 73 74 **P**3 4 8 **S** Partners HealthCare System, Inc., Boston, MA **N** Fallon Healthcare System, Worcester, MA; Partners HealthCare System, Boston, MA	23	10	819	34908	627	657777	2141	705037	290714	10902
MASSACHUSETTS MENTAL HEALTH CENTER, 74 Fenwood Road, Zip 02115–6196; tel. 617/734–1300; Jackie K. Moore, Ph.D., Chief Executive Officer (Nonreporting) **A**3 5 **S** Massachusetts Department of Mental Health, Boston, MA	12	22	27	—	—	—	—	—	—	—
✠ NEW ENGLAND BAPTIST HOSPITAL, 125 Parker Hill Avenue, Zip 02120–3297; tel. 617/754–5800; Alan H. Robbins, M.D., President (Total facility includes 18 beds in nursing home–type unit) **A**1 3 5 6 9 10 **F**1 2 3 4 5 7 8 10 11 12 13 15 16 17 18 19 20 21 22 23 24 25 26 27 28 29 30 31 32 33 34 35 37 38 39 40 41 42 43 44 45 46 48 49 50 51 52 53 54 55 56 57 58 59 60 61 62 63 64 65 66 67 68 69 70 71 72 73 74 **P**5 8 **S** CareGroup, Boston, MA **N** CareGroup, Boston, MA; Fallon Healthcare System, Worcester, MA	23	10	98	5989	98	—	—	85120	33598	1096
✠ NEW ENGLAND MEDICAL CENTER, 750 Washington Street, Zip 02111–1845; tel. 617/636–5000; Thomas F. O'Donnell, Jr., M.D., FACS, President and Chief Executive Officer (Total facility includes 21 beds in nursing home–type unit) **A**1 2 3 5 8 9 10 **F**3 4 5 7 8 10 11 12 13 15 16 17 18 19 20 21 22 23 25 26 27 28 29 30 31 34 35 37 38 39 40 41 42 43 44 45 46 47 49 51 52 53 54 55 56 57 58 59 60 61 63 64 65 66 67 68 69 70 71 73 74 **P**5 6 **S** Lifespan Corporation, Providence, RI **N** Lifespan, Providence, RI	23	10	349	14362	259	340588	1245	358273	142590	3989
✠ SHRINERS HOSPITALS FOR CHILDREN, SHRINERS BURNS HOSPITAL–BOSTON, (PEDIATRIC BURNS), 51 Blossom Street, Zip 02114–2699; tel. 617/722–3000; Robert F. Bories, Jr., FACHE, Administrator **A**1 3 **F**16 19 21 22 35 45 49 53 65 67 71 73 **S** Shriners Hospitals for Children, Tampa, FL	23	59	30	761	19	3421	—	—	—	246
✠ △ SPAULDING REHABILITATION HOSPITAL, 125 Nashua Street, Zip 02114–1198; tel. 617/573–7000; David E. Storto, Interim Chief Executive Officer (Total facility includes 37 beds in nursing home–type unit) **A**1 3 7 9 10 **F**2 3 12 17 19 20 21 22 25 26 27 28 29 30 32 34 35 39 41 45 46 48 49 50 53 54 55 56 57 58 60 63 64 65 66 71 73 **S** Partners HealthCare System, Inc., Boston, MA	23	46	284	4033	259	76395	—	—	—	1200

Hospital, Address, Telephone, Administrator, Approval, Facility, and Physician Codes, Health Care System, Network	Classi-fication Codes		Utilization Data					Expense (thousands) of dollars		
★ American Hospital Association (AHA) membership □ Joint Commission on Accreditation of Healthcare Organizations (JCAHO) accreditation + American Osteopathic Healthcare Association (AOHA) membership ○ American Osteopathic Association (AOA) accreditation △ Commission on Accreditation of Rehabilitation Facilities (CARF) accreditation Control codes 61, 63, 64, 71, 72 and 73 indicate hospitals listed by AOHA, but not registered by AHA. For definition of numerical codes, see page A4	Control	Service	Staffed Beds	Admissions	Census	Outpatient Visits	Births	Total	Payroll	Personnel
✠ ST. ELIZABETH'S MEDICAL CENTER OF BOSTON, 736 Cambridge Street, Zip 02135–2997; tel. 617/789–3000; Michael F. Collins, M.D., President (Total facility includes 17 beds in nursing home–type unit) **A**1 2 3 5 6 8 9 10 **F**1 2 3 4 7 8 10 11 12 14 15 16 17 18 19 20 21 22 23 25 26 28 29 30 31 32 33 34 35 37 38 39 40 41 42 43 44 45 46 49 51 52 54 55 56 57 58 59 60 61 64 65 66 67 70 71 72 73 74 **P**5 6 7 **S** Caritas Christi Health Care, Boston, MA **N** Caritas Christi Health Network, Boston, MA	21	10	238	13460	238	140874	1678	190702	78811	2353
□ VENCOR HOSPITAL–BOSTON, (ACUTE LONG TERM), 1515 Commonwealth Avenue, Zip 02135–3696; tel. 617/254–1100; Steven E. Levitsky, Administrator **A**1 10 **F**14 15 16 19 21 22 32 33 35 39 50 65 67 71 **S** Vencor, Incorporated, Louisville, KY	33	49	59	346	32	—	—	—	4757	129
✠ VETERANS AFFAIRS MEDICAL CENTER, Mailing Address: 150 South Huntington Avenue, Jamaica Plain Station, Zip 02130–4820; tel. 617/232–9500; Elwood J. Headley, M.D., Director **A**1 2 3 5 8 9 **F**3 5 8 10 11 15 18 19 20 21 22 24 25 27 28 29 30 31 32 33 34 35 37 39 41 42 44 45 46 49 51 52 54 55 56 58 60 64 65 67 69 71 73 74 **P**6 **S** Department of Veterans Affairs, Washington, DC	45	10	324	8033	239	369226	—	186566	97716	1846
BRAINTREE—Norfolk County										
✠ HEALTHSOUTH BRAINTREE REHABILITATION HOSPITAL, (Formerly Braintree Hospital), 250 Pond Street, Zip 02185–5391; tel. 781/848–5353; Ernest J. Broadbent, President and Chief Executive Officer **A**1 3 10 **F**5 12 19 27 35 41 42 46 48 49 50 54 64 65 66 67 71 73 **P**6 **S** HEALTHSOUTH Corporation, Birmingham, AL	33	46	187	2525	167	202438	—	64434	38870	1086
□ MASSACHUSETTS RESPIRATORY HOSPITAL, 2001 Washington Street, Zip 02184–8664; tel. 781/848–2600; Jay Mitchell, Chief Executive Officer **A**1 9 10 **F**28 30 32 34 36 39 41 46 49 52 54 59 64 65 67 73 **S** Quorum Health Group/Quorum Health Resources, Inc., Brentwood, TN	13	48	110	879	74	7000	—	20867	10699	264
BRIDGEWATER—Plymouth County										
BRIDGEWATER STATE HOSPITAL, 20 Administration Road, Zip 02324–3201; tel. 617/697–8161; Kenneth W. Nelson, Superintendent (Nonreporting)	12	22	350							
BRIGHTON—Suffolk County										
✠ ST. JOHN OF GOD HOSPITAL, 296 Allston Street, Zip 02146–1659; tel. 617/277–5750; William K. Brinkert, President (Nonreporting) **A**1 10 **S** Caritas Christi Health Care, Boston, MA **N** Caritas Christi Health Network, Boston, MA	21	48	31							
BROCKTON—Plymouth County										
✠ BROCKTON HOSPITAL, 680 Centre Street, Zip 02402–3395; tel. 508/941–7000; Norman B. Goodman, President and Chief Executive Officer (Total facility includes 26 beds in nursing home–type unit) **A**1 2 3 5 6 9 10 **F**3 4 7 8 10 11 12 13 14 15 16 17 18 19 21 22 23 26 28 29 30 31 32 33 34 35 37 39 40 41 42 44 46 49 51 52 53 54 55 56 57 58 59 60 63 64 65 66 67 71 72 73 74 **P**6 8	23	10	259	9888	145	94965	898	89605	—	1022
✠ BROCKTON–WEST ROXBURY VETERANS AFFAIRS MEDICAL CENTER, 940 Belmont Street, Zip 02401–5596; tel. 508/583–4500; Michael M. Lawson, Director (Total facility includes 149 beds in nursing home–type unit) (Nonreporting) **A**1 3 5 8 **S** Department of Veterans Affairs, Washington, DC	45	10	765							
✠ GOOD SAMARITAN MEDICAL CENTER, (Includes Good Samaritan Medical Center – Cushing Campus, 235 North Pearl Street, tel. 508/427–3000), 235 North Pearl Street, Zip 02401–1794; tel. 508/427–3000; Frank J. Larkin, President and Chief Executive Officer **A**1 2 5 9 10 **F**7 8 11 12 15 16 17 19 20 21 22 23 26 28 30 33 35 37 39 40 41 42 44 45 46 49 54 56 65 67 71 72 73 74 **P**5 **S** Caritas Christi Health Care, Boston, MA **N** Caritas Christi Health Network, Boston, MA	23	10	223	12058	155	—	1374	89416	40252	989
BROOKLINE—Norfolk County										
□ BOURNEWOOD HOSPITAL, 300 South Street, Zip 02167–3694; tel. 617/469–0300; Nasir A. Khan, M.D., Director **A**1 10 **F**2 3 14 15 16 26 34 52 53 54 55 56 57 58 59 65 67 **P**1	33	22	75	2374	61	2604	—	9200	5548	197
□ H. R. I. HOSPITAL, 227 Babcock Street, Zip 02146; tel. 617/731–3200; Roy A. Ettlinger, Chief Executive Officer (Nonreporting) **A**1 3 5 10 **S** Universal Health Services, Inc., King of Prussia, PA	33	22	51							
BURLINGTON—Middlesex County										
✠ LAHEY CLINIC, 41 Mall Road, Zip 01805–0001; tel. 781/744–5100; John A. Libertino, M.D., Chief Executive Officer **A**1 2 3 5 8 9 10 **F**4 5 8 10 11 12 13 14 15 16 17 18 19 21 22 23 25 26 27 28 29 30 31 32 34 35 37 39 41 42 43 44 45 46 48 49 51 52 53 54 55 56 57 58 60 61 63 64 65 66 67 69 70 71 72 73 74 **P**6 **N** Lahey Network, Burlington, MA; New England Health Partnership, Waltham, MA	23	10	298	14741	185	632454	—	234167	100416	2631
CAMBRIDGE—Middlesex County										
✠ CAMBRIDGE PUBLIC HEALTH COMMISSION, (Includes Cambridge Hospital, 1493 Cambridge Street, ; Somerville Hospital, 230 Highland Avenue, Somerville, Zip 02143; tel. 617/666–4400), 1493 Cambridge Street, Zip 02139–1099; tel. 617/498–1000; John G. O'Brien, Chief Executive Officer **A**1 3 5 6 9 10 **F**1 2 3 4 7 8 10 12 13 14 15 16 17 18 19 20 21 22 25 26 27 28 29 30 31 32 33 34 35 36 37 39 40 41 42 44 45 46 49 51 52 53 54 55 56 57 58 59 61 64 65 66 67 68 71 73 74 **P**6 8	16	10	275	9174	173	385856	621	146537	78612	1742
□ M. I. T. MEDICAL DEPARTMENT, 77 Massachusetts Avenue, Zip 02139–4307; tel. 617/253–4481; Arnold N. Weinberg, M.D., Director (Nonreporting) **A**1	23	11	18	—	—	—	—	—	—	—
✠ MOUNT AUBURN HOSPITAL, 330 Mount Auburn Street, Zip 02238; tel. 617/492–3500; Francis P. Lynch, President and Chief Executive Officer **A**1 2 3 5 8 9 10 **F**1 2 3 4 5 7 8 10 11 12 13 14 15 16 17 19 21 22 23 24 25 26 27 28 29 30 31 32 33 34 35 36 37 38 39 40 41 42 43 44 45 46 49 51 52 53 54 55 56 57 58 59 60 61 63 64 65 66 67 68 69 70 71 72 73 74 **P**5 6 7 **S** CareGroup, Boston, MA **N** CareGroup, Boston, MA	23	10	190	12386	128	122937	1217	125080	61576	1655

Hospital, Address, Telephone, Administrator, Approval, Facility, and Physician Codes, Health Care System, Network	Classi-fication Codes		Utilization Data					Expense (thousands) of dollars		
★ American Hospital Association (AHA) membership □ Joint Commission on Accreditation of Healthcare Organizations (JCAHO) accreditation + American Osteopathic Healthcare Association (AOHA) membership ○ American Osteopathic Association (AOA) accreditation △ Commission on Accreditation of Rehabilitation Facilities (CARF) accreditation Control codes 61, 63, 64, 71, 72 and 73 indicate hospitals listed by AOHA, but not registered by AHA. For definition of numerical codes, see page A4	Control	Service	Staffed Beds	Admissions	Census	Outpatient Visits	Births	Total	Payroll	Personnel

Hospital	Control	Service	Staffed Beds	Admissions	Census	Outpatient Visits	Births	Total	Payroll	Personnel
✠ STILLMAN INFIRMARY, HARVARD UNIVERSITY HEALTH SERVICES, 75 Mount Auburn Street, Zip 02138–4960; tel. 617/495–2010; David S. Rosenthal, M.D., Director (Nonreporting) **A**1 10	23	11	18	—	—	—	—	—	—	—
✠ △ YOUVILLE LIFECARE, 1575 Cambridge Street, Zip 02138–4398; tel. 617/876–4344; T. Richard Quigley, President and Chief Executive Officer (Total facility includes 140 beds in nursing home–type unit) **A**1 6 7 10 **F**6 12 15 16 17 26 30 34 42 48 49 51 54 57 64 65 67 73 **P**6 **S** Covenant Health Systems, Inc., Lexington, MA	21	46	286	2874	212	6800	0	45905	25112	617
CANTON—Norfolk County										
✠ MASSACHUSETTS HOSPITAL SCHOOL, 3 Randolph Street, Zip 02021–2397; tel. 781/828–2440; John H. Britt, Executive Director (Nonreporting) **A**1 5 10	12	56	110	—	—	—	—	—	—	—
CHELSEA—Suffolk County										
✠ LAWRENCE F. QUIGLEY MEMORIAL HOSPITAL, 91 Crest Avenue, Zip 02150–2199; tel. 617/884–5660; William D. Thompson, Commandant (Total facility includes 88 beds in nursing home–type unit) (Nonreporting) **A**1 10	12	49	159	—	—	—	—	—	—	—
CLINTON—Worcester County										
□ CLINTON HOSPITAL, 201 Highland Street, Zip 01510–1096; tel. 978/368–3000; Thomas Devins, Chief Executive Officer **A**1 5 9 10 **F**8 17 19 21 22 26 28 30 34 41 42 44 45 46 49 52 57 65 67 71 72 **P**6 8 **N** Fallon Healthcare System, Worcester, MA	23	10	44	1632	34	12172	—	11033	5705	193
CONCORD—Middlesex County										
✠ EMERSON HOSPITAL, 133 Old Road to Nine Acre Corner, Zip 01742–9120; tel. 978/369–1400; Geoffrey F. Cole, President and Chief Executive Officer (Nonreporting) **A**1 2 5 9 10	23	10	165	—	—	—	—	—	—	—
EVERETT—Middlesex County										
WHIDDEN MEMORIAL HOSPITAL See Hallmark Health System, Melrose										
FALL RIVER—Bristol County										
CHARLTON MEMORIAL HOSPITAL See Southcoast Hospitals Group										
✠ SAINT ANNE'S HOSPITAL, 795 Middle Street, Zip 02721–1798; tel. 508/674–5741; Michael W. Metzler, Acting President **A**1 2 9 10 **F**1 3 8 15 16 19 21 22 28 30 31 32 34 37 39 41 42 44 46 49 54 56 58 60 63 65 67 71 73 **P**3 5 6 7 **S** Caritas Christi Health Care, Boston, MA **N** Caritas Christi Health Network, Boston, MA	21	10	165	4755	76	151893	—	56146	23971	654
✠ △ SOUTHCOAST HOSPITALS GROUP, (Includes Charlton Memorial Hospital, 363 Highland Avenue, Zip 02720–3794; tel. 508/679–3131; St. Luke's Hospital of New Bedford, 101 Page Street, New Bedford, Zip 02740, Mailing Address: P.O. Box H–3000, Zip 02741–3000; tel. 508/997–1515; Tobey Hospital, 43 High Street, Wareham, Zip 02571; tel. 508/295–0880), 363 Highland Avenue, Zip 02720–3703; tel. 508/679–7013; Ronald B. Goodspeed, M.D., M.P.H., President **A**1 2 7 10 **F**3 4 6 7 8 10 11 12 13 14 15 16 17 18 19 21 22 23 24 25 26 28 29 30 31 32 33 34 35 37 39 40 41 42 44 45 46 48 49 52 54 55 56 57 58 59 60 61 63 64 65 66 67 68 71 72 73 74 **P**1 5 7	23	10	784	31512	500	587535	3665	284049	147410	—
FALMOUTH—Barnstable County										
✠ FALMOUTH HOSPITAL, 100 Ter Heun Drive, Zip 02540–2599; tel. 508/457–3500; Gail Freiswick, President and Chief Executive Officer **A**1 9 10 **F**1 3 4 6 7 8 10 12 14 15 16 17 19 21 22 23 26 27 28 29 30 31 32 33 35 37 40 41 42 44 46 48 49 52 56 58 59 60 64 65 67 71 72 73 74 **P**5 **S** Cape Cod Healthcare, Inc., Hyannis, MA **N** Cape Cod Healthcare, Inc., Hyannisport, MA	23	10	83	4825	—	53144	672	47087	21894	434
FITCHBURG—Worcester County										
HEALTH ALLIANCE–BURBANK HOSPITAL See Health Alliance Hospitals, Leominster										
FRAMINGHAM—Middlesex County										
✠ METROWEST MEDICAL CENTER, (Formerly Columbia MetroWest Medical Center), (Includes Framingham Union Hospital, 115 Lincoln Street, tel. 508/383–1000; Leonard Morse Hospital, 67 Union Street, Natick, Zip 01760; tel. 508/650–7000), 115 Lincoln Street, Zip 01702; tel. 508/383–1000; Thomas G. Hennessy, Chief Executive Officer (Nonreporting) **A**1 2 3 5 6 9 10 **S** Columbia/HCA Healthcare Corporation, Nashville, TN	33	10	398	—	—	—	—	—	—	—
GARDNER—Worcester County										
□ HEYWOOD HOSPITAL, 242 Green Street, Zip 01440–1373; tel. 978/632–3420; Daniel P. Moen, President and Chief Executive Officer **A**1 9 10 **F**1 3 5 7 8 12 15 16 17 18 19 21 22 24 25 26 27 28 29 30 31 32 33 34 35 36 37 39 40 41 42 44 45 46 49 51 52 56 57 58 64 65 68 71 73 **P**5 8	23	10	126	4283	72	134736	444	35429	17927	559
GLOUCESTER—Essex County										
ADDISON GILBERT HOSPITAL See Beverly Hospital, Beverly										
GREAT BARRINGTON—Berkshire County										
✠ FAIRVIEW HOSPITAL, 29 Lewis Avenue, Zip 01230–1713; tel. 413/528–0790; Claire L. Bowen, President **A**1 9 10 **F**7 8 12 15 16 17 19 20 21 22 25 26 28 29 30 31 32 33 34 35 37 39 40 41 42 44 46 49 54 55 56 61 64 65 66 67 71 73 74 **S** Berkshire Health Systems, Inc., Pittsfield, MA **N** Berkshire Health System, Pittsfield, MA	23	10	21	1344	15	—	169	15567	6165	164
GREENFIELD—Franklin County										
✠ FRANKLIN MEDICAL CENTER, 164 High Street, Zip 01301–2613; tel. 413/773–0211; Harlan J. Smith, President **A**1 2 9 10 **F**1 2 3 7 8 12 13 15 16 17 19 21 22 26 27 29 30 31 32 33 34 35 37 39 40 41 42 44 49 51 52 53 54 55 56 57 58 59 63 65 67 68 71 73 **P**3 5 6 7 8 **S** Baystate Health System, Inc., Springfield, MA **N** Baystate Health System, Springfield, MA	23	10	112	4686	—	141989	576	56797	27370	626

Hospital, Address, Telephone, Administrator, Approval, Facility, and Physician Codes, Health Care System, Network	Classi-fication Codes		Utilization Data					Expense (thousands) of dollars		
★ American Hospital Association (AHA) membership □ Joint Commission on Accreditation of Healthcare Organizations (JCAHO) accreditation + American Osteopathic Healthcare Association (AOHA) membership ○ American Osteopathic Association (AOA) accreditation △ Commission on Accreditation of Rehabilitation Facilities (CARF) accreditation Control codes 61, 63, 64, 71, 72 and 73 indicate hospitals listed by AOHA, but not registered by AHA. For definition of numerical codes, see page A4	Control	Service	Staffed Beds	Admissions	Census	Outpatient Visits	Births	Total	Payroll	Personnel

HAVERHILL—Essex County

BALDPATE HOSPITAL, 83 Baldpate Road, Zip 01833–2399; tel. 978/352–2131; Lucille M. Batal, Administrator (Nonreporting) **A**10	33	22	59	—	—	—	—	—	—	—
✠ HALE HOSPITAL, 140 Lincoln Avenue, Zip 01830–6798; tel. 978/374–2000; Robert J. Ingala, Chief Executive Officer **A**1 9 10 **F**7 8 10 11 12 14 15 16 17 19 21 22 23 28 29 30 32 34 35 37 39 40 41 42 44 45 49 53 54 56 57 58 61 63 65 67 68 71 73 74 **S** Quorum Health Group/Quorum Health Resources, Inc., Brentwood, TN **N** New England Health Partnership, Waltham, MA	14	10	113	4602	60	58700	553	37051	17490	464
✠ △ WHITTIER REHABILITATION HOSPITAL, 76 Summer Street, Zip 01830–5896; tel. 978/372–8000; Alfred Arcidi, M.D., President (Nonreporting) **A**1 7 10	33	46	60	—	—	—	—	—	—	—

HOLYOKE—Hampden County

| ✠ HOLYOKE HOSPITAL, 575 Beech Street, Zip 01040–2296; tel. 413/534–2500; Hank J. Porten, President **A**1 2 9 10 **F**3 7 8 11 12 13 14 15 16 17 18 19 21 22 24 25 26 27 28 29 30 31 32 33 34 35 37 39 40 41 42 44 45 46 49 51 52 53 54 55 56 57 58 59 60 61 63 64 65 67 68 71 73 74 **P**6 8 | 23 | 10 | 202 | 8189 | 136 | 158187 | 447 | 59992 | 30210 | 815 |
| ✠ SOLDIERS' HOME IN HOLYOKE, 110 Cherry Street, Zip 01040–7002; tel. 413/532–9475; Paul A. Morin, Superintendent (Total facility includes 238 beds in nursing home–type unit) (Nonreporting) **A**1 10 | 12 | 10 | 265 | — | — | — | — | — | — | — |

HYANNIS—Barnstable County

| ✠ CAPE COD HOSPITAL, 27 Park Street, Zip 02601–5203; tel. 508/771–1800; Gail M. Frieswick, Ed.D., President and Chief Executive Officer (Nonreporting) **A**1 2 9 10 **S** Cape Cod Healthcare, Inc., Hyannis, MA **N** Cape Cod Healthcare, Inc., Hyannisport, MA | 23 | 10 | 236 | — | — | — | — | — | — | — |

LAWRENCE—Essex County

| □ LAWRENCE GENERAL HOSPITAL, 1 General Street, Zip 01842–0389, Mailing Address: P.O. Box 189, Zip 01842–0389; tel. 978/683–4000; Joseph S. McManus, President and Chief Executive Officer **A**1 2 3 9 10 **F**7 8 10 11 14 15 16 17 19 22 23 25 28 29 30 31 32 33 34 35 37 40 41 44 46 60 61 63 65 67 68 71 72 73 74 **P**1 4 5 7 **N** Fallon Healthcare System, Worcester, MA | 23 | 10 | 191 | 8630 | 118 | — | 1433 | 77023 | 37147 | 916 |

LEEDS—Hampshire County

| ✠ VETERANS AFFAIRS MEDICAL CENTER, 421 North Main Street, Zip 01053–9764; tel. 413/584–4040; Robert McNamara, Director (Total facility includes 50 beds in nursing home–type unit) **A**1 9 **F**1 2 3 6 8 10 12 14 16 17 18 19 20 22 24 25 26 27 28 29 30 31 32 44 45 46 49 51 52 54 56 57 58 60 64 65 67 71 72 73 74 **S** Department of Veterans Affairs, Washington, DC | 45 | 82 | 167 | 2200 | 167 | 132894 | — | 57836 | 27727 | 669 |

LEOMINSTER—Worcester County

| ✠ HEALTH ALLIANCE HOSPITALS, (Includes Health Alliance–Burbank Hospital, 275 Nichols Road, Fitchburg, Zip 01420–8209; tel. 978/343–5000), 60 Hospital Road, Zip 01453–8004; tel. 978/466–2000; Douglas L. Fairfax, President and Chief Executive Officer (Total facility includes 289 beds in nursing home–type unit) **A**1 3 5 9 10 **F**1 3 7 8 10 12 14 15 16 17 18 19 21 22 26 28 30 31 32 33 34 35 36 37 40 41 42 44 46 48 49 51 52 53 54 56 57 58 59 61 64 65 66 67 68 70 71 72 73 74 **P**5 8 **N** Fallon Healthcare System, Worcester, MA | 23 | 10 | 451 | 8765 | 382 | 89308 | 1485 | 83269 | 40368 | 630 |

LOWELL—Middlesex County

| ✠ LOWELL GENERAL HOSPITAL, 295 Varnum Avenue, Zip 01854–2195; tel. 978/937–6000; Robert A. Donovan, President and Chief Executive Officer (Total facility includes 21 beds in nursing home–type unit) **A**1 2 9 10 **F**1 3 7 8 10 12 14 15 16 17 19 21 22 23 26 28 29 30 31 34 35 37 39 40 41 42 44 45 46 49 52 54 55 56 57 58 59 60 64 65 66 67 70 71 73 74 **P**8 | 23 | 10 | 231 | 9774 | 123 | 154394 | 2307 | 72776 | 35301 | 978 |
| ✠ SAINTS MEMORIAL MEDICAL CENTER, One Hospital Drive, Zip 01852–1389; tel. 978/458–1411; Thomas Clark, President and Chief Executive Officer (Nonreporting) **A**1 2 9 10 **N** Fallon Healthcare System, Worcester, MA | 23 | 10 | 170 | — | — | — | — | — | — | — |

LUDLOW—Hampden County

| ✠ △ HEALTHSOUTH REHABILITATION HOSPITAL OF WESTERN MASSACHUSETTS, (Formerly Rehabilitation Hospital of Western Massachusetts), 14 Chestnut Place, Zip 01056–3460; tel. 413/589–7581; Mark D. Kramer, Administrator (Nonreporting) **A**1 7 10 **S** HEALTHSOUTH Corporation, Birmingham, AL | 33 | 46 | 40 | — | — | — | — | — | — | — |

LYNN—Essex County

| ✠ ATLANTICARE MEDICAL CENTER, 500 Lynnfield Street, Zip 01904–1487; tel. 781/581–9200; Andrew J. Riddell, President and Chief Executive Officer (Total facility includes 24 beds in nursing home–type unit) (Nonreporting) **A**1 2 9 10 **S** Partners HealthCare System, Inc., Boston, MA **N** Lahey Network, Burlington, MA | 23 | 10 | 189 | — | — | — | — | — | — | — |

MARLBOROUGH—Middlesex County

| ✠ MARLBOROUGH HOSPITAL, 57 Union Street, Zip 01752–1297; tel. 508/481–5000; Anne Bourgeois, Interim Chief Executive Officer **A**1 5 9 10 **F**2 3 8 12 13 15 16 17 18 19 20 22 26 28 30 37 39 41 42 44 46 49 52 53 54 56 57 65 66 67 68 71 72 73 74 **P**5 8 **N** Continuum of Care Network, Marlborough, MA; Fallon Healthcare System, Worcester, MA | 23 | 10 | 66 | 3252 | 47 | 53722 | — | 30210 | 14929 | 364 |

MEDFIELD—Norfolk County

| ✠ MEDFIELD STATE HOSPITAL, 45 Hospital Road, Zip 02052–1099; tel. 508/359–7312; Theodore E. Kirousis, Area Director (Nonreporting) **A**1 10 **S** Massachusetts Department of Mental Health, Boston, MA | 12 | 22 | 212 | — | — | — | — | — | — | — |

Hospital, Address, Telephone, Administrator, Approval, Facility, and Physician Codes, Health Care System, Network	Classi-fication Codes		Utilization Data					Expense (thousands) of dollars		
★ American Hospital Association (AHA) membership □ Joint Commission on Accreditation of Healthcare Organizations (JCAHO) accreditation + American Osteopathic Healthcare Association (AOHA) membership ○ American Osteopathic Association (AOA) accreditation △ Commission on Accreditation of Rehabilitation Facilities (CARF) accreditation Control codes 61, 63, 64, 71, 72 and 73 indicate hospitals listed by AOHA, but not registered by AHA. For definition of numerical codes, see page A4	Control	Service	Staffed Beds	Admissions	Census	Outpatient Visits	Births	Total	Payroll	Personnel

MELROSE—Middlesex County

★ HALLMARK HEALTH SYSTEM, (Formerly UniCare Health System), (Includes Lawrence Memorial Hospital of Medford, 170 Governors Avenue, Medford, Zip 02155–1643; tel. 781/306–6000; Malden Hospital, 100 Hospital Road, Malden, Zip 02148–3591; tel. 617/322–7560; Melrose–Wakefield Hospital, 585 Lebanon Street, Zip 02176; tel. 617/979–3000; Whidden Memorial Hospital, 103 Garland Street, Everett, Zip 02149–5095), 585 Lebanon Street, Zip 02176–3298; tel. 781/979–3000; Richard S. Quinlan, President and Chief Executive Officer (Total facility includes 94 beds in nursing home–type unit) **A**1 2 6 9 10 **F**1 3 5 7 8 10 12 13 14 15 16 17 18 19 21 22 23 25 26 27 28 29 30 32 33 34 35 36 37 39 40 41 42 44 45 49 51 52 53 54 55 56 57 58 59 61 63 64 65 66 67 68 71 72 73 74 **P**1 5 ... 23 10 | 598 | 30192 | 404 | 316926 | 1788 | 236899 | 115976 | 2791

MELROSE–WAKEFIELD HOSPITAL See Hallmark Health System

METHUEN—Essex County

★ HOLY FAMILY HOSPITAL AND MEDICAL CENTER, 70 East Street, Zip 01844–4597; tel. 978/687–0151; William L. Lane, President (Total facility includes 19 beds in nursing home–type unit) **A**1 2 9 10 **F**3 7 8 10 11 12 13 14 15 16 17 18 19 20 21 22 23 25 26 28 29 30 31 32 33 34 35 37 38 39 40 41 42 44 45 46 49 51 52 53 54 55 56 57 58 59 60 63 64 65 66 67 68 69 71 72 73 74 **P**3 5 7 **S** Caritas Christi Health Care, Boston, MA **N** Caritas Christi Health Network, Boston, MA; Fallon Healthcare System, Worcester, MA ... 21 10 | 265 | 8469 | 133 | 78637 | 1149 | 64741 | 31282 | 902

MIDDLEBORO—Plymouth County

□ CRANBERRY SPECIALTY HOSPITAL OF PLYMOUTH COUNTY, 52 Oak Street, Zip 02346–2091; tel. 508/947–1000; John Scola, M.D., Interim Chief Executive Officer (Nonreporting) **A**1 10 ... 13 46 | 68 | — | — | — | — | — | — | —

MILFORD—Worcester County

★ MILFORD–WHITINSVILLE REGIONAL HOSPITAL, (Includes Whitinsville Medical Center, 18 Granite Street, Whitinsville, Zip 01588; tel. 508/234–6311), 14 Prospect Street, Zip 01757–3090; tel. 508/473–1190; Francis M. Saba, President and Chief Executive Officer (Nonreporting) **A**1 2 5 9 10 **N** Fallon Healthcare System, Worcester, MA ... 23 10 | 125 | — | — | — | — | — | — | —

MILTON—Norfolk County

★ MILTON HOSPITAL, 92 Highland Street, Zip 02186–3807; tel. 617/696–4600; George A. Geary, President (Total facility includes 32 beds in nursing home–type unit) **A**1 2 9 10 **F**8 11 12 14 15 16 17 19 21 22 28 29 30 34 37 39 41 42 44 46 49 60 63 64 65 66 71 73 **P**8 ... 23 10 | 137 | 4743 | 79 | 54886 | — | 36983 | 16921 | 561

NANTUCKET—Nantucket County

★ NANTUCKET COTTAGE HOSPITAL, 57 Prospect Street, Zip 02554–2799; tel. 508/228–1200; Lucille C. Giddings, R.N., CHE, President and Chief Executive Officer (Nonreporting) **A**1 9 10 ... 23 10 | 19 | — | — | — | — | — | — | —

NATICK—Middlesex County

LEONARD MORSE HOSPITAL See MetroWest Medical Center, Framingham

NEEDHAM—Norfolk County

★ DEACONESS–GLOVER HOSPITAL CORPORATION, 148 Chestnut Street, Zip 02192–2483; tel. 781/453–3000; John Dalton, President and Chief Executive Officer **A**1 2 9 10 **F**1 2 3 4 5 7 8 10 11 12 13 15 16 17 18 19 20 21 22 23 24 25 26 27 28 29 30 31 32 33 34 35 36 37 38 39 40 41 42 43 44 45 46 47 49 51 52 53 54 55 56 57 58 59 60 61 63 64 65 66 67 68 69 70 71 72 73 74 **P**3 5 7 8 **S** CareGroup, Boston, MA **N** CareGroup, Boston, MA; Fallon Healthcare System, Worcester, MA ... 23 10 | 41 | 2361 | 30 | 61500 | — | 21771 | 9829 | 296

NEW BEDFORD—Bristol County

ST. LUKE'S HOSPITAL OF NEW BEDFORD See Southcoast Hospitals Group, Fall River

NEWBURYPORT—Essex County

★ ANNA JAQUES HOSPITAL, 25 Highland Avenue, Zip 01950–3894; tel. 978/463–1000; Allan L. DesRosiers, President (Total facility includes 20 beds in nursing home–type unit) **A**1 9 10 **F**7 8 10 11 12 13 15 16 17 19 21 22 23 28 29 30 31 32 33 34 35 36 37 39 40 41 42 44 45 46 49 52 53 54 56 58 59 63 65 66 67 71 73 74 **P**5 7 ... 23 10 | 145 | 6419 | 98 | 99055 | 775 | 52935 | 26066 | 675

NEWTON LOWER FALLS—Middlesex County

★ NEWTON–WELLESLEY HOSPITAL, 2014 Washington Street, Zip 02162–1699; tel. 617/243–6000; John P. Bihldorff, President and Chief Executive Officer **A**1 2 3 5 9 10 **F**1 3 7 8 12 13 14 15 16 17 18 19 22 26 31 32 34 35 37 38 40 41 42 44 46 49 51 52 53 54 55 56 57 58 59 61 65 66 67 71 73 **P**1 5 ... 23 10 | 240 | 13509 | 156 | 84104 | 4338 | 129060 | 62804 | 1394

NORFOLK—Norfolk County

★ CARITAS SOUTHWOOD COMMUNITY HOSPITAL, (Formerly Southwood Community Hospital), 111 Dedham Street, Zip 02056–1664; tel. 508/668–0385; Delia O'Connor, President (Nonreporting) **A**1 2 9 10 **S** Caritas Christi Health Care, Boston, MA ... 23 10 | 182 | — | — | — | — | — | — | —

NORTH ADAMS—Berkshire County

★ NORTH ADAMS REGIONAL HOSPITAL, 71 Hospital Avenue, Zip 01247–2584; tel. 413/664–5505; John C. J. Cronin, President and Chief Executive Officer (Nonreporting) **A**1 2 9 10 ... 23 10 | 134 | — | — | — | — | — | — | —

NORTHAMPTON—Hampshire County

★ COOLEY DICKINSON HOSPITAL, 30 Locust Street, Zip 01061–5001, Mailing Address: P.O. Box 5001, Zip 01061–5001; tel. 413/582–2000; Craig N. Melin, President and Chief Executive Officer **A**1 2 9 10 **F**3 7 8 12 14 15 16 17 19 20 21 22 28 30 31 34 35 37 39 40 41 42 44 45 46 49 52 54 55 56 57 58 59 60 63 65 66 67 71 72 73 **P**6 8 ... 23 10 | 144 | 7564 | 85 | 158299 | 979 | 55460 | 27953 | 613

VETERANS AFFAIRS MEDICAL CENTER See Leeds

Hospital, Address, Telephone, Administrator, Approval, Facility, and Physician Codes, Health Care System, Network	Classi-fication Codes		Utilization Data					Expense (thousands) of dollars		
★ American Hospital Association (AHA) membership □ Joint Commission on Accreditation of Healthcare Organizations (JCAHO) accreditation + American Osteopathic Healthcare Association (AOHA) membership ○ American Osteopathic Association (AOA) accreditation △ Commission on Accreditation of Rehabilitation Facilities (CARF) accreditation Control codes 61, 63, 64, 71, 72 and 73 indicate hospitals listed by AOHA, but not registered by AHA. For definition of numerical codes, see page A4	Control	Service	Staffed Beds	Admissions	Census	Outpatient Visits	Births	Total	Payroll	Personnel

NORWOOD—Norfolk County

★ CARITAS NORWOOD HOSPITAL, (Formerly Norwood Hospital), 800 Washington Street, Zip 02062–3487; tel. 781/769–4000; Delia O'Connor, President (Total facility includes 41 beds in nursing home–type unit) **A**1 2 5 9 10 **F**1 3 7 8 10 12 15 16 19 20 21 22 23 24 25 26 27 28 29 30 31 32 33 34 35 37 39 40 41 42 44 46 49 50 52 54 55 56 57 58 59 60 63 64 65 67 68 71 72 73 **P**5 8 **S** Caritas Christi Health Care, Boston, MA
| | | 23 | 10 | 179 | 7343 | 85 | 74214 | 1085 | 69294 | 31735 | 2204 |

OAK BLUFFS—Dukes County

★ MARTHA'S VINEYARD HOSPITAL, Linton Lane, Zip 02557, Mailing Address: P.O. Box 1477, Zip 02557; tel. 508/693–0410; Charles S. Kinney, Chief Executive Officer **A**1 9 10 **F**1 3 6 7 8 12 14 15 17 18 19 22 27 29 30 31 32 33 34 36 37 39 40 41 42 44 49 51 53 54 55 56 57 58 61 62 65 66 67 71 73 74
| | | 23 | 10 | 14 | 1420 | 11 | 11486 | 129 | 16128 | 7948 | 198 |

PALMER—Hampden County

★ WING MEMORIAL HOSPITAL AND MEDICAL CENTERS, 40 Wright Street, Zip 01069–1138; tel. 413/283–7651; Richard H. Scheffer, President **A**1 2 5 9 10 **F**3 8 12 19 21 22 26 30 32 33 34 37 41 42 44 49 51 52 53 54 55 56 57 58 61 65 66 67 71 72 73 74 **P**6 **N** Lahey Network, Burlington, MA
| | | 23 | 10 | 46 | 1899 | 26 | 136100 | — | 29441 | 15683 | 448 |

PEABODY—Essex County

□ VENCOR HOSPITAL NORTH SHORE, (Formerly THC–Boston), 15 King Street, Zip 01960–4268; tel. 978/531–2900; Della Underwood, Chief Executive Officer (Nonreporting) **A**1 10 **S** Vencor, Incorporated, Louisville, KY
| | | 33 | 10 | 59 | — | — | — | — | — | — | — |

PEMBROKE—Plymouth County

PEMBROKE HOSPITAL, 199 Oak Street, Zip 02359–1953; tel. 781/826–8161; Michael P. Krupa, Ed.D., Chief Executive Officer (Nonreporting)
| | | 33 | 22 | 115 | — | — | — | — | — | — | — |

PITTSFIELD—Berkshire County

★ △ BERKSHIRE MEDICAL CENTER, (Includes Hillcrest Hospital, 165 Tor Court, Zip 01201–3099, Mailing Address: Box 1155, Zip 01202–1155; tel. 413/443–4761; Eugene A. Dellea, President and Chief Executive Officer), 725 North Street, Zip 01201–4124; tel. 413/447–2000; Ruth P. Blodgett, Chief Operating Officer **A**1 2 3 5 7 8 9 10 12 **F**2 3 4 6 7 8 10 12 13 15 16 17 18 19 20 21 22 26 28 30 31 32 34 35 37 38 39 40 41 42 44 45 46 48 49 51 52 53 54 55 56 57 58 59 60 64 65 66 70 71 72 73 74 **S** Berkshire Health Systems, Inc., Pittsfield, MA **N** Berkshire Health System, Pittsfield, MA
| | | 23 | 10 | 368 | 12629 | 224 | 105353 | 930 | 134423 | 65101 | — |

PLYMOUTH—Plymouth County

★ JORDAN HOSPITAL, 275 Sandwich Street, Zip 02360–2196; tel. 508/746–2001; Alan D. Knight, President and Chief Executive Officer **A**1 2 9 10 **F**1 2 3 4 7 8 11 12 15 16 17 18 19 21 22 23 27 28 29 30 31 32 33 34 35 37 39 40 41 42 43 44 45 46 49 52 53 54 56 60 64 65 66 67 68 71 73 74 **P**4 5 6 7 **S** Quorum Health Group/Quorum Health Resources, Inc., Brentwood, TN
| | | 23 | 10 | 119 | 6934 | 89 | 191551 | 835 | 66571 | 30238 | 598 |

POCASSET—Barnstable County

BARNSTABLE COUNTY HOSPITAL, 870 County Road, Zip 02559–2199; tel. 508/563–5941; Edward B. Leary, President (Nonreporting) **A**10
| | | 13 | 46 | 39 | — | — | — | — | — | — | — |

QUINCY—Norfolk County

★ QUINCY HOSPITAL, 114 Whitwell Street, Zip 02169–1899; tel. 617/773–6100; Jeffrey Doran, Chief Executive Officer **A**1 9 10 **F**3 7 8 10 12 15 16 17 19 21 22 26 27 28 30 31 32 33 34 35 36 37 39 40 41 42 44 46 52 54 55 56 57 58 59 60 61 64 65 67 71 72 73 74 **P**8 **S** Quorum Health Group/Quorum Health Resources, Inc., Brentwood, TN **N** New England Health Partnership, Waltham, MA
| | | 14 | 10 | 186 | 8184 | 131 | 87453 | 701 | 76537 | 33789 | 820 |

SALEM—Essex County

★ SALEM HOSPITAL, (Includes North Shore Children's Hospital, tel. 978/745–2100), 81 Highland Avenue, Zip 01970–2768; tel. 978/741–1200; Alexander Movahed, Acting President and Chief Executive Officer **A**1 2 3 5 9 10 **F**3 7 8 10 11 12 13 15 16 17 18 19 21 22 23 24 25 26 27 28 29 30 31 32 33 34 35 37 40 41 42 43 44 45 46 49 51 52 53 54 55 56 58 59 60 61 63 65 66 67 68 71 72 73 74 **P**1 3 6 **S** Partners HealthCare System, Inc., Boston, MA **N** Partners HealthCare System, Boston, MA
| | | 23 | 10 | 255 | 12186 | 154 | 415981 | 1726 | 138395 | 73330 | 1710 |

★ △ SHAUGHNESSY–KAPLAN REHABILITATION HOSPITAL, Dove Avenue, Zip 01970–2999; tel. 978/745–9000; Anthony Sciola, President and Chief Executive Officer (Total facility includes 40 beds in nursing home–type unit) **A**1 7 9 10 **F**3 7 8 10 11 12 14 16 19 21 22 24 25 26 27 28 29 30 31 32 33 34 37 40 41 42 44 45 46 48 49 51 52 53 54 55 56 58 59 60 61 63 65 66 67 68 71 72 73 74 **P**6 **S** Partners HealthCare System, Inc., Boston, MA **N** Partners HealthCare System, Boston, MA
| | | 23 | 46 | 160 | 2098 | 119 | — | — | 22008 | 10987 | 253 |

SOMERVILLE—Middlesex County

SOMERVILLE HOSPITAL See Cambridge Public Health Commission, Cambridge

SOUTH ATTLEBORO—Bristol County

□ FULLER MEMORIAL HOSPITAL, 200 May Street, Zip 02703–5599; tel. 508/761–8500; Landon Kite, President (Nonreporting) **A**1 9 10 **S** Universal Health Services, Inc., King of Prussia, PA
| | | 33 | 22 | 46 | — | — | — | — | — | — | — |

SOUTH WEYMOUTH—Norfolk County

★ SOUTH SHORE HOSPITAL, 55 Fogg Road, Zip 02190–2455; tel. 781/340–8000; David T. Hannan, President and Chief Executive Officer (Total facility includes 25 beds in nursing home–type unit) **A**1 2 9 10 **F**7 8 10 11 12 14 15 16 17 19 21 22 23 25 27 30 32 33 34 35 37 39 40 41 42 44 46 49 60 61 64 65 67 71 72 73 74 **P**1 2 6
| | | 23 | 10 | 307 | 16212 | 207 | 459039 | 3243 | 162202 | 80507 | 2046 |

Hospital, Address, Telephone, Administrator, Approval, Facility, and Physician Codes, Health Care System, Network	Classi- fication Codes		Utilization Data					Expense (thousands) of dollars		
★ American Hospital Association (AHA) membership □ Joint Commission on Accreditation of Healthcare Organizations (JCAHO) accreditation + American Osteopathic Healthcare Association (AOHA) membership ○ American Osteopathic Association (AOA) accreditation △ Commission on Accreditation of Rehabilitation Facilities (CARF) accreditation Control codes 61, 63, 64, 71, 72 and 73 indicate hospitals listed by AOHA, but not registered by AHA. For definition of numerical codes, see page A4	Control	Service	Staffed Beds	Admissions	Census	Outpatient Visits	Births	Total	Payroll	Personnel

SOUTHBRIDGE—Worcester County

✠ HARRINGTON MEMORIAL HOSPITAL, 100 South Street, Zip 01550–4045; tel. 508/765–9771; Richard M. Mangion, President and Chief Executive Officer **A**1 5 9 10 **F**1 3 4 5 6 7 8 10 11 12 14 15 16 17 18 19 20 21 22 23 24 25 26 27 28 30 31 32 33 34 35 36 37 39 40 41 42 43 44 45 46 49 50 51 52 53 54 55 56 57 58 59 60 61 62 63 65 66 67 68 69 70 71 73 74 **P**8 **N** Fallon Healthcare System, Worcester, MA	23	10	113	3839	48	211730	447	37352	21138	507

SPRINGFIELD—Hampden County

✠ BAYSTATE MEDICAL CENTER, 759 Chestnut Street, Zip 01199–0001; tel. 413/794–0000; Mark R. Tolosky, Chief Executive Officer **A**1 2 3 5 6 8 9 10 **F**3 4 6 7 8 9 10 11 12 13 14 15 16 17 19 20 21 22 23 24 25 26 27 28 30 31 32 33 34 35 37 38 39 40 41 42 43 44 45 46 47 48 49 51 52 53 54 55 56 57 58 59 60 61 63 64 65 67 68 69 70 71 72 73 74 **P**5 6 8 **S** Baystate Health System, Inc., Springfield, MA **N** Baystate Health System, Springfield, MA	23	10	685	29470	421	350553	5160	340628	148524	4643
✠ △ MERCY HOSPITAL, 271 Carew Street, Zip 01104–2398, Mailing Address: P.O. Box 9012, Zip 01102–9012; tel. 413/748–9000; Vincent J. McCorkle, President **A**1 2 7 9 10 **F**1 3 7 8 10 11 12 14 15 16 17 19 20 21 22 23 25 26 28 29 30 31 32 34 35 37 39 40 41 42 44 45 46 48 49 51 53 54 55 56 57 58 59 60 63 65 67 68 71 73 74 **S** Catholic Health East, Radnor, PA **N** Sisters of Providence Health System, Springfield, MA	21	10	228	9407	167	114422	620	95362	38144	1027
□ OLYMPUS SPECIALTY HOSPITAL–SPRINGFIELD, 1400 State Street, Zip 01109–2589; tel. 413/787–6700; Marilyn M. Riddle, Chief Executive Officer (Total facility includes 220 beds in nursing home–type unit) (Nonreporting) **A**1 5 10	14	49	394	—	—	—	—	—	—	—
✠ SHRINERS HOSPITALS FOR CHILDREN, SPRINGFIELD, 516 Carew Street, Zip 01104–2396; tel. 413/787–2000; Mark L. Niederpruem, Administrator **A**1 3 5 **P**6 **S** Shriners Hospitals for Children, Tampa, FL	23	57	40	881	20	14118	0	—	—	222

STOCKBRIDGE—Berkshire County

✠ AUSTEN RIGGS CENTER, 25 Main Street, Zip 01262–0962, Mailing Address: P.O. Box 962, Zip 01262–0962; tel. 413/298–5511; Edward R. Shapiro, M.D., Medical Director and Chief Executive Officer (Nonreporting) **A**1 3	23	22	47							

STONEHAM—Middlesex County

□ BOSTON REGIONAL MEDICAL CENTER, 5 Woodland Road, Zip 02180–1715, Mailing Address: P.O. Box 9102, Zip 02180–9102; tel. 781/979–7000; Charles S. Ricks, D.D.S., President and Chief Executive Officer (Nonreporting) **A**1 2 3 9 10 **N** Fallon Healthcare System, Worcester, MA	21	10	187							

STOUGHTON—Plymouth County

GOOD SAMARITAN MEDICAL CENTER See Brockton

✠ △ NEW ENGLAND SINAI HOSPITAL AND REHABILITATION CENTER, (REHABILITATION/LONG TERM ACUTE), 150 York Street, Zip 02072–1881; tel. 781/364–4850; Donald H. Goldberg, President (Total facility includes 16 beds in nursing home–type unit) **A**1 3 7 9 10 **F**1 5 12 15 16 20 28 33 34 39 42 48 49 53 64 65 66 67 73	23	49	147	1386	135	37804	0	36619	20873	527

TAUNTON—Bristol County

✠ MORTON HOSPITAL AND MEDICAL CENTER, 88 Washington Street, Zip 02780–2499; tel. 508/828–7000; Thomas C. Porter, President **A**1 2 9 10 **F**7 8 10 12 13 14 15 16 17 19 21 22 23 25 28 30 34 35 37 39 40 41 44 45 46 49 51 60 65 66 67 68 71 72 73 74	23	10	151	6192	87	157620	656	65282	30989	—
□ TAUNTON STATE HOSPITAL, 60 Hodges Avenue Extension, Zip 02780–3034, Mailing Address: P.O. Box 4007, Zip 02780–4007; tel. 508/824–7551; Katherine Chmiel, R.N., MSN, Administrator and Chief Operating Officer **A**1 10 **F**1 12 15 16 17 18 52 53 54 55 56 57 59 65 67 73 **S** Massachusetts Department of Mental Health, Boston, MA	12	22	188	379	18	0	0	—	—	—

TEWKSBURY—Middlesex County

✠ TEWKSBURY HOSPITAL, 365 East Street, Zip 01876–1998; tel. 978/851–7321; Raymond D. Sanzone, Executive Director **A**1 6 10 **F**1 2 3 15 16 17 19 20 22 23 26 27 28 30 31 32 33 35 39 41 42 52 53 54 55 56 57 58 59 60 62 65 67 70 73 **P**6 **S** Massachusetts Department of Mental Health, Boston, MA	12	48	730	430	604	—	—	34378	24767	—

WALTHAM—Middlesex County

✠ DEACONESS WALTHAM HOSPITAL, Hope Avenue, Zip 02254–9116; tel. 781/647–6000; Jeanette G. Clough, President and Chief Executive Officer (Total facility includes 21 beds in nursing home–type unit) **A**1 2 5 9 10 **F**2 3 7 8 11 12 13 14 15 16 17 18 19 20 21 22 26 28 29 30 31 32 33 36 37 40 41 42 44 45 46 49 52 53 54 55 56 57 58 59 60 61 64 65 66 67 68 70 71 72 73 74 **P**5 6 8 **S** CareGroup, Boston, MA **N** CareGroup, Boston, MA; Fallon Healthcare System, Worcester, MA	23	10	219	6709	92	66511	265	55543	30398	817
MIDDLESEX HOSPITAL See Olympus Specialty Hospital										
□ OLYMPUS SPECIALTY HOSPITAL, (Formerly Middlesex Hospital), 775 Trapelo Road, Zip 02254, Mailing Address: P.O. Box 9151, Zip 02254–9151; tel. 781/895–7000; Reva S. Tankle, Ph.D., Chief Executive Officer (Nonreporting) **A**1 10	13	48	120	—	—	—	—	—	—	—

WARE—Hampshire County

✠ MARY LANE HOSPITAL, 85 South Street, Zip 01082–1697; tel. 413/967–6211; Christine Shirtcliff, Executive Vice President **A**1 9 10 **F**1 3 7 8 12 15 16 17 19 21 22 27 28 29 30 32 33 34 37 39 40 41 42 44 45 46 49 54 58 61 65 67 68 71 72 73 74 **P**1 5 8 **S** Baystate Health System, Inc., Springfield, MA **N** Baystate Health System, Springfield, MA	23	10	34	1551	15	15530	208	15834	8161	222

Hospital, Address, Telephone, Administrator, Approval, Facility, and Physician Codes, Health Care System, Network	Classi-fication Codes		Utilization Data					Expense (thousands) of dollars		
★ American Hospital Association (AHA) membership □ Joint Commission on Accreditation of Healthcare Organizations (JCAHO) accreditation + American Osteopathic Healthcare Association (AOHA) membership ○ American Osteopathic Association (AOA) accreditation △ Commission on Accreditation of Rehabilitation Facilities (CARF) accreditation Control codes 61, 63, 64, 71, 72 and 73 indicate hospitals listed by AOHA, but not registered by AHA. For definition of numerical codes, see page A4	Control	Service	Staffed Beds	Admissions	Census	Outpatient Visits	Births	Total	Payroll	Personnel

WAREHAM—Plymouth County
TOBEY HOSPITAL See Southcoast Hospitals Group, Fall River

WEBSTER—Worcester County

✠ HUBBARD REGIONAL HOSPITAL, 340 Thompson Road, Zip 01570–0608; tel. 508/943–2600; Gerald J. Barbini, Administrator and Chief Executive Officer **A**1 9 10 **F**8 14 15 19 21 22 27 30 34 37 39 41 42 44 45 46 49 57 58 65 71 72 73 74 **P**3 7 **S** Quorum Health Group/Quorum Health Resources, Inc., Brentwood, TN **N** Fallon Healthcare System, Worcester, MA; New England Health Partnership, Waltham, MA	23	10	29	1479	18	48667	—	14358	6154	169

WELLESLEY—Norfolk County

□ CHARLES RIVER HOSPITAL, 203 Grove Street, Zip 02181–7413; tel. 781/304–2800; Juliette Fay, President and Chief Executive Officer (Nonreporting) **A**1 3 10 **S** Community Care Systems, Inc., Wellesley Hills, MA	33	22	62	—	—	—	—	—	—	—
SIMPSON INFIRMARY, WELLESLEY COLLEGE, Worcester Street, Zip 02181–8277; tel. 781/283–2810; Charlotte K. Sanner, M.D., Director Health Service **F**14 15 16 28 29 39 45 51 61 74 **P**3	23	11	11	81	1	7702	—	—	—	15

WESTBOROUGH—Worcester County

□ WESTBOROUGH STATE HOSPITAL, Lyman Street, Zip 01581–0288, Mailing Address: P.O. Box 288, Zip 01581–0288; tel. 508/366–4401; Theodore E. Kirousis, Area Director (Nonreporting) **A**1 10 **S** Massachusetts Department of Mental Health, Boston, MA	12	22	220	—	—	—	—	—	—	—

WESTFIELD—Hampden County

✠ NOBLE HOSPITAL, 115 West Silver Street, Zip 01086–1634; tel. 413/568–2811; George J. Koller, President and Chief Executive Officer **A**1 2 5 9 10 **F**2 8 14 15 16 19 21 22 28 29 30 32 33 35 37 39 41 42 44 45 46 48 49 54 55 56 59 65 67 71 73 **P**8	23	10	97	3024	57	79291	—	27372	14285	372

WESTWOOD—Norfolk County

WESTWOOD LODGE HOSPITAL, 45 Clapboardtree Street, Zip 02090–2930; tel. 781/762–7764; Michael P. Krupa, Ed.D., Chief Executive Officer (Nonreporting) **A**10	33	22	100	—	—	—	—	—	—	—

WHITINSVILLE—Worcester County
WHITINSVILLE MEDICAL CENTER See Milford–Whitinsville Regional Hospital, Milford

WINCHESTER—Middlesex County

✠ WINCHESTER HOSPITAL, 41 Highland Avenue, Zip 01890–9920; tel. 781/729–9000; Stephen R. Laverty, President and Chief Executive Officer **A**1 2 5 9 10 **F**7 8 12 14 15 16 17 19 20 21 22 25 26 27 28 29 30 32 33 34 35 36 37 39 40 41 42 44 45 46 49 51 60 61 63 64 65 67 68 71 72 73 74 **P**3 4 5 6 7 8	23	10	168	8518	109	307019	2064	92873	41971	—

WOBURN—Middlesex County

CHOATE HEALTH SYSTEMS, 23 Warren Avenue, Zip 01801–4979; tel. 781/933–6700 (Nonreporting) **A**10	33	22	21	—	—	—	—	—	—	—
□ △ HEALTHSOUTH NEW ENGLAND REHABILITATION HOSPITAL, (Formerly New England Rehabilitation Hospital), Two Rehabilitation Way, Zip 01801–6098; tel. 781/935–5050; Mary Moscato, Chief Executive Officer (Nonreporting) **A**1 7 9 10 **S** HEALTHSOUTH Corporation, Birmingham, AL	33	46	198	—	—	—	—	—	—	—
NEW ENGLAND REHABILITATION HOSPITAL See HEALTHSOUTH New England Rehabilitation Hospital										

WORCESTER—Worcester County

ADCARE HOSPITAL OF WORCESTER, 107 Lincoln Street, Zip 01605–2499; tel. 508/799–9000; David W. Hillis, President and Chief Executive Officer (Nonreporting) **A**10	33	82	88	—	—	—	—	—	—	—
□ △ FAIRLAWN REHABILITATION HOSPITAL, 189 May Street, Zip 01602–4399; tel. 508/791–6351; Peter M. Mantegazza, President and Chief Executive Officer **A**1 5 7 9 10 **F**12 15 25 26 34 45 46 48 49 65 73 **S** HEALTHSOUTH Corporation, Birmingham, AL	33	46	110	1662	96	17444	0	—	10211	313
✠ MEMORIAL HOSPITAL, (Formerly Memorial Health Care), 119 Belmont Street, Zip 01605–2982; tel. 508/793–6611; Peter H. Levine, M.D., President and Chief Executive Officer (Total facility includes 31 beds in nursing home–type unit) **A**1 2 3 5 8 9 10 12 **F**3 7 8 10 11 12 13 15 16 17 19 21 22 23 25 26 28 29 30 31 32 33 34 35 37 38 40 42 44 45 49 51 52 53 54 55 56 57 58 59 60 61 63 64 65 66 67 68 71 72 73 74 **P**2 8	23	10	375	21169	265	331478	3968	188190	86172	2581
✠ SAINT VINCENT HOSPITAL, 25 Winthrop Street, Zip 01604–4593; tel. 508/798–1234; Robert E. Maher, Jr., President and Chief Executive Officer (Nonreporting) **A**1 2 3 5 8 9 10 12 **S** TENET Healthcare Corporation, Santa Barbara, CA **N** Fallon Healthcare System, Worcester, MA	33	10	369	—	—	—	—	—	—	—
✠ UNIVERSITY OF MASSACHUSETTS MEDICAL CENTER, 55 Lake Avenue North, Zip 01655–0002; tel. 508/856–0011; Lin C. Wilder, Dr.PH, R.N., Director **A**1 2 3 5 8 9 10 **F**3 4 6 7 8 9 10 11 12 13 14 15 16 18 19 20 21 22 24 25 27 28 30 31 35 37 39 41 42 43 44 46 47 49 51 52 53 54 56 58 59 60 61 65 66 67 69 70 71 72 73 74 **P**4 **N** Fallon Healthcare System, Worcester, MA	12	10	339	17634	278	514788	—	269093	119342	—
□ WORCESTER STATE HOSPITAL, 305 Belmont Street, Zip 01604–1695; tel. 508/752–4681; Raymond Robinson, Chief Operating Officer (Nonreporting) **A**1 5 10 **S** Massachusetts Department of Mental Health, Boston, MA	12	22	176	—	—	—	—	—	—	—

Resident population 9,774 (in thousands)
Resident population in metro areas 82.5%
Birth rate per 1,000 population 14.5
65 years and over 12.4%
Percent of persons without health insurance 8.9%

Hospital, Address, Telephone, Administrator, Approval, Facility, and Physician Codes, Health Care System, Network	Classi-fication Codes		Utilization Data					Expense (thousands) of dollars		
★ American Hospital Association (AHA) membership ☐ Joint Commission on Accreditation of Healthcare Organizations (JCAHO) accreditation + American Osteopathic Healthcare Association (AOHA) membership ○ American Osteopathic Association (AOA) accreditation △ Commission on Accreditation of Rehabilitation Facilities (CARF) accreditation Control codes 61, 63, 64, 71, 72 and 73 indicate hospitals listed by AOHA, but not registered by AHA. For definition of numerical codes, see page A4	Control	Service	Staffed Beds	Admissions	Census	Outpatient Visits	Births	Total	Payroll	Personnel

ADDISON—Lenawee County

☐ ADDISON COMMUNITY HOSPITAL, 421 North Steer Street, Zip 49220–9409; tel. 517/547–6151; Trevor J. Dyksterhouse, Administrator (Nonreporting) **A**1 10 — 16 10 24 — — — — — — —

ALBION—Calhoun County

☐ TRILLIUM HOSPITAL, 809 West Erie Street, Zip 49224–1556; tel. 517/629–2191; Michael G. Boff, President **A**1 9 10 **F**7 8 11 12 14 15 16 17 19 20 21 22 26 28 29 30 32 33 34 35 37 39 40 41 44 48 51 53 54 55 56 57 58 59 63 65 71 72 73 **P**5 — 23 10 67 1599 16 74143 106 14084 6518 198

ALLEGAN—Allegan County

✠ ALLEGAN GENERAL HOSPITAL, 555 Linn Street, Zip 49010–1594; tel. 616/673–8424; James A. Klun, President **A**1 9 10 **F**8 11 12 14 15 16 19 21 22 28 32 33 34 35 37 39 40 41 42 44 45 46 49 51 52 54 55 56 58 59 65 66 67 71 72 73 **S** Quorum Health Group/Quorum Health Resources, Inc., Brentwood, TN **N** Hospital Network Inc., Kalamazoo, MI — 23 10 63 1843 19 39785 173 17496 7803 220

ALMA—Gratiot County

✠ △ GRATIOT COMMUNITY HOSPITAL, 300 East Warwick Drive, Zip 48801–1096; tel. 517/463–1101; Bob M. Baker, President and Chief Executive Officer (Nonreporting) **A**1 7 9 10 — 23 10 127 — — — — — — —

ALPENA—Alpena County

✠ ALPENA GENERAL HOSPITAL, 1501 West Chisholm Street, Zip 49707–1498; tel. 517/356–7390; John A. McVeety, Chief Executive Officer **A**1 2 9 10 **F**2 3 4 7 8 10 12 15 16 17 19 21 22 27 28 29 30 31 32 33 34 35 36 37 39 40 41 42 44 45 46 49 52 53 54 55 56 57 58 63 65 66 67 68 71 72 73 74 — 13 10 121 5697 72 65197 541 52565 25766 695

ANN ARBOR—Washtenaw County

✠ △ ST. JOSEPH MERCY HEALTH SYSTEM, (Includes St. Joseph Mercy Hospital), 5301 East Huron River Drive, Zip 48106, Mailing Address: P.O. Box 995, Zip 48106–0995; tel. 734/712–3456; Garry C. Faja, President and Chief Executive Officer **A**1 2 3 5 7 8 9 10 **F**1 2 3 4 5 7 8 10 11 12 13 14 15 16 17 19 20 21 22 25 26 27 28 29 30 31 32 33 34 35 37 39 40 41 42 43 44 45 46 48 49 51 52 53 54 55 56 57 58 59 60 63 65 66 67 68 70 71 72 73 74 **P**1 5 **S** Mercy Health Services, Farmington Hills, MI — 21 10 482 25709 344 475733 4001 320074 128281 —

☐ UNIVERSITY OF MICHIGAN HOSPITALS AND HEALTH CENTERS, 1500 East Medical Center Drive, Zip 48109; tel. 734/936–4000; Larry Warren, Executive Director **A**1 2 3 5 8 9 10 **F**2 3 4 5 7 8 9 10 11 12 13 14 15 16 17 18 19 20 21 22 23 24 25 26 28 29 30 31 32 34 35 36 37 38 39 40 41 42 43 44 45 46 47 48 49 50 51 52 53 54 55 56 57 58 60 61 63 65 66 67 69 70 71 72 73 74 **P**1 — 23 10 730 33761 575 1054547 2694 873817 431912 8072

✠ VETERANS AFFAIRS MEDICAL CENTER, 2215 Fuller Road, Zip 48105–2399; tel. 734/769–7100; James W. Roseborough, CHE, Director (Total facility includes 58 beds in nursing home–type unit) **A**1 3 5 8 **F**3 4 8 10 11 14 16 19 20 21 22 23 25 26 27 28 30 31 32 33 34 35 37 39 41 42 43 44 45 46 49 50 51 52 54 55 56 57 58 59 60 63 64 65 67 69 71 72 73 **S** Department of Veterans Affairs, Washington, DC — 45 10 203 5329 110 276474 — 114986 59492 1741

AUBURN HILLS—Oakland County

☐ HAVENWYCK HOSPITAL, 1525 University Drive, Zip 48326–2675; tel. 810/373–9200; Robert A. Kercorian, Chief Executive Officer **A**1 10 **F**12 16 18 30 39 46 52 53 54 55 56 57 58 59 65 67 **S** Ramsay Health Care, Inc., Coral Gables, FL — 33 22 120 3171 92 4118 — 11722 5128 186

BAD AXE—Huron County

✠ HURON MEMORIAL HOSPITAL, 1100 South Van Dyke Road, Zip 48413–9799; tel. 517/269–9521; James B. Gardner, President **A**1 9 10 **F**7 8 14 15 16 19 21 22 27 28 30 32 33 34 37 39 40 41 42 44 49 63 65 67 71 — 23 10 64 1896 20 46163 308 18945 8379 265

BATTLE CREEK—Calhoun County

✠ BATTLE CREEK HEALTH SYSTEM, (Includes Community Hospital, 183 West Street, Zip 49016; Fieldstone Center, 165 North Washington Avenue, Zip 49016; tel. 616/964–7121; Leila Hospital, 300 North Avenue, Zip 49016), 300 North Avenue, Zip 49016–3396; tel. 616/966–8000; Stephen L. Abbott, President and Chief Executive Officer (Total facility includes 141 beds in nursing home–type unit) **A**1 2 9 10 **F**2 3 4 6 7 8 10 12 14 15 16 17 18 19 21 22 26 27 28 29 30 32 33 34 35 37 39 40 41 42 44 45 49 52 53 54 55 56 57 59 60 61 63 64 65 66 67 68 71 72 73 74 **P**7 8 **S** Mercy Health Services, Farmington Hills, MI **N** Mercy Health Services – Michigan Region, Farmington Hills, MI; Battle Creek Health System, Battle Creek, MI — 23 10 421 12547 273 128519 1133 129047 55405 1418

✠ △ SOUTHWESTERN MICHIGAN REHABILITATION HOSPITAL, 183 West Street, Zip 49017–3424; tel. 616/965–3206; Diane D. Giannunzio, President **A**1 7 10 **F**48 49 — 23 46 30 356 12 24124 0 5138 1686 51

✠ VETERANS AFFAIRS MEDICAL CENTER, 5500 Armstrong Road, Zip 49016; tel. 616/966–5600; Michael K. Wheeler, Director (Total facility includes 170 beds in nursing home–type unit) **A**1 5 **F**3 8 12 15 16 17 19 20 25 27 28 30 31 32 33 34 37 41 46 48 49 51 52 54 55 57 58 64 65 67 71 73 74 **S** Department of Veterans Affairs, Washington, DC — 45 22 485 4112 456 109270 0 103822 58336 1298

Hospital, Address, Telephone, Administrator, Approval, Facility, and Physician Codes, Health Care System, Network	Classi-fication Codes		Utilization Data					Expense (thousands) of dollars		
★ American Hospital Association (AHA) membership □ Joint Commission on Accreditation of Healthcare Organizations (JCAHO) accreditation + American Osteopathic Healthcare Association (AOHA) membership ○ American Osteopathic Association (AOA) accreditation △ Commission on Accreditation of Rehabilitation Facilities (CARF) accreditation Control codes 61, 63, 64, 71, 72 and 73 indicate hospitals listed by AOHA, but not registered by AHA. For definition of numerical codes, see page A4	Control	Service	Staffed Beds	Admissions	Census	Outpatient Visits	Births	Total	Payroll	Personnel

BAY CITY—Bay County

✛ △ BAY MEDICAL CENTER, (Includes Bay Medical Center–West Campus, 3250 East Midland Road, Zip 48706; tel. 517/667–6750; Samaritan Health Center, 713 Ninth Street, Zip 48708; tel. 517/894–3799), 1900 Columbus Avenue, Zip 48708–6880; tel. 517/894–3000; Anthony W. Armstrong, President **A**1 2 7 9 10 12 13 **F**2 3 6 7 8 10 12 14 15 16 17 18 19 20 21 22 26 28 29 30 31 32 33 34 35 36 37 39 40 41 42 44 45 46 48 49 52 53 54 55 58 59 60 63 65 66 67 70 71 72 73 74 **P**6 8	23	10	341	15484	211	232331	1080	118040	54075	1696
BAY SPECIAL CARE, (Formerly Bay Special Care Center), (LONG TERM ACUTE CARE), 3250 East Midland Road, Zip 48706–2835, Mailing Address: 3250 East Midland Road, Suite 1, Zip 48706–2835; tel. 517/667–6802; Cheryl A. Burzynski, President **A**10 **F**2 3 7 8 10 11 12 17 18 19 21 22 26 30 32 33 35 36 37 39 40 41 42 44 45 46 48 49 51 52 53 54 55 56 57 58 59 60 63 65 66 71 72 73 74 **P**8	23	49	21	205	17	—	—	4644	1823	85

BERRIEN CENTER—Berrien County

LAKELAND MEDICAL CENTER, BERRIEN CENTER See Lakeland Medical Center–St. Joseph, Saint Joseph

BIG RAPIDS—Mecosta County

✛ MECOSTA COUNTY GENERAL HOSPITAL, 405 Winter Avenue, Zip 49307–2099; tel. 616/796–8691; Thomas E. Daugherty, Chief Executive Officer **A**1 9 10 **F**7 8 10 15 16 19 22 33 34 36 37 40 41 42 44 45 48 49 63 65 71 72 73 **P**7 **S** Quorum Health Group/Quorum Health Resources, Inc., Brentwood, TN	13	10	74	2401	27	77170	673	20350	8427	266

BRIGHTON—Livingston County

★ BRIGHTON HOSPITAL, 12851 East Grand River Avenue, Zip 48116–8596; tel. 810/227–1211; Ramon Royal, President **A**10 **F**2 3 14 15 16 39	23	82	83	1584	47	13198	—	7946	3955	144

CADILLAC—Wexford County

✛ MERCY HEALTH SERVICES–NORTH, 400 Hobart Street, Zip 49601–9596; tel. 616/876–7200; Michael J. Peterson, Interim President and Chief Executive Officer **A**1 9 10 **F**3 7 8 10 12 14 15 16 17 19 20 21 22 24 28 29 30 31 32 33 34 35 37 39 40 41 42 44 45 46 49 51 54 55 56 58 63 65 66 67 71 73 **P**1 2 3 4 5 6 7 8 **S** Mercy Health Services, Farmington Hills, MI **N** Mercy Health Services – Michigan Region, Farmington Hills, MI	21	10	79	4435	47	60126	491	38610	14787	566

CARO—Tuscola County

□ CARO CENTER, 2000 Chambers Road, Zip 48723–9240; tel. 517/673–3191; Rose Laskowski, R.N., Hospital Director **A**1 10 **F**3 4 5 7 8 9 10 11 12 15 16 18 19 20 21 22 23 26 30 31 32 33 35 37 39 40 42 43 44 45 46 49 52 53 54 55 56 57 58 59 60 61 65 67 69 70 71 74	12	22	204	359	1812	—	—	40072	17380	457
★ CARO COMMUNITY HOSPITAL, 401 North Hooper Street, Zip 48723–1476, Mailing Address: P.O. Box 71, Zip 48723–0071; tel. 517/673–3141; William P. Miller, President and Chief Executive Officer **A**9 10 **F**8 16 19 21 22 28 34 35 42 44 45 46 49 51 65 71 **P**6	16	10	15	730	7	43877	0	7268	2819	127

CARSON CITY—Montcalm County

+ ○ CARSON CITY HOSPITAL, 406 East Elm Street, Zip 48811–0879, Mailing Address: P.O. Box 879, Zip 48811–0879; tel. 517/584–3131; Bruce L. Traverse, President **A**9 10 11 12 13 **F**7 14 15 16 17 19 20 22 28 30 32 34 35 37 40 41 42 44 51 52 54 55 56 58 65 67 71 72 73 74 **P**6 **N** Butterworth Health System, Grand Rapids, MI	23	10	78	405	2	44619	405	19313	9727	391

CASS CITY—Tuscola County

✛ HILLS AND DALES GENERAL HOSPITAL, 4675 Hill Street, Zip 48726–1099; tel. 517/872–2121; Dee McKrow, Chief Executive Officer **A**1 9 10 **F**7 8 12 15 16 17 19 21 22 24 28 29 30 31 32 33 34 39 40 41 42 44 45 46 49 51 63 65 66 67 71 73 **P**5	23	10	47	902	10	26229	—	8386	4110	169

CHARLEVOIX—Charlevoix County

✛ CHARLEVOIX AREA HOSPITAL, 14700 Lake Shore Drive, Zip 49720–1931; tel. 616/547–4024; William Jackson, President **A**1 9 10 **F**7 8 14 15 20 22 28 30 37 40 41 44 49 65 66 71 73	23	10	33	1429	13	21765	202	11613	5476	180

CHARLOTTE—Eaton County

✛ HAYES–GREEN–BEACH MEMORIAL HOSPITAL, 321 East Harris Street, Zip 48813–1697; tel. 517/543–1050; Stephen W. Mapes, Chief Executive Officer **A**1 9 10 **F**7 8 15 16 17 19 21 22 24 28 30 34 36 39 40 41 42 44 46 49 65 66 67 71 73 **P**6	23	10	45	1588	14	39692	210	15991	9168	289

CHEBOYGAN—Cheboygan County

✛ COMMUNITY MEMORIAL HOSPITAL, 748 South Main Street, Zip 49721–2299, Mailing Address: P.O. Box 419, Zip 49721–0419; tel. 616/627–5601; Howard J. Purcell, Jr., President (Total facility includes 50 beds in nursing home–type unit) **A**1 9 10 **F**8 14 15 16 19 20 21 22 24 25 32 33 34 37 40 44 64 71 73 **P**8	23	10	92	2270	72	89689	238	20583	10515	331

CHELSEA—Washtenaw County

□ △ CHELSEA COMMUNITY HOSPITAL, 775 South Main Street, Zip 48118–1399; tel. 313/475–1311; Kathleen S. Griffiths, Interim President **A**1 3 5 7 9 10 **F**3 6 8 14 15 16 17 19 21 22 24 25 26 28 29 30 32 34 37 39 41 42 44 45 46 48 49 52 53 54 55 57 58 59 61 62 65 67 71 73 74	23	10	105	3170	61	110509	0	40409	19447	591

CLARE—Clare County

✛ ○ MIDMICHIGAN MEDICAL CENTER–CLARE, (Formerly MidMichigan Regional Medical Center–Clare), 104 West Sixth Street, Zip 48617–1409; tel. 517/386–9951; Lawrence F. Barco, President **A**1 9 10 11 **F**7 8 15 17 19 21 22 28 30 32 33 34 35 40 41 42 44 45 49 63 67 71 72 73 74 **P**3 4 8 **S** MidMichigan Health, Midland, MI	23	10	64	2335	23	32030	303	18404	8765	270

Hospital, Address, Telephone, Administrator, Approval, Facility, and Physician Codes, Health Care System, Network	Classi-fication Codes		Utilization Data					Expense (thousands) of dollars		
★ American Hospital Association (AHA) membership □ Joint Commission on Accreditation of Healthcare Organizations (JCAHO) accreditation + American Osteopathic Healthcare Association (AOHA) membership ○ American Osteopathic Association (AOA) accreditation △ Commission on Accreditation of Rehabilitation Facilities (CARF) accreditation Control codes 61, 63, 64, 71, 72 and 73 indicate hospitals listed by AOHA, but not registered by AHA. For definition of numerical codes, see page A4	Control	Service	Staffed Beds	Admissions	Census	Outpatient Visits	Births	Total	Payroll	Personnel

CLINTON TOWNSHIP—Macomb County

☒ ST. JOSEPH'S MERCY HOSPITALS AND HEALTH SERVICES, (Includes St. Joseph's Mercy Hospital–East, 215 North Avenue, Mount Clemens, Zip 48043; tel. 810/466–9300; St. Joseph's Mercy Hospital–West, 15855 19 Mile Road, Zip 48038; tel. 810/263–2300; St. Joseph's Mercy–North, 80650 North Van Dyke, Romeo, Zip 48065; tel. 810/798–3551), Jack Weiner, President and Chief Executive Officer **A**1 9 10 **F**3 6 7 8 10 11 12 13 15 16 17 19 21 22 26 27 28 29 30 31 32 33 34 35 36 37 39 40 41 42 44 45 46 48 49 52 54 55 56 57 58 59 60 61 64 65 67 68 71 72 73 74 **P**6 8 **S** Mercy Health Services, Farmington Hills, MI **N** Mercy Health Services – Michigan Region, Farmington Hills, MI; Henry Ford Health System, Detroit, MI | 23 | 10 | 298 | 14764 | 233 | 241191 | 1784 | 120723 | 56757 | 1719

COLDWATER—Branch County

☒ + ○ COMMUNITY HEALTH CENTER OF BRANCH COUNTY, 274 East Chicago Street, Zip 49036–2088; tel. 517/279–5489; Douglas L. Rahn, Chief Executive Officer **A**1 9 10 11 12 **F**3 7 8 10 14 16 19 21 22 28 29 30 31 32 33 35 37 40 41 42 44 49 51 52 54 55 56 57 58 59 63 65 67 70 71 72 73 **P**6 8 **S** Quorum Health Group/Quorum Health Resources, Inc., Brentwood, TN **N** Borgess Health Alliance, Kalamazoo, MI | 13 | 10 | 96 | 3697 | 40 | 83182 | 383 | 32132 | 14743 | 402

COMMERCE TOWNSHIP—Oakland County

☒ HURON VALLEY–SINAI HOSPITAL, (Formerly Huron Valley Hospital), 1 William Carls Drive, Zip 48382–1272; tel. 248/360–3300; Paul L. Broughton, FACHE, Senior Vice President **A**1 3 5 10 **F**7 8 10 14 15 19 21 22 28 30 31 34 37 39 40 42 44 45 46 65 67 71 73 **S** Detroit Medical Center, Detroit, MI **N** Detroit Medical Center, Detroit, MI | 23 | 10 | 140 | 8245 | 92 | 64262 | 1841 | 66380 | 23832 | —

CRYSTAL FALLS—Iron County

CRYSTAL FALLS COMMUNITY HOSPITAL See Iron County Community Hospital, Iron River

DEARBORN—Wayne County

☒ OAKWOOD HOSPITAL AND MEDICAL CENTER–DEARBORN, 18101 Oakwood Boulevard, Zip 48124–4093, Mailing Address: P.O. Box 2500, Zip 48123–2500; tel. 313/593–7000; Joseph Tasse, Administrator **A**1 2 3 5 8 9 10 **F**1 2 3 4 5 7 8 10 11 12 13 14 15 16 17 19 21 22 23 25 26 27 28 30 31 32 33 34 35 37 38 39 40 41 42 43 44 46 48 49 51 52 53 54 55 56 57 58 59 60 61 62 63 64 65 66 67 68 69 70 71 72 73 **P**5 7 **S** Oakwood Healthcare System, Dearborn, MI | 23 | 10 | 548 | 27892 | 419 | 654721 | 4667 | 301051 | 160020 | 3816

DECKERVILLE—Sanilac County

☒ DECKERVILLE COMMUNITY HOSPITAL, 3559 Pine Street, Zip 48427–0126, Mailing Address: P.O. Box 126, Zip 48427–0126; tel. 810/376–2835; Edward L. Gamache, Administrator **A**1 9 10 **F**14 15 16 19 22 28 29 30 39 41 42 45 46 67 71 73 **S** Mercy Health Services, Farmington Hills, MI | 23 | 10 | 17 | 272 | 2 | 13665 | — | 3331 | 1729 | 69

DETROIT—Wayne County

☒ △ CHILDREN'S HOSPITAL OF MICHIGAN, 3901 Beaubien Street, Zip 48201–9985; tel. 313/745–0073; Thomas M. Rozek, Senior Vice President **A**1 3 5 7 8 9 10 **F**9 10 12 13 14 15 16 17 18 19 20 22 25 27 28 29 30 31 34 35 38 39 41 42 43 44 45 46 47 48 49 50 51 64 65 67 68 69 70 71 72 73 **S** Detroit Medical Center, Detroit, MI **N** Detroit Medical Center, Detroit, MI | 23 | 50 | 245 | 13879 | 163 | 218467 | 0 | 172262 | 64550 | —

☒ DETROIT RECEIVING HOSPITAL AND UNIVERSITY HEALTH CENTER, 4201 St. Antoine Boulevard, Zip 48201–2194; tel. 313/745–3605; Leslie C. Bowman, Regional Administrator, Ancillary Services and Site Administrator **A**1 3 5 8 10 12 **F**4 7 8 9 10 11 12 17 18 19 21 22 23 27 28 29 30 31 32 34 35 37 39 41 42 43 44 46 49 50 51 52 54 56 57 58 60 65 67 70 71 72 73 **S** Detroit Medical Center, Detroit, MI **N** Detroit Medical Center, Detroit, MI | 23 | 10 | 278 | 12699 | 216 | 128452 | — | 164696 | 55853 | 1242

☒ ○ DETROIT RIVERVIEW HOSPITAL, 7733 East Jefferson Avenue, Zip 48214–2598; tel. 313/499–4000; Richard T. Young, President **A**1 9 10 11 12 **F**2 3 4 7 8 10 11 12 13 14 15 16 17 18 19 20 21 22 23 25 26 27 28 29 30 31 32 33 34 35 37 38 39 40 41 42 43 44 45 46 48 49 51 52 53 54 55 56 58 59 60 61 62 63 64 65 66 67 68 69 70 71 72 73 74 **P**5 6 8 **S** Sisters of St. Joseph Health System, Ann Arbor, MI **N** Saint John Health System, Detroit, MI; Detroit–Macomb Hospital Corp, Warren, MI | 23 | 10 | 262 | 12378 | 182 | 71518 | 1649 | 109587 | 54227 | 1061

☒ GRACE HOSPITAL, 6071 West Outer Drive, Zip 48235–2679; tel. 313/966–3525; Anne M. Regling, Regional Executive **A**1 3 5 8 9 10 12 **F**2 3 4 5 7 8 9 10 11 12 13 15 17 18 19 20 21 22 23 24 25 26 27 28 29 30 31 32 33 34 35 37 38 39 40 41 42 43 44 45 46 47 48 49 50 51 52 53 54 55 56 57 58 59 60 61 63 64 65 66 67 68 69 70 71 72 73 74 **P**5 6 8 **S** Detroit Medical Center, Detroit, MI **N** Detroit Medical Center, Detroit, MI | 23 | 10 | 343 | 17898 | 251 | 134925 | 2872 | 224184 | 73832 | 1779

☒ HARPER HOSPITAL, 3990 John R., Zip 48201–9027; tel. 313/745–8040; Paul L. Broughton, FACHE, Senior Vice President **A**1 2 3 5 8 9 10 12 **F**2 3 4 8 10 11 12 13 14 15 16 17 19 20 21 22 23 26 27 29 30 31 32 33 34 35 36 37 39 41 42 43 44 45 46 49 51 52 53 55 56 58 60 63 65 67 69 71 72 73 **S** Detroit Medical Center, Detroit, MI **N** Detroit Medical Center, Detroit, MI | 23 | 10 | 444 | 18110 | 327 | 199923 | 0 | 307369 | 95813 | —

☒ HENRY FORD HOSPITAL, 2799 West Grand Boulevard, Zip 48202–2689; tel. 313/876–2600; Stephen H. Velick, Chief Executive Officer **A**1 2 3 5 6 8 9 10 **F**1 2 3 4 5 6 7 8 9 10 11 12 13 14 15 16 17 18 19 20 21 22 23 24 25 26 27 28 29 30 31 32 33 34 35 36 37 38 39 40 41 42 43 44 45 46 49 50 51 52 53 54 55 56 57 58 59 60 61 63 64 65 66 67 68 69 70 71 72 73 74 **P**6 **S** Henry Ford Health System, Detroit, MI **N** Henry Ford Health System, Detroit, MI | 23 | 10 | 634 | 34423 | 497 | 749447 | 2437 | 355324 | 134788 | —

Hospital, Address, Telephone, Administrator, Approval, Facility, and Physician Codes, Health Care System, Network	Classi-fication Codes		Utilization Data					Expense (thousands) of dollars		
	Control	Service	Staffed Beds	Admissions	Census	Outpatient Visits	Births	Total	Payroll	Personnel

★ American Hospital Association (AHA) membership
□ Joint Commission on Accreditation of Healthcare Organizations (JCAHO) accreditation
+ American Osteopathic Healthcare Association (AOHA) membership
○ American Osteopathic Association (AOA) accreditation
△ Commission on Accreditation of Rehabilitation Facilities (CARF) accreditation
Control codes 61, 63, 64, 71, 72 and 73 indicate hospitals listed by AOHA, but not registered by AHA. For definition of numerical codes, see page A4

Hospital	Control	Service	Staffed Beds	Admissions	Census	Outpatient Visits	Births	Total	Payroll	Personnel
✠ HOLY CROSS HOSPITAL, 4777 East Outer Drive, Zip 48234–0401; tel. 313/369–9100; Michael F. Breen, President **A**1 9 10 **F**1 8 10 11 14 15 16 19 21 22 27 30 33 34 44 48 49 52 57 58 59 63 64 65 71 73 **P**4 5 8 **S** Sisters of St. Joseph Health System, Ann Arbor, MI **N** Saint John Health System, Detroit, MI	21	10	161	5470	114	45062	—	42276	21894	588
✠ HUTZEL HOSPITAL, 4707 St. Antoine Boulevard, Zip 48201–0154; tel. 313/745–7555; Phyllis Reynolds, R.N., Site Administrator (Nonreporting) **A**1 3 5 8 9 10 **S** Detroit Medical Center, Detroit, MI **N** Detroit Medical Center, Detroit, MI	23	10	243	—	—	—	—	—	—	—
✠ JOHN D. DINGELL VETERANS AFFAIRS MEDICAL CENTER, (Formerly Veterans Affairs Medical Center), 4646 John R. Street, Zip 48201–1932; tel. 313/576–1000; Carlos B. Lott, Jr., Director (Total facility includes 84 beds in nursing home–type unit) **A**1 2 3 5 8 **F**2 3 4 5 6 8 10 11 12 14 15 16 17 18 19 20 21 22 23 26 27 28 29 30 31 32 33 34 35 37 39 41 42 43 44 45 46 49 50 51 52 54 55 56 58 59 60 61 63 64 65 66 68 69 70 71 72 73 74 **P**6 **S** Department of Veterans Affairs, Washington, DC	45	10	271	5478	147	242989	0	—	—	1529
✠ MERCY HOSPITAL, 5555 Conner Avenue, Zip 48213–3499; tel. 313/579–4000; David Spivey, Interim Chief Executive Officer **A**1 3 9 10 **F**1 3 4 7 8 10 12 13 14 15 16 17 18 19 20 22 23 24 25 26 27 28 30 31 32 33 34 35 37 40 41 42 43 44 49 51 52 53 54 55 56 57 58 59 60 62 64 65 67 69 71 72 73 74 **P**5 6 8 **S** Mercy Health Services, Farmington Hills, MI **N** Mercy Health Services – Michigan Region, Farmington Hills, MI; Henry Ford Health System, Detroit, MI	21	10	248	10334	186	229104	921	104801	46280	1295
✠ △ REHABILITATION INSTITUTE OF MICHIGAN, 261 Mack Boulevard, Zip 48201–2495; tel. 313/745–1203; Bruce M. Gans, M.D., Senior Vice President **A**1 3 5 7 9 10 **F**3 4 5 7 8 9 10 11 12 13 14 15 16 17 19 20 21 22 23 24 25 26 27 28 29 30 31 32 33 34 35 37 38 39 40 41 42 43 44 45 46 47 48 49 50 51 52 53 54 55 56 57 58 59 60 61 63 64 65 66 67 69 70 71 72 73 74 **P**4 5 6 7 8 **S** Detroit Medical Center, Detroit, MI **N** Detroit Medical Center, Detroit, MI	23	46	96	1552	67	94097	0	43548	21776	504
✠ ○ △ SINAI HOSPITAL, 6767 West Outer Drive, Zip 48235–2899; tel. 313/493–6800; William Pinsky, M.D., Senior Vice President and Regional Executive **A**1 3 5 7 8 9 10 11 12 **F**3 4 5 7 8 10 11 12 13 14 15 16 17 18 19 20 21 22 23 24 25 26 27 28 29 30 31 32 33 34 35 37 38 39 40 41 42 43 44 45 46 47 48 49 50 51 52 53 54 55 56 57 58 59 60 61 63 65 66 67 69 70 71 72 73 74 **P**6 8 **S** Detroit Medical Center, Detroit, MI	23	10	446	20178	325	268437	3126	277718	144134	2939
✠ △ ST. JOHN HOSPITAL AND MEDICAL CENTER, (Includes St. John Hospital–Macomb Center, 26755 Ballard Road, Harrison Township, Zip 48045–2458; tel. 810/465–5501; David Sessions, President), 22101 Moross Road, Zip 48236–2172; tel. 313/343–4000; Timothy J. Grajewski, President and Chief Executive Officer **A**1 2 3 5 7 8 9 10 **F**2 3 4 6 7 8 10 11 12 13 14 15 16 17 18 19 20 21 22 23 25 26 27 28 29 30 31 32 33 34 35 36 37 38 39 40 41 42 43 44 45 46 48 49 51 52 53 54 55 56 57 58 59 60 61 62 65 66 67 68 69 70 71 72 73 74 **P**3 5 6 8 **S** Sisters of St. Joseph Health System, Ann Arbor, MI	21	10	662	29326	—	338484	3369	—	165831	—
✠ △ ST. JOHN HEALTH SYSTEM–SARATOGA CAMPUS, 15000 Gratiot Avenue, Zip 48205–1999; tel. 313/245–1200; Michael F. Breen, President **A**1 7 9 10 **F**8 12 14 15 16 17 19 21 22 25 26 27 28 30 31 37 39 42 44 45 48 49 63 65 71 73 **P**5 8 **S** Sisters of St. Joseph Health System, Ann Arbor, MI **N** Saint John Health System, Detroit, MI	23	10	154	3606	85	22338	1	31225	15318	598
DOWAGIAC—Cass County										
✠ LEE MEMORIAL HOSPITAL, 420 West High Street, Zip 49047–1907; tel. 616/782–8681; Fritz Fahrenbacher, Chief Executive Officer **A**1 9 10 **F**3 8 11 14 15 16 17 19 21 22 25 28 29 30 33 35 36 39 41 42 44 45 46 49 53 54 55 56 57 58 59 65 66 67 71 72 73 **P**6 8 **S** Sisters of St. Joseph Health System, Ann Arbor, MI **N** First Choice Network, Southhaven, MI; Borgess Health Alliance, Kalamazoo, MI	21	10	47	1958	22	22575	0	12357	5569	197
EAST CHINA—St. Clair County										
✠ RIVER DISTRICT HOSPITAL, 4100 South River Road, Zip 48054; tel. 810/329–7111; Frank W. Poma, President **A**1 9 10 **F**3 7 8 12 15 16 17 19 21 22 26 28 30 32 35 37 40 41 42 44 45 46 49 51 53 54 56 58 65 67 71 73 74 **P**6 8 **S** Sisters of St. Joseph Health System, Ann Arbor, MI **N** Saint John Health System, Detroit, MI; Port Huron Hospital/Blue Water Health Services, Port Huron, MI	23	10	68	2486	23	76984	595	23074	11636	306
EATON RAPIDS—Eaton County										
□ EATON RAPIDS COMMUNITY HOSPITAL, 1500 South Main Street, Zip 48827–0130, Mailing Address: P.O. Box 130, Zip 48827–0130; tel. 517/663–2671; Jack L. Denton, President **A**1 9 10 **F**8 12 14 15 16 19 22 28 30 34 35 36 39 41 42 44 46 51 56 65 71 72 73	23	10	21	644	7	26888	—	6865	3638	134
ESCANABA—Delta County										
✠ ST. FRANCIS HOSPITAL, 3401 Ludington Street, Zip 49829–1377; tel. 906/786–3311; Roger M. Burgess, Administrator **A**1 10 **F**7 8 15 16 17 19 22 26 28 29 30 32 33 34 35 37 40 41 42 44 45 49 51 65 66 67 71 72 73 74 **P**6 **S** OSF Healthcare System, Peoria, IL	23	10	66	3261	40	66670	412	37913	16818	415
FARMINGTON HILLS—Oakland County										
★ + ○ △ BOTSFORD GENERAL HOSPITAL, 28050 Grand River Avenue, Zip 48336–5933; tel. 248/471–8000; Gerson I. Cooper, President **A**7 9 10 11 12 13 **F**3 5 7 8 10 11 12 14 15 16 17 19 21 22 24 25 26 27 28 29 30 31 32 34 35 37 39 40 41 42 44 45 46 48 49 51 52 54 57 58 62 64 65 66 67 69 71 72 73 **P**5 6 7 **N** Great Lakes Health Network, Southfield, MI	23	10	328	12577	207	358240	886	153698	75331	1987

Hospital, Address, Telephone, Administrator, Approval, Facility, and Physician Codes, Health Care System, Network	Classification Codes		Utilization Data					Expense (thousands) of dollars		
	Control	Service	Staffed Beds	Admissions	Census	Outpatient Visits	Births	Total	Payroll	Personnel

★ American Hospital Association (AHA) membership
☐ Joint Commission on Accreditation of Healthcare Organizations (JCAHO) accreditation
+ American Osteopathic Healthcare Association (AOHA) membership
○ American Osteopathic Association (AOA) accreditation
△ Commission on Accreditation of Rehabilitation Facilities (CARF) accreditation
Control codes 61, 63, 64, 71, 72 and 73 indicate hospitals listed by AOHA, but not registered by AHA. For definition of numerical codes, see page A4

FERNDALE—Oakland County

★ KINGSWOOD HOSPITAL, 10300 West Eight Mile Road, Zip 48220–2198; tel. 248/398–3200; Glenn Black, Associate Vice President and Chief Operating Officer **A**1 3 10 **F**1 14 16 26 27 45 52 53 57 59 **S** Henry Ford Health System, Detroit, MI **N** Henry Ford Health System, Detroit, MI — 23 22 64 1785 40 7749 0 8723 4871 126

FLINT—Genesee County

★ HURLEY MEDICAL CENTER, One Hurley Plaza, Zip 48503–5993; tel. 810/257–9000; Glenn A. Fosdick, President and Chief Executive Officer **A**1 2 3 5 8 9 10 **F**3 7 8 9 10 11 12 13 14 15 16 17 18 19 20 21 22 24 25 26 27 28 29 30 31 32 33 34 35 37 38 39 40 41 42 44 45 46 47 48 49 51 52 53 54 55 56 57 58 59 60 61 63 64 65 66 67 69 70 71 72 73 74 **P**3 5 6 7 8 — 14 10 495 21327 310 312733 3655 231187 100456 2534

★ △ McLAREN REGIONAL MEDICAL CENTER, 401 South Ballenger Highway, Zip 48532–3685; tel. 810/342–2000; Philip A. Incarnati, President and Chief Executive Officer **A**1 2 3 5 7 8 9 10 **F**1 2 3 4 7 8 10 11 12 13 14 15 16 17 18 19 20 21 22 24 25 26 27 28 29 30 31 34 35 37 38 39 40 41 42 43 44 45 46 47 48 49 51 52 53 54 55 56 57 58 59 60 61 63 64 65 66 67 69 71 72 73 74 **P**6 — 23 10 436 17661 253 301766 1061 167381 76794 1749

FRANKFORT—Benzie County

★ PAUL OLIVER MEMORIAL HOSPITAL, 224 Park Avenue, Zip 49635–9658; tel. 616/352–9621; James D. Austin, CHE, Administrator (Total facility includes 40 beds in nursing home–type unit) **A**1 9 10 **F**8 14 15 16 17 19 21 22 26 28 30 32 33 34 35 41 44 46 49 53 56 57 58 59 60 61 64 65 66 67 71 72 73 74 **P**1 3 5 7 **S** Munson Healthcare, Traverse City, MI **N** Munson Healthcare, Traverse City, MI — 23 10 48 401 41 26437 — 6466 2136 85

FREMONT—Newaygo County

★ GERBER MEMORIAL HOSPITAL, 212 South Sullivan Street, Zip 49412–1596; tel. 616/924–3300; Ned B. Hughes, Jr., President **A**1 9 10 **F**7 8 14 15 16 17 18 22 26 30 32 34 37 39 40 41 42 44 45 46 49 52 54 55 56 57 58 65 66 67 71 72 73 74 **P**6 **N** Butterworth Health System, Grand Rapids, MI — 23 10 73 2368 29 67617 326 26844 13051 403

GARDEN CITY—Wayne County

+ ○ △ GARDEN CITY HOSPITAL, 6245 North Inkster Road, Zip 48135–4001; tel. 734/421–3300; Gary R. Ley, President and Chief Executive Officer **A**7 9 10 11 12 13 **F**2 3 7 8 10 11 12 14 15 16 17 19 22 27 28 29 33 34 35 37 39 40 41 42 44 46 48 49 51 60 65 66 67 71 72 73 **P**5 8 **N** Great Lakes Health Network, Southfield, MI — 23 10 253 10256 175 75508 802 93868 43680 1282

GAYLORD—Otsego County

★ OTSEGO MEMORIAL HOSPITAL, (Includes McReynolds Hall), 825 North Center Street, Zip 49735–1560; tel. 517/731–2216; John L. MacLeod, Administrator and Chief Executive Officer (Total facility includes 34 beds in nursing home–type unit) **A**1 9 10 **F**7 8 14 15 16 19 22 28 30 32 33 34 35 37 40 41 44 49 63 64 65 67 71 72 73 **P**6 8 — 23 10 87 1904 47 44334 246 15856 7608 278

GLADWIN—Gladwin County

★ MIDMICHIGAN MEDICAL CENTER–GLADWIN, (Formerly MidMichigan Regional Medical Center–Gladwin), 455 South Quarter Street, Zip 48624–1918; tel. 517/426–9286; Mark E. Bush, Executive Vice President **A**1 9 10 **F**15 16 17 19 22 28 30 34 41 44 46 49 51 67 71 72 73 **P**1 5 7 **S** MidMichigan Health, Midland, MI — 23 10 42 1450 17 37872 — 9879 4242 142

GRAND BLANC—Genesee County

★ + ○ △ GENESYS REGIONAL MEDICAL CENTER, One Genesys Parkway, Zip 48439–8066; tel. 810/606–6600; Elliot Joseph, President and Chief Executive Officer **A**1 2 3 5 7 9 10 11 12 13 **F**1 3 4 7 8 10 11 12 14 15 16 17 18 19 21 22 23 26 27 28 29 30 31 32 33 34 35 37 39 40 41 42 43 44 45 46 48 49 51 53 54 56 57 58 60 63 64 65 67 68 70 71 72 73 74 **P**1 6 7 **S** Sisters of St. Joseph Health System, Ann Arbor, MI — 21 10 386 25476 345 276816 2684 241156 121855 2668

GRAND HAVEN—Ottawa County

★ NORTH OTTAWA COMMUNITY HOSPITAL, 1309 Sheldon Road, Zip 49417–2488; tel. 616/842–3600; Richard Long, Interim Chief Executive Officer **A**1 9 10 **F**3 7 8 12 14 15 16 19 21 22 26 28 30 31 32 33 34 35 36 37 39 40 41 42 44 46 49 63 65 66 67 68 71 72 73 74 — 23 10 81 2630 27 158924 565 32042 14042 421

GRAND RAPIDS—Kent County

BLODGETT MEMORIAL MEDICAL CENTER See Spectrum Health–East Campus
BUTTERWORTH HOSPITAL See Spectrum Health–Downtown Campus

☐ FOREST VIEW HOSPITAL, 1055 Medical Park Drive S.E., Zip 49546–3671; tel. 616/942–9610; John F. Kuhn, Chief Executive Officer **A**1 10 **F**17 26 34 41 46 52 53 55 56 57 58 59 65 67 **S** Universal Health Services, Inc., King of Prussia, PA — 33 22 62 883 19 5850 0 5283 2637 85

★ KENT COMMUNITY HOSPITAL, 750 Fuller Avenue N.E., Zip 49503–1995; tel. 616/336–3300; Lori Portfleet, Chief Executive Officer (Total facility includes 338 beds in nursing home–type unit) (Nonreporting) **A**1 10 — 13 49 374 — — — — — — —

★ △ MARY FREE BED HOSPITAL AND REHABILITATION CENTER, 235 Wealthy S.E., Zip 49503–5299; tel. 616/242–0300; William H. Blessing, President **A**1 7 10 **F**15 16 19 21 25 27 32 34 35 39 41 45 48 49 65 67 71 73 — 23 46 80 867 51 33856 — 21554 13393 457

+ ○ △ METROPOLITAN HOSPITAL, 1919 Boston Street S.E., Zip 49506–4199, Mailing Address: P.O. Box 158, Zip 49501–0158; tel. 616/247–7200; Michael D. Faas, President and Chief Executive Officer **A**7 9 10 11 12 13 **F**1 3 4 7 8 10 12 14 15 16 17 19 21 22 23 24 25 26 28 29 30 31 32 33 34 35 37 39 40 41 42 44 48 49 51 53 54 55 56 57 58 59 60 61 63 64 65 66 67 70 71 73 74 **P**1 6 7 **N** Butterworth Health System, Grand Rapids, MI — 23 10 205 8311 116 210189 1221 82451 40103 988

Hospital, Address, Telephone, Administrator, Approval, Facility, and Physician Codes, Health Care System, Network	Classi-fication Codes		Utilization Data					Expense (thousands) of dollars		
★ American Hospital Association (AHA) membership □ Joint Commission on Accreditation of Healthcare Organizations (JCAHO) accreditation + American Osteopathic Healthcare Association (AOHA) membership ○ American Osteopathic Association (AOA) accreditation △ Commission on Accreditation of Rehabilitation Facilities (CARF) accreditation Control codes 61, 63, 64, 71, 72 and 73 indicate hospitals listed by AOHA, but not registered by AHA. For definition of numerical codes, see page A4	Control	Service	Staffed Beds	Admissions	Census	Outpatient Visits	Births	Total	Payroll	Personnel
⊠ PINE REST CHRISTIAN MENTAL HEALTH SERVICES, 300 68th Street S.E., Zip 49501–0165, Mailing Address: P.O. Box 165, Zip 49501–0165; tel. 616/455–5000; Daniel L. Holwerda, President and Chief Executive Officer **A**1 3 5 10 **F**3 4 7 8 9 10 11 12 13 14 15 16 17 19 21 22 25 26 29 30 32 35 37 38 40 42 43 44 45 46 47 50 52 53 54 55 56 57 58 59 60 61 63 64 65 71 72 73 **N** Butterworth Health System, Grand Rapids, MI	23	22	106	2386	53	89375	—	30170	17573	507
⊠ SAINT MARY'S HEALTH SERVICES, 200 Jefferson Avenue S.E., Zip 49503–4598; tel. 616/752–6090; David J. Ameen, President and Chief Executive Officer **A**1 2 3 5 9 10 **F**7 8 10 12 14 15 16 17 19 20 21 22 24 25 26 28 29 30 31 32 34 35 37 39 40 41 42 44 45 51 52 54 55 57 59 60 63 64 65 66 67 69 70 71 73 74 **P**3 **S** Mercy Health Services, Farmington Hills, MI **N** Mercy Health Services – Michigan Region, Farmington Hills, MI	21	10	287	12462	171	426905	1980	156164	66581	1825
⊠ SPECTRUM HEALTH–DOWNTOWN CAMPUS, (Formerly Butterworth Hospital), 100 Michigan Street N.E., Zip 49503–2551; tel. 616/391–1774; Philip H. McCorkle, Jr., Chief Executive Officer **A**1 2 3 5 8 9 10 **F**1 2 3 4 6 7 8 10 11 12 13 14 15 16 17 18 19 20 21 22 23 24 25 26 28 29 30 31 32 33 34 35 36 37 38 39 40 41 42 43 44 45 46 47 48 49 52 53 54 55 56 57 58 59 60 61 64 65 66 67 68 69 70 71 72 73 74 **P**5 6 8 **N** Butterworth Health System, Grand Rapids, MI	23	10	529	28011	376	627732	5691	284627	135011	4243
⊠ SPECTRUM HEALTH–EAST CAMPUS, (Formerly Blodgett Memorial Medical Center), (Includes Ferguson Campus, 72 Sheldon Boulevard S.E., Zip 49503–4294; tel. 616/356–4000), 1840 Welthy Street S.E., Zip 49506–2921; tel. 616/774–7444; Terrence Michael O'Rourke, President **A**1 2 3 5 8 9 10 **F**4 5 7 8 9 10 11 12 14 15 16 19 21 22 32 35 37 38 39 40 41 42 43 44 47 49 51 60 61 63 65 66 67 71 72 73 **P**5 6	23	10	332	16243	216	380389	3051	152202	68032	2009
GRAYLING—Crawford County										
★ MERCY HEALTH SERVICES NORTH–GRAYLING, 1100 Michigan Avenue, Zip 49738–1398; tel. 517/348–5461; Stephanie J. Riemer-Matuzak, Chief Operating Officer (Total facility includes 40 beds in nursing home–type unit) **A**9 10 **F**7 8 10 11 12 15 16 19 21 22 28 29 32 33 34 35 39 40 41 44 48 49 51 63 64 65 71 73 **P**8 **S** Mercy Health Services, Farmington Hills, MI **N** Mercy Health Services – Michigan Region, Farmington Hills, MI	21	10	98	2682	65	74709	252	27575	12297	403
GREENVILLE—Montcalm County										
⊠ UNITED MEMORIAL HOSPITAL ASSOCIATION, 615 South Bower Street, Zip 48838–2628; tel. 616/754–4691; Dennis G. Zielinski, Chief Executive Officer (Total facility includes 40 beds in nursing home–type unit) **A**1 9 10 **F**7 8 13 14 15 16 17 19 25 30 34 40 41 44 46 49 51 64 65 71 72 73 **P**3 **N** Butterworth Health System, Grand Rapids, MI	23	10	98	2234	57	79472	311	21912	7947	342
GROSSE POINTE—Wayne County										
⊠ BON SECOURS HOSPITAL, 468 Cadieux Road, Zip 48230–1592; tel. 313/343–1000; Michael Serilla, Acting Executive Vice President and Administrator (Total facility includes 200 beds in nursing home–type unit) **A**1 3 5 9 10 **F**3 7 8 10 15 16 17 18 19 21 22 24 25 26 27 28 29 30 31 32 33 35 36 37 39 40 42 44 45 46 49 51 63 64 65 67 71 73 74 **S** Bon Secours Health System, Inc., Marriottsville, MD	21	10	435	10620	334	95535	1360	96922	50585	1778
GROSSE POINTE FARMS—Wayne County										
⊠ HENRY FORD COTTAGE HOSPITAL OF GROSSE POINTE, 159 Kercheval Avenue, Zip 48236–3692; tel. 313/640–1000; Martin Monastersky, Interim Chief Executive Officer **A**1 3 9 10 **F**1 7 8 14 15 16 18 19 22 27 28 29 30 31 32 33 34 40 44 45 46 49 54 55 56 57 58 59 63 65 66 67 71 72 73 74 **P**6 **S** Henry Ford Health System, Detroit, MI **N** Henry Ford Health System, Detroit, MI	23	10	144	4501	74	192910	518	59169	30190	855
HANCOCK—Houghton County										
⊠ PORTAGE HEALTH SYSTEM, 200 Michigan Avenue, Zip 49930–1427; tel. 906/487–8000; James Bogan, Chief Executive Officer (Total facility includes 30 beds in nursing home–type unit) **A**1 9 10 **F**1 7 8 12 13 14 15 16 17 19 22 24 26 28 30 31 32 33 34 35 36 37 39 40 41 44 45 49 51 54 56 57 58 61 63 64 65 66 67 71 73 74 **P**6	23	10	74	1994	49	65043	378	22237	11797	329
HARBOR BEACH—Huron County										
★ HARBOR BEACH COMMUNITY HOSPITAL, 210 South First Street, Zip 48441–1236, Mailing Address: P.O. Box 40, Zip 48441–0040; tel. 517/479–3201; Pauline Siemen-Messing, R.N., President and Chief Executive Officer (Total facility includes 40 beds in nursing home–type unit) **A**9 10 **F**8 16 19 22 26 30 34 40 44 49 51 64 65 67 71 **P**6	23	10	61	475	42	17273	0	5559	2961	117
HARRISON TOWNSHIP—Macomb County										
ST. JOHN HOSPITAL–MACOMB CENTER See St. John Hospital and Medical Center, Detroit										
HASTINGS—Barry County										
□ PENNOCK HOSPITAL, 1009 West Green Street, Zip 49058–1790; tel. 616/945–3451; Daniel Hamilton, Chief Executive Officer **A**1 9 10 **F**7 8 11 12 14 15 16 19 21 22 24 26 28 29 30 32 33 34 35 37 39 40 41 42 44 45 46 49 56 62 63 65 66 67 71 73 **P**5	23	10	88	3127	41	123114	356	26781	11017	416
HILLSDALE—Hillsdale County										
⊠ HILLSDALE COMMUNITY HEALTH CENTER, 168 South Howell Street, Zip 49242–2081; tel. 517/437–4451; Charles A. Bianchi, President (Total facility includes 21 beds in nursing home–type unit) **A**1 9 10 **F**3 7 8 11 14 15 16 17 19 21 22 26 28 30 32 34 35 37 39 40 41 44 46 49 63 64 65 71 72 73 **N** Borgess Health Alliance, Kalamazoo, MI	23	10	74	2836	53	84320	339	20109	8099	269

Hospital, Address, Telephone, Administrator, Approval, Facility, and Physician Codes, Health Care System, Network	Classi-fication Codes		Utilization Data					Expense (thousands) of dollars		
	Control	Service	Staffed Beds	Admissions	Census	Outpatient Visits	Births	Total	Payroll	Personnel

★ American Hospital Association (AHA) membership
□ Joint Commission on Accreditation of Healthcare Organizations (JCAHO) accreditation
+ American Osteopathic Healthcare Association (AOHA) membership
○ American Osteopathic Association (AOA) accreditation
△ Commission on Accreditation of Rehabilitation Facilities (CARF) accreditation
Control codes 61, 63, 64, 71, 72 and 73 indicate hospitals listed by AOHA, but not registered by AHA. For definition of numerical codes, see page A4

HOLLAND—Ottawa County

✠ △ HOLLAND COMMUNITY HOSPITAL, 602 Michigan Avenue, Zip 49423–4999; tel. 616/392–5141; Judeth N. Javorek, R.N., President and Chief Executive Officer **A**1 7 9 10 **F**7 12 14 15 16 17 19 21 22 28 29 30 32 34 35 36 37 39 40 41 42 44 45 49 52 53 54 55 56 57 58 60 63 65 67 70 71 72 73 **P**8	23	10	163	8235	72	187162	1778	56552	25377	811

HOWELL—Livingston County

✠ MCPHERSON HOSPITAL, 620 Byron Road, Zip 48843–1093; tel. 517/545–6000; C. W. Lauderbach, Jr., Chief Operating Officer **A**1 9 10 **F**1 3 4 5 7 8 10 12 14 15 16 17 19 20 21 22 23 24 25 26 29 30 31 32 33 34 35 37 39 40 41 42 43 44 46 49 50 51 53 54 56 57 58 59 60 61 63 65 66 67 68 69 70 71 72 73 74 **P**2 5 7 8 **S** Mercy Health Services, Farmington Hills, MI **N** Mercy Health Services – Michigan Region, Farmington Hills, MI	21	10	45	3428	34	256764	740	42747	19875	555

IONIA—Ionia County

★ IONIA COUNTY MEMORIAL HOSPITAL, 479 Lafayette Street, Zip 48846–1834, Mailing Address: Box 1001, Zip 48846–1899; tel. 616/527–4200; Evonne G. Ulmer, Chief Executive Officer **A**9 10 **F**7 8 11 14 15 17 19 22 26 28 30 31 32 33 34 37 39 40 41 42 44 45 49 51 56 65 66 71 72 73 74 **P**6	23	10	55	1277	15	16198	181	11691	5196	159

IRON MOUNTAIN—Dickinson County

✠ DICKINSON COUNTY HEALTHCARE SYSTEM, 1721 South Stephenson Avenue, Zip 49801–3637; tel. 906/774–1313; John Schon, Administrator and Chief Executive Officer **A**1 9 10 **F**7 8 12 14 16 19 21 22 28 29 34 35 39 41 42 44 46 49 65 66 67 71 73	13	10	96	4405	52	112789	555	41364	19065	485
✠ VETERANS AFFAIRS MEDICAL CENTER, 325 East H. Street, Zip 49801–4792; tel. 906/774–3300; Thomas B. Arnold, Director (Total facility includes 40 beds in nursing home–type unit) **A**1 5 9 **F**3 8 12 17 19 20 21 22 26 27 30 31 33 34 37 39 42 44 45 46 49 51 58 64 65 71 72 73 74 **P**6 **S** Department of Veterans Affairs, Washington, DC	45	10	63	1253	52	64318	0	—	—	368

IRON RIVER—Iron County

✠ IRON COUNTY COMMUNITY HOSPITAL, (Includes Crystal Falls Community Hospital, 212 South Third Street, Crystal Falls, Zip 49920, Mailing Address: P.O. Box 60, Zip 49920–0060; tel. 906/875–6661), 1400 West Ice Lake Road, Zip 49935–9594; tel. 906/265–6121; David L. Hoff, Chief Executive Officer (Total facility includes 68 beds in nursing home–type unit) **A**1 9 10 **F**7 8 12 13 15 16 17 19 21 24 26 28 30 32 34 37 39 40 41 42 44 45 46 48 49 51 61 64 65 66 67 71 73 74	23	10	88	1598	85	36340	16	14594	6693	188

IRONWOOD—Gogebic County

✠ GRAND VIEW HOSPITAL, N10561 Grand View Lane, Zip 49938–9359; tel. 906/932–2525; Frederick Geissler, Chief Executive Officer **A**1 9 10 **F**7 11 14 15 16 17 19 21 22 28 32 33 34 39 40 41 42 44 45 49 61 65 66 71 73 74 **P**8 **N** Northern Lakes Health Consortium, Duluth, MN	23	10	52	2083	23	51904	211	15987	7035	203

ISHPEMING—Marquette County

□ BELL MEMORIAL HOSPITAL, 101 South Fourth Street, Zip 49849–2151; tel. 906/486–4431; Kevin P. Calhoun, President and Chief Executive Officer **A**1 9 10 **F**2 3 7 8 11 14 15 16 17 19 21 22 25 27 28 30 33 34 39 40 41 44 49 51 58 63 65 71 72 73 **P**3 6	23	10	30	1624	18	52558	212	14062	7188	217

JACKSON—Jackson County

★ + ○ DOCTORS HOSPITAL OF JACKSON, 110 North Elm Avenue, Zip 49202–3595; tel. 517/787–1440; Michael J. Falatko, President and Chief Executive Officer **A**9 10 11 **F**8 15 16 17 19 21 22 25 30 34 35 37 41 42 44 46 49 63 65 66 71 72 73 **N** Midwest Health Net, LLC., Fort Wayne, IN	23	10	46	1724	17	41491	—	18648	8370	271
□ DUANE L. WATERS HOSPITAL, 3857 Cooper Street, Zip 49201–7521; tel. 517/780–5600; Gerald De Voss, Acting Administrator **A**1 **F**15 16 20 22 29 31 34 41 44 46 52 54 56 64 65 67 **P**6	12	11	86	1264	71	4620	—	19240	9437	187
□ W. A. FOOTE MEMORIAL HOSPITAL, 205 North East Avenue, Zip 49201–1789; tel. 517/788–4800; Georgia R. Fojtasek, President and Chief Executive Officer **A**1 9 10 **F**2 3 7 8 10 11 12 14 15 16 17 18 19 21 22 24 26 28 29 30 32 33 34 35 36 37 39 40 41 42 44 45 46 48 49 51 52 53 54 55 56 57 58 59 63 65 66 67 71 73 74 **P**1 5	23	10	325	16613	198	366347	1820	122313	59451	2033

KALAMAZOO—Kalamazoo County

✠ △ BORGESS MEDICAL CENTER, 1521 Gull Road, Zip 49001–1640; tel. 616/226–4800; Randall Stasik, President and Chief Executive Officer (includes BORGESS–PIPP HEALTH CENTER, 411 Naomi Street, Plainwell, Zip 49080–9981; tel. 616/685–6811; Fritz Fahrenbacher, Vice President and Regional Hospital Administrator) **A**1 2 3 5 7 9 10 **F**3 4 5 7 8 10 11 12 14 15 16 17 18 19 20 21 22 23 24 25 26 28 29 30 31 32 33 34 35 37 39 40 41 42 43 44 45 46 48 49 51 52 53 54 55 56 57 58 59 60 63 65 66 67 69 71 72 73 74 **P**3 6 7 8 **S** Sisters of St. Joseph Health System, Ann Arbor, MI **N** Borgess Health Alliance, Kalamazoo, MI	21	10	390	17581	233	281547	1677	225768	90121	2192
✠ BRONSON METHODIST HOSPITAL, 252 East Lovell Street, Zip 49007–5345; tel. 616/341–6000; Frank J. Sardone, President and Chief Executive Officer **A**1 2 3 5 6 9 10 **F**2 3 4 6 7 8 9 10 11 12 13 14 15 16 17 18 19 20 21 23 24 25 26 27 28 29 30 31 32 33 34 35 37 38 39 40 41 42 43 44 45 46 47 48 49 51 52 53 54 55 56 57 58 59 60 61 62 63 64 65 66 67 68 70 71 72 73 74 **P**5 7 8 **S** Bronson Healthcare Group, Inc., Kalamazoo, MI **N** Hospital Network Inc., Kalamazoo, MI; Lakeland Regional Health System, St. Joseph, MI	23	10	307	15444	199	337243	2886	168258	72447	1993
□ KALAMAZOO REGIONAL PSYCHIATRIC HOSPITAL, 1312 Oakland Drive, Zip 49008–1205; tel. 616/337–3000; James Coleman, Director (Nonreporting) **A**1 10	12	22	220	—	—	—	—	—	—	—

Hospital, Address, Telephone, Administrator, Approval, Facility, and Physician Codes, Health Care System, Network	Classi-fication Codes		Utilization Data					Expense (thousands) of dollars		
★ American Hospital Association (AHA) membership □ Joint Commission on Accreditation of Healthcare Organizations (JCAHO) accreditation + American Osteopathic Healthcare Association (AOHA) membership ○ American Osteopathic Association (AOA) accreditation △ Commission on Accreditation of Rehabilitation Facilities (CARF) accreditation Control codes 61, 63, 64, 71, 72 and 73 indicate hospitals listed by AOHA, but not registered by AHA. For definition of numerical codes, see page A4	Control	Service	Staffed Beds	Admissions	Census	Outpatient Visits	Births	Total	Payroll	Personnel

KALKASKA—Kalkaska County

★ KALKASKA MEMORIAL HEALTH CENTER, 419 South Coral Street, Zip 49646–9438, Mailing Address: P.O. Box 249, Zip 49646–0249; tel. 616/258–7500; James D. Austin, CHE, Administrator (Total facility includes 68 beds in nursing home–type unit) **A**9 10 **F**15 16 28 34 49 58 64 65 67 72 73 74 **S** Munson Healthcare, Traverse City, MI **N** Munson Healthcare, Traverse City, MI

| | 16 | 10 | 76 | 190 | 68 | — | 0 | 4252 | 1979 | 89 |

L'ANSE—Baraga County

□ BARAGA COUNTY MEMORIAL HOSPITAL, 770 North Main Street, Zip 49946–1195; tel. 906/524–6166; John P. Tembreull, Administrator (Total facility includes 28 beds in nursing home–type unit) **A**1 9 10 **F**8 15 16 19 21 22 30 32 44 49 63 64 65 67 71

| | 13 | 10 | 52 | 1024 | 36 | 17807 | 0 | 8159 | 4130 | 136 |

LAKEVIEW—Montcalm County

□ KELSEY MEMORIAL HOSPITAL, 418 Washington Avenue, Zip 48850; tel. 517/352–7211; Richard Waller, Chief Executive Officer (Total facility includes 42 beds in nursing home–type unit) **A**1 10 **F**8 17 19 22 24 25 27 30 32 33 34 41 44 48 49 51 54 64 65 66 71 72 **S** Quorum Health Group/Quorum Health Resources, Inc., Brentwood, TN

| | 23 | 10 | 66 | 540 | 52 | 28180 | — | 10621 | 4947 | 206 |

LANSING—Ingham County

★ ○ △ INGHAM REGIONAL MEDICAL CENTER, (Formerly Michigan Capital Healthcare), (Includes Ingham Regional Medical Center, Greenlawn Campus, 401 West Greenlawn Avenue, tel. 517/334–2121; Ingham Regional Medical Center, Pennsylvania Campus, 2727 South Pennsylvania Avenue, Zip 48910; tel. 517/372–8220), 401 West Greenlawn Avenue, Zip 48910–2819; tel. 517/334–2121; Dennis M. Litos, President and Chief Executive Officer **A**1 3 5 7 8 9 10 11 12 13 **F**2 4 7 8 9 10 11 12 13 14 15 16 17 18 19 22 25 26 27 28 29 30 31 32 33 34 35 37 38 39 40 41 42 43 44 46 47 48 49 51 52 54 57 58 60 64 65 66 67 68 70 71 72 73 74 **P**3 7 8 **N** Ingham Regional Medical Center, Lansing, MI
INGHAM REGIONAL MEDICAL CENTER, GREENLAWN CAMPUS See Ingham Regional Medical Center
INGHAM REGIONAL MEDICAL CENTER, PENNSYLVANIA CAMPUS See Ingham Regional Medical Center

| | 23 | 10 | 364 | 14415 | 230 | 50631 | 828 | 172449 | 83131 | 2379 |

★ ○ △ SPARROW HEALTH SYSTEM, 1215 East Michigan Avenue, Zip 48912–1811, Mailing Address: P.O. Box 30480, Zip 48909–7980; tel. 517/483–2700; Joseph F. Damore, President and Chief Executive Officer **A**1 2 3 5 7 9 10 11 12 **F**2 3 4 6 7 8 9 10 11 12 14 15 16 17 18 19 21 22 23 24 26 28 29 30 32 33 34 35 36 37 38 39 40 41 42 43 44 46 47 48 49 51 52 53 54 55 56 57 58 59 60 61 63 65 67 68 70 71 72 73 74 **P**1 6

| | 23 | 10 | 354 | 20350 | 281 | 69756 | 4256 | 228802 | 114721 | 2748 |

★ ○ ST. LAWRENCE HOSPITAL AND HEALTHCARE SERVICES, 1210 West Saginaw Street, Zip 48915–1999; tel. 517/372–3610; Arthur Knueppel, President and Chief Executive Officer (Total facility includes 178 beds in nursing home–type unit) **A**1 2 3 5 9 10 11 12 **F**1 3 4 5 7 8 9 10 11 12 13 14 15 16 17 18 19 20 21 22 23 24 25 26 27 28 29 30 31 32 34 35 37 38 39 40 41 42 43 44 45 46 47 48 49 51 52 53 54 55 56 57 58 59 60 63 64 65 66 67 70 71 73 74 **P**4 5 6 8

| | 23 | 10 | 339 | 7844 | 270 | 174204 | 1093 | 75536 | 36118 | 1366 |

LAPEER—Lapeer County

□ LAPEER REGIONAL HOSPITAL, 1375 North Main Street, Zip 48446–1376; tel. 810/667–5500; Donald C. Kooy, President and Chief Executive Officer (Total facility includes 19 beds in nursing home–type unit) **A**1 9 10 **F**2 3 4 7 8 10 11 12 13 14 15 16 17 18 19 20 21 22 24 25 26 27 28 29 30 31 32 33 34 35 37 38 39 40 41 42 43 44 45 46 47 49 51 52 53 54 55 56 57 58 59 60 61 63 64 65 66 67 71 72 73 74 **P**4 6

| | 23 | 10 | 222 | 5817 | 445 | 73189 | 771 | 45005 | 20722 | 576 |

LAURIUM—Houghton County

★ KEWEENAW MEMORIAL MEDICAL CENTER, 205 Osceola Street, Zip 49913–2199; tel. 906/337–6500; Rick Wright, FACHE, CPA, President and Chief Executive Officer **A**1 9 10 **F**7 8 11 12 16 17 19 21 22 31 32 35 37 40 44 46 65 71 74 **P**6

| | 23 | 10 | 48 | 1534 | 18 | 29291 | 76 | 13730 | 7486 | 215 |

LINCOLN PARK—Wayne County

□ VENCOR HOSPITAL–DETROIT, 26400 West Outer Drive, Zip 48146–2088; tel. 313/594–6000; Deborah A. Sopo, Administrator **A**1 9 10 **F**10 16 22 27 37 65 67 **P**6 **S** Vencor, Incorporated, Louisville, KY

| | 33 | 10 | 114 | 538 | 72 | 0 | 0 | 16083 | 7789 | 251 |

LIVONIA—Wayne County

★ ST. MARY HOSPITAL, 36475 West Five Mile Road, Zip 48154–1988; tel. 734/655–4800; Sister Mary Renetta Rumpz, FACHE, President and Chief Executive Officer **A**1 9 10 **F**2 3 4 6 7 8 10 11 12 13 14 15 16 17 18 19 20 21 22 23 24 26 27 28 29 30 32 33 34 35 37 39 40 41 42 43 44 45 46 49 52 54 55 56 57 58 59 60 63 65 67 69 70 71 72 73 74 **P**4 5 8 **N** William Beaumont Hospital Corp, Royal Oak, MI

| | 21 | 10 | 253 | 11117 | 163 | 120471 | 1082 | 91951 | 46057 | 1124 |

LUDINGTON—Mason County

★ MEMORIAL MEDICAL CENTER OF WEST MICHIGAN, One Atkinson Drive, Zip 49431–1999; tel. 616/843–2591; Robert C. Marquardt, FACHE, President and Chief Executive Officer **A**10 **F**7 8 14 15 16 17 19 21 22 30 32 34 35 37 39 40 41 42 44 49 52 54 55 56 57 63 65 67 71 73 74 **P**6

| | 23 | 10 | 80 | 3208 | 41 | 68499 | 373 | 26651 | 12116 | 390 |

MADISON HEIGHTS—Oakland County

★ MADISON COMMUNITY HOSPITAL, 30671 Stephenson Highway, Zip 48071–1678; tel. 248/588–8000; Charles F. Pinkerman, Administrator **A**1 9 10 **F**8 15 16 19 22 26 27 28 30 32 37 41 44 46 49 52 56 57 59 65 67 68

| | 23 | 10 | 67 | 1306 | 26 | 42357 | 0 | 12085 | 6936 | 210 |

Hospital, Address, Telephone, Administrator, Approval, Facility, and Physician Codes, Health Care System, Network	Classi-fication Codes		Utilization Data					Expense (thousands) of dollars		
	Control	Service	Staffed Beds	Admissions	Census	Outpatient Visits	Births	Total	Payroll	Personnel

★ American Hospital Association (AHA) membership
□ Joint Commission on Accreditation of Healthcare Organizations (JCAHO) accreditation
+ American Osteopathic Healthcare Association (AOHA) membership
○ American Osteopathic Association (AOA) accreditation
△ Commission on Accreditation of Rehabilitation Facilities (CARF) accreditation
Control codes 61, 63, 64, 71, 72 and 73 indicate hospitals listed by AOHA, but not registered by AHA. For definition of numerical codes, see page A4

Hospital	Control	Service	Staffed Beds	Admissions	Census	Outpatient Visits	Births	Total	Payroll	Personnel
□ + ○ ST. JOHN HEALTH SYSTEM, OAKLAND HOSPITAL, (Formerly Oakland General Hospital), 27351 Dequindre, Zip 48071–3499; tel. 248/967–7000; Robert Deputat, President **A**1 9 10 11 12 13 **F**1 2 3 4 6 7 8 9 10 11 12 13 14 15 16 17 18 19 20 21 22 23 24 25 26 27 28 29 30 31 32 33 34 35 36 37 38 39 40 41 42 43 44 45 46 47 48 49 50 51 52 53 54 55 56 57 58 59 60 61 62 63 64 65 66 67 68 69 70 71 72 73 74 **P**4 5 6 7 8 **S** Sisters of St. Joseph Health System, Ann Arbor, MI **N** Saint John Health System, Detroit, MI; Great Lakes Health Network, Southfield, MI	21	10	166	6947	133	47135	—	63446	29601	915
MANISTEE—Manistee County										
WEST SHORE HOSPITAL, 1465 East Parkdale Avenue, Zip 49660–9785; tel. 616/398–1000; Burton O. Parks, III, Administrator **A**9 10 **F**7 8 11 12 14 15 16 17 19 21 22 24 28 29 30 32 33 35 39 40 41 42 44 45 46 49 51 63 65 67 71 73 74 **P**3 8	13	10	54	1700	20	37085	127	17215	8025	250
MANISTIQUE—Schoolcraft County										
✠ SCHOOLCRAFT MEMORIAL HOSPITAL, 500 Main Street, Zip 49854–0000; tel. 906/341–3200; David B. Jahn, Administrator and Chief Financial Officer **A**1 9 10 **F**2 3 4 7 8 9 10 11 14 15 16 17 18 19 20 21 22 23 24 26 27 28 29 30 31 32 33 34 35 36 37 38 39 40 41 42 43 44 45 46 47 48 49 51 52 53 54 55 56 57 58 59 60 63 64 65 66 67 70 71 72 73 74 **P**4	13	10	20	628	6	34134	117	8324	4721	129
MARLETTE—Sanilac County										
✠ MARLETTE COMMUNITY HOSPITAL, 2770 Main Street, Zip 48453–0307, Mailing Address: P.O. Box 307, Zip 48453–0307; tel. 517/635–4000; David S. McEwen, Chief Executive Officer (Total facility includes 43 beds in nursing home–type unit) **A**1 9 10 **F**1 13 14 15 16 17 18 19 20 21 22 26 28 29 30 33 34 36 39 42 44 45 46 48 49 62 64 65 66 67 71 **P**6 **S** Quorum Health Group/Quorum Health Resources, Inc., Brentwood, TN	23	10	91	1005	53	32582	—	16287	7664	321
MARQUETTE—Marquette County										
✠ △ MARQUETTE GENERAL HOSPITAL, 420 West Magnetic Street, Zip 49855–2794; tel. 906/225–4774; William Nemacheck, Chief Executive Officer **A**1 2 3 5 7 9 10 **F**2 3 4 5 7 8 10 11 13 14 15 16 17 18 19 21 22 23 26 28 29 30 32 33 34 35 37 38 39 40 41 42 43 44 45 46 48 49 51 52 53 54 55 56 57 58 60 65 66 67 70 71 73 74 **P**6 **N** Covenant Healthcare System, Inc., Milwaukee, WI	23	10	320	10039	161	321144	636	144177	72652	1780
MARSHALL—Calhoun County										
✠ OAKLAWN HOSPITAL, 200 North Madison Street, Zip 49068–1199; tel. 616/781–4271; Rob Covert, President and Chief Executive Officer **A**1 9 10 **F**3 5 7 8 12 14 15 16 17 19 21 22 24 29 30 31 32 33 34 35 36 37 39 40 41 44 45 46 49 52 54 55 56 57 58 59 61 63 65 66 67 71 73 **N** Hospital Network Inc., Kalamazoo, MI	23	10	94	2447	27	66772	537	26741	13299	376
MIDLAND—Midland County										
✠ △ MIDMICHIGAN MEDICAL CENTER–MIDLAND, (Formerly MidMichigan Regional Medical Center), 4005 Orchard Drive, Zip 48670; tel. 517/839–3000; David A. Reece, President **A**1 2 3 5 7 9 10 **F**7 8 10 11 12 15 16 19 20 21 22 25 26 27 28 29 30 31 32 33 34 35 36 37 39 40 41 42 44 45 46 48 49 51 52 54 55 56 57 58 59 60 64 65 66 67 71 72 73 74 **P**6 8 **S** MidMichigan Health, Midland, MI	23	10	221	10670	140	186208	1244	124748	54515	1447
MONROE—Monroe County										
✠ MERCY MEMORIAL HOSPITAL, 740 North Macomb Street, Zip 48161–9974, Mailing Address: P.O. Box 67, Zip 48161–0067; tel. 734/241–1700; Richard S. Hiltz, President and Chief Executive Officer (Total facility includes 70 beds in nursing home–type unit) **A**1 9 10 **F**1 2 3 4 5 6 7 8 9 10 11 12 13 14 15 16 17 18 19 20 21 22 23 24 25 26 27 28 29 30 31 32 33 34 35 36 37 38 39 40 41 42 43 44 45 46 47 48 49 50 51 52 53 54 55 56 57 58 59 60 61 62 63 64 65 66 67 68 69 70 71 72 73 74 **N** Lake Erie Health Alliance, Toledo, OH; Midwest Health Net, LLC., Fort Wayne, IN	23	10	243	9113	160	107408	939	63160	32183	889
MOUNT CLEMENS—Macomb County										
★ △ MOUNT CLEMENS GENERAL HOSPITAL, 1000 Harrington Boulevard, Zip 48043–2992; tel. 810/493–8000; Robert Milewski, President and Chief Executive Officer **A**9 10 11 12 13 **F**3 6 8 10 12 13 15 16 17 18 19 22 25 26 27 28 29 30 31 32 33 35 36 37 39 40 41 42 43 44 45 46 49 50 60 62 63 65 66 67 69 71 72 73 74 **N** Great Lakes Health Network, Southfield, MI	23	10	241	11335	149	84924	2831	152242	71378	1942
MOUNT PLEASANT—Isabella County										
✠ + ○ CENTRAL MICHIGAN COMMUNITY HOSPITAL, 1221 South Drive, Zip 48858–3234; tel. 517/772–6700; Mark A. Cwiek, President and Chief Executive Officer **A**1 9 10 11 **F**7 8 14 15 16 19 21 24 25 28 29 30 31 32 34 37 39 40 41 42 44 45 49 52 53 54 55 57 58 59 63 65 66 67 71 72 73 74 **P**6 8	23	10	118	3667	38	138616	452	37513	19839	638
MUNISING—Alger County										
□ MUNISING MEMORIAL HOSPITAL, 1500 Sand Point Road, Zip 49862–1406; tel. 906/387–4110; Carl J. Velte, Chief Executive Officer (Nonreporting) **A**1 9 10	23	10	40	—	—	—	—	—	—	—
MUSKEGON—Muskegon County										
□ HACKLEY HEALTH, 1700 Clinton Street, Zip 49443–3302, Mailing Address: P.O. Box 3302, Zip 49443–3302; tel. 616/726–3511; Gordon A. Mudler, President and Chief Executive Officer **A**1 2 9 10 **F**7 8 10 12 13 14 15 16 19 20 21 22 24 26 27 29 30 32 35 37 39 40 41 42 44 45 46 48 49 51 52 55 56 57 59 60 63 65 66 67 71 72 73 74 **P**5 6 7	23	10	195	8613	111	378798	1341	90827	41989	1122

Hospital, Address, Telephone, Administrator, Approval, Facility, and Physician Codes, Health Care System, Network	Classi-fication Codes		Utilization Data					Expense (thousands) of dollars		
★ American Hospital Association (AHA) membership □ Joint Commission on Accreditation of Healthcare Organizations (JCAHO) accreditation + American Osteopathic Healthcare Association (AOHA) membership ○ American Osteopathic Association (AOA) accreditation △ Commission on Accreditation of Rehabilitation Facilities (CARF) accreditation Control codes 61, 63, 64, 71, 72 and 73 indicate hospitals listed by AOHA, but not registered by AHA. For definition of numerical codes, see page A4	Control	Service	Staffed Beds	Admissions	Census	Outpatient Visits	Births	Total	Payroll	Personnel
✠ MERCY GENERAL HEALTH PARTNERS, 1500 East Sherman Boulevard, Zip 49443, Mailing Address: P.O. Box 358, Zip 49443–0358; tel. 616/739–3901; Roger Spoelman, President and Chief Executive Officer **A**1 9 10 12 **F**3 4 10 11 12 13 14 15 16 17 19 21 22 24 25 26 27 28 29 30 32 33 35 37 41 43 48 49 58 63 65 66 67 72 73 **P**1 5 6 8 **S** Mercy Health Services, Farmington Hills, MI **N** Mercy General Health Partners, Muskegon, MI	23	10	175	7093	104	283198	0	95434	38787	—
+ ○ MERCY GENERAL HEALTH PARTNERS–OAK AVENUE CAMPUS, 1700 Oak Avenue, Zip 49442–2407; tel. 616/773–3311; Roger Spoelman, Chief Executive Officer **A**9 10 11 12 13 **F**7 8 14 15 16 17 25 27 28 29 30 33 34 40 42 44 65 67 72 73 74 **P**1 5 6 8 **N** Mercy General Health Partners, Muskegon, MI; Mercy Health Services – Michigan Region, Farmington Hills, MI	23	10	20	2230	20	41954	1050	26170	11346	—
NEW BALTIMORE—Macomb County										
□ HARBOR OAKS HOSPITAL, 35031 23 Mile Road, Zip 48047–2097; tel. 810/725–5777; Gary J. LaHood, Administrator and Chief Executive Officer (Nonreporting) **A**1 10 **S** Pioneer Healthcare, Peabody, MA	32	22	64	—	—	—	—	—	—	—
NEWBERRY—Luce County										
✠ HELEN NEWBERRY JOY HOSPITAL, (Includes Helen Newberry Joy Hospital Annex), 502 West Harrie Street, Zip 49868–0070; tel. 906/293–9200; Wayne P. Hellerstedt, Chief Executive Officer (Total facility includes 48 beds in nursing home–type unit) **A**1 9 10 **F**7 13 19 21 23 24 26 29 33 41 43 46 52 60 63 64 66 **P**7	13	10	86	753	542	37259	1	10510	5492	193
NILES—Berrien County										
LAKELAND MEDICAL CENTER–NILES See Lakeland Medical Center–St. Joseph, Saint Joseph										
NORTHPORT—Leelanau County										
✠ LEELANAU MEMORIAL HEALTH CENTER, 215 South High Street, Zip 49670, Mailing Address: P.O. Box 217, Zip 49670–0217; tel. 616/386–0000; Jayne R. Bull, Administrator (Total facility includes 72 beds in nursing home–type unit) **A**1 10 **F**1 8 12 14 15 16 22 24 26 27 28 29 31 33 34 36 41 44 45 49 51 54 64 65 72 73 **S** Munson Healthcare, Traverse City, MI **N** Munson Healthcare, Traverse City, MI	23	10	91	299	68	12788	0	5327	2805	—
NORTHVILLE—Wayne County										
□ HAWTHORN CENTER, 18471 Haggerty Road, Zip 48167–9575; tel. 248/349–3000; Neil H. Wasserman, Chief Executive Officer and Chief Financial Officer **A**1 3 5 **F**20 52 53 65	12	52	118	185	92	0	—	20109	15251	312
□ NORTHVILLE PSYCHIATRIC HOSPITAL, 41001 West Seven Mile Road, Zip 48167–2698; tel. 810/349–1800; Ed Stovall, Administrative Officer **A**1 10 **F**6 12 14 15 16 20 22 52 55 57 65 67 73	12	22	427	592	375	0	0	53604	34280	864
ONTONAGON—Ontonagon County										
□ ONTONAGON MEMORIAL HOSPITAL, 601 Seventh Street, Zip 49953–1496; tel. 906/884–4134; Fred Nelson, Administrator (Total facility includes 46 beds in nursing home–type unit) **A**1 9 10 **F**8 12 15 16 17 19 20 21 22 26 28 29 30 34 36 39 41 44 51 53 64 65 66 **N** Northern Lakes Health Consortium, Duluth, MN	14	10	72	763	58	16472	0	7835	4090	152
OWOSSO—Shiawassee County										
✠ MEMORIAL HEALTHCARE CENTER, 826 West King Street, Zip 48867–2198; tel. 517/723–5211; Margaret S. Gulick, President and Chief Executive Officer (Total facility includes 16 beds in nursing home–type unit) **A**1 9 10 **F**3 7 8 11 12 13 14 15 16 17 18 19 21 22 25 27 28 29 30 32 33 35 36 37 39 40 41 42 44 46 48 49 52 53 54 56 57 58 59 63 64 65 66 67 68 71 72 73 74 **P**1 5	23	10	137	5529	78	258797	521	49980	28124	851
PAW PAW—Van Buren County										
✠ LAKEVIEW COMMUNITY HOSPITAL, 408 Hazen Street, Zip 49079–1019, Mailing Address: P.O. Box 209, Zip 49079–0209; tel. 616/657–3141; Sue E. Johnson–Phillippe, Chief Executive Officer (Total facility includes 120 beds in nursing home–type unit) **A**1 9 10 **F**7 8 12 14 15 16 17 19 20 22 26 30 32 33 34 35 37 39 40 41 44 45 49 52 54 55 57 59 61 64 65 67 71 72 73 74 **P**3 5 **S** Quorum Health Group/Quorum Health Resources, Inc., Brentwood, TN	16	10	168	1699	144	51683	—	21594	11035	392
PETOSKEY—Emmet County										
✠ NORTHERN MICHIGAN HOSPITAL, 416 Connable Avenue, Zip 49770–2297; tel. 616/348–4000; Jeffrey T. Wendling, President and Chief Executive Officer **A**1 2 9 10 **F**1 3 4 6 7 8 10 12 14 15 16 17 19 20 21 22 24 25 27 29 30 31 32 33 34 35 36 37 39 40 41 42 43 44 45 46 49 51 52 53 54 56 58 59 60 61 62 63 64 65 66 67 71 72 73 **P**7	23	10	261	8496	117	56514	881	80037	30616	915
PIGEON—Huron County										
✠ SCHEURER HOSPITAL, 170 North Caseville Road, Zip 48755–9704; tel. 517/453–3223; Dwight Gascho, President and Chief Executive Officer (Total facility includes 19 beds in nursing home–type unit) **A**1 9 10 **F**8 15 16 19 21 22 28 29 30 33 34 36 39 40 41 44 54 62 63 64 65 67 71 72 **P**6	23	10	47	688	26	31867	0	10181	5139	151
PLAINWELL—Allegan County										
BORGESS–PIPP HEALTH CENTER See Borgess Medical Center, Kalamazoo										
PONTIAC—Oakland County										
✠ NORTH OAKLAND MEDICAL CENTERS, 461 West Huron Street, Zip 48341–1651; tel. 248/857–7200; Robert L. Davis, President and Chief Executive Officer **A**1 3 5 9 10 **F**4 7 8 10 12 14 15 16 17 18 19 20 21 22 25 26 28 29 30 31 33 34 37 38 39 40 41 42 44 45 46 48 49 51 52 54 55 56 57 58 60 61 63 65 67 68 71 72 73 **P**8	23	10	222	9055	128	87870	1476	101966	47639	1165
+ ○ POH MEDICAL CENTER, (Formerly Pontiac Osteopathic Hospital), 50 North Perry Street, Zip 48342–2253; tel. 810/338–5000; Patrick Lamberti, Chief Executive Officer **A**9 10 11 12 13 **F**3 8 10 11 12 13 15 17 19 21 24 25 26 27 28 30 31 32 33 34 35 37 39 40 41 42 44 45 46 49 51 53 54 55 56 57 58 59 64 65 66 67 70 71 72 73 74 **P**5 8 **N** Great Lakes Health Network, Southfield, MI	23	10	149	6783	90	110790	0	80527	38396	1054

Hospital, Address, Telephone, Administrator, Approval, Facility, and Physician Codes, Health Care System, Network	Classi-fication Codes		Utilization Data					Expense (thousands) of dollars		
	Control	Service	Staffed Beds	Admissions	Census	Outpatient Visits	Births	Total	Payroll	Personnel

★ American Hospital Association (AHA) membership
☐ Joint Commission on Accreditation of Healthcare Organizations (JCAHO) accreditation
+ American Osteopathic Healthcare Association (AOHA) membership
○ American Osteopathic Association (AOA) accreditation
△ Commission on Accreditation of Rehabilitation Facilities (CARF) accreditation
Control codes 61, 63, 64, 71, 72 and 73 indicate hospitals listed by AOHA, but not registered by AHA. For definition of numerical codes, see page A4

PONTIAC OSTEOPATHIC HOSPITAL See POH Medical Center

Entry	Control	Service	Staffed Beds	Admissions	Census	Outpatient Visits	Births	Total	Payroll	Personnel
★ △ ST. JOSEPH MERCY OAKLAND, 900 Woodward Avenue, Zip 48341–2985; tel. 248/858–3000; Thomas L. Feurig, President and Chief Executive Officer **A**1 3 5 7 9 10 **F**2 3 4 6 7 8 10 11 12 13 14 15 16 17 19 21 22 25 26 27 28 29 30 31 32 33 34 35 36 37 38 39 40 41 42 43 44 46 47 48 49 52 53 54 55 56 57 58 59 60 61 62 64 65 66 67 70 71 72 73 74 **P**1 5 7 **S** Mercy Health Services, Farmington Hills, MI **N** Mercy Health Services – Michigan Region, Farmington Hills, MI; Henry Ford Health System, Detroit, MI	21	10	398	16642	260	282612	2531	177189	77226	2391

PORT HURON—St. Clair County

Entry	Control	Service	Staffed Beds	Admissions	Census	Outpatient Visits	Births	Total	Payroll	Personnel
★ △ MERCY HOSPITAL, 2601 Electric Avenue, Zip 48060; tel. 810/985–1510; Mary R. Trimmer, President and Chief Executive Officer **A**1 2 7 9 10 **F**4 8 10 12 14 15 16 17 19 21 22 28 30 31 32 33 34 35 37 39 41 42 43 44 45 46 48 49 60 63 65 66 67 71 73 74 **S** Mercy Health Services, Farmington Hills, MI **N** Mercy Health Services – Michigan Region, Farmington Hills, MI	21	10	119	4454	67	99111	—	45215	18905	611
★ PORT HURON HOSPITAL, 1221 Pine Grove Avenue, Zip 48061–5011; tel. 810/987–5000; Donald C. Fletcher, President and Chief Executive Officer **A**1 2 9 10 **F**3 4 7 8 10 11 12 14 15 16 17 19 20 21 22 26 29 30 31 34 35 37 40 42 43 44 45 46 49 52 54 55 56 57 59 63 65 66 67 71 73 74 **P**8 **S** Blue Water Health Services Corporation, Port Huron, MI **N** Saint John Health System, Detroit, MI; Port Huron Hospital/Blue Water Health Services, Port Huron, MI	23	10	175	8767	108	163637	1216	70040	32165	839

REED CITY—Osceola County

Entry	Control	Service	Staffed Beds	Admissions	Census	Outpatient Visits	Births	Total	Payroll	Personnel
★ REED CITY HOSPITAL CORPORATION, 7665 Patterson Road, Zip 49677–1122, Mailing Address: P.O. Box 75, Zip 49677–0075; tel. 616/832–3271; David M. Coates, Ph.D., President and Chief Executive Officer (Total facility includes 54 beds in nursing home–type unit) **A**1 9 10 **F**8 10 14 15 16 19 22 26 28 29 30 32 33 34 36 37 39 41 42 44 49 51 64 65 71 72 73 **P**8	23	10	83	1698	66	26141	—	14222	4991	167

ROCHESTER—Oakland County

Entry	Control	Service	Staffed Beds	Admissions	Census	Outpatient Visits	Births	Total	Payroll	Personnel
★ △ CRITTENTON HOSPITAL, 1101 West University Drive, Zip 48307–1831; tel. 248/652–5000; Dennis P. Markiewicz, Vice President, Hospital Operations **A**1 2 7 9 10 **F**7 8 10 11 14 15 16 19 21 22 24 27 28 29 30 32 33 34 35 37 39 40 41 42 44 45 46 48 49 52 54 55 56 57 58 59 60 63 65 66 67 71 72 73 74	23	10	227	11406	148	153433	1649	96722	43934	1286

ROGERS CITY—Presque Isle County

Entry	Control	Service	Staffed Beds	Admissions	Census	Outpatient Visits	Births	Total	Payroll	Personnel
☐ △ ROGERS CITY REHABILITATION HOSPITAL, 555 North Bradley Highway, Zip 49779–1599; tel. 517/734–7545; Nancy Dextrom, Executive Director (Nonreporting) **A**1 7 10	33	46	17	—	—	—	—	—	—	—

ROYAL OAK—Oakland County

Entry	Control	Service	Staffed Beds	Admissions	Census	Outpatient Visits	Births	Total	Payroll	Personnel
★ △ WILLIAM BEAUMONT HOSPITAL–ROYAL OAK, 3601 West Thirteen Mile Road, Zip 48073–6769; tel. 248/551–5000; John D. Labriola, Vice President and Director **A**1 2 3 5 7 8 9 10 **F**1 4 6 7 8 10 11 12 14 15 16 17 19 20 21 22 23 24 25 26 28 29 30 31 32 33 34 35 37 38 39 40 42 43 44 45 46 47 48 49 50 51 52 54 55 56 57 59 60 61 63 65 66 67 69 71 73 74 **P**7 8 **S** William Beaumont Hospital Corporation, Royal Oak, MI **N** William Beaumont Hospital Corp, Royal Oak, MI	23	10	859	45990	700	647591	5783	536143	252443	7534

SAGINAW—Saginaw County

Entry	Control	Service	Staffed Beds	Admissions	Census	Outpatient Visits	Births	Total	Payroll	Personnel
★ ALEDA E. LUTZ VETERANS AFFAIRS MEDICAL CENTER, 1500 Weiss Street, Zip 48602–5298; tel. 517/793–2340; Robert H. Sabin, Medical Center Director (Total facility includes 116 beds in nursing home–type unit) **A**1 5 9 **F**3 12 14 15 16 17 19 20 21 22 25 26 27 28 30 31 32 33 34 37 39 41 42 44 45 46 49 51 54 58 64 65 67 71 72 73 74 **S** Department of Veterans Affairs, Washington, DC	45	10	149	1897	112	69776	0	34946	23156	432
★ △ HEALTHSOURCE SAGINAW, (SPEC LONG TERM CARE REHAB PSYC), 3340 Hospital Road, Zip 48603–9623, Mailing Address: P.O. Box 6280, Zip 48608–6280; tel. 517/790–7700; Lester Heyboer, Jr., President and Chief Executive Officer (Total facility includes 213 beds in nursing home–type unit) **A**1 7 10 **F**3 15 20 26 39 41 45 46 48 49 52 53 54 55 57 58 64 65 67 73 **P**6	13	49	319	1575	214	13779	0	19481	10455	382
★ SAGINAW GENERAL HOSPITAL, 1447 North Harrison Street, Zip 48602–4785; tel. 517/771–4000; William J. Heath, President and Chief Executive Officer **A**1 3 5 9 10 **F**7 8 10 11 12 15 16 17 19 21 22 25 30 31 32 33 34 35 37 38 39 40 41 42 44 45 46 49 52 56 58 59 61 65 67 71 73 74 **P**1	23	10	234	10690	145	37000	3071	97130	44343	1178
★ △ ST. LUKE'S HOSPITAL, 700 Cooper Avenue, Zip 48602–5399; tel. 517/771–6001; Spencer Maidlow, President **A**1 3 5 7 9 10 **F**4 7 8 10 11 12 15 16 19 21 22 25 27 28 32 34 37 40 41 42 43 44 45 46 47 48 49 51 65 66 70 71 72 73 **P**1 6 7	23	10	288	13695	207	205560	751	131541	58739	1639
★ △ ST. MARY'S MEDICAL CENTER, 830 South Jefferson Avenue, Zip 48601–2594; tel. 517/776–8000; Frederic L. Fraizer, President and Chief Executive Officer **A**1 2 3 5 9 10 **F**4 8 9 10 11 14 15 16 17 19 21 22 25 27 28 30 34 35 37 39 40 43 44 45 46 49 54 56 60 63 65 67 70 71 73 74 **P**6 8 **S** Daughters of Charity National Health System, Saint Louis, MO	21	10	268	11850	190	165576	—	124544	53964	1449

SAINT IGNACE—Mackinac County

Entry	Control	Service	Staffed Beds	Admissions	Census	Outpatient Visits	Births	Total	Payroll	Personnel
MACKINAC STRAITS HOSPITAL AND HEALTH CENTER, 220 Burdette Street, Zip 49781–1792; tel. 906/643–8585; Mary E. Tamlyn, Administrator (Total facility includes 99 beds in nursing home–type unit) **A**9 10 **F**6 15 16 22 34 64 65 72	16	10	107	180	98	13902	0	7496	4256	270

SAINT JOHNS—Clinton County

Entry	Control	Service	Staffed Beds	Admissions	Census	Outpatient Visits	Births	Total	Payroll	Personnel
★ CLINTON MEMORIAL HOSPITAL, 805 South Oakland Street, Zip 48879–0260; tel. 517/224–6881; Paul E. McNamara, President **A**1 9 10 **F**7 8 14 15 16 17 19 22 24 26 28 30 32 33 34 35 36 40 41 42 44 49 65 66 71 72 73 **P**8	23	10	28	900	8	31556	85	17460	5262	177

Hospital, Address, Telephone, Administrator, Approval, Facility, and Physician Codes, Health Care System, Network	Classi-fication Codes		Utilization Data						Expense (thousands) of dollars		
★ American Hospital Association (AHA) membership □ Joint Commission on Accreditation of Healthcare Organizations (JCAHO) accreditation + American Osteopathic Healthcare Association (AOHA) membership ○ American Osteopathic Association (AOA) accreditation △ Commission on Accreditation of Rehabilitation Facilities (CARF) accreditation Control codes 61, 63, 64, 71, 72 and 73 indicate hospitals listed by AOHA, but not registered by AHA. For definition of numerical codes, see page A4	Control	Service	Staffed Beds	Admissions	Census	Outpatient Visits	Births	Total	Payroll	Personnel
□ RIVENDELL OF MICHIGAN, 101 West Townsend Road, Zip 48879–9200; tel. 517/224–1177; Michael Talmo, Chief Executive Officer (Nonreporting) **A**1 **S** Children's Comprehensive Services, Inc., Nashville, TN	33	22	63	—	—	—	—	—	—	—
SAINT JOSEPH—Berrien County										
⊞ △ LAKELAND MEDICAL CENTER–ST. JOSEPH, (Includes Lakeland Medical Center, Berrien Center, 6418 Dean's Hill Road, Berrien Center, Zip 49102–9704; tel. 616/471–7761; Lakeland Medical Center–Niles, 31 North St. Joseph Avenue, Niles, Zip 49120–2287; tel. 616/683–5510), 1234 Napier Avenue, Zip 49085–2112; tel. 616/983–8300; Joseph A. Wasserman, President and Chief Executive Officer (Total facility includes 193 beds in nursing home–type unit) **A**1 2 7 9 10 **F**3 4 7 8 10 12 14 15 16 17 19 20 21 22 25 26 28 30 31 32 34 35 36 37 39 40 41 42 43 44 48 49 52 54 56 58 59 60 64 65 66 67 71 73 **P**1 **N** Lakeland Regional Health System, St. Joseph, MI	23	10	608	15489	347	320145	2275	153958	67981	2200
SALINE—Washtenaw County										
⊞ SALINE COMMUNITY HOSPITAL, 400 West Russell Street, Zip 48176–1101; tel. 734/429–1500; Garry C. Faja, President and Chief Executive Officer **A**1 9 10 **F**2 3 8 12 14 15 17 19 20 21 22 28 30 31 33 34 41 44 49 65 67 71 73 **S** Mercy Health Services, Farmington Hills, MI **N** Mercy Health Services – Michigan Region, Farmington Hills, MI	21	10	47	1778	21	103208	—	21457	9160	241
SANDUSKY—Sanilac County										
★ MCKENZIE MEMORIAL HOSPITAL, 120 Delaware Street, Zip 48471–1087; tel. 810/648–3770; Joseph W. Weiler, President **A**9 10 **F**3 8 12 15 16 19 21 22 26 28 33 34 37 40 41 42 44 45 46 49 54 56 63 65 69 71 73 **P**6	23	10	25	978	8	18308	114	9704	4712	115
SAULT STE. MARIE—Chippewa County										
⊞ CHIPPEWA COUNTY WAR MEMORIAL HOSPITAL, 500 Osborn Boulevard, Zip 49783–4467; tel. 906/635–4460; Daniel Wakeman, Chief Executive Officer (Total facility includes 51 beds in nursing home–type unit) **A**1 9 10 **F**3 7 8 11 14 15 16 17 19 20 21 22 24 28 30 31 32 35 37 40 42 44 45 46 48 49 51 63 64 65 67 68 71 72 73 74 **P**5 6	23	10	86	2436	74	51596	408	25711	11538	388
SHELBY—Oceana County										
⊞ LAKESHORE COMMUNITY HOSPITAL, 72 South State Street, Zip 49455–1299; tel. 616/861–2156; Jay Bryan, Chief Executive Officer **A**1 9 10 **F**1 2 3 4 7 8 10 11 12 14 15 16 17 19 22 30 31 32 33 35 37 38 40 41 42 43 44 47 48 49 51 52 54 56 60 63 64 67 70 71 73 **P**4	23	10	24	814	7	21625	127	4758	2385	78
SHERIDAN—Montcalm County										
+ ○ SHERIDAN COMMUNITY HOSPITAL, 301 North Main Street, Zip 48884–9220, Mailing Address: P.O. Box 279, Zip 48884–0279; tel. 517/291–3261; Christopher Noland, Chief Executive Officer **A**9 10 11 **F**8 14 15 16 17 19 22 25 28 30 32 34 37 41 42 44 45 46 49 51 72 73	23	10	19	482	4	23164	—	5955	3213	108
SOUTH HAVEN—Van Buren County										
⊞ SOUTH HAVEN COMMUNITY HOSPITAL, 955 South Bailey Avenue, Zip 49090–9797; tel. 616/637–5271; Craig J. Marks, President and Chief Executive Officer **A**1 9 10 **F**7 8 15 16 19 30 32 35 37 40 41 42 44 48 49 71 73 **P**4 6 **N** Lakeland Regional Health System, St. Joseph, MI	16	10	10	1218	9	83936	336	12660	5646	175
SOUTHFIELD—Oakland County										
○ △ GREAT LAKES REHABILITATION HOSPITAL, 22401 Foster Winter Drive, Zip 48075–3708; tel. 248/483–5545; Teresa L. Thompson, R.N., Chief Operating Officer (Total facility includes 26 beds in nursing home–type unit) **A**7 9 10 11 **F**12 16 19 35 39 41 46 48 49 50 64 65 71 73	33	46	101	806	43	4095	—	9560	5207	181
⊞ PROVIDENCE HOSPITAL AND MEDICAL CENTERS, 16001 West Nine Mile Road, Zip 48075–4854, Mailing Address: Box 2043, Zip 48037–2043; tel. 248/424–3000; Brian M. Connolly, President and Chief Executive Officer **A**1 2 3 5 8 9 10 **F**1 3 4 7 8 10 11 12 13 14 15 16 17 19 21 22 25 26 28 29 30 31 32 33 34 35 37 38 39 40 41 42 43 44 45 46 48 49 51 52 54 55 56 58 59 60 65 66 67 70 71 72 73 74 **P**1 **S** Daughters of Charity National Health System, Saint Louis, MO	21	10	382	19242	273	1064727	3616	294892	130657	3066
⊞ STRAITH HOSPITAL FOR SPECIAL SURGERY, 23901 Lahser Road, Zip 48034–3296; tel. 248/357–3360; Gregory R. Hoose, Chief Executive Officer **A**1 9 10 **F**12 14 15 44 65	23	10	23	1052	13	5853	0	10021	4203	125
STANDISH—Arenac County										
□ STANDISH COMMUNITY HOSPITAL, 805 West Cedar Street, Zip 48658–9526, Mailing Address: P.O. Box 579, Zip 48658–0579; tel. 517/846–4521; Thomas G. Westhoff, Chief Executive Officer (Total facility includes 44 beds in nursing home–type unit) **A**1 9 10 **F**8 11 14 15 16 19 22 33 39 44 46 49 51 63 64 65 71 72	23	10	70	889	54	29557	0	11856	6930	268
STURGIS—St. Joseph County										
⊞ STURGIS HOSPITAL, 916 Myrtle, Zip 49091–2001; tel. 616/651–7824; David James, Chief Executive Officer **A**1 10 **F**7 8 11 12 14 15 16 17 18 19 20 21 22 24 25 28 29 30 32 33 34 35 36 37 39 40 41 42 44 45 46 49 51 63 65 67 71 73 **P**6 **S** Quorum Health Group/Quorum Health Resources, Inc., Brentwood, TN **N** Hospital Network Inc., Kalamazoo, MI	14	10	67	2300	22	70425	341	22895	10275	319
TAWAS CITY—Iosco County										
⊞ ST. JOSEPH HEALTH SYSTEM, (Formerly Tawas St. Joseph Hospital), 200 Hemlock Street, Zip 48763, Mailing Address: P.O. Box 659, Zip 48764–0659; tel. 517/362–3411; Paul R. Schmidt, CHE, President and Chief Executive Officer **A**1 9 10 **F**7 8 11 13 14 15 16 17 19 22 25 26 27 28 29 30 32 33 34 37 39 40 41 42 44 49 63 65 67 71 73 **S** Sisters of St. Joseph Health System, Ann Arbor, MI	21	10	60	2393	25	98950	309	23252	11203	457

Hospital, Address, Telephone, Administrator, Approval, Facility, and Physician Codes, Health Care System, Network	Classi-fication Codes		Utilization Data					Expense (thousands) of dollars		
★ American Hospital Association (AHA) membership □ Joint Commission on Accreditation of Healthcare Organizations (JCAHO) accreditation + American Osteopathic Healthcare Association (AOHA) membership ○ American Osteopathic Association (AOA) accreditation △ Commission on Accreditation of Rehabilitation Facilities (CARF) accreditation Control codes 61, 63, 64, 71, 72 and 73 indicate hospitals listed by AOHA, but not registered by AHA. For definition of numerical codes, see page A4	Control	Service	Staffed Beds	Admissions	Census	Outpatient Visits	Births	Total	Payroll	Personnel

TAYLOR—Wayne County

★ OAKWOOD HOSPITAL–HERITAGE CENTER, 10000 Telegraph Road, Zip 48180–3349; tel. 313/295–5000; Thomas E. Johnson, Vice President and Administrator **A**1 9 10 **F**1 2 3 4 5 6 7 8 9 10 11 12 13 14 15 16 17 18 19 20 21 22 25 26 27 28 30 31 32 33 34 35 36 37 38 39 41 42 44 46 48 49 50 51 52 53 54 55 56 57 58 59 60 61 62 63 64 65 66 67 68 69 70 71 72 73 **P**5 7 **S** Oakwood Healthcare System, Dearborn, MI | 23 | 10 | 257 | 8048 | 173 | 48792 | — | 66413 | 28469 | 763

TECUMSEH—Lenawee County

★ HERRICK MEMORIAL HOSPITAL, 500 East Pottawatamie Street, Zip 49286–2097; tel. 517/423–3834; Michael J. Mihora, Chief Executive Officer (Total facility includes 25 beds in nursing home–type unit) **A**1 9 10 **F**3 7 8 11 15 16 17 19 21 22 24 28 29 30 32 33 35 40 41 42 44 45 46 48 49 52 53 58 59 60 61 65 66 67 71 72 73 **P**7 8 | 23 | 10 | 94 | 2397 | 43 | 67654 | 221 | 20789 | 8286 | 312

THREE RIVERS—St. Joseph County

★ △ THREE RIVERS AREA HOSPITAL, 1111 West Broadway, Zip 49093–9362; tel. 616/278–1145; Matthew Chambers, Interim Chief Executive Officer **A**1 7 9 10 **F**7 8 12 15 16 17 19 21 22 24 28 30 31 32 33 34 35 37 39 41 42 44 45 46 48 49 54 61 65 67 71 73 74 **P**6 8 **S** Quorum Health Group/Quorum Health Resources, Inc., Brentwood, TN **N** Borgess Health Alliance, Kalamazoo, MI | 16 | 10 | 60 | 1652 | 24 | 42496 | 220 | 20576 | 8796 | 255

TRAVERSE CITY—Grand Traverse County

★ MUNSON MEDICAL CENTER, 1105 Sixth Street, Zip 49684–2386; tel. 616/935–5000; Ralph J. Cerny, President and Chief Executive Officer **A**1 2 3 7 9 10 12 13 **F**2 3 4 7 8 10 11 12 13 14 15 16 17 18 19 20 21 22 23 24 25 26 27 28 29 30 31 32 33 34 35 37 38 39 40 41 42 43 44 45 46 48 49 51 52 54 55 56 57 59 60 61 65 66 67 68 69 71 72 73 74 **P**7 8 **S** Munson Healthcare, Traverse City, MI | 23 | 10 | 368 | 16597 | 211 | 294302 | 1763 | 158680 | 76372 | 2035

TRENTON—Wayne County

★ OAKWOOD HOSPITAL SEAWAY CENTER, 5450 Fort Street, Zip 48183–4625; tel. 734/671–3800; Brian Peltz, Site Leader **A**1 9 10 **F**1 2 3 4 6 7 8 10 11 12 13 14 15 16 17 19 21 22 23 25 26 27 28 30 31 32 33 34 35 37 38 39 40 41 42 43 44 46 48 49 51 52 53 54 55 56 57 58 59 60 61 62 63 64 65 66 67 68 69 70 71 72 73 **P**5 7 **S** Oakwood Healthcare System, Dearborn, MI | 23 | 10 | 89 | 3355 | 39 | 50335 | 172 | 32362 | 12590 | 311

★ + ○ RIVERSIDE OSTEOPATHIC HOSPITAL, 150 Truax Street, Zip 48183–2151; tel. 734/676–4200; Dennis R. Lemanski, D.O., Vice President and Chief Administrative Officer **A**9 10 11 12 13 **F**7 8 10 11 12 14 15 16 17 18 19 21 22 24 26 27 28 29 30 31 32 33 34 35 36 37 39 40 41 42 44 45 46 49 52 54 55 56 57 60 61 63 65 66 67 70 71 73 74 **S** Henry Ford Health System, Detroit, MI **N** Great Lakes Health Network, Southfield, MI; Henry Ford Health System, Detroit, MI | 23 | 10 | 148 | 5905 | 80 | 112423 | 825 | 56398 | 25942 | 550

TROY—Oakland County

★ WILLIAM BEAUMONT HOSPITAL–TROY, 44201 Dequindre Road, Zip 48098–1198; tel. 248/828–5100; Eugene F. Michalski, Vice President and Director **A**1 3 9 10 **F**1 4 6 7 8 10 11 12 14 15 16 17 19 20 21 22 23 24 25 26 28 29 30 31 32 33 34 35 37 38 39 40 42 43 44 45 46 47 49 50 51 52 54 55 56 57 59 60 61 63 64 65 66 67 69 71 73 74 **P**7 8 **S** William Beaumont Hospital Corporation, Royal Oak, MI **N** William Beaumont Hospital Corp, Royal Oak, MI | 23 | 10 | 189 | 12355 | 154 | 372463 | 1734 | 125969 | 50240 | 1782

VICKSBURG—Kalamazoo County

★ △ BRONSON VICKSBURG HOSPITAL, 13326 North Boulevard, Zip 49097–1099; tel. 616/649–2321; Frank J. Sardone, President **A**1 7 9 10 **F**4 7 8 9 10 11 12 13 16 19 21 22 26 28 29 30 31 32 34 35 37 38 40 41 42 43 44 45 46 47 48 49 54 61 65 70 71 72 73 74 **S** Bronson Healthcare Group, Inc., Kalamazoo, MI **N** Hospital Network Inc., Kalamazoo, MI | 23 | 46 | 41 | 356 | 12 | 31099 | 0 | 7878 | 3096 | —

WARREN—Macomb County

□ ARBORVIEW HOSPITAL, 6902 Chicago Road, Zip 48092–4784; tel. 810/264–8875; Donald L. Warner, Chief Executive Officer **A**1 10 **F**15 16 52 53 54 55 56 57 58 59 **P**5 | 33 | 22 | 40 | 1049 | 15 | 0 | 0 | 4479 | 2171 | 66

★ + ○ △ BI-COUNTY COMMUNITY HOSPITAL, 13355 East Ten Mile Road, Zip 48089–2065; tel. 810/759–7300; Gary W. Popiel, Executive Vice President and Chief Executive Officer **A**7 9 10 11 12 13 **F**3 7 8 10 12 14 15 16 17 19 21 22 24 27 28 29 30 31 32 33 34 35 37 39 40 41 42 44 45 46 48 49 51 53 54 55 60 61 63 65 66 71 73 74 **P**1 6 **S** Henry Ford Health System, Detroit, MI **N** Great Lakes Health Network, Southfield, MI; Henry Ford Health System, Detroit, MI | 23 | 10 | 161 | 5859 | 93 | 115630 | 492 | 68389 | 32853 | 720

□ KERN HOSPITAL AND MEDICAL CENTER, (Formerly Kern Hospital for Special Surgery), 21230 Dequindre, Zip 48091–2287; tel. 810/427–1000; Manoj K. Prasad, M.D., Chief Executive Officer **A**1 9 10 **F**14 44 | 31 | 10 | 20 | 266 | 1 | 4183 | — | 4915 | 2553 | 83

★ △ MACOMB HOSPITAL CENTER, 11800 East Twelve Mile Road, Zip 48093–3494; tel. 810/573–5000; John E. Knox, President **A**1 2 7 9 10 **F**2 3 4 7 8 10 11 12 13 14 15 16 17 18 19 20 21 22 23 25 27 28 29 30 31 32 33 34 35 37 38 39 40 41 42 43 44 45 46 48 49 51 52 53 54 55 56 57 58 59 60 61 62 63 64 65 66 67 68 69 70 71 72 73 74 **P**4 5 6 8 **S** Sisters of St. Joseph Health System, Ann Arbor, MI **N** Saint John Health System, Detroit, MI; Detroit–Macomb Hospital Corp, Warren, MI | 23 | 10 | 296 | 12021 | 204 | — | 1293 | 106867 | 56671 | 1145

WATERVLIET—Berrien County

★ △ COMMUNITY HOSPITAL, Medical Park Drive, Zip 49098–0158, Mailing Address: P.O. Box 158, Zip 49098–0158; tel. 616/463–3111; Dennis Turney, Chief Executive Officer **A**1 7 9 10 **F**8 12 14 15 16 19 22 26 28 29 30 32 33 34 35 37 39 44 46 48 49 54 63 65 67 71 72 73 **P**1 **S** Quorum Health Group/Quorum Health Resources, Inc., Brentwood, TN **N** First Choice Network, Southhaven, MI; Borgess Health Alliance, Kalamazoo, MI | 23 | 10 | 54 | 1836 | 29 | 35919 | — | 15007 | 6953 | 241

Hospital, Address, Telephone, Administrator, Approval, Facility, and Physician Codes, Health Care System, Network	Classi-fication Codes		Utilization Data					Expense (thousands) of dollars		
★ American Hospital Association (AHA) membership □ Joint Commission on Accreditation of Healthcare Organizations (JCAHO) accreditation + American Osteopathic Healthcare Association (AOHA) membership ○ American Osteopathic Association (AOA) accreditation △ Commission on Accreditation of Rehabilitation Facilities (CARF) accreditation Control codes 61, 63, 64, 71, 72 and 73 indicate hospitals listed by AOHA, but not registered by AHA. For definition of numerical codes, see page A4	Control	Service	Staffed Beds	Admissions	Census	Outpatient Visits	Births	Total	Payroll	Personnel

WAYNE—Wayne County

✠ OAKWOOD HOSPITAL ANNAPOLIS CENTER, (Includes Oakwood Hospital Merriman Center–Westland, 2345 Merriman Road, Westland, Zip 48185; tel. 313/467–2300), 33155 Annapolis Road, Zip 48184–2493; tel. 313/467–4000; Mark Anthony, Vice President and Administrator **A**1 9 10 **F**1 2 3 4 6 7 8 10 11 12 13 14 15 16 17 18 19 21 22 23 25 26 27 28 30 31 32 33 34 35 37 38 39 40 41 42 43 44 46 48 49 51 52 53 54 55 56 57 58 59 60 61 62 63 64 65 66 67 68 69 71 72 73 **P**5 7 **S** Oakwood Healthcare System, Dearborn, MI

| | 23 | 10 | 219 | 7422 | 92 | 61940 | 682 | 59402 | 20670 | 561 |

WEST BRANCH—Ogemaw County

✠ TOLFREE MEMORIAL HOSPITAL, 335 East Houghton Avenue, Zip 48661–1199; tel. 517/345–3660; Douglas E. Pattullo, Chief Executive Officer **A**1 9 10 **F**7 11 15 16 19 22 32 33 34 39 40 42 44 71

| | 14 | 10 | 92 | 3456 | 40 | 42474 | 339 | 17323 | 7744 | 295 |

WESTLAND—Wayne County

OAKWOOD HOSPITAL MERRIMAN CENTER–WESTLAND See Oakwood Hospital Annapolis Center, Wayne

□ WALTER P. REUTHER PSYCHIATRIC HOSPITAL, 30901 Palmer Road, Zip 48185–5389; tel. 734/722–4500; Norma C. Josef, M.D., Director **A**1 10 **F**14 19 20 21 26 35 48 50 52 54 56 57 63 64 **P**5

| | 12 | 22 | 200 | 196 | 153 | — | — | 23705 | 13886 | 302 |

WYANDOTTE—Wayne County

✠ △ HENRY FORD WYANDOTTE HOSPITAL, 2333 Biddle Avenue, Zip 48192–4693; tel. 313/284–2400; William R. Alvin, President **A**1 7 9 10 **F**1 7 8 10 11 14 17 19 22 25 30 32 33 35 37 40 41 42 44 46 48 49 52 53 54 56 57 58 59 60 66 67 68 71 72 73 **P**6 **S** Henry Ford Health System, Detroit, MI **N** Henry Ford Health System, Detroit, MI

| | 23 | 10 | 355 | 14200 | 238 | — | 1027 | 113177 | 62028 | 1645 |

YPSILANTI—Washtenaw County

✠ OAKWOOD HOSPITAL BEYER CENTER–YPSILANTI, 135 South Prospect Street, Zip 48198–5693; tel. 734/484–2200; Richard Hillbom, Administrator **A**1 9 10 **F**1 2 3 4 6 7 8 10 11 12 13 14 15 16 17 19 21 22 23 25 26 27 28 30 31 32 33 34 35 37 38 40 41 42 43 44 45 46 48 49 51 52 53 54 55 56 57 58 59 60 61 62 63 64 65 66 67 68 69 71 72 73 **P**5 7 **S** Oakwood Healthcare System, Dearborn, MI

| | 23 | 10 | 57 | 3074 | 40 | 36849 | 206 | 26013 | 11216 | 320 |

ZEELAND—Ottawa County

✠ ZEELAND COMMUNITY HOSPITAL, 100 South Pine Street, Zip 49464–1619; tel. 616/772–4644; Henry A. Veenstra, President **A**1 9 10 **F**7 8 11 14 15 16 17 19 22 28 30 33 36 39 40 41 42 44 45 49 60 65 71 72 73 74 **P**4 8 **N** Butterworth Health System, Grand Rapids, MI

| | 23 | 10 | 55 | 1959 | 21 | 41158 | 313 | 16682 | 7760 | 250 |

Resident population 4,686 (in thousands)
Resident population in metro areas 69.4%
Birth rate per 1,000 population 14.1
65 years and over 12.4%
Percent of persons without health insurance 10.2%

Hospital, Address, Telephone, Administrator, Approval, Facility, and Physician Codes, Health Care System, Network	Classi-fication Codes		Utilization Data					Expense (thousands) of dollars		
★ American Hospital Association (AHA) membership □ Joint Commission on Accreditation of Healthcare Organizations (JCAHO) accreditation + American Osteopathic Healthcare Association (AOHA) membership ○ American Osteopathic Association (AOA) accreditation △ Commission on Accreditation of Rehabilitation Facilities (CARF) accreditation Control codes 61, 63, 64, 71, 72 and 73 indicate hospitals listed by AOHA, but not registered by AHA. For definition of numerical codes, see page A4	Control	Service	Staffed Beds	Admissions	Census	Outpatient Visits	Births	Total	Payroll	Personnel

ADA—Norman County

★ BRIDGES MEDICAL SERVICES, (Includes John Wimmer Memorial Home), 402 East Third Street, Zip 56510–0233, Mailing Address: P.O. Box 233, Zip 56510–0233; tel. 218/784–5000; Kyle Rasmussen, Administrator (Total facility includes 49 beds in nursing home–type unit) (Nonreporting) **A**9 10 — 14 10 63 — — — — — — —

| | 14 | 10 | 63 | — | — | — | — | — | — | — |

ADRIAN—Nobles County

★ ARNOLD MEMORIAL HEALTH CARE CENTER, (MEDICAL), 601 Louisiana Avenue, Zip 56110–0279, Mailing Address: Box 279, Zip 56110–0279; tel. 507/483–2668; Gerald E. Carl, Administrator (Total facility includes 41 beds in nursing home–type unit) **A**9 10 **F**1 2 3 6 7 26 28 32 33 34 49 64 71 **S** Sioux Valley Hospitals and Health System, Sioux Falls, SD

| | 15 | 49 | 50 | 79 | 41 | 1705 | 0 | 2106 | 1136 | 53 |

AITKIN—Aitkin County

★ RIVERWOOD HEALTH CARE CENTER, 301 Minnesota Avenue South, Zip 56431–1626; tel. 218/927–2121; Debra Boardman, Chief Executive Officer (Total facility includes 48 beds in nursing home–type unit) **A**9 10 **F**7 8 11 15 19 22 28 32 33 35 42 44 49 51 64 65 67 71 73 **P**8 **N** Northern Lakes Health Consortium, Duluth, MN

| | 23 | 10 | 68 | 946 | 53 | 23353 | 39 | 10543 | 5218 | 243 |

ALBANY—Stearns County

★ ALBANY AREA HOSPITAL AND MEDICAL CENTER, 300 Third Avenue, Zip 56307–9363; tel. 320/845–2121; Ben Koppelman, Administrator **A**9 10 **F**7 8 15 16 19 22 30 32 33 40 44 48 58 65 71 73 **P**6 **S** Catholic Health Initiatives, Denver, CO

| | 21 | 10 | 16 | 309 | 3 | 5133 | 43 | 3666 | 1784 | 77 |

ALBERT LEA—Freeborn County

✦ △ ALBERT LEA MEDICAL CENTER, (Formerly Naeve Hospital), 404 West Fountain Street, Zip 56007–2473; tel. 507/373–2384; Ronald A. Harmon, M.D., Chief Executive Officer **A**1 7 9 10 **F**7 8 15 16 17 19 21 22 28 32 33 34 35 36 37 39 40 41 42 44 46 48 54 65 67 71 **P**6 **S** Mayo Foundation, Rochester, MN

| | 23 | 10 | 72 | 2841 | 32 | 42550 | 445 | 23027 | 10976 | 361 |

ALEXANDRIA—Douglas County

✦ DOUGLAS COUNTY HOSPITAL, 111 17th Avenue East, Zip 56308–3798; tel. 320/762–1511; William G. Flaig, Administrator **A**1 9 10 **F**3 7 8 14 15 19 21 22 23 28 29 31 32 33 34 35 36 37 40 41 42 44 45 49 54 55 56 58 59 63 65 66 67 71 73

| | 13 | 10 | 110 | 3944 | 44 | 46280 | 509 | 30592 | 14178 | 336 |

ANOKA—Anoka County

□ ANOKA–METROPOLITAN REGIONAL TREATMENT CENTER, 3300 Fourth Avenue North, Zip 55303–1119; tel. 612/576–5500; Judith Krohn, Ph.D., Chief Executive Officer (Nonreporting) **A**1 10

| | 12 | 22 | 247 | — | — | — | — | — | — | — |

APPLETON—Swift County

APPLETON MUNICIPAL HOSPITAL AND NURSING HOME, 30 South Behl Street, Zip 56208–1699; tel. 320/289–2422; Mark E. Paulson, Administrator (Total facility includes 84 beds in nursing home–type unit) **A**9 10 **F**7 14 17 19 22 32 33 34 36 39 41 44 45 49 58 62 63 64 65 71 73 **P**7 **N** Minnesota Rural Health Cooperative, Willmar, MN

| | 14 | 10 | 104 | 406 | 85 | 8291 | 4 | 5443 | 2525 | 235 |

ARLINGTON—Sibley County

ARLINGTON MUNICIPAL HOSPITAL, 601 West Chandler Street, Zip 55307; tel. 507/964–2271; John Stindt, Administrator (Nonreporting) **A**9 10

| | 14 | 10 | 17 | — | — | — | — | — | — | — |

AURORA—St. Louis County

★ WHITE COMMUNITY HOSPITAL, 5211 Highway 110, Zip 55705–1599; tel. 218/229–2211; Cheryl A. High, Administrator (Total facility includes 69 beds in nursing home–type unit) **A**9 10 **F**7 16 17 22 26 28 30 31 34 36 42 44 49 60 64 65 66 67 **N** Northern Lakes Health Consortium, Duluth, MN

| | 23 | 10 | 85 | 336 | 68 | 5321 | — | 4255 | 2704 | 100 |

BAGLEY—Clearwater County

★ CLEARWATER HEALTH SERVICES, 203 Fourth Street N.W., Zip 56621–8307, Mailing Address: Rural Route 3, Box 46, Zip 56621–0046; tel. 218/694–6501; Larry Laudon, Administrator (Total facility includes 70 beds in nursing home–type unit) (Nonreporting) **A**9 10

| | 13 | 10 | 92 | — | — | — | — | — | — | — |

BAUDETTE—Lake of the Woods County

★ LAKEWOOD HEALTH CENTER, 600 South Main Avenue, Zip 56623, Mailing Address: Route 1, Box 2120, Zip 56623–2120; tel. 218/634–2120; SharRay Palm, President and Chief Executive Officer (Total facility includes 52 beds in nursing home–type unit) **A**9 10 **F**7 8 13 14 15 16 17 19 22 27 28 30 32 33 35 40 44 63 64 65 71 **S** Catholic Health Initiatives, Denver, CO **N**

| | 21 | 10 | 64 | 400 | 53 | 8347 | 29 | 5265 | 2585 | 109 |

BEMIDJI—Beltrami County

✦ NORTH COUNTRY REGIONAL HOSPITAL, 1100 West 38th Street, Zip 56601–9972; tel. 218/751–5430; Paul A. Miller, President and Chief Executive Officer (Total facility includes 78 beds in nursing home–type unit) **A**1 9 10 **F**4 7 8 12 14 15 16 17 19 21 22 28 29 30 32 33 34 35 37 39 40 41 42 44 45 49 62 64 65 67 71 73 **P**6

| | 23 | 10 | 162 | 5369 | 133 | 36572 | 782 | 40521 | 18205 | 594 |

BENSON—Swift County

★ SWIFT COUNTY–BENSON HOSPITAL, 1815 Wisconsin Avenue, Zip 56215–1653; tel. 320/843–4232; Frank Lawatsch, Chief Executive Officer **A**9 10 **F**7 8 11 15 16 19 22 28 32 33 34 35 36 37 39 40 41 42 44 49 54 58 64 65 67 71 **S** Brim, Inc., Portland, OR **N** Minnesota Rural Health Cooperative, Willmar, MN

| | 15 | 10 | 31 | 539 | 6 | 8603 | 25 | 3745 | 1633 | 410 |

Hospital, Address, Telephone, Administrator, Approval, Facility, and Physician Codes, Health Care System, Network	Classi-fication Codes		Utilization Data					Expense (thousands) of dollars		
★ American Hospital Association (AHA) membership □ Joint Commission on Accreditation of Healthcare Organizations (JCAHO) accreditation + American Osteopathic Healthcare Association (AOHA) membership ○ American Osteopathic Association (AOA) accreditation △ Commission on Accreditation of Rehabilitation Facilities (CARF) accreditation Control codes 61, 63, 64, 71, 72 and 73 indicate hospitals listed by AOHA, but not registered by AHA. For definition of numerical codes, see page A4	Control	Service	Staffed Beds	Admissions	Census	Outpatient Visits	Births	Total	Payroll	Personnel

BIGFORK—Itasca County

★ NORTHERN ITASCA HEALTH CARE CENTER, 258 Pine Tree Drive, Zip 56628, Mailing Address: P.O. Box 258, Zip 56628–0258; tel. 218/743–3177; Richard M. Ash, Chief Executive Officer (Total facility includes 40 beds in nursing home–type unit) **A**9 10 **F**1 6 7 8 15 16 19 20 22 26 28 32 33 34 40 41 42 44 49 62 64 65 66 67 71 73 **N** Northern Lakes Health Consortium, Duluth, MN; Itasca Partnership for Quality Healthcare, Grand Rapids, MN

| | 16 | 10 | 56 | 396 | 41 | 13028 | 24 | 6363 | 2768 | 109 |

BLUE EARTH—Faribault County

⊞ UNITED HOSPITAL DISTRICT, 515 South Moore Street, Zip 56013–2158, Mailing Address: P.O. Box 160, Zip 56013–0160; tel. 507/526–3273; Brian Kief, President **A**1 9 10 **F**7 8 15 16 17 19 22 26 27 28 30 31 32 33 34 35 36 37 39 40 41 44 45 49 53 54 55 58 65 67 71 **S** Allina Health System, Minneapolis, MN **N** Allina Health System, Minnetonka, MN; Quality Health Alliance, Mankato, MN

| | 16 | 10 | 24 | 1021 | 12 | 25939 | 29 | 9028 | 3597 | 144 |

BRAINERD—Crow Wing County

□ BRAINERD REGIONAL HUMAN SERVICES CENTER, 1777 Highway 18 East, Zip 56401–7389; tel. 218/828–2201; Harvey G. Caldwell, Administrator and Chief Executive Officer (Total facility includes 28 beds in nursing home–type unit) **A**1 10 **F**2 3 15 48 52 53 64 **P**6

| | 12 | 22 | 260 | 990 | 211 | 6450 | — | 28677 | 19538 | 545 |

□ ST. JOSEPH'S MEDICAL CENTER, 523 North Third Street, Zip 56401–3098; tel. 218/829–2861; Thomas K. Prusak, President **A**1 9 10 **F**2 3 7 8 11 12 15 16 19 21 22 28 29 30 31 32 33 34 35 39 40 41 42 44 46 48 49 52 53 54 55 56 58 59 60 65 66 67 71 73 **S** Benedictine Health System, Duluth, MN **N** Benedictine Health System, Duluth, MN

| | 21 | 10 | 162 | 5939 | 72 | 105938 | 623 | 44736 | 19475 | 489 |

BRECKENRIDGE—Wilkin County

★ ST. FRANCIS MEDICAL CENTER, 415 Oak Street, Zip 56520–1298; tel. 218/643–3000; David A. Nelson, President and Chief Executive Officer (Total facility includes 124 beds in nursing home–type unit) **A**9 10 **F**1 3 6 7 8 15 16 17 19 20 21 22 26 28 29 30 32 33 35 36 37 39 40 41 44 45 46 49 51 53 54 55 56 57 58 60 64 65 66 67 71 72 73 **S** Catholic Health Initiatives, Denver, CO

| | 21 | 10 | 171 | 1807 | 136 | 26964 | 295 | 16359 | 8021 | 301 |

BUFFALO—Wright County

⊞ BUFFALO HOSPITAL, 303 Catlin Street, Zip 55313–1947, Mailing Address: P.O. Box 609, Zip 55313–0609; tel. 612/682–7180; Mary Ellen Wells, Administrator **A**1 9 10 **F**1 7 8 9 11 14 15 16 17 19 21 22 26 27 28 29 30 32 33 34 35 37 39 40 41 42 44 45 46 49 55 56 65 66 67 71 73 **P**5 6 **S** Allina Health System, Minneapolis, MN **N** Allina Health System, Minnetonka, MN

| | 23 | 10 | 20 | 1884 | 15 | 26918 | 431 | 14605 | 7076 | 191 |

BURNSVILLE—Dakota County

⊞ FAIRVIEW RIDGES HOSPITAL, 201 East Nicollet Boulevard, Zip 55337–5799; tel. 612/892–2000; Mark M. Enger, Senior Vice President and Administrator **A**1 9 10 **F**3 7 8 14 15 16 17 19 21 22 32 33 34 35 37 40 41 42 44 45 46 48 49 51 54 65 66 67 71 73 74 **S** Fairview Hospital and Healthcare Services, Minneapolis, MN **N** Fairview Health System, Minneapolis, MN

| | 21 | 10 | 129 | 9507 | 78 | 64109 | 3063 | 58597 | 22611 | 556 |

CAMBRIDGE—Isanti County

⊞ CAMBRIDGE MEDICAL CENTER, 701 South Dellwood Street, Zip 55008–1920; tel. 612/689–7700; Lenny Libis, Administrator **A**1 9 10 **F**3 7 8 11 12 15 16 17 19 20 21 22 24 26 28 29 30 31 32 33 34 35 36 39 40 41 42 44 45 46 49 51 52 54 55 56 57 58 60 62 65 66 67 70 71 72 73 **P**8 **S** Allina Health System, Minneapolis, MN **N** Allina Health System, Minnetonka, MN

| | 23 | 10 | 81 | 3506 | 40 | 216405 | 459 | 45123 | 24716 | 586 |

CANBY—Yellow Medicine County

★ CANBY COMMUNITY HEALTH SERVICES, (Includes Senior Haven Convalescent Nursing Center), 112 St. Olaf Avenue South, Zip 56220–1433; tel. 507/223–7277; Robert J. Salmon, Chief Executive Officer (Total facility includes 75 beds in nursing home–type unit) **A**9 10 **F**7 8 15 17 19 21 22 26 27 28 29 30 32 33 34 35 36 37 39 40 41 42 44 49 53 62 64 65 66 67 71 73 **P**6 **S** Sioux Valley Hospitals and Health System, Sioux Falls, SD **N** Minnesota Rural Health Cooperative, Willmar, MN; Southwest Minnesota Health Alliance, Luverne, MN; Sioux Valley Health System, Sioux Falls, SD

| | 23 | 10 | 102 | 539 | 81 | 5763 | 38 | 6224 | 2985 | 129 |

CANNON FALLS—Goodhue County

★ COMMUNITY HOSPITAL, 1116 West Mill Street, Zip 55009–1898; tel. 507/263–4221; Randy Ulseth, Administrator **A**9 10 **F**1 2 3 4 5 6 7 8 9 10 11 12 13 14 17 18 19 20 21 22 23 24 25 26 27 28 29 30 31 32 33 34 35 36 37 39 40 41 42 43 44 45 46 47 48 49 50 51 52 53 54 55 56 57 58 60 61 62 63 64 65 66 67 68 69 70 71 72 73 74 **P**8

| | 16 | 10 | 21 | 458 | 4 | 3828 | 10 | 3832 | 1541 | 59 |

CASS LAKE—Cass County

⊞ U. S. PUBLIC HEALTH SERVICE INDIAN HOSPITAL, 7th Street and Grant Utley Avenue N.W., Zip 56633, Mailing Address: Rural Route 3, Box 211, Zip 56633; tel. 218/335–2293; Luella Brown, Service Unit Director (Nonreporting) **A**1 10 **S** U. S. Public Health Service Indian Health Service, Rockville, MD

| | 47 | 10 | 13 | — | — | — | — | — | — | — |

CLOQUET—Carlton County

★ CLOQUET COMMUNITY MEMORIAL HOSPITAL, 512 Skyline Boulevard, Zip 55720–1199; tel. 218/879–4641; James J. Carroll, Administrator (Total facility includes 88 beds in nursing home–type unit) **A**9 10 **F**7 8 12 19 22 28 30 32 34 35 36 37 39 40 41 42 44 45 46 49 64 65 67 71 72 73 **P**3 8 **N** Northern Lakes Health Consortium, Duluth, MN

| | 23 | 10 | 124 | 1325 | 98 | 23355 | 119 | 12738 | 6524 | 175 |

COOK—St. Louis County

★ COOK HOSPITAL AND CONVALESCENT NURSING CARE UNIT, 10 South Fifth Street East, Zip 55723–9745; tel. 218/666–5945; Allen J. Vogt, Administrator (Total facility includes 41 beds in nursing home–type unit) (Nonreporting) **A**9 10 **N** Northern Lakes Health Consortium, Duluth, MN

| | 16 | 10 | 55 | — | — | — | — | — | — | — |

Hospital, Address, Telephone, Administrator, Approval, Facility, and Physician Codes, Health Care System, Network	Classi-fication Codes		Utilization Data					Expense (thousands) of dollars		
	Control	Service	Staffed Beds	Admissions	Census	Outpatient Visits	Births	Total	Payroll	Personnel

★ American Hospital Association (AHA) membership
□ Joint Commission on Accreditation of Healthcare Organizations (JCAHO) accreditation
+ American Osteopathic Healthcare Association (AOHA) membership
○ American Osteopathic Association (AOA) accreditation
△ Commission on Accreditation of Rehabilitation Facilities (CARF) accreditation
Control codes 61, 63, 64, 71, 72 and 73 indicate hospitals listed by AOHA, but not registered by AHA. For definition of numerical codes, see page A4

COON RAPIDS—Anoka County

✠ MERCY HOSPITAL, 4050 Coon Rapids Boulevard, Zip 55433–2586; tel. 612/421–8888 **A**1 9 10 **F**2 3 4 7 8 10 11 12 14 15 16 17 18 19 21 22 23 24 27 28 32 33 35 36 37 39 40 41 42 43 44 45 46 49 52 53 54 55 56 57 58 60 63 65 67 68 70 71 72 73 **P**2 4 5 6 7 **S** Allina Health System, Minneapolis, MN — 23 | 10 | 192 | 12239 | 137 | 70522 | 2182 | 124075 | 54037 | 1316

CROOKSTON—Polk County

★ RIVERVIEW HEALTHCARE ASSOCIATION, 323 South Minnesota Street, Zip 56716–1600; tel. 218/281–9200; Thomas C. Lenertz, President and Chief Executive Officer (Total facility includes 162 beds in nursing home–type unit) **A**9 10 **F**1 2 3 7 8 15 16 17 19 20 21 22 26 28 29 30 31 32 33 37 40 41 44 45 46 49 56 64 65 66 67 70 71 73 — 23 | 10 | 234 | 1933 | 179 | 22237 | 122 | 16271 | 8599 | 474

CROSBY—Crow Wing County

★ CUYUNA REGIONAL MEDICAL CENTER, 320 East Main Street, Zip 56441–1690; tel. 218/546–7000; Thomas F. Reek, Chief Executive Officer (Total facility includes 130 beds in nursing home–type unit) **A**9 10 **F**7 8 15 16 19 22 26 28 30 31 32 33 34 35 37 40 41 42 44 49 64 65 66 71 73 **P**7 8 **N** Northern Lakes Health Consortium, Duluth, MN — 16 | 10 | 160 | 1369 | 140 | 44300 | 179 | 17302 | 8684 | 276

DAWSON—Lac Qui Parle County

JOHNSON MEMORIAL HEALTH SERVICES, 1282 Walnut Street, Zip 56232–2333; tel. 612/769–4323; Vern Silvernale, Administrator (Total facility includes 70 beds in nursing home–type unit) **A**9 10 **F**7 8 17 19 22 26 32 33 34 36 40 41 44 45 49 64 65 71 73 **P**6 **N** Minnesota Rural Health Cooperative, Willmar, MN — 16 | 10 | 93 | 355 | 71 | 3824 | 24 | 5291 | 3053 | 172

DEER RIVER—Itasca County

★ DEER RIVER HEALTHCARE CENTER, 1002 Comstock Drive, Zip 56636–9700; tel. 218/246–2900; Jeffrey Stampohar, Chief Executive Officer (Total facility includes 50 beds in nursing home–type unit) (Nonreporting) **A**9 10 **N** Northern Lakes Health Consortium, Duluth, MN; Itasca Partnership for Quality Healthcare, Grand Rapids, MN — 23 | 10 | 70 | — | — | — | — | — | — | —

DETROIT LAKES—Becker County

✠ ST. MARY'S REGIONAL HEALTH CENTER, 1027 Washington Avenue, Zip 56501–3598; tel. 218/847–5611; John H. Solheim, Chief Executive Officer (Total facility includes 100 beds in nursing home–type unit) **A**1 9 10 **F**7 8 10 12 15 16 17 19 21 22 26 27 28 30 32 33 34 35 37 39 40 41 42 44 46 49 60 62 64 65 66 67 69 71 73 74 **S** Benedictine Health System, Duluth, MN **N** Benedictine Health System, Duluth, MN — 21 | 10 | 163 | 2434 | 122 | 10809 | 378 | 14740 | 6600 | 151

DULUTH—St. Louis County

✠ △ MILLER DWAN MEDICAL CENTER, 502 East Second Street, Zip 55805–1982; tel. 218/727–8762; William H. Palmer, President **A**1 2 7 9 10 **F**3 6 9 12 14 15 16 17 18 19 21 23 26 28 31 34 35 37 39 41 42 44 45 46 48 49 52 53 55 56 57 58 59 60 65 67 71 73 **P**5 **N** Northern Lakes Health Consortium, Duluth, MN — 14 | 10 | 152 | 3412 | 71 | 76620 | 0 | 45822 | 22206 | 688

✠ ST. LUKE'S HOSPITAL, 915 East First Street, Zip 55805–2193; tel. 218/726–5555; John Strange, President and Chief Executive Officer **A**1 2 3 5 9 10 **F**3 4 7 8 10 11 12 14 15 16 19 20 21 22 23 28 30 31 32 33 34 35 37 39 40 41 42 43 44 49 51 52 53 54 55 56 57 58 59 60 63 65 67 70 71 72 73 **N** Northern Lakes Health Consortium, Duluth, MN — 23 | 10 | 256 | 7203 | 96 | 107440 | 827 | 88779 | 43895 | 973

✠ ST. MARY'S MEDICAL CENTER, 407 East Third Street, Zip 55805–1984; tel. 218/726–4000; Sister Kathleen Hofer, President **A**1 2 3 5 9 10 **F**2 3 4 5 6 7 8 9 10 11 14 15 16 17 18 19 20 21 22 23 24 27 29 30 31 32 33 34 35 36 37 38 39 40 41 42 43 44 45 46 47 48 49 51 52 53 54 55 56 57 58 59 60 61 62 63 64 65 66 67 70 71 72 73 **P**6 **S** Benedictine Health System, Duluth, MN **N** Benedictine Health System, Duluth, MN — 21 | 10 | 286 | 15830 | 209 | 95801 | 1458 | 142873 | 60481 | 1731

ELBOW LAKE—Grant County

★ GRANT COUNTY HEALTH CENTER, 930 First Street N.E., Zip 56531–4699; tel. 218/685–4461; Larry Rapp, Chief Medical and Executive Officer (Nonreporting) **A**9 10 — 23 | 10 | 15 | — | — | — | — | — | — | —

ELY—St. Louis County

★ ELY-BLOOMENSON COMMUNITY HOSPITAL, 328 West Conan Street, Zip 55731–1198; tel. 218/365–3271; John Fossum, Administrator (Total facility includes 99 beds in nursing home–type unit) **A**9 10 **F**1 7 8 11 15 17 19 21 22 32 33 34 35 36 39 40 44 49 64 65 67 71 72 73 **P**6 **N** Northern Lakes Health Consortium, Duluth, MN — 23 | 10 | 138 | 361 | 101 | 6001 | 50 | 8797 | 4857 | 268

FAIRMONT—Martin County

✠ FAIRMONT COMMUNITY HOSPITAL, (Includes Lutz Wing Convalescent and Nursing Care Unit), 835 Johnson Street, Zip 56031, Mailing Address: P.O. Box 835, Zip 56031–0835; tel. 507/238–4254; Gerry Gilbertson, President (Total facility includes 40 beds in nursing home–type unit) **A**1 9 10 **F**6 7 8 14 15 16 17 19 20 21 22 23 24 28 29 32 33 34 35 37 40 41 42 44 45 46 49 60 61 64 65 66 67 71 72 73 **N** Allina Health System, Minnetonka, MN — 23 | 10 | 92 | 1965 | 57 | 40258 | 285 | 16206 | 7326 | 191

FARIBAULT—Rice County

✠ DISTRICT ONE HOSPITAL, 631 S.E. First Street, Zip 55021–6345; tel. 507/334–6451; James N. Wolf, Chief Executive Officer **A**1 10 **F**7 8 10 15 16 19 20 21 22 28 30 32 33 35 36 37 39 40 41 42 44 45 65 66 67 71 72 73 — 16 | 10 | 64 | 2198 | 21 | 29281 | 411 | 16429 | 6925 | 204

FARIBAULT REGIONAL CENTER, 802 Circle Drive, Zip 55021–6399; tel. 507/332–3000; Bridget K. Stroud, Chief Executive Officer (Nonreporting) — 12 | 62 | 263 | — | — | — | — | — | — | —

Hospital, Address, Telephone, Administrator, Approval, Facility, and Physician Codes, Health Care System, Network	Classification Codes		Utilization Data					Expense (thousands) of dollars		
	Control	Service	Staffed Beds	Admissions	Census	Outpatient Visits	Births	Total	Payroll	Personnel

★ American Hospital Association (AHA) membership
☐ Joint Commission on Accreditation of Healthcare Organizations (JCAHO) accreditation
+ American Osteopathic Healthcare Association (AOHA) membership
○ American Osteopathic Association (AOA) accreditation
△ Commission on Accreditation of Rehabilitation Facilities (CARF) accreditation
Control codes 61, 63, 64, 71, 72 and 73 indicate hospitals listed by AOHA, but not registered by AHA. For definition of numerical codes, see page A4

☐ WILSON CENTER PSYCHIATRIC FACILITY FOR CHILDREN AND ADOLESCENTS, 1800 14th Street N.E., Zip 55021, Mailing Address: P.O. Box 917, Zip 55021–0917; tel. 507/334–5561; Kevin J. Mahoney, President (Nonreporting) **A**1 9	33	22	50	—	—	—	—	—	—	—
FARMINGTON—Dakota County										
★ SOUTH SUBURBAN MEDICAL CENTER, 3410–213th Street West, Zip 55024–1197; tel. 612/463–7825; Lee Larson, Chief Executive Officer (Total facility includes 65 beds in nursing home–type unit) (Nonreporting) **A**9 10 **S** Benedictine Health System, Duluth, MN **N** Benedictine Health System, Duluth, MN	23	10	95	—	—	—	—	—	—	—
FERGUS FALLS—Otter Tail County										
☐ FERGUS FALLS REGIONAL TREATMENT CENTER, Fir and Union Avenues, Zip 56537, Mailing Address: P.O. Box 157, Zip 56537–0157; tel. 218/739–7200; Michael Ackley, Administrator **A**1 10 **F**2 3 14 16 17 20 41 46 52 56 57 58 64 65 73 **P**6	12	22	269	1352	215	—	—	—	—	358
⊞ LAKE REGION HEALTHCARE CORPORATION, (Formerly Lake Region Hospital Corporation), 712 South Cascade Street, Zip 56537–2900, Mailing Address: P.O. Box 728, Zip 56538–0728; tel. 218/736–8000; Edward J. Mehl, Chief Executive Officer (Total facility includes 44 beds in nursing home–type unit) **A**1 9 10 **F**7 8 11 15 17 19 20 21 22 23 26 32 34 35 37 40 41 42 44 49 52 53 54 55 56 57 64 65 66 67 71 73	23	10	136	3321	90	32690	336	29176	14364	663
FOSSTON—Polk County										
★ FIRST CARE MEDICAL SERVICES, 900 South Hilligoss Boulevard East, Zip 56542–1599; tel. 218/435–1133; David Hubbard, Chief Executive Officer (Total facility includes 50 beds in nursing home–type unit) **A**9 10 **F**7 8 14 15 16 19 21 26 27 32 33 34 35 36 44 49 51 63 64 65 66 67 70 71 **P**5	23	10	71	617	54	48469	66	7934	4130	239
FRIDLEY—Anoka County										
★ UNITY HOSPITAL, 550 Osborne Road N.E., Zip 55432–2799; tel. 612/421–2222 **A**2 9 **F**2 3 7 8 10 12 14 15 16 17 18 19 21 22 23 27 28 29 30 32 33 35 36 37 39 40 41 42 43 44 45 46 49 51 52 53 54 55 56 57 58 59 60 63 64 65 67 68 70 71 72 73 **P**3 4 5 6 7 **S** Allina Health System, Minneapolis, MN	23	10	219	11187	121	—	1898	88880	40204	977
GLENCOE—McLeod County										
★ GLENCOE AREA HEALTH CENTER, 705 East 18th Street, Zip 55336–1499; tel. 320/864–3121; Jon D. Braband, Chief Executive Officer (Total facility includes 110 beds in nursing home–type unit) **A**9 10 **F**1 6 7 8 11 15 16 19 22 26 27 28 30 32 34 35 37 40 41 42 44 49 58 63 64 65 71 73 **S** HealthSystem Minnesota, Saint Louis Park, MN	14	10	149	1589	123	13721	169	14738	7040	347
GLENWOOD—Pope County										
★ GLACIAL RIDGE HOSPITAL, 10 Fourth Avenue S.E., Zip 56334–1898; tel. 320/634–4521; Douglas J. Reker, Administrator and Chief Executive Officer **A**9 10 **F**7 8 14 15 17 19 21 22 24 28 29 30 32 33 34 35 37 40 41 42 44 49 53 54 65 67 70 71 73 **P**6	16	10	19	515	5	9099	45	6101	3629	156
GOLDEN VALLEY—Hennepin County										
⊞ VENCOR HOSPITAL–MINNEAPOLIS, (Formerly Transitional Hospital Corporation of Minneapolis), 4101 Golden Valley Road, Zip 55422; tel. 612/588–2750; Patrick A. Auman, Ph.D., Chief Executive Officer (Nonreporting) **A**1 9 10 **S** Vencor, Incorporated, Louisville, KY	33	10	111	—	—	—	—	—	—	—
GRACEVILLE—Big Stone County										
GRACEVILLE HEALTH CENTER, 115 West Second Street, Zip 56240–0157, Mailing Address: P.O. Box 157, Zip 56240–0157; tel. 320/748–7223; Carollee Brinkman, Chief Executive Officer (Total facility includes 60 beds in nursing home–type unit) (Nonreporting) **A**9 10 **N** Minnesota Rural Health Cooperative, Willmar, MN	23	10	92	—	—	—	—	—	—	—
GRAND MARAIS—Cook County										
COOK COUNTY NORTH SHORE HOSPITAL, Gunflint Trail, Zip 55604, Mailing Address: P.O. Box 10, Zip 55604–0010; tel. 218/387–3040; Diane Pearson, Administrator (Total facility includes 47 beds in nursing home–type unit) **A**9 10 **F**7 8 11 17 22 32 33 40 49 64 65 71 73 **P**6 **N** Northern Lakes Health Consortium, Duluth, MN	16	10	57	309	46	10863	28	4777	2570	89
GRAND RAPIDS—Itasca County										
⊞ ITASCA MEDICAL CENTER, 126 First Avenue S.E., Zip 55744–3698; tel. 218/326–3401; Gary Kenner, President and Chief Executive Officer (Total facility includes 35 beds in nursing home–type unit) **A**1 9 10 **F**1 7 8 11 12 15 17 19 21 22 26 31 32 34 35 37 39 40 41 42 44 46 49 56 64 65 66 67 71 73 74 **S** Benedictine Health System, Duluth, MN **N** Benedictine Health System, Duluth, MN; Northern Lakes Health Consortium, Duluth, MN; Itasca Partnership for Quality Healthcare, Grand Rapids, MN	23	10	84	2733	59	34208	291	23836	12222	282
GRANITE FALLS—Yellow Medicine County										
⊞ GRANITE FALLS MUNICIPAL HOSPITAL AND MANOR, 345 Tenth Avenue, Zip 56241–1499; tel. 320/564–3111; George Gerlach, President (Total facility includes 64 beds in nursing home–type unit) **A**1 9 10 **F**8 14 15 16 17 19 22 28 30 31 32 33 35 36 40 44 46 49 62 63 64 65 71 **S** Allina Health System, Minneapolis, MN **N** Allina Health System, Minnetonka, MN; Minnesota Rural Health Cooperative, Willmar, MN	14	10	94	633	67	6174	1	7113	3819	207
HALLOCK—Kittson County										
KITTSON MEMORIAL HEALTHCARE CENTER, (Formerly Kittson Memorial Hospital), 1010 South Birch Street, Zip 56728, Mailing Address: P.O. Box 700, Zip 56728–0700; tel. 218/843–3612; Richard J. Failing, Chief Executive Officer (Total facility includes 88 beds in nursing home–type unit) **A**9 10 **F**8 11 15 16 19 22 27 32 33 35 39 40 44 49 64 65 71 **P**5 **N**	23	10	108	259	84	7794	13	4875	2620	234

Hospital, Address, Telephone, Administrator, Approval, Facility, and Physician Codes, Health Care System, Network	Classi-fication Codes		Utilization Data					Expense (thousands) of dollars		
★ American Hospital Association (AHA) membership □ Joint Commission on Accreditation of Healthcare Organizations (JCAHO) accreditation + American Osteopathic Healthcare Association (AOHA) membership ○ American Osteopathic Association (AOA) accreditation △ Commission on Accreditation of Rehabilitation Facilities (CARF) accreditation Control codes 61, 63, 64, 71, 72 and 73 indicate hospitals listed by AOHA, but not registered by AHA. For definition of numerical codes, see page A4	Control	Service	Staffed Beds	Admissions	Census	Outpatient Visits	Births	Total	Payroll	Personnel

HARMONY—Fillmore County

HARMONY COMMUNITY HOSPITAL, 815 South Main Avenue, Zip 55939–6625, Mailing Address: Route 1, Box 173, Zip 55939–0173; tel. 507/886–6544; Greg Braun, Administrator (Total facility includes 45 beds in nursing home–type unit) **A**9 10 **F**1 12 15 16 17 20 26 27 28 29 30 32 33 34 39 41 45 46 49 51 54 61 64 65 67 72 73 74 **P**3 6

	23	10	53	123	44	8593	0	2640	—	97

HASTINGS—Dakota County

□ REGINA MEDICAL CENTER, 1175 Nininger Road, Zip 55033–1098; tel. 612/480–4100; Lynn W. Olson, Administrator and Chief Executive Officer (Total facility includes 61 beds in nursing home–type unit) **A**1 9 10 **F**6 7 8 11 12 15 17 19 22 24 27 28 29 30 32 34 35 36 39 40 41 44 46 49 51 61 62 64 65 67 71 72 73 74 **P**4

	23	10	118	1847	76	22541	344	20066	11056	346

HENDRICKS—Lincoln County

★ HENDRICKS COMMUNITY HOSPITAL, 503 East Lincoln Street, Zip 56136–9598; tel. 507/275–3134; Kirk Stensrud, Administrator (Total facility includes 70 beds in nursing home–type unit) **A**9 10 **F**1 6 7 8 11 12 14 15 16 17 19 20 21 22 24 28 30 31 32 33 34 35 37 40 44 63 64 65 67 71 73 **N** Minnesota Rural Health Cooperative, Willmar, MN

	23	10	82	373	72	5778	28	4309	2114	121

HIBBING—St. Louis County

⊞ UNIVERSITY MEDICAL CENTER–MESABI, 750 East 34th Street, Zip 55746–4600; tel. 218/262–4881; Richard W. Dinter, Chief Operating Officer **A**1 9 10 **F**2 3 7 8 12 15 19 20 21 22 28 29 31 32 33 34 35 36 37 39 40 42 44 49 52 53 54 55 56 57 58 59 60 65 66 67 70 71 73 **P**5 **S** Fairview Hospital and Healthcare Services, Minneapolis, MN **N** Northern Lakes Health Consortium, Duluth, MN

	23	10	126	3686	47	55991	286	27931	12441	358

HUTCHINSON—McLeod County

⊞ HUTCHINSON AREA HEALTH CARE, 1095 Highway 15 South, Zip 55350–3182; tel. 320/234–5000; Philip G. Graves, President (Total facility includes 127 beds in nursing home–type unit) **A**1 9 10 **F**1 3 7 8 11 15 16 17 18 19 22 26 28 29 30 32 33 34 35 36 39 40 41 42 44 46 49 52 53 54 55 56 57 58 59 64 65 66 67 71 73 74 **S** Allina Health System, Minneapolis, MN **N** Allina Health System, Minnetonka, MN

	14	10	193	2636	144	40873	426	26870	12745	401

INTERNATIONAL FALLS—Koochiching County

⊞ FALLS MEMORIAL HOSPITAL, 1400 Highway 71, Zip 56649–2189; tel. 218/283–4481; Mary Klimp, Administrator and Chief Executive Officer **A**1 9 10 **F**7 8 11 14 15 16 17 19 20 21 22 28 30 32 33 35 37 40 42 44 46 48 49 56 64 65 71 73 **S** Quorum Health Group/Quorum Health Resources, Inc., Brentwood, TN **N** Northern Lakes Health Consortium, Duluth, MN

	23	10	35	1008	8	25074	115	7728	3242	107

IVANHOE—Lincoln County

★ DIVINE PROVIDENCE HEALTH CENTER, 312 East George Street, Zip 56142–0136, Mailing Address: P.O. Box G., Zip 56142–0136; tel. 507/694–1414; Patrick Branco, Administrator (Total facility includes 51 beds in nursing home–type unit) (Nonreporting) **A**9 10 **S** Avera Health, Yankton, SD **N** Minnesota Rural Health Cooperative, Willmar, MN

	23	10	79	—	—	—	—	—	—	—

JACKSON—Jackson County

★ JACKSON MEDICAL CENTER, 1430 North Highway, Zip 56143–1098; tel. 507/847–2420; Charlotte Heitkamp, Chief Executive Officer (Total facility includes 21 beds in nursing home–type unit) **A**9 10 **F**22 33 44 64 71 **P**6 **S** Sioux Valley Hospitals and Health System, Sioux Falls, SD

	14	10	41	430	24	10102	0	4007	1899	61

LAKE CITY—Wabasha County

⊞ LAKE CITY HOSPITAL, 904 South Lakeshore Drive, Zip 55041–1899; tel. 612/345–3321; Mark Rinehardt, Chief Executive Officer (Total facility includes 115 beds in nursing home–type unit) **A**1 9 10 **F**3 8 15 17 19 22 26 32 33 40 44 46 49 64 65 71 72 73

	14	10	144	700	109	4309	49	7664	4006	279

LE SUEUR—Le Sueur County

MINNESOTA VALLEY HEALTH CENTER, (Includes Gardenview Nursing Home), 621 South Fourth Street, Zip 56058–2203; tel. 507/665–3375; Jennifer D. Pfeffer, Administrator and Chief Executive Officer (Total facility includes 85 beds in nursing home–type unit) **A**9 10 **F**7 8 11 15 16 17 19 22 29 30 33 34 36 40 41 42 44 48 49 62 64 65 67 71 73 **P**3

	23	10	103	198	84	11484	22	4639	2469	126

LITCHFIELD—Meeker County

★ MEEKER COUNTY MEMORIAL HOSPITAL, 612 South Sibley Avenue, Zip 55355–3398; tel. 320/693–3242; Ronald E. Johnson, Administrator **A**9 10 **F**7 8 15 16 19 21 22 26 28 29 30 34 35 37 40 42 44 45 49 63 67 71

	13	10	38	1206	12	17489	189	7594	3314	103

LITTLE FALLS—Morrison County

⊞ ST. GABRIEL'S HOSPITAL, 815 Second Street S.E., Zip 56345–3596; tel. 320/632–5441; Larry A. Schulz, President and Chief Executive Officer (Total facility includes 150 beds in nursing home–type unit) **A**1 9 10 **F**1 3 6 7 8 12 15 16 17 19 20 21 22 24 26 27 28 30 31 32 33 34 35 37 39 40 41 42 44 45 46 49 53 54 55 56 57 58 59 62 63 64 65 66 67 70 71 73 **S** Catholic Health Initiatives, Denver, CO

	21	10	205	2277	162	50500	258	25755	11577	414

LONG PRAIRIE—Todd County

⊞ LONG PRAIRIE MEMORIAL HOSPITAL AND HOME, 20 Ninth Street S.E., Zip 56347–1404; tel. 320/732–2141; Clayton R. Peterson, President (Total facility includes 123 beds in nursing home–type unit) **A**1 9 10 **F**1 7 8 11 14 15 16 19 22 27 28 32 33 34 35 36 40 41 44 49 52 65 73 **P**3 **S** Allina Health System, Minneapolis, MN **N** Allina Health System, Minnetonka, MN

	23	10	141	733	110	19092	91	8982	4105	155

Hospital, Address, Telephone, Administrator, Approval, Facility, and Physician Codes, Health Care System, Network	Classi-fication Codes		Utilization Data					Expense (thousands) of dollars		Personnel
	Control	Service	Staffed Beds	Admissions	Census	Outpatient Visits	Births	Total	Payroll	

★ American Hospital Association (AHA) membership
□ Joint Commission on Accreditation of Healthcare Organizations (JCAHO) accreditation
+ American Osteopathic Healthcare Association (AOHA) membership
○ American Osteopathic Association (AOA) accreditation
△ Commission on Accreditation of Rehabilitation Facilities (CARF) accreditation
Control codes 61, 63, 64, 71, 72 and 73 indicate hospitals listed by AOHA, but not registered by AHA. For definition of numerical codes, see page A4

LUVERNE—Rock County

	Control	Service	Staffed Beds	Admissions	Census	Outpatient Visits	Births	Total	Payroll	Personnel
★ LUVERNE COMMUNITY HOSPITAL, 305 East Luverne Street, Zip 56156–2519, Mailing Address: P.O. Box 1019, Zip 56156–1019; tel. 507/283–2321; Gerald E. Carl, Administrator **A**9 10 **F**3 7 8 15 16 19 22 30 32 33 34 35 39 40 41 42 44 49 64 65 67 71 **P**3 **S** Sioux Valley Hospitals and Health System, Sioux Falls, SD **N** Southwest Minnesota Health Alliance, Luverne, MN	14	10	38	920	13	12048	130	6793	3114	132

MADELIA—Watonwan County

⊠ MADELIA COMMUNITY HOSPITAL, 121 Drew Avenue S.E., Zip 56062–1899; tel. 507/642–3255; Candace Fenske, R.N., Administrator **A**1 9 10 **F**7 14 15 16 17 19 20 21 22 28 29 32 33 34 36 40 41 44 45 49 64 65 71 **P**5	23	10	25	503	5	4145	39	2551	1171	47

MADISON—Lac Qui Parle County

★ MADISON HOSPITAL, (Formerly Lac Qui Parle Hospital of Madison), 820 Third Avenue, Zip 56256–1014, Mailing Address: P.O. Box 184, Zip 56256–0184; tel. 320/598–7556; Tom Richter, Chief Executive Officer **A**9 10 **F**7 8 19 22 28 30 32 33 34 35 36 40 44 49 65 71 **P**1 **N** Minnesota Rural Health Cooperative, Willmar, MN	23	10	12	246	2	640	15	1600	690	24

MAHNOMEN—Mahnomen County

MAHNOMEN HEALTH CENTER, 414 Jefferson Avenue, Zip 56557, Mailing Address: P.O. Box 396, Zip 56557–0396; tel. 218/935–2511; Craig Doughty, Chief Executive Officer (Total facility includes 48 beds in nursing home–type unit) **A**9 10 **F**8 11 17 19 22 24 26 28 30 31 33 34 35 39 44 46 48 49 51 53 64 65 71 **P**6	23	10	67	292	45	6042	—	3133	1613	136

MANKATO—Blue Earth County

⊠ IMMANUEL/ST. JOSEPH'S–MAYO HEALTH SYSTEM, 1025 Marsh Street, Zip 56001–4700, Mailing Address: P.O. Box 8673, Zip 56002–8673; tel. 507/625–4031; Douglas L. Wood, M.D., President; Jerome A. Crest, Executive Vice President **A**1 2 3 5 9 10 **F**3 7 8 10 12 15 16 17 19 20 21 22 23 28 29 30 31 32 33 34 35 37 39 40 41 42 44 45 49 52 53 54 55 56 57 58 59 60 63 65 67 71 73 74 **P**8 **S** Mayo Foundation, Rochester, MN	23	10	147	6903	84	62659	1046	50641	23503	679

MAPLEWOOD—Ramsey County

★ HEALTHEAST ST. JOHN'S HOSPITAL, 1575 Beam Avenue, Zip 55109; tel. 612/232–7000; William Knutson, Vice President and Administrator **A**3 5 9 10 **F**2 3 4 7 8 10 11 12 14 15 16 17 18 19 21 22 23 25 26 27 28 29 30 31 32 33 34 35 36 37 39 40 41 42 43 44 45 46 49 51 52 53 54 55 56 57 58 60 62 63 64 65 66 67 70 71 72 73 **P**1 6 8 **S** HealthEast, Saint Paul, MN **N** Healtheast, St. Paul, MN	23	10	163	12749	125	83216	2784	87143	37233	579

MARSHALL—Lyon County

★ WEINER MEMORIAL MEDICAL CENTER, 300 South Bruce Street, Zip 56258–1934; tel. 507/532–9661; James F. Hanko, Administrator and Chief Executive Officer (Total facility includes 76 beds in nursing home–type unit) **A**9 10 **F**1 6 7 8 14 15 16 17 19 20 22 24 26 27 28 29 30 31 32 33 34 35 37 39 40 41 42 44 45 49 56 57 58 62 64 65 67 71 72 73 **N** Minnesota Rural Health Cooperative, Willmar, MN; Affiliated Community Health Network, Inc., Willmar, MN	14	10	121	1807	88	14561	432	14085	7344	254

MELROSE—Stearns County

MELROSE AREA HOSPITAL, (Formerly Melrose Hospital and Pine Villa Nursing Home), 11 North Fifth Avenue West, Zip 56352–1098; tel. 320/256–4231; Joan Jackson, Administrator (Total facility includes 75 beds in nursing home–type unit) **A**9 10 **F**1 7 8 14 15 16 17 19 20 22 26 27 32 33 34 35 36 37 39 40 41 44 49 51 57 58 62 64 65 66 67 71 73 **P**5	14	10	87	433	80	8608	63	—	2599	111

MINNEAPOLIS—Hennepin County

⊠ △ ABBOTT NORTHWESTERN HOSPITAL, (Includes Sister Kenny Institute), 800 East 28th Street, Zip 55407–3799; tel. 612/863–4201; Mark Dixon, Administrator **A**1 2 3 5 7 9 10 **F**2 3 4 5 7 8 9 10 11 12 15 17 19 21 22 23 24 25 26 27 28 29 30 31 32 33 34 35 36 37 38 39 40 41 42 43 44 45 46 47 48 49 51 52 53 54 55 56 57 58 59 60 61 63 64 65 67 69 71 72 73 74 **P**5 6 8 **S** Allina Health System, Minneapolis, MN **N** Allina Health System, Minnetonka, MN	23	10	588	30343	436	—	3157	372066	162890	3335
□ CHILDREN'S HOSPITALS AND CLINICS, MINNEAPOLIS, (Formerly Children's Health Care, Minneapolis), 2525 Chicago Avenue South, Zip 55404–9976; tel. 612/813–6100; Brock D. Nelson, Chief Executive Officer (Nonreporting) **A**1 2 3 9 10	23	50	163	—	—	—	—	—	—	—
FAIRVIEW RIVERSIDE HOSPITAL See Fairview–University Medical Center										
⊠ FAIRVIEW SOUTHDALE HOSPITAL, 6401 France Avenue South, Zip 55435–2199; tel. 612/924–5000; Mark M. Enger, Senior Vice President and Administrator (Nonreporting) **A**1 2 9 10 **S** Fairview Hospital and Healthcare Services, Minneapolis, MN **N** Fairview Health System, Minneapolis, MN	23	10	355	—	—	—	—	—	—	—
⊠ FAIRVIEW–UNIVERSITY MEDICAL CENTER, (Includes Fairview Riverside Hospital, 2312 South Sixth Street, Zip 55454; St. Mary's Hospital and Rehabilitation Center, 2414 South Seventh Street, Zip 55454; tel. 612/338–2229; University of Minnesota Hospital and Clinic, 420 S.E. Delaware Street, Box 502, Zip 55455–0392; tel. 612/626–3000), 2450 Riverside Avenue, Zip 55454–1400; tel. 612/626–6685; Pamela L. Tibbetts, Senior Vice President and Administrator (Total facility includes 115 beds in nursing home–type unit) (Nonreporting) **A**1 2 3 5 6 8 9 10 **S** Fairview Hospital and Healthcare Services, Minneapolis, MN **N** Fairview Health System, Minneapolis, MN	23	10	1362	—	—	—	—	—	—	—
⊠ △ HENNEPIN COUNTY MEDICAL CENTER, 701 Park Avenue South, Zip 55415–1829; tel. 612/347–2121; John W. Bluford, Administrator (Nonreporting) **A**1 2 3 5 7 8 9 10	13	10	462	—	—	—	—	—	—	—

Hospital, Address, Telephone, Administrator, Approval, Facility, and Physician Codes, Health Care System, Network	Classi-fication Codes		Utilization Data						Expense (thousands) of dollars		
	Control	Service	Staffed Beds	Admissions	Census	Outpatient Visits	Births	Total	Payroll	Personnel

Legend:
★ American Hospital Association (AHA) membership
□ Joint Commission on Accreditation of Healthcare Organizations (JCAHO) accreditation
+ American Osteopathic Healthcare Association (AOHA) membership
○ American Osteopathic Association (AOA) accreditation
△ Commission on Accreditation of Rehabilitation Facilities (CARF) accreditation
Control codes 61, 63, 64, 71, 72 and 73 indicate hospitals listed by AOHA, but not registered by AHA. For definition of numerical codes, see page A4

Hospital	Control	Service	Staffed Beds	Admissions	Census	Outpatient Visits	Births	Total	Payroll	Personnel
★ PHILLIPS EYE INSTITUTE, 2215 Park Avenue, Zip 55404–3756; tel. 612/336–6000; Shari E. Levy, Administrator (Nonreporting) **A**1 10 **F**2 3 4 5 8 10 11 12 14 15 16 17 18 19 20 21 22 24 26 28 29 30 31 32 33 34 35 37 39 41 42 43 44 45 46 47 48 49 51 52 53 54 55 56 58 59 60 61 64 65 66 67 69 71 72 73 74 **S** Allina Health System, Minneapolis, MN **N** Allina Health System, Minnetonka, MN	23	45	10	643	2	13323	0	14017	4689	106
★ SHRINERS HOSPITALS FOR CHILDREN, TWIN CITIES, 2025 East River Parkway, Zip 55414–3696; tel. 612/335–5300; Laurence E. Johnson, Administrator **A**1 3 5 **F**15 19 34 35 39 44 45 46 49 53 65 67 71 73 **P**6 **S** Shriners Hospitals for Children, Tampa, FL	23	57	40	850	19	8437	—	—	—	159
ST. MARY'S HOSPITAL AND REHABILITATION CENTER See Fairview–University Medical Center										
UNIVERSITY OF MINNESOTA HOSPITAL AND CLINIC See Fairview–University Medical Center										
★ △ VETERANS AFFAIRS MEDICAL CENTER, One Veterans Drive, Zip 55417–2399; tel. 612/725–2000; Charles A. Milbrandt, Director **A**1 2 3 5 7 8 **F**1 2 3 4 5 6 8 10 11 12 15 16 17 18 19 20 21 22 24 25 26 27 28 29 30 31 32 34 35 37 39 41 42 43 44 45 46 48 49 50 51 52 54 55 56 58 59 60 64 65 67 69 71 72 73 74 **S** Department of Veterans Affairs, Washington, DC	45	10	471	10914	292	375137	—	228721	109160	2580
MONTEVIDEO—Chippewa County										
CHIPPEWA COUNTY MONTEVIDEO HOSPITAL, 824 North 11th Street, Zip 56265–1683; tel. 320/269–8877; Fred Knutson, Administrator (Nonreporting) **A**9 10 **N** Minnesota Rural Health Cooperative, Willmar, MN	15	10	29	—	—	—	—	—	—	—
MONTICELLO—Wright County										
★ MONTICELLO BIG LAKE HOSPITAL, 1013 Hart Boulevard, Zip 55362–8230; tel. 612/295–2945; Barbara Schwientek, Executive Director (Total facility includes 91 beds in nursing home–type unit) **A**1 9 10 **F**1 3 7 8 14 15 19 22 32 33 34 35 36 37 40 42 44 58 64 65 66 71 72	16	10	103	1094	98	12227	280	14169	6907	231
MOOSE LAKE—Carlton County										
★ MERCY HOSPITAL AND HEALTH CARE CENTER, 710 South Kenwood Avenue, Zip 55767–9405; tel. 218/485–4481; Dianne Mandernach, Chief Executive Officer (Total facility includes 94 beds in nursing home–type unit) (Nonreporting) **A**9 10 **N** Northern Lakes Health Consortium, Duluth, MN	16	10	119	—	—	—	—	—	—	—
MORA—Kanabec County										
★ KANABEC HOSPITAL, 300 Clark Street, Zip 55051–1590; tel. 320/679–1212; Thomas D. Kaufman, Administrator **A**1 9 10 **F**7 8 14 16 17 19 21 22 28 30 35 37 40 41 42 44 45 46 49 64 65 67 71 73 **P**5 **N**	13	10	35	1120	11	12108	160	8076	4038	116
MORRIS—Stevens County										
★ STEVENS COMMUNITY MEDICAL CENTER, 400 East First Street, Zip 56267–1407, Mailing Address: P.O. Box 660, Zip 56267–0660; tel. 320/589–1313; John Rau, President **A**1 9 10 **F**3 7 8 11 14 15 16 17 18 19 20 22 27 28 30 31 32 33 34 35 37 39 40 41 42 44 45 46 49 51 53 54 55 56 57 58 65 67 71 **P**6 **S** Allina Health System, Minneapolis, MN	23	10	39	1226	13	72780	90	12295	5827	171
NEW PRAGUE—Le Sueur County										
★ QUEEN OF PEACE HOSPITAL, 301 Second Street N.E., Zip 56071–1799; tel. 612/758–4431; Sister Jean Juenemann, Chief Executive Officer **A**1 9 10 **F**6 7 8 11 13 16 17 19 20 21 22 24 28 30 32 34 35 39 40 41 42 44 45 46 49 51 60 62 67 71 72 73	23	10	28	1315	11	65030	173	10873	5089	173
NEW ULM—Brown County										
★ NEW ULM MEDICAL CENTER, 1324 Fifth Street North, Zip 56073–1553, Mailing Address: P.O. Box 577, Zip 56073–0577; tel. 507/354–2111; David A. Grundstrom, President **A**1 9 10 **F**2 3 7 8 15 17 18 19 20 21 22 24 27 28 30 32 33 34 35 36 37 39 40 41 42 44 45 46 49 51 52 53 54 56 57 58 65 66 67 71 72 **P**3 **S** Allina Health System, Minneapolis, MN **N** Allina Health System, Minnetonka, MN; Quality Health Alliance, Mankato, MN	23	10	47	2237	23	56130	405	26059	9558	319
NORTHFIELD—Rice County										
★ NORTHFIELD HOSPITAL, (Includes H. O. DILLEY SKILLED NURSING FACILITY), 801 West First Street, Zip 55057–1697; tel. 507/645–6661; Kendall C. Bank, President (Total facility includes 40 beds in nursing home–type unit) **A**1 9 10 **F**7 8 11 14 15 16 19 20 22 28 30 32 33 34 35 36 39 40 41 42 44 45 46 49 51 64 65 66 67 71 73 **S** Allina Health System, Minneapolis, MN **N** Allina Health System, Minnetonka, MN	14	10	67	1841	50	18225	358	13028	6380	115
OLIVIA—Renville County										
★ RENVILLE COUNTY HOSPITAL, 611 East Fairview Avenue, Zip 56277–1397; tel. 320/523–1261; Dean G. Slagter, Administrator (Nonreporting) **A**9 10 **N** Minnesota Rural Health Cooperative, Willmar, MN	13	10	30	—	—	—	—	—	—	—
ONAMIA—Mille Lacs County										
★ MILLE LACS HEALTH SYSTEM, 200 North Elm Street, Zip 56359–7978; tel. 320/532–3154; Randall A. Farrow, President (Total facility includes 80 beds in nursing home–type unit) **A**1 9 10 **F**1 3 7 8 12 15 16 17 19 20 21 22 26 27 28 29 30 32 33 34 35 37 39 41 42 44 45 49 51 53 54 55 58 65 66 67 71 **P**6 **S** Allina Health System, Minneapolis, MN **N** Allina Health System, Minnetonka, MN; Northern Lakes Health Consortium, Duluth, MN	23	10	108	888	82	14175	84	11145	5321	112
ORTONVILLE—Big Stone County										
★ ORTONVILLE AREA HEALTH SERVICES, 750 Eastvold Avenue, Zip 56278–1133; tel. 320/839–2502; Michael R. Miller, Interim Administrator (Total facility includes 74 beds in nursing home–type unit) **A**9 10 **F**7 8 15 16 19 21 22 27 30 32 33 34 35 36 39 42 44 45 46 49 53 54 56 57 58 64 65 67 71 73 **S** Sioux Valley Hospitals and Health System, Sioux Falls, SD **N** Minnesota Rural Health Cooperative, Willmar, MN	14	10	105	582	96	14647	53	4502	2532	112

Hospital, Address, Telephone, Administrator, Approval, Facility, and Physician Codes, Health Care System, Network	Classification Codes		Utilization Data					Expense (thousands) of dollars		
	Control	Service	Staffed Beds	Admissions	Census	Outpatient Visits	Births	Total	Payroll	Personnel

★ American Hospital Association (AHA) membership
□ Joint Commission on Accreditation of Healthcare Organizations (JCAHO) accreditation
+ American Osteopathic Healthcare Association (AOHA) membership
○ American Osteopathic Association (AOA) accreditation
△ Commission on Accreditation of Rehabilitation Facilities (CARF) accreditation
Control codes 61, 63, 64, 71, 72 and 73 indicate hospitals listed by AOHA, but not registered by AHA. For definition of numerical codes, see page A4

OWATONNA—Steele County

✠ OWATONNA HOSPITAL, 903 Oak Street South, Zip 55060–3234; tel. 507/451–3850; Richard G. Slieter, Administrator **A**1 9 10 **F**7 8 12 14 15 16 19 21 22 28 30 32 33 35 36 37 40 44 49 52 54 55 56 57 58 65 66 67 71 **S** Allina Health System, Minneapolis, MN **N** Allina Health System, Minnetonka, MN
| 23 | 10 | 55 | 2024 | 22 | 27337 | 454 | 15749 | 6632 | 219 |

PARK RAPIDS—Hubbard County

✠ ST. JOSEPH'S AREA HEALTH SERVICES, 600 Pleasant Avenue, Zip 56470–1432; tel. 218/732–3311; David R. Hove, President and Chief Executive Officer **A**1 9 10 **F**7 8 15 16 19 21 22 30 32 33 35 37 40 44 49 63 65 71 **S** Catholic Health Initiatives, Denver, CO
| 21 | 10 | 40 | 1757 | 21 | 21881 | 143 | 14845 | 6836 | 222 |

PAYNESVILLE—Stearns County

★ PAYNESVILLE AREA HEALTH CARE SYSTEM, 200 First Street West, Zip 56362–1496; tel. 320/243–3767; William M. LaCroix, Administrator (Total facility includes 64 beds in nursing home–type unit) **A**9 10 **F**1 7 8 11 14 15 19 21 22 24 26 27 32 34 35 36 37 39 40 42 44 48 52 58 62 64 65 67 71 **P**8
| 16 | 10 | 94 | 637 | 69 | 13308 | 81 | 10644 | 4622 | 177 |

PERHAM—Otter Tail County

✠ PERHAM MEMORIAL HOSPITAL AND HOME, 665 Third Street S.W., Zip 56573–1199; tel. 218/346–4500; Chuck Hofius, Administrator (Total facility includes 102 beds in nursing home–type unit) (Nonreporting) **A**1 9 10
| 16 | 10 | 123 | — | — | — | — | — | — | — |

PIPESTONE—Pipestone County

PIPESTONE COUNTY MEDICAL CENTER, 911 Fifth Avenue S.W., Zip 56164; tel. 507/825–6125; Carl P. Vaagenes, Administrator (Total facility includes 43 beds in nursing home–type unit) (Nonreporting) **A**9 10 **S** Avera Health, Yankton, SD
| 13 | 10 | 76 | — | — | — | — | — | — | — |

PRINCETON—Sherburne County

✠ FAIRVIEW NORTHLAND REGIONAL HEALTH CARE, (Formerly Fairview Northland Regional Hospital), 911 Northland Drive, Zip 55371–2173; tel. 612/389–6300; Jeanne Lally, Senior Vice President and Administrator (Nonreporting) **A**1 9 10 **S** Fairview Hospital and Healthcare Services, Minneapolis, MN **N** Fairview Health System, Minneapolis, MN
| 23 | 10 | 41 | — | — | — | — | — | — | — |

RED WING—Goodhue County

✠ FAIRVIEW RED WING HOSPITAL, (Formerly St. John's Regional Health Center), 1407 West Fourth Street, Zip 55066–2198; tel. 612/388–6721; Craig Stockel, Interim Administrator (Nonreporting) **A**1 9 10 **S** Fairview Hospital and Healthcare Services, Minneapolis, MN **N**
| 23 | 10 | 68 | — | — | — | — | — | — | — |

REDLAKE—Beltrami County

✠ U.S. PUBLIC HEALTH SERVICE INDIAN HOSPITAL, Highway 1, Zip 56671; tel. 218/679–3912; Essimae Stevens, Service Unit Director (Nonreporting) **A**1 10 **S** U. S. Public Health Service Indian Health Service, Rockville, MD
| 47 | 10 | 23 | — | — | — | — | — | — | — |

REDWOOD FALLS—Redwood County

★ REDWOOD FALLS MUNICIPAL HOSPITAL, 100 Fallwood Road, Zip 56283–1828; tel. 507/637–2907; James E. Schulte, Administrator **A**9 10 **F**1 7 8 11 12 17 19 20 21 22 24 28 29 30 32 33 34 35 39 40 42 44 45 46 49 63 65 67 71 73 **N** Minnesota Rural Health Cooperative, Willmar, MN; Affiliated Community Health Network, Inc., Willmar, MN
| 14 | 10 | 35 | 962 | 8 | 10313 | 164 | 6150 | 3000 | 105 |

ROBBINSDALE—Hennepin County

✠ △ NORTH MEMORIAL MEDICAL CENTER, (Formerly North Memorial Health Care), 3300 Oakdale Avenue North, Zip 55422–2900; tel. 612/520–5200; Scott R. Anderson, President and Chief Executive Officer **A**1 2 3 5 7 9 10 **F**1 4 7 8 10 11 12 13 14 15 16 17 19 20 21 22 25 26 27 28 29 30 32 33 34 35 36 37 38 39 40 41 42 43 44 46 48 49 51 52 54 55 56 57 61 63 65 66 67 70 71 72 73 74 **P**1
| 23 | 10 | 374 | 21664 | 241 | 245711 | 3052 | 231094 | 114124 | 2749 |

ROCHESTER—Olmsted County

✠ OLMSTED MEDICAL CENTER, 1650 Fourth Street S.E., Zip 55904; tel. 507/285–8485; Dan Marren, FACHE, Chief Executive Officer **A**1 9 10 **F**7 15 19 22 24 36 37 40 43 71 73 **P**3
| 23 | 10 | 47 | 2021 | 15 | 18712 | 849 | 15291 | 6554 | — |

✠ ROCHESTER METHODIST HOSPITAL, 201 West Center Street, Zip 55902–3084; tel. 507/266–7890; John M. Panicek, Administrator (Nonreporting) **A**1 3 5 9 10 **S** Mayo Foundation, Rochester, MN **N** Mayo Foundation, Rochester, MN
| 23 | 10 | 335 | — | — | — | — | — | — | — |

✠ △ SAINT MARYS HOSPITAL, 1216 Second Street S.W., Zip 55902–1970; tel. 507/255–5123; John M. Panicek, Administrator (Nonreporting) **A**1 3 5 7 8 9 10 **S** Mayo Foundation, Rochester, MN **N** Mayo Foundation, Rochester, MN
| 23 | 10 | 797 | — | — | — | — | — | — | — |

ROSEAU—Roseau County

✠ ROSEAU AREA HOSPITAL AND HOMES, 715 Delmore Avenue, Zip 56751–1599; tel. 218/463–2500; David F. Hagen, President and Executive Officer (Total facility includes 104 beds in nursing home–type unit) **A**1 9 10 **F**7 8 10 11 12 13 14 15 16 19 21 22 28 30 32 33 34 35 39 41 42 44 45 49 58 60 63 64 65 67 71 73 **P**5 **N**
| 23 | 10 | 140 | 1176 | 132 | 18250 | 265 | 13439 | 7194 | 369 |

RUSH CITY—Chisago County

RUSH CITY HOSPITAL, 760 West Fourth Street, Zip 55069–9063; tel. 612/358–4708; Mark Lunseth, Administrator (Nonreporting) **A**9 10 **N** Northern Lakes Health Consortium, Duluth, MN
| 14 | 10 | 26 | — | — | — | — | — | — | — |

SAINT CLOUD—Stearns County

✠ ST. CLOUD HOSPITAL, 1406 Sixth Avenue North, Zip 56303–0016; tel. 320/251–2700; John Frobenius, President and Chief Executive Officer (Total facility includes 291 beds in nursing home–type unit) **A**1 2 3 9 10 **F**1 2 3 4 6 7 8 10 11 12 13 14 15 16 17 18 19 21 22 23 26 27 28 29 30 31 32 33 34 35 36 37 38 39 40 41 42 43 44 45 46 48 49 51 52 53 54 55 56 57 58 59 60 61 62 64 65 66 67 70 71 72 73 74 **P**3 6
| 21 | 10 | 616 | 15734 | 416 | 99917 | 2385 | 148207 | 69792 | 2303 |

Hospital, Address, Telephone, Administrator, Approval, Facility, and Physician Codes, Health Care System, Network	Classi-fication Codes		Utilization Data					Expense (thousands) of dollars		
	Control	Service	Staffed Beds	Admissions	Census	Outpatient Visits	Births	Total	Payroll	Personnel

★ American Hospital Association (AHA) membership
□ Joint Commission on Accreditation of Healthcare Organizations (JCAHO) accreditation
+ American Osteopathic Healthcare Association (AOHA) membership
○ American Osteopathic Association (AOA) accreditation
△ Commission on Accreditation of Rehabilitation Facilities (CARF) accreditation
Control codes 61, 63, 64, 71, 72 and 73 indicate hospitals listed by AOHA, but not registered by AHA. For definition of numerical codes, see page A4

✠ VETERANS AFFAIRS MEDICAL CENTER, 4801 Eighth Street North, Zip 56303–2099; tel. 320/252–1670; Barry I. Bahl, Associate Director (Total facility includes 220 beds in nursing home–type unit) **A**1 **F**1 2 3 6 8 12 19 20 26 30 33 34 35 39 41 44 46 49 51 52 56 57 58 59 64 65 67 71 73 74 **P**6 **S** Department of Veterans Affairs, Washington, DC	45	22	408	2580	386	124948	0	—	—	1004
SAINT JAMES—Watonwan County										
ST. JAMES HEALTH SERVICES, 1207 Sixth Avenue South, Zip 56081–2415; tel. 507/375–3261; Lee Holter, Chief Executive Officer **A**9 10 **F**6 7 8 15 16 17 19 20 21 22 28 30 32 33 35 39 40 44 45 46 49 51 65 67 71 **P**6 **N** Quality Health Alliance, Mankato, MN	23	10	24	305	4	25710	37	4732	2170	60
SAINT LOUIS PARK—Hennepin County										
□ △ METHODIST HOSPITAL HEALTHSYSTEM MINNESOTA, 6500 Excelsior Boulevard, Zip 55426–4702, Mailing Address: Box 650, Minneapolis, Zip 55440–0650; tel. 612/993–5000 **A**1 2 3 5 7 9 10 **F**3 4 5 6 7 8 10 11 12 14 15 17 18 19 20 22 23 25 26 28 29 30 31 32 33 34 35 37 39 40 41 42 43 44 45 46 49 51 53 54 55 56 57 58 59 60 61 64 65 66 67 68 69 71 72 73 **P**6 **S** HealthSystem Minnesota, Saint Louis Park, MN	23	10	349	22455	272	220697	3129	168610	75946	2150
SAINT PAUL—Ramsey County										
✠ CHILDREN'S HOSPITAL AND CLINICS, (Formerly Children's Health Care–St. Paul), 345 North Smith Avenue, Zip 55102–2392; tel. 612/220–6000; Brock D. Nelson, Chief Executive Officer (Nonreporting) **A**1 3 5 9 10	23	50	105	—	—	—	—	—	—	—
□ △ GILLETTE CHILDREN'S SPECIALTY HEALTHCARE, (PEDIATRIC SPECIALTY), 200 University Avenue East, Zip 55101–2598; tel. 612/291–2848; Margaret Perryman, Chief Executive Officer **A**1 3 5 7 9 10 **F**5 14 15 16 17 19 20 21 22 34 35 39 41 44 45 46 47 48 49 50 63 65 67 70 71 73 **P**4 7	23	59	48	1123	19	35292	0	28890	11839	298
✠ △ HEALTHEAST BETHESDA LUTHERAN HOSPITAL AND REHABILITATION CENTER, 559 Capitol Boulevard, Zip 55103–2101; tel. 612/232–2133; Scott Batulis, Vice President and Administrator (Nonreporting) **A**1 7 9 10 **S** HealthEast, Saint Paul, MN **N** Healtheast, St. Paul, MN	23	48	127	—	—	—	—	—	—	—
✠ HEALTHEAST ST. JOSEPH'S HOSPITAL, 69 West Exchange Street, Zip 55102–1053; tel. 612/232–3000; William Knutson, Vice President and Administrator **A**1 2 3 5 9 10 **F**1 3 4 7 8 10 11 12 14 15 16 17 18 19 21 22 23 25 26 27 28 29 30 31 32 33 34 35 36 37 39 40 41 42 43 44 45 46 48 49 51 52 53 54 55 56 57 58 60 63 64 65 66 67 70 71 72 73 **P**6 8 **S** HealthEast, Saint Paul, MN **N** Healtheast, St. Paul, MN	23	10	299	12048	150	61937	1381	110694	48145	895
✠ △ REGIONS HOSPITAL, (Formerly St. Paul–Ramsey Medical Center), 640 Jackson Street, Zip 55101–2595; tel. 612/221–3456; Terry S. Finzen, President **A**1 2 3 5 7 8 9 10 **F**3 4 5 7 8 9 10 11 17 18 19 20 21 22 25 26 29 31 32 33 34 35 37 38 40 41 42 43 44 46 47 48 49 51 52 53 54 56 57 58 61 65 70 71 72 73 74 **P**3 5 8 **N** HealthPartners, Minneapolis, MN ST. PAUL–RAMSEY MEDICAL CENTER See Regions Hospital	23	10	334	18645	273	304633	1799	208320	97966	2182
✠ UNITED HOSPITAL, 333 North Smith Street, Zip 55102–2389; tel. 612/220–8000; M. Barbara Balik, R.N., Ed.D., Administrator **A**1 2 3 5 9 10 **F**3 4 7 8 10 12 14 15 16 17 19 21 22 23 24 27 28 29 30 31 32 35 37 39 40 41 42 43 44 45 46 48 49 51 52 53 54 55 58 59 60 61 63 65 67 71 73 **S** Allina Health System, Minneapolis, MN **N** Allina Health System, Minnetonka, MN	23	10	407	23985	314	138689	4350	227970	95522	2179
SAINT PETER—Nicollet County										
★ COMMUNITY HOSPITAL AND HEALTH CARE CENTER, 618 West Broadway, Zip 56082–1327; tel. 507/931–2200; Colleen A. Spike, Interim Administrator (Total facility includes 85 beds in nursing home–type unit) (Nonreporting) **A**10 **S** Allina Health System, Minneapolis, MN MINNESOTA SECURITY HOSPITAL See St. Peter Regional Treatment Center	14	10	118	—	—	—	—	—	—	—
□ ST. PETER REGIONAL TREATMENT CENTER, (Includes Minnesota Security Hospital, Sheppard Drive, Zip 56082; tel. 507/931–7100), 100 Freeman Drive, Zip 56082–1599; tel. 507/931–7100; William L. Pedersen, Chief Executive Officer **A**1 9 10 **F**2 3 14 15 16 20 46 52 56 57 65 73 **N** Quality Health Alliance, Mankato, MN	12	22	432	874	357	—	—	38272	26968	651
SANDSTONE—Pine County										
PINE MEDICAL CENTER, 109 Court Avenue South, Zip 55072–5120; tel. 612/245–2212; Michael Hedrix, Administrator (Total facility includes 86 beds in nursing home–type unit) **A**9 10 **F**8 12 15 16 17 19 22 41 42 44 49 51 64 65 71 **P**6 **S** Benedictine Health System, Duluth, MN **N** Benedictine Health System, Duluth, MN; Northern Lakes Health Consortium, Duluth, MN	16	10	91	361	84	6919	—	6546	3261	198
SAUK CENTRE—Stearns County										
★ ST. MICHAEL'S HOSPITAL, 425 North Elm Street, Zip 56378–1010; tel. 320/352–2221; Delano Christianson, Administrator (Total facility includes 60 beds in nursing home–type unit) **A**9 10 **F**7 8 11 15 16 19 20 22 26 32 33 34 35 36 40 41 42 44 45 49 62 64 65 67 71 72 73	14	10	76	548	65	13286	67	6277	2966	121
SHAKOPEE—Scott County										
✠ ST. FRANCIS REGIONAL MEDICAL CENTER, 1455 St. Francis Avenue, Zip 55379–3380; tel. 612/403–3000; Venetia Kudrle, President (Nonreporting) **A**1 2 9 10 **S** Allina Health System, Minneapolis, MN **N** Benedictine Health System, Duluth, MN; Allina Health System, Minnetonka, MN	21	10	63	—	—	—	—	—	—	—
SLAYTON—Murray County										
★ MURRAY COUNTY MEMORIAL HOSPITAL, 2042 Juniper Avenue, Zip 56172–1016; tel. 507/836–6111; Jerry Bobeldyk, Administrator (Nonreporting) **A**9 10 **S** Sioux Valley Hospitals and Health System, Sioux Falls, SD **N** Southwest Minnesota Health Alliance, Luverne, MN; Sioux Valley Health System, Sioux Falls, SD	13	10	30	—	—	—	—	—	—	—

Hospital, Address, Telephone, Administrator, Approval, Facility, and Physician Codes, Health Care System, Network	Classi-fication Codes		Utilization Data					Expense (thousands) of dollars		
★ American Hospital Association (AHA) membership ☐ Joint Commission on Accreditation of Healthcare Organizations (JCAHO) accreditation + American Osteopathic Healthcare Association (AOHA) membership ○ American Osteopathic Association (AOA) accreditation △ Commission on Accreditation of Rehabilitation Facilities (CARF) accreditation Control codes 61, 63, 64, 71, 72 and 73 indicate hospitals listed by AOHA, but not registered by AHA. For definition of numerical codes, see page A4	Control	Service	Staffed Beds	Admissions	Census	Outpatient Visits	Births	Total	Payroll	Personnel

SLEEPY EYE—Brown County

SLEEPY EYE MUNICIPAL HOSPITAL, 400 Fourth Avenue N.W., Zip 56085–1109; tel. 507/794–3571; Chad Cooper, Administrator **A**9 10 **F**7 8 11 12 15 17 19 20 22 24 28 30 33 34 35 36 37 39 40 41 44 49 65 67 71 **N** Quality Health Alliance, Mankato, MN

| | 14 | 10 | 17 | 556 | 6 | 4258 | 0 | 2531 | 1149 | 49 |

SPRING GROVE—Houston County

TWEETEN LUTHERAN HEALTH CARE CENTER, 125 Fifth Avenue S.E., Zip 55974–1309; tel. 507/498–3211; Greg Braun, Administrator (Total facility includes 71 beds in nursing home–type unit) **A**9 10 **F**3 12 14 15 16 17 20 26 27 28 29 30 32 33 34 36 39 41 44 45 46 48 49 61 62 64 65 66 68 71 73 74 **P**6

| | 23 | 10 | 80 | 155 | 68 | 4708 | 0 | 3432 | 2094 | 185 |

SPRINGFIELD—Brown County

☐ SPRINGFIELD MEDICAL CENTER–MAYO HEALTH SYSTEM, (Formerly Springfield Community Hospital), 625 North Jackson Avenue, Zip 56087–1714, Mailing Address: P.O. Box 146, Zip 56087–0146; tel. 507/723–6201; Scott Thoreson, Administrator **A**1 9 10 **F**7 8 15 16 19 22 24 28 30 32 39 40 44 49 58 64 65 71 **N** Quality Health Alliance, Mankato, MN

| | 14 | 10 | 22 | 491 | 5 | 7008 | 49 | 2408 | 954 | 32 |

STAPLES—Wadena County

LAKEWOOD HEALTH SYSTEM, (Formerly Greater Staples Hospital and Care Center), 401 East Prairie Avenue, Zip 56479–9415; tel. 218/894–0300; Tim Rice, President (Total facility includes 100 beds in nursing home–type unit) **A**9 10 **F**7 8 14 15 16 19 22 26 27 28 30 32 33 35 41 44 45 46 49 64 65 67 71 **P**7

| | 16 | 10 | 140 | 965 | 107 | 14601 | 125 | 13780 | 6000 | 302 |

STARBUCK—Pope County

★ MINNEWASKA DISTRICT HOSPITAL, 610 West Sixth Street, Zip 56381, Mailing Address: P.O. Box 160, Zip 56381–0160; tel. 320/239–2201; Roxann A. Wellman, Chief Executive Officer **A**9 10 **F**7 8 14 15 16 17 18 19 22 26 27 28 32 33 34 35 36 37 39 40 41 42 44 62 64 65 71

| | 16 | 10 | 19 | 397 | 5 | 943 | 10 | 2081 | 1009 | 40 |

STILLWATER—Washington County

✠ LAKEVIEW HOSPITAL, 927 West Churchill Street, Zip 55082–5930; tel. 612/439–5330; Jeffrey J. Robertson, Chief Executive Officer **A**1 9 10 **F**7 8 11 15 16 17 19 21 22 28 30 32 33 34 35 37 39 40 41 42 44 45 46 49 65 66 67 68 71 73 74 **P**5

| | 23 | 10 | 23 | 2230 | 23 | 23812 | 662 | 26805 | 10990 | 299 |

THIEF RIVER FALLS—Pennington County

✠ NORTHWEST MEDICAL CENTER, 120 LaBree Avenue South, Zip 56701–2819; tel. 218/681–4240; Richard A. Spyhalski, Chief Executive Officer (Total facility includes 90 beds in nursing home–type unit) **A**1 9 10 **F**7 8 11 15 16 17 19 21 22 29 30 34 35 36 37 39 40 42 44 45 46 49 52 53 54 55 56 57 58 60 64 65 66 67 71 73 74

| | 23 | 10 | 158 | 2019 | 109 | 14217 | 233 | 17069 | 9563 | 309 |

TRACY—Lyon County

★ TRACY AREA MEDICAL SERVICES, (Formerly Tracy Municipal Hospital), 251 Fifth Street East, Zip 56175–1536; tel. 507/629–3200; Thomas J. Quinlivan, Administrator **A**9 10 **F**6 7 8 11 14 15 16 17 19 22 26 28 29 30 31 32 33 34 35 37 39 40 41 42 44 45 48 49 51 54 58 65 66 67 71 74 **P**5 **S** Sioux Valley Hospitals and Health System, Sioux Falls, SD **N** Southwest Minnesota Health Alliance, Luverne, MN; Sioux Valley Health System, Sioux Falls, SD

| | 14 | 10 | 24 | 567 | 5 | 12774 | 9 | 2722 | 1281 | 54 |

TWO HARBORS—Lake County

LAKE VIEW MEMORIAL HOSPITAL, 325 11th Avenue, Zip 55616–1298; tel. 218/834–7300; Brian J. Carlson, President and Chief Executive Officer (Total facility includes 50 beds in nursing home–type unit) **A**9 10 **F**3 7 14 15 40 44 49 64 65 70 71 73 **N** Northern Lakes Health Consortium, Duluth, MN

| | 23 | 10 | 66 | 492 | 55 | 7837 | 35 | 5012 | 2570 | 133 |

TYLER—Lincoln County

★ TYLER HEALTHCARE CENTER, 240 Willow Street, Zip 56178–0280; tel. 507/247–5521; James G. Blum, Interim Administrator (Total facility includes 43 beds in nursing home–type unit) **A**9 10 **F**1 7 8 15 16 19 22 24 26 32 33 35 36 40 44 49 58 64 67 71 **P**6 **S** Avera Health, Yankton, SD **N** Minnesota Rural Health Cooperative, Willmar, MN

| | 23 | 10 | 49 | 277 | 45 | 5922 | — | 3372 | 1772 | 118 |

VIRGINIA—St. Louis County

✠ △ VIRGINIA REGIONAL MEDICAL CENTER, 901 Ninth Street North, Zip 55792–2398; tel. 218/741–3340; Kyle Hopstad, Administrator (Total facility includes 116 beds in nursing home–type unit) **A**1 7 9 10 **F**4 7 8 10 14 15 16 19 21 22 23 26 28 30 32 34 35 37 40 42 44 48 64 65 66 67 71 73 **S** Quorum Health Group/Quorum Health Resources, Inc., Brentwood, TN **N** Northern Lakes Health Consortium, Duluth, MN

| | 14 | 10 | 190 | 3160 | 154 | 26433 | 283 | 27265 | 12120 | 347 |

WABASHA—Wabasha County

✠ ST. ELIZABETH HOSPITAL, 1200 Fifth Grand Boulevard West, Zip 55981–1098; tel. 612/565–4531; Thomas Crowley, President (Total facility includes 135 beds in nursing home–type unit) **A**1 9 10 **F**1 2 3 4 5 6 7 8 9 10 11 12 13 14 15 16 17 18 19 20 21 22 23 24 25 26 27 28 29 30 31 32 33 34 35 36 37 38 39 40 41 42 43 44 45 46 47 48 49 50 51 52 53 54 55 56 57 58 59 60 61 62 63 64 65 66 67 68 69 70 71 72 73 74 **P**1 2 3 4 5 6 7 8 **S** Marian Health System, Tulsa, OK

| | 21 | 10 | 160 | 744 | 141 | 19192 | 67 | 9593 | 4868 | 236 |

WACONIA—Carver County

✠ RIDGEVIEW MEDICAL CENTER, 500 South Maple Street, Zip 55387–1791; tel. 612/442–2191; Robert Stevens, President and Chief Executive Officer **A**1 9 10 **F**7 8 11 14 15 17 18 19 20 21 22 28 30 32 33 34 35 37 39 40 41 42 44 45 49 60 63 65 66 67 70 71 72 73 74

| | 14 | 10 | 90 | 5139 | 44 | 74839 | 964 | 39137 | 20374 | 531 |

Hospital, Address, Telephone, Administrator, Approval, Facility, and Physician Codes, Health Care System, Network	Classi-fication Codes		Utilization Data					Expense (thousands) of dollars		
	Control	Service	Staffed Beds	Admissions	Census	Outpatient Visits	Births	Total	Payroll	Personnel

★ American Hospital Association (AHA) membership
□ Joint Commission on Accreditation of Healthcare Organizations (JCAHO) accreditation
+ American Osteopathic Healthcare Association (AOHA) membership
○ American Osteopathic Association (AOA) accreditation
△ Commission on Accreditation of Rehabilitation Facilities (CARF) accreditation
Control codes 61, 63, 64, 71, 72 and 73 indicate hospitals listed by AOHA, but not registered by AHA. For definition of numerical codes, see page A4

WADENA—Wadena County

✚ TRI–COUNTY HOSPITAL, 415 Jefferson Street North, Zip 56482–1297; tel. 218/631–3510; Dennis C. Miley, Administrator **A**1 9 10 **F**7 8 11 14 15 16 17 19 21 22 26 28 30 32 33 34 35 36 37 39 40 41 42 44 45 49 53 54 58 64 65 66 67 71 73 **P**3	23	10	23	1384	18	11253	131	12146	5856	175

WARREN—Marshall County

★ NORTH VALLEY HEALTH CENTER, 109 South Minnesota Street, Zip 56762–1499; tel. 218/745–4211; Jon Linnell, Administrator **A**9 10 **F**8 11 13 15 16 17 19 22 24 28 29 30 32 35 37 39 41 44 45 48 49 66 71 73 **P**4 **N**	23	10	20	332	3	1872	0	3013	1769	53

WASECA—Waseca County

✚ WASECA AREA MEDICAL CENTER, 100 Fifth Avenue N.W., Zip 56093–2422; tel. 507/835–1210; Michael Milbrath, Administrator (Nonreporting) **A**1 9 10 **N** Quality Health Alliance, Mankato, MN	23	10	19	—	—	—	—	—	—	—

WESTBROOK—Cottonwood County

★ WESTBROOK HEALTH CENTER, 920 Bell Avenue, Zip 56183–9636, Mailing Address: P.O. Box 188, Zip 56183–0188; tel. 507/274–6121; Thomas J. Quinlivan, Administrator (Nonreporting) **A**10 **S** Sioux Valley Hospitals and Health System, Sioux Falls, SD **N** Sioux Valley Health System, Sioux Falls, SD	23	10	8	—	—	—	—	—	—	—

WHEATON—Traverse County

WHEATON COMMUNITY HOSPITAL, 401 12th Street North, Zip 56296–1099; tel. 320/563–8226; James J. Talley, Administrator **A**9 10 **F**7 11 12 14 15 16 17 19 20 21 22 24 27 28 29 30 32 33 34 35 37 39 40 41 42 44 46 48 49 52 53 54 55 57 58 63 64 67 71 73 **P**5	14	10	25	441	5	9167	19	3199	—	59

WILLMAR—Kandiyohi County

✚ RICE MEMORIAL HOSPITAL, 301 Becker Avenue S.W., Zip 56201–3395; tel. 320/235–4543; Lawrence J. Massa, Chief Executive Officer **A**1 2 9 10 **F**7 8 15 19 21 22 23 30 32 33 34 35 37 40 42 44 45 49 52 53 54 55 56 57 58 60 63 64 65 67 71 73 **N** Minnesota Rural Health Cooperative, Willmar, MN; Affiliated Community Health Network, Inc., Willmar, MN	14	10	207	4898	139	26185	756	45054	21450	633
□ WILLMAR REGIONAL TREATMENT CENTER, North Highway 71, Zip 56201–1128, Mailing Address: Box 1128, Zip 56201–1128; tel. 320/231–5100; Gregory G. Spartz, Chief Executive Officer (Nonreporting) **A**1 10 **N** Affiliated Community Health Network, Inc., Willmar, MN	12	22	375	—	—	—	—	—	—	—

WINDOM—Cottonwood County

★ WINDOM AREA HOSPITAL, Highways 60 and 71 North, Zip 56101, Mailing Address: P.O. Box 339, Zip 56101–0339; tel. 507/831–2400; J. Stephen Pautler, CHE, Administrator **A**9 10 **F**7 8 16 17 19 20 22 28 30 33 34 35 40 44 49 64 65 67 71 73 **P**6 **S** Sioux Valley Hospitals and Health System, Sioux Falls, SD **N** Southwest Minnesota Health Alliance, Luverne, MN; Sioux Valley Health System, Sioux Falls, SD	14	10	27	1019	11	12795	167	5139	1976	76

WINONA—Winona County

✚ COMMUNITY MEMORIAL HOSPITAL AND CONVALESCENT AND REHABILITATION UNIT, 855 Mankato Avenue, Zip 55987–4894, Mailing Address: P.O. Box 5600, Zip 55987–0600; tel. 507/454–3650; Patrick M. Booth, President (Total facility includes 104 beds in nursing home–type unit) **A**1 9 10 **F**1 2 6 7 8 10 11 15 16 17 19 21 22 23 24 26 28 30 32 33 35 37 39 40 41 44 45 46 49 51 52 53 54 55 56 57 60 63 64 65 67 71 73 **P**8	23	10	186	2980	129	—	445	25633	14137	534

WORTHINGTON—Nobles County

★ WORTHINGTON REGIONAL HOSPITAL, 1018 Sixth Avenue, Zip 56187–2202, Mailing Address: P.O. Box 997, Zip 56187–0997; tel. 507/372–2941; Melvin J. Platt, Administrator (Total facility includes 5 beds in nursing home–type unit) **A**10 **F**7 15 19 21 22 27 30 32 33 35 36 37 40 41 44 49 52 53 64 65 71 73 **S** Sioux Valley Hospitals and Health System, Sioux Falls, SD **N** Southwest Minnesota Health Alliance, Luverne, MN	14	10	66	2186	24	29757	322	14412	6660	202

WYOMING—Chisago County

✚ FAIRVIEW LAKES REGIONAL MEDICAL CENTER, 5200 Fairview Boulevard, Zip 55092–8013; tel. 612/982–7000; Daniel K. Anderson, Senior Vice President and Administrtor (Nonreporting) **A**1 9 10 **S** Fairview Hospital and Healthcare Services, Minneapolis, MN	23	10	38	—	—	—	—	—	—	—

ZUMBROTA—Goodhue County

✚ ZUMBROTA HEALTH CARE, 383 West Fifth Street, Zip 55992–1699; tel. 507/732–5131; Daniel Will, Administrator (Total facility includes 70 beds in nursing home–type unit) (Nonreporting) **A**1 9 10	23	10	94	—	—	—	—	—	—	—

MISSISSIPPI

Resident population 2,731 (in thousands)
Resident population in metro areas 35.0%
Birth rate per 1,000 population 15.7
65 years and over 12.3%
Percent of persons without health insurance 18.5%

Hospital, Address, Telephone, Administrator, Approval, Facility, and Physician Codes, Health Care System, Network	Classi-fication Codes		Utilization Data					Expense (thousands) of dollars		
	Control	Service	Staffed Beds	Admissions	Census	Outpatient Visits	Births	Total	Payroll	Personnel

★ American Hospital Association (AHA) membership
□ Joint Commission on Accreditation of Healthcare Organizations (JCAHO) accreditation
+ American Osteopathic Healthcare Association (AOHA) membership
○ American Osteopathic Association (AOA) accreditation
△ Commission on Accreditation of Rehabilitation Facilities (CARF) accreditation
Control codes 61, 63, 64, 71, 72 and 73 indicate hospitals listed by AOHA, but not registered by AHA. For definition of numerical codes, see page A4

Hospital	Control	Service	Staffed Beds	Admissions	Census	Outpatient Visits	Births	Total	Payroll	Personnel
ABERDEEN—Monroe County										
ABERDEEN–MONROE COUNTY HOSPITAL, 400 South Chestnut Street, Zip 39730–3335, Mailing Address: P.O. Box 747, Zip 39730–0747; tel. 601/369–2455; Frank Harrington, Administrator **A**9 10 **F**8 15 16 19 20 22 57 71 73 **P**5 6	15	10	27	602	14	4329	0	—	—	59
ACKERMAN—Choctaw County										
CHOCTAW COUNTY MEDICAL CENTER, 148 West Cherry Street, Zip 39735–0417, Mailing Address: P.O. Box 417, Zip 39735–0417; tel. 601/285–6235; Ouida Loper, Administrator (Total facility includes 66 beds in nursing home–type unit) **A**9 10 **F**22 64 65 **P**2	13	10	76	322	36	3551	0	—	—	118
AMORY—Monroe County										
⊞ GILMORE MEMORIAL HOSPITAL, 1105 Earl Frye Boulevard, Zip 38821–5500, Mailing Address: P.O. Box 459, Zip 38821–0459; tel. 601/256–7111; Robert F. Letson, President and Chief Executive Officer **A**1 9 10 **F**7 8 11 12 14 15 16 19 21 22 24 25 28 30 35 37 38 39 40 41 44 47 48 49 64 65 71 73 74 **P**8	23	10	95	3401	43	36275	807	—	—	378
BATESVILLE—Panola County										
SOUTH PANOLA COMMUNITY HOSPITAL, 155 Keating Road, Zip 38606, Mailing Address: P.O. Box 433, Zip 38606–0433; tel. 601/563–5611; Richard W. Manning, Administrator and Chief Executive Officer **A**9 10 **F**19 21 22 44 65 71 73 **P**3 7	13	10	70	1609	30	14630	0	4937	3172	102
BAY SAINT LOUIS—Hancock County										
⊞ HANCOCK MEDICAL CENTER, 149 Drinkwater Boulevard, Zip 39521–2790, Mailing Address: P.O. Box 2790, Zip 39521–2790; tel. 228/467–8600; Hal W. Leftwich, FACHE, Chief Executive Officer **A**1 9 10 **F**7 8 9 11 15 16 17 18 19 21 22 23 28 30 35 37 40 41 44 45 46 48 49 65 71 73 74 **P**8 **S** Quorum Health Group/Quorum Health Resources, Inc., Brentwood, TN	13	10	66	3598	44	35032	300	24275	9275	317
BAY SPRINGS—Jasper County										
JASPER GENERAL HOSPITAL, (Includes Jasper County Nursing Home), 15 A. South Sixth Street, Zip 39422–9738, Mailing Address: P.O. Box 527, Zip 39422–0527; tel. 601/764–2101; M. Kenneth Posey, FACHE, Administrator (Total facility includes 104 beds in nursing home–type unit) **A**9 10 **F**32 41 64 65 71	13	10	124	253	109	0	0	—	—	140
BELZONI—Humphreys County										
★ HUMPHREYS COUNTY MEMORIAL HOSPITAL, 500 CCC Road, Zip 39038–3806, Mailing Address: P.O. Box 510, Zip 39038–0510; tel. 601/247–3831; Debra L. Griffin, Administrator **A**9 10 **F**1 2 3 7 8 9 10 11 12 15 17 19 20 21 22 23 24 26 27 28 29 30 31 32 33 36 37 38 39 40 41 42 43 44 45 46 47 48 49 51 52 53 54 55 56 57 58 59 60 61 64 65 66 67 68 69 70 72 73 74	13	10	28	965	16	4597	1	—	—	109
BILOXI—Harrison County										
□ BILOXI REGIONAL MEDICAL CENTER, 150 Reynoir Street, Zip 39530–4199, Mailing Address: P.O. Box 128, Zip 39533–0128; tel. 601/432–1571; Joseph J. Mullany, Executive Director **A**1 2 9 10 **F**1 2 7 8 9 10 11 12 14 15 16 17 19 20 21 22 23 24 26 27 31 32 33 35 36 37 38 39 40 41 42 43 44 45 46 47 48 49 51 52 60 61 63 64 65 66 67 68 69 70 71 72 73 74 **P**5 8 **S** Health Management Associates, Naples, FL	33	10	153	6156	82	4170	570	35543	13390	439
⊞ GULF COAST MEDICAL CENTER, (Includes Gulf Oaks Hospital, 180–C Debuys Road, Zip 39531; tel. 601/388–0600; Hugh S. Simcoe, III, Administrator), 180–A Debuys Road, Zip 39531–4405; tel. 228/388–6711; Gary L. Stokes, Chief Executive Officer **A**1 9 10 **F**2 3 7 8 11 12 15 16 17 19 21 22 26 28 30 31 32 33 35 37 39 40 42 44 46 52 53 54 55 56 57 58 59 63 64 65 67 69 71 73 **P**1 2 4 5 6 8 **S** TENET Healthcare Corporation, Santa Barbara, CA	33	10	189	4104	74	44938	107	44340	23654	664
GULF OAKS HOSPITAL See Gulf Coast Medical Center										
⊞ VETERANS AFFAIRS MEDICAL CENTER, (Includes Veterans Affairs Medical Center, Gulfport Division, East Beach, Gulfport, Zip 39501; tel. 601/863–1972), 400 Veterans Avenue, Zip 39531–2410; tel. 228/388–5541; Julie A. Catellier, Director (Total facility includes 320 beds in nursing home–type unit) (Nonreporting) **A**1 2 3 5 9 **S** Department of Veterans Affairs, Washington, DC	45	10	510	—	—	—	—	—	—	—
BOONEVILLE—Prentiss County										
⊞ BAPTIST MEMORIAL HOSPITAL–BOONEVILLE, (Formerly Baptist Memorial Hospital), 100 Hospital Street, Zip 38829–3359; tel. 601/720–5000; Pamela W. Roberts, Administrator **A**1 9 10 **F**7 8 11 15 16 17 19 20 21 22 24 35 37 39 40 44 45 46 51 52 54 57 65 67 71 73 **P**1 3 7 **S** Baptist Memorial Health Care Corporation, Memphis, TN	21	10	103	2190	32	21553	58	12293	4625	218
BRANDON—Rankin County										
⊞ RANKIN MEDICAL CENTER, 350 Crossgates Boulevard, Zip 39042–2698; tel. 601/825–2811; Thomas Wiman, Executive Director **A**1 2 9 10 **F**5 6 8 11 18 19 21 22 24 25 28 29 30 32 35 37 41 42 44 46 47 49 51 52 57 62 63 65 71 73 **P**8 **S** Health Management Associates, Naples, FL	33	10	105	3916	59	59164	0	—	11504	560

Hospital, Address, Telephone, Administrator, Approval, Facility, and Physician Codes, Health Care System, Network	Classi-fication Codes		Utilization Data					Expense (thousands) of dollars		
★ American Hospital Association (AHA) membership □ Joint Commission on Accreditation of Healthcare Organizations (JCAHO) accreditation + American Osteopathic Healthcare Association (AOHA) membership ○ American Osteopathic Association (AOA) accreditation △ Commission on Accreditation of Rehabilitation Facilities (CARF) accreditation Control codes 61, 63, 64, 71, 72 and 73 indicate hospitals listed by AOHA, but not registered by AHA. For definition of numerical codes, see page A4	Control	Service	Staffed Beds	Admissions	Census	Outpatient Visits	Births	Total	Payroll	Personnel

BROOKHAVEN—Lincoln County

☒ KING'S DAUGHTERS HOSPITAL, 427 Highway 51 North, Zip 39601–2600, Mailing Address: P.O. Box 948, Zip 39602–0948; tel. 601/833–6011; Phillip L. Grady, Chief Executive Officer **A**1 9 10 **F**1 2 7 8 9 10 11 12 15 16 17 19 20 21 22 23 24 26 27 31 32 33 35 36 37 38 39 40 41 42 43 44 45 46 47 48 49 51 52 60 61 64 65 66 67 68 69 70 71 72 73 74 **P**3 **S** Quorum Health Group/Quorum Health Resources, Inc., Brentwood, TN	23	10	109	3761	50	15206	598	—	—	418

CALHOUN CITY—Calhoun County

HILLCREST HOSPITAL, 140 Burke–Calhoun City Road, Zip 38916–9690; tel. 601/628–6611; James P. Franklin, Administrator **A**9 10 **F**15 19 22 44 46 65 71	14	10	30	727	13	6857	0	2605	1107	51

CANTON—Madison County

MADISON COUNTY MEDICAL CENTER, Highway 16 East, Zip 39046, Mailing Address: P.O. Box 1607, Zip 39046–1607; tel. 601/859–1331; G. Wayne Schuler, Executive Director (Total facility includes 60 beds in nursing home–type unit) **A**9 10 **F**1 2 3 8 16 17 19 20 22 26 31 32 33 37 40 44 51 52 54 56 57 58 59 65 71 **P**6	13	10	127	1703	100	25209	372	12233	7412	282

CARTHAGE—Leake County

LEAKE MEMORIAL HOSPITAL, 300 Ellis Street, Zip 39051–0557, Mailing Address: P.O. Box 557, Zip 39051–0557; tel. 601/267–4511; Cindy Tadlock, Interim Administrator (Total facility includes 44 beds in nursing home–type unit) **A**9 10 **F**1 14 15 16 19 22 26 44 46 52 56 57 59 64 65 71 73 **P**6	33	10	76	1028	61	14770	0	—	—	143

CENTREVILLE—Wilkinson County

☒ FIELD MEMORIAL COMMUNITY HOSPITAL, 270 West Main Street, Zip 39631, Mailing Address: P.O. Box 639, Zip 39631–0639; tel. 601/645–5221; Brock A. Slabach, Administrator **A**1 9 10 **F**8 12 16 17 19 20 22 31 32 39 40 41 44 45 61 64 65 71 **S** Quorum Health Group/Quorum Health Resources, Inc., Brentwood, TN	13	10	66	1623	20	9019	92	—	—	132

CHARLESTON—Tallahatchie County

TALLAHATCHIE GENERAL HOSPITAL, 201 South Market, Zip 38921–2236, Mailing Address: P.O. Box 230, Zip 38921–0230; tel. 601/647–5535; F. W. Ergle, Jr., Administrator (Total facility includes 61 beds in nursing home–type unit) **A**9 10 **F**1 2 7 8 9 10 11 12 17 19 20 21 22 23 24 26 27 28 29 31 32 33 35 36 37 38 39 40 41 42 43 44 45 46 47 48 49 50 51 52 60 61 63 64 65 66 67 68 69 71 72 73 74 **P**8	13	10	77	611	66	2965	0	3606	2189	129

CLARKSDALE—Coahoma County

☒ NORTHWEST MISSISSIPPI REGIONAL MEDICAL CENTER, 1970 Hospital Drive, Zip 38614–7204, Mailing Address: P.O. Box 1218, Zip 38614–1218; tel. 601/624–3401; Roger C. LeDoux, Executive Director (Total facility includes 20 beds in nursing home–type unit) **A**1 5 9 10 **F**11 15 16 17 19 21 22 31 32 35 37 38 40 42 44 45 64 65 71 73 **S** Health Management Associates, Naples, FL	33	10	195	8047	123	24800	1175	—	—	611

CLEVELAND—Bolivar County

☒ BOLIVAR MEDICAL CENTER, (Formerly Bolivar County Hospital), Highway 8 East, Zip 38732–9722, Mailing Address: P.O. Box 1380, Zip 38732–1380; tel. 601/846–0061; Robert L. Hawley, Jr., Chief Executive Officer (Total facility includes 34 beds in nursing home–type unit) **A**1 9 10 **F**7 8 11 17 19 20 21 22 35 37 38 40 42 44 45 48 49 64 65 66 67 71 73 **P**2 8 **S** Quorum Health Group/Quorum Health Resources, Inc., Brentwood, TN	13	10	144	4807	110	14859	676	22654	11721	292

COLLINS—Covington County

□ COVINGTON COUNTY HOSPITAL, Sixth and Holly Streets, Zip 39428, Mailing Address: P.O. Box 1149, Zip 39428–1149; tel. 601/765–6711; Irving Hitt, Administrator **A**1 9 10 **F**7 8 11 12 14 15 16 17 19 20 21 22 26 32 33 35 37 38 40 44 45 46 48 49 52 57 64 65 71 73	13	10	82	1503	30	17743	211	8830	3554	141

COLUMBIA—Marion County

MARION GENERAL HOSPITAL, (Formerly Methodist Hospital of Marion County), 1560 Sumrall Road, Zip 39429–2654, Mailing Address: P.O. Box 630, Zip 39429–0630; tel. 601/736–6303; Jerry M. Howell, Chief Operating Officer **A**9 10 **F**1 2 7 8 9 10 11 12 15 17 19 20 21 22 23 27 31 32 33 35 36 37 38 40 41 43 44 46 47 48 49 51 52 60 61 65 66 69 71 72 73	13	10	79	1980	39	27146	0	11865	5883	219

COLUMBUS—Lowndes County

☒ BAPTIST MEMORIAL HOSPITAL–GOLDEN TRIANGLE, 2520 Fifth Street North, Zip 39703–2095, Mailing Address: P.O. Box 1307, Zip 39701–1307; tel. 601/244–1000; J. Stuart Mitchell, III, Administrator **A**1 9 10 **F**1 2 3 7 8 9 10 11 12 15 16 17 19 20 21 22 23 24 26 27 28 30 31 32 33 35 36 37 38 39 40 41 42 44 45 46 47 48 49 51 52 53 54 55 56 57 58 59 61 65 66 67 68 71 72 73 74 **P**3 **S** Baptist Memorial Health Care Corporation, Memphis, TN	21	10	328	8241	119	76950	1104	58781	21928	856
★ U. S. AIR FORCE HOSPITAL, 201 Independence, Suite 235, Zip 39701–5300; tel. 601/434–2297; Lieutenant Colonel Karen A. Bradway, MSC, USAF, Administrator (Nonreporting) **S** Department of the Air Force, Bowling AFB, DC	41	10	7	—	—	—	—	—	—	—

CORINTH—Alcorn County

☒ MAGNOLIA REGIONAL HEALTH CENTER, 611 Alcorn Drive, Zip 38834–9368; tel. 601/293–1000; Douglas Garner, Chief Executive Officer **A**1 9 10 **F**7 8 10 11 12 14 15 16 17 19 20 21 22 23 24 28 29 30 32 33 35 37 39 40 41 42 44 45 46 47 49 52 55 56 59 64 65 66 71 73 **P**5 **S** Quorum Health Group/Quorum Health Resources, Inc., Brentwood, TN	15	10	163	6636	108	70518	444	45085	17032	755

Hospital, Address, Telephone, Administrator, Approval, Facility, and Physician Codes, Health Care System, Network	Classi-fication Codes		Utilization Data					Expense (thousands) of dollars		
★ American Hospital Association (AHA) membership ☐ Joint Commission on Accreditation of Healthcare Organizations (JCAHO) accreditation + American Osteopathic Healthcare Association (AOHA) membership ○ American Osteopathic Association (AOA) accreditation △ Commission on Accreditation of Rehabilitation Facilities (CARF) accreditation Control codes 61, 63, 64, 71, 72 and 73 indicate hospitals listed by AOHA, but not registered by AHA. For definition of numerical codes, see page A4	Control	Service	Staffed Beds	Admissions	Census	Outpatient Visits	Births	Total	Payroll	Personnel

DE KALB—Kemper County

| KEMPER COMMUNITY HOSPITAL, Highway 39 & 16 Intersection, Zip 39328, Mailing Address: P.O. Box 246, Zip 39328–0246; tel. 601/743–5851; Kathryn Kneibert, Administrator (Total facility includes 19 beds in nursing home–type unit) **A**9 10 **F**15 16 33 52 57 64 **P**5 | 33 | 10 | 29 | 68 | 21 | 0 | 0 | — | — | 26 |

DURANT—Holmes County

| UNIVERSITY HOSPITAL AND CLINICS–DURANT, (Formerly University Hospital of Durant), 713 North West Avenue, Zip 39063–3007; tel. 601/653–3081; William D. McKinnon, FACHE, Administrator **A**10 **F**15 16 20 22 46 48 65 73 **P**6 | 12 | 10 | 29 | 781 | 14 | 7127 | 0 | — | — | 90 |

EUPORA—Webster County

| WEBSTER HEALTH SERVICES, 500 Highway 9 South, Zip 39744; tel. 601/258–6221; Harold H. Whitaker, Sr., Administrator (Total facility includes 33 beds in nursing home–type unit) **A**9 10 **F**6 8 15 16 17 19 21 22 24 28 29 30 32 33 44 45 46 48 60 64 65 67 71 **P**4 **S** North Mississippi Health Services, Inc., Tupelo, MS **N** North Mississippi Health Services, Tupelo, MS | 23 | 10 | 76 | 1516 | 55 | 10926 | 0 | 7082 | 3243 | 153 |

FAYETTE—Jefferson County

| JEFFERSON COUNTY HOSPITAL, 809 South Main Street, Zip 39069, Mailing Address: P.O. Box 577, Zip 39069–0577; tel. 601/786–3401; Virginia B. Robinson, Administrator **A**9 10 **F**15 16 17 22 35 45 46 52 64 65 71 73 74 | 13 | 10 | 30 | 658 | 14 | 2106 | 0 | — | — | 53 |

FOREST—Scott County

| LACKEY MEMORIAL HOSPITAL, 330 Broad Street, Zip 39074–0428, Mailing Address: P.O. Box 428, Zip 39074–0428; tel. 601/469–4151; Donna Riser, Administrator (Total facility includes 30 beds in nursing home–type unit) **A**10 **F**5 6 8 14 15 16 17 18 19 21 22 25 26 28 29 30 33 44 46 57 59 62 64 65 71 73 **P**5 | 23 | 10 | 64 | 1247 | 48 | 8179 | 0 | — | — | 141 |

GREENVILLE—Washington County

| ✠ DELTA REGIONAL MEDICAL CENTER, 1400 East Union Street, Zip 38703–3246, Mailing Address: P.O. Box 5247, Zip 38704–5247; tel. 601/378–3783; Barton A. Hove, Chief Executive Officer **A**1 9 10 **F**2 3 7 8 9 10 11 16 17 19 20 21 22 23 28 30 31 32 35 37 39 40 42 44 45 49 52 63 65 67 69 71 73 **P**8 **S** Quorum Health Group/Quorum Health Resources, Inc., Brentwood, TN | 13 | 10 | 159 | 5876 | 103 | 36473 | 580 | 42678 | 17407 | 790 |
| ✠ KING'S DAUGHTERS HOSPITAL, 300 Washington Avenue, Zip 38701–3614, Mailing Address: P.O. Box 1857, Zip 38702–1857; tel. 601/378–2020; Donald Joe Fisher, Administrator **A**1 9 10 **F**7 9 10 11 14 15 17 19 20 21 22 27 33 37 39 40 41 44 45 46 48 49 65 67 71 73 | 23 | 10 | 103 | 3093 | 43 | 48659 | 681 | 23278 | 10349 | 347 |

GREENWOOD—Leflore County

| ✠ GREENWOOD LEFLORE HOSPITAL, 1401 River Road, Zip 38930–4030, Mailing Address: Drawer 1410, Zip 38935–1410; tel. 601/459–7000; Terrell M. Cobb, Executive Director **A**1 9 10 **F**7 8 11 14 16 17 19 20 21 22 23 26 27 28 31 35 37 39 40 42 44 45 46 52 63 65 67 71 73 74 **P**6 8 | 15 | 10 | 213 | 8262 | 123 | 113959 | 766 | — | — | 858 |

GRENADA—Grenada County

| ✠ GRENADA LAKE MEDICAL CENTER, 960 Avent Drive, Zip 38901–5094; tel. 601/227–7101; Linda J. Gholston, Chief Executive Officer **A**1 9 10 **F**2 3 7 8 10 11 15 16 17 19 21 22 24 31 32 33 35 36 37 38 40 41 42 44 46 47 48 49 54 56 63 65 67 71 73 **P**8 | 13 | 10 | 122 | 5603 | 94 | 29852 | 739 | 25946 | 10394 | 465 |

GULFPORT—Harrison County

☐ BHC SAND HILL BEHAVIORAL HEALTHCARE, 11150 Highway 49 North, Zip 39503–4110; tel. 601/831–1700; David C. Bell, Chief Operating Officer **A**1 9 10 **F**2 3 9 10 11 12 16 17 20 22 27 31 35 37 46 52 53 54 55 56 58 59 65 67 68 71 **S** Behavioral Healthcare Corporation, Nashville, TN	33	22	60	839	30	0	0	—	—	155
COLUMBIA GARDEN PARK HOSPITAL See Garden Park Community Hospital										
✠ GARDEN PARK COMMUNITY HOSPITAL, (Formerly Columbia Garden Park Hospital), 1520 Broad Avenue, Zip 39501, Mailing Address: P.O. Box 1240, Zip 39502–1240; tel. 228/864–4210; William E. Peaks, Chief Executive Officer **A**1 9 10 **F**2 7 8 10 11 12 14 15 16 17 19 20 21 22 23 24 26 27 32 33 35 37 39 40 41 42 43 44 46 48 49 50 51 52 60 61 63 64 65 66 67 69 71 72 73 74 **P**5 6 7 8 **S** Columbia/HCA Healthcare Corporation, Nashville, TN	33	10	130	3546	58	22266	300	—	—	347
✠ △ MEMORIAL HOSPITAL AT GULFPORT, 4500 13th Street, Zip 39501–2569, Mailing Address: P.O. Box 1810, Zip 39502–1810; tel. 228/867–4000; W. R. Burton, Administrator **A**1 2 7 9 10 **F**3 7 8 10 11 12 15 16 17 18 19 21 22 23 25 27 28 29 30 31 33 35 37 38 40 41 42 43 44 46 47 48 49 51 52 54 55 56 58 59 61 63 65 66 71 72 73 74 **P**3 8 VETERANS AFFAIRS MEDICAL CENTER, GULFPORT DIVISION See Veterans Affairs Medical Center, Biloxi	15	10	313	14206	236	242494	1315	119748	47562	1634

HATTIESBURG—Forrest County

| ✠ FORREST GENERAL HOSPITAL, 6051 U.S. Highway 49, Zip 39401–7243, Mailing Address: P.O. Box 16389, Zip 39404–6389; tel. 601/288–7000; William C. Oliver, President **A**1 2 9 10 **F**2 3 6 7 8 10 11 12 14 15 16 17 19 20 21 22 23 28 29 30 32 33 35 37 38 39 40 41 42 43 44 45 46 48 49 52 53 54 55 56 58 59 60 63 64 65 66 67 69 71 73 74 **P**8
METHODIST HOSPITAL OF HATTIESBURG See Wesley Medical Center | 13 | 10 | 537 | 24632 | 379 | 122661 | 2764 | 146500 | 69633 | 2631 |
| ✠ WESLEY MEDICAL CENTER, (Formerly Methodist Hospital of Hattiesburg), 5001 Hardy Street, Zip 39402, Mailing Address: P.O. Box 16509, Zip 39404–6509; tel. 601/268–8000; William K. Ray, President and Chief Executive Officer **A**1 9 10 **F**7 8 10 11 12 14 15 16 19 21 22 23 24 27 32 33 35 37 38 40 41 42 44 46 47 48 49 52 64 65 66 67 68 71 72 73 74 **P**8 **S** Quorum Health Group/Quorum Health Resources, Inc., Brentwood, TN | 32 | 10 | 211 | 8376 | 127 | 77486 | 569 | — | — | 935 |

Hospital, Address, Telephone, Administrator, Approval, Facility, and Physician Codes, Health Care System, Network	Classi-fication Codes		Utilization Data					Expense (thousands) of dollars		
	Control	Service	Staffed Beds	Admissions	Census	Outpatient Visits	Births	Total	Payroll	Personnel

★ American Hospital Association (AHA) membership
☐ Joint Commission on Accreditation of Healthcare Organizations (JCAHO) accreditation
+ American Osteopathic Healthcare Association (AOHA) membership
○ American Osteopathic Association (AOA) accreditation
△ Commission on Accreditation of Rehabilitation Facilities (CARF) accreditation
Control codes 61, 63, 64, 71, 72 and 73 indicate hospitals listed by AOHA, but not registered by AHA. For definition of numerical codes, see page A4

HAZLEHURST—Copiah County

	Control	Service	Staffed Beds	Admissions	Census	Outpatient Visits	Births	Total	Payroll	Personnel
★ HARDY WILSON MEMORIAL HOSPITAL, 233 Magnolia Street, Zip 39083–2229, Mailing Address: P.O. Box 889, Zip 39083–0889; tel. 601/894–4541; L. Pat Moreland, Administrator **A**9 10 **F**8 19 20 22 27 40 52 57 65 67 71	13	10	49	1736	32	12522	225	—	—	129

HOLLY SPRINGS—Marshall County

MARSHALL COUNTY MEDICAL CENTER, (Formerly Holly Springs Memorial Hospital), 1430 East Salem, Zip 38635, Mailing Address: P.O. Box 6000, Zip 38634–6000; tel. 601/252–1212; Bill Renick, Administrator **A**10 **F**15 16 19 22 41 44 65 71 **S** NetCare Health Systems, Inc., Nashville, TN	23	10	40	964	15	23323	1	—	—	110

HOUSTON—Chickasaw County

☐ TRACE REGIONAL HOSPITAL, Highway 8 East, Zip 38851, Mailing Address: P.O. Box 626, Zip 38851–0626; tel. 601/456–3700; Bristol Messer, Chief Executive Officer **A**1 9 10 **F**2 3 8 11 16 19 21 22 24 28 29 30 31 37 39 44 52 57 65 71 **P**6 **S** NetCare Health Systems, Inc., Nashville, TN	33	10	84	2122	29	14168	3	—	—	164

INDIANOLA—Sunflower County

⊞ SOUTH SUNFLOWER COUNTY HOSPITAL, 121 East Baker Street, Zip 38751–2498; tel. 601/887–5235; H. J. Blessitt, Administrator **A**1 9 10 **F**7 11 19 21 22 37 40 44 65 71 **P**1	13	10	69	2028	24	9996	377	9369	4061	152

IUKA—Tishomingo County

☐ IUKA HOSPITAL, 1777 Curtis Drive, Zip 38852–1001, Mailing Address: P.O. Box 860, Zip 38852–0860; tel. 601/423–6051; George Hand, Interim Administrator **A**1 9 10 **F**8 11 12 14 15 16 17 19 21 22 24 25 27 28 29 30 32 33 37 39 41 44 45 46 49 65 67 68 71 73 **P**3 5 6 **S** North Mississippi Health Services, Inc., Tupelo, MS **N** North Mississippi Health Services, Tupelo, MS	23	10	48	1966	24	19548	0	—	—	116

JACKSON—Hinds County

☐ CHARTER BEHAVIORAL HEALTH SYSTEM, 3531 Lakeland Drive, Zip 39208–9794, Mailing Address: P.O. Box 4297, Zip 39296–4297; tel. 601/939–9030; Rick H. Gray, Ph.D., Chief Executive Officer **A**1 9 10 **F**2 3 15 18 22 52 53 54 55 56 57 58 59 65 **P**5 **S** Magellan Health Services, Atlanta, GA	33	22	111	2196	89	0	0	—	—	194
⊞ G.V. MONTGOMERY VETERANS AFFAIRS MEDICAL CENTER, 1500 East Woodrow Wilson Drive, Zip 39216–5199; tel. 601/364–1201; Richard P. Miller, Director (Total facility includes 120 beds in nursing home–type unit) (Nonreporting) **A**1 2 3 5 8 **S** Department of Veterans Affairs, Washington, DC	45	10	443	—	—	—	—	—	—	—
⊞ METHODIST HEALTHCARE, (Formerly Methodist Medical Center), 1850 Chadwick Drive, Zip 39204–3479, Mailing Address: P.O. Box 59001, Zip 39204–9001; tel. 601/376–1000; Cameron J. Welton, President and Chief Executive Officer **A**1 2 5 9 10 **F**7 8 10 11 14 15 16 17 19 21 22 23 28 29 30 31 32 33 35 37 38 39 40 42 43 44 45 46 47 48 49 51 52 54 58 63 64 65 67 71 73 74 **P**8 **S** Methodist Health Systems, Inc., Memphis, TN **N** Methodist Health Systems, Inc., Memphis, TN	23	10	319	12585	206	64463	1826	89823	34506	1392
METHODIST MEDICAL CENTER See Methodist Healthcare										
⊞ MISSISSIPPI BAPTIST MEDICAL CENTER, 1225 North State Street, Zip 39202–2002; tel. 601/968–1000; Kurt W. Metzner, President and Chief Executive Officer **A**1 2 3 5 9 10 **F**2 3 7 8 9 10 11 12 14 15 16 17 19 20 21 22 23 24 27 31 32 33 35 37 38 39 40 41 42 43 44 45 46 47 49 51 54 63 65 66 67 68 69 71 73 74 **P**7 8	23	10	569	18997	341	111325	781	173914	72683	2438
MISSISSIPPI CRIPPLED CHILDREN'S T. AND T. CENTER See University Hospitals and Clinics, University of Mississippi Medical Center										
⊞ MISSISSIPPI HOSPITAL RESTORATIVE CARE, 1225 North State Street, Zip 39202–2097, Mailing Address: P.O. Box 23695, Zip 39225–3695; tel. 601/968–1054; Michael Huseth, Chief Executive Officer **A**1 **F**2 6 10 11 12 14 15 16 17 18 20 21 22 23 24 25 27 28 29 30 31 32 33 35 37 39 41 42 43 45 47 54 63 65 66 67 71 73 74 **P**7 8	23	49	25	199	18	0	0	7643	3270	71
⊞ MISSISSIPPI METHODIST HOSPITAL AND REHABILITATION CENTER, 1350 Woodrow Wilson Drive, Zip 39216–5198; tel. 601/364–3462; Mark A. Adams, President and Chief Executive Officer **A**1 10 **F**2 12 14 15 16 17 19 27 32 35 39 41 44 45 46 48 49 65 67 71 73	23	46	121	1737	79	3355	0	—	—	586
☐ RIVER OAKS EAST–WOMAN'S PAVILION, 1026 North Flowood Drive, Zip 39208–9599, Mailing Address: P.O. Box 4546, Zip 39296–4546; tel. 601/932–1000; Carl Etter, Executive Director **A**1 9 10 **F**7 8 11 12 15 16 17 19 20 21 22 27 37 38 39 40 41 42 44 45 46 47 48 51 52 64 65 71 73 74 **S** Health Management Associates, Naples, FL	33	44	76	3164	40	351	1370	20456	8625	272
⊞ RIVER OAKS HOSPITAL, 1030 River Oaks Drive, Zip 39208–9729, Mailing Address: P.O. Box 5100, Zip 39296–5100; tel. 601/932–1030; John J. Cleary, President and Chief Executive Officer **A**1 10 **F**7 8 11 12 15 16 19 20 21 22 27 28 33 37 38 39 40 41 42 44 45 46 47 52 63 65 71 73 74 **S** Health Management Associates, Naples, FL	33	10	110	6845	76	15368	1425	52562	20755	678
⊞ ST. DOMINIC–JACKSON MEMORIAL HOSPITAL, 969 Lakeland Drive, Zip 39216–4699; tel. 601/982–0121; Claude W. Harbarger, President **A**1 2 3 5 9 10 **F**2 3 8 10 11 12 16 17 19 20 21 22 23 24 31 33 35 37 39 42 43 44 45 48 49 51 52 53 54 55 56 57 58 59 63 65 67 71 72 73 **P**8 **N**	23	10	571	13538	311	204072	0	102304	43978	1556
⊞ UNIVERSITY HOSPITALS AND CLINICS, UNIVERSITY OF MISSISSIPPI MEDICAL CENTER, (Includes Mississippi Crippled Children's T. and T. Center, 777 Lakeland Drive, Zip 39216; tel. 601/366–6442; Larry E. Tuminello, Director), 2500 North State Street, Zip 39216–4505; tel. 601/984–4100; Frederick Woodrell, Director **A**1 2 3 5 8 9 10 **F**8 9 10 11 12 15 16 19 20 21 22 23 31 35 37 38 39 40 41 42 43 44 45 46 47 48 49 51 52 54 55 56 57 58 61 63 64 65 66 67 68 69 70 71 73 **P**6 **S** Quorum Health Group/Quorum Health Resources, Inc., Brentwood, TN	12	10	576	23156	416	183227	3215	—	—	2863

Hospital, Address, Telephone, Administrator, Approval, Facility, and Physician Codes, Health Care System, Network	Classi-fication Codes		Utilization Data					Expense (thousands) of dollars		
	Control	Service	Staffed Beds	Admissions	Census	Outpatient Visits	Births	Total	Payroll	Personnel

★ American Hospital Association (AHA) membership
□ Joint Commission on Accreditation of Healthcare Organizations (JCAHO) accreditation
+ American Osteopathic Healthcare Association (AOHA) membership
○ American Osteopathic Association (AOA) accreditation
△ Commission on Accreditation of Rehabilitation Facilities (CARF) accreditation
Control codes 61, 63, 64, 71, 72 and 73 indicate hospitals listed by AOHA, but not registered by AHA. For definition of numerical codes, see page A4

KEESLER AFB—Harrison County

☒ U. S. AIR FORCE MEDICAL CENTER KEESLER, 301 Fisher Street, Room 1A132, Zip 39534–2519; tel. 228/377–6510; Colonel Paul Williamson, Administrator **A**1 2 3 5 **F**3 4 7 8 10 11 12 13 14 15 16 17 18 19 20 21 22 24 26 28 29 30 31 32 33 34 35 37 38 39 40 41 42 43 44 45 46 49 51 52 53 54 55 56 57 58 60 61 64 65 67 68 71 73 74 **P**6 **S** Department of the Air Force, Bowling AFB, DC

| | 41 | 10 | 135 | 6488 | 77 | 413128 | 800 | — | — | — |

KILMICHAEL—Montgomery County

KILMICHAEL HOSPITAL, 301 Lamar Avenue, Zip 39747–0188, Mailing Address: P.O. Box 188, Zip 39747–0188; tel. 601/262–4311; Clint Gee, III, Chief Executive Officer **A**9 10 **F**1 8 10 11 15 16 17 19 21 22 23 26 27 35 37 38 40 42 43 44 45 47 57 60 65 66 71 **P**8

| | 13 | 10 | 19 | 620 | 10 | 4401 | 0 | — | 878 | 47 |

KOSCIUSKO—Attala County

MONTFORT JONES MEMORIAL HOSPITAL, Highway 12 West, Zip 39090–3209, Mailing Address: Box 677, Zip 39090–0677; tel. 601/289–4311; Thomas Bland, Administrator **A**9 10 **F**2 8 11 15 19 20 21 22 26 33 37 40 44 47 48 49 57 65 71

| | 13 | 10 | 72 | 2210 | 45 | 20104 | 185 | 11468 | 4084 | 194 |

LAUREL—Jones County

☒ SOUTH CENTRAL REGIONAL MEDICAL CENTER, (Includes South Central Extended Care, Ivy Street, Ellisville, Zip 39437; tel. 601/477–9159), 1220 Jefferson Street, Zip 39440–4374, Mailing Address: P.O. Box 607, Zip 39441–0607; tel. 601/426–4000; G. Douglas Higginbotham, Executive Director **A**1 9 10 **F**2 7 8 11 14 15 16 17 19 20 21 22 23 24 26 28 29 30 32 33 35 37 39 40 41 42 44 45 46 48 49 52 57 63 64 65 66 67 70 71 73 74 **P**8

| | 13 | 10 | 285 | 9257 | 147 | 74034 | 1052 | 52496 | 23570 | 1161 |

LEXINGTON—Holmes County

☒ METHODIST HEALTHCARE MIDDLE MISSISSIPPI HOSPITAL, (Formerly Methodist Hospital of Middle Mississippi), 239 Bowling Green Road, Zip 39095–9332; tel. 601/834–1321; James K. Greer, Administrator **A**1 9 10 **F**7 8 19 21 22 27 40 44 46 65 71 73 **S** Methodist Health Systems, Inc., Memphis, TN **N** Methodist Health Systems, Inc., Memphis, TN
METHODIST HOSPITAL OF MIDDLE MISSISSIPPI See Methodist Healthcare Middle Mississippi Hospital

| | 23 | 10 | 80 | 2239 | 30 | 14133 | 122 | — | — | 135 |

LOUISVILLE—Winston County

WINSTON MEDICAL CENTER, 562 East Main Street, Zip 39339–2742, Mailing Address: P.O. Box 967, Zip 39339–0967; tel. 601/773–6211; W. Dale Saulters, Administrator (Total facility includes 120 beds in nursing home–type unit) **A**9 10 **F**8 11 19 22 37 44 57 64 65 71 73

| | 23 | 10 | 165 | 1397 | 143 | 18356 | 0 | — | — | 223 |

LUCEDALE—George County

GEORGE COUNTY HOSPITAL, 859 Winter Street, Zip 39452–6603, Mailing Address: P.O. Box 607, Zip 39452–0607; tel. 601/947–3161; Paul A. Gardner, CPA, Administrator **A**9 10 **F**1 2 7 8 9 11 12 15 16 17 19 21 22 24 26 27 32 33 35 36 37 38 39 40 41 42 44 45 46 47 48 49 51 52 61 64 65 66 67 68 70 71 72 73 74 **P**8

| | 13 | 10 | 53 | 2188 | 26 | 25315 | 145 | 9951 | 5820 | 253 |

MACON—Noxubee County

★ NOXUBEE GENERAL HOSPITAL, 606 North Jefferson Street, Zip 39341–2236, Mailing Address: P.O. Box 480, Zip 39341–0480; tel. 601/726–4231; Arthur Nester, Jr., Administrator (Total facility includes 60 beds in nursing home–type unit) **A**9 10 **F**2 8 9 11 15 20 22 27 31 37 38 40 44 47 48 52 64 65 70 73

| | 13 | 10 | 109 | 853 | 71 | 7211 | 0 | 5072 | 2548 | 122 |

MAGEE—Simpson County

MAGEE GENERAL HOSPITAL, 300 S.E. Third Avenue, Zip 39111–3698; tel. 601/849–5070; Althea H. Crumpton, Administrator **A**9 10 **F**19 21 22 28 30 31 44 65 71 73

| | 23 | 10 | 64 | 2288 | 33 | 26885 | 2 | — | — | 172 |

MAGNOLIA—Pike County

BEACHAM MEMORIAL HOSPITAL, 205 North Cherry Street, Zip 39652–2819; tel. 601/783–2351; Marilyn Speed, Administrator **A**9 10 **F**16 64 65 71

| | 23 | 10 | 37 | 1114 | 17 | 6827 | 0 | 3284 | 1540 | 73 |

MARKS—Quitman County

QUITMAN COUNTY HOSPITAL AND NURSING HOME, 340 Getwell Drive, Zip 38646–9785; tel. 601/326–8031; Richard E. Waller, M.D., Interim Administrator (Total facility includes 60 beds in nursing home–type unit) **A**9 10 **F**2 3 7 9 10 11 12 15 16 19 20 21 22 26 31 33 36 37 38 40 43 44 45 46 47 48 49 52 54 55 56 57 60 64 65 69 71 73

| | 33 | 10 | 96 | 900 | 81 | 9060 | 0 | — | — | 150 |

MCCOMB—Pike County

☒ SOUTHWEST MISSISSIPPI REGIONAL MEDICAL CENTER, 215 Marion Avenue, Zip 39648–2798, Mailing Address: P.O. Box 1307, Zip 39648–1307; tel. 601/249–5500; Norman M. Price, FACHE, Administrator **A**1 9 10 **F**7 8 10 11 15 16 17 19 20 21 22 26 28 30 32 35 37 40 44 45 46 48 49 63 64 65 67 70 71 73 74 **P**6

| | 15 | 10 | 120 | 7386 | 109 | 54887 | 807 | — | — | 1079 |

MEADVILLE—Franklin County

FRANKLIN COUNTY MEMORIAL HOSPITAL, Hospital Road, Zip 39653, Mailing Address: P.O. Box 636, Zip 39653–0636; tel. 601/384–5801; Semmes Ross, Jr., Administrator **A**9 10 **F**2 14 15 17 19 22 26 27 44 45 48 49 52 57 59 65 67 71

| | 13 | 10 | 42 | 845 | 22 | 3235 | 0 | — | — | 104 |

MENDENHALL—Simpson County

SIMPSON GENERAL HOSPITAL, 1842 Simpson Highway 49, Zip 39114–3592; tel. 601/847–2221; Wayne Harris, Administrator **A**9 10 **F**15 16 17 19 21 22 24 26 32 44 45 46 48 57 65 67 71 73 **P**5

| | 13 | 10 | 49 | 1301 | 29 | 11319 | 1 | 8537 | 3098 | 161 |

Hospital, Address, Telephone, Administrator, Approval, Facility, and Physician Codes, Health Care System, Network	Classi-fication Codes		Utilization Data					Expense (thousands) of dollars		
★ American Hospital Association (AHA) membership ☐ Joint Commission on Accreditation of Healthcare Organizations (JCAHO) accreditation + American Osteopathic Healthcare Association (AOHA) membership ○ American Osteopathic Association (AOA) accreditation △ Commission on Accreditation of Rehabilitation Facilities (CARF) accreditation Control codes 61, 63, 64, 71, 72 and 73 indicate hospitals listed by AOHA, but not registered by AHA. For definition of numerical codes, see page A4	Control	Service	Staffed Beds	Admissions	Census	Outpatient Visits	Births	Total	Payroll	Personnel

MERIDIAN—Lauderdale County

EAST MISSISSIPPI STATE HOSPITAL, 4555 Highland Park Drive, Zip 39307–5498, Mailing Address: Box 4128, West Station, Zip 39304–4128; tel. 601/482–6186; Ramiro J. Martinez, M.D., Director (Total facility includes 226 beds in nursing home–type unit) **F**2 12 14 15 16 20 26 46 52 53 57 64 65 73 **S** Mississippi State Department of Mental Health, Jackson, MS	12	22	633	1342	570	0	0	38310	22172	—
⊞ JEFF ANDERSON REGIONAL MEDICAL CENTER, 2124 14th Street, Zip 39301–4093; tel. 601/483–8811; Mark D. McPhail, Chief Executive Officer **A**1 9 10 **F**7 8 10 11 12 14 15 16 17 19 20 21 22 23 24 28 31 35 37 38 40 41 42 43 44 45 46 47 48 49 52 60 63 65 66 67 71 73 **P**7 8	23	10	260	8981	137	48430	711	—	—	771
☐ LAUREL WOOD CENTER, 5000 Highway 39 North, Zip 39303–1021; tel. 601/483–6211; John Chioco, Chief Executive Officer **A**1 10 **F**2 3 12 17 35 39 45 46 52 53 54 55 57 65 67 71 **P**6	33	22	79	660	29	0	0	—	—	120
⊞ RILEY MEMORIAL HOSPITAL, 1102 21st Avenue, Zip 39301–4096, Mailing Address: P.O. Box 1810, Zip 39302–1810; tel. 601/484–3590; Eric E. Weis, FACHE, Chief Executive Officer **A**1 9 10 **F**2 7 8 9 10 11 16 17 19 20 21 22 23 24 28 30 31 32 35 37 39 40 41 42 44 45 46 47 48 49 51 52 61 63 65 67 71 73 74 **P**1 8 **S** Health Management Associates, Naples, FL	23	10	180	7708	108	39647	544	—	—	709
⊞ RUSH FOUNDATION HOSPITAL, 1314 19th Avenue, Zip 39301–4195; tel. 601/483–0011; Wallace Strickland, Administrator **A**1 9 10 **F**1 2 6 7 8 9 10 11 12 15 16 17 18 19 20 21 22 23 24 25 26 27 28 29 30 31 32 33 36 37 38 39 40 41 42 43 44 45 46 47 49 51 52 60 61 63 64 65 66 67 68 69 71 72 73 74 **P**3 5 6 8	23	10	198	9180	128	17104	1192	75730	32304	1412

MONTICELLO—Lawrence County

LAWRENCE COUNTY HOSPITAL, Highway 84 East, Zip 39654–0788, Mailing Address: P.O. Box 788, Zip 39654–0788; tel. 601/587–4051; Deborah Roberts, Administrator **A**9 10 **F**2 9 11 17 20 21 22 32 37 38 45 46 57 65 71	13	10	53	1223	27	5786	0	4564	2525	143

NATCHEZ—Adams County

☐ NATCHEZ COMMUNITY HOSPITAL, 129 Jefferson Davis Boulevard, Zip 39120–5100, Mailing Address: P.O. Box 1203, Zip 39121–1203; tel. 601/445–6200; Raymond Bane, Executive Director **A**1 9 10 **F**7 8 11 14 16 19 21 22 23 28 30 31 35 37 40 42 44 46 49 65 71 73 **P**1 6 8 **S** Health Management Associates, Naples, FL	33	10	101	3342	42	26796	536	18263	7154	265
⊞ NATCHEZ REGIONAL MEDICAL CENTER, Seargent S. Prentiss Drive, Zip 39120, Mailing Address: P.O. Box 1488, Zip 39121–1488; tel. 601/443–2100; David M. Snyder, Executive Director and Chief Executive Officer **A**1 9 10 **F**7 8 11 14 15 16 19 21 22 23 35 37 39 40 41 42 44 49 51 64 65 71 73 74 **S** Quorum Health Group/Quorum Health Resources, Inc., Brentwood, TN	13	10	121	4461	69	14788	467	—	—	460

NEW ALBANY—Union County

⊞ BAPTIST MEMORIAL HOSPITAL–UNION COUNTY, 200 Highway 30 West, Zip 38652–3197; tel. 601/538–7631; John Tompkins, Administrator **A**1 9 10 **F**7 8 11 12 15 17 19 20 21 22 32 35 37 39 40 44 45 46 49 63 64 65 67 71 73 74 **S** Baptist Memorial Health Care Corporation, Memphis, TN	21	10	153	5928	66	34786	982	22187	8025	335

OCEAN SPRINGS—Jackson County

☐ OCEAN SPRINGS HOSPITAL, 3109 Bienville Boulevard, Zip 39564–4361; tel. 228/818–1111; Dwight Rimes, Administrator **A**1 9 **F**2 3 7 8 10 11 12 14 15 16 17 19 20 21 22 23 27 31 32 33 35 37 39 40 41 42 43 44 47 48 52 53 54 55 56 57 63 64 65 67 71 **P**3 8 **S** Singing River Hospital System, Pascagoula, MS	13	10	110	5017	75	88209	316	43706	17933	499

OKOLONA—Chickasaw County

★ OKOLONA COMMUNITY HOSPITAL, (Includes SHEARER–RICHARDSON MEMORIAL NURSING HOME), Rockwell Drive, Zip 38860–0420, Mailing Address: P.O. Box 420, Zip 38860–0420; tel. 601/447–3311; Brenda Wise, Administrator (Total facility includes 66 beds in nursing home–type unit) **A**9 10 **F**2 20 23 31 32 33 35 52 60 64 65 71 73	13	10	76	110	69	0	0	—	—	76

OLIVE BRANCH—De Soto County

☐ CHARTER PARKWOOD BEHAVIORAL HEALTH SYSTEM, 8135 Goodman Road, Zip 38654–2199; tel. 601/895–4900; M. Andrew Mayo, Chief Executive Officer **A**1 9 10 **F**2 3 11 12 15 16 17 20 22 24 27 33 35 37 39 42 45 47 50 52 53 54 55 56 58 59 63 64 65 67 68 71 72 74	33	22	66	1180	39	0	0	—	—	89

OXFORD—Lafayette County

⊞ BAPTIST MEMORIAL HOSPITAL–NORTH MISSISSIPPI, 2301 South Lamar Boulevard, Zip 38655–5338, Mailing Address: P.O. Box 946, Zip 38655–0946; tel. 601/232–8100; James Hahn, Administrator **A**1 9 10 **F**7 8 10 11 12 14 15 16 17 19 20 21 22 23 24 31 32 33 35 37 40 41 42 43 44 45 46 47 48 52 64 65 66 67 71 72 73 74 **P**3 4 5 **S** Baptist Memorial Health Care Corporation, Memphis, TN	23	10	158	9343	143	53413	770	53341	17181	774

PASCAGOULA—Jackson County

⊞ SINGING RIVER HOSPITAL, 2809 Denny Avenue, Zip 39581–5301; tel. 228/938–5000; James S. Kaigler, FACHE, Administrator **A**1 2 9 10 **F**2 3 7 8 10 11 12 14 15 16 17 19 20 21 22 23 27 28 29 30 31 32 33 35 37 39 40 41 42 43 44 47 48 52 53 54 55 56 57 63 64 65 67 71 **P**3 8 **S** Singing River Hospital System, Pascagoula, MS	13	10	297	12595	205	180889	980	111896	52179	1675

PHILADELPHIA—Neshoba County

⊞ CHOCTAW HEALTH CENTER, Highway 16 West, Zip 39350, Mailing Address: Route 7, Box R–50, Zip 39350; tel. 601/656–2211; Jim Wallace, Executive Director (Nonreporting) **A**1 10 **S** U. S. Public Health Service Indian Health Service, Rockville, MD	47	10	35	—	—	—	—	—	—	—

Hospital, Address, Telephone, Administrator, Approval, Facility, and Physician Codes, Health Care System, Network	Classi-fication Codes		Utilization Data					Expense (thousands) of dollars		
★ American Hospital Association (AHA) membership □ Joint Commission on Accreditation of Healthcare Organizations (JCAHO) accreditation + American Osteopathic Healthcare Association (AOHA) membership ○ American Osteopathic Association (AOA) accreditation △ Commission on Accreditation of Rehabilitation Facilities (CARF) accreditation Control codes 61, 63, 64, 71, 72 and 73 indicate hospitals listed by AOHA, but not registered by AHA. For definition of numerical codes, see page A4	Control	Service	Staffed Beds	Admissions	Census	Outpatient Visits	Births	Total	Payroll	Personnel
★ NESHOBA COUNTY GENERAL HOSPITAL, 1001 Holland Avenue, Zip 39350–2161, Mailing Address: P.O. Box 648, Zip 39350–0648; tel. 601/663–1200; Lawrence Graeber, Administrator (Total facility includes 118 beds in nursing home–type unit) **A**9 10 **F**8 19 22 26 27 31 33 35 44 57 64 65 71 73 **S** Quorum Health Group/Quorum Health Resources, Inc., Brentwood, TN	13	10	192	2154	150	30021	1	—	—	309
PICAYUNE—Pearl River County										
★ CROSBY MEMORIAL HOSPITAL, 801 Goodyear Boulevard, Zip 39466–3221, Mailing Address: P.O. Box 909, Zip 39466–0909; tel. 601/798–4711; Calvin Green, Administrator **A**9 10 **F**2 7 8 11 14 15 16 17 19 20 21 22 24 26 27 28 32 33 35 36 37 39 40 42 44 45 48 49 52 55 57 59 65 66 67 68 71 73 74 **P**8 **S** Quorum Health Group/Quorum Health Resources, Inc., Brentwood, TN	23	10	71	2839	39	34286	320	13880	6544	248
PONTOTOC—Pontotoc County										
PONTOTOC HOSPITAL AND EXTENDED CARE FACILITY, 176 South Main Street, Zip 38863–3311, Mailing Address: P.O. Box 790, Zip 38863–0790; tel. 601/489–5510; Fred B. Hood, Administrator (Total facility includes 44 beds in nursing home–type unit) **A**9 10 **F**8 14 15 16 17 20 22 27 32 33 36 39 45 46 48 49 64 65 67 71 73 **P**3 8 **S** North Mississippi Health Services, Inc., Tupelo, MS **N** North Mississippi Health Services, Inc., Tupelo, MS	23	10	71	644	58	11515	0	7000	3260	120
POPLARVILLE—Pearl River County										
PEARL RIVER COUNTY HOSPITAL, 305 West Moody Street, Zip 39470–7242, Mailing Address: P.O. Box 392, Zip 39470–0392; tel. 601/795–4543; Dorothy C. Bilbo, Administrator (Total facility includes 66 beds in nursing home–type unit) **A**9 10 **F**15 16 46 48 49 64 65 71 73	13	10	90	793	73	0	0	—	—	198
PORT GIBSON—Claiborne County										
★ CLAIBORNE COUNTY HOSPITAL, 123 McComb Avenue, Zip 39150–2915, Mailing Address: P.O. Box 1004, Zip 39150–1004; tel. 601/437–5141; Wanda C. Fleming, Administrator and Chief Executive Officer **A**9 10 **F**12 16 17 19 22 28 30 35 40 46 64 65 70 71 73	13	10	32	736	15	3712	31	4421	1328	66
PRENTISS—Jefferson Davis County										
PRENTISS REGIONAL HOSPITAL AND EXTENDED CARE FACILITIES, (Formerly Jefferson Davis County Hospital), 1102 Rose Street, Zip 39474; tel. 601/792–4276; Mike Boleware, Administrator (Total facility includes 60 beds in nursing home–type unit) **A**9 10 **F**2 3 8 11 12 14 15 16 17 19 20 22 26 39 41 45 46 48 54 55 57 64 65 71	23	10	101	520	68	13645	0	—	—	173
QUITMAN—Clarke County										
★ H. C. WATKINS MEMORIAL HOSPITAL, 605 South Archusa Avenue, Zip 39355–2398; tel. 601/776–6925; Thomas G. Bartlett, President and Chief Executive Officer (Total facility includes 11 beds in nursing home–type unit) **A**9 10 **F**2 8 11 12 19 21 22 32 33 35 37 44 49 52 64 65 71 **S** Quorum Health Group/Quorum Health Resources, Inc., Brentwood, TN	23	10	43	1114	33	6894	0	5527	2274	135
RICHTON—Perry County										
★ PERRY COUNTY GENERAL HOSPITAL, 206 Bay Avenue, Zip 39476, Mailing Address: Drawer Y., Zip 39476; tel. 601/788–6316; Bobby Welborn, Administrator (Total facility includes 66 beds in nursing home–type unit) **A**9 10 **F**17 20 22 30 32 44 48 64 65 71	13	10	88	364	71	4186	0	2877	2136	125
RIPLEY—Tippah County										
✦ TIPPAH COUNTY HOSPITAL, 1005 City Avenue North, Zip 38663–0499; tel. 601/837–9221; Jerry Green, Administrator (Total facility includes 40 beds in nursing home–type unit) **A**1 9 10 **F**8 11 15 16 19 21 22 26 27 31 33 37 44 47 64 65 71 **S** Baptist Memorial Health Care Corporation, Memphis, TN	13	10	110	1703	59	19414	0	8250	4154	189
RULEVILLE—Sunflower County										
NORTH SUNFLOWER COUNTY HOSPITAL, 840 North Oak Avenue, Zip 38771–0369, Mailing Address: P.O. Box 369, Zip 38771–0369; tel. 601/756–2711; Robert Crook, Administrator (Total facility includes 42 beds in nursing home–type unit) **A**9 10 **F**2 15 16 22 32 40 44 52 57 64 65 71 **P**1	13	10	86	1392	70	4563	15	—	—	209
SENATOBIA—Tate County										
□ SENATOBIA COMMUNITY HOSPITAL, 401 Getwell Drive, Zip 38668–2213, Mailing Address: P.O. Box 648, Zip 38668–0648; tel. 601/562–3100; Carol H. Hanes, Interim Chief Executive Officer **A**1 9 10 **F**7 8 12 16 19 20 22 26 31 33 40 44 45 46 48 52 65 71 **S** Paracelsus Healthcare Corporation, Houston, TX	33	10	52	1187	18	14067	141	10485	2913	127
SOUTHAVEN—De Soto County										
✦ △ BAPTIST MEMORIAL HOSPITAL–DESOTO, 7601 Southcrest Parkway, Zip 38671–4742; tel. 601/349–4000; Melvin E. Walker, Administrator (Total facility includes 90 beds in nursing home–type unit) **A**1 7 9 10 **F**2 7 8 10 11 12 15 16 17 19 20 21 22 23 24 26 31 32 33 35 37 38 39 40 41 42 43 44 45 46 48 49 51 52 60 63 64 65 66 67 71 72 73 74 **P**1 3 8 **S** Baptist Memorial Health Care Corporation, Memphis, TN	23	10	230	6143	158	40042	894	29658	12643	397
STARKVILLE—Oktibbeha County										
✦ OKTIBBEHA COUNTY HOSPITAL, 400 Hospital Road, Zip 39759–2163, Mailing Address: Drawer 1506, Zip 39760–1506; tel. 601/323–4320; Arthur C. Kelly, Administrator and Chief Executive Officer **A**1 9 10 **F**7 8 11 12 14 15 16 17 19 20 21 22 24 28 30 31 33 35 37 40 41 44 46 47 49 52 63 65 66 67 69 71 73	13	10	96	3502	47	142316	1112	22950	10591	349
TUPELO—Lee County										
✦ △ NORTH MISSISSIPPI MEDICAL CENTER, 830 South Gloster Street, Zip 38801–4934; tel. 601/841–3000; Jeffrey B. Barber, Dr.PH, President and Chief Executive Officer (Total facility includes 97 beds in nursing home–type unit) **A**1 2 5 7 9 10 **F**2 3 7 8 10 11 12 14 15 16 17 18 19 20 21 22 23 24 26 28 29 30 31 32 33 35 37 38 39 40 41 42 43 44 45 46 47 48 49 51 52 53 55 57 58 59 60 63 64 65 66 67 71 73 74 **P**3 6 **S** North Mississippi Health Services, Inc., Tupelo, MS **N** North Mississippi Health Services, Inc., Tupelo, MS	23	10	721	27094	520	110071	2305	225169	97083	3709

Hospital, Address, Telephone, Administrator, Approval, Facility, and Physician Codes, Health Care System, Network	Classi-fication Codes		Utilization Data					Expense (thousands) of dollars		
	Control	Service	Staffed Beds	Admissions	Census	Outpatient Visits	Births	Total	Payroll	Personnel

★ American Hospital Association (AHA) membership
□ Joint Commission on Accreditation of Healthcare Organizations (JCAHO) accreditation
+ American Osteopathic Healthcare Association (AOHA) membership
○ American Osteopathic Association (AOA) accreditation
△ Commission on Accreditation of Rehabilitation Facilities (CARF) accreditation
Control codes 61, 63, 64, 71, 72 and 73 indicate hospitals listed by AOHA, but not registered by AHA. For definition of numerical codes, see page A4

TYLERTOWN—Walthall County

WALTHALL COUNTY GENERAL HOSPITAL, 100 Hospital Drive, Zip 39667-2099; tel. 601/876-2122; Jimmy Graves, Administrator **A**9 10 **F**8 15 19 20 22 26 28 32 35 44 46 49 52 57 71 73

| | 13 | 10 | 49 | 1730 | 31 | 13927 | 0 | — | — | 125 |

UNION—Newton County

LAIRD HOSPITAL, 25117 Highway 15, Zip 39365-9099; tel. 601/774-8214; Georgia Buchanan, President **A**9 10 **F**8 19 21 22 32 37 41 44 46 48 49 63 65 71 73

| | 33 | 10 | 50 | 1746 | 29 | 16094 | 2 | — | — | 417 |

VICKSBURG—Warren County

COLUMBIA VICKSBURG MEDICAL CENTER See Vicksburg Medical Center

⊠ PARKVIEW REGIONAL MEDICAL CENTER, 100 McAuley Drive, Zip 39180-2897, Mailing Address: P.O. Box 590, Zip 39181-0590; tel. 601/631-2131; Harry Alvis, Chief Executive Officer (Total facility includes 31 beds in nursing home–type unit) **A**1 2 9 10 **F**2 7 8 11 12 19 21 22 23 24 32 35 37 39 40 41 44 45 49 52 57 58 64 65 66 67 71 72 73 **P**6 **S** Quorum Health Group/Quorum Health Resources, Inc., Brentwood, TN

| | 33 | 10 | 183 | 5838 | 120 | 70991 | 943 | 37132 | 13827 | 526 |

⊠ VICKSBURG MEDICAL CENTER, (Formerly Columbia Vicksburg Medical Center), 1111 Frontage Road, Zip 39181-5298; tel. 601/619-3800; Steve Roth, Chief Executive Officer **A**1 9 10 **F**1 2 3 7 8 9 10 11 12 14 16 17 19 20 21 22 23 24 26 27 31 32 33 35 36 37 38 39 40 41 42 43 44 45 46 47 48 49 51 52 53 54 55 56 57 58 59 60 61 64 65 66 67 68 69 71 72 73 74 **P**7 **S** Columbia/HCA Healthcare Corporation, Nashville, TN

| | 33 | 10 | 154 | 5116 | 96 | 23619 | 413 | 30248 | 13143 | 416 |

WATER VALLEY—Yalobusha County

YALOBUSHA GENERAL HOSPITAL, Highway 7 South, Zip 38965, Mailing Address: P.O. Box 728, Zip 38965-0728; tel. 601/473-1411; John R. Jones, Administrator (Total facility includes 59 beds in nursing home–type unit) **A**9 10 **F**12 14 19 20 39 41 48 64 65 71 73 **P**4

| | 13 | 10 | 91 | 716 | 70 | 287 | 0 | — | — | 125 |

WAYNESBORO—Wayne County

WAYNE GENERAL HOSPITAL, 950 Matthew Drive, Zip 39367-2590, Mailing Address: P.O. Box 1249, Zip 39367-1249; tel. 601/735-5151; Donald Hemeter, Administrator **A**9 10 **F**7 8 15 17 19 20 21 22 24 31 32 33 37 40 44 45 47 48 49 63 65 71 73

| | 13 | 10 | 80 | 4112 | 58 | 30100 | 322 | — | — | 337 |

WEST POINT—Clay County

CLAY COUNTY MEDICAL CENTER, 835 Medical Center Drive, Zip 39773-9320; tel. 601/495-2300; David M. Reid, Administrator **A**9 10 **F**7 8 11 15 16 17 19 20 21 22 24 33 37 39 40 41 42 44 45 46 48 49 51 61 65 66 67 71 73 74 **S** North Mississippi Health Services, Inc., Tupelo, MS **N** North Mississippi Health Services, Tupelo, MS

| | 23 | 10 | 60 | 3516 | 38 | 32179 | 392 | 13540 | 5922 | 212 |

WHITFIELD—Rankin County

★ MISSISSIPPI STATE HOSPITAL, Mailing Address: P.O. Box 157-A, Zip 39193-0157; tel. 601/351-8000; James G. Chastain, Director (Total facility includes 451 beds in nursing home–type unit) **F**2 7 8 9 10 11 12 15 17 19 20 21 22 23 27 31 35 37 38 40 41 42 43 44 45 46 47 48 49 52 53 54 55 56 57 58 59 60 61 64 65 69 71 73 74 **P**1 **S** Mississippi State Department of Mental Health, Jackson, MS

| | 12 | 22 | 1297 | 1407 | 1106 | 5551 | 0 | 73334 | 47273 | 1849 |

□ WHITFIELD MEDICAL SURGICAL HOSPITAL, Oak Circle, Zip 39193; tel. 601/351-8023; James I. Morton, FACHE, Administrator and Chief Executive Officer **A**1 10 **F**1 2 6 7 8 9 10 11 12 19 20 21 22 23 24 26 27 31 32 33 35 36 37 38 39 40 41 42 43 44 45 47 48 49 50 51 52 60 61 63 64 65 66 67 68 69 70 71 72 73 74

| | 12 | 10 | 43 | 492 | 21 | 5713 | 0 | — | — | 97 |

WIGGINS—Stone County

STONE COUNTY HOSPITAL, 1434 East Central Avenue, Zip 39577; tel. 601/928-6600; J. Clifton Quinn, Administrator **A**10 **F**1 8 11 14 15 16 17 19 21 26 33 37 41 44 49 52 57 59 65 66 71 73 **S** NetCare Health Systems, Inc., Nashville, TN

| | 33 | 10 | 50 | 1816 | 20 | 9524 | 0 | — | — | 189 |

WINONA—Montgomery County

TYLER HOLMES MEMORIAL HOSPITAL, 409 Tyler Holmes Drive, Zip 38967-1599; tel. 601/283-4114; Gregory S. Mullen, Administrator **A**9 10 **F**1 15 16 17 19 21 22 26 28 32 36 40 41 44 46 52 57 59 61 65 71 **P**8

| | 13 | 10 | 49 | 1399 | 26 | 16251 | 58 | 8442 | 2942 | 153 |

YAZOO CITY—Yazoo County

KING'S DAUGHTERS HOSPITAL, 823 Grand Avenue, Zip 39194-3233; tel. 601/746-2261; Noel W. Hart, Administrator **A**9 10 **F**8 11 14 16 19 20 22 24 28 31 33 37 44 46 65 71 73

| | 23 | 10 | 54 | 1731 | 32 | 37708 | 0 | — | — | 173 |

MISSOURI

Resident population 5,402 (in thousands)
Resident population in metro areas 68.1%
Birth rate per 1,000 population 13.9
65 years and over 13.8%
Percent of persons without health insurance 13.2%

Hospital, Address, Telephone, Administrator, Approval, Facility, and Physician Codes, Health Care System, Network	Classi-fication Codes		Utilization Data					Expense (thousands) of dollars		
★ American Hospital Association (AHA) membership □ Joint Commission on Accreditation of Healthcare Organizations (JCAHO) accreditation + American Osteopathic Healthcare Association (AOHA) membership ○ American Osteopathic Association (AOA) accreditation △ Commission on Accreditation of Rehabilitation Facilities (CARF) accreditation Control codes 61, 63, 64, 71, 72 and 73 indicate hospitals listed by AOHA, but not registered by AHA. For definition of numerical codes, see page A4	Control	Service	Staffed Beds	Admissions	Census	Outpatient Visits	Births	Total	Payroll	Personnel

ALBANY—Gentry County

★ GENTRY COUNTY MEMORIAL HOSPITAL, Clark and College Streets, Zip 64402–1499; tel. 660/726–3941; John W. Richmond, President and Chief Executive Officer (Total facility includes 10 beds in nursing home–type unit) **A**9 10 **F**8 12 15 16 17 19 20 21 22 26 27 28 29 30 32 33 34 35 37 41 42 44 45 46 48 49 51 61 63 64 65 66 67 69 71 73 74 **P**6 — 23 10 35 881 16 37862 0 6095 3033 113

APPLETON CITY—St. Clair County

ELLETT MEMORIAL HOSPITAL, 610 North Ohio Avenue, Zip 64724–1609; tel. 660/476–2111; Sandy Morlan, Administrator **A**9 10 **F**15 16 19 22 29 35 41 44 49 65 71 — 16 10 25 444 6 1993 0 1557 760 47

AURORA—Lawrence County

AURORA COMMUNITY HOSPITAL, 500 Porter Street, Zip 65605–2399; tel. 417/678–2122; Don Buchanan, Chief Operating Officer **A**9 10 **F**7 8 11 12 14 17 19 22 24 26 27 28 29 30 32 34 36 37 39 40 41 44 45 46 49 51 64 65 67 71 73 **P**6 — 14 10 38 1902 18 19851 309 9867 5405 226

BELTON—Cass County

★ RESEARCH BELTON HOSPITAL, 17065 South 71 Highway, Zip 64012–2165; tel. 816/348–1200; Daniel F. Sheehan, Administrator (Total facility includes 7 beds in nursing home–type unit) **A**9 **F**1 2 3 4 5 6 7 8 9 10 11 12 13 14 15 16 17 18 19 20 21 22 24 25 26 28 29 30 31 32 33 34 35 37 38 39 40 41 42 43 44 46 47 48 49 52 53 54 55 56 57 58 59 60 61 63 64 65 69 70 71 73 74 **P**1 **S** Health Midwest, Kansas City, MO **N** Health Midwest, Kansas City, MO — 23 10 47 1434 20 21442 0 13049 5396 145

BETHANY—Harrison County

HARRISON COUNTY COMMUNITY HOSPITAL, 2600 Miller Street, Zip 64424, Mailing Address: P.O. Box 428, Zip 64424–0428; tel. 660/425–2211; Dan P. Broyles, Administrator **A**9 10 **F**2 6 8 13 14 15 16 17 19 20 21 22 26 27 28 29 30 31 32 33 34 36 37 39 41 42 44 46 48 49 60 62 63 64 65 66 67 68 71 73 74 **P**5 — 16 10 23 730 6 24293 0 4091 1764 97

BLUE SPRINGS—Jackson County

⊡ △ ST. MARY'S HOSPITAL OF BLUE SPRINGS, 201 West R. D. Mize Road, Zip 64014; tel. 816/228–5900; N. Gary Wages, President and Chief Executive Officer (Total facility includes 10 beds in nursing home–type unit) **A**1 7 9 10 **F**4 6 7 8 10 11 12 14 15 16 17 19 20 21 22 24 25 26 28 29 30 31 32 33 34 35 37 38 39 40 41 42 43 44 45 46 48 49 60 63 64 65 66 67 71 72 73 **P**6 7 **S** Carondelet Health System, Saint Louis, MO **N** Carondelet Health, Kansas City, MO — 23 10 102 4349 61 48518 845 47078 20271 489

BOLIVAR—Polk County

⊡ CITIZENS MEMORIAL HOSPITAL, 1500 North Oakland, Zip 65613–3099; tel. 417/326–6000; Donald J. Babb, Chief Executive Officer **A**1 9 10 **F**7 8 14 15 16 17 19 21 22 26 27 28 29 30 31 32 33 34 35 37 39 40 41 42 44 46 49 52 56 57 58 64 65 67 70 71 73 74 **P**6 — 16 10 74 3124 34 28911 336 28931 14144 485

BOONVILLE—Cooper County

★ COOPER COUNTY MEMORIAL HOSPITAL, 17651 B. Highway, Zip 65233–2839, Mailing Address: P.O. Box 88, Zip 65233–0088; tel. 660/882–7461; Wilbert E. Meyer, Administrator and Chief Executive Officer (Total facility includes 24 beds in nursing home–type unit) **A**9 10 **F**8 12 14 15 16 17 19 22 28 29 30 32 34 35 39 41 44 49 54 64 65 67 71 73 — 13 10 49 660 30 15895 0 6639 3103 150

BRANSON—Taney County

⊡ SKAGGS COMMUNITY HEALTH CENTER, Business Highway 65 and Skaggs Road, Zip 65616–2035, Mailing Address: P.O. Box 650, Zip 65615–0650; tel. 417/335–7000; Bob D. Phillips, Administrator (Total facility includes 23 beds in nursing home–type unit) **A**1 9 10 **F**7 8 12 15 16 17 18 19 21 22 23 25 26 27 28 29 30 31 32 33 34 35 37 39 40 41 44 45 46 49 51 54 56 58 64 65 66 67 70 71 72 73 **P**8 — 23 10 99 4496 57 100168 426 36759 16178 588

BRIDGETON—St. Louis County

ST. VINCENT'S PSYCHIATRIC DIVISION See DePaul Health Center, Saint Louis

BROOKFIELD—Linn County

□ GENERAL JOHN J. PERSHING MEMORIAL HOSPITAL, 130 East Lockling Avenue, Zip 64628–0130, Mailing Address: P.O. Box 408, Zip 64628–0408; tel. 816/258–2222; Phil Hamilton, R.N., Chief Executive Officer **A**1 9 10 **F**8 12 14 17 19 22 24 28 29 30 31 32 33 35 39 40 42 44 46 49 51 65 71 73 — 23 10 34 905 8 54584 38 9490 4770 200

BUTLER—Bates County

BATES COUNTY MEMORIAL HOSPITAL, 615 West Nursery Street, Zip 64730–0370; tel. 660/679–4381; Bob S. Edwards, Jr., Chief Executive Officer (Total facility includes 12 beds in nursing home–type unit) **A**9 10 **F**7 8 12 14 16 19 21 22 24 28 29 30 32 33 34 35 37 39 40 41 44 45 46 49 64 65 66 71 73 — 13 10 52 1710 27 14860 23 9819 4302 146

CAMERON—Clinton County

CAMERON COMMUNITY HOSPITAL, 1015 West Fourth Street, Zip 64429–1498; tel. 816/632–2101; Joseph F. Abrutz, Jr., Administrator **A**9 10 **F**8 11 12 14 15 16 19 20 21 22 24 26 27 28 29 30 31 32 33 34 35 37 39 42 44 45 46 49 54 58 64 65 66 67 71 73 **P**6 — 23 10 39 1290 21 25203 0 14143 7374 266

Hospital, Address, Telephone, Administrator, Approval, Facility, and Physician Codes, Health Care System, Network	Classi-fication Codes		Utilization Data					Expense (thousands) of dollars		
	Control	Service	Staffed Beds	Admissions	Census	Outpatient Visits	Births	Total	Payroll	Personnel

★ American Hospital Association (AHA) membership
□ Joint Commission on Accreditation of Healthcare Organizations (JCAHO) accreditation
+ American Osteopathic Healthcare Association (AOHA) membership
○ American Osteopathic Association (AOA) accreditation
△ Commission on Accreditation of Rehabilitation Facilities (CARF) accreditation
Control codes 61, 63, 64, 71, 72 and 73 indicate hospitals listed by AOHA, but not registered by AHA. For definition of numerical codes, see page A4

CAPE GIRARDEAU—Cape Girardeau County

✠ SAINT FRANCIS MEDICAL CENTER, 211 St. Francis Drive, Zip 63703–8399; tel. 573/335–1251; James J. Sexton, President and Chief Executive Officer (Total facility includes 26 beds in nursing home–type unit) **A**1 2 10 **F**4 5 8 10 11 12 13 14 15 16 17 19 21 22 23 24 27 28 29 30 31 32 34 35 37 39 41 42 43 44 45 46 47 48 49 63 64 65 66 67 71 72 73 74 **P**8 ... `23 10 264 7162 124 55681 0 79621 33260 1074`

✠ SOUTHEAST MISSOURI HOSPITAL, 1701 Lacey Street, Zip 63701–5299; tel. 573/334–4822; James W. Wente, CPA, CHE, Administrator (Total facility includes 20 beds in nursing home–type unit) **A**1 2 6 10 **F**2 4 7 8 10 11 14 15 16 17 18 19 20 21 22 23 24 27 28 29 30 31 32 33 34 35 36 37 38 39 40 41 42 44 45 47 48 49 52 54 55 56 57 60 63 64 65 66 67 68 70 71 72 73 74 **P**8 ... `23 10 243 9905 140 117029 1517 89661 34502 1287`

CARROLLTON—Carroll County

CARROLL COUNTY MEMORIAL HOSPITAL, 1502 North Jefferson Street, Zip 64633–1999; tel. 816/542–1695; Jack L. Tindle, Chief Executive Officer **A**9 10 **F**8 14 15 19 22 29 32 34 41 42 44 46 71 ... `23 10 49 385 36 12287 0 3003 1495 68`

CARTHAGE—Jasper County

★ MCCUNE–BROOKS HOSPITAL, 627 West Centennial Avenue, Zip 64836–0677; tel. 417/358–8121; James W. McPheeters, III, Administrator (Total facility includes 7 beds in nursing home–type unit) **A**9 10 **F**8 19 21 22 28 29 30 32 33 35 36 37 44 49 52 57 64 65 66 67 71 **N** Carondelet Health, Kansas City, MO ... `14 10 70 1870 34 37781 0 16826 7504 311`

CASSVILLE—Barry County

SOUTH BARRY COUNTY MEMORIAL HOSPITAL, 94 Main Street, Zip 65625–1610; tel. 417/847–4115; Deborah Stubbs, Chief Executive Officer **A**9 10 **F**8 12 19 22 24 28 29 30 32 33 34 39 41 44 46 49 51 64 71 **P**1 5 ... `16 10 18 690 8 33053 0 6520 2588 118`

CHESTERFIELD—St. Louis County

✠ ST. LUKE'S HOSPITAL, 232 South Woods Mill Road, Zip 63017–3480; tel. 314/434–1500; George Tucker, M.D., President **A**1 2 3 5 9 10 **F**1 2 3 4 5 6 7 8 9 10 11 12 13 14 15 16 17 18 19 20 21 22 23 24 25 26 27 28 29 30 31 32 33 34 35 36 37 38 39 40 41 42 43 44 45 46 47 48 49 51 52 53 54 55 56 57 58 59 60 61 62 63 64 65 66 67 68 69 70 71 72 73 74 **P**6 7 8 **S** Sisters of Mercy Health System–St. Louis, Saint Louis, MO **N** Unity Health System, St. Louis, MO ... `23 10 369 17227 195 138676 2785 179237 84446 1946`

CHILLICOTHE—Livingston County

✠ HEDRICK MEDICAL CENTER, 100 Central Avenue, Zip 64601–1599; tel. 660/646–1480; R. Lynn Jackson, President and Chief Executive Officer **A**1 9 10 **F**7 8 12 14 15 16 17 18 19 22 28 29 30 32 33 34 35 36 37 39 40 41 42 44 45 46 55 58 64 65 67 71 73 **N** Health Midwest, Kansas City, MO ... `23 10 63 1491 21 24738 366 14747 6480 231`

CLINTON—Henry County

✠ GOLDEN VALLEY MEMORIAL HOSPITAL, 1600 North Second Street, Zip 64735–1197; tel. 660/885–5511; Randy S. Wertz, Administrator (Total facility includes 12 beds in nursing home–type unit) **A**1 9 10 **F**7 8 14 15 16 17 19 21 22 28 29 30 31 32 33 35 37 39 40 41 42 44 49 52 53 54 55 56 57 58 59 63 64 65 66 67 71 73 74 ... `16 10 106 3765 55 11124 341 23589 11011 411`

COLUMBIA—Boone County

✠ BOONE HOSPITAL CENTER, 1600 East Broadway, Zip 65201–5897; tel. 573/815–8000; Michael Shirk, President and Senior Executive Officer (Total facility includes 31 beds in nursing home–type unit) **A**1 2 3 5 9 10 **F**4 7 8 10 12 14 15 16 17 19 21 22 24 25 26 28 29 30 31 34 35 37 38 39 40 41 42 43 44 45 46 48 49 52 54 55 56 57 58 59 60 63 64 65 67 69 71 72 73 74 **P**3 5 8 **S** BJC Health System, Saint Louis, MO **N** BJC Health System, St. Louis, MO ... `23 10 313 13058 204 80517 1392 113983 44744 1277`

✠ △ COLUMBIA REGIONAL HOSPITAL, 404 Keene Street, Zip 65201–6698; tel. 573/875–9000; Bruce Eady, Chief Executive Officer **A**1 2 3 5 7 9 10 **F**4 7 8 10 12 14 15 16 18 19 20 21 22 23 26 28 29 30 31 32 33 34 35 37 39 40 41 42 44 45 46 48 49 50 52 53 57 60 63 64 65 66 67 69 71 72 73 74 **P**4 5 7 8 **S** TENET Healthcare Corporation, Santa Barbara, CA ... `33 10 265 5087 103 — 210 61795 19303 707`

ELLIS FISCHEL CANCER CENTER See University Hospitals and Clinics

✠ HARRY S. TRUMAN MEMORIAL VETERANS HOSPITAL, 800 Hospital Drive, Zip 65201–5297; tel. 573/814–6300; Gary L. Campbell, Director (Total facility includes 22 beds in nursing home–type unit) **A**1 3 5 8 **F**2 3 4 5 8 10 11 12 19 20 21 22 26 27 29 30 31 32 33 34 35 37 39 41 42 43 44 45 46 48 49 51 52 54 55 56 57 58 59 60 63 64 65 67 68 69 71 73 74 **P**6 **S** Department of Veterans Affairs, Washington, DC ... `45 10 131 4537 113 119602 0 78094 38229 935`

□ MID MISSOURI MENTAL HEALTH CENTER, 3 Hospital Drive, Zip 65201–5296; tel. 573/884–1300; Mark Stansberry, Superintendent **A**1 3 5 10 **F**14 15 16 29 52 53 54 55 56 57 58 59 **P**6 ... `12 22 69 1666 56 6376 0 14307 7260 262`

□ △ UNIVERSITY HOSPITALS AND CLINICS, (Includes Ellis Fischel Cancer Center, 115 Business Loop 70 West, Zip 65203; tel. 573/882–5460; Keith Weinhold, Director), One Hospital Drive, Zip 65212–0001; tel. 573/882–3737; Patsy J. Hart, Executive Director **A**1 2 3 5 7 8 9 10 **F**2 4 5 7 8 9 10 11 12 13 14 15 16 17 18 19 20 21 22 25 26 27 28 29 30 31 32 34 35 37 38 39 40 41 42 43 44 45 46 47 48 49 51 52 53 54 55 56 57 58 59 60 61 63 65 66 67 68 69 70 71 72 73 74 **P**1 ... `12 10 415 13464 244 408177 1569 227183 96669 3295`

CREVE COEUR—St. Louis County

BARNES–JEWISH WEST COUNTY HOSPITAL See Saint Louis

Hospital, Address, Telephone, Administrator, Approval, Facility, and Physician Codes, Health Care System, Network	Classi-fication Codes		Utilization Data					Expense (thousands) of dollars		
★ American Hospital Association (AHA) membership □ Joint Commission on Accreditation of Healthcare Organizations (JCAHO) accreditation + American Osteopathic Healthcare Association (AOHA) membership ○ American Osteopathic Association (AOA) accreditation △ Commission on Accreditation of Rehabilitation Facilities (CARF) accreditation Control codes 61, 63, 64, 71, 72 and 73 indicate hospitals listed by AOHA, but not registered by AHA. For definition of numerical codes, see page A4	Control	Service	Staffed Beds	Admissions	Census	Outpatient Visits	Births	Total	Payroll	Personnel

CRYSTAL CITY—Jefferson County

□ JEFFERSON MEMORIAL HOSPITAL, Highway 61 South, Zip 63019, Mailing Address: P.O. Box 350, Zip 63019–0350; tel. 314/933–1000; Mark S. Brodeur, Chief Executive Officer (Total facility includes 28 beds in nursing home–type unit) **A**1 9 10 **F**2 3 4 7 8 10 11 12 15 16 17 19 21 22 23 25 27 28 29 30 31 32 33 34 35 37 39 40 41 42 43 44 46 48 49 52 53 54 55 56 57 58 59 60 62 63 64 65 66 67 71 72 73 — 23 10 | 236 | 7389 | 122 | 75263 | 706 | 62463 | 29258 | 766

DEXTER—Stoddard County

DEXTER MEMORIAL HOSPITAL, 1200 North One Mile Road, Zip 63841–1099; tel. 573/624–5566; Randal Tennison, Administrator **A**9 10 **F**8 11 12 15 19 20 22 25 26 28 29 30 31 32 33 34 37 39 41 44 45 48 49 51 63 64 65 67 71 73 — 23 10 | 48 | 887 | 10 | 29225 | 1 | 9875 | 4635 | 182

DONIPHAN—Ripley County

RIPLEY COUNTY MEMORIAL HOSPITAL, 109 Plum Street, Zip 63935–1299; tel. 573/996–2141; Charles Ray Freeman, Administrator **A**9 10 **F**8 14 15 16 17 19 22 28 29 30 32 33 34 41 44 45 46 51 53 54 55 57 71 — 13 10 | 26 | 575 | 10 | 5526 | 0 | 4069 | 1905 | 94

EL DORADO SPRINGS—Cedar County

CEDAR COUNTY MEMORIAL HOSPITAL, 1401 South Park Street, Zip 64744–2096; tel. 417/876–2511; Jackie Boyles, Administrator **A**9 10 **F**7 8 14 15 16 19 22 28 29 32 40 41 46 49 64 65 71 73 74 — 13 10 | 34 | 924 | 10 | — | 88 | 1877 | 975 | 111

EXCELSIOR SPRINGS—Clay County

□ EXCELSIOR SPRINGS MEDICAL CENTER, 1700 Rainbow Boulevard, Zip 64024–1190; tel. 816/630–6081; Sally S. Nance, Chief Executive Officer (Total facility includes 80 beds in nursing home–type unit) **A**1 9 10 **F**6 8 12 14 15 16 17 19 20 22 26 27 28 29 30 32 33 34 35 36 37 39 41 42 44 45 46 49 51 64 65 67 71 73 — 14 10 | 105 | 816 | 80 | 15306 | 0 | 10617 | 5208 | 140

FAIRFAX—Atchison County

COMMUNITY HOSPITAL ASSOCIATION, Highway 59, Zip 64446–0107; tel. 660/686–2211; Larry S. Goodloe, Administrator **A**9 10 **F**7 8 11 19 20 22 29 30 32 33 34 35 37 39 40 41 42 44 46 49 58 64 65 71 — 23 10 | 44 | 867 | 21 | 12499 | 64 | 6453 | 2557 | 114

FARMINGTON—St. Francois County

+ ○ MINERAL AREA REGIONAL MEDICAL CENTER, 1212 Weber Road, Zip 63640–3309; tel. 573/756–4581; Kerry L. Noble, Chief Executive Officer **A**9 10 11 12 13 **F**1 2 3 7 8 14 15 16 17 18 19 20 22 27 28 29 30 31 32 34 35 37 39 40 41 42 44 45 46 49 53 54 55 56 57 58 59 64 65 66 67 70 71 73 **P**6 8 — 23 10 | 123 | 4003 | 50 | 97560 | 469 | 30837 | 12253 | 505

⊞ PARKLAND HEALTH CENTER, (Includes Parkland Health Center–Bonne Terre, 7245 Vo–Tech Road, Bonne Terre, Zip 63628; tel. 573/358–1400), 1101 West Liberty Street, Zip 63640–1997; tel. 573/756–6451; Richard L. Conklin, President **A**1 9 10 **F**3 4 7 8 12 14 15 16 19 20 21 22 25 28 29 30 32 33 34 35 36 37 39 40 41 42 44 45 46 49 51 53 54 55 56 57 58 63 65 66 69 71 73 **P**5 6 7 **S** BJC Health System, Saint Louis, MO **N** BJC Health System, St. Louis, MO — 23 10 | 94 | 3251 | 35 | 62123 | 395 | 29604 | 12109 | 442

□ SOUTHEAST MISSOURI MENTAL HEALTH CENTER, 1010 West Columbia, Zip 63640–2997; tel. 314/756–6792; Donald L. Barton, Superintendent **A**1 10 **F**28 29 34 39 41 45 46 52 54 65 67 73 — 12 22 | 206 | 1499 | 180 | 0 | 0 | 21260 | 14755 | 611

FLORISSANT—St. Louis County

CHRISTIAN HOSPITAL NORTHWEST See Christian Hospital Northeast–Northwest, Saint Louis

FORT LEONARD WOOD—Pulaski County

⊞ GENERAL LEONARD WOOD ARMY COMMUNITY HOSPITAL, 126 Missouri Avenue, Zip 65473–8952; tel. 573/596–0414; Lieutenant Colonel Julie Martin, Administrator **A**1 2 **F**1 2 3 4 5 6 7 8 9 10 11 12 13 14 15 16 17 18 19 20 21 22 23 24 25 26 27 28 29 30 31 32 33 34 35 36 37 38 39 40 41 42 43 44 45 46 47 48 49 50 51 52 53 54 55 56 57 58 59 60 61 62 63 64 65 66 67 68 69 70 71 72 73 74 **S** Department of the Army, Office of the Surgeon General, Falls Church, VA — 42 10 | 71 | 3477 | 36 | 238060 | 342 | 53307 | 22512 | 885

FREDERICKTOWN—Madison County

MADISON MEDICAL CENTER, 100 South Wood at West College, Zip 63645, Mailing Address: P.O. Box 431, Zip 63645–0431; tel. 573/783–3341; Floyd D. Bounds, Administrator (Total facility includes 123 beds in nursing home–type unit) **A**9 10 **F**8 14 15 16 17 19 22 29 30 32 34 37 39 40 41 44 46 49 51 64 65 71 — 13 10 | 159 | 372 | 113 | 17037 | 26 | 9051 | 4172 | 227

FULTON—Callaway County

□ CALLAWAY COMMUNITY HOSPITAL, 10 South Hospital Drive, Zip 65251–2513; tel. 573/642–3376; Gerald M. Torba, Chief Executive Officer **A**1 9 10 **F**6 8 13 14 15 16 17 19 22 24 25 28 29 30 32 34 37 39 40 41 42 44 46 49 58 65 67 71 73 — 23 10 | 31 | 1073 | 14 | 27479 | 112 | 10028 | 4114 | 158

□ FULTON STATE HOSPITAL, 600 East Fifth Street, Zip 65251–1798; tel. 573/592–4100; Stephen C. Reeves, Superintendent (Total facility includes 24 beds in nursing home–type unit) **A**1 10 **F**2 3 12 14 16 18 20 26 27 28 29 30 33 39 41 45 46 51 52 55 57 64 65 67 73 **P**6 — 12 22 | 508 | 741 | 440 | 0 | 0 | 52307 | 29861 | 1199

HANNIBAL—Marion County

□ HANNIBAL REGIONAL HOSPITAL, Highway 36 West, Zip 63401, Mailing Address: P.O. Box 551, Zip 63401–0551; tel. 573/248–1300; John C. Grossmeier, President and Chief Executive Officer **A**1 2 9 10 **F**7 8 10 14 15 16 17 18 19 20 21 22 23 28 29 30 31 32 34 35 37 39 40 41 44 46 49 52 54 55 56 57 58 59 61 63 65 66 67 71 73 74 **P**6 8 — 23 10 | 105 | 4859 | 64 | 59414 | 542 | 38536 | 15388 | 603

Hospital, Address, Telephone, Administrator, Approval, Facility, and Physician Codes, Health Care System, Network	Classi-fication Codes		Utilization Data					Expense (thousands) of dollars		
	Control	Service	Staffed Beds	Admissions	Census	Outpatient Visits	Births	Total	Payroll	Personnel

★ American Hospital Association (AHA) membership
□ Joint Commission on Accreditation of Healthcare Organizations (JCAHO) accreditation
+ American Osteopathic Healthcare Association (AOHA) membership
○ American Osteopathic Association (AOA) accreditation
△ Commission on Accreditation of Rehabilitation Facilities (CARF) accreditation
Control codes 61, 63, 64, 71, 72 and 73 indicate hospitals listed by AOHA, but not registered by AHA. For definition of numerical codes, see page A4

HARRISONVILLE—Cass County

✠ CASS MEDICAL CENTER, 1800 East Mechanic Street, Zip 64701–2099; tel. 816/884–3291; Alan Freeman, Administrator **A**1 9 10 **F**8 12 14 15 16 19 20 21 22 29 30 33 34 35 37 39 41 42 44 45 46 49 51 53 54 56 57 58 65 66 71 73 **P**7 **S** Health Midwest, Kansas City, MO **N** Health Midwest, Kansas City, MO | 13 | 10 | 42 | 1126 | 13 | 16593 | 0 | — | — | 162

HAYTI—Pemiscot County

PEMISCOT MEMORIAL HEALTH SYSTEM, Highway 61 and Reed, Zip 63851, Mailing Address: P.O. Box 489, Zip 63851–0489; tel. 573/359–1372; Darrell Jean, Administrator and Chief Executive Officer (Total facility includes 153 beds in nursing home–type unit) **A**10 **F**3 7 8 11 12 15 19 21 22 25 26 27 28 29 30 31 32 34 35 36 37 39 40 41 44 49 51 64 65 71 72 73 74 **P**6 8 | 13 | 10 | 216 | 4540 | 143 | 23259 | 209 | 23837 | 11111 | 636

HERMANN—Gasconade County

HERMANN AREA DISTRICT HOSPITAL, Mailing Address: P.O. Box 470, Zip 65041–0470; tel. 573/486–2191; Dan McKinney, Administrator **A**9 10 **F**8 12 15 16 17 19 20 22 28 29 30 32 33 34 35 36 39 40 42 44 46 49 64 65 71 73 **P**6 | 16 | 10 | 41 | 449 | 28 | 24978 | 22 | 4641 | 2108 | 98

HOUSTON—Texas County

TEXAS COUNTY MEMORIAL HOSPITAL, 1333 Sam Houston Boulevard, Zip 65483–2046; tel. 417/967–3311; William L. Sword, President and Chief Executive Officer **A**9 10 **F**7 8 12 14 16 19 20 22 24 25 27 28 29 30 31 32 33 34 36 37 39 40 41 44 45 46 49 51 64 65 71 73 **P**6 | 13 | 10 | 66 | 2225 | 25 | 10264 | 246 | 10007 | 5378 | 207

INDEPENDENCE—Jackson County

COLUMBIA INDEPENDENCE REGIONAL HEALTH CENTER See Independence Regional Health Center

✠ INDEPENDENCE REGIONAL HEALTH CENTER, (Formerly Columbia Independence Regional Health Center), 1509 West Truman Road, Zip 64050–3498; tel. 816/836–8100; Darrell W. Moore, Chief Executive Officer (Total facility includes 70 beds in nursing home–type unit) **A**1 2 9 10 **F**1 2 3 4 5 6 7 8 9 10 11 12 13 14 15 16 17 18 19 20 21 22 23 24 26 27 28 29 30 31 32 33 34 35 36 37 38 39 40 41 42 43 44 45 46 47 48 49 51 52 53 54 55 57 60 61 63 64 65 66 67 70 71 73 74 **P**5 6 **S** Columbia/HCA Healthcare Corporation, Nashville, TN | 33 | 10 | 329 | 9130 | 165 | 166229 | 457 | 80538 | 32234 | 938

✠ MEDICAL CENTER OF INDEPENDENCE, 17203 East 23rd Street, Zip 64057–1899; tel. 816/478–5000; Michael W. Chappelow, President and Chief Executive Officer (Total facility includes 9 beds in nursing home–type unit) **A**1 9 10 **F**1 2 3 4 5 7 8 9 10 11 12 13 14 15 16 17 18 19 20 21 22 23 24 25 26 27 28 29 30 31 32 33 34 35 36 37 38 39 40 41 42 43 44 45 46 47 48 49 51 52 53 54 55 56 57 58 59 60 61 63 64 65 66 67 68 69 70 71 73 74 **P**1 5 6 **S** Health Midwest, Kansas City, MO **N** Health Midwest, Kansas City, MO | 23 | 10 | 123 | 4507 | 58 | 41310 | 898 | 33710 | 14692 | 439

JEFFERSON CITY—Cole County

★ + ○ △ CAPITAL REGION MEDICAL CENTER–MADISON, 1125 Madison Street, Zip 65101–5227; tel. 573/635–7141; Edward F. Farnsworth, President (Total facility includes 16 beds in nursing home–type unit) **A**7 11 12 13 **F**1 3 4 7 8 10 12 13 14 15 16 17 18 19 21 22 23 24 25 26 28 29 30 31 32 33 34 35 36 37 39 40 41 42 43 44 45 46 48 49 53 54 55 56 57 58 59 60 63 64 65 66 67 71 72 73 **P**5 8 | 23 | 10 | 41 | 974 | 25 | 37549 | 337 | — | — | 1070

✠ CAPITAL REGION MEDICAL CENTER–SOUTHWEST, 1432 Southwest Boulevard, Zip 65109–4420, Mailing Address: P.O. Box 1128, Zip 65102–1128; tel. 573/635–6811; Edward F. Farnsworth, President **A**1 10 **F**1 3 4 7 8 10 12 13 14 15 16 17 18 19 21 22 23 24 25 26 28 29 30 31 32 33 34 35 36 37 39 40 41 42 43 44 45 46 48 49 52 53 54 55 56 57 58 59 60 63 64 65 66 67 71 72 73 **P**5 8 | 23 | 10 | 94 | 4989 | 70 | 46304 | 0 | 75386 | 33516 | 1070

✠ ST. MARYS HEALTH CENTER, 100 St. Marys Medical Plaza, Zip 65101–1601; tel. 573/761–7000; John S. Dubis, President **A**1 2 9 10 **F**4 7 8 10 12 14 15 16 17 18 19 20 21 22 24 28 29 30 31 32 33 34 35 37 39 40 41 42 43 44 45 46 48 49 51 52 53 54 55 56 57 58 59 60 63 64 65 67 70 71 72 73 74 **P**1 4 **S** SSM Health Care System, Saint Louis, MO | 23 | 10 | 151 | 8559 | 103 | 138367 | 1218 | 80268 | 32046 | 989

JOPLIN—Jasper County

✠ + ○ FREEMAN HEALTH SYSTEM, (Formerly Freeman Hospitals and Health System), (Includes Freeman Hospital East, 932 East 34th Street, Zip 64804–3999; Freeman Hospital West, 1102 West 32nd Street), 1102 West 32nd Street, Zip 64804–3599; tel. 417/623–2801; Gary D. Duncan, President and Chief Executive Officer (Total facility includes 32 beds in nursing home–type unit) (Nonreporting) **A**1 2 9 10 11 12 13 | 23 | 10 | 266 | — | — | — | — | — | — |

✠ △ ST. JOHN'S REGIONAL MEDICAL CENTER, 2727 McClelland Boulevard, Zip 64804–1694; tel. 417/781–2727; Robert G. Brueckner, President and Chief Executive Officer (Total facility includes 10 beds in nursing home–type unit) **A**1 2 7 9 10 **F**4 7 8 10 11 12 14 15 16 17 18 19 20 21 22 23 25 27 28 29 30 31 32 33 34 35 36 37 39 40 41 42 43 44 45 46 48 49 51 52 54 56 57 58 59 60 61 64 65 66 67 68 70 71 72 73 74 **P**1 **S** Catholic Health Initiatives, Denver, CO **N** Carondelet Health, Kansas City, MO | 23 | 10 | 367 | 14788 | 218 | 207663 | 780 | 142730 | 54928 | 1926

KANSAS CITY—Jackson County

✠ BAPTIST MEDICAL CENTER, 6601 Rockhill Road, Zip 64131–1197; tel. 816/276–7000; Michael S. McCoy, Interim President and Chief Executive Officer (Total facility includes 23 beds in nursing home–type unit) **A**1 2 3 5 9 10 **F**1 2 3 4 5 7 8 10 11 12 13 14 15 16 17 18 19 20 21 22 23 24 25 26 27 28 29 30 31 32 33 34 35 36 37 38 39 40 41 42 43 44 45 46 49 51 52 53 54 55 56 57 58 59 60 61 63 64 65 66 67 68 69 70 71 72 73 74 **P**1 4 5 7 **S** Health Midwest, Kansas City, MO **N** Health Midwest, Kansas City, MO | 23 | 10 | 315 | 11631 | 179 | 64704 | 1722 | 127999 | 49735 | 1287

Hospital, Address, Telephone, Administrator, Approval, Facility, and Physician Codes, Health Care System, Network	Classi-fication Codes		Utilization Data					Expense (thousands) of dollars		
	Control	Service	Staffed Beds	Admissions	Census	Outpatient Visits	Births	Total	Payroll	Personnel

★ American Hospital Association (AHA) membership
□ Joint Commission on Accreditation of Healthcare Organizations (JCAHO) accreditation
+ American Osteopathic Healthcare Association (AOHA) membership
○ American Osteopathic Association (AOA) accreditation
△ Commission on Accreditation of Rehabilitation Facilities (CARF) accreditation
　Control codes 61, 63, 64, 71, 72 and 73 indicate hospitals listed by AOHA, but not registered by AHA. For definition of numerical codes, see page A4

✠ CHILDREN'S MERCY HOSPITAL, 2401 Gillham Road, Zip 64108–9898; tel. 816/234–3000; Randall L. O'Donnell, Ph.D., President and Chief Executive Officer **A**1 2 3 5 8 9 10 **F**4 5 9 10 11 12 13 15 16 17 19 20 21 22 25 28 29 31 32 34 35 37 38 39 41 42 43 44 46 47 49 51 54 58 60 65 67 68 69 70 71 73 **P**4 5 6	23	50	167	7106	108	217348	0	147140	77389	1976
□ CRITTENTON, 10918 Elm Avenue, Zip 64134–4199; tel. 816/765–6600; Gary L. Watson, FACHE, Senior Executive Officer **A**1 10 **F**2 3 4 5 7 8 10 11 12 13 16 17 18 19 20 21 22 24 25 26 27 28 29 30 31 32 33 34 35 37 38 39 40 41 42 43 44 45 46 48 49 51 52 53 54 55 56 58 59 60 61 63 64 65 66 67 68 69 70 71 72 73 74 **P**6 8 **S** Saint Luke's Shawnee Mission Health System, Kansas City, MO	23	52	110	413	89	15370	0	—	—	178
✠ + ○　PARK LANE MEDICAL CENTER, 5151 Raytown Road, Zip 64133–2199; tel. 816/358–8000; Derell Taloney, President and Chief Executive Officer (Total facility includes 15 beds in nursing home–type unit) **A**1 9 10 11 12 13 **F**1 2 3 4 5 7 8 9 10 11 12 13 14 15 16 17 18 19 20 21 23 24 25 26 27 28 29 30 31 32 33 34 35 36 37 38 39 40 41 42 43 44 45 46 47 48 49 51 52 53 54 55 56 57 58 59 60 61 63 64 65 66 67 68 69 70 71 72 73 74 **P**1 4 5 7 **S** Health Midwest, Kansas City, MO **N** Health Midwest, Kansas City, MO	23	10	83	2193	38	80893	0	24886	11313	325
★ △　REHABILITATION INSTITUTE, 3011 Baltimore, Zip 64108–3465; tel. 816/751–7900; Ronald L. Herrick, President **A**7 9 10 **F**1 2 3 4 5 6 7 8 9 10 11 12 13 14 15 17 18 19 20 21 22 23 24 25 26 27 28 29 30 31 32 33 34 36 37 39 40 41 42 43 44 45 46 47 48 49 51 52 53 54 55 56 57 58 59 60 61 64 65 66 67 68 69 70 71 72 73 74 **P**2 5 8 **S** Health Midwest, Kansas City, MO **N** Health Midwest, Kansas City, MO	23	46	36	334	18	0	0	13226	7409	237
✠ RESEARCH MEDICAL CENTER, 2316 East Meyer Boulevard, Zip 64132–1199; tel. 816/276–4000; Steven R. Newton, Interim President and Chief Executive Officer (Total facility includes 35 beds in nursing home–type unit) **A**1 2 3 5 9 10 **F**1 2 3 4 5 7 8 9 10 11 12 13 14 15 16 17 18 19 20 21 22 23 24 25 26 27 28 29 30 31 32 33 34 35 36 37 38 39 40 41 42 43 44 45 46 47 48 49 51 52 53 54 55 56 57 58 59 60 61 63 64 65 66 67 68 69 70 71 72 73 74 **P**1 6 **S** Health Midwest, Kansas City, MO **N** Health Midwest, Kansas City, MO	23	10	491	14335	270	73039	1913	190236	80991	2365
✠ RESEARCH PSYCHIATRIC CENTER, 2323 East 63rd Street, Zip 64130–3495; tel. 816/444–8161; Todd Krass, Administrator and Chief Executive Officer **A**1 10 **F**1 2 3 4 5 6 7 8 9 10 11 12 13 15 16 17 18 19 20 22 23 24 25 26 27 28 29 30 31 32 33 34 35 37 38 39 40 41 42 43 44 45 46 47 48 49 51 52 53 54 55 56 57 58 59 60 61 62 64 65 66 67 68 69 70 71 72 73 74 **P**4 5 8 **S** Columbia/HCA Healthcare Corporation, Nashville, TN **N** Health Midwest, Kansas City, MO	33	22	100	1843	46	7821	0	9182	4459	140
✠ SAINT JOSEPH HEALTH CENTER, 1000 Carondelet Drive, Zip 64114–4673; tel. 816/942–4400; Richard M. Abell, President and Chief Executive Officer (Total facility includes 20 beds in nursing home–type unit) **A**1 2 5 9 10 **F**4 5 6 7 8 10 12 13 15 16 17 19 21 22 24 28 29 30 31 32 33 34 35 37 38 39 40 41 42 43 44 45 46 48 49 60 63 64 65 66 67 70 71 72 73 **P**1 3 4 5 6 7 **S** Carondelet Health System, Saint Louis, MO	23	10	257	10908	163	109692	1702	114108	46787	1142
✠ SAINT LUKE'S HOSPITAL, 4400 Wornall Road, Zip 64111–3238; tel. 816/932–2000; James M. Brophy, Senior Executive Officer (Total facility includes 30 beds in nursing home–type unit) **A**1 2 3 8 9 10 **F**2 3 4 5 7 8 10 11 12 13 14 15 16 17 18 19 20 21 22 23 24 25 26 27 28 29 30 31 32 33 34 35 37 38 39 40 42 43 44 45 46 48 49 51 52 53 54 55 56 57 58 59 60 61 63 64 65 66 67 68 69 70 71 72 73 74 **P**6 8 **S** Saint Luke's Shawnee Mission Health System, Kansas City, MO **N**	23	10	510	19903	341	180054	2737	244000	95661	2547
□ SAINT LUKE'S NORTHLAND HOSPITAL, 5830 N.W. Barry Road, Zip 64154–9988; tel. 816/932–2199; James M. Brophy, FACHE, Senior Executive Officer **A**1 **F**2 3 4 5 6 7 8 10 11 12 13 14 15 16 17 18 19 20 21 22 24 25 26 27 28 29 30 31 32 33 34 35 36 37 38 39 40 41 42 43 44 45 46 47 48 49 51 52 53 54 55 56 57 58 59 60 61 63 64 65 66 67 69 70 71 72 73 74 **P**6 8 **S** Saint Luke's Shawnee Mission Health System, Kansas City, MO	23	10	58	3238	33	40056	730	27325	11189	315
ST. MARY'S HOSPITAL See Trinity Lutheran Hospital										
✠ TRINITY LUTHERAN HOSPITAL, (Includes St. Mary's Hospital, 101 Memorial Drive, Zip 64108; tel. 816/751–4600), 3030 Baltimore Avenue, Zip 64108–3404; tel. 816/751–4600; Ronald A. Ommen, President and Chief Executive Officer (Total facility includes 30 beds in nursing home–type unit) **A**1 2 3 5 9 10 **F**1 2 3 4 5 7 8 10 11 12 14 15 16 17 18 19 21 22 23 24 25 26 27 28 29 30 31 32 34 35 36 37 38 39 40 41 42 43 44 45 46 48 49 51 52 53 54 55 56 57 58 59 60 61 62 64 65 66 67 69 70 71 72 73 74 **P**1 2 5 **S** Health Midwest, Kansas City, MO **N** Health Midwest, Kansas City, MO	23	10	334	7672	140	159429	0	—	—	1248
★ △　TRUMAN MEDICAL CENTER–EAST, 7900 Lee's Summit Road, Zip 64139–1241; tel. 816/373–4415; Donald R. Smithburg, Administrator (Total facility includes 212 beds in nursing home–type unit) **A**3 5 7 9 10 **F**3 7 8 10 11 12 13 14 15 16 17 18 19 20 21 22 25 26 27 29 30 31 32 34 35 37 38 39 40 41 42 44 45 46 47 48 49 51 52 53 54 55 56 57 58 59 61 64 65 66 70 71 73 74 **S** Truman Medical Center, Kansas City, MO	23	10	302	3800	241	99831	761	45385	21229	745
✠ TRUMAN MEDICAL CENTER–WEST, 2301 Holmes Street, Zip 64108–2677; tel. 816/556–3000; Rosa L. Miller, R.N., Administrator (Total facility includes 18 beds in nursing home–type unit) **A**1 2 3 5 8 9 10 **F**3 4 7 8 10 14 16 17 19 20 21 22 26 27 28 29 31 34 35 37 38 40 41 42 43 44 45 46 48 49 51 53 54 55 56 57 58 59 60 61 63 64 65 66 70 71 73 74 **P**6 7 **S** Truman Medical Center, Kansas City, MO	23	10	237	11154	184	249619	1867	113164	56011	—

Hospital, Address, Telephone, Administrator, Approval, Facility, and Physician Codes, Health Care System, Network	Classi-fication Codes		Utilization Data					Expense (thousands) of dollars		
	Control	Service	Staffed Beds	Admissions	Census	Outpatient Visits	Births	Total	Payroll	Personnel

★ American Hospital Association (AHA) membership
□ Joint Commission on Accreditation of Healthcare Organizations (JCAHO) accreditation
+ American Osteopathic Healthcare Association (AOHA) membership
○ American Osteopathic Association (AOA) accreditation
△ Commission on Accreditation of Rehabilitation Facilities (CARF) accreditation
Control codes 61, 63, 64, 71, 72 and 73 indicate hospitals listed by AOHA, but not registered by AHA. For definition of numerical codes, see page A4

Hospital	Control	Service	Staffed Beds	Admissions	Census	Outpatient Visits	Births	Total	Payroll	Personnel
□ TWO RIVERS PSYCHIATRIC HOSPITAL, 5121 Raytown Road, Zip 64133–2141; tel. 816/356–5688; Richard Failla, Chief Executive Officer **A**1 10 **F**12 14 16 17 18 26 27 29 39 41 45 46 52 53 54 55 56 57 59 65 67 **S** Universal Health Services, Inc., King of Prussia, PA	33	22	80	1171	36	0	0	8020	3323	115
□ VALUEMARK BEHAVIORAL HEALTHCARE SYSTEM OF KANSAS CITY, 4800 N.W. 88th Street, Zip 64154–2757; tel. 816/436–3900; John Hunter, Chief Executive Officer **A**1 10 **F**12 15 16 17 18 19 26 27 29 32 34 35 39 41 52 53 54 55 56 57 58 59 65 67 **S** ValueMark Healthcare Systems, Inc., Atlanta, GA	33	22	72	580	18	0	0	3760	2257	75
□ VENCOR HOSPITAL–KANSAS CITY, (VENTROLATOR LONG TERM CARE), 8701 Troost Avenue, Zip 64131–3495; tel. 816/995–2000; Suzanne R. Wilsey, Administrator (Total facility includes 16 beds in nursing home–type unit) **A**1 10 **F**12 14 16 19 21 22 27 29 33 34 35 37 39 41 42 45 46 49 50 52 57 60 63 64 65 67 71 73 **P**5 **S** Vencor, Incorporated, Louisville, KY	33	49	110	505	62	274	0	—	—	521
✶ VETERANS AFFAIRS MEDICAL CENTER, 4801 Linwood Boulevard, Zip 64128–2295; tel. 816/861–4700; Hugh F. Doran, Director **A**1 2 3 5 8 9 **F**1 2 3 4 6 8 9 10 11 12 16 17 18 19 20 21 22 23 26 28 29 30 31 32 33 34 35 37 39 41 42 43 44 45 46 48 49 51 52 54 55 56 57 58 59 60 63 64 65 67 71 73 74 **S** Department of Veterans Affairs, Washington, DC	45	10	165	5137	150	199304	0	—	65060	1106
□ WESTERN MISSOURI MENTAL HEALTH CENTER, 600 East 22nd Street, Zip 64108–2675; tel. 816/512–4000; Gloria Joseph, Superintendent **A**1 3 5 10 **F**2 3 6 15 18 19 21 22 24 27 29 35 39 45 46 52 53 54 55 56 57 58 63 65 67 71 73 **P**6	12	22	110	2429	81	7932	0	24162	16950	682
KENNETT—Dunklin County										
✶ TWIN RIVERS REGIONAL MEDICAL CENTER, 1301 First Street, Zip 63857–2508; tel. 573/888–4522; John W. Sanders, Chief Executive Officer **A**1 9 10 **F**7 8 11 12 13 14 15 16 17 19 21 22 23 24 25 27 28 29 30 32 33 34 35 37 40 41 42 44 48 49 52 53 56 65 66 71 73 **P**7 **S** TENET Healthcare Corporation, Santa Barbara, CA	33	10	118	3094	36	105660	332	25219	10086	374
KIRKSVILLE—Adair County										
□ + ○ NORTHEAST REGIONAL MEDICAL CENTER–JEFFERSON CAMPUS, (Formerly Kirksville Osteopatic Medical Center), (Includes Northeast Regional Medical Center–Patterson Campus, 112 East Patterson Avenue, tel. 660/785–1000), 315 South Osteopathy, Zip 63501–8599, Mailing Address: P.O. Box C8502, Zip 63501–8599; tel. 660/785–1100; Charles M. Boughton, Chief Executive Officer (Total facility includes 14 beds in nursing home–type unit) **A**1 9 10 11 12 13 **F**4 5 7 8 10 12 14 15 16 17 18 19 20 21 22 24 28 29 30 31 32 34 35 37 39 40 41 42 44 45 46 48 49 54 63 64 65 66 67 70 71 **P**5	33	10	164	4795	52	120692	538	39797	17761	715
LAKE SAINT LOUIS—St. Charles County										
★ ST. JOSEPH HOSPITAL WEST, 100 Medical Plaza, Zip 63367–1395; tel. 314/625–5200; Kevin F. Kast, President (Total facility includes 11 beds in nursing home–type unit) **A**9 10 **F**3 4 5 7 8 10 11 12 13 14 15 16 17 18 19 20 21 22 23 24 25 26 28 29 30 31 32 33 34 35 37 39 40 41 42 43 44 46 49 51 53 54 55 56 57 58 59 60 61 63 64 65 66 67 68 69 70 71 72 73 74 **P**1 2 4 6 7 **S** SSM Health Care System, Saint Louis, MO **N** SSM Health Care – Saint Louis, St. Louis, MO	23	10	100	2673	29	19797	438	20278	10046	197
LAMAR—Barton County										
★ BARTON COUNTY MEMORIAL HOSPITAL, Second and Gulf Streets, Zip 64759–0626; tel. 417/682–6081; Ronald Morton, Chief Executive Officer **A**9 10 **F**7 8 11 14 15 16 19 20 21 22 28 29 30 32 34 37 39 40 41 44 48 49 64 65 71	13	10	42	1180	16	25829	93	7742	3121	127
LEBANON—Laclede County										
✶ BREECH MEDICAL CENTER, 325 Harwood Avenue, Zip 65536–2317, Mailing Address: P.O. Box N., Zip 65536–2317; tel. 417/532–2136; Gary W. Pulsipher, Chief Executive Officer **A**1 9 10 **F**7 8 17 18 19 20 21 22 27 28 29 30 32 33 34 35 37 39 40 41 44 46 49 64 65 71 73 **S** Sisters of Mercy Health System–St. Louis, Saint Louis, MO	23	10	35	1683	16	21576	277	15883	6524	207
LEES SUMMIT—Jackson County										
✶ LEE'S SUMMIT HOSPITAL, 530 North Murray Road, Zip 64081–1497; tel. 816/251–7000; John L. Jacobson, President and Chief Executive Officer **A**1 9 10 **F**2 3 4 5 7 8 9 10 11 12 14 15 17 18 19 21 22 23 24 25 26 27 28 29 30 32 33 34 35 36 37 38 39 41 42 43 44 45 46 47 48 49 52 53 54 55 56 57 58 59 60 61 63 64 65 66 67 69 71 72 73 74 **P**4 5 7 8 **S** Health Midwest, Kansas City, MO **N** Health Midwest, Kansas City, MO	23	10	86	3098	38	52537	0	25278	11056	346
LEXINGTON—Lafayette County										
✶ LAFAYETTE REGIONAL HEALTH CENTER, 1500 State Street, Zip 64067–1199; tel. 660/259–2203; Jeffrey S. Tarrant, Administrator **A**1 9 10 **F**7 8 12 16 19 22 25 29 30 32 33 34 37 39 40 41 42 44 45 46 49 51 65 71 73 74 **P**4 **S** Health Midwest, Kansas City, MO **N** Health Midwest, Kansas City, MO	23	10	37	1713	20	34695	72	12432	4851	161
LIBERTY—Clay County										
✶ LIBERTY HOSPITAL, 2525 Glenn Hendren Drive, Zip 64069–1002, Mailing Address: P.O. Box 1002, Zip 64069–1002; tel. 816/792–7200; Joseph W. Crossett, Administrator (Total facility includes 20 beds in nursing home–type unit) **A**1 9 10 **F**5 7 8 10 15 16 17 19 21 22 23 26 27 28 29 30 32 33 34 35 36 37 38 39 40 41 42 44 48 49 60 64 65 67 70 71 73 **P**5	16	10	167	7540	109	65553	889	58721	25343	859
LOUISIANA—Pike County										
✶ PIKE COUNTY MEMORIAL HOSPITAL, 2305 West Georgia Street, Zip 63353–0020; tel. 573/754–5531; Pamm Hancock, Interim Administrator **A**1 9 10 **F**7 8 14 15 16 19 22 27 28 29 30 34 35 39 40 44 49 65 67 71 73 **P**8 **S** SSM Health Care System, Saint Louis, MO **N** SSM Health Care – Saint Louis, St. Louis, MO	13	10	25	844	8	22507	82	7556	3575	127

Hospital, Address, Telephone, Administrator, Approval, Facility, and Physician Codes, Health Care System, Network	Classi-fication Codes		Utilization Data					Expense (thousands) of dollars		
★ American Hospital Association (AHA) membership □ Joint Commission on Accreditation of Healthcare Organizations (JCAHO) accreditation + American Osteopathic Healthcare Association (AOHA) membership ○ American Osteopathic Association (AOA) accreditation △ Commission on Accreditation of Rehabilitation Facilities (CARF) accreditation Control codes 61, 63, 64, 71, 72 and 73 indicate hospitals listed by AOHA, but not registered by AHA. For definition of numerical codes, see page A4	Control	Service	Staffed Beds	Admissions	Census	Outpatient Visits	Births	Total	Payroll	Personnel

MACON—Macon County

SAMARITAN MEMORIAL HOSPITAL, 1205 North Jackson Street, Zip 63552; tel. 816/385-3151; Bernard A. Orman, Jr., Administrator **A**9 10 **F**3 5 7 8 12 14 15 16 17 18 19 22 24 26 27 28 29 30 31 32 33 34 39 40 41 42 44 45 49 51 52 56 57 59 65 66 67 71 74 **P**3 — 13 10 | 28 | 950 | 15 | 20695 | 67 | 8525 | 3506 | 161

MARSHALL—Saline County

★ FITZGIBBON HOSPITAL, 2305 South 65 Highway, Zip 65340-0250, Mailing Address: P.O. Box 250, Zip 65340-0250; tel. 660/886-7431; Ronald A. Ott, Chief Executive Officer (Total facility includes 13 beds in nursing home–type unit) **A**9 10 **F**7 8 15 16 17 19 21 22 24 27 28 29 30 32 33 34 35 37 39 40 41 44 46 49 53 54 57 58 59 64 65 66 67 71 73 74 **P**6 — 23 10 | 56 | 1953 | 26 | 82774 | 286 | 22590 | 10066 | 351

MARYVILLE—Nodaway County

✖ ST. FRANCIS HOSPITAL AND HEALTH SERVICES, 2016 South Main Street, Zip 64468-2693; tel. 660/562-2600; Michael Baumgartner, President **A**1 9 10 **F**7 8 12 15 16 18 19 20 21 22 27 28 29 30 31 32 33 34 35 39 40 42 44 49 51 52 54 55 56 57 58 59 64 65 67 71 73 **P**5 6 7 8 **S** SSM Health Care System, Saint Louis, MO — 23 10 | 54 | 1905 | 21 | 63758 | 276 | 14361 | 7244 | 311

MEMPHIS—Scotland County

○ SCOTLAND COUNTY MEMORIAL HOSPITAL, Sigler Avenue, Zip 63555, Mailing Address: Route 1, Box 53, Zip 63555; tel. 660/465-8511; Marcia R. Dial, Administrator **A**9 10 11 **F**5 7 8 12 13 14 15 16 17 18 19 20 22 25 26 28 29 30 32 33 34 37 39 40 41 42 44 45 46 48 49 51 64 65 66 67 71 74 **P**8 — 16 10 | 32 | 450 | 6 | 11876 | 37 | 3378 | 1417 | 87

MEXICO—Audrain County

✖ AUDRAIN MEDICAL CENTER, 620 East Monroe Street, Zip 65265-0858; tel. 573/581-1760; Charles P. Jansen, Administrator (Total facility includes 40 beds in nursing home–type unit) **A**1 9 10 **F**3 7 8 10 12 13 14 15 16 17 18 19 20 21 22 23 25 26 27 28 29 30 32 33 34 35 37 39 40 41 42 44 45 46 49 51 52 53 54 55 56 57 58 63 64 65 66 67 68 71 73 74 **P**2 — 23 10 | 154 | 4845 | 91 | 149414 | 246 | 47262 | 20772 | 653

MILAN—Sullivan County

★ ○ SULLIVAN COUNTY MEMORIAL HOSPITAL, 630 West Third Street, Zip 63556-1098; tel. 660/265-4212; Martha Gragg, Chief Executive Officer (Total facility includes 12 beds in nursing home–type unit) **A**10 11 **F**12 13 15 16 17 19 20 22 24 28 29 30 34 36 39 41 44 49 51 64 65 71 — 13 10 | 38 | 211 | 24 | 16658 | 0 | 2977 | 1520 | 82

MOBERLY—Randolph County

✖ MOBERLY REGIONAL MEDICAL CENTER, 1515 Union Avenue, Zip 65270-9449, Mailing Address: P.O. Box 3000, Zip 65270-3000; tel. 816/263-8400; Daniel E. McKay, Chief Executive Officer (Total facility includes 21 beds in nursing home–type unit) **A**1 9 10 **F**1 7 8 10 11 12 14 15 16 17 18 19 20 21 22 24 26 27 28 29 30 32 33 34 37 39 40 41 44 45 46 49 51 52 54 57 59 63 64 65 66 67 68 70 71 72 73 74 **S** Community Health Systems, Inc., Brentwood, TN — 33 10 | 93 | 3184 | 39 | 40937 | 291 | 19930 | 7097 | 259

MONETT—Barry County

COX–MONETT HOSPITAL, 801 Lincoln Avenue, Zip 65708-1698; tel. 417/235-3144; John Mentgen, Interim Administrator **A**9 10 **F**8 12 14 15 16 17 19 22 26 27 28 29 30 31 32 33 34 37 39 41 44 45 46 49 51 64 65 67 71 73 **P**1 3 — 23 10 | 53 | 1069 | 14 | 13602 | 0 | 7931 | 3745 | 184

MOUNT VERNON—Lawrence County

□ △ MISSOURI REHABILITATION CENTER, 600 North Main, Zip 65712-1099; tel. 417/466-3711; Charles A. Drewel, Director **A**1 7 10 **F**3 6 19 21 26 27 29 30 31 33 34 37 39 41 42 46 48 49 51 64 65 67 71 73 **P**6 — 12 10 | 136 | 517 | 71 | 23074 | 0 | 19935 | 11339 | 387

MOUNTAIN VIEW—Howell County

✖ ST. FRANCIS HOSPITAL, Highway 60, Zip 65548, Mailing Address: P.O. Box 82, Zip 65548-0082; tel. 417/934-2246; Sister M. Cornelia Blasko, Administrator **A**1 9 10 **F**8 14 15 16 19 22 29 32 33 34 39 49 64 65 70 71 72 **P**5 — 23 10 | 20 | 427 | 5 | 18762 | 0 | 3651 | 1531 | 79

NEOSHO—Newton County

FREEMAN NEOSHO HOSPITAL, 113 West Hickory Street, Zip 64850-1799; tel. 417/455-4352; Phil Willcoxon, Administrator **A**9 10 **F**2 3 4 5 7 8 9 10 11 12 13 17 19 20 21 22 26 27 28 29 30 31 32 33 34 35 37 38 39 40 41 42 43 44 45 46 47 48 49 51 52 53 54 55 56 57 58 59 60 61 63 64 65 66 70 71 72 73 74 **P**1 4 7 — 23 10 | 54 | 1888 | 31 | 37071 | 0 | 16379 | 4906 | 220

NEVADA—Vernon County

□ HEARTLAND BEHAVIORAL HEALTH SERVICES, 1500 West Ashland Street, Zip 64772-1710; tel. 417/667-2666; Ed Goosman, Chief Executive Officer **A**1 10 **F**26 29 52 53 54 55 56 57 59 65 **P**8 **S** Ramsay Health Care, Inc., Coral Gables, FL — 33 22 | 60 | 488 | 19 | — | 0 | 7968 | 3331 | 38

✖ NEVADA REGIONAL MEDICAL CENTER, 800 South Ash Street, Zip 64772-3223; tel. 417/667-3355; Michael L. Mullins, President (Total facility includes 10 beds in nursing home–type unit) **A**1 9 10 **F**7 8 14 15 17 19 22 25 27 28 29 30 31 32 33 34 35 36 37 39 40 41 44 46 49 64 65 71 73 **S** Quorum Health Group/Quorum Health Resources, Inc., Brentwood, TN — 14 10 | 97 | 2466 | 32 | 32166 | 347 | 16950 | 6822 | 277

NORTH KANSAS CITY—Clay County

✖ NORTH KANSAS CITY HOSPITAL, 2800 Clay Edwards Drive, Zip 64116-3281; tel. 816/691-2000; Nettie L. Agnew, R.N., Interim President and Chief Executive Officer (Total facility includes 39 beds in nursing home–type unit) **A**1 9 10 **F**2 3 4 7 8 9 10 11 12 14 15 16 17 18 19 20 21 22 23 28 29 30 32 33 34 35 36 37 38 39 40 41 42 43 44 46 47 48 49 52 54 55 56 57 58 59 60 63 64 65 67 70 71 72 73 **P**6 — 14 10 | 350 | 14196 | 241 | 82719 | 1499 | 126367 | 52684 | 1528

Hospital, Address, Telephone, Administrator, Approval, Facility, and Physician Codes, Health Care System, Network	Classification Codes		Utilization Data					Expense (thousands) of dollars		
	Control	Service	Staffed Beds	Admissions	Census	Outpatient Visits	Births	Total	Payroll	Personnel

★ American Hospital Association (AHA) membership
☐ Joint Commission on Accreditation of Healthcare Organizations (JCAHO) accreditation
+ American Osteopathic Healthcare Association (AOHA) membership
○ American Osteopathic Association (AOA) accreditation
△ Commission on Accreditation of Rehabilitation Facilities (CARF) accreditation
Control codes 61, 63, 64, 71, 72 and 73 indicate hospitals listed by AOHA, but not registered by AHA. For definition of numerical codes, see page A4

OSAGE BEACH—Camden County

★ LAKE OF THE OZARKS GENERAL HOSPITAL, 54 Hospital Drive, Zip 65065–9699; tel. 573/348–8000; Michael E. Henze, Chief Executive Officer (Total facility includes 12 beds in nursing home–type unit) **A**1 9 10 **F**4 7 8 10 12 14 15 16 17 19 20 21 22 23 28 29 30 32 33 34 35 37 39 40 41 42 43 44 45 46 49 63 64 65 66 67 71 73 74 **P**6

| | 23 | 10 | 96 | 3559 | 44 | 51671 | 569 | 38420 | 14810 | 569 |

OSCEOLA—St. Clair County

★ SAC–OSAGE HOSPITAL, Junction Highways 13 & Business 13, Zip 64776, Mailing Address: P.O. Box 426, Zip 64776–0426; tel. 417/646–8181; Terry E. Erwine, Administrator **A**1 9 10 **F**7 8 15 16 19 22 28 29 30 31 34 37 39 40 41 42 44 45 46 49 64 65 67 71 73

| | 16 | 10 | 47 | 1347 | 22 | 5669 | 47 | 5507 | 2745 | 116 |

PERRYVILLE—Perry County

☐ PERRY COUNTY MEMORIAL HOSPITAL, 434 North West Street, Zip 63775–1398; tel. 314/547–2536; Patrick E. Carron, CHE, Administrator **A**1 9 10 **F**1 7 8 12 14 15 16 17 18 19 22 23 24 25 26 27 28 29 30 32 33 34 35 39 40 41 42 44 49 53 58 63 64 65 66 67 68 71 72 73

| | 13 | 10 | 47 | 961 | 12 | 27896 | 176 | 11972 | 4905 | 217 |

PILOT KNOB—Iron County

★ ARCADIA VALLEY HOSPITAL, Highway 21, Zip 63663, Mailing Address: P.O. Box 548, Zip 63663–0548; tel. 573/546–3924; H. Clark Duncan, Administrator (Total facility includes 24 beds in nursing home–type unit) **A**1 9 10 **F**8 12 15 16 17 19 22 25 26 28 29 30 31 32 33 34 35 37 39 41 44 46 49 64 65 67 71 73 **P**8 **S** SSM Health Care System, Saint Louis, MO **N** SSM Health Care – Saint Louis, St. Louis, MO

| | 23 | 10 | 50 | 753 | 34 | 22533 | 0 | 8311 | 4010 | 149 |

POPLAR BLUFF—Butler County

☐ △ DOCTORS REGIONAL MEDICAL CENTER, 621 Pine Boulevard, Zip 63901; tel. 573/686–4111; Daniel R. Kelly, Chief Executive Officer (Total facility includes 10 beds in nursing home–type unit) **A**1 2 7 9 10 **F**2 3 7 8 12 14 15 16 17 18 19 20 21 22 23 24 25 28 29 30 31 32 33 34 35 37 39 40 41 42 44 45 48 49 51 52 53 54 55 56 57 58 59 64 65 66 67 71 72 73 74

| | 33 | 10 | 186 | 5592 | 77 | 10123 | 416 | 39136 | 13148 | 583 |

★ JOHN J. PERSHING VETERANS AFFAIRS MEDICAL CENTER, 1500 North Westwood Boulevard, Zip 63901–3318; tel. 573/686–4151; Nancy Arnold, Acting Director (Total facility includes 46 beds in nursing home–type unit) **A**1 9 **F**1 2 3 8 12 15 16 17 19 20 21 22 25 26 27 28 29 30 31 32 34 37 39 41 44 45 46 49 51 52 54 56 57 58 59 64 65 71 72 73 74 **P**6 **S** Department of Veterans Affairs, Washington, DC

| | 45 | 10 | 62 | 1256 | 59 | 68886 | 0 | 29581 | 13762 | 330 |

★ LUCY LEE HOSPITAL, 2620 North Westwood Boulevard, Zip 63901–2341, Mailing Address: P.O. Box 88, Zip 63901–2341; tel. 573/785–7721; Brian T. Flynn, Chief Executive Officer (Total facility includes 24 beds in nursing home–type unit) **A**1 2 10 **F**5 7 8 11 12 15 17 19 20 21 22 24 25 26 28 29 30 31 32 33 34 35 37 39 40 41 42 44 45 46 48 49 52 53 54 55 56 57 58 59 60 61 64 65 66 67 71 72 73 74 **P**1 7 **S** TENET Healthcare Corporation, Santa Barbara, CA

| | 33 | 10 | 185 | 7047 | 103 | 166352 | 1073 | 46537 | 15947 | 872 |

POTOSI—Washington County

WASHINGTON COUNTY MEMORIAL HOSPITAL, 300 Health Way, Zip 63664–1499; tel. 573/438–5451; William L. Schwarten, Administrator **A**9 10 **F**8 14 15 16 19 22 25 28 29 30 32 34 35 37 39 41 44 46 49 65 67 69 71 73 74

| | 13 | 10 | 42 | 482 | 6 | 25404 | 0 | 7866 | 3317 | 166 |

RICHMOND—Ray County

RAY COUNTY MEMORIAL HOSPITAL, 904 Wollard Boulevard, Zip 64085–2243; tel. 816/776–5432; Tommy L. Hicks, Administrator (Total facility includes 11 beds in nursing home–type unit) **A**9 10 **F**8 15 16 19 22 29 30 32 33 35 37 39 41 42 44 49 64 65 71 73

| | 13 | 10 | 50 | 1455 | 23 | 7496 | 0 | 9892 | 4717 | 154 |

ROLLA—Phelps County

★ ○ △ PHELPS COUNTY REGIONAL MEDICAL CENTER, 1000 West Tenth Street, Zip 65401–2905; tel. 573/364–3100; David Ross, Chief Executive Officer (Total facility includes 32 beds in nursing home–type unit) **A**1 7 9 10 11 12 **F**1 2 3 7 8 10 12 14 15 16 17 18 19 21 22 23 28 29 30 31 32 33 34 35 37 39 40 41 42 44 48 49 52 53 54 55 56 57 58 59 60 63 64 65 66 67 70 71 72 73 74 **P**3

| | 13 | 10 | 227 | 7294 | 113 | 46749 | 815 | 51736 | 20211 | 676 |

SAINT CHARLES—St. Charles County

☐ BHC SPIRIT OF ST. LOUIS HOSPITAL, 5931 Highway 94 South, Zip 63304–5601; tel. 314/441–7300; Gary L. Henry, Ph.D., Chief Executive Officer (Nonreporting) **A**1 9 10 **S** Behavioral Healthcare Corporation, Nashville, TN

| | 33 | 22 | 75 | — | — | — | — | — | — | — |

★ ST. JOSEPH HEALTH CENTER, 300 First Capitol Drive, Zip 63301–2835; tel. 314/947–5000; Kevin F. Kast, President (Total facility includes 19 beds in nursing home–type unit) **A**1 2 9 10 **F**1 2 3 4 5 6 7 8 9 10 11 12 13 14 15 16 17 18 19 20 21 22 23 24 25 26 28 29 30 31 32 33 34 35 37 38 39 40 41 42 43 44 46 47 48 49 51 52 53 54 55 56 57 58 59 60 61 63 64 65 66 67 68 69 70 71 72 73 74 **P**1 7 8 **S** SSM Health Care System, Saint Louis, MO **N** SSM Health Care – Saint Louis, St. Louis, MO; Carondelet Health, Kansas City, MO

| | 23 | 10 | 176 | 10218 | 138 | 43554 | 883 | 78973 | 35509 | 1010 |

SAINT JOSEPH—Buchanan County

★ △ HEARTLAND REGIONAL MEDICAL CENTER, (Includes Heartland Hospital East, 5325 Faraon Street, Zip 64506; Heartland Hospital West, 801 Faraon Street, Zip 64501; tel. 816/271–7111), 5325 Faraon Street, Zip 64506–3398; tel. 816/271–6000; Lowell C. Kruse, Chief Executive Officer (Total facility includes 210 beds in nursing home–type unit) **A**1 2 5 7 9 10 **F**4 5 7 8 10 11 12 14 15 16 17 18 19 21 22 24 25 27 28 30 31 33 34 37 39 40 41 42 43 44 45 46 48 49 51 52 54 55 56 57 60 64 65 66 70 71 73 74 **P**6 **N** Northwest Missouri Healthcare Agenda, Albany, MO

| | 23 | 10 | 494 | 15927 | 374 | 323687 | 1513 | 154257 | 67065 | — |

Hospital, Address, Telephone, Administrator, Approval, Facility, and Physician Codes, Health Care System, Network	Classi-fication Codes		Utilization Data					Expense (thousands) of dollars		
★ American Hospital Association (AHA) membership □ Joint Commission on Accreditation of Healthcare Organizations (JCAHO) accreditation + American Osteopathic Healthcare Association (AOHA) membership ○ American Osteopathic Association (AOA) accreditation △ Commission on Accreditation of Rehabilitation Facilities (CARF) accreditation Control codes 61, 63, 64, 71, 72 and 73 indicate hospitals listed by AOHA, but not registered by AHA. For definition of numerical codes, see page A4	Control	Service	Staffed Beds	Admissions	Census	Outpatient Visits	Births	Total	Payroll	Personnel

	Control	Service	Staffed Beds	Admissions	Census	Outpatient Visits	Births	Total	Payroll	Personnel
□ NORTHWEST MISSOURI PSYCHIATRIC REHABILITATION CENTER, (Formerly St. Joseph State Hospital), 3505 Frederick Avenue, Zip 64506; tel. 816/387–2300; Ron Dittemore, Ed.D., Superintendent **A**1 10 **F**15 29 52 53 54 55 56 64 65	12	22	108	191	114	60	0	17435	10610	410
SAINT LOUIS—St. Louis County										
⊞ ALEXIAN BROTHERS HOSPITAL, 3933 South Broadway, Zip 63118–9984; tel. 314/865–3333; Glenn Appelbaum, Senior Vice President (Total facility includes 40 beds in nursing home–type unit) **A**1 9 10 **F**2 3 4 5 7 8 9 10 11 12 13 14 15 16 17 18 19 21 22 25 26 27 28 29 30 31 32 33 34 35 36 37 38 39 40 41 42 43 44 45 46 47 48 49 51 52 53 54 55 56 57 58 59 60 63 64 65 66 67 70 71 72 73 74 **P**5 6 7 8 **S** Sisters of Mercy Health System–St. Louis, Saint Louis, MO **N** Unity Health System, St. Louis, MO	23	10	203	5243	91	39757	0	40509	18722	648
⊞ △ BARNES–JEWISH HOSPITAL, One Barnes–Jewish Hospital Plaza, Zip 63110–1094; tel. 314/362–5400; Peter L. Slavin, M.D., President **A**1 2 3 5 6 7 8 9 10 **F**2 3 4 5 7 8 9 10 11 12 13 14 15 16 17 18 19 20 21 22 23 24 25 26 27 28 29 30 31 32 33 34 35 36 37 38 39 40 41 42 43 44 45 46 47 48 49 50 51 52 53 54 55 56 57 58 59 60 61 62 63 64 65 66 67 68 69 70 71 72 73 74 **P**1 3 4 5 6 7 **S** BJC Health System, Saint Louis, MO **N** BJC Health System, St. Louis, MO	23	10	974	47759	766	287185	3878	656756	279447	8308
⊞ BARNES–JEWISH WEST COUNTY HOSPITAL, 12634 Olive Boulevard, Zip 63141–6354; tel. 314/996–8000; Gregory T. Wozniak, President (Total facility includes 10 beds in nursing home–type unit) **A**1 9 10 **F**1 2 3 4 5 6 7 8 9 10 11 12 13 14 15 16 17 18 19 20 21 22 23 24 25 26 27 28 29 30 31 32 33 34 35 36 37 38 39 40 41 42 43 44 45 46 47 48 49 50 51 52 53 54 55 56 57 58 59 60 61 62 63 64 65 66 67 68 69 70 71 72 73 74 **P**1 5 6 7 8 **S** BJC Health System, Saint Louis, MO **N** BJC Health System, St. Louis, MO	23	10	91	2772	41	34681	0	31705	8896	271
⊞ △ BETHESDA GENERAL HOSPITAL, 3655 Vista Avenue, Zip 63110–2594; tel. 314/772–9200; Joseph J. Brinker, Interim President (Total facility includes 28 beds in nursing home–type unit) **A**1 5 7 9 10 **F**1 4 6 8 10 12 14 17 19 21 22 23 26 27 28 29 30 32 33 34 35 36 37 39 41 42 44 46 48 49 50 52 54 55 56 57 58 59 60 62 63 64 65 67 71 73	23	10	118	810	35	1227	0	14769	6165	185
⊞ CARDINAL GLENNON CHILDREN'S HOSPITAL, 1465 South Grand Boulevard, Zip 63104–1095; tel. 314/577–5600; Douglas A. Ries, President **A**1 3 5 9 10 **F**2 3 4 5 6 9 10 12 13 14 15 16 17 18 19 20 21 22 23 25 27 28 29 30 31 32 33 34 35 38 39 41 42 43 44 45 46 47 48 49 50 51 52 53 54 55 56 58 59 60 63 65 66 67 68 69 70 71 72 73 74 **P**1 6 8 **S** SSM Health Care System, Saint Louis, MO **N** SSM Health Care – Saint Louis, St. Louis, MO	23	50	172	7729	110	150140	0	92873	38471	1150
⊞ △ CHRISTIAN HOSPITAL NORTHEAST–NORTHWEST, (Includes Christian Hospital Northwest, 1225 Graham Road, Florissant, Zip 63031; tel. 314/953–6000), 11133 Dunn Road, Zip 63136–6192; tel. 314/653–5000; W. R. Van Bokkelen, President and Senior Executive Officer (Total facility includes 26 beds in nursing home–type unit) **A**1 2 7 9 10 **F**3 4 7 8 10 11 12 14 15 16 17 18 19 20 21 22 24 26 28 29 30 31 32 33 34 35 36 37 39 41 42 43 44 45 46 48 49 50 51 53 54 55 56 57 58 59 60 61 62 63 64 65 66 67 68 69 70 71 72 73 74 **P**1 6 7 **S** BJC Health System, Saint Louis, MO **N** BJC Health System, St. Louis, MO	23	10	542	21760	332	146155	1822	200515	91800	2639
⊞ △ DEACONESS CENTRAL HOSPITAL, 6150 Oakland Avenue, Zip 63139–3297; tel. 314/768–3000; Glennon K. McFadden, Chief Executive Officer (Total facility includes 10 beds in nursing home–type unit) **A**1 2 3 5 7 9 10 12 **F**1 2 3 4 7 8 10 11 14 15 16 17 19 21 22 23 26 27 29 30 32 33 34 35 36 37 40 41 42 43 44 48 49 51 52 54 55 56 57 58 59 60 62 63 64 65 66 67 71 72 73 74 **P**1 6 7 8 **S** TENET Healthcare Corporation, Santa Barbara, CA	33	10	324	11747	185	89556	1924	128245	59196	1678
★ + ○ DEACONESS WEST HOSPITAL, (Formerly Deaconess Medical Center), (Includes Metropolitan Medical Center–West), 2345 Dougherty Ferry Road, Zip 63122–3313; tel. 314/768–3000; Joan D'Ambrose, Chief Executive Officer **A**9 10 11 12 13 **F**2 3 4 5 7 8 9 10 12 13 14 15 16 17 18 19 21 22 25 26 27 29 31 32 33 34 35 36 37 39 40 41 42 43 44 48 49 51 52 54 55 56 57 58 59 60 61 62 63 64 65 66 67 69 71 72 73 74 **P**6 7 8 **S** TENET Healthcare Corporation, Santa Barbara, CA	33	10	96	3045	46	27876	0	40700	16010	368
⊞ DEPAUL HEALTH CENTER, (Includes ST. ANNE'S SKILLED NURSING DIVISION; DePaul Hospital, Bridgeton, ; St. Vincent's Psychiatric Division, Bridgeton), 12303 DePaul Drive, Zip 63044–2588; tel. 314/344–6000; Robert G. Porter, President (Total facility includes 60 beds in nursing home–type unit) **A**1 2 9 10 **F**2 3 4 7 8 9 10 11 12 13 14 15 16 17 18 19 20 21 22 23 24 25 27 28 29 30 31 32 33 34 35 36 37 38 39 40 41 42 43 44 45 46 47 48 49 51 52 53 54 55 56 57 58 59 60 63 64 65 66 67 68 69 70 71 73 74 **P**1 3 4 6 **S** SSM Health Care System, Saint Louis, MO **N** SSM Health Care – Saint Louis, St. Louis, MO	21	10	282	11662	192	108246	912	106888	45768	1174
INCARNATE WORD HOSPITAL See Lafayette–Grand Hospital										
⊞ △ LAFAYETTE–GRAND HOSPITAL, (Formerly Incarnate Word Hospital), 3545 Lafayette Avenue, Zip 63104–9984; tel. 314/865–6500; Doug Doris, President and Chief Executive Officer **A**1 7 9 10 **F**8 10 12 14 15 16 17 19 21 22 26 27 28 29 30 32 33 34 35 37 42 44 48 49 52 56 57 58 59 62 64 65 71 73 **P**2 3 4 5 6 7 8 **S** TENET Healthcare Corporation, Santa Barbara, CA	33	10	214	4673	116	30707	0	42649	21638	795
⊞ LUTHERAN MEDICAL CENTER, 2639 Miami Street, Zip 63118–3999; tel. 314/772–1456; Clifford A. Yeager, Chief Executive Officer (Total facility includes 30 beds in nursing home–type unit) **A**1 6 9 10 **F**2 3 4 7 8 10 12 14 17 18 19 20 21 22 26 27 28 29 30 31 32 33 34 35 37 39 40 41 42 44 45 46 48 49 51 52 53 54 55 56 57 58 59 60 61 63 64 65 66 67 71 73 74 **P**6 **S** TENET Healthcare Corporation, Santa Barbara, CA	33	10	243	5667	127	161912	494	43013	20808	549
METROPOLITAN MEDICAL CENTER–WEST See Deaconess West Hospital										

Hospital, Address, Telephone, Administrator, Approval, Facility, and Physician Codes, Health Care System, Network	Classi-fication Codes		Utilization Data					Expense (thousands) of dollars		
	Control	Service	Staffed Beds	Admissions	Census	Outpatient Visits	Births	Total	Payroll	Personnel

American Hospital Association (AHA) membership
□ Joint Commission on Accreditation of Healthcare Organizations (JCAHO) accreditation
+ American Osteopathic Healthcare Association (AOHA) membership
○ American Osteopathic Association (AOA) accreditation
△ Commission on Accreditation of Rehabilitation Facilities (CARF) accreditation
Control codes 61, 63, 64, 71, 72 and 73 indicate hospitals listed by AOHA, but not registered by AHA. For definition of numerical codes, see page A4

Hospital	Control	Service	Staffed Beds	Admissions	Census	Outpatient Visits	Births	Total	Payroll	Personnel
□ METROPOLITAN ST. LOUIS PSYCHIATRIC CENTER, 5351 Delmar, Zip 63112–3198; tel. 314/877–0500; Gregory L. Dale, Chief Executive Officer **A**1 3 5 10 **F**1 2 3 6 12 17 18 20 22 29 35 39 41 45 46 52 55 56 57 58 59 64 65 73 **P**6	12	22	125	1821	106	5403	0	17972	10360	376
MISSOURI BAPTIST MEDICAL CENTER See Town and Country										
□ SAINT LOUIS UNIVERSITY HOSPITAL, 3635 Vista at Grand Boulevard, Zip 63110–0250, Mailing Address: P.O. Box 15250, Zip 63110–0250; tel. 314/577–8000; James Kimmey, M.D., M.P.H., Chairman and Chief Executive Officer **A**1 3 5 8 9 10 **F**1 4 5 8 10 11 14 15 19 20 21 22 23 26 28 29 30 31 34 35 37 39 41 42 43 44 45 46 49 50 51 52 53 54 55 56 57 58 59 60 61 63 65 67 69 70 71 73 **P**1 2 **S** TENET Healthcare Corporation, Santa Barbara, CA **N**	23	10	303	11688	202	129851	0	173646	72228	2029
⊞ SHRINERS HOSPITALS FOR CHILDREN, ST. LOUIS, 2001 South Lindbergh Boulevard, Zip 63131–3597; tel. 314/432–3600; Carolyn P. Golden, Administrator **A**1 3 5 **F**12 15 19 27 28 29 30 34 35 41 45 46 49 51 53 54 55 58 63 65 66 67 68 71 73 **S** Shriners Hospitals for Children, Tampa, FL	23	57	80	1900	30	12751	0	—	—	243
⊞ △ SSM REHAB, (Formerly SSM Rehabilitation Institute), 6420 Clayton Road, Suite 600, Zip 63117–1861; tel. 314/768–5300; Melinda Clark, President (Total facility includes 20 beds in nursing home–type unit) (Nonreporting) **A**1 7 9 10 **S** SSM Health Care System, Saint Louis, MO **N** SSM Health Care – Saint Louis, St. Louis, MO	21	46	78	—	—	—	—	—	—	—
⊞ ST. ANTHONY'S MEDICAL CENTER, 10010 Kennerly Road, Zip 63128–2185; tel. 314/525–1000; David P. Seifert, President (Total facility includes 96 beds in nursing home–type unit) **A**1 9 10 **F**1 2 3 4 5 7 8 9 10 11 12 13 14 15 16 17 18 19 20 21 22 23 24 25 26 27 28 29 30 31 32 33 34 35 36 37 38 39 40 41 42 43 44 45 46 47 48 49 51 52 53 54 55 56 57 58 59 60 61 63 64 65 66 67 68 69 70 71 72 73 74 **P**6 8 **S** Sisters of Mercy Health System–St. Louis, Saint Louis, MO **N** Unity Health System, St. Louis, MO	23	10	674	25623	424	148482	1250	175065	77232	2224
⊞ △ ST. JOHN'S MERCY MEDICAL CENTER, (Includes St. John's Mercy Hospital, 200 Madison Avenue, Washington, Zip 63090; tel. 314/239–8000), 615 South New Ballas Road, Zip 63141–8277; tel. 314/569–6000; Mark Weber, FACHE, President (Total facility includes 20 beds in nursing home–type unit) **A**1 2 3 5 7 8 9 10 **F**2 3 4 5 7 8 9 10 11 12 13 14 15 16 17 18 19 20 21 22 23 24 25 26 27 28 29 30 31 32 33 34 35 36 37 38 39 41 42 43 44 45 46 47 48 49 51 52 53 54 55 56 57 58 59 60 61 63 64 65 66 67 68 69 70 71 72 73 74 **P**1 2 6 **S** Sisters of Mercy Health System–St. Louis, Saint Louis, MO **N** Unity Health System, St. Louis, MO	23	10	913	36432	436	331051	7346	322805	145741	4258
⊞ ST. JOSEPH HOSPITAL OF KIRKWOOD, 525 Couch Avenue, Zip 63122–5594; tel. 314/966–1500; Carla S. Baum, President (Total facility includes 44 beds in nursing home–type unit) **A**1 2 9 10 **F**2 3 4 5 7 8 9 10 11 12 13 14 15 16 17 18 19 20 21 22 23 26 27 28 29 30 31 32 33 34 35 36 37 38 39 40 41 42 43 44 45 47 48 49 52 53 54 55 56 57 58 59 60 61 63 64 65 66 67 68 69 70 71 72 73 74 **P**1 **S** SSM Health Care System, Saint Louis, MO	23	10	213	6341	95	82330	795	55873	25167	734
⊞ ST. LOUIS CHILDREN'S HOSPITAL, (PEDIATRIC–GENERAL), One Children's Place, Zip 63110–1077; tel. 314/454–6000; Ted W. Frey, President **A**1 3 5 7 8 9 10 **F**2 3 4 5 6 7 8 9 10 11 12 13 14 15 16 17 18 19 20 21 22 23 24 25 26 27 28 29 30 31 32 33 34 35 36 37 38 39 40 41 42 43 44 45 46 47 48 49 50 51 52 53 54 55 56 57 58 59 60 61 62 63 64 65 66 67 68 69 70 71 72 73 74 **P**1 3 6 7 **S** BJC Health System, Saint Louis, MO **N** BJC Health System, St. Louis, MO	23	59	235	10353	149	119390	0	145736	62933	1606
□ ST. LOUIS PSYCHIATRIC REHABILITATION CENTER, (Formerly St. Louis State Hospital), 5300 Arsenal Street, Zip 63139–1494; tel. 314/644–8000; Robert O. Muether, Interim Superintendent **A**1 10 **F**12 20 24 29 30 39 52 54 55 65 73 **P**6	12	22	215	56	211	0	0	26029	15623	589
⊞ ST. MARY'S HEALTH CENTER, 6420 Clayton Road, Zip 63117–1811; tel. 314/768–8000; Michael E. Zilm, President (Total facility includes 50 beds in nursing home–type unit) **A**1 2 3 5 8 9 10 **F**2 3 4 5 7 8 10 11 12 13 14 15 16 17 18 19 20 21 22 23 24 25 26 27 28 29 30 31 32 33 34 35 36 37 38 39 40 41 42 43 44 45 46 47 48 49 51 52 53 54 55 56 57 58 59 60 61 63 64 65 66 67 68 69 71 72 73 74 **P**5 6 8 **S** SSM Health Care System, Saint Louis, MO **N** SSM Health Care – Saint Louis, St. Louis, MO	23	10	411	15240	259	143939	2465	139042	58657	1610
⊞ VETERANS AFFAIRS MEDICAL CENTER, 1 Jefferson Barracks Drive, Zip 63125–4199; tel. 314/652–4100; Linda Kurz, Acting Director (Total facility includes 153 beds in nursing home–type unit) **A**1 2 3 5 **F**2 3 4 5 8 10 12 14 15 16 18 19 21 22 24 26 29 31 32 34 35 37 41 46 49 50 52 54 56 57 58 59 60 63 64 65 69 71 73 **S** Department of Veterans Affairs, Washington, DC	45	10	383	8800	363	344086	0	—	—	2170
SAINT PETERS—St. Charles County										
⊞ BARNES–JEWISH ST. PETERS HOSPITAL, 10 Hospital Drive, Zip 63376–1659; tel. 314/916–9000; Carm Moceri, President (Total facility includes 8 beds in nursing home–type unit) **A**1 9 10 **F**7 8 10 12 14 15 16 17 19 21 22 26 27 28 29 30 31 32 33 34 35 39 40 41 42 44 49 63 64 65 66 67 71 72 73 74 **P**5 6 8 **S** BJC Health System, Saint Louis, MO **N** BJC Health System, St. Louis, MO	23	10	91	4193	43	81050	949	33145	14524	451
SALEM—Dent County										
SALEM MEMORIAL DISTRICT HOSPITAL, Highway 72 North, Zip 65560, Mailing Address: P.O. Box 774, Zip 65560; tel. 573/729–6626; Dennis P. Pryor, Administrator (Total facility includes 18 beds in nursing home–type unit) **A**9 10 **F**7 8 12 14 15 16 19 22 27 28 29 30 32 33 34 39 40 41 44 46 49 64 65 66 71 73	16	10	46	1268	34	16467	108	7882	3336	146

Hospital, Address, Telephone, Administrator, Approval, Facility, and Physician Codes, Health Care System, Network	Classi-fication Codes		Utilization Data					Expense (thousands) of dollars		
★ American Hospital Association (AHA) membership ☐ Joint Commission on Accreditation of Healthcare Organizations (JCAHO) accreditation + American Osteopathic Healthcare Association (AOHA) membership ○ American Osteopathic Association (AOA) accreditation △ Commission on Accreditation of Rehabilitation Facilities (CARF) accreditation Control codes 61, 63, 64, 71, 72 and 73 indicate hospitals listed by AOHA, but not registered by AHA. For definition of numerical codes, see page A4	Control	Service	Staffed Beds	Admissions	Census	Outpatient Visits	Births	Total	Payroll	Personnel

SEDALIA—Pettis County

☒ BOTHWELL REGIONAL HEALTH CENTER, 601 East 14th Street, Zip 65301–1706, Mailing Address: P.O. Box 1706, Zip 65302–1706; tel. 660/826–8833; James T. Rank, Administrator **A**1 9 10 **F**4 7 8 10 11 15 16 19 20 21 22 23 29 30 32 33 34 35 37 39 40 41 42 44 49 52 53 56 57 60 65 66 67 70 71 72 74

| | | 14 | 10 | 147 | 6007 | 80 | 38577 | 655 | 42040 | 19009 | 642 |

SIKESTON—Scott County

☐ MISSOURI DELTA MEDICAL CENTER, 1008 North Main Street, Zip 63801–5099; tel. 573/471–1600; Charles D. Ancell, President (Total facility includes 14 beds in nursing home–type unit) **A**1 9 10 **F**2 3 4 5 6 7 8 10 11 12 15 16 17 18 19 20 21 22 23 24 25 26 27 28 29 30 32 33 34 35 36 37 39 40 41 42 43 44 45 46 48 49 51 52 54 57 58 60 62 63 64 65 66 67 69 71 72 73 74 **P**8

| 23 | 10 | 158 | 5077 | 74 | 94235 | 487 | 34687 | 15668 | 572 |

SMITHVILLE—Clay County

☒ SAINT LUKE'S NORTHLAND HOSPITAL–SMITHVILLE CAMPUS, 601 South 169 Highway, Zip 64089–9334; tel. 816/532–3700; Don Sipes, Senior Executive Officer (Total facility includes 16 beds in nursing home–type unit) **A**1 9 10 **F**2 3 4 5 6 7 8 10 11 12 13 14 15 16 17 18 19 20 21 22 24 25 26 27 28 29 30 31 32 33 34 35 36 37 38 39 40 41 42 43 44 45 46 48 49 50 51 52 53 54 55 56 57 58 59 60 61 63 64 65 66 67 68 69 70 71 72 73 74 **P**6 8 **S** Saint Luke's Shawnee Mission Health System, Kansas City, MO

| 23 | 10 | 50 | 764 | 18 | 3156 | 0 | 11443 | 4630 | 143 |

SPRINGFIELD—Greene County

☒ ○ COLUMBIA HOSPITAL NORTH AND SOUTH, (Includes Columbia Hospital North, 2828 North National Street, Zip 65801, Mailing Address: Box 783, Jewell Station, Zip 65801–0783; tel. 417/869–5571; Columbia Hospital South), 3535 South National Avenue, Zip 65807–7399; tel. 417/882–4700; Michelle Fischer, Chief Executive Officer **A**1 10 11 **F**3 7 8 12 14 15 17 19 22 28 29 30 32 34 37 40 44 46 48 49 52 57 58 59 64 65 67 71 73 **S** Columbia/HCA Healthcare Corporation, Nashville, TN

| 33 | 10 | 150 | 3864 | 71 | 31124 | 274 | 39947 | 16805 | 438 |

☒ △ COX HEALTH SYSTEMS, (Includes Lester E. Cox Medical Center North, 1423 North Jefferson Avenue, Zip 65802; tel. 417/269–3000; Lester E. Cox Medical Center South, 3801 South National Avenue, Zip 65807; tel. 417/269–6000), 1423 North Jefferson Street, Zip 65802–1988; tel. 417/269–3000; Larry D. Wallis, President and Chief Executive Officer (Total facility includes 46 beds in nursing home–type unit) **A**1 2 3 6 7 9 10 **F**3 4 6 7 8 10 11 12 14 15 16 17 18 19 21 22 23 24 26 27 28 29 30 31 32 34 35 36 37 38 39 40 41 42 43 44 46 47 48 49 51 52 53 54 55 56 57 58 59 60 61 63 64 65 66 67 68 70 71 72 73 74 **P**1

| 23 | 10 | 659 | 24801 | 380 | 658025 | 3083 | — | — | 4026 |

☐ LAKELAND REGIONAL HOSPITAL, 440 South Market Street, Zip 65806–2090; tel. 417/865–5581; John William Thompson, Ph.D., President and Chief Executive Officer **A**1 10 **F**12 18 19 22 25 29 34 35 39 46 52 53 54 55 56 58 59 65 67 71 **P**5 6

| 33 | 22 | 94 | 1908 | 78 | 10145 | 0 | — | — | 191 |

☒ △ ST. JOHN'S REGIONAL HEALTH CENTER, 1235 East Cherokee Street, Zip 65804–2263; tel. 417/885–2000; Allen L. Shockley, President and Chief Executive Officer (Total facility includes 52 beds in nursing home–type unit) **A**1 2 6 7 10 **F**2 3 4 5 7 8 9 10 11 12 13 14 15 16 17 18 19 20 21 22 23 24 26 27 28 29 30 32 33 34 35 36 37 38 39 40 41 42 43 44 45 46 47 48 49 51 52 53 54 55 56 57 58 59 60 63 64 65 66 67 68 69 70 71 72 73 74 **P**6 **S** Sisters of Mercy Health System–St. Louis, Saint Louis, MO

| 23 | 10 | 758 | 29038 | 439 | 302594 | 2555 | 234534 | 107822 | 3876 |

☐ U. S. MEDICAL CENTER FOR FEDERAL PRISONERS, 1900 West Sunshine Street, Zip 65807–2240, Mailing Address: P.O. Box 4000, Zip 65808–4000; tel. 417/862–7041; R. H. Rison, Warden (Nonreporting) **A**1

| 48 | 10 | 587 | — | — | — | — | — | — | — |

STE. GENEVIEVE—Ste. Genevieve County

STE. GENEVIEVE COUNTY MEMORIAL HOSPITAL, Highways 61 and 32, Zip 63670–0468; tel. 573/883–2751; Joseph Moss, Administrator **A**9 10 **F**7 8 14 15 17 18 19 20 22 23 24 26 28 29 30 32 33 34 35 37 39 40 41 42 44 45 49 65 67 68 71 73

| 13 | 10 | 34 | 1409 | 19 | 42264 | 73 | 12250 | 5745 | 202 |

SULLIVAN—Crawford County

★ MISSOURI BAPTIST HOSPITAL OF SULLIVAN, 751 Sappington Bridge Road, Zip 63080–2354, Mailing Address: P.O. Box 190, Zip 63080–0190; tel. 573/468–4186; Davis D. Skinner, President (Total facility includes 6 beds in nursing home–type unit) **A**9 10 **F**7 8 12 14 15 16 17 18 19 20 21 22 26 27 28 29 30 31 32 33 34 35 37 39 40 41 42 44 45 46 49 51 56 58 64 65 71 73 **P**5 6 8 **S** BJC Health System, Saint Louis, MO **N** BJC Health System, St. Louis, MO

| 23 | 10 | 60 | 1604 | 19 | 67140 | 187 | 14512 | 6228 | 193 |

TOWN AND COUNTRY—St. Louis County

☒ MISSOURI BAPTIST MEDICAL CENTER, 3015 North Ballas Road, Zip 63131–2374; tel. 314/996–5000; Mark A. Eustis, President **A**1 2 6 9 10 **F**1 2 3 4 5 6 7 8 9 10 11 12 13 14 15 16 17 18 19 20 21 22 23 24 25 26 27 28 29 30 31 32 33 34 35 36 37 38 39 40 41 42 43 44 45 46 47 48 49 50 51 52 53 54 55 56 57 58 59 60 61 62 63 64 65 66 67 68 69 70 71 72 73 74 **P**1 5 6 7 8 **S** BJC Health System, Saint Louis, MO **N** BJC Health System, St. Louis, MO

| 23 | 10 | 360 | 15437 | 219 | 223678 | 2693 | 148878 | 63452 | 1923 |

TRENTON—Grundy County

☐ WRIGHT MEMORIAL HOSPITAL, 701 East First Street, Zip 64683–0648, Mailing Address: P.O. Box 628, Zip 64683–0628; tel. 660/359–5621; Ralph G. Goodrich, Senior Executive Officer **A**9 10 **F**7 8 11 14 15 16 17 19 22 26 27 28 29 30 32 33 34 35 37 39 40 41 42 44 49 51 56 58 64 65 71 73 **P**1 **S** Saint Luke's Shawnee Mission Health System, Kansas City, MO

| 23 | 10 | 48 | 786 | 8 | 22296 | 109 | 8389 | 4100 | 169 |

Hospital, Address, Telephone, Administrator, Approval, Facility, and Physician Codes, Health Care System, Network	Classi-fication Codes		Utilization Data					Expense (thousands) of dollars		

★ American Hospital Association (AHA) membership
□ Joint Commission on Accreditation of Healthcare Organizations (JCAHO) accreditation
+ American Osteopathic Healthcare Association (AOHA) membership
○ American Osteopathic Association (AOA) accreditation
△ Commission on Accreditation of Rehabilitation Facilities (CARF) accreditation
Control codes 61, 63, 64, 71, 72 and 73 indicate hospitals listed by AOHA, but not registered by AHA. For definition of numerical codes, see page A4

	Control	Service	Staffed Beds	Admissions	Census	Outpatient Visits	Births	Total	Payroll	Personnel

TROY—Lincoln County

□ LINCOLN COUNTY MEMORIAL HOSPITAL, 1000 East Cherry Street, Zip 63379–1599; tel. 314/528–8551; Floyd B. Dowell, Jr., Administrator (Total facility includes 8 beds in nursing home–type unit) **A**1 9 10 **F**8 11 12 15 16 17 19 20 21 22 23 25 28 29 30 32 33 34 35 37 39 41 44 45 46 49 64 65 66 67 71 **P**8

| 13 | 10 | 36 | 1573 | 23 | 38306 | 0 | 15046 | 7096 | 215 |

WARRENSBURG—Johnson County

□ WESTERN MISSOURI MEDICAL CENTER, 403 Burkarth Road, Zip 64093–3101; tel. 660/747–2500; Gregory B. Vinardi, President and Chief Executive Officer (Total facility includes 15 beds in nursing home–type unit) **A**1 9 10 **F**7 8 12 13 14 15 16 19 20 21 22 23 24 28 29 30 31 32 33 34 35 36 37 39 40 41 42 44 45 46 61 64 65 66 67 68 71 73 74

| 13 | 10 | 67 | 2398 | 32 | 42507 | 418 | 19325 | 8676 | 304 |

WASHINGTON—Franklin County

ST. JOHN'S MERCY HOSPITAL See St. John's Mercy Medical Center, Saint Louis

WENTZVILLE—St. Charles County

□ DOCTORS HOSPITAL, 500 Medical Drive, Zip 63385–0711; tel. 314/327–1000; Fred Woody, Chief Executive Officer (Total facility includes 27 beds in nursing home–type unit) **A**1 9 10 **F**7 8 12 14 15 16 19 21 22 23 26 28 29 30 32 33 34 35 37 39 40 41 42 44 46 49 52 56 57 63 64 65 67 70 71 72 73 74

| 33 | 10 | 94 | 1515 | 20 | 12920 | 134 | 13097 | 4671 | 152 |

WEST PLAINS—Howell County

⊞ OZARKS MEDICAL CENTER, 1100 Kentucky Avenue, Zip 65775–2029, Mailing Address: P.O. Box 1100, Zip 65775–1100; tel. 417/256–9111; Charles R. Brackney, President and Chief Executive Officer (Total facility includes 16 beds in nursing home–type unit) **A**1 9 10 **F**3 6 7 8 10 12 15 16 18 19 21 22 28 29 30 31 32 33 34 35 37 39 40 42 44 45 46 49 52 53 54 55 56 57 58 60 63 64 65 66 67 71 72 73 74 **P**8

| 23 | 10 | 120 | 5428 | 65 | 17840 | 701 | 46428 | 21775 | 829 |

WHITEMAN AFB—Johnson County

★ U. S. AIR FORCE CLINIC WHITEMAN, (Formerly U.S. Air Force Hospital Whiteman), 331 Sijan Avenue, Zip 65305–5001; tel. 660/687–1194; Lieutenant Colonel David Wilmot, USAF, MSC, Administrator **F**2 4 7 8 9 10 11 12 13 15 16 18 19 20 21 22 23 24 27 28 29 30 31 32 34 35 37 38 39 40 41 42 43 44 46 47 48 49 50 51 52 53 54 55 56 57 58 59 60 61 63 65 66 67 68 69 70 71 72 73 74 **P**1 7 **S** Department of the Air Force, Bowling AFB, DC
U.S. AIR FORCE HOSPITAL WHITEMAN See U. S. Air Force Clinic Whiteman

| 41 | 10 | 20 | 258 | 2 | 66599 | 155 | 17307 | 10982 | 168 |

MONTANA

Resident population 879 (in thousands)
Resident population in metro areas 23.8%
Birth rate per 1,000 population 12.9
65 years and over 13.2%
Percent of persons without health insurance 13.6%

Hospital, Address, Telephone, Administrator, Approval, Facility, and Physician Codes, Health Care System, Network	Classi-fication Codes		Utilization Data					Expense (thousands) of dollars		
	Control	Service	Staffed Beds	Admissions	Census	Outpatient Visits	Births	Total	Payroll	Personnel

★ American Hospital Association (AHA) membership
☐ Joint Commission on Accreditation of Healthcare Organizations (JCAHO) accreditation
＋ American Osteopathic Healthcare Association (AOHA) membership
◯ American Osteopathic Association (AOA) accreditation
△ Commission on Accreditation of Rehabilitation Facilities (CARF) accreditation
Control codes 61, 63, 64, 71, 72 and 73 indicate hospitals listed by AOHA, but not registered by AHA. For definition of numerical codes, see page A4

Hospital	Control	Service	Staffed Beds	Admissions	Census	Outpatient Visits	Births	Total	Payroll	Personnel
ANACONDA—Deer Lodge County										
★ COMMUNITY HOSPITAL OF ANACONDA, 401 West Pennsylvania Street, Zip 59711–1999; tel. 406/563–8500; Sam J. Allen, Administrator (Total facility includes 67 beds in nursing home–type unit) (Nonreporting) **A**9 10 **S** Quorum Health Group/Quorum Health Resources, Inc., Brentwood, TN	23	10	101	—	—	—	—	—	—	—
BAKER—Fallon County										
FALLON MEDICAL COMPLEX, 202 South 4th Street West, Zip 59313–0820, Mailing Address: P.O. Box 820, Zip 59313–0820; tel. 406/778–3331; David Espeland, Chief Executive Officer (Total facility includes 40 beds in nursing home–type unit) **A**9 10 **F**7 8 14 15 16 17 19 20 22 28 30 32 34 35 36 37 39 40 41 42 44 49 51 62 64 65 67 68 71 73 **P**6 8 **N** Montana Health Network, Inc., Miles City, MT	23	10	52	315	42	28307	19	4992	2571	124
BIG SANDY—Chouteau County										
★ BIG SANDY MEDICAL CENTER, Mailing Address: P.O. Box 530, Zip 59520–0530; tel. 406/378–2188; Harry Bold, Administrator (Total facility includes 22 beds in nursing home–type unit) **A**9 10 **F**15 16 22 32 34 49 64	23	10	30	50	19	5779	0	1066	557	31
BIG TIMBER—Sweet Grass County										
PIONEER MEDICAL CENTER, 301 West Seventh Avenue, Zip 59011, Mailing Address: P.O. Box 1228, Zip 59011–1228; tel. 406/932–4603; Cody Langbehn, Administrator (Total facility includes 52 beds in nursing home–type unit) **F**1 12 22 25 26 28 33 36 41 48 49 51 64 65 71	13	10	60	196	51	2159	0	2475	879	29
BILLINGS—Yellowstone County										
⊞ DEACONESS BILLINGS CLINIC, (Formerly Deaconess Medical Center), 2800 10th Avenue North, Zip 59101–0799, Mailing Address: P.O. Box 37000, Zip 59107–7000; tel. 406/657–4000; Nicholas J. Wolter, M.D., Chief Executive Officer (Total facility includes 125 beds in nursing home–type unit) **A**1 3 9 10 **F**4 8 10 12 13 14 15 16 17 18 19 21 22 25 26 27 28 29 30 31 34 35 37 39 41 42 43 44 45 46 49 51 52 53 54 55 56 57 58 59 60 63 64 65 66 67 70 71 73 74 **P**3 **N** Montana Health Network, Inc., Miles City, MT	23	10	219	9275	127	42058	0	160226	72855	1471
⊞ △ SAINT VINCENT HOSPITAL AND HEALTH CENTER, 1233 North 30th Street, Zip 59101–0165, Mailing Address: P.O. Box 35200, Zip 59107–5200; tel. 406/657–7000; Patrick M. Hermanson, Senior Executive Officer (Total facility includes 28 beds in nursing home–type unit) **A**1 7 9 10 **F**4 6 7 8 9 10 12 13 14 15 16 17 18 19 21 22 24 26 28 29 30 31 34 35 37 38 40 41 42 43 44 45 46 48 49 51 60 61 64 65 66 67 70 71 73 74 **P**6 **S** Sisters of Charity of Leavenworth Health Services Corporation, Leavenworth, KS	21	10	257	12720	178	114695	1971	109825	43300	1234
BOZEMAN—Gallatin County										
★ BOZEMAN DEACONESS HOSPITAL, 915 Highland Boulevard, Zip 59715–6999; tel. 406/585–5000; John A. Nordwick, President and Chief Executive Officer **A**9 10 **F**6 7 8 11 12 15 16 17 19 21 23 28 30 32 33 34 35 37 39 40 41 42 43 44 49 60 62 63 65 66 70 71 73	23	10	70	4016	38	61945	743	26273	10675	327
BROWNING—Glacier County										
⊞ U. S. PUBLIC HEALTH SERVICE BLACKFEET COMMUNITY HOSPITAL, Mailing Address: P.O. Box 760, Zip 59417–0760; tel. 406/338–6100; Reese Fisher, Service Unit Director (Nonreporting) **A**1 10 **S** U. S. Public Health Service Indian Health Service, Rockville, MD	47	10	25	—	—	—	—	—	—	—
BUTTE—Silver Bow County										
⊞ ST. JAMES COMMUNITY HOSPITAL, 400 South Clark Street, Zip 59701–2328, Mailing Address: P.O. Box 3300, Zip 59702–3300; tel. 406/723–2500; Robert Rodgers, Administrator and Senior Executive Officer **A**1 9 10 **F**12 15 16 17 19 20 21 22 23 24 26 28 29 30 34 35 37 40 42 44 45 46 49 60 63 64 65 66 67 70 71 73 **S** Sisters of Charity of Leavenworth Health Services Corporation, Leavenworth, KS	23	10	103	4296	61	38566	480	34950	13849	455
CHESTER—Liberty County										
LIBERTY COUNTY HOSPITAL AND NURSING HOME, Mailing Address: P.O. Box 705, Zip 59522–0705; tel. 406/759–5181; Douglas Faus, Administrator (Total facility includes 53 beds in nursing home–type unit) **A**9 10 **F**1 7 11 22 32 34 37 40 44 49 64 65 71	13	10	64	289	47	5527	19	2862	1432	72
CHOTEAU—Teton County										
TETON MEDICAL CENTER, 915 Fourth Street N.W., Zip 59422–9123; tel. 406/466–5763; Jay Pottenger, Administrator (Total facility includes 42 beds in nursing home–type unit) **A**9 10 **F**1 8 16 22 28 30 33 44 51 64	16	10	46	174	32	5441	0	2212	1152	62
CIRCLE—McCone County										
MCCONE COUNTY MEDICAL ASSISTANCE FACILITY, Mailing Address: P.O. Box 48, Zip 59215–0048; tel. 406/485–3381; Mack N. Simpson, Administrator (Total facility includes 38 beds in nursing home–type unit) (Nonreporting) **A**10 **N** Montana Health Network, Inc., Miles City, MT	23	10	40	—	—	—	—	—	—	—
COLUMBUS—Stillwater County										
STILLWATER COMMUNITY HOSPITAL, 44 West Fourth Avenue North, Zip 59019, Mailing Address: P.O. Box 959, Zip 59019–0959; tel. 406/322–5316; Tim Russell, Administrator (Total facility includes 9 beds in nursing home–type unit) (Nonreporting) **A**9 10 **N** Montana Health Network, Inc., Miles City, MT	23	10	23	—	—	—	—	—	—	—

Hospital, Address, Telephone, Administrator, Approval, Facility, and Physician Codes, Health Care System, Network	Classi-fication Codes		Utilization Data					Expense (thousands) of dollars		
	Control	Service	Staffed Beds	Admissions	Census	Outpatient Visits	Births	Total	Payroll	Personnel

★ American Hospital Association (AHA) membership
☐ Joint Commission on Accreditation of Healthcare Organizations (JCAHO) accreditation
+ American Osteopathic Healthcare Association (AOHA) membership
○ American Osteopathic Association (AOA) accreditation
△ Commission on Accreditation of Rehabilitation Facilities (CARF) accreditation
Control codes 61, 63, 64, 71, 72 and 73 indicate hospitals listed by AOHA, but not registered by AHA. For definition of numerical codes, see page A4.

CONRAD—Pondera County

★ PONDERA MEDICAL CENTER, 805 Sunset Boulevard, Zip 59425–1721, Mailing Address: P.O. Box 757, Zip 59425–0757; tel. 406/278–3211; Jim Robertson, Administrator (Total facility includes 59 beds in nursing home–type unit) **A**9 10 **F**1 7 8 15 16 20 22 28 32 33 40 41 44 49 64 70 71

| 13 | 10 | 79 | 651 | 63 | 7189 | 20 | 5664 | 2957 | 136 |

CROW AGENCY—Big Horn County

⊠ U. S. PUBLIC HEALTH SERVICE INDIAN HOSPITAL, Mailing Address: P.O. Box 9, Zip 59022–0009; tel. 406/638–2626; Tennyson Doney, Service Unit Director **A**1 10 **F**3 7 8 13 14 15 16 18 19 20 21 22 24 30 31 34 35 40 44 49 50 53 54 56 65 71 72 74 **P**6 **S** U. S. Public Health Service Indian Health Service, Rockville, MD

| 47 | 10 | 24 | 1503 | 13 | 105101 | 286 | 21939 | 9481 | 262 |

CULBERTSON—Roosevelt County

★ ROOSEVELT MEMORIAL MEDICAL CENTER, 818 Second Avenue East, Zip 59218, Mailing Address: P.O. Box 419, Zip 59218–0419; tel. 406/787–6281; Walter Busch, Administrator (Total facility includes 44 beds in nursing home–type unit) (Nonreporting) **A**10 **N** Montana Health Network, Inc., Miles City, MT

| 23 | 10 | 54 | — | — | — | — | — | — | — |

CUT BANK—Glacier County

★ GLACIER COUNTY MEDICAL CENTER, 802 Second Street S.E., Zip 59427–3331; tel. 406/873–2251; Allison Harvie, Acting Administrator (Total facility includes 39 beds in nursing home–type unit) **A**9 10 **F**7 8 15 19 20 22 31 32 34 37 40 42 44 56 64 65 71 73 **P**3 **S** Quorum Health Group/Quorum Health Resources, Inc., Brentwood, TN

| 13 | 10 | 59 | 479 | 46 | 11346 | 34 | 5075 | 2226 | 96 |

DEER LODGE—Powell County

★ POWELL COUNTY MEMORIAL HOSPITAL, 1101 Texas Avenue, Zip 59722–1828; tel. 406/846–2212; Connie Huber, R.N., Chief Executive Officer (Total facility includes 16 beds in nursing home–type unit) **A**9 10 **F**14 15 16 37 40 64 **S** Brim, Inc., Portland, OR

| 23 | 10 | 35 | 280 | 15 | 5705 | 17 | 3045 | 1414 | 66 |

DILLON—Beaverhead County

★ BARRETT MEMORIAL HOSPITAL, 1260 South Atlantic Street, Zip 59725–3597; tel. 406/683–3000; Jim D. Le Brun, Chief Executive Officer (Nonreporting) **A**9 10 **S** Brim, Inc., Portland, OR

| 16 | 10 | 31 | — | — | — | — | — | — | — |

ENNIS—Madison County

MADISON VALLEY HOSPITAL, 217 North Main Street, Zip 59729–0397, Mailing Address: P.O. Box 397, Zip 59729–0397; tel. 406/682–4222; Geri Wilson, Chief Executive Officer **A**9 10 **F**8 16 17 18 22 25 28 29 30 33 44 45 49 51 63 **P**5

| 16 | 10 | 9 | 165 | 2 | 831 | 0 | 1388 | 795 | 29 |

FORSYTH—Rosebud County

★ ROSEBUD HEALTH CARE CENTER, 383 North 17th Avenue, Zip 59327; tel. 406/356–2161; John M. Chioutsis, Chief Executive Officer (Total facility includes 55 beds in nursing home–type unit) **A**9 10 **F**8 11 15 26 28 30 32 37 44 64 67 71 73 **S** Brim, Inc., Portland, OR

| 23 | 10 | 75 | 345 | 57 | 9055 | 2 | 3878 | 1946 | 94 |

FORT BENTON—Chouteau County

MISSOURI RIVER MEDICAL CENTER, 1501 St. Charles Street, Zip 59442–0249, Mailing Address: P.O. Box 249, Zip 59442–0249; tel. 406/622–3331; Jay Pottenger, Administrator (Total facility includes 45 beds in nursing home–type unit) **A**9 10 **F**6 21 22 25 31 32 64 65 **P**6

| 16 | 10 | 52 | 205 | 40 | 7725 | 0 | 2895 | 1621 | 88 |

FORT HARRISON—Lewis and Clark County

⊠ VETERANS AFFAIRS HOSPITAL, Zip 59636; tel. 406/442–6410; Joseph Underkofler, Director **A**1 **F**3 4 8 11 12 19 20 21 22 24 25 26 27 28 29 30 31 34 35 37 39 41 42 44 45 46 49 51 52 54 55 57 58 65 67 71 72 73 74 **P**6 **S** Department of Veterans Affairs, Washington, DC

| 45 | 10 | 50 | 2132 | 45 | 55224 | 0 | — | — | 344 |

GLASGOW—Valley County

☐ FRANCES MAHON DEACONESS HOSPITAL, 621 Third Street South, Zip 59230–2699; tel. 406/228–4351; Randall G. Holom, Chief Executive Officer **A**1 3 9 10 **F**7 8 11 15 19 21 22 26 28 31 32 34 35 44 45 50 54 63 65 71 **P**3 **N** Montana Health Network, Inc., Miles City, MT

| 23 | 10 | 32 | 1135 | 12 | 27089 | 116 | 11730 | 4869 | 212 |

GLENDIVE—Dawson County

☐ GLENDIVE MEDICAL CENTER, 202 Prospect Drive, Zip 59330–1999; tel. 406/365–3306; Paul Hanson, Chief Executive Officer (Total facility includes 75 beds in nursing home–type unit) (Nonreporting) **A**1 9 10 **N** Montana Health Network, Inc., Miles City, MT

| 23 | 10 | 104 | — | — | — | — | — | — | — |

GREAT FALLS—Cascade County

⊠ △ BENEFIS HEALTH CARE, (Includes Benefis Health Care–East Campus, 1101 26th Street, Zip 59405; Benefis Health Care–West Campus, 500 15th Avenue South, Zip 59405, Mailing Address: P.O. Box 5013, Zip 59403–5013; tel. 406/727–3333), 500 15th Avenue South, Zip 59403–4389; tel. 406/455–5000; Lloyd V. Smith, President and Chief Executive Officer (Total facility includes 140 beds in nursing home–type unit) **A**1 2 7 9 10 **F**1 3 4 7 8 10 11 12 14 17 18 19 20 22 23 24 26 27 28 29 30 32 33 34 35 36 37 38 39 40 41 42 43 44 46 48 49 52 58 59 60 61 64 65 66 67 71 72 73 74 **S** Providence Services, Spokane, WA **N** Providence Services, Spokane, WA

| 23 | 10 | 477 | 12117 | 222 | 113933 | 1199 | 127693 | 57585 | 1712 |

HAMILTON—Ravalli County

★ MARCUS DALY MEMORIAL HOSPITAL, 1200 Westwood Drive, Zip 59840–2395; tel. 406/363–2211; John M. Bartos, Administrator (Nonreporting) **A**9 10

| 23 | 10 | 48 | — | — | — | — | — | — | — |

HARDIN—Big Horn County

★ BIG HORN COUNTY MEMORIAL HOSPITAL, 17 North Miles Avenue, Zip 59034–0430, Mailing Address: P.O. Box 430, Zip 59034–0430; tel. 406/665–2310; Raymond T. Hino, Chief Executive Officer (Total facility includes 37 beds in nursing home–type unit) (Nonreporting) **A**9 10 **S** Brim, Inc., Portland, OR

| 23 | 10 | 53 | — | — | — | — | — | — | — |

Hospital, Address, Telephone, Administrator, Approval, Facility, and Physician Codes, Health Care System, Network	Classi-fication Codes		Utilization Data					Expense (thousands) of dollars		
	Control	Service	Staffed Beds	Admissions	Census	Outpatient Visits	Births	Total	Payroll	Personnel

★ American Hospital Association (AHA) membership
□ Joint Commission on Accreditation of Healthcare Organizations (JCAHO) accreditation
+ American Osteopathic Healthcare Association (AOHA) membership
○ American Osteopathic Association (AOA) accreditation
△ Commission on Accreditation of Rehabilitation Facilities (CARF) accreditation
Control codes 61, 63, 64, 71, 72 and 73 indicate hospitals listed by AOHA, but not registered by AHA. For definition of numerical codes, see page A4

HARLEM—Blaine County

★ U. S. PUBLIC HEALTH SERVICE INDIAN HOSPITAL, Rural Route 1, Box 67, Zip 59526; tel. 406/353–3191; Charles D. Plumage, Director (Nonreporting) **A**10 **S** U. S. Public Health Service Indian Health Service, Rockville, MD
| 47 | 10 | 12 | — | — | — | — | — | — | — |

HARLOWTON—Wheatland County

★ WHEATLAND MEMORIAL HOSPITAL, 530 Third Street North, Zip 59036, Mailing Address: P.O. Box 287, Zip 59036–0287; tel. 406/632–4351; Craig E. Aasved, Administrator (Total facility includes 36 beds in nursing home–type unit) **A**9 10 **F**1 2 3 4 5 6 7 8 9 10 11 12 13 14 15 16 17 18 19 20 21 22 23 24 25 26 27 28 29 30 31 32 33 34 35 36 37 38 39 40 41 42 43 44 45 46 47 48 49 50 51 52 53 54 55 56 57 58 59 60 61 62 63 64 65 66 67 68 69 70 71 72 73 74 **P**1 7 8 **S** Quorum Health Group/Quorum Health Resources, Inc., Brentwood, TN
| 13 | 10 | 54 | 143 | 37 | 3224 | 0 | 3043 | 1637 | 75 |

HAVRE—Hill County

⊞ NORTHERN MONTANA HOSPITAL, 30 13th Street, Zip 59501–5222, Mailing Address: P.O. Box 1231, Zip 59501–1231; tel. 406/265–2211; David Henry, Chief Executive Officer (Total facility includes 153 beds in nursing home–type unit) **A**1 9 10 **F**1 2 3 6 7 8 11 12 13 14 15 16 17 18 19 21 22 24 25 28 29 30 32 33 34 35 39 40 41 44 45 46 49 51 52 54 55 56 57 58 59 61 64 65 66 67 68 71 72 73 74 **P**4 **S** Brim, Inc., Portland, OR
| 23 | 10 | 274 | 3459 | 75 | 34047 | 369 | 29174 | 14780 | 401 |

HELENA—Lewis and Clark County

⊞ SHODAIR CHILDREN'S HOSPITAL, 840 Helena Avenue, Zip 59601–3423, Mailing Address: P.O. Box 5539, Zip 59604–5539; tel. 406/444–7500; Jack Casey, Administrator **A**1 9 10 **F**15 16 52 53 55 58 59 61 64 65
| 23 | 52 | 66 | 119 | 28 | 6957 | 0 | 7013 | 4096 | 156 |

⊞ ST. PETER'S COMMUNITY HOSPITAL, 2475 Broadway, Zip 59601; tel. 406/442–2480; Robert W. Ladenburger, President **A**1 9 10 **F**7 8 10 12 14 15 16 17 19 21 22 28 29 30 31 32 33 34 35 36 38 39 40 41 42 44 45 46 49 52 54 55 56 57 58 59 60 63 64 65 67 71 73 **P**8
| 23 | 10 | 80 | 4759 | 40 | 71440 | 705 | 44889 | 20205 | 458 |

KALISPELL—Flathead County

⊞ △ KALISPELL REGIONAL MEDICAL CENTER, (Formerly Kalispell Regional Hospital), (Includes Pathways Treatment Center, 200 Heritage Way, Zip 59901; tel. 406/756–3950), 310 Sunnyview Lane, Zip 59901–3199; tel. 406/752–5111; Thomas W. Laux, President and Chief Executive Officer (Total facility includes 92 beds in nursing home–type unit) (Nonreporting) **A**1 7 9 10
| 23 | 10 | 242 | — | — | — | — | — | — | — |

LEWISTOWN—Fergus County

★ CENTRAL MONTANA MEDICAL CENTER, 408 Wendell Avenue, Zip 59457–2261, Mailing Address: P.O. Box 580, Zip 59457–0580; tel. 406/538–7711; David M. Faulkner, Chief Executive Officer and Administrator (Total facility includes 85 beds in nursing home–type unit) (Nonreporting) **A**9 10 **S** Quorum Health Group/Quorum Health Resources, Inc., Brentwood, TN **N** Montana Health Network, Inc., Miles City, MT
| 23 | 10 | 124 | — | — | — | — | — | — | — |

LIBBY—Lincoln County

★ ST. JOHN'S LUTHERAN HOSPITAL, 350 Louisiana Avenue, Zip 59923–2198; tel. 406/293–7761; Richard L. Palagi, Executive Director **A**9 10 **F**6 7 8 11 17 19 22 25 28 29 30 32 33 37 39 40 41 44 49 51 65 66 71 72 73 **P**6 7 **S** Brim, Inc., Portland, OR
| 23 | 10 | 26 | 1179 | 12 | 42095 | 113 | 7556 | 3837 | 140 |

LIVINGSTON—Park County

★ LIVINGSTON MEMORIAL HOSPITAL, 504 South 13th Street, Zip 59047–3798; tel. 406/222–3541; Richard V. Brown, Chief Executive Officer (Nonreporting) **A**9 10
| 23 | 10 | 35 | — | — | — | — | — | — | — |

MALTA—Phillips County

PHILLIPS COUNTY MEDICAL CENTER, (Formerly Phillips County Hospital), 417 South Fourth East, Zip 59538, Mailing Address: P.O. Box 640, Zip 59538–0640; tel. 406/654–1100; Larry E. Putnam, Administrator (Nonreporting) **A**9 10 **N** Montana Health Network, Inc., Miles City, MT
| 23 | 10 | 15 | — | — | — | — | — | — | — |

MILES CITY—Custer County

⊞ HOLY ROSARY HEALTH CENTER, 2600 Wilson Street, Zip 59301–5094; tel. 406/233–2600; H. Ray Gibbons, President and Chief Executive Officer (Total facility includes 107 beds in nursing home–type unit) **A**1 9 10 **F**2 3 7 8 11 12 13 14 15 16 17 19 21 22 24 27 28 30 32 35 36 37 39 40 42 44 48 49 52 53 54 55 56 57 58 63 64 65 67 71 73 **S** Sisters of Charity of Leavenworth Health Services Corporation, Leavenworth, KS **N** Montana Health Network, Inc., Miles City, MT
| 21 | 10 | 151 | 1764 | 100 | 27889 | 235 | 17395 | 6604 | 328 |

MISSOULA—Missoula County

⊞ △ COMMUNITY MEDICAL CENTER, 2827 Fort Missoula Road, Zip 59801; tel. 406/728–4100; Grant M. Winn, President (Nonreporting) **A**1 7 9 10 **S** Brim, Inc., Portland, OR
| 23 | 10 | 115 | — | — | — | — | — | — | — |

⊞ ST. PATRICK HOSPITAL, 500 West Broadway, Zip 59802–4096, Mailing Address: Box 4587, Zip 59806–4587; tel. 406/543–7271; Lawrence L. White, Jr., President (Total facility includes 18 beds in nursing home–type unit) **A**1 9 10 **F**2 3 4 10 12 14 15 16 17 19 21 22 23 24 27 29 30 32 33 34 35 36 37 39 41 42 43 44 45 49 52 53 54 55 56 57 58 59 60 63 64 65 66 67 68 69 70 71 72 73 **P**7 **S** Providence Services, Spokane, WA **N** Providence Services, Spokane, WA
| 21 | 10 | 213 | 9178 | 167 | 105137 | — | 83572 | 32437 | 1009 |

PHILIPSBURG—Granite County

GRANITE COUNTY MEMORIAL HOSPITAL AND NURSING HOME, Mailing Address: P.O. Box 729, Zip 59858–0729; tel. 406/859–3271; Doris White Gilbertson, Administrator (Total facility includes 28 beds in nursing home–type unit) (Nonreporting) **A**10
| 13 | 10 | 31 | — | — | — | — | — | — | — |

Hospital, Address, Telephone, Administrator, Approval, Facility, and Physician Codes, Health Care System, Network	Classi-fication Codes		Utilization Data					Expense (thousands) of dollars		
★ American Hospital Association (AHA) membership ☐ Joint Commission on Accreditation of Healthcare Organizations (JCAHO) accreditation + American Osteopathic Healthcare Association (AOHA) membership ○ American Osteopathic Association (AOA) accreditation △ Commission on Accreditation of Rehabilitation Facilities (CARF) accreditation Control codes 61, 63, 64, 71, 72 and 73 indicate hospitals listed by AOHA, but not registered by AHA. For definition of numerical codes, see page A4	Control	Service	Staffed Beds	Admissions	Census	Outpatient Visits	Births	Total	Payroll	Personnel

PLAINS—Sanders County

★ CLARK FORK VALLEY HOSPITAL, Mailing Address: P.O. Box 768, Zip 59859–0768; tel. 406/826–3601; Tom Mitchell, Chief Executive Officer (Total facility includes 28 beds in nursing home–type unit) (Nonreporting) **A**9 10

| | 23 | 10 | 44 | — | — | — | — | — | — | — |

PLENTYWOOD—Sheridan County

SHERIDAN MEMORIAL HOSPITAL, 440 West Laurel Avenue, Zip 59254–1596; tel. 406/765–1420; Ella Gutzke, Administrator (Total facility includes 78 beds in nursing home–type unit) **A**9 10 **F**7 8 12 15 16 19 22 26 28 30 31 32 34 36 37 40 41 44 46 49 51 64 65 67 68 71 73 **P**3 **N** Montana Health Network, Inc., Miles City, MT

| | 23 | 10 | 97 | 585 | 82 | 268 | 27 | 4945 | 2645 | 171 |

POLSON—Lake County

✠ ST. JOSEPH HOSPITAL, Skyline Drive and 14th Avenue, Zip 59860, Mailing Address: P.O. Box 1010, Zip 59860–1010; tel. 406/883–5377; John W. Glueckert, President **A**1 9 10 **F**7 8 15 19 22 24 32 40 44 65 73 **S** Providence Services, Spokane, WA **N** Providence Services, Spokane, WA

| | 21 | 10 | 22 | 587 | 4 | 20920 | 44 | 4919 | 2467 | 96 |

POPLAR—Roosevelt County

POPLAR COMMUNITY HOSPITAL See Northeast Montana Health Services, Wolf Point

RED LODGE—Carbon County

★ BEARTOOTH HOSPITAL AND HEALTH CENTER, (Formerly Carbon County Memorial Hospital and Nursing Home), 600 West 20th Street, Zip 59068, Mailing Address: P.O. Box 590, Zip 59068–0590; tel. 406/446–2345; Kelley Going, Administrator (Total facility includes 30 beds in nursing home–type unit) **A**9 10 **F**7 8 11 12 14 15 16 17 22 24 26 27 28 29 30 32 34 40 41 44 45 46 48 49 51 54 56 57 64 65 66 71 73 **P**5 **N** Montana Health Network, Inc., Miles City, MT

| | 23 | 10 | 52 | 463 | 30 | 7733 | 24 | 3646 | 1953 | 103 |

RONAN—Lake County

★ ST. LUKE COMMUNITY HOSPITAL, 107 Sixth Avenue S.W., Zip 59864–2634; tel. 406/676–4441; Shane Roberts, Administrator (Total facility includes 75 beds in nursing home–type unit) (Nonreporting) **A**9 10

| | 23 | 10 | 99 | — | — | — | — | — | — | — |

ROUNDUP—Musselshell County

★ ROUNDUP MEMORIAL HOSPITAL, 1202 Third Street West, Zip 59072–1816, Mailing Address: P.O. Box 40, Zip 59072–0040; tel. 406/323–2302; Dave McIvor, Administrator (Total facility includes 37 beds in nursing home–type unit) (Nonreporting) **A**9 10 **S** Brim, Inc., Portland, OR **N** Montana Health Network, Inc., Miles City, MT

| | 23 | 10 | 54 | — | — | — | — | — | — | — |

SCOBEY—Daniels County

DANIELS MEMORIAL HOSPITAL, 105 Fifth Avenue East, Zip 59263, Mailing Address: P.O. Box 400, Zip 59263–0400; tel. 406/487–2296; Glenn Haugo, Administrator (Total facility includes 48 beds in nursing home–type unit) (Nonreporting) **A**9 10 **N** Montana Health Network, Inc., Miles City, MT

| | 23 | 10 | 54 | — | — | — | — | — | — | — |

SHELBY—Toole County

MARIAS MEDICAL CENTER, (Formerly Toole County Hospital and Nursing Home), 640 Park Drive, Zip 59474–1663, Mailing Address: P.O. Box 915, Zip 59474–0915; tel. 406/434–3200; Jerry Morasko, Administrator (Total facility includes 68 beds in nursing home–type unit) (Nonreporting) **A**9 10
TOOLE COUNTY HOSPITAL AND NURSING HOME See Marias Medical Center

| | 13 | 10 | 88 | — | — | — | — | — | — | — |

SHERIDAN—Madison County

RUBY VALLEY HOSPITAL, 220 East Crofoot Street, Zip 59749, Mailing Address: P.O. Box 336, Zip 59749–0336; tel. 406/842–5453; Steve Lang, Administrator (Nonreporting) **A**9 10

| | 16 | 10 | 14 | — | — | — | — | — | — | — |

SIDNEY—Richland County

SIDNEY HEALTH CENTER, 216 14th Avenue S.W., Zip 59270–3586, Mailing Address: P.O. Box 1690, Zip 59270–1690; tel. 406/422–2100; Donald J. Rush, Chief Executive Officer (Total facility includes 93 beds in nursing home–type unit) **A**9 10 **F**1 8 11 19 21 22 24 30 32 33 35 36 40 42 44 49 64 65 71 73 **N** Montana Health Network, Inc., Miles City, MT

| | 23 | 10 | 135 | 1498 | 102 | 29943 | 141 | 16940 | 7517 | 344 |

SUPERIOR—Mineral County

★ MINERAL COMMUNITY HOSPITAL, Roosevelt and Brooklyn, Zip 59872, Mailing Address: P.O. Box 66, Zip 59872–0066; tel. 406/822–4841; Madelyn Faller, Chief Executive Officer (Total facility includes 20 beds in nursing home–type unit) (Nonreporting) **A**9 10 **S** Brim, Inc., Portland, OR

| | 23 | 10 | 30 | — | — | — | — | — | — | — |

TERRY—Prairie County

★ PRAIRIE COMMUNITY MEDICAL ASSISTANCE FACILITY, 312 South Adams Avenue, Zip 59349–0156, Mailing Address: P.O. Box 156, Zip 59349–0156; tel. 406/635–5511; James R. Mantz, Administrator (Total facility includes 19 beds in nursing home–type unit) **A**10 **F**8 13 15 22 26 28 36 51 64

| | 16 | 10 | 21 | 28 | 18 | 1978 | 0 | 1038 | 597 | 31 |

TOWNSEND—Broadwater County

BROADWATER HEALTH CENTER, 110 North Oak Street, Zip 59644–2306, Mailing Address: P.O. Box 519, Zip 59644–0519; tel. 406/266–3186; James Holcomb, Chief Executive Officer (Total facility includes 32 beds in nursing home–type unit) **A**9 10 **F**14 15 22 32 33 39 49 64 65 67

| | 23 | 10 | 42 | 147 | 34 | — | 0 | 2155 | 971 | 90 |

WARM SPRINGS—Deer Lodge County

MONTANA STATE HOSPITAL, Zip 59756; tel. 406/693–7000; Carl Keener, M.D., Medical Director (Nonreporting)

| | 12 | 10 | 32 | — | — | — | — | — | — | — |

WHITE SULPHUR SPRINGS—Cascade County

MOUNTAINVIEW MEDICAL CENTER, 16 West Main, Zip 59645, Mailing Address: P.O. Box Q, Zip 59645; tel. 406/547–3321; Greg Nielsen, Administrator (Total facility includes 31 beds in nursing home–type unit) **A**9 10 **F**13 26 28 39 49 64 **P**6

| | 23 | 10 | 37 | 145 | 24 | 514 | 0 | 2003 | 1123 | 45 |

Hospital, Address, Telephone, Administrator, Approval, Facility, and Physician Codes, Health Care System, Network	Classi-fication Codes		Utilization Data					Expense (thousands) of dollars		
	Control	Service	Staffed Beds	Admissions	Census	Outpatient Visits	Births	Total	Payroll	Personnel

★ American Hospital Association (AHA) membership
□ Joint Commission on Accreditation of Healthcare Organizations (JCAHO) accreditation
+ American Osteopathic Healthcare Association (AOHA) membership
○ American Osteopathic Association (AOA) accreditation
△ Commission on Accreditation of Rehabilitation Facilities (CARF) accreditation
Control codes 61, 63, 64, 71, 72 and 73 indicate hospitals listed by AOHA, but not registered by AHA. For definition of numerical codes, see page A4

WHITEFISH—Flathead County

★ NORTH VALLEY HOSPITAL, 6575 Highway 93 South, Zip 59937; tel. 406/863–2501; Kenneth E. S. Platou, Chief Executive Officer (Total facility includes 56 beds in nursing home–type unit) **A**9 10 **F**1 7 8 17 19 22 26 28 30 32 34 37 40 41 44 64 66 71 72 73 **P**5 8 **S** Quorum Health Group/Quorum Health Resources, Inc., Brentwood, TN

	23	10	99	1513	72	37824	193	13318	6366	221

WOLF POINT—Roosevelt County

NORTHEAST MONTANA HEALTH SERVICES, (Includes Poplar Community Hospital, H. and Court Avenue, Poplar, Zip 59255, Mailing Address: P.O. Box 38, Zip 59255; tel. 406/768–3452; Trinity Hospital, 315 Knapp Street, Zip 59201; tel. 406/653–2100; 315 Knapp Street, Zip 59201–1898; tel. 406/653–2110; Earl N. Sheehy, Chief Executive Officer (Total facility includes 82 beds in nursing home–type unit) **A**9 10 **F**1 7 8 15 16 19 22 26 27 28 30 36 37 40 42 44 45 46 62 64 65 71 **P**6 **N** Montana Health Network, Inc., Miles City, MT

	23	10	117	1049	75	17279	163	8319	4486	208

NEBRASKA

Resident population 1,657 (in thousands)
Resident population in metro areas 50.7%
Birth rate per 1,000 population 14.3
65 years and over 13.8%
Percent of persons without health insurance 11.4%

Hospital, Address, Telephone, Administrator, Approval, Facility, and Physician Codes, Health Care System, Network	Classification Codes		Utilization Data					Expense (thousands) of dollars		
	Control	Service	Staffed Beds	Admissions	Census	Outpatient Visits	Births	Total	Payroll	Personnel

★ American Hospital Association (AHA) membership
□ Joint Commission on Accreditation of Healthcare Organizations (JCAHO) accreditation
+ American Osteopathic Healthcare Association (AOHA) membership
○ American Osteopathic Association (AOA) accreditation
△ Commission on Accreditation of Rehabilitation Facilities (CARF) accreditation
Control codes 61, 63, 64, 71, 72 and 73 indicate hospitals listed by AOHA, but not registered by AHA. For definition of numerical codes, see page A4

Hospital, Address, Telephone, Administrator, Approval, Facility, and Physician Codes, Health Care System, Network	Control	Service	Staffed Beds	Admissions	Census	Outpatient Visits	Births	Total	Payroll	Personnel
AINSWORTH—Brown County										
BROWN COUNTY HOSPITAL, 945 East Zero Street, Zip 69210–1547; tel. 402/387–2800; Colleen Chapp, Interim Administrator **A**9 10 **F**7 8 11 15 19 22 32 34 37 40 44 48 49 64 65 71 **P**6 **N** North Central Hospital Nebraska Network, Osmond, NE	13	10	23	330	9	5160	30	—	1024	53
ALBION—Boone County										
★ BOONE COUNTY HEALTH CENTER, 723 West Fairview Street, Zip 68620–1725, Mailing Address: P.O. Box 151, Zip 68620–0151; tel. 402/395–2191; Gayle E. Primrose, Administrator **A**9 10 **F**2 3 7 8 11 15 16 17 19 22 24 25 26 28 30 31 32 33 34 35 37 39 40 41 42 44 45 48 49 51 52 53 54 55 57 58 65 66 67 71 73 **P**6 **N** Heartland Health Alliance, Lincoln, NE; Central Nebraska Primary Care Network, Ord, NE	13	10	20	811	8	79108	86	6688	3887	145
ALLIANCE—Box Butte County										
□ BOX BUTTE GENERAL HOSPITAL, 2101 Box Butte Avenue, Zip 69301–0810, Mailing Address: P.O. Box 810, Zip 69301–0810; tel. 308/762–6660; Terrance J. Padden, Administrator **A**1 9 10 **F**7 8 12 15 16 17 18 19 22 24 28 29 30 33 34 35 37 39 40 41 42 44 45 46 49 56 65 66 67 71 72 73 **P**8 **N** Western Nebraska Rural Health Care Network, Chadron, NE	13	10	44	684	9	16257	118	6189	2605	106
ALMA—Harlan County										
★ HARLAN COUNTY HOSPITAL, 717 North Brown Street, Zip 68920–0836, Mailing Address: P.O. Box 836, Zip 68920–0836; tel. 308/928–2151; Allen Van Driel, Administrator **A**9 10 **S** Great Plains Health Alliance, Inc., Phillipsburg, KS **N** Heartland Health Alliance, Lincoln, NE; Rural Health Partners, Lexington, NE; Great Plains Health Alliance, Phillipsburg, KS	13	10	25	224	13	7638	0	2263	1155	39
ATKINSON—Holt County										
WEST HOLT MEMORIAL HOSPITAL, 406 Legion Street, Zip 68713–0200, Mailing Address: Rural Route 1, Box 200, Zip 68713–0200; tel. 402/925–2811; Mel L. Snow, Administrator **A**9 10 **F**8 11 14 15 16 19 20 22 28 29 32 37 39 40 44 45 49 65 71 **P**3 6 **N** North Central Hospital Nebraska Network, Osmond, NE	23	10	18	320	3	9954	20	3440	1451	54
AUBURN—Nemaha County										
★ NEMAHA COUNTY HOSPITAL, 2022 13th Street, Zip 68305–1799; tel. 402/274–4366; Glen E. Krueger, Administrator **A**9 10 **F**8 17 19 22 28 34 35 37 42 44 49 64 65 71 73 **N** Heartland Health Alliance, Lincoln, NE	13	10	32	470	6	17532	2	3142	1509	64
AURORA—Hamilton County										
MEMORIAL HOSPITAL, 1423 Seventh Street, Zip 68818–1197; tel. 402/694–3171; Eldon A. Wall, Administrator (Total facility includes 53 beds in nursing home–type unit) **A**9 10 **F**7 8 11 15 22 28 30 32 33 34 36 37 39 40 41 42 44 49 64 65 66 71 **P**6 **N** Heartland Health Alliance, Lincoln, NE; Blue River Valley Health Network, Brainard, NE	23	10	78	654	56	14101	97	7006	4098	149
BASSETT—Rock County										
ROCK COUNTY HOSPITAL, 102 East South Street, Zip 68714, Mailing Address: P.O. Box 100, Zip 68714–0100; tel. 402/684–3366; David Stephenson, Administrator (Total facility includes 30 beds in nursing home–type unit) **A**9 10 **F**19 22 44 64 71 **N** North Central Hospital Nebraska Network, Osmond, NE	13	10	42	325	28	4526	—	2102	1030	73
BEATRICE—Gage County										
⊞ BEATRICE COMMUNITY HOSPITAL AND HEALTH CENTER, 1110 North Tenth Street, Zip 68310–2039, Mailing Address: P.O. Box 278, Zip 68310–0278; tel. 402/228–3344; Kenneth J. Zimmerman, Administrator (Total facility includes 87 beds in nursing home–type unit) **A**1 9 10 **F**7 8 11 12 15 16 17 19 20 21 22 23 26 28 30 31 32 33 34 35 36 37 40 41 42 44 45 46 49 51 54 62 64 65 66 67 68 71 73 **P**5 **N** Heartland Health Alliance, Lincoln, NE	23	10	143	1209	84	7694	193	15679	7866	319
BENKELMAN—Dundy County										
DUNDY COUNTY HOSPITAL, 1313 North Cheyenne Street, Zip 69021, Mailing Address: P.O. Box 626, Zip 69021–0626; tel. 308/423–2204; Robert L. Sheckler, Administrator **A**9 10 **F**8 13 15 17 19 21 22 24 27 28 29 30 35 37 40 41 42 43 44 63 71 73 74	13	10	14	310	4	7722	14	3036	1406	62
BLAIR—Washington County										
⊞ MEMORIAL COMMUNITY HOSPITAL AND HEALTH SYSTEM, (Formerly Memorial Community Hospital), 810 North 22nd Street, Zip 68008–1199, Mailing Address: P.O. Box 250, Zip 68008–0250; tel. 402/426–2182; Anton P. Zurbrugg, CHE, President and Chief Executive Officer **A**1 9 10 **F**7 8 14 15 16 17 18 19 22 28 30 32 33 34 35 36 39 40 41 42 44 45 46 49 64 65 67 71 73	23	10	33	944	9	31672	101	9437	5539	207
BRIDGEPORT—Morrill County										
MORRILL COUNTY COMMUNITY HOSPITAL, 1313 S. Street, Zip 69336–0579, Mailing Address: P.O. Box 579, Zip 69336–0579; tel. 308/262–1616; Julia Morrow, Administrator (Nonreporting) **A**9 10 **N** Western Nebraska Rural Health Care Network, Chadron, NE	13	10	20	—	—	—	—	—	—	—
BROKEN BOW—Custer County										
JENNIE M. MELHAM MEMORIAL MEDICAL CENTER, 145 Memorial Drive, Zip 68822–1378, Mailing Address: P.O. Box 250, Zip 68822–0250; tel. 308/872–6891; Michael J. Steckler, Chief Executive Officer (Total facility includes 77 beds in nursing home–type unit) **A**9 10 **F**6 7 15 19 22 24 30 32 33 34 35 44 62 64 65 71 **N** Heartland Health Alliance, Lincoln, NE	23	10	116	1099	84	9879	100	6661	3688	179

Hospital, Address, Telephone, Administrator, Approval, Facility, and Physician Codes, Health Care System, Network	Classi-fication Codes		Utilization Data					Expense (thousands) of dollars		
★ American Hospital Association (AHA) membership □ Joint Commission on Accreditation of Healthcare Organizations (JCAHO) accreditation + American Osteopathic Healthcare Association (AOHA) membership ○ American Osteopathic Association (AOA) accreditation △ Commission on Accreditation of Rehabilitation Facilities (CARF) accreditation Control codes 61, 63, 64, 71, 72 and 73 indicate hospitals listed by AOHA, but not registered by AHA. For definition of numerical codes, see page A4	Control	Service	Staffed Beds	Admissions	Census	Outpatient Visits	Births	Total	Payroll	Personnel

CALLAWAY—Custer County

★ CALLAWAY DISTRICT HOSPITAL, 211 Kimball, Zip 68825–0100, Mailing Address: P.O. Box 100, Zip 68825–0100; tel. 308/836–2228; Marvin Neth, Administrator **A**9 10 **F**11 15 16 19 22 33 37 40 44 71 **P**3

| | 16 | 10 | 12 | 242 | 3 | 5871 | 8 | 1296 | 558 | 26 |

CAMBRIDGE—Furnas County

★ TRI–VALLEY HEALTH SYSTEM, West Highway 6 and 34, Zip 69022–0488, Mailing Address: P.O. Box 488, Zip 69022–0488; tel. 308/697–3329; Kristopher H. Marwin, CHE, Chief Executive Officer (Total facility includes 36 beds in nursing home–type unit) **A**9 10 **F**7 8 11 12 14 15 16 17 19 22 24 25 27 28 32 33 34 36 37 39 40 42 44 45 49 51 62 64 65 66 67 71 **P**3 6 **S** Brim, Inc., Portland, OR **N** Heartland Health Alliance, Lincoln, NE; Rural Health Partners, Lexington, NE

| | 23 | 10 | 56 | 549 | 41 | 6905 | 68 | 8034 | 3827 | 176 |

CENTRAL CITY—Merrick County

LITZENBERG MEMORIAL COUNTY HOSPITAL, 1715 26th Street, Zip 68826–9620, Mailing Address: Route 2, Box 1, Zip 68826–0001; tel. 308/946–3015; Mike R. Bowman, Administrator (Total facility includes 45 beds in nursing home–type unit) **A**9 10 **F**6 7 8 14 15 16 19 21 22 24 27 32 36 42 44 48 49 64 65 66 71 73 **P**5

| | 13 | 10 | 66 | 618 | 50 | 11983 | 136 | 3992 | 1809 | 107 |

CHADRON—Dawes County

CHADRON COMMUNITY HOSPITAL, 821 Morehead Street, Zip 69337–2599; tel. 308/432–5586; Harold L. Krueger, Jr., Administrator **A**9 10 **F**6 7 8 12 13 15 16 17 18 19 22 28 30 31 32 33 39 40 44 48 61 62 64 65 71 73 **P**5 8 **N** Western Nebraska Rural Health Care Network, Chadron, NE

| | 23 | 10 | 32 | 756 | 14 | 6333 | 120 | 5997 | 2822 | 126 |

COLUMBUS—Platte County

⊠ COLUMBUS COMMUNITY HOSPITAL, 3020 18th Street, Zip 68601–4214, Mailing Address: P.O. Box 819, Zip 68602–0819; tel. 402/564–7118; Donald H. Zornes, Administrator (Total facility includes 19 beds in nursing home–type unit) **A**1 9 10 **F**7 8 10 11 15 16 17 19 20 21 22 23 28 30 31 32 33 34 35 36 37 38 39 40 41 44 45 46 49 64 65 67 71 73 **P**8

| | 23 | 10 | 54 | 2606 | 21 | 45965 | 451 | 16006 | 7596 | 260 |

COZAD—Dawson County

COZAD COMMUNITY HOSPITAL, 300 East 12th Street, Zip 69130–1505, Mailing Address: P.O. Box 108, Zip 69130–0108; tel. 308/784–2261; Lyle Davis, Administrator **A**9 10 **F**7 8 11 15 16 17 19 22 30 32 33 36 37 40 44 45 49 64 65 67 71 **P**6

| | 16 | 10 | 21 | 850 | 5 | 5787 | 49 | 4818 | 2523 | 94 |

CRAWFORD—Dawes County

LEGEND BUTTES HEALTH SERVICES, 11 Paddock Street, Zip 69339–1143, Mailing Address: P.O. Box 272, Zip 69339–0272; tel. 308/665–1770; Kim Engel, Chief Executive Officer **A**9 10 **F**15 16 19 22 24 30 31 32 34 40 44 51 61 64 65 **P**5 **N** Rapid City Regional Hospital System of Care, Rapid City, SD; Western Nebraska Rural Health Care Network, Chadron, NE

| | 14 | 10 | 11 | 99 | 2 | 1256 | — | 998 | 581 | 27 |

CREIGHTON—Knox County

CREIGHTON AREA HEALTH SERVICES, 1503 Main Street, Zip 68729–0186, Mailing Address: P.O. Box 186, Zip 68729–0186; tel. 402/358–3322; Paul Hurd, Chief Executive Officer (Total facility includes 47 beds in nursing home–type unit) **A**9 10 **F**1 7 8 15 16 17 19 22 27 28 30 32 34 35 37 39 40 41 42 44 64 65 67 71

| | 14 | 10 | 77 | 494 | 50 | 4523 | 15 | 3304 | 1678 | 87 |

CRETE—Saline County

★ CRETE MUNICIPAL HOSPITAL, 1540 Grove Street, Zip 68333–0220, Mailing Address: P.O. Box 220, Zip 68333–0220; tel. 402/826–6800; Joe Lohrman, Administrator (Total facility includes 22 beds in nursing home–type unit) **A**9 10 **F**7 8 14 19 22 28 32 33 42 44 49 64 71 73 **N** Heartland Health Alliance, Lincoln, NE; Blue River Valley Health Network, Brainard, NE

| | 14 | 10 | 57 | 631 | 44 | 6199 | 67 | 5008 | 2426 | 119 |

DAVID CITY—Butler County

BUTLER COUNTY HEALTH CARE CENTER, 372 South Ninth Street, Zip 68632–2199; tel. 402/367–3115; Roger Reamer, Administrator **A**9 10 **F**1 3 7 8 14 15 16 17 19 20 22 24 27 28 30 32 33 34 35 36 39 40 42 44 45 46 49 51 58 62 64 65 66 67 71 73 **N** Heartland Health Alliance, Lincoln, NE; Blue River Valley Health Network, Brainard, NE

| | 13 | 10 | 31 | 756 | 9 | 18843 | 115 | 3913 | 1952 | 80 |

FAIRBURY—Jefferson County

★ JEFFERSON COMMUNITY HEALTH CENTER, 2200 H. Street, Zip 68352–1119, Mailing Address: P.O. Box 277, Zip 68352–0277; tel. 402/729–3351; Bill Welch, Administrator (Total facility includes 41 beds in nursing home–type unit) **A**9 10 **F**7 8 10 13 15 17 19 22 24 26 28 29 30 32 33 35 40 41 42 44 45 49 64 65 66 67 71 73 **N** Heartland Health Alliance, Lincoln, NE

| | 23 | 10 | 65 | 538 | 46 | 6772 | 48 | 5584 | 2590 | 120 |

FALLS CITY—Richardson County

★ COMMUNITY MEDICAL CENTER, 2307 Barada Street, Zip 68355–1599; tel. 402/245–2428; Victor Lee, Chief Executive Officer and Administrator **A**9 10 **S** Great Plains Health Alliance, Inc., Phillipsburg, KS **N** Great Plains Health Alliance, Phillipsburg, KS

| | 23 | 10 | 35 | 1114 | 17 | 18468 | 66 | 6518 | 3163 | 121 |

FRANKLIN—Franklin County

★ FRANKLIN COUNTY MEMORIAL HOSPITAL, 1406 Q. Street, Zip 68939–0315, Mailing Address: P.O. Box 315, Zip 68939–0315; tel. 308/425–6221; Jerrell F. Gerdes, Administrator **A**9 10 **F**9 11 13 14 15 16 19 22 24 28 30 32 33 35 44 48 49 64 71 **P**6 **N** Heartland Health Alliance, Lincoln, NE; Rural Health Partners, Lexington, NE

| | 13 | 10 | 20 | 300 | 5 | 3126 | 2 | 2343 | 1320 | 64 |

FREMONT—Dodge County

⊠ FREMONT AREA MEDICAL CENTER, 450 East 23rd Street, Zip 68025–2387; tel. 402/721–1610; Vincent J. O'Connor, Jr., President and Chief Executive Officer (Total facility includes 162 beds in nursing home–type unit) **A**1 2 9 10 **F**1 7 8 11 15 17 19 21 22 26 27 28 29 30 31 32 33 34 35 37 39 40 41 42 44 45 46 48 49 60 63 64 65 66 67 71 72 73 **P**8

| | 13 | 10 | 262 | 3689 | 194 | 57144 | 398 | 36112 | 18621 | 575 |

Hospital, Address, Telephone, Administrator, Approval, Facility, and Physician Codes, Health Care System, Network	Classi-fication Codes		Utilization Data					Expense (thousands) of dollars		
	Control	Service	Staffed Beds	Admissions	Census	Outpatient Visits	Births	Total	Payroll	Personnel

★ American Hospital Association (AHA) membership
□ Joint Commission on Accreditation of Healthcare Organizations (JCAHO) accreditation
+ American Osteopathic Healthcare Association (AOHA) membership
○ American Osteopathic Association (AOA) accreditation
△ Commission on Accreditation of Rehabilitation Facilities (CARF) accreditation
Control codes 61, 63, 64, 71, 72 and 73 indicate hospitals listed by AOHA, but not registered by AHA. For definition of numerical codes, see page A4

FRIEND—Saline County

WARREN MEMORIAL HOSPITAL, 905 Second Street, Zip 68359–1198; tel. 402/947–2541; John Ramsay, Administrator (Total facility includes 58 beds in nursing home–type unit) **A**9 10 **F**1 15 21 22 28 32 33 34 36 44 49 64 71 **N** Blue River Valley Health Network, Brainard, NE — 14 10 73 79 57 5324 8 2092 1001 72

GENEVA—Fillmore County

FILLMORE COUNTY HOSPITAL, 1325 H. Street, Zip 68361–1325, Mailing Address: P.O. Box 193, Zip 68361–0193; tel. 402/759–3167; Larry Eichelberger, Administrator (Total facility includes 20 beds in nursing home–type unit) **A**9 10 **F**3 7 8 11 12 13 15 16 19 20 22 24 26 27 28 29 30 31 32 33 34 35 36 37 39 40 41 42 44 45 46 49 61 64 65 66 67 68 71 73 — 13 10 53 274 29 8360 31 3587 1631 75

GENOA—Nance County

GENOA COMMUNITY HOSPITAL, 706 Ewing Avenue, Zip 68640, Mailing Address: P.O. Box 310, Zip 68640–0310; tel. 402/993–2283; Wade Edwards, Administrator (Total facility includes 59 beds in nursing home–type unit) **A**9 10 **F**7 8 11 14 19 20 21 22 27 28 32 33 34 36 37 39 40 44 48 49 64 65 67 71 73 **P**3 6 — 14 10 79 142 56 4960 3 — 1607 69

GORDON—Sheridan County

★ GORDON MEMORIAL HOSPITAL DISTRICT, 300 East Eighth Street, Zip 69343–9990; tel. 308/282–0401; Gladys Phemister, Administrator (Total facility includes 50 beds in nursing home–type unit) **A**9 10 **F**1 3 8 11 16 17 19 22 28 30 32 37 40 44 49 61 64 71 **N** Western Nebraska Rural Health Care Network, Chadron, NE — 16 10 90 751 43 14860 24 4165 1991 141

GOTHENBURG—Dawson County

GOTHENBURG MEMORIAL HOSPITAL, 910 20th Street, Zip 69138–1237, Mailing Address: P.O. Box 469, Zip 69138–0469; tel. 308/537–3661; John H. Johnson, Chief Executive Officer (Total facility includes 37 beds in nursing home–type unit) **A**9 10 **F**7 8 19 22 24 28 29 32 33 34 37 40 44 45 48 64 67 71 **N** Heartland Health Alliance, Lincoln, NE; Rural Health Partners, Lexington, NE — 16 10 49 296 38 8774 52 — — 78

GRAND ISLAND—Hall County

GRAND ISLAND DIVISION See Veterans Affairs Greater Nebraska Health Care System, Lincoln

✠ SAINT FRANCIS MEDICAL CENTER, (Includes Saint Francis Memorial Health Center, 2116 West Faidley Avenue, Zip 68803, Mailing Address: P.O. Box 9804, Zip 68802; tel. 308/384–4600; 2620 West Faidley Avenue, Zip 68803–4297, Mailing Address: P.O. Box 9804, Zip 68802–9804; tel. 308/384–4600; Michael R. Gloor, FACHE, President and Chief Executive Officer (Total facility includes 36 beds in nursing home–type unit) **A**1 2 3 5 9 10 **F**2 3 7 8 10 11 15 16 17 19 20 21 22 23 27 28 30 32 33 34 35 37 38 39 40 41 42 44 45 49 54 58 60 62 64 65 66 67 71 73 **P**8 **S** Catholic Health Initiatives, Denver, CO — 23 10 198 6052 95 57657 914 55057 22175 622

GRANT—Perkins County

PERKINS COUNTY HEALTH SERVICES, (Includes GOLDEN OURS CONVALESCENT HOME), 900 Lincoln Avenue, Zip 69140–9799, Mailing Address: Rural Route 1, Box 26, Zip 69140–0026; tel. 308/352–7200; Carol A. Abbuhl, Chief Executive Officer (Total facility includes 64 beds in nursing home–type unit) **A**9 10 **F**11 19 22 26 28 32 40 42 44 49 64 65 67 71 — 16 10 84 603 60 7987 43 2304 1973 101

HASTINGS—Adams County

□ HASTINGS REGIONAL CENTER, 4200 West Second Street, Zip 68901–9700, Mailing Address: P.O. Box 579, Zip 68902–0579; tel. 402/463–2471; Michael J. Sheehan, Facility Administrator (Nonreporting) **A**1 10 — 12 49 232 — — — — — — —

✠ MARY LANNING MEMORIAL HOSPITAL, 715 North St. Joseph Avenue, Zip 68901–4497; tel. 402/463–4521; W. Michael Kearney, President (Total facility includes 15 beds in nursing home–type unit) **A**1 2 9 10 **N** Heartland Health Alliance, Lincoln, NE; Rural Health Partners, Lexington, NE — 23 10 125 5115 65 68432 599 38624 18956 686

HEBRON—Thayer County

★ THAYER COUNTY HEALTH SERVICES, 120 Park Avenue, Zip 68370–2019, Mailing Address: P.O. Box 49, Zip 68370–0049; tel. 402/768–6041; Larry E. Leaming, Administrator **A**9 10 **F**7 8 13 15 19 22 28 30 32 35 39 40 41 42 44 46 49 51 64 65 66 67 68 71 73 74 **P**6 — 13 10 18 506 4 17578 46 4204 1973 —

HENDERSON—York County

HENDERSON HEALTH CARE SERVICES, 1621 Front Street, Zip 68371–0217, Mailing Address: P.O. Box 217, Zip 68371–0217; tel. 402/723–4512; Calvin C. Graber, Chief Executive Officer (Total facility includes 41 beds in nursing home–type unit) **A**9 10 **F**1 6 7 8 11 14 15 16 17 19 22 24 26 27 30 32 33 34 36 37 40 42 44 46 49 62 64 65 66 67 71 **P**6 **N** Blue River Valley Health Network, Brainard, NE — 23 10 51 140 45 4039 20 3339 1869 85

HOLDREGE—Phelps County

✠ PHELPS MEMORIAL HEALTH CENTER, 1220 Miller Street, Zip 68949–1200, Mailing Address: P.O. Box 828, Zip 68949–0828; tel. 308/995–2211; Jerome Seigfried, Jr., Chief Executive Officer **A**1 9 10 **S** Quorum Health Group/Quorum Health Resources, Inc., Brentwood, TN **N** Heartland Health Alliance, Lincoln, NE; Rural Health Partners, Lexington, NE — 23 10 55 1535 17 16820 159 8932 4047 143

HUMBOLDT—Richardson County

COMMUNITY MEMORIAL HOSPITAL, 1128 Grand Avenue, Zip 68376–6019, Mailing Address: Rural Route 2, Box 34C, Zip 68376–9443; tel. 402/862–2231; Marlyn Reinitz, Administrator (Nonreporting) **A**9 10 — 23 10 20 — — — — — — —

Hospital, Address, Telephone, Administrator, Approval, Facility, and Physician Codes, Health Care System, Network	Classification Codes		Utilization Data					Expense (thousands) of dollars		
	Control	Service	Staffed Beds	Admissions	Census	Outpatient Visits	Births	Total	Payroll	Personnel

★ American Hospital Association (AHA) membership
☐ Joint Commission on Accreditation of Healthcare Organizations (JCAHO) accreditation
+ American Osteopathic Healthcare Association (AOHA) membership
○ American Osteopathic Association (AOA) accreditation
△ Commission on Accreditation of Rehabilitation Facilities (CARF) accreditation
Control codes 61, 63, 64, 71, 72 and 73 indicate hospitals listed by AOHA, but not registered by AHA. For definition of numerical codes, see page A4

IMPERIAL—Chase County

	Control	Service	Staffed Beds	Admissions	Census	Outpatient Visits	Births	Total	Payroll	Personnel
CHASE COUNTY COMMUNITY HOSPITAL, 600 West 12th Street, Zip 69033–0819, Mailing Address: P.O. Box 819, Zip 69033–0819; tel. 308/882–7111; James O'Neal, Administrator **A**9 10 **F**7 8 10 19 21 22 28 34 35 37 42 44 49 71 73 **N** Western Nebraska Rural Health Care Network, Chadron, NE	13	10	26	619	7	11405	55	2935	1393	64

KEARNEY—Buffalo County

	Control	Service	Staffed Beds	Admissions	Census	Outpatient Visits	Births	Total	Payroll	Personnel
✠ △ GOOD SAMARITAN HEALTH SYSTEMS, (Includes Richard H. Young Psychiatric Hospital, 4600 17th Avenue, Zip 68847; tel. 308/865–2000), 10 East 31st Street, Zip 68847–2926, Mailing Address: P.O. Box 1990, Zip 68848–1990; tel. 308/865–7100; William Wilson Hendrickson, President and Chief Executive Officer (Total facility includes 20 beds in nursing home–type unit) **A**1 2 3 5 7 9 10 **F**1 2 3 4 5 7 8 10 11 12 14 15 16 17 19 21 22 23 24 27 28 29 30 32 33 34 35 36 37 38 39 40 41 42 43 44 45 46 48 49 52 53 54 56 57 58 59 60 64 65 66 67 68 70 71 73 **P**6 8 **S** Catholic Health Initiatives, Denver, CO	21	10	267	8535	143	50907	815	92158	35956	1161

KIMBALL—Kimball County

	Control	Service	Staffed Beds	Admissions	Census	Outpatient Visits	Births	Total	Payroll	Personnel
KIMBALL COUNTY HOSPITAL, 505 South Burg Street, Zip 69145–1398; tel. 308/235–3621; Gerri Linn, Administrator **A**9 10 **F**15 19 22 27 30 32 40 41 44 49 51 71 73 74 **P**8 **N** Western Nebraska Rural Health Care Network, Chadron, NE	13	10	16	203	3	5941	18	2187	817	46

LEXINGTON—Dawson County

	Control	Service	Staffed Beds	Admissions	Census	Outpatient Visits	Births	Total	Payroll	Personnel
✠ TRI–COUNTY AREA HOSPITAL, 13th and Erie Streets, Zip 68850–0980, Mailing Address: P.O. Box 980, Zip 68850–0980; tel. 308/324–5651; Calvin A. Hiner, Administrator **A**1 9 10 **F**8 10 14 15 17 19 21 22 24 28 30 32 33 34 35 39 40 41 42 44 45 49 50 62 64 65 66 67 71 73 **N** Heartland Health Alliance, Lincoln, NE; Rural Health Partners, Lexington, NE	16	10	40	1426	15	28179	270	7477	3410	140

LINCOLN—Lancaster County

	Control	Service	Staffed Beds	Admissions	Census	Outpatient Visits	Births	Total	Payroll	Personnel
✠ BRYAN MEMORIAL HOSPITAL, 1600 South 48th Street, Zip 68506–1299; tel. 402/489–0200; R. Lynn Wilson, President (Total facility includes 20 beds in nursing home–type unit) **A**1 2 3 5 6 9 10 **F**4 7 8 10 11 12 15 19 21 22 23 28 29 30 31 32 34 35 37 40 42 43 44 52 54 63 64 65 66 67 69 71 73 **P**8 **N** Heartland Health Alliance, Lincoln, NE	23	10	296	14018	172	139741	1275	156543	58378	1916
LINCOLN DIVISION See Veterans Affairs Greater Nebraska Health Care System										
✠ LINCOLN GENERAL HOSPITAL, 2300 South 16th Street, Zip 68502–3781; tel. 402/475–1011; Arlan L. Stromberg, Administrator (Total facility includes 15 beds in nursing home–type unit) **A**1 2 3 5 9 10 **F**1 2 3 7 8 14 15 16 17 18 19 22 26 27 28 29 30 31 32 33 34 35 37 39 40 42 44 45 46 48 49 52 53 54 55 56 57 58 59 60 64 65 67 68 70 71 72 73 **P**7 8	14	10	226	7233	104	85404	801	64837	25507	871
☐ LINCOLN REGIONAL CENTER, West Prospector Place and Folsom, Zip 68522–2299, Mailing Address: P.O. Box 94949, Zip 68509–4949; tel. 402/471–4444; Barbara Ramsey, Ph.D., Chief Executive Officer **A**1 10 **F**14 15 16 20 27 41 52 53 54 55 56 57 58 59 65 67 73 **P**6	12	22	197	404	192	—	—	21195	13316	468
△ MADONNA REHABILITATION HOSPITAL, 5401 South Street, Zip 68506–2134; tel. 402/489–7102; Marsha Lommel Halpern, President and Chief Executive Officer (Total facility includes 126 beds in nursing home–type unit) **A**7 9 10 **F**1 12 14 15 16 17 25 27 30 32 34 41 45 46 48 49 64 65 67 73 **P**3	21	46	246	1641	213	20152	—	30421	20216	663
✠ ST. ELIZABETH COMMUNITY HEALTH CENTER, 555 South 70th Street, Zip 68510–2494; tel. 402/489–7181; Robert J. Lanik, President **A**1 2 3 5 9 10 **F**4 7 8 9 10 12 14 15 16 19 22 23 24 25 26 27 28 30 31 32 33 35 37 38 40 41 42 43 44 46 49 65 66 67 71 72 73 **P**6 7 **S** Catholic Health Initiatives, Denver, CO	21	10	136	6710	80	89396	1801	72244	28659	1059
✠ VETERANS AFFAIRS GREATER NEBRASKA HEALTH CARE SYSTEM, (Includes Grand Island Division, 2211 North Broadwell Avenue, Grand Island, Zip 68803–2196; tel. 308/382–3660; Lincoln Division, 600 South 70th Street, tel. 402/489–3802), 600 South 70th Street, Zip 68510–2493; tel. 402/489–3802; David Asper, Director (Total facility includes 76 beds in nursing home–type unit) **A**1 3 5 **F**1 2 3 8 11 12 15 16 17 18 19 20 21 22 23 26 27 28 29 30 31 32 33 34 35 37 39 41 42 44 45 46 49 51 52 54 57 58 60 61 65 67 71 73 74 **S** Department of Veterans Affairs, Washington, DC	45	10	147	2223	—	121181	0	—	—	—

LYNCH—Boyd County

	Control	Service	Staffed Beds	Admissions	Census	Outpatient Visits	Births	Total	Payroll	Personnel
★ NIOBRARA VALLEY HOSPITAL, Mailing Address: P.O. Box 118, Zip 68746–0118; tel. 402/569–2451; E. R. Testerman, Administrator **A**9 10 **F**6 7 19 22 26 28 30 32 34 39 40 44 45 49 61 64 71 **P**5 **N** North Central Hospital Nebraska Network, Osmond, NE	23	10	29	488	7	478	4	2196	—	46

MCCOOK—Red Willow County

	Control	Service	Staffed Beds	Admissions	Census	Outpatient Visits	Births	Total	Payroll	Personnel
✠ COMMUNITY HOSPITAL, 1301 East H. Street, Zip 69001–1328, Mailing Address: P.O. Box 1328, Zip 69001–1328; tel. 308/345–2650; Gary Bieganski, President **A**1 9 10 **F**7 8 14 15 17 19 21 22 28 30 32 35 37 40 44 45 49 64 65 71 73 74 **N** Heartland Health Alliance, Lincoln, NE; Rural Health Partners, Lexington, NE	23	10	44	1363	16	30876	149	11296	4801	152

MINDEN—Kearney County

	Control	Service	Staffed Beds	Admissions	Census	Outpatient Visits	Births	Total	Payroll	Personnel
★ KEARNEY COUNTY COMMUNITY HOSPITAL, 727 East First Street, Zip 68959–1700; tel. 308/832–1440; Doug Reiber, Administrator (Total facility includes 50 beds in nursing home–type unit) **A**9 10 **F**7 14 15 22 28 30 31 32 33 37 39 40 41 44 51 64 65 71 73 **P**3 6	13	10	122	184	51	7400	29	3770	2230	98

NEBRASKA CITY—Otoe County

	Control	Service	Staffed Beds	Admissions	Census	Outpatient Visits	Births	Total	Payroll	Personnel
★ ST. MARY'S HOSPITAL, 1314 Third Avenue, Zip 68410–1999; tel. 402/873–3321; Daniel J. Kelly, President and Chief Executive Officer **A**9 10 **F**3 7 8 15 16 19 22 32 33 35 36 40 41 44 46 49 63 64 65 66 71 73 **S** Catholic Health Initiatives, Denver, CO	21	10	28	529	9	25558	85	4425	1852	85

Hospital, Address, Telephone, Administrator, Approval, Facility, and Physician Codes, Health Care System, Network	Classi-fication Codes		Utilization Data					Expense (thousands) of dollars		
	Control	Service	Staffed Beds	Admissions	Census	Outpatient Visits	Births	Total	Payroll	Personnel

★ American Hospital Association (AHA) membership
□ Joint Commission on Accreditation of Healthcare Organizations (JCAHO) accreditation
+ American Osteopathic Healthcare Association (AOHA) membership
○ American Osteopathic Association (AOA) accreditation
△ Commission on Accreditation of Rehabilitation Facilities (CARF) accreditation
Control codes 61, 63, 64, 71, 72 and 73 indicate hospitals listed by AOHA, but not registered by AHA. For definition of numerical codes, see page A4.

NELIGH—Antelope County

★ ANTELOPE MEMORIAL HOSPITAL, 102 West Ninth Street, Zip 68756–0229, Mailing Address: P.O. Box 229, Zip 68756–0229; tel. 402/887–4151; Jack W. Green, Administrator **A**9 10 **F**7 8 15 17 19 22 24 30 32 34 40 42 44 45 46 49 64 65 71 **N** North Central Hospital Nebraska Network, Osmond, NE
| 23 | 10 | 45 | 700 | 15 | 11135 | 21 | 3888 | 1931 | 89 |

NORFOLK—Madison County

✠ FAITH REGIONAL HEALTH SERVICES, (Includes Lutheran Community Hospital, 2700 Norfolk Avenue, Zip 68701, Mailing Address: P.O. Box 869, Zip 68702–0869; tel. 402/371–4880; Our Lady of Lourdes Hospital, 1500 Koenigstein Avenue, Zip 68701–3698; tel. 402/371–3402), 2700 Norfolk Avenue, Zip 68702–0869, Mailing Address: P.O. BOX 869, Zip 68702–0869; tel. 402/644–7201; Robert L. Driewer, Chief Executive Officer **A**1 9 10 **S** Missionary Benedictine Sisters American Province, Norfolk, NE
| 23 | 10 | 115 | 5995 | 44 | 47012 | 922 | 42423 | 18739 | 745 |

LUTHERAN COMMUNITY HOSPITAL See Faith Regional Health Services

□ NORFOLK REGIONAL CENTER, 1700 North Victory Road, Zip 68701–6859, Mailing Address: P.O. Box 1209, Zip 68702–1209; tel. 402/370–3400 **A**1 10
| 12 | 22 | 174 | 393 | — | — | 0 | 13206 | 8494 | 308 |

OUR LADY OF LOURDES HOSPITAL See Faith Regional Health Services

NORTH PLATTE—Lincoln County

✠ GREAT PLAINS REGIONAL MEDICAL CENTER, 601 West Leota Street, Zip 69101–6598, Mailing Address: P.O. Box 1167, Zip 69103–1167; tel. 308/534–9310; Lucinda A. Bradley, President **A**1 2 3 5 9 10 **F**3 7 8 10 11 12 15 19 21 22 23 28 32 33 35 37 39 40 41 42 44 46 49 52 53 56 58 59 60 65 66 67 71 73 **P**8 **S** Quorum Health Group/Quorum Health Resources, Inc., Brentwood, TN **N** Heartland Health Alliance, Lincoln, NE; Rural Health Partners, Lexington, NE
| 23 | 10 | 99 | 4276 | 45 | 78221 | 515 | 40540 | 17083 | 513 |

O'NEILL—Holt County

✠ ST. ANTHONY'S HOSPITAL, Second and Adams Streets, Zip 68763–1597; tel. 402/336–2611; Ronald J. Cork, President and Chief Executive Officer **A**1 9 10 **F**7 8 12 15 16 17 18 19 20 22 26 28 29 30 31 32 34 35 39 40 42 44 49 54 61 65 66 67 71 73 **P**1 6 **S** Marycrest Health System, Denver, CO
| 21 | 10 | 29 | 768 | 5 | 14497 | 109 | 6618 | 2571 | 99 |

OAKLAND—Burt County

OAKLAND MEMORIAL HOSPITAL, 601 East Second Street, Zip 68045–1499; tel. 402/685–5601; Karen Vlach, Administrator **A**9 10 **F**8 12 15 16 19 22 28 30 32 33 34 35 36 37 39 41 42 44 46 51 64 71 73 **P**2 5
| 16 | 10 | 23 | 225 | 4 | — | 0 | 2254 | 1201 | 40 |

OFFUTT AFB—Sarpy County

✠ EHRLING BERGQUIST HOSPITAL, 2501 Capehart Road, Zip 68113–2160; tel. 402/294–7312; Colonel John R. Sheehan, USAF, MSC, Deputy Commander **A**1 3 5 **F**3 7 8 12 13 14 15 16 19 20 22 24 25 27 29 30 39 40 41 44 45 46 51 53 54 55 56 58 61 65 71 72 73 74 **S** Department of the Air Force, Bowling AFB, DC
| 41 | 10 | 45 | 2777 | 15 | 288568 | 626 | 58386 | — | — |

OGALLALA—Keith County

★ OGALLALA COMMUNITY HOSPITAL, 300 East Tenth Street, Zip 69153–1509; tel. 308/284–4011; Linda Morris, Administrator **A**9 10 **F**7 8 11 12 13 15 16 17 19 21 22 25 28 30 34 37 40 41 42 44 49 51 58 64 65 67 68 71 72 **P**6 **S** Lutheran Health Systems, Fargo, ND
| 23 | 10 | 29 | 779 | 8 | 25233 | 72 | 7586 | 4012 | 145 |

OMAHA—Douglas County

✠ ALEGENT HEALTH BERGAN MERCY MEDICAL CENTER, 7500 Mercy Road, Zip 68124; tel. 402/398–6060; Charles J. Marr, Chief Executive Officer (Total facility includes 241 beds in nursing home–type unit) **A**1 2 3 5 9 10 **F**1 2 3 4 5 7 8 10 11 12 15 16 17 18 19 20 21 22 24 25 26 27 28 29 30 31 32 33 34 35 36 37 38 39 40 41 42 43 44 45 46 48 49 50 51 52 53 54 55 56 57 58 59 60 61 62 63 64 65 66 67 68 71 72 73 74 **P**7 8 **S** Catholic Health Initiatives, Denver, CO **N** Alegent Health, Omaha, NE
| 21 | 10 | 646 | 14217 | 369 | 134053 | 2257 | 135701 | 55713 | 2732 |

✠ △ ALEGENT HEALTH IMMANUEL MEDICAL CENTER, 6901 North 72nd Street, Zip 68122–1799; tel. 402/572–2121; Charles J. Marr, Chief Executive Officer (Total facility includes 200 beds in nursing home–type unit) **A**1 2 5 7 9 10 **F**1 2 3 4 6 7 8 10 11 12 15 16 17 18 19 20 21 22 24 25 26 27 28 29 30 31 32 33 34 35 36 37 38 39 40 41 42 43 44 45 46 48 49 50 51 52 53 54 55 56 57 58 59 60 61 62 63 64 65 66 67 68 71 72 73 74 **P**7 8 **N** Alegent Health, Omaha, NE
| 23 | 10 | 542 | 11120 | 376 | 167076 | 851 | 137549 | 47334 | 1886 |

BISHOP CLARKSON MEMORIAL HOSPITAL See Nebraska Health System

□ BOYS TOWN NATIONAL RESEARCH HOSPITAL, 555 North 30th Street, Zip 68131–2198; tel. 402/498–6511; John K. Arch, Administrator **A**1 3 10 **F**16 21 34 44 46 51 53 73 **P**6
| 23 | 50 | 14 | 1301 | 4 | 107325 | 0 | — | — | 314 |

✠ CHILDREN'S HOSPITAL, 8301 Dodge Street, Zip 68114–4199; tel. 402/354–5400; Gary A. Perkins, President and Chief Executive Officer **A**1 3 5 9 10 **F**10 12 15 17 19 21 22 23 29 32 34 35 38 39 42 43 44 45 47 60 63 65 67 71 72 73 **P**8
| 23 | 50 | 100 | 5325 | 74 | 52921 | 0 | 58774 | 25038 | 686 |

○ DOUGLAS COUNTY HOSPITAL, 4102 Woolworth Avenue, Zip 68105–1899; tel. 402/444–7000; James C. Tourville, Administrator (Total facility includes 275 beds in nursing home–type unit) **A**10 11 **F**15 18 27 34 49 51 52 54 55 56 58 59 64 65 73
| 13 | 22 | 295 | 608 | 266 | 19720 | — | 13716 | 11155 | 453 |

✠ METHODIST RICHARD YOUNG, (Includes Richard H. Young Memorial Hospital), 415 South 25th Avenue, Zip 68131–3619; tel. 402/354–6600; Sandra C. Carson, FACHE, Senior Vice President **A**1 5 9 10 **F**2 3 4 7 8 9 10 11 12 13 15 17 18 19 20 21 22 23 25 26 27 28 29 30 32 33 34 35 37 38 39 40 41 42 43 47 48 49 51 52 53 54 55 56 57 58 59 60 61 62 63 64 65 66 67 69 70 72 73 74 **P**1 4 5 6 7
| 21 | 22 | 78 | 1443 | 57 | 27245 | 0 | 13935 | 7177 | 245 |

Hospital, Address, Telephone, Administrator, Approval, Facility, and Physician Codes, Health Care System, Network	Classification Codes		Utilization Data					Expense (thousands) of dollars		
	Control	Service	Staffed Beds	Admissions	Census	Outpatient Visits	Births	Total	Payroll	Personnel

★ American Hospital Association (AHA) membership
□ Joint Commission on Accreditation of Healthcare Organizations (JCAHO) accreditation
+ American Osteopathic Healthcare Association (AOHA) membership
○ American Osteopathic Association (AOA) accreditation
△ Commission on Accreditation of Rehabilitation Facilities (CARF) accreditation
   Control codes 61, 63, 64, 71, 72 and 73 indicate hospitals listed by AOHA, but not registered by AHA. For definition of numerical codes, see page A4

Hospital	Control	Service	Staffed Beds	Admissions	Census	Outpatient Visits	Births	Total	Payroll	Personnel
⊠ NEBRASKA HEALTH SYSTEM, (Includes Nebraska Health System (Formerly Bishop Clarkson Memorial Hospital), 4350 Dewey Avenue, ; Nebraska Health System (Formerly University of Nebraska Medical Center), 600 South 42nd Street, Zip 68198–4085; tel. 402/559–4000, 4350 Dewey Avenue, Zip 68105–1018; tel. 402/552–2040; Louis Burgher, M.D., Ph.D., President and Chief Executive Officer (Total facility includes 30 beds in nursing home–type unit) **A**1 2 3 5 8 9 10 **F**2 4 5 6 7 8 9 10 11 12 13 14 15 16 17 18 19 20 21 22 23 24 25 26 27 28 29 30 31 32 33 34 35 36 37 38 39 40 41 42 43 44 45 46 47 48 49 50 51 52 54 55 56 57 58 59 60 61 63 65 66 67 69 70 71 72 73 **P**4 7	23	10	516	20589	—	—	1895	—	105033	—
⊠ △ NEBRASKA METHODIST HOSPITAL, 8303 Dodge Street, Zip 68114–4199; tel. 402/354–4000; John Martin Fraser, President and Chief Executive Officer **A**1 2 3 7 9 10 **F**3 4 6 7 8 10 11 12 14 15 16 17 18 19 20 21 22 23 24 26 27 28 29 30 31 32 33 34 35 37 38 39 40 41 42 43 44 45 47 48 49 51 53 54 55 56 58 59 60 61 62 64 65 66 67 69 71 72 73 74 **P**6 7 8	23	10	310	13445	185	—	3231	141402	59560	2133
RICHARD H. YOUNG MEMORIAL HOSPITAL See Methodist Richard Young										
ST. JOSEPH CENTER FOR MENTAL HEALTH, 819 Dorcas Street, Zip 68108–1198; tel. 402/449–4000; Robert C. Caldwell, Chief Operating Officer **A**3 5 9 **F**3 14 16 52 53 54 55 56 57 58 59 65 67 73 **P**1 4 6 **S** TENET Healthcare Corporation, Santa Barbara, CA	33	22	70	1817	60	8897	—	11815	5740	179
⊠ ST. JOSEPH HOSPITAL, 601 North 30th Street, Zip 68131–2197; tel. 402/449–5021; J. Richard Stanko, President and Chief Executive Officer **A**1 2 3 5 8 10 **F**2 3 4 7 8 10 11 12 15 19 20 21 22 24 25 31 34 35 37 38 40 41 42 43 44 46 47 49 51 52 53 54 55 56 57 58 59 60 63 64 65 69 71 72 73 74 **P**2 7 8 **S** TENET Healthcare Corporation, Santa Barbara, CA	33	10	282	10115	159	53780	853	103018	34551	—
UNIVERSITY OF NEBRASKA MEDICAL CENTER See Nebraska Health System										
⊠ VETERANS AFFAIRS MEDICAL CENTER, 4101 Woolworth Avenue, Zip 68105–1873; tel. 402/449–0600; John J. Phillips, Director **A**1 3 5 8 **F**3 4 10 12 17 19 20 21 22 23 26 28 30 31 34 35 37 39 41 42 43 44 45 46 49 50 51 52 54 56 57 58 60 63 65 67 69 71 73 74 **P**1 **S** Department of Veterans Affairs, Washington, DC	45	10	122	3600	82	—	—	—	—	861
ORD—Valley County										
★ VALLEY COUNTY HOSPITAL, 217 Westridge Drive, Zip 68862–1675; tel. 308/728–3211; John E. Keelan, Chief Executive Officer and Administrator (Total facility includes 70 beds in nursing home–type unit) **A**9 10 **F**7 8 11 12 14 15 16 19 20 21 24 27 28 32 33 34 35 37 39 40 41 44 47 64 65 71 **N** Central Nebraska Primary Care Network, Ord, NE	13	10	96	756	73	13054	58	4674	2530	95
OSCEOLA—Polk County										
ANNIE JEFFREY MEMORIAL COUNTY HEALTH CENTER, 531 Beebe Street, Zip 68651, Mailing Address: P.O. Box 428, Zip 68651–0428; tel. 402/747–2031; Carol E. Jones, Administrator **A**9 10 **F**7 8 14 15 16 17 19 20 22 24 26 28 29 30 31 32 33 34 35 36 39 40 41 42 44 45 49 51 64 65 66 71 73 **P**5 6 8 **N** Blue River Valley Health Network, Brainard, NE	13	10	21	363	4	14775	24	2971	1603	66
OSHKOSH—Garden County										
GARDEN COUNTY HOSPITAL, 1100 West Second Street, Zip 69154, Mailing Address: P.O. Box 320, Zip 69154–0320; tel. 308/772–3283; Kelly Reece, Facility Manager (Total facility includes 36 beds in nursing home–type unit) (Nonreporting) **A**9 10 **N** Western Nebraska Rural Health Care Network, Chadron, NE	13	10	56	—	—	—	—	—	—	—
OSMOND—Pierce County										
★ OSMOND GENERAL HOSPITAL, 5th and Maple Street, Zip 68765–0429, Mailing Address: P.O. Box 429, Zip 68765–0429; tel. 402/748–3393; Celine Mlady, Chief Executive Officer **A**9 10 **F**1 8 15 19 22 28 30 32 33 34 35 36 44 49 64 65 71 **P**6 **N** North Central Hospital Nebraska Network, Osmond, NE	23	10	30	701	22	5542	—	2824	1539	63
PAPILLION—Sarpy County										
⊠ MIDLANDS COMMUNITY HOSPITAL, 11111 South 84th Street, Zip 68046–4157; tel. 402/593–3000; Diana Smalley, Chief Operating Officer **A**1 2 9 10 **F**2 3 4 7 8 10 12 16 19 21 22 26 28 32 34 35 37 40 41 42 43 44 45 49 52 53 54 55 56 57 58 59 60 63 64 65 66 70 71 72 73 **P**5	32	10	160	3228	47	29179	339	26343	11304	377
PAWNEE CITY—Pawnee County										
PAWNEE COUNTY MEMORIAL HOSPITAL, 600 I. Street, Zip 68420–3001, Mailing Address: P.O. Box 313, Zip 68420–0313; tel. 402/852–2231; James A. Kubik, Administrator **A**9 10	13	10	14	196	2	7707	2	2171	813	37
PENDER—Thurston County										
★ PENDER COMMUNITY HOSPITAL, 603 Earl Street, Zip 68047–0100, Mailing Address: P.O. Box 100, Zip 68047–0100; tel. 402/385–3083; Roger Mazour, Interim Administrator **A**9 10 **F**7 8 11 19 22 35 40 42 44 45 49 71 **P**7 **S** Mercy Health Services, Farmington Hills, MI	16	10	30	719	9	9185	61	3803	1557	75
PLAINVIEW—Pierce County										
PLAINVIEW PUBLIC HOSPITAL, 705 North Third Street, Zip 68769, Mailing Address: P.O. Box 489, Zip 68769–0489; tel. 402/582–4245; Donald T. Naiberk, Administrator and Chief Executive Officer (Nonreporting) **A**9 10 **N** North Central Hospital Nebraska Network, Osmond, NE	14	10	19	—	—	—	—	—	—	—
RED CLOUD—Webster County										
WEBSTER COUNTY COMMUNITY HOSPITAL, Sixth Avenue and Franklin Street, Zip 68970–0465; tel. 402/746–2291; Terry L. Hoffart, Administrator **A**9 10 **F**8 19 28 35 37 44 49 66 71 73 **P**3 **N** Heartland Health Alliance, Lincoln, NE; Rural Health Partners, Lexington, NE	13	10	16	255	4	752	—	1709	601	33

Hospital, Address, Telephone, Administrator, Approval, Facility, and Physician Codes, Health Care System, Network	Classification Codes		Utilization Data					Expense (thousands) of dollars		
	Control	Service	Staffed Beds	Admissions	Census	Outpatient Visits	Births	Total	Payroll	Personnel

★ American Hospital Association (AHA) membership
□ Joint Commission on Accreditation of Healthcare Organizations (JCAHO) accreditation
+ American Osteopathic Healthcare Association (AOHA) membership
○ American Osteopathic Association (AOA) accreditation
△ Commission on Accreditation of Rehabilitation Facilities (CARF) accreditation
Control codes 61, 63, 64, 71, 72 and 73 indicate hospitals listed by AOHA, but not registered by AHA. For definition of numerical codes, see page A4

SAINT PAUL—Howard County

★ HOWARD COUNTY COMMUNITY HOSPITAL, 1102 Kendall Street, Zip 68873–1536, Mailing Address: P.O. Box 406, Zip 68873–0406; tel. 308/754–4421; Russell W. Swigart, Administrator **A**9 10 **F**7 8 14 19 22 33 35 44 45 49 65 71 73	13	10	37	453	19	7434	37	2522	1273	67

SARGENT—Custer County

GOLI MEDICAL CENTER, (Formerly Sargent District Hospital), 1201 West Main Street, Zip 68874; tel. 308/527–3414; Rajitha Goli, M.D., Administrator and Chief Executive Officer (Nonreporting) **A**9 10	16	10	18	—	—	—	—	—	—	—

SCHUYLER—Colfax County

ALEGENT HEALTH–MEMORIAL HOSPITAL, 104 West 17th Street, Zip 68661–1396; tel. 402/352–2441; Al Klaasmeyer, Administrator (Total facility includes 31 beds in nursing home–type unit) **A**9 10 **F**7 8 12 15 16 17 22 26 28 30 31 32 34 36 38 39 40 42 44 48 49 56 64 65 66 67 71 **P**7 8 **N** Alegent Health, Omaha, NE	23	10	49	393	33	17380	84	5279	2370	118

SCOTTSBLUFF—Scotts Bluff County

⊞ REGIONAL WEST MEDICAL CENTER, 4021 Avenue B., Zip 69361–4695; tel. 308/635–3711; David M. Nitschke, President and Chief Executive Officer (Total facility includes 22 beds in nursing home–type unit) **A**1 2 3 5 9 10 **N** Western Nebraska Rural Health Care Network, Chadron, NE	23	10	202	6081	74	35703	669	52885	22675	754

SEWARD—Seward County

MEMORIAL HEALTH CARE SYSTEMS, 300 North Columbia Avenue, Zip 68434–9907; tel. 402/643–2971; Ronald D. Waltz, Chief Executive Officer (Total facility includes 120 beds in nursing home–type unit) **A**9 10 **F**1 7 8 12 15 16 17 19 22 26 27 28 30 32 33 34 35 39 44 45 46 49 64 65 66 71 73 **P**6 **N** Heartland Health Alliance, Lincoln, NE; Blue River Valley Health Network, Brainard, NE	23	10	154	620	127	16766	85	11043	6000	251

SIDNEY—Cheyenne County

★ MEMORIAL HEALTH CENTER, 645 Osage Street, Zip 69162–1799; tel. 308/254–5825; Rex D. Walk, Chief Executive Officer (Total facility includes 70 beds in nursing home–type unit) **A**9 10 **F**1 3 7 8 10 11 17 19 21 22 24 26 28 29 30 32 33 34 35 36 37 39 40 41 44 48 49 55 56 57 58 64 65 66 67 70 71 73 74 **N** Western Nebraska Rural Health Care Network, Chadron, NE; High Plains Rural Health Network, Fort Morgan, CO	23	10	102	1242	80	14958	111	9748	4995	—

SUPERIOR—Nuckolls County

BRODSTONE MEMORIAL HOSPITAL, 520 East Tenth Street, Zip 68978–1225, Mailing Address: P.O. Box 187, Zip 68978–0187; tel. 402/879–3281; Ronald D. Waggoner, Administrator and Chief Executive Officer **A**9 10 **F**7 8 19 22 27 32 33 34 35 36 37 40 41 44 49 64 65 71 **P**8 **N** Heartland Health Alliance, Lincoln, NE; Rural Health Partners, Lexington, NE	23	10	49	806	14	18820	56	5907	2355	104

SYRACUSE—Otoe County

COMMUNITY MEMORIAL HOSPITAL, 1579 Midland Street, Zip 68446–9732, Mailing Address: P.O. Box N., Zip 68446; tel. 402/269–2011; Ron Anderson, Administrator **A**9 10 **F**7 8 11 19 22 24 32 33 40 44 49 64 71 **N** Heartland Health Alliance, Lincoln, NE	16	10	18	239	2	—	—	2154	882	46

TECUMSEH—Johnson County

★ JOHNSON COUNTY HOSPITAL, 202 High Street, Zip 68450–0599, Mailing Address: P.O. Box 599, Zip 68450–0599; tel. 402/335–3361; Lavonne M. Rowe, Administrator **A**9 10 **F**1 7 8 14 15 16 17 19 22 28 30 32 33 34 37 40 41 42 44 49 51 63 71 **N** Heartland Health Alliance, Lincoln, NE	13	10	30	382	3	5344	32	2106	909	46

TILDEN—Antelope County

TILDEN COMMUNITY HOSPITAL, Second and Pine Streets, Zip 68781, Mailing Address: P.O. Box 340, Zip 68781–0340; tel. 402/368–5343; LuAnn Barr, Administrator (Nonreporting) **A**9 10	23	10	20	—	—	—	—	—	—	—

VALENTINE—Cherry County

CHERRY COUNTY HOSPITAL, Highway 12 and Green Street, Zip 69201–0410; tel. 402/376–2525; Brent A. Peterson, Administrator **A**9 10 **F**8 10 11 15 16 17 19 22 28 32 34 35 37 40 42 44 46 70 71 **P**6 **N** Heartland Health Alliance, Lincoln, NE	13	10	27	633	7	8107	176	4025	1778	69

WAHOO—Saunders County

SAUNDERS COUNTY HEALTH SERVICE, 805 West Tenth Street, Zip 68066–1102, Mailing Address: P.O. Box 185, Zip 68066–0185; tel. 402/443–4191; Michael Boyles, Administrator (Total facility includes 73 beds in nursing home–type unit) **A**9 10 **F**14 15 16 17 19 22 28 29 30 32 33 34 35 36 39 44 45 46 49 51 54 64 65 66 67 71 **P**6 **N** Blue River Valley Health Network, Brainard, NE	13	10	95	245	77	9619	0	5581	3233	138

WAYNE—Wayne County

PROVIDENCE MEDICAL CENTER, 1200 Providence Road, Zip 68787–1299; tel. 402/375–3800; Marcile Thomas, Administrator **A**9 10 **F**7 14 15 16 19 22 24 32 33 35 36 42 44 49 65 66 71 **S** Missionary Benedictine Sisters American Province, Norfolk, NE	21	10	34	955	11	9860	96	5047	2148	77

WEST POINT—Cuming County

★ ST. FRANCIS MEMORIAL HOSPITAL, 430 North Monitor Street, Zip 68788–1595; tel. 402/372–2404; Ronald O. Briggs, President (Total facility includes 70 beds in nursing home–type unit) **A**9 10 **F**6 7 8 15 19 22 24 32 33 34 40 44 48 49 71 73 **P**6 **S** Franciscan Sisters of Christian Charity HealthCare Ministry, Inc, Manitowoc, WI	21	10	97	683	74	60700	104	8070	4372	141

Hospital, Address, Telephone, Administrator, Approval, Facility, and Physician Codes, Health Care System, Network	Classi- fication Codes		Utilization Data					Expense (thousands) of dollars		
★ American Hospital Association (AHA) membership □ Joint Commission on Accreditation of Healthcare Organizations (JCAHO) accreditation + American Osteopathic Healthcare Association (AOHA) membership ○ American Osteopathic Association (AOA) accreditation △ Commission on Accreditation of Rehabilitation Facilities (CARF) accreditation Control codes 61, 63, 64, 71, 72 and 73 indicate hospitals listed by AOHA, but not registered by AHA. For definition of numerical codes, see page A4	Control	Service	Staffed Beds	Admissions	Census	Outpatient Visits	Births	Total	Payroll	Personnel

WINNEBAGO—Thurston County

✠ U. S. PUBLIC HEALTH SERVICE INDIAN HOSPITAL, Highway 7577, Zip 68071; tel. 402/878–2231; Donald Lee, Service Unit Director **A**1 10 **F**1 3 4 5 6 7 8 9 10 11 12 13 14 15 16 17 18 19 20 21 22 23 24 25 26 27 28 29 30 31 32 33 34 35 36 37 38 39 40 41 42 43 44 45 46 47 48 49 50 51 52 53 54 55 56 57 58 59 60 61 62 63 64 65 66 67 68 69 70 71 72 73 74 **P**8 **S** U. S. Public Health Service Indian Health Service, Rockville, MD	47	10	30	474	13	33069	—	7364	2910	—

YORK—York County

★ YORK GENERAL HOSPITAL, 2222 Lincoln Avenue, Zip 68467–1095; tel. 402/362–0445; Charles K. Schulz, Chief Executive Officer **A**9 10 **F**7 8 11 12 15 16 17 19 20 21 22 24 28 30 32 33 34 35 36 37 39 40 41 42 44 46 48 49 63 64 65 66 67 71 73 74 **P**5 **N** Heartland Health Alliance, Lincoln, NE; Blue River Valley Health Network, Brainard, NE	23	10	41	1198	14	31900	160	8749	4035	153

NEVADA

Resident population 1,677 (in thousands)
Resident population in metro areas 85.3%
Birth rate per 1,000 population 16.4
65 years and over 11.4%
Percent of persons without health insurance 15.6%

Hospital, Address, Telephone, Administrator, Approval, Facility, and Physician Codes, Health Care System, Network	Classification Codes		Utilization Data					Expense (thousands) of dollars		
	Control	Service	Staffed Beds	Admissions	Census	Outpatient Visits	Births	Total	Payroll	Personnel

★ American Hospital Association (AHA) membership
☐ Joint Commission on Accreditation of Healthcare Organizations (JCAHO) accreditation
+ American Osteopathic Healthcare Association (AOHA) membership
○ American Osteopathic Association (AOA) accreditation
△ Commission on Accreditation of Rehabilitation Facilities (CARF) accreditation
Control codes 61, 63, 64, 71, 72 and 73 indicate hospitals listed by AOHA, but not registered by AHA. For definition of numerical codes, see page A4

BATTLE MOUNTAIN—Lander County

Hospital	Control	Service	Staffed Beds	Admissions	Census	Outpatient Visits	Births	Total	Payroll	Personnel
BATTLE MOUNTAIN GENERAL HOSPITAL, 535 South Humboldt Street, Zip 89820–1988; tel. 702/635–2550; Kathy Ancho, Administrator (Nonreporting) **A**10	13	10	14	—	—	—	—	—	—	—

BOULDER CITY—Clark County

Hospital	Control	Service	Staffed Beds	Admissions	Census	Outpatient Visits	Births	Total	Payroll	Personnel
BOULDER CITY HOSPITAL, 901 Adams Boulevard, Zip 89005–2299; tel. 702/293–4111; Kim O. Crandell, Chief Executive Officer and Administrator (Total facility includes 47 beds in nursing home–type unit) (Nonreporting) **A**9 10	23	10	67	—	—	—	—	—	—	—

CARSON CITY—Carson City County

Hospital	Control	Service	Staffed Beds	Admissions	Census	Outpatient Visits	Births	Total	Payroll	Personnel
★ CARSON TAHOE HOSPITAL, 775 Fleischmann Way, Zip 89703, Mailing Address: P.O. Box 2168, Zip 89702–2168; tel. 702/882–1361; Steve Smith, Chief Executive Officer (Total facility includes 125 beds in nursing home–type unit) **A**1 9 10 **F**2 3 7 8 10 12 14 15 17 19 21 22 23 25 26 28 30 32 33 34 35 37 39 40 44 45 46 48 49 52 54 55 56 57 58 59 60 63 64 65 67 70 71 72 73	13	10	249	7931	179	88869	714	45034	24427	703

ELKO—Elko County

Hospital	Control	Service	Staffed Beds	Admissions	Census	Outpatient Visits	Births	Total	Payroll	Personnel
★ ELKO GENERAL HOSPITAL, 1297 College Avenue, Zip 89801–3499; tel. 702/753–1999; Anne Rieger, R.N., Administrator (Nonreporting) **A**1 9 10	13	10	50	—	—	—	—	—	—	—

ELY—White Pine County

Hospital	Control	Service	Staffed Beds	Admissions	Census	Outpatient Visits	Births	Total	Payroll	Personnel
☐ WILLIAM BEE RIRIE HOSPITAL, 1500 Avenue H., Zip 89301–2699; tel. 702/289–3001; Jack T. Wood, Administrator **A**1 9 10 **F**7 8 19 22 25 26 28 37 44 49 65 71 73	13	10	40	527	4	11050	73	6456	2379	85

FALLON—Churchill County

Hospital	Control	Service	Staffed Beds	Admissions	Census	Outpatient Visits	Births	Total	Payroll	Personnel
★ CHURCHILL COMMUNITY HOSPTIAL, 801 East Williams Avenue, Zip 89406–3052; tel. 702/423–3151; Jeffrey Feike, Administrator (Nonreporting) **A**1 9 10 **S** Lutheran Health Systems, Fargo, ND	23	10	40	—	—	—	—	—	—	—

HAWTHORNE—Mineral County

Hospital	Control	Service	Staffed Beds	Admissions	Census	Outpatient Visits	Births	Total	Payroll	Personnel
MOUNT GRANT GENERAL HOSPITAL, First and A. Street, Zip 89415, Mailing Address: P.O. Box 1510, Zip 89415–1510; tel. 702/945–2461; Richard Munger, Administrator (Total facility includes 20 beds in nursing home–type unit) (Nonreporting) **A**9 10	46	10	35	—	—	—	—	—	—	—

HENDERSON—Clark County

Hospital	Control	Service	Staffed Beds	Admissions	Census	Outpatient Visits	Births	Total	Payroll	Personnel
★ ST. ROSE DOMINICAN HOSPITAL, 102 Lake Mead Drive, Zip 89015–5524; tel. 702/564–2622; Rod A. Davis, President and Chief Executive Officer (Nonreporting) **A**1 9 10 **S** Catholic Healthcare West, San Francisco, CA **N** Catholic HealthCare West (CHW), San Francisco, CA	21	10	135	—	—	—	—	—	—	—

LAS VEGAS—Clark County

Hospital	Control	Service	Staffed Beds	Admissions	Census	Outpatient Visits	Births	Total	Payroll	Personnel
☐ BHC MONTEVISTA HOSPITAL, 5900 West Rochelle Avenue, Zip 89103–3327; tel. 702/364–1111; Darryl S. Dubroca, Chief Executive Officer and Administrator (Nonreporting) **A**1 10 **S** Behavioral Healthcare Corporation, Nashville, TN	33	22	80	—	—	—	—	—	—	—
☐ CHARTER BEHAVIORAL HEALTH SYSTEM OF NEVADA, 7000 West Spring Mountain Road, Zip 89117–3816; tel. 702/876–4357; Lynn M. Rosenbach, Chief Executive Officer (Nonreporting) **A**1 10 **S** Magellan Health Services, Atlanta, GA	33	22	84	—	—	—	—	—	—	—
★ △ COLUMBIA SUNRISE HOSPITAL AND MEDICAL CENTER, 3186 Maryland Parkway, Zip 89109–2306, Mailing Address: P.O. Box 98530, Zip 89193–8530; tel. 702/731–8000; Jerald F. Mitchell, President and Chief Executive Officer **A**1 2 5 7 9 10 **F**4 7 10 11 12 14 15 16 19 21 22 29 32 35 37 38 40 41 42 43 44 47 48 49 60 64 65 69 71 73 **S** Columbia/HCA Healthcare Corporation, Nashville, TN	33	10	671	37375	516	119462	5699	239458	100322	2620
★ COLUMBIA SUNRISE MOUNTAINVIEW HOSPITAL, 3100 North Tenaya Way, Zip 89128; tel. 702/255–5000; Mark J. Howard, President and Chief Executive Officer (Nonreporting) **A**10 **S** Columbia/HCA Healthcare Corporation, Nashville, TN	33	10	120	—	—	—	—	—	—	—
★ DESERT SPRINGS HOSPITAL, 2075 East Flamingo Road, Zip 89119–5121, Mailing Address: P.O. Box 19204, Zip 89132–9204; tel. 702/733–8800; Thomas L. Koenig, Chief Executive Officer (Nonreporting) **A**1 10 **S** Universal Health Services, Inc., King of Prussia, PA	33	10	225	—	—	—	—	—	—	—
★ MIKE O'CALLAGHAN FEDERAL HOSPITAL, 4700 Las Vegas Boulevard North, Suite 2419, Zip 89191–6601; tel. 702/653–2000; Colonel Jack A. Gupton, MSC, USAF, Administrator **A**1 **F**1 2 3 4 5 6 7 8 9 10 11 12 13 14 15 16 17 18 19 20 21 22 23 24 25 26 27 28 29 30 31 32 33 34 35 37 38 39 40 41 42 43 44 45 46 47 48 49 51 52 53 54 55 56 57 58 59 60 61 64 65 66 67 68 69 70 71 72 73 74 **P**1 **S** Department of the Air Force, Bowling AFB, DC	41	10	52	2892	21	214634	562	—	—	—
☐ THC–LAS VEGAS HOSPITAL, 5100 West Sahara Avenue, Zip 89102–3436; tel. 702/871–1418; Dale A. Kirby, Chief Executive Officer (Nonreporting) **A**1 10 **S** Transitional Hospitals Corporation, Las Vegas, NV	33	49	52	—	—	—	—	—	—	—
☐ UNIVERSITY MEDICAL CENTER, 1800 West Charleston Boulevard, Zip 89102–2386; tel. 702/383–2000; William R. Hale, Chief Executive Officer (Nonreporting) **A**1 2 3 5 10	13	10	506	—	—	—	—	—	—	—
☐ VALLEY HOSPITAL MEDICAL CENTER, 620 Shadow Lane, Zip 89106–4194; tel. 702/388–4000; Roger Collins, Chief Executive Officer and Managing Director (Nonreporting) **A**1 9 10 **S** Universal Health Services, Inc., King of Prussia, PA	33	10	365	—	—	—	—	—	—	—

Hospital, Address, Telephone, Administrator, Approval, Facility, and Physician Codes, Health Care System, Network	Classi-fication Codes		Utilization Data					Expense (thousands) of dollars		
★ American Hospital Association (AHA) membership □ Joint Commission on Accreditation of Healthcare Organizations (JCAHO) accreditation + American Osteopathic Healthcare Association (AOHA) membership ○ American Osteopathic Association (AOA) accreditation △ Commission on Accreditation of Rehabilitation Facilities (CARF) accreditation Control codes 61, 63, 64, 71, 72 and 73 indicate hospitals listed by AOHA, but not registered by AHA. For definition of numerical codes, see page A4	Control	Service	Staffed Beds	Admissions	Census	Outpatient Visits	Births	Total	Payroll	Personnel

LOVELOCK—Pershing County

★ PERSHING GENERAL HOSPITAL, 855 Sixth Street, Zip 89419, Mailing Address: P.O. Box 661, Zip 89419–0661; tel. 702/273–2621; Helen Woolley, Administrator (Total facility includes 25 beds in nursing home–type unit) (Nonreporting) **A**9 10 **S** Lutheran Health Systems, Fargo, ND

| | 16 | 10 | 34 | — | — | — | — | — | — | — |

NORTH LAS VEGAS—Clark County

⊞ LAKE MEAD HOSPITAL MEDICAL CENTER, 1409 East Lake Mead Boulevard, Zip 89030–7197; tel. 702/649–7711; Ernest Libman, Chief Executive Officer **A**1 10 **F**2 7 8 9 10 12 14 15 16 19 20 21 28 32 33 35 37 38 40 44 46 47 48 52 57 59 63 64 65 71 73 **S** TENET Healthcare Corporation, Santa Barbara, CA

| | 33 | 10 | 184 | 7699 | 120 | 53313 | 1364 | 56221 | 18421 | 571 |

OWYHEE—Elko County

⊞ U. S. PUBLIC HEALTH SERVICE OWYHEE COMMUNITY HEALTH FACILITY, Mailing Address: P.O. Box 130, Zip 89832–0130; tel. 702/757–2415; Walden Townsend, Service Unit Director (Nonreporting) **A**1 10 **S** U. S. Public Health Service Indian Health Service, Rockville, MD

| | 46 | 10 | 15 | — | — | — | — | — | — | — |

RENO—Washoe County

□ BHC WEST HILLS HOSPITAL, 1240 East Ninth Street, Zip 89512–2997, Mailing Address: P.O. Box 30012, Zip 89520–0012; tel. 702/323–0478; Pamela McCullough Broughton, Chief Executive Officer (Nonreporting) **A**1 3 5 10 **S** Behavioral Healthcare Corporation, Nashville, TN

| | 33 | 22 | 95 | — | — | — | — | — | — | — |

BHC WILLOW SPRINGS RESIDENTIAL TREATMENT CENTER, 690 Edison Way, Zip 89502–4135; tel. 702/858–3303; Robert Bartlett, Administrator **F**15 52 53 **P**8 **S** Behavioral Healthcare Corporation, Nashville, TN

| | 33 | 22 | 68 | 149 | 46 | — | — | 4940 | 2727 | 90 |

⊞ IOANNIS A. LOUGARIS VETERANS AFFAIRS MEDICAL CENTER, 1000 Locust Street, Zip 89520–0111; tel. 702/786–7200; Gary R. Whitfield, Director (Total facility includes 60 beds in nursing home–type unit) **A**1 3 5 **F**1 3 8 10 12 15 17 18 19 20 21 22 24 26 27 28 29 30 31 32 34 35 37 41 42 45 46 49 51 52 54 55 56 57 58 59 60 63 64 65 67 71 72 73 74 **S** Department of Veterans Affairs, Washington, DC

| | 45 | 10 | 146 | 3294 | 114 | 127015 | 0 | — | 30679 | 669 |

⊞ △ SAINT MARY'S REGIONAL MEDICAL CENTER, 235 West Sixth Street, Zip 89520–0108; tel. 702/323–2041; Jeff K. Bills, Chief Executive Officer (Total facility includes 16 beds in nursing home–type unit) **A**1 7 9 10 **F**2 3 4 7 8 10 11 12 13 15 16 17 19 20 21 22 23 24 25 28 29 30 32 33 34 35 37 38 39 40 41 42 43 44 46 48 49 63 64 65 67 68 71 72 73 74 **P**6 **N** Saint Mary's Health Network, Reno, NV

| | 21 | 10 | 276 | 12198 | 183 | 154562 | 2283 | 123415 | 55531 | 1431 |

⊞ WASHOE MEDICAL CENTER, 77 Pringle Way, Zip 89520–0109; tel. 702/328–4100; Robert B. Burn, President and Chief Executive Officer (Total facility includes 19 beds in nursing home–type unit) (Nonreporting) **A**1 2 3 5 9 10

| | 23 | 10 | 436 | — | — | — | — | — | — | — |

SPARKS—Washoe County

□ NEVADA MENTAL HEALTH INSTITUTE, 480 Galletti Way, Zip 89431–5574; tel. 702/688–2001; David Rosin, M.D., Medical Director **A**1 3 5 10 **F**6 12 34 52 55 56 57 58 59 65 **P**6

| | 12 | 22 | 52 | 1485 | 48 | 18991 | — | — | 6578 | 193 |

□ NORTHERN NEVADA MEDICAL CENTER, 2375 East Prater Way, Zip 89434–9645; tel. 702/331–7000; James R. Pagels, Chief Executive Officer and Managing Director **A**1 10 **F**8 12 14 15 16 17 19 21 22 26 27 28 29 30 34 35 37 39 44 46 49 51 52 54 55 56 57 58 59 65 66 71 72 73 **P**5 7 **S** Universal Health Services, Inc., King of Prussia, PA

| | 32 | 10 | 100 | 2250 | 40 | 39295 | — | 24470 | 8515 | 379 |

TONOPAH—Nye County

NYE REGIONAL MEDICAL CENTER, 825 South Main Street, Zip 89049, Mailing Address: P.O. Box 391, Zip 89049–0391; tel. 702/482–6233; Malinda Lewis, Administrator (Total facility includes 24 beds in nursing home–type unit) (Nonreporting) **A**9 10

| | 13 | 10 | 45 | — | — | — | — | — | — | — |

WINNEMUCCA—Humboldt County

★ HUMBOLDT GENERAL HOSPITAL, 118 East Haskell Street, Zip 89445–3299; tel. 702/623–5222; Byron Quinton, Administrator (Total facility includes 30 beds in nursing home–type unit) **A**9 10 **F**3 7 8 14 15 19 22 35 37 40 44 64 65 71 73 **P**5

| | 16 | 10 | 52 | 772 | 33 | 21742 | 328 | 9047 | 3735 | 138 |

YERINGTON—Lyon County

SOUTH LYON MEDICAL CENTER, Surprise at Whitacre Avenue, Zip 89447, Mailing Address: P.O. Box 940, Zip 89447–0940; tel. 702/463–2301; Joan S. Hall, R.N., Administrator (Total facility includes 30 beds in nursing home–type unit) (Nonreporting) **A**9 10

| | 23 | 10 | 44 | — | — | — | — | — | — | — |

NEW HAMPSHIRE

Resident population 1,177 (in thousands)
Resident population in metro areas 59.6%
Birth rate per 1,000 population 13.3
65 years and over 12.0%
Percent of persons without health insurance 9.5%

★ American Hospital Association (AHA) membership
□ Joint Commission on Accreditation of Healthcare Organizations (JCAHO) accreditation
+ American Osteopathic Healthcare Association (AOHA) membership
○ American Osteopathic Association (AOA) accreditation
△ Commission on Accreditation of Rehabilitation Facilities (CARF) accreditation
Control codes 61, 63, 64, 71, 72 and 73 indicate hospitals listed by AOHA, but not registered by AHA. For definition of numerical codes, see page A4

Hospital, Address, Telephone, Administrator, Approval, Facility, and Physician Codes, Health Care System, Network	Control	Service	Staffed Beds	Admissions	Census	Outpatient Visits	Births	Total	Payroll	Personnel
BERLIN—Coos County										
✚ ANDROSCOGGIN VALLEY HOSPITAL, 59 Page Hill Road, Zip 03570–3531; tel. 603/752–2200; Donald F. Saunders, President **A**1 9 10 **F**7 8 12 14 15 16 19 21 22 26 28 29 30 31 32 33 34 35 37 39 40 41 42 44 49 51 52 54 55 56 57 58 64 65 70 71 73 74 **P**3	23	10	64	2176	37	40750	121	19456	8405	251
CLAREMONT—Sullivan County										
✚ VALLEY REGIONAL HOSPITAL, 243 Elm Street, Zip 03743–2099; tel. 603/542–7771; Donald R. Holl, President **A**1 9 10 **F**1 3 7 8 12 13 15 16 17 18 19 21 22 23 24 25 26 27 28 29 30 32 33 34 35 37 39 40 41 42 44 45 49 51 52 54 55 56 57 58 59 63 64 65 66 67 68 70 71 72 73 74 **P**7 **N** Partners In Caring, Claremont, NH	23	10	43	1684	18	51900	207	22669	9315	318
COLEBROOK—Coos County										
★ UPPER CONNECTICUT VALLEY HOSPITAL, Corliss Lane, Zip 03576–9533, Mailing Address: RFD 2, Box 13, Zip 03576–9533; tel. 603/237–4971; Deanna S. Howard, Chief Executive Officer **A**9 10 **F**7 8 13 15 16 17 19 22 28 30 32 37 39 40 41 42 44 56 65 71 73	23	10	20	595	8	18583	53	5252	2371	119
CONCORD—Merrimack County										
✚ CONCORD HOSPITAL, 250 Pleasant Street, Zip 03301–2598; tel. 603/225–2711; Michael B. Green, President **A**1 2 3 5 9 10 **F**3 7 8 10 11 12 13 14 15 16 17 19 20 21 22 23 24 26 29 30 31 32 33 34 35 37 39 40 41 42 44 45 49 51 52 53 54 55 56 57 58 59 63 65 66 67 68 70 71 72 73 74 **P**6 7 **N** HealthLink, Laconia, NH	23	10	161	8926	112	175455	1273	90634	41993	1350
□ △ HEALTHSOUTH REHABILITATION HOSPITAL, 254 Pleasant Street, Zip 03301–2508; tel. 603/226–9800; Anne M. Fugagli, Administrator **A**1 7 10 **F**5 9 12 13 14 15 16 17 18 24 26 27 28 30 34 39 42 46 48 49 64 65 66 67 71 73 **S** HEALTHSOUTH Corporation, Birmingham, AL	33	46	50	905	43	7332	0	9128	4484	124
□ NEW HAMPSHIRE HOSPITAL, 36 Clinton Street, Zip 03301–3861; tel. 603/271–5200; Chester G. Batchelder, Superintendent (Total facility includes 99 beds in nursing home–type unit) **A**1 3 5 10 **F**14 15 16 20 26 28 31 39 41 45 46 52 53 54 55 57 64 65 67 73 **P**4 6	12	22	296	1299	236	0	—	41047	23398	851
DERRY—Rockingham County										
✚ PARKLAND MEDICAL CENTER, One Parkland Drive, Zip 03038–2750; tel. 603/432–1500; Scott W. Goodspeed, President and Chief Executive Officer **A**1 2 9 10 **F**7 8 12 17 19 22 27 28 30 32 34 35 39 41 42 44 45 49 57 65 67 71 73 74 **S** Columbia/HCA Healthcare Corporation, Nashville, TN	33	10	77	3138	39	66797	599	30132	12957	366
DOVER—Strafford County										
✚ WENTWORTH–DOUGLASS HOSPITAL, 789 Central Avenue, Zip 03820–2589; tel. 603/742–2801; Gregory J. Walker, Chief Executive Officer **A**1 2 9 10 **F**5 7 8 10 12 13 14 15 16 17 19 21 22 23 24 26 28 29 30 31 32 33 34 35 37 39 40 41 42 44 45 46 49 51 60 61 63 65 66 67 70 71 73 74 **P**5 8	23	10	104	4147	48	69553	617	49588	21731	623
DUBLIN—Cheshire County										
BEECH HILL HOSPITAL, New Harrisville Road, Zip 03444, Mailing Address: P.O. Box 254, Zip 03444–0254; tel. 603/563–8511; Linda J. Crumlin, Chief Executive Officer (Nonreporting) **A**9	23	82	70	—	—	—	—	—	—	—
EXETER—Rockingham County										
✚ EXETER HOSPITAL, 10 Buzell Avenue, Zip 03833–2515; tel. 603/778–7311; Kevin J. Callahan, President and Chief Executive Officer **A**1 2 9 10 **F**4 7 8 10 11 12 13 14 15 16 17 19 20 21 22 23 24 25 26 27 28 29 30 31 32 33 34 35 37 39 40 41 42 44 45 46 49 51 53 54 55 56 57 58 59 60 61 63 64 65 66 70 71 73 74 **P**1	23	10	80	4252	164	71800	820	55544	—	522
FRANKLIN—Merrimack County										
✚ FRANKLIN REGIONAL HOSPITAL, 15 Aiken Avenue, Zip 03235–1299; tel. 603/934–2060; Walter A. Strauch, Executive Director **A**1 9 10 **F**7 8 14 15 16 17 19 22 28 29 30 32 33 34 37 40 41 44 45 46 49 51 54 56 57 64 65 67 68 71 73 74 **P**6 8 **N** Caring Community Network of the Twin Rivers (CCNTR), Franklin, NH	23	10	49	1713	28	33143	118	17271	8733	239
GREENFIELD—Hillsborough County										
CROTCHED MOUNTAIN REHABILITATION CENTER, 1 Verney Drive, Zip 03047–5000; tel. 603/547–3311; Major W. Wheelock, President (Total facility includes 40 beds in nursing home–type unit) **F**6 12 20 24 27 28 39 48 49 53 65 73	23	46	101	32	102	0	—	20943	11947	448
HAMPSTEAD—Rockingham County										
□ HAMPSTEAD HOSPITAL, 218 East Road, Zip 03841–2228; tel. 603/329–5311; Phillip J. Kubiak, President **A**1 10 **F**3 6 15 16 18 19 22 25 26 34 35 45 52 53 54 56 57 58 59 65 67 71 **P**1 5 7	33	22	99	1397	42	—	—	10011	5813	155
HANOVER—Grafton County										
★ DARTMOUTH COLLEGE HEALTH SERVICE, 7 Rope Ferry Road, Zip 03755–1421; tel. 603/650–1400; John Turco, M.D., Director (Nonreporting)	23	11	10	—	—	—	—	—	—	—
KEENE—Cheshire County										
✚ △ CHESHIRE MEDICAL CENTER, 580 Court Street, Zip 03431–1718; tel. 603/355–2000; Robert J. Langlais, President and Chief Executive Officer **A**1 2 7 9 10 **F**1 7 8 11 12 14 15 16 17 18 19 20 21 22 23 24 27 28 29 30 31 32 33 34 35 36 37 39 40 41 42 44 45 46 48 49 52 53 54 55 56 57 58 59 60 63 65 66 67 70 71 73 74 **P**1	23	10	162	5024	77	59645	517	42867	19775	652

Hospital, Address, Telephone, Administrator, Approval, Facility, and Physician Codes, Health Care System, Network	Classi-fication Codes		Utilization Data					Expense (thousands) of dollars		
★ American Hospital Association (AHA) membership □ Joint Commission on Accreditation of Healthcare Organizations (JCAHO) accreditation + American Osteopathic Healthcare Association (AOHA) membership ○ American Osteopathic Association (AOA) accreditation △ Commission on Accreditation of Rehabilitation Facilities (CARF) accreditation Control codes 61, 63, 64, 71, 72 and 73 indicate hospitals listed by AOHA, but not registered by AHA. For definition of numerical codes, see page A4	Control	Service	Staffed Beds	Admissions	Census	Outpatient Visits	Births	Total	Payroll	Personnel

LACONIA—Belknap County

★ LAKES REGION GENERAL HOSPITAL, 80 Highland Street, Zip 03246–3298; tel. 603/524–3211; Thomas Clairmont, President **A**2 9 10 **F**1 3 4 7 8 10 12 13 14 15 16 17 19 20 22 23 24 26 28 30 31 33 34 35 37 40 41 42 44 45 49 52 53 54 55 56 57 63 65 67 70 71 72 73 74 **P**6 8 **N** HealthLink, Laconia, NH	23	10	117	5195	68	40937	551	53667	26476	763

LANCASTER—Coos County

✖ WEEKS MEMORIAL HOSPITAL, 173 Middle Street, Zip 03584; tel. 603/788–4911; Patsy Pilgrim, Chief Executive Officer **A**1 9 10 **F**7 8 12 14 15 16 17 19 21 22 26 28 29 30 31 32 33 34 37 39 40 41 42 44 46 49 56 65 66 67 68 71 73 **P**6	23	10	38	1152	17	61808	93	13060	7079	192

LEBANON—Grafton County

✖ ALICE PECK DAY MEMORIAL HOSPITAL, 125 Mascoma Street, Zip 03766–2650; tel. 603/448–3121; Robert A. Mesropian, President (Total facility includes 50 beds in nursing home–type unit) **A**1 9 10 **F**6 7 8 12 13 14 15 16 17 19 21 22 25 26 29 30 33 34 39 40 41 42 44 45 46 49 51 62 64 65 67 70 71 72 73 74 **P**8	23	10	82	742	57	44948	205	14105	7344	281
✖ MARY HITCHCOCK MEMORIAL HOSPITAL, One Medical Center Drive, Zip 03756–0001; tel. 603/650–5000; James W. Varnum, President **A**1 2 3 5 8 9 10 **F**3 4 7 8 10 11 12 14 15 16 17 19 20 21 22 23 26 27 28 29 30 31 32 33 34 35 36 37 38 39 40 41 42 43 44 45 46 47 48 49 51 52 53 54 56 57 58 59 60 61 63 65 66 67 69 70 71 72 73 74 **P**6 8 **N** HealthLink, Laconia, NH; Lahey Network, Burlington, MA	23	10	343	17577	244	329710	965	221270	79045	2539

LITTLETON—Grafton County

✖ LITTLETON REGIONAL HOSPITAL, 262 Cottage Street, Zip 03561–4101; tel. 603/444–7731; Robert S. Pearson, Administrator **A**1 2 9 10 **F**7 8 14 15 16 17 19 21 22 23 25 27 28 29 30 31 33 34 35 37 39 40 41 42 44 45 46 49 61 63 65 68 69 70 71 73 74 **S** Quorum Health Group/Quorum Health Resources, Inc., Brentwood, TN	23	10	49	1441	15	25837	232	16912	6798	224

MANCHESTER—Hillsborough County

✖ △ CATHOLIC MEDICAL CENTER, 100 McGregor Street, Zip 03102–3770; tel. 603/668–3545; Peter B. Davis, Interim Chief Executive Officer **A**1 7 9 10 **F**1 2 3 4 5 6 7 8 10 11 12 14 15 16 17 18 19 20 21 22 23 24 26 27 28 29 30 31 32 33 34 35 37 39 41 42 43 44 45 46 48 49 52 54 56 57 58 59 60 61 62 65 66 67 71 72 73 74 **P**7 8 **N** HealthLink, Laconia, NH	23	10	242	9281	162	91593	—	114652	38428	1039
✖ ELLIOT HOSPITAL, One Elliot Way, Zip 03103; tel. 603/669–5300; Peter B. Davis, Interim President and Chief Executive Officer **A**1 2 9 10 **F**1 3 4 5 6 7 8 10 11 12 13 14 15 16 17 18 19 20 21 22 23 24 26 27 28 29 30 31 32 33 34 35 37 38 39 40 41 42 43 44 45 46 49 51 52 54 55 56 57 58 59 60 61 62 63 65 66 67 70 71 72 73 74 **P**7 8 **N** HealthLink, Laconia, NH	23	10	238	9919	132	132000	2330	107980	41814	1156
✖ VETERANS AFFAIRS MEDICAL CENTER, 718 Smyth Road, Zip 03104–4098; tel. 603/624–4366; Paul J. McCool, Director (Total facility includes 120 beds in nursing home–type unit) **A**1 2 9 **F**1 2 3 4 5 6 8 10 12 14 15 16 17 19 20 21 22 24 25 26 27 28 29 30 31 32 33 34 37 39 41 42 44 45 46 49 51 54 55 56 57 58 61 63 64 65 67 71 72 73 74 **P**6 **S** Department of Veterans Affairs, Washington, DC	45	10	157	2018	140	102547	0	46804	22395	535

NASHUA—Hillsborough County

□ CHARTER BROOKSIDE BEHAVIORAL HEALTH SYSTEM OF NEW ENGLAND, 29 Northwest Boulevard, Zip 03063–4005; tel. 603/886–5000; Spencer Moore, Chief Executive Officer **A**1 10 **F**3 14 15 16 17 18 19 22 28 29 32 52 53 54 55 56 57 58 59 65 67 70 71 **S** Magellan Health Services, Atlanta, GA	33	22	100	510	78	935	0	2082	1533	160
✖ SOUTHERN NEW HAMPSHIRE REGIONAL MEDICAL CENTER, 8 Prospect Street, Zip 03060–3925, Mailing Address: P.O. Box 2014, Zip 03061–2014; tel. 603/577–2000; Thomas E. Wilhelmsen, Jr., President **A**1 2 9 10 **F**3 7 8 10 12 13 14 15 16 17 18 19 21 22 23 28 29 30 32 33 34 35 37 38 39 40 41 42 44 45 46 49 51 52 53 56 57 58 59 60 63 65 67 70 71 72 73 74 **P**3 6 8 **N** Lahey Network, Burlington, MA	23	10	147	6789	77	112019	1471	60157	28025	922
✖ △ ST. JOSEPH HOSPITAL (Formerly St. Joseph Healthcare), 172 Kinsley Street, Zip 03061; tel. 603/882–3000; Kenneth R. Ferron, Senior Vice President and Chief Operating Officer **A**1 2 6 7 9 10 **F**1 3 7 8 10 12 13 14 15 16 17 18 19 20 21 22 23 25 26 27 28 29 30 31 32 33 34 35 36 39 40 41 42 44 48 57 60 63 70 71 73 74 **P**6 8 **S** Covenant Health Systems, Inc., Lexington, MA **N** Saint Joseph Health Care, Nashua, NH	21	10	150	5808	81	105821	961	60290	28110	756

NEW LONDON—Merrimack County

★ NEW LONDON HOSPITAL, 270 County Road, Zip 03257–4570; tel. 603/526–2911; Alyson Pitman Giles, President and Chief Executive Officer (Total facility includes 58 beds in nursing home–type unit) **A**9 10 **F**7 8 12 13 14 15 16 17 18 19 20 22 24 25 28 30 32 33 34 35 36 37 39 40 41 42 44 45 49 51 61 64 65 66 67 71 72 73 74 **P**8	23	10	93	1331	73	113607	139	18379	9269	300

NORTH CONWAY—Carroll County

MEMORIAL HOSPITAL, 3073 Main Street, Zip 03860–5001, Mailing Address: P.O. Box 5001, Zip 03860–5001; tel. 603/356–5461; Gary R. Poquette, FACHE, Executive Director (Total facility includes 45 beds in nursing home–type unit) **A**9 10 **F**1 7 8 14 15 16 17 19 20 21 22 28 29 30 33 34 35 40 41 42 44 45 49 56 59 64 65 66 67 70 71 73 74 **P**3	23	10	80	1442	60	33063	235	16963	6716	205

PETERBOROUGH—Hillsborough County

✖ MONADNOCK COMMUNITY HOSPITAL, 452 Old Street Road, Zip 03458–1295; tel. 603/924–7191; Peter L. Gosline, Chief Executive Officer **A**1 9 10 **F**7 8 12 14 15 17 18 19 20 22 26 28 32 33 34 36 37 39 40 41 42 43 44 45 46 49 51 52 55 56 57 58 59 63 65 67 71 73 74	23	10	62	1715	23	63053	365	17627	7423	238

Hospital, Address, Telephone, Administrator, Approval, Facility, and Physician Codes, Health Care System, Network	Classi-fication Codes		Utilization Data					Expense (thousands) of dollars		
	Control	Service	Staffed Beds	Admissions	Census	Outpatient Visits	Births	Total	Payroll	Personnel

★ American Hospital Association (AHA) membership
□ Joint Commission on Accreditation of Healthcare Organizations (JCAHO) accreditation
+ American Osteopathic Healthcare Association (AOHA) membership
○ American Osteopathic Association (AOA) accreditation
△ Commission on Accreditation of Rehabilitation Facilities (CARF) accreditation
Control codes 61, 63, 64, 71, 72 and 73 indicate hospitals listed by AOHA, but not registered by AHA. For definition of numerical codes, see page A4

	Control	Service	Staffed Beds	Admissions	Census	Outpatient Visits	Births	Total	Payroll	Personnel
PLYMOUTH—Grafton County										
SPEARE MEMORIAL HOSPITAL, 16 Hospital Road, Zip 03264–1199; tel. 603/536–1120; David L. Pearse, Executive Director **A**9 10 **F**7 8 12 14 15 17 19 21 22 28 30 33 37 39 40 41 42 44 49 54 56 65 66 67 71 73 **P**8	23	10	33	1042	11	54101	82	11188	5855	171
PORTSMOUTH—Rockingham County										
✠ PORTSMOUTH REGIONAL HOSPITAL AND PAVILION, (Includes Portsmouth Pavilion), 333 Borthwick Avenue, Zip 03801–7004; tel. 603/436–5110; William J. Schuler, Chief Executive Officer **A**1 9 10 **F**3 4 7 8 10 12 17 18 19 21 22 23 24 26 28 30 32 33 34 35 41 42 44 49 53 56 57 58 59 63 65 71 72 73 **P**1 6 8 **S** Columbia/HCA Healthcare Corporation, Nashville, TN	33	10	179	7035	107	93887	876	—	—	623
ROCHESTER—Strafford County										
✠ FRISBIE MEMORIAL HOSPITAL, 11 Whitehall Road, Zip 03867–3297; tel. 603/332–5211; Alvin D. Felgar, President and Chief Executive Officer **A**1 2 9 10 **F**2 3 7 8 10 11 15 16 17 18 19 21 22 26 30 31 33 34 35 37 39 40 41 42 44 45 49 51 52 54 55 57 58 63 65 67 71 73 **P**3 5 6 8	23	10	88	3214	43	55730	532	31636	13565	399
SALEM—Rockingham County										
□ △ NORTHEAST REHABILITATION HOSPITAL, 70 Butler Street, Zip 03079; tel. 603/893–2900; John F. Prochilo, Chief Executive Officer and Administrator **A**1 7 10 **F**5 9 12 13 14 15 16 17 24 29 32 34 39 41 45 48 49 64 65 66 67 73	33	46	80	1183	63	92112	—	22106	15116	396
WOLFEBORO—Carroll County										
★ HUGGINS HOSPITAL, 240 South Main Street, Zip 03894–4411, Mailing Address: P.O. Box 912, Zip 03894–0912; tel. 603/569–7500; Leslie N. H. MacLeod, President (Total facility includes 27 beds in nursing home–type unit) **A**9 10 **F**1 6 7 8 16 17 19 20 21 22 26 28 30 34 37 39 40 41 44 49 62 64 65 67 71 73 74 **P**8	23	10	82	1910	56	50441	116	16121	—	251
WOODSVILLE—Grafton County										
✠ COTTAGE HOSPITAL, Swiftwater Road, Zip 03785–2001, Mailing Address: P.O. Box 2001, Zip 03785–2001; tel. 603/747–2761; Reginald J. Lavoie, Administrator **A**1 2 9 10 **F**7 8 15 16 19 22 36 37 40 41 42 44 49 54 65 71 72 73 74 **P**8	23	10	38	857	10	35756	77	9507	5303	154

NEW JERSEY

Resident population 8,053 (in thousands)
Resident population in metro areas 100%
Birth rate per 1,000 population 14.9
65 years and over 13.8%
Percent of persons without health insurance 16.7%

Hospital, Address, Telephone, Administrator, Approval, Facility, and Physician Codes, Health Care System, Network	Classi-fication Codes		Utilization Data					Expense (thousands) of dollars		
★ American Hospital Association (AHA) membership □ Joint Commission on Accreditation of Healthcare Organizations (JCAHO) accreditation + American Osteopathic Healthcare Association (AOHA) membership ○ American Osteopathic Association (AOA) accreditation △ Commission on Accreditation of Rehabilitation Facilities (CARF) accreditation Control codes 61, 63, 64, 71, 72 and 73 indicate hospitals listed by AOHA, but not registered by AHA. For definition of numerical codes, see page A4	Control	Service	Staffed Beds	Admissions	Census	Outpatient Visits	Births	Total	Payroll	Personnel

ANCORA—Atlantic County
□ ANCORA PSYCHIATRIC HOSPITAL, 202 Spring Garden Road, Zip 08037–9699; tel. 609/561–1700; Yvonne A. Pressley, Chief Executive Officer (Nonreporting) **A**1 10 **S** Division of Mental Health Services, Department of Human Services, State of New Jersey, Trenton, NJ — 12 22 625 — — — — — — —

ATLANTIC CITY—Atlantic County
✠ ATLANTIC CITY MEDICAL CENTER, 1925 Pacific Avenue, Zip 08401–6713; tel. 609/345–4000; David P. Tilton, President and Chief Executive Officer (Nonreporting) **A**1 3 9 10 **N** AtlantiCare Health System, Egg Harbor Township, NJ — 23 10 448 — — — — — — —

BAYONNE—Hudson County
✠ BAYONNE HOSPITAL, 29 East 29th Street, Zip 07002–4699; tel. 201/858–5000; Michael R. D'Agnes, President and Chief Executive Officer **A**1 2 6 9 10 **F**1 3 7 8 10 11 12 13 15 16 17 19 20 21 22 26 27 28 29 30 33 34 35 37 40 42 44 46 48 49 51 52 56 59 60 63 65 67 71 73 **P**5 7 **N** Qualcare Preferred Providers, Piscataway, NJ — 23 10 261 9352 203 — 564 79392 35068 939

BELLE MEAD—Somerset County
✠ CARRIER FOUNDATION, County Route 601, P.O. Box 147, Zip 08502–0147; tel. 908/281–1000; C. Richard Sarle, President and Chief Executive Officer **A**1 9 10 **F**2 3 16 49 52 53 54 55 56 57 58 59 65 73 **P**6 **N** Qualcare Preferred Providers, Piscataway, NJ — 23 22 132 2761 86 63530 0 24707 13108 520

BELLEVILLE—Essex County
✠ CLARA MAASS HEALTH SYSTEM, 1 Clara Maass Drive, Zip 07109–3557; tel. 973/450–2000; Thomas A. Biga, Executive Director (Total facility includes 179 beds in nursing home–type unit) (Nonreporting) **A**1 2 9 10 **S** Saint Barnabas Health Care System, Livingston, NJ **N** First Option Health Plan, Red Bank, NJ; Clara Maass Health System, Belleville, NJ — 23 10 644 — — — — — — —

BERKELEY HEIGHTS—Union County
★ RUNNELLS SPECIALIZED HOSPITAL, 40 Watchung Way, Zip 07922–2618; tel. 908/771–5700; Joseph W. Sharp, Administrator (Total facility includes 300 beds in nursing home–type unit) (Nonreporting) **A**9 10 — 13 49 345 — — — — — — —

BERLIN—Camden County
★ WEST JERSEY HOSPITAL–BERLIN, 100 Townsend Avenue, Zip 08009–9035; tel. 609/322–3200; Ellen Guarnieri, Acting Executive Director **A**9 **F**1 3 5 8 10 12 13 15 16 17 18 19 20 21 22 25 26 27 28 29 30 31 32 33 34 35 36 37 39 41 42 44 45 46 49 51 53 54 55 58 59 61 65 67 71 72 73 74 **P**5 7 **S** West Jersey Health System, Camden, NJ **N** First Option Health Plan, Red Bank, NJ — 23 10 79 3483 53 13012 0 26265 13683 278

BLACKWOOD—Camden County
□ CAMDEN COUNTY HEALTH SERVICES CENTER, Woodbury–Turnersville Road, Zip 08012–2799, Mailing Address: P.O. Box 1639, Zip 08012–2799; tel. 609/374–6500; Anthony Peters, Chief Executive Officer (Total facility includes 275 beds in nursing home–type unit) (Nonreporting) **A**1 3 9 10 — 13 49 422 — — — — — — —

BOONTON TOWNSHIP—Morris County
BOONTON TOWNSHIP CAMPUS See Northwest Covenant Medical Center, Denville

BRICK TOWNSHIP—Ocean County
BRICK HOSPITAL DIVISION See Meridian Health System, Neptune

BRIDGETON—Cumberland County
✠ SOUTH JERSEY HOSPITAL, (Includes South Jersey Hospital–Bridgeton, 333 Irving Avenue, tel. 609/451–6600; South Jersey Hospital–Elmer, West Front Street, Elmer, Zip 08318–0516, Mailing Address: P.O. Box 1090, Zip 08318–1090; tel. 609/358–2341; South Jersey Hospital–Millville, 1200 North High, Millville, Zip 08332–2586; tel. 609/825–3500), 333 Irving Avenue, Zip 08302–2100; tel. 609/451–6600; Paul S. Cooper, Chief Executive Officer **A**1 9 10 **F**3 7 8 12 14 15 16 17 18 19 20 21 22 24 25 29 30 32 33 34 35 37 39 40 41 42 44 45 46 49 52 53 54 55 56 57 58 59 60 65 66 67 68 71 72 **N** First Option Health Plan, Red Bank, NJ; Qualcare Preferred Providers, Piscataway, NJ; Fox Chase Network, Rockledge, PA — 23 10 375 11821 186 184144 779 102559 47925 1330

BROWNS MILLS—Burlington County
✠ DEBORAH HEART AND LUNG CENTER, (SPECIALTY HEART & LUNG CT), 200 Trenton Road, Zip 08015–1799; tel. 609/893–6611; John R. Ernst, Executive Director **A**1 3 5 9 10 13 **F**4 10 14 19 21 28 29 30 34 43 45 50 63 65 67 71 73 **P**6 — 23 49 161 5235 105 30200 0 — 65535 1376

CAMDEN—Camden County
✠ △ OUR LADY OF LOURDES MEDICAL CENTER, 1600 Haddon Avenue, Zip 08103–3117; tel. 609/757–3500; Alexander J. Hatala, President and Chief Executive Officer **A**1 3 5 7 9 10 12 **F**4 7 8 10 11 12 13 14 15 16 17 18 19 20 21 22 26 28 29 30 31 32 34 35 36 37 38 40 41 42 43 44 45 46 48 49 51 52 54 55 56 57 58 61 63 65 67 68 69 70 71 73 74 **P**6 7 **S** Catholic Health East, Radnor, PA **N** First Option Health Plan, Red Bank, NJ; Jefferson Health System, Radnor, PA — 21 10 306 14057 278 187373 1233 151936 66960 1886

Hospital, Address, Telephone, Administrator, Approval, Facility, and Physician Codes, Health Care System, Network	Classi-fication Codes		Utilization Data					Expense (thousands) of dollars		
★ American Hospital Association (AHA) membership ☐ Joint Commission on Accreditation of Healthcare Organizations (JCAHO) accreditation + American Osteopathic Healthcare Association (AOHA) membership ○ American Osteopathic Association (AOA) accreditation △ Commission on Accreditation of Rehabilitation Facilities (CARF) accreditation Control codes 61, 63, 64, 71, 72 and 73 indicate hospitals listed by AOHA, but not registered by AHA. For definition of numerical codes, see page A4	Control	Service	Staffed Beds	Admissions	Census	Outpatient Visits	Births	Total	Payroll	Personnel
☒ THE COOPER HEALTH SYSTEM, One Cooper Plaza, Zip 08103–1489; tel. 609/342–2000; Kevin G. Halpern, President and Chief Executive Officer **A**1 2 3 5 8 9 10 **F**3 4 5 8 10 11 12 13 14 15 16 17 18 19 21 22 24 25 26 27 28 29 30 31 32 33 34 35 37 38 40 41 42 43 44 45 46 47 49 51 52 53 54 57 58 60 61 62 63 65 66 67 68 69 70 71 73 74 **P**5 **N** Qualcare Preferred Providers, Piscataway, NJ	23	10	460	18695	272	520724	1952	296637	172605	3809
☒ WEST JERSEY HOSPITAL–CAMDEN, 1000 Atlantic Avenue, Zip 08104–1595; tel. 609/246–3000; Frederick M. Carey, Executive Director **A**1 2 3 5 9 10 **F**1 2 3 5 7 10 12 13 15 16 17 19 20 21 25 26 27 28 29 30 31 32 33 34 35 36 37 39 40 42 44 45 46 49 51 60 61 65 67 71 72 73 74 **P**5 7 **S** West Jersey Health System, Camden, NJ **N** First Option Health Plan, Red Bank, NJ; Qualcare Preferred Providers, Piscataway, NJ	23	10	117	5036	71	38192	0	48727	24263	536
CAPE MAY COURT HOUSE—Cape May County										
☒ BURDETTE TOMLIN MEMORIAL HOSPITAL, 2 Stone Harbor Boulevard, Zip 08210–9990; tel. 609/463–2000; Thomas L. Scott, FACHE, President and Chief Executive Officer **A**1 9 10 **F**3 7 8 14 15 16 17 19 20 21 22 27 28 30 32 34 35 37 40 42 44 45 46 49 55 65 67 71 73 **P**5 7 8 **N** First Option Health Plan, Red Bank, NJ; Cape Advantage Health Alliance, Cape May, NJ	23	10	206	9674	149	91836	633	66806	30022	926
CEDAR GROVE—Essex County										
☐ ESSEX COUNTY HOSPITAL CENTER, 125 Fairview Avenue, Zip 07009–1399; tel. 973/228–8200; Muriel M. Shore, Ed.D., R.N., Chief Executive Officer **A**1 9 10 **F**12 20 26 45 46 52 57 65 73	13	22	400	504	359	0	0	42023	25357	675
CHERRY HILL—Camden County										
★ + ○ KENNEDY MEMORIAL HOSPITALS–UNIVERSITY MEDICAL CENTER, (Includes Kennedy Memorial Hospital, 18 East Laurel Road, Stratford, Zip 08084; tel. 609/346–6000; Kennedy Memorial Hospital, 435 Hurffville–Cross Keys Road, Turnersville, Zip 08012; tel. 609/582–2500), 2201 Chapel Avenue West, Zip 08002–2048; tel. 609/488–6500; Joseph W. Devine, Vice President, Hospital Services **A**9 10 11 12 13 **F**2 3 6 7 8 10 11 12 13 14 15 16 17 18 19 20 21 22 23 24 25 26 27 28 29 30 31 32 33 34 35 36 37 38 39 40 41 42 44 45 46 49 51 52 53 54 55 56 57 58 59 61 63 64 65 66 67 68 70 71 73 74 **P**7	23	10	494	22416	318	355867	1840	179766	79769	2250
DENVILLE—Morris County										
☒ NORTHWEST COVENANT MEDICAL CENTER, (Includes Boonton Township Campus, 130 Powerville Road, Boonton Township, Zip 07005; tel. 201/625–6000; Denville Campus, 25 Pocono Road, Zip 07834; tel. 201/625–6000; Dover Campus, 24 Jardine Street, Dover, Zip 07801–3311; tel. 201/989–3000; Sussex Campus, 20 Walnut Street, Sussex, Zip 07461; tel. 201/702–2200), 25 Pocono Road, Zip 07834–2995; tel. 973/625–6000; Kathryn J. McDonagh, President and Chief Executive Officer (Total facility includes 97 beds in nursing home–type unit) (Nonreporting) **A**1 9 10 **S** Marian Health System, Tulsa, OK **N** Via Caritas Health System, Inc., Denville, NJ; Qualcare Preferred Providers, Piscataway, NJ	21	10	644	—						
DOVER—Morris County										
DOVER CAMPUS See Northwest Covenant Medical Center, Denville										
EAST ORANGE—Essex County										
☒ EAST ORANGE GENERAL HOSPITAL, 300 Central Avenue, Zip 07019–2819; tel. 973/672–8400; Mark Chastang, President and Chief Executive Officer (Nonreporting) **A**1 10 **N** First Option Health Plan, Red Bank, NJ	23	10	238	—	—	—	—	—	—	—
☒ VETERANS AFFAIRS NEW JERSEY HEALTH CARE SYSTEM, (Includes East Orange Division, 385 Tremont Avenue, tel. 973/676–1000; Lyons Division, 151 Knollcroft Road, Lyons, Zip 07939–9998; tel. 908/647–0180), 385 Tremont Avenue, Zip 07018–1095; tel. 973/676–1000; Kenneth H. Mizrach, Director (Total facility includes 390 beds in nursing home–type unit) (Nonreporting) **A**1 2 3 5 8 9 **S** Department of Veterans Affairs, Washington, DC	45	10	1702	—						
EDISON—Middlesex County										
★ △ JFK JOHNSON REHABILITATION INSTITUTE, 65 James Street, Zip 08818–3059; tel. 732/321–7050; Scott Gebhard, Senior Vice President Operations (Nonreporting) **A**7 10 **S** Solaris Health System, Edison, NJ	23	46	92	—	—	—	—	—	—	—
☒ JFK MEDICAL CENTER, 65 James Street, Zip 08818–3947; tel. 732/321–7000; John P. McGee, President and Chief Executive Officer (Nonreporting) **A**1 2 3 5 9 **S** Solaris Health System, Edison, NJ **N** First Option Health Plan, Red Bank, NJ	23	10	380	—	—	—	—	—	—	—
ROOSEVELT HOSPITAL, 1 Roosevelt Drive, Zip 08837–2333; tel. 908/321–6800; Thomas Lankey, Acting Superintendent and Chief Executive Officer (Total facility includes 536 beds in nursing home–type unit) (Nonreporting) **A**9 10	13	10	564	—	—	—	—	—	—	—
ELIZABETH—Union County										
☒ ELIZABETH GENERAL MEDICAL CENTER, 925 East Jersey Street, Zip 07201–2728; tel. 908/289–8600; David A. Fletcher, President and Chief Executive Officer (Total facility includes 136 beds in nursing home–type unit) **A**1 2 3 5 6 9 10 **F**1 2 3 7 8 10 12 15 16 17 18 19 20 21 22 26 28 29 30 31 33 34 37 39 40 41 42 44 45 49 51 52 53 54 55 56 57 58 59 60 64 65 67 71 73 74 **N** First Option Health Plan, Red Bank, NJ; Qualcare Preferred Providers, Piscataway, NJ	23	10	445	9315	323	240279	865	122008	61909	1603
☒ ST. ELIZABETH HOSPITAL, 225 Williamson Street, Zip 07202–3600; tel. 908/527–5000; Sister Elizabeth Ann Maloney, President and Chief Executive Officer **A**1 2 3 9 10 **F**3 7 8 10 11 12 13 14 15 16 17 19 21 22 24 25 26 27 28 30 31 34 35 37 39 40 41 42 44 45 49 54 60 63 67 68 71 73 74 **P**7 **N** The Mount Sinai Health System, New York, NY	21	10	256	12119	183	104684	1028	91156	41023	1058

Hospital, Address, Telephone, Administrator, Approval, Facility, and Physician Codes, Health Care System, Network	Classi-fication Codes		Utilization Data					Expense (thousands) of dollars		
★ American Hospital Association (AHA) membership □ Joint Commission on Accreditation of Healthcare Organizations (JCAHO) accreditation + American Osteopathic Healthcare Association (AOHA) membership ○ American Osteopathic Association (AOA) accreditation △ Commission on Accreditation of Rehabilitation Facilities (CARF) accreditation Control codes 61, 63, 64, 71, 72 and 73 indicate hospitals listed by AOHA, but not registered by AHA. For definition of numerical codes, see page A4	Control	Service	Staffed Beds	Admissions	Census	Outpatient Visits	Births	Total	Payroll	Personnel

ELMER—Salem County

SOUTH JERSEY HOSPITAL–ELMER See South Jersey Hospital, Bridgeton

ENGLEWOOD—Bergen County

★ ENGLEWOOD HOSPITAL AND MEDICAL CENTER, 350 Engle Street, Zip 07631–1898; tel. 201/894–3000; Daniel A. Kane, President and Chief Executive Officer **A**1 2 3 5 6 9 10 **F**8 10 12 14 15 16 17 19 20 22 28 29 30 31 32 33 34 35 37 38 40 42 44 45 46 49 51 52 59 60 61 65 66 67 68 71 73 **P**5 7 8 **N** The Mount Sinai Health System, New York, NY; First Option Health Plan, Red Bank, NJ | 23 | 10 | 321 | 21889 | 242 | 445744 | 2231 | 152060 | 73800 | 1671

FLEMINGTON—Hunterdon County

★ HUNTERDON MEDICAL CENTER, 2100 Wescott Drive, Zip 08822–4604; tel. 908/788–6100; Robert P. Wise, President and Chief Executive Officer **A**1 2 3 5 9 10 **F**1 3 7 8 10 12 14 15 16 17 18 19 21 22 23 24 25 26 28 29 30 31 32 33 34 35 36 37 39 40 41 42 44 45 46 49 51 52 53 54 55 56 57 58 59 61 65 66 67 69 71 73 74 **P**5 6 **N** First Option Health Plan, Red Bank, NJ; Qualcare Preferred Providers, Piscataway, NJ; Fox Chase Network, Rockledge, PA | 23 | 10 | 176 | 7555 | 105 | 236594 | 1291 | 78015 | 38907 | 1104

FLORHAM PARK—Morris County

★ ATLANTIC HEALTH SYSTEM, (Includes General Hospital Center at Passaic, 350 Boulevard, Passaic, Zip 07055–2800; tel. 973/365–4300; Marie Cassese, R.N., President; Morristown Memorial Hospital, 100 Madison Avenue, Morristown, Zip 07962–1956; tel. 973/971–5000; Jean M. McMahon, R.N., Vice President and General Manager; Mountainside Hospital, Bay and Highland Avenues, Montclair, Zip 07042–4898; tel. 973/429–6000; Robert A. Silver, Senior Vice President and General Manager; Overlook Hospital, 99 Beauvoir Avenue, Summit, Zip 07902–0220; tel. 908/522–2000; David H. Freed, Vice President and General Manager), 325 Columbia Turnpike, Zip 07932–1212, Mailing Address: P.O. Box 959, Zip 07932–0959; tel. 973/660–3100; Richard P. Oths, President and Chief Executive Officer **A**1 2 3 5 6 8 10 **F**2 3 4 5 7 8 10 11 12 13 15 16 17 18 19 20 21 22 24 25 26 27 28 29 30 31 32 33 34 35 36 37 38 39 40 41 42 43 44 45 46 47 48 49 51 52 53 54 55 56 57 58 59 60 61 64 65 66 67 68 70 71 72 73 74 **P**3 5 7 8 | 23 | 10 | 1559 | 67827 | 1058 | 978168 | 8554 | 686540 | 315308 | 7971

FREEHOLD—Monmouth County

★ CENTRASTATE MEDICAL CENTER, 901 West Main Street, Zip 07728–2549; tel. 732/431–2000; Thomas H. Litz, FACHE, President and Chief Executive Officer **A**1 9 10 **F**3 7 8 11 12 13 14 15 16 17 19 22 23 25 26 28 29 30 32 33 34 35 37 39 40 41 42 44 45 46 49 52 54 55 56 57 61 62 64 65 66 67 68 71 72 73 74 **P**5 8 **N** First Option Health Plan, Red Bank, NJ; Qualcare Preferred Providers, Piscataway, NJ | 23 | 10 | 240 | 9322 | 153 | 117292 | 1362 | 80758 | 36188 | 1133

GLEN GARDNER—Hunterdon County

□ SENATOR GARRET T. W. HAGEDORN GERO PSYCHIATRIC HOSPITAL, 200 Sanitorium Road, Zip 08826–9752; tel. 908/537–2141; Edna Volpe–Way, Chief Executive Officer (Nonreporting) **A**1 10 **S** Division of Mental Health Services, Department of Human Services, State of New Jersey, Trenton, NJ | 12 | 22 | 181 | — | — | — | — | — | — | —

GREYSTONE PARK—Morris County

★ GREYSTONE PARK PSYCHIATRIC HOSPITAL, Central Avenue, Zip 07950, Mailing Address: P.O. Box A., Zip 07950; tel. 973/538–1800; Michael Greenstein, Chief Executive Officer **A**1 9 10 **F**1 3 8 9 11 12 15 16 17 19 20 21 22 23 26 27 28 31 34 35 37 38 39 40 42 43 44 46 48 49 50 52 54 55 56 57 58 60 63 65 67 70 71 73 **P**6 **S** Division of Mental Health Services, Department of Human Services, State of New Jersey, Trenton, NJ | 12 | 22 | 605 | 418 | 572 | 0 | 0 | — | 41606 | 1106

HACKENSACK—Bergen County

★ HACKENSACK UNIVERSITY MEDICAL CENTER, (Includes Hasbrouck Heights Ambulatory Care Facility, Hasbrouck Heights), 30 Prospect Avenue, Zip 07601–1991; tel. 201/996–2000; John P. Ferguson, President and Chief Executive Officer **A**1 2 3 5 8 9 10 **F**3 4 5 7 8 10 11 12 13 14 15 16 17 18 19 20 21 22 24 25 26 27 28 29 30 31 32 33 34 35 36 37 38 39 40 41 42 43 44 45 46 47 49 51 52 53 54 55 56 57 58 59 60 61 65 66 67 68 69 70 71 72 73 74 **P**5 7 8 **N** Qualcare Preferred Providers, Piscataway, NJ | 23 | 10 | 629 | 47747 | 523 | 1396475 | 3656 | — | 176259 | 4125

HACKETTSTOWN—Warren County

★ HACKETTSTOWN COMMUNITY HOSPITAL, 651 Willow Grove Street, Zip 07840–1798; tel. 908/852–5100; Gene C. Milton, President and Chief Executive Officer **A**1 2 9 10 **F**3 7 8 12 14 15 16 19 20 21 22 24 26 28 29 30 32 33 34 35 36 39 41 42 44 45 46 49 65 66 67 71 73 74 **P**1 **N** First Option Health Plan, Red Bank, NJ | 21 | 10 | 106 | 4046 | 56 | 40191 | 558 | 31090 | 14095 | 471

HAMILTON—Mercer County

□ ROBERT WOOD JOHNSON UNIVERSITY HOSPITAL AT HAMILTON, One Hamilton Health Place, Zip 08690–3599; tel. 609/586–7900; Christy Stephenson, Chief Administrative Officer **A**1 9 10 **F**1 7 8 10 11 12 14 15 16 17 19 21 22 25 26 28 29 30 31 32 34 35 36 37 39 40 41 42 44 45 46 49 51 60 61 63 64 65 67 71 73 74 **P**6 7 **N** Qualcare Preferred Providers, Piscataway, NJ | 23 | 10 | 160 | 6332 | 96 | 58119 | 609 | 44773 | 17717 | 537

HAMMONTON—Atlantic County

★ WILLIAM B. KESSLER MEMORIAL HOSPITAL, 600 South White Horse Pike, Zip 08037–2099; tel. 609/561–6700; Warren E. Gager, Chief Executive Officer **A**1 9 10 **F**8 11 12 14 15 16 19 20 21 22 24 27 30 31 32 34 35 37 39 41 42 44 45 46 49 51 63 65 66 67 71 73 **N** First Option Health Plan, Red Bank, NJ | 23 | 10 | 84 | 3581 | 63 | — | — | 29158 | 17021 | 463

HOBOKEN—Hudson County

★ ST. MARY HOSPITAL, 308 Willow Avenue, Zip 07030–3889; tel. 201/418–1000; Robert S. Chaloner, President and Chief Executive Officer **A**1 3 9 10 **F**8 12 14 15 16 17 18 19 21 22 27 28 31 34 35 37 40 42 44 49 52 53 54 55 56 57 58 59 60 65 68 71 73 74 **P**7 8 **S** Franciscan Sisters of the Poor Health System, Inc., Latham, NY **N** Qualcare Preferred Providers, Piscataway, NJ | 21 | 10 | 136 | 8089 | 145 | 68494 | 933 | 77627 | 42926 | —

Hospital, Address, Telephone, Administrator, Approval, Facility, and Physician Codes, Health Care System, Network	Classi-fication Codes		Utilization Data					Expense (thousands) of dollars		
★ American Hospital Association (AHA) membership □ Joint Commission on Accreditation of Healthcare Organizations (JCAHO) accreditation + American Osteopathic Healthcare Association (AOHA) membership ○ American Osteopathic Association (AOA) accreditation △ Commission on Accreditation of Rehabilitation Facilities (CARF) accreditation Control codes 61, 63, 64, 71, 72 and 73 indicate hospitals listed by AOHA, but not registered by AHA. For definition of numerical codes, see page A4	Control	Service	Staffed Beds	Admissions	Census	Outpatient Visits	Births	Total	Payroll	Personnel

HOLMDEL—Monmouth County

★ BAYSHORE COMMUNITY HOSPITAL, 727 North Beers Street, Zip 07733–1598; tel. 732/739–5900; Thomas Goldman, President and Chief Executive Officer (Total facility includes 201 beds in nursing home–type unit) **A**1 9 10 **F**1 3 8 10 11 12 14 15 16 19 21 22 25 26 28 30 35 36 37 42 44 45 46 48 49 51 54 56 58 64 65 67 70 71 72 73 **P**5 6 7 8 **N** First Option Health Plan, Red Bank, NJ

| | 23 | 10 | 369 | 7741 | 374 | 45685 | 0 | 59499 | 27665 | 1147 |

IRVINGTON—Essex County

★ IRVINGTON GENERAL HOSPITAL, 832 Chancellor Avenue, Zip 07111–0709; tel. 973/399–6000; Paul A. Mertz, Executive Director **A**1 9 10 **F**7 8 10 12 15 16 17 19 21 22 26 27 28 30 31 33 34 35 37 38 40 41 42 43 44 46 49 52 53 60 65 69 71 73 74 **P**7 8 **S** Saint Barnabas Health Care System, Livingston, NJ **N** First Option Health Plan, Red Bank, NJ; Qualcare Preferred Providers, Piscataway, NJ

| | 23 | 10 | 123 | 4093 | 91 | 36172 | 0 | 36922 | 15160 | 370 |

JERSEY CITY—Hudson County

★ CHRIST HOSPITAL, 176 Palisade Avenue, Zip 07306–1196, Mailing Address: P.O. Box J–1, Zip 07306–1196; tel. 201/795–8200; Daniel R. Connell, President **A**1 2 6 9 10 12 13 **F**2 3 7 8 10 11 12 13 16 17 18 19 20 21 22 23 25 27 28 29 30 31 32 33 34 35 36 37 39 40 41 42 44 45 46 49 50 51 52 53 54 55 56 57 58 59 60 61 63 64 65 67 68 71 73 74 **P**3 5 8 **N** First Option Health Plan, Red Bank, NJ

| | 23 | 10 | 358 | 19574 | 279 | 404657 | 1125 | 118347 | 56955 | 1382 |

□ GREENVILLE HOSPITAL, 1825 John F. Kennedy Boulevard, Zip 07305–2198; tel. 201/547–6100; Jonathan M. Metsch, Dr.PH, President and Chief Executive Officer (Nonreporting) **A**1 9 10 **N** The Mount Sinai Health System, New York, NY

| | 23 | 10 | 86 | — | — | — | — | — | — | — |

★ JERSEY CITY MEDICAL CENTER, 50 Baldwin Avenue, Zip 07304–3199; tel. 201/915–2000; Jonathan M. Metsch, Dr.PH, President and Chief Executive Officer **A**1 3 5 9 10 **F**2 3 7 8 9 10 11 12 13 15 16 17 19 20 25 26 27 28 30 31 32 33 34 37 38 40 41 42 44 46 47 48 49 52 53 54 56 58 59 61 63 65 67 70 71 73 **P**4 7 **N** The Mount Sinai Health System, New York, NY

| | 23 | 10 | 332 | 16262 | 248 | 225553 | 2146 | 115314 | 83585 | — |

★ ST. FRANCIS HOSPITAL, 25 McWilliams Place, Zip 07302–1698; tel. 201/418–1000; Robert S. Chaloner, President and Chief Executive Officer **A**1 6 9 10 **F**8 11 12 14 15 16 17 19 20 22 26 27 28 35 37 41 44 48 49 52 57 58 60 65 71 73 **P**7 8 **S** Franciscan Sisters of the Poor Health System, Inc., Latham, NY **N** Qualcare Preferred Providers, Piscataway, NJ

| | 21 | 10 | 183 | 3847 | 101 | 25360 | 0 | 46325 | 23930 | 862 |

KEARNY—Hudson County

★ WEST HUDSON HOSPITAL, 206 Bergen Avenue, Zip 07032–3399; tel. 201/955–7051; Carmen Bruce Alecci, Executive Director (Total facility includes 46 beds in nursing home–type unit) (Nonreporting) **A**1 9 10 **S** Saint Barnabas Health Care System, Livingston, NJ **N** First Option Health Plan, Red Bank, NJ

| | 23 | 10 | 217 | — | — | — | — | — | — | — |

LAKEWOOD—Ocean County

★ KIMBALL MEDICAL CENTER, 600 River Avenue, Zip 08701–5281; tel. 732/363–1900; Joanne Carrocino, Executive Director **A**1 9 10 **F**1 2 3 4 6 7 8 10 11 12 13 14 15 16 17 18 19 20 21 22 24 25 26 27 28 29 30 31 32 33 34 35 36 37 39 40 41 42 44 45 46 49 51 52 54 55 56 57 58 59 60 61 64 65 66 67 68 71 72 73 74 **P**5 7 **S** Saint Barnabas Health Care System, Livingston, NJ **N** First Option Health Plan, Red Bank, NJ; Qualcare Preferred Providers, Piscataway, NJ

| | 23 | 10 | 248 | 10557 | 183 | 145676 | 1028 | 98278 | 45764 | 1172 |

LAWRENCEVILLE—Mercer County

★ △ ST. LAWRENCE REHABILITATION CENTER, 2381 Lawrenceville Road, Zip 08648; tel. 609/896–9500; Charles L. Brennan, Chief Executive Officer **A**1 7 10 **F**1 12 14 17 21 25 27 32 34 36 41 46 48 49 64 65 67 73 **N** Qualcare Preferred Providers, Piscataway, NJ

| | 21 | 46 | 116 | 1789 | 89 | 17627 | 0 | 16633 | 10141 | 300 |

LIVINGSTON—Essex County

★ ○ SAINT BARNABAS MEDICAL CENTER, 94 Old Short Hills Road, Zip 07039–5668; tel. 973/322–5000; Vincent D. Joseph, Executive Director (Nonreporting) **A**1 2 3 5 8 9 10 11 **S** Saint Barnabas Health Care System, Livingston, NJ **N** First Option Health Plan, Red Bank, NJ; Qualcare Preferred Providers, Piscataway, NJ

| | 23 | 10 | 615 | — | — | — | — | — | — | — |

LONG BRANCH—Monmouth County

★ MONMOUTH MEDICAL CENTER, 300 Second Avenue, Zip 07740–6303; tel. 732/222–5200; Frank J. Vozos, M.D., FACS, Executive Director (Nonreporting) **A**1 2 3 5 8 9 10 **S** Saint Barnabas Health Care System, Livingston, NJ **N** First Option Health Plan, Red Bank, NJ; Qualcare Preferred Providers, Piscataway, NJ

| | 23 | 10 | 435 | — | — | — | — | — | — | — |

LYONS—Somerset County

LYONS DIVISION See Veterans Affairs New Jersey Health Care System, East Orange

MANAHAWKIN—Ocean County

★ SOUTHERN OCEAN COUNTY HOSPITAL, 1140 Route 72 West, Zip 08050–2499; tel. 609/978–8910; Steven G. Littleson, President and Chief Executive Officer **A**1 2 9 10 **F**3 8 12 13 15 17 19 21 22 24 25 26 28 29 30 32 33 34 35 37 42 44 45 46 49 63 64 65 66 67 68 71 73 **P**1 5 7 **N** First Option Health Plan, Red Bank, NJ; Qualcare Preferred Providers, Piscataway, NJ

| | 23 | 10 | 134 | 5406 | 79 | 77836 | 0 | 43520 | 17050 | 0 |

MARLTON—Burlington County

★ WEST JERSEY HOSPITAL–MARLTON, 90 Brick Road, Zip 08053–9697; tel. 609/355–6000; Leroy J. Rosenberg, Executive Director **A**1 9 10 **F**1 2 3 5 7 8 10 12 13 15 16 17 19 20 21 22 25 26 27 28 29 30 31 32 36 37 38 39 40 41 42 44 45 46 49 51 60 61 65 67 71 72 73 74 **P**5 7 **S** West Jersey Health System, Camden, NJ **N** First Option Health Plan, Red Bank, NJ; Qualcare Preferred Providers, Piscataway, NJ

| | 23 | 10 | 163 | 7976 | 116 | 19930 | 0 | 59729 | 28190 | 593 |

Hospital, Address, Telephone, Administrator, Approval, Facility, and Physician Codes, Health Care System, Network	Classi-fication Codes		Utilization Data					Expense (thousands) of dollars		
★ American Hospital Association (AHA) membership □ Joint Commission on Accreditation of Healthcare Organizations (JCAHO) accreditation + American Osteopathic Healthcare Association (AOHA) membership ○ American Osteopathic Association (AOA) accreditation △ Commission on Accreditation of Rehabilitation Facilities (CARF) accreditation Control codes 61, 63, 64, 71, 72 and 73 indicate hospitals listed by AOHA, but not registered by AHA. For definition of numerical codes, see page A4	Control	Service	Staffed Beds	Admissions	Census	Outpatient Visits	Births	Total	Payroll	Personnel

MILLVILLE—Cumberland County

SOUTH JERSEY HOSPITAL–MILLVILLE See South Jersey Hospital, Bridgeton

MONTCLAIR—Essex County

✙ MONTCLAIR COMMUNITY HOSPITAL, 120 Harrison Avenue, Zip 07042–2498; tel. 973/744–7300; Emilie M. Murphy, R.N., Director (Nonreporting) **A**1 9 10 | 23 | 10 | 100 | — | — | — | — | — | — | —

MOUNTAINSIDE HOSPITAL See Atlantic Health System, Florham Park

MORRISTOWN—Morris County

MORRISTOWN MEMORIAL HOSPITAL See Atlantic Health System, Florham Park

MOUNT HOLLY—Burlington County

✙ MEMORIAL HOSPITAL OF BURLINGTON COUNTY, 175 Madison Avenue, Zip 08060–2099; tel. 609/267–0700; Chester B. Kaletkowski, President and Chief Executive Officer (Total facility includes 180 beds in nursing home–type unit) **A**1 2 3 5 9 10 **F**5 7 8 11 12 13 14 15 16 17 19 21 22 25 26 28 30 31 32 34 35 37 39 40 41 42 44 45 46 49 51 52 54 55 57 60 61 65 67 71 73 74 **P**2 4 5 7 **N** First Option Health Plan, Red Bank, NJ; Qualcare Preferred Providers, Piscataway, NJ | 23 | 10 | 549 | 16369 | 199 | 42829 | 1874 | 126464 | 53313 | —

MOUNTAINSIDE—Union County

✙ △ CHILDREN'S SPECIALIZED HOSPITAL, (Includes Children's Specialized Hospital–Ocean, 94 Stevens Road, Toms River, Zip 08755–1237; tel. 908/732–1100), 150 New Providence Road, Zip 07091–2590; tel. 908/301–5431; Richard B. Ahlfeld, President (Total facility includes 41 beds in nursing home–type unit) **A**1 7 10 **F**12 15 17 20 25 27 28 29 30 34 39 45 46 48 49 51 54 60 64 65 67 73 **N** Qualcare Preferred Providers, Piscataway, NJ | 23 | 56 | 117 | 304 | 79 | 91198 | 0 | 33197 | 18656 | 411

NEPTUNE—Monmouth County

✙ △ MERIDIAN HEALTH SYSTEM, (Includes Brick Hospital Division, 425 Jack Martin Boulevard, Brick Township, Zip 08724; tel. 908/840–2200; Jersey Shore Medical Center, 1945 Route 33, Zip 07754–0397; tel. 908/775–5500; Medical Center of Ocean County, 2121 Edgewater Place, Point Pleasant, Zip 08742–2290; tel. 908/892–1100; John T. Gribbin, President and Chief Executive Officer; Point Pleasant Hospital Division, 2121 Edgewater Place, Point Pleasant, Zip 08742; tel. 908/892–1100; Riverview Medical Center, 1 Riverview Plaza, Red Bank, Zip 07701–9982; tel. 908/741–2700; Paul S. Cohen, Executive Director and Chief Operating Officer), 1945 State Highway 33, Zip 07753; tel. 732/775–5500; John K. Lloyd, Chief Executive Officer (Nonreporting) **A**1 2 3 5 6 7 8 9 10 **N** Qualcare Preferred Providers, Piscataway, NJ | 23 | 10 | 1269 | | | | | | |

NEW BRUNSWICK—Middlesex County

HURTADO HEALTH CENTER, 11 Bishop Place, Zip 08901–1180; tel. 732/932–8429; Susan Skalsky, M.D., Director (Nonreporting) | 12 | 11 | 27 | | | | | | |

✙ ROBERT WOOD JOHNSON UNIVERSITY HOSPITAL, 1 Robert Wood Johnson Place, Zip 08903–2601; tel. 732/828–3000; Harvey A. Holzberg, President and Chief Executive Officer **A**1 2 3 5 8 9 10 **F**1 2 3 4 5 6 7 8 10 11 12 13 14 15 16 17 19 20 21 22 23 24 25 26 27 28 29 30 31 32 33 34 35 37 38 39 40 41 42 43 44 45 46 47 48 49 51 52 53 54 55 56 57 58 59 60 61 62 63 64 65 66 67 68 69 70 71 72 73 74 **P**4 5 7 8 **N** First Option Health Plan, Red Bank, NJ; Qualcare Preferred Providers, Piscataway, NJ | 23 | 10 | 430 | 29165 | 385 | 177123 | 1127 | 269745 | 110295 | —

✙ ST. PETER'S MEDICAL CENTER, 254 Easton Avenue, Zip 08901–1780, Mailing Address: P.O. Box 591, Zip 08903–0591; tel. 732/745–8600; John E. Matuska, President and Chief Executive Officer **A**1 2 3 5 9 10 **F**1 3 7 8 10 11 12 13 14 15 16 17 19 20 21 22 23 25 26 27 28 29 30 31 32 33 34 35 37 38 39 40 41 42 44 45 46 49 51 54 55 56 58 60 61 65 66 67 68 71 73 74 **P**1 2 7 **N** First Option Health Plan, Red Bank, NJ; Qualcare Preferred Providers, Piscataway, NJ | 21 | 10 | 406 | 21707 | 298 | 125593 | 5844 | 193460 | 92749 | 2223

NEWARK—Essex County

□ COLUMBUS HOSPITAL, 495 North 13th Street, Zip 07107–1397; tel. 973/268–1400; John G. Magliaro, President and Chief Executive Officer **A**1 9 10 **F**7 8 11 12 14 15 16 21 22 25 27 34 37 40 42 44 46 49 54 65 71 73 **P**5 7 **N** Qualcare Preferred Providers, Piscataway, NJ | 23 | 10 | 191 | 9509 | 131 | 66367 | 1134 | 75970 | 34439 | 745

✙ ○ NEWARK BETH ISRAEL MEDICAL CENTER, 201 Lyons Avenue, Zip 07112–2027; tel. 973/926–7000; Paul A. Mertz, Executive Director (Nonreporting) **A**1 2 3 5 8 10 11 12 13 **S** Saint Barnabas Health Care System, Livingston, NJ **N** First Option Health Plan, Red Bank, NJ; Qualcare Preferred Providers, Piscataway, NJ | 23 | 10 | 451 | — | — | — | — | — | — | —

□ SAINT JAMES HOSPITAL OF NEWARK, 155 Jefferson Street, Zip 07105; tel. 973/589–1300; Ceu Cirne–Neves, Administrator (Nonreporting) **A**1 3 9 10 **S** Cathedral Healthcare System, Inc., Newark, NJ | 21 | 10 | 189 | | | | | | |

□ SAINT MICHAEL'S MEDICAL CENTER, 268 Dr. Martin Luther King Jr. Boulevard, Zip 07102–2094; tel. 973/877–5000; Barbara Loughney, Acting Senior Vice President and Administrator **A**1 3 5 9 10 12 **F**3 4 6 7 8 10 12 13 14 15 16 17 18 19 20 21 22 24 25 26 27 28 29 30 31 32 33 34 35 39 40 41 42 43 44 45 46 49 50 51 53 54 58 59 60 63 65 66 67 71 73 74 **P**8 **S** Cathedral Healthcare System, Inc., Newark, NJ | 21 | 10 | 299 | 11663 | 208 | 80225 | 866 | 139482 | 59049 | 1202

✙ UNIVERSITY OF MEDICINE AND DENTISTRY OF NEW JERSEY–UNIVERSITY HOSPITAL, 150 Bergen Street, Zip 07103–2406; tel. 973/972–4300; William L. Vazquez, Vice President and Chief Executive Officer **A**1 2 3 5 8 9 10 **F**3 4 7 8 10 11 12 15 16 17 19 20 21 22 23 24 26 27 28 30 31 34 35 37 38 39 40 41 42 43 44 46 47 49 51 52 53 54 56 58 59 60 61 65 66 67 68 69 70 71 73 74 **P**5 **N** Qualcare Preferred Providers, Piscataway, NJ | 12 | 10 | 457 | 16987 | 340 | 304839 | 2202 | 322786 | 170956 | 3123

Hospital, Address, Telephone, Administrator, Approval, Facility, and Physician Codes, Health Care System, Network	Classi-fication Codes		Utilization Data					Expense (thousands) of dollars		
★ American Hospital Association (AHA) membership □ Joint Commission on Accreditation of Healthcare Organizations (JCAHO) accreditation + American Osteopathic Healthcare Association (AOHA) membership ○ American Osteopathic Association (AOA) accreditation △ Commission on Accreditation of Rehabilitation Facilities (CARF) accreditation Control codes 61, 63, 64, 71, 72 and 73 indicate hospitals listed by AOHA, but not registered by AHA. For definition of numerical codes, see page A4	Control	Service	Staffed Beds	Admissions	Census	Outpatient Visits	Births	Total	Payroll	Personnel

NEWTON—Sussex County

★ △ NEWTON MEMORIAL HOSPITAL, 175 High Street, Zip 07860–1004; tel. 973/383–2121; Dennis H. Collette, President and Chief Executive Officer **A**1 2 7 9 10 **F**3 7 8 12 14 15 16 17 18 19 20 21 22 27 28 29 30 31 32 35 36 37 39 40 41 42 44 45 46 48 49 52 53 54 55 56 57 58 59 61 63 65 67 71 73 **P**5 8 **N** First Option Health Plan, Red Bank, NJ
| | 23 | 10 | 162 | 8700 | 100 | 173827 | 920 | 54642 | 24528 | 585 |

NORTH BERGEN—Hudson County

★ PALISADES GENERAL HOSPITAL, 7600 River Road, Zip 07047–6217; tel. 201/854–5000; Bruce J. Markowitz, President and Chief Executive Officer (Nonreporting) **A**1 9 10 **N** Columbia Presbyterian Regional Network, New York, NY; First Option Health Plan, Red Bank, NJ; Qualcare Preferred Providers, Piscataway, NJ
| | 23 | 10 | 202 | — | — | — | — | — | — | — |

OLD BRIDGE—Middlesex County

OLD BRIDGE DIVISION See Raritan Bay Medical Center, Perth Amboy

ORANGE—Essex County

★ HOSPITAL CENTER AT ORANGE, (Includes New Jersey Orthopedic Hospital Unit, ; Orange Memorial Hospital Unit), 188 South Essex Avenue, Zip 07051; tel. 973/266–2200; James E. Romer, President and Chief Executive Officer **A**1 2 3 5 9 10 **F**8 12 15 17 19 22 27 28 29 30 34 35 36 39 40 41 42 44 45 46 49 51 60 61 63 65 66 67 71 73 74 **N** Qualcare Preferred Providers, Piscataway, NJ
| | 23 | 10 | 167 | 6248 | 137 | 127120 | 608 | 65135 | 33965 | 719 |

PARAMUS—Bergen County

★ BERGEN REGIONAL MEDICAL CENTER, (Formerly Bergen Pines County Hospital), 230 East Ridgewood Avenue, Zip 07652–4131; tel. 201/967–4000; Edward M. Lewis, Executive Director (Total facility includes 610 beds in nursing home–type unit) **A**1 3 5 6 9 10 **F**1 3 8 11 15 16 17 20 22 26 30 31 35 41 44 46 49 52 53 54 57 58 59 64 65 71 73
| | 13 | 10 | 1059 | 7953 | 880 | 66823 | 0 | 141895 | 72000 | 0 |

PASSAIC—Passaic County

★ BETH ISRAEL HOSPITAL, 70 Parker Avenue, Zip 07055–7000; tel. 973/365–5000; Jeffrey S. Moll, President and Chief Executive Officer (Total facility includes 13 beds in nursing home–type unit) **A**1 2 9 10 **F**8 10 11 12 13 14 15 16 17 19 21 22 26 27 28 29 30 31 32 33 34 35 37 39 41 42 44 45 46 49 51 59 60 61 63 64 65 67 68 71 72 73 74 **N** First Option Health Plan, Red Bank, NJ; Qualcare Preferred Providers, Piscataway, NJ
GENERAL HOSPITAL CENTER AT PASSAIC See Atlantic Health System, Florham Park
| | 23 | 10 | 223 | 6347 | 119 | 64149 | 0 | 49824 | 22965 | — |

★ ST. MARY'S HOSPITAL, 211 Pennington Avenue, Zip 07055–4698; tel. 973/470–3000; Patricia Peterson, President and Chief Executive Officer **A**1 9 10 **F**2 4 5 6 7 8 9 10 11 12 13 15 16 17 18 19 21 22 25 26 27 28 29 30 31 32 33 34 35 36 37 38 39 40 41 42 43 44 45 46 47 48 49 51 52 53 54 55 56 57 58 59 60 62 64 65 67 70 71 72 73 74 **P**1 5 **S** Marian Health System, Tulsa, OK **N** Via Caritas Health System, Inc., Denville, NJ
| | 21 | 10 | 229 | 5262 | 96 | 93686 | 831 | 52044 | 24237 | 741 |

PATERSON—Passaic County

★ BARNERT HOSPITAL, 680 Broadway Street, Zip 07514–1472; tel. 973/977–6600; Fred L. Lang, President and Chief Executive Officer **A**1 9 10 **F**1 3 6 7 8 14 15 16 17 19 21 22 26 27 28 29 30 31 34 36 37 40 41 42 44 45 46 49 51 52 53 54 55 56 58 59 63 65 67 68 71 73 74 **P**5 8 **N** First Option Health Plan, Red Bank, NJ
| | 23 | 10 | 190 | 7155 | 119 | 173653 | 773 | 63818 | 29358 | 703 |

★ ○ ST. JOSEPH'S HOSPITAL AND MEDICAL CENTER, 703 Main Street, Zip 07503–2691; tel. 973/754–2000; Sister Jane Frances Brady, Chief Executive Officer (Total facility includes 141 beds in nursing home–type unit) **A**1 2 3 5 8 9 10 11 12 **F**1 3 4 5 7 8 9 10 11 12 13 14 15 16 17 18 19 20 21 22 24 25 26 27 28 29 30 31 32 33 34 35 36 37 38 39 40 41 42 43 44 45 46 47 49 50 51 52 53 54 55 56 57 58 59 60 61 64 65 66 67 68 69 70 71 72 73 74 **P**1 5 7 **S** Marian Health System, Tulsa, OK **N** The Mount Sinai Health System, New York, NY; Seton Health Network, Inc., Paterson, NJ; First Option Health Plan, Red Bank, NJ; Via Caritas Health System, Inc., Denville, NJ; Qualcare Preferred Providers, Piscataway, NJ
| | 21 | 10 | 651 | 28974 | 433 | 347668 | 2734 | 279840 | 148204 | 3557 |

PEAPACK—Somerset County

★ △ MATHENY SCHOOL AND HOSPITAL, (Habilitation), Main Street, Zip 07977; tel. 908/234–0011; Robert Schonhorn, President **A**1 7 10 **F**1 6 12 15 16 17 20 27 32 34 49 51 54 64 65 73
| | 23 | 49 | 87 | 48 | 78 | 120 | 0 | 15255 | 9445 | 309 |

PERTH AMBOY—Middlesex County

★ RARITAN BAY MEDICAL CENTER, (Includes Old Bridge Division, One Hospital Plaza, Old Bridge, Zip 08857; tel. 732/360–1000; Perth Amboy Division, 530 New Brunswick Avenue, tel. 732/442–3700), 530 New Brunswick Avenue, Zip 08861–3685; tel. 732/442–3700; Keith H. McLaughlin, President and Chief Executive Officer **A**1 3 5 6 9 10 **F**2 3 6 7 8 10 11 12 14 15 16 17 18 19 21 22 23 27 28 29 31 32 33 34 35 36 37 39 40 42 44 49 51 52 54 55 56 58 61 63 65 67 68 71 73 **P**7 8 **N** Qualcare Preferred Providers, Piscataway, NJ
| | 23 | 10 | 415 | 13943 | 287 | 193944 | 854 | 137575 | 74677 | 1805 |

PHILLIPSBURG—Warren County

★ WARREN HOSPITAL, 185 Roseberry Street, Zip 08865–9955; tel. 908/859–6700; Jeffrey C. Goodwin, President and Chief Executive Officer **A**1 2 3 5 9 10 12 13 **F**3 4 7 8 9 10 11 12 14 15 16 17 18 19 20 21 22 25 26 27 29 30 31 32 33 34 35 36 37 38 39 40 41 42 43 44 45 46 47 49 51 52 53 54 56 57 58 59 60 65 66 67 68 69 70 71 73 **P**5 **N** Qualcare Preferred Providers, Piscataway, NJ
| | 23 | 10 | 214 | 8160 | 128 | 49794 | 333 | 56624 | 27820 | 845 |

Hospital, Address, Telephone, Administrator, Approval, Facility, and Physician Codes, Health Care System, Network	Classi-fication Codes		Utilization Data					Expense (thousands) of dollars		
★ American Hospital Association (AHA) membership ☐ Joint Commission on Accreditation of Healthcare Organizations (JCAHO) accreditation + American Osteopathic Healthcare Association (AOHA) membership ○ American Osteopathic Association (AOA) accreditation △ Commission on Accreditation of Rehabilitation Facilities (CARF) accreditation Control codes 61, 63, 64, 71, 72 and 73 indicate hospitals listed by AOHA, but not registered by AHA. For definition of numerical codes, see page A4	Control	Service	Staffed Beds	Admissions	Census	Outpatient Visits	Births	Total	Payroll	Personnel

PISCATAWAY—Middlesex County

UNIVERSITY OF MEDICINE AND DENTISTRY OF NEW JERSEY, UNIVERSITY BEHAVIORAL HEALTHCARE, 671 Hoes Lane, Zip 08854–5633, Mailing Address: P.O. Box 1392, Zip 08855–1392; tel. 732/235–5900; Christopher O. Kosseff, Acting Vice President and Chief Executive Officer (Nonreporting) **A**3 5 9 10

	12	22	64	—	—	—	—	—	—	—

PLAINFIELD—Union County

☒ MUHLENBERG REGIONAL MEDICAL CENTER, 1200 Park Avenue, Zip 07061; tel. 908/668–2000; John R. Kopicki, President and Chief Executive Officer (Total facility includes 23 beds in nursing home–type unit) **A**1 3 5 6 9 10 **F**1 3 7 8 10 11 12 14 15 16 17 19 21 22 27 28 29 30 31 32 33 35 37 39 40 41 42 44 45 46 49 51 52 53 54 55 56 57 58 59 60 63 64 65 67 69 71 72 73 **P**5 7 8 **S** Solaris Health System, Edison, NJ **N** First Option Health Plan, Red Bank, NJ

	23	10	314	13373	199	188513	1548	107585	53484	1517

POINT PLEASANT—Ocean County

MEDICAL CENTER OF OCEAN COUNTY See Meridian Health System, Neptune
POINT PLEASANT HOSPITAL DIVISION See Meridian Health System, Neptune

POMONA—Atlantic County

☒ △ BACHARACH REHABILITATION HOSPITAL, 61 West Jimmy Leeds Road, Zip 08240–0723, Mailing Address: P.O. Box 723, Zip 08240–0723; tel. 609/652–7000; Richard J. Kathrins, Administrator and Chief Executive Officer **A**1 2 7 10 **F**12 15 16 17 19 20 27 29 30 34 35 39 41 45 46 48 49 51 65 66 67 71 73 **P**6

	23	46	80	1476	66	40647	0	—	15091	397

POMPTON PLAINS—Morris County

☒ CHILTON MEMORIAL HOSPITAL, 97 West Parkway, Zip 07444–1696; tel. 973/831–5000; James J. Doyle, Jr., President and Chief Executive Officer **A**1 2 9 10 **F**7 8 10 12 13 14 15 16 17 19 20 21 22 25 26 28 29 30 31 32 33 34 35 37 39 40 41 42 44 45 47 49 51 52 53 54 55 56 57 60 63 65 66 67 71 72 73 74 **P**4 5 7 8 **N** First Option Health Plan, Red Bank, NJ

	23	10	256	14372	147	72204	1496	76257	34775	728

PRINCETON—Mercer County

☒ MEDICAL CENTER AT PRINCETON, (Includes Acute General Hospital, Merwick Unit–Extended Care and Rehabilitation, Princeton House Unit–Community Mental Health and Substance Abuse), 253 Witherspoon Street, Zip 08540–3213; tel. 609/497–4000; Dennis W. Doody, President and Chief Executive Officer (Total facility includes 93 beds in nursing home–type unit) **A**1 2 3 5 9 10 **F**1 2 3 7 8 10 11 12 14 15 16 17 18 19 20 21 22 26 27 28 29 30 31 32 33 34 37 39 40 41 42 44 46 48 49 52 54 55 56 57 58 59 60 63 64 65 67 71 73 **P**7 8 **N** First Option Health Plan, Red Bank, NJ

	23	10	392	16823	294	204898	1557	115260	56104	1783

RAHWAY—Union County

☒ RAHWAY HOSPITAL, 865 Stone Street, Zip 07065–2797; tel. 732/381–4200; Kirk C. Tice, President and Chief Executive Officer (Total facility includes 16 beds in nursing home–type unit) **A**1 9 10 **F**7 8 10 11 12 14 15 16 17 18 19 20 21 22 23 26 27 28 29 30 33 34 35 37 39 40 41 42 44 45 46 49 51 54 55 56 57 58 64 65 67 68 71 72 73 74 **P**1 5 **N** Qualcare Preferred Providers, Piscataway, NJ

	23	10	222	9725	173	63298	827	78263	36298	722

RED BANK—Monmouth County

RIVERVIEW MEDICAL CENTER See Meridian Health System, Neptune

RIDGEWOOD—Bergen County

☒ VALLEY HOSPITAL, 223 North Van Dien Avenue, Zip 07450–9982; tel. 201/447–8000; Michael W. Azzara, President **A**1 2 9 10 **F**2 3 4 7 8 10 11 12 13 14 15 16 17 19 20 21 22 25 26 28 29 30 31 32 33 34 36 37 38 39 40 41 42 43 44 45 46 49 51 52 53 54 55 56 57 58 59 60 61 65 66 67 68 71 72 73 74 **P**5 6 7 8 **N** Columbia Presbyterian Regional Network, New York, NY; First Option Health Plan, Red Bank, NJ

	23	10	412	37149	369	159478	3184	194013	99277	2257

SALEM—Salem County

☒ MEMORIAL HOSPITAL OF SALEM COUNTY, 310 Woodstown Road, Zip 08079–2080; tel. 609/935–1000; Denise R. Williams, President and Chief Executive Officer **A**1 2 9 10 **F**7 8 12 14 15 16 17 19 20 21 22 28 31 32 33 34 36 37 39 40 41 42 44 46 49 56 64 65 67 71 73 **P**5 6 **N** Qualcare Preferred Providers, Piscataway, NJ

	23	10	110	4734	67	77034	450	45014	21841	610

SECAUCUS—Hudson County

☐ MEADOWLANDS HOSPITAL MEDICAL CENTER, Meadowland Parkway, Zip 07096–1580; tel. 201/392–3100; Paul V. Cavalli, M.D., President **A**1 9 10 **F**2 3 7 8 10 11 12 13 15 17 18 19 20 21 22 24 26 27 28 29 30 31 32 35 37 39 40 41 42 44 46 48 49 52 53 54 55 56 57 58 61 63 65 67 70 71 73 74 **P**3 **N** The Mount Sinai Health System, New York, NY

	23	10	200	6446	90	70854	1113	49558	22890	—

SOMERS POINT—Atlantic County

☒ SHORE MEMORIAL HOSPITAL, 1 East New York Avenue, Zip 08244–2387; tel. 609/653–3500; Richard A. Pitman, President **A**1 2 9 10 **F**3 7 8 12 15 16 19 21 22 26 28 29 30 31 32 33 34 35 37 39 40 41 42 44 45 46 49 60 63 64 65 67 71 73 74 **P**5 7 **N** First Option Health Plan, Red Bank, NJ; Qualcare Preferred Providers, Piscataway, NJ

	23	10	195	10454	163	86192	1139	102200	45587	1256

SOMERVILLE—Somerset County

☒ SOMERSET MEDICAL CENTER, 110 Rehill Avenue, Zip 08876–2598; tel. 908/685–2200; Michael A. Turner, President and Chief Executive Officer **A**1 2 3 5 9 10 **F**3 7 8 10 11 12 14 15 16 17 19 21 22 23 26 28 30 31 32 33 35 37 39 40 41 42 44 46 49 51 52 54 55 56 57 58 59 65 67 71 74 **P**5 7 **N** First Option Health Plan, Red Bank, NJ; Qualcare Preferred Providers, Piscataway, NJ

	23	10	297	12689	191	124840	1126	107079	51502	1327

Hospital, Address, Telephone, Administrator, Approval, Facility, and Physician Codes, Health Care System, Network	Classi-fication Codes		Utilization Data					Expense (thousands) of dollars		
★ American Hospital Association (AHA) membership □ Joint Commission on Accreditation of Healthcare Organizations (JCAHO) accreditation + American Osteopathic Healthcare Association (AOHA) membership ○ American Osteopathic Association (AOA) accreditation △ Commission on Accreditation of Rehabilitation Facilities (CARF) accreditation Control codes 61, 63, 64, 71, 72 and 73 indicate hospitals listed by AOHA, but not registered by AHA. For definition of numerical codes, see page A4	Control	Service	Staffed Beds	Admissions	Census	Outpatient Visits	Births	Total	Payroll	Personnel

SOUTH AMBOY—Middlesex County

★ MEMORIAL MEDICAL CENTER AT SOUTH AMBOY, 540 Bordentown Avenue, Zip 08879–1598; tel. 732/721–1000; Irv J. Diamond, Chief Executive Officer (Nonreporting) **A**1 9 10 | 23 | 10 | 161 | — | — | — | — | — | — | —

STRATFORD—Camden County

KENNEDY MEMORIAL HOSPITAL See Kennedy Memorial Hospitals–University Medical Center, Cherry Hill

SUMMIT—Union County

□ CHARTER BEHAVIORAL HEALTH SYSTEM OF NEW JERSEY–SUMMIT, 19 Prospect Street, Zip 07902–0100; tel. 908/522–7000; James Gallagner, Chief Executive Officer (Nonreporting) **A**1 9 10 **S** Magellan Health Services, Atlanta, GA | 33 | 22 | 90 | — | — | — | — | — | — | —

OVERLOOK HOSPITAL See Atlantic Health System, Florham Park

SUSSEX—Sussex County

SUSSEX CAMPUS See Northwest Covenant Medical Center, Denville

TEANECK—Bergen County

★ HOLY NAME HOSPITAL, 718 Teaneck Road, Zip 07666–4281; tel. 201/833–3000; Michael Maron, President and Chief Executive Officer **A**1 2 3 6 9 10 **F**1 3 5 7 8 10 12 13 15 16 17 19 20 21 22 26 27 28 29 30 32 33 34 35 37 39 40 41 42 44 45 46 48 49 51 53 54 55 56 57 58 59 63 65 66 67 71 73 74 **P**6 8 **N** Columbia Presbyterian Regional Network, New York, NY; First Option Health Plan, Red Bank, NJ; Qualcare Preferred Providers, Piscataway, NJ | 23 | 10 | 312 | 20013 | 227 | 183305 | 1744 | 114819 | 60541 | 1503

TOMS RIVER—Ocean County

CHILDREN'S SPECIALIZED HOSPITAL–OCEAN See Children's Specialized Hospital, Mountainside

COMMUNITY KIMBALL HEALTH CARE SYSTEM See Community Medical Center

★ COMMUNITY MEDICAL CENTER, (Formerly Community Kimball Health Care System), 99 Route 37 West, Zip 08755–6423; tel. 732/240–8000; Kevin R. Burchill, Executive Director **A**1 2 9 10 **F**1 3 4 6 7 8 10 11 12 13 14 15 16 17 18 19 20 21 22 24 25 26 27 28 29 30 31 32 33 34 35 36 37 39 40 41 42 44 45 46 49 51 52 54 55 56 57 58 59 60 61 63 64 65 66 67 68 69 71 72 73 74 **P**4 5 **S** Saint Barnabas Health Care System, Livingston, NJ **N** First Option Health Plan, Red Bank, NJ; Qualcare Preferred Providers, Piscataway, NJ; Community/Kimball Health Care System, Toms River, NJ | 23 | 10 | 425 | 21474 | 311 | 236367 | 1948 | 185609 | 80356 | 2165

□ △ HEALTHSOUTH REHABILITATION HOSPITAL OF NEW JERSEY, 14 Hospital Drive, Zip 08755–6470; tel. 732/244–3100; Patricia Ostaszewski, Chief Executive Officer and Administrator (Total facility includes 63 beds in nursing home–type unit) **A**1 7 9 10 **F**6 12 19 21 25 35 41 45 46 48 49 58 59 64 65 66 67 71 73 **P**5 **S** HEALTHSOUTH Corporation, Birmingham, AL | 33 | 46 | 155 | 2498 | 131 | 31490 | 0 | 25200 | 15085 | 396

TRENTON—Mercer County

★ CAPITAL HEALTH SYSTEM, (Includes Capital Health System at Fuld, 750 Brunswick Avenue, Zip 08638–4174; tel. 609/394–6000; Capital Health System at Mercer), 446 Bellevue Avenue, Zip 08618–4597, Mailing Address: P.O. Box 1658, Zip 08607–1658; tel. 609/394–4000; Alireza Maghazehe, Interim President **A**1 2 3 5 6 9 10 **F**1 3 7 8 9 10 11 12 13 14 15 16 17 18 19 20 21 22 23 26 28 29 30 31 32 33 34 35 36 37 38 39 40 41 42 44 45 46 48 49 50 53 54 56 58 59 60 61 63 65 67 70 71 72 73 | 23 | 10 | 558 | 22834 | 346 | 404897 | 3328 | 221162 | 104687 | 2750

HELENE FULD MEDICAL CENTER See Capital Health System at Fuld

MERCER MEDICAL CENTER See Capital Health System at Mercer

★ ST. FRANCIS MEDICAL CENTER, 601 Hamilton Avenue, Zip 08629–1986; tel. 609/599–5000; Judith M. Persichilli, President and Chief Executive Officer **A**1 2 3 5 6 9 10 **F**4 7 8 10 12 14 15 16 17 19 21 22 23 26 27 28 29 30 31 32 33 34 35 36 42 43 44 45 46 49 51 54 55 56 58 59 60 63 65 67 68 71 72 73 74 **P**5 6 7 8 **S** Catholic Health Initiatives, Denver, CO **N** First Option Health Plan, Red Bank, NJ; Fox Chase Network, Rockledge, PA | 21 | 10 | 216 | 7385 | 126 | 140171 | 300 | 76522 | 38038 | 932

★ TRENTON PSYCHIATRIC HOSPITAL, Sullivan Way, Zip 08625, Mailing Address: P.O. Box 7500, West Trenton, Zip 08628–7500; tel. 609/633–1500; Joseph Jupin, Jr., Chief Executive Officer (Nonreporting) **A**1 3 9 10 **S** Division of Mental Health Services, Department of Human Services, State of New Jersey, Trenton, NJ | 12 | 22 | 379 | — | — | — | — | — | — | —

TURNERSVILLE—Camden County

KENNEDY MEMORIAL HOSPITAL See Kennedy Memorial Hospitals–University Medical Center, Cherry Hill

UNION—Union County

★ + ○ UNION HOSPITAL, 1000 Galloping Hill Road, Zip 07083–1652; tel. 908/687–1900; Kathryn W. Coyne, Executive Director and Chief Operating Officer **A**1 2 9 10 11 12 13 **F**1 8 11 12 14 15 17 19 20 21 22 25 26 27 28 29 30 31 34 37 39 41 42 44 45 46 49 64 65 66 71 72 73 **P**5 6 **S** Saint Barnabas Health Care System, Livingston, NJ **N** First Option Health Plan, Red Bank, NJ; Qualcare Preferred Providers, Piscataway, NJ | 23 | 10 | 148 | 5808 | 114 | 51167 | 0 | 63164 | 28828 | 788

VINELAND—Cumberland County

★ NEWCOMB MEDICAL CENTER, 65 South State Street, Zip 08360–4893; tel. 609/691–9000; Paul S. Cooper, Chief Executive Officer **A**1 2 9 10 **F**7 8 11 12 13 15 16 17 19 20 21 22 28 29 30 31 32 33 34 35 37 38 39 40 41 42 44 45 46 49 51 54 56 61 65 67 71 73 74 | 23 | 10 | 151 | 5648 | 79 | 82549 | 964 | 52809 | 24317 | 681

□ VINELAND DEVELOPMENTAL CENTER HOSPITAL, 1676 East Landis Avenue, Zip 08361–2992; tel. 609/696–6200; Judith L. Sisti, MS, Administrator **A**1 10 **F**8 19 20 21 22 23 27 34 35 42 44 49 51 54 56 57 58 59 65 71 **P**6 | 12 | 12 | 100 | 673 | 48 | 8721 | 0 | — | — | 229

Hospital, Address, Telephone, Administrator, Approval, Facility, and Physician Codes, Health Care System, Network	Classi-fication Codes		Utilization Data					Expense (thousands) of dollars		
★ American Hospital Association (AHA) membership □ Joint Commission on Accreditation of Healthcare Organizations (JCAHO) accreditation + American Osteopathic Healthcare Association (AOHA) membership ○ American Osteopathic Association (AOA) accreditation △ Commission on Accreditation of Rehabilitation Facilities (CARF) accreditation Control codes 61, 63, 64, 71, 72 and 73 indicate hospitals listed by AOHA, but not registered by AHA. For definition of numerical codes, see page A4	Control	Service	Staffed Beds	Admissions	Census	Outpatient Visits	Births	Total	Payroll	Personnel

VOORHEES—Camden County

★ WEST JERSEY HOSPITAL–VOORHEES, 101 Carnie Boulevard, Zip 08043–1597; tel. 609/325–3000; Joan T. Meyers, R.N., Executive Director **A**3 5 9 **F**1 2 3 5 7 8 10 12 13 15 16 17 19 20 21 22 25 26 27 28 29 30 31 32 33 34 37 38 39 40 41 42 44 45 46 49 51 60 61 65 67 71 72 73 74 **P**5 7 **S** West Jersey Health System, Camden, NJ **N** First Option Health Plan, Red Bank, NJ; Qualcare Preferred Providers, Piscataway, NJ
| 23 | 10 | 244 | 16142 | 190 | 38586 | 4983 | 100796 | 48277 | 1187 |

WAYNE—Passaic County

✠ WAYNE GENERAL HOSPITAL, 224 Hamburg Turnpike, Zip 07470–2100; tel. 973/942–6900; Kenneth H. Kozloff, Executive Director **A**1 9 10 **F**1 3 7 8 11 12 13 15 16 17 19 21 22 23 25 26 27 28 30 31 32 33 34 35 37 39 40 41 42 44 45 46 49 51 53 54 55 56 57 58 59 60 63 65 67 71 73 **P**5 8 **S** Saint Barnabas Health Care System, Livingston, NJ **N** Qualcare Preferred Providers, Piscataway, NJ
| 23 | 10 | 146 | 11119 | 125 | 155000 | 789 | 65018 | 29927 | 852 |

WEST ORANGE—Essex County

✠ △ KESSLER INSTITUTE FOR REHABILITATION, (Includes East Orange Facility, West Orange Facility, Saddle Brook Facility and Welkind Facility), 1199 Pleasant Valley Way, Zip 07052–1419; tel. 973/731–3600; Kenneth W. Aitchison, President and Chief Executive Officer **A**1 3 5 7 10 **F**15 16 48 67 71 73 **P**6 **N** Qualcare Preferred Providers, Piscataway, NJ
| 23 | 46 | 322 | 5474 | 272 | 148135 | — | — | — | 1087 |

WESTAMPTON TOWNSHIP—Burlington County

□ HAMPTON HOSPITAL, Rancocas Road, Zip 08073, Mailing Address: P.O. Box 7000, Zip 08073; tel. 609/267–7000; Michael Terwilliger, Acting Chief Executive Officer **A**1 10 **F**15 16 52 53 55 57 58 59 65 67 **P**6 **S** Hospital Group of America, Wayne, PA
| 33 | 22 | 100 | 2271 | 68 | 13405 | 0 | 17874 | 7685 | 202 |

WESTWOOD—Bergen County

✠ PASCACK VALLEY HOSPITAL, 250 Old Hook Road, Zip 07675–3181; tel. 201/358–3000; Louis R. Ycre, Jr., FACHE, President and Chief Executive Officer **A**1 2 9 10 **F**7 8 10 11 14 15 16 17 19 20 21 22 24 26 27 28 29 30 31 32 33 34 35 36 37 39 40 41 42 44 45 46 49 51 53 54 55 58 60 61 65 66 67 68 71 72 73 74 **P**1 4 5 7 **N** First Option Health Plan, Red Bank, NJ; Qualcare Preferred Providers, Piscataway, NJ
| 23 | 10 | 213 | 15882 | 141 | 113978 | 890 | 86305 | 40361 | 894 |

WILLINGBORO—Burlington County

★ ALLEGHENY UNIVERSITY HOSPITAL, RANCOCAS, (Formerly Graduate Health System–Rancocas), 218–A Sunset Road, Zip 08046–1162; tel. 609/835–2900; Joseph Flamini, President and Chief Executive Officer **A**2 9 10 12 **F**1 3 7 8 12 15 16 17 19 20 21 22 26 28 30 35 41 42 44 46 49 51 54 56 57 58 59 60 61 63 65 66 67 71 73 74 **S** Allegheny Health, Education and Research Foundation, Pittsburgh, PA
| 23 | 10 | 237 | 10403 | 171 | 113594 | 1300 | 87032 | 38564 | 858 |

WOODBRIDGE—Middlesex County

WOODBRIDGE DEVELOPMENT CENTER, Rahway Avenue, Zip 07095, Mailing Address: P.O. Box 189, Zip 07095; tel. 908/499–5951; Amy R. Bailon, M.D., Medical Director (Nonreporting)
| 12 | 12 | 125 | — | — | — | — | — | — | — |

WOODBURY—Gloucester County

✠ UNDERWOOD–MEMORIAL HOSPITAL, 509 North Broad Street, Zip 08096–1697, Mailing Address: P.O. Box 359, Zip 08096–0359; tel. 609/845–0100; Steven W. Jackmuff, President and Chief Executive Officer **A**1 3 9 10 **F**7 8 10 11 12 15 16 17 18 19 22 26 27 28 30 31 32 34 37 39 40 41 42 44 45 49 51 52 56 58 59 65 67 71 73 74 **N** First Option Health Plan, Red Bank, NJ; Qualcare Preferred Providers, Piscataway, NJ; Jefferson Health System, Radnor, PA
| 23 | 10 | 232 | 10701 | 154 | 97084 | 1209 | 81169 | 38337 | 1082 |

WYCKOFF—Bergen County

✠ RAMAPO RIDGE PSYCHIATRIC HOSPITAL, 301 Sicomac Avenue, Zip 07481–2194; tel. 201/848–5200; Douglas A. Struyk, President and Chief Executive Officer (Nonreporting) **A**1 10
| 23 | 22 | 80 | — | — | — | — | — | — | — |

NEW MEXICO

Resident population 1,730 (in thousands)
Resident population in metro areas 56.4%
Birth rate per 1,000 population 16.7
65 years and over 11.0%
Percent of persons without health insurance 22.3%

Hospital, Address, Telephone, Administrator, Approval, Facility, and Physician Codes, Health Care System, Network	Classification Codes		Utilization Data					Expense (thousands) of dollars		
	Control	Service	Staffed Beds	Admissions	Census	Outpatient Visits	Births	Total	Payroll	Personnel

★ American Hospital Association (AHA) membership
□ Joint Commission on Accreditation of Healthcare Organizations (JCAHO) accreditation
+ American Osteopathic Healthcare Association (AOHA) membership
○ American Osteopathic Association (AOA) accreditation
△ Commission on Accreditation of Rehabilitation Facilities (CARF) accreditation
Control codes 61, 63, 64, 71, 72 and 73 indicate hospitals listed by AOHA, but not registered by AHA. For definition of numerical codes, see page A4

ALAMOGORDO—Otero County

✶ GERALD CHAMPION MEMORIAL HOSPITAL, 1209 Ninth Street, Zip 88310–0597; Mailing Address: P.O. Box 597, Zip 88311–0597; tel. 505/439–2100; Carl W. Mantey, Administrator **A**1 9 10 **F**7 8 14 15 16 19 21 22 23 24 28 30 33 34 35 37 40 42 44 65 66 67 71 73 **P**5 **S** Quorum Health Group/Quorum Health Resources, Inc., Brentwood, TN	23	10	73	3424	34	56679	752	23620	7979	—

ALBUQUERQUE—Bernalillo County

★ CARRIE TINGLEY HOSPITAL, 1127 University Boulevard N.E., Zip 87102–1715; tel. 505/272–5200; Robert T. Maruca, Administrator **A**3 5 9 10 **F**2 3 4 7 8 9 10 11 12 13 17 18 19 22 25 26 28 29 30 31 32 33 34 35 37 38 39 40 41 42 43 44 45 46 47 48 49 51 52 53 54 55 56 58 59 60 61 64 65 66 67 68 69 70 71 72 73 74 **P**8 **S** University of New Mexico, Albuquerque, NM	12	56	18	412	9	13752	—	9617	4832	124
□ CHARTER HEIGHTS BEHAVIORAL HEALTH SYSTEM, (Includes Charter Heights Behavioral Health System Northeast, 103 Hospital Loop N.E., Zip 87109; Charter Heights Behavioral Health System Southeast, 5901 Zuni Road S.E., Zip 87108; tel. 505/265–8800), 103 Hospital Loop N.E., Zip 87109–2115; tel. 505/883–8777; Joel A. Hart, FACHE, Chief Executive Officer (Nonreporting) **A**1 9 10 **S** Magellan Health Services, Atlanta, GA	33	22	172	—	—	—	—	—	—	—
DESERT HILLS HOSPITAL, 5310 Sequoia Road N.W., Zip 87120–1249; tel. 505/836–7330; Kay Wade, President and Chief Executive Officer (Nonreporting)	33	22	35	—	—	—	—	—	—	—
□ △ HEALTHSOUTH REHABILITATION CENTER, 7000 Jefferson N.E., Zip 87109–4357; tel. 505/344–9478; Darby Brockette, Administrator (Nonreporting) **A**1 7 9 10 **S** HEALTHSOUTH Corporation, Birmingham, AL	33	46	60	—	—	—	—	—	—	—
□ LOVELACE HEALTH SYSTEM, 5400 Gibson Boulevard S.E., Zip 87108–4763; tel. 505/262–7000; Martin Hickey, M.D., Chief Executive Officer **A**1 2 3 5 9 10 **F**1 2 3 4 6 7 8 9 10 11 12 13 14 15 16 17 18 19 20 21 22 23 24 25 26 27 28 29 30 31 32 33 34 35 36 37 39 40 41 42 43 44 45 46 47 48 49 51 52 53 54 55 56 57 58 59 60 61 62 63 64 65 66 68 69 70 71 72 73 74 **N** Lovelace, Albuquerque, NM	33	10	197	9699	87	1061560	1928	348923	129811	—
□ MEMORIAL PSYCHIATRIC HOSPITAL, 806 Central Avenue S.E., Zip 87102–3671; Mailing Address: P.O. Box 26568, Zip 87125–6568; tel. 505/247–0220; Richard B. Hiester, Administrator (Nonreporting) **A**1 10	32	22	58	—	—	—	—	—	—	—
✶ PRESBYTERIAN HEALTHCARE SERVICES, (Formerly Presbyterian Hospital), 1100 Central Avenue S.E., Zip 87106–4934, Mailing Address: P.O. Box 26666, Zip 87125–6666; tel. 505/260–6333; James M. Minton, President and Chief Executive Officer **A**1 2 3 5 9 10 **F**2 3 4 5 7 8 10 11 12 13 14 15 16 17 18 19 21 22 23 24 25 26 27 28 29 30 32 33 34 35 36 37 38 39 40 41 42 43 44 46 47 48 49 51 52 53 54 55 56 57 58 59 60 63 64 65 66 67 69 70 71 72 73 74 **P**1 3 4 5 6 7 **S** Presbyterian Healthcare Services, Albuquerque, NM **N** Presbyterian HealthCare Services, Inc., Albuquerque, NM	23	10	344	26563	284	48449	4151	—	—	6081
★ PRESBYTERIAN KASEMAN HOSPITAL, 8300 Constitution Avenue N.E., Zip 87110–7624, Mailing Address: P.O. Box 26666, Zip 87125–6666; tel. 505/291–2000; Robert A. Garcia, Administrator (Nonreporting) **A**9 10 **S** Presbyterian Healthcare Services, Albuquerque, NM **N** Presbyterian HealthCare Services, Inc., Albuquerque, NM	23	10	120	—	—	—	—	—	—	—
★ PUBLIC HEALTH SERVICE INDIAN HOSPITAL, 801 Vassar Drive N.E., Zip 87106–2799; tel. 505/256–4000; Cheri Lyon, Service Unit Director (Nonreporting) **A**10 **S** U. S. Public Health Service Indian Health Service, Rockville, MD	47	10	28	—	—	—	—	—	—	—
✶ ST. JOSEPH MEDICAL CENTER, 601 Martin Luther King Drive N.E., Zip 87102, Mailing Address: P.O. Box 25555, Zip 87125–0555; tel. 505/727–8000; C. Vincent Townsend, Jr., Senior Vice President Hospital Group (Total facility includes 24 beds in nursing home–type unit) **A**1 2 5 9 10 **F**2 3 5 7 8 10 11 12 19 21 22 23 27 28 30 32 33 34 35 36 37 39 40 41 42 43 44 45 46 48 49 51 52 54 56 57 58 60 63 64 65 67 68 70 71 72 73 74 **P**5 **S** Catholic Health Initiatives, Denver, CO **N** Medical Network of New Mexico, Albuquerque, NM	21	10	228	10141	148	43267	—	83737	27332	—
✶ ST. JOSEPH NORTHEAST HEIGHTS HOSPITAL, 4701 Montgomery Boulevard N.E., Zip 87109–1251, Mailing Address: P.O. Box 25555, Zip 87125–0555; tel. 505/727–7800; Tony Struthers, Administrator **A**1 9 10 **F**4 7 8 10 11 12 19 21 22 23 27 30 32 33 34 35 36 37 39 40 42 43 44 46 49 51 54 56 57 58 60 61 63 65 67 68 71 72 73 74 **P**5 **S** Catholic Health Initiatives, Denver, CO **N** Medical Network of New Mexico, Albuquerque, NM	21	10	71	3839	36	39152	1272	20484	6995	—
★ △ ST. JOSEPH REHABILITATION HOSPITAL AND OUTPATIENT CENTER, 505 Elm Street N.E., Zip 87102–2500, Mailing Address: P.O. Box 25555, Zip 87125–5555; tel. 505/727–4700; Mary Lou Coors, Administrator (Total facility includes 17 beds in nursing home–type unit) **A**7 9 10 **F**4 7 8 10 11 12 19 21 22 27 28 30 32 33 34 35 36 37 39 40 41 42 43 44 45 46 48 49 51 54 56 57 58 60 61 63 64 65 67 68 70 71 72 73 74 **P**5 **S** Catholic Health Initiatives, Denver, CO **N** Medical Network of New Mexico, Albuquerque, NM	21	46	63	897	42	3495	—	13081	6161	—

Hospital, Address, Telephone, Administrator, Approval, Facility, and Physician Codes, Health Care System, Network	Classi-fication Codes		Utilization Data					Expense (thousands) of dollars		
★ American Hospital Association (AHA) membership □ Joint Commission on Accreditation of Healthcare Organizations (JCAHO) accreditation + American Osteopathic Healthcare Association (AOHA) membership ○ American Osteopathic Association (AOA) accreditation △ Commission on Accreditation of Rehabilitation Facilities (CARF) accreditation Control codes 61, 63, 64, 71, 72 and 73 indicate hospitals listed by AOHA, but not registered by AHA. For definition of numerical codes, see page A4	Control	Service	Staffed Beds	Admissions	Census	Outpatient Visits	Births	Total	Payroll	Personnel
✚ ST. JOSEPH WEST MESA HOSPITAL, 10501 Golf Course Road N.W., Zip 87114–5000, Mailing Address: P.O. Box 25555, Zip 87125–0555; tel. 505/727–2000; Mary Lou Coors, Administrator (Total facility includes 22 beds in nursing home–type unit) **A**1 9 10 **F**3 4 7 8 10 12 19 21 22 23 27 30 32 33 34 35 36 37 39 40 42 43 44 46 48 49 51 52 54 56 57 58 61 63 64 65 67 68 71 72 73 74 **P**5 **S** Catholic Health Initiatives, Denver, CO **N** Medical Network of New Mexico, Albuquerque, NM	21	10	92	2631	37	17480	542	17176	5780	—
✚ UNIVERSITY HOSPITAL, 2211 Lomas Boulevard N.E., Zip 87106–2745; tel. 505/272–2121; Stephen W. McKernan, Chief Executive Officer **A**1 2 3 5 8 9 10 **F**3 4 5 7 8 9 10 12 14 15 16 17 19 21 22 23 24 26 28 29 30 31 32 33 34 35 37 38 40 41 42 43 44 45 46 47 49 54 55 58 60 61 63 65 66 67 68 69 70 71 72 73 74 **S** University of New Mexico, Albuquerque, NM **N** University of New Mexico Health Science Center, Albuquerque, NM	12	10	263	19776	254	362424	3346	196619	81345	2745
★ UNIVERSITY OF NEW MEXICO CHILDREN'S PSYCHIATRIC HOSPITAL, 1001 Yale Boulevard N.E., Zip 87131–3830; tel. 505/272–2945; Christina B. Gunn, Chief Executive Officer (Nonreporting) **A**3 5 **S** University of New Mexico, Albuquerque, NM	12	52	53	—	—	—	—	—	—	—
★ UNIVERSITY OF NEW MEXICO MENTAL HEALTH CENTER, 2600 Marble N.E., Zip 87131–2600; tel. 505/272–2870; Christina B. Gunn, Chief Executive Officer (Nonreporting) **A**3 5 9 **S** University of New Mexico, Albuquerque, NM **N** University of New Mexico Health Science Center, Albuquerque, NM	13	22	60	—	—	—	—	—	—	—
□ VENCOR HOSPITAL – ALBUQUERQUE, (Formerly THC – Albuquerque), 700 High Street N.E., Zip 87102–2565; tel. 505/242–4444; Jean Koester, Chief Executive Officer **A**1 5 10 **F**12 14 15 22 26 27 28 37 41 65 67 **S** Transitional Hospitals Corporation, Las Vegas, NV	33	10	61	493	30	—	—	—	—	—
✚ VETERANS AFFAIRS MEDICAL CENTER, 1501 San Pedro S.E., Zip 87108–5138; tel. 505/265–1711; Norman E. Browne, Director (Total facility includes 47 beds in nursing home–type unit) **A**1 2 3 5 8 9 **F**1 2 3 4 5 8 10 12 17 18 19 20 21 22 23 25 26 27 28 29 30 31 32 33 34 35 37 39 41 42 43 44 45 46 48 49 51 52 54 55 56 58 59 63 64 65 67 71 73 74 **S** Department of Veterans Affairs, Washington, DC	45	10	261	7095	199	268892	—	141834	70059	1684
ARTESIA—Eddy County										
✚ ARTESIA GENERAL HOSPITAL, 702 North 13th Street, Zip 88210–1199; tel. 505/748–3333; Anthony J. Plantier, Administrator **A**1 9 10 **F**7 8 12 14 16 17 19 22 25 28 32 44 45 49 65 71 73 **S** Presbyterian Healthcare Services, Albuquerque, NM	16	10	20	561	6	2163	5	8020	4356	113
CANNON AFB—Curry County										
★ U. S. AIR FORCE HOSPITAL, 208 West Casablanca Avenue, Zip 88103–5300; tel. 505/784–6318; Major Douglas E. Anderson, MSC, USAF, Administrator (Nonreporting) **S** Department of the Air Force, Bowling AFB, DC	41	10	10	—	—	—	—	—	—	—
CARLSBAD—Eddy County										
✚ COLUMBIA MEDICAL CENTER OF CARLSBAD, 2430 West Pierce Street, Zip 88220–3597; tel. 505/887–4100; Thomas McClintock, Chief Executive Officer **A**1 9 10 **F**3 7 8 12 14 15 16 17 18 19 20 21 22 26 27 28 30 31 32 34 35 37 38 39 40 41 42 44 45 46 48 49 51 52 53 54 55 56 57 58 59 60 63 64 65 67 71 73 74 **P**8 **S** Columbia/HCA Healthcare Corporation, Nashville, TN	33	10	131	4569	56	59468	670	28624	12183	463
CLAYTON—Union County										
★ UNION COUNTY GENERAL HOSPITAL, 301 Harding Street, Zip 88415–3321, Mailing Address: P.O. Box 489, Zip 88415–0489; tel. 505/374–2585; W. C. McElhannon, Administrator **A**9 10 **F**7 8 11 14 15 16 22 28 32 34 35 37 40 41 42 44 49 64 70 **P**5 **S** Brim, Inc., Portland, OR	23	10	30	498	5	—	26	—	—	40
CLOVIS—Curry County										
✚ PLAINS REGIONAL MEDICAL CENTER, (Includes Plains Regional Medical Center–Portales, 1700 South Avenue O., Portales, Zip 88130, Mailing Address: P.O. Drawer 60, Zip 88130; tel. 505/356–4411), 2100 North Thomas Street, Zip 88101–9412, Mailing Address: P.O. Box 1688, Zip 88101–1688; tel. 505/769–2141; Dennis E. Headlee, Administrator (Nonreporting) **A**1 9 10 **S** Presbyterian Healthcare Services, Albuquerque, NM	21	10	84	—	—	—	—	—	—	—
CROWNPOINT—McKinley County										
✚ U. S. PUBLIC HEALTH SERVICE INDIAN HOSPITAL, Mailing Address: P.O. Box 358, Zip 87313–0358; tel. 505/786–5291; Anita Muneta, Chief Executive Officer (Nonreporting) **A**1 10 **S** U. S. Public Health Service Indian Health Service, Rockville, MD	44	10	32	—	—	—	—	—	—	—
DEMING—Luna County										
★ MIMBRES MEMORIAL HOSPITAL, 900 West Ash Street, Zip 88030–4098; tel. 505/546–2761; Timothy E. Schmidt, Chief Executive Officer (Total facility includes 70 beds in nursing home–type unit) (Nonreporting) **A**9 10 **S** Community Health Systems, Inc., Brentwood, TN	33	10	119	—	—	—	—	—	—	—
ESPANOLA—Rio Arriba County										
✚ ESPANOLA HOSPITAL, 1010 Spruce Street, Zip 87532–2746; tel. 505/753–7111; Marcella A. Romero, Administrator (Nonreporting) **A**1 9 10 **S** Presbyterian Healthcare Services, Albuquerque, NM	23	10	80	—	—	—	—	—	—	—
FARMINGTON—San Juan County										
✚ SAN JUAN REGIONAL MEDICAL CENTER, (Includes Interface Rehabilitation Hospital, 525 South Schwartz, Zip 87401; tel. 505/327–3422; Jeff Hamblen, Administrator), 801 West Maple Street, Zip 87401–5698; tel. 505/325–5011; Donald R. Carlson, President and Chief Executive Officer (Total facility includes 15 beds in nursing home–type unit) **A**1 2 9 10 **F**3 7 8 12 13 14 15 16 17 19 21 22 23 25 27 28 29 30 32 33 34 35 37 40 41 42 44 46 49 53 54 56 58 59 60 62 63 64 67 72 73 74	23	10	160	7798	108	87511	1071	68084	30310	815

Hospital, Address, Telephone, Administrator, Approval, Facility, and Physician Codes, Health Care System, Network	Classi-fication Codes		Utilization Data					Expense (thousands) of dollars		
★ American Hospital Association (AHA) membership ☐ Joint Commission on Accreditation of Healthcare Organizations (JCAHO) accreditation + American Osteopathic Healthcare Association (AOHA) membership ○ American Osteopathic Association (AOA) accreditation △ Commission on Accreditation of Rehabilitation Facilities (CARF) accreditation Control codes 61, 63, 64, 71, 72 and 73 indicate hospitals listed by AOHA, but not registered by AHA. For definition of numerical codes, see page A4	Control	Service	Staffed Beds	Admissions	Census	Outpatient Visits	Births	Total	Payroll	Personnel

FORT SUMNER—De Baca County

★ DEBACA GENERAL HOSPITAL, 500 North Tenth Street, Zip 88119, Mailing Address: P.O. Box 349, Zip 88119–0349; tel. 505/355–2414; Dick L. Stout, Chief Executive Officer and Administrator (Nonreporting) **A**9 10

| | 13 | 10 | 21 | — | — | — | — | — | — | — |

GALLUP—McKinley County

✠ GALLUP INDIAN MEDICAL CENTER, 516 East Nizhoni Boulevard, Zip 87301–5748, Mailing Address: P.O. Box 1337, Zip 87305–1337; tel. 505/722–1000; Timothy G. Fleming, M.D., Chief Executive Officer (Nonreporting) **A**1 10 **S** U. S. Public Health Service Indian Health Service, Rockville, MD

| | 47 | 10 | 99 | — | — | — | — | — | — | — |

✠ REHOBOTH MCKINLEY CHRISTIAN HOSPITAL, 1901 Red Rock Drive, Zip 87301–1901; tel. 505/863–7000; David J. Baltzer, President **A**1 9 10 **F**2 3 7 8 12 13 14 16 17 18 19 21 22 28 30 32 33 34 35 37 40 41 44 45 46 49 51 52 53 54 55 56 58 59 65 67 71 73 74 **P**5 6

| | 23 | 10 | 69 | 2814 | 61 | 64651 | 352 | 35452 | 18210 | 576 |

GRANTS—Cibola County

✠ CIBOLA GENERAL HOSPITAL, 1212 Bonita Avenue, Zip 87020–2104; tel. 505/287–4446; Polly Pine, Administrator **A**1 9 10 **F**7 15 16 19 22 28 37 40 44 45 46 65 71 **P**8 **S** Quorum Health Group/Quorum Health Resources, Inc., Brentwood, TN

| | 23 | 10 | 22 | 1159 | 8 | 9044 | 123 | 6771 | 2981 | 98 |

HOBBS—Lea County

✠ COLUMBIA LEA REGIONAL HOSPITAL, 5419 North Lovington Highway, Zip 88240–9125, Mailing Address: P.O. Box 3000, Zip 88240–3000; tel. 505/392–6581; Bill Gresco, Administrator (Nonreporting) **A**1 10 **S** Columbia/HCA Healthcare Corporation, Nashville, TN

| | 33 | 10 | 250 | — | — | — | — | — | — | — |

HOLLOMAN AFB—Otero County

✠ U. S. AIR FORCE HOSPITAL, 280 First Street, Zip 88330–8273; tel. 505/475–5587; Colonel Bruce P. Heseltine, MSC, USAF, Commander (Nonreporting) **A**1 **S** Department of the Air Force, Bowling AFB, DC

| | 41 | 10 | 7 | — | — | — | — | — | — | — |

KIRTLAND AFB—Bernalillo County

✠ U. S. AIR FORCE HOSPITAL–KIRTLAND, 1951 Second Street S.E., Zip 87117–5559; tel. 505/846–3547; Colonel Paul B. Christianson, USAF, Commander **A**1 3 5 **F**2 3 4 7 8 10 11 12 19 20 21 22 23 24 28 29 30 31 33 34 35 37 38 39 40 41 42 43 44 45 46 47 48 49 51 52 53 54 55 56 57 58 59 60 61 65 70 71 72 73 74 **P**1 3 5 **S** Department of the Air Force, Bowling AFB, DC

| | 41 | 10 | 15 | 1197 | 7 | 150351 | 0 | 18678 | — | 426 |

LAS CRUCES—Dona Ana County

☐ BHC MESILLA VALLEY HOSPITAL, 3751 Del Rey Boulevard, Zip 88012–8526, Mailing Address: P.O. Box 429, Zip 88004–0429; tel. 505/382–3500; Alison Druck, R.N., Ed.D., Interim Chief Executive Officer **A**1 10 **F**3 12 14 15 32 52 53 54 56 57 58 59 65 **P**5 **S** Behavioral Healthcare Corporation, Nashville, TN

| | 32 | 22 | 105 | 707 | 60 | — | — | 7775 | 3681 | — |

✠ MEMORIAL MEDICAL CENTER, 2450 South Telshor Boulevard, Zip 88011–5076; tel. 505/522–8641; Steven L. Smith, President and Chief Executive Officer (Total facility includes 15 beds in nursing home–type unit) **A**1 5 9 10 **F**4 7 8 10 12 15 19 21 22 28 32 35 37 40 42 43 44 49 50 52 56 60 64 65 70 71 72 73 74

| | 15 | 10 | 228 | 12034 | 152 | 115143 | 2579 | 99226 | 38683 | 1187 |

LAS VEGAS—San Miguel County

☐ LAS VEGAS MEDICAL CENTER, 3795 Hot Springs Boulevard, Zip 87701, Mailing Address: P.O. Box 1388, Zip 87701–1388; tel. 505/454–2100; Felix Alderele, Administrator (Total facility includes 166 beds in nursing home–type unit) **A**1 **F**12 14 15 16 20 27 32 41 48 52 53 54 56 57 58 64 65 73 **P**6

| | 12 | 22 | 367 | 653 | 306 | 63109 | — | — | 22749 | 929 |

✠ NORTHEASTERN REGIONAL HOSPITAL, 1235 Eighth Street, Zip 87701–4254, Mailing Address: P.O. Box 248, Zip 87701–0238; tel. 505/425–6751; Donna Beane, Interim Chief Executive Officer (Nonreporting) **A**1 9 10 **S** Brim, Inc., Portland, OR

| | 23 | 10 | 56 | — | — | — | — | — | — | — |

LOS ALAMOS—Los Alamos County

✠ LOS ALAMOS MEDICAL CENTER, 3917 West Road, Zip 87544–2293; tel. 505/662–4201; Paul J. Wilson, Administrator **A**1 9 10 **F**1 2 3 4 5 6 7 8 9 10 11 12 13 14 15 16 17 18 19 20 21 22 23 24 25 26 27 28 29 30 31 32 33 34 35 36 37 38 39 40 41 42 43 44 45 46 47 48 49 50 51 52 53 54 55 56 57 58 59 60 61 62 63 64 65 66 67 68 69 70 71 72 73 74 **P**3 5 7 8 **S** Lutheran Health Systems, Fargo, ND

| | 23 | 10 | 47 | 1573 | 15 | 43581 | 264 | 17309 | 6158 | 290 |

LOVINGTON—Lea County

✠ NOR–LEA GENERAL HOSPITAL, 1600 North Main Avenue, Zip 88260–2871; tel. 505/396–6611; David R. Jordan, Ph.D., Administrator and Chief Executive Officer **A**1 9 10 **F**1 2 3 4 5 6 7 8 9 11 12 13 15 16 17 18 19 20 21 22 23 24 25 26 27 28 29 30 31 32 33 34 35 36 37 38 39 40 41 42 43 44 45 46 47 48 49 50 51 52 53 54 55 56 57 58 59 60 61 62 63 64 65 66 67 68 69 70 71 72 73 74 **P**5 6 7 **S** Lubbock Methodist Hospital System, Lubbock, TX

| | 16 | 10 | 28 | 478 | 4 | 35080 | — | 5058 | 2192 | 95 |

MESCALERO—Otero County

✠ U. S. PUBLIC HEALTH SERVICE INDIAN HOSPITAL, Mailing Address: Box 210, Zip 88340–0210; tel. 505/671–4441; Joe Wahnee, Jr., Service Unit Director (Nonreporting) **A**1 10 **S** U. S. Public Health Service Indian Health Service, Rockville, MD

| | 47 | 10 | 13 | — | — | — | — | — | — | — |

PORTALES—Roosevelt County

PLAINS REGIONAL MEDICAL CENTER–PORTALES See Plains Regional Medical Center, Clovis

RATON—Colfax County

★ MINERS' COLFAX MEDICAL CENTER, (Includes Miners' Hospital of New Mexico), 200 Hospital Drive, Zip 87740–2099; tel. 505/445–3661; David Antle, Chief Executive Officer (Total facility includes 30 beds in nursing home–type unit) (Nonreporting) **A**9 10

| | 13 | 10 | 68 | — | — | — | — | — | — | — |

Hospital, Address, Telephone, Administrator, Approval, Facility, and Physician Codes, Health Care System, Network	Classi-fication Codes		Utilization Data					Expense (thousands) of dollars		
★ American Hospital Association (AHA) membership □ Joint Commission on Accreditation of Healthcare Organizations (JCAHO) accreditation + American Osteopathic Healthcare Association (AOHA) membership ○ American Osteopathic Association (AOA) accreditation △ Commission on Accreditation of Rehabilitation Facilities (CARF) accreditation Control codes 61, 63, 64, 71, 72 and 73 indicate hospitals listed by AOHA, but not registered by AHA. For definition of numerical codes, see page A4	Control	Service	Staffed Beds	Admissions	Census	Outpatient Visits	Births	Total	Payroll	Personnel

ROSWELL—Chaves County

✠ EASTERN NEW MEXICO MEDICAL CENTER, 405 West Country Club Road, Zip 88201–9981; tel. 505/622–8170; Ronald J. Shafer, President and Chief Executive Officer **A**1 3 9 10 **F**7 8 17 19 21 22 23 34 35 37 40 42 44 45 46 49 52 53 54 55 56 57 58 59 60 63 64 65 67 71 73 74	13	10	162	6378	78	85970	985	49445	18876	611
□ △ SOUTHERN NEW MEXICO REHABILITATION CENTER, (Includes Pecos Valley Lodge), 31 Gail Harris Avenue, Zip 88201–8134; tel. 505/347–5491; Dave Dryden, FACHE, Administrator **A**1 7 10 **F**2 3 12 31 48 49 65 **P**6	12	46	39	516	28	5070	—	7875	3203	121

RUIDOSO—Lincoln County

✠ LINCOLN COUNTY MEDICAL CENTER, 211 Sudderth Drive, Zip 88345–6043, Mailing Address: P.O. Box 8000, Zip 88345–8000; tel. 505/257–7381; Valerie Miller, Administrator **A**1 9 10 **F**7 8 12 15 16 17 19 20 22 24 28 30 34 37 40 41 42 44 46 49 71 73 **P**2 8 **S** Presbyterian Healthcare Services, Albuquerque, NM	23	10	38	825	6	46105	230	10537	5308	179

SAN FIDEL—Cibola County

✠ ACOMA–CANONCITO–LAGUNA HOSPITAL, Mailing Address: P.O. Box 130, Zip 87049–0130; tel. 505/552–6634; Richard L. Zephier, Ph.D., Service Unit Director **A**1 10 **F**3 8 12 13 14 15 16 17 18 20 22 25 26 27 28 29 30 34 36 39 41 45 46 49 51 53 54 58 61 64 65 66 67 68 71 72 74 **S** U. S. Public Health Service Indian Health Service, Rockville, MD	47	10	15	493	9	61845	—	—	—	—

SANTA FE—Santa Fe County

□ BHC PINON HILLS HOSPITAL, 313 Camino Alire, Zip 87501–2319; tel. 505/988–8003; Jerry Smith, Chief Executive Officer (Nonreporting) **A**1 10 **S** Behavioral Healthcare Corporation, Nashville, TN	33	22	34	—	—	—	—	—	—	—
✠ PHS SANTA FE INDIAN HOSPITAL, 1700 Cerrillos Road, Zip 87505–3554; tel. 505/988–9821; Lawrence A. Jordan, Director (Nonreporting) **A**1 10 **S** U. S. Public Health Service Indian Health Service, Rockville, MD	47	10	39	—	—	—	—	—	—	—
✠ △ ST. VINCENT HOSPITAL, 455 St. Michael's Drive, Zip 87505–7663, Mailing Address: P.O. Box 2107, Zip 87504–2107; tel. 505/983–3361; Ronald C. Winger, President and Chief Executive Officer **A**1 2 5 7 9 10 **F**3 7 10 11 12 15 17 18 19 20 21 22 23 24 28 30 31 32 33 35 37 39 40 42 44 46 48 49 50 52 53 54 55 56 58 59 60 64 65 67 68 70 71 72 73 **P**1 5 7	23	10	151	11216	136	127065	1529	86792	42077	1117

SANTA TERESA—Dona Ana County

□ ALLIANCE HOSPITAL OF SANTA TERESA, 100 Laura Court, Zip 88008, Mailing Address: P.O. Box 6, Las Cruces, Zip 88008–0006; tel. 505/589–0033; Michele Irwin, Administrator **A**1 10 **F**2 3 16 52 53 58 59 **S** Bowdon Corporate Offices, Atlanta, GA	33	22	72	500	23	2792	—	—	3719	138

SHIPROCK—San Juan County

✠ NORTHERN NAVAJO MEDICAL CENTER, Mailing Address: P.O. Box 160, Zip 87420–0160; tel. 505/368–6001; Dee Hutchison, Chief Executive Officer **A**1 10 **F**1 2 3 4 5 7 8 9 10 11 12 13 15 16 17 19 20 21 22 23 25 26 27 28 29 30 31 32 33 34 35 37 38 39 40 42 43 44 45 46 47 48 49 51 52 53 54 56 57 58 59 60 61 64 65 67 68 69 71 72 74 **P**6 **S** U. S. Public Health Service Indian Health Service, Rockville, MD	44	10	59	3235	32	178537	770	54868	28875	—

SILVER CITY—Grant County

✠ GILA REGIONAL MEDICAL CENTER, 1313 East 32nd Street, Zip 88061; tel. 505/538–4000; Jeffrey Carey, Administrator **A**1 9 10 **F**3 7 8 16 17 19 21 22 27 30 32 33 35 37 40 41 42 44 49 52 53 56 58 65 71 73 **P**3 5 **S** Quorum Health Group/Quorum Health Resources, Inc., Brentwood, TN	13	10	68	3646	34	65988	565	28348	14608	413

SOCORRO—Socorro County

✠ SOCORRO GENERAL HOSPITAL, 1202 Highway 60 West, Zip 87801, Mailing Address: P.O. Box 1009, Zip 87801–1009; tel. 505/835–1140; Jeff Dye, Administrator (Nonreporting) **A**1 9 10 **S** Presbyterian Healthcare Services, Albuquerque, NM	23	10	30	—	—	—	—	—	—	—

TAOS—Taos County

✠ HOLY CROSS HOSPITAL, 630 Paseo De Pueblo Sur, Zip 87571, Mailing Address: P.O. Box DD, Zip 87571; tel. 505/758–8883; Warren K. Spellman, Administrator (Nonreporting) **A**1 9 10 **S** Quorum Health Group/Quorum Health Resources, Inc., Brentwood, TN	23	10	42	—	—	—	—	—	—	—

TRUTH OR CONSEQUENCES—Sierra County

✠ SIERRA VISTA HOSPITAL, 800 East Ninth Avenue, Zip 87901–1961; tel. 505/894–2111; Domenica Rush, Administrator **A**1 9 10 **F**7 12 17 19 22 32 34 40 44 46 49 64 65 67 71	15	10	47	292	4	32325	22	5066	2168	106

TUCUMCARI—Quay County

★ DR. DAN C. TRIGG MEMORIAL HOSPITAL, 301 East Miel De Luna Avenue, Zip 88401–3810, Mailing Address: P.O. Box 608, Zip 88401–0608; tel. 505/461–0141; Dell Willis, Administrator (Nonreporting) **A**9 10 **S** Presbyterian Healthcare Services, Albuquerque, NM	23	10	37	—	—	—	—	—	—	—

ZUNI—McKinley County

✠ U. S. PUBLIC HEALTH SERVICE INDIAN HOSPITAL, Mailing Address: P.O. Box 467, Zip 87327–0467; tel. 505/782–4431; Jean Othole, Service Unit Director **A**1 10 **F**1 3 4 5 7 8 10 13 14 15 16 18 19 20 21 22 24 26 27 28 30 35 40 44 46 49 50 51 53 54 55 56 57 58 59 60 63 68 69 72 **S** U. S. Public Health Service Indian Health Service, Rockville, MD	47	10	37	877	9	59175	103	—	—	174

NEW YORK

Resident population 18,137 (in thousands)
Resident population in metro areas 91.7%
Birth rate per 1,000 population 15.3
65 years and over 13.4%
Percent of persons without health insurance 17.0%

Hospital, Address, Telephone, Administrator, Approval, Facility, and Physician Codes, Health Care System, Network	Classification Codes		Utilization Data					Expense (thousands) of dollars		
	Control	Service	Staffed Beds	Admissions	Census	Outpatient Visits	Births	Total	Payroll	Personnel

★ American Hospital Association (AHA) membership
□ Joint Commission on Accreditation of Healthcare Organizations (JCAHO) accreditation
+ American Osteopathic Healthcare Association (AOHA) membership
○ American Osteopathic Association (AOA) accreditation
△ Commission on Accreditation of Rehabilitation Facilities (CARF) accreditation
Control codes 61, 63, 64, 71, 72 and 73 indicate hospitals listed by AOHA, but not registered by AHA. For definition of numerical codes, see page A4

ALBANY—Albany County

Hospital, Address, Telephone, Administrator, Approval, Facility, and Physician Codes, Health Care System, Network	Control	Service	Staffed Beds	Admissions	Census	Outpatient Visits	Births	Total	Payroll	Personnel
✠ ALBANY MEDICAL CENTER, 43 New Scotland Avenue, Zip 12208–3478; tel. 518/262–3125; Thomas G. Foggo, Executive Vice President Care Delivery and General Director **A**1 2 3 5 8 9 10 12 **F**4 7 8 10 11 12 15 16 17 19 20 21 22 26 28 30 31 32 34 35 37 38 39 40 41 42 43 44 45 46 47 48 49 51 52 53 54 55 56 57 58 59 60 61 63 65 66 67 69 70 71 72 73 74 **P**6 **N** Greene County Rural Health Network, Catskill, NY	23	10	574	24255	459	342858	2271	275139	92480	2944
✠ CAPITAL DISTRICT PSYCHIATRIC CENTER, 75 New Scotland Avenue, Zip 12208–3474; tel. 518/447–9611; Jesse Nixon, Jr., Ph.D., Director (Nonreporting) **A**1 3 5 10 **S** New York State Department of Mental Health, Albany, NY	12	22	200	—	—	—	—	—	—	—
□ CHILD'S HOSPITAL, 25 Hackett Boulevard, Zip 12208–3499; tel. 518/242–1200; Stephen J. Lauko, Chief Executive Officer (Nonreporting) **A**1 3 5 9 10	23	45	20	—	—	—	—	—	—	—
✠ MEMORIAL HOSPITAL, 600 Northern Boulevard, Zip 12204–1083; tel. 518/471–3221; Norman E. Dascher, Jr., Vice President and Chief Operating Officer (Nonreporting) **A**1 6 9 10 **N** Shared Health Network, Inc., Albany, NY	23	10	165	—	—	—	—	—	—	—
✠ ST. PETER'S HOSPITAL, 315 South Manning Boulevard, Zip 12208–1789; tel. 518/525–1550; Steven P. Boyle, President and Chief Executive Officer **A**1 2 3 5 9 10 **F**3 4 7 8 10 11 12 13 14 15 16 17 18 19 20 21 22 25 26 27 28 29 30 31 32 33 34 35 36 37 38 39 40 41 42 43 44 45 46 48 49 51 54 63 65 67 68 71 72 73 74 **S** Catholic Health East, Radnor, PA **N** MercyCare Corporation, Albany, NY; Shared Health Network, Inc., Albany, NY	21	10	437	20757	340	430045	2414	160017	75553	—
✠ △ VETERANS AFFAIRS MEDICAL CENTER, 113 Holland Avenue, Zip 12208–3473; tel. 518/462–3311; Lawrence H. Flesh, M.D., Director (Total facility includes 50 beds in nursing home–type unit) **A**1 2 3 5 7 8 9 **F**1 3 4 8 10 11 12 17 18 19 20 21 22 25 26 28 29 30 31 32 33 34 35 37 39 41 42 44 45 46 48 49 50 51 52 54 55 56 57 58 59 60 63 64 65 67 71 73 74 **S** Department of Veterans Affairs, Washington, DC	45	10	154	4295	138	240474	0	—	78061	1418

ALEXANDRIA BAY—Jefferson County

Hospital	Control	Service	Staffed Beds	Admissions	Census	Outpatient Visits	Births	Total	Payroll	Personnel
□ E. J. NOBLE HOSPITAL SAMARITAN, 19 Fuller Street, Zip 13607; tel. 315/482–2511; Richard A. Brooks, Administrator and Chief Operating Officer (Total facility includes 27 beds in nursing home–type unit) (Nonreporting) **A**1 9 10 **N** Northern New York Rural Health Care Alliance, Watertown, NY	23	10	52	—	—	—	—	—	—	—

AMITYVILLE—Suffolk County

Hospital	Control	Service	Staffed Beds	Admissions	Census	Outpatient Visits	Births	Total	Payroll	Personnel
□ BRUNSWICK GENERAL HOSPITAL, (Includes Brunswick Hall, 80 Louden Avenue, Zip 11701–2735; tel. 516/789–7100; Brunswick Physical Medicine & Rehabilitation Hospital, 366 Broadway), 366 Broadway, Zip 11701–9820; tel. 516/789–7000; Benjamin M. Stein, M.D., President (Total facility includes 94 beds in nursing home–type unit) **A**1 9 10 **F**3 8 11 15 16 17 19 21 22 26 27 28 30 31 32 33 35 37 39 42 44 46 48 49 52 53 54 55 56 57 58 64 65 67 71 73 **N** Health First, New York, NY	33	10	474	7040	354	136272	0	76462	40550	982
□ SOUTH OAKS HOSPITAL, 400 Sunrise Highway, Zip 11701; tel. 516/264–4000; Patrick R. Martore, Chief Executive Officer (Nonreporting) **A**1 9 10	33	22	334	—	—	—	—	—	—	—

AMSTERDAM—Montgomery County

Hospital	Control	Service	Staffed Beds	Admissions	Census	Outpatient Visits	Births	Total	Payroll	Personnel
✠ AMSTERDAM MEMORIAL HOSPITAL, 4988 State Highway 30, Zip 12010–1699; tel. 518/842–3100; Cornelio R. Catena, President and Chief Executive Officer (Total facility includes 160 beds in nursing home–type unit) **A**1 9 10 **F**1 8 11 12 13 14 15 17 19 20 21 22 24 25 26 29 30 34 35 37 39 41 42 44 45 46 49 64 65 66 67 68 71 73 74 **S** Quorum Health Group/Quorum Health Resources, Inc., Brentwood, TN	23	10	242	2338	186	52078	—	29415	12224	—
✠ ST. MARY'S HOSPITAL, 427 Guy Park Avenue, Zip 12010–1095; tel. 518/842–1900; Peter E. Capobianco, President and Chief Executive Officer **A**1 9 10 **F**2 3 7 8 11 12 13 14 15 16 17 18 19 22 25 26 27 28 29 30 31 32 33 35 37 39 40 41 42 44 45 46 48 49 51 52 53 54 55 56 57 58 61 65 66 67 71 73 74 **P**8 **S** Carondelet Health System, Saint Louis, MO **N** Shared Health Network, Inc., Albany, NY	21	10	143	4941	84	170071	685	41395	22378	676

AUBURN—Cayuga County

Hospital	Control	Service	Staffed Beds	Admissions	Census	Outpatient Visits	Births	Total	Payroll	Personnel
✠ AUBURN MEMORIAL HOSPITAL, 17 Lansing Street, Zip 13021–1943; tel. 315/255–7011; Christopher J. Rogers, Administrator (Total facility includes 80 beds in nursing home–type unit) **A**1 5 9 10 **F**7 11 19 22 37 40 44 49 52 64 71 72 73	23	10	306	7694	223	106518	631	54073	27333	793

BATAVIA—Genesee County

Hospital	Control	Service	Staffed Beds	Admissions	Census	Outpatient Visits	Births	Total	Payroll	Personnel
✠ GENESEE MEMORIAL HOSPITAL, 127 North Street, Zip 14020–1697; tel. 716/343–6030; Douglas T. Jones, President and Chief Executive Officer **A**1 9 10 **F**7 8 11 15 16 19 22 25 27 28 29 30 33 34 37 39 40 41 42 44 45 51 61 65 67 71 73 74 **N** Lake Plains Community Care Network, Buffalo, NY	23	10	70	3086	53	106709	465	24339	10992	405
✠ ST. JEROME HOSPITAL, 16 Bank Street, Zip 14020–2260; tel. 716/343–3131; Charles W. Smith, Jr., Chief Executive Officer **A**1 9 10 **F**5 8 11 14 15 16 17 18 19 22 27 28 29 30 32 33 34 35 37 41 44 45 51 60 62 65 66 71 73 **N** Lake Plains Community Care Network, Buffalo, NY	21	10	96	2636	57	73003	—	22122	10178	372

Hospital, Address, Telephone, Administrator, Approval, Facility, and Physician Codes, Health Care System, Network	Classi-fication Codes		Utilization Data					Expense (thousands) of dollars		
★ American Hospital Association (AHA) membership □ Joint Commission on Accreditation of Healthcare Organizations (JCAHO) accreditation + American Osteopathic Healthcare Association (AOHA) membership ○ American Osteopathic Association (AOA) accreditation △ Commission on Accreditation of Rehabilitation Facilities (CARF) accreditation Control codes 61, 63, 64, 71, 72 and 73 indicate hospitals listed by AOHA, but not registered by AHA. For definition of numerical codes, see page A4	Control	Service	Staffed Beds	Admissions	Census	Outpatient Visits	Births	Total	Payroll	Personnel

Hospital	Control	Service	Staffed Beds	Admissions	Census	Outpatient Visits	Births	Total	Payroll	Personnel
✠ VETERANS AFFAIRS WESTERN NEW YORK HEALTHCARE SYSTEM–BATAVIA DIVISION, 222 Richmond Avenue, Zip 14020–1288; tel. 716/343–7500; Richard S. Droske, Director (Total facility includes 70 beds in nursing home–type unit) (Nonreporting) **A**1 5 9 **S** Department of Veterans Affairs, Washington, DC	45	10	158	—	—	—	—	—	—	—
BATH—Steuben County										
✠ IRA DAVENPORT MEMORIAL HOSPITAL, 7571 State Route 54, Zip 14810–9533; tel. 607/776–8500; James B. Watson, Chief Executive Officer (Total facility includes 120 beds in nursing home–type unit) **A**1 9 10 **F**1 3 7 8 15 16 17 19 20 22 26 30 31 34 37 40 42 44 49 51 64 65 67 71 73 74	23	10	186	2196	143	—	112	15961	7085	300
✠ VETERANS AFFAIRS MEDICAL CENTER, 76 Veterans Avenue, Zip 14810–0842; tel. 607/776–2111; Michael J. Sullivan, Director (Total facility includes 125 beds in nursing home–type unit) (Nonreporting) **A**1 9 **S** Department of Veterans Affairs, Washington, DC	45	10	615	—	—	—	—	—	—	—
BAY SHORE—Suffolk County										
✠ SOUTHSIDE HOSPITAL, 301 East Main Street, Zip 11706–8458; tel. 516/968–3000; Theodore A. Jospe, President (Nonreporting) **A**1 3 5 9 10 **S** North Shore– Long Island Jewish Health System, Manhasset, NY **N** North Shore Regional Health Systems, Manhasset, NY; First Choice Network, Inc., Mineola, NY	23	10	374	—	—	—	—	—	—	—
BEACON—Dutchess County										
✠ CRAIG HOUSE CENTER, Howland Avenue, Zip 12508; tel. 914/831–1200; Pamela Pohly, Administrator (Nonreporting) **A**1 10	33	22	61	—	—	—	—	—	—	—
BELLEROSE—Queens County, See New York City										
BETHPAGE—Nassau County										
□ MID–ISLAND HOSPITAL, 4295 Hempstead Turnpike, Zip 11714–5769; tel. 516/579–6000; Robert J. Reed, President (Nonreporting) **A**1 9 10	33	10	223	—	—	—	—	—	—	—
BINGHAMTON—Broome County										
BINGHAMTON GENERAL HOSPITAL See United Health Services Hospitals–Binghamton										
✠ BINGHAMTON PSYCHIATRIC CENTER, 425 Robinson Street, Zip 13901–4198; tel. 607/724–1391; Margaret R. Dugan, Executive Director **A**1 3 10 **F**15 16 20 25 39 46 52 57 58 65 73 **P**6 **S** New York State Department of Mental Health, Albany, NY	12	22	216	193	235	44585	—	—	—	551
✠ OUR LADY OF LOURDES MEMORIAL HOSPITAL, 169 Riverside Drive, Zip 13905–4198; tel. 607/798–5328; Michael G. Guley, President and Chief Executive Officer **A**1 2 9 10 **F**5 6 7 8 12 14 15 16 17 19 21 22 23 24 25 26 27 28 29 30 31 32 33 34 35 36 37 39 40 41 42 44 45 46 49 51 53 55 58 60 63 65 66 67 68 71 72 73 74 **P**5 6 7 **S** Daughters of Charity National Health System, Saint Louis, MO	21	10	184	9163	155	851262	1194	101394	46519	1256
✠ ○ UNITED HEALTH SERVICES HOSPITALS–BINGHAMTON, (Includes Binghamton General Hospital, ; Medicenter, 600 High Avenue, Endicott, Zip 13760; tel. 607/754–7171; Wilson Memorial Regional Medical Center, 33–57 Harrison Street, Johnson City, Zip 13790), 10–42 Mitchell Avenue, Zip 13903; tel. 607/763–6000; Matthew J. Salanger, President and Chief Executive Officer **A**1 3 5 8 9 10 11 **F**1 2 3 4 6 7 8 10 11 12 13 14 15 16 17 18 19 20 21 22 26 28 29 30 31 32 34 37 38 39 40 41 42 43 44 45 46 48 49 51 52 54 55 56 57 58 61 62 64 65 66 67 68 70 71 72 73 74 **P**1	23	10	516	19109	378	211117	1656	191718	78852	2387
BRENTWOOD—Suffolk County										
KINGS PARK PSYCHIATRIC CENTER See Pilgrim Psychiatric Center										
✠ PILGRIM PSYCHIATRIC CENTER, (Includes Kings Park Psychiatric Center, 998 Crooked Hill Road, tel. 516/761–3500; Alan M. Weinstock, MS, Chief Executive Officer), 998 Crooked Hill Road, Zip 11717–1087; tel. 516/761–3500; Kathleen Kelly, Chief Executive Officer (Nonreporting) **A**1 5 10 **S** New York State Department of Mental Health, Albany, NY	12	22	744	—	—	—	—	—	—	—
BROCKPORT—Monroe County										
✠ LAKESIDE MEMORIAL HOSPITAL, 156 West Avenue, Zip 14420–1286; tel. 716/637–3131; Robert W. Harris, President **A**1 9 10 **F**2 3 4 7 8 9 10 11 14 15 16 17 19 20 21 22 23 28 29 30 33 35 37 38 40 41 42 43 44 45 46 47 48 49 50 52 53 54 55 56 57 58 59 60 63 64 65 67 69 70 71	23	10	72	2878	55	14098	411	—	—	312
BRONX—Bronx County, See New York City										
BRONXVILLE—Westchester County										
✠ LAWRENCE HOSPITAL, 55 Palmer Avenue, Zip 10708–3491; tel. 914/787–1000; Roger G. Dvorak, President **A**1 2 9 10 **F**7 8 12 16 17 19 21 22 26 30 32 33 34 35 36 37 39 40 41 42 44 45 46 48 49 50 54 63 65 66 67 71 73 **P**5 8 **N** Health Star Network, Armonk, NY; The Excelcare System, Inc., Bronxville, NY; Columbia Presbyterian Regional Network, New York, NY	23	10	280	9196	164	—	1501	69470	36485	—
BROOKLYN—Kings County, See New York City										
BUFFALO—Erie County										
□ BRYLIN HOSPITALS, 1263 Delaware Avenue, Zip 14209–2497; tel. 716/886–8200; Leonard Pleskow, Chairman (Nonreporting) **A**1 9 10	33	22	150	—	—	—	—	—	—	—
✠ BUFFALO GENERAL HOSPITAL, (Includes Buffalo Columbus Hospital, 300 Niagara Street, Zip 14201; tel. 716/845–4300; Andres Garcia, Chief Executive Officer), 100 High Street, Zip 14203–1154; tel. 716/845–5600; Carrie B. Frank, President and Chief Executive Officer (Total facility includes 242 beds in nursing home–type unit) (Nonreporting) **A**1 3 5 8 9 10 **S** CGF Health System, Buffalo, NY **N** Buffalo General Health System, Buffalo, NY	23	10	965	—	—	—	—	—	—	—
✠ BUFFALO PSYCHIATRIC CENTER, 400 Forest Avenue, Zip 14213–1298; tel. 716/885–2261; George Molnar, M.D., Executive Director **A**1 10 **F**1 2 3 4 5 6 7 8 9 10 11 12 15 16 17 19 20 21 22 23 24 25 26 27 29 30 31 35 37 39 40 41 42 43 44 45 46 48 49 50 51 52 54 55 56 57 58 59 60 61 63 65 67 69 70 71 73 **P**1 **S** New York State Department of Mental Health, Albany, NY	12	22	260	163	306	56662	0	50850	35000	808

Hospital, Address, Telephone, Administrator, Approval, Facility, and Physician Codes, Health Care System, Network	Classi-fication Codes		Utilization Data					Expense (thousands) of dollars		
	Control	Service	Staffed Beds	Admissions	Census	Outpatient Visits	Births	Total	Payroll	Personnel

★ American Hospital Association (AHA) membership
☐ Joint Commission on Accreditation of Healthcare Organizations (JCAHO) accreditation
+ American Osteopathic Healthcare Association (AOHA) membership
○ American Osteopathic Association (AOA) accreditation
△ Commission on Accreditation of Rehabilitation Facilities (CARF) accreditation
Control codes 61, 63, 64, 71, 72 and 73 indicate hospitals listed by AOHA, but not registered by AHA. For definition of numerical codes, see page A4

Hospital	Control	Service	Staffed Beds	Admissions	Census	Outpatient Visits	Births	Total	Payroll	Personnel
☐ CHILDREN'S HOSPITAL, 219 Bryant Street, Zip 14222–2099; tel. 716/878–7000; Karen Blount, Vice President and Chief Operating Officer (Nonreporting) **A**1 3 5 9 10 **S** CGF Health System, Buffalo, NY	23	59	313	—	—	—	—	—	—	—
☐ ERIE COUNTY MEDICAL CENTER, 462 Grider Street, Zip 14215–3098; tel. 716/898–3000; Paul J. Candino, Chief Executive Officer (Total facility includes 156 beds in nursing home–type unit) **A**1 3 5 9 10 **F**3 4 8 10 12 13 14 15 16 17 18 19 20 21 22 25 26 27 28 30 31 32 33 34 35 39 41 42 43 44 49 51 53 54 55 56 57 58 63 65 67 69 70 71 73 74	13	10	417	12870	359	309688	0	180361	80420	1993
☐ MERCY HOSPITAL, 565 Abbott Road, Zip 14220–2095; tel. 716/826–7000; James W. Connolly, President and Chief Executive Officer (Total facility includes 74 beds in nursing home–type unit) **A**1 3 5 9 10 **F**2 3 4 6 7 8 9 10 11 12 14 15 17 18 19 20 21 22 23 25 26 27 28 29 30 31 32 33 34 35 36 37 38 39 40 41 42 43 44 45 46 47 48 49 51 52 53 54 55 56 57 58 59 60 61 62 63 64 65 66 67 68 69 71 72 73 74 **P**5 8 **S** Catholic Health East, Radnor, PA	21	10	290	13682	209	61413	2441	110266	52555	1497
☒ MILLARD FILLMORE HEALTH SYSTEM, (Includes Millard Fillmore Suburban Hospital, 1540 Maple Road, Williamsville, Zip 14221; tel. 716/688–3100), 3 Gates Circle, Zip 14209–9986; tel. 716/887–4600; Carol M. Cassell, Executive Vice President and Chief Operating Officer (Total facility includes 75 beds in nursing home–type unit) **A**1 3 5 6 8 9 10 **F**1 4 7 8 10 11 14 19 20 21 22 25 26 32 33 35 37 40 41 42 43 44 50 51 53 64 65 71 73 74 **S** CGF Health System, Buffalo, NY **N** Millard Fillmore Health System, Buffalo, NY	23	10	588	22802	395	242303	3056	227500	100123	
☐ ROSWELL PARK CANCER INSTITUTE, (COMPREHENSIVE CANCER CENTER), Elm and Carlton Streets, Zip 14263–0001; tel. 716/845–2300; David C. Hohn, M.D., President and Chief Executive Officer **A**1 2 3 5 8 9 10 **F**8 12 15 16 17 19 20 21 25 28 29 30 31 32 33 34 35 37 39 42 44 45 46 49 50 53 54 60 63 65 67 69 71 73 74 **P**6	12	49	137	5220	103	102533	—	142977	63664	2112
☐ SHEEHAN MEMORIAL HOSPITAL, 425 Michigan Avenue, Zip 14203–2297; tel. 716/848–2000; Olivia Smith–Blackwell, M.D., M.P.H., President and Chief Executive Officer (Nonreporting) **A**1 9 10	23	10	109	—	—	—	—	—	—	—
☒ SISTERS OF CHARITY HOSPITAL OF BUFFALO, 2157 Main Street, Zip 14214–2692; tel. 716/862–1000; Patrick J. Wiles, President and Chief Executive Officer (Total facility includes 80 beds in nursing home–type unit) **A**1 2 3 5 6 9 10 12 13 **F**2 3 7 8 11 12 14 15 16 17 18 19 20 21 22 25 26 28 29 30 32 33 34 35 37 39 40 41 42 44 45 46 48 49 51 60 61 64 65 71 72 73 74 **P**3 8 **S** Daughters of Charity National Health System, Saint Louis, MO	21	10	419	12219	232	372292	2689	107544	50478	1628
☒ VETERANS AFFAIRS WESTERN NEW YORK HEALTHCARE SYSTEM–BUFFALO DIVISION, 3495 Bailey Avenue, Zip 14215–1129; tel. 716/834–9200; William F. Feeley, Acting Director (Total facility includes 120 beds in nursing home–type unit) **A**1 2 3 5 8 9 **F**1 3 4 8 10 11 12 14 16 17 18 20 24 25 26 28 29 30 31 32 33 34 37 39 41 42 43 44 45 46 48 49 51 52 54 55 56 57 58 59 60 62 64 66 68 **S** Department of Veterans Affairs, Washington, DC	45	10	388	5614	230	363635	—	150300	84341	1718
☒ WESTERN NEW YORK CHILDREN'S PSYCHIATRIC CENTER, 1010 East and West Road, Zip 14224–3698; tel. 716/674–9730; Jed M. Cohen, Acting Executive Director **A**1 3 **F**12 13 17 18 20 25 27 29 30 45 46 52 53 54 55 56 58 65 67 73 **S** New York State Department of Mental Health, Albany, NY	12	52	46	86	39	8930	—	—	—	168
CAMBRIDGE—Washington County										
☐ MARY MCCLELLAN HOSPITAL, One Myrtle Avenue, Zip 12816–1098; tel. 518/677–2611; Kathleen Lacasse, Chief Executive Officer (Total facility includes 40 beds in nursing home–type unit) **A**1 9 10 **F**7 8 12 14 15 19 20 21 22 25 30 33 34 37 39 40 41 42 44 48 49 51 64 65 66 67 71 73 74 **P**5 6	23	10	114	1691	61	81917	156	16350	10066	294
CANANDAIGUA—Ontario County										
☒ F. F. THOMPSON HEALTH SYSTEM, 350 Parrish Street, Zip 14424–1793; tel. 716/396–6527; Linda M. Janczak, President and Chief Executive Officer (Total facility includes 188 beds in nursing home–type unit) **A**1 3 9 10 **F**1 7 8 12 14 15 16 17 19 21 22 25 28 29 30 33 34 35 37 39 40 41 42 44 45 49 64 65 66 67 71 72 73 74 **P**5 6	23	10	301	4448	245	146079	648	34284	23380	832
☒ VETERANS AFFAIRS MEDICAL CENTER, (LONG TERM MED AND PSYCHIATRY), 400 Fort Hill Avenue, Zip 14424–1197; tel. 716/396–3601; Stuart C. Collyer, Director (Total facility includes 196 beds in nursing home–type unit) **A**1 5 9 **F**2 3 12 16 17 19 20 26 27 28 30 31 32 33 39 41 44 46 49 51 52 54 55 56 57 58 59 64 65 67 71 73 74 **P**6 **S** Department of Veterans Affairs, Washington, DC	45	49	488	2034	490	93327	—	63152	40959	877
CARMEL—Putnam County										
ARMS ACRES, 75 Seminary Hill Road, Zip 10512–1921; tel. 914/225–3400; Edward Spauster, Ph.D., Executive Director (Nonreporting)	33	82	129	—	—	—	—	—	—	—
☒ PUTNAM HOSPITAL CENTER, Stoneleigh Avenue, Zip 10512–9948; tel. 914/279–5711; Rodney N. Hubbers, President and Chief Executive Officer (Nonreporting) **A**1 9 10 **N** Westchester Health Services Network, Mt Kisco, NY	23	10	164	—	—	—	—	—	—	—
CARTHAGE—Jefferson County										
☐ CARTHAGE AREA HOSPITAL, 1001 West Street, Zip 13619–9703; tel. 315/493–1000; Kenn C. Rishel, Administrator and Chief Executive Officer (Total facility includes 30 beds in nursing home–type unit) (Nonreporting) **A**1 9 10 **N** Northern New York Rural Health Care Alliance, Watertown, NY	23	10	78	—	—	—	—	—	—	—
CASTLE POINT—Dutchess County										
☒ VETERAN AFFAIRS HUDSON VALLEY HEALTH CARE SYSTEM–CASTLE POINT DIVISION, Mailing Address: P.O. Box 100, Montrose, Zip 10548–0100; tel. 914/831–2000; William D. Montague, Acting Medical Center Director (Total facility includes 113 beds in nursing home–type unit) (Nonreporting) **A**1 3 9 **S** Department of Veterans Affairs, Washington, DC	45	10	233	—	—	—	—	—	—	—

Hospital, Address, Telephone, Administrator, Approval, Facility, and Physician Codes, Health Care System, Network	Classi-fication Codes		Utilization Data					Expense (thousands) of dollars		
★ American Hospital Association (AHA) membership □ Joint Commission on Accreditation of Healthcare Organizations (JCAHO) accreditation + American Osteopathic Healthcare Association (AOHA) membership ○ American Osteopathic Association (AOA) accreditation △ Commission on Accreditation of Rehabilitation Facilities (CARF) accreditation Control codes 61, 63, 64, 71, 72 and 73 indicate hospitals listed by AOHA, but not registered by AHA. For definition of numerical codes, see page A4	Control	Service	Staffed Beds	Admissions	Census	Outpatient Visits	Births	Total	Payroll	Personnel

CHEEKTOWAGA—Erie County

✶ ST. JOSEPH HOSPITAL, 2605 Harlem Road, Zip 14225–4097; tel. 716/891–2400; Patrick J. Wiles, Chief Executive Officer **A**1 9 10 **F**4 7 8 11 12 14 15 16 17 19 22 25 28 29 30 31 32 33 35 36 37 39 41 42 43 44 45 46 49 50 51 60 63 65 69 71 73 74 **P**3 6 8 **S** Catholic Health East, Radnor, PA

| | 23 | 10 | 184 | 5321 | 99 | 155736 | — | 46377 | 22811 | 673 |

CLIFTON SPRINGS—Ontario County

✶ CLIFTON SPRINGS HOSPITAL AND CLINIC, 2 Coulter Road, Zip 14432–1189; tel. 315/462–1311; John P. Galati, President and Chief Executive Officer (Total facility includes 108 beds in nursing home–type unit) **A**1 9 10 **F**3 8 10 12 14 15 16 17 18 19 20 21 22 23 25 26 27 28 29 30 32 33 34 35 36 37 39 41 42 44 45 46 48 49 50 51 52 53 54 55 56 57 58 59 60 64 65 67 70 71 72 73 74 **P**5 7

| | 16 | 10 | 262 | 3006 | 168 | 127654 | 0 | 32507 | 16801 | 644 |

COBLESKILL—Schoharie County

□ BASSETT HOSPITAL OF SCHOHARIE COUNTY, 41 Grandview Drive, Zip 12043–1331; tel. 518/234–2511; Donald W. Massey, Administrator (Nonreporting) **A**1 9 10 **N** Bassett Healthcare, Cooperstown, NY

| | 23 | 10 | 40 | — | — | — | — | — | — | — |

COOPERSTOWN—Otsego County

✶ MARY IMOGENE BASSETT HOSPITAL, One Atwell Road, Zip 13326–1394; tel. 607/547–3100; William F. Streck, M.D., President and Chief Executive Officer **A**1 2 3 5 8 9 10 **F**7 8 10 12 14 15 16 19 20 21 22 25 29 30 31 34 35 37 39 40 41 42 44 45 46 49 51 52 53 54 55 56 58 59 60 61 63 65 66 67 70 71 73 **P**6 **N** Bassett Healthcare, Cooperstown, NY

| | 23 | 10 | 208 | 8044 | 108 | 425260 | 613 | 134064 | 73326 | 1918 |

CORNING—Steuben County

✶ CORNING HOSPITAL, 176 Denison Parkway East, Zip 14830–2899; tel. 607/937–7200; John E. Pignatore, President and Chief Executive Officer (Total facility includes 120 beds in nursing home–type unit) (Nonreporting) **A**1 9 10

| | 23 | 10 | 264 | — | — | — | — | — | — | — |

CORNWALL—Orange County

✶ CORNWALL HOSPITAL, 33 Laurel Avenue, Zip 12518–1499; tel. 914/534–7711; Val S. Gray, Executive Director **A**1 9 10 **F**8 15 16 17 19 20 22 26 27 28 29 30 35 37 42 44 49 52 54 56 57 63 65 67 68 71 73 **S** Greater Hudson Valley Health System, Newburgh, NY **N** Columbia Presbyterian Regional Network, New York, NY

| | 23 | 10 | 125 | 3902 | 82 | 43905 | — | 28889 | 15296 | 428 |

CORTLAND—Cortland County

✶ CORTLAND MEMORIAL HOSPITAL, 134 Homer Avenue, Zip 13045–0960; tel. 607/756–3500; Thomas H. Carman, President and Chief Executive Officer (Total facility includes 82 beds in nursing home–type unit) (Nonreporting) **A**1 9 10 **N** Cortland Area Rural Health Network, Cortland, NY

| | 23 | 10 | 259 | — | — | — | — | — | — | — |

CUBA—Allegany County

□ CUBA MEMORIAL HOSPITAL, 140 West Main Street, Zip 14727–1398; tel. 716/968–2000; Darlene D. Bainbridge, Interim Chief Executive Officer (Total facility includes 61 beds in nursing home–type unit) (Nonreporting) **A**1 3 9

| | 23 | 10 | 87 | — | — | — | — | — | — | — |

DANSVILLE—Livingston County

✶ NICHOLAS H. NOYES MEMORIAL HOSPITAL, 111 Clara Barton Street, Zip 14437–9527; tel. 716/335–6001; James Wissler, President and Chief Executive Officer **A**1 9 10 **F**8 15 16 17 19 22 28 30 34 35 36 39 42 44 49 51 53 54 55 57 58 65 68 71 72 73 74

| | 23 | 10 | 71 | 2360 | 30 | 90227 | 271 | 18877 | 8748 | 337 |

DOBBS FERRY—Westchester County

□ COMMUNITY HOSPITAL AT DOBBS FERRY, 128 Ashford Avenue, Zip 10522–1896; tel. 914/693–0700; Thomas E. Green, President and Chief Executive Officer (Nonreporting) **A**1 9 10

| | 23 | 10 | 50 | — | — | — | — | — | — | — |

DUNKIRK—Chautauqua County

✶ BROOKS MEMORIAL HOSPITAL, 529 Central Avenue, Zip 14048–2599; tel. 716/366–1111; Richard H. Ketcham, President **A**1 9 10 **F**7 8 17 19 21 22 25 26 28 29 30 32 35 36 37 40 41 42 44 46 49 60 65 71 73 **P**5

| | 23 | 10 | 133 | 3241 | 54 | 91831 | 478 | 25392 | 11242 | 366 |

EAST MEADOW—Nassau County

✶ NASSAU COUNTY MEDICAL CENTER, 2201 Hempstead Turnpike, Zip 11554–1854; tel. 516/572–0123; Jerald C. Newman, Vice President (Total facility includes 809 beds in nursing home–type unit) (Nonreporting) **A**1 2 3 5 8 9 10 **N** Health First, New York, NY

| | 13 | 10 | 1384 | — | — | — | — | — | — | — |

ELIZABETHTOWN—Essex County

✶ ELIZABETHTOWN COMMUNITY HOSPITAL, Park Street, Zip 12932–0277; tel. 518/873–6377; Douglas G. Cushing, Administrator (Nonreporting) **A**1 9 10 **N** Eastern Adirondack Health Care Network, Westport, NY

| | 23 | 10 | 25 | — | — | — | — | — | — | — |

ELLENVILLE—Ulster County

□ ELLENVILLE COMMUNITY HOSPITAL, Route 209, Zip 12428–0668, Mailing Address: P.O. Box 668, Zip 12428–0668; tel. 914/647–6400; Thomas H. Fletcher, Administrator (Nonreporting) **A**1 9 10

| | 23 | 10 | 31 | — | — | — | — | — | — | — |

ELMHURST—Queens County, See New York City

ELMIRA—Chemung County

✶ ARNOT OGDEN MEDICAL CENTER, 600 Roe Avenue, Zip 14905–1629; tel. 607/737–4100; Anthony J. Cooper, President and Chief Executive Officer (Total facility includes 40 beds in nursing home–type unit) **A**1 2 6 9 10 **F**4 7 8 10 11 12 15 16 17 19 21 22 25 26 27 28 29 30 31 34 35 37 38 39 40 41 42 43 44 45 46 49 51 54 60 61 63 64 65 67 68 70 71 72 73 74 **P**6

| | 23 | 10 | 259 | 7760 | 167 | — | 1334 | 85132 | 41706 | 1236 |

✶ ELMIRA PSYCHIATRIC CENTER, 100 Washington Street, Zip 14901–2898; tel. 607/737–4739; Bert W. Pyle, Jr., Director **A**1 10 **F**1 12 14 15 17 18 20 25 26 27 28 29 30 34 39 46 52 53 54 55 56 57 58 59 65 71 73 **P**1 **S** New York State Department of Mental Health, Albany, NY

| | 12 | 22 | 130 | 360 | 110 | — | — | — | — | 450 |

Hospital, Address, Telephone, Administrator, Approval, Facility, and Physician Codes, Health Care System, Network	Classi-fication Codes		Utilization Data					Expense (thousands) of dollars		
★ American Hospital Association (AHA) membership □ Joint Commission on Accreditation of Healthcare Organizations (JCAHO) accreditation + American Osteopathic Healthcare Association (AOHA) membership ○ American Osteopathic Association (AOA) accreditation △ Commission on Accreditation of Rehabilitation Facilities (CARF) accreditation Control codes 61, 63, 64, 71, 72 and 73 indicate hospitals listed by AOHA, but not registered by AHA. For definition of numerical codes, see page A4	Control	Service	Staffed Beds	Admissions	Census	Outpatient Visits	Births	Total	Payroll	Personnel
✶ ST. JOSEPH'S HOSPITAL, (Includes Twin Tiers Rehabilitation Center), 555 East Market Street, Zip 14902–1512; tel. 607/733–6541; Sister Marie Castagnaro, President and Chief Executive Officer (Total facility includes 31 beds in nursing home–type unit) **A**1 2 9 10 **F**3 8 9 11 12 14 15 16 17 18 19 21 22 23 26 28 30 31 33 34 35 37 39 41 42 44 45 46 48 49 51 52 54 55 56 57 58 62 64 65 66 67 69 70 71 73 **P**5 **S** Carondelet Health System, Saint Louis, MO	21	10	255	5174	150	89958	0	—	—	848
ENDICOTT—Broome County MEDICENTER See United Health Services Hospitals–Binghamton, Binghamton										
FAR ROCKAWAY—Queens County, See New York City										
FLUSHING—Queens County, See New York City										
FOREST HILLS—Queens County, See New York City										
FORT DRUM—Jefferson County WILCOX ARMY COMMUNITY HOSPITAL, Zip 13602–5004 (Nonreporting)	42	10	30	—	—	—	—	—	—	—
FULTON—Oswego County ✶ ALBERT LINDLEY LEE MEMORIAL HOSPITAL, 510 South Fourth Street, Zip 13069–2994; tel. 315/592–2224; Dennis A. Casey, Executive Director **A**1 9 10 **F**3 4 8 10 16 19 20 21 22 25 28 29 30 31 32 34 37 41 42 44 45 51 53 54 55 56 57 58 59 63 65 66 67 69 71 73 **N**	23	10	67	2401	45	42505	—	17230	8678	
GENEVA—Ontario County ✶ GENEVA GENERAL HOSPITAL, (Formerly Geneva Regional Health System), 196 North Street, Zip 14456–1694; tel. 315/787–4000; James J. Dooley, President (Total facility includes 343 beds in nursing home–type unit) **A**1 6 9 10 **F**1 2 4 7 8 10 12 13 14 15 16 17 19 20 21 22 25 26 27 28 29 30 31 32 33 34 35 36 37 39 40 41 42 44 45 46 48 49 54 56 62 64 65 67 68 69 71 72 73 74 **N** Four Lakes Rural Health Network, Geneva, NY	23	10	479	4848	395	262583	699	55313	24742	728
GLEN COVE—Nassau County ✶ NORTH SHORE UNIVERSITY HOSPITAL AT GLEN COVE, St. Andrews Lane, Zip 11542; tel. 516/674–7300; Mark R. Stenzler, Vice President Administration (Nonreporting) **A**1 2 3 5 9 10 **S** North Shore– Long Island Jewish Health System, Manhasset, NY **N** North Shore Regional Health Systems, Manhasset, NY	23	10	265	—	—	—	—	—	—	—
GLEN OAKS—Queens County, See New York City										
GLENS FALLS—Warren County □ GLENS FALLS HOSPITAL, 100 Park Street, Zip 12801–9898; tel. 518/792–3151; David G. Kruczlnicki, President and Chief Executive Officer (Nonreporting) **A**1 2 9 10 **N** Adirondack Rural Health Network, Glens Falls, NY; Shared Health Network, Inc., Albany, NY	23	10	410	—	—	—	—	—	—	—
GLOVERSVILLE—Fulton County □ NATHAN LITTAUER HOSPITAL AND NURSING HOME, 99 East State Street, Zip 12078–1293; tel. 518/725–8621; Thomas J. Dowd, President (Total facility includes 84 beds in nursing home–type unit) **A**1 5 9 10 **F**3 4 7 8 12 14 15 16 17 19 20 21 22 26 28 29 30 31 32 33 34 35 37 39 40 41 42 44 45 46 49 51 53 54 55 56 57 58 61 64 65 67 71 73 74 **N** Shared Health Network, Inc., Albany, NY	23	10	208	4291	142	139715	357	35450	18713	633
GOSHEN—Orange County ✶ ARDEN HILL HOSPITAL, 4 Harriman Drive, Zip 10924–2499; tel. 914/294–5441; Wayne Becker, Interim Chief Executive Officer **A**1 9 10 **F**2 7 8 11 12 14 15 16 17 19 21 22 27 28 30 33 34 35 37 39 40 41 42 44 45 49 52 53 54 55 56 57 58 59 63 65 67 71 73 74 **P**5 **N** The Mount Sinai Health System, New York, NY	23	10	174	6963	134	69843	728	45611	21468	605
GOUVERNEUR—St. Lawrence County □ EDWARD JOHN NOBLE HOSPITAL OF GOUVERNEUR, 77 West Barney Street, Zip 13642–1090; tel. 315/287–1000; Charles P. Conole, FACHE, Administrator **A**1 9 10 **F**7 8 9 11 12 13 14 15 16 17 18 19 20 21 22 26 28 29 30 32 33 34 35 37 38 39 40 41 42 43 44 45 46 47 49 52 53 54 56 57 60 61 64 65 70 71 74 **P**5 **N** Northern New York Rural Health Care Alliance, Watertown, NY	23	10	47	1495	24	25607	23	10111	5252	224
GOWANDA—Cattaraugus County □ TRI–COUNTY MEMORIAL HOSPITAL, 100 Memorial Drive, Zip 14070–1194; tel. 716/532–3377; Diane J. Osika, Interim Chief Executive Officer (Nonreporting) **A**1 9 10 **N** Buffalo General Health System, Buffalo, NY	23	10	48	—	—	—	—	—	—	—
GREENPORT—Suffolk County □ EASTERN LONG ISLAND HOSPITAL, 201 Manor Place, Zip 11944–1298; tel. 516/477–1000; John M. Gwiazda, President and Chief Executive Officer **A**1 9 10 **F**2 3 8 11 14 15 16 17 18 19 21 22 25 26 27 30 31 32 33 35 37 39 41 42 44 45 46 49 51 52 55 56 57 58 59 60 65 66 67 71 73 **N** First Choice Network, Inc., Mineola, NY	23	10	80	2414	58	11636	0	18610	9419	227
HAMILTON—Madison County ✶ COMMUNITY MEMORIAL HOSPITAL, Broad Street, Zip 13346–9518; tel. 315/824–1100; David Felton, Administrator (Total facility includes 40 beds in nursing home–type unit) (Nonreporting) **A**1 9 10 **N** Hamilton–Bassett–Crouse Rural Health Network, Hamilton, NY	23	10	84	—	—	—	—	—	—	—
HARRIS—Sullivan County □ COMMUNITY GENERAL HOSPITAL OF SULLIVAN COUNTY, Bushville Road, Zip 12742, Mailing Address: P.O. Box 800, Zip 12742–0800; tel. 914/794–3300; Martin I. Richman, Executive Director (Total facility includes 60 beds in nursing home–type unit) (Nonreporting) **A**1 9 10 **N** Sullivan County Rural Health Network, Harris, NY	23	10	304	—	—	—	—	—	—	—

Hospital, Address, Telephone, Administrator, Approval, Facility, and Physician Codes, Health Care System, Network	Classi-fication Codes		Utilization Data					Expense (thousands) of dollars		
★ American Hospital Association (AHA) membership □ Joint Commission on Accreditation of Healthcare Organizations (JCAHO) accreditation + American Osteopathic Healthcare Association (AOHA) membership ○ American Osteopathic Association (AOA) accreditation △ Commission on Accreditation of Rehabilitation Facilities (CARF) accreditation Control codes 61, 63, 64, 71, 72 and 73 indicate hospitals listed by AOHA, but not registered by AHA. For definition of numerical codes, see page A4	Control	Service	Staffed Beds	Admissions	Census	Outpatient Visits	Births	Total	Payroll	Personnel
HEMPSTEAD—Nassau County										
□ ISLAND MEDICAL CENTER, (Formerly Hempstead General Hospital Medical Center), 800 Front Street, Zip 11550–4600; tel. 516/560–1200; Alexander Skutzka, Chief Executive Officer (Nonreporting) **A**1 9 10	32	10	213	—	—	—	—	—	—	—
HOLLISWOOD—Queens County, See New York City										
HORNELL—Steuben County										
□ ST. JAMES MERCY HOSPITAL, 411 Canisteo Street, Zip 14843–2197; tel. 607/324–8000; Paul E. Shephard, President and Chief Executive Officer (Total facility includes 55 beds in nursing home–type unit) (Nonreporting) **A**1 6 9 10 **S** Catholic Health East, Radnor, PA	23	10	200	—	—	—	—	—	—	—
HUDSON—Columbia County										
⊞ COLUMBIA MEMORIAL HOSPITAL, (Includes Columbia–Greene Long Term Care, 161 Jefferson Heights, Catskill, Zip 12414; tel. 518/943–6363), 71 Prospect Avenue, Zip 12534–2900; tel. 518/828–8039; Jane Ehrlich, President and Chief Executive Officer (Total facility includes 120 beds in nursing home–type unit) **A**1 9 10 **F**7 8 15 16 19 20 21 22 26 33 34 37 40 41 42 44 46 49 51 52 54 60 64 65 67 71 72 73 **N** Greene County Rural Health Network, Catskill, NY	23	10	244	5945	223	—	479	46906	24040	647
HUNTINGTON—Suffolk County										
⊞ HUNTINGTON HOSPITAL, 270 Park Avenue, Zip 11743–2799; tel. 516/351–2200; J. Ronald Gaudreault, President and Chief Executive Officer (Nonreporting) **A**1 9 10 **S** North Shore– Long Island Jewish Health System, Manhasset, NY **N** North Shore Regional Health Systems, Manhasset, NY	23	10	269	—	—	—	—	—	—	—
HUNTINGTON STATION—Suffolk County										
⊞ SAGAMORE CHILDREN'S PSYCHIATRIC CENTER, 197 Half Hollow Road, Zip 11746; tel. 516/673–7700; Robert Schweitzer, Ed.D., Executive Director **A**1 **F**12 14 15 16 19 21 22 32 35 39 45 46 52 53 54 55 58 59 62 65 73 **S** New York State Department of Mental Health, Albany, NY	12	52	69	220	70	36886	0	—	—	242
ILION—Herkimer County										
MOHAWK VALLEY DIVISION See St. Luke's Memorial Hospital Center, Utica										
IRVING—Chautauqua County										
○ LAKE SHORE HOSPITAL, 845 Route 5 and 20, Zip 14081–9716; tel. 716/934–2654; James B. Foster, Chief Executive Officer (Total facility includes 160 beds in nursing home–type unit) **A**9 10 11 **F**1 8 12 15 17 19 22 30 32 33 34 35 37 44 45 49 52 56 64 65 69 71 73 **P**8 **N** Millard Fillmore Health System, Buffalo, NY	23	10	222	2049	203	38105	—	23380	10361	—
ITHACA—Tompkins County										
⊞ CAYUGA MEDICAL CENTER AT ITHACA, 101 Dates Drive, Zip 14850–1383; tel. 607/274–4011; Bonnie H. Howell, President and Chief Executive Officer **A**1 2 3 5 10 **F**7 8 12 13 14 15 16 17 18 19 21 22 24 25 28 30 31 32 33 34 35 36 37 39 40 41 42 44 46 48 49 52 54 56 60 63 65 66 67 71 72 73 74 **P**5 7 8	23	10	145	6135	91	—	770	—	—	623
JACKSON HEIGHTS—Queens County, See New York City										
JAMAICA—Queens County, See New York City										
JAMESTOWN—Chautauqua County										
⊞ WOMAN'S CHRISTIAN ASSOCIATION HOSPITAL, 207 Foote Avenue, Zip 14702–9975; tel. 716/487–0141; Mark E. Celmer, President and Chief Executive Officer **A**1 2 9 10 **F**2 3 8 12 14 15 16 17 18 19 20 21 22 23 25 27 28 29 30 33 34 35 36 37 39 40 41 42 44 45 46 48 49 51 52 53 54 55 56 57 58 59 60 65 66 67 68 71 73 74 **P**4 5 7 **N** Great Lakes Health Network, Erie, PA	23	10	301	10118	216	192178	817	74350	38407	1366
JOHNSON CITY—Broome County										
WILSON MEMORIAL REGIONAL MEDICAL CENTER See United Health Services Hospitals–Binghamton, Binghamton										
KATONAH—Westchester County										
⊞ FOUR WINDS HOSPITAL, 800 Cross River Road, Zip 10536–3549; tel. 914/763–8151; Samuel C. Klagsbrun, M.D., Executive Medical Director **A**1 10 **F**12 15 16 17 19 21 22 26 27 35 41 50 52 53 54 55 56 57 58 59 63 65 67 71 **P**3 4 7	33	22	150	1835	136	—	—	—	—	558
KENMORE—Erie County										
□ KENMORE MERCY HOSPITAL, 2950 Elmwood Avenue, Zip 14217–1390; tel. 716/447–6100; Sister Mary Joel Schimscheiner, Chief Executive Officer **A**1 9 10 **F**5 8 10 11 12 14 15 16 17 18 19 22 25 26 28 29 30 32 33 34 35 36 39 41 42 44 45 46 49 51 61 65 66 71 73 74 **P**5 **S** Massachusetts Department of Mental Health, Boston, MA	21	10	184	6934	133	167089	—	58858	26493	845
KINGSTON—Ulster County										
⊞ BENEDICTINE HOSPITAL, 105 Marys Avenue, Zip 12401–5894; tel. 914/338–2500; Thomas A. Dee, President and Chief Executive Officer (Nonreporting) **A**1 3 5 9 10	21	10	222	—	—	—	—	—	—	—
□ KINGSTON HOSPITAL, 396 Broadway, Zip 12401–4692; tel. 914/331–3131; Anthony P. Marmo, Chief Executive Officer (Nonreporting) **A**1 3 5 9 10 **S** Cross River HealthCare, Inc., Rhinebeck, NY	23	10	140	—	—	—	—	—	—	—
LACKAWANNA—Erie County										
⊞ OUR LADY OF VICTORY HOSPITAL, 55 Melroy Road, Zip 14218–1687; tel. 716/825–8000; John P. Davanzo, President and Chief Executive Officer (Total facility includes 10 beds in nursing home–type unit) (Nonreporting) **A**1 9 10	21	10	232	—	—	—	—	—	—	—
LEWISTON—Niagara County										
⊞ MOUNT ST. MARY'S HOSPITAL OF NIAGARA FALLS, 5300 Military Road, Zip 14092–1997; tel. 716/297–4800; Angelo G. Calbone, President and Chief Executive Officer (Nonreporting) **A**1 10 **S** Daughters of Charity National Health System, Saint Louis, MO	21	10	159	—	—	—	—	—	—	—

Hospital, Address, Telephone, Administrator, Approval, Facility, and Physician Codes, Health Care System, Network	Classification Codes		Utilization Data					Expense (thousands) of dollars		
	Control	Service	Staffed Beds	Admissions	Census	Outpatient Visits	Births	Total	Payroll	Personnel

★ American Hospital Association (AHA) membership
□ Joint Commission on Accreditation of Healthcare Organizations (JCAHO) accreditation
+ American Osteopathic Healthcare Association (AOHA) membership
○ American Osteopathic Association (AOA) accreditation
△ Commission on Accreditation of Rehabilitation Facilities (CARF) accreditation
Control codes 61, 63, 64, 71, 72 and 73 indicate hospitals listed by AOHA, but not registered by AHA. For definition of numerical codes, see page A4

LITTLE FALLS—Herkimer County

✠ LITTLE FALLS HOSPITAL, 140 Burwell Street, Zip 13365–1725; tel. 315/823–1000; David S. Armstrong, Jr., Administrator (Total facility includes 34 beds in nursing home–type unit) **A**1 9 10 **F**1 4 6 7 8 10 11 12 13 14 15 16 17 19 20 21 22 24 25 26 27 28 29 30 31 33 34 35 37 38 39 40 41 42 43 44 45 46 47 48 49 51 52 53 54 55 56 60 61 63 64 65 66 67 68 69 71 72 73 74 **P**5 **N** MoHawk Valley Network, Inc., Utica, NY	23	10	134	3589	93	64344	339	18569	9988	436

LITTLE NECK—Queens County, See New York City
LOCKPORT—Niagara County

✠ LOCKPORT MEMORIAL HOSPITAL, 521 East Avenue, Zip 14094–3299; tel. 716/514–5700; Michael J. Vlosky, President and Chief Executive Officer (Nonreporting) **A**1 9 10	23	10	134	—	—	—	—	—	—	—

LONG BEACH—Nassau County

✠ LONG BEACH MEDICAL CENTER, 455 East Bay Drive, Zip 11561–2300, Mailing Address: P.O. Box 300, Zip 11561–2300; tel. 516/897–1200; Martin F. Nester, Jr., Chief Executive Officer (Total facility includes 200 beds in nursing home–type unit) **A**1 9 10 12 13 **F**3 4 5 8 11 14 15 16 17 18 19 20 21 22 24 26 27 28 29 30 31 32 34 35 37 39 42 44 45 46 48 49 51 52 53 54 55 56 57 58 63 64 65 66 67 68 71 73 74 **P**1 **N** The Mount Sinai Health System, New York, NY	23	10	387	6194	351	186871	0	77628	41154	933

LONG ISLAND CITY—Queens County, See New York City
LOWVILLE—Lewis County

✠ LEWIS COUNTY GENERAL HOSPITAL, 7785 North State Street, Zip 13367–1297; tel. 315/376–5200; Ernest R. McNeely, Jr., Chief Executive Officer and Administrator (Total facility includes 160 beds in nursing home–type unit) **A**1 9 10 **F**1 7 8 15 16 19 21 22 27 28 30 34 37 40 41 44 45 46 49 51 64 65 66 67 71 73 74 **S** Brim, Inc., Portland, OR	13	10	214	2146	176	40884	285	21672	940	329

MALONE—Franklin County

✠ ALICE HYDE HOSPITAL ASSOCIATION, 115 Park Street, Zip 12953–0729, Mailing Address: P.O. Box 729, Zip 12953–0729; tel. 518/483–3000; John W. Johnson, President and Chief Executive Officer (Total facility includes 75 beds in nursing home–type unit) **A**1 9 10 **F**1 3 7 8 12 13 15 17 18 19 20 22 23 26 28 30 32 33 34 35 36 37 39 40 41 42 44 46 53 54 56 57 58 60 64 65 67 71 73	23	10	153	3611	174	69833	254	24702	12706	502

MANHASSET—Nassau County

MANHASSET AMBULATORY CARE PAVILION See Long Island Jewish Medical Center, New York

✠ NORTH SHORE UNIVERSITY HOSPITAL, 300 Community Drive, Zip 11030–3876; tel. 516/562–0100; John S. T. Gallagher, President and Chief Executive Officer (Total facility includes 253 beds in nursing home–type unit) (Nonreporting) **A**1 2 3 5 8 9 10 **S** North Shore– Long Island Jewish Health System, Manhasset, NY **N** North Shore Regional Health Systems, Manhasset, NY	23	10	958	—	—	—	—	—	—	—

MANHATTAN—New York County, See New York City
MARGARETVILLE—Delaware County

□ MARGARETVILLE MEMORIAL HOSPITAL, Route 28, Zip 12455, Mailing Address: P.O. Box 200, Zip 12455–0200; tel. 914/586–2631; Roger A. Masse, Chief Executive Officer **A**1 9 10 **F**8 19 21 22 28 34 37 44 49 65 67 71 73	23	10	22	540	9	25437	—	6276	3366	131

MASSENA—St. Lawrence County

□ MASSENA MEMORIAL HOSPITAL, One Hospital Drive, Zip 13662–1097; tel. 315/764–1711; Charles F. Fahd, II, Chief Executive Officer **A**1 9 10 **F**1 5 6 7 8 12 13 14 15 16 17 19 20 21 22 23 24 25 26 27 28 29 30 32 33 34 35 36 37 39 40 41 42 44 45 48 49 51 60 61 65 68 71 73 74 **P**5	14	10	40	3113	36	85833	261	20693	9792	289

MEDINA—Orleans County

✠ MEDINA MEMORIAL HOSPITAL, 200 Ohio Street, Zip 14103–1095; tel. 716/798–2000; Walter S. Becker, Administrator (Total facility includes 30 beds in nursing home–type unit) **A**1 9 10 **F**5 7 8 12 13 14 15 16 17 19 21 22 25 27 28 29 30 32 33 34 37 39 40 41 44 45 46 48 49 51 56 64 65 67 68 71 73 74 **P**3 5 **N** Lake Plains Community Care Network, Buffalo, NY	23	10	71	2402	38	—	254	20874	9389	—

MIDDLETOWN—Orange County

✠ △ HORTON MEDICAL CENTER, 60 Prospect Avenue, Zip 10940–4133; tel. 914/343–2424; Jeffrey D. Hirsch, Executive Vice President and Chief Operating Officer **A**1 2 7 9 10 **F**3 7 8 11 12 16 17 22 23 27 28 30 34 37 39 40 42 44 46 48 49 50 51 56 60 61 65 67 71 73 74 **P**1 5 **S** Greater Hudson Valley Health System, Newburgh, NY **N** Columbia Presbyterian Regional Network, New York, NY	23	10	171	9844	153	142126	1480	78722	39831	963
✠ MIDDLETOWN PSYCHIATRIC CENTER, 141 Monhagen Avenue, Zip 10940–6198; tel. 914/342–5511; James H. Bopp, Executive Director (Nonreporting) **A**1 3 10 **S** New York State Department of Mental Health, Albany, NY	12	22	271	—	—	—	—	—	—	—

MINEOLA—Nassau County

✠ WINTHROP–UNIVERSITY HOSPITAL, 259 First Street, Zip 11501; tel. 516/663–2200; Martin J. Delaney, President and Chief Executive Officer (Nonreporting) **A**1 2 3 5 8 9 10 **N** First Choice Network, Inc., Mineola, NY	23	10	518	—	—	—	—	—	—	—

MONTOUR FALLS—Schuyler County

✠ SCHUYLER HOSPITAL, 220 Steuben Street, Zip 14865–9709; tel. 607/535–7121; Robert Mincemoyer, President and Chief Executive Officer (Total facility includes 120 beds in nursing home–type unit) (Nonreporting) **A**1 9 10	23	10	169	—	—	—	—	—	—	—

MONTROSE—Westchester County

✠ VETERANS AFFAIRS HUDSON VALLEY HEALTH CARE SYSTEM–F.D. ROOSEVELT HOSPITAL, (Formerly Franklin Delano Roosevelt Veterans Affairs Hospital), Mailing Address: P.O. Box 100, Zip 10548–0100; tel. 914/737–4400; Michael A. Sabo, Director (Total facility includes 162 beds in nursing home–type unit) (Nonreporting) **A**1 3 5 **S** Department of Veterans Affairs, Washington, DC	45	22	550	—	—	—	—	—	—	—

Hospital, Address, Telephone, Administrator, Approval, Facility, and Physician Codes, Health Care System, Network	Classi-fication Codes		Utilization Data					Expense (thousands) of dollars		
	Control	Service	Staffed Beds	Admissions	Census	Outpatient Visits	Births	Total	Payroll	Personnel

★ American Hospital Association (AHA) membership
□ Joint Commission on Accreditation of Healthcare Organizations (JCAHO) accreditation
+ American Osteopathic Healthcare Association (AOHA) membership
○ American Osteopathic Association (AOA) accreditation
△ Commission on Accreditation of Rehabilitation Facilities (CARF) accreditation
Control codes 61, 63, 64, 71, 72 and 73 indicate hospitals listed by AOHA, but not registered by AHA. For definition of numerical codes, see page A4

MOUNT KISCO—Westchester County

Hospital	Control	Service	Staffed Beds	Admissions	Census	Outpatient Visits	Births	Total	Payroll	Personnel
✠ NORTHERN WESTCHESTER HOSPITAL CENTER, 400 Main Street, Zip 10549–3477; tel. 914/666–1200; Donald W. Davis, President **A**1 2 9 10 **F**15 16 19 21 28 29 30 31 33 35 39 40 41 42 44 45 46 49 52 53 54 55 56 57 60 61 65 66 71 73 74 **P**7 8 **N** Health Star Network, Armonk, NY; Westchester Health Services Network, Mt Kisco, NY	23	10	250	9221	148	58655	1764	80898	38137	898

MOUNT VERNON—Westchester County

Hospital	Control	Service	Staffed Beds	Admissions	Census	Outpatient Visits	Births	Total	Payroll	Personnel
□ MOUNT VERNON HOSPITAL, 12 North Seventh Avenue, Zip 10550–2098; tel. 914/664–8000; Richard L. Petrillo, M.D., Executive Director (Nonreporting) **A**1 3 5 6 9 10	23	10	182	—	—	—	—	—	—	—

NEW HAMPTON—Orange County

Hospital	Control	Service	Staffed Beds	Admissions	Census	Outpatient Visits	Births	Total	Payroll	Personnel
□ MID–HUDSON PSYCHIATRIC CENTER, Route 17M, Zip 10958, Mailing Address: P.O. Box 158, Zip 10958–0158; tel. 914/374–3171; Richard Bennett, Executive Director **A**1 10 **F**2 4 8 9 11 12 19 20 21 22 24 27 29 30 31 35 37 38 39 40 41 42 43 44 45 46 48 50 52 54 55 60 63 64 65 67 70 71 **P**6	12	22	279	273	292	—	—	—	—	—

NEW HYDE PARK—Queens County, See New York City

NEW ROCHELLE—Westchester County

Hospital	Control	Service	Staffed Beds	Admissions	Census	Outpatient Visits	Births	Total	Payroll	Personnel
✠ SOUND SHORE MEDICAL CENTER OF WESTCHESTER, 16 Guion Place, Zip 10802; tel. 914/632–5000; John R. Spicer, President and Chief Executive Officer **A**1 2 3 5 8 9 10 **F**1 3 7 8 12 13 14 15 16 17 18 19 21 22 26 27 28 29 31 32 33 34 35 36 37 38 39 40 41 42 44 45 46 48 49 51 53 54 55 56 57 58 60 61 63 64 65 66 67 68 69 70 71 72 73 **P**4 5 6 7 8 **N** Westchester Health Services Network, Mt Kisco, NY	23	10	259	10606	184	210740	1116	107706	50461	1149

NEW YORK (Includes all hospitals located within the five boroughs)
BRONX - Bronx County (Mailing Address - Bronx)
BROOKLYN - Kings County (Mailing Address - Brooklyn)
MANHATTAN - New York County (Mailing Address - New York)
QUEENS - Queens County (Mailing Addresses - Bellerose, Elmhurst, Far Rockaway, Flushing, Forest Hills, Glen Oaks, Holliswood, Jackson Heights, Jamaica, Little Neck, Long Island City, New Hyde Park, and Queens Village)
RICHMOND VALLEY - Richmond County (Mailing Address - Staten Island)
ABRAHAM JACOBI GENERAL CARE HOSPITAL AND PSYCHIATIC UNITS See Jacobi Medical Center
BAYLEY SETON CAMPUS See Sisters of Charity Medical Center

Hospital	Control	Service	Staffed Beds	Admissions	Census	Outpatient Visits	Births	Total	Payroll	Personnel
✠ BELLEVUE HOSPITAL CENTER, (Includes Bellevue Comprehensive General Care, Bellevue Physical Medicine and Rehabilitation Services, Bellevue Psychiatric Services, Bellevue Tuberculosis Services, Comprehensive Ambulatory Care Services: Level I Trauma Center), 462 First Avenue, Zip 10016–9198; tel. 212/562–4141; Carlos Perez, Executive Director **A**1 2 3 5 9 10 **F**1 2 3 4 8 10 11 12 13 14 15 16 17 18 19 20 21 22 23 26 27 28 29 30 31 34 37 38 39 40 41 42 43 44 45 46 47 48 49 51 52 53 54 55 56 57 58 59 60 61 65 67 68 70 71 72 73 74 **P**6 **S** New York City Health and Hospitals Corporation, New York, NY	14	10	888	24109	759	548960	1949	374766	225456	4952
✠ BETH ISRAEL MEDICAL CENTER, (Includes Beth Israel Medical Center–Kings Highway Division, 3201 Kings Highway, Zip 11234; tel. 718/252–3000; Beth Israel Medical Center–North Division, 170 East End Avenue, Zip 10128; tel. 212/870–9000), 281 First Avenue, Zip 10003–3803; tel. 212/420–2000; Matthew E. Fink, M.D., President and Chief Executive Officer **A**1 3 5 6 8 9 10 **F**2 3 4 5 7 8 10 11 12 13 14 15 16 17 18 19 20 21 22 25 26 28 29 30 31 32 33 34 35 37 38 39 40 41 42 43 44 45 46 47 48 49 50 51 52 53 54 55 56 57 58 59 60 61 63 64 65 66 67 68 71 72 73 74 **P**4 5 7 8 **S** Continuum Health Partners, New York, NY **N** Continuum Health Partners, Inc., New York, NY; Health First, New York, NY	23	10	1234	53004	1022	465247	5493	811192	394105	7757
BETH ISRAEL MEDICAL CENTER–KINGS HIGHWAY DIVISION See Beth Israel Medical Center										
✠ BRONX CHILDREN'S PSYCHIATRIC CENTER, 1000 Waters Place, Bronx, Zip 10461–2799; tel. 718/892–0808; E. Richard Feinberg, M.D., Executive Director (Nonreporting) **A**1 3 **S** New York State Department of Mental Health, Albany, NY	12	52	75	—	—	—	—	—	—	—
✠ BRONX PSYCHIATRIC CENTER, 1500 Waters Place, Bronx, Zip 10461–2796; tel. 718/931–0600; LeRoy Carmichael, Executive Director (Nonreporting) **A**1 3 5 10 **S** New York State Department of Mental Health, Albany, NY	12	22	658	—	—	—	—	—	—	—
✠ BRONX–LEBANON HOSPITAL CENTER, (Includes Concourse Division, 1650 Grand Concourse, Zip 10457; tel. 212/590–1800; Fulton Division, 1276 Fulton Avenue, Zip 10456; tel. 718/590–1800), 1276 Fulton Avenue, Bronx, Zip 10456–3499; tel. 718/590–1800; Miguel A. Fuentes, President and Chief Executive Officer (Nonreporting) **A**1 2 3 5 8 9 10 **N** Health First, New York, NY	23	10	576	—	—	—	—	—	—	—
□ BROOKDALE HOSPITAL MEDICAL CENTER, Linden Boulevard at Brookdale Plaza, Brooklyn, Zip 11212–3198; tel. 718/240–5000; Frank J. Maddalena, President and Chief Executive Officer (Total facility includes 448 beds in nursing home–type unit) **A**1 3 5 8 9 10 12 **F**1 4 6 7 8 10 11 12 15 16 17 19 20 21 22 23 25 26 27 28 30 31 32 33 34 35 36 37 38 40 41 42 44 46 47 49 51 53 54 55 56 57 58 59 60 61 62 64 65 66 67 68 70 71 73 **P**5 6 **N** The Mount Sinai Health System, New York, NY	23	10	973	24733	923	339009	2462	343160	188865	4087
✠ BROOKLYN HOSPITAL CENTER, (Includes Caledonian Campus, 100 Parkside Avenue, Zip 11226; tel. 718/940–2000; Downtown Campus, 121 DeKalb Avenue, Zip 11201), 121 DeKalb Avenue, Brooklyn, Zip 11201–5493; tel. 718/250–8005; Frederick D. Alley, President and Chief Executive Officer (Nonreporting) **A**1 2 3 5 8 9 10 **S** New York & Presbyterian Healthcare, New York, NY **N** NYU Medical Center, New York, NY; The Brooklyn Health Network, Brooklyn, NY; Health First, New York, NY	23	10	653	—	—	—	—	—	—	—

Hospital, Address, Telephone, Administrator, Approval, Facility, and Physician Codes, Health Care System, Network	Classification Codes		Utilization Data					Expense (thousands) of dollars		
★ American Hospital Association (AHA) membership □ Joint Commission on Accreditation of Healthcare Organizations (JCAHO) accreditation + American Osteopathic Healthcare Association (AOHA) membership ○ American Osteopathic Association (AOA) accreditation △ Commission on Accreditation of Rehabilitation Facilities (CARF) accreditation Control codes 61, 63, 64, 71, 72 and 73 indicate hospitals listed by AOHA, but not registered by AHA. For definition of numerical codes, see page A4	Control	Service	Staffed Beds	Admissions	Census	Outpatient Visits	Births	Total	Payroll	Personnel

BROOKLYN JEWISH DIVISION See Interfaith Medical Center										
★ CABRINI MEDICAL CENTER, 227 East 19th Street, Zip 10003–2600; tel. 212/995–6000; Jeffrey Frerichs, President and Chief Executive Officer (Nonreporting) **A**1 2 3 5 8 9 10 **N** The Mount Sinai Health System, New York, NY	21	10	493	—	—	—	—	—	—	—
CALEDONIAN CAMPUS See Brooklyn Hospital Center										
★ CALVARY HOSPITAL, 1740 Eastchester Road, Bronx, Zip 10461–2392; tel. 718/863–6900; Frank A. Calamari, President and Chief Executive Officer **A**1 9 10 **F**8 14 16 19 20 21 22 32 34 39 41 42 45 46 54 60 65 67 73 **N** Sisters of Charity Healthcare, Staten Island, NY	21	49	200	2418	175	19098	—	55628	31774	643
★ CATHOLIC MEDICAL CENTER OF BROOKLYN AND QUEENS, (Includes Holy Family Home, 1740 84th Street, Brooklyn, Zip 11214; tel. 718/232–3666; Mary Immaculate Hospital, 152–11 89th Avenue, Zip 11432; tel. 718/558–2000; Monsignor James H Fitzpatrick Pavilion for Skilled Nursing Care, 152–11 89th Avenue, Zip 11432; tel. 718/558–2800; St. John's Queens Hospital, tel. 718/558–1000; St. Joseph's Hospital, 158–40 79th Avenue, Flushing, Zip 11366; tel. 718/558–6200; St. Mary's Hospital of Brooklyn, 170 Buffalo Avenue, Brooklyn, Zip 11213; tel. 718/221–3000), 88–25 153rd Street, Jamaica, Zip 11432–3731; tel. 718/558–6900; William D. McGuire, President and Chief Executive Officer (Total facility includes 603 beds in nursing home–type unit) **A**1 2 3 5 6 8 9 10 **F**3 7 8 11 12 15 16 17 19 20 21 22 23 25 26 28 29 30 31 32 34 37 41 42 44 45 48 49 51 52 60 64 65 70 71 **P**6 **N** Continuum Health Partners, Inc., New York, NY	21	10	1585	42561	1317	1934860	4578	589301	290780	—
★ COLER MEMORIAL HOSPITAL, Roosevelt Island, Zip 10044; tel. 212/848–6000; Samuel Lehrfeld, Executive Director (Total facility includes 775 beds in nursing home–type unit) **A**1 10 **F**20 26 31 33 41 46 48 54 64 65 71 73 **S** New York City Health and Hospitals Corporation, New York, NY	14	48	1025	916	848	—	—	97245	55461	1316
CONCOURSE DIVISION See Bronx–Lebanon Hospital Center										
★ CONEY ISLAND HOSPITAL, 2601 Ocean Parkway, Brooklyn, Zip 11235–7795; tel. 718/616–3000; William Walsh, Executive Director **A**1 3 5 9 10 **F**3 4 5 7 8 10 11 12 14 15 16 17 18 19 20 21 22 23 25 26 27 28 30 31 32 34 35 37 39 40 41 42 43 44 46 48 49 51 52 53 54 55 56 57 58 59 60 61 65 67 68 69 70 71 73 74 **P**6 **S** New York City Health and Hospitals Corporation, New York, NY	14	10	442	16141	362	376359	1301	205738	116798	2603
CORNERSTONE OF MEDICAL ARTS CENTER HOSPITAL, 57 West 57th Street, Zip 10019–2802; tel. 212/755–0200; Norman J. Sokolow, President and Chief Executive Officer **A**9 **F**2	33	82	94	5001	86	16431	0	12800	6800	165
★ CREEDMOOR PSYCHIATRIC CENTER, Jamaica, Mailing Address: 80–45 Winchester Boulevard, Queens Village, Zip 11427–2199; tel. 718/264–3300; Charlotte Seltzer, Chief Executive Officer **A**1 3 10 **F**12 16 20 52 57 58 65 73 **S** New York State Department of Mental Health, Albany, NY	12	22	600	424	662	90106	—	—	—	1379
★ DOCTORS' HOSPITAL OF STATEN ISLAND, 1050 Targee Street, Staten Island, Zip 10304–4499; tel. 718/390–1400; Stephen N. F. Anderson, Director **A**1 9 10 **F**8 17 19 21 22 27 28 30 36 37 39 44 45 46 49 65 71 73	33	10	117	4501	68	14279	0	22937	10899	284
DOWNTOWN CAMPUS See Brooklyn Hospital Center										
★ △ ELMHURST HOSPITAL CENTER, 79–01 Broadway, Elmhurst, Zip 11373; tel. 718/334–4000; Pete Velez, Executive Director **A**1 2 3 5 7 8 9 10 **F**2 3 4 5 7 8 9 10 11 12 13 14 15 16 17 18 19 20 21 22 23 25 26 27 28 29 30 31 32 33 34 35 37 38 39 40 41 42 43 44 45 46 47 48 49 50 51 52 53 54 55 56 57 58 59 60 61 63 64 65 66 67 68 69 70 71 73 74 **P**5 6 7 8 **S** New York City Health and Hospitals Corporation, New York, NY **N** Queens Health Network, Elmhurst, NY; The Mount Sinai Health System, New York, NY	14	10	498	21135	443	565028	4370	292045	160172	3389
★ FLUSHING HOSPITAL MEDICAL CENTER, 45th Avenue at Parsons Boulevard, Flushing, Zip 11355–2100; tel. 718/670–5000; Stephen S. Mills, President and Chief Executive Officer (Nonreporting) **A**1 3 5 9 10 **S** New York & Presbyterian Healthcare, New York, NY **N** Preferred Health Network, Inc., Flushing, NY; The New York & Presbyterian Hospitals Care Network, Inc., New York, NY	23	10	321	—	—	—	—	—	—	—
FULTON DIVISION See Bronx–Lebanon Hospital Center										
★ △ GOLDWATER MEMORIAL HOSPITAL, Franklin D. Roosevelt Island, Zip 10044; tel. 212/318–8000; Samuel Lehrfeld, Executive Director (Total facility includes 544 beds in nursing home–type unit) **A**1 3 5 7 10 **F**19 22 26 31 41 46 48 54 64 65 71 73 **S** New York City Health and Hospitals Corporation, New York, NY	14	48	986	1123	877	—	—	96430	58708	1405
★ GRACIE SQUARE HOSPITAL, 420 East 76th Street, Zip 10021–3104; tel. 212/988–4400; Frank Bruno, Chief Executive Officer **A**1 9 10 **F**3 22 39 46 52 57 65 **P**1 5 **S** New York & Presbyterian Healthcare, New York, NY **N** The New York & Presbyterian Hospitals Care Network, Inc., New York, NY	23	22	100	2396	110	41549	—	21572	12466	294
★ △ HARLEM HOSPITAL CENTER, (Includes Harlem General Care Unit and Harlem Psychiatric Unit), 506 Lenox Avenue, Zip 10037–1894; tel. 212/939–1340; Linnette Webb, Senior Vice President and Executive Director **A**1 2 3 5 7 8 9 10 **F**1 3 4 5 6 7 8 9 10 11 12 13 15 16 17 18 19 20 21 22 23 25 26 27 28 29 30 31 32 34 35 36 37 38 39 40 41 42 43 44 45 46 47 48 49 50 51 52 53 54 55 56 57 58 59 60 61 63 65 67 68 69 70 71 72 73 74 **P**1 **S** New York City Health and Hospitals Corporation, New York, NY	14	10	380	15127	331	504232	1431	267332	153528	3217
HILLSIDE HOSPITAL See Long Island Jewish Medical Center										
★ HOLLISWOOD HOSPITAL, 87–37 Palermo Street, Holliswood, Zip 11423; tel. 718/776–8181; Jeffrey Borenstein, M.D., Chief Executive Officer and Medical Director (Nonreporting) **A**1 9 10	33	22	100	—	—	—	—	—	—	—

Hospital, Address, Telephone, Administrator, Approval, Facility, and Physician Codes, Health Care System, Network	Classi-fication Codes		Utilization Data					Expense (thousands) of dollars		
	Control	Service	Staffed Beds	Admissions	Census	Outpatient Visits	Births	Total	Payroll	Personnel

★ American Hospital Association (AHA) membership
□ Joint Commission on Accreditation of Healthcare Organizations (JCAHO) accreditation
+ American Osteopathic Healthcare Association (AOHA) membership
○ American Osteopathic Association (AOA) accreditation
△ Commission on Accreditation of Rehabilitation Facilities (CARF) accreditation
Control codes 61, 63, 64, 71, 72 and 73 indicate hospitals listed by AOHA, but not registered by AHA. For definition of numerical codes, see page A4

Hospital	Control	Service	Staffed Beds	Admissions	Census	Outpatient Visits	Births	Total	Payroll	Personnel
⊠ △ HOSPITAL FOR JOINT DISEASES ORTHOPEDIC INSTITUTE, 301 East 17th Street, Zip 10003–3890; tel. 212/598–6000; Victor H. Frankel, M.D., President **A**1 3 5 7 9 10 **F**4 5 7 8 10 11 12 14 15 16 17 19 20 21 22 23 24 25 26 28 29 30 31 34 35 37 39 40 41 42 44 45 46 47 48 49 51 52 54 55 56 57 60 61 63 65 66 67 69 71 72 73 74 **P**5 7 **N** NYU Medical Center, New York, NY	23	47	163	5694	122	69697	—	122099	51133	1156
⊠ HOSPITAL FOR SPECIAL SURGERY, 535 East 70th Street, Zip 10021–4898; tel. 212/606–1000; John R. Ahearn, Co–Chief Executive Officer **A**1 3 5 6 8 9 10 **F**1 2 3 4 5 6 7 8 9 10 11 12 13 14 15 16 17 18 19 20 21 22 23 24 25 26 27 28 29 30 31 32 33 34 35 36 37 38 39 40 41 42 43 44 45 46 47 48 49 50 51 52 53 54 55 56 57 58 59 60 61 63 64 65 66 67 68 69 70 71 72 73 74 **P**5 8 **S** New York & Presbyterian Healthcare, New York, NY **N** The New York & Presbyterian Hospitals Care Network, Inc., New York, NY	23	47	138	7040	99	162528	—	—	—	1401
□ INTERFAITH MEDICAL CENTER, (Includes Brooklyn Jewish Division, 555 Prospect Place, Zip 11238; tel. 718/935–7000; St. John's Episcopal Hospital Division, 1545 Atlantic Avenue, Zip 11213; tel. 718/604–6000), 555 Prospect Place, Brooklyn, Zip 11238–4299; tel. 718/935–7000; Corbett A. Price, Chief Executive Officer **A**1 3 5 6 9 10 **F**1 2 3 4 7 8 9 10 11 12 13 14 16 17 18 19 20 21 22 23 25 28 29 30 31 32 34 35 37 38 39 40 42 43 44 45 46 47 48 49 50 52 56 58 59 60 61 65 67 69 70 71 73 74 **P**5 6 **N** The Brooklyn Health Network, Brooklyn, NY; Health First, New York, NY	23	10	455	14913	388	254909	1088	171863	96984	2063
⊠ JACOBI MEDICAL CENTER, (Includes Abraham Jacobi General Care Hospital and Psychiatic Units, ; Van Etten Hospitals), Pelham Parkway South and Eastchester Road, Bronx, Zip 10461–1197; tel. 718/918–5000; Joseph S. Orlando, Executive Director **A**1 3 5 8 10 **F**1 3 7 8 9 11 12 13 14 15 16 17 18 19 20 21 22 28 29 30 31 32 34 35 37 38 39 40 41 42 44 45 46 47 48 49 51 52 53 54 55 56 58 60 61 65 67 68 70 71 73 74 **P**6 **S** New York City Health and Hospitals Corporation, New York, NY	14	10	485	19441	419	435372	2388	230231	167133	—
⊠ JAMAICA HOSPITAL MEDICAL CENTER, 8900 Van Wyck Expressway, Jamaica, Zip 11418–2832; tel. 718/206–6000; David P. Rosen, President **A**1 3 5 9 10 12 **F**7 8 10 12 14 15 16 17 19 20 21 22 24 25 26 27 28 30 32 34 35 37 40 41 42 44 46 47 48 49 51 52 53 54 55 56 57 58 59 61 63 65 67 70 71 72 73 74 **P**4 5 **N** NYU Medical Center, New York, NY; Health First, New York, NY	23	10	365	18672	346	281867	3059	204418	106810	2413
⊠ KINGS COUNTY HOSPITAL CENTER, 451 Clarkson Avenue, Brooklyn, Zip 11203–2097; tel. 718/245–3131; Jean G. Leon, R.N., Senior Vice President **A**1 2 3 5 9 10 **F**2 3 4 5 7 8 11 12 13 15 17 18 19 20 21 22 24 25 27 28 30 31 34 37 38 39 40 41 42 44 45 46 47 48 49 50 51 52 53 54 55 56 58 60 61 63 65 66 68 70 71 72 73 74 **P**6 **S** New York City Health and Hospitals Corporation, New York, NY	14	10	781	25516	652	700055	1954	307540	230796	—
KINGS HIGHWAY HOSPITAL CENTER See Beth Israel Medical Center										
⊠ KINGSBORO PSYCHIATRIC CENTER, 681 Clarkson Avenue, Brooklyn, Zip 11203–2199; tel. 718/221–7395; John Palmer, Ph.D., Director (Nonreporting) **A**1 3 5 10 **S** New York State Department of Mental Health, Albany, NY	12	22	400	—						
⊠ △ KINGSBROOK JEWISH MEDICAL CENTER, 585 Schenectady Avenue, Brooklyn, Zip 11203–1891; tel. 718/604–5000; Milton M. Gutman, Chief Executive Officer (Total facility includes 538 beds in nursing home–type unit) **A**1 3 5 7 9 10 **F**1 8 11 12 14 15 16 17 19 20 21 22 25 26 27 28 29 30 32 34 35 37 39 41 44 45 46 48 49 51 52 54 55 57 58 64 65 71 73 **P**5 **N** The Brooklyn Health Network, Brooklyn, NY; Health First, New York, NY	23	10	864	8951	813	88526	—	—	95040	—
⊠ LENOX HILL HOSPITAL, 100 East 77th Street, Zip 10021–1883; tel. 212/434–2000; Gladys George, President and Chief Executive Officer **A**1 3 5 8 9 10 **F**3 4 5 7 8 10 11 12 14 15 16 17 19 20 21 22 24 25 27 28 29 30 31 32 34 35 37 38 39 40 41 42 43 44 45 46 47 49 51 52 53 54 55 56 57 58 59 60 61 63 65 66 67 68 71 73 74 **P**5 7 8 **N** NYU Medical Center, New York, NY	23	10	652	28147	518	277050	3572	277935	149019	3100
⊠ LINCOLN MEDICAL AND MENTAL HEALTH CENTER, 234 East 149th Street, Bronx, Zip 10451–9998; tel. 718/579–5700; Lilliam Barrios–Paoli, Ph.D., Executive Director **A**1 3 9 10 **F**3 7 8 11 12 13 14 15 16 17 18 19 20 22 28 29 30 31 32 34 37 38 39 40 42 44 45 46 47 51 52 53 54 56 58 60 61 65 69 70 71 72 73 74 **P**5 **S** New York City Health and Hospitals Corporation, New York, NY	14	10	440	21004	335	550588	3311	275305	147417	3012
□ LONG ISLAND COLLEGE HOSPITAL, 339 Hicks Street, Brooklyn, Zip 11201–5509; tel. 718/780–1000; Donald F. Snell, President and Chief Executive Officer **A**1 2 3 5 8 9 10 **F**3 4 7 8 10 11 12 13 14 15 16 17 18 19 20 21 22 23 25 26 27 28 30 31 32 33 34 35 37 38 39 40 41 42 43 44 46 47 48 49 51 52 53 54 55 56 57 58 59 60 61 65 66 67 68 71 72 73 74 **P**5 6 **N** The Mount Sinai Health System, New York, NY	23	10	515	19068	324	213573	3010	—	128033	2640
⊠ LONG ISLAND JEWISH MEDICAL CENTER, (Formerly North Shore Long Island Medical Center), (Includes Hillside Hospital, 75–59 263rd Street, Glen Oaks, Zip 11004; tel. 718/470–8000; Long Island Jewish Medical Center, 270–05 76th Avenue, Zip 11040; tel. 718/470–7000; Manhasset Ambulatory Care Pavilion, 1554 Northern Boulevard, Manhasset, Zip 11030; tel. 516/365–2070; Schneider Children's Hospital, 270–05 76th Avenue, Zip 11040; tel. 718/470–3000), 270–05 76th Avenue, New Hyde Park, Zip 11040–1496; tel. 718/470–7000; David R. Dantzker, M.D., President and Chief Executive Officer (Nonreporting) **A**1 2 3 5 8 9 10 **S** North Shore– Long Island Jewish Health System, Manhasset, NY **N** North Shore Regional Health Systems, Manhasset, NY	23	10	804	—	—	—	—	—	—	—

Hospital, Address, Telephone, Administrator, Approval, Facility, and Physician Codes, Health Care System, Network	Classi-fication Codes		Utilization Data					Expense (thousands) of dollars		
★ American Hospital Association (AHA) membership □ Joint Commission on Accreditation of Healthcare Organizations (JCAHO) accreditation + American Osteopathic Healthcare Association (AOHA) membership ○ American Osteopathic Association (AOA) accreditation △ Commission on Accreditation of Rehabilitation Facilities (CARF) accreditation Control codes 61, 63, 64, 71, 72 and 73 indicate hospitals listed by AOHA, but not registered by AHA. For definition of numerical codes, see page A4	Control	Service	Staffed Beds	Admissions	Census	Outpatient Visits	Births	Total	Payroll	Personnel

	Control	Service	Staffed Beds	Admissions	Census	Outpatient Visits	Births	Total	Payroll	Personnel
✠ LUTHERAN MEDICAL CENTER, 150 55th Street, Brooklyn, Zip 11220–2570; tel. 718/630–7000; Joseph P. Cerni, President and Chief Executive Officer **A**1 3 5 9 10 12 **F**2 3 6 7 8 11 12 13 14 15 16 17 18 19 20 21 22 23 25 26 27 28 29 30 31 32 33 34 35 36 37 38 39 40 41 42 44 45 46 48 49 51 52 54 55 56 57 58 60 61 62 64 65 66 67 71 73 74 **P**5 **N** The Mount Sinai Health System, New York, NY	23	10	433	16650	310	—	—	—	—	2496
✠ MAIMONIDES MEDICAL CENTER, 4802 Tenth Avenue, Brooklyn, Zip 11219–2916; tel. 718/283–6000; Stanley Brezenoff, President **A**1 3 5 8 9 10 12 **F**1 4 7 8 10 11 12 13 14 15 16 17 18 19 20 21 22 25 26 27 28 30 31 32 34 35 37 38 39 40 41 42 43 44 46 49 51 52 53 54 55 56 57 58 59 61 63 65 66 67 68 69 71 72 73 74 **P**5 6 8 **N** Premier Preferred Care, New York, NY; The Mount Sinai Health System, New York, NY; Health First, New York, NY	23	10	705	30221	552	210764	4468	412891	211511	—
✠ MANHATTAN EYE, EAR AND THROAT HOSPITAL, 210 East 64th Street, Zip 10021–9885; tel. 212/838–9200; George A. Sarkar, Ph.D., JD, Executive Director (Nonreporting) **A**1 3 5 10	23	45	30	—	—	—	—	—	—	—
✠ MANHATTAN PSYCHIATRIC CENTER–WARD'S ISLAND, 600 East 125th Street, Zip 10035–9998; tel. 212/369–0500; Horace Belton, Executive Director (Nonreporting) **A**1 3 5 10 **S** New York State Department of Mental Health, Albany, NY	12	22	745	—	—	—	—	—	—	—
MARY IMMACULATE HOSPITAL See Catholic Medical Center of Brooklyn and Queens										
✠ MEMORIAL HOSPITAL FOR CANCER AND ALLIED DISEASES, (Cancer), 1275 York Avenue, Zip 10021–6094; tel. 212/639–2000; John R. Gunn, Executive Vice President **A**1 2 3 5 8 9 10 **F**8 12 14 15 16 17 19 20 21 25 28 29 30 31 34 35 37 39 42 44 45 46 49 50 54 58 60 63 65 67 69 71 72 73 **P**6	23	49	406	17621	344	247515	0	558948	190271	3698
✠ METROPOLITAN HOSPITAL CENTER, (Includes Metropolitan General Care Unit, Metropolitan Drug Detoxification and Metropolitan Psychiatric Unit), 1901 First Avenue, Zip 10029–7496; tel. 212/423–6262; Jose R. Sanchez, Executive Director **A**1 3 5 8 9 10 **F**1 2 3 7 8 10 11 12 13 14 15 16 17 18 19 20 21 22 25 26 27 28 29 30 31 32 34 35 37 38 39 40 41 42 44 45 46 47 48 49 51 52 53 54 55 56 57 58 59 60 61 63 65 71 73 74 **S** New York City Health and Hospitals Corporation, New York, NY	14	10	423	13286	361	405921	1776	214028	121490	2941
✠ MONTEFIORE MEDICAL CENTER, (Includes Jack D Weiler Hospital of Albert Einstein College of Medicine, 1825 Eastchester Road, Zip 10461–2373; tel. 718/904–2000; Loeb Center Nursing Rehabilitation, 111 East 210th Street), 111 East 210th Street, Bronx, Zip 10467–2490; tel. 718/920–4321; Spencer Foreman, M.D., President (Total facility includes 80 beds in nursing home–type unit) (Nonreporting) **A**1 2 3 5 8 9 10 **N** Health First, New York, NY	23	10	1027	—	—	—	—	—	—	—
✠ MOUNT SINAI MEDICAL CENTER, One Gustave L. Levy Place, Zip 10029–6574; tel. 212/241–6500; John W. Rowe, M.D., President (Nonreporting) **A**1 3 5 8 9 10 **N** The Mount Sinai Health System, New York, NY; Health First, New York, NY	23	10	1036	—	—	—	—	—	—	—
✠ △ NEW YORK AND PRESBYTERIAN HOSPITAL, (Includes New York Hospital, ; New York Hospital, Cornell University Medical Center, 525 East 68th Street, tel. 212/746–5454; New York Hospital, Westchester Division, ; Payne Whitney Psychiatric Clinic, ; Presbyterian Hospital in the City of New York, Columbia–Presbyterian Medical Center, Zip 10032–3784; tel. 212/305–2500), 525 East 68th Street, Zip 10021–4885; tel. 212/746–5454; David B. Skinner, M.D., Vice Chairman and Chief Executive Officer; William T. Speck, President and Chief Operating Officer **A**1 2 3 5 7 8 9 10 **F**1 2 3 4 5 6 7 8 9 10 11 12 13 14 15 16 17 18 19 20 21 22 23 24 25 26 27 28 29 30 31 32 33 34 35 36 37 38 39 40 41 42 43 44 45 46 47 48 49 50 51 52 53 54 55 56 57 58 59 60 61 63 64 65 66 67 68 69 70 71 72 73 74 **P**1 2 4 5 7 **S** New York & Presbyterian Healthcare, New York, NY	23	10	2038	78598	1778	1070547	9370	—	—	—
✠ NEW YORK COMMUNITY HOSPITAL, 2525 Kings Highway, Brooklyn, Zip 11229–1798; tel. 718/692–5300; Lin H. Mo, President and Chief Executive Officer (Nonreporting) **A**1 9 10 **S** New York & Presbyterian Healthcare, New York, NY **N** The New York & Presbyterian Hospitals Care Network, Inc., New York, NY	23	10	134	—	—	—	—	—	—	—
✠ NEW YORK EYE AND EAR INFIRMARY, 310 East 14th Street, Zip 10003–4201; tel. 212/979–4000; Joseph P. Corcoran, President and Chief Executive Officer **A**1 3 5 9 10 **F**12 13 14 17 19 23 30 34 44 60 69 70 71 73 **P**8	23	45	30	2331	13	166282	—	49669	25984	621
✠ NEW YORK HOSPITAL MEDICAL CENTER OF QUEENS, 56–45 Main Street, Flushing, Zip 11355–5000; tel. 718/670–1231; Stephen S. Mills, President and Chief Executive Officer **A**1 2 3 5 9 10 **F**3 4 8 9 10 11 12 13 14 15 16 17 18 19 20 21 22 24 25 26 27 28 29 30 31 32 33 34 35 37 39 40 41 42 43 44 45 46 47 49 51 52 54 58 60 61 64 65 66 67 69 70 71 72 73 74 **P**4 5 7 **S** New York & Presbyterian Healthcare, New York, NY **N** The New York & Presbyterian Hospitals Care Network, Inc., New York, NY	23	10	449	22632	385	243219	2429	261254	115593	—
NEW YORK HOSPITAL, CORNELL UNIVERSITY MEDICAL CENTER See New York and Presbyterian Hospital										
✠ NEW YORK METHODIST HOSPITAL, 506 Sixth Street, Brooklyn, Zip 11215–3645; tel. 718/780–3000; Mark J. Mundy, President and Chief Executive Officer **A**1 2 3 5 8 9 10 **F**2 3 4 5 7 8 9 10 11 12 13 16 17 19 20 21 22 23 25 26 27 28 29 30 31 32 34 35 37 38 39 40 41 42 43 44 46 47 48 49 51 52 53 54 55 57 58 59 60 61 63 64 65 66 67 68 69 70 71 72 73 74 **P**5 7 **S** New York & Presbyterian Healthcare, New York, NY **N** The New York & Presbyterian Hospitals Care Network, Inc., New York, NY	23	10	560	22383	493	268679	3378	239771	117765	2289

Hospital, Address, Telephone, Administrator, Approval, Facility, and Physician Codes, Health Care System, Network	Classi-fication Codes		Utilization Data					Expense (thousands) of dollars		
★ American Hospital Association (AHA) membership □ Joint Commission on Accreditation of Healthcare Organizations (JCAHO) accreditation + American Osteopathic Healthcare Association (AOHA) membership ○ American Osteopathic Association (AOA) accreditation △ Commission on Accreditation of Rehabilitation Facilities (CARF) accreditation Control codes 61, 63, 64, 71, 72 and 73 indicate hospitals listed by AOHA, but not registered by AHA. For definition of numerical codes, see page A4	Control	Service	Staffed Beds	Admissions	Census	Outpatient Visits	Births	Total	Payroll	Personnel
✦ NEW YORK STATE PSYCHIATRIC INSTITUTE, 722 West 168th Street, Zip 10032–2695; tel. 212/543–5000; John M. Oldham, M.D., Director (Nonreporting) **A**1 3 5 10 **S** New York State Department of Mental Health, Albany, NY	12	22	58	—	—	—	—	—	—	—
□ NEW YORK UNIVERSITY DOWNTOWN HOSPITAL, 170 William Street, Zip 10038–2649; tel. 212/312–5000; Leonard A. Aubrey, President and Chief Executive Officer **A**1 3 5 9 10 **F**3 7 8 12 14 15 16 17 19 22 25 26 28 29 30 31 32 34 37 38 39 40 44 45 46 49 51 65 66 71 73 **P**1 5 **N** NYU Medical Center, New York, NY	23	10	148	7861	120	76516	1788	95147	52671	1047
✦ NEW YORK UNIVERSITY HOSPITALS CENTER, (Includes Rusk Institute), 550 First Avenue, Zip 10016–4576; tel. 212/263–7300; Theresa A. Bischoff, Deputy Provost and Executive Vice President (Nonreporting) **A**1 3 5 8 9 10 **N** Health First, New York, NY	23	10	824	—	—	—	—	—	—	—
✦ NORTH CENTRAL BRONX HOSPITAL, 3424 Kossuth Avenue, Bronx, Zip 10467–2489; tel. 718/519–3500; Arthur Wagner, Chief Operating Officer **A**1 3 5 9 10 **F**1 2 3 7 8 9 10 11 12 13 14 15 16 17 18 19 20 21 22 26 28 29 30 31 32 34 35 37 38 39 40 41 42 44 45 46 47 48 49 51 52 53 54 56 58 65 67 68 70 71 73 74 **P**6 **S** New York City Health and Hospitals Corporation, New York, NY	14	10	268	10705	214	256544	3295	120743	82447	—
✦ NORTH GENERAL HOSPITAL, 1879 Madison Avenue, Zip 10035–2745; tel. 212/423–4000; Eugene McCabe, President (Nonreporting) **A**1 3 5 9 10	23	10	240	—	—	—	—	—	—	—
✦ NORTH SHORE UNIVERSITY HOSPITAL–FOREST HILLS, Flushing, Mailing Address: 102–01 66th Road, Zip 11375; tel. 718/830–4000; Andrew J. Mitchell, Vice President, Administration (Nonreporting) **A**1 2 3 5 9 10 **S** North Shore– Long Island Jewish Health System, Manhasset, NY **N** North Shore Regional Health Systems, Manhasset, NY	23	10	231	—	—	—	—	—	—	—
✦ OUR LADY OF MERCY MEDICAL CENTER, (Includes Florence D'Urso Pavilion, 1870 Pelham Parkway South, Zip 10461; tel. 212/430–6000), 600 East 233rd Street, Bronx, Zip 10466–2697; tel. 718/920–9000; Gary S. Horan, FACHE, President and Chief Executive Officer **A**1 2 3 5 8 9 10 **F**3 7 8 11 12 13 14 15 16 17 19 20 22 25 28 30 31 32 34 37 38 39 40 42 44 45 46 49 51 52 54 56 57 58 60 61 62 65 66 67 71 73 74 **S** Our Lady of Mercy Healthcare System, Inc., New York, NY **N** Sisters of Charity Healthcare, Staten Island, NY	21	10	508	16817	384	254316	3380	190102	106133	2362
□ PARKWAY HOSPITAL, Flushing, Mailing Address: 70–35 113th Street, Zip 11375; tel. 718/990–4100; Paul E. Svensson, Chief Executive Officer (Nonreporting) **A**1 9 10 **N** The Mount Sinai Health System, New York, NY	33	10	251	—	—	—	—	—	—	—
□ ○ PENINSULA HOSPITAL CENTER, 51–15 Beach Channel Drive, Far Rockaway, Zip 11691–1074; tel. 718/945–7100; Robert V. Levine, President and Chief Executive Officer **A**1 9 10 11 12 13 **F**8 11 15 16 17 18 19 20 21 22 26 27 28 30 32 33 34 35 37 41 42 44 45 46 49 51 54 56 60 63 65 67 69 70 71 73 **P**5 7 8 **N** Continuum Health Partners, Inc., New York, NY PRESBYTERIAN HOSPITAL IN THE CITY OF NEW YORK See New York and Presbyterian Hospital	23	10	235	5846	170	52526	—	65892	37185	1128
★ QUEENS CHILDREN'S PSYCHIATRIC CENTER, 74–03 Commonwealth Boulevard, Jamaica, Zip 11426–1890; tel. 718/264–4506; Gloria Faretra, M.D., Executive Director (Nonreporting) **S** New York State Department of Mental Health, Albany, NY	12	52	106	—	—	—	—	—	—	—
✦ QUEENS HOSPITAL CENTER, 82–68 164th Street, Jamaica, Zip 11432–1104; tel. 718/883–3000; Gladiola Sampson, Acting Executive Director **A**1 2 3 5 9 10 **F**2 3 4 7 8 10 12 13 14 16 17 19 20 21 22 25 26 31 32 34 35 37 38 40 42 43 44 46 48 49 51 52 53 54 56 57 58 59 60 63 65 67 68 71 73 74 **P**6 **S** New York City Health and Hospitals Corporation, New York, NY **N** Queens Health Network, Elmhurst, NY; The Mount Sinai Health System, New York, NY	14	10	292	12946	263	304409	1911	160737	108887	—
□ ROCKEFELLER UNIVERSITY HOSPITAL, 1230 York Avenue, Zip 10021–6399; tel. 212/327–8000; Emil Gotschlich, M.D., Vice President Medical Sciences (Nonreporting) **A**1 3 9 10	23	49	30	—	—	—	—	—	—	—
✦ SAINT VINCENT'S HOSPITAL AND MEDICAL CENTER OF NEW YORK, (Includes St. Vincent's Hospital, 275 North Street, Zip 10528; tel. 914/925–5300), 153 West 11th Street, Zip 10011–8397; tel. 212/604–7000; Karl P. Adler, M.D., President and Chief Executive Officer **A**1 2 3 5 6 8 9 10 **F**3 4 7 8 10 11 12 13 16 17 18 19 20 21 22 25 26 28 29 30 31 32 33 34 35 36 37 38 39 40 41 42 43 44 45 46 48 49 50 51 52 53 54 55 56 57 58 60 61 63 65 66 67 68 69 70 71 73 74 **P**1 5 7 **S** Sisters of Charity Healthcare, Staten Island, NY **N** Sisters of Charity Healthcare, Staten Island, NY SCHNEIDER CHILDREN'S HOSPITAL See Long Island Jewish Medical Center	21	10	622	22773	500	402777	1936	389525	198408	3456
✦ SISTERS OF CHARITY MEDICAL CENTER, (Includes Bayley Seton Campus, 75 Vanderbilt Avenue, Zip 10304–3850; tel. 718/354–6000; St Vincent's Campus, 355 Bard Avenue, tel. 718/876–1234), 355 Bard Avenue, Staten Island, Zip 10310–1699; tel. 718/876–1234; Dominick M. Stanzione, Chief Operating Officer and Executive Vice President **A**1 2 3 5 6 10 **F**1 3 4 5 6 7 8 10 11 12 13 14 15 16 17 18 19 20 21 22 23 25 26 27 28 29 30 31 32 33 34 35 37 38 39 40 41 42 43 44 45 46 47 48 49 51 52 53 54 55 56 57 58 59 60 61 62 64 65 66 67 68 69 70 71 72 73 74 **P**5 7 SOCIETY OF THE NEW YORK HOSP See New York and Presbyterian Hospital	21	10	628	26297	440	344937	3647	296758	125502	2581
✦ SOUTH BEACH PSYCHIATRIC CENTER, 777 Seaview Avenue, Staten Island, Zip 10305–3499; tel. 718/667–2300; Lucy Sarkis, M.D., Executive Director (Nonreporting) **A**1 10 **S** New York State Department of Mental Health, Albany, NY ST VINCENT'S MEDICAL CENTER See St Vincent's Campus	12	22	325	—	—	—	—	—	—	—

Hospital, Address, Telephone, Administrator, Approval, Facility, and Physician Codes, Health Care System, Network	Classi-fication Codes		Utilization Data					Expense (thousands) of dollars		
	Control	Service	Staffed Beds	Admissions	Census	Outpatient Visits	Births	Total	Payroll	Personnel

★ American Hospital Association (AHA) membership
□ Joint Commission on Accreditation of Healthcare Organizations (JCAHO) accreditation
+ American Osteopathic Healthcare Association (AOHA) membership
○ American Osteopathic Association (AOA) accreditation
△ Commission on Accreditation of Rehabilitation Facilities (CARF) accreditation
Control codes 61, 63, 64, 71, 72 and 73 indicate hospitals listed by AOHA, but not registered by AHA. For definition of numerical codes, see page A4

Hospital	Control	Service	Staffed Beds	Admissions	Census	Outpatient Visits	Births	Total	Payroll	Personnel
□ ○ ST. BARNABAS HOSPITAL, 183rd Street and Third Avenue, Bronx, Zip 10457–9998; tel. 718/960–9000; Ronald Gade, M.D., President (Nonreporting) **A**1 3 5 9 10 11 12 13 **N** The Mount Sinai Health System, New York, NY	23	10	458	—	—	—	—	—	—	—
□ ST. CLARE'S HOSPITAL AND HEALTH CENTER, 415 West 51st Street, Zip 10019–6394; tel. 212/586–1500; James A. Rutherford, President and Chief Executive Officer (Nonreporting) **A**1 9 10 12 **N** Sisters of Charity Healthcare, Staten Island, NY	21	10	236	—	—	—	—	—	—	—
ST. JOHN'S EPISCOPAL HOSPITAL DIVISION See Interfaith Medical Center										
★ ○ ST. JOHN'S EPISCOPAL HOSPITAL–SOUTH SHORE, 327 Beach 19th Street, Far Rockaway, Zip 11691–4424; tel. 718/869–7000; Paul J. Connor, III, Administrator (Nonreporting) **A**1 3 5 9 11 12 13 **S** Episcopal Health Services Inc., Uniondale, NY **N** Episcopal Health Services, Inc., Uniondale, NY; First Choice Network, Inc., Mineola, NY; The Mount Sinai Health System, New York, NY	21	10	314	—	—	—	—	—	—	—
ST. JOSEPH'S HOSPITAL See Catholic Medical Center of Brooklyn and Queens										
□ ST. LUKE'S–ROOSEVELT HOSPITAL CENTER, (Includes Roosevelt Hospital, 1000 Tenth Avenue, Zip 10019; tel. 212/523–4000; St. Luke's Hospital Center, 1111 Amsterdam Avenue, tel. 212/523–4000), 1111 Amsterdam Avenue, Zip 10025; tel. 212/523–4295; Ronald C. Ablow, M.D., President and Chief Executive Officer **A**1 3 5 8 9 10 **F**2 3 4 5 7 8 10 11 12 13 14 15 16 17 18 19 20 21 22 25 26 28 29 30 31 32 33 34 35 37 38 39 40 41 42 43 44 45 46 47 49 51 52 53 54 55 56 57 58 59 60 61 63 64 65 67 68 69 70 71 72 73 74 **P**4 5 8 **S** Continuum Health Partners, New York, NY **N** Continuum Health Partners, Inc., New York, NY	23	10	729	36367	692	484048	3839	593430	257157	5418
ST. MARY'S HOSPITAL OF BROOKLYN See Catholic Medical Center of Brooklyn and Queens										
□ △ STATEN ISLAND UNIVERSITY HOSPITAL, 475 Seaview Avenue, Staten Island, Zip 10305–9998; tel. 718/226–9000; Rick J. Varone, President (Nonreporting) **A**1 2 3 5 7 9 10 **S** North Shore– Long Island Jewish Health System, Manhasset, NY **N** North Shore Regional Health Systems, Manhasset, NY; The Mount Sinai Health System, New York, NY; Health First, New York, NY	23	10	617	—	—	—	—	—	—	—
UNION HOSPITAL OF THE BRONX, 260 East 188th Street, Bronx, Zip 10458; tel. 718/220–2020; Ronald Gade, M.D., President (Nonreporting) **A**9 10	23	10	197	—	—	—	—	—	—	—
★ UNIVERSITY HOSPITAL OF BROOKLYN–STATE UNIVERSITY OF NEW YORK HEALTH SCIENCE CENTER AT BROOKLYN, 445 Lenox Road, Brooklyn, Zip 11203–2098; tel. 718/270–2404; Percy Allen, II, FACHE, Vice President Hospital Affairs and Chief Executive Officer **A**1 2 3 5 8 9 10 **F**4 5 7 8 10 12 17 19 20 21 25 28 30 31 34 35 42 43 44 46 49 50 51 53 57 60 61 65 66 69 71 72 73 74 **N** Health First, New York, NY	12	10	376	11066	226	174736	2354	166116	101143	
VAN ETTEN HOSPITALS See Jacobi Medical Center										
★ VETERANS AFFAIRS MEDICAL CENTER, 800 Poly Place, Brooklyn, Zip 11209–7104; tel. 718/630–3500; Michael A. Sabo, Medical Director (Total facility includes 184 beds in nursing home–type unit) **A**1 3 5 8 **F**1 2 3 4 5 8 10 11 14 15 16 17 19 20 21 22 23 24 25 26 27 28 30 31 32 34 35 37 39 41 42 43 44 45 46 48 49 51 52 54 55 56 57 58 59 60 64 65 67 71 72 73 74 **P**6 **S** Department of Veterans Affairs, Washington, DC	45	10	496	6918	242	395000	—	193924	101715	
★ VETERANS AFFAIRS MEDICAL CENTER, 130 West Kingsbridge Road, Bronx, Zip 10468–3992; tel. 718/584–9000; Maryann Musumeci, Director (Total facility includes 120 beds in nursing home–type unit) **A**1 2 3 5 8 **F**2 3 8 10 11 12 16 17 19 20 22 23 25 26 28 30 31 32 33 34 35 37 39 42 44 45 46 48 49 51 52 54 56 57 58 63 64 65 67 71 72 73 74 **P**6 **S** Department of Veterans Affairs, Washington, DC **N** The Mount Sinai Health System, New York, NY	45	10	367	4838	213	265078	—	—	—	1564
★ VETERANS AFFAIRS MEDICAL CENTER, 423 East 23rd Street, Zip 10010–5050; tel. 212/686–7500; John J. Donnellan, Jr., Director **A**1 2 3 5 8 **F**1 2 3 4 6 8 10 11 16 17 18 19 20 21 22 23 24 25 26 27 28 29 30 31 32 33 34 35 37 39 41 42 43 44 45 46 48 49 51 52 53 54 55 56 57 58 60 63 64 65 67 71 73 74 **S** Department of Veterans Affairs, Washington, DC	45	10	257	6083	220	318028	—	173798	90618	1703
□ VICTORY MEMORIAL HOSPITAL, 9036 Seventh Avenue, Brooklyn, Zip 11228–3625; tel. 718/630–1234; Krishin L. Bhatia, Administrator (Total facility includes 150 beds in nursing home–type unit) (Nonreporting) **A**1 9 10 **N** Continuum Health Partners, Inc., New York, NY; The Brooklyn Health Network, Brooklyn, NY	23	10	410	—	—	—	—	—	—	—
□ WESTCHESTER SQUARE MEDICAL CENTER, 2475 St. Raymond Avenue, Bronx, Zip 10461–3198; tel. 718/430–7300; Alan Kopman, President and Chief Executive Officer **A**1 9 10 **F**11 19 22 27 34 35 37 42 44 49 65 71 73 **P**1 7	33	10	205	6792	157	39207	0	54473	26581	622
□ WESTERN QUEENS COMMUNITY HOSPITAL, 25–10 30th Avenue, Astoria Station, Long Island City, Zip 11102–2495; tel. 718/932–1000; Elliot J. Simon, FACHE, Chief Operating Officer (Nonreporting) **A**1 9 10 **N** The Mount Sinai Health System, New York, NY	33	10	208	—	—	—	—	—	—	—
★ WOODHULL MEDICAL AND MENTAL HEALTH CENTER, 760 Broadway Street, Brooklyn, Zip 11206–5383; tel. 718/963–8000; Cynthia Carrington–Murray, Executive Director **A**1 3 9 10 **F**3 7 8 11 12 14 15 16 17 18 19 20 21 22 25 26 27 28 29 30 31 34 37 39 40 41 42 44 45 46 47 48 49 51 52 53 54 55 56 57 58 61 65 67 68 71 73 74 **P**6 **S** New York City Health and Hospitals Corporation, New York, NY	14	10	439	16825	378	315935	1592	166932	118358	2528

Hospital, Address, Telephone, Administrator, Approval, Facility, and Physician Codes, Health Care System, Network	Classi-fication Codes		Utilization Data					Expense (thousands) of dollars		
★ American Hospital Association (AHA) membership □ Joint Commission on Accreditation of Healthcare Organizations (JCAHO) accreditation + American Osteopathic Healthcare Association (AOHA) membership ○ American Osteopathic Association (AOA) accreditation △ Commission on Accreditation of Rehabilitation Facilities (CARF) accreditation Control codes 61, 63, 64, 71, 72 and 73 indicate hospitals listed by AOHA, but not registered by AHA. For definition of numerical codes, see page A4	Control	Service	Staffed Beds	Admissions	Census	Outpatient Visits	Births	Total	Payroll	Personnel

⊠ ○ WYCKOFF HEIGHTS MEDICAL CENTER, 374 Stockholm Street, Brooklyn, Zip 11237–4099; tel. 718/963–7102; Dominick J. Gio, President and Chief Executive Officer **A**1 3 5 9 10 11 12 13 **F**7 8 11 15 16 17 19 20 21 22 26 27 28 30 31 32 34 37 38 39 40 42 44 46 47 49 51 60 65 67 71 72 73 **S** New York & Presbyterian Healthcare, New York, NY **N** Preferred Health Network, Inc., Flushing, NY; The New York & Presbyterian Hospitals Care Network, Inc., New York, NY	23	10	299	16032	437	149937	1380	183733	66280	—
NEWARK—Wayne County										
⊠ NEWARK–WAYNE COMMUNITY HOSPITAL, Driving Park Avenue, Zip 14513, Mailing Address: P.O. Box 111, Zip 14513–0111; tel. 315/332–2022; W. Neil Stroman, President (Total facility includes 160 beds in nursing home–type unit) **A**1 9 10 **F**1 7 8 12 16 19 20 21 22 24 26 28 30 33 35 37 39 40 41 44 49 52 54 56 57 58 61 64 65 71 73 74 **P**5 6 **S** Via Health, Rochester, NY **N** Via Health, Rochester, NY	33	10	241	2645	207	73881	302	29988	12898	554
NEWBURGH—Orange County										
□ ST. LUKE'S HOSPITAL, 70 Dubois Street, Zip 12550–4898, Mailing Address: P.O. Box 631, Zip 12550–0631; tel. 914/561–4400; Laurence E. Kelly, Executive Vice President and Administrator **A**1 9 10 **F**2 3 7 8 10 11 12 14 15 16 17 19 23 25 27 28 29 30 32 33 34 35 37 38 40 42 44 46 48 49 51 52 53 54 55 56 57 58 60 61 63 65 66 67 70 71 73 74 **S** Greater Hudson Valley Health System, Newburgh, NY **N** Columbia Presbyterian Regional Network, New York, NY	23	10	184	8897	118	102585	—	51932	25284	735
NEWFANE—Niagara County										
INTER–COMMUNITY MEMORIAL HOSPITAL, 2600 William Street, Zip 14108–1093; tel. 716/778–5111; Clare A. Haar, Chief Executive Officer **A**9 10 **F**7 8 11 14 15 16 17 19 20 21 22 25 26 28 29 30 32 34 35 37 39 40 41 42 44 45 49 51 61 65 71 72 73 74 **P**5 8	23	10	71	2187	29	56811	166	13779	6920	242
NIAGARA FALLS—Niagara County										
⊠ NIAGARA FALLS MEMORIAL MEDICAL CENTER, 621 Tenth Street, Zip 14302–0708, Mailing Address: P.O. Box 708, Zip 14302–0708; tel. 716/278–4000; Angelo G. Calbone, President and Chief Executive Officer (Nonreporting) **A**1 3 5 9 10	23	10	288	—	—	—	—	—	—	—
NORTH TARRYTOWN—Westchester County										
PHELPS MEMORIAL HOSPITAL CENTER See Sleepy Hollow										
NORTH TONAWANDA—Niagara County										
□ DE GRAFF MEMORIAL HOSPITAL, 445 Tremont Street, Zip 14120–0750, Mailing Address: P.O. Box 0750, Zip 14120–0750; tel. 716/694–4500; Marcia B. Gutfeld, Vice President and Chief Operating Officer (Total facility includes 80 beds in nursing home–type unit) (Nonreporting) **A**1 9 10 **S** CGF Health System, Buffalo, NY **N** Buffalo General Health System, Buffalo, NY	23	10	210	—	—	—	—	—	—	—
NORTHPORT—Suffolk County										
⊠ VETERANS AFFAIRS MEDICAL CENTER, (MED/SURG/PYCH/REHAB), 79 Middleville Road, Zip 11768–2293; tel. 516/261–4400; Mary A. Dowling, Director (Total facility includes 178 beds in nursing home–type unit) **A**1 2 3 5 8 **F**1 5 6 8 10 11 12 17 19 20 21 22 26 27 28 30 31 32 33 34 35 37 39 42 44 45 46 48 49 51 52 54 56 58 60 63 64 65 67 71 73 74 **S** Department of Veterans Affairs, Washington, DC	45	49	489	5026	460	295332	—	136410	94457	1573
NORWICH—Chenango County										
□ CHENANGO MEMORIAL HOSPITAL, 179 North Broad Street, Zip 13815–1097; tel. 607/337–4111; Frank W. Mirabito, President (Total facility includes 80 beds in nursing home–type unit) **A**1 9 10 **F**7 8 12 15 16 17 19 20 21 22 26 28 30 31 32 34 37 39 40 41 42 44 45 46 49 51 61 63 64 65 67 71 73 74 **P**6 7 8 **N** Chenango County Rural Health Network, Norwich, NY	23	10	138	2275	106	201418	302	31180	15082	511
NYACK—Rockland County										
⊠ NYACK HOSPITAL, North Midland Avenue, Zip 10960–1998; tel. 914/348–2000; Greger C. Anderson, President and Chief Executive Officer (Nonreporting) **A**1 2 9 10 **N** Columbia Presbyterian Regional Network, New York, NY	23	10	317	—	—	—	—	—	—	—
OCEANSIDE—Nassau County										
⊠ SOUTH NASSAU COMMUNITIES HOSPITAL, 2445 Oceanside Road, Zip 11572–1500; tel. 516/763–2030; Joseph A. Quagliata, Chief Administrative Officer **A**1 2 3 5 9 10 **F**4 7 8 9 10 11 13 14 15 16 17 19 20 21 22 26 27 28 29 30 31 32 33 35 37 38 39 41 42 43 44 45 46 47 49 51 52 53 54 55 56 57 58 59 60 63 65 66 67 68 69 70 71 73 74 **P**3 5 7	23	10	429	12316	283	170392	1220	101815	54524	—
OGDENSBURG—St. Lawrence County										
□ HEPBURN MEDICAL CENTER, 214 King Street, Zip 13669–1192; tel. 315/393–3600; Lorraine B. Kabot, FACHE, President and Chief Executive Officer (Total facility includes 29 beds in nursing home–type unit) **A**1 9 10 **F**4 7 8 14 15 16 17 18 19 21 22 23 24 25 26 28 29 30 31 33 34 35 39 40 42 44 45 46 49 51 52 54 55 56 58 60 63 64 65 67 69 71 73 74	23	10	149	4724	106	107122	384	31317	16160	—
⊠ ST. LAWRENCE PSYCHIATRIC CENTER, 1 Chimney Point Drive, Zip 13669–2291; tel. 315/393–3000; John R. Scott, Director **A**1 10 **F**3 4 5 6 7 8 10 12 13 18 19 20 21 22 23 24 28 31 32 33 35 36 42 43 44 45 46 49 50 52 53 54 55 56 57 58 59 60 63 69 70 71 73 **S** New York State Department of Mental Health, Albany, NY	12	22	175	326	177	9153	—	—	20291	—
OLEAN—Cattaraugus County										
⊠ OLEAN GENERAL HOSPITAL, 515 Main Street, Zip 14760–9912; tel. 716/373–2600; Robert A. Catalano, M.D., President and Chief Executive Officer **A**1 3 6 9 10 **F**7 8 9 11 12 15 16 18 19 21 22 23 30 32 33 35 38 39 40 41 42 44 45 46 47 49 52 54 56 57 63 64 65 67 71	23	10	209	6910	110	135570	619	44845	21574	—

Hospital, Address, Telephone, Administrator, Approval, Facility, and Physician Codes, Health Care System, Network	Classi-fication Codes		Utilization Data					Expense (thousands) of dollars		
★ American Hospital Association (AHA) membership □ Joint Commission on Accreditation of Healthcare Organizations (JCAHO) accreditation + American Osteopathic Healthcare Association (AOHA) membership ○ American Osteopathic Association (AOA) accreditation △ Commission on Accreditation of Rehabilitation Facilities (CARF) accreditation Control codes 61, 63, 64, 71, 72 and 73 indicate hospitals listed by AOHA, but not registered by AHA. For definition of numerical codes, see page A4	Control	Service	Staffed Beds	Admissions	Census	Outpatient Visits	Births	Total	Payroll	Personnel

ONEIDA—Madison County

| ✠ ONEIDA HEALTHCARE CENTER, 321 Genesee Street, Zip 13421–0321; tel. 315/363–6000; Richard G. Smith, Chief Executive Officer (Total facility includes 160 beds in nursing home–type unit) **A**1 9 10 **F**7 8 11 19 21 22 25 28 29 34 35 37 39 40 41 44 45 46 49 63 64 65 73 | 23 | 10 | 261 | 3133 | 198 | 102233 | 464 | 35351 | 16114 | 705 |

ONEONTA—Otsego County

| ✠ AURELIA OSBORN FOX MEMORIAL HOSPITAL, 1 Norton Avenue, Zip 13820–2697; tel. 607/432–2000; John R. Remillard, President (Total facility includes 131 beds in nursing home–type unit) **A**1 9 10 **F**1 7 8 11 15 16 17 18 19 21 22 24 25 26 28 30 32 33 34 35 36 37 39 40 41 42 44 45 46 49 51 52 54 55 56 57 58 60 63 64 65 71 73 74 **P**5 **S** Quorum Health Group/Quorum Health Resources, Inc., Brentwood, TN | 23 | 10 | 234 | 4331 | 204 | 137414 | 381 | 47004 | 21291 | 594 |

ORANGEBURG—Rockland County

| ✠ ROCKLAND CHILDREN'S PSYCHIATRIC CENTER, 599 Convent Road, Zip 10962; tel. 914/359–7400; Marcia Werby, Administrator (Nonreporting) **A**1 3 **S** New York State Department of Mental Health, Albany, NY | 12 | 52 | 54 | — | — | — | — | — | — | — |
| ✠ ROCKLAND PSYCHIATRIC CENTER, 140 Old Orangeburg Road, Zip 10962–0071; tel. 914/359–1000; James H. Bopp, Executive Director (Nonreporting) **A**1 5 10 **S** New York State Department of Mental Health, Albany, NY | 12 | 22 | 525 | — | — | — | — | — | — | — |

OSSINING—Westchester County

| OSSINING CORRECTIONAL FACILITIES HOSPITAL, 354 Hunter Street, Zip 10562–5498; tel. 914/941–0108; Benjamin I. Dyett, M.D., Director (Nonreporting) | 12 | 11 | 25 | — | — | — | — | — | — | — |
| □ STONY LODGE HOSPITAL, 40 Croton Dam Road, Zip 10562–2644, Mailing Address: P.O. Box 1250, Briarcliff Manor, Zip 10510–1250; tel. 914/941–7400; Kevin F. Czipo, Executive Director **A**1 10 **F**14 16 52 53 | 33 | 22 | 60 | 1071 | 50 | — | 0 | 9545 | 5225 | 188 |

OSWEGO—Oswego County

| ✠ OSWEGO HOSPITAL, 110 West Sixth Street, Zip 13126–9985; tel. 315/349–5511; Corte J. Spencer, Chief Executive Officer (Total facility includes 38 beds in nursing home–type unit) **A**1 9 10 **F**3 7 8 11 12 13 14 15 16 17 18 19 20 21 22 25 30 31 32 33 34 36 37 38 39 40 41 42 44 45 49 51 52 53 54 56 58 59 63 64 65 69 71 72 73 74 **N** | 23 | 10 | 192 | 3988 | 76 | 193925 | 714 | 34635 | 17346 | 534 |

PATCHOGUE—Suffolk County

| ✠ BROOKHAVEN MEMORIAL HOSPITAL MEDICAL CENTER, 101 Hospital Road, Zip 11772–9998; tel. 516/654–7100; Thomas Ockers, President and Chief Executive Officer (Nonreporting) **A**1 3 9 10 | 23 | 10 | 321 | — | — | — | — | — | — | — |

PEEKSKILL—Westchester County

| ✠ HUDSON VALLEY HOSPITAL CENTER, 1980 Crompond Road, Zip 10566–4182; tel. 914/737–9000; John C. Federspiel, President and Chief Executive Officer **A**1 9 10 **F**2 3 4 7 8 9 10 11 12 13 14 15 16 17 18 19 20 21 22 23 24 25 26 27 28 29 30 31 32 33 34 35 37 38 40 41 42 43 44 45 46 47 48 51 52 53 54 55 56 57 58 60 63 64 65 66 67 69 70 71 72 73 **P**5 8 **N** The Excelcare System, Inc., Bronxville, NY; Westchester Health Services Network, Mt Kisco, NY | 23 | 10 | 120 | 6065 | 84 | — | 1204 | 47269 | 22123 | 550 |

PENN YAN—Yates County

| ✠ SOLDIERS AND SAILORS MEMORIAL HOSPITAL OF YATES COUNTY, 418 North Main Street, Zip 14527–1085; tel. 315/531–2000; James J. Dooley, President and Chief Executive Officer (Total facility includes 152 beds in nursing home–type unit) (Nonreporting) **A**1 9 10 **N** Four Lakes Rural Health Network, Geneva, NY | 23 | 10 | 217 | — | — | — | — | — | — | — |

PLAINVIEW—Nassau County

| ✠ NORTH SHORE UNIVERSITY HOSPITAL AT PLAINVIEW, 888 Old Country Road, Zip 11803–4978; tel. 516/719–3000; Glenn Hirsch, Executive Vice President, Administration (Nonreporting) **A**1 2 9 10 **S** North Shore– Long Island Jewish Health System, Manhasset, NY **N** North Shore Regional Health Systems, Manhasset, NY | 33 | 10 | 279 | — | — | — | — | — | — | — |

PLATTSBURGH—Clinton County

| ✠ CHAMPLAIN VALLEY PHYSICIANS HOSPITAL MEDICAL CENTER, 75 Beekman Street, Zip 12901–1493; tel. 518/561–2000; Kevin J. Carroll, President (Total facility includes 54 beds in nursing home–type unit) **A**1 2 5 9 10 **F**7 8 10 11 12 13 15 16 19 20 21 22 23 24 25 28 30 32 33 34 35 36 37 40 41 42 44 46 49 51 52 56 60 64 65 67 70 71 72 73 74 **N** Eastern Adirondack Health Care Network, Westport, NY | 23 | 10 | 380 | 9551 | 236 | 191224 | 943 | 84154 | 41307 | 1229 |

POMONA—Rockland County

| □ DOCTOR ROBERT L. YEAGER HEALTH CENTER, (Includes Summit Park Hospital–Rockland County Infirmary), Sanatorium Road, Zip 10970–3554; tel. 914/364–2700; Peter T. Fella, Commissioner (Total facility includes 300 beds in nursing home–type unit) (Nonreporting) **A**1 10 | 13 | 49 | 408 | — | — | — | — | — | — | — |

PORT CHESTER—Westchester County

| ✠ UNITED HOSPITAL MEDICAL CENTER, 406 Boston Post Road, Zip 10573–7300; tel. 914/934–3000; Kevin Dahill, President and Chief Executive Officer (Total facility includes 40 beds in nursing home–type unit) **A**1 5 9 10 **F**1 2 3 7 8 11 12 14 15 16 17 18 19 20 21 22 26 27 28 29 30 31 32 33 34 35 36 38 39 40 41 42 44 46 49 52 53 54 56 57 58 59 60 63 64 65 67 71 73 **P**5 **S** New York & Presbyterian Healthcare, New York, NY **N** The Excelcare System, Inc., Bronxville, NY; The New York & Presbyterian Hospitals Care Network, Inc., New York, NY | 23 | 10 | 191 | 7387 | 161 | — | 909 | 68320 | 33773 | 752 |

PORT JEFFERSON—Suffolk County

| ✠ JOHN T. MATHER MEMORIAL HOSPITAL, 75 North Country Road, Zip 11777–2190; tel. 516/473–1320; Kenneth D. Roberts, President **A**1 2 9 10 **F**2 3 5 7 8 11 12 15 16 17 18 19 20 21 22 26 27 28 29 30 31 32 33 34 35 36 37 38 39 40 41 42 44 46 48 49 52 53 56 57 58 59 60 61 65 66 67 69 71 73 74 **P**8 | 23 | 10 | 248 | 9539 | 196 | 94083 | 0 | 86663 | 42285 | 1114 |

Hospital, Address, Telephone, Administrator, Approval, Facility, and Physician Codes, Health Care System, Network	Classi-fication Codes		Utilization Data					Expense (thousands) of dollars		
★ American Hospital Association (AHA) membership □ Joint Commission on Accreditation of Healthcare Organizations (JCAHO) accreditation + American Osteopathic Healthcare Association (AOHA) membership ○ American Osteopathic Association (AOA) accreditation △ Commission on Accreditation of Rehabilitation Facilities (CARF) accreditation Control codes 61, 63, 64, 71, 72 and 73 indicate hospitals listed by AOHA, but not registered by AHA. For definition of numerical codes, see page A4	Control	Service	Staffed Beds	Admissions	Census	Outpatient Visits	Births	Total	Payroll	Personnel

Hospital	Control	Service	Staffed Beds	Admissions	Census	Outpatient Visits	Births	Total	Payroll	Personnel
✠ ST. CHARLES HOSPITAL AND REHABILITATION CENTER, 200 Belle Terre Road, Zip 11777; tel. 516/474–6000; Barry T. Zeman, President and Chief Executive Officer (Nonreporting) **A**1 2 3 5 9 10 **N** First Choice Network, Inc., Mineola, NY	21	10	235	—	—	—	—	—	—	—
PORT JERVIS—Orange County										
✠ MERCY COMMUNITY HOSPITAL, 160 East Main Street, Zip 12771–2245, Mailing Address: P.O. Box 1014, Zip 12771–1014; tel. 914/856–5351; Marie T. Droege, Site Administrator (Total facility includes 46 beds in nursing home–type unit) **A**1 2 9 10 **F**7 8 12 14 15 16 17 19 20 22 28 30 31 32 34 35 37 39 40 42 44 46 49 52 54 56 60 64 65 67 71 73 **P**5 **S** Franciscan Sisters of the Poor Health System, Inc., Latham, NY **N** Tri–State Health System, Suffern, NY	21	10	187	3971	114	63983	224	33511	16304	551
POTSDAM—St. Lawrence County										
✠ CANTON–POTSDAM HOSPITAL, 50 Leroy Street, Zip 13676–1799; tel. 315/265–3300; Bruce C. Potter, President **A**1 9 10 **F**7 8 14 15 16 19 21 22 23 25 28 29 30 35 37 39 40 44 46 49 50 65 70 71 73	23	10	94	3757	64	95827	348	27184	13313	471
POUGHKEEPSIE—Dutchess County										
✠ HUDSON RIVER PSYCHIATRIC CENTER, Branch B., Zip 12601–1197; tel. 914/452–8000; James Regan, Ph.D., Chief Executive Officer (Nonreporting) **A**1 5 10 **S** New York State Department of Mental Health, Albany, NY	12	22	460	—	—	—	—	—	—	—
□ △ SAINT FRANCIS HOSPITAL, (Includes Saint Francis Hospital–Beacon, 60 Delavan Avenue, Beacon, Zip 12508; tel. 914/831–3500), 35 North Road, Zip 12601–1399; tel. 914/471–2000; Sister M. Ann Elizabeth, President **A**1 3 7 9 10 **F**2 3 7 8 10 11 12 13 14 15 16 17 19 20 21 22 23 26 27 28 29 30 31 32 33 34 35 37 38 39 40 41 42 43 44 45 46 48 49 51 52 53 54 55 56 57 58 60 61 63 65 66 67 68 69 70 71 72 73 74 **N** The Mount Sinai Health System, New York, NY	21	10	317	10496	258	248000	—	103559	51928	—
✠ VASSAR BROTHERS HOSPITAL, 45 Reade Place, Zip 12601–3990; tel. 914/454–8500; Ronald T. Mullahey, President **A**1 2 3 9 10 **F**7 8 10 11 12 14 15 16 17 19 20 21 22 27 28 30 31 32 33 34 37 38 39 40 42 44 45 46 60 61 65 67 71 73 74 **N** The Mount Sinai Health System, New York, NY	23	10	252	13473	199	154363	2586	95410	41474	987
QUEENS—Queens County, See New York City										
QUEENS VILLAGE—Queens County, See New York City										
RHINEBECK—Dutchess County										
✠ NORTHERN DUTCHESS HOSPITAL, 10 Springbrook Avenue, Zip 12572–5002, Mailing Address: P.O. Box 5002, Zip 12572–5002; tel. 914/876–3001; Michael C. Mazzarella, Chief Executive Officer **A**1 9 10 **F**2 4 7 8 9 10 11 12 15 16 18 19 20 21 22 24 26 27 30 31 32 33 34 35 37 39 40 41 42 43 44 45 46 48 49 52 53 54 55 56 57 58 59 60 62 64 65 67 69 71 73 **P**7 **S** Cross River HealthCare, Inc., Rhinebeck, NY	23	10	68	2652	43	—	574	21307	8965	—
RICHMOND VALLEY—Richmond County, See New York City										
RIVERHEAD—Suffolk County										
✠ CENTRAL SUFFOLK HOSPITAL, 1300 Roanoke Avenue, Zip 11901–2028; tel. 516/548–6000; Joseph F. Turner, President (Total facility includes 60 beds in nursing home–type unit) **A**1 9 10 **F**4 7 8 14 15 16 19 21 22 28 29 30 32 34 35 37 40 42 44 45 46 49 64 65 67 71 72 73 **P**7	23	10	196	4660	140	51414	222	51360	23996	621
ROCHESTER—Monroe County										
✠ GENESEE HOSPITAL, 224 Alexander Street, Zip 14607–4055; tel. 716/263–6000; William R. Holman, President (Total facility includes 40 beds in nursing home–type unit) (Nonreporting) **A**1 2 3 5 8 9 10 **S** Via Health, Rochester, NY **N** Via Health, Rochester, NY	23	10	305	—	—	—	—	—	—	—
✠ HIGHLAND HOSPITAL OF ROCHESTER, 1000 South Avenue, Zip 14620–2782; tel. 716/473–2200; Michael J. Weidner, President (Nonreporting) **A**1 2 3 5 9 10	23	10	225	—	—	—	—	—	—	—
□ MONROE COMMUNITY HOSPITAL, 435 East Henrietta Road, Zip 14620–4684; tel. 716/274–7100; Frank Tripodi, Executive Director (Total facility includes 566 beds in nursing home–type unit) (Nonreporting) **A**1 3 5 9 10	13	49	605	—	—	—	—	—	—	—
✠ PARK RIDGE HOSPITAL, 1555 Long Pond Road, Zip 14626–4182; tel. 716/723–7000; Martin E. Carlin, President **A**1 2 9 10 **F**1 3 6 7 8 10 11 12 13 14 15 16 17 18 19 20 21 22 24 26 28 30 31 32 33 34 35 36 37 39 40 41 42 43 44 45 46 48 49 51 52 53 54 55 56 57 58 59 61 62 64 65 66 67 68 69 70 71 72 73 74 **P**5 6 7 8 **S** Daughters of Charity National Health System, Saint Louis, MO **N** Unity Health System, Rochester, NY	23	10	259	8244	181	431424	—	88314	39816	1110
✠ ROCHESTER GENERAL HOSPITAL, 1425 Portland Avenue, Zip 14621–3099; tel. 716/338–4000; Richard S. Constantino, M.D., President **A**1 2 3 5 6 8 9 10 **F**1 4 7 8 9 10 11 12 13 17 18 19 20 21 22 23 25 26 27 28 30 31 32 33 34 35 37 38 40 41 42 43 44 48 49 51 52 53 56 57 58 59 60 61 64 65 66 67 69 70 71 72 73 74 **P**5 6 **S** Via Health, Rochester, NY **N** Via Health, Rochester, NY	23	10	526	24948	403	171499	2784	245482	117270	3011
✠ ROCHESTER PSYCHIATRIC CENTER, 1111 Elmwood Avenue, Zip 14620–3005; tel. 716/473–3230; Martin H. Von Holden, Executive Director **A**1 3 5 9 10 **F**12 14 15 16 52 53 55 57 65 67 73 **P**6 **S** New York State Department of Mental Health, Albany, NY	12	22	267	350	351	20000	—	—	—	—
✠ △ ST. MARY'S HOSPITAL, 89 Genesee Street, Zip 14611–3285; tel. 716/464–3000; Stewart Putnam, President **A**1 2 3 5 7 9 10 **F**1 2 3 6 7 8 10 11 12 13 14 15 16 17 18 19 20 21 22 24 26 28 30 31 32 33 34 35 37 39 40 41 42 44 45 46 48 49 51 52 53 54 55 56 57 58 59 61 62 64 65 66 67 68 71 72 73 74 **P**5 6 7 8 **S** Daughters of Charity National Health System, Saint Louis, MO **N** Unity Health System, Rochester, NY	21	10	218	5729	125	68558	593	94547	46938	1201

Hospital, Address, Telephone, Administrator, Approval, Facility, and Physician Codes, Health Care System, Network	Classi-fication Codes		Utilization Data					Expense (thousands) of dollars		
★ American Hospital Association (AHA) membership □ Joint Commission on Accreditation of Healthcare Organizations (JCAHO) accreditation + American Osteopathic Healthcare Association (AOHA) membership ○ American Osteopathic Association (AOA) accreditation △ Commission on Accreditation of Rehabilitation Facilities (CARF) accreditation Control codes 61, 63, 64, 71, 72 and 73 indicate hospitals listed by AOHA, but not registered by AHA. For definition of numerical codes, see page A4	Control	Service	Staffed Beds	Admissions	Census	Outpatient Visits	Births	Total	Payroll	Personnel
⊠ △ STRONG MEMORIAL HOSPITAL OF THE UNIVERSITY OF ROCHESTER, 601 Elmwood Avenue, Zip 14642–0002; tel. 716/275–2100; Steven I. Goldstein, General Director and Chief Executive Officer **A**1 3 5 7 8 9 10 **F**3 4 5 6 7 8 9 10 11 12 13 14 15 16 17 18 19 20 21 22 23 24 26 28 29 30 31 32 33 34 35 36 37 38 39 40 41 42 43 44 45 46 47 48 49 50 51 52 53 54 55 56 57 58 59 60 61 62 63 64 65 66 67 68 69 70 71 72 73 74 **P**1	23	10	644	25802	567	276923	3510	361439	173583	4514
ROCKVILLE CENTRE—Nassau County										
⊠ MERCY MEDICAL CENTER, 1000 North Village Avenue, Zip 11570–1098; tel. 516/255–0111; Vincent DiRubbio, President and Chief Executive Officer **A**1 2 3 9 10 **F**3 4 7 8 9 10 11 12 14 15 16 17 19 21 22 23 26 28 30 31 32 33 34 35 37 38 40 41 42 43 44 48 49 52 54 55 56 57 58 59 60 63 64 65 66 67 69 70 71 73 74 **P**6 8	21	10	387	13433	282	203961	1941	137163	62065	1735
ROME—Oneida County										
⊠ ROME MEMORIAL HOSPITAL, 1500 North James Street, Zip 13440–2898; tel. 315/338–7000; Alvin C. White, President and Chief Executive Officer (Total facility includes 82 beds in nursing home–type unit) **A**1 9 10 **F**3 7 8 12 13 14 15 16 19 21 22 28 30 31 34 36 37 39 40 41 44 45 46 49 60 64 65 66 71 73 74	23	10	203	5794	140	127691	624	38343	18961	699
ROSLYN—Nassau County										
⊠ ST. FRANCIS HOSPITAL, 100 Port Washington Boulevard, Zip 11576–1348; tel. 516/562–6000; Patrick J. Scollard, President and Chief Executive Officer **A**1 5 9 10 **F**3 4 7 8 10 11 12 14 15 16 17 19 20 21 22 24 28 29 30 32 33 34 35 36 37 39 41 42 43 44 45 46 47 49 50 54 56 57 58 59 60 63 65 66 67 69 71 73 74 **P**8 **N** Columbia Presbyterian Regional Network, New York, NY	23	10	279	14096	319	85290	—	191242	85782	—
RYE—Westchester County										
⊠ RYE HOSPITAL CENTER, 754 Boston Post Road, Zip 10580–2724; tel. 914/967–4567; Jack C. Schoenholtz, M.D., Medical Director and Administrator **A**1 10 **F**17 19 20 21 22 35 45 50 52 53 55 57 60 63 65 71 73	33	22	34	213	28	0	0	4861	2032	50
SARANAC LAKE—Franklin County										
⊠ ADIRONDACK MEDICAL CENTER, Lake Colby Drive, Zip 12983, Mailing Address: P.O. Box 471, Zip 12983–0471; tel. 518/891–4141; Chandler M. Ralph, Chief Executive Officer (Nonreporting) **A**1 9 10 **S** Brim, Inc., Portland, OR	23	10	100	—	—	—	—	—	—	—
SARATOGA SPRINGS—Saratoga County										
⊠ SARATOGA HOSPITAL, 211 Church Street, Zip 12866–1003; tel. 518/587–3222; David Andersen, President and Chief Executive Officer (Total facility includes 72 beds in nursing home–type unit) **A**1 9 10 **F**7 8 11 12 14 16 17 18 19 21 22 26 28 30 33 34 35 37 39 40 41 42 44 46 49 51 52 53 54 55 56 57 64 65 67 71 73 74 **P**5 **N** Shared Health Network, Inc., Albany, NY	23	10	201	6618	175	113090	716	49387	23397	763
SCHENECTADY—Schenectady County										
□ BELLEVUE WOMAN'S HOSPITAL, 2210 Troy Road, Zip 12309–4797; tel. 518/346–9400; Michael A. Mangini, Administrator and Chief Executive Officer (Nonreporting) **A**1 9 10	33	44	55	—	—	—	—	—	—	—
CONIFER PARK, 79 Glenridge Road, Zip 12302; tel. 518/399–6446; Jack Duffy, Executive Director **F**3 16 65 67 74 **P**6	33	82	225	2551	131	0	0	—	—	243
⊠ ELLIS HOSPITAL, 1101 Nott Street, Zip 12308–2487; tel. 518/243–4000; G. B. Serrill, President and Chief Executive Officer (Total facility includes 82 beds in nursing home–type unit) **A**1 2 3 5 6 9 10 **F**3 4 5 6 7 8 10 11 12 13 14 15 16 17 18 19 20 21 22 23 25 26 28 29 30 31 32 33 34 35 37 39 40 41 42 43 44 45 46 49 51 52 54 55 56 57 58 59 60 61 63 64 65 67 70 71 73 **S** Quorum Health Group/Quorum Health Resources, Inc., Brentwood, TN **N** Shared Health Network, Inc., Albany, NY	23	10	434	11808	307	230739	346	113218	53146	1639
□ ST. CLARE'S HOSPITAL OF SCHENECTADY, 600 McClellan Street, Zip 12304–1090; tel. 518/382–2000; Paul J. Chodkowski, President and Chief Executive Officer (Nonreporting) **A**1 3 5 9 10 12 **N** Shared Health Network, Inc., Albany, NY	21	10	200	—	—	—	—	—	—	—
⊠ △ SUNNYVIEW HOSPITAL AND REHABILITATION CENTER, 1270 Belmont Avenue, Zip 12308–2104; tel. 518/382–4500; Bradford M. Goodwin, President and Chief Executive Officer **A**1 3 5 7 9 10 **F**5 6 12 14 15 16 17 24 26 34 41 48 49 53 58 65 73 **P**5 6 **N** Shared Health Network, Inc., Albany, NY	23	46	104	1898	80	—	—	21921	13320	382
SEAFORD—Nassau County										
+ ○ MASSAPEQUA GENERAL HOSPITAL, 750 Hicksville Road, Zip 11783–1300, Mailing Address: P.O. Box 20, Zip 11783–0020; tel. 516/520–6000; John P. Breen, Chief Executive Officer (Nonreporting) **A**9 10 11 12 13	33	10	122	—	—	—	—	—	—	—
SIDNEY—Delaware County										
⊠ THE HOSPITAL, 43 Pearl Street West, Zip 13838–1399; tel. 607/561–2153; Russell A. Test, Administrator and Chief Executive Officer (Total facility includes 40 beds in nursing home–type unit) **A**1 9 10 **F**7 8 12 19 22 25 28 30 31 34 37 39 40 41 44 49 51 64 65 71 **S** Brim, Inc., Portland, OR	14	10	87	1726	62	42451	142	12920	6164	308
SLEEPY HOLLOW—Westchester County										
⊠ PHELPS MEMORIAL HOSPITAL CENTER, 701 North Broadway, Zip 10591–1096; tel. 914/366–3000; Keith F. Safian, President and Chief Executive Officer **A**1 9 10 **F**3 4 5 7 8 9 10 11 12 14 15 16 17 18 19 20 21 22 23 24 26 27 28 29 30 31 32 33 34 35 36 37 38 39 40 41 42 43 44 45 46 47 48 49 51 52 54 55 56 57 58 59 60 61 63 64 65 66 67 68 69 70 71 72 73 74 **P**1 5 **N** Health Star Network, Armonk, NY; The Excelcare System, Inc., Bronxville, NY; The Mount Sinai Health System, New York, NY	23	10	235	7584	150	119208	685	64783	36252	907

Hospital, Address, Telephone, Administrator, Approval, Facility, and Physician Codes, Health Care System, Network	Classi-fication Codes		Utilization Data					Expense (thousands) of dollars		
★ American Hospital Association (AHA) membership □ Joint Commission on Accreditation of Healthcare Organizations (JCAHO) accreditation + American Osteopathic Healthcare Association (AOHA) membership ○ American Osteopathic Association (AOA) accreditation △ Commission on Accreditation of Rehabilitation Facilities (CARF) accreditation Control codes 61, 63, 64, 71, 72 and 73 indicate hospitals listed by AOHA, but not registered by AHA. For definition of numerical codes, see page A4	Control	Service	Staffed Beds	Admissions	Census	Outpatient Visits	Births	Total	Payroll	Personnel

SMITHTOWN—Suffolk County

COMMUNITY HOSPITAL OF SMITHTOWN See St. John's Episcopal Medical Healthcare Center

✠ ST. JOHN'S EPISCOPAL HOSPITAL–SMITHTOWN, 50 Route 25–A, Zip 11787–1398; tel. 516/862–3000; Laura Righter, Regional Administrator (Nonreporting) **A**1 9 **S** Episcopal Health Services Inc., Uniondale, NY **N** Episcopal Health Services, Inc., Uniondale, NY; First Choice Network, Inc., Mineola, NY; The Mount Sinai Health System, New York, NY	21	10	366	—	—	—	—	—	—	—
□ ST. JOHN'S EPISCOPAL MEDICAL HEALTHCARE CENTER, (Formerly Community Hospital of Smithtown), 498 Smithtown By–Pass, Zip 11787–5018; tel. 516/361–4000; Michael Chiarello, Administrator (Nonreporting) **A**1 9 10	21	10	112	—	—	—	—	—	—	—

SODUS—Wayne County

✠ MYERS COMMUNITY HOSPITAL, 6600 Middle Road, Zip 14551–0310; tel. 315/483–3000; Jane Johnson, President and Chief Executive Officer **A**1 9 10 **F**7 8 11 12 16 17 19 22 28 30 37 40 44 45 46 49 66 67 71 73 74	23	10	32	1452	18	31445	230	11965	4654	189

SOUTHAMPTON—Suffolk County

□ SOUTHAMPTON HOSPITAL, 240 Meeting House Lane, Zip 11968–5090; tel. 516/726–8555; John J. Ferry, Jr., M.D., President and Chief Executive Officer (Nonreporting) **A**1 9 10 **N** First Choice Network, Inc., Mineola, NY	23	10	127	—	—	—	—	—	—	—

SPRINGVILLE—Erie County

□ BERTRAND CHAFFEE HOSPITAL, 224 East Main Street, Zip 14141–1497; tel. 716/592–2871; Roger A. Ford, Administrator (Nonreporting) **A**9 10	23	10	49	—	—	—	—	—	—	—

STAR LAKE—St. Lawrence County

★ CLIFTON–FINE HOSPITAL, Oswegatchie Trail, Zip 13690, Mailing Address: P.O. Box 10, Zip 13690–0010; tel. 315/848–3351; Rodney C. Boula, Administrator **A**9 10 **F**8 16 19 22 25 28 33 34 39 49 65 71	16	10	20	460	30	—	0	3214	1603	61

STATEN ISLAND—Richmond County, See New York City

STONY BROOK—Suffolk County

✠ UNIVERSITY HOSPITAL, State University of New York, Zip 11794–8410; tel. 516/689–8333; Michael A. Maffetone, Director and Chief Executive Officer **A**1 2 3 5 8 9 10 **F**4 7 8 9 10 11 12 13 14 15 16 17 18 19 20 21 22 25 26 28 29 30 31 34 35 37 38 39 40 41 42 43 44 45 46 47 49 51 52 53 54 55 56 57 58 59 60 61 63 64 65 66 67 68 69 70 71 72 73 74 **N** Health First, New York, NY	12	10	504	23999	370	306941	3546	302379	142000	5716

SUFFERN—Rockland County

□ GOOD SAMARITAN HOSPITAL, 255 Lafayette Avenue, Zip 10901–4869; tel. 914/368–5000; James A. Martin, Chief Executive Officer (Nonreporting) **A**1 9 10 **S** Franciscan Sisters of the Poor Health System, Inc., Latham, NY **N** Westchester Health Services Network, Mt Kisco, NY	21	10	308	—	—	—	—	—	—	—

SYOSSET—Nassau County

✠ NORTH SHORE UNIVERSITY HOSPITAL AT SYOSSET, 221 Jericho Turnpike, Zip 11791–4567; tel. 516/496–6400; Deborah Tascone, R.N., Vice President for Administration (Nonreporting) **A**1 3 9 10 **S** North Shore– Long Island Jewish Health System, Manhasset, NY **N** North Shore Regional Health Systems, Manhasset, NY	23	10	186	—	—	—	—	—	—	—

SYRACUSE—Onondaga County

□ BENJAMIN RUSH CENTER, 650 South Salina Street, Zip 13202–3524; tel. 315/476–2161; Norman J. Lesswing, Ph.D., Administrator and Chief Executive Officer (Nonreporting) **A**1 9 10	31	22	107	—	—	—	—	—	—	—
✠ COMMUNITY–GENERAL HOSPITAL OF GREATER SYRACUSE, 4900 Broad Road, Zip 13215; tel. 315/492–5011; Kent A. Arnold, President (Total facility includes 50 beds in nursing home–type unit) **A**1 3 5 9 10 **F**4 7 8 12 14 19 21 22 25 26 28 29 30 31 34 37 39 40 41 42 44 52 53 54 55 64 65 71 73 **P**5 6 7	12	10	322	10970	217	150644	1505	78911	36147	1143
✠ CROUSE HOSPITAL, 736 Irving Avenue, Zip 13210–1690; tel. 315/470–7111; Edward T. Wenzke, President and Chief Executive Officer **A**1 3 5 9 10 **F**1 2 3 4 5 6 7 8 9 10 11 12 13 14 15 16 17 18 19 20 21 22 23 24 25 26 27 28 29 30 31 32 33 34 35 36 37 38 39 40 41 42 43 44 45 46 47 48 49 50 51 52 53 54 55 56 57 58 59 60 61 62 63 64 65 66 67 68 69 70 71 72 73 74 **P**1 5 **N** Hamilton–Bassett–Crouse Rural Health Network, Hamilton, NY	23	10	500	22885	346	—	3638	159347	72539	—
✠ RICHARD H. HUTCHINGS PSYCHIATRIC CENTER, 620 Madison Street, Zip 13210–2319; tel. 315/473–4980; Bryan F. Rudes, Executive Director (Nonreporting) **A**1 3 5 10 **S** New York State Department of Mental Health, Albany, NY	12	22	184	—	—	—	—	—	—	—
□ ST. JOSEPH'S HOSPITAL HEALTH CENTER, 301 Prospect Avenue, Zip 13203–1895; tel. 315/448–5111; Theodore M. Pasinski, President (Nonreporting) **A**1 3 5 6 9 10 **S** Sisters of the 3rd Franciscan Order, Syracuse, NY	21	10	431	—	—	—	—	—	—	—
✠ UNIVERSITY HOSPITAL–SUNY HEALTH SCIENCE CENTER AT SYRACUSE, 750 East Adams Street, Zip 13210–2399; tel. 315/464–5540; Ben Moore, III, Executive Director **A**1 2 3 5 8 9 10 **F**4 8 9 10 11 12 15 16 17 19 20 21 22 23 25 26 28 29 30 31 34 35 37 39 41 42 43 44 45 46 47 48 49 52 53 54 55 56 57 58 59 60 61 63 65 66 67 68 69 70 71 72 73 74 **P**5 6 7	12	10	356	13986	291	255060	—	210496	103025	2739
✠ VETERANS AFFAIRS MEDICAL CENTER, 800 Irving Avenue, Zip 13210–2796; tel. 315/476–7461; Philip P. Thomas, Director (Total facility includes 50 beds in nursing home–type unit) (Nonreporting) **A**1 3 5 8 **S** Department of Veterans Affairs, Washington, DC	45	10	204	—	—	—	—	—	—	—

Hospital, Address, Telephone, Administrator, Approval, Facility, and Physician Codes, Health Care System, Network	Classi-fication Codes		Utilization Data					Expense (thousands) of dollars		
	Control	Service	Staffed Beds	Admissions	Census	Outpatient Visits	Births	Total	Payroll	Personnel

★ American Hospital Association (AHA) membership
□ Joint Commission on Accreditation of Healthcare Organizations (JCAHO) accreditation
+ American Osteopathic Healthcare Association (AOHA) membership
○ American Osteopathic Association (AOA) accreditation
△ Commission on Accreditation of Rehabilitation Facilities (CARF) accreditation
Control codes 61, 63, 64, 71, 72 and 73 indicate hospitals listed by AOHA, but not registered by AHA. For definition of numerical codes, see page A4

TICONDEROGA—Essex County

□ MOSES LUDINGTON HOSPITAL, Wicker Street, Zip 12883–1097; tel. 518/585–2831; Diane M. Hart, Chief Executive Officer (Nonreporting) **A**1 9 10 **N** Adirondack Rural Health Network, Glens Falls, NY	23	10	39	—	—	—	—	—	—	—

TROY—Rensselaer County

□ SAMARITAN HOSPITAL, 2215 Burdett Avenue, Zip 12180–2475; tel. 518/271–3300; Paul A. Milton, Chief Operating Officer (Nonreporting) **A**1 6 9 10 **N** Shared Health Network, Inc., Albany, NY; Northern New York Rural Health Care Alliance, Watertown, NY	23	10	272	—	—	—	—	—	—	—
⊠ SETON HEALTH SYSTEM, (Includes Seton Health System–Leonard Hospital, 74 New Turnpike Road, Zip 12182–1498; tel. 518/235–0310; Seton Health System–St. Mary's Hospital, 1300 Massachusetts Avenue, Zip 12180), 1300 Massachusetts Avenue, Zip 12180–1695; tel. 518/272–5000; Edward G. Murphy, M.D., President and Chief Executive Officer (Nonreporting) **A**1 9 10 **S** Daughters of Charity National Health System, Saint Louis, MO **N** Seton Health Care System, Troy, NY; Shared Health Network, Inc., Albany, NY	21	10	344	—	—	—	—	—	—	—

UTICA—Oneida County

⊠ FAXTON HOSPITAL, 1676 Sunset Avenue, Zip 13502–5475; tel. 315/738–6200; Andrew E. Peterson, President and Chief Executive Officer **A**1 2 9 10 **F**1 3 4 7 8 10 11 12 15 17 19 20 21 22 23 26 28 29 30 32 33 34 35 36 37 38 39 40 41 42 43 44 48 49 51 52 56 60 64 65 67 69 70 71 72 73 74 **P**3 **N** MoHawk Valley Network, Inc., Utica, NY	23	10	166	5300	109	97970	0	44657	19747	807
⊠ MOHAWK VALLEY PSYCHIATRIC CENTER, 1400 Noyes, Zip 13502–3803; tel. 315/797–6800; Sarah F. Rudes, Executive Director (Nonreporting) **A**1 10 **S** New York State Department of Mental Health, Albany, NY	12	22	614	—	—	—	—	—	—	—
⊠ ST. ELIZABETH MEDICAL CENTER, 2209 Genesee Street, Zip 13501–5999; tel. 315/798–8100; Sister Rose Vincent, President and Chief Executive Officer **A**1 3 6 9 10 12 **F**7 8 10 11 12 13 14 15 16 18 19 21 22 28 30 33 34 35 37 38 39 40 42 43 44 49 51 52 53 54 55 56 57 58 61 63 65 66 67 70 71 72 73 74 **P**6 **S** Sisters of the 3rd Franciscan Order, Syracuse, NY	21	10	176	7614	125	260182	0	62735	31537	1068
⊠ ST. LUKE'S MEMORIAL MEDICAL CENTER, (Includes Allen–Calder Skilled Nursing Facility; Mohawk Valley Division, 295 West Main Street, Ilion, Zip 13357–1599; tel. 315/895–7474), Mailing Address: P.O. Box 479, Zip 13503–0479; tel. 315/798–6000; Andrew E. Peterson, President and Chief Executive Officer (Total facility includes 124 beds in nursing home–type unit) **A**1 9 10 **F**1 4 7 8 10 11 12 14 15 16 19 20 21 22 25 26 28 29 30 31 32 33 34 35 37 40 41 42 44 46 49 51 52 60 63 64 65 70 71 73 74 **N** MoHawk Valley Network, Inc., Utica, NY	23	10	379	11421	317	133561	2067	60174	38117	1198

VALHALLA—Westchester County

⊠ BLYTHEDALE CHILDREN'S HOSPITAL, 95 Bradhurst Avenue, Zip 10595–1697; tel. 914/592–7555; Robert Stone, President **A**1 10 **F**14 15 16 20 24 28 29 30 32 34 41 45 46 49 53 54 55 58 65 66 67 71 73 **P**6	23	59	92	279	77	17244	—	22753	14169	362
□ WESTCHESTER MEDICAL CENTER, (Formerly Westchester County Medical Center), Valhalla Campus, Zip 10595; tel. 914/493–7000; Edward A. Stolzenberg, President and Chief Executive Officer (Nonreporting) **A**1 2 3 5 8 9 10 **N** Westchester Health Services Network, Mt Kisco, NY	13	10	657	—	—	—	—	—	—	—

VALLEY STREAM—Nassau County

⊠ FRANKLIN HOSPITAL MEDICAL CENTER, 900 Franklin Avenue, Zip 11580–2190; tel. 516/256–6000; Albert Dicker, President and Chief Executive Officer (Total facility includes 120 beds in nursing home–type unit) **A**1 2 9 10 **F**1 2 3 4 5 6 7 8 9 10 11 12 13 14 15 16 17 18 19 20 21 22 23 25 26 27 28 29 30 31 32 33 34 35 36 37 38 39 40 42 43 44 45 46 47 48 49 50 51 52 53 54 55 56 57 58 59 60 61 62 63 64 65 66 67 68 69 70 71 72 73 74 **P**5 8 **S** North Shore–Long Island Jewish Health System, Manhasset, NY **N** North Shore Regional Health Systems, Manhasset, NY	23	10	441	9607	335	33443	464	85292	39576	1083

WALTON—Delaware County

□ DELAWARE VALLEY HOSPITAL, 1 Titus Place, Zip 13856–1498; tel. 607/865–2100; David J. Polge, President and Chief Executive Officer **A**1 9 10 **F**7 8 15 17 19 21 22 25 26 27 28 30 33 39 41 42 44 49 61 63 65 67 71 73 74 **P**6	23	10	42	1513	24	31333	116	10644	5884	186

WARSAW—Wyoming County

□ WYOMING COUNTY COMMUNITY HOSPITAL, 400 North Main Street, Zip 14569–1097; tel. 716/786–2233; Lucille K. Sheedy, Administrator and Chief Executive Officer (Total facility includes 160 beds in nursing home–type unit) **A**1 9 10 **F**7 15 17 19 20 21 25 28 33 34 35 39 41 42 44 49 51 52 64 71 73 74 **P**8 **N** Lake Plains Community Care Network, Buffalo, NY	13	10	239	3203	207	64365	433	29911	13850	364

WARWICK—Orange County

⊠ ST. ANTHONY COMMUNITY HOSPITAL, 15–19 Maple Avenue, Zip 10990–5180; tel. 914/986–2276; R. Andrew Brothers, President and Chief Executive Officer (Nonreporting) **A**1 9 10 **S** Franciscan Sisters of the Poor Health System, Inc., Latham, NY **N** Tri–State Health System, Suffern, NY	21	10	73	—	—	—	—	—	—	—

WATERTOWN—Jefferson County

□ SAMARITAN MEDICAL CENTER, 830 Washington Street, Zip 13601–4066, Mailing Address: P.O. Box 517, Zip 13601–0517; tel. 315/785–4000; William P. Koughan, President and Chief Executive Officer (Nonreporting) **A**1 9 10	23	10	239	—	—	—	—	—	—	—

WELLSVILLE—Allegany County

⊠ JONES MEMORIAL HOSPITAL, 191 North Main Street, Zip 14895–1197, Mailing Address: P.O. Box 72, Zip 14895–0072; tel. 716/593–1100; William M. DiBerardino, FACHE, President and Chief Executive Officer **A**1 9 10 **F**7 8 12 15 16 19 21 22 28 29 30 35 36 39 41 42 44 45 46 49 51 65 66 67 68 74 **N** Allegany County Health Care Network, Wellsville, NY	23	10	70	3020	34	66691	412	20297	8689	292

Hospital, Address, Telephone, Administrator, Approval, Facility, and Physician Codes, Health Care System, Network	Classi-fication Codes		Utilization Data					Expense (thousands) of dollars		
★ American Hospital Association (AHA) membership □ Joint Commission on Accreditation of Healthcare Organizations (JCAHO) accreditation + American Osteopathic Healthcare Association (AOHA) membership ○ American Osteopathic Association (AOA) accreditation △ Commission on Accreditation of Rehabilitation Facilities (CARF) accreditation Control codes 61, 63, 64, 71, 72 and 73 indicate hospitals listed by AOHA, but not registered by AHA. For definition of numerical codes, see page A4	Control	Service	Staffed Beds	Admissions	Census	Outpatient Visits	Births	Total	Payroll	Personnel

WEST HAVERSTRAW—Rockland County

✠ HELEN HAYES HOSPITAL, Route 9W, Zip 10993–1195; tel. 914/947–3000; Magdalena Ramirez, Chief Executive Officer **A**1 3 5 9 10 **F**1 2 3 4 5 6 7 8 9 10 11 12 13 15 16 17 18 19 20 21 22 23 24 25 26 27 28 29 30 31 32 33 34 35 36 37 38 39 40 41 42 43 44 45 46 47 48 49 50 51 52 53 54 55 56 57 58 59 60 61 62 63 64 65 66 67 68 69 70 71 72 73 74 **P**6 **N** Columbia Presbyterian Regional Network, New York, NY	12	46	155	1986	123	31047	—	53200	22695	696

WEST ISLIP—Suffolk County

✠ GOOD SAMARITAN HOSPITAL MEDICAL CENTER, 1000 Montauk Highway, Zip 11795–4958; tel. 516/376–3000; Daniel P. Walsh, President (Total facility includes 100 beds in nursing home–type unit) (Nonreporting) **A**1 2 9 10 12 13	21	10	525	—	—	—	—	—	—	—

WEST POINT—Orange County

✠ KELLER ARMY COMMUNITY HOSPITAL, U.S. Military Academy, Zip 10996–1197; tel. 914/938–3305; Colonel Joseph FitzHarris, Commander (Nonreporting) **A**1 3 **S** Department of the Army, Office of the Surgeon General, Falls Church, VA	42	10	49	—	—	—	—	—	—	—

WESTFIELD—Chautauqua County

★ WESTFIELD MEMORIAL HOSPITAL, 189 East Main Street, Zip 14787–1195; tel. 716/326–4921; Barbara A. Malinowski, Administrator and Chief Executive Officer **A**9 10 **F**4 7 8 10 14 15 16 18 19 21 22 23 25 28 30 33 34 35 40 41 42 43 44 50 51 60 61 65 67 71 73 **P**1	23	10	32	865	10	34308	173	7119	3570	109

WHITE PLAINS—Westchester County

✠ △ BURKE REHABILITATION HOSPITAL, 785 Mamaroneck Avenue, Zip 10605–2593; tel. 914/597–2500; Mary Beth Walsh, M.D., Chief Executive Officer **A**1 5 7 9 10 **F**5 10 13 14 15 16 21 24 28 29 45 46 48 49 65 67 73 **P**5	23	46	150	2044	126	15636	0	36308	20052	—
NEW YORK HOSPITAL, WESTCHESTER DIVISION See New York and Presbyterian Hospital, New York										
□ ST. AGNES HOSPITAL, (Includes Children's Rehabilitation Center), 305 North Street, Zip 10605–2299; tel. 914/681–4500; Gary S. Horan, FACHE, President and Chief Executive Officer (Nonreporting) **A**1 3 5 9 10 **S** Our Lady of Mercy Healthcare System, Inc., New York, NY **N** Sisters of Charity Healthcare, Staten Island, NY	21	10	184	—	—	—	—	—	—	—
✠ WHITE PLAINS HOSPITAL CENTER, Davis Avenue, Zip 10601–4699; tel. 914/681–0600; Jon B. Schandler, President and Chief Executive Officer (Nonreporting) **A**1 2 5 9 10 **N** Health Star Network, Armonk, NY; Westchester Health Services Network, Mt Kisco, NY; Columbia Presbyterian Regional Network, New York, NY	23	10	301	—	—	—	—	—	—	—

WILLIAMSVILLE—Erie County

MILLARD FILLMORE SUBURBAN HOSPITAL See Millard Fillmore Health System, Buffalo										

YONKERS—Westchester County

✠ ST. JOHN'S RIVERSIDE HOSPITAL, 967 North Broadway, Zip 10701–1399; tel. 914/964–4444; James Foy, President and Chief Executive Officer **A**1 6 9 10 **F**3 7 8 10 14 15 16 17 19 21 22 24 27 28 29 30 31 32 33 34 35 37 39 40 41 42 43 44 45 49 51 60 61 65 66 67 68 71 73 74 **P**5 8 **N** Westchester Health Services Network, Mt Kisco, NY	23	10	273	10445	177	85703	1751	69641	39196	981
✠ ST. JOSEPH'S MEDICAL CENTER, 127 South Broadway, Zip 10701–4080; tel. 914/378–7000; Sister Mary Linehan, President **A**1 3 5 9 10 **F**1 3 4 7 8 14 15 16 17 19 21 22 25 26 27 29 30 31 32 33 34 35 37 39 41 42 44 45 46 47 49 51 52 53 54 55 56 57 58 59 60 63 64 65 67 69 71 72 73 74 **P**5 8 **S** Sisters of Charity Center, New York, NY **N** The Excelcare System, Inc., Bronxville, NY; Sisters of Charity Healthcare, Staten Island, NY	23	10	394	7051	157	—	—	77119	39758	946
✠ YONKERS GENERAL HOSPITAL, Two Park Avenue, Zip 10703–3497; tel. 914/964–7300; Tibisay A. Guzman, Executive Vice President and Chief Operating Officer **A**1 9 10 **F**2 3 14 15 16 17 18 19 21 31 34 37 41 42 44 45 46 54 60 63 65 71 73	23	10	190	5567	119	177138	0	38132	24064	656

NORTH CAROLINA

Resident population 7,425 (in thousands)
Resident population in metro areas 66.6%
Birth rate per 1,000 population 14.3
65 years and over 12.5%
Percent of persons without health insurance 16.0%

Hospital, Address, Telephone, Administrator, Approval, Facility, and Physician Codes, Health Care System, Network	Classi-fication Codes		Utilization Data					Expense (thousands) of dollars		
★ American Hospital Association (AHA) membership □ Joint Commission on Accreditation of Healthcare Organizations (JCAHO) accreditation + American Osteopathic Healthcare Association (AOHA) membership ○ American Osteopathic Association (AOA) accreditation △ Commission on Accreditation of Rehabilitation Facilities (CARF) accreditation Control codes 61, 63, 64, 71, 72 and 73 indicate hospitals listed by AOHA, but not registered by AHA. For definition of numerical codes, see page A4	Control	Service	Staffed Beds	Admissions	Census	Outpatient Visits	Births	Total	Payroll	Personnel

AHOSKIE—Hertford County

✠ ROANOKE–CHOWAN HOSPITAL, 500 South Academy Street, Zip 27910, Mailing Address: P.O. Box 1385, Zip 27910–1385; tel. 919/209–3000; Susan S. Lassiter, President and Chief Executive Officer **A**1 3 9 10 **F**7 8 10 12 13 15 16 19 20 21 22 24 28 30 32 33 35 37 40 41 42 44 46 49 51 52 54 56 57 58 65 67 71 72 73 **P**7 8 **N** Eastern Carolina Health Network, Greenville, NC — 23 10 | 124 | 4289 | 54 | 214485 | 446 | 28714 | 12304 | 581

ALBEMARLE—Stanly County

✠ STANLY MEMORIAL HOSPITAL, 301 Yadkin Street, Zip 28001, Mailing Address: P.O. Box 1489, Zip 28002–1489; tel. 704/984–4000; Roy M. Hinson, CHE, President and Chief Executive Officer **A**1 9 10 **F**1 7 8 10 11 12 15 19 20 21 22 23 26 28 30 31 32 34 35 36 37 39 40 41 42 44 45 46 48 49 51 52 53 55 56 57 64 65 66 67 71 73 **P**6 **N** Carolinas Hospital Network, Charlotte, NC; Central Carolina Rural Hospital Alliance, Albemarle, NC — 23 10 | 119 | 4415 | 60 | 64441 | 496 | 32675 | 12758 | 444

ANDREWS—Cherokee County

□ DISTRICT MEMORIAL HOSPITAL, 71 Whitaker Lane, Zip 28901–9229; tel. 704/321–1291; Daniel C. White, Chief Executive Officer (Total facility includes 25 beds in nursing home–type unit) **A**1 10 **F**1 8 12 14 15 16 17 19 20 21 22 24 28 29 30 35 37 41 42 44 45 46 49 51 64 65 67 71 73 **P**5 8 — 23 10 | 50 | 1166 | 36 | 17398 | — | 10157 | 5583 | 235

ASHEBORO—Randolph County

✠ RANDOLPH HOSPITAL, 364 White Oak Street, Zip 27204, Mailing Address: P.O. Box 1048, Zip 27204–1048; tel. 910/625–5151; Robert E. Morrison, President **A**1 9 10 **F**7 8 12 15 16 17 19 20 21 22 26 28 30 32 34 35 37 39 40 42 44 49 65 71 73 **P**3 — 23 10 | 104 | 4967 | 51 | 113688 | 586 | 36978 | 16870 | 638

ASHEVILLE—Buncombe County

□ CHARTER ASHEVILLE BEHAVIORAL HEALTH SYSTEM, 60 Caledonia Road, Zip 28803–2555, Mailing Address: P.O. Box 5534, Zip 28813–5534; tel. 704/253–3681; Tammy B. Wood, Chief Executive Officer **A**1 10 **F**2 3 12 14 16 18 25 34 46 52 53 54 55 56 57 58 59 65 **P**6 **S** Magellan Health Services, Atlanta, GA — 33 22 | 139 | 1891 | 53 | — | — | 11924 | 5219 | 168

✠ MISSION HOSPITAL, (Formerly Memorial Mission Medical Center), 509 Biltmore Avenue, Zip 28801–4690; tel. 704/255–4000; Robert F. Burgin, President and Chief Executive Officer **A**1 2 3 5 9 10 **F**1 4 6 7 8 10 11 12 13 14 15 16 17 19 20 21 22 23 24 25 26 27 28 29 30 31 32 33 34 35 37 38 39 40 41 42 43 44 45 46 47 48 49 52 53 56 57 58 59 60 61 62 63 64 65 67 70 71 73 74 **P**7 **S** Mission & St. Joseph's Health System, Asheville, NC **N** Mission & Saint Joseph Health System, Asheville, NC; Western North Carolina Health Network, Asheville, NC — 23 10 | 436 | 21817 | 315 | 170505 | 3263 | 222314 | 97094 | 2927

✠ ST. JOSEPH'S HOSPITAL, 428 Biltmore Avenue, Zip 28801–4502; tel. 704/255–3100; J. Lewis Daniels, President and Chief Executive Officer (Total facility includes 25 beds in nursing home–type unit) **A**1 2 9 10 **F**1 3 4 6 7 8 10 12 13 14 15 16 17 19 20 21 22 23 24 25 26 27 28 29 30 31 32 33 34 35 37 38 39 40 41 42 43 44 45 46 47 48 49 52 53 56 57 58 59 60 61 62 63 64 65 67 70 71 73 74 **P**7 **S** Mission & St. Joseph's Health System, Asheville, NC **N** Mission & Saint Joseph Health System, Asheville, NC; Western North Carolina Health Network, Asheville, NC — 21 10 | 275 | 10403 | 161 | 65431 | — | 89431 | 41283 | 1296

✠ △ THOMS REHABILITATION HOSPITAL, 68 Sweeten Creek Road, Zip 28803–1599, Mailing Address: P.O. Box 15025, Zip 28813–0025; tel. 704/274–2400; Charles D. Norvell, President **A**1 7 10 **F**12 14 15 16 17 26 28 30 34 39 41 46 48 49 65 67 73 **P**4 — 23 46 | 100 | 1187 | 62 | 34929 | — | 21523 | 13986 | 463

✠ VETERANS AFFAIRS MEDICAL CENTER, 1100 Tunnel Road, Zip 28805–2087; tel. 704/298–7911; James A. Christian, Director (Total facility includes 120 beds in nursing home–type unit) **A**1 3 5 9 **F**1 2 3 4 8 10 11 12 15 16 19 20 21 23 26 27 28 30 31 32 33 34 35 36 37 39 42 43 44 45 46 49 51 52 54 55 56 57 58 59 60 61 64 65 71 72 73 74 **P**6 **S** Department of Veterans Affairs, Washington, DC — 45 10 | 365 | 4066 | 145 | 101273 | — | — | 52713 | 1072

BANNER ELK—Avery County

□ CHARLES A. CANNON JR. MEMORIAL HOSPITAL, 805 Shawneehaw Avenue, Zip 28604–9724, Mailing Address: P.O. Box 8, Zip 28604–0008; tel. 704/898–5111; Edward C. Greene, Jr., Administrator (Total facility includes 10 beds in nursing home–type unit) **A**1 9 10 **F**7 8 11 19 21 22 28 30 33 37 40 44 52 56 57 64 65 71 73 **P**6 **N** Mountain States Healthcare Network, Johnson City, TN — 23 10 | 50 | 1525 | 22 | 16723 | 59 | 11256 | 4866 | 183

BELHAVEN—Beaufort County

PUNGO DISTRICT HOSPITAL, 202 East Water Street, Zip 27810–9998; tel. 919/943–2111; Thomas O. Miller, Administrator **A**9 10 **F**3 7 8 15 17 19 21 22 26 27 28 32 33 34 37 39 40 41 42 44 46 49 51 53 54 57 58 65 71 **N** Eastern Carolina Health Network, Greenville, NC — 23 10 | 42 | 1864 | 35 | 11743 | 39 | 8275 | 4398 | 197

BLACK MOUNTAIN—Buncombe County

□ JULIAN F. KEITH ALCOHOL AND DRUG ABUSE TREATMENT CENTER, (Formerly Alcohol and Drug Abuse Treatment Center), 301 Tabernacle Road, Zip 28711–2599; tel. 704/669–3402; William A. Rafter, Director (Nonreporting) **A**1 9 10 — 12 82 | 110 | — | — | — | — | — | — | —

Hospital, Address, Telephone, Administrator, Approval, Facility, and Physician Codes, Health Care System, Network	Classi-fication Codes		Utilization Data					Expense (thousands) of dollars		
★ American Hospital Association (AHA) membership □ Joint Commission on Accreditation of Healthcare Organizations (JCAHO) accreditation + American Osteopathic Healthcare Association (AOHA) membership ○ American Osteopathic Association (AOA) accreditation △ Commission on Accreditation of Rehabilitation Facilities (CARF) accreditation Control codes 61, 63, 64, 71, 72 and 73 indicate hospitals listed by AOHA, but not registered by AHA. For definition of numerical codes, see page A4	Control	Service	Staffed Beds	Admissions	Census	Outpatient Visits	Births	Total	Payroll	Personnel

BLOWING ROCK—Watauga County

✠ BLOWING ROCK HOSPITAL, (Includes Dr. Charles Davant Rehabilitation and Extended Care Center), Chestnut Street, Zip 28605–0148, Mailing Address: Box 148, Zip 28605–0148; tel. 704/295–3136; Patricia Gray, Administrator and Chief Executive Officer (Total facility includes 72 beds in nursing home–type unit) (Nonreporting) **A**1 9 10 **N** Wake Forest University Baptist Medical Center, Winston–Salem, NC

| | 23 | 10 | 100 | — | — | — | — | — | — | — |

BOILING SPRINGS—Cleveland County

CRAWLEY MEMORIAL HOSPITAL, 315 West College Avenue, Zip 28017, Mailing Address: P.O. Box 996, Zip 28017–0996; tel. 704/434–9466; Daphne Bridges, President (Total facility includes 45 beds in nursing home–type unit) **A**10 **F**15 34 37 44 49 65 73 **S** Carolinas HealthCare System, Charlotte, NC **N** Carolinas Hospital Network, Charlotte, NC

| | 23 | 10 | 51 | 111 | 46 | 1257 | 0 | 2435 | 1053 | 68 |

BOONE—Watauga County

✠ WATAUGA MEDICAL CENTER, Deerfield Road, Zip 28607–2600, Mailing Address: P.O. Box 2600, Zip 28607–2600; tel. 704/262–4100; Richard G. Sparks, President (Total facility includes 10 beds in nursing home–type unit) **A**1 2 10 **F**7 8 10 12 14 15 16 17 19 21 22 23 28 29 30 32 35 37 38 40 42 44 45 60 64 65 67 68 71 73 **P**3 8 **N** Carolinas Hospital Network, Charlotte, NC

| | 23 | 10 | 105 | 4822 | 58 | 43330 | 530 | 35695 | 15134 | 526 |

BREVARD—Transylvania County

✠ TRANSYLVANIA COMMUNITY HOSPITAL, Hospital Drive, Zip 28712–1116, Mailing Address: Box 1116, Zip 28712–1116; tel. 704/884–9111; Robert J. Bednarek, President and Chief Executive Officer (Nonreporting) **A**1 10 **N** Western North Carolina Health Network, Asheville, NC

| | 23 | 10 | 85 | — | — | — | — | — | — | — |

BRYSON CITY—Swain County

□ SWAIN COUNTY HOSPITAL, 45 Plateau Street, Zip 28713–6784; tel. 704/488–2155; Beverly Robinson, Administrator **A**1 9 10 **F**14 15 16 17 19 22 34 44 46 49 51 65 71 **P**8

| | 23 | 10 | 42 | 1021 | 38 | 15725 | — | 6675 | 3487 | 140 |

BURGAW—Pender County

★ PENDER MEMORIAL HOSPITAL, 507 Freemont Street, Zip 28425; tel. 910/259–5451; J. Larry Bishop, Chief Executive Officer (Total facility includes 43 beds in nursing home–type unit) (Nonreporting) **A**9 10 **S** Quorum Health Group/Quorum Health Resources, Inc., Brentwood, TN

| | 13 | 10 | 86 | — | — | — | — | — | — | — |

BURLINGTON—Alamance County

✠ ALAMANCE REGIONAL MEDICAL CENTER, 1240 Huffman Mill Road, Zip 27216–0202, Mailing Address: P.O. Box 202, Zip 27216–0202; tel. 336/538–7000; Thomas E. Ryan, President (Total facility includes 81 beds in nursing home–type unit) **A**1 2 9 10 **F**2 3 7 8 10 12 14 15 16 17 19 20 21 22 23 26 27 28 29 30 31 32 33 34 35 37 39 40 41 42 44 45 46 48 49 52 53 54 55 56 57 58 59 60 61 63 64 65 67 68 71 73 74 **P**5 7 **N** UNC Health Network, Chapel Hill, NC

| | 23 | 10 | 319 | 9417 | 195 | 96068 | 1206 | 84106 | 36144 | 1186 |

BUTNER—Granville County

□ JOHN UMSTEAD HOSPITAL, (Includes Alcohol and Drug Abuse Treatment Center, 205 West E. Street, Zip 27509; tel. 919/575–7928; Cliff Hood, Director), 1003 12th Street, Zip 27509–1626; tel. 919/575–7211; Patricia L. Christian, R.N., Ph.D., Director (Total facility includes 30 beds in nursing home–type unit) **A**1 3 5 10 **F**52 53 54 56 57 58

| | 12 | 22 | 593 | 4302 | — | 3339 | — | — | 39911 | — |

CAMP LEJEUNE—Onslow County

✠ NAVAL HOSPITAL, Mailing Address: P.O. Box 10100, Zip 28547–0100; tel. 450/451–4300; Captain Michael L. Cowan, MC, USN, Commanding Officer (Nonreporting) **A**1 **S** Department of Navy, Washington, DC

| | 43 | 10 | 166 | — | — | — | — | — | — | — |

CARY—Wake County

WESTERN WAKE MEDICAL CENTER See Wake Medical Center, Raleigh

CHAPEL HILL—Orange County

✠ UNIVERSITY OF NORTH CAROLINA HOSPITALS, (Includes North Carolina Children's and Women's Hospital; North Carolina Neurosciences Hospital), 101 Manning Drive, Zip 27514–4220; tel. 919/966–4131; Eric B. Munson, Executive Director **A**1 2 3 5 8 9 10 **F**2 4 5 7 8 9 10 11 12 13 14 15 16 17 18 19 20 21 22 23 24 25 26 28 29 30 31 32 34 35 37 38 39 40 41 42 43 44 45 46 47 48 49 51 52 53 54 55 56 57 58 60 61 63 64 65 66 67 69 70 71 72 73 74 **P**4 5 6 7 **N** Wake Forest University Baptist Medical Center, Winston–Salem, NC; UNC Health Network, Chapel Hill, NC

| | 12 | 10 | 654 | 26624 | 468 | 703614 | 2456 | 365881 | 166496 | 4577 |

CHARLOTTE—Mecklenburg County

AMETHYST, 1715 Sharon Road West, Zip 28210–5663, Mailing Address: P.O. Box 32861, Zip 28232–2861; tel. 704/554–8373; Steven G. Johnson, Administrator **F**1 2 3 4 5 6 7 8 9 10 11 12 13 15 16 17 18 19 20 21 22 23 24 25 26 27 28 29 30 31 32 33 34 35 36 37 38 39 40 41 42 43 44 45 46 47 48 49 50 51 52 53 54 55 56 57 58 59 60 61 63 64 65 66 67 68 69 70 71 72 73 74 **P**1 3 6

| | 16 | 82 | 94 | 497 | 32 | 14044 | 0 | — | — | 140 |

✠ CAROLINAS MEDICAL CENTER, 1000 Blythe Boulevard, Zip 28203–5871, Mailing Address: P.O. Box 32861, Zip 28232–2861; tel. 704/355–2000; Paul S. Franz, President **A**1 2 3 5 8 9 10 **F**1 2 3 4 5 6 7 8 9 10 11 12 13 14 15 17 18 19 20 21 22 23 24 25 26 27 28 29 30 31 32 34 35 36 37 38 39 40 41 42 43 44 45 46 47 48 49 50 51 52 53 54 55 56 57 58 59 60 61 63 64 65 66 67 68 69 70 71 72 73 74 **P**3 6 **S** Carolinas HealthCare System, Charlotte, NC **N** Carolinas Hospital Network, Charlotte, NC

| | 16 | 10 | 843 | 36704 | 619 | 311061 | 5449 | 460382 | 184204 | 6724 |

Hospital, Address, Telephone, Administrator, Approval, Facility, and Physician Codes, Health Care System, Network	Classification Codes		Utilization Data					Expense (thousands) of dollars		
	Control	Service	Staffed Beds	Admissions	Census	Outpatient Visits	Births	Total	Payroll	Personnel

★ American Hospital Association (AHA) membership
□ Joint Commission on Accreditation of Healthcare Organizations (JCAHO) accreditation
+ American Osteopathic Healthcare Association (AOHA) membership
○ American Osteopathic Association (AOA) accreditation
△ Commission on Accreditation of Rehabilitation Facilities (CARF) accreditation
Control codes 61, 63, 64, 71, 72 and 73 indicate hospitals listed by AOHA, but not registered by AHA. For definition of numerical codes, see page A4

Hospital	Control	Service	Staffed Beds	Admissions	Census	Outpatient Visits	Births	Total	Payroll	Personnel
⊠ △ CHARLOTTE INSTITUTE OF REHABILITATION, 1100 Blythe Boulevard, Zip 28203–5864; tel. 704/355–4300; Don Gabriel, Administrator **A**1 3 7 9 10 **F**1 2 3 4 5 6 7 8 9 10 11 12 13 15 16 17 18 19 20 21 22 23 25 26 27 28 29 30 31 32 34 35 36 37 38 39 40 41 42 43 44 45 46 47 48 49 50 51 52 53 54 55 56 57 58 59 61 63 64 65 66 67 69 70 71 72 73 74 **P**3 4 6 7 **S** Carolinas HealthCare System, Charlotte, NC **N** Carolinas Hospital Network, Charlotte, NC	16	46	133	1800	101	58737	—	31187	19898	—
□ CHARTER PINES BEHAVIORAL HEALTH SYSTEM, 3621 Randolph Road, Zip 28211–1337, Mailing Address: P.O. Box 221709, Zip 28222–1709; tel. 704/365–5368; Bruce Chambers, Ph.D., Chief Executive Officer (Nonreporting) **A**1 9 10 **S** Magellan Health Services, Atlanta, GA	33	22	60	—	—	—	—	—	—	—
⊠ △ MERCY HOSPITAL, 2001 Vail Avenue, Zip 28207–1289; tel. 704/379–5000; C. Curtis Copenhaver, Chief Executive Officer **A**1 6 7 9 10 **F**3 4 8 10 11 12 14 15 16 19 21 22 28 30 31 32 35 37 39 43 44 46 48 49 63 65 67 71 73 **S** Carolinas HealthCare System, Charlotte, NC **N** Carolinas Hospital Network, Charlotte, NC	16	10	244	7495	136	—	0	68760	30728	1053
⊠ PRESBYTERIAN HOSPITAL, 200 Hawthorne Lane, Zip 28204–2528, Mailing Address: P.O. Box 33549, Zip 28233–3549; tel. 704/384–4000; Thomas R. Revels, President and Chief Executive Officer (Total facility includes 12 beds in nursing home–type unit) **A**1 2 6 9 10 **F**3 4 5 7 8 10 11 12 13 15 17 18 19 21 22 23 25 27 28 29 30 31 32 33 34 35 37 38 39 40 41 42 43 44 45 46 47 49 51 52 53 54 55 56 57 58 59 60 61 63 64 65 67 70 71 73 74 **P**1 6 **S** Novant Health, Winston Salem, NC	23	10	551	29625	406	127618	4248	306487	128146	3548
PRESBYTERIAN SPECIALTY HOSPITAL, 1600 East Third Street, Zip 28204–3282, Mailing Address: P.O. Box 34425, Zip 28234–4425; tel. 704/384–6000; Chip Day, Acting Vice President (Nonreporting) **A**9 10 **S** Novant Health, Winston Salem, NC	23	45	15	—	—	—	—	—	—	—
⊠ PRESBYTERIAN–ORTHOPAEDIC HOSPITAL, 1901 Randolph Road, Zip 28207–1195; tel. 704/370–1549; Paul M. Jenson, Chief Executive Officer (Nonreporting) **A**1 9 10 **S** Novant Health, Winston Salem, NC	33	47	166	—	—	—	—	—	—	—
□ UNIVERSITY HOSPITAL, 8800 North Tryon Street, Zip 28262–8415, Mailing Address: P.O. Box 560727, Zip 28256–0727; tel. 704/548–6000; W. Spencer Lilly, Administrator **A**1 9 10 **F**4 6 7 8 10 12 14 16 19 20 21 22 24 28 29 30 31 32 34 35 37 38 39 40 41 42 43 44 49 50 51 53 54 55 56 57 58 59 60 61 63 65 66 67 69 70 71 72 73 74 **P**6 7 **S** Carolinas HealthCare System, Charlotte, NC **N** Carolinas Hospital Network, Charlotte, NC	16	10	115	5344	52	69517	1313	36182	15716	441
CHEROKEE—Swain County										
⊠ U. S. PUBLIC HEALTH SERVICE INDIAN HOSPITAL, Hospital Road, Zip 28719; tel. 704/497–9163; Janet Belcourt, Administrator **A**1 10 **F**3 8 12 13 14 15 16 17 20 22 25 26 27 28 30 32 34 39 41 45 49 51 53 58 61 65 67 68 71 74 **P**6 **S** U. S. Public Health Service Indian Health Service, Rockville, MD	44	10	28	1056	17	85904	0	—	—	—
CHERRY POINT—Craven County										
⊠ NAVAL HOSPITAL, Mailing Address: PSC Box 8023, Zip 28533–0023; tel. 919/466–0336; Captain Paul D. Garst, MC, USN, Commanding Officer (Nonreporting) **A**1 **S** Department of Navy, Washington, DC	43	10	23	—	—	—	—	—	—	—
CLINTON—Sampson County										
⊠ SAMPSON REGIONAL MEDICAL CENTER, (Formerly Sampson County Memorial Hospital), 607 Beaman Street, Zip 28328–2697, Mailing Address: Drawer 258, Zip 28329–0258; tel. 910/592–8511; Lee Pridgen, Jr., Administrator (Total facility includes 30 beds in nursing home–type unit) **A**1 9 10 **F**7 8 14 15 16 19 22 32 35 37 40 44 46 64 65 71 **N** UNC Health Network, Chapel Hill, NC	13	10	141	4080	74	54460	339	31187	15242	576
CLYDE—Haywood County										
⊠ HAYWOOD REGIONAL MEDICAL CENTER, 262 Leroy George Drive, Zip 28721–9434; tel. 704/456–7311; David O. Rice, President (Total facility includes 20 beds in nursing home–type unit) **A**1 9 10 **F**7 8 10 12 14 15 16 17 19 21 22 24 26 28 29 30 32 33 35 37 40 41 42 44 45 46 49 51 54 56 60 65 67 71 72 73 74 **P**3 8	13	10	200	5281	62	71589	318	45769	20193	714
COLUMBUS—Polk County										
□ ST. LUKE'S HOSPITAL, 220 Hospital Drive, Zip 28722–9473; tel. 704/894–3311; C. Cameron Highsmith, Jr., President and Chief Executive Officer **A**1 9 10 **F**12 14 16 19 21 22 26 28 30 37 39 44 46 52 56 57 58 64 65 71 73	23	10	73	2025	49	27931	—	14152	6629	367
CONCORD—Cabarrus County										
⊠ NORTHEAST MEDICAL CENTER, (Formerly Cabarrus Memorial Hospital), 920 Church Street North, Zip 28025–2983; tel. 704/783–3000; Laurence C. Hinsdale, President and Chief Executive Officer **A**1 2 3 5 6 9 10 **F**4 7 8 10 11 14 15 16 19 21 22 24 30 32 33 35 36 37 38 40 41 42 43 44 46 58 60 65 72 73 74 **P**3	23	10	342	14310	208	340677	1995	151308	70431	2125
CROSSNORE—Avery County										
⊠ SLOOP MEMORIAL HOSPITAL, One Crossnore Drive, Zip 28616, Mailing Address: Drawer 470, Zip 28616; tel. 704/733–9231; Edward C. Greene, Jr., President **A**1 9 10 **F**7 8 19 21 22 28 30 37 40 44 49 52 56 57 64 65 71 73 **P**6 **N** Mountain States Healthcare Network, Johnson City, TN	23	10	38	1608	19	24346	94	13116	6746	307
DANBURY—Stokes County										
★ STOKES–REYNOLDS MEMORIAL HOSPITAL, Mailing Address: P.O. Box 10, Zip 27016–0010; tel. 336/593–2831; Sandra D. Priddy, President (Total facility includes 40 beds in nursing home–type unit) **A**9 10 **F**3 8 14 15 16 19 22 25 33 37 44 57 64 65 71 72 73 74 **P**6 7 **N** Wake Forest University Baptist Medical Center, Winston–Salem, NC	21	10	93	1080	77	24053	—	11113	5258	232

Hospital, Address, Telephone, Administrator, Approval, Facility, and Physician Codes, Health Care System, Network	Classification Codes		Utilization Data					Expense (thousands) of dollars		
	Control	Service	Staffed Beds	Admissions	Census	Outpatient Visits	Births	Total	Payroll	Personnel

★ American Hospital Association (AHA) membership
□ Joint Commission on Accreditation of Healthcare Organizations (JCAHO) accreditation
+ American Osteopathic Healthcare Association (AOHA) membership
○ American Osteopathic Association (AOA) accreditation
△ Commission on Accreditation of Rehabilitation Facilities (CARF) accreditation
Control codes 61, 63, 64, 71, 72 and 73 indicate hospitals listed by AOHA, but not registered by AHA. For definition of numerical codes, see page A4.

DUNN—Harnett County

□ BETSY JOHNSON REGIONAL HOSPITAL, (Formerly Betsy Johnson Memorial Hospital), 800 Tilghman Drive, Zip 28334–5599, Mailing Address: Drawer 1706, Zip 28335–1706; tel. 910/892–7161; Shannon D. Brown, President **A**1 9 10 **F**7 8 14 15 17 19 22 28 30 34 35 37 40 44 46 49 65 67 71 73

| | 23 | 10 | 88 | 3642 | 39 | 50575 | 562 | 21645 | 10650 | 362 |

DURHAM—Durham County

✠ DUKE UNIVERSITY MEDICAL CENTER, (Includes Duke University Hospital), Erwin Road, Zip 27710, Mailing Address: P.O. Box 3708, Zip 27710–3708; tel. 919/684–8111; Michael D. Israel, Chief Executive Officer and Vice Chancellor **A**1 2 3 5 8 9 10 **F**2 4 5 7 8 9 10 11 12 13 15 16 17 19 20 21 22 23 24 26 28 29 30 31 34 35 37 38 39 40 41 42 43 44 45 46 47 48 49 50 51 52 53 54 55 56 57 58 59 60 61 63 65 66 67 68 69 70 71 72 73 74 **P**5 N Duke Health Network, Durham, NC

| | 23 | 10 | 839 | 35564 | 672 | 776435 | 2337 | 613414 | 234495 | — |

✠ DURHAM REGIONAL HOSPITAL, 3643 North Roxboro Road, Zip 27704–2763; tel. 919/470–4000; Richard L. Myers, President and Chief Executive Officer **A**1 3 5 6 9 10 **F**3 4 7 8 10 11 12 13 15 16 17 19 21 22 23 24 25 26 27 28 29 30 31 32 34 35 37 39 40 41 42 43 44 45 46 49 51 52 53 54 55 56 57 58 59 60 63 65 67 71 72 73 74 **P**1

| | 13 | 10 | 208 | 14056 | 176 | 82352 | 2384 | 118582 | 58150 | 1783 |

NORTH CAROLINA EYE AND EAR HOSPITAL, 1110 West Main Street, Zip 27701–2000; tel. 919/682–9341; H. Ed Jones, Chief Executive Officer (Nonreporting) **A**9 10

| | 33 | 45 | 24 | — | — | — | — | — | — | — |

✠ VETERANS AFFAIRS MEDICAL CENTER, 508 Fulton Street, Zip 27705–3897; tel. 919/286–0411; Michael B. Phaup, Director (Total facility includes 120 beds in nursing home–type unit) **A**1 3 5 8 9 **F**2 3 4 8 10 11 15 16 19 20 21 22 26 27 28 29 30 31 32 34 35 37 39 41 42 43 44 45 46 49 51 52 54 55 56 57 58 60 63 65 67 69 71 73 74 **S** Department of Veterans Affairs, Washington, DC

| | 45 | 10 | 330 | 8275 | 151 | 154679 | — | 137565 | 61144 | 1340 |

EDEN—Rockingham County

✠ MOREHEAD MEMORIAL HOSPITAL, 117 East King's Highway, Zip 27288–5299; tel. 336/623–9711; Robert Enders, President (Total facility includes 128 beds in nursing home–type unit) **A**1 9 10 **F**7 8 12 13 15 16 17 19 21 22 23 26 28 30 32 34 35 36 37 39 40 41 42 44 45 46 49 60 64 65 66 67 68 71 73 74 **P**6 8 **S** Quorum Health Group/Quorum Health Resources, Inc., Brentwood, TN **N** Wake Forest University Baptist Medical Center, Winston–Salem, NC; UNC Health Network, Chapel Hill, NC

| | 23 | 10 | 236 | 5452 | 185 | 94289 | 708 | 37885 | 17166 | 626 |

EDENTON—Chowan County

✠ CHOWAN HOSPITAL, 211 Virginia Road, Zip 27932–0629, Mailing Address: P.O. Box 629, Zip 27932–0629; tel. 919/482–8451; Barbara R. Cale, Administrator (Total facility includes 40 beds in nursing home–type unit) **A**1 9 10 **F**7 8 12 14 15 16 17 19 20 21 22 28 30 31 32 33 34 37 39 40 41 42 44 45 46 49 52 54 56 58 59 64 65 67 71 73 74 **P**3 **N** Eastern Carolina Health Network, Greenville, NC

| | 13 | 10 | 111 | 2649 | 63 | 22936 | 376 | 18746 | 9729 | 450 |

ELIZABETH CITY—Pasquotank County

✠ ALBEMARLE HOSPITAL, 1144 North Road Street, Zip 27909, Mailing Address: P.O. Box 1587, Zip 27906–1587; tel. 252/335–0531; Philip D. Bagby, President and Chief Executive Officer **A**1 9 10 **F**7 8 10 11 12 16 17 19 20 21 22 23 24 27 28 29 30 34 35 37 39 40 41 42 44 45 46 49 60 63 65 67 73 **N** Eastern Carolina Health Network, Greenville, NC

| | 13 | 10 | 145 | 7167 | 106 | 79690 | 734 | 47531 | 22144 | 723 |

ELIZABETHTOWN—Bladen County

✠ BLADEN COUNTY HOSPITAL, 501 South Poplar Street, Zip 28337–0398, Mailing Address: P.O. Box 398, Zip 28337–0398; tel. 910/862–5100; Leo A. Petit, Jr., Chief Executive Officer (Total facility includes 10 beds in nursing home–type unit) **A**1 9 10 **F**7 8 11 15 16 17 19 21 22 25 28 29 30 32 33 34 35 37 39 40 44 45 49 51 59 64 65 67 71 72 73 **P**6 8 **N** Bladen County Hospital, Elizabethtown, NC

| | 13 | 10 | 58 | 1843 | 31 | 29992 | 248 | 14490 | 6713 | 239 |

ELKIN—Surry County

✠ HUGH CHATHAM MEMORIAL HOSPITAL, Parkwood Drive, Zip 28621–0560, Mailing Address: P.O. Box 560, Zip 28621–0560; tel. 910/527–7000; Richard D. Osmus, Chief Executive Officer (Total facility includes 120 beds in nursing home–type unit) **A**1 9 10 **F**6 7 8 10 12 14 15 16 19 21 22 26 28 30 32 33 34 35 37 39 40 41 42 44 45 49 51 61 62 63 64 65 66 67 71 73 74 **P**1 **S** Quorum Health Group/Quorum Health Resources, Inc., Brentwood, TN **N** Wake Forest University Baptist Medical Center, Winston–Salem, NC

| | 23 | 10 | 201 | 4376 | 148 | 18679 | 265 | 31764 | 14065 | 510 |

ERWIN—Harnett County

✠ GOOD HOPE HOSPITAL, 410 Denim Drive, Zip 28339–0668, Mailing Address: P.O. Box 668, Zip 28339–0668; tel. 910/897–6151; Donald E. Annis, Chief Executive Officer **A**1 10 **F**11 16 17 19 21 22 28 29 30 32 33 35 44 49 51 52 54 55 56 57 65 66 67 71 73 **P**6 **S** Quorum Health Group/Quorum Health Resources, Inc., Brentwood, TN **N** UNC Health Network, Chapel Hill, NC

| | 23 | 10 | 72 | 2963 | 38 | 27047 | — | 13543 | 6433 | 266 |

FAYETTEVILLE—Cumberland County

✠ △ CAPE FEAR VALLEY HEALTH SYSTEM, 1638 Owen Drive, Zip 28304–3431, Mailing Address: P.O. Box 2000, Zip 28302–2000; tel. 910/609–4000; John T. Carlisle, Chief Executive Officer **A**1 2 3 5 7 9 10 **F**2 3 4 7 8 10 11 12 15 16 17 19 20 21 22 23 25 26 27 28 29 30 32 33 35 37 38 39 40 41 42 43 44 45 46 48 49 51 52 53 55 56 57 58 59 60 65 66 67 71 73 74 **P**6

| | 13 | 10 | 347 | 19026 | 316 | 287498 | 4207 | 180781 | 83474 | 3090 |

COLUMBIA HIGHSMITH–RAINEY MEMORIAL HOSPITAL See Highsmith–Rainey Memorial Hospital

Hospital, Address, Telephone, Administrator, Approval, Facility, and Physician Codes, Health Care System, Network	Classification Codes		Utilization Data					Expense (thousands) of dollars		
★ American Hospital Association (AHA) membership □ Joint Commission on Accreditation of Healthcare Organizations (JCAHO) accreditation + American Osteopathic Healthcare Association (AOHA) membership ○ American Osteopathic Association (AOA) accreditation △ Commission on Accreditation of Rehabilitation Facilities (CARF) accreditation Control codes 61, 63, 64, 71, 72 and 73 indicate hospitals listed by AOHA, but not registered by AHA. For definition of numerical codes, see page A4	Control	Service	Staffed Beds	Admissions	Census	Outpatient Visits	Births	Total	Payroll	Personnel

	Control	Service	Staffed Beds	Admissions	Census	Outpatient Visits	Births	Total	Payroll	Personnel
CUMBERLAND HOSPITAL, 3425 Melrose Road, Zip 28304–1695; tel. 910/609–3000; James P. Sprouse, Administrator (Nonreporting) **A**10	13	22	110	—	—	—	—	—	—	—
✚ HIGHSMITH–RAINEY MEMORIAL HOSPITAL, (Formerly Columbia Highsmith–Rainey Memorial Hospital), 150 Robeson Street, Zip 28301–5570; tel. 910/609–1000; Charles T. Adams, Interim Chief Executive Officer (Nonreporting) **A**1 9 10 **S** Columbia/HCA Healthcare Corporation, Nashville, TN	33	10	133	—	—	—	—	—	—	—
✚ VETERANS AFFAIRS MEDICAL CENTER, 2300 Ramsey Street, Zip 28301–3899; tel. 910/822–7059; Richard J. Baltz, Director (Total facility includes 39 beds in nursing home–type unit) **A**1 9 **F**1 3 8 14 15 16 17 19 20 21 22 24 26 27 28 29 30 31 32 33 34 37 39 41 44 46 48 49 51 52 55 56 57 58 64 65 67 71 73 74 **P**6 **S** Department of Veterans Affairs, Washington, DC	45	10	193	3867	105	140520	—	50312	25118	698
FLETCHER—Henderson County										
✚ PARK RIDGE HOSPITAL, Naples Road, Zip 28732, Mailing Address: P.O. Box 1569, Zip 28732–1569; tel. 704/684–8501; Michael V. Gentry, President **A**1 10 **F**7 8 10 11 12 14 15 19 21 22 23 32 33 37 39 40 41 44 45 46 52 53 56 57 58 59 65 67 71 73 **P**5 6 **S** Adventist Health System Sunbelt Health Care Corporation, Winter Park, FL	23	10	90	3500	51	34570	426	34968	16171	526
FORT BRAGG—Cumberland County										
✚ WOMACK ARMY MEDICAL CENTER, Normandy Drive, Zip 28307–5000; tel. 910/432–4802; Colonel Thomas H. Auer, Commander (Nonreporting) **A**1 3 5 **S** Department of the Army, Office of the Surgeon General, Falls Church, VA	42	10	173	—	—	—	—	—	—	—
FRANKLIN—Macon County										
✚ ANGEL MEDICAL CENTER, Riverview and White Oak Streets, Zip 28734, Mailing Address: P.O. Box 1209, Zip 28734–1209; tel. 704/524–8411; Michael E. Zuliani, Chief Executive Officer (Nonreporting) **A**1 9 10 **S** Quorum Health Group/Quorum Health Resources, Inc., Brentwood, TN **N** Wake Forest University Baptist Medical Center, Winston–Salem, NC	23	10	59	—	—	—	—	—	—	—
FUQUAY–VARINA—Wake County										
SOUTHERN WAKE HOSPITAL See Wake Medical Center, Raleigh										
GASTONIA—Gaston County										
✚ GASTON MEMORIAL HOSPITAL, 2525 Court Drive, Zip 28054–2142, Mailing Address: P.O. Box 1747, Zip 28053–1747; tel. 704/834–2000; Wayne F. Shovelin, President and Chief Executive Officer **A**1 2 9 10 **F**3 7 8 10 11 14 15 16 17 18 19 20 21 22 23 24 28 29 30 32 33 34 37 39 40 41 42 44 45 46 49 52 53 54 55 56 57 58 59 60 63 64 65 67 70 71 72 73 74	23	10	329	17157	241	109298	2228	122253	57613	1734
GOLDSBORO—Wayne County										
□ CHERRY HOSPITAL, Stevens Mill Road, Zip 27533–8000, Mailing Address: Caller Box 8000, Zip 27533–8000; tel. 919/731–3200; Liston G. Edwards, Director (Total facility includes 173 beds in nursing home–type unit) **A**1 3 5 10 **F**12 14 15 16 20 46 52 53 57 64 65 73 **P**6	12	22	662	2205	498	—	—	54375	40662	1261
✚ WAYNE MEMORIAL HOSPITAL, 2700 Wayne Memorial Drive, Zip 27534–8001, Mailing Address: P.O. Box 8001, Zip 27533–8001; tel. 919/736–1110; James W. Hubbell, President and Chief Executive Officer **A**1 2 9 10 **F**7 8 10 12 14 15 17 19 21 22 23 26 29 30 31 32 33 34 35 37 39 41 42 44 45 46 49 52 53 54 55 56 57 60 63 65 66 67 71 73 **N** Eastern Carolina Health Network, Greenville, NC	23	10	260	13408	183	86068	1320	77929	33205	1149
GREENSBORO—Guilford County										
□ CHARTER GREENSBORO BEHAVIORAL HEALTH SYSTEM, 700 Walter Reed Drive, Zip 27403–1129, Mailing Address: P.O. Box 10399, Zip 27404–0399; tel. 336/852–4821; Nancy Reaves, Chief Executive Officer (Nonreporting) **A**1 9 10 **S** Magellan Health Services, Atlanta, GA	33	22	68	—	—	—	—	—	—	—
✚ △ MOSES CONE HEALTH SYSTEM, (Formerly Moses H Cone Memorial Hospital), (Includes Moses H. Cone Memorial Hospital, 1200 North Elm Street, Zip 27401; tel. 910/574–7000; Wesley Long Community Hospital, 501 North Elam Avenue, Zip 27403–1199, Mailing Address: P.O. Box 2747, Zip 27402–2747; tel. 910/854–6100; Gary L. Park, President; Women's Hospital of Greensboro, 801 Green Valley Road, Zip 27408; tel. 910/574–6500), 1200 North Elm Street, Zip 27401–1020; tel. 336/832–1000; Dennis R. Barry, President (Total facility includes 290 beds in nursing home–type unit) **A**1 2 3 5 7 8 9 10 **F**4 5 7 8 10 11 12 14 15 16 17 19 20 21 22 23 25 26 28 29 30 31 32 33 34 35 37 38 39 40 41 42 43 44 45 46 48 49 52 54 55 57 59 60 61 63 64 65 66 67 70 71 72 73 74 **P**1 7 **N** North Carolina Health Network, Charlotte, NC	23	10	1066	38055	874	362301	5162	327564	151461	4150
□ VENCOR HOSPITAL–GREENSBORO, (MEDICALLY COMPLEX LONGTERM ACU), 2401 Southside Boulevard, Zip 27406–3311; tel. 336/271–2800; Leanne Fiorentino, Chief Executive Officer **A**1 10 **F**12 19 21 22 26 35 37 39 46 50 54 63 64 65 67 71 73 **S** Vencor, Incorporated, Louisville, KY	33	49	125	722	110	0	0	22905	11290	—
WESLEY LONG COMMUNITY HOSPITAL See Moses Cone Health System										
WOMEN'S HOSPITAL OF GREENSBORO See Moses Cone Health System										
GREENVILLE—Pitt County										
✚ △ PITT COUNTY MEMORIAL HOSPITAL–UNIVERSITY HEALTH SYSTEM OF EASTERN CAROLINA, 2100 Stantonsburg Road, Zip 27835–6028, Mailing Address: Box 6028, Zip 27835–6028; tel. 919/816–4451; Dave C. McRae, President and Chief Executive Officer **A**1 2 3 5 7 8 9 10 **F**4 7 8 9 10 11 12 13 14 15 16 17 19 20 21 22 24 25 27 30 31 32 33 34 35 37 38 39 40 41 42 43 44 45 46 47 48 49 51 52 53 54 55 56 57 58 59 60 61 63 64 65 67 69 70 71 72 73 74 **P**1 5 7 **N** Eastern Carolina Health Network, Greenville, NC	13	10	684	30725	561	139385	2950	308806	139056	4214

Hospital, Address, Telephone, Administrator, Approval, Facility, and Physician Codes, Health Care System, Network	Classi-fication Codes		Utilization Data					Expense (thousands) of dollars		
★ American Hospital Association (AHA) membership ☐ Joint Commission on Accreditation of Healthcare Organizations (JCAHO) accreditation + American Osteopathic Healthcare Association (AOHA) membership ○ American Osteopathic Association (AOA) accreditation △ Commission on Accreditation of Rehabilitation Facilities (CARF) accreditation Control codes 61, 63, 64, 71, 72 and 73 indicate hospitals listed by AOHA, but not registered by AHA. For definition of numerical codes, see page A4	Control	Service	Staffed Beds	Admissions	Census	Outpatient Visits	Births	Total	Payroll	Personnel
WALTER B. JONES ALCOHOL AND DRUG ABUSE TREATMENT CENTER, 2577 West Fifth Street, Zip 27834–7813; tel. 919/830–3426; Phillip A. Mooring, Director **A**10 **F**2 15 16 **P**6	12	82	76	1214	345	—	—	5782	3457	—
HAMLET—Richmond County										
☐ HAMLET HOSPITAL, Rice and Vance Streets, Zip 28345, Mailing Address: P.O. Box 1109, Zip 28345–1109; tel. 910/582–3611; Joe D. Howell, Executive Director (Nonreporting) **A**1 10 **S** Health Management Associates, Naples, FL	33	10	64	—	—	—	—	—	—	—
HENDERSON—Vance County										
⊠ △ MARIA PARHAM HOSPITAL, 566 Ruin Creek Road, Zip 27536–2957; tel. 252/438–4143; Philip S. Lakernick, President and Chief Executive Officer **A**1 7 9 10 **F**5 7 8 10 11 14 15 16 17 19 20 21 22 23 24 26 28 29 30 31 32 33 34 35 40 41 42 44 45 46 48 49 56 58 65 66 67 71 72 73 74 **P**8 **N** Duke Health Network, Durham, NC; UNC Health Network, Chapel Hill, NC	23	10	102	4394	55	71685	623	30643	12795	521
HENDERSONVILLE—Henderson County										
⊠ MARGARET R. PARDEE MEMORIAL HOSPITAL, 715 Fleming Street, Zip 28791–2563; tel. 828/696–1000; Frank J. Aaron, Jr., Chief Executive Officer (Total facility includes 40 beds in nursing home–type unit) **A**1 2 3 9 10 **F**1 7 8 11 12 14 15 16 17 19 21 22 23 26 28 29 30 32 34 35 36 37 40 41 42 44 45 46 49 51 52 54 55 56 57 58 59 60 61 63 64 65 67 71 72 73 74 **P**1 5 6 7 8 **N** Western North Carolina Health Network, Asheville, NC	13	10	223	7732	142	89119	392	64547	27748	994
HICKORY—Catawba County										
⊠ CATAWBA MEMORIAL HOSPITAL, 810 Fairgrove Church Road S.E., Zip 28602–9643; tel. 704/326–3000; J. Anthony Rose, President and Chief Executive Officer **A**1 9 10 **F**7 8 10 14 15 16 17 19 21 22 23 24 25 26 28 30 31 33 34 35 37 40 41 42 44 45 46 48 49 52 54 56 57 58 60 61 65 66 67 71 73 74 **P**8 **N** Carolinas Hospital Network, Charlotte, NC; Wake Forest University Baptist Medical Center, Winston–Salem, NC	13	10	189	7491	104	129360	1458	70821	32193	941
⊠ △ FRYE REGIONAL MEDICAL CENTER, (Includes Frye Regional Medical Center–South Campus, tel. 704/328–2226), 420 North Center Street, Zip 28601–5049; tel. 704/322–6070; Dennis Phillips, Chief Executive Officer (Nonreporting) **A**1 7 9 10 **S** TENET Healthcare Corporation, Santa Barbara, CA	33	10	355	—	—	—	—	—	—	—
HIGH POINT—Guilford County										
⊠ HIGH POINT REGIONAL HEALTH SYSTEM, 601 North Elm Street, Zip 27262–4398, Mailing Address: P.O. Box HP–5, Zip 27261; tel. 336/884–8400; Jeffrey S. Miller, President (Total facility includes 30 beds in nursing home–type unit) **A**1 2 9 10 **F**2 3 4 5 7 8 10 11 12 13 14 15 16 17 18 19 20 21 22 23 24 25 26 28 29 30 31 32 33 34 35 36 37 39 40 41 42 43 44 45 46 49 52 54 55 56 57 58 59 60 64 65 66 67 68 71 72 73 74 **P**3 5 8	23	10	342	16720	249	74603	1783	108787	47111	1498
HIGHLANDS—Macon County										
⊠ HIGHLANDS–CASHIERS HOSPITAL, Hospital Drive, Zip 28741, Mailing Address: P.O. Drawer 190, Zip 28741–0190; tel. 704/526–1200; Jack A. Calloway, Chief Executive Officer (Total facility includes 60 beds in nursing home–type unit) **A**1 10 **F**6 8 15 19 20 22 28 30 31 32 33 34 39 44 49 64 65 71 73	23	10	104	519	69	9319	—	7046	3706	144
JACKSONVILLE—Onslow County										
☐ BRYNN MARR BEHAVIORAL HEALTHCARE SYSTEM, 192 Village Drive, Zip 28546–7299; tel. 910/577–1400; Dale Armstrong, Chief Executive Officer (Nonreporting) **A**1 10 **S** Ramsay Health Care, Inc., Coral Gables, FL	33	22	76	—	—	—	—	—	—	—
⊠ ONSLOW MEMORIAL HOSPITAL, 317 Western Boulevard, Zip 28540, Mailing Address: P.O. Box 1358, Zip 28540–1358; tel. 910/577–2281; Douglas Kramer, Chief Executive Officer (Nonreporting) **A**1 9 10 **N** Eastern Carolina Health Network, Greenville, NC	16	10	133	—	—	—	—	—	—	—
JEFFERSON—Ashe County										
⊠ ASHE MEMORIAL HOSPITAL, 200 Hospital Avenue, Zip 28640; tel. 336/246–7101; R. D. Williams, Administrator and Chief Executive Officer (Total facility includes 60 beds in nursing home–type unit) **A**1 9 10 **F**7 8 14 15 16 19 22 24 28 29 34 35 39 40 41 44 45 49 64 65 71 73 **S** Quorum Health Group/Quorum Health Resources, Inc., Brentwood, TN **N** Wake Forest University Baptist Medical Center, Winston–Salem, NC	23	10	115	2030	86	32678	130	13706	5352	284
KENANSVILLE—Duplin County										
⊠ DUPLIN GENERAL HOSPITAL, 401 North Main Street, Zip 28349–9989, Mailing Address: P.O. Box 278, Zip 28349–0278; tel. 910/296–0941; Richard E. Harrell, President and Chief Executive Officer (Total facility includes 20 beds in nursing home–type unit) **A**1 9 10 **F**7 8 14 15 16 19 21 22 26 31 37 39 40 42 44 49 51 52 55 56 57 64 65 71 73 74 **P**6 **N** Eastern Carolina Health Network, Greenville, NC	23	10	80	3101	57	32179	585	15557	7565	324
KINGS MOUNTAIN—Cleveland County										
☐ KINGS MOUNTAIN HOSPITAL, 706 West King Street, Zip 28086–2708, Mailing Address: P.O. Box 339, Zip 28086–0339; tel. 704/739–3601; Hank Neal, Administrator (Total facility includes 10 beds in nursing home–type unit) **A**1 9 10 **F**8 11 14 19 22 37 38 44 47 49 52 56 64 65 71 73 **S** Carolinas HealthCare System, Charlotte, NC **N** Carolinas Hospital Network, Charlotte, NC	16	10	72	2191	39	29888	—	10270	4784	177
KINSTON—Lenoir County										
CASWELL CENTER, 2415 West Vernon Avenue, Zip 28501–3321; tel. 919/559–5222; Jim S. Woodall, Director **F**11 14 15 16 20 27 28 31 37 39 41 46 65 73	12	62	829	47	664	568	—	59195	41419	1717
⊠ LENOIR MEMORIAL HOSPITAL, 100 Airport Road, Zip 28501, Mailing Address: P.O. Box 1678, Zip 28503–1678; tel. 252/522–7171; Gary E. Black, President and Chief Executive Officer (Total facility includes 26 beds in nursing home–type unit) **A**1 2 9 10 **F**6 7 10 12 14 15 16 17 19 20 21 22 24 26 27 28 29 30 32 34 35 37 39 40 41 42 44 45 46 48 49 59 60 64 65 70 71 73 **N** Eastern Carolina Health Network, Greenville, NC	13	10	255	9401	154	63879	732	60740	26510	972

Hospital, Address, Telephone, Administrator, Approval, Facility, and Physician Codes, Health Care System, Network	Classi-fication Codes		Utilization Data					Expense (thousands) of dollars		
★ American Hospital Association (AHA) membership ☐ Joint Commission on Accreditation of Healthcare Organizations (JCAHO) accreditation + American Osteopathic Healthcare Association (AOHA) membership ○ American Osteopathic Association (AOA) accreditation △ Commission on Accreditation of Rehabilitation Facilities (CARF) accreditation Control codes 61, 63, 64, 71, 72 and 73 indicate hospitals listed by AOHA, but not registered by AHA. For definition of numerical codes, see page A4	Control	Service	Staffed Beds	Admissions	Census	Outpatient Visits	Births	Total	Payroll	Personnel

LAURINBURG—Scotland County

✠ SCOTLAND MEMORIAL HOSPITAL, 500 Lauchwood Drive, Zip 28352–5599; tel. 910/291–7000; Gregory C. Wood, Chief Executive Officer (Total facility includes 50 beds in nursing home–type unit) **A**1 9 10 **F**2 3 7 8 10 16 17 18 19 20 21 22 23 26 27 28 29 30 31 32 33 34 35 37 39 40 41 42 44 46 49 51 60 61 62 63 64 65 66 67 68 71 72 73 74 **P**8 **N** Carolinas Hospital Network, Charlotte, NC; UNC Health Network, Chapel Hill, NC

| | 23 | 10 | 174 | 4099 | 54 | 58674 | 532 | 36640 | 14965 | 595 |

LENOIR—Caldwell County

✠ CALDWELL MEMORIAL HOSPITAL, 321 Mulberry Street S.W., Zip 28645–5720, Mailing Address: P.O. Box 1890, Zip 28645–1890; tel. 704/757–5100; Frederick L. Soule, President and Chief Executive Officer (Total facility includes 10 beds in nursing home–type unit) **A**1 9 10 **F**7 8 10 12 14 15 16 17 19 21 22 24 27 28 30 32 33 34 35 37 40 41 42 44 45 49 59 64 65 66 67 71 72 73 74 **P**1 5 **N** Wake Forest University Baptist Medical Center, Winston–Salem, NC

| | 23 | 10 | 82 | 3932 | 36 | 144626 | 464 | 34731 | 17428 | 655 |

LEXINGTON—Davidson County

✠ LEXINGTON MEMORIAL HOSPITAL, 250 Hospital Drive, Zip 27292, Mailing Address: P.O. Box 1817, Zip 27293–1817; tel. 336/248–5161; John A. Cashion, FACHE, President **A**1 9 10 **F**3 7 8 10 14 15 19 22 25 29 30 32 34 35 37 39 40 41 42 44 45 46 49 51 53 54 55 56 58 59 63 65 67 71 72 73 **P**2 3 5 8 **N** Wake Forest University Baptist Medical Center, Winston–Salem, NC

| | 23 | 10 | 87 | 4161 | 48 | 72401 | 667 | 30354 | 14016 | 500 |

LINCOLNTON—Lincoln County

☐ LINCOLN MEDICAL CENTER, 200 Gamble Drive, Zip 28092–0677, Mailing Address: Box 677, Zip 28093–0677; tel. 704/735–3071; Peter W. Acker, President and Chief Executive Officer **A**1 9 10 **F**7 8 12 14 17 19 21 22 26 27 28 32 34 35 36 39 40 44 49 65 66 67 71 73 **N** Carolinas Hospital Network, Charlotte, NC

| | 23 | 10 | 75 | 3387 | 46 | 41091 | 431 | 30996 | 14802 | 510 |

LOUISBURG—Franklin County

☐ FRANKLIN REGIONAL MEDICAL CENTER, 100 Hospital Drive, Zip 27549–2256, Mailing Address: P.O. Box 609, Zip 27549–0609; tel. 919/496–5131; Thomas Hanenburg, Administrator **A**1 9 10 **F**8 10 12 16 17 19 22 23 25 28 32 35 37 44 52 56 65 66 67 71 73 **P**1 **S** Health Management Associates, Naples, FL

| | 33 | 10 | 85 | 2400 | 37 | — | — | — | — | — |

LUMBERTON—Robeson County

✠ SOUTHEASTERN REGIONAL MEDICAL CENTER, 300 West 27th Street, Zip 28358–3017, Mailing Address: P.O. Box 1408, Zip 28359–1408; tel. 910/671–5000; J. L. Welsh, Jr., President (Total facility includes 115 beds in nursing home–type unit) **A**1 9 10 **F**1 2 3 7 8 10 14 15 16 17 19 20 21 22 24 28 29 30 31 32 33 34 35 37 38 39 40 41 42 44 45 46 49 51 52 53 56 57 60 65 66 67 71 73 **P**8 **N** UNC Health Network, Chapel Hill, NC

| | 23 | 10 | 281 | 11696 | 200 | 161894 | 1585 | 82234 | 37201 | 1115 |

MARION—McDowell County

✠ MCDOWELL HOSPITAL, 100 Rankin Drive, Zip 28752–4989, Mailing Address: P.O. Box 730, Zip 28752–0730; tel. 828/659–5000; Jeffrey M. Judd, President and Chief Executive Officer **A**1 9 10 **F**7 8 14 17 19 21 22 23 24 25 30 37 42 44 45 46 49 63 65 67 71 73 74 **P**6 **N** Western North Carolina Health Network, Asheville, NC

| | 23 | 10 | 65 | 2788 | 32 | 39411 | 322 | 18247 | 8051 | 307 |

MATTHEWS—Mecklenburg County

☐ PRESBYTERIAN HOSPITAL–MATTHEWS, 1500 Matthews Township Parkway, Zip 28105, Mailing Address: P.O. Box 3310, Zip 28106–3310; tel. 704/384–6500; Mark R. Farmer, Vice President and Administrator (Nonreporting) **A**1 9 10 **S** Novant Health, Winston Salem, NC

| | 23 | 10 | 82 | — | — | — | — | — | — | — |

MCCAIN—Hoke County

MCCAIN CORRECTIONAL HOSPITAL, Mailing Address: P.O. Box 5118, Zip 28361–5118; tel. 910/944–2351; F. David Hubbard, Superintendent (Nonreporting)

| | 12 | 11 | 81 | — | — | — | — | — | — | — |

MOCKSVILLE—Davie County

✠ DAVIE COUNTY HOSPITAL, 223 Hospital Street, Zip 27028–2038, Mailing Address: P.O. Box 1209, Zip 27028–1209; tel. 336/751–8100; Mike Kimel, Administrator **A**1 9 10 **F**8 11 13 15 16 17 19 22 28 29 30 32 33 34 35 37 39 41 44 45 46 49 65 71 **P**3 6 7 8 **S** Novant Health, Winston Salem, NC

| | 23 | 10 | 30 | 888 | 13 | 14929 | — | 8391 | 4220 | 147 |

MONROE—Union County

✠ UNION REGIONAL MEDICAL CENTER, 600 Hospital Drive, Zip 28112–6000, Mailing Address: P.O. Box 5003, Zip 28111–5003; tel. 704/283–3100; John W. Roberts, President and Chief Executive Officer (Total facility includes 66 beds in nursing home–type unit) **A**1 3 9 10 **F**2 3 4 5 6 7 8 10 11 12 13 14 17 18 19 20 21 22 23 24 25 26 27 28 29 30 31 32 34 35 36 37 39 40 41 42 43 44 45 46 49 50 51 53 54 55 56 57 58 59 60 61 62 63 64 65 66 67 68 69 70 71 72 73 74 **P**5 **S** Carolinas HealthCare System, Charlotte, NC **N** Carolinas Hospital Network, Charlotte, NC; Central Carolina Rural Hospital Alliance, Albemarle, NC

| | 16 | 10 | 207 | 6103 | 131 | 68127 | 935 | 40934 | 19251 | 667 |

MOORESVILLE—Iredell County

☐ LAKE NORMAN REGIONAL MEDICAL CENTER, 610 East Center Avenue, Zip 28115, Mailing Address: P.O. Box 360, Zip 28115–0360; tel. 704/663–1113; P. Paul Smith, Jr., Executive Director **A**1 10 **F**7 8 10 12 14 15 16 17 19 21 22 25 26 28 30 32 34 35 36 37 39 42 44 45 46 49 65 67 69 71 73 74 **P**8 **S** Health Management Associates, Naples, FL

| | 33 | 10 | 100 | 3520 | 42 | 34304 | 328 | — | — | 319 |

MOREHEAD CITY—Carteret County

✠ CARTERET GENERAL HOSPITAL, 3500 Arendell Street, Zip 28557–2901, Mailing Address: P.O. Box 1619, Zip 28557–1619; tel. 919/247–1616; F. A. Odell, III, FACHE, President (Total facility includes 108 beds in nursing home–type unit) **A**1 9 10 **F**7 8 11 15 16 17 19 21 22 23 25 28 30 32 33 39 40 41 42 44 45 46 49 53 54 56 63 64 65 67 71 72 73 **P**3 4 **N** Eastern Carolina Health Network, Greenville, NC

| | 13 | 10 | 225 | 5282 | 177 | 61176 | 518 | 41830 | 19184 | — |

Hospital, Address, Telephone, Administrator, Approval, Facility, and Physician Codes, Health Care System, Network	Classi-fication Codes		Utilization Data					Expense (thousands) of dollars		
	Control	Service	Staffed Beds	Admissions	Census	Outpatient Visits	Births	Total	Payroll	Personnel

★ American Hospital Association (AHA) membership
□ Joint Commission on Accreditation of Healthcare Organizations (JCAHO) accreditation
+ American Osteopathic Healthcare Association (AOHA) membership
○ American Osteopathic Association (AOA) accreditation
△ Commission on Accreditation of Rehabilitation Facilities (CARF) accreditation
Control codes 61, 63, 64, 71, 72 and 73 indicate hospitals listed by AOHA, but not registered by AHA. For definition of numerical codes, see page A4

MORGANTON—Burke County

□ BROUGHTON HOSPITAL, 1000 South Sterling Street, Zip 28655–3999; tel. 704/433–2111; Seth P. Hunt, Jr., Director (Total facility includes 44 beds in nursing home–type unit) **A**1 10 **F**19 21 28 35 46 52 53 55 56 57 60 63 64 65 67 71 73 **P**6 — *12 22 632 3425 502 — — 85834 36909 1352*

✠ GRACE HOSPITAL, 2201 South Sterling Street, Zip 28655–4058; tel. 704/438–2000; V. Otis Wilson, Jr., President **A**1 9 10 **F**7 8 10 12 13 15 17 19 21 22 23 24 28 30 32 34 35 37 39 40 41 42 44 49 52 57 59 60 62 65 67 71 72 73 **P**1 — *23 10 149 5391 62 89717 753 46751 20255 618*

MOUNT AIRY—Surry County

✠ NORTHERN HOSPITAL OF SURRY COUNTY, 830 Rockford Street, Zip 27030–5365, Mailing Address: P.O. Box 1101, Zip 27030–1101; tel. 910/719–7000; William B. James, Chief Executive Officer (Total facility includes 13 beds in nursing home–type unit) **A**1 9 10 **F**7 8 10 12 15 17 19 20 22 25 26 28 29 30 32 33 34 35 37 40 41 42 44 45 49 52 56 59 63 64 65 67 71 73 74 **S** Quorum Health Group/Quorum Health Resources, Inc., Brentwood, TN **N** Wake Forest University Baptist Medical Center, Winston–Salem, NC — *16 10 115 4937 51 67423 720 36469 15999 603*

MURPHY—Cherokee County

✠ MURPHY MEDICAL CENTER, 4130 U.S. Highway 64 East, Zip 28906–7917; tel. 704/837–8161; Mike Stevenson, Administrator (Total facility includes 120 beds in nursing home–type unit) **A**1 10 **F**7 8 14 15 16 19 21 22 24 28 29 30 34 35 37 41 42 44 45 49 60 63 64 65 67 71 72 73 **P**5 **N** Western North Carolina Health Network, Asheville, NC — *23 10 170 2430 140 26005 244 19420 9030 365*

NEW BERN—Craven County

✠ △ CRAVEN REGIONAL MEDICAL AUTHORITY, 2000 Neuse Boulevard, Zip 28560–3499, Mailing Address: P.O. Box 12157, Zip 28561–2157; tel. 252/633–8111; Raymond Budrys, Chief Executive Officer **A**1 2 7 9 10 **F**4 7 8 10 11 12 14 19 21 22 25 26 27 28 29 30 31 32 34 35 37 39 40 41 42 43 44 48 49 52 55 56 57 59 60 63 64 65 66 71 73 74 **N** Eastern Carolina Health Network, Greenville, NC — *16 10 255 11883 178 118476 1221 103642 41418 1323*

NORTH WILKESBORO—Wilkes County

✠ WILKES REGIONAL MEDICAL CENTER, 1370 West D. Street, Zip 28659–3506, Mailing Address: P.O. Box 609, Zip 28659–0609; tel. 336/651–8100; David L. Henson, Chief Executive Officer (Total facility includes 10 beds in nursing home–type unit) (Nonreporting) **A**1 9 10 **N** Wake Forest University Baptist Medical Center, Winston–Salem, NC — *14 10 130 — — — — — — —*

OXFORD—Granville County

★ GRANVILLE MEDICAL CENTER, 1010 College Street, Zip 27565–2507, Mailing Address: Box 947, Zip 27565–0947; tel. 919/690–3000; Andrew Mannich, Administrator (Total facility includes 80 beds in nursing home–type unit) (Nonreporting) **A**9 10 **S** Quorum Health Group/Quorum Health Resources, Inc., Brentwood, TN **N** UNC Health Network, Chapel Hill, NC — *13 10 146 — — — — — — —*

PINEHURST—Moore County

✠ △ FIRSTHEALTH MOORE REGIONAL HOSPITAL, (Formerly Moore Regional Hospital), 35 Memorial Drive, Zip 28374, Mailing Address: P.O. Box 3000, Zip 28374–3000; tel. 910/215–1000; Charles T. Frock, President and Chief Executive Officer **A**1 2 7 9 10 **F**2 3 4 7 8 10 11 12 14 15 16 17 19 20 21 22 24 25 26 27 29 30 31 33 34 35 37 38 40 41 42 43 45 46 48 49 51 52 53 54 55 56 57 58 59 60 63 64 65 67 71 73 74 **P**5 7 **N** UNC Health Network, Chapel Hill, NC — *23 10 371 18381 278 105385 1521 137457 63446 1775*

PINEVILLE—Mecklenburg County

□ BHC CEDAR SPRING HOSPITAL, 9600 Pineville–Matthews Road, Zip 28134–7548; tel. 704/541–6676; Steven G. Johnson, Chief Executive Officer (Nonreporting) **A**1 10 — *33 22 70 — — — — — — —*

PLYMOUTH—Washington County

✠ WASHINGTON COUNTY HOSPITAL, 958 U.S. Highway 64 East, Zip 27962–9591; tel. 919/793–4135; Lawrence H. McAvoy, Administrator (Nonreporting) **A**1 9 10 **S** Quorum Health Group/Quorum Health Resources, Inc., Brentwood, TN **N** Eastern Carolina Health Network, Greenville, NC — *13 10 49 — — — — — — —*

RALEIGH—Wake County

CENTRAL PRISON HOSPITAL, 1300 Western Boulevard, Zip 27606–2148; tel. 919/733–0800; Robert Reardon, Hospital Services Administrator **F**3 16 19 20 21 22 31 33 35 44 48 49 52 56 58 59 64 **P**6 — *12 11 86 2023 49 34462 — — — 97*

COLUMBIA RALEIGH COMMUNITY HOSPITAL See Raleigh Community Hospital

□ DOROTHEA DIX HOSPITAL, 820 South Boylan Avenue, Zip 27603–2176; tel. 919/733–5324; Michael S. Pedneau, Director **A**1 3 5 10 **F**8 20 22 26 28 29 30 31 37 39 41 42 44 45 46 49 52 53 54 55 57 65 69 71 73 — *12 22 442 4284 383 — — 101175 39103 —*

✠ HOLLY HILL CHARTER BEHAVIORAL HEALTH SYSTEM, 3019 Falstaff Road, Zip 27610–1812; tel. 919/250–7000; James B. Brawley, Chief Executive Officer **A**1 9 10 **F**2 3 12 19 22 26 35 46 52 53 54 55 56 57 58 59 65 67 **S** Columbia/HCA Healthcare Corporation, Nashville, TN — *32 22 108 2582 58 0 — — — 123*

✠ RALEIGH COMMUNITY HOSPITAL, (Formerly Columbia Raleigh Community Hospital), 3400 Wake Forest Road, Zip 27609–7373, Mailing Address: P.O. Box 28280, Zip 27611–8280; tel. 919/954–3000; James E. Raynor, Chief Executive Officer **A**1 9 10 **F**3 7 12 14 15 17 19 21 22 23 24 30 31 32 34 35 37 39 40 41 42 44 45 49 52 53 54 57 58 59 64 65 66 71 73 **P**6 **S** Columbia/HCA Healthcare Corporation, Nashville, TN **N** Hospital Alliance for Community Health, Raleigh, NC — *33 10 151 5690 79 71152 753 — — 630*

Hospital, Address, Telephone, Administrator, Approval, Facility, and Physician Codes, Health Care System, Network	Classi- fication Codes		Utilization Data					Expense (thousands) of dollars		
★ American Hospital Association (AHA) membership □ Joint Commission on Accreditation of Healthcare Organizations (JCAHO) accreditation + American Osteopathic Healthcare Association (AOHA) membership ○ American Osteopathic Association (AOA) accreditation △ Commission on Accreditation of Rehabilitation Facilities (CARF) accreditation Control codes 61, 63, 64, 71, 72 and 73 indicate hospitals listed by AOHA, but not registered by AHA. For definition of numerical codes, see page A4	Control	Service	Staffed Beds	Admissions	Census	Outpatient Visits	Births	Total	Payroll	Personnel
✠ REX HEALTHCARE, 4420 Lake Boone Trail, Zip 27607–6599; tel. 919/783–3100; James W. Albright, President and Chief Executive Officer (Total facility includes 140 beds in nursing home–type unit) **A**1 2 9 10 **F**4 7 8 10 11 12 13 14 16 17 19 21 22 23 24 25 28 29 30 32 34 35 37 38 40 41 42 43 44 45 46 49 51 60 64 65 66 67 71 72 73 74 **P**1 6 **N** Hospital Alliance for Community Health, Raleigh, NC	23	10	522	27109	409	560038	5329	234886	78246	2855
WAKE COUNTY ALCOHOLISM TREATMENT CENTER, 3000 Falstaff Road, Zip 27610–1897; tel. 919/250–1500; Roy Nickell, Director Substance Abuse Services **A**9 10 **F**2 3 12 16 27 54 56 58 65 67 **P**5	13	82	34	854	28	15854	0	3666	3160	124
✠ △ WAKE MEDICAL CENTER, (Includes Eastern Wake Day Hospital, 320 Hospital Road, Zebulon, Zip 27597; tel. 919/269–7406; Southern Wake Hospital, 400 West Ranson Street, Fuquay–Varina, Zip 27526; tel. 919/552–2206; Western Wake Medical Center, 1900 Kildaire Farm Road, Cary, Zip 27511; tel. 919/233–2300), 3000 New Bern Avenue, Zip 27610–1295; tel. 919/250–8000; Raymond L. Champ, President (Total facility includes 37 beds in nursing home–type unit) **A**1 3 5 7 9 10 **F**4 5 7 8 10 11 12 13 15 16 17 19 20 21 22 24 25 27 28 30 31 32 34 35 37 38 39 40 41 42 43 44 45 46 47 48 49 51 63 64 65 66 67 70 71 72 73 74 **P**3 7 **N** Hospital Alliance for Community Health, Raleigh, NC; UNC Health Network, Chapel Hill, NC	23	10	633	29433	524	352019	3808	263537	115753	3290
REIDSVILLE—Rockingham County										
✠ ANNIE PENN HOSPITAL, 618 South Main Street, Zip 27320–5094; tel. 336/634–1010; Susan H. Fitzgibbon, President and Chief Executive Officer (Total facility includes 42 beds in nursing home–type unit) **A**1 9 10 **F**7 8 12 13 14 15 16 17 19 21 22 26 28 29 30 31 32 34 37 39 40 41 44 45 46 49 52 65 67 68 71 73 74	23	10	152	3753	84	66123	416	28670	12811	457
ROANOKE RAPIDS—Halifax County										
✠ HALIFAX REGIONAL MEDICAL CENTER, (Formerly Halifax Memorial Hospital), 250 Smith Church Road, Zip 27870–4914, Mailing Address: P.O. Box 1089, Zip 27870–1089; tel. 919/535–8011; M. E. Gilstrap, President and Chief Executive Officer **A**1 9 10 **F**7 8 12 14 15 17 19 20 21 22 23 28 30 31 34 35 36 37 40 42 44 45 46 49 51 52 53 55 56 57 58 60 63 65 67 71 72 73 74 **N** Eastern Carolina Health Network, Greenville, NC	23	10	158	8491	127	72134	756	47175	19293	705
ROCKINGHAM—Richmond County										
✠ RICHMOND MEMORIAL HOSPITAL, 925 Long Drive, Zip 28379–4815; tel. 910/417–3000; David G. Hohl, Chief Executive Officer (Total facility includes 45 beds in nursing home–type unit) **A**1 9 10 **F**7 8 10 12 14 15 16 17 19 22 23 26 28 29 30 32 34 35 37 40 41 44 45 49 64 65 67 68 71 73 74 **P**7 **N** Carolinas Hospital Network, Charlotte, NC; Central Carolina Rural Hospital Alliance, Albemarle, NC	23	10	129	5024	87	39848	496	32099	15613	596
ROCKY MOUNT—Nash County										
✠ NASH HEALTH CARE SYSTEMS, 2460 Curtis Ellis Drive, Zip 27804–2297; tel. 919/443–8000; Richard Kirk Toomey, President and Chief Executive Officer **A**1 2 9 10 **F**3 7 8 10 11 12 13 14 15 16 17 18 19 20 21 22 23 28 29 30 31 32 33 34 35 36 37 39 40 41 42 44 45 46 49 52 53 54 55 56 57 58 59 60 63 65 66 67 71 72 73 74 **P**6 7 **N** Eastern Carolina Health Network, Greenville, NC	13	10	279	11366	197	97206	1243	91793	41150	1406
ROXBORO—Person County										
✠ PERSON COUNTY MEMORIAL HOSPITAL, 615 Ridge Road, Zip 27573–4630; tel. 336/599–2121; Regis Cabonor, Administrator (Total facility includes 43 beds in nursing home–type unit) **A**1 9 10 **F**3 6 7 8 11 12 15 16 19 22 26 28 30 35 37 40 41 42 44 48 49 56 58 59 64 71 73	23	10	93	1783	56	35069	143	14851	6490	274
RUTHERFORDTON—Rutherford County										
✠ RUTHERFORD HOSPITAL, 288 South Ridgecrest Avenue, Zip 28139–3097; tel. 704/286–5000; Robert D. Jones, President (Total facility includes 150 beds in nursing home–type unit) **A**1 9 10 **F**1 7 8 10 14 15 16 19 21 22 23 28 30 32 34 35 37 40 41 42 44 45 46 49 50 52 54 55 56 64 65 71 73 **P**3 **S** Quorum Health Group/Quorum Health Resources, Inc., Brentwood, TN **N** Carolinas Hospital Network, Charlotte, NC; Western North Carolina Health Network, Asheville, NC; Wake Forest University Baptist Medical Center, Winston–Salem, NC	23	10	293	5206	213	70682	604	45228	20715	790
SALISBURY—Rowan County										
✠ ROWAN REGIONAL MEDICAL CENTER, 612 Mocksville Avenue, Zip 28144–2799; tel. 704/638–1000; James M. Freeman, Chief Executive Officer **A**1 9 10 **F**2 3 7 8 10 11 12 14 16 19 22 23 25 26 30 31 32 33 34 35 37 39 40 42 44 45 49 52 56 58 59 63 65 67 71 72 73 74 **P**1 **N** Wake Forest University Baptist Medical Center, Winston–Salem, NC	23	10	222	10001	143	56354	840	71193	31924	1044
✠ VETERANS AFFAIRS MEDICAL CENTER, 1601 Brenner Avenue, Zip 28144–2559; tel. 704/638–9000; Betty Bolin Brown, Ed.D., Acting Director (Total facility includes 120 beds in nursing home–type unit) **A**1 5 9 **F**2 3 4 8 10 13 14 15 18 19 20 21 22 23 24 25 26 28 29 30 31 32 33 34 35 37 41 42 43 44 45 46 48 49 51 52 54 56 57 58 63 64 65 67 71 73 74 **S** Department of Veterans Affairs, Washington, DC	45	22	612	3378	416	129088	0	104009	55542	1358
SANFORD—Lee County										
✠ CENTRAL CAROLINA HOSPITAL, 1135 Carthage Street, Zip 27330; tel. 919/774–2100; L. Glenn Davis, Executive Director **A**1 9 10 **F**7 8 10 12 16 19 21 22 23 31 32 33 34 35 36 37 39 40 41 42 44 46 52 65 71 73 **P**1 7 **S** TENET Healthcare Corporation, Santa Barbara, CA	33	10	137	5819	71	53131	898	31860	14233	535

Hospital, Address, Telephone, Administrator, Approval, Facility, and Physician Codes, Health Care System, Network	Classi-fication Codes		Utilization Data						Expense (thousands) of dollars		
★ American Hospital Association (AHA) membership □ Joint Commission on Accreditation of Healthcare Organizations (JCAHO) accreditation + American Osteopathic Healthcare Association (AOHA) membership ○ American Osteopathic Association (AOA) accreditation △ Commission on Accreditation of Rehabilitation Facilities (CARF) accreditation Control codes 61, 63, 64, 71, 72 and 73 indicate hospitals listed by AOHA, but not registered by AHA. For definition of numerical codes, see page A4	Control	Service	Staffed Beds	Admissions	Census	Outpatient Visits	Births	Total	Payroll	Personnel

SCOTLAND NECK—Halifax County

OUR COMMUNITY HOSPITAL, 921 Junior High Road, Zip 27874–0405, Mailing Address: Box 405, Zip 27874–0405; tel. 919/826–4144; Thomas K. Majure, Administrator (Total facility includes 60 beds in nursing home–type unit) (Nonreporting) **A**10	23	10	100	—	—	—	—	—	—	—

SEYMOUR JOHNSON AFB—Wayne County

✠ U. S. AIR FORCE HOSPITAL SEYMOUR JOHNSON, 1050 Jabara Avenue, Zip 27531–5300; tel. 919/736–5201; Colonel Michael Lischak, MC, USAF, Commander (Nonreporting) **A**1 9 **S** Department of the Air Force, Bowling AFB, DC	41	10	41	—	—	—	—	—	—	—

SHELBY—Cleveland County

✠ CLEVELAND REGIONAL MEDICAL CENTER, 201 Grover Street, Zip 28150–3940; tel. 704/487–3000; John Young, President and Chief Executive Officer (Total facility includes 120 beds in nursing home–type unit) (Nonreporting) **A**1 2 9 10 **S** Carolinas HealthCare System, Charlotte, NC **N** Carolinas Hospital Network, Charlotte, NC	13	10	296	—	—	—	—	—	—	—

SILER CITY—Chatham County

✠ CHATHAM HOSPITAL, West Third Street and Ivy Avenue, Zip 27344–2343, Mailing Address: P.O. Box 649, Zip 27344; tel. 919/663–2113; Woodrow W. Hathaway, Jr., Chief Executive Officer **A**1 9 10 **F**8 12 15 19 22 28 35 39 44 49 59 65 71 73 **S** Quorum Health Group/Quorum Health Resources, Inc., Brentwood, TN **N** UNC Health Network, Chapel Hill, NC	23	10	35	986	15	13874	—	7825	3240	126

SMITHFIELD—Johnston County

✠ JOHNSTON MEMORIAL HOSPITAL, 509 North Bright Leaf Boulevard, Zip 27577–1376, Mailing Address: P.O. Box 1376, Zip 27577–1376; tel. 919/934–8171; Leland E. Farnell, President **A**1 9 10 **F**7 8 14 15 16 19 20 21 22 23 25 28 30 32 33 34 35 36 37 40 42 44 49 51 52 54 56 57 65 67 68 71 72 73 **P**6 **S** Quorum Health Group/Quorum Health Resources, Inc., Brentwood, TN **N** UNC Health Network, Chapel Hill, NC	13	10	127	4840	62	146146	685	35237	16546	617

SOUTHPORT—Brunswick County

✠ J. ARTHUR DOSHER MEMORIAL HOSPITAL, 924 Howe Street, Zip 28461–3099; tel. 910/457–5271; Edgar Haywood, III, Administrator **A**1 10 **F**14 15 16 19 22 26 28 32 34 35 41 44 49 65 67 71	16	10	40	1286	14	12462	—	10953	4305	167

SPARTA—Alleghany County

✠ ALLEGHANY MEMORIAL HOSPITAL, (Formerly Alleghany County Memorial Hospital), 233 Doctors Street, Zip 28675–0009, Mailing Address: P.O. Box 9, Zip 28675–0009; tel. 336/372–5511; James Yarborough, Chief Executive Officer **A**1 9 10 **F**1 7 8 12 14 15 16 17 19 22 23 25 29 30 32 34 35 39 41 44 46 49 65 67 71 **P**1 5 **S** Quorum Health Group/Quorum Health Resources, Inc., Brentwood, TN **N** Wake Forest University Baptist Medical Center, Winston–Salem, NC	23	10	46	1421	19	11623	34	8005	4309	189

SPRUCE PINE—Mitchell County

□ SPRUCE PINE COMMUNITY HOSPITAL, 125 Hospital Drive, Zip 28777–3035, Mailing Address: P.O. Drawer 9, Zip 28777–0009; tel. 704/765–4201; Keith S. Holtsclaw, Chief Executive Officer **A**1 9 10 **F**7 8 11 12 14 15 16 17 19 22 24 28 30 32 33 41 42 44 49 51 56 65 71 72 73	23	10	40	1914	19	32063	129	11197	5789	232

STATESVILLE—Iredell County

✠ COLUMBIA DAVIS MEDICAL CENTER, 218 Old Mocksville Road, Zip 28625, Mailing Address: P.O. Box 1823, Zip 28687–1823; tel. 704/873–0281; G. Phillip Lotti, Chief Executive Officer **A**1 10 **F**3 7 8 10 11 12 14 15 16 17 19 21 22 23 24 26 28 30 31 32 34 35 37 39 40 41 42 44 45 49 51 52 54 55 56 57 58 59 63 64 65 66 67 71 72 73 74 **S** Columbia/HCA Healthcare Corporation, Nashville, TN	33	10	124	5094	61	23017	446	—	—	367
✠ IREDELL MEMORIAL HOSPITAL, 557 Brookdale Drive, Zip 28677–1828, Mailing Address: P.O. Box 1828, Zip 28687–1828; tel. 704/873–5661; S. Arnold Nunnery, President and Chief Executive Officer (Total facility includes 48 beds in nursing home–type unit) **A**1 2 9 10 **F**7 8 10 11 12 13 14 15 16 17 19 21 22 23 28 29 30 31 32 33 35 37 40 41 42 44 45 46 49 51 53 54 55 56 57 58 59 60 63 64 65 67 71 73 74 **N** Carolinas Hospital Network, Charlotte, NC	23	10	202	8490	131	108832	903	63980	31372	776

SUPPLY—Brunswick County

✠ COLUMBIA BRUNSWICK HOSPITAL, 1 Medical Center Drive, Zip 28462–3350, Mailing Address: P.O. Box 139, Zip 28462–0139; tel. 910/755–8121; C. Mark Gregson, Chief Executive Officer (Nonreporting) **A**1 9 10 **S** Columbia/HCA Healthcare Corporation, Nashville, TN	33	10	56	—	—	—	—	—	—	—

SYLVA—Jackson County

✠ HARRIS REGIONAL HOSPITAL, 68 Hospital Road, Zip 28779–2795; tel. 828/586–7000; Mark Leonard, Chief Executive Officer (Total facility includes 100 beds in nursing home–type unit) **A**1 9 10 **F**7 8 12 15 16 17 19 21 22 23 27 28 29 30 32 33 34 35 37 39 40 41 42 44 45 46 49 60 63 64 65 71 72 73 74 **P**7 8 **N** Western North Carolina Health Network, Asheville, NC	23	10	175	4346	141	39583	736	38857	18283	747

TARBORO—Edgecombe County

✠ HERITAGE HOSPITAL, (Formerly Columbia Heritage Hospital), 111 Hospital Drive, Zip 27886–2011; tel. 919/641–7700; Janet Mullaney, Chief Executive Officer (Total facility includes 10 beds in nursing home–type unit) **A**1 9 10 **F**4 7 8 10 11 12 16 19 20 21 22 23 25 31 32 33 34 35 36 37 38 39 40 41 42 43 44 45 46 47 48 49 50 52 53 54 55 56 57 58 59 60 61 63 64 65 66 67 69 70 71 73 **S** Columbia/HCA Healthcare Corporation, Nashville, TN **N** Eastern Carolina Health Network, Greenville, NC	33	10	127	4629	57	36432	672	22875	10171	373

Hospital, Address, Telephone, Administrator, Approval, Facility, and Physician Codes, Health Care System, Network	Classification Codes		Utilization Data					Expense (thousands) of dollars		
	Control	Service	Staffed Beds	Admissions	Census	Outpatient Visits	Births	Total	Payroll	Personnel

★ American Hospital Association (AHA) membership
☐ Joint Commission on Accreditation of Healthcare Organizations (JCAHO) accreditation
+ American Osteopathic Healthcare Association (AOHA) membership
○ American Osteopathic Association (AOA) accreditation
△ Commission on Accreditation of Rehabilitation Facilities (CARF) accreditation
Control codes 61, 63, 64, 71, 72 and 73 indicate hospitals listed by AOHA, but not registered by AHA. For definition of numerical codes, see page A4

TAYLORSVILLE—Alexander County

✠ ALEXANDER COMMUNITY HOSPITAL, 326 Third Street S.W., Zip 28681–3096; tel. 828/632–4282; Joe W. Pollard, Jr., Administrator **A**1 9 10 **F**2 3 4 8 9 10 11 14 15 16 17 19 21 22 23 30 32 33 35 37 39 41 42 43 44 46 47 48 49 52 53 54 55 56 57 58 59 60 64 65 67 70 71 73 **S** Quorum Health Group/Quorum Health Resources, Inc., Brentwood, TN **N** Wake Forest University Baptist Medical Center, Winston–Salem, NC — 23 10 36 974 9 12368 — 6738 2760 107

THOMASVILLE—Davidson County

✠ COMMUNITY GENERAL HOSPITAL OF THOMASVILLE, 207 Old Lexington Road, Zip 27360, Mailing Address: P.O. Box 789, Zip 27361–0789; tel. 336/472–2000; Lynn Ingram Boggs, President and Chief Executive Officer **A**1 9 10 **F**7 8 10 11 12 14 15 16 17 19 21 22 28 30 31 34 36 37 39 40 41 42 44 45 46 49 52 56 57 63 64 65 67 68 71 72 73 74 **P**5 **S** Novant Health, Winston Salem, NC — 23 10 128 4381 53 36032 613 25651 12390 471

TROY—Montgomery County

☐ FIRSTHEALTH MONTGOMERY MEMORIAL HOSPITAL, (Formerly Montgomery Memorial Hospital), 520 Allen Street, Zip 27371–2802, Mailing Address: P.O. Box 486, Zip 27371–0486; tel. 910/572–1301; Kerry A. Anderson, R.N., Administrator (Total facility includes 51 beds in nursing home–type unit) **A**1 9 10 **F**8 14 15 16 17 19 22 24 26 27 30 41 44 51 53 58 64 65 71 73 74 **P**3 — 23 10 67 782 53 44808 — 8672 4819 154

VALDESE—Burke County

✠ VALDESE GENERAL HOSPITAL, Mailing Address: P.O. Box 700, Zip 28690–0700; tel. 704/874–2251; Lloyd E. Wallace, President and Chief Executive Officer (Total facility includes 120 beds in nursing home–type unit) **A**1 2 10 **F**7 8 10 11 12 14 15 16 17 19 21 22 23 26 28 30 32 34 35 37 39 40 41 42 44 46 49 60 62 63 64 65 70 71 73 **P**8 **N** Carolinas Hospital Network, Charlotte, NC — 16 10 199 2994 154 31720 362 26619 11931 429

WADESBORO—Anson County

✠ ANSON COUNTY HOSPITAL AND SKILLED NURSING FACILITIES, 500 Morven Road, Zip 28170–2745; tel. 704/694–5131; Frederick G. Thompson, Ph.D., Administrator and Chief Executive Officer (Total facility includes 95 beds in nursing home–type unit) **A**1 9 10 **F**8 12 14 15 16 17 19 21 22 29 30 34 41 42 44 45 46 49 64 65 67 71 **N** Carolinas Hospital Network, Charlotte, NC — 13 10 125 1638 108 25188 — 13325 6780 320

WASHINGTON—Beaufort County

✠ BEAUFORT COUNTY HOSPITAL, 628 East 12th Street, Zip 27889–3498; tel. 919/975–4100; Kenneth E. Ragland, Administrator **A**1 9 10 **F**3 7 8 11 12 14 15 16 18 19 20 21 22 24 25 27 28 29 30 32 33 34 35 36 39 41 42 43 44 45 46 49 51 52 54 55 56 57 62 65 66 67 68 69 70 71 72 73 74 **P**3 5 **N** Eastern Carolina Health Network, Greenville, NC — 23 10 118 3659 55 44737 379 26660 12783 477

WHITEVILLE—Columbus County

✠ COLUMBUS COUNTY HOSPITAL, 500 Jefferson Street, Zip 28472–9987; tel. 910/642–8011; William S. Clark, Chief Executive Officer **A**1 9 10 **F**7 10 11 12 15 16 17 19 22 23 28 30 34 35 36 37 39 40 44 45 46 49 51 65 66 71 73 **S** Quorum Health Group/Quorum Health Resources, Inc., Brentwood, TN **N** UNC Health Network, Chapel Hill, NC — 23 10 117 5971 78 49435 474 33530 15689 537

WILLIAMSTON—Martin County

✠ MARTIN GENERAL HOSPITAL, 310 South McCaskey Road, Zip 27892–2150, Mailing Address: P.O. Box 1128, Zip 27892–1128; tel. 252/809–6121; George H. Brandt, Jr., Administrator (Nonreporting) **A**1 3 9 10 **N** Eastern Carolina Health Network, Greenville, NC — 13 10 49 — — — — — — —

WILMINGTON—New Hanover County

✠ CAPE FEAR MEMORIAL HOSPITAL, (Formerly Columbia Cape Fear Memorial Hospital), 5301 Wrightsville Avenue, Zip 28403–6599; tel. 910/452–8100; C. Mark Gregson, Chief Executive Officer (Nonreporting) **A**1 10 **S** Columbia/HCA Healthcare Corporation, Nashville, TN — 33 10 109 — — — — — — —

✠ △ NEW HANOVER REGIONAL MEDICAL CENTER, 2131 South 17th Street, Zip 28401–7483, Mailing Address: P.O. Box 9000, Zip 28402–9000; tel. 910/343–7000; William K. Atkinson, II, Ph.D., Chief Executive Officer **A**1 3 5 7 9 10 **F**2 3 4 7 8 10 11 12 15 16 17 18 19 20 22 25 26 27 28 29 30 31 32 33 34 35 37 38 39 40 42 43 44 45 48 49 51 52 53 54 55 58 59 60 61 63 65 67 68 69 70 71 73 74 **P**7 — 13 10 542 22529 366 265302 2571 216561 95932 3193

WILSON—Wilson County

✠ WILSON MEMORIAL HOSPITAL, 1705 South Tarboro Street, Zip 27893–3428; tel. 252/399–8040; Christopher T. Durrer, President and Chief Executive Officer **A**1 9 10 **F**7 8 10 12 14 15 16 17 19 20 22 23 28 29 32 33 34 35 36 37 40 41 42 44 45 46 49 52 53 54 55 56 58 65 67 71 73 **N** Eastern Carolina Health Network, Greenville, NC — 23 10 221 7866 118 118512 1189 59486 24273 796

WINDSOR—Bertie County

BERTIE COUNTY MEMORIAL HOSPITAL See Bertie Memorial Hospital

★ BERTIE MEMORIAL HOSPITAL, (Formerly Bertie County Memorial Hospital), 401 Sterlingworth Street, Zip 27983–1726, Mailing Address: P.O. Box 40, Zip 27983–1726; tel. 919/794–3141; Anthony F. Mullen, Administrator **A**9 10 **F**8 15 19 22 28 34 44 65 71 **N** Eastern Carolina Health Network, Greenville, NC — 23 10 49 472 25 17686 0 5046 2386 105

WINSTON–SALEM—Forsyth County

AMOS COTTAGE REHABILITATION HOSPITAL, 3325 Silas Creek Parkway, Zip 27103–3089; tel. 336/774–2400; Douglas M. Cody, Administrator **A**10 **F**12 17 34 39 45 46 49 65 73 **P**6 — 23 56 31 107 22 2325 — 4127 2381 103

Hospital, Address, Telephone, Administrator, Approval, Facility, and Physician Codes, Health Care System, Network	Classi- fication Codes		Utilization Data						Expense (thousands) of dollars		
★ American Hospital Association (AHA) membership □ Joint Commission on Accreditation of Healthcare Organizations (JCAHO) accreditation + American Osteopathic Healthcare Association (AOHA) membership ○ American Osteopathic Association (AOA) accreditation △ Commission on Accreditation of Rehabilitation Facilities (CARF) accreditation Control codes 61, 63, 64, 71, 72 and 73 indicate hospitals listed by AOHA, but not registered by AHA. For definition of numerical codes, see page A4	Control	Service	Staffed Beds	Admissions	Census	Outpatient Visits	Births	Total	Payroll	Personnel
□ CHARTER HOSPITAL OF WINSTON–SALEM, 3637 Old Vineyard Road, Zip 27104–4835; tel. 336/768–7710; Michael J. Carney, Chief Executive Officer (Nonreporting) **A**1 10 **S** Magellan Health Services, Atlanta, GA	33	22	99	—	—	—	—	—	—	—
✖ △ FORSYTH MEMORIAL HOSPITAL, 3333 Silas Creek Parkway, Zip 27103–3090; tel. 336/718–5000; Gregory J. Beier, President (Total facility includes 22 beds in nursing home–type unit) **A**1 2 3 5 7 9 10 **F**3 4 7 8 10 11 12 14 15 16 17 19 20 21 22 23 24 25 26 28 29 30 31 32 33 34 35 37 38 39 40 41 42 43 44 45 46 48 49 51 52 54 56 57 58 59 60 63 64 65 66 67 70 71 72 73 74 **P**6 8 **S** Novant Health, Winston Salem, NC	23	10	747	32604	572	95460	5815	123268	108240	4134
✖ MEDICAL PARK HOSPITAL, 1950 South Hawthorne Road, Zip 27103–3993, Mailing Address: P.O. Box 24728, Zip 27114–4728; tel. 910/718–0600; Eduard R. Koehler, Administrator **A**1 2 9 10 **F**2 3 4 7 8 10 11 12 14 15 16 17 19 20 21 22 24 25 26 27 28 29 30 31 32 33 34 35 37 38 39 40 41 42 43 44 45 46 48 49 51 52 54 55 56 57 58 59 60 63 64 65 66 67 71 72 73 74 **P**6 **S** Novant Health, Winston Salem, NC	23	10	59	2135	20	13052	—	21609	8511	240
✖ △ NORTH CAROLINA BAPTIST HOSPITAL, Medical Center Boulevard, Zip 27157; tel. 336/716–4745; Len B. Preslar, Jr., President and Chief Executive Officer **A**1 2 3 5 7 8 9 10 **F**3 4 5 8 9 10 11 12 13 14 15 16 17 19 20 21 22 23 24 25 26 28 29 30 31 32 34 35 37 38 40 43 44 45 46 47 48 49 50 51 52 53 54 55 56 57 58 59 60 61 63 64 65 66 67 69 70 71 73 74 **P**1 4 7 **N** Wake Forest University Baptist Medical Center, Winston–Salem, NC; UNC Health Network, Chapel Hill, NC	23	10	766	26329	555	97203	—	379180	173625	5446

YADKINVILLE—Yadkin County

✖ HOOTS MEMORIAL HOSPITAL, 624 West Main Street, Zip 27055–7804, Mailing Address: P.O. Box 68, Zip 27055–0068; tel. 336/679–2041; Lance C. Labine, President **A**1 9 10 **F**3 8 15 16 19 22 28 30 31 32 33 34 35 37 44 49 59 71 73 **P**6 **N** Wake Forest University Baptist Medical Center, Winston–Salem, NC	13	10	26	676	7	16951	—	5973	2869	100

ZEBULON—Wake County

EASTERN WAKE DAY HOSPITAL See Wake Medical Center, Raleigh

NORTH DAKOTA

Resident population 641 (in thousands)
Resident population in metro areas 42.1%
Birth rate per 1,000 population 13.5
65 years and over 14.5%
Percent of persons without health insurance 9.8%

Hospital, Address, Telephone, Administrator, Approval, Facility, and Physician Codes, Health Care System, Network	Classi-fication Codes		Utilization Data					Expense (thousands) of dollars		
	Control	Service	Staffed Beds	Admissions	Census	Outpatient Visits	Births	Total	Payroll	Personnel

★ American Hospital Association (AHA) membership
□ Joint Commission on Accreditation of Healthcare Organizations (JCAHO) accreditation
+ American Osteopathic Healthcare Association (AOHA) membership
○ American Osteopathic Association (AOA) accreditation
△ Commission on Accreditation of Rehabilitation Facilities (CARF) accreditation
Control codes 61, 63, 64, 71, 72 and 73 indicate hospitals listed by AOHA, but not registered by AHA. For definition of numerical codes, see page A4

Hospital	Control	Service	Staffed Beds	Admissions	Census	Outpatient Visits	Births	Total	Payroll	Personnel
ASHLEY—McIntosh County										
★ ASHLEY MEDICAL CENTER, 612 North Center Avenue, Zip 58413–0556; tel. 701/288–3433; Stephen H. Johnson, Administrator and Chief Executive Officer (Total facility includes 44 beds in nursing home–type unit) **A**9 10 **F**6 7 8 14 15 16 17 19 20 22 24 26 27 28 30 32 33 34 36 39 40 41 44 45 46 49 51 64 65 66 70 71 73 74	23	10	70	271	47	1729	1	3842	1933	102
BELCOURT—Rolette County										
⊠ U. S. PUBLIC HEALTH SERVICE INDIAN HOSPITAL, Mailing Address: P.O. Box 160, Zip 58316–0130; tel. 701/477–6111; Ray Grandbois, M.P.H., Service Unit Director (Nonreporting) **A**1 5 10 **S** U. S. Public Health Service Indian Health Service, Rockville, MD	47	10	42	—	—	—	—	—	—	—
BISMARCK—Burleigh County										
⊠ △ MEDCENTER ONE, 300 North Seventh Street, Zip 58501–4439, Mailing Address: P.O. Box 5525, Zip 58506–5525; tel. 701/323–6000; Terrance G. Brosseau, President and Chief Executive Officer (Total facility includes 22 beds in nursing home–type unit) **A**1 2 3 5 7 9 10 **F**2 3 4 5 7 8 10 11 12 13 14 15 16 17 18 19 20 21 22 23 24 26 27 28 29 30 31 32 33 34 35 36 37 38 39 40 41 42 43 44 45 46 47 48 49 51 52 53 54 55 56 57 58 59 60 61 62 63 64 65 66 67 68 69 70 71 73 74 **P**6 **N** Medcenter One, Bismarck, ND	23	10	231	7566	130	385006	600	128921	70396	2140
⊠ △ ST. ALEXIUS MEDICAL CENTER, 900 East Broadway, Zip 58501–4586, Mailing Address: P.O. Box 5510, Zip 58506–5510; tel. 701/224–7000; Richard A. Tschider, FACHE, Administrator and Chief Executive Officer **A**1 2 3 5 7 9 10 **F**3 4 5 7 8 10 12 13 14 15 16 17 18 19 20 21 22 23 24 26 27 28 29 30 31 32 33 34 35 37 38 39 40 41 42 43 44 45 47 48 49 51 52 53 54 55 56 57 58 59 61 64 65 66 67 70 71 72 73 74 **P**1 **S** Benedictine Sisters of the Annunciation, Bismarck, ND	21	10	269	9233	144	139893	1023	95446	45349	1315
BOTTINEAU—Bottineau County										
ST. ANDREW'S HEALTH CENTER, 316 Ohmer Street, Zip 58318–1018; tel. 701/228–2255; Keith Korman, President (Total facility includes 32 beds in nursing home–type unit) **A**5 9 10 **F**6 7 8 15 16 19 22 26 28 30 32 36 39 40 44 49 53 54 55 57 62 64 65 66 70 71 73 **P**5 **S** Sisters of Mary of the Presentation Health Corporation, Fargo, ND	23	10	67	455	45	6000	8	3533	1582	61
BOWMAN—Bowman County										
ST. LUKE'S TRI–STATE HOSPITAL, 202 Sixth Avenue S.W., Zip 58623–0009, Mailing Address: Drawer C., Zip 58623; tel. 701/523–5265; Jim Opdahl, Administrator (Nonreporting) **A**9 10	23	10	17	—	—	—	—	—	—	—
CANDO—Towner County										
★ TOWNER COUNTY MEDICAL CENTER, Highway 281 N, Box 6888, Zip 58324–0688; tel. 701/968–4411; Timothy J. Tracy, Chief Executive Officer (Total facility includes 10 beds in nursing home–type unit) (Nonreporting) **A**9 10	23	10	32	—	—	—	—	—	—	—
CARRINGTON—Foster County										
★ CARRINGTON HEALTH CENTER, 800 North Fourth Street, Zip 58421–1217; tel. 701/652–3141; Brian J. McDermott, Administrator (Total facility includes 40 beds in nursing home–type unit) **A**9 10 **F**7 8 15 16 19 22 26 28 30 32 34 35 44 49 51 64 65 67 71 73 **P**3 4 **S** Catholic Health Initiatives, Denver, CO	21	10	70	820	48	25775	51	7733	3227	127
CAVALIER—Pembina County										
★ PEMBINA COUNTY MEMORIAL HOSPITAL AND WEDGEWOOD MANOR, 301 Mountain Street East, Zip 58220–4015; tel. 701/265–8461; George A. Rohrich, Administrator (Total facility includes 60 beds in nursing home–type unit) **A**9 10 **F**7 8 12 15 16 17 19 22 27 28 30 32 35 36 37 39 40 42 44 46 49 51 62 64 65 71 **P**6 **S** Lutheran Health Systems, Fargo, ND	23	10	89	607	66	17592	46	6329	2937	109
COOPERSTOWN—Griggs County										
GRIGGS COUNTY HOSPITAL AND NURSING HOME, 1200 Roberts Avenue, Zip 58425, Mailing Address: P.O. Box 728, Zip 58425–0728; tel. 701/797–2221; Wayne Hendrickson, Interim Administrator (Total facility includes 58 beds in nursing home–type unit) (Nonreporting) **A**9 10 **N** MeritCare Health System, Fargo, ND	23	10	69	—	—	—	—	—	—	—
CROSBY—Divide County										
ST. LUKE'S HOSPITAL, 702 First Street Southwest, Zip 58730–0010; tel. 701/965–6384; Leslie O. Urvand, Administrator **A**9 10 **F**11 14 19 22 28 29 30 32 34 36 41 64 71 **P**6	23	10	29	342	7	1067	1	2334	947	44
DEVILS LAKE—Ramsey County										
⊠ MERCY HOSPITAL, 1031 Seventh Street, Zip 58301–2798; tel. 701/662–2131; Marlene Krein, President and Chief Executive Officer **A**1 9 10 **F**11 14 15 16 17 19 21 22 28 29 30 31 32 33 35 37 39 40 42 44 45 46 49 65 67 68 71 73 **P**5 **S** Catholic Health Initiatives, Denver, CO	21	10	35	1584	17	13475	244	10542	4896	166
DICKINSON—Stark County										
⊠ ST. JOSEPH'S HOSPITAL AND HEALTH CENTER, 30 Seventh Street West, Zip 58601–4399; tel. 701/225–7200; Greg Hanson, President and Chief Executive Officer **A**1 9 10 **F**7 8 15 16 17 19 21 22 24 30 32 33 34 35 36 37 40 41 44 46 49 52 53 54 55 56 57 58 59 63 65 66 67 71 73 **S** Catholic Health Initiatives, Denver, CO	21	10	90	2909	47	28879	357	23437	9991	360

Hospital, Address, Telephone, Administrator, Approval, Facility, and Physician Codes, Health Care System, Network	Classi-fication Codes		Utilization Data					Expense (thousands) of dollars		
★ American Hospital Association (AHA) membership □ Joint Commission on Accreditation of Healthcare Organizations (JCAHO) accreditation + American Osteopathic Healthcare Association (AOHA) membership ○ American Osteopathic Association (AOA) accreditation △ Commission on Accreditation of Rehabilitation Facilities (CARF) accreditation Control codes 61, 63, 64, 71, 72 and 73 indicate hospitals listed by AOHA, but not registered by AHA. For definition of numerical codes, see page A4	Control	Service	Staffed Beds	Admissions	Census	Outpatient Visits	Births	Total	Payroll	Personnel

ELGIN—Grant County

JACOBSON MEMORIAL HOSPITAL CARE CENTER, 601 East Street North, Zip 58533–0376; tel. 701/584–2792; Jacqueline Seibel, Administrator (Total facility includes 25 beds in nursing home–type unit) (Nonreporting) **A**9 10 **N** Medcenter One, Bismarck, ND

| | 23 | 10 | 50 | — | — | — | — | — | — | — |

FARGO—Cass County

□ △ DAKOTA HEARTLAND HEALTH SYSTEM, (Includes Dakota Heartland Health System–Island Park Campus, 510 Fourth Street South, Zip 58103; tel. 701/232–3331; Dakota Heartland Health System–South University Campus, 1720 South University Drive), 1720 South Univeristy Drive, Zip 58103–4994; tel. 701/280–4100; Louis Kauffman, President and Chief Executive Officer (Total facility includes 16 beds in nursing home–type unit) (Nonreporting) **A**1 2 3 5 7 9 10 **S** Paracelsus Healthcare Corporation, Houston, TX **N** Heartland Network, Inc., Fargo, ND

| | 32 | 10 | 203 | — | — | — | — | — | — | — |

✠ △ MERITCARE HEALTH SYSTEM, 720 Fourth Street North, Zip 58122–0002; tel. 701/234–6000; Roger Gilbertson, M.D., President (Total facility includes 24 beds in nursing home–type unit) **A**1 2 3 5 7 8 9 10 **F**4 7 8 10 11 12 14 15 16 19 21 22 23 24 26 28 29 30 31 32 33 34 35 37 38 39 40 41 42 43 44 45 46 47 48 49 51 52 53 54 55 56 57 58 59 60 61 63 65 66 69 70 71 72 73 74

| | 21 | 10 | 356 | 13698 | 210 | 51581 | 1571 | 129846 | 42862 | 1279 |

✠ VETERANS AFFAIRS MEDICAL AND REGIONAL OFFICE CENTER, 2101 Elm Street, Zip 58102–2498; tel. 701/232–3241; Douglas M. Kenyon, Director (Total facility includes 50 beds in nursing home–type unit) **A**1 3 5 **F**3 8 12 17 18 19 20 21 22 26 27 28 30 31 32 33 35 37 39 41 42 44 46 49 51 52 54 55 56 57 58 59 60 63 64 65 67 71 73 74 **S** Department of Veterans Affairs, Washington, DC

| | 45 | 10 | 125 | 2903 | 73 | 57861 | — | 46348 | 22183 | 586 |

FORT YATES—Sioux County

✠ U. S. PUBLIC HEALTH SERVICE INDIAN HOSPITAL, Mailing Address: P.O. Box J., Zip 58538; tel. 701/854–3831; Terry Pourier, Service Unit Director (Nonreporting) **A**1 5 10 **S** U. S. Public Health Service Indian Health Service, Rockville, MD

| | 47 | 10 | 14 | — | — | — | — | — | — | — |

GARRISON—McLean County

★ GARRISON MEMORIAL HOSPITAL, 407 Third Avenue S.E., Zip 58540–0039; tel. 701/463–2275; Richard Spilovoy, Administrator (Total facility includes 24 beds in nursing home–type unit) (Nonreporting) **A**5 9 10 **S** Benedictine Sisters of the Annunciation, Bismarck, ND

| | 21 | 10 | 54 | — | — | — | — | — | — | — |

GRAFTON—Walsh County

✠ UNITY MEDICAL CENTER, 164 West 13th Street, Zip 58237–1896; tel. 701/352–1620; Everett A. Butler, Chief Executive Officer **A**1 5 9 10 **F**7 8 15 17 19 22 28 29 30 32 33 34 35 40 41 42 44 49 51 54 65 67 70 71 73 **P**6

| | 23 | 10 | 17 | 480 | 8 | 27888 | 40 | 4796 | 2807 | 92 |

GRAND FORKS—Grand Forks County

✠ △ ALTRU HEALTH SYSTEM, (Includes Altru Hospital, 1200 South Columbia Road, tel. 701/780–5000; Altrua Health Institute, 1300 South Columbia Road, Mailing Address: P.O. Box 9017, Zip 58202; tel. 701/780–2311; 1000 South Columbia Road, Zip 58201; tel. 701/780–5000; Gregory Gerloff, Chief Executive Officer **A**1 2 3 5 7 9 10 **F**3 4 5 6 7 8 10 12 13 14 15 16 17 18 19 21 22 23 24 26 27 28 29 30 31 32 33 34 35 36 39 41 42 43 44 45 46 49 50 51 53 54 55 56 57 58 59 60 61 62 63 65 66 67 68 70 71 72 73 74 **P**2 **N** United Hospital, Grand Forks, ND
MEDICAL CENTER REHABILITATION HOSPITAL See Altrua Health Institute

| | 23 | 10 | 261 | 10112 | 147 | 86607 | 1143 | 155709 | 78535 | 2312 |

GRAND FORKS AFB—Grand Forks County

✠ U. S. AIR FORCE HOSPITAL, Grand Forks SAC, Zip 58205–6332, Mailing Address: Grand Forks SAC, 220 G. Street, Zip 58205–6332; tel. 701/747–5391; Lieutenant Colonel Robert J. Rennie, Administrator (Nonreporting) **A**1 5 **S** Department of the Air Force, Bowling AFB, DC

| | 41 | 10 | 15 | — | — | — | — | — | — | — |

HARVEY—Wells County

★ ST. ALOISIUS MEDICAL CENTER, 325 East Brewster Street, Zip 58341–1605; tel. 701/324–4651; Ronald J. Volk, President (Total facility includes 116 beds in nursing home–type unit) **A**5 9 10 **F**3 7 8 19 22 28 32 35 37 40 42 44 49 53 54 58 64 65 67 71 73 **S** Sisters of Mary of the Presentation Health Corporation, Fargo, ND

| | 21 | 10 | 165 | 692 | 131 | 6327 | 22 | 7071 | 3706 | 131 |

HAZEN—Mercer County

★ SAKAKAWEA MEDICAL CENTER, 510 Eighth Avenue N.E., Zip 58545–4637; tel. 701/748–2225; Ed Huyrsz, Administrator **A**5 9 10 **F**3 7 8 11 15 16 19 22 26 28 30 32 33 35 37 39 40 44 45 62 65 67 71 73 **P**6

| | 23 | 10 | 32 | 640 | 8 | 12678 | 57 | 4887 | 2372 | 113 |

HETTINGER—Adams County

□ WEST RIVER REGIONAL MEDICAL CENTER, 1000 Highway 12, Zip 58639–7530, Mailing Address: Rural Route 2, Box 124, Zip 58639–0124; tel. 701/567–4561; Jim K. Long, CPA, Administrator and Chief Executive Officer **A**1 5 9 10 **F**7 8 11 12 13 15 16 17 18 19 20 21 22 27 28 29 30 32 34 35 37 39 40 41 42 44 46 49 51 58 62 63 64 65 66 70 71 73 74 **P**3

| | 23 | 10 | 43 | 1581 | 20 | 8491 | 136 | 13356 | 4723 | 197 |

HILLSBORO—Traill County

HILLSBORO MEDICAL CENTER, (Formerly Hillsboro Community Hospital), 12 Third Street S.E., Zip 58045–4821, Mailing Address: P.O. Box 609, Zip 58045–0609; tel. 701/436–4501; Bruce D. Bowersox, Administrator (Total facility includes 50 beds in nursing home–type unit) (Nonreporting) **A**5 9 10

| | 23 | 10 | 74 | — | — | — | — | — | — | — |

JAMESTOWN—Stutsman County

✠ JAMESTOWN HOSPITAL, 419 Fifth Street N.E., Zip 58401–3360; tel. 701/252–1050; Richard W. Hall, President **A**1 5 9 10 **F**7 8 15 16 19 21 22 30 31 32 33 34 35 37 39 40 41 44 45 46 49 56 61 63 64 65 67 71 73

| | 23 | 10 | 56 | 1827 | 20 | 43199 | 261 | 12784 | 6368 | 214 |

Hospital, Address, Telephone, Administrator, Approval, Facility, and Physician Codes, Health Care System, Network	Classi-fication Codes		Utilization Data					Expense (thousands) of dollars		
	Control	Service	Staffed Beds	Admissions	Census	Outpatient Visits	Births	Total	Payroll	Personnel

★ American Hospital Association (AHA) membership
☐ Joint Commission on Accreditation of Healthcare Organizations (JCAHO) accreditation
+ American Osteopathic Healthcare Association (AOHA) membership
○ American Osteopathic Association (AOA) accreditation
△ Commission on Accreditation of Rehabilitation Facilities (CARF) accreditation
Control codes 61, 63, 64, 71, 72 and 73 indicate hospitals listed by AOHA, but not registered by AHA. For definition of numerical codes, see page A4

Hospital	Control	Service	Staffed Beds	Admissions	Census	Outpatient Visits	Births	Total	Payroll	Personnel
⊞ NORTH DAKOTA STATE HOSPITAL, 1024 23rd Street S.E., Zip 58402, Mailing Address: P.O. Box 476, Zip 58402–0476; tel. 701/253–3650; Alex Schweitzer, Superintendent and Chief Executive Officer **A**1 5 9 10 **F**2 14 15 16 52 53 54 55 56 57 58 59 64 **P**6	12	22	262	1657	216	—	—	26402	15300	—
KENMARE—Ward County										
★ KENMARE COMMUNITY HOSPITAL, (GENERAL MEDICAL SWING BEDS/LTC), 317 First Avenue N.W., Zip 58746–7104, Mailing Address: P.O. Box 697, Zip 58746–0697; tel. 701/385–4296; Verlin Buechler, President and Chief Executive Officer (Total facility includes 12 beds in nursing home–type unit) **A**9 10 **F**15 16 19 26 28 30 32 33 36 49 53 54 55 57 58 64 65 67 71 73 **S** Quorum Health Group/Quorum Health Resources, Inc., Brentwood, TN	21	49	42	100	38	4532	—	1971	1052	76
LANGDON—Cavalier County										
★ CAVALIER COUNTY MEMORIAL HOSPITAL, 909 Second Street, Zip 58249–2499; tel. 701/256–6180; Daryl J. Wilkens, Administrator **A**5 9 10 **F**7 8 11 15 19 22 29 30 32 33 34 37 39 40 42 44 49 51 63 65 **P**6	23	10	28	479	6	14418	25	2825	1545	68
LINTON—Emmons County										
LINTON HOSPITAL, 518 North Broadway, Zip 58552–7308, Mailing Address: P.O. Box 850, Zip 58552–0850; tel. 701/254–4511; Arlene Mack, Administrator **A**5 9 10 **F**16 32 36 37 40 44 49 65 70 73 **P**5	23	10	25	447	5	6485	19	3035	1722	61
LISBON—Ransom County										
★ LISBON MEDICAL CENTER, 905 Main Street, Zip 58054–0353, Mailing Address: P.O. Box 353, Zip 58054–0353; tel. 701/683–5241; Jack Jacobs, Administrator (Total facility includes 45 beds in nursing home–type unit) **A**5 9 10 **F**7 11 12 15 16 19 28 32 40 41 44 45 48 49 64 **S** Lutheran Health Systems, Fargo, ND	23	10	64	540	49	31512	28	5836	2980	
MAYVILLE—Traill County										
★ UNION HOSPITAL, 42 Sixth Avenue S.E., Zip 58257–1598; tel. 701/786–3800; James Mackay, Jr., Chief Executive Officer **A**5 9 10 **F**3 7 8 14 15 16 17 19 21 22 24 32 33 39 40 44 45 49 63 65 71 73	23	10	28	564	10	6558	27	2883	1427	57
MCVILLE—Nelson County										
COMMUNITY HOSPITAL IN NELSON COUNTY, Main Street, Zip 58254, Mailing Address: P.O. Box H., Zip 58254–0787; tel. 701/322–4328; Jim Opdahl, Administrator (Nonreporting) **A**9 10	23	10	19	—	—	—	—	—	—	—
MINOT—Ward County										
⊞ △ TRINITY MEDICAL CENTER, Burdick Expressway at Main Street, Zip 58701–5020, Mailing Address: P.O. Box 5020, Zip 58702–5020; tel. 701/857–5000; Terry G. Hoff, President (Total facility includes 294 beds in nursing home–type unit) **A**1 2 3 5 7 9 10 **F**1 3 4 7 8 10 12 13 14 15 16 17 19 21 22 23 24 25 26 28 30 31 32 33 34 35 37 38 39 40 41 42 43 44 45 46 48 49 51 53 54 55 56 57 58 59 62 63 64 65 66 67 68 70 71 72 73 74 **P**1 3 4 5 6	23	10	472	5385	390	38874	685	108233	56105	1057
⊞ U. S. AIR FORCE REGIONAL HOSPITAL, 10 Missile Avenue, Zip 58705–5024; tel. 701/723–5103; Colonel Robert C. Tollefson, Commander (Nonreporting) **A**1 5 **S** Department of the Air Force, Bowling AFB, DC	41	10	39	—	—	—	—	—	—	—
⊞ UNIMED MEDICAL CENTER, 407 3rd Street S.E., Zip 58702–5001; tel. 701/857–2000; James E. Richardson, FACHE, Interim Chief Executive Officer **A**1 2 3 5 9 10 **F**3 4 7 8 10 12 13 15 17 18 19 20 21 22 24 26 27 28 29 30 31 32 33 34 35 39 41 42 43 44 45 46 49 53 54 55 56 57 58 59 60 65 66 67 70 71 73 74 **P**7 **S** Quorum Health Group/Quorum Health Resources, Inc., Brentwood, TN	21	10	160	5309	75	56208	376	51083	21982	706
NORTHWOOD—Grand Forks County										
★ NORTHWOOD DEACONESS HEALTH CENTER, 4 North Park Street, Zip 58267–0190; tel. 701/587–6060; Larry E. Feickert, Chief Administrative Officer (Total facility includes 112 beds in nursing home–type unit) (Nonreporting) **A**9 10	21	10	124	—	—	—	—	—	—	—
OAKES—Dickey County										
⊞ OAKES COMMUNITY HOSPITAL, 314 South Eighth Street, Zip 58474–2099; tel. 701/742–3291; Sister Susan Marie Loeffen, President and Chief Executive Officer (Nonreporting) **A**1 9 10	21	10	30	—	—	—	—	—	—	—
PARK RIVER—Walsh County										
★ ST. ANSGAR'S HEALTH CENTER, 115 Vivian Street, Zip 58270–0708; tel. 701/284–7500; Michael D. Mahrer, President **A**9 10 **F**7 14 15 19 28 30 32 33 34 35 37 40 44 65 70 71 **P**5 **S** Catholic Health Initiatives, Denver, CO	21	10	20	564	10	8634	28	3251	1432	59
RICHARDTON—Stark County										
RICHARDTON HEALTH CENTER, 212 Third Avenue West, Zip 58652–7103, Mailing Address: P.O. Box H., Zip 58652; tel. 701/974–3304; Arlene Mack, Administrator (Total facility includes 23 beds in nursing home–type unit) **A**9 10 **F**11 14 15 16 22 24 26 27 29 36 38 40 65 71 73 **N** Medcenter One, Bismarck, ND	33	10	23	110	20	216	—	911	551	33
ROLLA—Rolette County										
PRESENTATION MEDICAL CENTER, 213 Second Avenue N.E., Zip 58367–7153, Mailing Address: P.O. Box 759, Zip 58367–0759; tel. 701/477–3161; Kimber Wraalstad, Chief Executive Officer (Total facility includes 48 beds in nursing home–type unit) **A**9 10 **F**7 8 13 19 22 28 30 32 34 36 37 40 41 42 44 45 49 53 54 57 58 64 65 66 71 73 74 **P**6 **S** Sisters of Mary of the Presentation Health Corporation, Fargo, ND	21	10	102	652	56	6797	101	6410	3443	149
RUGBY—Pierce County										
⊞ HEART OF AMERICA MEDICAL CENTER, Rugby Heights, Zip 58368, Mailing Address: P.O. Box 197, Zip 58368–0197; tel. 701/776–5261; Jerry E. Jurena, Executive Director (Total facility includes 198 beds in nursing home–type unit) **A**1 9 10 **F**3 7 19 21 22 26 28 31 32 33 34 36 37 39 40 41 44 49 62 64 65 66 67 71 73	23	10	236	866	206	14099	73	10633	5138	245

Hospital, Address, Telephone, Administrator, Approval, Facility, and Physician Codes, Health Care System, Network	Classi-fication Codes		Utilization Data					Expense (thousands) of dollars		
★ American Hospital Association (AHA) membership □ Joint Commission on Accreditation of Healthcare Organizations (JCAHO) accreditation + American Osteopathic Healthcare Association (AOHA) membership ○ American Osteopathic Association (AOA) accreditation △ Commission on Accreditation of Rehabilitation Facilities (CARF) accreditation Control codes 61, 63, 64, 71, 72 and 73 indicate hospitals listed by AOHA, but not registered by AHA. For definition of numerical codes, see page A4	Control	Service	Staffed Beds	Admissions	Census	Outpatient Visits	Births	Total	Payroll	Personnel

STANLEY—Mountrail County

MOUNTRAIL COUNTY MEDICAL CENTER, (Formerly Stanley Community Hospital), 502 Third Street S.E., Zip 58784–4323, Mailing Address: P.O. Box 399, Zip 58784–0399; tel. 701/628–2424; Mitch Leupp, Administrator (Nonreporting) **A**9 10

| | 23 | 10 | 25 | — | — | — | — | — | — | — |

TIOGA—Williams County

★ TIOGA MEDICAL CENTER, 810 North Welo Street, Zip 58852–0159, Mailing Address: P.O. Box 159, Zip 58852–0159; tel. 701/664–3305; Lowell D. Herfindahl, President and Chief Executive Officer (Total facility includes 30 beds in nursing home–type unit) **A**9 10 **F**7 8 15 19 21 22 26 28 32 37 40 42 57 64 65 70 71 73 **P**6

| | 23 | 10 | 59 | 450 | 33 | 7967 | 18 | 3356 | 1755 | 50 |

TURTLE LAKE—McLean County

COMMUNITY MEMORIAL HOSPITAL, 220 Fifth Avenue, Zip 58575, Mailing Address: P.O. Box 280, Zip 58575–0280; tel. 701/448–2331; Dale Aman, Administrator **A**9 10 **F**1 8 11 15 19 22 24 28 32 33 34 35 36 40 44 49 51 62 64 65 70 71 **P**6

| | 21 | 10 | 29 | 162 | 5 | 2465 | 0 | 1261 | 693 | 39 |

VALLEY CITY—Barnes County

⊞ MERCY HOSPITAL, 570 Chautauqua Boulevard, Zip 58072–3199; tel. 701/845–6400; Jane Bissel, President and Chief Executive Officer **A**1 9 10 **F**1 7 8 11 14 15 19 22 26 28 29 30 32 34 35 37 39 40 44 49 65 66 70 71 **S** Catholic Health Initiatives, Denver, CO

| | 21 | 10 | 50 | 944 | 38 | 14995 | 91 | 6885 | 3841 | 145 |

WATFORD CITY—McKenzie County

★ MCKENZIE COUNTY MEMORIAL HOSPITAL, 508 North Main Street, Zip 58854–7310, Mailing Address: P.O. Box 548, Zip 58854–0548; tel. 701/842–3000; Collette Anderson, Administrator **A**9 10 **F**7 11 15 19 22 24 28 30 32 39 40 44 49 64 66 71 **P**5 **N** Medcenter One, Bismarck, ND

| | 23 | 10 | 26 | 161 | 4 | 1091 | 6 | 1674 | 760 | 31 |

WILLISTON—Williams County

⊞ MERCY MEDICAL CENTER, 1301 15th Avenue West, Zip 58801–3896; tel. 701/774–7400; Duane D. Jerde, President and Chief Executive Officer **A**1 9 10 **F**2 3 7 8 12 15 19 21 22 23 24 28 30 32 33 34 35 37 39 40 41 42 44 45 46 49 52 53 54 55 56 57 58 59 60 63 64 65 66 67 71 73 74 **P**6 **S** Catholic Health Initiatives, Denver, CO

| | 21 | 10 | 105 | 2704 | 43 | — | 281 | 26073 | 12772 | 422 |

WISHEK—McIntosh County

★ WISHEK COMMUNITY HOSPITAL, 1007 Fourth Avenue South, Zip 58495, Mailing Address: P.O. Box 647, Zip 58495–0647; tel. 701/452–2326; C. Gary Kopp, Administrator **A**9 10 **F**11 14 15 16 19 21 24 25 30 32 34 37 44 45 48 49 64 65 70 71 **P**6 8

| | 23 | 10 | 22 | 390 | 4 | 12494 | 0 | 3865 | 2014 | 81 |

OHIO

Resident population 11,186 (in thousands)
Resident population in metro areas 81.2%
Birth rate per 1,000 population 14.0
65 years and over 13.4%
Percent of persons without health insurance 11.5%

Hospital, Address, Telephone, Administrator, Approval, Facility, and Physician Codes, Health Care System, Network	Classification Codes		Utilization Data					Expense (thousands) of dollars		
	Control	Service	Staffed Beds	Admissions	Census	Outpatient Visits	Births	Total	Payroll	Personnel

★ American Hospital Association (AHA) membership
□ Joint Commission on Accreditation of Healthcare Organizations (JCAHO) accreditation
+ American Osteopathic Healthcare Association (AOHA) membership
○ American Osteopathic Association (AOA) accreditation
△ Commission on Accreditation of Rehabilitation Facilities (CARF) accreditation
Control codes 61, 63, 64, 71, 72 and 73 indicate hospitals listed by AOHA, but not registered by AHA. For definition of numerical codes, see page A4

AKRON—Summit County

AKRON CITY HOSPITAL See Summa Health System

✠ AKRON GENERAL MEDICAL CENTER, 400 Wabash Avenue, Zip 44307–2433; tel. 330/384–6000; Alan J. Bleyer, President (Nonreporting) **A**1 2 3 5 9 10 **N** Northeast Ohio Health Network, Akron, OH	23	10	473	—	—	—	—	—	—	—
✠ CHILDREN'S HOSPITAL MEDICAL CENTER OF AKRON, One Perkins Square, Zip 44308–1062; tel. 330/379–8200; William H. Considine, President **A**1 3 5 8 9 10 **F**1 2 3 4 7 8 9 10 11 12 13 14 15 16 17 18 19 20 21 22 24 25 26 27 28 29 30 31 32 33 34 35 37 38 39 40 41 42 43 44 45 46 47 48 49 51 52 53 54 55 56 58 59 60 61 63 64 65 66 67 68 69 70 71 72 73 74 **P**8 **N** Northeast Ohio Health Network, Akron, OH; Cleveland Health Network, Independence, OH	23	50	200	7170	103	233087	1	113377	54354	1484
✠ △ EDWIN SHAW HOSPITAL FOR REHABILITATION, 1621 Flickinger Road, Zip 44312–4495; tel. 330/784–1271; Daniel K. Church, Ph.D., President and Chief Executive Officer (Total facility includes 49 beds in nursing home–type unit) **A**1 7 9 10 **F**2 3 14 15 17 20 34 36 46 48 49 64 65 67 73	15	46	139	2017	91	0	0	24630	13306	443
SAINT THOMAS HOSPITAL See Summa Health System										
✠ SUMMA HEALTH SYSTEM, (Includes Akron City Hospital, 525 East Market Street, Zip 44309–2090, Mailing Address: P.O. Box 2090, Zip 44309–2090; tel. 330/375–3000; Saint Thomas Hospital, 444 North Main Street, Zip 44310; tel. 330/375–3000), Albert F. Gilbert, Ph.D., President and Chief Executive Officer **A**1 2 3 5 6 8 9 10 **F**2 3 4 5 7 8 10 11 12 13 17 18 19 20 21 22 23 25 26 28 29 31 33 34 35 36 37 39 40 41 42 43 44 45 46 48 49 51 53 54 56 57 58 59 60 61 65 66 67 69 70 71 73 74 **N** Summa Health System, Akron, OH; Cleveland Health Network, Independence, OH; Summa Health System, Akron, OH	23	10	601	33446	456	463619	3707	—	—	—

ALLIANCE—Stark County

□ △ ALLIANCE COMMUNITY HOSPITAL, 264 East Rice Street, Zip 44601–4399; tel. 330/829–4000; Stanley W. Jonas, Chief Executive Officer (Total facility includes 78 beds in nursing home–type unit) **A**1 2 7 9 10 **F**7 8 12 14 15 17 19 21 22 23 25 26 28 29 30 32 33 34 35 36 37 39 40 41 42 44 45 46 48 49 51 64 65 66 67 71 72 73 74	23	10	206	4858	120	105186	597	41907	19304	715

AMHERST—Lorain County

✠ EMH AMHERST HOSPITAL, 254 Cleveland Avenue, Zip 44001–1699; tel. 440/988–6000; James L. Keegan, President and Chief Executive Officer (Nonreporting) **A**1 9 10 **N** Cleveland Health Network, Independence, OH; Comprehensive Healthcare of Ohio, Inc., Elyria, OH	23	10	71	—	—	—	—	—	—	—

ASHLAND—Ashland County

✠ SAMARITAN REGIONAL HEALTH SYSTEM, 1025 Center Street, Zip 44805–4098; tel. 419/289–0491; William C. Kelley, Jr., FACHE, President and Chief Executive Officer **A**1 9 10 **F**7 8 15 16 19 21 22 25 28 30 32 34 35 37 40 41 42 44 49 52 57 59 65 71 72 73	23	10	106	3401	35	115940	547	36797	14658	605

ASHTABULA—Ashtabula County

✠ ASHTABULA COUNTY MEDICAL CENTER, 2420 Lake Avenue, Zip 44004–4993; tel. 440/997–2262; R. D. Richardson, President and Chief Executive Officer **A**1 9 10 **F**3 7 8 14 15 16 19 21 22 27 31 32 33 34 35 37 40 41 42 44 46 49 51 52 53 54 55 56 57 58 59 63 64 65 66 71 73 **P**6 **N** Great Lakes Health Network, Erie, PA; Cleveland Health Network, Independence, OH	23	10	163	5290	78	130000	669	49316	22758	—

ATHENS—Athens County

✠ + O'BLENESS MEMORIAL HOSPITAL, 55 Hospital Drive, Zip 45701–2302; tel. 740/593–5551; Richard F. Castrop, President **A**1 9 10 12 13 **F**7 8 14 17 19 20 21 22 23 26 28 30 31 32 33 34 35 37 39 40 42 44 45 46 49 51 56 63 65 67 71 72 73	23	10	75	2696	29	60931	566	24432	10278	303
SOUTHEAST PSYCHIATRIC HOSPITAL See Appalachian Psychiatric Healthcare System, Cambridge										

BARBERTON—Summit County

✠ BARBERTON CITIZENS HOSPITAL, 155 Fifth Street N.E., Zip 44203–3398; tel. 330/745–1611; Ronald J. Elder, Chief Executive Officer (Total facility includes 46 beds in nursing home–type unit) (Nonreporting) **A**1 2 3 5 9 10 **S** Quorum Health Group/Quorum Health Resources, Inc., Brentwood, TN **N** Northeast Ohio Health Network, Akron, OH; Cleveland Health Network, Independence, OH	33	10	272	—	—	—	—	—	—	—

BARNESVILLE—Belmont County

✠ BARNESVILLE HOSPITAL ASSOCIATION, 639 West Main Street, Zip 43713–1096, Mailing Address: P.O. Box 309, Zip 43713–0309; tel. 740/425–3941; Richard L. Doan, Chief Executive Officer **A**1 9 10 **F**8 12 15 17 19 21 22 28 30 31 32 33 34 36 37 39 41 44 45 46 49 54 56 64 65 67 71 73 **P**6 **N** Ohio State Health Network, Columbus, OH	23	10	55	2169	32	31322	0	13616	6577	297

Hospital, Address, Telephone, Administrator, Approval, Facility, and Physician Codes, Health Care System, Network	Classi-fication Codes		Utilization Data					Expense (thousands) of dollars		
	Control	Service	Staffed Beds	Admissions	Census	Outpatient Visits	Births	Total	Payroll	Personnel

★ American Hospital Association (AHA) membership
□ Joint Commission on Accreditation of Healthcare Organizations (JCAHO) accreditation
+ American Osteopathic Healthcare Association (AOHA) membership
○ American Osteopathic Association (AOA) accreditation
△ Commission on Accreditation of Rehabilitation Facilities (CARF) accreditation
Control codes 61, 63, 64, 71, 72 and 73 indicate hospitals listed by AOHA, but not registered by AHA. For definition of numerical codes, see page A4

BATAVIA—Clermont County

□ CLERMONT MERCY HOSPITAL, 3000 Hospital Drive, Zip 45103–1998; tel. 513/732–8200; Karen S. Ehrat, Ph.D., President **A**1 9 10 **F**8 10 12 14 15 16 17 18 19 21 24 25 29 30 32 33 34 35 37 39 41 42 44 45 46 49 52 53 54 56 57 59 60 63 65 67 71 72 73 74 **P**6 8 **S** Catholic Healthcare Partners, Cincinnati, OH **N** Mercy Regional Health System, Greater Cincinnati, Cincinnati, OH	21	10	133	5026	59	178835	—	43205	19627	486

BEDFORD—Cuyahoga County

✠ UHHS BEDFORD MEDICAL CENTER, 44 Blaine Avenue, Zip 44146–2799; tel. 440/439–2000; Arlene A. Rak, R.N., President (Nonreporting) **A**1 2 9 10 **S** University Hospitals Health System, Cleveland, OH **N** University Hospitals Health System, Cleveland, OH	23	10	110							

BELLAIRE—Belmont County

✠ BELMONT COMMUNITY HOSPITAL, (Formerly City Hospital), 4697 Harrison Street, Zip 43906, Mailing Address: P.O. Box 653, Zip 43906–0653; tel. 740/671–1200; Gary R. Gould, FACHE, Chief Executive Officer **A**1 9 10 **F**4 7 8 10 19 21 22 24 25 27 32 33 34 35 37 40 41 42 43 44 48 49 52 53 60 65 66 71 73 **P**1 7	23	10	79	2377	35	34968	271	13669	7343	266

CITY HOSPITAL See Belmont Community Hospital

BELLEFONTAINE—Logan County

✠ MARY RUTAN HOSPITAL, 205 Palmer Avenue, Zip 43311–2298; tel. 937/592–4015; Ewing H. Crawfis, President (Nonreporting) **A**1 9 10 **N** Ohio State Health Network, Columbus, OH; West Central Ohio Regional Healthcare Alliance, Ltd., Lima, OH	23	10	72							

BELLEVUE—Sandusky County

✠ BELLEVUE HOSPITAL, 811 Northwest Street, Zip 44811, Mailing Address: P.O. Box 8004, Zip 44811–8004; tel. 419/483–4040; Michael K. Winthrop, President **A**1 2 9 10 **F**7 8 15 16 19 21 22 26 27 30 31 33 34 35 37 40 41 42 44 49 54 57 63 65 66 67 71 73 **P**7 8 **N** United Health Partners, Toledo, OH; Lake Erie Health Alliance, Toledo, OH	23	10	25	2136	21	34340	399	18959	8250	263

BOWLING GREEN—Wood County

✠ WOOD COUNTY HOSPITAL, 950 West Wooster Street, Zip 43402–2699; tel. 419/354–8900; Michael A. Miesle, Administrator **A**1 9 10 **F**7 8 10 14 16 19 21 22 23 28 31 33 34 35 36 37 39 40 41 42 44 49 58 63 65 66 71 73 **P**8 **N** United Health Partners, Toledo, OH; First Interhealth Network, Toledo, OH; Lake Erie Health Alliance, Toledo, OH	23	10	85	3233	38	67906	509	26229	12487	415

BRYAN—Williams County

□ COMMUNITY HOSPITALS OF WILLIAMS COUNTY, (Includes Bryan Hospital, 433 West High Street, Zip 43506; tel. 419/636–1131; Montpelier Hospital, Snyder and Lincoln Avenue, Montpelier, Zip 43543; tel. 419/485–3154), 433 West High Street, Zip 43506–1680; tel. 419/636–1131; Rusty O. Brunicardi, President (Nonreporting) **A**1 9 10	23	10	121							

BUCYRUS—Crawford County

✠ BUCYRUS COMMUNITY HOSPITAL, 629 North Sandusky Avenue, Zip 44820–0627, Mailing Address: Box 627, Zip 44820–0627; tel. 419/562–4677; Mark E. Marley, Chief Executive Officer **A**1 9 10 **F**8 14 15 16 19 21 22 28 30 32 33 35 36 37 39 42 44 49 51 63 65 71 73 **S** OhioHealth, Columbus, OH	23	10	47	922	11	39400	—	11189	3950	172

CADIZ—Harrison County

□ HARRISON COMMUNITY HOSPITAL, 951 East Market Street, Zip 43907–9749; tel. 740/942–4631; Terry Carson, Chief Executive Officer **A**1 9 10 **F**8 11 17 19 20 21 22 24 28 30 32 34 35 37 39 41 44 45 48 49 64 65 67 70 71 73 74	23	10	48	785	23	13590	—	6944	3224	123

CAMBRIDGE—Guernsey County

□ APPALACHIAN PSYCHIATRIC HEALTHCARE SYSTEM, (Includes Southeast Psychiatric Hospital, 100 Hospital Drive, Athens, Zip 45701–2301; tel. 614/594–5000; Mark F. McGee, M.D., Chief Clinical Officer), 66737 Old 21 Road North, Zip 43725–9298; tel. 740/439–1371; Stephen C. Pierson, Ph.D., Chief Executive Officer **A**1 9 10 **F**14 29 30 39 41 45 52 54 55 56 65 67 73	12	22	172	784	—	0	0	—	14202	—
✠ SOUTHEASTERN OHIO REGIONAL MEDICAL CENTER, 1341 North Clark Street, Zip 43725–0610, Mailing Address: P.O. Box 610, Zip 43725–0610; tel. 740/439–3561; Philip E. Hearing, President and Chief Executive Officer (Total facility includes 20 beds in nursing home–type unit) **A**1 2 9 10 **F**7 8 12 14 15 16 17 19 22 28 29 30 32 34 35 36 37 39 40 41 44 46 49 63 64 65 66 67 71 73 74 **P**6 8	23	10	113	4492	61	69947	331	35624	14911	701

CANTON—Stark County

✠ AULTMAN HOSPITAL, 2600 Sixth Street S.W., Zip 44710–1799; tel. 330/452–9911; Richard J. Pryce, President (Nonreporting) **A**1 2 3 5 6 9 10	23	10	736							
✠ △ MERCY MEDICAL CENTER, (Formerly Columbia Mercy Medical Center), 1320 Mercy Drive N.W., Zip 44708–2641; tel. 330/489–1000; Jack W. Topoleski, President and Chief Executive Officer **A**1 2 3 5 7 9 10 **F**3 4 7 8 10 11 12 14 15 16 17 19 21 22 24 26 27 28 30 32 33 34 35 37 38 39 40 41 42 43 44 45 46 48 49 50 52 53 54 55 56 57 58 59 60 63 65 66 68 69 70 71 72 73 74 **S** Columbia/HCA Healthcare Corporation, Nashville, TN	32	10	376	16549	254	449307	1812	142597	63886	2316

CHAGRIN FALLS—Cuyahoga County

✠ BHC WINDSOR HOSPITAL, 115 East Summit Street, Zip 44022–2750; tel. 440/247–5300; Donald K. Sykes, Jr., Chief Executive Officer **A**1 9 10 **F**1 2 3 25 34 49 52 53 54 55 56 57 58 59 60 67 **S** Behavioral Healthcare Corporation, Nashville, TN	33	22	50	914	23	702	0	—	—	54

Hospital, Address, Telephone, Administrator, Approval, Facility, and Physician Codes, Health Care System, Network	Classi-fication Codes		Utilization Data					Expense (thousands) of dollars		
	Control	Service	Staffed Beds	Admissions	Census	Outpatient Visits	Births	Total	Payroll	Personnel

★ American Hospital Association (AHA) membership
☐ Joint Commission on Accreditation of Healthcare Organizations (JCAHO) accreditation
+ American Osteopathic Healthcare Association (AOHA) membership
○ American Osteopathic Association (AOA) accreditation
△ Commission on Accreditation of Rehabilitation Facilities (CARF) accreditation
Control codes 61, 63, 64, 71, 72 and 73 indicate hospitals listed by AOHA, but not registered by AHA. For definition of numerical codes, see page A4

CHARDON—Geauga County

☐ △ HEATHER HILL HOSPITAL AND HEALTH CARE CENTER, (LONG TERM CARE HOSPITAL), 12340 Bass Lake Road, Zip 44024–8327; tel. 440/942–6424; Robert Glenn Harr, President (Total facility includes 194 beds in nursing home–type unit) **A**1 7 10 **F**1 12 14 15 17 19 21 26 27 29 30 32 33 34 35 39 41 45 48 49 57 58 64 65 66 67 71 73	23	49	250	1045	208	1516	—	21287	11342	384
✸ UHHS GEAUGA REGIONAL HOSPITAL, 13207 Ravenna Road, Zip 44024–9012; tel. 440/269–6000; Richard J. Frenchie, President and Chief Executive Officer (Total facility includes 21 beds in nursing home–type unit) **A**1 2 9 10 **F**7 8 11 12 14 15 16 19 20 21 22 28 30 32 33 34 35 37 39 40 41 42 44 45 46 49 63 64 65 66 67 71 73 74 **P**4 5 7 8 **S** University Hospitals Health System, Cleveland, OH **N** University Hospitals Health System, Cleveland, OH	23	10	122	4844	57	62248	736	35280	16083	376

CHILLICOTHE—Ross County

✸ ADENA HEALTH SYSTEM, 272 Hospital Road, Zip 45601–0708; tel. 740/779–7500; Allen V. Rupiper, President (Nonreporting) **A**1 10 **N** Community Hospitals of Ohio, Newark, OH; Mount Carmel Health System, Columbus, OH	23	10	156	—	—	—	—	—	—	—
✸ VETERANS AFFAIRS MEDICAL CENTER, 17273 State Route 104, Zip 45601–0999; tel. 740/773–1141; Michael W. Walton, Director (Total facility includes 167 beds in nursing home–type unit) **A**1 5 9 **F**1 2 3 8 12 15 17 19 20 21 22 26 27 28 29 30 31 32 33 35 37 41 44 46 49 51 52 54 55 56 57 58 64 65 67 71 73 74 **P**6 **S** Department of Veterans Affairs, Washington, DC	45	22	334	4410	232	109111	0	80088	43948	1124

CINCINNATI—Hamilton County

✸ BETHESDA NORTH HOSPITAL, 10500 Montgomery Road, Zip 45242–4415; tel. 513/745–1111; John S. Prout, President and Chief Executive Officer (Total facility includes 349 beds in nursing home–type unit) **A**1 9 10 **F**1 2 3 4 6 7 8 10 11 12 15 16 17 18 19 21 22 23 24 25 26 27 28 29 30 31 32 33 34 35 37 38 39 40 41 42 43 44 45 46 48 49 51 52 53 54 55 56 57 58 59 60 61 62 64 65 66 67 68 69 70 71 72 73 **P**3 7 **S** Bethesda Hospital, Inc., Cincinnati, OH **N** TriHealth, Cincinnati, OH	23	10	361	23150	221	261444	5537	199703	95286	3031
✸ △ BETHESDA OAK HOSPITAL, 619 Oak Street, Zip 45206–1690; tel. 513/569–6111; Linda D. Schaffner, R.N., Vice President and Administrator (Total facility includes 349 beds in nursing home–type unit) **A**1 2 3 5 7 9 10 **F**1 2 3 4 6 7 8 10 11 12 15 16 17 18 19 21 22 23 24 25 26 27 28 29 30 31 32 33 34 35 37 38 39 40 41 42 43 44 45 46 48 49 51 52 53 54 55 56 57 58 59 60 61 62 63 64 65 66 67 68 69 70 71 72 73 **P**3 7 **S** Bethesda Hospital, Inc., Cincinnati, OH **N** First Interhealth Network, Toledo, OH; TriHealth, Cincinnati, OH	23	10	361	23150	221	261444	5537	199703	95286	3031
✸ △ CHILDREN'S HOSPITAL MEDICAL CENTER, (Includes Division of Adolescent Medicine, Cincinnati Center for Developmental Disorders, and Convalescent Hospital for Children; Children's Hospital), 3333 Burnet Avenue, Zip 45229–3039; tel. 513/636–4200; James M. Anderson, President and Chief Executive Officer (Nonreporting) **A**1 2 3 5 7 8 9 10	23	50	279	—	—	—	—	—	—	—
✸ △ CHRIST HOSPITAL, 2139 Auburn Avenue, Zip 45219–2989; tel. 513/369–2000; Claus von Zychlin, Senior Executive Officer **A**1 2 3 5 6 7 9 10 **F**3 4 8 10 11 14 19 21 22 23 30 31 32 33 34 35 37 40 41 42 43 44 45 46 48 49 50 52 57 58 59 60 61 64 65 66 69 71 73 74 **P**1 6 **S** Health Alliance of Greater Cincinnati, Cincinnati, OH **N** The Healthcare Alliance of Greater Cincinnati, Cincinnati, OH; CHA Provider Network, Inc., Lexington, KY; Center Care, Bowling Green, KY	23	10	459	22455	285	148573	3574	244592	103098	2812
☐ △ DEACONESS HOSPITAL, 311 Straight Street, Zip 45219–1099; tel. 513/559–2100; E. Anthony Woods, President (Total facility includes 20 beds in nursing home–type unit) (Nonreporting) **A**1 7 9 10	23	10	219	—	—	—	—	—	—	—
✸ △ DRAKE CENTER, 151 West Galbraith Road, Zip 45216–1096; tel. 513/948–2500; Roberta J. Bradford, President and Chief Executive Officer (Total facility includes 186 beds in nursing home–type unit) **A**1 3 5 7 9 10 **F**2 8 12 14 15 16 17 20 22 24 26 27 30 34 36 37 38 39 41 46 48 49 52 64 65 66 67 70 73	23	46	286	1068	233	17189	0	42721	20093	589
✸ △ FRANCISCAN HOSPITAL–MOUNT AIRY CAMPUS, 2446 Kipling Avenue, Zip 45239–6650; tel. 513/853–5000; R. Christopher West, President (Total facility includes 20 beds in nursing home–type unit) (Nonreporting) **A**1 2 3 5 7 9 10 **S** Franciscan Sisters of the Poor Health System, Inc., Latham, NY	21	10	240	—	—	—	—	—	—	—
✸ FRANCISCAN HOSPITAL–WESTERN HILLS CAMPUS, 3131 Queen City Avenue, Zip 45238–2396; tel. 513/389–5000; R. Christopher West, President (Total facility includes 20 beds in nursing home–type unit) (Nonreporting) **A**1 2 7 9 10 **S** Franciscan Sisters of the Poor Health System, Inc., Latham, NY	21	10	226	—	—	—	—	—	—	—
✸ △ GOOD SAMARITAN HOSPITAL, 375 Dixmyth Avenue, Zip 45220–2489; tel. 513/872–1400; Sister Myra James Bradley, Chief Executive Officer (Total facility includes 15 beds in nursing home–type unit) **A**1 2 3 5 6 7 8 9 10 **F**1 2 3 4 6 7 8 10 11 12 15 16 17 18 19 21 22 23 24 25 26 27 28 29 30 31 32 33 34 35 37 38 39 40 41 42 43 44 45 46 48 49 51 52 53 54 55 56 57 58 59 60 61 62 63 64 65 66 67 68 69 70 71 72 73 **P**3 7 **S** Catholic Health Initiatives, Denver, CO **N** First Interhealth Network, Toledo, OH; TriHealth, Cincinnati, OH; Center Care, Bowling Green, KY	21	10	401	21821	265	128579	5273	196691	85565	2372
✸ △ JEWISH HOSPITAL KENWOOD, 4777 East Galbraith Road, Zip 45236; tel. 513/745–2200; Warren C. Falberg, Senior Executive Officer (Total facility includes 20 beds in nursing home–type unit) (Nonreporting) **A**1 2 3 5 7 9 10 **S** Health Alliance of Greater Cincinnati, Cincinnati, OH **N** The Healthcare Alliance of Greater Cincinnati, Cincinnati, OH; CHA Provider Network, Inc., Lexington, KY	23	10	437	—	—	—	—	—	—	—

Hospital, Address, Telephone, Administrator, Approval, Facility, and Physician Codes, Health Care System, Network	Classi-fication Codes		Utilization Data					Expense (thousands) of dollars		
	Control	Service	Staffed Beds	Admissions	Census	Outpatient Visits	Births	Total	Payroll	Personnel

★ American Hospital Association (AHA) membership
□ Joint Commission on Accreditation of Healthcare Organizations (JCAHO) accreditation
+ American Osteopathic Healthcare Association (AOHA) membership
○ American Osteopathic Association (AOA) accreditation
△ Commission on Accreditation of Rehabilitation Facilities (CARF) accreditation
Control codes 61, 63, 64, 71, 72 and 73 indicate hospitals listed by AOHA, but not registered by AHA. For definition of numerical codes, see page A4

Hospital	Control	Service	Staffed Beds	Admissions	Census	Outpatient Visits	Births	Total	Payroll	Personnel
□ MERCY HOSPITAL ANDERSON, 7500 State Road, Zip 45255–2492; tel. 513/624–4500; Karen S. Ehrat, Ph.D., President **A**1 2 9 10 **F**7 8 10 12 14 15 16 17 19 21 22 24 26 28 29 30 32 33 34 35 37 39 40 41 42 44 45 46 49 53 54 56 57 58 59 60 63 65 66 67 71 72 73 74 **P**8 **S** Catholic Healthcare Partners, Cincinnati, OH **N** Mercy Regional Health System, Greater Cincinnati, Cincinnati, OH	21	10	156	9140	86	107544	1798	70644	25519	653
PAULINE WARFIELD LEWIS CENTER, 1101 Summit Road, Zip 45237–2652; tel. 513/948–3600; Elizabeth Banks, Chief Executive Officer **A**9 10 **F**4 8 12 14 15 16 19 20 21 22 23 26 28 30 31 34 35 39 41 42 43 44 45 46 49 50 51 52 54 56 57 60 63 65 67 70 71 73 **P**6	12	22	228	515	138	0	0	27911	17394	336
✠ SHRINERS HOSPITALS FOR CHILDREN, SHRINERS BURNS HOSPITAL, CINCINNATI, (PEDIATRIC BURN INJURIES), 3229 Burnet Avenue, Zip 45229–3095; tel. 513/872–6000; Ronald R. Hitzler, Administrator **A**1 **F**9 12 19 21 35 41 44 45 46 50 54 56 63 65 67 69 71 73 **S** Shriners Hospitals for Children, Tampa, FL	23	59	30	831	22	4900	0	—	—	307
✠ UNIVERSITY HOSPITAL, 234 Goodman Street, Zip 45267–0700; tel. 513/558–1000; Elliot G. Cohen, Senior Executive Officer (Nonreporting) **A**1 2 3 5 8 9 10 **S** Health Alliance of Greater Cincinnati, Cincinnati, OH **N** The Healthcare Alliance of Greater Cincinnati, Cincinnati, OH; CHA Provider Network, Inc., Lexington, KY	12	10	418	—	—	—	—	—	—	—
✠ VETERANS AFFAIRS MEDICAL CENTER, 3200 Vine Street, Zip 45220–2288; tel. 513/475–6300; Gary N. Nugent, Medical Director (Total facility includes 64 beds in nursing home–type unit) **A**1 3 5 8 9 **F**1 2 3 4 5 7 8 10 11 12 17 18 19 20 21 22 26 27 31 32 34 35 37 39 41 42 43 44 45 46 49 51 52 54 56 57 58 60 64 65 71 73 74 **S** Department of Veterans Affairs, Washington, DC	45	10	250	6273	196	189202	—	100403	—	1238

CIRCLEVILLE—Pickaway County

Hospital	Control	Service	Staffed Beds	Admissions	Census	Outpatient Visits	Births	Total	Payroll	Personnel
✠ BERGER HEALTH SYSTEM, (Formerly Berger Hospital), 600 North Pickaway Street, Zip 43113–1499; tel. 740/474–2126; Brian R. Colfack, CHE, President and Chief Executive Officer **A**1 9 10 **F**8 14 15 16 17 19 21 22 27 28 29 30 32 33 34 35 37 39 40 41 42 44 45 46 48 49 63 65 66 67 71 72 73 74 **N** Community Hospitals of Ohio, Newark, OH; Mount Carmel Health System, Columbus, OH	15	10	70	2024	28		3	—	—	72

CLEVELAND—Cuyahoga County

Hospital	Control	Service	Staffed Beds	Admissions	Census	Outpatient Visits	Births	Total	Payroll	Personnel
CAMPUS HOSPITAL OF CLEVELAND, 18120 Puritas Road, Zip 44135–3896; tel. 216/476–0222; Joan Curran, Administrator **A**9 10 **F**3 12 18 20 22 52 56 58 59 65 67 **P**6	33	82	60	1050	20		—	6800	3000	63
CLEVELAND CAMPUS See Northcoast Behavioral Healthcare System, Northfield										
✠ △ CLEVELAND CLINIC HOSPITAL, 9500 Euclid Avenue, Zip 44195–5108; tel. 216/444–2200; Frank L. Lordeman, Chief Operating Officer **A**1 2 3 5 7 8 9 10 **F**3 4 5 7 8 9 10 11 12 14 15 16 17 19 20 21 22 23 24 25 26 27 28 29 30 31 32 33 34 35 37 38 39 40 41 42 43 44 45 46 47 48 49 50 51 52 53 54 55 56 57 58 59 60 61 63 64 65 66 67 69 70 71 72 73 74 **P**1 3 5 6 7 **N** Cleveland Health Network, Independence, OH	23	10	937	45179	731	1368303	2219	600619	283730	—
CLEVELAND PSYCHIATRIC INSTITUTE See Northcoast Behavioral Healthcare System, Northfield										
COLUMBIA ST. VINCENT CHARITY HOSPITAL See St. Vincent Charity Hospital										
□ DEACONESS HOSPITAL OF CLEVELAND, 4229 Pearl Road, Zip 44109–4218; tel. 216/459–6300; Wayne G. Deschambeau, Chief Executive Officer (Total facility includes 15 beds in nursing home–type unit) (Nonreporting) **A**1 2 9 10	32	10	212	—	—	—	—	—	—	—
✠ △ FAIRVIEW HOSPITAL, 18101 Lorain Avenue, Zip 44111–5656; tel. 216/476–4040; Thomas M. LaMotte, President and Chief Executive Officer (Total facility includes 35 beds in nursing home–type unit) **A**1 2 3 5 6 7 9 10 **F**1 4 5 7 8 10 11 12 14 15 16 17 19 21 22 23 24 26 27 28 29 30 32 33 34 35 36 37 38 39 40 41 42 43 44 45 46 48 49 51 54 56 57 58 59 60 63 65 66 67 70 71 72 73 74 **P**1 6 **S** Fairview Hospital System, Cleveland, OH **N** Cleveland Health Network, Independence, OH; Health Cleveland, Cleveland, OH	23	10	397	17226	247	322190	3337	151946	73784	2023
□ GRACE HOSPITAL, 2307 West 14th Street, Zip 44113–3698; tel. 216/687–1500; Robert P. Range, President and Chief Executive Officer **A**1 9 10 **F**8 14 15 16 26 27 28 29 30 32 34 37 39 41 44 45 46 49 51 65 71 72 73	23	10	25	166	21	20845	—	11005	5272	225
✠ HEALTH HILL HOSPITAL FOR CHILDREN, Mailing Address: 2801 Martin Luther King Jr. Drive, Zip 44104–3865; tel. 216/721–5400; Thomas A. Rathbone, President and Chief Executive Officer **A**1 10 **F**12 13 14 15 16 17 27 29 34 65 73 **P**6	23	56	46	256	22	7085	—	12898	7969	182
□ △ LUTHERAN HOSPITAL, 1730 West 25th Street, Zip 44113; tel. 216/696–4300; Jack E. Bell, Chief Operating Officer (Total facility includes 20 beds in nursing home–type unit) **A**1 3 7 9 10 **F**1 4 5 7 8 10 11 14 15 16 17 19 21 22 23 26 27 28 29 30 32 33 34 35 37 38 39 40 41 42 43 44 46 48 49 52 54 55 57 58 59 60 63 64 65 66 67 70 71 73 74 **P**1 6 **S** Fairview Hospital System, Cleveland, OH **N** Cleveland Health Network, Independence, OH; Health Cleveland, Cleveland, OH	23	10	204	4040	86	93054	0	42311	21583	626
□ MERIDIA HILLCREST HOSPITAL, 6780 Mayfield Road, Zip 44124–2202; tel. 216/449–4500; Catherine B. Leary, R.N., Chief Operating Officer (Nonreporting) **A**1 2 3 9 10 **S** Meridia Health System, Mayfield Village, OH **N** Merida Health System, Mayfield Village, OH; Cleveland Health Network, Independence, OH	23	10	263	—	—	—	—	—	—	—

Hospital, Address, Telephone, Administrator, Approval, Facility, and Physician Codes, Health Care System, Network	Classification Codes		Utilization Data					Expense (thousands) of dollars		
	Control	Service	Staffed Beds	Admissions	Census	Outpatient Visits	Births	Total	Payroll	Personnel

★ American Hospital Association (AHA) membership
□ Joint Commission on Accreditation of Healthcare Organizations (JCAHO) accreditation
+ American Osteopathic Healthcare Association (AOHA) membership
○ American Osteopathic Association (AOA) accreditation
△ Commission on Accreditation of Rehabilitation Facilities (CARF) accreditation
Control codes 61, 63, 64, 71, 72 and 73 indicate hospitals listed by AOHA, but not registered by AHA. For definition of numerical codes, see page A4

□ MERIDIA HURON HOSPITAL, 13951 Terrace Road, Zip 44112–4399; tel. 216/761–3300; Beverly Lozar, Chief Operating Officer (Total facility includes 20 beds in nursing home–type unit) **A**1 2 3 5 6 9 10 **F**4 5 7 8 10 11 12 13 14 15 16 17 19 21 22 25 26 27 28 29 30 31 33 34 35 36 37 38 40 41 42 43 44 45 46 49 51 52 54 55 56 57 58 59 60 61 63 64 65 66 67 68 70 71 72 73 74 **S** Meridia Health System, Mayfield Village, OH **N** Merida Health System, Mayfield Village, OH; Cleveland Health Network, Independence, OH	23	10	471	20660	293	209250	2811	193474	65601	1741
✖ △ METROHEALTH MEDICAL CENTER, 2500 MetroHealth Drive, Zip 44109–1998; tel. 216/778–7800; Terry R. White, President and Chief Executive Officer (Total facility includes 320 beds in nursing home–type unit) **A**1 2 3 5 6 7 8 9 10 **F**1 2 3 4 5 7 8 9 10 11 12 14 15 16 17 19 20 21 22 25 26 27 28 29 30 31 32 33 34 35 37 38 39 40 41 42 43 44 45 46 47 48 49 51 52 53 54 55 56 57 58 59 60 61 63 64 65 69 70 71 72 73 74 **P**6 **N** Cleveland Health Network, Independence, OH; The MetroHealth System, Cleveland, OH	13	10	803	19121	582	627022	3595	316771	164393	4864
✖ MT. SINAI MEDICAL CENTER, One Mt Sinai Drive, Zip 44106–4198; tel. 216/421–3400; Geoffrey Moebivs, Chief Operating Officer (Nonreporting) **A**1 2 3 5 8 9 10 **N** The Mount Sinai Health Care System, Cleveland, OH RAINBOW BABIES AND CHILDREN'S HOSPITAL See University Hospitals of Cleveland	23	10	344	—	—	—	—	—	—	—
✖ SAINT LUKE'S MEDICAL CENTER, 11311 Shaker Boulevard, Zip 44104–3805; tel. 216/368–7000; Jeffrey S. Jeney, President and Chief Executive Officer **A**1 3 5 8 9 10 **F**1 3 4 5 7 8 10 11 12 14 15 16 17 19 20 21 22 25 26 27 28 30 31 32 33 34 35 36 37 38 39 40 41 42 43 44 45 46 47 49 51 52 53 54 55 56 57 58 59 60 61 63 64 65 67 69 70 71 73 **P**7 **S** Columbia/HCA Healthcare Corporation, Nashville, TN **N** Saint Lukes Medical Center, Cleveland, OH	32	10	161	7622	105	120075	650	72028	34924	852
✖ SAINT MICHAEL HOSPITAL, 5163 Broadway Avenue, Zip 44127–1532; tel. 216/429–8000; Geoffrey D. Moebius, President and Chief Executive Officer (Total facility includes 55 beds in nursing home–type unit) (Nonreporting) **A**1 2 10	33	10	199	—	—	—	—	—	—	—
✖ ○ ST. JOHN WEST SHORE HOSPITAL, 29000 Center Ridge Road, Zip 44145–5219; tel. 440/835–8000; Fred M. DeGrandis, President and Chief Executive Officer (Nonreporting) **A**1 10 11 **S** Columbia/HCA Healthcare Corporation, Nashville, TN	33	10	183	—	—	—	—	—	—	—
✖ ST. VINCENT CHARITY HOSPITAL, (Formerly Columbia St. Vincent Charity Hospital), 2351 East 22nd Street, Zip 44115–3111; tel. 216/861–6200; Alan H. Channing, Chief Executive Officer (Nonreporting) **A**1 2 3 5 9 10 **S** Columbia/HCA Healthcare Corporation, Nashville, TN	33	10	266	—	—	—	—	—	—	—
✖ △ UNIVERSITY HOSPITALS OF CLEVELAND, (Includes Alfred and Norma Lerner Tower, Bolwell Health Center, Hanna Pavilion, Lakeside Hospital, Samuel Mather Pavilion; Rainbow Babies and Children's Hospital, ; University MacDonald Women's Hospital), 11100 Euclid Avenue, Zip 44106–2602; tel. 216/844–1000; Farah M. Walters, President and Chief Executive Officer (Total facility includes 50 beds in nursing home–type unit) **A**1 2 3 5 7 8 9 10 **F**2 3 4 5 7 8 10 11 12 13 14 16 17 18 19 20 21 22 23 24 25 26 27 28 29 30 31 32 33 34 35 37 38 39 40 41 42 43 44 45 46 47 48 49 50 51 52 53 54 55 56 57 58 59 60 61 63 64 65 66 67 68 69 70 71 72 73 74 **P**3 5 6 7 **S** University Hospitals Health System, Cleveland, OH **N** University Hospitals Health System, Cleveland, OH UNIVERSITY MACDONALD WOMEN'S HOSPITAL See University Hospitals of Cleveland	23	10	752	35674	566	642762	4850	—	—	5530
✖ VETERANS AFFAIRS MEDICAL CENTER, 10701 East Boulevard, Zip 44106–1702; tel. 216/791–3800; Richard S. Citron, Acting Director (Total facility includes 195 beds in nursing home–type unit) (Nonreporting) **A**1 3 5 8 9 **S** Department of Veterans Affairs, Washington, DC	45	10	817	—	—	—	—	—	—	—

COLDWATER—Mercer County

✖ MERCER COUNTY JOINT TOWNSHIP COMMUNITY HOSPITAL, 800 West Main Street, Zip 45828–1698; tel. 419/678–2341; James W. Isaacs, Chief Executive Officer **A**1 9 10 **F**7 8 15 16 19 21 22 25 28 30 32 33 35 37 40 41 42 44 46 63 65 66 67 71 72 73 **N** West Central Ohio Regional Healthcare Alliance, Ltd., Lima, OH; LutheranPreferred Network, Fort Wayne, IN	16	10	58	2320	25	138011	401	19620	8389	301

COLUMBUS—Franklin County

✖ ARTHUR G. JAMES CANCER HOSPITAL AND RESEARCH INSTITUTE, (ACUTE CARE CANCER HOSP AND RES), 300 West Tenth Avenue, Zip 43210–1240; tel. 614/293–5485; David E. Schuller, M.D., Chief Executive Officer **A**1 2 3 5 8 9 10 **F**3 4 5 7 8 9 10 11 12 13 14 15 16 17 19 20 21 22 24 25 26 28 29 30 31 32 33 34 35 37 38 39 41 42 43 44 45 46 48 49 51 52 53 54 55 56 57 58 59 60 61 63 65 66 67 69 70 71 **P**5 **N** Ohio State Health Network, Columbus, OH	12	49	120	5899	101	81897	—	95331	23900	921
✖ △ CHILDREN'S HOSPITAL, 700 Children's Drive, Zip 43205–2696; tel. 614/722–2000; Thomas N. Hansen, Acting Chief Executive Officer and Medical Director **A**1 2 3 5 7 9 10 **F**4 10 12 13 14 17 19 20 21 22 24 25 27 28 29 31 32 33 38 39 42 43 44 45 47 48 49 51 53 54 55 56 58 63 65 67 68 70 71 72 73 **P**8 COLUMBUS CAMPUS See Twin Valley Psychiatric System, Dayton	23	50	282	10523	155	305169	—	166956	72571	2482
□ △ COLUMBUS COMMUNITY HOSPITAL, 1430 South High Street, Zip 43207–1093; tel. 614/445–5000; Bobby Meadows, President and Chief Executive Officer (Nonreporting) **A**1 7 9 10	32	10	118	—	—	—	—	—	—	—
□ + ○ △ DOCTORS HOSPITAL, (Includes Doctors Hospital West, 5100 West Broad Street, Zip 43228; tel. 614/297–4000), 1087 Dennison Avenue, Zip 43201–3496; tel. 614/297–4000; Richard A. Vincent, President **A**1 7 9 10 11 12 13 **F**4 7 8 10 11 12 14 15 16 17 19 21 22 25 27 28 29 30 31 32 33 34 35 37 38 39 40 41 42 43 44 45 48 49 51 52 56 60 61 63 65 66 68 71 72 73 74 **P**8 **S** Doctors Hospital, Columbus, OH	23	10	337	14032	198	160129	1147	161279	67733	1006

Hospital, Address, Telephone, Administrator, Approval, Facility, and Physician Codes, Health Care System, Network	Classi-fication Codes		Utilization Data					Expense (thousands) of dollars		
★ American Hospital Association (AHA) membership □ Joint Commission on Accreditation of Healthcare Organizations (JCAHO) accreditation + American Osteopathic Healthcare Association (AOHA) membership ○ American Osteopathic Association (AOA) accreditation △ Commission on Accreditation of Rehabilitation Facilities (CARF) accreditation Control codes 61, 63, 64, 71, 72 and 73 indicate hospitals listed by AOHA, but not registered by AHA. For definition of numerical codes, see page A4	Control	Service	Staffed Beds	Admissions	Census	Outpatient Visits	Births	Total	Payroll	Personnel

✠ GRANT/RIVERSIDE METHODIST HOSPITALS–GRANT CAMPUS, 111 South Grant Avenue, Zip 43215–1898; tel. 614/566–9000; David P. Blom, President **A**1 2 3 5 8 9 10 **F**1 3 4 7 8 10 11 12 13 14 15 16 17 18 19 21 22 23 24 25 26 27 28 29 30 31 32 33 34 35 37 38 39 40 41 42 43 44 45 46 48 49 51 53 54 55 56 57 58 59 60 61 63 64 65 66 67 68 69 70 71 72 73 74 **P**1 2 3 4 5 6 7 8 **S** OhioHealth, Columbus, OH	21	10	470	18968	242	801665	3029	179776	73173	1765
✠ GRANT/RIVERSIDE METHODIST HOSPITALS–RIVERSIDE CAMPUS, 3535 Olentangy River Road, Zip 43214–3998; tel. 614/566–5000; David P. Blom, President **A**1 2 3 5 8 9 10 **F**1 2 3 4 7 8 10 11 12 13 14 15 16 17 19 20 21 22 23 24 25 26 27 28 29 30 31 32 33 34 35 37 38 39 40 41 42 43 44 45 46 48 49 51 52 53 54 55 56 57 58 59 60 61 63 64 65 66 67 68 70 71 72 73 74 **P**2 3 4 5 6 7 8 **S** OhioHealth, Columbus, OH	21	10	775	38062	497	198121	6157	351154	154838	4226
✠ MOUNT CARMEL HEALTH SYSTEM, (Includes Mount Carmel East Hospital, 6001 East Broad Street, Zip 43213; tel. 614/234–6000; Mount Carmel Medical Center, 793 West State Street, Zip 43222; tel. 614/234–5000; St. Ann's Hospital, 500 South Cleveland Avenue, Westerville, Zip 43081–8998; tel. 614/898–4000), Mailing Address: 793 West State Street, Zip 43222–1551; tel. 614/234–5423; Joseph Calvaruso, Interim Chief Executive Officer (Total facility includes 14 beds in nursing home–type unit) (Nonreporting) **A**1 2 3 5 9 10 **S** Holy Cross Health System Corporation, South Bend, IN **N** Mount Carmel Health System, Columbus, OH	21	10	929	—	—	—	—	—	—	—
✠ △ OHIO STATE UNIVERSITY MEDICAL CENTER, 410 West 10th Avenue, Zip 43210–1240; tel. 614/293–8000; R. Reed Fraley, Associate Vice President for Health Sciences and Chief Executive Officer **A**1 3 5 7 8 9 10 **F**3 4 5 7 8 9 10 11 12 14 15 16 17 19 20 21 22 23 24 25 26 28 29 30 31 32 33 34 35 37 38 39 40 41 42 43 44 45 46 48 49 51 52 53 54 55 56 57 58 59 60 61 63 64 65 66 67 69 70 71 72 73 74 **P**5 **N** Ohio State Health Network, Columbus, OH	12	10	553	24681	394	295786	3229	320417	124414	3639
✠ PARK MEDICAL CENTER, 1492 East Broad Street, Zip 43205–1546; tel. 614/251–3000; James L. Rieder, Chief Executive Officer (Total facility includes 20 beds in nursing home–type unit) **A**1 2 3 9 10 **F**2 3 4 6 8 10 12 14 16 19 21 22 24 26 27 28 29 32 35 37 41 42 44 45 49 51 52 57 60 64 65 67 71 72 73 74 **P**2 **S** Quorum Health Group/Quorum Health Resources, Inc., Brentwood, TN	33	10	165	6383	95	38539	—	—	—	513
CONNEAUT—Ashtabula County										
✠ UHHS BROWN MEMORIAL HOSPITAL, 158 West Main Road, Zip 44030–2039, Mailing Address: P.O. Box 648, Zip 44030–0648; tel. 440/593–1131; Carol Koellisch Drennen, R.N., President and Chief Executive Officer (Nonreporting) **A**1 9 10 **S** University Hospitals Health System, Cleveland, OH **N** Great Lakes Health Network, Erie, PA	23	10	51	—	—	—	—	—	—	—
COSHOCTON—Coshocton County										
□ COSHOCTON COUNTY MEMORIAL HOSPITAL, 1460 Orange Street, Zip 43812–6330, Mailing Address: P.O. Box 1330, Zip 43812–6330; tel. 614/622–6411; Gregory M. Nowak, Administrator (Total facility includes 61 beds in nursing home–type unit) (Nonreporting) **A**1 9 10 **N** Community Hospitals of Ohio, Newark, OH	23	10	151	—	—	—	—	—	—	—
CRESTLINE—Crawford County										
CRESTLINE HOSPITAL See MedCentral Health System, Mansfield										
CUYAHOGA FALLS—Summit County										
+ ○ CUYAHOGA FALLS GENERAL HOSPITAL, 1900 23rd Street, Zip 44223–1499; tel. 330/971–7000; Fred Anthony, President and Chief Executive Officer **A**9 10 11 12 13 **F**7 8 12 14 15 16 17 19 20 22 27 28 30 32 35 39 40 41 42 44 49 51 52 56 58 59 63 65 67 71 73 74 **P**3 8 **N** Northeast Ohio Health Network, Akron, OH	23	10	135	4369	58	18519	594	47634	22371	628
DAYTON—Montgomery County										
✠ CHILDREN'S MEDICAL CENTER, One Children's Plaza, Zip 45404–1815; tel. 937/226–8300; Laurence P. Harkness, President and Chief Executive Officer **A**1 3 5 8 9 10 **F**10 12 13 14 15 16 17 19 20 22 25 27 28 29 30 31 32 34 35 38 39 41 42 44 45 46 47 49 51 53 54 55 58 65 67 68 71 72 73	23	50	123	5793	79	201700	0	75372	34439	1091
DAYTON CAMPUS See Twin Valley Psychiatric System										
✠ △ FRANCISCAN MEDICAL CENTER–DAYTON CAMPUS, One Franciscan Way, Zip 45408–1498; tel. 937/229–6000; Duane L. Erwin, Chief Executive Officer (Total facility includes 30 beds in nursing home–type unit) **A**1 2 3 5 7 9 10 **F**1 4 6 7 8 10 11 12 14 15 16 17 19 20 21 22 24 25 26 27 29 30 31 32 34 35 36 37 38 39 40 41 42 43 44 45 46 48 49 51 52 53 54 55 56 57 58 59 60 61 62 64 65 66 67 70 71 72 73 74 **P**6 8 **S** Franciscan Sisters of the Poor Health System, Inc., Latham, NY	21	10	357	14900	245	279079	1026	143322	72409	1779
✠ GOOD SAMARITAN HOSPITAL AND HEALTH CENTER, 2222 Philadelphia Drive, Zip 45406–1813; tel. 937/278–2612; K. Douglas Deck, President and Chief Executive Officer **A**1 2 3 5 9 10 **F**3 4 6 7 8 9 10 11 12 14 15 16 17 18 19 20 21 22 23 24 25 26 28 29 30 31 32 34 35 37 38 39 40 41 42 43 44 45 46 48 49 51 52 53 54 55 56 57 58 59 60 62 63 64 65 66 67 68 69 70 71 72 73 74 **P**6 8 **S** Catholic Health Initiatives, Denver, CO	21	10	428	17002	238	197511	1525	168588	76564	2023
★ ○ GRANDVIEW HOSPITAL AND MEDICAL CENTER, (Includes Southview Hospital and Family Health Center, 1997 Miamisburg–Centerville Road, Zip 45459–3800; tel. 513/439–6000), 405 Grand Avenue, Zip 45405–4796; tel. 937/226–3200; Richard J. Minor, President **A**9 10 11 12 13 **F**3 4 7 8 10 12 13 14 15 16 17 18 19 21 22 23 25 28 29 30 31 32 33 34 35 36 39 41 42 43 44 45 46 49 51 54 55 56 57 58 59 63 65 66 67 68 69 72 73 74 **P**8	23	10	278	9677	145	107508	320	139608	65779	1636
KETTERING YOUTH SERVICES See Kettering Medical Center, Kettering										

	Classification Codes		Utilization Data					Expense (thousands) of dollars		
Hospital, Address, Telephone, Administrator, Approval, Facility, and Physician Codes, Health Care System, Network	Control	Service	Staffed Beds	Admissions	Census	Outpatient Visits	Births	Total	Payroll	Personnel

★ American Hospital Association (AHA) membership
□ Joint Commission on Accreditation of Healthcare Organizations (JCAHO) accreditation
+ American Osteopathic Healthcare Association (AOHA) membership
○ American Osteopathic Association (AOA) accreditation
△ Commission on Accreditation of Rehabilitation Facilities (CARF) accreditation
Control codes 61, 63, 64, 71, 72 and 73 indicate hospitals listed by AOHA, but not registered by AHA. For definition of numerical codes, see page A4

Hospital	Control	Service	Staffed Beds	Admissions	Census	Outpatient Visits	Births	Total	Payroll	Personnel
★ △ MIAMI VALLEY HOSPITAL, One Wyoming Street, Zip 45409–2763; tel. 937/208–8000; Thomas G. Breitenbach, Chief Executive Officer **A**1 2 3 5 7 8 9 10 **F**1 3 4 7 8 9 10 11 12 14 15 16 17 18 19 20 21 22 23 24 25 26 27 28 29 30 31 32 34 35 36 37 38 39 40 41 42 43 44 45 46 48 49 51 53 54 55 56 57 58 59 60 61 63 64 65 66 67 68 69 70 71 72 73 74 **P**6 8	23	10	714	28246	401	521176	5953	300251	124130	4005
□ TWIN VALLEY PSYCHIATRIC SYSTEM, (Includes Columbus Campus, 1960 West Broad Street, Columbus, Zip 43223–1295; tel. 614/752–0333; Dayton Campus, 2611 Wayne Avenue, tel. 937/258–0440), 2611 Wayne Avenue, Zip 45420–1800; tel. 937/258–0440; James Ignelzi, Chief Executive Officer (Nonreporting) **A**1 10	12	22	504	—	—	—	—	—	—	—
★ VETERANS AFFAIRS MEDICAL CENTER, 4100 West Third Street, Zip 45428–1002; tel. 937/268–6511; Steven M. Cohen, M.D., Director (Total facility includes 280 beds in nursing home–type unit) **A**1 3 5 8 9 **F**1 2 3 4 8 9 10 12 14 15 16 17 19 20 21 22 23 24 26 27 28 29 30 31 32 33 34 35 37 41 42 43 44 45 46 48 49 51 52 54 58 60 63 64 65 69 71 73 74 **S** Department of Veterans Affairs, Washington, DC	45	10	651	6062	610	208803	—	119173	75483	1672

DEFIANCE—Defiance County

Hospital	Control	Service	Staffed Beds	Admissions	Census	Outpatient Visits	Births	Total	Payroll	Personnel
★ DEFIANCE HOSPITAL, 1206 East Second Street, Zip 43512–2495; tel. 419/783–6955; Richard C. Sommer, Administrator **A**1 9 10 **F**7 8 11 15 16 19 20 21 22 27 28 29 30 31 32 34 35 37 40 41 42 44 52 55 56 57 58 59 63 65 71 73 **S** Quorum Health Group/Quorum Health Resources, Inc., Brentwood, TN **N** United Health Partners, Toledo, OH; Lake Erie Health Alliance, Toledo, OH; LutheranPreferred Network, Fort Wayne, IN	23	10	96	3128	35	32183	458	23817	9226	282

DELAWARE—Delaware County

Hospital	Control	Service	Staffed Beds	Admissions	Census	Outpatient Visits	Births	Total	Payroll	Personnel
□ △ GRADY MEMORIAL HOSPITAL, 561 West Central Avenue, Zip 43015–1485; tel. 740/369–8711; Everett P. Weber, Jr., President and Chief Executive Officer (Nonreporting) **A**1 2 7 9 10 **N** Community Hospitals of Ohio, Newark, OH	23	10	84	—	—	—	—	—	—	—

DENNISON—Tuscarawas County

Hospital	Control	Service	Staffed Beds	Admissions	Census	Outpatient Visits	Births	Total	Payroll	Personnel
★ TWIN CITY HOSPITAL, 819 North First Street, Zip 44621–1098; tel. 740/922–2800; Cheryl Hicks, Chief Executive Officer **A**1 9 10 **F**8 11 12 14 16 17 19 20 21 22 28 29 30 32 33 34 37 39 41 42 43 44 45 46 48 49 51 63 64 65 66 71 73 74 **P**7	23	10	30	535	7	67483	—	6070	2618	115

DOVER—Tuscarawas County

Hospital	Control	Service	Staffed Beds	Admissions	Census	Outpatient Visits	Births	Total	Payroll	Personnel
★ UNION HOSPITAL, 659 Boulevard, Zip 44622–2077; tel. 330/343–3311; William W. Harding, President and Chief Executive Officer **A**1 9 10 **F**7 8 14 15 16 17 19 21 22 28 30 32 33 34 35 36 37 39 40 42 44 49 53 54 55 56 57 58 63 65 66 67 71 73	23	10	102	4321	45	177261	796	34897	14851	511

EAST LIVERPOOL—Columbiana County

Hospital	Control	Service	Staffed Beds	Admissions	Census	Outpatient Visits	Births	Total	Payroll	Personnel
★ EAST LIVERPOOL CITY HOSPITAL, 425 West Fifth Street, Zip 43920–2498; tel. 330/385–7200; Melvin R. Creeley, President (Total facility includes 20 beds in nursing home–type unit) **A**1 9 10 **F**1 7 8 11 13 15 16 19 21 22 26 28 30 32 33 34 35 37 39 40 41 42 44 45 46 49 52 54 56 57 58 63 64 65 67 71 72 **P**8 **S** Quorum Health Group/Quorum Health Resources, Inc., Brentwood, TN	23	10	198	8621	87	—	401	37592	16275	416

ELYRIA—Lorain County

Hospital	Control	Service	Staffed Beds	Admissions	Census	Outpatient Visits	Births	Total	Payroll	Personnel
★ EMH REGIONAL MEDICAL CENTER, 630 East River Street, Zip 44035–5902; tel. 440/329–7500; Kevin C. Martin, Interim Chief Operating Officer **A**1 2 9 10 **F**2 4 7 8 10 11 15 16 19 21 22 23 25 26 28 30 32 33 34 35 37 39 40 41 42 43 44 49 51 52 55 56 59 63 65 66 67 69 71 72 73 74 **P**7 8 **N** Cleveland Health Network, Independence, OH; Comprehensive Healthcare of Ohio, Inc., Elyria, OH	23	10	296	11965	142	209660	1103	101216	36077	1100

EUCLID—Cuyahoga County

Hospital	Control	Service	Staffed Beds	Admissions	Census	Outpatient Visits	Births	Total	Payroll	Personnel
□ △ MERIDIA EUCLID HOSPITAL, 18901 Lake Shore Boulevard, Zip 44119–1090; tel. 216/531–9000; Denise Zeman, Chief Operating Officer (Total facility includes 40 beds in nursing home–type unit) **A**1 2 7 9 10 **F**7 8 10 12 13 14 16 17 19 21 22 25 26 29 30 31 34 35 37 38 40 41 44 45 46 48 49 52 54 64 65 66 67 71 72 73 74 **S** Meridia Health System, Mayfield Village, OH **N** Merida Health System, Mayfield Village, OH; Cleveland Health Network, Independence, OH	23	10	209	6736	148	47575	464	52505	22373	696

FAIRFIELD—Butler County

MERCY HOSPITAL OF FAIRFIELD See Mercy Hospital, Hamilton

FINDLAY—Hancock County

Hospital	Control	Service	Staffed Beds	Admissions	Census	Outpatient Visits	Births	Total	Payroll	Personnel
★ BLANCHARD VALLEY HEALTH ASSOCIATION SYSTEM, (Includes Blanchard Valley Regional Health Center–Bluffton Campus, 139 Garau Street, Bluffton, Zip 45817–0048; tel. 419/358–9010; Blanchard Valley Regional Health Center–Findlay Campus, 145 West Wallace Street, tel. 419/423–4500; Clifford R. Lehman, President), 145 West Wallace Street, Zip 45840–1299; tel. 419/423–4500; William E. Ruse, FACHE, President and Chief Executive Officer **A**1 9 10 **F**1 6 7 8 10 11 12 13 14 15 16 17 19 21 22 25 26 28 29 30 32 33 34 35 37 40 41 42 44 45 49 51 52 59 60 62 64 65 66 67 71 72 73 **P**6 **N** Great Lakes Health Network, Erie, PA	23	10	192	7740	84	157832	1303	57776	27083	831

FOSTORIA—Hancock County

Hospital	Control	Service	Staffed Beds	Admissions	Census	Outpatient Visits	Births	Total	Payroll	Personnel
★ FOSTORIA COMMUNITY HOSPITAL, 501 Van Buren Street, Zip 44830–0907, Mailing Address: P.O. Box 907, Zip 44830–0907; tel. 419/435–7734; Brad A. Higgins, President and Chief Executive Officer **A**1 3 9 10 **F**7 8 11 12 14 15 16 17 19 21 22 24 27 28 29 30 31 32 34 35 36 37 39 40 41 42 44 45 46 49 63 65 66 67 70 71 73 **N** United Health Partners, Toledo, OH	23	10	50	1237	11	33587	198	—	5562	209

FREMONT—Sandusky County

Hospital	Control	Service	Staffed Beds	Admissions	Census	Outpatient Visits	Births	Total	Payroll	Personnel
★ MEMORIAL HOSPITAL, 715 South Taft Avenue, Zip 43420–3200; tel. 419/332–7321; John A. Gorman, Chief Executive Officer **A**1 9 10 **F**1 7 8 15 16 17 19 21 22 27 28 29 30 32 33 34 35 36 37 39 40 41 42 44 45 49 52 54 55 57 58 59 65 71 73 74 **P**1 5 **S** Quorum Health Group/Quorum Health Resources, Inc., Brentwood, TN **N** United Health Partners, Toledo, OH; Lake Erie Health Alliance, Toledo, OH	23	10	132	3112	31	45076	476	31332	12353	386

Hospital, Address, Telephone, Administrator, Approval, Facility, and Physician Codes, Health Care System, Network	Classi-fication Codes		Utilization Data					Expense (thousands) of dollars		
★ American Hospital Association (AHA) membership □ Joint Commission on Accreditation of Healthcare Organizations (JCAHO) accreditation + American Osteopathic Healthcare Association (AOHA) membership ○ American Osteopathic Association (AOA) accreditation △ Commission on Accreditation of Rehabilitation Facilities (CARF) accreditation Control codes 61, 63, 64, 71, 72 and 73 indicate hospitals listed by AOHA, but not registered by AHA. For definition of numerical codes, see page A4	Control	Service	Staffed Beds	Admissions	Census	Outpatient Visits	Births	Total	Payroll	Personnel

GALION—Crawford County

☒ GALION COMMUNITY HOSPITAL, 269 Portland Way South, Zip 44833–2399; tel. 419/468–4841; Mark E. Marley, President and Chief Executive Officer (Total facility includes 33 beds in nursing home–type unit) (Nonreporting) **A**1 9 10 **S** OhioHealth, Columbus, OH

| | 23 | 10 | 108 | — | — | — | — | — | — | — |

GALLIPOLIS—Gallia County

☒ △ HOLZER MEDICAL CENTER, 100 Jackson Pike, Zip 45631–1563; tel. 740/446–5000; Charles I. Adkins, Jr., President **A**1 2 7 9 10 **F**7 8 11 12 17 19 21 22 23 24 25 26 28 29 30 32 33 35 37 40 41 42 44 46 48 49 58 60 63 64 65 67 69 71 73 74 **P**5 **N** Community Hospitals of Ohio, Newark, OH

| | 23 | 10 | 269 | 6335 | 83 | 58586 | 866 | 45925 | 18852 | 727 |

GARFIELD HEIGHTS—Cuyahoga County

☒ △ MARYMOUNT HOSPITAL, 12300 McCracken Road, Zip 44125–2975; tel. 216/581–0500; Thomas J. Trudell, President and Chief Executive Officer **A**1 2 6 7 9 10 **F**3 5 6 7 8 10 12 14 15 16 18 19 21 22 23 25 27 28 30 31 32 34 35 36 37 39 40 41 42 44 46 48 49 52 53 54 55 56 57 58 59 62 63 64 65 66 67 69 71 72 73 74 **P**1 3 6 7 **N** Cleveland Health Network, Independence, OH

| | 21 | 10 | 221 | 8572 | 136 | 104208 | 961 | 82262 | 36077 | 1028 |

GENEVA—Ashtabula County

☒ UHHS–MEMORIAL HOSPITAL OF GENEVA, 870 West Main Street, Zip 44041–1295; tel. 440/466–1141; Gerard D. Klein, Chief Executive Officer **A**1 9 10 **F**8 12 14 15 16 17 19 22 28 29 30 32 35 37 41 44 46 63 67 71 73 **P**7 **S** University Hospitals Health System, Cleveland, OH **N** University Hospitals Health System, Cleveland, OH

| | 23 | 10 | 35 | 816 | 10 | 34332 | — | 10597 | 4196 | 157 |

GEORGETOWN—Brown County

☒ BROWN COUNTY GENERAL HOSPITAL, 425 Home Street, Zip 45121–1407; tel. 937/378–6121; David T. Wallace, President and Chief Executive Officer **A**1 9 10 **F**3 7 8 14 19 21 22 28 32 33 35 37 40 41 42 44 45 46 53 54 55 56 57 58 59 63 65 69 71 73 **P**6 **S** Quorum Health Group/Quorum Health Resources, Inc., Brentwood, TN

| | 13 | 10 | 53 | 1621 | 15 | 48000 | 394 | 15569 | 6224 | 230 |

GREEN SPRINGS—Sandusky County

☒ △ ST. FRANCIS HEALTH CARE CENTRE, (LONG TERM CARE HOSPITAL), 401 North Broadway, Zip 44836–9653; tel. 419/639–2626; Dan Schwanke, Chief Executive Officer (Total facility includes 97 beds in nursing home–type unit) **A**1 7 9 10 **F**12 15 26 27 31 39 46 49 57 58 64 65 67 73 **P**1 **N** Lake Erie Health Alliance, Toledo, OH

| | 21 | 49 | 173 | 545 | 124 | 10192 | — | 15322 | 5964 | 234 |

GREENFIELD—Highland County

☒ △ GREENFIELD AREA MEDICAL CENTER, 545 South Street, Zip 45123–1400; tel. 937/981–2116; Mark E. Marchetti, Chief Executive Officer **A**1 7 9 10 **F**8 12 14 15 16 17 19 28 29 30 32 33 35 36 41 44 46 48 49 65 71 72 73 **S** Quorum Health Group/Quorum Health Resources, Inc., Brentwood, TN

| | 23 | 10 | 36 | 775 | 14 | 44181 | — | 9082 | 3607 | 115 |

GREENVILLE—Darke County

□ WAYNE HOSPITAL, 835 Sweitzer Street, Zip 45331–1077; tel. 937/548–1141; Raymond E. Laughlin, Jr., President and Chief Executive Officer (Total facility includes 73 beds in nursing home–type unit) **A**1 9 10 **F**7 15 17 19 21 22 34 35 44 45 49 65 68 71 73 **P**8

| | 23 | 10 | 92 | 2668 | 30 | 67969 | 419 | 22757 | 9993 | 305 |

HAMILTON—Butler County

☒ FORT HAMILTON–HUGHES MEMORIAL HOSPITAL, 630 Eaton Avenue, Zip 45013–2770; tel. 513/867–2000; James A. Kingsbury, President and Chief Executive Officer **A**1 2 9 10 **F**2 3 7 8 10 13 14 15 16 17 19 21 22 23 25 26 28 29 30 31 32 33 34 35 36 37 39 40 41 42 43 44 45 46 49 52 54 55 56 57 59 60 62 63 65 67 68 71 73 74 **P**7 8 **N** Community Hospitals of Ohio, Newark, OH

| | 23 | 10 | 179 | 8481 | 99 | 95111 | 1255 | 61337 | 25287 | 755 |

□ MERCY HOSPITAL, (Includes Mercy Hospital of Fairfield, 3000 Mack Road, Fairfield, ; Mercy Hospital of Hamilton, 100 Riverfront Plaza), 100 River Front Plaza, Zip 45011–2780, Mailing Address: P.O. Box 418, Zip 45012–0418; tel. 513/870–7080; David A. Ferrell, President (Total facility includes 53 beds in nursing home–type unit) **A**1 9 10 **F**4 6 7 8 10 12 14 15 16 17 19 21 22 24 25 26 27 28 29 30 32 33 34 35 36 37 39 40 41 42 44 45 46 48 49 53 54 55 56 57 59 60 63 64 65 67 71 72 73 74 **P**6 8 **S** Catholic Healthcare Partners, Cincinnati, OH **N** Mercy Regional Health System, Greater Cincinnati, Cincinnati, OH

| | 21 | 10 | 248 | 9868 | 142 | 165211 | 758 | 79479 | 32030 | 916 |

HICKSVILLE—Defiance County

☒ COMMUNITY MEMORIAL HOSPITAL, 208 North Columbus Street, Zip 43526–1299; tel. 419/542–6692; Deryl E. Gulliford, Ph.D., Administrator (Total facility includes 36 beds in nursing home–type unit) **A**1 9 10 **F**8 12 13 14 15 16 17 18 19 20 22 24 26 27 28 30 31 33 34 35 36 39 40 41 44 45 46 49 51 64 65 66 71 72 73 74 **P**6 7 **N** LutheranPreferred Network, Fort Wayne, IN; Sagamore Health Network, Inc., Carmel, IN

| | 16 | 10 | 36 | 558 | 4 | 22000 | 80 | — | — | 121 |

HILLSBORO—Highland County

☒ HIGHLAND DISTRICT HOSPITAL, 1275 North High Street, Zip 45133–8571; tel. 937/393–6100; Charles H. Bair, Chief Executive Officer **A**1 9 10 **F**7 8 12 14 15 16 17 19 22 32 35 40 41 42 44 46 49 65 66 68 71 73

| | 16 | 10 | 51 | 2236 | 23 | 47099 | 408 | 16570 | 7358 | 270 |

IRONTON—Lawrence County

□ RIVER VALLEY HEALTH SYSTEM, (Includes Behavioral Health–Portsmouth Campus, 2201 25th Street, Portsmouth, Zip 45662–3252; tel. 614/354–2804; Rick E. Harlow, Vice President Behavioral Health), 2228 South Ninth Street, Zip 45638–2526; tel. 614/532–3231; Terry L. Vanderhoof, President and Chief Executive Officer (Total facility includes 11 beds in nursing home–type unit) (Nonreporting) **A**1 9 10 **N** Ohio State Health Network, Columbus, OH

| | 13 | 10 | 219 | — | — | — | — | — | — | — |

Hospital, Address, Telephone, Administrator, Approval, Facility, and Physician Codes, Health Care System, Network	Classi-fication Codes		Utilization Data					Expense (thousands) of dollars		
	Control	Service	Staffed Beds	Admissions	Census	Outpatient Visits	Births	Total	Payroll	Personnel

★ American Hospital Association (AHA) membership
□ Joint Commission on Accreditation of Healthcare Organizations (JCAHO) accreditation
+ American Osteopathic Healthcare Association (AOHA) membership
○ American Osteopathic Association (AOA) accreditation
△ Commission on Accreditation of Rehabilitation Facilities (CARF) accreditation
Control codes 61, 63, 64, 71, 72 and 73 indicate hospitals listed by AOHA, but not registered by AHA. For definition of numerical codes, see page A4.

KENTON—Hardin County

★ HARDIN MEMORIAL HOSPITAL, 921 East Franklin Street, Zip 43326–2099, Mailing Address: P.O. Box 710, Zip 43326–0710; tel. 419/673–0761; Don J. Sabol, Chief Executive Officer **A**1 9 10 **F**1 3 4 5 7 8 12 13 14 15 16 17 18 19 20 21 22 23 26 27 28 29 30 31 32 33 34 35 36 37 39 40 41 42 43 44 45 46 49 50 51 53 54 55 56 57 58 59 60 61 63 65 66 67 70 71 73 74 **P**3 5 7 8 **S** OhioHealth, Columbus, OH	23	10	51	1791	22	45575	137	18052	8146	318

KETTERING—Montgomery County

★ KETTERING MEDICAL CENTER, (Includes Charles F. Kettering Memorial Hospital, 3535 Southern Boulevard, Zip 45429; tel. 513/298–4331; Kettering Youth Services, 5350 Lamme Road, Dayton, Zip 45439; tel. 513/299–9511; Sycamore Hospital, 2150 Leiter Road, Miamisburg, Zip 45342; tel. 513/866–0551), 3535 Southern Boulevard, Zip 45429–1221; tel. 937/298–4331; Francisco J. Perez, President and Chief Executive Officer **A**1 2 3 5 8 9 10 **F**3 4 5 6 7 8 10 11 12 14 15 16 17 19 21 22 23 24 26 27 28 29 30 32 34 35 37 38 39 40 41 42 43 44 45 46 49 50 51 52 53 54 55 56 57 58 59 60 62 63 65 66 67 71 72 73 74 **P**8	21	10	482	17552	255	131778	1737	220026	97742	2855

LAKEWOOD—Cuyahoga County

★ LAKEWOOD HOSPITAL, 14519 Detroit Avenue, Zip 44107–4383; tel. 216/521–4200; Revonda L. Shumaker, R.N., President and Chief Executive Officer (Total facility includes 45 beds in nursing home–type unit) **A**1 2 9 10 **F**1 2 3 4 5 7 8 9 10 11 12 13 14 15 16 17 18 19 20 21 22 23 24 25 26 27 28 29 30 31 32 33 34 35 36 37 38 39 40 41 42 43 44 45 46 47 48 49 50 51 52 53 54 55 56 57 58 59 60 61 63 64 65 66 67 68 69 70 71 72 73 74 **P**3 5 6 7 8 **N** Cleveland Health Network, Independence, OH	23	10	327	9930	161	136184	494	95493	40428	1139

LANCASTER—Fairfield County

★ △ FAIRFIELD MEDICAL CENTER, 401 North Ewing Street, Zip 43130–3371; tel. 740/687–8000; Creighton E. Likes, Jr., President and Chief Executive Officer (Total facility includes 24 beds in nursing home–type unit) **A**1 7 9 10 **F**7 8 10 12 14 16 17 18 19 21 22 24 25 26 28 29 30 32 34 35 37 39 40 41 42 44 46 48 49 51 52 55 56 57 58 59 60 64 65 66 67 70 71 73 **P**4	23	10	196	8804	97	228750	1318	79277	31695	1026

LIMA—Allen County

★ LIMA MEMORIAL HOSPITAL, 1001 Bellefontaine Avenue, Zip 45804–2894; tel. 419/228–3335; John B. White, President and Chief Executive Officer **A**1 2 9 10 **F**4 5 7 8 10 11 12 14 15 16 17 19 21 22 23 26 28 30 32 34 35 36 37 39 40 41 42 43 44 48 49 51 52 57 60 63 64 65 66 67 71 73 74 **P**7 8 **N** Lake Erie Health Alliance, Toledo, OH; Midwest Health Net, LLC., Fort Wayne, IN	23	10	236	7008	108	140725	568	75319	32118	938
□ OAKWOOD CORRECTIONAL FACILITY, 3200 North West Street, Zip 45801–2000; tel. 419/225–8052; M. Kay Northrup, Warden (Nonreporting) **A**1	12	22	186	—	—	—	—	—	—	—
□ △ ST. RITA'S MEDICAL CENTER, 730 West Market Street, Zip 45801–4670; tel. 419/227–3361; James P. Reber, President **A**1 2 7 9 10 **F**2 3 4 7 8 10 11 12 14 15 16 17 18 19 20 21 22 23 24 25 26 28 29 30 31 32 33 34 35 37 38 39 40 41 42 43 44 46 48 49 51 52 53 54 55 56 57 58 59 60 63 64 65 66 67 71 72 73 74 **P**8 **S** Catholic Healthcare Partners, Cincinnati, OH **N** Community Hospitals of Ohio, Newark, OH; West Central Ohio Regional Healthcare Alliance, Ltd., Lima, OH	21	10	312	11945	149	257488	1955	122484	54184	1679

LODI—Medina County

★ LODI COMMUNITY HOSPITAL, 225 Elyria Street, Zip 44254–1096; tel. 330/948–1222; Thomas L. Lockard, President and Chief Executive Officer (Total facility includes 7 beds in nursing home–type unit) (Nonreporting) **A**1 5 9 10	23	10	21							

LOGAN—Hocking County

★ HOCKING VALLEY COMMUNITY HOSPITAL, Route 2, State Route 664, Zip 43138–0966, Mailing Address: Box 966, Zip 43138–0966; tel. 740/385–5631; Larry Willard, Administrator (Total facility includes 30 beds in nursing home–type unit) **A**1 9 10 **F**7 8 12 14 15 16 19 22 28 30 35 37 41 42 44 45 49 51 52 58 63 64 65 66 67 71 73 74 **P**1 3 **N** Community Hospitals of Ohio, Newark, OH	13	10	92	1612	40	45520	105	—	6946	238

LONDON—Madison County

★ MADISON COUNTY HOSPITAL, 210 North Main Street, Zip 43140–1115; tel. 740/852–1372; Gary J. Lehman, President (Total facility includes 11 beds in nursing home–type unit) **A**1 9 10 **F**3 7 8 11 14 15 16 17 19 22 24 26 28 29 30 31 34 35 36 37 39 40 41 42 44 45 48 49 52 53 54 58 59 64 65 66 67 68 71 73 74	23	10	95	1808	36	22101	204	18325	7886	276

LORAIN—Lorain County

□ △ LORAIN COMMUNITY/ST. JOSEPH REGIONAL HEALTH CENTER, (Includes Lorain Community/St. Joseph Health Center—East Campus, 205 West 20th Street, Zip 44052–3794; tel. 216/233–1000; Lorain Community/St. Joseph Regional Health Center—West Campus, tel. 216/960–3000), 3700 Kolbe Road, Zip 44053–1697; tel. 216/960–3000; Brian C. Lockwood, President and Chief Executive Officer (Total facility includes 16 beds in nursing home–type unit) (Nonreporting) **A**1 2 7 9 10 **S** Catholic Healthcare Partners, Cincinnati, OH	23	10	303	—	—	—	—	—	—	—

MANSFIELD—Richland County

★ MEDCENTRAL HEALTH SYSTEM, (Includes Crestline Hospital, 700 Columbus Street, Crestline, Zip 44827; tel. 419/683–1212; Susan Brown, Nursing Director and Site Administrator; Mansfield Hospital, 335 Glessner Avenue, tel. 419/526–8000; Paul Kautz, M.D., Vice President and Chief Operating Officer; Shelby Hospital, 20 Morris Road, Shelby, Zip 44875–0608; tel. 419/342–5015; Ron Distl, Vice President and Chief Executive Officer), 335 Glessner Avenue, Zip 44903–2265; tel. 419/526–8000; James E. Meyer, President **A**1 2 6 9 10 **F**2 3 7 8 10 11 12 15 16 17 19 20 21 22 23 25 28 29 30 31 32 33 34 35 36 37 39 40 41 42 44 45 46 48 49 52 53 54 55 56 57 58 60 63 65 66 67 70 71 73 74 **P**5 7 8	23	10	307	11628	182	86323	1325	100144	48710	1465

Hospital, Address, Telephone, Administrator, Approval, Facility, and Physician Codes, Health Care System, Network	Classi-fication Codes		Utilization Data					Expense (thousands) of dollars		
★ American Hospital Association (AHA) membership □ Joint Commission on Accreditation of Healthcare Organizations (JCAHO) accreditation + American Osteopathic Healthcare Association (AOHA) membership ○ American Osteopathic Association (AOA) accreditation △ Commission on Accreditation of Rehabilitation Facilities (CARF) accreditation Control codes 61, 63, 64, 71, 72 and 73 indicate hospitals listed by AOHA, but not registered by AHA. For definition of numerical codes, see page A4	Control	Service	Staffed Beds	Admissions	Census	Outpatient Visits	Births	Total	Payroll	Personnel

✠ RICHLAND HOSPITAL, 1451 Lucas Road, Zip 44901–0637, Mailing Address: Box 637, Zip 44901–0637; tel. 419/589–5511; John Cochran, Administrator (Nonreporting) A1 9 10	23	22	92	—	—	—	—	—	—	—
MARIETTA—Washington County										
✠ △ MARIETTA MEMORIAL HOSPITAL, 401 Matthew Street, Zip 45750–1699; tel. 740/374–1400; Larry J. Unroe, President A1 7 9 10 F2 3 4 7 8 12 14 15 16 17 19 21 22 24 26 27 28 29 30 31 32 33 35 37 39 40 41 42 44 45 46 48 49 52 54 55 56 58 59 60 63 64 65 66 67 71 72 73 74 P8 N Community Hospitals of Ohio, Newark, OH	23	10	134	5508	69	135659	758	47992	21394	718
★ + ○ SELBY GENERAL HOSPITAL, 1106 Colegate Drive, Zip 45750–1323; tel. 740/373–0582; James J. Cliborne, Jr., Chief Executive Officer A9 10 11 12 13 F7 8 15 16 19 21 22 26 30 31 32 34 35 36 37 39 40 41 42 44 49 53 61 65 66 67 71 72 73 74 P8 S Quorum Health Group/Quorum Health Resources, Inc., Brentwood, TN	23	10	44	1703	21	33680	104	14482	5987	190
MARION—Marion County										
✠ △ MARION GENERAL HOSPITAL, 1000 McKinley Park Drive, Zip 43302–6397; tel. 740/383–8400; Frank V. Swinehart, President and Chief Executive Officer A1 2 7 9 10 F1 7 8 10 14 15 16 17 19 21 22 24 28 30 31 32 33 34 35 37 39 40 41 42 44 45 49 52 53 54 55 58 59 60 65 67 71 73 74 P7 8 S OhioHealth, Columbus, OH	23	10	148	5914	67	90757	1000	49949	22105	761
□ MEDCENTER HOSPITAL, 1050 Delaware Avenue, Zip 43302–6459; tel. 740/383–7706; Philip W. Smith, Jr., President A1 9 10 F8 10 12 15 16 17 19 21 22 30 32 34 35 37 41 42 44 48 49 65 67 71 73	23	10	83	3352	44	26612	—	28174	9499	21
MARTINS FERRY—Belmont County										
✠ EAST OHIO REGIONAL HOSPITAL, 90 North Fourth Street, Zip 43935–1648; tel. 740/633–1100; Brian K. Felici, Vice President and Administrator (Total facility includes 94 beds in nursing home–type unit) A1 9 10 F2 3 5 7 8 10 11 12 14 15 16 17 18 19 21 22 23 24 26 27 28 29 30 31 32 34 35 37 39 40 41 42 44 45 46 47 48 49 51 52 53 54 55 56 57 58 59 60 61 63 64 65 66 67 70 71 73 74 P6 8 S Allegheny Health, Education and Research Foundation, Pittsburgh, PA	23	10	178	3715	132	132400	—	38860	17493	467
MARYSVILLE—Union County										
□ MEMORIAL HOSPITAL, 500 London Avenue, Zip 43040–1594; tel. 937/644–6115; Danny L. Boggs, President and Chief Executive Officer (Total facility includes 95 beds in nursing home–type unit) A1 9 10 F7 8 12 14 15 16 19 21 22 24 27 28 30 32 34 35 36 37 39 40 41 42 44 46 49 63 64 65 66 67 71 73 P4 7	13	10	145	2407	101	85933	498	30128	15953	539
MASSILLON—Stark County										
★ + ○ DOCTORS HOSPITAL OF STARK COUNTY, 400 Austin Avenue N.W., Zip 44646–3554; tel. 330/837–7200; Thomas E. Cecconi, Chief Executive Officer A2 9 10 11 12 13 F7 8 10 12 14 15 16 19 21 22 23 26 27 30 32 34 35 37 39 40 41 42 44 45 48 49 51 52 54 57 59 61 63 65 67 71 73 74 P7 8 S Quorum Health Group/Quorum Health Resources, Inc., Brentwood, TN N Cleveland Health Network, Independence, OH	23	10	166	2736	35	62044	268	—	—	596
✠ △ MASSILLON COMMUNITY HOSPITAL, 875 Eighth Street N.E., Zip 44646–8503, Mailing Address: P.O. Box 805, Zip 44648–8503; tel. 330/832–8761; Mervin F. Strine, President and Chief Executive Officer (Total facility includes 20 beds in nursing home–type unit) A1 7 9 10 F3 4 7 8 10 11 12 15 16 17 19 20 21 22 23 26 28 29 30 31 32 34 35 37 39 40 41 42 44 45 46 48 49 63 64 65 67 71 73	23	10	179	5237	73	104774	279	40393	19289	685
□ MASSILLON PSYCHIATRIC CENTER, 3000 Erie Street, Zip 44646–7993, Mailing Address: Box 540, Zip 44648–0540; tel. 330/833–3135; Cathy L. Cincinat, Chief Executive Officer A1 10 F4 7 8 10 12 14 15 16 17 18 19 20 21 22 35 41 44 45 46 49 52 54 55 57 65 71 73 P6	12	22	189	1076	171	0	0	27683	17784	338
MAUMEE—Lucas County										
□ CHARTER HOSPITAL OF TOLEDO, 1725 Timber Line Road, Zip 43537–4015; tel. 419/891–9333; Dennis J. Sajdak, Chief Executive Officer (Nonreporting) A1 9 10 S Magellan Health Services, Atlanta, GA	33	52	38	—	—	—	—	—	—	—
✠ ST. LUKE'S HOSPITAL, 5901 Monclova Road, Zip 43537–1899; tel. 419/893–5911; Frank J. Bartell, III, President and Chief Executive Officer (Total facility includes 26 beds in nursing home–type unit) A1 2 9 10 F7 8 10 12 15 17 19 21 22 23 27 28 30 34 35 36 37 40 41 42 44 45 46 49 54 63 64 65 66 67 68 71 73 P8 N First Interhealth Network, Toledo, OH	23	10	153	8587	106	115705	292	74495	33239	936
MEDINA—Medina County										
✠ △ MEDINA GENERAL HOSPITAL, 1000 East Washington Street, Zip 44256–2170, Mailing Address: P.O. Box 427, Zip 44258–0427; tel. 330/725–1000; Gary D. Hallman, President and Chief Executive Officer A1 2 7 9 10 F7 8 12 13 14 15 17 19 20 21 22 28 30 32 33 34 35 37 39 40 41 42 44 49 51 61 65 66 67 71 73 74 P8 N Northeast Ohio Health Network, Akron, OH	23	10	118	4945	56	140782	880	50397	22559	—
MIAMISBURG—Montgomery County										
SYCAMORE HOSPITAL See Kettering Medical Center, Kettering										
MIDDLEBURG HEIGHTS—Cuyahoga County										
✠ SOUTHWEST GENERAL HEALTH CENTER, 18697 Bagley Road, Zip 44130–3497; tel. 440/816–8000; L. Jon Schurmeier, President and Chief Executive Officer (Nonreporting) A1 2 9 10	23	10	253	—	—	—	—	—	—	—

Hospital, Address, Telephone, Administrator, Approval, Facility, and Physician Codes, Health Care System, Network	Classi-fication Codes		Utilization Data					Expense (thousands) of dollars		
★ American Hospital Association (AHA) membership □ Joint Commission on Accreditation of Healthcare Organizations (JCAHO) accreditation + American Osteopathic Healthcare Association (AOHA) membership ○ American Osteopathic Association (AOA) accreditation △ Commission on Accreditation of Rehabilitation Facilities (CARF) accreditation Control codes 61, 63, 64, 71, 72 and 73 indicate hospitals listed by AOHA, but not registered by AHA. For definition of numerical codes, see page A4	Control	Service	Staffed Beds	Admissions	Census	Outpatient Visits	Births	Total	Payroll	Personnel

MIDDLETOWN—Butler County

★ △ MIDDLETOWN REGIONAL HOSPITAL, 105 McKnight Drive, Zip 45044–4838; tel. 513/424–2111; Douglas W. McNeill, FACHE, President and Chief Executive Officer **A**1 2 3 7 9 10 **F**5 8 10 11 12 13 15 16 17 19 21 22 23 24 28 29 30 32 33 34 35 36 37 38 39 40 41 42 44 46 48 49 50 52 53 54 55 56 57 58 59 63 71 73 74 **P**8 | 23 | 10 | 183 | 8446 | 96 | 134218 | 1084 | 73361 | 31508 | —

MILLERSBURG—Holmes County

□ JOEL POMERENE MEMORIAL HOSPITAL, 981 Wooster Road, Zip 44654–1094; tel. 330/674–1015; Peter Tuerpitz, Administrator and Chief Executive Officer **A**1 9 10 **F**7 8 11 15 19 20 22 32 35 37 40 41 44 49 65 71 73 **P**5 6 7 | 13 | 10 | 36 | 1940 | 17 | 23817 | 613 | 13287 | 5030 | 182

MONTPELIER—Williams County

MONTPELIER HOSPITAL See Community Hospitals of Williams County, Bryan

MOUNT GILEAD—Morrow County

★ MORROW COUNTY HOSPITAL, 651 West Marion Road, Zip 43338–1096; tel. 419/946–5015; Alan C. Pauley, Administrator (Total facility includes 38 beds in nursing home–type unit) **A**1 9 10 **F**1 7 8 14 15 17 19 21 22 28 30 32 34 35 36 37 39 40 41 42 44 49 51 64 65 66 71 73 **P**7 8 **S** OhioHealth, Columbus, OH | 13 | 10 | 75 | 1006 | 41 | 27145 | 141 | 11098 | 3963 | 147

MOUNT VERNON—Knox County

★ KNOX COMMUNITY HOSPITAL, 1330 Coshocton Road, Zip 43050–1495; tel. 740/393–9000; Robert G. Polahar, Chief Executive Officer **A**1 9 10 **F**7 16 19 22 32 35 36 37 40 42 44 46 52 59 65 71 73 **P**8 **S** Quorum Health Group/Quorum Health Resources, Inc., Brentwood, TN **N** Community Hospitals of Ohio, Newark, OH | 23 | 10 | 115 | 4148 | 45 | 45127 | 458 | 33999 | 12874 | 412

NAPOLEON—Henry County

★ HENRY COUNTY HOSPITAL, 11–600 State Road 424, Zip 43545–9399; tel. 419/592–4015; Robert J. Coholich, Chief Executive Officer **A**1 9 10 **F**3 7 8 11 12 14 15 19 20 22 24 28 29 30 34 35 37 39 40 41 42 44 45 46 49 53 58 64 65 66 71 73 74 **N** Lake Erie Health Alliance, Toledo, OH; Midwest Health Net, LLC., Fort Wayne, IN | 23 | 10 | 39 | 936 | 10 | 34528 | 152 | 9345 | 3812 | 122

NELSONVILLE—Athens County

+ ○ DOCTORS HOSPITAL OF NELSONVILLE, 1950 Mount Saint Mary Drive, Zip 45764–1193; tel. 614/753–1931; Mark R. Seckinger, Administrator (Total facility includes 45 beds in nursing home–type unit) (Nonreporting) **A**9 10 11 **S** Doctors Hospital, Columbus, OH | 23 | 10 | 70 | | | | | | |

NEWARK—Licking County

★ LICKING MEMORIAL HOSPITAL, 1320 West Main Street, Zip 43055–3699; tel. 740/348–4000; William J. Andrews, President **A**1 9 10 **F**3 7 8 10 11 12 14 15 16 17 19 21 22 28 31 32 35 37 41 42 44 45 49 52 54 55 56 57 58 59 61 63 65 67 71 73 74 **P**6 **N** Community Hospitals of Ohio, Newark, OH | 23 | 10 | 209 | 6804 | 69 | 177508 | 1060 | 48192 | 24622 | 1009

NORTHFIELD—Summit County

□ NORTHCOAST BEHAVIORAL HEALTHCARE SYSTEM, (Includes Cleveland Campus, 1708 Southpoint Drive, Cleveland, Zip 44109–1999; tel. 216/787–0500; George P. Gintoli, Chief Executive Officer; Northfield Campus, 1756 Sagamore Road, tel. 330/467–7131; Toledo Campus, 930 South Detroit Avenue, Toledo, Zip 43614–2701; tel. 419/381–1881; G. Terrence Smith, Chief Executive Officer), 1756 Sagamore Road, Zip 44067; tel. 330/467–7131; George P. Gintoli, Chief Executive Officer **A**1 3 5 10 **F**14 15 16 20 27 35 39 41 46 52 55 57 62 65 67 69 72 **P**6 | 12 | 22 | 429 | 2572 | 422 | 0 | 0 | — | — | 911

NORTHFIELD CAMPUS See Northcoast Behavioral Healthcare System
WESTERN RESERVE PSYCHIATRIC HOSPITAL See Northcoast Behavioral Healthcare System

NORWALK—Huron County

★ + ○ FISHER–TITUS MEDICAL CENTER, 272 Benedict Avenue, Zip 44857–2374; tel. 419/668–8101; Patrick J. Martin, President and Chief Executive Officer (Total facility includes 69 beds in nursing home–type unit) **A**1 2 9 10 11 **F**7 8 12 15 16 17 19 20 21 22 23 26 27 28 30 32 33 35 36 37 39 40 41 42 44 46 49 53 54 55 56 57 58 59 60 61 63 64 65 66 67 71 73 74 **P**2 7 **N** United Health Partners, Toledo, OH; Cleveland Health Network, Independence, OH; Lake Erie Health Alliance, Toledo, OH; Midwest Health Net, LLC., Fort Wayne, IN | 23 | 10 | 135 | 3621 | 94 | 58779 | 682 | 35649 | 16097 | 500

OAK HILL—Jackson County

★ OAK HILL COMMUNITY MEDICAL CENTER, 350 Charlotte Avenue, Zip 45656–1326; tel. 740/682–7717; Robert A. Bowers, Chief Executive Officer (Total facility includes 24 beds in nursing home–type unit) (Nonreporting) **A**1 9 10 | 23 | 10 | 68 | — | — | — | — | — | — | —

OBERLIN—Lorain County

★ ALLEN MEMORIAL HOSPITAL, 200 West Lorain Street, Zip 44074–1077; tel. 440/775–1211; James H. Schaum, President and Chief Executive Officer (Total facility includes 16 beds in nursing home–type unit) **A**1 9 10 **F**7 8 14 15 19 20 21 22 30 31 32 34 35 36 37 39 40 41 42 44 45 49 61 64 65 66 71 72 73 | 23 | 10 | 91 | 2064 | 28 | 21263 | 343 | 15575 | 6958 | 210

OREGON—Lucas County

□ ST. CHARLES MERCY HOSPITAL, (Formerly St. Charles Hospital), 2600 Navarre Avenue, Zip 43616–3297; tel. 419/698–7479; Cathleen K. Nelson, President and Chief Executive Officer **A**1 2 9 10 **F**3 4 7 8 10 11 12 14 15 16 17 19 21 22 23 24 25 26 27 28 29 30 31 32 33 34 35 36 37 39 40 41 42 43 44 45 49 50 51 52 53 54 56 57 58 59 60 62 63 64 65 66 67 68 69 70 71 72 73 74 **P**1 3 6 **S** Catholic Healthcare Partners, Cincinnati, OH **N** First Interhealth Network, Toledo, OH | 21 | 10 | 306 | 11399 | 174 | 202743 | 816 | 102414 | 53185 | 1692

Hospital, Address, Telephone, Administrator, Approval, Facility, and Physician Codes, Health Care System, Network	Control	Service	Staffed Beds	Admissions	Census	Outpatient Visits	Births	Total	Payroll	Personnel

ORRVILLE—Wayne County
☒ DUNLAP MEMORIAL HOSPITAL, 832 South Main Street, Zip 44667–2208; tel. 330/682–3010; Lynn V. Horner, President and Chief Executive Officer **A**1 9 10 **F**7 8 19 21 22 27 28 29 30 35 39 40 41 42 44 45 46 49 59 63 65 71 73 — 23 10 38 830 7 24862 276 9327 3353 134

OXFORD—Butler County
☒ MCCULLOUGH–HYDE MEMORIAL HOSPITAL, 110 North Poplar Street, Zip 45056–1292; tel. 513/523–2111; Richard A. Daniels, President and Chief Executive Officer **A**1 9 10 **F**7 8 11 12 14 15 16 17 19 21 22 27 28 30 33 34 35 36 37 39 40 42 44 49 63 65 66 67 71 72 73 **P**3 — 23 10 44 2637 21 51201 488 23239 10215 277

PAINESVILLE—Lake County
☒ △ LAKE HOSPITAL SYSTEM, 10 East Washington, Zip 44077–3472; tel. 216/354–2400; Cynthia Ann Moore–Hardy, President and Chief Executive Officer **A**1 2 7 9 10 **F**7 8 10 12 13 14 15 16 17 18 19 20 21 22 25 26 27 28 29 30 31 32 33 34 35 36 37 39 40 41 42 43 44 45 46 49 60 63 64 65 66 67 71 72 73 74 **P**1 3 **N** Lake Hospital System, Inc., Painesville, OH — 23 10 359 12910 168 358960 1423 129284 53191 1578

PARMA—Cuyahoga County
☒ △ PARMA COMMUNITY GENERAL HOSPITAL, 7007 Powers Boulevard, Zip 44129–5495; tel. 440/888–1800; Thomas A. Selden, President and Chief Executive Officer (Total facility includes 27 beds in nursing home–type unit) **A**1 2 7 9 10 **F**1 8 10 11 12 13 14 16 17 19 21 22 24 26 27 28 29 30 31 32 33 34 36 37 39 40 41 42 44 45 46 48 49 52 54 57 59 64 65 66 67 71 73 **P**1 7 **N** Cleveland Health Network, Independence, OH — 23 10 264 10768 185 103952 559 89233 40820 1262

PAULDING—Paulding County
☒ PAULDING COUNTY HOSPITAL, 11558 State Road 111, Zip 45879–9220; tel. 419/399–4080; Joseph M. Dorko, Chief Executive Officer **A**1 9 10 **F**7 8 19 21 22 28 30 32 34 35 36 39 40 41 44 49 51 64 71 72 73 **S** Quorum Health Group/Quorum Health Resources, Inc., Brentwood, TN **N** LutheranPreferred Network, Fort Wayne, IN; Midwest Health Net, LLC., Fort Wayne, IN — 13 10 51 774 7 29528 129 9759 4372 149

POMEROY—Meigs County
☒ VETERANS MEMORIAL HOSPITAL OF MEIGS COUNTY, 115 East Memorial Drive, Zip 45769–9572; tel. 740/992–2104; Robert Bowers, Administrator (Total facility includes 40 beds in nursing home–type unit) **A**1 9 10 **F**14 15 16 19 22 28 32 33 41 42 44 45 52 59 64 71 73 — 23 10 69 229 42 20374 — 6302 2622 —

PORT CLINTON—Ottawa County
☐ H. B. MAGRUDER MEMORIAL HOSPITAL, 615 Fulton Street, Zip 43452–2034; tel. 419/734–3131; David R. Norwine, President and Chief Executive Officer **A**1 9 10 **F**8 12 14 15 16 17 19 21 22 28 30 34 36 37 39 42 44 45 46 49 51 63 65 66 67 71 **P**6 8 **N** Lake Erie Health Alliance, Toledo, OH — 23 10 33 1662 15 74448 — 14417 6161 212

PORTSMOUTH—Scioto County
BEHAVIORAL HEALTH–PORTSMOUTH CAMPUS See River Valley Health System, Ironton
☒ △ SOUTHERN OHIO MEDICAL CENTER, (Includes Mercy Hospital, 1248 Kinneys Lane, Zip 45662; Scioto Memorial Hospital, 1805 27th Street, Zip 45662), 1805 27th Street, Zip 45662–2400; tel. 740/354–5000; Randal M. Arnett, President and Chief Executive Officer **A**1 7 9 10 12 **F**7 8 15 17 18 19 20 21 22 24 25 26 28 29 30 31 32 33 34 35 36 37 39 40 41 42 44 45 46 48 49 51 54 55 56 58 60 61 62 63 65 66 67 68 71 72 73 74 **P**3 6 **S** OhioHealth, Columbus, OH — 23 10 281 10996 158 197993 1576 92863 40839 1600

RAVENNA—Portage County
☒ ROBINSON MEMORIAL HOSPITAL, 6847 North Chestnut Street, Zip 44266–1204, Mailing Address: P.O. Box 1204, Zip 44266–1204; tel. 330/297–0811; Stephen Colecchi, President and Chief Executive Officer **A**1 2 5 9 10 **F**7 8 10 11 12 13 15 16 17 19 21 22 23 25 26 28 29 30 31 32 33 34 35 37 39 40 41 42 44 45 46 49 51 52 54 55 56 59 60 61 63 65 66 67 71 72 73 74 **P**6 **N** Northeast Ohio Health Network, Akron, OH — 13 10 131 8254 106 94650 888 82292 35618 1040

RICHMOND HEIGHTS—Cuyahoga County
★ + ○ PHS MT. SINAI MEDICAL CENTER EAST, (Formerly Richmond Heights General Hospital), 27100 Chardon Road, Zip 44143–1198; tel. 440/585–6500; Keith J. Petersen, Chief Executive Officer (Nonreporting) **A**9 10 11 12 13 **S** U. S. Public Health Service Indian Health Service, Rockville, MD — 23 10 98 — — — — — — —

ROCK CREEK—Ashtabula County
GLENBEIGH HEALTH SOURCES, Route 45, Zip 44084, Mailing Address: P.O. Box 298, Zip 44084–0298; tel. 440/563–3400; Patricia Weston–Hall, Executive Director **A**9 10 **F**2 3 15 16 **P**5 — 23 82 80 849 18 9222 — — — 55

SAINT CLAIRSVILLE—Belmont County
☐ BHC FOX RUN HOSPITAL, 67670 Traco Drive, Zip 43950–9375; tel. 614/695–2131; J. Frank Gallagher, III, Administrator (Nonreporting) **A**1 10 **S** Behavioral Healthcare Corporation, Nashville, TN — 33 22 65 — — — — — — —

SAINT MARYS—Auglaize County
☒ JOINT TOWNSHIP DISTRICT MEMORIAL HOSPITAL, 200 St. Clair Street, Zip 45885–2400; tel. 419/394–3387; James R. Chick, President (Total facility includes 23 beds in nursing home–type unit) **A**1 9 10 **F**7 8 12 15 17 19 21 22 25 27 28 30 32 33 34 35 37 40 41 44 46 49 51 64 65 67 71 73 **N** West Central Ohio Regional Healthcare Alliance, Ltd., Lima, OH — 23 10 91 4355 56 65645 333 30413 12650 467

SALEM—Columbiana County
☒ SALEM COMMUNITY HOSPITAL, 1995 East State Street, Zip 44460–0121; tel. 330/332–1551; Eugene Zentko, Administrator and Chief Executive Officer (Total facility includes 15 beds in nursing home–type unit) **A**1 5 9 10 **F**3 4 7 8 10 12 14 15 19 20 21 22 28 30 34 35 36 37 39 40 41 42 44 45 49 51 60 63 64 65 67 70 71 73 — 23 10 159 5736 72 84048 391 44694 22069 685

Hospital, Address, Telephone, Administrator, Approval, Facility, and Physician Codes, Health Care System, Network	Classi-fication Codes		Utilization Data					Expense (thousands) of dollars		
★ American Hospital Association (AHA) membership □ Joint Commission on Accreditation of Healthcare Organizations (JCAHO) accreditation + American Osteopathic Healthcare Association (AOHA) membership ○ American Osteopathic Association (AOA) accreditation △ Commission on Accreditation of Rehabilitation Facilities (CARF) accreditation Control codes 61, 63, 64, 71, 72 and 73 indicate hospitals listed by AOHA, but not registered by AHA. For definition of numerical codes, see page A4	Control	Service	Staffed Beds	Admissions	Census	Outpatient Visits	Births	Total	Payroll	Personnel

SANDUSKY—Erie County

□ + ○ △ FIRELANDS COMMUNITY HOSPITAL, 1101 Decatur Street, Zip 44870–3335; tel. 419/626–7400; Dennis A. Sokol, President and Chief Executive Officer (Nonreporting) **A**1 2 7 9 10 11 12 13 **N** Cleveland Health Network, Independence, OH; Lake Erie Health Alliance, Toledo, OH

| | 23 | 10 | 232 | — | — | — | — | — | — | — |

★ PROVIDENCE HOSPITAL, 1912 Hayes Avenue, Zip 44870–4736; tel. 419/621–7000; Sister Nancy Linenkugel, FACHE, President and Chief Executive Officer (Total facility includes 46 beds in nursing home–type unit) **A**1 2 6 9 10 **F**2 3 6 7 8 10 11 12 14 15 16 17 19 21 22 23 25 26 27 28 29 30 31 32 33 34 35 37 39 40 41 42 44 45 46 49 52 53 54 55 56 57 58 59 60 63 64 65 66 67 71 73 74 **P**3 8 **S** Franciscan Services Corporation, Sylvania, OH **N** United Health Partners, Toledo, OH

| | 21 | 10 | 180 | 3622 | 80 | 71459 | 245 | 40173 | 16802 | 557 |

SHELBY—Richland County

SHELBY HOSPITAL See MedCentral Health System, Mansfield

SIDNEY—Shelby County

★ WILSON MEMORIAL HOSPITAL, 915 West Michigan Street, Zip 45365–2491; tel. 937/498–2311; Thomas J. Boecker, President and Chief Executive Officer (Total facility includes 54 beds in nursing home–type unit) **A**1 9 10 **F**7 8 12 14 15 16 19 21 22 26 30 32 33 34 35 37 39 40 41 44 45 46 57 65 66 67 71 73 **P**6

| | 23 | 10 | 85 | 4068 | 88 | 87764 | 496 | 35157 | 15180 | 495 |

SPRINGFIELD—Clark County

★ COMMUNITY HOSPITAL, 2615 East High Street, Zip 45505–1422, Mailing Address: Box 1228, Zip 45501–1228; tel. 937/325–0531; Neal E. Kresheck, President (Total facility includes 41 beds in nursing home–type unit) **A**1 6 9 10 **F**6 7 8 10 11 12 13 14 15 16 17 19 21 22 24 26 27 28 29 30 31 32 33 34 35 36 37 39 40 41 42 44 45 46 49 51 60 63 64 65 66 67 68 71 72 73 74 **P**7

| | 23 | 10 | 201 | 9142 | 136 | 128530 | 1906 | 72569 | 31008 | 1124 |

□ △ MERCY MEDICAL CENTER, 1343 North Fountain Boulevard, Zip 45501–1380; tel. 937/390–5000; Teresa Richle, Interim Senior Vice President Acute Care Operations (Total facility includes 20 beds in nursing home–type unit) (Nonreporting) **A**1 5 7 9 10 **S** Catholic Healthcare Partners, Cincinnati, OH

| | 21 | 10 | 218 | — | — | — | — | — | — | — |

STEUBENVILLE—Jefferson County

★ TRINITY HEALTH SYSTEM, (Includes Trinity Medical Center East, 380 Summit Avenue, tel. 740/283–7000; Trinity Medical Center West, 400 Johnson Road, Zip 43952–2393; tel. 740/264–8000), 380 Summit Avenue, Zip 43952–2699; tel. 740/283–7000; Fred B. Brower, President and Chief Executive Officer **A**1 2 6 9 10 **F**2 3 7 8 10 11 14 15 16 17 19 20 22 23 24 27 28 30 32 33 34 35 36 37 40 41 42 44 48 49 51 52 53 56 57 58 59 60 63 64 65 66 67 71 72 73 74 **P**7 8 **S** Franciscan Services Corporation, Sylvania, OH

| | 23 | 10 | 347 | 10291 | 177 | 284997 | 695 | 109159 | 47020 | 1278 |

SYLVANIA—Lucas County

★ △ FLOWER HOSPITAL, 5200 Harroun Road, Zip 43560–2196; tel. 419/824–1444; Randall Kelley, Senior Vice President and Chief Operating Officer (Total facility includes 263 beds in nursing home–type unit) **A**1 2 3 5 7 9 10 **F**2 3 4 5 6 7 8 10 11 12 13 14 15 16 17 18 19 20 21 22 23 25 26 27 28 29 30 31 32 34 35 37 38 39 40 41 42 43 44 45 46 47 48 49 50 51 52 53 54 55 56 57 58 59 60 61 62 63 64 65 66 67 68 70 71 73 74 **P**6 7 8 **S** ProMedica Health System, Toledo, OH **N** First Interhealth Network, Toledo, OH; Lake Erie Health Alliance, Toledo, OH; Promedica Health System, Toledo, OH

| | 23 | 10 | 472 | 9434 | 379 | 64296 | 966 | 89187 | 41360 | 1392 |

TIFFIN—Seneca County

□ MERCY HOSPITAL, 485 West Market Street, Zip 44883–0727, Mailing Address: P.O. Box 727, Zip 44883–0727; tel. 419/447–3130; Mark Shugarman, President **A**1 9 10 **F**4 7 8 11 12 13 14 15 16 17 19 22 27 28 29 30 31 32 34 36 39 40 41 42 44 45 46 49 51 56 62 63 65 71 73 **P**8 **S** Catholic Healthcare Partners, Cincinnati, OH **N** United Health Partners, Toledo, OH; Lake Erie Health Alliance, Toledo, OH

| | 21 | 10 | 60 | 2554 | 25 | 63406 | 452 | 25312 | 10737 | 434 |

TOLEDO—Lucas County

★ △ MEDICAL COLLEGE OF OHIO HOSPITALS, 3000 Arlington Avenue, Zip 43614–5805; tel. 419/381–4172; Frank S. McCullough, M.D., President **A**1 2 3 5 7 8 10 **F**4 8 10 11 12 19 20 21 22 24 25 26 30 31 35 37 39 41 42 43 44 45 46 47 48 49 52 53 54 55 58 59 60 63 64 65 66 67 68 69 70 71 73 **P**4 **N** Lake Erie Health Alliance, Toledo, OH; Midwest Health Net, LLC., Fort Wayne, IN

| | 12 | 10 | 233 | 8181 | 160 | 203265 | — | 145419 | 59976 | 1746 |

NORTHWEST PSYCHIATRIC HOSPITAL See Northcoast Behavioral Healthcare System, Northfield

★ ○ RIVERSIDE MERCY HOSPITAL, (Formerly Riverside Hospital), 1600 North Superior Street, Zip 43604–2199; tel. 419/729–6000; Scott E. Shook, President (Total facility includes 12 beds in nursing home–type unit) (Nonreporting) **A**1 2 9 10 11 **S** Catholic Healthcare Partners, Cincinnati, OH

| | 23 | 10 | 162 | — | — | — | — | — | — | — |

□ ○ ST. VINCENT MERCY MEDICAL CENTER, 2213 Cherry Street, Zip 43608–2691; tel. 419/251–3232; Steven L. Mickus, President and Chief Executive Officer **A**1 2 3 5 6 9 10 11 12 13 **F**3 4 5 7 8 9 10 11 12 13 14 15 16 17 19 21 22 23 24 25 26 27 28 29 30 31 32 34 35 36 37 38 39 40 41 42 43 44 46 47 48 49 51 53 54 55 56 57 58 59 60 62 63 64 65 66 67 68 69 70 71 72 73 74 **P**8 **S** Catholic Healthcare Partners, Cincinnati, OH **N** United Health Partners, Toledo, OH; First Interhealth Network, Toledo, OH

| | 21 | 10 | 457 | 20333 | 305 | 263395 | 1812 | 284638 | 128610 | 3969 |

Hospital, Address, Telephone, Administrator, Approval, Facility, and Physician Codes, Health Care System, Network	Classi-fication Codes		Utilization Data					Expense (thousands) of dollars		
★ American Hospital Association (AHA) membership □ Joint Commission on Accreditation of Healthcare Organizations (JCAHO) accreditation + American Osteopathic Healthcare Association (AOHA) membership ○ American Osteopathic Association (AOA) accreditation △ Commission on Accreditation of Rehabilitation Facilities (CARF) accreditation Control codes 61, 63, 64, 71, 72 and 73 indicate hospitals listed by AOHA, but not registered by AHA. For definition of numerical codes, see page A4	Control	Service	Staffed Beds	Admissions	Census	Outpatient Visits	Births	Total	Payroll	Personnel

⊠ THE TOLEDO HOSPITAL, 2142 North Cove Boulevard, Zip 43606–3896; tel. 419/471–4000; Barbara Steele, President (Total facility includes 94 beds in nursing home–type unit) **A**1 2 3 5 8 9 10 **F**2 3 4 5 6 7 8 10 11 12 13 14 15 16 17 18 19 21 22 23 25 26 27 28 29 30 31 32 34 35 37 38 39 40 41 42 43 44 45 46 47 48 49 50 51 52 53 54 55 56 57 58 59 60 61 62 63 64 65 66 67 68 70 71 73 74 **P**6 7 8 **S** ProMedica Health System, Toledo, OH **N** Promedica Health System, Toledo, OH; Midwest Health Net, LLC., Fort Wayne, IN	23	10	673	24663	410	294965	3786	281055	127512	3291
TOLEDO CAMPUS See Northcoast Behavioral Healthcare System, Northfield										
TROY—Miami County										
⊠ △ UPPER VALLEY MEDICAL CENTER, (Includes Dettmer Hospital, 3130 North Dixie Highway, Zip 45373–1039; tel. 937/440–7500), 3130 North Dixie Highway, Zip 45373; tel. 937/440–7500; David J. Meckstroth, President and Chief Executive Officer (Total facility includes 18 beds in nursing home–type unit) **A**1 2 7 9 10 **F**2 3 4 7 8 10 12 13 15 16 17 18 19 21 22 25 27 28 29 30 31 32 34 35 36 37 39 40 41 42 44 45 46 48 49 52 53 54 55 56 57 58 59 60 62 65 66 67 68 71 72 73 74 **P**2 6	23	10	214	9533	—	142088	1104	—	43823	—
UPPER SANDUSKY—Wyandot County										
★ WYANDOT MEMORIAL HOSPITAL, 885 North Sandusky Avenue, Zip 43351–1098; tel. 419/294–4991; Joseph A. D'Ettorre, Chief Executive Officer **A**9 10 **F**7 8 11 12 15 16 19 21 22 33 34 35 40 41 42 44 46 56 63 71 73 **P**6 **N** Ohio State Health Network, Columbus, OH	16	10	31	944	10	36514	119	10077	3821	147
URBANA—Champaign County										
□ MERCY MEMORIAL HOSPITAL, 904 Scioto Street, Zip 43078–2200; tel. 937/653–5231; Richard Rogers, Senior Vice President (Nonreporting) **A**1 9 10 **S** Catholic Healthcare Partners, Cincinnati, OH	21	10	20	—	—	—	—	—	—	—
VAN WERT—Van Wert County										
⊠ VAN WERT COUNTY HOSPITAL, 1250 South Washington Street, Zip 45891–2599; tel. 419/238–2390; Mark J. Minick, President and Chief Executive Officer **A**1 9 10 **F**7 8 11 13 14 15 16 17 18 19 22 26 28 29 30 35 37 39 40 41 42 44 46 63 65 66 71 73 **P**1 7 8 **N** West Central Ohio Regional Healthcare Alliance, Ltd., Lima, OH; LutheranPreferred Network, Fort Wayne, IN; Midwest Health Net, LLC., Fort Wayne, IN	23	10	100	1775	15	101284	289	19298	7928	242
WADSWORTH—Medina County										
□ WADSWORTH–RITTMAN HOSPITAL, 195 Wadsworth Road, Zip 44281–9505; tel. 330/334–1504; James W. Brumlow, Jr., President and Chief Executive Officer (Nonreporting) **A**1 9 10 **N** Cleveland Health Network, Independence, OH	23	10	64	—	—	—	—	—	—	—
WARREN—Trumbull County										
FORUM HEALTH–TRUMBULL MEMORIAL HOSPITAL See Forum Health, Youngstown										
HILLSIDE REHABILITATION HOSPITAL See Forum Health, Youngstown										
□ ○ ST. JOSEPH HEALTH CENTER, 667 Eastland Avenue S.E., Zip 44484–4531; tel. 330/841–4000; Robert W. Shroder, Chief Operating Officer (Total facility includes 11 beds in nursing home–type unit) **A**1 2 9 10 11 12 13 **F**2 3 7 8 10 12 14 15 16 19 21 22 25 27 28 29 30 31 32 33 35 36 37 39 40 41 42 44 46 49 52 54 55 56 57 58 59 60 64 65 66 67 71 72 73 74 **P**1 **S** Catholic Healthcare Partners, Cincinnati, OH **N** Cleveland Health Network, Independence, OH	21	10	127	7143	83	121673	717	62581	23909	693
WARRENSVILLE HEIGHTS—Morgan County										
□ + ○ △ MERIDIA SOUTH POINTE HOSPITAL, 4110 Warrensville Center Road, Zip 44122–7099; tel. 216/491–6000; Kathleen A. Rice, Chief Operating Officer **A**1 2 7 9 10 11 12 13 **F**3 4 7 8 10 11 12 13 14 15 16 17 19 21 23 24 25 26 27 28 29 30 31 32 33 34 35 36 37 38 39 40 41 42 43 44 45 46 48 49 50 51 52 54 55 56 57 58 59 60 61 63 64 65 66 67 68 70 71 72 73 74 **S** Meridia Health System, Mayfield Village, OH **N** Merida Health System, Mayfield Village, OH	23	10	178	6566	94	100659	—	71431	26438	796
WASHINGTON COURT HOUSE—Lucas County										
⊠ FAYETTE COUNTY MEMORIAL HOSPITAL, 1430 Columbus Avenue, Zip 43160–1791; tel. 740/335–1210; Francis G. Albarano, Administrator **A**1 9 10 **F**7 8 12 14 15 17 19 20 21 22 27 28 29 30 32 33 34 35 36 37 39 40 41 42 44 46 49 56 65 66 68 71 73 **S** Quorum Health Group/Quorum Health Resources, Inc., Brentwood, TN	13	10	48	1474	15	61621	337	16116	6623	232
WAUSEON—Fulton County										
⊠ FULTON COUNTY HEALTH CENTER, 725 South Shoop Avenue, Zip 43567–1701; tel. 419/335–2015; E. Dean Beck, Administrator (Total facility includes 86 beds in nursing home–type unit) **A**1 2 9 10 **F**3 6 7 8 14 15 19 21 22 24 28 30 35 37 39 40 41 42 44 49 52 55 56 58 59 64 65 66 67 71 73 **N** United Health Partners, Toledo, OH; Lake Erie Health Alliance, Toledo, OH	23	10	172	2727	97	107323	351	24943	11454	427
WAVERLY—Pike County										
□ PIKE COMMUNITY HOSPITAL, 100 Dawn Lane, Zip 45690–9664; tel. 740/947–2186; Richard E. Sobota, President and Chief Executive Officer (Nonreporting) **A**1 9 10 **N** Ohio State Health Network, Columbus, OH	23	10	40	—	—	—	—	—	—	—
WEST UNION—Adams County										
□ ADAMS COUNTY HOSPITAL, 210 North Wilson Drive, Zip 45693–1574; tel. 937/544–5571; Philip S. Hanna, Administrator (Total facility includes 18 beds in nursing home–type unit) **A**1 9 10 **F**3 8 12 15 16 17 19 20 21 22 24 30 32 33 34 35 39 41 44 46 49 54 56 64 65 66 67 71 72 73	13	10	49	1285	30	39438	—	13440	5966	—
WESTERVILLE—Franklin County										
ST. ANN'S HOSPITAL See Mount Carmel Health System, Columbus										

Hospital, Address, Telephone, Administrator, Approval, Facility, and Physician Codes, Health Care System, Network	Classi-fication Codes		Utilization Data					Expense (thousands) of dollars		
★ American Hospital Association (AHA) membership □ Joint Commission on Accreditation of Healthcare Organizations (JCAHO) accreditation + American Osteopathic Healthcare Association (AOHA) membership ○ American Osteopathic Association (AOA) accreditation △ Commission on Accreditation of Rehabilitation Facilities (CARF) accreditation Control codes 61, 63, 64, 71, 72 and 73 indicate hospitals listed by AOHA, but not registered by AHA. For definition of numerical codes, see page A4	Control	Service	Staffed Beds	Admissions	Census	Outpatient Visits	Births	Total	Payroll	Personnel

WILLARD—Huron County

□ MERCY HOSPITAL–WILLARD, 110 East Howard Street, Zip 44890–1611; tel. 419/933–2931; James O. Detwiler, President **A**1 9 10 **F**7 8 15 16 19 22 23 28 29 30 32 33 34 35 36 37 40 41 42 44 45 49 58 63 65 66 67 71 73 **P**3 8 **S** Catholic Healthcare Partners, Cincinnati, OH **N** United Health Partners, Toledo, OH

	21	10	30	881	8	46268	171	12137	5184	194

WILLOUGHBY—Lake County

□ UHHS LAURELWOOD HOSPITAL, 35900 Euclid Avenue, Zip 44094–4648; tel. 440/953–3000; Farshid Afsarifard, Executive Director **A**1 9 10 **F**3 12 14 15 16 17 18 25 52 53 54 55 56 57 58 59 65 67 68 73 **P**5 6 **S** University Hospitals Health System, Cleveland, OH **N** The Mount Sinai Health Care System, Cleveland, OH

	23	22	160	1728	42	21333	—	9166	5120	228

WILMINGTON—Clinton County

⊞ CLINTON MEMORIAL HOSPITAL, 610 West Main Street, Zip 45177–2194; tel. 937/382–6611; Thomas F. Kurtz, Jr., President and Chief Executive Officer (Total facility includes 12 beds in nursing home–type unit) **A**1 2 3 9 10 **F**4 7 8 14 15 16 17 19 20 21 22 24 25 26 28 30 31 32 34 35 36 37 39 40 41 42 44 45 46 49 51 54 58 60 64 65 66 67 71 73 74 **P**1 3

	13	10	93	4298	48	124972	519	41229	18617	601

WOOSTER—Wayne County

□ WOOSTER COMMUNITY HOSPITAL, 1761 Beall Avenue, Zip 44691–2342; tel. 330/263–8100; William E. Sheron, Chief Executive Officer **A**1 2 9 10 **F**7 8 12 15 17 18 19 21 22 27 28 30 31 32 33 34 35 36 37 39 40 41 42 44 45 46 49 63 65 67 71 73 **P**3 **S** Quorum Health Group/Quorum Health Resources, Inc., Brentwood, TN

	14	10	90	4506	49	107976	705	34690	16723	530

WORTHINGTON—Franklin County

□ HARDING HOSPITAL, 445 East Granville Road, Zip 43085–3195; tel. 614/885–5381; S. R. Thorward, M.D., President and Chief Executive Officer **A**1 3 5 9 10 **F**3 12 22 25 26 34 52 54 56 57 58 59 65 67 74 **P**6

	23	22	36	1123	23	35134	—	14223	8617	279

WRIGHT–PATTERSON AFB—Greene County

⊞ U. S. AIR FORCE MEDICAL CENTER WRIGHT–PATTERSON, 4881 Sugar Maple Drive, Zip 45433–5529; tel. 937/257–0940; Brigadier General Earl W. Mabry, II, Commander (Nonreporting) **A**1 2 3 5 **S** Department of the Air Force, Bowling AFB, DC

	41	10	135	—	—	—	—	—	—	—

XENIA—Greene County

⊞ △ GREENE MEMORIAL HOSPITAL, 1141 North Monroe Drive, Zip 45385–1600; tel. 937/372–8011; Michael R. Stephens, President (Total facility includes 12 beds in nursing home–type unit) **A**1 2 5 7 9 10 **F**2 3 6 7 8 10 12 15 16 17 19 21 22 25 26 27 28 30 32 33 34 35 36 37 39 40 41 42 44 45 46 48 49 51 52 53 54 55 56 57 58 59 60 62 63 64 65 66 67 70 71 72 73 74 **P**6 7 8

	23	10	150	4486	66	119475	326	44853	17904	708

YOUNGSTOWN—Mahoning County

⊞ BHC BELMONT PINES HOSPITAL, 615 Churchill–Hubbard Road, Zip 44505–1379; tel. 330/759–2700; Edward Nasca, Chief Executive Officer (Nonreporting) **A**1 9 10 **S** Behavioral Healthcare Corporation, Nashville, TN

	33	22	77	—	—	—	—	—	—	—

⊞ △ FORUM HEALTH, (Formerly Western Reserve Care System), (Includes Forum Health–Trumbull Memorial Hospital, 1350 East Market Street, Warren, Zip 44482–6628; tel. 330/841–9011; Gary E. Kaatz, Chief Operating Officer; Hillside Rehabilitation Hospital, 8747 Squires Lane N.E., Warren, Zip 44484–1649; tel. 330/841–3700; Northside Medical Center, 500 Gypsy Lane, Zip 44501–0240; tel. 330/747–1444; Southside Medical Center, 345 Oak Hill Avenue, tel. 330/747–0777; Tod Children's Hospital, 500 Gypsy Lane, Zip 44501–0240; tel. 330/747–6700), 345 Oak Hill Avenue, Zip 44501–0990, Mailing Address: P.O. Box 990, Zip 44501–0990; tel. 330/747–0777; Charles A. Johns, President (Total facility includes 26 beds in nursing home–type unit) **A**1 2 3 7 8 9 10 **F**2 3 4 6 7 8 10 12 13 14 15 16 17 18 19 20 21 22 23 25 26 27 28 29 30 31 32 33 34 35 36 37 38 39 40 41 42 43 44 45 46 47 48 49 51 52 53 54 55 56 57 58 59 60 61 63 64 65 66 67 68 71 72 73 74 **P**8

	23	10	435	17066	268	209226	1639	193651	88048	2211

NORTHSIDE MEDICAL CENTER See Forum Health
SOUTHSIDE MEDICAL CENTER See Forum Health

□ ST. ELIZABETH HEALTH CENTER, 1044 Belmont Avenue, Zip 44501, Mailing Address: P.O. Box 1790, Zip 44501–1790; tel. 330/746–7211; Norman F. Gruber, Chief Operating Officer (Nonreporting) **A**1 2 3 5 6 8 9 10 **S** Catholic Healthcare Partners, Cincinnati, OH **N** Cleveland Health Network, Independence, OH

	21	10	318	—	—	—	—	—	—	—

TOD CHILDREN'S HOSPITAL See Forum Health
WESTERN RESERVE CARE SYSTEM See Forum Health

+ ○ YOUNGSTOWN OSTEOPATHIC HOSPITAL, 1319 Florencedale Avenue, Zip 44505–2795, Mailing Address: P.O. Box 1258, Zip 44501–1258; tel. 330/744–9200; John C. Weir, President and Chief Executive Officer (Nonreporting) **A**10 11 12 13

	23	10	88	—	—	—	—	—	—	—

ZANESVILLE—Muskingum County

⊞ △ GENESIS HEALTHCARE SYSTEM, (Includes Bethesda Hospital, 2951 Maple Avenue, Zip 43701–1465; tel. 614/454–4000; Charles D. Hunter, Executive Vice President and Chief Operating Officer; Good Samaritan Medical and Rehabilitation Center, 800 Forest Avenue), 800 Forest Avenue, Zip 43701–2881; tel. 740/454–5000; Thomas L. Sieber, President and Chief Executive Officer (Total facility includes 44 beds in nursing home–type unit) **A**1 2 7 9 10 **F**1 3 7 8 10 11 12 13 14 15 16 17 19 21 22 23 24 25 26 27 28 29 30 31 32 33 34 35 36 37 38 39 40 41 42 44 45 46 47 48 49 51 52 53 54 55 56 57 58 59 60 61 64 65 66 67 71 72 73 74 **P**8 **S** Franciscan Sisters of Christian Charity HealthCare Ministry, Inc, Manitowoc, WI **N** Community Hospitals of Ohio, Newark, OH

	21	10	429	16790	248	315508	2042	136075	62427	2145

OKLAHOMA

Resident population 3,317 (in thousands)
Resident population in metro areas 60.2%
Birth rate per 1,000 population 14.0
65 years and over 13.5%
Percent of persons without health insurance 17.0%

Hospital, Address, Telephone, Administrator, Approval, Facility, and Physician Codes, Health Care System, Network	Classi-fication Codes		Utilization Data					Expense (thousands) of dollars		
★ American Hospital Association (AHA) membership □ Joint Commission on Accreditation of Healthcare Organizations (JCAHO) accreditation + American Osteopathic Healthcare Association (AOHA) membership ○ American Osteopathic Association (AOA) accreditation △ Commission on Accreditation of Rehabilitation Facilities (CARF) accreditation Control codes 61, 63, 64, 71, 72 and 73 indicate hospitals listed by AOHA, but not registered by AHA. For definition of numerical codes, see page A4	Control	Service	Staffed Beds	Admissions	Census	Outpatient Visits	Births	Total	Payroll	Personnel

ADA—Pontotoc County

⊠ CARL ALBERT INDIAN HEALTH FACILITY, 1001 North Country Club Road, Zip 74820–2847; tel. 580/436–3980; Kenneth R. Ross, Administrator **A**1 10 **F**3 5 6 7 8 10 12 13 15 16 17 18 19 20 21 22 23 24 25 26 27 28 29 30 31 34 35 37 39 40 41 42 43 44 45 46 49 50 51 53 54 55 56 57 58 59 60 61 62 65 66 67 68 71 72 73 74 **P**1 6 **S** U. S. Public Health Service Indian Health Service, Rockville, MD	47	10	53	3018	28	196177	681	42601	14284	493
□ ROLLING HILLS HOSPITAL, 1000 Rolling Hills Lane, Zip 74820–9415; tel. 580/436–3600; Darnell Powell, Executive Director **A**1 10 **F**2 14 15 16 19 21 22 35 52 53 56 57 59 63 65 71	33	22	40	514	22	—	—	6077	2618	84
⊠ △ VALLEY VIEW REGIONAL HOSPITAL, 430 North Monta Vista, Zip 74820–4610; tel. 405/332–2323; Philip Fisher, President and Chief Executive Officer **A**1 2 7 9 10 **F**7 8 10 11 12 14 15 17 19 21 22 23 27 28 30 32 34 35 36 37 38 39 40 42 44 45 46 48 49 60 63 65 67 70 71 72 73	23	10	141	5536	79	50816	612	40817	15162	634

ALTUS—Jackson County

⊠ JACKSON COUNTY MEMORIAL HOSPITAL, 1200 East Pecan Street, Zip 73521–6192, Mailing Address: Box 8190, Zip 73522–8190; tel. 580/482–4781; William G. Wilson, President and Chief Executive Officer (Total facility includes 25 beds in nursing home–type unit) **A**1 9 10 **F**7 8 17 19 21 22 28 29 30 32 33 34 35 36 37 39 40 41 42 44 45 46 49 51 61 64 65 66 67 70 71 73	16	10	101	4320	70	37282	385	—		453
★ U. S. AIR FORCE HOSPITAL ALTUS, Altus AFB, Zip 73523–5005; tel. 580/481–5970; Colonel David L. Clark, USAF, Commander **F**8 14 16 20 40 44 46 51 55 58 71 **S** Department of the Air Force, Bowling AFB, DC	41	10	23	666	3	72642	184	—	10470	—

ALVA—Woods County

★ SHARE MEDICAL CENTER, 800 Share Drive, Zip 73717–3699, Mailing Address: P.O. Box 727, Zip 73717–0727; tel. 580/327–2800; Barbara Oestmann, Chief Executive Officer (Total facility includes 80 beds in nursing home–type unit) **A**9 10 **F**7 10 14 15 16 19 20 21 22 29 32 34 36 40 42 44 46 51 54 56 57 58 59 64 65 67 73 **S** Quorum Health Group/Quorum Health Resources, Inc., Brentwood, TN	16	10	117	872	72	11642	60	—		164

ANADARKO—Caddo County

ANADARKO MUNICIPAL HOSPITAL, 1002 Central Boulevard East, Zip 73005–4496; tel. 405/247–2551; Linda Whitlow, Administrator **A**9 10 **F**15 21 22 28 30 32 34 40 68 71 73	14	10	36	498	5	3169	9	3065	1214	69

ANTLERS—Pushmataha County

PUSHMATAHA COUNTY–TOWN OF ANTLERS HOSPITAL AUTHORITY, 510 East Main Street, Zip 74523–3262, Mailing Address: P.O. Box 518, Zip 74523–3262; tel. 580/298–3342; Les Alexander, Administrator (Nonreporting) **A**10	15	10	49	—	—	—	—	—		

ARDMORE—Carter County

⊠ MERCY MEMORIAL HEALTH CENTER, 1011 14th Street N.W., Zip 73401–1889; tel. 405/223–5400; Bobby G. Thompson, President and Chief Executive Officer **A**1 10 **F**3 7 8 10 12 14 15 16 19 20 21 22 23 26 28 29 30 31 32 34 35 40 41 42 44 45 46 48 49 52 54 55 56 57 59 60 64 65 67 71 73 **P**8 **S** Sisters of Mercy Health System–St. Louis, Saint Louis, MO **N** Mercy Health System, Oklahoma City, OK	21	10	199	6472	105	77377	678	45738	16217	827

ATOKA—Atoka County

★ ATOKA MEMORIAL HOSPITAL, 1501 South Virginia Avenue, Zip 74525–3298; tel. 580/889–3333; Bruce A. Bennett, Administrator and Chief Executive Officer **A**9 10 **F**11 12 14 15 16 19 22 28 30 32 34 49 66 71 73 **S** Quorum Health Group/Quorum Health Resources, Inc., Brentwood, TN	13	10	25	542	8	—	0	—		

BARTLESVILLE—Washington County

⊠ JANE PHILLIPS MEDICAL CENTER, 3500 East Frank Phillips Boulevard, Zip 74006–2409; tel. 918/333–7200; Larry Minden, Chief Executive Officer (Total facility includes 61 beds in nursing home–type unit) **A**1 2 5 9 10 **F**8 10 12 14 15 16 19 22 24 26 28 29 30 32 33 34 35 37 40 42 44 46 48 49 52 54 55 56 57 59 60 63 64 65 71 72 73 **P**4 7	23	10	219	6202	95	53944	765	49938	20277	656

BEAVER—Beaver County

BEAVER COUNTY MEMORIAL HOSPITAL, 212 East Eighth Street, Zip 73932, Mailing Address: P.O. Box 640, Zip 73932–0640; tel. 580/625–4551; La Vern Melton, Administrator **A**9 10 **F**8 22 27 28 44 65 66 73 **P**6	16	10	24	223	2	2541	33	1823	887	—

BETHANY—Oklahoma County

⊠ INTERGIS BETHANY HOSPITAL, (Formerly Columbia Bethany Hospital), 7600 N.W. 23rd Street, Zip 73008–4900; tel. 405/787–3450; David Lundquist, Chief Executive Officer **A**1 9 10 **F**4 10 12 14 15 16 17 19 22 26 28 29 30 32 33 34 37 44 46 48 49 52 53 64 65 67 71 72 73 **P**3 7 8 **S** INTEGRIS Health, Oklahoma City, OK	33	10	70	1866	36	16105	—	16926	6563	260

BLACKWELL—Kay County

★ BLACKWELL REGIONAL HOSPITAL, 710 South 13th Street, Zip 74631–3700; tel. 580/363–2311; Greg Martin, Administrator and Chief Executive Officer **A**9 10 **F**7 8 19 32 34 40 44 49 65 71 73 **P**7 **S** INTEGRIS Health, Oklahoma City, OK **N** Integris Health, Oklahoma City, OK	23	10	34	1274	16	10765	96	6605	2823	132

Hospital, Address, Telephone, Administrator, Approval, Facility, and Physician Codes, Health Care System, Network	Classi-fication Codes		Utilization Data					Expense (thousands) of dollars		
★ American Hospital Association (AHA) membership □ Joint Commission on Accreditation of Healthcare Organizations (JCAHO) accreditation + American Osteopathic Healthcare Association (AOHA) membership ○ American Osteopathic Association (AOA) accreditation △ Commission on Accreditation of Rehabilitation Facilities (CARF) accreditation Control codes 61, 63, 64, 71, 72 and 73 indicate hospitals listed by AOHA, but not registered by AHA. For definition of numerical codes, see page A4	Control	Service	Staffed Beds	Admissions	Census	Outpatient Visits	Births	Total	Payroll	Personnel

BOISE CITY—Cimarron County

CIMARRON MEMORIAL HOSPITAL, 100 South Ellis Street, Zip 73933; tel. 580/544–2501; Ronny Lathrop, Chief Executive Officer and Administrator (Total facility includes 41 beds in nursing home–type unit) **A**10 **F**1 7 8 22 25 28 32 39 40 44 64 71 **P**6 — 12 10 | 61 | 397 | 32 | 6151 | 64 | 8487 | 1545 | 77

BRISTOW—Creek County

★ BRISTOW MEMORIAL HOSPITAL, Seventh and Spruce Streets, Zip 74010, Mailing Address: P.O. Box 780, Zip 74010–0780; tel. 918/367–2215; William L. Legate, Administrator **A**9 10 **F**17 19 22 30 32 33 37 44 49 63 65 71 **P**6 — 23 10 | 17 | 298 | 3 | 28852 | 0 | 3031 | 1404 | —

BROKEN ARROW—Tulsa County

□ BROKEN ARROW MEDICAL CENTER, 3000 South Elm Place, Zip 74012–7952; tel. 918/455–3535; Bruce Switzer, Administrator **A**1 9 10 **F**15 19 21 22 27 32 37 39 41 42 44 48 49 65 71 73 — 23 10 | 71 | 1868 | 42 | 28357 | 2 | 20956 | 9651 | 343

BUFFALO—Harper County

★ HARPER COUNTY COMMUNITY HOSPITAL, Highway 64 North, Zip 73834, Mailing Address: P.O. Box 60, Zip 73834–0060; tel. 580/735–2555; P. Jane McDowell, Administrator **A**10 **F**8 15 17 22 28 29 30 33 36 39 40 44 46 49 71 — 13 10 | 25 | 323 | 5 | 1072 | 20 | 1435 | 753 | 49

CARNEGIE—Caddo County

★ CARNEGIE TRI–COUNTY MUNICIPAL HOSPITAL, 102 North Broadway, Zip 73015, Mailing Address: P.O. Box 97, Zip 73015–0097; tel. 580/654–1050; Phil Hawkins, Administrator (Nonreporting) **A**9 10 **N** First Health West, Lawton, OK — 14 10 | 28 | — | — | — | — | — | — | —

CHEYENNE—Roger Mills County

★ ROGER MILLS MEMORIAL HOSPITAL, Fifth and L. L Males Avenue, Zip 73628, Mailing Address: P.O. Box 219, Zip 73628–0219; tel. 580/497–3336; Marilyn Bryan, Administrator **A**9 10 **F**16 22 28 30 32 33 40 44 65 — 13 10 | 15 | 189 | 4 | 15044 | 5 | 2444 | 1400 | —

CHICKASHA—Grady County

✠ GRADY MEMORIAL HOSPITAL, 2220 North Iowa Avenue, Zip 73018–2738; tel. 405/224–2300; Roger R. Boid, Administrator (Total facility includes 11 beds in nursing home–type unit) **A**1 9 10 **F**11 12 19 20 21 22 28 31 32 34 37 39 40 41 44 49 56 63 64 67 71 73 — 16 10 | 147 | 3618 | 49 | 20455 | 414 | 24762 | 11267 | 374

CLAREMORE—Rogers County

✠ COLUMBIA CLAREMORE REGIONAL HOSPITAL, 1202 North Muskogee Place, Zip 74017–3036; tel. 918/341–2556; Ken Seidel, Executive Director (Nonreporting) **A**1 9 10 **S** Columbia/HCA Healthcare Corporation, Nashville, TN — 33 10 | 79 | — | — | — | — | — | — | —

✠ U. S. PUBLIC HEALTH SERVICE COMPREHENSIVE INDIAN HEALTH FACILITY, 101 South Moore Avenue, Zip 74017–5091; tel. 918/342–6434; John Daugherty, Jr., Service Unit Director **A**1 5 10 **F**15 16 20 22 34 37 40 44 49 51 61 65 71 **P**6 **S** U. S. Public Health Service Indian Health Service, Rockville, MD — 47 10 | 46 | 2276 | 27 | 160519 | 668 | — | 12993 | —

CLEVELAND—Pawnee County

CLEVELAND AREA HOSPITAL, 1401 West Pawnee Street, Zip 74020–3019; tel. 918/358–2501; Thomas Henton, President and Chief Executive Officer **A**9 10 **F**8 15 16 19 21 22 26 27 30 32 34 36 41 44 49 65 67 73 74 **S** Hillcrest HealthCare System, Tulsa, OK — 23 10 | 25 | 304 | 4 | 8450 | 0 | — | — | 89

CLINTON—Custer County

✠ INTERGRIS CLINTON REGIONAL HOSPITAL, (Formerly Clinton Regional Hospital), 100 North 30th Street, Zip 73601–3117, Mailing Address: P.O. Box 1569, Zip 73601–1569; tel. 580/323–2363; Jerry Jones, Administrator **A**1 9 10 **F**7 8 12 14 15 16 17 19 22 28 30 32 37 40 42 44 49 50 60 63 66 73 **S** INTEGRIS Health, Oklahoma City, OK **N** Integris Health, Oklahoma City, OK — 14 10 | 49 | 1555 | 18 | 16665 | 202 | 10951 | 4799 | 199

✠ U. S. PUBLIC HEALTH SERVICE INDIAN HOSPITAL, Mailing Address: Route 1, Box 3060, Zip 73601–9303; tel. 580/323–2884; Thedis V. Mitchell, Director (Nonreporting) **A**1 10 **S** U. S. Public Health Service Indian Health Service, Rockville, MD — 47 10 | 11 | — | — | — | — | — | — | —

COALGATE—Coal County

MARY HURLEY HOSPITAL, 6 North Covington Street, Zip 74538–2002; tel. 580/927–2327; Michael Shawn, Chief Executive Officer (Total facility includes 75 beds in nursing home–type unit) **A**9 10 **F**16 19 22 34 44 49 64 65 — 23 10 | 95 | 494 | 67 | — | 0 | 4906 | 2582 | 145

CORDELL—Washita County

★ CORDELL MEMORIAL HOSPITAL, 1220 North Glenn English Street, Zip 73632–2099; tel. 580/832–3339; Charles H. Greene, Jr., Administrator **A**10 **F**15 22 37 44 71 **N** First Health West, Lawton, OK — 14 10 | 28 | 484 | 5 | 4722 | 0 | 1980 | 940 | 45

CUSHING—Payne County

✠ CUSHING REGIONAL HOSPITAL, 1027 East Cherry Street, Zip 74023–4101, Mailing Address: P.O. Box 1409, Zip 74023–1409; tel. 918/225–2915; Ron Cackler, President and Chief Executive Officer **A**1 9 10 **F**1 3 12 15 17 19 21 22 25 26 28 29 30 32 33 36 37 40 41 42 44 45 46 49 52 54 55 56 57 58 59 64 65 66 67 71 73 **P**8 **S** Quorum Health Group/Quorum Health Resources, Inc., Brentwood, TN **N** Hillcrest Healthcare System, Tulsa, OK — 14 10 | 75 | 2497 | 39 | 18832 | 408 | 13877 | 5416 | 228

DRUMRIGHT—Creek County

★ DRUMRIGHT MEMORIAL HOSPITAL, 501 South Lou Allard Drive, Zip 74030–4899; tel. 918/352–2525; Jerry Jones, Administrator **A**9 10 **F**15 16 19 22 25 32 35 44 71 73 **P**1 4 5 8 **S** INTEGRIS Health, Oklahoma City, OK **N** Integris Health, Oklahoma City, OK — 23 10 | 15 | 516 | 7 | 4467 | 0 | 3997 | 2313 | 90

DUNCAN—Stephens County

✠ DUNCAN REGIONAL HOSPITAL, 1407 North Whisenant Drive, Zip 73533–1650, Mailing Address: P.O. Box 2000, Zip 73534–2000; tel. 580/252–5300; David Robertson, Chief Executive Officer (Total facility includes 16 beds in nursing home–type unit) **A**1 9 10 **F**7 8 11 13 14 15 16 17 19 21 22 29 30 32 33 35 37 39 40 41 44 45 48 49 64 65 66 71 73 **P**8 — 23 10 | 104 | 4043 | 53 | 49470 | 448 | 27308 | 12520 | 487

Hospital, Address, Telephone, Administrator, Approval, Facility, and Physician Codes, Health Care System, Network	Classi-fication Codes		Utilization Data					Expense (thousands) of dollars		
★ American Hospital Association (AHA) membership □ Joint Commission on Accreditation of Healthcare Organizations (JCAHO) accreditation + American Osteopathic Healthcare Association (AOHA) membership ○ American Osteopathic Association (AOA) accreditation △ Commission on Accreditation of Rehabilitation Facilities (CARF) accreditation Control codes 61, 63, 64, 71, 72 and 73 indicate hospitals listed by AOHA, but not registered by AHA. For definition of numerical codes, see page A4	Control	Service	Staffed Beds	Admissions	Census	Outpatient Visits	Births	Total	Payroll	Personnel

DURANT—Bryan County

□ MEDICAL CENTER OF SOUTHEASTERN OKLAHOMA, 1800 University Boulevard, Zip 74701–3006, Mailing Address: P.O. Box 1207, Zip 74702–1207; tel. 580/924–3080; Joshua Putter, Executive Director **A**1 9 10 **F**7 8 10 12 14 17 19 21 22 23 29 30 32 34 35 37 41 44 46 49 61 63 65 67 70 71 73 74 **S** Health Management Associates, Naples, FL — 33 10 103 5025 53 13853 632 — — 241

EDMOND—Oklahoma County

✠ EDMOND MEDICAL CENTER, (Formerly Columbia Edmond Medical Center), 1 South Bryant Street, Zip 73034–4798; tel. 405/359–5530; Stanley D. Tatum, Chief Executive Officer (Nonreporting) **A**1 9 10 **S** Columbia/HCA Healthcare Corporation, Nashville, TN **N** University Health Partners, Oklahoma City, OK — 33 10 75 — — — — — — —

HORIZON SPECIALTY HOSPITAL, 1100 East Ninth Street, Zip 73034–5755; tel. 405/341–8150; Joe Smithers, Administrator (Nonreporting) **A**10 — 33 49 43 — — — — — — —

EL RENO—Canadian County

★ PARK VIEW HOSPITAL, 2115 Parkview Drive, Zip 73036–2199, Mailing Address: P.O. Box 129, Zip 73036–0129; tel. 405/262–2640; Lex Smith, Administrator **A**9 10 **F**7 8 14 15 16 17 19 20 22 28 29 30 32 33 34 37 39 40 42 44 45 46 49 56 58 65 67 71 73 — 16 10 54 1744 22 17059 174 13011 7006 291

ELK CITY—Beckham County

✠ GREAT PLAINS REGIONAL MEDICAL CENTER, 1705 West Second Street, Zip 73644–4496, Mailing Address: P.O. Box 2339, Zip 73648–2339; tel. 580/225–2511; Tim Francis, Chief Executive Officer **A**1 9 10 **F**8 11 12 14 15 16 17 19 20 21 22 23 26 27 28 29 30 32 33 34 35 37 39 40 41 42 44 45 46 49 51 52 53 54 55 56 57 58 60 63 64 65 66 67 71 72 73 74 **P**8 — 23 10 78 2201 39 56104 186 20706 9122 366

ENID—Garfield County

□ INTEGRIS BASS BEHAVIORAL HEALTH SYSTEM, (Formerly Meadowlake Behavioral Health System), 2216 South Van Buren Street, Zip 73703–8299, Mailing Address: P.O. Box 5409, Zip 73702–5409; tel. 580/234–2220; James Hutchison, Director (Nonreporting) **A**1 **S** Ramsay Health Care, Inc., Coral Gables, FL — 33 22 50 — — — — — — —

✠ INTEGRIS BASS BAPTIST HEALTH CENTER, 600 South Monroe Street, Zip 73701, Mailing Address: P.O. Box 3168, Zip 73702–3168; tel. 580/233–2300; Wayne A. Sensor, Administrator **A**1 3 5 9 10 **F**2 10 12 15 19 21 22 26 28 29 30 31 32 33 34 35 36 37 39 40 41 42 44 46 48 49 52 54 55 56 57 60 63 64 66 67 71 72 73 74 **P**6 7 **S** INTEGRIS Health, Oklahoma City, OK **N** Integris Health, Oklahoma City, OK — 23 10 140 5357 86 44796 775 47645 18374 831

✠ △ ST. MARY'S MERCY HOSPITAL, 305 South Fifth Street, Zip 73701–5899, Mailing Address: Box 232, Zip 73702–0232; tel. 580/233–6100; Frank Lopez, FACHE, President and Chief Executive Officer **A**1 2 3 5 7 9 10 **F**7 8 10 12 14 15 16 17 19 21 22 23 24 31 34 35 36 37 40 42 44 48 49 65 71 73 **P**1 **S** Sisters of Mercy Health System–St. Louis, Saint Louis, MO **N** Mercy Health System, Oklahoma City, OK — 21 10 137 5270 94 69348 277 46040 16023 476

EUFAULA—Mcintosh County

COMMUNITY HOSPITAL–LAKEVIEW, 1 Hospital Drive, Zip 74432, Mailing Address: P.O. Box 629, Zip 74432–0629; tel. 918/689–2535; R. S. Smith, Chief Executive Officer **A**9 10 **F**8 14 15 16 19 21 22 28 32 34 44 46 67 71 73 — 33 10 33 517 4 5629 0 3527 1311 70

FAIRFAX—Osage County

★ FAIRFAX MEMORIAL HOSPITAL, Taft Avenue and Highway 18, Zip 74637, Mailing Address: P.O. Box 219, Zip 74637–0219; tel. 918/642–3291; Annabeth Murray, Administrator **A**9 10 **F**19 22 28 32 33 34 44 71 — 14 10 21 267 3 3038 0 2538 1179 53

FAIRVIEW—Major County

★ FAIRVIEW HOSPITAL, 523 East State Road, Zip 73737–1498; tel. 580/227–3721; Mark Harrel, Administrator (Nonreporting) **A**9 10 — 14 10 31 — — — — — — —

FORT SILL—Comanche County

✠ REYNOLDS ARMY COMMUNITY HOSPITAL, 4301 Mow–way Street, Zip 73503–6300; tel. 580/458–3000; Colonel Gary Ripple, Commander (Nonreporting) **A**1 **S** Department of the Army, Office of the Surgeon General, Falls Church, VA — 42 10 116 — — — — — — —

FORT SUPPLY—Woodward County

WESTERN STATE PSYCHIATRIC CENTER, Mailing Address: P.O. Box 1, Zip 73841–0001; tel. 580/766–2311; Steve Norwood, Director **A**10 **F**2 3 12 16 20 41 52 54 55 56 57 58 59 65 73 **P**6 **S** Oklahoma State Department of Mental Health and Substance Abuse Services, Oklahoma City, OK — 12 22 164 1132 797 42432 0 12990 7256 261

FREDERICK—Tillman County

★ MEMORIAL HOSPITAL, 319 East Josephine, Zip 73542–2299; tel. 580/335–7565; Doug Weaver, Chief Executive Officer (Nonreporting) **A**9 10 — 16 10 32 — — — — — — —

GROVE—Delaware County

✠ INTEGRIS GROVE GENERAL HOSPITAL, 1310 South Main Street, Zip 74344–1310; tel. 918/786–2243; Dee Renshaw, Administrator **A**1 9 10 **F**6 7 8 12 13 14 15 16 17 19 20 22 28 30 32 42 44 49 64 65 70 71 73 **P**1 5 7 **S** INTEGRIS Health, Oklahoma City, OK **N** Integris Health, Oklahoma City, OK — 23 10 72 3107 43 51565 155 21340 10387 392

GUTHRIE—Logan County

★ LOGAN HOSPITAL AND MEDICAL CENTER, Highway 33 West at Academy Road, Zip 73044, Mailing Address: P.O. Box 1017, Zip 73044–1017; tel. 405/282–6700; James R. Caton, Chief Executive Officer **A**9 10 **F**8 14 15 16 19 20 21 22 28 30 32 35 44 49 64 67 71 73 **S** Quorum Health Group/Quorum Health Resources, Inc., Brentwood, TN — 16 10 32 944 13 10032 0 8713 4366 118

Hospital, Address, Telephone, Administrator, Approval, Facility, and Physician Codes, Health Care System, Network	Classi-fication Codes		Utilization Data					Expense (thousands) of dollars		
	Control	Service	Staffed Beds	Admissions	Census	Outpatient Visits	Births	Total	Payroll	Personnel

★ American Hospital Association (AHA) membership
□ Joint Commission on Accreditation of Healthcare Organizations (JCAHO) accreditation
+ American Osteopathic Healthcare Association (AOHA) membership
○ American Osteopathic Association (AOA) accreditation
△ Commission on Accreditation of Rehabilitation Facilities (CARF) accreditation
Control codes 61, 63, 64, 71, 72 and 73 indicate hospitals listed by AOHA, but not registered by AHA. For definition of numerical codes, see page A4

GUYMON—Texas County

★ MEMORIAL HOSPITAL OF TEXAS COUNTY, 520 Medical Drive, Zip 73942–4438; tel. 580/338–6515; Kevin Cox, Interim Administrator **A**9 10 **F**7 8 12 13 14 15 17 18 19 21 22 28 29 30 31 32 33 35 36 37 39 40 44 46 49 66 71 74	13	10	35	1869	18	12016	242	9767	3653	234

HENRYETTA—Okmulgee County

★ HENRYETTA MEDICAL CENTER, Dewey Bartlett and Main Streets, Zip 74437, Mailing Address: P.O. Box 1269, Zip 74437–1269; tel. 918/652–4463; James P. Bailey, President and Chief Executive Officer **A**9 10 **F**8 12 13 14 15 16 17 18 19 20 22 26 27 28 29 30 31 32 35 36 39 41 42 44 45 46 49 52 54 55 56 57 58 62 67 71 73 **S** Quorum Health Group/Quorum Health Resources, Inc., Brentwood, TN	16	10	52	773	15	7799	0	5781	2561	153

HOBART—Kiowa County

★ ELKVIEW GENERAL HOSPITAL, 429 West Elm Street, Zip 73651–1699; tel. 580/726–3324; J. W. Finch, Jr., Administrator **A**9 10 **F**7 8 12 15 19 20 21 22 26 30 32 42 44 56 63 65 71 73 **N** First Health West, Lawton, OK	16	10	40	1308	17	7699	104	6138	3143	141

HOLDENVILLE—Hughes County

★ HOLDENVILLE GENERAL HOSPITAL, 100 Crestview Drive, Zip 74848–9700; tel. 405/379–6631; Joseph J. Mitchell, Chief Executive Officer and Administrator **A**9 10 **F**16 22 28 32 34 42 44 73 **S** Quorum Health Group/Quorum Health Resources, Inc., Brentwood, TN	14	10	27	790	9	19080	0	—	2270	100

HOLLIS—Harmon County

★ HARMON MEMORIAL HOSPITAL, 400 East Chestnut Street, Zip 73550–2030, Mailing Address: P.O. Box 791, Zip 73550–0791; tel. 580/688–3363; Al Allee, Administrator **A**9 10 **F**22 32 49 65 71 73 **N** First Health West, Lawton, OK	16	10	11	365	4	3163	0	1694	981	45

HUGO—Choctaw County

★ CHOCTAW MEMORIAL HOSPITAL, 1405 East Kirk Road, Zip 74743–3603; tel. 580/326–6414; Michael R. Morel, Administrator **A**9 10 **F**14 16 19 22 28 32 34 71 73 **S** INTEGRIS Health, Oklahoma City, OK **N** Integris Health, Oklahoma City, OK	15	10	38	1038	11	6066	0	4868	2128	111

IDABEL—Mccurtain County

★ MCCURTAIN MEMORIAL HOSPITAL, 1301 Lincoln Road, Zip 74745–7341; tel. 405/286–7623; Ronald Campbell, Administrator (Nonreporting) **A**9 10 **S** Quorum Health Group/Quorum Health Resources, Inc., Brentwood, TN	23	10	89	—	—	—	—	—	—	—

KINGFISHER—Kingfisher County

★ KINGFISHER REGIONAL HOSPITAL, 500 South Ninth Street, Zip 73750–3528, Mailing Address: P.O. Box 59, Zip 73750–0059; tel. 405/375–3141; Daryle Voss, Chief Executive Officer **A**9 10 **F**7 19 22 32 37 40 44 46 49 51 64 65 71 **P**6 **S** Quorum Health Group/Quorum Health Resources, Inc., Brentwood, TN	23	10	38	1156	12	47101	111	7891	3722	—

LAWTON—Comanche County

✠ COMANCHE COUNTY MEMORIAL HOSPITAL, 3401 Gore Boulevard, Zip 73505–0129, Mailing Address: Box 129, Zip 73502–0129; tel. 580/355–8620; Randall K. Segler, Chief Executive Officer **A**1 9 10 **F**2 3 4 7 8 10 11 12 14 15 16 19 20 21 22 28 29 30 31 32 35 37 39 40 41 42 43 44 46 48 49 52 53 56 57 58 59 60 63 64 65 66 67 68 70 71 72 73 74 **N** First Health West, Lawton, OK	16	10	343	7655	145	60147	1049	104015	43901	1439
MEMORIAL PAVILION, 1602 S.W. 82nd Street, Zip 73505–9099; tel. 580/536–0077; Jim Ivey, Administrator (Nonreporting) **A**10	33	22	99	—	—	—	—	—	—	—
✠ SOUTHWESTERN MEDICAL CENTER, (Formerly Columbia Southwestern Medical Center), 5602 S.W. Lee Boulevard, Zip 73505–9635, Mailing Address: P.O. Box 7290, Zip 73506–7290; tel. 580/531–4700; Thomas L. Rine, President and Chief Executive Officer **A**1 2 9 10 **F**7 10 12 14 15 16 17 19 21 22 26 28 30 32 34 35 37 40 42 44 48 49 51 52 57 60 65 70 71 72 73 74 **P**1 7 **S** Columbia/HCA Healthcare Corporation, Nashville, TN **N** University Health Partners, Oklahoma City, OK	33	10	139	4014	51	59061	447	36847	10861	453
✠ U. S. PUBLIC HEALTH SERVICE INDIAN HOSPITAL, 1515 Lawrie Tatum Road, Zip 73507–3099; tel. 580/353–0350; George E. Howell, Service Unit Director (Nonreporting) **A**1 10 **S** U. S. Public Health Service Indian Health Service, Rockville, MD	47	10	44	—	—	—	—	—	—	—

LINDSAY—Garvin County

LINDSAY MUNICIPAL HOSPITAL, Highway 19 West, Zip 73052, Mailing Address: P.O. Box 888, Zip 73052–0888; tel. 405/756–4321; Michelle Pierce, Interim Administrator (Nonreporting) **A**10	14	10	25	—	—	—	—	—	—	—

MADILL—Marshall County

MARSHALL MEMORIAL HOSPITAL, 1 Hospital Drive, Zip 73446, Mailing Address: P.O. Box 827, Zip 73446–0827; tel. 405/795–3384; Norma Howard, Administrator **A**10 **F**7 15 16 22 28 30 32 33 40 44 65 73 **S** INTEGRIS Health, Oklahoma City, OK **N** Integris Health, Oklahoma City, OK	13	10	25	831	10	7790	28	4589	2455	83

MANGUM—Greer County

MANGUM CITY HOSPITAL, One Wickersham Drive, Zip 73554, Mailing Address: P.O. Box 280, Zip 73554–0280; tel. 580/782–3353; Arthur H. Frable, Administrator **A**10 **F**7 14 15 19 32 40 70 71	14	10	24	597	8	169	40	3687	1849	72

MARIETTA—Love County

★ MERCY HEALTH LOVE COUNTY, (Formerly Love County Health Center), 300 Wanda Street, Zip 73448–1200; tel. 580/276–3347; Richard Barker, Administrator **A**10 **F**28 30 37 71	13	10	30	444	6	8425	0	3493	2314	73

MCALESTER—Pittsburg County

✠ △ MCALESTER REGIONAL HEALTH CENTER, One Clark Bass Boulevard, Zip 74501–4267, Mailing Address: P.O. Box 1228, Zip 74502–1228; tel. 918/426–1800; Joel W. Tate, FACHE, Chief Executive Officer **A**1 7 9 10 **F**3 4 6 7 8 10 11 12 15 16 17 18 19 20 21 22 23 27 28 29 30 31 32 33 34 35 36 37 39 40 41 42 44 45 46 48 49 53 54 56 58 59 63 64 65 66 67 71 73	23	10	181	4693	90	21662	557	34068	14136	627

Hospital, Address, Telephone, Administrator, Approval, Facility, and Physician Codes, Health Care System, Network	Classi-fication Codes		Utilization Data					Expense (thousands) of dollars		
★ American Hospital Association (AHA) membership □ Joint Commission on Accreditation of Healthcare Organizations (JCAHO) accreditation + American Osteopathic Healthcare Association (AOHA) membership ○ American Osteopathic Association (AOA) accreditation △ Commission on Accreditation of Rehabilitation Facilities (CARF) accreditation Control codes 61, 63, 64, 71, 72 and 73 indicate hospitals listed by AOHA, but not registered by AHA. For definition of numerical codes, see page A4	Control	Service	Staffed Beds	Admissions	Census	Outpatient Visits	Births	Total	Payroll	Personnel

MIAMI—Ottawa County

✚ INTEGRIS BAPTIST REGIONAL HEALTH CENTER, 200 Second Street S.W., Zip 74354–6830, Mailing Address: P.O. Box 1207, Zip 74355–1207; tel. 918/540–7100; Steven G. Kelly, Consolidated Administrator **A**1 9 10 **F**10 12 13 14 15 16 18 19 21 22 23 26 27 28 29 30 31 32 35 36 37 40 42 44 45 46 49 51 52 56 57 60 63 64 65 66 71 72 73 74 **P**1 2 3 4 5 7 8 **S** INTEGRIS Health, Oklahoma City, OK **N** Integris Health, Oklahoma City, OK	23	10	123	4939	73	30976	316	—	—	500
□ WILLOW CREST HOSPITAL, 130 A. Street S.W., Zip 74354–6800; tel. 918/542–1836; Anne G. Anthony, Administrator and Chief Executive Officer **A**1 10 **F**25 52 53 54 55 56 58 59 **P**3	33	22	50	208	31	1510	—	—	—	

MIDWEST CITY—Oklahoma County

✚ MIDWEST REGIONAL MEDICAL CENTER, (Formerly Midwest City Regional Medical Center), 2825 Parklawn Drive, Zip 73110–4258; tel. 405/737–4411; Martin D. Smith, Chief Operating Officer **A**1 2 9 10 **F**3 7 8 10 12 14 15 16 17 19 21 22 26 27 28 30 31 32 33 34 35 37 39 40 41 42 43 44 45 46 49 51 56 57 61 63 64 65 66 71 73 74 **S** Health Management Associates, Naples, FL	33	10	214	9747	133	—	914	75635	27409	905

MUSKOGEE—Muskogee County

✚ △ MUSKOGEE REGIONAL MEDICAL CENTER, 300 Rockefeller Drive, Zip 74401–5081; tel. 918/682–5501; Bill R. Kennedy, President and Chief Executive Officer **A**1 2 7 9 10 **F**10 12 14 15 16 19 20 21 22 23 28 29 30 32 34 35 37 39 40 41 42 44 46 48 49 57 58 59 60 65 68 71 72 73	16	10	225	10118	160	67713	935	59741	25177	895
✚ VETERANS AFFAIRS MEDICAL CENTER, 1011 Honor Heights Drive, Zip 74401–1399; tel. 918/683–3261; Allen J. Colston, Acting Director (Nonreporting) **A**1 3 5 **S** Department of Veterans Affairs, Washington, DC	45	10	99	—	—	—	—	—	—	

NORMAN—Cleveland County

□ GRIFFIN MEMORIAL HOSPITAL, 900 East Main Street, Zip 73071–5305, Mailing Address: P.O. Box 151, Zip 73070–0151; tel. 405/321–4880; Dave Statton, Interim Superintendent **A**1 3 5 10 **F**19 20 22 27 29 34 35 44 46 50 52 55 56 57 63 65 71 73 **P**6 **S** Oklahoma State Department of Mental Health and Substance Abuse Services, Oklahoma City, OK	12	22	182	1988	159	5904	0	24079	14560	544
J. D. MCCARTY CENTER FOR CHILDREN WITH DEVELOPMENTAL DISABILITIES, 1125 East Alameda, Zip 73071–5264; tel. 405/321–4830; Curtis A. Peters, Chief Executive Officer **A**10 **F**12 16 17 20 34 46 48 49 53 54 58 65 67 73	12	56	42	205	24	1105	—	—	1064	113
✚ NORMAN REGIONAL HOSPITAL, 901 North Porter Street, Zip 73071–6482, Mailing Address: P.O. Box 1308, Zip 73070–1308; tel. 405/321–1700; Max Lauderdale, Chief Executive Officer **A**1 2 9 10 **F**3 7 8 10 11 12 15 17 18 19 20 21 22 24 25 27 28 29 30 31 32 34 35 36 39 40 41 42 43 44 45 46 49 51 52 53 54 55 57 58 59 60 63 64 65 66 67 70 71 72 73 74 **P**1 6	16	10	250	11798	161	204700	1270	100245	44278	1493

NOWATA—Nowata County

JANE PHILLIPS NOWATA HEALTH CENTER, 237 South Locust Street, Zip 74048–0426, Mailing Address: P.O. Box 426, Zip 74048–0426; tel. 918/273–3102; Maggie Blevins, Administrator **A**9 10 **F**2 22 44 71 73	23	10	34	482	14	2500	0	1925	596	37

OKEENE—Blaine County

OKEENE MUNICIPAL HOSPITAL, 207 East F. Street, Zip 73763, Mailing Address: P.O. Box 489, Zip 73763–0489; tel. 405/822–4417; Debbie Howe, Administrator (Total facility includes 21 beds in nursing home–type unit) **A**9 10 **F**6 7 19 22 28 30 32 36 40 44 49 64 71	14	10	51	559	29	1733	78	3117	1729	95

OKEMAH—Okfuskee County

★ CREEK NATION COMMUNITY HOSPITAL, 309 North 14th Street, Zip 74859–2099; tel. 918/623–1424; Bert Robison, Chief Executive Officer (Nonreporting) **A**10 **S** U. S. Public Health Service Indian Health Service, Rockville, MD	47	10	34	—	—	—	—	—	—	

OKLAHOMA CITY—Oklahoma County

✚ BONE AND JOINT HOSPITAL, 1111 North Dewey Avenue, Zip 73103–2615; tel. 405/552–9100; James A. Hyde, Administrator (Nonreporting) **A**1 3 5 10 **S** SSM Health Care System, Saint Louis, MO	23	47	89	—	—	—	—	—	—	
CHILDREN'S HOSPITAL OF OKLAHOMA See The University Hospitals										
✚ DEACONESS HOSPITAL, 5501 North Portland Avenue, Zip 73112–2099; tel. 405/946–5581; Paul Dougherty, President and Chief Executive Officer (Total facility includes 22 beds in nursing home–type unit) **A**1 2 9 10 **F**1 3 4 5 6 7 8 10 12 14 15 16 17 19 20 21 22 23 24 25 26 28 29 30 32 33 36 37 39 40 41 42 43 44 45 46 48 49 51 52 53 54 55 56 57 58 59 60 61 62 64 65 67 71 73 74 **P**8	23	10	188	9340	136	—	1333	65935	29535	1088
□ △ HEALTHSOUTH REHABILITATION HOSPITAL, 700 N.W. Seventh Street, Zip 73102–1295; tel. 405/553–1192; Hank Ross, Chief Executive Officer (Nonreporting) **A**1 7 10 **S** HEALTHSOUTH Corporation, Birmingham, AL	33	46	46	—	—	—	—	—	—	
HIGH POINTE, 6501 N.E. 50th Street, Zip 73141–9613; tel. 405/424–3383; Charlene Arnett, Chief Executive Officer (Nonreporting) **A**10 **S** Century Healthcare Corporation, Tulsa, OK	33	22	68	—	—	—	—	—	—	
★ + ○ HILLCREST HEALTH CENTER, 2129 S.W. 59th Street, Zip 73119–7001; tel. 405/685–6671; Ray Brazier, President **A**9 10 11 12 13 **F**3 4 7 8 10 11 12 16 19 21 22 26 28 30 32 35 37 39 40 41 42 43 44 45 46 48 49 50 52 53 54 56 58 59 60 64 65 66 67 70 71 73 74 **P**8 **S** SSM Health Care System, Saint Louis, MO	23	10	172	4254	60	86208	793	46223	17641	526
✚ INTEGRIS BAPTIST MEDICAL CENTER, 3300 N.W. Expressway, Zip 73112–4481; tel. 405/949–3011; Thomas R. Rice, FACHE, President and Chief Operating Officer **A**1 2 3 5 9 10 **F**4 5 7 8 9 10 11 12 13 14 15 16 17 18 19 20 21 22 23 24 25 26 28 29 30 31 33 34 35 36 37 38 39 40 42 43 44 45 46 47 49 50 51 52 53 54 55 56 57 58 59 60 61 63 64 65 67 68 69 70 71 72 73 74 **S** INTEGRIS Health, Oklahoma City, OK **N** Integris Health, Oklahoma City, OK	23	10	401	23023	293	321349	2608	227005	79957	—

Hospital, Address, Telephone, Administrator, Approval, Facility, and Physician Codes, Health Care System, Network	Classification Codes		Utilization Data					Expense (thousands) of dollars		
	Control	Service	Staffed Beds	Admissions	Census	Outpatient Visits	Births	Total	Payroll	Personnel

★ American Hospital Association (AHA) membership
□ Joint Commission on Accreditation of Healthcare Organizations (JCAHO) accreditation
+ American Osteopathic Healthcare Association (AOHA) membership
○ American Osteopathic Association (AOA) accreditation
△ Commission on Accreditation of Rehabilitation Facilities (CARF) accreditation
Control codes 61, 63, 64, 71, 72 and 73 indicate hospitals listed by AOHA, but not registered by AHA. For definition of numerical codes, see page A4

⊠ △ INTEGRIS SOUTHWEST MEDICAL CENTER, 4401 South Western, Zip 73109–3441; tel. 405/636–7000; Thomas R. Rice, FACHE, President and Chief Operating Officer **A**1 2 7 9 10 **F**2 3 4 5 7 8 10 11 12 14 15 16 17 19 21 22 24 26 27 28 29 30 32 33 34 35 36 37 39 40 41 42 43 44 45 48 49 51 52 53 54 55 56 57 58 59 60 61 63 64 65 66 67 69 71 73 74 **P**1 7 **S** INTEGRIS Health, Oklahoma City, OK **N** Integris Health, Oklahoma City, OK	23	10	343	11183	226	66339	2079	104557	40877	1222
⊠ △ MERCY HEALTH CENTER, 4300 West Memorial Road, Zip 73120–8362; tel. 405/755–1515; Bruce F. Buchanan, FACHE, President and Chief Executive Officer **A**1 2 7 9 10 **F**1 3 4 7 8 10 11 12 15 16 17 18 19 21 22 24 26 27 28 29 30 31 32 33 34 35 36 37 38 39 40 41 42 43 44 45 47 48 49 52 53 54 56 58 59 60 64 65 67 71 73 74 **P**1 4 6 **S** Sisters of Mercy Health System–St. Louis, Saint Louis, MO **N** Mercy Health System, Oklahoma City, OK	21	10	326	12070	194	22271	1714	100885	45957	1575
□ NORTHWEST SURGICAL HOSPITAL, 9204 North May Avenue, Zip 73120–4419; tel. 405/848–1918; Dan Barnard, Chief Executive Officer **A**1 10 **F**15 22 44 66	33	10	9	400	2	1911	0	—	—	33
⊠ PRESBYTERIAN HOSPITAL, (Formerly Columbia Presbyterian Hospital), 700 N.E. 13th Street, Zip 73104–5070; tel. 405/271–5100; James O'Loughlin, Chief Executive Officer **A**1 2 3 5 9 10 **F**7 8 10 11 12 14 15 16 17 19 20 21 22 23 24 25 26 27 28 29 30 31 32 33 34 35 37 38 39 40 41 42 43 44 45 46 48 49 51 52 53 54 55 56 57 58 59 60 61 63 64 65 66 67 69 71 72 73 74 **P**1 5 7 **S** Columbia/HCA Healthcare Corporation, Nashville, TN **N** University Health Partners, Oklahoma City, OK	33	10	271	12935	189	46166	1313	114278	35009	1200
⊠ △ ST. ANTHONY HOSPITAL, 1000 North Lee Street, Zip 73102–1080, Mailing Address: P.O. Box 205, Zip 73101–0205; tel. 405/272–7000; Steven L. Hunter, President (Total facility includes 43 beds in nursing home–type unit) **A**1 2 3 5 7 9 10 **F**1 2 3 4 5 7 8 10 11 12 15 16 17 19 20 21 22 23 24 25 26 30 31 32 33 34 35 37 39 40 41 42 43 44 45 48 49 50 51 52 53 54 55 56 57 58 59 60 61 63 64 65 66 67 68 69 71 72 73 74 **P**8 **S** SSM Health Care System, Saint Louis, MO	21	10	408	12985	236	267222	996	130458	50979	—
⊠ THE UNIVERSITY HOSPITALS, (Includes Children's Hospital of Oklahoma, 940 N.E. 13th Street, Zip 73104; tel. 405/271–6165; University Hospital, Mailing Address: Box 26307, Zip 73126), 920 N.E. 13th Street, Zip 73104–5068, Mailing Address: P.O. Box 26307, Zip 73126–6307; tel. 405/271–5911; R. Timothy Coussons, M.D., President and Chief Executive Officer **A**1 2 3 5 8 9 10 **F**4 7 10 11 12 19 20 21 22 26 31 34 35 37 38 40 41 42 43 44 46 47 49 52 54 58 59 60 61 63 65 68 69 70 71 73 74 **N** University Health Partners, Oklahoma City, OK; University Hospitals, Oklahoma City, OK	12	10	295	14873	220	254616	2153	185877	68334	—
UNIVERSITY HOSPITAL See The University Hospitals										
⊠ VETERANS AFFAIRS MEDICAL CENTER, 921 N.E. 13th Street, Zip 73104–5028; tel. 405/270–0501; Steven J. Gentling, Director (Total facility includes 40 beds in nursing home–type unit) **A**1 3 5 8 **F**2 3 8 10 11 12 15 19 20 21 22 23 24 25 26 27 28 29 30 31 32 33 34 35 37 39 41 42 43 44 45 46 48 49 51 52 54 56 58 60 63 64 65 67 69 71 73 74 **P**6 **S** Department of Veterans Affairs, Washington, DC	45	10	208	6920	158	276668	—	136922	56211	1442
OKMULGEE—Okmulgee County										
GEORGE NIGH REHABILITATION INSTITUTE, 900 East Airport Road, Zip 74447–9762, Mailing Address: P.O. Box 1118, Zip 74447–1118; tel. 918/756–9211; Mitchell Townsend, Administrator (Total facility includes 5 beds in nursing home–type unit) **A**10 **F**15 16 19 21 34 35 41 48 49 64 65 71 73 **P**1	12	46	31	272	18	5293	0	—	2258	—
□ OMH MEDICAL CENTER, 1401 Morris Drive, Zip 74447–6419, Mailing Address: P.O. Box 1038, Zip 74447–1038; tel. 918/756–4233; David D. Rasmussen, Administrator **A**1 9 10 **F**15 16 19 21 28 30 32 40 44 45 52 57 58 63 65 71 72	23	10	66	2485	29	25234	440	—	6239	201
PAULS VALLEY—Garvin County										
□ PAULS VALLEY GENERAL HOSPITAL, 100 Valley Drive, Zip 73075–0368, Mailing Address: Box 368, Zip 73075–0368; tel. 405/238–5501; Charles Johnston, Administrator (Total facility includes 8 beds in nursing home–type unit) **A**1 9 10 **F**8 19 21 22 28 32 34 37 39 40 44 49 53 57 58 59 64 65 71	14	10	50	1582	22	28863	36	8600	4123	171
PAWHUSKA—Osage County										
PAWHUSKA HOSPITAL, 1101 East 15th Street, Zip 74056–1920; tel. 918/287–3232; Samuel T. Guild, Administrator (Nonreporting) **A**9 10	14	10	19	—	—	—	—	—	—	—
PAWNEE—Pawnee County										
★ PAWNEE MUNICIPAL HOSPITAL, 1212 Fourth Street, Zip 74058–4046, Mailing Address: P.O. Box 467, Zip 74058–0467; tel. 918/762–2577; John Ketring, Administrator **A**9 10 **F**8 14 15 19 22 28 32 44 49 63 73 **S** INTEGRIS Health, Oklahoma City, OK **N** Integris Health, Oklahoma City, OK	33	10	32	764	9	5100	0	3736	1645	77
PERRY—Noble County										
⊠ PERRY MEMORIAL HOSPITAL, 501 14th Street, Zip 73077–5099; tel. 580/336–3541; Judith K. Feuquay, Chief Executive Officer **A**1 10 **F**8 12 15 19 22 28 30 33 41 42 44 49 65 71 73 **P**8 **S** Quorum Health Group/Quorum Health Resources, Inc., Brentwood, TN	16	10	28	712	10	—	0	5008	2334	76
PONCA CITY—Kay County										
⊠ ST. JOSEPH REGIONAL MEDICAL CENTER OF NORTHERN OKLAHOMA, 14th Street and Hartford Avenue, Zip 74601–2035, Mailing Address: Box 1270, Zip 74602–1270; tel. 580/765–3321; Garry L. England, President and Chief Executive Officer (Total facility includes 10 beds in nursing home–type unit) (Nonreporting) **A**1 9 10 **S** Marian Health System, Tulsa, OK	21	10	88	—	—	—	—	—	—	—

Hospital, Address, Telephone, Administrator, Approval, Facility, and Physician Codes, Health Care System, Network	Classi-fication Codes		Utilization Data					Expense (thousands) of dollars		
★ American Hospital Association (AHA) membership □ Joint Commission on Accreditation of Healthcare Organizations (JCAHO) accreditation + American Osteopathic Healthcare Association (AOHA) membership ○ American Osteopathic Association (AOA) accreditation △ Commission on Accreditation of Rehabilitation Facilities (CARF) accreditation Control codes 61, 63, 64, 71, 72 and 73 indicate hospitals listed by AOHA, but not registered by AHA. For definition of numerical codes, see page A4	Control	Service	Staffed Beds	Admissions	Census	Outpatient Visits	Births	Total	Payroll	Personnel

POTEAU—Le Flore County

☒ EASTERN OKLAHOMA MEDICAL CENTER, 105 Wall Street, Zip 74953, Mailing Address: P.O. Box 1148, Zip 74953–1148; tel. 918/647–8161; Craig R. Cudworth, Chief Executive Officer **A**1 9 10 **F**7 8 19 21 22 23 26 27 28 30 32 33 34 37 39 40 42 44 45 49 53 55 63 65 71 73 **P**1 8 **S** Quorum Health Group/Quorum Health Resources, Inc., Brentwood, TN **N** Hillcrest Healthcare System, Tulsa, OK

| 23 | 10 | 72 | 1080 | 31 | — | 147 | 4112 | 2029 | 293 |

PRYOR—Mayes County

☒ MAYES COUNTY MEDICAL CENTER, 129 North Kentucky Street, Zip 74361–4211, Mailing Address: P.O. Box 278, Zip 74362–0278; tel. 918/825–1600; W. Charles Jordan, Administrator **A**1 9 10 **F**12 16 17 19 22 28 32 33 34 40 42 44 46 65 67 71 73 **P**6 7 **S** INTEGRIS Health, Oklahoma City, OK **N** Integris Health, Oklahoma City, OK

| 23 | 10 | 34 | 1118 | 14 | 16365 | 58 | 10377 | 5420 | 208 |

PURCELL—McClain County

★ PURCELL MUNICIPAL HOSPITAL, 1500 North Green Avenue, Zip 73080–1699, Mailing Address: P.O. Box 511, Zip 73080–0511; tel. 405/527–6524; Curtis R. Pryor, Administrator **A**9 10 **F**12 14 16 17 19 22 25 28 30 32 34 39 40 42 45 46 49 55 65 67 71 **S** Quorum Health Group/Quorum Health Resources, Inc., Brentwood, TN

| 14 | 10 | 16 | 1438 | 15 | 14472 | 92 | 7476 | 3164 | 140 |

SALLISAW—Sequoyah County

SEQUOYAH MEMORIAL HOSPITAL, 213 East Redwood Street, Zip 74955–2811, Mailing Address: P.O. Box 505, Zip 74955–0505; tel. 918/774–1100; Ruth Ann Roark, Administrator (Nonreporting) **A**10

| 15 | 10 | 41 | — | — | — | — | — | — | — |

SAPULPA—Creek County

□ BARTLETT MEMORIAL MEDICAL CENTER, 519 South Division Street, Zip 74066–4501, Mailing Address: P.O. Box 1368, Zip 74067–1368; tel. 918/224–4280; W. D. Robinson, Chief Executive Officer **A**1 9 10 **F**8 10 12 15 16 19 20 21 22 25 28 30 32 33 34 37 40 42 44 45 46 48 49 64 65 71 73 **P**5

| 23 | 10 | 113 | 2036 | 29 | 14768 | 70 | 14615 | 7053 | 297 |

SAYRE—Beckham County

★ SAYRE MEMORIAL HOSPITAL, 501 East Washington Street, Zip 73662, Mailing Address: P.O. Box 680, Zip 73662; tel. 580/928–5541; Larry Anderson, Administrator **A**9 10 **F**7 8 19 28 61 65 71 73 **P**2 **S** Quorum Health Group/Quorum Health Resources, Inc., Brentwood, TN

| 23 | 10 | 46 | 1045 | 12 | 10462 | 111 | 6347 | 3297 | 115 |

SEILING—Dewey County

SEILING HOSPITAL, Highway 60 N.E., Zip 73663, Mailing Address: P.O. Box 720, Zip 73663–0720; tel. 580/922–7361; Jane McDowell, Administrator **A**9 10 **F**19 22 28 32 44 49 71 **P**5

| 14 | 10 | 18 | 331 | 4 | 1097 | 0 | 1623 | 890 | — |

SEMINOLE—Seminole County

★ SEMINOLE MUNICIPAL HOSPITAL, 606 West Evans Street, Zip 74868–3897, Mailing Address: P.O. Box 2130, Zip 74818–2130; tel. 405/382–0600; Stephen R. Schoaps, Chief Executive Officer **A**9 10 **F**7 14 15 19 22 32 39 44 46 49 51 70 71 73 **S** Quorum Health Group/Quorum Health Resources, Inc., Brentwood, TN **N** University Health Partners, Oklahoma City, OK

| 14 | 10 | 39 | 657 | 7 | 10018 | 2 | 4191 | 1921 | 92 |

SHATTUCK—Ellis County

☒ NEWMAN MEMORIAL HOSPITAL, 905 South Main Street, Zip 73858–9602, Mailing Address: Box 279, Zip 73858–0279; tel. 580/938–2551; Gary W. Mitchell, Chief Executive Officer **A**1 9 10 **F**7 8 15 18 19 22 24 28 32 35 36 37 40 44 71 73 **P**8

| 23 | 10 | 27 | 1062 | 12 | 54050 | 108 | 8255 | 3696 | 159 |

SHAWNEE—Pottawatomie County

☒ MISSION HILL MEMORIAL HOSPITAL, 1900 South Gordon Cooper Drive, Zip 74801–8600; tel. 405/273–2240; Thomas G. Honaker, III, Administrator **A**1 9 10 **F**7 8 10 15 19 20 21 22 30 32 33 35 37 39 40 44 49 65 71 73 74 **P**4 8 **S** Brim, Inc., Portland, OR

| 32 | 10 | 49 | 1789 | 17 | 14765 | 252 | 9708 | 3998 | 167 |

☒ SHAWNEE REGIONAL HOSPITAL, 1102 West MacArthur Street, Zip 74801–1744; tel. 405/273–2270; Robert F. Maynard, Chief Executive Officer **A**1 2 9 10 **F**7 11 14 15 16 17 19 21 22 26 28 30 32 33 34 35 40 42 44 45 49 60 63 64 65 66 67 71 73 74

| 23 | 10 | 116 | 3879 | 49 | 48314 | 696 | 24813 | 10435 | 380 |

SPENCER—Oklahoma County

☒ INTEGRIS MENTAL HEALTH SYSTEM–WILLOW VIEW, 2601 North Spencer Road, Zip 73084–3699, Mailing Address: P.O. Box 11137, Oklahoma City, Zip 73136–0137; tel. 405/427–2441; Murali Krishna, M.D., President and Chief Operating Officer **A**1 10 **F**3 52 53 54 55 56 57 58 59 67 **S** INTEGRIS Health, Oklahoma City, OK

| 23 | 22 | 44 | 515 | 39 | 18952 | 0 | — | 5467 | 109 |

STIGLER—Haskell County

★ HASKELL COUNTY HEALTHCARE SYSTEM, 401 N.W. H. Street, Zip 74462–1625; tel. 918/967–4682; Stacy D. Holland, Administrator and Chief Executive Officer **A**9 10 **F**17 19 25 27 28 30 32 33 34 39 42 44 49 65 70 71 72 73 **P**5

| 13 | 10 | 31 | 670 | 10 | 7202 | 0 | 5746 | 3217 | 168 |

STILLWATER—Payne County

☒ STILLWATER MEDICAL CENTER, 1323 West Sixth Avenue, Zip 74074–4399, Mailing Address: P.O. Box 2408, Zip 74076–2408; tel. 405/372–1480; Jerry G. Moeller, President and Chief Executive Officer (Total facility includes 18 beds in nursing home–type unit) **A**1 9 10 **F**10 14 15 16 19 20 21 22 23 31 32 33 34 35 36 37 40 42 44 46 49 56 63 64 65 71 73 **P**8

| 16 | 10 | 92 | 4303 | 61 | 56280 | 787 | 36413 | 15030 | 526 |

STROUD—Lincoln County

★ STROUD MUNICIPAL HOSPITAL, Highway 66 West, Zip 74079, Mailing Address: P.O. Box 530, Zip 74079–0530; tel. 918/968–3571; James D. Moore, Administrator **A**9 10 **F**7 8 11 16 17 19 22 26 27 28 29 30 31 32 33 34 37 40 44 45 46 51 61 71 72 73 74 **P**5 **S** INTEGRIS Health, Oklahoma City, OK **N** Integris Health, Oklahoma City, OK

| 23 | 10 | 20 | 413 | 6 | 5030 | 14 | 3704 | 1712 | 94 |

Hospital, Address, Telephone, Administrator, Approval, Facility, and Physician Codes, Health Care System, Network	Classi-fication Codes		Utilization Data					Expense (thousands) of dollars		
	Control	Service	Staffed Beds	Admissions	Census	Outpatient Visits	Births	Total	Payroll	Personnel

★ American Hospital Association (AHA) membership
□ Joint Commission on Accreditation of Healthcare Organizations (JCAHO) accreditation
+ American Osteopathic Healthcare Association (AOHA) membership
○ American Osteopathic Association (AOA) accreditation
△ Commission on Accreditation of Rehabilitation Facilities (CARF) accreditation
Control codes 61, 63, 64, 71, 72 and 73 indicate hospitals listed by AOHA, but not registered by AHA. For definition of numerical codes, see page A4

SULPHUR—Murray County

ARBUCKLE MEMORIAL HOSPITAL, 2011 West Broadway Street, Zip 73086–4221; tel. 580/622–2161; Mike Pruitt, Administrator **A**9 10 **F**14 15 16 64	13	10	38	1320	15	3336	1	2817	1600	46

TAHLEQUAH—Cherokee County

✠ TAHLEQUAH CITY HOSPITAL, 1400 East Downing Street, Zip 74464–3324, Mailing Address: P.O. Box 1008, Zip 74465–1008; tel. 918/456–0641; L. Gene Matthews, Chief Executive Officer **A**1 9 10 **F**7 8 15 16 18 19 21 22 26 28 30 32 33 35 37 40 44 49 52 57 65 71 73 **S** Quorum Health Group/Quorum Health Resources, Inc., Brentwood, TN	16	10	74	2429	30	35756	258	16872	7690	315
✠ WILLIAM W. HASTINGS INDIAN HOSPITAL, 100 South Bliss Avenue, Zip 74464–3399; tel. 918/458–3100; Hickory Starr, Jr., Administrator **A**1 10 **F**7 15 19 20 22 28 31 34 37 39 40 44 52 53 54 55 56 57 58 63 73 **P**6 **S** U. S. Public Health Service Indian Health Service, Rockville, MD	47	10	60	3108	28	202739	1161	27790	14969	437

TALIHINA—La Flore County

✠ CHOCTAW NATION INDIAN HOSPITAL, Rural Route 2, Box 1725, Zip 74571–9517; tel. 918/567–2211; Rosemary Hooser, Administrator **A**1 10 **F**8 12 14 15 16 19 20 22 27 31 40 44 58 65 71 **P**6 **S** U. S. Public Health Service Indian Health Service, Rockville, MD	47	10	44	1196	13	51135	218	22608	10137	230

TINKER AFB—De Kalb County

✠ U. S. AIR FORCE HOSPITAL TINKER, 5700 Arnold Street, Zip 73145; tel. 405/736–2237; Colonel David D. Bissell, MC, USAF, Commander **A**1 **F**3 8 12 13 16 17 18 20 22 27 28 29 30 32 39 40 41 44 46 49 51 54 55 58 65 67 71 72 73 **S** Department of the Air Force, Bowling AFB, DC	41	10	25	2091	10	183841	577	23329	3933	571

TISHOMINGO—Johnston County

JOHNSTON MEMORIAL HOSPITAL, 1000 South Byrd Street, Zip 73460–3299; tel. 580/371–2327; Connie Pedersen, Interim Administrator (Nonreporting) **A**10	13	10	30	—	—	—	—	—	—	—

TULSA—Tulsa County

BROOKHAVEN HOSPITAL, 201 South Garnett Road, Zip 74128–1800; tel. 918/438–4257; Rolf B. Gainer, Chief Executive Officer and Administrator (Nonreporting) **A**10	31	22	40	—	—	—	—	—	—	—
✠ CHILDREN'S MEDICAL CENTER, 5300 East Skelly Drive, Zip 74135–6599, Mailing Address: Box 35648, Zip 74153–0648; tel. 918/664–6600; Gerard J. Rothlein, Jr., President and Chief Executive Officer (Nonreporting) **A**1 3 5 10 **S** Hillcrest HealthCare System, Tulsa, OK **N** Hillcrest Healthcare System, Tulsa, OK	23	59	108	—	—	—	—	—	—	—
✠ COLUMBIA DOCTORS HOSPITAL, 2323 South Harvard Avenue, Zip 74114–3370; tel. 918/744–4000; Anthony R. Young, President and Chief Executive Officer **A**1 10 **F**2 7 8 10 11 12 19 21 22 23 25 26 30 32 33 34 35 37 38 40 41 42 43 44 48 52 53 57 59 60 63 64 65 67 70 71 73 **P**1 7 **S** Columbia/HCA Healthcare Corporation, Nashville, TN **N** Eastern Oklahoma Health Network, Tulsa, OK	33	10	121	3287	61	26671	809	30623	9971	403
★ COLUMBIA SPECIALTY HOSPITAL OF TULSA, 2408 East 81st Street, 2500, Zip 74137–4210; tel. 918/491–2400; Kenneth Noteboom, Chief Executive Officer **A**10 **F**12 17 19 21 22 28 29 35 45 71 73 **S** Columbia/HCA Healthcare Corporation, Nashville, TN	33	49	45	208	16	0	0	—	—	54
✠ △ HILLCREST MEDICAL CENTER, 1120 South Utica, Zip 74104–4090; tel. 918/579–1000; Donald A. Lorack, Jr., President and Chief Executive Officer **A**1 2 3 5 7 9 10 **F**3 4 7 8 9 10 11 12 14 15 16 17 18 19 21 22 23 24 25 26 27 28 29 30 31 32 33 34 35 37 38 39 40 41 42 43 44 45 46 48 49 50 51 52 53 54 55 56 57 58 59 60 61 63 64 65 66 67 68 69 70 71 72 73 74 **P**1 5 6 7 **S** Hillcrest HealthCare System, Tulsa, OK **N** Hillcrest Healthcare System, Tulsa, OK; Eastern Oklahoma Health Network, Tulsa, OK	23	10	365	17577	256	102199	3698	159580	60201	2157
□ LAUREATE PSYCHIATRIC CLINIC AND HOSPITAL, 6655 South Yale Avenue, Zip 74136–3329; tel. 918/481–4000; John L. Fleming, M.D., Interim Chief Executive Officer (Nonreporting) **A**1 3 5 10	23	22	75	—	—	—	—	—	—	—
□ MEMORIAL MEDICAL CENTER AND CANCER TREATMENT CENTER–TULSA, 2408 East 81st Street, Zip 74137–4210; tel. 918/496–5000; Sandra Jackson, President **A**1 2 10 **F**12 14 15 16 19 21 27 28 30 34 35 37 39 44 45 46 49 60 63 67 73 **P**6 **S** Cancer Treatment Centers of America, Arlington Heights, IL	33	10	72	982	18	—	—	42827	11756	397
PARKSIDE HOSPITAL, 1620 East 12th Street, Zip 74120–5499; tel. 918/582–2131; Paul Greever, Chief Executive Officer **A**3 5 10 **F**1 2 3 12 14 17 18 30 54 55 56 58 59 65 73	23	52	40	1631	20	—	0	12643	7283	84
✠ SAINT FRANCIS HOSPITAL, 6161 South Yale Avenue, Zip 74136–1992; tel. 918/494–2200; Donna Rheault, Chief Operating Officer (Total facility includes 40 beds in nursing home–type unit) **A**1 2 3 5 8 9 10 **F**3 4 7 8 10 11 12 13 15 16 17 18 19 20 21 22 26 28 29 30 31 32 33 34 35 36 37 38 39 40 41 42 43 44 45 46 49 51 53 54 55 56 57 58 59 60 63 64 65 66 67 68 69 70 71 73 74 **P**6 8	23	10	606	29704	419	401765	3358	227896	96610	3596
□ SHADOW MOUNTAIN HOSPITAL, 6262 South Sheridan Road, Zip 74133–4099; tel. 918/492–8200; Nancy J. Cranton, Chief Executive Officer (Nonreporting) **A**1 **S** Healthcare America, Inc., Austin, TX	33	52	100	—	—	—	—	—	—	—
✠ △ ST. JOHN MEDICAL CENTER, 1923 South Utica Avenue, Zip 74104–5445; tel. 918/744–2345; Sister M. Therese Gottschalk, President **A**1 2 3 5 7 9 10 **F**1 2 3 4 7 8 10 11 12 14 15 16 17 18 19 20 21 22 23 24 25 26 27 28 29 30 31 32 33 34 35 37 38 39 40 41 42 43 44 45 47 48 49 52 54 55 56 57 58 59 60 62 64 65 66 67 69 70 71 72 73 74 **P**7 **S** Marian Health System, Tulsa, OK	21	10	552	21089	364	107186	2111	189977	70090	4370

Hospital, Address, Telephone, Administrator, Approval, Facility, and Physician Codes, Health Care System, Network	Classi-fication Codes		Utilization Data						Expense (thousands) of dollars		
★ American Hospital Association (AHA) membership □ Joint Commission on Accreditation of Healthcare Organizations (JCAHO) accreditation + American Osteopathic Healthcare Association (AOHA) membership ○ American Osteopathic Association (AOA) accreditation △ Commission on Accreditation of Rehabilitation Facilities (CARF) accreditation Control codes 61, 63, 64, 71, 72 and 73 indicate hospitals listed by AOHA, but not registered by AHA. For definition of numerical codes, see page A4	Control	Service	Staffed Beds	Admissions	Census	Outpatient Visits	Births	Total	Payroll	Personnel
✠ + ○ △ TULSA REGIONAL MEDICAL CENTER, (Formerly Columbia Tulsa Regional Medical Center), 744 West Ninth Street, Zip 74127–9990; tel. 918/599–5900; James M. MacCallum, President and Chief Executive Officer **A**1 7 9 10 11 12 13 **F**3 4 7 8 10 11 12 14 17 18 19 21 22 26 30 32 33 35 36 37 38 40 41 42 43 44 46 49 52 53 54 55 56 57 58 59 60 64 65 66 67 69 70 71 73 **P**7 8 **S** Columbia/HCA Healthcare Corporation, Nashville, TN	33	10	255	9594	158	79730	742	77119	33533	1200
VINITA—Craig County										
★ CRAIG GENERAL HOSPITAL, 735 North Foreman Street, Zip 74301–1418, Mailing Address: Box 326, Zip 74301–0326; tel. 918/256–7551; B. Joe Gunn, FACHE, Administrator and Chief Executive Officer **A**9 10 **F**7 8 11 12 15 16 19 21 22 28 30 32 34 35 36 40 42 44 49 65 67 71 73	16	10	28	1106	16	22484	123	8982	4037	153
□ EASTERN STATE HOSPITAL, Mailing Address: P.O. Box 69, Zip 74301–0069; tel. 918/256–7841; Karen Steed, Chief Executive Officer **A**1 10 **F**14 15 16 20 22 24 27 29 30 46 52 55 65 73 **P**6	12	22	290	1960	291	0	0	—	—	640
WAGONER—Wagoner County										
✠ WAGONER COMMUNITY HOSPITAL, (Formerly Columbia Wagoner Hospital), 1200 West Cherokee, Zip 74467–4681, Mailing Address: Box 407, Zip 74477–0407; tel. 918/485–5514; John W. Crawford, Chief Executive Officer **A**1 9 10 **F**7 8 14 15 16 18 19 21 22 24 26 28 29 30 31 32 34 37 39 40 42 44 45 46 49 51 52 53 54 55 56 58 65 71 73 74 **P**7 8 **S** Columbia/HCA Healthcare Corporation, Nashville, TN **N** Eastern Oklahoma Health Network, Tulsa, OK	33	10	100	2300	34	12952	126	14912	5751	145
WATONGA—Blaine County										
★ WATONGA MUNICIPAL HOSPITAL, 500 North Nash Boulevard, Zip 73772–0370, Mailing Address: Box 370, Zip 73772–0370; tel. 580/623–7211; Terry Buckner, Administrator **A**9 10 **F**11 15 19 22 26 29 32 33 34 44 49 51 71 **P**6 **S** Quorum Health Group/Quorum Health Resources, Inc., Brentwood, TN	16	10	24	744	9	5194	2	6415	3126	144
WAURIKA—Jefferson County										
★ JEFFERSON COUNTY HOSPITAL, Highway 70 and 81, Zip 73573, Mailing Address: P.O. Box 90, Zip 73573–0090; tel. 580/228–2344; Curtis R. Pryor, Administrator **A**9 10 **F**7 11 22 28 32 40 44 49 73 **N** First Health West, Lawton, OK	13	10	29	491	8	6469	1	—	1467	—
WEATHERFORD—Custer County										
★ SOUTHWESTERN MEMORIAL HOSPITAL, 215 North Kansas Street, Zip 73096–5499; tel. 580/772–5551; Ronnie D. Walker, President **A**9 10 **F**7 8 19 28 34 35 44 71 73 **N** First Health West, Lawton, OK	16	10	46	863	7	9463	226	4802	2175	89
WETUMKA—Hughes County										
WETUMKA GENERAL HOSPITAL, 325 South Washita, Zip 74883–5500; tel. 405/452–3276; Carolyn Keesee, Chief Executive Officer **A**10 **F**2 3 15 16 17 22 28 34 64 71	16	10	28	380	7	4351	0	3134	1742	78
WILBURTON—Latimer County										
LATIMER COUNTY GENERAL HOSPITAL, 806 Highway 2 North, Zip 74578–3698; tel. 918/465–2391; Jack Martin, Administrator **A**10 **F**19 28 32 **P**5	13	10	26	611	6	—	0	3261	1757	73
WOODWARD—Woodward County										
✠ WOODWARD HOSPITAL AND HEALTH CENTER, 900 17th Street, Zip 73801–2423; tel. 580/256–5511; Joel A. Hart, Administrator **A**1 9 10 **F**7 8 11 12 16 17 19 21 22 26 28 30 32 33 35 37 39 40 41 42 44 45 46 49 52 57 64 65 66 67 71 72 73 **P**5 7 8 **S** Quorum Health Group/Quorum Health Resources, Inc., Brentwood, TN	23	10	68	1908	31	—	252	16572	7050	275

OREGON

Resident population 3,243 (in thousands)
Resident population in metro areas 70.1%
Birth rate per 1,000 population 13.6
65 years and over 13.4%
Percent of persons without health insurance 15.3%

Hospital, Address, Telephone, Administrator, Approval, Facility, and Physician Codes, Health Care System, Network	Classi-fication Codes		Utilization Data					Expense (thousands) of dollars		
	Control	Service	Staffed Beds	Admissions	Census	Outpatient Visits	Births	Total	Payroll	Personnel

★ American Hospital Association (AHA) membership
□ Joint Commission on Accreditation of Healthcare Organizations (JCAHO) accreditation
+ American Osteopathic Healthcare Association (AOHA) membership
○ American Osteopathic Association (AOA) accreditation
△ Commission on Accreditation of Rehabilitation Facilities (CARF) accreditation
Control codes 61, 63, 64, 71, 72 and 73 indicate hospitals listed by AOHA, but not registered by AHA. For definition of numerical codes, see page A4.

ALBANY—Linn County
★ ALBANY GENERAL HOSPITAL, 1046 West Sixth Avenue, Zip 97321–1999; tel. 541/812–4000; Richard J. Delano, President **A**1 2 9 10 **F**7 10 15 17 19 21 22 28 29 30 32 33 34 35 37 39 40 41 42 44 46 49 54 59 60 65 66 67 68 70 71 72 73 74 **P**5 6 **N** Inter Community Health Network, Corvallis, OR; Health Future, Inc., Medford, OR — 23 10 71 3631 33 55692 684 28854 13079 401

ASHLAND—Jackson County
ASHLAND COMMUNITY HOSPITAL, 280 Maple Street, Zip 97520, Mailing Address: P.O. Box 98, Zip 97520; tel. 541/482–2441; James R. Watson, Administrator **A**9 10 **F**6 7 8 16 19 22 28 30 32 34 36 37 40 41 44 45 46 65 70 71 **P**5 **N** Health Future, Inc., Medford, OR — 23 10 37 1442 15 23603 295 14297 6826 201

ASTORIA—Clatsop County
★ COLUMBIA MEMORIAL HOSPITAL, 2111 Exchange Street, Zip 97103; tel. 503/325–4321; Terry O. Finklein, Chief Executive Officer **A**1 9 10 **F**7 8 16 17 19 21 22 28 30 32 33 34 37 39 40 41 42 44 49 65 67 68 70 71 73 74 **P**8 **N** Health Future, Inc., Medford, OR — 23 10 37 2155 17 41431 347 16446 7654 210

BAKER CITY—Baker County
□ ST. ELIZABETH HEALTH SERVICES, 3325 Pocahontas Road, Zip 97814; tel. 541/523–6461; Robert T. Mannix, Jr., President and Chief Operations Officer (Total facility includes 98 beds in nursing home–type unit) (Nonreporting) **A**1 9 10 **S** Catholic Health Initiatives, Denver, CO — 21 10 134 — — — — — — —

BANDON—Coos County
★ SOUTHERN COOS GENERAL HOSPITAL, 640 West Fourth, Zip 97411; tel. 541/347–2426; James A. Wathen, Chief Executive Officer **A**9 10 **F**8 14 15 17 20 22 32 34 44 49 65 71 — 16 10 18 161 2 8248 — 2550 1328 52

BEND—Deschutes County
★ ST. CHARLES MEDICAL CENTER, 2500 N.E. Neff Road, Zip 97701–6015; tel. 541/382–4321; James T. Lussier, President and Chief Executive Officer (Nonreporting) **A**1 2 3 9 10 **N** Central Oregon Hosp Network (CONET), Bend, OR; Health Future, Inc., Medford, OR — 23 10 181 — — — — — — —

BURNS—Harney County
HARNEY DISTRICT HOSPITAL, 557 West Washington Street, Zip 97720–1497; tel. 503/573–7281; David L. Harman, Administrator **A**9 10 **F**7 17 19 22 28 30 40 44 49 56 64 70 71 **P**5 **N** Central Oregon Hosp Network (CONET), Bend, OR — 16 10 36 394 3 14057 43 4254 1876 55

CLACKAMAS—Clackamas County
★ KAISER SUNNYSIDE MEDICAL CENTER, 10180 S.E. Sunnyside Road, Zip 97015–9303; tel. 503/571–4002; Alide Chase, Administrator **A**1 2 10 **F**2 3 4 7 8 9 10 11 12 13 16 18 19 20 21 22 23 24 26 27 28 29 30 31 32 33 34 35 37 38 39 40 41 42 43 44 45 46 47 48 49 50 52 53 54 55 56 57 58 59 60 61 63 64 65 66 67 69 70 71 72 73 74 **P**6 **S** Kaiser Foundation Hospitals, Oakland, CA **N** Oregon Health System in Collaboration, Lake Oswego, OR — 23 10 170 12037 121 270100 1766 — — —

COOS BAY—Coos County
★ BAY AREA HOSPITAL, 1775 Thompson Road, Zip 97420–2198; tel. 541/269–8111; Dale Jessup, President and Chief Executive Officer **A**1 2 9 10 **F**7 8 11 12 14 16 17 19 21 22 23 27 28 30 31 32 33 34 35 37 39 40 41 42 44 45 46 49 52 53 54 56 60 65 67 70 71 73 **P**5 **N** Health Future, Inc., Medford, OR — 16 10 114 6685 69 27365 562 48855 24584 647

COQUILLE—Coos County
COQUILLE VALLEY HOSPITAL, 940 East Fifth Street, Zip 97423; tel. 503/396–3101; Edna J. Cotner, Administrator **A**9 10 **F**7 8 14 15 16 22 32 40 44 67 71 **P**5 — 16 10 20 408 3 3215 69 3738 1479 59

CORVALLIS—Benton County
★ GOOD SAMARITAN HOSPITAL CORVALLIS, 3600 N.W. Samaritan Drive, Zip 97330, Mailing Address: P.O. Box 1068, Zip 97339; tel. 541/757–5111; Larry A. Mullins, President and Chief Executive Officer **A**1 2 9 10 **F**4 7 8 10 12 14 15 16 17 19 20 21 23 30 31 32 34 35 37 39 40 41 42 43 44 45 49 51 52 53 54 55 56 57 58 60 63 65 66 67 70 71 73 74 **P**6 **N** Inter Community Health Network, Corvallis, OR; Health Future, Inc., Medford, OR — 23 10 130 6597 72 144767 1973 65762 29550 761

COTTAGE GROVE—Lane County
★ COTTAGE GROVE HEALTHCARE COMMUNITY, 1340 Birch Avenue, Zip 97424; tel. 541/942–0511; William N. Wilber, Administrator (Total facility includes 40 beds in nursing home–type unit) (Nonreporting) **A**1 9 10 **S** Brim, Inc., Portland, OR — 23 10 67 — — — — — — —

DALLAS—Polk County
□ VALLEY COMMUNITY HOSPITAL, 550 S.E. Clay Street, Zip 97338, Mailing Address: P.O. Box 378, Zip 97338; tel. 503/623–8301; Stephen A. Bowles, President **A**1 9 10 **F**2 3 7 8 14 15 16 17 19 21 22 23 28 29 30 34 35 40 41 44 45 49 65 66 67 70 71 73 — 23 10 44 1291 12 25348 204 12004 6706 198

ENTERPRISE—Wallowa County
★ WALLOWA MEMORIAL HOSPITAL, 401 East First Street, Zip 97828, Mailing Address: P.O. Box 460, Zip 97828; tel. 541/426–3111; Kim Dahlman, Chief Executive Officer (Total facility includes 32 beds in nursing home–type unit) **A**9 10 **F**7 8 11 14 15 16 17 19 21 22 26 27 28 30 32 33 34 35 40 42 44 56 59 64 65 70 71 73 **P**5 — 16 10 55 518 34 11391 55 5654 2917 116

Hospital, Address, Telephone, Administrator, Approval, Facility, and Physician Codes, Health Care System, Network	Classi-fication Codes		Utilization Data					Expense (thousands) of dollars		
★ American Hospital Association (AHA) membership □ Joint Commission on Accreditation of Healthcare Organizations (JCAHO) accreditation + American Osteopathic Healthcare Association (AOHA) membership ○ American Osteopathic Association (AOA) accreditation △ Commission on Accreditation of Rehabilitation Facilities (CARF) accreditation Control codes 61, 63, 64, 71, 72 and 73 indicate hospitals listed by AOHA, but not registered by AHA. For definition of numerical codes, see page A4	Control	Service	Staffed Beds	Admissions	Census	Outpatient Visits	Births	Total	Payroll	Personnel

EUGENE—Lane County

☒ △ SACRED HEART MEDICAL CENTER, 1255 Hilyard Street, Zip 97401, Mailing Address: P.O. Box 10905, Zip 97440; tel. 541/686–7300; Judy Hodgson, Administrator **A**1 2 7 9 10 **F**4 7 8 10 11 12 14 15 16 17 19 21 22 24 25 26 28 29 30 32 33 34 35 37 38 40 41 42 43 44 45 48 49 52 56 60 61 65 67 70 71 72 73 74 **P**6 **S** PeaceHealth, Bellevue, WA **N** PeaceHealth, Bellevue, WA | 21 10 | 390 | 19621 | 238 | 254373 | 2470 | 186112 | 72955 | 2173

SERENITY LANE, 616 East 16th, Zip 97401; tel. 541/687–1110; Neil H. McNaughton, Executive Director and Administrator (Nonreporting) | 23 82 | 55 | — | — | — | — | — | — | —

FLORENCE—Lane County

☒ PEACE HARBOR HOSPITAL, 400 Ninth Street, Zip 97439, Mailing Address: P.O. Box 580, Zip 97439; tel. 541/997–8412; James Barnhart, Administrator **A**1 9 10 **F**7 8 14 15 16 19 21 22 30 32 33 35 37 40 44 45 49 65 70 71 73 **P**6 **S** PeaceHealth, Bellevue, WA **N** PeaceHealth, Bellevue, WA | 21 10 | 21 | 1142 | 12 | 25330 | 66 | 13572 | 6394 | 254

FOREST GROVE—Washington County

TUALITY FOREST GROVE HOSPITAL See Tuality Healthcare, Hillsboro

GOLD BEACH—Curry County

CURRY GENERAL HOSPITAL, 94220 Fourth Street, Zip 97444–9990; tel. 541/247–6621; Randall J. Scholten, Chief Executive Officer (Nonreporting) **A**9 10 | 12 10 | 24 | — | — | — | — | — | — | —

GRANTS PASS—Josephine County

☒ THREE RIVERS COMMUNITY HOSPITAL AND HEALTH CENTER–DIMMICK, 715 N.W. Dimmick Street, Zip 97526–1596; tel. 541/476–6831; Mark W. Folger, Senior Vice President **A**1 9 10 **F**7 8 11 15 16 17 19 21 22 23 24 28 29 30 32 33 34 35 37 39 40 41 44 45 46 49 51 54 56 65 67 68 70 71 72 73 **S** Asante Health System, Medford, OR **N** Health Future, Inc., Medford, OR | 23 10 | 87 | 3150 | 28 | 61068 | 565 | 24783 | 12605 | 311

□ THREE RIVERS COMMUNITY HOSPITAL AND HEALTH CENTER–WASHINGTON, 1505 N.W. Washington Boulevard, Zip 97526; tel. 541/479–7531; Mark W. Folger, Senior Vice President **A**1 9 10 **F**7 8 11 15 16 17 19 21 22 24 29 30 32 33 34 35 37 41 44 45 46 47 49 54 56 65 67 68 70 71 72 73 | 23 10 | 63 | 2798 | 29 | 70142 | 0 | 23458 | 10606 | 315

GRESHAM—Multnomah County

☒ LEGACY MOUNT HOOD MEDICAL CENTER, 24800 S.E. Stark, Zip 97030–0154; tel. 503/667–1122; Jane C. Cummins, Senior Vice President Clinical Operations **A**1 9 10 **F**2 3 7 8 15 17 19 21 22 27 28 30 32 33 35 37 40 41 42 44 45 46 49 60 65 67 71 73 74 **S** Legacy Health System, Portland, OR **N** Oregon Health System in Collaboration, Lake Oswego, OR; Legacy Health System, Portland, OR | 23 10 | 86 | 3779 | 35 | 42258 | 574 | 28996 | 13366 | 338

HEPPNER—Linn County

PIONEER MEMORIAL HOSPITAL, 564 East Pioneer Drive, Zip 97836, Mailing Address: P.O. Box 9, Zip 97836; tel. 503/676–9133; Kenneth A. Schmidt, President (Total facility includes 32 beds in nursing home–type unit) **A**10 **F**20 22 25 32 64 70 71 **P**5 **S** Adventist Health, Roseville, CA | 16 10 | 41 | 118 | 30 | 21711 | — | 4900 | 2423 | 91

HERMISTON—Umatilla County

☒ GOOD SHEPHERD COMMUNITY HOSPITAL, 610 N.W. 11th Street, Zip 97838–9696; tel. 541/567–6483; Dennis E. Burke, President **A**1 9 10 **F**7 8 14 15 16 19 22 28 30 32 34 35 37 40 44 45 46 51 65 67 70 71 73 **P**5 6 **N** Health Future, Inc., Medford, OR | 23 10 | 45 | 2307 | 20 | 36811 | 416 | 16941 | 7445 | 234

HILLSBORO—Washington County

TUALITY COMMUNITY HOSPITAL See Tuality Healthcare

☒ TUALITY HEALTHCARE, (Includes Tuality Community Hospital, 335 S.E. Eighth Avenue, Mailing Address: P.O. Box 309, Zip 97123; tel. 503/681–1111; Tuality Forest Grove Hospital, 1809 Maple Street, Forest Grove, Zip 97116–1995; tel. 503/357–2173), 335 S.E. Eighth Avenue, Zip 97123; tel. 503/681–1111; Richard Stenson, President (Total facility includes 22 beds in nursing home–type unit) **A**1 9 10 **F**3 4 7 8 10 12 13 14 16 17 19 21 22 23 24 25 26 27 28 29 30 32 33 34 35 37 39 40 41 42 44 45 49 52 57 58 59 65 66 67 71 72 73 74 **P**1 7 | 23 10 | 177 | 6595 | — | 102814 | 1325 | — | 19233 | —

HOOD RIVER—Hood River County

☒ HOOD RIVER MEMORIAL HOSPITAL, 13th and May Streets, Zip 97031, Mailing Address: P.O. Box 149, Zip 97031; tel. 541/386–3911; Tim Simmons, Chief Executive Officer (Nonreporting) **A**1 9 10 | 23 10 | 31 | — | — | — | — | — | — | —

JOHN DAY—Grant County

★ BLUE MOUNTAIN HOSPITAL, 170 Ford Road, Zip 97845; tel. 541/575–1311; David G. Triebes, Chief Executive Officer (Total facility includes 52 beds in nursing home–type unit) **A**9 10 **F**1 7 8 11 17 19 28 30 34 37 39 40 44 45 48 49 56 64 65 66 67 68 70 71 **P**5 8 **S** Brim, Inc., Portland, OR **N** Central Oregon Hosp Network (CONET), Bend, OR | 16 10 | 73 | 568 | 40 | 11443 | 78 | 6148 | 2917 | 61

KLAMATH FALLS—Klamath County

☒ MERLE WEST MEDICAL CENTER, 2865 Daggett Street, Zip 97601–1180; tel. 541/882–6311; Paul R. Stewart, President and Chief Executive Officer (Total facility includes 107 beds in nursing home–type unit) **A**1 2 3 9 10 **F**3 4 6 7 8 10 12 15 16 17 19 20 21 22 23 24 28 30 31 32 34 35 37 40 41 42 44 49 51 52 56 58 60 62 63 64 65 66 67 70 71 72 73 **P**5 **N** Health Future, Inc., Medford, OR | 23 10 | 238 | 7063 | 150 | 149886 | 794 | 56850 | 28158 | 946

LA GRANDE—Union County

☒ GRANDE RONDE HOSPITAL, 900 Sunset Drive, Zip 97850, Mailing Address: P.O. Box 3290, Zip 97850; tel. 541/963–8421; James A. Mattes, President (Total facility includes 14 beds in nursing home–type unit) **A**1 9 10 **F**7 8 12 14 15 16 19 21 22 23 24 32 33 35 37 39 40 41 42 44 49 63 64 65 67 70 71 73 **P**1 **N** Health Future, Inc., Medford, OR | 23 10 | 63 | 1992 | 18 | 36441 | 340 | 19945 | 9430 | 285

Hospital, Address, Telephone, Administrator, Approval, Facility, and Physician Codes, Health Care System, Network	Classi-fication Codes		Utilization Data					Expense (thousands) of dollars		
★ American Hospital Association (AHA) membership □ Joint Commission on Accreditation of Healthcare Organizations (JCAHO) accreditation + American Osteopathic Healthcare Association (AOHA) membership ○ American Osteopathic Association (AOA) accreditation △ Commission on Accreditation of Rehabilitation Facilities (CARF) accreditation Control codes 61, 63, 64, 71, 72 and 73 indicate hospitals listed by AOHA, but not registered by AHA. For definition of numerical codes, see page A4	Control	Service	Staffed Beds	Admissions	Census	Outpatient Visits	Births	Total	Payroll	Personnel

LAKEVIEW—Lake County

LAKE DISTRICT HOSPITAL, 700 South J. Street, Zip 97630–1679; tel. 503/947–2114; Richard T. Moore, Administrator (Total facility includes 47 beds in nursing home–type unit) (Nonreporting) **A**9 10 **N** Central Oregon Hosp Network (CONET), Bend, OR	16	10	68	—	—	—	—	—	—	—

LEBANON—Linn County

⊞ LEBANON COMMUNITY HOSPITAL, 525 North Santiam Highway, Zip 97355, Mailing Address: P.O. Box 739, Zip 97355–0739; tel. 541/258–2101; Steven W. Jasperson, Executive Vice President Operations **A**1 9 10 **F**7 8 14 15 17 19 22 24 28 29 32 33 34 35 37 40 41 44 49 65 67 70 71 73 **P**3 4 6 **N** Inter Community Health Network, Corvallis, OR; Health Future, Inc., Medford, OR	23	10	49	3298	30	57518	362	21172	11054	387

LINCOLN CITY—Lincoln County

⊞ NORTH LINCOLN HOSPITAL, 3043 N.E. 28th Street, Zip 97367–4523, Mailing Address: P.O. Box 767, Zip 97367–0767; tel. 541/994–3661; David C. Bigelow, Chief Executive Officer **A**1 9 10 **F**7 8 19 21 22 23 32 33 35 37 40 41 44 49 65 70 71 73 74 **P**1 5	16	10	28	1395	13	77408	187	19198	10083	267

MADRAS—Jefferson County

★ MOUNTAIN VIEW HOSPITAL DISTRICT, 470 N.E. A. Street, Zip 97741; tel. 541/475–3882; Ronald W. Barnes, Executive Director (Total facility includes 68 beds in nursing home–type unit) **A**9 10 **F**1 7 14 15 16 19 21 22 28 30 31 32 33 35 37 40 41 44 45 51 64 66 70 71 **P**5 **S** Brim, Inc., Portland, OR **N** Central Oregon Hosp Network (CONET), Bend, OR	16	10	102	1332	54	26434	201	10681	5531	194

MCMINNVILLE—Yamhill County

⊞ COLUMBIA WILLIAMETTE VALLEY MEDICAL CENTER, 2700 Three Mile Lane, Zip 97128–6498; tel. 503/472–6131; Rosemari Davis, Chief Executive Officer (Nonreporting) **A**1 9 10 **S** Columbia/HCA Healthcare Corporation, Nashville, TN	33	10	67	—	—	—	—	—	—	—

MEDFORD—Jackson County

⊞ PROVIDENCE MEDFORD MEDICAL CENTER, 1111 Crater Lake Avenue, Zip 97504–6241; tel. 541/732–5000; Charles T. Wright, Chief Executive, Southern Oregon Service Area (Total facility includes 18 beds in nursing home–type unit) (Nonreporting) **A**1 2 9 10 **S** Sisters of Providence Health System, Seattle, WA **N** Oregon Health System in Collaboration, Lake Oswego, OR; Providence Health System in Oregon, Portland, OR	21	10	140	—	—	—	—	—	—	—
⊞ ROGUE VALLEY MEDICAL CENTER, 2825 East Barnett Road, Zip 97504–8332; tel. 541/608–4900; Gary A. Sherwood, Executive Vice President **A**1 2 9 10 **F**2 3 4 7 10 11 12 14 15 16 17 19 21 22 23 26 27 28 29 30 31 32 33 34 35 37 38 39 40 41 42 43 44 45 46 47 49 51 52 56 57 60 64 65 67 69 70 71 73 74 **P**6 **S** Asante Health System, Medford, OR **N** Health Future, Inc., Medford, OR	23	10	249	11617	151	360870	1503	126223	56365	1610

MILWAUKIE—Clackamas County

⊞ PROVIDENCE MILWAUKIE HOSPITAL, 10150 S.E. 32nd Avenue, Zip 97222–6593; tel. 503/513–8300; Janice Burger, Operations Administrator **A**1 2 9 10 **F**1 2 3 4 5 7 8 9 10 11 15 16 17 19 20 22 23 24 26 29 31 32 33 34 35 37 38 40 41 42 43 44 47 48 49 51 52 53 56 57 58 60 64 65 66 67 69 70 71 72 73 74 **P**5 **S** Sisters of Providence Health System, Seattle, WA **N** Oregon Health System in Collaboration, Lake Oswego, OR; Providence Health System in Oregon, Portland, OR	21	10	56	2422	20	157351	420	25806	10124	273

NEWBERG—Yamhill County

⊞ PROVIDENCE NEWBERG HOSPITAL, 501 Villa Road, Zip 97132; tel. 503/537–1555; Mark W. Meinert, CHE, Chief Executive, Yamhill Service Area **A**1 9 10 **F**7 8 11 12 13 14 15 16 17 19 22 26 27 29 32 35 39 40 41 42 44 65 67 70 71 72 73 **P**5 **S** Sisters of Providence Health System, Seattle, WA **N** Oregon Health System in Collaboration, Lake Oswego, OR; Providence Health System in Oregon, Portland, OR	21	10	35	1367	11	65311	259	14953	6912	192

NEWPORT—Lincoln County

⊞ PACIFIC COMMUNITIES HEALTH DISTRICT, (Formerly Pacific Communities Hospital), 930 S.W. Abbey Street, Zip 97365–4820, Mailing Address: P.O. Box 945, Zip 97365–4820; tel. 541/265–2244; Michael R. Fraser, Administrator **A**1 10 **F**7 8 12 14 16 19 21 22 32 33 34 39 40 41 44 49 65 70 71 73 **P**5 6	16	10	41	1693	16	43322	223	19204	9179	271

ONTARIO—Malheur County

⊞ HOLY ROSARY MEDICAL CENTER, 351 S.W. Ninth Street, Zip 97914–2693; tel. 541/881–7000; Bruce Jensen, Chief Executive Officer and Team Leader **A**1 9 10 **F**7 8 11 14 15 16 19 21 22 28 30 31 32 33 35 40 42 44 45 46 49 63 70 71 73 **P**5 **S** Catholic Health Initiatives, Denver, CO	23	10	74	4031	34	55062	696	27644	11280	370

OREGON CITY—Clackamas County

⊞ WILLAMETTE FALLS HOSPITAL, 1500 Division Street, Zip 97045–1597; tel. 503/656–1631; Robert A. Steed, Administrator **A**1 2 9 10 **F**7 8 12 15 16 19 21 22 25 29 30 32 33 34 35 37 39 40 41 42 44 45 49 51 60 65 66 71 72 73 **P**5 8	23	10	91	5690	41	73879	1050	44772	21416	421

PENDLETON—Umatilla County

EASTERN OREGON PSYCHIATRIC CENTER, 2575 Westgate, Zip 97801; tel. 541/276–4511; Steve Shambaugh, Superintendent (Nonreporting) **A**10	12	22	60	—	—	—	—	—	—	—
⊞ ST. ANTHONY HOSPITAL, 1601 S.E. Court Avenue, Zip 97801–3297; tel. 541/276–5121; Jeffrey S. Drop, President and Chief Executive Officer **A**1 2 9 10 **F**7 8 11 12 14 15 17 19 20 21 22 23 24 26 28 29 30 32 33 34 35 37 38 39 40 41 42 44 46 49 51 63 65 67 70 71 73 **P**5 **S** Catholic Health Initiatives, Denver, CO	21	10	49	1901	17	20641	413	18622	7184	291

Hospital, Address, Telephone, Administrator, Approval, Facility, and Physician Codes, Health Care System, Network	Classi-fication Codes		Utilization Data					Expense (thousands) of dollars		
★ American Hospital Association (AHA) membership □ Joint Commission on Accreditation of Healthcare Organizations (JCAHO) accreditation + American Osteopathic Healthcare Association (AOHA) membership ○ American Osteopathic Association (AOA) accreditation △ Commission on Accreditation of Rehabilitation Facilities (CARF) accreditation Control codes 61, 63, 64, 71, 72 and 73 indicate hospitals listed by AOHA, but not registered by AHA. For definition of numerical codes, see page A4	Control	Service	Staffed Beds	Admissions	Census	Outpatient Visits	Births	Total	Payroll	Personnel

PORTLAND—Multnomah County

✶ ADVENTIST MEDICAL CENTER, 10123 S.E. Market, Zip 97216–2599; tel. 503/257–2500; Larry D. Dodds, President **A**1 2 9 10 **F**3 4 7 8 10 12 14 15 16 17 19 21 22 23 24 28 29 30 32 33 34 35 37 39 40 41 42 44 45 46 49 52 53 54 55 56 57 58 59 60 61 65 66 67 71 72 73 74 **P**5 7 **S** Adventist Health, Roseville, CA	21	10	278	8816	97	101298	1577	100827	46242	1421
DOERNBECHER CHILDREN'S HOSPITAL See Oregon Health Sciences University Hospital										
★ ○ EASTMORELAND HOSPITAL, 2900 S.E. Steele Street, Zip 97202; tel. 503/234–0411; Jack Brian Dusenbery, Chief Executive Officer (Nonreporting) **A**9 10 11 12 13	33	10	77	—	—	—	—	—	—	—
GOOD SAMARITAN HOSPITAL AND MEDICAL CENTER See Legacy Good Samaritan Hospital and Medical Center										
✶ △ LEGACY EMANUEL HOSPITAL AND HEALTH CENTER, 2801 North Gantenbein Avenue, Zip 97227–1674; tel. 503/413–2200; Stephani White, Vice President and Site Administrator **A**1 3 5 7 9 10 **F**1 2 3 4 7 8 9 10 11 12 13 14 16 17 19 21 22 23 24 25 26 28 29 30 31 32 33 34 35 36 37 38 39 40 41 42 43 44 45 46 47 48 49 51 52 53 54 56 57 58 59 60 61 63 64 65 66 67 69 70 71 72 73 74 **S** Legacy Health System, Portland, OR **N** Oregon Health System in Collaboration, Lake Oswego, OR; Legacy Health System, Portland, OR	23	10	350	17484	231	196534	2122	173817	80414	2232
✶ LEGACY GOOD SAMARITAN HOSPITAL AND MEDICAL CENTER, (Includes Good Samaritan Hospital and Medical Center, ; Rehabilitation Institute of Oregon), 1015 N.W. 22nd Avenue, Zip 97210; tel. 503/413–7711; John M. Mootry, Vice President and Site Administrator **A**1 2 3 5 9 10 **F**1 2 3 4 7 8 9 10 11 12 13 14 16 17 19 21 22 23 24 25 26 28 29 30 31 32 33 34 35 37 38 39 40 41 42 43 44 45 46 47 48 49 51 52 53 54 56 57 58 59 60 61 63 64 65 66 67 69 70 71 72 73 74 **S** Legacy Health System, Portland, OR **N** Oregon Health System in Collaboration, Lake Oswego, OR; Legacy Health System, Portland, OR	23	10	294	12226	175	270784	1643	149436	61721	1567
✶ OREGON HEALTH SCIENCES UNIVERSITY HOSPITAL, (Formerly University Hospital), (Includes Doernbecher Children's Hospital), 3181 S.W. Sam Jackson Park Road, Zip 97201–3098; tel. 503/494–8311; Roy G. Vinyard, Chief Administrative Officer **A**1 2 3 5 8 9 10 **F**3 4 5 7 8 9 10 11 12 13 15 16 17 18 19 20 21 22 23 24 25 26 28 29 30 31 32 33 34 35 37 38 39 40 41 42 43 44 45 46 47 48 49 51 52 53 54 55 56 57 58 60 61 63 64 65 66 67 68 69 70 71 72 73 74 **P**1 6 7 **N** Health Future, Inc., Medford, OR	16	10	361	19829	282	394681	2257	302307	114282	3671
□ PACIFIC GATEWAY HOSPITAL AND COUNSELING CENTER, 1345 S.E. Harney, Zip 97202; tel. 503/234–5353; George B. Rex, Chief Executive Officer (Nonreporting) **A**1 10 **S** Behavioral Healthcare Corporation, Nashville, TN	33	22	66	—	—	—	—	—	—	—
✶ △ PROVIDENCE PORTLAND MEDICAL CENTER, 4805 N.E. Glisan Street, Zip 97213–2967; tel. 503/215–1111; David T. Underriner, Operations Administrator (Total facility includes 20 beds in nursing home–type unit) **A**1 2 3 5 7 9 10 **F**1 3 4 5 6 7 8 10 11 12 13 14 15 16 17 18 19 21 22 23 24 25 26 27 28 29 31 32 33 34 35 37 38 39 40 41 42 43 44 45 48 49 51 52 53 54 55 56 57 58 59 60 61 62 64 65 66 67 68 69 71 72 73 74 **P**5 6 **S** Sisters of Providence Health System, Seattle, WA **N** Oregon Health System in Collaboration, Lake Oswego, OR; Providence Health System in Oregon, Portland, OR	21	10	380	21143	217	681634	2228	207167	86165	2370
✶ PROVIDENCE ST. VINCENT MEDICAL CENTER, 9205 S.W. Barnes Road, Zip 97225–6661; tel. 503/216–1234; Donald Elsom, Operations Administrator **A**1 2 3 5 9 10 **F**1 3 4 5 6 7 8 10 11 12 13 14 15 16 17 18 19 21 22 23 24 25 26 28 29 30 31 32 33 34 35 37 38 39 40 41 42 43 44 45 46 49 51 52 53 54 56 58 59 60 62 63 65 66 67 71 72 73 74 **P**4 5 6 **S** Sisters of Providence Health System, Seattle, WA **N** Oregon Health System in Collaboration, Lake Oswego, OR; Providence Health System in Oregon, Portland, OR	21	10	442	26919	298	405531	4877	246290	95674	2370
REHABILITATION INSTITUTE OF OREGON See Legacy Good Samaritan Hospital and Medical Center										
✶ SHRINERS HOSPITALS FOR CHILDREN, PORTLAND, 3101 S.W. Sam Jackson Park Road, Zip 97201; tel. 503/241–5090; Nancy Jones, Administrator (Nonreporting) **A**1 3 5 **S** Shriners Hospitals for Children, Tampa, FL	23	57	25	—	—	—	—	—	—	—
UNIVERSITY HOSPITAL See Oregon Health Sciences University Hospital										
✶ VETERANS AFFAIRS MEDICAL CENTER, 3710 S.W. U.S. Veterans Hospital Road, Zip 97201; tel. 503/220–8262; Michael E. Bays, Acting Chief Executive Officer (Total facility includes 72 beds in nursing home–type unit) **A**1 2 3 5 8 **F**1 2 3 4 8 10 11 12 14 15 16 19 20 21 22 24 25 26 27 28 29 30 31 32 33 34 37 39 41 42 43 46 48 49 51 52 54 55 56 57 58 59 63 64 65 66 67 69 71 73 74 **P**6 **S** Department of Veterans Affairs, Washington, DC	45	10	314	8408	163	289471	0	176241	86574	2074
✶ WOODLAND PARK HOSPITAL, 10300 N.E. Hancock, Zip 97220; tel. 503/257–5500; Kay Vetaly, Acting Chief Executive Officer (Nonreporting) **A**1 10	33	10	123	—	—	—	—	—	—	—

PRINEVILLE—Crook County

PIONEER MEMORIAL HOSPITAL, 1201 North Elm Street, Zip 97754; tel. 541/447–6254; Donald J. Wee, Executive Director **A**9 10 **F**7 8 15 16 17 19 22 28 29 30 32 33 34 37 39 40 44 49 65 67 70 71 73 **P**5 8 **S** Lutheran Health Systems, Fargo, ND **N** Central Oregon Hosp Network (CONET), Bend, OR	23	10	30	699	6	12602	96	8272	3791	110

REDMOND—Deschutes County

★ CENTRAL OREGON DISTRICT HOSPITAL, 1253 North Canal Boulevard, Zip 97756–1395; tel. 541/548–8131; James A. Diegel, CHE, Executive Director **A**9 10 **F**7 8 12 14 15 17 22 28 29 30 31 32 34 35 37 39 40 41 44 45 49 56 60 65 67 70 71 74 **P**3 5 7 **S** Lutheran Health Systems, Fargo, ND **N** Central Oregon Hosp Network (CONET), Bend, OR	16	10	48	1726	12	21036	320	13019	6285	204

Hospital, Address, Telephone, Administrator, Approval, Facility, and Physician Codes, Health Care System, Network	Classi- fication Codes		Utilization Data					Expense (thousands) of dollars		
★ American Hospital Association (AHA) membership □ Joint Commission on Accreditation of Healthcare Organizations (JCAHO) accreditation + American Osteopathic Healthcare Association (AOHA) membership ○ American Osteopathic Association (AOA) accreditation △ Commission on Accreditation of Rehabilitation Facilities (CARF) accreditation Control codes 61, 63, 64, 71, 72 and 73 indicate hospitals listed by AOHA, but not registered by AHA. For definition of numerical codes, see page A4	Control	Service	Staffed Beds	Admissions	Census	Outpatient Visits	Births	Total	Payroll	Personnel

REEDSPORT—Douglas County

LOWER UMPQUA HOSPITAL DISTRICT, 600 Ranch Road, Zip 97467–1795; tel. 541/271–2171; Sandra Reese, Administrator (Total facility includes 25 beds in nursing home–type unit) **A**9 10 **F**7 8 11 15 17 19 22 26 28 32 33 35 37 40 42 44 49 64 65 70 71 73	16	10	43	720	29	6150	42	7912	3602	99

ROSEBURG—Douglas County

✠ DOUGLAS COMMUNITY MEDICAL CENTER, (Formerly Columbia Douglas Medical Center), 738 West Harvard Avenue, Zip 97470–2996; tel. 541/440–2800; Ronald E. Yates, Chief Executive Officer (Nonreporting) **A**1 2 9 10 **S** Columbia/HCA Healthcare Corporation, Nashville, TN **N** Health Future, Inc., Medford, OR	33	10	88	—	—	—	—	—	—	—
✠ MERCY MEDICAL CENTER, 2700 Stewart Parkway, Zip 97470–1297; tel. 541/673–0611; Victor J. Fresolone, FACHE, President and Chief Executive Officer **A**1 2 9 10 **F**1 6 7 8 10 12 14 15 16 17 19 21 22 25 26 27 29 30 31 32 33 34 35 37 40 41 42 44 45 49 51 52 53 56 57 59 60 62 65 67 70 71 73 74 **P**3 7 **S** Catholic Health Initiatives, Denver, CO **N** Health Future, Inc., Medford, OR	21	10	95	7309	65	116797	802	43806	17325	625
✠ VETERANS AFFAIRS ROSEBURG HEALTHCARE SYSTEM, (Formerly Veterans Affairs Medical Center), 913 N.W. Garden Valley Boulevard, Zip 97470–6513; tel. 541/440–1000; Alan S. Perry, Director (Total facility includes 90 beds in nursing home–type unit) (Nonreporting) **A**1 **S** Department of Veterans Affairs, Washington, DC	45	10	229	—	—	—	—	—	—	—

SALEM—Marion County

□ OREGON STATE HOSPITAL, 2600 Center Street N.E., Zip 97310–0530; tel. 503/945–2870; Stanley F. Mazur–Hart, Ph.D., Superintendent (Nonreporting) **A**1 3 5 10	12	22	546	—	—	—	—	—	—	—
PSYCHIATRIC MEDICINE CENTER See Salem Hospital										
REGIONAL REHABILITATION CENTER See Salem Hospital										
✠ SALEM HOSPITAL, (Includes Psychiatric Medicine Center, 1127 Oak Street S.E., Zip 97301; Regional Rehabilitation Center, 2561 Center Street N.E., Zip 97301; tel. 503/370–5986), 665 Winter Street S.E., Zip 97301–3959, Mailing Address: Box 14001, Zip 97309–5014; tel. 503/370–5200; Dennis Noonan, President (Total facility includes 69 beds in nursing home–type unit) (Nonreporting) **A**1 2 9 10	23	10	429	—	—	—	—	—	—	—

SEASIDE—Clatsop County

✠ PROVIDENCE SEASIDE HOSPITAL, 725 South Wahanna Road, Zip 97138–7735; tel. 503/717–7000; Ronald Swanson, Chief Executive North Coast Service Area (Nonreporting) **A**1 10 **S** Sisters of Providence Health System, Seattle, WA **N** Oregon Health System in Collaboration, Lake Oswego, OR; Providence Health System in Oregon, Portland, OR	21	10	26	—	—	—	—	—	—	—

SILVERTON—Marion County

★ SILVERTON HOSPITAL, 342 Fairview Street, Zip 97381; tel. 503/873–1500; William E. Winter, Administrative Director **A**9 10 **F**7 8 11 17 19 22 25 27 28 29 30 34 37 40 41 44 45 46 64 67 70 71 73 **N** Health Future, Inc., Medford, OR	23	10	38	2433	21	37377	752	14146	6429	199

SPRINGFIELD—Lane County

✠ MCKENZIE–WILLAMETTE HOSPITAL, 1460 G. Street, Zip 97477–4197; tel. 541/726–4400; Roy J. Orr, President and Chief Executive Officer **A**1 9 10 **F**1 7 14 15 16 19 21 22 23 26 28 29 30 32 33 34 39 40 41 44 45 49 67 70 71 72 73 74 **P**1 5	23	10	105	7528	56	98805	922	48914	23004	609

STAYTON—Marion County

✠ SANTIAM MEMORIAL HOSPITAL, 1401 North 10th Avenue, Zip 97383; tel. 503/769–2175; Terry L. Fletchall, Administrator (Nonreporting) **A**1 9 10	23	10	40	—	—	—	—	—	—	—

THE DALLES—Wasco County

★ MID–COLUMBIA MEDICAL CENTER, 1700 East 19th Street, Zip 97058–3316; tel. 541/296–1111; Mark D. Scott, President **A**9 10 **F**6 7 8 10 13 14 15 16 17 19 22 23 24 27 28 30 31 32 33 35 37 39 40 41 42 44 45 65 67 70 71 72 73 74 **P**5 8 **N** Health Future, Inc., Medford, OR	23	10	49	2402	23	41758	252	24829	10933	431

TILLAMOOK—Tillamook County

✠ TILLAMOOK COUNTY GENERAL HOSPITAL, 1000 Third Street, Zip 97141–3430; tel. 503/842–4444; Wendell Hesseltine, President **A**1 9 10 **F**11 14 15 16 17 19 22 27 28 30 32 33 35 37 40 44 65 67 71 **S** Adventist Health, Roseville, CA	21	10	30	1630	2	32645	143	—	7855	205

TUALATIN—Clackamas County

✠ LEGACY MERIDIAN PARK HOSPITAL, 19300 S.W. 65th Avenue, Zip 97062–9741; tel. 503/692–1212; Jeff Cushing, Vice President and Site Administrator **A**1 2 9 10 **F**1 2 3 4 7 8 9 10 11 12 14 16 17 19 21 22 23 24 26 27 29 30 31 32 33 34 35 37 38 39 40 41 42 43 44 45 46 47 48 49 52 53 54 55 56 57 58 59 61 62 63 64 65 67 70 71 73 74 **S** Legacy Health System, Portland, OR **N** Oregon Health System in Collaboration, Lake Oswego, OR; Legacy Health System, Portland, OR	23	10	116	7499	63	57451	1308	46501	19493	525

PENNSYLVANIA

Resident population 12,019 (in thousands)
Resident population in metro areas 84.7%
Birth rate per 1,000 population 13.0
65 years and over 15.9%
Percent of persons without health insurance 9.5%

Hospital, Address, Telephone, Administrator, Approval, Facility, and Physician Codes, Health Care System, Network	Classi-fication Codes		Utilization Data					Expense (thousands) of dollars		
★ American Hospital Association (AHA) membership □ Joint Commission on Accreditation of Healthcare Organizations (JCAHO) accreditation + American Osteopathic Healthcare Association (AOHA) membership ○ American Osteopathic Association (AOA) accreditation △ Commission on Accreditation of Rehabilitation Facilities (CARF) accreditation Control codes 61, 63, 64, 71, 72 and 73 indicate hospitals listed by AOHA, but not registered by AHA. For definition of numerical codes, see page A4	Control	Service	Staffed Beds	Admissions	Census	Outpatient Visits	Births	Total	Payroll	Personnel

ABINGTON—Montgomery County

☒ ABINGTON MEMORIAL HOSPITAL, 1200 York Road, Zip 19001–3720; tel. 215/576–2000; Felix M. Pilla, President **A**1 2 3 5 6 9 10 **F**1 7 8 10 11 13 14 15 16 17 20 22 24 25 26 27 30 31 32 33 34 36 37 38 39 40 41 42 43 44 46 47 48 49 51 53 56 57 58 59 60 61 63 65 66 67 69 70 71 73 74 — 23 10 421 21288 313 326196 3289 237340 112086 2960

ALIQUIPPA—Beaver County

□ UPMC BEAVER VALLEY, 2500 Hospital Drive, Zip 15001–2123; tel. 724/857–1212; Thomas P. Timcho, President (Total facility includes 16 beds in nursing home–type unit) **A**1 9 10 **F**1 2 3 4 5 6 7 8 10 11 12 13 14 15 16 17 18 19 20 21 22 23 24 25 26 27 28 29 30 31 32 33 34 35 36 37 38 39 40 41 42 43 44 45 46 47 48 49 50 51 52 53 54 55 56 57 58 59 60 61 62 63 64 65 66 67 68 69 70 71 72 73 74 **P**1 5 6 7 **S** UPMC Health System, Pittsburgh, PA — 23 10 148 4955 87 18945 — 37821 18658 510

ALLENTOWN—Lehigh County

ALLENTOWN OSTEOPATHIC MEDICAL CENTER See St. Luke's Hospital, Bethlehem

□ ALLENTOWN STATE HOSPITAL, 1600 Hanover Avenue, Zip 18103–2408; tel. 610/740–3200; David W. Jay, Superintendent (Nonreporting) **A**1 9 10 — 12 22 415 — — — — — — —

□ △ GOOD SHEPHERD REHABILITATION HOSPITAL, 543 St. John Street, Zip 18103–3231; tel. 610/776–3120; Sara Gammon, President and Chief Executive Officer **A**1 7 9 10 **F**2 4 10 12 14 15 16 17 19 21 22 23 34 35 45 46 48 49 50 54 65 67 71 73 **P**6 — 23 46 75 1712 70 66924 — 28154 22511 527

☒ LEHIGH VALLEY HOSPITAL, Cedar Crest Boulevard and I–78, Zip 18103, Mailing Address: P.O. Box 689, Zip 18105–1556; tel. 610/402–8000; Elliot J. Sussman, M.D., President and Chief Executive Officer (Total facility includes 52 beds in nursing home–type unit) **A**1 2 3 5 8 9 10 12 **F**3 4 5 6 7 8 9 10 11 12 13 14 15 16 17 18 19 20 21 22 23 24 26 28 29 30 31 32 33 34 35 36 37 38 39 40 41 42 43 44 45 46 49 51 52 53 54 55 56 57 58 59 60 61 63 64 65 66 67 68 69 70 71 73 74 **P**6 8 — 23 10 659 29542 489 387179 3321 319600 138392 3602

☒ SACRED HEART HOSPITAL, 421 Chew Street, Zip 18102–3490; tel. 610/776–4500; Joseph M. Cimerola, FACHE, President and Chief Executive Officer (Total facility includes 22 beds in nursing home–type unit) **A**1 2 3 5 9 10 **F**4 7 8 10 11 12 13 14 15 16 17 18 20 22 25 26 27 28 29 30 31 32 33 34 37 38 39 40 41 42 44 45 46 49 50 51 52 54 55 56 57 58 60 64 65 67 68 69 72 73 74 **P**3 8 **N** Partnership for Community Health–Lehigh Valley, Allentown, PA; Sacred Heart Health Care System, Allentown, PA — 23 10 277 7802 126 135540 539 67452 25425 1088

ST LUKE'S HOSPITAL–ALLENTOWN CAMPUS See St. Luke's Hospital, Bethlehem

ALTOONA—Blair County

ALTOONA CENTER, 1515 Fourth Street, Zip 16601–4595; tel. 814/946–6900; Barry C. Benford, Director (Nonreporting) — 12 62 138 — — — — — — —

☒ ○ ALTOONA HOSPITAL, 620 Howard Avenue, Zip 16601–4899; tel. 814/946–2011; James W. Barner, President and Chief Executive Officer **A**1 2 3 5 6 9 10 11 12 **F**2 3 4 7 8 10 11 12 14 15 16 18 19 22 23 25 26 28 30 32 33 35 37 40 41 42 43 44 46 49 52 53 54 55 56 57 58 59 60 65 71 73 74 **P**1 — 23 10 199 12621 183 302171 1292 120728 54137 1363

☒ BON SECOURS–HOLY FAMILY REGIONAL HEALTH SYSTEM, 2500 Seventh Avenue, Zip 16602–2099; tel. 814/944–1681; David McConnell, Interim Chief Executive Officer (Total facility includes 15 beds in nursing home–type unit) **A**1 2 9 10 **F**7 8 14 15 16 17 19 21 22 27 28 30 31 32 33 35 37 40 41 44 45 46 48 49 52 54 57 58 59 60 64 65 66 67 71 73 74 **P**5 8 **S** Bon Secours Health System, Inc., Marriottsville, MD — 23 10 149 5383 100 101006 336 37707 16843 567

□ △ HEALTHSOUTH REHABILITATION HOSPITAL OF ALTOONA, 2005 Valley View Boulevard, Zip 16602–4598; tel. 814/944–3535; Michael A. Fenello, Administrator (Nonreporting) **A**1 7 9 10 **S** HEALTHSOUTH Corporation, Birmingham, AL — 33 46 70 — — — — — — —

☒ JAMES E. VAN ZANDT VETERANS AFFAIRS MEDICAL CENTER, 2907 Pleasant Valley Boulevard, Zip 16602–4377; tel. 814/943–8164; Gerald L. Williams, Director and Chief Executive Officer (Total facility includes 40 beds in nursing home–type unit) **A**1 **F**3 8 12 14 15 16 17 19 20 22 26 27 28 29 30 31 32 33 34 37 39 44 45 46 49 51 54 58 64 65 67 71 73 74 **P**6 **S** Department of Veterans Affairs, Washington, DC — 45 10 78 1513 39 65708 — 27791 14693 360

AMBLER—Montgomery County

□ HORSHAM CLINIC, 722 East Butler Pike, Zip 19002–2398; tel. 215/643–7800; David A. Baron, D.O., Medical Director (Nonreporting) **A**1 5 9 10 **S** Universal Health Services, Inc., King of Prussia, PA — 33 22 138 — — — — — — —

ASHLAND—Schuylkill County

□ ASHLAND REGIONAL MEDICAL CENTER, 101 Broad Street, Zip 17921–2198; tel. 717/875–2000; Michael J. Callan, Sr., Chief Executive Officer (Total facility includes 20 beds in nursing home–type unit) (Nonreporting) **A**1 9 10 — 23 10 97 — — — — — — —

Hospital, Address, Telephone, Administrator, Approval, Facility, and Physician Codes, Health Care System, Network	Classi-fication Codes		Utilization Data					Expense (thousands) of dollars		
★ American Hospital Association (AHA) membership □ Joint Commission on Accreditation of Healthcare Organizations (JCAHO) accreditation + American Osteopathic Healthcare Association (AOHA) membership ○ American Osteopathic Association (AOA) accreditation △ Commission on Accreditation of Rehabilitation Facilities (CARF) accreditation Control codes 61, 63, 64, 71, 72 and 73 indicate hospitals listed by AOHA, but not registered by AHA. For definition of numerical codes, see page A4	Control	Service	Staffed Beds	Admissions	Census	Outpatient Visits	Births	Total	Payroll	Personnel

BALA CYNWYD—Montgomery County

☒ MERCY HEALTH SYSTEM OF SOUTHEASTERN PENNSYLVANIA, (Includes Mercy Fitzgerald Hospital, 1500 South Lansdowne Avenue, Darby, Zip 19023; tel. 610/237-4020; Mercy Hospital of Philadelphia, 5301 Cedar Avenue, Philadelphia, Zip 19143; tel. 215/748-9000), One Bala Plaza, Suite 402, Zip 19004-1401; tel. 610/660-7440; Plato A. Marinakos, President and Chief Executive Officer **A**1 2 3 5 8 9 10 **F**2 4 7 8 10 11 12 13 14 15 16 17 18 19 22 23 25 28 29 30 31 32 33 34 35 36 37 38 39 40 41 42 44 46 48 49 52 54 55 56 57 58 60 64 65 67 71 73 74 **P**1 2 4 5 6 7 8 **S** Catholic Health East, Radnor, PA **N** Jefferson Health System, Radnor, PA | 21 | 10 | 504 | 22282 | 361 | 84533 | 1658 | 191657 | 93573 | — |

BEAVER—Beaver County

☒ THE MEDICAL CENTER, BEAVER, 1000 Dutch Ridge Road, Zip 15009-9727; tel. 724/728-7000; James C. Cooper, Chief Operating Officer (Total facility includes 34 beds in nursing home–type unit) **A**1 2 3 5 9 10 **F**4 5 7 8 10 15 16 17 19 20 21 22 23 25 26 28 29 30 31 32 33 34 35 37 39 40 41 42 43 44 45 46 49 51 52 54 56 57 59 60 61 63 64 65 67 71 73 74 **P**1 5 6 8 | 23 | 10 | 380 | 16434 | 264 | 335992 | 1476 | 141098 | 65323 | 1951 |

BENSALEM—Bucks County

LIVENGRIN FOUNDATION, 4833 Hulmeville Road, Zip 19020-3099; tel. 215/638-5200; Richard M. Pine, President and Chief Executive Officer (Nonreporting) | 23 | 82 | 76 | — | — | — | — | — | — | — |

BERWICK—Columbia County

☒ BERWICK HOSPITAL CENTER, 701 East 16th Street, Zip 18603-2316; tel. 717/759-5000; Thomas R. Sphatt, President and Chief Executive Officer (Total facility includes 240 beds in nursing home–type unit) **A**1 9 10 **F**2 3 7 8 12 14 15 16 17 19 21 22 25 26 27 28 30 32 33 34 35 37 40 41 42 44 46 49 58 63 64 65 66 67 71 73 **S** Quorum Health Group/Quorum Health Resources, Inc., Brentwood, TN | 23 | 10 | 340 | 3766 | 273 | 81903 | 276 | 32957 | 14670 | 657 |

BETHLEHEM—Northampton County

☒ MUHLENBERG HOSPITAL CENTER, 2545 Schoenersville Road, Zip 18017-7384; tel. 610/861-2200; William R. Mason, President **A**1 9 10 **F**4 7 8 9 10 11 12 14 15 16 17 19 20 21 22 25 27 28 29 30 32 33 34 35 37 38 40 41 42 43 44 45 46 47 48 49 52 56 57 58 59 60 63 64 65 70 71 73 74 **P**7 8 | 23 | 10 | 148 | 6098 | 105 | 113502 | — | 49451 | 21072 | 659 |

□ + ○ △ ST. LUKE'S HOSPITAL, (Includes St Luke's Hospital–Allentown Campus, 1736 Hamilton Street, Allentown, Zip 18104-5656; tel. 610/770-8300; John M. Sherwood, FACHE, President), 801 Ostrum Street, Zip 18015-1014; tel. 610/954-4000; Richard A. Anderson, President and Chief Executive Officer (Total facility includes 18 beds in nursing home–type unit) **A**1 2 3 5 6 7 8 9 10 11 12 13 **F**3 4 7 8 10 11 12 13 14 15 16 17 19 21 22 25 26 28 29 30 31 32 33 34 35 37 38 39 40 41 42 43 44 45 49 51 52 54 58 59 60 61 63 64 65 67 71 72 73 74 **P**8 | 23 | 10 | 560 | 23375 | 344 | 378457 | 2631 | 202314 | 93578 | 2291 |

BLOOMSBURG—Columbia County

☒ BLOOMSBURG HOSPITAL, 549 East Fair Street, Zip 17815-0340; tel. 717/387-2100; Robert J. Spinelli, Administrator and Chief Executive Officer **A**1 9 10 **F**2 3 7 8 14 15 17 19 21 22 27 28 29 30 32 33 34 35 37 40 41 42 44 46 52 54 55 56 58 59 65 67 71 73 | 23 | 10 | 117 | 3741 | 48 | 78575 | 565 | 24241 | 10101 | 370 |

BRADDOCK—Allegheny County

□ UPMC BRADDOCK, 400 Holland Avenue, Zip 15104-1599; tel. 412/636-5000; Richard Wilson Benfer, President (Nonreporting) **A**1 9 10 **S** UPMC Health System, Pittsburgh, PA | 23 | 10 | 227 | — | — | — | — | — | — | — |

BRADFORD—McKean County

☒ BRADFORD REGIONAL MEDICAL CENTER, 116 Interstate Parkway, Zip 16701-0218; tel. 814/368-4143; George E. Leonhardt, President and Chief Executive Officer (Total facility includes 95 beds in nursing home–type unit) **A**1 9 10 **F**7 8 14 15 16 17 19 21 22 23 24 25 26 28 30 31 32 33 34 35 37 39 40 41 42 44 45 46 49 51 52 53 54 55 56 57 58 60 63 64 65 66 67 71 73 **P**8 **N** Great Lakes Health Network, Erie, PA | 23 | 10 | 206 | 4520 | 158 | 138165 | 373 | 41720 | 18495 | 583 |

BRIDGEVILLE—Allegheny County

□ MAYVIEW STATE HOSPITAL, 1601 Mayview Road, Zip 15017-1547; tel. 412/257-6500; Shirley J. Dumpman, Superintendent (Total facility includes 93 beds in nursing home–type unit) **A**1 5 9 10 **F**14 20 52 57 65 **P**6 | 12 | 22 | 602 | 570 | 523 | 0 | 0 | 62703 | 38412 | 948 |

BRISTOL—Bucks County

☒ LOWER BUCKS HOSPITAL, 501 Bath Road, Zip 19007-3101; tel. 215/785-9200; Nathan Bosk, FACHE, Executive Director **A**1 3 9 10 **F**4 7 8 10 11 12 14 15 16 17 18 19 20 21 22 24 25 28 29 30 32 34 35 37 38 40 41 42 43 44 45 46 49 51 52 54 55 56 57 58 63 65 66 67 68 71 73 74 **P**1 5 **N** Temple University Health Network, Philadelphia, PA | 23 | 10 | 163 | 8877 | 118 | 149479 | 1383 | 66206 | 27229 | 873 |

BROOKVILLE—Jefferson County

☒ BROOKVILLE HOSPITAL, 100 Hospital Road, Zip 15825-1324; tel. 814/849-2312; Warren J. Bassett, FACHE, President **A**1 9 10 **F**7 8 11 14 15 16 17 19 20 21 22 28 30 32 39 40 41 44 45 49 63 65 66 69 71 **P**5 | 23 | 10 | 63 | 2137 | 24 | 87335 | 132 | 21216 | 8710 | 336 |

BROWNSVILLE—Fayette County

☒ BROWNSVILLE GENERAL HOSPITAL, 125 Simpson Road, Zip 15417-9699; tel. 724/785-7200; Richard D. Constantine, Chief Executive Officer (Total facility includes 21 beds in nursing home–type unit) **A**1 9 10 **F**8 15 16 17 19 21 22 23 26 28 29 30 31 33 35 37 39 41 44 45 46 49 52 54 57 60 64 65 67 71 73 **S** Quorum Health Group/Quorum Health Resources, Inc., Brentwood, TN | 23 | 10 | 115 | 3338 | 73 | 26328 | — | 20595 | 9182 | 280 |

Hospital, Address, Telephone, Administrator, Approval, Facility, and Physician Codes, Health Care System, Network	Classi-fication Codes		Utilization Data					Expense (thousands) of dollars		
★ American Hospital Association (AHA) membership □ Joint Commission on Accreditation of Healthcare Organizations (JCAHO) accreditation + American Osteopathic Healthcare Association (AOHA) membership ○ American Osteopathic Association (AOA) accreditation △ Commission on Accreditation of Rehabilitation Facilities (CARF) accreditation Control codes 61, 63, 64, 71, 72 and 73 indicate hospitals listed by AOHA, but not registered by AHA. For definition of numerical codes, see page A4	Control	Service	Staffed Beds	Admissions	Census	Outpatient Visits	Births	Total	Payroll	Personnel

BRYN MAWR—Montgomery County

BRYN MAWR COLLEGE INFIRMARY, Bryn Mawr College Campus, Zip 19010; tel. 610/526–7360; Kay Kerr, M.D., Medical Director (Nonreporting)	23	11	7	—	—	—	—	—	—	—
✠ BRYN MAWR HOSPITAL, 130 South Bryn Mawr Avenue, Zip 19010–3160; tel. 610/526–3000; Kenneth Hanover, President and Chief Executive Officer (Total facility includes 17 beds in nursing home–type unit) **A**1 2 3 5 9 10 **F**4 5 7 8 10 11 12 15 16 17 19 20 21 22 27 28 29 30 31 32 33 35 36 37 38 39 40 41 42 43 44 45 48 49 51 52 53 54 55 56 57 58 59 60 61 63 64 65 67 68 69 71 73 74 **P**1 3 5 7 8 **S** Jefferson Health System, Wayne, PA **N** Jefferson Health System, Radnor, PA	23	10	275	14703	204	121381	1994	138853	49594	1497

BUTLER—Butler County

✠ BUTLER HEALTH SYSTEM, 911 East Brady Street, Zip 16001–4646; tel. 724/284–4408; Joseph A. Stewart, Chief Executive Officer (Total facility includes 19 beds in nursing home–type unit) **A**1 9 10 **F**2 3 4 7 8 10 11 12 13 14 15 16 19 21 22 23 24 27 28 31 32 33 35 37 40 44 46 49 52 54 56 57 63 64 65 67 71 **P**4 5	23	10	251	9687	146	193961	993	68723	30430	968
✠ VETERANS AFFAIRS MEDICAL CENTER, (EXTENDED CARE PRIMARY MED CARE), 325 New Castle Road, Zip 16001–2480; tel. 724/287–4781; Michael E. Moreland, Director (Total facility includes 106 beds in nursing home–type unit) **A**1 9 **F**1 3 4 8 10 11 14 15 16 17 19 20 21 22 23 24 26 27 28 30 32 34 35 37 39 41 42 43 44 45 46 49 51 52 54 56 57 58 60 64 65 67 69 71 73 74 **P**6 **S** Department of Veterans Affairs, Washington, DC	45	49	200	1517	167	76211	—	37499	21322	481

CAMP HILL—Cumberland County

✠ HOLY SPIRIT HOSPITAL, 503 North 21st Street, Zip 17011–2288; tel. 717/763–2100; Sister Romaine Niemeyer, President **A**1 5 9 10 **F**2 3 4 7 8 10 12 15 16 17 18 19 21 22 27 28 29 30 31 32 33 34 35 37 38 39 40 41 42 44 46 51 52 53 54 55 56 57 58 59 60 63 65 67 68 69 71 73 74 **P**8	21	10	317	12278	186	131231	543	85637	44722	1490
STATE CORRECTIONAL INSTITUTION AT CAMP HILL, 2500 Lisbon Road, Zip 17011, Mailing Address: P.O. Box 200, Zip 17011–0200; tel. 717/737–4531; Kathy Montag, Administrator Health Care (Nonreporting)	12	49	34	—	—	—	—	—	—	—

CANONSBURG—Washington County

✠ ALLEGHENY UNIVERSITY HOSPITALS, CANONSBURG, (Formerly Canonsburg General Hospital), 100 Medical Boulevard, Zip 15317–9762; tel. 724/745–6100; Barbara A. Bensaia, Chief Executive Officer (Total facility includes 28 beds in nursing home–type unit) **A**1 9 10 **F**3 8 10 12 16 17 19 21 22 23 28 30 32 33 34 35 37 39 41 42 44 49 63 64 65 67 71 73 **P**1 **S** Allegheny Health, Education and Research Foundation, Pittsburgh, PA	23	10	120	3771	61	58716	—	27249	11399	328

CARBONDALE—Lackawanna County

✠ MARIAN COMMUNITY HOSPITAL, 100 Lincoln Avenue, Zip 18407–2170; tel. 717/281–1000; Sister Jean Coughlin, President and Chief Executive Officer **A**1 9 10 **F**8 12 14 15 16 17 19 21 22 26 28 29 30 31 32 34 35 37 41 42 44 45 49 52 56 57 65 67 69 71 73 **P**8	21	10	98	3848	61	52428	—	25543	10468	407

CARLISLE—Cumberland County

✠ CARLISLE HOSPITAL, 246 Parker Street, Zip 17013–3618; tel. 717/249–1212; Michael J. Halstead, President and Chief Executive Officer **A**1 9 10 **F**7 8 12 14 15 16 17 18 19 21 22 25 26 28 29 30 32 33 34 35 37 39 40 42 44 45 46 49 52 53 56 57 60 61 62 63 65 67 68 70 71 72 73 74 **P**7 8 **S** Quorum Health Group/Quorum Health Resources, Inc., Brentwood, TN	23	10	166	7121	95	147790	685	52142	24035	837

CENTRE HALL—Centre County

□ MEADOWS PSYCHIATRIC CENTER, Mailing Address: Rural Delivery 1, Box 259, Zip 16828–9798; tel. 814/364–2161; Joseph Barszczewski, Chief Executive Officer (Nonreporting) **A**1 9 10 **S** Universal Health Services, Inc., King of Prussia, PA	33	22	101	—	—	—	—	—	—	—

CHAMBERSBURG—Franklin County

✠ △ CHAMBERSBURG HOSPITAL, 112 North Seventh Street, Zip 17201–6005, Mailing Address: P.O. Box 6005, Zip 17201–6005; tel. 717/267–3000; Norman B. Epstein, President (Total facility includes 18 beds in nursing home–type unit) **A**1 2 7 9 10 **F**1 2 3 7 8 9 10 11 12 14 15 16 17 18 19 20 21 22 23 24 26 27 28 29 30 31 32 33 34 35 36 37 38 39 40 41 42 44 45 46 47 48 49 51 52 54 55 56 57 58 59 60 62 63 64 65 66 67 68 69 70 71 73 74 **P**6 8	23	10	217	10060	141	164903	1101	75282	37278	973

CHESTER—Delaware County

KEYSTONE CENTER, 2001 Providence Avenue, Zip 19013–5504; tel. 610/876–9000; Jimmy Patton, Chief Executive Officer and Managing Director (Nonreporting) **S** Universal Health Services, Inc., King of Prussia, PA	33	82	76	—	—	—	—	—	—	—

CLARION—Clarion County

★ + ○ CLARION HOSPITAL, One Hospital Drive, Zip 16214–8599; tel. 814/226–9500; John J. Shepard, President and Chief Executive Officer **A**9 10 11 12 13 **F**7 8 19 20 21 22 33 34 40 41 42 44 64 71 73 **S** Quorum Health Group/Quorum Health Resources, Inc., Brentwood, TN	23	10	86	3546	34	85189	372	21873	9212	359
□ CLARION PSYCHIATRIC CENTER, 2 Hospital Drive, Zip 16214, Mailing Address: Rural Delivery 3, Box 188, Zip 16214; tel. 814/226–9545; Michael R. Keefer, CHE, Administrator and Chief Executive Officer (Nonreporting) **A**1 9 10 **S** Universal Health Services, Inc., King of Prussia, PA	33	22	52	—	—	—	—	—	—	—

CLARKS SUMMIT—Lackawanna County

□ CLARKS SUMMIT STATE HOSPITAL, 1451 Hillside Drive, Zip 18411–9505; tel. 717/586–2011; Thomas P. Comerford, Jr., Superintendent (Total facility includes 167 beds in nursing home–type unit) (Nonreporting) **A**1 9 10	12	22	512	—	—	—	—	—	—	—

Hospital, Address, Telephone, Administrator, Approval, Facility, and Physician Codes, Health Care System, Network	Classi-fication Codes		Utilization Data					Expense (thousands) of dollars		
	Control	Service	Staffed Beds	Admissions	Census	Outpatient Visits	Births	Total	Payroll	Personnel

★ American Hospital Association (AHA) membership
□ Joint Commission on Accreditation of Healthcare Organizations (JCAHO) accreditation
+ American Osteopathic Healthcare Association (AOHA) membership
○ American Osteopathic Association (AOA) accreditation
△ Commission on Accreditation of Rehabilitation Facilities (CARF) accreditation
Control codes 61, 63, 64, 71, 72 and 73 indicate hospitals listed by AOHA, but not registered by AHA. For definition of numerical codes, see page A4

CLEARFIELD—Clearfield County

□ CLEARFIELD HOSPITAL, 809 Turnpike Avenue, Zip 16830–1232, Mailing Address: P.O. Box 992, Zip 16830–0992; tel. 814/765–5341; Stephen A. Wolfe, Chief Executive Officer **A**1 9 10 **F**7 8 10 12 14 15 16 17 19 21 22 23 25 28 29 30 32 33 34 35 37 39 40 41 42 44 45 46 49 51 60 63 64 65 66 67 71 73	23	10	92	4489	58	101317	503	43724	19590	596

COAL TOWNSHIP—Northumberland County

✚ SHAMOKIN AREA COMMUNITY HOSPITAL, 4200 Hospital Road, Zip 17866–9697; tel. 717/644–4200; Harold C. Warman, Jr., President and Chief Executive Officer (Total facility includes 15 beds in nursing home–type unit) **A**1 9 10 **F**8 12 14 15 16 17 19 21 22 26 27 28 30 31 33 35 37 41 44 46 49 54 57 59 63 64 65 66 67 71 73 **P**1	23	10	51	2099	31	68163	0	13109	5095	166

COALDALE—Schuylkill County

✚ MINER'S MEMORIAL MEDICAL CENTER, 360 West Ruddle Street, Zip 18218–0067, Mailing Address: P.O. Box 67, Zip 18218–0067; tel. 717/645–2131; William Crossin, Vice President Operations (Total facility includes 48 beds in nursing home–type unit) **A**1 9 10 **F**8 11 14 15 16 19 21 22 26 30 32 34 35 42 44 46 49 56 59 64 65 71 73	23	10	110	2265	76	35385	—	30363	11114	331

COATESVILLE—Chester County

✚ BRANDYWINE HOSPITAL, 201 Reeceville Road, Zip 19320–1536; tel. 610/383–8000; James H. Thornton, Jr., President and Chief Executive Officer (Total facility includes 20 beds in nursing home–type unit) **A**1 2 6 9 10 **F**7 8 10 12 13 14 15 16 17 18 19 20 21 24 25 26 27 28 29 30 31 32 33 34 35 36 37 39 40 41 42 44 45 46 49 50 51 52 56 57 59 60 61 63 64 65 66 67 68 70 71 72 73 74 **P**8	23	10	183	7504	104	80548	688	65773	28152	1064
✚ VETERANS AFFAIRS MEDICAL CENTER, 1400 Black Horse Hill Road, Zip 19320–2097; tel. 610/384–7711; Gary W. Devansky, Chief Executive Officer (Total facility includes 200 beds in nursing home–type unit) (Nonreporting) **A**1 9 **S** Department of Veterans Affairs, Washington, DC	45	22	710							

COLUMBIA—Lancaster County

✚ LANCASTER GENERAL HOSPITAL–SUSQUEHANNA DIVISION, 306 North Seventh Street, Zip 17512–2137, Mailing Address: P.O. Box 926, Zip 17512–0926; tel. 717/684–2841; Scott A. Berlucchi, President and Chief Executive Officer **A**1 9 10 **F**2 3 8 14 15 16 17 19 22 30 34 39 41 44 45 46 49 51 65 66 67 71 73 74 **P**5	23	10	79	1186	21	—	11	7779	3706	156

CONNELLSVILLE—Fayette County

✚ HIGHLANDS HOSPITAL, 401 East Murphy Avenue, Zip 15425–2700; tel. 724/628–1500; Michael J. Evans, Chief Executive Officer **A**1 9 10 **F**8 11 12 15 16 17 19 21 22 26 28 29 30 31 32 33 35 37 39 41 42 44 46 49 52 53 54 55 56 57 59 60 64 65 67 69 71 73 **P**8	23	10	92	3058	54	51893	—	19087	8472	265

CORRY—Erie County

✚ CORRY MEMORIAL HOSPITAL, 612 West Smith Street, Zip 16407–1152; tel. 814/664–4641; Joseph T. Hodges, President **A**1 9 10 **F**8 14 15 16 19 21 22 27 32 34 35 37 40 41 44 49 52 57 71 73 **P**7 **S** Quorum Health Group/Quorum Health Resources, Inc., Brentwood, TN **N** Great Lakes Health Network, Erie, PA	23	10	59	1787	22	37649	287	12197	4847	208

COUDERSPORT—Potter County

✚ CHARLES COLE MEMORIAL HOSPITAL, U.S. Route 6E, RR 1, Box 205, Zip 16915–9762; tel. 814/274–9300; David B. Acker, Chief Executive Officer (Total facility includes 55 beds in nursing home–type unit) **A**1 9 10 **F**3 8 11 12 14 15 16 17 19 21 22 24 25 28 30 32 33 34 35 40 41 44 46 49 50 51 53 54 55 56 57 58 63 64 65 66 71 73 74	23	10	125	2469	83	86023	283	28424	11063	439

DANVILLE—Montour County

□ DANVILLE STATE HOSPITAL, Route 11, Zip 17821–0700, Mailing Address: P.O. Box 700, Zip 17821–0700; tel. 717/271–4500; Paul J. Gritman, Superintendent (Total facility includes 60 beds in nursing home–type unit) **A**1 10 **F**1 2 3 4 5 6 7 8 9 10 11 12 13 17 18 19 20 21 22 23 24 25 26 27 28 29 30 31 32 33 34 35 36 37 38 39 40 41 42 43 44 45 46 47 48 49 50 51 52 53 54 55 56 57 58 59 60 61 62 63 64 65 66 67 68 69 70 71 72 73 74 **P**6	12	22	302	131	284	—	—	30280	18783	470
✚ ○ GEISINGER MEDICAL CENTER, 100 North Academy Avenue, Zip 17822–0150; tel. 717/271–6211; Nancy Rizzo, Senior Vice President, Operations (Nonreporting) **A**1 2 3 5 6 8 9 10 11 12 13 **S** Penn State Geisinger Health System, Harrisburg, PA **N** Geisinger Health System, Danville, PA	23	10	548	—	—	—	—	—	—	—

DEVON—Chester County

DEVEREUX FOUNDATION–FRENCH CENTER, 123 Old Lancaster Road, Zip 19333–1439, Mailing Address: P.O. Box 400, Zip 19333–0400; tel. 610/964–3215; Richard Warden, Executive Director (Total facility includes 84 beds in nursing home–type unit) (Nonreporting)	23	59	110							

DOWNINGTOWN—Chester County

★ ST. JOHN VIANNEY HOSPITAL, 151 Woodbine Road, Zip 19335–3057; tel. 610/269–2600; Louis D. Horvath, Administrator (Nonreporting) **A**9	21	22	54	—	—	—	—	—	—	—

DOYLESTOWN—Bucks County

✚ △ DOYLESTOWN HOSPITAL, 595 West State Street, Zip 18901–2597; tel. 215/345–2200; Richard A. Reif, President and Chief Executive Officer (Total facility includes 236 beds in nursing home–type unit) **A**1 7 9 10 **F**3 4 6 7 8 10 12 13 14 15 16 17 18 19 20 21 22 23 25 26 27 28 29 30 31 32 33 34 35 37 39 40 41 42 44 45 46 48 49 51 52 54 55 56 57 59 61 62 64 65 67 68 71 73 74 **P**5 6 8	23	10	432	9815	365	216927	1042	96633	45640	1569

Hospital, Address, Telephone, Administrator, Approval, Facility, and Physician Codes, Health Care System, Network	Classi-fication Codes		Utilization Data					Expense (thousands) of dollars		
	Control	Service	Staffed Beds	Admissions	Census	Outpatient Visits	Births	Total	Payroll	Personnel

★ American Hospital Association (AHA) membership
□ Joint Commission on Accreditation of Healthcare Organizations (JCAHO) accreditation
+ American Osteopathic Healthcare Association (AOHA) membership
○ American Osteopathic Association (AOA) accreditation
△ Commission on Accreditation of Rehabilitation Facilities (CARF) accreditation
Control codes 61, 63, 64, 71, 72 and 73 indicate hospitals listed by AOHA, but not registered by AHA. For definition of numerical codes, see page A4

□ FOUNDATIONS BEHAVIORAL HEALTH, 833 East Butler Avenue, Zip 18901–2298; tel. 215/345–0444; Ronald T. Bernstein, Chief Executive Officer (Nonreporting) **A**1 10	23	22	45	—	—	—	—	—	—	—

DREXEL HILL—Delaware County

⊠ ○ △ DELAWARE COUNTY MEMORIAL HOSPITAL, 501 North Lansdowne Avenue, Zip 19026–1114; tel. 610/284–8100; Joan K. Richards, President (Total facility includes 27 beds in nursing home–type unit) **A**1 2 5 7 9 10 11 12 **F**1 2 3 4 7 8 9 10 11 12 13 14 15 16 17 18 19 21 22 23 24 28 29 30 32 33 34 35 37 38 39 40 41 42 43 44 45 46 48 49 51 52 56 57 58 59 60 61 64 65 66 67 70 71 72 73 74 **S** Crozer–Keystone Health System, Springfield, PA **N** Crozer–Keystone Health System, Springfield, PA; Fox Chase Network, Rockledge, PA	23	10	231	10967	178	32183	1065	92943	34439	910

DU BOIS—Clearfield County

□ DUBOIS REGIONAL MEDICAL CENTER, 100 Hospital Avenue, Zip 15801–1499, Mailing Address: P.O. Box 447, Zip 15801–0447; tel. 814/371–2200; Raymond A. Graeca, President and Chief Executive Officer (Total facility includes 14 beds in nursing home–type unit) **A**1 2 9 10 **F**7 8 10 13 14 15 16 17 19 21 22 23 25 26 27 28 29 30 32 33 34 35 37 38 39 40 41 42 44 46 48 49 51 52 53 54 55 56 57 58 60 61 64 65 66 67 71 72 73 **P**6 8 **N** Community Benefits Strategy, DuBois, PA	23	10	203	7724	118	224679	620	66078	33229	975

EAGLEVILLE—Montgomery County

★ EAGLEVILLE HOSPITAL, 100 Eagleville Road, Zip 19408–0045, Mailing Address: P.O. Box 45, Zip 19408–0045; tel. 610/539–6000; Kendria Kurtz, Chief Executive Officer **A**9 10 **F**2 14 15 22 29 39 45 54 55 56 65 67 73 74 **P**6	23	82	126	2106	84	—	—	11562	6078	217

EAST STROUDSBURG—Monroe County

⊠ POCONO MEDICAL CENTER, 206 East Brown Street, Zip 18301–3006; tel. 717/421–4000; Marilyn R. Rettaliata, President and Chief Executive Officer (Total facility includes 73 beds in nursing home–type unit) **A**1 2 9 10 **F**7 8 11 13 15 19 21 22 25 30 31 37 39 40 41 42 44 45 46 49 52 56 60 64 65 67 71 73 74	23	10	215	9701	151	148948	909	67410	32447	818

EASTON—Northampton County

⊠ EASTON HOSPITAL, 250 South 21st Street, Zip 18042–3892; tel. 610/250–4000; Donna Mulholland, President and Chief Executive Officer **A**1 2 3 5 9 10 **F**4 7 8 10 12 15 16 17 19 20 21 22 28 29 30 31 32 33 34 35 36 37 38 39 40 41 42 43 44 45 46 48 49 54 56 59 60 63 65 67 71 73 74 **P**7 8	23	10	273	12972	226	222879	641	113797	53634	1641

ELKINS PARK—Montgomery County

⊠ ALLEGHENY UNIVERSITY HOSPITAL, ELKINS PARK, 60 East Township Line Road, Zip 19027–2220; tel. 215/663–6000; Margaret M. McGoldrick, President and Chief Executive Officer **A**1 3 5 9 10 **F**2 3 4 7 8 9 10 11 12 13 14 15 16 17 18 19 20 21 22 24 26 27 28 29 30 31 32 34 35 37 38 39 40 41 42 43 44 45 46 47 48 49 51 52 53 54 55 56 57 58 59 60 61 64 65 66 67 69 70 71 73 74 **P**6 7 **S** Allegheny Health, Education and Research Foundation, Pittsburgh, PA	23	10	151	7557	113	59630	1260	56824	22342	616

ELLWOOD CITY—Lawrence County

ELLWOOD CITY HOSPITAL, 724 Pershing Street, Zip 16117–1474; tel. 724/752–0081; Herbert S. Skuba, President (Total facility includes 23 beds in nursing home–type unit) (Nonreporting) **A**9 10	23	10	118	—	—	—	—	—	—	—

EPHRATA—Lancaster County

□ EPHRATA COMMUNITY HOSPITAL, 169 Martin Avenue, Zip 17522–1724, Mailing Address: P.O. Box 1002, Zip 17522–1002; tel. 717/733–0311; John M. Porter, Jr., President (Total facility includes 15 beds in nursing home–type unit) **A**1 9 10 **F**7 8 11 14 15 16 17 19 21 22 26 30 31 32 33 34 35 36 37 39 40 41 42 44 45 46 49 51 52 53 54 55 56 57 58 63 64 65 67 71 73 74 **P**6 8	23	10	124	5897	65	157943	556	41525	20608	724

ERIE—Erie County

⊠ HAMOT MEDICAL CENTER, 201 State Street, Zip 16550–0002; tel. 814/877–6000; John T. Malone, President and Chief Executive Officer (Total facility includes 35 beds in nursing home–type unit) **A**1 2 3 5 9 10 **F**2 3 4 6 7 8 10 11 12 13 14 15 16 17 18 19 21 22 23 24 26 27 28 29 30 31 32 33 34 35 36 37 38 39 40 41 42 43 44 45 46 49 50 51 52 53 54 55 56 57 58 59 60 61 62 63 64 65 66 67 68 70 71 72 73 74 **P**6 **N** Great Lakes Health Network, Erie, PA; Community Health Net, Erie, PA; Cleveland Health Network, Independence, OH	23	10	423	14984	223	107618	1462	134832	53380	2240
□ △ HEALTHSOUTH GREAT LAKES REHABILITATION HOSPITAL, 143 East Second Street, Zip 16507–1595; tel. 814/878–1200; William R. Fox, Chief Executive Officer (Nonreporting) **A**1 7 9 **S** HEALTHSOUTH Corporation, Birmingham, AL	33	46	108	—	—	—	—	—	—	—
□ △ HEALTHSOUTH LAKE ERIE INSTITUTE OF REHABILITATION, 137 West Second Street, Zip 16507–1403; tel. 814/453–5602; Louis M. Condrasky, Chief Operating Officer (Total facility includes 27 beds in nursing home–type unit) (Nonreporting) **A**1 7 9 10 **S** HEALTHSOUTH Corporation, Birmingham, AL	33	46	99	—	—	—	—	—	—	—
★ ○ METRO HEALTH CENTER, 252 West 11th Street, Zip 16501–1798; tel. 814/870–3400; Debra M. Dragovan, Chief Executive Officer **A**9 10 11 12 13 **F**7 8 14 15 16 19 21 22 30 34 35 37 40 41 44 46 63 65 71 73 **P**8 **S** Quorum Health Group/Quorum Health Resources, Inc., Brentwood, TN **N** Community Health Net, Erie, PA	23	10	112	2677	31	45255	196	19005	6850	244
+ ○ MILLCREEK COMMUNITY HOSPITAL, 5515 Peach Street, Zip 16509–2603; tel. 814/864–4031; Mary L. Eckert, President and Chief Executive Officer **A**9 10 11 12 13 **F**2 7 8 14 15 16 19 22 30 35 37 40 42 44 51 65 71 72 73 **N** Vantage Health Care Network, Inc., Meadville, PA	23	10	101	3521	39	49232	241	19298	7386	260

Hospital, Address, Telephone, Administrator, Approval, Facility, and Physician Codes, Health Care System, Network	Classi-fication Codes		Utilization Data					Expense (thousands) of dollars		
★ American Hospital Association (AHA) membership □ Joint Commission on Accreditation of Healthcare Organizations (JCAHO) accreditation + American Osteopathic Healthcare Association (AOHA) membership ○ American Osteopathic Association (AOA) accreditation △ Commission on Accreditation of Rehabilitation Facilities (CARF) accreditation Control codes 61, 63, 64, 71, 72 and 73 indicate hospitals listed by AOHA, but not registered by AHA. For definition of numerical codes, see page A4	Control	Service	Staffed Beds	Admissions	Census	Outpatient Visits	Births	Total	Payroll	Personnel

Hospital	Control	Service	Staffed Beds	Admissions	Census	Outpatient Visits	Births	Total	Payroll	Personnel
□ SAINT VINCENT HEALTH CENTER, 232 West 25th Street, Zip 16544–0001; tel. 814/452–5000; Sister Catherine Manning, President and Chief Executive Officer **A**1 3 5 6 9 10 **F**3 7 8 10 11 12 13 15 16 18 19 20 22 23 25 29 30 32 33 34 35 37 39 40 41 43 44 45 46 48 49 51 52 53 54 55 56 57 58 59 60 65 67 70 71 73 74 **P**6 **N** Vantage Health Care Network, Inc., Meadville, PA; Saint Vincent Health System, Erie, PA; Community Health Net, Erie, PA	23	10	453	15172	259	138274	1718	139581	55869	1842
✶ SHRINERS HOSPITALS FOR CHILDREN, ERIE, 1645 West 8th Street, Zip 16505–5007; tel. 814/875–8700; Richard W. Brzuz, Administrator **A**1 3 **F**5 15 28 34 41 46 48 49 65 71 73 **P**6 **S** Shriners Hospitals for Children, Tampa, FL	23	57	30	835	12	9364	—	—	—	117
✶ VETERANS AFFAIRS MEDICAL CENTER, 135 East 38th Street, Zip 16504–1559; tel. 814/868–6210; Stephen M. Lucas, Chief Executive Officer (Total facility includes 9 beds in nursing home–type unit) **A**1 **F**1 2 3 8 10 11 14 15 16 17 18 19 20 21 22 26 27 28 29 30 31 32 33 34 35 37 39 41 42 43 44 45 46 48 49 51 52 54 55 56 57 58 59 64 65 67 69 71 73 74 **P**6 **S** Department of Veterans Affairs, Washington, DC	45	10	74	1426	31	85674	0	41680	16082	409
EVERETT—Bedford County										
✶ UPMC BEDFORD MEMORIAL, (Formerly Memorial Hospital of Bedford County), 10455 Lincoln Highway, Zip 15537–4076; tel. 814/623–6161; James C. Vreeland, FACHE, President and Chief Executive Officer **A**1 9 10 **F**1 3 4 6 7 8 10 12 13 14 15 16 17 18 19 20 21 22 23 24 26 27 28 29 30 31 32 33 34 35 36 37 39 40 41 42 43 44 49 51 53 54 55 56 57 58 59 60 62 63 65 67 69 70 71 73 **P**8 **S** UPMC Health System, Pittsburgh, PA	23	10	59	1955	18	74053	252	18088	7925	277
FARRELL—Mercer County										
SHENANGO VALLEY CAMPUS See Horizon Hospital System, Greenville										
FORT WASHINGTON—Montgomery County										
□ NORTHWESTERN INSTITUTE, 450 Bethlehem Pike, Zip 19034–0209; tel. 215/641–5300; Joseph Roynan, Administrator (Nonreporting) **A**1 3 9 10	33	22	146	—	—	—	—	—	—	—
FRANKLIN—Venango County										
□ NORTHWEST MEDICAL CENTERS, (Includes Northwest Medical Center–Franklin Campus, 1 Spruce Street, Zip 16323; tel. 814/437–7000; Northwest Medical Center–Oil City Campus, 174 East Bissell Avenue, Oil City, Zip 16301–0568, Mailing Address: P.O. Box 1068, Zip 16301–0568; tel. 814/677–1711), 1 Spruce Street, Zip 16323–2544; tel. 814/437–7000; Neil E. Todhunter, Chief Executive Officer (Total facility includes 16 beds in nursing home–type unit) **A**1 2 9 10 **F**3 4 7 8 13 14 15 17 19 21 22 23 28 30 34 35 36 37 39 40 41 42 44 45 48 49 52 54 55 56 57 58 59 60 63 64 65 66 71 72 73 **P**6 7 8 **N** Vantage Health Care Network, Inc., Meadville, PA	23	10	189	8960	126	157692	433	61022	27797	888
GETTYSBURG—Adams County										
✶ GETTYSBURG HOSPITAL, 147 Gettys Street, Zip 17325–2534; tel. 717/334–2121; Steven W. Renner, President and Chief Executive Officer **A**1 9 10 **F**3 4 7 8 14 15 16 17 19 21 22 23 28 30 32 33 34 35 37 39 40 41 42 44 46 49 56 65 66 67 71 73 74 **P**8	23	10	76	4295	48	97859	5	36308	17272	495
GLENSIDE—Montgomery County										
✶ △ CHESTNUT HILL REHABILITATION HOSPITAL, 8601 Stenton Avenue, Zip 19038–8312; tel. 215/233–6200; James B. McCaslin, Director (Total facility includes 34 beds in nursing home–type unit) **A**1 7 10 **F**1 5 6 7 8 11 12 13 14 15 16 17 19 20 21 22 26 27 28 29 30 32 33 34 35 36 37 39 40 41 42 44 45 46 48 49 50 51 54 56 57 60 61 62 63 64 65 66 67 68 69 71 73 74 **P**4 5 7	23	46	91	1721	65	9404	—	13420	5770	227
GREENSBURG—Westmoreland County										
✶ WESTMORELAND REGIONAL HOSPITAL, 532 West Pittsburgh Street, Zip 15601–2282; tel. 724/832–4000; Joseph J. Peluso, President and Chief Executive Officer (Total facility includes 46 beds in nursing home–type unit) **A**1 2 3 9 10 **F**2 3 4 7 8 10 11 12 13 14 16 17 19 20 21 22 23 25 26 27 28 29 30 31 32 33 34 35 37 39 40 41 42 43 44 45 46 48 49 52 53 54 55 56 57 58 59 60 61 63 64 65 67 68 71 73 74 **P**1	23	10	345	13594	236	211600	719	96654	44424	1429
GREENVILLE—Mercer County										
□ ○ HORIZON HOSPITAL SYSTEM, (Includes Greenville Campus, 110 North Main Street, Zip 16125–1795; tel. 724/588–2100; Shenango Valley Campus, 2200 Memorial Drive, Farrell, Zip 16121–1398; tel. 724/981–3500), J. Larry Heinike, President and Chief Executive Officer (Total facility includes 38 beds in nursing home–type unit) **A**1 2 9 10 11 12 **F**2 3 5 7 8 10 12 13 14 15 16 17 19 20 21 22 23 24 25 26 27 28 29 30 32 33 34 35 37 39 40 41 42 44 45 46 48 49 54 55 56 57 58 60 61 63 64 65 66 67 68 71 72 73 74 **P**4 7 8 **N** Vantage Health Care Network, Inc., Meadville, PA	23	10	233	9340	134	197979	686	69462	31183	990
GROVE CITY—Mercer County										
□ + ○ UNITED COMMUNITY HOSPITAL, 631 North Broad Street Extension, Zip 16127–4603; tel. 412/458–5442; Robert J. Turner, Administrator (Total facility includes 20 beds in nursing home–type unit) **A**1 9 10 11 **F**3 7 8 14 15 16 17 19 21 22 28 30 32 33 34 35 37 39 40 41 42 44 45 49 56 63 64 65 67 70 71 73	23	10	104	3562	51	58827	291	24424	10433	350
HANOVER—York County										
HANOVER GENERAL HOSPITAL See Hanover Hospital										
✶ HANOVER HOSPITAL, (Formerly Hanover General Hospital), 300 Highland Avenue, Zip 17331–2297; tel. 717/637–3711; William R. Walb, President and Chief Executive Officer **A**1 9 10 **F**4 7 8 15 16 17 18 19 20 21 22 25 28 30 31 32 33 34 35 37 39 40 41 42 44 45 49 63 65 66 67 71 73 **P**8	23	10	113	5597	74	127618	610	48467	22111	630

Hospital, Address, Telephone, Administrator, Approval, Facility, and Physician Codes, Health Care System, Network	Classi-fication Codes		Utilization Data					Expense (thousands) of dollars		
★ American Hospital Association (AHA) membership □ Joint Commission on Accreditation of Healthcare Organizations (JCAHO) accreditation + American Osteopathic Healthcare Association (AOHA) membership ○ American Osteopathic Association (AOA) accreditation △ Commission on Accreditation of Rehabilitation Facilities (CARF) accreditation Control codes 61, 63, 64, 71, 72 and 73 indicate hospitals listed by AOHA, but not registered by AHA. For definition of numerical codes, see page A4	Control	Service	Staffed Beds	Admissions	Census	Outpatient Visits	Births	Total	Payroll	Personnel

HARRISBURG—Dauphin County

□ + ○ COMMUNITY GENERAL OSTEOPATHIC HOSPITAL, 4300 Londonderry Road, Zip 17109–5397, Mailing Address: P.O. Box 3000, Zip 17105–3000; tel. 717/652–3000; George R. Strohl, Jr., President **A**1 9 10 11 12 13 **F**8 14 15 19 21 22 30 33 36 37 39 41 42 44 45 49 65 71 73 | 23 | 10 | 99 | 4398 | 69 | 143995 | — | 48012 | 19906 | 568

□ EDGEWATER PSYCHIATRIC CENTER, 1829 North Front Street, Zip 17102–2213; tel. 717/238–8666; Stephen C. Blanchard, Director **A**1 9 10 **F**15 16 52 53 55 58 59 | 23 | 22 | 26 | 449 | 37 | 13039 | — | 12123 | 3297 | 125

□ HARRISBURG STATE HOSPITAL, Cameron and Maclay Streets, Zip 17105–1300, Mailing Address: Pouch A., Zip 17105–1300; tel. 717/772–7455; Bruce Darney, Superintendent (Nonreporting) **A**1 9 10 | 12 | 22 | 392 | — | | | | | |

PINNACLEHEALTH AT POLYCLINIC HOSPITAL See PinnacleHealth System

✠ PINNACLEHEALTH SYSTEM, (Includes PinnacleHealth at Harrisburg Hospital, 111 South Front Street, Zip 17101–2099; tel. 717/782–3131; Susan A. Edwards, Senior Vice President for Operations; PinnacleHealth at Polyclinic Hospital, 2601 North Third Street, Zip 17110–2098; tel. 717/782–4141; Susan A. Edwards, Senior Vice President for Operations; PinnacleHealth at Seidle Memorial Hospital, 120 South Filbert Street, Mechanicsburg, Zip 17055–6591; tel. 717/795–6760; Susan A. Edwards, Senior Vice President for Operations), 17 South Market Square, Zip 17101–2003, Mailing Address: P.O. Box 8700, Zip 17105–8700; tel. 717/782–5678; John S. Cramer, FACHE, President and Chief Executive Officer (Total facility includes 123 beds in nursing home–type unit) **A**1 2 3 5 9 10 **F**1 3 4 6 7 8 10 11 12 15 16 17 20 21 22 23 26 27 28 29 30 31 32 33 34 35 38 39 40 41 42 43 44 45 46 48 49 51 52 53 54 56 57 58 59 60 61 62 63 64 65 67 71 72 73 74 **P**1 3 5 6 7 | 23 | 10 | 775 | 30706 | 569 | 433800 | 4589 | 277163 | 127228 | 3767

HAVERFORD—Delaware County

□ HAVERFORD STATE HOSPITAL, 3500 Darby Road, Zip 19041–1018; tel. 610/526–2600; Frances L. Smith, R.N., MSN, Superintendent (Nonreporting) **A**1 9 10 | 12 | 22 | 340 | — | — | — | — | — | — | —

HAVERTOWN—Delaware County

□ MERCY COMMUNITY HOSPITAL, 2000 Old West Chester Pike, Zip 19083–2712; tel. 610/645–3600; Andrew E. Harris, Chief Executive Officer **A**1 9 10 **F**1 3 4 6 7 8 10 14 15 16 17 19 22 23 25 26 27 28 29 30 31 32 33 34 35 37 38 39 40 41 42 44 45 46 48 49 51 52 53 54 55 56 57 58 59 60 62 64 65 66 67 71 73 74 **P**8 **S** Catholic Health East, Radnor, PA | 23 | 10 | 107 | 3912 | 47 | 50880 | — | 26917 | 11566 | —

HAZLETON—Luzerne County

✠ HAZLETON GENERAL HOSPITAL, 700 East Broad Street, Zip 18201–6835; tel. 717/450–4357; E. Richard Moore, President **A**1 9 10 **F**7 8 12 14 15 16 17 19 21 22 24 27 28 29 30 31 32 34 35 36 37 39 40 41 42 44 45 46 49 51 52 54 55 56 57 61 63 64 65 67 71 73 74 | 23 | 10 | 152 | 5325 | 126 | 62885 | — | 33571 | 14053 | 555

✠ HAZLETON–ST. JOSEPH MEDICAL CENTER, 687 North Church Street, Zip 18201–3198; tel. 717/459–4444; Bernard C. Rudegeair, President and Chief Executive Officer (Total facility includes 11 beds in nursing home–type unit) **A**1 9 10 **F**2 3 7 8 13 14 15 16 17 19 21 22 23 24 25 27 28 30 32 33 34 35 36 37 39 40 41 42 44 45 48 49 52 54 55 56 57 58 59 63 64 65 67 71 73 74 | 21 | 10 | 120 | 4620 | 74 | 147622 | 511 | 34646 | 16415 | 551

HERSHEY—Dauphin County

✠ △ PENN STATE GEISINGER–MILTON S. HERSHEY MEDICAL CENTER, (Formerly Penn State University Hospital–Milton S. Hershey Medical Center), 500 University Drive, Zip 17033–0850, Mailing Address: P.O. Box 850, Zip 17033–0850; tel. 717/531–8521; Theodore E. Townsend, Senior Vice President, Operations **A**1 2 3 5 7 8 9 10 **F**3 4 5 7 8 10 12 14 15 16 17 19 21 22 23 24 25 26 28 29 30 31 32 34 35 37 38 39 40 41 42 43 44 45 46 47 48 49 51 52 53 54 55 56 57 58 59 60 61 63 65 66 67 69 70 71 72 73 74 **P**1 6 **S** Penn State Geisinger Health System, Harrisburg, PA | 23 | 10 | 451 | 20235 | 378 | 450839 | 1178 | 270654 | 123426 | 4782

PENN STATE UNIVERSITY HOSPITAL–MILTON S. HERSHEY MEDICAL CENTER See Penn State Geisinger–Milton S. Hershey Medical Center

HONESDALE—Wayne County

✠ WAYNE MEMORIAL HOSPITAL, 601 Park Street, Zip 18431–1445; tel. 717/253–8100; G. Richard Garman, Executive Director **A**1 9 10 **F**7 8 15 16 17 19 21 22 23 24 25 27 28 30 31 32 34 35 39 40 41 42 44 45 49 53 55 56 57 58 65 66 67 68 71 73 **P**8 | 23 | 10 | 95 | 4245 | 68 | 114326 | 478 | 31270 | 14203 | 527

HUNTINGDON—Huntingdon County

✠ J. C. BLAIR MEMORIAL HOSPITAL, 1225 Warm Springs Avenue, Zip 16652–2398; tel. 814/643–2290; Richard E. D'Alberto, Chief Executive Officer (Nonreporting) **A**1 9 10 **S** Quorum Health Group/Quorum Health Resources, Inc., Brentwood, TN | 23 | 10 | 104 | — | — | — | — | — | — | —

INDIANA—Indiana County

✠ INDIANA HOSPITAL, 835 Hospital Road, Zip 15701–3650, Mailing Address: P.O. Box 788, Zip 15701–0788; tel. 724/357–7000; Robert C. Parker, M.D., M.P.H., Acting Chief Executive Officer (Total facility includes 18 beds in nursing home–type unit) **A**1 9 10 **F**3 7 8 12 13 14 15 16 17 18 19 20 21 22 23 24 25 26 28 29 30 32 33 34 35 37 39 40 41 42 44 45 46 49 51 56 60 63 64 65 67 71 73 **P**6 | 23 | 10 | 155 | 6551 | 87 | 167116 | 696 | 50720 | 24996 | 730

JEANNETTE—Westmoreland County

□ JEANNETTE DISTRICT MEMORIAL HOSPITAL, 600 Jefferson Avenue, Zip 15644–2504; tel. 724/527–3551; Robert J. Bulger, President and Chief Executive Officer (Total facility includes 11 beds in nursing home–type unit) **A**1 9 10 **F**4 7 8 15 16 17 19 21 22 25 28 29 30 35 37 40 41 42 44 45 46 48 49 64 65 71 72 73 **P**8 **N** First Health Alliance, Pittsburgh, PA | 23 | 10 | 137 | 5534 | 86 | 77625 | 442 | 35351 | 16389 | 504

Hospital, Address, Telephone, Administrator, Approval, Facility, and Physician Codes, Health Care System, Network	Classi-fication Codes		Utilization Data					Expense (thousands) of dollars		
★ American Hospital Association (AHA) membership □ Joint Commission on Accreditation of Healthcare Organizations (JCAHO) accreditation + American Osteopathic Healthcare Association (AOHA) membership ○ American Osteopathic Association (AOA) accreditation △ Commission on Accreditation of Rehabilitation Facilities (CARF) accreditation Control codes 61, 63, 64, 71, 72 and 73 indicate hospitals listed by AOHA, but not registered by AHA. For definition of numerical codes, see page A4	Control	Service	Staffed Beds	Admissions	Census	Outpatient Visits	Births	Total	Payroll	Personnel
□ MONSOUR MEDICAL CENTER, 70 Lincoln Way East, Zip 15644–3167; tel. 724/527–1511; Michael N. J. Flinn, FACHE, Chief Executive Officer **A**1 9 10 **F**2 8 10 12 14 15 16 18 19 22 26 28 30 31 32 37 39 42 44 52 53 57 71 73	23	10	134	2539	64	53632	—	24093	11170	361
JERSEY SHORE—Lycoming County										
✦ JERSEY SHORE HOSPITAL, 1020 Thompson Street, Zip 17740–1729; tel. 717/398–0100; Louis A. Ditzel, Jr., President and Chief Executive Officer **A**1 9 10 **F**8 11 12 13 14 15 16 17 19 21 22 23 27 28 29 30 34 35 37 39 41 44 45 46 49 51 63 65 66 71 73 **P**6 **S** Quorum Health Group/Quorum Health Resources, Inc., Brentwood, TN	23	10	49	1483	15	44743	—	11333	4817	212
JOHNSTOWN—Cambria County										
GOOD SAMARITAN MEDICAL CENTER See Memorial Medical Center										
□ LEE HOSPITAL, 320 Main Street, Zip 15901–1694; tel. 814/533–0123; David R. Davis, President and Chief Executive Officer (Total facility includes 18 beds in nursing home–type unit) **A**1 2 9 10 **F**7 8 10 11 12 14 15 16 17 19 20 21 22 26 27 28 29 30 32 33 34 35 37 39 40 41 42 44 45 48 49 51 56 60 62 64 65 67 71 72 73 74 **P**8 **S** UPMC Health System, Pittsburgh, PA	23	10	224	8312	148	99915	447	71592	32070	1098
✦ MEMORIAL MEDICAL CENTER, (Includes Good Samaritan Medical Center, 1020 Franklin Street, Zip 15905–4186; tel. 814/533–1000), 1086 Franklin Street, Zip 15905–4398; tel. 814/534–9000; Steven E. Tucker, President (Total facility includes 73 beds in nursing home–type unit) (Nonreporting) **A**1 2 3 5 6 9 10 12	23	10	592	—	—	—	—	—	—	—
KANE—McKean County										
□ KANE COMMUNITY HOSPITAL, North Fraley Street, Zip 16735, Mailing Address: P.O. Box 778, Zip 16735–0778; tel. 814/837–8585; J. Gary Rhodes, Chief Executive Officer (Nonreporting) **A**1 9 10	23	10	36							
KINGSTON—Luzerne County										
NESBITT MEMORIAL HOSPITAL See Wyoming Valley Health Care System, Wilkes–Barre										
KITTANNING—Armstrong County										
□ ARMSTRONG COUNTY MEMORIAL HOSPITAL, One Nolte Drive, Zip 16201–8808; tel. 724/543–8500; Jack D. Hoard, President and Chief Executive Officer (Total facility includes 25 beds in nursing home–type unit) **A**1 2 9 10 **F**7 8 10 11 12 14 15 17 19 21 22 28 29 30 32 34 35 37 39 40 41 42 44 46 49 50 51 52 53 54 55 56 57 60 63 64 65 66 67 71 73 **P**5	23	10	210	6556	120	107318	475	44636	21099	728
LAFAYETTE HILL—Montgomery County										
□ EUGENIA HOSPITAL, 660 Thomas Road, Zip 19444–1199; tel. 215/836–7700; John P. Ash, FACHE, President and Chief Executive Officer (Nonreporting) **A**1 9 10	33	22	126							
LANCASTER—Lancaster County										
+ ○ COMMUNITY HOSPITAL OF LANCASTER, 1100 East Orange Street, Zip 17602–3218, Mailing Address: Box 3002, Zip 17604–3002; tel. 717/397–3711; Mark C. Barabas, President **A**9 10 11 12 13 **F**7 8 10 12 14 15 16 17 19 20 21 22 25 28 29 30 31 32 34 35 39 40 41 42 44 48 49 51 52 54 55 56 57 58 63 64 65 66 67 71 73 74 **P**8	23	10	152	5373	66	65824	710	38863	16583	741
□ △ LANCASTER GENERAL HOSPITAL, 555 North Duke Street, Zip 17602–2207, Mailing Address: P.O. Box 3555, Zip 17604–3555; tel. 717/290–5511; Mark A. Brazitis, President (Total facility includes 30 beds in nursing home–type unit) **A**1 2 3 5 6 7 9 10 **F**3 4 7 8 10 12 14 15 16 19 20 21 22 25 26 27 28 30 32 33 34 35 37 38 39 40 41 42 43 44 46 48 49 51 52 53 54 56 58 59 60 61 63 64 65 66 67 69 70 71 73 74	23	10	493	20910	286	423949	2830	203960	97561	2712
✦ △ ST. JOSEPH HOSPITAL, 250 College Avenue, Zip 17604; tel. 717/291–8211; John Kerr Tolmie, President and Chief Executive Officer (Total facility includes 19 beds in nursing home–type unit) (Nonreporting) **A**1 2 7 9 10 **S** Catholic Health Initiatives, Denver, CO	21	10	256	—	—	—	—	—	—	—
LANGHORNE—Bucks County										
+ ○ DELAWARE VALLEY MEDICAL CENTER, 200 Oxford Valley Road, Zip 19047–8304; tel. 215/949–5100; Carl E. Brown, President (Total facility includes 16 beds in nursing home–type unit) **A**9 10 11 12 13 **F**8 10 11 14 15 16 17 19 21 22 26 29 30 31 32 33 34 35 36 37 39 42 44 45 46 52 56 57 59 61 63 64 65 69 71 73	23	10	151	5809	92	—	—	50770	21671	659
✦ ST. MARY MEDICAL CENTER, Langhorne–Newtown Road, Zip 19047–1295; tel. 215/750–2000; Sister Clare Carty, President and Chief Executive Officer **A**1 2 9 10 **F**4 7 8 10 11 12 13 14 15 16 17 19 22 24 25 26 28 30 32 35 37 38 39 40 41 42 43 44 46 48 49 50 56 60 63 65 66 67 70 71 73 74 **P**1 6 7 **S** Catholic Health Initiatives, Denver, CO **N** Fox Chase Network, Rockledge, PA	21	10	270	11814	159	132887	1339	91705	40909	1019
LANSDALE—Montgomery County										
✦ NORTH PENN HOSPITAL, 100 Medical Campus Drive, Zip 19446–1200; tel. 215/368–2100; Robert H. McKay, President (Nonreporting) **A**1 2 9 10 **N** Fox Chase Network, Rockledge, PA	23	10	150	—	—	—	—	—	—	—
LATROBE—Westmoreland County										
✦ LATROBE AREA HOSPITAL, 121 West Second Avenue, Zip 15650–1096; tel. 724/537–1000; Douglas A. Clark, Executive Director (Total facility includes 20 beds in nursing home–type unit) **A**1 2 3 5 9 10 **F**5 7 8 10 11 12 13 14 15 16 17 18 19 21 22 24 25 27 28 29 30 31 32 33 34 35 37 39 40 41 42 44 45 49 51 52 53 54 55 56 58 59 60 63 64 65 67 68 71 73 74 **P**6	23	10	232	11981	149	250612	839	91652	49400	1286
LEBANON—Lebanon County										
✦ GOOD SAMARITAN HOSPITAL, Fourth and Walnut Streets, Zip 17042, Mailing Address: P.O. Box 1281, Zip 17042–1281; tel. 717/270–7500; Robert J. Longo, President and Chief Executive Officer (Total facility includes 19 beds in nursing home–type unit) **A**1 3 5 9 10 **F**3 4 7 8 10 12 14 15 16 17 18 19 20 21 22 24 27 30 31 32 33 34 35 37 39 40 41 42 44 46 48 49 51 53 54 55 56 57 58 59 60 63 64 65 66 67 71 72 73 74 **P**8	23	10	186	8989	137	157008	980	66120	29902	937

Hospital, Address, Telephone, Administrator, Approval, Facility, and Physician Codes, Health Care System, Network	Classi-fication Codes		Utilization Data					Expense (thousands) of dollars		
★ American Hospital Association (AHA) membership □ Joint Commission on Accreditation of Healthcare Organizations (JCAHO) accreditation + American Osteopathic Healthcare Association (AOHA) membership ○ American Osteopathic Association (AOA) accreditation △ Commission on Accreditation of Rehabilitation Facilities (CARF) accreditation Control codes 61, 63, 64, 71, 72 and 73 indicate hospitals listed by AOHA, but not registered by AHA. For definition of numerical codes, see page A4	Control	Service	Staffed Beds	Admissions	Census	Outpatient Visits	Births	Total	Payroll	Personnel

	Control	Service	Staffed Beds	Admissions	Census	Outpatient Visits	Births	Total	Payroll	Personnel
✠ VETERANS AFFAIRS MEDICAL CENTER, 1700 South Lincoln Avenue, Zip 17042–7529; tel. 717/272–6621; Leonard Washington, Jr., Director **A**1 3 5 9 **F**2 3 4 8 12 15 16 17 19 20 22 25 26 27 28 30 31 32 33 34 35 37 39 41 42 44 45 46 48 49 51 52 54 56 57 58 59 64 65 67 71 72 73 74 **P**6 **S** Department of Veterans Affairs, Washington, DC	45	10	369	2853	170	134413	—	79077	41277	1007
LEHIGHTON—Carbon County										
✠ GNADEN HUETTEN MEMORIAL HOSPITAL, 211 North 12th Street, Zip 18235–1138; tel. 610/377–1300; Robert J. Clark, FACHE, President and Chief Executive Officer (Total facility includes 91 beds in nursing home–type unit) **A**1 9 10 **F**7 8 14 15 16 17 19 20 21 22 25 26 27 28 30 32 33 35 36 37 39 40 41 42 44 45 46 49 51 52 53 54 55 56 57 59 61 64 65 67 71 73 74 **P**5 8	23	10	204	3847	147	124650	289	30329	14446	441
LEWISBURG—Union County										
EVANGELICAL COMMUNITY HOSPITAL, One Hospital Drive, Zip 17837–9314; tel. 717/522–2000; Michael Daniloff, President (Nonreporting) **A**9 10	23	10	115	—	—	—	—	—	—	—
U. S. PENITENTIARY INFIRMARY, Route 7, Zip 17837–9303; tel. 717/523–1251; Arnold Reyes, Administrator (Nonreporting)	48	11	17							
LEWISTOWN—Mifflin County										
✠ LEWISTOWN HOSPITAL, 400 Highland Avenue, Zip 17044–1198; tel. 717/248–5411; A. Gordon McAleer, President and Chief Executive Officer **A**1 2 9 10 12 **F**3 7 8 11 12 14 15 16 17 19 20 21 22 26 28 30 31 32 33 34 35 37 39 40 41 42 44 49 52 53 54 55 56 57 58 60 65 66 71 73 **P**6	23	10	179	7760	100	—	631	46068	22222	759
LOCK HAVEN—Clinton County										
✠ LOCK HAVEN HOSPITAL, 24 Cree Drive, Zip 17745–2699; tel. 717/893–5000; Gary R. Rhoads, President and Chief Executive Officer (Total facility includes 120 beds in nursing home–type unit) **A**1 9 10 **F**7 8 15 17 19 20 21 22 25 26 30 34 35 37 39 40 41 44 45 46 49 51 54 58 61 62 63 64 65 71 73 **P**5 8 **S** Quorum Health Group/Quorum Health Resources, Inc., Brentwood, TN	23	10	195	3379	141	48084	328	21266	9556	384
MALVERN—Chester County										
✠ △ BRYN MAWR REHABILITATION HOSPITAL, 414 Paoli Pike, Zip 19355–3311, Mailing Address: P.O. Box 3007, Zip 19355–3300; tel. 610/251–5400; Barry S. Rabner, President (Total facility includes 23 beds in nursing home–type unit) **A**1 7 9 10 **F**1 2 3 4 5 6 7 8 9 10 11 12 13 14 15 16 17 18 19 20 21 22 24 25 26 27 28 29 30 31 32 33 34 35 36 37 38 39 40 41 42 43 44 45 46 47 48 49 50 51 52 53 54 55 56 57 58 59 60 61 64 65 66 67 68 69 70 71 72 73 74 **S** Jefferson Health System, Wayne, PA **N** Jefferson Health System, Radnor, PA	23	46	141	2517	109	24985	—	31087	15731	510
DEVEREUX MAPLETON PSYCHIATRIC INSTITUTE–MAPLETON CENTER, 655 Sugartown Road, Zip 19355–0297, Mailing Address: Box 297, Zip 19355–0297; tel. 610/296–6923; Richard Warden, Executive Director (Nonreporting) **S** Devereux Foundation, Villanova, PA	23	22	13	—	—	—	—	—	—	—
MALVERN INSTITUTE, 940 King Road, Zip 19355–3167; tel. 610/647–0330; Thomas Cain, Administrator and Chief Executive Officer **A**9 **F**1 2 3 4 5 6 7 8 9 10 11 12 13 16 17 18 19 20 21 22 23 24 25 26 27 28 29 30 31 32 33 34 35 36 37 38 39 40 41 42 43 44 45 46 47 48 49 50 51 52 53 54 55 56 57 58 59 60 61 62 63 64 65 66 67 68 69 70 71 72 73 74	33	82	44	1402	37	1617	—	—	—	53
MCCONNELLSBURG—Fulton County										
★ FULTON COUNTY MEDICAL CENTER, 216 South First Street, Zip 17233–1399; tel. 717/485–6109; Robert B. Murray, III, Chief Executive Officer (Total facility includes 57 beds in nursing home–type unit) **A**9 10 **F**7 8 11 15 19 22 32 34 35 40 44 46 63 64 65 71	23	10	100	1177	74	82091	107	11666	5861	238
MCKEES ROCKS—Allegheny County										
✠ OHIO VALLEY GENERAL HOSPITAL, 25 Heckel Road, Zip 15136–1694; tel. 412/777–6161; William Provenzano, President **A**1 6 9 10 **F**4 7 8 10 12 13 14 15 16 17 18 19 20 21 22 23 24 25 26 28 29 30 32 33 34 35 36 37 39 40 41 42 44 45 46 49 51 61 65 67 71 72 73 **P**5 **S** Quorum Health Group/Quorum Health Resources, Inc., Brentwood, TN	23	10	103	4770	61	93700	455	39459	14553	441
MCKEESPORT—Allegheny County										
✠ MCKEESPORT HOSPITAL, 1500 Fifth Avenue, Zip 15132–2482; tel. 412/664–2000; Ronald H. Ott, President and Chief Executive Officer (Total facility includes 56 beds in nursing home–type unit) **A**1 3 5 9 10 **F**7 8 10 11 12 13 15 16 17 19 21 22 25 26 27 28 29 30 31 32 33 34 37 39 40 41 42 44 45 46 48 49 51 52 54 55 56 57 60 61 64 65 67 71 73 74 **S** UPMC Health System, Pittsburgh, PA	23	10	281	10242	207	94595	366	78159	38095	1243
MEADOWBROOK—Montgomery County										
□ HOLY REDEEMER HOSPITAL AND MEDICAL CENTER, 1648 Huntingdon Pike, Zip 19046–8099; tel. 215/947–3000; Mark T. Jones, President (Total facility includes 15 beds in nursing home–type unit) **A**1 5 9 10 **F**6 7 8 10 11 12 13 15 16 17 19 22 24 27 28 29 30 32 33 34 35 36 38 39 40 41 42 44 46 49 51 62 64 65 66 67 71 73 74 **P**6	23	10	232	11689	153	136855	1703	82953	33287	1102
MEADVILLE—Crawford County										
✠ MEADVILLE MEDICAL CENTER, (Includes Meadville City Hospital, 751 Liberty Street, Zip 16335; tel. 814/333–5000; Spencer Hospital, 1034 Grove Street, Zip 16335), 751 Liberty Street, Zip 16335–2555; tel. 814/333–5000; Anthony J. DeFail, President and Chief Executive Officer (Total facility includes 32 beds in nursing home–type unit) **A**1 2 9 10 **F**2 3 7 8 11 12 15 16 17 18 19 21 22 24 27 30 32 33 35 37 40 41 42 44 45 46 48 49 51 52 53 56 58 59 63 64 65 66 67 71 73 74 **P**3 7 8 **N** Vantage Health Care Network, Inc., Meadville, PA	23	10	238	8610	143	115193	592	59818	25362	816

Hospital, Address, Telephone, Administrator, Approval, Facility, and Physician Codes, Health Care System, Network	Classification Codes		Utilization Data					Expense (thousands) of dollars		
★ American Hospital Association (AHA) membership □ Joint Commission on Accreditation of Healthcare Organizations (JCAHO) accreditation + American Osteopathic Healthcare Association (AOHA) membership ○ American Osteopathic Association (AOA) accreditation △ Commission on Accreditation of Rehabilitation Facilities (CARF) accreditation Control codes 61, 63, 64, 71, 72 and 73 indicate hospitals listed by AOHA, but not registered by AHA. For definition of numerical codes, see page A4	Control	Service	Staffed Beds	Admissions	Census	Outpatient Visits	Births	Total	Payroll	Personnel

MECHANICSBURG—Cumberland County

□ △ HEALTHSOUTH REHABILITATION OF MECHANICSBURG, 175 Lancaster Boulevard, Zip 17055–2016, Mailing Address: P.O. Box 2016, Zip 17055–2016; tel. 717/691–3700; Melissa Kutz, Administrator and Chief Executive Officer (Nonreporting) **A**1 7 9 10 **S** HEALTHSOUTH Corporation, Birmingham, AL

| | 33 | 46 | 103 | — | — | — | — | — | — | — |

PINNACLEHEALTH AT SEIDLE MEMORIAL HOSPITAL See PinnacleHealth System, Harrisburg

MEDIA—Delaware County

✠ RIDDLE MEMORIAL HOSPITAL, 1068 West Baltimore Pike, Zip 19063–5177; tel. 610/566–9400; Donald L. Laughlin, President (Total facility includes 22 beds in nursing home–type unit) **A**1 2 9 10 **F**3 6 7 8 10 12 13 14 17 19 21 22 24 26 28 30 31 32 33 34 35 37 38 39 40 41 42 44 45 46 49 61 62 64 65 66 67 71 73 74 **P**6 7 **N** Jefferson Health System, Radnor, PA

| | 23 | 10 | 198 | 9209 | 118 | 75910 | 830 | 62343 | 29691 | 907 |

MEYERSDALE—Somerset County

✠ MEYERSDALE MEDICAL CENTER, 200 Hospital Drive, Zip 15552–1247; tel. 814/634–5911; Mary L. Libengood, Executive Director **A**1 9 10 **F**8 14 15 16 19 21 22 28 30 32 37 44 65 67 71 72 73 **P**6

| | 23 | 10 | 20 | 597 | 9 | 21207 | — | 4978 | 2407 | 107 |

MONONGAHELA—Washington County

✠ MONONGAHELA VALLEY HOSPITAL, 1163 Country Club Road, Rt 88, Zip 15063–1095; tel. 724/258–1000; Anthony M. Lombardi, President and Chief Executive Officer **A**1 2 9 10 **F**2 5 6 7 8 10 11 13 14 15 16 17 19 20 21 22 23 26 27 28 29 30 31 32 33 34 35 37 39 40 41 42 44 45 46 48 49 52 53 54 55 56 57 60 61 63 64 65 66 67 68 71 73 74 **P**8

| | 23 | 10 | 282 | 11201 | 194 | 179832 | 537 | 70086 | 32737 | 1037 |

MONROEVILLE—Allegheny County

✠ ALLEGHENY UNIVERSITY HOSPITALS, FORBES REGIONAL, (Formerly Forbes Regional Hospital), 2570 Haymaker Road, Zip 15146–3592; tel. 412/858–2000; Dana W. Ramish, President and Chief Executive Officer **A**1 2 3 5 9 10 **F**7 8 10 12 13 14 15 16 17 19 22 24 25 26 27 28 29 30 32 33 34 35 37 39 40 41 42 44 45 46 49 51 52 54 55 56 57 58 59 63 65 67 71 73 **P**5 6 **S** Allegheny Health, Education and Research Foundation, Pittsburgh, PA

| | 23 | 10 | 317 | 14311 | 214 | 80589 | 1331 | 97295 | 36542 | 1075 |

FORBES REGIONAL HOSPITAL See Allegheny University Hospitals, Forbes Regional

□ HEALTHSOUTH GREATER PITTSBURGH REHABILITATION HOSPITAL, 2380 McGinley Road, Zip 15146–4400; tel. 412/856–2400; Faith A. Deigan, Administrator **A**1 9 10 **F**15 16 34 48 49 **S** HEALTHSOUTH Corporation, Birmingham, AL

| | 33 | 46 | 89 | 1333 | 76 | 25752 | 0 | 20760 | 8742 | 271 |

MONTROSE—Susquehanna County

ENDLESS MOUNTAIN HEALTH SYSTEMS, 1 Grow Avenue, Zip 18801–1199; tel. 717/278–3801; Rex Catlin, Chief Executive Officer (Nonreporting) **A**9 10

| | 33 | 10 | 34 | — | — | — | — | — | — | — |

MOUNT GRETNA—Lebanon County

PHILHAVEN See Philhaven, Bahavioral Healthcare Services

□ PHILHAVEN, BAHAVIORAL HEALTHCARE SERVICES, (Formerly Philhaven), 283 South Butler Road, Zip 17064, Mailing Address: P.O. Box 550, Zip 17064–0550; tel. 717/273–8871; LaVern J. Yutzy, Chief Executive Officer **A**1 9 10 **F**14 15 32 52 53 54 55 56 57 58 59 65 73 74 **P**6

| | 21 | 22 | 83 | 1698 | 55 | 56324 | — | 23080 | 15021 | 520 |

MOUNT PLEASANT—Westmoreland County

✠ FRICK HOSPITAL, 508 South Church Street, Zip 15666–1790; tel. 724/547–1500; Rodney L. Gunderson, Executive Director and Chief Executive Officer (Total facility includes 18 beds in nursing home–type unit) **A**1 2 9 10 **F**7 8 10 11 12 14 15 16 17 18 19 20 21 22 26 28 29 30 31 32 34 35 37 39 40 41 42 44 45 46 49 52 53 54 55 56 57 58 59 60 63 64 65 66 67 69 71 73

| | 23 | 10 | 171 | 6374 | 97 | 96396 | 578 | 39656 | 19404 | 569 |

MUNCY—Lycoming County

MUNCY VALLEY HOSPITAL See Susquehanna Health System, Williamsport

NANTICOKE—Luzerne County

MERCY SPECIAL CARE HOSPITAL, 128 West Washington Street, Zip 18634–3198; tel. 717/735–5000; Robert D. Williams, Administrator (Nonreporting) **A**9 10 **S** Catholic Healthcare Partners, Cincinnati, OH

| | 23 | 49 | 38 | — | — | — | — | — | — | — |

NATRONA HEIGHTS—Allegheny County

✠ ALLEGHENY UNIVERSITY MEDICAL CENTER–ALLEGHENY VALLEY, (Formerly Allegheny Valley Hospital), 1301 Carlisle Street, Zip 15065–1192; tel. 724/224–5100; John R. England, President and Chief Executive Officer (Total facility includes 21 beds in nursing home–type unit) **A**1 2 9 10 **F**3 7 8 10 11 12 15 16 17 19 21 22 28 30 31 32 33 34 35 37 39 40 41 42 44 45 49 52 54 56 57 60 63 64 65 66 67 71 73 **P**2 8 **S** Allegheny Health, Education and Research Foundation, Pittsburgh, PA **N** SouthWest Integrated Delivery Network, Pittsburgh, PA

| | 23 | 10 | 268 | 9905 | 961 | 131323 | 608 | 69187 | 33585 | 930 |

NEW CASTLE—Lawrence County

✠ △ JAMESON HOSPITAL, (Formerly Jameson Memorial Hospital), 1211 Wilmington Avenue, Zip 16105–2595; tel. 724/658–9001; Thomas White, President and Chief Executive Officer (Total facility includes 20 beds in nursing home–type unit) **A**1 2 6 7 9 10 **F**7 8 10 11 12 13 14 15 16 17 19 20 21 22 23 26 28 30 32 34 35 37 39 40 41 42 44 45 48 49 59 60 61 63 64 65 66 67 71 72 73 74 **P**3 7 8

| | 23 | 10 | 183 | 6783 | 109 | 197891 | 597 | 62943 | 26636 | 995 |

JAMESON MEMORIAL HOSPITAL See Jameson Hospital

✠ ST. FRANCIS HOSPITAL OF NEW CASTLE, 1000 South Mercer Street, Zip 16101–4673; tel. 724/658–3511; Sister Donna Zwigart, FACHE, Chief Executive Officer (Total facility includes 45 beds in nursing home–type unit) **A**1 6 9 10 **F**2 3 5 8 11 14 15 16 19 21 22 23 26 28 29 30 31 32 33 34 35 39 40 41 42 44 45 46 48 49 52 53 54 55 56 57 58 59 60 61 62 63 64 65 67 71 73 74 **P**5 6 **S** St. Francis Health System, Pittsburgh, PA **N** Saint Francis Health System, Pittsburgh, PA

| | 23 | 10 | 193 | 4165 | 100 | 65255 | 115 | 31880 | 13380 | 527 |

Hospital, Address, Telephone, Administrator, Approval, Facility, and Physician Codes, Health Care System, Network	Classi-fication Codes		Utilization Data					Expense (thousands) of dollars		
★ American Hospital Association (AHA) membership □ Joint Commission on Accreditation of Healthcare Organizations (JCAHO) accreditation + American Osteopathic Healthcare Association (AOHA) membership ○ American Osteopathic Association (AOA) accreditation △ Commission on Accreditation of Rehabilitation Facilities (CARF) accreditation Control codes 61, 63, 64, 71, 72 and 73 indicate hospitals listed by AOHA, but not registered by AHA. For definition of numerical codes, see page A4	Control	Service	Staffed Beds	Admissions	Census	Outpatient Visits	Births	Total	Payroll	Personnel

NEW KENSINGTON—Westmoreland County

□ CITIZENS GENERAL HOSPITAL, 651 Fourth Avenue, Zip 15068–6591; tel. 724/337–3541; Robert E. Marino, Executive Director (Total facility includes 20 beds in nursing home–type unit) **A**1 2 6 9 10 **F**6 7 8 11 13 14 15 16 18 19 21 22 23 28 29 30 31 32 33 34 35 37 39 40 41 42 44 45 49 60 63 64 65 67 71 73

| | 23 | 10 | 120 | 5160 | 81 | 79689 | 276 | 40882 | 17176 | 540 |

NORRISTOWN—Montgomery County

□ MONTGOMERY COUNTY EMERGENCY SERVICE, 50 Beech Drive, Zip 19404, Mailing Address: Caller Box 3005, Zip 19404–3005; tel. 610/279–6100; Rocio Nell, M.D., Chief Executive Officer and Medical Director **A**1 10 **F**3 15 17 18 52 53 54 55 56 57 58 65 **P**6

| | 23 | 22 | 53 | 1963 | 43 | 848 | 0 | 6584 | 4779 | 153 |

🗷 MONTGOMERY HOSPITAL, 1301 Powell Street, Zip 19401, Mailing Address: P.O. Box 992, Zip 19404–0992; tel. 610/270–2000; Timothy M. Casey, President and Chief Executive Officer (Total facility includes 17 beds in nursing home–type unit) (Nonreporting) **A**1 2 3 5 9 10 **N** Fox Chase Network, Rockledge, PA

| | 23 | 10 | 256 | — | — | — | — | — | — | — |

□ NORRISTOWN STATE HOSPITAL, 1001 Sterigere Street, Zip 19401–5399; tel. 215/270–1000; Albert R. Di Dario, Superintendent **A**1 3 5 9 10 **F**14 20 24 46 52 57 65 73

| | 12 | 22 | 681 | 362 | 112 | — | — | 66529 | 43048 | 939 |

+ ○ SUBURBAN GENERAL HOSPITAL, 2701 DeKalb Pike, Zip 19401–1849; tel. 610/278–2000; Edward R. Solvibile, President (Nonreporting) **A**2 9 10 11 12 13

| | 23 | 10 | 106 | — | — | — | — | — | — | — |

🗷 VALLEY FORGE MEDICAL CENTER AND HOSPITAL, 1033 West Germantown Pike, Zip 19403–3998; tel. 610/539–8500; Marian W. Colcher, Interim Administrator (Nonreporting) **A**1 9 10

| | 33 | 10 | 70 | — | — | — | — | — | — | — |

NORTH WARREN—Warren County

□ WARREN STATE HOSPITAL, 33 Main Drive, Zip 16365–5099; tel. 814/723–5500; Carmen N. Ferranto, Superintendent **A**1 10 **F**8 14 16 19 20 22 32 35 37 42 44 45 46 48 49 52 57 65 70 71 73

| | 12 | 22 | 348 | 318 | 287 | 0 | — | — | — | 541 |

OAKDALE—Allegheny County

□ VENCOR HOSPITAL–PITTSBURGH, 7777 Steubenville Pike, Zip 15071–3409; tel. 412/494–5500; Patricia B. Speak, Administrator (Nonreporting) **A**1 10 **S** Vencor, Incorporated, Louisville, KY

| | 33 | 49 | 63 | — | — | — | — | — | — | — |

OIL CITY—Venango County

NORTHWEST MEDICAL CENTER–OIL CITY CAMPUS See Northwest Medical Centers, Franklin

OREFIELD—Lehigh County

★ NATIONAL HOSPITAL FOR KIDS IN CRISIS, 5300 Kids Peace Drive, Zip 18069–2044; tel. 610/799–8800; John P. Peter, Chief Executive Officer **A**9 10 **F**15 16 52 53 54 55 56 59 **P**6

| | 23 | 52 | 72 | 1012 | 50 | — | — | 13056 | 4694 | 163 |

PALMERTON—Carbon County

□ PALMERTON HOSPITAL, 135 Lafayette Avenue, Zip 18071–1598; tel. 610/826–3141; Peter L. Kern, President and Chief Executive Officer **A**1 9 10 **F**7 8 11 14 15 19 22 30 33 40 44 45 46 65 67 71

| | 23 | 10 | 70 | 2780 | 40 | 41214 | 186 | 17297 | 7682 | 272 |

PAOLI—Chester County

🗷 PAOLI MEMORIAL HOSPITAL, 255 West Lancaster Avenue, Zip 19301–1792; tel. 610/648–1204; Kenneth Hanover, President and Chief Executive Officer **A**1 2 9 10 **F**1 2 3 4 5 6 7 8 9 10 11 12 13 14 15 16 17 18 19 20 21 22 23 24 25 26 27 28 29 30 31 32 33 34 35 36 37 38 39 40 41 42 43 44 45 46 47 48 49 50 51 52 53 54 55 56 57 58 59 60 61 62 63 64 65 66 67 68 69 70 71 72 73 74 **P**1 3 5 6 7 8 **S** Jefferson Health System, Wayne, PA **N** Jefferson Health System, Radnor, PA; Fox Chase Network, Rockledge, PA

| | 23 | 10 | 137 | 7458 | 82 | 101692 | 710 | 51321 | 19648 | 579 |

PECKVILLE—Lackawanna County

MID–VALLEY HOSPITAL, 1400 South Main Street, Zip 18452–2098; tel. 717/383–5500; Gerard H. Warner, Jr., Chief Executive Officer **A**9 10 **F**8 14 15 16 17 19 21 22 28 30 32 33 34 37 39 42 44 46 49 65 71 73 **P**8

| | 23 | 10 | 57 | 1201 | 20 | 39375 | 0 | 9629 | 4027 | 167 |

PHILADELPHIA—Philadelphia County

□ ALBERT EINSTEIN MEDICAL CENTER, (Includes Moss Rehabilitation Hospital, 1200 West Tabor Road, Zip 19141–3099; tel. 215/456–9070), 5501 Old York Road, Zip 19141–3098; tel. 215/456–7890; Martin Goldsmith, President (Total facility includes 102 beds in nursing home–type unit) (Nonreporting) **A**1 2 3 5 8 9 10 13 **S** Albert Einstein Healthcare Network, Philadelphia, PA **N** Jefferson Health System, Radnor, PA; Albert Einstein Healthcare Network, Philadelphia, PA

| | 23 | 10 | 701 | — | — | — | — | — | — | — |

★ + ○ ALLEGHENY UNIVERSITY HOSPITAL, CITY AVENUE, (Formerly Graduate Health System–City Avenue), 4150 City Avenue, Zip 19131–1610; tel. 215/871–1000; Melvyn E. Smith, President (Nonreporting) **A**9 10 11 12 13 **S** Allegheny Health, Education and Research Foundation, Pittsburgh, PA

| | 23 | 10 | 195 | — | — | — | — | — | — | — |

🗷 ALLEGHENY UNIVERSITY HOSPITAL, GRADUATE, (Formerly Graduate Hospital), One Graduate Plaza, Zip 19146–1407; tel. 215/893–2000; Arnold Berman, M.D., President and Chief Executive Officer (Nonreporting) **A**1 2 3 5 8 9 10 **S** Allegheny Health, Education and Research Foundation, Pittsburgh, PA

| | 23 | 10 | 198 | — | — | — | — | — | — | — |

🗷 ALLEGHENY UNIVERSITY HOSPITAL, MEDICAL COLLEGE OF PENNSYLVANIA, (Includes Eastern Pennsylvania Psychiatric Institute, 3200 Henry Avenue, Zip 19129; tel. 215/842–4000), 3300 Henry Avenue, Zip 19129–1121; tel. 215/842–6000; Margaret M. McGoldrick, President and Chief Executive Officer **A**1 2 3 5 8 9 10 **F**2 3 4 7 8 9 10 11 12 13 14 15 16 17 18 19 20 21 22 24 26 27 28 29 30 31 32 34 35 37 38 39 40 41 42 43 44 45 46 47 48 49 51 52 53 54 55 56 57 58 59 60 61 64 65 66 67 69 70 71 73 74 **P**6 7 **S** Allegheny Health, Education and Research Foundation, Pittsburgh, PA

| | 23 | 10 | 401 | 15407 | 292 | 110162 | 1002 | 205047 | 85346 | 2148 |

Hospital, Address, Telephone, Administrator, Approval, Facility, and Physician Codes, Health Care System, Network	Classi-fication Codes		Utilization Data					Expense (thousands) of dollars		
	Control	Service	Staffed Beds	Admissions	Census	Outpatient Visits	Births	Total	Payroll	Personnel

★ The items below the header describe the symbols:

★ American Hospital Association (AHA) membership
□ Joint Commission on Accreditation of Healthcare Organizations (JCAHO) accreditation
+ American Osteopathic Healthcare Association (AOHA) membership
○ American Osteopathic Association (AOA) accreditation
△ Commission on Accreditation of Rehabilitation Facilities (CARF) accreditation
Control codes 61, 63, 64, 71, 72 and 73 indicate hospitals listed by AOHA, but not registered by AHA. For definition of numerical codes, see page A4

Hospital	Control	Service	Staffed Beds	Admissions	Census	Outpatient Visits	Births	Total	Payroll	Personnel
★ ○ ALLEGHENY UNIVERSITY HOSPITAL, PARKVIEW, (Formerly Parkview Hospital), 1331 East Wyoming Avenue, Zip 19124–3895; tel. 215/537–7400; Margaret M. McGoldrick, President and Chief Executive Officer (Total facility includes 19 beds in nursing home–type unit) (Nonreporting) **A**9 11 12 13 **S** Allegheny Health, Education and Research Foundation, Pittsburgh, PA	23	10	165	—	—	—	—	—	—	—
✚ ALLEGHENY UNIVERSITY HOSPITALS, HAHNEMANN, Broad and Vine Streets, Zip 19102–1192; tel. 215/762–7000; Margaret M. McGoldrick, President and Chief Executive Officer **A**1 2 3 5 8 9 10 **F**2 3 4 5 7 8 9 10 11 12 13 14 15 16 17 18 19 20 21 22 24 26 27 28 29 30 31 32 34 35 37 38 39 40 41 42 43 44 45 46 47 48 49 51 52 53 54 55 56 57 58 59 60 61 64 65 66 67 69 70 71 73 74 **P**6 7 **S** Allegheny Health, Education and Research Foundation, Pittsburgh, PA	23	10	427	19388	351	123965	1223	326584	127517	2887
□ BELMONT CENTER FOR COMPREHENSIVE TREATMENT, 4200 Monument Road, Zip 19131–1625; tel. 215/877–2000; Jack H. Dembow, General Director and Vice President (Nonreporting) **A**1 3 5 9 10 **S** Albert Einstein Healthcare Network, Philadelphia, PA **N** Albert Einstein Healthcare Network, Philadelphia, PA	23	22	146	—	—	—	—	—	—	—
□ CHARTER FAIRMOUNT INSTITUTE, 561 Fairthorne Avenue, Zip 19128–2499; tel. 215/487–4000; Paul B. Henry, Administrator (Nonreporting) **A**1 9 10 **S** Magellan Health Services, Atlanta, GA	33	22	146	—	—	—	—	—	—	—
✚ CHESTNUT HILL HEALTHCARE, (Formerly Chestnut Hill Hospital), 8835 Germantown Avenue, Zip 19118–2765; tel. 215/248–8200; Cary F. Leptuck, President **A**1 3 5 9 10 **F**7 8 11 12 13 15 16 17 19 21 22 29 33 35 36 37 40 41 42 44 46 49 51 60 65 71 73 74 **P**2 5 7	23	10	169	8519	101	101006	1192	53248	25217	845
□ CHILDREN'S HOSPITAL OF PHILADELPHIA, 34th Street and Civic Center Boulevard, Zip 19104–4399; tel. 215/590–1000; Edmond F. Notebaert, President **A**1 2 3 5 8 9 10 **F**4 10 11 12 13 14 15 16 17 19 20 21 22 25 28 29 30 31 32 34 35 38 39 42 43 44 45 46 47 48 49 51 52 53 54 55 56 58 59 60 65 67 68 69 70 71 73 **P**1	23	50	304	14815	202	310145	—	293149	120146	3114
□ CHILDREN'S SEASHORE HOUSE, 3405 Civic Center Boulevard, Zip 19104–4388; tel. 215/895–3600; Richard W. Shepherd, President and Chief Executive Officer **A**1 3 5 9 10 **F**14 15 19 21 25 27 34 35 48 49 53 54 65 73 **P**5	23	56	77	659	60	33349	—	38401	17097	488
EASTERN PENNSYLVANIA PSYCHIATRIC INSTITUTE See Allegheny University Hospital, Medical College of Pennsylvania										
✚ EPISCOPAL HOSPITAL, (Includes George L. Harrison Memorial House), 100 East Lehigh Avenue, Zip 19125–1098; tel. 215/427–7000; Mark T. Bateman, President and Chief Executive Officer (Total facility includes 35 beds in nursing home–type unit) **A**1 2 3 5 6 9 10 **F**3 4 7 8 10 12 14 15 16 17 19 20 21 22 25 26 27 28 29 30 31 32 34 35 37 38 39 40 41 42 43 44 45 46 49 51 54 63 64 65 67 68 71 72 73 74 **P**3	23	10	199	8478	164	119517	1229	88845	49716	1221
✚ FOX CHASE CANCER CENTER–AMERICAN ONCOLOGIC HOSPITAL, (ONCOLOGY), 7701 Burholme Avenue, Zip 19111–2412; tel. 215/728–6900; Robert C. Young, M.D., President **A**1 2 3 5 8 9 10 **F**8 12 14 15 17 18 19 20 21 28 29 30 31 32 33 34 35 37 39 41 42 44 45 46 49 54 60 65 67 69 71 73 74 **P**6 **N** Fox Chase Network, Rockledge, PA	23	49	74	3417	52	38485	—	56128	18273	521
✚ FRANKFORD HOSPITAL OF THE CITY OF PHILADELPHIA, (Includes Frankford Campus, Frankford Avenue and Wakeling Street, Zip 19124; tel. 215/831–2000; Torresdale Campus), Knights and Red Lion Roads, Zip 19114–1486; tel. 215/612–4000; Roy A. Powell, President **A**1 3 5 6 8 9 10 **F**2 3 7 8 12 13 14 15 16 17 19 21 22 23 24 25 26 27 28 29 30 31 32 34 35 37 38 39 40 41 42 44 45 46 48 49 51 59 60 61 64 65 67 70 71 73 74 **P**7 **N** Jefferson Health System, Radnor, PA	23	10	337	19263	265	178085	1825	161007	71789	—
FRIEDMAN HOSPITAL OF THE HOME FOR THE JEWISH AGED, 5301 Old York Road, Zip 19141–2996; tel. 215/456–2900; Frank Podietz, President (Total facility includes 538 beds in nursing home–type unit) **A**9 10 **F**1 2 3 4 5 6 7 8 9 10 11 12 13 15 16 17 18 19 20 21 22 23 24 25 26 27 28 29 30 31 32 33 34 35 36 37 38 39 40 41 42 43 44 45 46 47 48 49 50 51 52 53 54 55 56 57 58 59 60 61 62 63 64 65 66 67 68 69 70 71 72 73 74 **P**6	23	10	566	957	538	65517	—	49847	25124	824
✚ FRIENDS HOSPITAL, 4641 Roosevelt Boulevard, Zip 19124–2399; tel. 215/831–4600; Gary L. Gottlieb, M.D., Chief Executive Officer **A**1 3 9 10 **F**3 15 16 27 30 32 52 53 54 55 57 58 59 73 **P**6 7	23	22	192	4101	154	—	—	31440	19288	542
✚ GERMANTOWN HOSPITAL AND MEDICAL CENTER, One Penn Boulevard, Zip 19144–1498; tel. 215/951–8000; David A. Ricci, President and Chief Executive Officer (Total facility includes 22 beds in nursing home–type unit) **A**1 3 5 6 9 10 **F**7 8 15 16 19 21 22 26 27 28 29 30 32 33 34 35 37 39 40 41 42 44 46 49 51 60 63 64 65 67 68 71 73 74 **P**8 **N** Jefferson Health System, Radnor, PA	23	10	117	7042	102	73500	—	57499	27199	605
GIRARD MEDICAL CENTER See North Philadelphia Health System										
GRADUATE HEALTH SYSTEM–CITY AVENUE See Allegheny University Hospital, City Avenue										
GRADUATE HOSPITAL See Allegheny University Hospital, Graduate										
✚ △ HOSPITAL OF THE UNIVERSITY OF PENNSYLVANIA, 3400 Spruce Street, Zip 19104–4204; tel. 215/662–4000; Thomas E. Beeman, Senior Vice President, Operations **A**1 3 5 7 8 9 10 **F**2 3 4 5 7 8 10 11 12 14 15 16 17 18 19 20 21 22 23 25 26 28 29 30 31 32 33 34 35 37 38 39 40 41 42 43 44 45 46 48 49 50 51 52 53 54 55 56 57 58 59 60 61 63 64 65 66 67 69 70 71 73 74 **P**1 5 6 7 8 **N** University of Pennsylvania Health System, Philadelphia, PA	23	10	628	29923	530	489675	2422	579729	207680	7046

Hospital, Address, Telephone, Administrator, Approval, Facility, and Physician Codes, Health Care System, Network	Classi-fication Codes		Utilization Data					Expense (thousands) of dollars		
★ American Hospital Association (AHA) membership □ Joint Commission on Accreditation of Healthcare Organizations (JCAHO) accreditation + American Osteopathic Healthcare Association (AOHA) membership ○ American Osteopathic Association (AOA) accreditation △ Commission on Accreditation of Rehabilitation Facilities (CARF) accreditation Control codes 61, 63, 64, 71, 72 and 73 indicate hospitals listed by AOHA, but not registered by AHA. For definition of numerical codes, see page A4	Control	Service	Staffed Beds	Admissions	Census	Outpatient Visits	Births	Total	Payroll	Personnel
✠ JEANES HOSPITAL, 7600 Central Avenue, Zip 19111–2430; tel. 215/728–2000; G. Roger Martin, President and Chief Executive Officer (Total facility includes 24 beds in nursing home–type unit) **A**1 9 10 **F**1 7 8 12 14 15 16 17 19 21 22 24 26 28 30 32 33 35 37 38 39 40 41 42 44 46 49 60 61 64 65 66 67 71 73 74 **N** Temple University Health Network, Philadelphia, PA	23	10	212	9279	157	89650	601	76108	32585	964
□ JOHN F. KENNEDY MEMORIAL HOSPITAL, Langdon Street and Cheltenham Avenue, Zip 19124–1098; tel. 215/831–7000; James J. Nelson, Executive Director (Nonreporting) **A**1 9 10	23	10	141	—	—	—	—	—	—	—
□ KENSINGTON HOSPITAL, 136 West Diamond Street, Zip 19122–1707; tel. 215/426–8100; Eileen Hause, Chief Executive Officer **A**1 9 10 **F**3 8 15 16 20 31 44 51 58 65 71	23	10	45	2029	21	10822	—	5233	3168	99
✠ △ MAGEE REHABILITATION HOSPITAL, Six Franklin Plaza, Zip 19102–1177; tel. 215/587–3099; William E. Staas, Jr., President and Medical Director **A**1 3 7 9 10 **F**3 12 14 15 16 17 18 20 25 26 27 28 39 41 45 48 49 54 56 65 67 68 71 73 74 **P**4	23	46	96	1257	75	39739	—	30270	16379	429
METHODIST HOSPITAL See Thomas Jefferson University Hospital										
✠ △ NAZARETH HOSPITAL, 2601 Holme Avenue, Zip 19152–2096; tel. 215/335–6000; Daniel J. Sinnott, President and Chief Executive Officer (Total facility includes 29 beds in nursing home–type unit) **A**1 7 9 10 **F**7 8 11 12 14 15 16 17 19 21 22 27 28 30 31 32 34 35 37 38 39 40 41 42 44 45 46 48 49 52 54 56 57 60 63 64 65 67 71 73 74 **P**5 7 8 **S** Catholic Health Initiatives, Denver, CO	21	10	259	10179	166	154116	189	68426	31927	775
□ NEUMANN MEDICAL CENTER, 1741 Frankford Avenue, Zip 19125–2495; tel. 215/291–2000; Joseph C. Hare, President and Chief Executive Officer (Nonreporting) **A**1 9 10 **N** Temple University Health Network, Philadelphia, PA	23	10	166	—	—	—	—	—	—	—
□ NORTH PHILADELPHIA HEALTH SYSTEM, (Includes Girard Medical Center, Girard Avenue at Eighth Street, Zip 19122; tel. 215/787–2000; Gloria Zankwoski, Senior Vice President and Chief Executive Officer; St. Joseph's Hospital, 16th Street and Girard Avenue, tel. 215/787–9000; Catherine Kutzler, R.N., Senior Vice President and Chief Executive Officer), 16th Street and Girard Avenue, Zip 19130; tel. 215/787–9000; George J. Walmsley, III, President and Chief Executive Officer (Nonreporting) **A**1 5 9 10 12 13	23	10	315	—	—	—	—	—	—	—
□ NORTHEASTERN HOSPITAL OF PHILADELPHIA, 2301 East Allegheny Avenue, Zip 19134–4499; tel. 215/291–3000; Jeffrey L. Susi, Executive Director and Chief Executive Officer (Total facility includes 20 beds in nursing home–type unit) **A**1 2 5 6 9 10 **F**1 4 8 10 11 12 13 15 16 17 18 19 21 22 26 27 28 30 32 33 34 35 37 38 40 41 42 43 44 45 46 48 49 50 51 52 53 54 55 56 57 58 59 60 61 64 65 66 67 68 69 70 71 73 **P**4 5 6 **N** Temple University Health Network, Philadelphia, PA	23	10	159	6945	92	45159	799	45790	21367	544
PARKVIEW HOSPITAL See Allegheny University Hospital, Parkview										
✠ PENNSYLVANIA HOSPITAL, 800 Spruce Street, Zip 19107–6192; tel. 215/829–3000; John R. Ball, M.D., JD, President and Chief Executive Officer (Total facility includes 29 beds in nursing home–type unit) (Nonreporting) **A**1 3 5 8 9 10	23	10	414	—	—	—	—	—	—	—
□ PRESBYTERIAN MEDICAL CENTER OF THE UNIVERSITY OF PENNSYLVANIA HEALTH SYSTEM, 51 North 39th Street, Zip 19104–2640; tel. 215/662–8000; Michele M. Volpe, Executive Director (Total facility includes 20 beds in nursing home–type unit) (Nonreporting) **A**1 3 5 6 9 10 **N** University of Pennsylvania Health System, Philadelphia, PA	23	10	325	—	—	—	—	—	—	—
□ ROXBOROUGH MEMORIAL HOSPITAL, 5800 Ridge Avenue, Zip 19128–1737; tel. 215/483–9900; John J. Donnelly, Jr., President and Chief Executive Officer (Total facility includes 24 beds in nursing home–type unit) (Nonreporting) **A**1 6 9 10	23	10	129	—	—	—	—	—	—	—
✠ SHRINERS HOSPITALS FOR CHILDREN, PHILADELPHIA, 3551 North Broad Street, Zip 19140; tel. 215/430–4000; Sharon J. Rajnic, Administrator (Nonreporting) **A**1 3 5 **S** Shriners Hospitals for Children, Tampa, FL	23	57	80	—	—	—	—	—	—	—
✠ ○ ST. AGNES MEDICAL CENTER, 1900 South Broad Street, Zip 19145–2304; tel. 215/339–4100; Daniel J. Sinnott, President and Chief Executive Officer (Total facility includes 19 beds in nursing home–type unit) **A**1 3 5 9 10 11 **F**1 9 11 12 17 19 21 22 24 27 28 30 32 34 37 41 42 44 48 49 64 65 71 73 74 **P**5 7 8 **S** Catholic Health Initiatives, Denver, CO	21	10	172	5634	115	52626	—	54926	23059	537
✠ ST. CHRISTOPHER'S HOSPITAL FOR CHILDREN, Erie Avenue at Front Street, Zip 19134–1095; tel. 215/427–5000; Calvin Bland, President and Chief Executive Officer **A**1 3 5 8 9 10 **F**1 2 3 4 5 7 8 9 10 11 12 13 14 15 16 17 18 19 20 21 22 25 26 28 30 31 32 33 34 35 37 38 39 40 41 42 43 44 45 46 47 48 49 51 52 53 54 55 56 57 58 59 60 61 64 65 66 67 68 69 70 71 73 74 **P**6 7 **S** Allegheny Health, Education and Research Foundation, Pittsburgh, PA	23	50	183	11015	131	—	0	133131	55158	1229
ST. JOSEPH'S HOSPITAL See North Philadelphia Health System										
□ TEMPLE UNIVERSITY HOSPITAL, Broad and Ontario Streets, Zip 19140–5192; tel. 215/707–2000; Paul Boehringer, Executive Director (Total facility includes 16 beds in nursing home–type unit) (Nonreporting) **A**1 2 3 5 8 9 10 **N** Temple University Health Network, Philadelphia, PA	23	10	430	—	—	—	—	—	—	—

Hospital, Address, Telephone, Administrator, Approval, Facility, and Physician Codes, Health Care System, Network	Classification Codes		Utilization Data					Expense (thousands) of dollars		
	Control	Service	Staffed Beds	Admissions	Census	Outpatient Visits	Births	Total	Payroll	Personnel

★ American Hospital Association (AHA) membership
□ Joint Commission on Accreditation of Healthcare Organizations (JCAHO) accreditation
+ American Osteopathic Healthcare Association (AOHA) membership
○ American Osteopathic Association (AOA) accreditation
△ Commission on Accreditation of Rehabilitation Facilities (CARF) accreditation
Control codes 61, 63, 64, 71, 72 and 73 indicate hospitals listed by AOHA, but not registered by AHA. For definition of numerical codes, see page A4

Hospital	Control	Service	Staffed Beds	Admissions	Census	Outpatient Visits	Births	Total	Payroll	Personnel
⊞ △ THOMAS JEFFERSON UNIVERSITY HOSPITAL, (Includes Methodist Hospital, 2301 South Broad Street, Zip 19148; tel. 215/952–9000; Thomas Jefferson University Hospital–Ford Road Campus, 3905 Ford Road, Zip 19131; tel. 215/578–3630), 111 South 11th Street, Zip 19107–5096; tel. 215/955–7022; Thomas J. Lewis, President and Chief Executive Officer **A**1 2 3 5 6 7 8 9 10 **F**1 3 4 5 6 7 8 10 11 12 13 15 16 17 18 19 20 21 22 23 24 25 26 27 28 29 30 31 32 33 34 35 36 37 38 39 40 41 42 43 44 45 46 47 48 49 51 52 53 54 55 56 57 58 60 61 63 64 65 66 67 68 69 70 71 73 74 **P**2 3 4 7 8 **S** Jefferson Health System, Wayne, PA **N** Health Share, Philadelphia, PA; Jefferson Health System, Radnor, PA	23	10	686	30973	513	656548	3122	450104	222287	5285
□ VENCOR HOSPITAL–PHILADELPHIA, (ACUTE LONG TERM), 6129 Palmetto Street, Zip 19111–5729; tel. 215/722–8555; Debra Condon, Administrator **A**1 10 **F**22 37 65 71 **S** Vencor, Incorporated, Louisville, KY	33	49	52	279	37	—	—	10410	5255	137
⊞ VETERANS AFFAIRS MEDICAL CENTER, University and Woodland Avenues, Zip 19104–4594; tel. 215/823–5800; Earl F. Falast, Chief Executive Officer (Total facility includes 180 beds in nursing home–type unit) (Nonreporting) **A**1 3 5 8 9 **S** Department of Veterans Affairs, Washington, DC	45	10	656	—	—	—	—	—	—	—
⊞ WILLS EYE HOSPITAL, (EYE HOSPITAL), 900 Walnut Street, Zip 19107–5598; tel. 215/928–3000; D. McWilliams Kessler, Executive Director **A**1 3 5 9 10 **F**2 3 4 5 6 7 8 9 10 11 12 13 14 15 16 17 18 19 20 21 22 23 24 25 26 27 28 29 30 31 32 33 34 35 37 38 39 40 41 42 43 44 45 46 47 48 49 50 51 52 53 54 55 56 57 58 59 60 61 62 63 65 66 67 68 69 70 71 72 73 74 **N** Jefferson Health System, Radnor, PA	23	49	115	3905	43	62621	0	57370	23762	617

PHOENIXVILLE—Chester County

Hospital	Control	Service	Staffed Beds	Admissions	Census	Outpatient Visits	Births	Total	Payroll	Personnel
⊞ PHOENIXVILLE HOSPITAL, 140 Nutt Road, Zip 19460–0809, Mailing Address: P.O. Box 809, Zip 19460–0809; tel. 610/983–1000; Richard E. Seagrave, Executive Director and Chief Operating Officer **A**1 9 10 **F**7 8 10 11 13 14 15 16 17 19 20 21 26 30 31 32 33 35 37 39 40 41 42 44 46 49 54 55 56 61 63 65 66 71 73	23	10	106	6270	65	105282	1203	43166	19564	590

PITTSBURGH—Allegheny County

Hospital	Control	Service	Staffed Beds	Admissions	Census	Outpatient Visits	Births	Total	Payroll	Personnel
⊞ ALLEGHENY UNIVERSITY HOSPITALS WEST–FORBES METROPOLITAN, (Formerly Forbes Metropolitan Hospital), 225 Penn Avenue, Zip 15221–2173; tel. 412/247–2424; April A. Stevens, R.N., Vice President and Administrator (Nonreporting) **A**1 9 10 **S** Allegheny Health, Education and Research Foundation, Pittsburgh, PA	23	49	152	—	—	—	—	—	—	—
⊞ ALLEGHENY UNIVERSITY HOSPITALS, ALLEGHENY GENERAL, (Formerly Allegheny General Hospital), 320 East North Avenue, Zip 15212–4756; tel. 412/359–3131; Anthony M. Sanzo, President and Chief Executive Officer (Total facility includes 80 beds in nursing home–type unit) **A**1 2 3 5 8 9 10 **F**3 4 7 8 10 11 12 13 14 15 16 17 18 19 20 22 23 24 25 26 27 28 30 31 32 33 34 35 37 38 39 40 41 42 43 44 45 46 49 51 52 53 54 55 56 57 58 59 60 61 63 64 65 66 67 68 69 70 71 73 74 **P**8 **S** Allegheny Health, Education and Research Foundation, Pittsburgh, PA	23	10	569	30118	489	379970	1766	442717	160244	4215
★ CHILDREN'S HOME OF PITTSBURGH, 5618 Kentucky Avenue, Zip 15232–2696; tel. 412/441–4884; Pamela R. Schanwald, Chief Executive Officer (Nonreporting) **A**9 10	23	59	10	—	—	—	—	—	—	—
⊞ CHILDREN'S HOSPITAL OF PITTSBURGH, 3705 Fifth Avenue at De Soto Street, Zip 15213–2583; tel. 412/692–5325; Ronald L. Violi, President and Chief Executive Officer (Nonreporting) **A**1 2 3 5 8 9 10 **N** Tri–State Network, Pittsburgh, PA; University of Pittsburgh Medical Center, Pittsburgh, PA	23	50	235	—	—	—	—	—	—	—
EYE AND EAR HOSPITAL OF PITTSBURGH See UPMC–Presbyterian										
□ △ HEALTHSOUTH HARMARVILLE REHABILITATION HOSPITAL, Guys Run Road, Zip 15238–0460, Mailing Address: Box 11460, Guys Run Road, Zip 15238–0460; tel. 412/781–5700; Frank G. DeLisi, III, CHE, Chief Executive Officer and Director Operations (Total facility includes 40 beds in nursing home–type unit) (Nonreporting) **A**1 3 7 9 10 **S** HEALTHSOUTH Corporation, Birmingham, AL	33	46	202	—	—	—	—	—	—	—
⊞ MAGEE–WOMENS HOSPITAL, 300 Halket Street, Zip 15213–3180; tel. 412/641–1000; Irma E. Goertzen, President and Chief Executive Officer **A**1 2 3 5 8 9 10 **F**7 8 12 13 14 15 16 17 22 25 27 28 29 30 32 34 37 38 39 40 42 44 45 46 49 60 61 65 67 68 73 74 **P**6 8 **N** Tri–State Network, Pittsburgh, PA; University of Pittsburgh Medical Center, Pittsburgh, PA	23	44	277	13520	141	—	8384	114534	49902	1676
□ △ MERCY HOSPITAL OF PITTSBURGH, 1400 Locust Street, Zip 15219–5166; tel. 412/232–8111; Thomas J. Mattei, Chief Operating Officer (Total facility includes 37 beds in nursing home–type unit) (Nonreporting) **A**1 2 3 5 6 7 8 9 10 **S** Catholic Health East, Radnor, PA	23	10	493	—	—	—	—	—	—	—
□ MERCY PROVIDENCE HOSPITAL, 1004 Arch Street, Zip 15212–5294; tel. 412/323–5600; Thomas J. Mattei, Chief Operating Officer (Nonreporting) **A**1 9 10 **S** Catholic Health East, Radnor, PA	21	10	146	—	—	—	—	—	—	—
MONTEFIORE HOSPITAL See UPMC–Presbyterian										
PASSAVANT HOSPITAL See University of Pittsburgh Medical Center–Passavant										
PODIATRY HOSPITAL OF PITTSBURGH, 215 South Negley Avenue, Zip 15206–3522; tel. 412/661–0814; Joseph S. Noviello, Chief Executive Officer (Nonreporting) **A**9 10	23	49	13	—	—	—	—	—	—	—
⊞ △ REHABILITATION INSTITUTE OF PITTSBURGH, 6301 Northumberland Street, Zip 15217–1360; tel. 412/420–2400; John A. Wilson, President and Chief Executive Officer (Total facility includes 25 beds in nursing home–type unit) **A**1 7 9 10 **F**5 12 14 15 16 17 26 32 34 41 46 48 49 53 57 59 64 65 66 73	23	46	115	1581	85	—	—	24344	12946	411

Hospital, Address, Telephone, Administrator, Approval, Facility, and Physician Codes, Health Care System, Network	Classi-fication Codes		Utilization Data					Expense (thousands) of dollars		
★ American Hospital Association (AHA) membership □ Joint Commission on Accreditation of Healthcare Organizations (JCAHO) accreditation + American Osteopathic Healthcare Association (AOHA) membership ○ American Osteopathic Association (AOA) accreditation △ Commission on Accreditation of Rehabilitation Facilities (CARF) accreditation Control codes 61, 63, 64, 71, 72 and 73 indicate hospitals listed by AOHA, but not registered by AHA. For definition of numerical codes, see page A4	Control	Service	Staffed Beds	Admissions	Census	Outpatient Visits	Births	Total	Payroll	Personnel

✠ SHADYSIDE HOSPITAL, 5230 Centre Avenue, Zip 15232–1304; tel. 412/623–2121; Henry A. Mordoh, President (Total facility includes 145 beds in nursing home–type unit) **A**1 2 3 5 8 9 10 **F**3 4 6 7 8 10 11 13 14 15 16 17 18 19 21 22 25 26 27 28 30 31 32 33 34 35 37 39 40 41 42 43 44 46 49 51 53 54 55 56 57 58 59 60 61 62 64 65 66 67 68 69 70 71 73 74 **P**7 **S** UPMC Health System, Pittsburgh, PA **N** Fox Chase Network, Rockledge, PA	23	10	631	18921	426	206410	770	206815	81361	1998
□ SOUTH HILLS HEALTH SYSTEM, 565 Coal Valley Road, Zip 15236–0119, Mailing Address: Box 18119, Zip 15236–0119; tel. 412/469–5000; William R. Jennings, President and Chief Executive Officer (Total facility includes 74 beds in nursing home–type unit) (Nonreporting) **A**1 9 10 **N** Tri–State Network, Pittsburgh, PA	23	10	466	—	—	—	—	—	—	—
□ SOUTHWOOD PSYCHIATRIC HOSPITAL, 2575 Boyce Plaza Road, Zip 15241–3925; tel. 412/257–2290; Alan A. Axelson, M.D., Chief Executive Officer (Nonreporting) **A**1 9 **S** FHC Health Systems, Norfolk, VA	33	52	50	—	—	—	—	—	—	—
✠ ST. CLAIR MEMORIAL HOSPITAL, 1000 Bower Hill Road, Zip 15243–1899; tel. 412/561–4900; Benjamin E. Snead, President and Chief Executive Officer **A**1 2 9 10 **F**1 4 5 6 7 8 10 11 12 13 14 15 17 18 19 20 21 22 23 24 25 26 27 28 29 30 31 32 33 34 35 37 38 39 40 41 42 43 44 45 46 47 48 49 50 51 52 53 54 55 56 57 58 59 60 61 63 64 65 66 67 68 69 70 71 72 73 74 **P**1 3 8 **N** SouthWest Integrated Delivery Network, Pittsburgh, PA; Alpha Health Network, Pittsburgh, PA	23	10	266	11987	174	140683	1240	87036	41131	1141
✠ ○ ST. FRANCIS CENTRAL HOSPITAL, 1200 Centre Avenue, Zip 15219–3594; tel. 412/562–3000; Robin Z. Mohr, Chief Executive Officer (Total facility includes 19 beds in nursing home–type unit) **A**1 9 10 11 12 13 **F**2 3 4 5 7 8 10 11 12 13 14 17 18 19 20 21 22 23 25 26 27 28 29 30 31 32 34 35 37 39 40 41 42 43 44 45 46 48 49 51 52 53 54 55 56 57 58 59 60 61 62 63 64 65 66 67 68 71 72 73 74 **P**5 6 **S** St. Francis Health System, Pittsburgh, PA **N** Saint Francis Health System, Pittsburgh, PA	23	10	134	3951	65	52016	—	37010	14972	461
✠ △ ST. FRANCIS MEDICAL CENTER, 400 45th Street, Zip 15201–1198; tel. 412/622–4343; Sister Florence Brandt, Chief Executive Officer (Total facility includes 320 beds in nursing home–type unit) **A**1 2 3 5 6 7 8 9 10 **F**2 3 4 5 7 8 10 11 12 14 15 17 19 20 21 22 23 24 25 26 28 29 30 31 32 34 35 37 39 40 41 42 43 44 45 46 48 49 50 51 52 53 54 55 56 57 58 59 60 63 64 65 66 67 68 71 72 73 74 **P**8 **S** St. Francis Health System, Pittsburgh, PA	23	10	885	17787	634	304253	710	188504	84913	2586
STATE CORRECTIONAL INSTITUTION HOSPITAL, Doerr Street, Zip 15233, Mailing Address: Box 99901, Zip 15233; tel. 412/761–1955; Joseph Morrash, Administrator (Nonreporting)	12	11	27	—	—	—	—	—	—	—
□ SUBURBAN GENERAL HOSPITAL, 100 South Jackson Avenue, Zip 15202–3428; tel. 412/734–6000; Thomas H. Prickett, President and Chief Executive Officer (Total facility includes 26 beds in nursing home–type unit) (Nonreporting) **A**1 9 10	23	10	144	—	—	—	—	—	—	—
UNIVERISTY OF PITTSBURGH MEDICAL CENTER–SOUTHSIDE See UPMC South Side										
UNIVERSITY OF PITTSBURGH MEDICAL CENTER See UPMC–Presbyterian										
□ UNIVERSITY OF PITTSBURGH MEDICAL CENTER–PASSAVANT, (Formerly Passavant Hospital), 9100 Babcock Boulevard, Zip 15237–5842; tel. 412/367–6700; Ralph T. DeStefano, President and Chief Executive Officer (Total facility includes 24 beds in nursing home–type unit) **A**1 9 10 **F**4 6 7 8 10 11 12 15 16 17 19 21 22 26 28 29 30 32 34 35 37 39 40 41 42 43 44 45 46 49 51 53 54 55 56 57 58 59 60 61 62 63 64 65 66 67 69 71 72 73 74 **P**5 6 7 8 **S** UPMC Health System, Pittsburgh, PA	23	10	292	9700	139	150342	—	—	35696	1090
□ UPMC SOUTH SIDE, (Formerly Univeristy of Pittsburgh Medical Center–Southside), 2000 Mary Street, Zip 15203–2095; tel. 412/488–5550; George J. Korbakes, President **A**1 9 10 **F**1 2 3 4 5 6 7 8 10 11 12 13 14 15 16 17 18 19 20 21 22 23 24 25 26 27 28 29 30 31 32 33 34 35 36 37 38 39 40 41 42 43 44 45 46 47 48 49 50 51 52 53 54 55 56 57 58 59 60 61 62 63 64 65 66 67 68 69 70 71 72 73 74 **P**1 5 6 7 **S** UPMC Health System, Pittsburgh, PA	23	10	140	5050	105	20053	—	34394	16727	484
✠ UPMC–PRESBYTERIAN, (Formerly University of Pittsburgh Medical Center), (Includes Eye and Ear Hospital of Pittsburgh, 200 Lothrop Street, Zip 15213–2592; tel. 412/647–2345; Montefiore Hospital, 200 Lothrop Street, Zip 15213; tel. 412/647–2345; UPMC–Presbyterian Hospital, 200 Lothrop Street, Zip 15213; tel. 412/647–8650; Western Psychiatric Institute and Clinic, 3811 O'Hara Street, Zip 15213–2593; tel. 412/624–2100), Jeffrey A. Romoff, President **A**1 2 3 5 8 9 **F**1 2 3 4 5 6 7 8 10 11 12 13 14 15 16 17 18 19 20 21 22 23 24 25 26 27 28 29 30 31 32 33 34 35 36 37 38 39 40 41 42 43 44 45 46 48 49 50 51 52 53 54 55 56 57 58 59 60 61 63 64 65 66 67 68 69 70 71 72 73 74 **P**1 5 6 7 **S** UPMC Health System, Pittsburgh, PA **N** Tri–State Network, Pittsburgh, PA; University of Pittsburgh Medical Center, Pittsburgh, PA	23	10	840	31862	659	612321	—	561769	163538	6932
UPMC–PRESBYTERIAN HOSPITAL See UPMC–Presbyterian										
✠ UPMC–ST. MARGARET, (Formerly University of Pittsburgh Medical Center–St. Margaret), 815 Freeport Road, Zip 15215–3399; tel. 412/784–4000; Stanley J. Kevish, President (Total facility includes 22 beds in nursing home–type unit) **A**1 2 3 5 6 8 9 10 **F**5 6 8 10 15 16 17 19 20 21 22 25 26 28 29 30 31 32 33 34 35 37 39 41 42 44 45 46 48 49 56 57 58 60 62 64 65 66 67 71 73 **P**8 **S** UPMC Health System, Pittsburgh, PA **N** Tri–State Network, Pittsburgh, PA; University of Pittsburgh Medical Center, Pittsburgh, PA	23	10	223	8916	144	102262	—	85480	35130	968

Hospital, Address, Telephone, Administrator, Approval, Facility, and Physician Codes, Health Care System, Network	Classi-fication Codes		Utilization Data					Expense (thousands) of dollars		
★ American Hospital Association (AHA) membership □ Joint Commission on Accreditation of Healthcare Organizations (JCAHO) accreditation + American Osteopathic Healthcare Association (AOHA) membership ○ American Osteopathic Association (AOA) accreditation △ Commission on Accreditation of Rehabilitation Facilities (CARF) accreditation Control codes 61, 63, 64, 71, 72 and 73 indicate hospitals listed by AOHA, but not registered by AHA. For definition of numerical codes, see page A4	Control	Service	Staffed Beds	Admissions	Census	Outpatient Visits	Births	Total	Payroll	Personnel

☒ VETERANS AFFAIRS PITTSBURGH HEALTHCARE SYSTEM, (MEDICAL SURGICAL LONG TERM SER), (Includes Veterans Affairs Medical Center, 7180 Highland Drive, Zip 15206–1297; tel. 412/365–4900; Veterans Affairs Medical Center, University Drive C., tel. 412/688–6000), Delafield Road, Zip 15240–1001; tel. 412/784–3900; Thomas A. Cappello, Director (Total facility includes 300 beds in nursing home–type unit) **A**1 2 3 5 8 **F**1 3 4 5 6 8 9 10 11 12 16 17 18 19 20 21 22 23 24 26 27 28 29 30 31 32 34 35 37 39 40 41 42 43 44 45 46 49 50 51 52 54 55 56 57 58 59 60 63 64 65 67 69 71 73 74 **P**1 **S** Department of Veterans Affairs, Washington, DC	45	49	941	9435	768	341056	—	211353	113463	—
☒ WESTERN PENNSYLVANIA HOSPITAL, 4800 Friendship Avenue, Zip 15224–1722; tel. 412/578–5000; Charles M. O'Brien, Jr., President and Chief Executive Officer **A**1 2 3 5 6 8 9 10 **F**4 7 8 9 10 11 12 13 14 15 16 17 18 19 20 21 22 26 27 28 30 31 32 33 34 35 37 38 40 41 42 43 44 45 46 49 50 51 52 54 56 57 60 61 63 64 65 67 68 69 71 73 74 **P**7 8	23	10	455	18161	314	—	1672	203717	86926	2475
WESTERN PSYCHIATRIC INSTITUTE AND CLINIC See UPMC–Presbyterian										
PLEASANT GAP—Centre County										
□ △ HEALTHSOUTH NITTANY VALLEY REHABILITATION HOSPITAL, 550 West College Avenue, Zip 16823–8808; tel. 814/359–3421; Mary Jane Hawkins, Administrator and Chief Executive Officer (Nonreporting) **A**1 7 9 10 **S** HEALTHSOUTH Corporation, Birmingham, AL	33	46	88	—	—	—	—	—	—	—
POTTSTOWN—Montgomery County										
☒ POTTSTOWN MEMORIAL MEDICAL CENTER, 1600 East High Street, Zip 19464–5008; tel. 610/327–7000; John J. Buckley, President and Chief Executive Officer (Total facility includes 21 beds in nursing home–type unit) **A**1 2 9 10 **F**1 7 8 10 12 15 17 19 20 21 22 23 24 28 30 32 34 35 36 37 38 39 40 41 42 44 45 46 49 51 52 56 57 59 60 63 64 65 66 67 71 73 74 **P**6 **N** Jefferson Health System, Radnor, PA	23	10	212	9064	123	130477	836	70434	32793	920
POTTSVILLE—Schuylkill County										
☒ GOOD SAMARITAN REGIONAL MEDICAL CENTER, 700 East Norwegian Street, Zip 17901–2798; tel. 717/621–4000; Gino J. Pazzaglini, President and Chief Executive Officer **A**1 2 5 9 10 **F**3 4 7 8 11 12 14 15 16 19 22 26 28 30 31 32 33 34 35 36 37 39 40 41 42 44 45 46 65 67 71 73 74 **P**6 **S** Daughters of Charity National Health System, Saint Louis, MO	21	10	221	8318	133	137667	452	47549	22843	764
☒ △ POTTSVILLE HOSPITAL AND WARNE CLINIC, 420 South Jackson Street, Zip 17901–3692; tel. 717/621–5000; Donald R. Gintzig, President and Chief Executive Officer **A**1 2 6 7 9 10 **F**7 8 12 14 15 16 17 19 20 21 22 26 27 28 30 31 32 33 34 35 37 39 40 41 42 44 45 48 49 52 53 55 56 57 58 65 66 71 73 74 **S** Quorum Health Group/Quorum Health Resources, Inc., Brentwood, TN	23	10	196	6253	131	77280	482	45111	20578	719
PUNXSUTAWNEY—Jefferson County										
□ PUNXSUTAWNEY AREA HOSPITAL, 81 Hillcrest Drive, Zip 15767–2616; tel. 814/938–1800; Daniel D. Blough, Jr., Chief Executive Officer (Total facility includes 14 beds in nursing home–type unit) **A**1 9 10 **F**7 8 15 16 19 21 22 30 31 32 34 37 39 40 42 44 49 64 65 71	23	10	65	2297	33	85927	246	17490	7015	284
QUAKERTOWN—Bucks County										
□ ST. LUKE'S QUAKERTOWN HOSPITAL, 1021 Park Avenue, Zip 18951–1551; tel. 215/538–4500; Fred Sprissler, President and Chief Executive Officer **A**1 2 9 10 **F**3 8 15 17 19 22 23 26 27 28 30 31 37 41 42 44 49 52 53 54 58 64 65 67 71 73 74 **P**3 8	23	10	68	2570	37	37299	—	20164	8652	289
READING—Berks County										
☒ △ HEALTHSOUTH REHABILITATION HOSPITAL OF READING, (Formerly Reading Rehabilitation Hospital), 1623 Morgantown Road, Zip 19607–9455; tel. 610/796–6000; Teresa K. Stranko, Interim Administrator (Total facility includes 19 beds in nursing home–type unit) **A**1 3 7 9 10 **F**12 14 15 16 26 27 39 41 48 49 64 65 67 73 **S** HEALTHSOUTH Corporation, Birmingham, AL	21	46	95	1583	61	23759	—	18683	8241	408
☒ READING HOSPITAL AND MEDICAL CENTER, Sixth Avenue and Spruce Street, Zip 19611–1428, Mailing Address: P.O. Box 16052, Zip 19612–6052; tel. 610/378–6000; Charles Sullivan, President and Chief Executive Officer **A**1 2 5 6 9 10 **F**3 4 7 8 10 14 15 16 17 18 19 20 21 22 23 25 26 28 29 30 31 34 35 37 38 39 40 41 42 43 44 45 46 49 51 52 53 54 55 56 57 58 59 60 61 62 65 66 67 68 71 72 73 74 **P**8 **N** Fox Chase Network, Rockledge, PA	23	10	533	24529	368	537323	2760	203493	95199	2720
READING REHABILITATION HOSPITAL See HEALTHSOUTH Rehabilitation Hospital of Reading										
☒ ST. JOSEPH MEDICAL CENTER, Twelth and Walnut Streets, Zip 19603–0316, Mailing Address: P.O. Box 316, Zip 19603–0316; tel. 610/378–2000; Philip G. Dionne, President and Chief Executive Officer **A**1 2 3 5 9 10 12 **F**1 2 3 4 6 7 8 10 12 13 14 15 16 17 18 19 20 21 22 24 26 27 28 30 31 32 33 34 35 37 39 40 41 42 43 44 46 49 51 52 53 54 55 56 57 58 59 60 62 64 65 66 67 68 69 71 72 73 74 **P**1 5 8 **S** Catholic Health Initiatives, Denver, CO	23	10	243	10781	141	214372	924	84550	33926	1226
RENOVO—Clinton County										
BUCKTAIL MEDICAL CENTER, 1001 Pine Street, Zip 17764–1618; tel. 717/923–1000; Lennea F. Brown, Administrator (Total facility includes 41 beds in nursing home–type unit) (Nonreporting) **A**9 10	23	10	50	—	—	—	—	—	—	—
RIDGWAY—Elk County										
□ ELK COUNTY REGIONAL MEDICAL CENTER, 94 Hospital Street, Zip 15853; tel. 814/776–6111; Kenneth G. Turner, CHE, Chief Executive Officer **A**1 9 10 **F**7 8 14 15 16 19 21 22 28 30 33 34 36 37 39 40 41 42 44 49 51 52 55 56 57 65 67 71 73 74	23	10	51	1413	23	22748	64	10297	4696	178

Hospital, Address, Telephone, Administrator, Approval, Facility, and Physician Codes, Health Care System, Network	Classification Codes		Utilization Data					Expense (thousands) of dollars		
	Control	Service	Staffed Beds	Admissions	Census	Outpatient Visits	Births	Total	Payroll	Personnel

RIDLEY PARK—Delaware County
TAYLOR HOSPITAL See Crozer–Chester Medical Center, Upland

ROARING SPRING—Blair County
✠ NASON HOSPITAL, 105 Nason Drive, Zip 16673–1202; tel. 814/224–2141; John P. Kinney, President **A**1 5 9 10 **F**7 8 15 19 21 22 28 29 32 33 34 35 37 40 44 45 49 63 65 67 71 73 — 23 10 50 1775 21 44468 246 13745 5316 197

SAINT MARYS—Elk County
✠ ST. MARYS REGIONAL MEDICAL CENTER, 763 Johnsonburg Road, Zip 15857–3417; tel. 814/781–7500; Paul A. De Santis, President (Total facility includes 138 beds in nursing home–type unit) **A**1 9 10 **F**7 8 12 14 15 17 19 21 22 28 29 30 32 33 35 37 40 41 42 44 45 46 49 52 62 64 65 66 71 73 74 **N** Great Lakes Health Network, Erie, PA — 23 10 204 3363 166 60090 319 19040 13657 554

SAYRE—Bradford County
✠ ROBERT PACKER HOSPITAL, 1 Guthrie Square, Zip 18840–1698; tel. 717/888–6666; William F. Vanaskie, President **A**1 2 3 5 9 10 **F**1 4 5 6 7 8 10 12 13 14 15 16 17 19 20 22 23 24 26 27 28 29 30 31 32 33 34 35 39 40 42 43 44 45 49 51 52 54 56 57 58 59 60 62 63 65 67 68 70 71 73 74 **P**5 **S** Guthrie Healthcare System, Sayre, PA **N** Guthrie Healthcare System, Sayre, PA — 23 10 243 11502 164 57673 698 104382 37331 1229

SCRANTON—Lackawanna County
✠ △ ALLIED SERVICES REHABILITATION HOSPITAL, 475 Morgan Highway, Zip 18501; tel. 717/348–1300; James L. Brady, President **A**1 7 9 10 **F**1 3 5 6 12 13 14 16 17 18 24 25 26 27 28 29 30 31 32 34 39 41 42 45 46 49 54 55 57 58 59 62 65 66 67 73 74 — 23 46 107 2101 92 15644 0 28732 13656 475
✠ COMMUNITY MEDICAL CENTER, 1800 Mulberry Street, Zip 18510; tel. 717/969–8000; C. Richard Hartman, M.D., President and Chief Executive Officer (Total facility includes 18 beds in nursing home–type unit) **A**1 3 9 10 **F**1 4 7 8 10 11 12 13 14 15 16 17 18 19 21 22 23 25 26 27 28 29 30 33 34 35 37 38 39 40 41 42 43 44 45 46 49 51 52 53 54 55 56 57 58 59 60 61 64 65 67 68 70 71 72 73 74 **P**5 8 — 23 10 276 12151 194 108948 1777 92271 35909 1061
☐ MERCY HOSPITAL OF SCRANTON, 746 Jefferson Avenue, Zip 18501–1624; tel. 717/348–7100; John L. Nespoli, President and Chief Executive Officer (Total facility includes 22 beds in nursing home–type unit) **A**1 2 3 5 9 10 **F**4 7 8 10 11 12 16 17 19 21 22 23 24 28 29 32 33 34 35 37 40 42 43 44 49 51 60 63 64 65 67 71 73 74 **P**8 **S** Catholic Healthcare Partners, Cincinnati, OH — 21 10 285 11972 219 257780 858 97291 41773 1369
✠ MOSES TAYLOR HOSPITAL, 700 Quincy Avenue, Zip 18510–1724; tel. 717/340–2100; Harold E. Anderson, Chief Executive Officer (Total facility includes 32 beds in nursing home–type unit) **A**1 3 5 9 10 **F**8 12 15 19 21 22 23 26 32 33 34 35 37 41 42 44 45 46 49 52 57 64 65 71 73 **P**1 2 6 7 — 23 10 219 8094 179 86322 — 62996 23504 828

SELLERSVILLE—Bucks County
✠ △ GRAND VIEW HOSPITAL, 700 Lawn Avenue, Zip 18960–1576; tel. 215/453–4000; Stuart H. Fine, Chief Executive Officer (Total facility includes 20 beds in nursing home–type unit) **A**1 2 7 9 10 **F**2 7 8 11 12 13 15 16 17 18 19 21 22 23 24 26 28 29 30 31 32 33 34 36 37 40 41 42 44 45 46 49 52 53 54 56 57 58 59 60 63 64 65 67 71 73 74 **P**1 — 23 10 193 8756 122 132930 1132 67320 31723 1039

SEWICKLEY—Allegheny County
✠ △ D. T. WATSON REHABILITATION HOSPITAL, 301 Camp Meeting Road, Zip 15143–8773; tel. 412/741–9500; Robert N. Gibson, President and Chief Executive Officer **A**1 7 9 10 **F**12 16 48 49 65 **P**6 — 23 46 44 403 20 13100 — 11011 5564 56
✠ SEWICKLEY VALLEY HOSPITAL, (A DIVISION OF VALLEY MEDICAL FACILITIES), 720 Blackburn Road, Zip 15143–1459; tel. 412/741–6600; James C. Cooper, Chief Executive Officer (Total facility includes 18 beds in nursing home–type unit) **A**1 6 9 10 **F**4 7 8 10 12 15 16 17 19 21 22 26 28 29 30 31 32 33 34 36 37 40 41 42 44 48 52 53 54 55 56 57 58 59 60 64 65 67 71 73 74 **P**1 5 6 **N** SouthWest Integrated Delivery Network, Pittsburgh, PA — 23 10 186 10002 125 126829 838 86485 38192 1099

SHARON—Mercer County
✠ △ SHARON REGIONAL HEALTH SYSTEM, 740 East State Street, Zip 16146–3395; tel. 724/983–3911; Wayne W. Johnston, President and Chief Executive Officer (Total facility includes 40 beds in nursing home–type unit) **A**1 2 6 7 9 10 **F**3 7 8 10 11 13 15 16 17 19 21 22 23 24 25 26 28 29 30 32 33 34 35 37 39 40 41 42 44 45 48 49 51 52 53 54 55 56 57 58 59 60 63 64 65 66 67 71 72 73 74 **P**8 — 23 10 234 9172 155 292490 608 68003 29961 1186

SHICKSHINNY—Luzerne County
CLEAR BROOK LODGE, Bethel Road, Zip 18655, Mailing Address: Rural Delivery 2, Box 2166, Zip 18655; tel. 717/864–3116; Dave Lombard, President and Chief Executive Officer (Nonreporting) — 23 82 65 — — — — — — —

SOMERSET—Somerset County
✠ SOMERSET HOSPITAL CENTER FOR HEALTH, 225 South Center Avenue, Zip 15501–2088; tel. 814/443–5000; Michael J. Farrell, Chief Executive Officer (Total facility includes 15 beds in nursing home–type unit) **A**1 2 9 10 **F**1 3 7 8 10 13 14 15 16 17 19 20 21 22 23 26 28 29 30 31 32 33 34 35 37 39 40 41 42 44 46 49 52 53 54 55 56 57 58 59 64 65 66 67 71 72 73 74 **P**6 — 23 10 130 4829 77 118837 520 34019 14897 562

SPANGLER—Cambria County
✠ MINERS HOSPITAL NORTHERN CAMBRIA, 2205 Crawford Avenue, Zip 15775, Mailing Address: P.O. Box 490, Zip 15775–0490; tel. 814/948–7171; Roger P. Winn, Chief Executive Officer **A**1 9 10 **F**8 14 15 19 21 22 26 28 30 33 34 35 37 39 41 42 44 49 56 65 71 **S** Quorum Health Group/Quorum Health Resources, Inc., Brentwood, TN — 23 10 40 1614 20 43553 — 10978 4860 182

SPRINGFIELD—Delaware County
SPRINGFIELD HOSPITAL see Crozer–Chester Medical Center, Upland

Hospital, Address, Telephone, Administrator, Approval, Facility, and Physician Codes, Health Care System, Network	Classi-fication Codes		Utilization Data					Expense (thousands) of dollars		
★ American Hospital Association (AHA) membership □ Joint Commission on Accreditation of Healthcare Organizations (JCAHO) accreditation + American Osteopathic Healthcare Association (AOHA) membership ○ American Osteopathic Association (AOA) accreditation △ Commission on Accreditation of Rehabilitation Facilities (CARF) accreditation Control codes 61, 63, 64, 71, 72 and 73 indicate hospitals listed by AOHA, but not registered by AHA. For definition of numerical codes, see page A4	Control	Service	Staffed Beds	Admissions	Census	Outpatient Visits	Births	Total	Payroll	Personnel

STATE COLLEGE—Centre County

☒ CENTRE COMMUNITY HOSPITAL, 1800 East Park Avenue, Zip 16803–6797; tel. 814/231–7000; Lance H. Rose, FACHE, President **A**1 2 9 10 **F**7 8 11 14 15 16 17 19 21 22 23 28 30 31 32 33 34 35 37 39 40 41 42 44 46 49 52 54 56 57 60 61 63 65 71 73 — 23 | 10 | 167 | 8342 | 109 | 114623 | 1173 | 56680 | 26700 | 683

SUNBURY—Northumberland County

☒ SUNBURY COMMUNITY HOSPITAL, 350 North Eleventh Street, Zip 17801–0737; tel. 717/286–3333; Nicholas A. Prisco, Chief Executive Officer (Total facility includes 29 beds in nursing home–type unit) **A**1 9 10 **F**7 8 10 11 12 13 14 15 16 17 19 20 21 22 23 24 26 27 28 29 30 31 32 33 34 35 36 39 40 41 42 44 45 49 54 60 61 64 65 66 67 68 69 71 73 74 **P**8 — 23 | 10 | 101 | 3099 | 57 | 77295 | 149 | 21238 | 10455 | 379

SUSQUEHANNA—Susquehanna County

BARNES–KASSON COUNTY HOSPITAL, 400 Turnpike Street, Zip 18847–1638; tel. 717/853–3135; Sara C. Iveson, Executive Director (Total facility includes 58 beds in nursing home–type unit) **A**9 10 **F**7 8 12 13 16 17 19 20 22 27 30 32 34 35 36 37 40 41 42 44 45 49 51 63 64 65 68 71 73 — 23 | 10 | 105 | 1859 | 83 | 23205 | 127 | 11735 | 5959 | 214

TITUSVILLE—Crawford County

★ TITUSVILLE AREA HOSPITAL, 406 West Oak Street, Zip 16354–1499; tel. 814/827–1851; Anthony J. Nasralla, FACHE, President and Chief Executive Officer (Nonreporting) **A**9 10 **N** Vantage Health Care Network, Inc., Meadville, PA — 23 | 10 | 90 | — | — | — | — | — | — | —

TORRANCE—Westmoreland County

□ TORRANCE STATE HOSPITAL, Torrance Road, Zip 15779–0111; tel. 412/459–8000; Richard A. Stillwagon, Superintendent **A**1 10 **F**8 11 14 15 16 19 20 22 35 37 52 57 65 73 — 12 | 22 | 414 | 155 | 360 | 0 | 0 | 35472 | 18007 | 579

TOWANDA—Bradford County

★ MEMORIAL HOSPITAL, One Hospital Drive, Zip 18848–9702; tel. 717/265–2191; Gary A. Baker, President (Total facility includes 44 beds in nursing home–type unit) **A**9 10 **F**1 7 8 9 12 16 17 19 21 22 28 30 31 32 33 34 35 37 38 39 40 41 44 45 46 49 64 65 66 67 70 71 73 **S** Quorum Health Group/Quorum Health Resources, Inc., Brentwood, TN — 23 | 10 | 93 | 2165 | 69 | 25103 | 297 | 16001 | 7508 | 288

TREVOSE—Bucks County

□ EASTERN STATE SCHOOL AND HOSPITAL, 3740 Lincoln Highway, Zip 19047; tel. 215/953–6000 (Nonreporting) **A**1 5 9 10 — 12 | 52 | 157 | — | — | — | — | — | — | —

TROY—Bradford County

★ ○ TROY COMMUNITY HOSPITAL, 100 John Street, Zip 16947–1134; tel. 717/297–2121; Mark A. Webster, President **A**9 10 11 **F**1 4 6 7 8 11 12 14 15 19 20 21 22 23 24 26 27 28 29 30 32 33 35 37 40 41 42 43 44 45 46 47 49 50 52 54 55 58 60 61 63 64 65 66 67 70 71 73 74 **P**5 **S** Guthrie Healthcare System, Sayre, PA **N** Guthrie Healthcare System, Sayre, PA — 23 | 10 | 35 | 527 | 24 | 28645 | 2 | 9471 | 4542 | 98

TUNKHANNOCK—Wyoming County

☒ TYLER MEMORIAL HOSPITAL, 880 State Road 6 West, Zip 18657–9765; tel. 717/836–2161; William M. Milligan, Jr., President and Chief Executive Officer **A**1 2 9 10 **F**7 8 12 14 15 16 17 19 21 22 24 28 30 32 33 35 37 39 40 41 42 44 45 46 49 65 67 69 71 73 74 — 23 | 10 | 60 | 2795 | 28 | 41922 | 245 | 14467 | 6624 | 252

TYRONE—Blair County

☒ TYRONE HOSPITAL, One Hospital Drive, Zip 16686–1898; tel. 814/684–1255; Philip J. Stoner, Chief Executive Officer (Nonreporting) **A**1 9 10 **S** Quorum Health Group/Quorum Health Resources, Inc., Brentwood, TN — 23 | 10 | 59 | — | — | — | — | — | — | —

UNION CITY—Erie County

☒ UNION CITY MEMORIAL HOSPITAL, 130 North Main Street, Zip 16438–1094, Mailing Address: P.O. Box 111, Zip 16438–0111; tel. 814/438–1000; Thomas McLoughlin, President and Chief Executive Officer **A**1 9 10 **F**8 12 13 14 15 16 18 19 20 22 25 28 30 32 33 34 37 39 41 44 45 46 49 65 67 71 73 **P**3 7 **N** Saint Vincent Health System, Erie, PA — 23 | 10 | 23 | 761 | 12 | 17645 | 0 | 4975 | 2355 | 80

UNIONTOWN—Fayette County

☒ UNIONTOWN HOSPITAL, 500 West Berkeley Street, Zip 15401–5596; tel. 724/430–5000; Paul Bacharach, President and Chief Executive Officer (Total facility includes 38 beds in nursing home–type unit) **A**1 2 9 10 **F**7 8 14 15 16 19 21 22 23 30 32 33 34 35 37 39 40 42 44 46 49 63 64 65 71 73 **P**6 — 23 | 10 | 211 | 8978 | 126 | 167483 | 911 | 65313 | 28180 | 921

UPLAND—Delaware County

☒ ○ △ CROZER–CHESTER MEDICAL CENTER, (Includes Taylor Hospital, 175 East Chester Pike, Fidley Park, Zip 19078–2212; tel. 610/595–6000; Diane C. Miller, President and Chief Operating Officer, Springfield Hospital, 190 West Sproul Road, Springfield, Zip 19064–2097; tel. 610/328–8700; Gwendolyn A. Smith, R.N., Vice President), One Medical Center Boulevard, Zip 19013–3995; tel. 610/447–2000; Joan K. Richards, President (Total facility includes 47 beds in nursing home–type unit) **A**1 2 3 5 7 8 9 10 11 **F**1 3 4 7 8 9 10 11 12 13 14 15 16 17 19 20 21 22 23 24 26 27 28 29 30 31 32 33 34 35 36 37 38 39 40 41 42 43 44 45 46 47 48 49 50 51 52 54 55 56 57 58 59 60 61 63 64 65 66 67 68 69 70 71 72 73 74 **P**6 7 **S** Crozer–Keystone Health System, Springfield, PA **N** Crozer–Keystone Health System, Springfield, PA — 23 | 10 | 715 | 26855 | 424 | 97695 | 2516 | 308453 | 124870 | 3230

WARMINSTER—Bucks County

☒ ALLEGHENY UNIVERSITY HOSPITAL, BUCKS COUNTY, 225 Newtown Road, Zip 18974–5221; tel. 215/441–6600; Margaret M. McGoldrick, President and Chief Executive Officer **A**1 5 9 10 **F**2 3 4 7 8 9 10 11 12 13 14 15 16 17 18 19 20 21 22 24 26 27 28 29 30 31 32 34 35 37 38 40 41 42 43 44 45 46 47 48 49 51 52 53 54 55 56 57 58 59 60 61 64 65 66 67 69 70 71 73 74 **P**6 **S** Allegheny Health, Education and Research Foundation, Pittsburgh, PA — 23 | 10 | 135 | 6266 | 99 | 79005 | 508 | 45794 | 18581 | 538

Hospital, Address, Telephone, Administrator, Approval, Facility, and Physician Codes, Health Care System, Network	Classi-fication Codes		Utilization Data						Expense (thousands) of dollars		
★ American Hospital Association (AHA) membership □ Joint Commission on Accreditation of Healthcare Organizations (JCAHO) accreditation + American Osteopathic Healthcare Association (AOHA) membership ○ American Osteopathic Association (AOA) accreditation △ Commission on Accreditation of Rehabilitation Facilities (CARF) accreditation Control codes 61, 63, 64, 71, 72 and 73 indicate hospitals listed by AOHA, but not registered by AHA. For definition of numerical codes, see page A4	Control	Service	Staffed Beds	Admissions	Census	Outpatient Visits	Births	Total	Payroll	Personnel

WARREN—Warren County

WARREN GENERAL HOSPITAL, 2 Crescent Park West, Zip 16365–2111; tel. 814/723–3300; Alton M. Schadt, Executive Director (Total facility includes 16 beds in nursing home–type unit) **A**9 10 **F**3 7 8 14 19 21 22 23 28 29 30 32 33 34 35 37 40 41 44 46 49 51 52 56 60 63 64 65 66 71 73 **P**3 8 **N** Vantage Health Care Network, Inc., Meadville, PA — 23 10 105 3574 52 80295 353 29732 13458 504

WARREN STATE HOSPITAL See North Warren

WASHINGTON—Washington County

★ WASHINGTON HOSPITAL, 155 Wilson Avenue, Zip 15301–3336; tel. 724/225–7000; Telford W. Thomas, President and Chief Executive Officer (Total facility includes 17 beds in nursing home–type unit) **A**1 2 3 5 6 9 10 **F**4 7 8 10 11 12 13 14 15 16 17 19 20 21 22 23 25 26 28 29 30 32 33 34 35 37 39 40 41 42 43 44 45 49 51 52 54 55 56 57 60 61 63 64 65 66 67 68 71 73 74 **P**1 7 **N** University of Pittsburgh Medical Center, Pittsburgh, PA — 23 10 246 13162 189 413449 1026 123789 60281 1585

WAYNESBORO—Franklin County

★ WAYNESBORO HOSPITAL, 501 East Main Street, Zip 17268–2394; tel. 717/765–4000; Norman B. Epstein, President **A**1 5 9 10 **F**1 7 8 12 15 16 17 19 21 22 28 29 30 34 37 39 40 42 44 45 46 65 67 68 71 73 74 **P**8 — 23 10 62 2856 37 51906 395 23725 10699 313

WAYNESBURG—Greene County

★ GREENE COUNTY MEMORIAL HOSPITAL, Seventh Street and Bonar Avenue, Zip 15370–1697; tel. 412/627–3101; Raoul Walsh, Chief Executive Officer (Total facility includes 20 beds in nursing home–type unit) **A**1 9 10 **F**8 13 14 15 16 19 21 22 23 26 28 30 31 32 34 35 37 41 42 44 45 46 49 52 57 64 65 67 71 73 74 **P**1 **S** Quorum Health Group/Quorum Health Resources, Inc., Brentwood, TN — 23 10 55 2967 45 42828 — 23452 8375 298

WELLSBORO—Tioga County

★ SOLDIERS AND SAILORS MEMORIAL HOSPITAL, 32–36 Central Avenue, Zip 16901–1899; tel. 717/723–0100; Jan E. Fisher, R.N., Executive Director **A**1 9 10 **F**1 2 3 5 6 7 8 11 12 15 16 17 19 21 22 24 25 26 28 29 30 31 32 33 34 35 36 37 39 40 41 42 44 45 46 48 49 51 52 53 54 55 56 57 58 59 61 63 65 66 67 71 73 **P**4 5 **N** Laurel Health System, Wellsboro, PA — 23 10 103 3607 43 116163 289 21527 9836 342

WERNERSVILLE—Berks County

□ WERNERSVILLE STATE HOSPITAL, Route 422, Zip 19565–0300, Mailing Address: P.O. Box 300, Zip 19565–0300; tel. 610/670–4111; Kenneth W. Ehrhart, Acting Superintendent **A**1 9 10 **F**4 8 10 19 20 21 31 35 39 42 43 44 45 46 49 52 57 60 65 71 73 — 12 22 367 257 337 — — — — 542

WEST CHESTER—Chester County

★ CHESTER COUNTY HOSPITAL, 701 East Marshall Street, Zip 19380–4412; tel. 610/431–5000; H. L. Perry Pepper, President (Total facility includes 20 beds in nursing home–type unit) **A**1 2 6 9 10 **F**7 8 10 11 12 14 15 16 17 19 21 22 24 26 28 29 30 32 33 34 35 36 37 38 39 40 41 42 44 45 46 47 49 51 60 63 64 65 66 67 71 73 74 **P**4 6 7 8 — 23 10 215 10883 147 155488 2028 78682 35086 1073

WEST GROVE—Chester County

★ SOUTHERN CHESTER COUNTY MEDICAL CENTER, 1015 West Baltimore Pike, Zip 19390–9499; tel. 610/869–1000; Ralph A. Rossi, Jr., M.D., Interim President **A**1 9 10 **F**3 8 12 15 16 17 18 19 21 22 29 30 31 32 33 34 35 37 39 41 42 44 49 51 54 55 56 58 65 67 71 73 **P**1 — 23 10 46 2338 32 67525 — 24348 9975 390

WILKES–BARRE—Luzerne County

CLEAR BROOK MANOR, Road 10 East Northampton Street, Zip 18702; tel. 717/823–1171; Donald Noll, Director (Nonreporting) — 23 82 50 — — — — — — —

□ FIRST HOSPITAL WYOMING VALLEY, 149 Dana Street, Zip 18702–4825; tel. 717/829–7900; John Kasenchak, Administrator (Nonreporting) **A**1 9 10 — 33 22 96 — — — — — — —

★ △ JOHN HEINZ INSTITUTE OF REHABILITATION MEDICINE, 150 Mundy Street, Zip 18702–6830; tel. 717/826–3800; Thomas E. Pugh, Vice President Rehabilitation Services **A**1 7 9 10 **F**12 14 15 16 17 27 28 34 39 41 45 46 48 49 65 67 73 — 23 46 103 2156 97 99081 — — 14856 499

□ MERCY HOSPITAL OF WILKES–BARRE, 25 Church Street, Zip 18765–0999, Mailing Address: P.O. Box 658, Zip 18765–0658; tel. 717/826–3100; John L. Nespoli, President and Chief Executive Officer (Nonreporting) **A**1 9 10 **S** Catholic Healthcare Partners, Cincinnati, OH — 21 10 173 — — — — — — —

★ PENN STATE GEISINGER WYOMING VALLEY MEDICAL CENTER, 1000 East Mountain Drive, Zip 18711–0027; tel. 717/826–7300; Conrad W. Schintz, Senior Vice President Operations **A**1 2 9 10 **F**3 7 8 11 14 15 16 19 21 22 28 29 30 34 35 37 39 40 41 42 44 45 46 48 49 54 56 60 63 65 67 70 71 73 **P**3 6 8 **S** Penn State Geisinger Health System, Harrisburg, PA **N** Geisinger Health System, Danville, PA — 23 10 144 6172 90 171492 569 51094 19394 647

★ VETERANS AFFAIRS MEDICAL CENTER, 1111 East End Boulevard, Zip 18711–0026; tel. 717/824–3521; Reedes Hurt, Chief Executive Officer (Total facility includes 173 beds in nursing home–type unit) **A**1 2 3 5 9 **F**1 2 3 4 5 6 8 10 11 12 14 15 17 18 19 20 21 22 23 24 25 26 27 28 30 31 32 33 34 35 37 39 41 42 43 44 45 46 49 50 51 52 54 55 56 57 58 59 60 63 64 65 67 69 71 73 74 **S** Department of Veterans Affairs, Washington, DC — 45 10 315 3854 266 209127 — 84294 42928 1015

WILKES–BARRE GENERAL HOSPITAL See Wyoming Valley Health Care System

★ WYOMING VALLEY HEALTH CARE SYSTEM, (Includes Nesbitt Memorial Hospital, 562 Wyoming Avenue, Kingston, Zip 18704–3784; tel. 717/283–7000; Wilkes–Barre General Hospital, 575 North River Street, Zip 18764; tel. 717/829–8111); 575 North River Street, Zip 18764–0999; tel. 717/829–8111; Patricia Finan, Acting President and Chief Executive Officer **A**1 5 9 **F**2 3 4 6 7 8 10 11 12 13 14 15 16 17 19 20 21 22 23 24 25 27 28 29 30 32 33 34 35 37 39 40 41 42 43 44 46 49 52 53 54 55 56 57 58 59 60 62 63 64 65 66 67 68 71 72 73 74 **P**8 — 23 10 462 20540 356 448145 1801 190000 78461 2779

Hospital, Address, Telephone, Administrator, Approval, Facility, and Physician Codes, Health Care System, Network	Classi-fication Codes		Utilization Data					Expense (thousands) of dollars		
	Control	Service	Staffed Beds	Admissions	Census	Outpatient Visits	Births	Total	Payroll	Personnel

* ★ American Hospital Association (AHA) membership
* ☐ Joint Commission on Accreditation of Healthcare Organizations (JCAHO) accreditation
* + American Osteopathic Healthcare Association (AOHA) membership
* ○ American Osteopathic Association (AOA) accreditation
* △ Commission on Accreditation of Rehabilitation Facilities (CARF) accreditation
  Control codes 61, 63, 64, 71, 72 and 73 indicate hospitals listed by AOHA, but not registered by AHA. For definition of numerical codes, see page A4

WILLIAMSBURG—Blair County

| CHARTER BEHAVIORAL HEALTH SYSTEM AT COVE FORGE, New Beginnings Road, Zip 16693; tel. 814/832–2121; Jonathan Wolf, Chief Executive Officer (Nonreporting) **S** Magellan Health Services, Atlanta, GA | 33 | 82 | 100 | — | — | — | — | — | — | — |

WILLIAMSPORT—Lycoming County

| ⊠ △ SUSQUEHANNA HEALTH SYSTEM, (Includes Divine Providence Hospital, 1100 Grampian Boulevard, Zip 17701–1995; tel. 717/320–7006; Muncy Valley Hospital, 215 East Water Street, Muncy, Zip 17756–8700; tel. 717/546–8282; Williamsport Hospital and Medical Center, 777 Rural Avenue, Zip 17701–3198; tel. 717/321–1000; Steven P. Johnson, Senior Vice President and Chief Operating Officer Hospitals and LTC Operations), 1001 Grampian Boulevard, Zip 17701–1946; tel. 717/320–7000; Donald R. Creamer, President and Chief Executive Officer (Total facility includes 129 beds in nursing home–type unit) **A**1 2 3 5 7 9 10 **F**1 4 5 7 8 10 12 13 14 15 16 17 19 20 21 22 23 24 25 26 27 28 29 30 31 32 33 34 35 37 39 40 41 42 43 44 45 46 48 49 51 52 53 54 55 56 57 58 59 60 61 63 64 65 66 67 68 71 72 73 74 **P**3 7 8 | 23 | 10 | 501 | 15922 | 307 | 472574 | 1529 | 142360 | 60464 | 2042 |

WILLOW GROVE—Montgomery County

| ☐ HUNTINGTON HOSPITAL, 240 Fitzwatertown Road, Zip 19090–2399; tel. 215/657–4010; Alan I. Stevens, Administrator (Nonreporting) **A**1 9 10 | 23 | 22 | 31 | — | — | — | — | — | — | — |

WINDBER—Somerset County

| ☐ WINDBER HOSPITAL, 600 Somerset Avenue, Zip 15963–1331; tel. 814/467–6611; Nicholas Jacobs, Executive Director (Nonreporting) **A**1 9 10 | 23 | 10 | 67 | — | — | — | — | — | — | — |

WYNNEWOOD—Montgomery County

| ⊠ LANKENAU HOSPITAL, 100 Lancaster Avenue West, Zip 19096–3411; tel. 610/645–2000; William McCune, Senior Vice President, Operations (Total facility includes 22 beds in nursing home–type unit) **A**1 2 3 5 9 10 **F**4 7 8 10 12 14 15 16 17 19 20 21 22 28 29 30 31 32 33 34 35 37 38 39 40 41 42 43 44 45 46 49 51 54 56 57 60 63 64 65 66 67 68 69 71 73 **P**1 3 5 7 8 **S** Jefferson Health System, Wayne, PA **N** Jefferson Health System, Radnor, PA | 23 | 10 | 313 | 14860 | 232 | 119068 | 1683 | 161066 | 57228 | 1695 |

YORK—York County

☐ △ HEALTHSOUTH REHABILITATION HOSPITAL OF YORK, 1850 Normandie Drive, Zip 17404–1534; tel. 717/767–6941; Cheryl Fleming, Chief Executive Officer (Nonreporting) **A**1 7 9 10 **S** HEALTHSOUTH Corporation, Birmingham, AL	33	48	88	—	—	—	—	—	—	—
★ + ○ MEMORIAL HOSPITAL, 325 South Belmont Street, Zip 17403–2609, Mailing Address: P.O. Box 15118, Zip 17405–5118; tel. 717/843–8623; Sally J. Dixon, President and Chief Executive Officer **A**9 10 11 12 13 **F**7 8 10 12 14 15 16 17 19 21 22 23 25 26 28 30 31 32 33 34 35 36 37 39 40 41 42 44 45 49 51 52 53 56 57 60 63 65 66 67 71 73 **P**2	23	10	102	5825	76	67275	491	44369	21776	675
⊠ YORK HOSPITAL, 1001 South George Street, Zip 17405–3645; tel. 717/851–2345; Bruce M. Bartels, President **A**1 2 3 5 8 9 10 **F**3 4 7 8 10 11 12 14 15 16 17 18 19 20 21 22 23 25 26 28 30 31 32 33 34 35 37 38 39 40 41 42 43 44 45 46 49 51 52 53 54 55 56 57 58 59 60 61 63 65 67 68 69 70 71 72 73 74 **P**6 **S** York Health System, York, PA	23	10	430	23143	323	512272	2809	215390	104926	2893

RHODE ISLAND

Resident population 987 (in thousands)
Resident population in metro areas 93.8%
Birth rate per 1,000 population 13.5
65 years and over 15.8%
Percent of persons without health insurance 9.9%

Hospital, Address, Telephone, Administrator, Approval, Facility, and Physician Codes, Health Care System, Network	Classi-fication Codes		Utilization Data					Expense (thousands) of dollars		
★ American Hospital Association (AHA) membership □ Joint Commission on Accreditation of Healthcare Organizations (JCAHO) accreditation + American Osteopathic Healthcare Association (AOHA) membership ○ American Osteopathic Association (AOA) accreditation △ Commission on Accreditation of Rehabilitation Facilities (CARF) accreditation Control codes 61, 63, 64, 71, 72 and 73 indicate hospitals listed by AOHA, but not registered by AHA. For definition of numerical codes, see page A4	Control	Service	Staffed Beds	Admissions	Census	Outpatient Visits	Births	Total	Payroll	Personnel

CRANSTON—Providence County

□ ELEANOR SLATER HOSPITAL, (Includes Institute of Mental Health–Rhode Island Medical Center, Howard Avenue, Howard, Zip 02920, Mailing Address: Box 8281, Cranston, Zip 02920–0281; tel. 401/464–2495; Betty A. Fielder, Clinical Administrative Officer; Rhode Island Medical Center, Mailing Address: Box 8269, Zip 02920; tel. 401/464–3085), 111 Howard Avenue, Zip 02920–3001, Mailing Address: P.O. Box 8269, Zip 02920–8269; tel. 401/464–3085; Richard H. Freeman, Chief Executive Officer **A**1 3 9 10 **F**19 20 21 26 27 31 35 42 52 57 64 65 71 73 **P**6

| | | 12 | 48 | 457 | 292 | 486 | — | — | 100655 | 49484 | 1234 |

EAST PROVIDENCE—Providence County

✚ EMMA PENDLETON BRADLEY HOSPITAL, 1011 Veterans Memorial Parkway, Zip 02915–5099; tel. 401/434–3400; Daniel J. Wall, President and Chief Executive Officer (Nonreporting) **A**1 3 5 9 10 **S** Lifespan Corporation, Providence, RI **N** Lifespan, Providence, RI

| | | 23 | 52 | 60 | — | — | — | — | — | — | — |

HOWARD—Providence County

INSTITUTE OF MENTAL HEALTH–RHODE ISLAND MEDICAL CENTER See Eleanor Slater Hospital, Cranston

NEWPORT—Newport County

✚ △ NEWPORT HOSPITAL, 11 Friendship Street, Zip 02840–2299; tel. 401/846–6400; Arthur J. Sampson, President and Chief Executive Officer **A**1 2 7 9 10 **F**7 8 11 12 16 19 20 22 25 26 28 29 30 34 35 36 37 39 40 41 44 45 46 48 49 52 56 57 59 65 67 71 73 **P**3 6 7 **S** Lifespan Corporation, Providence, RI **N** Lifespan, Providence, RI

| | | 23 | 10 | 85 | 5837 | 81 | 94280 | 718 | 53237 | 24957 | 637 |

NORTH PROVIDENCE—Providence County

OUR LADY OF FATIMA HOSPITAL See St. Joseph Health Services of Rhode Island, Providence

PAWTUCKET—Providence County

✚ △ MEMORIAL HOSPITAL OF RHODE ISLAND, 111 Brewster Street, Zip 02860–4499; tel. 401/729–2000; Francis R. Dietz, President **A**1 2 3 5 7 8 9 10 **F**1 2 3 4 7 8 9 10 11 12 13 15 16 17 19 21 22 25 26 27 28 30 31 32 33 34 35 36 37 38 39 40 41 42 43 44 45 47 48 49 51 52 53 54 56 57 58 59 60 61 64 65 66 67 70 71 72 73 **P**8

| | | 23 | 10 | 195 | 7383 | 113 | 78024 | 750 | 103616 | 58305 | 1348 |

PROVIDENCE—Providence County

✚ BUTLER HOSPITAL, 345 Blackstone Boulevard, Zip 02906–4829; tel. 401/455–6200; Frank A. Delmonico, President and Chief Executive Officer **A**1 3 5 9 10 **F**2 3 7 8 10 11 12 15 17 18 19 21 25 26 27 28 29 30 31 32 33 35 37 38 39 42 44 45 46 48 49 51 52 53 54 55 56 57 58 59 61 63 65 67 68 71 73 74 **P**6 8 **S** Care New England Health System, Providence, RI **N** Care New England Health System, Providence, RI

| | | 23 | 22 | 105 | 4489 | 87 | 42870 | — | 34988 | 22418 | 494 |

✚ MIRIAM HOSPITAL, 164 Summit Avenue, Zip 02906–2895; tel. 401/793–2000; Steven D. Baron, President **A**1 2 3 5 8 9 10 **F**2 4 5 8 9 10 11 12 13 14 15 16 17 18 19 20 21 22 23 24 25 26 28 29 30 31 32 33 34 35 37 39 41 42 43 44 45 47 49 51 52 53 54 55 56 57 58 59 60 63 64 65 66 67 69 70 71 73 74 **P**3 4 5 7 8 **S** Lifespan Corporation, Providence, RI **N** Lifespan, Providence, RI

| | | 23 | 10 | 216 | 11348 | 168 | 174162 | 0 | 120956 | 53891 | 1313 |

✚ RHODE ISLAND HOSPITAL, 593 Eddy Street, Zip 02903–4900; tel. 401/444–4000; Steven D. Baron, President and Chief Executive Officer **A**1 2 3 5 8 9 10 **F**4 5 8 10 11 12 13 14 15 16 17 18 19 20 21 22 23 24 26 28 29 30 31 32 33 34 35 37 39 41 42 43 44 45 46 47 49 51 52 53 54 55 56 57 58 59 60 63 65 66 67 69 70 71 73 74 **P**3 4 5 6 7 8 **S** Lifespan Corporation, Providence, RI **N** Lifespan, Providence, RI

| | | 23 | 10 | 677 | 28632 | 477 | 481902 | — | 360213 | 162319 | 4517 |

✚ ROGER WILLIAMS MEDICAL CENTER, 825 Chalkstone Avenue, Zip 02908–4735; tel. 401/456–2000; Robert A. Urciuoli, President and Chief Executive Officer **A**1 2 3 5 8 9 10 **F**2 3 6 8 10 12 14 15 16 17 19 21 22 26 27 28 29 30 32 34 35 37 39 41 42 44 46 49 51 54 60 63 64 65 69 71 73 **P**3 5 8

| | | 23 | 10 | 152 | 7210 | 110 | 43344 | — | 85324 | 42178 | 1055 |

✚ ST. JOSEPH HEALTH SERVICES OF RHODE ISLAND, (Includes Our Lady of Fatima Hospital, 200 High Service Avenue, North Providence, Zip 02904; St. Joseph Hospital for Specialty Care, 21 Peace Street, Zip 02907; tel. 401/456–3000), 200 High Service Avenue, Zip 02904–5199; tel. 401/456–3000; H. John Keimig, President and Chief Executive Officer **A**1 6 9 10 **F**6 7 8 11 16 17 19 20 21 22 23 27 30 32 34 35 40 41 42 44 46 48 49 52 58 59 64 65 71 72 73 **P**8 **N** Saint Joseph Hospital, Providence, RI

| | | 21 | 10 | 307 | 11929 | 241 | 196944 | 430 | 116280 | 60170 | 1545 |

✚ VETERANS AFFAIRS MEDICAL CENTER, 830 Chalkstone Avenue, Zip 02908–4799; tel. 401/457–3042; Edward H. Seiler, Director **A**1 3 5 9 **F**1 3 4 8 10 12 16 17 18 19 20 21 22 25 26 27 28 31 32 33 34 35 37 41 42 43 44 46 49 52 54 55 56 57 58 61 63 64 65 67 69 71 72 73 74 **S** Department of Veterans Affairs, Washington, DC

| | | 45 | 10 | 78 | 3108 | 68 | 200945 | — | 68851 | 33602 | 737 |

✚ WOMEN AND INFANTS HOSPITAL OF RHODE ISLAND, 101 Dudley Street, Zip 02905–2499; tel. 401/274–1100; Thomas G. Parris, Jr., President **A**1 2 3 5 8 9 10 **F**2 3 4 5 7 8 10 11 12 13 16 17 18 19 20 21 22 23 24 25 26 27 28 29 30 31 32 33 34 35 37 38 39 40 41 42 43 44 45 46 47 48 49 51 52 53 54 55 56 57 58 59 61 63 65 66 67 68 70 71 73 74 **P**5 6 8 **S** Care New England Health System, Providence, RI **N** Care New England Health System, Providence, RI

| | | 23 | 44 | 197 | 13676 | 169 | 54952 | 8801 | 136918 | 71282 | 1849 |

Hospital, Address, Telephone, Administrator, Approval, Facility, and Physician Codes, Health Care System, Network	Classi-fication Codes		Utilization Data					Expense (thousands) of dollars		
★ American Hospital Association (AHA) membership □ Joint Commission on Accreditation of Healthcare Organizations (JCAHO) accreditation + American Osteopathic Healthcare Association (AOHA) membership ○ American Osteopathic Association (AOA) accreditation △ Commission on Accreditation of Rehabilitation Facilities (CARF) accreditation Control codes 61, 63, 64, 71, 72 and 73 indicate hospitals listed by AOHA, but not registered by AHA. For definition of numerical codes, see page A4	Control	Service	Staffed Beds	Admissions	Census	Outpatient Visits	Births	Total	Payroll	Personnel

WAKEFIELD—Washington County

✠ SOUTH COUNTY HOSPITAL, 100 Kenyon Avenue, Zip 02879–4299; tel. 401/782–8000; Patrick L. Muldoon, President and Chief Executive Officer **A**1 9 10 **F**7 8 11 12 13 15 16 17 19 20 21 22 26 28 29 30 31 32 33 34 35 36 37 39 40 41 42 44 45 46 49 51 56 59 63 65 66 67 71 72 73 74 **P**7 8 **N** Lifespan, Providence, RI

| | 23 | 10 | 100 | 4622 | 52 | 106051 | 596 | 42651 | 20384 | 533 |

WARWICK—Kent County

✠ △ KENT COUNTY MEMORIAL HOSPITAL, 455 Tollgate Road, Zip 02886–2770; tel. 401/737–7000; Robert E. Baute, M.D., President and Chief Executive Officer **A**1 2 7 9 10 **F**2 3 7 8 10 11 12 15 16 17 18 19 21 22 25 26 27 28 29 30 31 32 33 34 35 37 38 39 40 41 42 44 45 46 48 49 51 52 53 54 55 56 57 58 59 61 63 65 67 68 71 73 74 **P**6 8 **S** Care New England Health System, Providence, RI **N** Care New England Health System, Providence, RI

| | 23 | 10 | 317 | 14275 | 231 | 162753 | 1165 | 131696 | 70732 | 1625 |

WESTERLY—Washington County

✠ WESTERLY HOSPITAL, 25 Wells Street, Zip 02891–2934; tel. 401/596–6000; Michael K. Lally, President and Chief Executive Officer **A**1 9 10 **F**1 7 8 9 14 17 19 21 22 26 28 30 31 34 35 36 37 39 40 41 42 44 45 46 48 49 51 54 56 57 63 65 66 67 68 71 72 73 74 **P**6 8

| | 23 | 10 | 125 | 4225 | 55 | 270493 | 497 | 43405 | 19974 | 432 |

WOONSOCKET—Providence County

✠ LANDMARK MEDICAL CENTER, (Includes Landmark Medical Center–Fogarty Unit, Eddie Dowling Highway, North Smithfield, Zip 02896; tel. 401/766–0800; Landmark Medical Center–Woonsocket Unit, 115 Cass Avenue, Zip 02895; tel. 401/769–4100), 115 Cass Avenue, Zip 02895–4731; tel. 401/769–4100; Robert D. Walker, President and Chief Executive Officer (Total facility includes 19 beds in nursing home–type unit) **A**1 9 10 **F**7 8 11 15 16 19 21 22 26 28 29 30 32 33 34 35 37 39 40 41 42 44 45 48 49 52 53 54 55 56 57 58 63 64 65 67 71 72 73 **P**1 6 7

| | 23 | 10 | 173 | 7217 | 106 | 162810 | 378 | 73885 | 34674 | 765 |

SOUTH CAROLINA

Resident population 3,760 (in thousands)
Resident population in metro areas 69.7%
Birth rate per 1,000 population 14.2
65 years and over 12.1%
Percent of persons without health insurance 17.1%

Hospital, Address, Telephone, Administrator, Approval, Facility, and Physician Codes, Health Care System, Network	Control	Service	Staffed Beds	Admissions	Census	Outpatient Visits	Births	Total	Payroll	Personnel
ABBEVILLE—Abbeville County										
ABBEVILLE COUNTY MEMORIAL HOSPITAL, 901 West Greenwood Street, Zip 29620–0887, Mailing Address: P.O. Box 887, Zip 29620–0887; tel. 864/459–5011; Bruce P. Bailey, Administrator **A**9 10 **F**7 8 11 15 17 19 22 26 28 29 30 32 34 37 40 41 44 45 46 48 49 56 63 65 69 71 73 74 **P**1 **S** Quorum Health Group/Quorum Health Resources, Inc., Brentwood, TN **N** Premier Health Systems, Inc., Columbia, SC	13	10	48	1336	11	26051	99	8684	4534	204
AIKEN—Aiken County										
AIKEN REGIONAL MEDICAL CENTER, (Includes Aurora Pavilion, 655 Medical Park Drive, Zip 29801, Mailing Address: P.O. Box 1073, Zip 29802; tel. 803/641–5900), 202 University Parkway, Zip 29801–2757, Mailing Address: P.O. Box 1117, Zip 29802–1117; tel. 803/641–5000; Richard H. Satcher, Chief Executive Officer **A**1 2 9 10 **F**2 3 4 7 8 10 11 14 15 16 17 19 21 22 23 25 26 27 28 30 31 32 33 34 35 37 39 40 41 42 43 44 45 46 48 49 53 54 55 56 57 58 59 60 63 65 67 68 69 70 71 73 74 **P**4 **S** Universal Health Services, Inc., King of Prussia, PA	33	10	269	11508	144	172047	1106	84731	28639	789
ANDERSON—Anderson County										
ANDERSON AREA MEDICAL CENTER, 800 North Fant Street, Zip 29621–5793; tel. 864/261–1000; John A. Miller, Jr., President **A**1 2 3 5 9 10 **F**2 3 7 8 9 10 11 14 15 16 17 19 21 22 23 24 25 26 27 28 29 30 31 32 33 34 35 37 38 40 41 42 44 45 46 47 48 49 53 54 55 56 57 58 59 60 61 63 65 66 67 69 70 71 73 74 **P**4 5	23	10	371	16802	245	367030	1826	139113	65204	2209
BAMBERG—Bamberg County										
BAMBERG COUNTY MEMORIAL HOSPITAL AND NURSING CENTER, North and McGee Streets, Zip 29003–0507, Mailing Address: P.O. Box 507, Zip 29003–0507; tel. 803/245–4321; Warren E. Hammett, Administrator (Total facility includes 44 beds in nursing home–type unit) **A**1 9 10 **F**7 8 15 16 19 22 40 44 49 65 71 74 **N** Premier Health Systems, Inc., Columbia, SC	13	10	84	1310	62	11326	108	—	—	237
BARNWELL—Barnwell County										
BARNWELL COUNTY HOSPITAL, 2501 Reynolds Road, Zip 29812, Mailing Address: P.O. Box 588, Zip 29812–0588; tel. 803/259–1000; Tommy R. McDougal, Jr., Administrator and Chief Executive Officer **A**1 9 10 **F**8 16 17 19 21 22 26 28 29 30 31 33 34 37 44 45 48 49 65 71 73 **P**1 2 **N** Premier Health Systems, Inc., Columbia, SC; The Medical Resource Network, L.L.C., Atlanta, GA; University Health, Inc., Augusta, GA	13	10	27	906	15	12451	—	7089	2768	124
BEAUFORT—Beaufort County										
BEAUFORT MEMORIAL HOSPITAL, 955 Ribaut Road, Zip 29902–5441, Mailing Address: P.O. Box 1068, Zip 29901–1068; tel. 803/522–5200; David E. Brown, President and Chief Executive Officer (Total facility includes 44 beds in nursing home–type unit) **A**1 9 10 **F**7 8 14 15 16 17 19 21 22 23 24 28 29 30 31 32 33 34 35 37 39 40 41 44 45 46 49 54 55 56 57 59 63 65 66 69 71 73 74	13	10	170	6735	93	30195	1066	48031	21306	814
NAVAL HOSPITAL, 1 Pinckney Boulevard, Zip 29902–6148; tel. 803/525–5301; Captain Clint E. Adams, MC, USN, Commanding Officer **A**1 5 **F**2 3 4 5 6 7 8 9 10 11 13 17 18 19 21 22 23 24 26 27 28 29 30 31 32 33 34 35 36 37 38 39 40 41 42 43 44 45 46 47 48 49 50 51 52 53 54 55 56 57 58 60 61 65 66 67 69 70 71 73 74 **S** Department of Navy, Washington, DC	43	10	43	1438	11	287501	466	43490	25993	538
BENNETTSVILLE—Marlboro County										
MARLBORO PARK HOSPITAL, 1138 Cheraw Highway, Zip 29512–0738, Mailing Address: P.O. Box 738, Zip 29512–0738; tel. 803/479–2881; Stephen Chapman, Chief Executive Officer (Total facility includes 7 beds in nursing home–type unit) **A**1 9 10 **F**7 8 11 15 17 19 21 22 23 28 29 30 31 33 35 37 39 40 44 45 49 50 55 57 63 65 69 71 73 74 **P**5 8 **S** Community Health Systems, Inc., Brentwood, TN **N** Palmetto Community Health Network, Conway, SC; Premier Health Systems, Inc., Columbia, SC	32	10	105	2224	30	13701	205	17384	6936	228
CAMDEN—Kershaw County										
KERSHAW COUNTY MEDICAL CENTER, Haile and Roberts Streets, Zip 29020–7003, Mailing Address: P.O. Box 7003, Zip 29020–7003; tel. 803/432–4311; Donnie J. Weeks, President and Chief Executive Officer (Total facility includes 88 beds in nursing home–type unit) (Nonreporting) **A**1 9 10 **N** Carolina HealthChoice Network, Columbia, SC; Premier Health Systems, Inc., Columbia, SC	13	10	198	—	—	—	—	—	—	—
CHARLESTON—Charleston County										
BON SECOURS–ST. FRANCIS XAVIER HOSPITAL, 2095 Henry Tecklenburg Drive, Zip 29414–0001, Mailing Address: P.O. Box 160001, Zip 29414–0001; tel. 803/402–1000; Allen P. Carroll, Chief Executive Officer **A**1 9 10 **F**2 7 8 10 11 14 15 16 17 19 21 22 23 24 25 26 27 28 30 31 32 33 34 35 36 37 38 40 41 44 45 46 49 54 55 56 57 58 59 60 61 65 66 69 71 73 74 **P**4 **S** Bon Secours Health System, Inc., Marriottsville, MD **N** Premier Health Systems, Inc., Columbia, SC	21	10	145	5291	70	53978	823	50873	19791	573

Hospital, Address, Telephone, Administrator, Approval, Facility, and Physician Codes, Health Care System, Network	Classi-fication Codes		Utilization Data					Expense (thousands) of dollars		
	Control	Service	Staffed Beds	Admissions	Census	Outpatient Visits	Births	Total	Payroll	Personnel

★ American Hospital Association (AHA) membership
□ Joint Commission on Accreditation of Healthcare Organizations (JCAHO) accreditation
+ American Osteopathic Healthcare Association (AOHA) membership
○ American Osteopathic Association (AOA) accreditation
△ Commission on Accreditation of Rehabilitation Facilities (CARF) accreditation
Control codes 61, 63, 64, 71, 72 and 73 indicate hospitals listed by AOHA, but not registered by AHA. For definition of numerical codes, see page A4

Hospital	Control	Service	Staffed Beds	Admissions	Census	Outpatient Visits	Births	Total	Payroll	Personnel
✶ △ CHARLESTON MEMORIAL HOSPITAL, 326 Calhoun Street, Zip 29401–1189; tel. 803/953–8300; Agnes E. Arnold, R.N., CHE, Administrator **A**1 3 5 7 9 10 **F**4 8 10 11 16 17 19 22 23 31 32 35 37 45 49 54 56 60 65 69 71 73 74	13	10	117	1285	40	42585	—	38346	11177	376
□ CHARTER HOSPITAL OF CHARLESTON, 2777 Speissegger Drive, Zip 29405–8299; tel. 803/747–5830; Anne Battin, Administrator **A**1 10 **F**2 3 17 19 21 26 28 34 35 41 45 46 52 53 54 55 56 57 58 59 65 67 71 **S** Magellan Health Services, Atlanta, GA	33	22	70	714	15	2540	—	—	—	130
✶ COLUMBIA TRIDENT MEDICAL CENTER, 9330 Medical Plaza Drive, Zip 29406–9195; tel. 803/797–7000; Gene B. Wright, President and Chief Executive Officer **A**1 2 9 10 **F**2 4 7 8 9 10 11 15 16 17 19 21 22 23 24 26 28 29 30 31 32 33 34 35 37 38 39 40 41 42 43 44 45 46 47 48 49 53 55 56 57 58 59 60 63 65 66 67 69 70 71 73 74 **P**4 5 **S** Columbia/HCA Healthcare Corporation, Nashville, TN	33	10	273	13012	171	133737	1979	90543	—	1349
✶ △ MUSC MEDICAL CENTER OF MEDICAL UNIVERSITY OF SOUTH CAROLINA, 171 Ashley Avenue, Zip 29425–0950; tel. 843/792–2300; Stuart Smith, Vice President Clinical Operations and Chief Executive Officer **A**1 2 3 5 7 8 9 10 **F**2 3 4 5 6 7 8 9 10 11 13 14 15 16 17 18 19 20 21 22 23 24 25 26 27 28 29 30 31 32 33 34 35 36 37 38 39 40 41 42 43 44 45 46 47 48 49 50 51 52 53 54 55 56 57 58 59 60 61 62 63 65 66 67 68 69 70 71 73 74 NAVAL HOSPITAL See North Charleston	12	10	587	23999	407	471890	1940	351399	129897	3725
✶ ROPER HOSPITAL, 316 Calhoun Street, Zip 29401–1125; tel. 803/724–2000; Edward L. Berdick, President and Chief Executive Officer **A**1 2 6 9 10 **F**2 3 4 7 8 10 11 13 14 15 16 17 19 21 22 23 25 27 28 29 30 31 32 33 34 35 37 38 39 40 41 42 43 44 45 46 48 49 51 53 54 55 56 57 58 59 60 63 65 67 69 70 71 73 74 **P**2 6 **N** Premier Health Systems, Inc., Columbia, SC	23	10	380	15957	280	236759	1534	180478	61428	2285
✶ ROPER HOSPITAL NORTH, 2750 Speissegger Drive, Zip 29405–8294; tel. 803/744–2110; John C. Hales, Jr., FACHE, President and Chief Executive Officer **A**1 9 10 **F**2 3 4 8 9 10 11 13 14 15 16 17 18 19 20 21 22 23 25 26 27 28 29 30 31 32 33 34 35 37 38 39 40 41 42 43 44 45 46 47 48 49 51 53 54 55 56 57 58 59 60 63 65 67 69 70 71 74 **P**2 6	23	10	104	1715	36	52093	—	22722	6432	217
✶ VETERANS AFFAIRS MEDICAL CENTER, 109 Bee Street, Zip 29401–5703; tel. 803/577–5011; Dean S. Billik, Director **A**1 2 3 5 8 9 **F**2 3 4 8 10 11 17 19 20 21 22 26 28 30 31 32 33 34 35 37 41 43 45 46 48 49 51 52 54 55 56 57 58 59 60 63 65 69 71 73 74 **S** Department of Veterans Affairs, Washington, DC	45	10	105	4914	88	205564	—	—	54445	942
CHERAW—Chesterfield County										
✶ CHESTERFIELD GENERAL HOSPITAL, Highway 9 West, Zip 29520, Mailing Address: P.O. Box 151, Zip 29520–0151; tel. 803/537–7881; Chris Wolf, Chief Executive Officer (Total facility includes 7 beds in nursing home–type unit) **A**1 9 10 **F**6 7 8 11 13 14 15 16 17 19 21 22 23 26 27 28 29 30 31 32 33 34 35 37 38 39 40 41 44 45 46 47 48 49 51 63 65 69 71 73 **P**1 **S** Community Health Systems, Inc., Brentwood, TN **N** Palmetto Community Health Network, Conway, SC; Premier Health Systems, Inc., Columbia, SC	33	10	72	2192	26	30811	267	17518	6466	203
CHESTER—Chester County										
□ CHESTER COUNTY HOSPITAL AND NURSING CENTER, 1 Medical Park Drive, Zip 29706–9799; tel. 803/581–9400; Robert E. Waters, Chief Executive Officer (Total facility includes 100 beds in nursing home–type unit) (Nonreporting) **A**1 9 10 **N** Carolinas Hospital Network, Charlotte, NC; Premier Health Systems, Inc., Columbia, SC	13	10	170	—	—	—	—	—	—	—
CLINTON—Laurens County										
✶ LAURENS COUNTY HEALTHCARE SYSTEM, (Includes Laurens County Hospital, Mailing Address: P.O. Box 976, Zip 29325; tel. 803/833–9100), Highway 76 West, Zip 29325, Mailing Address: P.O. Box 976, Zip 29325–0976; tel. 864/833–9100; Michael A. Kozar, Chief Executive Officer (Total facility includes 131 beds in nursing home–type unit) **A**1 9 10 **F**7 8 11 13 14 15 16 17 19 21 22 23 28 29 30 31 32 33 34 35 37 39 44 45 46 49 55 56 65 67 69 71 74 **P**4 **S** Quorum Health Group/Quorum Health Resources, Inc., Brentwood, TN **N** Premier Health Systems, Inc., Columbia, SC	16	10	216	4000	179	49390	406	—	—	502
WHITTEN CENTER INFIRMARY, Whitten Center, Zip 29325, Mailing Address: Drawer 239, Zip 29325; tel. 864/833–2733; George Dellaportas, M.D., Director Professional Services (Nonreporting)	12	12	24	—	—	—	—	—	—	—
COLUMBIA—Richland County										
BAPTIST MEDICAL CENTER/COLUMBIA See Palmetto Baptist Medical Center/Columbia										
✶ COLUMBIA PROVIDENCE HOSPITAL, 2435 Forest Drive, Zip 29204–2098; tel. 803/256–5300; Larry R. Ellis, Interim Chief Executive Officer (Total facility includes 19 beds in nursing home–type unit) **A**1 9 10 **F**4 8 10 11 14 15 16 17 19 20 21 22 25 28 29 30 31 34 35 37 41 43 44 45 46 49 53 63 65 67 69 71 73 **S** Columbia/HCA Healthcare Corporation, Nashville, TN **N** Premier Health Systems, Inc., Columbia, SC	32	10	233	10650	184	63411	—	—	—	954
CRAFTS–FARROW STATE HOSPITAL, 7901 Farrow Road, Zip 29203–3299; tel. 803/935–7173; Samuel J. Boyd, Administrator (Nonreporting)	12	22	450	—	—	—	—	—	—	—
✶ △ HEALTHSOUTH REHABILITATION HOSPITAL, 2935 Colonial Drive, Zip 29203–6811; tel. 803/254–7777; Debbie W. Johnston, Director Operations **A**1 7 9 10 **F**15 17 24 26 27 34 39 41 45 46 48 49 65 66 67 71 73 **S** HEALTHSOUTH Corporation, Birmingham, AL **N** Premier Health Systems, Inc., Columbia, SC	33	46	87	1243	72	12841	—	15097	6986	222

Hospital, Address, Telephone, Administrator, Approval, Facility, and Physician Codes, Health Care System, Network	Classification Codes		Utilization Data					Expense (thousands) of dollars		
	Control	Service	Staffed Beds	Admissions	Census	Outpatient Visits	Births	Total	Payroll	Personnel

Approval key:
★ American Hospital Association (AHA) membership
□ Joint Commission on Accreditation of Healthcare Organizations (JCAHO) accreditation
+ American Osteopathic Healthcare Association (AOHA) membership
○ American Osteopathic Association (AOA) accreditation
△ Commission on Accreditation of Rehabilitation Facilities (CARF) accreditation
Control codes 61, 63, 64, 71, 72 and 73 indicate hospitals listed by AOHA, but not registered by AHA. For definition of numerical codes, see page A4

Hospital	Control	Service	Staffed Beds	Admissions	Census	Outpatient Visits	Births	Total	Payroll	Personnel
MIDLANDS CENTER, 8301 Farrow Road, Zip 29203–3294; tel. 803/935–7508; Ronald P. Childs, FACHE, Health Services Administrator (Nonreporting)	12	12	24	—	—	—	—	—	—	—
✠ PALMETTO BAPTIST MEDICAL CENTER/COLUMBIA, (Formerly Baptist Medical Center/Columbia), Taylor at Marion Street, Zip 29220; tel. 803/771–5010; James M. Bridges, Executive Vice President and Chief Operating Officer (Nonreporting) **A**1 2 9 10 **S** Palmetto Health Alliance, Columbia, SC **N** Premier Health Systems, Inc., Columbia, SC	21	10	387							
✠ PALMETTO RICHLAND MEMORIAL HOSPITAL, (Formerly Richland Memorial Hospital), Mailing Address: P.O. Box 2266, Zip 29203–2266; tel. 803/434–7000; Kester S. Freeman, Jr., Chief Executive Officer **A**1 2 3 5 8 9 10 **F**2 3 4 7 8 9 10 11 13 14 15 16 17 19 20 21 22 24 25 26 27 28 29 30 31 32 33 34 35 37 38 39 40 41 42 43 44 45 46 47 48 49 51 53 54 55 56 57 58 59 60 61 63 65 66 67 69 70 71 73 74 **N** Richland Community Health Partners, Columbia, SC	13	10	621	27855	520	311472	3059	332693	134268	4053
□ SOUTH CAROLINA STATE HOSPITAL, 2100 Bull Street, Zip 29202, Mailing Address: P.O. Box 119, Zip 29202–0119; tel. 803/734–6520; Jaime E. Condom, M.D., Director **A**1 **F**28 29 45 46 49 52 55 56 57 65 73	12	22	400	275	350			—	22398	615
✠ WILLIAM JENNINGS BRYAN DORN VETERANS HOSPITAL, 6439 Garners Ferry Road, Zip 29209–1639; tel. 803/776–4000; Brian Heckert, Director (Nonreporting) **A**1 2 3 5 **S** Department of Veterans Affairs, Washington, DC	45	10	342	—	—	—	—	—	—	—
✠ WILLIAM S. HALL PSYCHIATRIC INSTITUTE, 1800 Colonial Drive, Zip 29203–6827, Mailing Address: P.O. Box 202, Zip 29202–0202; tel. 803/734–7113; Donald W. Morgan, M.D., Director **A**1 3 5 10 **F**34 39 45 46 52 53 54 55 56 57 58 65 73	12	22	267	1055	182	—	—	—	21666	514
CONWAY—Horry County										
□ COASTAL CAROLINA HOSPITAL, 152 Waccamaw Medical Park Drive, Zip 29526–8922; tel. 803/347–7156; Dale Armstrong, Chief Executive Officer **A**1 10 **F**2 3 14 15 16 34 40 41 52 53 54 55 56 57 58 59 **P**5 **S** Ramsay Health Care, Inc., Coral Gables, FL	33	22	48	744	22	4951	—	6205	2868	124
✠ CONWAY HOSPITAL, 300 Singleton Ridge Road, Zip 29526, Mailing Address: P.O. Box 829, Zip 29528–0829; tel. 803/347–7111; Philip A. Clayton, President and Chief Executive Officer (Total facility includes 88 beds in nursing home–type unit) **A**1 9 10 **F**7 8 10 14 15 16 17 19 21 22 23 28 30 31 32 33 35 37 39 40 45 48 49 63 65 67 69 70 71 73 74 **N** Palmetto Community Health Network, Conway, SC	23	10	227	8102	168	75951	969	—	—	713
DARLINGTON—Darlington County										
WILSON MEDICAL CENTER See McLeod Regional Medical Center, Florence										
DILLON—Dillon County										
✠ SAINT EUGENE MEDICAL CENTER, (Formerly Saint Eugene Community Hospital), 301 East Jackson Street, Zip 29536–2509, Mailing Address: P.O. Box 1327, Zip 29536–1327; tel. 843/774–4111; Ronald W. Webb, President (Total facility includes 13 beds in nursing home–type unit) **A**1 9 10 **F**7 8 10 11 13 15 16 17 19 21 22 23 24 28 29 30 31 33 34 35 37 40 41 44 45 46 48 49 51 63 65 66 67 68 69 71 73 74 **P**1 5 **N** Palmetto Community Health Network, Conway, SC	23	10	111	4771	50	26990	302	—	—	307
EASLEY—Pickens County										
✠ PALMETTO BAPTIST MEDICAL CENTER EASLEY, 200 Fleetwood Drive, Zip 29640–2076, Mailing Address: P.O. Box 2129, Zip 29641–2129; tel. 864/855–7200; Roddey E. Gettys, III, Executive Vice President **A**1 9 10 **F**7 8 11 13 17 19 20 21 22 23 26 28 29 30 31 34 35 36 37 39 40 41 44 45 46 48 49 62 65 69 71 73 74 **S** Palmetto Health Alliance, Columbia, SC **N** Optimum Health Network, Greenville, SC; Premier Health Systems, Inc., Columbia, SC	23	10	93	3878	47	25964	695	31190	12825	453
EDGEFIELD—Edgefield County										
✠ EDGEFIELD COUNTY HOSPITAL, 300 Ridge Medical Plaza, Zip 29824; tel. 803/637–3174; W. Joseph Seel, Administrator **A**1 9 10 **F**8 13 15 16 17 19 22 26 27 28 29 30 32 33 39 41 45 48 49 51 65 67 68 69 71 74 **N** Premier Health Systems, Inc., Columbia, SC; Principal Health Care of Georgia, Atlanta, GA; The Medical Resource Network, L.L.C., Atlanta, GA; University Health, Inc., Augusta, GA	13	10	40	877	9	9949	—	6113	2826	144
FAIRFAX—Allendale County										
★ ALLENDALE COUNTY HOSPITAL, Highway 278 West, Zip 29827–0278, Mailing Address: Box 218, Zip 29827–0218; tel. 803/632–3311; M. K. Hiatt, Administrator (Total facility includes 44 beds in nursing home–type unit) **A**9 10 **F**7 8 15 16 19 22 28 31 33 40 41 44 49 65 69 71 74 **N** Premier Health Systems, Inc., Columbia, SC	13	10	80	738	49	20345	187	6037	2461	107
FLORENCE—Florence County										
✠ △ CAROLINAS HOSPITAL SYSTEM, (Includes Bruce Hospital System, 121 East Cedar Street, ; Florence General Hospital, 512 South Irby Street, Zip 29501–5210; tel. 803/661–3000), 121 East Cedar Street, Zip 29501, Mailing Address: P.O. Box 100550, Zip 29501–0550; tel. 803/661–3000; David A. McClellan, Chief Executive Officer (Total facility includes 44 beds in nursing home–type unit) **A**1 7 9 10 **F**2 3 4 8 10 11 13 14 15 16 17 19 20 21 22 24 25 26 27 28 29 30 31 32 33 34 35 37 38 39 40 41 43 44 45 47 48 49 51 53 55 57 58 60 62 63 65 66 67 69 71 73 74 **P**7 **S** Quorum Health Group/Quorum Health Resources, Inc., Brentwood, TN	33	10	360	13522	227	153552	—	123777	51160	1584
□ HEALTHSOUTH REHABILITATION HOSPITAL, 900 East Cheves Street, Zip 29506–2704; tel. 803/679–9000; Mark J. Stepanik, Interim Chief Executive Officer **A**1 9 10 **F**4 8 10 11 13 14 16 17 19 22 23 24 25 26 28 30 31 32 33 34 35 37 38 39 40 41 43 44 45 46 47 48 49 53 55 56 57 58 65 66 67 69 71 73 **S** HEALTHSOUTH Corporation, Birmingham, AL **N** Palmetto Community Health Network, Conway, SC	33	46	88	1116	64	11891	—	—	—	225

Hospital, Address, Telephone, Administrator, Approval, Facility, and Physician Codes, Health Care System, Network	Classi-fication Codes		Utilization Data					Expense (thousands) of dollars		
	Control	Service	Staffed Beds	Admissions	Census	Outpatient Visits	Births	Total	Payroll	Personnel

★ American Hospital Association (AHA) membership
□ Joint Commission on Accreditation of Healthcare Organizations (JCAHO) accreditation
+ American Osteopathic Healthcare Association (AOHA) membership
○ American Osteopathic Association (AOA) accreditation
△ Commission on Accreditation of Rehabilitation Facilities (CARF) accreditation
Control codes 61, 63, 64, 71, 72 and 73 indicate hospitals listed by AOHA, but not registered by AHA. For definition of numerical codes, see page A4.

✠ MCLEOD REGIONAL MEDICAL CENTER, (Includes Wilson Medical Center, 701 Cashua Ferry Road, Darlington, Zip 29532, Mailing Address: Box 1859, Zip 29540; tel. 803/395–1100; Debbie Locklair, Administrator), 555 East Cheves Street, Zip 29506–2617, Mailing Address: P.O. Box 100551, Zip 29501–0551; tel. 803/667–2000; J. Bruce Barragan, President and Chief Executive Officer **A**1 2 3 5 9 10 **F**2 3 4 7 8 9 10 11 13 15 17 18 19 20 21 22 23 24 25 26 27 28 29 30 31 32 33 34 35 37 38 39 40 41 42 43 44 45 46 47 48 49 50 51 52 53 54 55 56 57 58 59 60 63 65 66 67 68 69 70 71 73 74 **P**5 7 8 **N** Palmetto Community Health Network, Conway, SC	23	10	421	22222	326	201548	2002	201899	82269	2925
FORT JACKSON—Richland County										
✠ MONCRIEF ARMY COMMUNITY HOSPITAL, Mailing Address: P.O. Box 500, Zip 29207–5720; tel. 803/751–2284; Colonel Dale Carroll, Commander **A**1 2 **F**2 3 4 5 6 8 9 10 11 13 15 17 18 19 20 21 22 23 24 25 26 27 28 29 30 31 32 33 34 35 36 37 38 39 40 41 42 43 44 45 46 47 48 49 50 51 52 53 54 55 56 57 58 59 60 61 62 63 65 66 67 68 69 70 71 73 74 **P**5 **S** Department of the Army, Office of the Surgeon General, Falls Church, VA	42	10	69	2446	26	379617	—	—	—	846
GAFFNEY—Cherokee County										
□ UPSTATE CAROLINA MEDICAL CENTER, 1530 North Limestone Street, Zip 29340–4738; tel. 864/487–1500; Nancy C. Fodi, Executive Director **A**1 9 10 **F**8 11 14 15 17 19 21 22 24 28 29 30 32 33 34 35 37 40 41 44 45 46 48 49 65 66 71 73 74 **P**5 **S** Health Management Associates, Naples, FL **N** Premier Health Systems, Inc., Columbia, SC	33	10	125	3323	42	38047	321	22402	8758	303
GEORGETOWN—Georgetown County										
✠ GEORGETOWN MEMORIAL HOSPITAL, 606 Black River Road, Zip 29440–3368, Mailing Address: Drawer 1718, Zip 29442–1718; tel. 803/527–7000; Paul D. Gatens, Sr., Administrator **A**1 9 10 **F**2 5 7 8 9 10 11 14 15 16 17 19 21 22 23 24 25 28 29 30 31 34 35 37 39 40 41 42 44 45 46 47 48 49 54 56 59 60 61 63 65 66 69 70 71 73 74 **S** Quorum Health Group/Quorum Health Resources, Inc., Brentwood, TN **N** Premier Health Systems, Inc., Columbia, SC	23	10	131	7032	89	88518	710	45648	16048	535
GREENVILLE—Greenville County										
✠ GREENVILLE MEMORIAL HOSPITAL, 701 Grove Road, Zip 29605–4295; tel. 864/455–7000; J. Bland Burkhardt, Jr., Senior Vice President and Administrator (Total facility includes 48 beds in nursing home–type unit) **A**1 2 5 8 9 10 **F**2 3 4 5 7 8 10 11 13 14 15 16 17 18 19 21 22 24 25 26 27 28 29 30 31 32 33 34 35 37 38 39 40 41 42 43 44 45 46 47 48 49 50 51 53 54 55 56 57 58 59 60 61 63 65 66 67 68 69 70 71 73 74 **P**2 3 **S** Greenville Hospital System, Greenville, SC **N** Premier Health Systems, Inc., Columbia, SC; Greenville Hospital System, Greenville, SC	23	10	912	33624	634	492547	4456	—	—	4259
★ MARSHALL I. PICKENS HOSPITAL, 701 Grove Road, Zip 29605–5601; tel. 864/455–7834; Jack W. Bonner, M.D., Administrator and Medical Director (Nonreporting) **A**9 **S** Greenville Hospital System, Greenville, SC **N** Premier Health Systems, Inc., Columbia, SC; Greenville Hospital System, Greenville, SC	23	22	106	—	—	—	—	—	—	—
★ △ ROGER C. PEACE REHABILITATION HOSPITAL, 701 Grove Road, Zip 29605–4295; tel. 864/455–7000; Dennis C. Hollins, M.D., Ph.D., Administrator and Medical Director (Nonreporting) **A**7 9 **S** Greenville Hospital System, Greenville, SC **N** Premier Health Systems, Inc., Columbia, SC; Greenville Hospital System, Greenville, SC	23	46	50	—	—	—	—	—	—	—
✠ SHRINERS HOSPITALS FOR CHILDREN, GREENVILLE, 950 West Faris Road, Zip 29605–4277; tel. 864/271–3444; Gary F. Fraley, Administrator **A**1 3 5 **F**15 19 21 22 27 28 30 34 37 38 41 45 47 48 49 50 53 65 69 70 71 73 **P**5 **S** Shriners Hospitals for Children, Tampa, FL	23	57	60	1047	21	12622	—	—	—	199
✠ △ ST. FRANCIS HEALTH SYSTEM, One St. Francis Drive, Zip 29601–3207; tel. 864/255–1000; Richard C. Neugent, President **A**1 2 7 10 **F**2 3 4 8 10 11 15 16 17 19 21 22 23 24 25 28 29 30 31 32 33 34 35 37 38 39 40 41 42 43 44 45 46 48 49 52 53 55 57 58 59 60 63 65 66 67 69 71 73 74 **P**1 2 3 **N** Optimum Health Network, Greenville, SC; Saint Francis Health System, Greenville, SC	23	10	237	9212	158	184261	—	—	—	1366
W. J. BARGE MEMORIAL HOSPITAL, Wade Hampton Boulevard, Zip 29614; tel. 803/242–5100; William Brown, Administrator **F**7 22 34 35 40 44 49	23	11	79	1402	8	6820	49	2871	750	53
GREENWOOD—Greenwood County										
✠ SELF MEMORIAL HOSPITAL, 1325 Spring Street, Zip 29646–3860; tel. 864/227–4111; M. John Heydel, President and Chief Executive Officer **A**1 2 3 5 9 10 **F**2 3 7 8 10 11 13 14 15 16 17 18 19 20 21 22 23 24 25 26 28 29 30 31 32 33 34 35 37 38 39 40 41 42 44 45 46 47 49 51 53 54 55 56 57 58 60 63 65 66 67 68 69 70 71 73 74 **P**1 5 8 **N** Premier Health Systems, Inc., Columbia, SC	23	10	355	10971	176	146628	1643	88050	41086	1375
GREER—Greenville County										
★ ALLEN BENNETT HOSPITAL, (Includes Roger Huntington Nursing Center), 313 Memorial Drive, Zip 29650–1521; tel. 864/848–8130; Michael W. Massey, Administrator (Total facility includes 88 beds in nursing home–type unit) **A**9 10 **F**2 3 4 5 7 8 10 11 13 17 18 19 21 22 24 26 27 28 29 30 31 32 33 34 35 37 38 39 40 41 42 43 44 45 46 47 48 49 53 54 55 56 57 58 59 60 61 63 65 66 67 68 69 70 71 73 74 **P**2 3 **S** Greenville Hospital System, Greenville, SC **N** Premier Health Systems, Inc., Columbia, SC; Greenville Hospital System, Greenville, SC	23	10	146	3046	122	61047	337	26313	10339	297
□ CHARTER GREENVILLE BEHAVIORAL HEALTH SYSTEM, 2700 East Phillips Road, Zip 29650–4816; tel. 864/968–6300; William L. Callison, Chief Executive Officer **A**1 10 **F**2 3 14 15 16 34 53 54 55 56 57 58 59 **S** Magellan Health Services, Atlanta, GA **N** Optimum Health Network, Greenville, SC	33	22	66	2008	47	—	—	7710	—	108

Hospital, Address, Telephone, Administrator, Approval, Facility, and Physician Codes, Health Care System, Network	Classi-fication Codes		Utilization Data					Expense (thousands) of dollars		
★ American Hospital Association (AHA) membership □ Joint Commission on Accreditation of Healthcare Organizations (JCAHO) accreditation + American Osteopathic Healthcare Association (AOHA) membership ○ American Osteopathic Association (AOA) accreditation △ Commission on Accreditation of Rehabilitation Facilities (CARF) accreditation Control codes 61, 63, 64, 71, 72 and 73 indicate hospitals listed by AOHA, but not registered by AHA. For definition of numerical codes, see page A4	Control	Service	Staffed Beds	Admissions	Census	Outpatient Visits	Births	Total	Payroll	Personnel

HARTSVILLE—Darlington County

□ BYERLY HOSPITAL, 413 East Carolina Avenue, Zip 29550–4309; tel. 843/339–2100; Page Vaughan, Executive Director **A**1 10 **F**7 8 11 13 15 17 19 21 22 23 24 28 29 30 31 35 36 37 40 45 46 49 63 65 66 67 68 69 71 74 **S** Health Management Associates, Naples, FL **N** Palmetto Community Health Network, Conway, SC
| | 33 | 10 | 100 | 4414 | 52 | 36886 | 568 | 24045 | 8676 | 363 |

HILTON HEAD ISLAND—Beaufort County

✠ HILTON HEAD MEDICAL CENTER AND CLINICS, 25 Hospital Center Boulevard, Zip 29926–2738, Mailing Address: P.O. Box 21117, Zip 29925–1117; tel. 803/681–6122; Dennis Ray Bruns, President and Chief Executive Officer (Total facility includes 15 beds in nursing home–type unit) **A**1 9 10 **F**4 6 7 8 9 10 11 17 19 20 21 22 24 25 26 27 28 29 30 31 33 34 35 36 37 38 39 40 41 42 44 45 46 47 48 49 52 53 54 55 56 57 58 59 65 66 67 69 70 71 73 74 **S** TENET Healthcare Corporation, Santa Barbara, CA **N** Premier Health Systems, Inc., Columbia, SC; Principal Health Care of Georgia, Atlanta, GA
| | 32 | 10 | 79 | 4044 | 43 | 83963 | 376 | 39452 | 11190 | 395. |

KINGSTREE—Williamsburg County

★ CAROLINAS HOSPITAL SYSTEM–KINGSTREE, 500 Nelson Boulevard, Zip 29556–4027, Mailing Address: P.O. Drawer 568, Zip 29556–0568; tel. 803/354–9661; David T. Boucher, Chief Executive Officer **A**9 10 **F**7 8 11 14 15 16 17 19 20 22 28 29 30 31 33 34 35 37 40 41 44 45 46 49 65 69 71 73 74 **P**2 **S** Quorum Health Group/Quorum Health Resources, Inc., Brentwood, TN
| | 33 | 10 | 47 | 1583 | 15 | 23253 | 137 | 7807 | 3400 | 138 |

LAKE CITY—Florence County

✠ CAROLINAS HOSPITAL SYSTEM–LAKE CITY, 258 North Ron McNair Boulevard, Zip 29560–1029, Mailing Address: P.O. Box 1029, Zip 29560–1029; tel. 803/394–2036; Richard L. Gamber, Administrator **A**1 9 10 **F**8 17 19 22 24 26 28 29 30 31 33 34 35 36 39 41 44 45 46 49 65 66 69 71 73 74 **P**7 **S** Quorum Health Group/Quorum Health Resources, Inc., Brentwood, TN **N** Premier Health Systems, Inc., Columbia, SC
| | 33 | 10 | 40 | 1074 | 9 | 32909 | — | 9200 | 3698 | 172 |

LANCASTER—Lancaster County

✠ SPRINGS MEMORIAL HOSPITAL, 800 West Meeting Street, Zip 29720–2298; tel. 803/286–1214; Robert M. Luther, Chief Executive Officer **A**1 9 10 **F**2 3 7 8 10 11 15 16 17 19 21 22 23 28 30 31 32 33 34 35 37 40 41 44 45 48 49 60 65 67 69 71 73 74 **P**5 **S** Community Health Systems, Inc., Brentwood, TN
| | 33 | 10 | 137 | 5354 | 88 | 50575 | 627 | 48104 | 15886 | 485 |

LOCKHART—Union County

★ HOPE HOSPITAL, 102 Hope Drive, Zip 29364, Mailing Address: P.O. Box 280, Zip 29364–0280; tel. 864/545–6500; Mildred W. Purvis, Administrator **F**17 28 45
| | 13 | 10 | 10 | 134 | 3 | — | — | 610 | — | 12 |

LORIS—Horry County

✠ LORIS COMMUNITY HOSPITAL, 3655 Mitchell Street, Zip 29569–2827; tel. 803/716–7000; J. Timothy Browne, Chief Executive Officer (Total facility includes 88 beds in nursing home–type unit) **A**1 9 10 **F**7 8 11 14 15 16 17 19 21 22 28 30 31 34 35 37 40 41 44 45 46 49 63 65 69 70 71 **N** Palmetto Community Health Network, Conway, SC
| | 16 | 10 | 193 | 3564 | 129 | 63443 | 388 | 31860 | 12937 | 536 |

MANNING—Clarendon County

✠ CLARENDON MEMORIAL HOSPITAL, 10 Hospital Street, Zip 29102, Mailing Address: P.O. Box 550, Zip 29102–0550; tel. 803/435–8463; Edward R. Frye, Jr., Administrator **A**1 9 10 **F**7 8 10 11 14 15 16 17 18 19 20 21 22 25 26 29 30 31 32 33 34 35 36 37 39 40 44 45 49 54 65 68 71 73 74 **N** Carolina HealthChoice Network, Columbia, SC; Premier Health Systems, Inc., Columbia, SC
| | 16 | 10 | 56 | 2104 | 33 | 80988 | 303 | 17034 | 8294 | 322 |

MOUNT PLEASANT—Charleston County

✠ EAST COOPER REGIONAL MEDICAL CENTER, 1200 Johnnie Dodds Boulevard, Zip 29464–3294; tel. 803/881–0100; John F. Holland, President **A**1 9 10 **F**7 8 10 11 14 15 16 17 19 22 23 24 25 28 29 30 31 32 34 35 37 39 40 41 44 45 48 49 56 61 65 66 69 70 71 73 74 **P**4 **S** TENET Healthcare Corporation, Santa Barbara, CA **N** Premier Health Systems, Inc., Columbia, SC
| | 33 | 10 | 112 | 3834 | 41 | 68650 | 1226 | — | — | 409 |

MULLINS—Marion County

✠ MARION COUNTY MEDICAL CENTER, 2829 East Highway 76, Zip 29574, Mailing Address: P.O. Drawer 1150, Marion, Zip 29571–1150; tel. 803/431–2000; Thomas E. Fuller, Executive Director (Total facility includes 44 beds in nursing home–type unit) (Nonreporting) **A**1 9 10
| | 16 | 10 | 192 | — | — | — | — | — | — | — |

MYRTLE BEACH—Horry County

✠ COLUMBIA GRAND STRAND REGIONAL MEDICAL CENTER, 809 82nd Parkway, Zip 29572–1413; tel. 803/692–1100; Doug White, Chief Executive Officer (Total facility includes 18 beds in nursing home–type unit) **A**1 2 9 10 **F**4 7 8 10 11 13 14 15 16 17 19 21 22 23 24 25 26 28 29 30 31 32 33 34 35 37 39 40 41 43 44 45 46 48 49 60 63 65 66 67 69 70 71 73 74 **S** Columbia/HCA Healthcare Corporation, Nashville, TN
| | 33 | 10 | 205 | 10343 | 120 | 120950 | 646 | — | — | 769 |

NEWBERRY—Newberry County

✠ NEWBERRY COUNTY MEMORIAL HOSPITAL, 2669 Kinard Street, Zip 29108–0497, Mailing Address: P.O. Box 497, Zip 29108–0497; tel. 803/276–7570; Lynn W. Beasley, President and Chief Executive Officer **A**1 9 10 **F**7 8 11 13 15 16 17 19 21 22 28 29 30 31 37 39 40 44 45 47 49 65 69 71 73 74 **P**4 **S** Quorum Health Group/Quorum Health Resources, Inc., Brentwood, TN **N** Carolina HealthChoice Network, Columbia, SC; Premier Health Systems, Inc., Columbia, SC
| | 13 | 10 | 75 | 2039 | 27 | 30507 | 217 | 17089 | 6724 | 267 |

Hospital, Address, Telephone, Administrator, Approval, Facility, and Physician Codes, Health Care System, Network	Classi-fication Codes		Utilization Data					Expense (thousands) of dollars		
★ American Hospital Association (AHA) membership □ Joint Commission on Accreditation of Healthcare Organizations (JCAHO) accreditation + American Osteopathic Healthcare Association (AOHA) membership ○ American Osteopathic Association (AOA) accreditation △ Commission on Accreditation of Rehabilitation Facilities (CARF) accreditation Control codes 61, 63, 64, 71, 72 and 73 indicate hospitals listed by AOHA, but not registered by AHA. For definition of numerical codes, see page A4	Control	Service	Staffed Beds	Admissions	Census	Outpatient Visits	Births	Total	Payroll	Personnel

NORTH CHARLESTON—Charleston County

⊞ NAVAL HOSPITAL, 3600 Rivers Avenue, Zip 29405; tel. 803/743–7000; Captain Kathleen L. Martin, Commanding Officer **A**1 3 5 **F**8 12 15 16 19 20 21 24 28 29 30 32 35 39 40 41 44 45 49 51 52 58 61 63 65 66 71 72 73 **P**6 **S** Department of Navy, Washington, DC

| 43 | 10 | 32 | 1326 | 13 | 191386 | 0 | 34691 | 10483 | — |

ORANGEBURG—Orangeburg County

⊞ REGIONAL MEDICAL CENTER OF ORANGEBURG AND CALHOUN COUNTIES, 3000 St. Matthews Road, Zip 29118–1470; tel. 803/533–2200; Thomas C. Dandridge, President **A**1 2 9 10 **F**2 3 4 5 6 7 8 9 10 11 13 15 16 17 18 19 20 21 22 23 24 25 26 27 28 29 30 31 32 33 34 35 36 37 38 39 40 41 42 43 44 45 46 47 48 49 50 51 53 54 55 56 57 58 59 60 61 62 63 65 66 67 68 69 70 71 73 74 **P**5 **S** Quorum Health Group/Quorum Health Resources, Inc., Brentwood, TN

| 13 | 10 | 295 | 10244 | 157 | 46244 | 1393 | 72184 | 31165 | 1015 |

PICKENS—Pickens County

⊞ CANNON MEMORIAL HOSPITAL, 123 West G. Acker Drive, Zip 29671, Mailing Address: P.O. Box 188, Zip 29671–0188; tel. 864/878–4791; Norman G. Rentz, President and Chief Executive Officer **A**1 9 10 **F**8 11 13 14 17 19 22 26 28 29 30 31 34 37 44 45 49 65 69 71 **P**4 **N** Premier Health Systems, Inc., Columbia, SC

| 23 | 10 | 42 | 1040 | 14 | 26087 | — | 9331 | 3971 | 144 |

RIDGELAND—Jasper County

LOW COUNTRY GENERAL HOSPITAL, Highway 278, Zip 29936, Mailing Address: Drawer 400, Zip 29936–0400; tel. 803/726–8111; Jeffrey L. White, Chief Executive Officer **A**9 10 **F**2 3 4 5 6 7 8 9 10 11 13 15 17 18 19 20 21 22 23 24 25 26 27 28 29 30 31 32 33 34 35 36 37 38 39 40 41 42 43 44 45 46 47 48 49 50 51 52 53 54 55 56 57 58 59 60 61 62 63 65 66 67 68 69 70 71 73 74

| 23 | 10 | 31 | 662 | 8 | 6307 | 77 | 4263 | 2537 | 88 |

ROCK HILL—York County

⊞ PIEDMONT HEALTHCARE SYSTEM, 222 Herlong Avenue, Zip 29732–1952; tel. 803/329–1234; Paul A. Walker, President **A**1 9 10 **F**3 7 8 10 11 14 15 16 17 19 21 22 23 24 25 26 27 28 29 30 31 32 34 35 37 38 39 40 41 44 45 46 49 51 53 54 55 56 57 58 59 60 65 66 67 69 71 73 74 **P**3 **S** TENET Healthcare Corporation, Santa Barbara, CA

| 33 | 10 | 276 | 11910 | 162 | 101142 | 1420 | 87654 | 28493 | 1405 |

SENECA—Oconee County

⊞ OCONEE MEMORIAL HOSPITAL, (Includes Lila Doyle Nursing Care Facility), 298 Memorial Drive, Zip 29672; tel. 864/882–3351; W. H. Hudson, President (Total facility includes 79 beds in nursing home–type unit) **A**1 9 10 **F**7 8 11 13 15 16 17 19 21 22 23 28 30 31 33 34 35 37 41 44 45 49 65 67 69 71 73

| 23 | 10 | 195 | 6889 | 152 | 75753 | 587 | 50454 | 21173 | 813 |

SHAW AFB—Sumter County

⊞ U. S. AIR FORCE HOSPITAL SHAW, 431 Meadowlark Street, Zip 29152–5300; tel. 803/668–2559; Lieutenant Colonel Donald Taylor, Administrator **A**1 **F**2 3 4 7 8 9 10 11 13 14 15 16 17 18 19 20 22 23 24 28 29 30 34 35 37 38 39 40 41 42 43 44 45 46 47 48 49 50 51 52 53 54 55 56 58 59 60 61 63 65 66 67 68 69 71 73 74 **S** Department of the Air Force, Bowling AFB, DC

| 41 | 10 | 22 | 1255 | 7 | 136856 | 359 | — | — | 428 |

SIMPSONVILLE—Greenville County

★ HILLCREST HOSPITAL, 729 S.E. Main Street, Zip 29681–3280; tel. 864/967–6100; Mark Slyter, Administrator **A**9 10 **F**2 3 4 8 10 11 13 14 15 16 17 19 21 22 24 25 26 27 28 29 30 31 32 33 34 35 36 37 38 39 40 41 42 43 44 45 46 47 48 49 53 54 55 56 57 58 59 60 61 63 65 66 67 69 71 73 74 **P**2 3 **S** Greenville Hospital System, Greenville, SC **N** Premier Health Systems, Inc., Columbia, SC; Greenville Hospital System, Greenville, SC

| 23 | 10 | 46 | 1174 | 16 | 48584 | — | 15456 | 5382 | 131 |

SPARTANBURG—Spartanburg County

⊞ △ MARY BLACK HEALTH SYSTEM, 1700 Skylyn Drive, Zip 29307–1061, Mailing Address: P.O. Box 3217, Zip 29304–3217; tel. 864/573–3000; William W. Fox, Chief Executive Officer **A**1 7 9 10 **F**7 8 10 11 13 15 16 17 19 21 22 23 25 28 29 30 31 34 37 39 40 41 42 44 45 46 48 49 53 63 65 67 69 71 73 74 **P**1 2 3 **S** Quorum Health Group/Quorum Health Resources, Inc., Brentwood, TN **N** Optimum Health Network, Greenville, SC; Premier Health Systems, Inc., Columbia, SC

| 33 | 10 | 212 | 7454 | 107 | 120935 | 1297 | 63002 | 22595 | 671 |

⊞ SPARTANBURG REGIONAL MEDICAL CENTER, 101 East Wood Street, Zip 29303–3016; tel. 864/560–6000; Joseph Michael Oddis, President (Nonreporting) **A**1 2 3 5 9 10 **S** Spartanburg Regional Healthcare System, Spartanburg, SC

| 16 | 10 | 471 | — | — | — | — | — | — | — |

SUMMERVILLE—Dorchester County

★ SUMMERVILLE MEDICAL CENTER, 295 Midland Parkway, Zip 29485–8104; tel. 843/875–3993; Ian W. Watson, Chief Executive Officer (Nonreporting) **A**9 **S** Columbia/HCA Healthcare Corporation, Nashville, TN

| 33 | 10 | 99 | — | — | — | — | — | — | — |

SUMTER—Sumter County

⊞ TUOMEY REGIONAL MEDICAL CENTER, 129 North Washington Street, Zip 29150–4983; tel. 803/778–9000; Jay Cox, President and Chief Executive Officer (Nonreporting) **A**1 9 10 **S** Quorum Health Group/Quorum Health Resources, Inc., Brentwood, TN

| 23 | 10 | 206 | — | — | — | — | — | — | — |

TRAVELERS REST—Greenville County

□ SPRING BROOK BEHAVIORAL HEALTHCARE SYSTEM, (Formerly Chestnut Hill Psychiatric Hospital), One Chestnut Way, Zip 29690–1005, Mailing Address: P.O. Box 1005, Zip 29690–1005; tel. 864/834–8013; Shawn J. O'Connor, Chief Executive Officer **A**1 10 **F**17 19 21 22 25 26 27 29 34 35 45 48 49 52 53 54 55 56 57 58 59 65 70 71

| 33 | 22 | 44 | 198 | 10 | — | — | — | — | 61 |

Hospital, Address, Telephone, Administrator, Approval, Facility, and Physician Codes, Health Care System, Network	Classi-fication Codes		Utilization Data					Expense (thousands) of dollars		
★ American Hospital Association (AHA) membership □ Joint Commission on Accreditation of Healthcare Organizations (JCAHO) accreditation + American Osteopathic Healthcare Association (AOHA) membership ○ American Osteopathic Association (AOA) accreditation △ Commission on Accreditation of Rehabilitation Facilities (CARF) accreditation Control codes 61, 63, 64, 71, 72 and 73 indicate hospitals listed by AOHA, but not registered by AHA. For definition of numerical codes, see page A4	Control	Service	Staffed Beds	Admissions	Census	Outpatient Visits	Births	Total	Payroll	Personnel

UNION—Union County

⊞ WALLACE THOMSON HOSPITAL, 322 West South Street, Zip 29379–2857, Mailing Address: P.O. Box 789, Zip 29379–0789; tel. 864/429–2600; Harrell L. Connelly, Chief Executive Officer (Total facility includes 108 beds in nursing home–type unit) **A**1 9 10 **F**8 16 17 19 22 27 28 30 32 34 35 36 37 39 40 41 44 45 46 49 60 63 65 69 71 73 74 **P**5 **S** Quorum Health Group/Quorum Health Resources, Inc., Brentwood, TN	16	10	215	3838	158	39823	168	—	—	484

VARNVILLE—Hampton County

★ HAMPTON REGIONAL MEDICAL CENTER, 503 Carolina Avenue West, Zip 29944, Mailing Address: P.O. Box 338, Zip 29944–0338; tel. 803/943–2771; Dave H. Hamill, President and Chief Executive Officer **A**9 10 **F**8 17 19 22 28 29 30 34 44 45 49 65 69 71 73 74	23	10	36	511	6	7148	—	5647	2460	96

WALTERBORO—Colleton County

⊞ COLLETON MEDICAL CENTER, (Formerly Columbia Colleton Medical Center), 501 Robertson Boulevard, Zip 29488–5714; tel. 803/549–2000; Rebecca T. Brewer, CHE, Chief Executive Officer (Total facility includes 15 beds in nursing home–type unit) **A**1 9 10 **F**2 3 4 5 7 8 10 11 13 14 15 16 17 18 19 21 22 23 24 25 26 27 28 29 30 31 32 33 34 35 37 38 39 40 41 42 43 44 45 46 47 48 49 50 51 53 54 55 56 57 58 59 60 63 65 66 67 68 69 70 71 73 74 **P**1 2 6 8 **S** Columbia/HCA Healthcare Corporation, Nashville, TN	33	10	131	4003	77	39281	391	—	—	413

WEST COLUMBIA—Lexington County

□ CHARTER RIVERS BEHAVIORAL HEALTH SYSTEM, 2900 Sunset Boulevard, Zip 29169–3422; tel. 803/796–9911; Brooks Cagle, Chief Executive Officer (Nonreporting) **A**1 9 10 **S** Magellan Health Services, Atlanta, GA	33	22	80	—		—		—	—	
⊞ LEXINGTON MEDICAL CENTER, 2720 Sunset Boulevard, Zip 29169–4816; tel. 803/791–2000; Michael J. Biediger, President **A**1 9 10 **F**7 8 10 11 13 15 16 17 18 19 20 21 22 24 25 26 27 28 29 30 31 32 33 34 35 37 38 39 40 41 42 44 45 46 48 49 50 51 60 63 65 66 67 69 70 71 73 74 **P**4 **N** Premier Health Systems, Inc., Columbia, SC	16	10	283	13175	172	191413	2235	109280	45469	1424

WINNSBORO—Fairfield County

⊞ FAIRFIELD MEMORIAL HOSPITAL, 102 U.S. Highway 321 By–Pass North, Zip 29180, Mailing Address: P.O. Box 620, Zip 29180–0620; tel. 803/635–5548; Brent R. Lammers, Administrator **A**1 9 10 **F**8 14 15 16 17 19 22 28 29 32 33 34 39 44 45 49 65 67 69 71 73 **N** Carolina HealthChoice Network, Columbia, SC; Premier Health Systems, Inc., Columbia, SC	13	10	24	883	12	25459	—	8735	3909	184

WOODRUFF—Spartanburg County

★ B.J. WORKMAN MEMORIAL HOSPITAL, 751 East Georgia Street, Zip 29388, Mailing Address: P.O. Box 699, Zip 29388–0699; tel. 864/476–8122; G. Curtis Walker, R.N., Administrator (Nonreporting) **A**9 10 **S** Spartanburg Regional Healthcare System, Spartanburg, SC	13	10	32	—		—	—	—	—	—

SOUTH DAKOTA

Resident population 738 (in thousands)
Resident population in metro areas 33.0%
Birth rate per 1,000 population 14.6
65 years and over 14.4%
Percent of persons without health insurance 9.5%

Hospital, Address, Telephone, Administrator, Approval, Facility, and Physician Codes, Health Care System, Network	Classi-fication Codes		Utilization Data					Expense (thousands) of dollars		
★ American Hospital Association (AHA) membership □ Joint Commission on Accreditation of Healthcare Organizations (JCAHO) accreditation + American Osteopathic Healthcare Association (AOHA) membership ○ American Osteopathic Association (AOA) accreditation △ Commission on Accreditation of Rehabilitation Facilities (CARF) accreditation Control codes 61, 63, 64, 71, 72 and 73 indicate hospitals listed by AOHA, but not registered by AHA. For definition of numerical codes, see page A4	Control	Service	Staffed Beds	Admissions	Census	Outpatient Visits	Births	Total	Payroll	Personnel

ABERDEEN—Brown County

✠ △ ST. LUKE'S MIDLAND REGIONAL MEDICAL CENTER, 305 South State Street, Zip 57402–4450; tel. 605/622–5000; Dale J. Stein, President and Chief Executive Officer (Total facility includes 81 beds in nursing home–type unit) **A**1 2 7 9 10 **F**1 3 6 7 8 10 12 14 15 16 17 19 21 22 23 26 28 30 31 32 33 34 35 36 37 39 40 41 42 44 45 46 48 49 52 53 54 55 56 57 58 59 60 61 62 64 65 66 67 71 73 **P**6 7 **S** Avera Health, Yankton, SD — 21 10 258 6456 190 168959 713 61742 27420 758

ARMOUR—Douglas County

DOUGLAS COUNTY MEMORIAL HOSPITAL, 708 Eighth Street, Zip 57313–2102; tel. 605/724–2159; Angelia K. Henry, Administrator **A**9 10 **F**7 8 15 16 19 20 22 26 28 30 32 34 35 36 39 41 44 49 53 58 59 63 65 71 **N** Missouri Valley Health Network, Yankton, SD — 23 10 9 268 3 5161 15 1575 728 41

BOWDLE—Edmunds County

★ BOWDLE HOSPITAL, 9051 West Fifth Street, Zip 57428–0566; tel. 605/285–6146; Bryan Breitling, Administrator and Chief Executive Officer (Total facility includes 41 beds in nursing home–type unit) **A**9 10 **F**8 14 15 19 22 24 27 30 32 33 34 40 44 64 65 71 — 14 10 61 479 47 5996 13 3173 1603 87

BRITTON—Marshall County

MARSHALL COUNTY HEALTHCARE CENTER, (Formerly Marshall County Memorial Hospital), 413 Ninth Street, Zip 57430–0230, Mailing Address: Box 230, Zip 57430–0230; tel. 605/448–2253; Stephanie Lulewicz, Administrator **A**9 10 **F**6 8 15 16 19 22 28 30 32 71 73 **P**5 **S** Avera Health, Yankton, SD — 23 10 20 481 8 6183 — 2464 987 76

BROOKINGS—Brookings County

★ BROOKINGS HOSPITAL, 300 22nd Avenue, Zip 57006–2496; tel. 605/696–9000; David B. Johnson, Administrator (Total facility includes 79 beds in nursing home–type unit) **A**3 9 10 **F**7 12 14 16 17 19 22 26 27 28 30 32 33 35 36 37 39 40 44 45 46 64 67 71 73 — 14 10 140 2181 101 37201 306 14004 7687 198

BURKE—Gregory County

COMMUNITY MEMORIAL HOSPITAL, Eighth and Jackson, Zip 57523, Mailing Address: P.O. Box 319, Zip 57523–0319; tel. 605/775–2621; Carol A. Varland, Administrator (Nonreporting) **A**9 10 **N** Missouri Valley Health Network, Yankton, SD — 23 10 16 — — — — — — —

CANTON—Lincoln County

★ CANTON–INWOOD MEMORIAL HOSPITAL, 440 North Hiawatha Drive, Zip 57013–9404, Mailing Address: Rural Route 3, Box 7, Zip 57013–0007; tel. 605/987–2621; John Devick, Chief Executive Officer **A**9 10 **F**7 8 11 15 16 19 21 22 23 31 33 35 37 40 44 49 50 60 63 70 71 **S** Sioux Valley Hospitals and Health System, Sioux Falls, SD **N** Sioux Valley Health System, Sioux Falls, SD — 23 10 25 503 5 9211 38 2629 1196 64

CHAMBERLAIN—Brule County

★ MID DAKOTA HOSPITAL, 300 South Byron Boulevard, Zip 57325–9741; tel. 605/734–5511; Michael Penticoff, Administrator **A**9 10 **F**7 8 11 17 19 22 28 30 32 33 35 37 40 41 44 49 65 71 **S** Sioux Valley Hospitals and Health System, Sioux Falls, SD **N** Sioux Valley Health System, Sioux Falls, SD — 23 10 54 1355 14 8887 40 6543 3030 125

CLEAR LAKE—Deuel County

★ DEUEL COUNTY MEMORIAL HOSPITAL, (RURAL PRIMARY CARE HOSP), 701 Third Avenue South, Zip 57226–1037, Mailing Address: P.O. Box 1037, Zip 57226–1037; tel. 605/874–2141; Robert J. Salmon, Interim Administrator (Total facility includes 10 beds in nursing home–type unit) **A**9 10 **F**6 8 13 15 16 17 19 20 21 22 24 26 28 30 32 33 34 36 41 49 51 63 64 65 71 **P**6 **S** Sioux Valley Hospitals and Health System, Sioux Falls, SD — 23 49 16 195 3 4048 0 1498 831 36

CUSTER—Custer County

CUSTER COMMUNITY HOSPITAL, 1039 Montgomery Street, Zip 57730–1397; tel. 605/673–2229; Jason Petik, Administrator **A**9 10 **F**7 8 15 16 19 22 25 28 32 33 39 40 41 44 51 58 65 71 72 73 **P**7 8 **N** Rapid City Regional Hospital System of Care, Rapid City, SD — 23 10 10 180 3 17977 18 2467 1150 53

DE SMET—Kingsbury County

DE SMET MEMORIAL HOSPITAL, 306 Prairie Avenue S.W., Zip 57231–9499; tel. 605/854–3329; John L. Single, Chief Executive Officer and Administrator **A**9 10 **F**8 14 15 16 19 22 30 32 44 49 65 71 — 14 10 13 235 3 5605 — 870 467 —

DEADWOOD—Lawrence County

★ NORTHERN HILLS GENERAL HOSPITAL, 61 Charles Street, Zip 57732–1303; tel. 605/578–2313; Richard G. Soukup, Chief Executive Officer **A**9 10 **F**1 3 7 8 15 19 22 24 28 29 30 32 33 35 36 37 39 40 41 44 49 53 54 55 56 57 58 59 64 65 66 71 **N** Regional Hospital Healthcare Network, Deadwood, SD; Rapid City Regional Hospital System of Care, Rapid City, SD — 23 10 35 565 7 31693 52 5996 2944 110

DELL RAPIDS—Minnehaha County

DELL RAPIDS COMMUNITY HOSPITAL, 909 North Iowa Street, Zip 57022–1231; tel. 605/428–5431; Russ Nielsen, Administrator (Nonreporting) **A**9 10 — 23 10 19 — — — — — — —

Hospital, Address, Telephone, Administrator, Approval, Facility, and Physician Codes, Health Care System, Network	Classification Codes		Utilization Data					Expense (thousands) of dollars		
★ American Hospital Association (AHA) membership □ Joint Commission on Accreditation of Healthcare Organizations (JCAHO) accreditation + American Osteopathic Healthcare Association (AOHA) membership ○ American Osteopathic Association (AOA) accreditation △ Commission on Accreditation of Rehabilitation Facilities (CARF) accreditation Control codes 61, 63, 64, 71, 72 and 73 indicate hospitals listed by AOHA, but not registered by AHA. For definition of numerical codes, see page A4	Control	Service	Staffed Beds	Admissions	Census	Outpatient Visits	Births	Total	Payroll	Personnel

EAGLE BUTTE—Dewey County

⊠ U. S. PUBLIC HEALTH SERVICE INDIAN HOSPITAL, Mailing Address: P.O. Box 1012, Zip 57625–1012; tel. 605/964–3001; Orville Night Pipe, Service Unit Director **A**1 10 **F**1 3 4 5 6 7 8 10 12 13 14 15 16 17 18 19 20 21 22 23 24 25 26 27 28 29 30 31 32 33 34 35 36 39 40 41 42 43 44 45 46 49 50 51 53 54 55 56 57 58 59 60 61 62 63 65 66 67 68 69 70 71 72 73 74 **S** U. S. Public Health Service Indian Health Service, Rockville, MD — 44 10 27 866 9 60060 117 — — —

ELLSWORTH AFB—Meade County

⊠ U. S. AIR FORCE HOSPITAL, 2900 Doolittle Drive, Zip 57706; tel. 605/385–3201; Colonel Steven Sem, Commander (Nonreporting) **A**1 **S** Department of the Air Force, Bowling AFB, DC — 41 10 31

EUREKA—McPherson County

EUREKA COMMUNITY HOSPITAL, 410 Ninth Street, Zip 57437–0517; tel. 605/284–2661; Robert A. Dockter, Administrator **A**9 10 **F**6 8 15 16 17 19 22 32 35 44 49 65 66 71 **S** Avera Health, Yankton, SD — 23 10 9 204 2 7001 — 1051 493 30

FAULKTON—Faulk County

FAULK COUNTY MEMORIAL HOSPITAL, (RURAL PRIMARY CARE HOSPITAL), 911 St. John Street, Zip 57438, Mailing Address: P.O. Box 100, Zip 57438–0100; tel. 605/598–6263; Patricia Kadlec, Administrator **A**9 10 **F**6 12 14 15 16 17 22 27 28 30 32 34 37 39 41 46 49 51 62 64 65 — 13 49 19 170 6 5335 — 1286 640 28

FLANDREAU—Moody County

★ FLANDREAU MUNICIPAL HOSPITAL, 214 North Prairie Avenue, Zip 57028–1243; tel. 605/997–2433; Paul Bergman, Administrator **A**9 10 **F**8 15 16 19 21 22 32 33 34 41 44 49 71 **S** Avera Health, Yankton, SD — 14 10 18 353 4 6934 0 1987 904 44

FORT MEADE—Meade County

⊠ VETERANS AFFAIRS BLACK HILLS HEALTH CARE SYSTEM, (Includes Veterans Affairs Medical Center, 113 Comanche Road, ; Veterans Affairs Medical Center, 500 North Fifth Street, Hot Springs, Zip 57747; tel. 605/745–2052), 113 Comanche Road, Zip 57741–1099; tel. 605/347–2511; Peter P. Henry, Director (Total facility includes 110 beds in nursing home–type unit) **A**1 5 9 **F**2 3 4 5 8 10 12 14 15 17 18 19 20 21 22 23 26 27 28 29 30 31 32 33 34 35 36 37 39 41 42 43 44 46 48 49 51 52 54 56 57 58 60 64 65 69 71 73 74 **S** Department of Veterans Affairs, Washington, DC — 45 10 181 3217 185 169698 0 71806 39192 956

FREEMAN—Hutchinson County

★ FREEMAN COMMUNITY HOSPITAL, 510 East Eighth Street, Zip 57029–0370, Mailing Address: P.O. Box 370, Zip 57029–0370; tel. 605/925–4231; James M. Krehbiel, Chief Executive Officer (Total facility includes 59 beds in nursing home–type unit) **A**9 10 **F**1 7 8 14 15 16 17 19 22 26 27 28 29 30 32 33 34 35 36 37 39 40 41 42 44 45 48 49 62 63 64 65 66 67 71 73 **P**4 **N** Missouri Valley Health Network, Yankton, SD — 23 10 85 380 63 7901 29 4490 2343 61

GETTYSBURG—Potter County

★ GETTYSBURG MEDICAL CENTER, 606 East Garfield, Zip 57442–1398; tel. 605/765–2488; Mark Schmidt, Administrator (Total facility includes 54 beds in nursing home–type unit) (Nonreporting) **A**9 10 **S** Catholic Health Initiatives, Denver, CO — 23 10 61

GREGORY—Gregory County

★ GREGORY COMMUNITY HOSPITAL, 400 Park Street, Zip 57533–0400, Mailing Address: Box 408, Zip 57533–0408; tel. 605/835–8394; Carol A. Varland, Chief Executive Officer (Total facility includes 26 beds in nursing home–type unit) **A**9 10 **F**1 7 8 11 12 14 15 16 19 20 21 22 24 26 27 28 29 30 32 35 37 40 42 44 46 58 64 65 66 67 71 **S** Lutheran Health Systems, Fargo, ND **N** Missouri Valley Health Network, Yankton, SD — 23 10 84 802 68 20203 40 5907 2846 114

HOT SPRINGS—Fall River County

★ SOUTHERN HILLS GENERAL HOSPITAL, (Includes Castle Manor), 209 North 16th Street, Zip 57747–1375; tel. 605/745–3159; Eric Hanson, Administrator (Total facility includes 48 beds in nursing home–type unit) (Nonreporting) **A**9 10 **S** Lutheran Health Systems, Fargo, ND **N** Black Hills Healthcare Network, Spearfish, SD — 23 10 60

VETERANS AFFAIRS MEDICAL CENTER See Veterans Affairs Black Hills Health Care System, Fort Meade

HOVEN—Potter County

★ HOLY INFANT HOSPITAL, Main Street, Zip 57450–0158, Mailing Address: P.O. Box 158, Zip 57450–0158; tel. 605/948–2262; Jeff Marlette, Administrator (Nonreporting) **A**9 10 — 23 10 22

HURON—Beadle County

⊠ HURON REGIONAL MEDICAL CENTER, 172 Fourth Street S.E., Zip 57350–2590; tel. 605/353–6200; John L. Single, Chief Executive Officer **A**1 9 10 **F**7 8 14 15 19 21 22 24 30 32 33 34 35 37 39 40 41 44 45 49 56 65 66 71 73 74 **S** Quorum Health Group/Quorum Health Resources, Inc., Brentwood, TN — 23 10 61 2794 30 41358 273 18229 7420 243

LEMMON—Perkins County

FIVE COUNTIES HOSPITAL, (CRITICAL ACCESS HOSPITAL), 401 Sixth Avenue West, Zip 57638–1318, Mailing Address: P.O. Box 479, Zip 57638–0479; tel. 605/374–3871; Helen S. Lindquist, Administrator (Total facility includes 52 beds in nursing home–type unit) **A**9 10 **F**22 64 **N** Rapid City Regional Hospital System of Care, Rapid City, SD — 23 49 56 72 52 2888 — 1843 915 64

MADISON—Lake County

⊠ MADISON COMMUNITY HOSPITAL, 917 North Washington Avenue, Zip 57042–1696; tel. 605/256–6551; Tamara Miller, Administrator **A**1 9 10 **F**7 8 14 15 17 19 22 28 30 32 33 35 36 37 39 40 41 44 49 64 65 67 71 — 23 10 49 862 14 2652 68 5327 2819 108

Hospital, Address, Telephone, Administrator, Approval, Facility, and Physician Codes, Health Care System, Network	Classi-fication Codes		Utilization Data						Expense (thousands) of dollars		
	Control	Service	Staffed Beds	Admissions	Census	Outpatient Visits	Births		Total	Payroll	Personnel

★ American Hospital Association (AHA) membership
□ Joint Commission on Accreditation of Healthcare Organizations (JCAHO) accreditation
+ American Osteopathic Healthcare Association (AOHA) membership
○ American Osteopathic Association (AOA) accreditation
△ Commission on Accreditation of Rehabilitation Facilities (CARF) accreditation
Control codes 61, 63, 64, 71, 72 and 73 indicate hospitals listed by AOHA, but not registered by AHA. For definition of numerical codes, see page A4

MARTIN—Bennett County

BENNETT COUNTY COMMUNITY HOSPITAL, Merriman Star Route, Zip 57551, Mailing Address: P.O. Box 70D, Zip 57551; tel. 605/685–6622; James Haeder, Administrator (Total facility includes 48 beds in nursing home–type unit) **A**9 10 **F**7 8 22 28 29 32 34 40 49 64 — 13 10 | 68 | 415 | 50 | 1477 | 10 | 2934 | 1649 | 92

MILBANK—Grant County

□ ST. BERNARD'S PROVIDENCE HOSPITAL, (Includes St. William Home for the Aged), 901 East Virgil Avenue, Zip 57252–2124, Mailing Address: P.O. Box 432, Zip 57252–0432; tel. 605/432–4538; Sister Genevieve Karels, Administrator (Total facility includes 82 beds in nursing home–type unit) **A**1 9 10 **F**6 7 8 14 15 16 19 22 30 32 33 34 35 37 40 49 64 71 — 23 10 | 117 | 583 | 86 | 5962 | 43 | 5602 | 2416 | 142

MILLER—Hand County

★ HAND COUNTY MEMORIAL HOSPITAL, 300 West Fifth Street, Zip 57362–1238; tel. 605/853–2421; Clarence A. Lee, Administrator **A**9 10 **F**3 8 11 12 13 14 15 16 17 18 19 21 22 26 27 28 29 30 32 34 36 39 41 42 44 45 46 49 53 54 58 63 65 66 67 68 70 71 73 **P**1 3 4 5 6 7 8 **S** Avera Health, Yankton, SD — 23 10 | 23 | 530 | 7 | 3454 | 1 | 2565 | 1184 | 65

MITCHELL—Davison County

⌧ QUEEN OF PEACE HOSPITAL, 525 North Foster, Zip 57301–2999; tel. 605/995–2000; Ronald L. Jacobson, President and Chief Executive Officer (Total facility includes 84 beds in nursing home–type unit) **A**1 9 10 **F**1 3 7 8 12 14 15 16 17 19 22 23 24 26 27 28 30 32 33 34 35 36 37 39 40 41 42 44 45 49 56 62 64 65 66 67 71 73 74 **P**6 **S** Avera Health, Yankton, SD **N** Missouri Valley Health Network, Yankton, SD — 21 10 | 183 | 4139 | 132 | 70762 | 462 | 33327 | 15447 | 537

MOBRIDGE—Walworth County

★ MOBRIDGE REGIONAL HOSPITAL, 1401 Tenth Avenue West, Zip 57601–1199, Mailing Address: P.O. Box 580, Zip 57601–0580; tel. 605/845–3693; David Anderson, Chief Executive Officer **A**9 10 **F**7 8 14 15 16 19 22 24 26 28 29 30 31 32 34 35 37 40 44 45 49 56 57 65 66 67 71 — 23 10 | 48 | 809 | 8 | 8140 | 42 | 5466 | 2861 | 130

PARKSTON—Hutchinson County

★ ST. BENEDICT HEALTH CENTER, Glynn Drive, Zip 57366, Mailing Address: P.O. Box B., Zip 57366; tel. 605/928–3311; Gale Walker, Administrator (Total facility includes 75 beds in nursing home–type unit) **A**9 10 **F**6 7 8 11 15 16 17 19 22 24 26 28 29 30 32 33 34 36 37 40 42 44 49 51 64 65 66 67 71 73 **S** Avera Health, Yankton, SD **N** Missouri Valley Health Network, Yankton, SD — 21 10 | 105 | 659 | 58 | 20240 | 64 | 5375 | 2617 | 114

PHILIP—Haakon County

HANS P. PETERSON MEMORIAL HOSPITAL, 603 West Pine, Zip 57567, Mailing Address: P.O. Box 790, Zip 57567–0790; tel. 605/859–2511; David Dick, Administrator (Total facility includes 30 beds in nursing home–type unit) (Nonreporting) **A**9 10 **N** Rapid City Regional Hospital System of Care, Rapid City, SD — 23 10 | 50 | — | — | — | — | — | — | —

PIERRE—Hughes County

⌧ ST. MARY'S HOSPITAL, 800 East Dakota Avenue, Zip 57501–3313; tel. 605/224–3100; James D. M. Russell, Chief Executive Officer (Total facility includes 105 beds in nursing home–type unit) **A**1 9 10 **F**8 14 15 16 19 22 30 32 33 34 35 36 37 40 41 42 44 49 62 64 65 66 71 **P**5 **S** Catholic Health Initiatives, Denver, CO — 23 10 | 191 | 2825 | 118 | 15543 | 347 | 18844 | 9493 | 387

PINE RIDGE—Shannon County

⌧ U. S. PUBLIC HEALTH SERVICE INDIAN HOSPITAL, Mailing Address: P.O. Box 1201, Zip 57770–1201; tel. 605/867–5131; Vern F. Donnell, Service Unit Director (Nonreporting) **A**1 10 **S** U. S. Public Health Service Indian Health Service, Rockville, MD — 47 10 | 46 | — | — | — | — | — | — | —

PLATTE—Charles Mix County

★ PLATTE COMMUNITY MEMORIAL HOSPITAL, 609 East Seventh, Zip 57369–2123, Mailing Address: P.O. Box 200, Zip 57369–0200; tel. 605/337–3364; Mark Burket, Chief Executive Officer (Total facility includes 48 beds in nursing home–type unit) **A**9 10 **F**1 6 7 8 11 14 15 16 17 19 22 24 30 32 33 34 36 41 42 44 45 49 64 65 71 73 **S** Avera Health, Yankton, SD **N** Missouri Valley Health Network, Yankton, SD — 23 10 | 63 | 324 | 53 | 3419 | 21 | 3438 | 2128 | 49

RAPID CITY—Pennington County

⌧ INDIAN HEALTH SERVICE HOSPITAL, (Formerly Indian Health Service–Sioux San Hospital), 3200 Canyon Lake Drive, Zip 57702–8197; tel. 605/355–2280; James Cournoyer, Director **A**1 10 **F**1 2 3 4 5 6 7 8 9 10 11 12 13 15 16 17 18 19 20 21 22 27 28 29 30 31 33 34 35 37 38 39 40 42 43 44 47 48 49 50 52 53 54 55 56 57 58 59 60 63 64 65 67 69 71 72 73 74 **S** U. S. Public Health Service Indian Health Service, Rockville, MD — 47 10 | 32 | 604 | 11 | 60733 | 0 | 9854 | 5907 | —

⌧ RAPID CITY REGIONAL HOSPITAL SYSTEM OF CARE, (Formerly Rapid City Regional Hospital), 353 Fairmont Boulevard, Zip 57701–7393, Mailing Address: P.O. Box 6000, Zip 57709–6000; tel. 605/341–1000; Adil M. Ameer, President and Chief Executive Officer **A**1 2 3 5 9 10 **F**3 4 7 8 10 12 14 15 16 19 20 21 22 25 26 28 30 32 33 34 35 37 38 39 40 41 42 43 44 45 46 47 48 49 51 52 53 54 55 56 57 58 60 63 64 65 66 67 71 73 **P**1 6 7 **N** Rapid City Regional Hospital System of Care, Rapid City, SD — 23 10 | 368 | 14940 | 228 | 101488 | 1525 | 143081 | 62873 | 1715

REDFIELD—Spink County

COMMUNITY MEMORIAL HOSPITAL, 110 West Tenth Avenue, Zip 57469–0420, Mailing Address: P.O. Box 420, Zip 57469–0420; tel. 605/472–1111; Daniel Keierleber, Administrator **A**9 10 **F**7 8 14 16 19 22 26 30 32 34 36 37 40 41 44 46 49 51 64 71 **P**6 — 14 10 | 25 | 657 | 10 | 14751 | 13 | 3949 | 2285 | 90

Hospital, Address, Telephone, Administrator, Approval, Facility, and Physician Codes, Health Care System, Network	Classi- fication Codes		Utilization Data					Expense (thousands) of dollars		
★ American Hospital Association (AHA) membership □ Joint Commission on Accreditation of Healthcare Organizations (JCAHO) accreditation + American Osteopathic Healthcare Association (AOHA) membership ○ American Osteopathic Association (AOA) accreditation △ Commission on Accreditation of Rehabilitation Facilities (CARF) accreditation Control codes 61, 63, 64, 71, 72 and 73 indicate hospitals listed by AOHA, but not registered by AHA. For definition of numerical codes, see page A4	Control	Service	Staffed Beds	Admissions	Census	Outpatient Visits	Births	Total	Payroll	Personnel

ROSEBUD—Todd County

★ U. S. PUBLIC HEALTH SERVICE INDIAN HOSPITAL, Highway 18, Soldier Creek Road, Zip 57570; tel. 605/747–2231; Gayla J. Twiss, Service Unit Director **A**1 10 **F**3 4 7 8 9 10 11 12 13 14 15 16 17 18 19 20 21 22 23 24 27 28 29 30 31 32 33 34 35 37 38 39 40 41 42 43 44 45 46 47 48 49 50 52 53 54 56 57 58 59 60 61 63 64 65 66 67 69 71 72 74 **P**6 **S** U. S. Public Health Service Indian Health Service, Rockville, MD | 47 | 10 | 35 | 990 | 8 | 86887 | 53 | 14310 | 8452 | 213

SCOTLAND—Bon Homme County

★ LANDMANN–JUNGMAN MEMORIAL HOSPITAL, 600 Billars Street, Zip 57059–2026; tel. 605/583–2226; William H. Koellner, Administrator **A**9 10 **F**1 8 14 15 16 19 20 22 24 32 33 34 36 39 44 46 49 51 62 65 71 73 **N** Missouri Valley Health Network, Yankton, SD | 23 | 10 | 19 | 352 | 7 | 1434 | 8 | 2213 | 1175 | 57

SIOUX FALLS—Minnehaha County

CHILDRENS CARE HOSPITAL AND SCHOOL, (CHILDRENS SPECIALTY HOSP), 2501 West 26th Street, Zip 57105–2498; tel. 605/336–1840; Charisse S. Oland, President and Chief Executive Officer **F**12 16 17 25 27 34 48 49 64 65 73 | 23 | 59 | 96 | 30 | 71 | — | — | 10295 | 6521 | 177

★ △ MCKENNAN HOSPITAL, 800 East 21st Street, Zip 57105–1096, Mailing Address: P.O. Box 5045, Zip 57117–5045; tel. 605/322–8000; Fredrick Slunecka, President and Chief Executive Officer (Total facility includes 196 beds in nursing home–type unit) **A**1 2 3 5 7 9 10 **F**3 4 5 6 7 8 9 10 11 12 13 14 15 16 17 18 19 21 23 24 25 26 27 28 29 30 31 32 33 34 35 37 38 39 40 41 42 43 44 45 46 47 48 49 51 52 53 54 55 56 57 58 59 60 61 62 63 64 65 66 67 68 69 70 71 73 74 **P**1 6 **S** Avera Health, Yankton, SD **N** Affiliated Community Health Network, Inc., Willmar, MN | 21 | 10 | 521 | 14216 | 404 | 211191 | 1161 | 160327 | 70863 | 1794

★ ROYAL C. JOHNSON VETERANS MEMORIAL HOSPITAL, 2501 West 22nd Street, Zip 57105–1394, Mailing Address: P.O. Box 5046, Zip 57117–5046; tel. 605/336–3230; R. Vincent Crawford, Director (Total facility includes 73 beds in nursing home–type unit) **A**1 3 5 9 **F**1 2 3 11 12 15 16 17 19 20 21 22 26 27 28 29 30 31 32 33 34 35 37 39 41 42 44 45 46 48 49 51 52 54 56 57 58 59 64 65 67 71 73 74 **P**6 **S** Department of Veterans Affairs, Washington, DC | 45 | 10 | 131 | 2624 | 106 | 81600 | — | 49520 | 25255 | 632

★ △ SIOUX VALLEY HOSPITAL, (Includes Sioux Valley Behavioral Health, 2812 South Louise Avenue, Zip 57106–4309; tel. 605/361–8111), 1100 South Euclid Avenue, Zip 57105–0496, Mailing Address: P.O. Box 5039, Zip 57117–5039; tel. 605/333–1000; Becky Nelson, President **A**1 2 3 5 7 9 10 **F**4 7 8 10 11 12 13 14 15 16 17 18 19 20 21 22 24 25 26 27 28 29 30 31 32 33 34 35 37 39 40 41 42 43 44 45 46 47 48 49 51 53 54 55 56 58 61 65 66 67 70 71 72 73 74 **P**1 4 5 6 7 8 **S** Sioux Valley Hospitals and Health System, Sioux Falls, SD | 23 | 10 | 504 | 18081 | 295 | 150879 | 1958 | 191205 | 87303 | 3405

SISSETON—Roberts County

★ COTEAU DES PRAIRIES HOSPITAL, 205 Orchard Drive, Zip 57262–2398; tel. 605/698–7647; Bill Nelson, Administrator **A**9 10 **F**7 8 11 17 19 20 22 24 27 28 30 32 33 34 37 40 44 49 71 | 23 | 10 | 31 | 414 | 4 | 14550 | 126 | 2596 | 1164 | 56

★ U. S. PUBLIC HEALTH SERVICE INDIAN HOSPITAL, Chestnut Street, Zip 57262, Mailing Address: P.O. Box 189, Zip 57262–0189; tel. 605/698–7606; Richard Huff, Administrator **A**1 10 **F**1 3 4 5 6 7 8 10 12 13 14 15 16 17 18 19 20 21 22 23 24 26 27 28 29 30 31 32 33 34 35 36 39 41 42 43 44 46 49 50 51 53 54 55 56 58 59 60 61 62 63 65 66 67 68 69 71 72 73 74 **P**1 **S** U. S. Public Health Service Indian Health Service, Rockville, MD | 47 | 10 | 18 | 394 | 4 | 27751 | 0 | 6130 | 2494 | 24

SPEARFISH—Lawrence County

★ LOOKOUT MEMORIAL HOSPITAL, 1440 North Main Street, Zip 57783–1504; tel. 605/642–2617; Deb J. Krmpotic, R.N., Administrator **A**9 10 **F**1 6 7 8 11 12 14 15 16 19 21 22 27 28 30 32 33 34 35 36 37 39 40 41 42 44 45 46 49 51 62 63 64 65 66 67 71 73 **P**6 7 **S** Lutheran Health Systems, Fargo, ND **N** Black Hills Healthcare Network, Spearfish, SD | 23 | 10 | 32 | 1502 | 15 | 40572 | 265 | 9650 | 4057 | 190

STURGIS—Meade County

★ STURGIS COMMUNITY HEALTH CARE CENTER, 949 Harmon Street, Zip 57785–2452; tel. 605/347–2536; Deb J. Krmpotic, R.N., Administrator (Total facility includes 84 beds in nursing home–type unit) **A**9 10 **F**7 8 12 14 15 16 19 22 32 33 35 40 41 44 64 67 71 **S** Lutheran Health Systems, Fargo, ND **N** Black Hills Healthcare Network, Spearfish, SD | 23 | 10 | 114 | 962 | 94 | 19677 | 85 | 8156 | 3808 | 109

TYNDALL—Bon Homme County

★ ST. MICHAEL'S HOSPITAL, Douglas Street and Broadway, Zip 57066, Mailing Address: P.O. Box 27, Zip 57066–0027; tel. 605/589–3341; Carol Deurmier, Chief Executive Officer (Total facility includes 9 beds in nursing home–type unit) **A**10 **F**7 8 14 15 16 19 22 30 32 33 34 35 37 40 44 45 54 64 65 66 71 73 **N** Missouri Valley Health Network, Yankton, SD | 21 | 10 | 34 | 430 | 17 | 14345 | 28 | 2670 | 1432 | 56

VERMILLION—Clay County

★ SIOUX VALLEY VERMILLION CAMPUS, (Formerly Dakota Medical Center), 20 South Plum Street, Zip 57069–3346; tel. 605/624–2611; Larry W. Veitz, Chief Executive Officer (Total facility includes 66 beds in nursing home–type unit) **A**9 10 **F**3 7 8 10 14 16 17 19 22 28 29 30 32 33 35 37 39 40 41 42 44 45 46 49 64 65 66 67 71 73 **P**4 7 **S** Sioux Valley Hospitals and Health System, Sioux Falls, SD **N** Sioux Valley Health System, Sioux Falls, SD | 23 | 10 | 95 | 969 | 73 | 15530 | 57 | 6461 | 3104 | 82

VIBORG—Turner County

★ PIONEER MEMORIAL HOSPITAL, 315 North Washington Street, Zip 57070, Mailing Address: P.O. Box 368, Zip 57070–0368; tel. 605/326–5161; Georgia Pokorney, Chief Executive Officer (Total facility includes 52 beds in nursing home–type unit) **A**9 10 **F**1 3 4 6 7 8 10 11 15 19 20 21 22 24 26 28 32 33 34 35 36 37 38 39 40 41 42 43 44 45 47 49 51 62 64 65 66 67 70 71 74 **P**5 **S** Sioux Valley Hospitals and Health System, Sioux Falls, SD **N** Sioux Valley Health System, Sioux Falls, SD; Missouri Valley Health Network, Yankton, SD | 23 | 10 | 77 | 363 | 55 | 10035 | 2 | 3793 | 1866 | 91

Hospital, Address, Telephone, Administrator, Approval, Facility, and Physician Codes, Health Care System, Network	Classi-fication Codes		Utilization Data					Expense (thousands) of dollars		
	Control	Service	Staffed Beds	Admissions	Census	Outpatient Visits	Births	Total	Payroll	Personnel

★ American Hospital Association (AHA) membership
□ Joint Commission on Accreditation of Healthcare Organizations (JCAHO) accreditation
+ American Osteopathic Healthcare Association (AOHA) membership
○ American Osteopathic Association (AOA) accreditation
△ Commission on Accreditation of Rehabilitation Facilities (CARF) accreditation
Control codes 61, 63, 64, 71, 72 and 73 indicate hospitals listed by AOHA, but not registered by AHA. For definition of numerical codes, see page A4

WAGNER—Charles Mix County

★ WAGNER COMMUNITY MEMORIAL HOSPITAL, Third and Walnut, Zip 57380, Mailing Address: P.O. Box 280, Zip 57380–0280; tel. 605/384–3611; Arlene C. Bich, Administrator **A**9 10 **F**7 11 15 16 19 22 26 28 29 30 32 33 34 37 40 62 64 65 70 71 **N** Missouri Valley Health Network, Yankton, SD

	23	10	20	704	5	7005	1	2863	1268	51

WATERTOWN—Codington County

⊞ PRAIRIE LAKES HOSPITAL AND CARE CENTER, 400 Tenth Avenue N.W., Zip 57201–1599, Mailing Address: P.O. Box 1210, Zip 57201–1210; tel. 605/882–7000; Edmond L. Weiland, President and Chief Executive Officer (Total facility includes 51 beds in nursing home–type unit) **A**1 2 3 9 10 **F**7 8 14 15 16 17 19 22 29 32 33 34 35 37 39 40 41 42 44 45 46 49 54 56 58 64 65 66 71 73 74 **S** Sioux Valley Hospitals and Health System, Sioux Falls, SD

	23	10	122	2938	82	65898	637	26355	10272	362

WEBSTER—Day County

★ LAKE AREA HOSPITAL, North First Street, Zip 57274, Mailing Address: P.O. Box 489, Zip 57274–0489; tel. 605/345–3336; Donald J. Finn, Administrator **A**9 10 **F**7 8 11 12 15 16 19 21 22 28 30 31 34 40 44 45 49 71 **P**5 **S** Sioux Valley Hospitals and Health System, Sioux Falls, SD

	23	10	26	555	8	3811	0	3245	1342	62

WESSINGTON SPRINGS—Jerauld County

WESKOTA MEMORIAL MEDICAL CENTER, 604 First Street N.E., Zip 57382, Mailing Address: P.O. Box 429, Zip 57382; tel. 605/539–1201; Kayleen R. Lee, Chief Executive Officer **A**9 10 **F**7 15 19 22 30 32 44 49 71

	23	10	28	417	8	3870	18	1487	801	33

WINNER—Tripp County

★ WINNER REGIONAL HEALTHCARE CENTER, 745 East Eighth Street, Zip 57580–2677, Mailing Address: P.O. Box 745, Zip 57580–0745; tel. 605/842–7100; Robert Houser, Chief Executive Officer (Total facility includes 81 beds in nursing home–type unit) **A**9 10 **F**7 8 11 14 15 16 17 19 21 22 26 28 29 30 32 33 34 35 36 39 40 41 42 44 45 49 50 61 63 64 66 67 69 71 **S** Sioux Valley Hospitals and Health System, Sioux Falls, SD **N** Missouri Valley Health Network, Yankton, SD

	23	10	116	981	92	9056	148	8045	4319	117

YANKTON—Yankton County

⊞ △ SACRED HEART HEALTH SERVICES, 501 Summit Avenue, Zip 57078–3899; tel. 605/668–8000; Pamela J. Rezac, President and Chief Executive Officer (Total facility includes 113 beds in nursing home–type unit) **A**1 2 7 9 10 **F**1 3 4 6 7 8 10 11 12 13 14 15 16 17 19 20 21 22 23 24 25 26 27 28 29 30 31 32 33 34 35 36 37 38 39 40 41 42 44 45 46 48 49 51 53 54 55 56 57 58 59 60 61 62 64 65 66 67 68 69 71 72 73 74 **P**3 **S** Avera Health, Yankton, SD **N** Missouri Valley Health Network, Yankton, SD

	21	10	257	5064	176	22762	671	37679	16096	443

TENNESSEE

Resident population 5,368 (in thousands)
Resident population in metro areas 67.8%
Birth rate per 1,000 population 14.1
65 years and over 12.5%
Percent of persons without health insurance 15.2%

Hospital, Address, Telephone, Administrator, Approval, Facility, and Physician Codes, Health Care System, Network	Classi-fication Codes		Utilization Data					Expense (thousands) of dollars		
★ American Hospital Association (AHA) membership ☐ Joint Commission on Accreditation of Healthcare Organizations (JCAHO) accreditation + American Osteopathic Healthcare Association (AOHA) membership ○ American Osteopathic Association (AOA) accreditation △ Commission on Accreditation of Rehabilitation Facilities (CARF) accreditation Control codes 61, 63, 64, 71, 72 and 73 indicate hospitals listed by AOHA, but not registered by AHA. For definition of numerical codes, see page A4	Control	Service	Staffed Beds	Admissions	Census	Outpatient Visits	Births	Total	Payroll	Personnel

ASHLAND CITY—Cheatham County

★ COLUMBIA CHEATHAM MEDICAL CENTER, 313 North Main Street, Zip 37015–1358; tel. 615/792–3030; Rick Wallace, FACHE, Chief Executive Officer and Administrator **A**9 **F**12 14 15 16 19 22 28 32 33 45 46 49 51 54 56 57 65 66 71 73 **P**7 **S** Columbia/HCA Healthcare Corporation, Nashville, TN **N** Columbia Healthcare Network, Brentwood, TN

33	10	29	1491	15	15015	—	7792	2513	125

ATHENS—McMinn County

✠ ATHENS REGIONAL MEDICAL CENTER, (Formerly Columbia Athens Regional Medical Center), 1114 West Madison Avenue, Zip 37303–4150, Mailing Address: P.O. Box 250, Zip 37371–0250; tel. 423/745–1411; John R. Workman, Chief Executive Officer **A**1 9 10 **F**3 7 8 12 14 15 16 17 19 21 22 23 28 29 30 31 32 33 35 37 39 40 41 42 44 45 46 49 53 54 55 56 57 58 59 61 63 65 67 68 71 72 73 74 **S** Columbia/HCA Healthcare Corporation, Nashville, TN **N** Principal Health Care of Georgia, Atlanta, GA; Chattanooga Healthcare Network, Chattanooga, TN

33	10	97	2481	24	62150	352	15241	6424	229

BOLIVAR—Hardeman County

✠ BOLIVAR GENERAL HOSPITAL, (Formerly Bolivar Medical Center), 650 Nuckolls Road, Zip 38008–1500; tel. 901/658–3100; George L. Austin, Administrator (Nonreporting) **A**1 9 10 **S** West Tennessee Healthcare., Jackson, TN **N** West Tennessee Healthcare, Inc., Jackson, TN

23	10	47	—	—	—	—	—	—	—

BRISTOL—Sullivan County

✠ WELLMONT BRISTOL REGIONAL MEDICAL CENTER, (Formerly Bristol Regional Medical Center), 1 Medical Park Boulevard, Zip 37620–7430; tel. 423/844–4200; Randall M. Olson, Administrator (Total facility includes 30 beds in nursing home–type unit) **A**1 2 3 5 9 10 **F**1 4 6 7 8 10 11 12 14 15 16 17 19 20 21 22 23 24 25 26 28 29 30 31 32 33 34 35 36 37 39 40 41 42 43 44 46 49 51 52 55 56 57 58 59 60 63 64 65 66 67 70 71 72 73 74 **P**1 4 5 6 7 **S** Quorum Health Group/Quorum Health Resources, Inc., Brentwood, TN **N** Highlands Wellmont Health Network, Inc., Bristol, TN

23	10	339	12061	180	205754	693	106293	41906	1619

BROWNSVILLE—Haywood County

✠ METHODIST–HAYWOOD PARK HOSPITAL, 2545 North Washington Avenue, Zip 38012–1697; tel. 901/772–4110; Sandra Bailey, Administrator **A**1 9 10 **F**14 15 16 17 19 22 27 28 29 30 31 32 39 40 44 45 46 49 65 71 73 74 **P**3 6 7 8 **S** Methodist Health Systems, Inc., Memphis, TN

23	10	44	1392	14	13245	265	6399	2258	83

CAMDEN—Benton County

✠ CAMDEN GENERAL HOSPITAL, 175 Hospital Drive, Zip 38320–1617; tel. 901/584–6135; Billy Alred, Interim Administrator (Nonreporting) **A**1 9 10 **S** West Tennessee Healthcare., Jackson, TN **N** West Tennessee Healthcare, Inc., Jackson, TN

16	10	40	—	—	—	—	—	—	—

CARTHAGE—Smith County

CARTHAGE GENERAL HOSPITAL See Frank T. Rutherford Memorial Hospital

✠ FRANK T. RUTHERFORD MEMORIAL HOSPITAL, (Includes Carthage General Hospital, Highway 70 North, Zip 37030, Mailing Address: P.O. Box 319, Zip 37030–0319; Trousdale Medical Center, 500 Church Street, Hartsville, Zip 37074, Mailing Address: P.O. Box 319, Carthage, Zip 37030; tel. 615/374–2221), 130 Lebanon Highway, Zip 37030–2955, Mailing Address: P.O. Box 319, Zip 37030–0319; tel. 615/735–9815; Wayne Winfree, Chief Executive Officer **A**1 9 10 **F**7 8 12 15 19 22 28 32 44 45 51 65 67 71

23	10	54	2581	29	30526	54	14583	7068	—

✠ SMITH COUNTY MEMORIAL HOSPITAL, (Formerly Columbia Smith County Memorial Hospital), 158 Hospital Drive, Zip 37030–1096; tel. 615/735–1560; Jerry H. Futrell, Chief Executive Officer **A**1 9 10 **F**7 8 12 14 15 16 19 22 26 28 32 35 40 44 49 52 57 64 65 66 71 73 **P**8 **S** Columbia/HCA Healthcare Corporation, Nashville, TN

33	10	53	1688	22	18021	101	9890	3437	139

CELINA—Clay County

☐ CUMBERLAND RIVER HOSPITAL NORTH, (Includes Cumberland River Hospital South, 620 Hospital Drive, Gainesboro, Zip 38562–9573, Mailing Address: P.O. Box 36, Zip 38562–0036; tel. 931/268–0211), 100 Old Jefferson Street, Zip 38551; tel. 931/243–3581; Patrick J. Gray, Chief Executive Officer (Total facility includes 9 beds in nursing home–type unit) **A**1 9 10 **F**8 15 19 22 28 32 44 48 52 57 64 71 **S** Paracelsus Healthcare Corporation, Houston, TX

33	10	77	1943	31	152428	0	15688	7981	257

CENTERVILLE—Hickman County

☐ BAPTIST HICKMAN COMMUNITY HOSPITAL, 135 East Swan Street, Zip 37033–1446; tel. 615/729–4271; Jack M. Keller, Administrator (Total facility includes 40 beds in nursing home–type unit) **A**1 9 10 **F**8 14 15 16 19 22 28 30 32 33 34 49 59 64 65 71

23	10	65	519	18	9986	—	5966	2631	86

Hospital, Address, Telephone, Administrator, Approval, Facility, and Physician Codes, Health Care System, Network	Classi-fication Codes		Utilization Data					Expense (thousands) of dollars		
★ American Hospital Association (AHA) membership ☐ Joint Commission on Accreditation of Healthcare Organizations (JCAHO) accreditation + American Osteopathic Healthcare Association (AOHA) membership ○ American Osteopathic Association (AOA) accreditation △ Commission on Accreditation of Rehabilitation Facilities (CARF) accreditation Control codes 61, 63, 64, 71, 72 and 73 indicate hospitals listed by AOHA, but not registered by AHA. For definition of numerical codes, see page A4	Control	Service	Staffed Beds	Admissions	Census	Outpatient Visits	Births	Total	Payroll	Personnel

CHATTANOOGA—Hamilton County

★ COLUMBIA PARKRIDGE MEDICAL CENTER, (Includes Columbia East Ridge Hospital, 941 Spring Creek Road, East Ridge, Zip 37412, Mailing Address: P.O. Box 91229, Zip 37412–6229; tel. 423/894–7870; Brenda M. Waltz, CHE, Chief Executive Officer; Columbia Valley Hospital, 2200 Morris Hill Road, Zip 37421; tel. 423/894–4220), 2333 McCallie Avenue, Zip 37404–3285; tel. 423/698–6061; Christopher W. Dux, Chief Executive Officer (Total facility includes 28 beds in nursing home–type unit) **A**1 9 10 **F**1 2 3 4 7 8 10 12 14 15 16 18 19 20 21 22 23 24 26 28 30 31 32 33 34 35 37 38 39 40 41 42 43 44 45 46 49 52 53 54 55 56 57 58 59 61 64 65 66 67 71 72 73 74 **P**7 8 **S** Columbia/HCA Healthcare Corporation, Nashville, TN | 33 | 10 | 358 | 11493 | 161 | 65492 | 2001 | 74475 | 31673 | 926 |

COLUMBIA VALLEY HOSPITAL See Columbia Parkridge Medical Center

★ ERLANGER HEALTH SYSTEM, (Formerly Erlanger Medical Center), (Includes Erlanger North Hospital, 632 Morrison Springs Road, Zip 37415; tel. 615/778–3300; T. C. Thompson Children's Hospital, 910 Blackford Street, Zip 37403; tel. 615/778–6011; Willie D. Miller Eye Center), 975 East Third Street, Zip 37403–2112; tel. 423/778–7000; Dennis Pettigrew, Interim President and Chief Executive Officer **A**1 2 3 5 9 10 **F**3 4 7 8 9 10 11 12 15 16 17 18 19 20 21 22 23 24 25 26 27 28 30 32 34 35 37 38 40 41 42 43 44 46 47 49 51 52 53 54 55 57 58 59 60 61 63 65 66 67 69 70 71 72 73 74 **P**5 7 | 16 | 10 | 783 | 23265 | 315 | 449016 | 2588 | 259207 | 115853 | — |

☐ HEALTHSOUTH CHATTANOOGA REHABILITATION HOSPITAL, 2412 McCallie Avenue, Zip 37404–3398; tel. 423/698–0221; Susan Heath, Chief Executive Officer **A**1 10 **F**12 14 15 16 26 27 34 44 48 49 66 67 **P**2 **S** HEALTHSOUTH Corporation, Birmingham, AL | 33 | 46 | 69 | 1006 | 53 | 10610 | — | 9654 | 4973 | 181 |

★ MEMORIAL HEALTH CARE SYSTEM, (Formerly Memorial Hospital), 2525 De Sales Avenue, Zip 37404–3322; tel. 423/495–2525; L. Clark Taylor, Jr., President and Chief Executive Officer **A**1 2 5 9 10 **F**1 3 4 5 7 8 10 12 14 15 16 17 18 19 21 22 25 26 27 28 29 30 31 32 34 35 37 39 41 42 43 44 46 49 51 53 54 55 56 57 58 59 60 61 64 65 66 67 71 72 73 74 **P**1 7 **S** Catholic Health Initiatives, Denver, CO **N** Principal Health Care of Georgia, Atlanta, GA | 21 | 10 | 299 | 14301 | 215 | 140195 | — | 81507 | 52099 | 1694 |

★ MEMORIAL NORTH PARK HOSPITAL, (Formerly North Park Hospital), 2051 Hamill Road, Zip 37343–4096; tel. 423/870–6100; Sean S. McMurray, CHE, Administrator **A**1 9 10 **F**8 10 12 14 15 16 17 19 20 21 22 28 32 34 35 37 39 41 44 45 46 49 65 71 73 **S** Healthcorp of Tennessee, Inc., Chattanooga, TN **N** Principal Health Care of Georgia, Atlanta, GA | 23 | 10 | 83 | 2741 | 32 | 44268 | 0 | 37336 | 13961 | 521 |

☐ MOCCASIN BEND MENTAL HEALTH INSTITUTE, 100 Moccasin Bend Road, Zip 37405–4496; tel. 423/785–3400; Russell K. Vatter, Superintendent **A**1 10 **F**14 15 16 31 52 53 54 55 56 57 | 12 | 22 | 172 | 1478 | 149 | — | — | 17914 | 11633 | — |

★ △ SISKIN HOSPITAL FOR PHYSICAL REHABILITATION, One Siskin Plaza, Zip 37403–1306; tel. 423/634–1200; Robert P. Main, President and Chief Executive Officer **A**1 7 9 10 **F**12 15 16 17 19 20 21 22 25 26 27 32 34 35 39 41 44 48 49 64 65 66 67 70 71 73 **N** Principal Health Care of Georgia, Atlanta, GA | 23 | 46 | 80 | 1115 | 69 | — | — | 20996 | 10729 | 282 |

T. C. THOMPSON CHILDREN'S HOSPITAL See Erlanger Health System

☐ VENCOR HOSPITAL–CHATTANOOGA, 709 Walnut Street, Zip 37402–1961; tel. 423/266–7721; Steven E. McGraw, Administrator (Nonreporting) **A**1 10 **S** Vencor, Incorporated, Louisville, KY **N** Principal Health Care of Georgia, Atlanta, GA | 33 | 49 | 43 | — | — | — | — | — | — | — |

WILLIE D. MILLER EYE CENTER See Erlanger Health System

CLARKSVILLE—Montgomery County

★ CLARKSVILLE MEMORIAL HOSPITAL, 1771 Madison Street, Zip 37043–4900, Mailing Address: P.O. Box 3160, Zip 37043–3160; tel. 931/552–6622; James Lee Decker, President and Chief Executive Officer (Total facility includes 29 beds in nursing home–type unit) **A**1 9 10 **F**7 8 10 14 15 16 19 21 22 28 30 31 32 33 34 35 37 39 40 42 44 45 46 49 52 56 57 60 61 64 65 70 71 73 **P**2 5 **N** Center Care, Bowling Green, KY; Middle Tennessee Healthcare Network, Nashville, TN | 16 | 10 | 191 | 8789 | 108 | 85135 | 1224 | 67927 | 27403 | 962 |

CLEVELAND—Bradley County

★ BRADLEY MEMORIAL HOSPITAL, 2305 Chambliss Avenue N.W., Zip 37311, Mailing Address: P.O. Box 3060, Zip 37320–3060; tel. 423/559–6000; Jim Whitlock, Administrator **A**1 9 10 **F**7 8 10 12 14 15 16 17 19 21 22 23 28 30 32 33 34 35 37 39 40 41 42 44 49 52 56 58 59 65 67 71 73 74 **P**8 **N** Principal Health Care of Georgia, Atlanta, GA | 13 | 10 | 188 | 8010 | 87 | 90744 | 1109 | 62287 | 28377 | 884 |

★ CLEVELAND COMMUNITY HOSPITAL, 2800 Westside Drive N.W., Zip 37312–3599; tel. 423/339–4100; Phil Rowland, Chief Executive Officer (Nonreporting) **A**1 9 10 **S** Community Health Systems, Inc., Brentwood, TN **N** Principal Health Care of Georgia, Atlanta, GA | 33 | 10 | 70 | — | — | — | — | — | — | — |

COLUMBIA—Maury County

★ MAURY REGIONAL HOSPITAL, 1224 Trotwood Avenue, Zip 38401–4823; tel. 931/381–1111; William R. Walter, Administrator **A**1 9 10 **F**1 3 8 10 11 12 14 19 20 21 22 23 25 27 28 30 31 32 35 37 39 40 41 42 44 45 46 49 51 54 55 56 57 58 59 60 65 67 71 72 73 74 **N** Middle Tennessee Healthcare Network, Nashville, TN | 13 | 10 | 255 | 13309 | 148 | 126919 | 1565 | 97733 | 42626 | 1379 |

COOKEVILLE—Putnam County

★ COOKEVILLE REGIONAL MEDICAL CENTER, (Formerly Cookeville General Hospital), 142 West Fifth Street, Zip 38501–1760, Mailing Address: P.O. Box 340, Zip 38503–0340; tel. 931/528–2541; William M. Jennings, Administrator and Chief Operating Officer **A**1 9 10 **F**4 7 8 10 11 14 15 17 19 22 23 25 28 29 30 32 35 37 40 41 42 44 45 46 48 49 50 65 66 67 71 73 74 **P**7 **N** Center Care, Bowling Green, KY; Middle Tennessee Healthcare Network, Nashville, TN | 14 | 10 | 158 | 6843 | 79 | 96557 | 1096 | 54501 | 22344 | 850 |

Hospital, Address, Telephone, Administrator, Approval, Facility, and Physician Codes, Health Care System, Network	Classification Codes		Utilization Data					Expense (thousands) of dollars		
	Control	Service	Staffed Beds	Admissions	Census	Outpatient Visits	Births	Total	Payroll	Personnel

★ American Hospital Association (AHA) membership
□ Joint Commission on Accreditation of Healthcare Organizations (JCAHO) accreditation
+ American Osteopathic Healthcare Association (AOHA) membership
○ American Osteopathic Association (AOA) accreditation
△ Commission on Accreditation of Rehabilitation Facilities (CARF) accreditation
Control codes 61, 63, 64, 71, 72 and 73 indicate hospitals listed by AOHA, but not registered by AHA. For definition of numerical codes, see page A4

COPPERHILL—Polk County

□ COPPER BASIN MEDICAL CENTER, State Highway 68, Zip 37317, Mailing Address: P.O. Box 990, Zip 37317–0990; tel. 423/496–5511; Grady Scott, President and Chief Executive Officer **A**1 9 10 **F**8 14 16 19 22 34 45 46 51 65 71

| 23 | 10 | 40 | 1071 | 10 | 12073 | — | 4067 | 2257 | 92 |

COVINGTON—Tipton County

✠ BAPTIST MEMORIAL HOSPITAL–TIPTON, 1995 Highway 51 South, Zip 38019–3635; tel. 901/476–2621; Glenn Baker, Administrator **A**1 9 10 **F**7 8 14 15 16 19 22 32 33 38 39 40 44 45 51 63 66 71 **S** Baptist Memorial Health Care Corporation, Memphis, TN

| 23 | 10 | 48 | 2859 | 35 | — | 439 | 17629 | 6027 | 2337 |

CROSSVILLE—Cumberland County

✠ CUMBERLAND MEDICAL CENTER, 421 South Main Street, Zip 38555–5031; tel. 931/484–9511; Edwin S. Anderson, President (Total facility includes 16 beds in nursing home–type unit) **A**1 9 10 **F**7 8 10 11 12 14 15 16 19 22 23 24 28 29 32 35 37 39 40 41 42 44 45 49 51 60 64 65 67 71 73 **N** Middle Tennessee Healthcare Network, Nashville, TN

| 23 | 10 | 176 | 7235 | 93 | 59409 | 487 | 37912 | 18344 | 711 |

DAYTON—Rhea County

★ RHEA MEDICAL CENTER, 7900 Rhea County Highway, Zip 37321–5912; tel. 423/775–1121; Kennedy L. Croom, Jr., Administrator and Chief Executive Officer (Total facility includes 89 beds in nursing home–type unit) **A**9 10 **F**14 15 19 22 35 37 44 64 65 71 73 **S** Quorum Health Group/Quorum Health Resources, Inc., Brentwood, TN

| 13 | 10 | 131 | 1202 | 98 | 38804 | — | 11019 | 4638 | 240 |

DICKSON—Dickson County

✠ COLUMBIA HORIZON MEDICAL CENTER, 111 Highway 70 East, Zip 37055–2033; tel. 615/441–2357; Rick Wallace, FACHE, Chief Executive Officer and Administrator (Total facility includes 29 beds in nursing home–type unit) **A**1 9 10 **F**7 8 10 12 14 15 16 19 21 22 26 28 30 32 33 34 35 37 40 41 42 44 45 46 49 51 54 56 57 64 65 66 67 71 72 73 74 **P**7 **S** Columbia/HCA Healthcare Corporation, Nashville, TN **N** Columbia Healthcare Network, Brentwood, TN

| 33 | 10 | 169 | 5348 | 63 | 64834 | 447 | 38483 | 11568 | 396 |

DYERSBURG—Dyer County

✠ METHODIST HOSPITAL OF DYERSBURG, 400 Tickle Street, Zip 38024–3182; tel. 901/285–2410; Richard McCormick, Administrator **A**1 9 10 **F**7 8 12 14 15 19 20 21 22 23 27 28 30 32 33 34 35 37 40 44 45 46 49 60 65 71 73 **P**5 7 8 **S** Methodist Health Systems, Inc., Memphis, TN **N** Methodist Health Systems, Inc., Memphis, TN

| 23 | 10 | 105 | 3687 | 42 | 42382 | 500 | 30494 | 11106 | — |

EAST RIDGE—Hamilton County

COLUMBIA EAST RIDGE HOSPITAL See Columbia Parkridge Medical Center, Chattanooga

ELIZABETHTON—Carter County

✠ COLUMBIA SYCAMORE SHOALS HOSPITAL, 1501 West Elk Avenue, Zip 37643–1368; tel. 423/542–1300; Larry R. Jeter, Chief Executive Officer (Total facility includes 12 beds in nursing home–type unit) **A**1 9 10 **F**7 8 11 12 14 16 19 22 24 28 32 34 35 37 40 42 44 46 47 49 64 65 71 73 74 **P**5 7 8 **S** Columbia/HCA Healthcare Corporation, Nashville, TN

| 33 | 10 | 100 | 2315 | 28 | 56607 | 428 | 14526 | 5814 | 318 |

ERIN—Houston County

✠ COLUMBIA TRINITY HOSPITAL, 353 Main Street, Zip 37061–0489, Mailing Address: P.O. Box 489, Zip 37061–0489; tel. 931/289–4211; Jay Woodall, Chief Executive Officer **A**1 9 10 **F**7 8 12 14 15 16 17 19 22 28 40 41 44 49 52 54 57 65 66 70 71 **S** Columbia/HCA Healthcare Corporation, Nashville, TN

| 33 | 10 | 31 | 1350 | 12 | — | — | — | — | — |

ERWIN—Unicoi County

✠ UNICOI COUNTY MEMORIAL HOSPITAL, 100 Greenway Circle, Zip 37650–2196, Mailing Address: P.O. Box 802, Zip 37650–0802; tel. 423/743–3141; James L. McMackin, Chief Executive Officer (Total facility includes 46 beds in nursing home–type unit) **A**1 9 10 **F**8 14 15 16 17 19 22 28 30 32 39 41 44 49 64 65 66 71 **P**5 **N** Mountain States Healthcare Network, Johnson City, TN

| 16 | 10 | 84 | 1036 | 57 | 24998 | — | 9382 | 4067 | 184 |

ETOWAH—McMinn County

✠ WOODS MEMORIAL HOSPITAL DISTRICT, Highway 411 North, Zip 37331, Mailing Address: P.O. Box 410, Zip 37331–0410; tel. 423/263–3600; Phil Campbell, FACHE, Administrator (Total facility includes 88 beds in nursing home–type unit) (Nonreporting) **A**1 9 10

| 13 | 10 | 160 | — | — | — | — | — | — | — |

FAYETTEVILLE—Lincoln County

✠ LINCOLN COUNTY HEALTH FACILITIES, (Formerly Lincoln Regional Hospital), 700 West Maple Street, Zip 37334–3202; tel. 931/438–1111; Gary G. Kendrick, Chief Executive Officer **A**1 9 10 **F**7 8 15 17 19 21 22 24 26 27 28 32 33 34 35 37 40 41 42 44 49 67 71 73 **S** Quorum Health Group/Quorum Health Resources, Inc., Brentwood, TN

| 13 | 10 | 51 | 1812 | 21 | 29089 | 189 | 11238 | 5431 | 255 |

FRANKLIN—Williamson County

✠ WILLIAMSON MEDICAL CENTER, 2021 Carothers Road, Zip 37067–5822, Mailing Address: P.O. Box 681600, Zip 37068–1600; tel. 615/791–0500; Ronald G. Joyner, Chief Executive Officer **A**1 9 10 **F**3 7 8 10 15 19 21 22 23 28 30 33 34 35 37 40 42 44 46 49 54 56 63 65 66 67 71 72 73 **P**6 **N** Center Care, Bowling Green, KY; Middle Tennessee Healthcare Network, Nashville, TN

| 13 | 10 | 109 | 5197 | 61 | 92940 | 521 | 44997 | 18789 | 658 |

GAINESBORO—Jackson County

CUMBERLAND RIVER HOSPITAL SOUTH See Cumberland River Hospital North, Celina

Hospital, Address, Telephone, Administrator, Approval, Facility, and Physician Codes, Health Care System, Network	Classi-fication Codes		Utilization Data					Expense (thousands) of dollars		
	Control	Service	Staffed Beds	Admissions	Census	Outpatient Visits	Births	Total	Payroll	Personnel

★ American Hospital Association (AHA) membership
□ Joint Commission on Accreditation of Healthcare Organizations (JCAHO) accreditation
+ American Osteopathic Healthcare Association (AOHA) membership
○ American Osteopathic Association (AOA) accreditation
△ Commission on Accreditation of Rehabilitation Facilities (CARF) accreditation
Control codes 61, 63, 64, 71, 72 and 73 indicate hospitals listed by AOHA, but not registered by AHA. For definition of numerical codes, see page A4

GALLATIN—Sumner County

✠ SUMNER REGIONAL MEDICAL CENTER, 555 Hartsville Pike, Zip 37066–2449, Mailing Address: P.O. Box 1558, Zip 37066–1558; tel. 615/452–4210; William T. Sugg, President and Chief Executive Officer **A**1 9 10 **F**7 8 11 13 14 15 16 17 19 20 21 22 23 24 29 30 32 33 34 35 37 38 39 40 41 42 44 45 46 48 49 51 56 65 67 73 74 **N** Center Care, Bowling Green, KY; Middle Tennessee Healthcare Network, Nashville, TN
| 23 | 10 | 148 | 4476 | 61 | 80415 | 630 | 42771 | 17900 | 632 |

GERMANTOWN—Shelby County

□ △ BAPTIST REHABILITATION–GERMANTOWN, 2100 Exeter Road, Zip 38138; tel. 901/757–1350; Paula Gisler, Chief Executive Officer (Nonreporting) **A**1 7 9 10 **S** Baptist Memorial Health Care Corporation, Memphis, TN **N** Arkansas' FirstSource, Little Rock, AR
| 32 | 46 | 85 | — | — | — | — | — | — | — |

METHODIST HOSPITAL GERMANTOWN See Methodist Hospitals of Memphis, Memphis

GREENEVILLE—Greene County

✠ LAUGHLIN MEMORIAL HOSPITAL, 1420 Tusculum Boulevard, Zip 37745; tel. 423/787–5000; Charles H. Whitfield, Jr., President and Chief Executive Officer (Total facility includes 90 beds in nursing home–type unit) **A**1 9 10 **F**7 8 10 12 14 15 16 17 19 21 22 26 28 29 30 32 34 35 37 38 40 41 42 44 45 46 49 60 63 64 65 66 67 71 73 74 **N** Premier Health Network, Johnson City, TN
| 23 | 10 | 230 | 5099 | 147 | 44992 | 396 | 29862 | 11560 | 433 |

✠ TAKOMA ADVENTIST HOSPITAL, 401 Takoma Avenue, Zip 37743–4668; tel. 423/639–3151; Michael V. Gentry, President (Nonreporting) **A**1 9 10 **S** Adventist Health System Sunbelt Health Care Corporation, Winter Park, FL **N** Mountain States Healthcare Network, Johnson City, TN
| 21 | 10 | 80 | — | — | — | — | — | — | — |

HARRIMAN—Roane County

□ ROANE MEDICAL CENTER, 412 Devonia Street, Zip 37748–0489, Mailing Address: P.O. Box 489, Zip 37748–0489; tel. 423/882–1323; Jim Gann, Administrator **A**1 9 10 **F**7 8 10 15 16 17 19 22 24 28 30 35 37 40 44 67 71 73 **P**8
| 14 | 10 | 85 | 4536 | 47 | 50638 | 49 | 19412 | 8009 | 386 |

HARTSVILLE—Trousdale County

TROUSDALE MEDICAL CENTER See Frank T. Rutherford Memorial Hospital, Carthage

HENDERSONVILLE—Sumner County

★ HENDERSONVILLE HOSPITAL, (Formerly Columbia Hendersonville Hospital), 355 New Shackle Island Road, Zip 37075–2393; tel. 615/264–4000; Robert Klein, Chief Executive Officer (Total facility includes 10 beds in nursing home–type unit) **A**9 10 **F**7 8 10 12 14 15 16 17 19 21 22 26 28 29 30 32 33 34 35 37 40 44 46 49 50 51 64 65 66 67 71 72 73 74 **P**7 **S** Columbia/HCA Healthcare Corporation, Nashville, TN **N** Center Care, Bowling Green, KY; Columbia Healthcare Network, Brentwood, TN
| 33 | 10 | 67 | 2759 | 30 | 65928 | 503 | — | 8006 | 239 |

HERMITAGE—Davidson County

✠ SUMMIT MEDICAL CENTER, (Formerly Columbia Summit Medical Center), 5655 Frist Boulevard, Zip 37076–2053; tel. 615/316–3000; Bryan K. Dearing, Chief Executive Officer **A**1 9 10 **F**3 4 6 7 8 9 10 11 12 14 15 16 17 18 19 20 21 22 23 26 27 28 29 30 31 32 33 34 35 37 38 40 41 42 43 44 45 46 47 48 49 50 51 52 53 54 55 56 57 58 59 60 61 62 63 64 65 66 67 68 69 70 71 72 73 74 **P**5 7 8 **S** Columbia/HCA Healthcare Corporation, Nashville, TN **N** Columbia Healthcare Network, Brentwood, TN
| 33 | 10 | 204 | 9491 | 123 | 87946 | 1214 | 82402 | 26564 | 804 |

HUMBOLDT—Gibson County

✠ HUMBOLDT GENERAL HOSPITAL, 3525 Chere Carol Road, Zip 38343–3699; tel. 901/784–0301; Jeff Frieling, Administrator **A**1 9 10 **F**7 8 12 14 15 16 17 19 22 28 30 32 33 40 44 45 49 65 66 71 73 **S** West Tennessee Healthcare., Jackson, TN **N** West Tennessee Healthcare, Inc., Jackson, TN
| 15 | 10 | 44 | 1547 | 18 | 20612 | 187 | 5696 | 2554 | 107 |

HUNTINGDON—Carroll County

✠ BAPTIST MEMORIAL HOSPITAL–HUNTINGDON, 631 R. B. Wilson Drive, Zip 38344–1675; tel. 901/986–4461; Susan M. Breeden, Administrator **A**1 9 10 **F**7 8 12 15 16 17 19 21 22 24 28 29 30 31 32 34 35 37 41 44 46 49 58 67 71 73 **P**7 **S** Baptist Memorial Health Care Corporation, Memphis, TN
| 21 | 10 | 70 | 1950 | 24 | 19879 | 147 | 9389 | 3480 | 220 |

JACKSON—Madison County

✠ COLUMBIA REGIONAL HOSPITAL OF JACKSON, 367 Hospital Boulevard, Zip 38305–4518, Mailing Address: P.O. Box 3310, Zip 38303–0310; tel. 901/661–2000; Tim Brady, Chief Executive Officer **A**1 9 10 **F**4 7 8 10 11 12 16 17 19 20 21 22 23 26 30 32 34 35 37 40 42 44 45 46 49 60 64 65 71 73 74 **S** Columbia/HCA Healthcare Corporation, Nashville, TN
| 33 | 10 | 104 | 3313 | 50 | 11555 | 190 | 30234 | 11661 | 379 |

✠ △ JACKSON–MADISON COUNTY GENERAL HOSPITAL, 708 West Forest Avenue, Zip 38301–3855; tel. 901/425–5000; James T. Moss, President and Chief Executive Officer (Total facility includes 85 beds in nursing home–type unit) **A**1 2 3 5 7 9 10 **F**1 3 4 6 7 8 10 11 12 13 14 15 16 17 18 19 21 22 23 24 25 26 27 28 29 30 31 32 33 34 35 37 38 39 40 41 42 43 44 45 46 48 49 51 53 54 55 56 57 58 59 60 64 65 66 67 69 71 72 73 74 **P**1 6 7 **S** West Tennessee Healthcare., Jackson, TN **N** West Tennessee Healthcare, Inc., Jackson, TN
| 16 | 10 | 660 | 24828 | 447 | 151059 | 2767 | 195501 | 87069 | 3117 |

★ PATHWAYS OF TENNESSEE, 238 Summar Drive, Zip 38301–3982; tel. 901/935–8200; John D. Rudnick, Jr., FACHE, Executive Director **A**10 **F**2 3 4 6 8 10 11 12 13 14 15 16 17 18 19 21 22 25 26 28 29 30 32 33 34 35 37 38 39 40 41 42 43 44 45 46 47 48 49 50 51 52 53 54 55 56 57 58 59 60 61 63 64 65 66 67 71 72 73 74 **P**1 4 7 **S** West Tennessee Healthcare., Jackson, TN
| 23 | 22 | 47 | 924 | 21 | 76879 | — | 13314 | 7792 | 308 |

Hospital, Address, Telephone, Administrator, Approval, Facility, and Physician Codes, Health Care System, Network	Classi-fication Codes		Utilization Data					Expense (thousands) of dollars		
	Control	Service	Staffed Beds	Admissions	Census	Outpatient Visits	Births	Total	Payroll	Personnel

JAMESTOWN—Fentress County

☐ FENTRESS COUNTY GENERAL HOSPITAL, Highway 52 West, Zip 38556, Mailing Address: P.O. Box 1500, Zip 38556; tel. 615/879–8171; Curtis B. Courtney, Administrator (Total facility includes 13 beds in nursing home–type unit) (Nonreporting) **A**1 9 10 **S** Paracelsus Healthcare Corporation, Houston, TX
| | 33 | 10 | 73 | — | — | — | — | — | — | — |

JEFFERSON CITY—Jefferson County

☐ JEFFERSON MEMORIAL HOSPITAL, 1800 Bishop Avenue, Zip 37760–1992, Mailing Address: P.O. Box 560, Zip 37760–0560; tel. 423/475–2091; Michael C. Hicks, President and Chief Executive Officer (Nonreporting) **A**1 9 10 **S** Catholic Healthcare Partners, Cincinnati, OH
| | 15 | 10 | 51 | — | — | — | — | — | — | — |

JELLICO—Campbell County

✚ JELLICO COMMUNITY HOSPITAL, 188 Hospital Lane, Zip 37762–4400; tel. 423/784–7252; Jim Bunch, President and Chief Executive Officer **A**1 9 10 **F**7 8 12 14 15 16 17 19 21 22 26 27 28 29 31 35 37 39 40 41 44 45 46 49 58 65 71 72 73 **P**8 **S** Adventist Health System Sunbelt Health Care Corporation, Winter Park, FL
| | 21 | 10 | 54 | 1982 | 21 | 24350 | 241 | 15640 | 5297 | 108 |

JOHNSON CITY—Washington County

✚ COLUMBIA NORTH SIDE HOSPITAL, 401 Princeton Road, Zip 37601–2097, Mailing Address: P.O. Box 4900, Zip 37602–4900; tel. 423/854–5900; Eric Deaton, Chief Executive Officer **A**1 9 10 **F**3 4 7 8 10 12 14 15 16 18 19 21 22 23 24 28 29 30 31 32 33 34 35 37 39 41 42 43 44 45 49 51 54 56 58 59 60 64 65 66 67 68 69 70 71 72 73 74 **P**7 8 **S** Columbia/HCA Healthcare Corporation, Nashville, TN **N** Premier Health Network, Johnson City, TN
| | 33 | 10 | 127 | 3642 | 47 | 39557 | 0 | 26597 | 10367 | 315 |

★ △ JOHNSON CITY MEDICAL CENTER HOSPITAL, 400 North State of Franklin Road, Zip 37604–6094; tel. 423/431–6111; Dennis Vonderfecht, President and Chief Executive Officer **A**2 3 5 7 8 9 10 **F**2 3 4 7 8 10 12 13 14 15 16 17 18 19 20 21 22 23 24 25 26 27 28 29 30 31 32 33 34 35 37 38 39 40 41 42 43 44 45 46 47 48 49 51 52 53 54 55 56 58 59 60 63 64 65 66 67 68 69 70 71 72 73 74 **P**5 7 8 **N** Mountain States Healthcare Network, Johnson City, TN
| | 23 | 10 | 407 | 16466 | 274 | 134581 | 1227 | 148287 | 54588 | 2256 |

✚ JOHNSON CITY SPECIALTY HOSPITAL, (Formerly Columbia Johnson City Specialty Hospital), 203 East Watauga Avenue, Zip 37601–4651; tel. 423/926–1111; Lori Caudell Fatherree, Chief Executive Officer **A**1 9 10 **F**2 3 4 7 8 10 11 12 14 15 16 17 19 22 23 24 26 28 30 32 35 37 38 40 41 42 44 48 49 52 53 54 55 56 57 58 59 60 61 65 66 67 69 70 71 73 74 **P**4 5 7 8 **S** Columbia/HCA Healthcare Corporation, Nashville, TN **N** Premier Health Network, Johnson City, TN
| | 33 | 10 | 49 | 1165 | 8 | 13659 | 695 | 9967 | 3193 | 146 |

☐ △ NORTHEAST TENNESSEE REHABILITATION HOSPITAL, 2511 Wesley Street, Zip 37601–1723; tel. 423/283–0700; Dan Bolton, Chief Executive Officer **A**1 7 9 10 **F**5 12 14 16 17 19 28 29 34 35 39 41 48 49 54 55 60 65 66 67 **P**8
| | 32 | 46 | 60 | 484 | 30 | 3215 | 0 | 9569 | 4602 | 108 |

WOODRIDGE HOSPITAL, 403 State of Franklin Road, Zip 37604–6009; tel. 423/928–7111; Thomas J. De Martini, Administrator **A**3 5 9 10 **F**1 2 3 12 14 15 16 18 30 45 52 53 54 55 56 57 58 59 65 67 **P**6 **N** Mountain States Healthcare Network, Johnson City, TN
| | 23 | 22 | 65 | 3246 | 49 | 51167 | 0 | 14183 | 7723 | 144 |

KINGSPORT—Sullivan County

✚ COLUMBIA INDIAN PATH MEDICAL CENTER, (Includes Indian Path Pavilion, 2300 Pavilion Drive, Zip 37660–4672; tel. 423/378–7500), 2000 Brookside Drive, Zip 37660–4604; tel. 423/392–7000); Robert Bauer, Chief Executive Officer **A**1 9 10 **F**2 3 4 7 8 10 12 14 15 16 19 21 22 23 26 28 30 32 34 35 37 39 40 41 42 44 45 49 52 54 55 56 57 58 59 61 63 64 65 66 70 71 73 74 **P**5 7 8 **S** Columbia/HCA Healthcare Corporation, Nashville, TN
| | 33 | 10 | 220 | 5926 | 102 | 108037 | 278 | 46199 | 15886 | 573 |

☐ △ HEALTHSOUTH REHABILITATION HOSPITAL, 113 Cassel Drive, Zip 37660–3775; tel. 423/246–7240; Terry R. Maxhimer, Regional Vice President (Nonreporting) **A**1 7 9 10 **S** HEALTHSOUTH Corporation, Birmingham, AL
| | 33 | 46 | 50 | — | — | — | — | — | — | — |

INDIAN PATH PAVILION See Columbia Indian Path Medical Center

✚ WELLMONT HOLSTON VALLEY MEDICAL CENTER, (Formerly Holston Valley Hospital and Medical Center), West Ravine Street, Zip 37662–0224, Mailing Address: Box 238, Zip 37662–0224; tel. 423/224–4000; Louis H. Bremer, President and Chief Executive Officer (Total facility includes 35 beds in nursing home–type unit) **A**1 2 3 5 9 10 **F**1 4 7 8 10 11 12 14 15 16 17 19 20 21 22 23 24 25 26 28 29 30 31 32 33 34 35 37 38 39 40 41 42 43 44 46 47 49 51 52 54 55 56 57 58 59 60 63 64 65 66 67 69 70 71 72 73 74 **P**1 4 5 6 7 **S** Quorum Health Group/Quorum Health Resources, Inc., Brentwood, TN **N** CHA Provider Network, Inc., Lexington, KY; Premier Health Network, Johnson City, TN; Highlands Wellmont Health Network, Inc., Bristol, TN
| | 23 | 10 | 384 | 16398 | 243 | 139820 | 1630 | 149868 | 59520 | 1850 |

KNOXVILLE—Knox County

✚ △ BAPTIST HOSPITAL OF EAST TENNESSEE, 137 Blount Avenue S.E., Zip 37920–1643, Mailing Address: P.O. Box 1788, Zip 37901–1788; tel. 423/632–5011; Jon Foster, Executive Vice President and Administrator **A**1 2 7 9 10 **F**3 4 7 8 10 11 12 14 15 16 17 18 19 20 21 22 26 27 28 29 30 31 32 33 34 35 37 39 40 41 42 43 44 45 48 49 51 52 54 57 58 59 60 61 65 67 68 69 71 73 74 **P**8 **S** Baptist Health System of Tennessee, Knoxville, TN
| | 21 | 10 | 316 | 12677 | 208 | 99267 | 490 | 130713 | 53743 | — |

☐ EAST TENNESSEE CHILDREN'S HOSPITAL, 2018 Clinch Avenue, Zip 37916–2393, Mailing Address: P.O. Box 15010, Zip 37901–5010; tel. 423/541–8000; Robert F. Koppel, President and Chief Executive Officer **A**1 9 10 **F**10 15 16 19 22 32 34 35 38 39 41 42 44 45 46 47 49 51 53 60 65 70 71 73 **P**8
| | 23 | 50 | 103 | 5194 | 69 | 85083 | — | 45796 | 21634 | 859 |

Hospital, Address, Telephone, Administrator, Approval, Facility, and Physician Codes, Health Care System, Network	Classification Codes		Utilization Data					Expense (thousands) of dollars		
	Control	Service	Staffed Beds	Admissions	Census	Outpatient Visits	Births	Total	Payroll	Personnel

★ American Hospital Association (AHA) membership
□ Joint Commission on Accreditation of Healthcare Organizations (JCAHO) accreditation
+ American Osteopathic Healthcare Association (AOHA) membership
○ American Osteopathic Association (AOA) accreditation
△ Commission on Accreditation of Rehabilitation Facilities (CARF) accreditation
Control codes 61, 63, 64, 71, 72 and 73 indicate hospitals listed by AOHA, but not registered by AHA. For definition of numerical codes, see page A4.

Hospital	Control	Service	Staffed Beds	Admissions	Census	Outpatient Visits	Births	Total	Payroll	Personnel
★ △ FORT SANDERS REGIONAL MEDICAL CENTER, 1901 Clinch Avenue S.W., Zip 37916–2394; tel. 423/541–1111; James R. Burkhart, FACHE, Administrator (Total facility includes 24 beds in nursing home–type unit) **A**1 2 6 7 9 10 **F**2 3 4 7 8 10 11 12 14 15 16 17 18 19 21 22 23 24 25 26 27 28 30 31 32 33 34 35 37 39 40 41 42 43 44 45 46 48 49 52 53 54 55 56 57 58 59 60 61 63 64 65 66 67 68 71 73 74 **P**7 **S** Covenant Health, Nashville, TN **N** CHA Provider Network, Inc., Lexington, KY	23	10	410	17260	284	82984	2246	128703	50224	1782
★ FORT SANDERS–PARKWEST MEDICAL CENTER, 9352 Park West Boulevard, Zip 37923–4387, Mailing Address: P.O. Box 22993, Zip 37933–0993; tel. 423/694–5700; James R. Burkhart, FACHE, Administrator **A**1 2 9 10 **F**2 3 4 7 8 10 11 12 14 15 16 17 18 19 21 22 23 24 25 26 27 28 29 30 31 32 33 34 35 37 39 40 41 42 43 44 45 46 48 49 52 53 54 55 56 57 58 59 60 61 63 64 65 66 67 68 71 73 74 **P**7 **S** Covenant Health, Nashville, TN **N** CHA Provider Network, Inc., Lexington, KY	23	10	281	11170	150	87301	677	95296	31193	1094
□ LAKESHORE MENTAL HEALTH INSTITUTE, 5908 Lyons View Drive, Zip 37919–7598; tel. 423/450–5200; Richard Lee Thomas, Superintendent (Nonreporting) **A**1 10	12	22	277	—						
□ △ ST. MARY'S HEALTH SYSTEM, 900 East Oak Hill Avenue, Zip 37917–4556; tel. 423/545–8000; Richard C. Williams, President and Chief Executive Officer (Total facility includes 25 beds in nursing home–type unit) **A**1 2 3 7 9 10 **F**1 2 4 7 10 11 12 16 17 19 21 22 23 24 32 33 35 37 38 40 41 42 43 44 46 48 49 53 54 55 57 58 59 60 64 65 71 73 74 **P**1 2 5 6 7 **S** Catholic Healthcare Partners, Cincinnati, OH	21	10	300	13982	215	223134	1610	120383	51313	1565
★ UNIVERSITY OF TENNESSEE MEMORIAL HOSPITAL, 1924 Alcoa Highway, Zip 37920–6900; tel. 423/544–9000; Thomas M. Kish, Executive Director **A**1 2 3 9 10 **F**4 7 8 10 11 13 17 18 19 20 21 22 23 24 28 29 30 31 32 33 34 35 37 38 39 40 41 42 43 44 45 46 47 49 50 51 60 61 63 65 67 69 70 71 73 74 **P**7	12	10	439	20081	327	287824	3106	258676	113462	3522
LA FOLLETTE—Campbell County										
★ LA FOLLETTE MEDICAL CENTER, East Avenue, Zip 37766, Mailing Address: P.O. Box 1301, Zip 37766–1301; tel. 423/562–2211; Nicholas P. Lewis, Administrator (Total facility includes 98 beds in nursing home–type unit) **A**1 9 10 **F**8 14 19 22 32 34 41 44 49 51 58 59 64 65 71 73	14	10	161	3128	143	—	—	18787	9440	430
LAFAYETTE—Macon County										
★ MACON COUNTY GENERAL HOSPITAL, 204 Medical Drive, Zip 37083–1799, Mailing Address: P.O. Box 378, Zip 37083–0378; tel. 615/666–2147; Dennis A. Wolford, FACHE, Administrator **A**1 9 10 **F**14 15 16 19 22 28 30 44 51 65 71 **S** Quorum Health Group/Quorum Health Resources, Inc., Brentwood, TN **N** Center Care, Bowling Green, KY	23	10	43	994	11	—	0	4532	1805	76
LAWRENCEBURG—Lawrence County										
★ CROCKETT HOSPITAL, (Formerly Columbia Crockett Hospital), U.S. Highway 43 South, Zip 38464–0847, Mailing Address: P.O. Box 847, Zip 38464–0847; tel. 931/762–6571; Jack S. Buck, Chief Executive Officer **A**1 9 10 **F**7 8 10 12 13 14 15 16 17 18 19 20 21 22 28 29 30 34 35 37 39 40 41 44 45 46 48 49 51 65 66 67 68 71 73 74 **P**7 **S** Columbia/HCA Healthcare Corporation, Nashville, TN	33	10	98	2901	33	39642	171	15801	6124	198
LEBANON—Wilson County										
★ UNIVERSITY MEDICAL CENTER, (Includes McFarland Specialty Hospital, 500 Park Avenue, Zip 37087–3720; tel. 615/449–0500), 1411 Baddour Parkway, Zip 37087–2573; tel. 615/444–8262; Larry W. Keller, Chief Executive Officer **A**1 9 10 **F**7 8 10 12 15 19 21 22 28 29 30 32 34 35 37 39 40 41 42 44 46 48 49 52 54 55 56 57 59 60 63 64 65 66 71 73 74 **P**5 6 7 **S** TENET Healthcare Corporation, Santa Barbara, CA **N** Center Care, Bowling Green, KY	33	10	225	7184	105	67796	772	45733	20366	—
LEWISBURG—Marshall County										
□ MARSHALL MEDICAL CENTER, 1080 North Ellington Parkway, Zip 37091–2227, Mailing Address: P.O. Box 1609, Zip 37091–1609; tel. 931/359–6241; Steve C. Hoelscher, Administrator **A**1 10 **F**8 14 15 16 19 21 22 28 29 30 32 34 37 39 41 44 45 46 65 66 71 73	13	10	77	1413	14	28494	26	9460	4347	135
LEXINGTON—Henderson County										
★ METHODIST HOSPITAL OF LEXINGTON, 200 West Church Street, Zip 38351–2014; tel. 901/968–3646; Eugene Ragghianti, Administrator (Nonreporting) **A**1 9 10 **S** Methodist Health Systems, Inc., Memphis, TN **N** Methodist Health Systems, Inc., Memphis, TN	21	10	32	—	—	—	—	—	—	—
LINDEN—Perry County										
□ BAPTIST PERRY COMMUNITY HOSPITAL, (Formerly Baptist Perry Memorial Hospital), Highway 13 South, Zip 37096, Mailing Address: Route 10, Box 8, Zip 37096; tel. 931/589–2121; Gary C. Morse, Chief Executive Officer and Administrator (Nonreporting) **A**1 9 10	23	10	53	—	—	—	—	—	—	—
LIVINGSTON—Overton County										
★ COLUMBIA LIVINGSTON REGIONAL HOSPITAL, 315 Oak Street, Zip 38570, Mailing Address: P.O. Box 550, Zip 38570–0550; tel. 931/823–5611; Timothy W. McGill, Chief Executive Officer (Total facility includes 15 beds in nursing home–type unit) **A**1 9 10 **F**7 8 12 14 15 16 19 20 22 28 30 32 35 37 39 40 42 44 49 64 65 66 67 71 73 74 **P**7 8 **S** Columbia/HCA Healthcare Corporation, Nashville, TN	33	10	88	3751	45	30470	314	17843	6529	265
LOUDON—Loudon County										
★ FORT SANDERS LOUDON MEDICAL CENTER, 1125 Grove Street, Zip 37774–1512, Mailing Address: P.O. Box 217, Zip 37774–0217; tel. 423/458–8222; Ralph T. Williams, Administrator **A**1 9 10 **F**7 8 14 15 16 19 22 30 32 33 35 37 40 41 44 46 49 63 65 71 73 74 **P**6 **S** Covenant Health, Nashville, TN **N** CHA Provider Network, Inc., Lexington, KY	23	10	30	1481	13	15737	102	10446	4841	201

Hospital, Address, Telephone, Administrator, Approval, Facility, and Physician Codes, Health Care System, Network	Classi-fication Codes		Utilization Data					Expense (thousands) of dollars		
★ American Hospital Association (AHA) membership □ Joint Commission on Accreditation of Healthcare Organizations (JCAHO) accreditation + American Osteopathic Healthcare Association (AOHA) membership ○ American Osteopathic Association (AOA) accreditation △ Commission on Accreditation of Rehabilitation Facilities (CARF) accreditation Control codes 61, 63, 64, 71, 72 and 73 indicate hospitals listed by AOHA, but not registered by AHA. For definition of numerical codes, see page A4	Control	Service	Staffed Beds	Admissions	Census	Outpatient Visits	Births	Total	Payroll	Personnel

LOUISVILLE—Blount County

PENINSULA HOSPITAL, 2347 Jones Bend Road, Zip 37777–5213, Mailing Address: P.O. Box 2000, Zip 37777–2000; tel. 423/970–9800; David H. McReynolds, Chief Operating Officer and Administrator **A**9 10 **F**3 4 5 6 7 8 10 11 12 13 15 16 17 18 19 20 21 22 24 25 26 27 28 29 30 31 32 34 35 37 40 42 43 44 45 46 47 48 49 50 51 52 53 54 55 56 57 58 59 60 61 63 64 65 66 67 68 69 71 72 73 74 **N** CHA Provider Network, Inc., Lexington, KY	23	22	155	2709	75	15591	—	8459	4170	—

MADISON—Davidson County

COLUMBIA NASHVILLE MEMORIAL HOSPITAL See Nashville Memorial Hospital

✖ NASHVILLE MEMORIAL HOSPITAL, (Formerly Columbia Nashville Memorial Hospital), 612 West Due West Avenue, Zip 37115–4474; tel. 615/865–3511; Allyn R. Harris, Chief Executive Officer (Nonreporting) **A**1 2 5 9 10 **S** Columbia/HCA Healthcare Corporation, Nashville, TN **N** Center Care, Bowling Green, KY; Columbia Healthcare Network, Brentwood, TN	33	10	250	—	—	—	—	—	—	—
✖ △ TENNESSEE CHRISTIAN MEDICAL CENTER, (Includes Tennessee Christian Medical Center – Portland, 105 Redbud Drive, Portland, Zip 37148), 500 Hospital Drive, Zip 37115–5032; tel. 615/865–2373; Milton R. Siepman, Ph.D., President and Chief Executive Officer (Total facility includes 50 beds in nursing home–type unit) **A**1 7 9 10 **F**3 4 5 7 8 9 10 11 12 14 15 16 17 19 21 22 23 24 26 27 28 29 30 32 33 34 35 37 38 39 40 41 42 43 44 45 47 48 49 50 51 52 53 54 55 56 57 58 59 60 61 63 64 65 66 67 69 70 71 72 73 74 **P**1 3 5 7 **S** Adventist Health System Sunbelt Health Care Corporation, Winter Park, FL **N** Middle Tennessee Healthcare Network, Nashville, TN	21	10	281	7554	149	64375	293	56406	26316	791

MANCHESTER—Coffee County

★ COFFEE MEDICAL CENTER, 1001 McArthur Drive, Zip 37355–2455, Mailing Address: P.O. Box 1079, Zip 37355–1079; tel. 931/728–3586; Edward A. Perdue, Administrator (Total facility includes 72 beds in nursing home–type unit) **A**9 10 **F**8 17 19 22 26 33 34 40 41 44 49 64 65 67 71 73 **N** Center Care, Bowling Green, KY	16	10	122	817	79	10775	—	6554	2706	107
★ ○ MEDICAL CENTER OF MANCHESTER, 481 Interstate Drive, Zip 37355–3108, Mailing Address: P.O. Box 1409, Zip 37355–1409; tel. 931/728–6354; Margaret Hale, Chief Operating Officer (Nonreporting) **A**9 10 11 **S** TENET Healthcare Corporation, Santa Barbara, CA **N** Center Care, Bowling Green, KY	33	10	49	—	—	—	—	—	—	—

MARTIN—Weakley County

✖ VOLUNTEER GENERAL HOSPITAL, (Formerly Columbia Volunteer General Hospital), 161 Mount Pelia Road, Zip 38237–0967, Mailing Address: P.O. Box 967, Zip 38237–0967; tel. 901/587–4261; R. Coleman Foss, Chief Executive Officer **A**1 9 10 **F**7 8 12 13 15 16 17 19 21 22 23 24 28 30 32 34 35 37 39 40 42 44 45 46 49 65 66 67 71 73 **P**6 **S** Columbia/HCA Healthcare Corporation, Nashville, TN	33	10	65	2878	36	25450	381	18465	6351	184

MARYVILLE—Blount County

✖ BLOUNT MEMORIAL HOSPITAL, 907 East Lamar Alexander Parkway, Zip 37804–5016; tel. 423/983–7211; Joseph M. Dawson, Administrator **A**1 2 6 9 10 **F**3 4 7 8 10 11 12 13 14 15 16 17 18 19 21 22 23 24 25 28 30 31 32 33 34 35 37 39 40 41 42 44 46 49 52 54 55 56 58 59 60 63 65 66 67 70 71 73 **P**8	13	10	143	7935	98	146040	643	68972	29589	1120

MCKENZIE—Carroll County

✖ METHODIST HOSPITAL OF MCKENZIE, 161 Hospital Drive, Zip 38201–1636; tel. 901/352–4170; Randal E. Carson, Administrator **A**1 9 10 **F**7 8 15 16 19 22 24 27 28 32 33 39 40 44 49 64 65 66 71 73 **P**7 **S** Methodist Health Systems, Inc., Memphis, TN **N** Methodist Health Systems, Inc., Memphis, TN	21	10	27	1104	10	13858	324	7410	3530	125

MCMINNVILLE—Warren County

✖ RIVER PARK HOSPITAL, (Formerly Columbia River Park Hospital), 1559 Sparta Road, Zip 37110–1316; tel. 931/815–4000; Terry J. Gunn, Chief Executive Officer **A**1 9 10 **F**7 8 11 12 15 16 17 18 19 20 21 22 23 28 30 32 34 35 37 39 40 41 42 44 45 46 48 49 51 63 64 65 66 67 71 72 73 **P**7 **S** Columbia/HCA Healthcare Corporation, Nashville, TN **N** Columbia Healthcare Network, Brentwood, TN	33	10	86	4383	44	32670	448	19238	9090	338

MEMPHIS—Shelby County

✖ BAPTIST MEMORIAL HOSPITAL, (Includes Baptist Memorial Hospital East, 6019 Walnut Grove Road, Zip 38119; tel. 901/226–5000; Baptist Memorial Hospital Rehabilitation Center), 899 Madison Avenue, Zip 38146–0001; tel. 901/227–2727; Stephen Curtis Reynolds, President and Chief Executive Officer (Total facility includes 60 beds in nursing home–type unit) **A**1 2 3 5 6 9 10 **F**4 7 8 10 11 12 14 15 16 17 19 21 22 23 24 25 26 30 32 33 34 35 37 38 39 40 41 42 43 44 45 46 48 49 51 52 53 57 60 63 64 65 66 67 69 70 71 72 73 74 **P**2 8 **S** Baptist Memorial Health Care Corporation, Memphis, TN	21	10	1057	41789	730	200591	5101	398105	123064	3603
□ CHARTER LAKESIDE BEHAVIORAL HEALTH SYSTEM, 2911 Brunswick Road, Zip 38133–4199, Mailing Address: P.O. Box 341308, Zip 38134–1308; tel. 901/377–4700; Rob S. Waggener, Chief Executive Officer (Nonreporting) **A**1 9 10 **S** Magellan Health Services, Atlanta, GA	33	22	174	—	—	—	—	—	—	—
□ DELTA MEDICAL CENTER, (Formerly Eastwood Medical Center), 3000 Getwell Road, Zip 38118–2299; tel. 901/369–8500; Larry Walker, Chief Executive Officer **A**1 9 10 **F**2 3 8 17 19 21 22 26 28 29 30 34 35 37 39 42 44 51 52 56 57 58 59 63 65 67 71 73 **P**7	33	10	209	3410	90	22204	0	29385	—	—

EASTWOOD MEDICAL CENTER See Delta Medical Center

Hospital, Address, Telephone, Administrator, Approval, Facility, and Physician Codes, Health Care System, Network	Classi-fication Codes		Utilization Data					Expense (thousands) of dollars		
★ American Hospital Association (AHA) membership □ Joint Commission on Accreditation of Healthcare Organizations (JCAHO) accreditation + American Osteopathic Healthcare Association (AOHA) membership ○ American Osteopathic Association (AOA) accreditation △ Commission on Accreditation of Rehabilitation Facilities (CARF) accreditation Control codes 61, 63, 64, 71, 72 and 73 indicate hospitals listed by AOHA, but not registered by AHA. For definition of numerical codes, see page A4	Control	Service	Staffed Beds	Admissions	Census	Outpatient Visits	Births	Total	Payroll	Personnel

	Control	Service	Staffed Beds	Admissions	Census	Outpatient Visits	Births	Total	Payroll	Personnel
□ HEALTHSOUTH REHABILITATION HOSPITAL, 1282 Union Avenue, Zip 38104–3414; tel. 901/722–2000; Jerry Gray, Administrator **A**1 10 **F**12 15 48 49 65 **S** HEALTHSOUTH Corporation, Birmingham, AL	32	46	80	1600	77	16372	—	16134	8201	247
LE BONHEUR CHILDREN'S MEDICAL CENTER See Methodist Hospitals of Memphis										
□ MEMPHIS MENTAL HEALTH INSTITUTE, 865 Poplar Avenue, Zip 38105–4626, Mailing Address: P.O. Box 40966, Zip 38174–0966; tel. 901/524–1201; Elizabeth Banks, Superintendent **A**1 5 9 10 **F**2 3 20 26 39 45 46 52 55 56 57 65 67 73	12	22	135	1729	92	0	—	12061	7457	258
⊞ METHODIST HOSPITALS OF MEMPHIS, (Includes Le Bonheur Children's Medical Center, One Children's Plaza, Zip 38103–2893; tel. 901/572–3000; James E. Shmerling, President; Methodist Hospital Germantown, 7691 Poplar, Germantown, Zip 38138, Mailing Address: P.O. Box 381588, Zip 38138; tel. 901/754–6418; Methodist Hospitals of Memphis–Central, ; Methodist Hospitals of Memphis–South Unit, 1300 Wesley Drive, Zip 38116; tel. 901/346–3700; Cecelia Sawyer, Administrator; Methodist North–J. Harris Hospital, 3960 New Covington Pike, Zip 38128; tel. 901/372–5200; Tim Deaton, Administrator), 1265 Union Avenue, Zip 38104–3499; tel. 901/726–7000; Gary S. Shorb, President (Total facility includes 24 beds in nursing home–type unit) **A**1 2 3 5 6 9 10 **F**2 3 4 5 7 8 9 10 11 12 13 15 16 17 18 19 20 21 22 23 24 25 26 27 28 30 33 34 35 37 38 40 41 42 43 44 45 46 47 48 49 51 52 53 54 57 59 60 61 63 64 65 66 67 69 70 71 72 73 74 **P**6 7 8 **S** Methodist Health Systems, Inc., Memphis, TN **N** Methodist Health Systems, Inc., Memphis, TN	23	10	1232	58937	889	334183	7793	447262	205611	—
□ REGIONAL MEDICAL CENTER AT MEMPHIS, 877 Jefferson Avenue, Zip 38103–2897; tel. 901/545–7100; Bruce W. Steinhauer, M.D., President and Chief Executive Officer **A**1 2 3 5 6 8 9 10 **F**7 8 9 12 14 15 16 17 19 20 21 22 25 27 28 29 30 31 34 35 37 38 39 40 41 42 44 46 49 51 56 60 61 65 68 70 71 72 73 74	23	10	361	13983	233	134843	3269	182132	67521	2105
⊞ SAINT FRANCIS HOSPITAL, 5959 Park Avenue, Zip 38119–5198, Mailing Address: P.O. Box 171808, Zip 38187–1808; tel. 901/765–1000; David L. Archer, Chief Executive Officer (Total facility includes 197 beds in nursing home–type unit) **A**1 2 3 5 9 10 **F**1 2 3 4 7 8 10 11 12 16 19 21 22 23 24 32 33 34 35 37 38 39 40 41 42 43 44 46 48 49 51 52 53 58 59 60 64 65 70 71 73 74 **P**5 7 8 **S** TENET Healthcare Corporation, Santa Barbara, CA	33	10	506	17704	512	164975	2056	113516	50488	1574
⊞ △ ST. JOSEPH HOSPITAL AND HEALTH CENTERS, 220 Overton Avenue, Zip 38105–2789; tel. 901/577–2700; Joan M. Carlson, Administrator (Total facility includes 30 beds in nursing home–type unit) **A**1 3 6 7 9 10 **F**1 3 4 7 8 10 11 12 15 16 17 18 19 20 21 22 23 24 25 26 27 28 29 30 32 33 34 35 37 38 39 40 41 42 43 44 45 46 48 49 51 52 53 54 55 56 57 58 59 60 63 64 65 66 67 69 70 71 72 73 74 **P**2 8 **S** Baptist Memorial Health Care Corporation, Memphis, TN	21	10	295	8120	181	29587	—	61803	26470	1007
⊞ ST. JUDE CHILDREN'S RESEARCH HOSPITAL, (PEDIATRIC CATASTROPHIC DISEASE), 332 North Lauderdale Street, Zip 38105–2794; tel. 901/495–3300; Arthur W. Nienhuis, M.D., Director **A**1 2 3 5 9 10 **F**16 19 20 21 31 34 35 39 42 44 45 46 47 49 54 56 60 63 65 67 69 71 73 **P**6	23	59	54	2101	44	42744	—	155780	88569	1635
□ UNIVERSITY BEHAVIORAL HEALTH CENTER, 135 North Pauline Street, Zip 38105; tel. 901/448–2400; Stephen Wilensky, Executive Director **A**1 9 10 **F**3 52 53 54 55 56 57 58 59 **P**1	23	22	64	869	22	3002	—	5803	1858	98
□ UNIVERSITY OF TENNESSEE BOWLD HOSPITAL, 951 Court Avenue, Zip 38103–2898; tel. 901/448–4000; Jeffrey R. Woodside, M.D., Executive Director **A**1 2 3 5 9 10 **F**4 10 11 19 20 21 22 26 31 34 35 37 39 42 43 44 45 46 60 61 65 69 71 73	12	10	103	3710	68	25127	—	48427	17178	462
⊞ VETERANS AFFAIRS MEDICAL CENTER, 1030 Jefferson Avenue, Zip 38104–2193; tel. 901/523–8990; K. L. Mulholland, Jr., Director **A**1 2 3 5 8 **F**3 4 5 6 7 8 10 11 12 14 15 16 17 18 19 20 21 22 23 24 25 26 27 28 29 30 31 32 33 34 35 37 39 41 42 43 44 45 46 49 51 52 54 55 56 57 58 59 60 61 62 63 64 65 67 69 70 71 72 73 74 **P**6 **S** Department of Veterans Affairs, Washington, DC	45	10	376	8547	276	252836	—	142253	76770	1857
MILAN—Gibson County										
⊞ MILAN GENERAL HOSPITAL, (Formerly City of Milan Hospital), 4039 South Highland, Zip 38358; tel. 901/686–1591; Alfred P. Taylor, Administrator and Chief Executive Officer (Total facility includes 13 beds in nursing home–type unit) **A**1 9 10 **F**15 16 19 21 22 37 44 52 57 64 65 71 72 **S** West Tennessee Healthcare., Jackson, TN **N** West Tennessee Healthcare, Inc., Jackson, TN	14	10	62	1026	27	13849	—	7841	2878	116
MORRISTOWN—Hamblen County										
⊞ LAKEWAY REGIONAL HOSPITAL, 726 McFarland Street, Zip 37814–3990; tel. 423/586–2302; Robert B. Wampler, CPA, Chief Executive Officer **A**1 9 10 **F**7 8 11 12 15 19 21 22 23 28 30 34 35 37 39 40 42 44 46 48 49 64 65 66 71 73 74 **P**8 **S** Community Health Systems, Inc., Brentwood, TN **N** Mountain States Healthcare Network, Johnson City, TN	33	10	135	3153	48	29253	556	19660	5628	232
□ △ MORRISTOWN–HAMBLEN HOSPITAL, 908 West Fourth North Street, Zip 37816; tel. 423/586–4231; Richard L. Clark, Administrator and Chief Executive Officer (Nonreporting) **A**1 7 9 10 **N** Mountain States Healthcare Network, Johnson City, TN	23	10	143	—	—	—	—	—	—	—
MOUNTAIN HOME—Washington County										
⊞ JAMES H. QUILLEN VETERANS AFFAIRS MEDICAL CENTER, Zip 37684–4000; tel. 423/926–1171; Carl J. Gerber, M.D., Ph.D., Director (Total facility includes 120 beds in nursing home–type unit) **A**1 2 3 5 8 **F**1 3 4 5 6 8 10 11 12 14 16 17 18 19 20 21 22 24 25 26 27 28 29 30 31 32 33 34 35 36 37 39 41 42 43 44 45 46 49 51 52 54 55 56 57 58 59 60 62 64 65 67 69 71 73 74 **P**6 **S** Department of Veterans Affairs, Washington, DC	45	10	388	4797	262	213225	—	97101	56884	1361

Hospital, Address, Telephone, Administrator, Approval, Facility, and Physician Codes, Health Care System, Network	Classi-fication Codes		Utilization Data					Expense (thousands) of dollars		
★ American Hospital Association (AHA) membership □ Joint Commission on Accreditation of Healthcare Organizations (JCAHO) accreditation + American Osteopathic Healthcare Association (AOHA) membership ○ American Osteopathic Association (AOA) accreditation △ Commission on Accreditation of Rehabilitation Facilities (CARF) accreditation Control codes 61, 63, 64, 71, 72 and 73 indicate hospitals listed by AOHA, but not registered by AHA. For definition of numerical codes, see page A4	Control	Service	Staffed Beds	Admissions	Census	Outpatient Visits	Births	Total	Payroll	Personnel

MURFREESBORO—Rutherford County

✠ ALVIN C. YORK VETERANS AFFAIRS MEDICAL CENTER, 3400 Lebanon Pike, Zip 37129–1236; tel. 615/893–1360; R. Eugene Konik, Director (Total facility includes 150 beds in nursing home–type unit) **A**1 3 5 **F**1 2 3 4 8 10 12 15 16 17 19 20 21 22 25 26 28 30 32 33 34 35 37 41 42 43 44 46 49 50 51 52 54 55 56 57 58 63 64 65 67 71 73 74 **P**6 **S** Department of Veterans Affairs, Washington, DC	45	10	503	3623	412	152873	—	88417	49557	1145
✠ MIDDLE TENNESSEE MEDICAL CENTER, 400 North Highland Avenue, Zip 37130–3854, Mailing Address: P.O. Box 1178, Zip 37133–1178; tel. 615/849–4100; Arthur W. Hastings, President and Chief Executive Officer **A**1 9 10 **F**7 8 10 11 14 15 16 19 21 22 23 24 26 31 32 33 35 37 39 40 42 44 45 49 59 60 65 66 71 73 74 **P**5 **N** Middle Tennessee Healthcare Network, Nashville, TN	21	10	191	9815	108	80595	1710	66712	26802	850

NASHVILLE—Davidson County

✠ BAPTIST HOSPITAL, 2000 Church Street, Zip 37236–0002; tel. 615/329–5555; C. David Stringfield, President and Chief Executive Officer **A**1 2 3 5 9 10 **F**4 5 7 8 10 11 12 14 16 17 19 21 22 23 24 25 26 28 30 31 32 34 35 37 38 39 40 41 42 43 44 45 46 48 49 50 60 61 64 65 66 67 69 71 72 73 74 **P**5 7 **N** Center Care, Bowling Green, KY; Middle Tennessee Healthcare Network, Nashville, TN	23	10	545	28247	377	314529	4995	256363	97922	2925
COLUMBIA CENTENNIAL MEDICAL CENTER See Centennial Medical Center										
✠ △ CENTENNIAL MEDICAL CENTER AND PARTHENON PAVILION, (Formerly Columbia Centennial Medical Center), 2300 Patterson Street, Zip 37203–1528; tel. 615/342–1000; Larry Kloess, President (Total facility includes 24 beds in nursing home–type unit) (Nonreporting) **A**1 2 5 7 9 10 **S** Columbia/HCA Healthcare Corporation, Nashville, TN **N** Columbia Healthcare Network, Brentwood, TN	33	10	680	—	—	—	—	—	—	—
✠ COLUMBIA SOUTHERN HILLS MEDICAL CENTER, 391 Wallace Road, Zip 37211–4859; tel. 615/781–4000; Jeffrey Whitehorn, Chief Executive Officer (Total facility includes 20 beds in nursing home–type unit) **A**1 9 10 **F**1 2 3 4 5 7 8 10 11 12 13 14 15 16 17 18 19 20 21 22 23 24 25 26 28 29 30 31 32 33 34 35 37 38 39 40 41 42 43 44 45 48 49 50 51 52 53 54 55 56 57 58 59 63 64 65 66 70 71 73 74 **P**1 6 7 8 **S** Columbia/HCA Healthcare Corporation, Nashville, TN **N** Columbia Healthcare Network, Brentwood, TN	33	10	140	6405	75	57638	840	43618	18876	525
✠ METROPOLITAN NASHVILLE GENERAL HOSPITAL, 1818 Albion Street, Zip 37208; tel. 615/341–4490; John M. Stone, Director **A**1 2 3 5 6 9 10 **F**7 8 10 11 13 14 15 16 17 19 20 21 22 23 27 30 31 32 33 34 35 37 38 39 40 42 44 46 49 51 53 54 55 56 57 58 59 60 61 64 65 71 73	15	10	105	5218	76	106579	606	42796	23210	727
□ MIDDLE TENNESSEE MENTAL HEALTH INSTITUTE, 221 Stewarts Ferry Pike, Zip 37214–3325; tel. 615/902–7535; Joseph W. Carobene, Superintendent (Total facility includes 40 beds in nursing home–type unit) **A**1 3 10 **F**14 15 16 20 21 39 41 45 46 52 53 54 55 56 57 65 73	12	22	283	1645	199	—	—	28327	17320	680
★ NASHVILLE METROPOLITAN BORDEAUX HOSPITAL, 1414 County Hospital Road, Zip 37218–3001; tel. 615/862–7000; Wayne Hayes, Administrator (Total facility includes 525 beds in nursing home–type unit) **A**10 **F**15 20 26 27 28 41 46 64 65 67 73 **P**1	23	48	565	602	480	—	—	33810	17070	646
□ △ NASHVILLE REHABILITATION HOSPITAL, 610 Gallatin Road, Zip 37206–3225; tel. 615/226–4330; Jane Andrews, Administrator and Chief Executive Officer **A**1 7 9 10 **F**14 15 16 27 48 49 65 73	33	46	28	513	26	4456	—	8212	4441	145
✠ PSYCHIATRIC HOSPITAL AT VANDERBILT, 1601 23rd Avenue South, Zip 37212–3198; tel. 615/320–7770; Richard A. Bangert, Chief Executive Officer and Administrator **A**1 3 10 **F**3 15 16 17 19 21 22 35 50 52 53 54 55 56 57 58 59 62 70 71 **S** Columbia/HCA Healthcare Corporation, Nashville, TN **N** Columbia Healthcare Network, Brentwood, TN	32	22	88	2662	48	6533	0	9617	4735	167
✠ ST. THOMAS HOSPITAL, 4220 Harding Road, Zip 37205–2095, Mailing Address: P.O. Box 380, Zip 37202–0380; tel. 615/222–2111; John F. Tighe, President and Chief Executive Officer (Total facility includes 30 beds in nursing home–type unit) **A**1 2 3 5 9 10 **F**4 7 8 10 12 14 15 16 17 19 21 22 23 24 25 27 28 30 31 32 34 35 37 39 40 41 42 43 44 45 46 49 51 52 54 57 58 59 60 63 65 66 67 69 70 71 72 73 74 **P**1 3 5 6 7 **S** Daughters of Charity National Health System, Saint Louis, MO **N** Center Care, Bowling Green, KY; Middle Tennessee Healthcare Network, Nashville, TN; Saint Thomas Health Services, Nashville, TN	21	10	516	27273	422	136272	819	257047	106668	4257
✠ VANDERBILT UNIVERSITY HOSPITAL, 1161 21st Avenue South, Zip 37232–2102; tel. 615/322–5000; Norman B. Urmy, Executive Director (Total facility includes 23 beds in nursing home–type unit) **A**1 2 3 5 8 9 10 **F**1 4 5 7 8 9 10 11 12 17 18 19 21 22 23 24 26 29 30 31 32 33 34 35 37 38 39 40 41 42 43 44 45 46 47 49 50 51 52 53 54 55 56 57 58 59 60 61 63 64 65 66 67 69 70 71 72 73 74 **N** Middle Tennessee Healthcare Network, Nashville, TN; Saint Thomas Health Services, Nashville, TN	23	10	581	27243	410	518565	1253	370529	139803	4764
✠ VETERANS AFFAIRS MEDICAL CENTER, 1310 24th Avenue South, Zip 37212–2637; tel. 615/327–5332; William A. Mountcastle, Director **A**1 2 3 5 8 **F**1 2 3 4 8 10 11 12 14 15 16 17 18 19 20 21 22 25 26 28 29 30 31 32 33 34 35 37 39 41 42 43 44 45 46 48 49 50 51 52 56 57 58 59 60 62 63 64 65 67 69 71 73 74 **P**6 **S** Department of Veterans Affairs, Washington, DC	45	10	189	6011	141	188921	—	—	—	1592

NEWPORT—Cocke County

□ BAPTIST HOSPITAL OF COCKE COUNTY, 435 Second Street, Zip 37821–3799; tel. 423/625–2200; Wayne Buckner, Administrator (Total facility includes 56 beds in nursing home–type unit) **A**1 9 10 **F**7 8 11 15 16 19 20 21 22 26 28 29 30 34 35 39 40 41 44 45 46 49 61 64 65 71 73 **P**1 **S** Baptist Health System of Tennessee, Knoxville, TN	21	10	109	2567	79	35593	327	19107	7375	323

Hospital, Address, Telephone, Administrator, Approval, Facility, and Physician Codes, Health Care System, Network	Classi-fication Codes		Utilization Data					Expense (thousands) of dollars		
	Control	Service	Staffed Beds	Admissions	Census	Outpatient Visits	Births	Total	Payroll	Personnel

★ American Hospital Association (AHA) membership
□ Joint Commission on Accreditation of Healthcare Organizations (JCAHO) accreditation
+ American Osteopathic Healthcare Association (AOHA) membership
○ American Osteopathic Association (AOA) accreditation
△ Commission on Accreditation of Rehabilitation Facilities (CARF) accreditation
Control codes 61, 63, 64, 71, 72 and 73 indicate hospitals listed by AOHA, but not registered by AHA. For definition of numerical codes, see page A4

OAK RIDGE—Anderson County

□ METHODIST MEDICAL CENTER OF OAK RIDGE, 990 Oak Ridge Turnpike, Zip 37830–6976, Mailing Address: P.O. Box 2529, Zip 37831–2529; tel. 423/481–1000; George A. Mathews, President and Chief Executive Officer **A**1 2 9 10 **F**3 4 7 8 10 11 12 14 15 16 17 19 21 22 27 28 30 32 33 34 35 37 39 40 41 42 43 44 45 46 49 51 52 54 55 56 57 58 59 60 61 63 65 66 67 71 73 74 **P**7 **S** Covenant Health, Nashville, TN
| | 23 | 10 | 250 | 12675 | 181 | 170244 | 1044 | 98502 | 45128 | 1119 |

RIDGEVIEW PSYCHIATRIC HOSPITAL AND CENTER, 240 West Tyrone Road, Zip 37830–6571; tel. 423/482–1076; Robert J. Benning, Chief Executive Officer **A**10 **F**3 12 52 53 54 55 56 57 58 59 65 **P**6
| | 23 | 22 | 20 | 556 | 7 | 58263 | — | 6566 | 4090 | 159 |

ONEIDA—Scott County

✦ SCOTT COUNTY HOSPITAL, 18797 Alberta Avenue, Zip 37841–4939, Mailing Address: P.O. Box 4939, Zip 37841–4939; tel. 423/569–8521; Peter T. Petruzzi, Chief Executive Officer **A**1 9 10 **F**3 7 8 11 12 14 15 16 19 22 28 40 41 44 46 49 52 58 65 71 73 **S** Community Health Systems, Inc., Brentwood, TN
| | 33 | 10 | 91 | 2836 | 27 | 19238 | 106 | 9828 | 4556 | — |

PARIS—Henry County

✦ HENRY COUNTY MEDICAL CENTER, 301 Tyson Avenue, Zip 38242–4544, Mailing Address: Box 1030, Zip 38242–1030; tel. 901/644–8537; Thomas H. Gee, Administrator (Total facility includes 174 beds in nursing home–type unit) **A**1 9 10 **F**7 8 11 19 20 21 22 23 24 26 27 28 30 32 33 34 35 37 39 40 41 42 44 46 49 52 53 54 55 56 57 59 60 63 64 65 66 67 69 71 73 **P**5 **N** West Tennessee Healthcare, Inc., Jackson, TN
| | 16 | 10 | 271 | 4507 | 225 | 55827 | 326 | 28401 | 13593 | 567 |

PARSONS—Decatur County

DECATUR COUNTY GENERAL HOSPITAL, 969 Tennessee Avenue South, Zip 38363–0250, Mailing Address: Box 250, Zip 38363–0250; tel. 901/847–3031; Larry N. Lindsey, Administrator and Chief Executive Officer **A**9 10 **F**8 12 15 16 19 21 22 27 28 30 32 37 44 46 49 71 72 **N** West Tennessee Healthcare, Inc., Jackson, TN
| | 13 | 10 | 40 | 1303 | 20 | 4815 | 0 | 7467 | 3505 | 126 |

PIKEVILLE—Bledsoe County

□ BLEDSOE COUNTY GENERAL HOSPITAL, 128 Wheelertown Road, Zip 37367, Mailing Address: P.O. Box 699, Zip 37367–0699; tel. 423/447–2112; Gary Burton, Chief Executive Officer (Nonreporting) **A**1 9 10 **S** Paracelsus Healthcare Corporation, Houston, TX
| | 33 | 10 | 26 | — | — | — | — | — | — | — |

PORTLAND—Sumner County

TENNESSEE CHRISTIAN MEDICAL CENTER – PORTLAND See Tennessee Christian Medical Center, Madison

PULASKI—Giles County

✦ COLUMBIA HILLSIDE HOSPITAL, 1265 East College Street, Zip 38478–4541; tel. 931/363–7531; James H. Edmondson, Chief Executive Officer and Administrator **A**1 9 10 **F**12 15 16 19 21 22 28 35 39 40 41 44 52 57 65 71 **S** Columbia/HCA Healthcare Corporation, Nashville, TN
| | 16 | 10 | 80 | 2080 | 24 | 23209 | 178 | 10353 | 4749 | — |

RIPLEY—Lauderdale County

✦ BAPTIST MEMORIAL HOSPITAL–LAUDERDALE, 326 Asbury Road, Zip 38063–9701; tel. 901/635–1331; George S. Fray, Administrator **A**1 9 10 **F**2 3 8 15 16 19 22 26 28 30 32 33 34 37 39 44 45 46 49 52 54 55 56 57 65 71 73 74 **P**3 7 **S** Baptist Memorial Health Care Corporation, Memphis, TN
| | 21 | 10 | 70 | 1066 | 15 | 17811 | — | 7869 | 2976 | 151 |

ROGERSVILLE—Hawkins County

✦ HAWKINS COUNTY MEMORIAL HOSPITAL, 851 Locust Street, Zip 37857; tel. 423/272–2671; R. Frank Testerman, Administrator (Nonreporting) **A**1 9 10
| | 13 | 10 | 50 | — | — | — | — | — | — | — |

SAVANNAH—Hardin County

HARDIN COUNTY GENERAL HOSPITAL, 2006 Wayne Road, Zip 38372–2294; tel. 901/925–4954; Charlotte Burns, Administrator and Chief Executive Officer (Total facility includes 73 beds in nursing home–type unit) **A**9 10 **F**7 8 14 15 16 19 21 22 28 30 32 34 39 40 42 44 46 49 51 63 64 65 71 73 **P**8 **N** West Tennessee Healthcare, Inc., Jackson, TN
| | 13 | 10 | 123 | 1554 | 87 | 32210 | 195 | 9349 | 3797 | 241 |

SELMER—McNairy County

✦ MCNAIRY COUNTY GENERAL HOSPITAL, 705 East Poplar Avenue, Zip 38375–1748; tel. 901/645–3221; Rosamond M. Tyler, Administrator **A**1 9 10 **F**7 8 17 19 21 22 27 28 29 30 32 40 44 45 46 49 54 65 71 73 **N** West Tennessee Healthcare, Inc., Jackson, TN
| | 13 | 10 | 47 | 1287 | 13 | 20395 | 181 | — | 3131 | 145 |

SEVIERVILLE—Sevier County

✦ FORT SANDERS–SEVIER MEDICAL CENTER, 709 Middle Creek Road, Zip 37862–5016, Mailing Address: P.O. Box 8005, Zip 37864–8005; tel. 423/429–6100; Ralph T. Williams, Administrator (Total facility includes 54 beds in nursing home–type unit) **A**1 9 10 **F**7 8 10 12 15 19 20 21 22 28 30 32 33 34 35 37 40 41 44 45 49 63 64 67 71 73 **P**7 **S** Covenant Health, Nashville, TN **N** CHA Provider Network, Inc., Lexington, KY
| | 23 | 10 | 100 | 2253 | 77 | 62473 | 519 | 18558 | 7744 | 318 |

SEWANEE—Franklin County

EMERALD–HODGSON HOSPITAL See Southern Tennessee Medical Center, Winchester

SHELBYVILLE—Bedford County

□ BEDFORD COUNTY GENERAL HOSPITAL, 845 Union Street, Zip 37160–9971; tel. 931/685–5433; Richard L. Graham, Administrator (Total facility includes 107 beds in nursing home–type unit) **A**1 9 10 **F**7 8 12 13 14 15 16 19 22 28 29 30 31 32 34 35 39 40 41 42 44 46 49 64 65 68 69 71 73 **P**4 **N** Center Care, Bowling Green, KY; Middle Tennessee Healthcare Network, Nashville, TN
| | 13 | 10 | 180 | 2604 | 131 | 105679 | 310 | 18890 | 8032 | 375 |

Hospital, Address, Telephone, Administrator, Approval, Facility, and Physician Codes, Health Care System, Network	Classi-fication Codes		Utilization Data					Expense (thousands) of dollars		
★ American Hospital Association (AHA) membership □ Joint Commission on Accreditation of Healthcare Organizations (JCAHO) accreditation + American Osteopathic Healthcare Association (AOHA) membership ○ American Osteopathic Association (AOA) accreditation △ Commission on Accreditation of Rehabilitation Facilities (CARF) accreditation Control codes 61, 63, 64, 71, 72 and 73 indicate hospitals listed by AOHA, but not registered by AHA. For definition of numerical codes, see page A4	Control	Service	Staffed Beds	Admissions	Census	Outpatient Visits	Births	Total	Payroll	Personnel

SMITHVILLE—DeKalb County

☒ BAPTIST DEKALB HOSPITAL, 520 West Main Street, Zip 37166–0840, Mailing Address: P.O. Box 640, Zip 37166–0640; tel. 615/597–7171; Alan Markowitz, Ph.D., FACHE, Administrator and Chief Executive Officer **A**1 9 10 **F**7 8 10 12 15 16 19 21 22 26 28 29 30 35 37 40 42 44 46 49 51 59 61 65 66 67 71 **P**5 — 32 10 58 2064 20 12954 121 9280 4065 —

SOMERVILLE—Fayette County

★ METHODIST HEALTHCARE – FAYETTE HOSPITAL, (Formerly Methodist Hospital of Fayette), 214 Lakeview Drive, Zip 38068; tel. 901/465–0532; Michael Blome', Administrator **A**9 10 **F**2 3 4 5 6 7 8 9 10 11 12 13 14 15 16 17 19 21 22 23 24 25 26 27 28 29 30 31 32 33 34 35 37 38 39 40 41 42 43 44 45 46 47 48 49 51 52 53 54 55 56 57 58 59 60 63 64 65 67 69 71 72 73 **P**1 2 3 4 5 6 7 8 **S** Methodist Health Systems, Inc., Memphis, TN **N** Methodist Health Systems, Inc., Memphis, TN — 21 10 38 886 8 — 28 6987 2824 102

SOUTH PITTSBURG—Marion County

☒ COLUMBIA SOUTH PITTSBURG HOSPITAL, 210 West 12th Street, Zip 37380, Mailing Address: P.O. Box 349, Zip 37380–0349; tel. 423/837–6781; Phil Rowland, Chief Executive Officer (Nonreporting) **A**1 9 10 **S** Columbia/HCA Healthcare Corporation, Nashville, TN **N** Principal Health Care of Georgia, Atlanta, GA; Chattanooga Healthcare Network, Chattanooga, TN — 33 10 47 — — — — — — —

SPARTA—White County

☒ WHITE COUNTY COMMUNITY HOSPITAL, 401 Sewell Road, Zip 38583–1299; tel. 931/738–9211; Barry Keel, Chief Executive Officer **A**1 9 10 **F**8 11 12 15 16 19 22 26 28 37 39 40 44 46 48 49 52 57 65 66 73 **S** Community Health Systems, Inc., Brentwood, TN — 33 10 18 1349 15 17650 102 8168 3650 134

SPRINGFIELD—Robertson County

☒ NORTH CREST MEDICAL CENTER, 100 North Crest Drive, Zip 37172–2984; tel. 615/384–2411; William A. Kenley, President and Chief Executive Officer **A**1 9 10 **F**7 8 10 11 14 15 16 17 19 21 22 28 30 32 33 35 37 40 42 44 46 48 49 52 53 54 56 57 58 65 66 67 71 73 74 **N** Columbia Healthcare Network, Brentwood, TN — 23 10 60 3835 47 45750 517 31776 11247 410

SWEETWATER—Monroe County

☒ SWEETWATER HOSPITAL, 304 Wright Street, Zip 37874–2897; tel. 423/337–6171; Scott Bowman, Administrator **A**1 9 10 **F**7 15 19 22 32 40 44 49 65 73 — 23 10 59 2545 30 62942 206 15542 6282 —

TAZEWELL—Claiborne County

☒ CLAIBORNE COUNTY HOSPITAL, 1850 Old Knoxville Road, Zip 37879–3625, Mailing Address: P.O. Box 219, Zip 37879–0219; tel. 423/626–4211; Michael T. Hutchins, Administrator (Total facility includes 50 beds in nursing home–type unit) **A**1 9 10 **F**12 15 16 17 19 22 27 30 32 33 34 35 37 39 41 44 45 46 49 64 71 **N** CHA Provider Network, Inc., Lexington, KY — 13 10 110 3006 83 35055 3 13396 6594 323

TRENTON—Gibson County

☒ GIBSON GENERAL HOSPITAL, 200 Hospital Drive, Zip 38382–3300; tel. 901/855–7900; Kelly R. Yenawine, Administrator **A**1 9 10 **F**2 8 14 15 16 19 21 22 28 30 32 33 34 44 49 65 71 73 **P**1 **S** West Tennessee Healthcare., Jackson, TN **N** West Tennessee Healthcare, Inc., Jackson, TN — 15 10 42 818 9 16611 — 4111 2054 87

TULLAHOMA—Coffee County

☒ HARTON REGIONAL MEDICAL CENTER, 1801 North Jackson Street, Zip 37388–2201, Mailing Address: P.O. Box 460, Zip 37388–0460; tel. 931/393–3000; David C. Wilson, Chief Executive Officer (Nonreporting) **A**1 9 10 **S** TENET Healthcare Corporation, Santa Barbara, CA **N** Center Care, Bowling Green, KY — 33 10 137 — — — — — — —

UNION CITY—Obion County

☒ BAPTIST MEMORIAL HOSPITAL–UNION CITY, 1201 Bishop Street, Zip 38261–5403, Mailing Address: P.O. Box 310, Zip 38281–0310; tel. 901/884–8601; Mike Perryman, Administrator **A**1 9 10 **F**2 3 7 8 10 11 12 14 15 16 17 19 21 22 25 32 35 37 39 40 41 42 44 46 49 52 53 56 58 60 63 65 67 71 73 **S** Baptist Memorial Health Care Corporation, Memphis, TN — 23 10 133 4918 63 — 336 23298 8788 416

WAVERLY—Humphreys County

BAPTIST THREE RIVERS HOSPITAL, 451 Highway 13 South, Zip 37185–2149, Mailing Address: P.O. Box 437, Zip 37185–2149; tel. 931/296–4203; Donald W. James, DPH, Administrator (Total facility includes 10 beds in nursing home–type unit) **A**9 10 **F**8 14 15 16 19 22 28 30 44 46 51 64 65 71 73 — 32 10 52 710 9 22901 0 5767 2276 81

WAYNESBORO—Wayne County

□ WAYNE MEDICAL CENTER, 103 J. V. Mangubat Drive, Zip 38485, Mailing Address: P.O. Box 580, Zip 38485–0580; tel. 931/722–5411; Shirley Harder, Chief Executive Officer **A**1 9 10 **F**7 8 15 19 22 33 44 49 65 71 — 23 10 32 1309 13 14649 50 5507 2212 117

WESTERN INSTITUTE—Hardeman County

□ WESTERN MENTAL HEALTH INSTITUTE, Highway 64 West, Zip 38074; tel. 901/658–5141; Elizabeth Littlefield, Ed.D., Superintendent **A**1 10 **F**52 53 56 57 — 12 22 247 1006 248 — — 21603 14345 —

WINCHESTER—Franklin County

☒ SOUTHERN TENNESSEE MEDICAL CENTER, (Formerly Columbia Southern Tennessee Medical Center), (Includes Emerald–Hodgson Hospital, University Avenue, Sewanee, Zip 37375; tel. 615/598–5691), 185 Hospital Road, Zip 37398–2468; tel. 931/967–8200; Michael W. Garfield, Administrator (Total facility includes 66 beds in nursing home–type unit) (Nonreporting) **A**1 9 10 **S** Columbia/HCA Healthcare Corporation, Nashville, TN **N** Center Care, Bowling Green, KY — 33 10 128 — — — — — — —

Hospital, Address, Telephone, Administrator, Approval, Facility, and Physician Codes, Health Care System, Network	Classi-fication Codes		Utilization Data					Expense (thousands) of dollars		
★ American Hospital Association (AHA) membership □ Joint Commission on Accreditation of Healthcare Organizations (JCAHO) accreditation + American Osteopathic Healthcare Association (AOHA) membership ○ American Osteopathic Association (AOA) accreditation △ Commission on Accreditation of Rehabilitation Facilities (CARF) accreditation Control codes 61, 63, 64, 71, 72 and 73 indicate hospitals listed by AOHA, but not registered by AHA. For definition of numerical codes, see page A4	Control	Service	Staffed Beds	Admissions	Census	Outpatient Visits	Births	Total	Payroll	Personnel

WOODBURY—Cannon County

☒ COLUMBIA STONES RIVER HOSPITAL, 324 Doolittle Road, Zip 37190–1139; tel. 615/563–4001; Bill Patterson, Interim Administrator **A**1 9 10 **F**8 12 14 15 19 21 22 26 28 29 30 32 35 39 41 42 44 46 49 51 52 57 63 65 71 73 **S** Columbia/HCA Healthcare Corporation, Nashville, TN **N** Columbia Healthcare Network, Brentwood, TN

33	10	55	1386	17	11683	0	7040	3234	105

TEXAS

Resident population 19,439 (in thousands)
Resident population in metro areas 84.1%
Birth rate per 1,000 population 17.5
65 years and over 10.2%
Percent of persons without health insurance 24.3%

Hospital, Address, Telephone, Administrator, Approval, Facility, and Physician Codes, Health Care System, Network	Classi-fication Codes		Utilization Data					Expense (thousands) of dollars		
★ American Hospital Association (AHA) membership □ Joint Commission on Accreditation of Healthcare Organizations (JCAHO) accreditation + American Osteopathic Healthcare Association (AOHA) membership ○ American Osteopathic Association (AOA) accreditation △ Commission on Accreditation of Rehabilitation Facilities (CARF) accreditation Control codes 61, 63, 64, 71, 72 and 73 indicate hospitals listed by AOHA, but not registered by AHA. For definition of numerical codes, see page A4	Control	Service	Staffed Beds	Admissions	Census	Outpatient Visits	Births	Total	Payroll	Personnel

ABILENE—Taylor County

✠ ABILENE REGIONAL MEDICAL CENTER, 6250 Highway 83–84 at Antilley Road, Zip 79606–5299; tel. 915/695–9900; Woody Gilliland, Chief Executive Officer (Total facility includes 20 beds in nursing home–type unit) **A**1 9 10 **F**4 7 8 10 11 12 14 15 16 17 19 21 22 24 25 26 28 29 30 32 34 35 37 38 39 40 42 43 44 45 46 49 51 61 63 64 65 67 71 73 74 **P**3 7 **S** Quorum Health Group/Quorum Health Resources, Inc., Brentwood, TN	33	10	160	6504	93	30246	963	54167	21347	731
✠ △ HENDRICK HEALTH SYSTEM, 1242 North 19th Street, Zip 79601–2316; tel. 915/670–2000; Michael C. Waters, FACHE, President (Total facility includes 49 beds in nursing home–type unit) **A**1 7 9 10 **F**4 5 6 7 8 10 11 12 15 16 17 19 20 21 22 23 24 25 26 27 28 29 30 31 32 33 34 35 37 39 40 41 42 43 44 45 46 47 48 49 51 56 60 62 63 64 65 66 67 70 71 73 74 **P**6 8 **N** The Heart Network of Texas, Irving, TX	21	10	376	13661	232	128090	1327	131441	57347	2411
✠ U. S. AIR FORCE HOSPITAL, 7th Medical Group, Dyess AFB, Zip 79607–1367; tel. 915/696–5429; Major Robin M. King, Administrator (Nonreporting) **A**1 **S** Department of the Air Force, Bowling AFB, DC	41	10	20	—	—	—	—	—	—	—

ALICE—Jim Wells County

✠ COLUMBIA ALICE PHYSICIANS AND SURGEONS HOSPITAL, 300 East Third Street, Zip 78332–4794; tel. 512/664–4376; Abraham Martinez, Chief Executive Officer (Nonreporting) **A**1 9 10 **S** Columbia/HCA Healthcare Corporation, Nashville, TN **N** Columbia Healthcare – South Texas Division, Corpus Christi, TX	33	10	123							

ALPINE—Brewster County

★ BIG BEND REGIONAL MEDICAL CENTER, 801 East Brown Street, Zip 79830–3209; tel. 915/837–3447; Don Edd Green, Chief Executive Officer **A**9 10 **F**1 3 7 8 12 13 14 15 16 17 18 19 25 26 27 28 30 31 32 34 36 39 40 44 45 46 49 51 53 54 55 56 57 58 61 62 64 65 67 68 69 70 71 73 **S** Community Health Systems, Inc., Brentwood, TN **N** Permian Basin Rural Health Network, Fort Stockton, TX	16	10	32	1609	11	51397	185	7854	4160	134

ALVIN—Brazoria County

★ COLUMBIA ALVIN MEDICAL CENTER, 301 Medic Lane, Zip 77511–5597; tel. 281/331–6141; Donald A. Shaffett, Chief Executive Officer (Total facility includes 14 beds in nursing home–type unit) (Nonreporting) **A**9 10 **S** Columbia/HCA Healthcare Corporation, Nashville, TN	33	10	86	—	—	—	—	—	—	—

AMARILLO—Potter County

✠ △ BAPTIST ST. ANTHONY HEALTH SYSTEM, 1600 Wallace Boulevard, Zip 79106–1799; tel. 806/358–5800; John D. Hicks, President and Chief Executive Officer (Total facility includes 86 beds in nursing home–type unit) **A**1 2 3 5 7 9 10 **F**4 7 8 10 11 12 14 15 16 17 19 20 21 22 23 26 27 28 30 32 33 34 35 36 37 39 40 41 42 43 44 45 46 48 49 51 63 65 66 69 71 72 73 74 **P**3 7	21	10	454	21887		123076	1404	—	63554	
✠ NORTHWEST TEXAS HEALTHCARE SYSTEM, (Includes Psychiatric Pavilion, 7201 Evans, Zip 79106), 1501 South Coulter Avenue, Zip 79106–1790, Mailing Address: P.O. Box 1110, Zip 79175–1110; tel. 806/354–1000; Michael A. Callahan, Chief Executive Officer **A**1 3 5 10 **F**3 4 7 8 10 12 13 14 15 16 17 18 19 20 21 22 24 25 26 29 30 31 32 34 35 37 38 39 40 41 42 43 44 45 46 47 49 51 52 53 54 55 56 57 58 59 63 64 65 66 67 71 73 74 **P**6 **S** Universal Health Services, Inc., King of Prussia, PA PSYCHIATRIC PAVILION See Northwest Texas Healthcare System	33	10	334	15216	212	227724	2781	148473	48850	1566
✠ VETERANS AFFAIRS MEDICAL CENTER, 6010 Amarillo Boulevard West, Zip 79106–1992; tel. 806/354–7801; Wallace M. Hopkins, FACHE, Director (Total facility includes 120 beds in nursing home–type unit) (Nonreporting) **A**1 2 3 5 **S** Department of Veterans Affairs, Washington, DC	45	10	218	—	—	—	—	—	—	—

ANAHUAC—Chambers County

BAYSIDE COMMUNITY HOSPITAL, 200 Hospital Drive, Zip 77514, Mailing Address: P.O. Box 398, Zip 77514–0398; tel. 409/267–3143; Stephen M. Goode, Executive Director **A**9 10 **F**22 28 32 36 43 **P**6	16	10	12	187	2	6407	0	—	—	54

ANDREWS—Andrews County

✠ PERMIAN GENERAL HOSPITAL, Northeast By–Pass, Zip 79714, Mailing Address: P.O. Box 2108, Zip 79714–2108; tel. 915/523–2200; Randy R. Richards, Chief Executive Officer **A**1 9 10 **F**7 8 12 14 15 16 17 18 19 20 21 22 24 28 30 32 34 35 38 39 40 41 44 45 49 51 65 67 70 71 73 **P**7 **N** Lubbock Methodist Hospital System, Lubbock, TX; Permian Basin Rural Health Network, Fort Stockton, TX	13	10	71	1472	14	15439	288	11725	5269	193

ANGLETON—Brazoria County

✠ ANGLETON–DANBURY GENERAL HOSPITAL, 132 East Hospital Drive, Zip 77515–4197; tel. 409/849–7721; David A. Bleakney, Administrator **A**1 9 10 **F**7 8 10 12 14 15 16 19 21 22 24 28 29 30 31 34 35 37 40 44 45 46 49 65 66 67 71 73 **P**8 **N** Memorial/Sisters of Charity Health Network, Houston, TX	16	10	24	2991	23	29249	467	18415	6017	236

ANSON—Jones County

★ ANSON GENERAL HOSPITAL, 101 Avenue J., Zip 79501–2198; tel. 915/823–3231; Dudley R. White, Administrator (Total facility includes 8 beds in nursing home–type unit) **A**9 10 **F**19 20 22 24 32 44 49 71 73 **P**3 8 **N** Lubbock Methodist Hospital System, Lubbock, TX	14	10	30	804	12	20701	1	4910	2570	133

Hospital, Address, Telephone, Administrator, Approval, Facility, and Physician Codes, Health Care System, Network	Classi-fication Codes		Utilization Data					Expense (thousands) of dollars		
★ American Hospital Association (AHA) membership □ Joint Commission on Accreditation of Healthcare Organizations (JCAHO) accreditation + American Osteopathic Healthcare Association (AOHA) membership ○ American Osteopathic Association (AOA) accreditation △ Commission on Accreditation of Rehabilitation Facilities (CARF) accreditation Control codes 61, 63, 64, 71, 72 and 73 indicate hospitals listed by AOHA, but not registered by AHA. For definition of numerical codes, see page A4	Control	Service	Staffed Beds	Admissions	Census	Outpatient Visits	Births	Total	Payroll	Personnel

ARANSAS PASS—San Patricio County

✠ COLUMBIA NORTH BAY HOSPITAL, 1711 West Wheeler Avenue, Zip 78336–4536; tel. 512/758–8585; Steve Sutherlin, Chief Executive Officer **A**1 9 10 **F**1 7 12 15 16 19 22 28 30 34 35 37 40 44 51 52 57 58 59 65 71 73 **P**7 8 **S** Columbia/HCA Healthcare Corporation, Nashville, TN **N** Columbia Healthcare – South Texas Division, Corpus Christi, TX	33	10	69	1947	24	15286	180	16269	7041	189

ARLINGTON—Tarrant County

✠ ARLINGTON MEMORIAL HOSPITAL, 800 West Randol Mill Road, Zip 76012–2503; tel. 817/548–6100; Wayne N. Clark, President and Chief Executive Officer **A**1 9 10 **F**4 7 8 10 11 12 14 15 16 17 19 21 22 23 24 33 34 35 37 38 39 40 41 42 43 44 45 49 60 65 71 73 74 **P**1 **S** Texas Health Resources, Irving, TX **N** Southwest Preferred Network, Dallas, TX	23	10	375	15564	189	97001	2731	101565	43486	1449
□ BHC MILLWOOD HOSPITAL, 1011 North Cooper Street, Zip 76011–5517; tel. 817/261–3121; Wayne Hallford, Chief Executive Officer **A**1 9 10 **F**3 12 22 25 27 34 46 52 53 54 56 58 59 65 67 **P**8 **S** Behavioral Healthcare Corporation, Nashville, TN	33	22	80	1266	28	3813	0	6026	3084	102
✠ COLUMBIA MEDICAL CENTER OF ARLINGTON, 3301 Matlock Road, Zip 76015–2998; tel. 817/465–3241; John A. Fromhold, Chief Executive Officer **A**1 9 10 **F**1 2 3 4 7 8 10 12 14 15 17 19 20 21 22 26 27 28 29 30 31 32 33 34 35 37 38 39 40 41 42 43 44 45 46 48 49 52 53 54 55 56 57 58 59 64 65 71 73 74 **P**5 7 **S** Columbia/HCA Healthcare Corporation, Nashville, TN	33	10	178	7706	101	60631	1900	70044	22426	737
□ △ HEALTHSOUTH REHABILITATION HOSPITAL OF ARLINGTON, 3200 Matlock Road, Zip 76015–2911; tel. 817/468–4000; S. Denise Borroni, Administrator and Chief Executive Officer **A**1 7 10 **F**8 10 12 19 22 24 25 26 32 35 41 44 48 49 62 65 66 73 **S** HEALTHSOUTH Corporation, Birmingham, AL	33	46	60	788	40	6511	0	10664	4175	137
□ VENCOR ARLINGTON, TEXAS, (Formerly THC – Arlington), 1000 North Cooper Street, Zip 76011–5540; tel. 817/543–0200; A. C. Buchanan, Administrator **A**1 10 **F**12 14 16 17 22 26 28 37 41 64 65 **S** Transitional Hospitals Corporation, Las Vegas, NV	33	10	75	506	40	789	0	14617	7049	159

ASPERMONT—Stonewall County

★ STONEWALL MEMORIAL HOSPITAL, U.S. Highway 380 & 83 North, Zip 79502, Mailing Address: Drawer C., Zip 79502; tel. 940/989–3551; Scott A. Anderson, Administrator (Total facility includes 2 beds in nursing home–type unit) **A**9 10 **F**12 15 16 22 28 32 33 34 41 58 64	16	10	16	155	2	4730	0	1705	825	47

ATHENS—Henderson County

✠ EAST TEXAS MEDICAL CENTER ATHENS, 2000 South Palestine Street, Zip 75751–5610; tel. 903/675–2216; Patrick L. Wallace, Administrator **A**1 9 10 **F**8 15 19 21 22 23 27 28 30 32 33 37 40 42 44 49 65 66 67 70 71 **P**7 **S** East Texas Medical Center Regional Healthcare System, Tyler, TX **N** Healthcare Partners of East Texas, Inc., Tyler, TX	23	10	108	5181	54	93285	782	33348	12553	367

ATLANTA—Cass County

★ ATLANTA MEMORIAL HOSPITAL, Highway 77 at South Williams, Zip 75551, Mailing Address: P.O. Box 1049, Zip 75551–1049; tel. 903/799–3000; Tom Crow, Administrator **A**9 10 **F**1 7 8 9 10 11 15 17 19 20 22 26 27 28 30 32 34 37 39 40 42 43 44 45 47 49 52 57 59 61 64 65 70 71 72 73 **P**8 **N** Regional Healthcare Alliance, Tyler, TX	16	10	50	2287	31	18273	166	9403	4456	233
BROOKS HOSPITAL, 230 North Louise Street, Zip 75551–2589, Mailing Address: P.O. Box 1069, Zip 75551–1069; tel. 903/796–2873; Jesse Brooks, M.D., Administrator **F**1 2 3 4 5 6 7 8 9 10 11 12 13 17 18 19 20 21 22 23 24 25 26 27 28 29 30 31 32 33 34 35 36 37 38 39 40 41 42 43 44 45 46 47 48 49 50 51 52 53 54 55 56 57 58 59 60 61 62 63 64 65 66 67 68 69 70 71 72 73 74 **P**1 2 3 4 5 6 7 8	33	10	22	355	5	163	0	1800	818	58

AUSTIN—Travis County

✠ AUSTIN DIAGNOSTIC MEDICAL CENTER, 12221 MoPac Expressway North, Zip 78758–2483; tel. 512/901–1000; Charles F. Sexton, Interim Chief Executive Officer (Total facility includes 18 beds in nursing home–type unit) **A**1 10 **F**1 2 3 4 7 8 10 11 12 14 15 16 17 18 19 21 22 23 24 25 27 28 29 30 31 32 34 35 37 38 39 40 41 42 43 44 45 46 48 49 52 53 54 55 57 58 59 60 61 63 64 65 66 67 68 69 71 72 73 74 **P**1 3 7 8 **S** Columbia/HCA Healthcare Corporation, Nashville, TN	32	10	141	7403	91	168141	746	57934	25840	843
□ AUSTIN STATE HOSPITAL, 4110 Guadalupe Street, Zip 78751–4296; tel. 512/452–0381; Diane Faucher, Superintendent **A**1 3 10 **F**11 20 37 39 40 52 53 55 56 57 65 73	12	22	328	1878	261	—	—	38013	20903	789
BHC SHOAL CREEK HOSPITAL See Seton Shoal Creek Hospital										
✠ BRACKENRIDGE HOSPITAL, (Includes CHILDREN'S HOSPITAL OF AUSTIN), 601 East 15th Street, Zip 78701–1996; tel. 512/476–6461; John C. Brindley, Chief Executive Officer **A**1 2 3 9 10 **F**4 7 8 9 10 11 12 13 15 16 17 18 19 21 23 25 26 27 28 29 30 31 32 34 35 37 39 40 41 42 43 44 46 47 49 51 53 54 56 60 61 63 64 65 66 67 69 70 71 72 73 74 **P**5 6 7 8 **S** Daughters of Charity National Health System, Saint Louis, MO	23	10	291	13937	177	148710	2781	126838	51320	1192
□ △ BROWN SCHOOLS REHABILITATION CENTER, (Formerly Healthcare Rehabilitation Center), 1106 West Dittmar, Zip 78745–9990, Mailing Address: P.O. Box 150459, Zip 78715–0459; tel. 512/444–4835; James G. Dalzell, Chief Executive Officer **A**1 7 10 **F**12 16 34 39 41 45 46 49 52 53 55 58 59 65 **S** Healthcare America, Inc., Austin, TX	33	46	96	117	72	4114	0	15352	9367	386
□ CHARTER BEHAVIORAL HEALTH SYSTEM OF AUSTIN, 8402 Cross Park Drive, Zip 78754–4588, Mailing Address: P.O. Box 140585, Zip 78714–0585; tel. 870/837–1800; Armin Steege, Chief Executive Officer **A**1 9 10 **F**3 12 14 15 16 19 21 25 35 46 52 54 55 56 58 59 65 67 71 **P**5 7 **S** Magellan Health Services, Atlanta, GA	32	22	40	900	17	4038	—	6078	2743	76

Hospital, Address, Telephone, Administrator, Approval, Facility, and Physician Codes, Health Care System, Network	Classi-fication Codes		Utilization Data					Expense (thousands) of dollars		
★ American Hospital Association (AHA) membership □ Joint Commission on Accreditation of Healthcare Organizations (JCAHO) accreditation + American Osteopathic Healthcare Association (AOHA) membership ○ American Osteopathic Association (AOA) accreditation △ Commission on Accreditation of Rehabilitation Facilities (CARF) accreditation Control codes 61, 63, 64, 71, 72 and 73 indicate hospitals listed by AOHA, but not registered by AHA. For definition of numerical codes, see page A4	Control	Service	Staffed Beds	Admissions	Census	Outpatient Visits	Births	Total	Payroll	Personnel
CHRISTOPHER HOUSE, 2820 East Martin Luther King, Zip 78702; tel. 512/370–8500; Carol Cody, Administrator (Nonreporting)	23	49	15	—	—	—	—	—	—	—
✖ COLUMBIA ST. DAVID'S SOUTH HOSPITAL, 901 West Ben White Boulevard, Zip 78704–6903; tel. 512/447–2211; Richard W. Klusmann, Chief Executive Officer **A**1 9 10 **F**4 7 8 10 12 15 19 21 22 23 28 33 34 35 42 43 44 49 60 65 67 71 73 74 **P**1 7 **S** Columbia/HCA Healthcare Corporation, Nashville, TN **N** Columbia Saint David's Health Network, Austin, TX	33	10	164	7785	103	199812	938	67367	26631	611
□ △ HEALTHSOUTH REHABILITATION HOSPITAL OF AUSTIN, 1215 Red River Street, Zip 78701, Mailing Address: P.O. Box 13366, Zip 78711–3366; tel. 512/474–5700; William O. Mitchell, Jr., Chief Executive Officer (Total facility includes 20 beds in nursing home–type unit) **A**1 7 9 10 **F**12 15 16 46 48 49 64 67 73 **S** HEALTHSOUTH Corporation, Birmingham, AL	33	46	80	1525	64	30182	—	—	7143	247
OAKS PSYCHIATRIC HEALTH SYSTEM, 1407 West Stassney Lane, Zip 78745–2998; tel. 512/464–0400; Mack Wigley, Chief Executive Officer (Nonreporting) **S** Healthcare America, Inc., Austin, TX	33	22	118							
✖ SETON MEDICAL CENTER, 1201 West 38th Street, Zip 78705–1056; tel. 512/324–1000; John C. Brindley, Chief Executive Officer **A**1 2 9 10 **F**4 7 8 10 11 12 13 15 16 17 19 21 22 23 25 26 27 28 29 30 31 32 33 34 35 36 37 38 39 40 41 42 43 44 46 47 49 51 53 54 56 60 61 63 64 65 66 67 69 70 71 72 73 74 **P**5 6 7 8 **S** Daughters of Charity National Health System, Saint Louis, MO	23	10	472	25745	336	317658	6212	204619	83950	2265
□ SETON SHOAL CREEK HOSPITAL, (Formerly BHC Shoal Creek Hospital), 3501 Mills Avenue, Zip 78731–6391; tel. 512/452–0361; Gail M. Oberta, Administrator and Chief Executive Officer **A**1 9 10 **F**3 15 16 19 21 26 27 34 35 52 53 57 58 59 **P**1 **S** Daughters of Charity National Health System, Saint Louis, MO	33	22	118	1785	37	9923	—	—	—	71
□ SPECIALTY HOSPITAL OF AUSTIN, 4207 Burnet Road, Zip 78756–3396; tel. 512/706–1900; William R. Cook, Chief Executive Officer (Nonreporting) **A**1 10	33	49	71							
✖ ST. DAVID'S MEDICAL CENTER, (Formerly Columbia St. David's Hospital), 919 East 32nd Street, Zip 78705–2709, Mailing Address: P.O. Box 4039, Zip 78765–4039; tel. 512/476–7111; Cole C. Eslyn, Chief Executive Officer **A**1 2 9 10 **F**1 2 3 4 7 8 10 12 14 15 16 17 18 19 21 22 23 24 25 27 28 29 30 31 32 34 35 36 37 38 39 40 41 42 43 44 45 46 48 49 52 53 54 55 56 57 58 59 60 61 63 64 65 66 67 68 69 71 72 73 74 **P**1 3 7 8 **S** Columbia/HCA Healthcare Corporation, Nashville, TN **N** Columbia Saint David's Health Network, Austin, TX	32	10	296	20554	201	70121	4363	120084	44899	1492
✖ ST. DAVID'S PAVILION, 1025 East 32nd Street, Zip 78765; tel. 512/867–5800; Cole C. Eslyn, Chief Executive Officer **A**1 9 10 **F**1 3 4 7 8 10 11 12 14 15 16 18 19 21 22 23 24 25 26 27 28 29 30 31 32 33 35 36 37 38 39 40 41 42 43 44 45 46 48 49 52 53 54 55 57 58 59 60 61 63 64 65 66 67 69 71 72 73 74 **P**1 3 7 8 **S** Columbia/HCA Healthcare Corporation, Nashville, TN **N** Columbia Saint David's Health Network, Austin, TX	32	22	38	1525	27	5716	0	8516	2774	81
✖ △ ST. DAVID'S REHABILITATION CENTER, 1005 East 32nd Street, Zip 78705–2705, Mailing Address: P.O. Box 4270, Zip 78765–4270; tel. 512/867–5100; Cole C. Eslyn, Chief Executive Officer (Total facility includes 37 beds in nursing home–type unit) **A**1 7 9 10 **F**1 3 4 7 8 10 11 12 14 15 16 18 19 21 22 23 24 25 26 27 28 29 30 31 32 34 35 36 37 38 39 40 41 42 43 44 45 46 48 49 53 54 55 57 58 59 60 61 63 64 65 66 67 69 71 72 73 74 **P**1 3 7 8 **S** Columbia/HCA Healthcare Corporation, Nashville, TN **N** Columbia Saint David's Health Network, Austin, TX	32	46	104	1858	75	29854	—	18562	9503	257
AZLE—Tarrant County										
✖ HARRIS METHODIST NORTHWEST, 108 Denver Trail, Zip 76020–3697; tel. 817/444–8600; Larry Thompson, Vice President and Administrator **A**1 9 10 **F**8 15 16 19 22 30 34 41 44 49 64 65 66 71 **S** Texas Health Resources, Irving, TX **N** The Heart Network of Texas, Irving, TX; North Texas Healthcare Network, Dallas, TX	21	10	44	1204	14	20975	0	11094	4336	154
BALLINGER—Runnels County										
BALLINGER MEMORIAL HOSPITAL, 608 Avenue B., Zip 76821–2499; tel. 915/365–2531; Robert E. Vernor, Administrator **A**9 10 **F**14 15 16 22 24 28 31 32 65 71	16	10	16	439	6	9023	0	2357	1182	74
BAY CITY—Matagorda County										
✖ MATAGORDA GENERAL HOSPITAL, 1115 Avenue G., Zip 77414–3544; tel. 409/245–6383; Wendell H. Baker, Jr., Chief Executive Officer **A**1 9 10 **F**4 7 8 10 12 13 15 16 18 19 21 22 23 24 26 28 30 31 32 33 34 35 37 39 40 44 48 49 54 57 65 67 70 71 73 74 **P**5 8 **S** Matagorda County Hospital District, Bay City, TX	16	10	67	2600	24	22346	415	18945	9802	432
BAYTOWN—Harris County										
□ BAYCOAST MEDICAL CENTER, 1700 James Bowie Drive, Zip 77520–3386, Mailing Address: P.O. Box 1451, Zip 77520–1451; tel. 713/420–6100; Frank T. Beirne, President and Chief Executive Officer (Nonreporting) **A**1 9 10 **S** Paracelsus Healthcare Corporation, Houston, TX	33	10	191	—	—	—	—	—	—	—
✖ SAN JACINTO METHODIST HOSPITAL, 4401 Garth Road, Zip 77521–3160; tel. 281/420–8600; William Simmons, President and Chief Executive Officer (Total facility includes 45 beds in nursing home–type unit) **A**1 3 5 9 10 **F**1 3 4 7 8 10 12 15 18 19 20 21 22 23 26 27 28 30 32 34 35 37 39 40 41 42 44 45 46 48 49 51 52 54 55 56 57 58 59 60 63 64 65 67 69 71 73 **P**7 8 **S** Methodist Health Care System, Houston, TX **N** Gulf Coast Provider Network, Houston, TX	21	10	231	9707	151	149201	1230	74016	28768	1085

Hospital, Address, Telephone, Administrator, Approval, Facility, and Physician Codes, Health Care System, Network	Classi-fication Codes		Utilization Data					Expense (thousands) of dollars		
	Control	Service	Staffed Beds	Admissions	Census	Outpatient Visits	Births	Total	Payroll	Personnel

★ American Hospital Association (AHA) membership
□ Joint Commission on Accreditation of Healthcare Organizations (JCAHO) accreditation
+ American Osteopathic Healthcare Association (AOHA) membership
○ American Osteopathic Association (AOA) accreditation
△ Commission on Accreditation of Rehabilitation Facilities (CARF) accreditation
Control codes 61, 63, 64, 71, 72 and 73 indicate hospitals listed by AOHA, but not registered by AHA. For definition of numerical codes, see page A4

BEAUMONT—Jefferson County

Hospital	Control	Service	Staffed Beds	Admissions	Census	Outpatient Visits	Births	Total	Payroll	Personnel
★ BAPTIST HOSPITAL OF SOUTHEAST TEXAS, College and 11th Streets, Zip 77701, Mailing Address: Drawer 1591, Zip 77704–1591; tel. 409/835–3781; David N. Parmer, President and Chief Executive Officer (Total facility includes 31 beds in nursing home–type unit) **A**1 5 9 10 **F**4 7 8 10 12 14 15 16 17 19 21 22 23 27 28 29 30 32 33 35 37 39 41 42 43 44 45 46 47 49 51 60 64 65 67 71 72 73 74 **P**5 8	23	10	172	6664	118	47569	0	55530	17750	733
★ COLUMBIA BEAUMONT MEDICAL CENTER, (Includes Fannin Pavilion of Beaumont Regional Medical Center, 3250 Fannin Street, Zip 77701; tel. 409/833–1411), 3080 College, Zip 77701–4689, Mailing Address: P.O. Box 5817, Zip 77726–5817; tel. 409/833–1411; Luis G. Silva, Chief Executive Officer and Regional Administrator **A**1 9 10 **F**3 7 8 12 14 15 16 19 20 22 26 27 28 30 31 32 35 37 38 40 41 42 44 45 52 53 54 55 56 57 58 59 64 65 67 71 73 74 **P**3 7 8 **S** Columbia/HCA Healthcare Corporation, Nashville, TN	33	10	364	6031	96	34513	1253	38326	17777	513
FANNIN PAVILION OF BEAUMONT REGIONAL MEDICAL CENTER See Columbia Beaumont Medical Center										
□ △ HEALTHSOUTH REHABILITATION HOSPITAL OF BEAUMONT, (Formerly Southeast Texas Rehabilitation Hospital), 3340 Plaza 10 Boulevard, Zip 77707; tel. 409/835–0835; David J. Holly, Chief Executive Officer (Total facility includes 18 beds in nursing home–type unit) **A**1 7 10 **F**12 17 19 24 25 27 28 32 34 35 48 49 65 67 71 73 **P**5 **S** HEALTHSOUTH Corporation, Birmingham, AL	32	46	60	815	48	18104	—	13542	6277	156
SOUTHEAST TEXAS REHABILITATION HOSPITAL See HEALTHSOUTH Rehabilitation Hospital of Beaumont										
★ ST. ELIZABETH HOSPITAL, 2830 Calder Avenue, Zip 77702, Mailing Address: P.O. Box 5405, Zip 77726–5405; tel. 409/892–7171; Sister Mary Fatima McCarthy, Administrator (Total facility includes 27 beds in nursing home–type unit) **A**1 2 5 9 10 **F**4 7 8 10 11 12 13 14 15 16 17 19 20 21 22 24 26 27 28 29 30 31 32 33 34 35 37 38 39 40 41 42 43 44 45 46 47 48 49 51 60 63 64 65 67 70 71 72 73 74 **P**3 5 6 7 8 **S** Sisters of Charity of the Incarnate Word Healthcare System, Houston, TX **N** SouthEast Texas Integrated Community Health Network, Houston, TX	21	10	468	21832	361	164820	2315	168974	72968	2265

BEDFORD—Tarrant County

Hospital	Control	Service	Staffed Beds	Admissions	Census	Outpatient Visits	Births	Total	Payroll	Personnel
★ HARRIS METHODIST–HEB, (Includes Harris Methodist–Springwood, 1608 Hospital Parkway, Zip 76022; tel. 817/355–7700), 1600 Hospital Parkway, Zip 76022–6913, Mailing Address: P.O. Box 669, Zip 76095–0669; tel. 817/685–4000; Jack McCabe, Senior Vice President and Administrator (Total facility includes 15 beds in nursing home–type unit) **A**1 2 9 10 **F**2 3 4 7 8 10 12 14 15 16 17 18 19 21 22 23 24 28 30 31 32 34 35 37 39 40 41 42 43 44 45 46 48 49 52 53 54 55 56 57 58 59 60 64 65 67 71 73 74 **P**2 5 7 **S** Texas Health Resources, Irving, TX **N** The Heart Network of Texas, Irving, TX; North Texas Healthcare Network, Dallas, TX	21	10	177	10241	110	64989	1795	87104	35284	1076

BEEVILLE—Bee County

Hospital	Control	Service	Staffed Beds	Admissions	Census	Outpatient Visits	Births	Total	Payroll	Personnel
□ SPOHN BEE COUNTY HOSPITAL, 1500 East Houston Street, Zip 78102; tel. 512/354–2125; Andrew E. Anderson, Jr., Administrator **A**1 9 10 **F**8 14 15 16 19 22 28 34 35 37 40 44 45 46 49 57 65 70 71 73 **P**1 3 4 5 6 7	21	10	66	3970	39	53811	431	19153	8603	421

BELLVILLE—Austin County

Hospital	Control	Service	Staffed Beds	Admissions	Census	Outpatient Visits	Births	Total	Payroll	Personnel
□ BELLVILLE GENERAL HOSPITAL, 44 North Cummings Street, Zip 77418–1347; tel. 409/865–3141; Bob Ellzey, Administrator **A**1 9 10 **F**8 12 19 21 22 26 28 30 32 33 34 35 44 49 60 65 71 73	16	10	32	923	11	10840	119	6120	2478	109

BIG LAKE—Reagan County

Hospital	Control	Service	Staffed Beds	Admissions	Census	Outpatient Visits	Births	Total	Payroll	Personnel
REAGAN MEMORIAL HOSPITAL, 805 North Main Street, Zip 76932–3999; tel. 915/884–2561; Ron Galloway, Administrator (Total facility includes 48 beds in nursing home–type unit) **A**9 10 **F**15 22 24 26 30 32 49 64 66 **N** Permian Basin Rural Health Network, Fort Stockton, TX	16	10	62	70	31	1354	1	2427	1203	60

BIG SPRING—Howard County

Hospital	Control	Service	Staffed Beds	Admissions	Census	Outpatient Visits	Births	Total	Payroll	Personnel
□ BIG SPRING STATE HOSPITAL, Lamesa Highway, Zip 79720, Mailing Address: P.O. Box 231, Zip 79721–0231; tel. 915/267–8216; Edward Moughon, Superintendent **A**1 10 **F**14 15 16 17 18 19 20 22 26 35 44 45 49 52 53 55 56 57 65 71 **P**5 **N** Permian Basin Rural Health Network, Fort Stockton, TX	12	22	292	829	242	—	—	27498	15681	650
★ SCENIC MOUNTAIN MEDICAL CENTER, 1601 West 11th Place, Zip 79720–4198; tel. 915/263–1211; Kenneth W. Randall, Chief Executive Officer **A**1 9 10 **F**7 8 10 12 14 16 19 21 22 27 28 31 32 34 35 40 41 44 46 49 52 57 63 64 65 71 73 **P**7 8 **S** Community Health Systems, Inc., Brentwood, TN **N** Permian Basin Rural Health Network, Fort Stockton, TX	33	10	120	4451	60	18064	279	22764	8480	285
★ VETERANS AFFAIRS MEDICAL CENTER, 300 Veterans Boulevard, Zip 79720–5500; tel. 915/263–7361; Cary D. Brown, Director (Total facility includes 40 beds in nursing home–type unit) (Nonreporting) **A**1 2 3 5 **S** Department of Veterans Affairs, Washington, DC **N** Permian Basin Rural Health Network, Fort Stockton, TX	45	10	189							

BONHAM—Fannin County

Hospital	Control	Service	Staffed Beds	Admissions	Census	Outpatient Visits	Births	Total	Payroll	Personnel
★ NORTHEAST MEDICAL CENTER, 504 Lipscomb Boulevard, Zip 75418–4096, Mailing Address: P.O. Drawer C., Zip 75418–4096; tel. 903/583–8585; Glenn E. Lowery, Chief Executive Officer (Total facility includes 10 beds in nursing home–type unit) **A**1 9 10 **F**8 12 14 15 19 21 22 28 32 34 37 41 44 49 60 64 65 71 73 **S** Community Health Systems, Inc., Brentwood, TN	32	10	48	1463	25	16724	1	11699	5075	142
★ SAM RAYBURN MEMORIAL VETERANS CENTER, 1201 East Ninth Street, Zip 75418–4091; tel. 903/583–2111; Charles C. Freeman, Director (Total facility includes 120 beds in nursing home–type unit) (Nonreporting) **A**1 **S** Department of Veterans Affairs, Washington, DC	45	10	374	—	—	—	—	—	—	—

Hospital, Address, Telephone, Administrator, Approval, Facility, and Physician Codes, Health Care System, Network	Classi-fication Codes		Utilization Data					Expense (thousands) of dollars		
★ American Hospital Association (AHA) membership □ Joint Commission on Accreditation of Healthcare Organizations (JCAHO) accreditation + American Osteopathic Healthcare Association (AOHA) membership ○ American Osteopathic Association (AOA) accreditation △ Commission on Accreditation of Rehabilitation Facilities (CARF) accreditation Control codes 61, 63, 64, 71, 72 and 73 indicate hospitals listed by AOHA, but not registered by AHA. For definition of numerical codes, see page A4	Control	Service	Staffed Beds	Admissions	Census	Outpatient Visits	Births	Total	Payroll	Personnel

BORGER—Hutchinson County

✠ GOLDEN PLAINS COMMUNITY HOSPITAL, 200 South McGee Street, Zip 79007–0495; tel. 806/273–1100; Norman Lambert, Chief Executive Officer **A**1 9 10 **F**7 8 12 15 16 19 22 28 32 34 35 37 39 40 44 46 49 65 67 70 71 73

| | 16 | 10 | 49 | 1208 | 11 | 18316 | 127 | 10365 | 4422 | 156 |

BOWIE—Montague County

★ BOWIE MEMORIAL HOSPITAL, 705 East Greenwood Avenue, Zip 76230–3199; tel. 940/872–1126; Joyce Crumpler, R.N., Administrator **A**9 10 **F**14 15 16 19 22 28 32 33 37 44 49 65 70 71 **N** Texoma Health Network, Wichita Falls, TX

| | 16 | 10 | 44 | 1188 | 17 | 42038 | — | 8474 | 4358 | 180 |

BRADY—McCulloch County

HEART OF TEXAS MEMORIAL HOSPITAL, Nine Road, Zip 76825–1150, Mailing Address: P.O. Box 1150, Zip 76825–1150; tel. 915/597–2901; Windell M. McCord, Administrator **A**9 10 **F**19 22 24 28 32 44 49 51 70 71 73

| | 16 | 10 | 27 | 594 | 9 | 7588 | 0 | 3328 | 1628 | 89 |

BRECKENRIDGE—Stephens County

STEPHENS MEMORIAL HOSPITAL, 200 South Geneva Street, Zip 76424–4799; tel. 817/559–2241; James Reese, CHE, Administrator **A**9 10 **F**7 8 15 16 19 22 24 26 28 30 32 34 36 40 41 42 44 49 51 65 70 71

| | 13 | 10 | 33 | 915 | 11 | 31510 | 57 | 5559 | 2781 | 122 |

BRENHAM—Washington County

✠ TRINITY COMMUNITY MEDICAL CENTER OF BRENHAM, 700 Medical Parkway, Zip 77833–5498; tel. 409/836–6173; John L. Simms, President and Chief Executive Officer **A**1 9 10 **F**7 14 15 16 19 26 28 32 37 40 44 49 60 65 71 73 **S** Franciscan Services Corporation, Sylvania, OH

| | 21 | 10 | 60 | 2317 | 26 | 25339 | 315 | 16217 | 6843 | — |

BROWNFIELD—Terry County

✠ BROWNFIELD REGIONAL MEDICAL CENTER, 705 East Felt, Zip 79316–3439; tel. 806/637–3551; Mike Click, Administrator **A**1 9 10 **F**7 8 14 15 16 17 19 22 24 28 29 30 31 32 34 40 44 46 49 65 69 70 71 73 **N** Lubbock Methodist Hospital System, Lubbock, TX

| | 16 | 10 | 42 | 704 | 9 | 41958 | 99 | 7610 | 4068 | 166 |

BROWNSVILLE—Cameron County

✠ BROWNSVILLE MEDICAL CENTER, 1040 West Jefferson Street, Zip 78520–5829, Mailing Address: Box 3590, Zip 78523–3590; tel. 956/544–1400; Tim A. Joslin, Chief Executive Officer **A**1 9 10 **F**4 7 8 10 12 15 16 19 22 23 24 28 30 32 33 35 37 38 40 41 43 44 45 49 51 53 54 55 56 57 58 59 64 65 70 71 73 74 **P**3 4 7 8 **S** TENET Healthcare Corporation, Santa Barbara, CA

| | 32 | 10 | 196 | 9470 | 151 | 83111 | 1792 | 60269 | 23741 | 814 |

✠ VALLEY REGIONAL MEDICAL CENTER, 1 Ted Hunt Boulevard, Zip 78521–7899, Mailing Address: P.O. Box 3710, Zip 78521–3710; tel. 956/831–9611; David Butler, Chief Executive Officer **A**1 9 10 **F**4 7 8 10 11 12 14 15 16 17 19 21 22 25 27 28 30 32 34 35 37 38 39 40 41 43 44 46 48 49 64 65 67 71 73 74 **P**5 7 **S** Columbia/HCA Healthcare Corporation, Nashville, TN **N** Columbia Healthcare – South Texas Division, Corpus Christi, TX

| | 32 | 10 | 183 | 7373 | 101 | 67867 | 2153 | 46339 | 18341 | 564 |

BROWNWOOD—Brown County

✠ COLUMBIA BROWNWOOD REGIONAL MEDICAL CENTER, 1501 Burnet Drive, Zip 76801–5933, Mailing Address: P.O. Box 760, Zip 76804–0760; tel. 915/646–8541; Art Layne, Administrator and Chief Executive Officer (Total facility includes 20 beds in nursing home–type unit) **A**1 9 10 **F**7 8 10 12 14 15 16 17 19 21 22 23 24 25 26 28 30 32 33 34 35 36 37 39 40 41 42 44 45 46 48 49 51 52 54 57 60 63 64 65 67 71 73 74 **P**7 **S** Columbia/HCA Healthcare Corporation, Nashville, TN

| | 33 | 10 | 164 | 7285 | 99 | 129127 | 767 | 43402 | 17362 | 612 |

BRYAN—Brazos County

✠ ST. JOSEPH REGIONAL HEALTH CENTER, 2801 Franciscan Drive, Zip 77802–2599; tel. 409/776–3777; Sister Gretchen Kunz, President and Chief Executive Officer (Total facility includes 25 beds in nursing home–type unit) **A**1 3 5 9 10 **F**3 4 7 8 10 11 12 14 15 16 17 19 21 22 23 25 26 28 29 30 31 32 33 34 35 37 39 40 41 42 43 44 45 46 48 49 54 55 56 58 60 63 64 65 67 71 72 73 **P**8 **S** Franciscan Services Corporation, Sylvania, OH

| | 21 | 10 | 237 | 12438 | 151 | 162851 | 2261 | 101386 | 39714 | 1442 |

BURLESON—Johnson County

✠ HUGULEY MEMORIAL MEDICAL CENTER, 11801 South Freeway, Zip 76028, Mailing Address: P.O. Box 6337, Fort Worth, Zip 76115–6337; tel. 817/293–9110; Peter M. Weber, President and Chief Executive Officer (Total facility includes 33 beds in nursing home–type unit) **A**1 10 **F**3 7 8 10 11 12 13 14 15 16 17 19 21 22 23 24 25 26 28 29 30 32 33 34 35 37 39 40 41 42 44 45 46 49 51 52 53 54 55 56 57 58 59 60 62 63 64 65 67 69 71 73 74 **P**1 3 5 6 7 **S** Adventist Health System Sunbelt Health Care Corporation, Winter Park, FL

| | 21 | 10 | 169 | 7488 | 103 | 96508 | 1057 | 67598 | 26237 | 1047 |

BURNET—Burnet County

✠ SETON HIGHLAND LAKES, (Formerly Highland Lakes Medical Center), Highway 281 South, Zip 78611, Mailing Address: P.O. Box 840, Zip 78611–0840; tel. 512/756–6000; Terry R. Andris, CHE, Administrator and Vice President Operations **A**1 9 10 **F**8 19 21 22 33 34 42 44 59 65 71

| | 16 | 10 | 33 | 1039 | 11 | 12266 | 1 | 8620 | 3459 | — |

CALDWELL—Burleson County

★ BURLESON ST. JOSEPH HEALTH CENTER, 1101 Woodson Drive, Zip 77836–1052, Mailing Address: P.O. Drawer 360, Zip 77836–0360; tel. 409/567–3245; William H. Craig, President and Chief Executive Officer **A**9 10 **F**8 13 14 15 16 17 19 21 22 25 26 28 29 30 32 34 44 46 49 65 71 73 **P**5 7 8 **S** Franciscan Services Corporation, Sylvania, OH

| | 21 | 10 | 30 | 345 | 6 | 12418 | 0 | 5729 | 2450 | 74 |

CAMERON—Milam County

CENTRAL TEXAS HOSPITAL, 806 North Crockett Avenue, Zip 76520–2599; tel. 254/697–6591; Louis West, President **A**9 10 **F**8 14 19 22 27 28 30 32 37 44 49 57 59 71 73 **S** NetCare Health Systems, Inc., Nashville, TN **N** Central Texas Rural Health Network, Harrietsville, TX; Brazo's Valley Health Network, Waco, TX

| | 23 | 10 | 34 | 395 | 6 | 13926 | 2 | 3370 | 1337 | 59 |

Hospital, Address, Telephone, Administrator, Approval, Facility, and Physician Codes, Health Care System, Network	Classi-fication Codes		Utilization Data					Expense (thousands) of dollars		
★ American Hospital Association (AHA) membership □ Joint Commission on Accreditation of Healthcare Organizations (JCAHO) accreditation + American Osteopathic Healthcare Association (AOHA) membership ○ American Osteopathic Association (AOA) accreditation △ Commission on Accreditation of Rehabilitation Facilities (CARF) accreditation Control codes 61, 63, 64, 71, 72 and 73 indicate hospitals listed by AOHA, but not registered by AHA. For definition of numerical codes, see page A4	Control	Service	Staffed Beds	Admissions	Census	Outpatient Visits	Births	Total	Payroll	Personnel

CANADIAN—Hemphill County

HEMPHILL COUNTY HOSPITAL, 1020 South Fourth Street, Zip 79014–3315; tel. 806/323–6422; Robert Ezzell, Administrator **A**9 **F**1 8 12 17 18 21 22 26 32 33 34 36 49 51 65 70 71	16	10	19	181	4	13754	0	3528	1623	69

CANYON—Randall County

⊞ PALO DURO HOSPITAL, 2 Hospital Drive, Zip 79015–3199; tel. 806/655–7751; Larry Baggett, Administrator **A**1 9 10 **F**3 8 12 15 16 19 20 22 26 27 28 32 34 36 39 41 44 45 49 52 54 55 65 66 71 73	16	10	19	483	4	78314	0	6880	2880	110

CARRIZO SPRINGS—Dimmit County

DIMMIT COUNTY MEMORIAL HOSPITAL, 704 Hospital Drive, Zip 78834–3836; tel. 210/876–2424; Ernest Flores, Jr., Administrator **A**9 10 **F**7 14 15 16 19 22 28 32 34 40 44 61 70 71 **N** Southwest Texas Rural Health Alliance, San Antonio, TX	13	10	35	1077	11	13712	144	5807	2781	120

CARROLLTON—Denton County

⊞ TRINITY MEDICAL CENTER, 4343 North Josey Lane, Zip 75010–4691; tel. 972/492–1010; Craig E. Sims, President (Total facility includes 12 beds in nursing home–type unit) **A**1 9 10 **F**4 7 8 10 12 14 15 16 17 19 20 21 22 23 25 26 28 29 30 32 33 34 35 37 38 39 40 41 42 43 44 45 49 54 61 63 64 65 66 67 71 73 74 **P**5 **S** TENET Healthcare Corporation, Santa Barbara, CA	33	10	149	5182	49	73880	1741	45873	14253	392

CARTHAGE—Panola County

□ EAST TEXAS MEDICAL CENTER CARTHAGE, (Formerly Panola General Hospital), 409 Cottage Road, Zip 75633–1466, Mailing Address: P.O. Box 549, Zip 75633–0549; tel. 903/693–3841; Gary Mikeal Hudson, Administrator **A**1 9 10 **F**8 16 19 22 32 37 44 65 71 73 **N** Healthcare Partners of East Texas, Inc., Tyler, TX; Regional Healthcare Alliance, Tyler, TX	33	10	30	849	12	28749	—	8200	3612	—

CENTER—Shelby County

□ MEMORIAL HOSPITAL OF CENTER, (Formerly Memorial Hospital), 602 Hurst Street, Zip 75935–3414, Mailing Address: P.O. Box 1749, Zip 75935–1749; tel. 409/598–2781; Robert V. Deen, Chief Executive Officer **A**1 9 10 **F**8 12 15 16 19 21 22 30 32 33 40 44 49 64 65 70 71 73 **P**8 **S** Park Healthcare Company, Nashville, TN **N** Healthcare Partners of East Texas, Inc., Tyler, TX	33	10	42	1265	12	38787	137	10272	3629	146

CENTER POINT—Kerr County

□ STARLITE VILLAGE HOSPITAL, Elm Pass Road, Zip 78010, Mailing Address: P.O. Box 317, Zip 78010–0317; tel. 210/634–2212; Chas H. Williams, M.D., Administrator **A**1 10 **F**3 22 34 39 52 56 57 58 59 65 67 **P**5	33	82	42	1236	19	4335	—	3030	1607	65

CHANNELVIEW—Harris County

SUN BELT REGIONAL MEDICAL CENTER EAST See Columbia East Houston Medical Center, Houston										

CHILDRESS—Childress County

□ CHILDRESS REGIONAL MEDICAL CENTER, Highway 83 North, Zip 79201, Mailing Address: P.O. Box 1030, Zip 79201–1030; tel. 940/937–6371; Frances T. Smith, Administrator **A**1 9 10 **F**8 12 13 14 15 16 17 19 21 22 26 27 28 29 30 31 32 33 34 39 40 44 45 46 49 51 65 66 67 70 71 73 74	16	10	35	1062	11	26379	221	7795	3879	168

CHILLICOTHE—Hardeman County

CHILLICOTHE HOSPITAL DISTRICT, 303 Avenue I., Zip 79225, Mailing Address: P.O. Box 370, Zip 79225–0370; tel. 817/852–5131; Linda Hall, Administrator **A**9 10 **F**12 15 16 19 21 22 28 30 32 35 44 65 69 70 71 73 **N** Texoma Health Network, Wichita Falls, TX	16	10	12	88	1	366	—	1184	612	24

CLARKSVILLE—Red River County

⊞ EAST TEXAS MEDICAL CENTER–CLARKSVILLE, Highway 82 West, Zip 75426, Mailing Address: P.O. Box 1270, Zip 75426–1270; tel. 903/427–3851; Terry Cutler, Executive Director **A**1 9 10 **F**8 14 15 19 22 28 30 34 37 39 44 45 46 49 65 67 70 71 **P**8 **S** East Texas Medical Center Regional Healthcare System, Tyler, TX	16	10	36	1755	17	17478	0	6772	2800	120

CLEBURNE—Johnson County

⊞ WALLS REGIONAL HOSPITAL, 201 Walls Drive, Zip 76031–1008; tel. 817/641–2551; Brent D. Magers, FACHE, Chief Executive Officer and Administrator (Total facility includes 12 beds in nursing home–type unit) **A**1 9 10 **F**3 4 7 8 10 12 13 14 15 16 17 19 21 22 23 24 26 27 28 29 30 31 32 33 34 35 37 39 40 41 42 43 44 45 46 49 51 53 54 55 56 58 59 61 63 64 65 66 67 69 70 71 73 74 **P**5 **S** Texas Health Resources, Irving, TX **N** The Heart Network of Texas, Irving, TX; North Texas Healthcare Network, Dallas, TX	21	10	112	3752	44	93059	608	28774	11250	367

CLEVELAND—Liberty County

⊞ CLEVELAND REGIONAL MEDICAL CENTER, 300 East Crockett Street, Zip 77327–4062, Mailing Address: P.O. Box 1688, Zip 77328–1688; tel. 281/593–1811; Don Willie, Chief Executive Officer (Total facility includes 11 beds in nursing home–type unit) **A**1 9 10 **F**7 8 10 12 15 16 19 21 22 28 30 32 33 34 35 37 39 40 41 42 44 46 49 54 64 65 71 73 **P**7 **S** Community Health Systems, Inc., Brentwood, TN	32	10	115	3469	43	29049	418	23128	9566	286

CLIFTON—Bosque County

★ GOODALL–WITCHER HOSPITAL, 101 South Avenue T., Zip 76634–1897, Mailing Address: P.O. Box 549, Zip 76634–0549; tel. 254/675–8322; Jim B. Smith, President and Chief Executive Officer (Total facility includes 30 beds in nursing home–type unit) **A**9 10 **F**7 8 15 19 21 22 30 32 34 37 40 44 49 64 65 70 71 73 **P**3 **N** Central Texas Rural Health Network, Harrietsville, TX; Brazo's Valley Health Network, Waco, TX	23	10	70	1287	14	6177	249	11215	4652	192

Hospital, Address, Telephone, Administrator, Approval, Facility, and Physician Codes, Health Care System, Network	Classi-fication Codes		Utilization Data					Expense (thousands) of dollars		
★ American Hospital Association (AHA) membership ☐ Joint Commission on Accreditation of Healthcare Organizations (JCAHO) accreditation + American Osteopathic Healthcare Association (AOHA) membership ○ American Osteopathic Association (AOA) accreditation △ Commission on Accreditation of Rehabilitation Facilities (CARF) accreditation Control codes 61, 63, 64, 71, 72 and 73 indicate hospitals listed by AOHA, but not registered by AHA. For definition of numerical codes, see page A4	Control	Service	Staffed Beds	Admissions	Census	Outpatient Visits	Births	Total	Payroll	Personnel

COLEMAN—Coleman County

COLEMAN COUNTY MEDICAL CENTER, 310 South Pecos Street, Zip 76834–4159; tel. 915/625–2135; Michael Morris, Administrator **A**9 10 **F**14 15 16 21 22 24 30 32 34 36 39 44 49 61 73	16	10	23	1108	10	4414	8	3713	1748	119

COLLEGE STATION—Brazos County

✠ COLUMBIA MEDICAL CENTER, 1604 Rock Prairie Road, Zip 77845–8345, Mailing Address: P.O. Box 10000, Zip 77842–3500; tel. 409/764–5100; Thomas W. Jackson, Chief Executive Officer (Total facility includes 10 beds in nursing home–type unit) **A**1 5 9 10 **F**4 7 8 10 11 12 14 16 17 19 21 22 23 24 30 31 32 34 35 37 38 40 41 42 43 44 48 49 61 64 71 **P**8 **S** Columbia/HCA Healthcare Corporation, Nashville, TN	33	10	119	3214	35	52050	591	25845	10558	318

COLORADO CITY—Mitchell County

★ MITCHELL COUNTY HOSPITAL, 1543 Chestnut Street, Zip 79512–3998; tel. 915/728–3431; Roland K. Rickard, Administrator **A**9 10 **F**7 8 15 16 19 21 24 29 30 32 33 40 44 49 64 65 67 70 71 **P**5 **S** Lubbock Methodist Hospital System, Lubbock, TX **N** Lubbock Methodist Hospital System, Lubbock, TX	16	10	25	825	9	—	62	9345	5270	

COLUMBUS—Colorado County

COLUMBUS COMMUNITY HOSPITAL, 110 Shult Drive, Zip 78934–3010, Mailing Address: P.O. Box 865, Zip 78934–0865; tel. 409/732–2371; Robert Thomas, Administrator (Nonreporting) **A**9 10	23	10	36	—	—	—	—	—	—	—

COMANCHE—Comanche County

COMANCHE COMMUNITY HOSPITAL, 211 South Austin Street, Zip 76442–3224; tel. 915/356–5241; W. Evan Moore, Administrator **A**9 10 **F**15 19 21 22 24 32 34 40 49 51 56 65 67 70 71 **N** Lubbock Methodist Hospital System, Lubbock, TX	16	10	18	420	7	8647	5	4216	2244	101

COMMERCE—Hunt County

PRESBYTERIAN HOSPITAL OF COMMERCE See Hunt Memorial Hospital District, Greenville										

CONROE—Montgomery County

✠ COLUMBIA CONROE REGIONAL MEDICAL CENTER, 504 Medical Boulevard, Zip 77304, Mailing Address: P.O. Box 1538, Zip 77305–1538; tel. 409/539–1111; Edward W. Myers, Chief Executive Officer (Total facility includes 12 beds in nursing home–type unit) **A**1 3 9 10 **F**4 7 8 10 11 12 14 15 16 19 21 22 23 26 27 28 29 30 32 33 34 35 37 38 39 40 41 42 43 44 45 48 49 51 54 60 63 64 65 67 70 71 73 74 **P**7 8 **S** Columbia/HCA Healthcare Corporation, Nashville, TN	33	10	242	11399	148	97131	1815	69535	30573	844

CORPUS CHRISTI—Nueces County

☐ CHARTER BEHAVIORAL HEALTH SYSTEM–CORPUS CHRISTI, 3126 Rodd Field Road, Zip 78414–3901; tel. 512/993–8893; John S. Lacy, Chief Executive Officer **A**1 9 10 **F**3 15 16 17 52 53 54 55 56 57 58 59 **S** Magellan Health Services, Atlanta, GA	32	22	80	1358	28	5582	—	8443	2973	79
✠ COLUMBIA BAY AREA MEDICAL CENTER, 7101 South Padre Island Drive, Zip 78412–4999; tel. 512/985–1200; Kirk G. Wilson, Chief Executive Officer **A**1 9 10 12 13 **F**3 4 7 8 10 12 15 16 19 21 22 25 26 28 32 33 35 37 38 39 40 41 42 43 44 45 51 53 54 55 56 57 58 60 63 64 65 66 67 71 73 74 **P**5 7 8 **S** Columbia/HCA Healthcare Corporation, Nashville, TN **N** Columbia Healthcare – South Texas Division, Corpus Christi, TX	32	10	149	6867	86	51784	1922	54981	20450	605
✠ COLUMBIA BAYVIEW PSYCHIATRIC CENTER, 6226 Saratoga Boulevard, Zip 78414–3421; tel. 512/993–9700; Janie L. Harwood, Chief Executive Officer **A**1 9 10 **F**3 4 5 6 7 8 9 10 11 12 14 15 16 17 18 19 21 22 23 24 25 26 28 29 30 31 32 35 37 38 40 42 43 44 47 48 49 50 51 52 53 54 55 56 57 58 59 60 63 64 70 71 73 74 **P**8 **S** Columbia/HCA Healthcare Corporation, Nashville, TN **N** Columbia Healthcare – South Texas Division, Corpus Christi, TX	33	22	40	1283	26	4297	0	6141	3372	107
✠ COLUMBIA DOCTORS REGIONAL MEDICAL CENTER, 3315 South Alameda Street, Zip 78411–1883, Mailing Address: P.O. Box 3828, Zip 78463–3828; tel. 512/857–1501; Steven Woerner, Chief Executive Officer (Total facility includes 26 beds in nursing home–type unit) **A**1 9 10 **F**2 3 4 7 8 10 11 12 14 15 16 17 18 19 20 21 22 23 25 27 28 29 30 31 32 33 34 35 37 38 39 40 41 42 43 44 45 46 48 49 52 53 54 55 56 57 58 59 60 61 64 65 66 67 68 69 71 73 74 **P**3 5 7 8 **S** Columbia/HCA Healthcare Corporation, Nashville, TN **N** Columbia Healthcare – South Texas Division, Corpus Christi, TX	32	10	237	11431	150	31695	2625	64836	25674	1207
✠ COLUMBIA NORTHWEST HOSPITAL, 13725 Farm to Market Road 624, Zip 78410–5199; tel. 512/767–4500; Winston Borland, Chief Executive Officer **A**1 9 10 **F**8 15 19 20 21 22 24 25 28 31 32 34 37 41 44 48 63 64 65 66 67 71 **S** Columbia/HCA Healthcare Corporation, Nashville, TN **N** Columbia Healthcare – South Texas Division, Corpus Christi, TX	33	10	63	2287	36	260508	0	34608	16749	683
✠ △ COLUMBIA REHABILITATION HOSPITAL, 6226 Saratoga Boulevard, Zip 78414–3499; tel. 512/991–9690; John Krogness, Chief Executive Officer **A**1 7 9 10 **F**2 3 4 7 8 10 12 15 16 19 20 21 22 25 26 27 28 29 30 31 32 34 35 37 38 39 40 41 42 43 44 45 48 49 52 53 54 55 56 57 58 59 64 65 69 71 73 74 **P**5 8 **S** Columbia/HCA Healthcare Corporation, Nashville, TN **N** Columbia Healthcare – South Texas Division, Corpus Christi, TX	32	46	40	622	26	5172	0	8519	4531	127
✠ DRISCOLL CHILDREN'S HOSPITAL, 3533 South Alameda Street, Zip 78411–1785, Mailing Address: P.O. Box 6530, Zip 78466–6530; tel. 512/694–5000; J. E. Ted Stibbards, Ph.D., President and Chief Executive Officer **A**1 3 5 9 10 **F**4 5 10 12 14 15 16 17 19 21 22 25 27 28 29 30 31 32 33 34 35 38 39 41 42 43 44 45 46 47 48 49 51 53 54 60 63 65 66 67 68 71 72 73 74 **N** SouthEast Texas Hospital System, Dallas, TX	23	50	188	7023	121	93937	—	69158	32095	1138

Hospital, Address, Telephone, Administrator, Approval, Facility, and Physician Codes, Health Care System, Network	Classi-fication Codes		Utilization Data					Expense (thousands) of dollars		
★ American Hospital Association (AHA) membership □ Joint Commission on Accreditation of Healthcare Organizations (JCAHO) accreditation + American Osteopathic Healthcare Association (AOHA) membership ○ American Osteopathic Association (AOA) accreditation △ Commission on Accreditation of Rehabilitation Facilities (CARF) accreditation Control codes 61, 63, 64, 71, 72 and 73 indicate hospitals listed by AOHA, but not registered by AHA. For definition of numerical codes, see page A4	Control	Service	Staffed Beds	Admissions	Census	Outpatient Visits	Births	Total	Payroll	Personnel

★ NAVAL HOSPITAL, 10651 E. Street, Zip 78419–5131; tel. 512/961–2685; Captain N. J. Lescavage, Commanding Officer (Nonreporting) **S** Department of Navy, Washington, DC	43	10	25	—	—	—	—	—	—	—
✠ △ SPOHN HEALTH SYSTEM, 1702 Santa Fe, Zip 78404; tel. 512/881–3000; Jake Henry, Jr., President (Total facility includes 66 beds in nursing home–type unit) **A**1 2 7 9 10 **F**4 7 8 10 11 12 14 15 16 17 19 21 22 24 26 27 28 29 30 31 32 33 34 35 37 39 40 41 42 43 44 45 46 48 49 51 52 57 60 64 65 66 67 71 73 74 **P**1 3 4 5 6 7 **S** Incarnate Word Health Services, San Antonio, TX	21	10	489	18846	306	150885	1994	143279	58203	1797
✠ SPOHN MEMORIAL HOSPITAL, 2606 Hospital Boulevard, Zip 78405–1818, Mailing Address: Box 5280, Zip 78465–5280; tel. 512/902–4000; Steven R. Kamber, Vice President and Administrator (Total facility includes 23 beds in nursing home–type unit) **A**1 3 9 10 **F**4 5 7 8 9 10 11 12 14 15 16 17 18 19 20 21 22 24 26 27 28 29 30 31 32 33 34 35 37 39 40 42 43 44 45 46 49 50 51 52 53 54 55 56 57 58 59 60 63 64 65 66 67 68 69 71 72 73 74 **P**1 3 4 5 6 7	21	10	245	8357	146	169036	902	95328	38050	1188
CORSICANA—Navarro County										
✠ NAVARRO REGIONAL HOSPITAL, (Formerly Columbia Navarro Regional Hospital), 3201 West Highway 22, Zip 75110; tel. 903/872–4861; Nancy A. Byrnes, President and Chief Executive Officer **A**1 9 10 **F**4 7 8 10 12 14 15 16 19 20 22 23 27 28 30 31 32 35 39 40 41 42 44 48 49 57 64 65 71 73 **P**3 7 8 **S** Columbia/HCA Healthcare Corporation, Nashville, TN	33	10	144	3990	60	44696	491	29817	10333	339
CRANE—Crane County										
★ CRANE MEMORIAL HOSPITAL, 1310 South Alford Street, Zip 79731–3899; tel. 915/558–3555; Stan Wiley, Administrator **A**9 10 **F**8 14 15 16 22 27 28 29 30 34 39 44 51 71 72 **N** Permian Basin Rural Health Network, Fort Stockton, TX	13	10	28	188	2	6451	0	2554	1090	34
CROCKETT—Houston County										
✠ EAST TEXAS MEDICAL CENTER CROCKETT, 1100 Loop 304 East, Zip 75835–1810; tel. 409/544–2002; Nelda K. Welch, Administrator **A**1 9 10 **F**7 8 13 14 15 16 17 19 21 22 25 27 28 30 34 37 39 40 41 42 44 46 48 49 51 63 65 66 67 70 71 73 **P**7 **S** East Texas Medical Center Regional Healthcare System, Tyler, TX	23	10	54	2316	28	37104	132	13608	6306	221
CROSBYTON—Crosby County										
★ CROSBYTON CLINIC HOSPITAL, 710 West Main Street, Zip 79322–2143; tel. 806/675–2382; Michael Johnson, Administrator and Chief Executive Officer **A**9 10 **F**2 3 4 7 8 10 11 12 15 16 17 18 19 20 21 22 24 28 29 30 32 34 35 37 38 39 40 41 42 43 44 45 46 47 48 49 51 52 53 54 55 57 58 59 60 64 65 71 73 74 **P**6 **S** St. Joseph Health System, Orange, CA	23	10	35	885	12	20755	0	5026	2360	102
CUERO—De Witt County										
✠ CUERO COMMUNITY HOSPITAL, 2550 North Esplanade Street, Zip 77954–4716; tel. 512/275–6191; James E. Buckner, Jr., Administrator **A**1 9 10 **F**7 8 14 15 16 19 21 22 25 28 30 31 32 34 35 37 39 40 41 44 45 49 51 63 65 70 73 **N** SouthEast Texas Hospital System, Dallas, TX	16	10	45	2469	32	138666	157	18166	7821	375
DALHART—Dallam County										
□ COON MEMORIAL HOSPITAL AND HOME, 1411 Denver Avenue, Zip 79022–4809; tel. 806/249–4571; Leroy Schaffner, Chief Executive Officer **A**1 9 10 **F**7 14 15 19 22 26 28 32 33 34 36 40 44 45 49 70 71 73	16	10	28	468	4	12870	18	5099	2047	77
DALLAS—Dallas County										
A. WEBB ROBERTS HOSPITAL See Baylor University Medical Center										
★ BAYLOR CENTER FOR RESTORATIVE CARE, 3504 Swiss Avenue, Zip 75204–6224; tel. 214/820–9700; Gerry Brueckner, R.N., Executive Director **A**9 10 **F**3 4 5 7 8 10 11 12 13 14 15 16 17 19 21 22 23 24 25 26 28 30 31 32 33 34 35 37 38 41 42 43 44 45 46 47 48 49 50 52 53 54 56 57 58 59 60 61 63 64 65 66 67 69 70 71 73 74 **P**3 5 7 8 **S** Baylor Health Care System, Dallas, TX **N** Baylor Health Care System Network, Dallas, TX; North Texas Health Network, Irving, TX; North Texas Healthcare Network, Dallas, TX	23	10	72	678	58	0	0	9175	4495	153
★ △ BAYLOR INSTITUTE FOR REHABILITATION, 3505 Gaston Avenue, Zip 75246–2018; tel. 214/826–7030; Judith C. Waterston, Executive Director **A**3 7 10 **F**2 3 4 5 7 8 9 10 11 12 14 15 16 17 19 21 22 23 24 25 26 27 28 29 30 31 32 33 34 35 37 38 39 40 41 42 43 44 45 46 47 48 49 51 52 53 56 57 58 60 61 64 65 66 67 69 70 71 73 74 **P**5 7 **S** Baylor Health Care System, Dallas, TX **N** North Texas Health Network, Irving, TX; North Texas Healthcare Network, Dallas, TX	21	46	92	1589	78	7923	0	19683	10029	269
✠ BAYLOR UNIVERSITY MEDICAL CENTER, (Includes A. Webb Roberts Hospital, ; Erik and Margaret Jonsson Hospital, ; George W. Truett Memorial Hospital, ; Karl and Esther Hoblitzelle Memorial Hospital), 3500 Gaston Avenue, Zip 75246–2088; tel. 214/820–0111; M. Tim Parris, Executive Vice President and Chief Operating Officer **A**1 2 3 5 8 9 10 **F**3 4 5 7 8 10 11 12 15 17 18 19 20 21 22 23 24 26 28 29 30 31 32 33 34 35 36 37 38 39 40 41 42 43 44 45 46 47 48 49 50 54 55 56 57 58 59 60 61 63 64 65 66 67 69 70 71 73 74 **P**1 **S** Baylor Health Care System, Dallas, TX **N** Baylor Health Care System Network, Dallas, TX; The Heart Network of Texas, Irving, TX; Regional Healthcare Alliance, Tyler, TX; North Texas Health Network, Irving, TX; North Texas Healthcare Network, Dallas, TX	21	10	873	35659	585	384270	4085	415740	159174	4967
✠ CHARLTON METHODIST HOSPITAL, 3500 West Wheatland Road, Zip 75222, Mailing Address: Box 225357, Zip 75222–5357; tel. 214/947–7500; Kim N. Hollon, FACHE, Executive Director **A**1 3 9 10 **F**7 8 14 15 16 17 19 21 22 23 24 25 26 28 30 31 37 39 40 42 44 49 51 56 64 65 66 67 70 71 73 74 **S** Methodist Hospitals of Dallas, Dallas, TX	23	10	134	8186	103	93228	1514	50439	22842	707

Hospital, Address, Telephone, Administrator, Approval, Facility, and Physician Codes, Health Care System, Network	Classification Codes		Utilization Data					Expense (thousands) of dollars		
★ American Hospital Association (AHA) membership □ Joint Commission on Accreditation of Healthcare Organizations (JCAHO) accreditation + American Osteopathic Healthcare Association (AOHA) membership ○ American Osteopathic Association (AOA) accreditation △ Commission on Accreditation of Rehabilitation Facilities (CARF) accreditation Control codes 61, 63, 64, 71, 72 and 73 indicate hospitals listed by AOHA, but not registered by AHA. For definition of numerical codes, see page A4	Control	Service	Staffed Beds	Admissions	Census	Outpatient Visits	Births	Total	Payroll	Personnel

Hospital	Control	Service	Staffed Beds	Admissions	Census	Outpatient Visits	Births	Total	Payroll	Personnel
✶ CHILDREN'S MEDICAL CENTER OF DALLAS, 1935 Motor Street, Zip 75235–7794; tel. 214/640–2000; George D. Farr, President and Chief Executive Officer **A**1 2 3 5 8 9 10 **F**4 10 12 13 14 15 16 17 19 20 21 22 25 27 28 30 31 32 34 35 39 41 42 43 44 45 46 47 49 51 52 53 54 55 56 58 59 63 65 66 67 69 70 71 72 73 **N** Regional Healthcare Alliance, Tyler, TX	23	50	224	12337	157	214326	—	171569	82597	2034
✶ ○ COLUMBIA MEDICAL CENTER–DALLAS SOUTHWEST, 2929 South Hampton Road, Zip 75224–3026; tel. 214/330–4611; James B. Warren, Chief Executive Officer **A**1 9 10 11 12 13 **F**1 2 3 4 5 6 7 8 9 10 11 12 13 14 15 16 17 18 19 20 21 22 23 24 25 26 27 28 29 30 31 32 33 34 35 36 37 38 39 40 41 42 43 44 45 46 47 48 49 50 51 52 53 54 55 56 57 58 59 60 61 62 63 64 65 66 67 68 69 70 71 72 73 74 **P**1 5 7 **S** Columbia/HCA Healthcare Corporation, Nashville, TN **N** Saint Paul Medical Center Affiliate Network, Dallas, TX	32	10	104	2364	29	28072	72	20775	8621	249
✶ DALLAS COUNTY HOSPITAL DISTRICT–PARKLAND HEALTH AND HOSPITAL SYSTEM, 5201 Harry Hines Boulevard, Zip 75235–7731; tel. 214/590–8000; Ron J. Anderson, M.D., President and Chief Executive Officer **A**1 2 3 5 8 9 10 **F**4 5 7 9 10 11 12 14 15 16 17 18 19 20 21 22 23 25 26 28 29 30 31 34 35 37 38 39 40 41 42 43 44 45 46 48 49 51 52 54 55 56 57 58 59 60 61 63 65 67 68 69 70 71 73 74	16	10	691	39180	526	757944	13578	517814	196082	6397
✶ DOCTORS HOSPITAL OF DALLAS, 9440 Poppy Drive, Zip 75218–3694; tel. 214/324–6100; Robert S. Freymuller, Chief Executive Officer (Total facility includes 18 beds in nursing home–type unit) **A**1 9 10 **F**2 4 7 8 9 10 11 12 14 15 16 17 19 20 21 22 23 26 27 28 29 30 31 32 33 34 35 37 38 40 41 42 43 44 45 46 47 48 49 52 56 57 59 60 63 64 65 66 67 70 71 72 73 74 **P**5 7 **S** TENET Healthcare Corporation, Santa Barbara, CA	32	10	197	7867	128	43544	494	57060	23092	663
ERIK AND MARGARET JONSSON HOSPITAL See Baylor University Medical Center										
GEORGE W. TRUETT MEMORIAL HOSPITAL See Baylor University Medical Center										
□ GREEN OAKS HOSPITAL, 7808 Clodus Fields Drive, Zip 75251–2206; tel. 214/991–9504; Dennis Wade, Administrator **A**1 9 **F**2 3 14 15 16 41 52 56 57 58 59 67 **P**8	32	22	106	3274	60	13040	0	—	7445	47
□ △ HEALTHSOUTH MEDICAL CENTER, 2124 Research Row, Zip 75235–2504; tel. 214/904–6100; Robert M. Smart, Area Manager and Chief Executive Officer **A**1 7 10 **F**5 12 14 15 16 19 21 22 25 26 27 30 32 34 44 45 46 48 49 54 65 66 67 71 73 **S** HEALTHSOUTH Corporation, Birmingham, AL	33	46	106	1013	51	7649	—	18809	8542	250
KARL AND ESTHER HOBLITZELLE MEMORIAL HOSPITAL See Baylor University Medical Center										
★ MARY SHIELS HOSPITAL, 3515 Howell Street, Zip 75204–2895; tel. 214/443–3000; Rob Shiels, Administrator **A**9 10 **F**34 44 45 46 49	33	10	15	337	2	2427	—	5837	2882	64
✶ △ MEDICAL CITY DALLAS HOSPITAL, (Formerly Columbia Medical City at Medical City Dallas), 7777 Forest Lane, Zip 75230–2598; tel. 972/566–7000; Stephen Corbeil, President and Chief Executive Officer (Total facility includes 34 beds in nursing home–type unit) **A**1 2 7 9 10 **F**3 4 7 8 10 11 12 14 16 17 18 19 20 21 22 23 25 26 28 29 30 31 32 33 34 35 37 38 39 40 41 42 43 44 45 46 47 48 49 50 51 53 54 55 56 57 58 59 60 61 63 64 65 66 67 69 71 73 74 **P**5 7 **S** Columbia/HCA Healthcare Corporation, Nashville, TN	33	10	511	21692	312	65313	3963	233925	76767	2298
✶ METHODIST MEDICAL CENTER, 1441 North Beckley Avenue, Zip 75203–1201, Mailing Address: Box 655999, Zip 75265–5999; tel. 214/947–8181; John W. Carver, FACHE, Executive Director **A**1 2 3 5 7 8 9 10 **F**4 7 8 10 11 12 14 15 16 17 19 21 22 23 24 25 26 27 28 29 30 31 32 33 34 35 37 38 39 40 41 42 43 44 45 46 48 49 51 60 61 63 64 65 66 67 69 70 71 73 74 **P**1 7 **S** Methodist Hospitals of Dallas, Dallas, TX	23	10	375	14624	258	136530	2256	135794	61121	1685
□ △ NORTH DALLAS REHABILITATION HOSPITAL, 8383 Meadow Road, Zip 75231–3798; tel. 214/891–0880; Brian F. Wells, Administrator and Chief Executive Officer **A**1 7 10 **F**13 14 15 16 26 27 32 33 34 39 48 49 54 64 65 67 71 73	33	46	36	250	11	54	0	—	—	45
PEDIATRIC CENTER FOR RESTORATIVE CARE, 3301 Swiss Avenue, Zip 75204–6219; tel. 214/828–4747; Geraldine Brueckner, Administrator **A**10 **F**3 4 7 8 9 10 11 12 13 15 16 17 19 21 24 25 26 27 28 29 30 31 32 33 34 35 37 38 41 42 43 44 45 46 47 48 49 50 53 54 55 56 57 59 61 63 64 65 66 67 69 71 73 74 **P**1 3 5 7 **N** North Texas Health Network, Irving, TX	23	50	17	153	11	8955	0	4385	2420	71
✶ △ PRESBYTERIAN HOSPITAL OF DALLAS, 8200 Walnut Hill Lane, Zip 75231–4402; tel. 214/345–6789; Mark H. Merrill, Executive Director (Total facility includes 78 beds in nursing home–type unit) **A**1 2 3 5 7 9 10 **F**2 3 4 5 6 7 8 10 11 12 13 14 15 16 17 18 19 21 22 23 24 25 26 27 28 29 30 31 32 33 34 35 36 37 38 39 40 41 42 43 44 45 46 48 49 50 51 52 53 54 55 56 57 58 59 60 61 62 63 64 65 66 67 68 69 71 72 73 74 **P**2 5 6 8 **S** Texas Health Resources, Irving, TX **N** Presbyterian Healthcare System, Dallas, TX; Regional Healthcare Alliance, Tyler, TX; North Texas Healthcare Network, Dallas, TX	23	10	655	25600	319	243207	4811	238070	105022	3149
✶ RHD MEMORIAL MEDICAL CENTER, Seven Medical Parkway, Zip 75381, Mailing Address: P.O. Box 819094, Zip 75381–9094; tel. 972/247–1000; Craig E. Sims, President and Chief Executive Officer **A**1 10 **F**4 7 8 10 12 14 15 16 17 19 20 21 22 23 25 26 28 29 30 32 33 34 35 37 39 40 41 42 43 44 45 49 54 61 63 65 66 67 71 73 74 **P**5 **S** TENET Healthcare Corporation, Santa Barbara, CA	33	10	150	4118	47	50165	440	50292	13055	412
✶ ST. PAUL MEDICAL CENTER, 5909 Harry Hines Boulevard, Zip 75235–6285; tel. 214/879–1000; Frank Tiedemann, President and Chief Executive Officer **A**1 2 3 5 8 9 10 **F**3 4 5 7 8 10 11 12 13 15 16 17 19 21 22 23 24 25 26 27 28 29 30 31 32 33 34 35 37 38 40 41 42 43 44 46 49 52 53 54 55 56 57 58 59 60 61 64 65 67 69 71 73 74 **P**2 3 5 7 **S** Texas Health Resources, Irving, TX	21	10	308	12878	201	122137	2416	73799	58674	1544

Hospital, Address, Telephone, Administrator, Approval, Facility, and Physician Codes, Health Care System, Network	Classi-fication Codes		Utilization Data					Expense (thousands) of dollars		
★ American Hospital Association (AHA) membership ▫ Joint Commission on Accreditation of Healthcare Organizations (JCAHO) accreditation + American Osteopathic Healthcare Association (AOHA) membership ○ American Osteopathic Association (AOA) accreditation △ Commission on Accreditation of Rehabilitation Facilities (CARF) accreditation Control codes 61, 63, 64, 71, 72 and 73 indicate hospitals listed by AOHA, but not registered by AHA. For definition of numerical codes, see page A4	Control	Service	Staffed Beds	Admissions	Census	Outpatient Visits	Births	Total	Payroll	Personnel

Hospital	Control	Service	Staffed Beds	Admissions	Census	Outpatient Visits	Births	Total	Payroll	Personnel
⊠ TEXAS SCOTTISH RITE HOSPITAL FOR CHILDREN, 2222 Welborn Street, Zip 75219–0567; Mailing Address: Box 190567, Zip 75219–0567; tel. 214/559–5000; J. C. Montgomery, Jr., President **A**1 3 5 **F**5 19 20 28 34 39 41 45 46 65 67 71 73 **P**6	23	57	64	2322	25	40359	0	42324	—	556
▫ TIMBERLAWN MENTAL HEALTH SYSTEM, 4600 Samuell Boulevard, Zip 75228–6800; Mailing Address: P.O. Box 151489, Zip 75315–1489; tel. 214/381–7181; Debra S. Lowrance, R.N., Chief Executive Officer and Managing Director **A**1 3 9 10 **F**2 3 12 15 17 22 26 46 52 53 54 55 56 57 58 59 62 67 **P**6 **S** Universal Health Services, Inc., King of Prussia, PA	33	22	124	2578	63	—	0	11245	5465	194
▫ ○ TRI-CITY HEALTH CENTRE, 7525 Scyene Road, Zip 75227–5677; tel. 214/381–7171; Patti Griffith, R.N., Administrator and Chief Executive Officer **A**1 10 11 12 13 **F**3 7 8 10 14 15 16 17 19 21 22 25 26 27 28 30 34 35 37 39 40 42 44 46 49 52 57 58 63 65 71 72 73	23	10	131	3247	46	28946	535	31971	10212	320
▫ VENCOR HOSPITAL–DALLAS, (LONG TERM ACUTE CARE), 1600 Abrams Road, Zip 75214–4499; tel. 214/818–2400; Dorothy J. Elford, Executive Director and Chief Executive Officer **A**1 9 10 **F**22 37 65 **S** Vencor, Incorporated, Louisville, KY	32	49	51	273	34	7	0	9795	5121	253
⊠ VETERANS AFFAIRS NORTH TEXAS HEALTH CARE SYSTEM, (Formerly Veterans Affairs Medical Center), 4500 South Lancaster Road, Zip 75216–7167; tel. 214/376–5451; Alan G. Harper, Director (Total facility includes 120 beds in nursing home–type unit) (Nonreporting) **A**1 2 3 5 8 **S** Department of Veterans Affairs, Washington, DC	45	10	557	—	—	—	—	—	—	—
▫ △ ZALE LIPSHY UNIVERSITY HOSPITAL, 5151 Harry Hines Boulevard, Zip 75235–7786; tel. 214/590–3000; Robert B. Smith, President and Chief Executive Officer **A**1 3 5 7 8 9 10 **F**4 8 10 12 14 15 19 22 28 29 30 32 34 37 41 42 43 44 45 46 48 50 52 54 56 57 59 64 65 67 71 73	23	10	147	5410	108	8615	0	84878	25142	722
DE LEON—Comanche County										
⊠ DE LEON HOSPITAL, 407 South Texas Avenue, Zip 76444–1947, Mailing Address: P.O. Box 319, Zip 76444–0319; tel. 254/893–2011; Michael K. Hare, Administrator **A**1 9 10 **F**8 14 15 22 28 32 34 42 44 46 49 58 65 71 73 **S** Brim, Inc., Portland, OR **N** Lubbock Methodist Hospital System, Lubbock, TX	16	10	14	797	12	25711	1	4688	2257	84
DE SOTO—Dallas County										
▫ CEDARS HOSPITAL, 2000 North Old Hickory Trail, Zip 75115–2242; tel. 972/298–7323; Don Johnson, Administrator **A**1 9 10 **F**3 14 15 16 26 34 45 52 53 54 55 56 57 58 59 65 **N** Saint Paul Medical Center Affiliate Network, Dallas, TX; Brazo's Valley Health Network, Waco, TX	33	22	76	825	26	3742	0	7203	2981	90
▫ HAVEN HOSPITAL, 800 Kirnwood Drive, Zip 75115–2092; tel. 972/709–3700; Sheila C. Kelly, R.N., MS, Chief Executive Officer **A**1 9 10 **F**3 15 16 52 53 56 57 58 59 60 **S** Ramsay Health Care, Inc., Coral Gables, FL	33	22	51	682	37	5739	0	6177	2755	112
DECATUR—Wise County										
⊠ DECATUR COMMUNITY HOSPITAL, 2000 South FM 51, Zip 76234–9295; tel. 940/627–5921; Steve Summers, Administrator (Total facility includes 10 beds in nursing home–type unit) **A**1 9 10 **F**7 8 12 14 15 19 21 22 24 28 30 32 34 37 40 41 44 49 64 65 68 70 71 73	16	10	49	2606	23	71348	525	15026	7331	276
DEL RIO—Val Verde County										
⊠ VAL VERDE REGIONAL MEDICAL CENTER, (Formerly Val Verde Memorial Hospital), 801 Bedell Avenue, Zip 78840–4185, Mailing Address: P.O. Box 1527, Zip 78840–1527; tel. 830/775–8566; Don Griffin, Chief Executive Officer **A**1 9 10 **F**7 8 10 12 15 16 19 21 22 28 30 32 33 34 35 36 37 39 40 44 45 46 49 51 65 70 71 73 74 **P**5 **N** Memorial/Sisters of Charity Health Network, Houston, TX; Southwest Texas Rural Health Alliance, San Antonio, TX	16	10	76	3289	37	41906	889	20652	9049	361
DENISON—Grayson County										
⊠ TEXOMA HEALTHCARE SYSTEM, 1000 Memorial Drive, Zip 75020–2035, Mailing Address: P.O. Box 890, Zip 75021–9988; tel. 903/416–4000; Arthur L. Hohenberger, FACHE, President and Chief Executive Officer **A**1 2 9 10 **F**3 4 7 8 10 11 12 14 15 16 17 19 21 26 27 28 29 30 32 33 34 35 37 39 40 41 42 43 44 45 46 48 49 51 52 53 54 56 57 58 59 60 65 66 67 71 73 74 **P**3 5 **N** The Heart Network of Texas, Irving, TX	23	10	205	7396	108	60516	403	71218	28785	—
DENTON—Denton County										
⊠ COLUMBIA MEDICAL CENTER OF DENTON, 4405 North Interstate 35, Zip 76207–3499; tel. 940/566–4000; Bob J. Haley, Chief Executive Officer (Total facility includes 25 beds in nursing home–type unit) **A**1 9 10 **F**4 7 8 10 12 16 17 19 20 21 22 23 27 28 30 32 33 34 35 36 37 40 41 42 43 44 48 49 52 57 59 60 64 65 71 72 73 **S** Columbia/HCA Healthcare Corporation, Nashville, TN	33	10	271	6128	99	64289	862	47404	20540	693
⊠ DENTON COMMUNITY HOSPITAL, 207 North Bonnie Brae Street, Zip 76201–3798; tel. 940/898–7000; Timothy Charles, Chief Executive Officer **A**1 9 10 **F**14 19 21 22 28 30 31 32 35 37 42 44 49 56 63 64 65 66 67 71 73 74 **P**5 **S** NetCare Health Systems, Inc., Nashville, TN	33	10	110	5099	59	37670	736	29025	11583	431
DENVER CITY—Yoakum County										
★ YOAKUM COUNTY HOSPITAL, 412 Mustang Avenue, Zip 79323–2750, Mailing Address: P.O. Drawer 1130, Zip 79323–1130; tel. 806/592–5484; Edward Rodgers, Chief Executive Officer (Total facility includes 3 beds in nursing home–type unit) **A**9 10 **F**6 15 17 28 29 30 32 37 40 44 49 65 70 71 73 **P**5 **S** St. Joseph Health System, Orange, CA	13	10	24	484	4	16192	101	4133	1387	60
DIMMITT—Castro County										
PLAINS MEMORIAL HOSPITAL, 310 West Halsell Street, Zip 79027–1846, Mailing Address: P.O. Box 278, Zip 79027–0278; tel. 806/647–2191; Joseph F. Sloan, CHE, Chief Executive Officer **A**9 10 **F**8 12 14 15 21 22 28 32 33 36 40 44 49 65 70 71	16	10	30	401	3	38567	61	5443	2435	118

Hospital, Address, Telephone, Administrator, Approval, Facility, and Physician Codes, Health Care System, Network	Classi-fication Codes		Utilization Data					Expense (thousands) of dollars		
★ American Hospital Association (AHA) membership □ Joint Commission on Accreditation of Healthcare Organizations (JCAHO) accreditation + American Osteopathic Healthcare Association (AOHA) membership ○ American Osteopathic Association (AOA) accreditation △ Commission on Accreditation of Rehabilitation Facilities (CARF) accreditation Control codes 61, 63, 64, 71, 72 and 73 indicate hospitals listed by AOHA, but not registered by AHA. For definition of numerical codes, see page A4	Control	Service	Staffed Beds	Admissions	Census	Outpatient Visits	Births	Total	Payroll	Personnel

DUMAS—Moore County

★ MOORE COUNTY HOSPITAL DISTRICT, (Formerly Memorial Hospital), 224 East Second Street, Zip 79029–3808; tel. 806/935–7171; Scott R. Brown, Administrator and Chief Executive Officer (Nonreporting) **A**9 10 **N** Lubbock Methodist Hospital System, Lubbock, TX

| 16 | 10 | 51 | — | — | — | — | — | — | — |

EAGLE LAKE—Colorado County

⊞ RICE MEDICAL CENTER, 600 South Austin Road, Zip 77434–3298, Mailing Address: P.O. Box 277, Zip 77434–0277; tel. 409/234–5571; David N. Keith, Chief Executive Officer **A**1 9 10 **F**7 8 14 15 16 19 22 28 32 35 40 42 44 46 49 70 71 73 **P**6

| 16 | 10 | 31 | 513 | 5 | 14043 | 117 | 5240 | 2323 | 93 |

EAGLE PASS—Maverick County

★ FORT DUNCAN MEDICAL CENTER, 350 South Adams Street, Zip 78852; tel. 830/757–7501; Don Spaulding, Administrator and Chief Executive Officer **A**6 9 10 **F**1 3 6 7 8 13 15 18 19 20 24 25 26 27 28 29 30 31 32 33 34 35 36 37 39 40 41 44 45 49 54 55 56 61 62 65 67 69 70 71 73 **S** Quorum Health Group/Quorum Health Resources, Inc., Brentwood, TN

| 16 | 10 | 69 | 4271 | 46 | 75925 | 911 | 22313 | 8224 | 289 |

EASTLAND—Eastland County

EASTLAND MEMORIAL HOSPITAL, 304 South Daugherty Street, Zip 76448–2609, Mailing Address: P.O. Box 897, Zip 76448–0897; tel. 254/629–2601; John Yeary, Administrator **A**9 10 **F**8 15 16 19 21 22 24 26 28 29 30 34 40 44 49 67 70 71 73

| 16 | 10 | 38 | 1418 | 14 | 17914 | 128 | 5874 | 2864 | 130 |

EDEN—Concho County

CONCHO COUNTY HOSPITAL, 614 Eaker Street, Zip 76837, Mailing Address: Drawer L., Zip 76837; tel. 915/869–5911; Joe Brosig, Administrator **A**9 10 **F**14 15 22 70 73 **P**5

| 16 | 10 | 20 | 257 | 3 | — | 0 | 1422 | 1005 | 41 |

EDINBURG—Hidalgo County

⊞ EDINBURG HOSPITAL, 333 West Freddy Gonzalez Drive, Zip 78539–6199; tel. 956/383–6211; Leon J. Belila, Administrator **A**1 9 10 **F**1 2 4 7 8 10 12 14 15 16 17 19 21 22 24 28 29 30 32 34 35 37 38 39 40 41 42 43 44 45 46 47 48 49 51 52 53 54 55 56 57 58 59 60 61 63 64 65 66 67 70 71 73 74 **P**1 3 7 **S** Universal Health Services, Inc., King of Prussia, PA

| 33 | 10 | 139 | 5454 | 60 | 22089 | 1434 | 18053 | 13795 | 446 |

EDNA—Jackson County

JACKSON COUNTY HOSPITAL, 1013 South Wells Street, Zip 77957–4098; tel. 512/782–5241; Marcella V. Henke, Administrator and Chief Executive Officer **A**9 10 **F**14 15 16 19 22 32 34 44 57 71 73 **N** SouthEast Texas Hospital System, Dallas, TX

| 16 | 10 | 31 | 393 | 5 | 31850 | — | 4939 | 1493 | 62 |

EL CAMPO—Wharton County

⊞ EL CAMPO MEMORIAL HOSPITAL, 303 Sandy Corner Road, Zip 77437–9535; tel. 409/543–6251; Steve Gularte, Administrator (Nonreporting) **A**1 9 10 **N** SouthEast Texas Hospital System, Dallas, TX

| 16 | 10 | 42 | — | — | — | — | — | — | — |

EL PASO—El Paso County

★ COLUMBIA BEHAVIORAL CENTER, 1155 Idaho Street, Zip 79902–1699; tel. 915/544–4000; Serena Pickman, Administrator **A**9 **F**3 4 7 8 9 10 11 12 14 15 16 18 19 20 21 22 23 24 25 26 27 28 30 31 32 33 34 35 37 38 39 40 41 42 43 44 45 46 47 48 49 52 53 54 55 56 57 58 59 60 63 64 65 66 67 69 71 73 74 **P**1 7 **S** Columbia/HCA Healthcare Corporation, Nashville, TN

| 32 | 22 | 25 | 788 | 9 | — | 0 | 5304 | 2214 | 48 |

⊞ COLUMBIA MEDICAL CENTER–EAST, 10301 Gateway West, Zip 79925–7798; tel. 915/595–9000; Douglas A. Matney, Senior Vice President Operations (Total facility includes 29 beds in nursing home–type unit) **A**1 9 10 **F**2 3 4 7 8 9 10 11 12 16 18 19 20 21 22 23 24 25 26 27 28 29 30 31 32 33 34 35 37 38 39 40 41 42 43 44 45 46 47 48 49 52 53 54 55 56 57 58 59 60 63 64 65 66 67 68 69 71 73 74 **P**5 7 8 **S** Columbia/HCA Healthcare Corporation, Nashville, TN

| 32 | 10 | 299 | 14065 | 210 | 105399 | 2204 | 109769 | 40634 | 1084 |

⊞ COLUMBIA MEDICAL CENTER–WEST, 1801 North Oregon Street, Zip 79902–3591; tel. 915/521–1776; Hank Hernandez, Chief Executive Officer (Total facility includes 18 beds in nursing home–type unit) **A**1 9 10 **F**2 3 4 7 8 9 10 11 12 14 15 16 18 19 20 21 22 23 24 25 26 27 28 30 31 32 33 34 35 37 38 39 40 41 42 43 44 45 46 47 48 49 52 53 54 55 56 57 58 59 60 63 64 65 66 67 69 71 73 74 **P**1 7 **S** Columbia/HCA Healthcare Corporation, Nashville, TN

| 32 | 10 | 221 | 8950 | 131 | 92046 | 1343 | 94710 | 32169 | 824 |

★ △ COLUMBIA REHABILITATION HOSPITAL, 300 Waymore Drive, Zip 77902–1628; tel. 915/577–2600; Cristina Huerta, Administrative Director (Nonreporting) **A**7 **S** Columbia/HCA Healthcare Corporation, Nashville, TN

| 33 | 46 | 40 | — | — | — | — | — | — | — |

⊞ PROVIDENCE MEMORIAL HOSPITAL, 2001 North Oregon Street, Zip 79902–3368; tel. 915/577–6011; L. Marcus Fry, Jr., Chief Executive Officer (Total facility includes 61 beds in nursing home–type unit) **A**1 2 5 9 10 **F**4 7 8 10 11 12 15 16 17 19 21 22 25 28 29 30 31 32 33 34 35 36 37 38 39 40 41 42 43 44 45 46 47 49 51 60 61 63 64 65 66 67 69 71 73 74 **P**7 8 **S** TENET Healthcare Corporation, Santa Barbara, CA

| 32 | 10 | 378 | 16063 | 234 | 156952 | 3477 | 148310 | 55976 | 1706 |

□ R. E. THOMASON GENERAL HOSPITAL, 4815 Alameda Avenue, Zip 79905–2794, Mailing Address: P.O. Box 20009, Zip 79998–0009; tel. 915/544–1200; Pete T. Duarte, Chief Executive Officer **A**1 2 3 5 9 10 **F**4 8 10 14 15 16 17 19 20 21 22 23 27 28 31 33 35 37 38 39 40 41 42 43 44 45 46 47 49 51 54 60 61 63 65 66 68 71 73 **P**6

| 16 | 10 | 277 | 12455 | 182 | 371266 | 4880 | 113521 | 40581 | 1356 |

⊞ △ RIO VISTA PHYSICAL REHABILITATION HOSPITAL, (Formerly Rio Vista Rehabilitation Hospital), 1740 Curie Drive, Zip 79902–2900; tel. 915/544–3399; Patsy A. Parker, Administrator and Chief Executive Officer (Total facility includes 27 beds in nursing home–type unit) **A**1 7 9 10 **F**4 5 7 8 9 10 11 12 14 15 16 17 19 21 22 25 27 28 30 32 33 34 35 36 37 38 39 40 41 42 43 44 46 47 48 49 60 63 64 65 69 71 73 74 **P**3 5 7 8 **S** TENET Healthcare Corporation, Santa Barbara, CA

| 33 | 46 | 100 | 1422 | 59 | 32149 | — | 21205 | 11370 | 408 |

Hospital, Address, Telephone, Administrator, Approval, Facility, and Physician Codes, Health Care System, Network	Classi-fication Codes		Utilization Data					Expense (thousands) of dollars		
	Control	Service	Staffed Beds	Admissions	Census	Outpatient Visits	Births	Total	Payroll	Personnel

★ American Hospital Association (AHA) membership
☐ Joint Commission on Accreditation of Healthcare Organizations (JCAHO) accreditation
+ American Osteopathic Healthcare Association (AOHA) membership
○ American Osteopathic Association (AOA) accreditation
△ Commission on Accreditation of Rehabilitation Facilities (CARF) accreditation
Control codes 61, 63, 64, 71, 72 and 73 indicate hospitals listed by AOHA, but not registered by AHA. For definition of numerical codes, see page A4

⊠ SIERRA MEDICAL CENTER, 1625 Medical Center Drive, Zip 79902–5044; tel. 915/747–4000; L. Marcus Fry, Jr., Chief Executive Officer **A**1 2 9 10 **F**4 7 8 10 11 12 15 16 17 19 20 21 22 28 29 30 31 32 33 34 35 36 37 38 39 40 41 42 43 44 45 46 47 48 49 60 63 64 65 66 67 69 71 73 74 **P**7 8 **S** TENET Healthcare Corporation, Santa Barbara, CA	32	10	328	11493	155	101385	2403	127799	38492	1243
☐ SOUTHWESTERN GENERAL HOSPITAL, 1221 North Cotton, Zip 79902–3096; tel. 915/496–9600; Stephen J. Campbell, Administrator **A**1 9 10 **F**7 8 11 15 16 17 19 21 22 28 30 34 35 40 44 49 63 65 71 74	32	10	102	1926	21	22220	137	13912	6083	219
⊠ WILLIAM BEAUMONT ARMY MEDICAL CENTER, 5005 North Piedras Street, Zip 79920–5001; tel. 915/569–2121; Colonel Jimmy Sanders, Chief of Staff (Nonreporting) **A**1 2 3 5 **S** Department of the Army, Office of the Surgeon General, Falls Church, VA	42	10	209	—	—	—	—	—	—	—
ELDORADO—Schleicher County										
SCHLEICHER COUNTY MEDICAL CENTER, 305 Mertzon Highway, Zip 76936, Mailing Address: Box V., Zip 76936; tel. 915/853–2507; Jim B. Roddie, Administrator (Total facility includes 8 beds in nursing home–type unit) **A**9 **F**1 22 28 45 49 64 65 70 73 **P**6	16	10	16	73	6	4933	0	1353	647	43
ELECTRA—Wichita County										
ELECTRA MEMORIAL HOSPITAL, 1207 South Bailey Street, Zip 76360–3221, Mailing Address: P.O. Box 1112, Zip 76360–1112; tel. 940/495–3981; Jan A. Reed, CPA, Administrator and Chief Executive Officer **A**9 10 **F**8 13 15 19 21 22 26 28 30 32 34 41 44 51 61 64 65 66 70 71 73 74 **N** Texoma Health Network, Wichita Falls, TX	16	10	23	639	8	18042	0	3053	1520	75
FAIRFIELD—Freestone County										
FAIRFIELD MEMORIAL HOSPITAL, 125 Newman Street, Zip 75840–1499; tel. 903/389–2121; Milton W. Meadows, Administrator **A**9 10 **F**7 8 15 19 21 22 25 28 30 33 37 40 44 64 **N** Healthcare Partners of East Texas, Inc., Tyler, TX; Regional Healthcare Alliance, Tyler, TX	16	10	20	512	7	7893	25	3969	1608	72
FLORESVILLE—Wilson County										
WILSON MEMORIAL HOSPITAL, 1301 Hospital Boulevard, Zip 78114–2798; tel. 830/393–3122; Robert Duffield, Administrator **A**9 10 **F**8 14 17 19 21 22 28 30 32 33 34 39 44 46 49 65 67 71 73 **N** Southwest Texas Rural Health Alliance, San Antonio, TX	16	10	30	561	9	47186	0	5430	2471	94
FORT HOOD—Bell County										
⊠ DARNALL ARMY COMMUNITY HOSPITAL, 36000 Darnall Loop, Zip 76544–4752; tel. 254/288–8000; Colonel Kenneth L. Farmer, Jr., Commander **A**1 2 3 5 **F**1 2 3 4 7 8 10 11 12 13 14 15 16 17 18 19 20 21 22 23 24 25 26 27 28 29 30 31 32 33 34 35 37 38 39 40 41 42 43 44 45 46 47 48 49 51 52 53 54 55 56 57 58 59 60 61 64 65 66 67 70 71 72 73 74 **P**5 6 8 **S** Department of the Army, Office of the Surgeon General, Falls Church, VA	42	10	117	12209	86	813369	3038	118076	51986	1477
FORT STOCKTON—Pecos County										
⊠ PECOS COUNTY MEMORIAL HOSPITAL, Sanderson Highway, Zip 79735, Mailing Address: P.O. Box 1648, Zip 79735–1648; tel. 915/336–2241; David B. Shaw, Administrator and Chief Executive Officer **A**1 9 10 **F**7 12 13 14 15 16 17 19 22 24 28 29 30 32 34 39 40 44 45 46 49 51 61 65 67 70 71 72 73 **N** Lubbock Methodist Hospital System, Lubbock, TX; Permian Basin Rural Health Network, Fort Stockton, TX	13	10	31	1079	10	34805	188	10167	4641	182
FORT WORTH—Tarrant County										
☐ ALL SAINTS EPISCOPAL HOSPITAL OF FORT WORTH, 1400 Eighth Avenue, Zip 76104–4192, Mailing Address: P.O. Box 31, Zip 76101–0031; tel. 817/926–2544; James P. Schuessler, President and Chief Executive Officer **A**1 2 9 10 **F**3 4 7 8 10 11 12 14 15 16 17 19 21 22 24 25 26 27 28 29 30 32 33 34 35 37 38 39 40 41 42 43 44 45 46 48 49 52 53 54 55 56 57 58 59 60 61 64 65 66 67 69 71 72 73 74 **P**1 3 4 5 7	23	10	267	12033	163	67703	1292	107491	42093	1183
ALL SAINTS HOSPITAL–CITYVIEW, 7100 Oakmont Boulevard, Zip 76132–3999; tel. 817/346–5870; Larry Robertson, Senior Vice President and Administrator **F**1 2 3 4 7 8 10 11 12 13 14 15 16 17 19 20 21 22 24 26 28 29 30 32 33 34 35 37 38 39 40 41 42 43 44 45 46 48 49 51 52 53 54 55 56 57 58 59 60 63 64 65 66 67 71 72 73 74 **P**5 6 7	23	10	43	1882	15	25801	749	14885	5457	164
☐ COOK CHILDREN'S MEDICAL CENTER, 801 Seventh Avenue, Zip 76104–2796; tel. 817/885–4000; Russell K. Tolman, President **A**1 3 9 10 **F**10 12 13 14 15 16 17 18 19 20 21 22 25 27 28 29 30 31 32 34 35 38 39 41 42 43 44 45 46 47 48 49 51 52 53 55 56 58 59 60 63 65 66 67 68 69 70 71 72 73 **P**3 4 6	23	50	181	7085	119	128628	0	120596	46992	1546
★ HARRIS CONTINUED CARE HOSPITAL, (LONG–TERM ACUTE CARE), 1301 Pennsylvania Avenue, 4th Floor, Zip 76104–2190, Mailing Address: P.O. Box 3471, Zip 76113–3471; tel. 817/878–5500; Larry Thompson, Administrator **A**10 **F**2 3 4 7 8 10 11 12 13 16 17 18 19 21 22 23 24 26 27 28 29 30 31 32 33 34 35 37 38 39 40 41 42 43 44 45 46 48 49 50 52 53 54 55 56 58 59 60 61 63 64 65 66 67 69 70 71 72 73 74 **P**2 5 7 **S** Texas Health Resources, Irving, TX **N** The Heart Network of Texas, Irving, TX; North Texas Healthcare Network, Dallas, TX	21	49	10	68	7	0	0	5622	1419	24
⊠ HARRIS METHODIST FORT WORTH, 1301 Pennsylvania Avenue, Zip 76104–2895; tel. 817/882–2000; Barclay E. Berdan, Chief Executive Officer (Total facility includes 19 beds in nursing home–type unit) **A**1 2 3 9 10 **F**2 3 4 7 8 10 11 12 14 15 16 17 18 19 20 21 22 23 24 25 26 27 28 29 30 31 32 33 34 35 37 38 39 40 41 42 43 44 45 46 47 48 49 51 52 53 54 55 56 57 58 60 61 63 64 65 66 67 69 70 71 72 73 74 **P**3 5 **S** Texas Health Resources, Irving, TX **N** The Heart Network of Texas, Irving, TX; North Texas Healthcare Network, Dallas, TX	21	10	511	23029	335	98989	4942	201813	82487	2587

Hospital, Address, Telephone, Administrator, Approval, Facility, and Physician Codes, Health Care System, Network	Classi-fication Codes		Utilization Data					Expense (thousands) of dollars		
★ American Hospital Association (AHA) membership ☐ Joint Commission on Accreditation of Healthcare Organizations (JCAHO) accreditation + American Osteopathic Healthcare Association (AOHA) membership ○ American Osteopathic Association (AOA) accreditation △ Commission on Accreditation of Rehabilitation Facilities (CARF) accreditation Control codes 61, 63, 64, 71, 72 and 73 indicate hospitals listed by AOHA, but not registered by AHA. For definition of numerical codes, see page A4	Control	Service	Staffed Beds	Admissions	Census	Outpatient Visits	Births	Total	Payroll	Personnel

✠ HARRIS METHODIST SOUTHWEST, 6100 Harris Parkway, Zip 76132–4199; tel. 817/346–5050; David B. Rowe, Vice President and Administrator (Total facility includes 8 beds in nursing home–type unit) **A**1 9 10 **F**2 3 4 7 8 10 11 12 13 14 15 16 17 18 19 21 22 23 24 26 27 28 29 30 31 32 33 34 35 37 38 39 40 41 42 43 44 45 46 47 48 49 50 51 52 53 54 55 56 57 58 59 60 61 62 63 64 65 66 67 68 69 70 71 72 73 74 **P**2 3 5 7 8 **S** Texas Health Resources, Irving, TX **N** The Heart Network of Texas, Irving, TX; North Texas Healthcare Network, Dallas, TX	21	10	75	4571	40	62304	1671	36487	13106	454
☐ △ HEALTHSOUTH REHABILITATION HOSPITAL OF FORT WORTH, 1212 West Lancaster Avenue, Zip 76102–4510; tel. 817/870–2336; Laura J. Lycan, Administrator and Chief Executive Officer **A**1 7 9 10 **F**12 16 27 32 34 41 42 48 49 54 65 66 67 **S** HEALTHSOUTH Corporation, Birmingham, AL	33	46	60	607	33	7564	—	—	3921	114
☐ △ HEALTHSOUTH REHABILITATION HOSPITAL–CITYVIEW, (Formerly Fort Worth Rehabilitation Hospital), 6701 Oakmont Boulevard, Zip 76132–2957; tel. 817/370–4700; Robert L. McNew, Chief Executive Officer **A**1 7 9 10 **F**12 14 15 22 25 26 27 32 34 46 48 49 66 67 **S** HEALTHSOUTH Corporation, Birmingham, AL	33	46	62	648	41	6854	—	12386	5008	144
JOHN PETER SMITH HOSPITAL See Tarrant County Hospital District										
☐ + ○ △ OSTEOPATHIC MEDICAL CENTER OF TEXAS, 1000 Montgomery Street, Zip 76107–2691; tel. 817/731–4311; Ron Stephen, Executive Vice President and Administrator (Total facility includes 19 beds in nursing home–type unit) **A**1 7 9 10 11 12 13 **F**4 7 8 10 11 12 13 14 15 16 17 19 21 22 24 26 27 28 30 31 32 34 35 37 39 40 41 42 43 44 46 48 49 52 53 54 55 56 57 59 61 64 65 66 70 71 72 73 **P**1 5 7	23	10	205	7529	149	72429	667	79626	30257	806
✠ △ PLAZA MEDICAL CENTER OF FORT WORTH, (Formerly Columbia Plaza Medical Center of Fort Worth), 900 Eighth Avenue, Zip 76104–3986; tel. 817/336–2100; Stephen Bernstein, FACHE, Chief Executive Officer **A**1 7 9 10 **F**2 4 6 7 8 9 10 11 12 16 17 19 20 21 22 23 24 26 27 29 30 31 32 33 34 35 37 38 39 40 41 42 43 44 45 46 47 48 49 51 52 53 54 55 56 57 58 59 60 61 63 64 65 66 71 73 74 **P**5 7 **S** Columbia/HCA Healthcare Corporation, Nashville, TN	33	10	306	10365	159	26177	946	93523	33413	733
☐ TARRANT COUNTY HOSPITAL DISTRICT, (Includes John Peter Smith Hospital), 1500 South Main Street, Zip 76104–4941; tel. 817/921–3431; Anthony J. Alcini, President and Chief Executive Officer (Total facility includes 16 beds in nursing home–type unit) **A**1 3 5 6 9 10 **F**4 8 10 12 13 14 15 16 17 18 19 21 22 25 27 28 30 31 32 34 35 37 38 40 41 42 43 44 46 49 51 52 54 55 56 57 58 59 61 63 64 67 68 69 71 72 73 74 **P**3 8 **S** Tarrant County Hospital District, Fort Worth, TX	16	10	375	18956	234	298331	4635	193162	71494	2766
TARRANT COUNTY PSYCHIATRIC CENTER, 1527 Hemphill Street, Zip 76104–4789; tel. 817/923–6467; Connie Oliverson Perra, Director (Nonreporting)	16	22	39	—	—	—	—	—	—	—
THC – FORT WORTH See Vencor Hospital–Fort Worth Southwest										
TRINITY SPRINGS PAVILION–EAST, 1500 South Main Street, Zip 76104–4917; tel. 817/927–3636; Robert N. Bourassa, Executive Director (Nonreporting) **S** Tarrant County Hospital District, Fort Worth, TX	16	52	34	—	—	—	—	—	—	—
VENCOR HOSPITAL–FORT WORTH SOUTHWEST, (Formerly THC – Fort Worth), (LONG TERM ACUTE CARE), 7800 Oakmont Boulevard, Zip 76132–4299; tel. 817/346–0094; Barbara Schmidt, Administrator **A**9 **F**12 16 19 21 22 27 31 33 34 35 37 39 41 49 64 65 70 71 **S** Transitional Hospitals Corporation, Las Vegas, NV	33	49	80	456	41	601	0	13312	6723	107
FREDERICKSBURG—Gillespie County										
✠ HILL COUNTRY MEMORIAL HOSPITAL, 1020 Kerrville Road, Zip 78624, Mailing Address: P.O. Box 835, Zip 78624–0835; tel. 830/997–4353; Jeff A. Bourgeois, Chief Executive Officer **A**1 9 10 **F**7 8 15 16 19 21 22 23 24 30 32 33 35 37 39 40 41 42 44 46 49 63 64 65 66 67 70 71 73 **P**8 **N** Southwest Texas Rural Health Alliance, San Antonio, TX	23	10	59	3284	39	47162	403	22663	10094	422
FRIONA—Parmer County										
PARMER COUNTY COMMUNITY HOSPITAL, 1307 Cleveland Street, Zip 79035–1121; tel. 806/247–2754; Bill J. Neely, Administrator **A**9 10 **F**8 15 19 22 30 32 33 34 36 71	23	10	34	327	2	7114	0	3307	1497	23
GAINESVILLE—Cooke County										
GAINESVILLE MEMORIAL HOSPITAL, 1016 Ritchey Street, Zip 76240–3539; tel. 940/665–1751; William S. Abbott, Administrator (Total facility includes 10 beds in nursing home–type unit) **A**9 10 **F**7 8 14 15 16 17 18 19 22 28 30 32 33 35 36 39 44 49 65 71 73 **P**8	16	10	50	2077	19	—	308	12874	6960	290
GALVESTON—Galveston County										
✠ SHRINERS HOSPITALS FOR CHILDREN, GALVESTON BURNS INSTITUTE, (PEDIATRIC BURNS), 815 Market Street, Zip 77550–2725; tel. 409/770–6600; John A. Swartwout, Administrator **A**1 3 5 **F**9 10 19 34 35 44 54 65 71 73 **S** Shriners Hospitals for Children, Tampa, FL	23	59	30	996	16	2723	0	22166	8341	259
✠ UNIVERSITY OF TEXAS MEDICAL BRANCH HOSPITALS, 301 University Boulevard, Zip 77555–0138; tel. 409/772–1011; James F. Arens, M.D., Chief Executive Officer **A**1 2 3 5 8 9 10 **F**1 4 5 7 8 9 10 11 12 15 16 17 19 20 21 22 23 24 25 26 27 28 29 30 31 32 33 34 35 37 38 39 40 41 42 43 44 45 46 47 48 49 51 52 53 54 55 56 57 58 59 60 61 63 65 66 68 69 71 72 73 74 **P**5 6 7 **S** University of Texas System, Austin, TX **N** Gulf Health Network, Galveston, TX	12	10	884	32670	555	788159	4182	426744	174921	5495

Hospital, Address, Telephone, Administrator, Approval, Facility, and Physician Codes, Health Care System, Network	Classi-fication Codes		Utilization Data					Expense (thousands) of dollars		
★ American Hospital Association (AHA) membership □ Joint Commission on Accreditation of Healthcare Organizations (JCAHO) accreditation + American Osteopathic Healthcare Association (AOHA) membership ○ American Osteopathic Association (AOA) accreditation △ Commission on Accreditation of Rehabilitation Facilities (CARF) accreditation Control codes 61, 63, 64, 71, 72 and 73 indicate hospitals listed by AOHA, but not registered by AHA. For definition of numerical codes, see page A4	Control	Service	Staffed Beds	Admissions	Census	Outpatient Visits	Births	Total	Payroll	Personnel

GARLAND—Dallas County

✠ BAYLOR MEDICAL CENTER AT GARLAND, 2300 Marie Curie Boulevard, Zip 75042–5706; tel. 972/487–5000; John B. McWhorter, III, Executive Director (Total facility includes 20 beds in nursing home–type unit) **A**1 3 9 10 **F**4 7 8 10 11 12 15 16 17 19 20 21 22 24 25 26 28 29 30 31 32 33 34 35 37 39 41 42 43 44 45 46 47 48 49 50 51 53 54 55 56 60 61 63 64 65 66 67 68 69 70 71 73 74 **P**6 7 8 **S** Baylor Health Care System, Dallas, TX **N** Baylor Health Care System Network, Dallas, TX; North Texas Health Network, Irving, TX; North Texas Healthcare Network, Dallas, TX	23	10	170	8776	116	131508	1492	68650	29413	953
✠ GARLAND COMMUNITY HOSPITAL, 2696 West Walnut Street, Zip 75042–6499; tel. 972/276–7116; K. Dwayne Ray, Administrator and Chief Executive Officer **A**1 9 10 **F**3 15 16 17 19 21 22 26 27 28 30 32 35 37 39 41 44 49 52 54 55 56 57 58 59 63 65 67 71 73 **S** TENET Healthcare Corporation, Santa Barbara, CA	33	10	113	2568	42	61878	—	28876	11239	375

GATESVILLE—Coryell County

□ CORYELL MEMORIAL HOSPITAL, 1507 West Main Street, Zip 76528–1098, Mailing Address: P.O. Box 659, Zip 76528–0659; tel. 254/248–6300; David Byrom, Administrator (Total facility includes 24 beds in nursing home–type unit) **A**1 9 10 **F**14 15 22 27 32 33 37 44 49 51 62 65 67 71 73 **P**2	16	10	48	893	14	54333	0	9996	5260	243

GEORGETOWN—Williamson County

✠ GEORGETOWN HEALTHCARE SYSTEM, (Formerly Georgetown Hospital), 2000 Scenic Drive, Zip 78626–7793; tel. 512/930–5338; Kenneth W. Poteete, President and Chief Executive Officer (Total facility includes 9 beds in nursing home–type unit) **A**1 9 10 **F**7 8 10 14 15 16 19 21 22 28 30 32 34 35 37 39 40 41 42 44 49 64 65 66 67 70 71 73	23	10	65	3056	30	38868	711	22373	10951	393

GLEN ROSE—Somervell County

✠ GLEN ROSE MEDICAL CENTER, 1021 Holden Street, Zip 76043–4937, Mailing Address: P.O. Box 2099, Zip 76043–2099; tel. 254/897–2215; Gary A. Marks, Administrator **A**1 9 10 **F**14 15 16 19 22 44 49 60 62 63 70	13	10	16	635	6	14164	—	6541	2565	136

GONZALES—Gonzales County

MEMORIAL HOSPITAL, Highway 90A By–Pass, Zip 78629, Mailing Address: P.O. Box 587, Zip 78629–0587; tel. 830/672–7581; Douglas Langley, Administrator **A**9 10 **F**8 14 15 16 17 18 19 22 28 29 30 32 34 37 39 40 41 42 44 46 49 51 65 66 67 70 71 73 **N** Southwest Texas Rural Health Alliance, San Antonio, TX	16	10	35	1088	13	19200	131	8563	3944	173
✠ △ WARM SPRINGS REHABILITATION HOSPITAL, Mailing Address: P.O. Box 58, Zip 78629–0058; tel. 830/672–6592; John W. Davis, Administrator **A**1 7 9 10 **F**15 16 32 41 48 49 65 **N** Southwest Texas Rural Health Alliance, San Antonio, TX	23	46	68	651	44	13356	—	9261	4193	195

GRAHAM—Young County

GRAHAM GENERAL HOSPITAL, 1301 Montgomery Road, Zip 76450–4224, Mailing Address: P.O. Box 1390, Zip 76450–1390; tel. 940/549–3400; Blake Kretz, Administrator **A**9 10 **F**7 8 15 16 19 22 26 28 30 32 33 34 35 36 40 41 42 44 57 64 65 70 71 73 **P**5 7	14	10	40	1660	16	89700	236	11140	5004	223

GRANBURY—Hood County

✠ LAKE GRANBURY MEDICAL CENTER, (Formerly Hood General Hospital), 1310 Paluxy Road, Zip 76048–5699; tel. 817/573–2683; John V. Villanueva, Chief Executive Officer (Nonreporting) **A**1 9 10 **S** Community Health Systems, Inc., Brentwood, TN	33	10	49	—	—	—	—	—	—	—

GRAND PRAIRIE—Dallas County

✠ + ○ DALLAS–FORT WORTH MEDICAL CENTER, 2709 Hospital Boulevard, Zip 75051–1083; tel. 972/641–5000; Robert A. Ficken, Chief Executive Officer (Total facility includes 11 beds in nursing home–type unit) **A**1 9 10 11 12 13 **F**4 7 8 10 12 15 16 17 19 21 22 23 24 25 26 27 28 30 32 34 35 37 38 39 40 41 44 46 48 49 51 52 57 64 65 71 73 74 **P**5 **S** Quorum Health Group/Quorum Health Resources, Inc., Brentwood, TN **N** Saint Paul Medical Center Affiliate Network, Dallas, TX	23	10	162	4683	66	70753	956	40300	16419	553

GRAND SALINE—Van Zandt County

★ COZBY–GERMANY HOSPITAL, 707 North Waldrip Street, Zip 75140–1555; tel. 903/962–4242; William Rowton, Chief Executive Officer **A**9 10 **F**8 19 20 22 26 32 33 34 44 49 59 65 70 71 **N** Healthcare Partners of East Texas, Inc., Tyler, TX; Regional Healthcare Alliance, Tyler, TX	23	10	26	315	3	—	1	2896	1520	56

GRAPEVINE—Tarrant County

✠ BAYLOR MEDICAL CENTER AT GRAPEVINE, 1650 West College Street, Zip 76051–1650; tel. 817/329–2500; Mark C. Hood, Executive Director (Total facility includes 9 beds in nursing home–type unit) (Nonreporting) **A**1 9 10 **S** Baylor Health Care System, Dallas, TX **N** Baylor Health Care System Network, Dallas, TX; North Texas Health Network, Irving, TX; North Texas Healthcare Network, Dallas, TX	21	10	68	—	—	—	—	—	—	—
□ CHARTER GRAPEVINE BEHAVIORAL HEALTH SYSTEM, 2300 William D. Tate Avenue, Zip 76051–9964; tel. 817/481–1900; Michael V. Lee, Chief Executive Officer **A**1 9 10 **F**1 3 12 16 19 22 27 34 35 46 48 52 53 54 55 56 57 58 59 65 67 70 71 **S** Magellan Health Services, Atlanta, GA	32	22	80	1789	33	11120	0	10895	3114	82

GREENVILLE—Hunt County

□ GLEN OAKS HOSPITAL, 301 East Division, Zip 75401–4199; tel. 903/454–6000; Thomas E. Rourke, Administrator **A**1 9 10 **F**2 3 15 46 52 53 54 55 56 57 58 59 68 **S** Universal Health Services, Inc., King of Prussia, PA	33	22	54	962	21	1860	—	4137	2324	81

Hospital, Address, Telephone, Administrator, Approval, Facility, and Physician Codes, Health Care System, Network	Classification Codes		Utilization Data					Expense (thousands) of dollars		
★ American Hospital Association (AHA) membership □ Joint Commission on Accreditation of Healthcare Organizations (JCAHO) accreditation + American Osteopathic Healthcare Association (AOHA) membership ○ American Osteopathic Association (AOA) accreditation △ Commission on Accreditation of Rehabilitation Facilities (CARF) accreditation Control codes 61, 63, 64, 71, 72 and 73 indicate hospitals listed by AOHA, but not registered by AHA. For definition of numerical codes, see page A4	Control	Service	Staffed Beds	Admissions	Census	Outpatient Visits	Births	Total	Payroll	Personnel

	Control	Service	Staffed Beds	Admissions	Census	Outpatient Visits	Births	Total	Payroll	Personnel
✠ HUNT MEMORIAL HOSPITAL DISTRICT, (Includes Presbyterian Hospital of Commerce, 2900 Sterling Hart Drive, Commerce, Zip 75428; tel. 903/886–3161; Presbyterian Hospital of Greenville, 4215 Joe Ramsey Boulevard, Zip 75401), 4215 Joe Ramsey Boulevard East, Zip 75401–7899, Mailing Address: P.O. Drawer 1059, Zip 75403–1059; tel. 903/408–5000; Richard Carter, Chief Executive Officer **A**1 9 10 **F**7 8 12 14 15 16 19 21 22 28 29 30 32 34 35 39 41 44 49 64 65 67 71 72 73 **P**8 **N** Presbyterian Healthcare System, Dallas, TX	16	10	145	5844	60	90613	0	38792	17607	563
GROESBECK—Limestone County										
LIMESTONE MEDICAL CENTER, 701 McClintic Street, Zip 76642–2105; tel. 254/729–3281; Penny Gray, Administrator and Chief Executive Officer **A**9 10 **F**1 15 16 19 28 32 34 35 39 46 49 51 57 59 61 66 73 **N** Central Texas Rural Health Network, Harrietsville, TX; Brazo's Valley Health Network, Waco, TX	16	10	15	208	2	15338	0	3999	2175	75
GROVES—Jefferson County										
★ + ○ DOCTORS HOSPITAL, 5500 39th Street, Zip 77619–9805; tel. 409/962–5733; John Isbell, Chief Executive Officer **A**9 10 11 12 13 **F**3 4 7 8 10 12 14 15 19 21 22 26 28 30 32 34 35 37 41 42 43 44 46 49 51 52 53 57 59 60 63 64 65 66 70 71 73 **P**8 **S** Quorum Health Group/Quorum Health Resources, Inc., Brentwood, TN	23	10	78	2337	25	14680	0	21274	6033	197
HALE CENTER—Hale County										
✠ HI-PLAINS HOSPITAL, 203 West Fourth Street, Zip 79041, Mailing Address: P.O. Box 1260, Zip 79041–1260; tel. 806/839–2471; Michael J. Keller, Administrator (Total facility includes 44 beds in nursing home–type unit) **A**1 9 10 **F**7 14 15 16 17 19 24 26 28 29 30 32 40 44 49 61 65 66 70 71 **P**8	23	10	84	488	47	2445	89	4999	2533	60
HALLETTSVILLE—Lavaca County										
LAVACA MEDICAL CENTER, 1400 North Texana Street, Zip 77964–2099; tel. 512/798–3671; James Vanek, Administrator (Nonreporting) **A**9 10 **N** SouthEast Texas Hospital System, Dallas, TX	16	10	36	—	—	—	—	—	—	—
HAMLIN—Jones County										
HAMLIN MEMORIAL HOSPITAL, 632 Northwest Second Street, Zip 79520–3831, Mailing Address: P.O. Box 400, Zip 79520–0400; tel. 915/576–3646; Charley C. Latham, Administrator **A**9 10 **F**15 16 19 22 28 32 33 35 36 44 71 **P**6	16	10	23	376	6	1665	2	2426	1247	60
HARLINGEN—Cameron County										
□ RIO GRANDE STATE CENTER, 1401 South Rangerville Road, Zip 78552–7638; tel. 956/425–8900; Sonia Hernandez-Keeble, Director **A**1 9 **F**24 28 31 39 45 46 52 55 56 57 65 67 73	12	22	60	948	39	—	—	10916	5654	346
✠ SOUTH TEXAS HOSPITAL, 1301 Rangerville Road, Zip 78552–7609, Mailing Address: P.O. Box 592, Zip 78551–0592; tel. 956/423–3420; James N. Elkins, FACHE, Director **A**1 10 **F**8 12 14 15 16 17 19 20 21 27 28 29 30 34 35 39 41 44 45 46 49 51 65 71 73 74 **P**6 **S** Texas Department of Health, Austin, TX	12	10	84	573	32	28880	—	14542	6222	305
✠ VALLEY BAPTIST MEDICAL CENTER, 2101 Pease Street, Zip 78550–8307, Mailing Address: P.O. Drawer 2588, Zip 78551–2588; tel. 956/389–1100; Ben M. McKibbens, President (Total facility includes 60 beds in nursing home–type unit) **A**1 2 5 9 10 **F**4 7 8 10 11 12 13 15 16 17 18 19 22 23 26 28 29 30 32 33 35 37 38 39 40 41 42 43 44 45 47 48 49 60 71 **P**3 8	21	10	363	19405	217	106273	3938	154353	61646	2032
HASKELL—Haskell County										
HASKELL MEMORIAL HOSPITAL, 1 North Avenue N., Zip 79521–5499, Mailing Address: P.O. Box 1117, Zip 79521–1117; tel. 817/864–2621; Bill Nemir, Administrator **A**9 10 **F**14 15 16 19 22 24 27 28 29 30 32 33 36 44 46 49 66 71 73 **P**1	16	10	30	376	5	1965	0	2606	1087	—
HEMPHILL—Sabine County										
★ SABINE COUNTY HOSPITAL, Highway 83 West, Zip 75948, Mailing Address: P.O. Box 750, Zip 75948–0750; tel. 409/787–3300; Edith McCauley, Administrator (Nonreporting) **A**9 10	16	10	36	—	—	—	—	—	—	—
HENDERSON—Rusk County										
✠ HENDERSON MEMORIAL HOSPITAL, 300 Wilson Street, Zip 75652–5956; tel. 903/657–7541; George T. Roberts, Jr., Chief Executive Officer (Total facility includes 16 beds in nursing home–type unit) **A**1 9 10 **F**7 8 12 15 16 19 20 22 28 29 30 31 32 34 35 37 39 40 44 45 46 49 63 64 65 70 71 74 **P**8 **S** Quorum Health Group/Quorum Health Resources, Inc., Brentwood, TN **N** Healthcare Partners of East Texas, Inc., Tyler, TX; Regional Healthcare Alliance, Tyler, TX	23	10	96	3326	42	59852	382	19574	9166	339
HENRIETTA—Clay County										
CLAY COUNTY MEMORIAL HOSPITAL, 310 West South Street, Zip 76365–3399; tel. 940/538–5621; Edward E. Browning, Chief Executive Officer and Administrator **A**9 10 **F**7 19 22 26 30 32 34 44 49 57 70 71 **P**8 **N** Texoma Health Network, Wichita Falls, TX	13	10	24	345	5	6510	—	3123	1465	61
HEREFORD—Deaf Smith County										
✠ HEREFORD REGIONAL MEDICAL CENTER, 801 East Third Street, Zip 79045–5727, Mailing Address: P.O. Box 1858, Zip 79045–1858; tel. 806/364–2141; George N. Parsley, Administrator **A**1 9 10 **F**6 7 8 10 12 13 14 15 16 17 18 19 20 21 22 24 26 28 30 31 32 33 34 35 36 37 40 41 42 43 44 45 46 49 53 54 55 56 57 58 59 60 65 67 70 71 73 74 **N** Lubbock Methodist Hospital System, Lubbock, TX	16	10	39	1178	11	28421	304	10783	5497	208

Hospital, Address, Telephone, Administrator, Approval, Facility, and Physician Codes, Health Care System, Network	Classi-fication Codes		Utilization Data					Expense (thousands) of dollars		
	Control	Service	Staffed Beds	Admissions	Census	Outpatient Visits	Births	Total	Payroll	Personnel

★ American Hospital Association (AHA) membership
□ Joint Commission on Accreditation of Healthcare Organizations (JCAHO) accreditation
+ American Osteopathic Healthcare Association (AOHA) membership
○ American Osteopathic Association (AOA) accreditation
△ Commission on Accreditation of Rehabilitation Facilities (CARF) accreditation
Control codes 61, 63, 64, 71, 72 and 73 indicate hospitals listed by AOHA, but not registered by AHA. For definition of numerical codes, see page A4

HILLSBORO—Hill County

★ HILL REGIONAL HOSPITAL, 101 Circle Drive, Zip 76645–2670; tel. 254/582–8425; Jan McClure, Chief Executive Officer (Total facility includes 23 beds in nursing home–type unit) **A**1 9 10 **F**7 12 15 16 19 22 26 30 34 35 37 40 41 44 45 46 52 57 64 70 71 73 **S** Community Health Systems, Inc., Brentwood, TN **N** Central Texas Rural Health Network, Harrietsville, TX; Brazo's Valley Health Network, Waco, TX … 33 10 92 1958 24 20435 209 9617 3947 128

HONDO—Medina County

MEDINA COMMUNITY HOSPITAL, 3100 Avenue East, Zip 78861–3599; tel. 210/741–4677; Richard D. Arnold, Administrator **A**9 10 **F**7 12 14 15 19 21 24 27 28 29 32 34 40 41 42 44 46 49 70 71 **P**4 **N** Southwest Texas Rural Health Alliance, San Antonio, TX … 15 10 27 916 8 93604 164 14171 6656 264

HOUSTON—Harris County

★ AMERICAN TRANSITIONAL HOSPITAL, (LONG TERM ACUTE CARE), 6447 Main Street, Zip 77030, Mailing Address: 6500 Fannin Street, Suite 907, Zip 77030; tel. 713/791–9393; Ron J. MacLaren, Administrator and Chief Executive Officer **A**1 10 **F**12 16 19 20 21 22 32 33 35 39 41 42 44 46 49 50 60 63 65 67 71 **S** American Transitional Hospitals, Inc., Franklin, TN … 33 49 58 488 36 0 0 11304 4086 127

□ ATH HEIGHTS HOSPITAL, 1917 Ashland Street, Zip 77008–3994; tel. 713/861–6161; Patrick W. Gandy, Chief Executive Officer **A**1 9 10 **F**12 19 22 37 48 65 71 **S** American Transitional Hospitals, Inc., Franklin, TN … 33 10 170 946 88 — — 22682 8941 233

BEN TAUB GENERAL HOSPITAL See Harris County Hospital District

CASA, A SPECIAL HOSPITAL, (SUB ACUTE CARE), 1803 Old Spanish Trail, Zip 77054–2001; tel. 713/796–2272; Gretchen Thorp, R.N., Administrator **A**10 **F**6 12 15 31 42 65 73 … 32 49 40 601 19 0 0 2645 1063 47

★ COLUMBIA BELLAIRE MEDICAL CENTER, 5314 Dashwood Street, Zip 77081–4689; tel. 713/512–1200; Walter Leleux, Chief Executive Officer (Total facility includes 15 beds in nursing home–type unit) **A**1 9 10 **F**1 3 7 8 12 14 15 16 17 19 21 22 23 26 27 28 30 35 37 40 41 42 44 49 52 54 55 56 57 58 59 64 65 67 70 71 73 74 **P**5 7 8 **S** Columbia/HCA Healthcare Corporation, Nashville, TN **N** Gulf Coast Provider Network, Houston, TX … 33 10 202 5662 89 40387 1625 46835 16009 467

★ COLUMBIA DOCTORS HOSPITAL AIRLINE, 5815 Airline Drive, Zip 77076–4996; tel. 713/695–6041; Joe G. Baldwin, Chief Executive Officer (Nonreporting) **A**1 9 **S** Columbia/HCA Healthcare Corporation, Nashville, TN … 32 10 114 — — — — — — —

★ COLUMBIA EAST HOUSTON MEDICAL CENTER, (Includes Sun Belt Regional Medical Center East, 15101 East Freeway, Channelview, Zip 77530; tel. 713/452–1511), 13111 East Freeway, Zip 77015; tel. 713/455–6911; Merrily Walters, Administrator **A**1 9 10 **F**7 8 10 11 12 14 15 16 19 20 21 22 26 28 30 31 32 33 34 35 37 39 40 41 42 44 46 49 51 52 54 57 65 71 72 73 74 **P**5 **S** Columbia/HCA Healthcare Corporation, Nashville, TN … 33 10 179 5749 64 57910 1144 47760 19985 —

★ COLUMBIA NORTH HOUSTON MEDICAL CENTER, 233 West Parker Road, Zip 77076–2999; tel. 713/697–2831; Joe G. Baldwin, Chief Executive Officer **A**1 9 10 **F**3 4 7 8 10 12 14 15 16 19 20 22 23 24 25 26 27 28 29 30 32 33 34 35 37 39 40 41 42 43 44 45 46 48 49 52 55 57 58 59 64 65 66 67 70 71 73 74 **P**5 7 8 **S** Columbia/HCA Healthcare Corporation, Nashville, TN … 33 10 197 11834 139 61485 1670 52616 23801 720

★ △ COLUMBIA ROSEWOOD MEDICAL CENTER, 9200 Westheimer Road, Zip 77063–3599; tel. 713/780–7900; Pat Currie, Chief Executive Officer (Total facility includes 18 beds in nursing home–type unit) **A**1 7 9 10 **F**3 4 5 7 8 10 12 14 16 18 19 20 21 22 23 24 26 27 28 30 31 32 33 34 35 37 39 40 41 42 43 44 48 49 51 52 53 54 55 56 57 58 59 60 63 64 65 66 67 71 73 74 **P**7 8 **S** Columbia/HCA Healthcare Corporation, Nashville, TN **N** Gulf Coast Provider Network, Houston, TX … 33 10 184 5337 76 42166 478 41279 15807 358

COLUMBIA SPRING BRANCH MEDICAL CENTER See Spring Branch Medical Center

★ COLUMBIA TEXAS ORTHOPEDIC HOSPITAL, 7401 South Main Street, Zip 77030–4509; tel. 713/799–8600; John J. Jackson, Chief Executive Officer **A**1 9 10 **F**2 3 4 5 7 8 10 11 12 13 14 16 17 18 19 22 23 24 25 26 27 28 30 32 35 37 38 39 41 42 43 44 46 47 48 49 50 52 53 54 55 56 57 58 59 60 61 64 65 66 67 68 69 71 72 73 74 **P**1 5 7 **S** Columbia/HCA Healthcare Corporation, Nashville, TN … 32 47 49 1631 18 26119 0 21490 8412 251

★ △ COLUMBIA WEST HOUSTON MEDICAL CENTER, 12141 Richmond Avenue, Zip 77082–2499; tel. 281/558–3444; Jeffrey S. Holland, Chief Executive Officer (Total facility includes 18 beds in nursing home–type unit) **A**1 7 9 10 **F**3 4 7 8 10 11 12 14 19 21 22 26 28 29 30 32 33 34 35 37 38 39 40 41 42 43 44 46 48 49 52 57 64 65 66 71 73 74 **P**5 8 **S** Columbia/HCA Healthcare Corporation, Nashville, TN **N** Gulf Coast Provider Network, Houston, TX … 33 10 169 6161 83 50285 1216 43738 17898 524

COLUMBIA WOMAN'S HOSPITAL OF TEXAS See Woman's Hospital of Texas

□ CYPRESS CREEK HOSPITAL, 17750 Cali Drive, Zip 77090–2700; tel. 713/586–7600; Terry Scovill, Administrator **A**1 9 10 **F**3 22 52 53 54 55 56 57 58 59 67 **S** Healthcare America, Inc., Austin, TX … 33 22 94 1376 36 6359 0 6513 3628 —

★ △ CYPRESS FAIRBANKS MEDICAL CENTER, 10655 Steepletop Drive, Zip 77065–4297; tel. 281/890–4285; Bill Klier, Chief Executive Officer (Total facility includes 14 beds in nursing home–type unit) **A**1 7 9 10 **F**2 7 8 10 12 19 21 22 28 29 30 31 32 34 35 37 40 41 44 46 49 50 52 63 64 65 66 67 71 73 74 **S** TENET Healthcare Corporation, Santa Barbara, CA **N** Gulf Coast Provider Network, Houston, TX … 33 10 133 6041 54 60484 948 54970 22064 616

★ DIAGNOSTIC CENTER HOSPITAL, 6447 Main Street, Zip 77030–1595; tel. 713/790–0790; William A. Gregory, Chief Executive Officer (Total facility includes 25 beds in nursing home–type unit) **A**1 9 10 **F**2 4 7 8 9 10 11 12 15 16 17 19 20 21 22 23 24 26 27 28 30 31 32 33 34 35 37 38 39 40 41 42 43 44 45 46 47 48 49 50 52 54 55 57 58 60 61 63 64 65 66 67 69 71 73 **P**1 3 **S** Methodist Health Care System, Houston, TX … 23 10 109 3601 69 — 0 38906 14152 413

Hospital, Address, Telephone, Administrator, Approval, Facility, and Physician Codes, Health Care System, Network	Classi-fication Codes		Utilization Data					Expense (thousands) of dollars		
★ American Hospital Association (AHA) membership □ Joint Commission on Accreditation of Healthcare Organizations (JCAHO) accreditation + American Osteopathic Healthcare Association (AOHA) membership ○ American Osteopathic Association (AOA) accreditation △ Commission on Accreditation of Rehabilitation Facilities (CARF) accreditation Control codes 61, 63, 64, 71, 72 and 73 indicate hospitals listed by AOHA, but not registered by AHA. For definition of numerical codes, see page A4	Control	Service	Staffed Beds	Admissions	Census	Outpatient Visits	Births	Total	Payroll	Personnel
✸ DOCTORS HOSPITAL–TIDWELL, (Formerly Yale Clinic and Hospital), 510 West Tidwell Road, Zip 77091–4399; tel. 713/691–1111; John H. Styles, Jr., Administrator (Nonreporting) **A**1 9 10	33	10	43	—	—	—	—	—	—	—
□ FOREST SPRINGS HOSPITAL, 1120 Cypress Station, Zip 77090–3031; tel. 281/893–7200; Deo Shanker, CPA, Chief Executive Officer **A**1 9 **F**2 3 19 21 27 35 52 53 54 55 56 57 58 59 65 **S** Cambridge International, Inc,, Houston, TX	33	22	48	293	7	861	0	2484	—	72
□ GULF PINES BEHAVIORAL HEALTH SERVICES, 205 Hollow Tree Lane, Zip 77090–2801; tel. 713/537–0700; Lawrence Story, Chief Executive Officer and Administrator (Nonreporting) **A**1 9 10 **S** Children's Comprehensive Services, Inc., Nashville, TN	33	22	140	—	—	—	—	—	—	—
□ HARRIS COUNTY HOSPITAL DISTRICT, (Includes Ben Taub General Hospital, 1504 Taub Loop, Zip 77030; tel. 713/793–2300; William M. Adams, Senior Vice President; Lyndon B Johnson General Hospital, 5656 Kelley, Zip 77026; tel. 713/636–5000; Margo Hilliard, M.D., Senior Vice President; Quentin Mease Hospital, 3601 North MacGregor, Zip 77004; tel. 713/528–1499; William M. Adams, Senior Vice President), 2525 Holly Hall Street, Zip 77054–4108, Mailing Address: P.O. Box 66769, Zip 77266–6769; tel. 713/746–6403; Lois Jean Moore, President and Chief Executive Officer (Total facility includes 24 beds in nursing home–type unit) **A**1 3 5 8 9 10 **F**3 4 7 8 10 11 12 14 15 16 17 18 19 20 21 22 23 25 26 27 30 31 32 34 35 37 38 40 42 43 44 47 48 49 52 56 58 59 60 61 63 64 65 67 68 70 71 73 **P**6	16	10	926	41268	644	896100	12020	432110	164279	5064
✸ HARRIS COUNTY PSYCHIATRIC CENTER, 2800 South MacGregor Way, Zip 77021–1000, Mailing Address: P.O. Box 20249, Zip 77225–0249; tel. 713/741–5000; Robert W. Guynn, M.D., Executive Director **A**1 3 5 9 10 **F**3 12 14 15 16 19 21 27 35 41 46 50 52 53 54 55 56 57 58 63 65 67 71 73 **S** University of Texas System, Austin, TX	12	22	250	5429	182	0	0	30635	14786	418
✸ △ HEALTHSOUTH HOUSTON REHABILITATION INSTITUTE, (Formerly Houston Rehabilitation Institute), 17506 Red Oak Drive, Zip 77090–7721, Mailing Address: P.O. Box 73684, Zip 77273–3684; tel. 281/580–1212; Anne R. Leon, Chief Executive Officer (Total facility includes 14 beds in nursing home–type unit) (Nonreporting) **A**1 7 9 10 **S** HEALTHSOUTH Corporation, Birmingham, AL	33	46	80	—	—	—	—	—	—	—
✸ HERMANN HOSPITAL, 6411 Fannin, Zip 77030–1501; tel. 713/704–4000; Lynn Walts, R.N., Dr.PH, President and Chief Executive Officer (Total facility includes 15 beds in nursing home–type unit) **A**1 3 5 8 9 10 **F**4 7 8 9 10 11 12 14 15 16 17 19 20 21 22 25 26 27 28 30 31 32 34 35 37 38 39 40 41 42 43 44 45 46 47 48 49 50 51 56 61 63 64 65 66 67 68 69 70 71 72 73 74 **P**7 8 **S** Memorial Herman Healthcare System, Houston, TX **N** Gulf Coast Provider Network, Houston, TX	23	10	624	24018	421	300092	2187	352243	118979	3659
✸ HOUSTON NORTHWEST MEDICAL CENTER, 710 FM 1960 West, Zip 77090–3496; tel. 281/440–1000; James Kelly, Chief Executive Officer (Total facility includes 20 beds in nursing home–type unit) **A**1 2 9 10 **F**3 4 7 8 10 12 15 16 17 19 20 21 22 23 24 28 29 30 31 32 33 34 35 37 38 40 41 42 43 44 45 46 49 52 53 54 55 56 57 58 59 60 61 64 65 67 71 72 73 74 **P**7 8 **S** TENET Healthcare Corporation, Santa Barbara, CA **N** Gulf Coast Provider Network, Houston, TX HOUSTON REHABILITATION INSTITUTE See HEALTHSOUTH Houston Rehabilitation Institute	32	10	383	17661	194	351041	3633	141251	56269	1168
□ INTRACARE MEDICAL CENTER HOSPITAL, 7601 Fannin Street, Zip 77054–1905; tel. 713/790–0949; Alice Hiniker, Ph.D., Administrator **A**1 9 10 **F**3 19 21 27 35 52 53 54 55 56 58 59 65 **S** Cambridge International, Inc,, Houston, TX LYNDON B JOHNSON GENERAL HOSPITAL See Harris County Hospital District MEMORIAL HOSPITAL NORTHWEST See Memorial Hospital Southwest MEMORIAL HOSPITAL SOUTHEAST See Memorial Hospital Southwest	33	22	100	767	25	5742	0	6390	2695	106
✸ MEMORIAL HOSPITAL SOUTHWEST, (Includes Memorial Hospital Northwest, 1635 North Loop West, Zip 77008; tel. 713/867–3380; Memorial Hospital Southeast, 11800 Astoria, Zip 77089; tel. 281/929–6100), 7600 Beechnut, Zip 77074–1850; tel. 713/776–5000; James E. Eastham, Vice President and Chief Executive Officer (Total facility includes 41 beds in nursing home–type unit) **A**1 2 3 5 9 10 **F**2 3 4 6 7 8 10 11 12 14 15 16 17 19 21 22 23 25 26 27 28 29 30 31 32 33 34 35 37 38 39 40 41 42 43 44 45 46 48 49 51 52 53 54 55 56 57 58 59 60 62 63 64 65 66 67 68 70 71 72 73 74 **P**3 4 7 **S** Memorial Herman Healthcare System, Houston, TX **N** Memorial/Sisters of Charity Health Network, Houston, TX	23	10	490	22063	315	101016	3654	161885	54991	1521
✸ MEMORIAL HOSPITAL–MEMORIAL CITY, 920 Frostwood Drive, Zip 77024–9173; tel. 713/932–3000; Jerel T. Humphrey, Vice President, Chief Executive Officer and Administrator (Total facility includes 24 beds in nursing home–type unit) **A**1 2 6 9 10 **F**2 3 4 6 7 8 10 11 12 14 15 16 17 19 21 22 23 25 26 27 28 29 30 31 32 33 34 35 37 38 39 40 41 42 43 44 45 46 48 49 51 52 53 54 55 56 57 58 59 60 62 63 64 65 66 67 68 70 71 72 73 74 **P**3 4 7 **S** Memorial Herman Healthcare System, Houston, TX **N** Memorial/Sisters of Charity Health Network, Houston, TX	23	10	316	15724	175	74331	3172	104286	29968	914
MEMORIAL REHABILITATION HOSPITAL, 3043 Gessner Drive, Zip 77080–2597; tel. 713/462–2515; Roger Truskoloski, Administrator, Chief Executive Officer and Vice President (Total facility includes 24 beds in nursing home–type unit) **F**2 3 4 6 7 8 10 11 12 14 15 16 17 19 21 22 23 25 26 27 28 29 30 31 32 33 34 35 37 38 39 40 41 42 43 44 45 46 48 49 51 52 53 54 55 56 57 58 59 60 62 63 64 65 66 67 68 70 71 72 73 74 **P**3 4 7 **S** Memorial Herman Healthcare System, Houston, TX	23	46	106	772	46	1064	0	13116	4188	152

Hospital, Address, Telephone, Administrator, Approval, Facility, and Physician Codes, Health Care System, Network	Classi-fication Codes		Utilization Data					Expense (thousands) of dollars		
	Control	Service	Staffed Beds	Admissions	Census	Outpatient Visits	Births	Total	Payroll	Personnel

★ American Hospital Association (AHA) membership
□ Joint Commission on Accreditation of Healthcare Organizations (JCAHO) accreditation
+ American Osteopathic Healthcare Association (AOHA) membership
○ American Osteopathic Association (AOA) accreditation
△ Commission on Accreditation of Rehabilitation Facilities (CARF) accreditation
Control codes 61, 63, 64, 71, 72 and 73 indicate hospitals listed by AOHA, but not registered by AHA. For definition of numerical codes, see page A4

Hospital	Control	Service	Staffed Beds	Admissions	Census	Outpatient Visits	Births	Total	Payroll	Personnel
⊞ MEMORIAL SPRING SHADOWS GLEN, 2801 Gessner, Zip 77080–2599; tel. 713/462–4000; G. Jerry Mueck, Vice President, Chief Executive Officer and Administrator **A**1 9 **F**2 3 4 6 7 8 10 11 12 14 15 16 17 19 21 22 23 25 26 27 28 29 30 31 32 33 34 35 37 38 39 40 41 42 43 44 45 46 48 49 51 52 53 54 55 56 57 58 59 60 62 63 64 65 66 67 68 70 71 72 73 74 **P**3 4 7 **S** Memorial Herman Healthcare System, Houston, TX **N** Memorial/Sisters of Charity Health Network, Houston, TX	23	22	108	2043	51	706	—	14378	5733	215
NORTHSIDE GENERAL HOSPITAL, 2807 Little York Road, Zip 77093–3495; tel. 713/697–7777; Carole A. Veloso, President and Chief Executive Officer **A**9 10 **F**12 14 15 16 17 19 21 22 28 34 37 42 44 46 49 61 65 70 71	33	10	39	1685	18	4880	0	9602	3244	163
⊞ △ PARK PLAZA HOSPITAL, 1313 Hermann Drive, Zip 77004–7092; tel. 713/527–5000; Robert L. Quist, Chief Executive Officer (Total facility includes 40 beds in nursing home–type unit) **A**1 2 3 5 7 9 10 **F**4 7 8 10 12 14 15 16 17 19 21 22 26 28 30 31 32 34 35 37 40 41 42 43 44 45 46 48 49 52 57 60 61 63 64 65 67 71 73 **P**1 5 7 **S** TENET Healthcare Corporation, Santa Barbara, CA	32	10	370	8974	181	53406	868	80866	30372	939
QUENTIN MEASE HOSPITAL See Harris County Hospital District										
□ RIVERSIDE GENERAL HOSPITAL, 3204 Ennis Street, Zip 77004–3299; tel. 713/526–2441; Earnest Gibson, III, Administrator (Nonreporting) **A**1 9 10	23	82	56	—	—	—	—	—	—	—
SAM HOUSTON MEMORIAL HOSPITAL See Spring Branch Medical Center										
⊞ SHARPSTOWN GENERAL HOSPITAL, 6700 Bellaire at Tarnef, Zip 77074–4999, Mailing Address: P.O. Box 740389, Zip 77274–0389; tel. 713/774–7611; Steve Altmiller, Chief Executive Officer **A**1 9 10 **F**4 7 8 10 11 12 14 15 16 17 19 20 21 22 25 26 27 28 30 31 32 33 34 35 36 37 38 39 40 41 42 43 44 46 49 51 52 53 54 56 57 59 60 65 66 67 71 73 74 **P**5 7 8 **S** TENET Healthcare Corporation, Santa Barbara, CA	33	10	120	3594	47	66947	1080	29820	14843	395
⊞ SHRINERS HOSPITALS FOR CHILDREN, HOUSTON, 6977 Main Street, Zip 77030–3701; tel. 713/797–1616; Steven B. Reiter, Administrator **A**1 3 5 **F**5 9 12 17 19 20 22 27 28 34 35 39 44 45 48 49 51 54 64 65 67 71 73 **P**6 **S** Shriners Hospitals for Children, Tampa, FL	23	57	40	673	17	10091	—	—	—	171
⊞ SPECIALTY HOSPITAL OF HOUSTON, (LONG TERM ACUTE CARE), 5556 Gasmer Drive, Zip 77035–4598; tel. 713/551–5300; Shelley R. Cochran, Interim Chief Executive Officer **A**1 10 **F**4 8 10 12 14 15 16 19 21 22 24 26 30 31 35 37 39 41 42 43 44 45 46 49 50 51 60 63 64 65 67 71	33	49	54	247	26	—	—	9812	4046	116
⊞ △ SPRING BRANCH MEDICAL CENTER, (Formerly Columbia Spring Branch Medical Center), (Includes Sam Houston Memorial Hospital, 1615 Hillendahl, Zip 77055; tel. 713/932–5500), 8850 Long Point Road, Zip 77055–3082; tel. 713/467–6555; Pat Currie, Chief Executive Officer (Total facility includes 25 beds in nursing home–type unit) (Nonreporting) **A**1 2 7 9 10 **S** Columbia/HCA Healthcare Corporation, Nashville, TN **N** Gulf Coast Provider Network, Houston, TX	33	10	345	—	—	—	—	—	—	—
⊞ △ ST. JOSEPH HOSPITAL, 1919 LaBranch Street, Zip 77002; tel. 713/757–1000; Sally E. Jeffcoat, Administrator (Total facility includes 29 beds in nursing home–type unit) **A**1 2 3 5 7 9 10 **F**3 4 7 8 10 11 12 13 14 15 16 17 18 19 21 22 23 24 26 28 29 30 31 32 33 34 35 37 38 39 40 41 42 43 44 45 46 48 49 51 52 54 55 56 57 59 60 61 63 64 65 66 67 68 70 71 72 73 **P**1 4 5 6 7 **S** Sisters of Charity of the Incarnate Word Healthcare System, Houston, TX **N** SouthEast Texas Integrated Community Health Network, Houston, TX	23	10	481	18426	273	—	4641	—	70557	2253
⊞ ST. LUKE'S EPISCOPAL HOSPITAL, 6720 Bertner Avenue, Zip 77030–2697; Mailing Address: Box 20269, Zip 77225–0269; tel. 713/791–2011; Michael K. Jhin, President and Chief Executive Officer **A**1 2 3 5 8 9 10 **F**4 7 8 10 11 12 14 15 17 19 21 22 25 28 29 30 32 34 35 37 39 40 41 42 43 44 45 46 48 49 51 54 56 61 63 65 67 68 69 71 73 74 **P**5 7 8	21	10	621	29320	430	183126	2523	354849	132784	—
⊞ TEXAS CHILDREN'S HOSPITAL, 6621 Fannin Street, Zip 77030–2399, Mailing Address: Box 300630, Zip 77230–0630; tel. 713/770–1000; Mark A. Wallace, Executive Director and Chief Executive Officer **A**1 3 5 8 9 10 **F**4 5 10 12 13 14 15 16 17 19 20 21 22 24 25 29 30 31 32 34 35 38 39 41 42 43 44 45 46 47 49 50 51 54 55 58 60 63 65 66 67 68 69 70 71 72 73 **P**5 7	23	50	374	18937	314	336680	0	259012	117025	2908
⊞ △ THE INSTITUTE FOR REHABILITATION AND RESEARCH, 1333 Moursund, Zip 77030–3405; tel. 713/799–5000; Louisa F. Adelung, President and Chief Executive Officer (Nonreporting) **A**1 3 5 7 9 10	23	46	92	—	—	—	—	—	—	—
⊞ △ THE METHODIST HOSPITAL, 6565 Fannin Street, Zip 77030–2707; tel. 713/790–3311; R. G. Girotto, Executive Vice President and Chief Operating Officer (Total facility includes 25 beds in nursing home–type unit) **A**1 2 3 5 7 8 9 10 **F**2 3 4 5 7 8 10 11 12 14 15 16 17 18 19 20 21 22 26 28 29 30 31 32 33 34 35 37 39 40 41 42 43 44 45 46 48 49 50 51 52 54 55 56 57 58 59 60 61 62 63 64 65 66 67 69 71 73 74 **P**2 3 5 **S** Methodist Health Care System, Houston, TX	23	10	900	32908	747	286211	2875	458476	168763	6458
⊞ TWELVE OAKS HOSPITAL, 4200 Portsmouth Street, Zip 77027–6899; tel. 713/623–2500; Steve Altmiller, Chief Executive Officer (Total facility includes 15 beds in nursing home–type unit) **A**1 9 10 **F**2 3 4 7 8 10 11 12 15 16 17 19 21 22 26 27 28 29 30 31 32 35 37 38 40 42 43 44 45 46 48 49 52 53 54 55 56 57 58 59 60 61 64 65 67 71 73 74 **P**1 2 3 4 5 6 7 8 **S** TENET Healthcare Corporation, Santa Barbara, CA	32	10	213	4955	105	17483	—	42596	17038	465
□ UNIVERSITY OF TEXAS M. D. ANDERSON CANCER CENTER, (ONCOLOGY COMPREHENSIVE CANCER), 1515 Holcombe Boulevard, Box 506, Zip 77030–4009; tel. 713/792–6000; John Mendelsohn, M.D., President **A**1 2 3 5 8 9 10 **F**8 12 14 15 16 17 19 20 21 25 28 29 30 34 35 37 39 41 42 44 45 46 48 49 50 53 54 55 56 58 60 63 65 67 69 71 73 **P**5 6 **S** University of Texas System, Austin, TX	12	49	417	15955	320	451185	0	659067	325973	7460

Hospital, Address, Telephone, Administrator, Approval, Facility, and Physician Codes, Health Care System, Network	Classi-fication Codes		Utilization Data					Expense (thousands) of dollars		
★ American Hospital Association (AHA) membership □ Joint Commission on Accreditation of Healthcare Organizations (JCAHO) accreditation + American Osteopathic Healthcare Association (AOHA) membership ○ American Osteopathic Association (AOA) accreditation △ Commission on Accreditation of Rehabilitation Facilities (CARF) accreditation Control codes 61, 63, 64, 71, 72 and 73 indicate hospitals listed by AOHA, but not registered by AHA. For definition of numerical codes, see page A4	Control	Service	Staffed Beds	Admissions	Census	Outpatient Visits	Births	Total	Payroll	Personnel
⊠ VENCOR HOSPITAL–HOUSTON, (LONG TERM ACUTE CARE), 6441 Main Street, Zip 77030–1596; tel. 713/790–0500; Bob Stein, Executive Director **A**1 9 10 **F**12 22 26 34 39 46 67 **S** Vencor, Incorporated, Louisville, KY	33	49	96	526	58	0	0	15109	7405	217
⊠ VETERANS AFFAIRS MEDICAL CENTER, 2002 Holcombe Boulevard, Zip 77030–4298; tel. 713/791–1414; David Whatley, Director (Total facility includes 120 beds in nursing home–type unit) (Nonreporting) **A**1 3 5 8 **S** Department of Veterans Affairs, Washington, DC	45	10	859	—	—	—	—	—	—	—
□ WEST OAKS HOSPITAL, 6500 Hornwood Drive, Zip 77074–5095; tel. 713/995–0909; Terry Scovill, Chief Executive Officer **A**1 9 10 **F**1 2 3 6 15 16 26 27 34 39 52 53 54 55 56 57 58 59 65 **S** Healthcare America, Inc., Austin, TX	33	22	144	3616	60	10508	0	10294	5699	78
⊠ WOMAN'S HOSPITAL OF TEXAS, (Formerly Columbia Woman's Hospital of Texas), 7600 Fannin Street, Zip 77054–1900; tel. 713/790–1234; Linda B. Russell, Chief Executive Officer **A**1 5 9 10 **F**2 3 4 7 8 9 12 19 21 22 23 24 25 26 27 30 31 32 34 35 37 38 39 40 41 42 43 44 45 46 47 48 49 51 52 53 54 55 56 57 58 59 60 64 65 66 71 73 74 **P**7 8 **S** Columbia/HCA Healthcare Corporation, Nashville, TN **N** Gulf Coast Provider Network, Houston, TX YALE CLINIC AND HOSPITAL See Doctors Hospital–Tidwell	33	44	156	10251	124	20493	6314	63980	28186	727
HUMBLE—Harris County										
□ △ HEALTHSOUTH REHABILITATION HOSPITAL, 19002 McKay Drive, Zip 77338–5701; tel. 281/446–6148; Darrell L. Pile, Administrator (Total facility includes 12 beds in nursing home–type unit) **A**1 7 10 **F**12 14 15 16 19 21 22 25 26 27 34 35 39 44 45 46 48 49 64 65 66 67 71 73 **S** HEALTHSOUTH Corporation, Birmingham, AL	33	46	58	602	30	5974	0	7059	3515	134
⊠ NORTHEAST MEDICAL CENTER HOSPITAL, 18951 Memorial North, Zip 77338–4297; tel. 281/540–7700; Syble F. Missildine, Administrator (Total facility includes 16 beds in nursing home–type unit) **A**1 2 9 10 **F**1 3 4 5 6 7 8 10 11 12 13 15 16 17 18 19 20 21 22 23 24 25 26 27 28 29 30 31 32 33 34 35 36 37 38 39 40 41 42 43 44 45 46 49 51 53 54 55 56 57 58 59 60 61 62 63 64 65 66 67 68 69 70 71 72 73 74 **P**1 5 8	16	10	171	8399	101	98038	1195	68075	26709	759
HUNT—Kerr County										
LA HACIENDA TREATMENT CENTER, FM 1340, Zip 78024, Mailing Address: P.O. Box 1, Zip 78024–0001; tel. 830/238–4222; Frank J. Sadlack, Ph.D., Executive Director **F**3 12 16 17 22 24 30 31 39 41 45 46 54 56 67 **P**1	32	82	97	1116	38	13555	—	7865	3542	146
HUNTSVILLE—Walker County										
⊠ HUNTSVILLE MEMORIAL HOSPITAL, 3000 I–45, Zip 77340, Mailing Address: P.O. Box 4001, Zip 77342–4001; tel. 409/291–3411; Ralph E. Beaty, Administrator (Total facility includes 11 beds in nursing home–type unit) **A**1 6 9 10 **F**7 8 14 16 19 21 22 23 25 28 29 30 32 34 35 37 40 41 44 49 64 65 66 67 70 71 73 **S** Quorum Health Group/Quorum Health Resources, Inc., Brentwood, TN **N** Healthcare Partners of East Texas, Inc., Tyler, TX	23	10	130	3120	37	73379	492	27458	12388	353
IRAAN—Pecos County										
□ PECOS COUNTY GENERAL HOSPITAL, 305 West Fifth Street, Zip 79744, Mailing Address: P.O. Box 665, Zip 79744–2057; tel. 915/639–2871; David B. Shaw, Administrator and Chief Executive Officer **A**1 9 10 **F**14 15 16 22 28 30 34 39 44 45 49 51 65 70 71 **N** Lubbock Methodist Hospital System, Lubbock, TX; Permian Basin Rural Health Network, Fort Stockton, TX	13	10	13	272	3	5688	0	2441	583	26
IRVING—Dallas County										
AMERICAN TRANSITIONAL HOSPITAL–DALLAS/FORT WORTH, (LONG TERM ACUTE CARE), 1745 West Irving Boulevard, Zip 75061–7111; tel. 972/488–9167; LouAnn O. Mathews, Administrator **A**10 **F**22 51 65 **S** American Transitional Hospitals, Inc., Franklin, TN	33	49	36	156	11	0	0	5115	1698	116
⊠ BAYLOR MEDICAL CENTER AT IRVING, (Formerly Irving Healthcare System), 1901 North MacArthur Boulevard, Zip 75061–2291; tel. 972/579–8100; H. J. Macfarland, FACHE, Executive Director (Total facility includes 18 beds in nursing home–type unit) (Nonreporting) **A**1 2 9 10 **S** Baylor Health Care System, Dallas, TX **N** Baylor Health Care System Network, Dallas, TX	21	10	231	—	—	—	—	—	—	—
JACKSBORO—Jack County										
FAITH COMMUNITY HOSPITAL, 717 Magnolia Street, Zip 76458–1111; tel. 940/567–6633; Don Hopkins, Administrator **A**9 10 **F**28 32 41 44 49 64 65 70 71 **P**6 **N** Texoma Health Network, Wichita Falls, TX	16	10	18	500	4	18087	—	3064	1374	68
JACKSONVILLE—Cherokee County										
★ EAST TEXAS MEDICAL CENTER JACKSONVILLE, (Formerly Nan Travis Memorial Hospital), 501 South Ragsdale Street, Zip 75766–2413; tel. 903/586–3000; Steve Bowen, President (Total facility includes 18 beds in nursing home–type unit) **A**9 10 **F**7 8 15 17 19 20 22 24 25 28 30 32 34 35 41 42 43 44 46 49 57 65 66 67 71 74 **N** Healthcare Partners of East Texas, Inc., Tyler, TX	23	10	74	2616	36	39374	340	21002	10249	305
JASPER—Jasper County										
⊠ JASPER MEMORIAL HOSPITAL, 1275 Marvin Hancock Drive, Zip 75951–4995; tel. 409/384–5461; George N. Miller, Jr., Administrator **A**1 6 9 10 **F**7 8 12 14 15 16 17 18 19 22 25 26 28 29 30 31 32 34 35 37 40 44 45 46 49 51 65 70 71 73 **P**5 7 8 **S** Sisters of Charity of the Incarnate Word Healthcare System, Houston, TX	21	10	54	2616	19	33243	490	11550	6064	227
LAKES REGIONAL MEDICAL CENTER, 1001 Dickerson Drive, Zip 75951–5110, Mailing Address: P.O. Box 1990, Zip 75951–1990; tel. 409/384–2575; Spencer Guimarin, Administrator **A**9 10 **F**1 7 8 15 16 19 20 22 32 33 34 44 45 46 49 50 65 71 73 **P**5	33	10	35	1145	17	26943	18	5979	2980	127

Hospital, Address, Telephone, Administrator, Approval, Facility, and Physician Codes, Health Care System, Network	Classi-fication Codes		Utilization Data					Expense (thousands) of dollars		
★ American Hospital Association (AHA) membership □ Joint Commission on Accreditation of Healthcare Organizations (JCAHO) accreditation + American Osteopathic Healthcare Association (AOHA) membership ○ American Osteopathic Association (AOA) accreditation △ Commission on Accreditation of Rehabilitation Facilities (CARF) accreditation Control codes 61, 63, 64, 71, 72 and 73 indicate hospitals listed by AOHA, but not registered by AHA. For definition of numerical codes, see page A4	Control	Service	Staffed Beds	Admissions	Census	Outpatient Visits	Births	Total	Payroll	Personnel

JOURDANTON—Atascosa County

□ TRI–CITY COMMUNITY HOSPITAL, Highway 97 East, Zip 78026, Mailing Address: P.O. Box 189, Zip 78026–0189; tel. 512/769–3515; S. Allen Smith, Administrator **A**1 9 10 **F**8 16 18 19 20 21 22 26 28 30 32 33 34 35 41 42 44 46 49 57 58 66 67 71 72 **P**5 **N** Southwest Texas Rural Health Alliance, San Antonio, TX	32	10	30	1772	18	114332	0	16609	6855	346

JUNCTION—Kimble County

KIMBLE HOSPITAL, 2101 Main Street, Zip 76849–2101; tel. 915/446–3321; Jamie R. Jacoby, Administrator **A**9 10 **F**24 32 34 70 71 **N** Southwest Texas Rural Health Alliance, San Antonio, TX	16	10	16	305	3	19194	—	2792	1272	52

KATY—Fort Bend County

✚ KATY MEDICAL CENTER, (Formerly Columbia Katy Medical Center), 5602 Medical Center Drive, Zip 77494–6399; tel. 281/392–1111; Brian S. Barbe, Chief Executive Officer **A**1 9 10 **F**7 8 10 12 16 19 20 21 22 28 29 30 31 32 33 34 35 36 37 40 41 43 44 53 54 55 56 57 58 59 60 65 66 67 69 70 71 73 74 **P**5 8 **S** Columbia/HCA Healthcare Corporation, Nashville, TN	33	10	73	4004	32	41081	675	19796	9292	268

KAUFMAN—Kaufman County

✚ PRESBYTERIAN HOSPITAL OF KAUFMAN, 850 Highway 243 West, Zip 75142–9998, Mailing Address: P.O. Box 310, Zip 75142–0310; tel. 972/932–7200; Michael J. McBride, CHE, Executive Director (Total facility includes 6 beds in nursing home–type unit) (Nonreporting) **A**1 9 10 **S** Texas Health Resources, Irving, TX **N** Presbyterian Healthcare System, Dallas, TX; Regional Healthcare Alliance, Tyler, TX; North Texas Healthcare Network, Dallas, TX	23	10	68	—	—	—	—	—	—	—

KENEDY—Karnes County

OTTO KAISER MEMORIAL HOSPITAL, 3349 South Highway 181, Zip 78119–5240; tel. 830/583–3401; Harold L. Boening, Administrator **A**9 10 **F**19 22 32 37 44 49 71 **N** Southwest Texas Rural Health Alliance, San Antonio, TX	16	10	30	332	4	33145	0	3309	1310	82

KERMIT—Winkler County

MEMORIAL HOSPITAL, 821 Jeffee Drive, Zip 79745–4696, Mailing Address: Drawer H., Zip 79745–6008; tel. 915/586–5864; Judene Willhelm, Administrator (Nonreporting) **A**9 10 **N** Permian Basin Rural Health Network, Fort Stockton, TX	13	10	16	—	—	—	—	—	—	—

KERRVILLE—Kerr County

□ KERRVILLE STATE HOSPITAL, 721 Thompson Drive, Zip 78028–5154; tel. 830/896–2211; Gloria P. Olsen, Ph.D., Superintendent **A**1 10 **F**14 15 16 20 22 26 30 39 45 52 56 57 65 67 73	12	22	224	528	175	—	—	24762	14880	634
KERVILLE DIVISION See South Texas Veterans Health Care System, San Antonio										
✚ SID PETERSON MEMORIAL HOSPITAL, 710 Water Street, Zip 78028–5398; tel. 830/896–4200; Frederick W. Hall, Jr., Administrator (Total facility includes 25 beds in nursing home–type unit) **A**1 9 10 **F**4 7 8 12 14 15 16 19 21 22 23 28 30 32 34 35 37 40 41 42 44 45 46 49 62 64 65 71 73 74 **P**8 **N** Southwest Texas Rural Health Alliance, San Antonio, TX	23	10	115	5325	78	28750	417	28885	14616	527

KILGORE—Gregg County

★ ROY H. LAIRD MEMORIAL HOSPITAL, 1612 South Henderson Boulevard, Zip 75662–3594; tel. 903/984–3505; Roderick G. La Grone, President **A**9 10 **F**7 8 19 21 22 26 30 32 34 35 37 39 40 44 45 71 73 74 **N** Healthcare Partners of East Texas, Inc., Tyler, TX; Regional Healthcare Alliance, Tyler, TX	14	10	51	1456	11	22102	361	11518	5285	—

KILLEEN—Bell County

✚ METROPLEX HOSPITAL, 2201 South Clear Creek Road, Zip 76542–9305; tel. 254/526–7523; Kenneth A. Finch, Chief Executive Officer (Total facility includes 13 beds in nursing home–type unit) **A**1 9 10 **F**7 8 10 12 14 15 16 17 19 21 22 28 29 30 32 35 37 39 40 41 42 44 45 46 49 52 53 54 55 56 57 59 63 64 65 67 71 73 **S** Adventist Health System Sunbelt Health Care Corporation, Winter Park, FL **N** Metroplex Health Network, Kileen, TX	21	10	213	6275	86	69195	699	50485	18573	721

KINGSVILLE—Kleberg County

✚ SPOHN KLEBERG MEMORIAL HOSPITAL, 1311 General Cavazos Boulevard, Zip 78363–1197, Mailing Address: P.O. Box 1197, Zip 78363–1197; tel. 512/595–1661; Ernesto M. Flores, Jr., Administrator (Total facility includes 15 beds in nursing home–type unit) **A**1 9 10 **F**7 8 10 12 14 16 17 19 21 22 25 28 30 31 32 33 34 35 37 39 40 43 44 46 49 60 64 65 67 68 71 72 73 74 **P**1 3 4 5 6 7 **S** Incarnate Word Health Services, San Antonio, TX	21	10	100	6245	70	—	470	28567	13124	421

KINGWOOD—Harris County

□ CHARTER BEHAVIORAL HEALTH SYSTEM, 2001 Ladbrook Drive, Zip 77339–3004; tel. 281/358–4501; Mark Micheletti, Chief Executive Officer (Nonreporting) **A**1 9 10 **S** Magellan Health Services, Atlanta, GA	33	22	80	—	—	—	—	—	—	—
✚ COLUMBIA KINGWOOD MEDICAL CENTER, 22999 U.S. Highway 59, Zip 77339; tel. 281/359–7500; Charles D. Schuetz, Chief Executive Officer **A**1 9 10 **F**2 3 4 6 7 8 9 10 11 12 13 14 15 16 17 18 19 21 22 23 24 25 26 27 28 29 30 31 32 33 34 35 36 37 38 39 40 41 42 43 44 45 46 47 48 49 50 51 52 53 54 55 56 57 58 59 60 61 62 63 64 65 66 67 68 69 70 71 72 73 74 **P**1 2 5 7 **S** Columbia/HCA Healthcare Corporation, Nashville, TN	33	10	152	7020	89	45343	893	47918	18804	543

LA GRANGE—Fayette County

✚ FAYETTE MEMORIAL HOSPITAL, 543 North Jackson Street, Zip 78945–2040; tel. 409/968–3166; William F. O'Brien, Chief Executive Officer and Administrator **A**1 9 10 **F**7 8 12 14 15 16 17 19 22 26 28 29 30 32 33 39 40 41 42 44 46 49 51 65 71 73 74	23	10	45	2104	26	55772	285	13119	5492	244

Hospital, Address, Telephone, Administrator, Approval, Facility, and Physician Codes, Health Care System, Network	Classification Codes		Utilization Data					Expense (thousands) of dollars		
★ American Hospital Association (AHA) membership □ Joint Commission on Accreditation of Healthcare Organizations (JCAHO) accreditation + American Osteopathic Healthcare Association (AOHA) membership ○ American Osteopathic Association (AOA) accreditation △ Commission on Accreditation of Rehabilitation Facilities (CARF) accreditation Control codes 61, 63, 64, 71, 72 and 73 indicate hospitals listed by AOHA, but not registered by AHA. For definition of numerical codes, see page A4	Control	Service	Staffed Beds	Admissions	Census	Outpatient Visits	Births	Total	Payroll	Personnel

LACKLAND AFB—Bexar County

★ WILFORD HALL MEDICAL CENTER, 2200 Bergquist Drive, Zip 78236–5300; tel. 210/292–7353; Colonel Arthur E. Aenchbacher, Jr., Administrator (Nonreporting) A1 2 3 5 S Department of the Air Force, Bowling AFB, DC

| | 41 | 10 | 715 | — | — | — | — | — | — | — |

LAKE JACKSON—Brazoria County

★ △ BRAZOSPORT MEMORIAL HOSPITAL, 100 Medical Drive, Zip 77566–9983; tel. 409/297–4411; Wesley W. Oswald, Chief Executive Officer A1 2 7 9 10 F2 3 7 8 10 12 15 16 19 21 22 23 30 32 35 36 37 40 41 42 44 48 49 52 53 56 57 58 59 60 64 65 67 71 73 74 P8 S Quorum Health Group/Quorum Health Resources, Inc., Brentwood, TN

| | 23 | 10 | 156 | 4922 | 61 | 62835 | 737 | 35256 | 15256 | 495 |

LAMESA—Dawson County

□ MEDICAL ARTS HOSPITAL, 1600 North Bryan Avenue, Zip 79331; tel. 806/872–2183; Arla Jeffcoat, Administrator A1 9 10 F7 8 15 16 17 19 22 28 30 32 34 40 44 46 49 65 70 71 73 N Lubbock Methodist Hospital System, Lubbock, TX; Permian Basin Rural Health Network, Fort Stockton, TX

| | 13 | 10 | 44 | 580 | 6 | 15941 | 79 | 7151 | 3770 | 187 |

LANCASTER—Dallas County

★ COLUMBIA MEDICAL CENTER AT LANCASTER, 2600 West Pleasant Run Road, Zip 75146–1199; tel. 972/223–9600; Ernest C. Lynch, III, Chief Executive Officer A1 9 10 F2 3 4 7 8 9 10 11 12 13 16 17 19 20 21 22 23 25 26 27 28 29 30 31 32 33 34 35 37 38 39 40 41 42 43 44 46 47 48 49 52 53 54 55 56 57 58 59 61 63 64 65 66 67 69 70 71 72 73 74 P5 7 S Columbia/HCA Healthcare Corporation, Nashville, TN

| | 33 | 10 | 74 | 2431 | 34 | 25708 | 120 | 17012 | 8518 | 212 |

LAREDO—Webb County

★ COLUMBIA DOCTORS HOSPITAL OF LAREDO, 500 East Mann Road, Zip 78041–2699; tel. 956/723–1131; Benjamin Everett, Chief Executive Officer (Total facility includes 6 beds in nursing home–type unit) A1 9 10 F8 15 16 19 20 21 22 28 30 32 34 35 37 39 40 42 44 46 49 60 63 64 65 71 72 73 74 P8 S Columbia/HCA Healthcare Corporation, Nashville, TN N Columbia Healthcare – South Texas Division, Corpus Christi, TX

| | 32 | 10 | 107 | 6075 | 68 | 66007 | 2036 | 33152 | 13767 | 555 |

★ MERCY REGIONAL MEDICAL CENTER, 1515 Logan Avenue, Zip 78040–4617, Mailing Address: Drawer 2068, Zip 78044–2068; tel. 956/718–6222; Mark S. Stauder, President and Chief Executive Officer (Total facility includes 47 beds in nursing home–type unit) A1 9 10 F4 7 8 10 11 12 13 14 15 16 17 19 21 22 25 27 28 30 31 32 34 35 37 38 39 40 43 44 45 47 48 49 63 64 71 72 73 74 P8 S Sisters of Mercy Health System–St. Louis, Saint Louis, MO

| | 21 | 10 | 320 | 13877 | 210 | — | 3564 | 100317 | 37347 | 1368 |

LEAGUE CITY—Galveston County

□ DEVEREUX TEXAS TREATMENT NETWORK, 1150 Devereux Drive, Zip 77573–2043; tel. 713/335–1000; L. Gail Atkinson, Executive Director A1 9 10 F2 3 12 13 15 16 17 18 20 22 24 25 30 32 34 39 45 46 51 52 53 54 55 56 57 58 59 65 67 68 70 S Devereux Foundation, Villanova, PA

| | 23 | 22 | 88 | 539 | 45 | 3150 | 0 | 9995 | 5292 | 160 |

LEVELLAND—Hockley County

★ METHODIST HOSPITAL–LEVELLAND, 1900 South College Avenue, Zip 79336–6508; tel. 806/894–4963; Jerry Osburn, Administrator A1 9 10 F7 8 14 15 16 17 19 20 21 22 28 29 30 31 32 33 34 36 37 39 44 45 46 49 51 53 54 55 56 57 58 59 65 70 71 73 P7 S Lubbock Methodist Hospital System, Lubbock, TX

| | 21 | 10 | 44 | 1388 | 15 | 20276 | 241 | 10141 | 3794 | — |

LEWISVILLE—Denton County

★ MEDICAL CENTER OF LEWISVILLE, (Formerly Columbia Medical Center), 500 West Main, Zip 75057–3699; tel. 972/420–1000; Raymond M. Dunning, Jr., Chief Executive Officer A1 9 10 F4 7 8 19 22 32 33 35 37 40 41 42 44 49 64 65 66 67 71 73 74 S Columbia/HCA Healthcare Corporation, Nashville, TN

| | 33 | 10 | 116 | 6567 | 74 | 54848 | 1137 | 52068 | 17700 | 557 |

LIBERTY—Liberty County

LIBERTY–DAYTON HOSPITAL, 1353 North Travis Street, Zip 77575–1353; tel. 409/336–7316; Mynette Dennis, R.N., Administrator A9 10 F12 19 20 30 32 33 34 44 71 73

| | 33 | 10 | 29 | 897 | 9 | 8155 | 0 | 6664 | 2571 | 103 |

LIBERTY HILL—Williamson County

MERIDELL ACHIEVEMENT CENTER, 12550 West Highway 29, Zip 78642, Mailing Address: P.O. Box 87, Zip 78642–0087; tel. 800/366–8656; Scott McAvoy, Managing Director (Nonreporting) S Universal Health Services, Inc., King of Prussia, PA

| | 33 | 52 | 78 | — | — | — | — | — | — | — |

LINDEN—Cass County

LINDEN MUNICIPAL HOSPITAL, North Kaufman Street, Zip 75563–5235, Mailing Address: P.O. Box 32, Zip 75563–0032; tel. 903/756–5561; C. Edward Anderson, Administrator A9 10 F8 16 19 20 22 32 37 44 46 48 49 57 58 59 64 71 N Healthcare Partners of East Texas, Inc., Tyler, TX; Regional Healthcare Alliance, Tyler, TX

| | 16 | 10 | 39 | 864 | 14 | 3374 | 0 | 4848 | 2488 | 104 |

LITTLEFIELD—Lamb County

★ LAMB HEALTHCARE CENTER, 1500 South Sunset, Zip 79339–4899; tel. 806/385–6411; Randall A. Young, Administrator A1 9 10 F7 15 16 19 22 28 30 32 33 34 36 39 40 44 45 46 64 65 70 71 74 S Lubbock Methodist Hospital System, Lubbock, TX N Lubbock Methodist Hospital System, Lubbock, TX

| | 13 | 10 | 40 | 1032 | 16 | 10572 | 118 | 5828 | 2574 | 116 |

LIVINGSTON—Polk County

MEMORIAL MEDICAL CENTER–LIVINGSTON, 602 East Church Street, Zip 77351–1257, Mailing Address: P.O. Box 1257, Zip 77351–1257; tel. 409/327–4381; James C. Dickson, Administrator A9 10 F7 8 15 19 22 28 30 34 44 71 73 N Healthcare Partners of East Texas, Inc., Tyler, TX

| | 23 | 10 | 28 | 1299 | 9 | 27872 | 149 | 8040 | 3592 | — |

Hospital, Address, Telephone, Administrator, Approval, Facility, and Physician Codes, Health Care System, Network	Classi-fication Codes		Utilization Data					Expense (thousands) of dollars		
★ American Hospital Association (AHA) membership ☐ Joint Commission on Accreditation of Healthcare Organizations (JCAHO) accreditation + American Osteopathic Healthcare Association (AOHA) membership ○ American Osteopathic Association (AOA) accreditation △ Commission on Accreditation of Rehabilitation Facilities (CARF) accreditation Control codes 61, 63, 64, 71, 72 and 73 indicate hospitals listed by AOHA, but not registered by AHA. For definition of numerical codes, see page A4	Control	Service	Staffed Beds	Admissions	Census	Outpatient Visits	Births	Total	Payroll	Personnel

LLANO—Llano County

⊞ LLANO MEMORIAL HOSPITAL, 200 West Ollie Street, Zip 78643–2628; tel. 915/247–5040; Ernest Parisi, Administrator and Chief Executive Officer **A**1 9 10 **F**7 8 15 16 17 19 21 22 28 30 32 33 40 41 42 44 49 51 65 71 73 **P**4	13	10	30	1562	22	—	286	13085	5387	221

LOCKNEY—Floyd County

W. J. MANGOLD MEMORIAL HOSPITAL, 320 North Main Street, Zip 79241–0037, Mailing Address: Box 37, Zip 79241–0037; tel. 806/652–3373; Robin Satterwhite, Administrator **A**9 10 **F**7 19 22 28 34 40 44 49 51 61 70 71	16	10	27	580	6	19103	135	3200	1607	80

LONGVIEW—Gregg County

COLUMBIA LONGVIEW REGIONAL MEDICAL CENTER See Longview Regional Medical Center

⊞ △ GOOD SHEPHERD MEDICAL CENTER, 700 East Marshall Avenue, Zip 75601–5571; tel. 903/236–2000; Jerry D. Adair, President and Chief Executive Officer (Total facility includes 26 beds in nursing home–type unit) **A**1 7 9 10 **F**4 7 8 10 12 14 15 16 17 19 20 21 22 23 25 26 27 28 29 30 31 32 34 35 37 39 40 41 42 43 44 45 46 48 49 51 56 59 63 64 65 66 69 71 73 74 **P**1 **N** Healthcare Partners of East Texas, Inc., Tyler, TX; Good Sheperd Health Network, Longview, TX; Regional Healthcare Alliance, Tyler, TX	23	10	323	15543	233	140549	1797	121325	50877	1709
⊞ LONGVIEW REGIONAL MEDICAL CENTER, (Formerly Columbia Longview Regional Medical Center), 2901 North Fourth Street, Zip 75605–5191, Mailing Address: P.O. Box 14000, Zip 75607–4000; tel. 903/758–1818; Velinda Stevens, Chief Executive Officer (Total facility includes 20 beds in nursing home–type unit) **A**1 9 10 **F**4 7 8 10 12 15 17 18 19 20 21 22 23 24 28 30 32 34 35 37 39 40 41 42 43 44 45 46 48 49 60 63 64 65 66 67 71 73 74 **P**7 8 **S** Columbia/HCA Healthcare Corporation, Nashville, TN	33	10	164	4066	65	45926	323	42255	19037	498

LUBBOCK—Lubbock County

☐ CHARTER PLAINS BEHAVIORAL HEALTH SYSTEM, 801 North Quaker Avenue, Zip 79416–2408, Mailing Address: P.O. Box 10560, Zip 79408–0560; tel. 806/744–5505; Earl W. Balzen, R.N., Chief Executive Officer and Administrator **A**1 5 9 10 **F**3 12 34 46 52 53 54 56 57 58 59 65 67 **S** Magellan Health Services, Atlanta, GA	32	22	80	786	16	3950	0	4876	2018	86
⊞ HIGHLAND MEDICAL CENTER, 2412 50th Street, Zip 79412–2494; tel. 806/788–4060; David Conejo, Chief Executive Officer (Total facility includes 12 beds in nursing home–type unit) **A**1 2 9 10 **F**7 8 12 14 15 16 17 19 20 21 22 26 28 29 30 34 35 37 39 40 41 42 44 45 46 48 49 51 61 64 65 67 69 71 72 73 74 **P**5 7 **S** Community Health Systems, Inc., Brentwood, TN	33	10	76	1953	26	20595	369	15845	5991	220
☐ HORIZON SPECIALTY HOSPITAL, 1409 9th Street, Zip 79401–2601; tel. 806/767–9133; Steve Grappe, Administrator **A**1 9 10 **F**12 27 65	33	46	30	178	14	0	0	5339	1712	68
★ METHODIST CHILDREN'S HOSPITAL, 3610 21st Street, Zip 79410–1218; tel. 806/784–5040; George H. McCleskey, President and Chief Executive Officer **A**9 10 **F**4 8 10 12 14 15 16 19 21 22 23 24 30 31 32 35 38 41 42 43 44 45 47 49 60 65 69 70 71 **S** Lubbock Methodist Hospital System, Lubbock, TX	21	50	65	1909	22	15862	0	11994	3547	64
⊞ △ METHODIST HOSPITAL, 3615 19th Street, Zip 79410–1201, Mailing Address: Box 1201, Zip 79408–1201; tel. 806/792–1011; George H. McCleskey, President and Chief Executive Officer **A**1 2 6 7 9 10 **F**4 7 8 10 11 14 15 16 17 19 21 22 23 24 26 30 31 32 35 37 39 40 41 42 43 44 45 48 49 60 64 65 67 69 70 71 73 74 **S** Lubbock Methodist Hospital System, Lubbock, TX	21	10	520	20821	355	93844	1415	236192	87963	2191
⊞ SOUTH PARK HOSPITAL, 6610 Quaker Avenue, Zip 79413–5938; tel. 806/791–8000; D. Clinton Matthews, Chief Executive Officer (Nonreporting) **A**1 9 10	33	10	101	—	—	—	—	—	—	—
⊞ △ ST. MARY OF THE PLAINS HOSPITAL, 4000 24th Street, Zip 79410–1894; tel. 806/796–6000; Charley O. Trimble, President and Chief Executive Officer **A**1 2 3 5 7 9 10 **F**4 7 8 10 11 12 14 15 16 17 19 20 21 22 28 29 30 31 32 34 35 37 38 40 41 42 43 44 45 46 47 48 52 56 59 60 64 65 67 71 73 74 **P**5 6 8 **S** St. Joseph Health System, Orange, CA	21	10	410	14464	267	483285	1085	181782	51848	2024
⊞ UNIVERSITY MEDICAL CENTER, 602 Indiana Avenue, Zip 79415–3364, Mailing Address: P.O. Box 5980, Zip 79408–5980; tel. 806/743–3111; James P. Courtney, President and Chief Executive Officer **A**1 2 3 5 9 10 **F**4 7 8 9 10 11 12 15 17 19 21 22 23 28 29 30 31 35 37 38 39 40 41 42 43 44 46 47 48 49 56 60 63 64 65 66 67 69 70 71 73 74 **P**7	16	10	318	15548	184	150493	2011	84296	40845	1692

LUFKIN—Angelina County

⊞ COLUMBIA WOODLAND HEIGHTS MEDICAL CENTER, 500 Gaslight Boulevard, Zip 75901–3157, Mailing Address: P.O. Box 150610, Zip 75915–0610; tel. 409/634–8311; Don H. McBride, Chief Executive Officer **A**1 9 10 **F**4 7 8 10 11 12 15 16 19 21 22 23 25 28 30 32 34 35 39 40 43 44 45 46 49 64 65 66 71 73 74 **P**5 8 **S** Columbia/HCA Healthcare Corporation, Nashville, TN	32	10	110	5413	74	55547	656	34517	12484	423
⊞ MEMORIAL MEDICAL CENTER OF EAST TEXAS, 1201 West Frank Avenue, Zip 75904–3357, Mailing Address: P.O. Box 1447, Zip 75902–1447; tel. 409/634–8111; Gary Lex Whatley, President and Chief Executive Officer (Total facility includes 30 beds in nursing home–type unit) **A**1 2 9 10 **F**1 7 8 10 12 14 15 16 17 18 19 21 22 23 24 26 27 28 29 30 31 32 34 35 37 39 40 41 42 44 45 46 48 49 51 52 54 55 56 57 58 59 60 64 65 66 67 71 72 73 74 **P**5 6 7 8 **N** Healthcare Partners of East Texas, Inc., Tyler, TX	23	10	233	9599	147	143798	602	60305	23321	867

LULING—Caldwell County

★ EDGAR B. DAVIS MEMORIAL HOSPITAL, 130 Hays Street, Zip 78648–3207, Mailing Address: P.O. Box 510, Zip 78648–0510; tel. 830/875–5643; Neal Kelley, Administrator (Total facility includes 6 beds in nursing home–type unit) **A**9 10 **F**8 15 16 19 21 22 27 28 34 35 44 49 56 57 58 64 65 71 **P**8 **N** Southwest Texas Rural Health Alliance, San Antonio, TX	14	10	21	1011	11	31894	106	6363	2761	124

Hospital, Address, Telephone, Administrator, Approval, Facility, and Physician Codes, Health Care System, Network	Classification Codes		Utilization Data					Expense (thousands) of dollars		
★ American Hospital Association (AHA) membership □ Joint Commission on Accreditation of Healthcare Organizations (JCAHO) accreditation + American Osteopathic Healthcare Association (AOHA) membership ○ American Osteopathic Association (AOA) accreditation △ Commission on Accreditation of Rehabilitation Facilities (CARF) accreditation Control codes 61, 63, 64, 71, 72 and 73 indicate hospitals listed by AOHA, but not registered by AHA. For definition of numerical codes, see page A4	Control	Service	Staffed Beds	Admissions	Census	Outpatient Visits	Births	Total	Payroll	Personnel

MADISONVILLE—Madison County

★ MADISON ST. JOSEPH HEALTH CENTER, (Formerly St. Francis Health Center), 100 West Cross Street, Zip 77864–0698, Mailing Address: Box 698, Zip 77864–0698; tel. 409/348–2631; James P. Gibson, President and Chief Executive Officer **A**1 9 10 **F**7 8 14 15 16 19 20 21 22 25 28 30 32 33 34 40 44 49 51 58 64 65 71 73 **P**6 **S** Franciscan Services Corporation, Sylvania, OH	21	10	35	1064	15	39839	101	9735	5011	247

MANSFIELD—Tarrant County

□ VENCOR HOSPITAL–FORT WORTH SOUTH, (Includes Vencor Hospital – Fort Worth West, 815 Eighth Avenue, Fort Worth, Zip 76104; tel. 817/332–4812), 1802 Highway 157 North, Zip 76063–9555; tel. 817/473–6101; Bill Grey, Administrator **A**1 9 10 **F**12 14 19 22 26 35 37 44 49 65 71 **S** Vencor, Incorporated, Louisville, KY	33	10	67	404	36	27	0	10395	4932	140

MARLIN—Falls County

CENTRAL TEXAS VETERANS AFFAIRS HEALTH CARE SYSTEM, MARLIN INTEGRATED CLINICAL FACILITY See Central Texas Veterans Affairs Healthcare System, Temple

FALLS COMMUNITY HOSPITAL AND CLINIC, (GENERAL MEDICAL), 322 Coleman Street, Zip 76661–2358, Mailing Address: Box 60, Zip 76661–0060; tel. 254/803–3561; Willis L. Reese, Administrator **A**9 10 **F**1 3 4 5 6 7 8 10 12 13 15 16 17 18 19 20 21 22 23 24 25 26 27 28 29 30 31 32 33 34 35 36 39 41 42 43 44 45 46 49 50 51 53 54 55 56 57 58 59 60 61 62 63 65 66 67 68 69 70 71 72 73 74 **P**5 **N** Central Texas Rural Health Network, Harrietsville, TX; Brazo's Valley Health Network, Waco, TX	23	49	32	1258	14	53364	0	5674	2107	112

MARSHALL—Harrison County

★ MARSHALL REGIONAL MEDICAL CENTER, 811 South Washington Avenue, Zip 75670–5336, Mailing Address: P.O. Box 1599, Zip 75671–1599; tel. 903/927–6000; Thomas N. Cammack, Jr., Chief Executive Officer (Total facility includes 10 beds in nursing home–type unit) **A**1 9 10 **F**7 8 12 15 16 17 19 21 22 23 28 30 31 32 34 35 37 39 40 41 42 44 46 49 64 65 71 73 **P**3 7 8 **N** Regional Healthcare Alliance, Tyler, TX	23	10	103	3935	45	71045	605	28190	11401	412

MCALLEN—Hidalgo County

□ CHARTER PALMS BEHAVIORAL HEALTH SYSTEM, 1421 East Jackson Avenue, Zip 78501–1602, Mailing Address: P.O. Box 5239, Zip 78502–5239; tel. 956/631–5421; Leslie Bingham, Chief Executive Officer (Nonreporting) **A**1 9 10 **S** Magellan Health Services, Atlanta, GA	33	22	80	—	—	—	—	—	—	—
★ COLUMBIA RIO GRANDE REGIONAL HOSPITAL, 101 East Ridge Road, Zip 78503–1299; tel. 956/632–6000; Randall M. Everts, Chief Executive Officer **A**1 9 10 **F**4 7 8 10 11 12 17 19 20 21 22 23 24 25 26 28 29 30 34 35 37 38 39 40 41 42 43 44 46 48 49 60 64 65 67 71 73 74 **P**8 **S** Columbia/HCA Healthcare Corporation, Nashville, TN **N** Columbia Healthcare – South Texas Division, Corpus Christi, TX	32	10	267	10747	136	73924	2007	61001	22745	766
□ MCALLEN MEDICAL CENTER, 301 West Expressway 83, Zip 78503; tel. 956/632–4000; Daniel P. McLean, Executive Director **A**1 3 9 10 **F**4 7 8 10 12 14 15 16 19 21 22 23 24 28 29 30 32 34 35 37 38 39 40 41 42 43 44 45 46 47 48 49 51 52 53 54 55 56 57 58 59 60 61 63 64 65 66 67 71 73 **P**3 7 8 **S** Universal Health Services, Inc., King of Prussia, PA	33	10	451	21980	363	79345	5932	128955	55159	1560

MCCAMEY—Upton County

MCCAMEY HOSPITAL, Highway 305 South, Zip 79752, Mailing Address: P.O. Box 1200, Zip 79752–1200; tel. 915/652–8626; Bill Boswell, Chief Executive Officer (Total facility includes 30 beds in nursing home–type unit) **A**9 10 **F**15 16 22 28 32 34 44 49 64 **N** Permian Basin Rural Health Network, Fort Stockton, TX	16	10	46	82	28	24727	0	4385	2071	44

MCKINNEY—Collin County

★ MEDICAL CENTER OF MCKINNEY, (Formerly Columbia Medical Center of McKinney), (Includes Westpark Surgery Center, 130 South Central Expressway, Zip 75070; tel. 972/548–5300), 1800 North Graves Street, Zip 75069–3499; tel. 972/548–3000; Dale Mulder, Chief Executive Officer **A**1 9 10 **F**7 8 12 15 16 19 22 23 26 28 32 34 35 41 42 44 46 57 65 71 72 73 74 **S** Columbia/HCA Healthcare Corporation, Nashville, TN	32	10	155	6275	87	84225	1032	43651	18454	612

NORTH TEXAS MEDICAL CENTER–WESTPARK CAMPUS See Westpark Surgery Center

MEMPHIS—Hall County

HALL COUNTY HOSPITAL, 1800 North Boykin Drive, Zip 79245–2039; tel. 806/259–3504; Jody Dixon, Administrator **A**9 10 **F**28 32 33 39 45 70 71 73 **P**6	16	10	20	316	3	6056	0	1867	1019	55

MESQUITE—Dallas County

□ MEDICAL CENTER OF MESQUITE, 1011 North Galloway Avenue, Zip 75149–2433; tel. 214/320–7000; Terry J. Fontenot, Administrator **A**1 9 10 **F**4 7 8 10 11 12 14 15 16 17 19 21 22 29 30 32 33 35 37 38 39 40 42 43 44 49 54 63 64 65 71 73 74 **P**5 **S** Paracelsus Healthcare Corporation, Houston, TX **N** Saint Paul Medical Center Affiliate Network, Dallas, TX; Brazo's Valley Health Network, Waco, TX	33	10	176	5492	73	48150	441	48225	17563	495
□ MESQUITE COMMUNITY HOSPITAL, 3500 Interstate 30, Zip 75150–2696; tel. 972/698–3300; Raymond P. De Blasi, Chief Executive Officer (Total facility includes 13 beds in nursing home–type unit) **A**1 9 10 **F**7 8 10 15 16 19 20 21 22 26 31 32 33 34 35 37 39 40 44 49 52 57 64 65 67 71 73	33	10	128	5800	67	48071	1427	32847	14376	450

MEXIA—Limestone County

★ PARKVIEW REGIONAL HOSPITAL, 312 East Glendale Street, Zip 76667–3608; tel. 254/562–5332; William E. Price, Interim Administrator **A**1 9 10 **F**7 8 12 14 15 16 17 19 21 22 28 29 30 32 34 35 37 40 41 44 45 46 48 49 51 65 66 70 71 73 **P**4 **S** Province Healthcare Corporation, Brentwood, TN **N** Central Texas Rural Health Network, Harrietsville, TX; Brazo's Valley Health Network, Waco, TX	33	10	44	1420	—	22877	157	11405	4167	168

Hospital, Address, Telephone, Administrator, Approval, Facility, and Physician Codes, Health Care System, Network	Classi-fication Codes		Utilization Data					Expense (thousands) of dollars		
★ American Hospital Association (AHA) membership □ Joint Commission on Accreditation of Healthcare Organizations (JCAHO) accreditation + American Osteopathic Healthcare Association (AOHA) membership ○ American Osteopathic Association (AOA) accreditation △ Commission on Accreditation of Rehabilitation Facilities (CARF) accreditation Control codes 61, 63, 64, 71, 72 and 73 indicate hospitals listed by AOHA, but not registered by AHA. For definition of numerical codes, see page A4	Control	Service	Staffed Beds	Admissions	Census	Outpatient Visits	Births	Total	Payroll	Personnel

MIDLAND—Midland County

☒ △ MEMORIAL HOSPITAL AND MEDICAL CENTER, (Includes Memorial Rehabilitation Hospital, Zip 79704; tel. 915/697–5200), 2200 West Illinois Avenue, Zip 79701–6499; tel. 915/685–1111; Harold Rubin, President and Chief Executive Officer (Total facility includes 17 beds in nursing home–type unit) **A**1 2 5 7 9 10 **F**4 7 8 10 12 13 14 15 16 17 19 21 22 23 25 27 28 29 30 33 34 35 37 39 40 41 42 43 44 48 49 51 56 60 64 65 66 67 70 71 72 73 74 **P**8 **N** Permian Basin Rural Health Network, Fort Stockton, TX — 16 10 245 10240 173 114460 1467 110276 36428 1189

□ WESTWOOD MEDICAL CENTER, 4214 Andrews Highway, Zip 79703–4861; tel. 915/522–2273; Michael S. Potter, President and Chief Executive Officer **A**1 9 10 **F**7 8 10 12 15 16 19 21 28 31 32 37 39 40 44 46 49 63 67 71 72 73 **P**7 **S** Paracelsus Healthcare Corporation, Houston, TX — 33 10 80 2429 25 37090 316 27512 8101 265

MINERAL WELLS—Palo Pinto County

★ PALO PINTO GENERAL HOSPITAL, 400 S.W. 25th Avenue, Zip 76067–9685; tel. 940/325–7891; Guy Hazlett, II, FACHE, Chief Executive Officer **A**9 10 **F**4 7 8 12 13 14 15 16 19 21 22 29 30 32 33 35 36 37 39 40 44 45 46 49 51 65 66 67 71 73 74 — 16 10 44 2820 32 30122 387 20928 9804 —

MISSION—Hidalgo County

☒ MISSION HOSPITAL, 900 South Bryan Road, Zip 78572–6613; tel. 956/580–9000; Paul H. Ballard, Chief Executive Officer **A**1 9 10 **F**7 8 12 14 15 16 17 19 21 22 28 29 30 32 35 37 40 41 44 45 46 49 51 60 65 71 73 **P**3 7 8 **S** Quorum Health Group/Quorum Health Resources, Inc., Brentwood, TN — 23 10 110 5189 67 30552 1090 35219 14511 537

MISSOURI CITY—Fort Bend County

☒ FORT BEND MEDICAL CENTER, (Formerly Columbia Fort Bend Hospital), 3803 FM 1092 at Highway 6, Zip 77459; tel. 281/403–4800; Jeffrey S. Holland, Chief Executive Officer (Total facility includes 5 beds in nursing home–type unit) **A**1 9 10 **F**2 3 4 5 6 7 8 9 10 11 12 13 14 16 17 18 19 20 21 22 23 24 25 26 28 29 30 31 32 33 34 35 36 37 38 39 40 41 42 43 44 45 46 47 48 49 52 53 54 55 56 57 58 59 60 64 65 66 67 68 69 71 72 73 74 **P**5 7 8 **S** Columbia/HCA Healthcare Corporation, Nashville, TN — 33 10 65 3068 35 28730 481 21545 8957 327

MONAHANS—Ward County

☒ WARD MEMORIAL HOSPITAL, 406 South Gary Street, Zip 79756–4798; tel. 915/943–2511; Ray Mason, Interim Chief Executive Officer **A**1 9 10 **F**1 3 4 5 6 7 8 10 12 13 14 15 16 17 18 19 20 21 22 23 24 25 26 27 28 29 30 31 32 33 34 35 36 39 40 41 42 43 44 45 46 49 50 51 53 54 55 56 57 58 59 60 61 62 63 64 65 66 67 68 69 70 71 72 73 74 **N** Permian Basin Rural Health Network, Fort Stockton, TX — 13 10 49 958 9 11905 29 6483 3825 167

MORTON—Cochran County

★ COCHRAN MEMORIAL HOSPITAL, 201 East Grant Street, Zip 79346–3444; tel. 806/266–5565; Paul McKinney, Administrator **A**9 10 **F**15 28 32 51 70 **P**5 **N** Lubbock Methodist Hospital System, Lubbock, TX — 16 10 30 51 2 4742 0 2219 1190 56

MOUNT PLEASANT—Titus County

☒ TITUS REGIONAL MEDICAL CENTER, 2001 North Jefferson Avenue, Zip 75455–2398; tel. 903/577–6000; Steven K. Jacobson, Chief Executive Officer (Total facility includes 20 beds in nursing home–type unit) **A**1 9 10 **F**7 8 10 11 15 16 17 19 21 22 28 30 32 34 35 37 39 40 41 44 48 49 64 65 70 71 73 74 **P**8 **S** Quorum Health Group/Quorum Health Resources, Inc., Brentwood, TN **N** Healthcare Partners of East Texas, Inc., Tyler, TX; Regional Healthcare Alliance, Tyler, TX — 16 10 165 5605 72 143245 1073 43266 18725 652

MOUNT VERNON—Franklin County

☒ EAST TEXAS MEDICAL CENTER–MOUNT VERNON, Highway 37 South, Zip 75457, Mailing Address: P.O. Box 477, Zip 75457–0477; tel. 903/537–4552; Jerry Edwards, CHE, Administrator **A**1 9 10 **F**8 12 13 15 16 17 19 20 22 26 27 28 29 30 32 34 39 44 49 51 57 70 71 72 **P**7 8 **S** East Texas Medical Center Regional Healthcare System, Tyler, TX **N** Healthcare Partners of East Texas, Inc., Tyler, TX — 23 10 30 699 7 71835 0 6068 2921 103

MUENSTER—Cooke County

MUENSTER MEMORIAL HOSPITAL, 605 North Maple Street, Zip 76252–2424, Mailing Address: P.O. Box 370, Zip 76252–0370; tel. 817/759–2271; Jack R. Endres, Administrator **A**9 10 **F**7 8 15 19 20 21 22 28 30 32 33 34 40 44 49 65 67 70 71 — 16 10 18 399 4 17922 75 3305 1746 65

MULESHOE—Bailey County

★ MULESHOE AREA MEDICAL CENTER, 708 South First Street, Zip 79347–3627; tel. 806/272–4524; Jim G. Bone, Interim Administrator (Total facility includes 54 beds in nursing home–type unit) **A**9 10 **F**7 8 19 25 28 29 30 32 33 35 40 44 64 70 71 73 **S** Lubbock Methodist Hospital System, Lubbock, TX **N** Lubbock Methodist Hospital System, Lubbock, TX — 16 10 79 580 56 15469 49 4461 2134 150

NACOGDOCHES—Nacogdoches County

☒ NACOGDOCHES MEDICAL CENTER, 4920 N.E. Stallings, Zip 75961–1200, Mailing Address: P.O. Box 631604, Zip 75963–1604; tel. 409/568–3380; Glenn A. Robinson, Director **A**1 9 10 **F**4 7 8 10 12 15 16 19 21 22 23 30 32 33 34 35 37 40 41 42 43 44 46 49 60 64 65 67 71 73 **P**5 **S** TENET Healthcare Corporation, Santa Barbara, CA **N** Regional Healthcare Alliance, Tyler, TX — 32 10 113 6070 71 32767 697 34043 13830 509

☒ △ NACOGDOCHES MEMORIAL HOSPITAL, 1204 North Mound Street, Zip 75961–4061; tel. 409/568–8521; Gary J. Blan, FACHE, President and Chief Executive Officer (Total facility includes 14 beds in nursing home–type unit) **A**1 7 9 10 **F**4 7 8 10 14 15 16 19 22 28 30 31 32 33 34 35 37 40 41 42 43 44 45 48 49 64 65 67 71 73 **P**8 **N** Healthcare Partners of East Texas, Inc., Tyler, TX — 16 10 153 5441 84 38596 844 44540 18383 647

Hospital, Address, Telephone, Administrator, Approval, Facility, and Physician Codes, Health Care System, Network	Classi-fication Codes		Utilization Data					Expense (thousands) of dollars		
★ American Hospital Association (AHA) membership □ Joint Commission on Accreditation of Healthcare Organizations (JCAHO) accreditation + American Osteopathic Healthcare Association (AOHA) membership ○ American Osteopathic Association (AOA) accreditation △ Commission on Accreditation of Rehabilitation Facilities (CARF) accreditation Control codes 61, 63, 64, 71, 72 and 73 indicate hospitals listed by AOHA, but not registered by AHA. For definition of numerical codes, see page A4	Control	Service	Staffed Beds	Admissions	Census	Outpatient Visits	Births	Total	Payroll	Personnel

	Control	Service	Staffed Beds	Admissions	Census	Outpatient Visits	Births	Total	Payroll	Personnel
□ PINELANDS HOSPITAL, 4632 Northeast Stallings Drive, Zip 75961–1617, Mailing Address: P.O. Box 1004, Zip 79563–1004; tel. 409/560–5900; Steve Scott, Chief Operating Officer **A**1 9 10 **F**12 15 17 18 26 52 53 54 55 56 57 58 59 65 67 **P**1 5 7 **N** Healthcare Partners of East Texas, Inc., Tyler, TX; Regional Healthcare Alliance, Tyler, TX	33	22	38	540	16	2117	—	3787	1836	41
NASSAU BAY—Harris County										
✠ ST. JOHN HOSPITAL, 18300 St. John Drive, Zip 77058; tel. 281/333–5503; Thomas Permetti, Administrator (Total facility includes 24 beds in nursing home–type unit) **A**1 9 10 **F**2 3 4 5 7 8 9 10 11 12 14 15 16 17 18 19 21 22 24 27 28 30 31 32 33 34 35 36 37 38 39 40 41 42 44 45 46 47 48 49 50 51 52 53 54 55 56 57 58 59 60 61 63 64 65 66 67 69 71 72 73 74 **P**3 5 7 8 **S** Sisters of Charity of the Incarnate Word Healthcare System, Houston, TX **N** SouthEast Texas Integrated Community Health Network, Houston, TX	23	10	135	4493	36	83783	739	40389	15728	561
NAVASOTA—Grimes County										
CLC–NAVASOTA REGIONAL HOSPITAL See Grimes St. Joseph Health Center										
GRIMES ST. JOSEPH HEALTH CENTER, (Formerly CLC–Navasota Regional Hospital), 210 South Judson Street, Zip 77868–3704, Mailing Address: P.O. Box 1390, Zip 77868–1390; tel. 409/825–6585; Molly Hurst, Administrative Director (Total facility includes 12 beds in nursing home–type unit) **A**9 **F**12 14 15 16 17 22 39 45 49 64 65 71 73 **P**8	21	10	30	706	13	5833	0	3863	1539	64
NEDERLAND—Jefferson County										
✠ MID–JEFFERSON HOSPITAL, Highway 365 and 27th Street, Zip 77627–6288, Mailing Address: P.O. Box 1917, Zip 77627–1917; tel. 409/727–2321; Wilson J. Weber, Chief Executive Officer (Total facility includes 18 beds in nursing home–type unit) **A**1 5 9 10 **F**7 8 12 13 15 16 17 19 21 22 28 29 30 31 32 34 37 40 44 45 46 51 64 71 73 74 **P**3 7 **S** TENET Healthcare Corporation, Santa Barbara, CA	32	10	138	3092	37	59021	488	21307	7749	257
NEW BRAUNFELS—Comal County										
✠ MCKENNA MEMORIAL HOSPITAL, 600 North Union Avenue, Zip 78130; tel. 830/606–9111; M. Ray Harris, Jr., President and Chief Executive Officer **A**1 9 10 **F**7 8 12 15 16 17 19 20 21 22 23 24 25 27 28 30 32 33 34 35 37 39 40 41 42 44 45 46 48 49 51 54 56 58 63 64 65 71 72 73 74 **P**1 **N** Southwest Texas Rural Health Alliance, San Antonio, TX	23	10	84	4842	51	54987	712	33073	15590	547
NOCONA—Montague County										
★ NOCONA GENERAL HOSPITAL, 100 Park Street, Zip 76255–3616; tel. 940/825–3235; Jamers Brasier, Administrator **A**9 10 **F**8 12 15 16 19 20 22 26 28 32 34 39 40 41 42 44 49 51 58 65 70 71 73 **N** Texoma Health Network, Wichita Falls, TX	16	10	36	1011	12	20652	92	6051	2839	111
NORTH RICHLAND HILLS—Tarrant County										
✠ COLUMBIA NORTH HILLS HOSPITAL, 4401 Booth Calloway Road, Zip 76180–7399; tel. 817/284–1431; Randy Moresi, Chief Executive Officer (Total facility includes 14 beds in nursing home–type unit) **A**1 9 10 **F**4 7 8 10 11 12 15 16 19 21 22 23 24 28 29 30 32 33 34 35 37 39 40 41 42 43 44 45 46 48 49 64 65 67 71 73 74 **P**5 **S** Columbia/HCA Healthcare Corporation, Nashville, TN	32	10	133	5614	70	54578	979	42766	18566	518
ODESSA—Ector County										
✠ MEDICAL CENTER HOSPITAL, 500 West Fourth Street, Zip 79761–5059, Mailing Address: P.O. Drawer 7239, Zip 79760–7239; tel. 915/640–4000; J. Michael Stephans, Administrator (Total facility includes 25 beds in nursing home–type unit) **A**1 2 3 5 9 10 **F**4 7 8 10 11 12 16 17 19 21 22 23 25 30 33 34 35 37 38 39 40 42 43 44 46 49 50 51 53 56 58 59 60 63 64 65 71 73 **P**8 **N** Permian Basin Rural Health Network, Fort Stockton, TX	16	10	335	12093	226	124505	1472	124032	44473	1613
✠ ODESSA REGIONAL HOSPITAL, 520 East Sixth Street, Zip 79761–4565, Mailing Address: P.O. Box 4859, Zip 79760–4859; tel. 915/334–8200; Lex A. Guinn, Chief Executive Officer **A**1 9 10 **F**7 8 10 12 14 15 16 19 22 27 28 29 30 32 34 36 37 38 39 40 44 45 46 65 67 70 71 73 74 **P**7 **S** TENET Healthcare Corporation, Santa Barbara, CA	32	44	100	4075	43	68519	1424	27165	10208	356
OLNEY—Young County										
★ HAMILTON HOSPITAL, 903 West Hamilton Street, Zip 76374–1725, Mailing Address: P.O. Box 158, Zip 76374–0158; tel. 940/564–5521; William R. Smith, Administrator (Nonreporting) **A**9 10 **N** Texoma Health Network, Wichita Falls, TX	16	10	46	—	—	—	—	—	—	—
ORANGE—Orange County										
□ BAPTIST HOSPITAL–ORANGE, 608 Strickland Drive, Zip 77630–4717; tel. 409/883–9361; Kevin T. Coleman, Administrator (Total facility includes 16 beds in nursing home–type unit) **A**1 9 10 **F**7 8 12 14 15 16 17 19 21 22 26 27 28 30 31 32 34 35 37 40 41 44 48 49 64 65 66 67 71 72 73 74 **P**1	23	10	118	4122	60	52525	192	31250	9974	453
PALACIOS—Matagorda County										
★ WAGNER GENERAL HOSPITAL, 310 Green Street, Zip 77465–3214, Mailing Address: P.O. Box 859, Zip 77465–0859; tel. 512/972–2511; Kevin Hecht, Director **A**9 10 **F**4 7 8 10 11 12 13 15 16 18 19 21 22 23 24 26 28 30 31 32 33 34 35 37 39 44 48 49 51 52 54 57 61 65 67 70 71 74 **P**5 6 **S** Matagorda County Hospital District, Bay City, TX	16	10	6	5	0	3945	0	1024	717	20
PALESTINE—Anderson County										
□ MEMORIAL MOTHER FRANCES HOSPITAL, (Formerly Memorial Hospital), 4000 South Loop 256, Zip 75801–8467, Mailing Address: P.O. Box 4070, Zip 75802–4070; tel. 903/731–5000; Stephen M. Erixon, Chief Executive Officer **A**1 9 10 **F**11 19 21 22 28 30 32 34 35 39 40 44 45 46 48 52 57 63 65 66 71 **P**3 4 7 **S** Province Healthcare Corporation, Brentwood, TN	32	10	84	3273	45	45188	303	—	—	390

Hospital, Address, Telephone, Administrator, Approval, Facility, and Physician Codes, Health Care System, Network	Classi-fication Codes		Utilization Data					Expense (thousands) of dollars		
★ American Hospital Association (AHA) membership □ Joint Commission on Accreditation of Healthcare Organizations (JCAHO) accreditation + American Osteopathic Healthcare Association (AOHA) membership ○ American Osteopathic Association (AOA) accreditation △ Commission on Accreditation of Rehabilitation Facilities (CARF) accreditation Control codes 61, 63, 64, 71, 72 and 73 indicate hospitals listed by AOHA, but not registered by AHA. For definition of numerical codes, see page A4	Control	Service	Staffed Beds	Admissions	Census	Outpatient Visits	Births	Total	Payroll	Personnel

Hospital	Control	Service	Staffed Beds	Admissions	Census	Outpatient Visits	Births	Total	Payroll	Personnel
⊠ △ TRINITY VALLEY MEDICAL CENTER, 2900 South Loop 256, Zip 75801–6958; tel. 903/731–1000; Larry C. Bozeman, Chief Executive Officer (Total facility includes 12 beds in nursing home–type unit) **A**1 7 9 10 **F**7 8 10 12 16 19 20 21 22 23 27 28 30 32 34 35 37 40 41 44 45 46 48 49 52 55 56 57 63 64 65 67 70 71 73 74 **S** TENET Healthcare Corporation, Santa Barbara, CA **N** Healthcare Partners of East Texas, Inc., Tyler, TX	33	10	150	4391	55	63799	627	33447	12259	394
PAMPA—Gray County										
⊠ COLUMBIA MEDICAL CENTER OF PAMPA, One Medical Plaza, Zip 79065; tel. 806/665–3721; J. Phillip Young, President and Chief Executive Officer **A**1 9 10 **F**7 8 10 12 15 16 19 21 22 23 26 28 30 32 34 35 39 41 44 46 49 57 61 65 66 67 71 73 **P**1 7 **S** Columbia/HCA Healthcare Corporation, Nashville, TN	33	10	107	3174	45	10839	275	25047	11253	379
PARIS—Lamar County										
⊠ MCCUISTION REGIONAL MEDICAL CENTER, 865 Deshong Drive, Zip 75462–2097, Mailing Address: P.O. Box 160, Zip 75461–0160; tel. 903/737–1111; Anthony A. Daigle, Executive Director **A**1 9 10 **F**7 8 10 11 12 14 15 16 17 19 21 22 23 24 27 28 29 30 31 32 33 34 35 37 40 41 42 44 45 46 49 60 65 66 67 71 73 74 **P**1 **S** Texas Health Resources, Irving, TX **N** Presbyterian Healthcare System, Dallas, TX	23	10	158	6539	67	46874	740	32799	13209	480
⊠ ST. JOSEPH'S HOSPITAL AND HEALTH CENTER, 820 Clarksville Street, Zip 75460–9070, Mailing Address: P.O. Box 9070, Zip 75461–9070; tel. 903/785–4521; Monty E. McLaurin, President **A**1 9 10 **F**4 8 10 12 14 15 16 19 21 22 23 24 26 28 29 30 31 32 33 34 35 37 39 41 42 43 44 46 48 49 51 52 54 55 56 57 58 59 60 65 66 67 71 73 **P**3 7 8 **S** Incarnate Word Health Services, San Antonio, TX **N** Southwest Preferred Network, Dallas, TX	21	10	175	7350	121	45160	0	48613	19694	0
PASADENA—Harris County										
⊠ COLUMBIA BAYSHORE MEDICAL CENTER, 4000 Spencer Highway, Zip 77504–1294; tel. 713/359–2000; Russell Meyers, Chief Executive Officer **A**1 2 9 10 **F**3 4 7 8 10 11 12 14 15 16 17 19 20 21 22 25 26 27 28 29 31 32 33 35 37 40 41 42 43 44 45 46 48 49 51 52 54 55 56 58 59 60 61 64 65 66 67 68 70 71 72 73 74 **P**4 5 7 8 **S** Columbia/HCA Healthcare Corporation, Nashville, TN **N** Gulf Coast Provider Network, Houston, TX	33	10	280	12910	175	123689	1719	89055	31888	1021
□ MEMORIAL HOSPITAL PASADENA, 906 East Southmore Avenue, Zip 77502–1124, Mailing Address: P.O. Box 1879, Zip 77502–1879; tel. 713/477–0411; Dennis M. Knox, Vice President and Chief Executive Officer (Total facility includes 22 beds in nursing home–type unit) **A**1 9 10 **F**2 3 4 6 7 8 10 11 12 14 15 16 17 19 21 22 23 25 26 27 28 29 30 31 32 33 34 35 37 38 39 40 41 42 43 44 45 46 48 49 51 52 53 54 55 56 57 58 59 60 62 63 64 65 66 67 68 70 71 72 73 74 **P**3 4 7 **S** Memorial Herman Healthcare System, Houston, TX	23	10	173	2955	39	25688	1176	36303	14306	425
PEARSALL—Frio County										
FRIO HOSPITAL, 320 Berry Ranch Road, Zip 78061–3998; tel. 210/334–3617; Alan D. Holmes, Chief Executive Officer **A**9 10 **F**7 15 16 19 22 28 32 35 44 49 70 71 **N** Southwest Texas Rural Health Alliance, San Antonio, TX	23	10	22	882	9	14638	230	5571	2621	108
PECOS—Reeves County										
★ REEVES COUNTY HOSPITAL, 2323 Texas Street, Zip 79772–7338; tel. 915/447–3551; Charles N. Butts, Interim Chief Executive Officer **A**9 10 **F**7 14 19 22 28 32 37 40 44 46 65 70 **S** Lubbock Methodist Hospital System, Lubbock, TX **N** Permian Basin Rural Health Network, Fort Stockton, TX	16	10	44	791	8	12119	124	5969	2439	105
PERRYTON—Ochiltree County										
OCHILTREE GENERAL HOSPITAL, 3101 Garrett Drive, Zip 79070–5393; tel. 806/435–3606; Wallace N. Boyd, Administrator **A**9 10 **F**7 8 12 15 17 19 21 22 28 29 30 32 33 34 36 37 40 44 49 65 67 70 71 73 74 **P**1	16	10	45	957	11	20175	174	5984	2985	105
PITTSBURG—Camp County										
⊠ EAST TEXAS MEDICAL CENTER PITTSBURG, 414 Quitman Street, Zip 75686–1032; tel. 903/856–6663; W. Perry Henderson, Administrator **A**1 9 10 **F**1 8 19 21 22 25 32 44 70 71 73 **P**3 5 **S** East Texas Medical Center Regional Healthcare System, Tyler, TX **N** Healthcare Partners of East Texas, Inc., Tyler, TX	23	10	43	1156	17	84992	—	9720	4688	173
PLAINVIEW—Hale County										
⊠ METHODIST HOSPITAL PLAINVIEW, 2601 Dimmitt Road, Zip 79072–1833; tel. 806/296–5531; Joe S. Langford, Administrator **A**1 9 10 **F**2 3 7 8 10 12 14 15 16 17 18 19 20 21 22 23 25 28 30 31 32 34 35 36 37 39 40 41 42 44 45 46 49 51 52 53 54 55 56 57 58 59 65 66 67 70 71 72 73 **P**3 7 **S** Lubbock Methodist Hospital System, Lubbock, TX	21	10	100	2350	29	71420	456	—	—	287
PLANO—Collin County										
⊠ COLUMBIA MEDICAL CENTER OF PLANO, 3901 West 15th Street, Zip 75075–7799; tel. 972/596–6800; Harvey L. Fishero, President and Chief Executive Officer (Total facility includes 20 beds in nursing home–type unit) **A**1 2 9 10 **F**4 7 8 10 11 12 14 15 16 17 18 19 21 22 23 24 28 30 31 32 33 34 35 37 38 40 42 43 44 45 46 49 60 64 65 66 67 71 73 74 **P**3 7 **S** Columbia/HCA Healthcare Corporation, Nashville, TN	33	10	265	13878	160	60912	3798	113957	39527	1026
⊠ △ HEALTHSOUTH REHABILITATION HOSPITAL–PLANO, (Formerly Plano Rehabilitation Hospital), 2800 West 15th Street, Zip 75075–7526; tel. 972/612–9000; Laurence J. Frayne, Chief Executive Officer **A**1 7 10 **F**1 5 12 15 16 19 21 24 27 32 35 39 41 48 49 50 54 58 63 65 66 73 **P**5 **S** HEALTHSOUTH Corporation, Birmingham, AL PLANO REHABILITATION HOSPITAL See HEALTHSOUTH Rehabilitation Hospital–Plano	32	46	62	868	51	40398	—	15842	8114	311

Hospital, Address, Telephone, Administrator, Approval, Facility, and Physician Codes, Health Care System, Network	Classi-fication Codes		Utilization Data					Expense (thousands) of dollars		
★ American Hospital Association (AHA) membership □ Joint Commission on Accreditation of Healthcare Organizations (JCAHO) accreditation + American Osteopathic Healthcare Association (AOHA) membership ○ American Osteopathic Association (AOA) accreditation △ Commission on Accreditation of Rehabilitation Facilities (CARF) accreditation Control codes 61, 63, 64, 71, 72 and 73 indicate hospitals listed by AOHA, but not registered by AHA. For definition of numerical codes, see page A4	Control	Service	Staffed Beds	Admissions	Census	Outpatient Visits	Births	Total	Payroll	Personnel

	Control	Service	Staffed Beds	Admissions	Census	Outpatient Visits	Births	Total	Payroll	Personnel
✠ PRESBYTERIAN HOSPITAL OF PLANO, 6200 West Parker Road, Zip 75093–7914; tel. 972/608–8000; Philip M. Wentworth, FACHE, Executive Director **A**1 9 10 **F**7 8 12 14 15 16 17 19 21 22 23 27 28 29 30 32 33 34 35 37 39 40 44 46 49 61 63 64 65 66 71 72 73 74 **P**8 **S** Texas Health Resources, Irving, TX **N** Presbyterian Healthcare System, Dallas, TX; North Texas Health Network, Irving, TX; North Texas Healthcare Network, Dallas, TX	23	10	91	6425	57	45160	1842	52522	19099	536
PORT ARTHUR—Jefferson County										
✠ PARK PLACE MEDICAL CENTER, 3050 39th Street, Zip 77642–5535, Mailing Address: P.O. Box 1648, Zip 77641–1648; tel. 409/983–4951; Wilson J. Weber, Chief Executive Officer (Total facility includes 21 beds in nursing home–type unit) **A**1 9 10 **F**4 7 8 10 12 15 16 17 19 21 22 23 27 28 29 30 34 35 37 38 40 41 42 43 44 45 46 48 51 60 64 65 67 71 72 73 74 **P**3 7 **S** TENET Healthcare Corporation, Santa Barbara, CA	32	10	219	4626	77	25731	528	36951	12915	451
✠ ST. MARY HOSPITAL, 3600 Gates Boulevard, Zip 77642–3601, Mailing Address: P.O. Box 3696, Zip 77643–3696; tel. 409/985–7431; Jeffrey Webster, Chief Executive Officer (Total facility includes 20 beds in nursing home–type unit) **A**1 3 5 9 10 **F**4 7 8 10 12 13 14 15 16 17 19 20 21 22 24 25 27 29 30 32 33 34 35 39 41 42 43 44 46 49 51 54 56 57 58 59 60 65 67 71 73 74 **P**1 3 4 5 6 7 8 **S** Sisters of Charity of the Incarnate Word Healthcare System, Houston, TX **N** SouthEast Texas Integrated Community Health Network, Houston, TX	21	10	211	9140	122	93578	725	65681	25937	765
PORT LAVACA—Calhoun County										
✠ MEMORIAL MEDICAL CENTER, 815 North Virginia Street, Zip 77979–3025, Mailing Address: P.O. Box 25, Zip 77979–0025; tel. 512/552–6713; Bob L. Bybee, President and Chief Executive Officer **A**1 9 10 **F**7 14 15 16 19 22 26 28 30 32 33 35 37 38 40 44 45 57 65 71 **N** SouthEast Texas Hospital System, Dallas, TX	13	10	56	1587	18	27265	254	13102	6161	235
QUANAH—Hardeman County										
HARDEMAN COUNTY MEMORIAL HOSPITAL, 402 Mercer Street, Zip 79252–4026, Mailing Address: P.O. Box 90, Zip 79252–0090; tel. 940/663–2795; Charles Hurt, Administrator **A**9 10 **F**15 19 22 27 32 34 44 65 70 71 73 **P**6 **N** Texoma Health Network, Wichita Falls, TX	16	10	23	233	4	22413	—	2375	1247	68
QUITMAN—Wood County										
□ EAST TEXAS MEDICAL CENTER–WOOD COUNTY AT QUITMAN, (Formerly Wood County Central Hospital), 117 Winnsboro Street, Zip 75783–2144, Mailing Address: P.O. Box 1000, Zip 75783–1000; tel. 903/763–4505; Marion W. Stanberry, Administrator **A**1 9 10 **F**7 8 12 14 15 16 19 21 22 28 30 34 42 44 46 49 67 70 71 73 **P**2 3 7 8 **N** Healthcare Partners of East Texas, Inc., Tyler, TX; Regional Healthcare Alliance, Tyler, TX	16	10	30	1197	14	12056	113	6545	2724	106
RANKIN—Upton County										
RANKIN HOSPITAL DISTRICT, 1105 Elizabeth Street, Zip 79778, Mailing Address: P.O. Box 327, Zip 79778–0327; tel. 915/693–2443; John Paul Loyless, Administrator **A**9 10 **F**14 15 16 17 22 32 34 39 40 44 46 51 71 73 **N** Permian Basin Rural Health Network, Fort Stockton, TX	16	10	20	39	0	13237	2	2057	1117	31
REFUGIO—Refugio County										
✠ REFUGIO COUNTY MEMORIAL HOSPITAL, 107 Swift Street, Zip 78377–2425; tel. 512/526–2321; Bill Jones, Administrator **A**1 9 10 **F**14 15 16 17 19 22 25 31 34 36 39 44 45 46 49 51 63 **P**6 **N** SouthEast Texas Hospital System, Dallas, TX	16	10	20	320	4	13832	0	5200	1905	91
RICHARDSON—Dallas County										
□ BAYLOR RICHARDSON MEDICAL CENTER, 401 West Campbell Road, Zip 75080–3499; tel. 972/498–4000; Ronald L. Boring, President and Chief Executive Officer (Total facility includes 16 beds in nursing home–type unit) **A**1 9 10 **F**2 3 4 7 8 9 10 11 12 17 18 19 21 22 23 25 26 28 29 30 31 32 33 34 35 37 38 39 40 41 42 43 44 45 46 47 48 49 52 53 54 55 56 57 58 59 60 61 63 64 65 66 67 68 69 70 71 72 73 74 **P**5 6 7 8 **N** Baylor Health Care System Network, Dallas, TX; North Texas Healthcare Network, Dallas, TX	16	10	113	5263	53	49523	691	42075	16283	490
RICHMOND—Fort Bend County										
□ POLLY RYON MEMORIAL HOSPITAL, 1705 Jackson Street, Zip 77469–3289; tel. 281/341–3000; Sam L. Steffee, Executive Director and Chief Executive Officer (Total facility includes 34 beds in nursing home–type unit) **A**1 9 10 **F**7 8 14 19 21 22 31 32 33 34 35 37 40 41 44 46 49 64 65 66 67 70 71 73 **P**5 8 **N** Memorial/Sisters of Charity Health Network, Houston, TX; Gulf Coast Provider Network, Houston, TX	16	10	145	4267	61	36353	704	28109	11606	363
RIO GRANDE CITY—Starr County										
★ STARR COUNTY MEMORIAL HOSPITAL, Rural Route 1, Zip 78582–9801, Mailing Address: P.O. Box 78, Zip 78582–0078; tel. 956/487–5561; Thalia H. Munoz, Administrator **A**9 10 **F**7 14 15 16 19 20 40 44 65 70 71 73	16	10	44	2069	20	10548	869	8922	4319	185
ROCKDALE—Milam County										
RICHARDS MEMORIAL HOSPITAL, 1700 Brazos Street, Zip 76567–2517, Mailing Address: Drawer 1010, Zip 76567–1010; tel. 512/446–2513; Edward F. Lynch, Administrator (Total facility includes 10 beds in nursing home–type unit) **A**9 10 **F**8 19 22 25 26 28 32 33 34 44 49 52 57 59 70 71 73 **P**5	16	10	47	588	9	17787	1	4398	1757	82
ROTAN—Fisher County										
FISHER COUNTY HOSPITAL DISTRICT, Roby Highway, Zip 79546, Mailing Address: Drawer F., Zip 79546; tel. 915/735–2256; Ella Raye Helms, Administrator (Total facility includes 7 beds in nursing home–type unit) **A**9 10 **F**8 13 15 16 17 19 24 28 30 32 34 39 44 49 51 64 65 70 71 73 **P**4 6 **S** Lubbock Methodist Hospital System, Lubbock, TX **N** Lubbock Methodist Hospital System, Lubbock, TX	16	10	20	357	10	36097	0	4497	2104	90

Hospital, Address, Telephone, Administrator, Approval, Facility, and Physician Codes, Health Care System, Network	Classification Codes		Utilization Data					Expense (thousands) of dollars		
	Control	Service	Staffed Beds	Admissions	Census	Outpatient Visits	Births	Total	Payroll	Personnel

★ American Hospital Association (AHA) membership
□ Joint Commission on Accreditation of Healthcare Organizations (JCAHO) accreditation
+ American Osteopathic Healthcare Association (AOHA) membership
○ American Osteopathic Association (AOA) accreditation
△ Commission on Accreditation of Rehabilitation Facilities (CARF) accreditation
Control codes 61, 63, 64, 71, 72 and 73 indicate hospitals listed by AOHA, but not registered by AHA. For definition of numerical codes, see page A4.

ROUND ROCK—Williamson County

★ ROUND ROCK HOSPITAL, 2400 Round Rock Avenue, Zip 78681–4097; tel. 512/341–1000; Deborah L. Ryle, Chief Executive Officer **A**1 9 10 **F**7 12 14 15 16 19 22 23 28 29 30 34 37 40 42 44 49 64 65 71 73 74 **P**7 8 **S** Columbia/HCA Healthcare Corporation, Nashville, TN **N** Columbia Saint David's Health Network, Austin, TX

| 32 | 10 | 65 | 3744 | 40 | 42555 | 941 | 23813 | 9718 | 261 |

ROWLETT—Rockwall County

★ LAKE POINTE MEDICAL CENTER, 6800 Scenic Drive, Zip 75088, Mailing Address: P.O. Box 1550, Zip 75030–1550; tel. 972/412–2273; Kenneth R. Teel, Administrator **A**1 9 10 **F**7 8 11 12 13 16 17 19 20 22 24 28 29 32 33 34 35 39 40 41 42 44 45 49 64 65 66 67 71 72 73 74 **P**8 **S** TENET Healthcare Corporation, Santa Barbara, CA

| 33 | 10 | 88 | 4822 | 45 | 83465 | 538 | 30668 | 12844 | 343 |

RUSK—Cherokee County

□ EAST TEXAS MEDICAL CENTER RUSK, 500 North Bonner Street, Zip 75785, Mailing Address: P.O. Box 317, Zip 75785–0317; tel. 903/683–2273; Brenda Copley, Acting Administrator **A**1 9 10 **F**8 12 14 15 16 17 19 21 22 24 26 28 29 30 31 32 34 39 41 44 45 46 49 51 65 67 70 71 73 **P**7 **S** East Texas Medical Center Regional Healthcare System, Tyler, TX **N** Healthcare Partners of East Texas, Inc., Tyler, TX

| 23 | 10 | 25 | 628 | 5 | 13202 | 0 | 7380 | 3387 | 172 |

□ RUSK STATE HOSPITAL, Jacksonville Highway North, Zip 75785, Mailing Address: P.O. Box 318, Zip 75785–0318; tel. 903/683–3421; Harold R. Parrish, Superintendent **A**1 10 **F**14 15 16 19 20 21 26 27 28 30 31 35 44 45 46 52 54 55 56 57 65 67 71 73

| 12 | 22 | 386 | 2004 | 353 | — | — | 35363 | 21238 | 958 |

SAN ANGELO—Tom Green County

★ △ COLUMBIA MEDICAL CENTER OF SAN ANGELO, 3501 Knickerbocker Road, Zip 76904–7698; tel. 915/949–9511; Gregory R. Angle, President and Chief Executive Officer **A**1 2 7 9 10 **F**4 7 8 10 12 13 17 21 22 23 24 25 26 28 29 30 32 33 35 37 38 39 40 41 42 43 44 45 46 48 49 51 63 64 65 66 67 71 72 73 74 **P**3 5 7 8 **S** Columbia/HCA Healthcare Corporation, Nashville, TN

| 33 | 10 | 143 | 5665 | 74 | 42645 | 806 | 41250 | 15208 | 593 |

□ RIVER CREST HOSPITAL, 1636 Hunters Glen Road, Zip 76901–5016; tel. 915/949–5722; Larry Grimes, Managing Director **A**1 9 10 **F**3 12 13 15 16 17 19 21 22 26 27 28 30 35 41 46 49 50 52 53 54 55 56 57 58 59 63 65 67 68 71 **P**5 **S** Universal Health Services, Inc., King of Prussia, PA

| 33 | 22 | 80 | 1354 | 25 | 2693 | — | 4296 | 2114 | 56 |

★ △ SHANNON MEDICAL CENTER, (Includes Shannon Medical Center– St. John's Campus, 2018 Pulliam Street, Zip 76905–5197; tel. 915/659–7100), 120 East Harris Street, Zip 76903–5976; tel. 915/653–6741; John Geanes, President and Chief Executive Officer (Total facility includes 13 beds in nursing home–type unit) **A**1 2 7 9 10 **F**2 3 4 7 8 10 11 12 14 15 16 17 19 21 22 23 24 25 27 28 29 30 32 34 35 37 40 41 42 43 44 45 46 48 49 52 53 54 55 56 57 58 59 60 63 64 65 66 67 71 72 73 74 **P**3

| 23 | 10 | 219 | 10725 | 136 | 64262 | 1356 | 65852 | 25634 | 1132 |

SAN ANTONIO—Bexar County

★ BAPTIST MEDICAL CENTER, 111 Dallas Street, Zip 78205–1230; tel. 210/297–7000; Fred R. Mills, President and Chief Executive Officer (Total facility includes 31 beds in nursing home–type unit) **A**1 2 3 5 6 9 10 **F**2 3 4 7 8 10 11 12 14 15 16 17 19 20 21 23 26 28 29 30 31 33 34 35 37 38 39 40 41 42 43 44 45 46 48 49 52 54 55 56 57 59 60 63 64 65 67 69 70 71 73 74 **P**3 7 8 **S** Baptist Health System, San Antonio, TX

| 21 | 10 | 480 | 16687 | 298 | 69031 | 2020 | 125315 | 57321 | 1582 |

★ BROOKE ARMY MEDICAL CENTER, Fort Sam Houston, Zip 78234–6200; tel. 210/916–4141; Colonel Joseph P. Gonzales, MS, USA, Chief of Staff (Nonreporting) **A**1 2 3 5 9 **S** Department of the Army, Office of the Surgeon General, Falls Church, VA

| 42 | 10 | 464 | — | — | — | — | — | — | — |

□ CHARTER REAL BEHAVIORAL HEALTH SYSTEM, 8550 Huebner Road, Zip 78240–1897, Mailing Address: P.O. Box 380157, Zip 78280–0157; tel. 210/699–8585; Robert Quintanilla, Chief Executive Officer **A**1 9 10 **F**1 3 12 14 15 16 25 26 27 31 34 39 41 46 52 53 54 55 56 57 58 59 65 67 **S** Magellan Health Services, Atlanta, GA

| 32 | 22 | 90 | 1490 | 32 | 6690 | 0 | 6847 | 2987 | 82 |

□ △ HEALTHSOUTH REHABILITATION INSTITUTE OF SAN ANTONIO, 9119 Cinnamon Hill, Zip 78240–5401; tel. 210/691–0737; Diane B. Lampe, Administrator and Chief Executive Officer **A**1 7 9 10 **F**5 12 14 15 16 19 21 25 26 27 32 35 41 42 44 46 48 49 50 63 65 66 67 71 73 **S** HEALTHSOUTH Corporation, Birmingham, AL

| 33 | 46 | 108 | 1406 | 70 | 15313 | 0 | 17501 | 6771 | 240 |

□ HORIZON SPECIALTY HOSPITAL, (LONG TERM ACUTE CARE), 7310 Oak Manor Drive, Zip 78229–4509; tel. 210/308–0261; Peggy Wood, Administrator **A**1 10 **F**12 14 16 17 19 21 26 28 31 32 33 35 39 45 46 48 50 63 65 71

| 33 | 49 | 30 | 200 | 15 | — | — | 5689 | 1468 | 56 |

★ METHODIST AMBULATORY SURGERY HOSPITAL, 9150 Huebner Road, Zip 78240–1545; tel. 210/691–0800; Elaine F. Morris, Administrator (Total facility includes 16 beds in nursing home–type unit) **A**1 10 **F**2 4 7 8 10 11 12 17 18 19 21 22 23 24 25 26 27 28 29 30 32 33 34 35 37 38 39 40 41 42 43 44 45 46 47 48 49 51 52 54 55 57 60 61 64 65 66 67 69 70 71 73 74 **P**8 **S** Columbia/HCA Healthcare Corporation, Nashville, TN

| 33 | 10 | 37 | 641 | 10 | 13511 | — | 13185 | 4692 | 177 |

★ METHODIST WOMEN'S AND CHILDREN'S HOSPITAL, 8109 Fredericksburg Road, Zip 78229–3383; tel. 210/692–5000; Janet Porter, President and Chief Executive Officer **A**1 9 **F**2 3 4 7 8 10 11 12 13 14 15 16 17 18 19 21 22 23 25 26 27 28 29 30 31 32 34 35 37 38 39 40 41 42 43 44 45 46 47 48 49 52 53 54 55 56 57 58 59 60 61 63 64 65 66 67 69 70 71 72 73 74 **P**2 5 7 8 **S** Columbia/HCA Healthcare Corporation, Nashville, TN **N** Methodist Healthcare System of San Antonio, Ltd., San Antonio, TX

| 32 | 10 | 150 | 7325 | 69 | 58266 | 4307 | 35321 | 17260 | 442 |

Hospital, Address, Telephone, Administrator, Approval, Facility, and Physician Codes, Health Care System, Network	Classi-fication Codes		Utilization Data					Expense (thousands) of dollars		
	Control	Service	Staffed Beds	Admissions	Census	Outpatient Visits	Births	Total	Payroll	Personnel

★ American Hospital Association (AHA) membership
☐ Joint Commission on Accreditation of Healthcare Organizations (JCAHO) accreditation
+ American Osteopathic Healthcare Association (AOHA) membership
○ American Osteopathic Association (AOA) accreditation
△ Commission on Accreditation of Rehabilitation Facilities (CARF) accreditation
Control codes 61, 63, 64, 71, 72 and 73 indicate hospitals listed by AOHA, but not registered by AHA. For definition of numerical codes, see page A4

Hospital	Control	Service	Staffed Beds	Admissions	Census	Outpatient Visits	Births	Total	Payroll	Personnel
✠ METROPOLITAN METHODIST HOSPITAL, 1310 McCullough Avenue, Zip 78212–2617; tel. 210/208–2200; Mark L. Bernard, Chief Executive Officer (Total facility includes 16 beds in nursing home–type unit) **A**1 9 10 **F**2 3 4 5 7 8 10 11 12 13 14 15 16 17 18 19 20 21 22 23 24 25 26 27 28 29 30 31 32 33 35 37 38 39 40 41 42 43 44 45 46 47 48 49 52 53 54 55 57 58 59 60 61 63 64 65 66 67 69 70 71 72 73 74 **P**5 6 7 8 **S** Columbia/HCA Healthcare Corporation, Nashville, TN **N** Methodist Healthcare System of San Antonio, Ltd., San Antonio, TX	32	10	237	11489	127	36449	2692	57520	25299	742
☐ MISSION VISTA BEHAVIORAL HEALTH SYSTEM, 14747 Jones Maltsberger, Zip 78247–3713; tel. 210/490–0000; Holly Minis, Chief Executive Officer **A**1 9 10 **F**3 12 14 15 16 18 22 26 34 45 46 52 54 56 57 58 59 65 67 **P**6 **S** Ramsay Health Care, Inc., Coral Gables, FL	33	22	16	624	12	5229	0	3221	1597	29
☐ NIX HEALTH CARE SYSTEM, 414 Navarro Street, Zip 78205–2522; tel. 210/271–1800; John F. Strieby, President and Chief Executive Officer (Total facility includes 17 beds in nursing home–type unit) **A**1 3 9 10 **F**4 7 8 10 14 19 21 26 28 30 32 33 34 35 37 39 40 41 42 43 44 45 46 49 52 57 59 60 63 64 65 66 67 69 71 73 74 **P**5 7	33	10	132	3242	55	—	576	—	—	617
NORTH CENTRAL BAPTIST HOSPITAL, 520 Madison Oak Drive, Zip 78258–3912; Dan Brown, Administrator **F**2 3 4 7 8 10 11 14 15 16 17 19 20 21 22 23 26 28 29 30 31 32 33 34 35 37 38 39 40 41 42 43 44 45 47 48 49 52 54 57 59 60 63 64 65 67 69 70 71 73 74 **P**3 7 8 **S** Baptist Health System, San Antonio, TX	21	10	88	2833	29	26835	430	24386	10236	421
NORTHEAST BAPTIST HOSPITAL, 8811 Village Drive, Zip 78217–5440; tel. 210/653–2330; Dan Brown, Administrator **F**2 3 4 7 8 10 11 12 13 14 15 16 17 19 20 21 22 23 26 28 29 30 31 32 33 34 35 37 38 39 40 41 42 43 44 45 46 47 48 49 52 53 54 55 56 57 58 59 60 61 63 64 65 67 69 70 71 73 74 **P**3 7 8 **S** Baptist Health System, San Antonio, TX	21	10	234	9740	130	54184	1900	71697	31615	1001
✠ NORTHEAST METHODIST HOSPITAL, 12412 Judson Road, Zip 78233–3272, Mailing Address: P.O. Box 659510, Zip 78265–9510; tel. 210/650–4949; Mark L. Bernard, Chief Executive Officer (Total facility includes 10 beds in nursing home–type unit) **A**1 9 10 **F**2 3 4 5 7 8 10 11 12 13 14 15 16 17 18 19 20 21 22 23 24 25 26 27 28 29 30 31 32 33 34 35 37 38 39 40 41 42 43 44 45 46 47 48 49 52 53 54 55 56 57 58 59 60 61 63 64 65 66 67 69 71 72 73 74 **P**5 6 7 8 **S** Columbia/HCA Healthcare Corporation, Nashville, TN **N** Methodist Healthcare System of San Antonio, Ltd., San Antonio, TX	32	10	117	3667	52	45731	2	30522	12021	334
✠ SAN ANTONIO COMMUNITY HOSPITAL, 8026 Floyd Curl Drive, Zip 78229–3915; tel. 210/692–8110; James C. Scoggin, Jr., Chief Executive Officer **A**1 3 5 9 10 **F**2 3 4 7 8 10 11 12 13 14 15 16 17 18 19 20 21 22 23 25 26 27 28 29 30 31 32 33 34 35 37 38 39 40 41 42 43 44 45 46 47 48 49 52 54 55 56 57 58 59 60 61 63 64 65 66 67 69 70 71 72 73 74 **P**5 7 8 **S** Columbia/HCA Healthcare Corporation, Nashville, TN **N** Methodist Healthcare System of San Antonio, Ltd., San Antonio, TX	32	10	291	6724	106	74621	—	58469	23520	603
☐ SAN ANTONIO STATE HOSPITAL, 6711 South New Braunfels, Zip 78223–3009, Mailing Address: Box 23991, Highland Hills Station, Zip 78223–0991; tel. 210/531–7711; Robert C. Arizpe, Superintendent **A**1 10 **F**6 8 12 17 18 20 22 27 28 29 30 34 45 46 49 52 53 54 55 56 58 65 67 73 **P**6	12	22	423	2234	372	0	—	47265	27969	1252
✠ △ SANTA ROSA HEALTH CARE CORPORATION, 519 West Houston Street, Zip 78207–3108; tel. 210/704–2011; William C. Finlayson, President and Chief Execuctive Officer **A**1 2 3 5 7 9 10 **F**2 3 4 5 7 8 10 11 12 13 14 15 16 17 18 19 20 21 22 26 27 28 29 30 31 32 33 34 35 37 38 39 40 41 42 43 44 45 46 47 48 49 51 52 53 54 55 56 57 58 59 60 61 63 64 65 66 67 68 69 71 72 73 74 **S** Incarnate Word Health Services, San Antonio, TX **N** Primary CareNet of Texas, San Antonio, TX	21	10	608	21363	895	152697	3127	193303	83299	2615
✠ SOUTH TEXAS VETERANS HEALTH CARE SYSTEM, (Includes Kerrville Division, 3600 Memorial Boulevard, Kerrville, Zip 78028; tel. 210/896–2020; San Antonio Division, 7400 Merton Minter Boulevard, tel. 210/617–5140; Jose R. Coronado, FACHE, Director), 7400 Merton Minter Boulevard, Zip 78284–5799; tel. 210/617–5140; Jose R. Coronado, FACHE, Director (Total facility includes 274 beds in nursing home–type unit) (Nonreporting) **A**1 2 5 8 **S** Department of Veterans Affairs, Washington, DC	45	10	1112	—	—	—	—	—	—	—
SOUTHEAST BAPTIST HOSPITAL, 4214 East Southcross Boulevard, Zip 78222–3740; tel. 210/297–3000; Kevin Walters, Administrator **F**2 3 4 7 8 10 12 14 15 16 17 19 20 21 22 23 26 28 29 30 31 32 33 34 35 37 38 40 41 42 43 44 45 46 48 49 52 53 54 55 56 57 59 60 61 63 64 65 67 69 70 71 73 74 **P**3 7 8 **S** Baptist Health System, San Antonio, TX	21	10	153	6051	83	40474	558	39523	19133	524
✠ △ SOUTHWEST GENERAL HOSPITAL, 7400 Barlite Boulevard, Zip 78224–1399; tel. 210/921–2000; Keith Swinney, Chief Executive Officer (Total facility includes 23 beds in nursing home–type unit) **A**1 7 10 **F**7 12 15 16 17 19 29 32 33 34 35 37 40 41 42 44 45 46 48 49 52 54 56 57 64 65 67 71 **S** TENET Healthcare Corporation, Santa Barbara, CA	33	10	223	6813	105	51747	951	47112	25537	770
SOUTHWEST MENTAL HEALTH CENTER, 8535 Tom Slick, Zip 78229–3363; tel. 210/616–0300; Sharon M. Stanush, President (Nonreporting) **A**3 5 9	23	52	80	—	—	—	—	—	—	—
✠ SOUTHWEST TEXAS METHODIST HOSPITAL, 7700 Floyd Curl Drive, Zip 78229–3993; tel. 210/575–4000; James C. Scoggin, Jr., Chief Executive Officer **A**1 2 3 5 9 10 **F**2 3 4 5 7 8 10 11 12 13 14 15 16 17 18 19 20 21 22 23 25 26 27 28 29 30 31 32 33 34 35 37 38 39 40 41 42 43 44 45 46 47 48 49 52 54 55 56 57 58 59 60 61 63 64 65 66 67 69 70 71 72 73 74 **P**2 5 7 8 **S** Columbia/HCA Healthcare Corporation, Nashville, TN **N** Methodist Healthcare System of San Antonio, Ltd., San Antonio, TX	32	10	585	25498	377	101410	3687	199738	85070	2626

Hospital, Address, Telephone, Administrator, Approval, Facility, and Physician Codes, Health Care System, Network	Classi-fication Codes		Utilization Data					Expense (thousands) of dollars		
★ American Hospital Association (AHA) membership ☐ Joint Commission on Accreditation of Healthcare Organizations (JCAHO) accreditation + American Osteopathic Healthcare Association (AOHA) membership ○ American Osteopathic Association (AOA) accreditation △ Commission on Accreditation of Rehabilitation Facilities (CARF) accreditation Control codes 61, 63, 64, 71, 72 and 73 indicate hospitals listed by AOHA, but not registered by AHA. For definition of numerical codes, see page A4	Control	Service	Staffed Beds	Admissions	Census	Outpatient Visits	Births	Total	Payroll	Personnel

☐ ST. LUKE'S BAPTIST HOSPITAL, 7930 Floyd Curl Drive, Zip 78229–0100; tel. 210/692–8703; John Penn Krause, Administrator (Total facility includes 30 beds in nursing home–type unit) **A**1 3 5 9 **F**2 3 4 7 8 10 11 12 14 15 16 17 19 20 21 22 23 26 28 29 30 31 33 34 35 37 38 39 40 41 42 43 44 45 46 48 49 52 54 55 57 59 60 63 64 65 67 69 71 73 **P**3 7 8 **S** Baptist Health System, San Antonio, TX	21	10	219	6886	95	20982	0	56764	20770	615
✸ TEXAS CENTER FOR INFECTIOUS DISEASE, 2303 S.E. Military Drive, Zip 78223–3597; tel. 210/534–8857; James N. Elkins, FACHE, Director **A**1 9 10 **F**14 15 16 19 20 21 22 24 27 31 34 39 41 44 45 46 51 54 65 71 73 **P**1 **S** Texas Department of Health, Austin, TX	12	33	109	204	67	8998	—	13397	7219	309
✸ UNIVERSITY HEALTH SYSTEM, (Includes University Health Center – Downtown, tel. 210/358–3400; University Hospital, tel. 210/358–4000), 4502 Medical Drive, Zip 78229–4493; tel. 210/358–4000; John A. Guest, President and Chief Executive Officer **A**1 2 3 5 8 10 **F**4 7 8 10 11 12 13 14 16 17 18 19 20 21 22 25 26 28 29 30 31 35 37 38 39 40 41 42 43 44 45 46 47 48 49 51 52 53 54 55 56 57 58 60 61 63 64 65 67 69 70 71 72 73 74	16	10	547	19218	312	474273	2908	299207	99053	4158
✸ △ WARM SPRINGS AND BAPTIST REHABILITATION HOSPITAL, 5101 Medical Drive, Zip 78229–6098; tel. 210/616–0100; James L. Ashbaugh, Regional Director of Operations **A**1 3 7 10 **F**12 13 15 16 24 27 28 32 34 41 48 49 65 67 73 **P**7	23	46	62	1208	55	20594	0	15830	6172	222
SAN AUGUSTINE—San Augustine County										
MEMORIAL MEDICAL CENTER OF SAN AUGUSTINE, 511 East Hospital Street, Zip 75972–2121, Mailing Address: P.O. Box 658, Zip 75972–0658; tel. 409/275–3446; Terry Napper, Administrator **A**9 10 **F**8 11 12 14 15 16 17 20 24 27 28 30 32 34 37 40 44 46 48 49 51 52 64 65 71 **P**6 7 8	23	10	15	564	5	—	1	3508	1829	90
SAN BENITO—Cameron County										
✸ DOLLY VINSANT MEMORIAL HOSPITAL, 400 East U.S. Highway 77, Zip 78586–5310, Mailing Address: P.O. Box 42, Zip 78586–0042; tel. 956/399–1313; R. William Warren, Chairman and Chief Executive Officer **A**1 9 10 **F**19 21 22 28 34 39 44 45 49 71 73	33	10	49	1146	12	12157	—	7922	3282	148
SAN MARCOS—Hays County										
✸ CENTRAL TEXAS MEDICAL CENTER, 1301 Wonder World Drive, Zip 78666–7544; tel. 512/353–8979; Kenneth Bacon, President and Chief Executive Officer (Total facility includes 9 beds in nursing home–type unit) **A**1 9 10 **F**7 8 10 12 14 15 16 17 20 21 22 24 28 29 30 32 33 35 39 40 41 44 45 46 49 50 64 65 66 67 71 73 **P**6 8 **S** Adventist Health System Sunbelt Health Care Corporation, Winter Park, FL **N** Southwest Texas Rural Health Alliance, San Antonio, TX	21	10	109	4207	48	56981	828	36635	12462	429
SAN MARCOS TREATMENT CENTER, Bert Brown Road, Zip 78667–0768, Mailing Address: P.O. Box 768, Zip 78667–0768; tel. 512/396–8500; Mack Wigley, Chief Executive Officer (Nonreporting) **S** Healthcare America, Inc., Austin, TX	33	22	152	—	—	—	—	—	—	—
SEGUIN—Guadalupe County										
✸ GUADALUPE VALLEY HOSPITAL, 1215 East Court Street, Zip 78155–5189; tel. 830/379–2411; Don L. Richey, Administrator (Total facility includes 15 beds in nursing home–type unit) **A**1 9 10 **F**3 7 8 12 14 15 18 19 21 22 23 26 31 32 33 34 35 37 40 42 44 45 46 49 53 55 57 58 63 64 65 66 67 70 71 73 **P**1 **N** Southwest Texas Rural Health Alliance, San Antonio, TX	15	10	90	4694	60	64920	669	32052	15348	596
SEMINOLE—Gaines County										
★ MEMORIAL HOSPITAL, 209 N.W. Eighth Street, Zip 79360–3447; tel. 915/758–5811; Steve Beck, Chief Executive Officer and Administrator **A**9 10 **F**3 7 8 12 13 14 15 16 17 18 19 20 21 22 24 26 27 28 29 30 31 32 33 34 35 36 39 40 41 44 45 46 49 50 51 53 54 55 56 58 59 61 63 65 66 67 70 71 73 **N** Permian Basin Rural Health Network, Fort Stockton, TX	16	10	33	818	8	27585	154	9424	3152	—
SEYMOUR—Baylor County										
★ SEYMOUR HOSPITAL, 200 Stadium Drive, Zip 76380–2344; tel. 940/888–5572; Charles Norris, Administrator **A**9 10 **F**1 19 22 26 27 28 30 32 34 37 40 41 44 49 59 64 65 67 70 71 **P**6 **N** Texoma Health Network, Wichita Falls, TX	16	10	34	640	46	7817	46	4633	—	128
SHAMROCK—Wheeler County										
SHAMROCK GENERAL HOSPITAL, 1000 South Main Street, Zip 79079–2896; tel. 806/256–2114; Allen P. Alberty, Chief Executive Officer (Total facility includes 7 beds in nursing home–type unit) **A**9 10 **F**12 13 14 22 32 33 44 63 64 73	16	10	20	333	10	31610	3	3097	1498	71
SHEPPARD AFB—Wichita County										
✸ U. S. AIR FORCE REGIONAL HOSPITAL–SHEPPARD, 149 Hart Street, Suite 1, Zip 76311–3478; tel. 940/676–2010; Colonel Richard D. Maddox, Administrator **A**1 **F**2 3 8 11 12 13 15 16 17 18 19 20 22 24 27 28 29 30 35 37 38 39 40 41 44 45 46 47 48 49 51 52 53 54 55 56 58 61 65 67 68 71 73 74 **P**6 8 **S** Department of the Air Force, Bowling AFB, DC	41	10	80	2977	41	200983	333	52967	24590	—
SHERMAN—Grayson County										
✸ COLUMBIA MEDICAL CENTER OF SHERMAN, 1111 Gallagher Road, Zip 75090–1798; tel. 903/870–7000; John F. Adams, Chief Executive Officer (Total facility includes 22 beds in nursing home–type unit) **A**1 9 10 **F**7 8 12 15 19 21 22 23 26 28 29 30 31 32 33 34 35 37 40 41 42 44 45 46 48 49 50 52 57 63 64 65 67 71 73 74 **P**1 7 **S** Columbia/HCA Healthcare Corporation, Nashville, TN	33	10	160	2456	45	—	279	31019	10344	336
✸ △ WILSON N. JONES REGIONAL HEALTH SYSTEM, 500 North Highland Avenue, Zip 75092–7354, Mailing Address: P.O. Box 1258, Zip 75091–1258; tel. 903/870–4611; Harry F. Barnes, FACHE, President and Chief Executive Officer (Total facility includes 29 beds in nursing home–type unit) (Nonreporting) **A**1 7 9 10	23	10	197	—	—	—	—	—	—	—

Hospital, Address, Telephone, Administrator, Approval, Facility, and Physician Codes, Health Care System, Network	Classi-fication Codes		Utilization Data					Expense (thousands) of dollars		
	Control	Service	Staffed Beds	Admissions	Census	Outpatient Visits	Births	Total	Payroll	Personnel

American Hospital Association (AHA) membership
□ Joint Commission on Accreditation of Healthcare Organizations (JCAHO) accreditation
+ American Osteopathic Healthcare Association (AOHA) membership
○ American Osteopathic Association (AOA) accreditation
△ Commission on Accreditation of Rehabilitation Facilities (CARF) accreditation
Control codes 61, 63, 64, 71, 72 and 73 indicate hospitals listed by AOHA, but not registered by AHA. For definition of numerical codes, see page A4

SILSBEE—Hardin County

★ COLUMBIA SILSBEE DOCTORS HOSPITAL, Highway 418, Zip 77656, Mailing Address: P.O. Box 1208, Zip 77656–1208; tel. 409/385–5531; David Cottey, Chief Executive Officer (Total facility includes 13 beds in nursing home–type unit) **A**9 10 **F**8 12 15 19 22 25 28 32 34 37 44 46 49 51 64 65 71 73 **P**5 **S** Columbia/HCA Healthcare Corporation, Nashville, TN

33	10	59	1915	25	82218	—	15925	6348	215

SMITHVILLE—Bastrop County

SMITHVILLE HOSPITAL, Ninth and Mills Streets, Zip 78957, Mailing Address: P.O. Box 359, Zip 78957–0359; tel. 512/237–3214; James W. Langford, Administrator (Nonreporting) **A**9 10

| 16 | 10 | 27 | — | — | — | — | — | — | — |

SNYDER—Scurry County

✠ D. M. COGDELL MEMORIAL HOSPITAL, 1700 Cogdell Boulevard, Zip 79549–6198; tel. 915/573–6374; Jeff Reecer, Chief Executive Officer (Total facility includes 41 beds in nursing home–type unit) (Nonreporting) **A**1 9 10 **S** St. Joseph Health System, Orange, CA

| 13 | 10 | 72 | — | — | — | — | — | — | — |

SONORA—Sutton County

LILLIAN M. HUDSPETH MEMORIAL HOSPITAL, 308 Hudspeth Avenue, Zip 76950–3399, Mailing Address: P.O. Box 455, Zip 76950–0455; tel. 915/387–2521; Joe Hendrus, Administrator **A**9 10 **F**14 15 22 28 70

| 16 | 10 | 13 | 190 | 1 | 28503 | 1 | 1530 | 667 | 38 |

SPEARMAN—Hansford County

★ HANSFORD HOSPITAL, (MEDICAL ONLY), 707 South Roland Street, Zip 79081–3441; tel. 806/659–2535; Anne Snow, Administrator (Total facility includes 84 beds in nursing home–type unit) **A**9 10 **F**8 13 14 15 16 17 22 26 27 28 30 32 33 34 36 41 42 48 49 64 65 71 73 74

| 16 | 49 | 97 | 249 | 2 | 17835 | 0 | 2788 | 1242 | 61 |

STAMFORD—Jones County

STAMFORD MEMORIAL HOSPITAL, Highway 6 East, Zip 79553, Mailing Address: P.O. Box 911, Zip 79553–0911; tel. 915/773–2725; Craig Haterius, Administrator **A**9 10 **F**15 19 20 22 24 32 44 71 **P**5

| 16 | 10 | 35 | 337 | 4 | 5543 | 1 | 3089 | 1128 | 79 |

STANTON—Martin County

MARTIN COUNTY HOSPITAL DISTRICT, 610 North St. Peter Street, Zip 79782, Mailing Address: P.O. Box 640, Zip 79782–0640; tel. 915/756–3345; Rick Jacobus, Administrator **A**9 10 **F**15 16 22 40 44 70 71 **P**5 **N** Permian Basin Rural Health Network, Fort Stockton, TX

| 16 | 10 | 26 | 380 | 5 | 3465 | 25 | 3557 | 1533 | 57 |

STEPHENVILLE—Erath County

✠ HARRIS METHODIST–ERATH COUNTY, 411 North Belknap Street, Zip 76401–3415, Mailing Address: P.O. Box 1399, Zip 76401–1399; tel. 254/965–1500; Ronald E. Dorris, Administrator **A**1 9 10 **F**7 15 16 19 22 23 26 28 29 30 31 32 33 35 37 39 40 41 42 44 46 49 51 65 67 70 71 73 74 **P**2 5 7 **S** Texas Health Resources, Irving, TX **N** The Heart Network of Texas, Irving, TX; North Texas Healthcare Network, Dallas, TX

| 21 | 10 | 75 | 3124 | 34 | 13481 | 430 | 17114 | 6223 | 217 |

SULPHUR SPRINGS—Hopkins County

✠ HOPKINS COUNTY MEMORIAL HOSPITAL, 115 Airport Road, Zip 75482–0115; tel. 903/885–7671; Richard L. Goddard, Chief Executive Officer **A**1 9 10 **F**7 8 14 15 16 19 22 28 30 31 32 33 34 40 44 46 49 59 64 65 70 71 **N** Baylor Health Care System Network, Dallas, TX; Regional Healthcare Alliance, Tyler, TX

| 16 | 10 | 94 | 4027 | 39 | 47920 | 843 | 18819 | 8598 | 345 |

SWEENY—Brazoria County

□ SWEENY COMMUNITY HOSPITAL, 305 North McKinney Street, Zip 77480–2895; tel. 409/548–3311; Herbert A. Turk, FACHE, Administrator **A**1 9 10 **F**14 19 22 32 35 36 37 44 46 49 57 65 67 71 73

| 16 | 10 | 19 | 247 | 2 | 3600 | — | 6065 | 2789 | 101 |

SWEETWATER—Nolan County

✠ ROLLING PLAINS MEMORIAL HOSPITAL, 200 East Arizona Street, Zip 79556–7199, Mailing Address: P.O. Box 690, Zip 79556–0690; tel. 915/235–1701; Thomas F. Kennedy, Administrator **A**1 9 10 **F**7 8 14 15 16 19 20 22 24 26 31 32 33 34 35 37 40 44 49 65 70 71 73

| 16 | 10 | 54 | 1616 | 26 | 22027 | 213 | 10540 | 4699 | 199 |

TAHOKA—Lynn County

LYNN COUNTY HOSPITAL DISTRICT, Brownfield Highway, Zip 79373–1310, Mailing Address: Box 1310, Zip 79373–1310; tel. 806/998–4533; Louise Landers, Administrator (Nonreporting) **A**9 10

| 16 | 10 | 24 | — | — | — | — | — | — | — |

TAYLOR—Williamson County

□ JOHNS COMMUNITY HOSPITAL, 305 Mallard Lane, Zip 76574–1208; tel. 512/352–7611; Ernest Balla, Administrator **A**1 9 10 **F**8 14 15 19 21 22 27 28 30 32 34 37 44 45 49 51 64 65 71 **P**6

| 23 | 10 | 46 | 1267 | 28 | 21036 | — | 8438 | 4370 | 152 |

TEMPLE—Bell County

✠ CENTRAL TEXAS VETERANS AFFAIRS HEALTHCARE SYSTEM, (Includes Central Texas Veterans Affairs Health Care System, 4800 Memorial Drive, Waco, Zip 76711–1397; tel. 817/752–6581; Central Texas Veterans Affairs Health Care System, Marlin Integrated Clinical Facility, 1016 Ward Street, Marlin, Zip 76661–2162; tel. 817/778–4811; Olin E. Teague Veterans' Center, 1901 South First Street, Zip 76504; tel. 817/778–4811), 1901 South First Street, Zip 76504–7493; tel. 254/778–4811; Dean Billick, Director (Total facility includes 320 beds in nursing home–type unit) (Nonreporting) **A**1 2 3 5 **S** Department of Veterans Affairs, Washington, DC

| 45 | 10 | 1852 | — | — | — | — | — | — | — |

✠ KING'S DAUGHTERS HOSPITAL, 1901 S.W. H. K. Dodgen Loop, Zip 76502–1896; tel. 254/771–8600; Tucker Bonner, President (Total facility includes 8 beds in nursing home–type unit) **A**1 9 10 **F**7 14 15 16 19 20 21 22 23 27 28 30 31 32 33 34 35 37 39 40 41 42 44 45 49 56 63 64 65 67 71 73 **P**1 **N** Brazo's Valley Health Network, Waco, TX
OLIN E. TEAGUE VETERANS' CENTER See Central Texas Veterans Affairs Healthcare System

| 23 | 10 | 96 | 2797 | 32 | 35057 | 467 | 24144 | 10021 | 342 |

Hospital, Address, Telephone, Administrator, Approval, Facility, and Physician Codes, Health Care System, Network	Classi-fication Codes		Utilization Data					Expense (thousands) of dollars		
	Control	Service	Staffed Beds	Admissions	Census	Outpatient Visits	Births	Total	Payroll	Personnel

★ American Hospital Association (AHA) membership
□ Joint Commission on Accreditation of Healthcare Organizations (JCAHO) accreditation
+ American Osteopathic Healthcare Association (AOHA) membership
○ American Osteopathic Association (AOA) accreditation
△ Commission on Accreditation of Rehabilitation Facilities (CARF) accreditation
Control codes 61, 63, 64, 71, 72 and 73 indicate hospitals listed by AOHA, but not registered by AHA. For definition of numerical codes, see page A4

Hospital	Control	Service	Staffed Beds	Admissions	Census	Outpatient Visits	Births	Total	Payroll	Personnel
⊞ △ SCOTT AND WHITE MEMORIAL HOSPITAL, 2401 South 31st Street, Zip 76508–0002; tel. 254/724–2111; Dick Sweeden, Administrator (Total facility includes 38 beds in nursing home–type unit) **A**1 2 3 5 7 8 9 10 **F**1 3 4 7 8 10 11 12 14 15 16 17 19 20 21 22 23 25 26 27 28 29 30 31 32 33 35 37 38 40 41 42 43 44 45 46 47 48 49 52 53 54 56 57 58 59 60 61 64 65 66 67 69 71 72 73 74	23	10	439	21145	311	98578	2230	199086	89362	3173
TERRELL—Kaufman County										
⊞ MEDICAL CENTER AT TERRELL, (Formerly Columbia Medical Center at Terrell), 1551 Highway 34 South, Zip 75160–4833; tel. 972/563–7611; Ronald J. Ensor, Chief Executive Officer **A**1 9 10 **F**7 8 12 15 16 19 21 22 34 35 37 39 40 41 44 45 46 48 49 64 71 73 **S** Columbia/HCA Healthcare Corporation, Nashville, TN **N** North Texas Health Network, Irving, TX	33	10	130	2796	40	30995	183	18915	7189	253
□ TERRELL STATE HOSPITAL, 1200 East Brin Street, Zip 75160–2938, Mailing Address: P.O. Box 70, Zip 75160–0070; tel. 972/563–6452; Beatrice Butler, Superintendent **A**1 3 5 9 10 **F**1 3 4 5 6 7 8 9 10 11 12 13 14 15 16 17 18 19 20 21 22 23 25 26 27 28 29 30 31 34 35 36 37 38 39 40 41 42 43 44 45 46 47 48 49 50 52 53 54 55 56 57 58 59 60 63 65 67 68 71 73 **P**6	12	22	425	1798	340	—	—	41572	22312	—
TEXARKANA—Bowie County										
□ △ HEALTHSOUTH REHABILITATION HOSPITAL OF TEXARKANA, 515 West 12th Street, Zip 75501–4416; tel. 903/793–0088; Jeffrey A. Livingston, Chief Executive Officer **A**1 7 9 10 **F**14 15 16 22 46 48 49 65 66 **S** HEALTHSOUTH Corporation, Birmingham, AL	33	46	60	966	50	11162	0	10539	5064	222
⊞ MEDICAL ARTS HOSPITAL, 2501 College Drive, Zip 75501–2703, Mailing Address: P.O. Box 6045, Zip 75505–6045; tel. 903/798–5200; Jerry Kincade, Chief Executive Officer **A**1 5 9 10 **F**8 12 14 16 19 20 21 22 25 26 28 30 32 34 37 39 42 44 45 46 49 51 64 65 66 71 73 **P**4 7 8 **S** Columbia/HCA Healthcare Corporation, Nashville, TN	33	10	59	690	9	12035	—	14532	7786	232
⊞ △ ST. MICHAEL HEALTH CARE CENTER, (Includes St. Michael Rehabilitation Hospital, 2400 St. Michael Drive, Zip 75503; tel. 903/614–4000; Chris Karam, Administrator), 2600 St. Michael Drive, Zip 75503–2372; tel. 903/614–2009; Don A. Beeler, Chief Executive Officer (Total facility includes 44 beds in nursing home–type unit) **A**1 2 7 9 10 **F**4 7 8 10 11 12 15 16 17 19 21 22 24 25 27 28 30 32 33 34 35 37 39 40 41 42 43 44 46 48 49 57 58 60 64 65 66 73 **P**3 7 8 **S** Sisters of Charity of the Incarnate Word Healthcare System, Houston, TX **N** Healthcare Partners of East Texas, Inc., Tyler, TX	21	46	80	1071	62	0	0	17035	7190	243
⊞ WADLEY REGIONAL MEDICAL CENTER, 1000 Pine Street, Zip 75501–5170, Mailing Address: Box 1878, Zip 75504–1878; tel. 903/798–8000; Hugh R. Hallgren, President and Chief Executive Officer **A**1 2 5 9 10 **F**4 7 8 10 12 13 15 16 17 19 21 22 23 27 28 29 30 31 32 33 34 35 37 38 39 40 41 42 43 44 45 46 49 50 60 63 64 65 71 72 73 74 **P**8 **N** The Heart Network of Texas, Irving, TX	23	10	325	12614	169	111208	1767	88171	36318	958
TEXAS CITY—Galveston County										
⊞ △ COLUMBIA MAINLAND MEDICAL CENTER, 6801 E. F. Lowry Expressway, Zip 77591; tel. 409/938–5000; Alice G. Adams, Administrator **A**1 5 7 9 10 **F**4 7 8 10 11 12 14 15 16 18 19 20 21 22 26 28 29 30 31 32 33 34 35 37 39 40 41 42 43 44 45 46 48 49 51 52 54 55 56 57 58 59 60 61 64 65 67 71 72 73 74 **P**1 5 **S** Columbia/HCA Healthcare Corporation, Nashville, TN	33	10	175	6485	88	96143	611	51044	17880	552
THE WOODLANDS—Montgomery County										
⊞ MEMORIAL HOSPITAL–THE WOODLANDS, 9250 Pinecroft Drive, Zip 77380–3225; tel. 281/364–2300; Steve Sanders, Vice President, Chief Executive Officer and Administrator **A**1 9 **F**2 3 4 6 7 8 10 11 12 14 15 16 17 19 21 22 23 25 26 27 28 29 30 31 32 33 34 35 37 38 39 40 41 42 43 44 45 46 48 49 51 52 53 54 55 56 57 58 59 60 62 63 64 65 66 67 68 70 71 72 73 74 **P**3 4 7 **S** Memorial Herman Healthcare System, Houston, TX **N** Memorial/Sisters of Charity Health Network, Houston, TX	23	10	68	4673	38	35080	1613	22497	9061	315
THROCKMORTON—Throckmorton County										
THROCKMORTON COUNTY MEMORIAL HOSPITAL, 802 North Minter Street, Zip 76483, Mailing Address: P.O. Box 729, Zip 76483–0729; tel. 940/849–2151; Charles Norris, Administrator **A**9 10 **F**22 27 44 59 67 **N** Texoma Health Network, Wichita Falls, TX	15	10	20	169	—	2812	0	—	—	—
TOMBALL—Harris County										
⊞ △ TOMBALL REGIONAL HOSPITAL, 605 Holderrieth Street, Zip 77375–0889, Mailing Address: Box 889, Zip 77377–0889; tel. 281/351–1623; Robert F. Schaper, President and Chief Executive Officer (Total facility includes 15 beds in nursing home–type unit) **A**1 7 9 10 **F**4 7 8 10 11 12 15 16 19 21 22 23 24 29 30 32 33 34 35 37 39 40 42 43 44 45 46 48 49 52 54 56 57 58 59 64 65 66 71 73 **P**8 **N** Memorial/Sisters of Charity Health Network, Houston, TX	16	10	114	6132	90	72633	532	55722	19087	762
TRINITY—Trinity County										
EAST TEXAS MEDICAL CENTER TRINITY, (Formerly Trinity Memorial Hospital), 900 Prospect Drive, Zip 75862–0471, Mailing Address: P.O. Box 471, Zip 75862–0471; tel. 409/594–3541; James C. Whitmire, CHE, Administrator **A**9 10 **F**22 32 33 34 65 73	16	10	22	567	9	8135	—	3435	1880	74
TULIA—Swisher County										
★ SWISHER MEMORIAL HOSPITAL DISTRICT, 539 Southeast Second, Zip 79088–2403, Mailing Address: P.O. Box 808, Zip 79088–0808; tel. 806/995–3581; Tony Staynings, Chief Executive Officer **A**9 10 **F**19 21 22 28 30 32 33 34 41 49 64 65 71 73 **S** St. Joseph Health System, Orange, CA	16	10	25	166	6	2003	0	2916	1419	65

Hospital, Address, Telephone, Administrator, Approval, Facility, and Physician Codes, Health Care System, Network	Classi-fication Codes		Utilization Data					Expense (thousands) of dollars		
★ American Hospital Association (AHA) membership □ Joint Commission on Accreditation of Healthcare Organizations (JCAHO) accreditation + American Osteopathic Healthcare Association (AOHA) membership ○ American Osteopathic Association (AOA) accreditation △ Commission on Accreditation of Rehabilitation Facilities (CARF) accreditation Control codes 61, 63, 64, 71, 72 and 73 indicate hospitals listed by AOHA, but not registered by AHA. For definition of numerical codes, see page A4	Control	Service	Staffed Beds	Admissions	Census	Outpatient Visits	Births	Total	Payroll	Personnel

TYLER—Smith County

DOCTORS MEMORIAL HOSPITAL, 1400 West Southwest Loop 323, Zip 75701; tel. 903/561–3771; Olie E. Clem, Chief Executive Officer **A**9 10 **F**4 10 12 15 19 22 26 28 32 35 42 43 44 46 49 60 70 71 **P**7 8 **N** Healthcare Partners of East Texas, Inc., Tyler, TX · 23 · 10 · 46 · 1397 · 17 · 6855 · 155 · 7546 · 3767 · 116

□ EAST TEXAS MEDICAL CENTER REHABILITATION CENTER, 701 Olympic Plaza Circle, Zip 75701–1996; tel. 903/596–3000; Eddie L. Howard, Vice President and Chief Operating Officer **A**1 10 **F**2 3 4 5 7 8 10 11 12 15 16 19 21 24 25 26 27 28 29 30 31 32 34 35 37 39 40 41 42 43 44 45 48 49 52 53 54 55 56 57 58 59 60 61 64 65 66 67 69 70 71 73 74 **P**7 **S** East Texas Medical Center Regional Healthcare System, Tyler, TX · 23 · 46 · 49 · 824 · 40 · 132936 · — · — · 7976 · —

⊠ △ EAST TEXAS MEDICAL CENTER TYLER, (Includes East Texas Medical Center Behavioral Health Center, 4101 University Boulevard, Zip 75701–6600; tel. 903/566–8668), 1000 South Beckham Street, Zip 75701–1996, Mailing Address: Box 6400, Zip 75711–6400; tel. 903/597–0351 (Total facility includes 34 beds in nursing home–type unit) **A**1 2 7 9 10 **F**4 7 8 10 11 12 14 16 19 21 22 26 28 30 32 34 35 37 39 40 41 42 43 44 46 49 52 53 54 55 56 57 58 59 60 63 64 65 66 69 70 71 72 73 **P**6 7 8 **S** East Texas Medical Center Regional Healthcare System, Tyler, TX · 23 · 10 · 351 · 17001 · 233 · 178284 · 589 · 175451 · 64340 · 2926

EAST TEXAS MEDICAL CENTER–PSYCHIATRIC CENTER See East Texas Medical Center Behavioral Health Center

□ △ HEALTHSOUTH REHABILITATION HOSPITAL–TYLER, 3131 Troup Highway, Zip 75701–8352; tel. 903/510–7000; Thomas J. Cook, Chief Executive Officer **A**1 7 10 **F**12 14 15 16 19 21 27 28 30 34 35 39 41 46 48 49 65 66 67 71 73 **S** HEALTHSOUTH Corporation, Birmingham, AL **N** Regional Healthcare Alliance, Tyler, TX · 32 · 46 · 63 · 828 · 49 · 7437 · — · 11449 · 5452 · 142

⊠ TRINITY MOTHER FRANCES HEALTH SYSTEM, 800 East Dawson, Zip 75701–2093; tel. 903/593–8441; J. Lindsey Bradley, Jr., FACHE, President and Chief Administrative Officer **A**1 2 3 9 10 **F**4 7 8 10 11 12 13 14 15 16 17 18 19 21 22 23 24 25 28 29 30 31 32 34 35 37 40 41 42 43 44 45 46 49 51 60 61 63 64 65 66 67 68 70 71 72 73 74 **P**5 6 8 **N** The Heart Network of Texas, Irving, TX; Regional Healthcare Alliance, Tyler, TX · 23 · 10 · 274 · 15343 · 202 · 168076 · 2354 · 176961 · 64058 · 1873

⊠ UNIVERSITY OF TEXAS HEALTH CENTER AT TYLER, Gladewater Highway, Zip 75708, Mailing Address: P.O. Box 2003, Zip 75710–2003; tel. 903/877–3451; Ronald F. Garvey, M.D., Chief Administrative Officer and Director (Total facility includes 50 beds in nursing home–type unit) **A**1 9 10 **F**4 8 10 12 16 21 22 26 31 34 37 39 41 42 43 44 45 49 51 53 60 64 65 71 73 **P**6 **S** University of Texas System, Austin, TX **N** Regional Healthcare Alliance, Tyler, TX · 12 · 10 · 167 · 3435 · 83 · 108589 · 0 · 62923 · 35525 · 1234

UVALDE—Uvalde County

UVALDE COUNTY HOSPITAL AUTHORITY, 1025 Garner Field Road, Zip 78801–1025; tel. 830/278–6251; Ben M. Durr, Administrator **A**9 10 **F**7 8 10 12 15 16 19 21 22 25 28 32 33 34 35 37 40 41 44 45 49 65 70 71 72 73 **N** Southwest Texas Rural Health Alliance, San Antonio, TX · 16 · 10 · 51 · 3456 · 29 · 47277 · 593 · 15915 · 7041 · 318

VAN HORN—Culberson County

CULBERSON HOSPITAL DISTRICT, Eisenhower–Farm Market Road 2185, Zip 79855, Mailing Address: P.O. Box 609, Zip 79855–0609; tel. 915/283–2760; Joe Wright, Administrator (Nonreporting) **A**9 10 · 16 · 10 · 25 · — · — · — · — · — · — · —

VERNON—Wilbarger County

□ WILBARGER GENERAL HOSPITAL, 920 Hillcrest Drive, Zip 76384–3196; tel. 817/552–9351; Larry Parsons, Administrator **A**1 9 10 **F**7 12 14 15 16 19 21 22 28 32 34 40 44 45 46 49 65 67 71 74 **P**5 · 16 · 10 · 49 · 1937 · 26 · 89203 · 104 · 9452 · 3863 · 196

VICTORIA—Victoria County

⊠ CITIZENS MEDICAL CENTER, 2701 Hospital Drive, Zip 77901–5749; tel. 512/572–5113; David P. Brown, Administrator **A**1 2 9 10 **F**4 7 8 10 11 12 14 15 16 17 18 19 20 21 22 23 25 26 28 29 30 31 32 33 34 35 37 39 41 42 43 44 45 46 49 50 52 54 55 56 57 59 60 63 64 65 67 71 73 **P**8 **N** SouthEast Texas Hospital System, Dallas, TX · 13 · 10 · 231 · 8409 · 136 · 58268 · 0 · 66668 · 24370 · 974

⊠ DETAR HOSPITAL, (Formerly Columbia Detar Hospital), 506 East San Antonio Street, Zip 77901–6060, Mailing Address: Box 2089, Zip 77902–2089; tel. 512/575–7441; William R. Blanchard, Chief Executive Officer (Total facility includes 16 beds in nursing home–type unit) **A**1 9 10 **F**3 4 7 8 10 11 12 14 15 16 19 22 24 26 27 28 29 30 32 34 35 39 40 41 42 43 44 45 46 48 49 52 53 54 55 56 57 58 64 65 67 71 73 74 **P**3 7 **S** Columbia/HCA Healthcare Corporation, Nashville, TN · 33 · 10 · 217 · 7212 · 96 · 114414 · 1351 · 49330 · 20784 · 709

□ VICTORIA REGIONAL MEDICAL CENTER, 101 Medical Drive, Zip 77904–3198; tel. 512/573–6100; J. Michael Mastej, Chief Executive Officer and Managing Director **A**1 9 10 **F**3 7 12 14 15 16 19 21 22 28 29 30 31 34 37 40 44 45 46 49 52 53 54 55 56 57 58 59 65 67 71 73 **P**5 **S** Universal Health Services, Inc., King of Prussia, PA **N** SouthEast Texas Hospital System, Dallas, TX · 33 · 10 · 156 · 3793 · 49 · 45910 · 493 · 29079 · 10749 · 376

WACO—McLennan County

CENTRAL TEXAS VETERANS AFFAIRS HEALTH CARE SYSTEM See Central Texas Veterans Affairs Healthcare System, Temple

⊠ △ HILLCREST BAPTIST MEDICAL CENTER, 3000 Herring Avenue, Zip 76708–3299, Mailing Address: Box 5100, Zip 76708–0100; tel. 254/202–2000; Richard E. Scott, President **A**1 2 3 5 7 9 10 **F**1 4 5 7 8 10 11 12 13 15 16 17 19 21 22 23 26 27 28 29 30 31 32 33 34 35 37 38 39 40 41 42 43 44 45 46 48 49 51 56 60 63 65 66 67 68 70 71 72 73 74 **P**3 6 7 8 **N** The Heart Network of Texas, Irving, TX; Brazo's Valley Health Network, Waco, TX · 21 · 10 · 272 · 13602 · 173 · 213811 · 3080 · 105303 · 42038 · 1641

Hospital, Address, Telephone, Administrator, Approval, Facility, and Physician Codes, Health Care System, Network	Classification Codes		Utilization Data					Expense (thousands) of dollars		
★ American Hospital Association (AHA) membership □ Joint Commission on Accreditation of Healthcare Organizations (JCAHO) accreditation + American Osteopathic Healthcare Association (AOHA) membership ○ American Osteopathic Association (AOA) accreditation △ Commission on Accreditation of Rehabilitation Facilities (CARF) accreditation Control codes 61, 63, 64, 71, 72 and 73 indicate hospitals listed by AOHA, but not registered by AHA. For definition of numerical codes, see page A4	Control	Service	Staffed Beds	Admissions	Census	Outpatient Visits	Births	Total	Payroll	Personnel

	Control	Service	Staffed Beds	Admissions	Census	Outpatient Visits	Births	Total	Payroll	Personnel
☒ PROVIDENCE HEALTH CENTER, 6901 Medical Parkway, Zip 76712–7998, Mailing Address: P.O. Box 2589, Zip 76702–2589; tel. 254/751–4000; Kent A. Keahey, President and Chief Executive Officer **A**1 2 3 5 9 10 **F**3 4 6 7 8 10 11 13 14 15 16 17 18 19 21 22 23 26 27 28 30 31 32 33 34 35 39 40 42 43 44 49 51 53 54 55 56 57 58 59 60 63 65 67 71 73 74 **P**8 **S** Daughters of Charity National Health System, Saint Louis, MO	21	10	170	7343	94	57317	260	57614	22102	787
WAXAHACHIE—Ellis County										
☒ BAYLOR MEDICAL CENTER–ELLIS COUNTY, (Includes Baylor Medical Center – Ellis County, 803 West Lampasas Street, Ennis, Zip 75119; tel. 972/875–0900), 1405 West Jefferson Street, Zip 75165–2275; tel. 972/923–7000; James Michael Lee, Executive Director **A**1 9 10 **F**7 8 15 19 22 24 27 30 32 35 36 37 39 40 41 42 44 49 64 65 66 71 73 **S** Baylor Health Care System, Dallas, TX **N** Baylor Health Care System Network, Dallas, TX; North Texas Healthcare Network, Dallas, TX	23	10	91	5182	55	72063	1067	38931	16987	569
WEATHERFORD—Parker County										
☒ CAMPBELL HEALTH SYSTEM, 713 East Anderson Street, Zip 76086–9971; tel. 817/596–8751; John B. Millstead, Chief Executive Officer **A**1 9 10 **F**7 8 14 15 16 17 19 21 22 23 24 28 30 31 32 33 34 36 37 39 40 41 44 49 65 67 70 71 73 **P**1 **S** Quorum Health Group/Quorum Health Resources, Inc., Brentwood, TN **N** Lubbock Methodist Hospital System, Lubbock, TX	16	10	78	3260	29	53533	591	24647	9726	384
WEBSTER—Harris County										
☒ COLUMBIA CLEAR LAKE REGIONAL MEDICAL CENTER, 500 Medical Center Boulevard, Zip 77598–4286; tel. 281/338–3110; Donald A. Shaffett, Chief Executive Officer (Total facility includes 39 beds in nursing home–type unit) **A**1 2 9 10 **F**4 7 8 10 11 12 14 15 16 19 21 22 23 30 32 33 34 35 37 38 39 40 42 43 44 45 46 48 49 52 57 60 61 64 65 71 73 **P**1 5 **S** Columbia/HCA Healthcare Corporation, Nashville, TN **N** Gulf Coast Provider Network, Houston, TX	33	10	415	16212	176	129732	2993	90809	33441	1027
WEIMAR—Colorado County										
□ COLORADO–FAYETTE MEDICAL CENTER, 400 Youens Drive, Zip 78962–9561; tel. 409/725–9531; Randy Bacus, Chief Executive Officer (Total facility includes 14 beds in nursing home–type unit) **A**1 9 10 **F**8 12 15 16 19 22 28 32 34 41 44 49 64 65 71 73 **P**5	23	10	52	1955	35	32516	—	11901	479	162
WELLINGTON—Collingsworth County										
COLLINGSWORTH GENERAL HOSPITAL, 1014 15th Street, Zip 79095–3704; tel. 806/447–2521; S. Beth Caison, Administrator **A**9 10 **F**8 12 13 14 15 16 19 22 26 28 30 32 34 44 46 51 71 74 **P**6	16	10	20	362	6	22390	0	2925	1351	59
WESLACO—Hidalgo County										
☒ KNAPP MEDICAL CENTER, 1401 East Eighth Street, Zip 78596–6640, Mailing Address: P.O. Box 1110, Zip 78599–1110; tel. 956/968–8567; Robert W. Vanderveer, Administrator **A**1 9 10 **F**7 8 15 16 17 19 20 21 26 27 28 30 32 33 34 35 37 39 40 42 44 45 46 49 63 65 67 70 71 73 74 **P**3	23	10	215	10201	114	55484	1963	63953	24395	938
WEST—McLennan County										
□ WEST COMMUNITY HOSPITAL, 501 Meadow Drive, Zip 76691–1018, Mailing Address: P.O. Box 478, Zip 76691–0478; tel. 817/826–7000; Betty York, Executive Director **A**1 9 10 **F**14 15 16 19 22 32 44 46 51 65 71 73 **P**8 **N** Central Texas Rural Health Network, Harrietsville, TX; Brazo's Valley Health Network, Waco, TX	16	10	21	290	7	14913	0	—	—	61
WHARTON—Wharton County										
☒ GULF COAST MEDICAL CENTER, (Formerly Columbia Gulf Coast Medical Center), 1400 Highway 59, Zip 77488–3004, Mailing Address: P.O. Box 3004, Zip 77488–3004; tel. 409/532–2500; Michael D. Murphy, Chief Executive Officer (Total facility includes 20 beds in nursing home–type unit) **A**1 2 9 10 **F**7 10 12 14 15 16 19 21 22 28 30 32 33 34 37 40 41 42 44 45 46 48 60 63 64 65 67 71 73 74 **S** Columbia/HCA Healthcare Corporation, Nashville, TN	33	10	161	3968	59	76405	643	28282	13137	423
WHEELER—Wheeler County										
PARKVIEW HOSPITAL, 1000 Sweetwater Street, Zip 79096, Mailing Address: P.O. Box 1030, Zip 79096–1030; tel. 806/826–5581; B. W. Robertson, Administrator **A**9 10 **F**8 14 15 16 17 19 22 32 46 64 65 71	16	10	23	442	6	952	0	2760	1429	67
WHITNEY—Hill County										
LAKE WHITNEY MEDICAL CENTER, 200 North San Jacinto Street, Zip 76692–2388, Mailing Address: P.O. Box 458, Zip 76692–0458; tel. 254/694–3165; Ruth Ann Crow, Administrator (Nonreporting) **A**9 10 **N** Central Texas Rural Health Network, Harrietsville, TX; Brazo's Valley Health Network, Waco, TX	16	10	48	—	—	—	—	—	—	—
WICHITA FALLS—Wichita County										
□ RED RIVER HOSPITAL, 1505 Eighth Street, Zip 76301–3106; tel. 940/322–3171; Ricky Powell, Chief Executive Officer **A**1 9 10 **F**15 19 20 22 26 52 53 54 55 56 57 58 59 65 **S** Children's Comprehensive Services, Inc., Nashville, TN	33	22	50	926	25	5073	0	4608	2127	70
☒ UNITED REGIONAL HEALTH CARE SYSTEM, (Includes United Regional Health Care System–Eighth Street Campus, 1600 Eighth Street, Zip 76301–3164; United Regional Health Care System–Eleventh Street Campus, 1600 11th Street, Zip 76301–9988; tel. 940/720–0055; David D. Whitaker, FACHE, President and Chief Operating Officer), 1600 Eighth Street, Zip 76310; tel. 940/720–0055; Jeffrey E. Hausler, Vice Chairman and Chief Executive Officer (Total facility includes 37 beds in nursing home–type unit) **A**1 2 3 5 9 10 **F**4 7 8 10 11 12 13 14 15 16 17 19 20 21 22 23 26 27 28 29 30 31 32 34 35 37 39 40 41 42 43 44 46 49 60 61 63 65 67 68 71 72 73 74 **P**5 7 8 UNITED REGIONAL HEALTH CARE SYSTEM–EIGHTH STREET CAMPUS See United Regional Health Care System	23	10	429	14436	—	101770	1825	—	43661	—

Hospital, Address, Telephone, Administrator, Approval, Facility, and Physician Codes, Health Care System, Network	Classi-fication Codes		Utilization Data					Expense (thousands) of dollars		
★ American Hospital Association (AHA) membership □ Joint Commission on Accreditation of Healthcare Organizations (JCAHO) accreditation + American Osteopathic Healthcare Association (AOHA) membership ○ American Osteopathic Association (AOA) accreditation △ Commission on Accreditation of Rehabilitation Facilities (CARF) accreditation Control codes 61, 63, 64, 71, 72 and 73 indicate hospitals listed by AOHA, but not registered by AHA. For definition of numerical codes, see page A4	Control	Service	Staffed Beds	Admissions	Census	Outpatient Visits	Births	Total	Payroll	Personnel

UNITED REGIONAL HEALTH CARE SYSTEM–ELEVENTH STREET CAMPUS See United Regional Health Care System										
□ WICHITA FALLS STATE HOSPITAL, 6515 Lake Road, Zip 76308–5419, Mailing Address: Box 300, Zip 76307–0300; tel. 817/692–1220; James E. Smith, Superintendent **A**1 10 **F**15 16 20 39 41 45 46 52 53 57 65 73 **P**6	12	22	389	1224	345	—	—	37831	22790	1188
WINNIE—Chambers County										
□ MEDICAL CENTER OF WINNIE, Broadway at Campbell Road, Zip 77665, Mailing Address: P.O. Box 208, Zip 77665–0208; tel. 409/296–2131; J. L. Flotte', Chief Executive Officer (Nonreporting) **A**1 9 10	23	10	49	—	—	—	—	—	—	—
WINNSBORO—Wood County										
✸ PRESBYTERIAN HOSPITAL OF WINNSBORO, 719 West Coke Road, Zip 75494–3098, Mailing Address: P.O. Box 628, Zip 75494–0628; tel. 903/342–5227; Dan Noteware, Executive Director (Total facility includes 8 beds in nursing home–type unit) **A**1 9 10 **F**8 12 17 19 21 22 28 29 30 35 37 39 42 44 46 49 64 67 71 73 **S** Texas Health Resources, Irving, TX **N** Healthcare Partners of East Texas, Inc., Tyler, TX; Presbyterian Healthcare System, Dallas, TX; Regional Healthcare Alliance, Tyler, TX; North Texas Healthcare Network, Dallas, TX	23	10	50	1078	15	27829	0	—	—	132
WINTERS—Runnels County										
NORTH RUNNELS HOSPITAL, East Highway 53, Zip 79567, Mailing Address: P.O. Box 185, Zip 79567–0185; tel. 915/754–4553; Jeffrey Turner, Interim Administrator **A**9 10 **F**9 19 22 28 30 32 33 44 71	16	10	21	218	2	21398	—	2855	1611	71
WOODVILLE—Tyler County										
TYLER COUNTY HOSPITAL, 1100 West Bluff Street, Zip 75979–4799, Mailing Address: P.O. Box 549, Zip 75979–0549; tel. 409/283–8141; James W. Gainey, R.N., Administrator **A**6 9 10 **F**7 8 14 19 22 28 30 32 34 40 44 70 71 73	16	10	26	1025	13	16036	0	4997	2313	108
YOAKUM—Lavaca County										
✸ YOAKUM COMMUNITY HOSPITAL, 1200 Carl Ramert Drive, Zip 77995–4198, Mailing Address: P.O. Box 753, Zip 77995–0753; tel. 512/293–2321; Elwood E. Currier, Jr., CHE, Administrator **A**1 9 10 **F**7 8 12 14 16 17 19 20 22 26 28 30 32 34 35 37 39 40 41 44 45 49 57 65 66 67 68 70 71 73 **N** SouthEast Texas Hospital System, Dallas, TX	23	10	30	1071	14	—	132	8666	3895	153

UTAH

Resident population 2,059 (in thousands)
Resident population in metro areas 77.3%
Birth rate per 1,000 population 20.1
65 years and over 8.8%
Percent of persons without health insurance 12.0%

Hospital, Address, Telephone, Administrator, Approval, Facility, and Physician Codes, Health Care System, Network	Classi-fication Codes		Utilization Data					Expense (thousands) of dollars		
★ American Hospital Association (AHA) membership ☐ Joint Commission on Accreditation of Healthcare Organizations (JCAHO) accreditation + American Osteopathic Healthcare Association (AOHA) membership ○ American Osteopathic Association (AOA) accreditation △ Commission on Accreditation of Rehabilitation Facilities (CARF) accreditation Control codes 61, 63, 64, 71, 72 and 73 indicate hospitals listed by AOHA, but not registered by AHA. For definition of numerical codes, see page A4	Control	Service	Staffed Beds	Admissions	Census	Outpatient Visits	Births	Total	Payroll	Personnel
AMERICAN FORK—Utah County										
⊠ AMERICAN FORK HOSPITAL, 170 North 1100 East, Zip 84003–9787; tel. 801/763–3300; Keith N. Alexander, Administrator and Chief Operating Officer **A**1 9 10 **F**3 4 7 8 10 11 12 14 15 17 18 19 21 22 24 28 29 30 32 35 39 40 41 42 43 44 45 46 49 51 53 54 55 56 58 59 60 64 65 66 67 70 71 73 74 **P**5 6 **S** Intermountain Health Care, Inc., Salt Lake City, UT **N** Intermountain HealthCare/Amerinet, Salt Lake City, UT	23	10	66	4622	27	85671	2299	21809	10217	—
BEAVER—Beaver County										
BEAVER VALLEY HOSPITAL, 85 North 400 East, Zip 84713, Mailing Address: P.O. Box 1670, Zip 84713–1670; tel. 435/438–2531; Craig Val Davidson, CHE, Administrator (Total facility includes 24 beds in nursing home–type unit) **A**9 10 **F**7 14 15 16 20 22 32 44 46 49 65 66 71 73	14	10	36	711	28	6312	84	3977	1759	83
BOUNTIFUL—Davis County										
⊠ LAKEVIEW HOSPITAL, 630 East Medical Drive, Zip 84010–4996; tel. 801/292–6231; Craig Preston, Chief Executive Officer **A**1 9 10 **F**3 4 7 8 10 11 12 15 16 18 19 21 22 24 26 28 29 30 32 34 35 37 39 40 41 42 44 46 49 52 53 54 55 56 57 58 59 61 64 65 66 67 71 73 74 **P**5 **S** Columbia/HCA Healthcare Corporation, Nashville, TN	33	10	128	3567	40	29232	746	32339	12374	467
BRIGHAM CITY—Box Elder County										
★ BRIGHAM CITY COMMUNITY HOSPITAL, (Formerly Columbia Brigham City CommunityHospital), 950 South Medical Drive, Zip 84302–3090; tel. 435/734–4200; Tad A. Morley, Chief Executive Officer **A**9 10 **F**2 3 4 7 8 10 11 12 14 15 16 19 21 22 23 28 32 34 35 37 38 39 40 41 42 43 44 46 47 49 52 53 56 58 59 60 64 65 71 73 **S** Columbia/HCA Healthcare Corporation, Nashville, TN	33	10	21	1433	10	28218	512	—	—	165
CEDAR CITY—Iron County										
★ VALLEY VIEW MEDICAL CENTER, 595 South 75 East, Zip 84720–3462; tel. 435/586–6587; Craig M. Smedley, Administrator **A**9 10 **F**7 8 12 15 16 19 21 22 28 32 37 40 41 44 51 64 65 71 **P**6 **S** Intermountain Health Care, Inc., Salt Lake City, UT **N** Intermountain HealthCare/Amerinet, Salt Lake City, UT	23	10	36	1897	13	68013	580	—	5688	198
DELTA—Millard County										
★ DELTA COMMUNITY MEDICAL CENTER, 126 South White Sage Avenue, Zip 84624–8937; tel. 801/864–5591; James E. Beckstrand, Administrator **A**9 10 **F**1 3 6 7 8 14 17 18 22 26 28 29 32 33 39 40 44 45 46 48 49 53 54 55 56 57 58 64 66 71 73 74 **P**6 7 **S** Intermountain Health Care, Inc., Salt Lake City, UT **N** Intermountain HealthCare/Amerinet, Salt Lake City, UT	23	10	20	376	4	5585	100	3018	1290	—
FILLMORE—Millard County										
★ FILLMORE COMMUNITY MEDICAL CENTER, 674 South Highway 99, Zip 84631–5013; tel. 801/743–5591; James E. Beckstrand, Administrator **A**9 10 **F**7 8 11 14 15 18 22 26 28 29 32 33 34 37 39 40 44 45 47 48 49 51 64 65 71 73 **P**6 **S** Intermountain Health Care, Inc., Salt Lake City, UT **N** Intermountain HealthCare/Amerinet, Salt Lake City, UT	23	10	20	248	13	31302	56	2677	1110	53
GUNNISON—Sanpete County										
★ GUNNISON VALLEY HOSPITAL, 64 East 100 North, Zip 84634, Mailing Address: P.O. Box 759, Zip 84634–0759; tel. 435/528–7246; Greg Rosenvall, Administrator **A**9 10 **F**3 7 8 13 15 19 21 22 25 29 30 32 34 44 49 51 67 71 **S** Rural Health Management Corporation, Nephi, UT	16	10	21	929	9	32425	161	6085	2595	110
HEBER CITY—Wasatch County										
★ WASATCH COUNTY HOSPITAL, 55 South 500 East, Zip 84032–1999; tel. 801/654–2500; Randall K. Probst, Administrator **A**9 10 **F**7 12 14 15 16 17 20 22 26 28 29 30 32 36 39 44 45 46 51 66 67 71 73 **S** Intermountain Health Care, Inc., Salt Lake City, UT **N** Intermountain HealthCare/Amerinet, Salt Lake City, UT	23	10	20	538	5	20591	137	4130	1622	39
HILL AFB—Davis County										
⊠ U. S. AIR FORCE HOSPITAL, 7321 11th Street, Zip 84056–5012; tel. 801/777–5457; Lieutenant Colonel Steven H. Regner, Commander **A**1 9 **F**8 12 13 16 20 24 25 28 29 30 34 39 41 44 45 46 49 51 54 58 71 72 73 **P**6 **S** Department of the Air Force, Bowling AFB, DC	41	10	15	637	4	127779	—	—	—	—
KANAB—Kane County										
KANE COUNTY HOSPITAL, 355 North Main Street, Zip 84741–3238; tel. 801/644–5811; Mike Sinclair, Administrator **A**9 10 **F**7 19 22 32 34 40 44 73 **P**6	16	10	38	366	17	6872	36	3684	1856	90
LAYTON—Davis County										
☐ DAVIS HOSPITAL AND MEDICAL CENTER, 1600 West Antelope Drive, Zip 84041–1142; tel. 801/825–9561; Bruce A. Baldwin, Chief Executive Officer **A**1 9 10 **F**4 7 8 10 14 15 16 17 19 21 22 26 28 29 30 33 34 37 38 39 40 42 44 45 46 49 52 57 58 59 60 64 65 66 71 72 74 **P**6 **S** Paracelsus Healthcare Corporation, Houston, TX	33	10	126	5887	55	68542	1855	29832	13582	428

Hospital, Address, Telephone, Administrator, Approval, Facility, and Physician Codes, Health Care System, Network	Classi-fication Codes		Utilization Data					Expense (thousands) of dollars		
	Control	Service	Staffed Beds	Admissions	Census	Outpatient Visits	Births	Total	Payroll	Personnel

★ American Hospital Association (AHA) membership
□ Joint Commission on Accreditation of Healthcare Organizations (JCAHO) accreditation
+ American Osteopathic Healthcare Association (AOHA) membership
○ American Osteopathic Association (AOA) accreditation
△ Commission on Accreditation of Rehabilitation Facilities (CARF) accreditation
Control codes 61, 63, 64, 71, 72 and 73 indicate hospitals listed by AOHA, but not registered by AHA. For definition of numerical codes, see page A4

LOGAN—Cache County

⊠ LOGAN REGIONAL HOSPITAL, 1400 North 500 East, Zip 84341–2455; tel. 435/752–2050; Richard Smith, Administrator (Total facility includes 15 beds in nursing home–type unit) **A**1 9 10 **F**3 7 8 10 11 12 15 16 19 21 22 24 26 28 29 30 32 33 34 35 37 39 40 41 42 44 45 49 51 52 53 54 56 57 58 59 64 65 66 67 68 71 72 73 74 **P**6 7 **S** Intermountain Health Care, Inc., Salt Lake City, UT
23 | 10 | 112 | 7260 | 63 | 163261 | 2171 | 43977 | 21292 | 607

MILFORD—Beaver County

★ MILFORD VALLEY MEMORIAL HOSPITAL, 451 North Main Street, Zip 84751–0640, Mailing Address: P.O. Box 640, Zip 84751–0640; tel. 801/387–2411; John E. Gledhill, Administrator (Nonreporting) **A**9 10 **S** Rural Health Management Corporation, Nephi, UT
16 | 10 | 34 | — | — | — | — | — | — | —

MOAB—Grand County

★ ALLEN MEMORIAL HOSPITAL, 719 West 400 North Street, Zip 84532–2297, Mailing Address: P.O. Box 998, Zip 84532–0998; tel. 435/259–7191; Charles A. Davis, Administrator **A**9 10 **F**7 14 19 22 28 30 32 33 40 44 46 65 70 71 **S** Rural Health Management Corporation, Nephi, UT
16 | 10 | 38 | 646 | 5 | 11381 | 91 | 6068 | 2651 | 119

MONTICELLO—San Juan County

★ SAN JUAN HOSPITAL, 364 West First North, Zip 84535, Mailing Address: P.O. Box 308, Zip 84535–0308; tel. 435/587–2116; Craig Ambrosiani, Executive Director (Total facility includes 10 beds in nursing home–type unit) **A**9 10 **F**7 14 15 20 22 25 44 64 71 72 **P**5
16 | 10 | 35 | 560 | 12 | 3936 | 148 | 5680 | 2358 | 95

MOUNT PLEASANT—Sanpete County

★ SANPETE VALLEY HOSPITAL, 1100 South Medical Drive, Zip 84647–2222; tel. 435/462–2441; George Winn, Administrator **A**9 10 **F**7 8 12 14 15 16 17 19 22 28 30 32 33 39 44 46 49 64 71 **P**6 **S** Intermountain Health Care, Inc., Salt Lake City, UT **N** Intermountain HealthCare/Amerinet, Salt Lake City, UT
23 | 10 | 20 | 541 | 10 | 65368 | 101 | 4868 | 1751 | 82

NEPHI—Juab County

★ CENTRAL VALLEY MEDICAL CENTER, 549 North 400 East, Zip 84648–1226; tel. 801/623–1242; Mark R. Stoddard, President **A**9 10 **F**8 19 22 28 30 32 34 39 40 44 49 51 64 71 **P**6 **S** Rural Health Management Corporation, Nephi, UT
23 | 10 | 22 | 518 | 4 | 21971 | 83 | 6593 | 2316 | 101

OGDEN—Weber County

⊠ COLUMBIA OGDEN REGIONAL MEDICAL CENTER, 5475 South 500 East, Zip 84405–6978; tel. 801/479–2111; Steven B. Bateman, Chief Executive Officer **A**1 2 9 10 **F**3 4 7 8 10 11 12 13 14 15 16 17 18 19 20 21 22 24 26 28 29 30 31 32 34 35 37 38 39 40 41 42 43 44 45 46 48 49 51 52 53 54 55 56 57 58 59 60 64 65 67 68 70 71 72 73 74 **P**5 6 7 8 **S** Columbia/HCA Healthcare Corporation, Nashville, TN
33 | 10 | 179 | 6655 | 77 | 53619 | 1852 | — | — | 713

⊠ MCKAY–DEE HOSPITAL CENTER, 3939 Harrison Boulevard, Zip 84409–2386, Mailing Address: Box 9370, Zip 84409–0370; tel. 801/398–2800; Thomas F. Hanrahan, Chief Executive Officer **A**1 2 3 5 9 10 **F**2 3 4 7 8 10 11 12 14 15 17 18 19 21 22 24 25 26 28 29 30 31 32 33 34 35 37 38 39 40 41 42 43 44 45 48 49 51 52 53 54 55 56 57 58 59 61 64 65 66 67 70 71 72 73 74 **S** Intermountain Health Care, Inc., Salt Lake City, UT **N** Intermountain HealthCare/Amerinet, Salt Lake City, UT
23 | 10 | 293 | 12719 | 141 | 388616 | 2831 | 125984 | 57616 | 1830

OREM—Utah County

★ OREM COMMUNITY HOSPITAL, 331 North 400 West, Zip 84057–1999; tel. 801/224–4080; Kim Nielsen, Administrator and Chief Operating Officer **A**9 10 **F**4 7 8 10 11 12 13 14 15 16 17 18 19 20 21 22 24 25 26 28 29 30 31 32 33 34 35 36 37 38 39 40 41 42 43 44 45 46 48 49 51 52 53 54 55 56 57 58 60 61 64 65 66 67 68 70 71 72 73 74 **P**6 **S** Intermountain Health Care, Inc., Salt Lake City, UT **N** Intermountain HealthCare/Amerinet, Salt Lake City, UT
23 | 10 | 20 | 1489 | 6 | 53872 | 1065 | 8133 | 3787 | —

PANGUITCH—Garfield County

★ GARFIELD MEMORIAL HOSPITAL AND CLINICS, 200 North 400 East, Zip 84759, Mailing Address: P.O. Box 389, Zip 84759–0389; tel. 435/676–8811; Eric Packer, Administrator (Total facility includes 30 beds in nursing home–type unit) **A**9 10 **F**7 12 15 17 22 25 32 39 40 44 46 48 64 65 71 73 **P**6 **S** Intermountain Health Care, Inc., Salt Lake City, UT **N** Intermountain HealthCare/Amerinet, Salt Lake City, UT
23 | 10 | 44 | 513 | 28 | 29567 | 52 | 3989 | 1597 | 58

PAYSON—Utah County

★ MOUNTAIN VIEW HOSPITAL, 1000 East 100 North, Zip 84651–1690; tel. 801/465–9201; Kevin Johnson, Chief Executive Officer **A**9 10 **F**4 7 8 10 12 19 21 22 26 28 30 32 35 37 40 41 44 45 46 48 52 53 54 55 56 57 58 59 64 65 70 71 73 74 **S** Columbia/HCA Healthcare Corporation, Nashville, TN
33 | 10 | 123 | 4085 | 39 | 56073 | 1189 | 31770 | 10260 | 392

PRICE—Carbon County

★ CASTLEVIEW HOSPITAL, 300 North Hospital Drive, Zip 84501–4200; tel. 801/637–4800; L. Allen Penry, Chief Executive Officer (Total facility includes 10 beds in nursing home–type unit) (Nonreporting) **A**9 10 **S** Columbia/HCA Healthcare Corporation, Nashville, TN
33 | 10 | 84 | — | — | — | — | — | — | —

PROVO—Utah County

□ UTAH STATE HOSPITAL, 1300 East Center Street, Zip 84606–3554, Mailing Address: P.O. Box 270, Zip 84603–0270; tel. 801/344–4200; Mark I. Payne, Superintendent **A**1 10 **F**14 15 16 20 26 41 52 53 55 56 57 65 73 **P**6
12 | 22 | 343 | 332 | 304 | — | — | — | 16873 | —

⊠ △ UTAH VALLEY REGIONAL MEDICAL CENTER, 1034 North 500 West, Zip 84604–3337; tel. 801/373–7850; Chris Coons, Chief Operating Officer (Total facility includes 14 beds in nursing home–type unit) **A**1 2 3 7 9 10 **F**4 7 8 10 11 12 13 14 15 16 17 18 19 20 21 22 24 25 26 28 29 30 31 32 33 34 35 36 37 38 39 40 41 42 43 44 45 46 48 49 51 52 53 54 55 56 57 58 60 61 64 65 66 67 68 70 71 72 73 74 **P**6 **S** Intermountain Health Care, Inc., Salt Lake City, UT **N** Intermountain HealthCare/Amerinet, Salt Lake City, UT
23 | 10 | 314 | 17964 | 191 | 307790 | 4111 | 145095 | 66838 | —

Hospital, Address, Telephone, Administrator, Approval, Facility, and Physician Codes, Health Care System, Network	Classi-fication Codes		Utilization Data					Expense (thousands) of dollars		
★ American Hospital Association (AHA) membership □ Joint Commission on Accreditation of Healthcare Organizations (JCAHO) accreditation + American Osteopathic Healthcare Association (AOHA) membership ○ American Osteopathic Association (AOA) accreditation △ Commission on Accreditation of Rehabilitation Facilities (CARF) accreditation Control codes 61, 63, 64, 71, 72 and 73 indicate hospitals listed by AOHA, but not registered by AHA. For definition of numerical codes, see page A4	Control	Service	Staffed Beds	Admissions	Census	Outpatient Visits	Births	Total	Payroll	Personnel

RICHFIELD—Sevier County

★ SEVIER VALLEY HOSPITAL, 1100 North Main Street, Zip 84701–1843; tel. 435/896–8271; Gary E. Beck, Administrator **A**1 9 10 **F**7 8 12 14 15 16 17 19 21 22 28 30 32 33 34 35 39 40 41 44 48 49 51 64 65 71 73 **P**3 5 6 **S** Intermountain Health Care, Inc., Salt Lake City, UT **N** Intermountain HealthCare/Amerinet, Salt Lake City, UT	23	10	27	1384	11	29542	258	9494	3390	154

ROOSEVELT—Duchesne County

★ UINTAH BASIN MEDICAL CENTER, 250 West 300 North, 75–2, Zip 84066; tel. 435/722–6163; Bradley D. LeBaron, Administrator **A**9 10 **F**7 8 11 12 14 15 16 17 19 21 24 28 30 32 33 35 37 40 44 49 51 66 67 71 73 **P**5 7 8	13	10	42	1987	15	31494	356	16449	6135	253

SAINT GEORGE—Washington County

★ DIXIE REGIONAL MEDICAL CENTER, 544 South 400 East, Zip 84770–3799; tel. 435/634–4000; L. Steven Wilson, Administrator **A**1 2 9 10 **F**4 7 8 10 11 15 16 17 19 21 22 27 28 30 32 33 34 35 39 40 41 42 44 45 46 49 50 51 52 54 60 61 63 65 66 67 68 69 71 72 73 74 **P**5 **S** Intermountain Health Care, Inc., Salt Lake City, UT **N** Intermountain HealthCare/Amerinet, Salt Lake City, UT	23	10	149	8479	80	209595	1728	56095	21266	785

SALT LAKE CITY—Salt Lake County

□ BHC OLYMPUS VIEW HOSPITAL, 1430 East 4500 South, Zip 84117–4208; tel. 801/272–8000; Barry W. Woodward, Administrator (Nonreporting) **A**1 10 **S** Behavioral Healthcare Corporation, Nashville, TN	33	22	82	—	—	—	—	—	—	—
★ COTTONWOOD HOSPITAL MEDICAL CENTER, 5770 South 300 East, Zip 84107–6186; tel. 801/262–3461; Douglas R. Fonnesbeck, Administrator **A**1 2 9 10 **F**1 2 3 4 5 6 7 8 9 10 11 12 13 14 15 16 17 18 19 20 21 22 23 24 25 26 27 28 29 30 31 32 33 34 35 36 37 39 40 41 42 43 44 45 46 47 48 49 51 52 53 54 55 56 57 58 59 60 61 62 63 64 65 66 67 68 69 70 71 72 73 74 **P**3 4 5 6 **S** Intermountain Health Care, Inc., Salt Lake City, UT **N** Intermountain HealthCare/Amerinet, Salt Lake City, UT	23	10	148	10538	81	304750	3226	89678	33198	1127
HIGHLAND RIDGE HOSPITAL, 4578 Highland Drive, Zip 84117–4200; tel. 801/272–9851; Robert H. Boswell, Administrator (Nonreporting) **S** Pioneer Healthcare, Peabody, MA	33	82	34	—	—	—	—	—	—	—
★ △ LDS HOSPITAL, Eighth Avenue and C. Street, Zip 84143–0001; tel. 801/321–1100; Richard M. Cagen, Chief Executive Officer and Administrator (Total facility includes 32 beds in nursing home–type unit) **A**1 2 3 5 7 9 10 **F**3 4 7 8 10 11 12 14 15 16 17 18 19 21 22 24 25 26 28 30 31 32 33 34 35 37 38 40 41 42 43 44 45 46 47 48 49 51 52 53 54 55 56 57 58 59 60 61 64 65 66 67 69 70 71 72 73 74 **P**4 6 **S** Intermountain Health Care, Inc., Salt Lake City, UT	23	10	412	25518	305	630366	4296	246850	106096	3081
□ PIONEER VALLEY HOSPITAL, 3460 South Pioneer Parkway, Zip 84120–2648; tel. 801/964–3100; Brian Mottishaw, Chief Executive Officer (Total facility includes 19 beds in nursing home–type unit) **A**1 2 9 10 **F**3 4 7 8 10 12 13 15 17 18 19 20 21 22 23 24 25 26 28 30 31 32 33 34 35 39 41 42 43 44 45 49 53 54 55 56 57 58 63 65 66 67 69 71 72 73 74 **P**8 **S** Paracelsus Healthcare Corporation, Houston, TX	33	10	104	3622	35	38157	675	—	—	377
★ PRIMARY CHILDREN'S MEDICAL CENTER, (PED MED SURG REHAB PSYCH), 100 North Medical Drive, Zip 84113–1100; tel. 801/588–2000; Joseph R. Horton, Chief Executive Officer and Administrator **A**1 3 5 9 10 **F**2 3 4 5 7 8 10 11 12 13 14 15 17 19 20 21 22 24 25 26 30 31 32 34 35 37 38 39 40 41 42 43 44 45 46 47 48 49 51 52 53 54 55 56 57 58 59 60 61 63 64 65 66 67 69 70 71 72 73 74 **S** Intermountain Health Care, Inc., Salt Lake City, UT **N** Intermountain HealthCare/Amerinet, Salt Lake City, UT	23	59	183	9505	149	100348	—	129430	60674	1787
□ SALT LAKE REGIONAL MEDICAL CENTER, 1050 East South Temple, Zip 84102–1599; tel. 801/350–4111; Kay Matsumura, Chief Executive Officer **A**1 2 3 5 9 10 **F**4 7 8 10 12 14 15 16 17 19 21 22 23 24 26 27 28 29 30 31 32 33 34 35 37 38 39 40 41 42 43 44 45 46 48 49 50 51 56 63 64 65 66 67 70 71 73 74 **P**5 7 8 **S** Paracelsus Healthcare Corporation, Houston, TX	33	10	200	6305	64	159704	1766	47806	20344	695
★ SHRINERS HOSPITALS FOR CHILDREN–INTERMOUNTAIN, Fairfax Road and Virginia Street, Zip 84103–4399; tel. 801/536–3500; J. Craig Patchin, Administrator **A**1 3 5 **F**12 19 34 35 39 41 47 49 54 65 67 71 73 **P**5 6 **S** Shriners Hospitals for Children, Tampa, FL	23	57	40	987	22	5600	0	—	—	179
★ ST. MARK'S HOSPITAL, (Formerly Columbia St. Mark's Hospital), 1200 East 3900 South, Zip 84124–1390; tel. 801/268–7111; John Hanshaw, Chief Executive Officer **A**1 2 3 9 10 **F**4 7 8 10 11 12 14 15 16 17 19 21 22 23 25 26 27 28 29 30 32 34 35 37 39 40 41 42 43 44 45 46 48 52 53 55 58 59 60 61 63 64 65 71 72 73 74 **P**4 5 7 **S** Columbia/HCA Healthcare Corporation, Nashville, TN	33	10	205	14465	149	146457	2730	95833	32273	1148
★ △ UNIVERSITY OF UTAH HOSPITALS AND CLINICS, 50 North Medical Drive, Zip 84132–0002; tel. 801/581–2380; Christine St. Andre, Executive Director **A**1 2 3 5 7 8 9 10 **F**4 6 7 8 9 10 11 12 14 15 16 17 18 19 20 21 22 23 25 26 28 29 30 31 32 34 35 37 38 40 41 42 43 44 45 46 48 49 51 52 53 54 55 56 57 58 59 60 61 64 65 66 67 68 69 70 71 72 73 74 **P**5	12	10	380	16647	302	31412	2849	241842	98138	3516
□ UNIVERSITY OF UTAH NEUROPSYCHIATRIC INSTITUTE, 501 Chipeta Way, Zip 84108–1225; tel. 801/583–2500; Ross Van Vranken, Chief Executive Officer **A**1 3 5 10 **F**1 2 3 12 14 15 16 17 19 21 26 35 45 46 52 53 54 55 56 57 58 59 65 67 68 **P**5 8	23	22	90	1848	60	15571	—	13993	6773	228
★ VETERANS AFFAIRS MEDICAL CENTER, 500 Foothill Drive, Zip 84148–0002; tel. 801/582–1565; James R. Floyd, Medical Center Director **A**1 2 3 5 8 9 **F**3 4 8 10 12 14 15 16 17 18 19 20 21 22 23 24 25 26 27 28 29 30 31 32 33 34 35 37 39 41 42 43 44 45 46 48 49 50 51 52 54 55 56 57 58 60 61 63 64 65 67 69 71 73 74 **S** Department of Veterans Affairs, Washington, DC	45	10	180	5563	131	193012	—	122637	59424	1476

Hospital, Address, Telephone, Administrator, Approval, Facility, and Physician Codes, Health Care System, Network	Classi-fication Codes		Utilization Data					Expense (thousands) of dollars		
	Control	Service	Staffed Beds	Admissions	Census	Outpatient Visits	Births	Total	Payroll	Personnel

Approval codes legend:
★ American Hospital Association (AHA) membership
□ Joint Commission on Accreditation of Healthcare Organizations (JCAHO) accreditation
+ American Osteopathic Healthcare Association (AOHA) membership
○ American Osteopathic Association (AOA) accreditation
△ Commission on Accreditation of Rehabilitation Facilities (CARF) accreditation
Control codes 61, 63, 64, 71, 72 and 73 indicate hospitals listed by AOHA, but not registered by AHA. For definition of numerical codes, see page A4

SANDY—Salt Lake County

☒ ALTA VIEW HOSPITAL, 9660 South 1300 East, Zip 84094–3793; tel. 801/576–2600; Wes Thompson, Administrator and Chief Executive Officer **A**1 9 10 **F**1 2 3 4 5 6 7 8 9 10 11 12 13 14 15 16 17 18 19 20 21 22 23 24 25 26 27 28 29 30 31 32 33 34 35 36 37 38 39 40 41 42 43 44 45 46 47 48 49 51 52 53 54 55 56 57 58 59 60 61 62 63 64 65 66 67 68 69 70 71 72 73 74 **P**3 4 5 6 **S** Intermountain Health Care, Inc., Salt Lake City, UT **N** Intermountain HealthCare/Amerinet, Salt Lake City, UT — 23 10 70 4723 31 157286 1821 35304 16290 489

□ △ HEALTHSOUTH REHABILITATION HOSPITAL OF UTAH, 8074 South 1300 East, Zip 84094–0743; tel. 801/561–3400; Richard M. Richards, Administrator (Total facility includes 36 beds in nursing home–type unit) (Nonreporting) **A**1 7 10 **S** HEALTHSOUTH Corporation, Birmingham, AL — 33 46 73 — — — — — — —

TOOELE—Tooele County

★ TOOELE VALLEY REGIONAL MEDICAL CENTER, 211 South 100 East, Zip 84074–2794; tel. 435/882–1697; Mark F. Dalley, Chief Executive Officer (Total facility includes 84 beds in nursing home–type unit) (Nonreporting) **A**9 10 **S** Rural Health Management Corporation, Nephi, UT — 13 10 122 — — — — — — —

TREMONTON—Box Elder County

★ BEAR RIVER VALLEY HOSPITAL, 440 West 600 North, Zip 84337–2497; tel. 801/257–7441; Robert F. Jex, Administrator (Total facility includes 38 beds in nursing home–type unit) **A**9 10 **F**7 12 14 15 17 20 22 32 33 40 44 46 49 58 64 73 **P**3 **S** Intermountain Health Care, Inc., Salt Lake City, UT **N** Intermountain HealthCare/Amerinet, Salt Lake City, UT — 23 10 58 548 40 8238 47 2353 1253 32

VERNAL—Uintah County

☒ COLUMBIA ASHLEY VALLEY MEDICAL CENTER, 151 West 200 North, Zip 84078–1907; tel. 435/789–3342; Ronald J. Perry, Chief Executive Officer **A**1 9 10 **F**7 8 11 15 16 19 24 28 30 31 32 35 37 38 40 41 44 46 66 70 71 73 **P**7 **S** Columbia/HCA Healthcare Corporation, Nashville, TN — 33 10 29 1278 10 28735 277 11728 4910 197

WEST JORDAN—Salt Lake County

COPPER HILLS YOUTH CENTER, (Formerly Rivendell Psychiatric Center), 5899 West Rivendell Drive, Zip 84088–5700, Mailing Address: P.O. Box 459, Zip 84084–0459; tel. 801/561–3377; Sandy Podley, Chief Executive Officer (Nonreporting) **A**10 **S** Children's Comprehensive Services, Inc., Nashville, TN — 33 52 80 — — — — — — —

□ JORDAN VALLEY HOSPITAL, 3580 West 9000 South, Zip 84088–8811; tel. 801/561–8888; Jeffrey J. Manley, Chief Executive Officer **A**1 9 10 **F**7 8 14 15 16 19 21 22 23 25 28 30 32 34 37 40 44 46 63 65 71 73 74 **P**1 6 7 8 **S** Paracelsus Healthcare Corporation, Houston, TX — 33 10 50 2810 19 45324 1308 21340 8014 280

WOODS CROSS—Davis County

□ BENCHMARK BEHAVIORAL HEALTH SYSTEMS, 592 West 1350 South, Zip 84087–1665; tel. 801/299–5300; Richard O. Hurt, Ph.D., Chief Executive Officer **A**1 9 10 **F**1 2 14 15 16 22 52 53 57 58 59 65 67 **P**8 **S** Ramsay Health Care, Inc., Coral Gables, FL — 33 22 68 53 71 1175 — 6930 3649 248

VERMONT

Resident population 589 (in thousands)
Resident population in metro areas 27.2%
Birth rate per 1,000 population 12.7
65 years and over 12.1%
Percent of persons without health insurance 11.1%

Hospital, Address, Telephone, Administrator, Approval, Facility, and Physician Codes, Health Care System, Network	Classi-fication Codes		Utilization Data					Expense (thousands) of dollars		
	Control	Service	Staffed Beds	Admissions	Census	Outpatient Visits	Births	Total	Payroll	Personnel

★ American Hospital Association (AHA) membership
□ Joint Commission on Accreditation of Healthcare Organizations (JCAHO) accreditation
+ American Osteopathic Healthcare Association (AOHA) membership
○ American Osteopathic Association (AOA) accreditation
△ Commission on Accreditation of Rehabilitation Facilities (CARF) accreditation
Control codes 61, 63, 64, 71, 72 and 73 indicate hospitals listed by AOHA, but not registered by AHA. For definition of numerical codes, see page A4

BARRE—Washington County

★ CENTRAL VERMONT MEDICAL CENTER, Fisher Road, Zip 05641–9060, Mailing Address: P.O. Box 547, Zip 05641–0547; tel. 802/371–4100; Daria V. Mason, Chief Executive Officer (Total facility includes 153 beds in nursing home–type unit) **A**1 9 10 **F**7 8 11 14 15 16 17 19 20 21 22 23 27 28 30 31 34 35 37 39 40 41 42 44 45 46 49 51 52 54 56 57 58 61 64 65 66 71 72 73 74 **P**3 4 7 8

| | 23 | 10 | 275 | 4273 | 204 | 25751 | 478 | 43306 | 19773 | 526 |

BENNINGTON—Bennington County

★ SOUTHWESTERN VERMONT MEDICAL CENTER, 100 Hospital Drive East, Zip 05201–5013; tel. 802/442–6361; Harvey M. Yorke, President and Chief Executive Officer **A**1 2 9 10 **F**1 2 3 4 7 8 10 11 12 14 15 16 17 19 21 22 25 26 27 28 30 32 33 34 35 37 39 40 41 42 44 45 46 48 49 51 52 53 54 55 56 57 58 59 60 63 64 65 66 67 69 70 71 72 73 74 **P**5 6 8

| | 23 | 10 | 90 | 4652 | 50 | 121489 | 435 | 39752 | 19001 | 581 |

BRATTLEBORO—Windham County

★ BRATTLEBORO MEMORIAL HOSPITAL, 9 Belmont Avenue, Zip 05301–3498; tel. 802/257–0341; Brian R. Mitteer, President **A**1 9 10 **F**7 8 11 14 15 16 17 19 21 22 24 28 30 31 35 37 39 40 41 42 44 46 49 63 65 67 71 73

| | 23 | 10 | 61 | 2730 | 31 | 59584 | 364 | 23025 | 9410 | 273 |

★ BRATTLEBORO RETREAT, 75 Linden Street, Zip 05301–4807, Mailing Address: P.O. Box 803, Zip 05302–0803; tel. 802/257–7785; Richard T. Palmisano, II, R.N., MS, Chief Executive Officer (Total facility includes 117 beds in nursing home–type unit) **A**1 3 5 10 **F**2 3 12 15 34 52 53 54 55 56 57 58 59 64 **P**6 7

| | 23 | 22 | 219 | 2161 | 170 | 14923 | 0 | 31366 | 18090 | 630 |

BURLINGTON—Chittenden County

★ FLETCHER ALLEN HEALTH CARE, (Includes Fanny Allen Campus, 101 College Parkway, Colchester, Zip 05446–3035; tel. 802/655–1234; Medical Center Hospital Campus, Colchester Avenue, Zip 05401; tel. 802/656–2345), 111 Colchester Avenue, Zip 05401–1429; tel. 802/656–2345; William V. Boettcher, Chief Executive Officer **A**1 2 3 5 8 9 10 **F**2 3 4 7 8 9 10 11 12 13 14 15 16 17 18 19 20 21 22 23 25 26 28 29 30 31 32 33 34 35 37 38 39 40 41 42 43 44 45 46 47 48 49 51 52 53 54 55 56 57 58 59 60 63 64 65 66 67 69 70 71 72 73 **P**1 8 **N** Fletcher Allen Health Care, Burlington, VT

| | 23 | 10 | 382 | 19429 | 331 | 271610 | 2488 | 227370 | 105522 | 3773 |

MIDDLEBURY—Addison County

★ PORTER HOSPITAL, 75 South Street, Zip 05753–8606; tel. 802/388–4701; James L. Daily, President (Total facility includes 118 beds in nursing home–type unit) **A**1 9 10 **F**8 14 16 17 19 21 22 26 28 30 35 37 39 40 42 44 45 46 49 51 63 64 65 67 71 73 74

| | 23 | 10 | 163 | 1604 | 124 | 58848 | 338 | 20112 | 9287 | 497 |

MORRISVILLE—Lamoille County

★ COPLEY HOSPITAL, Washington Highway, Zip 05661–9209, Mailing Address: RD 3, Box 760, Zip 05661–9209; tel. 802/888–4231; Carolyn C. Roberts, President **A**1 9 10 **F**7 8 11 14 15 16 17 19 21 22 28 29 30 33 34 36 37 39 40 42 44 46 48 49 53 56 58 64 65 66 67 71 73 **P**8

| | 23 | 10 | 43 | 1681 | 21 | 45628 | 279 | 16266 | 7480 | 259 |

NEWPORT—Orleans County

★ NORTH COUNTRY HOSPITAL AND HEALTH CENTER, 189 Prouty Drive, Zip 05855–9329; tel. 802/334–7331; Sidney A. Toll, President **A**1 9 10 **F**7 8 11 15 17 19 21 22 28 29 33 35 37 39 40 41 42 44 45 46 49 51 58 65 67 71 73 74 **P**6

| | 23 | 10 | 27 | 2163 | 20 | 60127 | 258 | 21271 | 11137 | 316 |

RANDOLPH—Orange County

★ GIFFORD MEDICAL CENTER, 44 South Main Street, Zip 05060, Mailing Address: P.O. Box 2000, Zip 05060–2000; tel. 802/728–4441; David H. Gregg, Jr., President (Total facility includes 42 beds in nursing home–type unit) **A**1 2 9 10 **F**3 6 7 8 11 12 13 14 15 16 17 18 19 21 22 25 26 27 28 29 30 31 32 33 34 37 39 40 41 42 44 45 46 49 51 53 54 55 56 57 58 61 64 65 67 68 71 72 73 74 **P**6

| | 23 | 10 | 94 | 1337 | 56 | 22901 | 249 | 16929 | 8984 | 306 |

RUTLAND—Rutland County

★ RUTLAND REGIONAL MEDICAL CENTER, 160 Allen Street, Zip 05701–4595; tel. 802/775–7111; Thomas W. Huebner, President and Chief Executive Officer **A**1 2 9 10 **F**4 6 7 8 12 13 14 15 16 19 21 22 23 28 30 31 34 35 37 39 40 41 42 44 45 46 48 49 52 54 55 56 58 59 60 63 65 66 67 70 71 72 73 **P**5 8

| | 23 | 10 | 84 | 6800 | 93 | 101624 | 632 | 65097 | 31271 | — |

SAINT ALBANS—Franklin County

★ NORTHWESTERN MEDICAL CENTER, 131 Fairfield Street, Zip 05478–1734, Mailing Address: P.O. Box 1370, Zip 05478–1370; tel. 802/524–5911; Peter A. Hofstetter, Chief Executive Officer **A**1 2 9 10 **F**7 8 12 14 15 16 17 19 22 28 29 30 34 36 37 39 40 41 44 45 46 49 51 65 67 71 72 73 **P**8 **S** Quorum Health Group/Quorum Health Resources, Inc., Brentwood, TN

| | 23 | 10 | 70 | 2387 | 25 | 23819 | 721 | 22633 | 10296 | 284 |

SAINT JOHNSBURY—Caledonia County

★ NORTHEASTERN VERMONT REGIONAL HOSPITAL, Hospital Drive, Zip 05819–9962, Mailing Address: P.O. Box 905, Zip 05819–9962; tel. 802/748–8141; Paul R. Bengtson, Chief Executive Officer **A**1 9 10 **F**7 8 14 15 16 17 19 21 22 29 30 31 34 37 39 40 41 42 44 45 46 49 53 54 56 58 63 65 66 67 71 72 73 74 **P**7 **S** Quorum Health Group/Quorum Health Resources, Inc., Brentwood, TN

| | 23 | 10 | 64 | 1775 | 18 | 59317 | 262 | 19029 | 7456 | 234 |

Hospital, Address, Telephone, Administrator, Approval, Facility, and Physician Codes, Health Care System, Network	Classi-fication Codes		Utilization Data					Expense (thousands) of dollars		
★ American Hospital Association (AHA) membership □ Joint Commission on Accreditation of Healthcare Organizations (JCAHO) accreditation + American Osteopathic Healthcare Association (AOHA) membership ○ American Osteopathic Association (AOA) accreditation △ Commission on Accreditation of Rehabilitation Facilities (CARF) accreditation Control codes 61, 63, 64, 71, 72 and 73 indicate hospitals listed by AOHA, but not registered by AHA. For definition of numerical codes, see page A4	Control	Service	Staffed Beds	Admissions	Census	Outpatient Visits	Births	Total	Payroll	Personnel

SPRINGFIELD—Windsor County

⊞ SPRINGFIELD HOSPITAL, 25 Ridgewood Road, Zip 05156–2003, Mailing Address: P.O. Box 2003, Zip 05156–2003; tel. 802/885–2151; Glenn D. Cordner, Chief Executive Officer **A**1 9 10 **F**7 8 12 14 15 16 19 21 22 25 26 28 31 34 35 37 39 40 41 42 44 49 52 56 63 65 67 71 72 73 **P**4 7	23	10	69	1990	21	43154	215	20850	7772	258

TOWNSHEND—Windham County

★ GRACE COTTAGE HOSPITAL, (Includes Stratton House Nursing Home), Route 35, Zip 05353–0216, Mailing Address: P.O. Box 216, Zip 05353–0126; tel. 802/365–7357; Albert LaRochelle, Administrator (Total facility includes 30 beds in nursing home–type unit) **A**9 10 **F**1 7 16 22 27 33 36 40 41 44 49 51 58 64 65 73 **P**6	23	10	47	408	36	8360	14	3393	1918	90

WATERBURY—Washington County

VERMONT STATE HOSPITAL, 103 South Main Street, Zip 05671–2501; tel. 802/241–1000; Bertold Francke, M.D., Interim Executive Director (Nonreporting) **A**9 10	12	22	70	—	—	—	—	—	—	—

WHITE RIVER JUNCTION—Windsor County

⊞ VETERANS AFFAIRS MEDICAL CENTER, North Hartland Road, Zip 05009–0001; tel. 802/295–9363; Gary M. De Gasta, Director **A**1 3 5 8 9 **F**1 2 3 4 5 6 7 8 10 12 14 15 16 17 18 19 20 21 22 25 26 27 28 29 30 31 32 33 34 35 37 39 41 42 43 44 45 46 48 49 51 52 54 55 56 57 58 59 60 61 64 65 67 71 73 74 **P**6 **S** Department of Veterans Affairs, Washington, DC	45	10	60	2745	64	107226	—	60498	29849	587

WINDSOR—Windsor County

★ MOUNT ASCUTNEY HOSPITAL AND HEALTH CENTER, Rural Route 1, Box 6, Zip 05089–9702; tel. 802/674–6711; Richard Slusky, Administrator (Total facility includes 66 beds in nursing home–type unit) **A**9 10 **F**8 12 14 15 16 17 20 22 26 27 29 30 31 32 33 34 36 37 39 41 44 45 46 48 49 54 56 58 64 65 67 71 73 **P**6	23	10	99	1046	85	16855	—	11652	5750	250

VIRGINIA

Resident population 6,734 (in thousands)
Resident population in metro areas 77.7%
Birth rate per 1,000 population 14.5
65 years and over 11.2%
Percent of persons without health insurance 12.5%

Hospital, Address, Telephone, Administrator, Approval, Facility, and Physician Codes, Health Care System, Network	Classi-fication Codes		Utilization Data					Expense (thousands) of dollars		
★ American Hospital Association (AHA) membership □ Joint Commission on Accreditation of Healthcare Organizations (JCAHO) accreditation + American Osteopathic Healthcare Association (AOHA) membership ○ American Osteopathic Association (AOA) accreditation △ Commission on Accreditation of Rehabilitation Facilities (CARF) accreditation Control codes 61, 63, 64, 71, 72 and 73 indicate hospitals listed by AOHA, but not registered by AHA. For definition of numerical codes, see page A4	Control	Service	Staffed Beds	Admissions	Census	Outpatient Visits	Births	Total	Payroll	Personnel

ABINGDON—Washington County

☒ JOHNSTON MEMORIAL HOSPITAL, 351 North Court Street, Zip 24210–2921; tel. 540/676–7000; Clark R. Beil, Chief Executive Officer **A**1 2 9 10 **F**3 4 7 8 10 12 14 15 16 17 19 20 21 22 25 26 27 28 30 31 32 33 34 35 37 38 39 40 41 42 44 45 46 49 51 56 57 59 63 65 66 67 69 71 72 73 74 **P**1 6 8 **N** Mountain States Healthcare Network, Johnson City, TN | 23 | 10 | 135 | 4596 | 60 | 71524 | 696 | 33808 | 13971 | 547

ALEXANDRIA—Independent City County

☒ INOVA ALEXANDRIA HOSPITAL, 4320 Seminary Road, Zip 22304–1594; tel. 703/504–3000; H. Patrick Walters, President **A**1 2 3 5 9 10 **F**2 3 4 6 7 8 10 11 12 13 14 15 16 17 19 21 22 25 26 28 29 30 31 32 34 35 37 38 39 40 41 42 43 44 45 46 47 48 49 51 52 53 54 55 56 57 58 59 60 61 63 64 65 66 67 68 69 70 71 72 73 74 **P**2 5 7 **S** Inova Health System, Springfield, VA | 23 | 10 | 300 | 14731 | 206 | 114308 | 3360 | 109243 | — | 1353

☒ △ INOVA MOUNT VERNON HOSPITAL, 2501 Parker's Lane, Zip 22306–3209; tel. 703/664–7000; Susan Herbert, Administrator **A**1 2 3 7 9 10 **F**1 3 4 6 7 8 10 11 12 13 14 15 16 17 19 21 22 23 25 26 27 28 29 30 31 32 33 34 35 36 37 38 39 40 41 42 43 44 45 46 47 48 49 51 52 53 54 55 56 57 58 59 60 61 63 64 65 66 67 68 69 70 71 72 73 74 **P**1 2 7 8 **S** Inova Health System, Springfield, VA **N** Inova Health System, Springfield, VA | 23 | 10 | 229 | 8258 | 148 | 60464 | 0 | 77378 | 33122 | 747

ARLINGTON—Arlington County

☒ ARLINGTON HOSPITAL, 1701 North George Mason Drive, Zip 22205–3698; tel. 703/558–5000; James B. Cole, President and Chief Executive Officer **A**1 2 3 5 9 10 **F**3 4 7 8 10 11 14 15 16 17 19 21 22 26 28 29 30 31 34 35 37 40 41 42 43 44 46 49 50 52 56 57 58 59 60 63 65 67 71 73 | 32 | 10 | 282 | 13261 | 174 | 110796 | 2764 | 106446 | 45778 | 1152

☒ △ COLUMBIA PENTAGON CITY HOSPITAL, (Formerly National Hospital Medical Center), 2455 Army Navy Drive, Zip 22206–2999; tel. 703/920–6700; Thomas Anderson, Chief Executive Officer **A**1 5 7 9 10 **F**1 3 5 7 8 12 14 15 16 17 18 19 21 23 24 25 26 27 28 29 30 31 32 34 35 37 39 41 42 43 44 45 46 48 49 50 51 53 54 55 56 57 58 59 60 62 65 66 67 68 71 72 73 74 **P**4 5 7 8 **S** Columbia/HCA Healthcare Corporation, Nashville, TN | 33 | 10 | 102 | 1782 | 34 | 32461 | 0 | 29611 | 12500 | 371

□ HOSPICE OF NORTHERN VIRGINIA, 4715 North 15th Street, Zip 22205; tel. 703/525–7070; David J. English, President and Chief Executive Officer (Nonreporting) **A**1 10 | 23 | 49 | 15 | — | — | — | — | — | — | —

NATIONAL HOSPITAL MEDICAL CENTER See Columbia Pentagon City Hospital

☒ VENCOR HOSPITAL–ARLINGTON, 601 South Carlin Springs Road, Zip 22204–1096; tel. 703/671–1200; Robert S. Davis, III, CHE, Administrator (Nonreporting) **A**1 5 9 10 **S** Vencor, Incorporated, Louisville, KY | 33 | 10 | 206 | | | | | | |

BEDFORD—Independent City County

☒ CARILION BEDFORD MEMORIAL HOSPITAL, 1613 Oakwood Street, Zip 24523–0688, Mailing Address: P.O. Box 688, Zip 24523–0688; tel. 540/586–2441; Howard Ainsley, Director (Total facility includes 111 beds in nursing home–type unit) (Nonreporting) **A**1 9 10 **S** Carilion Health System, Roanoke, VA **N** Carilion Health System, Roanoke, VA | 23 | 10 | 161 | | | | | | |

BIG STONE GAP—Wise County

☒ LONESOME PINE HOSPITAL, 1990 Holton Avenue East, Zip 24219–0230; tel. 540/523–3111; Paul A. Bishop, Administrator **A**1 9 10 **F**7 8 14 15 16 17 19 21 22 26 28 30 32 33 34 35 40 42 44 46 49 63 65 71 73 74 **P**1 4 5 6 7 **S** Quorum Health Group/Quorum Health Resources, Inc., Brentwood, TN **N** CHA Provider Network, Inc., Lexington, KY; Highlands Wellmont Health Network, Inc., Bristol, TN | 23 | 10 | 54 | 1822 | 21 | 21449 | 196 | 14056 | 6126 | 218

BLACKSBURG—Montgomery County

☒ MONTGOMERY REGIONAL HOSPITAL, (Formerly Columbia Montgomery Regional Hospital), 3700 South Main Street, Zip 24060–7081, Mailing Address: P.O. Box 90004, Zip 24062–9004; tel. 540/953–5101; David R. Williams, Chief Executive Officer (Total facility includes 11 beds in nursing home–type unit) **A**1 9 10 **F**2 3 4 7 8 10 11 12 14 15 16 17 18 19 21 22 23 24 26 28 29 30 31 32 33 34 35 37 38 39 40 41 42 43 44 45 46 47 48 49 51 52 53 54 55 56 57 58 59 60 61 63 64 65 66 67 70 71 72 73 74 **P**8 **S** Columbia/HCA Healthcare Corporation, Nashville, TN | 33 | 10 | 105 | 4256 | 43 | 93951 | 633 | 30290 | 13420 | 435

BURKEVILLE—Nottoway County

□ PIEDMONT GERIATRIC HOSPITAL, (GERIATRIC PSYCHIATRY), Mailing Address: P.O. Box 427, Zip 23922–0427; tel. 804/767–4401; Willard R. Pierce, Jr., Director **A**1 9 10 **F**19 20 22 25 26 27 35 41 46 52 55 57 60 65 67 71 73 **S** Virginia Department of Mental Health, Richmond, VA | 12 | 49 | 210 | 117 | 184 | — | — | 15088 | 9403 | 381

CATAWBA—Roanoke County

□ CATAWBA HOSPITAL, Mailing Address: P.O. Box 200, Zip 24070–0200; tel. 540/375–4200; James S. Reinhard, M.D., Director **A**1 9 10 **F**14 15 16 19 20 26 35 45 46 52 57 65 73 **P**6 | 12 | 22 | 218 | 452 | 169 | — | — | 11479 | 8627 | 336

CHARLOTTESVILLE—Independent City County

□ CHARTER BEHAVIORAL HEALTH SYSTEM OF CHARLOTTESVILLE, 2101 Arlington Boulevard, Zip 22903–1593; tel. 804/977–1120; Wayne Adams, Chief Executive Officer (Nonreporting) **A**1 9 10 **S** Magellan Health Services, Atlanta, GA **N** Virginia Health Network, Richmond, VA | 33 | 22 | 62 | — | — | — | — | — | — | —

Hospital, Address, Telephone, Administrator, Approval, Facility, and Physician Codes, Health Care System, Network	Classi-fication Codes		Utilization Data					Expense (thousands) of dollars		
★ American Hospital Association (AHA) membership □ Joint Commission on Accreditation of Healthcare Organizations (JCAHO) accreditation + American Osteopathic Healthcare Association (AOHA) membership ○ American Osteopathic Association (AOA) accreditation △ Commission on Accreditation of Rehabilitation Facilities (CARF) accreditation Control codes 61, 63, 64, 71, 72 and 73 indicate hospitals listed by AOHA, but not registered by AHA. For definition of numerical codes, see page A4	Control	Service	Staffed Beds	Admissions	Census	Outpatient Visits	Births	Total	Payroll	Personnel
✠ MARTHA JEFFERSON HOSPITAL, 459 Locust Avenue, Zip 22902–9940; tel. 804/982–7000; James E. Haden, President and Chief Executive Officer **A**1 2 9 10 **F**7 8 12 14 16 17 19 20 21 22 23 24 25 26 27 28 29 30 31 32 33 34 35 37 39 40 41 42 44 45 46 49 51 60 63 64 65 66 67 71 72 73 74 **P**7 8 **N** Virginia Health Network, Richmond, VA	23	10	156	9148	95	90625	1406	75288	36633	980
✠ UNIVERSITY OF VIRGINIA MEDICAL CENTER, Jefferson Park Avenue, Zip 22908, Mailing Address: P.O. Box 10050, Zip 22906–0050; tel. 804/924–0211; Michael J. Halseth, Executive Director **A**1 2 3 5 8 9 10 **F**4 5 7 8 9 10 11 13 15 16 18 19 20 21 22 23 25 26 27 28 29 30 31 32 33 34 35 37 38 39 40 41 42 43 44 45 46 47 48 49 51 52 53 54 55 56 57 58 59 60 61 63 65 66 67 68 69 70 71 72 73 74 **P**3 **N** Central Virginia Health Network, Richmond, VA	12	10	594	27737	454	488359	1452	431330	149784	5003
CHESAPEAKE—Independent City County										
✠ CHESAPEAKE GENERAL HOSPITAL, 736 Battlefield Boulevard North, Zip 23320–4941, Mailing Address: P.O. Box 2028, Zip 23327–2028; tel. 757/547–8121; Donald S. Buckley, FACHE, President **A**1 2 5 9 10 **F**1 4 6 7 8 10 12 14 15 16 17 19 21 22 23 24 26 27 28 29 30 31 32 33 34 35 36 37 39 40 42 44 45 46 49 52 54 55 57 59 60 61 63 65 66 67 71 73 74 **N** Virginia Health Network, Richmond, VA	16	10	260	13943	203	138404	2993	97659	42580	1379
CLINTWOOD—Dickenson County										
DICKENSON COUNTY MEDICAL CENTER, Hospital Drive, Zip 24228, Mailing Address: P.O. Box 1390, Zip 24228–1390; tel. 540/926–0300; Benjamin A. Peak, Chief Executive Officer (Nonreporting) **A**9 10	33	10	41	—	—	—	—	—	—	—
CULPEPER—Culpeper County										
✠ CULPEPER MEMORIAL HOSPITAL, 501 Sunset Lane, Zip 22701–3917, Mailing Address: Box 592, Zip 22701–0592; tel. 540/829–4100; H. Lee Kirk, Jr., President and Chief Executive Officer **A**1 9 10 **F**2 7 8 12 14 15 16 17 19 20 22 24 28 29 30 32 33 34 35 37 40 41 42 44 46 48 49 52 54 55 56 57 58 59 63 65 67 71 **P**7 8	23	10	70	3301	34	34688	309	23103	11256	430
DANVILLE—Independent City County										
✠ DANVILLE REGIONAL MEDICAL CENTER, 142 South Main Street, Zip 24541–2922; tel. 804/799–2100; Larry T. DePriest, President (Total facility includes 60 beds in nursing home–type unit) **A**1 2 3 5 6 9 10 **F**2 3 6 7 8 10 11 12 14 15 16 17 19 21 22 28 29 30 31 32 34 35 37 39 40 41 42 44 45 46 48 49 51 52 54 55 56 58 59 60 61 62 63 64 65 67 71 72 73 74 **P**6 8	23	10	252	11494	159	290513	1123	94035	36216	1150
□ SOUTHERN VIRGINIA MENTAL HEALTH INSTITUTE, 382 Taylor Drive, Zip 24541–4023; tel. 804/799–6220; Constance N. Fletcher, Ph.D., Director (Nonreporting) **A**1 9 10 **S** Virginia Department of Mental Health, Richmond, VA	12	22	96	—	—	—	—	—	—	—
EMPORIA—Independent City County										
✠ GREENSVILLE MEMORIAL HOSPITAL, 214 Weaver Avenue, Zip 23847–1482; tel. 804/348–2000; Rosemary C. Check, Chief Executive Officer (Total facility includes 65 beds in nursing home–type unit) **A**1 9 10 **F**7 8 12 14 16 19 21 22 27 28 30 32 34 35 37 40 42 44 45 46 49 63 64 65 71 73 **S** Quorum Health Group/Quorum Health Resources, Inc., Brentwood, TN **N** Virginia Health Network, Richmond, VA	23	10	144	3262	105	41706	132	19494	8939	336
FAIRFAX—Independent City County										
✠ INOVA FAIR OAKS HOSPITAL, 3600 Joseph Siewick Drive, Zip 22033–1709; tel. 703/391–3600; Steven E. Brown, Administrator (Nonreporting) **A**1 2 5 9 10 **S** Inova Health System, Springfield, VA **N** Inova Health System, Springfield, VA	23	10	133	—	—	—	—	—	—	—
FALLS CHURCH—Independent City County										
✠ DOMINION HOSPITAL, 2960 Sleepy Hollow Road, Zip 22044–2001; tel. 703/536–2000; Barbara D. S. Hekimian, Chief Executive Officer (Nonreporting) **A**1 9 10 **S** Columbia/HCA Healthcare Corporation, Nashville, TN	33	22	100	—	—	—	—	—	—	—
✠ INOVA FAIRFAX HOSPITAL, 3300 Gallows Road, Zip 22042–3300; tel. 703/698–1110; Jolene Tornabeni, Administrator **A**1 2 3 5 8 9 10 **F**1 2 3 4 6 7 8 10 11 12 13 16 17 19 21 22 25 28 29 30 31 32 34 35 36 37 38 39 40 41 42 43 44 45 46 47 49 51 52 53 54 55 56 57 58 59 60 61 63 64 65 66 67 68 69 70 71 72 73 74 **P**1 4 6 7 8 **S** Inova Health System, Springfield, VA **N** Inova Health System, Springfield, VA	23	10	656	44583	572	140976	9623	385571	170409	3910
□ NORTHERN VIRGINIA MENTAL HEALTH INSTITUTE, 3302 Gallows Road, Zip 22042–3398; tel. 703/207–7111; John Russotto, Facility Director (Nonreporting) **A**1 9 10 **S** Virginia Department of Mental Health, Richmond, VA	12	22	62	—	—	—	—	—	—	—
FARMVILLE—Prince Edward County										
✠ SOUTHSIDE COMMUNITY HOSPITAL, 800 Oak Street, Zip 23901–1199; tel. 804/392–8811; John H. Greer, President **A**1 9 10 **F**7 8 14 15 16 19 20 22 32 35 37 40 41 42 44 45 46 49 65 66 71 73 **S** Carilion Health System, Roanoke, VA	23	10	88	4555	46	40000	380	25888	12057	415
FISHERSVILLE—Augusta County										
□ AUGUSTA HEALTH CARE, 96 Medical Center Drive, Zip 22939, Mailing Address: P.O. Box 1000, Zip 22939–1000; tel. 540/932–4000; Richard H. Graham, President and Chief Executive Officer **A**1 2 10 **F**3 7 8 10 12 14 15 16 17 19 20 21 22 23 24 26 27 28 29 30 31 32 33 34 35 37 39 40 41 42 44 45 46 48 49 51 52 53 54 55 56 57 58 59 63 64 65 66 67 71 73 **P**8	23	10	221	11486	143	220888	952	85422	37887	1284
□ △ WOODROW WILSON REHABILITATION CENTER, Mailing Address: P.O. Box 1500, Zip 22939–1500; tel. 540/332–7000; David J. Schwemer, Administrator (Nonreporting) **A**1 7 10	12	46	30	—	—	—	—	—	—	—
FORT BELVOIR—Fairfax County										
✠ DEWITT ARMY COMMUNITY HOSPITAL, 9501 Farrell Road, Zip 22060–5901; tel. 703/805–0510; Colonel Stephen L. Jones, Commander (Nonreporting) **A**1 3 5 **S** Department of the Army, Office of the Surgeon General, Falls Church, VA	42	10	62	—	—	—	—	—	—	—

Hospital, Address, Telephone, Administrator, Approval, Facility, and Physician Codes, Health Care System, Network	Classification Codes		Utilization Data					Expense (thousands) of dollars		
	Control	Service	Staffed Beds	Admissions	Census	Outpatient Visits	Births	Total	Payroll	Personnel

★ American Hospital Association (AHA) membership
□ Joint Commission on Accreditation of Healthcare Organizations (JCAHO) accreditation
+ American Osteopathic Healthcare Association (AOHA) membership
○ American Osteopathic Association (AOA) accreditation
△ Commission on Accreditation of Rehabilitation Facilities (CARF) accreditation
Control codes 61, 63, 64, 71, 72 and 73 indicate hospitals listed by AOHA, but not registered by AHA. For definition of numerical codes, see page A4

FRANKLIN—Independent City County

⊠ SOUTHAMPTON MEMORIAL HOSPITAL, 100 Fairview Drive, Zip 23851–1206, Mailing Address: P.O. Box 817, Zip 23851–0817; tel. 757/569–6100; Edward J. Patnesky, President and Chief Executive Officer (Total facility includes 131 beds in nursing home–type unit) **A**1 9 10 **F**3 6 7 8 12 14 15 16 19 21 22 23 26 28 30 32 33 34 35 37 39 40 41 42 44 46 49 55 57 62 64 65 66 67 71 73 74 **N** Virginia Health Network, Richmond, VA

		Control	Service	Staffed Beds	Admissions	Census	Outpatient Visits	Births	Total	Payroll	Personnel
SOUTHAMPTON MEMORIAL HOSPITAL		23	10	203	3006	165	50016	246	27001	12110	470

FREDERICKSBURG—Independent City County

⊠ MARY WASHINGTON HOSPITAL, 1001 Sam Perry Boulevard, Zip 22401–3354; tel. 540/899–1100; Fred M. Rankin, III, President and Chief Executive Officer **A**1 2 9 10 **F**2 3 4 6 7 8 10 11 12 13 14 15 16 17 18 19 21 22 23 25 26 27 28 29 30 31 32 33 34 35 36 37 38 39 40 41 42 43 44 45 46 49 52 53 54 55 56 57 58 59 60 62 63 64 65 67 68 71 72 73 **P**5 8

Hospital		Control	Service	Staffed Beds	Admissions	Census	Outpatient Visits	Births	Total	Payroll	Personnel
MARY WASHINGTON HOSPITAL		23	10	328	16079	205	155379	2298	129806	51129	1579

FRONT ROYAL—Warren County

⊠ WARREN MEMORIAL HOSPITAL, 1000 Shenandoah Avenue, Zip 22630–3598; tel. 540/636–0300; Charlie M. Horton, President (Total facility includes 40 beds in nursing home–type unit) **A**1 9 10 **F**7 8 16 19 22 28 32 34 37 40 41 44 45 63 64 65 67 71 73 74 **P**5 8 **S** Valley Health System, Winchester, VA **N** Valley Health System, Winchester, VA

Hospital		Control	Service	Staffed Beds	Admissions	Census	Outpatient Visits	Births	Total	Payroll	Personnel
WARREN MEMORIAL HOSPITAL		23	10	95	1781	63	—	143	17512	8054	270

GALAX—Independent City County

⊠ TWIN COUNTY REGIONAL HOSPITAL, 200 Hospital Drive, Zip 24333–2283; tel. 540/236–8181; Marcus G. Kuhn, President and Chief Executive Officer **A**1 9 10 **F**7 8 11 12 19 21 22 24 32 33 34 40 41 44 45 46 49 52 54 56 58 59 65 67 71 **P**5 **N** Wake Forest University Baptist Medical Center, Winston–Salem, NC

Hospital		Control	Service	Staffed Beds	Admissions	Census	Outpatient Visits	Births	Total	Payroll	Personnel
TWIN COUNTY REGIONAL HOSPITAL		23	10	118	4744	50	41051	432	31462	13818	526

GLOUCESTER—Gloucester County

□ RIVERSIDE WALTER REED HOSPITAL, 7519 Hospital Drive, Zip 23061–4178, Mailing Address: P.O. Box 1130, Zip 23061–1130; tel. 804/693–8800; Grady W. Philips, III, Vice President and Administrator **A**1 9 10 **F**1 2 3 4 6 7 8 10 11 12 13 14 15 16 17 18 19 21 22 23 24 25 26 27 28 29 30 31 32 33 34 35 37 39 40 41 42 43 44 45 46 48 49 51 52 53 54 55 56 57 58 59 60 61 62 63 64 65 66 67 70 71 72 73 74 **P**6 **S** Riverside Health System, Newport News, VA **N** Virginia Health Network, Richmond, VA

Hospital		Control	Service	Staffed Beds	Admissions	Census	Outpatient Visits	Births	Total	Payroll	Personnel
RIVERSIDE WALTER REED HOSPITAL		23	10	71	1964	33	84222	—	15323	7255	—

GRUNDY—Buchanan County

⊠ BUCHANAN GENERAL HOSPITAL, Mailing Address: Route 5, Box 20, Zip 24614–9611; tel. 540/935–1000; John West, Administrator **A**1 9 10 **F**8 14 15 19 21 22 23 28 30 32 35 37 42 44 49 65 71 73 **P**8 **S** Quorum Health Group/Quorum Health Resources, Inc., Brentwood, TN

Hospital		Control	Service	Staffed Beds	Admissions	Census	Outpatient Visits	Births	Total	Payroll	Personnel
BUCHANAN GENERAL HOSPITAL		23	10	144	4734	56	62539	—	21147	9554	353

HAMPTON—Independent City County

COLUMBIA PENINSULA CENTER FOR BEHAVIORAL HEALTH See Peninsula Behavioral Center

⊠ PENINSULA BEHAVIORAL CENTER, (Formerly Columbia Peninsula Center for Behavioral Health), 2244 Executive Drive, Zip 23666–2430; tel. 757/827–1001; Steuart A. Kimmeth, Chief Executive Officer **A**1 9 10 **F**12 15 16 19 35 52 53 54 55 56 57 59 65 **P**6 **S** Columbia/HCA Healthcare Corporation, Nashville, TN

Hospital		Control	Service	Staffed Beds	Admissions	Census	Outpatient Visits	Births	Total	Payroll	Personnel
PENINSULA BEHAVIORAL CENTER		33	22	90	2028	34	1556	—	6073	3630	144

⊠ SENTARA HAMPTON GENERAL HOSPITAL, 3120 Victoria Boulevard, Zip 23661–1585, Mailing Address: Drawer 640, Zip 23669–0640; tel. 757/727–7000; Russell Kenwood, Administrator **A**1 2 9 10 **F**1 2 3 4 6 7 8 9 10 11 12 13 14 15 16 17 19 20 21 22 23 24 25 26 27 28 29 30 31 32 33 34 35 36 37 39 40 41 42 43 44 45 46 48 49 51 52 53 54 55 56 57 58 59 60 61 62 63 64 65 66 67 69 70 71 72 73 74 **P**5 6 7 **S** Sentara Health System, Norfolk, VA **N** Sentara Health System, Norfolk, VA

Hospital		Control	Service	Staffed Beds	Admissions	Census	Outpatient Visits	Births	Total	Payroll	Personnel
SENTARA HAMPTON GENERAL HOSPITAL		23	10	198	8928	146	158254	1028	66779	24059	794

⊠ U. S. AIR FORCE HOSPITAL, 45 Pine Street, Zip 23665–2080; tel. 757/764–6825; Colonel Glenn R. Willauer, Administrator (Nonreporting) **A**1 **S** Department of the Air Force, Bowling AFB, DC

Hospital		Control	Service	Staffed Beds	Admissions	Census	Outpatient Visits	Births	Total	Payroll	Personnel
U. S. AIR FORCE HOSPITAL		41	10	59	—	—	—	—	—	—	—

⊠ VETERANS AFFAIRS MEDICAL CENTER, 100 Emancipation Drive, Zip 23667–0001; tel. 757/722–9961; William G. Wright, Director (Total facility includes 120 beds in nursing home–type unit) (Nonreporting) **A**1 2 3 5 8 **S** Department of Veterans Affairs, Washington, DC

Hospital		Control	Service	Staffed Beds	Admissions	Census	Outpatient Visits	Births	Total	Payroll	Personnel
VETERANS AFFAIRS MEDICAL CENTER		45	10	670	—	—	—	—	—	—	—

HARRISONBURG—Independent City County

⊠ ROCKINGHAM MEMORIAL HOSPITAL, 235 Cantrell Avenue, Zip 22801–3293; tel. 540/433–4100; Carter Melton, President **A**1 2 9 10 **F**3 7 8 10 12 13 14 15 16 17 18 19 20 21 22 23 24 25 28 29 30 31 32 33 34 35 39 41 42 44 45 46 49 54 55 56 57 58 59 60 63 65 66 67 68 71 73 74 **P**7 8

Hospital		Control	Service	Staffed Beds	Admissions	Census	Outpatient Visits	Births	Total	Payroll	Personnel
ROCKINGHAM MEMORIAL HOSPITAL		23	10	265	12086	152	114457	1657	88309	42166	1260

HOPEWELL—Independent City County

⊠ JOHN RANDOLPH MEDICAL CENTER, (Formerly Columbia John Randolph Medical Center), 411 West Randolph Road, Zip 23860, Mailing Address: P.O. Box 971, Zip 23860; tel. 804/541–1600; Daniel J. Wetta, Jr., Chief Executive Officer (Total facility includes 124 beds in nursing home–type unit) **A**1 9 10 **F**2 3 4 7 8 10 11 12 13 14 15 16 17 18 19 21 22 23 24 25 26 28 29 30 31 32 33 34 35 36 37 38 39 40 41 42 43 44 45 46 47 48 49 51 52 53 54 55 56 57 58 59 60 63 64 65 66 67 68 69 71 72 73 74 **P**1 5 7 **S** Columbia/HCA Healthcare Corporation, Nashville, TN **N** Preferred Care of Richmond, Richmond, VA

Hospital		Control	Service	Staffed Beds	Admissions	Census	Outpatient Visits	Births	Total	Payroll	Personnel
JOHN RANDOLPH MEDICAL CENTER		33	10	271	7812	213	83097	573	45348	21982	884

HOT SPRINGS—Bath County

★ BATH COUNTY COMMUNITY HOSPITAL, Mailing Address: Drawer Z, Zip 24445; tel. 540/839–7000; Harry M. Lowd, III, Director **A**9 10 **F**8 12 15 16 17 20 22 28 29 30 32 33 34 36 37 39 44 45 46 49 54 56 65 67 71 73

Hospital		Control	Service	Staffed Beds	Admissions	Census	Outpatient Visits	Births	Total	Payroll	Personnel
BATH COUNTY COMMUNITY HOSPITAL		23	10	25	510	7	15103	0	5353	2398	84

Hospital, Address, Telephone, Administrator, Approval, Facility, and Physician Codes, Health Care System, Network	Classi-fication Codes		Utilization Data					Expense (thousands) of dollars		
★ American Hospital Association (AHA) membership □ Joint Commission on Accreditation of Healthcare Organizations (JCAHO) accreditation + American Osteopathic Healthcare Association (AOHA) membership ○ American Osteopathic Association (AOA) accreditation △ Commission on Accreditation of Rehabilitation Facilities (CARF) accreditation Control codes 61, 63, 64, 71, 72 and 73 indicate hospitals listed by AOHA, but not registered by AHA. For definition of numerical codes, see page A4	Control	Service	Staffed Beds	Admissions	Census	Outpatient Visits	Births	Total	Payroll	Personnel

KILMARNOCK—Lancaster County

★ RAPPAHANNOCK GENERAL HOSPITAL, 101 Harris Drive, Zip 22482, Mailing Address: P.O. Box 1449, Zip 22482–1449; tel. 804/435–8000; James M. Holmes, President and Chief Executive Officer (Nonreporting) **A**9 10 **N** Central Virginia Health Network, Richmond, VA
| | | 23 | 10 | 76 | — | — | — | — | — | — | — |

LEBANON—Russell County

✶ RUSSELL COUNTY MEDICAL CENTER, Carroll and Tate Streets, Zip 24266–4510; tel. 540/889–1224; Jerry E. Lowery, Executive Director **A**1 9 10 **F**8 11 12 14 15 19 22 23 28 30 32 35 39 40 41 42 44 52 54 56 57 59 63 65 70 71 73 74 **S** Community Health Systems, Inc., Brentwood, TN
| | | 33 | 10 | 78 | 3251 | 42 | 59063 | 26 | 15793 | 6391 | 264 |

LEESBURG—Loudoun County

□ CHARTER BEHAVIORAL HEALTH SYSTEM AT SPRINGWOOD, 42009 Charter Springwood Lane, Zip 20176–6269; tel. 703/777–0800; Craig S. Juengling, Chief Executive Officer (Nonreporting) **A**1 9 10 **S** Magellan Health Services, Atlanta, GA
| | | 33 | 22 | 77 | — | — | — | — | — | — | — |

★ GRAYDON MANOR, 801 Childrens Center Road, Zip 22075–2598; tel. 703/777–3485; Bernard Haberlein, Executive Director **F**16 52 53 55 58
| | | 23 | 52 | 41 | 59 | 39 | 3737 | — | 5117 | 3265 | 100 |

✶ LOUDOUN HOSPITAL CENTER, 44045 Riverside Parkway, Zip 20176–2799; tel. 703/858–6000; G. T. Dunlop Ecker, President and Chief Executive Officer (Total facility includes 100 beds in nursing home–type unit) **A**1 2 9 10 **F**3 7 8 12 14 15 16 17 19 21 22 25 26 29 30 31 33 34 35 36 37 39 40 41 42 44 45 49 52 53 54 55 56 57 58 59 60 61 63 65 67 71 72 73 **P**6 8
| | | 23 | 10 | 112 | 4923 | 61 | 48295 | 878 | — | 19536 | 505 |

LEXINGTON—Independent City County

★ STONEWALL JACKSON HOSPITAL, 1 Health Circle, Zip 24450–2492; tel. 540/462–1200; William Mahone, V, Administrator (Total facility includes 50 beds in nursing home–type unit) **A**9 10 **F**7 8 14 15 16 19 21 22 27 28 30 32 33 34 36 37 39 40 41 44 46 49 63 64 65 71 73 **S** Carilion Health System, Roanoke, VA
| | | 23 | 10 | 130 | 2002 | 69 | 42233 | 213 | 15624 | 7191 | 323 |

LOW MOOR—Alleghany County

✶ COLUMBIA ALLEGHANY REGIONAL HOSPITAL, One ARH Lane, Zip 24457, Mailing Address: P.O. Box 7, Zip 24457–0007; tel. 540/862–6200; Ward W. Stevens, CHE, Chief Executive Officer (Nonreporting) **A**1 9 10 12 13 **S** Columbia/HCA Healthcare Corporation, Nashville, TN
| | | 33 | 10 | 196 | — | — | — | — | — | — | — |

LURAY—Page County

✶ PAGE MEMORIAL HOSPITAL, 200 Memorial Drive, Zip 22835–1005; tel. 540/743–4561; Donald J. Morgan, Administrator **A**1 9 10 **F**8 14 15 17 19 22 28 30 32 33 35 39 44 45 46 49 63 65 67 71 73 74 **P**6
| | | 23 | 10 | 54 | 1482 | 16 | 38977 | — | 10163 | 5109 | 193 |

LYNCHBURG—Independent City County

✶ LYNCHBURG GENERAL HOSPITAL, 1901 Tate Springs Road, Zip 24501–1167; tel. 804/947–3000; L. Darrell Powers, Senior Vice President (Total facility includes 130 beds in nursing home–type unit) **A**1 2 5 6 9 10 **F**1 2 3 4 8 10 11 14 15 16 17 18 19 20 21 22 23 24 25 26 28 29 30 32 33 34 35 37 38 40 41 42 43 44 48 49 52 53 54 55 56 57 58 59 60 63 64 65 67 71 72 73 74 **P**6 7 8 **S** Centra Health, Inc., Lynchburg, VA
| | | 23 | 10 | 350 | 12132 | 296 | 100323 | 0 | 96458 | 45898 | 1108 |

✶ △ VIRGINIA BAPTIST HOSPITAL, 3300 Rivermont Avenue, Zip 24503–9989; tel. 804/947–4000; Thomas C. Jividen, Senior Vice President (Total facility includes 36 beds in nursing home–type unit) **A**1 5 7 9 10 **F**1 3 4 8 10 11 14 15 16 17 18 19 20 21 22 23 24 25 26 27 28 29 30 31 32 33 34 35 37 38 40 41 42 43 44 48 49 52 53 54 55 56 57 58 59 60 63 64 65 67 68 71 72 73 74 **P**8 **S** Centra Health, Inc., Lynchburg, VA
| | | 23 | 10 | 326 | 9324 | 195 | 38404 | 2271 | 76711 | 42706 | 1017 |

MADISON HEIGHTS—Amherst County

CENTRAL VIRGINIA TRAINING CENTER, 210 East Colony Road, Zip 24572–2005, Mailing Address: P.O. Box 1098, Lynchburg, Zip 24505–1098; tel. 804/947–6326; Judy Dudley, Director (Total facility includes 104 beds in nursing home–type unit) (Nonreporting) **A**10 **S** Virginia Department of Mental Health, Richmond, VA
| | | 12 | 62 | 1112 | — | — | — | — | — | — | — |

MANASSAS—Independent City County

✶ PRINCE WILLIAM HOSPITAL, 8700 Sudley Road, Zip 20110–4418, Mailing Address: Box 2610, Zip 20108–0867; tel. 703/369–8000; Kenneth B. Swenson, President **A**1 2 9 10 **F**3 7 8 12 14 15 16 17 19 22 23 24 30 32 34 35 37 38 39 40 41 42 44 45 46 49 53 54 55 56 57 58 59 65 71
| | | 23 | 10 | 131 | 7326 | 74 | 85263 | 1464 | 55317 | 24358 | 706 |

MARION—Smyth County

✶ SMYTH COUNTY COMMUNITY HOSPITAL, 700 Park Boulevard, Zip 24354–3526, Mailing Address: P.O. Box 880, Zip 24354–0880; tel. 540/782–1234; Roger W. Cooper, President (Total facility includes 125 beds in nursing home–type unit) **A**1 9 10 **F**3 6 7 8 19 21 22 23 28 30 32 35 40 42 44 45 49 63 64 65 71
| | | 23 | 10 | 285 | 3407 | 154 | 45259 | 316 | 28462 | 13843 | 545 |

□ SOUTHWESTERN VIRGINIA MENTAL HEALTH INSTITUTE, 502 East Main Street, Zip 24354–3390; tel. 540/783–1200; Gerald E. Deans, Director (Nonreporting) **A**1 9 10 **S** Virginia Department of Mental Health, Richmond, VA
| | | 12 | 22 | 266 | — | — | — | — | — | — | — |

MARTINSVILLE—Independent City County

✶ MEMORIAL HOSPITAL OF MARTINSVILLE AND HENRY COUNTY, 320 Hospital Drive, Zip 24112–1981, Mailing Address: Box 4788, Zip 24115–4788; tel. 540/666–7200; Joseph Roach, Chief Executive Officer **A**1 2 9 10 **F**7 8 10 11 14 15 16 19 21 22 23 28 29 30 31 32 33 37 39 40 41 42 44 45 46 49 52 54 55 56 57 59 60 63 65 67 71 73 **S** Quorum Health Group/Quorum Health Resources, Inc., Brentwood, TN **N** Wake Forest University Baptist Medical Center, Winston–Salem, NC
| | | 23 | 10 | 152 | 6660 | 89 | 177879 | 529 | 51657 | 23049 | 767 |

Hospital, Address, Telephone, Administrator, Approval, Facility, and Physician Codes, Health Care System, Network	Classi-fication Codes		Utilization Data					Expense (thousands) of dollars		
	Control	Service	Staffed Beds	Admissions	Census	Outpatient Visits	Births	Total	Payroll	Personnel

★ American Hospital Association (AHA) membership
□ Joint Commission on Accreditation of Healthcare Organizations (JCAHO) accreditation
+ American Osteopathic Healthcare Association (AOHA) membership
○ American Osteopathic Association (AOA) accreditation
△ Commission on Accreditation of Rehabilitation Facilities (CARF) accreditation
Control codes 61, 63, 64, 71, 72 and 73 indicate hospitals listed by AOHA, but not registered by AHA. For definition of numerical codes, see page A4

NASSAWADOX—Northampton County

Hospital	Control	Service	Staffed Beds	Admissions	Census	Outpatient Visits	Births	Total	Payroll	Personnel
⊞ SHORE MEMORIAL HOSPITAL, (Formerly Northampton–Accomack Memorial Hospital), 9507 Hospital Avenue, Zip 23413–1821, Mailing Address: P.O. Box 17, Zip 23413–0017; tel. 757/442–8000; Richard A. Brvenik, President and Chief Executive Officer (Total facility includes 13 beds in nursing home–type unit) **A**1 5 9 10 **F**3 7 8 12 13 14 15 16 17 18 19 20 21 25 26 27 28 30 31 32 33 34 35 36 37 39 40 41 42 44 45 46 49 51 52 53 54 55 56 57 58 59 61 63 64 65 66 67 68 69 70 71 72 73 74 **P**4 6	23	10	123	5066	88	46586	460	29497	13666	507

NEW KENT—New Kent County

Hospital	Control	Service	Staffed Beds	Admissions	Census	Outpatient Visits	Births	Total	Payroll	Personnel
□ △ CUMBERLAND, A BROWN SCHOOLS HOSPITAL FOR CHILDREN AND ADOLESCENTS, 9407 Cumberland Road, Zip 23124–2029; tel. 804/966–2242; Elizabeth B. Woodard, Chief Executive Officer **A**1 7 10 **F**16 21 48 52 53 64 65 **S** Healthcare America, Inc., Austin, TX	33	56	84	148	78	544	—	12829	6003	212

NEWPORT NEWS—Independent City County

Hospital	Control	Service	Staffed Beds	Admissions	Census	Outpatient Visits	Births	Total	Payroll	Personnel
COLONIAL HOSPITAL See Woodside Hospital										
⊞ MARY IMMACULATE HOSPITAL, (Includes St. Francis Nursing Center), 2 Bernardine Drive, Zip 23602–4499; tel. 757/886–6000; Cynthia B. Farrand, Executive Vice President (Total facility includes 115 beds in nursing home–type unit) **A**1 3 5 9 10 **F**3 7 8 10 12 14 15 16 17 19 20 21 22 25 27 28 29 30 31 32 33 34 35 37 38 39 40 41 42 44 45 49 59 63 64 65 67 71 72 73 74 **P**1 7 8 **S** Bon Secours Health System, Inc., Marriottsville, MD **N** Central Virginia Health Network, Richmond, VA	21	10	225	6381	173	96015	1393	44161	16442	519
⊞ MCDONALD ARMY COMMUNITY HOSPITAL, Jefferson Avenue, Fort Eustis, Zip 23604–5548; tel. 757/314–7501; Colonel George Weightman, Commander (Nonreporting) **A**1 **S** Department of the Army, Office of the Surgeon General, Falls Church, VA	42	10	30	—	—	—	—	—	—	—
NEWPORT NEWS GENERAL HOSPITAL, 5100 Marshall Avenue, Zip 23605–2600, Mailing Address: P.O. Box 5769, Zip 23605–5769; tel. 804/247–7200; Lissa B. Hays, Chief Operating Officer (Nonreporting) **A**5 9 10	23	10	126							
⊞ RIVERSIDE REGIONAL MEDICAL CENTER, (Includes Riverside Psychiatric Institute), 500 J. Clyde Morris Boulevard, Zip 23601–1976; tel. 757/594–2000; Gerald R. Brink, President and Chief Executive Officer **A**1 2 3 5 6 9 10 **F**1 2 3 4 6 7 8 10 11 12 13 14 15 16 17 18 19 20 21 22 23 24 25 26 27 28 29 30 31 32 33 34 35 37 39 40 41 42 43 44 45 46 48 49 51 52 53 54 55 56 57 58 59 60 61 62 63 64 65 66 67 70 71 72 73 74 **P**6 **S** Riverside Health System, Newport News, VA **N** Virginia Health Network, Richmond, VA	23	10	576	17850	246	250755	2332	147606	55140	—
□ WOODSIDE HOSPITAL, (Formerly Colonial Hospital), 17579 Warwick Boulevard, Zip 23603–1343; tel. 757/888–0400; Robert J. Lehmann, Chief Executive Officer (Nonreporting) **A**1 9 10	33	22	68							

NORFOLK—Independent City County

Hospital	Control	Service	Staffed Beds	Admissions	Census	Outpatient Visits	Births	Total	Payroll	Personnel
⊞ BON SECOURS–DEPAUL MEDICAL CENTER, 150 Kingsley Lane, Zip 23505–4650; tel. 757/889–5000; David McCombs, Executive Vice President and Administrator (Nonreporting) **A**1 2 3 5 6 9 10 **S** Bon Secours Health System, Inc., Marriottsville, MD **N** Virginia Health Network, Richmond, VA; DePaul Medical Center Group, Norfolk, VA	21	10	202							
⊞ CHILDREN'S HOSPITAL OF THE KING'S DAUGHTERS, 601 Children's Lane, Zip 23507–1971; tel. 757/668–7700; Robert I. Bonar, Jr., President and Chief Executive Officer **A**1 2 3 5 9 10 **F**10 14 16 19 21 22 31 32 34 35 38 39 41 42 43 44 46 47 49 51 65 67 69 71 **P**1 5 7 8 **N** Virginia Health Network, Richmond, VA	23	50	146	5729	125	121365	—	89033	39942	1338
★ LAKE TAYLOR HOSPITAL, 1309 Kempsville Road, Zip 23502–2286; tel. 757/461–5001; David B. Tate, Jr., President and Chief Executive Officer (Total facility includes 226 beds in nursing home–type unit) **A**9 10 **F**14 20 31 54 57 64 65 73 **S** Riverside Health System, Newport News, VA	16	48	330	467	243	—	—	13752	6850	303
□ NORFOLK COMMUNITY HOSPITAL, 2539 Corprew Avenue, Zip 23504–3994; tel. 757/628–1400; Phillip D. Brooks, President (Nonreporting) **A**1 5 9 10	23	10	103	—	—	—	—	—	—	—
□ NORFOLK PSYCHIATRIC CENTER, 860 Kempsville Road, Zip 23502–3980; tel. 757/461–4565; Diane Carvalho, Administrator (Nonreporting) **A**1 9 10 **S** Magellan Health Services, Atlanta, GA	33	22	77							
★ SENTARA LEIGH HOSPITAL, 830 Kempsville Road, Zip 23502–3981; tel. 757/466–6000; Darleen S. Anderson, R.N., MSN, Site Administrator **A**3 5 9 10 **F**1 2 3 4 6 7 8 9 10 11 12 13 14 15 16 17 18 19 21 22 23 24 25 26 27 28 29 30 31 32 33 34 35 36 37 39 40 41 42 43 44 45 46 48 49 51 52 53 54 55 56 57 58 59 60 61 62 63 64 65 66 67 69 70 71 72 73 74 **P**5 6 7 **S** Sentara Health System, Norfolk, VA **N** Sentara Health System, Norfolk, VA	23	10	217	10597	131	—	1614	67994	27570	926
⊞ SENTARA NORFOLK GENERAL HOSPITAL, 600 Gresham Drive, Zip 23507–1999; tel. 757/668–3000; Mark R. Gavens, President **A**1 2 3 5 6 8 9 10 **F**1 2 3 4 6 7 8 9 10 11 12 13 14 15 16 17 18 19 21 22 23 24 25 26 27 28 29 30 31 32 33 34 35 36 37 39 40 41 42 43 44 45 46 48 49 50 51 52 53 54 55 56 57 58 59 60 61 62 63 64 65 66 67 69 70 71 72 73 74 **P**5 6 7 **S** Sentara Health System, Norfolk, VA **N** Sentara Health System, Norfolk, VA	23	10	495	21645	355	191354	2414	216809	72375	2709

NORTON—Independent City County

Hospital	Control	Service	Staffed Beds	Admissions	Census	Outpatient Visits	Births	Total	Payroll	Personnel
□ NORTON COMMUNITY HOSPITAL, 100 15th Street N.W., Zip 24273–1699; tel. 540/679–9700; Jerry Kincade, Chief Executive Officer **A**1 9 10 **F**7 8 12 14 15 16 17 19 20 21 22 23 24 25 26 28 30 31 32 33 34 35 37 39 40 41 44 45 46 49 51 63 65 66 67 68 71 72 73 74 **P**6 8 **N** Highlands Wellmont Health Network, Inc., Bristol, TN	23	10	51	4264	48	55253	429	23429	9685	283

Hospital, Address, Telephone, Administrator, Approval, Facility, and Physician Codes, Health Care System, Network	Classi-fication Codes		Utilization Data					Expense (thousands) of dollars		
	Control	Service	Staffed Beds	Admissions	Census	Outpatient Visits	Births	Total	Payroll	Personnel

American Hospital Association (AHA) membership
Joint Commission on Accreditation of Healthcare Organizations (JCAHO) accreditation
American Osteopathic Healthcare Association (AOHA) membership
American Osteopathic Association (AOA) accreditation
Commission on Accreditation of Rehabilitation Facilities (CARF) accreditation
Control codes 61, 63, 64, 71, 72 and 73 indicate hospitals listed by AOHA, but not registered by AHA. For definition of numerical codes, see page A4

★ ST. MARY'S HOSPITAL, Third Street N.E., Zip 24273–1131, Mailing Address: P.O. Box 620, Zip 24273–0620; tel. 540/679–9100; Gary L. DelForge, Administrator (Total facility includes 66 beds in nursing home–type unit) **A**9 10 **F**3 7 8 12 13 15 16 19 20 21 22 25 26 28 29 30 32 34 35 37 40 41 42 44 45 46 52 54 55 56 57 58 63 64 65 67 71 73	23	10	133	2559	69	42303	93	18872	7027	343
PEARISBURG—Giles County										
✠ CARILION GILES MEMORIAL HOSPITAL, 1 Taylor Avenue, Zip 24134–1932; tel. 540/921–6000; Morris D. Reece, Administrator (Total facility includes 21 beds in nursing home–type unit) **A**1 9 10 **F**8 12 14 15 16 17 19 21 22 27 28 29 30 32 33 34 35 37 39 41 42 44 45 46 49 50 51 53 54 55 56 57 58 59 60 61 62 63 64 65 66 67 68 69 71 72 73 74 **P**1 2 3 4 5 6 7 8 **S** Carilion Health System, Roanoke, VA **N** Carilion Health System, Roanoke, VA	23	10	53	1357	37	17334	—	12568	6276	237
PENNINGTON GAP—Lee County										
✠ LEE COUNTY COMMUNITY HOSPITAL, West Morgan Avenue, Zip 24277, Mailing Address: P.O. Box 70, Zip 24277–0070; tel. 540/546–1440; James L. Davis, Chief Executive Officer (Nonreporting) **A**1 9 10 **N** Mountain States Healthcare Network, Johnson City, TN	23	10	80	—	—	—	—	—	—	—
PETERSBURG—Independent City County										
□ CENTRAL STATE HOSPITAL, 26317 West Washington Street, Zip 23803, Mailing Address: P.O. Box 4030, Zip 23803–4030; tel. 804/524–7000; James C. Bumpas, Director (Nonreporting) **A**1 5 9 10	12	22	526	—	—	—	—	—	—	—
✠ POPLAR SPRINGS HOSPITAL, 350 Poplar Drive, Zip 23805–4657; tel. 804/733–6874; Anthony J. Vadella, Chief Executive Officer (Nonreporting) **A**1 9 10 **N** Preferred Care of Richmond, Richmond, VA	33	22	100	—	—	—	—	—	—	—
✠ SOUTHSIDE REGIONAL MEDICAL CENTER, 801 South Adams Street, Zip 23803–5133; tel. 804/862–5000; David S. Dunham, President (Total facility includes 20 beds in nursing home–type unit) **A**1 6 9 10 **F**7 8 10 12 14 15 16 19 20 21 22 23 25 28 29 30 32 34 35 37 39 40 41 42 44 45 46 49 52 53 54 55 56 57 59 60 63 64 65 67 71 72 73 **P**7 8 **S** Quorum Health Group/Quorum Health Resources, Inc., Brentwood, TN **N** Central Virginia Health Network, Richmond, VA	16	10	267	11629	174	151852	1279	80606	38338	1335
PORTSMOUTH—Independent City County										
✠ △ MARYVIEW HOSPITAL, (Formerly Bon Secours–Maryview Medical Center), 3636 High Street, Zip 23707–3236; tel. 757/398–2200; Wayne Jones, Executive Vice President and Administrator (Total facility includes 120 beds in nursing home–type unit) **A**1 2 3 5 7 9 10 **F**3 8 10 11 14 15 16 17 18 19 21 22 23 25 30 32 33 34 35 37 39 40 41 42 44 49 52 53 54 55 56 58 59 60 63 65 66 67 71 72 73 **P**1 **S** Bon Secours Health System, Inc., Marriottsville, MD **N** Virginia Health Network, Richmond, VA	23	10	321	13556	190	50411	753	96327	40936	1391
✠ NAVAL MEDICAL CENTER, 620 John Paul Jones Circle, Zip 23708–2197; tel. 757/953–7424; Rear Admiral Marion Balsam, MC, USN, Commander **A**1 2 3 5 **F**3 4 5 8 10 11 12 14 15 16 19 20 21 23 24 25 28 29 30 31 34 35 37 38 39 40 41 42 44 45 46 49 50 51 52 54 56 58 59 60 61 63 65 66 71 72 73 74 **S** Department of Navy, Washington, DC	43	10	310	25453	207	1832797	2497	—	—	—
PULASKI—Independent City County										
✠ PULASKI COMMUNITY HOSPITAL, (Formerly Columbia Pulaski Community Hospital), 2400 Lee Highway, Zip 24301–0759, Mailing Address: P.O. Box 759, Zip 24301–0759; tel. 540/994–8100; Jack Nunley, Chief Executive Officer (Total facility includes 12 beds in nursing home–type unit) **A**1 9 10 **F**7 8 12 14 15 16 19 21 22 27 28 30 32 35 37 40 41 42 44 45 56 60 63 64 65 70 71 73 **P**8 **S** Columbia/HCA Healthcare Corporation, Nashville, TN	33	10	62	3498	48	50747	101	21394	9673	372
RADFORD—Independent City County										
✠ △ CARILION RADFORD COMMUNITY HOSPITAL, 700 Randolph Street, Zip 24141–2430; tel. 540/731–2000; Virginia Ousley, Director (Total facility includes 27 beds in nursing home–type unit) **A**1 7 9 10 **F**7 8 10 13 15 16 17 19 20 22 23 24 26 27 28 29 30 31 32 34 35 36 37 39 40 41 42 44 45 49 51 53 54 55 56 57 58 59 63 64 65 67 70 71 72 73 74 **P**8 **S** Carilion Health System, Roanoke, VA **N** Carilion Health System, Roanoke, VA	23	10	122	4703	73	52985	759	40169	15719	—
✠ CARILION SAINT ALBANS HOSPITAL, Route 11, Lee Highway, Zip 24143, Mailing Address: P.O. Box 3608, Zip 24143–3608; tel. 540/639–2481; Janet McKinney Crawford, Administrator **A**1 9 10 **F**3 12 15 16 52 53 54 56 57 58 59 65 73 **P**8 **S** Carilion Health System, Roanoke, VA **N** Carilion Health System, Roanoke, VA	23	22	66	1671	27	10330	—	9270	4589	150
RESTON—Fairfax County										
✠ COLUMBIA RESTON HOSPITAL CENTER, 1850 Town Center Parkway, Zip 20190–3298; tel. 703/689–9023; William A. Adams, President and Chief Executive Officer **A**1 2 5 9 10 **F**7 8 10 12 14 15 16 19 22 23 24 30 32 35 37 39 40 41 42 44 49 51 65 66 73 **P**1 4 5 **S** Columbia/HCA Healthcare Corporation, Nashville, TN	33	10	121	7894	83	85585	1964	46491	21744	583
RICHLANDS—Tazewell County										
✠ COLUMBIA CLINCH VALLEY MEDICAL CENTER, 2949 West Front Street, Zip 24641–2099; tel. 540/596–6000; James W. Thweatt, Chief Executive Officer (Total facility includes 22 beds in nursing home–type unit) **A**1 9 10 **F**3 7 8 10 11 12 14 15 17 19 20 21 22 23 28 29 30 31 32 34 35 37 39 40 41 42 44 45 46 48 58 60 63 64 65 67 71 73 **S** Columbia/HCA Healthcare Corporation, Nashville, TN **N** Mountain States Healthcare Network, Johnson City, TN	33	10	200	6451	77	30610	575	35366	11394	460
RICHMOND—Independent City County										
✠ BON SECOURS ST. MARY'S HOSPITAL, (Formerly St. Mary's Hospital), 5801 Bremo Road, Zip 23226–1900; tel. 804/285–2011; Ann E. Honeycutt, Executive Vice President and Administrator (Nonreporting) **A**1 2 3 5 9 10 **S** Bon Secours Health System, Inc., Marriottsville, MD **N** Virginia Health Network, Richmond, VA; Central Virginia Health Network, Richmond, VA	21	10	391	—	—	—	—	—	—	—

Hospital, Address, Telephone, Administrator, Approval, Facility, and Physician Codes, Health Care System, Network	Classi-fication Codes		Utilization Data					Expense (thousands) of dollars		
	Control	Service	Staffed Beds	Admissions	Census	Outpatient Visits	Births	Total	Payroll	Personnel

★ American Hospital Association (AHA) membership
□ Joint Commission on Accreditation of Healthcare Organizations (JCAHO) accreditation
+ American Osteopathic Healthcare Association (AOHA) membership
○ American Osteopathic Association (AOA) accreditation
△ Commission on Accreditation of Rehabilitation Facilities (CARF) accreditation
Control codes 61, 63, 64, 71, 72 and 73 indicate hospitals listed by AOHA, but not registered by AHA. For definition of numerical codes, see page A4

Hospital	Control	Service	Staffed Beds	Admissions	Census	Outpatient Visits	Births	Total	Payroll	Personnel
⊠ BON SECOURS–RICHMOND COMMUNITY HOSPITAL, 1500 North 28th Street, Zip 23223–5396, Mailing Address: Box 27184, Zip 23261–7184; tel. 804/225–1700; Samuel F. Lillard, Executive Vice President and Administrator (Total facility includes 20 beds in nursing home–type unit) **A**1 9 10 **F**2 4 7 8 10 11 12 14 15 17 19 21 22 25 26 28 29 30 31 32 33 34 35 37 38 39 40 41 42 43 44 46 47 49 52 55 56 60 61 62 63 64 65 71 73 **P**1 6 **S** Bon Secours Health System, Inc., Marriottsville, MD **N** Virginia Health Network, Richmond, VA; Central Virginia Health Network, Richmond, VA	23	10	232	7380	131	51171	—	79742	31560	1184
⊠ BON SECOURS–STUART CIRCLE, 413 Stuart Circle, Zip 23220–3799; tel. 804/358–7051; Edward Gerardo, Interim Executive Vice President and Administrator (Nonreporting) **A**1 9 10 **S** Bon Secours Health System, Inc., Marriottsville, MD **N** Virginia Health Network, Richmond, VA; Central Virginia Health Network, Richmond, VA	21	10	158	—	—	—	—	—	—	—
□ CAPITOL MEDICAL CENTER, (Formerly Metropolitan Hospital), 701 West Grace Street, Zip 23220–4191; tel. 804/775–4100; Priscilla J. Shuler, Chief Executive Officer **A**1 9 10 **F**8 15 16 17 19 22 28 30 32 34 35 37 41 44 52 56 57 65 66 71 73 **P**7 **S** Paracelsus Healthcare Corporation, Houston, TX	32	10	104	3550	78	203828	0	35237	18033	476
□ CHARTER WESTBROOK BEHAVIORAL HEALTH SYSTEM, 1500 Westbrook Avenue, Zip 23227–3399; tel. 804/266–9671; Stephen P. Fahey, Administrator (Nonreporting) **A**1 9 10 **S** Magellan Health Services, Atlanta, GA **N** Virginia Health Network, Richmond, VA	33	22	210	—	—	—	—	—	—	—
⊠ △ CHILDREN'S HOSPITAL, 2924 Brook Road, Zip 23220–1298; tel. 804/321–7474; Leslie G. Wyatt, Administrator **A**1 3 5 7 9 **F**12 14 20 27 34 39 44 46 48 49 53 58 65 67 71	23	50	36	445	9	27621	—	13151	6304	181
⊠ △ CHIPPENHAM AND JOHNSTON–WILLIS HOSPITALS, (Includes Chippenham Medical Center, 7101 Jahnke Road, Zip 23225; tel. 804/320–3911; Johnston–Willis Hospital, 1401 Johnston–Willis Drive, Zip 23235; tel. 804/330–2000), 7101 Jahnke Road, Zip 23225–4044; tel. 804/320–3911; Marilyn B. Tavenner, Chief Executive Officer **A**1 2 3 5 7 9 10 **F**1 3 4 7 8 10 11 12 13 14 15 16 17 18 19 20 21 22 23 24 26 27 28 29 30 31 32 33 34 35 37 39 40 41 42 43 44 45 46 49 51 53 54 55 56 57 58 59 60 61 63 64 65 66 67 71 73 74 **S** Columbia/HCA Healthcare Corporation, Nashville, TN **N** Preferred Care of Richmond, Richmond, VA	33	10	487	27369	410	279761	3457	—	—	2709
□ △ HEALTHSOUTH MEDICAL CENTER, 7700 East Parham Road, Zip 23294–4301; tel. 804/747–5600; Charles A. Stark, CHE, Administrator, Chief Executive and Regional Vice President **A**1 5 7 10 **F**5 8 10 12 14 15 16 17 19 20 21 22 23 25 26 27 28 29 30 31 32 33 34 35 37 39 41 42 44 45 46 48 49 51 54 55 56 57 58 63 65 66 67 71 73 74 **S** HEALTHSOUTH Corporation, Birmingham, AL	33	10	147	4163	72	25352	—	40030	15018	425
□ HEALTHSOUTH REHABILITATION HOSPITAL OF VIRGINIA, 5700 Fitzhugh Avenue, Zip 23226–1800; tel. 804/288–5700; Jeff Ruskan, Administrator (Nonreporting) **A**1 10 **S** HEALTHSOUTH Corporation, Birmingham, AL	33	46	40	—	—	—	—	—	—	—
⊠ HENRICO DOCTORS' HOSPITAL, 1602 Skipwith Road, Zip 23229–5298; tel. 804/289–4500; Patrick W. Farrell, Chief Executive Officer **A**1 2 9 10 **F**1 2 3 4 7 8 10 11 12 14 15 16 17 19 21 22 23 24 25 26 28 29 30 32 33 34 35 36 37 38 39 40 41 42 43 44 46 47 48 49 52 53 54 55 56 57 58 59 60 61 63 64 65 66 67 69 71 72 73 74 **P**5 6 7 8 **S** Columbia/HCA Healthcare Corporation, Nashville, TN **N** Preferred Care of Richmond, Richmond, VA	33	10	340	14588	208	121772	3028	109090	46053	—
⊠ HUNTER HOLMES MCGUIRE VETERANS AFFAIRS MEDICAL CENTER, 1201 Broad Rock Boulevard, Zip 23249–0002; tel. 804/675–5000; James W. Dudley, Director (Total facility includes 80 beds in nursing home–type unit) (Nonreporting) **A**1 2 3 5 8 **S** Department of Veterans Affairs, Washington, DC	45	10	616	—	—	—	—	—	—	—
JOHNSTON–WILLIS HOSPITAL See Chippenham and Johnston–Willis Hospitals										
⊠ △ MEDICAL COLLEGE OF VIRGINIA HOSPITALS, VIRGINIA COMMONWEALTH UNIVERSITY, 401 North 12th Street, Zip 23219, Mailing Address: P.O. Box 980510, Zip 23298–0510; tel. 804/828–9000; Carl R. Fischer, Associate Vice President and Chief Executive Officer **A**1 2 3 5 7 8 9 10 **F**3 4 7 8 9 10 11 12 14 15 16 17 18 19 20 21 22 23 25 26 27 29 30 31 32 34 35 37 38 40 41 42 43 44 45 46 47 48 49 51 52 53 54 56 57 58 59 60 61 63 65 66 68 69 70 71 72 73 74 **P**4 **N** Virginia Health Network, Richmond, VA	16	10	702	28490	507	307306	2361	411738	183821	4589
⊠ MEMORIAL REGIONAL MEDICAL CENTER, 1300 Westwood Avenue, Zip 23227–4699, Mailing Address: P.O. Box 26783, Zip 23261–6783; tel. 804/264–6436; Michael Robinson, Executive Vice President and Administrator (Total facility includes 20 beds in nursing home–type unit) (Nonreporting) **A**1 2 5 6 9 10 **S** Bon Secours Health System, Inc., Marriottsville, MD **N** Virginia Health Network, Richmond, VA; Central Virginia Health Network, Richmond, VA	23	10	272	—	—	—	—	—	—	—
METROPOLITAN HOSPITAL See Capitol Medical Center										
⊠ RETREAT HOSPITAL, 2621 Grove Avenue, Zip 23220–4308; tel. 804/254–5100; Paul L. Baldwin, Chief Operating Officer (Nonreporting) **A**1 2 9 10 **S** Columbia/HCA Healthcare Corporation, Nashville, TN **N** Preferred Care of Richmond, Richmond, VA	33	10	146	—	—	—	—	—	—	—
⊠ RICHMOND EYE AND EAR HOSPITAL, 1001 East Marshall Street, Zip 23219–1993; tel. 804/775–4500; William E. Holmes, Chief Executive Officer (Nonreporting) **A**1 9 10 **S** Quorum Health Group/Quorum Health Resources, Inc., Brentwood, TN	23	45	32	—	—	—	—	—	—	—
□ △ SHELTERING ARMS REHABILITATION HOSPITAL, 1311 Palmyra Avenue, Zip 23227–4418; tel. 804/342–4100; Michael J. McDonnell, Interim Chief Executive Officer **A**1 7 9 10 **F**12 17 25 34 46 48 49 65 66 73 **P**6 **N** Virginia Health Network, Richmond, VA; Central Virginia Health Network, Richmond, VA	23	46	40	965	34	54549	—	21517	13481	310
ST. MARY'S HOSPITAL See Bon Secours St. Mary's Hospital										

Hospital, Address, Telephone, Administrator, Approval, Facility, and Physician Codes, Health Care System, Network	Classi-fication Codes		Utilization Data					Expense (thousands) of dollars		
★ American Hospital Association (AHA) membership ☐ Joint Commission on Accreditation of Healthcare Organizations (JCAHO) accreditation + American Osteopathic Healthcare Association (AOHA) membership ○ American Osteopathic Association (AOA) accreditation △ Commission on Accreditation of Rehabilitation Facilities (CARF) accreditation Control codes 61, 63, 64, 71, 72 and 73 indicate hospitals listed by AOHA, but not registered by AHA. For definition of numerical codes, see page A4	Control	Service	Staffed Beds	Admissions	Census	Outpatient Visits	Births	Total	Payroll	Personnel
☐ VALUEMARK WEST END BEHAVIORAL HEALTHCARE SYSTEM, 12800 West Creek Parkway, Zip 23238–1116; tel. 804/784–2200; James D. McBeath, Chief Executive Officer (Nonreporting) **A**1 9 10 **S** ValueMark Healthcare Systems, Inc., Atlanta, GA	33	22	84	—	—	—	—	—	—	—
ROANOKE—Independent City County										
★△ CARILION MEDICAL CENTER, (Formerly Carilion Roanoke Memorial Hospital), (Includes Carilion Roanoke Community Hospital, 101 Elm Avenue S.E., Zip 24013–2230, Mailing Address: P.O. Box 12946, Zip 24029–2946; tel. 540/985–8000; Roanoke Memorial Rehabilitation Center, South Jefferson and McClanahan Streets, Mailing Address: P.O. Box 13367, Zip 24033), Belleview at Jefferson Street, Zip 24014, Mailing Address: P.O. Box 13367, Zip 24033–3367; tel. 540/981–7000; Lucas A. Snipes, FACHE, Director **A**1 2 3 5 6 7 9 10 **F**2 3 4 7 8 10 11 12 13 14 15 16 17 18 19 20 21 22 23 24 25 26 27 28 29 30 31 32 33 34 35 37 38 39 40 41 42 43 44 45 46 47 48 49 51 52 53 54 55 56 57 58 59 60 61 63 64 65 66 67 68 70 71 72 73 74 **P**2 8 **S** Carilion Health System, Roanoke, VA **N** Carilion Health System, Roanoke, VA	23	10	646	28990	451	—	2761	310555	105000	3599
ROCKY MOUNT—Franklin County										
★ CARILION FRANKLIN MEMORIAL HOSPITAL, 180 Floyd Avenue, Zip 24151–1389; tel. 540/483–5277; Matthew J. Perry, Director **A**1 9 10 **F**7 8 11 15 16 17 19 22 30 32 33 39 40 41 42 44 49 65 67 71 73 **P**2 7 8 **S** Carilion Health System, Roanoke, VA **N** Carilion Health System, Roanoke, VA	23	10	37	2454	20	23200	250	14986	6137	229
SALEM—Independent City County										
COLUMBIA LEWIS–GALE MEDICAL CENTER See Lewis–Gale Medical Center										
★△ LEWIS–GALE MEDICAL CENTER, (Formerly Columbia Lewis–Gale Medical Center), 1900 Electric Road, Zip 24153–7494; tel. 540/776–4000; William B. Downey, Administrator (Nonreporting) **A**1 2 7 9 10 **S** Columbia/HCA Healthcare Corporation, Nashville, TN	33	10	521	—	—	—	—	—	—	—
LEWIS–GALE PSYCHIATRIC CENTER See Lewis–Gale Pavilion										
MOUNT REGIS CENTER, 405 Kimball Avenue, Zip 24153–6299; tel. 703/389–4761; Gail S. Basham, Chief Operating Officer (Nonreporting) **S** Pioneer Healthcare, Peabody, MA	23	82	25	—	—	—	—	—	—	—
★ VETERANS AFFAIRS MEDICAL CENTER, 1970 Roanoke Boulevard, Zip 24153; tel. 540/982–2463; Stephen L. Lemons, Ed.D., Director (Total facility includes 90 beds in nursing home–type unit) **A**1 2 3 5 8 **F**1 2 3 4 8 10 12 14 15 16 17 19 20 21 22 23 25 26 27 28 29 30 31 32 34 35 37 39 41 42 43 44 45 46 49 51 52 54 55 56 57 58 59 60 63 64 65 67 69 71 73 74 **S** Department of Veterans Affairs, Washington, DC	45	10	313	5575	297	214304	—	102491	56773	1292
SOUTH BOSTON—Independent City County										
★ HALIFAX REGIONAL HOSPITAL, 2204 Wilborn Avenue, Zip 24592–1638; tel. 804/575–3100; Chris A. Lumsden, Administrator (Total facility includes 19 beds in nursing home–type unit) **A**1 9 10 **F**7 8 10 12 14 15 16 17 19 20 21 28 29 30 31 32 34 35 37 40 41 44 45 46 49 59 63 64 65 71 73 **P**7 8 **S** Quorum Health Group/Quorum Health Resources, Inc., Brentwood, TN	23	10	157	5746	259	47381	573	43897	17756	677
SOUTH HILL—Mecklenburg County										
★ COMMUNITY MEMORIAL HEALTHCENTER, 125 Buena Vista Circle, Zip 23970–0090, Mailing Address: P.O. Box 90, Zip 23970–0090; tel. 804/447–3151; R. Michael Berryman, President (Total facility includes 161 beds in nursing home–type unit) **A**1 9 10 **F**2 3 7 8 11 12 13 14 15 16 17 18 19 21 22 24 26 27 28 30 31 32 33 34 36 39 40 41 42 44 45 46 49 52 54 56 57 58 59 63 64 65 66 67 71 72 73 **P**8 **N** Virginia Health Network, Richmond, VA; Central Virginia Health Network, Richmond, VA	23	10	284	5623	231	55069	250	36634	16472	603
STAUNTON—Independent City County										
DE JARNETTE CENTER, 1355 Richmond Road, Zip 24401–1091, Mailing Address: Box 2309, Zip 24402–2309; tel. 540/332–2100; Andrea C. Newsome, FACHE, Director (Nonreporting) **A**3 9 **S** Virginia Department of Mental Health, Richmond, VA	12	59	60	—	—	—	—	—	—	—
☐ WESTERN STATE HOSPITAL, 1301 Richmond Avenue, Zip 24401–9146, Mailing Address: P.O. Box 2500, Zip 24402–2500; tel. 540/332–8000; Lynwood F. Harding, Director **A**1 9 10 **F**2 4 5 8 9 10 11 12 19 20 21 22 23 26 27 30 31 35 37 39 40 41 42 43 44 46 48 49 50 52 57 60 63 65 67 69 71 73 **S** Virginia Department of Mental Health, Richmond, VA	12	22	432	859	422	0	—	39229	25295	882
STUART—Patrick County										
★ PATRICK COMMUNITY MEMORIAL HOSPITAL, (Formerly R J Reynolds–Patrick County Memorial Hospital), Mailing Address: Route 2, Box 71, Zip 24171–9512; tel. 540/694–3151; John M. Faulkner, FACHE, President and Chief Executive Officer (Total facility includes 25 beds in nursing home–type unit) **A**1 9 10 **F**7 8 14 15 16 17 19 22 28 30 32 33 36 37 39 40 41 44 46 49 64 65 71 73 **N** Wake Forest University Baptist Medical Center, Winston–Salem, NC	23	10	59	1166	35	38132	104	9234	4648	219
SUFFOLK—Independent City County										
★ LOUISE OBICI MEMORIAL HOSPITAL, 1900 North Main Street, Zip 23434–4323, Mailing Address: P.O. Box 1100, Zip 23439–1100; tel. 757/934–4000; William C. Giermak, President and Chief Executive Officer **A**1 2 5 6 9 10 **F**7 8 10 15 16 17 19 22 27 28 30 31 32 34 35 36 37 39 40 41 42 44 45 46 49 52 54 55 59 60 65 67 71 73 74 **N** Virginia Health Network, Richmond, VA	23	10	160	7313	104	86452	888	52029	28831	793
TAPPAHANNOCK—Essex County										
☐ RIVERSIDE TAPPAHANNOCK HOSPITAL, Mailing Address: Route 2, Box 612, Zip 22560; tel. 804/443–3311; Elizabeth J. Martin, Vice President and Administrator (Total facility includes 25 beds in nursing home–type unit) **A**1 9 10 **F**8 10 12 14 15 16 17 19 21 22 23 24 27 28 29 30 32 34 35 37 39 41 44 45 46 48 49 51 64 65 66 67 71 72 73 **P**6 **S** Riverside Health System, Newport News, VA **N** Virginia Health Network, Richmond, VA	23	10	100	1956	47	44233	—	10601	6094	—

Hospital, Address, Telephone, Administrator, Approval, Facility, and Physician Codes, Health Care System, Network	Classi-fication Codes		Utilization Data					Expense (thousands) of dollars		
★ American Hospital Association (AHA) membership ☐ Joint Commission on Accreditation of Healthcare Organizations (JCAHO) accreditation + American Osteopathic Healthcare Association (AOHA) membership ○ American Osteopathic Association (AOA) accreditation △ Commission on Accreditation of Rehabilitation Facilities (CARF) accreditation Control codes 61, 63, 64, 71, 72 and 73 indicate hospitals listed by AOHA, but not registered by AHA. For definition of numerical codes, see page A4	Control	Service	Staffed Beds	Admissions	Census	Outpatient Visits	Births	Total	Payroll	Personnel

TAZEWELL—Tazewell County

★ TAZEWELL COMMUNITY HOSPITAL, 141 Ben Bolt Avenue, Zip 24651–9700; tel. 540/988–2506; Craig B. James, Administrator **A**9 10 **F**8 15 19 22 30 32 34 35 44 46 71 73 **S** Carilion Health System, Roanoke, VA

| | 23 | 10 | 42 | 1240 | 15 | 23042 | 0 | 8034 | 3284 | 143 |

VIRGINIA BEACH—Independent City County

✖ SENTARA BAYSIDE HOSPITAL, 800 Independence Boulevard, Zip 23455–6076; tel. 757/363–6100; Virginia Bogue, Site Administrator **A**1 5 9 10 **F**1 2 3 4 6 7 8 9 10 11 12 13 14 15 16 17 18 19 21 22 23 24 25 26 27 28 29 30 31 32 33 34 35 36 37 39 40 41 42 43 44 45 46 48 49 51 52 53 54 55 56 57 58 59 60 61 62 63 64 65 66 67 69 70 71 72 73 74 **P**5 6 7 **S** Sentara Health System, Norfolk, VA **N** Sentara Health System, Norfolk, VA

| | 23 | 10 | 116 | 5947 | 70 | — | 1176 | 39842 | 12591 | 496 |

✖ VIRGINIA BEACH GENERAL HOSPITAL, 1060 First Colonial Road, Zip 23454–9000; tel. 757/481–8000; Robert L. Graves, Administrator **A**1 2 3 5 9 10 **F**4 7 8 10 11 12 14 15 16 17 18 19 21 22 23 24 25 28 29 30 31 32 33 34 35 37 38 39 40 41 42 43 44 45 49 56 60 61 63 64 65 66 67 69 70 71 72 73 **P**6 7 8 **N** Tidewater Health Care, Virginia Beach, VA; Virginia Health Network, Richmond, VA

| | 23 | 10 | 274 | 11895 | 155 | 155282 | 2007 | 90600 | 37765 | 1081 |

WARRENTON—Fauquier County

✖ FAUQUIER HOSPITAL, 500 Hospital Drive, Zip 20186–3099; tel. 540/347–2550; Rodger H. Baker, President and Chief Executive Officer **A**1 9 10 **F**6 7 8 12 14 15 16 17 19 21 22 28 29 30 32 33 34 35 37 39 40 41 42 44 45 46 49 63 65 67 71 73 **P**6

| | 23 | 10 | 83 | 4302 | 45 | 51642 | 484 | 35625 | 16914 | 553 |

WILLIAMSBURG—Independent City County

☐ EASTERN STATE HOSPITAL, Mailing Address: P.O. Box 8791, Zip 23187–8791; tel. 757/253–5161; John M. Favret, Director (Total facility includes 310 beds in nursing home–type unit) (Nonreporting) **A**1 5 9 10 **S** Virginia Department of Mental Health, Richmond, VA

| | 12 | 22 | 727 | — | — | — | — | — | — | — |

✖ WILLIAMSBURG COMMUNITY HOSPITAL, 301 Monticello Avenue, Zip 23187–8700, Mailing Address: Box 8700, Zip 23187–8700; tel. 757/259–6000; Les A. Donahue, President and Chief Executive Officer **A**1 5 9 10 **F**3 7 8 9 10 12 14 15 16 17 18 19 20 21 22 23 25 26 27 28 29 30 32 33 34 35 36 37 38 39 40 41 42 44 45 47 48 49 51 54 55 56 58 60 63 65 66 67 71 72 73 74 **P**4 **S** Sentara Health System, Norfolk, VA **N** Virginia Health Network, Richmond, VA; Sentara Health System, Norfolk, VA

| | 23 | 10 | 119 | 5995 | 60 | 112666 | 829 | 50126 | 20676 | 714 |

WINCHESTER—Independent City County

✖ WINCHESTER MEDICAL CENTER, 1840 Amherst Street, Zip 22601–2540, Mailing Address: P.O. Box 3340, Zip 22604–3340; tel. 540/722–8000; George B. Caley, President **A**1 2 9 10 **F**4 7 8 10 11 12 14 15 16 19 21 23 28 29 30 32 33 35 36 37 38 39 40 41 42 43 44 46 48 49 52 53 56 58 59 60 63 65 67 69 71 72 73 **P**5 7 8 **S** Valley Health System, Winchester, VA **N** Valley Health System, Winchester, VA

| | 23 | 10 | 392 | 20457 | 279 | 183516 | 1747 | 140284 | 62808 | 1677 |

WOODBRIDGE—Prince William County

✖ POTOMAC HOSPITAL, 2300 Opitz Boulevard, Zip 22191–3399; tel. 703/670–1313; William Mason Moss, President **A**1 2 9 10 **F**6 7 8 10 11 12 14 15 16 17 19 21 22 28 29 30 31 32 33 34 35 37 38 39 40 41 42 44 46 49 51 52 54 55 56 57 58 59 60 62 63 65 67 71 73 74 **P**5

| | 23 | 10 | 153 | 7533 | 76 | 105333 | 1779 | 59666 | 26639 | 649 |

WOODSTOCK—Shenandoah County

✖ SHENANDOAH MEMORIAL HOSPITAL, 759 South Main Street, Zip 22664–1127, Mailing Address: P.O. Box 508, Zip 22664–0508; tel. 540/459–4021; Floyd Heater, Chief Executive Officer (Total facility includes 34 beds in nursing home–type unit) **A**1 9 10 **F**3 4 7 8 10 12 14 15 16 17 19 21 22 23 27 28 30 32 34 35 37 39 40 41 44 45 46 49 50 52 53 54 55 56 57 58 59 60 63 64 65 66 68 69 70 71 73

| | 23 | 10 | 129 | 2586 | 65 | 123719 | 174 | 20336 | 8820 | 356 |

WYTHEVILLE—Wythe County

★ WYTHE COUNTY COMMUNITY HOSPITAL, 600 West Ridge Road, Zip 24382–1099; tel. 540/228–0200; Larry H. Chewning, III, Chief Executive Officer (Total facility includes 8 beds in nursing home–type unit) **A**2 9 10 **F**7 8 11 12 13 14 15 16 17 19 21 22 23 25 26 27 28 29 30 32 33 34 35 37 39 40 41 42 44 45 46 48 49 52 53 54 55 56 58 61 64 65 66 67 71 73 74 **S** Carilion Health System, Roanoke, VA

| | 23 | 10 | 82 | 2632 | 32 | 46913 | 245 | 19950 | 9055 | 338 |

WASHINGTON

Resident population 5,610 (in thousands)
Resident population in metro areas 82.9%
Birth rate per 1,000 population 14.5
65 years and over 11.6%
Percent of persons without health insurance 13.5%

Hospital, Address, Telephone, Administrator, Approval, Facility, and Physician Codes, Health Care System, Network	Classification Codes		Utilization Data					Expense (thousands) of dollars		
	Control	Service	Staffed Beds	Admissions	Census	Outpatient Visits	Births	Total	Payroll	Personnel

★ American Hospital Association (AHA) membership
□ Joint Commission on Accreditation of Healthcare Organizations (JCAHO) accreditation
+ American Osteopathic Healthcare Association (AOHA) membership
○ American Osteopathic Association (AOA) accreditation
△ Commission on Accreditation of Rehabilitation Facilities (CARF) accreditation
Control codes 61, 63, 64, 71, 72 and 73 indicate hospitals listed by AOHA, but not registered by AHA. For definition of numerical codes, see page A4

	Control	Service	Staffed Beds	Admissions	Census	Outpatient Visits	Births	Total	Payroll	Personnel
ABERDEEN—Grays Harbor County										
⊠ GRAYS HARBOR COMMUNITY HOSPITAL, 915 Anderson Drive, Zip 98520; tel. 360/532–8330; Michael J. Madden, Administrator (Total facility includes 60 beds in nursing home–type unit) **A**1 9 10 **F**2 3 7 12 16 19 21 22 25 32 35 37 40 42 44 45 49 54 56 64 65 70 71 73 **P**8	23	10	172	4384	104	47987	523	39991	18979	481
ANACORTES—Skagit County										
★ ISLAND HOSPITAL, 1211 24th Street, Zip 98221–2590; tel. 360/299–1300; C. Philip Sandifer, Administrator **A**2 9 10 **F**7 8 12 14 15 16 19 21 22 24 28 29 30 31 32 34 35 37 39 40 42 44 45 46 49 51 65 67 68 70 71 73 74 **P**8	16	10	43	2037	19	49268	253	25069	12755	299
ARLINGTON—Snohomish County										
⊠ CASCADE VALLEY HOSPITAL, NORTH SNOHOMISH COUNTY HEALTH SYSTEM, 330 South Stillaguamish Avenue, Zip 98223–1642; tel. 360/435–2133; Robert D. Campbell, Jr., Administrator **A**1 9 10 **F**7 8 12 15 19 22 34 35 37 40 42 44 71 74 **P**5 7 8	16	10	48	1794	15	30433	382	18993	8533	289
AUBURN—King County										
□ AUBURN REGIONAL MEDICAL CENTER, (Formerly Auburn General Hospital), 202 North Division, Plaza One, Zip 98001–4908; tel. 253/833–7711; Michael M. Gherardini, Chief Executive Officer and Managing Director (Nonreporting) **A**1 2 9 10 **S** Universal Health Services, Inc., King of Prussia, PA	33	10	100	—	—	—	—	—	—	—
BELLEVUE—King County										
⊠ OVERLAKE HOSPITAL MEDICAL CENTER, 1035 116th Avenue N.E., Zip 98004; tel. 425/688–5000; Kenneth D. Graham, President and Chief Executive Officer **A**1 2 9 10 **F**4 7 10 11 12 14 15 16 17 19 21 22 24 25 26 34 35 37 39 40 41 42 43 44 46 48 49 52 53 54 56 57 59 60 65 67 70 71 72 73 74 **P**6	23	10	233	13838	145	98975	3015	109636	49800	1271
BELLINGHAM—Whatcom County										
⊠ ST. JOSEPH HOSPITAL, 2901 Squalicum Parkway, Zip 98225–1898; tel. 360/734–5400; Nancy J. Bitting, Chief Executive Officer **A**1 2 9 10 **F**1 2 3 4 7 10 11 16 17 19 21 22 27 28 35 37 40 41 42 43 44 48 49 52 54 57 60 65 66 70 71 72 73 **S** PeaceHealth, Bellevue, WA **N** PeaceHealth, Bellevue, WA; Dominican Network, Spokane, WA	23	10	206	11019	119	—	1801	93159	40910	1088
BREMERTON—Kitsap County										
⊠ HARRISON MEMORIAL HOSPITAL, 2520 Cherry Street, Zip 98310–4270; tel. 360/377–3911; David W. Gitch, President and Chief Executive Officer **A**1 2 9 10 **F**4 7 10 12 14 15 16 17 19 21 22 23 25 26 27 28 30 31 32 33 34 35 37 39 40 41 42 44 45 46 49 52 53 54 55 56 57 58 60 61 65 67 70 71 72 73 74 **P**1	23	10	252	12168	127	59442	1785	83248	40898	1040
⊠ NAVAL HOSPITAL, Boone Road, Zip 98312–1898; tel. 360/475–4000; Captain Gregg S. Parker, Commanding Officer (Nonreporting) **A**1 3 5 **S** Department of Navy, Washington, DC	43	10	76	—	—	—	—	—	—	—
BREWSTER—Okanogan County										
★ OKANOGAN–DOUGLAS COUNTY HOSPITAL, 703 Northwest Second, Zip 98812; Mailing Address: P.O. Box 577, Zip 98812; tel. 509/689–2517; Howard M. Gamble, Administrator **A**9 10 **F**7 8 11 16 19 28 29 30 34 37 40 44 47 49 65 66 70 71	16	10	43	1023	9	11516	185	6593	3391	133
BURIEN—King County										
⊠ △ HIGHLINE COMMUNITY HOSPITAL, (Includes Highline Specialty Center, 12844 Military Road Fork, Tukwila, Zip 98168; Mark Benedum, Administrator), 16251 Sylvester Road S.W., Zip 98166; tel. 206/244–9970; Paul Tucker, Administrator (Total facility includes 30 beds in nursing home–type unit) (Nonreporting) **A**1 2 7 10	23	10	203	—	—	—	—	—	—	—
CENTRALIA—Lewis County										
⊠ PROVIDENCE CENTRALIA HOSPITAL, 914 South Scheuber Road, Zip 98531; tel. 360/736–2803; Mitzi VandeWege, Interim Administrator (Total facility includes 63 beds in nursing home–type unit) **A**1 2 9 10 **F**3 6 7 8 11 12 14 15 16 17 19 20 21 22 26 28 29 30 31 32 33 34 35 39 40 41 42 44 45 46 48 49 51 62 64 65 66 67 71 72 73 74 **P**8 **S** Sisters of Providence Health System, Seattle, WA	21	10	206	4567	84	107027	601	39836	20671	514
CHELAN—Chelan County										
LAKE CHELAN COMMUNITY HOSPITAL, 503 East Highland Avenue, Zip 98816, Mailing Address: Box 908, Zip 98816; tel. 509/682–2531; Moe Chaudry, Chief Executive Officer (Nonreporting) **A**9 10	16	10	30	—	—	—	—	—	—	—
CHEWELAH—Stevens County										
★ ST. JOSEPH'S HOSPITAL, 500 East Webster Street, Zip 99109, Mailing Address: P.O. Box 197, Zip 99109; tel. 509/935–8211; Gary V. Peck, Chief Executive Officer (Total facility includes 40 beds in nursing home–type unit) **A**9 10 **F**7 8 14 15 16 17 21 28 29 30 34 40 41 44 46 49 51 56 64 65 66 67 70 71 73 **P**5 8 **S** Providence Services, Spokane, WA **N** Providence Services, Spokane, WA	21	10	65	945	48	14457	60	7413	3392	106
CLARKSTON—Asotin County										
□ TRI–STATE MEMORIAL HOSPITAL, 1221 Highland Avenue, Zip 99403–0189, Mailing Address: P.O. Box 189, Zip 99403–0189; tel. 509/758–5511; Joseph K. Lillard, Administrator **A**1 9 10 **F**6 8 11 14 15 16 17 19 22 32 33 34 37 42 44 62 65 67 69 71 **P**8	23	10	40	1228	15	29368	—	13777	5209	201

Hospital, Address, Telephone, Administrator, Approval, Facility, and Physician Codes, Health Care System, Network	Classi-fication Codes		Utilization Data					Expense (thousands) of dollars		
★ American Hospital Association (AHA) membership ☐ Joint Commission on Accreditation of Healthcare Organizations (JCAHO) accreditation + American Osteopathic Healthcare Association (AOHA) membership ○ American Osteopathic Association (AOA) accreditation △ Commission on Accreditation of Rehabilitation Facilities (CARF) accreditation Control codes 61, 63, 64, 71, 72 and 73 indicate hospitals listed by AOHA, but not registered by AHA. For definition of numerical codes, see page A4	Control	Service	Staffed Beds	Admissions	Census	Outpatient Visits	Births	Total	Payroll	Personnel

COLFAX—Whitman County

★ WHITMAN HOSPITAL AND MEDICAL CENTER, 1200 West Fairview, Zip 99111–5252; tel. 509/397–3435; Gordon C. McLean, Administrator (Nonreporting) **A**9 10	13	10	32	—	—	—	—	—	—	—

COLVILLE—Stevens County

✠ MOUNT CARMEL HOSPITAL, 982 East Columbia Street, Zip 99114–0351; Mailing Address: Box 351, Zip 99114–0351; tel. 509/684–2561; Gloria Cooper, Chief Executive Officer **A**1 3 9 10 **F**7 8 12 14 15 16 19 22 34 37 40 41 44 45 46 49 56 67 70 71 **P**8 **S** Providence Services, Spokane, WA **N** Dominican Network, Spokane, WA; Providence Services, Spokane, WA	21	10	33	1560	13	27107	233	11748	5353	161

COUPEVILLE—Island County

✠ WHIDBEY GENERAL HOSPITAL, 101 North Main Street, Zip 98239–0400, Mailing Address: Box 400, Zip 98239–0400; tel. 360/678–5151; Robert Zylstra, Administrator (Nonreporting) **A**1 2 9 10	16	10	51	—	—	—	—	—	—	—

DAVENPORT—Lincoln County

★ LINCOLN HOSPITAL, 10 Nichols Street, Zip 99122; tel. 509/725–7101; Victor Vander Does, Administrator (Total facility includes 71 beds in nursing home–type unit) **A**9 10 **F**6 7 8 13 15 16 17 19 20 26 27 28 30 31 39 40 41 44 46 49 64 65 70 71 **N** Lincoln County Public Health Coalition, Davenport, WA; Columbian Basin Health Network, Mead, WA	16	10	104	670	83	9316	36	7580	4027	174

DAYTON—Columbia County

DAYTON GENERAL HOSPITAL, 1012 South Third Street, Zip 99328; tel. 509/382–2531; Oral R. Compson, Administrator (Nonreporting) **A**9 10	16	10	18	—	—	—	—	—	—	—

DEER PARK—Spokane County

★ DEER PARK HEALTH CENTER AND HOSPITAL, East 1015 D. Street, Zip 99006, Mailing Address: P.O. Box 742, Zip 99006; tel. 509/276–5061; Cathy Simchuk, Chief Operating Officer **A**9 10 **F**1 2 3 4 5 6 7 8 9 10 11 12 13 14 16 17 19 21 23 25 26 29 32 33 34 35 37 38 41 42 43 44 45 46 47 48 49 50 51 52 53 54 55 56 57 58 59 60 61 63 64 65 67 69 71 72 73 74 **P**5 6 **S** Providence Services, Spokane, WA **N** Dominican Network, Spokane, WA	21	10	26	412	15	—	28	3682	2027	44

EDMONDS—Snohomish County

✠ STEVENS HEALTHCARE, 21601 76th Avenue West, Zip 98026–7506; tel. 425/640–4000; Steve C. McCary, President and Chief Executive Officer **A**1 2 9 10 **F**1 4 7 8 10 12 16 17 18 19 20 21 22 25 26 27 28 29 30 31 34 35 37 39 40 41 42 44 45 46 49 51 52 53 54 55 56 57 58 65 66 67 70 71 73 74 **P**1 6 7 **N** Health Washington, Seattle, WA	16	10	134	8201	87	355659	1612	91839	42506	1046

ELLENSBURG—Kittitas County

KITTITAS VALLEY COMMUNITY HOSPITAL, 603 South Chestnut Street, Zip 98926; tel. 509/962–7302; Eric Jensen, Administrator **A**3 9 10 **F**7 8 11 15 16 17 19 22 26 32 33 35 36 37 39 40 41 44 49 65 67 70 71 73	16	10	37	1588	14	40794	265	13486	6644	185

ENUMCLAW—King County

COMMUNITY MEMORIAL HOSPITAL, 1450 Battersby Avenue, Zip 98022, Mailing Address: P.O. Box 218, Zip 98022–0218; tel. 360/825–2505; Dennis A. Popp, Administrator and Chief Executive Officer (Nonreporting) **A**9 10	23	10	29	—	—	—	—	—	—	—

EPHRATA—Grant County

★ COLUMBIA BASIN HOSPITAL, 200 Southeast Boulevard, Zip 98823–1997; tel. 509/754–4631; Allen L. Beach, Administrator (Total facility includes 29 beds in nursing home–type unit) **A**9 10 **F**8 15 16 20 21 22 38 39 49 64 65 66 67 71 **P**6 **N** Columbian Basin Health Network, Mead, WA	16	10	58	140	29	12914	1	4953	2691	91

EVERETT—Snohomish County

✠ △ PROVIDENCE GENERAL MEDICAL CENTER, (Includes Providence General Medical Center – Colby Campus, 14th and Colby Avenue, Mailing Address: P.O. Box 1147, Zip 98206; tel. 206/261–2000; Providence General Medical Center – Pacific Campus, Pacific and Nassau Streets, Zip 98201; tel. 206/258–7123), 1321 Colby Street, Zip 98206, Mailing Address: P.O. Box 1067, Zip 98206–1067; tel. 425/261–2000; Mel Pyne, Administrator (Total facility includes 12 beds in nursing home–type unit) **A**1 2 7 9 10 **F**2 3 4 7 8 10 12 14 15 16 19 21 22 24 25 26 28 29 30 31 32 33 34 35 37 39 40 41 42 43 44 45 46 48 49 50 51 53 56 60 63 65 66 67 68 70 71 73 74 **S** Sisters of Providence Health System, Seattle, WA	23	10	311	17244	179	428171	3236	152477	64699	1617

FAIRCHILD AFB—Spokane County

★ U. S. AIR FORCE HOSPITAL, 701 Hospital Loop, Zip 99011–8701; tel. 509/247–5217; Major Stuart R. Cowles, MSC, Administrator (Nonreporting) **S** Department of the Air Force, Bowling AFB, DC	41	10	35	—	—	—	—	—	—	—

FEDERAL WAY—King County

★ ST. FRANCIS HOSPITAL, 34515 Ninth Avenue South, Zip 98003–9710; tel. 253/927–9700; Mike Fitzgerald, Chief Financial Officer **A**2 9 10 **F**4 7 8 9 10 12 13 15 16 17 19 21 22 23 25 28 29 30 32 33 34 35 37 38 39 40 41 42 43 44 48 49 52 53 55 56 57 63 64 65 67 68 70 71 72 73 74 **P**1 5 7 **S** Catholic Health Initiatives, Denver, CO	21	10	77	5180	44	55401	1705	44877	18080	402

FORKS—Clallam County

FORKS COMMUNITY HOSPITAL, 530 Bogachiel Way, Zip 98331–9699; tel. 360/374–6271; Janet A. Hays, Administrator (Total facility includes 36 beds in nursing home–type unit) (Nonreporting) **A**9 10	16	10	53	—	—	—	—	—	—	—

GOLDENDALE—Klickitat County

KLICKITAT VALLEY HOSPITAL, 310 South Roosevelt, Zip 98620, Mailing Address: P.O. Box 5, Zip 98620; tel. 509/773–4022; Ron Ingraham, Administrator **A**3 9 10 **F**3 7 8 15 18 19 20 22 27 28 31 32 33 34 35 39 40 41 44 46 49 51 53 54 56 57 58 59 65 67 68 69 71 72 **P**3 5 8	16	10	27	528	3	15690	59	4558	2391	73

Hospital, Address, Telephone, Administrator, Approval, Facility, and Physician Codes, Health Care System, Network	Classi-fication Codes		Utilization Data					Expense (thousands) of dollars		
★ American Hospital Association (AHA) membership □ Joint Commission on Accreditation of Healthcare Organizations (JCAHO) accreditation + American Osteopathic Healthcare Association (AOHA) membership ○ American Osteopathic Association (AOA) accreditation △ Commission on Accreditation of Rehabilitation Facilities (CARF) accreditation Control codes 61, 63, 64, 71, 72 and 73 indicate hospitals listed by AOHA, but not registered by AHA. For definition of numerical codes, see page A4	Control	Service	Staffed Beds	Admissions	Census	Outpatient Visits	Births	Total	Payroll	Personnel

GRAND COULEE—Grant County

★ COULEE COMMUNITY HOSPITAL, 411 Fortuyn Road, Zip 99133–8718; tel. 509/633–1753; Charlotte Lang, Administrator (Total facility includes 29 beds in nursing home–type unit) (Nonreporting) **A**9 10 **S** Brim, Inc., Portland, OR **N** Columbian Basin Health Network, Mead, WA
— 16 10 48 — — — — — — —

ILWACO—Pacific County

★ OCEAN BEACH HOSPITAL, Mailing Address: Drawer H., Zip 98624; tel. 360/642–3181; Pamela Ott, R.N., Administrator (Nonreporting) **A**9 10
16 10 14 — — — — — — —

KENNEWICK—Benton County

⊞ KENNEWICK GENERAL HOSPITAL, 900 South Auburn Street, Zip 99336–0128, Mailing Address: Box 6128, Zip 99336; tel. 509/586–6111; Tom Nielsen, Administrator (Nonreporting) **A**1 2 9 10 **S** Quorum Health Group/Quorum Health Resources, Inc., Brentwood, TN
16 10 70 — — — — — — —

KIRKLAND—King County

□ BHC FAIRFAX HOSPITAL, 10200 N.E. 132nd Street, Zip 98034; tel. 425/821–2000; Michelle Egerer, Chief Executive Officer (Nonreporting) **A**1 9 10 **S** Behavioral Healthcare Corporation, Nashville, TN
33 22 133 — — — — — — —

⊞ EVERGREEN COMMUNITY HEALTH CENTER, (Formerly Evergreen Hospital Medical Center), 12040 N.E. 128th Street, Zip 98034; tel. 425/899–1000; Andrew Fallat, FACHE, Chief Executive Officer (Total facility includes 17 beds in nursing home–type unit) **A**1 2 9 10 **F**1 4 7 8 10 11 12 13 14 15 16 17 19 21 22 23 24 26 27 28 29 30 32 33 34 35 37 39 40 41 42 44 45 46 47 49 51 54 56 57 58 60 61 63 64 65 67 68 70 71 72 73 **P**6 **N** Health Washington, Seattle, WA; PeaceHealth, Bellevue, WA
16 10 149 9709 79 155534 2925 92986 42475 1152

LAKEWOOD—Pierce County

⊞ ST. CLARE HOSPITAL, 11315 Bridgeport Way S.W., Zip 98499–0998, Mailing Address: P.O. Box 99998, Zip 98499–0998; tel. 253/588–1711; Mike Fitzgerald, Chief Financial Officer **A**1 10 **F**2 3 4 6 7 8 9 10 11 12 14 15 16 17 18 19 20 21 22 23 25 26 28 29 30 31 32 33 34 35 37 38 39 40 41 42 43 44 45 46 47 48 49 52 53 54 55 56 57 58 59 60 61 64 65 66 67 68 69 70 71 72 73 74 **P**5 6 7 8 **S** Catholic Health Initiatives, Denver, CO
21 10 60 3435 34 45139 601 35176 13961 258

LONGVIEW—Cowlitz County

⊞ ST. JOHN MEDICAL CENTER, 1614 East Kessler Boulevard, Zip 98632, Mailing Address: P.O. Box 3002, Zip 98632–0302; tel. 360/423–1530; Doug Doorn, Chief Financial Officer **A**1 2 9 10 **F**2 3 6 7 8 10 11 12 14 15 16 17 18 19 20 22 27 34 35 37 39 40 41 42 43 44 45 46 49 51 52 56 59 60 65 67 69 70 71 72 73 74 **P**6 **S** PeaceHealth, Bellevue, WA **N** PeaceHealth, Bellevue, WA
23 10 171 10139 110 84768 1160 83867 38720 1164

MCCLEARY—Grays Harbor County

★ MARK REED HOSPITAL, 322 South Birch Street, Zip 98557; tel. 360/495–3244; Jean E. Roberts, Administrator (Nonreporting) **A**9 10 **S** Sisters of Providence Health System, Seattle, WA
16 10 7 — — — — — — —

MEDICAL LAKE—Spokane County

□ EASTERN STATE HOSPITAL, Mailing Address: P.O. Box A., Zip 99022–0045; tel. 509/299–4351; C. Jan Gregg, Chief Executive Officer **A**1 10 **F**14 15 16 20 27 45 46 52 54 55 56 57 65 73 **P**6
12 22 302 816 283 — — 39965 23636 568

MONROE—Snohomish County

⊞ VALLEY GENERAL HOSPITAL, 14701 179th S.E., Zip 98272, Mailing Address: P.O. Box 646, Zip 98272–0646; tel. 360/794–7497; Eric Buckland, CHE, Chief Executive Officer **A**1 9 10 **F**2 3 7 8 11 15 16 19 21 24 28 30 31 34 37 40 44 46 49 53 56 58 65 66 67 68 71 73
16 10 70 2089 29 24369 387 17257 7425 216

MORTON—Lewis County

★ MORTON GENERAL HOSPITAL, 521 Adams Street, Zip 98356, Mailing Address: Drawer C., Zip 98356–0019; tel. 360/496–5112; Mike Lee, Superintendent (Total facility includes 30 beds in nursing home–type unit) (Nonreporting) **A**9 10 **S** Sisters of Providence Health System, Seattle, WA
16 10 50 — — — — — — —

MOSES LAKE—Grant County

⊞ SAMARITAN HEALTHCARE, 801 East Wheeler Road, Zip 98837–1899; tel. 509/765–5606; Keith J. Baldwin, Administrator **A**1 9 10 **F**7 11 15 16 17 19 21 22 28 29 30 34 35 37 39 40 41 44 45 46 49 51 65 66 67 70 71 73 **P**4 8 **N** Columbian Basin Health Network, Mead, WA
16 10 50 2708 20 27161 1003 23001 11287 338

MOUNT VERNON—Skagit County

⊞ AFFILIATED HEALTH SERVICES, (Includes Skagit Valley Hospital, 1415 Kincaid Street, Mailing Address: P.O. Box 1376, Zip 98273–1376; tel. 360/424–4111; Gregg A. Davidson, Associate Administrator and Chief Operating Officer; United General Hospital, 1971 Highway 20, Sedro Woolley, Zip 98284, Mailing Address: P.O. Box 1376, Zip 98273–1376; tel. 360/856–6021), 1415 Kincaid Street, Zip 98274, Mailing Address: P.O. Box 1376, Zip 98273–1376; tel. 360/424–4111; Patrick R. Mahoney, Administrator and Chief Executive Officer **A**1 2 9 10 **F**4 5 7 8 10 11 12 14 15 16 17 19 21 22 23 26 28 29 30 32 33 34 35 36 37 39 40 41 42 44 46 49 52 54 56 57 58 59 60 63 65 67 70 71 73 74
16 10 161 7127 71 107254 1233 74983 — —

NEWPORT—Pend Oreille County

NEWPORT COMMUNITY HOSPITAL, 714 West Pine, Zip 99156; tel. 509/447–2441; John R. White, Administrator (Total facility includes 50 beds in nursing home–type unit) (Nonreporting) **A**9 10
16 10 74 — — — — — — —

OAK HARBOR—Island County

⊞ NAVAL HOSPITAL, 3475 North Saratoga Street, Zip 98278–8800; tel. 360/257–9500; Captain Michael W. Benway, Commanding Officer (Nonreporting) **A**1 **S** Department of Navy, Washington, DC
43 10 25 — — — — — — —

Hospital, Address, Telephone, Administrator, Approval, Facility, and Physician Codes, Health Care System, Network	Classi-fication Codes		Utilization Data					Expense (thousands) of dollars		
★ American Hospital Association (AHA) membership □ Joint Commission on Accreditation of Healthcare Organizations (JCAHO) accreditation + American Osteopathic Healthcare Association (AOHA) membership ○ American Osteopathic Association (AOA) accreditation △ Commission on Accreditation of Rehabilitation Facilities (CARF) accreditation Control codes 61, 63, 64, 71, 72 and 73 indicate hospitals listed by AOHA, but not registered by AHA. For definition of numerical codes, see page A4	Control	Service	Staffed Beds	Admissions	Census	Outpatient Visits	Births	Total	Payroll	Personnel

ODESSA—Lincoln County

★ ODESSA MEMORIAL HOSPITAL, 502 East Amende, Zip 99159, Mailing Address: P.O. Box 368, Zip 99159–0368; tel. 509/982–2611; Carol Schott, Administrator (Total facility includes 23 beds in nursing home–type unit) (Nonreporting) **A**9 10 **N** Lincoln County Public Health Coalition, Davenport, WA

| | 16 | 10 | 40 | — | — | — | — | — | — | — |

OLYMPIA—Thurston County

🕸 CAPITAL MEDICAL CENTER, (Formerly Columbia Capital Medical Center), 3900 Capital Mall Drive S.W., Zip 98502–8654, Mailing Address: P.O. Box 19002, Zip 98507–0013; tel. 360/754–5858; Garry L. Gause, Chief Executive Officer (Total facility includes 9 beds in nursing home–type unit) (Nonreporting) **A**1 2 9 10 **S** Columbia/HCA Healthcare Corporation, Nashville, TN
COLUMBIA CAPITAL MEDICAL CENTER See Capital Medical Center

| | 33 | 10 | 104 | — | — | — | — | — | — | — |

🕸 △ PROVIDENCE ST. PETER HOSPITAL, 413 Lilly Road N.E., Zip 98506–5116; tel. 360/491–9480; C. Scott Bond, Administrator **A**1 2 3 5 7 9 10 **F**3 4 7 8 10 11 12 15 17 18 19 20 21 22 23 24 25 26 27 28 29 30 31 32 33 34 35 37 39 40 41 42 43 44 45 46 48 49 51 52 53 54 55 56 57 58 59 60 63 65 67 70 71 73 **P**8 **S** Sisters of Providence Health System, Seattle, WA

| | 21 | 10 | 327 | 14635 | 157 | 218601 | 2015 | 140781 | 69746 | 1837 |

OMAK—Okanogan County

★ MID–VALLEY HOSPITAL, 810 Valley Way Road, Zip 98841, Mailing Address: Box 793, Zip 98841; tel. 509/826–1760; Michael D. Billing, Administrator **A**3 9 10 **F**7 12 14 15 16 19 22 35 37 40 44 46 49 51 **N** Columbian Basin Health Network, Mead, WA

| | 16 | 10 | 32 | 1306 | 4 | 12402 | 260 | 10972 | 5580 | 163 |

OTHELLO—Adams County

★ OTHELLO COMMUNITY HOSPITAL, 315 North 14th Street, Zip 99344; tel. 509/488–2636; Jerry Lane, Administrator **A**9 10 **F**7 8 19 22 28 34 36 40 41 44 71 **P**5 **N** Columbian Basin Health Network, Mead, WA

| | 16 | 10 | 32 | 848 | 5 | 21444 | 364 | 5406 | 2921 | 76 |

PASCO—Franklin County

🕸 LOURDES MEDICAL CENTER, (Formerly Our Lady of Lourdes Health Center), 520 North Fourth Avenue, Zip 99301, Mailing Address: P.O. Box 2568, Zip 99302; tel. 509/547–7704; Thomas Corley, Chief Executive Officer (Total facility includes 21 beds in nursing home–type unit) **A**1 2 9 10 **F**2 3 7 8 11 14 15 16 17 22 23 32 33 37 40 41 44 45 48 49 51 52 53 54 55 56 57 58 59 64 65 66 67 70 71 73 **P**4 5 6 7 8 **S** Carondelet Health System, Saint Louis, MO
OUR LADY OF LOURDES HEALTH CENTER See Lourdes Medical Center

| | 21 | 10 | 132 | 3793 | 51 | 93499 | 588 | 34727 | 15846 | 446 |

POMEROY—Garfield County

GARFIELD COUNTY MEMORIAL HOSPITAL, 66th North Sixth Street, Zip 99347–0880, Mailing Address: P.O. Box 880, Zip 99347; tel. 509/843–1591; Harry Aubert, Administrator (Total facility includes 40 beds in nursing home–type unit) (Nonreporting) **A**9 10

| | 16 | 10 | 54 | — | — | — | — | — | — | — |

PORT ANGELES—Clallam County

□ OLYMPIC MEMORIAL HOSPITAL, 939 Caroline Street, Zip 98362–3997; tel. 360/417–7000; Tom Stegbauer, Administrator **A**1 2 9 10 **F**7 8 11 12 14 15 16 17 19 20 21 22 23 24 25 27 28 29 30 32 34 37 39 40 41 42 44 45 46 49 51 60 61 65 67 70 71 73 74 **P**3 7 8

| | 16 | 10 | 64 | 4895 | 44 | 87399 | 614 | 39760 | 19602 | 492 |

PORT TOWNSEND—Jefferson County

★ JEFFERSON GENERAL HOSPITAL, 834 Sheridan, Zip 98368; tel. 360/385–2200; Victor J. Dirksen, Administrator **A**10 **F**7 8 10 11 12 13 15 16 17 19 21 22 23 24 27 28 29 30 31 32 33 37 39 40 41 44 45 48 49 65 66 67 68 71 73 **P**8

| | 16 | 10 | 35 | 1597 | 12 | 33995 | 139 | — | 7104 | 207 |

PROSSER—Benton County

★ PROSSER MEMORIAL HOSPITAL, 723 Memorial Street, Zip 99350–1593; tel. 509/786–2222; John E. Rohrer, Administrator (Total facility includes 36 beds in nursing home–type unit) **A**9 10 **F**7 8 22 26 31 32 40 41 42 44 49 64 65 71 73 74

| | 16 | 10 | 62 | 672 | 35 | 13488 | 396 | 8139 | 3719 | 125 |

PULLMAN—Whitman County

□ PULLMAN MEMORIAL HOSPITAL, N.E. 1125 Washington Avenue, Zip 99163–4742; tel. 509/332–2541; Scott K. Adams, Chief Executive Officer **A**1 9 10 **F**1 2 3 4 5 6 7 8 9 10 11 12 14 15 16 17 18 19 20 21 23 24 25 26 27 28 29 30 31 32 33 34 35 36 37 38 39 40 41 42 43 44 45 46 47 48 49 50 51 53 54 55 56 57 58 59 60 61 62 63 64 65 66 67 68 69 70 71 72 73 74 **P**3 8 **S** Brim, Inc., Portland, OR

| | 16 | 10 | 36 | 1069 | 8 | 36178 | 274 | 12437 | 5294 | 154 |

PUYALLUP—Pierce County

🕸 △ GOOD SAMARITAN COMMUNITY HEALTHCARE, 407 14th Avenue S.E., Zip 98372–0192, Mailing Address: Box 1247, Zip 98371–0192; tel. 253/848–6661; David K. Hamry, President **A**1 2 7 9 10 **F**1 6 7 11 12 14 15 16 17 18 19 21 22 24 25 26 28 29 30 32 33 34 37 38 39 40 41 42 44 45 46 48 49 51 53 54 55 56 57 58 59 60 62 63 65 66 67 68 70 71 72 73 **P**1 6 7

| | 21 | 10 | 211 | 9005 | 118 | 435965 | 1410 | 110013 | 65355 | 1649 |

QUINCY—Grant County

QUINCY VALLEY MEDICAL CENTER, 908 Tenth Avenue S.W., Zip 98848; tel. 509/787–3531; Arne Seim, Interim Administrator (Total facility includes 22 beds in nursing home–type unit) (Nonreporting) **A**9 10 **N** Columbian Basin Health Network, Mead, WA

| | 13 | 10 | 38 | — | — | — | — | — | — | — |

REDMOND—King County

★ THE EASTSIDE HOSPITAL, 2700 152nd Avenue N.E., Zip 98052–5560; tel. 425/883–5151; Patricia Kennedy–Scott, Northern Region Vice President (Nonreporting) **N** Group Health Cooperative of Puget Sound, Seattle, WA

| | 23 | 10 | 125 | — | — | — | — | — | — | — |

Hospital, Address, Telephone, Administrator, Approval, Facility, and Physician Codes, Health Care System, Network	Classi-fication Codes		Utilization Data					Expense (thousands) of dollars		
	Control	Service	Staffed Beds	Admissions	Census	Outpatient Visits	Births	Total	Payroll	Personnel

★ American Hospital Association (AHA) membership
□ Joint Commission on Accreditation of Healthcare Organizations (JCAHO) accreditation
+ American Osteopathic Healthcare Association (AOHA) membership
○ American Osteopathic Association (AOA) accreditation
△ Commission on Accreditation of Rehabilitation Facilities (CARF) accreditation
Control codes 61, 63, 64, 71, 72 and 73 indicate hospitals listed by AOHA, but not registered by AHA. For definition of numerical codes, see page A4

RENTON—King County

★ VALLEY MEDICAL CENTER, 400 South 43rd Street, Zip 98055–9987; tel. 425/228–3450; Richard D. Roodman, Chief Executive Officer (Total facility includes 39 beds in nursing home–type unit) **A**1 2 3 5 9 10 **F**3 4 7 8 10 11 12 13 14 15 16 17 18 19 21 22 23 24 25 27 28 29 30 31 34 35 37 39 40 41 42 44 46 49 51 52 54 56 58 60 64 65 67 68 70 71 73 74 **P**1 6 — 16 — 10 — 196 — 14941 — 146 — 311495 — 2988 — 124789 — 58101 — 1416

| | 16 | 10 | 196 | 14941 | 146 | 311495 | 2988 | 124789 | 58101 | 1416 |

REPUBLIC—Ferry County

FERRY COUNTY MEMORIAL HOSPITAL, 36 Klondike Road, Zip 99166; tel. 509/775–3333; Nancy McIntyre, Administrator (Total facility includes 14 beds in nursing home–type unit) **A**9 10 **F**7 8 12 13 15 16 17 18 19 20 26 27 29 30 31 32 33 36 37 39 40 41 44 45 46 49 51 53 54 55 56 57 58 59 61 62 64 65 66 67 68 70 71 73 74

| | 16 | 10 | 25 | 315 | 15 | 7202 | 5 | 2935 | 1343 | 62 |

RICHLAND—Benton County

CARONDELET BEHAVIORAL HEALTH CENTER See Lourdes Counseling Center

★ KADLEC MEDICAL CENTER, 888 Swift Boulevard, Zip 99352–9974; tel. 509/946–4611; Marcel Loh, President and Chief Executive Officer **A**1 2 9 10 **F**1 7 8 10 12 14 15 19 20 21 22 31 32 35 37 38 39 40 41 42 44 45 46 48 49 51 60 65 70 71 73 **S** Quorum Health Group/Quorum Health Resources, Inc., Brentwood, TN

| | 23 | 10 | 124 | 6055 | 67 | 65759 | 1334 | 62152 | 25632 | 552 |

★ LOURDES COUNSELING CENTER, (Formerly Carondelet Behavioral Health Center), 1175 Carondelet Drive, Zip 99352–1175; tel. 509/943–9104; Thomas Corley, Chief Executive Officer (Nonreporting) **A**1 9 10 **S** Carondelet Health System, Saint Louis, MO

| | 21 | 22 | 32 | — | — | — | — | — | — | — |

RITZVILLE—Adams County

EAST ADAMS RURAL HOSPITAL, 903 South Adams Street, Zip 99169–2298; tel. 509/659–1200; James G. Parrish, Administrator (Nonreporting) **A**9 10 **N** Columbian Basin Health Network, Mead, WA

| | 16 | 10 | 17 | — | — | — | — | — | — | — |

SEATTLE—King County

★ △ CHILDREN'S HOSPITAL AND REGIONAL MEDICAL CENTER, 4800 Sand Point Way N.E., Zip 98105, Mailing Address: Box 5371, Zip 98105–0371; tel. 206/526–2000; Treuman Katz, President and Chief Executive Officer **A**1 2 3 5 7 8 9 10 **F**5 10 12 13 14 15 16 17 19 20 21 22 28 29 31 32 34 35 38 39 42 43 44 45 47 48 49 51 52 53 54 55 56 58 59 60 61 65 66 67 68 69 70 71 72 73 **P**6

| | 23 | 50 | 208 | 10840 | 152 | 145795 | — | 143296 | 59403 | 1703 |

★ △ HARBORVIEW MEDICAL CENTER, 325 Ninth Avenue, Box 359717, Zip 98104–2499; tel. 206/731–3000; David E. Jaffe, Executive Director and Chief Executive Officer **A**1 3 5 7 8 9 10 **F**2 3 4 5 7 8 9 10 11 12 13 15 16 17 18 19 20 21 22 23 25 26 27 28 30 31 34 35 37 38 39 40 41 42 43 44 45 46 47 48 49 50 51 52 53 54 55 56 57 58 59 60 65 66 67 68 69 70 71 72 73 74 **P**3

| | 13 | 10 | 334 | 13245 | 273 | 339365 | 0 | 245910 | 113862 | — |

★ △ NORTHWEST HOSPITAL, 1550 North 115th Street, Zip 98133–8498; tel. 206/364–0500; James D. Hart, President (Total facility includes 42 beds in nursing home–type unit) (Nonreporting) **A**1 2 3 7 9 10

| | 23 | 10 | 238 | — | — | — | — | — | — | — |

★ △ PROVIDENCE SEATTLE MEDICAL CENTER, 500 17th Avenue, Zip 98122, Mailing Address: P.O. Box 34008, Zip 98124–1008; tel. 206/320–2000; Nancy A. Giunto, Operations Administrator (Total facility includes 54 beds in nursing home–type unit) **A**1 2 3 5 7 9 10 **F**1 4 6 7 8 10 11 12 14 15 16 17 19 20 21 22 23 26 27 29 30 31 32 33 34 35 37 39 40 41 42 43 44 45 46 48 49 51 52 54 55 56 57 58 59 60 61 63 64 65 66 67 68 71 72 73 74 **P**6 **S** Sisters of Providence Health System, Seattle, WA

| | 21 | 10 | 334 | 15696 | 187 | 102641 | 1946 | 168045 | 78118 | 1593 |

□ REGIONAL HOSPITAL FOR RESPIRATORY AND COMPLEX CARE, 12844 Military Road South, Zip 98168; tel. 206/248–4548; James C. Cannon, Administrator and Chief Executive Officer (Nonreporting) **A**1 10

| | 23 | 49 | 27 | — | — | — | — | — | — | — |

□ SCHICK SHADEL HOSPITAL, 12101 Ambaum Boulevard S.W., Zip 98146–2699, Mailing Address: Box 48149, Zip 98148–0149; tel. 206/244–8100; Mary Ellen Stewart, Administrator (Nonreporting) **A**1 9 10

| | 33 | 82 | 63 | — | — | — | — | — | — | — |

★ SWEDISH HEALTH SERVICES, (Includes Swedish Medical Center–Ballard, Northwest Market and Barnes, Zip 98107–1507, Mailing Address: Box 70707, Zip 98107; tel. 206/782–2700), 747 Broadway Avenue, Zip 98122–4307; tel. 206/386–6000; Richard H. Peterson, President and Chief Executive Officer (Nonreporting) **A**1 2 3 5 9 10 **N** Health Washington, Seattle, WA

| | 23 | 10 | 597 | — | — | — | — | — | — | — |

★ △ UNIVERSITY OF WASHINGTON MEDICAL CENTER, 1959 Northeast Pacific Street, Box 356151, Zip 98195–6151; tel. 206/548–3300; Robert H. Muilenburg, Executive Director **A**1 2 3 5 7 8 9 10 **F**4 5 7 8 10 14 15 16 19 20 21 22 23 25 28 29 30 31 34 35 38 39 40 41 42 43 44 45 46 48 49 50 51 52 54 55 56 57 58 59 60 61 63 65 66 69 71 72 73 74 **P**6

| | 12 | 10 | 398 | 15112 | 263 | 292476 | 1636 | 276308 | 114026 | 3085 |

□ VENCOR SEATTLE HOSPITAL, (Formerly THC–Seattle Hospital), 10560 Fifth Avenue N.E., Zip 98125–0977; tel. 206/364–2050; Deborah L. Abrams, Chief Executive Officer (Nonreporting) **A**1 9 10 **S** Vencor, Incorporated, Louisville, KY

| | 33 | 10 | 30 | — | — | — | — | — | — | — |

★ VETERANS AFFAIRS PUGET SOUND HEALTH CARE SYSTEM, (Includes Veterans Affairs Puget Sound Health Care System–American Lake Division, Tacoma, Zip 98493; tel. 206/582–8440), 1660 South Columbian Way, Zip 98108–1597; tel. 206/762–1010; Timothy B. Williams, Director (Total facility includes 132 beds in nursing home–type unit) (Nonreporting) **A**1 3 5 8 9 **S** Department of Veterans Affairs, Washington, DC

| | 45 | 10 | 557 | — | — | — | — | — | — | — |

★ △ VIRGINIA MASON MEDICAL CENTER, 1100 Ninth Avenue, Zip 98101, Mailing Address: P.O. Box 900, Zip 98111–0900; tel. 206/223–6600; J. Michael Rona, Vice President and Executive Administrator **A**1 2 3 5 7 9 10 **F**1 3 4 7 8 10 11 12 14 15 16 17 19 21 22 23 25 26 27 28 29 30 31 32 34 35 37 39 40 41 42 43 44 45 46 48 49 51 53 54 55 56 57 58 59 60 61 64 65 66 67 69 71 72 73 74 **P**6

| | 23 | 10 | 272 | 16231 | 218 | 41424 | — | 378671 | 198206 | 4107 |

Hospital, Address, Telephone, Administrator, Approval, Facility, and Physician Codes, Health Care System, Network	Classi-fication Codes		Utilization Data					Expense (thousands) of dollars		
★ American Hospital Association (AHA) membership □ Joint Commission on Accreditation of Healthcare Organizations (JCAHO) accreditation + American Osteopathic Healthcare Association (AOHA) membership ○ American Osteopathic Association (AOA) accreditation △ Commission on Accreditation of Rehabilitation Facilities (CARF) accreditation Control codes 61, 63, 64, 71, 72 and 73 indicate hospitals listed by AOHA, but not registered by AHA. For definition of numerical codes, see page A4	Control	Service	Staffed Beds	Admissions	Census	Outpatient Visits	Births	Total	Payroll	Personnel

SEDRO WOOLLEY—Skagit County
UNITED GENERAL HOSPITAL See Affiliated Health Services, Mount Vernon

SHELTON—Mason County

□ MASON GENERAL HOSPITAL, 901 Mountainview Drive, Zip 98584, Mailing Address: P.O. Box 1668, Zip 98584; tel. 360/426–1611; G. Robert Appel, Administrator (Nonreporting) **A**1 9 10	16	10	68	—	—	—	—	—	—	—

SOUTH BEND—Pacific County

WILLAPA HARBOR HOSPITAL, 800 Alder Street, Zip 98586–0438, Mailing Address: P.O. Box 438, Zip 98586–0438; tel. 360/875–5526; Carole Halsan, Interim Administrator (Nonreporting) **A**9 10	16	10	18	—	—	—	—	—	—	—

SPOKANE—Spokane County

□ DEACONESS MEDICAL CENTER–SPOKANE, 800 West Fifth Avenue, Zip 99204, Mailing Address: P.O. Box 248, Zip 99210–0248; tel. 509/458–5800; Thomas J. Zellers, Chief Operating Officer **A**1 2 3 5 9 10 **F**2 3 4 7 8 9 10 11 12 14 15 16 17 18 19 21 22 23 24 26 27 29 30 31 32 35 37 38 39 40 41 42 43 44 45 46 47 48 49 52 53 54 55 56 57 58 60 63 64 65 66 69 70 71 72 73 74 **S** Empire Health Services, Spokane, WA	23	10	388	12409	161	—	2471	131450	51132	1234
⊞ HOLY FAMILY HOSPITAL, North 5633 Lidgerwood Avenue, Zip 99207; tel. 509/482–0111; Ronald J. Schurra, Chief Executive Officer **A**1 2 9 10 **F**1 2 4 7 8 9 10 11 12 15 16 19 21 22 23 26 27 28 29 30 32 35 37 38 39 40 41 42 43 44 45 46 47 48 49 51 52 53 54 55 56 57 58 59 60 63 64 65 66 67 68 69 70 71 72 73 74 **P**7 8 **S** Providence Services, Spokane, WA **N** Dominican Network, Spokane, WA; Providence Services, Spokane, WA	21	10	206	8546	91	69966	1137	61137		
⊞ SACRED HEART MEDICAL CENTER, West 101 Eighth Avenue, Zip 99220, Mailing Address: P.O. Box 2555, Zip 99220; tel. 509/455–3040; Ryland P. Davis, President (Nonreporting) **A**1 2 3 5 9 10 **S** Providence Services, Spokane, WA **N** Providence Services, Spokane, WA	21	10	607							
⊞ SHRINERS HOSPITALS FOR CHILDREN–SPOKANE, 911 West Fifth Avenue, Zip 99204–2901, Mailing Address: P.O. Box 2472, Zip 99210–2472; tel. 509/455–7844; Charles R. Young, Administrator **A**1 3 **F**12 15 17 20 34 39 49 65 73 **S** Shriners Hospitals for Children, Tampa, FL	23	57	30	718	12	7241	0		—	129
△ ST. LUKES REHABILITATION INSTITUTE, 711 South Cowley Street, Zip 99202; tel. 509/838–4771; Debra D. Hanks, Administrator (Nonreporting) **A**7 9 10	23	46	72	—	—	—	—	—	—	—
□ VALLEY HOSPITAL AND MEDICAL CENTER, 12606 East Mission Avenue, Zip 99216–9969; tel. 509/924–6650; Michael T. Liepman, Chief Operating Officer (Nonreporting) **A**1 2 9 10 **S** Empire Health Services, Spokane, WA	23	10	117							
⊞ VETERANS AFFAIRS MEDICAL CENTER, North 4815 Assembly Street, Zip 99205–6197; tel. 509/327–0200; Joseph M. Manley, Director (Total facility includes 60 beds in nursing home–type unit) (Nonreporting) **A**1 **S** Department of Veterans Affairs, Washington, DC	45	10	192							

SUNNYSIDE—Yakima County

★ + ○ SUNNYSIDE COMMUNITY HOSPITAL, 10th and Tacoma Avenue, Zip 98944, Mailing Address: P.O. Box 719, Zip 98944–0719; tel. 509/837–1650; Jon D. Smiley, Chief Executive Officer **A**2 9 10 11 **F**7 8 11 19 20 21 22 23 28 29 30 32 33 39 40 42 44 45 46 51 65 67 70 71 73 **P**4 **S** Brim, Inc., Portland, OR	23	10	34	2013	18	44908	584	16299	6858	200

TACOMA—Pierce County

□ ALLENMORE HOSPITAL, South 19th and Union Avenue, Zip 98405, Mailing Address: P.O. Box 11414, Zip 98411–0414; tel. 253/572–2323; Charles Hoffman, Vice President **A**1 9 **F**1 4 7 8 10 11 12 13 14 17 18 19 20 21 22 23 25 26 28 29 30 31 32 33 34 35 37 38 39 40 41 42 43 44 45 46 49 50 51 56 57 60 63 65 67 68 69 70 71 72 73 74 **P**5 6 **S** MultiCare Health System, Tacoma, WA **N** Multicare Health System, Tacoma, WA	23	10	72	2991	34	71535	—	37216	15618	414
⊞ MADIGAN ARMY MEDICAL CENTER, Zip 98431–5000; tel. 253/968–1110; Brigadier General George J. Brown, M.D., Commanding General **A**1 2 3 5 **F**3 4 7 8 10 11 12 13 14 15 16 17 19 20 21 22 24 25 26 27 28 29 30 31 34 35 37 38 39 40 41 42 43 44 45 46 47 49 50 51 52 54 56 57 58 60 61 63 65 66 67 71 72 73 74 **S** Department of the Army, Office of the Surgeon General, Falls Church, VA	42	10	181	14748	128	833000	1946	—	124000	2831
□ MARY BRIDGE CHILDREN'S HOSPITAL AND HEALTH CENTER, 317 Martin Luther King Jr. Way, Zip 98405–0299, Mailing Address: Box 5299, Zip 98405–0299; tel. 253/552–1400; William B. Connoley, President and Chief Executive Officer **A**1 3 5 9 10 **F**1 4 7 8 10 11 12 13 17 18 19 21 22 23 25 26 28 29 30 31 32 33 34 35 37 38 39 40 41 42 43 44 47 49 50 54 60 63 65 67 68 70 71 72 73 74 **P**5 6 **S** MultiCare Health System, Tacoma, WA **N** Health Washington, Seattle, WA; Multicare Health System, Tacoma, WA	23	50	72	3065	30	156320	—	30862	14539	348
⊞ PUGET SOUND HOSPITAL, 215 South 36th Street, Zip 98408, Mailing Address: P.O. Box 11412, Zip 98411–0412; tel. 253/474–0561; Bruce Brandler, Administrator **A**1 9 10 **F**1 2 12 19 22 37 41 44 48 49 51 52 56 57 58 59 65 71 73 **P**8	33	10	140	3512	64	109519	—	25236	11273	258
ST. CLARE HOSPITAL See Lakewood										
⊞ △ ST. JOSEPH MEDICAL CENTER, 1717 South J. Street, Zip 98405, Mailing Address: P.O. Box 2197, Zip 98401–2197; tel. 253/627–4101; Joseph W. Wilczek, President and Chief Executive Officer **A**1 2 7 9 10 **F**2 4 6 7 8 9 10 11 12 14 15 16 17 18 19 20 21 22 23 24 25 26 28 29 30 31 32 33 34 35 36 37 39 40 41 42 43 44 45 46 48 49 51 52 54 56 57 58 59 60 61 63 64 65 67 69 71 72 73 74 **P**5 8 **S** Catholic Health Initiatives, Denver, CO	21	10	271	14966	176	86948	2750	173355	68761	2341

Hospital, Address, Telephone, Administrator, Approval, Facility, and Physician Codes, Health Care System, Network	Classi-fication Codes		Utilization Data					Expense (thousands) of dollars		
	Control	Service	Staffed Beds	Admissions	Census	Outpatient Visits	Births	Total	Payroll	Personnel
★ American Hospital Association (AHA) membership □ Joint Commission on Accreditation of Healthcare Organizations (JCAHO) accreditation + American Osteopathic Healthcare Association (AOHA) membership ○ American Osteopathic Association (AOA) accreditation △ Commission on Accreditation of Rehabilitation Facilities (CARF) accreditation Control codes 61, 63, 64, 71, 72 and 73 indicate hospitals listed by AOHA, but not registered by AHA. For definition of numerical codes, see page A4										
✠ TACOMA GENERAL HOSPITAL, 315 Martin Luther King Jr. Way, Zip 98405–0299, Mailing Address: P.O. Box 5299, Zip 98405–0299; tel. 253/552–1000; William B. Connoley, President and Chief Executive Officer **A**1 2 3 5 9 10 **F**1 4 7 8 10 11 12 13 17 18 19 21 22 24 25 26 28 29 30 31 32 33 34 35 37 38 40 41 42 43 44 45 46 47 49 50 51 60 63 65 67 68 70 71 72 73 74 **P**5 6 **S** MultiCare Health System, Tacoma, WA **N** Health Washington, Seattle, WA; Multicare Health System, Tacoma, WA	23	10	282	13890	166	300738	3211	141803	53809	1292
VETERANS AFFAIRS PUGET SOUND HEALTH CARE SYSTEM–AMERICAN LAKE DIVISION See Veterans Affairs Puget Sound Health Care System, Seattle										
□ WESTERN STATE HOSPITAL, 9601 Steilacoom Boulevard S.W., Zip 98498; tel. 253/582–8900; Jerry L. Dennis, M.D., Chief Executive Officer (Nonreporting) **A**1 9 10	12	22	835	—	—	—	—	—	—	—
TONASKET—Okanogan County										
NORTH VALLEY HOSPITAL, Second and Western, Zip 98855, Mailing Address: P.O. Box 488, Zip 98855; tel. 509/486–2151; Warner H. Bartleson, Administrator (Total facility includes 70 beds in nursing home–type unit) (Nonreporting) **A**9 10	16	10	92	—	—	—	—	—	—	—
TOPPENISH—Yakima County										
✠ PROVIDENCE TOPPENISH HOSPITAL, 502 West Fourth Avenue, Zip 98948, Mailing Address: P.O. Box 672, Zip 98948–0672; tel. 509/865–3105; Steve Burdick, Administrator **A**1 9 10 **F**8 14 15 16 19 21 22 32 33 34 37 40 41 44 46 51 65 70 71 73 **P**6 **S** Sisters of Providence Health System, Seattle, WA	21	10	48	2037	17	59513	606	13392	5979	162
VANCOUVER—Clark County										
✠ △ SOUTHWEST WASHINGTON MEDICAL CENTER, (Includes Vancouver Memorial Campus, 3400 Main Street, Zip 98663; tel. 206/696–5000), 400 N.E. Mother Joseph Place, Zip 98664, Mailing Address: P.O. Box 1600, Zip 98668; tel. 360/256–2000; Geoffrey N. Lang, President and Chief Executive Officer (Nonreporting) **A**1 2 3 7 9 10	23	10	297	—	—	—	—	—	—	—
WALLA WALLA—Walla Walla County										
✠ JONATHAN M. WAINWRIGHT MEMORIAL VETERANS AFFAIRS MEDICAL CENTER, 77 Wainwright Drive, Zip 99362–3994; tel. 509/525–5200; George Marnell, Director (Total facility includes 30 beds in nursing home–type unit) **A**1 **F**2 3 15 16 19 20 22 30 34 37 41 44 46 49 51 52 54 58 59 64 65 71 73 74 **P**6 **S** Department of Veterans Affairs, Washington, DC	45	10	76	1313	34	45408	—	—	—	316
✠ △ ST. MARY MEDICAL CENTER, 401 West Poplar Street, Zip 99362, Mailing Address: Box 1477, Zip 99362–0312; tel. 509/525–3320; John A. Isely, President **A**1 2 7 9 10 **F**7 8 14 19 22 28 30 31 32 35 37 38 39 40 41 42 44 48 49 52 56 58 60 70 71 73 74 **P**6 **S** Providence Services, Spokane, WA **N** Providence Services, Spokane, WA	21	10	134	3380	39	56389	450	39767	18192	572
STATE PENITENTIARY HOSPITAL, Mailing Address: Box 520, Zip 99362; tel. 509/525–3610; Barbara Croft, Health Care Manager (Nonreporting)	12	11	36	—	—	—	—	—	—	—
★ WALLA WALLA GENERAL HOSPITAL, 1025 South Second Avenue, Zip 99362, Mailing Address: Box 1398, Zip 99362; tel. 509/525–0480; Rodney T. Applegate, President (Nonreporting) **A**2 9 10 **S** Adventist Health, Roseville, CA	21	10	72	—	—	—	—	—	—	—
WENATCHEE—Chelan County										
✠ CENTRAL WASHINGTON HOSPITAL, 1300 Fuller Street, Zip 98801–1948, Mailing Address: Box 1887, Zip 98807–1887; tel. 509/662–1511; John T. Evans, Jr., President and Chief Executive Officer (Nonreporting) **A**1 9 10	23	10	154	—	—	—	—	—	—	—
WHITE SALMON—Klickitat County										
SKYLINE HOSPITAL, 211 Skyline Drive, Zip 98672–0099, Mailing Address: Box 99, Zip 98672–0099; tel. 509/493–1101; Lynn Milnes, Administrator and Chief Executive Officer **A**9 10 **F**7 8 9 10 11 15 16 22 28 32 33 34 37 38 40 44 47 51 64 70 **P**5	16	10	24	655	5	11335	109	5701	3106	100
YAKIMA—Yakima County										
✠ PROVIDENCE YAKIMA MEDICAL CENTER, 110 South Ninth Avenue, Zip 98902–3397; tel. 509/575–5000; Richard Brown, Operations Administrator (Total facility includes 12 beds in nursing home–type unit) **A**1 2 3 9 10 **F**4 7 8 10 11 15 16 17 19 21 22 23 28 29 30 32 33 34 35 37 40 41 42 43 44 45 46 48 49 51 62 63 64 65 67 70 71 73 74 **P**4 5 **S** Sisters of Providence Health System, Seattle, WA	21	10	190	6395	77	244254	545	79859	33639	1055
✠ YAKIMA VALLEY MEMORIAL HOSPITAL, 2811 Tieton Drive, Zip 98902–3799; tel. 509/575–8000; Richard W. Linneweh, Jr., President and Chief Executive Officer **A**1 2 3 9 10 **F**7 8 10 11 12 13 14 15 16 17 19 21 22 23 28 29 30 32 33 34 35 37 38 39 40 41 42 44 45 46 49 52 54 56 58 59 60 63 65 66 67 70 71 73 74	23	10	210	10458	109	168616	2444	81467	33292	—

WEST VIRGINIA

Resident population 1,816 (in thousands)
Resident population in metro areas 41.8%
Birth rate per 1,000 population 11.7
65 years and over 15.2%
Percent of persons without health insurance 14.9%

Hospital, Address, Telephone, Administrator, Approval, Facility, and Physician Codes, Health Care System, Network	Classification Codes		Utilization Data					Expense (thousands) of dollars		
	Control	Service	Staffed Beds	Admissions	Census	Outpatient Visits	Births	Total	Payroll	Personnel

★ American Hospital Association (AHA) membership
☐ Joint Commission on Accreditation of Healthcare Organizations (JCAHO) accreditation
+ American Osteopathic Healthcare Association (AOHA) membership
○ American Osteopathic Association (AOA) accreditation
△ Commission on Accreditation of Rehabilitation Facilities (CARF) accreditation
Control codes 61, 63, 64, 71, 72 and 73 indicate hospitals listed by AOHA, but not registered by AHA. For definition of numerical codes, see page A4

Hospital	Control	Service	Staffed Beds	Admissions	Census	Outpatient Visits	Births	Total	Payroll	Personnel
BECKLEY—Raleigh County										
☐ BECKLEY APPALACHIAN REGIONAL HOSPITAL, 306 Stanaford Road, Zip 25801–3142; tel. 304/255–3000; David R. Lyon, Administrator **A**1 9 10 **F**1 3 4 8 11 12 15 16 17 18 19 21 22 26 28 29 30 31 32 35 37 39 42 44 45 49 52 53 54 55 56 57 58 59 63 65 71 73 **P**6 **S** Appalachian Regional Healthcare, Lexington, KY **N** Partners in Health Network, Inc., Charleston, WV; CHA Provider Network, Inc., Lexington, KY	23	10	173	6815	115	20868	—	31751	14102	607
✸ BECKLEY HOSPITAL, 1007 South Oakwood Avenue, Zip 25801–5999; tel. 304/256–1200; Albert M. Tieche, Jr., Administrator (Nonreporting) **A**1 9 **S** Columbia/HCA Healthcare Corporation, Nashville, TN	33	10	52	—	—	—	—	—	—	—
✸ COLUMBIA RALEIGH GENERAL HOSPITAL, 1710 Harper Road, Zip 25801–3397; tel. 304/256–4100; Brent A. Marsteller, Chief Executive Officer (Total facility includes 18 beds in nursing home–type unit) **A**1 9 10 12 **F**7 8 10 12 15 16 19 20 21 22 23 25 28 30 32 33 34 35 37 38 39 41 42 44 45 52 64 65 67 70 71 72 73 **P**7 **S** Columbia/HCA Healthcare Corporation, Nashville, TN	33	10	275	11401	152	77775	1796	60897	25195	888
✸ VETERANS AFFAIRS MEDICAL CENTER, 200 Veterans Avenue, Zip 25801–6499; tel. 304/255–2121; Gerard P. Husson, Director (Total facility includes 42 beds in nursing home–type unit) (Nonreporting) **A**1 **S** Department of Veterans Affairs, Washington, DC	45	10	112	—	—	—	—	—	—	—
BERKELEY SPRINGS—Morgan County										
★ MORGAN COUNTY WAR MEMORIAL HOSPITAL, 1124 Fairfax Street, Zip 25411–1718; tel. 304/258–1234; David A. Sweeney, FACHE, Administrator (Total facility includes 16 beds in nursing home–type unit) **A**9 10 **F**8 15 16 22 27 30 32 34 39 44 45 46 49 64 65 71 73 **S** Valley Health System, Winchester, VA	13	10	44	1107	32	23260	0	7375	2837	119
BLUEFIELD—Mercer County										
✸ BLUEFIELD REGIONAL MEDICAL CENTER, 500 Cherry Street, Zip 24701–3390; tel. 304/327–1100; Eugene P. Pawlowski, President **A**1 9 10 **F**7 8 10 11 12 13 14 15 16 19 21 22 24 30 32 34 35 37 39 40 41 42 44 45 49 50 60 63 64 65 71 72 73 **P**8 **N** Southern Virginia Rural Health Network, Princeton, WV	23	10	265	8534	137	114701	802	62331	26150	909
✸ COLUMBIA ST. LUKE'S HOSPITAL, 1333 Southview Drive, Zip 24701–4399, Mailing Address: P.O. Box 1190, Zip 24701–1190; tel. 304/327–2900; Barry A. Papania, President and Chief Executive Officer **A**1 9 10 **F**8 12 14 15 16 19 21 22 23 26 30 32 35 37 39 41 44 49 54 56 63 65 67 71 73 **P**5 7 **S** Columbia/HCA Healthcare Corporation, Nashville, TN	33	10	79	1968	27	23875	—	13677	5187	200
BUCKEYE—Pocahontas County										
★ POCAHONTAS MEMORIAL HOSPITAL, Mailing Address: Rural Route 2, Box 52 W., Zip 24924; tel. 304/799–7400; Alavin R. Lawson, JD, Chief Executive Officer **A**9 10 **F**14 15 16 19 21 26 28 29 30 32 34 41 44 45 46 49 51 64 65 71 72 73	13	10	27	770	14	27131	3	4119	1648	91
BUCKHANNON—Upshur County										
✸ ST. JOSEPH'S HOSPITAL, Amalia Drive, Zip 26201–2222; tel. 304/473–2000; Wayne B. Griffith, FACHE, Chief Executive Officer (Total facility includes 16 beds in nursing home–type unit) **A**1 3 9 10 **F**2 7 8 12 14 15 16 17 19 22 28 32 33 34 35 37 40 42 44 46 49 52 56 57 58 59 64 65 67 71 73 **P**7 8	23	10	95	2890	43	55733	216	17689	7001	292
CHARLESTON—Kanawha County										
✸ △ CHARLESTON AREA MEDICAL CENTER, (Includes General Division, 501 Morris Street, Zip 25301, Mailing Address: Box 1393, Zip 25325; tel. 304/348–5432; Memorial Division, 3200 Maccorkle Avenue S.E., Zip 25304; tel. 304/348–5432; Women and Children's Hospital, 800 Pennsylvania Avenue, Zip 25302; tel. 304/348–5432), 501 Morris Street, Zip 25301–1300, Mailing Address: P.O. Box 1547, Zip 25326–1547; tel. 304/348–5432; Robert L. Savage, President and Chief Executive Officer (Total facility includes 19 beds in nursing home–type unit) **A**1 2 3 5 7 8 9 10 12 **F**2 3 4 5 6 7 8 10 11 12 13 14 15 16 17 18 19 20 21 22 23 24 25 26 27 28 29 30 31 32 33 34 35 36 37 38 39 40 41 42 43 44 45 46 47 48 49 51 52 54 55 56 57 58 59 60 61 63 64 65 66 67 68 69 70 71 72 73 74 **P**3 4 7 **S** Camcare, Inc., Charleston, WV **N** Partners in Health Network, Inc., Charleston, WV	23	10	818	35749	584	307550	2693	397889	146514	4625
✸ EYE AND EAR CLINIC OF CHARLESTON, 1306 Kanawha Boulevard East, Zip 25301, Mailing Address: P.O. Box 2271, Zip 25328–2271; tel. 304/343–4371; W. Allen Shelton, II, Administrator and Chief Executive Officer (Nonreporting) **A**1 9 10	33	45	26	—	—	—	—	—	—	—
GENERAL DIVISION See Charleston Area Medical Center										
✸ HIGHLAND HOSPITAL, 300 56th Street S.E., Zip 25304–2361, Mailing Address: P.O. Box 4107, Zip 25364–4107; tel. 304/926–1600; David M. McWatters, Administrator **A**1 5 9 10 **F**3 12 13 14 16 17 28 29 30 32 34 39 52 53 54 55 56 57 58 59 65 67	23	22	50	823	25	—	0	7082	3577	127
MEMORIAL DIVISION See Charleston Area Medical Center										
✸ SAINT FRANCIS HOSPITAL, 333 Laidley Street, Zip 25301–1628, Mailing Address: P.O. Box 471, Zip 25322–0471; tel. 304/347–6500; David R. Sirk, President and Chief Executive Officer (Total facility includes 30 beds in nursing home–type unit) (Nonreporting) **A**1 9 10 **S** Columbia/HCA Healthcare Corporation, Nashville, TN	33	10	155	—	—	—	—	—	—	—
WOMEN AND CHILDREN'S HOSPITAL See Charleston Area Medical Center										

Hospital, Address, Telephone, Administrator, Approval, Facility, and Physician Codes, Health Care System, Network	Classi-fication Codes		Utilization Data					Expense (thousands) of dollars		
★ American Hospital Association (AHA) membership □ Joint Commission on Accreditation of Healthcare Organizations (JCAHO) accreditation + American Osteopathic Healthcare Association (AOHA) membership ○ American Osteopathic Association (AOA) accreditation △ Commission on Accreditation of Rehabilitation Facilities (CARF) accreditation Control codes 61, 63, 64, 71, 72 and 73 indicate hospitals listed by AOHA, but not registered by AHA. For definition of numerical codes, see page A4	Control	Service	Staffed Beds	Admissions	Census	Outpatient Visits	Births	Total	Payroll	Personnel

CLARKSBURG—Harrison County

⊞ LOUIS A. JOHNSON VETERANS AFFAIRS MEDICAL CENTER, 1 Medical Center Drive, Zip 26301–4199; tel. 304/623–3461; Michael W. Neusch, FACHE, Director (Nonreporting) **A**1 2 3 5 9 **S** Department of Veterans Affairs, Washington, DC

| | 45 | 10 | 160 | — | — | — | — | — | — | |

⊞ UNITED HOSPITAL CENTER, Route 19 South, Zip 26301, Mailing Address: P.O. Box 1680, Zip 26302–1680; tel. 304/624–2121; Bruce C. Carter, President **A**1 2 3 5 9 10 12 13 **F**3 7 8 10 11 12 14 16 19 20 21 22 23 25 30 32 33 34 35 37 39 40 41 42 44 45 46 49 51 52 53 54 55 56 57 58 59 60 63 64 65 67 71 73 74 **P**6 8 **S** West Virginia United Health System, Fairmont, WV **N** Webster Memorial/United Hospital Center EACH/RPCH Network, Webster Springs, WV; Health Partners Network, Inc., Fairmont, WV; Integrated Provider Network, Morgantown, WV

| | 23 | 10 | 309 | 11886 | 167 | 265672 | 859 | 91710 | 39407 | 1249 |

ELKINS—Randolph County

⊞ DAVIS MEMORIAL HOSPITAL, Gorman Avenue and Reed Street, Zip 26241, Mailing Address: P.O. Box 1484, Zip 26241–1484; tel. 304/636–3300; Robert L. Hammer, II, Chief Executive Officer **A**1 9 10 **F**2 3 4 6 7 8 9 10 11 16 19 21 22 23 26 27 28 29 30 31 32 33 34 35 36 37 38 39 40 41 42 43 44 46 47 48 49 50 52 53 54 55 56 57 58 59 60 63 64 65 69 70 71 73 **P**7 8

| | 23 | 10 | 115 | 5769 | 73 | 148708 | 524 | 43249 | 17614 | 617 |

FAIRMONT—Marion County

⊞ FAIRMONT GENERAL HOSPITAL, 1325 Locust Avenue, Zip 26554–1435; tel. 304/367–7100; Richard W. Graham, FACHE, President (Total facility includes 61 beds in nursing home–type unit) **A**1 9 10 **F**2 3 7 8 10 11 12 14 15 16 17 19 21 22 23 28 29 30 32 35 36 39 40 41 42 44 46 49 52 53 54 55 56 57 58 59 63 64 65 66 67 71 73 74 **P**4 7 8 **S** Quorum Health Group/Quorum Health Resources, Inc., Brentwood, TN

| | 23 | 10 | 224 | 6624 | 148 | 140179 | 588 | 48553 | 20708 | 768 |

GASSAWAY—Braxton County

★ BRAXTON COUNTY MEMORIAL HOSPITAL, 100 Hoylman Drive, Zip 26624–9308; tel. 304/364–5156; Tony E. Atkins, Administrator **A**9 10 **F**8 13 15 16 17 19 21 22 24 28 31 32 34 44 65 71 73 74 **S** Camcare, Inc., Charleston, WV **N** Partners in Health Network, Inc., Charleston, WV

| | 23 | 10 | 30 | 949 | 8 | 21535 | 5 | 6500 | 3393 | — |

GLEN DALE—Marshall County

⊞ REYNOLDS MEMORIAL HOSPITAL, 800 Wheeling Avenue, Zip 26038–1697; tel. 304/845–3211; John Sicurella, Chief Executive Officer (Total facility includes 20 beds in nursing home–type unit) **A**1 6 9 10 **F**1 3 7 8 15 16 17 19 21 22 24 26 28 29 30 32 33 34 35 37 39 40 41 42 44 45 46 49 53 54 55 56 57 58 59 60 63 64 65 70 71 73 **P**8

| | 23 | 10 | 140 | 3251 | 54 | 71796 | 133 | 28439 | 12307 | 430 |

GRAFTON—Taylor County

□ GRAFTON CITY HOSPITAL, 500 Market Street, Zip 26354–1187; tel. 304/265–0400; Gary R. Willmon, Administrator (Total facility includes 72 beds in nursing home–type unit) **A**1 9 10 **F**8 11 12 14 15 16 19 21 22 24 25 26 28 29 30 32 33 34 37 39 42 44 45 46 49 51 54 64 65 66 70 71 72 73 74 **P**3

| | 14 | 10 | 106 | 2377 | 83 | 19776 | — | 9116 | 4009 | 247 |

GRANTSVILLE—Calhoun County

MINNIE HAMILTON HEALTHCARE CENTER, High Street, Zip 26147, Mailing Address: Route 1, Box 1A, Zip 26147; tel. 304/354–9244; Barbara Lay, Administrator **A**9 **F**8 13 14 15 16 17 18 19 21 22 28 30 34 39 45 49 51 65 71 **N** Partners in Health Network, Inc., Charleston, WV

| | 23 | 10 | 15 | 486 | 4 | 19717 | 0 | 4182 | 2340 | 108 |

HINTON—Summers County

□ SUMMERS COUNTY APPALACHIAN REGIONAL HOSPITAL, Terrace Street, Zip 25951, Mailing Address: Drawer 940, Zip 25951–0940; tel. 304/466–1000; Clyde E. Bolton, Administrator (Total facility includes 24 beds in nursing home–type unit) **A**1 9 10 **F**8 12 14 15 16 17 19 22 28 30 34 35 37 44 46 48 49 51 64 65 70 71 73 74 **S** Appalachian Regional Healthcare, Lexington, KY **N** Partners in Health Network, Inc., Charleston, WV; CHA Provider Network, Inc., Lexington, KY

| | 23 | 10 | 65 | 873 | 34 | 63430 | — | 8765 | 3088 | 145 |

HUNTINGTON—Cabell County

⊞ CABELL HUNTINGTON HOSPITAL, 1340 Hal Greer Boulevard, Zip 25701–0195; tel. 304/526–2000; W. Don Smith, II, President and Chief Executive Officer (Total facility includes 15 beds in nursing home–type unit) **A**1 3 5 9 10 **F**4 7 8 9 15 16 19 20 21 22 23 28 29 30 31 32 33 34 35 37 38 39 40 41 42 44 45 46 47 49 51 60 61 63 64 65 67 69 70 71 73 74 **P**8 **N** CHA Provider Network, Inc., Lexington, KY

| | 23 | 10 | 293 | 14648 | 186 | 203890 | 2297 | 106300 | 47358 | 1383 |

⊞ COLUMBIA RIVER PARK HOSPITAL, 1230 Sixth Avenue, Zip 25701–2312, Mailing Address: P.O. Box 1875, Zip 25719–1875; tel. 304/526–9111; Scott C. Stamm, Chief Executive Officer **A**1 9 10 **F**1 17 18 22 28 30 52 53 54 55 56 57 58 59 **S** Columbia/HCA Healthcare Corporation, Nashville, TN

| | 33 | 22 | 165 | 1929 | 50 | — | — | 9574 | 4041 | 128 |

□ △ HEALTHSOUTH HUNTINGTON REHABILITATION HOSPITAL, 6900 West Country Club Drive, Zip 25705–2000; tel. 304/733–1060; Homer Fowler, Chief Operating Officer **A**1 7 10 **F**34 42 45 48 73 **S** HEALTHSOUTH Corporation, Birmingham, AL **N** CHA Provider Network, Inc., Lexington, KY

| | 33 | 46 | 40 | 694 | 37 | 6446 | 0 | 7965 | 4490 | — |

⊞ ST. MARY'S HOSPITAL, 2900 First Avenue, Zip 25702–1272; tel. 304/526–1234; J. Thomas Jones, Executive Director (Total facility includes 20 beds in nursing home–type unit) **A**1 2 3 5 6 9 10 **F**2 4 7 8 10 11 12 15 16 17 19 21 22 23 26 28 29 30 31 32 34 35 37 39 40 41 42 43 44 45 46 49 52 53 54 55 56 57 59 60 63 64 65 67 70 71 73 74 **P**2 8 **N** CHA Provider Network, Inc., Lexington, KY

| | 21 | 10 | 440 | 16391 | 265 | 116596 | 721 | 133614 | 55799 | 1618 |

Hospital, Address, Telephone, Administrator, Approval, Facility, and Physician Codes, Health Care System, Network	Classi-fication Codes		Utilization Data					Expense (thousands) of dollars		
★ American Hospital Association (AHA) membership □ Joint Commission on Accreditation of Healthcare Organizations (JCAHO) accreditation + American Osteopathic Healthcare Association (AOHA) membership ○ American Osteopathic Association (AOA) accreditation △ Commission on Accreditation of Rehabilitation Facilities (CARF) accreditation Control codes 61, 63, 64, 71, 72 and 73 indicate hospitals listed by AOHA, but not registered by AHA. For definition of numerical codes, see page A4	Control	Service	Staffed Beds	Admissions	Census	Outpatient Visits	Births	Total	Payroll	Personnel

⊞ VETERANS AFFAIRS MEDICAL CENTER, 1540 Spring Valley Drive, Zip 25704–9300; tel. 304/429–6741; David N. Pennington, Chief Executive Officer (Nonreporting) **A**1 3 5 9 **S** Department of Veterans Affairs, Washington, DC	45	10	170	—	—	—	—	—	—	—
HURRICANE—Putnam County										
⊞ PUTNAM GENERAL HOSPITAL, 1400 Hospital Drive, Zip 25526–9210, Mailing Address: P.O. Box 900, Zip 25526–0900; tel. 304/757–1700; Patsy Hardy, Administrator **A**1 9 10 **F**8 12 14 15 16 18 19 21 23 28 30 32 33 34 35 37 41 44 46 49 65 66 71 73 **P**7 **S** Columbia/HCA Healthcare Corporation, Nashville, TN	33	10	64	2588	37	3024	0	18445	7719	261
KEYSER—Mineral County										
□ POTOMAC VALLEY HOSPITAL, 167 South Mineral Street, Zip 26726–2699; tel. 304/788–3141; Larry Abrams, Administrator **A**1 9 10 **F**11 14 19 21 22 29 30 31 32 33 37 44 49 63 65 67 71 73	33	10	42	1996	18	48729	0	12215	4260	188
KINGWOOD—Preston County										
⊞ PRESTON MEMORIAL HOSPITAL, 300 South Price Street, Zip 26537–1495; tel. 304/329–1400; Charles Lonchar, President and Chief Executive Officer **A**1 9 10 **F**2 3 7 8 12 17 19 22 24 28 30 32 34 35 40 41 44 49 63 65 71 73 74 **P**8 **S** Quorum Health Group/Quorum Health Resources, Inc., Brentwood, TN	23	10	60	1186	16	50101	152	10657	4743	226
LOGAN—Logan County										
★ GUYAN VALLEY HOSPITAL, 396 Dingess Street, Zip 25601–3695; tel. 304/792–1700; Phillip Belchek, Administrator (Nonreporting)	23	10	43	—	—	—	—	—	—	—
□ LOGAN GENERAL HOSPITAL, 20 Hospital Drive, Zip 25601–3473; tel. 304/792–1101; C. David Morrison, President **A**1 10 12 13 **F**8 15 16 19 21 22 30 34 41 42 44 49 54 55 56 58 65 71 73 **P**6	23	10	132	7115	91	204508	520	72515	39184	927
MADISON—Boone County										
⊞ BOONE MEMORIAL HOSPITAL, 701 Madison Avenue, Zip 25130–1699; tel. 304/369–1230; Tommy H. Mullins, Administrator **A**1 9 10 **F**14 15 16 19 21 22 32 33 44 45 49 64 65 71 73 **N** Partners in Health Network, Inc., Charleston, WV; CHA Provider Network, Inc., Lexington, KY	13	10	38	611	13	33461	0	5892	2528	117
MAN—Logan County										
□ MAN ARH HOSPITAL, 700 East McDonald Avenue, Zip 25635–1011; tel. 304/583–8421; Louis G. Roe, Jr., Administrator **A**1 9 10 **F**8 12 14 15 16 17 19 21 22 25 28 29 30 31 32 34 35 37 44 45 46 49 54 56 58 65 71 73 **P**6 **S** Appalachian Regional Healthcare, Lexington, KY **N** Partners in Health Network, Inc., Charleston, WV; CHA Provider Network, Inc., Lexington, KY	23	10	42	846	8	52991	—	11992	5816	236
MARTINSBURG—Berkeley County										
⊞ CITY HOSPITAL, Dry Run Road, Zip 25401, Mailing Address: P.O. Box 1418, Zip 25402–1418; tel. 304/264–1000; Peter L. Mulford, Administrator (Total facility includes 19 beds in nursing home–type unit) **A**1 2 9 10 **F**1 3 7 8 12 16 17 22 23 24 28 30 34 37 40 41 42 44 45 46 49 52 56 57 58 60 63 64 65 66 67 71 73 74 **P**1 **S** Quorum Health Group/Quorum Health Resources, Inc., Brentwood, TN	23	10	163	6778	108	117194	796	47045	19228	607
⊞ VETERANS AFFAIRS MEDICAL CENTER, Charles Town Road, Zip 25401–0205; tel. 304/263–0811; Francis Citro, Jr., M.D., Acting Director (Total facility includes 150 beds in nursing home–type unit) (Nonreporting) **A**1 3 5 9 **S** Department of Veterans Affairs, Washington, DC	45	10	370	—	—	—	—	—	—	—
MONTGOMERY—Fayette County										
⊞ MONTGOMERY GENERAL HOSPITAL, 401 Sixth Avenue, Zip 25136–0270, Mailing Address: P.O. Box 270, Zip 25136–0270; tel. 304/442–5151; William R. Laird, IV, President and Chief Executive Officer (Total facility includes 44 beds in nursing home–type unit) **A**1 10 **F**8 12 16 19 22 28 30 32 34 35 37 44 46 49 51 64 65 71 73 **P**6 **N** Partners in Health Network, Inc., Charleston, WV	23	10	99	1666	61	57531	0	21321	9547	298
MORGANTOWN—Monongalia County										
□ CHESTNUT RIDGE HOSPITAL, 930 Chestnut Ridge Road, Zip 26505–2854; tel. 304/293–4000; Lawrence J. Drake, Chief Executive Officer **A**1 5 9 10 **F**2 9 11 15 19 21 22 35 37 38 40 47 48 52 53 54 56 57 58 59 70 71 **P**6 **S** Ramsay Health Care, Inc., Coral Gables, FL	33	22	70	1216	45	3706	0	7958	3024	150
□ △ HEALTHSOUTH MOUNTAIN REGIONAL REHABILITATION HOSPITAL, 1160 Van Voorhis, Zip 26505–3435; tel. 304/598–1100; Sharon Nero, Chief Executive Officer **A**1 7 10 **F**5 12 13 14 16 17 30 34 39 41 42 48 49 65 66 74 **S** HEALTHSOUTH Corporation, Birmingham, AL	33	46	80	1148	75	9369	—	17843	7370	233
⊞ MONONGALIA GENERAL HOSPITAL, 1200 J. D. Anderson Drive, Zip 26505–3486; tel. 304/598–1200; Robert P. Ritz, Chief Executive Officer (Total facility includes 20 beds in nursing home–type unit) **A**1 3 5 9 10 **F**4 6 7 8 10 11 12 13 14 15 16 17 19 21 22 23 24 25 28 30 31 32 33 34 35 37 39 42 43 44 46 49 51 54 60 61 62 63 65 66 67 71 72 73 74 **S** Quorum Health Group/Quorum Health Resources, Inc., Brentwood, TN	23	10	205	7755	111	130883	548	70401	28453	968
⊞ WEST VIRGINIA UNIVERSITY HOSPITALS, Medical Center Drive, Zip 26506–4749; tel. 304/598–4000; Bruce McClymonds, President **A**1 2 3 5 8 9 10 **F**2 3 4 7 8 10 11 12 17 18 19 20 21 22 23 25 26 28 29 30 31 32 33 34 35 37 38 40 41 42 43 44 45 46 47 48 49 50 51 52 53 54 55 56 57 58 59 60 61 63 64 65 66 67 69 70 71 73 74 **P**6 8 **S** West Virginia United Health System, Fairmont, WV **N** Health Partners Network, Inc., Fairmont, WV; Integrated Provider Network, Morgantown, WV	23	10	331	12827	230	369419	1291	181061	67724	2235
NEW MARTINSVILLE—Wetzel County										
⊞ WETZEL COUNTY HOSPITAL, 3 East Benjamin Drive, Zip 26155–2758; tel. 304/455–8000; C. Thomas Long, Chief Executive Officer **A**1 9 10 **F**7 8 13 14 15 16 17 19 21 22 28 32 34 37 39 40 41 44 45 46 49 65 67 70 71 73	13	10	51	1642	15	11247	163	14578	5663	183

Hospital, Address, Telephone, Administrator, Approval, Facility, and Physician Codes, Health Care System, Network	Classi-fication Codes		Utilization Data					Expense (thousands) of dollars		
★ American Hospital Association (AHA) membership ☐ Joint Commission on Accreditation of Healthcare Organizations (JCAHO) accreditation + American Osteopathic Healthcare Association (AOHA) membership ○ American Osteopathic Association (AOA) accreditation △ Commission on Accreditation of Rehabilitation Facilities (CARF) accreditation Control codes 61, 63, 64, 71, 72 and 73 indicate hospitals listed by AOHA, but not registered by AHA. For definition of numerical codes, see page A4	Control	Service	Staffed Beds	Admissions	Census	Outpatient Visits	Births	Total	Payroll	Personnel

OAK HILL—Fayette County

⊞ PLATEAU MEDICAL CENTER, 430 Main Street, Zip 25901–3455; tel. 304/469–8600; David L. Brash, Administrator (Total facility includes 11 beds in nursing home–type unit) **A**1 9 10 **F**8 12 13 14 15 16 17 19 20 21 22 27 32 34 35 37 44 45 46 49 64 65 71 73 **P**6 **S** Camcare, Inc., Charleston, WV **N** Partners in Health Network, Inc., Charleston, WV

| | 33 | 10 | 79 | 2541 | 37 | 50176 | 0 | 15238 | 7370 | 305 |

PARKERSBURG—Wood County

⊞ CAMDEN–CLARK MEMORIAL HOSPITAL, 800 Garfield Avenue, Zip 26101–5378, Mailing Address: P.O. Box 718, Zip 26102–0718; tel. 304/424–2111; Thomas J. Corder, President and Chief Executive Officer (Total facility includes 25 beds in nursing home–type unit) **A**1 2 9 10 **F**7 8 12 14 15 16 17 19 21 22 23 24 28 29 30 32 33 34 35 39 40 41 42 44 45 46 49 60 63 64 65 67 71 73 74 **P**7 **N** Mid–Ohio Valley Rural Health Network, Parkersburg, WV

| | 23 | 10 | 345 | 10574 | 142 | 200751 | 797 | 75598 | 31104 | 1051 |

☐ △ HEALTHSOUTH WESTERN HILLS REGIONAL REHABILITATION HOSPITAL, 3 Western Hills Drive, Zip 26101–8122, Mailing Address: P.O. Box 1428, Zip 26102–1428; tel. 304/420–1300; Thomas Heller, Administrator (Nonreporting) **A**1 7 10 **S** HEALTHSOUTH Corporation, Birmingham, AL

| | 33 | 46 | 40 | — | | | | | | |

⊞ ST. JOSEPH'S HOSPITAL, 1824 Murdoch Avenue, Zip 26101–3246, Mailing Address: P.O. Box 327, Zip 26102–0327; tel. 304/424–4111; Stephens M. Mundy, Chief Executive Officer (Total facility includes 20 beds in nursing home–type unit) **A**1 9 10 **F**2 3 7 8 10 11 12 14 15 16 17 19 22 23 25 26 27 28 29 30 31 32 34 35 37 39 40 41 42 44 45 46 48 49 52 53 55 56 57 59 63 64 65 66 67 71 72 73 74 **P**7

| | 32 | 10 | 294 | 8259 | 119 | 146726 | 620 | — | 21258 | 699 |

PETERSBURG—Grant County

★ GRANT MEMORIAL HOSPITAL, Route 55 West, Zip 26847, Mailing Address: P.O. Box 1019, Zip 26847–1019; tel. 304/257–1026; Robert L. Harman, Administrator (Total facility includes 10 beds in nursing home–type unit) **A**9 10 **F**7 8 12 13 15 17 19 21 22 26 28 29 30 32 33 34 37 40 42 44 49 58 64 65 70 71 74 **N** Eastern Panhandle Integrated Delivery System, Petersburg, WV

| | 13 | 10 | 65 | 2509 | 38 | 67272 | 279 | 16188 | 7289 | 323 |

PHILIPPI—Barbour County

BROADDUS HOSPITAL, College Hill, Zip 26416–1051; tel. 304/457–1760; Susannah Higgins, Chief Executive Officer (Total facility includes 60 beds in nursing home–type unit) **A**9 **F**8 12 13 14 15 16 17 19 22 26 27 28 30 32 33 34 42 44 49 51 54 64 65 73 74

| | 23 | 10 | 72 | 434 | 61 | 22027 | 1 | 5638 | 2924 | 146 |

POINT PLEASANT—Mason County

⊞ PLEASANT VALLEY HOSPITAL, 2520 Valley Drive, Zip 25550–2083; tel. 304/675–4340; Michael G. Sellards, Executive Director (Total facility includes 100 beds in nursing home–type unit) (Nonreporting) **A**1 2 9 10

| | 23 | 10 | 201 | — | — | — | — | — | — | — |

PRINCETON—Mercer County

☐ △ HEALTHSOUTH SOUTHERN HILLS REHABILITATION HOSPITAL, 120 Twelfth Street, Zip 24740–2312; tel. 304/487–8000; Timothy Mitchell, Administrator (Nonreporting) **A**1 7 10 **S** HEALTHSOUTH Corporation, Birmingham, AL

| | 33 | 46 | 40 | — | — | — | — | — | — | — |

⊞ PRINCETON COMMUNITY HOSPITAL, 12th Street, Zip 24740–1369, Mailing Address: P.O. Box 1369, Zip 24740–1369; tel. 304/487–7000; Daniel C. Dunmyer, Chief Executive Officer (Total facility includes 23 beds in nursing home–type unit) (Nonreporting) **A**1 2 9 10 **N** Southern Virginia Rural Health Network, Princeton, WV

| | 14 | 10 | 206 | — | — | — | — | — | — | — |

RANSON—Jefferson County

⊞ JEFFERSON MEMORIAL HOSPITAL, 300 South Preston Street, Zip 25438–1699; tel. 304/728–1600; Jon D. Applebaum, Administrator **A**1 5 9 10 **F**7 8 14 15 16 17 19 21 22 28 30 32 33 34 35 37 39 40 41 42 44 45 46 54 65 66 67 70 71 72 73 **P**8

| | 23 | 10 | 52 | 2222 | 23 | 21169 | 209 | 17856 | 8515 | 303 |

RICHWOOD—Nicholas County

RICHWOOD AREA COMMUNITY HOSPITAL, Riverside Addition, Zip 26261; tel. 304/846–2573; D. Parker Haddix, Chief Executive Officer **A**9 **F**13 22 28 34 44 51 64 71 73 **N** Partners in Health Network, Inc., Charleston, WV

| | 23 | 10 | 25 | 209 | 1 | 10298 | — | 1334 | 705 | 38 |

RIPLEY—Jackson County

⊞ JACKSON GENERAL HOSPITAL, Pinnell Street, Zip 25271, Mailing Address: P.O. Box 720, Zip 25271–0720; tel. 304/372–2731; Richard L. Rohaley, President and Chief Executive Officer **A**1 9 10 **F**7 8 11 15 16 19 21 22 28 32 34 37 40 41 44 49 65 66 71 72 **N** Partners in Health Network, Inc., Charleston, WV

| | 23 | 10 | 82 | 2760 | 36 | 45620 | 156 | 20427 | 4273 | 324 |

ROMNEY—Hampshire County

HAMPSHIRE MEMORIAL HOSPITAL, 549 Center Avenue, Zip 26757–1199; tel. 304/822–4561; Roberta D. McCauley, Chief Executive Officer (Total facility includes 30 beds in nursing home–type unit) **A**9 10 **F**8 14 15 16 19 22 30 31 44 49 64 65 71 **P**4

| | 33 | 10 | 47 | 681 | 35 | 31459 | — | 6206 | 2360 | 100 |

RONCEVERTE—Greenbrier County

⊞ GREENBRIER VALLEY MEDICAL CENTER, 202 Maplewood Avenue, Zip 24970–0497, Mailing Address: P.O. Box 497, Zip 24970–0497; tel. 304/647–4411; James B. Wood, Chief Executive Officer **A**1 9 10 **F**7 8 12 14 16 19 21 22 23 26 28 29 30 33 34 35 37 39 40 42 44 45 46 49 60 63 65 71 73 **S** Columbia/HCA Healthcare Corporation, Nashville, TN

| | 33 | 10 | 122 | 4392 | 57 | 36090 | 451 | 24366 | 9460 | 388 |

SISTERSVILLE—Tyler County

SISTERSVILLE GENERAL HOSPITAL, 314 South Wells Street, Zip 26175–1098; tel. 304/652–2611; Lynn McCormick, Administrator **A**9 **F**8 15 16 22 24 28 30 32 33 41 44 49 64 65 71 73 **N** Mid–Ohio Valley Rural Health Network, Parkersburg, WV

| | 14 | 10 | 12 | 199 | 2 | 27906 | 0 | 3770 | 1936 | 92 |

Hospital, Address, Telephone, Administrator, Approval, Facility, and Physician Codes, Health Care System, Network	Classi-fication Codes		Utilization Data					Expense (thousands) of dollars		
★ American Hospital Association (AHA) membership □ Joint Commission on Accreditation of Healthcare Organizations (JCAHO) accreditation + American Osteopathic Healthcare Association (AOHA) membership ○ American Osteopathic Association (AOA) accreditation △ Commission on Accreditation of Rehabilitation Facilities (CARF) accreditation Control codes 61, 63, 64, 71, 72 and 73 indicate hospitals listed by AOHA, but not registered by AHA. For definition of numerical codes, see page A4	Control	Service	Staffed Beds	Admissions	Census	Outpatient Visits	Births	Total	Payroll	Personnel

SOUTH CHARLESTON—Kanawha County

☒ THOMAS MEMORIAL HOSPITAL, 4605 MacCorkle Avenue S.W., Zip 25309–1398; tel. 304/766–3600; Stephen P. Dexter, Chief Executive Officer **A**1 3 5 9 10 **F**3 7 8 11 14 15 16 17 19 21 22 24 26 27 28 29 30 32 33 34 35 36 37 39 40 41 42 44 45 49 52 53 54 55 56 57 58 59 60 63 65 67 71 72 73 74 **P**7

| | 23 | 10 | 200 | 8162 | 118 | 189816 | 548 | 67265 | 27198 | 802 |

SPENCER—Roane County

☒ ROANE GENERAL HOSPITAL, 200 Hospital Drive, Zip 25276–1060; tel. 304/927–6200; Andrew Mazon, III, Administrator and Chief Executive Officer (Total facility includes 9 beds in nursing home–type unit) **A**1 9 10 **F**1 7 8 17 19 21 22 28 30 32 34 40 44 45 64 65 71 73 **N** Partners in Health Network, Inc., Charleston, WV

| | 23 | 10 | 55 | 1131 | 24 | 24457 | 163 | 11569 | 5943 | 225 |

SUMMERSVILLE—Nicholas County

★ SUMMERSVILLE MEMORIAL HOSPITAL, 400 Fairview Heights Road, Zip 26651–0400; tel. 304/872–2891; David Lackey, Administrator (Total facility includes 52 beds in nursing home–type unit) **A**9 10 **F**4 7 8 11 14 17 19 21 22 25 26 30 34 35 37 40 42 44 45 49 64 65 67 70 71 72 73

| | 14 | 10 | 109 | 2009 | 77 | 52024 | 185 | 18942 | 8224 | 363 |

WEBSTER SPRINGS—Webster County

★ WEBSTER COUNTY MEMORIAL HOSPITAL, 324 Miller Mountain Drive, Zip 26288–1087; tel. 304/847–5682; Stephen M. Gavalchik, Administrator (Nonreporting) **A**9 **N** Webster Memorial/United Hospital Center EACH/RPCH Network, Webster Springs, WV

| | 13 | 10 | 6 | — | — | — | — | — | — | — |

WEIRTON—Brooke County

☒ WEIRTON MEDICAL CENTER, 601 Colliers Way, Zip 26062–5091; tel. 304/797–6000; Donald Muhlenthaler, FACHE, President and Chief Executive Officer (Total facility includes 33 beds in nursing home–type unit) **A**1 9 10 **F**7 8 10 11 13 14 15 16 17 19 20 21 22 23 24 25 26 27 28 29 30 31 32 33 34 35 39 40 41 42 44 45 49 52 53 54 55 56 57 58 59 63 64 65 66 67 69 70 71 73 **P**1 **N** Tri-State Community Care Network, Weirton, WV

| | 23 | 10 | 240 | 6961 | 112 | 100160 | 270 | 47386 | 21342 | 690 |

WESTON—Lewis County

☒ STONEWALL JACKSON MEMORIAL HOSPITAL, Mailing Address: Route 4, Box 10, Zip 26452; tel. 304/269–8000; David D. Shaffer, Chief Executive Officer (Total facility includes 10 beds in nursing home–type unit) **A**1 9 10 **F**7 8 15 16 19 22 28 30 32 35 40 41 42 44 45 46 49 64 65 66 70 71 73 **P**8

| | 23 | 10 | 70 | 3173 | 45 | 67699 | 265 | 16029 | 7261 | 273 |

□ WILLIAM R. SHARPE JR. HOSPITAL, Route 33 West, Zip 26452, Mailing Address: P.O. Drawer 1127, Zip 26452–1127; tel. 304/269–1210; Jack C. Clohan, Jr., Administrator **A**1 5 10 **F**14 15 16 26 27 45 46 52 54 55 56 57 65 67 73 **P**6

| | 12 | 22 | 150 | 1254 | 119 | 1 | 1 | 21137 | 8338 | 417 |

WHEELING—Ohio County

☒ OHIO VALLEY MEDICAL CENTER, 2000 Eoff Street, Zip 26003–3870; tel. 304/234–0123; Thomas P. Galinski, President and Chief Executive Officer (Total facility includes 172 beds in nursing home–type unit) **A**1 2 3 5 9 10 12 13 **F**3 5 7 8 10 11 12 14 15 16 17 18 19 21 22 23 24 25 26 27 28 29 30 31 32 34 35 37 39 40 41 42 44 45 47 48 49 51 52 53 54 55 56 57 58 59 60 61 63 64 65 66 67 71 73 74 **P**6 8 **S** Allegheny Health, Education and Research Foundation, Pittsburgh, PA

| | 23 | 10 | 385 | 7599 | 249 | 111117 | 535 | 67370 | 28527 | 1150 |

☒ WHEELING HOSPITAL, 1 Medical Park, Zip 26003–0708; tel. 304/243–3000; Donald H. Hofreuter, M.D., Administrator and Chief Executive Officer **A**1 2 3 5 9 10 **F**3 4 7 8 10 11 12 13 15 16 17 19 20 21 22 23 24 26 27 28 29 30 31 32 34 35 37 39 40 41 42 43 44 45 46 49 51 53 54 55 56 57 58 59 60 63 65 66 67 70 71 72 73 74 **P**7 8

| | 23 | 10 | 276 | 10694 | 138 | 212531 | 1144 | 106896 | 44839 | 1485 |

WILLIAMSON—Mingo County

□ WILLIAMSON MEMORIAL HOSPITAL, 859 Alderson Street, Zip 25661–3215, Mailing Address: P.O. Box 1980, Zip 25661–1980; tel. 304/235–2500; James Arp, Administrator **A**1 9 10 **F**7 8 12 15 16 19 21 22 23 28 30 31 32 34 35 37 39 42 44 46 48 71 **S** Health Management Associates, Naples, FL

| | 33 | 10 | 76 | 3964 | 46 | 32879 | 221 | 18202 | 7716 | 334 |

WISCONSIN

Resident population 5,170 (in thousands)
Resident population in metro areas 67.9%
Birth rate per 1,000 population 13.4
65 years and over 13.3%
Percent of persons without health insurance 8.4%

Hospital, Address, Telephone, Administrator, Approval, Facility, and Physician Codes, Health Care System, Network	Classification Codes		Utilization Data					Expense (thousands) of dollars		
	Control	Service	Staffed Beds	Admissions	Census	Outpatient Visits	Births	Total	Payroll	Personnel

★ American Hospital Association (AHA) membership
□ Joint Commission on Accreditation of Healthcare Organizations (JCAHO) accreditation
+ American Osteopathic Healthcare Association (AOHA) membership
○ American Osteopathic Association (AOA) accreditation
△ Commission on Accreditation of Rehabilitation Facilities (CARF) accreditation
Control codes 61, 63, 64, 71, 72 and 73 indicate hospitals listed by AOHA, but not registered by AHA. For definition of numerical codes, see page A4

AMERY—Polk County

✠ APPLE RIVER HOSPITAL, 230 Deronda Street, Zip 54001–1407; tel. 715/268–7151; Michael Karuschak, Jr., Administrator **A**1 9 10 **F**7 8 11 16 19 21 22 29 32 33 34 35 37 39 40 42 44 45 48 49 61 64 65 66 71 **S** Quorum Health Group/Quorum Health Resources, Inc., Brentwood, TN
| | 23 | 10 | 4 | 1110 | 12 | 13431 | 111 | 8592 | 3371 | 121 |

ANTIGO—Langlade County

□ LANGLADE MEMORIAL HOSPITAL, 112 East Fifth Avenue, Zip 54409–2796; tel. 715/623–2331; David R. Schneider, Executive Director **A**1 9 10 **F**1 2 3 4 7 8 9 10 11 12 16 19 21 22 26 29 32 33 34 35 36 37 38 40 42 43 44 45 47 49 52 53 54 55 56 57 58 59 61 63 64 65 71 **P**7
| | 21 | 10 | 49 | 1835 | 21 | 28565 | 227 | 16802 | 7637 | 251 |

APPLETON—Outagamie County

✠ APPLETON MEDICAL CENTER, 1818 North Meade Street, Zip 54911–3496; tel. 920/731–4101; Paul E. Macek, Senior Vice President **A**1 2 3 5 9 10 **F**2 3 4 6 7 8 10 11 12 14 16 18 19 21 22 23 24 26 29 32 34 35 36 37 38 39 40 41 42 43 44 45 46 48 49 52 53 54 55 56 57 58 59 60 61 62 64 65 66 69 70 71 72 74 **P**6 8 **S** United Health Group, Appleton, WI
| | 23 | 10 | 146 | 7252 | 86 | 86591 | 1222 | 72596 | 31155 | 757 |

✠ △ ST. ELIZABETH HOSPITAL, 1506 South Oneida Street, Zip 54915–1397; tel. 920/738–2000; Otto L. Cox, President and Chief Executive Officer **A**1 2 3 5 7 10 **F**1 2 3 4 5 6 7 8 9 10 11 12 18 19 21 22 23 26 29 32 33 34 35 36 37 38 39 40 41 42 43 44 45 46 47 48 49 52 53 54 55 56 57 58 59 60 61 62 63 64 65 66 70 71 74 **S** Wheaton Franciscan Services, Inc., Wheaton, IL **N** Affinity Health System, Inc., Oshkosh, WI
| | 21 | 10 | 166 | 7796 | 88 | 160235 | 1246 | 66838 | 29466 | 869 |

ARCADIA—Trempealeau County

✠ FRANCISCAN SKEMP HEALTHCARE–ARCADIA CAMPUS, 464 South St. Joseph Avenue, Zip 54612–1401; tel. 608/323–3341; Robert M. Tracey, Administrator (Total facility includes 75 beds in nursing home–type unit) **A**1 10 **F**2 3 7 14 16 18 19 22 26 29 32 33 34 40 41 44 45 46 49 52 58 61 64 65 66 71 **P**8 **S** Franciscan Skemp Healthcare, La Crosse, WI **N** Franciscan Skemp Healthcare, LaCrosse, WI
| | 21 | 10 | 101 | 348 | 70 | 19491 | 59 | — | — | — |

ASHLAND—Ashland County

✠ MEMORIAL MEDICAL CENTER, 1615 Maple Lane, Zip 54806–3689; tel. 715/682–4563; Daniel J. Hymans, President **A**1 9 10 **F**2 3 7 8 11 14 19 21 22 25 26 29 30 33 34 35 37 39 40 41 42 44 45 48 49 52 53 54 55 56 57 58 59 61 63 64 65 66 67 71 73
| | 23 | 10 | 101 | 3344 | 40 | 29101 | 335 | 24831 | 12714 | 368 |

BALDWIN—St. Croix County

★ BALDWIN HOSPITAL, 730 10th Avenue, Zip 54002–0045; tel. 715/684–3311; Richard L. Range, Administrator **A**9 10 **F**7 8 11 13 17 19 20 22 26 27 28 29 30 32 33 34 35 37 39 40 41 42 44 45 46 48 49 51 61 64 65 66 67 68 71 73
| | 23 | 10 | 27 | 1090 | 10 | 24906 | 63 | 7909 | 3336 | 111 |

BARABOO—Sauk County

✠ ST. CLARE HOSPITAL AND HEALTH SERVICES, 707 14th Street, Zip 53913–1597; tel. 608/356–5561; David B. Jordahl, FACHE, President **A**1 3 10 **F**2 3 7 8 11 12 14 17 18 19 20 21 22 24 26 29 30 31 32 33 34 35 36 37 39 40 41 42 44 45 46 49 53 58 61 63 64 65 66 67 71 73 **S** SSM Health Care System, Saint Louis, MO **N** Health Care Network of Wisconsin (HCN), Brookfield, WI
| | 21 | 10 | 76 | 2642 | 27 | 48333 | 296 | 20174 | 9471 | 254 |

BARRON—Barron County

□ BARRON MEMORIAL MEDICAL CENTER AND SKILLED NURSING FACILITY, 1222 Woodland Avenue, Zip 54812–1798; tel. 715/537–3186; Mark D. Wilson, Administrator (Total facility includes 50 beds in nursing home–type unit) **A**1 9 10 **F**7 8 9 11 12 14 16 17 19 22 24 29 30 34 36 37 39 40 41 44 45 46 47 49 51 54 55 56 57 58 61 62 64 65 66 67 71 72 73 **S** Mayo Foundation, Rochester, MN **N** Luther/Midelfort/Mayo Health System, Eau Claire, WI
| | 23 | 10 | 92 | 1220 | 61 | 21453 | 64 | 8104 | 3997 | 132 |

BEAVER DAM—Dodge County

✠ BEAVER DAM COMMUNITY HOSPITALS, 707 South University Avenue, Zip 53916–3089; tel. 920/887–7181; John R. Landdeck, President (Total facility includes 123 beds in nursing home–type unit) **A**1 9 10 **F**2 8 11 14 16 19 22 26 29 32 33 34 35 36 37 39 40 41 42 44 45 46 48 49 52 61 64 65 66 71 72 74
| | 23 | 10 | 216 | 3066 | 144 | 66000 | 394 | — | — | — |

BELOIT—Rock County

□ △ BELOIT MEMORIAL HOSPITAL, 1969 West Hart Road, Zip 53511–2299; tel. 608/364–5011; Gregory K. Britton, President and Chief Executive Officer **A**1 7 9 10 **F**2 3 4 5 7 8 9 10 11 12 17 18 19 20 21 22 23 25 26 27 28 29 30 31 32 33 34 35 37 38 39 40 41 42 43 44 45 46 47 48 49 50 51 52 53 54 55 56 57 58 59 60 61 63 64 65 66 67 69 70 71 72 73 74 **P**1
| | 23 | 10 | 124 | 4895 | 68 | 126528 | 652 | 45723 | 21399 | 691 |

BERLIN—Green Lake County

□ COMMUNITY HEALTH NETWORK, (Includes Berlin Memorial Hospital, Juliette Manor Nursing Home, Community Clinics), 225 Memorial Drive, Zip 54923–1295; tel. 920/361–1313; Craig W. C. Schmidt, President and Chief Executive Officer (Total facility includes 114 beds in nursing home–type unit) **A**1 2 9 10 **F**2 3 4 6 7 8 9 10 11 12 14 16 19 21 22 24 25 26 29 32 33 34 35 36 37 39 40 41 42 44 45 47 48 49 52 53 54 55 56 57 58 59 61 62 63 64 65 66 70 71 72 74 **P**6 8 **N** Partners Health System, Inc., Berlin, WI
| | 23 | 10 | 187 | 2129 | 124 | 37125 | 227 | — | — | — |

Hospital, Address, Telephone, Administrator, Approval, Facility, and Physician Codes, Health Care System, Network	Classi-fication Codes		Utilization Data					Expense (thousands) of dollars		
	Control	Service	Staffed Beds	Admissions	Census	Outpatient Visits	Births	Total	Payroll	Personnel

★ American Hospital Association (AHA) membership
□ Joint Commission on Accreditation of Healthcare Organizations (JCAHO) accreditation
+ American Osteopathic Healthcare Association (AOHA) membership
○ American Osteopathic Association (AOA) accreditation
△ Commission on Accreditation of Rehabilitation Facilities (CARF) accreditation
Control codes 61, 63, 64, 71, 72 and 73 indicate hospitals listed by AOHA, but not registered by AHA. For definition of numerical codes, see page A4

BLACK RIVER FALLS—Jackson County

□ BLACK RIVER MEMORIAL HOSPITAL, 711 West Adams Street, Zip 54615–9113; tel. 715/284–5361; Stanley J. Gaynor, Chief Executive Officer and Administrator **A**1 3 9 10 **F**2 3 7 12 19 22 26 28 29 30 34 35 36 40 41 44 45 49 52 54 61 64 65 66 67 70 71 72 73

	23	10	38	1029	11	8370	146	6933	3301	121

BLOOMER—Chippewa County

★ BLOOMER COMMUNITY MEMORIAL HOSPITAL AND THE MAPLEWOOD, 1501 Thompson Street, Zip 54724–1299; tel. 715/568–2000; John Perushek, Administrator (Total facility includes 75 beds in nursing home–type unit) **A**1 9 10 **F**1 7 8 9 14 16 19 21 22 26 32 33 34 40 41 42 44 48 49 53 54 56 57 58 61 64 65 71 74 **P**8 **S** Mayo Foundation, Rochester, MN **N** Luther/Midelfort/Mayo Health System, Eau Claire, WI

	23	10	101	594	77	8091	42	—	—	—

BOSCOBEL—Grant County

BOSCOBEL AREA HEALTH CARE, 205 Parker Street, Zip 53805–1698; tel. 608/375–4112; Steven T. Moburg, Administrator (Total facility includes 79 beds in nursing home–type unit) **A**10 **F**1 2 3 7 8 16 17 18 19 20 22 25 26 27 28 29 30 32 34 40 41 42 44 45 49 51 52 53 54 55 56 57 58 59 61 64 65 67 71 72 73 **P**5 6

	23	10	125	1240	75	9296	60	9445	3463	162

BROOKFIELD—Waukesha County

★ △ ELMBROOK MEMORIAL HOSPITAL, 19333 West North Avenue, Zip 53045–4198; tel. 414/785–2000; Kimry A. Johnsrud, President **A**1 7 9 10 **F**2 3 4 5 6 7 8 10 11 12 18 19 21 22 23 25 26 29 31 32 33 34 35 36 37 38 39 40 41 42 43 44 45 46 48 49 52 53 54 55 56 57 58 59 60 61 62 63 65 66 69 70 71 74 **P**2 5 7 8 **S** Wheaton Franciscan Services, Inc., Wheaton, IL **N** Health Care Network of Wisconsin (HCN), Brookfield, WI; Covenant Healthcare System, Inc., Milwaukee, WI

	21	10	136	6195	70	70078	982	52422	20921	454

BURLINGTON—Racine County

★ MEMORIAL HOSPITAL CORPORATION OF BURLINGTON, 252 McHenry Street, Zip 53105–1828; tel. 414/763–2411; Loren J. Anderson, President and Chief Executive Officer **A**1 9 10 **F**8 9 10 11 12 16 18 19 21 22 23 26 29 34 35 37 39 40 41 42 44 45 46 48 56 61 64 65 71 74 **P**4 5 6 **S** Aurora Health Care, Milwaukee, WI **N** Health Care Network of Wisconsin (HCN), Brookfield, WI; Aurora Health Care, Milwaukee, WI

	23	10	87	3065	31	74090	545	30815	12311	367

CHILTON—Calumet County

★ CALUMET MEDICAL CENTER, 614 Memorial Drive, Zip 53014–1597; tel. 920/849–2386; Joseph L. Schumacher, Administrator **A**1 9 10 **F**3 8 10 11 12 16 17 18 19 20 21 22 26 28 29 30 32 33 34 35 36 37 39 41 42 44 45 46 47 49 51 53 54 55 56 57 58 59 61 64 65 66 67 70 71 73 74

	23	10	53	664	8	30925	0	9064	4180	145

CHIPPEWA FALLS—Chippewa County

★ ST. JOSEPH'S HOSPITAL, 2661 County Highway I., Zip 54729–1498; tel. 715/723–1811; David B. Fish, Executive Vice President **A**1 9 10 **F**2 3 7 8 11 12 14 16 19 21 22 26 29 32 33 34 36 37 39 40 41 42 44 45 46 47 56 61 64 65 71 **S** Hospital Sisters Health System, Springfield, IL

	21	10	127	3524	55	54950	397	27660	13852	471

COLUMBUS—Columbia County

★ COLUMBUS COMMUNITY HOSPITAL, 1515 Park Avenue, Zip 53925–1618; tel. 920/623–2200; Miles Meyer, Administrator **A**1 10 **F**7 8 9 11 12 14 16 17 19 21 22 26 28 29 30 34 37 39 40 41 42 44 45 47 49 61 63 64 65 67 71 72 73 74

	23	10	34	1663	21	21450	110	11467	5056	153

CUBA CITY—Grant County

CUBA CITY MEDICAL CENTER See Southwest Health Center, Platteville

CUMBERLAND—Barron County

□ CUMBERLAND MEMORIAL HOSPITAL, 1110 Seventh Avenue, Zip 54829, Mailing Address: P.O. Box 37, Zip 54829–0037; tel. 715/822–2741; James M. O'Keefe, Administrator (Total facility includes 71 beds in nursing home–type unit) **A**1 10 **F**2 7 12 13 16 17 19 20 21 22 26 27 28 29 30 34 35 39 40 41 42 44 45 46 52 54 56 57 58 61 62 63 64 65 66 67 68 70 71 73 **P**5 6 **N** Northern Lakes Health Consortium, Duluth, MN

	23	10	131	1518	86	8024	68	8056	4489	176

DARLINGTON—Lafayette County

MEMORIAL HOSPITAL OF LAFAYETTE COUNTY, 800 Clay Street, Zip 53530–1228, Mailing Address: P.O. Box 70, Zip 53530–0070; tel. 608/776–4466; Sherry Kudronowicz, Administrator **A**10 **F**2 3 7 8 14 17 19 22 26 29 34 35 40 44 45 46 48 49 52 56 61 64 65 67 71

	13	10	28	438	3	16456	60	4075	1494	55

DODGEVILLE—Iowa County

★ MEMORIAL HOSPITAL OF IOWA COUNTY, 825 South Iowa Street, Zip 53533–1999; tel. 608/935–2711; Ray Marmorstone, Administrator (Total facility includes 44 beds in nursing home–type unit) **A**1 9 10 **F**1 7 8 11 12 16 19 22 26 29 32 33 34 35 37 39 40 41 42 44 45 46 47 48 49 61 64 65 66 71 72 74 **S** Brim, Inc., Portland, OR

	23	10	84	1446	50	33679	216	—	—	—

DURAND—Pepin County

CHIPPEWA VALLEY HOSPITAL AND OAKVIEW CARE CENTER, 1220 Third Avenue West, Zip 54736–1600, Mailing Address: P.O. Box 224, Zip 54736–0224; tel. 715/672–4211; Douglas R. Peterson, President and Chief Executive Officer (Total facility includes 58 beds in nursing home–type unit) **A**9 10 **F**7 8 19 22 24 26 27 29 34 36 39 40 44 45 48 49 61 64 65 71 **S** Adventist Health System Sunbelt Health Care Corporation, Winter Park, FL

	21	10	81	689	53	9531	34	6001	2392	111

EAGLE RIVER—Vilas County

★ EAGLE RIVER MEMORIAL HOSPITAL, 201 Hospital Road, Zip 54521–8835; tel. 715/479–7411; Patricia L. Richardson, President and Chief Operating Officer **A**9 10 **F**2 3 6 7 8 11 12 13 14 16 17 19 20 21 22 24 27 28 29 30 32 33 34 35 36 37 39 40 41 42 44 45 46 48 49 51 52 61 62 64 65 66 67 68 71 73 74

	23	10	9	492	6	17591	0	6176	2889	102

Hospital, Address, Telephone, Administrator, Approval, Facility, and Physician Codes, Health Care System, Network	Classi-fication Codes		Utilization Data					Expense (thousands) of dollars		
	Control	Service	Staffed Beds	Admissions	Census	Outpatient Visits	Births	Total	Payroll	Personnel

★ American Hospital Association (AHA) membership
☐ Joint Commission on Accreditation of Healthcare Organizations (JCAHO) accreditation
+ American Osteopathic Healthcare Association (AOHA) membership
○ American Osteopathic Association (AOA) accreditation
△ Commission on Accreditation of Rehabilitation Facilities (CARF) accreditation
Control codes 61, 63, 64, 71, 72 and 73 indicate hospitals listed by AOHA, but not registered by AHA. For definition of numerical codes, see page A4

EAU CLAIRE—Eau Claire County

Entry	Control	Service	Staffed Beds	Admissions	Census	Outpatient Visits	Births	Total	Payroll	Personnel
☐ LUTHER HOSPITAL, 1221 Whipple Street, Zip 54702–4105; tel. 715/838–3311; William Rupp, M.D., President and Chief Executive Officer **A**1 2 3 5 9 10 **F**3 4 7 8 9 10 11 12 19 21 22 24 29 32 33 34 35 37 38 39 40 41 42 43 44 45 46 47 48 52 53 54 55 56 57 58 59 60 61 63 64 65 66 69 70 71 74 **S** Mayo Foundation, Rochester, MN **N** Luther/Midelfort/Mayo Health System, Eau Claire, WI; Mayo Foundation, Rochester, MN	23	10	182	7837	95	111141	886	70845	29597	1034
★ △ SACRED HEART HOSPITAL, 900 West Clairemont Avenue, Zip 54701–5105; tel. 715/839–4121; Stephen F. Ronstrom, Executive Vice President **A**1 2 3 5 7 9 10 **F**7 8 10 11 12 16 18 19 21 22 23 24 25 26 28 29 30 32 33 34 35 36 37 38 39 40 41 42 44 45 46 47 48 49 52 53 54 55 56 57 58 59 60 61 62 63 64 65 67 70 71 73 74 **S** Hospital Sisters Health System, Springfield, IL	21	10	261	7249	92	93627	755	58075	26228	757

EDGERTON—Rock County

Entry	Control	Service	Staffed Beds	Admissions	Census	Outpatient Visits	Births	Total	Payroll	Personnel
MEMORIAL COMMUNITY HOSPITAL, 313 Stoughton Road, Zip 53534–1198; tel. 608/884–3441; Charles E. Bruhn, Chief Executive Officer (Total facility includes 61 beds in nursing home–type unit) **A**9 10 **F**8 11 12 14 17 19 20 22 27 29 30 32 33 34 35 36 37 39 41 42 44 45 46 47 48 49 51 61 62 63 64 65 66 67 71 72 73 74 **P**5 7 **S** Brim, Inc., Portland, OR	23	10	115	980	76	17646	0	27831	13645	247

ELKHORN—Walworth County

Entry	Control	Service	Staffed Beds	Admissions	Census	Outpatient Visits	Births	Total	Payroll	Personnel
★ LAKELAND MEDICAL CENTER, West 3985 County Road NN, Zip 53121, Mailing Address: P.O. Box 1002, Zip 53121–1002; tel. 414/741–2000; Kathy Skowlund, Administrator **A**1 9 10 **F**2 3 7 8 11 12 16 19 21 22 26 29 32 33 34 35 37 39 40 41 42 44 45 46 52 53 54 56 58 59 61 63 64 65 66 71 72 74 **P**5 **S** Aurora Health Care, Milwaukee, WI **N** Aurora Health Care, Milwaukee, WI	23	10	78	3464	40	56451	459	32382	13417	417

FOND DU LAC—Fond Du Lac County

Entry	Control	Service	Staffed Beds	Admissions	Census	Outpatient Visits	Births	Total	Payroll	Personnel
☐ △ AGNESIAN HEALTHCARE, 430 East Division Street, Zip 54935–0385; tel. 920/929–2300; Robert A. Fale, President **A**1 2 7 9 10 **F**1 2 3 4 5 7 8 10 11 12 16 18 19 21 22 23 26 29 31 32 33 34 35 36 37 39 40 41 42 43 44 45 48 49 52 53 54 55 56 57 58 59 60 61 63 64 65 66 70 71 72 74 **P**3 **N** Health Care Network of Wisconsin (HCN), Brookfield, WI	21	10	161	6481	78	186131	1001	85525	33131	838

FORT ATKINSON—Jefferson County

Entry	Control	Service	Staffed Beds	Admissions	Census	Outpatient Visits	Births	Total	Payroll	Personnel
★ FORT ATKINSON MEMORIAL HEALTH SERVICES, 611 East Sherman Avenue, Zip 53538–1998; tel. 920/568–5000; John C. Albaugh, President and Chief Executive Officer (Total facility includes 28 beds in nursing home–type unit) **A**1 9 10 **F**3 7 8 9 11 12 16 17 19 21 22 23 24 25 26 28 29 30 32 33 34 35 37 39 40 41 42 44 45 46 47 48 49 54 58 61 63 64 65 66 67 68 71 72 73 74 **P**6 7	23	10	102	3909	42	93397	445	36635	17480	516

FRIENDSHIP—Adams County

Entry	Control	Service	Staffed Beds	Admissions	Census	Outpatient Visits	Births	Total	Payroll	Personnel
☐ ADAMS COUNTY MEMORIAL HOSPITAL AND NURSING CARE UNIT, 402 West Lake Street, Zip 53934–9699, Mailing Address: P.O. Box 40, Zip 53934–0040; tel. 608/339–3331; Steven R. Nockerts, Administrator and Chief Executive Officer (Total facility includes 18 beds in nursing home–type unit) **A**1 9 10 **F**1 2 3 8 12 14 16 18 19 22 25 26 27 29 30 32 33 34 35 39 41 42 44 45 48 49 55 56 57 58 61 64 65 66 71 **P**5	23	10	58	798	26	34948	0	8851	4540	160

GRANTSBURG—Burnett County

Entry	Control	Service	Staffed Beds	Admissions	Census	Outpatient Visits	Births	Total	Payroll	Personnel
BURNETT MEDICAL CENTER, 257 West St. George Avenue, Zip 54840–7827; tel. 715/463–5353; Timothy J. Wick, Chief Executive Officer (Total facility includes 53 beds in nursing home–type unit) **A**9 10 **F**1 7 8 14 16 17 19 21 22 26 29 30 34 35 37 39 40 41 42 44 45 46 48 49 61 64 65 66 67 71 72 **S** Brim, Inc., Portland, OR **N** Health Care Network of Wisconsin (HCN), Brookfield, WI	23	10	70	745	58	9464	51	5589	2559	117

GREEN BAY—Brown County

Entry	Control	Service	Staffed Beds	Admissions	Census	Outpatient Visits	Births	Total	Payroll	Personnel
★ BELLIN HOSPITAL, 744 South Webster Avenue, Zip 54301–3581, Mailing Address: P.O. Box 23400, Zip 54305–3400; tel. 920/433–3500; George Kerwin, President **A**1 9 10 **F**4 7 8 10 11 14 16 17 19 21 23 24 25 27 28 29 30 32 33 34 35 37 39 40 41 42 43 44 45 46 61 63 64 65 66 71 72 73 **P**5 6	21	10	167	9099	94	310127	1809	106741	52286	1493
☐ BELLIN PSYCHIATRIC CENTER, 301 East St. Joseph Street, Zip 54301–2241, Mailing Address: P.O. Box 23725, Zip 54305–3725; tel. 920/433–3630; Robert W. Fry, President **A**1 10 **F**2 3 11 14 17 19 21 25 26 28 29 30 34 35 37 45 48 50 52 53 54 55 56 57 58 59 61 63 64 65 67 71 73	21	22	60	1277	26	12643	0	6592	3432	101
BROWN COUNTY MENTAL HEALTH CENTER, 2900 St. Anthony Drive, Zip 54311–5899; tel. 414/468–1136; Mark Quam, Executive Director **A**10 **F**2 3 12 17 18 34 39 52 53 54 55 56 57 58 61 64 65 67 73	13	22	74	1500	32	14819	0	6832	4102	134
★ ST. MARY'S HOSPITAL MEDICAL CENTER, 1726 Shawano Avenue, Zip 54303–3282; tel. 920/498–4200; James G. Coller, Executive Vice President and Administrator **A**1 10 **F**7 8 11 16 17 19 21 22 24 27 28 29 30 33 34 35 36 37 39 40 42 44 45 46 47 51 56 61 63 64 65 67 70 71 73 **S** Hospital Sisters Health System, Springfield, IL	21	10	119	4585	49	80576	595	40675	17745	456
★ △ ST. VINCENT HOSPITAL, 835 South Van Buren Street, Zip 54307–3508, Mailing Address: P.O. Box 13508, Zip 54307–3508; tel. 920/433–0111; Joseph J. Neidenbach, Administrator and Executive Vice President **A**1 2 7 9 10 **F**4 7 8 10 11 13 16 17 19 20 21 22 23 26 27 28 29 30 32 33 34 35 36 37 38 39 40 41 42 44 45 46 48 49 51 60 61 63 64 65 66 67 68 70 71 73 **P**2 **S** Hospital Sisters Health System, Springfield, IL	21	10	298	11806	170	100472	1535	113692	55288	1541

GREENFIELD—Milwaukee County

Entry	Control	Service	Staffed Beds	Admissions	Census	Outpatient Visits	Births	Total	Payroll	Personnel
☐ THC–MILWAUKEE, 5017 South 110th Street, Zip 53228; tel. 414/427–8282; Lee Jaeger, Chief Executive Officer **A**1 9 10 **F**12 16 19 20 21 22 26 27 29 35 37 42 45 46 48 57 61 64 65 71 **S** Transitional Hospitals Corporation, Las Vegas, NV	33	10	34	215	26	1	0	10436	3544	100

Hospital, Address, Telephone, Administrator, Approval, Facility, and Physician Codes, Health Care System, Network	Classi-fication Codes		Utilization Data					Expense (thousands) of dollars		
★ American Hospital Association (AHA) membership ☐ Joint Commission on Accreditation of Healthcare Organizations (JCAHO) accreditation + American Osteopathic Healthcare Association (AOHA) membership ○ American Osteopathic Association (AOA) accreditation △ Commission on Accreditation of Rehabilitation Facilities (CARF) accreditation Control codes 61, 63, 64, 71, 72 and 73 indicate hospitals listed by AOHA, but not registered by AHA. For definition of numerical codes, see page A4	Control	Service	Staffed Beds	Admissions	Census	Outpatient Visits	Births	Total	Payroll	Personnel

HARTFORD—Washington County

☒ HARTFORD MEMORIAL HOSPITAL, 1032 East Sumner Street, Zip 53027–1698; tel. 414/673–2300; Mark Schwartz, Administrator **A**1 9 10 **F**1 7 8 11 12 14 16 17 19 21 22 24 26 27 29 30 32 33 34 35 36 37 39 40 41 42 44 45 49 61 63 64 65 66 67 70 71 73 74 **S** Aurora Health Care, Milwaukee, WI **N** Health Care Network of Wisconsin (HCN), Brookfield, WI; Aurora Health Care, Milwaukee, WI

| 23 | 10 | 71 | 1706 | 32 | 51614 | 242 | 18829 | 8268 | 275 |

HAYWARD—Sawyer County

☒ HAYWARD AREA MEMORIAL HOSPITAL AND NURSING HOME, Mailing Address: Route 3, Box 3999, Zip 54843–3999; tel. 715/634–8911; Barbara A. Peickert, R.N., Chief Executive Officer (Total facility includes 76 beds in nursing home–type unit) **A**1 9 10 **F**7 8 16 17 19 21 22 26 28 29 30 33 34 40 41 42 44 45 56 61 63 64 65 67 71 73 **N** Northern Lakes Health Consortium, Duluth, MN

| 23 | 10 | 117 | 1242 | 83 | 25100 | 113 | 8567 | 4120 | 160 |

HAZEL GREEN—Grant County

HAZEL GREEN HOSPITAL See Southwest Health Center, Platteville

HILLSBORO—Vernon County

☒ ST. JOSEPH'S MEMORIAL HOSPITAL AND NURSING HOME, 400 Water Avenue, Zip 54634–0527, Mailing Address: P.O. Box 527, Zip 54634–0527; tel. 608/489–2211; Nancy Bauman, Chief Executive Officer (Total facility includes 65 beds in nursing home–type unit) **A**1 10 **F**7 8 12 19 21 22 26 29 34 35 36 39 40 41 42 44 45 48 49 54 56 57 61 64 65 66 70 71 **S** Brim, Inc., Portland, OR

| 21 | 10 | 85 | 263 | 42 | 25835 | 41 | — | — | — |

HUDSON—St. Croix County

☐ HUDSON MEDICAL CENTER, 400 Wisconsin Street, Zip 54016–1600; tel. 715/386–9321; John W. Marnell, Chief Executive Officer **A**1 9 10 **F**1 3 7 8 11 12 14 16 17 19 21 22 24 26 27 28 29 30 32 33 34 35 36 37 39 40 41 42 44 45 46 48 49 54 61 64 65 66 67 71 73 **P**4 **N** Health Care Network of Wisconsin (HCN), Brookfield, WI

| 23 | 10 | 39 | 1112 | 19 | 16610 | 151 | 8754 | 4157 | 139 |

JANESVILLE—Rock County

☒ MERCY HEALTH SYSTEM, 1000 Mineral Point Avenue, Zip 53545–5003, Mailing Address: P.O. Box 5003, Zip 53547–5003; tel. 608/756–6000; Javon R. Bea, President and Chief Executive Officer (Total facility includes 22 beds in nursing home–type unit) **A**1 3 9 10 **F**1 2 3 4 5 6 7 8 10 12 14 16 18 19 21 22 23 24 25 26 29 31 32 33 34 35 36 37 38 39 40 41 42 43 44 45 46 48 49 52 53 54 55 56 57 58 59 60 61 62 63 64 65 66 70 71 72 74 **P**6 **N** Southern Wisconsin Health Care System, Janesville, WI

| 23 | 10 | 238 | 9075 | 124 | 440230 | 1317 | — | — | — |

KENOSHA—Kenosha County

☒ KENOSHA HOSPITAL AND MEDICAL CENTER, 6308 Eighth Avenue, Zip 53143–5082; tel. 414/656–2011; Richard O. Schmidt, Jr., President, Chief Executive Officer and General Counsel **A**1 9 10 **F**4 5 7 8 10 11 12 14 16 19 21 22 23 24 25 26 29 31 32 33 34 35 36 37 38 39 40 41 42 43 44 45 46 48 49 56 61 63 64 65 66 69 70 71 72 74 **P**6 8 **S** Horizon Healthcare, Inc., Milwaukee, WI **N** Horizon Healthcare, Inc., Milwaukee, WI

| 23 | 10 | 116 | 6066 | 62 | 111227 | 934 | 65378 | 32407 | 752 |

☒ ST. CATHERINE'S HOSPITAL, 3556 Seventh Avenue, Zip 53140–2595; tel. 414/656–3011; Robert M. Lovell, Interim Chief Executive Officer **A**1 2 3 9 10 **F**2 3 7 8 9 10 11 12 14 16 17 18 19 21 22 25 26 28 29 30 32 33 34 35 36 37 38 39 40 41 42 44 45 46 47 48 49 52 54 55 56 57 58 59 60 61 63 64 65 66 67 69 70 71 73 74 **P**8 **S** Wheaton Franciscan Services, Inc., Wheaton, IL **N** Health Care Network of Wisconsin (HCN), Brookfield, WI

| 21 | 10 | 148 | 5964 | 77 | 148847 | 740 | 48435 | 20874 | 629 |

KEWAUNEE—Kewaunee County

★ ST. MARY'S KEWAUNEE AREA MEMORIAL HOSPITAL, 810 Lincoln Street, Zip 54216–1140, Mailing Address: P.O. Box 217, Zip 54216–0217; tel. 920/388–2210; Steven H. Spencer, Administrator (Nonreporting) **A**9 10 **S** Aurora Health Care, Milwaukee, WI **N** Aurora Health Care, Milwaukee, WI

| 23 | 10 | 17 | — | — | — | — | — | — | — |

LA CROSSE—La Crosse County

☒ FRANCISCAN SKEMP HEALTHCARE–LA CROSSE CAMPUS, 700 West Avenue South, Zip 54601–4783; tel. 608/785–0940; Brian C. Campion, M.D., Chief Executive Officer **A**1 2 3 10 **F**2 3 4 6 7 8 9 10 11 12 13 16 17 18 19 20 21 22 23 24 26 27 28 29 30 32 33 34 35 36 37 38 39 40 41 42 43 44 45 46 47 49 51 52 53 54 55 56 57 58 59 60 61 62 64 65 66 67 68 70 71 72 73 74 **S** Franciscan Skemp Healthcare, La Crosse, WI **N** Franciscan Skemp Healthcare, LaCrosse, WI

| 21 | 10 | 213 | 8701 | 107 | 75465 | 728 | 65914 | 30938 | 900 |

☒ △ LUTHERAN HOSPITAL–LA CROSSE, 1910 South Avenue, Zip 54601–9980; tel. 608/785–0530; John N. Katrana, Ph.D., Chief Administrative Officer **A**1 2 5 7 8 9 10 **N** Lutheran Health System, LaCrosse, WI

| 12 | 10 | 286 | 13442 | — | 106966 | 1556 | — | — | — |

LADYSMITH—Rusk County

RUSK COUNTY MEMORIAL HOSPITAL AND NURSING HOME, 900 College Avenue West, Zip 54848–2116; tel. 715/532–5561; J. Michael Shaw, Administrator (Total facility includes 99 beds in nursing home–type unit) **A**10 **F**2 3 7 8 9 11 13 17 19 20 22 26 27 28 29 30 34 37 38 39 40 42 44 45 48 52 53 54 55 56 57 58 59 61 64 65 67 70 71 73

| 13 | 10 | 134 | 1126 | 103 | 22899 | 110 | 9965 | 4531 | 153 |

LANCASTER—Grant County

☒ GRANT REGIONAL HEALTH CENTER, (Formerly Lancaster Memorial Hospital), 507 South Monroe Street, Zip 53813–2099; tel. 608/723–2143; Larry D. Rentfro, FACHE, Chief Executive Officer **A**1 10 **F**7 8 14 16 19 22 24 25 26 28 29 30 32 33 34 35 37 39 40 41 44 45 48 51 61 64 65 66 71 72 73 74 **P**5 **S** Brim, Inc., Portland, OR

| 23 | 10 | 28 | 741 | 6 | 25322 | 93 | 6400 | 2671 | 106 |

Hospital, Address, Telephone, Administrator, Approval, Facility, and Physician Codes, Health Care System, Network	Classi-fication Codes		Utilization Data					Expense (thousands) of dollars		
	Control	Service	Staffed Beds	Admissions	Census	Outpatient Visits	Births	Total	Payroll	Personnel

★ American Hospital Association (AHA) membership
□ Joint Commission on Accreditation of Healthcare Organizations (JCAHO) accreditation
+ American Osteopathic Healthcare Association (AOHA) membership
○ American Osteopathic Association (AOA) accreditation
△ Commission on Accreditation of Rehabilitation Facilities (CARF) accreditation
Control codes 61, 63, 64, 71, 72 and 73 indicate hospitals listed by AOHA, but not registered by AHA. For definition of numerical codes, see page A4

MADISON—Dane County

□ MENDOTA MENTAL HEALTH INSTITUTE, 301 Troy Drive, Zip 53704–1599; tel. 608/243–2500; Steve Watters, Chief Executive Officer **A**1 3 5 10 **F**2 12 13 17 18 20 22 25 26 27 28 29 30 34 39 45 46 51 52 53 55 56 57 58 61 64 65 67 68 73	12	22	257	659	229	11772	0	38206	23378	662
⊞ △ MERITER HOSPITAL, (Includes Meriter–Capitol), 202 South Park Street, Zip 53715–1599; tel. 608/267–6000; Terri L. Potter, President and Chief Executive Officer **A**1 3 5 7 10 **F**1 3 4 5 6 7 8 9 10 11 12 13 16 17 19 20 21 22 23 24 25 26 28 29 30 32 33 34 35 36 37 38 39 40 41 42 43 44 45 46 47 48 49 52 53 54 55 56 57 58 59 60 61 64 65 66 67 71 73 74	23	10	378	14860	206	142470	3244	151988	62924	1534
⊞ ST. MARYS HOSPITAL MEDICAL CENTER, 707 South Mills Street, Zip 53715–0450; tel. 608/251–6100; Gerald W. Lefert, President **A**1 3 5 10 **F**1 4 7 8 10 11 12 13 17 18 19 20 21 22 23 24 25 26 27 28 29 30 32 33 34 35 37 38 39 40 41 43 44 45 46 47 49 51 52 53 54 55 56 57 59 60 61 64 65 66 67 68 70 71 73 **P**5 8 **S** SSM Health Care System, Saint Louis, MO **N** MEDACOM Tri-State, Oakbrook, IL; Health Care Network of Wisconsin (HCN), Brookfield, WI	23	10	332	16987	218	38278	2905	133493	54499	1258
⊞ △ UNIVERSITY OF WISCONSIN HOSPITAL AND CLINICS, (Includes University of Wisconsin Children's Hospital), 600 Highland Avenue, Zip 53792–0002; tel. 608/263–6400; Gordon M. Derzon, Chief Executive Officer **A**1 3 5 7 8 9 10 **F**3 4 5 8 9 10 11 12 13 14 16 17 19 20 21 22 23 24 25 26 28 29 30 31 32 34 35 37 39 40 41 42 43 44 45 46 47 48 49 50 51 52 53 54 55 56 57 58 60 61 63 64 65 66 67 69 70 71 72 73 74 **N** University of Wisconsin Hospitals and Clinics, Madison, WI	23	10	478	20319	344	423658	0	300171	122219	3769
⊞ WILLIAM S. MIDDLETON MEMORIAL VETERANS HOSPITAL, 2500 Overlook Terrace, Zip 53705–2286; tel. 608/256–1901; Nathan L. Geraths, Director (Nonreporting) **A**1 3 5 **S** Department of Veterans Affairs, Washington, DC	45	10	200	—	—	—	—	—	—	—

MANITOWOC—Manitowoc County

⊞ △ HOLY FAMILY MEMORIAL MEDICAL CENTER, 2300 Western Avenue, Zip 54220, Mailing Address: P.O. Box 1450, Zip 54221–1450; tel. 920/684–2011; Daniel B. McGinty, President and Chief Executive Officer **A**1 7 9 10 **F**1 2 3 7 8 10 11 12 14 16 17 19 21 22 23 25 26 28 29 30 32 33 34 35 36 37 39 40 41 42 44 45 48 49 50 51 52 55 56 58 59 60 61 63 64 65 66 67 68 71 73 **P**6 **S** Franciscan Sisters of Christian Charity HealthCare Ministry, Inc, Manitowoc, WI	21	10	176	5913	80	150042	473	56388	27249	807

MARINETTE—Marinette County

□ BAY AREA MEDICAL CENTER, 3100 Shore Drive, Zip 54143–4297; tel. 715/735–6621; Rick Ament, President and Chief Executive Officer **A**1 9 10 **F**3 7 8 11 12 18 19 21 22 25 26 27 28 29 30 34 35 37 40 41 42 44 45 46 49 52 54 55 57 60 61 63 64 65 66 71 73 **P**6	23	10	115	4375	52	44941	424	33765	15684	383

MARSHFIELD—Wood County

NORWOOD HEALTH CENTER, 1600 North Chestnut Avenue, Zip 54449–1499; tel. 715/384–2188; Randy Bestul, Administrator **A**10 **F**12 52 53 57 58 61 64 65	13	22	19	537	8	0	0	1488	890	44
⊞ △ SAINT JOSEPH'S HOSPITAL, 611 St. Joseph Avenue, Zip 54449–1898; tel. 715/387–1713; Michael A. Schmidt, President and Chief Executive Officer **A**1 2 3 5 7 10 **F**2 3 4 5 6 7 9 10 11 13 14 16 17 19 21 22 23 25 26 28 29 30 31 32 33 34 35 36 37 38 39 40 41 42 43 44 45 46 47 48 49 52 53 56 57 58 59 60 61 63 64 65 66 67 69 70 71 73 74 **P**8 **S** Marian Health System, Tulsa, OK	21	10	524	16258	252	132721	1176	161924	57243	1594

MAUSTON—Juneau County

MILE BLUFF MEDICAL CENTER, 1050 Division Street, Zip 53948–1997; tel. 608/847–6161; Daniel N. Manders, President and Chief Executive Officer (Total facility includes 60 beds in nursing home–type unit) **A**3 10 **F**7 8 16 19 21 22 25 26 28 29 30 32 33 34 35 39 40 41 42 44 45 46 49 61 62 63 64 65 66 71 72 73 **P**6	23	10	97	1983	76	47909	203	18611	9825	266

MEDFORD—Taylor County

⊞ MEMORIAL HOSPITAL OF TAYLOR COUNTY, (Includes Memorial Nursing Home), 135 South Gibson Street, Zip 54451–1696; tel. 715/748–8100; Greg Roraff, President and Chief Executive Officer (Total facility includes 104 beds in nursing home–type unit) **A**1 9 10 **F**1 6 7 8 11 16 17 19 21 22 28 29 30 32 34 35 37 40 41 44 45 46 49 51 54 56 61 63 64 65 67 71 73 **P**4 **N** Community Health Care, Inc., Wausau, WI	23	10	153	1062	113	24590	155	—	—	169

MENOMONEE FALLS—Waukesha County

⊞ △ COMMUNITY MEMORIAL HOSPITAL, W180 N8085 Town Hall Road, Zip 53051, Mailing Address: P.O. Box 408, Zip 53052–0408; tel. 414/251–1000; Robert Eugene Drisner, President and Chief Executive Officer **A**1 2 7 9 10 **F**2 3 4 5 6 7 8 9 10 11 12 14 16 17 18 19 21 22 23 24 25 26 27 28 29 30 32 33 34 35 36 37 38 39 40 41 42 43 44 45 47 48 49 52 53 54 55 56 57 58 59 60 61 64 65 66 67 70 71 73 74 **S** Horizon Healthcare, Inc., Milwaukee, WI **N** Health Care Network of Wisconsin (HCN), Brookfield, WI; Horizon Healthcare, Inc., Milwaukee, WI	23	10	142	6609	80	48323	917	56786	25830	813

MENOMONIE—Dunn County

□ MYRTLE WERTH HOSPITAL–MAYO HEALTH SYSTEM, 2321 Stout Road, Zip 54751–2397; tel. 715/235–5531; Thomas Miller, III, Chief Executive Officer **A**1 3 9 10 **F**7 8 11 16 19 21 22 26 28 29 30 34 35 37 39 40 41 44 45 48 61 63 64 65 66 67 71	23	10	55	1490	13	29937	273	8975	4197	159

Hospital, Address, Telephone, Administrator, Approval, Facility, and Physician Codes, Health Care System, Network	Classi-fication Codes		Utilization Data					Expense (thousands) of dollars		
★ American Hospital Association (AHA) membership □ Joint Commission on Accreditation of Healthcare Organizations (JCAHO) accreditation + American Osteopathic Healthcare Association (AOHA) membership ○ American Osteopathic Association (AOA) accreditation △ Commission on Accreditation of Rehabilitation Facilities (CARF) accreditation Control codes 61, 63, 64, 71, 72 and 73 indicate hospitals listed by AOHA, but not registered by AHA. For definition of numerical codes, see page A4	Control	Service	Staffed Beds	Admissions	Census	Outpatient Visits	Births	Total	Payroll	Personnel

MEQUON—Ozaukee County

✚ ST. MARY'S HOSPITAL OZAUKEE, 13111 North Port Washington Road, Zip 53097–2416; tel. 414/243–7300; Therese B. Pandl, Senior Vice President and Chief Operating Officer **A**1 9 10 **F**2 3 4 5 7 8 9 10 11 12 13 14 16 17 18 19 22 25 26 27 28 29 30 32 33 34 35 37 38 39 40 41 42 43 44 45 46 47 48 49 51 52 53 54 55 56 57 58 59 61 64 65 66 67 70 71 72 73 74 **P**5 6 **S** Daughters of Charity National Health System, Saint Louis, MO **N** Columbia – St. Mary's, Inc., Milwaukee, WI; Horizon Healthcare, Inc., Milwaukee, WI

| | 21 | 10 | 82 | 4283 | 50 | 137453 | 671 | 41327 | 20111 | 707 |

MERRILL—Lincoln County

✚ GOOD SAMARITAN HEALTH CENTER OF MERRILL, 601 Center Avenue South, Zip 54452–3404; tel. 715/536–5511; Michael Hammer, President and Chief Executive Officer **A**1 9 10 **F**1 3 4 5 7 8 9 10 11 12 13 14 17 18 19 20 21 22 23 26 28 29 30 32 33 34 35 36 37 38 39 40 41 42 44 45 47 49 51 53 54 55 56 57 58 59 61 64 65 66 67 68 70 71 73 74 **S** Catholic Health Initiatives, Denver, CO

| | 21 | 10 | 63 | 1511 | 21 | 43453 | 169 | 11420 | 5247 | 168 |

MILWAUKEE—Milwaukee County

CHARTER HOSPITAL OF MILWAUKEE, 11101 West Lincoln Avenue, Zip 53227–1166; tel. 414/327–3000; Robert Kwech, Chief Executive Officer (Nonreporting) **A**9 10 **S** Magellan Health Services, Atlanta, GA

| | 33 | 22 | 80 | — | — | — | — | — | — | — |

✚ CHILDREN'S HOSPITAL OF WISCONSIN, 9000 West Wisconsin Avenue, Zip 53226–4810, Mailing Address: P.O. Box 1997, Zip 53201–1997; tel. 414/266–2000; Jon E. Vice, President and Chief Executive Officer **A**1 3 5 8 9 10 **F**4 5 9 10 11 12 13 16 17 19 20 21 22 23 25 27 28 29 30 31 32 33 34 35 37 38 39 41 42 43 44 45 46 47 48 49 51 52 53 54 56 58 60 61 63 64 65 66 67 68 69 70 71 72 73 **P**4 **N** Health Care Network of Wisconsin (HCN), Brookfield, WI

| | 23 | 50 | 222 | 17416 | 167 | 209735 | 0 | 151923 | 54267 | 1433 |

✚ CLEMENT J. ZABLOCKI VETERANS AFFAIRS MEDICAL CENTER, 5000 West National Avenue, Zip 53295; tel. 414/384–2000; Glen W. Grippen, Director (Total facility includes 196 beds in nursing home–type unit) (Nonreporting) **A**1 2 3 5 8 **S** Department of Veterans Affairs, Washington, DC

| | 45 | 10 | 566 | — | — | — | — | — | — | — |

✚ △ COLUMBIA HOSPITAL, 2025 East Newport Avenue, Zip 53211–2990; tel. 414/961–3300; Susan Henckel, Executive Vice President and Chief Executive Officer **A**1 2 3 5 7 9 10 **F**2 3 4 5 7 8 9 10 11 12 14 16 18 19 21 22 23 24 25 26 29 31 32 33 34 35 37 38 39 40 41 42 43 44 45 46 47 48 49 52 53 54 55 56 57 58 59 60 61 63 64 65 66 70 71 72 74 **P**6 **S** Horizon Healthcare, Inc., Milwaukee, WI **N** Health Care Network of Wisconsin (HCN), Brookfield, WI; Columbia – St. Mary's, Inc., Milwaukee, WI; Horizon Healthcare, Inc., Milwaukee, WI

| | 23 | 10 | 334 | 10646 | 157 | 239054 | 1024 | 125396 | 52048 | 1410 |

✚ △ FROEDTERT MEMORIAL LUTHERAN HOSPITAL, 9200 West Wisconsin Avenue, Zip 53226–3596, Mailing Address: P.O. Box 26099, Zip 53226–3596; tel. 414/259–3000; William D. Petasnick, President **A**1 2 3 5 7 8 9 10 **F**1 3 4 5 7 8 10 11 12 14 16 19 21 22 23 25 26 29 31 32 33 34 35 36 37 39 40 41 42 43 44 45 46 48 49 52 54 55 56 57 58 60 61 62 63 64 65 66 69 70 71 72 74 **S** Horizon Healthcare, Inc., Milwaukee, WI **N** Health Care Network of Wisconsin (HCN), Brookfield, WI; Horizon Healthcare, Inc., Milwaukee, WI

| | 23 | 10 | 472 | 17665 | 348 | 346763 | 411 | 264910 | 70786 | 2093 |

✚ MILWAUKEE COUNTY MENTAL HEALTH DIVISION, 9455 Watertown Plank Road, Zip 53226–3559; tel. 414/257–6995; M. Kathleen Eilers, Administrator (Total facility includes 200 beds in nursing home–type unit) **A**1 3 5 10 **F**2 3 7 9 11 12 14 18 19 20 21 22 25 26 27 29 30 31 34 35 38 39 40 42 44 46 47 48 49 51 52 53 56 57 58 59 61 64 65 70 71 72 73

| | 13 | 22 | 380 | 4346 | 369 | 17595 | 0 | 99353 | 42729 | 1261 |

MILWAUKEE PSYCHIATRIC HOSPITAL See Wauwatosa

○ NORTHWEST GENERAL HOSPITAL, 5310 West Capitol Drive, Zip 53216–2299; tel. 414/447–8543; C. Dennis Barr, President and Chief Executive Officer **A**10 11 **F**2 3 8 12 13 17 19 21 22 27 28 29 30 34 35 37 39 41 42 44 45 48 49 61 63 64 65 67 71 72 73

| | 23 | 10 | 98 | 2197 | 29 | 32456 | 0 | 12146 | 6304 | 222 |

✚ △ SACRED HEART REHABILITATION INSTITUTE, 2350 North Lake Drive, Zip 53211–4507, Mailing Address: P.O. Box 392, Zip 53201–0392; tel. 414/298–6700; William H. Lange, Administrator and Senior Vice President **A**1 7 10 **F**12 14 16 19 21 25 26 29 34 35 39 41 45 46 48 49 54 57 61 64 65 66 71 **P**1 5 6 **S** Daughters of Charity National Health System, Saint Louis, MO **N** Columbia – St. Mary's, Inc., Milwaukee, WI

| | 21 | 46 | 69 | 891 | 40 | 10086 | 0 | 18588 | 9863 | 336 |

✚ △ SINAI SAMARITAN MEDICAL CENTER, (Includes Sinai Samaritan Medical Center–East Campus, 945 North 12th Street, Zip 53233; Sinai Samaritan Medical Center–West Campus, 2000 West Kilbourn Avenue, Zip 53233; tel. 414/344–8800), 945 North 12th Street, Zip 53233–1337, Mailing Address: P.O. Box 342, Zip 53201–0342; tel. 414/219–2000; Leonard E. Wilk, Administrator **A**1 2 3 5 7 8 9 10 **F**1 2 3 4 5 8 10 11 12 13 14 16 17 18 19 20 21 22 23 24 25 26 27 28 29 30 31 32 33 34 35 36 37 38 39 40 41 42 43 44 45 46 47 48 49 51 52 53 54 55 56 57 58 59 60 61 63 64 65 66 67 68 69 70 71 72 73 74 **P**4 6 **S** Aurora Health Care, Milwaukee, WI **N** Health Care Network of Wisconsin (HCN), Brookfield, WI; Aurora Health Care, Milwaukee, WI

| | 23 | 10 | 354 | 15730 | 200 | 292667 | 4127 | 192563 | 68872 | 1894 |

✚ △ ST. FRANCIS HOSPITAL, 3237 South 16th Street, Zip 53215–4592; tel. 414/647–5000; Gregory A. Banaszynski, President **A**1 2 5 7 9 10 **F**2 3 4 5 6 7 8 10 11 12 14 16 18 19 21 22 23 25 26 29 32 33 34 35 36 37 38 39 40 41 42 43 44 45 46 48 49 52 53 54 55 56 57 58 59 60 61 62 63 64 65 66 70 71 72 74 **P**5 6 7 8 **S** Wheaton Franciscan Services, Inc., Wheaton, IL **N** Felician Health Care, Inc., Chicago, IL; Health Care Network of Wisconsin (HCN), Brookfield, WI; Covenant Healthcare System, Inc., Milwaukee, WI

| | 23 | 10 | 265 | 10658 | 155 | 97029 | 1385 | 103171 | 40001 | 1241 |

Hospital, Address, Telephone, Administrator, Approval, Facility, and Physician Codes, Health Care System, Network	Classi-fication Codes		Utilization Data					Expense (thousands) of dollars		
★ American Hospital Association (AHA) membership ☐ Joint Commission on Accreditation of Healthcare Organizations (JCAHO) accreditation + American Osteopathic Healthcare Association (AOHA) membership ○ American Osteopathic Association (AOA) accreditation △ Commission on Accreditation of Rehabilitation Facilities (CARF) accreditation Control codes 61, 63, 64, 71, 72 and 73 indicate hospitals listed by AOHA, but not registered by AHA. For definition of numerical codes, see page A4	Control	Service	Staffed Beds	Admissions	Census	Outpatient Visits	Births	Total	Payroll	Personnel

✠ ST. JOSEPH'S HOSPITAL, 5000 West Chambers Street, Zip 53210–9988; tel. 414/447–2000; Jon L. Wachs, President (Total facility includes 28 beds in nursing home–type unit) **A**1 2 3 5 9 10 **F**1 2 3 4 5 6 7 8 9 10 11 12 13 17 18 19 21 22 23 24 25 26 27 28 29 30 31 32 33 34 35 37 38 39 40 41 42 43 44 45 46 47 48 49 51 52 53 54 55 56 57 58 59 60 61 63 64 65 66 67 68 69 70 71 73 74 **P**5 7 **S** Wheaton Franciscan Services, Inc., Wheaton, IL **N** Health Care Network of Wisconsin (HCN), Brookfield, WI; Covenant Healthcare System, Inc., Milwaukee, WI	21	10	595	21177	323	153058	3841	166911	69320	2149
✠ △ ST. LUKE'S MEDICAL CENTER, (Includes St. Luke's South Shore, 5900 South Lake Drive, Cudahy, Zip 53110–8903; tel. 414/769–9000; Lee Jaeger, Administrator), 2900 West Oklahoma Avenue, Zip 53215–4330, Mailing Address: P.O. Box 2901, Zip 53201–2901; tel. 414/649–6000; Mark S. Wiener, Administrator **A**1 2 3 5 7 8 9 10 **F**1 2 3 4 5 7 8 10 11 12 14 16 18 19 21 22 23 24 25 26 29 31 32 33 34 35 36 37 38 39 40 41 42 43 44 45 46 47 48 49 52 53 54 55 56 57 58 59 60 61 63 64 65 66 69 70 71 72 74 **P**4 6 **S** Aurora Health Care, Milwaukee, WI **N** Health Care Network of Wisconsin (HCN), Brookfield, WI; Aurora Health Care, Milwaukee, WI	23	10	777	31273	478	377847	1443	385623	122133	3407
✠ ST. MARY'S HOSPITAL, 2323 North Lake Drive, Zip 53211–9682, Mailing Address: P.O. Box 503, Zip 53201–0503; tel. 414/291–1000; Charles C. Lobeck, Chief Executive Officer **A**1 2 3 5 9 10 **F**3 4 7 8 9 10 11 12 14 16 17 18 19 21 22 25 26 27 28 29 30 32 34 35 37 38 39 40 41 42 43 44 45 51 53 54 57 58 59 61 63 64 65 66 67 71 72 73 74 **P**5 6 **S** Daughters of Charity National Health System, Saint Louis, MO **N** Health Care Network of Wisconsin (HCN), Brookfield, WI; Columbia – St. Mary's, Inc., Milwaukee, WI; Horizon Healthcare, Inc., Milwaukee, WI	21	10	257	8762	128	297705	2348	125930	57742	1629
✠ △ ST. MICHAEL HOSPITAL, 2400 West Villard Avenue, Zip 53209–4999; tel. 414/527–8000; Jeffrey K. Jenkins, President (Total facility includes 11 beds in nursing home–type unit) **A**1 2 3 5 7 9 10 **F**2 3 4 7 8 10 11 12 13 14 16 18 19 20 21 22 23 24 25 26 27 28 29 30 32 33 34 35 37 38 39 40 41 42 43 44 45 46 48 49 51 52 53 54 55 56 57 58 59 60 61 63 64 65 66 67 68 69 70 71 72 73 74 **P**6 7 **S** Wheaton Franciscan Services, Inc., Wheaton, IL **N** Health Care Network of Wisconsin (HCN), Brookfield, WI; Covenant Healthcare System, Inc., Milwaukee, WI	21	10	155	8806	129	95520	884	84650	34123	952
VENCOR HOSPITAL–MILWAUKEE, 5700 West Layton Avenue, Zip 53202; tel. 414/325–5900; E. Kay Gray, Interim Administrator **A**10 **F**6 10 12 16 17 19 21 22 26 27 32 35 37 39 45 46 49 50 54 57 64 65 **S** Vencor, Incorporated, Louisville, KY	33	10	51	230	26	4	0	—	—	23
MONROE—Green County										
☐ THE MONROE CLINIC, 515 22nd Avenue, Zip 53566–1598; tel. 608/324–1000; Kenneth Blount, President and Chief Executive Officer **A**1 9 10 **F**3 5 7 8 10 11 14 16 17 18 19 21 22 23 24 25 26 28 29 30 32 33 34 35 37 39 40 41 42 44 45 46 47 48 49 51 53 54 56 57 58 61 63 64 65 66 67 71 72 73 74 **P**6 8	21	10	117	3519	39	211754	374	54783	29445	695
NEENAH—Winnebago County										
✠ △ THEDA CLARK MEDICAL CENTER, 130 Second Street, Zip 54956–2883, Mailing Address: P.O. Box 2021, Zip 54957–2021; tel. 920/729–3100; Paul E. Macek, Senior Vice President **A**1 7 9 10 **F**2 3 4 5 6 7 8 10 11 12 13 14 16 17 18 19 21 22 23 24 25 26 28 29 30 32 34 35 36 37 38 39 40 41 42 43 44 45 46 48 49 51 52 53 54 55 56 57 58 59 60 61 62 64 65 66 67 68 69 70 71 72 73 74 **P**6 8 **S** United Health Group, Appleton, WI	23	10	216	8954	127	59715	1492	70770	33028	821
NEILLSVILLE—Clark County										
MEMORIAL MEDICAL CENTER, (Includes Neillsville Memorial Home), 216 Sunset Place, Zip 54456–1799; tel. 715/743–3101; Glen E. Grady, Administrator (Total facility includes 140 beds in nursing home–type unit) **A**9 10 **F**3 6 7 8 16 19 21 22 25 26 29 32 34 35 39 40 41 42 44 45 46 61 62 64 65 71 72 **P**6	23	10	169	1082	135	47228	30	—	—	
NEW LONDON—Outagamie County										
✠ NEW LONDON FAMILY MEDICAL CENTER, 1405 Mill Street, Zip 54961–2155, Mailing Address: P.O. Box 307, Zip 54961–0307; tel. 920/982–5330; Paul E. Gurgel, President and Chief Executive Officer **A**1 9 10 **F**7 8 11 16 19 22 26 29 30 34 35 37 39 40 41 44 45 48 49 61 64 67 71 72	23	10	39	1242	13	52097	159	9639	4357	126
NEW RICHMOND—St. Croix County										
★ HOLY FAMILY HOSPITAL, 535 Hospital Road, Zip 54017–1495; tel. 715/246–2101; Jean M. Needham, President **A**9 10 **F**7 8 11 12 17 18 19 21 22 24 26 28 29 30 32 33 34 35 36 37 39 40 41 42 44 45 46 49 61 63 64 65 66 67 71 73	21	10	20	1343	12	11469	147	6609	3154	98
OCONOMOWOC—Waukesha County										
MEMORIAL HOSPITAL OCONOMOWOC See Oconomowoc Memorial Hospital										
✠ △ OCONOMOWOC MEMORIAL HOSPITAL, (Formerly Memorial Hospital Oconomowoc), 791 Summit Avenue, Zip 53066–3896; tel. 414/569–9400; Douglas Guy, President and Chief Executive Officer **A**1 7 9 10 **F**1 2 3 6 7 8 11 14 16 19 21 22 24 26 29 31 32 33 34 35 37 39 40 41 42 44 45 46 48 49 56 61 63 64 65 70 71 74 **P**6 **S** Horizon Healthcare, Inc., Milwaukee, WI **N** Health Care Network of Wisconsin (HCN), Brookfield, WI; Horizon Healthcare, Inc., Milwaukee, WI	23	10	73	2916	29	81184	490	32443	15069	398
☐ ROGERS MEMORIAL HOSPITAL, 34700 Valley Road, Zip 53066–4599; tel. 414/646–4411; David L. Moulthrop, Ph.D., President and Chief Executive Officer **A**1 9 10 **F**3 12 14 16 17 18 19 20 25 26 27 28 29 30 34 35 39 45 46 51 52 53 54 55 56 57 58 59 61 64 65 67 68	23	22	90	972	58	5633	0	11581	6339	182

Hospital, Address, Telephone, Administrator, Approval, Facility, and Physician Codes, Health Care System, Network	Classi-fication Codes		Utilization Data					Expense (thousands) of dollars		
★ American Hospital Association (AHA) membership □ Joint Commission on Accreditation of Healthcare Organizations (JCAHO) accreditation + American Osteopathic Healthcare Association (AOHA) membership ○ American Osteopathic Association (AOA) accreditation △ Commission on Accreditation of Rehabilitation Facilities (CARF) accreditation Control codes 61, 63, 64, 71, 72 and 73 indicate hospitals listed by AOHA, but not registered by AHA. For definition of numerical codes, see page A4	Control	Service	Staffed Beds	Admissions	Census	Outpatient Visits	Births	Total	Payroll	Personnel

OCONTO—Oconto County

★ OCONTO MEMORIAL HOSPITAL, 405 First Street, Zip 54153–1299; tel. 920/834–8800; Lee W. Bennett, Chief Executive Officer and Chief Financial Officer **A**9 10 **F**1 3 4 5 6 7 8 10 12 13 17 18 19 20 21 22 24 26 27 28 29 30 32 33 34 35 36 39 43 44 45 46 51 53 54 55 56 57 58 59 60 61 62 64 65 66 67 68 71 74

	23	10	17	362	5	12839	0	3087	1547	52

OCONTO FALLS—Oconto County

COMMUNITY MEMORIAL HOSPITAL, 855 South Main Street, Zip 54154–1296; tel. 920/846–3444; Jim Van Dornick, Administrator **A**10 **F**3 7 8 12 19 22 25 26 29 32 34 35 37 39 40 41 44 45 46 47 48 49 61 64 65 66 70 71 72 74 **P**5 8 **N** Health Care Network of Wisconsin (HCN), Brookfield, WI

	23	10	26	876	11	46065	47	8966	4410	145

OSCEOLA—Polk County

OSCEOLA MEDICAL CENTER, 301 River Street, Zip 54020, Mailing Address: P.O. Box 218, Zip 54020–0218; tel. 715/294–2111; Jeffrey K. Meyer, Administrator and Chief Executive Officer (Total facility includes 40 beds in nursing home–type unit) **A**9 10 **F**7 8 11 19 22 29 32 33 34 37 40 41 42 44 45 46 48 49 61 64 65 71 **P**5

	23	10	59	538	46	18033	61	—	—	—

OSHKOSH—Winnebago County

✠ △ MERCY MEDICAL CENTER, 631 Hazel Street, Zip 54901–4680, Mailing Address: P.O. Box 1100, Zip 54902–1100; tel. 920/236–2000; Otto L. Cox, President and Chief Executive Officer **A**1 2 3 7 9 10 **F**3 4 5 7 8 9 10 11 12 18 19 21 22 23 25 26 29 32 33 34 35 36 37 40 41 42 43 44 45 46 47 48 49 52 53 54 55 56 57 58 61 63 64 65 66 70 71 72 **P**6 **S** Marian Health System, Tulsa, OK **N** Affinity Health System, Inc., Oshkosh, WI

	21	10	221	8084	114	356205	797	80600	36115	967

OSSEO—Trempealeau County

OSSEO AREA HOSPITAL AND NURSING HOME, 13025 Eighth Street, Zip 54758, Mailing Address: P.O. Box 70, Zip 54758–0070; tel. 715/597–3121; Bradley D. Groseth, Administrator (Total facility includes 61 beds in nursing home–type unit) **A**10 **F**11 19 22 26 29 32 33 34 37 41 44 45 46 47 49 61 62 64 65 69 71 **P**8 **S** Mayo Foundation, Rochester, MN **N** Luther/Midelfort/Mayo Health System, Eau Claire, WI

	23	10	79	213	57	9324	0	—	—	—

PARK FALLS—Price County

✠ FLAMBEAU HOSPITAL, 98 Sherry Avenue, Zip 54552–1467, Mailing Address: P.O. Box 310, Zip 54552–0310; tel. 715/762–2484; Curtis A. Johnson, Administrator **A**1 10 **F**7 8 11 12 16 17 19 21 22 24 26 27 28 29 30 32 33 34 36 37 39 40 41 44 45 46 48 49 51 61 63 65 66 67 71 72 73 **S** Marian Health System, Tulsa, OK **N** Marshfield Clinic's Regional System, Marshfield, WI; Northern Lakes Health Consortium, Duluth, MN

	23	10	42	1145	13	24911	105	9643	4535	183

PHELPS—Vilas County

NORTHWOODS HOSPITAL, 2383 State Highway 17, Zip 54554–9472, Mailing Address: P.O. Box 126, Zip 54554–0126; tel. 715/545–2313; Judson Schultz, Executive Director (Total facility includes 77 beds in nursing home–type unit) **A**9 10 **F**8 14 16 26 29 32 34 39 41 44 45 46 48 49 61 62 64 65 71 72

	23	10	82	125	69	5215	0	—	—	—

PLATTEVILLE—Grant County

★ SOUTHWEST HEALTH CENTER, (Includes Cuba City Medical Center, 808 South Washington Street, Cuba City, Zip 53807; tel. 608/744–2161; Hazel Green Hospital, 2110 Church Street, Hazel Green, Zip 53811; tel. 608/854–2231), 1100 Fifth Avenue, Zip 53818–1299; tel. 608/348–2331; Anne K. Klawiter, President and Chief Executive Officer (Total facility includes 105 beds in nursing home–type unit) **A**10 **F**6 7 8 16 19 22 26 29 32 34 35 36 39 40 44 45 61 64 65 71 **S** Brim, Inc., Portland, OR

	23	10	138	1298	115	19162	161	—	—	—

PLYMOUTH—Sheboygan County

★ VALLEY VIEW MEDICAL CENTER, 901 Reed Street, Zip 53073–2409; tel. 920/893–1771; T. Gregg Watson, Administrator (Total facility includes 60 beds in nursing home–type unit) **A**9 10 **F**7 8 11 12 14 16 19 21 22 26 29 32 33 34 35 36 37 39 40 41 42 44 45 46 48 49 61 62 63 64 65 70 71 72 74 **S** Aurora Health Care, Milwaukee, WI **N** Health Care Network of Wisconsin (HCN), Brookfield, WI; Aurora Health Care, Milwaukee, WI

	23	10	98	1166	71	27804	149	—	—	—

PORT WASHINGTON—Ozaukee County

ST. MARY'S HOSPITAL OZAUKEE See Mequon

PORTAGE—Columbia County

✠ DIVINE SAVIOR HOSPITAL AND NURSING HOME, 1015 West Pleasant Street, Zip 53901–9987, Mailing Address: P.O. Box 387, Zip 53901–0387; tel. 608/742–4131; Michael Decker, President and Chief Executive Officer (Total facility includes 111 beds in nursing home–type unit) **A**1 10 **F**2 3 7 8 11 16 17 19 20 21 22 25 26 28 29 30 32 34 35 36 37 39 40 41 42 44 45 46 48 49 51 56 61 63 64 65 66 67 70 71 73

	21	10	160	1903	123	38875	185	19601	9156	354

PRAIRIE DU CHIEN—Crawford County

✠ PRAIRIE DU CHIEN MEMORIAL HOSPITAL, 705 East Taylor Street, Zip 53821–2196; tel. 608/326–2431; Harold W. Brown, Chief Executive Officer **A**1 9 10 **F**1 2 3 6 7 8 11 12 14 16 17 19 22 26 28 29 30 32 33 34 35 36 37 39 40 41 42 44 45 46 49 53 54 56 58 59 61 62 65 67 68 71 **N** Mississippi Valley Health Partnership, Prairie du Chien, WI

	23	10	43	1746	33	18620	159	11267	5869	194

PRAIRIE DU SAC—Sauk County

✠ SAUK PRAIRIE MEMORIAL HOSPITAL, 80 First Street, Zip 53578–1550; tel. 608/643–3311; Bobbe Teigen, Administrator **A**1 10 **F**2 7 8 11 12 14 16 19 21 22 24 25 26 29 31 32 33 34 35 36 37 39 40 41 42 44 45 48 49 54 56 57 61 63 64 65 66 70 71 72 **P**8

	23	10	36	2300	21	36349	207	20931	9681	303

Hospital, Address, Telephone, Administrator, Approval, Facility, and Physician Codes, Health Care System, Network	Classi-fication Codes		Utilization Data					Expense (thousands) of dollars		
★ American Hospital Association (AHA) membership □ Joint Commission on Accreditation of Healthcare Organizations (JCAHO) accreditation + American Osteopathic Healthcare Association (AOHA) membership ○ American Osteopathic Association (AOA) accreditation △ Commission on Accreditation of Rehabilitation Facilities (CARF) accreditation Control codes 61, 63, 64, 71, 72 and 73 indicate hospitals listed by AOHA, but not registered by AHA. For definition of numerical codes, see page A4	Control	Service	Staffed Beds	Admissions	Census	Outpatient Visits	Births	Total	Payroll	Personnel

RACINE—Racine County

☒ △ SAINT MARY'S MEDICAL CENTER, 3801 Spring Street, Zip 53405–1690; tel. 414/636–4011; Edward P. Demeulenaere, President and Chief Executive Officer **A**1 2 3 7 9 10 **F**2 3 4 7 8 10 11 12 14 16 19 21 22 23 24 25 26 29 32 33 34 35 37 38 39 40 41 42 43 44 45 46 47 48 49 52 53 54 55 56 57 58 59 60 61 64 65 66 71 72 74 **P**6 **S** Wheaton Franciscan Services, Inc., Wheaton, IL **N** All Saints Healthcare System, Racine, WI — 21 10 196 8975 123 184616 0 84007 35516 1278

★ ST. LUKE'S MEMORIAL HOSPITAL, 1320 Wisconsin Avenue, Zip 53403–1987; tel. 414/636–2011; Edward P. Demeulenaere, President and Chief Executive Officer (Total facility includes 41 beds in nursing home–type unit) **A**5 9 10 **F**2 3 4 7 10 11 12 14 16 19 21 22 23 24 26 29 32 33 34 35 38 39 40 41 42 43 44 45 46 47 48 49 52 53 54 55 56 57 58 59 60 61 64 65 66 71 72 74 **P**6 **S** Wheaton Franciscan Services, Inc., Wheaton, IL **N** Health Care Network of Wisconsin (HCN), Brookfield, WI; All Saints Healthcare System, Racine, WI — 23 10 183 2676 117 89449 1959 — — —

REEDSBURG—Sauk County

□ REEDSBURG AREA MEDICAL CENTER, 2000 North Dewey Street, Zip 53959–1097; tel. 608/524–6487; George L. Johnson, President (Total facility includes 50 beds in nursing home–type unit) **A**1 10 **F**4 7 8 10 11 12 16 17 18 19 21 22 24 28 29 30 32 33 34 35 36 37 39 40 41 42 44 45 47 49 51 61 64 65 66 67 70 71 72 73 — 23 10 88 1874 66 36482 173 16880 7704 239

RHINELANDER—Oneida County

☒ SACRED HEART–ST. MARY'S HOSPITALS, (Includes Sacred Heart Hospital, 216 North Seventh Street, Tomahawk, Zip 54487; tel. 715/453–7700; St. Mary's Hospital, 1044 Kabel Avenue, Zip 54501; tel. 715/369–6600), 1044 Kabel Avenue, Zip 54501–3998; Mailing Address: P.O. Box 20, Zip 54501–0020; tel. 715/369–6600; Kevin J. O'Donnell, President and Chief Executive Officer **A**1 10 **F**2 3 7 8 11 12 13 16 17 19 22 23 24 26 29 32 33 34 35 36 37 39 40 41 42 44 45 46 49 51 52 53 54 55 56 57 58 59 60 61 63 64 65 66 67 68 71 73 **S** Marian Health System, Tulsa, OK — 21 10 47 4735 55 42657 404 36614 18530 593

RICE LAKE—Barron County

☒ LAKEVIEW MEDICAL CENTER, 1100 North Main Street, Zip 54868–1238; tel. 715/234–1515; Edward H. Wolf, Chief Executive Officer **A**1 9 10 **F**7 11 16 17 19 22 24 26 28 29 30 32 33 34 35 36 37 39 40 41 42 44 45 49 61 63 64 65 66 67 71 73 **N** Northern Lakes Health Consortium, Duluth, MN — 23 10 69 2659 27 21377 435 18986 9362 261

RICHLAND CENTER—Richland County

□ RICHLAND HOSPITAL, 431 North Park Street, Zip 53581–1899; tel. 608/647–6321; Thomas J. Werner, Administrator **A**1 10 **F**3 7 8 10 11 19 21 22 26 29 32 33 34 36 37 39 40 41 42 44 45 54 55 56 58 61 64 65 66 70 71 — 23 10 38 1510 16 14939 172 12199 5802 198

RIPON—Fond Du Lac County

☒ RIPON MEDICAL CENTER, 933 Newbury Street, Zip 54971–1798, Mailing Address: P.O. Box 390, Zip 54971–0390; tel. 920/748–3101; Jon W. Baker, Chief Executive Officer **A**1 9 10 **F**7 8 11 12 16 19 21 22 24 26 27 28 29 30 34 35 39 40 41 42 44 45 46 47 49 51 54 58 61 63 64 65 66 67 70 71 72 73 74 **S** Brim, Inc., Portland, OR — 23 10 29 1105 11 28717 84 10017 4133 130

RIVER FALLS—St. Croix County

☒ RIVER FALLS AREA HOSPITAL, 1629 East Division Street, Zip 54022–1571; tel. 715/425–6155; Sharon Whelan, President **A**1 9 10 **F**7 11 14 16 19 21 22 24 26 29 32 33 34 35 36 37 39 40 44 45 46 47 48 49 61 64 65 66 71 72 **P**6 8 **S** Allina Health System, Minneapolis, MN **N** Allina Health System, Minnetonka, MN — 23 10 36 995 9 9865 212 9519 3689 97

SAINT CROIX FALLS—Polk County

□ ST. CROIX VALLEY MEMORIAL HOSPITAL, 204 South Adams Street, Zip 54024–9400; tel. 715/483–3261; Steve L. Urosevich, Chief Executive Officer **A**1 9 10 **F**2 3 6 7 8 11 13 17 18 19 20 21 22 24 26 28 29 30 32 33 34 35 37 40 41 42 44 45 46 47 52 53 54 56 57 58 61 63 64 65 66 67 68 70 71 73 74 **N** Health Care Network of Wisconsin (HCN), Brookfield, WI — 23 10 69 1959 16 26352 303 12027 5660 171

SHAWANO—Shawano County

☒ SHAWANO MEDICAL CENTER, 309 North Bartlette Street, Zip 54166–0477; tel. 715/526–2111; John J. Kestly, Administrator **A**1 9 10 **F**7 8 10 11 14 16 17 19 21 22 26 28 29 30 32 33 34 35 37 39 40 44 45 46 48 56 61 63 64 65 66 67 71 73 74 **P**5 **S** Brim, Inc., Portland, OR — 23 10 46 2478 25 38818 361 15687 6743 226

SHEBOYGAN—Sheboygan County

☒ △ SHEBOYGAN MEMORIAL MEDICAL CENTER, 2629 North Seventh Street, Zip 53083–4998; tel. 920/451–5000; T. Gregg Watson, Administrator **A**1 2 7 9 10 **F**2 3 5 7 8 10 11 12 16 19 21 22 23 26 29 34 35 37 39 40 41 42 44 45 46 47 48 49 52 53 54 55 56 57 58 61 63 64 65 66 70 71 74 **S** Aurora Health Care, Milwaukee, WI **N** Health Care Network of Wisconsin (HCN), Brookfield, WI; Aurora Health Care, Milwaukee, WI — 23 10 138 5133 55 47910 935 34799 15334 506

☒ △ ST. NICHOLAS HOSPITAL, 1601 North Taylor Drive, Zip 53081–2496; tel. 920/459–8300; Michael J. Stenger, Executive Vice President and Administrator **A**1 2 7 9 10 **F**3 7 8 10 11 12 13 14 16 17 18 19 20 21 22 23 24 25 26 27 28 29 30 32 33 34 35 36 37 39 40 41 42 44 45 48 49 51 54 56 58 60 61 63 64 65 66 67 68 69 70 71 72 73 74 **P**5 **S** Hospital Sisters Health System, Springfield, IL **N** Covenant Healthcare System, Inc., Milwaukee, WI — 21 10 185 3139 40 57719 324 31463 11867 432

SHELL LAKE—Washburn County

□ INDIANHEAD MEDICAL CENTER, 113 Fourth Avenue West, Zip 54871; tel. 715/468–7833; Paul Naglosky, Administrator **A**1 9 10 **F**7 11 19 22 26 29 32 34 35 37 40 42 44 45 46 61 64 65 69 71 — 33 10 49 645 7 6477 31 3118 1422 61

Hospital, Address, Telephone, Administrator, Approval, Facility, and Physician Codes, Health Care System, Network	Classi-fication Codes		Utilization Data					Expense (thousands) of dollars		
★ American Hospital Association (AHA) membership □ Joint Commission on Accreditation of Healthcare Organizations (JCAHO) accreditation + American Osteopathic Healthcare Association (AOHA) membership ○ American Osteopathic Association (AOA) accreditation △ Commission on Accreditation of Rehabilitation Facilities (CARF) accreditation Control codes 61, 63, 64, 71, 72 and 73 indicate hospitals listed by AOHA, but not registered by AHA. For definition of numerical codes, see page A4	Control	Service	Staffed Beds	Admissions	Census	Outpatient Visits	Births	Total	Payroll	Personnel

SPARTA—Monroe County

☒ FRANCISCAN SKEMP HEALTHCARE–SPARTA CAMPUS, 310 West Main Street, Zip 54656–2171; tel. 608/269–2132; William P. Sexton, Administrator (Total facility includes 30 beds in nursing home–type unit) **A**1 10 **F**2 7 8 12 14 16 19 22 26 29 32 33 34 39 40 41 44 45 46 49 61 64 65 66 70 71 74 **S** Franciscan Skemp Healthcare, La Crosse, WI **N** Franciscan Skemp Healthcare, LaCrosse, WI — 21 10 60 756 35 35534 139 — — —

SPOONER—Washburn County

☒ COMMUNITY MEMORIAL HOSPITAL AND NURSING HOME, 819 Ash Street, Zip 54801–1299; tel. 715/635–2111; Michael Schafer, Chief Executive Officer (Total facility includes 90 beds in nursing home–type unit) **A**1 9 10 **F**2 7 8 11 12 16 17 19 21 22 26 27 28 29 32 33 34 36 37 40 41 42 44 45 48 50 61 63 64 65 66 67 71 73 **S** Brim, Inc., Portland, OR **N** Northern Lakes Health Consortium, Duluth, MN — 23 10 136 1015 99 18663 87 8546 4303 133

STANLEY—Chippewa County

☒ VICTORY MEDICAL CENTER, 230 East Fourth Avenue, Zip 54768–1298; tel. 715/644–5571; Cynthia Eichman, Chief Executive Officer and Administrator (Total facility includes 86 beds in nursing home–type unit) **A**1 10 **F**1 8 11 16 19 21 22 25 28 29 30 34 37 39 41 44 45 46 49 51 56 61 64 65 66 67 69 71 72 73 **P**6 **S** Marian Health System, Tulsa, OK — 21 10 127 667 87 19668 5 8333 3677 187

STEVENS POINT—Portage County

☒ SAINT MICHAEL'S HOSPITAL, 900 Illinois Avenue, Zip 54481–3196; tel. 715/346–5000; Jeffrey L. Martin, President and Chief Executive Officer **A**1 9 10 **F**2 7 8 11 14 16 17 19 21 22 23 25 26 28 29 30 33 34 35 36 37 38 39 40 41 42 44 45 46 47 49 51 52 53 54 55 56 57 61 63 64 65 66 71 73 **S** Marian Health System, Tulsa, OK — 21 10 104 4329 44 56012 755 38446 15605 465

STOUGHTON—Dane County

□ STOUGHTON HOSPITAL ASSOCIATION, 900 Ridge Street, Zip 53589–1896; tel. 608/873–6611; Terrence Brenny, President **A**1 9 10 **F**1 8 11 13 14 17 19 20 22 26 27 28 29 30 31 32 33 34 35 37 41 42 44 45 46 48 49 51 52 54 57 61 63 64 65 66 67 68 71 72 73 — 23 10 40 1222 14 32743 0 12149 5228 171

STURGEON BAY—Door County

☒ DOOR COUNTY MEMORIAL HOSPITAL, 330 South 16th Place, Zip 54235–1495; tel. 920/743–5566; Gerald M. Worrick, President and Administrator (Total facility includes 30 beds in nursing home–type unit) **A**1 9 10 **F**1 3 4 7 8 10 11 14 16 19 20 21 22 25 26 28 29 30 31 32 33 34 35 37 39 40 41 42 43 44 45 46 48 49 51 53 54 55 61 64 65 67 69 70 71 72 73 **P**6 — 23 10 77 2036 52 35452 184 24126 12482 323

SUPERIOR—Douglas County

□ ST. MARY'S HOSPITAL OF SUPERIOR, 3500 Tower Avenue, Zip 54880–5395; tel. 715/392–8281; Terry Jacobson, Acting Administrator **A**1 9 10 **F**11 12 13 14 16 17 19 20 21 22 27 28 29 30 32 34 35 37 39 41 42 44 45 46 48 49 51 61 64 65 67 68 71 73 **S** Benedictine Health System, Duluth, MN **N** Health Care Network of Wisconsin (HCN), Brookfield, WI; Benedictine Health System, Duluth, MN — 23 10 42 1429 15 45677 0 11743 5528 170

TOMAH—Monroe County

□ TOMAH MEMORIAL HOSPITAL, 321 Butts Avenue, Zip 54660–1412; tel. 608/372–2181; Philip Stuart, Administrator **A**1 9 10 **F**2 3 7 9 11 12 13 16 17 19 22 26 28 29 32 33 34 35 36 38 39 40 41 42 44 45 52 61 63 64 65 66 67 71 72 **P**5 **N** Lutheran Health System, LaCrosse, WI — 23 10 45 1019 11 23011 167 8754 4054 144

☒ VETERANS AFFAIRS MEDICAL CENTER, 500 East Veterans Street, Zip 54660; tel. 608/372–3971; Stan Johnson, Medical Center Director (Total facility includes 100 beds in nursing home–type unit) (Nonreporting) **A**1 **S** Department of Veterans Affairs, Washington, DC — 45 22 569 — — — — — — —

TOMAHAWK—Lincoln County

SACRED HEART HOSPITAL See Sacred Heart–St. Mary's Hospitals, Rhinelander

TWO RIVERS—Manitowoc County

☒ TWO RIVERS COMMUNITY HOSPITAL AND HAMILTON MEMORIAL HOME, 2500 Garfield Street, Zip 54241–2399; tel. 920/793–1178; Steven H. Spencer, Administrator (Total facility includes 85 beds in nursing home–type unit) **A**1 9 10 **F**7 8 10 11 12 14 19 22 25 26 29 32 33 34 35 36 37 39 40 41 44 45 46 47 48 49 61 64 65 71 **S** Aurora Health Care, Milwaukee, WI **N** Aurora Health Care, Milwaukee, WI — 23 10 138 1709 99 20944 273 — — —

VIROQUA—Vernon County

VERNON MEMORIAL HOSPITAL, 507 South Main Street, Zip 54665–2096; tel. 608/637–2101; Garith W. Steiner, Chief Executive Officer **A**10 **F**2 3 7 8 12 13 14 16 17 19 22 24 26 28 29 30 32 33 34 39 40 41 42 44 45 46 49 54 55 56 57 58 61 64 65 66 67 70 71 73 — 23 10 21 1501 14 22367 161 12193 6254 193

WATERTOWN—Dodge County

☒ WATERTOWN MEMORIAL HOSPITAL, 125 Hospital Drive, Zip 53098–3384; tel. 920/261–4210; John P. Kosanovich, President **A**1 10 **F**1 3 6 7 8 11 12 13 16 17 19 21 22 25 26 29 30 32 33 34 35 36 37 39 40 41 44 45 46 47 49 56 58 61 63 64 65 66 67 70 71 72 73 74 **P**6 8 — 23 10 45 2234 25 78435 333 22585 10804 281

WAUKESHA—Waukesha County

☒ △ WAUKESHA MEMORIAL HOSPITAL, 725 American Avenue, Zip 53188–5099; tel. 414/544–2011; Rexford W. Titus, III, President and Chief Executive Officer **A**1 2 3 5 7 9 10 **F**2 3 4 6 7 8 9 10 11 12 14 19 21 22 23 25 26 29 32 33 34 35 36 37 38 39 40 41 42 43 44 45 47 48 49 52 53 54 55 56 57 58 59 60 61 62 63 64 65 66 70 71 72 74 **P**1 6 7 **N** Health Care Network of Wisconsin (HCN), Brookfield, WI; Waukesha Hospital System, Inc., Waukesha, WI — 23 10 307 11766 157 223484 2124 132650 49546 1156

Hospital, Address, Telephone, Administrator, Approval, Facility, and Physician Codes, Health Care System, Network	Classi-fication Codes		Utilization Data					Expense (thousands) of dollars		
★ American Hospital Association (AHA) membership □ Joint Commission on Accreditation of Healthcare Organizations (JCAHO) accreditation + American Osteopathic Healthcare Association (AOHA) membership ○ American Osteopathic Association (AOA) accreditation △ Commission on Accreditation of Rehabilitation Facilities (CARF) accreditation Control codes 61, 63, 64, 71, 72 and 73 indicate hospitals listed by AOHA, but not registered by AHA. For definition of numerical codes, see page A4	Control	Service	Staffed Beds	Admissions	Census	Outpatient Visits	Births	Total	Payroll	Personnel

WAUPACA—Waupaca County

★ RIVERSIDE MEDICAL CENTER, 800 Riverside Drive, Zip 54981–1999; tel. 715/258–1000; Jan V. Carrell, Chief Executive Officer **A**1 9 10 **F**7 8 9 10 11 19 21 22 23 26 29 34 35 37 40 41 42 44 45 46 47 48 61 63 64 65 71 74 **S** Quorum Health Group/Quorum Health Resources, Inc., Brentwood, TN
| | 23 | 10 | 36 | 1531 | 14 | 45700 | 231 | 15020 | 6696 | 210 |

WAUPUN—Fond Du Lac County

★ WAUPUN MEMORIAL HOSPITAL, 620 West Brown Street, Zip 53963–1799; tel. 920/324–5581; James E. Baer, FACHE, President **A**1 9 10 **F**5 7 8 11 16 17 19 21 22 23 25 26 28 29 30 32 33 34 35 36 37 39 40 41 44 45 47 49 51 61 64 65 67 68 71 73 **N** Health Care Network of Wisconsin (HCN), Brookfield, WI
| | 21 | 10 | 49 | 1084 | 10 | 34045 | 127 | 12344 | 5135 | 165 |

WAUSAU—Marathon County

NORTH CENTRAL HEALTH CARE FACILITIES, 1100 Lakeview Drive, Zip 54403–6799; tel. 715/848–4600; Tim Steller, Chief Executive Officer (Total facility includes 356 beds in nursing home–type unit) **A**10 **F**2 3 12 17 19 22 25 26 27 29 34 35 39 45 48 49 52 53 54 55 56 57 58 59 61 64 65 67 73
| | 13 | 22 | 406 | 1288 | 368 | 107525 | 0 | 42167 | 22358 | 609 |

★ △ WAUSAU HOSPITAL, 333 Pine Ridge Boulevard, Zip 54401–4187, Mailing Address: P.O. Box 1847, Zip 54402–1847; tel. 715/847–2121; Paul A. Spaude, President and Chief Executive Officer **A**1 2 3 5 7 9 10 **F**2 3 4 7 8 9 10 11 16 19 21 22 23 25 26 28 29 30 32 33 34 35 37 39 40 41 42 43 44 45 46 47 48 49 52 53 54 56 57 58 59 60 61 63 64 65 67 70 71 73 **P**6 **N** Community Health Care, Inc., Wausau, WI
| | 23 | 10 | 216 | 11225 | 143 | 75185 | 1458 | 105468 | 42394 | 1254 |

WAUWATOSA—Milwaukee County

+ ○ LAKEVIEW HOSPITAL, 10010 West Blue Mound Road, Zip 53226; tel. 414/259–7200; J. E. Race, Administrator and Chief Executive Officer (Nonreporting) **A**9 10 11 12 **N** Covenant Healthcare System, Inc., Milwaukee, WI
| | 23 | 10 | 72 | — | — | — | — | — | — | — |

★ MILWAUKEE PSYCHIATRIC HOSPITAL, 1220 Dewey Avenue, Zip 53213–2598; tel. 414/454–6600; James A. Moore, Administrator **A**1 3 5 9 10 **F**1 2 3 4 5 6 7 9 10 11 12 13 14 16 17 18 19 20 21 22 23 24 25 26 27 28 29 30 31 32 33 34 35 36 38 39 40 41 42 43 44 45 46 47 48 49 50 51 52 53 54 55 56 57 58 59 60 61 62 63 64 65 66 67 68 70 71 72 73 74 **P**6 **S** Aurora Health Care, Milwaukee, WI **N** Aurora Health Care, Milwaukee, WI
| | 23 | 22 | 75 | 1904 | 30 | 25879 | 0 | 13650 | 5735 | 172 |

WEST ALLIS—Milwaukee County

□ CHARTER BEHAVIORAL HEALTH SYSTEM OF MILWAUKEE/WEST ALLIS, 11101 West Lincoln Avenue, Zip 53227; tel. 414/327–3000; Robert Kwech, Chief Executive Officer (Nonreporting) **A**1
| | 33 | 22 | 80 | — | — | — | — | — | — | — |

★ WEST ALLIS MEMORIAL HOSPITAL, 8901 West Lincoln Avenue, Zip 53227–0901, Mailing Address: P.O. Box 27901, Zip 53227–0901; tel. 414/328–6000; Richard A. Kellar, Administrator **A**1 2 9 10 **F**1 2 3 4 5 6 7 8 10 11 12 16 17 18 19 21 22 23 24 25 27 29 30 31 32 33 34 35 36 37 38 39 40 41 42 43 44 45 48 49 52 53 54 55 56 57 58 59 60 61 63 64 65 66 67 71 72 73 74 **P**2 4 5 6 **S** Aurora Health Care, Milwaukee, WI **N** Health Care Network of Wisconsin (HCN), Brookfield, WI; Aurora Health Care, Milwaukee, WI
| | 23 | 10 | 199 | 8693 | 120 | 130772 | 1069 | 86529 | 40081 | 911 |

WEST BEND—Washington County

★ ST. JOSEPH'S COMMUNITY HOSPITAL OF WEST BEND, 551 South Silverbrook Drive, Zip 53095–3898; tel. 414/334–5533; Gregory T. Burns, Executive Director **A**1 9 10 **F**2 7 8 11 12 13 14 16 17 18 19 21 22 23 25 26 28 29 30 34 35 36 37 39 40 41 42 44 45 47 49 52 54 57 61 63 64 65 67 68 70 71 **P**6 **N** Health Care Network of Wisconsin (HCN), Brookfield, WI
| | 23 | 10 | 121 | 4966 | 55 | 46168 | 690 | 27379 | 13288 | 384 |

WHITEHALL—Trempealeau County

TRI–COUNTY MEMORIAL HOSPITAL, 18601 Lincoln Street, Zip 54773–0065, Mailing Address: P.O. Box 65, Zip 54773–0065; tel. 715/538–4361; Ronald B. Fields, President (Total facility includes 110 beds in nursing home–type unit) **A**9 10 **F**3 4 5 6 7 8 10 11 14 16 17 19 20 21 22 26 27 28 29 30 31 32 33 34 35 36 37 39 41 42 43 44 45 46 48 49 50 51 53 54 55 56 57 58 59 60 61 63 64 65 66 67 68 69 71 73 74 **N** Lutheran Health System, LaCrosse, WI
| | 23 | 10 | 148 | 561 | 92 | 9949 | 0 | 6442 | 3275 | 159 |

WILD ROSE—Waushara County

WILD ROSE COMMUNITY MEMORIAL HOSPITAL, 601 Grove Avenue, Zip 54984, Mailing Address: P.O. Box 243, Zip 54984–0243; tel. 414/622–3257; Donald Caves, President **A**9 10 **F**2 3 6 8 9 12 17 18 19 22 26 27 28 29 30 32 33 34 37 39 40 41 44 45 48 49 51 53 54 56 57 58 61 65 66 67 68 71 73 74 **N** Partners Health System, Inc., Berlin, WI
| | 23 | 10 | 26 | 443 | 4 | 12613 | 30 | 4073 | 1601 | 78 |

WINNEBAGO—Winnebago County

□ WINNEBAGO MENTAL HEALTH INSTITUTE, Mailing Address: P.O. Box 9, Zip 54985–0009; tel. 414/235–4910; Joann O'Connor, Director **A**1 3 10 **F**2 4 7 8 10 11 19 22 24 29 35 40 41 44 45 46 47 48 50 52 53 55 56 61 63 64 65 70 71 72
| | 12 | 22 | 330 | 831 | 247 | 276 | 0 | 32787 | 20311 | 676 |

WISCONSIN RAPIDS—Wood County

★ RIVERVIEW HOSPITAL ASSOCIATION, (Includes Riverview Manor), 410 Dewey Street, Zip 54494–4724, Mailing Address: P.O. Box 8080, Zip 54495–8080; tel. 715/423–6060; Celse A. Berard, President (Total facility includes 118 beds in nursing home–type unit) **A**1 9 10 **F**2 7 8 11 13 14 17 19 20 21 22 26 29 30 34 35 36 37 39 40 42 44 45 47 48 49 51 52 54 61 63 64 65 66 67 70 71
| | 23 | 10 | 197 | 3476 | 141 | 31475 | 592 | 29939 | 14002 | 435 |

WOODRUFF—Oneida County

★ HOWARD YOUNG MEDICAL CENTER, 240 Maple Street, Zip 54568, Mailing Address: P.O. Box 470, Zip 54568–0470; tel. 715/356–8000; Patricia L. Richardson, President and Chief Executive Officer **A**1 9 10 **F**3 6 7 8 9 11 12 13 17 18 19 20 21 22 23 24 25 26 27 28 29 30 32 33 34 35 37 39 40 41 42 44 45 46 47 48 49 51 56 58 61 63 65 66 67 68 71 73
| | 23 | 10 | 65 | 4174 | 46 | 32350 | 263 | 37313 | 16361 | 518 |

WYOMING

Resident population 480 (in thousands)
Resident population in metro areas 29.8%
Birth rate per 1,000 population 13.5
65 years and over 11.2%
Percent of persons without health insurance 13.5%

Hospital, Address, Telephone, Administrator, Approval, Facility, and Physician Codes, Health Care System, Network	Classi- fication Codes		Utilization Data					Expense (thousands) of dollars		
	Control	Service	Staffed Beds	Admissions	Census	Outpatient Visits	Births	Total	Payroll	Personnel

★ American Hospital Association (AHA) membership
☐ Joint Commission on Accreditation of Healthcare Organizations (JCAHO) accreditation
+ American Osteopathic Healthcare Association (AOHA) membership
○ American Osteopathic Association (AOA) accreditation
△ Commission on Accreditation of Rehabilitation Facilities (CARF) accreditation
Control codes 61, 63, 64, 71, 72 and 73 indicate hospitals listed by AOHA, but not registered by AHA. For definition of numerical codes, see page A4

AFTON—Lincoln County

★ STAR VALLEY HOSPITAL, 110 Hospital Lane, Zip 83110, Mailing Address: P.O. Box 579, Zip 83110–0579; tel. 307/886–5800; Alberto Vasquez, Administrator (Total facility includes 24 beds in nursing home–type unit) **A**9 10 **F**7 8 12 15 16 22 25 28 30 32 34 40 44 46 49 51 64 65 71 73 **P**6 **S** Intermountain Health Care, Inc., Salt Lake City, UT	16	10	39	551	3	25936	94	3712	2047	71

BUFFALO—Johnson County

☐ JOHNSON COUNTY MEMORIAL HOSPITAL, 497 West Lott Street, Zip 82834–1691; tel. 307/684–5521; Sandy Ward, Administrator (Total facility includes 54 beds in nursing home–type unit) **A**1 9 10 **F**8 19 22 26 28 32 33 35 37 40 44 45 49 64 65 71	16	10	69	591	50	12967	60	6884	3598	128

CASPER—Natrona County

⊞ △ WYOMING MEDICAL CENTER, 1233 East Second Street, Zip 82601–2988; tel. 307/577–7201; Michael E. Schrader, President and Chief Executive Officer **A**1 3 7 9 10 **F**3 4 7 8 10 12 13 14 15 16 17 19 21 22 23 25 27 28 30 31 32 34 35 37 39 40 41 42 43 44 45 46 48 49 51 52 54 55 56 58 59 60 61 65 67 71 73 74 **P**6 **N** Wyoming Integrated Network, Casper, WY	23	10	194	7681	91	64707	935	76916	32206	1051

CHEYENNE—Laramie County

★ U. S. AIR FORCE HOSPITAL, 6900 Alden Drive, Zip 82005–3913; tel. 307/773–2045; Major Angela D. Fowler, MSC, USAF, Administrator (Nonreporting) **A**9 **S** Department of the Air Force, Bowling AFB, DC	41	10	15	—	—	—	—	—	—	—
⊞ UNITED MEDICAL CENTER, (Includes De Paul Hospital, 2600 East 18th Street, Zip 82001–5511; tel. 307/634–2273), 214 East 23rd Street, Zip 82001–3790; tel. 307/634–2273; Jon M. Gates, Chief Executive Officer **A**1 3 9 10 **F**2 3 4 7 8 10 11 12 15 16 17 19 21 22 23 24 28 30 35 37 40 41 42 43 44 46 48 49 52 53 54 55 56 57 58 59 60 63 64 65 67 71 73	13	10	170	7244	85	167454	838	58247	25018	834
⊞ VETERANS AFFAIRS MEDICAL CENTER, 2360 East Pershing Boulevard, Zip 82001–5392; tel. 307/778–7550; Richard Fry, Acting Director (Total facility includes 50 beds in nursing home–type unit) (Nonreporting) **A**1 9 **S** Department of Veterans Affairs, Washington, DC	45	10	125	—	—	—	—	—	—	—

CODY—Park County

⊞ WEST PARK HOSPITAL, 707 Sheridan Avenue, Zip 82414; tel. 307/527–7501; Douglas A. McMillan, Administrator and Chief Executive Officer (Total facility includes 88 beds in nursing home–type unit) **A**1 9 10 **F**2 3 7 8 15 17 19 21 22 26 27 28 32 33 34 35 37 39 40 41 42 44 45 46 48 49 52 53 54 55 56 57 58 64 65 66 67 71 73 **S** Quorum Health Group/Quorum Health Resources, Inc., Brentwood, TN	16	10	171	1446	14	—	205	22975	10576	332

DOUGLAS—Converse County

CONVERSE COUNTY MEMORIAL HOSPITAL See Memorial Hospital of Converse County

★ MEMORIAL HOSPITAL OF CONVERSE COUNTY, (Formerly Converse County Memorial Hospital), 111 South Fifth Street, Zip 82633–2490; tel. 307/358–2122; Fred F. Schroeder, Administrator **A**9 10 **F**1 2 3 4 5 6 7 8 9 10 11 12 13 15 16 17 18 19 20 22 24 26 28 30 31 32 33 34 35 36 37 38 39 40 41 42 43 44 45 46 47 48 49 52 62 64 65 66 67 68 69 70 71 73 74 **P**5	13	10	34	385	4	23205	75	5789	2616	106

EVANSTON—Uinta County

⊞ EVANSTON REGIONAL HOSPITAL, 190 Arrowhead Drive, Zip 82930–9266; tel. 307/789–3636; Robert W. Allen, Administrator **A**1 9 10 **F**7 8 12 15 16 17 19 20 22 28 29 30 32 33 35 37 39 40 44 46 49 65 67 70 71 73 **S** Intermountain Health Care, Inc., Salt Lake City, UT	23	10	38	1235	10	45860	294	9978	3486	122
WYOMING STATE HOSPITAL, 830 Highway 150 South, Zip 82931–5341, Mailing Address: P.O. Box 177, Zip 82931–0177; tel. 307/789–3464; Pablo Hernandez, M.D., Administrator **A**10 **F**3 6 12 14 15 16 17 20 34 41 45 52 53 54 55 56 57 58 65 67 73	12	22	122	441	104	0	0	15321	8878	399

GILLETTE—Campbell County

⊞ CAMPBELL COUNTY MEMORIAL HOSPITAL, 501 South Burma Avenue, Zip 82716–3426, Mailing Address: P.O. Box 3011, Zip 82717–3011; tel. 307/682–8811; David Crow, Chief Executive Officer **A**1 9 10 **F**3 7 8 11 12 14 15 16 17 18 19 22 28 32 35 36 37 39 40 41 42 44 45 46 47 49 52 53 55 56 57 58 59 65 66 67 71 73 **P**8	23	10	79	2384	24	74840	428	29325	12556	350

JACKSON—Teton County

☐ ST. JOHN'S HOSPITAL AND LIVING CENTER, 625 East Broadway Street, Zip 83001, Mailing Address: P.O. Box 428, Zip 83001–0428; tel. 307/733–3636; John Valiante, Chief Executive Officer **A**1 9 10 **F**7 14 16 17 19 22 28 32 33 34 35 37 39 40 42 44 45 46 48 49 51 56 59 64 65 67 71 73 **N** Community Health Care Network, Jackson, WY	16	10	102	2064	70	24268	291	29565	12900	555

KEMMERER—Lincoln County

★ SOUTH LINCOLN MEDICAL CENTER, 711 Onyx Street, Zip 83101–3214, Mailing Address: P.O. Box 390, Zip 83101–0390; tel. 307/877–4401; Marla Shelby, Administrator and Chief Executive Officer **A**9 10 **F**7 8 20 22 28 32 34 40 44 64 65 71 **P**6	16	10	16	210	4	18172	16	3696	1788	79

Hospital, Address, Telephone, Administrator, Approval, Facility, and Physician Codes, Health Care System, Network	Classi-fication Codes		Utilization Data					Expense (thousands) of dollars		
★ American Hospital Association (AHA) membership □ Joint Commission on Accreditation of Healthcare Organizations (JCAHO) accreditation + American Osteopathic Healthcare Association (AOHA) membership ○ American Osteopathic Association (AOA) accreditation △ Commission on Accreditation of Rehabilitation Facilities (CARF) accreditation Control codes 61, 63, 64, 71, 72 and 73 indicate hospitals listed by AOHA, but not registered by AHA. For definition of numerical codes, see page A4	Control	Service	Staffed Beds	Admissions	Census	Outpatient Visits	Births	Total	Payroll	Personnel

LANDER—Fremont County

⊞ LANDER VALLEY MEDICAL CENTER, 1320 Bishop Randall Drive, Zip 82520–3996; tel. 307/332–4420; Andrew Gramlich, Chief Executive Officer (Total facility includes 21 beds in nursing home–type unit) (Nonreporting) **A**1 9 10	33	10	102	—	—	—	—	—	—	—

LARAMIE—Albany County

⊞ IVINSON MEMORIAL HOSPITAL, 255 North 30th Street, Zip 82070–5195; tel. 307/742–2141; J. Michael Boyd, Chief Executive Officer (Total facility includes 13 beds in nursing home–type unit) **A**1 9 10 **F**7 8 14 15 16 17 18 19 21 22 23 28 30 33 35 37 39 40 41 44 46 48 49 52 53 54 55 56 57 58 64 65 67 68 71 73 **P**5 8 **N** Wyoming Integrated Network, Casper, WY	16	10	65	3113	27	35078	481	26384	11316	365

LOVELL—Big Horn County

★ NORTH BIG HORN HOSPITAL, 1115 Lane 12, Zip 82431–9580, Mailing Address: P.O. Box 518, Zip 82431–0518; tel. 307/548–2771; Kent Kellersberger, Chief Executive Officer (Total facility includes 95 beds in nursing home–type unit) **A**9 10 **F**1 8 11 12 14 15 16 17 22 24 26 28 30 31 32 34 37 39 44 45 46 49 51 64 65 66 67 71 73	16	10	116	383	87	8843	—	7054	3640	177

LUSK—Niobrara County

NIOBRARA COUNTY HOSPITAL DISTRICT, 939 Ballencee Avenue, Zip 82225, Mailing Address: P.O. Box 780, Zip 82225–0780; tel. 307/334–2711; Gary W. Robertson, Administrator (Total facility includes 36 beds in nursing home–type unit) (Nonreporting) **A**9 10 **S** Quorum Health Group/Quorum Health Resources, Inc., Brentwood, TN	16	10	46	—	—	—	—	—	—	—

NEWCASTLE—Weston County

WESTON COUNTY HEALTH SERVICES, (Formerly Weston County Memorial Hospital), 1124 Washington Street, Zip 82701–2996; tel. 307/746–4491; Jack Brinkers, CHE, Administrator (Total facility includes 51 beds in nursing home–type unit) **A**9 10 **F**7 8 11 14 15 16 19 22 28 32 35 37 39 40 44 49 64 67 71 **N** Rapid City Regional Hospital System of Care, Rapid City, SD	13	10	73	352	47	9714	51	4565	2228	104
WESTON COUNTY MEMORIAL HOSPITAL See Weston County Health Services										

POWELL—Park County

⊞ POWELL HOSPITAL, 777 Avenue H., Zip 82435–2296; tel. 307/754–2267; Rod Barton, Chief Executive Officer (Total facility includes 100 beds in nursing home–type unit) **A**1 9 10 **F**7 8 12 14 15 16 17 19 21 22 26 28 30 32 33 34 35 37 39 40 41 44 46 49 51 64 65 66 67 71 73 **P**1 4 7 **S** Brim, Inc., Portland, OR	23	10	140	1053	105	14806	220	11270	6014	245

RAWLINS—Carbon County

□ MEMORIAL HOSPITAL OF CARBON COUNTY, 2221 West Elm Street, Zip 82301–5108; tel. 307/324–2221; Richard Johnson, Chief Executive Officer (Total facility includes 10 beds in nursing home–type unit) **A**1 9 10 **F**14 15 16 19 22 24 28 30 35 37 44 45 49 64 66 71	13	10	45	1288	12	6614	2	12738	5179	182

RIVERTON—Fremont County

⊞ COLUMBIA RIVERTON MEMORIAL HOSPITAL, 2100 West Sunset Drive, Zip 82501–2274; tel. 307/856–4161; Doug Crabtree, Chief Executive Officer **A**1 9 10 **F**7 8 11 14 15 19 21 22 23 28 30 31 32 33 34 35 37 39 40 44 45 46 49 65 70 71 73 **P**7 **S** Columbia/HCA Healthcare Corporation, Nashville, TN	33	10	59	1699	18	26854	236	11813	4979	242

ROCK SPRINGS—Sweetwater County

⊞ MEMORIAL HOSPITAL OF SWEETWATER COUNTY, 1200 College Drive, Zip 82901–5868, Mailing Address: Box 1359, Zip 82902–1359; tel. 307/362–3711; John M. Ferry, Executive Director **A**1 9 10 **F**7 8 14 15 16 19 22 28 29 35 36 37 39 40 41 44 45 49 56 65 66 71 73	13	10	99	2270	21	70513	534	20986	8922	312

SHERIDAN—Sheridan County

□ MEMORIAL HOSPITAL OF SHERIDAN COUNTY, 1401 West Fifth Street, Zip 82801–2799; tel. 307/672–1000; T. Marvin Goldman, Administrator **A**1 9 10 **F**7 8 11 14 15 19 21 22 23 28 32 33 35 37 40 42 44 46 49 56 60 65 67 71 73	13	10	60	2687	32	38400	311	21477	10370	350
⊞ VETERANS AFFAIRS MEDICAL CENTER, 1898 Fort Road, Zip 82801–8320; tel. 307/672–3473; Maureen Humphrey, Director (Total facility includes 50 beds in nursing home–type unit) **A**1 **F**2 3 8 11 15 16 19 20 21 22 26 27 28 30 32 34 35 39 41 44 45 46 49 51 52 54 56 57 58 60 64 65 67 71 73 74 **P**6 **S** Department of Veterans Affairs, Washington, DC	45	22	204	1858	155	34215	0	—	—	422

SUNDANCE—Crook County

CROOK COUNTY MEDICAL SERVICES DISTRICT, 713 Oak Street, Zip 82729, Mailing Address: P.O. Box 517, Zip 82729–0517; tel. 307/283–3501; Don A. Nelson, Administrator (Total facility includes 32 beds in nursing home–type unit) **A**9 10 **F**1 14 15 16 22 28 32 33 34 45 46 49 64 65 71 73 **P**6	16	10	48	244	38	7374	—	3488	1934	85

THERMOPOLIS—Hot Springs County

⊞ HOT SPRINGS COUNTY MEMORIAL HOSPITAL, 150 East Arapahoe Street, Zip 82443–2498; tel. 307/864–3121; Edward G. Leake, Chief Executive Officer **A**1 9 10 **F**7 8 11 15 19 22 28 32 34 35 37 39 40 41 44 45 48 63 65 71 73	13	10	49	1120	11	15718	72	6476	2806	109

TORRINGTON—Goshen County

⊞ COMMUNITY HOSPITAL, 2000 Campbell Drive, Zip 82240–1597; tel. 307/532–4181; Charles Myers, Administrator **A**1 9 10 **F**7 8 11 12 16 17 19 22 26 28 30 32 34 35 36 37 39 42 44 49 64 65 66 67 71 **S** Lutheran Health Systems, Fargo, ND	23	10	36	1391	21	32092	137	6926	2902	160

WHEATLAND—Platte County

⊞ PLATTE COUNTY MEMORIAL HOSPITAL, 201 14th Street, Zip 82201–3201, Mailing Address: P.O. Box 848, Zip 82201–0848; tel. 307/322–3636; Dana K. Barnett, Administrator (Total facility includes 43 beds in nursing home–type unit) **A**1 9 10 **F**7 8 12 14 15 16 19 22 28 29 32 34 35 37 40 44 64 65 71 73 **S** Lutheran Health Systems, Fargo, ND	23	10	86	1028	66	27511	97	5289	2416	149

Hospital, Address, Telephone, Administrator, Approval, Facility, and Physician Codes, Health Care System, Network	Classi-fication Codes		Utilization Data					Expense (thousands) of dollars		
★ American Hospital Association (AHA) membership □ Joint Commission on Accreditation of Healthcare Organizations (JCAHO) accreditation + American Osteopathic Healthcare Association (AOHA) membership ○ American Osteopathic Association (AOA) accreditation △ Commission on Accreditation of Rehabilitation Facilities (CARF) accreditation Control codes 61, 63, 64, 71, 72 and 73 indicate hospitals listed by AOHA, but not registered by AHA. For definition of numerical codes, see page A4	Control	Service	Staffed Beds	Admissions	Census	Outpatient Visits	Births	Total	Payroll	Personnel

WORLD—Washakie County

✈ WASHAKIE MEMORIAL HOSPITAL, 400 South 15th Street, Zip 82401–3531, Mailing Address: P.O. Box 700, Zip 82401–0700; tel. 307/347–3221; James Kiser, Administrator **A**1 9 10 **F**7 8 12 14 15 16 17 19 22 28 29 30 32 36 39 40 41 44 45 46 48 49 51 64 65 67 68 71 73 **P**3 **S** Lutheran Health Systems, Fargo, ND

	23	10	30	997	10	37628	96	7714	3690	124

Hospital, Address, Telephone, Administrator, Approval, Facility, and Physician Codes, Health Care System, Network	Classi-fication Codes		Utilization Data					Expense (thousands) of dollars		
★ American Hospital Association (AHA) membership □ Joint Commission on Accreditation of Healthcare Organizations (JCAHO) accreditation + American Osteopathic Healthcare Association (AOHA) membership ○ American Osteopathic Association (AOA) accreditation △ Commission on Accreditation of Rehabilitation Facilities (CARF) accreditation Control codes 61, 63, 64, 71, 72 and 73 indicate hospitals listed by AOHA, but not registered by AHA. For definition of numerical codes, see page A4	Control	Service	Staffed Beds	Admissions	Census	Outpatient Visits	Births	Total	Payroll	Personnel

AMERICAN SAMOA

PAGO PAGO—American Samoa County

LYNDON B. JOHNSON TROPICAL MEDICAL CENTER, Zip 96799; tel. 684/633–1222; Iotamo T. Saleapaga, M.D., Director Health (Nonreporting) **A**10	12	10	125	—	—	—	—	—	—	—

GUAM

AGANA—Guam County

⊞ U. S. NAVAL HOSPITAL, Mailing Address: PSC 490, Box 7607, FPO, AP, Zip 96538–1600; tel. 671/344–9340; Captain David Wheeler, Sr., Chief Executive Officer (Nonreporting) **A**1 **S** Department of Navy, Washington, DC	43	10	55	—	—	—	—	—	—	—

TAMUNING—Guam County

GUAM MEMORIAL HOSPITAL AUTHORITY, 850 Governor Carlos G. Camacho Road, Zip 96911; tel. 671/647–2211; Tyrone J. Taitano, Administrator (Total facility includes 29 beds in nursing home–type unit) (Nonreporting)	16	10	186	—	—	—	—	—	—	—

MARSHALL ISLANDS

KWAJALEIN ISLAND—Marshall Islands County

KWAJALEIN HOSPITAL, Mailing Address: Box 1702, APO, AP, Zip 96555–5000; tel. 805/355–2225; Mike Mathews, Administrator (Nonreporting) **S** Department of the Army, Office of the Surgeon General, Falls Church, VA	42	10	14	—	—	—	—	—	—	—

PUERTO RICO

AGUADILLA—Aguadilla County

⊞ AGUADILLA GENERAL HOSPITAL, Carr Aguadilla San Juan, Zip 00605, Mailing Address: P.O. Box 4036, Zip 00605; tel. 787/891–3000; William Rodriguez Castro, Executive Director (Nonreporting) **A**1 9 10 **S** Puerto Rico Department of Health, San Juan, PR	12	10	110	—	—	—	—	—	—	—

AIBONITO—Aibonito County

★ MENNONITE GENERAL HOSPITAL, Jose Vasquez, Zip 00705, Mailing Address: P.O. Box 1379, Zip 00705; tel. 787/735–8001; Domingo Torres Zayas, CHE, Executive Director **A**9 10 **F**14 15 16 19 22 33 34 35 37 39 44 49 65 71 72 73 **P**5	23	10	211	13961	169	102829	1623	34547	13494	886

ARECIBO—Arecibo County

★ ARECIBO REGIONAL HOSPITAL, 129 San Luis Avenue, Zip 00612, Mailing Address: P.O. Box 202, Zip 00613; tel. 787/878–7272; Samuel Monroig, Administrator (Nonreporting) **A**9 10 **S** Puerto Rico Department of Health, San Juan, PR	12	10	183	—	—	—	—	—	—	—
HOSPITAL DR. SUSONI, 55 Nicomedes Rivera Street, Zip 00612, Mailing Address: P.O. Box 145200, Zip 00614; tel. 787/878–1010; Hector Barreto, M.D., Director (Nonreporting) **A**9 10	33	10	138	—	—	—	—	—	—	—
★ HOSPITAL EL BUEN PASTOR, 52 De Diego, Zip 00612, Mailing Address: P.O. Box 413, Zip 00612; tel. 787/878–2730; Julio Galarce, Administrator (Nonreporting)	33	10	72	—	—	—	—	—	—	—

ARROYO—Arroyo County

★ LAFAYETTE HOSPITAL, Central Lafayette, Zip 00714, Mailing Address: P.O. Box 207, Zip 00714; tel. 787/839–3232; Francisco Santiago–Vega, Consultor (Nonreporting) **A**9 10	33	10	30	—	—	—	—	—	—	—

Hospital, Address, Telephone, Administrator, Approval, Facility, and Physician Codes, Health Care System, Network	Classi-fication Codes		Utilization Data					Expense (thousands) of dollars		
★ American Hospital Association (AHA) membership □ Joint Commission on Accreditation of Healthcare Organizations (JCAHO) accreditation + American Osteopathic Healthcare Association (AOHA) membership ○ American Osteopathic Association (AOA) accreditation △ Commission on Accreditation of Rehabilitation Facilities (CARF) accreditation Control codes 61, 63, 64, 71, 72 and 73 indicate hospitals listed by AOHA, but not registered by AHA. For definition of numerical codes, see page A4	Control	Service	Staffed Beds	Admissions	Census	Outpatient Visits	Births	Total	Payroll	Personnel

BAYAMON—Bayamon County

Hospital	Control	Service	Staffed Beds	Admissions	Census	Outpatient Visits	Births	Total	Payroll	Personnel
⊞ HOSPITAL HERMANOS MELENDEZ, Route 2, KM 11–7, Zip 00960, Mailing Address: P.O. Box 306, Zip 00960; tel. 787/785–9784; Tomas Martinez, Administrator **A**1 9 10 **F**8 10 11 16 19 22 37 44 49 63 71 73 **P**8	33	10	211	15265	184	45619	1852	—	—	954
★ HOSPITAL MATILDE BRENES, Extension Hermanas Davila, Zip 00960, Mailing Address: P.O. Box 2957, Zip 00960; tel. 809/786–6315; Manuel J. Vazquez, Administrator (Nonreporting) **A**9 10	33	10	95	—	—	—	—	—	—	—
⊞ HOSPITAL SAN PABLO, Calle San Cruz 70, Zip 00961, Mailing Address: P.O. Box 236, Zip 00960; tel. 787/740–4747; Jorge De Jesus, Executive Director **A**1 3 5 9 10 **F**4 7 8 10 11 12 16 19 22 23 34 37 38 39 40 42 43 44 45 65 71 73 **S** Universal Health Services, Inc., King of Prussia, PA	33	10	362	21431	296	186293	2057	45797	24189	—
⊞ HOSPITAL UNIVERSITARIO DR. RAMON RUIZ ARNAU, Avenue Laurel, Santa Juanita, Zip 00956; tel. 787/787–5151; Iris J. Vazquez Rosario, Executive Director (Nonreporting) **A**1 3 5 9 10 **S** Puerto Rico Department of Health, San Juan, PR	16	10	372	—	—	—	—	—	—	—
⊞ MEPSI CENTER, Carretera Numero 2 K. 8–2, Zip 00959–6089, Mailing Address: Carretera Numero 2 K. 8–2, Zip 00960–6089; tel. 787/793–3030; Manuel G. Mendez, Operating Trustee **A**1 9 10 **F**2 14 15 16 19 35 41 45 46 49 52 53 55 56 57 59 63 65	33	22	450	3502	157	—	—	15772	6604	259

CAGUAS—Caguas County

Hospital	Control	Service	Staffed Beds	Admissions	Census	Outpatient Visits	Births	Total	Payroll	Personnel
⊞ CAGUAS REGIONAL HOSPITAL, Carretera Caguas A. Cidra, Zip 00725, Mailing Address: P.O. Box 5729, Zip 00726; tel. 787/744–2500; Noemi Davis Marte, M.D., Medical Director (Nonreporting) **A**1 3 5 9 10	12	10	256	—	—	—	—	—	—	—
□ HOSPITAL INTERAMERICANO DE MEDICINA AVANZADA, Avenida Luis Munoz Marin, Zip 00726, Mailing Address: Apartado 4980, Zip 00726; tel. 787/743–3434; Carlos M. Pineiro, President (Nonreporting) **A**1 9 10	32	10	300	—	—	—	—	—	—	—

CAROLINA—Carolina County

Hospital	Control	Service	Staffed Beds	Admissions	Census	Outpatient Visits	Births	Total	Payroll	Personnel
⊞ HOSPITAL DR. FEDERICO TRILLA, 65th Infanteria, KM 8 3, Zip 00984, Mailing Address: P.O. Box 3869, Zip 00984; tel. 787/757–1800; Ivon Millon, Chief Executive Officer (Nonreporting) **A**1 3 5 9 10	33	10	220	—	—	—	—	—	—	—

CASTANER—Lares County

Hospital	Control	Service	Staffed Beds	Admissions	Census	Outpatient Visits	Births	Total	Payroll	Personnel
★ CASTANER GENERAL HOSPITAL, KM 64–2, Route 135, Zip 00631, Mailing Address: P.O. Box 1003, Zip 00631; tel. 787/829–5010; Domingo Monroig, Administrator (Nonreporting) **A**9 10	23	10	24	—	—	—	—	—	—	—

CAYEY—Cayey County

Hospital	Control	Service	Staffed Beds	Admissions	Census	Outpatient Visits	Births	Total	Payroll	Personnel
★ HOSPITAL MENONITA DE CAYEY, 4 H. Mendoza Street, Zip 00737, Mailing Address: P.O. Box 373130, Zip 00737; tel. 787/738–2181; Domingo Torres–Zayas, Executive Director (Nonreporting) **A**9 10	23	10	50	—	—	—	—	—	—	—

CIDRA—Cidra County

Hospital	Control	Service	Staffed Beds	Admissions	Census	Outpatient Visits	Births	Total	Payroll	Personnel
⊞ FIRST HOSPITAL PANAMERICANO, State Road 787 KM 1 5, Zip 00739, Mailing Address: P.O. Box 1398, Zip 00739; tel. 787/739–5555; Jorge Torres, Executive Director (Nonreporting) **A**1 5 10 **S** FHC Health Systems, Norfolk, VA	33	22	165	—	—	—	—	—	—	—

FAJARDO—Fajardo County

Hospital	Control	Service	Staffed Beds	Admissions	Census	Outpatient Visits	Births	Total	Payroll	Personnel
★ DOCTORS GUBERN'S HOSPITAL, (Includes Dr. Gubern's Hospital, General Valero Avenue 267 & 261, Mailing Address: Box 846, Zip 00738; tel. 809/792–3495; Antonio R. Barcelo, Director), 110 Antonio R. Barcelo, Zip 00738, Mailing Address: P.O. Box 846, Zip 00738–0846; tel. 787/863–0669; Edwin Sueiro, Executive Director (Nonreporting) **A**9 10 **S** United Medical Corporation, Windermere, FL	33	10	51	—	—	—	—	—	—	—
□ DR. JOSE RAMOS LEBRON HOSPITAL, General Valero Avenue, #194, Zip 00738, Mailing Address: P.O. Box 1283, Zip 00738–1283; tel. 787/863–0505; Victor R. Marrero, Executive Administrator (Nonreporting) **A**1 9 10 **S** Universal Health Services, Inc., King of Prussia, PA	33	10	180	—	—	—	—	—	—	—

GUAYAMA—Guayama County

Hospital	Control	Service	Staffed Beds	Admissions	Census	Outpatient Visits	Births	Total	Payroll	Personnel
⊞ DR. ALEJANDRO BUITRAGO–GUAYAMA AREA HOSPITAL, Avenue Pedro Albesus, Zip 00784, Mailing Address: Call Box 1006, Zip 00785–1006; tel. 787/864–4300; Carlos Rodriguez Mateo, M.D., Medical Director (Nonreporting) **A**1 9 10	12	10	155	—	—	—	—	—	—	—
★ HOSPITAL SANTA ROSA, Veterans Avenue, Zip 00784, Mailing Address: P.O. Box 10008, Zip 00785; tel. 787/864–0101; Humberto M. Monserrate, Administrator **A**9 10 **F**7 10 16 19 22 35 37 40 71 **P**1	23	10	89	4718	48	63034	628	5189	3167	—

HUMACAO—Humacao County

Hospital	Control	Service	Staffed Beds	Admissions	Census	Outpatient Visits	Births	Total	Payroll	Personnel
□ FONT MARTELO HOSPITAL, 3 Font Martelo Street, Zip 00792, Mailing Address: P.O. Box 639, Zip 00792–0639; tel. 787/852–2424; Julio A. Ortiz, M.D., Chairman (Nonreporting) **A**1 9 10	33	10	64	—	—	—	—	—	—	—
HOSPITAL DR. DOMINGUEZ, 300 Font Martelo Street, Zip 00791, Mailing Address: P.O. Box 699, Zip 00792; tel. 787/852–0505; Rogelio Diaz–Reyes, Administrator (Nonreporting) **A**9 10	33	10	54	—	—	—	—	—	—	—
★ HOSPITAL SUB–REGIONAL DR. VICTOR R. NUNEZ, Avenida Tejas, Expreso Cruz Ortiz Stella, Zip 00791; tel. 787/852–2727; Ahmed Alvarez Pabon, Executive Director **A**10 **F**2 3 4 5 8 9 10 11 12 13 14 15 16 17 18 19 20 21 22 23 28 29 30 31 34 35 37 38 39 40 41 42 43 44 45 46 47 48 49 51 52 53 54 55 56 57 58 59 60 61 64 65 69 70 71 73 **P**8	33	10	84	1266	46	43621	1360	16396	6859	550
★ RYDER MEMORIAL HOSPITAL, 355 Font Martelo Street, Zip 00792, Mailing Address: P.O. Box 859, Zip 00792–0859; tel. 787/852–0768; Saturnino Pena Flores, Executive Director (Total facility includes 62 beds in nursing home–type unit) (Nonreporting) **A**9 10	23	10	209	—	—	—	—	—	—	—

Hospital, Address, Telephone, Administrator, Approval, Facility, and Physician Codes, Health Care System, Network	Classi-fication Codes		Utilization Data					Expense (thousands) of dollars		
★ American Hospital Association (AHA) membership □ Joint Commission on Accreditation of Healthcare Organizations (JCAHO) accreditation + American Osteopathic Healthcare Association (AOHA) membership ○ American Osteopathic Association (AOA) accreditation △ Commission on Accreditation of Rehabilitation Facilities (CARF) accreditation Control codes 61, 63, 64, 71, 72 and 73 indicate hospitals listed by AOHA, but not registered by AHA. For definition of numerical codes, see page A4	Control	Service	Staffed Beds	Admissions	Census	Outpatient Visits	Births	Total	Payroll	Personnel

MANATI—Manati County

★ CLINICA SAN AGUSTIN, Route 2, KM 49–5, Zip 00674, Mailing Address: P.O. Box 991, Zip 00674; tel. 787/854–2091; Astrid Abreu, Administrator **A**9 10 **F**15 16 22 39 44 45 51 58 65 71 **P**5 8

| | 33 | 10 | 12 | 1453 | 15 | — | 43 | 2632 | 793 | |

☒ DOCTORS CENTER, KM 47–7, Zip 00674, Mailing Address: P.O. Box 30532, Zip 00674; tel. 787/854–1795; Carla Blanco, Administrator (Nonreporting) **A**1 3 9 10

| | 33 | 10 | 150 | — | — | — | — | — | — | |

MAYAGUEZ—Mayaguez County

☒ BELLA VISTA HOSPITAL, State Road 349, Zip 00680, Mailing Address: P.O. Box 1750, Zip 00681; tel. 787/834–6000; Samuel Leonor, Chief Executive Officer (Nonreporting) **A**1 3 9 10 **S** Adventist Health System Sunbelt Health Care Corporation, Winter Park, FL

| | 21 | 10 | 157 | — | — | — | — | — | — | |

CLINICA ESPANOLA, Barrio La Quinta, Zip 00680, Mailing Address: P.O. Box 490, Zip 00681–0490; tel. 787/832–0442; Emigdio Inigo–Agostini, M.D., Board President (Nonreporting) **A**9 10

| | 33 | 10 | 69 | — | — | — | — | — | — | |

☒ DR. RAMON E. BETANCES HOSPITAL–MAYAGUEZ MEDICAL CENTER BRANCH, 410 Hostos Avenue, Zip 00680; tel. 787/834–8686; Maria Del Pilar Rodriguez, Administrator (Nonreporting) **A**1 3 5 10

| | 12 | 10 | 253 | — | — | — | — | — | — | |

★ HOSPITAL PEREA, 15 Basora Street, Zip 00681, Mailing Address: P.O. Box 170, Zip 00681; tel. 787/834–0101; Ramon Lopez, Administrator (Nonreporting) **A**10 **S** United Medical Corporation, Windermere, FL

| | 33 | 10 | 82 | — | — | — | — | — | — | |

PONCE—Ponce County

☒ DR. PILA'S HOSPITAL, Avenida Las Americas, Zip 00731, Mailing Address: P.O. Box 1910, Zip 00733–1910; tel. 787/848–5600; Miguel J. Bustelo, Executive Director **A**1 3 5 9 10 **F**7 8 15 16 19 20 21 22 28 32 34 35 37 40 44 49 51 63 65 71

| | 23 | 10 | 177 | 9882 | 142 | 49107 | 826 | 34539 | 10724 | — |

☒ HOSPITAL DE DAMAS, Ponce by Pass, Zip 00731; tel. 787/840–8686; Roberto A. Rentas, Administrator (Total facility includes 28 beds in nursing home–type unit) (Nonreporting) **A**1 3 5 9 10

| | 23 | 10 | 334 | — | — | — | — | — | — | |

☒ HOSPITAL EPISCOPAL SAN LUCAS, Guadalupe Street, Zip 00731, Mailing Address: P.O. Box 2027, Zip 00733; tel. 787/840–4545; Guillermo J. Martin, Executive Director **A**1 3 5 10 **F**4 7 8 10 11 15 16 19 21 22 27 34 37 38 40 43 44 46 49 63 64 65 71 **P**8

| | 21 | 10 | 168 | 7853 | 127 | 26800 | 488 | — | — | |

☒ HOSPITAL ONCOLOGICO ANDRES GRILLASCA, Centro Medico De Ponce, Zip 00733, Mailing Address: P.O. Box 1324, Zip 00733; tel. 787/848–0800; Angel M. Franceschi, Administrator (Nonreporting) **A**1 2 3 5 9 10

| | 23 | 49 | 53 | — | — | — | — | — | — | |

☒ PONCE REGIONAL HOSPITAL, 917 Tito Castro Avenue, Zip 00731; tel. 787/844–2080; Julio Andino Rodriguez, Executive Director (Nonreporting) **A**1 3 5 9 10 **S** Puerto Rico Department of Health, San Juan, PR

| | 12 | 10 | 407 | — | — | — | — | — | — | |

SAN GERMAN—San German County

☒ HOSPITAL DE LA CONCEPCION, 41 Luna Street, Zip 00683, Mailing Address: P.O. Box 285, Zip 00683–0285; tel. 787/892–1860; Jaime F. Maestre Grau, Executive Director (Nonreporting) **A**1 2 3 5 9 10

| | 21 | 10 | 167 | — | — | — | — | — | — | |

SAN JUAN—San Juan County

☒ ASHFORD PRESBYTERIAN COMMUNITY HOSPITAL, 1451 Ashford Avenue Condado, Zip 00907, Mailing Address: P.O. Box 9020032, Zip 00902–0032; tel. 787/721–2160; Jose Cora, Executive Director (Nonreporting) **A**1 9 10

| | 23 | 10 | 180 | — | — | — | — | — | — | |

☒ AUXILIO MUTUO HOSPITAL, Ponce De Leon Avenue, Zip 00919, Mailing Address: P.O. Box 191227, Zip 00919–1227; tel. 787/758–2000; Ivan E. Colon, Administrator (Nonreporting) **A**1 3 9 10

| | 23 | 10 | 402 | — | — | — | — | — | — | |

☒ BHC HOSPITAL SAN JUAN CAPESTRANO, Mailing Address: Rural Route 2, Box 11, Zip 00926; tel. 787/760–0222; Laura Vargas, Administrator (Nonreporting) **A**1 10 **S** Behavioral Healthcare Corporation, Nashville, TN

| | 33 | 22 | 88 | — | — | — | — | — | — | |

DOCTORS HOSPITAL, 1395 San Rafael Street, Zip 00910, Mailing Address: Box 11338, Santurce Station, Zip 00910; tel. 809/723–2950; Georgina Mattei de Collazo, Executive Director (Nonreporting) **A**9 10

| | 33 | 10 | 96 | — | — | — | — | — | — | |

☒ FUNDACION HOSPITAL METROPOLITAN, 1785 Route 21, Caparra, Zip 00922, Mailing Address: P.O. Box 11981, Zip 00922; tel. 787/793–6200; Racheline A. Gonzalez, Administrator (Nonreporting) **A**1 9

| | 23 | 10 | 119 | — | — | — | — | — | — | |

★ HATO REY COMMUNITY HOSPITAL, Mailing Address: 435 Ponce De Leon, Hato Rey, Zip 00917; tel. 787/754–0909; Jorge De Jesus, Executive Director (Nonreporting) **A**9 10 **S** United Medical Corporation, Windermere, FL

| | 33 | 10 | 105 | — | — | — | — | — | — | |

☒ HOSPITAL DEL MAESTRO, 550 Sergio Cuevas, Zip 00918, Mailing Address: P.O. Box 364708, Zip 00936–4708; tel. 787/758–8383; Maria Mercedes Rivera, Administrator **A**1 10 **F**7 8 10 11 19 21 22 27 32 33 34 38 40 42 43 44 45 48 49 65 67 71 73

| | 23 | 10 | 247 | 9831 | 149 | 28063 | 925 | 16445 | 9039 | 603 |

☒ HOSPITAL PAVIA, 1462 Asia Street, Zip 00909, Mailing Address: Box 11137, Santurce Station, Zip 00910; tel. 787/727–6060; Jorge De Jesus, Executive Director (Nonreporting) **A**1 9 10 **S** United Medical Corporation, Windermere, FL

| | 33 | 10 | 183 | — | — | — | — | — | — | |

★ HOSPITAL SAN FRANCISCO, 371 De Diego Avenue, Zip 00923, Mailing Address: P.O. Box 29025, Zip 00929–0025; tel. 787/767–2528; Domingo Nevarez, Executive Director (Nonreporting) **A**10 **S** Universal Health Services, Inc., King of Prussia, PA

| | 33 | 10 | 160 | — | — | — | — | — | — | |

☒ I. GONZALEZ MARTINEZ ONCOLOGIC HOSPITAL, (ONCOLOGY), Puerto Rico Medical Center, Hato Rey, Zip 00935, Mailing Address: P.O. Box 191811, Zip 00919–1811; tel. 787/765–2382; Celia Molano, Executive Director **A**1 3 5 9 10 **F**8 12 19 20 21 29 34 35 37 42 44 48 49 60 65 71 73

| | 23 | 49 | 80 | 1828 | 33 | 28996 | — | 10031 | 4633 | — |

Hospital, Address, Telephone, Administrator, Approval, Facility, and Physician Codes, Health Care System, Network	Classi-fication Codes		Utilization Data					Expense (thousands) of dollars		
★ American Hospital Association (AHA) membership □ Joint Commission on Accreditation of Healthcare Organizations (JCAHO) accreditation + American Osteopathic Healthcare Association (AOHA) membership ○ American Osteopathic Association (AOA) accreditation △ Commission on Accreditation of Rehabilitation Facilities (CARF) accreditation Control codes 61, 63, 64, 71, 72 and 73 indicate hospitals listed by AOHA, but not registered by AHA. For definition of numerical codes, see page A4	Control	Service	Staffed Beds	Admissions	Census	Outpatient Visits	Births	Total	Payroll	Personnel

	Control	Service	Staffed Beds	Admissions	Census	Outpatient Visits	Births	Total	Payroll	Personnel
★ INDUSTRIAL HOSPITAL, Puerto Rico Medical Center, Zip 00936, Mailing Address: P.O. Box 5028, Zip 00936; tel. 787/764–3660; Evelyn Vargas, Administrator (Nonreporting) **A**3 5	12	10	125	—	—	—	—	—	—	—
★ SAN CARLOS GENERAL HOSPITAL, 1822 Ponce De Leon Avenue, Zip 00919, Mailing Address: Call Box 8410, Zip 00910–8410; tel. 787/727–5858; Pedro Gonzalez, Executive Director (Total facility includes 8 beds in nursing home–type unit) (Nonreporting) **A**9 10	33	10	66	—	—	—	—	—	—	—
★ SAN JORGE CHILDREN'S HOSPITAL, 258 San Jorge Avenue, Zip 00912; tel. 787/727–1000; Domingo Cruz Vivaldi, Administrator (Nonreporting) **A**9 **S** United Medical Corporation, Windermere, FL	33	50	85	—	—	—	—	—	—	—
⊞ SAN JUAN CITY HOSPITAL, Puerto Rico Medical Center, Zip 00928, Mailing Address: Apartado 21405, Rio Piedras, Zip 00928; tel. 787/766–2222; Maritza Espinosa, Chief Executive Officer **A**1 3 5 10 **F**1 2 3 4 5 6 7 8 9 10 11 12 13 14 15 16 17 18 19 20 21 22 23 24 26 28 29 30 31 32 33 34 35 36 37 38 39 40 41 42 43 44 45 46 47 48 49 50 51 52 53 54 55 56 57 58 59 60 61 62 63 65 66 67 68 69 70 71 72 73 74 **P**6	14	10	264	11778	175	63605	3815	44426	14193	—
★ STATE PSYCHIATRIC HOSPITAL, Monacillos Avenue, Zip 00936, Mailing Address: Call Box 2100, Caparra Heights Station, Zip 00922–2100; tel. 787/766–4646; Guadalupe Alvarez, Administrator (Nonreporting) **A**3 **S** Puerto Rico Department of Health, San Juan, PR	12	22	425	—	—	—	—	—	—	—
★ U. S. NAVAL HOSPITAL, Roosevelt Roads, Mailing Address: P.O. Box 3007, FPO, AA, Zip 34051–8100; tel. 787/865–5762; Captain G. R. Brown, Commanding Officer (Nonreporting) **S** Department of Navy, Washington, DC	43	10	35	—	—	—	—	—	—	—
⊞ UNIVERSITY HOSPITAL, Puerto Rico Medical Center, Rio Piedras Station, Zip 00935; tel. 787/754–3654; Roberto Hernandez, Administrator (Nonreporting) **A**1 2 3 5 9 10 **S** Puerto Rico Department of Health, San Juan, PR	12	10	297	—	—	—	—	—	—	—
⊞ UNIVERSITY PEDIATRIC HOSPITAL, Mailing Address: Call Box 191079, Zip 00910–1079; tel. 787/756–3198; Sylvia Mercado, Chief Executive Officer (Nonreporting) **A**1 3 5 9 10	12	50	135	—	—	—	—	—	—	—
⊞ VETERANS AFFAIRS MEDICAL CENTER, One Veterans Plaza, Zip 00927–5800; tel. 787/766–5665; James A. Palmer, Director (Total facility includes 120 beds in nursing home–type unit) (Nonreporting) **A**1 2 3 5 8 **S** Department of Veterans Affairs, Washington, DC	45	10	693	—	—	—	—	—	—	—
VEGA BAJA—Vega Baja County										
★ WILMA N. VAZQUEZ MEDICAL CENTER, KM 395 Road 2, Call Box 7001, Zip 00694; tel. 787/858–1580; Ramon J. Vilar, Administrator (Total facility includes 68 beds in nursing home–type unit) (Nonreporting) **A**9 10	33	10	150	—	—	—	—	—	—	—
YAUCO—Yauco County										
⊞ HOSPITAL DE AREA DE YAUCO, Carretera 128 KM 1 0, Zip 00698, Mailing Address: P.O. Box 68, Zip 00698; tel. 787/856–2105; Miguel A. Solivan, Executive Director **A**1 5 10 **F**8 20 22 37 39 40 44 54 65 71	12	10	123	4977	52	64433	992	11933	5959	391

VIRGIN ISLANDS

CHRISTIANSTED—St. Croix County

	Control	Service	Staffed Beds	Admissions	Census	Outpatient Visits	Births	Total	Payroll	Personnel
⊞ GOVERNOR JUAN F. LOUIS HOSPITAL, 4007 Estate Diamond Ruby, Zip 00820–4421; tel. 340/778–6311; George H. McCoy, Chief Executive Officer (Total facility includes 20 beds in nursing home–type unit) **A**1 10 **F**7 12 14 15 16 17 19 20 22 37 40 44 45 49 51 52 54 55 56 57 60 64 65 71	12	10	130	6248	—	25529	1085	—	—	—

SAINT THOMAS—St. Thomas County

	Control	Service	Staffed Beds	Admissions	Census	Outpatient Visits	Births	Total	Payroll	Personnel
ROY LESTER SCHNEIDER HOSPITAL, 9048 Sugar Estate, Charlotte Amalie, Zip 00802; tel. 809/776–8311; Judy Magras, Acting Chief Executive Officer (Nonreporting) **A**10	12	10	133	—	—	—	—	—	—	—

U.S. Government Hospitals
Outside the United States, by Area

GERMANY

Heidelberg: ★ U. S. Army Hospital, APO, AE 09014
Landstuhl: ★ Landstuhl Army Regional Medical Center, APO, AE 09180
Wurzburg: ★ U. S. Army Hospital, APO, USAMEDDAC Wurzburg, AE 09244

ICELAND

Keflavilk: ★ U. S. Naval Hospital–Keflavilk, FPO, PSC 1003, Box 8, AE 09728–0308

ITALY

Naples: ★ U. S. Naval Hospital, FPO, AE 09619

JAPAN

Yokosuka: ★ U. S. Naval Hospital, FPO, Box 1487, AP 96350

KOREA

Seoul: ★ U. S. Army Community Hospital Seoul, APO, AP 96205
Yongsan: Medcom 18th Commander, Facilities Division Eamc L EM, APO, AP 96205

PANAMA

Ancon: ★ Gorgas Army Hospital, APO, AA 34004

SPAIN

Rota: ★ U. S. Naval Hospital, Rota, FPO, PSC 819, Box 18, AE 09645–2500

TAIWAN

Taipei: U. S. Naval Hospital Taipei, Taipei, No 300 Shin–Pai Road, Sec 2

★Indicates membership in the American Hospital Association

This section is an index of all hospitals in alphabetical order by hospital name, followed by the city, state and page reference to the hospital's listing in Section A.

C

D

DEACONESS MEDICAL CENTER–SPOKANE, SPOKANE, WA, p. A450
DEACONESS WALTHAM HOSPITAL, WALTHAM, MA, p. A206
DEACONESS WEST HOSPITAL, SAINT LOUIS, MO, p. A249
DEACONESS–GLOVER HOSPITAL CORPORATION, NEEDHAM, MA, p. A204
DEACONESS–NASHOBA HOSPITAL, AYER, MA, p. A199
DEARBORN COUNTY HOSPITAL, LAWRENCEBURG, IN, p. A143
DEATON SPECIALTY HOSPITAL AND HOME, BALTIMORE, MD, p. A193
DEBACA GENERAL HOSPITAL, FORT SUMNER, NM, p. A282
DEBORAH HEART AND LUNG CENTER, BROWNS MILLS, NJ, p. A271
DECATUR COMMUNITY HOSPITAL, DECATUR, TX, p. A404
DECATUR COUNTY GENERAL HOSPITAL, PARSONS, TN, p. A392
DECATUR COUNTY HOSPITAL, LEON, IA, p. A152
DECATUR COUNTY HOSPITAL, OBERLIN, KS, p. A163
DECATUR COUNTY MEMORIAL HOSPITAL, GREENSBURG, IN, p. A140
DECATUR GENERAL HOSPITAL, DECATUR, AL, p. A13
DECATUR GENERAL HOSPITAL–WEST, DECATUR, AL, p. A13
DECATUR HOSPITAL, DECATUR, GA, p. A105
DECATUR MEMORIAL HOSPITAL, DECATUR, IL, p. A125
DECHAIRO HOSPITAL, WESTMORELAND, KS, p. A167
DECKERVILLE COMMUNITY HOSPITAL, DECKERVILLE, MI, p. A210
DEER PARK HEALTH CENTER AND HOSPITAL, DEER PARK, WA, p. A446
DEER RIVER HEALTHCARE CENTER, DEER RIVER, MN, p. A224
DEER'S HEAD CENTER, SALISBURY, MD, p. A197
DEERING HOSPITAL, MIAMI, FL, p. A90
DEFIANCE HOSPITAL, DEFIANCE, OH, p. A326
DEKALB BAPTIST MEDICAL CENTER, FORT PAYNE, AL, p. A14
DEKALB MEDICAL CENTER, DECATUR, GA, p. A105
DEKALB MEMORIAL HOSPITAL, AUBURN, IN, p. A137
DEL AMO HOSPITAL, TORRANCE, CA, p. A65
DEL E. WEBB MEMORIAL HOSPITAL, SUN CITY WEST, AZ, p. A26
DELANO REGIONAL MEDICAL CENTER, DELANO, CA, p. A41
DELAWARE COUNTY MEMORIAL HOSPITAL, MANCHESTER, IA, p. A152
DELAWARE COUNTY MEMORIAL HOSPITAL, DREXEL HILL, PA, p. A353
DELAWARE PSYCHIATRIC CENTER, NEW CASTLE, DE, p. A78
DELAWARE VALLEY HOSPITAL, WALTON, NY, p. A302
DELAWARE VALLEY MEDICAL CENTER, LANGHORNE, PA, p. A356
DELL RAPIDS COMMUNITY HOSPITAL, DELL RAPIDS, SD, p. A378
DELNOR–COMMUNITY HOSPITAL, GENEVA, IL, p. A127
DELRAY MEDICAL CENTER, DELRAY BEACH, FL, p. A84
DELTA COMMUNITY MEDICAL CENTER, DELTA, UT, p. A430
DELTA COUNTY MEMORIAL HOSPITAL, DELTA, CO, p. A69
DELTA MEDICAL CENTER, MEMPHIS, TN, p. A389
DELTA MEMORIAL HOSPITAL, DUMAS, AR, p. A30
DELTA REGIONAL MEDICAL CENTER, GREENVILLE, MS, p. A235
DENTON COMMUNITY HOSPITAL, DENTON, TX, p. A404
DENVER HEALTH MEDICAL CENTER, DENVER, CO, p. A69
DEPAUL HEALTH CENTER, SAINT LOUIS, MO, p. A249
DEPAUL/TULANE BEHAVIORAL HEALTH CENTER, NEW ORLEANS, LA, p. A184
DEQUINCY MEMORIAL HOSPITAL, DEQUINCY, LA, p. A180
DES MOINES GENERAL HOSPITAL, DES MOINES, IA, p. A149
DESERT HILLS CENTER FOR YOUTH AND FAMILIES, TUCSON, AZ, p. A27
DESERT HILLS HOSPITAL, ALBUQUERQUE, NM, p. A280
DESERT REGIONAL MEDICAL CENTER, PALM SPRINGS, CA, p. A55
DESERT SAMARITAN MEDICAL CENTER, MESA, AZ, p. A23
DESERT SPRINGS HOSPITAL, LAS VEGAS, NV, p. A266
DESERT VALLEY HOSPITAL, VICTORVILLE, CA, p. A66
DESERT VISTA BEHAVIORAL HEALTH SERVICES, MESA, AZ, p. A23
DESOTO MEMORIAL HOSPITAL, ARCADIA, FL, p. A81
DETAR HOSPITAL, VICTORIA, TX, p. A427
DETROIT RECEIVING HOSPITAL AND UNIVERSITY HEALTH CENTER, DETROIT, MI, p. A210
DETROIT RIVERVIEW HOSPITAL, DETROIT, MI, p. A210
DEUEL COUNTY MEMORIAL HOSPITAL, CLEAR LAKE, SD, p. A378
DEVEREUX FOUNDATION–FRENCH CENTER, DEVON, PA, p. A352
DEVEREUX GEORGIA TREATMENT NETWORK, KENNESAW, GA, p. A108
DEVEREUX HOSPITAL AND CHILDREN'S CENTER OF FLORIDA, MELBOURNE, FL, p. A90
DEVEREUX MAPLETON PSYCHIATRIC INSTITUTE–MAPLETON CENTER, MALVERN, PA, p. A357

DEVEREUX TEXAS TREATMENT NETWORK, LEAGUE CITY, TX, p. A415
DEWITT ARMY COMMUNITY HOSPITAL, FORT BELVOIR, VA, p. A437
DEWITT CITY HOSPITAL, DE WITT, AR, p. A30
DEWITT COMMUNITY HOSPITAL, DE WITT, IA, p. A149
DEXTER MEMORIAL HOSPITAL, DEXTER, MO, p. A243
DIAGNOSTIC CENTER HOSPITAL, HOUSTON, TX, p. A410
DICKENSON COUNTY MEDICAL CENTER, CLINTWOOD, VA, p. A437
DICKINSON COUNTY HEALTHCARE SYSTEM, IRON MOUNTAIN, MI, p. A214
DICKINSON COUNTY MEMORIAL HOSPITAL, SPIRIT LAKE, IA, p. A155
DIMMIT COUNTY MEMORIAL HOSPITAL, CARRIZO SPRINGS, TX, p. A400
DISTRICT MEMORIAL HOSPITAL, ANDREWS, NC, p. A304
DISTRICT OF COLUMBIA GENERAL HOSPITAL, WASHINGTON, DC, p. A79
DISTRICT ONE HOSPITAL, FARIBAULT, MN, p. A224
DIVINE PROVIDENCE HEALTH CENTER, IVANHOE, MN, p. A226
DIVINE SAVIOR HOSPITAL AND NURSING HOME, PORTAGE, WI, p. A464
DIXIE REGIONAL MEDICAL CENTER, SAINT GEORGE, UT, p. A432
DOCTOR ROBERT L. YEAGER HEALTH CENTER, POMONA, NY, p. A298
DOCTOR'S MEMORIAL HOSPITAL, PERRY, FL, p. A94
DOCTORS CENTER, MANATI, PR, p. A473
DOCTORS COMMUNITY HOSPITAL, LANHAM, MD, p. A196
DOCTORS GUBERN'S HOSPITAL, FAJARDO, PR, p. A472
DOCTORS HOSPITAL, SPRINGFIELD, IL, p. A135
DOCTORS HOSPITAL, WENTZVILLE, MO, p. A252
DOCTORS HOSPITAL, COLUMBUS, OH, p. A324
DOCTORS HOSPITAL, SAN JUAN, PR, p. A473
DOCTORS HOSPITAL, GROVES, TX, p. A409
DOCTORS HOSPITAL OF DALLAS, DALLAS, TX, p. A403
DOCTORS HOSPITAL OF HYDE PARK, CHICAGO, IL, p. A122
DOCTORS HOSPITAL OF JACKSON, JACKSON, MI, p. A214
DOCTORS HOSPITAL OF JEFFERSON, METAIRIE, LA, p. A183
DOCTORS HOSPITAL OF MANTECA, MANTECA, CA, p. A52
DOCTORS HOSPITAL OF NELSONVILLE, NELSONVILLE, OH, p. A330
DOCTORS HOSPITAL OF SARASOTA, SARASOTA, FL, p. A96
DOCTORS HOSPITAL OF STARK COUNTY, MASSILLON, OH, p. A329
DOCTORS HOSPITAL OF WEST COVINA, WEST COVINA, CA, p. A67
DOCTORS HOSPITAL–TIDWELL, HOUSTON, TX, p. A411
DOCTORS MEDICAL CENTER, MODESTO, CA, p. A52
DOCTORS MEDICAL CENTER–PINOLE CAMPUS, PINOLE, CA, p. A56
DOCTORS MEDICAL CENTER–SAN PABLO CAMPUS, SAN PABLO, CA, p. A62
DOCTORS MEMORIAL HOSPITAL, BONIFAY, FL, p. A81
DOCTORS MEMORIAL HOSPITAL, TYLER, TX, p. A427
DOCTORS REGIONAL MEDICAL CENTER, POPLAR BLUFF, MO, p. A248
DOCTORS' HOSPITAL OF SHREVEPORT, SHREVEPORT, LA, p. A186
DOCTORS' HOSPITAL OF STATEN ISLAND, NEW YORK, NY, p. A292
DODGE COUNTY HOSPITAL, EASTMAN, GA, p. A106
DOLLY VINSANT MEMORIAL HOSPITAL, SAN BENITO, TX, p. A424
DOMINICAN SANTA CRUZ HOSPITAL, SANTA CRUZ, CA, p. A62
DOMINION HOSPITAL, FALLS CHURCH, VA, p. A437
DONALSONVILLE HOSPITAL, DONALSONVILLE, GA, p. A105
DOOLY MEDICAL CENTER, VIENNA, GA, p. A113
DOOR COUNTY MEMORIAL HOSPITAL, STURGEON BAY, WI, p. A466
DORCHESTER GENERAL HOSPITAL, CAMBRIDGE, MD, p. A195
DORMINY MEDICAL CENTER, FITZGERALD, GA, p. A106
DOROTHEA DIX HOSPITAL, RALEIGH, NC, p. A311
DOS PALOS MEMORIAL HOSPITAL, DOS PALOS, CA, p. A41
DOUGLAS COMMUNITY MEDICAL CENTER, ROSEBURG, OR, p. A348
DOUGLAS COUNTY HOSPITAL, ALEXANDRIA, MN, p. A222
DOUGLAS COUNTY HOSPITAL, OMAHA, NE, p. A262
DOUGLAS COUNTY MEMORIAL HOSPITAL, ARMOUR, SD, p. A378
DOWN EAST COMMUNITY HOSPITAL, MACHIAS, ME, p. A191
DOWNEY COMMUNITY HOSPITAL FOUNDATION, DOWNEY, CA, p. A41
DOYLESTOWN HOSPITAL, DOYLESTOWN, PA, p. A352
DR. ALEJANDRO BUITRAGO–GUAYAMA AREA HOSPITAL, GUAYAMA, PR, p. A472
DR. DAN C. TRIGG MEMORIAL HOSPITAL, TUCUMCARI, NM, p. A283
DR. JOHN WARNER HOSPITAL, CLINTON, IL, p. A125

DR. JOSE RAMOS LEBRON HOSPITAL, FAJARDO, PR, p. A472
DR. PILA'S HOSPITAL, PONCE, PR, p. A473
DR. RAMON E. BETANCES HOSPITAL–MAYAGUEZ MEDICAL CENTER BRANCH, MAYAGUEZ, PR, p. A473
DRAKE CENTER, CINCINNATI, OH, p. A322
DREW MEMORIAL HOSPITAL, MONTICELLO, AR, p. A33
DRISCOLL CHILDREN'S HOSPITAL, CORPUS CHRISTI, TX, p. A401
DRUMRIGHT MEMORIAL HOSPITAL, DRUMRIGHT, OK, p. A336
DUANE L. WATERS HOSPITAL, JACKSON, MI, p. A214
DUBOIS REGIONAL MEDICAL CENTER, DU BOIS, PA, p. A353
DUKE UNIVERSITY MEDICAL CENTER, DURHAM, NC, p. A307
DUKES MEMORIAL HOSPITAL, PERU, IN, p. A144
DUNCAN REGIONAL HOSPITAL, DUNCAN, OK, p. A336
DUNDY COUNTY HOSPITAL, BENKELMAN, NE, p. A258
DUNLAP MEMORIAL HOSPITAL, ORRVILLE, OH, p. A331
DUNN MEMORIAL HOSPITAL, BEDFORD, IN, p. A137
DUNWOODY MEDICAL CENTER, ATLANTA, GA, p. A101
DUPLIN GENERAL HOSPITAL, KENANSVILLE, NC, p. A309
DURHAM REGIONAL HOSPITAL, DURHAM, NC, p. A307
DWIGHT D. EISENHOWER VETERANS AFFAIRS MEDICAL CENTER, LEAVENWORTH, KS, p. A161
DWIGHT DAVID EISENHOWER ARMY MEDICAL CENTER, FORT GORDON, GA, p. A106

E

E. A. CONWAY MEDICAL CENTER, MONROE, LA, p. A184
E. J. NOBLE HOSPITAL SAMARITAN, ALEXANDRIA BAY, NY, p. A284
EAGLE RIVER MEMORIAL HOSPITAL, EAGLE RIVER, WI, p. A458
EAGLEVILLE HOSPITAL, EAGLEVILLE, PA, p. A353
EARL K. LONG MEDICAL CENTER, BATON ROUGE, LA, p. A178
EARLY MEMORIAL HOSPITAL, BLAKELY, GA, p. A102
EAST ADAMS RURAL HOSPITAL, RITZVILLE, WA, p. A449
EAST ALABAMA MEDICAL CENTER, OPELIKA, AL, p. A17
EAST BAY HOSPITAL, RICHMOND, CA, p. A57
EAST CARROLL PARISH HOSPITAL, LAKE PROVIDENCE, LA, p. A183
EAST COOPER REGIONAL MEDICAL CENTER, MOUNT PLEASANT, SC, p. A375
EAST JEFFERSON GENERAL HOSPITAL, METAIRIE, LA, p. A183
EAST LIVERPOOL CITY HOSPITAL, EAST LIVERPOOL, OH, p. A326
EAST LOS ANGELES DOCTORS HOSPITAL, LOS ANGELES, CA, p. A48
EAST LOUISIANA STATE HOSPITAL, JACKSON, LA, p. A181
EAST MISSISSIPPI STATE HOSPITAL, MERIDIAN, MS, p. A238
EAST MORGAN COUNTY HOSPITAL, BRUSH, CO, p. A68
EAST OHIO REGIONAL HOSPITAL, MARTINS FERRY, OH, p. A329
EAST ORANGE GENERAL HOSPITAL, EAST ORANGE, NJ, p. A272
EAST PASCO MEDICAL CENTER, ZEPHYRHILLS, FL, p. A99
EAST POINTE HOSPITAL, LEHIGH ACRES, FL, p. A89
EAST TENNESSEE CHILDREN'S HOSPITAL, KNOXVILLE, TN, p. A387
EAST TEXAS MEDICAL CENTER ATHENS, ATHENS, TX, p. A396
EAST TEXAS MEDICAL CENTER CARTHAGE, CARTHAGE, TX, p. A400
EAST TEXAS MEDICAL CENTER CROCKETT, CROCKETT, TX, p. A402
EAST TEXAS MEDICAL CENTER JACKSONVILLE, JACKSONVILLE, TX, p. A413
EAST TEXAS MEDICAL CENTER PITTSBURG, PITTSBURG, TX, p. A420
EAST TEXAS MEDICAL CENTER REHABILITATION CENTER, TYLER, TX, p. A427
EAST TEXAS MEDICAL CENTER RUSK, RUSK, TX, p. A422
EAST TEXAS MEDICAL CENTER TRINITY, TRINITY, TX, p. A426
EAST TEXAS MEDICAL CENTER TYLER, TYLER, TX, p. A427
EAST TEXAS MEDICAL CENTER–CLARKSVILLE, CLARKSVILLE, TX, p. A400
EAST TEXAS MEDICAL CENTER–MOUNT VERNON, MOUNT VERNON, TX, p. A418
EAST TEXAS MEDICAL CENTER–WOOD COUNTY AT QUITMAN, QUITMAN, TX, p. A421
EASTERN LONG ISLAND HOSPITAL, GREENPORT, NY, p. A288
EASTERN MAINE MEDICAL CENTER, BANGOR, ME, p. A189
EASTERN NEW MEXICO MEDICAL CENTER, ROSWELL, NM, p. A283
EASTERN OKLAHOMA MEDICAL CENTER, POTEAU, OK, p. A341
EASTERN OREGON PSYCHIATRIC CENTER, PENDLETON, OR, p. A346
EASTERN OZARKS REGIONAL HEALTH SYSTEM, CHEROKEE VILLAGE, AR, p. A29
EASTERN PLUMAS DISTRICT HOSPITAL, PORTOLA, CA, p. A56

F

GOODLAND REGIONAL MEDICAL CENTER, GOODLAND, KS, p. A159
GORDON HOSPITAL, CALHOUN, GA, p. A103
GORDON MEMORIAL HOSPITAL DISTRICT, GORDON, NE, p. A260
GOSHEN GENERAL HOSPITAL, GOSHEN, IN, p. A140
GOTHENBURG MEMORIAL HOSPITAL, GOTHENBURG, NE, p. A260
GOTTLIEB MEMORIAL HOSPITAL, MELROSE PARK, IL, p. A130
GOVE COUNTY MEDICAL CENTER, QUINTER, KS, p. A164
GOVERNOR JUAN F. LOUIS HOSPITAL, CHRISTIANSTED, VI, p. A474
GRACE COTTAGE HOSPITAL, TOWNSHEND, VT, p. A435
GRACE HOSPITAL, DETROIT, MI, p. A210
GRACE HOSPITAL, MORGANTON, NC, p. A311
GRACE HOSPITAL, CLEVELAND, OH, p. A323
GRACEVILLE HEALTH CENTER, GRACEVILLE, MN, p. A225
GRACEWOOD STATE SCHOOL AND HOSPITAL, GRACEWOOD, GA, p. A107
GRACIE SQUARE HOSPITAL, NEW YORK, NY, p. A292
GRADY GENERAL HOSPITAL, CAIRO, GA, p. A103
GRADY MEMORIAL HOSPITAL, ATLANTA, GA, p. A101
GRADY MEMORIAL HOSPITAL, DELAWARE, OH, p. A326
GRADY MEMORIAL HOSPITAL, CHICKASHA, OK, p. A336
GRAFTON CITY HOSPITAL, GRAFTON, WV, p. A453
GRAHAM COUNTY HOSPITAL, HILL CITY, KS, p. A160
GRAHAM GENERAL HOSPITAL, GRAHAM, TX, p. A408
GRAHAM HOSPITAL, CANTON, IL, p. A121
GRANADA HILLS COMMUNITY HOSPITAL, LOS ANGELES, CA, p. A49
GRAND RIVER HOSPITAL DISTRICT, RIFLE, CO, p. A72
GRAND VIEW HOSPITAL, IRONWOOD, MI, p. A214
GRAND VIEW HOSPITAL, SELLERSVILLE, PA, p. A365
GRANDE RONDE HOSPITAL, LA GRANDE, OR, p. A345
GRANDVIEW HOSPITAL AND MEDICAL CENTER, DAYTON, OH, p. A325
GRANITE COUNTY MEMORIAL HOSPITAL AND NURSING HOME, PHILIPSBURG, MT, p. A255
GRANITE FALLS MUNICIPAL HOSPITAL AND MANOR, GRANITE FALLS, MN, p. A225
GRANT COUNTY HEALTH CENTER, ELBOW LAKE, MN, p. A224
GRANT MEMORIAL HOSPITAL, PETERSBURG, WV, p. A455
GRANT REGIONAL HEALTH CENTER, LANCASTER, WI, p. A460
GRANT/RIVERSIDE METHODIST HOSPITALS–GRANT CAMPUS, COLUMBUS, OH, p. A325
GRANT/RIVERSIDE METHODIST HOSPITALS–RIVERSIDE CAMPUS, COLUMBUS, OH, p. A325
GRANVILLE MEDICAL CENTER, OXFORD, NC, p. A311
GRAPE COMMUNITY HOSPITAL, HAMBURG, IA, p. A151
GRATIOT COMMUNITY HOSPITAL, ALMA, MI, p. A208
GRAYDON MANOR, LEESBURG, VA, p. A439
GRAVETTE MEDICAL CENTER HOSPITAL, GRAVETTE, AR, p. A31
GRAYS HARBOR COMMUNITY HOSPITAL, ABERDEEN, WA, p. A445
GREAT LAKES REHABILITATION HOSPITAL, SOUTHFIELD, MI, p. A219
GREAT PLAINS REGIONAL MEDICAL CENTER, NORTH PLATTE, NE, p. A262
GREAT PLAINS REGIONAL MEDICAL CENTER, ELK CITY, OK, p. A337
GREATER BALTIMORE MEDICAL CENTER, BALTIMORE, MD, p. A193
GREATER BRIDGEPORT COMMUNITY MENTAL HEALTH CENTER, BRIDGEPORT, CT, p. A74
GREATER COMMUNITY HOSPITAL, CRESTON, IA, p. A149
GREATER EL MONTE COMMUNITY HOSPITAL, SOUTH EL MONTE, CA, p. A64
GREATER SOUTHEAST COMMUNITY HOSPITAL, WASHINGTON, DC, p. A79
GREELEY COUNTY HOSPITAL, TRIBUNE, KS, p. A166
GREEN HOSPITAL OF SCRIPPS CLINIC, LA JOLLA, CA, p. A46
GREEN OAKS HOSPITAL, DALLAS, TX, p. A403
GREENBRIER BEHAVIORAL HEALTH SYSTEM, COVINGTON, LA, p. A180
GREENBRIER HOSPITAL, BROOKSVILLE, FL, p. A82
GREENBRIER VALLEY MEDICAL CENTER, RONCEVERTE, WV, p. A455
GREENE COUNTY GENERAL HOSPITAL, LINTON, IN, p. A143
GREENE COUNTY HOSPITAL, EUTAW, AL, p. A14
GREENE COUNTY MEDICAL CENTER, JEFFERSON, IA, p. A152
GREENE COUNTY MEMORIAL HOSPITAL, WAYNESBURG, PA, p. A367
GREENE MEMORIAL HOSPITAL, XENIA, OH, p. A334
GREENFIELD AREA MEDICAL CENTER, GREENFIELD, OH, p. A327
GREENLEAF CENTER, FORT OGLETHORPE, GA, p. A106
GREENLEAF CENTER, VALDOSTA, GA, p. A112
GREENSVILLE MEMORIAL HOSPITAL, EMPORIA, VA, p. A437
GREENVIEW REGIONAL HOSPITAL, BOWLING GREEN, KY, p. A168

GREENVILLE HOSPITAL, JERSEY CITY, NJ, p. A274
GREENVILLE MEMORIAL HOSPITAL, GREENVILLE, SC, p. A374
GREENWELL SPRINGS HOSPITAL, GREENWELL SPRINGS, LA, p. A181
GREENWICH HOSPITAL, GREENWICH, CT, p. A74
GREENWOOD COUNTY HOSPITAL, EUREKA, KS, p. A159
GREENWOOD LEFLORE HOSPITAL, GREENWOOD, MS, p. A235
GREGORY COMMUNITY HOSPITAL, GREGORY, SD, p. A379
GRENADA LAKE MEDICAL CENTER, GRENADA, MS, p. A235
GREYSTONE PARK PSYCHIATRIC HOSPITAL, GREYSTONE PARK, NJ, p. A273
GRIFFIN HOSPITAL, DERBY, CT, p. A74
GRIFFIN MEMORIAL HOSPITAL, NORMAN, OK, p. A339
GRIGGS COUNTY HOSPITAL AND NURSING HOME, COOPERSTOWN, ND, p. A316
GRIMES ST. JOSEPH HEALTH CENTER, NAVASOTA, TX, p. A419
GRINNELL REGIONAL MEDICAL CENTER, GRINNELL, IA, p. A151
GRISELL MEMORIAL HOSPITAL DISTRICT ONE, RANSOM, KS, p. A165
GRITMAN MEDICAL CENTER, MOSCOW, ID, p. A118
GROSSMONT HOSPITAL, LA MESA, CA, p. A46
GROVE HILL MEMORIAL HOSPITAL, GROVE HILL, AL, p. A15
GRUNDY COUNTY MEMORIAL HOSPITAL, GRUNDY CENTER, IA, p. A151
GUADALUPE VALLEY HOSPITAL, SEGUIN, TX, p. A424
GUAM MEMORIAL HOSPITAL AUTHORITY, TAMUNING, GU, p. A471
GULF BREEZE HOSPITAL, GULF BREEZE, FL, p. A86
GULF COAST HOSPITAL, FORT MYERS, FL, p. A85
GULF COAST MEDICAL CENTER, PANAMA CITY, FL, p. A93
GULF COAST MEDICAL CENTER, BILOXI, MS, p. A233
GULF COAST MEDICAL CENTER, WHARTON, TX, p. A428
GULF COAST TREATMENT CENTER, FORT WALTON BEACH, FL, p. A85
GULF PINES BEHAVIORAL HEALTH SERVICES, HOUSTON, TX, p. A411
GULF PINES HOSPITAL, PORT SAINT JOE, FL, p. A95
GUNDRY–GLASS HOSPITAL, BALTIMORE, MD, p. A193
GUNNISON VALLEY HOSPITAL, GUNNISON, CO, p. A71
GUNNISON VALLEY HOSPITAL, GUNNISON, UT, p. A430
GUTHRIE COUNTY HOSPITAL, GUTHRIE CENTER, IA, p. A151
GUTTENBERG MUNICIPAL HOSPITAL, GUTTENBERG, IA, p. A151
GUYAN VALLEY HOSPITAL, LOGAN, WV, p. A454

H

H. B. MAGRUDER MEMORIAL HOSPITAL, PORT CLINTON, OH, p. A331
H. C. WATKINS MEMORIAL HOSPITAL, QUITMAN, MS, p. A239
H. DOUGLAS SINGER MENTAL HEALTH AND DEVELOPMENTAL CENTER, ROCKFORD, IL, p. A134
H. LEE MOFFITT CANCER CENTER AND RESEARCH INSTITUTE, TAMPA, FL, p. A97
H. R. I. HOSPITAL, BROOKLINE, MA, p. A201
H.S.C. MEDICAL CENTER, MALVERN, AR, p. A33
HABERSHAM COUNTY MEDICAL CENTER, DEMOREST, GA, p. A105
HACKENSACK UNIVERSITY MEDICAL CENTER, HACKENSACK, NJ, p. A273
HACKETTSTOWN COMMUNITY HOSPITAL, HACKETTSTOWN, NJ, p. A273
HACKLEY HEALTH, MUSKEGON, MI, p. A216
HADLEY MEMORIAL HOSPITAL, WASHINGTON, DC, p. A79
HALE COUNTY HOSPITAL, GREENSBORO, AL, p. A15
HALE HOSPITAL, HAVERHILL, MA, p. A203
HALIFAX COMMUNITY HEALTH SYSTEM, DAYTONA BEACH, FL, p. A83
HALIFAX REGIONAL HOSPITAL, SOUTH BOSTON, VA, p. A443
HALIFAX REGIONAL MEDICAL CENTER, ROANOKE RAPIDS, NC, p. A312
HALL COUNTY HOSPITAL, MEMPHIS, TX, p. A417
HALL–BROOKE HOSPITAL, A DIVISION OF HALL–BROOKE FOUNDATION, WESTPORT, CT, p. A77
HALLMARK HEALTH SYSTEM, MELROSE, MA, p. A204
HALSTEAD HOSPITAL, HALSTEAD, KS, p. A159
HAMILTON CENTER, TERRE HAUTE, IN, p. A146
HAMILTON COUNTY HOSPITAL, SYRACUSE, KS, p. A166
HAMILTON COUNTY PUBLIC HOSPITAL, WEBSTER CITY, IA, p. A156
HAMILTON HOSPITAL, OLNEY, TX, p. A419
HAMILTON MEDICAL CENTER, JASPER, FL, p. A88
HAMILTON MEDICAL CENTER, DALTON, GA, p. A105
HAMILTON MEMORIAL HOSPITAL DISTRICT, MCLEANSBORO, IL, p. A130
HAMLET HOSPITAL, HAMLET, NC, p. A309
HAMLIN MEMORIAL HOSPITAL, HAMLIN, TX, p. A409
HAMMOND–HENRY HOSPITAL, GENESEO, IL, p. A127

HAMOT MEDICAL CENTER, ERIE, PA, p. A353
HAMPSHIRE MEMORIAL HOSPITAL, ROMNEY, WV, p. A455
HAMPSTEAD HOSPITAL, HAMPSTEAD, NH, p. A268
HAMPTON HOSPITAL, WESTAMPTON TOWNSHIP, NJ, p. A279
HAMPTON REGIONAL MEDICAL CENTER, VARNVILLE, SC, p. A377
HANCOCK COUNTY MEMORIAL HOSPITAL, BRITT, IA, p. A147
HANCOCK MEDICAL CENTER, BAY SAINT LOUIS, MS, p. A233
HANCOCK MEMORIAL HOSPITAL, SPARTA, GA, p. A111
HANCOCK MEMORIAL HOSPITAL AND HEALTH SERVICES, GREENFIELD, IN, p. A140
HAND COUNTY MEMORIAL HOSPITAL, MILLER, SD, p. A380
HANFORD COMMUNITY MEDICAL CENTER, HANFORD, CA, p. A44
HANNIBAL REGIONAL HOSPITAL, HANNIBAL, MO, p. A243
HANOVER HOSPITAL, HANOVER, KS, p. A160
HANOVER HOSPITAL, HANOVER, PA, p. A354
HANS P. PETERSON MEMORIAL HOSPITAL, PHILIP, SD, p. A380
HANSFORD HOSPITAL, SPEARMAN, TX, p. A425
HARBOR BEACH COMMUNITY HOSPITAL, HARBOR BEACH, MI, p. A213
HARBOR HOSPITAL CENTER, BALTIMORE, MD, p. A193
HARBOR OAKS HOSPITAL, NEW BALTIMORE, MI, p. A217
HARBOR VIEW MERCY HOSPITAL, FORT SMITH, AR, p. A31
HARBORVIEW MEDICAL CENTER, SEATTLE, WA, p. A449
HARDEMAN COUNTY MEMORIAL HOSPITAL, QUANAH, TX, p. A421
HARDIN COUNTY GENERAL HOSPITAL, ROSICLARE, IL, p. A134
HARDIN COUNTY GENERAL HOSPITAL, SAVANNAH, TN, p. A392
HARDIN MEMORIAL HOSPITAL, ELIZABETHTOWN, KY, p. A169
HARDIN MEMORIAL HOSPITAL, KENTON, OH, p. A328
HARDING HOSPITAL, WORTHINGTON, OH, p. A334
HARDTNER MEDICAL CENTER, OLLA, LA, p. A186
HARDY WILSON MEMORIAL HOSPITAL, HAZLEHURST, MS, p. A236
HARFORD MEMORIAL HOSPITAL, HAVRE DE GRACE, MD, p. A196
HARLAN ARH HOSPITAL, HARLAN, KY, p. A171
HARLAN COUNTY HOSPITAL, ALMA, NE, p. A258
HARLEM HOSPITAL CENTER, NEW YORK, NY, p. A292
HARMON MEMORIAL HOSPITAL, HOLLIS, OK, p. A338
HARMONY COMMUNITY HOSPITAL, HARMONY, MN, p. A226
HARMS MEMORIAL HOSPITAL DISTRICT, AMERICAN FALLS, ID, p. A116
HARNEY DISTRICT HOSPITAL, BURNS, OR, p. A344
HARPER COUNTY COMMUNITY HOSPITAL, BUFFALO, OK, p. A336
HARPER HOSPITAL, DETROIT, MI, p. A210
HARRINGTON MEMORIAL HOSPITAL, SOUTHBRIDGE, MA, p. A206
HARRIS CONTINUED CARE HOSPITAL, FORT WORTH, TX, p. A406
HARRIS COUNTY HOSPITAL DISTRICT, HOUSTON, TX, p. A411
HARRIS COUNTY PSYCHIATRIC CENTER, HOUSTON, TX, p. A411
HARRIS HOSPITAL, NEWPORT, AR, p. A33
HARRIS METHODIST FORT WORTH, FORT WORTH, TX, p. A406
HARRIS METHODIST NORTHWEST, AZLE, TX, p. A397
HARRIS METHODIST SOUTHWEST, FORT WORTH, TX, p. A407
HARRIS METHODIST–ERATH COUNTY, STEPHENVILLE, TX, p. A425
HARRIS METHODIST–HEB, BEDFORD, TX, p. A398
HARRIS REGIONAL HOSPITAL, SYLVA, NC, p. A313
HARRISBURG MEDICAL CENTER, HARRISBURG, IL, p. A128
HARRISBURG STATE HOSPITAL, HARRISBURG, PA, p. A355
HARRISON COMMUNITY HOSPITAL, CADIZ, OH, p. A321
HARRISON COUNTY COMMUNITY HOSPITAL, BETHANY, MO, p. A241
HARRISON COUNTY HOSPITAL, CORYDON, IN, p. A138
HARRISON MEMORIAL HOSPITAL, CYNTHIANA, KY, p. A169
HARRISON MEMORIAL HOSPITAL, BREMERTON, WA, p. A445
HARRY S. TRUMAN MEMORIAL VETERANS HOSPITAL, COLUMBIA, MO, p. A242
HART COUNTY HOSPITAL, HARTWELL, GA, p. A107
HARTFORD HOSPITAL, HARTFORD, CT, p. A74
HARTFORD MEMORIAL HOSPITAL, HARTFORD, WI, p. A460
HARTGROVE HOSPITAL, CHICAGO, IL, p. A122
HARTON REGIONAL MEDICAL CENTER, TULLAHOMA, TN, p. A393
HARTSELLE MEDICAL CENTER, HARTSELLE, AL, p. A15
HARVARD MEMORIAL HOSPITAL, HARVARD, IL, p. A128
HASKELL COUNTY HEALTHCARE SYSTEM, STIGLER, OK, p. A341
HASKELL MEMORIAL HOSPITAL, HASKELL, TX, p. A409
HASTINGS REGIONAL CENTER, HASTINGS, NE, p. A260
HATO REY COMMUNITY HOSPITAL, SAN JUAN, PR, p. A473
HAVASU SAMARITAN REGIONAL HOSPITAL, LAKE HAVASU CITY, AZ, p. A23
HAVEN HOSPITAL, DE SOTO, TX, p. A404
HAVENWYCK HOSPITAL, AUBURN HILLS, MI, p. A208

HOFFMAN ESTATES MEDICAL CENTER, HOFFMAN ESTATES, IL, p. A129
HOLDENVILLE GENERAL HOSPITAL, HOLDENVILLE, OK, p. A338
HOLLAND COMMUNITY HOSPITAL, HOLLAND, MI, p. A214
HOLLISWOOD HOSPITAL, NEW YORK, NY, p. A292
HOLLY HILL CHARTER BEHAVIORAL HEALTH SYSTEM, RALEIGH, NC, p. A311
HOLLY SPRINGS MEMORIAL HOSPITAL, HOLLY SPRINGS, MS, p. A236
HOLLYWOOD COMMUNITY HOSPITAL OF HOLLYWOOD, LOS ANGELES, CA, p. A49
HOLLYWOOD MEDICAL CENTER, LOS ANGELES, FL, p. A86
HOLLYWOOD PAVILION, LOS ANGELES, FL, p. A86
HOLMES REGIONAL MEDICAL CENTER, MELBOURNE, FL, p. A90
HOLTON COMMUNITY HOSPITAL, HOLTON, KS, p. A160
HOLY CROSS HOSPITAL, FORT LAUDERDALE, FL, p. A84
HOLY CROSS HOSPITAL, CHICAGO, IL, p. A122
HOLY CROSS HOSPITAL, DETROIT, MI, p. A211
HOLY CROSS HOSPITAL, TAOS, NM, p. A283
HOLY CROSS HOSPITAL OF SILVER SPRING, SILVER SPRING, MD, p. A197
HOLY FAMILY HEALTH SERVICES, ESTHERVILLE, IA, p. A150
HOLY FAMILY HOSPITAL, SPOKANE, WA, p. A450
HOLY FAMILY HOSPITAL, NEW RICHMOND, WI, p. A463
HOLY FAMILY HOSPITAL AND MEDICAL CENTER, METHUEN, MA, p. A204
HOLY FAMILY MEDICAL CENTER, DES PLAINES, IL, p. A125
HOLY FAMILY MEMORIAL MEDICAL CENTER, MANITOWOC, WI, p. A461
HOLY INFANT HOSPITAL, HOVEN, SD, p. A379
HOLY NAME HOSPITAL, TEANECK, NJ, p. A278
HOLY REDEEMER HOSPITAL AND MEDICAL CENTER, MEADOWBROOK, PA, p. A357
HOLY ROSARY HEALTH CENTER, MILES CITY, MT, p. A255
HOLY ROSARY MEDICAL CENTER, ONTARIO, OR, p. A346
HOLY SPIRIT HOSPITAL, CAMP HILL, PA, p. A351
HOLYOKE HOSPITAL, HOLYOKE, MA, p. A203
HOLZER MEDICAL CENTER, GALLIPOLIS, OH, p. A327
HOMER MEMORIAL HOSPITAL, HOMER, LA, p. A181
HOMESTEAD HOSPITAL, HOMESTEAD, FL, p. A86
HONOKAA HOSPITAL, HONOKAA, HI, p. A114
HOOD MEMORIAL HOSPITAL, AMITE, LA, p. A178
HOOD RIVER MEMORIAL HOSPITAL, HOOD RIVER, OR, p. A345
HOOPESTON COMMUNITY MEMORIAL HOSPITAL, HOOPESTON, IL, p. A129
HOOTS MEMORIAL HOSPITAL, YADKINVILLE, NC, p. A315
HOPE HOSPITAL, LOCKHART, SC, p. A375
HOPEDALE MEDICAL COMPLEX, HOPEDALE, IL, p. A129
HOPKINS COUNTY MEMORIAL HOSPITAL, SULPHUR SPRINGS, TX, p. A425
HORIZON HOSPITAL SYSTEM, GREENVILLE, PA, p. A354
HORIZON SPECIALTY HOSPITAL, EDMOND, OK, p. A337
HORIZON SPECIALTY HOSPITAL, LUBBOCK, TX, p. A416
HORIZON SPECIALTY HOSPITAL, SAN ANTONIO, TX, p. A422
HORN MEMORIAL HOSPITAL, IDA GROVE, IA, p. A151
HORSHAM CLINIC, AMBLER, PA, p. A349
HORTON HEALTH FOUNDATION, HORTON, KS, p. A160
HORTON MEDICAL CENTER, MIDDLETOWN, NY, p. A290
HOSPICE OF NORTHERN VIRGINIA, ARLINGTON, VA, p. A436
HOSPICE OF PALM BEACH COUNTY, WEST PALM BEACH, FL, p. A99
HOSPITAL CENTER AT ORANGE, ORANGE, NJ, p. A276
HOSPITAL DE AREA DE YAUCO, YAUCO, PR, p. A474
HOSPITAL DE DAMAS, PONCE, PR, p. A473
HOSPITAL DE LA CONCEPCION, SAN GERMAN, PR, p. A473
HOSPITAL DEL MAESTRO, SAN JUAN, PR, p. A473
HOSPITAL DISTRICT NUMBER FIVE OF HARPER COUNTY, HARPER, KS, p. A160
HOSPITAL DISTRICT NUMBER SIX OF HARPER COUNTY, ANTHONY, KS, p. A157
HOSPITAL DR. DOMINGUEZ, HUMACAO, PR, p. A472
HOSPITAL DR. FEDERICO TRILLA, CAROLINA, PR, p. A472
HOSPITAL DR. SUSONI, ARECIBO, PR, p. A471
HOSPITAL EL BUEN PASTOR, ARECIBO, PR, p. A471
HOSPITAL EPISCOPAL SAN LUCAS, PONCE, PR, p. A473
HOSPITAL FOR JOINT DISEASES ORTHOPEDIC INSTITUTE, NEW YORK, NY, p. A293
HOSPITAL FOR SICK CHILDREN, WASHINGTON, DC, p. A79
HOSPITAL FOR SPECIAL CARE, NEW BRITAIN, CT, p. A75
HOSPITAL FOR SPECIAL SURGERY, NEW YORK, NY, p. A293
HOSPITAL HERMANOS MELENDEZ, BAYAMON, PR, p. A472
HOSPITAL INTERAMERICANO DE MEDICINA AVANZADA, CAGUAS, PR, p. A472
HOSPITAL MATILDE BRENES, BAYAMON, PR, p. A472
HOSPITAL MENONITA DE CAYEY, CAYEY, PR, p. A472
HOSPITAL OF SAINT RAPHAEL, NEW HAVEN, CT, p. A75
HOSPITAL OF THE CALIFORNIA INSTITUTION FOR MEN, CHINO, CA, p. A39

HOSPITAL OF THE UNIVERSITY OF PENNSYLVANIA, PHILADELPHIA, PA, p. A360
HOSPITAL ONCOLOGICO ANDRES GRILLASCA, PONCE, PR, p. A473
HOSPITAL PAVIA, SAN JUAN, PR, p. A473
HOSPITAL PEREA, MAYAGUEZ, PR, p. A473
HOSPITAL SAN FRANCISCO, SAN JUAN, PR, p. A473
HOSPITAL SAN PABLO, BAYAMON, PR, p. A472
HOSPITAL SANTA ROSA, GUAYAMA, PR, p. A472
HOSPITAL SUB-REGIONAL DR. VICTOR R. NUNEZ, HUMACAO, PR, p. A472
HOSPITAL UNIVERSITARIO DR. RAMON RUIZ ARNAU, BAYAMON, PR, p. A472
HOT SPRINGS COUNTY MEMORIAL HOSPITAL, THERMOPOLIS, WY, p. A469
HOULTON REGIONAL HOSPITAL, HOULTON, ME, p. A190
HOUSTON MEDICAL CENTER, WARNER ROBINS, GA, p. A113
HOUSTON NORTHWEST MEDICAL CENTER, HOUSTON, TX, p. A411
HOWARD COMMUNITY HOSPITAL, KOKOMO, IN, p. A142
HOWARD COUNTY COMMUNITY HOSPITAL, SAINT PAUL, NE, p. A264
HOWARD COUNTY GENERAL HOSPITAL, COLUMBIA, MD, p. A195
HOWARD MEMORIAL HOSPITAL, NASHVILLE, AR, p. A33
HOWARD UNIVERSITY HOSPITAL, WASHINGTON, DC, p. A79
HOWARD YOUNG MEDICAL CENTER, WOODRUFF, WI, p. A467
HUBBARD REGIONAL HOSPITAL, WEBSTER, MA, p. A207
HUDSON MEDICAL CENTER, HUDSON, WI, p. A460
HUDSON RIVER PSYCHIATRIC CENTER, POUGHKEEPSIE, NY, p. A299
HUDSON VALLEY HOSPITAL CENTER, PEEKSKILL, NY, p. A298
HUERFANO MEDICAL CENTER, WALSENBURG, CO, p. A73
HUEY P. LONG MEDICAL CENTER, PINEVILLE, LA, p. A186
HUGGINS HOSPITAL, WOLFEBORO, NH, p. A270
HUGH CHATHAM MEMORIAL HOSPITAL, ELKIN, NC, p. A307
HUGHSTON SPORTS MEDICINE HOSPITAL, COLUMBUS, GA, p. A104
HUGULEY MEMORIAL MEDICAL CENTER, BURLESON, TX, p. A399
HUHUKAM MEMORIAL HOSPITAL, SACATON, AZ, p. A26
HUMBOLDT COUNTY MEMORIAL HOSPITAL, HUMBOLDT, IA, p. A151
HUMBOLDT GENERAL HOSPITAL, WINNEMUCCA, NV, p. A267
HUMBOLDT GENERAL HOSPITAL, HUMBOLDT, TN, p. A386
HUMPHREYS COUNTY MEMORIAL HOSPITAL, BELZONI, MS, p. A233
HUNT MEMORIAL HOSPITAL DISTRICT, GREENVILLE, TX, p. A409
HUNTER HOLMES MCGUIRE VETERANS AFFAIRS MEDICAL CENTER, RICHMOND, VA, p. A442
HUNTERDON MEDICAL CENTER, FLEMINGTON, NJ, p. A273
HUNTINGTON EAST VALLEY HOSPITAL, GLENDORA, CA, p. A44
HUNTINGTON HOSPITAL, HUNTINGTON, NY, p. A289
HUNTINGTON HOSPITAL, WILLOW GROVE, PA, p. A368
HUNTINGTON MEMORIAL HOSPITAL, PASADENA, CA, p. A55
HUNTINGTON MEMORIAL HOSPITAL, HUNTINGTON, IN, p. A141
HUNTSVILLE HOSPITAL, HUNTSVILLE, AL, p. A15
HUNTSVILLE MEMORIAL HOSPITAL, HUNTSVILLE, TX, p. A413
HURLEY MEDICAL CENTER, FLINT, MI, p. A212
HURON MEMORIAL HOSPITAL, BAD AXE, MI, p. A208
HURON REGIONAL MEDICAL CENTER, HURON, SD, p. A379
HURON VALLEY-SINAI HOSPITAL, COMMERCE TOWNSHIP, MI, p. A210
HURTADO HEALTH CENTER, NEW BRUNSWICK, NJ, p. A275
HUTCHESON MEDICAL CENTER, FORT OGLETHORPE, GA, p. A106
HUTCHINSON AREA HEALTH CARE, HUTCHINSON, MN, p. A226
HUTCHINSON HOSPITAL CORPORATION, HUTCHINSON, KS, p. A160
HUTZEL HOSPITAL, DETROIT, MI, p. A211

I

I. GONZALEZ MARTINEZ ONCOLOGIC HOSPITAL, HATO REY, PR, p. A473
IBERIA GENERAL HOSPITAL AND MEDICAL CENTER, NEW IBERIA, LA, p. A184
IDAHO ELKS REHABILITATION HOSPITAL, BOISE, ID, p. A116
IDAHO FALLS RECOVERY CENTER, IDAHO FALLS, ID, p. A117
ILLINI COMMUNITY HOSPITAL, PITTSFIELD, IL, p. A133
ILLINI HOSPITAL, SILVIS, IL, p. A134
ILLINOIS MASONIC MEDICAL CENTER, CHICAGO, IL, p. A122
ILLINOIS VALLEY COMMUNITY HOSPITAL, PERU, IL, p. A133
IMMANUEL/ST. JOSEPH'S-MAYO HEALTH SYSTEM, MANKATO, MN, p. A227

IMPACT DRUG AND ALCOHOL TREATMENT CENTER, PASADENA, CA, p. A55
IMPERIAL POINT MEDICAL CENTER, FORT LAUDERDALE, FL, p. A85
INDEPENDENCE REGIONAL HEALTH CENTER, INDEPENDENCE, MO, p. A244
INDIAN HEALTH SERVICE HOSPITAL, RAPID CITY, SD, p. A380
INDIAN RIVER MEMORIAL HOSPITAL, VERO BEACH, FL, p. A99
INDIAN VALLEY HOSPITAL DISTRICT, GREENVILLE, CA, p. A44
INDIANA HOSPITAL, INDIANA, PA, p. A355
INDIANHEAD MEDICAL CENTER, SHELL LAKE, WI, p. A465
INDUSTRIAL HOSPITAL, SAN JUAN, PR, p. A474
INGALLS HOSPITAL, HARVEY, IL, p. A128
INGHAM REGIONAL MEDICAL CENTER, LANSING, MI, p. A215
INLAND HOSPITAL, WATERVILLE, ME, p. A192
INLAND VALLEY REGIONAL MEDICAL CENTER, WILDOMAR, CA, p. A67
INNER HARBOUR HOSPITALS, DOUGLASVILLE, GA, p. A105
INOVA ALEXANDRIA HOSPITAL, ALEXANDRIA, VA, p. A436
INOVA FAIR OAKS HOSPITAL, FAIRFAX, VA, p. A437
INOVA FAIRFAX HOSPITAL, FALLS CHURCH, VA, p. A437
INOVA MOUNT VERNON HOSPITAL, ALEXANDRIA, VA, p. A436
INTEGRIS BAPTIST MEDICAL CENTER, OKLAHOMA CITY, OK, p. A339
INTEGRIS BAPTIST REGIONAL HEALTH CENTER, MIAMI, OK, p. A339
INTEGRIS BASS BEHAVIORAL HEALTH SYSTEM, ENID, OK, p. A337
INTEGRIS BASS BAPTIST HEALTH CENTER, ENID, OK, p. A337
INTEGRIS GROVE GENERAL HOSPITAL, GROVE, OK, p. A337
INTEGRIS MENTAL HEALTH SYSTEM-WILLOW VIEW, SPENCER, OK, p. A341
INTEGRIS SOUTHWEST MEDICAL CENTER, OKLAHOMA CITY, OK, p. A340
INTER-COMMUNITY MEMORIAL HOSPITAL, NEWFANE, NY, p. A297
INTERFAITH MEDICAL CENTER, NEW YORK, NY, p. A293
INTERGIS BETHANY HOSPITAL, BETHANY, OK, p. A335
INTERGRIS CLINTON REGIONAL HOSPITAL, CLINTON, OK, p. A336
INTRACARE MEDICAL CENTER HOSPITAL, HOUSTON, TX, p. A411
IOANNIS A. LOUGARIS VETERANS AFFAIRS MEDICAL CENTER, RENO, NV, p. A267
IONIA COUNTY MEMORIAL HOSPITAL, IONIA, MI, p. A214
IOWA LUTHERAN HOSPITAL, DES MOINES, IA, p. A149
IOWA MEDICAL AND CLASSIFICATION CENTER, OAKDALE, IA, p. A153
IOWA METHODIST MEDICAL CENTER, DES MOINES, IA, p. A150
IRA DAVENPORT MEMORIAL HOSPITAL, BATH, NY, p. A285
IREDELL MEMORIAL HOSPITAL, STATESVILLE, NC, p. A313
IRELAND ARMY COMMUNITY HOSPITAL, FORT KNOX, KY, p. A170
IRON COUNTY COMMUNITY HOSPITAL, IRON RIVER, MI, p. A214
IROQUOIS MEMORIAL HOSPITAL AND RESIDENT HOME, WATSEKA, IL, p. A136
IRVINE MEDICAL CENTER, IRVINE, CA, p. A45
IRVINGTON GENERAL HOSPITAL, IRVINGTON, NJ, p. A274
IRWIN ARMY COMMUNITY HOSPITAL, FORT RILEY, KS, p. A159
IRWIN COUNTY HOSPITAL, OCILLA, GA, p. A110
ISHAM HEALTH CENTER, ANDOVER, MA, p. A199
ISLAND HOSPITAL, ANACORTES, WA, p. A445
ISLAND MEDICAL CENTER, HEMPSTEAD, NY, p. A289
ITASCA MEDICAL CENTER, GRAND RAPIDS, MN, p. A225
IUKA HOSPITAL, IUKA, MS, p. A236
IVINSON MEMORIAL HOSPITAL, LARAMIE, WY, p. A469

J

J. ARTHUR DOSHER MEMORIAL HOSPITAL, SOUTHPORT, NC, p. A313
J. C. BLAIR MEMORIAL HOSPITAL, HUNTINGDON, PA, p. A355
J. D. MCCARTY CENTER FOR CHILDREN WITH DEVELOPMENTAL DISABILITIES, NORMAN, OK, p. A339
J. F. K. MEDICAL CENTER, ATLANTIS, FL, p. A81
J. PAUL JONES HOSPITAL, CAMDEN, AL, p. A12
JACKSON BROOK INSTITUTE, SOUTH PORTLAND, ME, p. A192
JACKSON COUNTY HOSPITAL, SCOTTSBORO, AL, p. A18
JACKSON COUNTY HOSPITAL, EDNA, TX, p. A405
JACKSON COUNTY MEMORIAL HOSPITAL, ALTUS, OK, p. A335
JACKSON COUNTY PUBLIC HOSPITAL, MAQUOKETA, IA, p. A152
JACKSON GENERAL HOSPITAL, RIPLEY, WV, p. A455
JACKSON HOSPITAL, MARIANNA, FL, p. A90
JACKSON HOSPITAL AND CLINIC, MONTGOMERY, AL, p. A16
JACKSON MEDICAL CENTER, JACKSON, MN, p. A226
JACKSON MEMORIAL HOSPITAL, MIAMI, FL, p. A90

N

P

Q

R

RHEA MEDICAL CENTER, DAYTON, TN, p. A385
RHODE ISLAND HOSPITAL, PROVIDENCE, RI, p. A369
RICE COUNTY HOSPITAL DISTRICT NUMBER ONE, LYONS, KS, p. A162
RICE MEDICAL CENTER, EAGLE LAKE, TX, p. A405
RICE MEMORIAL HOSPITAL, WILLMAR, MN, p. A232
RICHARD H. HUTCHINGS PSYCHIATRIC CENTER, SYRACUSE, NY, p. A301
RICHARD L. ROUDEBUSH VETERANS AFFAIRS MEDICAL CENTER, INDIANAPOLIS, IN, p. A141
RICHARDS MEMORIAL HOSPITAL, ROCKDALE, TX, p. A421
RICHARDSON MEDICAL CENTER, RAYVILLE, LA, p. A186
RICHARDTON HEALTH CENTER, RICHARDTON, ND, p. A318
RICHLAND HOSPITAL, MANSFIELD, OH, p. A329
RICHLAND HOSPITAL, RICHLAND CENTER, WI, p. A465
RICHLAND MEMORIAL HOSPITAL, OLNEY, IL, p. A132
RICHLAND PARISH HOSPITAL–DELHI, DELHI, LA, p. A180
RICHMOND EYE AND EAR HOSPITAL, RICHMOND, VA, p. A442
RICHMOND MEMORIAL HOSPITAL, ROCKINGHAM, NC, p. A312
RICHMOND MEMORIAL HOSPITAL, RICHMOND, VA, p. A442
RICHMOND STATE HOSPITAL, RICHMOND, IN, p. A145
RICHWOOD AREA COMMUNITY HOSPITAL, RICHWOOD, WV, p. A455
RIDDLE MEMORIAL HOSPITAL, MEDIA, PA, p. A358
RIDEOUT MEMORIAL HOSPITAL, MARYSVILLE, CA, p. A52
RIDGECREST HOSPITAL, CLAYTON, GA, p. A104
RIDGECREST REGIONAL HOSPITAL, RIDGECREST, CA, p. A57
RIDGEVIEW INSTITUTE, SMYRNA, GA, p. A111
RIDGEVIEW MEDICAL CENTER, WACONIA, MN, p. A231
RIDGEVIEW PSYCHIATRIC HOSPITAL AND CENTER, OAK RIDGE, TN, p. A392
RILEY MEMORIAL HOSPITAL, MERIDIAN, MS, p. A238
RINGGOLD COUNTY HOSPITAL, MOUNT AYR, IA, p. A153
RIO GRANDE STATE CENTER, HARLINGEN, TX, p. A409
RIO VISTA PHYSICAL REHABILITATION HOSPITAL, EL PASO, TX, p. A405
RIPLEY COUNTY MEMORIAL HOSPITAL, DONIPHAN, MO, p. A243
RIPON MEDICAL CENTER, RIPON, WI, p. A465
RIVENDELL BEHAVIORAL HEALTH SERVICES, BENTON, AR, p. A29
RIVENDELL OF MICHIGAN, SAINT JOHNS, MI, p. A219
RIVER CREST HOSPITAL, SAN ANGELO, TX, p. A422
RIVER DISTRICT HOSPITAL, EAST CHINA, MI, p. A211
RIVER FALLS AREA HOSPITAL, RIVER FALLS, WI, p. A465
RIVER OAKS EAST–WOMAN'S PAVILION, JACKSON, MS, p. A236
RIVER OAKS HOSPITAL, NEW ORLEANS, LA, p. A185
RIVER OAKS HOSPITAL, JACKSON, MS, p. A236
RIVER PARISHES HOSPITAL, LA PLACE, LA, p. A182
RIVER PARK HOSPITAL, MCMINNVILLE, TN, p. A389
RIVER VALLEY HEALTH SYSTEM, IRONTON, OH, p. A327
RIVER WEST MEDICAL CENTER, PLAQUEMINE, LA, p. A186
RIVEREDGE HOSPITAL, FOREST PARK, IL, p. A127
RIVERLAND MEDICAL CENTER, FERRIDAY, LA, p. A180
RIVERSIDE COMMUNITY HOSPITAL, RIVERSIDE, CA, p. A57
RIVERSIDE COUNTY REGIONAL MEDICAL CENTER, MORENO VALLEY, CA, p. A53
RIVERSIDE GENERAL HOSPITAL, HOUSTON, TX, p. A412
RIVERSIDE HEALTH SYSTEM, WICHITA, KS, p. A167
RIVERSIDE MEDICAL CENTER, KANKAKEE, IL, p. A129
RIVERSIDE MEDICAL CENTER, FRANKLINTON, LA, p. A180
RIVERSIDE MEDICAL CENTER, WAUPACA, WI, p. A467
RIVERSIDE MERCY HOSPITAL, TOLEDO, OH, p. A332
RIVERSIDE OSTEOPATHIC HOSPITAL, TRENTON, MI, p. A220
RIVERSIDE REGIONAL MEDICAL CENTER, NEWPORT NEWS, VA, p. A440
RIVERSIDE TAPPAHANNOCK HOSPITAL, TAPPAHANNOCK, VA, p. A443
RIVERSIDE WALTER REED HOSPITAL, GLOUCESTER, VA, p. A438
RIVERVALLEY BEHAVIORAL HEALTH HOSPITAL, OWENSBORO, KY, p. A175
RIVERVIEW HEALTHCARE ASSOCIATION, CROOKSTON, MN, p. A224
RIVERVIEW HOSPITAL, NOBLESVILLE, IN, p. A144
RIVERVIEW HOSPITAL ASSOCIATION, WISCONSIN RAPIDS, WI, p. A467
RIVERVIEW HOSPITAL FOR CHILDREN, MIDDLETOWN, CT, p. A75
RIVERVIEW REGIONAL MEDICAL CENTER, GADSDEN, AL, p. A14
RIVERWOOD HEALTH CARE CENTER, AITKIN, MN, p. A222
ROANE GENERAL HOSPITAL, SPENCER, WV, p. A456
ROANE MEDICAL CENTER, HARRIMAN, TN, p. A386
ROANOKE–CHOWAN HOSPITAL, AHOSKIE, NC, p. A304
ROBERT F. KENNEDY MEDICAL CENTER, HAWTHORNE, CA, p. A45
ROBERT PACKER HOSPITAL, SAYRE, PA, p. A365
ROBERT WOOD JOHNSON UNIVERSITY HOSPITAL, NEW BRUNSWICK, NJ, p. A275

ROBERT WOOD JOHNSON UNIVERSITY HOSPITAL AT HAMILTON, HAMILTON, NJ, p. A273
ROBINSON MEMORIAL HOSPITAL, RAVENNA, OH, p. A331
ROCHELLE COMMUNITY HOSPITAL, ROCHELLE, IL, p. A133
ROCHESTER GENERAL HOSPITAL, ROCHESTER, NY, p. A299
ROCHESTER METHODIST HOSPITAL, ROCHESTER, MN, p. A229
ROCHESTER PSYCHIATRIC CENTER, ROCHESTER, NY, p. A299
ROCK COUNTY HOSPITAL, BASSETT, NE, p. A258
ROCK CREEK CENTER, LEMONT, IL, p. A130
ROCKCASTLE HOSPITAL AND RESPIRATORY CARE CENTER, MOUNT VERNON, KY, p. A175
ROCKDALE HOSPITAL, CONYERS, GA, p. A104
ROCKEFELLER UNIVERSITY HOSPITAL, NEW YORK, NY, p. A295
ROCKFORD CENTER, NEWARK, DE, p. A78
ROCKFORD MEMORIAL HOSPITAL, ROCKFORD, IL, p. A134
ROCKINGHAM MEMORIAL HOSPITAL, HARRISONBURG, VA, p. A438
ROCKLAND CHILDREN'S PSYCHIATRIC CENTER, ORANGEBURG, NY, p. A298
ROCKLAND PSYCHIATRIC CENTER, ORANGEBURG, NY, p. A298
ROCKVILLE GENERAL HOSPITAL, VERNON ROCKVILLE, CT, p. A76
ROGER C. PEACE REHABILITATION HOSPITAL, GREENVILLE, SC, p. A374
ROGER MILLS MEMORIAL HOSPITAL, CHEYENNE, OK, p. A336
ROGER WILLIAMS MEDICAL CENTER, PROVIDENCE, RI, p. A369
ROGERS CITY REHABILITATION HOSPITAL, ROGERS CITY, MI, p. A218
ROGERS MEMORIAL HOSPITAL, OCONOMOWOC, WI, p. A463
ROGUE VALLEY MEDICAL CENTER, MEDFORD, OR, p. A346
ROLLING HILLS HOSPITAL, ADA, OK, p. A335
ROLLING PLAINS MEMORIAL HOSPITAL, SWEETWATER, TX, p. A425
ROME MEMORIAL HOSPITAL, ROME, NY, p. A300
ROOSEVELT HOSPITAL, EDISON, NJ, p. A272
ROOSEVELT MEMORIAL MEDICAL CENTER, CULBERTSON, MT, p. A254
ROOSEVELT WARM SPRINGS INSTITUTE FOR REHABILITATION, WARM SPRINGS, GA, p. A113
ROPER HOSPITAL, CHARLESTON, SC, p. A372
ROPER HOSPITAL NORTH, CHARLESTON, SC, p. A372
ROSE MEDICAL CENTER, DENVER, CO, p. A69
ROSEAU AREA HOSPITAL AND HOMES, ROSEAU, MN, p. A229
ROSEBUD HEALTH CARE CENTER, FORSYTH, MT, p. A254
ROSELAND COMMUNITY HOSPITAL, CHICAGO, IL, p. A124
ROSWELL PARK CANCER INSTITUTE, BUFFALO, NY, p. A286
ROUND ROCK HOSPITAL, ROUND ROCK, TX, p. A422
ROUNDUP MEMORIAL HOSPITAL, ROUNDUP, MT, p. A256
ROUTT MEMORIAL HOSPITAL, STEAMBOAT SPRINGS, CO, p. A72
ROWAN REGIONAL MEDICAL CENTER, SALISBURY, NC, p. A312
ROXBOROUGH MEMORIAL HOSPITAL, PHILADELPHIA, PA, p. A361
ROY H. LAIRD MEMORIAL HOSPITAL, KILGORE, TX, p. A414
ROY LESTER SCHNEIDER HOSPITAL, SAINT THOMAS, VI, p. A474
ROYAL C. JOHNSON VETERANS MEMORIAL HOSPITAL, SIOUX FALLS, SD, p. A381
RUBY VALLEY HOSPITAL, SHERIDAN, MT, p. A256
RUMFORD COMMUNITY HOSPITAL, RUMFORD, ME, p. A191
RUNNELLS SPECIALIZED HOSPITAL, BERKELEY HEIGHTS, NJ, p. A271
RUSH CITY HOSPITAL, RUSH CITY, MN, p. A229
RUSH COUNTY HEALTHCARE CENTER, LA CROSSE, KS, p. A161
RUSH FOUNDATION HOSPITAL, MERIDIAN, MS, p. A238
RUSH MEMORIAL HOSPITAL, RUSHVILLE, IN, p. A145
RUSH NORTH SHORE MEDICAL CENTER, SKOKIE, IL, p. A134
RUSH–COPLEY MEMORIAL HOSPITAL, AURORA, IL, p. A120
RUSH–PRESBYTERIAN–ST. LUKE'S MEDICAL CENTER, CHICAGO, IL, p. A124
RUSK COUNTY MEMORIAL HOSPITAL AND NURSING HOME, LADYSMITH, WI, p. A460
RUSK STATE HOSPITAL, RUSK, TX, p. A422
RUSSELL COUNTY HOSPITAL, RUSSELL SPRINGS, KY, p. A176
RUSSELL COUNTY MEDICAL CENTER, LEBANON, VA, p. A439
RUSSELL HOSPITAL, ALEXANDER CITY, AL, p. A11
RUSSELL REGIONAL HOSPITAL, RUSSELL, KS, p. A165
RUTHERFORD HOSPITAL, RUTHERFORDTON, NC, p. A312
RUTLAND REGIONAL MEDICAL CENTER, RUTLAND, VT, p. A434
RYDER MEMORIAL HOSPITAL, HUMACAO, PR, p. A472
RYE HOSPITAL CENTER, RYE, NY, p. A300

S

SABETHA COMMUNITY HOSPITAL, SABETHA, KS, p. A165
SABINE COUNTY HOSPITAL, HEMPHILL, TX, p. A409

SABINE MEDICAL CENTER, MANY, LA, p. A183
SAC–OSAGE HOSPITAL, OSCEOLA, MO, p. A248
SACRED HEART HEALTH SERVICES, YANKTON, SD, p. A382
SACRED HEART HOSPITAL, CHICAGO, IL, p. A124
SACRED HEART HOSPITAL, CUMBERLAND, MD, p. A195
SACRED HEART HOSPITAL, ALLENTOWN, PA, p. A349
SACRED HEART HOSPITAL, EAU CLAIRE, WI, p. A459
SACRED HEART HOSPITAL OF PENSACOLA, PENSACOLA, FL, p. A94
SACRED HEART MEDICAL CENTER, EUGENE, OR, p. A345
SACRED HEART MEDICAL CENTER, SPOKANE, WA, p. A450
SACRED HEART REHABILITATION INSTITUTE, MILWAUKEE, WI, p. A462
SACRED HEART–ST. MARY'S HOSPITALS, RHINELANDER, WI, p. A465
SADDLEBACK MEMORIAL MEDICAL CENTER, LAGUNA HILLS, CA, p. A46
SAGAMORE CHILDREN'S PSYCHIATRIC CENTER, HUNTINGTON STATION, NY, p. A289
SAGE MEMORIAL HOSPITAL, GANADO, AZ, p. A23
SAGINAW GENERAL HOSPITAL, SAGINAW, MI, p. A218
SAINT AGNES MEDICAL CENTER, FRESNO, CA, p. A43
SAINT ALPHONSUS REGIONAL MEDICAL CENTER, BOISE, ID, p. A116
SAINT ANNE'S HOSPITAL, FALL RIVER, MA, p. A202
SAINT ANTHONY HOSPITAL, CHICAGO, IL, p. A124
SAINT ANTHONY MEDICAL CENTER, ROCKFORD, IL, p. A134
SAINT ANTHONY MEMORIAL HEALTH CENTERS, MICHIGAN CITY, IN, p. A143
SAINT ANTHONY'S HEALTH CENTER, ALTON, IL, p. A120
SAINT BARNABAS MEDICAL CENTER, LIVINGSTON, NJ, p. A274
SAINT BERNARD HOSPITAL AND HEALTH CARE CENTER, CHICAGO, IL, p. A124
SAINT EUGENE MEDICAL CENTER, DILLON, SC, p. A373
SAINT FRANCIS HOSPITAL, POUGHKEEPSIE, NY, p. A299
SAINT FRANCIS HOSPITAL, TULSA, OK, p. A342
SAINT FRANCIS HOSPITAL, MEMPHIS, TN, p. A390
SAINT FRANCIS HOSPITAL, CHARLESTON, WV, p. A452
SAINT FRANCIS HOSPITAL AND HEALTH CENTER, BLUE ISLAND, IL, p. A121
SAINT FRANCIS HOSPITAL AND MEDICAL CENTER, HARTFORD, CT, p. A74
SAINT FRANCIS MEDICAL CENTER, PEORIA, IL, p. A133
SAINT FRANCIS MEDICAL CENTER, CAPE GIRARDEAU, MO, p. A242
SAINT FRANCIS MEDICAL CENTER, GRAND ISLAND, NE, p. A260
SAINT FRANCIS MEMORIAL HOSPITAL, SAN FRANCISCO, CA, p. A60
SAINT JAMES HOSPITAL, PONTIAC, IL, p. A133
SAINT JAMES HOSPITAL OF NEWARK, NEWARK, NJ, p. A275
SAINT JOHN HOSPITAL, LEAVENWORTH, KS, p. A162
SAINT JOHN'S HEALTH SYSTEM, ANDERSON, IN, p. A137
SAINT JOHN'S HOSPITAL AND HEALTH CENTER, SANTA MONICA, CA, p. A63
SAINT JOSEPH COMMUNITY HOSPITAL, NEW HAMPTON, IA, p. A153
SAINT JOSEPH HEALTH CENTER, KANSAS CITY, MO, p. A245
SAINT JOSEPH HOSPITAL, EUREKA, CA, p. A42
SAINT JOSEPH HOSPITAL, BELVIDERE, IL, p. A121
SAINT JOSEPH HOSPITAL & HEALTH CENTER, KOKOMO, IN, p. A142
SAINT JOSEPH'S HOSPITAL, MARSHFIELD, WI, p. A461
SAINT JOSEPH'S HOSPITAL OF ATLANTA, ATLANTA, GA, p. A101
SAINT JOSEPH'S HOSPITAL OF MARSHALL COUNTY, PLYMOUTH, IN, p. A144
SAINT LOUIS UNIVERSITY HOSPITAL, SAINT LOUIS, MO, p. A250
SAINT LOUISE HOSPITAL, MORGAN HILL, CA, p. A53
SAINT LUKE INSTITUTE, SILVER SPRING, MD, p. A198
SAINT LUKE'S HOSPITAL, KANSAS CITY, MO, p. A245
SAINT LUKE'S MEDICAL CENTER, CLEVELAND, OH, p. A324
SAINT LUKE'S NORTHLAND HOSPITAL, KANSAS CITY, MO, p. A245
SAINT LUKE'S NORTHLAND HOSPITAL–SMITHVILLE CAMPUS, SMITHVILLE, MO, p. A251
SAINT MARGARET MERCY HEALTHCARE CENTERS, HAMMOND, IN, p. A140
SAINT MARY MEDICAL CENTER, LONG BEACH, CA, p. A48
SAINT MARY OF NAZARETH HOSPITAL CENTER, CHICAGO, IL, p. A124
SAINT MARY'S HEALTH SERVICES, GRAND RAPIDS, MI, p. A213
SAINT MARY'S MEDICAL CENTER, RACINE, WI, p. A465
SAINT MARY'S REGIONAL MEDICAL CENTER, RUSSELLVILLE, AR, p. A34
SAINT MARY'S REGIONAL MEDICAL CENTER, RENO, NV, p. A267
SAINT MARYS HOSPITAL, ROCHESTER, MN, p. A229
SAINT MICHAEL HOSPITAL, CLEVELAND, OH, p. A324

T

U

V

VICKSBURG MEDICAL CENTER, VICKSBURG, MS, p. A240
VICTOR VALLEY COMMUNITY HOSPITAL, VICTORVILLE, CA, p. A66
VICTORIA REGIONAL MEDICAL CENTER, VICTORIA, TX, p. A427
VICTORY MEDICAL CENTER, STANLEY, WI, p. A466
VICTORY MEMORIAL HOSPITAL, WAUKEGAN, IL, p. A136
VICTORY MEMORIAL HOSPITAL, NEW YORK, NY, p. A296
VILLA FELICIANA MEDICAL COMPLEX, JACKSON, LA, p. A181
VILLA MARIA HOSPITAL, NORTH MIAMI, FL, p. A92
VILLAVIEW COMMUNITY HOSPITAL, SAN DIEGO, CA, p. A60
VILLE PLATTE MEDICAL CENTER, VILLE PLATTE, LA, p. A188
VINELAND DEVELOPMENTAL CENTER HOSPITAL, VINELAND, NJ, p. A278
VIRGINIA BAPTIST HOSPITAL, LYNCHBURG, VA, p. A439
VIRGINIA BEACH GENERAL HOSPITAL, VIRGINIA BEACH, VA, p. A444
VIRGINIA GAY HOSPITAL, VINTON, IA, p. A155
VIRGINIA MASON MEDICAL CENTER, SEATTLE, WA, p. A449
VIRGINIA REGIONAL MEDICAL CENTER, VIRGINIA, MN, p. A231
VOLUNTEER GENERAL HOSPITAL, MARTIN, TN, p. A389

W

W. A. FOOTE MEMORIAL HOSPITAL, JACKSON, MI, p. A214
W. J. BARGE MEMORIAL HOSPITAL, GREENVILLE, SC, p. A374
W. J. MANGOLD MEMORIAL HOSPITAL, LOCKNEY, TX, p. A416
WABASH COUNTY HOSPITAL, WABASH, IN, p. A146
WABASH GENERAL HOSPITAL DISTRICT, MOUNT CARMEL, IL, p. A131
WABASH VALLEY HOSPITAL, WEST LAFAYETTE, IN, p. A146
WADLEY REGIONAL MEDICAL CENTER, TEXARKANA, TX, p. A426
WADSWORTH–RITTMAN HOSPITAL, WADSWORTH, OH, p. A333
WAGNER COMMUNITY MEMORIAL HOSPITAL, WAGNER, SD, p. A382
WAGNER GENERAL HOSPITAL, PALACIOS, TX, p. A419
WAGONER COMMUNITY HOSPITAL, WAGONER, OK, p. A343
WAHIAWA GENERAL HOSPITAL, WAHIAWA, HI, p. A115
WAKE COUNTY ALCOHOLISM TREATMENT CENTER, RALEIGH, NC, p. A312
WAKE MEDICAL CENTER, RALEIGH, NC, p. A312
WALDO COUNTY GENERAL HOSPITAL, BELFAST, ME, p. A189
WALKER BAPTIST MEDICAL CENTER, JASPER, AL, p. A15
WALLA WALLA GENERAL HOSPITAL, WALLA WALLA, WA, p. A451
WALLACE THOMSON HOSPITAL, UNION, SC, p. A377
WALLOWA MEMORIAL HOSPITAL, ENTERPRISE, OR, p. A344
WALLS REGIONAL HOSPITAL, CLEBURNE, TX, p. A400
WALTER B. JONES ALCOHOL AND DRUG ABUSE TREATMENT CENTER, GREENVILLE, NC, p. A309
WALTER KNOX MEMORIAL HOSPITAL, EMMETT, ID, p. A117
WALTER O. BOSWELL MEMORIAL HOSPITAL, SUN CITY, AZ, p. A26
WALTER OLIN MOSS REGIONAL MEDICAL CENTER, LAKE CHARLES, LA, p. A182
WALTER P. REUTHER PSYCHIATRIC HOSPITAL, WESTLAND, MI, p. A221
WALTER REED ARMY MEDICAL CENTER, WASHINGTON, DC, p. A79
WALTHALL COUNTY GENERAL HOSPITAL, TYLERTOWN, MS, p. A240
WALTON MEDICAL CENTER, MONROE, GA, p. A109
WALTON REGIONAL HOSPITAL, DE FUNIAK SPRINGS, FL, p. A83
WALTON REHABILITATION HOSPITAL, AUGUSTA, GA, p. A102
WAMEGO CITY HOSPITAL, WAMEGO, KS, p. A166
WARD MEMORIAL HOSPITAL, MONAHANS, TX, p. A418
WARM SPRINGS AND BAPTIST REHABILITATION HOSPITAL, SAN ANTONIO, TX, p. A424
WARM SPRINGS REHABILITATION HOSPITAL, GONZALES, TX, p. A408
WARRACK MEDICAL CENTER HOSPITAL, SANTA ROSA, CA, p. A63
WARREN G. MAGNUSON CLINICAL CENTER, NATIONAL INSTITUTES OF HEALTH, BETHESDA, MD, p. A195
WARREN GENERAL HOSPITAL, WARREN, PA, p. A367
WARREN HOSPITAL, PHILLIPSBURG, NJ, p. A276
WARREN MEMORIAL HOSPITAL, FRIEND, NE, p. A260
WARREN MEMORIAL HOSPITAL, FRONT ROYAL, VA, p. A438
WARREN STATE HOSPITAL, NORTH WARREN, PA, p. A359
WASATCH COUNTY HOSPITAL, HEBER CITY, UT, p. A430
WASECA AREA MEDICAL CENTER, WASECA, MN, p. A232
WASHAKIE MEMORIAL HOSPITAL, WORLAND, WY, p. A470
WASHINGTON ADVENTIST HOSPITAL, TAKOMA PARK, MD, p. A198
WASHINGTON COUNTY HOSPITAL, NASHVILLE, IL, p. A131
WASHINGTON COUNTY HOSPITAL, WASHINGTON, IA, p. A155
WASHINGTON COUNTY HOSPITAL, WASHINGTON, KS, p. A166

WASHINGTON COUNTY HOSPITAL, PLYMOUTH, NC, p. A311
WASHINGTON COUNTY HOSPITAL ASSOCIATION, HAGERSTOWN, MD, p. A196
WASHINGTON COUNTY INFIRMARY AND NURSING HOME, CHATOM, AL, p. A13
WASHINGTON COUNTY MEMORIAL HOSPITAL, SALEM, IN, p. A145
WASHINGTON COUNTY MEMORIAL HOSPITAL, POTOSI, MO, p. A248
WASHINGTON COUNTY REGIONAL HOSPITAL, SANDERSVILLE, GA, p. A111
WASHINGTON HOSPITAL, WASHINGTON, PA, p. A367
WASHINGTON HOSPITAL CENTER, WASHINGTON, DC, p. A80
WASHINGTON MEDICAL CENTER, CULVER CITY, CA, p. A40
WASHINGTON REGIONAL MEDICAL CENTER, FAYETTEVILLE, AR, p. A30
WASHINGTON TOWNSHIP HEALTH CARE DISTRICT, FREMONT, CA, p. A43
WASHINGTON–ST. TAMMANY REGIONAL MEDICAL CENTER, BOGALUSA, LA, p. A179
WASHOE MEDICAL CENTER, RENO, NV, p. A267
WATAUGA MEDICAL CENTER, BOONE, NC, p. A305
WATERBURY HOSPITAL, WATERBURY, CT, p. A77
WATERTOWN MEMORIAL HOSPITAL, WATERTOWN, WI, p. A466
WATONGA MUNICIPAL HOSPITAL, WATONGA, OK, p. A343
WATSONVILLE COMMUNITY HOSPITAL, WATSONVILLE, CA, p. A66
WAUKESHA MEMORIAL HOSPITAL, WAUKESHA, WI, p. A466
WAUPUN MEMORIAL HOSPITAL, WAUPUN, WI, p. A467
WAUSAU HOSPITAL, WAUSAU, WI, p. A467
WAVERLY MUNICIPAL HOSPITAL, WAVERLY, IA, p. A155
WAYNE COUNTY HOSPITAL, CORYDON, IA, p. A148
WAYNE COUNTY HOSPITAL, MONTICELLO, KY, p. A174
WAYNE GENERAL HOSPITAL, WAYNESBORO, MS, p. A240
WAYNE GENERAL HOSPITAL, WAYNE, NJ, p. A279
WAYNE HOSPITAL, GREENVILLE, OH, p. A327
WAYNE MEDICAL CENTER, WAYNESBORO, TN, p. A393
WAYNE MEMORIAL HOSPITAL, JESUP, GA, p. A108
WAYNE MEMORIAL HOSPITAL, GOLDSBORO, NC, p. A308
WAYNE MEMORIAL HOSPITAL, HONESDALE, PA, p. A355
WEBSTER COUNTY COMMUNITY HOSPITAL, RED CLOUD, NE, p. A263
WEBSTER COUNTY MEMORIAL HOSPITAL, WEBSTER SPRINGS, WV, p. A456
WEBSTER HEALTH SERVICES, EUPORA, MS, p. A235
WEDOWEE HOSPITAL, WEDOWEE, AL, p. A19
WEED ARMY COMMUNITY HOSPITAL, FORT IRWIN, CA, p. A42
WEEKS MEMORIAL HOSPITAL, LANCASTER, NH, p. A269
WEINER MEMORIAL MEDICAL CENTER, MARSHALL, MN, p. A227
WEIRTON MEDICAL CENTER, WEIRTON, WV, p. A456
WEISBROD MEMORIAL HOSPITAL, EADS, CO, p. A70
WELBORN MEMORIAL BAPTIST HOSPITAL, EVANSVILLE, IN, p. A139
WELLINGTON REGIONAL MEDICAL CENTER, WEST PALM BEACH, FL, p. A99
WELLMONT BRISTOL REGIONAL MEDICAL CENTER, BRISTOL, TN, p. A383
WELLMONT HOLSTON VALLEY MEDICAL CENTER, KINGSPORT, TN, p. A387
WELLS COMMUNITY HOSPITAL, BLUFFTON, IN, p. A137
WELLSPRING FOUNDATION, BETHLEHEM, CT, p. A74
WELLSTAR COBB HOSPITAL, AUSTELL, GA, p. A102
WELLSTAR DOUGLAS HOSPITAL, DOUGLASVILLE, GA, p. A105
WELLSTAR KENNESTONE HOSPITAL, MARIETTA, GA, p. A109
WELLSTAR PAULDING HOSPITAL, DALLAS, GA, p. A105
WELLSTAR WINDY HILL HOSPITAL, MARIETTA, GA, p. A109
WELSH GENERAL HOSPITAL, WELSH, LA, p. A188
WENTWORTH–DOUGLASS HOSPITAL, DOVER, NH, p. A268
WERNERSVILLE STATE HOSPITAL, WERNERSVILLE, PA, p. A367
WESKOTA MEMORIAL MEDICAL CENTER, WESSINGTON SPRINGS, SD, p. A382
WESLEY MEDICAL CENTER, WICHITA, KS, p. A167
WESLEY MEDICAL CENTER, HATTIESBURG, MS, p. A235
WESLEY REHABILITATION HOSPITAL, WICHITA, KS, p. A167
WESLEY WOODS GERIATRIC HOSPITAL, ATLANTA, GA, p. A101
WEST ALLIS MEMORIAL HOSPITAL, WEST ALLIS, WI, p. A467
WEST ANAHEIM MEDICAL CENTER, ANAHEIM, CA, p. A36
WEST BOCA MEDICAL CENTER, BOCA RATON, FL, p. A81
WEST CALCASIEU CAMERON HOSPITAL, SULPHUR, LA, p. A187
WEST CARROLL MEMORIAL HOSPITAL, OAK GROVE, LA, p. A186
WEST CENTRAL COMMUNITY HOSPITAL, CLINTON, IN, p. A138
WEST COMMUNITY HOSPITAL, WEST, TX, p. A428
WEST FELICIANA PARISH HOSPITAL, SAINT FRANCISVILLE, LA, p. A186
WEST FLORIDA REGIONAL MEDICAL CENTER, PENSACOLA, FL, p. A94
WEST GEORGIA HEALTH SYSTEM, LA GRANGE, GA, p. A108

WEST HOLT MEMORIAL HOSPITAL, ATKINSON, NE, p. A258
WEST HUDSON HOSPITAL, KEARNY, NJ, p. A274
WEST JEFFERSON MEDICAL CENTER, MARRERO, LA, p. A183
WEST JERSEY HOSPITAL–BERLIN, BERLIN, NJ, p. A271
WEST JERSEY HOSPITAL–CAMDEN, CAMDEN, NJ, p. A272
WEST JERSEY HOSPITAL–MARLTON, MARLTON, NJ, p. A274
WEST JERSEY HOSPITAL–VOORHEES, VOORHEES, NJ, p. A279
WEST OAKS HOSPITAL, HOUSTON, TX, p. A413
WEST PACES MEDICAL CENTER, ATLANTA, GA, p. A102
WEST PARK HOSPITAL, CODY, WY, p. A468
WEST RIVER REGIONAL MEDICAL CENTER, HETTINGER, ND, p. A317
WEST SHORE HOSPITAL, MANISTEE, MI, p. A216
WEST SIDE DISTRICT HOSPITAL, TAFT, CA, p. A64
WEST SUBURBAN HOSPITAL MEDICAL CENTER, OAK PARK, IL, p. A132
WEST VALLEY MEDICAL CENTER, CALDWELL, ID, p. A116
WEST VIRGINIA UNIVERSITY HOSPITALS, MORGANTOWN, WV, p. A454
WESTBOROUGH STATE HOSPITAL, WESTBOROUGH, MA, p. A207
WESTBRIDGE TREATMENT CENTER, PHOENIX, AZ, p. A25
WESTBROOK COMMUNITY HOSPITAL, WESTBROOK, ME, p. A192
WESTBROOK HEALTH CENTER, WESTBROOK, MN, p. A232
WESTCHESTER GENERAL HOSPITAL, MIAMI, FL, p. A91
WESTCHESTER MEDICAL CENTER, VALHALLA, NY, p. A302
WESTCHESTER SQUARE MEDICAL CENTER, NEW YORK, NY, p. A296
WESTERLY HOSPITAL, WESTERLY, RI, p. A370
WESTERN ARIZONA REGIONAL MEDICAL CENTER, BULLHEAD CITY, AZ, p. A22
WESTERN BAPTIST HOSPITAL, PADUCAH, KY, p. A175
WESTERN MARYLAND CENTER, HAGERSTOWN, MD, p. A196
WESTERN MEDICAL CENTER HOSPITAL ANAHEIM, ANAHEIM, CA, p. A36
WESTERN MEDICAL CENTER–SANTA ANA, SANTA ANA, CA, p. A62
WESTERN MENTAL HEALTH INSTITUTE, WESTERN INSTITUTE, TN, p. A393
WESTERN MISSOURI MEDICAL CENTER, WARRENSBURG, MO, p. A252
WESTERN MISSOURI MENTAL HEALTH CENTER, KANSAS CITY, MO, p. A246
WESTERN NEW YORK CHILDREN'S PSYCHIATRIC CENTER, BUFFALO, NY, p. A286
WESTERN PENNSYLVANIA HOSPITAL, PITTSBURGH, PA, p. A364
WESTERN PLAINS REGIONAL HOSPITAL, DODGE CITY, KS, p. A158
WESTERN QUEENS COMMUNITY HOSPITAL, NEW YORK, NY, p. A296
WESTERN STATE HOSPITAL, HOPKINSVILLE, KY, p. A171
WESTERN STATE HOSPITAL, STAUNTON, VA, p. A443
WESTERN STATE HOSPITAL, TACOMA, WA, p. A451
WESTERN STATE PSYCHIATRIC CENTER, FORT SUPPLY, OK, p. A337
WESTFIELD MEMORIAL HOSPITAL, WESTFIELD, NY, p. A303
WESTLAKE REGIONAL HOSPITAL, COLUMBIA, KY, p. A169
WESTMORELAND REGIONAL HOSPITAL, GREENSBURG, PA, p. A354
WESTON COUNTY HEALTH SERVICES, NEWCASTLE, WY, p. A469
WESTSIDE REGIONAL MEDICAL CENTER, PLANTATION, FL, p. A94
WESTVIEW HOSPITAL, INDIANAPOLIS, IN, p. A141
WESTWOOD LODGE HOSPITAL, WESTWOOD, MA, p. A207
WESTWOOD MEDICAL CENTER, MIDLAND, TX, p. A418
WETUMKA GENERAL HOSPITAL, WETUMKA, OK, p. A343
WETZEL COUNTY HOSPITAL, NEW MARTINSVILLE, WV, p. A454
WHEATLAND MEMORIAL HOSPITAL, HARLOWTON, MT, p. A255
WHEATON COMMUNITY HOSPITAL, WHEATON, MN, p. A232
WHEELER COUNTY HOSPITAL, GLENWOOD, GA, p. A107
WHEELING HOSPITAL, WHEELING, WV, p. A456
WHIDBEY GENERAL HOSPITAL, COUPEVILLE, WA, p. A446
WHITE COMMUNITY HOSPITAL, AURORA, MN, p. A222
WHITE COUNTY COMMUNITY HOSPITAL, SPARTA, TN, p. A393
WHITE COUNTY MEDICAL CENTER, SEARCY, AR, p. A35
WHITE COUNTY MEDICAL CENTER, CARMI, IL, p. A121
WHITE COUNTY MEMORIAL HOSPITAL, MONTICELLO, IN, p. A143
WHITE MEMORIAL MEDICAL CENTER, LOS ANGELES, CA, p. A51
WHITE MOUNTAIN REGIONAL MEDICAL CENTER, SPRINGERVILLE, AZ, p. A26
WHITE PLAINS HOSPITAL CENTER, WHITE PLAINS, NY, p. A303
WHITE RIVER MEDICAL CENTER, BATESVILLE, AR, p. A29
WHITESBURG APPALACHIAN REGIONAL HOSPITAL, WHITESBURG, KY, p. A177

Y

Z

This section is an index of the key health care professionals for the hospitals and/or health care systems listed in this publication. The index is in alphabetical order, by individual, followed by the title, institutional affiliation, city, state and page reference to the hospital and/or health care system listing in section A and/or B.

A

AARON Jr., Frank J., Chief Executive Officer, Margaret R. Pardee Memorial Hospital, Hendersonville, NC, p. A309

AASVED, Craig E., Administrator, Wheatland Memorial Hospital, Harlowton, MT, p. A255

ABBOTT, Stephen L., President and Chief Executive Officer, Battle Creek Health System, Battle Creek, MI, p. A208

ABBOTT, William S., Administrator, Gainesville Memorial Hospital, Gainesville, TX, p. A407

ABBUHL, Carol A., Chief Executive Officer, Perkins County Health Services, Grant, NE, p. A260

ABELL, Richard M., President and Chief Executive Officer, Saint Joseph Health Center, Kansas City, MO, p. A245

ABLOW, Ronald C., M.D., President and Chief Executive Officer, St. Luke's–Roosevelt Hospital Center, New York, NY, p. A296

ABRAMS, Deborah L., Chief Executive Officer, Vencor Seattle Hospital, Seattle, WA, p. A449

ABRAMS, Larry, Administrator, Potomac Valley Hospital, Keyser, WV, p. A454

ABREU, Astrid, Administrator, Clinica San Agustin, Manati, PR, p. A473

ABRUTZ Jr., Joseph F., Administrator, Cameron Community Hospital, Cameron, MO, p. A241

ACKER, David B., Chief Executive Officer, Charles Cole Memorial Hospital, Coudersport, PA, p. A352

ACKER, Peter W., President and Chief Executive Officer, Lincoln Medical Center, Lincolnton, NC, p. A310

ACKLEY, Michael, Administrator, Fergus Falls Regional Treatment Center, Fergus Falls, MN, p. A225

ACKLEY, Richard Michael, Administrator and Chief Executive Officer, Forest Hospital, Des Plaines, IL, p. A125

ADAIR, Jerry D., President and Chief Executive Officer, Good Shepherd Medical Center, Longview, TX, p. A416

ADAMS, Alice G., Administrator, Columbia Mainland Medical Center, Texas City, TX, p. A426

ADAMS, Charles T., Interim Chief Executive Officer, Highsmith–Rainey Memorial Hospital, Fayetteville, NC, p. A308

ADAMS, Daniel F., President and Chief Executive Officer, Presbyterian Intercommunity Hospital, Whittier, CA, p. A67

ADAMS, Harry F., Administrator, Washington Medical Center, Culver City, CA, p. A40

ADAMS, Jerry W., President, Sumter Regional Hospital, Americus, GA, p. A100

ADAMS, John F., Chief Executive Officer, Columbia Medical Center of Sherman, Sherman, TX, p. A424

ADAMS, Judy, Administrator and Chief Executive Officer, Little River Memorial Hospital, Ashdown, AR, p. A29

ADAMS, Mark, Chief Executive Officer, West Valley Medical Center, Caldwell, ID, p. A116

ADAMS, Mark A., President and Chief Executive Officer, Mississippi Methodist Hospital and Rehabilitation Center, Jackson, MS, p. A236

ADAMS, Richard, Ph.D., Administrator, BHC Cedar Vista Hospital, Fresno, CA, p. A43

ADAMS, Scott K., Chief Executive Officer, Pullman Memorial Hospital, Pullman, WA, p. A448

ADAMS, Wayne, Chief Executive Officer, Charter Behavioral Health System of Charlottesville, Charlottesville, VA, p. A436

ADAMS, William A., President and Chief Executive Officer, Columbia Reston Hospital Center, Reston, VA, p. A441

ADAMS, Nancy R., Commander, Tripler Army Medical Center, Honolulu, HI, p. A114

ADAMS, Clint E., USN, Commanding Officer, Naval Hospital, Beaufort, SC, p. A371

ADDISON, Wilfred J., President and Chief Executive Officer, Inland Hospital, Waterville, ME, p. A192

ADELUNG, Louisa F., President and Chief Executive Officer, The Institute for Rehabilitation and Research, Houston, TX, p. A412

ADKINS Jr., Charles I., President, Holzer Medical Center, Gallipolis, OH, p. A327

ADLER, Karl P., M.D., President and Chief Executive Officer, Saint Vincent's Hospital and Medical Center of New York, New York, NY, p. A295

AENCHBACHER Jr., Arthur E., Administrator, Wilford Hall Medical Center, Lackland AFB, TX, p. A415

AFSARIFARD, Farshid, Executive Director, UHHS Laurelwood Hospital, Willoughby, OH, p. A334

AGNEW, Nettie L., R.N., Interim President and Chief Executive Officer, North Kansas City Hospital, North Kansas City, MO, p. A247

AHEARN, John R., Co–Chief Executive Officer, Hospital for Special Surgery, New York, NY, p. A293

AHLFELD, Richard B., President, Children's Specialized Hospital, Mountainside, NJ, p. A275

AINSLEY, Howard, Director, Carilion Bedford Memorial Hospital, Bedford, VA, p. A436

AINSWORTH, Larry K., President and Chief Executive Officer, St. Joseph Hospital, Orange, CA, p. A55

AITCHISON, Kenneth W., President and Chief Executive Officer, Kessler Institute for Rehabilitation, West Orange, NJ, p. A279

AKERS, Cynthia O., R.N., Administrator, Hamilton County Hospital, Syracuse, KS, p. A166

ALBARANO, Francis G., Administrator, Fayette County Memorial Hospital, Washington Court House, OH, p. A333

ALBAUGH, John C., President and Chief Executive Officer, Fort Atkinson Memorial Health Services, Fort Atkinson, WI, p. A459

ALBERT, Anna, Chief Executive Officer, U. S. Public Health Service Phoenix Indian Medical Center, Phoenix, AZ, p. A25

ALBERTY, Allen P., Chief Executive Officer, Shamrock General Hospital, Shamrock, TX, p. A424

ALBRIGHT, James W., President and Chief Executive Officer, Rex Healthcare, Raleigh, NC, p. A312

ALCHESAY–NACHU, Carla, Service Unit Director, U. S. Public Health Service Indian Hospital, Whiteriver, AZ, p. A27

ALCINI, Anthony J.

President and Chief Executive Officer, Tarrant County Hospital District, Fort Worth, TX, p. A407

President and Chief Executive Officer, Tarrant County Hospital District, Fort Worth, TX, p. B143

ALDERELE, Felix, Administrator, Las Vegas Medical Center, Las Vegas, NM, p. A282

ALDRED, Richard, Chief Administrative Officer, St. Dominic's Hospital, Manteca, CA, p. A52

ALECCI, Carmen Bruce, Executive Director, West Hudson Hospital, Kearny, NJ, p. A274

ALEMAN, Ralph A., Chief Executive Officer, Cedars Medical Center, Miami, FL, p. A90

ALEXANDER, Keith N., Administrator and Chief Operating Officer, American Fork Hospital, American Fork, UT, p. A407

ALEXANDER, Les, Administrator, Pushmataha County–Town of Antlers Hospital Authority, Antlers, OK, p. A335

ALEXANDER, Michael, Administrator, Clinch Memorial Hospital, Homerville, GA, p. A107

ALLEE, Al, Administrator, Harmon Memorial Hospital, Hollis, OK, p. A338

ALLEN, Richard L., Chief Executive Officer, Mid–America Rehabilitation Hospital, Overland Park, KS, p. A164

ALLEN, Robert W., Administrator, Evanston Regional Hospital, Evanston, WY, p. A468

ALLEN, Sam J., Administrator, Community Hospital of Anaconda, Anaconda, MT, p. A253

ALLEN, Terry H., Executive Director, 45th Street Mental Health Center, West Palm Beach, FL, p. A99

ALLEN, Timothy, Chief Executive Officer, Charter Behavioral Health System of Southern California/Mission Viejo, Mission Viejo, CA, p. A52

ALLEN, Greg, USAF, Administrator, U. S. Air Force Hospital, Edwards AFB, CA, p. A41

ALLEN, David M., MSC, Administrator, U. S. Air Force Hospital Dover, Dover, DE, p. A78

ALLEN II, Percy, FACHE, Vice President Hospital Affairs and Chief Executive Officer, University Hospital of Brooklyn–State University of New York Health Science Center at Brooklyn, New York, NY, p. A296

ALLEY, Frederick D., President and Chief Executive Officer, Brooklyn Hospital Center, New York, NY, p. A291

ALLEY, Richard S.

Regional Vice President and Administrator, Arrowhead Community Hospital and Medical Center, Glendale, AZ, p. A23

Chief Executive Officer, Phoenix Baptist Hospital and Medical Center, Phoenix, AZ, p. A25

ALLEY, Carl M., MSC, Deputy Commander and Administrator, U. S. Air Force Hospital Robins, Robins AFB, GA, p. A110

ALLMAN, Roger J., Chief Executive Officer, King's Daughters' Hospital, Madison, IN, p. A143

ALRED, Billy, Interim Administrator, Camden General Hospital, Camden, TN, p. A383

ALTMILLER, Steve

Chief Executive Officer, Sharpstown General Hospital, Houston, TX, p. A412

Chief Executive Officer, Twelve Oaks Hospital, Houston, TX, p. A412

ALTON, Aaron, President, Sisters of Mary of the Presentation Health Corporation, Fargo, ND, p. B138

ALVAREZ, Frank D., Chief Executive Officer, Maricopa Medical Center, Phoenix, AZ, p. A25

ALVAREZ, Guadalupe, Administrator, State Psychiatric Hospital, San Juan, PR, p. A474

ALVIN, William R., President, Henry Ford Wyandotte Hospital, Wyandotte, MI, p. A221

ALVIS, Harry, Chief Executive Officer, Parkview Regional Medical Center, Vicksburg, MS, p. A240

AMAN, Dale, Administrator, Community Memorial Hospital, Turtle Lake, ND, p. A319

AMBROSIANI, Craig, Executive Director, San Juan Hospital, Monticello, UT, p. A431

AMEEN, David J., President and Chief Executive Officer, Saint Mary's Health Services, Grand Rapids, MI, p. A213

AMEER, Adil M., President and Chief Executive Officer, Rapid City Regional Hospital System of Care, Rapid City, SD, p. A380

AMENT, Rick, President and Chief Executive Officer, Bay Area Medical Center, Marinette, WI, p. A461

AMOS, James L., President, Margaret Mary Community Hospital, Batesville, IN, p. A137

AMOS, Helen, President and Chief Executive Officer, Mercy Medical Center, Baltimore, MD, p. A194

AMSTUTZ, Terry L., CHE, Chief Executive Officer and Administrator, Medical Center of Calico Rock, Calico Rock, AR, p. A29

ANAEBONAM, Nneka, Administrator, Isham Health Center, Andover, MA, p. A199

ANASTASIO, Lance W., President, Winter Haven Hospital, Winter Haven, FL, p. A99

ANCELL, Charles D., President, Missouri Delta Medical Center, Sikeston, MO, p. A251

ANCHO, Kathy, Administrator, Battle Mountain General Hospital, Battle Mountain, NV, p. A266

ANDERSEN, David, President and Chief Executive Officer, Saratoga Hospital, Saratoga Springs, NY, p. A300

ANDERSEN, Edward, President and Chief Executive Officer, CGH Medical Center, Sterling, IL, p. A135

ANDERSON, C. Edward, Administrator, Linden Municipal Hospital, Linden, TX, p. A415

ANDERSON, Collette, Administrator, McKenzie County Memorial Hospital, Watford City, ND, p. A319

ANDERSON, Daniel K., Senior Vice President and Administrtor, Fairview Lakes Regional Medical Center, Wyoming, MN, p. A232

ANDERSON, Darleen S., MSN, Site Administrator, Sentara Leigh Hospital, Norfolk, VA, p. A440

ANDERSON, David, Chief Executive Officer, Mobridge Regional Hospital, Mobridge, SD, p. A380

ANDERSON, David S., FACHE, Administrator, Lassen Community Hospital, Susanville, CA, p. A64

ANDERSON, Donald A., President and Chief Executive Officer, Everglades Regional Medical Center, Pahokee, FL, p. A93

ANDERSON, Duane H., Chief Executive Officer, Payson Regional Medical Center, Payson, AZ, p. A24

ANDERSON, Edwin S., President, Cumberland Medical Center, Crossville, TN, p. A385

ANDERSON, Greger C., President and Chief Executive Officer, Nyack Hospital, Nyack, NY, p. A297

ANDERSON, H. William, Administrator, Baxter County Regional Hospital, Mountain Home, AR, p. A33

ANDERSON, Harold E., Chief Executive Officer, Moses Taylor Hospital, Scranton, PA, p. A365

ANDERSON, J. Kendall, President and Chief Executive Officer, Mount Diablo Medical Center, Concord, CA, p. A40

ANDERSON, James M., President and Chief Executive Officer, Children's Hospital Medical Center, Cincinnati, OH, p. A322

ANDERSON, John, Chief Executive Officer, Columbia Four Rivers Medical Center, Selma, AL, p. A18

ANDERSON, Kerry A., R.N., Administrator, FirstHealth Montgomery Memorial Hospital, Troy, NC, p. A314

ANDERSON, Larry, Administrator, Sayre Memorial Hospital, Sayre, OK, p. A341

ANDERSON, Loren J., President and Chief Executive Officer, Memorial Hospital Corporation of Burlington, Burlington, WI, p. A458

ANDERSON, Melinda, Administrator, Olive View–UCLA Medical Center, Los Angeles, CA, p. A50

ANDERSON, Paul J., Administrator, Winneshiek County Memorial Hospital, Decorah, IA, p. A149

ANDERSON, Richard A., President and Chief Executive Officer, St. Luke's Hospital, Bethlehem, PA, p. A350

ANDERSON, Ron, Administrator, Community Memorial Hospital, Syracuse, NE, p. A264

ANDERSON, Ron J., M.D., President and Chief Executive Officer, Dallas County Hospital District–Parkland Health and Hospital System, Dallas, TX, p. A403

ANDERSON, Scott A., Administrator, Stonewall Memorial Hospital, Aspermont, TX, p. A396

ANDERSON, Scott R., President and Chief Executive Officer, North Memorial Medical Center, Robbinsdale, MN, p. A229

ANDERSON, Stephen N. F., Director, Doctors' Hospital of Staten Island, New York, NY, p. A292

ANDERSON, Thomas, Chief Executive Officer, Columbia Pentagon City Hospital, Arlington, VA, p. A436

ANDERSON, William H., Administrator and Chief Executive Officer, South Florida Baptist Hospital, Plant City, FL, p. A94

ANDERSON, Douglas E., USAF, Administrator, U. S. Air Force Hospital, Cannon AFB, NM, p. A281

ANDERSON, Mary Jo, Senior Vice President, Hospital Operations, Scripps Health, San Diego, CA, p. B135

ANDERSON Jr., Andrew E., Administrator, Spohn Bee County Hospital, Beeville, TX, p. A398

ANDERSON Jr., E. Ratcliffe, M.D., Executive Director, Truman Medical Center, Kansas City, MO, p. B146

ANDREWS, Jane, Administrator and Chief Executive Officer, Nashville Rehabilitation Hospital, Nashville, TN, p. A391

ANDREWS, Norman J., Chief Executive Officer, Oak Valley District Hospital, Oakdale, CA, p. A54

ANDREWS, William J., President, Licking Memorial Hospital, Newark, OH, p. A330

ANDREWS, Mary Ann, President and Chief Executive Officer, Sisters of Charity of St. Augustine Health System, Cleveland, OH, p. B137

ANDRIS, Terry R., CHE, Administrator and Vice President Operations, Seton Highland Lakes, Burnet, TX, p. A399

ANDRON, Thomas, Chief Executive Officer, Kremmling Memorial Hospital, Kremmling, CO, p. A71

ANDRUS, Michael G., Administrator and Chief Executive Officer, Franklin County Medical Center, Preston, ID, p. A118

ANDRUS, Terry W., President, East Alabama Medical Center, Opelika, AL, p. A17

ANEL, Manuel, M.D., Administrator and Chief Executive Officer, Long Beach Doctors Hospital, Long Beach, CA, p. A47

ANGELO, Ralph R., Acting Director, Veterans Affairs Medical Center, Augusta, GA, p. A102

ANGERMEIER, Ingo, FACHE, Administrator and Chief Executive Officer, LSU Medical Center–University Hospital, Shreveport, LA, p. A187

ANGLE, Gregory R., President and Chief Executive Officer, Columbia Medical Center of San Angelo, San Angelo, TX, p. A422

ANNIS, Donald E., Chief Executive Officer, Good Hope Hospital, Erwin, NC, p. A307

ANSLEY, Nancy J., Executive Director and Chief Financial Officer, The Retreat, Sunrise, FL, p. A97

ANTHONY, Anne G., Administrator and Chief Executive Officer, Willow Crest Hospital, Miami, OK, p. A339

ANTHONY, Fred, President and Chief Executive Officer, Cuyahoga Falls General Hospital, Cuyahoga Falls, OH, p. A325

ANTHONY, Mark, Vice President and Administrator, Oakwood Hospital Annapolis Center, Wayne, MI, p. A221

ANTLE, David, Chief Executive Officer, Miners' Colfax Medical Center, Raton, NM, p. A282

ANTWINE, Brenda, Administrator, HEALTHSOUTH Rehabilitation Hospital of Jonesboro, Jonesboro, AR, p. A32

APPEL, G. Robert, Administrator, Mason General Hospital, Shelton, WA, p. A450

APPEL, Harley B., Chief Executive Officer, Community Memorial Hospital, Marysville, KS, p. A162

APPELBAUM, Glenn, Senior Vice President, Alexian Brothers Hospital, Saint Louis, MO, p. A249

APPLEBAUM, Jon D., Administrator, Jefferson Memorial Hospital, Ranson, WV, p. A455

APPLEGATE, Rodney T., President, Walla Walla General Hospital, Walla Walla, WA, p. A451

APRATO, Peter P., Administrator and Chief Operating Officer, Robert F. Kennedy Medical Center, Hawthorne, CA, p. A45

ARBUCKLE, Barry, Ph.D.
Chief Executive Officer, Orange Coast Memorial Medical Center, Fountain Valley, CA, p. A43
Chief Executive Officer, Saddleback Memorial Medical Center, Laguna Hills, CA, p. A46

ARCH, John K., Administrator, Boys Town National Research Hospital, Omaha, NE, p. A262

ARCHBELL, Larry J., Vice President Operations, University Community Hospital–Carrollwood, Tampa, FL, p. A98

ARCHER, David L., Chief Executive Officer, Saint Francis Hospital, Memphis, TN, p. A390

ARCHER, Kenneth W., Administrator, Gooding County Memorial Hospital, Gooding, ID, p. A117

ARCHER III, William R., M.D., Commissioner, Texas Department of Health, Austin, TX, p. B146

ARCIDI, Alfred, M.D., President, Whittier Rehabilitation Hospital, Haverhill, MA, p. A203

ARENS, James F., M.D., Chief Executive Officer, University of Texas Medical Branch Hospitals, Galveston, TX, p. A407

ARISMENDI, Luis, M.D., Administrator, Dameron Hospital, Stockton, CA, p. A64

ARIZPE, Robert C., Superintendent, San Antonio State Hospital, San Antonio, TX, p. A423

ARMOUR, James, Administrator, Jackson County Hospital, Scottsboro, AL, p. A18

ARMSTRONG, Anthony W., President, Bay Medical Center, Bay City, MI, p. A209

ARMSTRONG, Dale
Chief Executive Officer, Brynn Marr Behavioral Healthcare System, Jacksonville, NC, p. A309
Chief Executive Officer, Coastal Carolina Hospital, Conway, SC, p. A373

ARMSTRONG Jr., David S., Administrator, Little Falls Hospital, Little Falls, NY, p. A290

ARNETT, Charlene, Chief Executive Officer, High Pointe, Oklahoma City, OK, p. A339

ARNETT, Randal M., President and Chief Executive Officer, Southern Ohio Medical Center, Portsmouth, OH, p. A331

ARNOLD, Agnes E., CHE, Administrator, Charleston Memorial Hospital, Charleston, SC, p. A372

ARNOLD, Kent A., President, Community–General Hospital of Greater Syracuse, Syracuse, NY, p. A301

ARNOLD, Margo, Administrator, West Side District Hospital, Taft, CA, p. A64

ARNOLD, Nancy, Acting Director, John J. Pershing Veterans Affairs Medical Center, Poplar Bluff, MO, p. A248

ARNOLD, Richard D., Administrator, Medina Community Hospital, Hondo, TX, p. A410

ARNOLD, Thomas B., Director, Veterans Affairs Medical Center, Iron Mountain, MI, p. A214

ARP, James, Administrator, Williamson Memorial Hospital, Williamson, WV, p. A456

ASAY, Grant, Chief Executive Officer, Sitka Community Hospital, Sitka, AK, p. A21

ASH, James L.
President and Chief Executive Officer, Cottage Health System, Santa Barbara, CA, p. B91
President and Chief Executive Officer, Santa Barbara Cottage Hospital, Santa Barbara, CA, p. A62
Chief Executive Officer, Santa Ynez Valley Cottage Hospital, Solvang, CA, p. A63

ASH, John P., FACHE, President and Chief Executive Officer, Eugenia Hospital, Lafayette Hill, PA, p. A356

ASH, Richard M., Chief Executive Officer, Northern Itasca Health Care Center, Bigfork, MN, p. A223

ASHBAUGH, James L., Regional Director of Operations, Warm Springs and Baptist Rehabilitation Hospital, San Antonio, TX, p. A424

ASHCRAFT, Steven F., Interim Administrator, ARH Regional Medical Center, Hazard, KY, p. A171

ASHJIAN, Lee, Chief Executive Officer, Cary Medical Center, Caribou, ME, p. A190

ASHKIN, David, M.D., Medical Executive Director, A. G. Holley State Hospital, Lantana, FL, p. A89

ASPER, David, Director, Veterans Affairs Greater Nebraska Health Care System, Lincoln, NE, p. A261

ASSELL, William C., President and Chief Executive Officer, St. Joseph's Mercy Hospital, Centerville, IA, p. A148

ATKINS, Tony E., Administrator, Braxton County Memorial Hospital, Gassaway, WV, p. A453

ATKINSON, Allan, Administrator, Belmond Community Hospital, Belmond, IA, p. A147

ATKINSON, L. Gail, Executive Director, Devereux Texas Treatment Network, League City, TX, p. A415

ATKINSON, Robert P., President and Chief Executive Officer, Jefferson Regional Medical Center, Pine Bluff, AR, p. A34

ATKINSON II, William K., Ph.D., Chief Executive Officer, New Hanover Regional Medical Center, Wilmington, NC, p. A314

ATZROTT, Allan Earl, President, Prince George's Hospital Center, Cheverly, MD, p. A195

AUBERT, Harry, Administrator, Garfield County Memorial Hospital, Pomeroy, WA, p. A448

AUBREY, Leonard A., President and Chief Executive Officer, New York University Downtown Hospital, New York, NY, p. A295

AUER, Thomas H., Commander, Womack Army Medical Center, Fort Bragg, NC, p. A308

AUMAN, Patrick A., Ph.D., Chief Executive Officer, Vencor Hospital–Minneapolis, Golden Valley, MN, p. A225

AUSMAN, Dan F., Chief Executive Officer, Monterey Park Hospital, Monterey Park, CA, p. A53

AUSTIN, George L., Administrator, Bolivar General Hospital, Bolivar, TN, p. A383

AUSTIN, James D., CHE
Administrator, Kalkaska Memorial Health Center, Kalkaska, MI, p. A215
Administrator, Paul Oliver Memorial Hospital, Frankfort, MI, p. A212

AUSTIN, Robert S., President, Gunnison Valley Hospital, Gunnison, CO, p. A71

AVERS, John M., Chief Executive Officer, White County Memorial Hospital, Monticello, IN, p. A143

AXELSON, Alan A., M.D., Chief Executive Officer, Southwood Psychiatric Hospital, Pittsburgh, PA, p. A363

AYRES, Larry J., Administrator and Chief Executive Officer, Pointe Coupee General Hospital, New Roads, LA, p. A185

AZZARA, Michael W., President, Valley Hospital, Ridgewood, NJ, p. A277

B

BABB, Donald J., Chief Executive Officer, Citizens Memorial Hospital, Bolivar, MO, p. A241

BACHARACH, Paul, President and Chief Executive Officer, Uniontown Hospital, Uniontown, PA, p. A366

BACIARELLI, Renato V., Administrator, Mercy Medical Center, Durango, CO, p. A70

BACON, Kenneth, President and Chief Executive Officer, Central Texas Medical Center, San Marcos, TX, p. A424

BACUS, Randy, Chief Executive Officer, Colorado–Fayette Medical Center, Weimar, TX, p. A428

BADGER Jr., Theodore J., Chief Executive Officer, Beauregard Memorial Hospital, De Ridder, LA, p. A180

BAER, James E., FACHE, President, Waupun Memorial Hospital, Waupun, WI, p. A467

BAGBY, Philip D., President and Chief Executive Officer, Albemarle Hospital, Elizabeth City, NC, p. A307

BAGGETT, Larry, Administrator, Palo Duro Hospital, Canyon, TX, p. A400

BAGLEY, Douglas D., Executive Director, LAC–University of Southern California Medical Center, Los Angeles, CA, p. A49

BAHL, Barry I., Associate Director, Veterans Affairs Medical Center, Saint Cloud, MN, p. A230

BAILEY, Bruce P., Administrator, Abbeville County Memorial Hospital, Abbeville, SC, p. A371

BAILEY, David, Chief Executive Officer, Kokomo Rehabilitation Hospital, Kokomo, IN, p. A142

BAILEY, Frederick R., Chief Executive Officer, North Fulton Regional Hospital, Roswell, GA, p. A110

BAILEY, James P., President and Chief Executive Officer, Henryetta Medical Center, Henryetta, OK, p. A338

BAILEY, Owen, Administrator, Thomas Hospital, Fairhope, AL, p. A14

BAILEY, Sandra, Administrator, Methodist–Haywood Park Hospital, Brownsville, TN, p. A383

BAILON, Amy R., M.D., Medical Director, Woodbridge Development Center, Woodbridge, NJ, p. A279

BAINBRIDGE, Darlene D., Interim Chief Executive Officer, Cuba Memorial Hospital, Cuba, NY, p. A287

BAIR, Charles H., Chief Executive Officer, Highland District Hospital, Hillsboro, OH, p. A327

BAIRD, Marvin L., Executive Director, Adams County Memorial Hospital, Decatur, IN, p. A138

BAKER, Bob M., President and Chief Executive Officer, Gratiot Community Hospital, Alma, MI, p. A208

BAKER, Gary A., President, Memorial Hospital, Towanda, PA, p. A366

BAKER, Glenn, Administrator, Baptist Memorial Hospital–Tipton, Covington, TN, p. A385

BAKER, Harry M., Chief Executive Officer, Cross County Hospital, Wynne, AR, p. A35

BAKER, Jeannie, Administrator, Shands at Starke, Starke, FL, p. A97

BAKER, John A., Chief Executive Officer, Methodist Behavioral Resources, New Orleans, LA, p. A185

BAKER, Jon W., Chief Executive Officer, Ripon Medical Center, Ripon, WI, p. A465

BAKER, Rod L., President and Chief Executive Officer, Parrish Medical Center, Titusville, FL, p. A98

BAKER, Rodger H., President and Chief Executive Officer, Fauquier Hospital, Warrenton, VA, p. A444

BAKER, Ronald J., Administrator, Kiowa County Memorial Hospital, Greensburg, KS, p. A159

BAKER Jr., Wendell H.
District Administrator, Matagorda County Hospital District, Bay City, TX, p. B116
Chief Executive Officer, Matagorda General Hospital, Bay City, TX, p. A397

BAKST, Michael D., Ph.D., Executive Director, Community Memorial Hospital of San Buenaventura, Ventura, CA, p. A66

BALCH, Charles M., M.D., President and Chief Executive Officer, City of Hope National Medical Center, Duarte, CA, p. A41

BALDWIN, Bruce A., Chief Executive Officer, Davis Hospital and Medical Center, Layton, UT, p. A430

BALDWIN, Gilda
Chief Executive Officer, Southern Winds Hospital, Hialeah, FL, p. A86
Chief Executive Officer, Westchester General Hospital, Miami, FL, p. A91

BALDWIN, Joe G.
Chief Executive Officer, Columbia Doctors Hospital Airline, Houston, TX, p. A410
Chief Executive Officer, Columbia North Houston Medical Center, Houston, TX, p. A410

BALDWIN, Keith J., Administrator, Samaritan Healthcare, Moses Lake, WA, p. A447

BALDWIN, Paul L., Chief Operating Officer, Retreat Hospital, Richmond, VA, p. A442

BALIK, M. Barbara, Ed.D., Administrator, United Hospital, Saint Paul, MN, p. A230

BALKCOM, Charles, President, Candler County Hospital, Metter, GA, p. A109

BALL, Donald M., President, Jackson Hospital and Clinic, Montgomery, AL, p. A16

BALL, John R., JD, President and Chief Executive Officer, Pennsylvania Hospital, Philadelphia, PA, p. A361

BALLA, Ernest, Administrator, Johns Community Hospital, Taylor, TX, p. A425

BALLANTYNE III, Reginald M., President, PMH Health Resources, Inc., Phoenix, AZ, p. B125

BALLARD, Paul H., Chief Executive Officer, Mission Hospital, Mission, TX, p. A418

BALLARD, Susan, Administrator, Menifee Valley Medical Center, Sun City, CA, p. A64

BALSAM, Marion, USN, Commander, Naval Medical Center, Portsmouth, VA, p. A441

BALTZ, Richard J., Director, Veterans Affairs Medical Center, Fayetteville, NC, p. A308

BALTZER, David J., President, Rehoboth McKinley Christian Hospital, Gallup, NM, p. A282

BALZEN, Earl W., R.N., Chief Executive Officer and Administrator, Charter Plains Behavioral Health System, Lubbock, TX, p. A416

BAN Jr., Albert, Administrator, Thomasville Infirmary, Thomasville, AL, p. A18

BANASZYNSKI, Gregory A., President, St. Francis Hospital, Milwaukee, WI, p. A462

BANE, Raymond, Executive Director, Natchez Community Hospital, Natchez, MS, p. A238

BANGERT, Richard A., Chief Executive Officer and Administrator, Psychiatric Hospital at Vanderbilt, Nashville, TN, p. A391

BANK, Kendall C., President, Northfield Hospital, Northfield, MN, p. A228

BANKS, Elizabeth
Superintendent, Memphis Mental Health Institute, Memphis, TN, p. A390
Chief Executive Officer, Pauline Warfield Lewis Center, Cincinnati, OH, p. A323

BARABAS, Mark C., President, Community Hospital of Lancaster, Lancaster, PA, p. A356

BARBAKOW, Jeffrey, Chairman and Chief Executive Officer, TENET Healthcare Corporation, Santa Barbara, CA, p. B143

BARBATO, Anthony L., M.D., President and Chief Executive Officer, Loyola University Medical Center, Maywood, IL, p. A130

BARBE, Brian S., Chief Executive Officer, Katy Medical Center, Katy, TX, p. A414

BARBER, Jeffrey B., Dr.PH
President and Chief Executive Officer, North Mississippi Health Services, Inc., Tupelo, MS, p. B122
President and Chief Executive Officer, North Mississippi Medical Center, Tupelo, MS, p. A239

BARBER, Mike, Facility Service Integrator, Clovis Community Medical Center, Clovis, CA, p. A40

BARBER, Steve, Administrator, Dorminy Medical Center, Fitzgerald, GA, p. A106

BARBINI, Gerald J., Administrator and Chief Executive Officer, Hubbard Regional Hospital, Webster, MA, p. A207

BARCO, Lawrence F., President, MidMichigan Medical Center–Clare, Clare, MI, p. A209

BARKER, Richard, Administrator, Mercy Health Love County, Marietta, OK, p. A338

BARLOW, Rulon J., Administrator, Central Peninsula General Hospital, Soldotna, AK, p. A21

BARNARD, Dan, Chief Executive Officer, Northwest Surgical Hospital, Oklahoma City, OK, p. A340

BARNER, James W., President and Chief Executive Officer, Altoona Hospital, Altoona, PA, p. A349

BARNES, Harry F., FACHE, President and Chief Executive Officer, Wilson N. Jones Regional Health System, Sherman, TX, p. A424

BARNES, Mary Ann, Administrator, Kaiser Foundation Hospital, Los Angeles, CA, p. A49

BARNES, Ronald W., Executive Director, Mountain View Hospital District, Madras, OR, p. A346

BARNETT, Dana K., Administrator, Platte County Memorial Hospital, Wheatland, WY, p. A469

BARNETT, Gary L., President and Chief Executive Officer, Central Kansas Medical Center, Great Bend, KS, p. A159

BARNETT, Rick J., Executive Vice President and Chief Operating Officer, Mercy Medical Center Mount Shasta, Mount Shasta, CA, p. A53

BARNETT, Timothy, Chief Executive Officer, Yavapai Regional Medical Center, Prescott, AZ, p. A26

BARNETTE, Chris W.
President and Chief Executive Officer, Baton Rouge General Medical Center, Baton Rouge, LA, p. A178
President and Chief Executive Officer, General Health System, Baton Rouge, LA, p. B101

BARNHART, James, Administrator, Peace Harbor Hospital, Florence, OR, p. A345

BARON, David A., D.O., Medical Director, Horsham Clinic, Ambler, PA, p. A349

BARON, Steven D.
President, Miriam Hospital, Providence, RI, p. A369
President and Chief Executive Officer, Rhode Island Hospital, Providence, RI, p. A369

BARR, C. Dennis, President and Chief Executive Officer, Northwest General Hospital, Milwaukee, WI, p. A462

BARR, LuAnn, Administrator, Tilden Community Hospital, Tilden, NE, p. A264

BARRAGAN, J. Bruce, President and Chief Executive Officer, McLeod Regional Medical Center, Florence, SC, p. A374

BARRETO, Hector, M.D., Director, Hospital Dr. Susoni, Arecibo, PR, p. A471

BARRETT, Susan
President and Chief Executive Officer, Mercy Health System of Kansas, Fort Scott, KS, p. A159
President and Chief Executive Officer, Mercy Hospitals of Kansas, Independence, KS, p. A160

BARRETTE, Paul R., Chief Executive Officer, Maine Coast Memorial Hospital, Ellsworth, ME, p. A190

BARRIOS–PAOLI, Lilliam, Ph.D., Executive Director, Lincoln Medical and Mental Health Center, New York, NY, p. A293

BARRON, Steven R., President and Chief Executive Officer, Alexian Brothers Hospital, San Jose, CA, p. A61

BARROW, William F., President and Chief Executive Officer, De Soto Regional Health System, Mansfield, LA, p. A183

BERGMAN, Paul, Administrator, Flandreau Municipal Hospital, Flandreau, SD, p. A379

BERGREN, Jeff, Chief Executive Officer and Administrator, BHC Streamwood Hospital, Streamwood, IL, p. A135

BERHOW, John, President, McCray Memorial Hospital, Kendallville, IN, p. A142

BERKLEY, Ralph B., Administrator, Illinois Valley Community Hospital, Peru, IL, p. A133

BERLUCCHI, Scott A., President and Chief Executive Officer, Lancaster General Hospital–Susquehanna Division, Columbia, PA, p. A352

BERMAN, Arnold, M.D., President and Chief Executive Officer, Allegheny University Hospital, Graduate, Philadelphia, PA, p. A359

BERMAN, Seth, Executive Director, Hall–Brooke Hospital, A Division of Hall–Brooke Foundation, Westport, CT, p. A77

BERNARD, Mark L.
Chief Executive Officer, Metropolitan Methodist Hospital, San Antonio, TX, p. A423
Chief Executive Officer, Northeast Methodist Hospital, San Antonio, TX, p. A423

BERNARD, Patricia, R.N., Administrator, Osborne County Memorial Hospital, Osborne, KS, p. A164

BERNARD, Peter J.
President and Chief Executive Officer, Caritas Medical Center, Louisville, KY, p. A173
President and Chief Executive Officer, Caritas Peace Center, Louisville, KY, p. A173

BERND, David L., President and Chief Executive Officer, Sentara Health System, Norfolk, VA, p. B135

BERNSTEIN, Martin B., Chief Executive Officer, Northern Maine Medical Center, Fort Kent, ME, p. A190

BERNSTEIN, Ronald T., Chief Executive Officer, Foundations Behavioral Health, Doylestown, PA, p. A353

BERNSTEIN, Stephen, FACHE, Chief Executive Officer, Plaza Medical Center of Fort Worth, Fort Worth, TX, p. A407

BERO, Joan A., Regional Vice President and Chief Operating Officer, Saint Louise Hospital, Morgan Hill, CA, p. A53

BERRETT, Britt, Chief Executive Officer, Sharp Chula Vista Medical Center, Chula Vista, CA, p. A39

BERRYMAN, R. Michael, President, Community Memorial Healthcenter, South Hill, VA, p. A443

BERTEAU, Robert, Chief Executive Officer, ValueMark Behavioral Healthcare System of Florida, Orlando, FL, p. A93

BERTRAM, Donna L., R.N., Administrator, Penrose–St. Francis Health Services, Colorado Springs, CO, p. A69

BERTSCH, Darrold, Administrator, Central Arizona Medical Center, Florence, AZ, p. A23

BESON, James, Commander, Weed Army Community Hospital, Fort Irwin, CA, p. A42

BESTUL, Randy, Administrator, Norwood Health Center, Marshfield, WI, p. A461

BESWICK, Melinda D., President and Chief Executive Officer, California Hospital Medical Center, Los Angeles, CA, p. A48

BETJEMANN, John H., President, Methodist Hospitals, Gary, IN, p. A140

BETTENDORF, Felix, President, Alexian Brothers Health System, Inc., Elk Grove Village, IL, p. B65

BETTS, Peter J., President and Chief Executive Officer, East Jefferson General Hospital, Metairie, LA, p. A183

BEVERLY, Douglas H., CHE, Chief Operating Officer, St. Clair Regional Hospital, Pell City, AL, p. A17

BEVERLY, Ken B., President and Chief Executive Officer, Archbold Medical Center, Thomasville, GA, p. B67

BEVINS, O. David, Chief Executive Officer, Kentucky River Medical Center, Jackson, KY, p. A171

BEYER, Robert L., President and Chief Executive Officer, St. Joseph's Medical Center, South Bend, IN, p. A145

BHATIA, Krishin L., Administrator, Victory Memorial Hospital, New York, NY, p. A296

BIANCHI, Charles A., President, Hillsdale Community Health Center, Hillsdale, MI, p. A213

BICH, Arlene C., Administrator, Wagner Community Memorial Hospital, Wagner, SD, p. A382

BICKLING, J. Allan, Chief Executive Officer, Edward W. McCready Memorial Hospital, Crisfield, MD, p. A195

BIEDIGER, Michael J., President, Lexington Medical Center, West Columbia, SC, p. A377

BIEGANSKI, Gary, President, Community Hospital, McCook, NE, p. A261

BIERMAN, Ronald L., Chief Executive Officer, HEALTHSOUTH Northern Kentucky Rehabilitation Hospital, Covington, KY, p. A169

BIESTER Jr., Doris J., Chief Executive Officer, Children's Hospital, Denver, CO, p. A69

BIGA, Cathleen D., President and Chief Executive Officer, La Grange Memorial Hospital, La Grange, IL, p. A129

BIGA, Thomas A., Executive Director, Clara Maass Health System, Belleville, NJ, p. A271

BIGELOW, David C., Chief Executive Officer, North Lincoln Hospital, Lincoln City, OR, p. A346

BIGLEY, Robert F., Administrator, Dale Medical Center, Ozark, AL, p. A17

BIGOGNO, James C., FACHE, President and Chief Executive Officer, Howard Community Hospital, Kokomo, IN, p. A142

BIHLDORFF, John P., President and Chief Executive Officer, Newton–Wellesley Hospital, Newton Lower Falls, MA, p. A204

BILBO, Dorothy C., Administrator, Pearl River County Hospital, Poplarville, MS, p. A239

BILL, Charles E., CHE, Chief Executive Officer, Cobre Valley Community Hospital, Claypool, AZ, p. A22

BILLICK, Dean, Director, Central Texas Veterans Affairs Healthcare System, Temple, TX, p. A425

BILLIK, Dean S., Director, Veterans Affairs Medical Center, Charleston, SC, p. A372

BILLING, Michael D., Administrator, Mid–Valley Hospital, Omak, WA, p. A448

BILLS, Jeff K., Chief Executive Officer, Saint Mary's Regional Medical Center, Reno, NV, p. A267

BILLS, Robert C., President and Vice Chairman, Valley Presbyterian Hospital, Los Angeles, CA, p. A51

BING, William W., Administrator, Morehouse General Hospital, Bastrop, LA, p. A178

BINGHAM, John, Administrator, Magic Valley Regional Medical Center, Twin Falls, ID, p. A119

BINGHAM, Leslie, Chief Executive Officer, Charter Palms Behavioral Health System, McAllen, TX, p. A417

BIRCHELL, Bruce K., Chief Executive Officer, Morton County Health System, Elkhart, KS, p. A158

BIRD, Kim B., Administrator, Lifecare Hospitals, Shreveport, LA, p. A187

BIRDZELL, JoAnn
President and Chief Executive Officer, St. Catherine Hospital, East Chicago, IN, p. A139
President and Chief Executive Officer, St. Elizabeth's Hospital, Chicago, IL, p. A124

BIRDZELL, John R., FACHE, Chief Executive Officer, Bedford Regional Medical Center, Bedford, IN, p. A137

BISCARO, Ron, Administrator, St. Francis Medical Center of Santa Barbara, Santa Barbara, CA, p. A62

BISCHALANEY, George, Interim President and Chief Executive Officer, Eden Medical Center, Castro Valley, CA, p. A39

BISCHOFF, Theresa A., Deputy Provost and Executive Vice President, New York University Hospitals Center, New York, NY, p. A295

BISCONE, Mark A., Executive Director, Waldo County General Hospital, Belfast, ME, p. A189

BISHOP, J. Larry, Chief Executive Officer, Pender Memorial Hospital, Burgaw, NC, p. A305

BISHOP, Marvin O., Administrator, Weisbrod Memorial Hospital, Eads, CO, p. A70

BISHOP, Paul A., Administrator, Lonesome Pine Hospital, Big Stone Gap, VA, p. A436

BISSEL, Jane, President and Chief Executive Officer, Mercy Hospital, Valley City, ND, p. A319

BISSELL, David D., USAF, Commander, U. S. Air Force Hospital Tinker, Tinker AFB, OK, p. A342

BITTING, Nancy J., Chief Executive Officer, St. Joseph Hospital, Bellingham, WA, p. A445

BLACK, Gary E., President and Chief Executive Officer, Lenoir Memorial Hospital, Kinston, NC, p. A309

BLACK, Glenn, Associate Vice President and Chief Operating Officer, Kingswood Hospital, Ferndale, MI, p. A212

BLACK, Sharon S., R.N., Administrator and Chief Operating Officer, HEALTHSOUTH Rehabilitation Hospital of South Louisiana, Baton Rouge, LA, p. A178

BLAIR, David L., President, Twin Cities Hospital, Niceville, FL, p. A92

BLAIR, John E., President and Chief Executive Officer, Ravenswood Hospital Medical Center, Chicago, IL, p. A123

BLAIR, Mardian J., President, Adventist Health System Sunbelt Health Care Corporation, Winter Park, FL, p. B64

BLAKLEY, Scott F., Administrator, Brentwood Behavioral Healthcare, Shreveport, LA, p. A186

BLAN, Gary J., FACHE, President and Chief Executive Officer, Nacogdoches Memorial Hospital, Nacogdoches, TX, p. A418

BLANCHARD, Stephen C., Director, Edgewater Psychiatric Center, Harrisburg, PA, p. A355

BLANCHARD, William R., Chief Executive Officer, Detar Hospital, Victoria, TX, p. A427

BLANCHETTE, Edward A., M.D., Director, Connecticut Department of Correction's Hospital, Somers, CT, p. A76

BLANCO, Carla, Administrator, Doctors Center, Manati, PR, p. A473

BLAND, Calvin, President and Chief Executive Officer, St. Christopher's Hospital for Children, Philadelphia, PA, p. A361

BLAND, Edward C., Chief Executive Officer, Colusa Community Hospital, Colusa, CA, p. A40

BLAND, Thomas, Administrator, Montfort Jones Memorial Hospital, Kosciusko, MS, p. A237

BLASBAND, Charles A., Chief Executive Officer, Citrus Memorial Hospital, Inverness, FL, p. A87

BLASKO, M. Cornelia, Administrator, St. Francis Hospital, Mountain View, MO, p. A247

BLASKO Jr., Joseph, President and Chief Executive Officer, Incarnate Word Health Services, San Antonio, TX, p. B108

BLEAKNEY, David A., Administrator, Angleton–Danbury General Hospital, Angleton, TX, p. A395

BLEIBERG, Ephram, M.D., President and Chief of Staff, C. F. Menninger Memorial Hospital, Topeka, KS, p. A166

BLESSING, William H., President, Mary Free Bed Hospital and Rehabilitation Center, Grand Rapids, MI, p. A212

BLESSITT, H. J., Administrator, South Sunflower County Hospital, Indianola, MS, p. A236

BLEVINS, Maggie, Administrator, Jane Phillips Nowata Health Center, Nowata, OK, p. A339

BLEYER, Alan J., President, Akron General Medical Center, Akron, OH, p. A320

BLODGETT, Ruth P., Chief Operating Officer, Berkshire Medical Center, Pittsfield, MA, p. A205

BLOM, David P.
President, Grant/Riverside Methodist Hospitals–Grant Campus, Columbus, OH, p. A325
President, Grant/Riverside Methodist Hospitals–Riverside Campus, Columbus, OH, p. A325

BLOME', Michael, Administrator, Methodist Healthcare – Fayette Hospital, Somerville, TN, p. A393

BLOUGH Jr., Daniel D., Chief Executive Officer, Punxsutawney Area Hospital, Punxsutawney, PA, p. A364

BLOUNT, Karen, Vice President and Chief Operating Officer, Children's Hospital, Buffalo, NY, p. A286

BLOUNT, Kenneth, President and Chief Executive Officer, The Monroe Clinic, Monroe, WI, p. A463

BLUFORD, John W., Administrator, Hennepin County Medical Center, Minneapolis, MN, p. A227

BLUM, James G., Interim Administrator, Tyler Healthcare Center, Tyler, MN, p. A231

BOARDMAN, Debra, Chief Executive Officer, Riverwood Health Care Center, Aitkin, MN, p. A222

BOBBS, Kathy, Chief Executive Officer, Columbia Riverview Medical Center, Gonzales, LA, p. A180

BOBELDYK, Jerry, Administrator, Murray County Memorial Hospital, Slayton, MN, p. A230

BOECKER, Thomas J., President and Chief Executive Officer, Wilson Memorial Hospital, Sidney, OH, p. A332

BOEHRINGER, Paul, Executive Director, Temple University Hospital, Philadelphia, PA, p. A361

BOENING, Harold L., Administrator, Otto Kaiser Memorial Hospital, Kenedy, TX, p. A414

BOETTCHER, William V., Chief Executive Officer, Fletcher Allen Health Care, Burlington, VT, p. A434

BOFF, Michael G., President, Trillium Hospital, Albion, MI, p. A208

BOGAN, James, Chief Executive Officer, Portage Health System, Hancock, MI, p. A213

BOGGS, Danny L., President and Chief Executive Officer, Memorial Hospital, Marysville, OH, p. A329

BOGGS, Lynn Ingram, President and Chief Executive Officer, Community General Hospital of Thomasville, Thomasville, NC, p. A314

BOGGS, Michael S., Chief Executive Officer, Coliseum Medical Centers, Macon, GA, p. A108

BOGGUS Jr., Solon, Interim Chief Executive Officer, Columbia Olympia Fields Osteopathic Hospital and Medical Center, Olympia Fields, IL, p. A132

BOGUE, Virginia, Site Administrator, Sentara Bayside Hospital, Virginia Beach, VA, p. A444

BOHL, Jim, President and Chief Executive Officer, Doctors Hospital, Springfield, IL, p. A135

BOID, Roger R., Administrator, Grady Memorial Hospital, Chickasha, OK, p. A336

BOLD, Harry, Administrator, Big Sandy Medical Center, Big Sandy, MT, p. A253

BOLEWARE, Mike, Administrator, Prentiss Regional Hospital and Extended Care Facilities, Prentiss, MS, p. A239

BOLTON, Clyde E., Administrator, Summers County Appalachian Regional Hospital, Hinton, WV, p. A453

BOLTON, Dan, Chief Executive Officer, Northeast Tennessee Rehabilitation Hospital, Johnson City, TN, p. A387

BOMAR, Betsy, Chief Executive Officer, Clearwater Community Hospital, Clearwater, FL, p. A82

BONAR Jr., Robert I., President and Chief Executive Officer, Children's Hospital of the King's Daughters, Norfolk, VA, p. A440

BOND, C. Scott, Administrator, Providence St. Peter Hospital, Olympia, WA, p. A448

BONE, Jim G., Interim Administrator, Muleshoe Area Medical Center, Muleshoe, TX, p. A418

BONNER, Jack W., M.D., Administrator and Medical Director, Marshall I. Pickens Hospital, Greenville, SC, p. A374

BONNER, Tucker, President, King's Daughters Hospital, Temple, TX, p. A425

BONNETT, Joseph E., Executive Vice President and Chief Executive Officer, Freeport Memorial Hospital, Freeport, IL, p. A127

BOONE, Richard, Executive Director, Crawford Memorial Hospital, Van Buren, AR, p. A35

BOOR, Leon J., Chief Executive Officer, Memorial Hospital, Abilene, KS, p. A157

BOOTH, Patrick M., President, Community Memorial Hospital and Convalescent and Rehabilitation Unit, Winona, MN, p. A232

BOOTH, Peter G., President, Henrietta D. Goodall Hospital, Sanford, ME, p. A191

BOPP, James H.
Executive Director, Middletown Psychiatric Center, Middletown, NY, p. A290
Executive Director, Rockland Psychiatric Center, Orangeburg, NY, p. A298

BORDELON, Olive, Chief Executive Officer, St. Frances Cabrini Hospital, Alexandria, LA, p. A178

BORENSTEIN, Jeffrey, M.D., Chief Executive Officer and Medical Director, Holliswood Hospital, New York, NY, p. A292

BORIES Jr., Robert F., FACHE, Administrator, Shriners Hospitals for Children, Shriners Burns Hospital–Boston, Boston, MA, p. A200

BORING, Ronald L., President and Chief Executive Officer, Baylor Richardson Medical Center, Richardson, TX, p. A421

BORLAND, Winston, Chief Executive Officer, Columbia Northwest Hospital, Corpus Christi, TX, p. A401

BORRONI, S. Denise, Administrator and Chief Executive Officer, HEALTHSOUTH Rehabilitation Hospital of Arlington, Arlington, TX, p. A396

BOSK, Nathan, FACHE, Executive Director, Lower Bucks Hospital, Bristol, PA, p. A350

BOSSARD, Karen L., Administrator, Greene County Medical Center, Jefferson, IA, p. A152

BOSTICK, Roy D., Director, E. A. Conway Medical Center, Monroe, LA, p. A184

BOSTON, Edward D., Chief Executive Officer, Huntsville Hospital, Huntsville, AL, p. A15

BOSWELL, Bill, Chief Executive Officer, McCamey Hospital, McCamey, TX, p. A417

BOSWELL, Robert H., Administrator, Highland Ridge Hospital, Salt Lake City, UT, p. A432

BOUCHER, David T., Chief Executive Officer, Carolinas Hospital System–Kingstree, Kingstree, SC, p. A375

BOUFFARD, Rodney, Superintendent, Augusta Mental Health Institute, Augusta, ME, p. A189

BOUGHTON, Charles M., Chief Executive Officer, Northeast Regional Medical Center–Jefferson Campus, Kirksville, MO, p. A246

BOUIS, Charles, President and Chief Executive Officer, Edward A. Utlaut Memorial Hospital, Greenville, IL, p. A128

BOULA, Rodney C., Administrator, Clifton–Fine Hospital, Star Lake, NY, p. A301

BOULENGER, Bo, Chief Executive Officer, Homestead Hospital, Homestead, FL, p. A86

BOUNDS, Floyd D., Administrator, Madison Medical Center, Fredericktown, MO, p. A243

BOURASSA, Robert N., Executive Director, Trinity Springs Pavilion–East, Fort Worth, TX, p. A407

BOURGEOIS, Anne, Interim Chief Executive Officer, Marlborough Hospital, Marlborough, MA, p. A203

BOURGEOIS, Jeff A., Chief Executive Officer, Hill Country Memorial Hospital, Fredericksburg, TX, p. A407

BOURGEOIS Jr., Milton D., Administrator, St. Anne General Hospital, Raceland, LA, p. A186

BOVENDER Jr., Jack O., President and Chief Operating Officer, Columbia/HCA Healthcare Corporation, Nashville, TN, p. B81

BOWEN, Claire L., President, Fairview Hospital, Great Barrington, MA, p. A202

BOWEN, Steve, President, East Texas Medical Center Jacksonville, Jacksonville, TX, p. A413

BOWER, Roger H., USAF, Commander, U. S. Air Force Hospital, MacDill AFB, FL, p. A89

BOWERS, Robert, Administrator, Veterans Memorial Hospital of Meigs County, Pomeroy, OH, p. A331

BOWERS, Robert A., Chief Executive Officer, Oak Hill Community Medical Center, Oak Hill, OH, p. A330

BOWERSOX, Bruce D., Administrator, Hillsboro Medical Center, Hillsboro, ND, p. A317

BOWLES, Stephen A., President, Valley Community Hospital, Dallas, OR, p. A344

BOWLING, John S., President and Chief Executive Officer, South Georgia Medical Center, Valdosta, GA, p. A112

BOWMAN, Leslie C., Regional Administrator, Ancillary Services and Site Administrator, Detroit Receiving Hospital and University Health Center, Detroit, MI, p. A210

BOWMAN, Mike R., Administrator, Litzenberg Memorial County Hospital, Central City, NE, p. A259

BOWMAN, Scott, Administrator, Sweetwater Hospital, Sweetwater, TN, p. A393

BOYD, Charles E., Administrator, Doctors' Hospital of Shreveport, Shreveport, LA, p. A186

BOYD, Christopher L., Chief Executive Officer and Managing Director, Inland Valley Regional Medical Center, Wildomar, CA, p. A67

BOYD, J. Michael, Chief Executive Officer, Ivinson Memorial Hospital, Laramie, WY, p. A469

BOYD, Samuel J., Administrator, Crafts–Farrow State Hospital, Columbia, SC, p. A372

BOYD, Wallace N., Administrator, Ochiltree General Hospital, Perryton, TX, p. A420

BOYER, Gregory E., Chief Executive Officer, Wellington Regional Medical Center, West Palm Beach, FL, p. A99

BOYLE, Steven P., President and Chief Executive Officer, St. Peter's Hospital, Albany, NY, p. A284

BOYLES, Jackie, Administrator, Cedar County Memorial Hospital, El Dorado Springs, MO, p. A243

BOYLES, Michael, Administrator, Saunders County Health Service, Wahoo, NE, p. A264

BOZEMAN, Larry C., Chief Executive Officer, Trinity Valley Medical Center, Palestine, TX, p. A420

BRABAND, Jon D., Chief Executive Officer, Glencoe Area Health Center, Glencoe, MN, p. A225

BRACHT, Gerald E., Vice President and Administrator, Scripps Memorial Hospital–Encinitas, Encinitas, CA, p. A42

BRACKIN, D. Wayne, Chief Executive Officer, South Miami Hospital, Miami, FL, p. A91

BRACKNEY, Charles R., President and Chief Executive Officer, Ozarks Medical Center, West Plains, MO, p. A252

BRADEL, William T., Executive Director, Sacred Heart Hospital, Cumberland, MD, p. A195

BRADFORD, Roberta J., President and Chief Executive Officer, Drake Center, Cincinnati, OH, p. A322

BRADLEY, David K., Chief Executive Officer, Geary Community Hospital, Junction City, KS, p. A161

BRADLEY, Lucinda A., President, Great Plains Regional Medical Center, North Platte, NE, p. A262

BRADLEY, Myra James, Chief Executive Officer, Good Samaritan Hospital, Cincinnati, OH, p. A322

BRADLEY Jr., J. Lindsey, FACHE, President and Chief Administrative Officer, Trinity Mother Frances Health System, Tyler, TX, p. A427

BRADSHAW, Dorothy A., Director, Deer's Head Center, Salisbury, MD, p. A197

BRADWAY, Karen A., USAF, Administrator, U. S. Air Force Hospital, Columbus, MS, p. A234

BRADY, Barry, Administrator, Van Buren County Memorial Hospital, Clinton, AR, p. A30

BRADY, James L., President, Allied Services Rehabilitation Hospital, Scranton, PA, p. A365

BRADY, Keith D., Chief Executive Officer and Administrator, Southern Inyo County Local Health Care District, Lone Pine, CA, p. A47

BRADY, Patrick R., Administrator, Sutter Solano Medical Center, Vallejo, CA, p. A66

BRADY, Tim, Chief Executive Officer, Columbia Regional Hospital of Jackson, Jackson, TN, p. A386

BRADY, Jane Frances, Chief Executive Officer, St. Joseph's Hospital and Medical Center, Paterson, NJ, p. A276

BRAILSFORD, Tammie McMann, Administrator, Saint Mary Medical Center, Long Beach, CA, p. A48

BRAMLETT Jr., E. Chandler
President and Chief Executive Officer, Infirmary Health System, Inc., Mobile, AL, p. B109
President and Chief Executive Officer, Mobile Infirmary Medical Center, Mobile, AL, p. A16

BRANAMAN, A. Ray, Administrator, Mary Breckinridge Hospital, Hyden, KY, p. A171

BRANCO, Patrick, Administrator, Divine Providence Health Center, Ivanhoe, MN, p. A226

BRANDLER, Bruce, Administrator, Puget Sound Hospital, Tacoma, WA, p. A450

BRANDON, David, Chief Executive Officer, Fayette Memorial Hospital, Connersville, IN, p. A138

BRANDT, Stephen, President and Chief Executive Officer, West Florida Regional Medical Center, Pensacola, FL, p. A94

BRANDT, Florence, Chief Executive Officer, St. Francis Medical Center, Pittsburgh, PA, p. A363

BRANDT Jr., George H., Administrator, Martin General Hospital, Williamston, NC, p. A314

BRANTLEY, Cheryl Y., Administrator, South Florida Evaluation and Treatment Center, Miami, FL, p. A91

BRASEL, James B., Administrator, Shriners Hospitals for Children, Honolulu, Honolulu, HI, p. A114

BRASH, David L., Administrator, Plateau Medical Center, Oak Hill, WV, p. A455

BRASIER, Jamers, Administrator, Nocona General Hospital, Nocona, TX, p. A419

BRASS, Alan W., FACHE, President and Chief Executive Officer, ProMedica Health System, Toledo, OH, p. B126

BRAUN, Greg
Administrator, Harmony Community Hospital, Harmony, MN, p. A226
Administrator, Tweeten Lutheran Health Care Center, Spring Grove, MN, p. A231
BRAWLEY, James B., Chief Executive Officer, Holly Hill Charter Behavioral Health System, Raleigh, NC, p. A311
BRAY, Donald C., President and Chief Executive Officer, University Hospital, Augusta, GA, p. A102
BRAZIER, Ray, President, Hillcrest Health Center, Oklahoma City, OK, p. A339
BRAZITIS, Mark A., President, Lancaster General Hospital, Lancaster, PA, p. A356
BREAUX, Kenneth, Chief Executive Officer, Randolph County Medical Center, Pocahontas, AR, p. A34
BREEDEN, James L., Administrator, Kaiser Foundation Hospital, Los Angeles, CA, p. A49
BREEDEN, Susan M., Administrator, Baptist Memorial Hospital–Huntingdon, Huntingdon, TN, p. A386
BREEN, John P., Chief Executive Officer, Massapequa General Hospital, Seaford, NY, p. A300
BREEN, Michael F.
President, Holy Cross Hospital, Detroit, MI, p. A211
President, St. John Health System–Saratoga Campus, Detroit, MI, p. A211
BREGANT Jr., Robert E., Administrator, Ransom Memorial Hospital, Ottawa, KS, p. A164
BREHE, Deborah, Chief Executive Officer, Mission Bay Hospital, San Diego, CA, p. A59
BREITENBACH, Thomas G., Chief Executive Officer, Miami Valley Hospital, Dayton, OH, p. A326
BREITLING, Bryan, Administrator and Chief Executive Officer, Bowdle Hospital, Bowdle, SD, p. A378
BREMER, Louis H., President and Chief Executive Officer, Wellmont Holston Valley Medical Center, Kingsport, TN, p. A387
BRENNAN, Charles L., Chief Executive Officer, St. Lawrence Rehabilitation Center, Lawrenceville, NJ, p. A274
BRENNAN, Donald A., President and Chief Executive Officer, Daughters of Charity National Health System, Saint Louis, MO, p. B92
BRENNY, Terrence, President, Stoughton Hospital Association, Stoughton, WI, p. A466
BREON, Richard C., President and Chief Executive Officer, St. Mary's Medical Center of Evansville, Evansville, IN, p. A139
BRESSANELLI, Leo A., President and Chief Executive Officer, Genesis Medical Center, Davenport, IA, p. A149
BRETT, C. William, Ph.D., President and Chief Executive Officer, Windmoor Healthcare of Clearwater, Clearwater, FL, p. A82
BREWER, Gary L., Chief Executive Officer, Valley View Hospital, Glenwood Springs, CO, p. A70
BREWER, Jeff, President, Walker Baptist Medical Center, Jasper, AL, p. A15
BREWER, Rebecca T., CHE, Chief Executive Officer, Colleton Medical Center, Walterboro, SC, p. A377
BREWER, Sally, Chief Executive Officer, Memorial Hospital at Exeter, Exeter, CA, p. A42
BREWER, Victor F., Administrator, Good Samaritan Hospital, Bakersfield, CA, p. A37
BREXLER, James L., Chief Executive Officer, Oakwood Healthcare System, Dearborn, MI, p. B122
BREZENOFF, Stanley, President, Maimonides Medical Center, New York, NY, p. A294
BRIDGES, Daphne, President, Crawley Memorial Hospital, Boiling Springs, NC, p. A305
BRIDGES, James M., Executive Vice President and Chief Operating Officer, Palmetto Baptist Medical Center/Columbia, Columbia, SC, p. A373
BRIGGS, Ronald O., President, St. Francis Memorial Hospital, West Point, NE, p. A264
BRILEY, Ellen, Administrator and Chief Executive Officer, Elba General Hospital, Elba, AL, p. A14
BRIMHALL, Dennis C., President, University of Colorado Hospital, Denver, CO, p. A70
BRINDLEY, John C.
Chief Executive Officer, Brackenridge Hospital, Austin, TX, p. A396
Chief Executive Officer, Seton Medical Center, Austin, TX, p. A397

BRINGHURST, John F., Administrator, Petersburg Medical Center, Petersburg, AK, p. A21
BRINK, Gerald R., President and Chief Executive Officer, Riverside Regional Medical Center, Newport News, VA, p. A440
BRINKER, Joseph J., Interim President, Bethesda General Hospital, Saint Louis, MO, p. A249
BRINKERS, Jack, CHE, Administrator, Weston County Health Services, Newcastle, WY, p. A469
BRINKERT, William K., President, St. John of God Hospital, Brighton, MA, p. A201
BRINKMAN, Carollee, Chief Executive Officer, Graceville Health Center, Graceville, MN, p. A225
BRITT, John H., Executive Director, Massachusetts Hospital School, Canton, MA, p. A202
BRITTON, Gregory K., President and Chief Executive Officer, Beloit Memorial Hospital, Beloit, WI, p. A457
BROADBENT, Ernest J., President and Chief Executive Officer, HEALTHSOUTH Braintree Rehabilitation Hospital, Braintree, MA, p. A201
BROCCOLINO, Victor A., President and Chief Executive Officer, Howard County General Hospital, Columbia, MD, p. A195
BROCK, John D., Chief Executive Officer, Spring View Hospital, Lebanon, KY, p. A172
BROCKELMAN, Rodney, Administrator, Jewell County Hospital, Mankato, KS, p. A162
BROCKETTE, Darby, Administrator, HEALTHSOUTH Rehabilitation Center, Albuquerque, NM, p. A280
BROCKMANN, William F., President and Chief Executive Officer, Caylor–Nickel Medical Center, Bluffton, IN, p. A137
BRODEUR, Mark S., Chief Executive Officer, Jefferson Memorial Hospital, Crystal City, MO, p. A243
BRODY, Robert J., President and Chief Executive Officer, St. Francis Hospital and Health Centers, Beech Grove, IN, p. A137
BRODY, Sue G.
President and Chief Executive Officer, Bayfront Medical Center, Saint Petersburg, FL, p. A95
President and Chief Executive Officer, St. Anthony's Hospital, Saint Petersburg, FL, p. A96
BROGAN, Alanna, Chief Operating Officer, Petaluma Valley Hospital, Petaluma, CA, p. A56
BROOKHART, Duane, Ph.D., President and Chief Executive Officer, Northridge Medical Center, Prattville, AL, p. A17
BROOKS, Jesse, M.D., Administrator, Brooks Hospital, Atlanta, TX, p. A396
BROOKS, Phillip D., President, Norfolk Community Hospital, Norfolk, VA, p. A440
BROOKS, Richard A., Administrator and Chief Operating Officer, E. J. Noble Hospital Samaritan, Alexandria Bay, NY, p. A284
BROOKS, William P., Superintendent, Winfield State Hospital and Training Center, Winfield, KS, p. A167
BROOKS III, J. Milton, Administrator, Pineville Community Hospital Association, Pineville, KY, p. A176
BROPHY, James M., Senior Executive Officer, Saint Luke's Hospital, Kansas City, MO, p. A245
BROPHY, James M., FACHE, Senior Executive Officer, Saint Luke's Northland Hospital, Kansas City, MO, p. A245
BROSIG, Joe, Administrator, Concho County Hospital, Eden, TX, p. A405
BROSSEAU, Terrance G., President and Chief Executive Officer, MedCenter One, Bismarck, ND, p. A316
BROTHERS, R. Andrew, President and Chief Executive Officer, St. Anthony Community Hospital, Warwick, NY, p. A302
BROTMAN, Martin, M.D., President and Chief Executive Officer, California Pacific Medical Center, San Francisco, CA, p. A60
BROUGHTON, Pamela McCullough, Chief Executive Officer, BHC West Hills Hospital, Reno, NV, p. A267
BROUGHTON, Paul L., FACHE
Senior Vice President, Harper Hospital, Detroit, MI, p. A210
Senior Vice President, Huron Valley–Sinai Hospital, Commerce Township, MI, p. A210
BROWER, Fred B., President and Chief Executive Officer, Trinity Health System, Steubenville, OH, p. A332

BROWN, Betty Bolin, Ed.D., Acting Director, Veterans Affairs Medical Center, Salisbury, NC, p. A312
BROWN, Carl D., Administrator, Lakeview Community Hospital, Eufaula, AL, p. A14
BROWN, Carl E., President, Delaware Valley Medical Center, Langhorne, PA, p. A356
BROWN, Cary D., Director, Veterans Affairs Medical Center, Big Spring, TX, p. A398
BROWN, Dan
Administrator, North Central Baptist Hospital, San Antonio, TX, p. A423
Administrator, Northeast Baptist Hospital, San Antonio, TX, p. A423
BROWN, David E., President and Chief Executive Officer, Beaufort Memorial Hospital, Beaufort, SC, p. A371
BROWN, David P., Administrator, Citizens Medical Center, Victoria, TX, p. A427
BROWN, Donald G., Chief Executive Officer, Community Memorial Hospital, Monmouth, IL, p. A131
BROWN, Fred L., President and Chief Executive Officer, BJC Health System, Saint Louis, MO, p. B72
BROWN, H. Thomas, Administrator, Cobb Memorial Hospital, Royston, GA, p. A111
BROWN, Harold W., Chief Executive Officer, Prairie Du Chien Memorial Hospital, Prairie Du Chien, WI, p. A464
BROWN, Lennea F., Administrator, Bucktail Medical Center, Renovo, PA, p. A364
BROWN, Luella, Service Unit Director, U. S. Public Health Service Indian Hospital, Cass Lake, MN, p. A223
BROWN, Mary W., Executive Vice President and Director, Ochsner Foundation Hospital, New Orleans, LA, p. A185
BROWN, Murray L., Administrator, Neosho Memorial Regional Medical Center, Chanute, KS, p. A157
BROWN, Patricia W., Executive Director, Savannas Hospital, Port St. Lucie, FL, p. A95
BROWN, Rex H., President, Hillsboro Area Hospital, Hillsboro, IL, p. A128
BROWN, Richard, Operations Administrator, Providence Yakima Medical Center, Yakima, WA, p. A451
BROWN, Richard V., Chief Executive Officer, Livingston Memorial Hospital, Livingston, MT, p. A255
BROWN, Richard W., President and Chief Executive Officer, Health Midwest, Kansas City, MO, p. B104
BROWN, Scott R., Administrator and Chief Executive Officer, Moore County Hospital District, Dumas, TX, p. A405
BROWN, Shannon D., President, Betsy Johnson Regional Hospital, Dunn, NC, p. A307
BROWN, Steven E., Administrator, Inova Fair Oaks Hospital, Fairfax, VA, p. A437
BROWN, Terry, Administrator and Chief Executive Officer, HEALTHSOUTH Lakeshore Rehabilitation Hospital, Birmingham, AL, p. A12
BROWN, William, Administrator, W. J. Barge Memorial Hospital, Greenville, SC, p. A374
BROWN, George J., M.D., Commanding General, Madigan Army Medical Center, Tacoma, WA, p. A450
BROWN, G. R., Commanding Officer, U. S. Naval Hospital, Roosevelt Roads, PR, p. A474
BROWNE, J. Timothy, Chief Executive Officer, Loris Community Hospital, Loris, SC, p. A375
BROWNE, Norman E., Director, Veterans Affairs Medical Center, Albuquerque, NM, p. A281
BROWNING, Edward E., Chief Executive Officer and Administrator, Clay County Memorial Hospital, Henrietta, TX, p. A409
BROWNLEE, Walter W., President, Jefferson County Hospital, Fairfield, IA, p. A150
BROYLES, Dan P., Administrator, Harrison County Community Hospital, Bethany, MO, p. A241
BRUCE, Sandra B., President and Chief Executive Officer, Saint Alphonsus Regional Medical Center, Boise, ID, p. A116
BRUECKNER, Geraldine, Administrator, Pediatric Center for Restorative Care, Dallas, TX, p. A403
BRUECKNER, Gerry, R.N., Executive Director, Baylor Center for Restorative Care, Dallas, TX, p. A402
BRUECKNER, Robert G., President and Chief Executive Officer, St. John's Regional Medical Center, Joplin, MO, p. A244

BRUHN, Charles E., Chief Executive Officer, Memorial Community Hospital, Edgerton, WI, p. A459

BRUM, Joseph G., President and Chief Executive Officer, Henry Medical Center, Stockbridge, GA, p. A112

BRUMITT, Jerry D., President and Chief Executive Officer, Saint John's Health System, Anderson, IN, p. A137

BRUMLOW Jr., James W., President and Chief Executive Officer, Wadsworth–Rittman Hospital, Wadsworth, OH, p. A333

BRUNDIGE, James E., Administrator, Haxtun Hospital District, Haxtun, CO, p. A71

BRUNICARDI, Rusty O., President, Community Hospitals of Williams County, Bryan, OH, p. A321

BRUNO, Frank, Chief Executive Officer, Gracie Square Hospital, New York, NY, p. A292

BRUNS, Dennis Ray, President and Chief Executive Officer, Hilton Head Medical Center and Clinics, Hilton Head Island, SC, p. A375

BRVENIK, Richard A., President and Chief Executive Officer, Shore Memorial Hospital, Nassawadox, VA, p. A440

BRYAN, Jay, Chief Executive Officer, Lakeshore Community Hospital, Shelby, MI, p. A219

BRYAN, Marilyn, Administrator, Roger Mills Memorial Hospital, Cheyenne, OK, p. A336

BRYAN–WILLIAMS, Margaret, Administrator, Shriners Hospitals for Children, Northern California, Sacramento, CA, p. A58

BRZUZ, Richard W., Administrator, Shriners Hospitals for Children, Erie, Erie, PA, p. A354

BUCHANAN, A. C., Administrator, Vencor Arlington, Texas, Arlington, TX, p. A396

BUCHANAN, Bruce F., FACHE, President and Chief Executive Officer, Mercy Health Center, Oklahoma City, OK, p. A340

BUCHANAN, Don, Chief Operating Officer, Aurora Community Hospital, Aurora, MO, p. A241

BUCHANAN, Georgia, President, Laird Hospital, Union, MS, p. A240

BUCK, Jack S., Chief Executive Officer, Crockett Hospital, Lawrenceburg, TN, p. A388

BUCKLAND, Eric, CHE, Chief Executive Officer, Valley General Hospital, Monroe, WA, p. A447

BUCKLEY, Donald S., FACHE, President, Chesapeake General Hospital, Chesapeake, VA, p. A437

BUCKLEY, Howard R., President, Mercy Hospital Portland, Portland, ME, p. A191

BUCKLEY, Jeffrey L., President and Chief Executive Officer, Gateway Regional Health System, Mount Sterling, KY, p. A175

BUCKLEY, John J., President and Chief Executive Officer, Pottstown Memorial Medical Center, Pottstown, PA, p. A364

BUCKLEY Jr., John J., President, Southern Illinois Hospital Services, Carbondale, IL, p. B140

BUCKNER, Terry, Administrator, Watonga Municipal Hospital, Watonga, OK, p. A343

BUCKNER, Wayne, Administrator, Baptist Hospital of Cocke County, Newport, TN, p. A391

BUCKNER Jr., James E., Administrator, Cuero Community Hospital, Cuero, TX, p. A402

BUDDE, Dale G., President, Marycrest Health System, Denver, CO, p. B116

BUDNICK, Michael J., Administrator and Chief Executive Officer, Gibson General Hospital, Princeton, IN, p. A145

BUDRYS, Raymond, Chief Executive Officer, Craven Regional Medical Authority, New Bern, NC, p. A311

BUECHLER, Verlin, President and Chief Executive Officer, Kenmare Community Hospital, Kenmare, ND, p. A318

BUHRMANN, Henry J., President and Chief Executive Officer, Marin General Hospital, Greenbrae, CA, p. A44

BULGER, Robert J., President and Chief Executive Officer, Jeannette District Memorial Hospital, Jeannette, PA, p. A355

BULL, Jayne R., Administrator, Leelanau Memorial Health Center, Northport, MI, p. A217

BULLARD, Elizabeth A., Administrator, Madison Parish Hospital, Tallulah, LA, p. A187

BULLOCK, Scott B., President, MaineGeneral Medical Center–Waterville Campus, Waterville, ME, p. A192

BUMPAS, James C., Director, Central State Hospital, Petersburg, VA, p. A441

BUNCH, Jim, President and Chief Executive Officer, Jellico Community Hospital, Jellico, TN, p. A387

BUNCH, Jimm, Chief Executive Officer, Memorial Hospital, Manchester, KY, p. A174

BUNKER, Stephen P., President and Chief Operating Officer, Holmes Regional Medical Center, Melbourne, FL, p. A90

BURCHILL, Kevin R., Executive Director, Community Medical Center, Toms River, NJ, p. A278

BURD, Ronald P., President and Chief Executive Officer, Devereux Foundation, Villanova, PA, p. B98

BURDEN, Susan, Acting Chief Executive Officer, College Hospital Costa Mesa, Costa Mesa, CA, p. A40

BURDICK, Steve, Administrator, Providence Toppenish Hospital, Toppenish, WA, p. A451

BURDIN Jr., John J., President and Chief Executive Officer, Lafayette General Medical Center, Lafayette, LA, p. A182

BURFEIND, Raymond F., President, Covenant Medical Center, Waterloo, IA, p. A155

BURFITT, Gregory H., President and Chief Executive Officer, Brookwood Medical Center, Birmingham, AL, p. A11

BURGER, Janice, Operations Administrator, Providence Milwaukie Hospital, Milwaukie, OR, p. A346

BURGESS, Roger M., Administrator, St. Francis Hospital, Escanaba, MI, p. A211

BURGHER, Louis, Ph.D., President and Chief Executive Officer, Nebraska Health System, Omaha, NE, p. A263

BURGIN, Robert F., President and Chief Executive Officer, Mission Hospital, Asheville, NC, p. A304

BURGIO, David E., FACHE, President and Chief Executive Officer, Berea Hospital, Berea, KY, p. A168

BURKE, Dennis E., President, Good Shepherd Community Hospital, Hermiston, OR, p. A345

BURKET, Mark, Chief Executive Officer, Platte Community Memorial Hospital, Platte, SD, p. A380

BURKHARD, Thomas, Commanding Officer, Naval Hospital, Camp Pendleton, CA, p. A38

BURKHARDT Jr., J. Bland, Senior Vice President and Administrator, Greenville Memorial Hospital, Greenville, SC, p. A374

BURKHART, James R., FACHE
Administrator, Fort Sanders Regional Medical Center, Knoxville, TN, p. A388
Administrator, Fort Sanders–Parkwest Medical Center, Knoxville, TN, p. A388

BURN, Robert B., President and Chief Executive Officer, Washoe Medical Center, Reno, NV, p. A267

BURNETTE, W. Scott, Chief Executive Officer, Effingham Hospital, Springfield, GA, p. A111

BURNS, Charlotte, Administrator and Chief Executive Officer, Hardin County General Hospital, Savannah, TN, p. A392

BURNS, Dennis R., Administrator and Chief Executive Officer, Sonoma Valley Hospital, Sonoma, CA, p. A63

BURNS, Gregory T., Executive Director, St. Joseph's Community Hospital of West Bend, West Bend, WI, p. A467

BURNS, Randall P., Director and Chief Executive Officer, Alaska Psychiatric Hospital, Anchorage, AK, p. A20

BURROUGHS, Michael R., President and Chief Executive Officer, Northlake Regional Medical Center, Atlanta, GA, p. A101

BURTON, Gary, Chief Executive Officer, Bledsoe County General Hospital, Pikeville, TN, p. A392

BURTON, W. R., Administrator, Memorial Hospital at Gulfport, Gulfport, MS, p. A235

BURZYNSKI, Cheryl A., President, Bay Special Care, Bay City, MI, p. A209

BUSBIN, Patsy, Acting Chief Executive Officer, Bacon County Hospital, Alma, GA, p. A100

BUSCH, Walter, Administrator, Roosevelt Memorial Medical Center, Culbertson, MT, p. A254

BUSER, Kenneth R., President and Chief Executive Officer, Union Memorial Hospital, Baltimore, MD, p. A194

BUSH, Mark E., Executive Vice President, MidMichigan Medical Center–Gladwin, Gladwin, MI, p. A212

BUSHMAIER, Jim E., Administrator and Chief Executive Officer, Stuttgart Regional Medical Center, Stuttgart, AR, p. A35

BUSTELO, Miguel J., Executive Director, Dr. Pila's Hospital, Ponce, PR, p. A473

BUTIKOFER, Lon D., Ph.D., Administrator and Chief Executive Officer, Delaware County Memorial Hospital, Manchester, IA, p. A152

BUTLER, Beatrice, Superintendent, Terrell State Hospital, Terrell, TX, p. A426

BUTLER, David, Chief Executive Officer, Valley Regional Medical Center, Brownsville, TX, p. A399

BUTLER, Everett A., Chief Executive Officer, Unity Medical Center, Grafton, ND, p. A317

BUTLER, Frank, Director, University of Kentucky Hospital, Lexington, KY, p. A172

BUTLER, Peter W., President and Chief Executive Officer, Methodist Health Care System, Houston, TX, p. B119

BUTLER, Richard E., Chief Executive Officer, Western Medical Center–Santa Ana, Santa Ana, CA, p. A62

BUTLER, Ronald G., Chief Executive Officer, Columbia Eastern Idaho Regional Medical Center, Idaho Falls, ID, p. A117

BUTLER, Jeffrey L., Administrator, Malcolm Grow Medical Center, Andrews AFB, MD, p. A193

BUTLER, Joe W.
Deputy Commander and Administrator, Bayne–Jones Army Community Hospital, Fort Polk, LA, p. A180
Deputy Commander Administration, Martin Army Community Hospital, Fort Benning, GA, p. A106

BUTTS, Charles N., Interim Chief Executive Officer, Reeves County Hospital, Pecos, TX, p. A420

BUTTS, Donald E., Chief Executive Officer, Gulf Coast Medical Center, Panama City, FL, p. A93

BUURMAN, Rita K., Chief Executive Officer, Sabetha Community Hospital, Sabetha, KS, p. A165

BYBEE, Bob L., President and Chief Executive Officer, Memorial Medical Center, Port Lavaca, TX, p. A421

BYRNE, Frank D., M.D., President, Parkview Hospital, Fort Wayne, IN, p. A139

BYRNES, Nancy A., President and Chief Executive Officer, Navarro Regional Hospital, Corsicana, TX, p. A402

BYROM, David, Administrator, Coryell Memorial Hospital, Gatesville, TX, p. A408

C

CABONOR, Regis, Administrator, Person County Memorial Hospital, Roxboro, NC, p. A312

CACKLER, Ron, President and Chief Executive Officer, Cushing Regional Hospital, Cushing, OK, p. A336

CAGEN, Richard M., Chief Executive Officer and Administrator, LDS Hospital, Salt Lake City, UT, p. A432

CAGLE, Brooks, Chief Executive Officer, Charter Rivers Behavioral Health System, West Columbia, SC, p. A377

CAHILL, Patricia A., President and Chief Executive Officer, Catholic Health Initiatives, Denver, CO, p. B77

CAIN, Margaret C., Chief Executive Officer, Columbia North Suburban Medical Center, Thornton, CO, p. A73

CAIN, R. Mark, Executive Director, Southwest Hospital, Little Rock, AR, p. A32

CAIN, Thomas, Administrator and Chief Executive Officer, Malvern Institute, Malvern, PA, p. A357

CAISON, S. Beth, Administrator, Collingsworth General Hospital, Wellington, TX, p. A428

CALAMARI, Frank A., President and Chief Executive Officer, Calvary Hospital, New York, NY, p. A292

CALBONE, Angelo G.
President and Chief Executive Officer, Mount St. Mary's Hospital of Niagara Falls, Lewiston, NY, p. A289
President and Chief Executive Officer, Niagara Falls Memorial Medical Center, Niagara Falls, NY, p. A297

CALDERIN, Carolina, Chief Executive Officer, Pan American Hospital, Miami, FL, p. A91

CALDERONE, John, Ph.D., Chief Executive Officer, Corona Regional Medical Center, Corona, CA, p. A40

CALDWELL, Darren, Chief Executive Officer, Drew Memorial Hospital, Monticello, AR, p. A33

CALDWELL, Harvey G., Administrator and Chief Executive Officer, Brainerd Regional Human Services Center, Brainerd, MN, p. A223

CALDWELL, Robert C., Chief Operating Officer, St. Joseph Center for Mental Health, Omaha, NE, p. A263

CALE, Barbara R., Administrator, Chowan Hospital, Edenton, NC, p. A307

CALEY, George B., President, Winchester Medical Center, Winchester, VA, p. A444

CALHOUN, Kevin P., President and Chief Executive Officer, Bell Memorial Hospital, Ishpeming, MI, p. A214

CALICO, Forrest, M.D., President, Appalachian Regional Healthcare, Lexington, KY, p. B67

CALLAHAN, Keith L., Executive Vice President and Administrator, St. Mary's Hospital, Decatur, IL, p. A125

CALLAHAN, Kevin J., President and Chief Executive Officer, Exeter Hospital, Exeter, NH, p. A268

CALLAHAN, Michael A., Chief Executive Officer, Northwest Texas Healthcare System, Amarillo, TX, p. A395

CALLAN Sr., Michael J., Chief Executive Officer, Ashland Regional Medical Center, Ashland, PA, p. A349

CALLISON, William L., Chief Executive Officer, Charter Greenville Behavioral Health System, Greer, SC, p. A374

CALLOWAY, Jack A., Chief Executive Officer, Highlands–Cashiers Hospital, Highlands, NC, p. A309

CALTRIDER, Jerry, Administrator, Bradford Health Services at Oak Mountain, Pelham, AL, p. A17

CALVARUSO, Joseph, Interim Chief Executive Officer, Mount Carmel Health System, Columbus, OH, p. A325

CAMERON, Marie, FACHE, President and Chief Executive Officer, Southwest Hospital and Medical Center, Atlanta, GA, p. A101

CAMMACK Jr., Thomas N., Chief Executive Officer, Marshall Regional Medical Center, Marshall, TX, p. A417

CAMPBELL, Bruce C., President and Chief Executive Officer, Illinois Masonic Medical Center, Chicago, IL, p. A122

CAMPBELL, C. Scott, Executive Director, Bulloch Memorial Hospital, Statesboro, GA, p. A112

CAMPBELL, David J., President and Chief Executive Officer, Detroit Medical Center, Detroit, MI, p. B98

CAMPBELL, Deborah, Administrator, Thomas H. Boyd Memorial Hospital, Carrollton, IL, p. A121

CAMPBELL, Gary L., Director, Harry S. Truman Memorial Veterans Hospital, Columbia, MO, p. A242

CAMPBELL, H. Neil, Chief Executive Officer, Children's Comprehensive Services, Inc., Nashville, TN, p. B81

CAMPBELL, Phil, FACHE, Administrator, Woods Memorial Hospital District, Etowah, TN, p. A385

CAMPBELL, Rita A., Executive Vice President and Chief Executive Officer, Western Arizona Regional Medical Center, Bullhead City, AZ, p. A22

CAMPBELL, Ronald, Administrator, McCurtain Memorial Hospital, Idabel, OK, p. A338

CAMPBELL, Stephen J., Administrator, Southwestern General Hospital, El Paso, TX, p. A406

CAMPBELL, Wayne, Chief Executive Officer, Fort Walton Beach Medical Center, Fort Walton Beach, FL, p. A85

CAMPBELL, William E., Ph.D., Superintendent, Glenwood State Hospital School, Glenwood, IA, p. A151

CAMPBELL Jr., Robert D., Administrator, Cascade Valley Hospital, North Snohomish County Health System, Arlington, WA, p. A445

CAMPION, Brian C., M.D.
President and Chief Executive Officer, Franciscan Skemp Healthcare, La Crosse, WI, p. B101
Chief Executive Officer, Franciscan Skemp Healthcare–La Crosse Campus, La Crosse, WI, p. A460

CANDINO, Paul J., Chief Executive Officer, Erie County Medical Center, Buffalo, NY, p. A286

CANISIA, M., Administrator, Saint Francis Medical Center, Peoria, IL, p. A133

CANNINGTON, H. D., Chief Executive Officer, Doctor's Memorial Hospital, Perry, FL, p. A94

CANNON, James C., Administrator and Chief Executive Officer, Regional Hospital for Respiratory and Complex Care, Seattle, WA, p. A449

CANTRELL, Gary, President and Chief Executive Officer, Lawnwood Regional Medical Center, Fort Pierce, FL, p. A85

CANTWELL, Jerry, Administrator, Delta County Memorial Hospital, Delta, CO, p. A69

CAPOBIANCO, Peter E., President and Chief Executive Officer, St. Mary's Hospital, Amsterdam, NY, p. A284

CAPONI, Vincent C., President and Chief Executive Officer, St. Vincent's Hospital, Birmingham, AL, p. A12

CAPPELLO, Thomas A., Director, Veterans Affairs Pittsburgh Healthcare System, Pittsburgh, PA, p. A364

CARALIS, George P., President and Chief Executive Officer, Alta Bates Medical Center–Ashby Campus, Berkeley, CA, p. A38

CARBONE, Davide M., Chief Executive Officer, Aventura Hospital and Medical Center, Miami, FL, p. A90

CARDA, Timothy L.
Administrator and Chief Executive Officer, Buena Park Medical Center, Buena Park, CA, p. A38
Chief Executive Officer, Tustin Hospital, Tustin, CA, p. A65

CAREY, Frederick M., Executive Director, West Jersey Hospital–Camden, Camden, NJ, p. A272

CAREY, Jeffrey, Administrator, Gila Regional Medical Center, Silver City, NM, p. A283

CARL, Gerald E.
Administrator, Arnold Memorial Health Care Center, Adrian, MN, p. A222
Administrator, Luverne Community Hospital, Luverne, MN, p. A227

CARLBERG, Duane A., President and Chief Executive Officer, Windham Community Memorial Hospital, Willimantic, CT, p. A77

CARLE, Chris, Administrator, St. Elizabeth Medical Center–Grant County, Williamstown, KY, p. A177

CARLIN, Martin E., President, Park Ridge Hospital, Rochester, NY, p. A299

CARLISLE, John T., Chief Executive Officer, Cape Fear Valley Health System, Fayetteville, NC, p. A307

CARLSON, Brian J., President and Chief Executive Officer, Lake View Memorial Hospital, Two Harbors, MN, p. A231

CARLSON, Donald R., President and Chief Executive Officer, San Juan Regional Medical Center, Farmington, NM, p. A281

CARLSON, Greg L., President and Chief Executive Officer, Owensboro Mercy Health System, Owensboro, KY, p. A175

CARLSON, Joan M., Administrator, St. Joseph Hospital and Health Centers, Memphis, TN, p. A390

CARLSON, Roland R., Chief Executive Officer, Sandwich Community Hospital, Sandwich, IL, p. A134

CARLSON, Stephen G., President and Chief Operating Officer, Flagstaff Medical Center, Flagstaff, AZ, p. A22

CARLSTEDT, Nancy S., President, Bloomington Hospital, Bloomington, IN, p. A137

CARMAN, Robert O., President, Wuesthoff Hospital, Rockledge, FL, p. A95

CARMAN, Thomas H., President and Chief Executive Officer, Cortland Memorial Hospital, Cortland, NY, p. A287

CARMEN, Robert G., President and Chief Executive Officer, Glendale Adventist Medical Center, Glendale, CA, p. A44

CARMICHAEL, LeRoy, Executive Director, Bronx Psychiatric Center, New York, NY, p. A291

CARMONA, Richard, M.D., Chief Executive Officer, Kino Community Hospital, Tucson, AZ, p. A27

CARNEY, Christopher M., President and Chief Executive Officer, Bon Secours Health System, Inc., Marriottsville, MD, p. B73

CARNEY, David J., Chief Executive Officer, Southwest Georgia Regional Medical Center, Cuthbert, GA, p. A104

CARNEY, Michael J., Chief Executive Officer, Charter Hospital of Winston–Salem, Winston–Salem, NC, p. A315

CAROBENE, Joseph W., Superintendent, Middle Tennessee Mental Health Institute, Nashville, TN, p. A391

CAROSELLI, Joseph P., Administrator, Idaho Elks Rehabilitation Hospital, Boise, ID, p. A116

CARPENTER, David R., FACHE, Senior Vice President and Administrator, Scottsdale Healthcare–Osborn, Scottsdale, AZ, p. A26

CARR, C. Larry, President, Bakersfield Memorial Hospital, Bakersfield, CA, p. A37

CARR, Wiley N., President and Chief Executive Officer, Porter Memorial Hospital, Valparaiso, IN, p. A146

CARRAWAY, Robert M., M.D., Chairman and Chief Executive Officer, Carraway Methodist Health System, Birmingham, AL, p. B77

CARRELL, Jan V., Chief Executive Officer, Riverside Medical Center, Waupaca, WI, p. A467

CARRIER, Patrick Brian, Administrator, Opelousas General Hospital, Opelousas, LA, p. A186

CARRINGTON–MURRAY, Cynthia, Executive Director, Woodhull Medical and Mental Health Center, New York, NY, p. A296

CARROCINO, Joanne, Executive Director, Kimball Medical Center, Lakewood, NJ, p. A274

CARROLL, Allen P., Chief Executive Officer, Bon Secours–St. Francis Xavier Hospital, Charleston, SC, p. A371

CARROLL, James J., Administrator, Cloquet Community Memorial Hospital, Cloquet, MN, p. A223

CARROLL, Kevin J., President, Champlain Valley Physicians Hospital Medical Center, Plattsburgh, NY, p. A298

CARROLL, Michael W., Administrator, Richland Parish Hospital–Delhi, Delhi, LA, p. A180

CARROLL, Dale, Commander, Moncrief Army Community Hospital, Fort Jackson, SC, p. A374

CARRON, Patrick E., CHE, Administrator, Perry County Memorial Hospital, Perryville, MO, p. A248

CARSON, Mitchell C., President, Ball Memorial Hospital, Muncie, IN, p. A144

CARSON, Randal E., Administrator, Methodist Hospital of McKenzie, McKenzie, TN, p. A389

CARSON, Sandra C., FACHE, Senior Vice President, Methodist Richard Young, Omaha, NE, p. A262

CARSON, Terry, Chief Executive Officer, Harrison Community Hospital, Cadiz, OH, p. A321

CARTER, Bruce C., President, United Hospital Center, Clarksburg, WV, p. A453

CARTER, Michael C., Chief Executive Officer, Anaheim Memorial Medical Center, Anaheim, CA, p. A36

CARTER, Richard, Chief Executive Officer, Hunt Memorial Hospital District, Greenville, TX, p. A409

CARTY, Clare, President and Chief Executive Officer, St. Mary Medical Center, Langhorne, PA, p. A356

CARVALHO, Diane, Administrator, Norfolk Psychiatric Center, Norfolk, VA, p. A440

CARVER, John W., FACHE, Executive Director, Methodist Medical Center, Dallas, TX, p. A403

CARY, Roger C., President and Chief Executive Officer, Midwestern Regional Medical Center, Zion, IL, p. A136

CASEY, Dennis A., Executive Director, Albert Lindley Lee Memorial Hospital, Fulton, NY, p. A288

CASEY, Jack, Administrator, Shodair Children's Hospital, Helena, MT, p. A255

CASEY, Timothy M., President and Chief Executive Officer, Montgomery Hospital, Norristown, PA, p. A359

CASEY, William J.
Administrator, Kingsburg District Hospital, Kingsburg, CA, p. A46
Chief Executive Officer, Sanger General Hospital, Sanger, CA, p. A62

CASEY, Lynn, President and Chief Executive Officer, St. Mary's Hospital and Medical Center, Grand Junction, CO, p. A71

CASHION, John A., FACHE, President, Lexington Memorial Hospital, Lexington, NC, p. A310

CASSELL, Carol M., Executive Vice President and Chief Operating Officer, Millard Fillmore Health System, Buffalo, NY, p. A286

CLARK, Robert J., FACHE, President and Chief Executive Officer, Gnaden Huetten Memorial Hospital, Lehighton, PA, p. A357

CLARK, Thomas, President and Chief Executive Officer, Saints Memorial Medical Center, Lowell, MA, p. A203

CLARK, Wayne N., President and Chief Executive Officer, Arlington Memorial Hospital, Arlington, TX, p. A396

CLARK, William S., Chief Executive Officer, Columbus County Hospital, Whiteville, NC, p. A314

CLARK, David L., USAF, Commander, U. S. Air Force Hospital Altus, Altus, OK, p. A335

CLARK Jr., Ralph, President, Helen Keller Hospital, Sheffield, AL, p. A18

CLARKE, Richard W., Chief Executive Officer, Emanuel County Hospital, Swainsboro, GA, p. A112

CLARKE, Robert T.
President and Chief Executive Officer, Memorial Health System, Springfield, IL, p. B117
President and Chief Executive Officer, Memorial Medical Center, Springfield, IL, p. A135

CLASSEN, Howard H., Chief Executive Officer, Natividad Medical Center, Salinas, CA, p. A58

CLAY, James L., Director, Central Alabama Veteran Affairs Health Care System, Montgomery, AL, p. A16

CLAYTON, Kent G.
Chief Executive Officer, Coastal Communities Hospital, Santa Ana, CA, p. A62
Chief Executive Officer, Santa Ana Hospital Medical Center, Santa Ana, CA, p. A62

CLAYTON, Philip A., President and Chief Executive Officer, Conway Hospital, Conway, SC, p. A373

CLEARWATER, William J., Vice President and Administrator, St. John's Pleasant Valley Hospital, Camarillo, CA, p. A38

CLEARY, John J., President and Chief Executive Officer, River Oaks Hospital, Jackson, MS, p. A236

CLEM, Olie E., Chief Executive Officer, Doctors Memorial Hospital, Tyler, TX, p. A427

CLEMENT, Mark C., President and Chief Executive Officer, Holy Cross Hospital, Chicago, IL, p. A122

CLEMENTS, Larry E., Administrator, Wildwood Lifestyle Center and Hospital, Wildwood, GA, p. A113

CLENDENIN, Philip A., Chief Executive Officer, Greenview Regional Hospital, Bowling Green, KY, p. A168

CLIBORNE Jr., James J., Chief Executive Officer, Selby General Hospital, Marietta, OH, p. A329

CLICK, Mike, Administrator, Brownfield Regional Medical Center, Brownfield, TX, p. A399

CLINE, Phillip E., Administrator, Providence Kodiak Island Medical Center, Kodiak, AK, p. A21

CLOHAN Jr., Jack C., Administrator, William R. Sharpe Jr. Hospital, Weston, WV, p. A456

CLOUGH, Jeanette G., President and Chief Executive Officer, Deaconess Waltham Hospital, Waltham, MA, p. A206

COATES, Cliff, Chief Executive Officer, Sutter Medical Center, Santa Rosa, Santa Rosa, CA, p. A63

COATES, David M., Ph.D., President and Chief Executive Officer, Reed City Hospital Corporation, Reed City, MI, p. A218

COATS, Rodney M., President and Chief Executive Officer, Washington County Memorial Hospital, Salem, IN, p. A145

COBB, Terrell M., Executive Director, Greenwood Leflore Hospital, Greenwood, MS, p. A235

COCHRAN, Barry S.
President, Cherokee Baptist Medical Center, Centre, AL, p. A13
President, DeKalb Baptist Medical Center, Fort Payne, AL, p. A14

COCHRAN, Gloria, Administrator, Burke County Hospital, Waynesboro, GA, p. A113

COCHRAN, John, Administrator, Richland Hospital, Mansfield, OH, p. A329

COCHRAN, Shelley R., Interim Chief Executive Officer, Specialty Hospital of Houston, Houston, TX, p. A412

CODY, Carol, Administrator, Christopher House, Austin, TX, p. A397

CODY, Douglas M., Administrator, Amos Cottage Rehabilitation Hospital, Winston-Salem, NC, p. A314

COE, William G., Executive Vice President and Chief Executive Officer, La Paz Regional Hospital, Parker, AZ, p. A24

COHEN, Bruce M., M.D., President and Psychiatrist-in-Chief, McLean Hospital, Belmont, MA, p. A199

COHEN, Elliot G., Senior Executive Officer, University Hospital, Cincinnati, OH, p. A323

COHEN, Jed M., Acting Executive Director, Western New York Children's Psychiatric Center, Buffalo, NY, p. A286

COHEN, Kenneth B., Director, Riverside County Regional Medical Center, Moreno Valley, CA, p. A53

COHEN, Philip A., Chief Executive Officer, Garfield Medical Center, Monterey Park, CA, p. A53

COHEN, Steven M., M.D., Director, Veterans Affairs Medical Center, Dayton, OH, p. A326

COHOLICH, Robert J., Chief Executive Officer, Henry County Hospital, Napoleon, OH, p. A330

COKER Jr., Robert J., Administrator, Greene County Hospital, Eutaw, AL, p. A14

COLBY, Dan, President and Chief Executive Officer, Harvard Memorial Hospital, Harvard, IL, p. A128

COLCHER, Marian W., Interim Administrator, Valley Forge Medical Center and Hospital, Norristown, PA, p. A359

COLE, Geoffrey F., President and Chief Executive Officer, Emerson Hospital, Concord, MA, p. A202

COLE, James B., President and Chief Executive Officer, Arlington Hospital, Arlington, VA, p. A436

COLE, James M., President and Chief Executive Officer, Cleo Wallace Centers Hospital, Westminster, CO, p. A73

COLECCHI, Stephen, President and Chief Executive Officer, Robinson Memorial Hospital, Ravenna, OH, p. A331

COLEMAN, Dan C., President and Chief Executive Officer, John C. Lincoln Health Network, Phoenix, AZ, p. A24

COLEMAN, Dennis E., President and Chief Executive Officer, Granada Hills Community Hospital, Los Angeles, CA, p. A49

COLEMAN, James, Director, Kalamazoo Regional Psychiatric Hospital, Kalamazoo, MI, p. A214

COLEMAN, Kevin T., Administrator, Baptist Hospital-Orange, Orange, TX, p. A419

COLFACK, Brian R., CHE, President and Chief Executive Officer, Berger Health System, Circleville, OH, p. A323

COLLER, James G., Executive Vice President and Administrator, St. Mary's Hospital Medical Center, Green Bay, WI, p. A459

COLLETTE, Dennis H., President and Chief Executive Officer, Newton Memorial Hospital, Newton, NJ, p. A276

COLLIER, C. Thomas, President and Chief Executive Officer, Sierra Nevada Memorial Hospital, Grass Valley, CA, p. A44

COLLING, Kenneth F., Senior Vice President and Area Manager, Kaiser Foundation Hospital, San Diego, CA, p. A59

COLLINS, Dale, President and Chief Executive Officer, Baptist Health System of Tennessee, Knoxville, TN, p. B69

COLLINS, James L., M.D., Clinical Director', Crownsville Hospital Center, Crownsville, MD, p. A195

COLLINS, Jeffrey A., Chief Executive Officer, Sun Coast Hospital, Largo, FL, p. A89

COLLINS, Michael F., M.D.
President, Caritas Christi Health Care, Boston, MA, p. B76
President, St. Elizabeth's Medical Center of Boston, Boston, MA, p. A201

COLLINS, Michael L., Chief Executive Officer, Seven Rivers Community Hospital, Crystal River, FL, p. A83

COLLINS, Roger, Chief Executive Officer and Managing Director, Valley Hospital Medical Center, Las Vegas, NV, p. A266

COLLINS, Thomas J., President and Chief Executive Officer, Memorial Health Services, Long Beach, CA, p. B117

COLLYER, Stuart C., Director, Veterans Affairs Medical Center, Canandaigua, NY, p. A286

COLON, Ivan E., Administrator, Auxilio Mutuo Hospital, San Juan, PR, p. A473

COLSTON, Allen J., Acting Director, Veterans Affairs Medical Center, Muskogee, OK, p. A339

COLVERT, Charles C., President, Shelby Baptist Medical Center, Alabaster, AL, p. A11

COLVIN, James E., Executive Director, Devereux Hospital and Children's Center of Florida, Melbourne, FL, p. A90

COLVIN, Robert A., President and Chief Executive Officer, Memorial Health System, Savannah, GA, p. A111

COLWELL, Loretto Marie, President, St. Francis Hospital and Medical Center, Topeka, KS, p. A166

COMER, W. Jefferson, FACHE, Chief Executive Officer, Northwest Medical Center, Tucson, AZ, p. A27

COMERFORD Jr., Thomas P., Superintendent, Clarks Summit State Hospital, Clarks Summit, PA, p. A351

COMPSON, Oral R., Administrator, Dayton General Hospital, Dayton, WA, p. A446

COMSTOCK, John M., Chief Executive Officer, Sioux Valley Memorial Hospital, Cherokee, IA, p. A148

CONDOM, Jaime E., M.D., Director, South Carolina State Hospital, Columbia, SC, p. A373

CONDON, Debra, Administrator, Vencor Hospital-Philadelphia, Philadelphia, PA, p. A362

CONDRASKY, Louis M., Chief Operating Officer, HEALTHSOUTH Lake Erie Institute of Rehabilitation, Erie, PA, p. A353

CONEJO, David, Chief Executive Officer, Highland Medical Center, Lubbock, TX, p. A416

CONELL, Marge, R.N., Administrator, Ellinwood District Hospital, Ellinwood, KS, p. A158

CONGER, Rex D., President and Chief Executive Officer, Iroquois Memorial Hospital and Resident Home, Watseka, IL, p. A136

CONKLIN, Richard L., President, Parkland Health Center, Farmington, MO, p. A243

CONN, Kevin R., Administrator, HEALTHSOUTH Sunrise Rehabilitation Hospital, Fort Lauderdale, FL, p. A84

CONNELL, Daniel R., President, Christ Hospital, Jersey City, NJ, p. A274

CONNELL, Joe M., Chief Executive Officer, Lake Wales Medical Centers, Lake Wales, FL, p. A88

CONNELLY, Harrell L., Chief Executive Officer, Wallace Thomson Hospital, Union, SC, p. A377

CONNELLY, Michael D., President and Chief Executive Officer, Catholic Healthcare Partners, Cincinnati, OH, p. B79

CONNOLEY, William B.
President and Chief Executive Officer, Mary Bridge Children's Hospital and Health Center, Tacoma, WA, p. A450
President, MultiCare Health System, Tacoma, WA, p. B120
President and Chief Executive Officer, Tacoma General Hospital, Tacoma, WA, p. A451

CONNOLLY, Brian M., President and Chief Executive Officer, Providence Hospital and Medical Centers, Southfield, MI, p. A219

CONNOLLY, James W., President and Chief Executive Officer, Mercy Hospital, Buffalo, NY, p. A286

CONNOR III, Paul J., Administrator, St. John's Episcopal Hospital-South Shore, New York, NY, p. A296

CONOLE, Charles P., FACHE, Administrator, Edward John Noble Hospital of Gouverneur, Gouverneur, NY, p. A288

CONSIDINE, William H., President, Children's Hospital Medical Center of Akron, Akron, OH, p. A320

CONSTANTINE, Richard D., Chief Executive Officer, Brownsville General Hospital, Brownsville, PA, p. A350

CONSTANTINO, Richard S., M.D., President, Rochester General Hospital, Rochester, NY, p. A299

CONTE, Richard L., Chief Executive Officer and Chairman of the Board, Transitional Hospitals Corporation, Las Vegas, NV, p. B146

CONTE, William A., Director, Edith Nourse Rogers Memorial Veterans Hospital, Bedford, MA, p. A199

CONTI, Vincent S., President and Chief Executive Officer, Maine Medical Center, Portland, ME, p. A191

CONWAY, Jerry, Chief Executive Officer, BHC Vista Del Mar Hospital, Ventura, CA, p. A66

CONZEMIUS, James D., President, Flagler Hospital, Saint Augustine, FL, p. A95

COOK, E. Tim, Chief Executive Officer, Osceola Medical Center, Kissimmee, FL, p. A88

COOK, Jack M., President and Chief Executive Officer, Health Alliance of Greater Cincinnati, Cincinnati, OH, p. B103

COOK, Richard P., Chief Executive Officer, Columbia Fairview Park Hospital, Dublin, GA, p. A105

COOK, Thomas J., Chief Executive Officer, HEALTHSOUTH Rehabilitation Hospital–Tyler, Tyler, TX, p. A427

COOK, William R., Chief Executive Officer, Specialty Hospital of Austin, Austin, TX, p. A397

COONS, Chris, Chief Operating Officer, Utah Valley Regional Medical Center, Provo, UT, p. A431

COOPER, Anthony J., President and Chief Executive Officer, Arnot Ogden Medical Center, Elmira, NY, p. A287

COOPER, Chad, Administrator, Sleepy Eye Municipal Hospital, Sleepy Eye, MN, p. A231

COOPER, Gerson I., President, Botsford General Hospital, Farmington Hills, MI, p. A211

COOPER, Gloria, Chief Executive Officer, Mount Carmel Hospital, Colville, WA, p. A446

COOPER, James C.
    Chief Executive Officer, Sewickley Valley Hospital, (A Division of Valley Medical Facilities), Sewickley, PA, p. A365
    Chief Operating Officer, The Medical Center, Beaver, Beaver, PA, p. A350

COOPER, Maxine T.
    Chief Executive Officer, Chapman Medical Center, Orange, CA, p. A54
    Chief Executive Officer, Placentia–Linda Hospital, Placentia, CA, p. A56

COOPER, Paul S.
    Chief Executive Officer, Newcomb Medical Center, Vineland, NJ, p. A278
    Chief Executive Officer, South Jersey Hospital, Bridgeton, NJ, p. A271

COOPER, Robert, Chief Executive Officer, Marshalltown Medical and Surgical Center, Marshalltown, IA, p. A153

COOPER, Roger W., President, Smyth County Community Hospital, Marion, VA, p. A439

COORS, Mary Lou
    Administrator, St. Joseph Rehabilitation Hospital and Outpatient Center, Albuquerque, NM, p. A280
    Administrator, St. Joseph West Mesa Hospital, Albuquerque, NM, p. A281

COPELAN, H. Neil, President and Chief Executive Officer, South Fulton Medical Center, East Point, GA, p. A106

COPENHAVER, C. Curtis, Chief Executive Officer, Mercy Hospital, Charlotte, NC, p. A306

COPLEY, Brenda, Acting Administrator, East Texas Medical Center Rusk, Rusk, TX, p. A422

CORA, Jose, Executive Director, Ashford Presbyterian Community Hospital, San Juan, PR, p. A473

CORBEIL, Stephen, President and Chief Executive Officer, Medical City Dallas Hospital, Dallas, TX, p. A403

CORBETT, Clifford L., President and Chief Executive Officer, Morris Hospital, Morris, IL, p. A131

CORCORAN, Joseph P., President and Chief Executive Officer, New York Eye and Ear Infirmary, New York, NY, p. A294

CORDER, Thomas J., President and Chief Executive Officer, Camden–Clark Memorial Hospital, Parkersburg, WV, p. A455

CORDNER, Glenn D., Chief Executive Officer, Springfield Hospital, Springfield, VT, p. A435

CORDOVA, Richard, Executive Director, San Francisco General Hospital Medical Center, San Francisco, CA, p. A60

COREY, Jack M., President, DeKalb Memorial Hospital, Auburn, IN, p. A137

CORK, Ronald J., President and Chief Executive Officer, St. Anthony's Hospital, O'Neill, NE, p. A262

CORLEY, Thomas
    Chief Executive Officer, Lourdes Counseling Center, Richland, WA, p. A449
    Chief Executive Officer, Lourdes Medical Center, Pasco, WA, p. A448

CORLEY, William E., President, Community Hospitals Indianapolis, Indianapolis, IN, p. A141

CORNISH, Helen K., Director, Veterans Affairs Medical Center–Lexington, Lexington, KY, p. A172

CORONADO, Jose R., FACHE, Director, South Texas Veterans Health Care System, San Antonio, TX, p. A423

CORVINO, Frank A., President and Chief Executive Officer, Greenwich Hospital, Greenwich, CT, p. A74

CORY, Clarence, President, Ottumwa Regional Health Center, Ottumwa, IA, p. A154

COSTA, Mark, President, Little Company of Mary Hospital, Torrance, CA, p. A65

COSTELLO Jr., Michael J., Chief Executive Officer, Santa Teresita Hospital, Duarte, CA, p. A41

COTNER, Edna J., Administrator, Coquille Valley Hospital, Coquille, OR, p. A344

COTTEY, David, Chief Executive Officer, Columbia Silsbee Doctors Hospital, Silsbee, TX, p. A425

COUCH, Ken, President, Summit Hospital Corporation, Atlanta, GA, p. B142

COUGHLIN, Jean, President and Chief Executive Officer, Marian Community Hospital, Carbondale, PA, p. A351

COURAGE Jr., Kenneth F., Chief Executive Officer, Psychiatric Institute of Washington, Washington, DC, p. A79

COURNOYER, James, Director, Indian Health Service Hospital, Rapid City, SD, p. A380

COURTIER, Steven, Chief Executive Officer, Hollywood Community Hospital of Hollywood, Los Angeles, CA, p. A49

COURTNEY, Curtis B., Administrator, Fentress County General Hospital, Jamestown, TN, p. A387

COURTNEY, Hattie, Administrator, Gladys Spellman Specialty Hospital and Nursing Center, Hyattsville, MD, p. A196

COURTNEY, James P., President and Chief Executive Officer, University Medical Center, Lubbock, TX, p. A416

COUSER, David G., FACHE, Administrator, Audubon County Memorial Hospital, Audubon, IA, p. A147

COUSSONS, R. Timothy, M.D., President and Chief Executive Officer, The University Hospitals, Oklahoma City, OK, p. A340

COVA, Charles J., Executive Vice President, Marian Medical Center, Santa Maria, CA, p. A62

COVERT, Michael H., FACHE, President and Chief Executive Officer, Sarasota Memorial Hospital, Sarasota, FL, p. A96

COVERT, Rob, President and Chief Executive Officer, Oaklawn Hospital, Marshall, MI, p. A216

COVEY, Laird, Interim President, Northern Cumberland Memorial Hospital, Bridgton, ME, p. A190

COVINGTON, Steven, Superintendent, Madison State Hospital, Madison, IN, p. A143

COWAN, Connie, Administrator and Chief Executive Officer, Beverly Specialty Hospitals–HMC, Houston, TX, p. A410

COWAN, Michael L., USN, Commanding Officer, Naval Hospital, Camp Lejeune, NC, p. A305

COWLES, Stuart R., MSC, Administrator, U. S. Air Force Hospital, Fairchild AFB, WA, p. A446

COX, Jay, President and Chief Executive Officer, Tuomey Regional Medical Center, Sumter, SC, p. A376

COX, Keith, CHE, Chief Executive Officer, Charter Behavioral Health System, Mobile, AL, p. A16

COX, Kevin, Interim Administrator, Memorial Hospital of Texas County, Guymon, OK, p. A338

COX, Leigh, Administrator, Navapache Regional Medical Center, Show Low, AZ, p. A26

COX, Otto L.
    President and Chief Executive Officer, Mercy Medical Center, Oshkosh, WI, p. A464
    President and Chief Executive Officer, St. Elizabeth Hospital, Appleton, WI, p. A457

COX Sr., Arthur J., Director, Florida Center for Addictions and Dual Disorders, Avon Park, FL, p. A81

COYNE, Kathryn W., Executive Director and Chief Operating Officer, Union Hospital, Union, NJ, p. A278

CRABTREE, Doug, Chief Executive Officer, Columbia Riverton Memorial Hospital, Riverton, WY, p. A469

CRAIG, Larry, Chief Executive Officer, Jane Todd Crawford Hospital, Greensburg, KY, p. A170

CRAIG, William H., President and Chief Executive Officer, Burleson St. Joseph Health Center, Caldwell, TX, p. A399

CRAIGIN, Jane, Chief Executive Officer, St. Vincent Williamsport Hospital, Williamsport, IN, p. A146

CRAIN, Stephen L.
    President, St Mary Medical Plaza, South Bend, IN, p. A145
    President and Chief Executive Officer, St. Joseph Community Hospital, Mishawaka, IN, p. A143

CRAMER, John S., FACHE, President and Chief Executive Officer, PinnacleHealth System, Harrisburg, PA, p. A355

CRANDALL, David, President and Chief Executive Officer, Hospital for Special Care, New Britain, CT, p. A75

CRANDELL, Kim O., Chief Executive Officer and Administrator, Boulder City Hospital, Boulder City, NV, p. A266

CRANE, Margaret W., Chief Executive Officer, Barlow Respiratory Hospital, Los Angeles, CA, p. A48

CRANSTON, Henry J., Chief Executive Officer, HEALTHSOUTH Sea Pines Rehabilitation Hospital, Melbourne, FL, p. A90

CRANTON, Nancy J., Chief Executive Officer, Shadow Mountain Hospital, Tulsa, OK, p. A342

CRAWFIS, Ewing H., President, Mary Rutan Hospital, Bellefontaine, OH, p. A321

CRAWFORD, David E., FACHE, Executive Vice President and Chief Operating Officer, Medical Center East, Birmingham, AL, p. A12

CRAWFORD, Janet McKinney, Administrator, Carilion Saint Albans Hospital, Radford, VA, p. A441

CRAWFORD, John W., Chief Executive Officer, Wagoner Community Hospital, Wagoner, OK, p. A343

CRAWFORD, R. Vincent, Director, Royal C. Johnson Veterans Memorial Hospital, Sioux Falls, SD, p. A381

CREAMER, Donald R., President and Chief Executive Officer, Susquehanna Health System, Williamsport, PA, p. A368

CREEDEN Jr., Francis V.
    President and Chief Executive Officer, Providence Medical Center, Kansas City, KS, p. A161
    President and Chief Executive Officer, Saint John Hospital, Leavenworth, KS, p. A162

CREELEY, Melvin R., President, East Liverpool City Hospital, East Liverpool, OH, p. A326

CRESS, Michael D., Administrator, Vencor Hospital–San Diego, San Diego, CA, p. A60

CREST, Jerome A., Executive Vice President, Immanuel/St. Joseph's–Mayo Health System, Mankato, MN, p. A227

CREWS, James C., President and Chief Executive Officer, Samaritan Health System, Phoenix, AZ, p. B134

CRIPE, Kimberly C., Chief Executive Officer, Children's Hospital of Orange County, Orange, CA, p. A55

CROFT, Barbara, Health Care Manager, State Penitentiary Hospital, Walla Walla, WA, p. A451

CRONBERG, Chris, Chief Executive Officer, Northern Cochise Community Hospital, Willcox, AZ, p. A28

CRONE, William G., President and Chief Executive Officer, Naples Community Hospital, Naples, FL, p. A91

CRONEN, Kathleen, Chief Executive Officer, Charter North Star Behavioral Health System, Anchorage, AK, p. A20

CRONIN, John C. J., President and Chief Executive Officer, North Adams Regional Hospital, North Adams, MA, p. A204

CROOK, Robert, Administrator, North Sunflower County Hospital, Ruleville, MS, p. A239

CROOM Jr., Kennedy L., Administrator and Chief Executive Officer, Rhea Medical Center, Dayton, TN, p. A385

CROSSETT, Joseph W., Administrator, Liberty Hospital, Liberty, MO, p. A246

CROSSIN, William, Vice President Operations, Miner's Memorial Medical Center, Coaldale, PA, p. A352

CROUCH, Matthew, Chief Executive Officer, Charter Anchor Hospital, Atlanta, GA, p. A100

CROW, David, Chief Executive Officer, Campbell County Memorial Hospital, Gillette, WY, p. A468

CROW, Ruth Ann, Administrator, Lake Whitney Medical Center, Whitney, TX, p. A428

CROW, Tom, Administrator, Atlanta Memorial Hospital, Atlanta, TX, p. A396

CROWDER, Jerry W., President and Chief Executive Officer, Bradford Health Services, Birmingham, AL, p. B73

CROWDER, Harvey R., Commander, U. S. Air Force Hospital, Panama City, FL, p. A93

CROWELL, Eric, President and Chief Executive Officer, Trinity Medical Center–West Campus, Rock Island, IL, p. A134

CROWELL, Lynn, Chief Executive Officer, Howard Memorial Hospital, Nashville, AR, p. A33

CROWLEY, Jane Durney, Chief Executive Officer, Liberty Medical Center, Baltimore, MD, p. A194
President and Chief Executive Officer, Bon Secour Baltimore Health System, Baltimore, MD, p. A193

CROWLEY, Thomas, President, St. Elizabeth Hospital, Wabasha, MN, p. A231

CROWTHER, Bruce K., President and Chief Executive Officer, Northwest Community Healthcare, Arlington Heights, IL, p. A120

CRUICKSHANK, James A., Chief Executive Officer, University Hospital and Medical Center, Tamarac, FL, p. A97

CRUMLIN, Linda J., Chief Executive Officer, Beech Hill Hospital, Dublin, NH, p. A268

CRUMPLER, Joyce, R.N., Administrator, Bowie Memorial Hospital, Bowie, TX, p. A399

CRUMPTON, Althea H., Administrator, Magee General Hospital, Magee, MS, p. A237

CUCCI, Edward A., President and Chief Executive Officer, Swedish Covenant Hospital, Chicago, IL, p. A124

CUDWORTH, Craig R., Chief Executive Officer, Eastern Oklahoma Medical Center, Poteau, OK, p. A341

CULBERSON, David, Chief Executive Officer, West Anaheim Medical Center, Anaheim, CA, p. A36

CULLEN, James J., President, Hospital of Saint Raphael, New Haven, CT, p. A75

CULLEN, Sheila M., Acting Director, Veterans Affairs Medical Center, San Francisco, CA, p. A61

CULLEY, James R., Administrator, Valdez Community Hospital, Valdez, AK, p. A21

CULVERN, Rita, Administrator, Jefferson Hospital, Louisville, GA, p. A108

CUMMING, Irene M., Chief Executive Officer, University of Kansas Medical Center, Kansas City, KS, p. A161

CUMMINGS, Bruce D., Chief Executive Officer, Blue Hill Memorial Hospital, Blue Hill, ME, p. A189

CUMMINS, Jane C., Senior Vice President Clinical Operations, Legacy Mount Hood Medical Center, Gresham, OR, p. A345

CURE, DeAnn K., Chief Executive Officer, Kit Carson County Memorial Hospital, Burlington, CO, p. A68

CURLEY, Terrence A., Executive Director, Selma District Hospital, Selma, CA, p. A63

CURRAN, Joan, Administrator, Campus Hospital of Cleveland, Cleveland, OH, p. A323

CURRIE, Pat
Chief Executive Officer, Columbia Rosewood Medical Center, Houston, TX, p. A410
Chief Executive Officer, Spring Branch Medical Center, Houston, TX, p. A412

CURRIER Jr., Elwood E., CHE, Administrator, Yoakum Community Hospital, Yoakum, TX, p. A429

CURRY, Robert H., Senior Vice President and Chief Executive Officer, Thunderbird Samaritan Medical Center, Glendale, AZ, p. A23

CURTIS, Jeff, President and Chief Executive Officer, H.S.C. Medical Center, Malvern, AR, p. A33

CUSANO, Philip D.
President and Chief Executive Officer, St. Joseph Medical Center, Stamford, CT, p. A76
President and Chief Executive Officer, Stamford Hospital, Stamford, CT, p. A76

CUSHING, Douglas G., Administrator, Elizabethtown Community Hospital, Elizabethtown, NY, p. A287

CUSHING, Jeff, Vice President and Site Administrator, Legacy Meridian Park Hospital, Tualatin, OR, p. A348

CUSTER–MITCHELL, Marilyn J., Administrator, West Central Community Hospital, Clinton, IN, p. A138

CUTHBERT, Garda, Administrator, Oneida County Hospital, Malad City, ID, p. A117

CUTLER, Terry, Executive Director, East Texas Medical Center–Clarksville, Clarksville, TX, p. A400

CWIEK, Mark A., President and Chief Executive Officer, Central Michigan Community Hospital, Mount Pleasant, MI, p. A216

CZIPO, Kevin F., Executive Director, Stony Lodge Hospital, Ossining, NY, p. A298

D

D'AGNES, Michael R., President and Chief Executive Officer, Bayonne Hospital, Bayonne, NJ, p. A271

D'AGOSTINO, James P., Executive Director, Mount San Rafael Hospital, Trinidad, CO, p. A73

D'ALBERTO, Richard E., Chief Executive Officer, J. C. Blair Memorial Hospital, Huntingdon, PA, p. A355

D'AMBROSE, Joan, Chief Executive Officer, Deaconess West Hospital, Saint Louis, MO, p. A249

D'ERAMO, David, President and Chief Executive Officer, Saint Francis Hospital and Medical Center, Hartford, CT, p. A74

D'ETTORRE, Joseph A., Chief Executive Officer, Wyandot Memorial Hospital, Upper Sandusky, OH, p. A333

DAGUE, James O., President, Goshen General Hospital, Goshen, IN, p. A140

DAHILL, Kevin, President and Chief Executive Officer, United Hospital Medical Center, Port Chester, NY, p. A298

DAHLBERG, Edwin E., President, St. Luke's Regional Medical Center, Boise, ID, p. A116

DAHLMAN, Kim, Chief Executive Officer, Wallowa Memorial Hospital, Enterprise, OR, p. A344

DAIGLE, Anthony A., Executive Director, McCuistion Regional Medical Center, Paris, TX, p. A420

DAIKEN, Michael E., Administrator, DeQuincy Memorial Hospital, DeQuincy, LA, p. A180

DAILEY, Deborah S., President and Chief Executive Officer, Hospice of Palm Beach County, West Palm Beach, FL, p. A99

DAILEY, Doug, Chief Executive Officer, Florence Hospital, Florence, AL, p. A14

DAILY, James L., President, Porter Hospital, Middlebury, VT, p. A434

DAL CIELO, William J., Chief Executive Officer, Alameda Hospital, Alameda, CA, p. A36

DALE, Gregory L., Chief Executive Officer, Metropolitan St. Louis Psychiatric Center, Saint Louis, MO, p. A250

DALLEY, Mark F., Chief Executive Officer, Tooele Valley Regional Medical Center, Tooele, UT, p. A433

DALTON, John, President and Chief Executive Officer, Deaconess–Glover Hospital Corporation, Needham, MA, p. A204

DALTON Jr., James E., President and Chief Executive Officer, Quorum Health Group/Quorum Health Resources, Inc., Brentwood, TN, p. B127

DALY, Michael J., President, Baystate Health System, Inc., Springfield, MA, p. B71

DALZELL, James G., Chief Executive Officer, Brown Schools Rehabilitation Center, Austin, TX, p. A396

DAMORE, Joseph F., President and Chief Executive Officer, Sparrow Health System, Lansing, MI, p. A215

DAMPIER, Bobby H., Chief Executive Officer, Regional Medical Center of Hopkins County, Madisonville, KY, p. A174

DANDRIDGE, Thomas C., President, Regional Medical Center of Orangeburg and Calhoun Counties, Orangeburg, SC, p. A376

DANIEL, Steven G., Administrator, Bob Wilson Memorial Grant County Hospital, Ulysses, KS, p. A166

DANIEL, William E., Administrator, Baptist Meriwether Hospital, Warm Springs, GA, p. A113

DANIEL, William W., Chief Executive Officer, Pioneers Memorial Healthcare District, Brawley, CA, p. A38

DANIELS, Gary J., Ph.D., Superintendent, Parsons State Hospital and Training Center, Parsons, KS, p. A164

DANIELS, Gary R., President, Penobscot Bay Medical Center, Rockport, ME, p. A191

DANIELS, J. Lewis, President and Chief Executive Officer, St. Joseph's Hospital, Asheville, NC, p. A304

DANIELS, John D., President and Chief Executive Officer, St. Luke's Regional Medical Center, Sioux City, IA, p. A155

DANIELS, Richard A., President and Chief Executive Officer, McCullough–Hyde Memorial Hospital, Oxford, OH, p. A331

DANILOFF, Michael, President, Evangelical Community Hospital, Lewisburg, PA, p. A357

DANTZKER, David R., M.D., President and Chief Executive Officer, Long Island Jewish Medical Center, New York, NY, p. A293

DARBY, Renate, Interim Chief Executive Officer, Santa Rosa Medical Center, Milton, FL, p. A91

DARLING, J. Rudy, President and Chief Executive Officer, Carroll Regional Medical Center, Berryville, AR, p. A29

DARNEY, Bruce, Superintendent, Harrisburg State Hospital, Harrisburg, PA, p. A355

DASCHER Jr., Norman E., Vice President and Chief Operating Officer, Memorial Hospital, Albany, NY, p. A284

DATTALO, Thomas J., Chief Executive Officer, Riveredge Hospital, Forest Park, IL, p. A127

DAUGHERTY, Charles R., Administrator, Baptist Memorial Hospital, Forrest City, AR, p. A31

DAUGHERTY, Thomas E., Chief Executive Officer, Mecosta County General Hospital, Big Rapids, MI, p. A209

DAUGHERTY Jr., John, Service Unit Director, U. S. Public Health Service Comprehensive Indian Health Facility, Claremore, OK, p. A336

DAVANZO, John P., President and Chief Executive Officer, Our Lady of Victory Hospital, Lackawanna, NY, p. A289

DAVE, Bashker J., M.D., Superintendent, Mental Health Institute, Independence, IA, p. A151

DAVIDGE, Robert C., President and Chief Executive Officer, Our Lady of the Lake Regional Medical Center, Baton Rouge, LA, p. A179

DAVIDSON, Craig Val, CHE, Administrator, Beaver Valley Hospital, Beaver, UT, p. A430

DAVIS, Aleen S., Chief Executive Officer, Charter Behavioral Health System of Atlanta at Peachford, Atlanta, GA, p. A100

DAVIS, Charles A., Administrator, Allen Memorial Hospital, Moab, UT, p. A431

DAVIS, David R., President and Chief Executive Officer, Lee Hospital, Johnstown, PA, p. A356

DAVIS, Donald W., President, Northern Westchester Hospital Center, Mount Kisco, NY, p. A291

DAVIS, Gary, Service Unit Director, U. S. Public Health Service Indian Hospital, Parker, AZ, p. A24

DAVIS, Glen C., Administrator, Grady General Hospital, Cairo, GA, p. A103

DAVIS, Hervey, Administrator, Dr. John Warner Hospital, Clinton, IL, p. A125

DAVIS, James L., Chief Executive Officer, Lee County Community Hospital, Pennington Gap, VA, p. A441

DAVIS, John W., Administrator, Warm Springs Rehabilitation Hospital, Gonzales, TX, p. A408

DAVIS, L. Glenn, Executive Director, Central Carolina Hospital, Sanford, NC, p. A312

DAVIS, Lary, President, Sonora Community Hospital, Sonora, CA, p. A63

DAVIS, Lyle, Administrator, Cozad Community Hospital, Cozad, NE, p. A259

DAVIS, Michael J., Ph.D., Superintendent, Woodward State Hospital–School, Woodward, IA, p. A156

DAVIS, Pamela Meyer, President and Chief Executive Officer, Edward Hospital, Naperville, IL, p. A131

DAVIS, Paul, Administrator, Gove County Medical Center, Quinter, KS, p. A164

DAVIS, Peter B.
Interim Chief Executive Officer, Catholic Medical Center, Manchester, NH, p. A269
Interim President and Chief Executive Officer, Elliot Hospital, Manchester, NH, p. A269

DAVIS, Robert L., President and Chief Executive Officer, North Oakland Medical Centers, Pontiac, MI, p. A217

DAVIS, Rod A., President and Chief Executive Officer, St. Rose Dominican Hospital, Henderson, NV, p. A266

DAVIS, Ronald D., Chief Executive Officer, Washington County Hospital, Washington, IA, p. A155

DAVIS, Rosemari, Chief Executive Officer, Columbia Williamette Valley Medical Center, McMinnville, OR, p. A346

DAVIS, Ryland P., President, Sacred Heart Medical Center, Spokane, WA, p. A450

DAVIS, Donald T., Commander, U. S. Air Force Hospital, Vandenberg AFB, CA, p. A66

DAVIS, M. Adrian, Ph.D., President and Chief Executive Officer, Memorial Hospital and Health Care Center, Jasper, IN, p. A142

DAVIS III, Robert S., CHE, Administrator, Vencor Hospital–Arlington, Arlington, VA, p. A436

DAVIS Jr., Ray H., Chief Executive Officer, Calais Regional Hospital, Calais, ME, p. A190

DAWES, Christopher G., President, Lucile Salter Packard Children's Hospital at Stanford, Palo Alto, CA, p. A55

DAWES, Dennis W., President, Hendricks Community Hospital, Danville, IN, p. A138

DAWSON, George W., President, Centra Health, Inc., Lynchburg, VA, p. B81

DAWSON, Joseph M., Administrator, Blount Memorial Hospital, Maryville, TN, p. A389

DAWSON, Lynn, Chief Executive Officer, Spalding Rehabilitation Hospital, Aurora, CO, p. A68

DAY, Chip, Acting Vice President, Presbyterian Specialty Hospital, Charlotte, NC, p. A306

DAY, Robert, Ph.D., Superintendent, Kansas Neurological Institute, Topeka, KS, p. A166

DE BLASI, Raymond P., Chief Executive Officer, Mesquite Community Hospital, Mesquite, TX, p. A417

DE GASTA, Gary M., Director, Veterans Affairs Medical Center, White River Junction, VT, p. A435

DE JEAN, Julie, Administrator and Chief Executive Officer, Kansas Rehabilitation Hospital, Topeka, KS, p. A166

DE JESUS, Jorge
   Executive Director, Hato Rey Community Hospital, San Juan, PR, p. A473
   Executive Director, Hospital Pavia, San Juan, PR, p. A473
   Executive Director, Hospital San Pablo, Bayamon, PR, p. A472

DE MARTINI, Thomas J., Administrator, Woodridge Hospital, Johnson City, TN, p. A387

DE MELECIO, Carmen Feliciano, M.D., Secretary of Health, Puerto Rico Department of Health, San Juan, PR, p. B126

DE NARVAEZ, Denny, Chief Executive Officer, Florida Medical Center Hospital, Fort Lauderdale, FL, p. A84

DE SANTIS, Paul A., President, St. Marys Regional Medical Center, Saint Marys, PA, p. A365

DE VOSS, Gerald, Acting Administrator, Duane L. Waters Hospital, Jackson, MI, p. A214

DEAN, Harrison M., Senior Vice President and Administrator, Baptist Memorial Medical Center, North Little Rock, AR, p. A34

DEAN, Rhonda, Chief Executive Officer, El Dorado Hospital, Tucson, AZ, p. A27

DEANS, Gerald E., Director, Southwestern Virginia Mental Health Institute, Marion, VA, p. A439

DEARING, Bryan K., Chief Executive Officer, Summit Medical Center, Hermitage, TN, p. A386

DEARTH, Jim, M.D., Chief Executive Officer, Children's Hospital of Alabama, Birmingham, AL, p. A12

DEATON, Eric, Chief Executive Officer, Columbia North Side Hospital, Johnson City, TN, p. A387

DEBOER, Michael D., President and Chief Executive Officer, Baptist Medical Center, Montgomery, AL, p. A16

DEBRUCE, Lucinda
   Chief Executive Officer, Charter Behavioral Health System of Little Rock, Maumelle, AR, p. A33
   Administrator, Charter Behavioral Health System of Northwest Arkansas, Fayetteville, AR, p. A30

DECK, K. Douglas, President and Chief Executive Officer, Good Samaritan Hospital and Health Center, Dayton, OH, p. A325

DECKER, Dale A., Chief Executive Officer, Sierra Vista Community Hospital, Sierra Vista, AZ, p. A26

DECKER, James Lee, President and Chief Executive Officer, Clarksville Memorial Hospital, Clarksville, TN, p. A384

DECKER, Michael, President and Chief Executive Officer, Divine Savior Hospital and Nursing Home, Portage, WI, p. A464

DEDIC, Ronald J., President and Chief Executive Officer, Highland Community Hospital, Belvidere, IL, p. A120

DEE, Thomas A., President and Chief Executive Officer, Benedictine Hospital, Kingston, NY, p. A289

DEEMS, Andrew W., President and Chief Executive Officer, Eisenhower Memorial Hospital and Betty Ford Center at Eisenhower, Rancho Mirage, CA, p. A57

DEEN, Robert V., Chief Executive Officer, Memorial Hospital of Center, Center, TX, p. A400

DEFAIL, Anthony J., President and Chief Executive Officer, Meadville Medical Center, Meadville, PA, p. A357

DEFAUW, Thomas David, President and Chief Executive Officer, Rockford Memorial Hospital, Rockford, IL, p. A134

DEGEORGE–SMITH, Ellen, Director, Veterans Affairs Central Iowa Health Care System, Des Moines, IA, p. A150

DEGINA Jr., Anthony M., Chief Executive Officer, Plantation General Hospital, Plantation, FL, p. A94

DEGRAAF, Douglas P., Chief Executive Officer, Winter Park Memorial Hospital, Winter Park, FL, p. A99

DEGRANDIS, Fred M., President and Chief Executive Officer, St. John West Shore Hospital, Cleveland, OH, p. A324

DEIGAN, Faith A., Administrator, HEALTHSOUTH Greater Pittsburgh Rehabilitation Hospital, Monroeville, PA, p. A358

DEIKER, Tom, Ph.D., Superintendent, Mental Health Institute, Cherokee, IA, p. A148

DEL MAURO, Ronald, President and Chief Executive Officer, Saint Barnabas Health Care System, Livingston, NJ, p. B134

DELA CRUZ, Romel, Administrator, Honokaa Hospital, Honokaa, HI, p. A114

DELANEY, Martin J., President and Chief Executive Officer, Winthrop–University Hospital, Mineola, NY, p. A290

DELANO, Richard J., President, Albany General Hospital, Albany, OR, p. A344

DELFORGE, Gary L., Administrator, St. Mary's Hospital, Norton, VA, p. A441

DELISI III, Frank G., CHE, Chief Executive Officer and Director Operations, HEALTHSOUTH Harmarville Rehabilitation Hospital, Pittsburgh, PA, p. A362

DELLAPORTAS, George, M.D., Director Professional Services, Whitten Center Infirmary, Clinton, SC, p. A372

DELLAROCCO, Paul J., President and Chief Executive Officer, Franciscan Children's Hospital and Rehabilitation Center, Boston, MA, p. A200

DELMONICO, Frank A., President and Chief Executive Officer, Butler Hospital, Providence, RI, p. A369

DEMBOW, Jack H., General Director and Vice President, Belmont Center for Comprehensive Treatment, Philadelphia, PA, p. A360

DEMEULENAERE, Edward P.
   President and Chief Executive Officer, Saint Mary's Medical Center, Racine, WI, p. A465
   President and Chief Executive Officer, St. Luke's Memorial Hospital, Racine, WI, p. A465

DEMORALES, Jon, Executive Director, Atascadero State Hospital, Atascadero, CA, p. A37

DENARDO, John J., Director, Veterans Affairs Edward Hines, Jr. Hospital, Hines, IL, p. A128

DENEY, Robert, Chief Executive Officer, Charter Behavioral Health System–Palm Springs, Cathedral City, CA, p. A39

DENNIS, Daniel, Administrator, Wray Community District Hospital, Wray, CO, p. A73

DENNIS, Jerry L., M.D., Chief Executive Officer, Western State Hospital, Tacoma, WA, p. A451

DENNIS, Mynette, R.N., Administrator, Liberty–Dayton Hospital, Liberty, TX, p. A415

DENTON, Jack L., President, Eaton Rapids Community Hospital, Eaton Rapids, MI, p. A211

DENTON, Mary M., Administrator, La Salle General Hospital, Jena, LA, p. A181

DEPRIEST, Larry T., President, Danville Regional Medical Center, Danville, VA, p. A437

DEPUTAT, Robert, President, St. John Health System, Oakland Hospital, Madison Heights, MI, p. A216

DERKS, Darla, Administrator, Behavioral Healthcare–Columbus, Columbus, IN, p. A138

DERZON, Gordon M., Chief Executive Officer, University of Wisconsin Hospital and Clinics, Madison, WI, p. A461

DESANTIS, Daniel, Administrator, Sierra–Kings District Hospital, Reedley, CA, p. A57

DESCHAINE, Terry, Chief Executive Officer, Fredonia Regional Hospital, Fredonia, KS, p. A159

DESCHAMBEAU, Wayne G., Chief Executive Officer, Deaconess Hospital of Cleveland, Cleveland, OH, p. A323

DESROSIERS, Allan L., President, Anna Jaques Hospital, Newburyport, MA, p. A204

DESTEFANO, Joseph A., Chief Executive Officer, Alta District Hospital, Dinuba, CA, p. A41

DESTEFANO, Ralph T., President and Chief Executive Officer, University of Pittsburgh Medical Center–Passavant, Pittsburgh, PA, p. A363

DETWILER, James O., President, Mercy Hospital–Willard, Willard, OH, p. A334

DEURMIER, Carol, Chief Executive Officer, St. Michael's Hospital, Tyndall, SD, p. A381

DEUTSCH, Mel D., Administrator, Larkin Community Hospital, South Miami, FL, p. A97

DEVANSKY, Gary W., Chief Executive Officer, Veterans Affairs Medical Center, Coatesville, PA, p. A352

DEVICK, John, Chief Executive Officer, Canton–Inwood Memorial Hospital, Canton, SD, p. A378

DEVILLE, Linda, Chief Executive Officer, Ville Platte Medical Center, Ville Platte, LA, p. A188

DEVINE, Joseph W., Vice President, Hospital Services, Kennedy Memorial Hospitals–University Medical Center, Cherry Hill, NJ, p. A272

DEVINS, Thomas, Chief Executive Officer, Clinton Hospital, Clinton, MA, p. A202

DEVITT, ValGene, President and Chief Executive Officer, Ukiah Valley Medical Center, Ukiah, CA, p. A65

DEVOCELLE, Frank H., President and Chief Executive Officer, Olathe Medical Center, Olathe, KS, p. A163

DEXTER, Stephen P., Chief Executive Officer, Thomas Memorial Hospital, South Charleston, WV, p. A456

DEXTROM, Nancy, Executive Director, Rogers City Rehabilitation Hospital, Rogers City, MI, p. A218

DEYOUNG, Andrew, Administrator, St. Bernard's Behavioral Health, Jonesboro, AR, p. A32

DI DARIO, Albert R., Superintendent, Norristown State Hospital, Norristown, PA, p. A359

DIAL, Marcia R., Administrator, Scotland County Memorial Hospital, Memphis, MO, p. A247

DIAMOND, Eugene C., President and Chief Executive Officer, Saint Margaret Mercy Healthcare Centers, Hammond, IN, p. A140

DIAMOND, Irv J., Chief Executive Officer, Memorial Medical Center at South Amboy, South Amboy, NJ, p. A278

DIAZ, Consuelo C., Chief Executive Officer, LAC–Rancho Los Amigos Medical Center, Downey, CA, p. A41

DIAZ–REYES, Rogelio, Administrator, Hospital Dr. Dominguez, Humacao, PR, p. A472

DIBERARDINO, William M., FACHE, President and Chief Executive Officer, Jones Memorial Hospital, Wellsville, NY, p. A302

DICAPO, Joseph R., Chief Executive Officer, Columbia Medical Center, Baton Rouge, LA, p. A178

DICESARE, Gayle, President and Chief Officer, RiverValley Behavioral Health Hospital, Owensboro, KY, p. A175

DICICCO, Chris, Chief Executive Officer, Doctors Medical Center, Modesto, CA, p. A52

DICK, David, Administrator, Hans P. Peterson Memorial Hospital, Philip, SD, p. A380

DICKER, Albert, President and Chief Executive Officer, Franklin Hospital Medical Center, Valley Stream, NY, p. A302

DICKSON, James C., Administrator, Memorial Medical Center–Livingston, Livingston, TX, p. A415

DICKSON, James J., Administrator and Chief Executive Officer, Coalinga Regional Medical Center, Coalinga, CA, p. A40

DICKSON, Thomas C., Executive Vice President and Chief Operating Officer, Del E. Webb Memorial Hospital, Sun City West, AZ, p. A26

DIEGEL, James A., CHE, Executive Director, Central Oregon District Hospital, Redmond, OR, p. A347

DIETZ, Brian E., FACHE, Executive Vice President, Saint Joseph's Hospital of Marshall County, Plymouth, IN, p. A144

DIETZ, Francis R., President, Memorial Hospital of Rhode Island, Pawtucket, RI, p. A369

DIFEDERICO, William, President, Athol Memorial Hospital, Athol, MA, p. A199

DIFRANCO, Vincent, Chief Executive Officer, Wills Memorial Hospital, Washington, GA, p. A113

DILLARD, Evan S., President, Marion Baptist Medical Center, Hamilton, AL, p. A15

DILLENSCHNEIDER, Grace Anne, General Superior, Sisters of the 3rd Franciscan Order, Syracuse, NY, p. B139

DILLON, Jerry D., President and Chief Executive Officer, Century Healthcare Corporation, Tulsa, OK, p. B81

DILLON, John M., Chief Executive Officer, Paris Community Hospital, Paris, IL, p. A132

DINTER, Richard W., Chief Operating Officer, University Medical Center–Mesabi, Hibbing, MN, p. A226

DIONNE, Philip G., President and Chief Executive Officer, St. Joseph Medical Center, Reading, PA, p. A364

DIRKSEN, Victor J., Administrator, Jefferson General Hospital, Port Townsend, WA, p. A448

DIRUBBIO, Vincent, President and Chief Executive Officer, Mercy Medical Center, Rockville Centre, NY, p. A300

DITTEMORE, Ron, Ed.D., Superintendent, Northwest Missouri Psychiatric Rehabilitation Center, Saint Joseph, MO, p. A249

DITZEL Jr., Louis A., President and Chief Executive Officer, Jersey Shore Hospital, Jersey Shore, PA, p. A356

DIX, Dexter D., Director, Veterans Affairs Medical Center, Wilmington, DE, p. A78

DIXON, Jody, Administrator, Hall County Hospital, Memphis, TX, p. A417

DIXON, Mark, Administrator, Abbott Northwestern Hospital, Minneapolis, MN, p. A227

DIXON, Robert, President and Chief Executive Officer, Riverside Health System, Wichita, KS, p. A167

DIXON, Sally J., President and Chief Executive Officer, Memorial Hospital, York, PA, p. A368

DIXON, Stephen E.
President and Chief Executive Officer, La Palma Intercommunity Hospital, La Palma, CA, p. A46
President and Chief Executive Officer, Martin Luther Hospital, Anaheim, CA, p. A36

DIXON, Thomas D., Administrator, John and Mary Kirby Hospital, Monticello, IL, p. A131

DIZNEY, Donald R., Chairman, United Medical Corporation, Windermere, FL, p. B148

DOAN, Richard L., Chief Executive Officer, Barnesville Hospital Association, Barnesville, OH, p. A320

DOBBS, Steve, Chief Executive Officer, Fawcett Memorial Hospital, Port Charlotte, FL, p. A95

DOCKTER, Robert A., Administrator, Eureka Community Hospital, Eureka, SD, p. A379

DODDS, Larry D., President, Adventist Medical Center, Portland, OR, p. A347

DOHERTY, Thomas C., Medical Center Director, Veterans Affairs Medical Center, Miami, FL, p. A91

DOISE, Daryl J., Administrator, Columbia Doctors' Hospital of Opelousas, Opelousas, LA, p. A186

DOLINS, David, President, Beth Israel Deaconess Medical Center, Boston, MA, p. A199

DOMANICO, Lee, Chief Executive Officer, USC University Hospital, Los Angeles, CA, p. A51

DONAHUE, Les A., President and Chief Executive Officer, Williamsburg Community Hospital, Williamsburg, VA, p. A444

DONAHUE, Patrick, Administrator, Union County Methodist Hospital, Morganfield, KY, p. A175

DONALSON III, Walter P., President and Chief Executive Officer, Garrett County Memorial Hospital, Oakland, MD, p. A197

DONEY, Tennyson, Service Unit Director, U. S. Public Health Service Indian Hospital, Crow Agency, MT, p. A254

DONLIN, Michael, Chief Executive Officer, Floyd Valley Hospital, Le Mars, IA, p. A152

DONNELL, Vern F., Service Unit Director, U. S. Public Health Service Indian Hospital, Pine Ridge, SD, p. A380

DONNELLAN Jr., John J., Director, Veterans Affairs Medical Center, New York, NY, p. A296

DONNELLY, Leo J., Executive Director, The Friary of Baptist Health Center, Gulf Breeze, FL, p. A86

DONNELLY Jr., John J., President and Chief Executive Officer, Roxborough Memorial Hospital, Philadelphia, PA, p. A361

DONOVAN, Robert A., President and Chief Executive Officer, Lowell General Hospital, Lowell, MA, p. A203

DOODY, Dennis W., President and Chief Executive Officer, Medical Center at Princeton, Princeton, NJ, p. A277

DOOLEY, James J.
President, Geneva General Hospital, Geneva, NY, p. A288
President and Chief Executive Officer, Soldiers and Sailors Memorial Hospital of Yates County, Penn Yan, NY, p. A298

DOOLEY, Jerry, Chief Executive Officer, Terre Haute Regional Hospital, Terre Haute, IN, p. A146

DOOLEY, Mark, Chief Executive Officer, Charter Behavioral Health Systems, Lafayette, IN, p. A142

DOORDAN, Martin L., President, Anne Arundel Medical Center, Annapolis, MD, p. A193

DOORN, Doug, Chief Financial Officer, St. John Medical Center, Longview, WA, p. A447

DORAN, Dennis J., President and Chief Executive Officer, Provena United Samaritans Medical Center, Danville, IL, p. A125

DORAN, Hugh F., Director, Veterans Affairs Medical Center, Kansas City, MO, p. A246

DORAN, Jeffrey, Chief Executive Officer, Quincy Hospital, Quincy, MA, p. A205

DORIS, Doug, President and Chief Executive Officer, Lafayette–Grand Hospital, Saint Louis, MO, p. A249

DORKO, Joseph M., Chief Executive Officer, Paulding County Hospital, Paulding, OH, p. A331

DORRIS, Ronald E., Administrator, Harris Methodist–Erath County, Stephenville, TX, p. A425

DORSEY, Lawrence T., Administrator, University Medical Center, Lafayette, LA, p. A182

DOTSON, Philip E., Administrator and Chief Executive Officer, Athens–Limestone Hospital, Athens, AL, p. A11

DOTY, Elizabeth A., Administrator, Regional Health Services of Howard County, Cresco, IA, p. A149

DOUGHERTY, Paul, President and Chief Executive Officer, Deaconess Hospital, Oklahoma City, OK, p. A339

DOUGHERTY Jr., Cary M., Chief Operating Officer, LSU Medical Center Health Care Services Division, Baton Rouge, LA, p. B112

DOUGHTY, Craig, Chief Executive Officer, Mahnomen Health Center, Mahnomen, MN, p. A227

DOVER, James F., Administrator and Executive Vice President, St. Mary's Hospital, Streator, IL, p. A135

DOWD, Thomas J., President, Nathan Littauer Hospital and Nursing Home, Gloversville, NY, p. A288

DOWDELL, Thomas C., Executive Director, Memorial Hospital and Medical Center of Cumberland, Cumberland, MD, p. A195

DOWELL Jr., Floyd B., Administrator, Lincoln County Memorial Hospital, Troy, MO, p. A252

DOWLING, Mary A., Director, Veterans Affairs Medical Center, Northport, NY, p. A297

DOWN, Philip, President, Doctors Community Hospital, Lanham, MD, p. A196

DOWNEY, William B., Administrator, Lewis–Gale Medical Center, Salem, VA, p. A443

DOWNING, Samuel W., Chief Executive Officer, Salinas Valley Memorial Hospital, Salinas, CA, p. A58

DOWNS, Martin, Facility Director, Lincoln Developmental Center, Lincoln, IL, p. A130

DOYLE Jr., James J., President and Chief Executive Officer, Chilton Memorial Hospital, Pompton Plains, NJ, p. A277

DOZORETZ, Ronald I., M.D., Chairman, FHC Health Systems, Norfolk, VA, p. B100

DRAGOVAN, Debra M., Chief Executive Officer, Metro Health Center, Erie, PA, p. A353

DRAKE, Lawrence J., Chief Executive Officer, Chestnut Ridge Hospital, Morgantown, WV, p. A454

DRENNEN, Carol Koellisch, R.N., President and Chief Executive Officer, UHHS Brown Memorial Hospital, Conneaut, OH, p. A325

DREW, John A., President and Chief Executive Officer, Athens Regional Medical Center, Athens, GA, p. A100

DREW, W. David
President and Chief Executive Officer, Atchison Hospital, Atchison, KS, p. A157
Interim Administrator, Jefferson County Memorial Hospital, Winchester, KS, p. A167

DREWA, Marcus E.
President, Methodist Health System, Jacksonville, FL, p. B119
President and Chief Executive Officer, Methodist Medical Center, Jacksonville, FL, p. A87

DREWEL, Charles A., Director, Missouri Rehabilitation Center, Mount Vernon, MO, p. A247

DRIEWER, Robert L., Chief Executive Officer, Faith Regional Health Services, Norfolk, NE, p. A262

DRISNER, Robert Eugene, President and Chief Executive Officer, Community Memorial Hospital, Menomonee Falls, WI, p. A461

DROBOT, Michael D., President and Chief Executive Officer, Pacific Hospital of Long Beach, Long Beach, CA, p. A48

DROEGE, Marie T., Site Administrator, Mercy Community Hospital, Port Jervis, NY, p. A299

DROP, Jeffrey S., President and Chief Executive Officer, St. Anthony Hospital, Pendleton, OR, p. A346

DROSKE, Richard S., Director, Veterans Affairs Western New York Healthcare System–Batavia Division, Batavia, NY, p. A285

DRUCK, Alison, Ed.D., Interim Chief Executive Officer, BHC Mesilla Valley Hospital, Las Cruces, NM, p. A282

DRUCKER, Steven C., President, Loretto Hospital, Chicago, IL, p. A123

DRUE, Margi, Administrator, Kahi Mohala, Ewa Beach, HI, p. A114

DRYDEN, Dave, FACHE, Administrator, Southern New Mexico Rehabilitation Center, Roswell, NM, p. A283

DUARTE, Pete T., Chief Executive Officer, R. E. Thomason General Hospital, El Paso, TX, p. A405

DUBIS, John S., President, St. Marys Health Center, Jefferson City, MO, p. A244

DUBROCA, Darryl S., Chief Executive Officer and Administrator, BHC Montevista Hospital, Las Vegas, NV, p. A266

DUDLEY, James W., Director, Hunter Holmes McGuire Veterans Affairs Medical Center, Richmond, VA, p. A442

DUDLEY, Judy, Director, Central Virginia Training Center, Madison Heights, VA, p. A439

DUFFIELD, Robert, Administrator, Wilson Memorial Hospital, Floresville, TX, p. A406

DUFFY, Charles, President, Decatur County Memorial Hospital, Greensburg, IN, p. A140

DUFFY, Jack, Executive Director, Conifer Park, Schenectady, NY, p. A300

DUGAN, Margaret R., Executive Director, Binghamton Psychiatric Center, Binghamton, NY, p. A285

DUKE, Lance B., FACHE
President and Chief Executive Officer, Phenix Regional Hospital, Phenix City, AL, p. A17
President and Chief Executive Officer, The Medical Center, Columbus, GA, p. A104

DUKES, Annie L., JD, Chief Executive Officer and Administrator, Southeast Colorado Hospital and Long Term Care, Springfield, CO, p. A72

DUMPMAN, Shirley J., Superintendent, Mayview State Hospital, Bridgeville, PA, p. A350

DUNCAN, Gary D., President and Chief Executive Officer, Freeman Health System, Joplin, MO, p. A244

DUNCAN, H. Clark, Administrator, Arcadia Valley Hospital, Pilot Knob, MO, p. A248

DUNHAM, David S., President, Southside Regional Medical Center, Petersburg, VA, p. A441

DUNMYER, Daniel C., Chief Executive Officer, Princeton Community Hospital, Princeton, WV, p. A455

DUNN, Joseph W., Ph.D.
Chief Executive Officer, Daniel Freeman Marina Hospital, Venice, CA, p. A45
Chief Executive Officer, Daniel Freeman Memorial Hospital, Inglewood, CA, p. A45

DUNNE, Deborah, Administrator, Scripps Hospital–East County, El Cajon, CA, p. A41

DUNNING Jr., Raymond M., Chief Executive Officer, Medical Center of Lewisville, Lewisville, TX, p. A415

DUPPER, Frank F., President, Adventist Health, Roseville, CA, p. B64

DUPUIS, Burton, Administrator, Gary Memorial Hospital, Breaux Bridge, LA, p. A179

DURHAM, Jeffrey L., Chief Executive Officer, Mediplex Rehabilitation Hospital, Bowling Green, KY, p. A168

DURR, Ben M., Administrator, Uvalde County Hospital Authority, Uvalde, TX, p. A427

DURRER, Christopher T., President and Chief Executive Officer, Wilson Memorial Hospital, Wilson, NC, p. A314

DUSENBERY, Jack Brian, Chief Executive Officer, Eastmoreland Hospital, Portland, OR, p. A347

DUTCHER, Phillip C.
Interim President, Good Samaritan Medical Center, West Palm Beach, FL, p. A99
President and Chief Executive Officer, St. Mary's Hospital, West Palm Beach, FL, p. A99

DUTREY, Susan, Administrator, Decatur County Hospital, Leon, IA, p. A152

DUX, Christopher W., Chief Executive Officer, Columbia Parkridge Medical Center, Chattanooga, TN, p. A384

DVORAK, Roger G., President, Lawrence Hospital, Bronxville, NY, p. A285

DWOZAN, C. Richard, President, Habersham County Medical Center, Demorest, GA, p. A105

DYAR, David C., President and Administrator, Westview Hospital, Indianapolis, IN, p. A141

DYE, Jeff, Administrator, Socorro General Hospital, Socorro, NM, p. A283

DYER, Paul F., President, Chowchilla District Memorial Hospital, Chowchilla, CA, p. A39

DYER, Rebecca J., Administrator, Union General Hospital, Blairsville, GA, p. A102

DYETT, Benjamin I., M.D., Director, Ossining Correctional Facilities Hospital, Ossining, NY, p. A298

DYKES, Bradford W., Chief Executive Officer, Perry County Memorial Hospital, Tell City, IN, p. A146

DYKES Sr., Kenneth E., Administrator and Chief Executive Officer, Gulf Pines Hospital, Port Saint Joe, FL, p. A95

DYKSTERHOUSE, Trevor J., Administrator, Addison Community Hospital, Addison, MI, p. A208

DYKSTRA, Janet, Chief Executive Officer, Osceola Community Hospital, Sibley, IA, p. A154

E

EADY, Bruce, Chief Executive Officer, Columbia Regional Hospital, Columbia, MO, p. A242

EAGAR Jr., Dan M., Administrator, Bessemer Carraway Medical Center, Bessemer, AL, p. A11

EASTHAM, James E., Vice President and Chief Executive Officer, Memorial Hospital Southwest, Houston, TX, p. A411

EATON, Fred R., Administrator, Bannock Regional Medical Center, Pocatello, ID, p. A118

EAZELL, Dale E., Ph.D., President and Chief Executive Officer, Casa Colina Hospital for Rehabilitative Medicine, Pomona, CA, p. A56

EBERLE, Douglas W., President and Chief Executive Officer, St. Elizabeth Medical Center, Lafayette, IN, p. A142

ECHELARD, Paul D., Administrator, Pinecrest Rehabilitation Hospital, Delray Beach, FL, p. A84

ECKENHOFF, Edward A., President and Chief Executive Officer, National Rehabilitation Hospital, Washington, DC, p. A79

ECKER, G. T. Dunlop, President and Chief Executive Officer, Loudoun Hospital Center, Leesburg, VA, p. A439

ECKERT, Mary L., President and Chief Executive Officer, Millcreek Community Hospital, Erie, PA, p. A353

ECTON, Doris, Administrator and Chief Executive Officer, Nicholas County Hospital, Carlisle, KY, p. A169

EDMISSON, Jete, President and Chief Executive Officer, Illini Community Hospital, Pittsfield, IL, p. A133

EDMONDSON, James H., Chief Executive Officer and Administrator, Columbia Hillside Hospital, Pulaski, TN, p. A392

EDWARDS, Jerry, CHE, Administrator, East Texas Medical Center–Mount Vernon, Mount Vernon, TX, p. A418

EDWARDS, John R., Chief Executive Officer, Pacific Alliance Medical Center, Los Angeles, CA, p. A50

EDWARDS, Liston G., Director, Cherry Hospital, Goldsboro, NC, p. A308

EDWARDS, Mark, Chief Executive Officer, Massac Memorial Hospital, Metropolis, IL, p. A131

EDWARDS, Samuel, Administrator, Ventura County Medical Center, Ventura, CA, p. A66

EDWARDS, Thomas I., President and Chief Executive Officer, Chatuge Regional Hospital and Nursing Home, Hiawassee, GA, p. A107

EDWARDS, Wade, Administrator, Genoa Community Hospital, Genoa, NE, p. A260

EDWARDS, Robert E., Administrator and Deputy Commander, U. S. Air Force Hospital, Davis–Monthan AFB, AZ, p. A22

EDWARDS Jr., Bob S., Chief Executive Officer, Bates County Memorial Hospital, Butler, MO, p. A241

EGERER, Michelle, Chief Executive Officer, BHC Fairfax Hospital, Kirkland, WA, p. A447

EHRAT, Karen S., Ph.D.
President, Clermont Mercy Hospital, Batavia, OH, p. A321
President, Mercy Hospital Anderson, Cincinnati, OH, p. A323

EHRHARDT, Bill E., Executive Director, Bowdon Corporate Offices, Atlanta, GA, p. B73

EHRHART, Kenneth W., Acting Superintendent, Wernersville State Hospital, Wernersville, PA, p. A367

EHRLICH, Jane, President and Chief Executive Officer, Columbia Memorial Hospital, Hudson, NY, p. A289

EICHELBERGER, Larry, Administrator, Fillmore County Hospital, Geneva, NE, p. A260

EICHER, Kim D., President and Chief Executive Officer, Rehabilitation Hospital of Indiana, Indianapolis, IN, p. A141

EICHMAN, Cynthia, Chief Executive Officer and Administrator, Victory Medical Center, Stanley, WI, p. A466

EILERMAN, Ted, President, St. Elizabeth Medical Center, Granite City, IL, p. A127

EILERS, M. Kathleen, Administrator, Milwaukee County Mental Health Division, Milwaukee, WI, p. A462

EISENMANN, Claudia A., Director Operations, HEALTHSOUTH Rehabilitation Hospital of Fort Smith, Fort Smith, AR, p. A31

EISNER, Nina W., Chief Executive Officer, The Pavilion, Champaign, IL, p. A122

ELDER, Ronald J., Chief Executive Officer, Barberton Citizens Hospital, Barberton, OH, p. A320

ELDREDGE, Clifford M., President and Chief Executive Officer, Vail Valley Medical Center, Vail, CO, p. A73

ELDRIDGE, Ruth A., R.N., Regional Vice President, Administration, Broward General Medical Center, Fort Lauderdale, FL, p. A84

ELEGANT, Bruce M., President and Chief Executive Officer, Oak Park Hospital, Oak Park, IL, p. A132

ELFORD, Dorothy J., Executive Director and Chief Executive Officer, Vencor Hospital–Dallas, Dallas, TX, p. A404

ELHAJ, Ali A., Chief Executive Officer, Charter Ridge Hospital, Lexington, KY, p. A172

ELIZABETH, M. Ann, President, Saint Francis Hospital, Poughkeepsie, NY, p. A299

ELKINS, James N., FACHE
Director, South Texas Hospital, Harlingen, TX, p. A409
Director, Texas Center for Infectious Disease, San Antonio, TX, p. A424

ELLERMANN, Michael P., Administrator, Washington County Hospital, Nashville, IL, p. A131

ELLIOTT, Maurice W., President, Methodist Health Systems, Inc., Memphis, TN, p. B119

ELLIS, Dan, Administrator, Horn Memorial Hospital, Ida Grove, IA, p. A151

ELLIS, Elmer G., President and Chief Executive Officer, East Texas Medical Center Regional Healthcare System, Tyler, TX, p. B99

ELLIS, Larry R., Interim Chief Executive Officer, Columbia Providence Hospital, Columbia, SC, p. A372

ELLZEY, Bob, Administrator, Bellville General Hospital, Bellville, TX, p. A398

ELROD, James K., President, Willis–Knighton Medical Center, Shreveport, LA, p. A187

ELSOM, Donald, Operations Administrator, Providence St. Vincent Medical Center, Portland, OR, p. A347

EMGE, Joann, Chief Executive Officer, Sparta Community Hospital, Sparta, IL, p. A134

EMMONS, Bobby B., Administrator, Fleming County Hospital, Flemingsburg, KY, p. A170

ENDERS, Robert, President, Morehead Memorial Hospital, Eden, NC, p. A307

ENDRES, Jack R., Administrator, Muenster Memorial Hospital, Muenster, TX, p. A418

ENGEL, Kim, Chief Executive Officer, Legend Buttes Health Services, Crawford, NE, p. A259

ENGELKEN, Joseph T., Chief Executive Officer, Community Hospital Onaga, Onaga, KS, p. A163

ENGER, Mark M.
Senior Vice President and Administrator, Fairview Ridges Hospital, Burnsville, MN, p. A223
Senior Vice President and Administrator, Fairview Southdale Hospital, Minneapolis, MN, p. A227

ENGHOLM, Kari L., Administrator, Humboldt County Memorial Hospital, Humboldt, IA, p. A151

ENGLAND, Garry L., President and Chief Executive Officer, St. Joseph Regional Medical Center of Northern Oklahoma, Ponca City, OK, p. A340

ENGLAND, John R., President and Chief Executive Officer, Allegheny University Medical Center–Allegheny Valley, Natrona Heights, PA, p. A358

ENGLERTH, Ladonna, Administrator, East Carroll Parish Hospital, Lake Providence, LA, p. A183

ENGLISH, David J., President and Chief Executive Officer, Hospice of Northern Virginia, Arlington, VA, p. A436

ENSOR, Ronald J., Chief Executive Officer, Medical Center at Terrell, Terrell, TX, p. A426

EPSTEIN, Norman B.
President, Chambersburg Hospital, Chambersburg, PA, p. A351
President, Waynesboro Hospital, Waynesboro, PA, p. A367

ERB, Myrna, Administrator, Adair County Memorial Hospital, Greenfield, IA, p. A151

ERGLE Jr., F. W., Administrator, Tallahatchie General Hospital, Charleston, MS, p. A234

ERICH, Kevin R., Administrator, Frank R. Howard Memorial Hospital, Willits, CA, p. A67

ERICKSON, Tyler, Administrator, Montrose Memorial Hospital, Montrose, CO, p. A72

ERIXON, Stephen M., Chief Executive Officer, Memorial Mother Frances Hospital, Palestine, TX, p. A419

ERMSHAR, Edwin L.
President and Chief Executive Officer, Lindsay District Hospital, Lindsay, CA, p. A47
President and Chief Executive Officer, Sierra View District Hospital, Porterville, CA, p. A56

ERNE, Michael H.
Senior Vice President and Administrator, St. Anthony Central Hospital, Denver, CO, p. A70
Chief Executive Officer, St. Anthony North Hospital, Westminster, CO, p. A73

ERNST, John R., Executive Director, Deborah Heart and Lung Center, Browns Mills, NJ, p. A271

ERWIN, Duane L., Chief Executive Officer, Franciscan Medical Center–Dayton Campus, Dayton, OH, p. A325

ERWINE, Terry E., Administrator, Sac–Osage Hospital, Osceola, MO, p. A248

ESLYN, Cole C.
Chief Executive Officer, St. David's Medical Center, Austin, TX, p. A397
Chief Executive Officer, St. David's Pavilion, Austin, TX, p. A397
Chief Executive Officer, St. David's Rehabilitation Center, Austin, TX, p. A397

ESPELAND, David, Chief Executive Officer, Fallon Medical Complex, Baker, MT, p. A253

ESPINOSA, Maritza, Chief Executive Officer, San Juan City Hospital, San Juan, PR, p. A474

ESTRADA, Ted R., Chief Executive Officer, Los Angeles Community Hospital, Los Angeles, CA, p. A49

ETHEREDGE, H. Rex, President and Chief Executive Officer, Memorial Hospital of Jacksonville, Jacksonville, FL, p. A87

ETTER, Carl, Executive Director, River Oaks East–Woman's Pavilion, Jackson, MS, p. A236

ETTLINGER, Roy A.
Chief Executive Officer, Arbour Hospital, Boston, MA, p. A199
Chief Executive Officer, H. R. I. Hospital, Brookline, MA, p. A201

EUSTIS, Mark A., President, Missouri Baptist Medical Center, Town and Country, MO, p. A251

EVANS, Michael J., Chief Executive Officer, Highlands Hospital, Connellsville, PA, p. A352

EVANS Jr., John T., President and Chief Executive Officer, Central Washington Hospital, Wenatchee, WA, p. A451

EVERETT, Benjamin, Chief Executive Officer, Columbia Doctors Hospital of Laredo, Laredo, TX, p. A415

EVERTS, Randall M., Chief Executive Officer, Columbia Rio Grande Regional Hospital, McAllen, TX, p. A417

EWELL, Bobby E., Executive Director, Professional Rehabilitation Hospital, Ferriday, LA, p. A180

EZZELL, Robert, Administrator, Hemphill County Hospital, Canadian, TX, p. A400

F

FAAS, Michael D., President and Chief Executive Officer, Metropolitan Hospital, Grand Rapids, MI, p. A212

FAGERSTROM, Charles, Vice President, Norton Sound Regional Hospital, Nome, AK, p. A21

FAHD II, Charles F., Chief Executive Officer, Massena Memorial Hospital, Massena, NY, p. A290

FAHEY, Stephen P., Administrator, Charter Westbrook Behavioral Health System, Richmond, VA, p. A442

FAHLE, LeRoy D., Interim President and Chief Executive Officer, Sarah Bush Lincoln Health System, Mattoon, IL, p. A130

FAHRENBACHER, Fritz, Chief Executive Officer, Lee Memorial Hospital, Dowagiac, MI, p. A211

FAILE, Gene, Chief Executive Officer, Glades General Hospital, Belle Glade, FL, p. A81

FAILING, Ann C., President, Church Hospital Corporation, Baltimore, MD, p. A193

FAILING, Richard J., Chief Executive Officer, Kittson Memorial Healthcare Center, Hallock, MN, p. A225

FAILLA, Richard, Chief Executive Officer, Two Rivers Psychiatric Hospital, Kansas City, MO, p. A246

FAIRFAX, Douglas L., President and Chief Executive Officer, Health Alliance Hospitals, Leominster, MA, p. A203

FAIRMAN, John A., Executive Director, District of Columbia General Hospital, Washington, DC, p. A79

FAJA, Garry C.
President and Chief Executive Officer, Saline Community Hospital, Saline, MI, p. A219
President and Chief Executive Officer, St. Joseph Mercy Health System, Ann Arbor, MI, p. A208

FAJT, John D., Executive Director, Putnam County Hospital, Greencastle, IN, p. A140

FALAST, Earl F., Chief Executive Officer, Veterans Affairs Medical Center, Philadelphia, PA, p. A362

FALATKO, Michael J., President and Chief Executive Officer, Doctors Hospital of Jackson, Jackson, MI, p. A214

FALBERG, Warren C., Senior Executive Officer, Jewish Hospital Kenwood, Cincinnati, OH, p. A322

FALE, Randall J., FACHE, President and Chief Executive Officer, St. Joseph's Regional Health Center, Hot Springs, AR, p. A31

FALE, Robert A., President, Agnesian HealthCare, Fond Du Lac, WI, p. A459

FALLAT, Andrew, FACHE, Chief Executive Officer, Evergreen Community Health Center, Kirkland, WA, p. A447

FALLER, Madelyn, Chief Executive Officer, Mineral Community Hospital, Superior, MT, p. A256

FAMA, Cheryl A., Administrator, Vice President and Chief Operating Officer, Saint Francis Memorial Hospital, San Francisco, CA, p. A60

FANNING Jr., Robert R., Chief Executive Officer, Beverly Hospital, Beverly, MA, p. A199

FANTASIA, Sam, Director, Division of Administration and Financial Services, St. Elizabeths Hospital, Washington, DC, p. A79

FARBER, Nancy D., Chief Executive Officer, Washington Township Health Care District, Fremont, CA, p. A43

FARETRA, Gloria, M.D., Executive Director, Queens Children's Psychiatric Center, New York, NY, p. A295

FARMER, Mark R., Vice President and Administrator, Presbyterian Hospital–Matthews, Matthews, NC, p. A310

FARMER Jr., Kenneth L., Commander, Darnall Army Community Hospital, Fort Hood, TX, p. A406

FARNELL, Leland E., President, Johnston Memorial Hospital, Smithfield, NC, p. A313

FARNSWORTH, Edward F.
President, Capital Region Medical Center–Madison, Jefferson City, MO, p. A244
President, Capital Region Medical Center–Southwest, Jefferson City, MO, p. A244

FARR, George D., President and Chief Executive Officer, Children's Medical Center of Dallas, Dallas, TX, p. A403

FARRAND, Cynthia B., Executive Vice President, Mary Immaculate Hospital, Newport News, VA, p. A440

FARRELL, Michael J., Chief Executive Officer, Somerset Hospital Center for Health, Somerset, PA, p. A365

FARRELL, Patrick W., Chief Executive Officer, Henrico Doctors' Hospital, Richmond, VA, p. A442

FARRELL Sr., John T., President and Chief Executive Officer, St. Joseph Medical Center of Fort Wayne, Fort Wayne, IN, p. A139

FARRINGTON, Jack N., Ph.D., Executive Vice President, Episcopal Health Services Inc., Uniondale, NY, p. B100

FARRIS, James R., CHE, Chief Executive Officer, Wabash General Hospital District, Mount Carmel, IL, p. A131

FARROW, Randall A., President, Mille Lacs Health System, Onamia, MN, p. A228

FARROW, Shelby, Administrator, California Medical Facility, Vacaville, CA, p. A65

FATHERREE, Lori Caudell, Chief Executive Officer, Johnson City Specialty Hospital, Johnson City, TN, p. A387

FAUCHER, Diane, Superintendent, Austin State Hospital, Austin, TX, p. A396

FAULK, A. Donald, FACHE, President, Medical Center of Central Georgia, Macon, GA, p. A108

FAULKNER, David M., Chief Executive Officer and Administrator, Central Montana Medical Center, Lewistown, MT, p. A255

FAULKNER, John M., FACHE, President and Chief Executive Officer, Patrick County Memorial Hospital, Stuart, VA, p. A443

FAULWELL, James A., Administrator, Grundy County Memorial Hospital, Grundy Center, IA, p. A151

FAUS, Douglas, Administrator, Liberty County Hospital and Nursing Home, Chester, MT, p. A253

FAUST, Bill D., Administrator, Floyd County Memorial Hospital, Charles City, IA, p. A148

FAVRET, John M., Director, Eastern State Hospital, Williamsburg, VA, p. A444

FAWZY, Fawzy I., M.D., Medical Director, University of California Los Angeles Neuropsychiatric Hospital, Los Angeles, CA, p. A51

FAY, Juliette, President and Chief Executive Officer, Charles River Hospital, Wellesley, MA, p. A207

FEARS, John R., Director, Carl T. Hayden Veterans Affairs Medical Center, Phoenix, AZ, p. A24

FECHTEL Jr., Edward J., President and Chief Executive Officer, St. Mary's Hospital, Athens, GA, p. A100

FEDERSPIEL, John C., President and Chief Executive Officer, Hudson Valley Hospital Center, Peekskill, NY, p. A298

FEDYK, Mark F., Administrator, Morrison Community Hospital, Morrison, IL, p. A131

FEELEY, William F., Acting Director, Veterans Affairs Western New York Healthcare System–Buffalo Division, Buffalo, NY, p. A286

FEICKERT, Larry E., Chief Administrative Officer, Northwood Deaconess Health Center, Northwood, ND, p. A318

FEIKE, Jeffrey, Administrator, Churchill Community Hosptial, Fallon, NV, p. A266

FEILER, Kenneth H., President and Chief Executive Officer, Rose Medical Center, Denver, CO, p. A69

FEINBERG, E. Richard, M.D., Executive Director, Bronx Children's Psychiatric Center, New York, NY, p. A291

FEIT, Marcelina, President and Chief Executive Officer, Valley Memorial Hospital, Livermore, CA, p. A47

FEIT, Marcy
Chief Executive Officer, ValleyCare Health System, Pleasanton, CA, p. B151
Chief Executive Officer, ValleyCare Medical Center, Pleasanton, CA, p. A56

FELDMAN, Mitchell S., Chief Executive Officer, Delray Medical Center, Delray Beach, FL, p. A84

FELDT, Roger D., FACHE, President and Chief Executive Officer, Saline Memorial Hospital, Benton, AR, p. A29

FELGAR, Alvin D., President and Chief Executive Officer, Frisbie Memorial Hospital, Rochester, NH, p. A270

FELICI, Brian K., Vice President and Administrator, East Ohio Regional Hospital, Martins Ferry, OH, p. A329

FELLA, Peter T., Commissioner, Doctor Robert L. Yeager Health Center, Pomona, NY, p. A298

FELLMAN, Randall E., USAF, Commanding Officer, U. S. Air Force Hospital Mountain Home, Mountain Home AFB, ID, p. A118

FELTON, David, Administrator, Community Memorial Hospital, Hamilton, NY, p. A288

FENCEL, Michael M., Chief Executive Officer, Brandon Regional Medical Center, Brandon, FL, p. A82

FENELLO, Michael A., Administrator, HEALTHSOUTH Rehabilitation Hospital of Altoona, Altoona, PA, p. A349

FENSKE, Candace, R.N., Administrator, Madelia Community Hospital, Madelia, MN, p. A227

FENTON, John V.
Chief Executive Officer, Brotman Medical Center, Culver City, CA, p. A40
Chief Executive Officer, Midway Hospital Medical Center, Los Angeles, CA, p. A49

FERGUSON, James E., Chief Executive Officer, BHC College Meadows Hospital, Lenexa, KS, p. A162

FERGUSON, John P., President and Chief Executive Officer, Hackensack University Medical Center, Hackensack, NJ, p. A273

FERRANTE, Anthony A., M.D., President and Chief Executive Officer, Elmcrest Psychiatric Institute, Portland, CT, p. A76

FERRANTO, Carmen N., Superintendent, Warren State Hospital, North Warren, PA, p. A359

FERRELL, David A., President, Mercy Hospital, Hamilton, OH, p. A327

FERRON, Kenneth R., Senior Vice President and Chief Operating Officer, St. Joseph Hospital, Nashua, NH, p. A269

FERRY, John M., Executive Director, Memorial Hospital of Sweetwater County, Rock Springs, WY, p. A469

FERRY, Thomas P., Administrator and Chief Executive, Alfred I.duPont Hospital for Children, Wilmington, DE, p. A78

FERRY Jr., John J., M.D., President and Chief Executive Officer, Southampton Hospital, Southampton, NY, p. A301

FEUQUAY, Judith K., Chief Executive Officer, Perry Memorial Hospital, Perry, OK, p. A340

FEURER, Russell E., Chief Executive, Good Shepherd Hospital, Barrington, IL, p. A120

FEURIG, Thomas L., President and Chief Executive Officer, St. Joseph Mercy Oakland, Pontiac, MI, p. A218

FICKEN, Robert A., Chief Executive Officer, Dallas–Fort Worth Medical Center, Grand Prairie, TX, p. A408

FICKES, Cathy, R.N., Chief Executive Officer, Mission Community Hospital–San Fernando Campus, San Fernando, CA, p. A60

FICKLIN, Dennis E., Chief Executive Officer, Family Health West, Fruita, CO, p. A70

FIDLER, John E., FACHE, Chief Executive Officer, Chico Community Hospital, Chico, CA, p. A39

FIDUCIA, Karen A., Interim Chief Executive Officer, Thibodaux Regional Medical Center, Thibodaux, LA, p. A187

FIELD, Carol, Senior Corporate Director and Administrator, Carondelet Holy Cross Hospital, Nogales, AZ, p. A24

FIELDS, Ronald B., President, Tri-County Memorial Hospital, Whitehall, WI, p. A467

FIKE, Ruthita J.
Administrator, Littleton Adventist Hospital, Littleton, CO, p. A71
Administrator, Porter Adventist Hospital, Denver, CO, p. A69

FINAN, Patricia, Acting President and Chief Executive Officer, Wyoming Valley Health Care System, Wilkes–Barre, PA, p. A367

FINAN Jr., John J., President and Chief Executive Officer, Franciscan Missionaries of Our Lady Health System, Inc., Baton Rouge, LA, p. B100

FINCH, Kenneth A., Chief Executive Officer, Metroplex Hospital, Killeen, TX, p. A414

FINCH Jr., J. W., Administrator, Elkview General Hospital, Hobart, OK, p. A338

FINE, Stuart H., Chief Executive Officer, Grand View Hospital, Sellersville, PA, p. A365

FINK, Matthew E., M.D., President and Chief Executive Officer, Beth Israel Medical Center, New York, NY, p. A291

FINKLEIN, Terry O., Chief Executive Officer, Columbia Memorial Hospital, Astoria, OR, p. A344

FINLAYSON, William C., President and Chief Executive Officer, Santa Rosa Health Care Corporation, San Antonio, TX, p. A423

FINLEY, Ed, Administrator, Wichita County Hospital, Leoti, KS, p. A162

FINN, Donald J., Administrator, Lake Area Hospital, Webster, SD, p. A382

FINNEGAN, Andrew J., CHE, Administrator, Brooks County Hospital, Quitman, GA, p. A110

FINNEGAN, Jay, Chief Executive Officer, Oak Hill Hospital, Spring Hill, FL, p. A97

FINUCANE, Mark, Director Health, Los Angeles County–Department of Health Services, Los Angeles, CA, p. B112

FINZEN, Terry S., President, Regions Hospital, Saint Paul, MN, p. A230

FIORENTINO, Leanne, Chief Executive Officer, Vencor Hospital–Greensboro, Greensboro, NC, p. A308

FISCHER, Carl R., Associate Vice President and Chief Executive Officer, Medical College of Virginia Hospitals, Virginia Commonwealth University, Richmond, VA, p. A442

FISCHER, Joseph, Chief Executive Officer, BHC Pinnacle Pointe Hospital, Little Rock, AR, p. A32

FISCHER, Michelle, Chief Executive Officer, Columbia Hospital North and South, Springfield, MO, p. A251

FISCHER, Robert W., President, Northwest Hospital Center, Randallstown, MD, p. A197

FISH, David B., Executive Vice President, St. Joseph's Hospital, Chippewa Falls, WI, p. A458

FISH, Robert H., President and Chief Executive Officer, Santa Rosa Memorial Hospital, Santa Rosa, CA, p. A63

FISHER, Donald Joe, Administrator, King's Daughters Hospital, Greenville, MS, p. A235

FISHER, Jan E., R.N., Executive Director, Soldiers and Sailors Memorial Hospital, Wellsboro, PA, p. A367

FISHER, Philip, President and Chief Executive Officer, Valley View Regional Hospital, Ada, OK, p. A335

FISHER, Reese, Service Unit Director, U. S. Public Health Service Blackfeet Community Hospital, Browning, MT, p. A253

FISHERO, Harvey L., President and Chief Executive Officer, Columbia Medical Center of Plano, Plano, TX, p. A420

FITCH Sr., Carl W., President and Chief Executive Officer, Wesley Medical Center, Wichita, KS, p. A167

FITZGERALD, Mike
Chief Financial Officer, St. Clare Hospital, Lakewood, WA, p. A447
Chief Financial Officer, St. Francis Hospital, Federal Way, WA, p. A446

FITZGIBBON, Susan H., President and Chief Executive Officer, Annie Penn Hospital, Reidsville, NC, p. A312

FITZHARRIS, Joseph, Commander, Keller Army Community Hospital, West Point, NY, p. A303

FITZPATRICK, Daniel, Chief Executive Officer, Harlan ARH Hospital, Harlan, KY, p. A171

FITZPATRICK, James G., Administrator, Kossuth Regional Health Center, Algona, IA, p. A147

FLAHERTY, Tom, Assistant Administrator, Los Angeles County Central Jail Hospital, Los Angeles, CA, p. A49

FLAIG, William G., Administrator, Douglas County Hospital, Alexandria, MN, p. A222

FLAKE, Glenn M., Executive Director, Newnan Hospital, Newnan, GA, p. A110

FLAMINI, Joseph, President and Chief Executive Officer, Allegheny University Hospital, Rancocas, Willingboro, NJ, p. A279

FLEMING, Cheryl, Chief Executive Officer, HEALTHSOUTH Rehabilitation Hospital of York, York, PA, p. A368

FLEMING, John L., M.D., Interim Chief Executive Officer, Laureate Psychiatric Clinic and Hospital, Tulsa, OK, p. A342

FLEMING, Timothy G., M.D., Chief Executive Officer, Gallup Indian Medical Center, Gallup, NM, p. A282

FLEMING, Wanda C., Administrator and Chief Executive Officer, Claiborne County Hospital, Port Gibson, MS, p. A239

FLESH, Lawrence H., M.D., Director, Veterans Affairs Medical Center, Albany, NY, p. A284

FLESSNER, Arnold, Administrator, Waverly Municipal Hospital, Waverly, IA, p. A155

FLETCHALL, Terry L., Administrator, Santiam Memorial Hospital, Stayton, OR, p. A348

FLETCHER, Allen P., President, Northeast Alabama Regional Medical Center, Anniston, AL, p. A11

FLETCHER, Constance N., Ph.D., Director, Southern Virginia Mental Health Institute, Danville, VA, p. A437

FLETCHER, David A., President and Chief Executive Officer, Elizabeth General Medical Center, Elizabeth, NJ, p. A272

FLETCHER, Donald C.
President and Chief Executive Officer, Blue Water Health Services Corporation, Port Huron, MI, p. B73
President and Chief Executive Officer, Port Huron Hospital, Port Huron, MI, p. A218

FLETCHER, Thomas H., Administrator, Ellenville Community Hospital, Ellenville, NY, p. A287

FLINN, Michael N. J., FACHE, Chief Executive Officer, Monsour Medical Center, Jeannette, PA, p. A356

FLORES, Saturnino Pena, Executive Director, Ryder Memorial Hospital, Humacao, PR, p. A472

FLORES Jr., Ernest, Administrator, Dimmit County Memorial Hospital, Carrizo Springs, TX, p. A400

FLORES Jr., Ernesto M., Administrator, Spohn Kleberg Memorial Hospital, Kingsville, TX, p. A414

FLOTTE', J. L., Chief Executive Officer, Medical Center of Winnie, Winnie, TX, p. A429

FLOWERS, Randel, Ph.D., Administrator, Clinton County Hospital, Albany, KY, p. A168

FLOYD, James R., Medical Center Director, Veterans Affairs Medical Center, Salt Lake City, UT, p. A432

FLYNN, Brian T., Chief Executive Officer, Lucy Lee Hospital, Poplar Bluff, MO, p. A248

FLYNN, Patrick D., President and Chief Executive Officer, Washington Regional Medical Center, Fayetteville, AR, p. A30

FLYNN Jr., James H., President and Chief Executive Officer, Franciscan Sisters of the Poor Health System, Inc., Latham, NY, p. B101

FODI, Nancy C., Executive Director, Upstate Carolina Medical Center, Gaffney, SC, p. A374

FOGGO, Thomas G., Executive Vice President Care Delivery and General Director, Albany Medical Center, Albany, NY, p. A284

FOJTASEK, Georgia R., President and Chief Executive Officer, W. A. Foote Memorial Hospital, Jackson, MI, p. A214

FOLGER, Mark W.
Senior Vice President, Three Rivers Community Hospital and Health Center–Dimmick, Grants Pass, OR, p. A345
Senior Vice President, Three Rivers Community Hospital and Health Center–Washington, Grants Pass, OR, p. A345

FONNESBECK, Douglas R., Administrator, Cottonwood Hospital Medical Center, Salt Lake City, UT, p. A432

FONTANEZ, Carmen I., Chief Executive Officer, Columbia Woodland Hospital, Hoffman Estates, IL, p. A129

FONTENOT, Teri G., President and Chief Executive Officer, Woman's Hospital, Baton Rouge, LA, p. A179

FONTENOT, Terry J., Administrator, Medical Center of Mesquite, Mesquite, TX, p. A417

FORD, Karen, Chief Executive Officer, Sabine Medical Center, Many, LA, p. A183

FORD, Ken, Administrator, Tattnall Memorial Hospital, Reidsville, GA, p. A110

FORD, Raymond L., President and Chief Executive Officer, Glenwood Regional Medical Center, West Monroe, LA, p. A188

FORD, Roger A., Administrator, Bertrand Chaffee Hospital, Springville, NY, p. A301

FORD, W. Raymond C., Chief Executive Officer, Specialty Hospital Jacksonville, Jacksonville, FL, p. A87

FOREMAN, Robert, Associate Administrator, Brooksville Regional Hospital, Brooksville, FL, p. A82

FOREMAN, Spencer, M.D., President, Montefiore Medical Center, New York, NY, p. A294

FORMIGONI, Ugo, Metro–West Network Manager, John J. Madden Mental Health Center, Hines, IL, p. A128

FORNOFF, Gerald A., Chief Executive Officer, Lakeside Hospital, Metairie, LA, p. A183

FOSDICK, Glenn A., President and Chief Executive Officer, Hurley Medical Center, Flint, MI, p. A212

FOSS, R. Coleman, Chief Executive Officer, Volunteer General Hospital, Martin, TN, p. A389

FOSSUM, John, Administrator, Ely–Bloomenson Community Hospital, Ely, MN, p. A224

FOSTER, Allen, Administrator, Mizell Memorial Hospital, Opp, AL, p. A17

FOSTER, James B., Chief Executive Officer, Lake Shore Hospital, Irving, NY, p. A289

FOSTER, Jon, Executive Vice President and Administrator, Baptist Hospital of East Tennessee, Knoxville, TN, p. A387

FOSTER, Randall S., Administrator and Chief Executive Officer, LAC–King–Drew Medical Center, Los Angeles, CA, p. A49

FOSTER, Robert T., Deputy Commander for Administration, Ireland Army Community Hospital, Fort Knox, KY, p. A170

FOSTER Jr., Charles L., FACHE, President and Chief Executive Officer, West Georgia Health System, La Grange, GA, p. A108

FOUGEROUSE, Frank G., President and Chief Executive Officer, Wirth Regional Hospital, Oakland City, IN, p. A144

FOWLER, Homer, Chief Operating Officer, HEALTHSOUTH Huntington Rehabilitation Hospital, Huntington, WV, p. A453

FOWLER, Angela D., USAF, Administrator, U. S. Air Force Hospital, Cheyenne, WY, p. A468

FOX, David S.
President, Behavioral Health Center, Winfield, IL, p. A136
President, Central DuPage Hospital, Winfield, IL, p. A136

FOX, Ted, Administrator and Chief Executive Officer, El Centro Regional Medical Center, El Centro, CA, p. A41

FOX, William R., Chief Executive Officer, HEALTHSOUTH Great Lakes Rehabilitation Hospital, Erie, PA, p. A353

FOX, William W., Chief Executive Officer, Mary Black Health System, Spartanburg, SC, p. A376

FOY, James, President and Chief Executive Officer, St. John's Riverside Hospital, Yonkers, NY, p. A303

FRABLE, Arthur H., Administrator, Mangum City Hospital, Mangum, OK, p. A338

FRAGALA, M. Richard, M.D., Superintendent, Clifton T. Perkins Hospital Center, Jessup, MD, p. A196

FRAIZER, Frederic L., President and Chief Executive Officer, St. Mary's Medical Center, Saginaw, MI, p. A218

FRALEY, Gary F., Administrator, Shriners Hospitals for Children, Greenville, Greenville, SC, p. A374

FRALEY, R. Reed, Associate Vice President for Health Sciences and Chief Executive Officer, Ohio State University Medical Center, Columbus, OH, p. A325

FRANCES, Richard J., M.D., President and Medical Director, Silver Hill Hospital, New Canaan, CT, p. A75

FRANCESCHI, Angel M., Administrator, Hospital Oncologico Andres Grillasca, Ponce, PR, p. A473

FRANCIS, Talton L., FACHE, Administrator, Russell Regional Hospital, Russell, KS, p. A165

FRANCIS, Tim, Chief Executive Officer, Great Plains Regional Medical Center, Elk City, OK, p. A337

FRANCKE, Bertold, M.D., Interim Executive Director, Vermont State Hospital, Waterbury, VT, p. A435

FRANDSEN, Jeff, Chief Executive Officer, Columbia Palm Drive Hospital, Sebastopol, CA, p. A63

FRANK, Carrie B., President and Chief Executive Officer, Buffalo General Hospital, Buffalo, NY, p. A285

FRANK, Iris C., Administrator, Sutter Maternity and Surgery Center of Santa Cruz, Santa Cruz, CA, p. A62

FRANK, Merrill A., Chief Executive Officer, Rangely District Hospital, Rangely, CO, p. A72

FRANKEL, Victor H., M.D., President, Hospital for Joint Diseases Orthopedic Institute, New York, NY, p. A293

FRANKENFIELD, Sheri, Chief Executive Officer, Jay County Hospital, Portland, IN, p. A144

FRANKLIN, James P., Administrator, Hillcrest Hospital, Calhoun City, MS, p. A234

FRANZ, Charles C., Chief Executive Officer, South Peninsula Hospital, Homer, AK, p. A20

FRANZ, Paul S., President, Carolinas Medical Center, Charlotte, NC, p. A305

FRARACCIO, Robert D., Administrator, Clark Regional Medical Center, Winchester, KY, p. A177

FRASCHETTI, Robert J., President and Chief Executive Officer, St. Jude Medical Center, Fullerton, CA, p. A43

FRASER, James, Interim Chief Executive Officer, Davenport Medical Center, Davenport, IA, p. A149

FRASER, John Martin, President and Chief Executive Officer, Nebraska Methodist Hospital, Omaha, NE, p. A263

FRASER, Michael R., Administrator, Pacific Communities Health District, Newport, OR, p. A346

FRAY, George S., Administrator, Baptist Memorial Hospital–Lauderdale, Ripley, TN, p. A392

FRAYNE, Laurence J., Chief Executive Officer, HEALTHSOUTH Rehabilitation Hospital–Plano, Plano, TX, p. A420

FREDERIC, Donald J., Chief Executive Officer, Crossroads Community Hospital, Mount Vernon, IL, p. A131

FREEBORN, Lisa J., R.N., Administrator, Wamego City Hospital, Wamego, KS, p. A166

FREEBURG, Eric, Administrator, Memorial Hospital, Chester, IL, p. A122

FREELAND, Franklin, Ed.D., Chief Executive Officer, Fort Defiance Indian Health Service Hospital, Fort Defiance, AZ, p. A23

FREEMAN, Alan, Administrator, Cass Medical Center, Harrisonville, MO, p. A244

FREEMAN, Carol B., Chief Executive Officer, Columbia Huntington Beach Hospital and Medical Center, Huntington Beach, CA, p. A45

FREEMAN, Charles C., Director, Sam Rayburn Memorial Veterans Center, Bonham, TX, p. A398

FREEMAN, Charles Ray, Administrator, Ripley County Memorial Hospital, Doniphan, MO, p. A243

FREEMAN, James M., Chief Executive Officer, Rowan Regional Medical Center, Salisbury, NC, p. A312

FREEMAN, Richard H., Chief Executive Officer, Eleanor Slater Hospital, Cranston, RI, p. A369

FREEMAN Jr., Kester S., Chief Executive Officer, Palmetto Richland Memorial Hospital, Columbia, SC, p. A373

FREISWICK, Gail, President and Chief Executive Officer, Falmouth Hospital, Falmouth, MA, p. A202

FRENCH, Douglas D., President and Chief Executive Officer, St. Vincent Hospitals and Health Services, Indianapolis, IN, p. A141

FRENCH III, George E., Chief Executive Officer, Minden Medical Center, Minden, LA, p. A184

FRENCHIE, Richard J., President and Chief Executive Officer, UHHS Geauga Regional Hospital, Chardon, OH, p. A322

FRERICHS, Jeffrey, President and Chief Executive Officer, Cabrini Medical Center, New York, NY, p. A292

FRESOLONE, Victor J., FACHE, President and Chief Executive Officer, Mercy Medical Center, Roseburg, OR, p. A348

FREY, Ted W., President, St. Louis Children's Hospital, Saint Louis, MO, p. A250

FREYMULLER, Robert S., Chief Executive Officer, Doctors Hospital of Dallas, Dallas, TX, p. A403

FRIED, Jeffrey M., FACHE, President and Chief Executive Officer, Beebe Medical Center, Lewes, DE, p. A78

FRIEDELL, Peter E., M.D., President, Jackson Park Hospital and Medical Center, Chicago, IL, p. A122

FRIEDLANDER, John E., President and Chief Executive Officer, CGF Health System, Buffalo, NY, p. B81

FRIEDMAN, Diane, R.N., President and Chief Executive Officer, Provena Covenant Medical Center, Urbana, IL, p. A135

FRIEDMAN, Steven H., Ph.D., Executive Vice President, Methodist Hospital of Chicago, Chicago, IL, p. A123

FRIEL, John P., President and Chief Executive Officer, Watsonville Community Hospital, Watsonville, CA, p. A66

FRIELING, Jeff, Administrator, Humboldt General Hospital, Humboldt, TN, p. A386

FRIES, Jack, President, St. Luke's Hospital, San Francisco, CA, p. A60

FRIESWICK, Gail M., Ed.D., President and Chief Executive Officer, Cape Cod Hospital, Hyannis, MA, p. A203

FRIGO, John S., President, Rush North Shore Medical Center, Skokie, IL, p. A134

FRITTS, Rosemary, Administrator, Pike County Memorial Hospital, Murfreesboro, AR, p. A33

FRITZ, Michael H., President, Carle Foundation Hospital, Urbana, IL, p. A135

FROBENIUS, John, President and Chief Executive Officer, St. Cloud Hospital, Saint Cloud, MN, p. A229

FROCK, Charles T., President and Chief Executive Officer, FirstHealth Moore Regional Hospital, Pinehurst, NC, p. A311

FROMHOLD, John A., Chief Executive Officer, Columbia Medical Center of Arlington, Arlington, TX, p. A396

FRONZA Jr., Leo F., President and Chief Executive Officer, Elmhurst Memorial Hospital, New York, IL, p. A126

FRY, Richard, Acting Director, Veterans Affairs Medical Center, Cheyenne, WY, p. A468

FRY, Robert W., President, Bellin Psychiatric Center, Green Bay, WI, p. A459

FRY, Willis F., Executive Director, Broadlawns Medical Center, Des Moines, IA, p. A149

FRY Jr., L. Marcus
Chief Executive Officer, Providence Memorial Hospital, El Paso, TX, p. A405
Chief Executive Officer, Sierra Medical Center, El Paso, TX, p. A406

FRYE Jr., Edward R., Administrator, Clarendon Memorial Hospital, Manning, SC, p. A375

FUENTES, Miguel A., President and Chief Executive Officer, Bronx–Lebanon Hospital Center, New York, NY, p. A291

FUGAGLI, Anne M., Administrator, Healthsouth Rehabilitation Hospital, Concord, NH, p. A268

FUHRMAN, Andrew, Chief Executive Officer, BHC Fort Lauderdale Hospital, Fort Lauderdale, FL, p. A84

FULFORD, Richard C., Administrator, Gulf Breeze Hospital, Gulf Breeze, FL, p. A86

FULKS, Jerry, Chief Executive Officer, Lanier Park Hospital, Gainesville, GA, p. A107

FULL, James M., Chief Executive Officer, Randolph County Hospital and Health Services, Winchester, IN, p. A146

FULLER, David W., Chief Executive Officer, Lane Memorial Hospital, Zachary, LA, p. A188

FULLER, Thomas E., Executive Director, Marion County Medical Center, Mullins, SC, p. A375

FUMAI, Frank L., President and Chief Executive Officer, Cathedral Healthcare System, Inc., Newark, NJ, p. B77

FUNK, Lawrence J., Executive Administrator, Laguna Honda Hospital and Rehabilitation Center, San Francisco, CA, p. A60

FUQUA, David G., R.N., Chief Executive Officer, Marshall County Hospital, Benton, KY, p. A168

FURSTMAN, Marc A., Chief Executive Officer, Los Angeles Metropolitan Medical Center, Los Angeles, CA, p. A49

FUTRELL, Jerry H., Chief Executive Officer, Smith County Memorial Hospital, Carthage, TN, p. A383

G

GABARRO, Ralph, Chief Executive Officer, Mayo Regional Hospital, Dover–Foxcroft, ME, p. A190

GABOW, Patricia A., M.D., Chief Executive Officer and Medical Director, Denver Health Medical Center, Denver, CO, p. A69

GABRIEL, Don, Administrator, Charlotte Institute of Rehabilitation, Charlotte, NC, p. A306

GADE, Ronald, M.D.
President, St. Barnabas Hospital, New York, NY, p. A296
President, Union Hospital of the Bronx, New York, NY, p. A296

GAFFNEY, Betty, Administrator, St. Joseph Memorial Hospital, Murphysboro, IL, p. A131

GAGEN, Thomas C., Administrator, Scripps Memorial Hospital–La Jolla, La Jolla, CA, p. A46

GAGER, Warren E., Chief Executive Officer, William B. Kessler Memorial Hospital, Hammonton, NJ, p. A273

GAINER, Rolf B., Chief Executive Officer and Administrator, Brookhaven Hospital, Tulsa, OK, p. A342

GAINEY, James W., R.N., Administrator, Tyler County Hospital, Woodville, TX, p. A429

GAINTNER, J. Richard, M.D., Chief Executive Officer, Shands HealthCare, Gainesville, FL, p. B135

GALARCE, Julio, Administrator, Hospital El Buen Pastor, Arecibo, PR, p. A471

GALATI, John P., President and Chief Executive Officer, Clifton Springs Hospital and Clinic, Clifton Springs, NY, p. A287

GALES, Larry V., Administrator, Stanton County Health Care Facility, Johnson, KS, p. A161

GALINSKI, Thomas P., President and Chief Executive Officer, Ohio Valley Medical Center, Wheeling, WV, p. A456

GALLAGHER, John S. T.
President and Chief Executive Officer, North Shore University Hospital, Manhasset, NY, p. A290
Co–President and Chief Executive Officer, North Shore– Long Island Jewish Health System, Manhasset, NY, p. B122

GALLAGHER, Michael R., Interim President and Chief Executive Officer, Sharon Hospital, Sharon, CT, p. A76

GALLAGHER III, J. Frank, Administrator, BHC Fox Run Hospital, Saint Clairsville, OH, p. A331

GALLAGNER, James, Chief Executive Officer, Charter Behavioral Health System of New Jersey–Summit, Summit, NJ, p. A278

GALLATI, Todd, Chief Executive Officer, Lake City Medical Center, Lake City, FL, p. A88

GALLIN, John I., M.D., Director, Warren G. Magnuson Clinical Center, National Institutes of Health, Bethesda, MD, p. A195

GALLOWAY, Ron, Administrator, Reagan Memorial Hospital, Big Lake, TX, p. A398

GAMACHE, Edward L., Administrator, Deckerville Community Hospital, Deckerville, MI, p. A210

GAMBER, Richard L., Administrator, Carolinas Hospital System–Lake City, Lake City, SC, p. A375

GAMBLE, Howard M., Administrator, Okanogan–Douglas County Hospital, Brewster, WA, p. A445

GAMBLE, Joe E., Chief Executive Officer, White County Medical Center, Carmi, IL, p. A121

GAMBRELL Jr., Edward C., Administrator, Stephens County Hospital, Toccoa, GA, p. A112

GAMEL, Richard B., Chief Executive Officer, Citizens Medical Center, Colby, KS, p. A158

GAMMIERE, Thomas A., Vice President and Administrator, Scripps Hospital–Chula Vista, Chula Vista, CA, p. A39

GAMMON, Sara, President and Chief Executive Officer, Good Shepherd Rehabilitation Hospital, Allentown, PA, p. A349

GANDY, Patrick W., Chief Executive Officer, ATH Heights Hospital, Houston, TX, p. A410

GANN, Jim, Administrator, Roane Medical Center, Harriman, TN, p. A386

GANNON, Frank R., Administrator and Regional Vice President, HEALTHSOUTH Medical Center, Birmingham, AL, p. A12

GANS, Bruce M., M.D., Senior Vice President, Rehabilitation Institute of Michigan, Detroit, MI, p. A211

GANTZ, Daniel L., President, Fayette County Hospital and Long Term Care, Vandalia, IL, p. A136

GARBER, Jeff, Administrator and Chief Executive Officer, HEALTHSOUTH Rehabilitation Hospital of Sarasota, Sarasota, FL, p. A96

GARCIA, Louis O., President and Chief Executive Officer, Columbia Medical Center of Aurora, Aurora, CO, p. A68

GARCIA, Martha, Chief Executive Officer, Coral Gables Hospital, Coral Gables, FL, p. A83

GARCIA, Robert A., Administrator, Presbyterian Kaseman Hospital, Albuquerque, NM, p. A280

GARDNER, James B., President, Huron Memorial Hospital, Bad Axe, MI, p. A208

GARDNER, Jonathan H., Chief Executive Officer, Veterans Affairs Medical Center, Tucson, AZ, p. A27

GARDNER, Paul A., CPA, Administrator, George County Hospital, Lucedale, MS, p. A237

GARDNER Jr., James E., Chief Executive Officer, St. Patrick Hospital of Lake Charles, Lake Charles, LA, p. A182

GARFIELD, Michael W., Administrator, Southern Tennessee Medical Center, Winchester, TN, p. A393

GARFUNKEL, Sanford M., Medical Center Director, Veterans Affairs Medical Center, Washington, DC, p. A79

GARLEB, Pat, Administrator, Hospital of the California Institution for Men, Chino, CA, p. A39

GARMAN, G. Richard, Executive Director, Wayne Memorial Hospital, Honesdale, PA, p. A355

GARNER, Douglas, Chief Executive Officer, Magnolia Regional Health Center, Corinth, MS, p. A234

GARNER, Gerald J., Chairman of the Board, Coast Plaza Doctors Hospital, Norwalk, CA, p. A54

GARRETT, Vernon G., Chief Executive Officer, BHC Intermountain Hospital, Boise, ID, p. A116

GARRIGAN, Michael E., President and Chief Executive Officer, St. Francis Hospital, Columbus, GA, p. A104

GARST, Paul D., USN, Commanding Officer, Naval Hospital, Cherry Point, NC, p. A306

GARVEY, Ronald F., M.D., Chief Administrative Officer and Director, University of Texas Health Center at Tyler, Tyler, TX, p. A427

GASCHO, Dwight, President and Chief Executive Officer, Scheurer Hospital, Pigeon, MI, p. A217

GAST, Edwin A., Administrator, Grand River Hospital District, Rifle, CO, p. A72

GASTON, Richard, Administrator, Macon Northside Hospital, Macon, GA, p. A108

GATENS Sr., Paul D., Administrator, Georgetown Memorial Hospital, Georgetown, SC, p. A374

GATES, Jon M., Chief Executive Officer, United Medical Center, Cheyenne, WY, p. A468

GATES, Monica P., Chief Executive Officer, Slidell Memorial Hospital and Medical Center, Slidell, LA, p. A187

GATES, Truman L., Chief Executive Officer, Community Hospital of Los Gatos, Los Gatos, CA, p. A51

GATHRIGHT, Dan
Senior Vice President and Administrator, Baptist Medical Center Arkadelphia, Arkadelphia, AR, p. A29
Vice President and Administrator, Baptist Medical Center Heber Springs, Heber Springs, AR, p. A31

GATMAITAN, Alfonso W., Chief Executive Officer, Tipton County Memorial Hospital, Tipton, IN, p. A146

GATRELL, Cloyd B., Commander, Munson Army Health Center, Fort Leavenworth, KS, p. A159

GAUDREAULT, J. Ronald, President and Chief Executive Officer, Huntington Hospital, Huntington, NY, p. A289

GAUSE, Garry L., Chief Executive Officer, Capital Medical Center, Olympia, WA, p. A448

GAVALCHIK, Stephen M., Administrator, Webster County Memorial Hospital, Webster Springs, WV, p. A456

GAVENS, Mark R., President, Sentara Norfolk General Hospital, Norfolk, VA, p. A440

GAYNOR, Stanley J., Chief Executive Officer and Administrator, Black River Memorial Hospital, Black River Falls, WI, p. A458

GEANES, John, President and Chief Executive Officer, Shannon Medical Center, San Angelo, TX, p. A422

GEARY, George A., President, Milton Hospital, Milton, MA, p. A204

GEBHARD, Scott, Senior Vice President Operations, JFK Johnson Rehabilitation Institute, Edison, NJ, p. A272

GEE, Roland D., Chief Executive Officer, Guttenberg Municipal Hospital, Guttenberg, IA, p. A151

GEE, Thomas H., Administrator, Henry County Medical Center, Paris, TN, p. A392

GEE III, Clint, Chief Executive Officer, Kilmichael Hospital, Kilmichael, MS, p. A237

GEHANT, David P., President and Chief Executive Officer, Boulder Community Hospital, Boulder, CO, p. A68

GEISSLER, Frederick, Chief Executive Officer, Grand View Hospital, Ironwood, MI, p. A214

GELLER, Harold S., Administrator, Jackson County Public Hospital, Maquoketa, IA, p. A152

GENTLING, Steven J., Director, Veterans Affairs Medical Center, Oklahoma City, OK, p. A340

GENTRY, Lee, President, Lawrence Memorial Hospital, Walnut Ridge, AR, p. A35

GENTRY, Michael V.
President, Park Ridge Hospital, Fletcher, NC, p. A308
President, Takoma Adventist Hospital, Greeneville, TN, p. A386

GEORGE, Dennis L., Chief Executive Officer, Coffey County Hospital, Burlington, KS, p. A157

GEORGE, Gladys, President and Chief Executive Officer, Lenox Hill Hospital, New York, NY, p. A293

GEPFORD, Jon W., President and Chief Executive Officer, Parkview Hospital, Brunswick, ME, p. A190

GERARDO, Edward, Interim Executive Vice President and Administrator, Bon Secours–Stuart Circle, Richmond, VA, p. A442

GERATHS, Nathan L., Director, William S. Middleton Memorial Veterans Hospital, Madison, WI, p. A461

GERBER, Carl J., Ph.D., Director, James H. Quillen Veterans Affairs Medical Center, Mountain Home, TN, p. A390

GERDES, Jerrell F., Administrator, Franklin County Memorial Hospital, Franklin, NE, p. A259

GERLACH, George, President, Granite Falls Municipal Hospital and Manor, Granite Falls, MN, p. A225

GERLACH, John R., Chief Executive Officer/Administrator, DeKalb Medical Center, Decatur, GA, p. A105

GERLACH, Matthew S., Chief Executive Officer and President, Beverly Hospital, Montebello, CA, p. A53

GERLOFF, Gregory, Chief Executive Officer, Altru Health System, Grand Forks, ND, p. A317

GETTYS III, Roddey E., Executive Vice President, Palmetto Baptist Medical Center Easley, Easley, SC, p. A373

GHERARDINI, Michael M., Chief Executive Officer and Managing Director, Auburn Regional Medical Center, Auburn, WA, p. A445

GHEZZI, Lee, Administrator, Windmoor Healthcare of Miami, Miami, FL, p. A91

GHOLSTON, Linda J., Chief Executive Officer, Grenada Lake Medical Center, Grenada, MS, p. A235

GIANNUNZIO, Diane D., President, Southwestern Michigan Rehabilitation Hospital, Battle Creek, MI, p. A208

GIBBONS, H. Ray, President and Chief Executive Officer, Holy Rosary Health Center, Miles City, MT, p. A255

GIBBS, Henry T., Administrator, Bleckley Memorial Hospital, Cochran, GA, p. A104

GIBSON, James P., President and Chief Executive Officer, Madison St. Joseph Health Center, Madisonville, TX, p. A417

GIBSON, Robert N., President and Chief Executive Officer, D. T. Watson Rehabilitation Hospital, Sewickley, PA, p. A365

GIBSON, Thomas J., Administrator, University of South Alabama Knollwood Park Hospital, Mobile, AL, p. A16

GIBSON III, Earnest, Administrator, Riverside General Hospital, Houston, TX, p. A412

GIDDINGS, Lucille C., CHE, President and Chief Executive Officer, Nantucket Cottage Hospital, Nantucket, MA, p. A204

GIEDD, James L., Administrator, Phillips County Hospital, Phillipsburg, KS, p. A164

GIERMAK, William C., President and Chief Executive Officer, Louise Obici Memorial Hospital, Suffolk, VA, p. A443

GIESECKE, Stephan A., MSC, Commander, U. S. Air Force Hospital Moody, Moody AFB, GA, p. A109

GILBERT, Albert F., Ph.D., President and Chief Executive Officer, Summa Health System, Akron, OH, p. A320

GILBERT, Brian D., Administrator, Wrangell General Hospital and Long Term Care Facility, Wrangell, AK, p. A21

GILBERT, Thomas D., President and Chief Executive Officer, Dunwoody Medical Center, Atlanta, GA, p. A101

GILBERT, William L., Chief Executive Officer, San Jose Medical Center, San Jose, CA, p. A61

GILBERTSON, Doris White, Administrator, Granite County Memorial Hospital and Nursing Home, Philipsburg, MT, p. A255

GILBERTSON, Gerry, President, Fairmont Community Hospital, Fairmont, MN, p. A224

GILBERTSON, Roger, M.D., President, MeritCare Health System, Fargo, ND, p. A317

GILES, Alyson Pitman, President and Chief Executive Officer, New London Hospital, New London, NH, p. A269

GILLIARD, Ronald M., FACHE, Administrator, Mitchell County Hospital, Camilla, GA, p. A103

GILLIHAN, Kerry G., President and Chief Executive Officer, Cardinal Hill Rehabilitation Hospital, Lexington, KY, p. A172

GILLILAND, Jerry E., President, Park Healthcare Company, Nashville, TN, p. B124

GILLILAND, Woody, Chief Executive Officer, Abilene Regional Medical Center, Abilene, TX, p. A395

GILLMAN, Jerry, President and Chief Executive Officer, Thompson Memorial Medical Center, Burbank, CA, p. A38

GILLS, Karl B., Administrator, North Colorado Medical Center, Greeley, CO, p. A71

GILMORE, Beverly, Chief Executive Officer, Columbia South Valley Hospital, Gilroy, CA, p. A44

GILROY, Gretchen, President and Chief Executive Officer, St. Francis Medical Center–West, Ewa Beach, HI, p. A114

GILSTRAP, M. E., President and Chief Executive Officer, Halifax Regional Medical Center, Roanoke Rapids, NC, p. A312

GINTOLI, George P., Chief Executive Officer, Northcoast Behavioral Healthcare System, Northfield, OH, p. A330

GINTZIG, Donald R., President and Chief Executive Officer, Pottsville Hospital and Warne Clinic, Pottsville, PA, p. A364

GIO, Dominick J., President and Chief Executive Officer, Wyckoff Heights Medical Center, New York, NY, p. A297

GIROTTO, R. G., Executive Vice President and Chief Operating Officer, The Methodist Hospital, Houston, TX, p. A412

GISLER, Paula, Chief Executive Officer, Baptist Rehabilitation–Germantown, Germantown, TN, p. A386

GITCH, David W., President and Chief Executive Officer, Harrison Memorial Hospital, Bremerton, WA, p. A445

GIUNTO, Nancy A., Operations Administrator, Providence Seattle Medical Center, Seattle, WA, p. A449

GLASS, Sheldon D., M.D., President, Gundry–Glass Hospital, Baltimore, MD, p. A193

GLASSCOCK, Gary M., Administrator, Lloyd Noland Hospital and Health System, Fairfield, AL, p. A14

GLATT, Marie Damian, President, Sisters of Charity of Leavenworth Health Services Corporation, Leavenworth, KS, p. B137

GLAVIS, Edward S., Administrator, Kaiser Foundation Hospital, Fresno, CA, p. A43

GLEDHILL, John E., Administrator, Milford Valley Memorial Hospital, Milford, UT, p. A431

GLOOR, Michael R., FACHE, President and Chief Executive Officer, Saint Francis Medical Center, Grand Island, NE, p. A260

GLOSSY, Bernard, President, Verdugo Hills Hospital, Glendale, CA, p. A44

GLUECKERT, John W., President, St. Joseph Hospital, Polson, MT, p. A256

GODDARD, Christopher M., Administrator, Marcum and Wallace Memorial Hospital, Irvine, KY, p. A171

GODDARD, Richard L., Chief Executive Officer, Hopkins County Memorial Hospital, Sulphur Springs, TX, p. A425

GOERING, Melvin, Chief Executive Officer, Prairie View, Newton, KS, p. A163

GOERTZEN, Irma E., President and Chief Executive Officer, Magee–Womens Hospital, Pittsburgh, PA, p. A362

GOESER, Stephen L., Administrator, Shelby County Myrtue Memorial Hospital, Harlan, IA, p. A151

GOFF, David W., President and Chief Executive Officer, Valley Health System, Winchester, VA, p. B151

GOFF, James A., FACHE, Director, Veterans Affairs Palo Alto Health Care System, Palo Alto, CA, p. A55

GOING, Kelley, Administrator, Beartooth Hospital and Health Center, Red Lodge, MT, p. A256

GOLD, Larry M., President and Chief Executive Officer, Connecticut Children's Medical Center, Hartford, CT, p. A74

GOLD, Richard, Chief Executive Officer, West Boca Medical Center, Boca Raton, FL, p. A81

GOLDBACH, Peter D., M.D., Chief Executive Officer, Symmes Hospital and Medical Center, Arlington, MA, p. A199

GOLDBERG, Donald H., President, New England Sinai Hospital and Rehabilitation Center, Stoughton, MA, p. A206

GOLDBERG, Edward M., President and Chief Executive Officer, Hoffman Estates Medical Center, Hoffman Estates, IL, p. A129

GOLDEN, Carolyn P., Administrator, Shriners Hospitals for Children, St. Louis, Saint Louis, MO, p. A250

GOLDFARB, Saul, Chief Executive Officer, Gateways Hospital and Mental Health Center, Los Angeles, CA, p. A48

GOLDMAN, T. Marvin, Administrator, Memorial Hospital of Sheridan County, Sheridan, WY, p. A469

GOLDMAN, Thomas, President and Chief Executive Officer, Bayshore Community Hospital, Holmdel, NJ, p. A274

GOLDSMITH, Martin
President, Albert Einstein Healthcare Network, Philadelphia, PA, p. B65
President, Albert Einstein Medical Center, Philadelphia, PA, p. A359

GOLDSTEIN, Gary W., M.D., President, Kennedy Krieger Children's Hospital, Baltimore, MD, p. A194

GOLDSTEIN, Steven, Ph.D., President and Chief Executive Officer, Chestnut Lodge Hospital, Rockville, MD, p. A197

GOLDSTEIN, Steven I., General Director and Chief Executive Officer, Strong Memorial Hospital of the University of Rochester, Rochester, NY, p. A300

GOLI, Rajitha, M.D., Administrator and Chief Executive Officer, Goli Medical Center, Sargent, NE, p. A264

GOLSON, Allen, Chief Executive Officer, Palmyra Medical Centers, Albany, GA, p. A100

GONZALES, Joseph P., USA, Chief of Staff, Brooke Army Medical Center, San Antonio, TX, p. A422

GONZALEZ, Arthur A., Dr.PH, President and Chief Executive Officer, Schumpert Medical Center, Shreveport, LA, p. A187

GONZALEZ, Pedro, Executive Director, San Carlos General Hospital, San Juan, PR, p. A474

GONZALEZ, Racheline A., Administrator, Fundacion Hospital Metropolitan, Caparra, PR, p. A473

GONZALEZ, Sonia I., R.N., Chief Operating Officer, Spring Hill Regional Hospital, Spring Hill, FL, p. A97

GOODE, Galen, Chief Executive Officer, Hamilton Center, Terre Haute, IN, p. A146

GOODE, Stephen M., Executive Director, Bayside Community Hospital, Anahuac, TX, p. A395

GOODLOE, Larry S., Administrator, Community Hospital Association, Fairfax, MO, p. A243

GOODMAN, Carol L., Administrator and Chief Executive Officer, Union County Hospital District, Anna, IL, p. A120

GOODMAN, Norman B., President and Chief Executive Officer, Brockton Hospital, Brockton, MA, p. A201

GOODMAN, Terry, Executive Director, Miami Jewish Home and Hospital for Aged, Miami, FL, p. A91

GOODRICH, Ralph G., Senior Executive Officer, Wright Memorial Hospital, Trenton, MO, p. A251

GOODSPEED, Ronald B., M.P.H., President, Southcoast Hospitals Group, Fall River, MA, p. A202

GOODSPEED, Scott W., President and Chief Executive Officer, Parkland Medical Center, Derry, NH, p. A268

GOODWIN, Bradford M., President and Chief Executive Officer, Sunnyview Hospital and Rehabilitation Center, Schenectady, NY, p. A300

GOODWIN, Jeffrey C., President and Chief Executive Officer, Warren Hospital, Phillipsburg, NJ, p. A276

GOODWIN, Phillip H., President, Camcare, Inc., Charleston, WV, p. B75

GOODWIN, Robert P., President and Chief Executive Officer, Lourdes Hospital, Paducah, KY, p. A175

GOOSMAN, Ed, Chief Executive Officer, Heartland Behavioral Health Services, Nevada, MO, p. A247

GORDON, Michael L., President and Chief Executive Officer, Woodlawn Hospital, Rochester, IN, p. A145

GORDON, William G., Chief Executive Officer, Barton Memorial Hospital, South Lake Tahoe, CA, p. A64

GORE, Gary R., Administrator, Marshall Medical Center North, Guntersville, AL, p. A15

GORMAN, John A., Chief Executive Officer, Memorial Hospital, Fremont, OH, p. A326

GOSLINE, Peter L., Chief Executive Officer, Monadnock Community Hospital, Peterborough, NH, p. A269

GOSS, Allan S., Director, Veterans Affairs Medical Center, Alexandria, LA, p. A178

GOTSCHLICH, Emil, M.D., Vice President Medical Sciences, Rockefeller University Hospital, New York, NY, p. A295

GOTTLIEB, Gary L., M.D., Chief Executive Officer, Friends Hospital, Philadelphia, PA, p. A360

GOTTSCHALK, M. Therese
President, Marian Health System, Tulsa, OK, p. B115
President, St. John Medical Center, Tulsa, OK, p. A342

GOULD, Gary R., FACHE, Chief Executive Officer, Belmont Community Hospital, Bellaire, OH, p. A321

GOULET, Diana L., Chief Executive Officer, BHC Canyon Ridge Hospital, Chino, CA, p. A39

GOUX, Rene, Chief Executive Officer, Jo Ellen Smith Medical Center, New Orleans, LA, p. A184

GOVIER, George A., President and Chief Executive Officer, Mercy Medical Center, Redding, CA, p. A57

GOWING, Robert E.
Interim Administrator, Atmore Community Hospital, Atmore, AL, p. A11
Administrator, Jay Hospital, Jay, FL, p. A88

GRABER, Calvin C., Chief Executive Officer, Henderson Health Care Services, Henderson, NE, p. A260

GRADY, Glen E., Administrator, Memorial Medical Center, Neillsville, WI, p. A463

GRADY, Phillip L., Chief Executive Officer, King's Daughters Hospital, Brookhaven, MS, p. A234

GRAEBER, Lawrence, Administrator, Neshoba County General Hospital, Philadelphia, MS, p. A239

GRAECA, Raymond A., President and Chief Executive Officer, DuBois Regional Medical Center, Du Bois, PA, p. A353

GRAFF, Sylvester, President and Chief Executive Officer, Queen of Angels–Hollywood Presbyterian Medical Center, Los Angeles, CA, p. A50

GRAGG, Martha, Chief Executive Officer, Sullivan County Memorial Hospital, Milan, MO, p. A247

GRAH, John A., Administrator, Williamson ARH Hospital, South Williamson, KY, p. A176

GRAHAM, George W., President, Torrance Memorial Medical Center, Torrance, CA, p. A65

GRAHAM, John A., President and Chief Executive Officer, Sherman Hospital, Elgin, IL, p. A126

GRAHAM, Kenneth D., President and Chief Executive Officer, Overlake Hospital Medical Center, Bellevue, WA, p. A445

GRAHAM, Larry M., Chief Executive Officer, Chalmette Medical Center, Chalmette, LA, p. A179

GRAHAM, Richard H., President and Chief Executive Officer, Augusta Health Care, Fishersville, VA, p. A437

GRAHAM, Richard L., Administrator, Bedford County General Hospital, Shelbyville, TN, p. A392

GRAHAM, Richard W., FACHE, President, Fairmont General Hospital, Fairmont, WV, p. A453

GRAJEWSKI, Timothy J., President and Chief Executive Officer, St. John Hospital and Medical Center, Detroit, MI, p. A211

GRAMLEY, Thomas S., Administrator, South Florida State Hospital, Pembroke Pines, FL, p. A94

GRAMLICH, Andrew, Chief Executive Officer, Lander Valley Medical Center, Lander, WY, p. A469

GRAND, Gary S., Chief Executive Officer, Central Louisiana State Hospital, Pineville, LA, p. A186

GRANDBOIS, Ray, M.P.H., Service Unit Director, U. S. Public Health Service Indian Hospital, Belcourt, ND, p. A316

GRANGER, Keith, President and Chief Executive Officer, Flowers Hospital, Dothan, AL, p. A13

GRAPPE, Steve, Administrator, Horizon Specialty Hospital, Lubbock, TX, p. A416

GRAVES, Jimmy, Administrator, Walthall County General Hospital, Tylertown, MS, p. A240

GRAVES, John T., President and Chief Executive Officer, St. Joseph's Hospital, Huntingburg, IN, p. A141

GRAVES, Philip G., President, Hutchinson Area Health Care, Hutchinson, MN, p. A226

GRAVES, Robert L., Administrator, Virginia Beach General Hospital, Virginia Beach, VA, p. A444

GRAY, David L., President, Hardin Memorial Hospital, Elizabethtown, KY, p. A169

GRAY, E. Kay, Interim Administrator, Vencor Hospital–Milwaukee, Milwaukee, WI, p. A463

GRAY, Jerry, Administrator, HEALTHSOUTH Rehabilitation Hospital, Memphis, TN, p. A390

GRAY, Patricia, Administrator and Chief Executive Officer, Blowing Rock Hospital, Blowing Rock, NC, p. A305

GRAY, Patrick J., Chief Executive Officer, Cumberland River Hospital North, Celina, TN, p. A383

GRAY, Penny, Administrator and Chief Executive Officer, Limestone Medical Center, Groesbeck, TX, p. A409

GRAY, Rick H., Ph.D., Chief Executive Officer, Charter Behavioral Health System, Jackson, MS, p. A236

GRAY, Val S., Executive Director, Cornwall Hospital, Cornwall, NY, p. A287

GRAY Jr., Clinton, Administrator, Maniilaq Health Center, Kotzebue, AK, p. A21

GRAY Jr., George H., Director, Veterans Affairs Medical Center, Little Rock, AR, p. A33

GRAYBILL, Scott R., Chief Executive Officer and Administrator, Community Hospital of Bremen, Bremen, IN, p. A138

GREEN, Calvin, Administrator, Crosby Memorial Hospital, Picayune, MS, p. A239

GREEN, Don Edd, Chief Executive Officer, Big Bend Regional Medical Center, Alpine, TX, p. A395

GREEN, Jack W., Administrator, Antelope Memorial Hospital, Neligh, NE, p. A262

GREEN, Jerry, Administrator, Tippah County Hospital, Ripley, MS, p. A239

GREEN, John H., Administrator, West Feliciana Parish Hospital, Saint Francisville, LA, p. A186

GREEN, Michael B., President, Concord Hospital, Concord, NH, p. A268

GREEN, Patrick, Administrator, Morgan Memorial Hospital, Madison, GA, p. A109

GREEN, Thomas E., President and Chief Executive Officer, Community Hospital at Dobbs Ferry, Dobbs Ferry, NY, p. A287

GREEN, Warren A., President and Chief Executive Officer, Sinai Hospital of Baltimore, Baltimore, MD, p. A194

GREENBERG, Herman R., Administrator, Maxwell Hospital, Montgomery, AL, p. A17

GREENE, A. Hugh, Executive Vice President and Chief Operating Officer, Baptist Medical Center, Jacksonville, FL, p. A87

GREENE, William M., FACHE, President, Santa Paula Memorial Hospital, Santa Paula, CA, p. A63

GREENE Jr., Charles H., Administrator, Cordell Memorial Hospital, Cordell, OK, p. A336

GREENE Jr., Edward C.
Administrator, Charles A. Cannon Jr. Memorial Hospital, Banner Elk, NC, p. A304
President, Sloop Memorial Hospital, Crossnore, NC, p. A306

GREENSPAN, Benn, President and Chief Executive Officer, Mount Sinai Hospital Medical Center of Chicago, Chicago, IL, p. A123

GREENSTEIN, Michael, Chief Executive Officer, Greystone Park Psychiatric Hospital, Greystone Park, NJ, p. A273

GREENWELL, Maryann J.
Chief Executive Officer, Ridgecrest Hospital, Clayton, GA, p. A104
Chief Executive Officer, Woodridge Hospital, Clayton, GA, p. A104

GREENWOOD, Kay, MS, Facility Director, North Alabama Regional Hospital, Decatur, AL, p. A13

GREER, James K., Administrator, Methodist Healthcare Middle Mississippi Hospital, Lexington, MS, p. A237

GREER, John H., President, Southside Community Hospital, Farmville, VA, p. A437

GREEVER, Paul, Chief Executive Officer, Parkside Hospital, Tulsa, OK, p. A342

GREGG, C. Jan, Chief Executive Officer, Eastern State Hospital, Medical Lake, WA, p. A447

GREGG Jr., David H., President, Gifford Medical Center, Randolph, VT, p. A434

GREGORY, Mary Jo, Chief Executive Officer, Tempe St. Luke's Hospital, Tempe, AZ, p. A27

GREGORY, Samuel S., Administrator, Upson Regional Medical Center, Thomaston, GA, p. A112

GREGORY, William A., Chief Executive Officer, Diagnostic Center Hospital, Houston, TX, p. A410

GREGSON, C. Mark
Chief Executive Officer, Cape Fear Memorial Hospital, Wilmington, NC, p. A314
Chief Executive Officer, Columbia Brunswick Hospital, Supply, NC, p. A313

GRESCO, Bill, Administrator, Columbia Lea Regional Hospital, Hobbs, NM, p. A282

GREY, Bill, Administrator, Vencor Hospital–Fort Worth South, Mansfield, TX, p. A417

GREY, Joel E.
Administrator, Sutter Auburn Faith Community Hospital, Auburn, CA, p. A37
Chief Executive Officer, Sutter Roseville Medical Center, Roseville, CA, p. A58

GRIFFIN, Debra L., Administrator, Humphreys County Memorial Hospital, Belzoni, MS, p. A233

GRIFFIN, Don, Ph.D., President and Chief Executive Officer, Regional Medical Center–Bayonet Point, Hudson, FL, p. A87

GRIFFIN, Don, Chief Executive Officer, Val Verde Regional Medical Center, Del Rio, TX, p. A404

GRIFFITH, Dennis, Vice President, Decatur General Hospital–West, Decatur, AL, p. A13

GRIFFITH, Patti, R.N., Administrator and Chief Executive Officer, Tri–City Health Centre, Dallas, TX, p. A404

GRIFFITH, Richard L., President and Chief Executive Officer, Queen's Health Systems, Honolulu, HI, p. B127

GRIFFITH, Wayne B., FACHE, Chief Executive Officer, St. Joseph's Hospital, Buckhannon, WV, p. A452

GRIFFITHS, Claudia N., President, Casa Grande Regional Medical Center, Casa Grande, AZ, p. A22

GRIFFITHS, Kathleen S., Interim President, Chelsea Community Hospital, Chelsea, MI, p. A209

GRIMES, Larry, Managing Director, River Crest Hospital, San Angelo, TX, p. A422

GRIMES, Teresa F., Administrator, Vaughn Jackson Medical Center, Jackson, AL, p. A15

GRIMES III, Thomas F., Executive Vice President and Chief Operating Officer, St. Elizabeth Community Hospital, Red Bluff, CA, p. A57

GRIMM, Steve, Chief Executive Officer, North Georgia Medical Center, Ellijay, GA, p. A106

GRIPPEN, Glen W., Director, Clement J. Zablocki Veterans Affairs Medical Center, Milwaukee, WI, p. A462

GRISSLER, Brian G., President and Chief Executive Officer, Suburban Hospital, Bethesda, MD, p. A194

GRISWOLD, Rosanne U., Chief Executive Officer, Charlotte Hungerford Hospital, Torrington, CT, p. A76

GRITMAN, Paul J., Superintendent, Danville State Hospital, Danville, PA, p. A352

GRONEWALD, John E., Chief Operating Officer, Ridgeview Institute, Smyrna, GA, p. A111

GROSETH, Bradley D., Administrator, Osseo Area Hospital and Nursing Home, Osseo, WI, p. A464

GROSS, Dan, Chief Executive Officer, Sharp Memorial Hospital, San Diego, CA, p. A59

GROSS, Diane S., Administrator, Holton Community Hospital, Holton, KS, p. A160

GROSS, Joseph W., President and Chief Executive Officer, St. Elizabeth Medical Center–North, Covington, KY, p. A169

GROSS, Kevin, Chief Executive Officer, Columbia Presbyterian–St. Luke's Medical Center, Denver, CO, p. A69

GROSSMEIER, John C., President and Chief Executive Officer, Hannibal Regional Hospital, Hannibal, MO, p. A243

GROVER Sr., Bradley K., FACHE
Chief Executive Officer, Northside Hospital and Heart Institute, Saint Petersburg, FL, p. A96
President and Chief Executive Officer, St. Petersburg Medical Center, Saint Petersburg, FL, p. A96

GRUBER, Norman F., Chief Operating Officer, St. Elizabeth Health Center, Youngstown, OH, p. A334

GRUNDSTROM, David A., President, New Ulm Medical Center, New Ulm, MN, p. A228

GRUSSING, Mel, Administrator, LAC–High Desert Hospital, Lancaster, CA, p. A47

GUARNIERI, Ellen, Acting Executive Director, West Jersey Hospital–Berlin, Berlin, NJ, p. A271

GUENTHER, Charles, Administrator, Eastern Plumas District Hospital, Portola, CA, p. A56

GUEST, John A., President and Chief Executive Officer, University Health System, San Antonio, TX, p. A424

GUILD, Samuel T., Administrator, Pawhuska Hospital, Pawhuska, OK, p. A340

GUIMARIN, Spencer, Administrator, Lakes Regional Medical Center, Jasper, TX, p. A413

GUINN, Lex A., Chief Executive Officer, Odessa Regional Hospital, Odessa, TX, p. A419

GULARTE, Steve, Administrator, El Campo Memorial Hospital, El Campo, TX, p. A405

GULEY, Michael G., President and Chief Executive Officer, Our Lady of Lourdes Memorial Hospital, Binghamton, NY, p. A285

GULICK, Margaret S., President and Chief Executive Officer, Memorial Healthcare Center, Owosso, MI, p. A217

GULLIFORD, Deryl E., Ph.D., Administrator, Community Memorial Hospital, Hicksville, OH, p. A327

GUNDERSON, Rodney L., Executive Director and Chief Executive Officer, Frick Hospital, Mount Pleasant, PA, p. A358

GUNN, B. Joe, FACHE, Administrator and Chief Executive Officer, Craig General Hospital, Vinita, OK, p. A343

GUNN, Christina B.
Chief Executive Officer, University of New Mexico Children's Psychiatric Hospital, Albuquerque, NM, p. A281
Chief Executive Officer, University of New Mexico Mental Health Center, Albuquerque, NM, p. A281

GUNN, John R., Executive Vice President, Memorial Hospital for Cancer and Allied Diseases, New York, NY, p. A294

GUNN, Terry J., Chief Executive Officer, River Park Hospital, McMinnville, TN, p. A389

GUPTON, Jack A., USAF, Administrator, Mike O'Callaghan Federal Hospital, Las Vegas, NV, p. A266

GURGEL, Paul E., President and Chief Executive Officer, New London Family Medical Center, New London, WI, p. A463

GUSTAFSON, Philip P., Administrator, San Ramon Regional Medical Center, San Ramon, CA, p. A62

GUTFELD, Marcia B., Vice President and Chief Operating Officer, De Graff Memorial Hospital, North Tonawanda, NY, p. A297

GUTHMILLER, Martin W., Administrator, Orange City Municipal Hospital, Orange City, IA, p. A153

GUTHRIE, Deborah S., Chief Executive Officer, Columbia Parkway Medical Center, Lithia Springs, GA, p. A108

GUTHRIE, Denise, Chief Executive Officer, Charter Cypress Behavioral Health System, Lafayette, LA, p. A182

GUTMAN, Milton M., Chief Executive Officer, Kingsbrook Jewish Medical Center, New York, NY, p. A293

GUTZKE, Ella, Administrator, Sheridan Memorial Hospital, Plentywood, MT, p. A256

GUY, Alan C., President and Chief Executive Officer, Covenant Health, Nashville, TN, p. B91

GUY, Douglas, President and Chief Executive Officer, Oconomowoc Memorial Hospital, Oconomowoc, WI, p. A463

GUYNN, Robert W., M.D., Executive Director, Harris County Psychiatric Center, Houston, TX, p. A411

GUZMAN, Tibisay A., Executive Vice President and Chief Operating Officer, Yonkers General Hospital, Yonkers, NY, p. A303

GWIAZDA, John M., President and Chief Executive Officer, Eastern Long Island Hospital, Greenport, NY, p. A288

GYSIN, Joyce, Administrator, Surprise Valley Community Hospital, Cedarville, CA, p. A39

H

HAAR, Clare A., Chief Executive Officer, Inter–Community Memorial Hospital, Newfane, NY, p. A297

HABERLEIN, Bernard, Executive Director, Graydon Manor, Leesburg, VA, p. A439

HACHTEN II, Richard A., Chief Executive Officer, Alegent Health Mercy Hospital, Council Bluffs, IA, p. A149

HACKER, Richard, Interim Administrator, Russell County Hospital, Russell Springs, KY, p. A176

HADDIX, D. Parker, Chief Executive Officer, Richwood Area Community Hospital, Richwood, WV, p. A455

HADEN, James E., President and Chief Executive Officer, Martha Jefferson Hospital, Charlottesville, VA, p. A437

HAEDER, James, Administrator, Bennett County Community Hospital, Martin, SD, p. A380

HAGEL, Sonja, Chief Executive Officer, North Hollywood Medical Center, Los Angeles, CA, p. A50

HAGEN, David F., President and Executive Officer, Roseau Area Hospital and Homes, Roseau, MN, p. A229

HAHN, James, Administrator, Baptist Memorial Hospital–North Mississippi, Oxford, MS, p. A238

HAILS, Robert, Chief Executive Officer, Charter Beacon, Fort Wayne, IN, p. A139

HALE, Margaret, Chief Operating Officer, Medical Center of Manchester, Manchester, TN, p. A389

HALE, William R., Chief Executive Officer, University Medical Center, Las Vegas, NV, p. A266

HALES Jr., John C., FACHE, President and Chief Executive Officer, Roper Hospital North, Charleston, SC, p. A372

HALEY, Bob J., Chief Executive Officer, Columbia Medical Center of Denton, Denton, TX, p. A404

HALKO, Mavis B., Administrator, Lakeshore Community Hospital, Dadeville, AL, p. A13

HALL, Amanda M., Administrator, Smith Hospital, Hahira, GA, p. A107

HALL, Cindy, Administrator, Eastern Ozarks Regional Health System, Cherokee Village, AR, p. A29

HALL, Dennis A., President, Baptist Health System, Birmingham, AL, p. B69

HALL, Diane S., Administrator, Bullock County Hospital, Union Springs, AL, p. A18

HALL, Herbert L., Chief Executive Officer, Wellspring Foundation, Bethlehem, CT, p. A74

HALL, Joan S., R.N., Administrator, South Lyon Medical Center, Yerington, NV, p. A267

HALL, Kim, Chief Executive Officer, Charter Behavioral Health System–Glendale, Glendale, AZ, p. A23

HALL, Linda, Administrator, Chillicothe Hospital District, Chillicothe, TX, p. A400

HALL, Marcia K., Chief Executive Officer, Sharp Coronado Hospital, Coronado, CA, p. A40

HALL, Richard W., President, Jamestown Hospital, Jamestown, ND, p. A317

HALL, Roger L., Chief Executive Officer, North Okaloosa Medical Center, Crestview, FL, p. A83

HALL Jr., Frederick W., Administrator, Sid Peterson Memorial Hospital, Kerrville, TX, p. A414

HALLFORD, Wayne, Chief Executive Officer, BHC Millwood Hospital, Arlington, TX, p. A396

HALLGREN, Hugh R., President and Chief Executive Officer, Wadley Regional Medical Center, Texarkana, TX, p. A426

HALLMAN, Gary D., President and Chief Executive Officer, Medina General Hospital, Medina, OH, p. A329

HALLMAN, Susan, Administrator, Inner Harbour Hospitals, Douglasville, GA, p. A105

HALLONQUIST, Frances A., Chief Executive Officer, Kapiolani Medical Center for Women and Children, Honolulu, HI, p. A114

HALM, Barry J., President and Chief Executive Officer, Benedictine Health System, Duluth, MN, p. B72

HALPERN, Kevin G., President and Chief Executive Officer, The Cooper Health System, Camden, NJ, p. A272

HALPERN, Marsha Lommel, President and Chief Executive Officer, Madonna Rehabilitation Hospital, Lincoln, NE, p. A261

HALSAN, Carole, Interim Administrator, Willapa Harbor Hospital, South Bend, WA, p. A450

HALSETH, Michael J., Executive Director, University of Virginia Medical Center, Charlottesville, VA, p. A437

HALSTEAD, Michael J., President and Chief Executive Officer, Carlisle Hospital, Carlisle, PA, p. A351

HAMILL, Dave H., President and Chief Executive Officer, Hampton Regional Medical Center, Varnville, SC, p. A377

HAMILTON, Daniel, Chief Executive Officer, Pennock Hospital, Hastings, MI, p. A213

HAMILTON, Phil, R.N., Chief Executive Officer, General John J. Pershing Memorial Hospital, Brookfield, MO, p. A241

HAMILTON, Richard C., Administrator, Eldora Regional Medical Center, Eldora, IA, p. A150

HAMM, David, Interim Chief Executive Officer, Exempla Saint Joseph Hospital, Denver, CO, p. A69

HAMMACK, Stanley K., Administrator, USA Children's and Women's Hospital, Mobile, AL, p. A16

HAMMER, Michael, President and Chief Executive Officer, Good Samaritan Health Center of Merrill, Merrill, WI, p. A462

HAMMER, Pat, Chief Executive Officer, Ten Broeck Hospital, Louisville, KY, p. A174

HAMMER, David L., MC, Commander, U. S. Air Force Academy Hospital, USAF Academy, CO, p. A73

HAMMER II, Robert L., Chief Executive Officer, Davis Memorial Hospital, Elkins, WV, p. A453

HAMMETT, Warren E., Administrator, Bamberg County Memorial Hospital and Nursing Center, Bamberg, SC, p. A371

HAMMOND, Joe, Administrator, Eureka Springs Hospital, Eureka Springs, AR, p. A30

HAMNER, David, Administrator, Hardtner Medical Center, Olla, LA, p. A186

HAMRY, David K., President, Good Samaritan Community Healthcare, Puyallup, WA, p. A448

HANCOCK, Barbara, Interim Administrator, State Hospital North, Orofino, ID, p. A118

HANCOCK, Edward H., President, Nanticoke Memorial Hospital, Seaford, DE, p. A78

HANCOCK, Pamm, Interim Administrator, Pike County Memorial Hospital, Louisiana, MO, p. A246

HAND, George, Interim Administrator, Iuka Hospital, Iuka, MS, p. A236

HANENBURG, Thomas, Administrator, Franklin Regional Medical Center, Louisburg, NC, p. A310

HANES, Carol H., Interim Chief Executive Officer, Senatobia Community Hospital, Senatobia, MS, p. A239

HANKO, James F., Administrator and Chief Executive Officer, Weiner Memorial Medical Center, Marshall, MN, p. A227

HANKS, Debra D., Administrator, St. Lukes Rehabilitation Institute, Spokane, WA, p. A450

HANKS, Sheridan, Administrator, Georgiana Doctors Hospital, Georgiana, AL, p. A15

HANLEY, Richard, Chief Executive Officer, Down East Community Hospital, Machias, ME, p. A191

HANNA, Philip S., Administrator, Adams County Hospital, West Union, OH, p. A333

HANNAN, David T., President and Chief Executive Officer, South Shore Hospital, South Weymouth, MA, p. A205

HANNIG, Virgil
   Senior Vice President and Administrator, Franklin Hospital and Skilled Nursing Care Unit, Benton, IL, p. A121
   Administrator, Herrin Hospital, Herrin, IL, p. A128
   Senior Vice President and Administrator, United Mine Workers of America Union Hospital, West Frankfort, IL, p. A136

HANOVER, Kenneth
   President and Chief Executive Officer, Bryn Mawr Hospital, Bryn Mawr, PA, p. A351
   President and Chief Executive Officer, Paoli Memorial Hospital, Paoli, PA, p. A359

HANRAHAN, Thomas F., Chief Executive Officer, McKay–Dee Hospital Center, Ogden, UT, p. A431

HANSEN, Edwin L., Vice President, Yukon–Kuskokwim Delta Regional Hospital, Bethel, AK, p. A20

HANSEN, Irwin C., President and Chief Executive Officer, Summit Medical Center, Oakland, CA, p. A54

HANSEN, Thomas N., Acting Chief Executive Officer and Medical Director, Children's Hospital, Columbus, OH, p. A324

HANSHAW, John, Chief Executive Officer, St. Mark's Hospital, Salt Lake City, UT, p. A432

HANSON, Bryant R., President and Chief Executive Officer, Floyd Memorial Hospital and Health Services, New Albany, IN, p. A144

HANSON, Craig, Administrator, St. Luke Hospital, Marion, KS, p. A162

HANSON, Eric, Administrator, Southern Hills General Hospital, Hot Springs, SD, p. A379

HANSON, Greg, President and Chief Executive Officer, St. Joseph's Hospital and Health Center, Dickinson, ND, p. A316

HANSON, Jerry, Administrator and Chief Executive Officer, Crawford County Hospital District One, Girard, KS, p. A159

HANSON, Marlin, Administrator, Marshall Medical Center South, Boaz, AL, p. A12

HANSON, Paul, Chief Executive Officer, Glendive Medical Center, Glendive, MT, p. A254

HANSON, Timothy H., President and Chief Executive Officer, HealthEast, Saint Paul, MN, p. B105

HANYAK, Diana C., Chief Executive Officer, Charter Behavioral Health System of Southern California–Corona, Corona, CA, p. A40

HARBARGER, Claude W., President, St. Dominic–Jackson Memorial Hospital, Jackson, MS, p. A236

HARBIN, Henry, M.D., President and Chief Executive Officer, Magellan Health Services, Atlanta, GA, p. B114

HARCOURT Jr., John P., President and Chief Executive Officer, Healthcare America, Inc., Austin, TX, p. B104

HARDER, Shirley, Chief Executive Officer, Wayne Medical Center, Waynesboro, TN, p. A393

HARDIN, Richard R., Chief Executive Officer, Desert Hills Center for Youth and Families, Tucson, AZ, p. A27

HARDING, John R., President and Chief Executive Officer, Florida Hospital Heartland Division, Sebring, FL, p. A96

HARDING, Lynwood F., Director, Western State Hospital, Staunton, VA, p. A443

HARDING, William W., President and Chief Executive Officer, Union Hospital, Dover, OH, p. A326

HARDY, Patsy, Administrator, Putnam General Hospital, Hurricane, WV, p. A454

HARDY, Stephen L., Ph.D., Facility Director, Chester Mental Health Center, Chester, IL, p. A122

HARDY, J. Thomas, Commanding Officer, Irwin Army Community Hospital, Fort Riley, KS, p. A159

HARE, Joseph C., President and Chief Executive Officer, Neumann Medical Center, Philadelphia, PA, p. A361

HARE, Michael K., Administrator, De Leon Hospital, De Leon, TX, p. A404

HARENSKI, Robert J., Chief Executive Officer, Antelope Valley Hospital, Lancaster, CA, p. A47

HARKINS, William D., President and Chief Executive Officer, Ancilla Systems Inc., Hobart, IN, p. B67

HARKNESS, Laurence P., President and Chief Executive Officer, Children's Medical Center, Dayton, OH, p. A325

HARLAN, Thomas M., Chief Executive Officer, Chinese Hospital, San Francisco, CA, p. A60

HARMAN, David L., Administrator, Harney District Hospital, Burns, OR, p. A344

HARMAN, Gerald M., Executive Vice President, St. Elizabeth's Hospital, Belleville, IL, p. A120

HARMAN, Richmond M., President and Chief Executive Officer, Martin Memorial Health Systems, Stuart, FL, p. A97

HARMAN, Robert L., Administrator, Grant Memorial Hospital, Petersburg, WV, p. A455

HARMON, Ronald A., M.D., Chief Executive Officer, Albert Lea Medical Center, Albert Lea, MN, p. A222

HARMS, Charles F., Administrator, McKee Medical Center, Loveland, CO, p. A72

HARPER, Alan G., Director, Veterans Affairs North Texas Health Care System, Dallas, TX, p. A404

HARPER, John D., President, South Shore Hospital, Chicago, IL, p. A124

HARR, Robert Glenn, President, Heather Hill Hospital and Health Care Center, Chardon, OH, p. A322

HARREL, Mark, Administrator, Fairview Hospital, Fairview, OK, p. A337

HARRELL, David E., Chief Executive Officer, Georgia Baptist Health Care System, Atlanta, GA, p. B102

HARRELL, Richard E., President and Chief Executive Officer, Duplin General Hospital, Kenansville, NC, p. A309

HARRINGTON, Frank, Administrator, Aberdeen–Monroe County Hospital, Aberdeen, MS, p. A233

HARRINGTON, Joseph P., Chief Executive Officer, Lodi Memorial Hospital, Lodi, CA, p. A47

HARRINGTON, Michael L., Executive Vice President and Administrator, Bon Secours–St. Joseph Hospital, Port Charlotte, FL, p. A95

HARRINGTON, Timothy, President, Victory Memorial Hospital, Waukegan, IL, p. A136

HARRINGTON Jr., Allan, Chief Executive Officer, Tucson General Hospital, Tucson, AZ, p. A27

HARRINGTON Jr., John L., FACHE, Administrator, Vencor Hospital–Phoenix, Phoenix, AZ, p. A25

HARRINGTON Jr., Russell D., President, Baptist Health, Little Rock, AR, p. B68

HARRIS, Allyn R., Chief Executive Officer, Nashville Memorial Hospital, Madison, TN, p. A389

HARRIS, Andrew E., Chief Executive Officer, Mercy Community Hospital, Havertown, PA, p. A355

HARRIS, Frank W., President and Chief Executive Officer, Russell Hospital, Alexander City, AL, p. A11

HARRIS, Robert L., President and Chief Executive Officer, Ingalls Hospital, Harvey, IL, p. A128

HARRIS, Robert W., President, Lakeside Memorial Hospital, Brockport, NY, p. A285

HARRIS, Wayne, Administrator, Simpson General Hospital, Mendenhall, MS, p. A237

HARRIS Jr., M. Ray, President and Chief Executive Officer, McKenna Memorial Hospital, New Braunfels, TX, p. A419

HARROD, Pat, Chief Executive Officer, Charter Behavioral Health System of Paducah, Paducah, KY, p. A175

HARRYMAN, John D., Executive Director, Charlotte Regional Medical Center, Punta Gorda, FL, p. A95

HART, Diane M., Chief Executive Officer, Moses Ludington Hospital, Ticonderoga, NY, p. A302

HART, James D., President, Northwest Hospital, Seattle, WA, p. A449

HART, Joel A., FACHE, Chief Executive Officer, Charter Heights Behavioral Health System, Albuquerque, NM, p. A280

HART, Joel A., Administrator, Woodward Hospital and Health Center, Woodward, OK, p. A343

HART, Noel W., Administrator, King's Daughters Hospital, Yazoo City, MS, p. A240

HART, Patsy J., Executive Director, University Hospitals and Clinics, Columbia, MO, p. A242

HART, Steven, Commanding Officer, Naval Hospital, Lemoore, CA, p. A47

HARTLEY, H. William, Chief Executive Officer, Rush Memorial Hospital, Rushville, IN, p. A145

HARTMAN, C. Richard, M.D., President and Chief Executive Officer, Community Medical Center, Scranton, PA, p. A365

HARVIE, Allison, Acting Administrator, Glacier County Medical Center, Cut Bank, MT, p. A254

HARWOOD, Janie L., Chief Executive Officer, Columbia Bayview Psychiatric Center, Corpus Christi, TX, p. A401

HASTINGS, Arthur W., President and Chief Executive Officer, Middle Tennessee Medical Center, Murfreesboro, TN, p. A391

HASTINGS, G. Richard, President and Chief Executive Officer, Saint Luke's Shawnee Mission Health System, Kansas City, MO, p. B134

HATALA, Alexander J., President and Chief Executive Officer, Our Lady of Lourdes Medical Center, Camden, NJ, p. A271

HATCHER, John M., President, Whitley Memorial Hospital, Columbia City, IN, p. A138

HATERIUS, Craig, Administrator, Stamford Memorial Hospital, Stamford, TX, p. A425

HATHAWAY Jr., Woodrow W., Chief Executive Officer, Chatham Hospital, Siler City, NC, p. A313

HAUG, William F., FACHE, President and Chief Executive Officer, Motion Picture and Television Fund Hospital and Residential Services, Los Angeles, CA, p. A50

HAUGH, Diana, MS, Superintendent, Larue D. Carter Memorial Hospital, Indianapolis, IN, p. A141

HAUGO, Glenn, Administrator, Daniels Memorial Hospital, Scobey, MT, p. A256

HAUSE, Eileen, Chief Executive Officer, Kensington Hospital, Philadelphia, PA, p. A361

HAUSLER, Jeffrey E., Vice Chairman and Chief Executive Officer, United Regional Health Care System, Wichita Falls, TX, p. A428

HAWKINS, Leslie A., Chief Executive Officer, Mount Desert Island Hospital, Bar Harbor, ME, p. A189

HAWKINS, Mary Jane, Administrator and Chief Executive Officer, HEALTHSOUTH Nittany Valley Rehabilitation Hospital, Pleasant Gap, PA, p. A364

HAWKINS, Phil, Administrator, Carnegie Tri–County Municipal Hospital, Carnegie, OK, p. A336

HAWKINS, Robert L., Superintendent, Colorado Mental Health Institute at Pueblo, Pueblo, CO, p. A72

HAWKINSON, Curtis, Chief Executive Officer, Keefe Memorial Hospital, Cheyenne Wells, CO, p. A68

HAWLEY, Jess, Administrator, Syringa General Hospital, Grangeville, ID, p. A117

HAWLEY Jr., Robert L., Chief Executive Officer, Bolivar Medical Center, Cleveland, MS, p. A234

HAWTHORNE, Connie, Chief Executive Officer, Medical Center Shoals, Muscle Shoals, AL, p. A17

HAWTHORNE, Douglas D., President and Chief Executive Officer, Texas Health Resources, Irving, TX, p. B146

HAYES, Billy, Administrator, Baptist Hospital, Worth County, Sylvester, GA, p. A112

HAYES, David R., President, Taylor County Hospital, Campbellsville, KY, p. A169

HAYES, Howard A., President and Chief Executive Officer, St. Joseph Regional Medical Center, Lewiston, ID, p. A117

HAYES, James M., Administrator, Hamilton Memorial Hospital District, McLeansboro, IL, p. A130

HAYES, T. Farrell, President, Healthcorp of Tennessee, Inc., Chattanooga, TN, p. B105

HAYES, Thomas P.
Chief Executive Officer, Fremont Medical Center, Yuba City, CA, p. A67
Chief Executive Officer, Fremont–Rideout Health Group, Yuba City, CA, p. B101
Chief Executive Officer, Rideout Memorial Hospital, Marysville, CA, p. A52

HAYES, Wayne, Administrator, Nashville Metropolitan Bordeaux Hospital, Nashville, TN, p. A391

HAYS, Cheryl, Administrator, Lawrence Baptist Medical Center, Moulton, AL, p. A17

HAYS, Janet A., Administrator, Forks Community Hospital, Forks, WA, p. A446

HAYS, Lissa B., Chief Operating Officer, Newport News General Hospital, Newport News, VA, p. A440

HAYWARD, John, President and Chief Executive Officer, PeaceHealth, Bellevue, WA, p. B125

HAYWOOD, Thomas L., Chief Executive Officer, Southeast Arizona Medical Center, Douglas, AZ, p. A22

HAYWOOD III, Edgar, Administrator, J. Arthur Dosher Memorial Hospital, Southport, NC, p. A313

HAZLETT II, Guy, FACHE, Chief Executive Officer, Palo Pinto General Hospital, Mineral Wells, TX, p. A418

HEAD, William C., USAF, Administrator, U. S. Air Force Regional Hospital, Eglin AFB, FL, p. A84

HEADDING, John, Chief Administrative Officer, Mercy Hospital and Health Services, Merced, CA, p. A52

HEADLEE, Dennis E., Administrator, Plains Regional Medical Center, Clovis, NM, p. A281

HEADLEY, Elwood J., M.D., Director, Veterans Affairs Medical Center, Boston, MA, p. A201

HEARD, William C., Administrator and Chief Executive Officer, Cumberland Hall Hospital, Hopkinsville, KY, p. A171

HEARING, Philip E., President and Chief Executive Officer, Southeastern Ohio Regional Medical Center, Cambridge, OH, p. A321

HEATER, Floyd, Chief Executive Officer, Shenandoah Memorial Hospital, Woodstock, VA, p. A444

HEATH, Susan, Chief Executive Officer, HEALTHSOUTH Chattanooga Rehabilitation Hospital, Chattanooga, TN, p. A384

HEATH, William J., President and Chief Executive Officer, Saginaw General Hospital, Saginaw, MI, p. A218

HEATHERLY, Neil, Chief Executive Officer, Columbia Metropolitan Hospital, Atlanta, GA, p. A100

HEATHERLY, Wayne S., Chief Executive Officer, Columbia Regional Medical Center, Montgomery, AL, p. A16

HECHT, Kevin, Director, Wagner General Hospital, Palacios, TX, p. A419

HECK III, George L., President and Chief Executive Officer, Coffee Regional Medical Center, Douglas, GA, p. A105

HECKERT, Brian, Director, William Jennings Bryan Dorn Veterans Hospital, Columbia, SC, p. A373

HECKERT Jr., Robert James, MSC, Chief of Staff, Walter Reed Army Medical Center, Washington, DC, p. A79

HEDRIX, Michael, Administrator, Pine Medical Center, Sandstone, MN, p. A230

HEIN, Joyce Grove, Chief Executive Officer, Lakewood Medical Center, Morgan City, LA, p. A184

HEINIKE, J. Larry, President and Chief Executive Officer, Horizon Hospital System, Greenville, PA, p. A354

HEISE, Patrick B., Chief Executive Officer, Community Memorial Hospital, Staunton, IL, p. A135

HEITKAMP, Charlotte, Chief Executive Officer, Jackson Medical Center, Jackson, MN, p. A226

HEKIMIAN, Barbara D. S., Chief Executive Officer, Dominion Hospital, Falls Church, VA, p. A437

HELIN, Ernie, Chief Executive Officer, Ashley County Medical Center, Crossett, AR, p. A30

HELLER, Thomas, Administrator, HEALTHSOUTH Western Hills Regional Rehabilitation Hospital, Parkersburg, WV, p. A455

HELLERSTEDT, Wayne P., Chief Executive Officer, Helen Newberry Joy Hospital, Newberry, MI, p. A217

HELLYER, Nancy R., R.N., Chief Executive Officer, Columbia Grant Hospital, Chicago, IL, p. A122

HELM, Michael D., President, Sparks Regional Medical Center, Fort Smith, AR, p. A31

HELMS, Ella Raye, Administrator, Fisher County Hospital District, Rotan, TX, p. A421

HELZER, James D., Administrator, Veterans Home of California, Yountville, CA, p. A67

HEMETER, Donald, Administrator, Wayne General Hospital, Waynesboro, MS, p. A240

HENCKEL, Susan, Executive Vice President and Chief Executive Officer, Columbia Hospital, Milwaukee, WI, p. A462

HENDERSON, Cynthia T., M.P.H., Hospital Director and Chief Operating Officer, Oak Forest Hospital of Cook County, Oak Forest, IL, p. A132

HENDERSON, Donald, Chief Executive Officer, Byrd Regional Hospital, Leesville, LA, p. A183

HENDERSON, W. Perry, Administrator, East Texas Medical Center Pittsburg, Pittsburg, TX, p. A420

HENDRICKSON, Wayne, Interim Administrator, Griggs County Hospital and Nursing Home, Cooperstown, ND, p. A316

HENDRICKSON, William Wilson, President and Chief Executive Officer, Good Samaritan Health Systems, Kearney, NE, p. A261

HENDRIX, Wayne, President, Kosciusko Community Hospital, Warsaw, IN, p. A146

HENDRUS, Joe, Administrator, Lillian M. Hudspeth Memorial Hospital, Sonora, TX, p. A425

HENGER, Robert E., Administrator, Carraway Northwest Medical Center, Winfield, AL, p. A19

HENIKOFF, Leo M.
President and Chief Executive Officer, Rush–Presbyterian–St. Luke's Medical Center, Chicago, IL, p. A124
President, Rush–Presbyterian–St. Luke's Medical Center, Chicago, IL, p. B134

HENKE, Marcella V., Administrator and Chief Executive Officer, Jackson County Hospital, Edna, TX, p. A405

HENLEY, Darryl E., Administrator, Dos Palos Memorial Hospital, Dos Palos, CA, p. A41

HENNESSY, Thomas G., Chief Executive Officer, MetroWest Medical Center, Framingham, MA, p. A202

HENNEY, Jane E., M.D., Vice President Health Sciences, University of New Mexico, Albuquerque, NM, p. B150

HENRY, Angelia K., Administrator, Douglas County Memorial Hospital, Armour, SD, p. A378

HENRY, David, Chief Executive Officer, Northern Montana Hospital, Havre, MT, p. A255

HENRY, Gary L., Ph.D., Chief Executive Officer, BHC Spirit of St. Louis Hospital, Saint Charles, MO, p. A248

HENRY, Paul B., Administrator, Charter Fairmount Institute, Philadelphia, PA, p. A360

HENRY, Peter P., Director, Veterans Affairs Black Hills Health Care System, Fort Meade, SD, p. A379

HENRY, Terry, Interim Administrator, University Medical Center, Fresno, CA, p. A43

HENRY Jr., Jake, President, Spohn Health System, Corpus Christi, TX, p. A402

HENRY Sr., John Dunklin, FACHE
Chief Executive Officer, Crawford Long Hospital of Emory University, Atlanta, GA, p. A100
Chief Executive Officer, Emory University Hospital, Atlanta, GA, p. A101

HENSLER, Paul J., Chief Executive Officer, Sutter Lakeside Hospital, Lakeport, CA, p. A46

HENSLEY, Dana S.
President, Birmingham Baptist Medical Center–Montclair Campus, Birmingham, AL, p. A11
President and Chief Executive Officer, Birmingham Baptist Medical Center–Princeton, Birmingham, AL, p. A11

HENSON, Blair W., Administrator, Florala Memorial Hospital, Florala, AL, p. A14

HENSON, Carl, Administrator, Minidoka Memorial Hospital and Extended Care Facility, Rupert, ID, p. A118

HENSON, David L., Chief Executive Officer, Wilkes Regional Medical Center, North Wilkesboro, NC, p. A311

HENSON, James C., President, United Hospital Corporation, Memphis, TN, p. B148

HENSON, John S., President, Baptist Regional Medical Center, Corbin, KY, p. A169

HENTON, Thomas, President and Chief Executive Officer, Cleveland Area Hospital, Cleveland, OK, p. A336

HENZE, Michael E., Chief Executive Officer, Lake of the Ozarks General Hospital, Osage Beach, MO, p. A248

HERBERT, Susan, Administrator, Inova Mount Vernon Hospital, Alexandria, VA, p. A436

HERFINDAHL, Lowell D., President and Chief Executive Officer, Tioga Medical Center, Tioga, ND, p. A319

HERMAN, Bernard J., President and Chief Executive Officer, Mercy Healthcare–Bakersfield, Bakersfield, CA, p. A37

HERMAN, Paul, Chief Executive Officer, San Luis Valley Regional Medical Center, Alamosa, CO, p. A68

HERMANSON, Patrick M., Senior Executive Officer, Saint Vincent Hospital and Health Center, Billings, MT, p. A253

HERNANDEZ, Hank, Chief Executive Officer, Columbia Medical Center–West, El Paso, TX, p. A405

HERNANDEZ, Leonard, Administrator and Chief Executive Officer, Plainville Rural Hospital District Number One, Plainville, KS, p. A164

HERNANDEZ, Pablo, M.D., Administrator, Wyoming State Hospital, Evanston, WY, p. A468

HERNANDEZ, Roberto, Administrator, University Hospital, San Juan, PR, p. A474

HERNANDEZ–KEEBLE, Sonia, Director, Rio Grande State Center, Harlingen, TX, p. A409

HERRICK, Ronald L., President, Rehabilitation Institute, Kansas City, MO, p. A245

HERRING, Michael S., Administrator, Samuel Simmonds Memorial Hospital, Barrow, AK, p. A20

HERRON, John M., Administrator, Baptist North Hospital, Cumming, GA, p. A104

HERRON, Thomas L., FACHE, President and Chief Executive Officer, Largo Medical Center, Largo, FL, p. A89

HERVEY, Roger D., Administrator, Galena–Stauss Hospital, Galena, IL, p. A127

HERZOG, Paul F., President and Chief Executive Officer, Bethany Medical Center, Kansas City, KS, p. A161

HESELTINE, Bruce P., USAF, Commander, U. S. Air Force Hospital, Holloman AFB, NM, p. A282

HESS, Carolyn K., Administrator, Grape Community Hospital, Hamburg, IA, p. A151

HESS, Roy E., Executive Vice President and Administrator, Bon Secours–Venice Hospital, Venice, FL, p. A98

HESSELMANN, Thomas J., President and Chief Executive Officer, Samaritan Health System, Clinton, IA, p. A148

HESSELTINE, Wendell, President, Tillamook County General Hospital, Tillamook, OR, p. A348

HESTER, Forrest G., President and Chief Executive Officer, Abraham Lincoln Memorial Hospital, Lincoln, IL, p. A130

HETLAGE, C. Kennon, Administrator, Memorial Regional Hospital, Los Angeles, FL, p. A86

HEUSER, Keith E., Chief Executive Officer, Memorial Hospital, Carthage, IL, p. A121

HEYBOER Jr., Lester, President and Chief Executive Officer, HealthSource Saginaw, Saginaw, MI, p. A218

HEYDE, Jorge A., CHE, Administrator, GlenOaks Hospital, Glendale Heights, IL, p. A127

HEYDEL, M. John, President and Chief Executive Officer, Self Memorial Hospital, Greenwood, SC, p. A374

HEYDT, Stuart, M.D., Chief Executive Officer, Penn State Geisinger Health System, Harrisburg, PA, p. B125

HIATT, M. K., Administrator, Allendale County Hospital, Fairfax, SC, p. A373

HIBBS, Cathryn A., Chief Executive Officer, Southwest Hospital, Louisville, KY, p. A174

HICKEY, Martin, M.D., Chief Executive Officer, Lovelace Health System, Albuquerque, NM, p. A280

HICKS, Alex, Acting Chief Executive Officer, Gadsden Community Hospital, Quincy, FL, p. A95

HICKS, Cheryl, Chief Executive Officer, Twin City Hospital, Dennison, OH, p. A326

HICKS, John D., President and Chief Executive Officer, Baptist St. Anthony Health System, Amarillo, TX, p. A395

HICKS, John R., President and Chief Executive Officer, Platte Valley Medical Center, Brighton, CO, p. A68

HICKS, Kevin J., Chief Executive Officer, Overland Park Regional Medical Center, Overland Park, KS, p. A164

HICKS, Michael C., President and Chief Executive Officer, Jefferson Memorial Hospital, Jefferson City, TN, p. A387

HICKS, Tommy L., Administrator, Ray County Memorial Hospital, Richmond, MO, p. A248

HIDDE, A. John, President and Chief Executive Officer, Good Samaritan Hospital, Vincennes, IN, p. A146

HIESTER, Richard B., Administrator, Memorial Psychiatric Hospital, Albuquerque, NM, p. A280

HIETPAS, Bernard G.
Chief Executive Officer, Glenn Medical Center, Willows, CA, p. A67
Administrator, Seneca District Hospital, Chester, CA, p. A39

HIGGINBOTHAM, G. Douglas, Executive Director, South Central Regional Medical Center, Laurel, MS, p. A237

HIGGINS, Brad A., President and Chief Executive Officer, Fostoria Community Hospital, Fostoria, OH, p. A326

HIGGINS, Susannah, Chief Executive Officer, Broaddus Hospital, Philippi, WV, p. A455

HIGH, Cheryl A., Administrator, White Community Hospital, Aurora, MN, p. A222

HIGHSMITH Jr., C. Cameron, President and Chief Executive Officer, St. Luke's Hospital, Columbus, NC, p. A306

HILL, David L., President and Chief Executive Officer, Wahiawa General Hospital, Wahiawa, HI, p. A115

HILL, James C., Chief Executive Officer, Charter Behavioral Health System of Tampa Bay, Tampa, FL, p. A97

HILL, Jim, Chief Executive Officer, Charter Behavioral Health System of Tampa Bay at Largo, Largo, FL, p. A89

HILL, Kent D., Director, Veterans Affairs Medical and Regional Office Center, Wichita, KS, p. A167

HILL, Robert B., President, Bethesda Memorial Hospital, Boynton Beach, FL, p. A81

HILL, Thomas E.
Chief Executive Officer, WellStar Cobb Hospital, Austell, GA, p. A102
Chief Executive Officer, WellStar Douglas Hospital, Douglasville, GA, p. A105
Chief Executive Officer, WellStar Health System, Austell, GA, p. B153
Chief Executive Officer, WellStar Kennestone Hospital, Marietta, GA, p. A109
Chief Executive Officer, WellStar Paulding Hospital, Dallas, GA, p. A105
Chief Executive Officer, WellStar Windy Hill Hospital, Marietta, GA, p. A109

HILL, Timothy E., Chief Executive Officer, North Arkansas Regional Medical Center, Harrison, AR, p. A31

HILL, John, FACHE, Administrator, David Grant Medical Center, Travis AFB, CA, p. A65

HILLBOM, Richard, Administrator, Oakwood Hospital Beyer Center–Ypsilanti, Ypsilanti, MI, p. A221

HILLENMEYER, John, President and Chief Executive Officer, Orlando Regional Healthcare System, Orlando, FL, p. B123

HILLIS, David W., President and Chief Executive Officer, Adcare Hospital of Worcester, Worcester, MA, p. A207

HILTZ, Richard S., President and Chief Executive Officer, Mercy Memorial Hospital, Monroe, MI, p. A216

HINCHEY, Paul P.
President and Chief Executive Officer, Candler Hospital, Savannah, GA, p. A111
President and Chief Executive Officer, St. Joseph's Hospital, Savannah, GA, p. A111

HINDS, Bob, Executive Director, Bradford Health Services at Huntsville, Madison, AL, p. A16

HINER, Calvin A., Administrator, Tri–County Area Hospital, Lexington, NE, p. A261

HINIKER, Alice, Ph.D., Administrator, Intracare Medical Center Hospital, Houston, TX, p. A411

HINO, Raymond T., Chief Executive Officer, Big Horn County Memorial Hospital, Hardin, MT, p. A254

HINSDALE, Laurence C., President and Chief Executive Officer, NorthEast Medical Center, Concord, NC, p. A306

HINSON, Roy M., CHE, President and Chief Executive Officer, Stanly Memorial Hospital, Albemarle, NC, p. A304

HINTON, J. Philip, M.D., President and Chief Executive Officer, Fresno Community Hospital and Medical Center, Fresno, CA, p. A43

HINTON, James H., President and Chief Executive Officer, Presbyterian Healthcare Services, Albuquerque, NM, p. B125

HINTON, Philip, M.D., Chief Executive Officer, Community Hospitals of Central California, Fresno, CA, p. B90

HIRSCH, Glenn, Executive Vice President, Administration, North Shore University Hospital at Plainview, Plainview, NY, p. A298

HIRSCH, Jeffrey D., Executive Vice President and Chief Operating Officer, Horton Medical Center, Middletown, NY, p. A290

HIRT, Fred D., President and Chief Executive Officer, Mount Sinai Medical Center, Miami Beach, FL, p. A91

HITT, Irving, Administrator, Covington County Hospital, Collins, MS, p. A234

HITZLER, Ronald R., Administrator, Shriners Hospitals for Children, Shriners Burns Hospital, Cincinnati, Cincinnati, OH, p. A323

HOARD, Jack D., President and Chief Executive Officer, Armstrong County Memorial Hospital, Kittanning, PA, p. A356

HODGE Jr., Joseph T., Facility Administrator, Central State Hospital, Milledgeville, GA, p. A109

HODGES, Joseph T., President, Corry Memorial Hospital, Corry, PA, p. A352

HODGES, Linda L., R.N., Associate Administrator, Green Hospital of Scripps Clinic, La Jolla, CA, p. A46

HODGSON, Judy, Administrator, Sacred Heart Medical Center, Eugene, OR, p. A345

HOELSCHER, Steve C., Administrator, Marshall Medical Center, Lewisburg, TN, p. A388

HOFER, Kathleen, President, St. Mary's Medical Center, Duluth, MN, p. A224

HOFF, David L., Chief Executive Officer, Iron County Community Hospital, Iron River, MI, p. A214

HOFF, Terry G., President, Trinity Medical Center, Minot, ND, p. A318

HOFFART, Terry L., Administrator, Webster County Community Hospital, Red Cloud, NE, p. A263

HOFFMAN, Charles, Vice President, Allenmore Hospital, Tacoma, WA, p. A450

HOFIUS, Chuck, Administrator, Perham Memorial Hospital and Home, Perham, MN, p. A229

HOFREUTER, Donald H., M.D., Administrator and Chief Executive Officer, Wheeling Hospital, Wheeling, WV, p. A456

HOFSTETTER, Peter A., Chief Executive Officer, Northwestern Medical Center, Saint Albans, VT, p. A434

HOGAN, Karen C., Administrator and Chief Executive Officer, San Diego County Psychiatric Hospital, San Diego, CA, p. A59

HOGAN, Ronald C., Superintendent, Georgia Regional Hospital at Atlanta, Decatur, GA, p. A105

HOGUE, John, Administrator, Covina Valley Community Hospital, West Covina, CA, p. A67

HOHENBERGER, Arthur L., FACHE, President and Chief Executive Officer, Texoma Healthcare System, Denison, TX, p. A404

HOHL, David G., Chief Executive Officer, Richmond Memorial Hospital, Rockingham, NC, p. A312

HOHN, David C., M.D., President and Chief Executive Officer, Roswell Park Cancer Institute, Buffalo, NY, p. A286

HOIDEL, David, Chief Executive Officer, DePaul/Tulane Behavioral Health Center, New Orleans, LA, p. A184

HOLCOMB, David M., President and Chief Executive Officer, Jennie Edmundson Memorial Hospital, Council Bluffs, IA, p. A149

HUNT, Roger S., President and Chief Executive Officer, Via Health, Rochester, NY, p. B152

HUNT, William, Chief Operating Officer, Woodland Memorial Hospital, Woodland, CA, p. A67

HUNT Jr., Seth P., Director, Broughton Hospital, Morganton, NC, p. A311

HUNTER, David C., Chief Executive Officer, Wabash County Hospital, Wabash, IN, p. A146

HUNTER, John, Chief Executive Officer, ValueMark Behavioral Healthcare System of Kansas City, Kansas City, MO, p. A246

HUNTER, Steven L., President, St. Anthony Hospital, Oklahoma City, OK, p. A340

HUPFELD, Stanley F., President and Chief Executive Officer, INTEGRIS Health, Oklahoma City, OK, p. B109

HURD, Paul, Chief Executive Officer, Creighton Area Health Services, Creighton, NE, p. A259

HURST, Molly, Administrative Director, Grimes St. Joseph Health Center, Navasota, TX, p. A419

HURSTELL, Stanley E., Administrator, Leonard J. Chabert Medical Center, Houma, LA, p. A181

HURT, Charles, Administrator, Hardeman County Memorial Hospital, Quanah, TX, p. A421

HURT, Reedes, Chief Executive Officer, Veterans Affairs Medical Center, Wilkes–Barre, PA, p. A367

HURT, Richard O., Ph.D., Chief Executive Officer, Benchmark Behavioral Health Systems, Woods Cross, UT, p. A433

HURZELER, Rosemary Johnson, President and Chief Executive Officer, The Connecticut Hospice, Branford, CT, p. A74

HUSETH, Michael, Chief Executive Officer, Mississippi Hospital Restorative Care, Jackson, MS, p. A236

HUSSON, Gerard P., Director, Veterans Affairs Medical Center, Beckley, WV, p. A452

HUTCHENRIDER, Ken, President and Chief Executive Officer, Western Plains Regional Hospital, Dodge City, KS, p. A158

HUTCHINS, Joe T., Chief Executive Officer, Barrow Medical Center, Winder, GA, p. A113

HUTCHINS, Michael T., Administrator, Claiborne County Hospital, Tazewell, TN, p. A393

HUTCHISON, Dee, Chief Executive Officer, Northern Navajo Medical Center, Shiprock, NM, p. A283

HUTCHISON, James, Director, Integris Bass Behavioral Health System, Enid, OK, p. A337

HUYRSZ, Ed, Administrator, Sakakawea Medical Center, Hazen, ND, p. A317

HYDE, James A., Administrator, Bone and Joint Hospital, Oklahoma City, OK, p. A339

HYER, Julie, President and Chief Executive Officer, Dominican Santa Cruz Hospital, Santa Cruz, CA, p. A62

HYMANS, Daniel J., President, Memorial Medical Center, Ashland, WI, p. A457

HYNES, John J., President and Chief Executive Officer, Care New England Health System, Providence, RI, p. B75

I

IGNELZI, James, Chief Executive Officer, Twin Valley Psychiatric System, Dayton, OH, p. A326

INCARNATI, Philip A., President and Chief Executive Officer, McLaren Regional Medical Center, Flint, MI, p. A212

INGALA, Robert J., Chief Executive Officer, Hale Hospital, Haverhill, MA, p. A203

INGHAM, Ray, President and Chief Executive Officer, Witham Memorial Hospital, Lebanon, IN, p. A143

INGRAHAM, Ron, Administrator, Klickitat Valley Hospital, Goldendale, WA, p. A446

INIGO-AGOSTINI, Emigdio, M.D., Board President, Clinica Espanola, Mayaguez, PR, p. A473

IRBY, Frank, Chief Executive Officer, Raulerson Hospital, Okeechobee, FL, p. A92

IRWIN, Michele, Administrator, Alliance Hospital of Santa Teresa, Santa Teresa, NM, p. A283

IRWIN Jr., Richard M., President and Chief Executive Officer, Health Central, Ocoee, FL, p. A92

ISAACS, James W., Chief Executive Officer, Mercer County Joint Township Community Hospital, Coldwater, OH, p. A324

ISBELL, John, Chief Executive Officer, Doctors Hospital, Groves, TX, p. A409

ISELY, John A., President, St. Mary Medical Center, Walla Walla, WA, p. A451

ISRAEL, Michael D., Chief Executive Officer and Vice Chancellor, Duke University Medical Center, Durham, NC, p. A307

IVERSEN, Dale E., President and Chief Executive Officer, Warrack Medical Center Hospital, Santa Rosa, CA, p. A63

IVES, R. Wayne, Administrator, San Vicente Hospital, Los Angeles, CA, p. A50

IVESON, Sara C., Executive Director, Barnes–Kasson County Hospital, Susquehanna, PA, p. A366

IVEY, Jim, Administrator, Memorial Pavilion, Lawton, OK, p. A338

J

JACKMAN, Marley D., Administrator, Twin Falls Clinic Hospital, Twin Falls, ID, p. A119

JACKMUFF, Steven W., President and Chief Executive Officer, Underwood–Memorial Hospital, Woodbury, NJ, p. A279

JACKSON, Fred L., Chief Executive Officer, King's Daughters' Medical Center, Ashland, KY, p. A168

JACKSON, Joan, Administrator, Melrose Area Hospital, Melrose, MN, p. A227

JACKSON, John J., Chief Executive Officer, Columbia Texas Orthopedic Hospital, Houston, TX, p. A410

JACKSON, R. Lynn, President and Chief Executive Officer, Hedrick Medical Center, Chillicothe, MO, p. A242

JACKSON, Sandra, President, Memorial Medical Center and Cancer Treatment Center–Tulsa, Tulsa, OK, p. A342

JACKSON, Thomas W., Chief Executive Officer, Columbia Medical Center, College Station, TX, p. A401

JACKSON, Valerie A.
Chief Executive Officer, East Pointe Hospital, Lehigh Acres, FL, p. A89
Chief Executive Officer, Gulf Coast Hospital, Fort Myers, FL, p. A85

JACKSON, William, President, Charlevoix Area Hospital, Charlevoix, MI, p. A209

JACOBS, Jack, Administrator, Lisbon Medical Center, Lisbon, ND, p. A318

JACOBS, Nicholas, Executive Director, Windber Hospital, Windber, PA, p. A368

JACOBS, Selby, M.P.H., Director, Connecticut Mental Health Center, New Haven, CT, p. A75

JACOBSEN, David P., Administrator, Tehachapi Hospital, Tehachapi, CA, p. A64

JACOBSON, John L., President and Chief Executive Officer, Lee's Summit Hospital, Lees Summit, MO, p. A246

JACOBSON, Rod, Administrator, Bear Lake Memorial Hospital, Montpelier, ID, p. A118

JACOBSON, Ronald L., President and Chief Executive Officer, Queen of Peace Hospital, Mitchell, SD, p. A380

JACOBSON, Steven K., Chief Executive Officer, Titus Regional Medical Center, Mount Pleasant, TX, p. A418

JACOBSON, Terry, Acting Administrator, St. Mary's Hospital of Superior, Superior, WI, p. A466

JACOBUS, Rick, Administrator, Martin County Hospital District, Stanton, TX, p. A425

JACOBY, Jamie R., Administrator, Kimble Hospital, Junction, TX, p. A414

JAEGER, Lee, Chief Executive Officer, THC–Milwaukee, Greenfield, WI, p. A459

JAFFE, David E., Executive Director and Chief Executive Officer, Harborview Medical Center, Seattle, WA, p. A449

JAHN, David B., Administrator and Chief Financial Officer, Schoolcraft Memorial Hospital, Manistique, MI, p. A216

JAMES, Craig B., Administrator, Tazewell Community Hospital, Tazewell, VA, p. A444

JAMES, David, Chief Executive Officer, Sturgis Hospital, Sturgis, MI, p. A219

JAMES, Donald W., DPH, Administrator, Baptist Three Rivers Hospital, Waverly, TN, p. A393

JAMES, Lisa, Administrator, Wesley Rehabilitation Hospital, Wichita, KS, p. A167

JAMES, William B., Chief Executive Officer, Northern Hospital of Surry County, Mount Airy, NC, p. A311

JAMES Jr., George H., President and Chief Executive Officer, Memorial Hospital, Seymour, IN, p. A145

JANCZAK, Linda M., President and Chief Executive Officer, F. F. Thompson Health System, Canandaigua, NY, p. A286

JANSEN, Charles P., Administrator, Audrain Medical Center, Mexico, MO, p. A247

JARM, Timothy L., President, Jewish Hospital–Shelbyville, Shelbyville, KY, p. A176

JARRETT, James L., Administrator, Wheeler County Hospital, Glenwood, GA, p. A107

JASPERSON, Steven W., Executive Vice President Operations, Lebanon Community Hospital, Lebanon, OR, p. A346

JAUDES, Paula Kienberger, M.D., President and Chief Executive Officer, LaRabida Children's Hospital and Research Center, Chicago, IL, p. A123

JAVOREK, Judeth N., R.N., President and Chief Executive Officer, Holland Community Hospital, Holland, MI, p. A214

JAY, David W., Superintendent, Allentown State Hospital, Allentown, PA, p. A349

JEAN, Darrell, Administrator and Chief Executive Officer, Pemiscot Memorial Health System, Hayti, MO, p. A244

JEANMARD, William C., Chief Executive Officer, Allen Parish Hospital, Kinder, LA, p. A182

JEFFCOAT, Arla, Administrator, Medical Arts Hospital, Lamesa, TX, p. A415

JEFFCOAT, Sally E., Administrator, St. Joseph Hospital, Houston, TX, p. A412

JENEY, Jeffrey S., President and Chief Executive Officer, Saint Luke's Medical Center, Cleveland, OH, p. A324

JENKINS, Jeffrey K., President, St. Michael Hospital, Milwaukee, WI, p. A463

JENNINGS, William M., Administrator and Chief Operating Officer, Cookeville Regional Medical Center, Cookeville, TN, p. A384

JENNINGS, William R., President and Chief Executive Officer, South Hills Health System, Pittsburgh, PA, p. A363

JENSEN, Bruce, Chief Executive Officer and Team Leader, Holy Rosary Medical Center, Ontario, OR, p. A346

JENSEN, Eric, Administrator, Kittitas Valley Community Hospital, Ellensburg, WA, p. A446

JENSON, Paul M., Chief Executive Officer, Presbyterian–Orthopaedic Hospital, Charlotte, NC, p. A306

JERDE, Duane D., President and Chief Executive Officer, Mercy Medical Center, Williston, ND, p. A319

JERNIGAN Jr., Robert F., Administrator, South Baldwin Regional Medical Center, Foley, AL, p. A14

JERVIS, Charles R., Director, San Bernardino County Medical Center, San Bernardino, CA, p. A59

JESIOLOWSKI, Craig A., Chief Executive Officer, Gibson Community Hospital, Gibson City, IL, p. A127

JESSUP, Dale, President and Chief Executive Officer, Bay Area Hospital, Coos Bay, OR, p. A344

JETER, John H., M.D., President and Chief Executive Officer, Hays Medical Center, Hays, KS, p. A160

JETER, Larry R., Chief Executive Officer, Columbia Sycamore Shoals Hospital, Elizabethton, TN, p. A385

JEX, Robert F., Administrator, Bear River Valley Hospital, Tremonton, UT, p. A433

JHIN, Michael K., President and Chief Executive Officer, St. Luke's Episcopal Hospital, Houston, TX, p. A412

JIVIDEN, Thomas C., Senior Vice President, Virginia Baptist Hospital, Lynchburg, VA, p. A439

JOHANSON, Blair R., Administrator, Charter Behavioral Health System/Central Georgia, Macon, GA, p. A108

JOHN, Roger S., President and Chief Executive Officer, Great Plains Health Alliance, Inc., Phillipsburg, KS, p. B102

JOHN, Susie, M.D., Chief Executive Officer, Tuba City Indian Medical Center, Tuba City, AZ, p. A27

JOHNS, Charles A., President, Forum Health, Youngstown, OH, p. A334

JOHNSON, Curtis A., Administrator, Flambeau Hospital, Park Falls, WI, p. A464

JOHNSON, David B., Administrator, Brookings Hospital, Brookings, SD, p. A378

JOHNSON, Dennis B., Administrator, Tri County Baptist Hospital, La Grange, KY, p. A172

JOHNSON, Don, Administrator, Cedars Hospital, De Soto, TX, p. A404

JOHNSON, Doyle K., Administrator, Mercy Hospital, Moundridge, KS, p. A163

JOHNSON, Elizabeth, Chief Executive Officer, Sage Memorial Hospital, Ganado, AZ, p. A23

JOHNSON, Eugene, President and Chief Executive Officer, Satilla Regional Medical Center, Waycross, GA, p. A113

JOHNSON, George L., President, Reedsburg Area Medical Center, Reedsburg, WI, p. A465

JOHNSON, James K., Senior Executive Officer, Anderson County Hospital, Garnett, KS, p. A159

JOHNSON, Jane, President and Chief Executive Officer, Myers Community Hospital, Sodus, NY, p. A301

JOHNSON, John C., Chief Executive Officer, Holy Cross Hospital, Fort Lauderdale, FL, p. A84

JOHNSON, John H., Chief Executive Officer, Gothenburg Memorial Hospital, Gothenburg, NE, p. A260

JOHNSON, John W., President and Chief Executive Officer, Alice Hyde Hospital Association, Malone, NY, p. A290

JOHNSON, Karen E., Administrator, Hartgrove Hospital, Chicago, IL, p. A122

JOHNSON, Karl E., Chief Executive Officer, Mount Graham Community Hospital, Safford, AZ, p. A26

JOHNSON, Kevin, Chief Executive Officer, Mountain View Hospital, Payson, UT, p. A431

JOHNSON, L. Barney, President and Chief Executive Officer, Harbor Hospital Center, Baltimore, MD, p. A193

JOHNSON, LaQuita, Chief Executive Officer, Oakdale Community Hospital, Oakdale, LA, p. A186

JOHNSON, Laurence E., Administrator, Shriners Hospitals for Children, Twin Cities, Minneapolis, MN, p. A228

JOHNSON, Michael, Administrator and Chief Executive Officer, Crosbyton Clinic Hospital, Crosbyton, TX, p. A402

JOHNSON, Paul H., President and Chief Executive Officer, Gaylord Hospital, Wallingford, CT, p. A77

JOHNSON, Richard, Chief Executive Officer, Memorial Hospital of Carbon County, Rawlins, WY, p. A469

JOHNSON, Ronald E., Administrator, Meeker County Memorial Hospital, Litchfield, MN, p. A226

JOHNSON, Stan, Medical Director, Veterans Affairs Medical Center, Tomah, WI, p. A466

JOHNSON, Stephen H., Administrator and Chief Executive Officer, Ashley Medical Center, Ashley, ND, p. A316

JOHNSON, Steven G.
Administrator, Amethyst, Charlotte, NC, p. A305
Chief Executive Officer, BHC Cedar Spring Hospital, Pineville, NC, p. A311

JOHNSON, Steven M.
President, Citizens Baptist Medical Center, Talladega, AL, p. A18
President, Coosa Valley Baptist Medical Center, Sylacauga, AL, p. A18

JOHNSON, Thomas E., Vice President and Administrator, Oakwood Hospital–Heritage Center, Taylor, MI, p. A220

JOHNSON, Thomas M., Chief Executive Officer, Kaweah Delta Healthcare District, Visalia, CA, p. A66

JOHNSON, Van R., President and Chief Executive Officer, Sutter Health, Sacramento, CA, p. B142

JOHNSON, Viola L., Chief Executive Officer, Huhukam Memorial Hospital, Sacaton, AZ, p. A26

JOHNSON, William D., President, Lee Memorial Health System, Fort Myers, FL, p. A85

JOHNSON–PHILLIPPE, Sue E., Chief Executive Officer, LakeView Community Hospital, Paw Paw, MI, p. A217

JOHNSRUD, Kimry A., President, Elmbrook Memorial Hospital, Brookfield, WI, p. A458

JOHNSTON, Charles, Administrator, Pauls Valley General Hospital, Pauls Valley, OK, p. A340

JOHNSTON, Debbie W., Director Operations, HEALTHSOUTH Rehabilitation Hospital, Columbia, SC, p. A372

JOHNSTON, R. Joe, President and Chief Executive Officer, Dukes Memorial Hospital, Peru, IN, p. A144

JOHNSTON, Wayne W., President and Chief Executive Officer, Sharon Regional Health System, Sharon, PA, p. A365

JOINER, H. Glenn, Chief Executive Officer, T. J. Samson Community Hospital, Glasgow, KY, p. A170

JOLLY, Jay P., Administrator and Chief Executive Officer, Clay County Hospital, Brazil, IN, p. A138

JONAS, Stuart W., Chief Executive Officer, Alliance Community Hospital, Alliance, OH, p. A320

JONES, Bill, Administrator, Refugio County Memorial Hospital, Refugio, TX, p. A421

JONES, Carol E., Administrator, Annie Jeffrey Memorial County Health Center, Osceola, NE, p. A263

JONES, Donald J., Administrator, Vaughan Chilton Medical Center, Clanton, AL, p. A13

JONES, Douglas T., President and Chief Executive Officer, Genesee Memorial Hospital, Batavia, NY, p. A284

JONES, Dwayne, Chief Executive Officer, Fairchild Medical Center, Yreka, CA, p. A67

JONES, H. Ed, Chief Executive Officer, North Carolina Eye and Ear Hospital, Durham, NC, p. A307

JONES, J. Thomas, Executive Director, St. Mary's Hospital, Huntington, WV, p. A453

JONES, James S., Director, Veterans Affairs Medical Center, Danville, IL, p. A125

JONES, Jerry
Administrator, Drumright Memorial Hospital, Drumright, OK, p. A336
Administrator, Intergris Clinton Regional Hospital, Clinton, OK, p. A336

JONES, John R., Administrator, Yalobusha General Hospital, Water Valley, MS, p. A240

JONES, Lowell
President, Marymount Medical Center, London, KY, p. A173
Chief Executive Officer, Our Lady of the Way Hospital, Martin, KY, p. A174

JONES, Mark T., President, Holy Redeemer Hospital and Medical Center, Meadowbrook, PA, p. A357

JONES, Nancy, Administrator, Shriners Hospitals for Children, Portland, Portland, OR, p. A347

JONES, Robert D., President, Rutherford Hospital, Rutherfordton, NC, p. A312

JONES, Robert T., M.D., President and Chief Executive Officer, Hutcheson Medical Center, Fort Oglethorpe, GA, p. A106

JONES, Wayne, Executive Vice President and Administrator, Maryview Hospital, Portsmouth, VA, p. A441

JONES, Stephen L., Commander, DeWitt Army Community Hospital, Fort Belvoir, VA, p. A437

JORDAHL, David B., FACHE, President, St. Clare Hospital and Health Services, Baraboo, WI, p. A457

JORDAN, Bobby, Chief Executive Officer, Winn Parish Medical Center, Winnfield, LA, p. A188

JORDAN, David R., Ph.D., Administrator and Chief Executive Officer, Nor–Lea General Hospital, Lovington, NM, p. A282

JORDAN, J. Larry, Administrator, Homer Memorial Hospital, Homer, LA, p. A181

JORDAN, Lawrence A., Director, PHS Santa Fe Indian Hospital, Santa Fe, NM, p. A283

JORDAN, Linda U., Administrator, Clay County Hospital, Ashland, AL, p. A11

JORDAN, Sheila M., R.N., Administrator, Monrovia Community Hospital, Monrovia, CA, p. A52

JORDAN, W. Charles, Administrator, Mayes County Medical Center, Pryor, OK, p. A341

JOSE, Sharon L., R.N., Vice President, Hospital Operations, Pioneer Hospital, Artesia, CA, p. A37

JOSEF, Norma C., M.D., Director, Walter P. Reuther Psychiatric Hospital, Westland, MI, p. A221

JOSEPH, Elliot, President and Chief Executive Officer, Genesys Regional Medical Center, Grand Blanc, MI, p. A212

JOSEPH, Gloria, Superintendent, Western Missouri Mental Health Center, Kansas City, MO, p. A246

JOSEPH, Michael G., Chief Executive Officer, Westside Regional Medical Center, Plantation, FL, p. A94

JOSEPH, Vincent D., Executive Director, Saint Barnabas Medical Center, Livingston, NJ, p. A274

JOSLIN, Tim A., Chief Executive Officer, Brownsville Medical Center, Brownsville, TX, p. A399

JOSPE, Theodore A., President, Southside Hospital, Bay Shore, NY, p. A285

JOYCE, Michael P., President and Chief Executive Officer, Columbia Medical Center–Port St. Lucie, Port St. Lucie, FL, p. A95

JOYNER, Ronald G., Chief Executive Officer, Williamson Medical Center, Franklin, TN, p. A385

JUBINSKY, Linda, Chief Executive Officer, Columbia Peachtree Regional Hospital, Newnan, GA, p. A110

JUDD, Jeffrey M., President and Chief Executive Officer, McDowell Hospital, Marion, NC, p. A310

JUDD, Russell V., Chief Executive Officer, Barstow Community Hospital, Barstow, CA, p. A37

JUENEMANN, Jean, Chief Executive Officer, Queen of Peace Hospital, New Prague, MN, p. A228

JUENGLING, Craig S.
Chief Executive Officer, Charter Behavioral Health System at Springwood, Leesburg, VA, p. A439
Chief Executive Officer, Charter Behavioral Health System of Maryland at Potomac Ridge, Rockville, MD, p. A197

JUPIN Jr., Joseph, Chief Executive Officer, Trenton Psychiatric Hospital, Trenton, NJ, p. A278

JURENA, Jerry E., Executive Director, Heart of America Medical Center, Rugby, ND, p. A318

K

KABOT, Lorraine B., FACHE, President and Chief Executive Officer, Hepburn Medical Center, Ogdensburg, NY, p. A297

KADLEC, Patricia, Administrator, Faulk County Memorial Hospital, Faulkton, SD, p. A379

KAIGLER, James S., FACHE, Administrator, Singing River Hospital, Pascagoula, MS, p. A238

KAJIWARA, Gary K., President and Chief Executive Officer, Kuakini Medical Center, Honolulu, HI, p. A114

KALETKOWSKI, Chester B., President and Chief Executive Officer, Memorial Hospital of Burlington County, Mount Holly, NJ, p. A275

KALLEN–ZURY, Karen, Chief Executive Officer, Hollywood Pavilion, Los Angeles, FL, p. A86

KAMBER, Steven R., Vice President and Administrator, Spohn Memorial Hospital, Corpus Christi, TX, p. A402

KANE, Daniel A., President and Chief Executive Officer, Englewood Hospital and Medical Center, Englewood, NJ, p. A273

KANNADY, Donald L., Administrator, Bunkie General Hospital, Bunkie, LA, p. A179

KANTOS, Craig A., Chief Executive Officer, Millinocket Regional Hospital, Millinocket, ME, p. A191

KARELS, Genevieve, Administrator, St. Bernard's Providence Hospital, Milbank, SD, p. A380

KARPF, Michael, M.D., Vice Provost Hospital System and Director Medical Center, University of California Los Angeles Medical Center, Los Angeles, CA, p. A51

KARUSCHAK Jr., Michael, Administrator, Apple River Hospital, Amery, WI, p. A457

KASENCHAK, John, Administrator, First Hospital Wyoming Valley, Wilkes–Barre, PA, p. A367

KASPERIK, Donald J., Commander, Winn Army Community Hospital, Hinesville, GA, p. A107

KAST, Kevin F.
President, St. Joseph Health Center, Saint Charles, MO, p. A248
President, St. Joseph Hospital West, Lake Saint Louis, MO, p. A246

KASTELIC, Sumiyo E., Director, University of California San Diego Medical Center, San Diego, CA, p. A59

KATHRINS, Richard J., Administrator and Chief Executive Officer, Bacharach Rehabilitation Hospital, Pomona, NJ, p. A277

KATRANA, John N., Ph.D., Chief Administrative Officer, Lutheran Hospital–La Crosse, La Crosse, WI, p. A460

KATSUDA, Frank, Administrator, Memorial Hospital of Gardena, Gardena, CA, p. A44

KATZ, Steven E., M.D., President, Jackson Brook Institute, South Portland, ME, p. A192

KATZ, Stuart A., FACHE, Administrator, Hawarden Community Hospital, Hawarden, IA, p. A151

KATZ, Treuman, President and Chief Executive Officer, Children's Hospital and Regional Medical Center, Seattle, WA, p. A449

KAUFFMAN, Louis, President and Chief Executive Officer, Dakota Heartland Health System, Fargo, ND, p. A317

KAUFMAN, Alan G., Director, Division of Mental Health Services, Department of Human Services, State of New Jersey, Trenton, NJ, p. B99

KAUFMAN, Thomas D., Administrator, Kanabec Hospital, Mora, MN, p. A228

KAYLER, R. S., USN, Commanding Officer, Naval Hospital, Twentynine Palms, CA, p. A65

KEAHEY, Kent A., President and Chief Executive Officer, Providence Health Center, Waco, TX, p. A428

KEARNEY, Daniel, Chief Executive Officer, Charter Behavioral Health System–Orlando, Kissimmee, FL, p. A88

KEARNEY, W. Michael, President, Mary Lanning Memorial Hospital, Hastings, NE, p. A260

KEARS, David J., Director, Alameda County Health Care Services Agency, San Leandro, CA, p. B65

KEATON, Charles H., President and Chief Executive Officer, West Paces Medical Center, Atlanta, GA, p. A102

KECK, Wade E.
Chief Executive Officer, Memorial Health Services, Adel, GA, p. B117
Chief Executive Officer, Memorial Hospital of Adel, Adel, GA, p. A100

KEEFER, Michael R., CHE, Administrator and Chief Executive Officer, Clarion Psychiatric Center, Clarion, PA, p. A351

KEEGAN, James L., President and Chief Executive Officer, EMH Amherst Hospital, Amherst, OH, p. A320

KEEHAN, Carol, President, Providence Hospital, Washington, DC, p. A79

KEEL, Barry, Chief Executive Officer, White County Community Hospital, Sparta, TN, p. A393

KEEL, Deborah C., Chief Executive Officer, Kenner Regional Medical Center, Kenner, LA, p. A182

KEELAN, John E., Chief Executive Officer and Administrator, Valley County Hospital, Ord, NE, p. A263

KEELEY, Brian E., President and Chief Executive Officer, Baptist Health System of South Florida, Miami, FL, p. B69

KEEN, Robert C., CHE, President and Chief Executive Officer, Hancock Memorial Hospital and Health Services, Greenfield, IN, p. A140

KEENE, Lee D., Administrator, Rockcastle Hospital and Respiratory Care Center, Mount Vernon, KY, p. A175

KEENER, Carl, M.D., Medical Director, Montana State Hospital, Warm Springs, MT, p. A256

KEESEE, Carolyn, Chief Executive Officer, Wetumka General Hospital, Wetumka, OK, p. A343

KEIERLEBER, Daniel, Administrator, Community Memorial Hospital, Redfield, SD, p. A380

KEIMIG, H. John, President and Chief Executive Officer, St. Joseph Health Services of Rhode Island, Providence, RI, p. A369

KEIR, Douglas C., Chief Executive Officer, McDuffie County Hospital, Thomson, GA, p. A112

KEITH, David N., Chief Executive Officer, Rice Medical Center, Eagle Lake, TX, p. A405

KELLAR, Richard A., Administrator, West Allis Memorial Hospital, West Allis, WI, p. A467

KELLER, Jack M., Administrator, Baptist Hickman Community Hospital, Centerville, TN, p. A383

KELLER, Larry W., Chief Executive Officer, University Medical Center, Lebanon, TN, p. A388

KELLER, Michael J., Administrator, Hi–Plains Hospital, Hale Center, TX, p. A409

KELLERSBERGER, Kent, Chief Executive Officer, North Big Horn Hospital, Lovell, WY, p. A469

KELLEY, Neal, Administrator, Edgar B. Davis Memorial Hospital, Luling, TX, p. A416

KELLEY, Randall, Senior Vice President and Chief Operating Officer, Flower Hospital, Sylvania, OH, p. A332

KELLEY, Robert C., President and Chief Executive Officer, Madera Community Hospital, Madera, CA, p. A51

KELLEY Jr., William C., FACHE, President and Chief Executive Officer, Samaritan Regional Health System, Ashland, OH, p. A320

KELLIE, Karen J., President, McCall Memorial Hospital, McCall, ID, p. A117

KELLISON, Jay R., Chief Executive Officer, BHC Walnut Creek Hospital, Walnut Creek, CA, p. A66

KELLOGG, Richard E., Acting Commissioner, Virginia Department of Mental Health, Richmond, VA, p. B152

KELLY, Arthur C., Administrator and Chief Executive Officer, Oktibbeha County Hospital, Starkville, MS, p. A239

KELLY, Daniel J., President and Chief Executive Officer, St. Mary's Hospital, Nebraska City, NE, p. A261

KELLY, Daniel R., Chief Executive Officer, Doctors Regional Medical Center, Poplar Bluff, MO, p. A248

KELLY, Frank J., President and Chief Executive Officer, Danbury Hospital, Danbury, CT, p. A74

KELLY, James, Chief Executive Officer, Houston Northwest Medical Center, Houston, TX, p. A411

KELLY, Jeffrey R., President and Chief Executive Officer, Deaconess–Nashoba Hospital, Ayer, MA, p. A199

KELLY, Kathleen, Chief Executive Officer, Pilgrim Psychiatric Center, Brentwood, NY, p. A285

KELLY, Laurence E., Executive Vice President and Administrator, St. Luke's Hospital, Newburgh, NY, p. A297

KELLY, Sheila C., MS, Chief Executive Officer, Haven Hospital, De Soto, TX, p. A404

KELLY, Steven G., Consolidated Administrator, Integris Baptist Regional Health Center, Miami, OK, p. A339

KELLY, Timothy J., M.D., President, Fairbanks Hospital, Indianapolis, IN, p. A141

KELLY Jr., Winfield M., President and Chief Executive Officer, Dimensions Health Corporation, Largo, MD, p. B99

KENDRICK, Gary G., Chief Executive Officer, Lincoln County Health Facilities, Fayetteville, TN, p. A385

KENLEY, William A., President and Chief Executive Officer, North Crest Medical Center, Springfield, TN, p. A393

KENNEDY, Bill R., President and Chief Executive Officer, Muskogee Regional Medical Center, Muskogee, OK, p. A339

KENNEDY, Christopher S., President and Chief Operating Officer, Health First/Cape Canaveral Hospital, Cocoa Beach, FL, p. A83

KENNEDY, Thomas F., Administrator, Rolling Plains Memorial Hospital, Sweetwater, TX, p. A425

KENNEDY III, Thomas D., President and Chief Executive Officer, Bristol Hospital, Bristol, CT, p. A74

KENNEDY–SCOTT, Patricia, Northern Region Vice President, The Eastside Hospital, Redmond, WA, p. A448

KENNER, Gary, President and Chief Executive Officer, Itasca Medical Center, Grand Rapids, MN, p. A225

KENWOOD, Russell, Administrator, Sentara Hampton General Hospital, Hampton, VA, p. A438

KENYON, Douglas M., Director, Veterans Affairs Medical and Regional Office Center, Fargo, ND, p. A317

KERCORIAN, Robert A., Chief Executive Officer, Havenwyck Hospital, Auburn Hills, MI, p. A208

KERINS Sr., James J., Administrator, Caverna Memorial Hospital, Horse Cave, KY, p. A171

KERN, Cynthia L., Administrator, Edgemont Hospital, Los Angeles, CA, p. A48

KERN, Peter L., President and Chief Executive Officer, Palmerton Hospital, Palmerton, PA, p. A359

KERNER, Michael K., President and Chief Executive Officer, Columbia Augusta Medical Center, Augusta, GA, p. A102

KERR, Kay, M.D., Medical Director, Bryn Mawr College Infirmary, Bryn Mawr, PA, p. A351

KERR, Michael, Administrator, Bellwood General Hospital, Bellflower, CA, p. A37

KERVIN, David D., Administrator, Richardson Medical Center, Rayville, LA, p. A186

KERWIN, George, President, Bellin Hospital, Green Bay, WI, p. A459

KESSEN, Donald J., Administrator and Chief Executive Officer, Rawlins County Health Center, Atwood, KS, p. A157

KESSLER, D. McWilliams, Executive Director, Wills Eye Hospital, Philadelphia, PA, p. A362

KESSLER, Renee, Executive Vice President and Chief Operating Officer, St. Joseph Medical Center, Towson, MD, p. A198

KESSLER, William E., President, Saint Anthony's Health Center, Alton, IL, p. A120

KESTLY, John J., Administrator, Shawano Medical Center, Shawano, WI, p. A465

KETCHAM, Michael S., Administrator, Manning Regional Healthcare Center, Manning, IA, p. A152

KETCHAM, Richard H., President, Brooks Memorial Hospital, Dunkirk, NY, p. A287

KETRING, John, Administrator, Pawnee Municipal Hospital, Pawnee, OK, p. A340

KEVISH, Stanley J., President, UPMC–St. Margaret, Pittsburgh, PA, p. A363

KHAN, Nasir A., M.D., Director, Bournewood Hospital, Brookline, MA, p. A201

KIEF, Brian, President, United Hospital District, Blue Earth, MN, p. A223

KIEFER, Joseph N., Administrator, Helen Ellis Memorial Hospital, Tarpon Springs, FL, p. A98

KIELANOWICZ, Marie, Provincial Superior, Sisters of the Holy Family of Nazareth–Sacred Heart Province, Des Plaines, IL, p. B140

KIELMAN, Richard C., President and Chief Executive Officer, Dickinson County Memorial Hospital, Spirit Lake, IA, p. A155

KIELY, Robert Gerard, President and Chief Executive Officer, Middlesex Hospital, Middletown, CT, p. A75

KILEY, Dennis, President, Gordon Hospital, Calhoun, GA, p. A103

KIMEL, Mike, Administrator, Davie County Hospital, Mocksville, NC, p. A310

KIMMETH, Steuart A., Chief Executive Officer, Peninsula Behavioral Center, Hampton, VA, p. A438

KIMMEY, James, M.P.H., Chairman and Chief Executive Officer, Saint Louis University Hospital, Saint Louis, MO, p. A250

KINCADE, Jerry
Chief Executive Officer, Medical Arts Hospital, Texarkana, TX, p. A426
Chief Executive Officer, Norton Community Hospital, Norton, VA, p. A440

KINDEL, Dave, President and Chief Executive Officer, Southwest Medical Center, Liberal, KS, p. A162

KINDRED, Bryan, Chief Executive Officer, DCH Health System, Tuscaloosa, AL, p. B92

KINDRED, Bryan N., President and Chief Executive Officer, DCH Regional Medical Center, Tuscaloosa, AL, p. A18

KING, Dennis P., President, Acadia Hospital, Bangor, ME, p. A189

KING, John G., President and Chief Executive Officer, Legacy Health System, Portland, OR, p. B111

KING, Keith R., Chief Executive Officer, Winona Memorial Hospital, Indianapolis, IN, p. A141

KING, Larry R., Administrator, Washington–St. Tammany Regional Medical Center, Bogalusa, LA, p. A179

KING, Michael, Administrator, Winslow Memorial Hospital, Winslow, AZ, p. A28

KING, Robin M., Administrator, U. S. Air Force Hospital, Abilene, TX, p. A395

KINGSBURY, James A., President and Chief Executive Officer, Fort Hamilton–Hughes Memorial Hospital, Hamilton, OH, p. A327

KINNEY, Charles S., Chief Executive Officer, Martha's Vineyard Hospital, Oak Bluffs, MA, p. A205

KINNEY, John P., President, Nason Hospital, Roaring Spring, PA, p. A365

KIRBY, Dale A., Chief Executive Officer, THC–Las Vegas Hospital, Las Vegas, NV, p. A266

KIRK, Brian, Chief Executive Officer, Sheridan County Hospital, Hoxie, KS, p. A160

KIRK, Warren J.
Administrator, Citrus Valley Medical Center Inter–Community Campus, Covina, CA, p. A40
Administrator and Chief Operating Officer, Citrus Valley Medical Center–Queen of the Valley Campus, West Covina, CA, p. A67

KIRK Jr., H. Lee, President and Chief Executive Officer, Culpeper Memorial Hospital, Culpeper, VA, p. A437

KIRK Jr., William R., President and Chief Executive Officer, Kent & Queen Anne's Hospital, Chestertown, MD, p. A195

KIRN, Galen, Administrator, California Mens Colony Hospital, San Luis Obispo, CA, p. A61

KIROUSIS, Theodore E.
Area Director, Medfield State Hospital, Medfield, MA, p. A203
Area Director, Westborough State Hospital, Westborough, MA, p. A207

KIRSCHNER, Sidney, President and Chief Executive Officer, Northside Hospital, Atlanta, GA, p. A101

KISER, Greg, Chief Executive Officer, Three Rivers Medical Center, Louisa, KY, p. A173

KISER, James, Administrator, Washakie Memorial Hospital, Worland, WY, p. A470

KISH, Thomas M., Executive Director, University of Tennessee Memorial Hospital, Knoxville, TN, p. A388

KITE, Landon, President, Fuller Memorial Hospital, South Attleboro, MA, p. A205

KIZER, Kenneth W., M.P.H., Under Secretary for Health, Department of Veterans Affairs, Washington, DC, p. B95

KLAASMEYER, Al, Administrator, Alegent Health–Memorial Hospital, Schuyler, NE, p. A264

KLAGSBRUN, Samuel C., M.D., Executive Medical Director, Four Winds Hospital, Katonah, NY, p. A289

KLAWITER, Anne K., President and Chief Executive Officer, Southwest Health Center, Platteville, WI, p. A464

KLEIN, Ann, Executive Director, Recovery Inn of Menlo Park, Menlo Park, CA, p. A52

KLEIN, Gerard D., Chief Executive Officer, UHHS–Memorial Hospital of Geneva, Geneva, OH, p. A327

KLEIN, Robert, Chief Executive Officer, Hendersonville Hospital, Hendersonville, TN, p. A386

KLEIN, Steven M., President and Chief Executive Officer, North Shore Medical Center, Miami, FL, p. A91

KLIER, Bill, Chief Executive Officer, Cypress Fairbanks Medical Center, Houston, TX, p. A410

KLIMA, Dennis E.
President and Chief Executive Officer, Bayhealth Medical Center, Dover, DE, p. B70
President and Chief Executive Officer, Bayhealth Medical Center, Dover, DE, p. A78

KLIMP, Mary, Administrator and Chief Executive Officer, Falls Memorial Hospital, International Falls, MN, p. A226

KLINT, Robert B., M.D., President and Chief Executive Officer, SwedishAmerican Health System, Rockford, IL, p. A134

KLUN, James A., President, Allegan General Hospital, Allegan, MI, p. A208

KLUSMANN, Richard W., Chief Executive Officer, Columbia St. David's South Hospital, Austin, TX, p. A397

KLUTTS, Robert, Chief Executive Officer, Touchette Regional Hospital, Centreville, IL, p. A121

KLUTTZ, James K., President and Chief Executive Officer, Frederick Memorial Hospital, Frederick, MD, p. A196

KNAPP, Dennis L., President, Cameron Memorial Community Hospital, Angola, IN, p. A137

KNAUSS, Albert C., President and Chief Executive Officer, Marion General Hospital, Marion, IN, p. A143

KNEIBERT, Kathryn, Administrator, Kemper Community Hospital, De Kalb, MS, p. A235

KNIGHT, Alan D., President and Chief Executive Officer, Jordan Hospital, Plymouth, MA, p. A205

KNIGHT, Jimmy M., Administrator and Chief Executive Officer, Corcoran District Hospital, Corcoran, CA, p. A40

KNIGHT, Robert, Chief Executive Officer, Kern Valley Hospital District, Lake Isabella, CA, p. A46

KNIGHT, Russell M., President and Chief Executive Officer, Mercy Health Center, Dubuque, IA, p. A150

KNOBLE, James K., President, Methodist Medical Center of Illinois, Peoria, IL, p. A133

KNOX, Dennis M., Vice President and Chief Executive Officer, Memorial Hospital Pasadena, Pasadena, TX, p. A420

KNOX, John E., President, Macomb Hospital Center, Warren, MI, p. A220

KNOX, Jud, President, York Hospital, York, ME, p. A192

KNUTSON, Fred, Administrator, Chippewa County Montevideo Hospital, Montevideo, MN, p. A228

KNUTSON, William
Vice President and Administrator, HealthEast St. John's Hospital, Maplewood, MN, p. A227
Vice President and Administrator, HealthEast St. Joseph's Hospital, Saint Paul, MN, p. A230

KOBAN Jr., Michael A., Chief Executive Officer, NetCare Health Systems, Inc., Nashville, TN, p. B120

KOBAYASHI, Bertrand, Deputy Director, State of Hawaii, Department of Health, Honolulu, HI, p. B141

KOEHLER, Eduard R., Administrator, Medical Park Hospital, Winston–Salem, NC, p. A315

KOELLNER, William H., Administrator, Landmann–Jungman Memorial Hospital, Scotland, SD, p. A381

KOENIG, Scott, Chief Executive Officer, Columbia Lakeview Regional Medical Center, Covington, LA, p. A179

KOENIG, Thomas L., Chief Executive Officer, Desert Springs Hospital, Las Vegas, NV, p. A266

KOESTER, Jean, Chief Executive Officer, Vencor Hospital – Albuquerque, Albuquerque, NM, p. A281

KOLLARS, Tim, Administrator and Chief Executive Officer, Lincoln Hospital Medical Center, Los Angeles, CA, p. A49

KOLLER, George J., President and Chief Executive Officer, Noble Hospital, Westfield, MA, p. A207

KONIK, R. Eugene, Director, Alvin C. York Veterans Affairs Medical Center, Murfreesboro, TN, p. A391

KOOY, Donald C., President and Chief Executive Officer, Lapeer Regional Hospital, Lapeer, MI, p. A215

KOPICKI, John R., President and Chief Executive Officer, Muhlenberg Regional Medical Center, Plainfield, NJ, p. A277

KOPMAN, Alan, President and Chief Executive Officer, Westchester Square Medical Center, New York, NY, p. A296

KOPP, C. Gary, Administrator, Wishek Community Hospital, Wishek, ND, p. A319

KOPPEL, Robert F., President and Chief Executive Officer, East Tennessee Children's Hospital, Knoxville, TN, p. A387

KOPPELMAN, Ben, Administrator, Albany Area Hospital and Medical Center, Albany, MN, p. A222

KORBAKES, George J., President, UPMC South Side, Pittsburgh, PA, p. A363

KORBELAK, Kathleen M., President and Chief Executive Officer, Saint Joseph Hospital & Health Center, Kokomo, IN, p. A142

KORDICK, Jill, Administrator, Madison County Memorial Hospital, Winterset, IA, p. A156

KORMAN, Keith, President, St. Andrew's Health Center, Bottineau, ND, p. A316

KORNEFF, Allen R., President and Chief Executive Officer, Downey Community Hospital Foundation, Downey, CA, p. A41

KOSANOVICH, John P., President, Watertown Memorial Hospital, Watertown, WI, p. A466

KOSCHALKE, Patricia Ann, President and Chief Executive Officer, Holy Family Medical Center, Des Plaines, IL, p. A125

KOSSEFF, Christopher O., Acting Vice President and Chief Executive Officer, University of Medicine and Dentistry of New Jersey, University Behavioral Healthcare, Piscataway, NJ, p. A277

KOUGHAN, William P., President and Chief Executive Officer, Samaritan Medical Center, Watertown, NY, p. A302

KOWAL, Robert P., President, Greater Baltimore Medical Center, Baltimore, MD, p. A193

KOWALSKI, Richard S., Administrator and Chief Executive Officer, St. Mary Medical Center, Galesburg, IL, p. A127

KOZAI, Gerald T., Administrator and Chief Operating Officer, St. Francis Medical Center, Lynwood, CA, p. A51

KOZAR, Michael A., Chief Executive Officer, Laurens County Healthcare System, Clinton, SC, p. A372

KOZLOFF, Kenneth H., Executive Director, Wayne General Hospital, Wayne, NJ, p. A279

KRABBENHOFT, Kelby K., President, Sioux Valley Hospitals and Health System, Sioux Falls, SD, p. B136

KRAGE, Oliver D., President and Chief Executive Officer, Roseland Community Hospital, Chicago, IL, p. A124

KRAMER, Douglas, Chief Executive Officer, Onslow Memorial Hospital, Jacksonville, NC, p. A309

KRAMER, Mark D., Administrator, Healthsouth Rehabilitation Hospital of Western Massachusetts, Ludlow, MA, p. A203

KRAMER, Richard J., President and Chief Executive Officer, Catholic Healthcare West, San Francisco, CA, p. B80

KRAMER, Thomas H., President, Deaconess Hospital, Evansville, IN, p. A139

KRASS, Todd, Administrator and Chief Executive Officer, Research Psychiatric Center, Kansas City, MO, p. A245

KRAUSE, John Penn, Administrator, St. Luke's Baptist Hospital, San Antonio, TX, p. A424

KREHBIEL, James M., Chief Executive Officer, Freeman Community Hospital, Freeman, SD, p. A379

KREIN, Marlene, President and Chief Executive Officer, Mercy Hospital, Devils Lake, ND, p. A316

KRESHECK, Neal E., President, Community Hospital, Springfield, OH, p. A332

KRETZ, Blake, Administrator, Graham General Hospital, Graham, TX, p. A408

KREUZER, Jay E., FACHE, President, Saint Francis Hospital and Health Center, Blue Island, IL, p. A121

KREVANS, Sarah
Administrator, Kaiser Foundation Hospital, Sacramento, CA, p. A58
Administrator, Kaiser Foundation Hospital, Sacramento, CA, p. A58

KREYKES, William, President and Chief Executive Officer, Lifespan Corporation, Providence, RI, p. B111

KRIEGER, Robert M., Chief Executive Officer, Orange Park Medical Center, Orange Park, FL, p. A92

KRISHNA, Murali, M.D., President and Chief Operating Officer, Integris Mental Health System–Willow View, Spencer, OK, p. A341

KRMPOTIC, Deb J., R.N.
Administrator, Lookout Memorial Hospital, Spearfish, SD, p. A381
Administrator, Sturgis Community Health Care Center, Sturgis, SD, p. A381

KROELL Jr., H. Scott, Chief Executive Officer, Liberty Regional Medical Center, Hinesville, GA, p. A107

KROESE, Robert D., Chief Executive Officer, Pella Regional Health Center, Pella, IA, p. A154

KROGNESS, John, Chief Executive Officer, Columbia Rehabilitation Hospital, Corpus Christi, TX, p. A401

KROHN, Judith, Ph.D., Chief Executive Officer, Anoka–Metropolitan Regional Treatment Center, Anoka, MN, p. A222

KRONENBERG, Irving, President and Executive Director, Hebrew Home and Hospital, West Hartford, CT, p. A77

KRUCKEBERG, Karl, Director, Alton Mental Health Center, Alton, IL, p. A120

KRUCZLNICKI, David G., President and Chief Executive Officer, Glens Falls Hospital, Glens Falls, NY, p. A288

KRUEGER, Glen E., Administrator, Nemaha County Hospital, Auburn, NE, p. A258

KRUEGER Jr., Harold L., Administrator, Chadron Community Hospital, Chadron, NE, p. A259

KRUPA, Michael P., Ed.D.
Chief Executive Officer, Pembroke Hospital, Pembroke, MA, p. A205
Chief Executive Officer, Westwood Lodge Hospital, Westwood, MA, p. A207

KRUSE, Lowell C., Chief Executive Officer, Heartland Regional Medical Center, Saint Joseph, MO, p. A248

KUBIAK, Phillip J., President, Hampstead Hospital, Hampstead, NH, p. A268

KUBIK, James A., Administrator, Pawnee County Memorial Hospital, Pawnee City, NE, p. A263

KUCZKOWSKI, Claire, Administrator, John C. Fremont Healthcare District, Mariposa, CA, p. A52

KUDRLE, Venetia, President, St. Francis Regional Medical Center, Shakopee, MN, p. A230

KUDRONOWICZ, Sherry, Administrator, Memorial Hospital of Lafayette County, Darlington, WI, p. A458

KUHN, John F., Chief Executive Officer, Forest View Hospital, Grand Rapids, MI, p. A212

KUHN, Marcus G., President and Chief Executive Officer, Twin County Regional Hospital, Galax, VA, p. A438

KUHN, Rebecca C., R.N., President and Chief Executive Officer, Paradise Valley Hospital, Phoenix, AZ, p. A25

KUNZ, Susan, Administrator, Teton Valley Hospital, Driggs, ID, p. A117

KUNZ, Gretchen, President and Chief Executive Officer, St. Joseph Regional Health Center, Bryan, TX, p. A399

KURTZ, Kendria, Chief Executive Officer, Eagleville Hospital, Eagleville, PA, p. A353

KURTZ, Myers R., Administrator, G. Pierce Wood Memorial Hospital, Arcadia, FL, p. A81

KURTZ Jr., Thomas F., President and Chief Executive Officer, Clinton Memorial Hospital, Wilmington, OH, p. A334

KURZ, Linda, Acting Director, Veterans Affairs Medical Center, Saint Louis, MO, p. A250

KUSS, B. Ann, Chief Executive Officer and Managing Director, River Parishes Hospital, La Place, LA, p. A182

KUTSUDA, Frank, Administrator and Chief Executive Officer, East Los Angeles Doctors Hospital, Los Angeles, CA, p. A48

KUTZ, Melissa, Administrator and Chief Executive Officer, HEALTHSOUTH Rehabilitation of Mechanicsburg, Mechanicsburg, PA, p. A358

KUYKENDALL, George A., President and Chief Executive Officer, San Antonio Community Hospital, Upland, CA, p. A65

KWECH, Robert
Chief Executive Officer, Charter Behavioral Health System of Milwaukee/West Allis, West Allis, WI, p. A467
Chief Executive Officer, Charter Hospital of Milwaukee, Milwaukee, WI, p. A462

L

LA GRONE, Roderick G., President, Roy H. Laird Memorial Hospital, Kilgore, TX, p. A414

LAABS, Allison C., Executive Vice President and Administrator, St. John's Hospital, Springfield, IL, p. A135

LABARCA, Laurie, Chief Operating Officer, Via Christi Rehabilitation Center, Wichita, KS, p. A167

LABINE, Lance C., President, Hoots Memorial Hospital, Yadkinville, NC, p. A315

LABONTE, Frank, FACHE, Administrator, Shriners Hospitals for Children, Los Angeles, Los Angeles, CA, p. A50

LABRIOLA, John D., Vice President and Director, William Beaumont Hospital–Royal Oak, Royal Oak, MI, p. A218

LACASSE, Kathleen, Chief Executive Officer, Mary McClellan Hospital, Cambridge, NY, p. A286

LACKEY, David, Administrator, Summersville Memorial Hospital, Summersville, WV, p. A456

LACKEY, Tom O., Administrator, North Jackson Hospital, Bridgeport, AL, p. A12

LACONTE, Norman H., President and Chief Executive Officer, Proctor Hospital, Peoria, IL, p. A133

LACROIX, William M., Administrator, Paynesville Area Health Care System, Paynesville, MN, p. A229

LACY, Edward L., Administrator, McGehee–Desha County Hospital, McGehee, AR, p. A33

LACY, John S., Chief Executive Officer, Charter Behavioral Health System–Corpus Christi, Corpus Christi, TX, p. A401

LACY, Leslie, Administrator, Cheyenne County Hospital, Saint Francis, KS, p. A165

LADENBURGER, Robert W., President, St. Peter's Community Hospital, Helena, MT, p. A255

LAFFOON, David C., CHE, Chief Executive Officer, Central Arkansas Hospital, Searcy, AR, p. A34

LAHOOD, Gary J., Administrator and Chief Executive Officer, Harbor Oaks Hospital, New Baltimore, MI, p. A217

LAIBLE, Ray, Administrative Director, State Hospital South, Blackfoot, ID, p. A116

LAIRD, Michael J., Administrator and Chief Executive Officer, Pana Community Hospital, Pana, IL, p. A132

LAIRD IV, William R., President and Chief Executive Officer, Montgomery General Hospital, Montgomery, WV, p. A454

LAKE, Robin E., Chief Executive Officer, Harris Hospital, Newport, AR, p. A33

LAKE, Thomas E., Chief Executive Officer, Pioneers Hospital of Rio Blanco County, Meeker, CO, p. A72

LAKERNICK, Philip S., President and Chief Executive Officer, Maria Parham Hospital, Henderson, NC, p. A309

LALLY, Jeanne, Senior Vice President and Administrator, Fairview Northland Regional Health Care, Princeton, MN, p. A229

LALLY, Michael K., President and Chief Executive Officer, Westerly Hospital, Westerly, RI, p. A370

LAMB, Brent, Administrator, Van Nuys Hospital, Los Angeles, CA, p. A51

LAMBERT, Norman, Chief Executive Officer, Golden Plains Community Hospital, Borger, TX, p. A399

LAMBERT, Terry R., Chief Executive Officer, Newman Memorial County Hospital, Emporia, KS, p. A158

LAMBERTI, Patrick, Chief Executive Officer, POH Medical Center, Pontiac, MI, p. A217

LAMMERS, Brent R., Administrator, Fairfield Memorial Hospital, Winnsboro, SC, p. A377

LAMOTTE, Thomas M., President and Chief Executive Officer, Fairview Hospital, Cleveland, OH, p. A323

LAMOUREUX, Bruce, Chief Executive Officer, Saint John's Hospital and Health Center, Santa Monica, CA, p. A63

LAMPE, Diane B., Administrator and Chief Executive Officer, HEALTHSOUTH Rehabilitation Institute of San Antonio, San Antonio, TX, p. A422

LAND, Trudy, Chief Executive Officer, Lakeland Medical Center, New Orleans, LA, p. A185

LANDDECK, John R., President, Beaver Dam Community Hospitals, Beaver Dam, WI, p. A457

LANDERS, Louise, Administrator, Lynn County Hospital District, Tahoka, TX, p. A425

LANDRENEAU, Doug, Administrator, Welsh General Hospital, Welsh, LA, p. A188

LANDRY, Ray A., Administrator, Abbeville General Hospital, Abbeville, LA, p. A178

LANE, Jerry, Administrator, Othello Community Hospital, Othello, WA, p. A448

LANE, Michael, Administrator and Chief Executive Officer, Greenleaf Center, Valdosta, GA, p. A112

LANE, William L., President, Holy Family Hospital and Medical Center, Methuen, MA, p. A204

LANG, Charlotte, Administrator, Coulee Community Hospital, Grand Coulee, WA, p. A447

LANG, Fred L., President and Chief Executive Officer, Barnert Hospital, Paterson, NJ, p. A276

LANG, Geoffrey N., President and Chief Executive Officer, Southwest Washington Medical Center, Vancouver, WA, p. A451

LANG, Steve, Administrator, Ruby Valley Hospital, Sheridan, MT, p. A256

LANGBEHN, Cody, Administrator, Pioneer Medical Center, Big Timber, MT, p. A253

LANGE, William H., Administrator and Senior Vice President, Sacred Heart Rehabilitation Institute, Milwaukee, WI, p. A462

LANGFORD, James W., Administrator, Smithville Hospital, Smithville, TX, p. A425

LANGFORD, Joe S., Administrator, Methodist Hospital Plainview, Plainview, TX, p. A420

LANGLAIS, Robert J., President and Chief Executive Officer, Cheshire Medical Center, Keene, NH, p. A268

LANGLEY, Douglas, Administrator, Memorial Hospital, Gonzales, TX, p. A408

LANGMEAD, Paula A., Superintendent, Springfield Hospital Center, Sykesville, MD, p. A198

LANIK, Robert J., President, St. Elizabeth Community Health Center, Lincoln, NE, p. A261

LANKEY, Thomas, Acting Superintendent and Chief Executive Officer, Roosevelt Hospital, Edison, NJ, p. A272

LARCEN, Stephen W., Ph.D., Chief Executive Officer, Natchaug Hospital, Mansfield Center, CT, p. A75

LARET, Mark R., Executive Director, University of California, Irvine Medical Center, Orange, CA, p. A55

LARKIN, Donald N., Chief Executive Officer, San Gorgonio Memorial Hospital, Banning, CA, p. A37

LARKIN, Frank J., President and Chief Executive Officer, Good Samaritan Medical Center, Brockton, MA, p. A201

LAROCHELLE, Albert, Administrator, Grace Cottage Hospital, Townshend, VT, p. A435

LARSON, Dale, Chief Executive Officer, Doctors Memorial Hospital, Bonifay, FL, p. A81

LARSON, Gary E., Chief Executive Officer, Illini Hospital, Silvis, IL, p. A134

LARSON, James R., President and Chief Executive Officer, Hi–Desert Medical Center, Joshua Tree, CA, p. A45

LARSON, Lee, Chief Executive Officer, South Suburban Medical Center, Farmington, MN, p. A225

LARSON II, George V., Chief Executive Officer, Melissa Memorial Hospital, Holyoke, CO, p. A71

LARSSON, Randi, Chief Operating Officer and Administrator, Sharp Cabrillo Hospital, San Diego, CA, p. A59

LASKOWSKI, Rose, R.N., Hospital Director, Caro Center, Caro, MI, p. A209

LASSITER, Susan S., President and Chief Executive Officer, Roanoke–Chowan Hospital, Ahoskie, NC, p. A304

LATHAM, Charley C., Administrator, Hamlin Memorial Hospital, Hamlin, TX, p. A409

LATHREN, James E., President and Chief Executive Officer, Georgia Baptist Medical Center, Atlanta, GA, p. A101

LATHROP, Ronny, Chief Executive Officer and Administrator, Cimarron Memorial Hospital, Boise City, OK, p. A336

LAUDERBACH Jr., C. W., Chief Operating Officer, McPherson Hospital, Howell, MI, p. A214

LAUDERDALE, Max, Chief Executive Officer, Norman Regional Hospital, Norman, OK, p. A339

LAUDICK, Paul E.
President and Chief Executive Officer, Memorial Medical Center, Woodstock, IL, p. A136
President and Chief Executive Officer, Northern Illinois Medical Center, McHenry, IL, p. A130

LAUDON, Larry, Administrator, Clearwater Health Services, Bagley, MN, p. A222

LAUER, Paula, Operations Manager, Dechairo Hospital, Westmoreland, KS, p. A167

LAUGHLIN, Donald L., President, Riddle Memorial Hospital, Media, PA, p. A358

LAUGHLIN Jr., Raymond E., President and Chief Executive Officer, Wayne Hospital, Greenville, OH, p. A327

LAUGHNAN, Woody J., Chief Executive Officer, Modoc Medical Center, Alturas, CA, p. A36

LAUKO, Stephen J., Chief Executive Officer, Child's Hospital, Albany, NY, p. A284

LAURI, John P., President and Chief Executive Officer, Tri-City Medical Center, Oceanside, CA, p. A54

LAUX, Thomas W., President and Chief Executive Officer, Kalispell Regional Medical Center, Kalispell, MT, p. A255

LAVENDER, Tunisia, R.N., Chief Operating Officer, Pickens County Medical Center, Carrollton, AL, p. A12

LAVERTY, Stephen R., President and Chief Executive Officer, Winchester Hospital, Winchester, MA, p. A207

LAVOIE, Reginald J., Administrator, Cottage Hospital, Woodsville, NH, p. A270

LAWATSCH, Frank, Chief Executive Officer, Swift County–Benson Hospital, Benson, MN, p. A222

LAWRENCE, David M., M.D., Chairman and Chief Executive Officer, Kaiser Foundation Hospitals, Oakland, CA, p. B111

LAWRENCE Jr., J. David, Chief Executive Officer, BJC Medical Center, Commerce, GA, p. A104

LINEHAN, Mary, President, St. Joseph's Medical Center, Yonkers, NY, p. A303

LINENKUGEL, Nancy, FACHE, President and Chief Executive Officer, Providence Hospital, Sandusky, OH, p. A332

LINGENFELTER, Wayne M., Ed.D., Administrator and Chief Executive Officer, Vencor Hospital–San Leandro, San Leandro, CA, p. A61

LINGLE, Robert L., Executive Director, Singing River Hospital System, Pascagoula, MS, p. B136

LINGOR, John Daniel, President and Chief Executive Officer, Mount Carmel Medical Center, Pittsburg, KS, p. A164

LINN, Gerri, Administrator, Kimball County Hospital, Kimball, NE, p. A261

LINNELL, Jon, Administrator, North Valley Health Center, Warren, MN, p. A232

LINNEWEH Jr., Richard W., President and Chief Executive Officer, Yakima Valley Memorial Hospital, Yakima, WA, p. A451

LINTJER, Gregory W., President, Elkhart General Hospital, Elkhart, IN, p. A139

LIPSTEIN, Steven, President and Chief Operating Officer, University of Chicago Hospitals, Chicago, IL, p. A124

LISCHAK, Michael, USAF, Commander, U. S. Air Force Hospital Seymour Johnson, Seymour Johnson AFB, NC, p. A313

LISTER, Susan, Chief Executive Officer, Charter Winds Hospital, Athens, GA, p. A100

LITOS, Dennis M., President and Chief Executive Officer, Ingham Regional Medical Center, Lansing, MI, p. A215

LITTLEFIELD, Elizabeth, Ed.D., Superintendent, Western Mental Health Institute, Western Institute, TN, p. A393

LITTLESON, Steven G., President and Chief Executive Officer, Southern Ocean County Hospital, Manahawkin, NJ, p. A274

LITTRELL, Nancy, Chief Executive Officer, Woodford Hospital, Versailles, KY, p. A177

LITZ, Thomas H., FACHE, President and Chief Executive Officer, Centrastate Medical Center, Freehold, NJ, p. A273

LIVERMORE, Craig A., President and Chief Executive Officer, Delnor–Community Hospital, Geneva, IL, p. A127

LIVINGSTON, Jeffrey A., Chief Executive Officer, HEALTHSOUTH Rehabilitation Hospital of Texarkana, Texarkana, TX, p. A426

LLOYD, John K., Chief Executive Officer, Meridian Health System, Neptune, NJ, p. A275

LOBECK, Charles C., Chief Executive Officer, St. Mary's Hospital, Milwaukee, WI, p. A463

LOCKARD, Thomas L., President and Chief Executive Officer, Lodi Community Hospital, Lodi, OH, p. A328

LOCKWOOD, Brian C., President and Chief Executive Officer, Lorain Community/St. Joseph Regional Health Center, Lorain, OH, p. A328

LOEBIG Jr., Wilfred F., President and Chief Executive Officer, Wheaton Franciscan Services, Inc., Wheaton, IL, p. B153

LOEFFEN, Susan Marie, President and Chief Executive Officer, Oakes Community Hospital, Oakes, ND, p. A318

LOEWEN, Harold C., President, Oaklawn Psychiatric Center, Inc., Goshen, IN, p. A140

LOGE, Frank J., Director, University of California, Davis Medical Center, Sacramento, CA, p. A58

LOGUE, John W., Executive Vice President and Chief Operating Officer, St. Vincent's Medical Center, Jacksonville, FL, p. A87

LOH, Marcel, President and Chief Executive Officer, Kadlec Medical Center, Richland, WA, p. A449

LOHRMAN, Joe, Administrator, Crete Municipal Hospital, Crete, NE, p. A259

LOMBARD, Dave, President and Chief Executive Officer, Clear Brook Lodge, Shickshinny, PA, p. A365

LOMBARDI, Anthony M., President and Chief Executive Officer, Monongahela Valley Hospital, Monongahela, PA, p. A358

LONCHAR, Charles, President and Chief Executive Officer, Preston Memorial Hospital, Kingwood, WV, p. A454

LONG, C. Thomas, Chief Executive Officer, Wetzel County Hospital, New Martinsville, WV, p. A454

LONG, Charles H., Chief Executive Officer, Columbia De Queen Regional Medical Center, De Queen, AR, p. A30

LONG, Faye, Administrator, Caldwell Memorial Hospital, Columbia, LA, p. A179

LONG, Jim K., CPA, Administrator and Chief Executive Officer, West River Regional Medical Center, Hettinger, ND, p. A317

LONG, Lawrence C., Chief Executive Officer, Tahoe Forest Hospital District, Truckee, CA, p. A65

LONG, Max, Chief Executive Officer, Walter Knox Memorial Hospital, Emmett, ID, p. A117

LONG, Richard, Interim Chief Executive Officer, North Ottawa Community Hospital, Grand Haven, MI, p. A212

LONGACRE, Leslie, Executive Director and Chief Executive Officer, South Lake Hospital, Clermont, FL, p. A82

LONGO, Robert J., President and Chief Executive Officer, Good Samaritan Hospital, Lebanon, PA, p. A356

LOPER, Ouida, Administrator, Choctaw County Medical Center, Ackerman, MS, p. A233

LOPEZ, Frank, FACHE, President and Chief Executive Officer, St. Mary's Mercy Hospital, Enid, OK, p. A337

LOPEZ, Ramon, Administrator, Hospital Perea, Mayaguez, PR, p. A473

LOPMAN, Abe, Executive Director, Orlando Regional Medical Center, Orlando, FL, p. A93

LORACK Jr., Donald A.
President and Chief Executive Officer, Hillcrest HealthCare System, Tulsa, OK, p. B107
President and Chief Executive Officer, Hillcrest Medical Center, Tulsa, OK, p. A342

LORDEMAN, Frank L., Chief Operating Officer, Cleveland Clinic Hospital, Cleveland, OH, p. A323

LORE, John S., President and Chief Executive Officer, Sisters of St. Joseph Health System, Ann Arbor, MI, p. B139

LOSOFF, Martin, President and Chief Operating Officer, Rush–Copley Memorial Hospital, Aurora, IL, p. A120

LOTHE, Eric L., President and Chief Executive Officer, Skiff Medical Center, Newton, IA, p. A153

LOTT Jr., Carlos B., Director, John D. Dingell Veterans Affairs Medical Center, Detroit, MI, p. A211

LOTTI, G. Phillip, Chief Executive Officer, Columbia Davis Medical Center, Statesville, NC, p. A313

LOUGHNEY, Barbara, Acting Senior Vice President and Administrator, Saint Michael's Medical Center, Newark, NJ, p. A275

LOUISE, Stella, President and Chief Executive Officer, Saint Mary of Nazareth Hospital Center, Chicago, IL, p. A124

LOVEDAY, William J., President and Chief Executive Officer, Clarian Health Partners, Indianapolis, IN, p. A141

LOVELL, Robert M., Interim Chief Executive Officer, St. Catherine's Hospital, Kenosha, WI, p. A460

LOVELL Jr., Charles D., Chief Executive Officer, Muhlenberg Community Hospital, Greenville, KY, p. A170

LOVETT, Juanice, Chief Executive Officer, Sharp Healthcare Murrieta, Murrieta, CA, p. A53

LOVING, David E., Chief Executive Officer, Edge Regional Medical Center, Troy, AL, p. A18

LOWD III, Harry M., Director, Bath County Community Hospital, Hot Springs, VA, p. A438

LOWE, Phillip, Chief Executive Officer, St. Vincent General Hospital, Leadville, CO, p. A71

LOWERY, Glenn E., Chief Executive Officer, Northeast Medical Center, Bonham, TX, p. A398

LOWERY, Jerry E., Executive Director, Russell County Medical Center, Lebanon, VA, p. A439

LOWRANCE, Debra S., R.N., Chief Executive Officer and Managing Director, Timberlawn Mental Health System, Dallas, TX, p. A404

LOWRY, James R., FACHE, Chief Executive Officer, Colquitt Regional Medical Center, Moultrie, GA, p. A109

LOYLESS, John Paul, Administrator, Rankin Hospital District, Rankin, TX, p. A421

LOZAR, Beverly, Chief Operating Officer, Meridia Huron Hospital, Cleveland, OH, p. A324

LUCAS, Stephen M., Chief Executive Officer, Veterans Affairs Medical Center, Erie, PA, p. A354

LUCHTEFELD, Daniel J., Director, Eastern State Hospital, Lexington, KY, p. A172

LUCK Jr., James V., M.D., Chief Executive Officer and Medical Director, Orthopaedic Hospital, Los Angeles, CA, p. A50

LUDEKE, Max L., FACHE, President and Chief Executive Officer, Wood River Township Hospital, Wood River, IL, p. A136

LUKE, Lesile P., Chief Executive Officer, Crawford Memorial Hospital, Robinson, IL, p. A133

LUKER, Patricia, Chief Executive Officer, Franklin Foundation Hospital, Franklin, LA, p. A180

LULEWICZ, Stephanie, Administrator, Marshall County Healthcare Center, Britton, SD, p. A378

LUMSDEN, Chris A., Administrator, Halifax Regional Hospital, South Boston, VA, p. A443

LUND, Mark, Superintendent, Mental Health Institute, Clarinda, IA, p. A148

LUND, Robert S., Administrator, Kaiser Foundation Hospital–Riverside, Riverside, CA, p. A57

LUNDQUIST, David, Chief Executive Officer, Intergis Bethany Hospital, Bethany, OK, p. A335

LUNDSTROM, Greg, Administrator and Chief Executive Officer, Lindsborg Community Hospital, Lindsborg, KS, p. A162

LUNSETH, Mark, Administrator, Rush City Hospital, Rush City, MN, p. A229

LUNSFORD, W. Bruce, Board Chairman, President and Chief Executive Officer, Vencor, Incorporated, Louisville, KY, p. B151

LUSE, Robert H., Chief Executive Officer, Mariners Hospital, Tavernier, FL, p. A98

LUSSIER, James T., President and Chief Executive Officer, St. Charles Medical Center, Bend, OR, p. A344

LUTHER, Robert M., Chief Executive Officer, Springs Memorial Hospital, Lancaster, SC, p. A375

LUTJEMEIER, Everett, Administrator, Washington County Hospital, Washington, KS, p. A166

LYBARGER, William A., Administrator, Cedar Vale Community Hospital, Cedar Vale, KS, p. A157

LYCAN, Laura J., Administrator and Chief Executive Officer, HEALTHSOUTH Rehabilitation Hospital of Fort Worth, Fort Worth, TX, p. A407

LYNCH, Edward F., Administrator, Richards Memorial Hospital, Rockdale, TX, p. A421

LYNCH, Francis P., President and Chief Executive Officer, Mount Auburn Hospital, Cambridge, MA, p. A201

LYNCH III, Ernest C., Chief Executive Officer, Columbia Medical Center at Lancaster, Lancaster, TX, p. A415

LYON, Cheri, Service Unit Director, Public Health Service Indian Hospital, Albuquerque, NM, p. A280

LYON, David R., Administrator, Beckley Appalachian Regional Hospital, Beckley, WV, p. A452

LYONS, James F., President and Chief Executive Officer, Cape Cod Healthcare, Inc., Hyannis, MA, p. B75

LYONS, Richard D., President and Chief Executive Officer, Northridge Hospital and Medical Center, Sherman Way Campus, Los Angeles, CA, p. A50

LYSINGER, R. Craig, Administrator, Wabash Valley Hospital, West Lafayette, IN, p. A146

M

MAAS, Lawrence A., Administrator, Sutter Davis Hospital, Davis, CA, p. A41

MABRY, Jerry D., Executive Director, National Park Medical Center, Hot Springs, AR, p. A31

MABRY II, Earl W., Commander, U. S. Air Force Medical Center Wright–Patterson, Wright–Patterson AFB, OH, p. A334

MAC DEVITT, Robert E., Chief Executive Officer, Labette County Medical Center, Parsons, KS, p. A164

MACCALLUM, James M., President and Chief Executive Officer, Tulsa Regional Medical Center, Tulsa, OK, p. A343

MACDOWELL, Barry S., President, Reid Hospital and Health Care Services, Richmond, IN, p. A145

MACEK, Paul E.
Senior Vice President, Appleton Medical Center, Appleton, WI, p. A457
Senior Vice President, Theda Clark Medical Center, Neenah, WI, p. A463

MACFARLAND, H. J., FACHE, Executive Director, Baylor Medical Center at Irving, Irving, TX, p. A413

MACGARD, Elizabeth, Chief Executive Officer, Mendocino Coast District Hospital, Fort Bragg, CA, p. A42

MACK, Arlene
Administrator, Linton Hospital, Linton, ND, p. A318
Administrator, Richardton Health Center, Richardton, ND, p. A318

MACKAY Jr., James, Chief Executive Officer, Union Hospital, Mayville, ND, p. A318

MACKE, Anita, Administrator, Meadowbrook Hospital, Gardner, KS, p. A159

MACLAREN, Ron J., Chief Executive Officer, American Transitional Hospital, Houston, TX, p. A410

MACLEOD, John L., Administrator and Chief Executive Officer, Otsego Memorial Hospital, Gaylord, MI, p. A212

MACLEOD, Leslie N. H., President, Huggins Hospital, Wolfeboro, NH, p. A270

MACRI, William P., Chief Executive Officer, Franklin–Simpson Memorial Hospital, Franklin, KY, p. A170

MADDALENA, Frank J., President and Chief Executive Officer, Brookdale Hospital Medical Center, New York, NY, p. A291

MADDEN, Michael J.
Administrator, Grays Harbor Community Hospital, Aberdeen, WA, p. A445
Chief Executive Los Angeles Service Area, Providence Holy Cross Medical Center, Los Angeles, CA, p. A50
Chief Executive Los Angeles Service Area, Providence Saint Joseph Medical Center, Burbank, CA, p. A38

MADDEN, Patrick J., President and Chief Executive Officer, Sacred Heart Hospital of Pensacola, Pensacola, FL, p. A94

MADDOCK, Dan S., President, Taylor Regional Hospital, Hawkinsville, GA, p. A107

MADDOX, Jim L., Chief Administrative Officer, North Logan Mercy Hospital, Paris, AR, p. A34

MADDOX, Richard D., Administrator, U. S. Air Force Regional Hospital–Sheppard, Sheppard AFB, TX, p. A424

MAESTRE GRAU, Jaime F., Executive Director, Hospital De La Concepcion, San German, PR, p. A473

MAFFETONE, Michael A., Director and Chief Executive Officer, University Hospital, Stony Brook, NY, p. A301

MAGARIAN–MORSE, Myda, Administrator and Chief Operating Officer, St. Vincent Medical Center, Los Angeles, CA, p. A51

MAGEE, James L., Executive Director, Piggott Community Hospital, Piggott, AR, p. A34

MAGERS, Brent D., FACHE, Chief Executive Officer and Administrator, Walls Regional Hospital, Cleburne, TX, p. A400

MAGHAZEHE, Alireza, Interim President, Capital Health System, Trenton, NJ, p. A278

MAGLIARO, John G., President and Chief Executive Officer, Columbus Hospital, Newark, NJ, p. A275

MAGOON, Patrick M., President and Chief Executive Officer, Children's Memorial Hospital, Chicago, IL, p. A122

MAGRAS, Judy, Acting Chief Executive Officer, Roy Lester Schneider Hospital, Saint Thomas, VI, p. A474

MAHADEVAN, Dev, Administrator, Kaiser Foundation Hospital, Los Angeles, CA, p. A49

MAHAFFEY, Robert, Administrator, Heart of Florida Regional Medical Center, Davenport, FL, p. A83

MAHAN, Stephen, Chief Executive Officer, Ocala Regional Medical Center, Ocala, FL, p. A92

MAHER, Robert J., President, Our Lady of Bellefonte Hospital, Ashland, KY, p. A168

MAHER Jr., Robert E., President and Chief Executive Officer, Saint Vincent Hospital, Worcester, MA, p. A207

MAHN, Edward F., Chief Executive Officer, Ketchikan General Hospital, Ketchikan, AK, p. A21

MAHONE V, William, Administrator, Stonewall Jackson Hospital, Lexington, VA, p. A439

MAHONEY, Kevin J., President, Wilson Center Psychiatric Facility for Children and Adolescents, Faribault, MN, p. A225

MAHONEY, Michael P., President and Chief Executive Officer, St. Rose Hospital, Hayward, CA, p. A45

MAHONEY, Patrick R., Administrator and Chief Executive Officer, Affiliated Health Services, Mount Vernon, WA, p. A447

MAHRER, Michael D., President, St. Ansgar's Health Center, Park River, ND, p. A318

MAIDLOW, Spencer, President, St. Luke's Hospital, Saginaw, MI, p. A218

MAIER, Harry R., President, Memorial Hospital, Belleville, IL, p. A120

MAIER, Vonnie, President and Chief Executive Officer, Huerfano Medical Center, Walsenburg, CO, p. A73

MAIN, Robert P., President and Chief Executive Officer, Siskin Hospital for Physical Rehabilitation, Chattanooga, TN, p. A384

MAJURE, Thomas K., Administrator, Our Community Hospital, Scotland Neck, NC, p. A313

MAKI, James W., Chief Executive Officer, Huntington East Valley Hospital, Glendora, CA, p. A44

MAKOWSKI, Peter E., President and Chief Executive Officer, Citrus Valley Health Partners, Covina, CA, p. B81

MALINOWSKI, Barbara A., Administrator and Chief Executive Officer, Westfield Memorial Hospital, Westfield, NY, p. A303

MALINOWSKI, Mary Norberta, President, St. Joseph Hospital, Bangor, ME, p. A189

MALLAH, Isaac, President and Chief Executive Officer, St. Joseph's Hospital, Tampa, FL, p. A98

MALONE, John T., President and Chief Executive Officer, Hamot Medical Center, Erie, PA, p. A353

MALONEY, Elizabeth Ann, President and Chief Executive Officer, St. Elizabeth Hospital, Elizabeth, NJ, p. A272

MAMOON, Wendy, Chief Executive Officer, Rock Creek Center, Lemont, IL, p. A130

MANCHUR, Fred, President, San Joaquin Community Hospital, Bakersfield, CA, p. A37

MANCINI, Dorothy J., R.N., Regional Vice President Administration, Imperial Point Medical Center, Fort Lauderdale, FL, p. A85

MANDERNACH, Dianne, Chief Executive Officer, Mercy Hospital and Health Care Center, Moose Lake, MN, p. A228

MANDERS, Daniel N., President and Chief Executive Officer, Mile Bluff Medical Center, Mauston, WI, p. A461

MANDSAGER, Richard, M.D., Director, U. S. Public Health Service Alaska Native Medical Center, Anchorage, AK, p. A20

MANGINI, Michael A., Administrator and Chief Executive Officer, Bellevue Woman's Hospital, Schenectady, NY, p. A300

MANGION, Richard M., President and Chief Executive Officer, Harrington Memorial Hospital, Southbridge, MA, p. A204

MANGOLD, Larry K., Interim President and Chief Executive Officer, Wilcox Memorial Hospital, Lihue, HI, p. A115

MANLEY, Jeffrey J., Chief Executive Officer, Jordan Valley Hospital, West Jordan, UT, p. A433

MANLEY, Joseph M., Director, Veterans Affairs Medical Center, Spokane, WA, p. A450

MANLEY, Warren, Administrator, Camden Medical Center, Saint Marys, GA, p. A111

MANNICH, Andrew, Administrator, Granville Medical Center, Oxford, NC, p. A311

MANNING, Richard W., Administrator and Chief Executive Officer, South Panola Community Hospital, Batesville, MS, p. A233

MANNING, Catherine, President and Chief Executive Officer, Saint Vincent Health Center, Erie, PA, p. A354

MANNIX Jr., Robert T., President and Chief Operations Officer, St. Elizabeth Health Services, Baker City, OR, p. A344

MANSFIELD, Jodi J., Senior Vice President and Chief Operating Officer, Shands at the University of Florida, Gainesville, FL, p. A86

MANSON, Lisa, Administrator, Central Community Hospital, Elkader, IA, p. A150

MANTEGAZZA, Peter M., President and Chief Executive Officer, Fairlawn Rehabilitation Hospital, Worcester, MA, p. A207

MANTEY, Carl W., Administrator, Gerald Champion Memorial Hospital, Alamogordo, NM, p. A280

MANTZ, James R., Administrator, Prairie Community Medical Assistance Facility, Terry, MT, p. A256

MANUEL, Mark L., Administrator, Eunice Regional Medical Center, Eunice, LA, p. A180

MAPES, Stephen W., Chief Executive Officer, Hayes–Green–Beach Memorial Hospital, Charlotte, MI, p. A209

MAPLES, Ruth, Executive Director, Lanterman Developmental Center, Pomona, CA, p. A56

MARCELINE, Alex M., Chief Executive Officer, Palms West Hospital, Loxahatchee, FL, p. A89

MARCHETTI, Mark E., Chief Executive Officer, Greenfield Area Medical Center, Greenfield, OH, p. A327

MARCOS, Luis R., M.D., President, New York City Health and Hospitals Corporation, New York, NY, p. B121

MARIE, Donna, Executive Vice President and Chief Executive Officer, Resurrection Medical Center, Chicago, IL, p. A123

MARINAKOS, Plato A., President and Chief Executive Officer, Mercy Health System of Southeastern Pennsylvania, Bala Cynwyd, PA, p. A350

MARINO, Robert E., Executive Director, Citizens General Hospital, New Kensington, PA, p. A359

MARION, Ben, Chief Executive Officer, Turning Point Hospital, Moultrie, GA, p. A109

MARK, Richard J., President and Chief Executive Officer, St. Mary's Hospital, East St. Louis, IL, p. A126

MARKHAM, Patricia, Administrator, Cass County Memorial Hospital, Atlantic, IA, p. A147

MARKIEWICZ, Dennis P., Vice President, Hospital Operations, Crittenton Hospital, Rochester, MI, p. A218

MARKOS, Dennis R., Chief Executive Officer, Ed Fraser Memorial Hospital, MacClenny, FL, p. A89

MARKOWITZ, Alan, FACHE, Administrator and Chief Executive Officer, Baptist DeKalb Hospital, Smithville, TN, p. A393

MARKOWITZ, Bruce J., President and Chief Executive Officer, Palisades General Hospital, North Bergen, NJ, p. A276

MARKS, Craig J., President and Chief Executive Officer, South Haven Community Hospital, South Haven, MI, p. A219

MARKS, Gary A., Administrator, Glen Rose Medical Center, Glen Rose, TX, p. A408

MARKUM, Lind, Administrator, Del Puerto Hospital, Patterson, CA, p. A56

MARLETTE, Jeff, Administrator, Holy Infant Hospital, Hoven, SD, p. A379

MARLEY, Mark E.
Chief Executive Officer, Bucyrus Community Hospital, Bucyrus, OH, p. A321
President and Chief Executive Officer, Galion Community Hospital, Galion, OH, p. A327

MARMO, Anthony P., Chief Executive Officer, Kingston Hospital, Kingston, NY, p. A289

MARMORSTONE, Ray, Administrator, Memorial Hospital of Iowa County, Dodgeville, WI, p. A458

MARNELL, George, Director, Jonathan M. Wainwright Memorial Veterans Affairs Medical Center, Walla Walla, WA, p. A451

MARNELL, John W., Chief Executive Officer, Hudson Medical Center, Hudson, WI, p. A460

MAROHN, Harold G., Acting Chief Executive Officer, BHC Belmont Hills Hospital, Belmont, CA, p. A38

MARON, Michael, President and Chief Executive Officer, Holy Name Hospital, Teaneck, NJ, p. A278

MARONEY, George, Administrator, Memorial Hospital of Carbondale, Carbondale, IL, p. A121

MARQUARDT, Robert C., FACHE, President and Chief Executive Officer, Memorial Medical Center of West Michigan, Ludington, MI, p. A215

MARQUARDT, Dennis, USAF, Commander, U. S. Air Force Hospital, Shreveport, LA, p. A187

MARQUETTE Jr., Gerald Joseph, Administrator, Coffeyville Regional Medical Center, Coffeyville, KS, p. A158

MARQUEZ, Michael, Chief Executive Officer, Manatee Memorial Hospital, Bradenton, FL, p. A82

MARR, Charles J.
Chief Executive Officer, Alegent Health Bergan Mercy Medical Center, Omaha, NE, p. A262
Chief Executive Officer, Alegent Health Immanuel Medical Center, Omaha, NE, p. A262

MARREN, Dan, FACHE, Chief Executive Officer, Olmsted Medical Center, Rochester, MN, p. A229

MARRERO, Victor R., Executive Administrator, Dr. Jose Ramos Lebron Hospital, Fajardo, PR, p. A472

MARSHALL, Bob, Administrator, Charter North Star Hospital and Counseling Center, Anchorage, AK, p. A20

MARSHALL, John A., President and Chief Executive Officer, Suburban Hospital, Louisville, KY, p. A174

MARSHALL, Mike, Chief Executive Officer, HEALTHSOUTH Rehabilitation Hospital of Tallahassee, Tallahassee, FL, p. A97

MARSTELLER, Brent A., Chief Executive Officer, Columbia Raleigh General Hospital, Beckley, WV, p. A452

MARTE, Noemi Davis, M.D., Medical Director, Caguas Regional Hospital, Caguas, PR, p. A472

MARTIN, Andria, MS, Director and Vice President Operations, University of Connecticut Health Center, John Dempsey Hospital, Farmington, CT, p. A74

MARTIN, D. Wayne, President and Chief Executive Officer, Crisp Regional Hospital, Cordele, GA, p. A104

MARTIN, Elizabeth J., Vice President and Administrator, Riverside Tappahannock Hospital, Tappahannock, VA, p. A443

MARTIN, G. Roger, President and Chief Executive Officer, Jeanes Hospital, Philadelphia, PA, p. A361

MARTIN, Greg, Administrator and Chief Executive Officer, Blackwell Regional Hospital, Blackwell, OK, p. A335

MARTIN, Guillermo J., Executive Director, Hospital Episcopal San Lucas, Ponce, PR, p. A473

MARTIN, Jack, Administrator, Latimer County General Hospital, Wilburton, OK, p. A343

MARTIN, James A., Chief Executive Officer, Good Samaritan Hospital, Suffern, NY, p. A301

MARTIN, Jeffrey L., President and Chief Executive Officer, Saint Michael's Hospital, Stevens Point, WI, p. A466

MARTIN, Kevin C., Interim Chief Operating Officer, EMH Regional Medical Center, Elyria, OH, p. A326

MARTIN, Neil
President and Chief Executive Officer, Redwood Memorial Hospital, Fortuna, CA, p. A42
President and Chief Executive Officer, Saint Joseph Hospital, Eureka, CA, p. A42

MARTIN, Norm, President and Chief Executive Officer, Parkview Community Hospital Medical Center, Riverside, CA, p. A57

MARTIN, Patrick J., President and Chief Executive Officer, Fisher–Titus Medical Center, Norwalk, OH, p. A330

MARTIN, Kathleen L., Commanding Officer, Naval Hospital, North Charleston, SC, p. A376

MARTIN, Julie, Administrator, General Leonard Wood Army Community Hospital, Fort Leonard Wood, MO, p. A243

MARTIN–SHAW, Carolyn, President, Saint Joseph Community Hospital, New Hampton, IA, p. A153

MARTINEZ, Abraham, Chief Executive Officer, Columbia Alice Physicians and Surgeons Hospital, Alice, TX, p. A395

MARTINEZ, Charles, Ph.D., Chief Executive Officer, Community Hospital of Huntington Park, Huntington Park, CA, p. A45

MARTINEZ, Ramiro J., M.D., Director, East Mississippi State Hospital, Meridian, MS, p. A238

MARTINEZ, Tomas, Administrator, Hospital Hermanos Melendez, Bayamon, PR, p. A472

MARTINEZ Jr., Fred, Chief Executive Officer, St. Charles Parish Hospital, Luling, LA, p. A183

MARTINEZ–LOPEZ, Lester, Director Health Services, Colonel Florence A. Blanchfield Army Community Hospital, Fort Campbell, KY, p. A170

MARTINSEN, Eric, President, Paradise Valley Hospital, National City, CA, p. A53

MARTORE, Patrick R., Chief Executive Officer, South Oaks Hospital, Amityville, NY, p. A284

MARUCA, Robert T., Administrator, Carrie Tingley Hospital, Albuquerque, NM, p. A280

MARWIN, Kristopher H., CHE, Chief Executive Officer, Tri–Valley Health System, Cambridge, NE, p. A259

MASCHING, Frances Marie, President, OSF Healthcare System, Peoria, IL, p. B123

MASON, Bill A., President, Springhill Memorial Hospital, Mobile, AL, p. A16

MASON, Daria V., Chief Executive Officer, Central Vermont Medical Center, Barre, VT, p. A434

MASON, Ray, Interim Chief Executive Officer, Ward Memorial Hospital, Monahans, TX, p. A418

MASON, Stephen D., Administrator, Northwest Florida Community Hospital, Chipley, FL, p. A82

MASON, William R., President, Muhlenberg Hospital Center, Bethlehem, PA, p. A350

MASSA, Lawrence J., Chief Executive Officer, Rice Memorial Hospital, Willmar, MN, p. A232

MASSE, Roger A., Chief Executive Officer, Margaretville Memorial Hospital, Margaretville, NY, p. A290

MASSEY, Donald W., Administrator, Bassett Hospital of Schoharie County, Cobleskill, NY, p. A287

MASSEY, Michael W., Administrator, Allen Bennett Hospital, Greer, SC, p. A374

MASTEJ, J. Michael, Chief Executive Officer and Managing Director, Victoria Regional Medical Center, Victoria, TX, p. A427

MASTERSON, David, Chief Executive Officer, Blackford County Hospital, Hartford City, IN, p. A140

MASTRANGELO, Anthony G., Executive Vice President and Chief Executive Officer, St. Joseph's Hospital, Highland, IL, p. A128

MATARELLI, Steven A., Administrator, Vencor Hospital–Chicago North, Chicago, IL, p. A125

MATEO, Carlos Rodriguez, M.D., Medical Director, Dr. Alejandro Buitrago–Guayama Area Hospital, Guayama, PR, p. A472

MATHER, Kelly, Chief Executive Officer, San Leandro Hospital, San Leandro, CA, p. A61

MATHEWS, George A., President and Chief Executive Officer, Methodist Medical Center of Oak Ridge, Oak Ridge, TN, p. A392

MATHEWS, LouAnn O., Administrator, American Transitional Hospital–Dallas/Fort Worth, Irving, TX, p. A413

MATHEWS, Mike, Administrator, Kwajalein Hospital, Kwajalein Island, MH, p. A471

MATHEWS, Thomas C., Administrator, Bartow Memorial Hospital, Bartow, FL, p. A81

MATNEY, Douglas A., Senior Vice President Operations, Columbia Medical Center–East, El Paso, TX, p. A405

MATSUMURA, Kay, Chief Executive Officer, Salt Lake Regional Medical Center, Salt Lake City, UT, p. A432

MATTEI, Thomas J.
Chief Operating Officer, Mercy Hospital of Pittsburgh, Pittsburgh, PA, p. A362
Chief Operating Officer, Mercy Providence Hospital, Pittsburgh, PA, p. A362

MATTEI DE COLLAZO, Georgina, Executive Director, Doctors Hospital, San Juan, PR, p. A473

MATTES, James A., President, Grande Ronde Hospital, La Grande, OR, p. A345

MATTHEWS, Clint, Chief Executive Officer, Palm Beach Gardens Medical Center, Palm Beach Gardens, FL, p. A93

MATTHEWS, D. Clinton, Chief Executive Officer, South Park Hospital, Lubbock, TX, p. A416

MATTHEWS, L. Gene, Chief Executive Officer, Tahlequah City Hospital, Tahlequah, OK, p. A342

MATTINGLY, Bernie, Chief Executive Officer, Burbon Community Hospital, Paris, KY, p. A175

MATTISON, Kenneth R., President and Chief Executive Officer, Florida Hospital Waterman, Eustis, FL, p. A84

MATUSKA, John E., President and Chief Executive Officer, St. Peter's Medical Center, New Brunswick, NJ, p. A275

MAURER, Gregory L., Administrator, Elmore Medical Center, Mountain Home, ID, p. A118

MAXHIMER, Terry R., Regional Vice President, HEALTHSOUTH Rehabilitation Hospital, Kingsport, TN, p. A387

MAY, Bill, Chief Executive Officer, Allen County Hospital, Iola, KS, p. A161

MAY, Maurice I., President, Hebrew Rehabilitation Center for Aged, Boston, MA, p. A200

MAYA, Victor, Chief Executive Officer, Kendall Medical Center, Miami, FL, p. A90

MAYNARD, Robert F., Chief Executive Officer, Shawnee Regional Hospital, Shawnee, OK, p. A341

MAYO, Jim L., Administrator, Baptist Medical Center–Nassau, Fernandina Beach, FL, p. A84

MAYO, M. Andrew, Chief Executive Officer, Charter Parkwood Behavioral Health System, Olive Branch, MS, p. A238

MAZON III, Andrew, Administrator and Chief Executive Officer, Roane General Hospital, Spencer, WV, p. A456

MAZOUR, Roger, Interim Administrator, Pender Community Hospital, Pender, NE, p. A263

MAZUR–HART, Stanley F., Ph.D., Superintendent, Oregon State Hospital, Salem, OR, p. A348

MAZZARELLA, Michael C.
Chief Executive Officer, Cross River HealthCare, Inc., Rhinebeck, NY, p. B91
Chief Executive Officer, Northern Dutchess Hospital, Rhinebeck, NY, p. A299

MAZZUCA, Philip J., Executive Director, Parkway Medical Center Hospital, Decatur, AL, p. A13

MCAFEE Jr., James T., Chairman, President and Chief Executive Officer, ValueMark Healthcare Systems, Inc., Atlanta, GA, p. B151

MCALEER, A. Gordon, President and Chief Executive Officer, Lewistown Hospital, Lewistown, PA, p. A357

MCALLISTER, C. C., President and Chief Executive Officer, Ouachita Medical Center, Camden, AR, p. A29

MCAVOY, Lawrence H., Administrator, Washington County Hospital, Plymouth, NC, p. A311

MCAVOY, Scott, Managing Director, Meridell Achievement Center, Liberty Hill, TX, p. A415

MCBEATH, James D., Chief Executive Officer, ValueMark West End Behavioral Healthcare System, Richmond, VA, p. A443

MCBEE, Marie, Chief Executive Officer, Charter Behavioral Health System at Warwick Manor, East New Market, MD, p. A195

MCBRIDE, Don H., Chief Executive Officer, Columbia Woodland Heights Medical Center, Lufkin, TX, p. A416

MCBRIDE, Michael J., CHE, Executive Director, Presbyterian Hospital of Kaufman, Kaufman, TX, p. A414

MCCABE, Eugene, President, North General Hospital, New York, NY, p. A295

MCCABE, Jack, Senior Vice President and Administrator, Harris Methodist–HEB, Bedford, TX, p. A398

MCCABE, Steve, Chief Executive Officer, Hill Crest Behavioral Health Services, Birmingham, AL, p. A12

MCCABE Jr., Patrick, Executive Director, Levi Hospital, Hot Springs National Park, AR, p. A31

MCCALL, Gerald A., Administrator, Kaiser Foundation Hospital, Anaheim, CA, p. A36

MCCARTHY, Bridget, President, Mercy American River/Mercy San Juan Hospital, Carmichael, CA, p. A39

MCCARTHY, Mary Fatima, Administrator, St. Elizabeth Hospital, Beaumont, TX, p. A398

MCCARY, Steve C., President and Chief Executive Officer, Stevens Healthcare, Edmonds, WA, p. A446

MCCASLIN, James B., Director, Chestnut Hill Rehabilitation Hospital, Glenside, PA, p. A354

MCCAULEY, Edith, Administrator, Sabine County Hospital, Hemphill, TX, p. A409

MCCAULEY, Roberta D., Chief Executive Officer, Hampshire Memorial Hospital, Romney, WV, p. A455

MCCLELLAN, David A., Chief Executive Officer, Carolinas Hospital System, Florence, SC, p. A373

MCCLESKEY, George H.
President and Chief Executive Officer, Lubbock Methodist Hospital System, Lubbock, TX, p. B113
President and Chief Executive Officer, Methodist Children's Hospital, Lubbock, TX, p. A416
President and Chief Executive Officer, Methodist Hospital, Lubbock, TX, p. A416

MCCLINTOCK, Thomas, Chief Executive Officer, Columbia Medical Center of Carlsbad, Carlsbad, NM, p. A281

MCCLINTOCK, William T., FACHE, Chief Executive Officer, Boundary Community Hospital, Bonners Ferry, ID, p. A116

MCCLURE, Jan, Chief Executive Officer, Hill Regional Hospital, Hillsboro, TX, p. A410

MCCLYMONDS, Bruce, President, West Virginia University Hospitals, Morgantown, WV, p. A454

MCCOMBS, David, Executive Vice President and Administrator, Bon Secours–DePaul Medical Center, Norfolk, VA, p. A440

MCCONAHY, Richard L., Chief Executive Officer, Middle Georgia Hospital, Macon, GA, p. A108

MCCONKEY, David M., Chief Executive, Good Samaritan Hospital, Downers Grove, IL, p. A126

MCCONNELL, David, Interim Chief Executive Officer, Bon Secours–Holy Family Regional Health System, Altoona, PA, p. A349

MCCOOL, Paul J., Director, Veterans Affairs Medical Center, Manchester, NH, p. A269

MCCORD, Windell M., Administrator, Heart of Texas Memorial Hospital, Brady, TX, p. A399

MCCORKLE, Vincent J., President, Mercy Hospital, Springfield, MA, p. A206

MCCORKLE Jr., Philip H., Chief Executive Officer, Spectrum Health–Downtown Campus, Grand Rapids, MI, p. A213

MCCORMACK, J. David, Executive Director, Riverview Regional Medical Center, Gadsden, AL, p. A14

MCCORMICK, James, Superintendent, Richmond State Hospital, Richmond, IN, p. A145

MCCORMICK, John J., Chief Executive Officer, San Bernardino Mountains Community Hospital District, Lake Arrowhead, CA, p. A46

MCCORMICK, Lynn, Administrator, Sistersville General Hospital, Sistersville, WV, p. A455

MCCORMICK, Richard, Administrator, Methodist Hospital of Dyersburg, Dyersburg, TN, p. A385

MCCOY, George H., Chief Executive Officer, Governor Juan F. Louis Hospital, Christiansted, VI, p. A474

MCCOY, L. Kent, President, Huntington Memorial Hospital, Huntington, IN, p. A141

MCCOY, Michael S., Interim President and Chief Executive Officer, Baptist Medical Center, Kansas City, MO, p. A244

MCCOY, Mike, Chief Executive Officer, Saint Mary's Regional Medical Center, Russellville, AR, p. A34

MCCOY, Sherman P., Executive Director and Chief Executive Officer, Howard University Hospital, Washington, DC, p. A79

MCCRACKEN, Clyde T., Administrator, Ness County Hospital Number Two, Ness City, KS, p. A163

MCCRAY, Cindy M., Administrator and Director Nursing, Hospital District Number Six of Harper County, Anthony, KS, p. A157

MCCULLOUGH, Frank S., M.D., President, Medical College of Ohio Hospitals, Toledo, OH, p. A332

MCCUNE, William, Senior Vice President, Operations, Lankenau Hospital, Wynnewood, PA, p. A368

MCDANIEL, John P., Chief Executive Officer, Medlantic Healthcare Group, Washington, DC, p. B116

MCDERMOTT, Brian J., Administrator, Carrington Health Center, Carrington, ND, p. A316

MCDONAGH, Kathryn J., President and Chief Executive Officer, Northwest Covenant Medical Center, Denville, NJ, p. A272

MCDONALD, William A., President and Chief Executive Officer, Miami Children's Hospital, Miami, FL, p. A90

MCDONNELL, Michael J., Interim Chief Executive Officer, Sheltering Arms Rehabilitation Hospital, Richmond, VA, p. A442

MCDOUGAL Jr., Tommy R., Administrator and Chief Executive Officer, Barnwell County Hospital, Barnwell, SC, p. A371

MCDOWELL, James W., President and Chief Executive Officer, St. Mary's Hospital, Centralia, IL, p. A121

MCDOWELL, Jane, Administrator, Seiling Hospital, Seiling, OK, p. A341

MCDOWELL, P. Jane, Administrator, Harper County Community Hospital, Buffalo, OK, p. A336

MCELHANNON, W. C., Administrator, Union County General Hospital, Clayton, NM, p. A281

MCEWEN, David S., Chief Executive Officer, Marlette Community Hospital, Marlette, MI, p. A216

MCFADDEN, Glennon K., Chief Executive Officer, Deaconess Central Hospital, Saint Louis, MO, p. A249

MCFADDEN, Pamela J., President and Chief Executive Officer, North Coast Health Care Centers, Santa Rosa, CA, p. A63

MCGEACHEY, Edward J., President and Chief Executive Officer, Southern Maine Medical Center, Biddeford, ME, p. A189

MCGEE, John P.
President and Chief Executive Officer, JFK Medical Center, Edison, NJ, p. A272
President and Chief Executive Officer, Solaris Health System, Edison, NJ, p. B140

MCGILL, Richard M., Administrator, Hale County Hospital, Greensboro, AL, p. A15

MCGILL, Timothy W., Chief Executive Officer, Columbia Livingston Regional Hospital, Livingston, TN, p. A388

MCGINTY, Daniel B., President and Chief Executive Officer, Holy Family Memorial Medical Center, Manitowoc, WI, p. A461

MCGLASHAN, Thomas H., M.D., Director, Yale Psychiatric Institute, New Haven, CT, p. A75

MCGLEW, Timothy, Chief Executive Officer, Alhambra Hospital, Alhambra, CA, p. A36

MCGOLDRICK, Margaret M.
President and Chief Executive Officer, Allegheny University Hospital, Bucks County, Warminster, PA, p. A366
President and Chief Executive Officer, Allegheny University Hospital, Elkins Park, Elkins Park, PA, p. A353
President and Chief Executive Officer, Allegheny University Hospital, Medical College of Pennsylvania, Philadelphia, PA, p. A359
President and Chief Executive Officer, Allegheny University Hospital, Parkview, Philadelphia, PA, p. A360
President and Chief Executive Officer, Allegheny University Hospitals, Hahnemann, Philadelphia, PA, p. A360

MCGOUGH, Susan, Administrator, Memorial Hospital, Weiser, ID, p. A119

MCGOWAN, Donna, R.N., Administrator, Lane County Hospital, Dighton, KS, p. A158

MCGOWAN, George, FACHE, Chief Executive Officer, Blount Memorial Hospital, Oneonta, AL, p. A17

MCGRATH, Denise B., Chief Executive Officer, HEALTHSOUTH Treasure Coast Rehabilitation Hospital, Vero Beach, FL, p. A99

MCGRAW, Steven E., Administrator, Vencor Hospital–Chattanooga, Chattanooga, TN, p. A384

MCGRIFF III, W. A., President and Chief Executive Officer, University Medical Center, Jacksonville, FL, p. A87

MCGUIRE, William D., President and Chief Executive Officer, Catholic Medical Center of Brooklyn and Queens, New York, NY, p. A292

MCINTYRE, Nancy, Administrator, Ferry County Memorial Hospital, Republic, WA, p. A449

MCINTYRE, Kathleen, President, Little Company of Mary Hospital and Health Care Centers, Evergreen Park, IL, p. A126

MCIVOR, Dave, Administrator, Roundup Memorial Hospital, Roundup, MT, p. A256

MCKAY, Daniel E., Chief Executive Officer, Moberly Regional Medical Center, Moberly, MO, p. A247

MCKAY, Robert H., President, North Penn Hospital, Lansdale, PA, p. A356

MCKELVEY, Cornelius, Interim Chief Executive Officer, Holy Cross Hospital of Silver Spring, Silver Spring, MD, p. A197

MCKERNAN, Stephen W., Chief Executive Officer, University Hospital, Albuquerque, NM, p. A281

MCKIBBENS, Ben M., President, Valley Baptist Medical Center, Harlingen, TX, p. A409

MCKINNEY, Dan, Administrator, Hermann Area District Hospital, Hermann, MO, p. A244

MCKINNEY, Jim, President, Brim, Inc., Portland, OR, p. B73

MCKINNEY, Paul, Administrator, Cochran Memorial Hospital, Morton, TX, p. A418

MCKINNEY Jr., Buck, Chief Executive Officer, Kiowa District Hospital, Kiowa, KS, p. A161

MCKINNON, Ronald A., Administrator, Benson Hospital, Benson, AZ, p. A22

MCKINNON, William D., FACHE, Administrator, University Hospital and Clinics–Durant, Durant, MS, p. A235

MCKLEM, Patricia A., Medical Center Director, Veterans Affairs Medical Center, Prescott, AZ, p. A25

MCKNEW, Linda A., R.N., Administrator, Shands at Lake Shore, Lake City, FL, p. A88

MCKROW, Dee, Chief Executive Officer, Hills and Dales General Hospital, Cass City, MI, p. A209

MCLAUGHLIN, Keith H., President and Chief Executive Officer, Raritan Bay Medical Center, Perth Amboy, NJ, p. A276

MCLAURIN, Monty E., President, St. Joseph's Hospital and Health Center, Paris, TX, p. A420

MCLEAN, Daniel P., Executive Director, McAllen Medical Center, McAllen, TX, p. A417

MCLEAN, Gordon C., Administrator, Whitman Hospital and Medical Center, Colfax, WA, p. A446

MCLEOD, Richard D., Administrator, Owen County Memorial Hospital, Owenton, KY, p. A175

MCLOUGHLIN, Thomas, President and Chief Executive Officer, Union City Memorial Hospital, Union City, PA, p. A366

MCMACKIN, James L., Chief Executive Officer, Unicoi County Memorial Hospital, Erwin, TN, p. A385

MCMACKIN, Kent W., Chief Executive Officer, Fannin Regional Hospital, Blue Ridge, GA, p. A103

MCMANUS, Joseph S., President and Chief Executive Officer, Lawrence General Hospital, Lawrence, MA, p. A203

MCMANUS, Michael Thomas, President, St. Clement Health Services, Red Bud, IL, p. A133

MCMEEKIN, John C., President and Chief Executive Officer, Crozer–Keystone Health System, Springfield, PA, p. B91

MCMILLAN, Douglas A., Administrator and Chief Executive Officer, West Park Hospital, Cody, WY, p. A468

MCMILLIN, Alan E., Chief Executive Officer, Women and Children's Hospital–Lake Charles, Lake Charles, LA, p. A183

MCMULLEN, Ronald B., President, Alton Memorial Hospital, Alton, IL, p. A120

MCMURDO, Timothy B., Chief Executive Officer, San Mateo County General Hospital, San Mateo, CA, p. A61

MCMURRAY, Sean S., CHE, Administrator, Memorial North Park Hospital, Chattanooga, TN, p. A384

MCMURRY, Patricia, Chief Executive Officer, New England Rehabilitation Hospital of Portland, Portland, ME, p. A191

MCMURTRY, Roger, Chief Mental Health Bureau, Mississippi State Department of Mental Health, Jackson, MS, p. B119

MCNAIR, Mike H., Chief Executive Officer, Hartselle Medical Center, Hartselle, AL, p. A15

MCNAMARA, Paul E., President, Clinton Memorial Hospital, Saint Johns, MI, p. A218

MCNAMARA, Robert, Director, Veterans Affairs Medical Center, Leeds, MA, p. A203

MCNAUGHTON, Neil H., Executive Director and Administrator, Serenity Lane, Eugene, OR, p. A345

MCNEELY Jr., Ernest R., Chief Executive Officer and Administrator, Lewis County General Hospital, Lowville, NY, p. A290

MCNEIL, Greg R., Administrator, Dallas County Hospital, Fordyce, AR, p. A31

MCNEILL, Douglas W., FACHE, President and Chief Executive Officer, Middletown Regional Hospital, Middletown, OH, p. A330

MCNEW, Robert L., Chief Executive Officer, HEALTHSOUTH Rehabilitation Hospital–Cityview, Fort Worth, TX, p. A407

MCPHAIL, Mark D., Chief Executive Officer, Jeff Anderson Regional Medical Center, Meridian, MS, p. A238

MCPHEETERS III, James W., Administrator, McCune–Brooks Hospital, Carthage, MO, p. A242

MCPHERSON, Rodney, Administrator, Delta Memorial Hospital, Dumas, AR, p. A30

MCQUEEN, Elbert T., Chief Executive Officer, HEALTHSOUTH Central Georgia Rehabilitation Hospital, Macon, GA, p. A108

MCRAE, Arnold F., Administrator and Chief Executive Officer, HEALTHSOUTH Rehabilitation Hospital of Montgomery, Montgomery, AL, p. A16

MCRAE, Dave C., President and Chief Executive Officer, Pitt County Memorial Hospital–University Health System of Eastern Carolina, Greenville, NC, p. A308

MCRAE, Margaret S., Site Administrator, Cleveland Clinic Hospital, Fort Lauderdale, FL, p. A84

MCREE, Matt, Administrator, Hart County Hospital, Hartwell, GA, p. A107

MCREYNOLDS, David H., Chief Operating Officer and Administrator, Peninsula Hospital, Louisville, TN, p. A389

MCVEETY, John A., Chief Executive Officer, Alpena General Hospital, Alpena, MI, p. A208

MCWATERS Jr., Joe H., Administrator and Chief Executive Officer, First Hospital Vallejo, Vallejo, CA, p. A66

MCWATTERS, David M., Administrator, Highland Hospital, Charleston, WV, p. A452

MCWHORTER III, John B., Executive Director, Baylor Medical Center at Garland, Garland, TX, p. A408

MEADE, Robert, Chief Executive Officer, Pasco Community Hospital, Dade City, FL, p. A83

MEADES, LeVern, Acting Administrator, Lallie Kemp Medical Center, Independence, LA, p. A181

MEADOWS, Bobby, President and Chief Executive Officer, Columbus Community Hospital, Columbus, OH, p. A324

MEADOWS, Milton W., Administrator, Fairfield Memorial Hospital, Fairfield, TX, p. A406

MEAGHER, Thomas J., Chief Operating Officer, HEALTHSOUTH Bakersfield Rehabilitation Hospital, Bakersfield, CA, p. A37

MEARIAN, Chase, Administrator, Sierra Valley District Hospital, Loyalton, CA, p. A51

MECHLER, Kathleen, Chief Executive Officer, Mountain Crest Hospital, Fort Collins, CO, p. A70

MECHTENBERG, David A., Chief Executive Officer, Ridgecrest Regional Hospital, Ridgecrest, CA, p. A57

MECKLENBURG, Gary A., President and Chief Executive Officer, Northwestern Memorial Hospital, Chicago, IL, p. A123

MECKSTROTH, David J., President and Chief Executive Officer, Upper Valley Medical Center, Troy, OH, p. A333

MEDILL, Delmar J., Interim Chief Executive Officer, Jackson Parish Hospital, Jonesboro, LA, p. A181

MEEHAN, John J., President and Chief Executive Officer, Hartford Hospital, Hartford, CT, p. A74

MEEKER, Timothy L., Executive Director, Sonoma Developmental Center, Eldridge, CA, p. A41

MEGARA, John J., Chief Executive Officer, Anacapa Hospital, Port Hueneme, CA, p. A56

MEHL, Edward J., Chief Executive Officer, Lake Region Healthcare Corporation, Fergus Falls, MN, p. A225

MEIBERT, Kenneth A., Chief Executive Officer, BHC Sierra Vista Hospital, Sacramento, CA, p. A58

MEIER, Ernie, President and Chief Executive Officer, Alaska Regional Hospital, Anchorage, AK, p. A20

MEINERT, Mark W., CHE, Chief Executive, Yamhill Service Area, Providence Newberg Hospital, Newberg, OR, p. A346

MEIS, Fred J., Administrator and Chief Executive Officer, Graham County Hospital, Hill City, KS, p. A160

MELBY, Bernette A., Executive Director, University Health Services, Amherst, MA, p. A199

MELBY, Gina, Chief Executive Officer, Columbia Northwest Medical Center, Pompano Beach, FL, p. A94

MELCHIORRE Jr., Joseph E., CHE, Executive Administrator, Shriners Hospitals for Children, Tampa, FL, p. B135

MELIN, Craig N., President and Chief Executive Officer, Cooley Dickinson Hospital, Northampton, MA, p. A204

MELTON, Carter, President, Rockingham Memorial Hospital, Harrisonburg, VA, p. A438

MELTON, John W., Chief Executive Officer, Columbia East Montgomery Medical Center, Montgomery, AL, p. A16

MELTON, La Vern, Administrator, Beaver County Memorial Hospital, Beaver, OK, p. A335

MELTON, S. Dean, President and Chief Executive Officer, Morgan County Memorial Hospital, Martinsville, IN, p. A143

MENAUGH, John E., Chief Executive Officer, Sutter Coast Hospital, Crescent City, CA, p. A40

MENDELSOHN, John, M.D., President, University of Texas M. D. Anderson Cancer Center, Houston, TX, p. A412

MENDEZ, Lincoln S., Chief Executive Officer, HEALTHSOUTH Doctors' Hospital, Coral Gables, FL, p. A83

MENDEZ, Manuel G., Operating Trustee, Mepsi Center, Bayamon, PR, p. A472

MENTGEN, John, Interim Administrator, Cox–Monett Hospital, Monett, MO, p. A247

MERCADO, Sylvia, Chief Executive Officer, University Pediatric Hospital, San Juan, PR, p. A474

MEREDITH, Stephen L., Chief Executive Officer, Twin Lakes Regional Medical Center, Leitchfield, KY, p. A172

MERRILL, Mark H., Executive Director, Presbyterian Hospital of Dallas, Dallas, TX, p. A403

MERTZ, Paul A.
Executive Director, Irvington General Hospital, Irvington, NJ, p. A274
Executive Director, Newark Beth Israel Medical Center, Newark, NJ, p. A275

MERWIN, Robert W., Chief Executive Officer, Mills–Peninsula Health Services, Burlingame, CA, p. A38

MESMER, Keith, Interim Administrator, Hazel Hawkins Memorial Hospital, Hollister, CA, p. A45

MESROPIAN, Robert A., President, Alice Peck Day Memorial Hospital, Lebanon, NH, p. A269

MESSER, Barbara, R.N., Administrator, Capistrano by the Sea Hospital, Dana Point, CA, p. A41

MESSER, Bristol, Chief Executive Officer, Trace Regional Hospital, Houston, MS, p. A236

MESSING, Fred M., Chief Executive Officer, Baptist Hospital of Miami, Miami, FL, p. A90

MESSMER, Joseph, President and Chief Executive Officer, Mercy Medical Center, Nampa, ID, p. A118

METIVIER, Roland, Chief Executive Officer, Las Encinas Hospital, Pasadena, CA, p. A55

METSCH, Jonathan M., Dr.PH
President and Chief Executive Officer, Greenville Hospital, Jersey City, NJ, p. A274
President and Chief Executive Officer, Jersey City Medical Center, Jersey City, NJ, p. A274

METZLER, Michael W., Acting President, Saint Anne's Hospital, Fall River, MA, p. A202

METZNER, Kurt W., President and Chief Executive Officer, Mississippi Baptist Medical Center, Jackson, MS, p. A236

MEYER, Eugene W., President and Chief Executive Officer, Lawrence Memorial Hospital, Lawrence, KS, p. A161

MEYER, Frederick C., President and Chief Executive Officer, Southern California Healthcare Systems, Pasadena, CA, p. B140

MEYER, James E., President, MedCentral Health System, Mansfield, OH, p. A328

MEYER, Jeffrey K., Administrator and Chief Executive Officer, Osceola Medical Center, Osceola, WI, p. A464

MEYER, Marlis, Interim Director, Veterans Affairs Medical Center, Lake City, FL, p. A88

MEYER, Miles, Administrator, Columbus Community Hospital, Columbus, WI, p. A458

MEYER, Ralph H., FACHE, President and Chief Executive Officer, Guthrie Healthcare System, Sayre, PA, p. B103

MEYER, Robert F., M.D.
Chief Executive Officer, Samaritan Behavioral Health Center–Scottsdale, Scottsdale, AZ, p. A26
Chief Executive Officer, Samaritan–Wendy Paine O'Brien Treatment Center, Phoenix, AZ, p. A25

MEYER, Wilbert E., Administrator and Chief Executive Officer, Cooper County Memorial Hospital, Boonville, MO, p. A241

MEYERS, Joan T., R.N., Executive Director, West Jersey Hospital–Voorhees, Voorhees, NJ, p. A279

MEYERS, Mark, President and Chief Executive Officer, Columbia West Hills Medical Center, Los Angeles, CA, p. A48

MEYERS, Russell, Chief Executive Officer, Columbia Bayshore Medical Center, Pasadena, TX, p. A420

MICHAEL, Barry, Chief Executive Officer, Meadows Regional Medical Center, Vidalia, GA, p. A113

MICHAEL, Max, M.D., Chief Executive Officer and Medical Director, Cooper Green Hospital, Birmingham, AL, p. A12

MICHALSKI, Eugene F., Vice President and Director, William Beaumont Hospital–Troy, Troy, MI, p. A220

MICHELETTI, Mark, Chief Executive Officer, Charter Behavioral Health System, Kingwood, TX, p. A414

MICHELL, Dyer T., President, Munroe Regional Medical Center, Ocala, FL, p. A92

MICKOSEFF, Tecla A., Administrator, LAC–Harbor–University of California at Los Angeles Medical Center, Torrance, CA, p. A65

MICKUS, Steven L., President and Chief Executive Officer, St. Vincent Mercy Medical Center, Toledo, OH, p. A332

MIDDLEBROOK, Randy, Chief Executive Officer and Administrator, Aspen Valley Hospital District, Aspen, CO, p. A68

MIDKIFF, Stephen L., Executive Director, Sebastian River Medical Center, Sebastian, FL, p. A96

MIESLE, Michael A., Administrator, Wood County Hospital, Bowling Green, OH, p. A321

MIGUEL, Hortense, R.N., Service Unit Director, U. S. Public Health Service Indian Hospital, Winterhaven, CA, p. A67

MIHORA, Michael J., Chief Executive Officer, Herrick Memorial Hospital, Tecumseh, MI, p. A220

MIKLAS, Joanne P., Ph.D., Superintendent, Gracewood State School and Hospital, Gracewood, GA, p. A107

MILANES, Carlos, Executive Vice President and Administrator, Palm Springs General Hospital, Hialeah, FL, p. A86

MILBRANDT, Charles A., Director, Veterans Affairs Medical Center, Minneapolis, MN, p. A228

MILBRATH, Michael, Administrator, Waseca Area Medical Center, Waseca, MN, p. A232

MILES, Paul V., Administrator, Middlesboro Appalachian Regional Hospital, Middlesboro, KY, p. A174

MILEWSKI, Robert, President and Chief Executive Officer, Mount Clemens General Hospital, Mount Clemens, MI, p. A216

MILEY, Dennis C., Administrator, Tri–County Hospital, Wadena, MN, p. A232

MILLBURG, Charles L., CHE, Chief Executive Officer, Shenandoah Memorial Hospital, Shenandoah, IA, p. A154

MILLER, Alan B., President and Chief Executive Officer, Universal Health Services, Inc., King of Prussia, PA, p. B149

MILLER, Blaine K., Administrator, Minneola District Hospital, Minneola, KS, p. A163

MILLER, Charles R.
Chief Executive Officer, Northwest Iowa Health Center, Sheldon, IA, p. A154
President and Chief Operating Officer, Paracelsus Healthcare Corporation, Houston, TX, p. B124

MILLER, Emil P., Chief Executive Officer, North Ridge Medical Center, Fort Lauderdale, FL, p. A85

MILLER, George E., Chief Executive Officer, North Monroe Hospital, Monroe, LA, p. A184

MILLER, Jeffrey S., President, High Point Regional Health System, High Point, NC, p. A309

MILLER, Kevin J., Chief Executive Officer, Medical Center of Southern Indiana, Charlestown, IN, p. A138

MILLER, Kimberly J., Administrator, Mitchell County Regional Health Center, Osage, IA, p. A153

MILLER, Michael R., Interim Administrator, Ortonville Area Health Services, Ortonville, MN, p. A228

MILLER, Paul A., President and Chief Executive Officer, North Country Regional Hospital, Bemidji, MN, p. A222

MILLER, Richard, Administrator and Chief Executive Officer, Norton County Hospital, Norton, KS, p. A163

MILLER, Richard P.
Director, G.V. Montgomery Veterans Affairs Medical Center, Jackson, MS, p. A236
President and Chief Executive Officer, West Jersey Health System, Camden, NJ, p. B153

MILLER, Robert, Chief Executive Officer, Henry County Health Center, Mount Pleasant, IA, p. A153

MILLER, Rosa L., R.N., Administrator, Truman Medical Center–West, Kansas City, MO, p. A245

MILLER, Tamara, Administrator, Madison Community Hospital, Madison, SD, p. A379

MILLER, Thomas D., Chief Executive Officer, Lutheran Hospital of Indiana, Fort Wayne, IN, p. A139

MILLER, Thomas O., Administrator, Pungo District Hospital, Belhaven, NC, p. A304

MILLER, Valerie, Administrator, Lincoln County Medical Center, Ruidoso, NM, p. A283

MILLER, Wayne T., Administrator, Behavioral Healthcare of Northern Indiana, Plymouth, IN, p. A144

MILLER, William P., President and Chief Executive Officer, Caro Community Hospital, Caro, MI, p. A209

MILLER, Mark A., Deputy Commander, Fox Army Health Center, Redstone Arsenal, AL, p. A17

MILLER III, Thomas, Chief Executive Officer, Myrtle Werth Hospital–Mayo Health System, Menomonie, WI, p. A461

MILLER Jr., George N., Administrator, Jasper Memorial Hospital, Jasper, TX, p. A413

MILLER Jr., John A., President, Anderson Area Medical Center, Anderson, SC, p. A371

MILLIGAN Jr., William M., President and Chief Executive Officer, Tyler Memorial Hospital, Tunkhannock, PA, p. A366

MILLIRONS, Dennis C., President and Chief Executive Officer, Riverside Medical Center, Kankakee, IL, p. A129

MILLON, Ivon, Chief Executive Officer, Hospital Dr. Federico Trilla, Carolina, PR, p. A472

MILLS, Fred R.
President and Chief Executive Officer, Baptist Health System, San Antonio, TX, p. B69
President and Chief Executive Officer, Baptist Medical Center, San Antonio, TX, p. A422

MILLS, Stephen S.
President and Chief Executive Officer, Flushing Hospital Medical Center, New York, NY, p. A292
President and Chief Executive Officer, New York Hospital Medical Center of Queens, New York, NY, p. A294

MILLSTEAD, John B., Chief Executive Officer, Campbell Health System, Weatherford, TX, p. A428

MILNES, Lynn, Administrator and Chief Executive Officer, Skyline Hospital, White Salmon, WA, p. A451

MILTON, Gene C., President and Chief Executive Officer, Hackettstown Community Hospital, Hackettstown, NJ, p. A273

MILTON, Paul A., Chief Operating Officer, Samaritan Hospital, Troy, NY, p. A302

MINCEMOYER, Robert, President and Chief Executive Officer, Schuyler Hospital, Montour Falls, NY, p. A290

MINDEN, Larry, Chief Executive Officer, Jane Phillips Medical Center, Bartlesville, OK, p. A335

MINER, Charles B., President and Chief Executive Officer, Meridia Health System, Mayfield Village, OH, p. B118

MINER, Greg, Administrator, Loring Hospital, Sac City, IA, p. A154

MINICK, Mark J., President and Chief Executive Officer, Van Wert County Hospital, Van Wert, OH, p. A333

MINIS, Holly, Chief Executive Officer, Mission Vista Behavioral Health System, San Antonio, TX, p. A423

MINKIN, Robert A., CHE, President and Chief Executive Officer, Desert Regional Medical Center, Palm Springs, CA, p. A55

MINNICK, Peggy, Administrator, BHC Alhambra Hospital, Rosemead, CA, p. A58

MINNIS, Vernon, Chief Executive Officer, Hospital District Number Five of Harper County, Harper, KS, p. A160

MINNIX Jr., William L., President and Chief Executive Officer, Wesley Woods Geriatric Hospital, Atlanta, GA, p. A101

MINOR, Richard J., President, Grandview Hospital and Medical Center, Dayton, OH, p. A325

MINTON, James M., President and Chief Executive Officer, Presbyterian Healthcare Services, Albuquerque, NM, p. A280

MIRABITO, Frank W., President, Chenango Memorial Hospital, Norwich, NY, p. A297

MISENER, Kenneth T., Vice President and Chief Operating Officer, Fairview Hospital System, Cleveland, OH, p. B100

MISHELL, Jeffrey, M.D., Chief Executive Officer, Precedent Health Center, Denver, CO, p. A69

MISHLER, Sheila, Chief Executive Officer, BHC Valle Vista Hospital, Greenwood, IN, p. A140

MISSILDINE, Syble F., Administrator, Northeast Medical Center Hospital, Humble, TX, p. A413

MITCHELL, David M., Chief Executive Officer, Avoyelles Hospital, Marksville, LA, p. A183

MITCHELL, Andrew J., Vice President, Administration, North Shore University Hospital–Forest Hills, New York, NY, p. A295

MITCHELL, Gary W., Chief Executive Officer, Newman Memorial Hospital, Shattuck, OK, p. A341

MITCHELL, Jay, Chief Executive Officer, Massachusetts Respiratory Hospital, Braintree, MA, p. A201

MITCHELL, Jerald F., President and Chief Executive Officer, Columbia Sunrise Hospital and Medical Center, Las Vegas, NV, p. A266

MITCHELL, Jon K., FACHE, President and Chief Executive Officer, Asante Health System, Medford, OR, p. B67

MITCHELL, Joseph J., Chief Executive Officer and Administrator, Holdenville General Hospital, Holdenville, OK, p. A338

MITCHELL, Joseph K., Administrator, Tuolumne General Hospital, Sonora, CA, p. A63

MITCHELL, Karlene, President, Wedowee Hospital, Wedowee, AL, p. A19

MITCHELL, Sidney E., Executive Director, University of Illinois at Chicago Medical Center, Chicago, IL, p. A125

MITCHELL, Thedis V., Director, U. S. Public Health Service Indian Hospital, Clinton, OK, p. A336

MITCHELL, Timothy, Administrator, HEALTHSOUTH Southern Hills Rehabilitation Hospital, Princeton, WV, p. A455

MITCHELL, Tom, Chief Executive Officer, Clark Fork Valley Hospital, Plains, MT, p. A256

MITCHELL III, J. Stuart, Administrator, Baptist Memorial Hospital–Golden Triangle, Columbus, MS, p. A234

MITCHELL Jr., William O., Chief Executive Officer, HEALTHSOUTH Rehabilitation Hospital of Austin, Austin, TX, p. A397

MITCHENER Jr., Charles, Chief Executive Officer, Jacksonville Hospital, Jacksonville, AL, p. A15

MITRICK, Joseph, Administrator, Baptist Medical Center–Beaches, Jacksonville Beach, FL, p. A87

MITTEER, Brian R., President, Brattleboro Memorial Hospital, Brattleboro, VT, p. A434

MIZRACH, Kenneth H., Director, Veterans Affairs New Jersey Health Care System, East Orange, NJ, p. A272

MLADY, Celine, Chief Executive Officer, Osmond General Hospital, Osmond, NE, p. A263

MO, Lin H., President and Chief Executive Officer, New York Community Hospital, New York, NY, p. A294

MOAKLER, Thomas J., Chief Executive Officer, Houlton Regional Hospital, Houlton, ME, p. A190

MOBURG, Steven T., Administrator, Boscobel Area Health Care, Boscobel, WI, p. A458

MOCERI, Carm, President, Barnes–Jewish St. Peters Hospital, Saint Peters, MO, p. A250

MODDERMAN, Melvin E., Administrator, Lincoln Trail Behavioral Health System, Radcliff, KY, p. A176

MOEBIUS, Geoffrey D., President and Chief Executive Officer, Saint Michael Hospital, Cleveland, OH, p. A324

MOEBIVS, Geoffrey, Chief Operating Officer, Mt. Sinai Medical Center, Cleveland, OH, p. A324

MOELLER, Jerry G., President and Chief Executive Officer, Stillwater Medical Center, Stillwater, OK, p. A341

MOEN, Daniel P., President and Chief Executive Officer, Heywood Hospital, Gardner, MA, p. A202

MOEN, Robert A., President and Chief Executive Officer, Emanuel Medical Center, Turlock, CA, p. A65

MOHR, Robin Z., Chief Executive Officer, St. Francis Central Hospital, Pittsburgh, PA, p. A363

MOLANO, Celia, Executive Director, I. Gonzalez Martinez Oncologic Hospital, Hato Rey, PR, p. A473

MOLL, Jeffrey S., President and Chief Executive Officer, Beth Israel Hospital, Passaic, NJ, p. A276

MOLNAR, George, M.D., Executive Director, Buffalo Psychiatric Center, Buffalo, NY, p. A285

MONARDO, Greg, President and Chief Executive Officer, Davies Medical Center, San Francisco, CA, p. A60

MONASTERSKY, Martin, Interim Chief Executive Officer, Henry Ford Cottage Hospital of Grosse Pointe, Grosse Pointe Farms, MI, p. A213

MONE, Thomas D., President and Chief Executive Officer, San Gabriel Valley Medical Center, San Gabriel, CA, p. A61

MONGAN, James J., M.D., President, Massachusetts General Hospital, Boston, MA, p. A200

MONGE, Peter W., President and Chief Executive Officer, Montgomery General Hospital, Olney, MD, p. A197

MONNAHAN, John E., President and Senior Executive Officer, Clay County Hospital, Flora, IL, p. A127

MONROIG, Domingo, Administrator, Castaner General Hospital, Castaner, PR, p. A472

MONROIG, Samuel, Administrator, Arecibo Regional Hospital, Arecibo, PR, p. A471

MONSERRATE, Humberto M., Administrator, Hospital Santa Rosa, Guayama, PR, p. A472

MONTAG, Kathy, Administrator Health Care, State Correctional Institution at Camp Hill, Camp Hill, PA, p. A351

MONTAGUE, William D., Acting Medical Center Director, Veteran Affairs Hudson Valley Health Care System–Castle Point Division, Castle Point, NY, p. A286

MONTGOMERY II, Raymond W., President and Chief Executive Officer, White County Medical Center, Searcy, AR, p. A35

MONTGOMERY Jr., J. C., President, Texas Scottish Rite Hospital for Children, Dallas, TX, p. A404

MONTION, Robert M., Chief Executive Officer, Tulare District Hospital, Tulare, CA, p. A65

MOONEY, Jimmy, Chief Executive Officer, Willingway Hospital, Statesboro, GA, p. A112

MOORE, Darrell W., Chief Executive Officer, Independence Regional Health Center, Independence, MO, p. A244

MOORE, Duncan, President and Chief Executive Officer, Tallahassee Memorial Regional Medical Center, Tallahassee, FL, p. A97

MOORE, E. Richard, President, Hazleton General Hospital, Hazleton, PA, p. A355

MOORE, Gary M., President and Chief Executive Officer, DeSoto Memorial Hospital, Arcadia, FL, p. A81

MOORE, Jackie K., Ph.D., Chief Executive Officer, Massachusetts Mental Health Center, Boston, MA, p. A200

MOORE, James A., Administrator, Milwaukee Psychiatric Hospital, Wauwatosa, WI, p. A467

MOORE, James D., Administrator, Stroud Municipal Hospital, Stroud, OK, p. A341

MOORE, Jason H., President and Chief Executive Officer, John D. Archbold Memorial Hospital, Thomasville, GA, p. A112

MOORE, John, Administrator, Hiawatha Community Hospital, Hiawatha, KS, p. A160

MOORE, Joseph L.
Director, Veterans Affairs Chicago Health Care System–Lakeside Division, Chicago, IL, p. A125
Director, Veterans Affairs Chicago Health Care System–West Side Division, Chicago, IL, p. A125

MOORE, Lois Jean, President and Chief Executive Officer, Harris County Hospital District, Houston, TX, p. A411

MOORE, Mindy S., Administrator, Vencor Hospital–Brea, Brea, CA, p. A38

MOORE, Richard T., Administrator, Lake District Hospital, Lakeview, OR, p. A346

MOORE, Robert J., CHE, Chief Executive Officer, Pekin Hospital, Pekin, IL, p. A132

MOORE, Sarah, Vice President, Medical Center at Scottsville, Scottsville, KY, p. A176

MOORE, Spencer, Chief Executive Officer, Charter Brookside Behavioral Health System of New England, Nashua, NH, p. A269

MOORE, T. Jerald, President and Chief Executive Officer, American Transitional Hospitals, Inc., Franklin, TN, p. B67

MOORE, Terence F., President, MidMichigan Health, Midland, MI, p. B119

MOORE, Terry L., Chief Executive Officer, Englewood Community Hospital, Englewood, FL, p. A84

MOORE, W. Evan, Administrator, Comanche Community Hospital, Comanche, TX, p. A401

MOORE III, Ben, Executive Director, University Hospital–SUNY Health Science Center at Syracuse, Syracuse, NY, p. A301

MOORE–HARDY, Cynthia Ann, President and Chief Executive Officer, Lake Hospital System, Painesville, OH, p. A331

MOORHEAD, J. David, M.D., President, Loma Linda University Medical Center, Loma Linda, CA, p. A47

MOORING, Phillip A., Director, Walter B. Jones Alcohol and Drug Abuse Treatment Center, Greenville, NC, p. A309

MOOTRY, John M., Vice President and Site Administrator, Legacy Good Samaritan Hospital and Medical Center, Portland, OR, p. A347

MORASKO, Jerry, Administrator, Marias Medical Center, Shelby, MT, p. A256

MORASKO, Robert A., Chief Executive Officer, Shoshone Medical Center, Kellogg, ID, p. A117

MORDOH, Henry A., President, Shadyside Hospital, Pittsburgh, PA, p. A363

MOREL, Michael R., Administrator, Choctaw Memorial Hospital, Hugo, OK, p. A338

MORELAND, L. Pat, Administrator, Hardy Wilson Memorial Hospital, Hazlehurst, MS, p. A236

MORELAND, Michael E., Director, Veterans Affairs Medical Center, Butler, PA, p. A351

MORESI, Randy, Chief Executive Officer, Columbia North Hills Hospital, North Richland Hills, TX, p. A419

MORGAN, Charles R., Administrator, Wayne Memorial Hospital, Jesup, GA, p. A108

MORGAN, Craig, Administrator, Knox County Hospital, Barbourville, KY, p. A168

MORGAN, Donald J., Administrator, Page Memorial Hospital, Luray, VA, p. A439

MORGAN, Donald W., M.D., Director, William S. Hall Psychiatric Institute, Columbia, SC, p. A373

MORGAN, James E., Director, Huey P. Long Medical Center, Pineville, LA, p. A186

MORGAN, John, President, Gottlieb Memorial Hospital, Melrose Park, IL, p. A130

MORGAN, Michael L., President and Chief Executive Officer, St. Edward Mercy Medical Center, Fort Smith, AR, p. A31

MORIN, Paul A., Superintendent, Soldiers' Home in Holyoke, Holyoke, MA, p. A203

MORLAN, Sandy, Administrator, Ellett Memorial Hospital, Appleton City, MO, p. A241

MORLEY, Tad A., Chief Executive Officer, Brigham City Community Hospital, Brigham City, UT, p. A430

MORRASH, Joseph, Administrator, State Correctional Institution Hospital, Pittsburgh, PA, p. A363

MORRIS, Elaine F., Administrator, Methodist Ambulatory Surgery Hospital, San Antonio, TX, p. A422

MORRIS, Joe, Chief Executive Officer, Kootenai Medical Center, Coeur D'Alene, ID, p. A117

MORRIS, Leigh E., President, La Porte Hospital and Health Services, La Porte, IN, p. A142

MORRIS, Linda, Administrator, Ogallala Community Hospital, Ogallala, NE, p. A262

MORRIS, Michael, Administrator, Coleman County Medical Center, Coleman, TX, p. A401

MORRIS, Monica, Chief Executive Officer, Conejos County Hospital, La Jara, CO, p. A71

MORRIS, Randall R., Administrator, West Carroll Memorial Hospital, Oak Grove, LA, p. A186

MORRIS, Robert, M.D., Administrator, Hilo Medical Center, Hilo, HI, p. A114

MORRISON, Ann, R.N., Chief Executive Officer, Sebasticook Valley Hospital, Pittsfield, ME, p. A191

MORRISON, C. David, President, Logan General Hospital, Logan, WV, p. A454

MORRISON, Robert E., President, Randolph Hospital, Asheboro, NC, p. A304

MORROW, Julia, Administrator, Morrill County Community Hospital, Bridgeport, NE, p. A258

MORSE, Gary C., Chief Executive Officer and Administrator, Baptist Perry Community Hospital, Linden, TN, p. A388

MORTON, James I., FACHE, Administrator and Chief Executive Officer, Whitfield Medical Surgical Hospital, Whitfield, MS, p. A240

MORTON, Ronald, Chief Executive Officer, Barton County Memorial Hospital, Lamar, MO, p. A246

MOSCATO, Mary, Chief Executive Officer, HEALTHSOUTH New England Rehabilitation Hospital, Woburn, MA, p. A207

MOSES, Jon, Administrator, Wood River Medical Center, Los Angeles, ID, p. A119

MOSS, Dwayne, Administrator, L. V. Stabler Memorial Hospital, Greenville, AL, p. A15

MOSS, James T.
President and Chief Executive Officer, Jackson–Madison County General Hospital, Jackson, TN, p. A386
President, West Tennessee Healthcare., Jackson, TN, p. B153

MOSS, Joseph, Administrator, Ste. Genevieve County Memorial Hospital, Ste. Genevieve, MO, p. A251

MOSS, Paul E., President, Milford Hospital, Milford, CT, p. A75

MOSS, Rod, Chief Executive Officer, HEALTHSOUTH Rehabilitation Hospital of North Alabama, Huntsville, AL, p. A15

MOSS, William Mason, President, Potomac Hospital, Woodbridge, VA, p. A444

MOTTISHAW, Brian, Chief Executive Officer, Pioneer Valley Hospital, Salt Lake City, UT, p. A432

MOTZER, Earl James, FACHE, Chief Executive Officer, The James B. Haggin Memorial Hospital, Harrodsburg, KY, p. A171

MOUGHON, Edward, Superintendent, Big Spring State Hospital, Big Spring, TX, p. A398

MOULTHROP, David L., Ph.D., President and Chief Executive Officer, Rogers Memorial Hospital, Oconomowoc, WI, p. A463

MOUNTCASTLE, William A., Director, Veterans Affairs Medical Center, Nashville, TN, p. A391

MOVAHED, Alexander, Acting President and Chief Executive Officer, Salem Hospital, Salem, MA, p. A205

MROSS, Charles D., President and Chief Executive Officer, Franklin Square Hospital Center, Baltimore, MD, p. A193

MUDLER, Gordon A., President and Chief Executive Officer, Hackley Health, Muskegon, MI, p. A216

MUECK, G. Jerry, Vice President, Chief Executive Officer and Administrator, Memorial Spring Shadows Glen, Houston, TX, p. A412

MUELLER, Jens, Chairman, Pacific Health Corporation, Long Beach, CA, p. B123

MUETHER, Robert O., Interim Superintendent, St. Louis Psychiatric Rehabilitation Center, Saint Louis, MO, p. A250

MUETZEL, Hal, Chief Executive Officer, South Bay Hospital, Sun City Center, FL, p. A97

MUHLENTHALER, Donald, FACHE, President and Chief Executive Officer, Weirton Medical Center, Weirton, WV, p. A456

MUILENBURG, Robert H., Executive Director, University of Washington Medical Center, Seattle, WA, p. A449

MULDER, Dale, Chief Executive Officer, Medical Center of McKinney, McKinney, TX, p. A417

MULDOON, Patrick L., President and Chief Executive Officer, South County Hospital, Wakefield, RI, p. A370

MULFORD, Peter L., Administrator, City Hospital, Martinsburg, WV, p. A454

MULHOLLAND, Donna, President and Chief Executive Officer, Easton Hospital, Easton, PA, p. A353

MULHOLLAND Jr., K. L., Director, Veterans Affairs Medical Center, Memphis, TN, p. A390

MULL, Connie, Chief Executive Officer, Cedar Springs Psychiatric Hospital, Colorado Springs, CO, p. A68

MULLAHEY, Ronald T., President, Vassar Brothers Hospital, Poughkeepsie, NY, p. A299

MULLANEY, Garrell S., Superintendent, Connecticut Valley Hospital, Middletown, CT, p. A75

MULLANEY, Janet, Chief Executive Officer, Heritage Hospital, Tarboro, NC, p. A313

MULLANY, Joseph J., Executive Director, Biloxi Regional Medical Center, Biloxi, MS, p. A233

MULLEN, Anthony F., Administrator, Bertie Memorial Hospital, Windsor, NC, p. A314

MULLEN, Gregory S., Administrator, Tyler Holmes Memorial Hospital, Winona, MS, p. A240

MULLEN, Robert L., Administrator, Rice County Hospital District Number One, Lyons, KS, p. A162

MULLER, A. Gary, FACHE, Administrator and Regional Vice President, Coral Springs Medical Center, Coral Springs, FL, p. A83

MULLER, Ralph W., Chief Executive Officer, University of Chicago Health System, Chicago, IL, p. B150

MULLER, Thomas W., M.D., Superintendent, Northwest Georgia Regional Hospital, Rome, GA, p. A110

MULLINS, Charles B., Executive Vice Chancellor, University of Texas System, Austin, TX, p. B150

MULLINS, Larry A., President and Chief Executive Officer, Good Samaritan Hospital Corvallis, Corvallis, OR, p. A344

MULLINS, Michael L., President, Nevada Regional Medical Center, Nevada, MO, p. A247

MULLINS, Tommy H., Administrator, Boone Memorial Hospital, Madison, WV, p. A454

MUNDY, Mark J., President and Chief Executive Officer, New York Methodist Hospital, New York, NY, p. A294

MUNDY, Stephens M., Chief Executive Officer, St. Joseph's Hospital, Parkersburg, WV, p. A455

MUNETA, Anita, Chief Executive Officer, U. S. Public Health Service Indian Hospital, Crownpoint, NM, p. A281

MUNGER, Richard, Administrator, Mount Grant General Hospital, Hawthorne, NV, p. A266

MUNOZ, Thalia H., Administrator, Starr County Memorial Hospital, Rio Grande City, TX, p. A421

MUNSON, Eric B., Executive Director, University of North Carolina Hospitals, Chapel Hill, NC, p. A305

MUNTEL, Edward G., Ph.D., President and Chief Executive Officer, Children's Psychiatric Hospital of Northern Kentucky, Covington, KY, p. A169

MUNTZ, Timothy, President, St. Margaret's Hospital, Spring Valley, IL, p. A135

MURPHY, Edward G., M.D., President and Chief Executive Officer, Seton Health System, Troy, NY, p. A302

MURPHY, Emilie M., R.N., Director, Montclair Community Hospital, Montclair, NJ, p. A275

MURPHY, Horace W., President and Chief Executive Officer, Washington County Hospital Association, Hagerstown, MD, p. A196

MURPHY, Jim, Chief Executive Officer, Knoxville Area Community Hospital, Knoxville, IA, p. A152

MURPHY, Joyce A., President, Carney Hospital, Boston, MA, p. A200

MURPHY, Michael, President and Chief Executive Officer, Sharp Healthcare, San Diego, CA, p. B135

MURPHY, Michael D., Chief Executive Officer, Gulf Coast Medical Center, Wharton, TX, p. A428

MURPHY, Michael W., Ph.D., Director, Veterans Affairs Northern Indiana Health Care System, Fort Wayne, IN, p. A139

MURPHY, Peter J., President and Chief Executive Officer, St. James Hospital and Health Centers, Chicago Heights, IL, p. A125

MURPHY, Christina, President and Chief Executive Officer, Sisters of Charity of the Incarnate Word Healthcare System, Houston, TX, p. B137

MURPHY III, Frank V., President and Chief Executive Officer, Morton Plant Hospital, Clearwater, FL, p. A82

MURRAY, Annabeth, Administrator, Fairfax Memorial Hospital, Fairfax, OK, p. A337

MURRAY, Joan, R.N., Administrator, St. James Parish Hospital, Lutcher, LA, p. A183

MURRAY, T. Michael, President, South Coast Medical Center, South Laguna, CA, p. A64

MURRAY, Thomas J., President, St. Joseph Hospital, Lexington, KY, p. A172

MURRAY III, Robert B., Chief Executive Officer, Fulton County Medical Center, McConnellsburg, PA, p. A357

MURRELL, Joe, Administrator, Vencor Hospital–LaGrange, LaGrange, IN, p. A143

MUSUMECI, Maryann, Director, Veterans Affairs Medical Center, New York, NY, p. A296

MUTCH, Patrick F., President, Laurel Regional Hospital, Laurel, MD, p. A197

MYERS, Charles, Administrator, Community Hospital, Torrington, WY, p. A469

MYERS, Donna L., Administrator and Chief Executive Officer, Rush County Healthcare Center, La Crosse, KS, p. A161

MYERS, Edward W., Chief Executive Officer, Columbia Conroe Regional Medical Center, Conroe, TX, p. A401

MYERS, Gary, Administrator, Mammoth Hospital, Mammoth Lakes, CA, p. A51

MYERS, Richard L., President and Chief Executive Officer, Durham Regional Hospital, Durham, NC, p. A307

MYNARK, Richard H., Administrator, Pulaski Memorial Hospital, Winamac, IN, p. A146

N

NABORS, Charles E., Chief Executive Officer and Administrator, Bryan W. Whitfield Memorial Hospital, Demopolis, AL, p. A13

NACHTMAN, Frank, Administrator, Marshall Hospital, Placerville, CA, p. A56

NAGELVOORT, Clarence A., President and Chief Executive Officer, Norwegian–American Hospital, Chicago, IL, p. A123

NAGLOSKY, Paul, Administrator, Indianhead Medical Center, Shell Lake, WI, p. A465

NAIBERK, Donald T., Administrator and Chief Executive Officer, Plainview Public Hospital, Plainview, NE, p. A263

NAKAYAMA, Makoto, President and Chief Executive Officer, Long Beach Community Medical Center, Long Beach, CA, p. A47

NANCE, Sally S., Chief Executive Officer, Excelsior Springs Medical Center, Excelsior Springs, MO, p. A243

NAPIER, Randy L., President and Chief Executive Officer, Southern Indiana Rehabilitation Hospital, New Albany, IN, p. A144

NAPPER, Rick, Chief Executive Officer, Crittenden County Hospital, Marion, KY, p. A174

NAPPER, Terry, Administrator, Memorial Medical Center of San Augustine, San Augustine, TX, p. A424

NARBUTAS, Virgis, Administrator, Vencor Hospital–Ontario, Ontario, CA, p. A54

NARUM, Larry, President, Provena Saint Joseph Hospital, Elgin, IL, p. A126

NASCA, Edward, Chief Executive Officer, BHC Belmont Pines Hospital, Youngstown, OH, p. A334

NASRALLA, Anthony J., FACHE, President and Chief Executive Officer, Titusville Area Hospital, Titusville, PA, p. A366

NATHAN, David G., M.D., President, Dana–Farber Cancer Institute, Boston, MA, p. A200

NATZKE, Kenneth J., Administrator, St. Joseph Medical Center, Bloomington, IL, p. A121

NAY, Clifford D., Executive Director, Scott Memorial Hospital, Scottsburg, IN, p. A145

NEAL, Hank, Administrator, Kings Mountain Hospital, Kings Mountain, NC, p. A309

NEAL, John C., Administrator, Mercy Hospital–Turner Memorial, Ozark, AR, p. A34

NEALE, Ada, Acting Director, Veterans Affairs Medical Center, Fresno, CA, p. A43

NEAMAN, Mark R., President and Chief Executive Officer, Evanston Hospital, Evanston, IL, p. A126

NEEDHAM, Jean M., President, Holy Family Hospital, New Richmond, WI, p. A463

NEEDMAN, Herbert G., Administrator and Chief Executive Officer, Temple Community Hospital, Los Angeles, CA, p. A51

NEELY, Bill J., Administrator, Parmer County Community Hospital, Friona, TX, p. A407

NEELY, Cindy, Administrator and Chief Executive Officer, Maude Norton Memorial City Hospital, Columbus, KS, p. A158

NEFF, Mark J., President and Chief Executive Officer, St. Claire Medical Center, Morehead, KY, p. A175

NEIDENBACH, Joseph J., Administrator and Executive Vice President, St. Vincent Hospital, Green Bay, WI, p. A459

NELL, Rocio, M.D., Chief Executive Officer and Medical Director, Montgomery County Emergency Service, Norristown, PA, p. A359

NELSON, Becky, President, Sioux Valley Hospital, Sioux Falls, SD, p. A381

NELSON, Bill, Administrator, Coteau Des Prairies Hospital, Sisseton, SD, p. A381

NELSON, Brock D.
Chief Executive Officer, Children's Hospital and Clinics, Saint Paul, MN, p. A230
Chief Executive Officer, Children's Hospitals and Clinics, Minneapolis, Minneapolis, MN, p. A227

NELSON, Cathleen K., President and Chief Executive Officer, St. Charles Mercy Hospital, Oregon, OH, p. A330

NELSON, David A., President and Chief Executive Officer, St. Francis Medical Center, Breckenridge, MN, p. A223

NELSON, Don A., Administrator, Crook County Medical Services District, Sundance, WY, p. A469

NELSON, Fred, Administrator, Ontonagon Memorial Hospital, Ontonagon, MI, p. A217

NELSON, James J., Executive Director, John F. Kennedy Memorial Hospital, Philadelphia, PA, p. A361

NELSON, James O., Administrator, Buena Vista County Hospital, Storm Lake, IA, p. A155

NELSON, Kenneth W., Superintendent, Bridgewater State Hospital, Bridgewater, MA, p. A201

NELSON, R. A., USN, Commander, Naval Medical Center, San Diego, CA, p. A59

NEMACHECK, William, Chief Executive Officer, Marquette General Hospital, Marquette, MI, p. A216

NEMIR, Bill, Administrator, Haskell Memorial Hospital, Haskell, TX, p. A409

NERO, Marshall L., Chief Executive Officer, Elmore Community Hospital, Wetumpka, AL, p. A19

NERO, Sharon, Chief Executive Officer, HEALTHSOUTH Mountain Regional Rehabilitation Hospital, Morgantown, WV, p. A454

NESPOLI, John L.
President and Chief Executive Officer, Mercy Hospital of Scranton, Scranton, PA, p. A365
President and Chief Executive Officer, Mercy Hospital of Wilkes–Barre, Wilkes–Barre, PA, p. A367

NESTER Jr., Arthur, Administrator, Noxubee General Hospital, Macon, MS, p. A237

NESTER Jr., Martin F., Chief Executive Officer, Long Beach Medical Center, Long Beach, NY, p. A290

NETH, Marvin, Administrator, Callaway District Hospital, Callaway, NE, p. A259

NETHERLAND, Ann, Chief Executive Officer, Franklin Medical Center, Winnsboro, LA, p. A188

NEUGENT, Richard C., President, St. Francis Health System, Greenville, SC, p. A374

NEUMANN, Charles, Chief Executive Officer, Atlantic General Hospital, Berlin, MD, p. A194

NEUSCH, Michael W., FACHE, Director, Louis A. Johnson Veterans Affairs Medical Center, Clarksburg, WV, p. A453

NEVAREZ, Domingo, Executive Director, Hospital San Francisco, San Juan, PR, p. A473

NEVILL, David, President and Chief Executive Officer, Halstead Hospital, Halstead, KS, p. A159

NEWBERRY, R. Alan, President and Chief Executive Officer, Peninsula Regional Medical Center, Salisbury, MD, p. A197

NEWBOLD, Philip A., President and Chief Executive Officer, Memorial Hospital of South Bend, South Bend, IN, p. A145

NEWCOMB, Sherrie, Administrator, Jenkins Community Hospital, Jenkins, KY, p. A171

NEWMAN, Delores, MS, Network Manager, Metro South Network, Tinley Park Mental Health Center, Tinley Park, IL, p. A135

NEWMAN, Douglas, Administrator, Stafford District Hospital, Stafford, KS, p. A166

NEWMAN, Jerald C., Vice President, Nassau County Medical Center, East Meadow, NY, p. A287

NEWMAN, Robert G., M.D., Chief Executive Officer, Continuum Health Partners, New York, NY, p. B91

NEWMAN, Stephen L., M.D., President and Chief Executive Officer, Audubon Hospital, Louisville, KY, p. A173

NEWSOME, Andrea C., FACHE, Director, De Jarnette Center, Staunton, VA, p. A443

NEWTON, Steven R., Interim President and Chief Executive Officer, Research Medical Center, Kansas City, MO, p. A245

NG, Vincent, Director, Veterans Affairs Connecticut Healthcare System–West Haven Division, West Haven, CT, p. A77

NICHOLS, Hugh, Administrator, Vaughan Perry Hospital, Marion, AL, p. A16

NICHOLS, Mark, Chief Executive Officer, Columbia Polk General Hospital, Cedartown, GA, p. A103

NICHOLS, Ralph, Superintendent, Evansville State Hospital, Evansville, IN, p. A139

NICKELL, Roy, Director Substance Abuse Services, Wake County Alcoholism Treatment Center, Raleigh, NC, p. A312

NICKENS III, John R., Chief Executive Officer, Century City Hospital, Los Angeles, CA, p. A48

NICKERSON, Ruth Marie, President and Chief Executive Officer, Saint Agnes Medical Center, Fresno, CA, p. A43

NICO, Vincent O., Regional Vice President, HEALTHSOUTH Rehabilitation Hospital, Largo, FL, p. A89

NIDA, Jerry, M.D., Commissioner of Health, Oklahoma State Department of Mental Health and Substance Abuse Services, Oklahoma City, OK, p. B123

NIEDERPRUEM, Mark L., Administrator, Shriners Hospitals for Children, Springfield, Springfield, MA, p. A206

NIEHM, Sandy, Administrator, Council Community Hospital and Nursing Home, Council, ID, p. A117

NIELSEN, Greg, Administrator, Mountainview Medical Center, White Sulphur Springs, MT, p. A256

NIELSEN, Kim, Administrator and Chief Operating Officer, Orem Community Hospital, Orem, UT, p. A431

NIELSEN, Russ, Administrator, Dell Rapids Community Hospital, Dell Rapids, SD, p. A378

NIELSEN, Tom, Administrator, Kennewick General Hospital, Kennewick, WA, p. A447

NIEMEYER, Romaine, President, Holy Spirit Hospital, Camp Hill, PA, p. A351

NIENHUIS, Arthur W., M.D., Director, St. Jude Children's Research Hospital, Memphis, TN, p. A390

NIGHT PIPE, Orville, Service Unit Director, U. S. Public Health Service Indian Hospital, Eagle Butte, SD, p. A379

NILLES, Edward L., President and Chief Executive Officer, Bradley County Medical Center, Warren, AR, p. A35

NISSEN, David C., Chief Executive Officer, Charter Springs Hospital, Ocala, FL, p. A92

NITSCHKE, David M., President and Chief Executive Officer, Regional West Medical Center, Scottsbluff, NE, p. A264

NIXON Jr., Jesse, Ph.D.
Director, Capital District Psychiatric Center, Albany, NY, p. A284
Director, New York State Department of Mental Health, Albany, NY, p. B121

NOBLE, Kerry L., Chief Executive Officer, Mineral Area Regional Medical Center, Farmington, MO, p. A243

NOBLE, Stephen H., President, Accord Health Care Corporation, Clearwater, FL, p. B64

NOCE Jr., Walter W., President and Chief Executive Officer, Childrens Hospital of Los Angeles, Los Angeles, CA, p. A48

NOCELLA, Kiki, Administrator, Avalon Municipal Hospital and Clinic, Avalon, CA, p. A37
NOCKERTS, Steven R., Administrator and Chief Executive Officer, Adams County Memorial Hospital and Nursing Care Unit, Friendship, WI, p. A459
NOHRE, Allen S., Chief Executive Officer, Desert Vista Behavioral Health Services, Mesa, AZ, p. A23
NOLAN, Michael J., Chief Executive Officer, Ascension Hospital, Gonzales, LA, p. A180
NOLAND, Christopher, Chief Executive Officer, Sheridan Community Hospital, Sheridan, MI, p. A219
NOLL, Donald, Director, Clear Brook Manor, Wilkes–Barre, PA, p. A367
NOONAN, Dennis, President, Salem Hospital, Salem, OR, p. A348
NORDWICK, John A., President and Chief Executive Officer, Bozeman Deaconess Hospital, Bozeman, MT, p. A253
NORDWICK, Thomas, President and Chief Executive Officer, Holy Family Health Services, Estherville, IA, p. A150
NOREM, Kathryn J., Executive Director, Starke Memorial Hospital, Knox, IN, p. A142
NOREN, Mary K.
    Superintendent, Eastern Shore Hospital Center, Cambridge, MD, p. A195
    Chief Executive Officer, Upper Shore Community Mental Health Center, Chestertown, MD, p. A195
NORMAN, Jeffrey K., Chief Executive Officer, PMH Health Services Network, Phoenix, AZ, p. A25
NORMAN, Paul Michael, President, East Pasco Medical Center, Zephyrhills, FL, p. A99
NORRIS, Charles
    Administrator, Seymour Hospital, Seymour, TX, p. A424
    Administrator, Throckmorton County Memorial Hospital, Throckmorton, TX, p. A426
NORRIS, Doug, Chief Operating Officer, Western Medical Center Hospital Anaheim, Anaheim, CA, p. A36
NORRIS, Gail B., Administrator, Telfair County Hospital, McRae, GA, p. A109
NORRIS, Jim, Executive Director, St. Cloud Hospital, A Division of Orlando Regional Healthcare System, Saint Cloud, FL, p. A95
NORRIS, Jim, Interim Chief Executive Officer, Continuum, Kendallville, IN, p. B91
NORTH, Joel E., Administrator, Baptist Memorial Hospital–Osceola, Osceola, AR, p. A34
NORTHRUP, M. Kay, Warden, Oakwood Correctional Facility, Lima, OH, p. A328
NORTON, Charles R., Administrator, Biggs–Gridley Memorial Hospital, Gridley, CA, p. A44
NORVELL, Charles D., President, Thoms Rehabilitation Hospital, Asheville, NC, p. A304
NORWINE, David R., President and Chief Executive Officer, H. B. Magruder Memorial Hospital, Port Clinton, OH, p. A331
NORWOOD, Steve, Director, Western State Psychiatric Center, Fort Supply, OK, p. A337
NOSACKA, Mark, Chief Executive Officer, River West Medical Center, Plaquemine, LA, p. A186
NOTEBAERT, Edmond F., President, Children's Hospital of Philadelphia, Philadelphia, PA, p. A360
NOTEBOOM, Kenneth, Chief Executive Officer, Columbia Specialty Hospital of Tulsa, Tulsa, OK, p. A342
NOTEWARE, Dan, Executive Director, Presbyterian Hospital of Winnsboro, Winnsboro, TX, p. A429
NOVAK, Edward, President and Chief Executive Officer, Sacred Heart Hospital, Chicago, IL, p. A124
NOVIELLO, Joseph S., Chief Executive Officer, Podiatry Hospital of Pittsburgh, Pittsburgh, PA, p. A362
NOWAK, Gregory M., Administrator, Coshocton County Memorial Hospital, Coshocton, OH, p. A325
NOWAK, Martin, Interim Executive Director, University of Alabama Hospital, Birmingham, AL, p. A12
NUGENT, Gary N., Medical Director, Veterans Affairs Medical Center, Cincinnati, OH, p. A323
NUNAMAKER, E. Michael, President and Chief Executive Officer, Mercy Health Center of Manhattan, New York, KS, p. A162
NUNLEY, Jack, Chief Executive Officer, Pulaski Community Hospital, Pulaski, VA, p. A441

NUNNERY, S. Arnold, President and Chief Executive Officer, Iredell Memorial Hospital, Statesville, NC, p. A313
NURKIN, Harry A., Ph.D., President and Chief Executive Officer, Carolinas HealthCare System, Charlotte, NC, p. B76
NYP, Randall G., President and Chief Executive Officer, Via Christi Regional Medical Center, Wichita, KS, p. A167

O

O'BRIEN, John, Administrator, Ellsworth Municipal Hospital, Iowa Falls, IA, p. A152
O'BRIEN, John G., Chief Executive Officer, Cambridge Public Health Commission, Cambridge, MA, p. A201
O'BRIEN, Michael C., Administrator, Sarah D. Culbertson Memorial Hospital, Rushville, IL, p. A134
O'BRIEN, William F., Chief Executive Officer and Administrator, Fayette Memorial Hospital, La Grange, TX, p. A414
O'BRIEN Jr., Charles M., President and Chief Executive Officer, Western Pennsylvania Hospital, Pittsburgh, PA, p. A364
O'CONNELL, John W., President, Franciscan Services Corporation, Sylvania, OH, p. B101
O'CONNELL, Rick, Chief Executive Officer, Lucerne Medical Center, Orlando, FL, p. A93
O'CONNOR, Delia
    President, Caritas Norwood Hospital, Norwood, MA, p. A205
    President, Caritas Southwood Community Hospital, Norfolk, MA, p. A204
O'CONNOR, Joann, Director, Winnebago Mental Health Institute, Winnebago, WI, p. A467
O'CONNOR, Shawn J., Chief Executive Officer, Spring Brook Behavioral Healthcare System, Travelers Rest, SC, p. A376
O'CONNOR, William D., President and Chief Executive Officer, Rehabilitation Hospital of the Pacific, Honolulu, HI, p. A114
O'CONNOR Jr., Vincent J., President and Chief Executive Officer, Fremont Area Medical Center, Fremont, NE, p. A259
O'DONNELL, Kevin J., President and Chief Executive Officer, Sacred Heart–St. Mary's Hospitals, Rhinelander, WI, p. A465
O'DONNELL, Randall L., Ph.D., President and Chief Executive Officer, Children's Mercy Hospital, Kansas City, MO, p. A245
O'DONNELL Jr., Thomas F., FACS, President and Chief Executive Officer, New England Medical Center, Boston, MA, p. A200
O'GRADY Jr., Michael J., President and Chief Executive Officer, Indian River Memorial Hospital, Vero Beach, FL, p. A99
O'HARA, Gene L., Administrator, Providence Alaska Medical Center, Anchorage, AK, p. A20
O'KEEFE, James M., Administrator, Cumberland Memorial Hospital, Cumberland, WI, p. A458
O'LOUGHLIN, James, Chief Executive Officer, Presbyterian Hospital, Oklahoma City, OK, p. A340
O'MALLEY, Dennis, President, Craig Hospital, Englewood, CO, p. A70
O'NEAL, James, Administrator, Chase County Community Hospital, Imperial, NE, p. A261
O'NEIL, John D., Executive Vice President and Administrator, St. Mary's Hospital Warrick, Boonville, IN, p. A137
O'ROURKE, Terrence Michael, President, Spectrum Health–East Campus, Grand Rapids, MI, p. A213
O'SHAUGHNESSY, Jon C., President and Chief Executive Officer, Lake Cumberland Regional Hospital, Somerset, KY, p. A176
O'SHEA, James E., Administrator, Greenbrier Hospital, Brooksville, FL, p. A82
OAKEY, James A., President and Chief Executive Officer, Helix Health, Lutherville Timonium, MD, p. B107
OBERTA, Gail M., Administrator and Chief Executive Officer, Seton Shoal Creek Hospital, Austin, TX, p. A397

OCHS, David, Administrator, Saint James Hospital, Pontiac, IL, p. A133
OCHS, Kristine, R.N., Administrator, Grisell Memorial Hospital District One, Ransom, KS, p. A165
OCKERS, Thomas, President and Chief Executive Officer, Brookhaven Memorial Hospital Medical Center, Patchogue, NY, p. A298
ODDIS, Joseph Michael
    President, Spartanburg Regional Healthcare System, Spartanburg, SC, p. B140
    President, Spartanburg Regional Medical Center, Spartanburg, SC, p. A376
ODELL III, F. A., FACHE, President, Carteret General Hospital, Morehead City, NC, p. A310
OESTMANN, Barbara, Chief Executive Officer, Share Medical Center, Alva, OK, p. A335
OGLESBY, Darrell M., Administrator, Putnam General Hospital, Eatonton, GA, p. A106
OKINAKA, Cynthia, Administrator, St. Francis Medical Center, Honolulu, HI, p. A114
OLAND, Charisse S., President and Chief Executive Officer, Childrens Care Hospital and School, Sioux Falls, SD, p. A381
OLDHAM, John M., M.D., Director, New York State Psychiatric Institute, New York, NY, p. A295
OLIVER, William C., President, Forrest General Hospital, Hattiesburg, MS, p. A235
OLIVERIUS, Maynard F.
    President and Chief Executive Officer, Stormont–Vail HealthCare, Topeka, KS, p. A166
    President and Chief Executive Officer, Stormont–Vail HealthCare, Topeka, KS, p. B142
OLSEN, Gloria P., Ph.D., Superintendent, Kerrville State Hospital, Kerrville, TX, p. A414
OLSEN, Robert T., CHE, President and Chief Executive Officer, Yuma Regional Medical Center, Yuma, AZ, p. A28
OLSON, JoAline, R.N., President, St. Helena Hospital, Deer Park, CA, p. A41
OLSON, Lynn W., Administrator and Chief Executive Officer, Regina Medical Center, Hastings, MN, p. A226
OLSON, Nathan C., President and Chief Executive Officer, Hammond–Henry Hospital, Geneseo, IL, p. A127
OLSON, Neva M., Chief Executive Officer, Samuel Mahelona Memorial Hospital, Kapaa, HI, p. A115
OLSON, Randall M., Administrator, Wellmont Bristol Regional Medical Center, Bristol, TN, p. A383
OMMEN, Ronald A., President and Chief Executive Officer, Trinity Lutheran Hospital, Kansas City, MO, p. A245
ONO, Sidney, Administrator, Desert Valley Hospital, Victorville, CA, p. A66
OPDAHL, Jim
    Administrator, Community Hospital in Nelson County, McVille, ND, p. A318
    Administrator, St. Luke's Tri–State Hospital, Bowman, ND, p. A316
OPPEGARD, Stanley C., Vice President and Chief Operating Officer, Methodist Hospital, Sacramento, CA, p. A58
ORAVEC Jr., Andrew, Administrator, Community Hospital of New Port Richey, New Port Richey, FL, p. A92
ORFGEN, Lynn C., Chief Executive Officer, St. Charles General Hospital, New Orleans, LA, p. A185
ORLANDO, Joseph S., Executive Director, Jacobi Medical Center, New York, NY, p. A293
ORMAN Jr., Bernard A., Administrator, Samaritan Memorial Hospital, Macon, MO, p. A247
ORME, Cliff, Executive Director, Valley Hospital, Palmer, AK, p. A21
ORMOND, Evalyn
    Administrator, Sterlington Hospital, Sterlington, LA, p. A187
    Administrator, Union General Hospital, Farmerville, LA, p. A180
ORR, Jon, Administrator, Mountain View Hospital, Gadsden, AL, p. A14
ORR, Lindell W., Chief Executive Officer, Blake Medical Center, Bradenton, FL, p. A82
ORR, Roy J., President and Chief Executive Officer, McKenzie–Willamette Hospital, Springfield, OR, p. A348

ORR, Steven R., Chairman and Chief Executive Officer, Lutheran Health Systems, Fargo, ND, p. B113

ORRICK, Charles H., Administrator, Donalsonville Hospital, Donalsonville, GA, p. A105

ORTENZIO, Robert, President and Chief Executive Officer, Continental Medical Systems, Inc., Mechanicsburg, PA, p. B90

ORTIZ, Julio A., M.D., Chairman, Font Martelo Hospital, Humacao, PR, p. A472

OSBORNE, David W., President and Chief Executive Officer, Norwalk Hospital, Norwalk, CT, p. A76

OSBORNE, Doug, Facility Administrator, Georgia Regional Hospital at Savannah, Savannah, GA, p. A111

OSBORNE, Edward J., Chief Executive Officer, ValueMark–Brawner Behavioral Healthcare System–North, Smyrna, GA, p. A111

OSBURN, Jerry, Administrator, Methodist Hospital–Levelland, Levelland, TX, p. A415

OSIKA, Diane J., Interim Chief Executive Officer, Tri–County Memorial Hospital, Gowanda, NY, p. A288

OSMUS, Richard D., Chief Executive Officer, Hugh Chatham Memorial Hospital, Elkin, NC, p. A307

OSSE, John M., Administrator, Mitchell County Hospital, Beloit, KS, p. A157

OSTASZEWSKI, Patricia, Chief Executive Officer and Administrator, HEALTHSOUTH Rehabilitation Hospital of New Jersey, Toms River, NJ, p. A278

OSWALD, Wesley W., Chief Executive Officer, Brazosport Memorial Hospital, Lake Jackson, TX, p. A415

OTAKE, Stanley, Chief Executive Officer, Bellflower Medical Center, Bellflower, CA, p. A37

OTHOLE, Jean, Service Unit Director, U. S. Public Health Service Indian Hospital, Zuni, NM, p. A283

OTHS, Richard P., President and Chief Executive Officer, Atlantic Health System, Florham Park, NJ, p. A273

OTT, Pamela, R.N., Administrator, Ocean Beach Hospital, Ilwaco, WA, p. A447

OTT, Ronald A., Chief Executive Officer, Fitzgibbon Hospital, Marshall, MO, p. A247

OTT, Ronald H., President and Chief Executive Officer, McKeesport Hospital, McKeesport, PA, p. A357

OTTEN, Jeffrey, President, Brigham and Women's Hospital, Boston, MA, p. A200

OUSLEY, Virginia, Director, Carilion Radford Community Hospital, Radford, VA, p. A441

OWEN, Ed, Chief Executive Officer, BHC Fremont Hospital, Fremont, CA, p. A43

OWEN, Ronald S., Chief Executive Officer, Southeast Alabama Medical Center, Dothan, AL, p. A13

OWEN, Terry, Chief Executive Officer, Emory–Adventist Hospital, Smyrna, GA, p. A111

OWENS, Ben E., President, St. Bernards Regional Medical Center, Jonesboro, AR, p. A32

OWENS, Craig A., President and Chief Executive Officer, Marcus J. Lawrence Medical Center, Cottonwood, AZ, p. A22

P

PAAP, Antonie H., President and Chief Executive Officer, Children's Hospital Oakland, Oakland, CA, p. A54

PABON, Ahmed Alvarez, Executive Director, Hospital Sub–Regional Dr. Victor R. Nunez, Humacao, PR, p. A472

PACINI, Carol, Provincialate Superior, Little Company of Mary Sisters Healthcare System, Evergreen Park, IL, p. B112

PACKER, Eric, Administrator, Garfield Memorial Hospital and Clinics, Panguitch, UT, p. A431

PACKER, Richard, Administrator, Cassia Regional Medical Center, Burley, ID, p. A116

PACKNETT, Michael J., President and Chief Executive Officer, St. Mary–Rogers Memorial Hospital, Rogers, AR, p. A34

PADDEN, Terrance J., Administrator, Box Butte General Hospital, Alliance, NE, p. A258

PAGE, Dan B., President, Greenleaf Health Systems, Inc., Chattanooga, TN, p. B103

PAGE, David R., President and Chief Executive Officer, Fairview Hospital and Healthcare Services, Minneapolis, MN, p. B100

PAGE, Susan M., President and Chief Executive Officer, Pratt Regional Medical Center, Pratt, KS, p. A164

PAGELS, James R., Chief Executive Officer and Managing Director, Northern Nevada Medical Center, Sparks, NV, p. A267

PALAGI, Richard L., Executive Director, St. John's Lutheran Hospital, Libby, MT, p. A255

PALM, SharRay, President and Chief Executive Officer, Lakewood Health Center, Baudette, MN, p. A222

PALMER, James A., Director, Veterans Affairs Medical Center, San Juan, PR, p. A474

PALMER, John, Ph.D., Director, Kingsboro Psychiatric Center, New York, NY, p. A293

PALMER, William H., President, Miller Dwan Medical Center, Duluth, MN, p. A224

PALMISANO II, Richard T., MS, Chief Executive Officer, Brattleboro Retreat, Brattleboro, VT, p. A434

PANDL, Therese B., Senior Vice President and Chief Operating Officer, St. Mary's Hospital Ozaukee, Mequon, WI, p. A462

PANICEK, John M.

Administrator, Rochester Methodist Hospital, Rochester, MN, p. A229

Administrator, Saint Marys Hospital, Rochester, MN, p. A229

PANIS, Reggie, President, Villaview Community Hospital, San Diego, CA, p. A60

PAPANIA, Barry A., President and Chief Executive Officer, Columbia St. Luke's Hospital, Bluefield, WV, p. A452

PARENTE, William D., Director and Chief Executive Officer, Santa Monica–UCLA Medical Center, Santa Monica, CA, p. A63

PARIS, David, Administrator, George E. Weems Memorial Hospital, Apalachicola, FL, p. A81

PARIS, Gregory A., Administrator, Monroe County Hospital, Albia, IA, p. A147

PARIS, Herbert, President, Mid Coast Hospital, Bath, ME, p. A189

PARISI, Ernest, Administrator and Chief Executive Officer, Llano Memorial Hospital, Llano, TX, p. A416

PARKER, Douglas M., Chief Executive Officer, Northside Hospital – Cherokee, Canton, GA, p. A103

PARKER, Douglas W., Chief Executive Officer, St. Vincent–North Rehabilitation Hospital, Sherwood, AR, p. A35

PARKER, Patsy A., Administrator and Chief Executive Officer, Rio Vista Physical Rehabilitation Hospital, El Paso, TX, p. A405

PARKER, Phillip L.

Administrator, D. W. McMillan Memorial Hospital, Brewton, AL, p. A12

Administrator, Escambia County Health Care Authority, Brewton, AL, p. B100

PARKER, Robert C., M.P.H., Acting Chief Executive Officer, Indiana Hospital, Indiana, PA, p. A355

PARKER, Scott S., President, Intermountain Health Care, Inc., Salt Lake City, UT, p. B109

PARKER, Tim, Chief Executive Officer, Miami Heart Institute and Medical Center, Miami, FL, p. A91

PARKER, Gregg S., Commanding Officer, Naval Hospital, Bremerton, WA, p. A445

PARKS, Ralph L., Administrator and Chief Executive Officer, Victor Valley Community Hospital, Victorville, CA, p. A66

PARKS III, Burton O., Administrator, West Shore Hospital, Manistee, MI, p. A216

PARMER, David N., President and Chief Executive Officer, Baptist Hospital of Southeast Texas, Beaumont, TX, p. A398

PARRIS, M. Tim, Executive Vice President and Chief Operating Officer, Baylor University Medical Center, Dallas, TX, p. A402

PARRIS, Y. C., Director, Veterans Affairs Medical Center, Birmingham, AL, p. A12

PARRIS Jr., Thomas G., President, Women and Infants Hospital of Rhode Island, Providence, RI, p. A369

PARRISH, Harold R., Superintendent, Rusk State Hospital, Rusk, TX, p. A422

PARRISH, James G., Administrator, East Adams Rural Hospital, Ritzville, WA, p. A449

PARSLEY, George N., Administrator, Hereford Regional Medical Center, Hereford, TX, p. A409

PARSONS, Ann C., Interim Administrator, St. Vincent Mercy Hospital, Elwood, IN, p. A139

PARSONS, Larry, Administrator, Wilbarger General Hospital, Vernon, TX, p. A427

PARTON, Gerald L., Chief Executive Officer, Doctors Hospital of Jefferson, Metairie, LA, p. A183

PASINSKI, Theodore M., President, St. Joseph's Hospital Health Center, Syracuse, NY, p. A301

PASSAMA, Gary J., President and Chief Executive Officer, NorthBay Healthcare System, Fairfield, CA, p. B122

PATCHIN, J. Craig, Administrator, Shriners Hospitals for Children–Intermountain, Salt Lake City, UT, p. A432

PATE, Alfred S., Director, Veterans Affairs Medical Center, North Chicago, IL, p. A132

PATNESKY, Edward J., President and Chief Executive Officer, Southampton Memorial Hospital, Franklin, VA, p. A438

PATOUT, John P., Administrator, Vermilion Hospital, Lafayette, LA, p. A182

PATSEY, Lois K., Administrator and Chief Executive Officer, East Bay Hospital, Richmond, CA, p. A57

PATTEN, Bill, Administrator, Sedgwick County Health Center, Julesburg, CO, p. A71

PATTERSON, Bill, Interim Administrator, Columbia Stones River Hospital, Woodbury, TN, p. A394

PATTERSON, Donald E., Administrator, Siloam Spring Memorial Hospital, Siloam Springs, AR, p. A35

PATTERSON, Mike, Administrator, Sylvan Grove Hospital, Jackson, GA, p. A108

PATTON, David W., Chief Executive Officer, Maui Memorial Hospital, Wailuku, HI, p. A115

PATTON, Jimmy, Chief Executive Officer and Managing Director, Keystone Center, Chester, PA, p. A351

PATTULLO, Douglas E., Chief Executive Officer, Tolfree Memorial Hospital, West Branch, MI, p. A221

PATZ, Stephen M., Chief Executive Officer, Parkway Regional Medical Center, North Miami Beach, FL, p. A92

PAUGH, J. William, President and Chief Executive Officer, St. Joseph Hospital, Augusta, GA, p. A102

PAUL, Kevin, Administrator, Dooly Medical Center, Vienna, GA, p. A113

PAULEY, Alan C., Administrator, Morrow County Hospital, Mount Gilead, OH, p. A330

PAULSON, Mark E., Administrator, Appleton Municipal Hospital and Nursing Home, Appleton, MN, p. A222

PAUTLER, J. Stephen, CHE, Administrator, Windom Area Hospital, Windom, MN, p. A232

PAWLAK, Paul, President and Chief Executive Officer, Silver Cross Hospital, Joliet, IL, p. A129

PAWLOWSKI, Eugene P., President, Bluefield Regional Medical Center, Bluefield, WV, p. A452

PAYNE, Mark I., Superintendent, Utah State Hospital, Provo, UT, p. A431

PAZZAGLINI, Gino J., President and Chief Executive Officer, Good Samaritan Regional Medical Center, Pottsville, PA, p. A364

PEAK, Benjamin A., Chief Executive Officer, Dickenson County Medical Center, Clintwood, VA, p. A437

PEAK, James G., Director, Memorial Hospital and Manor, Bainbridge, GA, p. A102

PEAKS, William E., Chief Executive Officer, Garden Park Community Hospital, Gulfport, MS, p. A235

PEARSE, David L., Executive Director, Speare Memorial Hospital, Plymouth, NH, p. A270

PEARSON, Bruce E., Vice President and Chief Executive Officer, Desert Samaritan Medical Center, Mesa, AZ, p. A23

PEARSON, Diane, Administrator, Cook County North Shore Hospital, Grand Marais, MN, p. A225

PEARSON, Gerald P., President, Provena Health, Frankfort, IL, p. B126

PEARSON, Robert S., Administrator, Littleton Regional Hospital, Littleton, NH, p. A269

PEARSON, Roger W., Administrator, Ellsworth County Hospital, Ellsworth, KS, p. A158

PECEVICH, Mark, M.D., Superintendent, Spring Grove Hospital Center, Baltimore, MD, p. A194

PECK, Gary V., Chief Executive Officer, St. Joseph's Hospital, Chewelah, WA, p. A445

PECK, Richard H., Administrator, Eliza Coffee Memorial Hospital, Florence, AL, p. A14

PECK, Theresa
President and Chief Executive Officer, Catholic Health Partners, Chicago, IL, p. B79
President and Chief Executive Officer, Columbus Hospital, Chicago, IL, p. A122
President and Chief Executive Officer, Saint Anthony Hospital, Chicago, IL, p. A124
President and Chief Executive Officer, St. Joseph Hospital, Chicago, IL, p. A124

PEDERSEN, Connie, Interim Administrator, Johnston Memorial Hospital, Tishomingo, OK, p. A342

PEDERSEN, William L., Chief Executive Officer, St. Peter Regional Treatment Center, Saint Peter, MN, p. A230

PEDNEAU, Michael S., Director, Dorothea Dix Hospital, Raleigh, NC, p. A311

PEED, Nancy, Administrator, Peach Regional Medical Center, Fort Valley, GA, p. A106

PEEK, Scott, Administrator, Chambers Memorial Hospital, Danville, AR, p. A30

PEEPLES, Lewis T., Chief Executive Officer, Jennie Stuart Medical Center, Hopkinsville, KY, p. A171

PEICKERT, Barbara A., R.N., Chief Executive Officer, Hayward Area Memorial Hospital and Nursing Home, Hayward, WI, p. A460

PELHAM, Judith, President and Chief Executive Officer, Mercy Health Services, Farmington Hills, MI, p. B118

PELLEGRINO, Cynthia Miller, Director and Chief Executive Officer, Western Maryland Center, Hagerstown, MD, p. A196

PELLETIER, Nancy, Interim Administrator, Charles A. Dean Memorial Hospital, Greenville, ME, p. A190

PELLEY, Catherine M., President and Chief Executive Officer, St. Mary Regional Medical Center, Apple Valley, CA, p. A36

PELTZ, Brian, Site Leader, Oakwood Hospital Seaway Center, Trenton, MI, p. A220

PELUSO, Joseph J., President and Chief Executive Officer, Westmoreland Regional Hospital, Greensburg, PA, p. A354

PEMBERTON, Thomas Paul, Chief Executive Officer, Tallahassee Community Hospital, Tallahassee, FL, p. A97

PENLAND, Victoria M.
Administrator and Chief Operating Officer, Palomar Medical Center, Escondido, CA, p. A42
President and Chief Executive Officer, Palomar Pomerado Health System, San Diego, CA, p. B124

PENNINGTON, David N., Chief Executive Officer, Veterans Affairs Medical Center, Huntington, WV, p. A454

PENRY, L. Allen, Chief Executive Officer, Castleview Hospital, Price, UT, p. A431

PENTICOFF, Michael, Administrator, Mid Dakota Hospital, Chamberlain, SD, p. A378

PENTZ, Thomas R.
Chief Executive Officer, Atlantic Medical Center–Daytona, Daytona Beach, FL, p. A83
Chief Executive Officer, Atlantic Medical Center–Ormond, Ormond Beach, FL, p. A93

PEPPER, H. L. Perry, President, Chester County Hospital, West Chester, PA, p. A367

PERDUE, Edward A., Administrator, Coffee Medical Center, Manchester, TN, p. A389

PEREZ, Carlos, Executive Director, Bellevue Hospital Center, New York, NY, p. A291

PEREZ, Francisco J., President and Chief Executive Officer, Kettering Medical Center, Kettering, OH, p. A328

PEREZ, George, Executive Vice President and Chief Operating Officer, Walter O. Boswell Memorial Hospital, Sun City, AZ, p. A26

PERFETTO, Patricia, MSN, Executive Director, Willough at Naples, Naples, FL, p. A91

PERIALAS–GRADY, Sophia, Chief Executive Officer, Atlantic Shores Hospital, Fort Lauderdale, FL, p. A84

PERKINS, Gary A., President and Chief Executive Officer, Children's Hospital, Omaha, NE, p. A262

PERMETTI, Thomas, Administrator, St. John Hospital, Nassau Bay, TX, p. A419

PERNAU, James O., Administrator, Sterling Regional Medcenter, Sterling, CO, p. A73

PERRA, Connie Oliverson, Director, Tarrant County Psychiatric Center, Fort Worth, TX, p. A407

PERREAULT, Robert A., Director, Veterans Affairs Medical Center, Decatur, GA, p. A105

PERRY, Alan S., Director, Veterans Affairs Roseburg Healthcare System, Roseburg, OR, p. A348

PERRY, George H., Ph.D., Chief Executive Officer, Bayou Oaks Behavioral Health System, Houma, LA, p. A181

PERRY, Matthew J., Director, Carilion Franklin Memorial Hospital, Rocky Mount, VA, p. A443

PERRY, Michael J., Chief Executive Officer, Charter Behavioral Health System of Northwest Indiana, Hobart, IN, p. A140

PERRY, Mike, Chief Executive Officer, Westbridge Treatment Center, Phoenix, AZ, p. A25

PERRY, Ronald J., Chief Executive Officer, Columbia Ashley Valley Medical Center, Vernal, UT, p. A433

PERRYMAN, Margaret, Chief Executive Officer, Gillette Children's Specialty Healthcare, Saint Paul, MN, p. A230

PERRYMAN, Mike, Administrator, Baptist Memorial Hospital–Union City, Union City, TN, p. A393

PERSICHILLI, Judith M., President and Chief Executive Officer, St. Francis Medical Center, Trenton, NJ, p. A278

PERUSHEK, John, Administrator, Bloomer Community Memorial Hospital and the MapleWood, Bloomer, WI, p. A458

PETASNICK, William D., President, Froedtert Memorial Lutheran Hospital, Milwaukee, WI, p. A462

PETER, John P., Chief Executive Officer, National Hospital for Kids in Crisis, Orefield, PA, p. A359

PETERS, Anthony, Chief Executive Officer, Camden County Health Services Center, Blackwood, NJ, p. A271

PETERS, Curtis A., Chief Executive Officer, J. D. McCarty Center for Children With Developmental Disabilities, Norman, OK, p. A339

PETERS, Douglas S., President and Chief Executive Officer, Jefferson Health System, Wayne, PA, p. B110

PETERS, J. Robert, Executive Director, Memorial Hospital, Colorado Springs, CO, p. A68

PETERSEN, Gary L., Administrator, Crawford County Memorial Hospital, Denison, IA, p. A149

PETERSEN, Keith J., Chief Executive Officer, PHS Mt. Sinai Medical Center East, Richmond Heights, OH, p. A331

PETERSEN, Thomas A., Vice President and Chief Operating Officer, Mercy General Hospital, Sacramento, CA, p. A58

PETERSON, Andrew E.
President and Chief Executive Officer, Faxton Hospital, Utica, NY, p. A302
President and Chief Executive Officer, St. Luke's Memorial Hospital Center, Utica, NY, p. A302

PETERSON, Brent A., Administrator, Cherry County Hospital, Valentine, NE, p. A264

PETERSON, Bruce D., Administrator, Mercer County Hospital, Aledo, IL, p. A120

PETERSON, Clayton R., President, Long Prairie Memorial Hospital and Home, Long Prairie, MN, p. A226

PETERSON, David A., President and Chief Executive Officer, Aroostook Medical Center, Presque Isle, ME, p. A191

PETERSON, Douglas R., President and Chief Executive Officer, Chippewa Valley Hospital and Oakview Care Center, Durand, WI, p. A458

PETERSON, Leland W., President and Chief Executive Officer, Sun Health Corporation, Sun City, AZ, p. B142

PETERSON, Michael J., Interim President and Chief Executive Officer, Mercy Health Services–North, Cadillac, MI, p. A209

PETERSON, Patricia, President and Chief Executive Officer, St. Mary's Hospital, Passaic, NJ, p. A276

PETERSON, Randy, President and Chief Executive Officer, Salina Regional Health Center, Salina, KS, p. A165

PETERSON, Richard H., President and Chief Executive Officer, Swedish Health Services, Seattle, WA, p. A449

PETERSON, Robert M., Administrator, Bingham Memorial Hospital, Blackfoot, ID, p. A116

PETERSON, Ronald R.
President, Johns Hopkins Bayview Medical Center, Baltimore, MD, p. A193
President, Johns Hopkins Health System, Baltimore, MD, p. B111
President, Johns Hopkins Hospital, Baltimore, MD, p. A193

PETERSON, William D., Administrator, Herington Municipal Hospital, Herington, KS, p. A160

PETIK, Jason, Administrator, Custer Community Hospital, Custer, SD, p. A378

PETIT Jr., Leo A., Chief Executive Officer, Bladen County Hospital, Elizabethtown, NC, p. A307

PETRE, Patrick A., Chief Executive Officer, San Dimas Community Hospital, San Dimas, CA, p. A60

PETRILLO, Richard L., M.D., Executive Director, Mount Vernon Hospital, Mount Vernon, NY, p. A291

PETRUZZI, Peter T., Chief Executive Officer, Scott County Hospital, Oneida, TN, p. A392

PETTIGREW, Dennis, Interim President and Chief Executive Officer, Erlanger Health System, Chattanooga, TN, p. A384

PETTINGILL, Richard R.
Administrator, Kaiser Foundation Hospital, San Francisco, CA, p. A60
Administrator, Kaiser Foundation Hospital, San Rafael, CA, p. A62
Administrator, Kaiser Foundation Hospital, South San Francisco, CA, p. A64

PETTRY, Harvey H., President and Chief Executive Officer, Richland Memorial Hospital, Olney, IL, p. A132

PEZZOLI, Robert E., President and Chief Executive Officer, St. Agnes Healthcare, Baltimore, MD, p. A194

PFEFFER, Jennifer D., Administrator and Chief Executive Officer, Minnesota Valley Health Center, Le Sueur, MN, p. A226

PFEIFFER, James A.
Chief Administrative Officer, Mease Countryside Hospital, Safety Harbor, FL, p. A95
Vice President and Chief Operating Officer, Mease Hospital Dunedin, Dunedin, FL, p. A84

PFITZER, Anthony D., Administrator, St. Anthony's Memorial Hospital, Effingham, IL, p. A126

PHAUP, Michael B., Director, Veterans Affairs Medical Center, Durham, NC, p. A307

PHELPS, David E., President and Chief Executive Officer, Berkshire Health Systems, Inc., Pittsfield, MA, p. B72

PHELPS, M. Randell, Administrator, Memorial Hospital, Craig, CO, p. A69

PHEMISTER, Gladys, Administrator, Gordon Memorial Hospital District, Gordon, NE, p. A260

PHILIPS III, Grady W., Vice President and Administrator, Riverside Walter Reed Hospital, Gloucester, VA, p. A438

PHILLIPS, Andrew J., Ed.D., Superintendent, Cedarcrest Hospital, Newington, CT, p. A76

PHILLIPS, Arthur J., Administrator, Caribou Memorial Hospital and Nursing Home, Soda Springs, ID, p. A118

PHILLIPS, Bob D., Administrator, Skaggs Community Health Center, Branson, MO, p. A241

PHILLIPS, Dennis, Chief Executive Officer, Frye Regional Medical Center, Hickory, NC, p. A309

PHILLIPS, John F., Administrator, Gravette Medical Center Hospital, Gravette, AR, p. A31

PHILLIPS, John J., Director, Veterans Affairs Medical Center, Omaha, NE, p. A263

PHILLIPS, Randall, President and Chief Executive Officer, Princeton Hospital, Orlando, FL, p. A93

PICHE, William K., Chief Executive Officer, Good Samaritan Hospital, San Jose, CA, p. A61

PICKMAN, Serena, Administrator, Columbia Behavioral Center, El Paso, TX, p. A405

PIEPER, Blaine, Administrator, Ohio County Hospital, Hartford, KY, p. A171

PIERCE, Michelle, Interim Administrator, Lindsay Municipal Hospital, Lindsay, OK, p. A338

PIERCE, Peggy, Administrator, Calhoun Memorial Hospital, Arlington, GA, p. A100

PIERCE, Randolph J., President and Chief Executive Officer, Boca Raton Community Hospital, Boca Raton, FL, p. A81

PIERCE Jr., Willard R., Director, Piedmont Geriatric Hospital, Burkeville, VA, p. A436

PIERETTI, Larry, President and Chief Executive Officer, Southwest Florida Regional Medical Center, Fort Myers, FL, p. A85

PIERROT, Alan H., M.D., Chief Executive Officer, Fresno Surgery Center–The Hospital for Surgery, Fresno, CA, p. A43

PIERSON, Richard, Executive Director, Clinical Programs, University Hospital of Arkansas, Little Rock, AR, p. A33

PIERSON, Stephen C., Ph.D., Chief Executive Officer, Appalachian Psychiatric Healthcare System, Cambridge, OH, p. A321

PIFER, George, President, Feather River Hospital, Paradise, CA, p. A55

PIGNATORE, John E., President and Chief Executive Officer, Corning Hospital, Corning, NY, p. A287

PILE, Darrell L., Administrator, HEALTHSOUTH Rehabilitation Hospital, Humble, TX, p. A413

PILGRIM, Patsy, Chief Executive Officer, Weeks Memorial Hospital, Lancaster, NH, p. A269

PILKINGTON III, Albert, Administrator and Chief Executive Officer, Mena Medical Center, Mena, AR, p. A33

PILLA, Felix M., President, Abington Memorial Hospital, Abington, PA, p. A349

PINCKNEY, Frank D., President, Greenville Hospital System, Greenville, SC, p. B103

PINE, Polly, Administrator, Cibola General Hospital, Grants, NM, p. A282

PINE, Richard M., President and Chief Executive Officer, Livengrin Foundation, Bensalem, PA, p. A350

PINEIRO, Carlos M., President, Hospital Interamericano De Medicina Avanzada, Caguas, PR, p. A472

PINKERMAN, Charles F., Administrator, Madison Community Hospital, Madison Heights, MI, p. A215

PINKHAM, Margaret G., President and Chief Executive Officer, St. Andrews Hospital and Healthcare Center, Boothbay Harbor, ME, p. A189

PINSKY, William, M.D., Senior Vice President and Regional Executive, Sinai Hospital, Detroit, MI, p. A211

PIPICELLI, Thomas P., President and Chief Executive Officer, William W. Backus Hospital, Norwich, CT, p. A76

PIPKIN, Barry, Chief Executive Officer and Managing Director, Bridgeway, North Little Rock, AR, p. A34

PIRIZ, J. E., Administrator, Memorial Hospital Pembroke, Pembroke Pines, FL, p. A94

PITCHFORD, Harold, Executive Director, Porterville Developmental Center, Porterville, CA, p. A56

PITMAN, Richard A., President, Shore Memorial Hospital, Somers Point, NJ, p. A277

PITTMAN, Deanna, Administrator, Wilson County Hospital, Neodesha, KS, p. A163

PIVIROTTO, Gregory A., President and Chief Executive Officer, University Medical Center, Tucson, AZ, p. A27

PLANTIER, Anthony J., Administrator, Artesia General Hospital, Artesia, NM, p. A281

PLATOU, Kenneth E. S., Chief Executive Officer, North Valley Hospital, Whitefish, MT, p. A257

PLATT, Anne, Administrator, East Morgan County Hospital, Brush, CO, p. A68

PLATT, C. James, Administrator, Fort Madison Community Hospital, Fort Madison, IA, p. A151

PLATT, Melvin J., Administrator, Worthington Regional Hospital, Worthington, MN, p. A232

PLESKOW, Leonard, Chairman, Brylin Hospitals, Buffalo, NY, p. A285

PLOWDEN, Moultrie D., CHE, President, Randolph County Hospital, Roanoke, AL, p. A18

PLUMAGE, Charles D., Director, U. S. Public Health Service Indian Hospital, Harlem, MT, p. A255

PLUMMER, Josh, Administrator, Calhoun–Liberty Hospital, Blountstown, FL, p. A81

POASTER, Larry B., Ph.D., Director, Stanislaus Behavioral Health Center, Modesto, CA, p. A52

PODIETZ, Frank, President, Friedman Hospital of the Home for the Jewish Aged, Philadelphia, PA, p. A360

PODLEY, Sandy, Chief Executive Officer, Copper Hills Youth Center, West Jordan, UT, p. A433

POEHLING, Jerry, Interim Administrator, Spencer Municipal Hospital, Spencer, IA, p. A155

POHLY, Pamela, Administrator, Craig House Center, Beacon, NY, p. A285

POHREN, Allen E., Administrator, Montgomery County Memorial Hospital, Red Oak, IA, p. A154

POKORNEY, Georgia, Chief Executive Officer, Pioneer Memorial Hospital, Viborg, SD, p. A381

POLAHAR, Robert G., Chief Executive Officer, Knox Community Hospital, Mount Vernon, OH, p. A330

POLGE, David J., President and Chief Executive Officer, Delaware Valley Hospital, Walton, NY, p. A302

POLHEBER, Richard, Chief Executive Officer, Page Hospital, Page, AZ, p. A24

POLL, Max, President and Chief Executive Officer, Scottsdale Healthcare, Scottsdale, AZ, p. B135

POLLA, Dale E., Administrator, Harms Memorial Hospital District, American Falls, ID, p. A116

POLLARD Jr., Joe W., Administrator, Alexander Community Hospital, Taylorsville, NC, p. A314

POLLOCK, Rusty, President and Chief Executive Officer, Rehabilitation Institute at Santa Barbara, Santa Barbara, CA, p. A62

POLUNAS, David M., Administrator and Chief Executive Officer, Heart of Florida Behavioral Center, Lakeland, FL, p. A88

POMA, Frank W., President, River District Hospital, East China, MI, p. A211

POOLE, Karen, Interim Chief Executive Officer, San Clemente Hospital and Medical Center, San Clemente, CA, p. A59

POOR, George W., President and Chief Executive Officer, Memorial Hospital, Logansport, IN, p. A143

POORTEN, Kevin P., Vice President and Chief Executive Officer, Havasu Samaritan Regional Hospital, Lake Havasu City, AZ, p. A23

POPE, James W., Chief Executive Officer, Orange County Hospital, Paoli, IN, p. A144

POPIEL, Gary W., Executive Vice President and Chief Executive Officer, Bi–County Community Hospital, Warren, MI, p. A220

POPP, Dennis A., Administrator and Chief Executive Officer, Community Memorial Hospital, Enumclaw, WA, p. A446

POQUETTE, Gary R., FACHE, Executive Director, Memorial Hospital, North Conway, NH, p. A269

PORTEN, Hank J., President, Holyoke Hospital, Holyoke, MA, p. A203

PORTER, Greg, Administrator and Chief Executive Officer, Cordova Community Medical Center, Cordova, AK, p. A20

PORTER, Janet, President and Chief Executive Officer, Methodist Women's and Children's Hospital, San Antonio, TX, p. A422

PORTER, John T., President and Chief Executive Officer, Avera Health, Yankton, SD, p. B68

PORTER, Robert G., President, DePaul Health Center, Saint Louis, MO, p. A249

PORTER, Ronald W., Chief Executive Officer, U.S. FamilyCare Medical Center, Montclair, CA, p. A53

PORTER, Thomas C., President, Morton Hospital and Medical Center, Taunton, MA, p. A206

PORTER Jr., John M., President, Ephrata Community Hospital, Ephrata, PA, p. A353

PORTEUS, Robert W., President and Chief Executive Officer, Carlinville Area Hospital, Carlinville, IL, p. A121

PORTFLEET, Lori, Chief Executive Officer, Kent Community Hospital, Grand Rapids, MI, p. A212

POSEY, M. Kenneth, FACHE, Administrator, Jasper General Hospital, Bay Springs, MS, p. A233

POSTON, Stuart, President, Murray–Calloway County Hospital, Murray, KY, p. A175

POTEETE, Kenneth W., President and Chief Executive Officer, Georgetown Healthcare System, Georgetown, TX, p. A408

POTTENGER, Jay
    Administrator, Missouri River Medical Center, Fort Benton, MT, p. A254
    Administrator, Teton Medical Center, Choteau, MT, p. A253

POTTER, Bruce C., President, Canton–Potsdam Hospital, Potsdam, NY, p. A299

POTTER, Michael S., President and Chief Executive Officer, Westwood Medical Center, Midland, TX, p. A418

POTTER, Terri L., President and Chief Executive Officer, Meriter Hospital, Madison, WI, p. A461

POURIER, Terry, Service Unit Director, U. S. Public Health Service Indian Hospital, Fort Yates, ND, p. A317

POWELL, Darnell, Executive Director, Rolling Hills Hospital, Ada, OK, p. A335

POWELL, Denny W., Chief Executive Officer, Columbia Medical Center Phoenix, Phoenix, AZ, p. A24

POWELL, Ricky, Chief Executive Officer, Red River Hospital, Wichita Falls, TX, p. A428

POWELL, Roy A., President, Frankford Hospital of the City of Philadelphia, Philadelphia, PA, p. A360

POWELL Jr., Boone, President, Baylor Health Care System, Dallas, TX, p. B70

POWERS, L. Darrell, Senior Vice President, Lynchburg General Hospital, Lynchburg, VA, p. A439

POWERS, Michael K., Administrator, Fairbanks Memorial Hospital, Fairbanks, AK, p. A20

POWERS, Terry C., Administrator, Fort Logan Hospital, Stanford, KY, p. A177

PRASAD, Manoj K., M.D., Chief Executive Officer, Kern Hospital and Medical Center, Warren, MI, p. A220

PRESLAR Jr., Len B., President and Chief Executive Officer, North Carolina Baptist Hospital, Winston–Salem, NC, p. A315

PRESSLEY, Yvonne A., Chief Executive Officer, Ancora Psychiatric Hospital, Ancora, NJ, p. A271

PRESTON, Craig, Chief Executive Officer, Lakeview Hospital, Bountiful, UT, p. A430

PRIBYL, Stephen J., USAF, Administrator, Scott Medical Center, Scott AFB, IL, p. A134

PRICE, Corbett A., Chief Executive Officer, Interfaith Medical Center, New York, NY, p. A293

PRICE, Floyd N., Administrator, Grove Hill Memorial Hospital, Grove Hill, AL, p. A15

PRICE, Norman M., FACHE, Administrator, Southwest Mississippi Regional Medical Center, McComb, MS, p. A237

PRICE, William E., Interim Administrator, Parkview Regional Hospital, Mexia, TX, p. A417

PRICE Jr., Eston, Administrator, Evans Memorial Hospital, Claxton, GA, p. A103

PRICE Jr., Warren T.
    Chief Executive Officer, East Louisiana State Hospital, Jackson, LA, p. A181
    Chief Executive Officer, Greenwell Springs Hospital, Greenwell Springs, LA, p. A181

PRICKETT, Thomas H., President and Chief Executive Officer, Suburban General Hospital, Pittsburgh, PA, p. A363

PRIDDY, Sandra D., President, Stokes–Reynolds Memorial Hospital, Danbury, NC, p. A306

PRIDGEN Jr., Lee, Administrator, Sampson Regional Medical Center, Clinton, NC, p. A306

PRIMEAUX, Elizabeth A., Chief Executive Officer, Greater El Monte Community Hospital, South El Monte, CA, p. A64

PRIMROSE, Gayle E., Administrator, Boone County Health Center, Albion, NE, p. A258

PRISCO, Nicholas A., Chief Executive Officer, Sunbury Community Hospital, Sunbury, PA, p. A366

PRISELAC, Thomas M., President and Chief Executive Officer, Cedars–Sinai Medical Center, Los Angeles, CA, p. A48

PRISTER, James Richard, President, R. M. Specialty Hospital, Hinsdale, IL, p. A128

PRITCHARD, Eugene, President, Condell Medical Center, Libertyville, IL, p. A130

PRITCHETT, Beverly, Executive Officer, Department of the Army, Office of the Surgeon General, Falls Church, VA, p. B94

PROBST, Randall K., Administrator, Wasatch County Hospital, Heber City, UT, p. A430

PROCHILO, John F., Chief Executive Officer and Administrator, Northeast Rehabilitation Hospital, Salem, NH, p. A270

PROCTOR, Randy, Superintendent, Osawatomie State Hospital, Osawatomie, KS, p. A163

PROPHIT, Alice M., Chief Executive Officer, North Louisiana Rehabilitation Hospital, Ruston, LA, p. A186

PROUT, John S.
President and Chief Executive Officer, Bethesda Hospital, Inc., Cincinnati, OH, p. B72
President and Chief Executive Officer, Bethesda North Hospital, Cincinnati, OH, p. A322

PROVENZANO, William, President, Ohio Valley General Hospital, McKees Rocks, PA, p. A357

PRUITT, Mike, Administrator, Arbuckle Memorial Hospital, Sulphur, OK, p. A342

PRUSAK, Thomas K., President, St. Joseph's Medical Center, Brainerd, MN, p. A223

PRYCE, Richard J., President, Aultman Hospital, Canton, OH, p. A321

PRYOR, Curtis R.
Administrator, Jefferson County Hospital, Waurika, OK, p. A343
Administrator, Purcell Municipal Hospital, Purcell, OK, p. A341

PRYOR, Dennis P., Administrator, Salem Memorial District Hospital, Salem, MO, p. A250

PUCKETT, Ralph A., USN, Commanding Officer, Naval Hospital, Patuxent River, MD, p. A197

PUGH, Richard E., President and Chief Executive Officer, New Milford Hospital, New Milford, CT, p. A76

PUGH, Thomas E., Vice President Rehabilitation Services, John Heinz Institute of Rehabilitation Medicine, Wilkes–Barre, PA, p. A367

PUGLISI Jr., Frank J., Executive Director, Contra Costa Regional Medical Center, Martinez, CA, p. A52

PULLMAN, Jay, Chief Executive Officer, Rehabilitation Hospital of Baton Rouge, Baton Rouge, LA, p. A179

PULSIPHER, Gary W., Chief Executive Officer, Breech Medical Center, Lebanon, MO, p. A246

PUNG, Dawn S., Administrator, Kau Hospital, Pahala, HI, p. A115

PURCELL Jr., Howard J., President, Community Memorial Hospital, Cheboygan, MI, p. A209

PURVIS, Jay, Acting Chief Executive Officer, Fairfield Memorial Hospital, Fairfield, IL, p. A127

PURVIS, Mildred W., Administrator, Hope Hospital, Lockhart, SC, p. A375

PUTNAM, Larry E., Administrator, Phillips County Medical Center, Malta, MT, p. A255

PUTNAM, Stewart, President, St. Mary's Hospital, Rochester, NY, p. A299

PUTTER, Joshua, Executive Director, Medical Center of Southeastern Oklahoma, Durant, OK, p. A337

PYLE, Joseph, Administrator, Meadow Wood Behavioral Health System, New Castle, DE, p. A78

PYLE Jr., Bert W., Director, Elmira Psychiatric Center, Elmira, NY, p. A287

PYNE, Mel, Administrator, Providence General Medical Center, Everett, WA, p. A446

Q

QUAGLIATA, Joseph A., Chief Administrative Officer, South Nassau Communities Hospital, Oceanside, NY, p. A297

QUAM, Mark, Executive Director, Brown County Mental Health Center, Green Bay, WI, p. A459

QUAYE, Beverly, Administrator, Tustin Rehabilitation Hospital, Tustin, CA, p. A65

QUIGLEY, T. Richard, President and Chief Executive Officer, Youville Lifecare, Cambridge, MA, p. A202

QUINLAN, Richard S., President and Chief Executive Officer, Hallmark Health System, Melrose, MA, p. A204

QUINLIVAN, Thomas J.
Administrator, Tracy Area Medical Services, Tracy, MN, p. A231
Administrator, Westbrook Health Center, Westbrook, MN, p. A232

QUINN, J. Clifton, Administrator, Stone County Hospital, Wiggins, MS, p. A240

QUINN, Robert G., FACHE, Administrator, U. S. Air Force Hospital, Beale AFB, CA, p. A37

QUINTANILLA, Robert, Chief Executive Officer, Charter Real Behavioral Health System, San Antonio, TX, p. A422

QUINTON, Byron, Administrator, Humboldt General Hospital, Winnemucca, NV, p. A267

QUIST, Robert L., Chief Executive Officer, Park Plaza Hospital, Houston, TX, p. A412

R

RAAB, Daniel J., President and Chief Executive Officer, St. Vincent Memorial Hospital, Taylorville, IL, p. A135

RABNER, Barry S., President, Bryn Mawr Rehabilitation Hospital, Malvern, PA, p. A357

RABUKA, Mickey, Administrator, Murray Medical Center, Chatsworth, GA, p. A103

RACE, J. E., Administrator and Chief Executive Officer, Lakeview Hospital, Wauwatosa, WI, p. A467

RAFFERTY, Patrick W., Administrator, Doctors Hospital of Manteca, Manteca, CA, p. A52

RAFTER, William A., Director, Julian F. Keith Alcohol and Drug Abuse Treatment Center, Black Mountain, NC, p. A304

RAGGHIANTI, Eugene, Administrator, Methodist Hospital of Lexington, Lexington, TN, p. A388

RAGLAND, James H., Administrator, Marengo Memorial Hospital, Marengo, IA, p. A152

RAGLAND, Kenneth E., Administrator, Beaufort County Hospital, Washington, NC, p. A314

RAHN, Douglas L., Chief Executive Officer, Community Health Center of Branch County, Coldwater, MI, p. A210

RAJNIC, Sharon J., Administrator, Shriners Hospitals for Children, Philadelphia, Philadelphia, PA, p. A361

RAK, Arlene A., R.N., President, UHHS Bedford Medical Center, Bedford, OH, p. A321

RALEY, Ana, Administrator, Hadley Memorial Hospital, Washington, DC, p. A79

RALPH, Chandler M., Chief Executive Officer, Adirondack Medical Center, Saranac Lake, NY, p. A300

RALPH, Stephen A., President and Chief Executive Officer, Huntington Memorial Hospital, Pasadena, CA, p. A55

RAMIREZ, Magdalena, Chief Executive Officer, Helen Hayes Hospital, West Haverstraw, NY, p. A303

RAMISH, Dana W., President and Chief Executive Officer, Allegheny University Hospitals, Forbes Regional, Monroeville, PA, p. A358

RAMPAGE, Bruce E., President and Chief Executive Officer, Saint Anthony Memorial Health Centers, Michigan City, IN, p. A143

RAMSAY, John, Administrator, Warren Memorial Hospital, Friend, NE, p. A260

RAMSEY, Barbara, Ph.D., Chief Executive Officer, Lincoln Regional Center, Lincoln, NE, p. A261

RANDALL, Kenneth W., Chief Executive Officer, Scenic Mountain Medical Center, Big Spring, TX, p. A398

RANDALL, Malcom, Director, Veterans Affairs Medical Center, Gainesville, FL, p. A86

RANEY, James Edward, President and Chief Executive Officer, United Health Group, Appleton, WI, p. B148

RANGE, Richard L., Administrator, Baldwin Hospital, Baldwin, WI, p. A457

RANGE, Robert P., President and Chief Executive Officer, Grace Hospital, Cleveland, OH, p. A323

RANK, James T., Administrator, Bothwell Regional Health Center, Sedalia, MO, p. A251

RANKIN III, Fred M., President and Chief Executive Officer, Mary Washington Hospital, Fredericksburg, VA, p. A438

RANSDELL, Hart, Chief Executive Officer, Jupiter Medical Center, Jupiter, FL, p. A88

RANSDELL, Lewis A., Administrator, Vencor Hospital–Fort Lauderdale, Fort Lauderdale, FL, p. A85

RAPAPORT, Gary D., Chief Executive Officer, Sutter Tracy Community Hospital, Tracy, CA, p. A65

RAPOPORT, Morton I., M.D., President and Chief Executive Officer, University of Maryland Medical System, Baltimore, MD, p. A194

RAPP, Larry, Chief Medical and Executive Officer, Grant County Health Center, Elbow Lake, MN, p. A224

RAPP, Phillip J., President and Chief Executive Officer, St. Francis at Salina, Salina, KS, p. A165

RASH, Marty, President and Chief Executive Officer, Province Healthcare Corporation, Brentwood, TN, p. B126

RASMUSSEN, David D., Administrator, OMH Medical Center, Okmulgee, OK, p. A340

RASMUSSEN, Kyle, Administrator, Bridges Medical Services, Ada, MN, p. A222

RASMUSSEN, William C., Administrator, Valley Community Hospital, Santa Maria, CA, p. A63

RATHBONE, Thomas A., President and Chief Executive Officer, Health Hill Hospital for Children, Cleveland, OH, p. A323

RAU, John, President, Stevens Community Medical Center, Morris, MN, p. A228

RAY, K. Dwayne, Administrator and Chief Executive Officer, Garland Community Hospital, Garland, TX, p. A408

RAY, William K., President and Chief Executive Officer, Wesley Medical Center, Hattiesburg, MS, p. A235

RAYNOR, James E., Chief Executive Officer, Raleigh Community Hospital, Raleigh, NC, p. A311

READ, J. Larry, President, St. Luke's Hospital, Jacksonville, FL, p. A87

READ, Timothy A., Administrator, Morris County Hospital, Council Grove, KS, p. A158

REAMER, Roger, Administrator, Butler County Health Care Center, David City, NE, p. A259

REAMEY, Kirk, Administrator, Magnolia Hospital, Magnolia, AR, p. A33

REARDON, Robert, Hospital Services Administrator, Central Prison Hospital, Raleigh, NC, p. A311

REARDON, Timothy F., FACHE, Chief Executive Officer, Yuma District Hospital, Yuma, CO, p. A73

REASBECK, Suzanne, President and Chief Executive Officer, Flaget Memorial Hospital, Bardstown, KY, p. A168

REAVES, Nancy, Chief Executive Officer, Charter Greensboro Behavioral Health System, Greensboro, NC, p. A308

REBER, James P., President, St. Rita's Medical Center, Lima, OH, p. A328

REDDISH, Robert R., Administrator and Chief Executive Officer, Chicot Memorial Hospital, Lake Village, AR, p. A32

REDDOCH Jr., James F., Director, Bryce Hospital, Tuscaloosa, AL, p. A18

REECE, David A., President, MidMichigan Medical Center–Midland, Midland, MI, p. A216

REECE, Kelly, Facility Manager, Garden County Hospital, Oshkosh, NE, p. A263

REECE, Morris D., Administrator, Carilion Giles Memorial Hospital, Pearisburg, VA, p. A441

REECER, Jeff, Chief Executive Officer, D. M. Cogdell Memorial Hospital, Snyder, TX, p. A425

REED, Harold, Administrator, Fayette Medical Center, Fayette, AL, p. A14

REED, Jan A., CPA, Administrator and Chief Executive Officer, Electra Memorial Hospital, Electra, TX, p. A406

REED, Joy, R.N., Administrator, Ottawa County Health Center, Minneapolis, KS, p. A163

REED, Robert J., President, Mid–Island Hospital, Bethpage, NY, p. A285

REED, Ronald R., President and Chief Executive Officer, Mercy Hospital, Iowa City, IA, p. A151

REED, Steven B., President and Chief Executive Officer, Columbia Women's Hospital–Indianapolis, Indianapolis, IN, p. A141

REED, Timothy A., Administrator, Kaiser Foundation Hospital–Bellflower, Bellflower, CA, p. A37

REEDER, Steve, Chief Executive Officer, Helena Regional Medical Center, Helena, AR, p. A31

REEK, Thomas F., Chief Executive Officer, Cuyuna Regional Medical Center, Crosby, MN, p. A224

REES, Ron R., President and Chief Executive Officer, Halifax Community Health System, Daytona Beach, FL, p. A83

REESE, James, CHE, Administrator, Stephens Memorial Hospital, Breckenridge, TX, p. A399

REESE, Sandra, Administrator, Lower Umpqua Hospital District, Reedsport, OR, p. A348

REESE, Willis L., Administrator, Falls Community Hospital and Clinic, Marlin, TX, p. A417

REEVES, Luther E., Chief Executive Officer, Appling Healthcare System, Baxley, GA, p. A102

REEVES, Stephen C., Superintendent, Fulton State Hospital, Fulton, MO, p. A243

REGAN, James, Ph.D., Chief Executive Officer, Hudson River Psychiatric Center, Poughkeepsie, NY, p. A299

REGEHR, Stan, President and Chief Executive Officer, Memorial Hospital, McPherson, KS, p. A162

REGLING, Anne M., Regional Executive, Grace Hospital, Detroit, MI, p. A210

REGNER, Steven H., Commander, U. S. Air Force Hospital, Hill AFB, UT, p. A430

REIBER, Doug, Administrator, Kearney County Community Hospital, Minden, NE, p. A261

REID, David M., Administrator, Clay County Medical Center, West Point, MS, p. A240

REIF, Richard A., President and Chief Executive Officer, Doylestown Hospital, Doylestown, PA, p. A352

REINER, Steven S., Administrator, Kearny County Hospital, Lakin, KS, p. A161

REINERTSEN, James, M.D., Chief Executive Officer, CareGroup, Boston, MA, p. B75

REINHARD, James S., M.D., Director, Catawba Hospital, Catawba, VA, p. A436

REINHARDT, J. Rudy, Administrator, Hendry Regional Medical Center, Clewiston, FL, p. A83

REINITZ, Marlyn, Administrator, Community Memorial Hospital, Humboldt, NE, p. A260

REITER, Steven B., Administrator, Shriners Hospitals for Children, Houston, Houston, TX, p. A412

REITINGER, Thomas A., President and Chief Executive Officer, Mercy Hospital Medical Center, Des Moines, IA, p. A150

REKER, Douglas J., Administrator and Chief Executive Officer, Glacial Ridge Hospital, Glenwood, MN, p. A225

REMBIS, Michael A., FACHE, Chief Executive Officer, John F. Kennedy Memorial Hospital, Indio, CA, p. A45

REMBOLDT, Darwin R., President and Chief Executive Officer, Hanford Community Medical Center, Hanford, CA, p. A44

REMILLARD, John R., President, Aurelia Osborn Fox Memorial Hospital, Oneonta, NY, p. A298

RENANDER, Dennis J., President and Chief Executive Officer, Galesburg Cottage Hospital, Galesburg, IL, p. A127

RENFORD, Edward J., President and Chief Executive Officer, Grady Memorial Hospital, Atlanta, GA, p. A101

RENICK, Bill, Administrator, Holly Springs Memorial Hospital, Holly Springs, MS, p. A236

RENNER, Steven W., President and Chief Executive Officer, Gettysburg Hospital, Gettysburg, PA, p. A354

RENNIE, Robert J., Administrator, U. S. Air Force Hospital, Grand Forks AFB, ND, p. A317

RENSHAU, Dee, Administrator, Integris Grove General Hospital, Grove, OK, p. A337

RENTAS, Roberto A., Administrator, Hospital De Damas, Ponce, PR, p. A473

RENTFRO, Larry D., FACHE, Chief Executive Officer, Grant Regional Health Center, Lancaster, WI, p. A460

RENTZ, Norman G., President and Chief Executive Officer, Cannon Memorial Hospital, Pickens, SC, p. A376

RESNICK, Peter V., Executive Director, Dearborn County Hospital, Lawrenceburg, IN, p. A143

RETTALIATA, Marilyn R., President and Chief Executive Officer, Pocono Medical Center, East Stroudsburg, PA, p. A353

REVELS, Thomas R., President and Chief Executive Officer, Presbyterian Hospital, Charlotte, NC, p. A306

REX, George B., Chief Executive Officer, Pacific Gateway Hospital and Counseling Center, Portland, OR, p. A347

REYES, Arnold, Administrator, U. S. Penitentiary Infirmary, Lewisburg, PA, p. A357

REYES, Phillip W., M.D., Co–Medical Executive Director, Molokai General Hospital, Kaunakakai, HI, p. A115

REYNOLDS, Phyllis, R.N., Site Administrator, Hutzel Hospital, Detroit, MI, p. A211

REYNOLDS, Stephen Curtis
President and Chief Executive Officer, Baptist Memorial Health Care Corporation, Memphis, TN, p. B70
President and Chief Executive Officer, Baptist Memorial Hospital, Memphis, TN, p. A389

REZAC, Pamela J., President and Chief Executive Officer, Sacred Heart Health Services, Yankton, SD, p. A382

RHEAULT, Donna, Chief Operating Officer, Saint Francis Hospital, Tulsa, OK, p. A342

RHEAULT, LeRoy E., President and Chief Executive Officer, Via Christi Health System, Wichita, KS, p. B152

RHINE, Scott, Administrator and Chief Executive Officer, Lompoc District Hospital, Lompoc, CA, p. A47

RHINEHART, Jennie, Administrator, Community Hospital, Tallassee, AL, p. A18

RHOADS, Gary R., President and Chief Executive Officer, Lock Haven Hospital, Lock Haven, PA, p. A357

RHODES, J. Gary, Chief Executive Officer, Kane Community Hospital, Kane, PA, p. A356

RICCI, David A., President and Chief Executive Officer, Germantown Hospital and Medical Center, Philadelphia, PA, p. A360

RICE, Alan J., President, Simi Valley Hospital and Health Care Services, Simi Valley, CA, p. A63

RICE, David O., President, Haywood Regional Medical Center, Clyde, NC, p. A306

RICE, Kathleen A., Chief Operating Officer, Meridia South Pointe Hospital, Warrensville Heights, OH, p. A333

RICE, Thomas R., FACHE
President and Chief Operating Officer, Integris Baptist Medical Center, Oklahoma City, OK, p. A339
President and Chief Operating Officer, Integris Southwest Medical Center, Oklahoma City, OK, p. A340

RICE, Tim, President, Lakewood Health System, Staples, MN, p. A231

RICHARD, Robert J., Administrator, People's Memorial Hospital of Buchanan County, Independence, IA, p. A151

RICHARDS, Joan K.
President, Crozer–Chester Medical Center, Upland, PA, p. A366
President, Delaware County Memorial Hospital, Drexel Hill, PA, p. A353

RICHARDS, Randy R., Chief Executive Officer, Permian General Hospital, Andrews, TX, p. A395

RICHARDS, Richard M., Administrator, HEALTHSOUTH Rehabilitation Hospital of Utah, Sandy, UT, p. A433

RICHARDS, Tom, Facility Director, Choate Mental Health and Developmental Center, Anna, IL, p. A120

RICHARDSON, A. D., Administrator, Hood Memorial Hospital, Amite, LA, p. A178

RICHARDSON, Darrel C., Chief Operating Officer, Kanakanak Hospital, Dillingham, AK, p. A20

RICHARDSON, J. E., Chief Executive Officer, Savoy Medical Center, Mamou, LA, p. A183

RICHARDSON, James E., FACHE, Interim Chief Executive Officer, UniMed Medical Center, Minot, ND, p. A318

RICHARDSON, Mark D., President and Chief Executive Officer, Burlington Medical Center, Burlington, IA, p. A147

RICHARDSON, Patricia L.
President and Chief Operating Officer, Eagle River Memorial Hospital, Eagle River, WI, p. A458
President and Chief Executive Officer, Howard Young Medical Center, Woodruff, WI, p. A467

RICHARDSON, R. D., President and Chief Executive Officer, Ashtabula County Medical Center, Ashtabula, OH, p. A320

RICHARDSON, William T., President and Chief Executive Officer, Tift General Hospital, Tifton, GA, p. A112

RICHEY, Don L., Administrator, Guadalupe Valley Hospital, Seguin, TX, p. A424

RICHLE, Teresa, Interim Senior Vice President Acute Care Operations, Mercy Medical Center, Springfield, OH, p. A332

RICHMAN, Martin I., Executive Director, Community General Hospital of Sullivan County, Harris, NY, p. A288

RICHMOND, John W., President and Chief Executive Officer, Gentry County Memorial Hospital, Albany, MO, p. A241

RICHTER, Tom, Chief Executive Officer, Madison Hospital, Madison, MN, p. A227

RICKARD, Roland K., Administrator, Mitchell County Hospital, Colorado City, TX, p. A401

RICKS, Charles S., D.D.S., President and Chief Executive Officer, Boston Regional Medical Center, Stoneham, MA, p. A206

RIDDELL, Andrew J., President and Chief Executive Officer, Atlanticare Medical Center, Lynn, MA, p. A203

RIDDLE, Brian L., Chief Executive Officer, Oconee Regional Medical Center, Milledgeville, GA, p. A109

RIDDLE, Marilyn M., Chief Executive Officer, Olympus Specialty Hospital–Springfield, Springfield, MA, p. A206

RIDENOUR, Richard T., USN, Commander, National Naval Medical Center, Bethesda, MD, p. A194

RIDLEY, Keith R., Chief Executive Officer, Kahuku Hospital, Kahuku, HI, p. A114

RIEDER, James L., Chief Executive Officer, Park Medical Center, Columbus, OH, p. A325

RIEDMANN, Gary P., President and Chief Executive Officer, St. Anthony Regional Hospital, Carroll, IA, p. A147

RIEGE, Michael J., Chief Executive Officer, Virginia Gay Hospital, Vinton, IA, p. A155

RIEGER, Anne, R.N., Administrator, Elko General Hospital, Elko, NV, p. A266

RIEMER–MATUZAK, Stephanie J., Chief Operating Officer, Mercy Health Services North–Grayling, Grayling, MI, p. A213

RIES, Douglas A., President, Cardinal Glennon Children's Hospital, Saint Louis, MO, p. A249

RIES, William G., President, Lake Forest Hospital, Lake Forest, IL, p. A129

RIGDON, Henry, Executive Vice President, Northeast Georgia Medical Center, Gainesville, GA, p. A107

RIGHTER, Laura, Regional Administrator, St. John's Episcopal Hospital–Smithtown, Smithtown, NY, p. A301

RIGSBY, John P., Administrator, Garrard County Memorial Hospital, Lancaster, KY, p. A172

RILEY, Carolyn E., Chief Executive Officer, Monroe County Medical Center, Tompkinsville, KY, p. A177

RILEY, Rex, President and Chief Executive Officer, Valley Children's Hospital, Fresno, CA, p. A43

RILEY, Vernette, Administrator and Chief Executive Officer, Dallas County Hospital, Perry, IA, p. A154

RIMES, Dwight, Administrator, Ocean Springs Hospital, Ocean Springs, MS, p. A238

RINE, Thomas L., President and Chief Executive Officer, Southwestern Medical Center, Lawton, OK, p. A338

RINEHARDT, Mark, Chief Executive Officer, Lake City Hospital, Lake City, MN, p. A226

RINKER, Franklin M., President and Chief Executive Officer, Promina Gwinnett Hospital System, Lawrenceville, GA, p. A108

RIORDAN, William J., President and Chief Executive Officer, St. Vincent's Medical Center, Bridgeport, CT, p. A74

RIPPLE, Gary, Commander, Reynolds Army Community Hospital, Fort Sill, OK, p. A337

RISER, Donna, Administrator, Lackey Memorial Hospital, Forest, MS, p. A235

RISHEL, Kenn C., Administrator and Chief Executive Officer, Carthage Area Hospital, Carthage, NY, p. A286

RISK, Richard R., President and Chief Executive Officer, Advocate Health Care, Oak Brook, IL, p. B65

RISON, R. H., Warden, U. S. Medical Center for Federal Prisoners, Springfield, MO, p. A251

RITER, Pamela M., R.N., Administrator, Vencor Hospital–St Petersburg, Saint Petersburg, FL, p. A96

RITZ, Robert P., Chief Executive Officer, Monongalia General Hospital, Morgantown, WV, p. A454

RIVERA, Maria Mercedes, Administrator, Hospital Del Maestro, San Juan, PR, p. A473

RIZZO, Nancy, Senior Vice President, Operations, Geisinger Medical Center, Danville, PA, p. A352

ROACH, Joseph, Chief Executive Officer, Memorial Hospital of Martinsville and Henry County, Martinsville, VA, p. A439

ROADMAN II, Charles H., Surgeon General, Department of the Air Force, Bowling AFB, DC, p. B93

ROARK, Ruth Ann, Administrator, Sequoyah Memorial Hospital, Sallisaw, OK, p. A341

ROBBINS, Alan H., M.D., President, New England Baptist Hospital, Boston, MA, p. A200

ROBBINS, B. C., Superintendent, Georgia Mental Health Institute, Atlanta, GA, p. A101

ROBBINS, Wes, Chief Executive Officer, Charter by–the–Sea Behavioral Health System, Saint Simons Island, GA, p. A111

ROBERSON, Madeleine L.
Chief Executive Officer, Medical Center of Southwest Louisiana, Lafayette, LA, p. A182
Chief Executive Officer, Women's and Children's Hospital, Lafayette, LA, p. A182

ROBERTS, Carolyn C., President, Copley Hospital, Morrisville, VT, p. A434

ROBERTS, Deborah, Administrator, Lawrence County Hospital, Monticello, MS, p. A238

ROBERTS, Jean E., Administrator, Mark Reed Hospital, McCleary, WA, p. A447

ROBERTS, John W., President and Chief Executive Officer, Union Regional Medical Center, Monroe, NC, p. A310

ROBERTS, Jonathan, Dr.PH, Chief Executive Officer, Earl K. Long Medical Center, Baton Rouge, LA, p. A178

ROBERTS, Kenneth D., President, John T. Mather Memorial Hospital, Port Jefferson, NY, p. A298

ROBERTS, Pamela W., Administrator, Baptist Memorial Hospital–Booneville, Booneville, MS, p. A233

ROBERTS, Robert D., Interim President and Chief Executive Officer, Pacific Coast Hospital, San Francisco, CA, p. A60

ROBERTS, Shane, Administrator, St. Luke Community Hospital, Ronan, MT, p. A256

ROBERTS, Shirley R., Administrator, Washington County Regional Hospital, Sandersville, GA, p. A111

ROBERTS Jr., George T., Chief Executive Officer, Henderson Memorial Hospital, Henderson, TX, p. A409

ROBERTSON, B. W., Administrator, Parkview Hospital, Wheeler, TX, p. A428

ROBERTSON, David, Chief Executive Officer, Duncan Regional Hospital, Duncan, OK, p. A336

ROBERTSON, Gary W., Administrator, Niobrara County Hospital District, Lusk, WY, p. A469

ROBERTSON, Jeffrey J., Chief Executive Officer, Lakeview Hospital, Stillwater, MN, p. A231

ROBERTSON, Jim, Administrator, Pondera Medical Center, Conrad, MT, p. A254

ROBERTSON, Larry, Senior Vice President and Administrator, All Saints Hospital–Cityview, Fort Worth, TX, p. A406

ROBERTSON, Thomas L., President and Chief Executive Officer, Carilion Health System, Roanoke, VA, p. B76

ROBERTSON, William G., Senior Executive Officer, Shawnee Mission Medical Center, Shawnee Mission, KS, p. A165

ROBINSON, Beverly, Administrator, Swain County Hospital, Bryson City, NC, p. A305

ROBINSON, Brian C., Chief Executive Officer, North Florida Regional Medical Center, Gainesville, FL, p. A85

ROBINSON, Edward P., Administrator, Community Hospital, Munster, IN, p. A144

ROBINSON, Glenn A., Director, Nacogdoches Medical Center, Nacogdoches, TX, p. A418

ROBINSON, Margaret, Administrator, Anamosa Community Hospital, Anamosa, IA, p. A147

ROBINSON, Michael, Executive Vice President and Administrator, Richmond Memorial Hospital, Richmond, VA, p. A442

ROBINSON, Patrick C., M.D., Administrator, Walter Olin Moss Regional Medical Center, Lake Charles, LA, p. A182

ROBINSON, Phillip D., Chief Executive Officer, J. F. K. Medical Center, Atlantis, FL, p. A81

ROBINSON, Raymond, Chief Operating Officer, Worcester State Hospital, Worcester, MA, p. A207

ROBINSON, Richard F., Director, Veterans Affairs Medical Center, Fayetteville, AR, p. A30

ROBINSON, Richard H., Chief Executive Officer, Irvine Medical Center, Irvine, CA, p. A45

ROBINSON, Virginia B., Administrator, Jefferson County Hospital, Fayette, MS, p. A235

ROBINSON, W. D., Chief Executive Officer, Bartlett Memorial Medical Center, Sapulpa, OK, p. A341

ROBISON, Bert, Chief Executive Officer, Creek Nation Community Hospital, Okemah, OK, p. A339

ROBY, William J., Executive Vice President, Mountain Manor Treatment Center, Emmitsburg, MD, p. A196

ROCKER, Watson W., President and Chief Executive Officer, Jenkins County Hospital, Millen, GA, p. A109

ROCKLAGE, Mary Roch, President and Chief Executive Officer, Sisters of Mercy Health System–St. Louis, Saint Louis, MO, p. B138

ROCKWOOD Jr., John M., President, Munson Healthcare, Traverse City, MI, p. B120

RODDIE, Jim B., Administrator, Schleicher County Medical Center, Eldorado, TX, p. A406

RODGERS, Edward, Chief Executive Officer, Yoakum County Hospital, Denver City, TX, p. A404

RODGERS, Robert, Administrator and Senior Executive Officer, St. James Community Hospital, Butte, MT, p. A253

RODRIGUEZ, Julio Andino, Executive Director, Ponce Regional Hospital, Ponce, PR, p. A473

RODRIGUEZ, Maria Del Pilar, Administrator, Dr. Ramon E. Betances Hospital–Mayaguez Medical Center Branch, Mayaguez, PR, p. A473

RODRIGUEZ, Roy, M.D., Chief Executive Officer, Bayview Hospital and Mental Health System, Chula Vista, CA, p. A39

ROE Jr., Louis G., Administrator, Man ARH Hospital, Man, WV, p. A454

ROEBACK, Jason, President, Frazier Rehabilitation Center, Louisville, KY, p. A173

ROEDER, John R., President, Providence Hospital, Mobile, AL, p. A16

ROGERS, Bryan R., President and Chief Executive Officer, Foothill Presbyterian Hospital–Morris L. Johnston Memorial, Glendora, CA, p. A44

ROGERS, Charles L., President, Cushing Memorial Hospital, Leavenworth, KS, p. A161

ROGERS, Christopher J., Administrator, Auburn Memorial Hospital, Auburn, NY, p. A284

ROGERS, Richard, Senior Vice President, Mercy Memorial Hospital, Urbana, OH, p. A333

ROGERSON, Russell E., Warden, Iowa Medical and Classification Center, Oakdale, IA, p. A153

ROGOLS, Kevin L., President and Chief Executive Officer, Finley Hospital, Dubuque, IA, p. A150

ROHALEY, Richard L., President and Chief Executive Officer, Jackson General Hospital, Ripley, WV, p. A455

ROHRER, John E., Administrator, Prosser Memorial Hospital, Prosser, WA, p. A448

ROHRICH, George A., Administrator, Pembina County Memorial Hospital and Wedgewood Manor, Cavalier, ND, p. A316

ROJEK, Kenneth J., Chief Executive, Lutheran General Hospital, Park Ridge, IL, p. A132

ROMER, James E., President and Chief Executive Officer, Hospital Center at Orange, Orange, NJ, p. A276

ROMERO, Dudley, President and Chief Executive Officer, Our Lady of Lourdes Regional Medical Center, Lafayette, LA, p. A182

ROMERO, Marcella A., Administrator, Espanola Hospital, Espanola, NM, p. A281

ROMOFF, Jeffrey A.
President, UPMC Health System, Pittsburgh, PA, p. B150
President, UPMC–Presbyterian, Pittsburgh, PA, p. A363

RONA, J. Michael, Vice President and Executive Administrator, Virginia Mason Medical Center, Seattle, WA, p. A449

RONSTROM, Stephen F., Executive Vice President, Sacred Heart Hospital, Eau Claire, WI, p. A459

ROODMAN, Richard D., Chief Executive Officer, Valley Medical Center, Renton, WA, p. A449

ROONEY, Ronald K., President, Arkansas Methodist Hospital, Paragould, AR, p. A34

ROOT, Darwin E., Administrator, Harrison Memorial Hospital, Cynthiana, KY, p. A169

RORAFF, Greg, President and Chief Executive Officer, Memorial Hospital of Taylor County, Medford, WI, p. A461

ROSASCO Jr., Edward J., President, Mercy Hospital, Miami, FL, p. A90

ROSE, J. Anthony, President and Chief Executive Officer, Catawba Memorial Hospital, Hickory, NC, p. A309

ROSE, Lance H., FACHE, President, Centre Community Hospital, State College, PA, p. A366

ROSE, Renee, President and Chief Executive Officer, Horizon Healthcare, Inc., Milwaukee, WI, p. B108

ROSEBOROUGH, James W., CHE, Director, Veterans Affairs Medical Center, Ann Arbor, MI, p. A208

ROSEN, David P., President, Jamaica Hospital Medical Center, New York, NY, p. A293

ROSENBACH, Lynn M., Chief Executive Officer, Charter Behavioral Health System of Nevada, Las Vegas, NV, p. A266

ROSENBERG, Leroy J., Executive Director, West Jersey Hospital–Marlton, Marlton, NJ, p. A274

ROSENTHAL, David S., M.D., Director, Stillman Infirmary, Harvard University Health Services, Cambridge, MA, p. A202

ROSENVALL, Greg, Administrator, Gunnison Valley Hospital, Gunnison, UT, p. A430

ROSIN, David, M.D., Medical Director, Nevada Mental Health Institute, Sparks, NV, p. A267

ROSS, David, Chief Executive Officer, Phelps County Regional Medical Center, Rolla, MO, p. A248

ROSS, David J., Chief Executive Officer, White Mountain Regional Medical Center, Springerville, AZ, p. A26

ROSS, David Z., Acting Chief Executive Officer, Levindale Hebrew Geriatric Center and Hospital, Baltimore, MD, p. A194

ROSS, Hank, Chief Executive Officer, HEALTHSOUTH Rehabilitation Hospital, Oklahoma City, OK, p. A339

ROSS, Harvey, Executive Director and Chief Executive Officer, Mediplex Rehabilitation–Denver, Thornton, CO, p. A73

ROSS, James E., FACHE
Chief Executive Officer, Deaton Specialty Hospital and Home, Baltimore, MD, p. A193
Chief Executive Officer, James Lawrence Kernan Hospital, Baltimore, MD, p. A193

ROSS, Joseph P.
President and Chief Executive Officer, Dorchester General Hospital, Cambridge, MD, p. A195
President and Chief Executive Officer, Memorial Hospital at Easton Maryland, Easton, MD, p. A195

ROSS, Kenneth R., Administrator, Carl Albert Indian Health Facility, Ada, OK, p. A335

ROSS, Zeff, Administrator, Memorial Hospital West, Pembroke Pines, FL, p. A94

ROSS Jr., Semmes, Administrator, Franklin County Memorial Hospital, Meadville, MS, p. A237

ROSSETTI, Stephen J., Ph.D., President and Chief Executive Officer, Saint Luke Institute, Silver Spring, MD, p. A198

ROSSFELD, John
Administrator, Bascom Palmer Eye Institute–Anne Bates Leach Eye Hospital, Miami, FL, p. A90
Administrator, University of Miami Hospital and Clinics, Miami, FL, p. A91

ROSSI, L. J., M.D., Chief Executive Officer, Hopedale Medical Complex, Hopedale, IL, p. A129

ROSSI Jr., Ralph A., M.D., Interim President, Southern Chester County Medical Center, West Grove, PA, p. A367

ROSSIO, Gary J., Acting Director, Veterans Affairs Medical Center, San Diego, CA, p. A60

ROTH, Steve, Chief Executive Officer, Vicksburg Medical Center, Vicksburg, MS, p. A240

ROTH, William, Chief Executive Officer, HEALTHSOUTH Chesapeake Rehabilitation Hospital, Salisbury, MD, p. A197

ROTHLEIN Jr., Gerard J., President and Chief Executive Officer, Children's Medical Center, Tulsa, OK, p. A342

ROTHSTEIN, Ruth M.
  Chief, Cook County Bureau of Health Services, Chicago, IL, p. B91
  Hospital Director, Cook County Hospital, Chicago, IL, p. A122
ROURKE, Thomas E., Administrator, Glen Oaks Hospital, Greenville, TX, p. A408
ROUSH, Sharon L., Chief Executive Officer, Columbia Hospital, West Palm Beach, FL, p. A99
ROWE, David B., Vice President and Administrator, Harris Methodist Southwest, Fort Worth, TX, p. A407
ROWE, Gary L., President and Chief Executive Officer, St. Catherine Hospital, Garden City, KS, p. A159
ROWE, John W., M.D., President, Mount Sinai Medical Center, New York, NY, p. A294
ROWE, Lavonne M., Administrator, Johnson County Hospital, Tecumseh, NE, p. A264
ROWLAND, Phil
  Chief Executive Officer, Cleveland Community Hospital, Cleveland, TN, p. A384
  Chief Executive Officer, Columbia South Pittsburg Hospital, South Pittsburg, TN, p. A393
ROWTON, William, Chief Executive Officer, Cozby–Germany Hospital, Grand Saline, TX, p. A408
ROYAL, Ramon, President, Brighton Hospital, Brighton, MI, p. A209
ROYNAN, Joseph, Administrator, Northwestern Institute, Fort Washington, PA, p. A354
ROZEK, Thomas M., Senior Vice President, Children's Hospital of Michigan, Detroit, MI, p. A210
RUBENSTEIN, David A., Chief Operating Officer, Dwight David Eisenhower Army Medical Center, Fort Gordon, GA, p. A106
RUBIN, Harold, President and Chief Executive Officer, Memorial Hospital and Medical Center, Midland, TX, p. A418
RUCKDESCHEL, John C., M.D., Director and Chief Executive Officer, H. Lee Moffitt Cancer Center and Research Institute, Tampa, FL, p. A97
RUDEGEAIR, Bernard C., President and Chief Executive Officer, Hazleton–St. Joseph Medical Center, Hazleton, PA, p. A355
RUDES, Bryan F., Executive Director, Richard H. Hutchings Psychiatric Center, Syracuse, NY, p. A301
RUDES, Sarah F., Executive Director, Mohawk Valley Psychiatric Center, Utica, NY, p. A302
RUDNICK Jr., John D., FACHE, Executive Director, Pathways of Tennessee, Jackson, TN, p. A386
RUELAS, Raul D., M.D., Administrator, Gulf Coast Treatment Center, Fort Walton Beach, FL, p. A85
RUFFIN, Edward W., Administrator, Columbia Coliseum Psychiatric Hospital, Macon, GA, p. A108
RUFFNER, John
  Administrator, Hemet Valley Medical Center, Hemet, CA, p. A45
  Interim Chief Executive Officer, Valley Health System, Hemet, CA, p. B151
RUMLEY, Darrell, Service Unit Director and Chief Executive Officer, U. S. Public Health Service Indian Hospital, Sells, AZ, p. A26
RUMPZ, Mary Renetta, FACHE, President and Chief Executive Officer, St. Mary Hospital, Livonia, MI, p. A215
RUNDIO, Robert A.
  Executive Director of Hospital Operations, Mesa Lutheran Hospital, Mesa, AZ, p. A24
  Executive Director of Hospital Operations, Valley Lutheran Hospital, Mesa, AZ, p. A24
RUPIPER, Allen V., President, Adena Health System, Chillicothe, OH, p. A322
RUPP, William, M.D., President and Chief Executive Officer, Luther Hospital, Eau Claire, WI, p. A459
RUPPERT, James C., Regional Administrator, Alegent Health Mercy Hospital, Corning, IA, p. A148
RUSE, William E., FACHE, President and Chief Executive Officer, Blanchard Valley Health Association System, Findlay, OH, p. A326
RUSH, Domenica, Administrator, Sierra Vista Hospital, Truth or Consequences, NM, p. A283
RUSH, Donald J., Chief Executive Officer, Sidney Health Center, Sidney, MT, p. A256
RUSHING, R. Lynn, Chief Executive Officer, Brook Lane Psychiatric Center, Hagerstown, MD, p. A196

RUSKAN, Jeff, Administrator, HEALTHSOUTH Rehabilitation Hospital of Virginia, Richmond, VA, p. A442
RUSSEL, Kimberly A., President and Chief Executive Officer, Mary Greeley Medical Center, Ames, IA, p. A147
RUSSELL, Bill, Chief Operating Officer and Administrator, Fair Oaks Hospital, Delray Beach, FL, p. A84
RUSSELL, Daniel F., President and Chief Executive Officer, Catholic Health East, Radnor, PA, p. B77
RUSSELL, James D. M., Chief Executive Officer, St. Mary's Hospital, Pierre, SD, p. A380
RUSSELL, Linda B., Chief Executive Officer, Woman's Hospital of Texas, Houston, TX, p. A413
RUSSELL, Mark R., President and Chief Executive Officer, Hospital Group of America, Wayne, PA, p. B108
RUSSELL, Tim, Administrator, Stillwater Community Hospital, Columbus, MT, p. A253
RUSSELL, Webster T., Chief Executive Officer, South Central Kansas Regional Medical Center, Arkansas City, KS, p. A157
RUSSOTTO, John, Facility Director, Northern Virginia Mental Health Institute, Falls Church, VA, p. A437
RUTENBERG, Jack, Administrator, Villa Maria Hospital, North Miami, FL, p. A92
RUTHERFORD, James A., President and Chief Executive Officer, St. Clare's Hospital and Health Center, New York, NY, p. A296
RUTKOWSKI, Robert, Chief Executive, South Suburban Hospital, Hazel Crest, IL, p. A128
RUTTER, David E., Administrator, Mahaska County Hospital, Oskaloosa, IA, p. A154
RUYLE, W. Kenneth, Director, Veterans Affairs Medical Center, Tuscaloosa, AL, p. A18
RUZYCKI, Frank C., Executive Director, Roosevelt Warm Springs Institute for Rehabilitation, Warm Springs, GA, p. A113
RYAN, Michael G., President and Chief Executive Officer, St. Francis Specialty Hospital, Monroe, LA, p. A184
RYAN, Michael J., Administrator, Nemaha Valley Community Hospital, Seneca, KS, p. A165
RYAN, Thomas E., President, Alamance Regional Medical Center, Burlington, NC, p. A305
RYAN, Mary Jean, President and Chief Executive Officer, SSM Health Care System, Saint Louis, MO, p. B140
RYBA, Thomas L., Chief Executive Officer, Charter Savannah Behavioral Health System, Savannah, GA, p. A111
RYLE, Deborah L., Chief Executive Officer, Round Rock Hospital, Round Rock, TX, p. A422

S

SABA, Francis M., President and Chief Executive Officer, Milford–Whitinsville Regional Hospital, Milford, MA, p. A204
SABIN, Margaret D., Chief Executive Officer, Routt Memorial Hospital, Steamboat Springs, CO, p. A72
SABIN, Robert H., Medical Center Director, Aleda E. Lutz Veterans Affairs Medical Center, Saginaw, MI, p. A218
SABO, Michael A.
  Director, Veterans Affairs Hudson Valley Health Care System–F.D. Roosevelt Hospital, Montrose, NY, p. A290
  Medical Director, Veterans Affairs Medical Center, New York, NY, p. A296
SABOL, Don J., Chief Executive Officer, Hardin Memorial Hospital, Kenton, OH, p. A328
SACCO, Frank V., FACHE, Chief Executive Officer, Memorial Healthcare System, Los Angeles, FL, p. B117
SACK, Michael V., President and Chief Executive Officer, Union Hospital, Elkton, MD, p. A195
SACKETT, John, Administrator, Avista Adventist Hospital, Louisville, CO, p. A72
SACKETT, Walter, Senior Vice President and Administrator, St. Mary–Corwin Medical Center, Pueblo, CO, p. A72

SADAU, Ernie W., President and Chief Executive Officer, Hinsdale Hospital, Hinsdale, IL, p. A128
SADLACK, Frank J., Ph.D., Executive Director, La Hacienda Treatment Center, Hunt, TX, p. A413
SADLER, Blair L., President, Children's Hospital and Health Center, San Diego, CA, p. A59
SADVARY, Thomas J., FACHE, Senior Vice President and Administrator, Scottsdale Healthcare–Shea, Scottsdale, AZ, p. A26
SAFIAN, Keith F., President and Chief Executive Officer, Phelps Memorial Hospital Center, Sleepy Hollow, NY, p. A300
SAGO, Glenn R., Administrator, Arkansas State Hospital, Little Rock, AR, p. A32
SAINER, Elliot A., President and Chief Executive Officer, College Health Enterprises, Cerritos, CA, p. B81
SAJDAK, Dennis J., Chief Executive Officer, Charter Hospital of Toledo, Maumee, OH, p. A329
SALA Jr., Anthony S., Chief Executive Officer, Highland Hospital, Shreveport, LA, p. A187
SALANGER, Matthew J., President and Chief Executive Officer, United Health Services Hospitals–Binghamton, Binghamton, NY, p. A285
SALBER, M. Agnes, Prioress, Missionary Benedictine Sisters American Province, Norfolk, NE, p. B119
SALEAPAGA, Iotamo T., M.D., Director Health, Lyndon B. Johnson Tropical Medical Center, Pago Pago, AS, p. A471
SALISBURY, Roger, Administrator, Hodgeman County Health Center, Jetmore, KS, p. A161
SALMON, Robert J.
  Chief Executive Officer, Canby Community Health Services, Canby, MN, p. A223
  Interim Administrator, Deuel County Memorial Hospital, Clear Lake, SD, p. A378
SALVANT, Darlene, Chief Executive Officer, BHC East Lake Hospital, New Orleans, LA, p. A184
SAMET, Kenneth A., President, Washington Hospital Center, Washington, DC, p. A80
SAMPLE, James L., Chief Executive Officer, Columbia Andalusia Hospital, Andalusia, AL, p. A11
SAMPSON, Arthur J., President and Chief Executive Officer, Newport Hospital, Newport, RI, p. A369
SAMPSON, Gladiola, Acting Executive Director, Queens Hospital Center, New York, NY, p. A295
SANCHEZ, Jose R., Executive Director, Metropolitan Hospital Center, New York, NY, p. A294
SANCHEZ, Roberto, Administrator, Lower Florida Keys Health System, Key West, FL, p. A88
SANDER, Larry J., FACHE, Director, Veterans Affairs Medical Center–Louisville, Louisville, KY, p. A174
SANDERS, John W., Chief Executive Officer, Twin Rivers Regional Medical Center, Kennett, MO, p. A246
SANDERS, Steve, Vice President, Chief Executive Officer and Administrator, Memorial Hospital–The Woodlands, The Woodlands, TX, p. A426
SANDERS, Jimmy, Chief of Staff, William Beaumont Army Medical Center, El Paso, TX, p. A406
SANDIFER, C. Philip, Administrator, Island Hospital, Anacortes, WA, p. A445
SANDLIN, Keith, Chief Executive Officer, Columbia Cartersville Medical Center, Cartersville, GA, p. A103
SANGER, William A., President and Chief Executive Officer, Cancer Treatment Centers of America, Arlington Heights, IL, p. B75
SANNER, Charlotte K., M.D., Director Health Service, Simpson Infirmary, Wellesley College, Wellesley, MA, p. A207
SANTIAGO–VEGA, Francisco, Consultor, Lafayette Hospital, Arroyo, PR, p. A471
SANZO, Anthony M.
  President and Chief Executive Officer, Allegheny Health, Education and Research Foundation, Pittsburgh, PA, p. B65
  President and Chief Executive Officer, Allegheny University Hospitals, Allegheny General, Pittsburgh, PA, p. A362
SANZONE, Raymond D., Executive Director, Tewksbury Hospital, Tewksbury, MA, p. A206

SARDONE, Frank J.
President and Chief Executive Officer, Bronson Healthcare Group, Inc., Kalamazoo, MI, p. B75
President and Chief Executive Officer, Bronson Methodist Hospital, Kalamazoo, MI, p. A214
President, Bronson Vicksburg Hospital, Vicksburg, MI, p. A220

SARKAR, George A., JD, Executive Director, Manhattan Eye, Ear and Throat Hospital, New York, NY, p. A294

SARKIS, Lucy, M.D., Executive Director, South Beach Psychiatric Center, New York, NY, p. A295

SARLE, C. Richard, President and Chief Executive Officer, Carrier Foundation, Belle Mead, NJ, p. A271

SASSER, L. Wayne, Vice President and Administrator, Crenshaw Baptist Hospital, Luverne, AL, p. A15

SATALA, Taylor, Service Unit Director, U. S. Public Health Services Indian Hospital, Keams Canyon, AZ, p. A23

SATCHER, Richard H., Chief Executive Officer, Aiken Regional Medical Center, Aiken, SC, p. A371

SATO, James, Chief Executive Officer, Bear Valley Community Hospital, Big Bear Lake, CA, p. A38

SATTERWHITE, Robin, Administrator, W. J. Mangold Memorial Hospital, Lockney, TX, p. A416

SATZGER, Bruce G., Administrator and Chief Executive Officer, Commmunity Hospital of San Bernardino, San Bernardino, CA, p. A59

SAUCIER, George J., Chief Executive Officer, Northshore Regional Medical Center, Slidell, LA, p. A187

SAULS, Randy, Administrator, Louis Smith Memorial Hospital, Lakeland, GA, p. A108

SAULTERS, W. Dale, Administrator, Winston Medical Center, Louisville, MS, p. A237

SAUNDERS, Donald F., President, Androscoggin Valley Hospital, Berlin, NH, p. A268

SAVAGE, Robert L., President and Chief Executive Officer, Charleston Area Medical Center, Charleston, WV, p. A452

SCHADT, Alton M., Executive Director, Warren General Hospital, Warren, PA, p. A367

SCHAENGOLD, Phillip S., JD, Chief Executive Officer, George Washington University Hospital, Washington, DC, p. A79

SCHAFER, Michael, Chief Executive Officer, Community Memorial Hospital and Nursing Home, Spooner, WI, p. A466

SCHAFFER, Arnold R., President and Chief Executive Officer, Glendale Memorial Hospital and Health Center, Glendale, CA, p. A44

SCHAFFNER, Leroy, Chief Executive Officer, Coon Memorial Hospital and Home, Dalhart, TX, p. A402

SCHAFFNER, Linda D., R.N., Vice President and Administrator, Bethesda Oak Hospital, Cincinnati, OH, p. A322

SCHANDLER, Jon B., President and Chief Executive Officer, White Plains Hospital Center, White Plains, NY, p. A303

SCHANWALD, Pamela R., Chief Executive Officer, Children's Home of Pittsburgh, Pittsburgh, PA, p. A362

SCHAPER, Robert F., President and Chief Executive Officer, Tomball Regional Hospital, Tomball, TX, p. A426

SCHAPPELL, Martin, Chief Executive Officer, Charter Glade Behavioral Health System, Fort Myers, FL, p. A85

SCHAUM, James H., President and Chief Executive Officer, Allen Memorial Hospital, Oberlin, OH, p. A330

SCHAUMBURG, John, Administrator, Lanai Community Hospital, Lanai City, HI, p. A115

SCHEFFER, Richard H., President, Wing Memorial Hospital and Medical Centers, Palmer, MA, p. A205

SCHERLIN, Marlys, Chief Executive Officer, Greater Community Hospital, Creston, IA, p. A149

SCHERR, Morris L., Executive Vice President, Taylor Manor Hospital, Ellicott City, MD, p. A196

SCHERTZ, David A.
Administrator, Saint Anthony Medical Center, Rockford, IL, p. A134
Administrator, Saint Joseph Hospital, Belvidere, IL, p. A121

SCHIMSCHEINER, Mary Joel, Chief Executive Officer, Kenmore Mercy Hospital, Kenmore, NY, p. A289

SCHINTZ, Conrad W., Senior Vice President Operations, Penn State Geisinger Wyoming Valley Medical Center, Wilkes–Barre, PA, p. A367

SCHLAUTMAN, Jacolyn M., Executive Vice President, St. Joseph's Hospital, Breese, IL, p. A121

SCHLEGELMILCH, Kurt W., M.D., Director, Veterans Affairs Medical Center, Grand Junction, CO, p. A71

SCHLEUSS, Cheryl M., Chief Executive Officer, Greenbrier Behavioral Health System, Covington, LA, p. A180

SCHMELTER, Robert, President, Community Hospital of Ottawa, Ottawa, IL, p. A132

SCHMIDT, Barbara, Administrator, Vencor Hospital–Fort Worth Southwest, Fort Worth, TX, p. A407

SCHMIDT, Craig W. C., President and Chief Executive Officer, Community Health Network, Berlin, WI, p. A457

SCHMIDT, Gene E., President, Hutchinson Hospital Corporation, Hutchinson, KS, p. A160

SCHMIDT, Kenneth A., President, Pioneer Memorial Hospital, Heppner, OR, p. A345

SCHMIDT, Mark, Administrator, Gettysburg Medical Center, Gettysburg, SD, p. A379

SCHMIDT, Michael A., President and Chief Executive Officer, Saint Joseph's Hospital, Marshfield, WI, p. A461

SCHMIDT, Paul R., CHE, President and Chief Executive Officer, St. Joseph Health System, Tawas City, MI, p. A219

SCHMIDT, Richard T., Executive Director, Decatur Hospital, Decatur, GA, p. A105

SCHMIDT, Steve
Administrator and Chief Executive Officer, Lancaster Community Hospital, Lancaster, CA, p. A47
Chief Executive Officer, Redding Medical Center, Redding, CA, p. A57

SCHMIDT, Timothy E., Chief Executive Officer, Mimbres Memorial Hospital, Deming, NM, p. A281

SCHMIDT Jr., Richard O., President, Chief Executive Officer and General Counsel, Kenosha Hospital and Medical Center, Kenosha, WI, p. A460

SCHMOYER, Carol, Administrator, Wickenburg Regional Hospital, Wickenburg, AZ, p. A27

SCHNEDLER, Lisa Wagner, Administrator, Van Buren County Hospital, Keosauqua, IA, p. A152

SCHNEIDER, Carol, Chief Executive, Christ Hospital and Medical Center, Oak Lawn, IL, p. A132

SCHNEIDER, Charles F., President, Day Kimball Hospital, Putnam, CT, p. A76

SCHNEIDER, Cynthia K., Administrator, Greeley County Hospital, Tribune, KS, p. A166

SCHNEIDER, David R., Executive Director, Langlade Memorial Hospital, Antigo, WI, p. A457

SCHNEIDER, Mark E., Chief Executive Officer, Rivendell Behavioral Health Services, Benton, AR, p. A29

SCHNEIDER, Thomas R., Administrator, Shriners Hospitals for Children, Shreveport, Shreveport, LA, p. A187

SCHOAPS, Stephen R., Chief Executive Officer, Seminole Municipal Hospital, Seminole, OK, p. A341

SCHOEN, William J., Chairman and Chief Executive Officer, Health Management Associates, Naples, FL, p. B103

SCHOENHOLTZ, Jack C., M.D., Medical Director and Administrator, Rye Hospital Center, Rye, NY, p. A300

SCHOLTEN, Randall J., Chief Executive Officer, Curry General Hospital, Gold Beach, OR, p. A345

SCHON, John, Administrator and Chief Executive Officer, Dickinson County Healthcare System, Iron Mountain, MI, p. A214

SCHONHORN, Robert, President, Matheny School and Hospital, Peapack, NJ, p. A276

SCHOTT, Carol, Administrator, Odessa Memorial Hospital, Odessa, WA, p. A448

SCHRADER, Michael E., President and Chief Executive Officer, Wyoming Medical Center, Casper, WY, p. A468

SCHREEG, Timothy M., President and Chief Executive Officer, Jasper County Hospital, Rensselaer, IN, p. A145

SCHROEDER, Edward G., President and Chief Executive Officer, St. Joseph's Medical Center, Stockton, CA, p. A64

SCHROEDER, Fred F., Administrator, Memorial Hospital of Converse County, Douglas, WY, p. A468

SCHROFFEL, Bruce, Chief Operating Officer, University of California San Francisco Medical Center, San Francisco, CA, p. A60

SCHRUPP, Richard, President and Chief Executive Officer, Mercy Hospital of Franciscan Sisters, Oelwein, IA, p. A153

SCHUBERT, John D., Administrator and Chief Executive Officer, Pinckneyville Community Hospital, Pinckneyville, IL, p. A133

SCHUESSLER, James P., President and Chief Executive Officer, All Saints Episcopal Hospital of Fort Worth, Fort Worth, TX, p. A406

SCHUETZ, Charles D., Chief Executive Officer, Columbia Kingwood Medical Center, Kingwood, TX, p. A414

SCHULER, G. Wayne, Executive Director, Madison County Medical Center, Canton, MS, p. A234

SCHULER, William J., Chief Executive Officer, Portsmouth Regional Hospital and Pavilion, Portsmouth, NH, p. A270

SCHULLER, David E., M.D., Chief Executive Officer, Arthur G. James Cancer Hospital and Research Institute, Columbus, OH, p. A324

SCHULTE, James E., Administrator, Redwood Falls Municipal Hospital, Redwood Falls, MN, p. A229

SCHULTZ, Judson, Executive Director, Northwoods Hospital, Phelps, WI, p. A464

SCHULTZ, Michael, President, Redbud Community Hospital, Clearlake, CA, p. A40

SCHULTZ, Steve, President, Eye Foundation Hospital, Birmingham, AL, p. A12

SCHULZ, Charles K., Chief Executive Officer, York General Hospital, York, NE, p. A265

SCHULZ, Larry A., President and Chief Executive Officer, St. Gabriel's Hospital, Little Falls, MN, p. A226

SCHUMACHER, Joseph L., Administrator, Calumet Medical Center, Chilton, WI, p. A458

SCHURMAN, Bruce A., President, Marianjoy Rehabilitation Hospital and Clinics, Wheaton, IL, p. A136

SCHURMEIER, L. Jon, President and Chief Executive Officer, Southwest General Health Center, Middleburg Heights, OH, p. A329

SCHURRA, Ronald J., Chief Executive Officer, Holy Family Hospital, Spokane, WA, p. A450

SCHUSTER, Emmett, Administrator and Chief Executive Officer, Greenwood County Hospital, Eureka, KS, p. A159

SCHWANKE, Dan, Chief Executive Officer, St. Francis Health Care Centre, Green Springs, OH, p. A327

SCHWARTEN, William L., Administrator, Washington County Memorial Hospital, Potosi, MO, p. A248

SCHWARTZ, John N., Chief Executive Officer, Trinity Hospital, Chicago, IL, p. A124

SCHWARTZ, Mark, Administrator, Hartford Memorial Hospital, Hartford, WI, p. A460

SCHWARTZ, Michael J., President, Alexian Brothers Medical Center, Elk Grove Village, IL, p. A126

SCHWARZ, Donald E., President and Chief Executive Officer, Jewish Memorial Hospital and Rehabilitation Center, Boston, MA, p. A200

SCHWEITZER, Alex, Superintendent and Chief Executive Officer, North Dakota State Hospital, Jamestown, ND, p. A318

SCHWEITZER, Robert, Ed.D., Executive Director, Sagamore Children's Psychiatric Center, Huntington Station, NY, p. A289

SCHWEMER, David J., Administrator, Woodrow Wilson Rehabilitation Center, Fishersville, VA, p. A437

SCHWIENTEK, Barbara, Executive Director, Monticello Big Lake Hospital, Monticello, MN, p. A228

SCHWIND, Mary, MS, Chief Executive Officer, Healdsburg General Hospital, Healdsburg, CA, p. A45

SCIOLA, Anthony, President and Chief Executive Officer, Shaughnessy–Kaplan Rehabilitation Hospital, Salem, MA, p. A205

SCOGGIN Jr., James C.
Chief Executive Officer, San Antonio Community Hospital, San Antonio, TX, p. A423
Chief Executive Officer, Southwest Texas Methodist Hospital, San Antonio, TX, p. A423

SCOLA, John, M.D., Interim Chief Executive Officer, Cranberry Specialty Hospital of Plymouth County, Middleboro, MA, p. A204

SCOLLARD, Patrick J., President and Chief Executive Officer, St. Francis Hospital, Roslyn, NY, p. A300

SCOTT, Camille, Administrator, Benewah Community Hospital, Saint Maries, ID, p. A118

SCOTT, Charles F.
President and Chief Executive Officer, Memorial Hospital of Tampa, Tampa, FL, p. A98
President, Town and Country Hospital, Tampa, FL, p. A98

SCOTT, Grady, President and Chief Executive Officer, Copper Basin Medical Center, Copperhill, TN, p. A385

SCOTT, John R., Director, St. Lawrence Psychiatric Center, Ogdensburg, NY, p. A297

SCOTT, Mark D., President, Mid–Columbia Medical Center, The Dalles, OR, p. A348

SCOTT, Richard E., President, Hillcrest Baptist Medical Center, Waco, TX, p. A427

SCOTT, Steve, Chief Operating Officer, Pinelands Hospital, Nacogdoches, TX, p. A419

SCOTT, Thomas L., FACHE, President and Chief Executive Officer, Burdette Tomlin Memorial Hospital, Cape May Court House, NJ, p. A272

SCOVILL, Terry
Administrator, Cypress Creek Hospital, Houston, TX, p. A410
Chief Executive Officer, West Oaks Hospital, Houston, TX, p. A413

SCURR, David J., Superintendent, Mental Health Institute, Mount Pleasant, IA, p. A153

SEABERG, Lynn, Administrator and Chief Executive Officer, Indian Valley Hospital District, Greenville, CA, p. A44

SEAGRAVE, Richard E., Executive Director and Chief Operating Officer, Phoenixville Hospital, Phoenixville, PA, p. A362

SEAL, Ronald, President and Chief Executive Officer, Marion Memorial Hospital, Marion, IL, p. A130

SEALE, Corey A., Chief Executive Officer, Fallbrook Hospital District, Fallbrook, CA, p. A42

SEAVER, Roger E., President and Chief Executive Officer, Northridge Hospital Medical Center–Roscoe Boulevard Campus, Los Angeles, CA, p. A50

SECKINGER, Mark R., Administrator, Doctors Hospital of Nelsonville, Nelsonville, OH, p. A330

SEEL, W. Joseph, Administrator, Edgefield County Hospital, Edgefield, SC, p. A373

SEELY, E. T., Administrator, Ferrell Hospital, Eldorado, IL, p. A126

SEGLER, Randall K., Chief Executive Officer, Comanche County Memorial Hospital, Lawton, OK, p. A338

SEIBEL, Jacqueline, Administrator, Jacobson Memorial Hospital Care Center, Elgin, ND, p. A317

SEIDEL, Ken, Executive Director, Columbia Claremore Regional Hospital, Claremore, OK, p. A336

SEIDLER, Richard A., FACHE, Chief Executive Officer, Allen Memorial Hospital, Waterloo, IA, p. A155

SEIFERT, David P., President, St. Anthony's Medical Center, Saint Louis, MO, p. A250

SEIGFREID Jr., Jerome, Chief Executive Officer, Phelps Memorial Health Center, Holdrege, NE, p. A260

SEILER, Edward H., Director, Veterans Affairs Medical Center, Providence, RI, p. A369

SEILER, Steven L., Senior Vice President and Chief Executive Officer, Good Samaritan Regional Medical Center, Phoenix, AZ, p. A24

SEIM, Arne, Interim Administrator, Quincy Valley Medical Center, Quincy, WA, p. A448

SEITZ, J. H., Administrator, Salem Hospital, Hillsboro, KS, p. A160

SELBERG, Jeffrey D.
President and Chief Executive Officer, Exempla Healthcare, Inc., Denver, CO, p. B100
President and Chief Executive Officer, Exempla Lutheran Medical Center, Wheat Ridge, CO, p. A73

SELDEN, Thomas A., President and Chief Executive Officer, Parma Community General Hospital, Parma, OH, p. A331

SELLARDS, Michael G., Executive Director, Pleasant Valley Hospital, Point Pleasant, WV, p. A455

SELTZER, Charlotte, Chief Executive Officer, Creedmoor Psychiatric Center, New York, NY, p. A292

SELZ, Timothy P., President and Chief Executive Officer, Provena Saint Therese Medical Center, Waukegan, IL, p. A136

SELZER, Stephen R., President and Chief Executive Officer, Southwest Memorial Hospital, Cortez, CO, p. A69

SEM, Steven, Commander, U. S. Air Force Hospital, Ellsworth AFB, SD, p. A379

SENNEFF, Robert G., Chief Executive Officer, DeWitt Community Hospital, De Witt, IA, p. A149

SENSOR, Wayne A., Administrator, Integris Bass Baptist Health Center, Enid, OK, p. A337

SERILLA, Michael, Acting Executive Vice President and Administrator, Bon Secours Hospital, Grosse Pointe, MI, p. A213

SERNULKA, John M., President and Chief Executive Officer, Carroll County General Hospital, Westminster, MD, p. A198

SERRILL, G. B., President and Chief Executive Officer, Ellis Hospital, Schenectady, NY, p. A300

SEWARD Jr., James P., Chief Executive Officer, Berrien County Hospital, Nashville, GA, p. A110

SEXTON, Charles F., Interim Chief Executive Officer, Austin Diagnostic Medical Center, Austin, TX, p. A396

SEXTON, J. Dennis, President, All Children's Hospital, Saint Petersburg, FL, p. A95

SEXTON, James J., President and Chief Executive Officer, Saint Francis Medical Center, Cape Girardeau, MO, p. A242

SEXTON, William P., Administrator, Franciscan Skemp Healthcare–Sparta Campus, Sparta, WI, p. A466

SEYMOUR, James A., Regional Administrator, Alegent Health Community Memorial Hospital, Missouri Valley, IA, p. A153

SHAFER, Ronald J., President and Chief Executive Officer, Eastern New Mexico Medical Center, Roswell, NM, p. A283

SHAFFER, David D., Chief Executive Officer, Stonewall Jackson Memorial Hospital, Weston, WV, p. A456

SHAFFETT, Donald A.
Chief Executive Officer, Columbia Alvin Medical Center, Alvin, TX, p. A395
Chief Executive Officer, Columbia Clear Lake Regional Medical Center, Webster, TX, p. A428

SHAMBAUGH, Steve, Superintendent, Eastern Oregon Psychiatric Center, Pendleton, OR, p. A346

SHANKER, Deo, CPA, Chief Executive Officer, Forest Springs Hospital, Houston, TX, p. A411

SHANKLE, John, Interim Chief Executive Officer, North Baldwin Hospital, Bay Minette, AL, p. A11

SHAPIRO, Edward R., M.D., Medical Director and Chief Executive Officer, Austen Riggs Center, Stockbridge, MA, p. A206

SHAPIRO, Marcia S., Chief Executive Officer, Chicago Lakeshore Hospital, Chicago, IL, p. A122

SHARFSTEIN, Steven S., M.D., President, Medical Director and Chief Executive Officer, Sheppard and Enoch Pratt Hospital, Baltimore, MD, p. A194

SHARMA, Timothy, M.D., President, Cambridge International, Inc,, Houston, TX, p. B75

SHARP, Joseph, Acting Administrator, Orange County Community Hospital of Buena Park, Buena Park, CA, p. A38

SHARP, Joseph W., Administrator, Runnells Specialized Hospital, Berkeley Heights, NJ, p. A271

SHARPE, Diane, Chief Executive Officer, ValueMark Pine Grove Behavioral Healthcare System, Los Angeles, CA, p. A51

SHAW, David B.
Administrator and Chief Executive Officer, Pecos County General Hospital, Iraan, TX, p. A413
Administrator and Chief Executive Officer, Pecos County Memorial Hospital, Fort Stockton, TX, p. A406

SHAW, Doug, Administrator, Mad River Community Hospital, Arcata, CA, p. A36

SHAW, Douglas E., President, Jewish Hospital, Louisville, KY, p. A173

SHAW, J. Michael, Administrator, Rusk County Memorial Hospital and Nursing Home, Ladysmith, WI, p. A460

SHAW, Phil, Executive Director, Spalding Regional Hospital, Griffin, GA, p. A107

SHAW, Robert C., Administrator and Chief Executive Officer, Columbia Los Robles Hospital and Medical Center, Thousand Oaks, CA, p. A64

SHAWN, Michael, Chief Executive Officer, Mary Hurley Hospital, Coalgate, OK, p. A336

SHEAR, Bruce A., President and Chief Executive Officer, Pioneer Healthcare, Peabody, MA, p. B125

SHECKLER, Robert L., Administrator, Dundy County Hospital, Benkelman, NE, p. A258

SHEEDY, Lucille K., Administrator and Chief Executive Officer, Wyoming County Community Hospital, Warsaw, NY, p. A302

SHEEHAN, Daniel F., Administrator, Research Belton Hospital, Belton, MO, p. A241

SHEEHAN, Michael J., Facility Administrator, Hastings Regional Center, Hastings, NE, p. A260

SHEEHAN, John R., MSC, Deputy Commander, Ehrling Bergquist Hospital, Offutt AFB, NE, p. A262

SHEEHY, Earl N., Chief Executive Officer, Northeast Montana Health Services, Wolf Point, MT, p. A257

SHEETZ, Douglas A., Chief Executive Officer, Keokuk County Health Center, Sigourney, IA, p. A154

SHELBY, Dennis R., Chief Executive Officer, HEALTHSOUTH Rehabilitation Hospital, Fayetteville, AR, p. A30

SHELBY, Marla, Administrator and Chief Executive Officer, South Lincoln Medical Center, Kemmerer, WY, p. A468

SHELDON, Lyle Ernest
Executive Vice President and Chief Operating Officer, Fallston General Hospital, Fallston, MD, p. A196
President and Chief Executive Officer, Harford Memorial Hospital, Havre De Grace, MD, p. A196
President and Chief Executive Officer, Upper Chesapeake Health System, Fallston, MD, p. B151

SHELTON, Frank, President, Union Hospital, Terre Haute, IN, p. A146

SHELTON II, W. Allen, Administrator and Chief Executive Officer, Eye and Ear Clinic of Charleston, Charleston, WV, p. A452

SHEMBERGER, Kaylor E., President and Chief Executive Officer, Chandler Regional Hospital, Chandler, AZ, p. A22

SHEPARD, John J., President and Chief Executive Officer, Clarion Hospital, Clarion, PA, p. A351

SHEPARD, R. Coert, President, Anderson Hospital, Maryville, IL, p. A130

SHEPHARD, Paul E., President and Chief Executive Officer, St. James Mercy Hospital, Hornell, NY, p. A289

SHEPHERD, Richard W., President and Chief Executive Officer, Children's Seashore House, Philadelphia, PA, p. A360

SHERON, William E., Chief Executive Officer, Wooster Community Hospital, Wooster, OH, p. A334

SHERROD, Rhonda, Administrator, Shands at Live Oak, Live Oak, FL, p. A89

SHERVINGTON, Walter W., M.D., Chief Executive Officer, New Orleans Adolescent Hospital, New Orleans, LA, p. A185

SHERWOOD, Gary A., Executive Vice President, Rogue Valley Medical Center, Medford, OR, p. A346

SHIELDS, Lena L., Chief Executive, Bethany Hospital, Chicago, IL, p. A122

SHIELS, Rob, Administrator, Mary Shiels Hospital, Dallas, TX, p. A403

SHIMONO, Jiro R., Director, Delaware Psychiatric Center, New Castle, DE, p. A78

SHIPPY, Janice, R.N., Administrator, Sedan City Hospital, Sedan, KS, p. A165

SHIRK, Michael, President and Senior Executive Officer, Boone Hospital Center, Columbia, MO, p. A242

SHIRTCLIFF, Christine, Executive Vice President, Mary Lane Hospital, Ware, MA, p. A206

SHOCKLEY, Allen L., President and Chief Executive Officer, St. John's Regional Health Center, Springfield, MO, p. A251

SHOOK, Scott E., President, Riverside Mercy Hospital, Toledo, OH, p. A332

SHORB, Gary S., President, Methodist Hospitals of Memphis, Memphis, TN, p. A390

SHORE, Muriel M., R.N., Chief Executive Officer, Essex County Hospital Center, Cedar Grove, NJ, p. A272

SHOVELIN, Wayne F., President and Chief Executive Officer, Gaston Memorial Hospital, Gastonia, NC, p. A308

SHRODER, Robert W., Chief Operating Officer, St. Joseph Health Center, Warren, OH, p. A333

SHUFF, R. Lindsay, Administrator, Greenleaf Center, Fort Oglethorpe, GA, p. A106

SHUGARMAN, Mark, President, Mercy Hospital, Tiffin, OH, p. A332

SHULER, Priscilla J., Chief Executive Officer, Capitol Medical Center, Richmond, VA, p. A442

SHUMAKER, Revonda L., R.N., President and Chief Executive Officer, Lakewood Hospital, Lakewood, OH, p. A328

SHYAVITZ, Linda, President and Chief Executive Officer, Sturdy Memorial Hospital, Attleboro, MA, p. A199

SICURELLA, John, Chief Executive Officer, Reynolds Memorial Hospital, Glen Dale, WV, p. A453

SIEBER, Thomas L., President and Chief Executive Officer, Genesis HealthCare System, Zanesville, OH, p. A334

SIEGEL, Bruce, M.P.H., President and Chief Executive Officer, Tampa General Healthcare, Tampa, FL, p. A98

SIEGEL, Patricia, Senior Vice President and Area Manager, Kaiser Foundation Hospital, Fontana, CA, p. A42

SIEGWALD–MAYS, Cheryl, Administrator, Columbia Behavioral Health Center, Miami, FL, p. A90

SIEMEN–MESSING, Pauline, R.N., President and Chief Executive Officer, Harbor Beach Community Hospital, Harbor Beach, MI, p. A213

SIEMERS, Thomas R., Chief Executive Officer, Rebsamen Regional Medical Center, Jacksonville, AR, p. A32

SIEPMAN, Milton R., Ph.D., President and Chief Executive Officer, Tennessee Christian Medical Center, Madison, TN, p. A389

SILLEN, Robert, Executive Director, Santa Clara Valley Medical Center, San Jose, CA, p. A61

SILLS, Doug, President and Chief Executive Officer, Central Florida Regional Hospital, Sanford, FL, p. A96

SILVA, Luis G., Chief Executive Officer and Regional Administrator, Columbia Beaumont Medical Center, Beaumont, TX, p. A398

SILVA, William G., Executive Director, Metropolitan State Hospital, Norwalk, CA, p. A54

SILVER, Jack B., M.P.H., Chief Executive Officer, Arizona State Hospital, Phoenix, AZ, p. A24

SILVER, Richard A., Director, James A. Haley Veterans Hospital, Tampa, FL, p. A97

SILVERNALE, Vern, Administrator, Johnson Memorial Health Services, Dawson, MN, p. A224

SILVIA, Clarence J., President, Bradley Memorial Hospital and Health Center, Southington, CT, p. A76

SIMCHUK, Cathy, Chief Operating Officer, Deer Park Health Center and Hospital, Deer Park, WA, p. A446

SIMMONS, Randy, Administrator, Davis County Hospital, Bloomfield, IA, p. A147

SIMMONS, Stephen H.
Senior Administrator, University of South Alabama Hospitals, Mobile, AL, p. B150
Administrator, University of South Alabama Medical Center, Mobile, AL, p. A16

SIMMONS, Tim, Chief Executive Officer, Hood River Memorial Hospital, Hood River, OR, p. A345

SIMMONS, W. Clay, Executive Director, Bradford Health Services at Birmingham, Birmingham, AL, p. A11

SIMMONS, William, President and Chief Executive Officer, San Jacinto Methodist Hospital, Baytown, TX, p. A397

SIMMS, John L., President and Chief Executive Officer, Trinity Community Medical Center of Brenham, Brenham, TX, p. A399

SIMON, Elliot J., FACHE, Chief Operating Officer, Western Queens Community Hospital, New York, NY, p. A296

SIMON, Mary Alvera, Administrator, Mercy Hospital of Scott County, Waldron, AR, p. A35

SIMONIN, Steve J., Chief Executive Officer, Community Memorial Hospital, Clarion, IA, p. A148

SIMPATICO, Thomas, M.D., Facility Director and Network System Manager, Chicago–Read Mental Health Center, Chicago, IL, p. A122

SIMPSON, Mack N., Administrator, McCone County Medical Assistance Facility, Circle, MT, p. A253

SIMPSON, Tim, Administrator, Vencor–North Florida, Green Cove Springs, FL, p. A86

SIMS, Craig E.
President and Chief Executive Officer, RHD Memorial Medical Center, Dallas, TX, p. A403
President, Trinity Medical Center, Carrollton, TX, p. A400

SIMS, Norman L., USAF, Commander, U. S. Air Force Hospital Little Rock, Jacksonville, AR, p. A32

SIMS Jr., John H., Director, Veterans Affairs Medical Center, Togus, ME, p. A192

SINCLAIR, Mike, Administrator, Kane County Hospital, Kanab, UT, p. A430

SINGLE, John L.
Chief Executive Officer and Administrator, De Smet Memorial Hospital, De Smet, SD, p. A378
Chief Executive Officer, Huron Regional Medical Center, Huron, SD, p. A379

SINGLETON, J. Knox, President, Inova Health System, Springfield, VA, p. B109

SINNOTT, Daniel J.
President and Chief Executive Officer, Nazareth Hospital, Philadelphia, PA, p. A361
President and Chief Executive Officer, St. Agnes Medical Center, Philadelphia, PA, p. A361
President and Chief Executive Officer, St. Francis Hospital, Wilmington, DE, p. A78

SIPES, Don, Senior Executive Officer, Saint Luke's Northland Hospital–Smithville Campus, Smithville, MO, p. A251

SIPKOSKI, Michael, Executive Vice President and Chief Executive Officer, St. Francis Hospital, Litchfield, IL, p. A130

SIRK, David R., President and Chief Executive Officer, Saint Francis Hospital, Charleston, WV, p. A452

SISSON, William G., President, Central Baptist Hospital, Lexington, KY, p. A172

SISTI, Judith L., MS, Administrator, Vineland Developmental Center Hospital, Vineland, NJ, p. A278

SISTO, Dennis, Acting President and Chief Executive Officer, Queen of the Valley Hospital, Napa, CA, p. A53

SKALSKY, Susan, M.D., Director, Hurtado Health Center, New Brunswick, NJ, p. A275

SKELLEY, Dennis B., President and Chief Executive Officer, Walton Rehabilitation Hospital, Augusta, GA, p. A102

SKINNER, David B., M.D.
President and Chief Executive Officer, New York & Presbyterian Healthcare, New York, NY, p. B120
Vice Chairman and Chief Executive Officer, New York and Presbyterian Hospital, New York, NY, p. A294

SKINNER, Davis D., President, Missouri Baptist Hospital of Sullivan, Sullivan, MO, p. A251

SKINNER, Sandra, Chief Executive Officer, First Health, Inc., Batesville, MS, p. B100

SKOGSBERGH, James H.
President, Iowa Lutheran Hospital, Des Moines, IA, p. A149
President, Iowa Methodist Medical Center, Des Moines, IA, p. A150

SKOMOROCH, Orianna A., Chief Executive Officer, Kauai Veterans Memorial Hospital, Waimea, HI, p. A115

SKOWLUND, Kathy, Administrator, Lakeland Medical Center, Elkhorn, WI, p. A459

SKUBA, Herbert S., President, Ellwood City Hospital, Ellwood City, PA, p. A353

SKUTZKA, Alexander, Chief Executive Officer, Island Medical Center, Hempstead, NY, p. A289

SKVAREK, Joann A., Executive Vice President, Edgewater Medical Center, Chicago, IL, p. A122

SLABACH, Brock A., Administrator, Field Memorial Community Hospital, Centreville, MS, p. A234

SLAGTER, Dean G., Administrator, Renville County Hospital, Olivia, MN, p. A228

SLAUBAUGH, D. Ray, President, Graham Hospital, Canton, IL, p. A121

SLAVEN, Terrence, Interim President and Chief Executive Officer, Phoenix Children's Hospital, Phoenix, AZ, p. A25

SLAVIN, Peter L., M.D., President, Barnes–Jewish Hospital, Saint Louis, MO, p. A249

SLIETER, Richard G., Administrator, Owatonna Hospital, Owatonna, MN, p. A229

SLOAN, Gary
Chief Executive Officer, Doctors Medical Center–Pinole Campus, Pinole, CA, p. A56
Chief Executive Officer, Doctors Medical Center–San Pablo Campus, San Pablo, CA, p. A62

SLOAN, Joseph F., CHE, Chief Executive Officer, Plains Memorial Hospital, Dimmitt, TX, p. A404

SLOAN, Robert L., Chief Executive Officer, Sibley Memorial Hospital, Washington, DC, p. A79

SLUNECKA, Fredrick, President and Chief Executive Officer, McKennan Hospital, Sioux Falls, SD, p. A381

SLUSKY, Richard, Administrator, Mount Ascutney Hospital and Health Center, Windsor, VT, p. A435

SLYTER, Mark, Administrator, Hillcrest Hospital, Simpsonville, SC, p. A376

SMALL, Marilyn, Acting Site Executive Officer, Veterans Affairs Medical Center, Marion, IL, p. A130

SMALL, Sandra
Administrator, Kaiser Foundation Hospital, Walnut Creek, CA, p. A66
Administrator, Kaiser Foundation Hospital and Rehabilitation Center, Vallejo, CA, p. A66

SMALLEY, Diana, Chief Operating Officer, Midlands Community Hospital, Papillion, NE, p. A263

SMART, Dalton L., Administrator, Jennings Community Hospital, North Vernon, IN, p. A144

SMART, Michael, Chief Executive Officer, Alameda County Medical Center–Highland Campus, Oakland, CA, p. A54

SMART, Michael G., Administrator, Alameda County Medical Center, San Leandro, CA, p. A61

SMART, Robert M., Area Manager and Chief Executive Officer, HEALTHSOUTH Medical Center, Dallas, TX, p. A403

SMEDLEY, Craig M., Administrator, Valley View Medical Center, Cedar City, UT, p. A430

SMIGELSKI, Daniel R., Chief Executive Officer, Gritman Medical Center, Moscow, ID, p. A118

SMILEY, Jon D., Chief Executive Officer, Sunnyside Community Hospital, Sunnyside, WA, p. A450

SMILEY, W. David, Chief Executive Officer, San Joaquin Valley Rehabilitation Hospital, Fresno, CA, p. A43

SMITH, Alex B., Ph.D., Executive Director, Terrebonne General Medical Center, Houma, LA, p. A181

SMITH, Bernadette
Chief Operating Officer, Seton Medical Center, Daly City, CA, p. A40
Chief Operating Officer, Seton Medical Center Coastside, Moss Beach, CA, p. A53

SMITH, C. W., President and Chief Executive Officer, Parkview Medical Center, Pueblo, CO, p. A72

SMITH, Charles M., M.D.
President and Chief Executive Officer, Christiana Care Corporation, Wilmington, DE, p. B81
President and Chief Executive Officer, Christiana Hospital, Newark, DE, p. A78
President and Chief Executive Officer, Wilmington Hospital, Wilmington, DE, p. A78

SMITH, Connie, Chief Executive Officer, The Medical Center at Bowling Green, Bowling Green, KY, p. A168

SMITH, David M., FACHE, President and Chief Executive Officer, West Jefferson Medical Center, Marrero, LA, p. A183

SMITH, Dennis H.
Director, VA Maryland Health Care System–Fort Howard Division, Fort Howard, MD, p. A196
Director, Veterans Affairs Maryland Health Care System–Baltimore Division, Baltimore, MD, p. A194
Director, Veterans Affairs Maryland Health Care System–Perry Point Division, Perry Point, MD, p. A197

SMITH, F. Curtis, President, Massachusetts Eye and Ear Infirmary, Boston, MA, p. A200

SMITH, Frances L., MSN, Superintendent, Haverford State Hospital, Haverford, PA, p. A355

SMITH, Frances T., Administrator, Childress Regional Medical Center, Childress, TX, p. A400

SMITH, Gordon, Administrator, Merrill Pioneer Community Hospital, Rock Rapids, IA, p. A154

SMITH, Gwendolyn A., R.N., Vice President, Springfield Hospital, Springfield, PA, p. A366

SMITH, H. Gerald, President and Chief Executive Officer, St. Francis Medical Center, Monroe, LA, p. A184

SMITH, Harlan J., President, Franklin Medical Center, Greenfield, MA, p. A202

SMITH, Harley, Chief Executive Officer, Colorado River Medical Center, Needles, CA, p. A54

SMITH, James E., Superintendent, Wichita Falls State Hospital, Wichita Falls, TX, p. A429

SMITH, Jeffrey H., Ph.D., Superintendent, Logansport State Hospital, Logansport, IN, p. A143

SMITH, Jerry, Chief Executive Officer, BHC Pinon Hills Hospital, Santa Fe, NM, p. A283

SMITH, Jim B., President and Chief Executive Officer, Goodall–Witcher Hospital, Clifton, TX, p. A400

SMITH, Joe E., Administrator and Chief Executive Officer, DeWitt City Hospital, De Witt, AR, p. A30

SMITH, Johnson L., Chief Executive Officer and Administrator, St. Anthony's Healthcare Center, Morrilton, AR, p. A33

SMITH, Joseph S., Chief Executive Officer, Boone County Hospital, Boone, IA, p. A147

SMITH, Kathleen, Executive Director, Friendly Hills Regional Medical Center, La Habra, CA, p. A46

SMITH, Lex, Administrator, Park View Hospital, El Reno, OK, p. A337

SMITH, Lloyd V., President and Chief Executive Officer, Benefis Health Care, Great Falls, MT, p. A254

SMITH, Martin D., Chief Operating Officer, Midwest Regional Medical Center, Midwest City, OK, p. A339

SMITH, Melvyn E., President, Allegheny University Hospital, City Avenue, Philadelphia, PA, p. A359

SMITH, Meredith H., Administrator, Dodge County Hospital, Eastman, GA, p. A106

SMITH, Michael N., Director Healthcare Services, San Joaquin General Hospital, French Camp, CA, p. A43

SMITH, R. S., Chief Executive Officer, Community Hospital–Lakeview, Eufaula, OK, p. A337

SMITH, Randy, Interim Administrator, Jackson Hospital, Marianna, FL, p. A90

SMITH, Raymond N., Chief Executive Officer, Community Hospital of Gardena, Gardena, CA, p. A44

SMITH, Richard, Administrator, Logan Regional Hospital, Logan, UT, p. A431

SMITH, Richard G., Chief Executive Officer, Oneida Healthcare Center, Oneida, NY, p. A298

SMITH, Robbie, Administrator, Higgins General Hospital, Bremen, GA, p. A103

SMITH, Robert B., President and Chief Executive Officer, Zale Lipshy University Hospital, Dallas, TX, p. A404

SMITH, Robert L., President and Chief Executive Officer, Decatur General Hospital, Decatur, AL, p. A13

SMITH, S. Allen, Administrator, Tri–City Community Hospital, Jourdanton, TX, p. A414

SMITH, Steve, Chief Executive Officer, Carson Tahoe Hospital, Carson City, NV, p. A266

SMITH, Steven L., President and Chief Executive Officer, Memorial Medical Center, Las Cruces, NM, p. A282

SMITH, Stuart, Vice President Clinical Operations and Chief Executive Officer, MUSC Medical Center of Medical University of South Carolina, Charleston, SC, p. A372

SMITH, Terry J., Administrator, Bibb Medical Center, Centreville, AL, p. A13

SMITH, Thomas G., Chief Executive Officer, Parkview Hospital of Topeka, Topeka, KS, p. A166

SMITH, Thomas W., President and Chief Executive Officer, Ephraim McDowell Regional Medical Center, Danville, KY, p. A169

SMITH, Timothy
President and Chief Executive Officer, Fountain Valley Regional Hospital and Medical Center, Fountain Valley, CA, p. A42
President and Chief Executive Officer, Garden Grove Hospital and Medical Center, Garden Grove, CA, p. A43

SMITH, Todd A., Chief Executive Officer, Charter Behavioral Health System of Southern California–Charter Oak, Covina, CA, p. A40

SMITH, Tommy J., President and Chief Executive Officer, Baptist Healthcare System, Louisville, KY, p. B70

SMITH, W. David, Director, Veterans Affairs Medical Center, Fort Lyon, CO, p. A70

SMITH, Wayne T., President and Chief Executive Officer, Community Health Systems, Inc., Brentwood, TN, p. B89

SMITH, William C., Chief Executive Officer, Livingston Hospital and Healthcare Services, Salem, KY, p. A176

SMITH, William R., Administrator, Hamilton Hospital, Olney, TX, p. A419

SMITH II, W. Don, President and Chief Executive Officer, Cabell Huntington Hospital, Huntington, WV, p. A453

SMITH Jr., Charles W., Chief Executive Officer, St. Jerome Hospital, Batavia, NY, p. A284

SMITH Jr., P. Paul, Executive Director, Lake Norman Regional Medical Center, Mooresville, NC, p. A310

SMITH Jr., Philip W., President, MedCenter Hospital, Marion, OH, p. A329

SMITH–BLACKWELL, Olivia, M.P.H., President and Chief Executive Officer, Sheehan Memorial Hospital, Buffalo, NY, p. A286

SMITHBURG, Donald R., Administrator, Truman Medical Center–East, Kansas City, MO, p. A245

SMITHERS, Joe, Administrator, Horizon Specialty Hospital, Edmond, OK, p. A337

SMITHHISLER, John, CHE, Chief Executive Officer, Centinela Hospital Medical Center, Inglewood, CA, p. A45

SMITHMIER, Kenneth L., President and Chief Executive Officer, Decatur Memorial Hospital, Decatur, IL, p. A125

SNEAD, Benjamin E., President and Chief Executive Officer, St. Clair Memorial Hospital, Pittsburgh, PA, p. A363

SNEDIGAR, Rudy, Chief Executive Officer, Clarinda Regional Health Center, Clarinda, IA, p. A148

SNELL, Donald F., President and Chief Executive Officer, Long Island College Hospital, New York, NY, p. A293

SNIPES, Lucas A., FACHE, Director, Carilion Medical Center, Roanoke, VA, p. A443

SNOW, Anne, Administrator, Hansford Hospital, Spearman, TX, p. A425

SNOW, Mel L., Administrator, West Holt Memorial Hospital, Atkinson, NE, p. A258

SNYDER, David M., Executive Director and Chief Executive Officer, Natchez Regional Medical Center, Natchez, MS, p. A238

SOBOTA, Richard E., President and Chief Executive Officer, Pike Community Hospital, Waverly, OH, p. A333

SODERBLOM, Alan, Administrator, Loma Linda University Behavioral Medicine Center, Redlands, CA, p. A57

SODOMKA, Patricia, FACHE, Executive Director, Medical College of Georgia Hospital and Clinics, Augusta, GA, p. A102

SOILEAU, Joseph L., Chief Executive Officer, South Cameron Memorial Hospital, Cameron, LA, p. A179

SOKOL, Dennis A., President and Chief Executive Officer, Firelands Community Hospital, Sandusky, OH, p. A332

SOKOLOW, Norman J., President and Chief Executive Officer, Cornerstone of Medical Arts Center Hospital, New York, NY, p. A292

SOLARE, Frank A., President and Chief Executive Officer, Thorek Hospital and Medical Center, Chicago, IL, p. A124

SOLHEIM, John H., Chief Executive Officer, St. Mary's Regional Health Center, Detroit Lakes, MN, p. A224

SOLIVAN, Miguel A., Executive Director, Hospital De Area De Yauco, Yauco, PR, p. A474

SOLNIT, Albert J., M.D., Commissioner, Connecticut State Department of Mental Health, Hartford, CT, p. B90

SOLVIBILE, Edward R., President, Suburban General Hospital, Norristown, PA, p. A359

SOMMER, Richard C., Administrator, Defiance Hospital, Defiance, OH, p. A326

SONDECKER, James, Administrator, St. Joseph's Behavioral Health Center, Stockton, CA, p. A64

SONDUCK, Allan C., President and Chief Executive Officer, Provena St. Mary's Hospital, Kankakee, IL, p. A129

SOPO, Deborah A., Administrator, Vencor Hospital–Detroit, Lincoln Park, MI, p. A215

SOUKUP, Richard G., Chief Executive Officer, Northern Hills General Hospital, Deadwood, SD, p. A378

SOULE, Frederick L., President and Chief Executive Officer, Caldwell Memorial Hospital, Lenoir, NC, p. A310

SOYUGENC, Marjorie Z., President and Chief Executive Officer, Welborn Memorial Baptist Hospital, Evansville, IN, p. A139

SPAETH, Ronald G., President and Chief Executive Officer, Highland Park Hospital, Highland Park, IL, p. A128

SPANG, A. James, Administrator, Shriners Hospitals for Children–Chicago, Chicago, IL, p. A124

SPARKMAN, Dena C., Administrator, McDowell ARH Hospital, McDowell, KY, p. A174

SPARKMAN, Ronald L., Administrator, Carraway Burdick West Medical Center, Haleyville, AL, p. A15

SPARKS, Julian, Board Chairman, Marshall County Health Care Authority, Guntersville, AL, p. B116

SPARKS, Richard G., President, Watauga Medical Center, Boone, NC, p. A305

SPARROW, William T., Chief Executive Officer, BHC San Luis Rey Hospital, Encinitas, CA, p. A42

SPARTZ, Gregory G., Chief Executive Officer, Willmar Regional Treatment Center, Willmar, MN, p. A232

SPAUDE, Paul A., President and Chief Executive Officer, Wausau Hospital, Wausau, WI, p. A467

SPAULDING, Don, Administrator and Chief Executive Officer, Fort Duncan Medical Center, Eagle Pass, TX, p. A405

SPAUSTER, Edward, Ph.D., Executive Director, Arms Acres, Carmel, NY, p. A286

SPEAK, Patricia B., Administrator, Vencor Hospital–Pittsburgh, Oakdale, PA, p. A359

SPEARS, Leonard J., Vice President and Chief Executive Officer, American Legion Hospital, Crowley, LA, p. A180

SPECK, William T., President and Chief Operating Officer, New York and Presbyterian Hospital, New York, NY, p. A294

SPEED, Marilyn, Administrator, Beacham Memorial Hospital, Magnolia, MS, p. A237

SPELLMAN, Warren K., Administrator, Holy Cross Hospital, Taos, NM, p. A283

SPENCER, Corte J., Chief Executive Officer, Oswego Hospital, Oswego, NY, p. A298

SPENCER, Herman J., Administrator, Northern Inyo Hospital, Bishop, CA, p. A38

SPENCER, Steven H.
Administrator, St. Mary's Kewaunee Area Memorial Hospital, Kewaunee, WI, p. A460
Administrator, Two Rivers Community Hospital and Hamilton Memorial Home, Two Rivers, WI, p. A466

SPERO, Barry M., President, Masonic Geriatric Healthcare Center, Wallingford, CT, p. A77

SPHATT, Thomas R., President and Chief Executive Officer, Berwick Hospital Center, Berwick, PA, p. A350

SPICER, John R., President and Chief Executive Officer, Sound Shore Medical Center of Westchester, New Rochelle, NY, p. A291

SPIKE, Colleen A., Interim Administrator, Community Hospital and Health Care Center, Saint Peter, MN, p. A230

SPILLMAN, Eugene, Executive Director, Natchitoches Parish Hospital, Natchitoches, LA, p. A184

SPILOVOY, Richard, Administrator, Garrison Memorial Hospital, Garrison, ND, p. A317

SPINELLI, Robert J., Administrator and Chief Executive Officer, Bloomsburg Hospital, Bloomsburg, PA, p. A350

SPITLER III, William H., President, Perry Memorial Hospital, Princeton, IL, p. A133

SPIVEY, David, Interim Chief Executive Officer, Mercy Hospital, Detroit, MI, p. A211

SPIVEY, Sue, Administrator, Irwin County Hospital, Ocilla, GA, p. A110

SPOELMAN, Roger
President and Chief Executive Officer, Mercy General Health Partners, Muskegon, MI, p. A217
Chief Executive Officer, Mercy General Health Partners–Oak Avenue Campus, Muskegon, MI, p. A217

SPRAY, William Russell, Chief Executive Officer, Gadsden Regional Medical Center, Gadsden, AL, p. A14

SPRENGER, Gordon M., Executive Officer, Allina Health System, Minneapolis, MN, p. B66

SPRINGER, Kay H., Administrator, Steele Memorial Hospital, Salmon, ID, p. A118

SPRISSLER, Fred, President and Chief Executive Officer, St. Luke's Quakertown Hospital, Quakertown, PA, p. A364

SPROUSE, James P., Administrator, Cumberland Hospital, Fayetteville, NC, p. A308

SPYHALSKI, Richard A., Chief Executive Officer, Northwest Medical Center, Thief River Falls, MN, p. A231

ST. ANDRE, Christine, Executive Director, University of Utah Hospitals and Clinics, Salt Lake City, UT, p. A432

ST. CLAIR, Marvin O., Administrator, Hawaii State Hospital, Kaneohe, HI, p. A115

ST. CLAIR, Nelson L., President, Riverside Health System, Newport News, VA, p. B133

STAAS Jr., William E., President and Medical Director, Magee Rehabilitation Hospital, Philadelphia, PA, p. A361

STACEY, Bryan, Administrator, Ashland Health Center, Ashland, KS, p. A157

STACEY, Rulon F., President and Chief Executive Officer, Poudre Valley Hospital, Fort Collins, CO, p. A70

STACK, Edward A., President and Chief Executive Officer, Behavioral Healthcare Corporation, Nashville, TN, p. B71

STAHELSKI, David H., Senior Vice President Hospital Operations, Manchester, CT, p. A75
Senior Vice President Hospital Operations, Rockville General Hospital, Vernon Rockville, CT, p. A76

STAMM, Scott C., Chief Executive Officer, Columbia River Park Hospital, Huntington, WV, p. A453

STAMPOHAR, Jeffrey, Chief Executive Officer, Deer River Healthcare Center, Deer River, MN, p. A224

STANBERRY, Marion W., Administrator, East Texas Medical Center–Wood County at Quitman, Quitman, TX, p. A421

STANKO, J. Richard, President and Chief Executive Officer, St. Joseph Hospital, Omaha, NE, p. A263

STANLEY, Robert R., Chief Executive Officer, Iberia General Hospital and Medical Center, New Iberia, LA, p. A184

STANSBERRY, Mark, Superintendent, Mid Missouri Mental Health Center, Columbia, MO, p. A242

STANUSH, Sharon M., President, Southwest Mental Health Center, San Antonio, TX, p. A423

STANZIONE, Dominick M., Chief Operating Officer and Executive Vice President, Sisters of Charity Medical Center, New York, NY, p. A295

STAPLES, Nancy, MS, Administrator, Elgin Mental Health Center, Elgin, IL, p. A126

STARK, Charles A., CHE, Administrator, Chief Executive and Regional Vice President, HEALTHSOUTH Medical Center, Richmond, VA, p. A442

STARK, David, Interim Administrator, Clarke County Hospital, Osceola, IA, p. A154

STARNES, Gregory D., Chief Executive Officer, Culver Union Hospital, Crawfordsville, IN, p. A138

STARR, Gerald A.
Chief Executive Officer, Delano Regional Medical Center, Delano, CA, p. A41
Chief Executive Officer, Kern Medical Center, Bakersfield, CA, p. A37

STARR Jr., Hickory, Administrator, William W. Hastings Indian Hospital, Tahlequah, OK, p. A342

STASIK, Randall, President and Chief Executive Officer, Borgess Medical Center, Kalamazoo, MI, p. A214

STATTON, Dave, Interim Superintendent, Griffin Memorial Hospital, Norman, OK, p. A339

STATUTO, Richard, Chief Executive Officer, St. Joseph Health System, Orange, CA, p. B141

STAUDER, Mark S., President and Chief Executive Officer, Mercy Regional Medical Center, Laredo, TX, p. A415

STAYNINGS, Tony, Chief Executive Officer, Swisher Memorial Hospital District, Tulia, TX, p. A426

STECKLER, Michael J., Chief Executive Officer, Jennie M. Melham Memorial Medical Center, Broken Bow, NE, p. A258

STEED, Karen, Chief Executive Officer, Eastern State Hospital, Vinita, OK, p. A343

STEED, Larry N., Administrator, Tanner Medical Center–Villa Rica, Villa Rica, GA, p. A113

STEED, Robert A., Administrator, Willamette Falls Hospital, Oregon City, OR, p. A346

STEEGE, Armin, Chief Executive Officer, Charter Behavioral Health System of Austin, Austin, TX, p. A396

STEELE, Barbara, President, The Toledo Hospital, Toledo, OH, p. A333

STEFFEE, Sam L., Executive Director and Chief Executive Officer, Polly Ryon Memorial Hospital, Richmond, TX, p. A421

STEGBAUER, Tom, Administrator, Olympic Memorial Hospital, Port Angeles, WA, p. A448

STEIDER, Norman D., President, Memorial Hospital of Michigan City, Michigan City, IN, p. A143

STEIN, Benjamin M., M.D., President, Brunswick General Hospital, Amityville, NY, p. A284

STEIN, Bob, Executive Director, Vencor Hospital–Houston, Houston, TX, p. A413

STEIN, Dale J., President and Chief Executive Officer, St. Luke's Midland Regional Medical Center, Aberdeen, SD, p. A378

STEIN, Gary M., President and Chief Executive Officer, Touro Infirmary, New Orleans, LA, p. A185

STEIN, Norman V., President, University Community Hospital, Tampa, FL, p. A98

STEIN, Sheldon J., Chief Operating Officer, Mt. Washington Pediatric Hospital, Baltimore, MD, p. A194

STEINER, Garith W., Chief Executive Officer, Vernon Memorial Hospital, Viroqua, WI, p. A466

STEINER, Keith M., Administrator, Madison Memorial Hospital, Rexburg, ID, p. A118

STEINHAUER, Bruce W., M.D., President and Chief Executive Officer, Regional Medical Center at Memphis, Memphis, TN, p. A390

STEINHOFF, Earl J., Chief Executive Officer, Prowers Medical Center, Lamar, CO, p. A71

STEITZ, David P., Chief Executive Officer, Frankfort Regional Medical Center, Frankfort, KY, p. A170

STELLER, Tim, Chief Executive Officer, North Central Health Care Facilities, Wausau, WI, p. A467

STENBERG, Scott, Chief Executive Officer, Sutter Amador Hospital, Jackson, CA, p. A45

STENGER, Michael J., Executive Vice President and Administrator, St. Nicholas Hospital, Sheboygan, WI, p. A465

STENSON, Richard, President, Tuality Healthcare, Hillsboro, OR, p. A345

STENSRUD, Kirk, Administrator, Hendricks Community Hospital, Hendricks, MN, p. A226

STENZLER, Mark R., Vice President Administration, North Shore University Hospital at Glen Cove, Glen Cove, NY, p. A288

STEPANIK, Mark J., Interim Chief Executive Officer, HEALTHSOUTH Rehabilitation Hospital, Florence, SC, p. A373

STEPHANS, J. Michael, Administrator, Medical Center Hospital, Odessa, TX, p. A419

STEPHEN, Ron, Executive Vice President and Administrator, Osteopathic Medical Center of Texas, Fort Worth, TX, p. A407

STEPHENS, Michael D., President and Chief Executive Officer, Hoag Memorial Hospital Presbyterian, Newport Beach, CA, p. A54

STEPHENS, Michael R., President, Greene Memorial Hospital, Xenia, OH, p. A334

STEPHENS, Terry A., Executive Director, Sierra Tucson, Tucson, AZ, p. A27

STEPHENS Jr., Jack T., President and Chief Executive Officer, Lakeland Regional Medical Center, Lakeland, FL, p. A88

STEPHENSON, Christy, Chief Administrative Officer, Robert Wood Johnson University Hospital at Hamilton, Hamilton, NJ, p. A273

STEPHENSON, David, Administrator, Rock County Hospital, Bassett, NE, p. A258

STEPP, Merle E., President and Chief Executive Officer, Clark Memorial Hospital, Jeffersonville, IN, p. A142

STERN, Ron, Chief Executive Officer, Palmetto General Hospital, Hialeah, FL, p. A86

STEVENS, Alan I., Administrator, Huntington Hospital, Willow Grove, PA, p. A368

STEVENS, April A., R.N., Vice President and Administrator, Allegheny University Hospitals West–Forbes Metropolitan, Pittsburgh, PA, p. A362

STEVENS, Essimae, Service Unit Director, U.S. Public Health Service Indian Hospital, Redlake, MN, p. A229

STEVENS, Robert, President and Chief Executive Officer, Ridgeview Medical Center, Waconia, MN, p. A231

STEVENS, Velinda, Chief Executive Officer, Longview Regional Medical Center, Longview, TX, p. A416

STEVENS, Ward W., CHE, Chief Executive Officer, Columbia Alleghany Regional Hospital, Low Moor, VA, p. A439

STEVENS Jr., Vernon R., Administrator, Riverland Medical Center, Ferriday, LA, p. A180

STEVENSON, Kevin, Chief Executive Officer, Lakeview Rehabilitation Hospital, Elizabethtown, KY, p. A169

STEVENSON, Mike, Administrator, Murphy Medical Center, Murphy, NC, p. A311

STEWART, Charles L., Administrator, Northport Hospital–DCH, Northport, AL, p. A17

STEWART, Christine R., President and Chief Executive Officer, Northwest Medical Center, Russellville, AL, p. A18

STEWART, Diane Gail, Administrator, Sutter Center for Psychiatry, Sacramento, CA, p. A58

STEWART, Joseph A., Chief Executive Officer, Butler Health System, Butler, PA, p. A351

STEWART, Lawrence C., Director, Veterans Affairs Medical Center, Long Beach, CA, p. A48

STEWART, Mary Ellen, Administrator, Schick Shadel Hospital, Seattle, WA, p. A449

STEWART, Paul R., President and Chief Executive Officer, Merle West Medical Center, Klamath Falls, OR, p. A345

STEWART, Shirley A., President and Chief Executive Officer, Tulane University Hospital and Clinic, New Orleans, LA, p. A185

STIBBARDS, J. E. Ted, Ph.D., President and Chief Executive Officer, Driscoll Children's Hospital, Corpus Christi, TX, p. A401

STILLWAGON, Richard A., Superintendent, Torrance State Hospital, Torrance, PA, p. A366

STILLWELL, James M., Director, Impact Drug and Alcohol Treatment Center, Pasadena, CA, p. A55

STINDT, John, Administrator, Arlington Municipal Hospital, Arlington, MN, p. A222

STOCK, Greg K., Chief Executive Officer, Northwest Medical Center, Springdale, AR, p. A35

STOCKEL, Craig, Interim Administrator, Fairview Red Wing Hospital, Red Wing, MN, p. A229

STOCKTON, Eddy R., Administrator, Wayne County Hospital, Monticello, KY, p. A174

STODDARD, Mark R.
President, Central Valley Medical Center, Nephi, UT, p. A431
President, Rural Health Management Corporation, Nephi, UT, p. B133

STOKER, Teresa, Executive Director, Hillside Hospital, Atlanta, GA, p. A101

STOKES, Barry S., President and Chief Executive Officer, Edward White Hospital, Saint Petersburg, FL, p. A96

STOKES, Gary L., Chief Executive Officer, Gulf Coast Medical Center, Biloxi, MS, p. A233

STOLL, Dale D., Chief Executive Officer, Arkansas Valley Regional Medical Center, La Junta, CO, p. A71

STOLZENBERG, Edward A., President and Chief Executive Officer, Westchester Medical Center, Valhalla, NY, p. A302

STONE, John M., Director, Metropolitan Nashville General Hospital, Nashville, TN, p. A391

STONE, Ken, Administrator, Vencor Hospital – Central Tampa, Tampa, FL, p. A98

STONE, Robert, President, Blythedale Children's Hospital, Valhalla, NY, p. A302

STONE, Thomas J., Administrator, St. Tammany Parish Hospital, Covington, LA, p. A180

STONER, Philip J., Chief Executive Officer, Tyrone Hospital, Tyrone, PA, p. A366

STORDAHL, Dean R., Director, Jerry L. Pettis Memorial Veterans Medical Center, Loma Linda, CA, p. A47

STORTO, David E., Interim Chief Executive Officer, Spaulding Rehabilitation Hospital, Boston, MA, p. A200

STORY, Lawrence, Chief Executive Officer and Administrator, Gulf Pines Behavioral Health Services, Houston, TX, p. A411

STOUT, Dick L., Chief Executive Officer and Administrator, DeBaca General Hospital, Fort Sumner, NM, p. A282

STOVALL, Ed, Administrative Officer, Northville Psychiatric Hospital, Northville, MI, p. A217

STRANGE, John, President and Chief Executive Officer, St. Luke's Hospital, Duluth, MN, p. A224

STRANKO, Teresa K., Interim Administrator, HEALTHSOUTH Rehabilitation Hospital of Reading, Reading, PA, p. A364

STRASSHEIM, Dale S., President, BroMenn Healthcare, Normal, IL, p. A131

STRAUCH, Walter A., Executive Director, Franklin Regional Hospital, Franklin, NH, p. A268

STRECK, William F., M.D., President and Chief Executive Officer, Mary Imogene Bassett Hospital, Cooperstown, NY, p. A287

STREET, Jackie, President, Idaho Falls Recovery Center, Idaho Falls, ID, p. A117

STRICKLAND, Wallace, Administrator, Rush Foundation Hospital, Meridian, MS, p. A238

STRIEBY, John F., President and Chief Executive Officer, Nix Health Care System, San Antonio, TX, p. A423

STRINE, Mervin F., President and Chief Executive Officer, Massillon Community Hospital, Massillon, OH, p. A329

STRINGFIELD, C. David, President and Chief Executive Officer, Baptist Hospital, Nashville, TN, p. A391

STROHL Jr., George R., President, Community General Osteopathic Hospital, Harrisburg, PA, p. A355

STROMAN, W. Neil, President, Newark–Wayne Community Hospital, Newark, NY, p. A297

STROMBERG, Arlan L., Administrator, Lincoln General Hospital, Lincoln, NE, p. A261

STROTE, Ted, Administrator, Stevens County Hospital, Hugoton, KS, p. A160

STROUD, Bridget K., Chief Executive Officer, Faribault Regional Center, Faribault, MN, p. A224

STRUTHERS, Tony, Administrator, St. Joseph Northeast Heights Hospital, Albuquerque, NM, p. A280

STRUXNESS, Ronald E., Executive Vice President and Chief Executive Officer, Our Lady of the Resurrection Medical Center, Chicago, IL, p. A123

STRUYK, Douglas A., President and Chief Executive Officer, Ramapo Ridge Psychiatric Hospital, Wyckoff, NJ, p. A279

STUART, Philip, Administrator, Tomah Memorial Hospital, Tomah, WI, p. A466

STUBBS, Deborah, Chief Executive Officer, South Barry County Memorial Hospital, Cassville, MO, p. A242

STUDER, Quinton, President, Baptist Hospital, Pensacola, FL, p. A94

STUENKEL, Kurt, FACHE, President and Chief Executive Officer, Floyd Medical Center, Rome, GA, p. A110

STYLES Jr., John H., Administrator, Doctors Hospital–Tidwell, Houston, TX, p. A411

SUDDERS, Marylou, Commissioner, Massachusetts Department of Mental Health, Boston, MA, p. B116

SUEIRO, Edwin, Executive Director, Doctors Gubern's Hospital, Fajardo, PR, p. A472

SUGG, William T., President and Chief Executive Officer, Sumner Regional Medical Center, Gallatin, TN, p. A386

SUGIYAMA, Deborah
President, NorthBay Medical Center, Fairfield, CA, p. A42
President, Vacavalley Hospital, Vacaville, CA, p. A65

SULLIVAN, Charles, President and Chief Executive Officer, Reading Hospital and Medical Center, Reading, PA, p. A364

SULLIVAN, John, Chief Executive Officer, St. Francis Hospital, Evanston, IL, p. A126

SULLIVAN, Michael J., Director, Veterans Affairs Medical Center, Bath, NY, p. A285

SUMMERHILL, Ron, Administrator, Harbor View Mercy Hospital, Fort Smith, AR, p. A31

SUMMERS, Steve, Administrator, Decatur Community Hospital, Decatur, TX, p. A404

SUMMERS, William L., Executive Director, Patton State Hospital, Patton, CA, p. A56

SUMMERSETT III, James A., FACHE, President and Chief Executive Officer, Conway Regional Medical Center, Conway, AR, p. A30

SURFUS, Dianne, Interim Chief Executive Officer, Wells Community Hospital, Bluffton, IN, p. A137

SUSI, Jeffrey L., Executive Director and Chief Executive Officer, Northeastern Hospital of Philadelphia, Philadelphia, PA, p. A361

SUSSMAN, Elliot J., M.D., President and Chief Executive Officer, Lehigh Valley Hospital, Allentown, PA, p. A349

SUSSMAN, Michael H., President and Chief Executive Officer, Pacifica Hospital, Huntington Beach, CA, p. A45

SUTHERLIN, Steve, Chief Executive Officer, Columbia North Bay Hospital, Aransas Pass, TX, p. A396

SUTTERER, Larry J., USAF, Administrator, U. S. Air Force Regional Hospital, Elmendorf AFB, AK, p. A20

SVENSSON, Paul E., Chief Executive Officer, Parkway Hospital, New York, NY, p. A295

SWANSON, Lucille W., Ph.D., Acting Director, Veterans Affairs Medical Center, West Palm Beach, FL, p. A99

SWANSON, Ronald, Chief Executive North Coast Service Area, Providence Seaside Hospital, Seaside, OR, p. A348

SWARTWOUT, John A., Administrator, Shriners Hospitals for Children, Galveston Burns Institute, Galveston, TX, p. A407

SWEARINGEN, Lawrence L., President and Chief Executive Officer, Blessing Hospital, Quincy, IL, p. A133

SWEEDEN, Dick, Administrator, Scott and White Memorial Hospital, Temple, TX, p. A426

SWEENEY, David A., FACHE, Administrator, Morgan County War Memorial Hospital, Berkeley Springs, WV, p. A452

SWENSON, Kenneth B., President, Prince William Hospital, Manassas, VA, p. A439

SWIGART, Russell W., Administrator, Howard County Community Hospital, Saint Paul, NE, p. A264

SWINDLE, Dean, Chief Executive Officer, Concord Hospital, Baton Rouge, LA, p. A178

SWINDLING, William, Commanding Officer, U. S. Air Force Hospital, Patrick AFB, FL, p. A93

SWINEHART, Frank V., President and Chief Executive Officer, Marion General Hospital, Marion, OH, p. A329

SWINIARSKI, Wayne A., FACHE, Chief Executive Officer, West Calcasieu Cameron Hospital, Sulphur, LA, p. A187

SWINNEY, Keith, Chief Executive Officer, Southwest General Hospital, San Antonio, TX, p. A423

SWISHER, Charles D., Executive Director, Kendrick Memorial Hospital, Mooresville, IN, p. A144

SWITZER, Bruce, Administrator, Broken Arrow Medical Center, Broken Arrow, OK, p. A336

SWORD, William L., President and Chief Executive Officer, Texas County Memorial Hospital, Houston, MO, p. A244

SYKES Jr., Donald K., Chief Executive Officer, BHC Windsor Hospital, Chagrin Falls, OH, p. A321

SYPNIEWSKI, Al, Administrator, Baptist Memorial Hospital–Blytheville, Blytheville, AR, p. A29

T

TADLOCK, Cindy, Interim Administrator, Leake Memorial Hospital, Carthage, MS, p. A234

TAITANO, Tyrone J., Administrator, Guam Memorial Hospital Authority, Tamuning, GU, p. A471

TALLEY, James J., Administrator, Wheaton Community Hospital, Wheaton, MN, p. A232

TALLY, James E., Ph.D.
President and Chief Executive Officer, Egleston Children's Hospital at Emory University, Atlanta, GA, p. A101
President and Chief Executive Officer, Scottish Rite Children's Medical Center, Atlanta, GA, p. A101

TALMO, Michael, Chief Executive Officer, Rivendell of Michigan, Saint Johns, MI, p. A219

TALONEY, Derell, President and Chief Executive Officer, Park Lane Medical Center, Kansas City, MO, p. A245

TAMAR, Earl, Chief Operating Officer, Acute Care Services, Cape Coral Hospital, Cape Coral, FL, p. A82

TAMLYN, Mary E., Administrator, Mackinac Straits Hospital and Health Center, Saint Ignace, MI, p. A218

TAMME, Paula, Chief Executive Officer, Central State Hospital, Louisville, KY, p. A173

TAMME, Susan Stout, President, Baptist Hospital East, Louisville, KY, p. A173

TAN, Bienvenido, M.D., Chief Executive Officer, Newhall Community Hospital, Newhall, CA, p. A54

TAN-LACHICA, Nieves, M.D., Superintendent, Andrew McFarland Mental Health Center, Springfield, IL, p. A135

TANKLE, Reva S., Ph.D., Chief Executive Officer, Olympus Specialty Hospital, Waltham, MA, p. A206

TANNER, Anthony J., Executive Vice President, HEALTHSOUTH Corporation, Birmingham, AL, p. B105

TANNER, Gale V., Administrator, Monroe County Hospital, Forsyth, GA, p. A106

TANNER, Laurence A., President and Chief Executive Officer, New Britain General Hospital, New Britain, CT, p. A75

TARBET, Michele T., R.N., Chief Executive Officer, Grossmont Hospital, La Mesa, CA, p. A46

TARR, Judith, Chief Executive Officer, Miles Memorial Hospital, Damariscotta, ME, p. A190

TARRANT, Jeffrey S., Administrator, Lafayette Regional Health Center, Lexington, MO, p. A246

TASCONE, Deborah, R.N., Vice President for Administration, North Shore University Hospital at Syosset, Syosset, NY, p. A301

TASSE, Joseph, Administrator, Oakwood Hospital and Medical Center–Dearborn, Dearborn, MI, p. A210

TATE, Joel W., FACHE, Chief Executive Officer, McAlester Regional Health Center, McAlester, OK, p. A338

TATE Jr., David B., President and Chief Executive Officer, Lake Taylor Hospital, Norfolk, VA, p. A440

TATUM, Stanley D., Chief Executive Officer, Edmond Medical Center, Edmond, OK, p. A337

TAUSSIG, Lynn M., M.D., President and Chief Executive Officer, National Jewish Medical and Research Center, Denver, CO, p. A69

TAVARY, Jim, Chief Executive Officer and Administrator, Copper Queen Community Hospital, Bisbee, AZ, p. A22

TAVENNER, Marilyn B., Chief Executive Officer, Chippenham and Johnston–Willis Hospitals, Richmond, VA, p. A442

TAVERNIER, Patrice L., Administrator, Fishermen's Hospital, Marathon, FL, p. A89

TAYLOR, Alfred P., Administrator and Chief Executive Officer, Milan General Hospital, Milan, TN, p. A390

TAYLOR, Dennis A., Administrator, North Bay Medical Center, New Port Richey, FL, p. A92

TAYLOR, James H., President and Chief Executive Officer, University of Louisville Hospital, Louisville, KY, p. A174

TAYLOR, Meredith, Administrator, Vencor Hospital–Sacramento, Folsom, CA, p. A42

TAYLOR, Steven L., Chief Executive Officer, Harrison County Hospital, Corydon, IN, p. A138

TAYLOR, Donald, Administrator, U. S. Air Force Hospital Shaw, Shaw AFB, SC, p. A376

TAYLOR Jr., L. Clark, President and Chief Executive Officer, Memorial Health Care System, Chattanooga, TN, p. A384

TEAGUE, M. E., Chief Executive Officer, Louisiana State Hospitals, New Orleans, LA, p. B112

TEEL, Kenneth R., Administrator, Lake Pointe Medical Center, Rowlett, TX, p. A422

TSCHIDER, Richard A., FACHE, Administrator and Chief Executive Officer, St. Alexius Medical Center, Bismarck, ND, p. A316

TSO, Ronald, Chief Executive Officer, Chinle Comprehensive Health Care Facility, Chinle, AZ, p. A22

TUCKER, Edgar, Director, Colmery–O'Neil Veterans Affairs Medical Center, Topeka, KS, p. A166

TUCKER, Edgar L., Director, Dwight D. Eisenhower Veterans Affairs Medical Center, Leavenworth, KS, p. A161

TUCKER, George, M.D., President, St. Luke's Hospital, Chesterfield, MO, p. A242

TUCKER, Joseph R., President, St. Claude Medical Center, New Orleans, LA, p. A185

TUCKER, Paul, Administrator, Highline Community Hospital, Burien, WA, p. A445

TUCKER, Steven E., President, Memorial Medical Center, Johnstown, PA, p. A356

TUERPITZ, Peter, Administrator and Chief Executive Officer, Joel Pomerene Memorial Hospital, Millersburg, OH, p. A330

TULLMAN, Stephen M., Administrator, Alliant Hospitals, Louisville, KY, p. A173

TUNGATE, Rex A., Administrator, Westlake Regional Hospital, Columbia, KY, p. A169

TURCO, John, M.D., Director, Dartmouth College Health Service, Hanover, NH, p. A268

TURK, Herbert A., FACHE, Administrator, Sweeny Community Hospital, Sweeny, TX, p. A425

TURLEY, Frank, Ph.D., Executive Director, Napa State Hospital, Napa, CA, p. A53

TURNBULL, James, Administrator and Chief Executive Officer, Clara Barton Hosptial, Hoisington, KS, p. A160

TURNER, Howard D., Chief Executive Officer, Heart of the Rockies Regional Medical Center, Salida, CO, p. A72

TURNER, Jeffrey, Interim Administrator, North Runnels Hospital, Winters, TX, p. A429

TURNER, Joseph F., President, Central Suffolk Hospital, Riverhead, NY, p. A299

TURNER, Kenneth G., CHE, Chief Executive Officer, Elk County Regional Medical Center, Ridgway, PA, p. A364

TURNER, Mark, Chief Executive Officer, Ojai Valley Community Hospital, Ojai, CA, p. A54

TURNER, Michael A., President and Chief Executive Officer, Somerset Medical Center, Somerville, NJ, p. A277

TURNER, Robert J., Administrator, United Community Hospital, Grove City, PA, p. A354

TURNEY, Brian, Chief Executive Officer, Kingman Regional Medical Center, Kingman, AZ, p. A23

TURNEY, Dennis, Chief Executive Officer, Community Hospital, Watervliet, MI, p. A220

TUTEN, Amelia, R.N., Administrator, Hamilton Medical Center, Jasper, FL, p. A88

TUTEN, E. Allen, Administrator, Lincoln General Hospital, Ruston, LA, p. A186

TWISS, Gayla J., Service Unit Director, U. S. Public Health Service Indian Hospital, Rosebud, SD, p. A381

TYLER, Rosamond M., Administrator, McNairy County General Hospital, Selmer, TN, p. A392

TYRER, Ronald T.
Interim Chief Executive Officer, Georgetown Community Hospital, Georgetown, KY, p. A170
Interim Chief Executive Officer, Meadoview Regional Medical Center, Maysville, KY, p. A174

TYSON, Bernard J.
Administrator, Kaiser Foundation Hospital, Hayward, CA, p. A45
Administrator, Kaiser Foundation Hospital, Oakland, CA, p. A54

U

UFFER, Mark H., Chief Executive Officer, St. Luke Medical Center, Pasadena, CA, p. A56

UHLING, Casey, Administrator, St. Mary's Hospital, Cottonwood, ID, p. A117

ULAND, Jonas S., Executive Director, Greene County General Hospital, Linton, IN, p. A143

ULICNY, Gary R., Ph.D., President and Chief Executive Officer, Shepherd Center, Atlanta, GA, p. A101

ULLIAN, Elaine S., President and Chief Executive Officer, Boston Medical Center, Boston, MA, p. A199

ULMER, Evonne G., Chief Executive Officer, Ionia County Memorial Hospital, Ionia, MI, p. A214

ULSETH, Randy, Administrator, Community Hospital, Cannon Falls, MN, p. A223

UMBDENSTOCK, Richard J., President and Chief Executive Officer, Providence Services, Spokane, WA, p. B126

UNDERKOFLER, Joseph, Director, Veterans Affairs Hospital, Fort Harrison, MT, p. A254

UNDERRINER, David T., Operations Administrator, Providence Portland Medical Center, Portland, OR, p. A347

UNDERWOOD, Della, Chief Executive Officer, Vencor Hospital North Shore, Peabody, MA, p. A205

UNDERWOOD, Jay, Chief Executive Officer, HEALTHSOUTH Rehabilitation Institute of Tucson, Tucson, AZ, p. A27

UNROE, Larry J., President, Marietta Memorial Hospital, Marietta, OH, p. A329

UNRUH, Greg, Chief Executive Officer, Scott County Hospital, Scott City, KS, p. A165

UOMO, Paul Dell, President and Chief Executive Officer, Greater Hudson Valley Health System, Newburgh, NY, p. B102

URCIUOLI, Robert A., President and Chief Executive Officer, Roger Williams Medical Center, Providence, RI, p. A369

URMY, Norman B., Executive Director, Vanderbilt University Hospital, Nashville, TN, p. A391

UROSEVICH, Steve L., Chief Executive Officer, St. Croix Valley Memorial Hospital, Saint Croix Falls, WI, p. A465

URSO, Susan, Administrator, Mendota Community Hospital, Mendota, IL, p. A131

URVAND, Leslie O., Administrator, St. Luke's Hospital, Crosby, ND, p. A316

USHIJIMA, Arthur A., President and Chief Executive Officer, Queen's Medical Center, Honolulu, HI, p. A114

V

VAAGENES, Carl P., Administrator, Pipestone County Medical Center, Pipestone, MN, p. A229

VADELLA, Anthony J., Chief Executive Officer, Poplar Springs Hospital, Petersburg, VA, p. A441

VALDESPINO, Gustavo, Chief Executive Officer, Suburban Medical Center, Paramount, CA, p. A55

VALDESPINO, Gustavo A.
Chief Executive Officer, Lakewood Regional Medical Center, Lakewood, CA, p. A46
Chief Executive Officer, Los Alamitos Medical Center, Los Alamitos, CA, p. A48

VALENTINE, Billy M., Director, Overton Brooks Veterans Affairs Medical Center, Shreveport, LA, p. A187

VALIANTE, John, Chief Executive Officer, St. John's Hospital and Living Center, Jackson, WY, p. A468

VALLIANT, Robert F., Administrator, Bartlett Regional Hospital, Juneau, AK, p. A21

VAN BOKKELEN, W. R., President and Senior Executive Officer, Christian Hospital Northeast–Northwest, Saint Louis, MO, p. A249

VAN DORNICK, Jim, Administrator, Community Memorial Hospital, Oconto Falls, WI, p. A464

VAN DRIEL, Allen, Administrator, Harlan County Hospital, Alma, NE, p. A258

VAN ETTEN, Peter, President and Chief Executive Officer, Stanford University Hospital, Stanford, CA, p. A64

VAN GORDER, Chris D., Chief Executive Officer, Long Beach Memorial Medical Center, Long Beach, CA, p. A47

VAN STRATEN, Elizabeth, President and Chief Executive Officer, Saint Bernard Hospital and Health Care Center, Chicago, IL, p. A124

VAN VORST, Charles B., President and Chief Executive Officer, Mercy Hospital and Medical Center, Chicago, IL, p. A123

VAN VRANKEN, Ross, Chief Executive Officer, University of Utah Neuropsychiatric Institute, Salt Lake City, UT, p. A432

VANASKIE, William F., President, Robert Packer Hospital, Sayre, PA, p. A365

VANDENBERG, Patricia, President and Chief Executive Officer, Holy Cross Health System Corporation, South Bend, IN, p. B107

VANDENBROEK, Deborah, President and Chief Executive Officer, Marian Health Center, Sioux City, IA, p. A155

VANDER DOES, Victor, Administrator, Lincoln Hospital, Davenport, WA, p. A446

VANDERGRIFT, Patricia, Administrator, BHC St. Johns River Hospital, Jacksonville, FL, p. A87

VANDERHOOF, Terry L., President and Chief Executive Officer, River Valley Health System, Ironton, OH, p. A327

VANDERVEER, Robert W., Administrator, Knapp Medical Center, Weslaco, TX, p. A428

VANDERVORT, Darryl L., President and Chief Executive Officer, Katherine Shaw Bethea Hospital, Dixon, IL, p. A125

VANDEWEGE, Mitzi, Interim Administrator, Providence Centralia Hospital, Centralia, WA, p. A445

VANEK, James, Administrator, Lavaca Medical Center, Hallettsville, TX, p. A409

VANOURNY, Stephen E., M.D., President and Chief Executive Officer, St. Luke's Hospital, Cedar Rapids, IA, p. A148

VARGAS, Evelyn, Administrator, Industrial Hospital, San Juan, PR, p. A474

VARGAS, Laura, Administrator, BHC Hospital San Juan Capestrano, San Juan, PR, p. A473

VARLAND, Carol A.
Administrator, Community Memorial Hospital, Burke, SD, p. A378
Chief Executive Officer, Gregory Community Hospital, Gregory, SD, p. A379

VARNUM, James W., President, Mary Hitchcock Memorial Hospital, Lebanon, NH, p. A269

VARONE, Rick J., President, Staten Island University Hospital, New York, NY, p. A296

VASKELIS, Glenna L., Administrator, Sequoia Hospital, Redwood City, CA, p. A57

VASQUEZ, Alberto, Administrator, Star Valley Hospital, Afton, WY, p. A468

VATTER, Russell K., Superintendent, Moccasin Bend Mental Health Institute, Chattanooga, TN, p. A384

VAUGHAN, Page, Executive Director, Byerly Hospital, Hartsville, SC, p. A375

VAUGHT, Richard H., Administrator, William Newton Memorial Hospital, Winfield, KS, p. A167

VAZQUEZ, Manuel J., Administrator, Hospital Matilde Brenes, Bayamon, PR, p. A472

VAZQUEZ, William L., Vice President and Chief Executive Officer, University of Medicine and Dentistry of New Jersey–University Hospital, Newark, NJ, p. A275

VAZQUEZ ROSARIO, Iris J., Executive Director, Hospital Universitario Dr. Ramon Ruiz Arnau, Bayamon, PR, p. A472

VEENSTRA, Henry A., President, Zeeland Community Hospital, Zeeland, MI, p. A221

VEITZ, Larry W., Chief Executive Officer, Sioux Valley Vermillion Campus, Vermillion, SD, p. A381

VELEZ, Pete, Executive Director, Elmhurst Hospital Center, New York, NY, p. A292

VELICK, Stephen H., Chief Executive Officer, Henry Ford Hospital, Detroit, MI, p. A210

VELLINGA, David H., President and Chief Executive Officer, North Iowa Mercy Health Center, Mason City, IA, p. A153

VELOSO, Carole A., President and Chief Executive Officer, Northside General Hospital, Houston, TX, p. A412

VELTE, Carl J., Chief Executive Officer, Munising Memorial Hospital, Munising, MI, p. A216

VENTURA, N. Lawrence, Superintendent, Bangor Mental Health Institute, Bangor, ME, p. A189

VERMAELEN, Elizabeth A., President, Sisters of Charity Center, New York, NY, p. B137

W

WALTON, Dorcas, Administrator, Kaiser Foundation Hospital, Santa Rosa, CA, p. A63

WALTON, Michael W., Director, Veterans Affairs Medical Center, Chillicothe, OH, p. A322

WALTS, Lynn, Dr.PH, President and Chief Executive Officer, Hermann Hospital, Houston, TX, p. A411

WALTZ, Ronald D., Chief Executive Officer, Memorial Health Care Systems, Seward, NE, p. A264

WALZ, George, CHE, Chief Executive Officer, Breckinridge Memorial Hospital, Hardinsburg, KY, p. A171

WALZ, Patrick, Chief Executive Officer, Community Hospital Medical Center, Phoenix, AZ, p. A24

WAMPLER, Robert B., CPA, Chief Executive Officer, Lakeway Regional Hospital, Morristown, TN, p. A390

WANGER, David S., Chief Executive Officer, General Hospital, Eureka, CA, p. A42

WARD, Sandy, Administrator, Johnson County Memorial Hospital, Buffalo, WY, p. A468

WARDEN, Gail L., President and Chief Executive Officer, Henry Ford Health System, Detroit, MI, p. B107

WARDEN, Richard
Executive Director, Devereux Foundation–French Center, Devon, PA, p. A352
Executive Director, Devereux Mapleton Psychiatric Institute–Mapleton Center, Malvern, PA, p. A357

WARMAN Jr., Harold C., President and Chief Executive Officer, Shamokin Area Community Hospital, Coal Township, PA, p. A352

WARNER, Donald L., Chief Executive Officer, Arborview Hospital, Warren, MI, p. A220

WARNER Jr., Gerard H., Chief Executive Officer, Mid–Valley Hospital, Peckville, PA, p. A359

WARREN, James B., Chief Executive Officer, Columbia Medical Center–Dallas Southwest, Dallas, TX, p. A403

WARREN, Larry, Executive Director, University of Michigan Hospitals and Health Centers, Ann Arbor, MI, p. A208

WARREN, R. William, Chairman and Chief Executive Officer, Dolly Vinsant Memorial Hospital, San Benito, TX, p. A424

WARREN, Richard A., Chief Executive Officer, Camino Healthcare, Mountain View, CA, p. A53

WARREN, Roger J., M.D., Administrator, Hanover Hospital, Hanover, KS, p. A160

WASHINGTON Jr., Leonard, Director, Veterans Affairs Medical Center, Lebanon, PA, p. A357

WASSERMAN, Joseph A., President and Chief Executive Officer, Lakeland Medical Center–St. Joseph, Saint Joseph, MI, p. A219

WASSERMAN, Neil H., Chief Executive Officer and Chief Financial Officer, Hawthorn Center, Northville, MI, p. A217

WASSON, Ted D., President and Chief Executive Officer, William Beaumont Hospital Corporation, Royal Oak, MI, p. B154

WATERHOUSE, Blake E., M.D., Chief Executive Officer, Straub Clinic and Hospital, Honolulu, HI, p. A114

WATERS, Michael C., FACHE, President, Hendrick Health System, Abilene, TX, p. A395

WATERS, Robert E., Chief Executive Officer, Chester County Hospital and Nursing Center, Chester, SC, p. A372

WATERS, W. Charles, President, Newton Medical Center, Newton, KS, p. A163

WATERSTON, Judith C., Executive Director, Baylor Institute for Rehabilitation, Dallas, TX, p. A402

WATFORD, Rodney C., Administrator, Early Memorial Hospital, Blakely, GA, p. A102

WATHEN, James A., Chief Executive Officer, Southern Coos General Hospital, Bandon, OR, p. A344

WATKINS, John R., Chief Executive Officer, Vencor Hospital – New Orleans, New Orleans, LA, p. A185

WATSON, Duffy, President and Chief Executive Officer, Henry Mayo Newhall Memorial Hospital, Valencia, CA, p. A66

WATSON, Gary L., FACHE, Senior Executive Officer, Crittenton, Kansas City, MO, p. A245

WATSON, Ian W., Chief Executive Officer, Summerville Medical Center, Summerville, SC, p. A376

WATSON, James B., Chief Executive Officer, Ira Davenport Memorial Hospital, Bath, NY, p. A285

WATSON, James R., Administrator, Ashland Community Hospital, Ashland, OR, p. A344

WATSON, Lorraine, Ph.D., Chief Executive Officer, Charter Behavioral Health System of San Diego, San Diego, CA, p. A59

WATSON, Randy J., Administrator, Charter Forest Behavioral Health System, Shreveport, LA, p. A186

WATSON, T. Gregg
Administrator, Sheboygan Memorial Medical Center, Sheboygan, WI, p. A465
Administrator, Valley View Medical Center, Plymouth, WI, p. A464

WATSON, Virgil, Administrator, Sumner County Hospital District One, Caldwell, KS, p. A157

WATTERS, Steve, Chief Executive Officer, Mendota Mental Health Institute, Madison, WI, p. A461

WAUGH, Patrick D., Chief Executive Officer, St. Luke's Behavioral Health Center, Phoenix, AZ, p. A25

WEADICK, James F., Administrator and Chief Executive Officer, Newton General Hospital, Covington, GA, p. A104

WEARMOUTH, Chris, Administrator, Nature Coast Regional Health Network, Williston, FL, p. A99

WEATHERLY, Jesse O., President, Cullman Regional Medical Center, Cullman, AL, p. A13

WEAVER, Doug, Chief Executive Officer, Memorial Hospital, Frederick, OK, p. A337

WEAVER, Thomas H., FACHE, Director, Veterans Affairs Medical Center, Bay Pines, FL, p. A81

WEBB, Linnette, Senior Vice President and Executive Director, Harlem Hospital Center, New York, NY, p. A292

WEBB, Ronald W., President, Saint Eugene Medical Center, Dillon, SC, p. A373

WEBB Jr., Charles L., Administrator, Charter louisville Behavioral Health System, Louisville, KY, p. A173

WEBER, Mark, FACHE, President, St. John's Mercy Medical Center, Saint Louis, MO, p. A250

WEBER, Peter M., President and Chief Executive Officer, Huguley Memorial Medical Center, Burleson, TX, p. A399

WEBER, Wilson J.
Chief Executive Officer, Mid–Jefferson Hospital, Nederland, TX, p. A419
Chief Executive Officer, Park Place Medical Center, Port Arthur, TX, p. A421

WEBER Jr., Everett P., President and Chief Executive Officer, Grady Memorial Hospital, Delaware, OH, p. A326

WEBSTER, Jeffrey, Chief Executive Officer, St. Mary Hospital, Port Arthur, TX, p. A421

WEBSTER, Mark A., President, Troy Community Hospital, Troy, PA, p. A366

WEBSTER, William W., Chief Executive Officer, St. Luke's Medical Center, Phoenix, AZ, p. A25

WEE, Donald J., Executive Director, Pioneer Memorial Hospital, Prineville, OR, p. A347

WEEKS, Donnie J., President and Chief Executive Officer, Kershaw County Medical Center, Camden, SC, p. A371

WEEKS, Steven Douglas
Senior Vice President and Administrator, Baptist Medical Center, Little Rock, AR, p. A32
Senior Vice President and Administrator, Baptist Rehabilitation Institute, Little Rock, AR, p. A32

WEEMS, Nadine L., Administrator, Perry Hospital, Perry, GA, p. A110

WEIDNER, Michael J., President, Highland Hospital of Rochester, Rochester, NY, p. A299

WEIGHTMAN, George, Commander, McDonald Army Community Hospital, Newport News, VA, p. A440

WEILAND, Edmond L., President and Chief Executive Officer, Prairie Lakes Hospital and Care Center, Watertown, SD, p. A382

WEILER, Joseph W., President, McKenzie Memorial Hospital, Sandusky, MI, p. A219

WEINBAUM, Barry G., Chief Executive Officer, Alvarado Hospital Medical Center, San Diego, CA, p. A59

WEINBERG, Arnold N., M.D., Director, M. I. T. Medical Department, Cambridge, MA, p. A201

WEINER, David Stephen, President, Children's Hospital, Boston, MA, p. A200

WEINER, Jack, President and Chief Executive Officer, St. Joseph's Mercy Hospitals and Health Services, Clinton Township, MI, p. A210

WEINSTEIN, Stephen M., Chief Executive Officer, Doctors Hospital of Hyde Park, Chicago, IL, p. A122

WEIR, John C., President and Chief Executive Officer, Youngstown Osteopathic Hospital, Youngstown, OH, p. A334

WEIR, Silas M., Chief Executive Officer, Centura Special Care Hospital, Denver, CO, p. A69

WEIS, Eric E., FACHE, Chief Executive Officer, Riley Memorial Hospital, Meridian, MS, p. A238

WEISS, Thomas M., Chief Executive Officer, Columbia Medical Center of Huntsville, Huntsville, AL, p. A15

WELBORN, Bobby, Administrator, Perry County General Hospital, Richton, MS, p. A239

WELCH, Bill, Administrator, Jefferson Community Health Center, Fairbury, NE, p. A259

WELCH, Nelda K., Administrator, East Texas Medical Center Crockett, Crockett, TX, p. A402

WELCH, Reynold R., Chief Executive Officer, Anaheim General Hospital, Anaheim, CA, p. A36

WELDING, Theodore, Chief Executive Officer, Vencor Hospital–Coral Gables, Coral Gables, FL, p. A83

WELLINGER, M. Rosita, President and Chief Executive Officer, St. Francis Health System, Pittsburgh, PA, p. B141

WELLMAN, Roxann A., Chief Executive Officer, Minnewaska District Hospital, Starbuck, MN, p. A231

WELLS, Brian F., Administrator and Chief Executive Officer, North Dallas Rehabilitation Hospital, Dallas, TX, p. A403

WELLS, Mary Ellen, Administrator, Buffalo Hospital, Buffalo, MN, p. A223

WELLS, Scott, Interim Chief Executive Officer, Franklin General Hospital, Hampton, IA, p. A151

WELSH, John H., Chief Executive Officer, Rumford Community Hospital, Rumford, ME, p. A191

WELSH Jr., J. L., President, Southeastern Regional Medical Center, Lumberton, NC, p. A310

WELTON, Cameron J., President and Chief Executive Officer, Methodist Healthcare, Jackson, MS, p. A236

WENDLING, Jeffrey T., President and Chief Executive Officer, Northern Michigan Hospital, Petoskey, MI, p. A217

WENTE, James W., CHE, Administrator, Southeast Missouri Hospital, Cape Girardeau, MO, p. A242

WENTWORTH, Philip M., FACHE, Executive Director, Presbyterian Hospital of Plano, Plano, TX, p. A421

WENTZ, Robert J., President and Chief Executive Officer, Oroville Hospital, Oroville, CA, p. A55

WENZKE, Edward T., President and Chief Executive Officer, Crouse Hospital, Syracuse, NY, p. A301

WERBY, Marcia, Administrator, Rockland Children's Psychiatric Center, Orangeburg, NY, p. A298

WERNER, Thomas J., Administrator, Richland Hospital, Richland Center, WI, p. A465

WERNER, Thomas L., President, Florida Hospital, Orlando, FL, p. A92

WERNICK, Joel, President and Chief Executive Officer, Phoebe Putney Memorial Hospital, Albany, GA, p. A100

WERTZ, Randy S., Administrator, Golden Valley Memorial Hospital, Clinton, MO, p. A242

WESOLOWSKI, Jaime A., Chief Executive Officer, Meadowcrest Hospital, Gretna, LA, p. A181

WESP, James H., Administrator, Vencor Hospital–Louisville, Louisville, KY, p. A174

WEST, John, Administrator, Buchanan General Hospital, Grundy, VA, p. A438

WEST, Louis, President, Central Texas Hospital, Cameron, TX, p. A399

WEST, R. Christopher
President, Franciscan Hospital–Mount Airy Campus, Cincinnati, OH, p. A322
President, Franciscan Hospital–Western Hills Campus, Cincinnati, OH, p. A322

WESTFALL, Bernard G., President and Chief Executive Officer, West Virginia United Health System, Fairmont, WV, p. B153

WESTHOFF, Thomas G., Chief Executive Officer, Standish Community Hospital, Standish, MI, p. A219

WESTIN, Charles A., FACHE, Administrator, Republic County Hospital, Belleville, KS, p. A157

WESTON–HALL, Patricia, Executive Director, Glenbeigh Health Sources, Rock Creek, OH, p. A331

WETTA Jr., Daniel J., Chief Executive Officer, John Randolph Medical Center, Hopewell, VA, p. A438

WHALEN, David, President and Chief Executive Officer, Putnam Community Medical Center, Palatka, FL, p. A93

WHATLEY, David, Director, Veterans Affairs Medical Center, Houston, TX, p. A413

WHATLEY, Gary Lex, President and Chief Executive Officer, Memorial Medical Center of East Texas, Lufkin, TX, p. A416

WHEAT, Richard L., Chief Financial Officer, Clearwater Valley Hospital, Orofino, ID, p. A118

WHEELER, Michael K., Director, Veterans Affairs Medical Center, Battle Creek, MI, p. A208

WHEELER Sr., David, Chief Executive Officer, U. S. Naval Hospital, Agana, GU, p. A471

WHEELOCK, Major W., President, Crotched Mountain Rehabilitation Center, Greenfield, NH, p. A268

WHELAN, Sharon, President, River Falls Area Hospital, River Falls, WI, p. A465

WHELAN–WILLIAMS, Sue, Site Administrator, South Seminole Hospital, Longwood, FL, p. A89

WHIPKEY, Neil, Administrator, Campbellton Graceville Hospital, Graceville, FL, p. A86

WHIPPLE, Ingrid L., Chief Executive Officer, BHC Heritage Oaks Hospital, Sacramento, CA, p. A58

WHITAKER, E. Berton, President and Chief Executive Officer, Southeast Georgia Regional Medical Center, Brunswick, GA, p. A103

WHITAKER, James B., President, Circles of Care, Melbourne, FL, p. A90

WHITAKER Sr., Harold H., Administrator, Webster Health Services, Eupora, MS, p. A235

WHITE, Alvin C., President and Chief Executive Officer, Rome Memorial Hospital, Rome, NY, p. A300

WHITE, Dale A., Chief Executive Officer, Horton Health Foundation, Horton, KS, p. A160

WHITE, Daniel C., Chief Executive Officer, District Memorial Hospital, Andrews, NC, p. A304

WHITE, Daryl Sue, R.N., Managing Director, River Oaks Hospital, New Orleans, LA, p. A185

WHITE, Doug, Chief Executive Officer, Columbia Grand Strand Regional Medical Center, Myrtle Beach, SC, p. A375

WHITE, Dudley R., Administrator, Anson General Hospital, Anson, TX, p. A395

WHITE, James W., Chief Executive Officer, Columbia Springhill Medical Center, Springhill, LA, p. A187

WHITE, Jeffrey L., Chief Executive Officer, Low Country General Hospital, Ridgeland, SC, p. A376

WHITE, John B., President and Chief Executive Officer, Lima Memorial Hospital, Lima, OH, p. A328

WHITE, John R., Administrator, Newport Community Hospital, Newport, WA, p. A447

WHITE, Kevin A., Administrator, Medicine Lodge Memorial Hospital, Medicine Lodge, KS, p. A163

WHITE, Mary M., President and Chief Executive Officer, Swedish Medical Center, Englewood, CO, p. A70

WHITE, Stephani, Vice President and Site Administrator, Legacy Emanuel Hospital and Health Center, Portland, OR, p. A347

WHITE, Terry R., President and Chief Executive Officer, MetroHealth Medical Center, Cleveland, OH, p. A324

WHITE, Thomas, President and Chief Executive Officer, Jameson Hospital, New Castle, PA, p. A358

WHITE, Thomas M., President, Empire Health Services, Spokane, WA, p. B99

WHITE Jr., Lawrence L., President, St. Patrick Hospital, Missoula, MT, p. A255

WHITEHORN, Jeffrey, Chief Executive Officer, Columbia Southern Hills Medical Center, Nashville, TN, p. A391

WHITELEY, Earl S., CHE, Chief Executive Officer, Medical Center Enterprise, Enterprise, AL, p. A14

WHITFIELD, Gary R., Director, Ioannis A. Lougaris Veterans Affairs Medical Center, Reno, NV, p. A267

WHITFIELD Jr., Charles H., President and Chief Executive Officer, Laughlin Memorial Hospital, Greeneville, TN, p. A386

WHITING, Joseph K., Executive Vice President and Chief Operating Officer, Bayhealth Medical Center, Milford Memorial Campus, Milford, DE, p. A78

WHITLOCK, Jim, Administrator, Bradley Memorial Hospital, Cleveland, TN, p. A384

WHITLOW, Linda, Administrator, Anadarko Municipal Hospital, Anadarko, OK, p. A335

WHITMIRE, James C., CHE, Administrator, East Texas Medical Center Trinity, Trinity, TX, p. A426

WHITNEY, Harry E., Interim President and Chief Executive Officer, Santa Marta Hospital, Los Angeles, CA, p. A50

WHITTINGTON, Terry G., Chief Executive Officer and Administrator, Bogalusa Community Medical Center, Bogalusa, LA, p. A179

WICK, Timothy J., Chief Executive Officer, Burnett Medical Center, Grantsburg, WI, p. A459

WIDENER, Stephen G., President and Chief Executive Officer, Chestatee Regional Hospital, Dahlonega, GA, p. A105

WIEBE, John F., Chief Executive Officer, Clay County Hospital, Clay Center, KS, p. A158

WIENER, Mark S., Administrator, St. Luke's Medical Center, Milwaukee, WI, p. A463

WIESNER, Gerald, Vice President and Chief Operating Officer, Miami County Medical Center, Paola, KS, p. A164

WIGGINS, Gary K., Chief Executive Officer, Central Valley General Hospital, Hanford, CA, p. A44

WIGGINS, Louise, Chief Executive Officer and Administrator, Summit Hospital of Northwest Louisiana, Bossier City, LA, p. A179

WIGGINS, Stephen P., Director, Western State Hospital, Hopkinsville, KY, p. A171

WIGLEY, Mack
   Chief Executive Officer, Oaks Psychiatric Health System, Austin, TX, p. A397
   Chief Executive Officer, San Marcos Treatment Center, San Marcos, TX, p. A424

WILBER, William N., Administrator, Cottage Grove Healthcare Community, Cottage Grove, OR, p. A344

WILCZEK, Joseph W., President and Chief Executive Officer, St. Joseph Medical Center, Tacoma, WA, p. A450

WILDER, Lin C., R.N., Director, University of Massachusetts Medical Center, Worcester, MA, p. A207

WILDER, Steven S., President and Chief Executive Officer, Central Community Hospital, Clifton, IL, p. A125

WILENSKY, Stephen, Executive Director, University Behavioral Health Center, Memphis, TN, p. A390

WILES, Patrick J.
   President and Chief Executive Officer, Sisters of Charity Hospital of Buffalo, Buffalo, NY, p. A286
   Chief Executive Officer, St. Joseph Hospital, Cheektowaga, NY, p. A287

WILES, Paul M., President, Novant Health, Winston Salem, NC, p. B122

WILEY, Stan, Administrator, Crane Memorial Hospital, Crane, TX, p. A402

WILFORD, Dan S., President, Memorial Herman Healthcare System, Houston, TX, p. B117

WILFORD, Ned B., President and Chief Executive Officer, Hamilton Medical Center, Dalton, GA, p. A105

WILHELM, Mary Eileen, President and Chief Executive Officer, Mercy Medical, Daphne, AL, p. A13

WILHELMSEN Jr., Thomas E., President, Southern New Hampshire Regional Medical Center, Nashua, NH, p. A269

WILK, Leonard E., Administrator, Sinai Samaritan Medical Center, Milwaukee, WI, p. A462

WILKENS, Daryl J., Administrator, Cavalier County Memorial Hospital, Langdon, ND, p. A318

WILKERSON, Larry D., Chief Executive Officer, Augusta Medical Complex, Augusta, KS, p. A157

WILKINS, Patricia S., Administrator, North Caddo Medical Center, Vivian, LA, p. A188

WILKINS, William W., President and Chief Executive Officer, OhioHealth, Columbus, OH, p. B123

WILKINSON, Gary L., Director, Veterans Affairs Medical Center, Iowa City, IA, p. A152

WILKINSON, Steven D., President and Chief Executive Officer, Menorah Medical Center, Overland Park, KS, p. A164

WILL, Daniel, Administrator, Zumbrota Health Care, Zumbrota, MN, p. A232

WILLARD, Larry, Administrator, Hocking Valley Community Hospital, Logan, OH, p. A328

WILLAUER, Glenn R., Administrator, U. S. Air Force Hospital, Hampton, VA, p. A438

WILLCOXON, Phil, Administrator, Freeman Neosho Hospital, Neosho, MO, p. A247

WILLERT, Todd, Administrator, Story County Hospital and Long Term Care Facility, Nevada, IA, p. A153

WILLERT, St. Joan
   President and Chief Executive Officer, Carondelet St. Joseph's Hospital, Tucson, AZ, p. A27
   President and Chief Executive Officer, Carondelet St. Mary's Hospital, Tucson, AZ, p. A27

WILLETT, Allan Brock, M.D., Director, Colorado Mental Health Institute at Fort Logan, Denver, CO, p. A69

WILLETT, Richard, Chief Executive Officer, Redington–Fairview General Hospital, Skowhegan, ME, p. A192

WILLHELM, Judene, Administrator, Memorial Hospital, Kermit, TX, p. A414

WILLIAMS, Chas H., M.D., Administrator, Starlite Village Hospital, Center Point, TX, p. A400

WILLIAMS, Cindy, FACHE, Administrator, Carraway Methodist Medical Center, Birmingham, AL, p. A12

WILLIAMS, David R., Chief Executive Officer, Montgomery Regional Hospital, Blacksburg, VA, p. A436

WILLIAMS, Denise R., President and Chief Executive Officer, Memorial Hospital of Salem County, Salem, NJ, p. A277

WILLIAMS, Gerald L., Director and Chief Executive Officer, James E. Van Zandt Veterans Affairs Medical Center, Altoona, PA, p. A349

WILLIAMS, John G.
   President and Chief Executive Officer, O'Connor Hospital, San Jose, CA, p. A61
   President, St. Mary's Medical Center, San Francisco, CA, p. A60

WILLIAMS, Miriam K., Administrator, Charter Hospital of Pasco, Lutz, FL, p. A89

WILLIAMS, Oreta, Administrator, Jeff Davis Hospital, Hazlehurst, GA, p. A107

WILLIAMS, R. D., Administrator and Chief Executive Officer, Ashe Memorial Hospital, Jefferson, NC, p. A309

WILLIAMS, Ralph T.
   Administrator, Fort Sanders Loudon Medical Center, Loudon, TN, p. A388
   Administrator, Fort Sanders–Sevier Medical Center, Sevierville, TN, p. A392

WILLIAMS, Richard C., President and Chief Executive Officer, St. Mary's Health System, Knoxville, TN, p. A388

WILLIAMS, Robert B.
   Administrator, Florida State Hospital, Chattahoochee, FL, p. A82
   Administrator, Shands at AGH, Gainesville, FL, p. A85

WILLIAMS, Robert D., Administrator, Mercy Special Care Hospital, Nanticoke, PA, p. A358

WILLIAMS, Roby D., Administrator, Hardin County General Hospital, Rosiclare, IL, p. A134

WILLIAMS, Roger, Chief Executive Officer, Carroll County Hospital, Carrollton, KY, p. A169

WILLIAMS, Stephen A., President, Alliant Health System, Louisville, KY, p. B66

WILLIAMS, Timothy B., Director, Veterans Affairs Puget Sound Health Care System, Seattle, WA, p. A449

WILLIAMS, Trude, R.N., Administrator, Pacifica Hospital of the Valley, Los Angeles, CA, p. A50

WILLIAMS III, Raymond, President and Chief Executive Officer, Sumner Regional Medical Center, Wellington, KS, p. A166

WILLIAMS Jr., Elton L., CPA, President, Lake Charles Memorial Hospital, Lake Charles, LA, p. A182

WILLIAMS Jr., John F., M.D., Director, Wishard Health Services, Indianapolis, IN, p. A142

WILLIAMSON, Paul, Administrator, U. S. Air Force Medical Center Keesler, Keesler AFB, MS, p. A237

WILLIE, Don, Chief Executive Officer, Cleveland Regional Medical Center, Cleveland, TX, p. A400

WILLIS, Dell, Administrator, Dr. Dan C. Trigg Memorial Hospital, Tucumcari, NM, p. A283

WILLIS, Yvonne, Administrator, Bowdon Area Hospital, Bowdon, GA, p. A103

WILLMAN, Arthur C., Vice President Operations, Searhc MT. Edgecumbe Hospital, Sitka, AK, p. A21

WILLMON, Gary R., Administrator, Grafton City Hospital, Grafton, WV, p. A453

WILLS, Andrew, Chief Executive Officer, Estes Park Medical Center, Estes Park, CO, p. A70

WILMOT, Helen
Administrator, Kaiser Foundation Hospital, Redwood City, CA, p. A57
Administrator, Kaiser Foundation Hospital, Santa Clara, CA, p. A62

WILMOT, David, MSC, Administrator, U. S. Air Force Clinic Whiteman, Whiteman AFB, MO, p. A252

WILSEY, Suzanne R., Administrator, Vencor Hospital–Kansas City, Kansas City, MO, p. A246

WILSON, Asa B., Administrator, Decatur County Hospital, Oberlin, KS, p. A163

WILSON, Bill D., Administrator, Wayne County Hospital, Corydon, IA, p. A148

WILSON, Bob L., Administrator, Villa Feliciana Medical Complex, Jackson, LA, p. A181

WILSON, David C., Chief Executive Officer, Harton Regional Medical Center, Tullahoma, TN, p. A393

WILSON, Geri, Chief Executive Officer, Madison Valley Hospital, Ennis, MT, p. A254

WILSON, Hugh D.
Chief Executive Officer, Columbia Doctors Hospital, Columbus, GA, p. A104
Chief Executive Officer, Hughston Sports Medicine Hospital, Columbus, GA, p. A104

WILSON, Jim, President and Chief Executive Officer, Susan B. Allen Memorial Hospital, El Dorado, KS, p. A158

WILSON, John A., President and Chief Executive Officer, Rehabilitation Institute of Pittsburgh, Pittsburgh, PA, p. A362

WILSON, John M.
President, Bay Harbor Hospital, Los Angeles, CA, p. A48
President, San Pedro Peninsula Hospital, Los Angeles, CA, p. A50

WILSON, Kirk G., Chief Executive Officer, Columbia Bay Area Medical Center, Corpus Christi, TX, p. A401

WILSON, L. Steven, Administrator, Dixie Regional Medical Center, Saint George, UT, p. A432

WILSON, Mark D., Administrator, Barron Memorial Medical Center and Skilled Nursing Facility, Barron, WI, p. A457

WILSON, Nancy, Senior Vice President and Regional Administrator, Scripps Mercy Hospital, San Diego, CA, p. A59

WILSON, Paul J., Administrator, Los Alamos Medical Center, Los Alamos, NM, p. A282

WILSON, R. Lynn, President, Bryan Memorial Hospital, Lincoln, NE, p. A261

WILSON, Ralph J., Administrator, Red Bay Hospital, Red Bay, AL, p. A17

WILSON, Stephen K., President and Chief Executive Officer, Genesis Rehabilitation Hospital, Jacksonville, FL, p. A87

WILSON, William G., President and Chief Executive Officer, Jackson County Memorial Hospital, Altus, OK, p. A335

WILSON Jr., V. Otis, President, Grace Hospital, Morganton, NC, p. A311

WILTERMOOD, Michael C., Administrator, St. Benedicts Family Medical Center, Jerome, ID, p. A117

WIMAN, Thomas, Executive Director, Rankin Medical Center, Brandon, MS, p. A233

WINFREE, Wayne, Chief Executive Officer, Frank T. Rutherford Memorial Hospital, Carthage, TN, p. A383

WINFREY, Robert C., President and Chief Operating Officer, Greater Southeast Community Hospital, Washington, DC, p. A79

WINGER, Ronald C., President and Chief Executive Officer, St. Vincent Hospital, Santa Fe, NM, p. A283

WINKLER, Gordon W., Administrator, Ringgold County Hospital, Mount Ayr, IA, p. A153

WINN, George, Administrator, Sanpete Valley Hospital, Mount Pleasant, UT, p. A431

WINN, Grant M., President, Community Medical Center, Missoula, MT, p. A255

WINN, Roger P., Chief Executive Officer, Miners Hospital Northern Cambria, Spangler, PA, p. A365

WINSLOW, F. Scott, President and Chief Executive Officer, Columbia Michael Reese Hospital and Medical Center, Chicago, IL, p. A122

WINTER, Jeffrey P., Chief Executive Officer, Riverside Community Hospital, Riverside, CA, p. A57

WINTER, William E., Administrative Director, Silverton Hospital, Silverton, OR, p. A348

WINTHROP, Michael K., President, Bellevue Hospital, Bellevue, OH, p. A321

WISBY, Diane, President and Chief Executive Officer, Goleta Valley Cottage Hospital, Santa Barbara, CA, p. A62

WISE, Brenda, Administrator, Okolona Community Hospital, Okolona, MS, p. A238

WISE, Franklin E., Administrator, Fulton County Hospital, Salem, AR, p. A34

WISE, Jerry R., Administrator, Stewart–Webster Hospital, Richland, GA, p. A110

WISE, Robert P., President and Chief Executive Officer, Hunterdon Medical Center, Flemington, NJ, p. A273

WISEMAN, Richard J., Ph.D., Superintendent, Riverview Hospital for Children, Middletown, CT, p. A75

WISSINK, Gerald L., President and Chief Executive Officer, Baptist Hospitals and Health Systems, Inc., Phoenix, AZ, p. B70

WISSLER, James, President and Chief Executive Officer, Nicholas H. Noyes Memorial Hospital, Dansville, NY, p. A287

WISSMAN, William W., Interim Executive Director, Dunn Memorial Hospital, Bedford, IN, p. A137

WITT, Stephen, Chief Executive Officer, College Hospital, Cerritos, CA, p. A39

WOERNER, Steven, Chief Executive Officer, Columbia Doctors Regional Medical Center, Corpus Christi, TX, p. A401

WOLF, Chris, Chief Executive Officer, Chesterfield General Hospital, Cheraw, SC, p. A372

WOLF, Edward H., Chief Executive Officer, Lakeview Medical Center, Rice Lake, WI, p. A465

WOLF, James N., Chief Executive Officer, District One Hospital, Faribault, MN, p. A224

WOLF, Jonathan, Chief Executive Officer, Charter Behavioral Health System at Cove Forge, Williamsburg, PA, p. A368

WOLF, Laura J., President, Franciscan Sisters of Christian Charity HealthCare Ministry, Inc, Manitowoc, WI, p. B101

WOLFE, Philip R., Chief Executive Officer, N. T. Enloe Memorial Hospital, Chico, CA, p. A39

WOLFE, Stephen A., Chief Executive Officer, Clearfield Hospital, Clearfield, PA, p. A352

WOLFF, Ronald V., President and Chief Executive Officer, Bay Medical Center, Panama City, FL, p. A93

WOLFORD, Dennis A., FACHE, Administrator, Macon County General Hospital, Lafayette, TN, p. A388

WOLIN, Harry, Administrator and Chief Executive Officer, Mason District Hospital, Havana, IL, p. A128

WOLTER, Nicholas J., M.D., Chief Executive Officer, Deaconess Billings Clinic, Billings, MT, p. A253

WOOD, Alice, Director, Richard L. Roudebush Veterans Affairs Medical Center, Indianapolis, IN, p. A141

WOOD, Douglas L., M.D., President, Immanuel/St. Joseph's–Mayo Health System, Mankato, MN, p. A227

WOOD, Gregory C., Chief Executive Officer, Scotland Memorial Hospital, Laurinburg, NC, p. A310

WOOD, Jack T., Administrator, William Bee Ririe Hospital, Ely, NV, p. A266

WOOD, James B., Chief Executive Officer, Greenbrier Valley Medical Center, Ronceverte, WV, p. A455

WOOD, James R., Chairman and Chief Executive Officer, Maryland General Hospital, Baltimore, MD, p. A194

WOOD, Kenneth R., Administrator, Johnson Regional Medical Center, Clarksville, AR, p. A29

WOOD, Peggy, Administrator, Horizon Specialty Hospital, San Antonio, TX, p. A422

WOOD, Sharon R., Administrator, Veterans Home and Hospital, Rocky Hill, CT, p. A76

WOOD, Tammy B., Chief Executive Officer, Charter Asheville Behavioral Health System, Asheville, NC, p. A304

WOODALL, Jay, Chief Executive Officer, Columbia Trinity Hospital, Erin, TN, p. A385

WOODALL, Jim S., Director, Caswell Center, Kinston, NC, p. A309

WOODALL, Marsha, Interim Chief Executive Officer, Caldwell County Hospital, Princeton, KY, p. A176

WOODARD, Elizabeth B., Chief Executive Officer, Cumberland, A Brown Schools Hospital for Children and Adolescents, New Kent, VA, p. A440

WOODRELL, Frederick, Director, University Hospitals and Clinics, University of Mississippi Medical Center, Jackson, MS, p. A236

WOODS, Daniel J., Chief Executive Officer, Sartori Memorial Hospital, Cedar Falls, IA, p. A148

WOODS, E. Anthony, President, Deaconess Hospital, Cincinnati, OH, p. A322

WOODSIDE, Jeffrey R., M.D., Executive Director, University of Tennessee Bowld Hospital, Memphis, TN, p. A390

WOODWARD, Barry W., Administrator, BHC Olympus View Hospital, Salt Lake City, UT, p. A432

WOODY, Fred, Chief Executive Officer, Doctors Hospital, Wentzville, MO, p. A252

WOOLLEY, Helen, Administrator, Pershing General Hospital, Lovelock, NV, p. A267

WOOLSLAYER, Richard N., Chief Executive Officer, Arroyo Grande Community Hospital, Arroyo Grande, CA, p. A36

WOOTEN, Richard L., President and Chief Executive Officer, Leesburg Regional Medical Center, Leesburg, FL, p. A89

WORKMAN, Dennis, M.D., Medical Director, Charter Behavioral Health System of Atlanta, Atlanta, GA, p. A100

WORKMAN, John R., Chief Executive Officer, Athens Regional Medical Center, Athens, TN, p. A383

WORLEY, Steve, President and Chief Executive Officer, Children's Hospital, New Orleans, LA, p. A184

WORRELL, Robert, Chief Executive Officer, Redgate Memorial Hospital, Long Beach, CA, p. A48

WORRICK, Gerald M., President and Administrator, Door County Memorial Hospital, Sturgeon Bay, WI, p. A466

WORSHAM, Sharon, Administrator, Charter Centennial Peaks Behavioral Health System, Louisville, CO, p. A72

WOZNIAK, Gregory T., President, Barnes–Jewish West County Hospital, Saint Louis, MO, p. A249

WRAALSTAD, Kimber, Chief Executive Officer, Presentation Medical Center, Rolla, ND, p. A318

WRAY, Christine R., Chief Executive Officer, St. Mary's Hospital, Leonardtown, MD, p. A197

WRIGHT, Brenda, Acting Administrator, McLean County Health Center, Calhoun, KY, p. A168

WRIGHT, Charles T., Chief Executive, Southern Oregon Service Area, Providence Medford Medical Center, Medford, OR, p. A346

WRIGHT, Gene B., President and Chief Executive Officer, Columbia Trident Medical Center, Charleston, SC, p. A372

WRIGHT, Joe, Administrator, Culberson Hospital District, Van Horn, TX, p. A427

WRIGHT, Rick, CPA, President and Chief Executive Officer, Keweenaw Memorial Medical Center, Laurium, MI, p. A215

WRIGHT, Roy W., President and Chief Executive Officer, Des Moines General Hospital, Des Moines, IA, p. A149

WRIGHT, Skip, Administrator, Vencor Hospital–Atlanta, Atlanta, GA, p. A101

WRIGHT, William G., Director, Veterans Affairs Medical Center, Hampton, VA, p. A438

WRIGHT, Margaret, President, Palos Community Hospital, Palos Heights, IL, p. A132

WRIGHT–GRIGGS, Stephanie, Chief Operating Officer, Provident Hospital of Cook County, Chicago, IL, p. A123

WYATT, Leslie G., Administrator, Children's Hospital, Richmond, VA, p. A442

WYNN, Chester A., President and Chief Executive Officer, Passavant Area Hospital, Jacksonville, IL, p. A129

X

XINIS, James J., President and Chief Executive Officer, Calvert Memorial Hospital, Prince Frederick, MD, p. A197

Y

YAGER, Jolene, R.N., Administrator, Lincoln County Hospital, Lincoln, KS, p. A162

YARBOROUGH, James, Chief Executive Officer, Alleghany Memorial Hospital, Sparta, NC, p. A313

YARBROUGH, Kathy, Interim Administrator, Trinity Hospital, Weaverville, CA, p. A66

YARBROUGH, Mary G., President and Chief Executive Officer, St. Joseph's Hospital and Medical Center, Phoenix, AZ, p. A25

YATES, Ronald E., Chief Executive Officer, Douglas Community Medical Center, Roseburg, OR, p. A348

YCRE Jr., Louis R., FACHE, President and Chief Executive Officer, Pascack Valley Hospital, Westwood, NJ, p. A279

YEAGER, Clifford A., Chief Executive Officer, Lutheran Medical Center, Saint Louis, MO, p. A249

YEARY, John, Administrator, Eastland Memorial Hospital, Eastland, TX, p. A405

YENAWINE, Kelly R., Administrator, Gibson General Hospital, Trenton, TN, p. A393

YIM, Herbert K., Administrator, Kohala Hospital, Kohala, HI, p. A115

YOCHUM, Richard E., President, Pomona Valley Hospital Medical Center, Pomona, CA, p. A56

YOKOBOSKY Jr., Walter J., Chief Executive Officer, Rockford Center, Newark, DE, p. A78

YORK, Betty, Executive Director, West Community Hospital, West, TX, p. A428

YORKE, Harvey M., President and Chief Executive Officer, Southwestern Vermont Medical Center, Bennington, VT, p. A434

YOSHIOKA, James T., President, UniHealth, Burbank, CA, p. B148

YOSKO, Kathleen C., President and Chief Executive Officer, Schwab Rehabilitation Hospital and Care Network, Chicago, IL, p. A124

YOUNG, Anthony R., President and Chief Executive Officer, Columbia Doctors Hospital, Tulsa, OK, p. A342

YOUNG, Charles R., Administrator, Shriners Hospitals for Children–Spokane, Spokane, WA, p. A450

YOUNG, J. Phillip, President and Chief Executive Officer, Columbia Medical Center of Pampa, Pampa, TX, p. A420

YOUNG, John, President and Chief Executive Officer, Cleveland Regional Medical Center, Shelby, NC, p. A313

YOUNG, Randall A., Administrator, Lamb Healthcare Center, Littlefield, TX, p. A415

YOUNG, Richard T., President, Detroit Riverview Hospital, Detroit, MI, p. A210

YOUNG, Robert C., M.D., President, Fox Chase Cancer Center–American Oncologic Hospital, Philadelphia, PA, p. A360

YOUNG Jr., Frederick C., President, Pendleton Memorial Methodist Hospital, New Orleans, LA, p. A185

YOUNG Jr., William W., President, Central Maine Medical Center, Lewiston, ME, p. A190

YOUREE, James H., Chief Executive Officer, French Hospital Medical Center, San Luis Obispo, CA, p. A61

YUTZY, LaVern J., Chief Executive Officer, Philhaven, Bahavioral Healthcare Services, Mount Gretna, PA, p. A358

Z

ZACCAGNINO, Joseph A., President and Chief Executive Officer, Yale–New Haven Hospital, New Haven, CT, p. A75

ZACHARY, Beth D., Chief Operating Officer, White Memorial Medical Center, Los Angeles, CA, p. A51

ZAGER, Joe, Chief Executive Officer, Monroe County Hospital, Monroeville, AL, p. A16

ZANFINI, Gaetano, Chief Executive Officer, Brea Community Hospital, Brea, CA, p. A38

ZASTROW, Allan, FACHE, Chief Executive Officer, Keokuk Area Hospital, Keokuk, IA, p. A152

ZAYAS, Domingo Torres, CHE, Executive Director, Mennonite General Hospital, Aibonito, PR, p. A471

ZECHMAN Jr., Edwin K., President and Chief Executive Officer, Children's National Medical Center, Washington, DC, p. A79

ZEH, Brian R., Executive Director, Clinton County Hospital, Frankfort, IN, p. A140

ZELLERS, Thomas J., Chief Operating Officer, Deaconess Medical Center–Spokane, Spokane, WA, p. A450

ZEMAN, Barry T., President and Chief Executive Officer, St. Charles Hospital and Rehabilitation Center, Port Jefferson, NY, p. A299

ZEMAN, Denise, Chief Operating Officer, Meridia Euclid Hospital, Euclid, OH, p. A326

ZENTKO, Eugene, Administrator and Chief Executive Officer, Salem Community Hospital, Salem, OH, p. A331

ZEPEDA, Susan G., Ph.D., Chief Executive Officer, San Luis Obispo General Hospital, San Luis Obispo, CA, p. A61

ZEPHIER, Richard L., Ph.D., Service Unit Director, Acoma–Canoncito–Laguna Hospital, San Fidel, NM, p. A283

ZIELINSKI, Dennis G., Chief Executive Officer, United Memorial Hospital Association, Greenville, MI, p. A213

ZILM, Michael E., President, St. Mary's Health Center, Saint Louis, MO, p. A250

ZIMMERMAN, Kenneth J., Administrator, Beatrice Community Hospital and Health Center, Beatrice, NE, p. A258

ZIMMERMAN, Nancy, Administrator, Comanche County Hospital, Coldwater, KS, p. A158

ZIOMEK, Janice, Administrator, Moreno Valley Community Hospital, Moreno Valley, CA, p. A53

ZORNES, Donald H., Administrator, Columbus Community Hospital, Columbus, NE, p. A259

ZUBER, Eugene, Administrator, Newport Hospital and Clinic, Newport, AR, p. A34

ZUBKOFF, William, Ph.D., Chief Executive Officer, South Shore Hospital and Medical Center, Miami Beach, FL, p. A91

ZULIANI, Michael E., Chief Executive Officer, Angel Medical Center, Franklin, NC, p. A308

ZUMWALT, Roger C., Executive Director, Community Hospital, Grand Junction, CO, p. A70

ZURBRUGG, Anton P., CHE, President and Chief Executive Officer, Memorial Community Hospital and Health System, Blair, NE, p. A258

ZWIGART, Donna, FACHE, Chief Executive Officer, St. Francis Hospital of New Castle, New Castle, PA, p. A358

ZYLSTRA, Robert, Administrator, Whidbey General Hospital, Coupeville, WA, p. A446

AHA Membership Categories

The American Hospital Association is primarily an organization of hospitals and related institutions. Its object, according to its bylaws, is "to promote high–quality health care and health services for all the people through leadership in the development of public policy, leadership in the representation and advocacy of hospital and health care organization interests, and leadership in the provision of services to assist hospitals and health care organizations in meeting the health care needs of their communities."

The major source of income for the AHA is its membership dues, which are established by the membership through the House of Delegates. The types of membership and the basis for dues for each type are described in the following paragraphs.

Institutional Members

Type I–A and I–B, Hospitals

General and special hospitals that care for patients with conditions requiring a comparatively short stay. Type I–A includes short–term hospitals that are freestanding or which are operating units of health care systems not holding type III membership. Type I–B are short–term hospitals that are operating units of health care systems holding type III membership.

Type II–A and II–B, Hospitals

All other hospitals that provide inpatient care. Type II–A includes long–term hospitals that are freestanding or which are operating units of health care systems not holding type III membership. Type II–B includes longer–term hospitals that are operating units of health care systems holding type III membership.

Type III, Health Care Systems

Only those organizations (corporate headquarters, or similar entity) operating two or more hospitals or a single hospital owning, leasing, or sponsoring at least three operating entities of nonhospital preacute and postacute health care organizations can be classified as type III institutions. Headquarters of health care systems are eligible for type III membership when 90 percent of their owned, leased, managed, or sponsored hospitals are AHA members.

Membership dues are computed individually for each hospital and are based on total reported operating expenses for the most recent 12–month period. Type III members pay no dues other than those dues paid by their type B member units.

Type IV, Nonhospital Preacute and Postacute Health Care Organizations

Type IV–A, and IV–B organizations are defined as nonhospital preacute and postacute organizations that are responsible for delivery or delivery and financing of health care services. Health care delivery, for purposes of this definition, is the availability of professional health care staff during all hours of the organization's operations. Type IV–C members shall be limited to educational organizations.

Provisional Members

Hospitals that are in the planning or construction stage and that, on completion, will be eligible for institutional membership type I or type II. Provisional membership may also be granted to applicant institutions that cannot, at present, meet the requirements of type I or type II membership.

Government Institution Group Members

Groups of government hospitals operated by the same unit of government may obtain institutional membership under a group plan. Membership dues are based on a special schedule set forth in the bylaws of the AHA.

Contracting Hospitals

The AHA also provides membership services to certain hospitals that are prevented from holding membership because of legal or other restrictions. Contracting hospitals pay dues on the same basis as if they were classified as type I or II members.

Associate Members

Associate members are organizations interested in the objectives of the AHA but not eligible for institution membership. Membership dues are a fixed annual sum, depending on the location (inside or outside the United States and Canada) of the organization.

Types I and II

Hospitals

U.S. hospitals and hospitals in areas associated with the U.S. that are type I (short–term) or type II (long–term) members of the American Hospital Association are included in the list of hospitals in section A. Canadian types I and II members of the American Hospital Association are listed below.

Canada

ALBERTA

Edmonton: MISERICORDIA COMMUNITY HEALTH CENTRE, 16940 87th Avenue, Zip T5R 4H5; tel. 403/930–5611; Douglas C. Perry, M.D., Chief Corporate Officer
ROYAL ALEXANDRA HOSPITAL, 10240 Kingsway, Zip T5H 3V9; tel. 403/477–4111; Brian Spooner, Chief Operating Officer
Lamont: LAMONT HEALTH CARE CENTRE, 5216–53rd Street, Zip T0B 2R0; tel. 403/895–2211; Harold James, Chief Executive Officer
St. Albert: STURGEON COMMUNITY HEALTH CENTRE, 201 Boudreau Road, Zip T8N 6C4; tel. 403/460–6200; Wendy Hill, Network Administrator
Stony Plain: STONY PLAIN MUNICIPAL HOSPITAL, 4800 55th Avenue, Zip T7Z 1P9; tel. 403/963–2241; Myrene Couves, Administrator

BRITISH COLUMBIA

Langley: LANGLEY MEMORIAL HOSPITAL, 22051 Fraser Highway, Zip V3A 4H4; tel. 604/534–4121; Pat E. Zanon, President and Chief Executive Officer
Vancouver: BRITISH COLUMBIA'S CHILDREN'S HOSPITAL, 4480 Oak Street, Zip V6H 3V4; tel. 604/875–2345; John H. Tegenfeldt, President

MANITOBA

Portage La Prarie: PORTAGE DISTRICT GENERAL HOSPITAL, 524 Fifth Street S.E., Zip R1N 3A8; tel. 204/239–2211; Garry C. Mattin, Executive Director
Winnipeg: RIVERVIEW HEALTH CENTRE, 1 Morley Avenue East, Zip R3L 2P4; tel. 204/452–3411; Norman R. Kasian, President

ST. BONIFACE GENERAL HOSPITAL, 409 Tache Avenue, Zip R2H 2A6; tel. 204/233–8563; Kenneth Tremblay, President and Chief Executive Officer
VICTORIA GENERAL HOSPITAL, 2340 Pembina Highway, Zip R3T 2E8; tel. 204/269–3570; Marion Suski, President and Chief Executive Officer

NOVA SCOTIA

North Sydney: NORTHSIDE HARBOR VIEW HOSPITAL, P.O. Box 399, Zip B2A 3M4; tel. 902/794–8521; Mary S. MacIsaac, Chief Executive Officer
Sydney: CAPE BRETON REGIONAL HOSPITAL, 1482 George Street, Zip B1P 1P3; tel. 902/567–8000; John Malcom, Chief Executive Officer

ONTARIO

Brantford: ST. JOSEPH'S HOSPITAL, 99 Wayne Gretzky Parkway, Zip N3S 6T6; tel. 519/753–8641; Romeo Cercone, President and Chief Executive Officer
Guelph: HOMEWOOD HEALTH CENTER, 150 Delhi Street, Zip N1E 6K9; tel. 519/824–1010; Ronald A. Pond, M.D., President and Chief Executive Officer
London: ST. MARYS' HOSPITAL CAMPUS, P.O. Box 5777, Zip N6A 1Y6; tel. 613/646–6000; Philip C. Hassen, President
North York: BAYCREST CENTRE–GERIATRIC CARE, 3560 Bathurst Street, Zip M6A 2E1; tel. 416/789–5131; Stephen W. Herbert, President and Chief Executive Officer
Ottawa: ROYAL OTTAWA HOSPITAL, 1145 Carling Avenue, Zip K1Z 7K4; tel. 613/722–6521; George F. Langill, Executive Director
Parry Sound: WEST PARRY SOUND HEALTH CENTRE, 10 James Street, Zip P2A 1T3; tel. 705/746–9321; Norman Maciver, Chief Executive Officer
Renfrew: RENFREW VICTORIA HOSPITAL, 499 Raglan Street North, Zip K7V 1P6; tel. 613/432–4851; Randy V. Penney, Executive Director
Strathroy: STRATHROY MIDDLESEX GENERAL HOSPITAL, 395 Carrie Street, Zip N7G 3C9; tel. 519/245–1550; Thomas M. Enright, Executive Director

Sudbury: SUDBURY MEMORIAL HOSPITAL, 865 Regent Street South, Zip P3E 3Y9; tel. 705/671–1000; Esko J. Vainio, Executive Director
Thornhill: SHOULDICE HOSPITAL, P.O. Box 370, Zip L3T 4A3; tel. 905/889–1125; Alan O'Dell, Administrator
Toronto: DOCTORS HOSPITAL, 45 Brunswick Avenue, Zip M5S 5411; tel. 416/923–5411; Brian McFarlane, President and Chief Executive Officer
MOUNT SINAI HOSPITAL, 600 University Avenue, Zip M5G 1X5; tel. 416/596–4200; Theodore J. Freedman, President and Chief Executive Officer
REHABILITATION INSTITUTE OF TORONTO, 550 University Avenue, Zip M5G 2A2; tel. 416/597–5111; Clifford A. Nordal, President and Chief Executive Officer
ST. JOSEPH'S HEALTH CENTRE, 30 the Queensway, Zip M6R 1B5; tel. 416/534–9531; Marilyn Bruner, President and Chief Executive Officer
WOMEN'S COLLEGE HOSPITAL, 76 Grenville Street, Zip M5S 1B2; tel. 416/323–6400; Patricia Campbell, President and Chief Executive Officer

QUEBEC

Montreal: HOPITAL NOTRE DAME, 1560 Rue Sherbrooke Est, Zip H2L 4M1; tel. 514/281–6000; David Levine, Director General
MONTREAL CHILDREN'S HOSPITAL, 2300 Tupper Street, Zip H3H 1P3; tel. 514/934–4400; Elizabeth Riley, Executive Director
MOUNT SINAI HOSPITAL CENTER, 5690 Cavendish Cote St–Luc', Zip H4W 1S7; tel. 514/369–2222; Joseph Rothbart, Executive Director
Sherbrooke: SHERBROOKE HOSPITAL, 375 Argyle Street, Zip J1J 3H5; tel. 819/569–3661; Daniel Bergeron, Director General

Type III

Health Care Systems

Health Care Systems that are type III members of the American Hospital Association are included in the lists of health care systems in section B of this guide. Membership is indicated by a star (★) preceding the name of the system.

Type IV

Type IV members of the American Hospital Association include Nonhospital Precute and Postacute Health Care Organizations. These organizations are responsible for delivery or delivery and financing of health care services.

Type IV members also include Associated University Programs in Health Administration and Hospital Schools of Nursing.

Associated University Programs in Health Administration

ALABAMA

Birmingham: UNIVERSITY OF ALABAMA AT BIRMINGHAM, 1675 University Boulevard, Zip 35294–3361; tel. 205/934–5661; Charles L. Joiner, Ph.D., Dean

ARIZONA

Tempe: SCHOOL OF HEALTH ADMINISTRATION AND POLICY, ARIZONA STATE UNIVERSITY, P.O. Box 874506, Zip 85287–4506; tel. 602/965–7778; Frank G. Williams, Ph.D., Professor

CALIFORNIA

Los Angeles: UCLA SCHOOL OF PUBLIC HEALTH, P.O. Box 951772, Zip 90095–1772; tel. 310/825–2594; Thomas Rice, M.D., Administrator

San Francisco: GOLDEN GATE UNIVERSITY, 536 Mission Street, General Library, Zip 94105; tel. 415/442–0777; Steven Dunlap, Assistant Librarian

DISTRICT OF COLUMBIA

Washington: SCHOOL OF PUBLIC HEALTH AND HEALTH SERVICES, THE GEORGE WASHINGTON UNIVERSITY, 600 21st Street N.W., Zip 20052; tel. 202/676–6220; Richard F. Southby, Ph.D., Associate Dean Health Services

GEORGIA

Atlanta: GEORGIA STATE UNIVERSITY, INSTITUTE OF HEALTH ADMINISTRATION, University Plaza, Zip 30303; tel. 404/651–2000; Everett A. Johnson, Director

ILLINOIS

Carbondale: SOUTHERN ILLINOIS UNIVERSITY, COLLEGE OF APPLIED SCIENCES AND ARTS, Zip 62901; tel. 618/536–6682; Frederic L. Morgan, Ph.D., Chair Health Care Professions

Chicago: UNIVERSITY OF CHICAGO, GRADUATE PROGRAM IN HEALTH ADMINISTRATION AND POLICY, 969 East 60th Street, Zip 60637; tel. 312/753–4191; Edward Lawlor, Ph.D., Director

Evanston: HEALTH SERVICE MANAGEMENT PROGRAM, KELLOGG GRADUATE SCHOOL OF MANAGEMENT, NORTHWESTERN UNIVERSITY, 2001 Sheridan Road, Zip 60208; tel. 847/492–5540; Joel Shalowitz, M.D., Professor and Director

University Park: PROGRAM IN HEALTH SERVICE ADMINISTRATION, SCHOOL OF HEALTH PROFESSIONS, GOVERNORS STATE UNIVERSITY, Zip 60466; tel. 847/534–4030; Sang–O Rhee, Chairman

IOWA

Calmar: NORTHEAST IOWA COMMUNITY COLLEGE, Box 400, Zip 52132; tel. 319/562–3263; Melinda Hanson, R.N., Chairperson Health and Human Services

Iowa City: GRADUATE PROGRAM IN HOSPITAL AND HEALTH ADMINISTRATION, UNIVERSITY OF IOWA, 2700 Steindler Building, Zip 52242; tel. 319/356–2593; Douglas Wakefield, Ph.D., Interim Head

MARYLAND

Bethesda: NAVAL SCHOOL OF HEALTH SCIENCES, Naval Medical Command, National Region, Zip 20889–5611; tel. 301/295–1251; Captain Harry Coffey, Commanding Officer

MISSOURI

Saint Louis: PROGRAM IN HOSPITAL AND HEALTH CARE ADMINISTRATION, ST. LOUIS UNIVERSITY, 3525 Caroline Street, Zip 63104; tel. 314/577–8000; Michael Counte, Ph.D., Chairman

WASHINGTON UNIVERSITY, SCHOOL OF MEDICINE, 4547 Clayton Avenue, Zip 63110; tel. 314/362–2477; James O. Hepner, Ph.D., Director Health Administration Program

NEW YORK

Valhalla: NEW YORK MEDICAL COLLEGE, Administration Building, Zip 10595; tel. 914/347–5044; Father Harry C. Barrett, M.P.H., President and Chief Executive Officer

OHIO

Columbus: GRADUATE PROGRAM IN HEALTH SERVICES MANAGEMENT AND POLICY, OHIO STATE UNIVERSITY, 1583 Perry Street, Room 246 Samp, Zip 43210; tel. 614/292–9708; Stephen F. Loebs, Ph.D., Chairman and Associate Professor

OKLAHOMA

Oklahoma City: UNIVERSITY OF OKLAHOMA HEALTH SCIENCE CENTER, DEPARTMENT OF HEALTH ADMINISTRATION AND POLICY, P.O. Box 26901, Zip 73104; tel. 405/271–2114; Keith Curtis, Associate Professor and Interim Chair

PENNSYLVANIA

Philadelphia: TEMPLE UNIVERSITY, DEPARTMENT OF HEALTH ADMINISTRATION, SCHOOL OF BUSINESS ADMINISTRATION, Zip 19122–6083; tel. 215/787–8082; William Aaronson, Professor and Chairman

University Park: PENNSYLVANIA STATE UNIVERSITY, 116 Henderson Building, Zip 16802; tel. 814/863–2859; Diane Brannon, Ph.D., Interim Department Head, Health Policy and Administration

TEXAS

Fort Sam Houston: ARMY–BAYLOR UNIVERSITY PROGRAM IN HEALTH CARE ADMINISTRATION, Academy of Health Sciences–USA, Zip 78234; tel. 512/221–5009

San Antonio: OUR LADY OF THE LAKE UNIVERSITY – GRADUATE PROGRAM IN HEALTH CARE MANAGEMENT, 411 S.W. 24th Street, Zip 78207–4666; tel. 210/434–6711; Paul Brooke, M.D., Health Care Coordinator

TRINITY UNIVERSITY, 715 Stadium Drive, Suite 58, Zip 78212–7200; tel. 210/736–8107; Niccie McKay, Ph.D., Chairman

Sheppard AFB: U. S. AIR FORCE SCHOOL OF HEALTH CARE SCIENCES, Building 1900, MSTL/114, Academic Library, Zip 76311; tel. 817/851–2511

PUERTO RICO

San Juan: SCHOOL OF PUBLIC HEALTH, P.O. Box 5067, Zip 00936; tel. 809/767–9626; Orlando Nieves, Dean

Hospital Schools of Nursing

ARKANSAS

Little Rock: BAPTIST MEDICAL SYSTEM School of Nursing
Pine Bluff: JEFFERSON REGIONAL MEDICAL CENTER School of Nursing

CALIFORNIA

Los Angeles: LOS ANGELES COUNTY–UNIVERSITY OF SOUTHERN CALIFORNIA MEDICAL CENTER School of Nursing

CONNECTICUT

Bridgeport: ST. VINCENT'S COLLEGE
Hartford: SAINT FRANCIS HOSPITAL AND MEDICAL CENTER School of Nursing
Middletown: MIDDLESEX MEMORIAL HOSPITAL ONA M. WILCOX School of Nursing

DELAWARE

Lewes: BEEBE MEDICAL CENTER School of Nursing

FLORIDA

Miami: JAMES M. JACKSON MEMORIAL HOSPITAL School of Nursing

GEORGIA

Atlanta: GEORGIA BAPTIST MEDICAL CENTER School of Nursing

ILLINOIS

Canton: GRAHAM HOSPITAL School of Nursing
Chicago: RAVENSWOOD HOSPITAL MEDICAL CENTER School of Nursing
Danville: LAKEVIEW MEDICAL CENTER School of Nursing
Peoria: METHODIST HOSPITAL OF CENTRAL ILLINOIS School of Nursing

INDIANA

Lafayette: ST. ELIZABETH HOSPITAL MEDICAL CENTER School of Nursing

IOWA

Des Moines: IOWA METHODIST HOSPITAL School of Nursing
MERCY HOSPITAL MEDICAL CENTER School of Nursing
Sioux City: ST. LUKE'S REGIONAL MEDICAL CENTER School of Nursing

LOUISIANA

Baton Rouge: BATON ROUGE GENERAL MEDICAL CENTER School of Nursing
OUR LADY OF LAKE REGIONAL MEDICAL CENTER School of Nursing

MARYLAND

Baltimore: UNION MEMORIAL HOSPITAL School of Nursing
Easton: MEMORIAL HOSPITAL AT EASTON MARYLAND School of Nursing

MASSACHUSETTS

Boston: NEW ENGLAND BAPTIST HOSPITAL School of Nursing
Brockton: BROCKTON HOSPITAL School of Nursing
Medford: LAWRENCE MEMORIAL HOSPITAL OF MEDFORD School of Nursing
Springfield: BAYSTATE MEDICAL CENTER School of Nursing

MICHIGAN

Detroit: HENRY FORD HOSPITAL School of Nursing
Kalamazoo: BRONSON METHODIST HOSPITAL School of Nursing

MISSOURI

Saint Louis: BARNES HOSPITAL School of Nursing
LUTHERAN MEDICAL CENTER School of Nursing
Springfield: LESTER E. COX MEDICAL CENTERS School of Nursing
ST JOHN'S School of Nursing
Town & Country: MISSOURI BAPTIST MEDICAL CENTER School of Nursing

NEBRASKA

Lincoln: BRYAN MEMORIAL HOSPITAL School of Nursing

NEW JERSEY

Camden: OUR LADY OF LOURDES MEDICAL CENTER School of Nursing
Elizabeth: ELIZABETH GENERAL MEDICAL CENTER School of Nursing
Englewood: ENGLEWOOD HOSPITAL AND MEDICAL CENTER School of Nursing
Jersey City: CHRIST HOSPITAL School of Nursing
Montclair: MOUNTAINSIDE HOSPITAL School of Nursing
Neptune: ANN MAY School of Nursing
Plainfield: MUHLENBERG REGIONAL MEDICAL CENTER School of Nursing
Teaneck: HOLY NAME HOSPITAL School of Nursing
Trenton: HELENE FULD MEDICAL CENTER School of Nursing
MERCER MEDICAL CENTER School of Nursing
ST. FRANCIS MEDICAL CENTER School of Nursing

NEW YORK

Buffalo: SISTERS OF CHARITY HOSPITAL School of Nursing
Elmira: ARNOT–OGDEN MEMORIAL HOSPITAL School of Nursing
New York: ST. VINCENT'S HOSPITAL AND MEDICAL CENTER OF NEW YORK School of Nursing
Staten Island: ST. VINCENT'S MEDICAL CENTER School of Nursing
Utica: ST. ELIZABETH HOSPITAL School of Nursing
Yonkers: ST. JOHN'S RIVERSIDE HOSPITAL COCHRAN School of Nursing

NORTH CAROLINA

Charlotte: MERCY HOSPITAL School of Nursing
PRESBYTERIAN HOSPITAL School of Nursing
Concord: CABARRUS MEMORIAL HOSPITAL School of Nursing
Durham: WATTS School of Nursing

NORTH DAKOTA

Bismarck: MEDCENTER ONE School of Nursing
Minot: TRINITY MEDICAL CENTER School of Nursing

OHIO

Akron: AKRON CITY HOSPITAL IDABELLE FIRESTONE School of Nursing
SUMMA ST. THOMAS School of Nursing
Canton: AULTMAN HOSPITAL School of Nursing
Cincinnati: CHRIST HOSPITAL School of Nursing
GOOD SAMARITAN HOSPITAL School of Nursing
Cleveland: FAIRVIEW GENERAL HOSPITAL School of Nursing

Sandusky: PROVIDENCE HOSPITAL School of Nursing
Springfield: COMMUNITY HOSPITAL OF SPRINGFIELD AND CLARK COUNTY School of Nursing

PENNSYLVANIA

Altoona: ALTOONA HOSPITAL School of Nursing
Johnstown: CONEMAUGH VALLEY MEMORIAL HOSPITAL School of Nursing
New Castle: JAMESON MEMORIAL HOSPITAL School of Nursing
ST. FRANCIS HOSPITAL OF NEW CASTLE School of Nursing
Philadelphia: EPISCOPAL HOSPITAL School of Nursing
GERMANTOWN HOSPITAL AND MEDICAL CENTER School of Nursing
METHODIST HOSPITAL School of Nursing
Pittsburgh: SHADYSIDE HOSPITAL School of Nursing
ST. FRANCIS MEDICAL CENTER School of Nursing
ST. MARGARET MEMORIAL HOSPITAL LOUISE SUYDAM MCCLINTIC School of Nursing
WESTERN PENNSYLVANIA HOSPITAL School of Nursing
Pottsville: POTTSVILLE HOSPITAL AND WARNE CLINIC School of Nursing
Sewickley: SEWICKLEY VALLEY HOSPITAL School of Nursing
Sharon: SHARON REGIONAL HEALTH SYSTEM School of Nursing
Washington: WASHINGTON HOSPITAL School of Nursing
West Chester: CHESTER COUNTY HOSPITAL School of Nursing

RHODE ISLAND

North Providence: ST. JOSEPH HOSPITAL School of Nursing

TENNESSEE

Knoxville: FORT SANDERS REGIONAL MEDICAL CENTER School of Nursing
Memphis: BAPTIST MEMORIAL HOSPITAL School of Nursing
METHODIST HOSPITALS OF MEMPHIS–CENTRAL School of Nursing
ST. JOSEPH HOSPITAL School of Nursing

TEXAS

Lubbock: METHODIST HOSPITAL School of Nursing
San Antonio: BAPTIST MEDICAL CENTER School of Nursing

VIRGINIA

Danville: MEMORIAL HOSPITAL OF DANVILLE School of Nursing
Lynchburg: LYNCHBURG GENERAL–MARSHALL LODGE HOSPITAL School of Nursing
Newport News: RIVERSIDE REGIONAL MEDICAL CENTER School of Nursing
Norfolk: DEPAUL MEDICAL CENTER School of Nursing
SENTARA NORFOLK GENERAL HOSPITAL School of Nursing
Petersburg: SOUTHSIDE REGIONAL MEDICAL CENTER School of Nursing
Richmond: RICHMOND MEMORIAL HOSPITAL School of Nursing
Suffolk: OBICI HOSPITAL School of Nursing

WEST VIRGINIA

Huntington: ST. MARY'S HOSPITAL School of Nursing

Nonhospital Preacute and Postacute Care Facilities

ALABAMA

Birmingham: HEALTH PARTNERS OF ALABAMA, INC., 600 Beacon Parkway West, Zip 35209; tel. 205/941–1012; Jim Ludwig, President and Chief Executive Officer
Fort McClellan: NOBLE ARMY HEALTH CLINIC, Zip 36205–5083; tel. 205/848–2232

ALASKA

Anchorage: DEPARTMENT OF VETERANS AFFAIRS ALASKA MEDICAL AND REGIONAL OFFICE CENTER, 2925 Debarr Road, Zip 99508–2989; tel. 907/257–6930; Alonzo M. Poteet, III, Director

ARIZONA

Phoenix: CAMELBACK FAMILY MEDICINE, 5040 North 15th Avenue, Zip 85015; tel. 602/238–3314; Jeffrey K. Norman, Chief Executive Officer
JESSE OWENS MEMORIAL MEDICAL CENTER, 325 East Baseline Road, Zip 85040; tel. 602/238–3314; Jeffrey K. Norman, Chief Executive Officer
PMH FAMILY HEALTH CENTER–WEST MCDOWELL, 5030 West McDowell Road, Zip 85035; tel. 602/2383314; Jeffrey K. Norman, Chief Executive Officer

ARKANSAS

Little Rock: CENTRAL ARKANSAS RADIATION THERAPY INSTITUTE, P.O. Box 55050, Zip 72215; tel. 501/664–8573; Janice E. Burford, President and Chief Executive Officer

CALIFORNIA

Long Beach: NAVAL MEDICAL CLINIC, Reeves Avenue, Building 831, Zip 90822–5073; tel. 562/521–4201; Captain J. M. Lamdin, Commanding Officer
Los Angeles: DEPARTMENT OF VETERANS AFFAIRS, OUTPATIENT CLINIC, 351 East Temple Street, Room A–102, Zip 90012; tel. 213/253–5000; Jules Morevac, Ph.D., Director
Port Hueneme: NAVAL MEDICAL CLINIC, Zip 93043; tel. 805/982–4501
San Francisco: VETERANS AFFAIRS OUTPATIENT CLINIC, 4150 Clement Street, Zip 94121; tel. 415/221–4810; Lawrence C. Stewart, Director
Sepulveda: VETERANS AFFAIRS MEDICAL CENTER, 16111 Plummer Street, Zip 91343; tel. 818/891–7711; Perry C. Norman, Director

CONNECTICUT

Stamford: THE REHABILITATION CENTER, 26 Palmer's Hill Road, Zip 06902; tel. 203/325–1544; Kathleen Murphy, President

DELAWARE

New Castle: CHRISTIANA CARE VISITING NURSE ASSOCIATION, One Reads Way, Zip 19720; tel. 302/323–8200
SCHWEIZER'S THERAPY AND REHABILITATION, 100 Corporate Commons, Suite 1, Zip 19720
Newark: CHRISTIANA CARE IMAGING CENTER, 4751 Ogletown–Stanton Road, Zip 19718
CHRISTIANA SURGICENTER, 4755 Ogletown–Stanton Road, Zip 19718
Wilmington: EUGENE DUPONT PREVENTIVE MEDICINE AND REHABILITATION INSTITUTE
INFUSION SERVICES OF DELAWARE, 1701 Rockland Road, Suite 102, Zip 19803

FLORIDA

Key West: NAVAL REGIONAL MEDICAL CLINIC, Roosevelt Boulevard, Zip 33040; tel. 305/293–4500; Captain F. L. Anzalone, Officer–in–Charge

Miami: VITAS HEALTHCARE CORPORATION, 100 South Biscayne Boulevard, Zip 33131; tel. 305/374–4143; Hugh Westbrook, Chairman and Chief Executive Officer
Pompano Beach: COLUMBIA POMPANO BEACH MEDICAL CENTER, 600 S.W. Third Street, Zip 33060–6979; tel. 954/782–2000
Riverview: TAMPA BAY ACADEMY, 12012 Boyette Road, Zip 33569; tel. 813/677–6700; Edward C. Hoefle, Administrator

HAWAII

Honolulu: VETERANS AFFAIRS MEDICAL REGIONAL OFFICE, P.O. Box 50188, Zip 96850; tel. 808/541–1582
Pearl Harbor: NAVAL REGIONAL MEDICAL CLINIC, Box 121, Building 1750, Zip 96860–5080; tel. 808/471–3025; Captain Robert Murphy, M.D., MSC, USN, Commanding Officer

INDIANA

Kendallville: COMPRECARE HOME HEALTH AND HOSPICE, P.O. Box 517, Zip 46755–0517; tel. 219/347–6340; Marilyn Alligood, R.N., Chief Executive Officer
NOBLE COUNTY EMERGENCY MEDICAL SERVICES, P.O. Box 249, Zip 46755–0249; tel. 219/347–6307; Kim Bloomfield, Chief Executive Officer
OCCUPATIONAL HEALTH MANAGEMENT, P.O. Box 249, Zip 46755–0249; tel. 219/347–6309; Marylyn Asher, Chief Executive Officer

KANSAS

Wichita: U. S. AIR FORCE HOSPITAL, 59570 Leavenworth Street, Suite 6E4, Zip 67221–5300; tel. 316/652–5000; Lieutenant Colonel Bruce A. Harma, Administrator

LOUISIANA

New Orleans: NAVAL MEDICAL CLINIC, Zip 70142; tel. 504/678–2400; Lieutenant Colonel Deborah Auth, Director, Administration

MARYLAND

Annapolis: NAVAL MEDICAL CLINIC, Zip 21402; tel. 410/293–1330
Fort George G Meade: KIMBROUGH ARMY COMMUNITY HOSPITAL, Zip 20755; tel. 301/677–4171; Colonel David W. Roberts, Commanding Officer

MASSACHUSETTS

Falmouth: GOSNOLD ON CAPE COD, 200 Ter Heun Drive, Box CC, Zip 02540; tel. 508/540–6550; Raymond Tamasi, Chief Executive Officer

MICHIGAN

Port Huron: TRI–HOSPITAL E.M.S., 309 Grand River Street, Zip 48060; tel. 313/985–7115; Ken Cummings, Chief Executive Officer
WILLOW ENTERPRISES, INC., 1221 Pine Grove Avenue, Zip 48060; tel. 313/989–3737; James B. Bridge, Chief Executive Officer
Sault Sainte Marie: SAULT SAINTE MARIE TRIBAL HEALTH AND HUMAN SERVICES CENTER, 2864 Ashmun Street, Zip 49783; tel. 906/495–5651; Russell Vizina, Division Director Health

MISSOURI

Independence: SURGI–CARE CENTER OF INDEPENDENCE, 2311 Redwood Avenue, Zip 64057; tel. 816/373–7995; Michael W. Chappelow, President and Chief Executive Officer

MONTANA

Malmstrom AFB: U. S. AIR FORCE CLINIC, Zip 59402–5300; tel. 406/731–3863; Lieutenant Colonel Gary D. McMannon, FACHE, USAF, Administrator

NEVADA

Las Vegas: VETERANS AFFAIRS–OUTPATIENT CLINIC, 1703 West Charleston Boulevard, Zip 89102; tel. 702/389–3700; Ramon J. Reevey, Director

NEW HAMPSHIRE

Portsmouth: NAVAL MEDICAL CLINIC, Building H–1, Zip 03801; tel. 207/439–1000; Captain F. M. Richardson, Commanding Officer

NEW JERSEY

Fort Monmouth: PATTERSON ARMY HEALTH CLINIC, Zip 07703–5607; tel. 908/532–1266; Colonel Dolores Loew, Commander

NEW MEXICO

Fort Bayard: FORT BAYARD MEDICAL CENTER, P.O. Box 36219, Zip 88036; tel. 505/537–3302; Marquita George, Administrator

NEW YORK

Lake Placid: CAMELOT, 50 Riverside Drive, Zip 12946; tel. 518/523–3605; Father Carlos J. Caguiat, FACHE, Vice President
New York: STATE UNIVERSITY OF NEW YORK, UNIVERSITY OPTOMETRIC CENTER, 100 East 24th Street, Zip 10010; tel. 212/780–4930; Richard C. Weber, Executive Director
Rochester: ROCHESTER REHABILITATION CENTER, 1000 Elmwood Avenue, Zip 14620; tel. 716/271–2520; George H. Gieselman, President

NORTH CAROLINA

Winston Salem: QUALCHOICE OF NORTH CAROLINA, INC., 2000 West First Street, Suite 210, Zip 27104; tel. 910/716–0900; Douglas G. Cueny, President

OHIO

Cleveland: KAISER PERMANENTE, 1001 Lakeside, Zip 44114; tel. 216/362–2000; Greg Palmer, Chief Executive Officer
Columbus: VETERANS AFFAIRS OUTPATIENT CLINIC, 2090 Kenny Road, Zip 43221; tel. 614/469–5663; Troy E. Page, Director

OKLAHOMA

Enid: U. S. AIR FORCE CLINIC, Vance AFB, Building 810, Zip 73705–5000; tel. 405/249–7494; Lieutenant Colonel Andrew F. Love, MSC, USAF, Commander Medical Group

OREGON

Portland: BESS KAISER FOUNDATION HOSPITAL, 5055 North Greeley Avenue, Zip 97217–3591; tel. 503/285–9321; Alide Chase, Administrator

PENNSYLVANIA

Chester: COMMUNITY HOSPITAL, DIVISION OF THE CROZER–CHESTER MEDICAL CENTER, Ninth and Wilson Streets, Zip 19013–2098; tel. 610/494–0700; Joan K. Richards, President

---

Pittsburgh: HEALTH ASSISTANCE PROGRAM FOR PERSONNEL IN INDUSTRY, 4221 Penn Avenue, Zip 15224; tel. 412/622–4994; Eugene Ginchereau, M.D., Director

York: SOUTH CENTRAL PREFERRED, 1803 Mount Rose Avenue, Zip 17403; tel. 717/741–9511; Charles H. Chodroff, M.D., Executive Director

YORK HEALTH CARE SERVICES, 1001 South George Street, Zip 17405; tel. 717/851–2121; Brian A. Gragnolati, President

YORK HEALTH SYSTEM MEDICAL GROUP, Zip 17403; tel. 717/741–8125; William R. Richards, Executive Director

RHODE ISLAND

Newport: NAVAL HOSPITAL, Zip 02841–1002; tel. 401/841–3915; Captain C. Henderson, III, MSC, USN, Commanding Officer

TEXAS

El Paso: VETERANS AFFAIRS HEALTHCARE CENTER, 5001 North Piedras Street, Zip 79930–4211; tel. 915/564–6100; Edward Valenzuela, Director

Houston: CHAMPION'S RESIDENTIAL TREATMENT CENTER, 14320 Walters Road, Zip 77014; tel. 713/537–5050; Brad Thompson, Chief Executive Officer

San Antonio: U. S. AIR FORCE CLINIC BROOKS, Building 615, Zip 78235–5300; tel. 210/536–2087; Major Edward M. Jenkins, Administrator

VIRGINIA

Fort Lee: KENNER ARMY HEALTH CLINIC, 700 24th Street, Zip 23801–1716; tel. 804/734–9256

Quantico: NAVAL REGIONAL MEDICAL CLINIC, Zip 22134; tel. 703/640–2236; Captain William L. Roach, Jr., MSC, USN, Commanding Officer

WISCONSIN

Green Bay: UNITY HOSPICE, P.O. Box 28345, Zip 54324–8345; tel. 920/494–0225; Donald Seibel, Executive Director

Milwaukee: EYE INSTITUTE–MEDICAL COLLEGE OF WISCONSIN, 925 North 87th Street, Zip 53226–3595; tel. 414/456–7800; James N. Browne, Chief Executive Officer

Provisional

The listing includes organizations that, as of April 1998, were in the planning or construction stage and that, on completion, will be eligible for institutional membership of type I or II. Some hospitals are granted provisional membership for reasons related to other Association requirements. Hospitals classified as provisional members for reasons other than being under construction are indicated by a bullet (•).

ARIZONA

Phoenix: MAYO CLINIC HOSPITAL, 13400 East Shea Boulevard, Zip 85259; tel. 602/301–8367; Thomas C. Bour, Administrator

Ambulatory Centers and Home Care Agencies

United States

ARIZONA

RAYMOND W. BLISS ARMY HEALTH CENTER, Fort Huachuca, Zip 85613–7040; tel. 520/533–2350; Major Christopher Hale, Deputy Commander

CONNECTICUT

NAVAL HOSPITAL, 1 Wahoo Drive, Box 600, Groton, Zip 06349–5600; tel. 860/694–3261; Captain Kathleen Hiatt, Deputy Commanding Officer

FLORIDA

NEMOURS CHILDREN'S CLINIC, 807 Nira Street, Jacksonville, Zip 32207; tel. 904/390–3600; Barry P. Sales, Administrator

NEW YORK

WESTFALL SURGERY CENTER, 919 Westfall Road, Rochester, Zip 14618; tel. 716/256–1330; Gary J. Scott, Administrative Director

PENNSYLVANIA

CRAIG HOUSE–TECHNOMA, 751 North Negley Avenue, Pittsburgh, Zip 15206; tel. 412/361–2801; Richard L. Kerchnner, Administrator

WISCONSIN

CURATIVE REHABILITATION SERVICES, 1000 North 92nd Street, Wauwatosa, Zip 53226; tel. 414/259–1414; Robert H. Coons, Jr., President

Philippines

DEPARTMENT OF VETERANS AFFAIRS, OUTPATIENT CLINIC, Manila, Zip 96440; tel. 632/521–7116

Blue Cross Plans

United States

ARIZONA

BLUE CROSS AND BLUE SHIELD OF ARIZONA, Box 13466, Phoenix, Zip 85002–3466; tel. 602/864–4400; Robert B. Bulla, President and Chief Executive Officer

FLORIDA

BLUE CROSS AND BLUE SHIELD OF FLORIDA, INC., P.O. Box 1798, Jacksonville, Zip 32231–0014; tel. 904/791–8081; William E. Flaherty, Chairman and Chief Executive Officer

NEW YORK

BLUE CROSS AND BLUE SHIELD OF CENTRAL NEW YORK, Box 4809, Syracuse, Zip 13221–4809; tel. 315/448–3902; Albert F. Antonini, President and Chief Executive Officer

OKLAHOMA

BLUE CROSS AND BLUE SHIELD OF OKLAHOMA, Box 3283, Tulsa, Zip 74102; tel. 918/583–0861; Ronald F. King, President and Chief Executive Officer

PENNSYLVANIA

CAPITAL BLUE CROSS, 2500 Elmerton Avenue, Harrisburg, Zip 17110; tel. 717/541–7000; James M. Mead, President

HIGHMARK BLUE CROSS BLUE SHIELD, 120 Fifth Avenue Place, Suite 3014, Pittsburgh, Zip 15222; tel. 412/255–7000; Sandra R. Tomlinson, Chief Executive Officer

INDEPENDENCE BLUE CROSS, 1901 Market Street, Philadelphia, Zip 19103; tel. 215/241–3300; Denise Dodd, Manager

TEXAS

BLUE CROSS AND BLUE SHIELD OF TEXAS, INC., Box 655730, Dallas, Zip 75265–5730; tel. 214/766–6900; Rogers Coleman, M.D., President

Shared Services Organizations

INDIANA

HOLY CROSS SERVICES CORPORATION, Saint Mary's, Lourdes Hall, Notre Dame, Zip 46556–5014; tel. 219/283–4600; David L. Burk, Chief Executive Officer

TEXAS

TEXAS HOSPITAL ASSOCIATION, P.O. Box 15587, Austin, Zip 78761–5587; tel. 512/465–1000; Terry Townsend, President and Chief Executive Officer

Other Associate Members

U.S. government hospitals in areas outside the United States that are members of the American Hospital Association are not shown here, but are included in the list of such hospitals in section A of this guide, where membership is indicated by a star (★) preceeding the name of the individual hospital.

UNITED STATES

Architecture:

BURT HILL KOSAR RITTELMANN ASSOCIATES, 400 Morgan Center, Butler, Pennsylvania Zip 16001–5977; tel. 412/285–4761; John E. Brock, Principal

EARL SWENSSON ASSOCIATES, INC., 2100 West End Avenue, Suite 1200, Nashville, Tennessee Zip 37203; tel. 615/329–9445; Richard L. Miller, President

LEGAT MEDICAL ARCHITECTS, 24 North Chapel, Waukegan, Illinois Zip 60085; tel. 847/605–0234; Casimir Frankiewicz, President

MARSHALL CRAFT ASSOCIATES, INC., 6112 York Road, Baltimore, Maryland Zip 21212; tel. 301/532–3131; Richard S. Abbott, Secretary

MATTHEI AND COLIN ASSOCIATES, 332 South Michigan Avenue, Suite 614, Chicago, Illinois Zip 60604; tel. 312/939–4002; Ronald G. Kobold, Managing Partner

SVERDRUP FACILITIES CORPORATION, 801 North 11th Street, Saint Louis, Missouri Zip 63101–1015; tel. 314/997–0300; Nicholas J. Varrone, Vice President

THE RITCHIE ORGANIZATION, 80 Bridge Street, Newton, Massachusetts Zip 02158; tel. 617/969–9400; Wendell R. Morgan, Jr., President

WILLIAM A. BERRY & SON, INC., 100 Conifer Hill Drive, Danvers, Massachusetts Zip 01923; tel. 978/774–1057; Ronda Paradis, Vice President

Bank:

BANK OF TOKYO–MITSUBISHI, 1251 Avenue of the Americas, 12, New York, New York Zip 10020–1104; tel. 212/782–4329; John Beckwith, Vice President

Behavioral Health Center:

DEVEREUX–VICTORIA, 120 David Wade Drive, Victoria, Texas Zip 77902–2666; tel. 512/575–8271; L. Gail Atkinson, Executive Director

Communication Systems Org:

SOUTHWESTERN BELL, One Bell Center, Room 11–E–2, Saint Louis, Missouri Zip 63101–3099; tel. 314/235–2446; William C. Winter, Manager Market Healthcare

Construction Firm:

HBE CORPORATION, P.O. Box 419039, Saint Louis, Missouri Zip 63141; tel. 314/567–9000; Mike Dolan, Executive Vice President

LEO A. DALY COMPANY, 8600 Indian Hills Drive, Omaha, Nebraska Zip 68114; tel. 402/391–8111; James M. Ingram, Senior Vice President

Consulting Firm:

A.P.M., INCORPORATED, 1675 Broadway, 18th Floor, New York, New York Zip 10019; tel. 212/903–9300; Karen Flaherty, Coordinator Marketing

ARAMARK HEALTHCARE SUPPORT SERVICES, 1101 Market Street, Philadelphia, Pennsylvania Zip 19107; tel. 215/238–3000; Constance B. Girard–diCarlo, President

ARTHUR ANDERSEN & COMPANY, 33 West Monroe Street, Chicago, Illinois Zip 60603; tel. 312/580–0033; Edward Giniat, Director

CAMPBELL WILSON, 9400 Central Expressway, Suite 613, Dallas, Texas Zip 75231; tel. 214/373–7077; Danna J. Wilson, Principal

CHI SYSTEMS, INC., 130 South First Street, Ann Arbor, Michigan Zip 48104; tel. 313/761–3912; Karl G. Bartscht, Chief Executive Officer

COOPERS & LYBRAND, L.L.P., 203 North LaSalle Street, Chicago, Illinois Zip 60601; tel. 312/701–5893; Robert McDonald, Chairman, National Healthcare Industry

DAVIES CONSULTING, INC., 6935 Wisconsin Avenue, Suite 600, Chevy Chase, Maryland Zip 20815; tel. 301/652–4535; Mercedes Sanchez, Principal, Healthcare Practice

ERNST AND YOUNG, 2001 Market Street, Suite 4000, Philadelphia, Pennsylvania Zip 19103–7096; tel. 215/448–5000; Thomas K. Shaffert, Partner

HAMILTON–KSA, 1355 Peachtree Street N.E., Suite 900, Atlanta, Georgia Zip 30309–0900; tel. 404/892–0321; W. Barry Moore, National Director

HBO & COMPANY, 301 Perimeter Center North, Atlanta, Georgia Zip 30346; tel. 404/393–6000; Pat Hamby, Director Regulatory Affairs and Standards

HEALTH DIMENSIONS, 7100 Northland Circle, Suite 205, Minneapolis, Minnesota Zip 55428; Betty Ziebarth, Director

HEALTHCARE FINANCIAL ENTERPRISES, INC., 1475 West Cypress Creek Road, 204, Fort Lauderdale, Florida Zip 33309; tel. 954/772–7878; Peter A. Carvalho, President

HEIDRICK AND STRUGGLES, 233 South Wacker, Suite 7000, Chicago, Illinois Zip 60606; tel. 312/372–8811; Richard P. Gustafson, Partner

JURAN INSTITUTE, 11 River Road, Wilton, Connecticut Zip 06897; tel. 203/834–1700; Sally Georgen Archer, Account Executive

MARSHALL ERDMAN & ASSOCIATES, INC., 5117 University Avenue, Madison, Wisconsin Zip 53705; tel. 608/238–0211; Ron R. Halverson, Senior Vice President Sales and Marketing

MCFAUL & LYONS, INC., 306 Horizon Center, Trenton, New Jersey Zip 08691; tel. 609/588–4900; William McFaul, Chairman of the Board

PRESS, GANEY ASSOCIATES, INC., 404 Columbia Place, South Bend, Indiana Zip 46601; tel. 219/232–3387; Dennis W. Heck, FACHE, Vice President, Corporate Development

RURAL HEALTH CONSULTANTS, 2500 West Sixth, Suite H., Lawrence, Kansas Zip 66049; tel. 913/832–8778; Tina Shoemaker, Senior Consultant

TIBER GROUP, INC., 200 South Wacker Drive, Suite 2620, Chicago, Illinois Zip 60601; tel. 312/609–9935; Madeline Chulumovich, Manager Research and Development

TOWERS PERRIN, 100 Summit Lake Drive, Valhalla, New York Zip 10595; tel. 212/309–3400; Leslie Tobias, Information Specialist

VICTOR KRAMER COMPANY, INC., 405 Murray Hill Parkway, Suite 1040, Rutherford, New Jersey Zip 07070; tel. 201/935–0414; Thomas Mara, President

WEST HUDSON AND COMPANY, INC., 5230 Pacific Concourse Drive, Suite 400, Beverly Hills, California Zip 90210–4507; tel. 310/297–4200; Adrianne Court, Operations Manager

WHITMAN GARVEY, INC., 1191 Second Avenue, Suite 1800, Seattle, Washington Zip 98101–2939; tel. 206/628–3763; James T. Whitman, President

YAFFE AND COMPANY, INC., 2119 Caves Road, Owings Mills, Maryland Zip 21117; tel. 301/332–1166; Rian M. Yaffe, President

Educational Services:

CALIFORNIA COLLEGE FOR HEALTH SCIENCES, 222 West 24th Street, National City, California Zip 91950; tel. 619/477–4800; Dale K. Bean, Program Director

Facilities Management:

AMERICAN UTILITIES, P.O. Box 1214, Orem, Utah Zip 84059–1214; Ellen Burkett, President

JOHNSON CONTROLS, INC., 3354 Perimeter Hill Drive, Suite 105, Nashville, Tennessee Zip 37211–3667; tel. 615/333–9304; C. Patrick Hardwick, Business Development Manager

SCRIBCOR, INC., 400 North Michigan Avenue, Suite 415, Chicago, Illinois Zip 60611; tel. 312/923–8000; Stephen T. Kardel, President

SERVICEMASTER COMPANY, One Servicemaster Way, Downers Grove, Illinois Zip 60515; tel. 708/964–1300; C. William Pollard, Chairman

Health Care Alliance:

PREMIER, INC., 3 Westbrook Corporate Center, 9th Floor, Westchester, Illinois Zip 60154–5735; tel. 708/409–4100; Alan Weinstein, President

UNIVERSITY HEALTH SYSTEM OF NEW JERSEY, 154 West State Street, Trenton, New Jersey Zip 08608; tel. 609/656–9600; Thomas E. Terrill, Ph.D., President

UNIVERSITY HEALTHSYSTEM CONSORTIUM, INC., 2001 Spring Road, Suite 700, Oak Brook, Illinois Zip 60523; tel. 630/954–1700; Robert J. Baker, President and Chief Executive Officer

VHA, INC., P.O. Box 140909, Irving, Texas Zip 75014–0909; tel. 972/830–0000; C. Thomas Smith, President and Chief Executive Officer

Information Systems:

3M HEALTH INFORMATION SYSTEMS, P.O. Box 57900, Murray, Utah Zip 84157; tel. 801/265–4400; Scott Slivka, Marketing Manager

FIRST COAST SYSTEMS, 6430 Southpoint Parkway, Suite 250, Jacksonville, Florida Zip 32216–0978; tel. 904/296–4200; Charles R. Gibbs, President

H.C.I.A., INC., 300 East Lombard Street, Baltimore, Maryland Zip 21202; tel. 410/576–9600; Jean Chenoweth, Senior Vice President Industry Relations

IMS AMERICA, LTD., 660 West Germantown Pike, Plymouth Meeting, Pennsylvania Zip 19462; tel. 610/834–5000; Ann Murphy, Senior Information Manager

PHAMIS, INC., 401 Second Avenue South, Suite 200, Seattle, Washington Zip 98154–1144; tel. 206/622–9558; Frank Sample, President and Chief Executive Officer

SUPERIOR CONSULTANT COMPANY, INC., 4000 Town Center, Suite 1100, Southfield, Michigan Zip 48075; tel. 810/386–8300; Richard D. Helppie, President

VECTOR RESEARCH, INC., P.O. Box 1506, Ann Arbor, Michigan Zip 48106; tel. 313/973–9210; Kevin J. Dombkowski, Program Scientist

Insurance Broker:

AETNA RETIREMENT SERVICES, 151 Farmington Avenue–TNA1, Hartford, Connecticut Zip 06156; tel. 860/273–2826; Robert H. Barley, Vice President

HEALTHCARE UNDERWRITERS MUTUAL INSURANCE COMPANY, 8 British American Boulevard, Latham, New York Zip 12110; tel. 518/786–2700; Gerald J. Cassidy, President and Chief Executive Officer

LOCKTON COMPANIES, 7400 State Line Road, Prairie Village, Kansas Zip 66208; tel. 913/676–9546; Becky Sullivan, Vice President Unit Manager

PHICO INSURANCE COMPANY, P.O. Box 85, Mechanicsburg, Pennsylvania Zip 17055–0085; tel. 717/766–1122; Barry Persofsky, President and Chief Executive Officer

PRINCIPAL FINANCIAL GROUP, 711 High Street, Des Moines, Iowa Zip 50392–4620; tel. 515/247–5222; Joan Burns, Technical Senior Consultant

VALIC, 2919 Allen Parkway (L13–05), Houston, Texas Zip 77019; tel. 713/831–5311; Carol Melville, Associate Director Healthcare Marketing

Investment Broker:

STEPHENS, INC., 111 Center Street, Little Rock, Arkansas Zip 72201; tel. 501/377–8125; Nancy Weaver, Research Analyst

Manufacturer/Supplier:

ABBOTT LABORATORIES, One Abbott Park Road, Abbott Park, Illinois Zip 60064; tel. 847/937–2692; William M. Dwyer, Senior Director Strategic Marketing

ALM SURGICAL EQUIPMENT, INC., 1820 North Lemon Street, Anaheim, California Zip 92801–1009; tel. 714/578–1234; George E. Crispin, President

AMGEN, 1840 Dehavilland Drive, Department 631, Thousand Oaks, California Zip 91320–1789; tel. 805/499–5725; Teresa Romney, Revenue Analyst

BAXTER INTERNATIONAL, INC., One Baxter Parkway, 32W, Deerfield, Illinois Zip 60015; tel. 800/940–6511; Vernon Louck, Jr., Chief Executive Officer

BFI MEDICAL WASTE SYSTEMS, 757 North Eldridge, Houston, Texas Zip 77077; tel. 713/870–7013; Mike Archer, Director Medical Services

BOSTON SCIENTIFIC CORPORATION, One Boston Scientific Place, Natick, Massachusetts Zip 01760; tel. 508/972–4406; John Abele, Chairman

DIAGNOSTIC HEALTH SERVICES, 2777 Stemmons Freeway, Suite 1525, Dallas, Texas Zip 75207; tel. 214/634–0403; James Kirker, Vice President

FIELDCREST CANNON, INC., P.O. Box 107, Kannapolis, North Carolina Zip 28081; tel. 704/939–2000; J. G. Coles, Vice President

GENERAL ELECTRIC MEDICAL SYSTEMS, P.O. Box 414, W–451, Milwaukee, Wisconsin Zip 53201–0414; tel. 414/544–3287; Frank Cheng, Manager Market and Group Analysis

HILL–ROM, 1069 State Route 46 East, Batesville, Indiana Zip 47006; tel. 812/934–8285; Fay Bohlke, Marketing

IMMUNEX CORPORATION, 51 University Street, Seattle, Washington Zip 98101; tel. 206/587–0430; Michael L. Kleinberg, Director Professional Services

INTERMEDICS, INC., 4000 Technology Drive, Angleton, Texas Zip 77515; tel. 409/848–4000; Richard R. Ames, Vice President Sales

MANAGEMENT SCIENCE ASSOCIATES, INC., 4801 Cliff Avenue, Independence, Missouri Zip 64055; tel. 816/795–1947; Kenneth J. McDonald, President

MERCK U. S. HUMAN HEALTH, WP35–150, West Point, Pennsylvania Zip 19486; tel. 215/652–5000; Phyllis Rausch, Marketing Associate

MILCARE, INC., A. HERMAN MILLER COMPANY, 8500 Byron Road, Zeeland, Michigan Zip 49464; tel. 616/654–8000; David Reid, Senior Vice President and General Manager

NEMSCHOFF CHAIRS, INC., P.O. Box 129, Sheboygan, Wisconsin Zip 53082–0129; tel. 920/459–1216; David Stinson, Vice President

PFIZER U.S. PHARMACEUTICALS GROUP, 235 East 42nd Street, New York, New York Zip 10017; tel. 212/573–7877; Daniel J. Coakley, Director Trade Development and Industry Affairs

PROCTER & GAMBLE, Two Procter & Gamble Plaza, Cincinnati, Ohio Zip 45202; tel. 513/983–6248; James L. Knepler, Manager Patient Care Professional Relations Health Care Products

SIGMA–TAU PHARMACEUTICALS, INC., 800 South Frederick Avenue, Suite 300, Gaithersburg, Maryland Zip 20877; tel. 301/948–1041; C. Kenneth Mehrling, Executive Vice President and General Manager

W. W. GRAINGER, INC., 333 Knightsbridge Parkway, Lincolnshire, Illinois Zip 60069; tel. 847/913–8333; Kolleen K. Schulze, Associate Marketing Manager

ZENECA PHARMACEUTICALS GROUP, P.O. Box 15437, Wilmington, Delaware Zip 19850–5437; tel. 302/886–3167; Zahirr Ladhani, Strategy Manager

Metro Health Care Assn:

HEALTHCARE ASSOCIATION OF SOUTHERN CALIFORNIA, 201 North Figueroa Street, 4th Floor, Los Angeles, California Zip 90071–3322; tel. 213/538–0700; James D. Barber, President

Other:

ADVISORY BOARD COMPANY, 600 New Hampshire Avenue N.W., Washington, District of Columbia Zip 20037–2403; tel. 202/672–5600; David Bradley, President

AMERICA'S BLOOD CENTERS, 725 15th Street N.W., Suite 700, Washington, District of Columbia Zip 20005; tel. 202/393–5725; Jim MacPherson, Executive Director

AMERICAN ASSOCIATION OF NURSE ANESTHETISTS, 222 South Prospect Avenue, Park Ridge, Illinois Zip 60068–4001; tel. 847/692–7050; John F. Garde, Executive Director

AMERICAN BOARD OF MEDICAL SPECIALTIES, 1007 Church Street, Suite 404, Evanston, Illinois Zip 60201–5913; tel. 847/491–9091; J. Lee Dockery, M.D., Executive Vice President

AMERICAN ELECTRIC POWER, P.O. Box 2021, Roanoke, Virginia Zip 24022; tel. 540/985–2750; Jon F. Williams, Healthcare Segment Manager

AMERICAN HEALTH PROPERTIES, INC., 6400 South Fiddlers Green Circle, Suite 1800, Englewood, Colorado Zip 80111–4961; tel. 303/796–9793; Greg Schonert, Vice President

AMERICAN SOCIETY OF HOSPITAL PHARMACISTS, 7272 Wisconsin Avenue, Bethesda, Maryland Zip 20814; tel. 301/657–3000; Joseph A. Oddis, Executive Vice President

ARMED FORCES INSTITUTE OF PATHOLOGY, 6825 16th Street N.W., Building 54, Washington, District of Columbia Zip 20306–6000; tel. 202/782–2100; Colonel Michael Dickerson, Director

ARMED FORCES MEDICAL LIBRARY, 5109 Leesburg Pike, Room 670, Falls Church, Virginia Zip 22041–3258; tel. 703/756–8028; D. Zehnpfennig, Administrative Librarian

ASSOCIATION OF OPERATING ROOM NURSES, 2170 South Parker Road, Suite 300, Denver, Colorado Zip 80231–5711; tel. 303/755–6304; Sara Katsh, Librarian

ASSOCIATION OF UNIVERSITY PROGRAMS IN HEALTH ADMINISTRATION, 1911 North Fort Myer Drive, Suite 503, Arlington, Virginia Zip 22209; tel. 703/524–0511; Henry Fernandez, President

BARRY, BETTE AND LED DUKE, INC., 52 Corporate Circle, Albany, New York Zip 12203; tel. 518/452–8200; Robert E. Bale, Vice President Medical Facilities

BEECH STREET, 173 Technology, Irvine, California Zip 92618; tel. 714/727–1359; Doreen Corwin, Vice President Network Development

BERGEN, BRUNSWICK CORPORATION, 4000 Metropolitan Drive, Orange, California Zip 92868; tel. 714/385–6903; Shannon Jager, Librarian

BIOMATRIX, INC., 65 Railroad Avenue, Ridgefield, New Jersey Zip 07657; tel. 201/945–9550; Barbara A. Rohan, Vice President Public Policy and Reimbursement

BLUE CROSS AND BLUE SHIELD ASSOCIATION, 225 North Michigan Avenue, Chicago, Illinois Zip 60601–7680; tel. 312/440–6000; Patrick G. Hays, President

BLUE SHIELD OF CALIFORNIA, 6701 Center Drive West, Suite 800, Los Angeles, California Zip 90045; tel. 310/568–5460; Alan Puzarne, Senior Vice President and Chief Executive Southern Region

BLUE CROSS AND BLUE SHIELD OF THE ROCHESTER AREA, 150 East Main Street, Rochester, New York Zip 14647; tel. 716/454–1700; Howard J. Berman, President and Chief Executive Officer

BROADCAST MUSIC, INC., 10 Music Square East, Nashville, Tennessee Zip 37203–4399; tel. 615/401–2000; Kathryn D. Crow, Director Industry Relations

CES/WAY INTERNATIONAL, INC., 5308 Ashbrook, Houston, Texas Zip 77081; tel. 713/666–3541; Michael D. Leach, President and Chief Executive Officer

CIGNA HEALTHCARE–BRISTOL CUSTOMER CLAIM SERVICES CENTER, 32 Valley Street, Level B., Bristol, Connecticut Zip 06010; tel. 860/585–4212; Linda S. Martinelli, Financial Analyst

CONNECTICUT HOSPITAL ASSOCIATION, Box 90, Wallingford, Connecticut Zip 06492–0090; tel. 203/265–7611; Dennis P. May, President

COPELCO CAPITAL, INC., 700 East Gate Drive, Mount Laurel, New Jersey Zip 08054; tel. 800/257–8451; Kevin Ward, Division Manager

COUNTRY VILLA HEALTH SERVICES, 4551 Glencoe Avenue, 3rd Floor, Marina Del Rey, California Zip 90292; tel. 310/574–3733; John H. Libby, Executive Vice President

CURBELL, INC., ELECTRONICS DIVISION, 7 Cobham Drive, Orchard Park, New York Zip 14127–4180; tel. 716/667–3377; Michael P. Donovan, Marketing Manager

DELMARVA FOUNDATION FOR MEDICAL CARE, INC., 9240 Centreville Road, Easton, Maryland Zip 21601; tel. 410/822–0697; Timothy G. Jones, Chief Financial Officer

DELOITTE & TOUCHE, 250 East Fifth Street, Suite 2100, Cincinnati, Ohio Zip 45202; tel. 513/723–3228; Julie Lange, Manager Marketing

DEPARTMENT OF AIR FORCE MEDICAL SERVICE, HQ USAF/SG, Bolling AFB, District of Columbia Zip 20332–6188; tel. 202/545–6700

DEPARTMENT OF THE ARMY, OFFICE OF THE SURGEON GENERAL, Washington, District of Columbia Zip 20310; tel. 202/690–6467; Commander James Bemberg, Administrative Officer

DEPARTMENT OF THE NAVY, BUREAU OF MEDICINE AND SURGERY, 2300 East Street N.W., Washington, District of Columbia Zip 20372–5300; tel. 202/433–4475

DEPARTMENT OF VETERANS AFFAIRS, 301 Howard Street, Suite 700, San Francisco, California Zip 94105; Linda Pierce, Director, Sierra Pacific Network

DEPARTMENT OF VETERANS AFFAIRS, 810 Vermont Avenue N.W., Washington, District of Columbia Zip 20420; tel. 202/273–5400; Jesse Brown, Secretary

DHHS, PUBLIC HEALTH SERVICE, DIVISION OF INDIAN HEALTH, HEALTH CARE ADMINISTRATION BRANCH, 5600 Fisher Lane, Room 6A–25, Rockville, Maryland Zip 20857; tel. 301/443–1085; Susanne Caviness, M.D., Chief Patient Registration and Quality Management

DIABETES TREATMENT CENTERS OF AMERICA, One Burton Hills Boulevard, Suite 300, Nashville, Tennessee Zip 37215; tel. 615/665–1133; Kathryn J. Kirk, Senior Vice President

DIAMOND CRYSTAL SPECIALTY FOODS, INC., 10 Burlington Avenue, Wilmington, Massachusetts Zip 01887–3997; tel. 978/944–3977; Denise C. Kelly, Marketing Manager

DIVERSIFIED INVESTMENT ADVISORS, 4 Manhattanville Road, Purchase, New York Zip 10577; tel. 914/697–8552; Cherith Harrison, Vice President

DU PONT CORIAN, P.O. Box 80702, Room 1243, Wilmington, Delaware Zip 19880–0702; tel. 302/999–5447; John Burr, Marketing Manager

EDAP TECHNOMED, INC., Two Burlington Woods, Burlington, Massachusetts Zip 01803; tel. 781/221–1601; Christine Meehan, Vice President Marketing

EMERGENCY CONSULTANTS, INC., 2240 South Airport Road, Traverse City, Michigan Zip 49684; tel. 800/253–1795; James Johnson, M.D., President

EMERGENCY PRACTICE ASSOCIATES, P.O. Box 1260, Waterloo, Iowa Zip 50706; tel. 319/236–3858; Margo Grimm, Chief Executive Officer

ENERGY PACIFIC, 633 West Fifth Street, 48th Floor, Los Angeles, California Zip 90071–2006; tel. 760/753–1670; Ted Pena, National Account Executive

ENVIRO GUARD, LTD., P.O. Box 13666, Research Triangle Pk, North Carolina Zip 27709–3666; tel. 919/363–0550; Dan Farmer, Technical Director

EXECUTIVE RISK MANAGEMENT ASSOCIATES, 82 Hopmeadow Street, Simsbury, Connecticut Zip 06070; tel. 203/244–8900; Paul Romano, Manager

GROUP HEALTH INC., 441 Ninth Avenue, 8th Floor, New York, New York Zip 10001–1601; tel. 212/615–0966; Laurie Nordone, Director

GUIDANT CORPORATION/CPI, 4100 Hamline Avenue North, Saint Paul, Minnesota Zip 55112; tel. 612/582–4017; Eva R. Shipley, Supervisor, Library Information Center

HARVARD PILGRIM HEALTH CARE, 10 Brookline Place West, Brookline, Massachusetts Zip 02146; tel. 617/730–4747; Patricia Harriell, Director Health Care Policy

HAWAII MEDICAL SERVICE ASSOCIATION, P.O. Box 860, Honolulu, Hawaii Zip 96808–0860; tel. 808/948–5482; Waynette Wong–Chu, Manager Facility Reimbursement

HAWAII STATE DEPARTMENT OF HEALTH, 3675 Kilauea Avenue, Honolulu, Hawaii Zip 96816; tel. 808/961–4255; Bertrand Kobayashi, Deputy Director

HEALTH CARE PROPERTY INVESTORS, INC., 10990 Wilshire Boulevard, Suite 1200, Newport Beach, California Zip 92660–1875; tel. 213/473–1990; Kenneth B. Roath, President and Chief Executive Officer

HEALTH MANAGEMENT SYSTEMS, INC., 401 Park Avenue South, New York, New York Zip 10016; tel. 212/685–4545; Mark D. Mandel, Vice President Marketing

HEALTH PARTNERS OF PHILADELPHIA, 4700 Wissahickon Avenue, Suite 118, Philadelphia, Pennsylvania Zip 19144–4283; tel. 215/849–9606; Barbara Plager, President and Chief Executive Officer

HEALTHCARE FINANCIAL PARTNERS, 2 Wisconsin Circle, 4th Floor, Chevy Case, Maryland Zip 20815; tel. 301/961–1640; Carolyn Small, Marketing Manager

HEALTHTEK SOLUTIONS, INC., 999 Waterside Drive, Suite 1910, Norfolk, Virginia Zip 23510; tel. 757/625–0800; Anthony Montville, President

INNOVATIVE SURGICAL CONCEPTS, INC., 1841 South Grand Avenue, Schofield, Wisconsin Zip 54476; tel. 715/359–1869; Michele Hahn, Executive Vice President

INTERNATIONAL ASSOCIATION FOR HEALTHCARE SECURITY AND SAFETY, P.O. Box 637, Lombard, Illinois Zip 60148; tel. 630/953–0990; Nancy Felesena, Executive Assistant

J. STEPHENS MAYHUGH AND ASSOCIATES, INC., P.O. Box 3276, Baton Rouge, Louisiana Zip 70821–3276; tel. 800/426–2349; Janet Stephens Mayhugh, Chief Executive Officer

JANZEN, JOHNSTON AND ROCKWELL, EMERGENCY MEDICINE MANAGEMENT SERVICES, INC., 4551 Glencoe Avenue, Suite 260, Marina Del Rey, California Zip 90292; tel. 310/301–2030; Richard W. Sanders, Vice President Marketing

KANSAS HEALTH FOUNDATION, 309 East Douglas, Wichita, Kansas Zip 67202; tel. 316/262–7676; Don Stewart, Vice President and Senior Advisor

M D ANDERSON CANCER CENTER OUTREACH CORPORATION, 7505 South Main Street, Suite 250, Houston, Texas Zip 77030; tel. 713/794–5000; Robert N. Shaw, President

MCDONALD'S CORPORATION, 711 Jorie Boulevard, Dept 093, Oak Brook, Illinois Zip 60521; tel. 708/575–3000; Laura Ramirez, Senior Manager Specials

MEDICAL PROTECTIVE COMPANY, 5814 Reed Road, Fort Wayne, Indiana Zip 46835; tel. 219/486–0424; Kathleen M. Roman, Director Risk Management

MODERN HEALTHCARE, 740 North Rush Street, Chicago, Illinois Zip 60611; tel. 312/368–6644; Charles S. Lauer, Corporate Vice President

MORRISON HEALTH CARE, INC., 1955 Lake Park Drive, Suite 400, Smyrna, Georgia Zip 30080–8855; tel. 770/437–3300; Glenn Davenport, President and Chief Executive Officer

NATIONAL HEALTHCARE LINEN SERVICES, 1420 Peachtree Street N.E., Atlanta, Georgia Zip 30309; tel. 404/853–6142; William Gallagher, Business Manager

NAVAL REGIONAL MEDICAL CENTER, PSC 1005, Box 36, FPO, APO/FPO Europe Zip 09593–0136

NETCO COMMUNICATIONS CORPORATION, 6100 West 110th Street, Minneapolis, Minnesota Zip 55438; tel. 612/886–5119; Kelly J. Brown, Director Medical Products

NIPSCO INDUSTRIES HEALTH CARE MARKETING AND SALES, 5265 Hohman Avenue, Hammond, Indiana Zip 46320; tel. 219/647–6413; John McKee, Manager Health Care Segment

OLYMPUS AMERICA, INC., 2 Corporte Center Drive, Melville, New York Zip 11747; tel. 516/844–5000; Steven K. Wendt, Senior Manager National Accounts

OWEN HEALTHCARE, INC., 9800 Centre Parkway, Suite 1100, Houston, Texas Zip 77036; tel. 713/777–8173; Pam Robinson, Communications Coordinator

PMR CORPORATION, 501 Washington Street, 5th Floor, San Diego, California Zip 92103; tel. 619/610–4052; Sue Erskine, Executive Vice President

RABOBANK INTERNATIONAL, 300 South Wacker Drive, Suite 3500, Chicago, Illinois Zip 60606; tel. 312/408–8213; Lydia Crowson, Vice President

REHABCARE GROUP, INC., 7733 Forsyth Boulevard, Suite 1700, Saint Louis, Missouri Zip 63105–1817; tel. 314/863–7422; Keith L. Goding, Executive Vice President and Chief Development Officer

RENFREW CENTER, 475 Spring Lane, Philadelphia, Pennsylvania Zip 19128; tel. 215/482–5353; Samuel Menaged, President

RURAL/METRO CORPORATION, 8401 East Indian School Road, Scottsdale, Arizona Zip 85251; tel. 602/994–3886; Michel A. Sucher, M.D., Vice President, Medical Affairs

SAINT JOSEPH'S CARE GROUP, INC., P.O. Box 1935, South Bend, Indiana Zip 46634; tel. 219/237–7111; Robert L. Beyer, President and Chief Executive Officer

SHARED MEDICAL SYSTEMS, 51 Valley Stream Parkway, Malvern, Pennsylvania Zip 19355; tel. 215/296–6300; Susan B. West, Manager Communications

SPECIALTY LABORATORIES, INC., 2211 Michigan Avenue, Santa Monica, California Zip 90404; tel. 310/828–6543; Susan Bailey, Marketing Manager

SPECTRUM COMPREHENSIVE CARE, INC., 12300 Ford Road, Suite 300, Dallas, Texas Zip 75234; tel. 972/243–6279; Joseph Rosenfield, President and Chief Executive Officer

STEPHENS, LYNN, KLEIN AND MCNICHOLAS, P.A., 9130 South Dadeland Boulevard, Miami, Florida Zip 33156; tel. 305/670–3700; Oscar J. Cabanas, Partner

SYNDICATED OFFICE SYSTEMS, 3 Imperial Promenade, Suite 1100, Santa Ana, California Zip 92707; tel. 714/438–6500; Arnold M. Robin, President

SYNTELLECT, INC., 20401 North 29th Avenue, Phoenix, Arizona Zip 85027; tel. 602/789–2834; Robyn Cochran, Product Marketing Manager–Healthcare

TCG DEVELOPMENT, LLC, 305 Madison Avenue, Suite 2033, New York, New York Zip 10165; tel. 212/972–2829; John P. Cole, President and Chief Executive Officer

TERRY S. WARD AND ASSOCIATES, 5300 Hollister, Suite 200, Houston, Texas Zip 77040; tel. 713/690–1000; Terry S. Ward, President

TEXAS MEDICAL CENTER, 406 Jesse Jones Library Building, Houston, Texas Zip 77030–3303; tel. 713/791–8805; Richard E. Wainerdi, President

THE RENFREW CENTER, 7700 Renfrew Lane, Coconut Creek, Florida Zip 33073; tel. 305/698–9222; Barbara Peterson, Executive Director

TOSHIBA AMERICA MEDICAL SYSTEMS, INC., 2441 Michelle Drive, Tustin, California Zip 92680; tel. 714/730–5000; Catherine M. Eilts, Corporate Marketing and Public Relations Manager

TRANSLOGIC CORPORATION, 10825 East 47th Avenue, Denver, Colorado Zip 80239; tel. 800/525–1841; Jim Patrician, President

U. S. AIR FORCE SCHOOL OF AEROSPACE MEDICINE, USAFSAM–CCE, Brooks AFB, Texas Zip 78235–5301; tel. 512/536–3342

U. S. ARMY MEDICAL COMMAND, Fort Sam Houston, Texas Zip 78234; tel. 210/221–1211

UNITED HOSPITAL FUND OF NEW YORK, 350 Fifth Avenue, 23rd Floor, New York, New York Zip 10118; tel. 212/494–0700; James R. Tallon, Jr., President

VANDERWEIL ENGINEERS, 1055 Maitland Ctr Commons Boulevard, Maitland, Florida Zip 32751; tel. 407/660–0088; Ron Graham, Construction Administrator

VETERANS AFFAIRS CENTRAL REGION OFFICE, P.O. Box 134002, Ann Arbor, Michigan Zip 48113–4002; Linda Belton, Network Director

VETERANS AFFAIRS EASTERN REGION OFFICE, 9600 North Point Road, Fort Howard, Maryland Zip 21052

VETERANS AFFAIRS SOUTHERN REGION, 1461 Lakeover Road, Jackson, Mississippi Zip 39213; tel. 601/364–7920; John R. Higgins, M.D., Network Director

WINSTAR TELECOMMUNICATIONS, INC., 101 North Wacker Drive, Suite 1950, Chicago, Illinois Zip 60606; tel. 312/673–9400; Jill Buckenmeyer, National Account Manager

Preferred Provider Org:

U.S.A. MANAGED CARE ORGANIZATION, 7301 North 16th Street, Suite 201, Phoenix, Arizona Zip 85020; tel. 602/371–3880; Karen Bass, Vice President and Chief Administrative Officer

School of Nursing:

NORTHEASTERN HOSPITAL OF PHILADELPHIA SCHOOL OF NURSING, 2301 East Allegheny Avenue, Philadelphia, Pennsylvania Zip 19134; tel. 215/291–3000; Shirley L. Hickman, Ph.D., Director School of Nursing

State Agency for Health:

OFFICE OF HOSPITAL AND PATIENT DATA SYSTEMS–WASHINGTON STATE DEPARTMENT OF HEALTH, P.O. Box 47811, Olympia, Washington Zip 98504–7811; tel. 206/705–6000; Hank Brown, Acting Office Director

CANADA

Other:

DARCOR CASTERS, 7 Staffordshire Place, Toronto, Ontario Zip M8W 1T1; tel. 416/255–8563; Cyril J. Muhic, Regional Sales Manager

DESJARDINS LIFE INSURANCE, 200 Avenue Des Commandeurs, Levis, Quebec Zip G6V 6R2; tel. 800/465–6390; Louise Des Ormeaux, Director

ST. JOSEPH'S HEALTH CARE SYSTEM, P.O. Box 155, LCD 1, Hamilton, Ontario Zip L8L 7V7; tel. 905/528–0138; Brian Guest, Executive Director

FOREIGN

AUSTRALIA

Other:

CEDAR COURT REHABILITATION HOSPITAL, 888 Toorak Road, Camberwell, Victoria, Zip 3124; Rodney G. Nissen, General Manager

THE VICTORIAN HEALTHCARE ASSOCIATION LIMITED, P.O. Box 365, South Melbourne, Zip 3205; tel. 613/266–3691; John Popper, Managing Director

BAHRAIN

Other:

INTERNATIONAL HOSPITAL OF BAHRAIN, P.O. Box 1084, Manama, F. S. Zeerah, M.D., President

BERMUDA

Other:

KING EDWARD VII MEMORIAL HOSPITAL, P.O. Box HM1023, Hamilton, L. Keitha Bassett, Health Sciences Librarian

BRAZIL

Consulting Firm:

HOSPITALIUM–PLANNING AND HOSPITAL ADMINISTRATION, Rua Dos Pinheiros, 498–CJ, 61, San Paulo, Zip 05422–000; Edson G. Santos, Director and Partner

Other:

CLINICA SAO VICENTE, Rua Joao Borges 204 – Gavea, Dogue, Luiz Roberto Londres, President

PRONTOBABY–HOSPITAL DA CRIANGA, Rua Adolfo Mota No 81, Rio De Janeiro, Mario Eduardo Gulmarseo Viana, Director

CHILE

School of Medicine:

PONTIFICIA UNIVERSIDAD CATOLICA DE CHILE FACULTAD DE MEDICINA, Lira 44, Santiago, Jamie Bellolio Rodriguez, Economic Vice Dean–Faculty of Medicine

COLUMBIA

Other:

FUNDACION SANTA FE DE BOGOTA, Calle 116 9–02, Santa Fe De Bogota, Ana Catalina Vesquez Quintero, Manager

GREECE

Other:

DIAGNOSTIC AND THERAPEUTIC CENTRE OF ATHENS HYGEIA, S A, 4 Erythrou Stavrou & Kifissiap, Athens, C. Kitsionas, Executive Director

IASO S.A. DIAGNOSTIC THERAPEUTIC AND RESEARCH CENTER, OBSTETRICS AND GYNECOLOGY HOSPITAL, 37–39 Kifissias Avenue, Maroussi Athens, Zip 15123; Constantin Mavros, Ph.D., Managing Director and Chief Executive Officer

ISRAEL

Other:

HADASSAH MEDICAL ORGANIZATION, Box 12000, Jerusalem, Zip 91120; Shmuel Penchas, M.D., Director General

S.A.R.E.L. SUPPLIES AND SERVICES FOR MEDICINE LTD., 15 Yehuda & Noah Mozes Street, Tel Aviv, Moshe Modai, Ph.D., Chief Executive Officer

JAPAN

Consulting Firm:

SYSTEM ENVIRONMENTAL RESEARCH INSTITUTE, CO., Kishiya Boulevard, 1–13–35 Hirao, Chuo–ku, Fukuoka, Zip 810; Yukitoshi Yamamoto, President

Other:

NAVAL REGIONAL MEDICAL CENTER, FPO, Zip 96362

LEBANON

Other:

AMERICAN UNIVERSITY OF BEIRUT MEDICAL CENTER, 850 Third Avenue, 18th Floor, New York, Zip 10022; Dieter Kuntz, Executive Director
SAINT GEORGE HOSPITAL, P.O. Box 166378, Beirut, Ziad Kamel, Assistant Director

MALAYSIA

Other:

JOHOR SPECIALIST HOSPITAL, 39–B, Jalan Abdul Samad, 80100 Johor Bahru, tel. 07/227–8118; Puan Siti Sa'diah Sa–Diah Bakir, Director and Administrator

MEXICO

Other:

HOSPITAL MEXICO–AMERICANO, Calle Colomos 2110, Guadalajara, Omar Nicolas Aguilar, M.D., General Manager
SHRINERS HOSPITAL FOR CHILDREN, Suchil 152, Colonel El Rosario, Mexico City, Carmen G. Solorzano, Administrator

UNIVERSIDAD AUTONOMA DE GUADALAJARA, Av Patria 1201 Lomas Del Valle, Guadalajara, tel. 210/366–1611; Ricardo Del Castillo, Associate Dean, Foreign Students

Other Inpatient Care:

OASIS HOSPITAL, 2247 San Diego Avenue, Suite 235, San Ysidro, Zip 92143; tel. 800/700–1850; Francisco Contreras, Director

PERU

Other:

ASOCIACION BENEFICA ANGLO AMERICANA, Avenue Alfredo Salazar 3 Era, Lima 27, Gonzalo Garrido–Lecca, Director
SOUTHERN PERU COPPER CORPORATION, 1612 N.W. 84th Avenue, Miami, Zip 33126–1032; Rod G. Guzman, Medical Division Superintendent

PHILIPPINES

Other:

ST. LUKE'S MEDICAL CENTER, 279 East Rodriguez Sr Boulevard, Quezon City, Jose F. G. Ledesma, Chief Executive Officer

SAUDI ARABIA

Other:

AL–SALAMA HOSPITAL, Pr Abdallah Street, Jeddah; Mailing Address: P.O. Box 40030, Jeddah, Atef S. Salloum, M.D., Director Development and Planning
AL THOMAIRY GENERAL HOSPITAL, P.O. Box 996, Dhahran 31932, Ahmed Al Kuwaiti, Director
MUHAMMAD S BASHARAHIL HOSPITAL, P.O. Box 10505, Makkah, Sameer M. Basharahil, Vice President

SAUDI ARAMCO MEDICAL SERVICES, 9009 West Loop South, MS–549, Houston, Zip 77096; Harris Worchel, Supervisor Information and Image Services

SPAIN

Other:

ESCUELA INTERNACIONAL DE ALTA DIRECCION HOSPITALARIO, Alcala 114, 1, Madrid 28009, Enrique Marochi Rodriguez, Chairman

TAIWAN

Other:

CHANG GUNG MEMORIAL HOSPITAL, 199 Tun Hwa North Road, Taipei, Yi–Chou Chuang, Director Administration Center
NATIONAL TAIWAN UNIVERSITY HOSPITAL, 7 Chung–Shan South Road, Taipei, Tung–Yuan Tai, M.D., Director

TURKEY

Other:

AMERICAN HOSPITAL OF ISTANBUL, 1101 Post Oak Boulevard, Suite 9B, Houston, Zip 77056; George D. Roundtree, Chief Executive Officer
BAYRAKTAR GAYRIMENKUL GELLSTIRME A. S., Buyukdere Caddesi, 106, Esentepe–Istanbul, A. Oktay Cini, M.D., Vice President
ISTANBUL MEMORIAL MEDICAL CENTER, Caglayan Vatan Caddesi, 2/5, Istanbul, Zip 80340; Sarper Tanli, M.D., Medical Director

UNITED ARAB EMIRATES

Other:

AMERICAN HOSPITAL–DUBAI, P.O. Box 59, Dubai, Saeed M. Almulla, Chairman

B

**Networks,
Health Care Systems
and Alliances**

Section B

Introduction

This section includes listings for networks, health care systems and alliances.

Networks

The *AHA Guide* shows listings of networks. A network is defined as a group of hospitals, physicians, other providers, insurers and/or community agencies that work together to coordinate and deliver a broad spectrum of services to their community. Organizations listed represent the lead or hub of the network activity. Networks are listed by state, then alphabetically by name including participating partners.

The network identification process has purposely been designed to capture networks of varying organization type. Sources include but are not limited to the following: *AHA Annual Survey,* national, state and metropolitan associations, national news and periodical searches, and the networks and their health care providers themselves. Therefore, networks are included regardless of whether a hospital or healthcare system is the network lead. When an individual hospital does appear in the listing, it is indicative of the role the hospital plays as the network lead. In addition, the network listing is **not** mutually exclusive of the hospital, health care system or alliance listings within this publication.

Networks are very fluid in their composition as goals evolve and partners change. Therefore, some of the networks included in this listing may have dissolved, reformed, or simply been renamed as this section was being produced for publication.

The network identification process is an ongoing and responsive initiative. As more information is collected and validated, it will be made available in other venues, in addition to the *AHA Guide.* For more information concerning the network identification process, please contact Healthcare InfoSource, Inc. a subsidiary of the American Hospital Association at 312/422–2100.

Health Care Systems

To reflect the diversity that exists among health care organizations, this publication uses the term health care system to identify both multihospital and diversified single hospital systems.

Multihospital Systems

A multihospital health care system is two or more hospitals owned, leased, sponsored, or contract managed by a central organization.

Single Hospital Systems

Single, freestanding member hospitals may be categorized as health care systems by bringing into Type IV–A membership three or more, and at least 25 percent, of their owned or leased non–hospital preacute and postacute health care organizations. (For purposes of definition, health care delivery is the availability of professional healthcare staff during all hours of the organization's operations). Type IV–A organizations provide, or provide and finance, diagnostic, therapeutic, and/or consultative patient or client services that normally precede or follow acute, inpatient, hospitalization; or that serve to prevent or substitute for such hospitalization. These services are provided in either a freestanding facility not eligible for licensure as a hospital understate statue or through one that is a subsidiary of a hospital.

The first part of this section is an alphabetical list of multihospital health care systems. Each system listed contains two or more hospitals, which are listed under the system by state. Data for this section were compiled from the 1997 *Annual Survey* and the membership information base as published in section A of the *AHA Guide.*

One of the following codes appears after the name of each system listed to indicate the type of organizational control reported by that system:

CC   Catholic (Roman) church–related system, not–for–profit

CO   Other church–related system, not–for–profit

NP   Other not–for–profit system, including nonfederal, governmental systems

IO   Investor–owned, for profit system

FG   Federal Government

One of the following codes appears after the name of each hospital to indicate how that hospital is related to the system:

O   Owned

L   Leased

S   Sponsored

CM   Contract–managed

The second part of this section lists health care systems indexed geographically by state and city. Every effort has been made to be as inclusive and accurate as possible. However, as in all efforts of this type, there may be omissions. For further information, write to the section for Health Care Systems, American Hospital Association, One North Franklin, Chicago, IL 60606–3401.

Alliances

An alliance is a formal organization, usually owned by shareholders/members, that works on behalf of its individual members in the provision of services and products and in the promotion of activities and ventures. The organization functions under a set of bylaws or other written rules to which each member agrees to abide.

Alliances are listed alphabetically by name. Its members are listed alphabetically by state, city, and then by member name.

ALABAMA

ALABAMA HEALTH SERVICES
48 Medical Park East Drive, Suite 450, Birmingham, AL 35235-2407; tel. 205/838-3999; Robert C. Chapman, President & Chief Executive Officer

BLOUNT MEMORIAL HOSPITAL, 1000 Lincoln Avenue, Oneonta, AL, Zip 35121-2534, Mailing Address: P.O. Box 1000, Zip 35121-1000; tel. 205/625-3511; George McGowan, FACHE, Chief Executive Officer

BROOKWOOD MEDICAL CENTER, 2010 Brookwood Medical Center Drive, Birmingham, AL, Zip 35209; tel. 205/877-1000; Gregory H. Burfitt, President and Chief Executive Officer

LLOYD NOLAND HOSPITAL AND HEALTH SYSTEM, 701 Lloyd Noland Parkway, Fairfield, AL, Zip 35064-2699; tel. 205/783-5106; Gary M. Glasscock, Administrator

MEDICAL CENTER EAST, 50 Medical Park East Drive, Birmingham, AL, Zip 35235-9987; tel. 205/838-3000; David E. Crawford, FACHE, Executive Vice President and Chief Operating Officer

ST. CLAIR REGIONAL HOSPITAL, 2805 Hospital Drive, Pell City, AL, Zip 35125-1499; tel. 205/338-3301; Douglas H. Beverly, CHE, Chief Operating Officer

BAPTIST HEALTH SYSTEM
P.O. Box 830605, Birmingham, AL 35283-0605; tel. 205/715-5000; Carl Sather, Senior Vice President

BIRMINGHAM BAPTIST MEDICAL CENTER–MONTCLAIR CAMPUS, 800 Montclair Road, Birmingham, AL, Zip 35213-1984; tel. 205/592-1000; Dana S. Hensley, President

BIRMINGHAM BAPTIST MEDICAL CENTER–PRINCETON, 701 Princeton Avenue S.W., Birmingham, AL, Zip 35211-1305; tel. 205/783-3000; Dana S. Hensley, President and Chief Executive Officer

CHEROKEE BAPTIST MEDICAL CENTER, 400 Northwood Drive, Centre, AL, Zip 35960-1023; tel. 205/927-5531; Barry S. Cochran, President

CITIZENS BAPTIST MEDICAL CENTER, 604 Stone Avenue, Talladega, AL, Zip 35160-2217, Mailing Address: P.O. Box 978, Zip 35161-0978; tel. 205/362-8111; Steven M. Johnson, President

COOSA VALLEY BAPTIST MEDICAL CENTER, 315 West Hickory Street, Sylacauga, AL, Zip 35150-2996; tel. 205/249-5000; Steven M. Johnson, President

CULLMAN REGIONAL MEDICAL CENTER, 1912 Alabama Highway 157, Cullman, AL, Zip 35055, Mailing Address: P.O. Box 1108, Zip 35056-1108; tel. 205/737-2000; Jesse O. Weatherly, President

DEKALB BAPTIST MEDICAL CENTER, 200 Medical Center Drive, Fort Payne, AL, Zip 35967, Mailing Address: P.O. Box 680778, Zip 35968-0778; tel. 205/845-3150; Barry S. Cochran, President

LAWRENCE BAPTIST MEDICAL CENTER, 202 Hospital Street, Moulton, AL, Zip 35650-0039, Mailing Address: P.O. Box 39, Zip 35650-0039; tel. 205/974-2200; Cheryl Hays, Administrator

MARION BAPTIST MEDICAL CENTER, 1256 Military Street South, Hamilton, AL, Zip 35570-5001; tel. 205/921-6200; Evan S. Dillard, President

SHELBY BAPTIST MEDICAL CENTER, 1000 First Street North, Alabaster, AL, Zip 35007-0488, Mailing Address: Box 488, Zip 35007-0488; tel. 205/620-8100; Charles C. Colvert, President

WALKER BAPTIST MEDICAL CENTER, 3400 Highway 78 East, Jasper, AL, Zip 35501-8956, Mailing Address: P.O. Box 3547, Zip 35502-3547; tel. 205/387-4000; Jeff Brewer, President

HEALTHGROUP OF ALABAMA, L.L.C.
P.O. Box 1246, Madison, AL 35758; tel. 205/772-4155; Edward D. Boston, Chief Executive Officer

ATHENS–LIMESTONE HOSPITAL, 700 West Market Street, Athens, AL, Zip 35611-2457, Mailing Address: P.O. Box 999, Zip 35612-0999; tel. 205/233-9292; Philip E. Dotson, Administrator and Chief Executive Officer

DECATUR GENERAL HOSPITAL, 1201 Seventh Street S.E., Decatur, AL, Zip 35601, Mailing Address: P.O. Box 2239, Zip 35609-2239; tel. 205/341-2000; Robert L. Smith, President and Chief Executive Officer

DECATUR GENERAL HOSPITAL–WEST, 2205 Beltline Road S.W., Decatur, AL, Zip 35601-3687, Mailing Address: P.O. Box 2240, Zip 35609-2240; tel. 205/350-1450; Dennis Griffith, Vice President

ELIZA COFFEE MEMORIAL HOSPITAL, 205 Marengo Street, Florence, AL, Zip 35630-6033, Mailing Address: P.O. Box 818, Zip 35631-0818; tel. 256/768-9191; Richard H. Peck, Administrator

HUNTSVILLE HOSPITAL, 101 Sivley Road, Huntsville, AL, Zip 35801-4470; tel. 256/517-8020; Edward D. Boston, Chief Executive Officer

PROVIDER OF RURAL HEALTH NETWORK
P.O. Box 11126, Montgomery, AL 36111; tel. 334/260-8600; Tommy McDougal, President

BRYAN W. WHITFIELD MEMORIAL HOSPITAL, Highway 80 West, Demopolis, AL, Zip 36732, Mailing Address: P.O. Box 890, Zip 36732-0890; tel. 334/289-4000; Charles E. Nabors, Chief Executive Officer and Administrator

UNIVERSITY OF ALABAMA HOSPITAL/UAB HEALTH SYSTEM
701 South 20th Street, Suite 720, Birmingham, AL 35233; tel. 205/934-5199; Dr. Michael Geheb, Chief Executive Officer

UNIVERSITY OF ALABAMA HOSPITAL, 619 South 19th Street, Birmingham, AL, Zip 35233-6505; tel. 205/934-4011; Martin Nowak, Interim Executive Director

ALASKA

KETCHIKAN GENERAL HOSPITAL
3100 Tongass Avenue, Ketchikan, AK 99901; tel. 907/225-5171; Ed Mahn, President

NORTON SOUND REGIONAL HOSPITAL, Bering Straits, Nome, AK, Zip 99762, Mailing Address: P.O. Box 966, Zip 99762-0966; tel. 907/443-3311; Charles Fagerstrom, Vice President

ARIZONA

ARIZONA VOLUNTARY HOSPITAL FEDERATION
1430 West Broadway, Suite A110, Tempe, AZ 85282; tel. 602/968-5622; Lew Harper, Network Contact

CASA GRANDE REGIONAL MEDICAL CENTER, 1800 East Florence Boulevard, Casa Grande, AZ, Zip 85222-5399; tel. 520/426-6300; Claudia N. Griffiths, President

CHANDLER REGIONAL HOSPITAL, 475 South Dobson Road, Chandler, AZ, Zip 85224-4230; tel. 602/963-4561; Kaylor E. Shemberger, President and Chief Executive Officer

FLAGSTAFF MEDICAL CENTER, 1200 North Beaver Street, Flagstaff, AZ, Zip 86001-3198; tel. 520/779-3366; Stephen G. Carlson, President and Chief Operating Officer

KINGMAN REGIONAL MEDICAL CENTER, 3269 Stockton Hill Road, Kingman, AZ, Zip 86401-3691; tel. 520/757-0602; Brian Turney, Chief Executive Officer

PAYSON REGIONAL MEDICAL CENTER, 807 South Ponderosa Street, Payson, AZ, Zip 85541-5599; tel. 520/474-3222; Duane H. Anderson, Chief Executive Officer

PMH HEALTH SERVICES NETWORK, 1201 South Seventh Avenue, Phoenix, AZ, Zip 85007-3995; tel. 602/258-5111; Jeffrey K. Norman, Chief Executive Officer

UNIVERSITY MEDICAL CENTER, 1501 North Campbell Avenue, Tucson, AZ, Zip 85724-0002; tel. 520/694-0111; Gregory A. Pivirotto, President and Chief Executive Officer

YAVAPAI REGIONAL MEDICAL CENTER, 1003 Willow Creek Road, Prescott, AZ, Zip 86301-1668; tel. 520/445-2700; Timothy Barnett, Chief Executive Officer

YUMA REGIONAL MEDICAL CENTER, 2400 South Avenue A., Yuma, AZ, Zip 85364-7170; tel. 520/344-2000; Robert T. Olsen, CHE, President and Chief Executive Officer

BAPTIST HOSPITALS AND HEALTH SYSTEMS
2224 West Northern Avenue, D-300, Phoenix, AZ 85021; tel. 602/864-5260; Michael L. Purvis, Executive Vice President

ARROWHEAD COMMUNITY HOSPITAL AND MEDICAL CENTER, 18701 North 67th Avenue, Glendale, AZ, Zip 85308-5722; tel. 602/561-1000; Richard S. Alley, Regional Vice President and Administrator

PHOENIX BAPTIST HOSPITAL AND MEDICAL CENTER, 2000 West Bethany Home Road, Phoenix, AZ, Zip 85015-2110; tel. 602/249-0212; Richard S. Alley, Chief Executive Officer

WESTERN ARIZONA REGIONAL MEDICAL CENTER, 2735 Silver Creek Road, Bullhead City, AZ, Zip 86442-8303; tel. 520/763-2273; Rita A. Campbell, Executive Vice President and Chief Executive Officer

CARONDELET HEALTH NETWORK, INC.
1601 West Saint Mary's Road, Tucson, AZ 85745; tel. 602/622-5833; Sister Saint Joan Willert, President & Chief Executive Officer

CARONDELET HOLY CROSS HOSPITAL, 1171 Target Range Road, Nogales, AZ, Zip 85621-2496; tel. 520/287-2771; Carol Field, Senior Corporate Director and Administrator

CARONDELET ST. JOSEPH'S HOSPITAL, 350 North Wilmot Road, Tucson, AZ, Zip 85711-2678; tel. 520/296-3211; Sister St. Joan Willert, President and Chief Executive Officer

CARONDELET ST. MARY'S HOSPITAL, 1601 West St. Mary's Road, Tucson, AZ, Zip 85745-2682; tel. 520/622-5833; Sister St. Joan Willert, President and Chief Executive Officer

LUTHERAN HEALTHCARE NETWORK
500 West Tenth Place, Mesa, AZ 85201; tel. 602/461-2157; Don Evans, Chief Executive Officer

MESA LUTHERAN HOSPITAL, 525 West Brown Road, Mesa, AZ, Zip 85201-3299; tel. 602/834-1211; Robert A. Rundio, Executive Director of Hospital Operations

VALLEY LUTHERAN HOSPITAL, 6644 Baywood Avenue, Mesa, AZ, Zip 85206-1797; tel. 602/981-2000; Robert A. Rundio, Executive Director of Hospital Operations

MARICOPA INTEGRATED HEALTH SYSTEM
2601 East Roosevelt Street, Phoenix, AZ 85008; tel. 602/267-5011; Frank D. Alvarez, Chief Executive Officer

MARICOPA MEDICAL CENTER, 2601 East Roosevelt Street, Phoenix, AZ, Zip 85008-4956, Mailing Address: P.O. Box 5099, Zip 85010-5099; tel. 602/267-5111; Frank D. Alvarez, Chief Executive Officer

NORTHERN ARIZONA HEALTHCARE
1200 North Beaver Street, Flagstaff, AZ 86001; tel. 520/779-3366; Joseph M. Kortum, President and Chief Executive Officer

FLAGSTAFF MEDICAL CENTER, 1200 North Beaver Street, Flagstaff, AZ, Zip 86001-3198; tel. 520/779-3366; Stephen G. Carlson, President and Chief Operating Officer

MARCUS J. LAWRENCE MEDICAL CENTER, 202 South Willard Street, Cottonwood, AZ, Zip 86326-4170; tel. 520/634-2251; Craig A. Owens, President and Chief Executive Officer

SAINT LUKES HEALTH SYSTEM
1800 East Van Buren Street, Phoenix, AZ 85006; tel. 602/784-5509; Tom Salerno, Chief Executive Officer

ST. LUKE'S BEHAVIORAL HEALTH CENTER, 1800 East Van Buren, Phoenix, AZ, Zip 85006-3742; tel. 602/251-8484; Patrick D. Waugh, Chief Executive Officer

ST. LUKE'S MEDICAL CENTER, 1800 East Van Buren Street, Phoenix, AZ, Zip 85006-3742; tel. 602/251-8100; William W. Webster, Chief Executive Officer

TEMPE ST. LUKE'S HOSPITAL, 1500 South Mill Avenue, Tempe, AZ, Zip 85281-6699; tel. 602/784-5510; Mary Jo Gregory, Chief Executive Officer

SAMARITAN HEALTH SERVICES
1441 North 12th Street, Phoenix, AZ 85006; tel. 602/230-1555; Phyllis Biedess, President

COLORADO RIVER MEDICAL CENTER, 1401 Bailey Avenue, Needles, CA, Zip 92363; tel. 760/326-4531; Harley Smith, Chief Executive Officer

DESERT SAMARITAN MEDICAL CENTER, 1400 South Dobson Road, Mesa, AZ, Zip 85202-9879; tel. 602/835-3000; Bruce E. Pearson, Vice President and Chief Executive Officer

GOOD SAMARITAN REGIONAL MEDICAL CENTER, 1111 East McDowell Road, Phoenix, AZ, Zip 85006-2666, Mailing Address: P.O. Box 2989, Zip 85062-2989; tel. 602/239-2000; Steven L. Seiler, Senior Vice President and Chief Executive Officer

HAVASU SAMARITAN REGIONAL HOSPITAL, 101 Civic Center Lane, Lake Havasu City, AZ, Zip 86403-5683; tel. 520/855-8185; Kevin P. Poorten, Vice President and Chief Executive Officer

MARYVALE SAMARITAN MEDICAL CENTER, 5102 West Campbell Avenue, Phoenix, AZ, Zip 85031-1799; tel. 602/848-5000; Connie Beldon, Senior Administrator

SAMARITAN BEHAVIORAL HEALTH CENTER–SCOTTSDALE, 7575 East Earll Drive, Scottsdale, AZ, Zip 85251-6998; tel. 602/941-7500; Robert F. Meyer, M.D., Chief Executive Officer

SAMARITAN–WENDY PAINE O'BRIEN TREATMENT CENTER, 5055 North 34th Street, Phoenix, AZ, Zip 85018-1498; tel. 602/955-6200; Robert F. Meyer, M.D., Chief Executive Officer

SAN CLEMENTE HOSPITAL AND MEDICAL CENTER, 654 Camino De Los Mares, San Clemente, CA, Zip 92673; tel. 714/496-1122; Karen Poole, Interim Chief Executive Officer

THUNDERBIRD SAMARITAN MEDICAL CENTER, 5555 West Thunderbird Road, Glendale, AZ, Zip 85306-4696; tel. 602/588-5555; Robert H. Curry, Senior Vice President and Chief Executive Officer

WHITE MOUNTAIN REGIONAL MEDICAL CENTER, 118 South Mountain Avenue, Springerville, AZ, Zip 85938, Mailing Address: P.O. Box 880, Zip 85938-0880; tel. 520/333-4368; David J. Ross, Chief Executive Officer

SUN HEALTH CORPORATION
13180 North 103rd Drive, Sun City, AZ 85351; tel. 602/876-5301; Leland W. Peterson, President & CEO

DEL E. WEBB MEMORIAL HOSPITAL, 14502 West Meeker Boulevard, Sun City West, AZ, Zip 85375-5299, Mailing Address: P.O. Box 5169, Sun City, Zip 85375-5169; tel. 602/214-4000; Thomas C. Dickson, Executive Vice President and Chief Operating Officer

WALTER O. BOSWELL MEMORIAL HOSPITAL, 10401 West Thunderbird Boulevard, Sun City, AZ, Zip 85351-3092, Mailing Address: P.O. Box 1690, Zip 85372-1690; tel. 602/876-5356; George Perez, Executive Vice President and Chief Operating Officer

TMC HEALTHCARE ADMINISTRATION
5301 East Grant Road, Tucson, AZ 85712; tel. 520/327-5461; Darrell P. Thorpe, M.D., President & Chief Executive Officer

PALO VERDE MENTAL HEALTH SERVICES, 2695 North Craycroft, Tucson, AZ, Zip 85712-2244; tel. 520/324-5438

ARKANSAS

ARKANSAS NETWORK
5106 McClanahan, Suite E., North Little Rock, AR 72116; tel. 501/666-1200; Mike Gross, Network Director

BATES MEDICAL CENTER, 602 North Walton Boulevard, Bentonville, AR, Zip 72712; tel. 501/273-2481; Thomas P. O'Neal, Executive Vice President and Chief Operating Officer

CHICOT MEMORIAL HOSPITAL, 2729 Highway 65 and 82 South, Lake Village, AR, Zip 71653, Mailing Address: P.O. Box 512, Zip 71653-0512; tel. 870/265-5351; Robert R. Reddish, Administrator and Chief Executive Officer

DELTA MEMORIAL HOSPITAL, 300 East Pickens Street, Dumas, AR, Zip 71639-2710, Mailing Address: P.O. Box 887, Zip 71639-0887; tel. 870/382-4303; Rodney McPherson, Administrator

HOWARD MEMORIAL HOSPITAL, 800 West Leslie Street, Nashville, AR, Zip 71852-0381, Mailing Address: Box 381, Zip 71852-0381; tel. 870/845-4400; Lynn Crowell, Chief Executive Officer

MENA MEDICAL CENTER, 311 North Morrow Street, Mena, AR, Zip 71953-2516; tel. 501/394-6100; Albert Pilkington, III, Administrator and Chief Executive Officer

NORTHWEST MEDICAL CENTER, 609 West Maple Avenue, Springdale, AR, Zip 72764-5394, Mailing Address: P.O. Box 47, Zip 72765-0047; tel. 501/751-5711; Greg K. Stock, Chief Executive Officer

OUACHITA MEDICAL CENTER, 638 California Street, Camden, AR, Zip 71701-4699, Mailing Address: P.O. Box 797, Zip 71701-0797; tel. 870/836-1000; C. C. McAllister, President and Chief Executive Officer

REBSAMEN REGIONAL MEDICAL CENTER, 1400 West Braden Street, Jacksonville, AR, Zip 72076-3788; tel. 501/985-7000; Thomas R. Siemers, Chief Executive Officer

SALINE MEMORIAL HOSPITAL, 1 Medical Park Drive, Benton, AR, Zip 72015-3354; tel. 501/776-6000; Roger D. Feldt, FACHE, President and Chief Executive Officer

SILOAM SPRING MEMORIAL HOSPITAL, 205 East Jefferson Street, Siloam Springs, AR, Zip 72761-3697; tel. 501/524-4141; Donald E. Patterson, Administrator

ST. VINCENT INFIRMARY MEDICAL CENTER, Two St. Vincent Circle, Little Rock, AR, Zip 72205-5499; tel. 501/660-3000; Diana T. Hueter, President and Chief Executive Officer

ARKANSAS' FIRSTSOURCE
P.O. Box 2181, Little Rock, AR 72203-2181; tel. 501/378-2000; Mike Brown, Executive Director

ARKANSAS CHILDREN'S HOSPITAL, 800 Marshall Street, Little Rock, AR, Zip 72202-3591; tel. 501/320-1100; Jonathan R. Bates, M.D., President and Chief Executive Officer

ARKANSAS METHODIST HOSPITAL, 900 West Kingshighway, Paragould, AR, Zip 72450-5942, Mailing Address: P.O. Box 339, Zip 72451-0339; tel. 870/239-7000; Ronald K. Rooney, President

BAPTIST MEDICAL CENTER, 9601 Interstate 630, Exit 7, Little Rock, AR, Zip 72205-7299; tel. 501/202-2000; Steven Douglas Weeks, Senior Vice President and Administrator

BAPTIST MEDICAL CENTER ARKADELPHIA, 3050 Twin Rivers Drive, Arkadelphia, AR, Zip 71923-4299; tel. 870/245-1100; Dan Gathright, Senior Vice President and Administrator

BAPTIST MEDICAL CENTER HEBER SPRINGS, 2319 Highway 110 West, Heber Springs, AR, Zip 72543; tel. 501/206-3000; Dan Gathright, Vice President and Administrator

BAPTIST MEMORIAL HOSPITAL–BLYTHEVILLE, 1520 North Division Street, Blytheville, AR, Zip 72315, Mailing Address: P.O. Box 108, Zip 72316-0108; tel. 870/838-7300; Al Sypniewski, Administrator

BAPTIST MEMORIAL HOSPITAL–FORREST CITY, 1601 Newcastle Road, Forrest City, AR, Zip 72335, Mailing Address: P.O. Box 667, Zip 72336-0667; tel. 870/633-2020

BAPTIST MEMORIAL HOSPITAL–OSCEOLA, 611 West Lee Avenue, Osceola, AR, Zip 72370-3001, Mailing Address: P.O. Box 607, Zip 72370-0607; tel. 870/563-7000; Joel E. North, Administrator

BAPTIST MEMORIAL MEDICAL CENTER, One Pershing Circle, North Little Rock, AR, Zip 72114-1899; tel. 501/202-3000; Harrison M. Dean, Senior Vice President and Administrator

BAPTIST REHABILITATION INSTITUTE, 9601 Interstate 630, Exit 7, Little Rock, AR, Zip 72205-7249; tel. 501/202-7000; Steven Douglas Weeks, Senior Vice President and Administrator

BAPTIST REHABILITATION–GERMANTOWN, 2100 Exeter Road, Germantown, TN, Zip 38138; tel. 901/757-1350; Paula Gisler, Chief Executive Officer

BAXTER COUNTY REGIONAL HOSPITAL, 624 Hospital Drive, Mountain Home, AR, Zip 72653-2954; tel. 870/424-1000; H. William Anderson, Administrator

BOONEVILLE COMMUNITY HOSPITAL, 880 West Main Street, Booneville, AR, Zip 72927-3420, Mailing Address: P.O. Box 290, Zip 72927-0290; tel. 501/675-2800; Robert R. Bash, Administrator

BRADLEY COUNTY MEDICAL CENTER, 404 South Bradley Street, Warren, AR, Zip 71671; tel. 870/226-3731; Edward L. Nilles, President and Chief Executive Officer

CARROLL REGIONAL MEDICAL CENTER, 214 Carter Street, Berryville, AR, Zip 72616-4303; tel. 870/423-3355; J. Rudy Darling, President and Chief Executive Officer

CHAMBERS MEMORIAL HOSPITAL, Highway 10 at Detroit, Danville, AR, Zip 72833, Mailing Address: P.O. Box 639, Zip 72833-0639; tel. 501/495-2241; Scott Peek, Administrator

CHICOT MEMORIAL HOSPITAL, 2729 Highway 65 and 82 South, Lake Village, AR, Zip 71653, Mailing Address: P.O. Box 512, Zip 71653-0512; tel. 870/265-5351; Robert R. Reddish, Administrator and Chief Executive Officer

COLUMBIA DE QUEEN REGIONAL MEDICAL CENTER, 1306 Collin Raye Drive, De Queen, AR, Zip 71832-2198; tel. 501/584-4111; Charles H. Long, Chief Executive Officer

COLUMBIA MEDICAL PARK HOSPITAL, 2001 South Main Street, Hope, AR, Zip 71801-8194; tel. 870/777-2323; Jimmy Leopard, Chief Executive Officer

CONWAY REGIONAL MEDICAL CENTER, 2302 College Avenue, Conway, AR, Zip 72032-6297; tel. 501/329-3831; James A. Summersett, III, FACHE, President and Chief Executive Officer

CRAWFORD MEMORIAL HOSPITAL, East Main & South 20th Streets, Van Buren, AR, Zip 72956, Mailing Address: P.O. Box 409, Zip 72956-0409; tel. 501/474-3401; Richard Boone, Executive Director

CRITTENDEN MEMORIAL HOSPITAL, 200 Tyler Avenue, West Memphis, AR, Zip 72301-4223, Mailing Address: P.O. Box 2248, Zip 72303-2248; tel. 501/735-1500; Ross Hooper, Chief Executive Officer

CROSS COUNTY HOSPITAL, 310 South Falls Boulevard, Wynne, AR, Zip 72396-3013, Mailing Address: P.O. Box 590, Zip 72396-0590; tel. 870/238-3300; Harry M. Baker, Chief Executive Officer

DELTA MEMORIAL HOSPITAL, 300 East Pickens Street, Dumas, AR, Zip 71639-2710, Mailing Address: P.O. Box 887, Zip 71639-0887; tel. 870/382-4303; Rodney McPherson, Administrator

DEWITT CITY HOSPITAL, Highway 1 and Madison Street, De Witt, AR, Zip 72042, Mailing Address: P.O. Box 32, Zip 72042-0032; tel. 870/946-3571; Joe E. Smith, Administrator and Chief Executive Officer

Section B

DREW MEMORIAL HOSPITAL, 778 Scogin Drive, Monticello, AR, Zip 71655–5728; tel. 870/367–2411; Darren Caldwell, Chief Executive Officer

EASTERN OZARKS REGIONAL HEALTH SYSTEM, 122 South Allegheny Drive, Cherokee Village, AR, Zip 72529–7300; tel. 870/257–4101; Cindy Hall, Administrator

EUREKA SPRINGS HOSPITAL, 24 Norris Street, Eureka Springs, AR, Zip 72632–3541; tel. 501/253–7400; Joe Hammond, Administrator

FULTON COUNTY HOSPITAL, Highway 9, Salem, AR, Zip 72576, Mailing Address: P.O. Box 517, Zip 72576–0517; tel. 501/895–2691; Franklin E. Wise, Administrator

GRAVETTE MEDICAL CENTER HOSPITAL, 1101 Jackson Street S.W., Gravette, AR, Zip 72736–0470, Mailing Address: P.O. Box 470, Zip 72736–0470; tel. 501/787–5291; John F. Phillips, Administrator

H.S.C. MEDICAL CENTER, 1001 Schneider Drive, Malvern, AR, Zip 72104–4828; tel. 501/337–4911; Jeff Curtis, President and Chief Executive Officer

HARBOR VIEW MERCY HOSPITAL, 10301 Mayo Road, Fort Smith, AR, Zip 72903–1631, Mailing Address: P.O. Box 17000, Zip 72917–7000; tel. 501/484–5550; Ron Summerhill, Administrator

HARRIS HOSPITAL, 1205 McLain Street, Newport, AR, Zip 72112–3533; tel. 870/523–8911; Robin E. Lake, Chief Executive Officer

HEALTHSOUTH REHABILITATION HOSPITAL OF JONESBORO, 1201 Fleming Avenue, Jonesboro, AR, Zip 72401–4311, Mailing Address: P.O. Box 1680, Zip 72403–1680; tel. 870/932–0440; Brenda Antwine, Administrator

HELENA REGIONAL MEDICAL CENTER, 1801 Martin Luther king Drive, Helena, AR, Zip 72342, Mailing Address: P.O. Box 788, Zip 72342–0788; tel. 870/338–5800; Steve Reeder, Chief Executive Officer

HOWARD MEMORIAL HOSPITAL, 800 West Leslie Street, Nashville, AR, Zip 71852–0381, Mailing Address: Box 381, Zip 71852–0381; tel. 870/845–4400; Lynn Crowell, Chief Executive Officer

JEFFERSON REGIONAL MEDICAL CENTER, 1515 West 42nd Avenue, Pine Bluff, AR, Zip 71603–7089; tel. 870/541–7100; Robert P. Atkinson, President and Chief Executive Officer

JOHNSON REGIONAL MEDICAL CENTER, 1100 East Poplar Street, Clarksville, AR, Zip 72830–4419, Mailing Address: P.O. Box 738, Zip 72830–0738; tel. 501/754–5454; Kenneth R. Wood, Administrator

LAWRENCE MEMORIAL HOSPITAL, 1309 West Main, Walnut Ridge, AR, Zip 72476–1430, Mailing Address: P.O. Box 839, Zip 72476–0839; tel. 501/886–1200; Lee Gentry, President

LITTLE RIVER MEMORIAL HOSPITAL, Fifth and Locke Streets, Ashdown, AR, Zip 71822–0577, Mailing Address: P.O. Box 577, Zip 71822–0577; tel. 870/898–5011; Judy Adams, Administrator and Chief Executive Officer

MAGNOLIA HOSPITAL, 101 Hospital Drive, Magnolia, AR, Zip 71753–2416, Mailing Address: Box 629, Zip 71753–0629; tel. 870/235–3000; Kirk Reamey, Administrator

MCGEHEE–DESHA COUNTY HOSPITAL, 900 South Third, McGehee, AR, Zip 71654–0351, Mailing Address: Box 351, Zip 71654–0351; tel. 501/222–5600; Edward L. Lacy, Administrator

MEDICAL CENTER OF CALICO ROCK, 103 Grasse Street, Calico Rock, AR, Zip 72519, Mailing Address: P.O. Box 438, Zip 72519–0438; tel. 870/297–3726; Terry L. Amstutz, CHE, Chief Executive Officer and Administrator

MEDICAL CENTER OF SOUTH ARKANSAS, 700 West Grove Street, El Dorado, AR, Zip 71730–4416, Mailing Address: P.O. Box 1998, Zip 71731–1998; tel. 870/864–3200; Luther J. Lewis, Chief Executive Officer

MENA MEDICAL CENTER, 311 North Morrow Street, Mena, AR, Zip 71953–2516; tel. 501/394–6100; Albert Pilkington, III, Administrator and Chief Executive Officer

MERCY HOSPITAL OF SCOTT COUNTY, Highways 71 and 80, Waldron, AR, Zip 72958–9984, Mailing Address: Box 2230, Zip 72958–2230; tel. 501/637–4135; Sister Mary Alvera Simon, Administrator

MERCY HOSPITAL–TURNER MEMORIAL, 801 West River Street, Ozark, AR, Zip 72949–3000; tel. 501/667–4138; John C. Neal, Administrator

NEWPORT HOSPITAL AND CLINIC, 2000 McLain Street, Newport, AR, Zip 72112–3697; tel. 870/523–6721; Eugene Zuber, Administrator

NORTH ARKANSAS REGIONAL MEDICAL CENTER, 620 North Willow Street, Harrison, AR, Zip 72601–2994; tel. 870/365–2000; Timothy E. Hill, Chief Executive Officer

NORTH LOGAN MERCY HOSPITAL, 500 East Academy, Paris, AR, Zip 72855–4099; tel. 501/963–6101; Jim L. Maddox, Chief Administrative Officer

OUACHITA MEDICAL CENTER, 638 California Street, Camden, AR, Zip 71701–4699, Mailing Address: P.O. Box 797, Zip 71701–0797; tel. 870/836–1000; C. C. McAllister, President and Chief Executive Officer

PIGGOTT COMMUNITY HOSPITAL, 1206 Gordon Duckworth Drive, Piggott, AR, Zip 72454–1911; tel. 870/598–3881; James L. Magee, Executive Director

PIKE COUNTY MEMORIAL HOSPITAL, 315 East 13th Street, Murfreesboro, AR, Zip 71958–9541; tel. 870/285–3182; Rosemary Fritts, Administrator

RANDOLPH COUNTY MEDICAL CENTER, 2801 Medical Center Drive, Pocahontas, AR, Zip 72455–9497; tel. 870/892–4511; Kenneth Breaux, Chief Executive Officer

REBSAMEN REGIONAL MEDICAL CENTER, 1400 West Braden Street, Jacksonville, AR, Zip 72076–3788; tel. 501/985–7000; Thomas R. Siemers, Chief Executive Officer

SAINT MARY'S REGIONAL MEDICAL CENTER, 1808 West Main Street, Russellville, AR, Zip 72801–2724; tel. 501/968–2841; Mike McCoy, Chief Executive Officer

SALINE MEMORIAL HOSPITAL, 1 Medical Park Drive, Benton, AR, Zip 72015–3354; tel. 501/776–6000; Roger D. Feldt, FACHE, President and Chief Executive Officer

SILOAM SPRING MEMORIAL HOSPITAL, 205 East Jefferson Street, Siloam Springs, AR, Zip 72761–3697; tel. 501/524–4141; Donald E. Patterson, Administrator

ST. ANTHONY'S HEALTHCARE CENTER, 4 Hospital Drive, Morrilton, AR, Zip 72110–4510; tel. 501/354–3512; Johnson L. Smith, Chief Executive Officer and Administrator

ST. BERNARD'S BEHAVIORAL HEALTH, 2712 East Johnson Avenue, Jonesboro, AR, Zip 72401–1874; tel. 870/932–2800; Andrew DeYoung, Administrator

ST. BERNARDS REGIONAL MEDICAL CENTER, 224 East Matthews Street, Jonesboro, AR, Zip 72401–3156, Mailing Address: P.O. Box 9320, Zip 72403–9320; tel. 870/972–4100; Ben E. Owens, President

ST. EDWARD MERCY MEDICAL CENTER, 7301 Rogers Avenue, Fort Smith, AR, Zip 72903–4189, Mailing Address: P.O. Box 17000, Zip 72917–7000; tel. 501/484–6000; Michael L. Morgan, President and Chief Executive Officer

ST. JOSEPH'S REGIONAL HEALTH CENTER, 300 Werner Street, Hot Springs, AR, Zip 71913–6448; tel. 501/622–1000; Randall J. Fale, FACHE, President and Chief Executive Officer

ST. MARY–ROGERS MEMORIAL HOSPITAL, 1200 West Walnut Street, Rogers, AR, Zip 72756–3599; tel. 501/636–0200; Michael J. Packnett, President and Chief Executive Officer

STONE COUNTY MEDICAL CENTER, Highway 14 East, Mountain View, AR, Zip 72560, Mailing Address: P.O. Box 510, Zip 72560–0510; tel. 870/269–4361; Stanley Townsend, Administrator

STUTTGART REGIONAL MEDICAL CENTER, North Buerkle Road, Stuttgart, AR, Zip 72160, Mailing Address: P.O. Box 1905, Zip 72160–1905; tel. 870/673–3511; Jim E. Bushmaier, Administrator and Chief Executive Officer

VAN BUREN COUNTY MEMORIAL HOSPITAL, Highway 65 South, Clinton, AR, Zip 72031, Mailing Address: P.O. Box 206, Zip 72031–0206; tel. 501/745–2401; Barry Brady, Administrator

WASHINGTON REGIONAL MEDICAL CENTER, 1125 North College Avenue, Fayetteville, AR, Zip 72703–1994; tel. 501/442–1000; Patrick D. Flynn, President and Chief Executive Officer

WHITE COUNTY MEDICAL CENTER, 3214 East Race, Searcy, AR, Zip 72143–4847; tel. 501/268–6121; Raymond W. Montgomery, II, President and Chief Executive Officer

WHITE RIVER MEDICAL CENTER, 1710 Harrison Street, Batesville, AR, Zip 72501–2197, Mailing Address: P.O. Box 2197, Zip 72503–2197; tel. 870/793–1200; Gary Bebow, Administrator and Chief Executive Officer

BAPTIST HEALTH
9601 Interstate 630, Exit 7, Little Rock, AR 72205; tel. 501/227–2015; Dewey Freeman, Vice President

BAPTIST MEDICAL CENTER, 9601 Interstate 630, Exit 7, Little Rock, AR, Zip 72205–7299; tel. 501/202–2000; Steven Douglas Weeks, Senior Vice President and Administrator

BAPTIST MEDICAL CENTER ARKADELPHIA, 3050 Twin Rivers Drive, Arkadelphia, AR, Zip 71923–4299; tel. 870/245–1100; Dan Gathright, Senior Vice President and Administrator

BAPTIST MEMORIAL MEDICAL CENTER, One Pershing Circle, North Little Rock, AR, Zip 72114–1899; tel. 501/202–3000; Harrison M. Dean, Senior Vice President and Administrator

BAPTIST REHABILITATION INSTITUTE, 9601 Interstate 630, Exit 7, Little Rock, AR, Zip 72205–7249; tel. 501/202–7000; Steven Douglas Weeks, Senior Vice President and Administrator

SAINT EDWARD MERCY MEDICAL CENTER
7301 Rogers Avenue, Fort Smith, AR 72917–7000; tel. 501/484–6000; Larry Goss, Vice President

HARBOR VIEW MERCY HOSPITAL, 10301 Mayo Road, Fort Smith, AR, Zip 72903–1631, Mailing Address: P.O. Box 17000, Zip 72917–7000; tel. 501/484–5550; Ron Summerhill, Administrator

MERCY HOSPITAL OF SCOTT COUNTY, Highways 71 and 80, Waldron, AR, Zip 72958–9984, Mailing Address: Box 2230, Zip 72958–2230; tel. 501/637–4135; Sister Mary Alvera Simon, Administrator

MERCY HOSPITAL–TURNER MEMORIAL, 801 West River Street, Ozark, AR, Zip 72949–3000; tel. 501/667–4138; John C. Neal, Administrator

NORTH LOGAN MERCY HOSPITAL, 500 East Academy, Paris, AR, Zip 72855–4099; tel. 501/963–6101; Jim L. Maddox, Chief Administrative Officer

ST. EDWARD MERCY MEDICAL CENTER, 7301 Rogers Avenue, Fort Smith, AR, Zip 72903–4189, Mailing Address: P.O. Box 17000, Zip 72917–7000; tel. 501/484–6000; Michael L. Morgan, President and Chief Executive Officer

CALIFORNIA

ADVENTIST HEALTH SYSTEM–LOMA LINDA
11161 Anderson Street, Loma Linda, CA 92350; tel. 909/824–4540; B. Lyn Behrens, MB, BS, President

LOMA LINDA UNIVERSITY BEHAVIORAL MEDICINE CENTER, 1710 Barton Road, Redlands, CA, Zip 92373; tel. 909/793–9333; Alan Soderblom, Administrator

LOMA LINDA UNIVERSITY MEDICAL CENTER, 11234 Anderson Street, Loma Linda, CA, Zip 92354–2870, Mailing Address: P.O. Box 2000, Zip 92354–0200; tel. 909/824–0800; J. David Moorhead, M.D., President

Section B

ADVENTIST HEALTH–NORTHERN CALIFORNIA
    363 Highland Avenue, Deer Park, CA 94576;
    tel. 707/963–6240; Everett Gooch,
    President & Chief Executive Officer

FEATHER RIVER HOSPITAL, 5974 Pentz Road,
    Paradise, CA, Zip 95969–5593;
    tel. 530/877–9361; George Pifer, President

FRANK R. HOWARD MEMORIAL HOSPITAL, 1 Madrone
    Street, Willits, CA, Zip 95490;
    tel. 707/459–6801; Kevin R. Erich,
    Administrator

ST. HELENA HOSPITAL, 650 Sanitarium Road, Deer
    Park, CA, Zip 94576, Mailing Address: P.O. Box
    250, Zip 94576; tel. 707/963–3611; JoAline
    Olson, R.N., President

UKIAH VALLEY MEDICAL CENTER, 275 Hospital Drive,
    Ukiah, CA, Zip 95482; tel. 707/462–3111;
    ValGene Devitt, President and Chief Executive
    Officer

ADVENTIST HEALTH–SOUTHERN CALIFORNIA
    1509 Wilson Terrace, Glendale, CA 91206;
    tel. 818/409–8300; Bob Carmen, President &
    Chief Executive Officer

GLENDALE ADVENTIST MEDICAL CENTER, 1509
    Wilson Terrace, Glendale, CA, Zip 91206–4007;
    tel. 818/409–8000; Robert G. Carmen,
    President and Chief Executive Officer

SIMI VALLEY HOSPITAL AND HEALTH CARE
    SERVICES, 2975 North Sycamore Drive, Simi
    Valley, CA, Zip 93065–1277;
    tel. 805/527–2462; Alan J. Rice, President

WHITE MEMORIAL MEDICAL CENTER, 1720 Cesar E.
    Chavez Avenue, Los Angeles, CA,
    Zip 90033–2481; tel. 213/268–5000; Beth D.
    Zachary, Chief Operating Officer

CATHOLIC HEALTHCARE WEST (CHW)
    1700 Montgomery Street, Suite 300, San
    Francisco, CA 94111; tel. 415/438–5500;
    Debbie Cantu, Director of Corporate
    Communications

DOMINICAN SANTA CRUZ HOSPITAL, 1555 Soquel
    Drive, Santa Cruz, CA, Zip 95065–1794;
    tel. 408/462–7700; Sister Julie Hyer, President
    and Chief Executive Officer

MARK TWAIN ST. JOSEPH'S HOSPITAL, 768 Mountain
    Ranch Road, San Andreas, CA,
    Zip 95249–9710; tel. 209/754–2515; Michael
    P. Lawson, Administrator

MERCY AMERICAN RIVER/MERCY SAN JUAN
    HOSPITAL, 6501 Coyle Avenue, Carmichael, CA,
    Zip 95608, Mailing Address: P.O. Box 479,
    Zip 95608; tel. 916/537–5000; Sister Bridget
    McCarthy, President

MERCY GENERAL HOSPITAL, 4001 J. Street,
    Sacramento, CA, Zip 95819;
    tel. 916/453–4950; Thomas A. Petersen, Vice
    President and Chief Operating Officer

MERCY HEALTHCARE–BAKERSFIELD, 2215 Truxtun
    Avenue, Bakersfield, CA, Zip 93301, Mailing
    Address: Box 119, Zip 93302;
    tel. 805/632–5000; Bernard J. Herman,
    President and Chief Executive Officer

MERCY HOSPITAL AND HEALTH SERVICES, 2740 M.
    Street, Merced, CA, Zip 95340–2880;
    tel. 209/384–6444; John Headding, Chief
    Administrative Officer

MERCY HOSPITAL OF FOLSOM, 1650 Creekside
    Drive, Folsom, CA, Zip 95630–3405;
    tel. 916/983–7400; Donald C. Hudson, Vice
    President and Chief Operating Officer

MERCY MEDICAL CENTER, 2175 Rosaline Avenue,
    Redding, CA, Zip 96001, Mailing Address: Box
    496009, Zip 96049–6009; tel. 916/225–6000;
    George A. Govier, President and Chief Executive
    Officer

MERCY MEDICAL CENTER MOUNT SHASTA, 914 Pine
    Street, Mount Shasta, CA, Zip 96067, Mailing
    Address: P.O. Box 239, Zip 96067–0239;
    tel. 530/926–6111; Rick J. Barnett, Executive
    Vice President and Chief Operating Officer

METHODIST HOSPITAL, 7500 Hospital Drive,
    Sacramento, CA, Zip 95823–5477;
    tel. 916/423–3000; Stanley C. Oppegard, Vice
    President and Chief Operating Officer

O'CONNOR HOSPITAL, 2105 Forest Avenue, San
    Jose, CA, Zip 95128–1471; tel. 408/947–2500;
    John G. Williams, President and Chief Executive
    Officer

ROBERT F. KENNEDY MEDICAL CENTER, 4500 West
    116th Street, Hawthorne, CA, Zip 90250;
    tel. 310/973–1711; Peter P. Aprato,
    Administrator and Chief Operating Officer

SAINT FRANCIS MEMORIAL HOSPITAL, 900 Hyde
    Street, San Francisco, CA, Zip 94109, Mailing
    Address: Box 7726, Zip 94120–7726;
    tel. 415/353–6000; Cheryl A. Fama,
    Administrator, Vice President and Chief
    Operating Officer

SAINT LOUISE HOSPITAL, 18500 Saint Louise Drive,
    Morgan Hill, CA, Zip 95037; tel. 408/779–1500;
    Joan A. Bero, Regional Vice President and Chief
    Operating Officer

SAINT MARY MEDICAL CENTER, 1050 Linden Avenue,
    Long Beach, CA, Zip 90801, Mailing Address:
    P.O. Box 887, Zip 90801; tel. 562/491–9000;
    Tammie McMann Brailsford, Administrator

SEQUOIA HOSPITAL, 170 Alameda De Las Pulgas,
    Redwood City, CA, Zip 94062–2799;
    tel. 650/369–5811; Glenna L. Vaskelis,
    Administrator

SETON MEDICAL CENTER, 1900 Sullivan Avenue,
    Daly City, CA, Zip 94015; tel. 650/992–4000;
    Bernadette Smith, Chief Operating Officer

SETON MEDICAL CENTER COASTSIDE, 600 Marine
    Boulevard, Moss Beach, CA, Zip 94038;
    tel. 650/728–5521; Bernadette Smith, Chief
    Operating Officer

SIERRA NEVADA MEMORIAL HOSPITAL, 155 Glasson
    Way, Grass Valley, CA, Zip 95945–5792, Mailing
    Address: P.O. Box 1029, Zip 95945–5792;
    tel. 530/274–6000; C. Thomas Collier,
    President and Chief Executive Officer

ST. BERNARDINE MEDICAL CENTER, 2101 North
    Waterman Avenue, San Bernardino, CA,
    Zip 92404; tel. 909/883–8711; Margo Walter,
    Administrator and Chief Operating Officer

ST. DOMINIC'S HOSPITAL, 1777 West Yosemite
    Avenue, Manteca, CA, Zip 95337;
    tel. 209/825–3500; Richard Aldred, Chief
    Administrative Officer

ST. ELIZABETH COMMUNITY HOSPITAL, 2550 Sister
    Mary Columba Drive, Red Bluff, CA,
    Zip 96080–4397; tel. 530/529–8005; Thomas
    F. Grimes, III, Executive Vice President and Chief
    Operating Officer

ST. FRANCIS MEDICAL CENTER, 3630 East Imperial
    Highway, Lynwood, CA, Zip 90262;
    tel. 310/603–6000; Gerald T. Kozai,
    Administrator and Chief Operating Officer

ST. JOHN'S PLEASANT VALLEY HOSPITAL, 2309
    Antonio Avenue, Camarillo, CA,
    Zip 93010–1459; tel. 805/389–5800; William J.
    Clearwater, Vice President and Administrator

ST. JOHN'S REGIONAL MEDICAL CENTER, 1600
    North Rose Avenue, Oxnard, CA, Zip 93030;
    tel. 805/988–2500; James R. Hoss, President
    and Chief Operating Officer

ST. JOSEPH'S BEHAVIORAL HEALTH CENTER, 2510
    North California Street, Stockton, CA,
    Zip 95204–5568; tel. 209/948–2100; James
    Sondecker, Administrator

ST. JOSEPH'S HOSPITAL AND MEDICAL CENTER, 350
    West Thomas Road, Phoenix, AZ,
    Zip 85013–4496, Mailing Address: P.O. Box
    2071, Zip 85001–2071; tel. 602/406–3100;
    Mary G. Yarbrough, President and Chief
    Executive Officer

ST. JOSEPH'S MEDICAL CENTER, 1800 North
    California Street, Stockton, CA,
    Zip 95204–6088, Mailing Address: P.O. Box
    213008, Zip 95213–9008; tel. 209/943–2000;
    Edward G. Schroeder, President and Chief
    Executive Officer

ST. MARY'S MEDICAL CENTER, 450 Stanyan Street,
    San Francisco, CA, Zip 94117–1079;
    tel. 415/668–1000; John G. Williams, President

ST. ROSE DOMINICAN HOSPITAL, 102 Lake Mead
    Drive, Henderson, NV, Zip 89015–5524;
    tel. 702/564–2622; Rod A. Davis, President and
    Chief Executive Officer

ST. VINCENT MEDICAL CENTER, 2131 West Third
    Street, Los Angeles, CA, Zip 90057–0992,
    Mailing Address: P.O. Box 57992, Zip 90057;
    tel. 213/484–7111; Myda Magarian–Morse,
    Administrator and Chief Operating Officer

WOODLAND MEMORIAL HOSPITAL, 1325 Cottonwood
    Street, Woodland, CA, Zip 95695–5199;
    tel. 530/662–3961; William Hunt, Chief
    Operating Officer

CEDARS–SINAI HEALTH SYSTEM
    8700 Beverly Boulevard, Los Angeles, CA
    90048; tel. 310/855–5000; Thomas M.
    Priselac, President & Chief Executive Officer

CEDARS–SINAI MEDICAL CENTER, 8700 Beverly
    Boulevard, Los Angeles, CA, Zip 90048–1865,
    Mailing Address: Box 48750, Zip 90048–0750;
    tel. 310/855–5000; Thomas M. Priselac,
    President and Chief Executive Officer

EAST BAY MEDICAL NETWORK
    2000 Powell Street, 9th Floor, Emeryville, CA
    94608; tel. 510/450–9850; Blake Kirk,
    Provider Relations

ALAMEDA HOSPITAL, 2070 Clinton Avenue, Alameda,
    CA, Zip 94501; tel. 510/522–3700; William J.
    Dal Cielo, Chief Executive Officer

ALTA BATES MEDICAL CENTER–ASHBY CAMPUS,
    2450 Ashby Avenue, Berkeley, CA, Zip 94705;
    tel. 510/204–4444; George P. Caralis,
    President and Chief Executive Officer

MOUNT DIABLO MEDICAL CENTER, 2540 East Street,
    Concord, CA, Zip 94520, Mailing Address: P.O.
    Box 4110, Zip 94524–4110;
    tel. 925/682–8200; J. Kendall Anderson,
    President and Chief Executive Officer

PATTON STATE HOSPITAL, 3102 East Highland
    Avenue, Patton, CA, Zip 92369;
    tel. 909/425–7000; William L. Summers,
    Executive Director

SAN LEANDRO HOSPITAL, 13855 East 14th Street,
    San Leandro, CA, Zip 94578–0398;
    tel. 510/667–4510; Kelly Mather, Chief
    Executive Officer

SUTTER DELTA MEDICAL CENTER, 3901 Lone Tree
    Way, Antioch, CA, Zip 94509;
    tel. 925/779–7200; Linda Horn, Administrator

WASHINGTON TOWNSHIP HEALTH CARE DISTRICT,
    2000 Mowry Avenue, Fremont, CA,
    Zip 94538–1716; tel. 510/797–1111; Nancy D.
    Farber, Chief Executive Officer

ESSENTIAL HEALTHCARE NETWORK
    525 North Garfield Park, Monterey Park, CA
    91754; tel. 818/573–2222; A. Schaffer,
    Acting Executive Director

COMMUNITY HOSPITAL OF HUNTINGTON PARK, 2623
    East Slauson Avenue, Huntington Park, CA,
    Zip 90255; tel. 213/583–1931; Charles
    Martinez, Ph.D., Chief Executive Officer

GARFIELD MEDICAL CENTER, 525 North Garfield
    Avenue, Monterey Park, CA, Zip 91754;
    tel. 626/573–2222; Philip A. Cohen, Chief
    Executive Officer

GREATER EL MONTE COMMUNITY HOSPITAL, 1701
    South Santa Anita Avenue, South El Monte, CA,
    Zip 91733–9918; tel. 626/579–7777; Elizabeth
    A. Primeaux, Chief Executive Officer

PACIFIC ALLIANCE MEDICAL CENTER, 531 West
    College Street, Los Angeles, CA,
    Zip 90012–2385; tel. 213/624–8411; John R.
    Edwards, Chief Executive Officer

QUEEN OF ANGELS–HOLLYWOOD PRESBYTERIAN
    MEDICAL CENTER, 1300 North Vermont Avenue,
    Los Angeles, CA, Zip 90027–0069;
    tel. 213/413–3000; Sylvester Graff, President
    and Chief Executive Officer

ROBERT F. KENNEDY MEDICAL CENTER, 4500 West
    116th Street, Hawthorne, CA, Zip 90250;
    tel. 310/973–1711; Peter P. Aprato,
    Administrator and Chief Operating Officer

SANTA MARTA HOSPITAL, 319 North Humphreys
    Avenue, Los Angeles, CA, Zip 90022–1499;
    tel. 213/266–6500; Harry E. Whitney, Interim
    President and Chief Executive Officer

ST. FRANCIS MEDICAL CENTER, 3630 East Imperial
    Highway, Lynwood, CA, Zip 90262;
    tel. 310/603–6000; Gerald T. Kozai,
    Administrator and Chief Operating Officer

Section B

SUBURBAN MEDICAL CENTER, 16453 South Colorado Avenue, Paramount, CA, Zip 90723; tel. 562/531–3110; Gustavo Valdespino, Chief Executive Officer

FREMONT–RIDEOUT HEALTH GROUP
970 Plumas Street, Yuba City, CA 95991;
tel. 530/751–9526; Deborah Coulter,
Community Relation Director

FREMONT MEDICAL CENTER, 970 Plumas Street, Yuba City, CA 95991; tel. 530/751–4000; Thomas P. Hayes, Chief Executive Officer

RIDEOUT MEMORIAL HOSPITAL, 726 Fourth Street, Marysville, CA, Zip 95901–2128, Mailing Address: Box 2128, Zip 95901–2128; tel. 916/749–4300; Thomas P. Hayes, Chief Executive Officer

FRIENDLY HILLS HEALTHCARE NETWORK
931 South Beach, LaHabra, CA 90631;
tel. 310/694–4711; Albert Barnett, M.D.,
Chairman & Chief Executive Officer

FRIENDLY HILLS REGIONAL MEDICAL CENTER, 1251 West Lambert Road, La Habra, CA, Zip 90631; tel. 562/694–3838; Kathleen Smith, Executive Director

ST. JUDE MEDICAL CENTER, 101 East Valencia Mesa Drive, Fullerton, CA, Zip 92635; tel. 714/992–3000; Robert J. Fraschetti, President and Chief Executive Officer

HEALTH FIRST NETWORK
4020 5th Avenue, 3rd Floor, San Diego, CA 92103; tel. 619/293–0986; Roger Burke, President

PALOMAR MEDICAL CENTER, 555 East Valley Parkway, Escondido, CA, Zip 92025–3084; tel. 760/739–3000; Victoria M. Penland, Administrator and Chief Operating Officer

POMERADO HOSPITAL, 15615 Pomerado Road, Poway, CA, Zip 92064; tel. 619/485–4600; Marvin W. Levenson, M.D., Administrator and Chief Operating Officer

INTERMOUNTAIN RURAL HEALTH NETWORK
228 McDowell Street, Alturas, CA 96101;
tel. 530/233–4704; Donna Donald, Director

INDIAN VALLEY HOSPITAL DISTRICT, 184 Hot Springs Road, Greenville, CA, Zip 95947; tel. 530/284–7191; Lynn Seaberg, Administrator and Chief Executive Officer

MAYERS MEMORIAL HOSPITAL DISTRICT, Highway 299 East, Fall River Mills, CA, Zip 96028, Mailing Address: Box 459, Zip 96028; tel. 530/336–5511; Judi Beck, Administrator

MODOC MEDICAL CENTER, 228 McDowell Street, Alturas, CA, Zip 96101; tel. 916/233–5131; Woody J. Laughnan, Chief Executive Officer

SURPRISE VALLEY COMMUNITY HOSPITAL, Main and Washington Streets, Cedarville, CA, Zip 96104, Mailing Address: P.O. Box 246, Zip 96104–0246; tel. 530/279–6111; Joyce Gysin, Administrator

KAISER FOUNDATION HEALTH PLAN OF NORTHERN CALIFORNIA
1950 Franklin Street, Oakland, CA 94612;
tel. 510/987–1000; David Pockell, Executive Regional Vice President

KAISER FOUNDATION HOSPITAL, 2425 Geary Boulevard, San Francisco, CA, Zip 94115; tel. 415/202–2000; Richard R. Pettingill, Administrator

KAISER FOUNDATION HOSPITAL, 280 West MacArthur Boulevard, Oakland, CA, Zip 94611; tel. 510/987–1000; Bernard J. Tyson, Administrator

KAISER FOUNDATION HOSPITAL, 1425 South Main Street, Walnut Creek, CA, Zip 94596; tel. 510/295–4000; Sandra Small, Administrator

KAISER FOUNDATION HOSPITAL, 27400 Hesperian Boulevard, Hayward, CA, Zip 94545–4297; tel. 510/784–4313; Bernard J. Tyson, Administrator

KAISER FOUNDATION HOSPITAL, 1150 Veterans Boulevard, Redwood City, CA, Zip 94063–2087; tel. 650/299–2000; Helen Wilmot, Administrator

KAISER FOUNDATION HOSPITAL, 6600 Bruceville Road, Sacramento, CA, Zip 95823; tel. 916/688–2430; Sarah Krevans, Administrator

KAISER FOUNDATION HOSPITAL, 99 Montecillo Road, San Rafael, CA, Zip 94903–3397; tel. 415/444–2000; Richard R. Pettingill, Administrator

KAISER FOUNDATION HOSPITAL, 900 Kiely Boulevard, Santa Clara, CA, Zip 95051–5386; tel. 408/236–6400; Helen Wilmot, Administrator

KAISER FOUNDATION HOSPITAL, 1200 El Camino Real, South San Francisco, CA, Zip 94080–3299; tel. 650/742–2547; Richard R. Pettingill, Administrator

KAISER FOUNDATION HOSPITAL AND REHABILITATION CENTER, 975 Sereno Drive, Vallejo, CA, Zip 94589; tel. 707/651–1000; Sandra Small, Administrator

REDDING MEDICAL CENTER, 1100 Butte Street, Redding, CA, Zip 96001–0853, Mailing Address: Box 496072, Zip 96049–6072; tel. 530/244–5454; Steve Schmidt, Chief Executive Officer

LITTLE COMPANY OF MARY HEALTH SERVICES
4101 Torrance Boulevard, Torrance, CA 90503; tel. 310/540–7676; James Lester, President

LITTLE COMPANY OF MARY HOSPITAL, 4101 Torrance Boulevard, Torrance, CA, Zip 90503–4698; tel. 310/540–7676; Mark Costa, President

SAN PEDRO PENINSULA HOSPITAL, 1300 West Seventh Street, San Pedro, CA, Zip 90732; tel. 310/832–3311; John M. Wilson, President

NORTHBAY HEALTHCARE SYSTEM
1200 B. Gale Wilson Boulevard, Fairfield, CA 94533; tel. 707/429–3600; Gary J. Passama, President & Chief Executive Officer

NORTHBAY MEDICAL CENTER, 1200 B. Gale Wilson Boulevard, Fairfield, CA, Zip 94533–3587; tel. 707/429–3600; Deborah Sugiyama, President

VACAVALLEY HOSPITAL, 1000 Nut Tree Road, Vacaville, CA, Zip 95687; tel. 707/429–7717; Deborah Sugiyama, President

NORTHERN SIERRA RURAL HEALTH NETWORK
P.O. Box 224, Downieville, CA 95936–0224;
tel. 530/289–0135; Speranza Avram,
Executive Director

LASSEN COMMUNITY HOSPITAL, 560 Hospital Lane, Susanville, CA, Zip 96130–4809; tel. 530/257–5325; David S. Anderson, FACHE, Administrator

SIERRA VALLEY DISTRICT HOSPITAL, 700 Third Street, Loyalton, CA, Zip 96118, Mailing Address: Box 178, Zip 96118; tel. 530/993–1225; Chase Mearian, Administrator

PROVIDENCE HEALTH SYSTEM IN CALIFORNIA
501 South Buena Vista Street, Burbank, CA 91505; tel. 818/843–5111; Michael Madden, CEO

PROVIDENCE HOLY CROSS MEDICAL CENTER, 15031 Rinaldi Street, Mission Hills, CA, Zip 91345–1285; tel. 818/365–8051; Michael J. Madden, Chief Executive Los Angeles Service Area

PROVIDENCE SAINT JOSEPH MEDICAL CENTER, 501 South Buena Vista Street, Burbank, CA, Zip 91505–4866; tel. 818/843–5111; Michael J. Madden, Chief Executive Los Angeles Service Area

SAINT JOSEPH HEALTH SYSTEM
440 South Batavia Street, Orange, CA 92668–3995; tel. 714/997–7690; Jim Dake, Manager of Technical Services

QUEEN OF THE VALLEY HOSPITAL, 1000 Trancas Street, Napa, CA, Zip 94558, Mailing Address: Box 2340, Zip 94558; tel. 707/252–4411; Dennis Sisto, Acting President and Chief Executive Officer

REDWOOD MEMORIAL HOSPITAL, 3300 Renner Drive, Fortuna, CA, Zip 95540; tel. 707/725–3361; Neil Martin, President and Chief Executive Officer

SAINT JOSEPH HOSPITAL, 2700 Dolbeer Street, Eureka, CA, Zip 95501; tel. 707/269–4223; Neil Martin, President and Chief Executive Officer

SANTA ROSA MEMORIAL HOSPITAL, 1165 Montgomery Drive, Santa Rosa, CA, Zip 95405, Mailing Address: Box 522, Zip 95402; tel. 707/546–3210; Robert H. Fish, President and Chief Executive Officer

ST. MARY REGIONAL MEDICAL CENTER, 18300 Highway 18, Apple Valley, CA, Zip 92307–0725, Mailing Address: Box 7025, Zip 92307–0725; tel. 760/242–2311; Catherine M. Pelley, President and Chief Executive Officer

ST. JOSEPH HOSPITAL, 1100 West Stewart Drive, Orange, CA, Zip 92668, Mailing Address: P.O. Box 5600, Zip 92613–5600; tel. 714/633–9111; Larry K. Ainsworth, President and Chief Executive Officer

ST. JUDE MEDICAL CENTER, 101 East Valencia Mesa Drive, Fullerton, CA, Zip 92635; tel. 714/992–3000; Robert J. Fraschetti, President and Chief Executive Officer

SCRIPPSHEALTH
4275 Campus Point Court, San Diego, CA 92121; tel. 619/678–6111; Kay Alexander, Executive Assistant

GREEN HOSPITAL OF SCRIPPS CLINIC, 10666 North Torrey Pines Road, La Jolla, CA, Zip 92037–1093; tel. 619/455–9100; Linda L. Hodges, R.N., Associate Administrator

SCRIPPS HOSPITAL–CHULA VISTA, 435 H. Street, Chula Vista, CA, Zip 91912–1537, Mailing Address: P.O. Box 1537, Zip 91910–1537; tel. 619/691–7000; Thomas A. Gammiere, Vice President and Administrator

SCRIPPS HOSPITAL–EAST COUNTY, 1688 East Main Street, El Cajon, CA, Zip 92021; tel. 619/593–5600; Deborah Dunne, Administrator

SCRIPPS MEMORIAL HOSPITAL–ENCINITAS, 354 Santa Fe Drive, Encinitas, CA, Zip 92024, Mailing Address: P.O. Box 230817, Zip 92023; tel. 760/753–6501; Gerald E. Bracht, Vice President and Administrator

SCRIPPS MEMORIAL HOSPITAL–LA JOLLA, 9888 Genesee Avenue, La Jolla, CA, Zip 92037–1276, Mailing Address: P.O. Box 28, Zip 92038–0028; tel. 619/626–4123; Thomas C. Gagen, Administrator

SCRIPPS MERCY HOSPITAL, 4077 Fifth Avenue, San Diego, CA, Zip 92103–2180; tel. 619/260–7101; Nancy Wilson, Senior Vice President and Regional Administrator

SHARP HEALTHCARE
3131 Berger Avenue, Suite 100, San Diego, CA 92123; tel. 619/541–4000; Mike Murphy, President & Chief Executive Officer

GROSSMONT HOSPITAL, 5555 Grossmont Center Drive, La Mesa, CA, Zip 91942, Mailing Address: Box 158, Zip 91944–0158; tel. 619/465–0711; Michele T. Tarbet, R.N., Chief Executive Officer

SHARP CABRILLO HOSPITAL, 3475 Kenyon Street, San Diego, CA, Zip 92110–5067; tel. 619/221–3400; Randi Larsson, Chief Operating Officer and Administrator

SHARP CHULA VISTA MEDICAL CENTER, 751 Medical Center Court, Chula Vista, CA, Zip 91911, Mailing Address: Box 1297, Zip 91912; tel. 619/482–5800; Britt Berrett, Chief Executive Officer

SHARP HEALTHCARE MURRIETA, 25500 Medical Center Drive, Murrieta, CA, Zip 92562–5966; tel. 909/696–6000; Juanice Lovett, Chief Executive Officer

SHARP MEMORIAL HOSPITAL, 7901 Frost Street, San Diego, CA, Zip 92123–2788; tel. 619/541–3400; Dan Gross, Chief Executive Officer

SOUTHERN CALIFORNIA HEALTHCARE SYSTEMS
1300 East Green Street, Pasadena, CA 91106;
tel. 818/397–2900; Frederick C. Meyer,
President & Chief Executive Officer

Section B

BEVERLY HOSPITAL, 309 West Beverly Boulevard, Montebello, CA, Zip 90640; tel. 213/726-1222; Matthew S. Gerlach, Chief Executive Officer and President

HUNTINGTON EAST VALLEY HOSPITAL, 150 West Alosta Avenue, Glendora, CA, Zip 91740-4398; tel. 626/335-0231; James W. Maki, Chief Executive Officer

HUNTINGTON MEMORIAL HOSPITAL, 100 West California Boulevard, Pasadena, CA, Zip 91105, Mailing Address: P.O. Box 7013, Zip 91109-7013; tel. 626/397-5000; Stephen A. Ralph, President and Chief Executive Officer

METHODIST HOSPITAL OF SOUTHERN CALIFORNIA, 300 West Huntington Drive, Arcadia, CA, Zip 91007, Mailing Address: P.O. Box 60016, Zip 91066-6016; tel. 626/445-4441; Dennis M. Lee, President

VERDUGO HILLS HOSPITAL, 1812 Verdugo Boulevard, Glendale, CA, Zip 91208; tel. 818/790-7100; Bernard Glossy, President

SUTTER-CHS
P.O. Box 160727, Sacramento, CA 95816; tel. 916/733-8800; Van Johnson, President & Chief Executive Officer

ALTA BATES MEDICAL CENTER-ASHBY CAMPUS, 2450 Ashby Avenue, Berkeley, CA, Zip 94705; tel. 510/204-4444; George P. Caralis, President and Chief Executive Officer

CALIFORNIA PACIFIC MEDICAL CENTER, 2333 Buchanan Street, San Francisco, CA, Zip 94115, Mailing Address: P.O. Box 7999, Zip 94120; tel. 415/563-4321; Martin Brotman, M.D., President and Chief Executive Officer

DAMERON HOSPITAL, 525 West Acacia Street, Stockton, CA, Zip 95203; tel. 209/944-5550; Luis Arismendi, M.D., Administrator

EDEN MEDICAL CENTER, 20103 Lake Chabot Road, Castro Valley, CA, Zip 94546; tel. 510/537-1234; George Bischalaney, Interim President and Chief Executive Officer

MARIN GENERAL HOSPITAL, 250 Bon Air Road, Greenbrae, CA, Zip 94904, Mailing Address: Box 8010, San Rafael, Zip 94912-8010; tel. 415/925-7000; Henry J. Buhrmann, President and Chief Executive Officer

MEMORIAL HOSPITALS ASSOCIATION, Modesto, CA, Mailing Address: P.O. Box 942, Zip 95353; tel. 209/526-4500; David P. Benn, President and Chief Executive Officer

MILLS-PENINSULA HEALTH SERVICES, 1783 El Camino Real, Burlingame, CA, Zip 94010-3205; tel. 650/696-5400; Robert W. Merwin, Chief Executive Officer

NOVATO COMMUNITY HOSPITAL, 1625 Hill Road, Novato, CA, Zip 94947, Mailing Address: P.O. Box 1108, Zip 94948; tel. 415/897-3111; Anne Hosfeld, Chief Administrative Officer

OAK VALLEY DISTRICT HOSPITAL, 350 South Oak Street, Oakdale, CA, Zip 95361; tel. 209/847-3011; Norman J. Andrews, Chief Executive Officer

SUTTER AMADOR HOSPITAL, 810 Court Street, Jackson, CA, Zip 95642-2379; tel. 209/223-7500; Scott Stenberg, Chief Executive Officer

SUTTER AUBURN FAITH COMMUNITY HOSPITAL, 11815 Education Street, Auburn, CA, Zip 95604, Mailing Address: Box 8992, Zip 95604-8992; tel. 916/888-4518; Joel E. Grey, Administrator

SUTTER CENTER FOR PSYCHIATRY, 7700 Folsom Boulevard, Sacramento, CA, Zip 95826-2608; tel. 916/386-3000; Diane Gail Stewart, Administrator

SUTTER COAST HOSPITAL, 800 East Washington Boulevard, Crescent City, CA, Zip 95531; tel. 707/464-8511; John E. Menaugh, Chief Executive Officer

SUTTER COMMUNITY HOSPITALS, 5151 F. Street, Sacramento, CA, Zip 95819-3295; tel. 916/454-3333; Lou Lazatin, Chief Executive Officer

SUTTER DAVIS HOSPITAL, 2000 Sutter Place, Davis, CA, Zip 95616, Mailing Address: P.O. Box 1617, Zip 95617; tel. 530/756-6440; Lawrence A. Maas, Administrator

SUTTER DELTA MEDICAL CENTER, 3901 Lone Tree Way, Antioch, CA, Zip 94509; tel. 925/779-7200; Linda Horn, Administrator

SUTTER LAKESIDE HOSPITAL, 5176 Hill Road East, Lakeport, CA, Zip 95453-6111; tel. 707/262-5001; Paul J. Hensler, Chief Executive Officer

SUTTER MEDICAL CENTER, SANTA ROSA, 3325 Chanate Road, Santa Rosa, CA, Zip 95404; tel. 707/576-4000; Cliff Coates, Chief Executive Officer

SUTTER MERCED MEDICAL CENTER, 301 East 13th Street, Merced, CA, Zip 95340-6211; tel. 209/385-7000; Brian S. Bentley, Administrator

SUTTER ROSEVILLE MEDICAL CENTER, One Medical Plaza, Roseville, CA, Zip 95661-3477; tel. 916/781-1000; Joel E. Grey, Chief Executive Officer

SUTTER SOLANO MEDICAL CENTER, 300 Hospital Drive, Vallejo, CA, Zip 94589-2517, Mailing Address: P.O. Box 3189, Zip 94589; tel. 707/554-4444; Patrick R. Brady, Administrator

SUTTER TRACY COMMUNITY HOSPITAL, 1420 North Tracy Boulevard, Tracy, CA, Zip 95376-3497; tel. 209/835-1500; Gary D. Rapaport, Chief Executive Officer

TENET HEALTHCARE CORPORATION
3820 State Street, Santa Barbara, CA 93105; tel. 805/563-7000; Jeffrey C. Barbakow, Chairman & Chief Executive Officer

ALVARADO HOSPITAL MEDICAL CENTER, 6655 Alvarado Road, San Diego, CA, Zip 92120-5298; tel. 619/287-3270; Barry G. Weinbaum, Chief Executive Officer

CENTURY CITY HOSPITAL, 2070 Century Park East, Los Angeles, CA, Zip 90067; tel. 310/553-6211; John R. Nickens, III, Chief Executive Officer

COMMUNITY HOSPITAL OF LOS GATOS, 815 Pollard Road, Los Gatos, CA, Zip 95030; tel. 408/378-6131; Truman L. Gates, Chief Executive Officer

DOCTORS HOSPITAL OF MANTECA, 1205 East North Street, Manteca, CA, Zip 95336, Mailing Address: Box 191, Zip 95336; tel. 209/823-3111; Patrick W. Rafferty, Administrator

DOCTORS MEDICAL CENTER, 1441 Florida Avenue, Modesto, CA, Zip 95350-4418, Mailing Address: P.O. Box 4138, Zip 95352-4138; tel. 209/578-1211; Chris DiCicco, Chief Executive Officer

DOCTORS MEDICAL CENTER-PINOLE CAMPUS, 2151 Appian Way, Pinole, CA, Zip 94564; tel. 510/724-5000; Gary Sloan, Chief Executive Officer

GARDEN GROVE HOSPITAL AND MEDICAL CENTER, 12601 Garden Grove Boulevard, Garden Grove, CA, Zip 92843-1959; tel. 714/741-2700; Timothy Smith, President and Chief Executive Officer

GARFIELD MEDICAL CENTER, 525 North Garfield Avenue, Monterey Park, CA, Zip 91754; tel. 626/573-2222; Philip A. Cohen, Chief Executive Officer

IRVINE MEDICAL CENTER, 16200 Sand Canyon Avenue, Irvine, CA, Zip 92618-3714; tel. 714/753-2000; Richard H. Robinson, Chief Executive Officer

JOHN F. KENNEDY MEMORIAL HOSPITAL, 47-111 Monroe Street, Indio, CA, Zip 92201, Mailing Address: P.O. Drawer LLLL, Zip 92202-2558; tel. 760/347-6191; Michael A. Rembis, FACHE, Chief Executive Officer

LAKEWOOD REGIONAL MEDICAL CENTER, 3700 East South Street, Lakewood, CA, Zip 90712; tel. 562/531-2550; Gustavo A. Valdespino, Chief Executive Officer

LOS ALAMITOS MEDICAL CENTER, 3751 Katella Avenue, Los Alamitos, CA, Zip 90720; tel. 562/598-1311; Gustavo A. Valdespino, Chief Executive Officer

NORTH HOLLYWOOD MEDICAL CENTER, 12629 Riverside Drive, North Hollywood, CA, Zip 91607-3495; tel. 818/980-9200; Sonja Hagel, Chief Executive Officer

PLACENTIA-LINDA HOSPITAL, 1301 Rose Drive, Placentia, CA, Zip 92870; tel. 714/993-2000; Maxine T. Cooper, Chief Executive Officer

REDDING MEDICAL CENTER, 1100 Butte Street, Redding, CA, Zip 96001-0853, Mailing Address: Box 496072, Zip 96049-6072; tel. 530/244-5454; Steve Schmidt, Chief Executive Officer

SAN DIMAS COMMUNITY HOSPITAL, 1350 West Covina Boulevard, San Dimas, CA, Zip 91773-0308; tel. 909/599-6811; Patrick A. Petre, Chief Executive Officer

SAN RAMON REGIONAL MEDICAL CENTER, 6001 Norris Canyon Road, San Ramon, CA, Zip 94583; tel. 925/275-9200; Philip P. Gustafson, Administrator

SIERRA VISTA REGIONAL MEDICAL CENTER, 1010 Murray Street, San Luis Obispo, CA, Zip 93405, Mailing Address: Box 1367, Zip 93406-1367; tel. 805/546-7600; Harold E. Chilton, Chief Executive Officer

TWIN CITIES COMMUNITY HOSPITAL, 1100 Las Tablas Road, Templeton, CA, Zip 93465; tel. 805/434-3500; Harold E. Chilton, Chief Executive Officer

UNIHEALTH
4100 West Alameda, Burbank, CA 91505; tel. 818/238-6000; Terry Hartshorn, President

CALIFORNIA HOSPITAL MEDICAL CENTER, 1401 South Grand Avenue, Los Angeles, CA, Zip 90015-3063; tel. 213/748-2411; Melinda D. Beswick, President and Chief Executive Officer

GLENDALE MEMORIAL HOSPITAL AND HEALTH CENTER, 1420 South Central Avenue, Glendale, CA, Zip 91204-2594; tel. 818/502-1900; Arnold R. Schaffer, President and Chief Executive Officer

LA PALMA INTERCOMMUNITY HOSPITAL, 7901 Walker Street, La Palma, CA, Zip 90623-5850, Mailing Address: P.O. Box 5850, Buena Park, Zip 90622; tel. 714/670-7400; Stephen E. Dixon, President and Chief Executive Officer

LINDSAY DISTRICT HOSPITAL, 740 North Sequoia Avenue, Lindsay, CA, Zip 93247, Mailing Address: Box 40, Zip 93247; tel. 209/562-4955; Edwin L. Ermshar, President and Chief Executive Officer

LONG BEACH COMMUNITY MEDICAL CENTER, 1720 Termino Avenue, Long Beach, CA, Zip 90804; tel. 562/498-1000; Makoto Nakayama, President and Chief Executive Officer

MARTIN LUTHER HOSPITAL, 1830 West Romneya Drive, Anaheim, CA, Zip 92801-1854; tel. 714/491-5200; Stephen E. Dixon, President and Chief Executive Officer

NORTHRIDGE HOSPITAL AND MEDICAL CENTER, SHERMAN WAY CAMPUS, 14500 Sherman Circle, Van Nuys, CA, Zip 91405; tel. 818/997-0101; Richard D. Lyons, President and Chief Executive Officer

NORTHRIDGE HOSPITAL MEDICAL CENTER-ROSCOE BOULEVARD CAMPUS, 18300 Roscoe Boulevard, Northridge, CA, Zip 91328; tel. 818/885-8500; Roger E. Seaver, President and Chief Executive Officer

SAN GABRIEL VALLEY MEDICAL CENTER, 438 West Las Tunas Drive, San Gabriel, CA, Zip 91776, Mailing Address: P.O. Box 1507, Zip 91778-1507; tel. 626/289-5454; Thomas D. Mone, President and Chief Executive Officer

SANTA MONICA-UCLA MEDICAL CENTER, 1250 16th Street, Santa Monica, CA, Zip 90404-1200; tel. 310/319-4000; William D. Parente, Director and Chief Executive Officer

COLORADO

CENTURA PENROSE-ST FRANCIS HEALTH SERVICES 2215 N. Cascade Avenue, P.O. Box 7021, Colorado Springs, CO 80933; tel. 719/776-5000; Donna L. Bertram, Administrator

PENROSE-ST. FRANCIS HEALTH SERVICES, Colorado Springs, CO, Donna L. Bertram, R.N., Administrator

COLUMBIA – HEALTH ONE
4643 South Ulster Street, Suite 1200,
Englewood, CO 80237; tel. 303/788–2500;
Molly Hagen, Director Planning

COLUMBIA MEDICAL CENTER OF AURORA, 1501
South Potomac Street, Aurora, CO,
Zip 80012–5499; tel. 303/695–2600; Louis O.
Garcia, President and Chief Executive Officer

COLUMBIA NORTH SUBURBAN MEDICAL CENTER,
9191 Grant Street, Thornton, CO,
Zip 80229–4341; tel. 303/451–7800; Margaret
C. Cain, Chief Executive Officer

COLUMBIA PRESBYTERIAN–ST. LUKE'S MEDICAL
CENTER, 1719 East 19th Avenue, Denver, CO,
Zip 80218–1281; tel. 303/839–6000; Kevin
Gross, Chief Executive Officer

ROSE MEDICAL CENTER, 4567 East Ninth Avenue,
Denver, CO, Zip 80220–3941;
tel. 303/320–2121; Kenneth H. Feiler, President
and Chief Executive Officer

SWEDISH MEDICAL CENTER, 501 East Hampden
Avenue, Englewood, CO, Zip 80110–0101;
tel. 303/788–5000; Mary M. White, President
and Chief Executive Officer

COMMUNITY HEALTH PROVIDERS ORGANIZATION
2021 North 12th Street, Grand Junction, CO
81501; tel. 970/256–6200; Roger C. Zumwalt,
Chief Executive Officer

COMMUNITY HOSPITAL, 2021 North 12th Street,
Grand Junction, CO, Zip 81501–2999;
tel. 970/242–0920; Roger C. Zumwalt,
Executive Director

EXEMPLA
600 Grant Street, Denver, CO 80203–3525;
tel. 303/813–5000; Jeffrey Selberg, Chief
Operating Officer

EXEMPLA LUTHERAN MEDICAL CENTER, 8300 West
38th Avenue, Wheat Ridge, CO,
Zip 80033–6005; tel. 303/425–4500; Jeffrey
D. Selberg, President and Chief Executive Officer

EXEMPLA SAINT JOSEPH HOSPITAL, 1835 Franklin
Street, Denver, CO, Zip 80218–1191;
tel. 303/837–7111; David Hamm, Interim Chief
Executive Officer

SPALDING REHABILITATION HOSPITAL, 900 Potomac
Street, Aurora, CO, Zip 80011–6716;
tel. 303/367–1166; Lynn Dawson, Chief
Executive Officer

HEALTH & MEDICAL NETWORK OF COLORADO
555 East Pikes Peak, Suite 108, Colorado
Springs, CO 80903; tel. 719/475–5025; Ron
Burnside, President & Chief Executive Officer

MEMORIAL HOSPITAL, 1400 East Boulder Street,
Colorado Springs, CO, Zip 80909–5599, Mailing
Address: Box 1326, Zip 80901–1326;
tel. 719/365–5000; J. Robert Peters, Executive
Director

HIGH PLAINS RURAL HEALTH NETWORK
218 East Kiowa Avenue, Fort Morgan, CO
80701; tel. 303/867–6195; Peter Caplan,
Executive Director

CHEYENNE COUNTY HOSPITAL, 210 West First
Street, Saint Francis, KS, Zip 67756, Mailing
Address: P.O. Box 547, Zip 67756–0547;
tel. 785/332–2104; Leslie Lacy, Administrator

COLORADO PLAINS MEDICAL CENTER, 1000 Lincoln
Street, Fort Morgan, CO, Zip 80701–3298;
tel. 970/867–3391; Thomas Thomson,
Administrator and Chief Executive Officer

EAST MORGAN COUNTY HOSPITAL, 2400 West
Edison Street, Brush, CO, Zip 80723–1640;
tel. 970/842–5151; Anne Platt, Administrator

ESTES PARK MEDICAL CENTER, 555 Prospect
Avenue, Estes Park, CO, Zip 80517, Mailing
Address: P.O. Box 2740, Zip 80517;
tel. 970/586–2317; Andrew Wills, Chief
Executive Officer

HAXTUN HOSPITAL DISTRICT, 235 West Fletcher
Street, Haxtun, CO, Zip 80731–0308, Mailing
Address: Box 308, Zip 80731–0308;
tel. 970/774–6123; James E. Brundige,
Administrator

HAYS MEDICAL CENTER, 2220 Canterbury Road,
Hays, KS, Zip 67601–2342, Mailing Address:
P.O. Box 8100, Zip 67601–8100;
tel. 785/623–5113; John H. Jeter, M.D.,
President and Chief Executive Officer

KEEFE MEMORIAL HOSPITAL, 602 North Sixth Street
West, Cheyenne Wells, CO, Zip 80810, Mailing
Address: P.O. Box 578, Zip 80810–0578;
tel. 719/767–5661; Curtis Hawkinson, Chief
Executive Officer

KIT CARSON COUNTY MEMORIAL HOSPITAL, 286
16th Street, Burlington, CO, Zip 80807–1697;
tel. 719/346–5311; DeAnn K. Cure, Chief
Executive Officer

LINCOLN COMMUNITY HOSPITAL AND NURSING
HOME, 111 Sixth Street, Hugo, CO, Zip 80821,
Mailing Address: P.O. Box 248,
Zip 80821–0248; tel. 719/743–2421; Mary L.
Thompson, Administrator

MELISSA MEMORIAL HOSPITAL, 505 South Baxter
Avenue, Holyoke, CO, Zip 80734–1496;
tel. 970/854–2241; George V. Larson, II, Chief
Executive Officer

MEMORIAL HEALTH CENTER, 645 Osage Street,
Sidney, NE, Zip 69162–1799;
tel. 308/254–5825; Rex D. Walk, Chief
Executive Officer

NORTH COLORADO MEDICAL CENTER, 1801 16th
Street, Greeley, CO, Zip 80631–5199;
tel. 970/350–6000; Karl B. Gills, Administrator

PROWERS MEDICAL CENTER, 401 Kendall Drive,
Lamar, CO, Zip 81052–3993;
tel. 719/336–4343; Earl J. Steinhoff, Chief
Executive Officer

RAWLINS COUNTY HEALTH CENTER, 707 Grant
Street, Atwood, KS, Zip 67730–4700, Mailing
Address: Box 47, Zip 67730–4700;
tel. 785/626–3211; Donald J. Kessen,
Administrator and Chief Executive Officer

STERLING REGIONAL MEDCENTER, 615 Fairhurst
Street, Sterling, CO, Zip 80751–4523, Mailing
Address: P.O. Box 3500, Zip 80751–3500;
tel. 970/522–0122; James O. Pernau,
Administrator

WRAY COMMUNITY DISTRICT HOSPITAL, 1017 West
7th Street, Wray, CO, Zip 80758–1420;
tel. 970/332–4811; Daniel Dennis, Administrator

YUMA DISTRICT HOSPITAL, 910 South Main Street,
Yuma, CO, Zip 80759–3098, Mailing Address:
P.O. Box 306, Zip 80759–0306;
tel. 970/848–5405; Timothy F. Reardon,
FACHE, Chief Executive Officer

KIDSMART HEALTH PARTNERS
600 Grant Street, Suite 404, Denver, CO
80203; tel. 303/839–1552; Doug Paschal,
COO

CHILDREN'S HOSPITAL, 1056 East 19th Avenue,
Denver, CO, Zip 80218–1088;
tel. 303/861–8888; Doris J. Biester, Jr., Chief
Executive Officer

QUORUM HEALTH NETWORK OF COLORADO
4450 Arapahoe Avenue, Suite 200, Boulder,
CO 80303; tel. 303/440–5511; John Leavitt,
Executive Director

GRAND RIVER HOSPITAL DISTRICT, 701 East Fifth
Street, Rifle, CO, Zip 81650–2970, Mailing
Address: P.O. Box 912, Zip 81650–0912;
tel. 970/625–1510; Edwin A. Gast,
Administrator

PIONEERS HOSPITAL OF RIO BLANCO COUNTY, 345
Cleveland Street, Meeker, CO, Zip 81641–0000;
tel. 970/878–5047; Thomas E. Lake, Chief
Executive Officer

CONNECTICUT

CONNECTICUT HEALTH SYSTEM, INC.
80 Seymour Street, Hartford, CT 06102–5037;
tel. 860/545–5000; John Meehan, President &
Chief Executive Officer

GAYLORD HOSPITAL, Gaylord Farm Road, Wallingford,
CT, Zip 06492, Mailing Address: P.O. Box 400,
Zip 06492; tel. 203/284–2800; Paul H.
Johnson, President and Chief Executive Officer

HOSPITAL OF SAINT RAPHAEL, 1450 Chapel Street,
New Haven, CT, Zip 06511–1450;
tel. 203/789–3000; James J. Cullen, President

EASTERN CONNECTICUT HEALTH NETWORK
71 Haynes Street, Manchester, CT 06040;
tel. 203/872–0501; Michael Gallacher,
President

MANCHESTER MEMORIAL HOSPITAL, 71 Haynes
Street, Manchester, CT, Zip 06040–4188;
tel. 860/646–1222

ROCKVILLE GENERAL HOSPITAL, 31 Union Street,
Vernon Rockville, CT, Zip 06066–3160;
tel. 860/872–0501

SAINT FRANCIS PHYSICIAN HOSPITAL ORGANIZATION
1000 Asylum Avenue – Suite 3214, Hartford,
CT 06105–1299; tel. 860/714–5606; Jess
Kupec, PHO President

SAINT FRANCIS HOSPITAL AND MEDICAL CENTER,
114 Woodland Street, Hartford, CT,
Zip 06105–1299; tel. 860/714–4000; David
D'Eramo, President and Chief Executive Officer

SAINT MARY'S HOSPITAL
56 Franklin Street, Waterbury, CT 06706;
tel. 203/597–3238; Jack Dobbins, Executive
Vice President

SAINT FRANCIS HOSPITAL AND MEDICAL CENTER,
114 Woodland Street, Hartford, CT,
Zip 06105–1299; tel. 860/714–4000; David
D'Eramo, President and Chief Executive Officer

ST. MARY'S HOSPITAL, 56 Franklin Street, Waterbury,
CT, Zip 06706–1200; tel. 203/574–6000;
Sister Marguerite Waite, President and Chief
Executive Officer

DELAWARE

MEDICAL CENTER OF DELAWARE FOUNDATION
P.O. Box 1668, Wilmington, DE 19899;
tel. 302/733–1321; James F. Caldas,
Executive Vice President

CHRISTIANA HOSPITAL, 4755 Ogletown–Stanton
Road, Newark, DE, Zip 19718;
tel. 302/733–1000; Charles M. Smith, M.D.,
President and Chief Executive Officer

NANTICOKE HEALTH SERVICES
801 Middleford Road, Seaford, DE 19973;
tel. 302/629–6611; Edward H. Hancock,
President

NANTICOKE MEMORIAL HOSPITAL, 801 Middleford
Road, Seaford, DE, Zip 19973–3698;
tel. 302/629–6611; Edward H. Hancock,
President

DISTRICT OF COLUMBIA

MEDLANTIC HEALTHCARE GROUP
100 Irving Street, NorthWest, Washington, DC
20010; tel. 202/877–7800; Ken Samet,
President

NATIONAL REHABILITATION HOSPITAL, 102 Irving
Street N.W., Washington, DC, Zip 20010–2949;
tel. 202/877–1000; Edward A. Eckenhoff,
President and Chief Executive Officer

WASHINGTON HOSPITAL CENTER, 110 Irving Street
N.W., Washington, DC, Zip 20010–2975;
tel. 202/877–7000; Kenneth A. Samet,
President

FLORIDA

ADVENTIST HEALTH SYSTEM
111 North Orlando Avenue, Winter Park, FL
32789–3675; tel. 407/647–4400; Mardian J.
Blair, President

EAST PASCO MEDICAL CENTER, 7050 Gall
Boulevard, Zephyrhills, FL, Zip 33541–1399;
tel. 813/788–0411; Paul Michael Norman,
President

FLORIDA HOSPITAL, 601 East Rollins Street, Orlando,
FL, Zip 32803–1489; tel. 407/896–6611;
Thomas L. Werner, President

FLORIDA HOSPITAL HEARTLAND DIVISION, 4200
Sun'n Lake Boulevard, Sebring, FL, Zip 33872,
Mailing Address: P.O. Box 9400, Zip 33872;
tel. 941/314–4466; John R. Harding, President
and Chief Executive Officer

Section B

FLORIDA HOSPITAL WATERMAN, 201 North Eustis Street, Eustis, FL, Zip 32726–3488, Mailing Address: P.O. Box B., Zip 32727–0377; tel. 352/589–3333; Kenneth R. Mattison, President and Chief Executive Officer

ALLEGANY HEALTH SYSTEM
6200 Courtney Campbell Causeway, Tampa, FL 33607–1458; tel. 813/281–9098; Debbie Coakley, Network Contact

ST. ANTHONY'S HOSPITAL, 1200 Seventh Avenue North, Saint Petersburg, FL, Zip 33705–1388, Mailing Address: P.O. Box 12588, Zip 33733–2588; tel. 813/825–1100; Sue G. Brody, President and Chief Executive Officer

ST. JOSEPH'S HOSPITAL, 3001 West Martin Luther King Boulevard, Tampa, FL, Zip 33607–6387, Mailing Address: P.O. Box 4227, Zip 33677–4227; tel. 813/870–4000; Isaac Mallah, President and Chief Executive Officer

ST. MARY'S HOSPITAL, 901 45th Street, West Palm Beach, FL, Zip 33407–2495, Mailing Address: P.O. Box 24620, Zip 33416–4620; tel. 561/844–6300; Phillip C. Dutcher, President and Chief Executive Officer

BAPTIST HEALTH CARE, INC.
P.O. Box 17500, Pensacola, FL 32501; tel. 850/469–2338; David Sjoberg, Vice President of Planning

ATMORE COMMUNITY HOSPITAL, 401 Medical Park Drive, Atmore, AL, Zip 36502–3091; tel. 334/368–2500; Robert E. Gowing, Interim Administrator

BAPTIST HOSPITAL, 1000 West Moreno, Pensacola, FL, Zip 32501–2393, Mailing Address: P.O. Box 17500, Zip 32522–7500; tel. 850/469–2313; Quinton Studer, President

D. W. MCMILLAN MEMORIAL HOSPITAL, 1301 Belleville Avenue, Brewton, AL, Zip 36426–1306, Mailing Address: P.O. Box 908, Zip 36427–0908; tel. 334/867–8061; Phillip L. Parker, Administrator

GULF BREEZE HOSPITAL, 1110 Gulf Breeze Parkway, Gulf Breeze, FL, Zip 32561, Mailing Address: P.O. Box 159, Zip 32562; tel. 850/934–2000; Richard C. Fulford, Administrator

JAY HOSPITAL, 221 South Alabama Street, Jay, FL, Zip 32565–1070, Mailing Address: P.O. Box 397, Zip 32565–0397; tel. 850/675–8000; Robert E. Gowing, Administrator

MIZELL MEMORIAL HOSPITAL, 702 Main Street, Opp, AL, Zip 36467–1626, Mailing Address: P.O. Box 1010, Zip 36467–1010; tel. 334/493–3541; Allen Foster, Administrator

BAPTIST/ST. VINCENT'S HEALTH SYSTEM
1301 Riverplace Boulevard, Jacksonville, FL 32207; tel. 904/202–4000; William C. Mason, Chief Executive Officer

BAPTIST MEDICAL CENTER, 800 Prudential Drive, Jacksonville, FL, Zip 32207–8203; tel. 904/202–2000; A. Hugh Greene, Executive Vice President and Chief Operating Officer

BAPTIST MEDICAL CENTER–BEACHES, 1350 13th Avenue South, Jacksonville Beach, FL, Zip 32250–3205; tel. 904/247–2900; Joseph Mitrick, Administrator

BAPTIST MEDICAL CENTER–NASSAU, 1250 South 18th Street, Fernandina Beach, FL, Zip 32034–3098; tel. 904/321–3501; Jim L. Mayo, Administrator

ST. VINCENT'S MEDICAL CENTER, 1800 Barrs Street, Jacksonville, FL, Zip 32204–2982, Mailing Address: P.O. Box 2982, Zip 32203–2982; tel. 904/308–7300; John W. Logue, Executive Vice President and Chief Operating Officer

BAYCARE HEALTH NETWORK, INC.
17757 U.S. Highway 19 North, Suite 100, Clearwater, FL 34624; tel. 813/535–3335; John K. Vretas, President & Chief Executive Officer

ALL CHILDREN'S HOSPITAL, 801 Sixth Street South, Saint Petersburg, FL, Zip 33701–4899; tel. 813/898–7451; J. Dennis Sexton, President

BAYFRONT MEDICAL CENTER, 701 Sixth Street South, Saint Petersburg, FL, Zip 33701–4891; tel. 813/823–1234; Sue G. Brody, President and Chief Executive Officer

BROOKSVILLE REGIONAL HOSPITAL, 55 Ponce De Leon Boulevard, Brooksville, FL, Zip 34601–0037, Mailing Address: P.O. Box 37, Zip 34605–0037; tel. 352/796–5111; Robert Foreman, Associate Administrator

EAST PASCO MEDICAL CENTER, 7050 Gall Boulevard, Zephyrhills, FL, Zip 33541–1399; tel. 813/788–0411; Paul Michael Norman, President

MANATEE MEMORIAL HOSPITAL, 206 Second Street East, Bradenton, FL, Zip 34208–1000; tel. 941/746–5111; Michael Marquez, Chief Executive Officer

MEASE COUNTRYSIDE HOSPITAL, 3231 McMullen–Booth Road, Safety Harbor, FL, Zip 34695–1098, Mailing Address: P.O. 1098, Zip 34695–1098; tel. 813/725–6111; James A. Pfeiffer, Chief Administrative Officer

MEASE HOSPITAL DUNEDIN, 601 Main Street, Dunedin, FL, Zip 34698–5891, Mailing Address: P.O. Box 760, Zip 34697–0760; tel. 813/733–1111; James A. Pfeiffer, Vice President and Chief Operating Officer

MORTON PLANT HOSPITAL, 323 Jeffords Street, Clearwater, FL, Zip 34616–3892, Mailing Address: Box 210, Zip 34617–0210; tel. 813/462–7000; Frank V. Murphy, III, President and Chief Executive Officer

NORTH BAY MEDICAL CENTER, 6600 Madison Street, New Port Richey, FL, Zip 34652–1900; tel. 813/842–8468; Dennis A. Taylor, Administrator

SOUTH FLORIDA BAPTIST HOSPITAL, 301 North Alexander Street, Plant City, FL, Zip 33566–9058, Mailing Address: Drawer H., Zip 33564–9058; tel. 813/757–1200; William H. Anderson, Administrator and Chief Executive Officer

SPRING HILL REGIONAL HOSPITAL, 10461 Quality Drive, Spring Hill, FL, Zip 34609; tel. 352/688–8200; Sonia I. Gonzalez, R.N., Chief Operating Officer

ST. ANTHONY'S HOSPITAL, 1200 Seventh Avenue North, Saint Petersburg, FL, Zip 33705–1388, Mailing Address: P.O. Box 12588, Zip 33733–2588; tel. 813/825–1100; Sue G. Brody, President and Chief Executive Officer

ST. JOSEPH'S HOSPITAL, 3001 West Martin Luther King Boulevard, Tampa, FL, Zip 33607–6387, Mailing Address: P.O. Box 4227, Zip 33677–4227; tel. 813/870–4000; Isaac Mallah, President and Chief Executive Officer

UNIVERSITY COMMUNITY HOSPITAL, 3100 East Fletcher Avenue, Tampa, FL, Zip 33613–4688; tel. 813/971–6000; Norman V. Stein, President

UNIVERSITY COMMUNITY HOSPITAL–CARROLLWOOD, 7171 North Dale Mabry Highway, Tampa, FL, Zip 33614–2699; tel. 813/558–8001; Larry J. Archbell, Vice President Operations

COLUMBIA/HCA EAST FLORIDA DIVISION
2111 Glenwood Drive, Suite 100, Winter Park, FL 32792–3309; tel. 407/646–7505; Joseph R. Swedish, President

AVENTURA HOSPITAL AND MEDICAL CENTER, 20900 Biscayne Boulevard, Miami, FL, Zip 33180–1407; tel. 305/682–7100; Davide M. Carbone, Chief Executive Officer

CEDARS MEDICAL CENTER, 1400 N.W. 12th Avenue, Miami, FL, Zip 33136–1003; tel. 305/325–5511; Ralph A. Aleman, Chief Executive Officer

CENTRAL FLORIDA REGIONAL HOSPITAL, 1401 West Seminole Boulevard, Sanford, FL, Zip 32771–6764; tel. 407/321–4500; Doug Sills, President and Chief Executive Officer

COLUMBIA MEDICAL CENTER–PORT ST. LUCIE, 1800 S.E. Tiffany Avenue, Port St. Lucie, FL, Zip 34952–7580; tel. 561/335–4000; Michael P. Joyce, President and Chief Executive Officer

COLUMBIA NORTHWEST MEDICAL CENTER, 2801 North State Road 7, Pompano Beach, FL, Zip 33063–5727, Mailing Address: P.O. Box 639002, Margate, Zip 33063–9002; tel. 954/978–4000; Gina Melby, Chief Executive Officer

DEERING HOSPITAL, 9333 S.W. 152nd Street, Miami, FL, Zip 33157–1780; tel. 305/256–5100; Jude Torchia, Chief Executive Officer

KENDALL MEDICAL CENTER, 11750 Bird Road, Miami, FL, Zip 33175–3530; tel. 305/223–3000; Victor Maya, Chief Executive Officer

LAWNWOOD REGIONAL MEDICAL CENTER, 1700 South 23rd Street, Fort Pierce, FL, Zip 34950–0188; tel. 561/461–4000; Gary Cantrell, President and Chief Executive Officer

LUCERNE MEDICAL CENTER, 818 Main Lane, Orlando, FL, Zip 32801; tel. 407/649–6111; Rick O'Connell, Chief Executive Officer

MEMORIAL HOSPITAL PEMBROKE, 2301 University Drive, Pembroke Pines, FL, Zip 33024; tel. 954/962–9650; J. E. Piriz, Administrator

MIAMI HEART INSTITUTE AND MEDICAL CENTER, 4701 Meridian Avenue, Miami, FL, Zip 33140–2910; tel. 305/674–3114; Tim Parker, Chief Executive Officer

OSCEOLA MEDICAL CENTER, 700 West Oak Street, Kissimmee, FL, Zip 34741–4996, Mailing Address: P.O. Box 422589, Zip 34742–2589; tel. 407/846–2266; E. Tim Cook, Chief Executive Officer

PALMS WEST HOSPITAL, 13001 Southern Boulevard, Loxahatchee, FL, Zip 33470–1150; tel. 561/798–3300; Alex M. Marceline, Chief Executive Officer

PLANTATION GENERAL HOSPITAL, 401 N.W. 42nd Avenue, Plantation, FL, Zip 33317–2882; tel. 954/587–5010; Anthony M. Degina, Jr., Chief Executive Officer

RAULERSON HOSPITAL, 1796 Highway 441 North, Okeechobee, FL, Zip 34972, Mailing Address: P.O. Box 1307, Zip 34973–1307; tel. 941/763–2151; Frank Irby, Chief Executive Officer

UNIVERSITY HOSPITAL AND MEDICAL CENTER, 7201 North University Drive, Tamarac, FL, Zip 33321–2996; tel. 954/721–2200; James A. Cruickshank, Chief Executive Officer

WESTSIDE REGIONAL MEDICAL CENTER, 8201 West Broward Boulevard, Plantation, FL, Zip 33324–9937; tel. 954/473–6600; Michael G. Joseph, Chief Executive Officer

WINTER PARK MEMORIAL HOSPITAL, 200 North Lakemont Avenue, Winter Park, FL, Zip 32792–3273; tel. 407/646–7000; Douglas P. DeGraaf, Chief Executive Officer

COLUMBIA/HCA NORTH FLORIDA DIVISION
1705 Metropolitan Boulevard, Suite 201, Tallahassee, FL 32308; tel. 850/253–0343; Jim Slack, President

FORT WALTON BEACH MEDICAL CENTER, 1000 Mar–Walt Drive, Fort Walton Beach, FL, Zip 32547–6795; tel. 850/862–1111; Wayne Campbell, Chief Executive Officer

GULF COAST MEDICAL CENTER, 449 West 23rd Street, Panama City, FL, Zip 32405–4593, Mailing Address: P.O. Box 15309, Zip 32406–5309; tel. 850/769–8341; Donald E. Butts, Chief Executive Officer

MEMORIAL HOSPITAL OF JACKSONVILLE, 3625 University Boulevard South, Jacksonville, FL, Zip 32216–4240, Mailing Address: P.O. Box 16325, Zip 32216–6325; tel. 904/399–6111; H. Rex Etheredge, President and Chief Executive Officer

NORTH FLORIDA REGIONAL MEDICAL CENTER, 6500 Newberry Road, Gainesville, FL, Zip 32605–4392, Mailing Address: P.O. Box 147006, Zip 32614–7006; tel. 352/333–4000; Brian C. Robinson, Chief Executive Officer

OCALA REGIONAL MEDICAL CENTER, 1431 S.W. First Avenue, Ocala, FL, Zip 34474–4058, Mailing Address: P.O. Box 2200, Zip 34478–2200; tel. 352/401–1000; Stephen Mahan, Chief Executive Officer

ORANGE PARK MEDICAL CENTER, 2001 Kingsley Avenue, Orange Park, FL, Zip 32073–5156; tel. 904/276–8500; Robert M. Krieger, Chief Executive Officer

PUTNAM COMMUNITY MEDICAL CENTER, Highway 20 West, Palatka, FL, Zip 32177, Mailing Address: P.O. Box 778, Zip 32178–0778; tel. 904/328–5711; David Whalen, President and Chief Executive Officer

SPECIALTY HOSPITAL JACKSONVILLE, 4901 Richard Street, Jacksonville, FL, Zip 32207; tel. 904/737–3120; W. Raymond C. Ford, Chief Executive Officer

TALLAHASSEE COMMUNITY HOSPITAL, 2626 Capital Medical Boulevard, Tallahassee, FL, Zip 32308–4499; tel. 850/656–5000; Thomas Paul Pemberton, Chief Executive Officer

TWIN CITIES HOSPITAL, 2190 Highway 85 North, Niceville, FL, Zip 32578–1045; tel. 850/678–4131; David L. Blair, President

WEST FLORIDA REGIONAL MEDICAL CENTER, 8383 North Davis Highway, Pensacola, FL, Zip 32514–6088, Mailing Address: P.O. Box 18900, Zip 32523–8900; tel. 850/494–4000; Stephen Brandt, President and Chief Executive Officer

COLUMBIA/HCA WEST FLORIDA DIVISION
6200 Courtney Campbell Causeway, Tampa, FL 33607; tel. 813/286–6000; J. Daniel Miller, President

BARTOW MEMORIAL HOSPITAL, 1239 East Main Street, Bartow, FL, Zip 33830–5005, Mailing Address: Box 1050, Zip 33830–1050; tel. 941/533–8111; Thomas C. Mathews, Administrator

BLAKE MEDICAL CENTER, 2020 59th Street West, Bradenton, FL, Zip 34209–4669, Mailing Address: P.O. Box 25004, Zip 34206–5004; tel. 941/792–6611; Lindell W. Orr, Chief Executive Officer

BRANDON REGIONAL MEDICAL CENTER, 119 Oakfield Drive, Brandon, FL, Zip 33511–5799; tel. 813/681–5551; Michael M. Fencel, Chief Executive Officer

CLEARWATER COMMUNITY HOSPITAL, 1521 Druid Road East, Clearwater, FL, Zip 34616–6193, Mailing Address: P.O. Box 9068, Zip 34618–9068; tel. 813/447–4571; Betsy Bomar, Chief Executive Officer

COMMUNITY HOSPITAL OF NEW PORT RICHEY, 5637 Marine Parkway, New Port Richey, FL, Zip 34652–4331, Mailing Address: P.O. Box 996, Zip 34656–0996; tel. 813/848–1733; Andrew Oravec, Jr., Administrator

DOCTORS HOSPITAL OF SARASOTA, 5731 Bee Ridge Road, Sarasota, FL, Zip 34233–5056; tel. 941/342–1100; William C. Lievense, President and Chief Executive Officer

EAST POINTE HOSPITAL, 1500 Lee Boulevard, Lehigh Acres, FL, Zip 33936–4897; tel. 941/369–2101; Valerie A. Jackson, Chief Executive Officer

EDWARD WHITE HOSPITAL, 2323 Ninth Avenue North, Saint Petersburg, FL, Zip 33713–6898, Mailing Address: P.O. Box 12018, Zip 33733–2018; tel. 813/323–1111; Barry S. Stokes, President and Chief Executive Officer

ENGLEWOOD COMMUNITY HOSPITAL, 700 Medical Boulevard, Englewood, FL, Zip 34223–3978; tel. 941/475–6571; Terry L. Moore, Chief Executive Officer

FAWCETT MEMORIAL HOSPITAL, 21298 Olean Boulevard, Port Charlotte, FL, Zip 33952–6765, Mailing Address: P.O. Box 4028, Punta Gorda, Zip 33949–4028; tel. 941/629–1181; Steve Dobbs, Chief Executive Officer

GULF COAST HOSPITAL, 13681 Doctors Way, Fort Myers, FL, Zip 33912–4309; tel. 941/768–5000; Valerie A. Jackson, Chief Executive Officer

LARGO MEDICAL CENTER, 201 14th Street S.W., Largo, FL, Zip 33770–3133, Mailing Address: P.O. Box 2905, Zip 33779–2905; tel. 813/588–5200; Thomas L. Herron, FACHE, President and Chief Executive Officer

NORTHSIDE HOSPITAL AND HEART INSTITUTE, 6000 49th Street North, Saint Petersburg, FL, Zip 33709–2145; tel. 813/521–4411; Bradley K. Grover, Sr., FACHE, Chief Executive Officer

OAK HILL HOSPITAL, 11375 Cortez Boulevard, Spring Hill, FL, Zip 34611, Mailing Address: P.O. Box 5300, Zip 34611–5300; tel. 352/596–6632; Jay Finnegan, Chief Executive Officer

REGIONAL MEDICAL CENTER–BAYONET POINT, 14000 Fivay Road, Hudson, FL, Zip 34667–7199; tel. 813/863–2411; Don Griffin, Ph.D., President and Chief Executive Officer

SOUTH BAY HOSPITAL, 4016 State Road 674, Sun City Center, FL, Zip 33573–5298; tel. 813/634–3301; Hal Muetzel, Chief Executive Officer

ST. PETERSBURG MEDICAL CENTER, 6500 38th Avenue North, Saint Petersburg, FL, Zip 33710–1629; tel. 813/384–1414; Bradley K. Grover, Sr., FACHE, President and Chief Executive Officer

WEST FLORIDA REGIONAL MEDICAL CENTER, 8383 North Davis Highway, Pensacola, FL, Zip 32514–6088, Mailing Address: P.O. Box 18900, Zip 32523–8900; tel. 850/494–4000; Stephen Brandt, President and Chief Executive Officer

COMMUNITY HEALTH NETWORK OF INDIAN RIVER COUNTY
1000 36th Street, Vero Beach, FL 32960; tel. 561/563–4668; Michael J. O'Grady, CEO & President

INDIAN RIVER MEMORIAL HOSPITAL, 1000 36th Street, Vero Beach, FL, Zip 32960–6592; tel. 561/567–4311; Michael J. O'Grady, Jr., President and Chief Executive Officer

DIMENSIONS HEALTH/BAPTIST HEALTH SYSTEMS
8900 North Kendall Drive, Miami, FL 33176; tel. 305/596–1960; Brian Keeley, President

BAPTIST HOSPITAL OF MIAMI, 8900 North Kendall Drive, Miami, FL, Zip 33176–2197; tel. 305/596–6503; Fred M. Messing, Chief Executive Officer

HOMESTEAD HOSPITAL, 160 N.W. 13th Street, Homestead, FL, Zip 33030–4299; tel. 305/248–3232; Bo Boulenger, Chief Executive Officer

MARINERS HOSPITAL, 50 High Point Road, Tavernier, FL, Zip 33070–2031; tel. 305/852–4418; Robert H. Luse, Chief Executive Officer

SOUTH MIAMI HOSPITAL, 6200 S.W. 73rd Street, Miami, FL, Zip 33143–9990; tel. 305/661–4611; D. Wayne Brackin, Chief Executive Officer

FLORIDA HEALTH CHOICE
5300 West Atlantic Avenue, Suite 302, Del Ray Beach, FL 33486; tel. 407/496–0505; D. Nat West, President

BETHESDA MEMORIAL HOSPITAL, 2815 South Seacrest Boulevard, Boynton Beach, FL, Zip 33435–7995; tel. 561/737–7733; Robert B. Hill, President

BOCA RATON COMMUNITY HOSPITAL, 800 Meadows Road, Boca Raton, FL, Zip 33486–2368; tel. 561/393–4002; Randolph J. Pierce, President and Chief Executive Officer

GOOD SAMARITAN MEDICAL CENTER, Flagler Drive at Palm Beach Lakes Boulevard, West Palm Beach, FL, Zip 33401–3499; tel. 561/655–5511; Phillip C. Dutcher, Interim President

HOLY CROSS HOSPITAL, 4725 North Federal Highway, Fort Lauderdale, FL, Zip 33308–4668, Mailing Address: P.O. Box 23460, Zip 33307–3460; tel. 954/771–8000; John C. Johnson, Chief Executive Officer

MARTIN MEMORIAL HEALTH SYSTEMS, 300 S.E. Hospital Drive, Stuart, FL, Zip 34994, Mailing Address: P.O. Box 9010, Zip 34995–9010; tel. 561/223–5945; Richmond M. Harman, President and Chief Executive Officer

MEMORIAL REGIONAL HOSPITAL, 3501 Johnson Street, Hollywood, FL, Zip 33021–5421; tel. 954/987–2000; C. Kennon Hetlage, Administrator

ST. MARY'S HOSPITAL, 901 45th Street, West Palm Beach, FL, Zip 33407–2495, Mailing Address: P.O. Box 24620, Zip 33416–4620; tel. 561/844–6300; Phillip C. Dutcher, President and Chief Executive Officer

FLORIDA HOSPITAL HEALTH NETWORK
601 East Rollins Street, Orlando, FL 32803; tel. 407/896–6611; Thomas L. Werner, President

FLORIDA HOSPITAL, 601 East Rollins Street, Orlando, FL, Zip 32803–1489; tel. 407/896–6611; Thomas L. Werner, President

FLORIDA HOSPITAL WATERMAN, 201 North Eustis Street, Eustis, FL, Zip 32726–3488, Mailing Address: P.O. Box B., Zip 32727–0377; tel. 352/589–3333; Kenneth R. Mattison, President and Chief Executive Officer

GENESIS HEALTH, INC.
3627 University Boulevard South, Jacksonville, FL 32216; tel. 904/391–1201; Douglas Baer, Vice President

GENESIS REHABILITATION HOSPITAL, 3599 University Boulevard South, Jacksonville, FL, Zip 32216–4211, Mailing Address: P.O. Box 16406, Zip 32245–6406; tel. 904/858–7600; Stephen K. Wilson, President and Chief Executive Officer

HOLY CROSS HEALTH MINISTRIES
4725 North Federal Highway, Ft Lauderdale, FL 33308; tel. 954/771–8000; John Johnson, CEO

HOLY CROSS HOSPITAL, 4725 North Federal Highway, Fort Lauderdale, FL, Zip 33308–4668, Mailing Address: P.O. Box 23460, Zip 33307–3460; tel. 954/771–8000; John C. Johnson, Chief Executive Officer

LAKE OKEECHOBEE RURAL HEALTH NETWORK
1500 NorthWest Avenue L., Belle Glade, FL 33430; tel. 561/993–4221; Andrew Behrman, Executive Director

EVERGLADES REGIONAL MEDICAL CENTER, 200 South Barfield Highway, Pahokee, FL, Zip 33476–1897; tel. 407/924–5200; Donald A. Anderson, President and Chief Executive Officer

GLADES GENERAL HOSPITAL, 1201 South Main Street, Belle Glade, FL, Zip 33430–4911; tel. 561/996–6571; Gene Faile, Chief Executive Officer

HENDRY REGIONAL MEDICAL CENTER, 500 West Sugarland Highway, Clewiston, FL, Zip 33440–3094; tel. 941/983–9121; J. Rudy Reinhardt, Administrator

J. F. K. MEDICAL CENTER, 5301 South Congress Avenue, Atlantis, FL, Zip 33462–1197; tel. 561/965–7300; Phillip D. Robinson, Chief Executive Officer

MARTIN MEMORIAL HEALTH SYSTEMS, 300 S.E. Hospital Drive, Stuart, FL, Zip 34994, Mailing Address: P.O. Box 9010, Zip 34995–9010; tel. 561/223–5945; Richmond M. Harman, President and Chief Executive Officer

ST. MARY'S HOSPITAL, 901 45th Street, West Palm Beach, FL, Zip 33407–2495, Mailing Address: P.O. Box 24620, Zip 33416–4620; tel. 561/844–6300; Phillip C. Dutcher, President and Chief Executive Officer

MED CONNECT
4901 NorthWest 17th Way, Suite 304, Ft Lauderdale, FL 33309; tel. 305/938–9755; Bill Gil, Chief Executive Officer

FLORIDA MEDICAL CENTER HOSPITAL, 5000 West Oakland Park Boulevard, Fort Lauderdale, FL, Zip 33313–1585; tel. 954/735–6000; Denny De Narvaez, Chief Executive Officer

GOOD SAMARITAN MEDICAL CENTER, Flagler Drive at Palm Beach Lakes Boulevard, West Palm Beach, FL, Zip 33401–3499; tel. 561/655–5511; Phillip C. Dutcher, Interim President

NORTH RIDGE MEDICAL CENTER, 5757 North Dixie Highway, Fort Lauderdale, FL, Zip 33334–4182, Mailing Address: P.O. Box 23160, Zip 33307; tel. 954/776–6000; Emil P. Miller, Chief Executive Officer

PALM BEACH GARDENS MEDICAL CENTER, 3360 Burns Road, Palm Beach Gardens, FL, Zip 33410–4304; tel. 561/622–1411; Clint Matthews, Chief Executive Officer

Section B

PALMS WEST HOSPITAL, 13001 Southern Boulevard, Loxahatchee, FL, Zip 33470–1150; tel. 561/798–3300; Alex M. Marceline, Chief Executive Officer

PLANTATION GENERAL HOSPITAL, 401 N.W. 42nd Avenue, Plantation, FL, Zip 33317–2882; tel. 954/587–5010; Anthony M. Degina, Jr., Chief Executive Officer

ST. MARY'S HOSPITAL, 901 45th Street, West Palm Beach, FL, Zip 33407–2495, Mailing Address: P.O. Box 24620, Zip 33416–4620; tel. 561/844–6300; Phillip C. Dutcher, President and Chief Executive Officer

MEMORIAL HEALTHCARE SYSTEM
3501 Johnson Street, Hollywood, FL 33021; tel. 954/967–2918; Paul Betz, Administrative Resident

MEMORIAL HOSPITAL PEMBROKE, 2301 University Drive, Pembroke Pines, FL, Zip 33024; tel. 954/962–9650; J. E. Piriz, Administrator

MEMORIAL HOSPITAL WEST, 703 North Flamingo Road, Pembroke Pines, FL, Zip 33028; tel. 954/436–5000; Zeff Ross, Administrator

MEMORIAL REGIONAL HOSPITAL, 3501 Johnson Street, Hollywood, FL, Zip 33021–5421; tel. 954/987–2000; C. Kennon Hetlage, Administrator

METHODIST HEALTH SYSTEMS
580 West Eighth Street, Jacksonville, FL 32209; tel. 904/798–8000; Marcus Drewa, President

METHODIST MEDICAL CENTER, 580 West Eighth Street, Jacksonville, FL, Zip 32209–6553; tel. 904/798–8000; Marcus E. Drewa, President and Chief Executive Officer

MID–FLORIDA MEDICAL SERVICES, INC.
200 Avenue 'F', Northeast, Winter Haven, FL 33881; tel. 941/293–1121; Lance Anastasio, President

LAKE WALES MEDICAL CENTERS, 410 South 11th Street, Lake Wales, FL, Zip 33853–4256, Mailing Address: P.O. Box 3460, Zip 33859–3460; tel. 941/676–1433; Joe M. Connell, Chief Executive Officer

WINTER HAVEN HOSPITAL, 200 Avenue F. N.E., Winter Haven, FL, Zip 33881–4193; tel. 941/297–1899; Lance W. Anastasio, President

MORTON PLANT MEASE HEALTH CARE
833 Milwaukee Avenue, Dunedin, FL 34698; tel. 813/734–6498; Ginger Lay, Director, Managed Care

MEASE COUNTRYSIDE HOSPITAL, 3231 McMullen–Booth Road, Safety Harbor, FL, Zip 34695–1098, Mailing Address: P.O. 1098, Zip 34695–1098; tel. 813/725–6111; James A. Pfeiffer, Chief Administrative Officer

MEASE HOSPITAL DUNEDIN, 601 Main Street, Dunedin, FL, Zip 34698–5891, Mailing Address: P.O. Box 760, Zip 34697–0760; tel. 813/733–1111; James A. Pfeiffer, Vice President and Chief Operating Officer

MORTON PLANT HOSPITAL, 323 Jeffords Street, Clearwater, FL, Zip 34616–3892, Mailing Address: Box 210, Zip 34617–0210; tel. 813/462–7000; Frank V. Murphy, III, President and Chief Executive Officer

ORLANDO REGIONAL HEALTHCARE SYSTEM
1414 Kuhl Avenue, Orlando, FL 32806; tel. 407/841–5111; Gary Strack, Chairman & Chief Executive Officer

ORLANDO REGIONAL MEDICAL CENTER, 1414 Kuhl Avenue, Orlando, FL, Zip 32806–2093; tel. 407/841–5111; Abe Lopman, Executive Director

SOUTH LAKE HOSPITAL, 847 Eighth Street, Clermont, FL, Zip 34711–2196; tel. 352/394–4071; Leslie Longacre, Executive Director and Chief Executive Officer

SOUTH SEMINOLE HOSPITAL, 555 West State Road 434, Longwood, FL, Zip 32750–4999; tel. 407/767–1200; Sue Whelan–Williams, Site Administrator

ST. CLOUD HOSPITAL, A DIVISION OF ORLANDO REGIONAL HEALTHCARE SYSTEM, 2906 17th Street, Saint Cloud, FL, Zip 34769–6099; tel. 407/892–2135; Jim Norris, Executive Director

PANHANDLE AREA HEALTH NETWORK
2954–A Penn Avenue, Marianna, FL 32446; tel. 850/482–9298; Lucia Maxwell, Executive Director

CALHOUN–LIBERTY HOSPITAL, 424 Burns Avenue, Blountstown, FL, Zip 32424–1097; tel. 850/674–5411; Josh Plummer, Administrator

CAMPBELLTON GRACEVILLE HOSPITAL, 5429 College Drive, Graceville, FL, Zip 32440; tel. 850/263–4431; Neil Whipkey, Administrator

DOCTORS MEMORIAL HOSPITAL, 401 East Byrd Avenue, Bonifay, FL, Zip 32425–3007, Mailing Address: P.O. Box 188, Zip 32425–0188; tel. 850/547–1120; Dale Larson, Chief Executive Officer

JACKSON HOSPITAL, 4250 Hospital Drive, Marianna, FL, Zip 32446–1939, Mailing Address: P.O. Box 1608, Zip 32447–1608; tel. 850/526–2200; Randy Smith, Interim Administrator

NORTHWEST FLORIDA COMMUNITY HOSPITAL, 1360 Brickyard Road, Chipley, FL, Zip 32428–6303, Mailing Address: P.O. Box 889, Zip 32428–0889; tel. 850/638–1610; Stephen D. Mason, Administrator

TENET SOUTH FLORIDA HEALTH SYSTEM NETWORK
500 West Cypress Creek Road, Suite 370, Fort Lauderdale, FL 33309; tel. 954/351–7757; Don Steigman, Senior Vice President

CORAL GABLES HOSPITAL, 3100 Douglas Road, Coral Gables, FL, Zip 33134–6990; tel. 305/445–8461; Martha Garcia, Chief Executive Officer

DELRAY MEDICAL CENTER, 5352 Linton Boulevard, Delray Beach, FL, Zip 33484–6580; tel. 561/498–4440; Mitchell S. Feldman, Chief Executive Officer

FAIR OAKS HOSPITAL, 5440 Linton Avenue, Delray Beach, FL, Zip 33484–6578; tel. 561/495–1000; Bill Russell, Chief Operating Officer and Administrator

FLORIDA MEDICAL CENTER HOSPITAL, 5000 West Oakland Park Boulevard, Fort Lauderdale, FL, Zip 33313–1585; tel. 954/735–6000; Denny De Narvaez, Chief Executive Officer

HIALEAH HOSPITAL, 651 East 25th Street, Hialeah, FL, Zip 33013–3878; tel. 305/693–6100; Clifford J. Bauer, Chief Executive Officer

HOLLYWOOD MEDICAL CENTER, 3600 Washington Street, Hollywood, FL, Zip 33021–8216; tel. 954/966–4500; Holly Lerner, Chief Executive Officer

NORTH RIDGE MEDICAL CENTER, 5757 North Dixie Highway, Fort Lauderdale, FL, Zip 33334–4182, Mailing Address: P.O. Box 23160, Zip 33307; tel. 954/776–6000; Emil P. Miller, Chief Executive Officer

PALM BEACH GARDENS MEDICAL CENTER, 3360 Burns Road, Palm Beach Gardens, FL, Zip 33410–4304; tel. 561/622–1411; Clint Matthews, Chief Executive Officer

PALMETTO GENERAL HOSPITAL, 2001 West 68th Street, Hialeah, FL, Zip 33016–1898; tel. 305/823–5000; Ron Stern, Chief Executive Officer

PALMS OF PASADENA HOSPITAL, 1501 Pasadena Avenue South, Saint Petersburg, FL, Zip 33707–3798; tel. 813/381–1000; John D. Bartlett, Chief Executive Officer

PARKWAY REGIONAL MEDICAL CENTER, 160 N.W. 170th Street, North Miami Beach, FL, Zip 33169–5576; tel. 305/654–5050; Stephen M. Patz, Chief Executive Officer

TOWN AND COUNTRY HOSPITAL, 6001 Webb Road, Tampa, FL, Zip 33615–3291; tel. 813/885–6666; Charles F. Scott, President

WEST BOCA MEDICAL CENTER, 21644 State Road 7, Boca Raton, FL, Zip 33428–1899; tel. 561/488–8000; Richard Gold, Chief Executive Officer

THE HEALTH ADVANTAGE NETWORK
2111 Glenwood Drive, Suite 202, Winter Park, FL 32792; tel. 407/646–7800; Elizabeth Abely, Network Contact

ATLANTIC MEDICAL CENTER–DAYTONA, 400 North Clyde Morris Boulevard, Daytona Beach, FL, Zip 32114–2770, Mailing Address: P.O. Box 9000, Zip 32120–9000; tel. 904/239–5000; Thomas R. Pentz, Chief Executive Officer

AVENTURA HOSPITAL AND MEDICAL CENTER, 20900 Biscayne Boulevard, Miami, FL, Zip 33180–1407; tel. 305/682–7100; Davide M. Carbone, Chief Executive Officer

BLAKE MEDICAL CENTER, 2020 59th Street West, Bradenton, FL, Zip 34209–4669, Mailing Address: P.O. Box 25004, Zip 34206–5004; tel. 941/792–6611; Lindell W. Orr, Chief Executive Officer

BRANDON REGIONAL MEDICAL CENTER, 119 Oakfield Drive, Brandon, FL, Zip 33511–5799; tel. 813/681–5551; Michael M. Fencel, Chief Executive Officer

CEDARS MEDICAL CENTER, 1400 N.W. 12th Avenue, Miami, FL, Zip 33136–1003; tel. 305/325–5511; Ralph A. Aleman, Chief Executive Officer

CENTRAL FLORIDA REGIONAL HOSPITAL, 1401 West Seminole Boulevard, Sanford, FL, Zip 32771–6764; tel. 407/321–4500; Doug Sills, President and Chief Executive Officer

CLEARWATER COMMUNITY HOSPITAL, 1521 Druid Road East, Clearwater, FL, Zip 34616–6193, Mailing Address: P.O. Box 9068, Zip 34618–9068; tel. 813/447–4571; Betsy Bomar, Chief Executive Officer

COLUMBIA MEDICAL CENTER–PORT ST. LUCIE, 1800 S.E. Tiffany Avenue, Port St. Lucie, FL, Zip 34952–7580; tel. 561/335–4000; Michael P. Joyce, President and Chief Executive Officer

COLUMBIA NORTHWEST MEDICAL CENTER, 2801 North State Road 7, Pompano Beach, FL, Zip 33063–5727, Mailing Address: P.O. Box 639002, Margate, Zip 33063–9002; tel. 954/978–4000; Gina Melby, Chief Executive Officer

COMMUNITY HOSPITAL OF NEW PORT RICHEY, 5637 Marine Parkway, New Port Richey, FL, Zip 34652–4331, Mailing Address: P.O. Box 996, Zip 34656–0996; tel. 813/848–1733; Andrew Oravec, Jr., Administrator

DEERING HOSPITAL, 9333 S.W. 152nd Street, Miami, FL, Zip 33157–1780; tel. 305/256–5100; Jude Torchia, Chief Executive Officer

DOCTORS HOSPITAL OF SARASOTA, 5731 Bee Ridge Road, Sarasota, FL, Zip 34233–5056; tel. 941/342–1100; William C. Lievense, President and Chief Executive Officer

EAST POINTE HOSPITAL, 1500 Lee Boulevard, Lehigh Acres, FL, Zip 33936–4897; tel. 941/369–2101; Valerie A. Jackson, Chief Executive Officer

EDWARD WHITE HOSPITAL, 2323 Ninth Avenue North, Saint Petersburg, FL, Zip 33713–6898, Mailing Address: P.O. Box 12018, Zip 33733–2018; tel. 813/323–1111; Barry S. Stokes, President and Chief Executive Officer

ENGLEWOOD COMMUNITY HOSPITAL, 700 Medical Boulevard, Englewood, FL, Zip 34223–3978; tel. 941/475–6571; Terry L. Moore, Chief Executive Officer

FAWCETT MEMORIAL HOSPITAL, 21298 Olean Boulevard, Port Charlotte, FL, Zip 33952–6765, Mailing Address: P.O. Box 4028, Punta Gorda, Zip 33949–4028; tel. 941/629–1181; Steve Dobbs, Chief Executive Officer

FORT WALTON BEACH MEDICAL CENTER, 1000 Mar–Walt Drive, Fort Walton Beach, FL, Zip 32547–6795; tel. 850/862–1111; Wayne Campbell, Chief Executive Officer

GULF COAST HOSPITAL, 13681 Doctors Way, Fort Myers, FL, Zip 33912–4309; tel. 941/768–5000; Valerie A. Jackson, Chief Executive Officer

GULF COAST MEDICAL CENTER, 449 West 23rd Street, Panama City, FL, Zip 32405–4593, Mailing Address: P.O. Box 15309, Zip 32406–5309; tel. 850/769–8341; Donald E. Butts, Chief Executive Officer

HAMILTON MEDICAL CENTER, 506 N.W. Fourth Street, Jasper, FL, Zip 32052; tel. 904/792-7200; Amelia Tuten, R.N., Administrator

KENDALL MEDICAL CENTER, 11750 Bird Road, Miami, FL, Zip 33175-3530; tel. 305/223-3000; Victor Maya, Chief Executive Officer

LAKE CITY MEDICAL CENTER, 1701 West U.S. Highway 90, Lake City, FL, Zip 32055-3718; tel. 904/752-2922; Todd Gallati, Chief Executive Officer

LARGO MEDICAL CENTER, 201 14th Street S.W., Largo, FL, Zip 33770-3133, Mailing Address: P.O. Box 2905, Zip 33779-2905; tel. 813/588-5200; Thomas L. Herron, FACHE, President and Chief Executive Officer

LAWNWOOD REGIONAL MEDICAL CENTER, 1700 South 23rd Street, Fort Pierce, FL, Zip 34950-4168; tel. 561/461-4000; Gary Cantrell, President and Chief Executive Officer

LUCERNE MEDICAL CENTER, 818 Main Lane, Orlando, FL, Zip 32801; tel. 407/649-6111; Rick O'Connell, Chief Executive Officer

MEMORIAL HOSPITAL OF JACKSONVILLE, 3625 University Boulevard South, Jacksonville, FL, Zip 32216-4240, Mailing Address: P.O. Box 16325, Zip 32216-6325; tel. 904/399-6111; H. Rex Etheredge, President and Chief Executive Officer

MEMORIAL HOSPITAL PEMBROKE, 2301 University Drive, Pembroke Pines, FL, Zip 33024; tel. 954/962-9650; J. E. Piriz, Administrator

MIAMI HEART INSTITUTE AND MEDICAL CENTER, 4701 Meridian Avenue, Miami, FL, Zip 33140-2910; tel. 305/674-3114; Tim Parker, Chief Executive Officer

NORTH FLORIDA REGIONAL MEDICAL CENTER, 6500 Newberry Road, Gainesville, FL, Zip 32605-4392, Mailing Address: P.O. Box 147006, Zip 32614-7006; tel. 352/333-4000; Brian C. Robinson, Chief Executive Officer

NORTH OKALOOSA MEDICAL CENTER, 151 Redstone Avenue S.E., Crestview, FL, Zip 32539-6026; tel. 850/689-8100; Roger L. Hall, Chief Executive Officer

NORTHSIDE HOSPITAL AND HEART INSTITUTE, 6000 49th Street North, Saint Petersburg, FL, Zip 33709-2145; tel. 813/521-4411; Bradley K. Grover, Sr., FACHE, Chief Executive Officer

OAK HILL HOSPITAL, 11375 Cortez Boulevard, Spring Hill, FL, Zip 34611, Mailing Address: P.O. Box 5300, Zip 34611-5300; tel. 352/596-6632; Jay Finnegan, Chief Executive Officer

OCALA REGIONAL MEDICAL CENTER, 1431 S.W. First Avenue, Ocala, FL, Zip 34474-4058, Mailing Address: P.O. Box 2200, Zip 34478-2200; tel. 352/401-1000; Stephen Mahan, Chief Executive Officer

ORANGE PARK MEDICAL CENTER, 2001 Kingsley Avenue, Orange Park, FL, Zip 32073-5156; tel. 904/276-8500; Robert M. Krieger, Chief Executive Officer

OSCEOLA MEDICAL CENTER, 700 West Oak Street, Kissimmee, FL, Zip 34741-4996, Mailing Address: P.O. Box 422589, Zip 34742-2589; tel. 407/846-2266; E. Tim Cook, Chief Executive Officer

PALMS WEST HOSPITAL, 13001 Southern Boulevard, Loxahatchee, FL, Zip 33470-1150; tel. 561/798-3300; Alex M. Marceline, Chief Executive Officer

PASCO COMMUNITY HOSPITAL, 13100 Fort King Road, Dade City, FL, Zip 33525-5294; tel. 352/521-1100; Robert Meade, Chief Executive Officer

PLANTATION GENERAL HOSPITAL, 401 N.W. 42nd Avenue, Plantation, FL, Zip 33317-2882; tel. 954/587-5010; Anthony M. Degina, Jr., Chief Executive Officer

PUTNAM COMMUNITY MEDICAL CENTER, Highway 20 West, Palatka, FL, Zip 32177, Mailing Address: P.O. Box 778, Zip 32178-0778; tel. 904/328-5711; David Whalen, President and Chief Executive Officer

RAULERSON HOSPITAL, 1796 Highway 441 North, Okeechobee, FL, Zip 34972, Mailing Address: P.O. Box 1307, Zip 34973-1307; tel. 941/763-2151; Frank Irby, Chief Executive Officer

REGIONAL MEDICAL CENTER-BAYONET POINT, 14000 Fivay Road, Hudson, FL, Zip 34667-7199; tel. 813/863-2411; Don Griffin, Ph.D., President and Chief Executive Officer

SANTA ROSA MEDICAL CENTER, 1450 Berryhill Road, Milton, FL, Zip 32570-4028, Mailing Address: P.O. Box 648, Zip 32572-0648; tel. 850/626-7762; Renate Darby, Interim Chief Executive Officer

SOUTH BAY HOSPITAL, 4016 State Road 674, Sun City Center, FL, Zip 33573-5298; tel. 813/634-3301; Hal Muetzel, Chief Executive Officer

SOUTH SEMINOLE HOSPITAL, 555 West State Road 434, Longwood, FL, Zip 32750-4999; tel. 407/767-1200; Sue Whelan-Williams, Site Administrator

SOUTHWEST FLORIDA REGIONAL MEDICAL CENTER, 2727 Winkler Avenue, Fort Myers, FL, Zip 33901-9396; tel. 941/939-1147; Larry Pieretti, President and Chief Executive Officer

SPECIALTY HOSPITAL JACKSONVILLE, 4901 Richard Street, Jacksonville, FL, Zip 32207; tel. 904/737-3120; W. Raymond C. Ford, Chief Executive Officer

ST. PETERSBURG MEDICAL CENTER, 6500 38th Avenue North, Saint Petersburg, FL, Zip 33710-1629; tel. 813/384-1414; Bradley K. Grover, Sr., FACHE, President and Chief Executive Officer

TALLAHASSEE COMMUNITY HOSPITAL, 2626 Capital Medical Boulevard, Tallahassee, FL, Zip 32308-4499; tel. 850/656-5000; Thomas Paul Pemberton, Chief Executive Officer

TWIN CITIES HOSPITAL, 2190 Highway 85 North, Niceville, FL, Zip 32578-1045; tel. 850/678-4131; David L. Blair, President

UNIVERSITY HOSPITAL AND MEDICAL CENTER, 7201 North University Drive, Tamarac, FL, Zip 33321-2996; tel. 954/721-2200; James A. Cruickshank, Chief Executive Officer

WEST FLORIDA REGIONAL MEDICAL CENTER, 8383 North Davis Highway, Pensacola, FL, Zip 32514-6088, Mailing Address: P.O. Box 18900, Zip 32523-8900; tel. 850/494-4000; Stephen Brandt, President and Chief Executive Officer

WESTSIDE REGIONAL MEDICAL CENTER, 8201 West Broward Boulevard, Plantation, FL, Zip 33324-9937; tel. 954/473-6600; Michael G. Joseph, Chief Executive Officer

WINTER PARK MEMORIAL HOSPITAL, 200 North Lakemont Avenue, Winter Park, FL, Zip 32792-3273; tel. 407/646-7000; Douglas P. DeGraaf, Chief Executive Officer

GEORGIA

CANDLER HEALTH SYSTEM
5353 Reynolds Street, Savannah, GA 31412; tel. 912/692-2018; Thomas E. Hassett, Chief Executive Officer

APPLING HEALTHCARE SYSTEM, 301 East Tollison Street, Baxley, GA, Zip 31513-2898; tel. 912/367-9841; Luther E. Reeves, Chief Executive Officer

CANDLER COUNTY HOSPITAL, Cedar Road, Metter, GA, Zip 30439, Mailing Address: P.O. Box 597, Zip 30439-0597; tel. 912/685-5741; Charles Balkcom, President

CANDLER HOSPITAL, 5353 Reynolds Street, Savannah, GA, Zip 31405-6013, Mailing Address: P.O. Box 9787, Zip 31412-9787; tel. 912/692-6000; Paul P. Hinchey, President and Chief Executive Officer

EFFINGHAM HOSPITAL, 459 Highway 119 South, Springfield, GA, Zip 31329-3021, Mailing Address: P.O. Box 386, Zip 31329-0386; tel. 912/754-6451; W. Scott Burnette, Chief Executive Officer

EMORY UNIVERSITY HOSPITAL, 1364 Clifton Road N.E., Atlanta, GA, Zip 30322-1102; tel. 404/727-7021; John Dunklin Henry, Sr., FACHE, Chief Executive Officer

LIBERTY REGIONAL MEDICAL CENTER, 112 East Oglethorpe Boulevard, Hinesville, GA, Zip 31313-3600, Mailing Address: P.O. Box 919, Zip 31313-0919; tel. 912/369-9400; H. Scott Kroell, Jr., Chief Executive Officer

MEADOWS REGIONAL MEDICAL CENTER, 1703 Meadows Lane, Vidalia, GA, Zip 30474-8915, Mailing Address: P.O. Box 1048, Zip 30474-1048; tel. 912/537-8921; Barry Michael, Chief Executive Officer

WILLINGWAY HOSPITAL, 311 Jones Mill Road, Statesboro, GA, Zip 30458-4765; tel. 912/764-6236; Jimmy Mooney, Chief Executive Officer

CHATTAHOOCHEE HEALTH NETWORK
P.O. Box 3274, Gainesville, GA 30503-3274; tel. 770/503-3552; R. Fleming Weaver, Executive Director

LANIER PARK HOSPITAL, 675 White Sulphur Road, Gainesville, GA, Zip 30505, Mailing Address: P.O. Box 1354, Zip 30503-1354; tel. 770/503-3000; Jerry Fulks, Chief Executive Officer

COLUMBUS REGIONAL HEALTHCARE SYSTEM, INC.
P.O. Box 790, Columbus, GA 31902-0790; tel. 706/660-6110; Larry Sanders, Chairman & Chief Executive Officer

PHENIX REGIONAL HOSPITAL, 1707 21st Avenue, Phenix City, AL, Zip 36867-3753, Mailing Address: P.O. Box 190, Zip 36868-0190; tel. 334/291-8502; Lance B. Duke, FACHE, President and Chief Executive Officer

THE MEDICAL CENTER, 710 Center Street, Columbus, GA, Zip 31902, Mailing Address: P.O. Box 951, Zip 31902-0951; tel. 706/571-1000; Lance B. Duke, FACHE, President and Chief Executive Officer

COMMUNITY HEALTHCARE NETWORK
707 Center Street, Suite 400, Columbus, GA 31902-0790; tel. 706/660-6110; Kevin Sass, Executive Director & Vice President

BAPTIST MERIWETHER HOSPITAL, 5995 Spring Street, Warm Springs, GA, Zip 31830, Mailing Address: P.O. Box 8, Zip 31830-0008; tel. 706/655-3331; William E. Daniel, Administrator

SOUTHWEST GEORGIA REGIONAL MEDICAL CENTER, 109 Randolph Street, Cuthbert, GA, Zip 31740-1338; tel. 912/732-2181; David J. Carney, Chief Executive Officer

THE MEDICAL CENTER, 710 Center Street, Columbus, GA, Zip 31902, Mailing Address: P.O. Box 951, Zip 31902-0951; tel. 706/571-1000; Lance B. Duke, FACHE, President and Chief Executive Officer

WEST GEORGIA HEALTH SYSTEM, 1514 Vernon Road, La Grange, GA, Zip 30240-4199; tel. 706/882-1411; Charles L. Foster, Jr., FACHE, President and Chief Executive Officer

GEORGIA 1ST, INC.
150 E. Ponce de Leon Avenue Suite 490, Decatur, GA 30030; tel. 404/778-4939; Russ Toal, President & Chief Executive Officer

APPLING HEALTHCARE SYSTEM, 301 East Tollison Street, Baxley, GA, Zip 31513-2898; tel. 912/367-9841; Luther E. Reeves, Chief Executive Officer

ATHENS REGIONAL MEDICAL CENTER, 1199 Prince Avenue, Athens, GA, Zip 30606-2793; tel. 706/549-9977; John A. Drew, President and Chief Executive Officer

BROOKS COUNTY HOSPITAL, 903 North Court Street, Quitman, GA, Zip 31643-1315, Mailing Address: P.O. Box 5000, Zip 31643-5000; tel. 912/263-4171; Andrew J. Finnegan, CHE, Administrator

CAMDEN MEDICAL CENTER, 2000 Dan Proctor Drive, Saint Marys, GA, Zip 31558, Mailing Address: 2000 Dan Proctor Dirve, Zip 31558; tel. 912/576-4200; Warren Manley, Administrator

CANDLER COUNTY HOSPITAL, Cedar Road, Metter, GA, Zip 30439, Mailing Address: P.O. Box 597, Zip 30439–0597; tel. 912/685–5741; Charles Balkcom, President

CANDLER HOSPITAL, 5353 Reynolds Street, Savannah, GA, Zip 31405–6013, Mailing Address: P.O. Box 9787, Zip 31412–9787; tel. 912/692–6000; Paul P. Hinchey, President and Chief Executive Officer

COLUMBIA EASTSIDE MEDICAL CENTER, 1700 Medical Way, Snellville, GA, Zip 30078, Mailing Address: P.O. Box 587, Zip 30078–0587; tel. 770/979–0200; Les Beard, Chief Executive Officer

COLUMBIA FAIRVIEW PARK HOSPITAL, 200 Industrial Boulevard, Dublin, GA, Zip 31021–2997, Mailing Address: P.O. Box 1408, Zip 31040–1408; tel. 912/275–2000; Richard P. Cook, Chief Executive Officer

CRAWFORD LONG HOSPITAL OF EMORY UNIVERSITY, 550 Peachtree Street N.E., Atlanta, GA, Zip 30365–2225; tel. 404/686–4411; John Dunklin Henry, Sr., FACHE, Chief Executive Officer

CRISP REGIONAL HOSPITAL, 902 North Seventh Street, Cordele, GA, Zip 31015–5007; tel. 912/276–3100; D. Wayne Martin, President and Chief Executive Officer

EARLY MEMORIAL HOSPITAL, 630 Columbia Street, Blakely, GA, Zip 31723–1798; tel. 912/723–4241; Rodney C. Watford, Administrator

EFFINGHAM HOSPITAL, 459 Highway 119 South, Springfield, GA, Zip 31329–3021, Mailing Address: P.O. Box 386, Zip 31329–0386; tel. 912/754–6451; W. Scott Burnette, Chief Executive Officer

EGLESTON CHILDREN'S HOSPITAL AT EMORY UNIVERSITY, 1405 Clifton Road N.E., Atlanta, GA, Zip 30322–1101; tel. 404/325–6000; James E. Tally, Ph.D., President and Chief Executive Officer

ELBERT MEMORIAL HOSPITAL, 4 Medical Drive, Elberton, GA, Zip 30635–1897; tel. 706/283–3151; Ronald J. Vigus, Interim Chief Executive Officer

EMORY UNIVERSITY HOSPITAL, 1364 Clifton Road N.E., Atlanta, GA, Zip 30322–1102; tel. 404/727–7021; John Dunklin Henry, Sr., FACHE, Chief Executive Officer

EMORY–ADVENTIST HOSPITAL, 3949 South Cobb Drive S.E., Smyrna, GA, Zip 30080–6300; tel. 770/434–0710; Terry Owen, Chief Executive Officer

FLOYD MEDICAL CENTER, 304 Turner McCall Boulevard, Rome, GA, Zip 30165–2734, Mailing Address: P.O. Box 233, Zip 30162–0233; tel. 706/802–2000; Kurt Stuenkel, FACHE, President and Chief Executive Officer

GRADY GENERAL HOSPITAL, 1155 Fifth Street S.E., Cairo, GA, Zip 31728–3142, Mailing Address: P.O. Box 360, Zip 31728–0360; tel. 912/377–1150; Glen C. Davis, Administrator

HABERSHAM COUNTY MEDICAL CENTER, Highway 441, Demorest, GA, Zip 30535, Mailing Address: P.O. Box 37, Zip 30535–0037; tel. 706/754–2161; C. Richard Dwozan, President

HIGGINS GENERAL HOSPITAL, 200 Allen Memorial Drive, Bremen, GA, Zip 30110–2012, Mailing Address: P.O. Box 655, Zip 30110–0655; tel. 770/537–5851; Robbie Smith, Administrator

HOUSTON MEDICAL CENTER, 1601 Watson Boulevard, Warner Robins, GA, Zip 31093–3431, Mailing Address: Box 2886, Zip 31099–2886; tel. 912/922–4281; Arthur P. Christie, Administrator

JOHN D. ARCHBOLD MEMORIAL HOSPITAL, Gordon Avenue at Mimosa Drive, Thomasville, GA, Zip 31792–6113, Mailing Address: P.O. Box 1018, Zip 31799–1018; tel. 912/228–2000; Jason H. Moore, President and Chief Executive Officer

LIBERTY REGIONAL MEDICAL CENTER, 112 East Oglethorpe Boulevard, Hinesville, GA, Zip 31313–3600, Mailing Address: P.O. Box 919, Zip 31313–0919; tel. 912/369–9400; H. Scott Kroell, Jr., Chief Executive Officer

LOUIS SMITH MEMORIAL HOSPITAL, 852 West Thigpen Avenue, Lakeland, GA, Zip 31635–1099; tel. 912/482–3110; Randy Sauls, Administrator

MEDICAL CENTER OF CENTRAL GEORGIA, 777 Hemlock Street, Macon, GA, Zip 31201–2155, Mailing Address: P.O. Box 6000, Zip 31208–6000; tel. 912/633–1000; A. Donald Faulk, FACHE, President

MEDICAL COLLEGE OF GEORGIA HOSPITAL AND CLINICS, 1120 15th Street, Augusta, GA, Zip 30912–5000; tel. 706/721–0211; Patricia Sodomka, FACHE, Executive Director

MITCHELL COUNTY HOSPITAL, 90 Stephens Street, Camilla, GA, Zip 31730–1899, Mailing Address: P.O. Box 639, Zip 31730–0639; tel. 912/336–5284; Ronald M. Gilliard, FACHE, Administrator

NEWTON GENERAL HOSPITAL, 5126 Hospital Drive, Covington, GA, Zip 30209; tel. 770/786–7053; James F. Weadick, Administrator and Chief Executive Officer

NORTH FULTON REGIONAL HOSPITAL, 3000 Hospital Boulevard, Roswell, GA, Zip 30076–9930; tel. 770/751–2500; Frederick R. Bailey, Chief Executive Officer

NORTHEAST GEORGIA MEDICAL CENTER, 743 Spring Street N.E., Gainesville, GA, Zip 30501–3899; tel. 770/535–3553; Henry Rigdon, Executive Vice President

NORTHSIDE HOSPITAL, 1000 Johnson Ferry Road N.E., Atlanta, GA, Zip 30342–1611; tel. 404/851–8000; Sidney Kirschner, President and Chief Executive Officer

OCONEE REGIONAL MEDICAL CENTER, 821 North Cobb Street, Milledgeville, GA, Zip 31061–2351, Mailing Address: P.O. Box 690, Zip 31061–0690; tel. 912/454–3500; Brian L. Riddle, Chief Executive Officer

PALMYRA MEDICAL CENTERS, 2000 Palmyra Road, Albany, GA, Zip 31701–1528, Mailing Address: P.O. Box 1908, Zip 31702–1908; tel. 912/434–2000; Allen Golson, Chief Executive Officer

SOUTH GEORGIA MEDICAL CENTER, 2501 North Patterson Street, Valdosta, GA, Zip 31602–1735, Mailing Address: P.O. Box 1727, Zip 31603–1727; tel. 912/333–1000; John S. Bowling, President and Chief Executive Officer

SOUTHEAST GEORGIA REGIONAL MEDICAL CENTER, 3100 Kemble Avenue, Brunswick, GA, Zip 31520–4252, Mailing Address: P.O. Box 1518, Zip 31521–1518; tel. 912/264–7000; E. Berton Whitaker, President and Chief Executive Officer

SOUTHERN REGIONAL MEDICAL CENTER, 11 Upper Riverdale Road S.W., Riverdale, GA, Zip 30274–2600; tel. 770/991–8000; Eugene A. Leblond, FACHE, President and Chief Executive Officer

SPALDING REGIONAL HOSPITAL, 601 South Eighth Street, Griffin, GA, Zip 30224–4294, Mailing Address: P.O. Drawer V., Zip 30224–1168; tel. 770/228–2721; Phil Shaw, Executive Director

SUMTER REGIONAL HOSPITAL, 100 Wheatley Drive, Americus, GA, Zip 31709–3799; tel. 912/924–6011; Jerry W. Adams, President

TANNER MEDICAL CENTER, 705 Dixie Street, Carrollton, GA, Zip 30117–3818; tel. 770/836–9666; Loy M. Howard, Chief Executive Officer

TANNER MEDICAL CENTER–VILLA RICA, 601 Dallas Road, Villa Rica, GA, Zip 30180–1202, Mailing Address: P.O. Box 638, Zip 30180–0638; tel. 770/459–7100; Larry N. Steed, Administrator

THE MEDICAL CENTER, 710 Center Street, Columbus, GA, Zip 31902, Mailing Address: P.O. Box 951, Zip 31902–0951; tel. 706/571–1000; Lance B. Duke, FACHE, President and Chief Executive Officer

TIFT GENERAL HOSPITAL, 901 East 18th Street, Tifton, GA, Zip 31794–3648, Mailing Address: Drawer 747, Zip 31793–0747; tel. 912/382–7120; William T. Richardson, President and Chief Executive Officer

UPSON REGIONAL MEDICAL CENTER, 801 West Gordon Street, Thomaston, GA, Zip 30286–2831, Mailing Address: P.O. Box 1059, Zip 30286–1059; tel. 706/647–8111; Samuel S. Gregory, Administrator

WALTON MEDICAL CENTER, 330 Alcovy Street, Monroe, GA, Zip 30655–2140, Mailing Address: P.O. Box 1346, Zip 30655–1346; tel. 770/267–8461; Edgar L. Belcher, Administrator

WEST GEORGIA HEALTH SYSTEM, 1514 Vernon Road, La Grange, GA, Zip 30240–4199; tel. 706/882–1411; Charles L. Foster, Jr., FACHE, President and Chief Executive Officer

GRADY HEALTH SYSTEM
80 Butler Street, Atlanta, GA 30335; tel. 404/616–4307; Edward Renford, President

GRADY MEMORIAL HOSPITAL, 80 Butler Street S.E., Atlanta, GA, Zip 30335–3801, Mailing Address: P.O. Box 26189, Zip 30335–3801; tel. 404/616–4252; Edward J. Renford, President and Chief Executive Officer

PRINCIPAL HEALTH CARE OF GEORGIA
3715 Northside Parkway – Suite 4300, Atlanta, GA 30327; tel. 404/231–9911; Ken Bryant, Executive Director

APPLING HEALTHCARE SYSTEM, 301 East Tollison Street, Baxley, GA, Zip 31513–2898; tel. 912/367–9841; Luther E. Reeves, Chief Executive Officer

ATHENS REGIONAL MEDICAL CENTER, 1114 West Madison Avenue, Athens, TN, Zip 37303–4150, Mailing Address: P.O. Box 250, Zip 37371–0250; tel. 423/745–1411; John R. Workman, Chief Executive Officer

BERRIEN COUNTY HOSPITAL, 1221 East McPherson Street, Nashville, GA, Zip 31639–2326, Mailing Address: P.O. Box 665, Zip 31639–0665; tel. 912/686–7471; James P. Seward, Jr., Chief Executive Officer

BRADLEY MEMORIAL HOSPITAL, 2305 Chambliss Avenue N.W., Cleveland, TN, Zip 37311, Mailing Address: P.O. Box 3060, Zip 37320–3060; tel. 423/559–6000; Jim Whitlock, Administrator

BULLOCH MEMORIAL HOSPITAL, 500 East Grady Street, Statesboro, GA, Zip 30458–5105, Mailing Address: P.O. Box 1048, Zip 30459–1048; tel. 912/486–1000; C. Scott Campbell, Executive Director

BURKE COUNTY HOSPITAL, 351 Liberty Street, Waynesboro, GA, Zip 30830–9686; tel. 706/554–4435; Gloria Cochran, Administrator

CANDLER COUNTY HOSPITAL, Cedar Road, Metter, GA, Zip 30439, Mailing Address: P.O. Box 597, Zip 30439–0597; tel. 912/685–5741; Charles Balkcom, President

CANDLER HOSPITAL, 5353 Reynolds Street, Savannah, GA, Zip 31405–6013, Mailing Address: P.O. Box 9787, Zip 31412–9787; tel. 912/692–6000; Paul P. Hinchey, President and Chief Executive Officer

CLEVELAND COMMUNITY HOSPITAL, 2800 Westside Drive N.W., Cleveland, TN, Zip 37312–3599; tel. 423/339–4100; Phil Rowland, Chief Executive Officer

COBB MEMORIAL HOSPITAL, 577 Franklin Springs Street, Royston, GA, Zip 30662–3909, Mailing Address: P.O. Box 589, Zip 30662–0589; tel. 706/245–5034; H. Thomas Brown, Administrator

COLISEUM MEDICAL CENTERS, 350 Hospital Drive, Macon, GA, Zip 31213; tel. 912/765–7000; Michael S. Boggs, Chief Executive Officer

COLUMBIA CARTERSVILLE MEDICAL CENTER, 960 Joe Frank Harris Parkway, Cartersville, GA, Zip 30120, Mailing Address: P.O. Box 200008, Zip 30120–9001; tel. 770/382–1530; Keith Sandlin, Chief Executive Officer

COLUMBIA DOCTORS HOSPITAL, 616 19th Street, Columbus, GA, Zip 31901–1528, Mailing Address: P.O. Box 2188, Zip 31902–2188; tel. 706/571–4262; Hugh D. Wilson, Chief Executive Officer

COLUMBIA EAST RIDGE HOSPITAL, 941 Spring Creek Road, East Ridge, TN, Zip 37412, Mailing Address: P.O. Box 91229, Zip 37412–6229; tel. 423/894–7870; Brenda M. Waltz, CHE, Chief Executive Officer

COLUMBIA FAIRVIEW PARK HOSPITAL, 200 Industrial Boulevard, Dublin, GA, Zip 31021–2997, Mailing Address: P.O. Box 1408, Zip 31040–1408; tel. 912/275–2000; Richard P. Cook, Chief Executive Officer

COLUMBIA PEACHTREE REGIONAL HOSPITAL, 60 Hospital Road, Newnan, GA, Zip 30264, Mailing Address: P.O. Box 2228, Zip 30264–2228; tel. 770/253–1912; Linda Jubinsky, Chief Executive Officer

COLUMBIA SOUTH PITTSBURG HOSPITAL, 210 West 12th Street, South Pittsburg, TN, Zip 37380, Mailing Address: P.O. Box 349, Zip 37380–0349; tel. 423/837–6781; Phil Rowland, Chief Executive Officer

DECATUR HOSPITAL, 450 North Candler Street, Decatur, GA, Zip 30030–2671, Mailing Address: P.O. Box 40, Zip 30031–0040; tel. 404/377–0221; Richard T. Schmidt, Executive Director

DEKALB MEDICAL CENTER, 2701 North Decatur Road, Decatur, GA, Zip 30033–5995; tel. 404/501–1000; John R. Gerlach, Chief Executive Officer/Administrator

DODGE COUNTY HOSPITAL, 715 Griffin Street S.W., Eastman, GA, Zip 31023–2223, Mailing Address: P.O. Box 4309, Zip 31023–4309; tel. 912/374–4000; Meredith H. Smith, Administrator

DOOLY MEDICAL CENTER, 1300 Union Street, Vienna, GA, Zip 31092–7541, Mailing Address: P.O. Box 278, Zip 31092–0278; tel. 912/268–4141; Kevin Paul, Administrator

EDGEFIELD COUNTY HOSPITAL, 300 Ridge Medical Plaza, Edgefield, SC, Zip 29824; tel. 803/637–3174; W. Joseph Seel, Administrator

EFFINGHAM HOSPITAL, 459 Highway 119 South, Springfield, GA, Zip 31329–3021, Mailing Address: P.O. Box 386, Zip 31329–0386; tel. 912/754–6451; W. Scott Burnette, Chief Executive Officer

EGLESTON CHILDREN'S HOSPITAL AT EMORY UNIVERSITY, 1405 Clifton Road N.E., Atlanta, GA, Zip 30322–1101; tel. 404/325–6000; James E. Tally, Ph.D., President and Chief Executive Officer

EMANUEL COUNTY HOSPITAL, 117 Kite Road, Swainsboro, GA, Zip 30401–3231, Mailing Address: P.O. Box 879, Zip 30401–0879; tel. 912/237–9911; Richard W. Clarke, Chief Executive Officer

FLOYD MEDICAL CENTER, 304 Turner McCall Boulevard, Rome, GA, Zip 30165–2734, Mailing Address: P.O. Box 233, Zip 30162–0233; tel. 706/802–2000; Kurt Stuenkel, FACHE, President and Chief Executive Officer

GORDON HOSPITAL, 1035 Red Bud Road, Calhoun, GA, Zip 30701–2082, Mailing Address: P.O. Box 12938, Zip 30703–7013; tel. 706/629–2895; Dennis Kiley, President

HART COUNTY HOSPITAL, Gibson and Cade Streets, Hartwell, GA, Zip 30643–0280, Mailing Address: P.O. Box 280, Zip 30643–0280; tel. 706/856–6100; Matt McRee, Administrator

HIGGINS GENERAL HOSPITAL, 200 Allen Memorial Drive, Bremen, GA, Zip 30110–2012, Mailing Address: P.O. Box 655, Zip 30110–0655; tel. 770/537–5851; Robbie Smith, Administrator

HILTON HEAD MEDICAL CENTER AND CLINICS, 25 Hospital Center Boulevard, Hilton Head Island, SC, Zip 29926–2738, Mailing Address: P.O. Box 21117, Zip 29925–1117; tel. 803/681–6122; Dennis Ray Bruns, President and Chief Executive Officer

HUTCHESON MEDICAL CENTER, 100 Gross Crescent Circle, Fort Oglethorpe, GA, Zip 30742–3669; tel. 706/858–2000; Robert T. Jones, M.D., President and Chief Executive Officer

JEFFERSON HOSPITAL, 1067 Peachtree Street, Louisville, GA, Zip 30434–1599; tel. 912/625–7000; Rita Culvern, Administrator

LIBERTY REGIONAL MEDICAL CENTER, 112 East Oglethorpe Boulevard, Hinesville, GA, Zip 31313–3600, Mailing Address: P.O. Box 919, Zip 31313–0919; tel. 912/369–9400; H. Scott Kroell, Jr., Chief Executive Officer

LOUIS SMITH MEMORIAL HOSPITAL, 852 West Thigpen Avenue, Lakeland, GA, Zip 31635–1099; tel. 912/482–3110; Randy Sauls, Administrator

MCDUFFIE COUNTY HOSPITAL, 521 Hill Street S.W., Thomson, GA, Zip 30824–2199; tel. 706/595–1411; Douglas C. Keir, Chief Executive Officer

MEADOWS REGIONAL MEDICAL CENTER, 1703 Meadows Lane, Vidalia, GA, Zip 30474–8915, Mailing Address: P.O. Box 1048, Zip 30474–1048; tel. 912/537–8921; Barry Michael, Chief Executive Officer

MEMORIAL HEALTH CARE SYSTEM, 2525 De Sales Avenue, Chattanooga, TN, Zip 37404–3322; tel. 423/495–2525; L. Clark Taylor, Jr., President and Chief Executive Officer

MEMORIAL HEALTH SYSTEM, 4700 Waters Avenue, Savannah, GA, Zip 31404–6283, Mailing Address: P.O. Box 23089, Zip 31403–3089; tel. 912/350–8000; Robert A. Colvin, President and Chief Executive Officer

MEMORIAL HOSPITAL AND MANOR, 1500 East Shotwell Street, Bainbridge, GA, Zip 31717–4294; tel. 912/246–3500; James G. Peak, Director

MEMORIAL NORTH PARK HOSPITAL, 2051 Hamill Road, Chattanooga, TN, Zip 37343–4096; tel. 423/870–6100; Sean S. McMurray, CHE, Administrator

NEWTON GENERAL HOSPITAL, 5126 Hospital Drive, Covington, GA, Zip 30209; tel. 770/786–7053; James F. Weadick, Administrator and Chief Executive Officer

NORTH GEORGIA MEDICAL CENTER, 1362 South Main Street, Ellijay, GA, Zip 30540–0346, Mailing Address: P.O. Box 2239, Zip 30540–0346; tel. 706/276–4741; Steve Grimm, Chief Executive Officer

NORTHEAST GEORGIA MEDICAL CENTER, 743 Spring Street N.E., Gainesville, GA, Zip 30501–3899; tel. 770/535–3553; Henry Rigdon, Executive Vice President

NORTHSIDE HOSPITAL, 1000 Johnson Ferry Road N.E., Atlanta, GA, Zip 30342–1611; tel. 404/851–8000; Sidney Kirschner, President and Chief Executive Officer

NORTHSIDE HOSPITAL – CHEROKEE, 201 Hospital Road, Canton, GA, Zip 30114–2408, Mailing Address: P.O. Box 906, Zip 30114–0906; tel. 770/720–5100; Douglas M. Parker, Chief Executive Officer

OCONEE REGIONAL MEDICAL CENTER, 821 North Cobb Street, Milledgeville, GA, Zip 31061–2351, Mailing Address: P.O. Box 690, Zip 31061–0690; tel. 912/454–3500; Brian L. Riddle, Chief Executive Officer

PALMYRA MEDICAL CENTERS, 2000 Palmyra Road, Albany, GA, Zip 31701–1528, Mailing Address: P.O. Box 1908, Zip 31702–1908; tel. 912/434–2000; Allen Golson, Chief Executive Officer

PHENIX REGIONAL HOSPITAL, 1707 21st Avenue, Phenix City, AL, Zip 36867–3753, Mailing Address: P.O. Box 190, Zip 36868–0190; tel. 334/291–8502; Lance B. Duke, FACHE, President and Chief Executive Officer

PIEDMONT HOSPITAL, 1968 Peachtree Road N.W., Atlanta, GA, Zip 30309–1231; tel. 404/605–5000; Richard B. Hubbard, III, President and Chief Executive Officer

PROMINA GWINNETT HOSPITAL SYSTEM, Lawrenceville, GA, Mailing Address: P.O. Box 348, Zip 30246–0348; tel. 770/995–4321; Franklin M. Rinker, President and Chief Executive Officer

PUTNAM GENERAL HOSPITAL, Lake Oconee Parkway, Eatonton, GA, Zip 31024–4330, Mailing Address: Box 4330, Zip 31024–4330; tel. 706/485–2711; Darrell M. Oglesby, Administrator

RIDGECREST HOSPITAL, 393 Ridgecrest Circle, Clayton, GA, Zip 30525; tel. 706/782–4297; Maryann J. Greenwell, Chief Executive Officer

ROCKDALE HOSPITAL, 1412 Milstead Avenue N.E., Conyers, GA, Zip 30207–9990; tel. 770/918–3000; Nelson Toebbe, Chief Executive Officer

SATILLA REGIONAL MEDICAL CENTER, 410 Darling Avenue, Waycross, GA, Zip 31501–5246, Mailing Address: P.O. Box 139, Zip 31502–0139; tel. 912/283–3030; Eugene Johnson, President and Chief Executive Officer

SCOTTISH RITE CHILDREN'S MEDICAL CENTER, 1001 Johnson Ferry Road N.E., Atlanta, GA, Zip 30342–1600; tel. 404/256–5252; James E. Tally, Ph.D., President and Chief Executive Officer

SHEPHERD CENTER, 2020 Peachtree Road N.W., Atlanta, GA, Zip 30309–1465; tel. 404/352–2020; Gary R. Ulicny, Ph.D., President and Chief Executive Officer

SISKIN HOSPITAL FOR PHYSICAL REHABILITATION, One Siskin Plaza, Chattanooga, TN, Zip 37403–1306; tel. 423/634–1200; Robert P. Main, President and Chief Executive Officer

SOUTH FULTON MEDICAL CENTER, 1170 Cleveland Avenue, East Point, GA, Zip 30344; tel. 404/305–3500; H. Neil Copelan, President and Chief Executive Officer

SOUTH GEORGIA MEDICAL CENTER, 2501 North Patterson Street, Valdosta, GA, Zip 31602–1735, Mailing Address: P.O. Box 1727, Zip 31603–1727; tel. 912/333–1000; John S. Bowling, President and Chief Executive Officer

SOUTHEAST ALABAMA MEDICAL CENTER, 1108 Ross Clark Circle, Dothan, AL, Zip 36301–3024, Mailing Address: P.O. Box 6987, Zip 36302–6987; tel. 334/793–8111; Ronald S. Owen, Chief Executive Officer

SOUTHEAST GEORGIA REGIONAL MEDICAL CENTER, 3100 Kemble Avenue, Brunswick, GA, Zip 31520–4252, Mailing Address: P.O. Box 1518, Zip 31521–1518; tel. 912/264–7000; E. Berton Whitaker, President and Chief Executive Officer

SOUTHERN REGIONAL MEDICAL CENTER, 11 Upper Riverdale Road S.W., Riverdale, GA, Zip 30274–2600; tel. 770/991–8000; Eugene A. Leblond, FACHE, President and Chief Executive Officer

SPALDING REGIONAL HOSPITAL, 601 South Eighth Street, Griffin, GA, Zip 30224–4294, Mailing Address: P.O. Drawer V., Zip 30224–1168; tel. 770/228–2721; Phil Shaw, Executive Director

ST. MARY'S HOSPITAL, 1230 Baxter Street, Athens, GA, Zip 30606–3791; tel. 706/548–7581; Edward J. Fechtel, Jr., President and Chief Executive Officer

STEPHENS COUNTY HOSPITAL, 2003 Falls Road, Toccoa, GA, Zip 30577–9700; tel. 706/886–6841; Edward C. Gambrell, Jr., Administrator

SUMTER REGIONAL HOSPITAL, 100 Wheatley Drive, Americus, GA, Zip 31709–3799; tel. 912/924–6011; Jerry W. Adams, President

TANNER MEDICAL CENTER, 705 Dixie Street, Carrollton, GA, Zip 30117–3818; tel. 770/836–9666; Loy M. Howard, Chief Executive Officer

TANNER MEDICAL CENTER–VILLA RICA, 601 Dallas Road, Villa Rica, GA, Zip 30180–1202, Mailing Address: P.O. Box 638, Zip 30180–0638; tel. 770/459–7100; Larry N. Steed, Administrator

TAYLOR REGIONAL HOSPITAL, Macon Highway, Hawkinsville, GA, Zip 31036, Mailing Address: P.O. Box 1297, Zip 31036–1297; tel. 912/783–0200; Dan S. Maddock, President

THE MEDICAL CENTER, 710 Center Street, Columbus, GA, Zip 31902, Mailing Address: P.O. Box 951, Zip 31902–0951; tel. 706/571–1000; Lance B. Duke, FACHE, President and Chief Executive Officer

UNIVERSITY HOSPITAL, 1350 Walton Way, Augusta, GA, Zip 30901–2629; tel. 706/722–9011; Donald C. Bray, President and Chief Executive Officer

UPSON REGIONAL MEDICAL CENTER, 801 West Gordon Street, Thomaston, GA, Zip 30286–2831, Mailing Address: P.O. Box 1059, Zip 30286–1059; tel. 706/647–8111; Samuel S. Gregory, Administrator

VENCOR HOSPITAL–CHATTANOOGA, 709 Walnut Street, Chattanooga, TN, Zip 37402–1961; tel. 423/266–7721; Steven E. McGraw, Administrator

WALTON REHABILITATION HOSPITAL, 1355 Independence Drive, Augusta, GA, Zip 30901–1037; tel. 706/724–7746; Dennis B. Skelley, President and Chief Executive Officer

WASHINGTON COUNTY REGIONAL HOSPITAL, 610 Sparta Highway, Sandersville, GA, Zip 31082–1362, Mailing Address: P.O. Box 636, Zip 31082–0636; tel. 912/552–3901; Shirley R. Roberts, Administrator

WAYNE MEMORIAL HOSPITAL, 865 South First Street, Jesup, GA, Zip 31598, Mailing Address: P.O. Box 408, Zip 31598–0408; tel. 912/427–6811; Charles R. Morgan, Administrator

WELLSTAR COBB HOSPITAL, 3950 Austell Road, Austell, GA, Zip 30106–1121; tel. 770/732–4000; Thomas E. Hill, Chief Executive Officer

WELLSTAR DOUGLAS HOSPITAL, 8954 Hospital Drive, Douglasville, GA, Zip 30134–2282; tel. 770/949–1500; Thomas E. Hill, Chief Executive Officer

WELLSTAR PAULDING HOSPITAL, 600 West Memorial Drive, Dallas, GA, Zip 30132–1335; tel. 770/445–4411; Thomas E. Hill, Chief Executive Officer

WELLSTAR WINDY HILL HOSPITAL, 2540 Windy Hill Road, Marietta, GA, Zip 30067–8632; tel. 770/644–1000; Thomas E. Hill, Chief Executive Officer

PROMINA HEALTH SYSTEM, INC.
2000 South Park Place, Atlanta, GA 30339; tel. 770/956–6455; Mike Britain, Director, System Planning

DECATUR HOSPITAL, 450 North Candler Street, Decatur, GA, Zip 30030–2671, Mailing Address: P.O. Box 40, Zip 30031–0040; tel. 404/377–0221; Richard T. Schmidt, Executive Director

DEKALB MEDICAL CENTER, 2701 North Decatur Road, Decatur, GA, Zip 30033–5995; tel. 404/501–1000; John R. Gerlach, Chief Executive Officer/Administrator

PIEDMONT HOSPITAL, 1968 Peachtree Road N.W., Atlanta, GA, Zip 30309–1231; tel. 404/605–5000; Richard B. Hubbard, III, President and Chief Executive Officer

PROMINA GWINNETT HOSPITAL SYSTEM, Lawrenceville, GA, Mailing Address: P.O. Box 348, Zip 30246–0348; tel. 770/995–4321; Franklin M. Rinker, President and Chief Executive Officer

SOUTHERN REGIONAL MEDICAL CENTER, 11 Upper Riverdale Road S.W., Riverdale, GA, Zip 30274–2600; tel. 770/991–8000; Eugene A. Leblond, FACHE, President and Chief Executive Officer

WELLSTAR COBB HOSPITAL, 3950 Austell Road, Austell, GA, Zip 30106–1121; tel. 770/732–4000; Thomas E. Hill, Chief Executive Officer

WELLSTAR DOUGLAS HOSPITAL, 8954 Hospital Drive, Douglasville, GA, Zip 30134–2282; tel. 770/949–1500; Thomas E. Hill, Chief Executive Officer

WELLSTAR KENNESTONE HOSPITAL, 677 Church Street, Marietta, GA, Zip 30060–1148; tel. 770/793–5000; Thomas E. Hill, Chief Executive Officer

WELLSTAR PAULDING HOSPITAL, 600 West Memorial Drive, Dallas, GA, Zip 30132–1335; tel. 770/445–4411; Thomas E. Hill, Chief Executive Officer

WELLSTAR WINDY HILL HOSPITAL, 2540 Windy Hill Road, Marietta, GA, Zip 30067–8632; tel. 770/644–1000; Thomas E. Hill, Chief Administrator

SAINT JOSEPH'S HOSPITAL OF ATLANTA
5665 Peachtree, Dunwoody Road, Northeast, Atlanta, GA 30342; tel. 404/851–7543; Brian Tisher, Planning Specialist

SAINT JOSEPH'S HOSPITAL OF ATLANTA, 5665 Peachtree Dunwoody Road N.E., Atlanta, GA, Zip 30342–1764; tel. 404/851–7001; Brue Chandler, President and Chief Executive Officer

THE MEDICAL RESOURCE NETWORK, L.L.C.
900 Circle 75 Parkway, Suite 1400, Atlanta, GA 30339; tel. 770/980–2340; David Record, Executive Vice President & COO

APPLING HEALTHCARE SYSTEM, 301 East Tollison Street, Baxley, GA, Zip 31513–2898; tel. 912/367–9841; Luther E. Reeves, Chief Executive Officer

ATHENS REGIONAL MEDICAL CENTER, 1199 Prince Avenue, Athens, GA, Zip 30606–2793; tel. 706/549–9977; John A. Drew, President and Chief Executive Officer

BARNWELL COUNTY HOSPITAL, 2501 Reynolds Road, Barnwell, SC, Zip 29812, Mailing Address: P.O. Box 588, Zip 29812–0588; tel. 803/259–1000; Tommy R. McDougal, Jr., Administrator and Chief Executive Officer

BERRIEN COUNTY HOSPITAL, 1221 East McPherson Street, Nashville, GA, Zip 31639–2326, Mailing Address: P.O. Box 665, Zip 31639–0665; tel. 912/686–7471; James P. Seward, Jr., Chief Executive Officer

BROOKS COUNTY HOSPITAL, 903 North Court Street, Quitman, GA, Zip 31643–1315, Mailing Address: P.O. Box 5000, Zip 31643–5000; tel. 912/263–4171; Andrew J. Finnegan, CHE, Administrator

BURKE COUNTY HOSPITAL, 351 Liberty Street, Waynesboro, GA, Zip 30830–9686; tel. 706/554–4435; Gloria Cochran, Administrator

CALHOUN MEMORIAL HOSPITAL, 209 Academy & Carswell Streets, Arlington, GA, Zip 31713, Mailing Address: Drawer R., Zip 31713; tel. 912/725–4272; Peggy Pierce, Administrator

CANDLER COUNTY HOSPITAL, Cedar Road, Metter, GA, Zip 30439, Mailing Address: P.O. Box 597, Zip 30439–0597; tel. 912/685–5741; Charles Balkcom, President

CANDLER HOSPITAL, 5353 Reynolds Street, Savannah, GA, Zip 31405–6013, Mailing Address: P.O. Box 9787, Zip 31412–9787; tel. 912/692–6000; Paul P. Hinchey, President and Chief Executive Officer

CHEROKEE BAPTIST MEDICAL CENTER, 400 Northwood Drive, Centre, AL, Zip 35960–1023; tel. 205/927–5531; Barry S. Cochran, President

CRISP REGIONAL HOSPITAL, 902 North Seventh Street, Cordele, GA, Zip 31015–5007; tel. 912/276–3100; D. Wayne Martin, President and Chief Executive Officer

DECATUR HOSPITAL, 450 North Candler Street, Decatur, GA, Zip 30030–2671, Mailing Address: P.O. Box 40, Zip 30031–0040; tel. 404/377–0221; Richard T. Schmidt, Executive Director

DEKALB MEDICAL CENTER, 2701 North Decatur Road, Decatur, GA, Zip 30033–5995; tel. 404/501–1000; John R. Gerlach, Chief Executive Officer/Administrator

DODGE COUNTY HOSPITAL, 715 Griffin Street S.W., Eastman, GA, Zip 31023–2223, Mailing Address: P.O. Box 4309, Zip 31023–4309; tel. 912/374–4000; Meredith H. Smith, Administrator

DONALSONVILLE HOSPITAL, Hospital Circle, Donalsonville, GA, Zip 31745, Mailing Address: P.O. Box 677, Zip 31745–0677; tel. 912/524–5217; Charles H. Orrick, Administrator

DOOLY MEDICAL CENTER, 1300 Union Street, Vienna, GA, Zip 31092–7541, Mailing Address: P.O. Box 278, Zip 31092–0278; tel. 912/268–4141; Kevin Paul, Administrator

EARLY MEMORIAL HOSPITAL, 630 Columbia Street, Blakely, GA, Zip 31723–1798; tel. 912/723–4241; Rodney C. Watford, Administrator

EDGEFIELD COUNTY HOSPITAL, 300 Ridge Medical Plaza, Edgefield, SC, Zip 29824; tel. 803/637–3174; W. Joseph Seel, Administrator

EFFINGHAM HOSPITAL, 459 Highway 119 South, Springfield, GA, Zip 31329–3021, Mailing Address: P.O. Box 386, Zip 31329–0386; tel. 912/754–6451; W. Scott Burnette, Chief Executive Officer

EGLESTON CHILDREN'S HOSPITAL AT EMORY UNIVERSITY, 1405 Clifton Road N.E., Atlanta, GA, Zip 30322–1101; tel. 404/325–6000; James E. Tally, Ph.D., President and Chief Executive Officer

EMANUEL COUNTY HOSPITAL, 117 Kite Road, Swainsboro, GA, Zip 30401–3231, Mailing Address: P.O. Box 879, Zip 30401–0879; tel. 912/237–9911; Richard W. Clarke, Chief Executive Officer

FLOYD MEDICAL CENTER, 304 Turner McCall Boulevard, Rome, GA, Zip 30165–2734, Mailing Address: P.O. Box 233, Zip 30162–0233; tel. 706/802–2000; Kurt Stuenkel, FACHE, President and Chief Executive Officer

GORDON HOSPITAL, 1035 Red Bud Road, Calhoun, GA, Zip 30701–2082, Mailing Address: P.O. Box 12938, Zip 30703–7013; tel. 706/629–2895; Dennis Kiley, President

GRADY GENERAL HOSPITAL, 1155 Fifth Street S.E., Cairo, GA, Zip 31728–3142, Mailing Address: P.O. Box 360, Zip 31728–0360; tel. 912/377–1150; Glen C. Davis, Administrator

HAMILTON MEDICAL CENTER, 1200 Memorial Drive, Dalton, GA, Zip 30720–2529, Mailing Address: P.O. Box 1168, Zip 30722–1168; tel. 706/272–6000; Ned B. Wilford, President and Chief Executive Officer

HEALTHSOUTH CENTRAL GEORGIA REHABILITATION HOSPITAL, 3351 Northside Drive, Macon, GA, Zip 31210–2591; tel. 912/471–3536; Elbert T. McQueen, Chief Executive Officer

HIGGINS GENERAL HOSPITAL, 200 Allen Memorial Drive, Bremen, GA, Zip 30110–2012, Mailing Address: P.O. Box 655, Zip 30110–0655; tel. 770/537–5851; Robbie Smith, Administrator

HOUSTON MEDICAL CENTER, 1601 Watson Boulevard, Warner Robins, GA, Zip 31093–3431, Mailing Address: Box 2886, Zip 31099–2886; tel. 912/922–4281; Arthur P. Christie, Administrator

JEFFERSON HOSPITAL, 1067 Peachtree Street, Louisville, GA, Zip 30434–1599; tel. 912/625–7000; Rita Culvern, Administrator

JOHN D. ARCHBOLD MEMORIAL HOSPITAL, Gordon Avenue at Mimosa Drive, Thomasville, GA, Zip 31792–6113, Mailing Address: P.O. Box 1018, Zip 31799–1018; tel. 912/228–2000; Jason H. Moore, President and Chief Executive Officer

LIBERTY REGIONAL MEDICAL CENTER, 112 East Oglethorpe Boulevard, Hinesville, GA, Zip 31313–3600, Mailing Address: P.O. Box 919, Zip 31313–0919; tel. 912/369–9400; H. Scott Kroell, Jr., Chief Executive Officer

MCDUFFIE COUNTY HOSPITAL, 521 Hill Street S.W., Thomson, GA, Zip 30824–2199; tel. 706/595–1411; Douglas C. Keir, Chief Executive Officer

MEDICAL CENTER OF CENTRAL GEORGIA, 777 Hemlock Street, Macon, GA, Zip 31201–2155, Mailing Address: P.O. Box 6000, Zip 31208–6000; tel. 912/633–1000; A. Donald Faulk, FACHE, President

MINNIE G. BOSWELL MEMORIAL HOSPITAL, 1201 Siloam Highway, Greensboro, GA, Zip 30642–2811, Mailing Address: P.O. Box 329, Zip 30642–0329; tel. 706/453–7331; Earnest E. Benton, Chief Executive Officer

MITCHELL COUNTY HOSPITAL, 90 Stephens Street, Camilla, GA, Zip 31730–1899, Mailing Address: P.O. Box 639, Zip 31730–0639; tel. 912/336–5284; Ronald M. Gilliard, FACHE, Administrator

Section B

MONROE COUNTY HOSPITAL, 88 Martin Luther King Jr. Drive, Forsyth, GA, Zip 31029–1682, Mailing Address: P.O. Box 1068, Zip 31029–1068; tel. 912/994–2521; Gale V. Tanner, Administrator

NORTHEAST GEORGIA MEDICAL CENTER, 743 Spring Street N.E., Gainesville, GA, Zip 30501–3899; tel. 770/535–3553; Henry Rigdon, Executive Vice President

NORTHSIDE HOSPITAL, 1000 Johnson Ferry Road N.E., Atlanta, GA, Zip 30342–1611; tel. 404/851–8000; Sidney Kirschner, President and Chief Executive Officer

OCONEE REGIONAL MEDICAL CENTER, 821 North Cobb Street, Milledgeville, GA, Zip 31061–2351, Mailing Address: P.O. Box 690, Zip 31061–0690; tel. 912/454–3500; Brian L. Riddle, Chief Executive Officer

PEACH REGIONAL MEDICAL CENTER, 601 North Camellia Boulevard, Fort Valley, GA, Zip 31030–4599; tel. 912/825–8691; Nancy Peed, Administrator

PERRY HOSPITAL, 1120 Morningside Drive, Perry, GA, Zip 31069–2906, Mailing Address: Drawer 1004, Zip 31069–1004; tel. 912/987–3600; Nadine L. Weems, Administrator

PHENIX REGIONAL HOSPITAL, 1707 21st Avenue, Phenix City, AL, Zip 36867–3753, Mailing Address: P.O. Box 190, Zip 36868–0190; tel. 334/291–8502; Lance B. Duke, FACHE, President and Chief Executive Officer

PHOEBE PUTNEY MEMORIAL HOSPITAL, 417 Third Avenue, Albany, GA, Zip 31701–1828, Mailing Address: P.O. Box 1828, Zip 31703–1828; tel. 912/883–1800; Joel Wernick, President and Chief Executive Officer

PIEDMONT HOSPITAL, 1968 Peachtree Road N.W., Atlanta, GA, Zip 30309–1231; tel. 404/605–5000; Richard B. Hubbard, III, President and Chief Executive Officer

PUTNAM GENERAL HOSPITAL, Lake Oconee Parkway, Eatonton, GA, Zip 31024–4330, Mailing Address: Box 4330, Zip 31024–4330; tel. 706/485–2711; Darrell M. Oglesby, Administrator

SHEPHERD CENTER, 2020 Peachtree Road N.W., Atlanta, GA, Zip 30309–1465; tel. 404/352–2020; Gary R. Ulicny, Ph.D., President and Chief Executive Officer

SOUTH FULTON MEDICAL CENTER, 1170 Cleveland Avenue, East Point, GA, Zip 30344; tel. 404/305–3500; H. Neil Copelan, President and Chief Executive Officer

SOUTH GEORGIA MEDICAL CENTER, 2501 North Patterson Street, Valdosta, GA, Zip 31602–1735, Mailing Address: P.O. Box 1727, Zip 31603–1727; tel. 912/333–1000; John S. Bowling, President and Chief Executive Officer

SOUTHWEST GEORGIA REGIONAL MEDICAL CENTER, 109 Randolph Street, Cuthbert, GA, Zip 31740–1338; tel. 912/732–2181; David J. Carney, Chief Executive Officer

TAYLOR REGIONAL HOSPITAL, Macon Highway, Hawkinsville, GA, Zip 31036, Mailing Address: P.O. Box 1297, Zip 31036–1297; tel. 912/783–0200; Dan S. Maddock, President

THE MEDICAL CENTER, 710 Center Street, Columbus, GA, Zip 31902, Mailing Address: P.O. Box 951, Zip 31902–0951; tel. 706/571–1000; Lance B. Duke, FACHE, President and Chief Executive Officer

UNIVERSITY HOSPITAL, 1350 Walton Way, Augusta, GA, Zip 30901–2629; tel. 706/722–9011; Donald C. Bray, President and Chief Executive Officer

UPSON REGIONAL MEDICAL CENTER, 801 West Gordon Street, Thomaston, GA, Zip 30286–2831, Mailing Address: P.O. Box 1059, Zip 30286–1059; tel. 706/647–8111; Samuel S. Gregory, Administrator

WELLSTAR COBB HOSPITAL, 3950 Austell Road, Austell, GA, Zip 30106–1121; tel. 770/732–4000; Thomas E. Hill, Chief Executive Officer

WELLSTAR DOUGLAS HOSPITAL, 8954 Hospital Drive, Douglasville, GA, Zip 30134–2282; tel. 770/949–1500; Thomas E. Hill, Chief Executive Officer

WELLSTAR KENNESTONE HOSPITAL, 677 Church Street, Marietta, GA, Zip 30060–1148; tel. 770/793–5000; Thomas E. Hill, Chief Executive Officer

WELLSTAR PAULDING HOSPITAL, 600 West Memorial Drive, Dallas, GA, Zip 30132–1335; tel. 770/445–4411; Thomas E. Hill, Chief Executive Officer

WELLSTAR WINDY HILL HOSPITAL, 2540 Windy Hill Road, Marietta, GA, Zip 30067–8632; tel. 770/644–1000; Thomas E. Hill, Chief Executive Officer

WILLINGWAY HOSPITAL, 311 Jones Mill Road, Statesboro, GA, Zip 30458–4765; tel. 912/764–6236; Jimmy Mooney, Chief Executive Officer

UNIVERSITY HEALTH, INC.
1350 Walton Way, Augusta, GA 30901; tel. 706/722–9011; Donald C. Bray, President/CEO

BARNWELL COUNTY HOSPITAL, 2501 Reynolds Road, Barnwell, SC, Zip 29812, Mailing Address: P.O. Box 588, Zip 29812–0588; tel. 803/259–1000; Tommy R. McDougal, Jr., Administrator and Chief Executive Officer

BURKE COUNTY HOSPITAL, 351 Liberty Street, Waynesboro, GA, Zip 30830–9686; tel. 706/554–4435; Gloria Cochran, Administrator

EDGEFIELD COUNTY HOSPITAL, 300 Ridge Medical Plaza, Edgefield, SC, Zip 29824; tel. 803/637–3174; W. Joseph Seel, Administrator

EMANUEL COUNTY HOSPITAL, 117 Kite Road, Swainsboro, GA, Zip 30401–3231, Mailing Address: P.O. Box 879, Zip 30401–0879; tel. 912/237–9911; Richard W. Clarke, Chief Executive Officer

JEFFERSON HOSPITAL, 1067 Peachtree Street, Louisville, GA, Zip 30434–1599; tel. 912/625–7000; Rita Culvern, Administrator

MCDUFFIE COUNTY HOSPITAL, 521 Hill Street S.W., Thomson, GA, Zip 30824–2199; tel. 706/595–1411; Douglas C. Keir, Chief Executive Officer

MINNIE G. BOSWELL MEMORIAL HOSPITAL, 1201 Siloam Highway, Greensboro, GA, Zip 30642–2811, Mailing Address: P.O. Box 329, Zip 30642–0329; tel. 706/453–7331; Earnest E. Benton, Chief Executive Officer

UNIVERSITY HOSPITAL, 1350 Walton Way, Augusta, GA, Zip 30901–2629; tel. 706/722–9011; Donald C. Bray, President and Chief Executive Officer

WILLS MEMORIAL HOSPITAL, 120 Gordon Street, Washington, GA, Zip 30673–1602, Mailing Address: P.O. Box 370, Zip 30673–0370; tel. 706/678–2151; Vincent DiFranco, Chief Executive Officer

HAWAII

PACIFIC HEALTH CARE
1946 Young Street, Honolulu, HI 96826; tel. 808/547–9712; Gary Kajiwara, President & Chief Executive Officer

KUAKINI MEDICAL CENTER, 347 North Kuakini Street, Honolulu, HI, Zip 96817–2381; tel. 808/536–2236; Gary K. Kajiwara, President and Chief Executive Officer

ST. FRANCIS MEDICAL CENTER, 2230 Liliha Street, Honolulu, HI, Zip 96817–9979, Mailing Address: P.O. Box 30100, Zip 96820–0100; tel. 808/547–6011; Cynthia Okinaka, Administrator

QUEENS HEALTH SYSTEMS
1301 Punchbowl Street, Honolulu, HI 96813; tel. 808/532–6100; Richard Griffith, President & Chief Executive Officer

MOLOKAI GENERAL HOSPITAL, Kaunakakai, HI, Mailing Address: P.O. Box 408, Zip 96748–0408; tel. 808/553–5331; Phillip W. Reyes, M.D., Co–Medical Executive Director

QUEEN'S MEDICAL CENTER, 1301 Punchbowl Street, Honolulu, HI, Zip 96813; tel. 808/538–9011; Arthur A. Ushijima, President and Chief Executive Officer

IDAHO

NORTH IDAHO RURAL HEALTH NETWORK
700 Ironwood Drive, Suite 220, Coeur d'Alene, ID 83814; tel. 208/666–3212; Richard McMaster, Executive Director

BENEWAH COMMUNITY HOSPITAL, 229 South Seventh Street, Saint Maries, ID, Zip 83861–1894; tel. 208/245–5551; Camille Scott, Administrator

BONNER GENERAL HOSPITAL, 520 North Third Avenue, Sandpoint, ID, Zip 83864–0877, Mailing Address: Box 1448, Zip 83864–0877; tel. 208/263–1441; Gene Tomt, FACHE, Chief Executive Officer

BOUNDARY COMMUNITY HOSPITAL, 6640 Kaniksu Street, Bonners Ferry, ID, Zip 83805–7532, Mailing Address: HCR 61, Box 61A, Zip 83805–9500; tel. 208/267–3141; William T. McClintock, FACHE, Chief Executive Officer

KOOTENAI MEDICAL CENTER, 2003 Lincoln Way, Coeur D'Alene, ID, Zip 83814–2677; tel. 208/666–2000; Joe Morris, Chief Executive Officer

SHOSHONE MEDICAL CENTER, 3 Jacobs Gulch, Kellogg, ID, Zip 83837–2096; tel. 208/784–1221; Robert A. Morasko, Chief Executive Officer

SOUTH CENTRAL HEALTH NETWORK
P.O. Box 547, Twin Falls, ID 83303; tel. 208/734–5900; Connie Perry, Project Coordinator

GOODING COUNTY MEMORIAL HOSPITAL, 1120 Montana Street, Gooding, ID, Zip 83330–1858; tel. 208/934–4433; Kenneth W. Archer, Administrator

MAGIC VALLEY REGIONAL MEDICAL CENTER, 650 Addison Avenue West, Twin Falls, ID, Zip 83301–5444, Mailing Address: P.O. Box 409, Zip 83303–0409; tel. 208/737–2000; John Bingham, Administrator

MINIDOKA MEMORIAL HOSPITAL AND EXTENDED CARE FACILITY, 1224 Eighth Street, Rupert, ID, Zip 83350–1599; tel. 208/436–0481; Carl Henson, Administrator

ST. BENEDICTS FAMILY MEDICAL CENTER, 709 North Lincoln Avenue, Jerome, ID, Zip 83338–1851, Mailing Address: P.O. Box 586, Zip 83338–0586; tel. 208/324–4301; Michael C. Wiltermood, Administrator

TWIN FALLS CLINIC HOSPITAL, 666 Shoshone Street East, Twin Falls, ID, Zip 83301–6168, Mailing Address: P.O. Box 1233, Zip 83301–1233; tel. 208/733–3700; Marley D. Jackman, Administrator

WOOD RIVER MEDICAL CENTER, Sun Valley Road, Sun Valley, ID, Zip 83353, Mailing Address: P.O. Box 86, Zip 83353–0086; tel. 208/622–3333; Jon Moses, Administrator

ILLINOIS

ADVOCATE HEALTH CARE
2025 Windsor Drive, Oak Brook, IL 60523; tel. 630/572–9393; Richard R. Risk, President & CEO

BETHANY HOSPITAL, 3435 West Van Buren Street, Chicago, IL, Zip 60624–3399; tel. 773/265–7700; Lena L. Shields, Chief Executive

CHRIST HOSPITAL AND MEDICAL CENTER, 4440 West 95th Street, Oak Lawn, IL, Zip 60453–2699; tel. 708/425–8000; Carol Schneider, Chief Executive

GOOD SAMARITAN HOSPITAL, 3815 Highland Avenue, Downers Grove, IL, Zip 60515–1590; tel. 630/275–5900; David M. McConkey, Chief Executive

GOOD SHEPHERD HOSPITAL, 450 West Highway 22, Barrington, IL, Zip 60010–1901; tel. 847/381–9600; Russell E. Feurer, Chief Executive

LUTHERAN GENERAL HOSPITAL, 1775 Dempster Street, Park Ridge, IL, Zip 60068–1174; tel. 847/723–2210; Kenneth J. Rojek, Chief Executive

RAVENSWOOD HOSPITAL MEDICAL CENTER, 4550 North Winchester Avenue, Chicago, IL, Zip 60640–5205; tel. 773/878–4300; John E. Blair, President and Chief Executive Officer

SOUTH SUBURBAN HOSPITAL, 17800 South Kedzie Avenue, Hazel Crest, IL, Zip 60429–0989; tel. 708/799–8000; Robert Rutkowski, Chief Executive

TRINITY HOSPITAL, 2320 East 93rd Street, Chicago, IL, Zip 60617–3982; tel. 773/978–2000; John N. Schwartz, Chief Executive Officer

TRINITY MEDICAL CENTER–WEST CAMPUS, 2701 17th Street, Rock Island, IL, Zip 61201–5393; tel. 309/779–5000; Eric Crowell, President and Chief Executive Officer

CATHOLIC HEALTH PARTNERS
2520 North Lakeview Avenue, Chicago, IL 60614; tel. 312/883–7300; Sister Theresa Peck, Chief Exectuve Officer

COLUMBUS HOSPITAL, 2520 North Lakeview Avenue, Chicago, IL, Zip 60614–1895; tel. 773/388–7300; Sister Theresa Peck, President and Chief Executive Officer

SAINT ANTHONY HOSPITAL, 2875 West 19th Street, Chicago, IL, Zip 60623–3596; tel. 773/521–1710; Sister Theresa Peck, President and Chief Executive Officer

ST. JOSEPH HOSPITAL, 2900 North Lake Shore Drive, Chicago, IL, Zip 60657–6274; tel. 773/665–3000; Sister Theresa Peck, President and Chief Executive Officer

CENTEGRA HEALTH SYSTEM
4309 Medical Center Drive, Suite B202, McHenry, IL 60090; tel. 815/759–8100; Gail Bumgarner, Vice President

MEMORIAL MEDICAL CENTER, Highway 14 and Doty Road, Woodstock, IL, Zip 60098–3797, Mailing Address: P.O. Box 1990, Zip 60098–1990; tel. 815/338–2500; Paul E. Laudick, President and Chief Executive Officer

NORTHERN ILLINOIS MEDICAL CENTER, 4201 Medical Center Drive, McHenry, IL, Zip 60050–9506; tel. 815/759–8110; Paul E. Laudick, President and Chief Executive Officer

FAMILY HEALTH NETWORK, INC.
910 W. Van Buren – 6th Floor, Chicago, IL 60607; tel. 312/491–1956; Philip C. Bradley, President & CEO

DOCTORS HOSPITAL OF HYDE PARK, 5800 South Stony Island Avenue, Chicago, IL, Zip 60637–2099; tel. 773/643–9200; Stephen M. Weinstein, Chief Executive Officer

ILLINOIS MASONIC MEDICAL CENTER, 836 West Wellington Avenue, Chicago, IL, Zip 60657–5193; tel. 773/975–1600; Bruce C. Campbell, President and Chief Executive Officer

MERCY HOSPITAL AND MEDICAL CENTER, 2525 South Michigan Avenue, Chicago, IL, Zip 60616–2477; tel. 312/567–2000; Charles B. Van Vorst, President and Chief Executive Officer

MOUNT SINAI HOSPITAL MEDICAL CENTER OF CHICAGO, California Avenue and 15th Street, Chicago, IL, Zip 60608–1610; tel. 773/542–2000; Benn Greenspan, President and Chief Executive Officer

NORWEGIAN–AMERICAN HOSPITAL, 1044 North Francisco Avenue, Chicago, IL, Zip 60622–2794; tel. 773/292–8200; Clarence A. Nagelvoort, President and Chief Executive Officer

ROSELAND COMMUNITY HOSPITAL, 45 West 111th Street, Chicago, IL, Zip 60628–4294; tel. 773/995–3000; Oliver D. Krage, President and Chief Executive Officer

RUSH–PRESBYTERIAN–ST. LUKE'S MEDICAL CENTER, 1653 West Congress Parkway, Chicago, IL, Zip 60612–3833; tel. 312/942–5000; Leo M. Henikoff, President and Chief Executive Officer

SAINT BERNARD HOSPITAL AND HEALTH CARE CENTER, 326 west 64th Street, Chicago, IL, Zip 60621; tel. 773/962–3900; Sister Elizabeth Van Straten, President and Chief Executive Officer

SAINT MARY OF NAZARETH HOSPITAL CENTER, 2233 West Division Street, Chicago, IL, Zip 60622–3086; tel. 312/770–2000; Sister Stella Louise, President and Chief Executive Officer

SCHWAB REHABILITATION HOSPITAL AND CARE NETWORK, 1401 South California Boulevard, Chicago, IL, Zip 60608–1612; tel. 773/522–2010; Kathleen C. Yosko, President and Chief Executive Officer

FELICIAN HEALTH CARE, INC.
3800 Peterson Avenue, Chicago, IL 60659; tel. 414/647–5622; Sister Mary Clarette, CSSF

ST. FRANCIS HOSPITAL, 3237 South 16th Street, Milwaukee, WI, Zip 53215–4592; tel. 414/647–5000; Gregory A. Banaszynski, President

ST. MARY'S HOSPITAL, 400 North Pleasant Avenue, Centralia, IL, Zip 62801–3091; tel. 618/532–6731; James W. McDowell, President and Chief Executive Officer

FREEPORT REGIONAL HEALTH PLAN
1045 West Stephenson Street, Freeport, IL 61032; tel. 815/235–0272; Shelly Dunham, Provider and Member Service Coordinator

FREEPORT MEMORIAL HOSPITAL, 1045 West Stephenson Street, Freeport, IL, Zip 61032–4899; tel. 815/235–4131; Joseph E. Bonnett, Executive Vice President and Chief Executive Officer

MEDACOM TRI-STATE
1315 West 22nd Street, Suite 300, Oakbrook, IL 60521; tel. 630/954–1880; Elizabeth Kerr, Network Coordinator

BETHANY HOSPITAL, 3435 West Van Buren Street, Chicago, IL, Zip 60624–3399; tel. 773/265–7700; Lena L. Shields, Chief Executive

CHRIST HOSPITAL AND MEDICAL CENTER, 4440 West 95th Street, Oak Lawn, IL, Zip 60453–2699; tel. 708/425–8000; Carol Schneider, Chief Executive

DELNOR–COMMUNITY HOSPITAL, 300 Randall Road, Geneva, IL, Zip 60134–4200; tel. 630/208–3000; Craig A. Livermore, President and Chief Executive Officer

GENESIS MEDICAL CENTER, 1227 East Rusholme Street, Davenport, IA, Zip 52803–2498; tel. 319/421–1000; Leo A. Bressanelli, President and Chief Executive Officer

GOOD SAMARITAN HOSPITAL, 3815 Highland Avenue, Downers Grove, IL, Zip 60515–1590; tel. 630/275–5900; David M. McConkey, Chief Executive

GOOD SAMARITAN REGIONAL HEALTH CENTER, 605 North 12th Street, Mount Vernon, IL, Zip 62864–2899; tel. 618/242–4600; Leo F. Childers, Jr., FACHE, President

GOOD SHEPHERD HOSPITAL, 450 West Highway 22, Barrington, IL, Zip 60010–1901; tel. 847/381–9600; Russell E. Feurer, Chief Executive

LA GRANGE MEMORIAL HOSPITAL, 5101 South Willow Spring Road, La Grange, IL, Zip 60525–2680; tel. 708/352–1200; Cathleen D. Biga, President and Chief Executive Officer

LOYOLA UNIVERSITY MEDICAL CENTER, 2160 South First Avenue, Maywood, IL, Zip 60153–5585; tel. 708/216–9000; Anthony L. Barbato, M.D., President and Chief Executive Officer

PROVENA SAINT JOSEPH HOSPITAL, 77 North Airlite Street, Elgin, IL, Zip 60123–4912; tel. 847/695–3200; Larry Narum, President

PROVENA SAINT JOSEPH MEDICAL CENTER, 333 North Madison Street, Joliet, IL, Zip 60435–6595; tel. 815/725–7133; David W. Benfer, President and Chief Executive Officer

PROVENA SAINT THERESE MEDICAL CENTER, 2615 Washington Street, Waukegan, IL, Zip 60085–4988; tel. 847/249–3900; Timothy P. Selz, President and Chief Executive Officer

PROVENA UNITED SAMARITANS MEDICAL CENTER, 812 North Logan, Danville, IL, Zip 61832–3788; tel. 217/442–6300; Dennis J. Doran, President and Chief Executive Officer

SAINT FRANCIS HOSPITAL AND HEALTH CENTER, 12935 South Gregory Street, Blue Island, IL, Zip 60406–2470; tel. 708/597–2000; Jay E. Kreuzer, FACHE, President

SOUTH SUBURBAN HOSPITAL, 17800 South Kedzie Avenue, Hazel Crest, IL, Zip 60429–0989; tel. 708/799–8000; Robert Rutkowski, Chief Executive

ST. JAMES HOSPITAL AND HEALTH CENTERS, 1423 Chicago Road, Chicago Heights, IL, Zip 60411–3483; tel. 708/756–1000; Peter J. Murphy, President and Chief Executive Officer

ST. MARYS HOSPITAL MEDICAL CENTER, 707 South Mills Street, Madison, WI, Zip 53715–0450; tel. 608/251–6100; Gerald W. Lefert, President

SWEDISHAMERICAN HEALTH SYSTEM, 1313 East State Street, Rockford, IL, Zip 61104; tel. 815/968–4400; Robert B. Klint, M.D., President and Chief Executive Officer

TRINITY HOSPITAL, 2320 East 93rd Street, Chicago, IL, Zip 60617–3982; tel. 773/978–2000; John N. Schwartz, Chief Executive Officer

MERCER COUNTY COMMUNITY CARE NETWORK
409 NorthWest Ninth Avenue, Aledo, IL 61231; tel. 309/582–5301; Bruce D. Peterson, CEO

MERCER COUNTY HOSPITAL, 409 N.W. Ninth Avenue, Aledo, IL, Zip 61231–1296; tel. 309/582–5301; Bruce D. Peterson, Administrator

NORTHWESTERN HEALTHCARE NETWORK
980 North Michigan Avenue, Suite 1500, Chicago, IL 60611; tel. 312/335–6000; Amy Kosifas, Assistant Vice President–Planning

CHILDREN'S MEMORIAL HOSPITAL, 2300 Children's Plaza, Chicago, IL, Zip 60614–3394; tel. 773/880–4000; Patrick M. Magoon, President and Chief Executive Officer

EVANSTON HOSPITAL, 2650 Ridge Avenue, Evanston, IL, Zip 60201–1797; tel. 847/570–2000; Mark R. Neaman, President and Chief Executive Officer

HIGHLAND PARK HOSPITAL, 718 Glenview Avenue, Highland Park, IL, Zip 60035–2497; tel. 847/480–3905; Ronald G. Spaeth, President and Chief Executive Officer

INGALLS HOSPITAL, One Ingalls Drive, Harvey, IL, Zip 60426–3591; tel. 708/333–2300; Robert L. Harris, President and Chief Executive Officer

NORTHWEST COMMUNITY HEALTHCARE, 800 West Central Road, Arlington Heights, IL, Zip 60005–2392; tel. 847/618–1000; Bruce K. Crowther, President and Chief Executive Officer

NORTHWESTERN MEMORIAL HOSPITAL, Superior Street and Fairbanks Court, Chicago, IL, Zip 60611–2950; tel. 312/908–2000; Gary A. Mecklenburg, President and Chief Executive Officer

SILVER CROSS HOSPITAL, 1200 Maple Road, Joliet, IL, Zip 60432–1497; tel. 815/740–1100; Paul Pawlak, President and Chief Executive Officer

SWEDISH COVENANT HOSPITAL, 5145 North California Avenue, Chicago, IL, Zip 60625–3688; tel. 773/878–8200; Edward A. Cucci, President and Chief Executive Officer

RUSH SYSTEM FOR HEALTH
820 West Jackson, Suite 200, Chicago, IL 60607; tel. 312/831–9858; Patricia Dillon, Associate Director

HOLY FAMILY MEDICAL CENTER, 100 North River Road, Des Plaines, IL, Zip 60016–1255; tel. 847/297–1800; Sister Patricia Ann Koschalke, President and Chief Executive Officer

ILLINOIS MASONIC MEDICAL CENTER, 836 West Wellington Avenue, Chicago, IL, Zip 60657–5193; tel. 773/975–1600; Bruce C. Campbell, President and Chief Executive Officer

LAKE FOREST HOSPITAL, 660 North Westmoreland Road, Lake Forest, IL, Zip 60045–1696; tel. 847/234–5600; William G. Ries, President

OAK PARK HOSPITAL, 520 South Maple Avenue, Oak Park, IL, Zip 60304–1097; tel. 708/383–9300; Bruce M. Elegant, President and Chief Executive Officer

RIVERSIDE MEDICAL CENTER, 350 North Wall Street, Kankakee, IL, Zip 60901–0749; tel. 815/933–1671; Dennis C. Millirons, President and Chief Executive Officer

RUSH NORTH SHORE MEDICAL CENTER, 9600 Gross Point Road, Skokie, IL, Zip 60076–1257; tel. 847/677–9600; John S. Frigo, President

RUSH–COPLEY MEMORIAL HOSPITAL, 2000 Ogden Avenue, Aurora, IL, Zip 60504–4206; tel. 630/978–6200; Martin Losoff, President and Chief Operating Officer

RUSH–PRESBYTERIAN–ST. LUKE'S MEDICAL CENTER, 1653 West Congress Parkway, Chicago, IL, Zip 60612–3833; tel. 312/942–5000; Leo M. Henikoff, President and Chief Executive Officer

SERVANTCOR
335 East Fifth Avenue, Clifton, IL 60927; tel. 815/937–2034; Joseph F. Feth, President

CENTRAL COMMUNITY HOSPITAL, 335 East Fifth Avenue, Clifton, IL, Zip 60927, Mailing Address: P.O. Box 68, Zip 60927–0068; tel. 815/694–2392; Steven S. Wilder, President and Chief Executive Officer

PROVENA COVENANT MEDICAL CENTER, 1400 West Park Street, Urbana, IL, Zip 61801–2396; tel. 217/337–2000; Diane Friedman, R.N., President and Chief Executive Officer

PROVENA ST. MARY'S HOSPITAL, 500 West Court Street, Kankakee, IL, Zip 60901–3661; tel. 815/937–2400; Allan C. Sonduck, President and Chief Executive Officer

SWEDISHAMERICAN HEALTH SYSTEM
1313 East State Street, Rockford, IL 61104; tel. 815/968–4400; Kathy Humansen, Management Engineering

SWEDISHAMERICAN HEALTH SYSTEM, 1313 East State Street, Rockford, IL, Zip 61104; tel. 815/968–4400; Robert B. Klint, M.D., President and Chief Executive Officer

SYNERGON HEALTH SYSTEM
520 South Maple Avenue, Oak Park, IL 60304; tel. 708/660–2060; Julie Stasiak, Director of Planning

OAK PARK HOSPITAL, 520 South Maple Avenue, Oak Park, IL, Zip 60304–1097; tel. 708/383–9300; Bruce M. Elegant, President and Chief Executive Officer

THE CARLE FOUNDATION
611 West Park Street, Urbana, IL 61801; tel. 217/383–3311; Karen Shelby, Network Contact

CARLE FOUNDATION HOSPITAL, 611 West Park Street, Urbana, IL, Zip 61801–2595; tel. 217/383–3311; Michael H. Fritz, President

THE PAVILION, 809 West Church Street, Champaign, IL, Zip 61820; tel. 217/373–1700; Nina W. Eisner, Chief Executive Officer

UNIFIED HEALTH CARE NETWORK
2160 South 1st Avenue, Building 105, Room 3922, Maywood, IL 60153; tel. 708/216–9190; Burton VanderLaan, M.D., President

LOYOLA UNIVERSITY MEDICAL CENTER, 2160 South First Avenue, Maywood, IL, Zip 60153–5585; tel. 708/216–9000; Anthony L. Barbato, M.D., President and Chief Executive Officer

OUR LADY OF THE RESURRECTION MEDICAL CENTER, 5645 West Addison Street, Chicago, IL, Zip 60634–4455; tel. 773/282–7000; Ronald E. Struxness, Executive Vice President and Chief Executive Officer

RESURRECTION MEDICAL CENTER, 7435 West Talcott Avenue, Chicago, IL, Zip 60631–3746; tel. 773/774–8000; Sister Donna Marie, Executive Vice President and Chief Executive Officer

SAINT BERNARD HOSPITAL AND HEALTH CARE CENTER, 326 west 64th Street, Chicago, IL, Zip 60621; tel. 773/962–3900; Sister Elizabeth Van Straten, President and Chief Executive Officer

SAINT FRANCIS MEDICAL CENTER, 530 N.E. Glen Oak Avenue, Peoria, IL, Zip 61637; tel. 309/655–2000; Sister M. Canisia, Administrator

SAINT JAMES HOSPITAL, 610 East Water Street, Pontiac, IL, Zip 61764–2194; tel. 815/842–2828; David Ochs, Administrator

SAINT MARY OF NAZARETH HOSPITAL CENTER, 2233 West Division Street, Chicago, IL, Zip 60622–3086; tel. 312/770–2000; Sister Stella Louise, President and Chief Executive Officer

UNIVERSITY OF CHICAGO HOSPITALS & HEALTH SYSTEM
5841 South Maryland Avenue, Chicago, IL 60637; tel. 773/702–1000; Ralph Muller, President

LOUIS A. WEISS MEMORIAL HOSPITAL, 4646 North Marine Drive, Chicago, IL, Zip 60640–1501; tel. 773/878–8700; Gregory A. Cierlik, President and Chief Executive Officer

UNIVERSITY OF CHICAGO HOSPITALS, 5841 South Maryland Avenue, Chicago, IL, Zip 60637–1470; tel. 773/702–1000; Steven Lipstein, President and Chief Operating Officer

INDIANA

ANCILLA SYSTEMS, INC.
1000 South Lake Park Avenue, Hobart, IN 46342; tel. 219/947–8500; William D. Harkins, President

ST. CATHERINE HOSPITAL, 4321 Fir Street, East Chicago, IN, Zip 46312–3097; tel. 219/392–7000; JoAnn Birdzell, President and Chief Executive Officer

ST. ELIZABETH'S HOSPITAL, 1431 North Claremont Avenue, Chicago, IL, Zip 60622–1791; tel. 773/278–2000; JoAnn Birdzell, President and Chief Executive Officer

ST. JOSEPH MEDICAL CENTER OF FORT WAYNE, 700 Broadway, Fort Wayne, IN, Zip 46802–1493; tel. 219/425–3000; John T. Farrell, Sr., President and Chief Executive Officer

ST. MARY'S HOSPITAL, 129 North Eighth Street, East St. Louis, IL, Zip 62201–2999; tel. 618/274–1900; Richard J. Mark, President and Chief Executive Officer

ST. MARY'S MEDICAL CENTER OF EVANSVILLE, 3700 Washington Avenue, Evansville, IN, Zip 47750; tel. 812/485–4000; Richard C. Breon, President and Chief Executive Officer

CAYLOR–NICKEL HEALTH NETWORK
One Caylor–Nickel Square, Bluffton, IN 46714; tel. 219/824–3500; William F. Brockman, Chief Executive Officer

CAYLOR–NICKEL MEDICAL CENTER, One Caylor–Nickel Square, Bluffton, IN, Zip 46714–2529; tel. 219/824–3500; William F. Brockmann, President and Chief Executive Officer

JAY COUNTY HOSPITAL, 500 West Votaw Street, Portland, IN, Zip 47371–1322; tel. 219/726–7131; Sheri Frankenfield, Chief Executive Officer

RANDOLPH COUNTY HOSPITAL AND HEALTH SERVICES, 325 South Oak Street, Winchester, IN, Zip 47394–2235, Mailing Address: P.O. Box 407, Zip 47394–0407; tel. 765/584–9001; James M. Full, Chief Executive Officer

COMMUNITY HEALTH ALLIANCE
707 North Michigan Street, Suite 100, South Bend, IN 46601; tel. 219/284–1825; David Sage, Chief Operating Officer

ELKHART GENERAL HOSPITAL, 600 East Boulevard, Elkhart, IN, Zip 46514–2499, Mailing Address: P.O. Box 1329, Zip 46515–1329; tel. 219/294–2621; Gregory W. Lintjer, President

LA PORTE HOSPITAL AND HEALTH SERVICES, 1007 Lincolnway, La Porte, IN, Zip 46352–0250, Mailing Address: P.O. Box 250, Zip 46350–0250; tel. 219/326–1234; Leigh E. Morris, President

LUTHERAN HOSPITAL OF INDIANA, 7950 West Jefferson Boulevard, Fort Wayne, IN, Zip 46804–1677; tel. 219/435–7001; Thomas D. Miller, Chief Executive Officer

HOLY CROSS HEALTH SYSTEM
3606 East Jefferson Boulevard, South Bend, IN 46615–3097; tel. 219/233–8558; Sister Pat Vandenburg, President & Chief Executive Officer

SAINT JOHN'S HEALTH SYSTEM, 2015 Jackson Street, Anderson, IN, Zip 46016–4339; tel. 765/649–2511; Jerry D. Brumitt, President and Chief Executive Officer

SAINT JOSEPH'S HOSPITAL OF MARSHALL COUNTY, 1915 Lake Avenue, Plymouth, IN, Zip 46563–9905, Mailing Address: P.O. Box 670, Zip 46563–9905; tel. 219/936–3181; Brian E. Dietz, FACHE, Executive Vice President

ST. JOSEPH'S MEDICAL CENTER, 801 East LaSalle, South Bend, IN, Zip 46617–2800, Mailing Address: P.O. Box 1935, Zip 46634–1935; tel. 219/237–7111; Robert L. Beyer, President and Chief Executive Officer

LUTHERANPREFERRED NETWORK
7950 West Jefferson Boulevard, Fort Wayne, IN 46804; tel. 219/435–7001; Michael Schatzlein, Vice President

ADAMS COUNTY MEMORIAL HOSPITAL, 805 High Street, Decatur, IN, Zip 46733–2311, Mailing Address: P.O. Box 151, Zip 46733–0151; tel. 219/724–2145; Marvin L. Baird, Executive Director

BLACKFORD COUNTY HOSPITAL, 503 East Van Cleve Street, Hartford City, IN, Zip 47348–1897; tel. 765/348–0300; David Masterson, Chief Executive Officer

CAMERON MEMORIAL COMMUNITY HOSPITAL, 416 East Maumee Street, Angola, IN, Zip 46703–2015; tel. 219/665–2141; Dennis L. Knapp, President

CAYLOR–NICKEL MEDICAL CENTER, One Caylor–Nickel Square, Bluffton, IN, Zip 46714–2529; tel. 219/824–3500; William F. Brockmann, President and Chief Executive Officer

COMMUNITY MEMORIAL HOSPITAL, 208 North Columbus Street, Hicksville, OH, Zip 43526–1299; tel. 419/542–6692; Deryl E. Gulliford, Ph.D., Administrator

DEFIANCE HOSPITAL, 1206 East Second Street, Defiance, OH, Zip 43512–2495; tel. 419/783–6955; Richard C. Sommer, Administrator

DEKALB MEMORIAL HOSPITAL, 1316 East Seventh Street, Auburn, IN, Zip 46706–2515, Mailing Address: P.O. Box 542, Zip 46706–0542; tel. 219/925–4600; Jack M. Corey, President

DUKES MEMORIAL HOSPITAL, 275 West 12th Street, Peru, IN, Zip 46970–1698; tel. 765/473–6621; R. Joe Johnston, President and Chief Executive Officer

HUNTINGTON MEMORIAL HOSPITAL, 1215 Etna Avenue, Huntington, IN, Zip 46750–3696; tel. 219/356–3000; L. Kent McCoy, President

INDIANA UNIVERSITY MEDICAL CENTER, 550 North University Boulevard, Indianapolis, IN, Zip 46202–5262; tel. 317/274–5000

JAY COUNTY HOSPITAL, 500 West Votaw Street, Portland, IN, Zip 47371–1322; tel. 219/726–7131; Sheri Frankenfield, Chief Executive Officer

KOSCIUSKO COMMUNITY HOSPITAL, 2101 East Dubois Drive, Warsaw, IN, Zip 46580–3288; tel. 219/267–3200; Wayne Hendrix, President

LUTHERAN HOSPITAL OF INDIANA, 7950 West Jefferson Boulevard, Fort Wayne, IN, Zip 46804–1677; tel. 219/435–7001; Thomas D. Miller, Chief Executive Officer

MCCRAY MEMORIAL HOSPITAL, 951 East Hospital Drive, Kendallville, IN, Zip 46755–2293, Mailing Address: P.O. Box 249, Zip 46755–0249; tel. 219/347–1100; John Berhow, President

Section B

MERCER COUNTY JOINT TOWNSHIP COMMUNITY HOSPITAL, 800 West Main Street, Coldwater, OH, Zip 45828–1698; tel. 419/678–2341; James W. Isaacs, Chief Executive Officer

PAULDING COUNTY HOSPITAL, 11558 State Road 111, Paulding, OH, Zip 45879–9220; tel. 419/399–4080; Joseph M. Dorko, Chief Executive Officer

VAN WERT COUNTY HOSPITAL, 1250 South Washington Street, Van Wert, OH, Zip 45891–2599; tel. 419/238–2390; Mark J. Minick, President and Chief Executive Officer

WABASH COUNTY HOSPITAL, 710 North East Street, Wabash, IN, Zip 46992–1924, Mailing Address: P.O. Box 548, Zip 46992–0548; tel. 219/563–3131; David C. Hunter, Chief Executive Officer

WELLS COMMUNITY HOSPITAL, 1100 South Main Street, Bluffton, IN, Zip 46714–3697; tel. 219/824–3210; Dianne Surfus, Interim Chief Executive Officer

METHODIST HOSPITAL OF INDIANA
P.O. Box 1367, Indianapolis, IN 46202;
tel. 317/929–2000; William J. Loveday,
President & Chief Executive Officer

METHODIST HOSPITAL OF INDIANA, 1701 North Senate Boulevard, Indianapolis, IN, Zip 46202, Mailing Address: I. 65 at 21st Street, P.O. Box 1367, Zip 46206–1367; tel. 317/929–2000

REHABILITATION HOSPITAL OF INDIANA, 4141 Shore Drive, Indianapolis, IN, Zip 46254–2607; tel. 317/329–2000; Kim D. Eicher, President and Chief Executive Officer

MIDWEST HEALTH NET, LLC.
6202 Constitution Drive, Fort Wayne, IN
46804; tel. 219/436–7879; Thomas C. Henry,
President

BEDFORD REGIONAL MEDICAL CENTER, 2900 West 16th Street, Bedford, IN, Zip 47421–3583; tel. 812/275–1200; John R. Birdzell, FACHE, Chief Executive Officer

CAMERON MEMORIAL COMMUNITY HOSPITAL, 416 East Maumee Street, Angola, IN, Zip 46703–2015; tel. 219/665–2141; Dennis L. Knapp, President

CAYLOR–NICKEL MEDICAL CENTER, One Caylor–Nickel Square, Bluffton, IN, Zip 46714–2529; tel. 219/824–3500; William F. Brockmann, President and Chief Executive Officer

CLINTON COUNTY HOSPITAL, 1300 South Jackson Street, Frankfort, IN, Zip 46041–3394, Mailing Address: P.O. Box 669, Zip 46041–0669; tel. 765/659–4731; Brian R. Zeh, Executive Director

COMMUNITY HOSPITAL OF ANDERSON AND MADISON COUNTY, 1515 North Madison Avenue, Anderson, IN, Zip 46011–3453; tel. 765/642–8011

DECATUR COUNTY MEMORIAL HOSPITAL, 720 North Lincoln Street, Greensburg, IN, Zip 47240–1398; tel. 812/663–4331; Charles Duffy, President

DEKALB MEMORIAL HOSPITAL, 1316 East Seventh Street, Auburn, IN, Zip 46706–2515, Mailing Address: P.O. Box 542, Zip 46706–0542; tel. 219/925–4600; Jack M. Corey, President

DOCTORS HOSPITAL OF JACKSON, 110 North Elm Avenue, Jackson, MI, Zip 49202–3595; tel. 517/787–1440; Michael J. Falatko, President and Chief Executive Officer

DUKES MEMORIAL HOSPITAL, 275 West 12th Street, Peru, IN, Zip 46970–1698; tel. 765/473–6621; R. Joe Johnston, President and Chief Executive Officer

FISHER–TITUS MEDICAL CENTER, 272 Benedict Avenue, Norwalk, OH, Zip 44857–2374; tel. 419/668–8101; Patrick J. Martin, President and Chief Executive Officer

GREENE COUNTY GENERAL HOSPITAL, Rural Route 1, Box 1000, Linton, IN, Zip 47441–9457; tel. 812/847–2281; Jonas S. Uland, Executive Director

HANCOCK MEMORIAL HOSPITAL AND HEALTH SERVICES, 801 North State Street, Greenfield, IN, Zip 46140–1270, Mailing Address: P.O. Box 827, Zip 46140–0827; tel. 317/462–5544; Robert C. Keen, Ph.D., CHE, President and Chief Executive Officer

HENRY COUNTY HOSPITAL, 11–600 State Road 424, Napoleon, OH, Zip 43545–9399; tel. 419/592–4015; Robert J. Coholich, Chief Executive Officer

HENRY COUNTY MEMORIAL HOSPITAL, 1000 North 16th Street, New Castle, IN, Zip 47362–4319, Mailing Address: P.O. Box 490, Zip 47362–0490; tel. 765/521–0890; Jack Basler, President

HOWARD COMMUNITY HOSPITAL, 3500 South La Fountain Street, Kokomo, IN, Zip 46904–9011; tel. 765/453–0702; James C. Bigogno, FACHE, President and Chief Executive Officer

HUNTINGTON MEMORIAL HOSPITAL, 1215 Etna Avenue, Huntington, IN, Zip 46750–3696; tel. 219/356–3000; L. Kent McCoy, President

JOHNSON MEMORIAL HOSPITAL, 1125 West Jefferson Street, Franklin, IN, Zip 46131–2140, Mailing Address: P.O. Box 549, Zip 46131–0549; tel. 317/736–3300; Gregg A. Bechtold, President and Chief Executive Officer

KOSCIUSKO COMMUNITY HOSPITAL, 2101 East Dubois Drive, Warsaw, IN, Zip 46580–3288; tel. 219/267–3200; Wayne Hendrix, President

LIMA MEMORIAL HOSPITAL, 1001 Bellefontaine Avenue, Lima, OH, Zip 45804–2894; tel. 419/228–3335; John B. White, President and Chief Executive Officer

MCCRAY MEMORIAL HOSPITAL, 951 East Hospital Drive, Kendallville, IN, Zip 46755–2293, Mailing Address: P.O. Box 249, Zip 46755–0249; tel. 219/347–1100; John Berhow, President

MEDICAL COLLEGE OF OHIO HOSPITALS, 3000 Arlington Avenue, Toledo, OH, Zip 43614–5805; tel. 419/381–4172; Frank S. McCullough, M.D., President

MERCY MEMORIAL HOSPITAL, 740 North Macomb Street, Monroe, MI, Zip 48161–9974, Mailing Address: P.O. Box 67, Zip 48161–0067; tel. 734/241–1700; Richard S. Hiltz, President and Chief Executive Officer

METHODIST HOSPITAL OF INDIANA, 1701 North Senate Boulevard, Indianapolis, IN, Zip 46202, Mailing Address: I. 65 at 21st Street, P.O. Box 1367, Zip 46206–1367; tel. 317/929–2000

MORGAN COUNTY MEMORIAL HOSPITAL, 2209 John R. Wooden Drive, Martinsville, IN, Zip 46151–1840, Mailing Address: P.O. Box 1717, Zip 46151–1717; tel. 765/342–8441; S. Dean Melton, President and Chief Executive Officer

PARKVIEW HOSPITAL, 2200 Randallia Drive, Fort Wayne, IN, Zip 46805–4699; tel. 219/484–6636; Frank D. Byrne, M.D., President

PAULDING COUNTY HOSPITAL, 11558 State Road 111, Paulding, OH, Zip 45879–9220; tel. 419/399–4080; Joseph M. Dorko, Chief Executive Officer

RANDOLPH COUNTY HOSPITAL AND HEALTH SERVICES, 325 South Oak Street, Winchester, IN, Zip 47394–2235, Mailing Address: P.O. Box 407, Zip 47394–0407; tel. 765/584–9001; James M. Full, Chief Executive Officer

RIVERVIEW HOSPITAL, 395 Westfield Road, Noblesville, IN, Zip 46060–1425, Mailing Address: P.O. Box 220, Zip 46061–0220; tel. 317/773–0760; Seward Horner, President

ST MARY MEDICAL PLAZA, 2515 East Jefferson Boulevard, South Bend, IN, Zip 46615–2691; tel. 219/288–8311; Stephen L. Crain, President

ST. CATHERINE HOSPITAL, 4321 Fir Street, East Chicago, IN, Zip 46312–3097; tel. 219/392–7000; JoAnn Birdzell, President and Chief Executive Officer

ST. ELIZABETH'S HOSPITAL, 1431 North Claremont Avenue, Chicago, IL, Zip 60622–1791; tel. 773/278–2000; JoAnn Birdzell, President and Chief Executive Officer

ST. JOSEPH MEDICAL CENTER OF FORT WAYNE, 700 Broadway, Fort Wayne, IN, Zip 46802–1493; tel. 219/425–3000; John T. Farrell, Sr., President and Chief Executive Officer

ST. MARY MEDICAL CENTER, 1500 South Lake Park Avenue, Hobart, IN, Zip 46342–6699; tel. 219/942–0551; Milton Triana, President and Chief Executive Officer

ST. MARY'S HOSPITAL, 129 North Eighth Street, East St. Louis, IL, Zip 62201–2999; tel. 618/274–1900; Richard J. Mark, President and Chief Executive Officer

THE TOLEDO HOSPITAL, 2142 North Cove Boulevard, Toledo, OH, Zip 43606–3896; tel. 419/471–4000; Barbara Steele, President

TIPTON COUNTY MEMORIAL HOSPITAL, 1000 South Main Street, Tipton, IN, Zip 46072–9799; tel. 765/675–8500; Alfonso W. Gatmaitan, Chief Executive Officer

VAN WERT COUNTY HOSPITAL, 1250 South Washington Street, Van Wert, OH, Zip 45891–2599; tel. 419/238–2390; Mark J. Minick, President and Chief Executive Officer

WABASH COUNTY HOSPITAL, 710 North East Street, Wabash, IN, Zip 46992–1924, Mailing Address: P.O. Box 548, Zip 46992–0548; tel. 219/563–3131; David C. Hunter, Chief Executive Officer

WELLS COMMUNITY HOSPITAL, 1100 South Main Street, Bluffton, IN, Zip 46714–3697; tel. 219/824–3210; Dianne Surfus, Interim Chief Executive Officer

WESTVIEW HOSPITAL, 3630 Guion Road, Indianapolis, IN, Zip 46222–1699; tel. 317/924–6661; David C. Dyar, President and Administrator

WHITE COUNTY MEMORIAL HOSPITAL, 1101 O'Connor Boulevard, Monticello, IN, Zip 47960–1698; tel. 219/583–7111; John M. Avers, Chief Executive Officer

WHITLEY MEMORIAL HOSPITAL, 353 North Oak Street, Columbia City, IN, Zip 46725–1623; tel. 219/244–6191; John M. Hatcher, President

WITHAM MEMORIAL HOSPITAL, 1124 North Lebanon Street, Lebanon, IN, Zip 46052–1776, Mailing Address: P.O. Box 1200, Zip 46052–3005; tel. 765/482–2700; Ray Ingham, President and Chief Executive Officer

PARKVIEW HEALTH SYSTEM
146 Chestnut Street, Fort Wayne, IN 46805;
tel. 219/484–6636; David Ridderheim,
President & Chief Executive Officer

HUNTINGTON MEMORIAL HOSPITAL, 1215 Etna Avenue, Huntington, IN, Zip 46750–3696; tel. 219/356–3000; L. Kent McCoy, President

PARKVIEW HOSPITAL, 2200 Randallia Drive, Fort Wayne, IN, Zip 46805–4699; tel. 219/484–6636; Frank D. Byrne, M.D., President

WHITLEY MEMORIAL HOSPITAL, 353 North Oak Street, Columbia City, IN, Zip 46725–1623; tel. 219/244–6191; John M. Hatcher, President

SAGAMORE HEALTH NETWORK, INC.
11555 North Meridian, Suite 400, Carmel, IN
46032; tel. 317/573–2903; William R. Ealy,
President

ADAMS COUNTY MEMORIAL HOSPITAL, 805 High Street, Decatur, IN, Zip 46733–2311, Mailing Address: P.O. Box 151, Zip 46733–0151; tel. 219/724–2145; Marvin L. Baird, Executive Director

CAMERON MEMORIAL COMMUNITY HOSPITAL, 416 East Maumee Street, Angola, IN, Zip 46703–2015; tel. 219/665–2141; Dennis L. Knapp, President

CLAY COUNTY HOSPITAL, 1206 East National Avenue, Brazil, IN, Zip 47834–2797; tel. 812/448–2675; Jay P. Jolly, Administrator and Chief Executive Officer

CLINTON COUNTY HOSPITAL, 1300 South Jackson Street, Frankfort, IN, Zip 46041–3394, Mailing Address: P.O. Box 669, Zip 46041–0669; tel. 765/659–4731; Brian R. Zeh, Executive Director

COMMUNITY HOSPITAL OF BREMEN, 411 South Whitlock Street, Bremen, IN, Zip 46506–1699; tel. 219/546–2211; Scott R. Graybill, Chief Executive Officer and Administrator

Section B

COMMUNITY MEMORIAL HOSPITAL, 208 North Columbus Street, Hicksville, OH, Zip 43526–1299; tel. 419/542–6692; Deryl E. Gulliford, Ph.D., Administrator

DUKES MEMORIAL HOSPITAL, 275 West 12th Street, Peru, IN, Zip 46970–1698; tel. 765/473–6621; R. Joe Johnston, President and Chief Executive Officer

DUNN MEMORIAL HOSPITAL, 1600 23rd Street, Bedford, IN, Zip 47421–4704; tel. 812/275–3331; William W. Wissman, Interim Executive Director

FAIRBANKS HOSPITAL, 8102 Clearvista Parkway, Indianapolis, IN, Zip 46256–4698; tel. 317/849–8222; Timothy J. Kelly, M.D., President

FLOYD MEMORIAL HOSPITAL AND HEALTH SERVICES, 1850 State Street, New Albany, IN, Zip 47150–4997; tel. 812/949–5500; Bryant R. Hanson, President and Chief Executive Officer

GIBSON GENERAL HOSPITAL, 1808 Sherman Drive, Princeton, IN, Zip 47670–1043; tel. 812/385–3401; Michael J. Budnick, Administrator and Chief Executive Officer

GREENE COUNTY GENERAL HOSPITAL, Rural Route 1, Box 1000, Linton, IN, Zip 47441–9457; tel. 812/847–2281; Jonas S. Uland, Executive Director

HANCOCK MEMORIAL HOSPITAL AND HEALTH SERVICES, 801 North State Street, Greenfield, IN, Zip 46140–1270, Mailing Address: P.O. Box 827, Zip 46140–0827; tel. 317/462–5544; Robert C. Keen, Ph.D., CHE, President and Chief Executive Officer

HENDRICKS COMMUNITY HOSPITAL, 1000 East Main Street, Danville, IN, Zip 46122–0409, Mailing Address: P.O. Box 409, Zip 46122–0409; tel. 317/745–4451; Dennis W. Dawes, President

HENRY COUNTY MEMORIAL HOSPITAL, 1000 North 16th Street, New Castle, IN, Zip 47362–4319, Mailing Address: P.O. Box 490, Zip 47362–0490; tel. 765/521–0890; Jack Basler, President

HUNTINGTON MEMORIAL HOSPITAL, 1215 Etna Avenue, Huntington, IN, Zip 46750–3696; tel. 219/356–3000; L. Kent McCoy, President

INDIANA UNIVERSITY MEDICAL CENTER, 550 North University Boulevard, Indianapolis, IN, Zip 46202–5262; tel. 317/274–5000

JOHNSON MEMORIAL HOSPITAL, 1125 West Jefferson Street, Franklin, IN, Zip 46131–2140, Mailing Address: P.O. Box 549, Zip 46131–0549; tel. 317/736–3300; Gregg A. Bechtold, President and Chief Executive Officer

KENDRICK MEMORIAL HOSPITAL, 1201 Hadley Road N.W., Mooresville, IN, Zip 46158–1789; tel. 317/831–1160; Charles D. Swisher, Executive Director

KOSCIUSKO COMMUNITY HOSPITAL, 2101 East Dubois Drive, Warsaw, IN, Zip 46580–3288; tel. 219/267–3200; Wayne Hendrix, President

LA PORTE HOSPITAL AND HEALTH SERVICES, 1007 Lincolnway, La Porte, IN, Zip 46352–0250, Mailing Address: P.O. Box 250, Zip 46350–0250; tel. 219/326–1234; Leigh E. Morris, President

MARY SHERMAN HOSPITAL, 320 North Section Street, Sullivan, IN, Zip 47882–1239, Mailing Address: P.O. Box 10, Zip 47882–0010; tel. 812/268–4311; Thomas J. Hudgins, Administrator

MCCRAY MEMORIAL HOSPITAL, 951 East Hospital Drive, Kendallville, IN, Zip 46755–2293, Mailing Address: P.O. Box 249, Zip 46755–0249; tel. 219/347–1100; John Berhow, President

MEDICAL CENTER OF SOUTHERN INDIANA, 2200 Market Street, Charlestown, IN, Zip 47111–0069, Mailing Address: P.O. Box 69, Zip 47111–0069; tel. 812/256–3301; Kevin J. Miller, Chief Executive Officer

MEMORIAL HOSPITAL, 1101 Michigan Avenue, Logansport, IN, Zip 46947–7013, Mailing Address: P.O. Box 7013, Zip 46947–7013; tel. 219/753–7541; George W. Poor, President and Chief Executive Officer

METHODIST HOSPITAL OF INDIANA, 1701 North Senate Boulevard, Indianapolis, IN, Zip 46202, Mailing Address: I. 65 at 21st Street, P.O. Box 1367, Zip 46206–1367; tel. 317/929–2000

MORGAN COUNTY MEMORIAL HOSPITAL, 2209 John R. Wooden Drive, Martinsville, IN, Zip 46151–1840, Mailing Address: P.O. Box 1717, Zip 46151–1717; tel. 765/342–8441; S. Dean Melton, President and Chief Executive Officer

OAKLAWN PSYCHIATRIC CENTER, INC., 330 Lakeview Drive, Goshen, IN, Zip 46526–9365, Mailing Address: P.O. Box 809, Zip 46527–0809; tel. 219/533–1234; Harold C. Loewen, President

ORANGE COUNTY HOSPITAL, 642 West Hospital Road, Paoli, IN, Zip 47454–0499, Mailing Address: P.O. Box 499, Zip 47454–0499; tel. 812/723–2811; James W. Pope, Chief Executive Officer

PARKVIEW HOSPITAL, 2200 Randallia Drive, Fort Wayne, IN, Zip 46805–4699; tel. 219/484–6636; Frank D. Byrne, M.D., President

PULASKI MEMORIAL HOSPITAL, 616 East 13th Street, Winamac, IN, Zip 46996–1117; tel. 219/946–6131; Richard H. Mynark, Administrator

PUTNAM COUNTY HOSPITAL, 1542 Bloomington Street, Greencastle, IN, Zip 46135–2297; tel. 765/653–5121; John D. Fajt, Executive Director

RANDOLPH COUNTY HOSPITAL AND HEALTH SERVICES, 325 South Oak Street, Winchester, IN, Zip 47394–2235, Mailing Address: P.O. Box 407, Zip 47394–0407; tel. 765/584–9001; James M. Full, Chief Executive Officer

REHABILITATION HOSPITAL OF INDIANA, 4141 Shore Drive, Indianapolis, IN, Zip 46254–2607; tel. 317/329–2000; Kim D. Eicher, President and Chief Executive Officer

RIVERVIEW HOSPITAL, 395 Westfield Road, Noblesville, IN, Zip 46060–1425, Mailing Address: P.O. Box 220, Zip 46061–0220; tel. 317/773–0760; Seward Horner, President

RUSH MEMORIAL HOSPITAL, 1300 North Main Street, Rushville, IN, Zip 46173–1198; tel. 765/932–4111; H. William Hartley, Chief Executive Officer

SAINT ANTHONY MEMORIAL HEALTH CENTERS, 301 West Homer Street, Michigan City, IN, Zip 46360–4358; tel. 219/879–8511; Bruce E. Rampage, President and Chief Executive Officer

SAINT JOHN'S HEALTH SYSTEM, 2015 Jackson Street, Anderson, IN, Zip 46016–4339; tel. 765/649–2511; Jerry D. Brumitt, President and Chief Executive Officer

SAINT JOSEPH'S HOSPITAL OF MARSHALL COUNTY, 1915 Lake Avenue, Plymouth, IN, Zip 46563–9905, Mailing Address: P.O. Box 670, Zip 46563–9905; tel. 219/936–3181; Brian E. Dietz, FACHE, Executive Vice President

SAINT MARGARET MERCY HEALTHCARE CENTERS, 5454 Hohman Avenue, Hammond, IN, Zip 46320–1999; tel. 219/933–2074; Eugene C. Diamond, President and Chief Executive Officer

ST MARY MEDICAL PLAZA, 2515 East Jefferson Boulevard, South Bend, IN, Zip 46615–2691; tel. 219/288–8311; Stephen L. Crain, President

ST. ANTHONY MEDICAL CENTER, 1201 South Main Street, Crown Point, IN, Zip 46307–8483; tel. 219/738–2100; Stephen O. Leurck, President and Chief Executive Officer

ST. CATHERINE HOSPITAL, 4321 Fir Street, East Chicago, IN, Zip 46312–3097; tel. 219/392–7000; JoAnn Birdzell, President and Chief Executive Officer

ST. FRANCIS HOSPITAL AND HEALTH CENTERS, 1600 Albany Street, Beech Grove, IN, Zip 46107–1593; tel. 317/787–3311; Robert J. Brody, President and Chief Executive Officer

ST. JOSEPH MEDICAL CENTER OF FORT WAYNE, 700 Broadway, Fort Wayne, IN, Zip 46802–1493; tel. 219/425–3000; John T. Farrell, Sr., President and Chief Executive Officer

ST. JOSEPH'S MEDICAL CENTER, 801 East LaSalle, South Bend, IN, Zip 46617–2800, Mailing Address: P.O. Box 1935, Zip 46634–1935; tel. 219/237–7111; Robert L. Beyer, President and Chief Executive Officer

ST. MARY MEDICAL CENTER, 1500 South Lake Park Avenue, Hobart, IN, Zip 46342–6699; tel. 219/942–0551; Milton Triana, President and Chief Executive Officer

ST. MARY'S HOSPITAL WARRICK, 1116 Millis Avenue, Boonville, IN, Zip 47601–0629, Mailing Address: Box 629, Zip 47601–0629; tel. 812/897–4800; John D. O'Neil, Executive Vice President and Administrator

ST. MARY'S MEDICAL CENTER OF EVANSVILLE, 3700 Washington Avenue, Evansville, IN, Zip 47750; tel. 812/485–4000; Richard C. Breon, President and Chief Executive Officer

ST. VINCENT HOSPITALS AND HEALTH SERVICES, 2001 West 86th Street, Indianapolis, IN, Zip 46260–1991, Mailing Address: P.O. Box 40970, Zip 46240–0970; tel. 317/338–2345; Douglas D. French, President and Chief Executive Officer

ST. VINCENT MERCY HOSPITAL, 1331 South A. Street, Elwood, IN, Zip 46036–1942; tel. 765/552–4600; Ann C. Parsons, Interim Administrator

STARKE MEMORIAL HOSPITAL, 102 East Culver Road, Knox, IN, Zip 46534–2299; tel. 219/772–6231; Kathryn J. Norem, Executive Director

TIPTON COUNTY MEMORIAL HOSPITAL, 1000 South Main Street, Tipton, IN, Zip 46072–9799; tel. 765/675–8500; Alfonso W. Gatmaitan, Chief Executive Officer

UNION HOSPITAL, 1606 North Seventh Street, Terre Haute, IN, Zip 47804–2780; tel. 812/238–7000; Frank Shelton, President

WABASH COUNTY HOSPITAL, 710 North East Street, Wabash, IN, Zip 46992–1924, Mailing Address: P.O. Box 548, Zip 46992–0548; tel. 219/563–3131; David C. Hunter, Chief Executive Officer

WELLS COMMUNITY HOSPITAL, 1100 South Main Street, Bluffton, IN, Zip 46714–3697; tel. 219/824–3210; Dianne Surfus, Interim Chief Executive Officer

WESTVIEW HOSPITAL, 3630 Guion Road, Indianapolis, IN, Zip 46222–1699; tel. 317/924–6661; David C. Dyar, President and Administrator

WHITE COUNTY MEMORIAL HOSPITAL, 1101 O'Connor Boulevard, Monticello, IN, Zip 47960–1698; tel. 219/583–7111; John M. Avers, Chief Executive Officer

WHITLEY MEMORIAL HOSPITAL, 353 North Oak Street, Columbia City, IN, Zip 46725–1623; tel. 219/244–6191; John M. Hatcher, President

WITHAM MEMORIAL HOSPITAL, 1124 North Lebanon Street, Lebanon, IN, Zip 46052–1776, Mailing Address: P.O. Box 1200, Zip 46052–3005; tel. 765/482–2700; Ray Ingham, President and Chief Executive Officer

SAINT VINCENT HOSPITALS AND HEALTH SERVICES, INC.
2001 West 86th Street, Indianapolis, IN 40970; tel. 317/338–7000; Douglas D. French, President & Chief Executive Officer

JENNINGS COMMUNITY HOSPITAL, 301 Henry Street, North Vernon, IN, Zip 47265–1097; tel. 812/346–6200; Dalton L. Smart, Administrator

SAINT JOSEPH HOSPITAL & HEALTH CENTER, 1907 West Sycamore Street, Kokomo, IN, Zip 46904–9010, Mailing Address: P.O. Box 9010, Zip 46904–9010; tel. 765/452–5611; Kathleen M. Korbelak, President and Chief Executive Officer

ST. VINCENT MERCY HOSPITAL, 1331 South A. Street, Elwood, IN, Zip 46036–1942; tel. 765/552–4600; Ann C. Parsons, Interim Administrator

ST. VINCENT WILLIAMSPORT HOSPITAL, 412 North Monroe Street, Williamsport, IN, Zip 47993–0215; tel. 765/762–2496; Jane Craigin, Chief Executive Officer

SELECT HEALTH NETWORK
P.O. Box 1197, South Bend, IN 46624;
tel. 219/237-7822; Len Strzelecki, Chief
Executive Officer

ST. JOSEPH'S MEDICAL CENTER, 801 East LaSalle,
South Bend, IN, Zip 46617-2800, Mailing
Address: P.O. Box 1935, Zip 46634-1935;
tel. 219/237-7111; Robert L. Beyer, President
and Chief Executive Officer

SUBURBAN HEALTH ORGANIZATION
2780 Waterfront Parkway East Drive,
Indianapolis, IN 46214; tel. 317/692-5222;
Julie M. Carmichael, President

CLINTON COUNTY HOSPITAL, 1300 South Jackson
Street, Frankfort, IN, Zip 46041-3394, Mailing
Address: P.O. Box 669, Zip 46041-0669;
tel. 765/659-4731; Brian R. Zeh, Executive
Director

HANCOCK MEMORIAL HOSPITAL AND HEALTH
SERVICES, 801 North State Street, Greenfield,
IN, Zip 46140-1270, Mailing Address: P.O. Box
827, Zip 46140-0827; tel. 317/462-5544;
Robert C. Keen, Ph.D., CHE, President and Chief
Executive Officer

HENDRICKS COMMUNITY HOSPITAL, 1000 East Main
Street, Danville, IN, Zip 46122-0409, Mailing
Address: P.O. Box 409, Zip 46122-0409;
tel. 317/745-4451; Dennis W. Dawes, President

HENRY COUNTY MEMORIAL HOSPITAL, 1000 North
16th Street, New Castle, IN, Zip 47362-4319,
Mailing Address: P.O. Box 490,
Zip 47362-0490; tel. 765/521-0890; Jack
Basler, President

JOHNSON MEMORIAL HOSPITAL, 1125 West
Jefferson Street, Franklin, IN, Zip 46131-2140,
Mailing Address: P.O. Box 549,
Zip 46131-0549; tel. 317/736-3300; Gregg A.
Bechtold, President and Chief Executive Officer

MORGAN COUNTY MEMORIAL HOSPITAL, 2209 John
R. Wooden Drive, Martinsville, IN,
Zip 46151-1840, Mailing Address: P.O. Box
1717, Zip 46151-1717; tel. 765/342-8441; S.
Dean Melton, President and Chief Executive
Officer

RIVERVIEW HOSPITAL, 395 Westfield Road,
Noblesville, IN, Zip 46060-1425, Mailing
Address: P.O. Box 220, Zip 46061-0220;
tel. 317/773-0760; Seward Horner, President

TIPTON COUNTY MEMORIAL HOSPITAL, 1000 South
Main Street, Tipton, IN, Zip 46072-9799;
tel. 765/675-8500; Alfonso W. Gatmaitan, Chief
Executive Officer

WESTVIEW HOSPITAL, 3630 Guion Road, Indianapolis,
IN, Zip 46222-1699; tel. 317/924-6661; David
C. Dyar, President and Administrator

WITHAM MEMORIAL HOSPITAL, 1124 North Lebanon
Street, Lebanon, IN, Zip 46052-1776, Mailing
Address: P.O. Box 1200, Zip 46052-3005;
tel. 765/482-2700; Ray Ingham, President and
Chief Executive Officer

IOWA

GENESIS HEALTH SYSTEM
1227 East Rushmore Street, Davenport, IA
52803; tel. 319/326-6512; Leo Bressanelli,
Chief Executive Officer

DEWITT COMMUNITY HOSPITAL, 1118 11th Street,
De Witt, IA, Zip 52742-1296;
tel. 319/659-4200; Robert G. Senneff, Chief
Executive Officer

GENESIS MEDICAL CENTER, 1227 East Rusholme
Street, Davenport, IA, Zip 52803-2498;
tel. 319/421-1000; Leo A. Bressanelli,
President and Chief Executive Officer

ILLINI HOSPITAL, 801 Hospital Road, Silvis, IL,
Zip 61282-1893; tel. 309/792-9363; Gary E.
Larson, Chief Executive Officer

MERCY NETWORK OF HEALTH SERVICES
400 University Drive, Des Moines, IA 50309;
tel. 515/247-8372; Sara Drobnick, Vice
President

ADAIR COUNTY MEMORIAL HOSPITAL, 609 S.E. Kent
Street, Greenfield, IA, Zip 50849-9454;
tel. 515/743-2123; Myrna Erb, Administrator

AUDUBON COUNTY MEMORIAL HOSPITAL, 515
Pacific Street, Audubon, IA, Zip 50025-1099;
tel. 712/563-2611; David G. Couser, FAAMA,
FACHE, Administrator

DAVIS COUNTY HOSPITAL, 507 North Madison Street,
Bloomfield, IA, Zip 52537-1299;
tel. 515/664-2145; Randy Simmons,
Administrator

HAMILTON COUNTY PUBLIC HOSPITAL, 800 Ohio
Street, Webster City, IA, Zip 50595-2824,
Mailing Address: P.O. Box 430,
Zip 50595-0430; tel. 515/832-9400; Roger W.
Lenz, Administrator

MANNING REGIONAL HEALTHCARE CENTER, 410
Main Street, Manning, IA, Zip 51455-1093;
tel. 712/653-2072; Michael S. Ketcham,
Administrator

MERCY HOSPITAL MEDICAL CENTER, 400 University
Avenue, Des Moines, IA, Zip 50314-3190;
tel. 515/247-4278; Thomas A. Reitinger,
President and Chief Executive Officer

MONROE COUNTY HOSPITAL, RR 3, Box 311-11,
Albia, IA, Zip 52531; tel. 515/932-2134;
Gregory A. Paris, Administrator

RINGGOLD COUNTY HOSPITAL, 211 Shellway Drive,
Mount Ayr, IA, Zip 50854-1299;
tel. 515/464-3226; Gordon W. Winkler,
Administrator

ST. ANTHONY REGIONAL HOSPITAL, South Clark
Street, Carroll, IA, Zip 51401;
tel. 712/792-8231; Gary P. Riedmann,
President and Chief Executive Officer

ST. JOSEPH'S MERCY HOSPITAL, 1 St. Joseph's
Drive, Centerville, IA, Zip 52544;
tel. 515/437-3411; William C. Assell, President
and Chief Executive Officer

STORY COUNTY HOSPITAL AND LONG TERM CARE
FACILITY, 630 Sixth Street, Nevada, IA,
Zip 50201-2266; tel. 515/382-2111; Todd
Willert, Administrator

WAYNE COUNTY HOSPITAL, 417 South East Street,
Corydon, IA, Zip 50060-1860, Mailing Address:
P.O. Box 305, Zip 50060-0305;
tel. 515/872-2260; Bill D. Wilson, Administrator

NORTH IOWA MERCY HEALTH NETWORK
84 Beaumont Drive, Mason City, IA 50401;
tel. 515/424-7481; David Ross, President

BELMOND COMMUNITY HOSPITAL, 403 First Street
S.E., Belmond, IA, Zip 50421-1201, Mailing
Address: P.O. Box 326, Zip 50421-0326;
tel. 515/444-3223; Allan Atkinson,
Administrator

ELDORA REGIONAL MEDICAL CENTER, 2413
Edgington Avenue, Eldora, IA, Zip 50627-1541;
tel. 515/858-5416; Richard C. Hamilton,
Administrator

FRANKLIN GENERAL HOSPITAL, 1720 Central Avenue
East, Hampton, IA, Zip 50441-1859;
tel. 515/456-5000; Scott Wells, Interim Chief
Executive Officer

HANCOCK COUNTY MEMORIAL HOSPITAL, 531 First
Street N.W., Britt, IA, Zip 50423-0068, Mailing
Address: P.O. Box 68, Zip 50423-0068;
tel. 515/843-3801; Harriet Thompson,
Administrator

KOSSUTH REGIONAL HEALTH CENTER, 1515 South
Phillips Street, Algona, IA, Zip 50511-3649;
tel. 515/295-2451; James G. Fitzpatrick,
Administrator

MITCHELL COUNTY REGIONAL HEALTH CENTER, 616
North Eighth Street, Osage, IA,
Zip 50461-1498; tel. 515/732-3781; Kimberly
J. Miller, Administrator

NORTH IOWA MERCY HEALTH CENTER, 1000 Fourth
Street S.W., Mason City, IA, Zip 50401-2800;
tel. 515/422-7000; David H. Vellinga, President
and Chief Executive Officer

REGIONAL HEALTH SERVICES OF HOWARD COUNTY,
235 Eighth Avenue West, Cresco, IA,
Zip 52136-1098; tel. 319/547-2101; Elizabeth
A. Doty, Administrator

ST LUKES/IOWA HEALTH SYSTEM
700 East University Avenue, Des Moines, IA
50316; tel. 515/263-5399; Barry C. Spear,
Vice President of System Development

IOWA METHODIST MEDICAL CENTER, 1200 Pleasant
Street, Des Moines, IA, Zip 50309-9976;
tel. 515/241-6212; James H. Skogsbergh,
President

MARENGO MEMORIAL HOSPITAL, 300 West May
Street, Marengo, IA, Zip 52301-1261, Mailing
Address: P.O. Box 228, Zip 52301-0228;
tel. 319/642-5543; James H. Ragland,
Administrator

VIRGINIA GAY HOSPITAL, 502 North Ninth Avenue,
Vinton, IA, Zip 52349-2299;
tel. 319/472-6200; Michael J. Riege, Chief
Executive Officer

KANSAS

COMMUNITY HEALTH ALLIANCE
Route 1, Box 1, Winchester, KS 66097;
tel. 816/276-7580; Steven Ashcroft,
Administrator

COMMUNITY HOSPITAL ONAGA, 120 West Eighth
Street, Onaga, KS, Zip 66521-0120;
tel. 785/889-4272; Joseph T. Engelken, Chief
Executive Officer

COMMUNITY MEMORIAL HOSPITAL, 708 North 18th
Street, Marysville, KS, Zip 66508-1399;
tel. 913/562-2311; Harley B. Appel, Chief
Executive Officer

GEARY COMMUNITY HOSPITAL, Ash and St. Mary's
Road, Junction City, KS, Zip 66441, Mailing
Address: P.O. Box 490, Zip 66441-0490;
tel. 785/238-4131; David K. Bradley, Chief
Executive Officer

HOLTON COMMUNITY HOSPITAL, 510 Kansas
Avenue, Holton, KS, Zip 66436-1545;
tel. 913/364-2116; Diane S. Gross,
Administrator

HORTON HEALTH FOUNDATION, 240 West 18th
Street, Horton, KS, Zip 66439-1245;
tel. 785/486-2642; Dale A. White, Chief
Executive Officer

JEFFERSON COUNTY MEMORIAL HOSPITAL, 408
Delaware Street, Winchester, KS,
Zip 66097-4002, Mailing Address: Rural Route
1, Box 1, Zip 66097-0001; tel. 913/774-4340;
W. David Drew, Interim Administrator

MERCY HEALTH CENTER OF MANHATTAN, Manhattan,
KS, Mailing Address: 1823 College Avenue,
Zip 66502-3381; E. Michael Nunamaker,
President and Chief Executive Officer

MORRIS COUNTY HOSPITAL, 600 North Washington
Street, Council Grove, KS, Zip 66846-1499,
Mailing Address: P.O. Box 275,
Zip 66846-0275; tel. 316/767-6811; Jim
Reagan, M.D., Administrator

NEMAHA VALLEY COMMUNITY HOSPITAL, 1600
Community Drive, Seneca, KS, Zip 66538-9758;
tel. 785/336-6181; Michael J. Ryan,
Administrator

ST. FRANCIS HOSPITAL AND MEDICAL CENTER,
1700 West Seventh Street, Topeka, KS,
Zip 66606-1690; tel. 913/295-8000; Sister
Loretto Marie Colwell, President

GREAT PLAINS HEALTH ALLIANCE
P.O. Box 366, Phillipsburg, KS 67661;
tel. 913/543-2111; Roger John, President

ASHLAND HEALTH CENTER, 709 Oak Street, Ashland,
KS, Zip 67831, Mailing Address: P.O. Box 188,
Zip 67831; tel. 316/635-2241; Bryan Stacey,
Administrator

CHEYENNE COUNTY HOSPITAL, 210 West First
Street, Saint Francis, KS, Zip 67756, Mailing
Address: P.O. Box 547, Zip 67756-0547;
tel. 785/332-2104; Leslie Lacy, Administrator

COMMUNITY MEDICAL CENTER, 2307 Barada Street,
Falls City, NE, Zip 68355-1599;
tel. 402/245-2428; Victor Lee, Chief Executive
Officer and Administrator

ELLINWOOD DISTRICT HOSPITAL, 605 North Main
Street, Ellinwood, KS, Zip 67526-1440;
tel. 316/564-2548; Marge Conell, R.N.,
Administrator

FREDONIA REGIONAL HOSPITAL, 1527 Madison
Street, Fredonia, KS, Zip 66736-1751, Mailing
Address: P.O. Box 579, Zip 66736-0579;
tel. 316/378-2121; Terry Deschaine, Chief
Executive Officer

GREELEY COUNTY HOSPITAL, 506 Third Street, Tribune, KS, Zip 67879, Mailing Address: P.O. Box 338, Zip 67879–0338; tel. 316/376–4221; Cynthia K. Schneider, Administrator

GRISELL MEMORIAL HOSPITAL DISTRICT ONE, 210 South Vermont, Ransom, KS, Zip 67572–0268, Mailing Address: P.O. Box 268, Zip 67572–0268; tel. 785/731–2231; Kristine Ochs, R.N., Administrator

HARLAN COUNTY HOSPITAL, 717 North Brown Street, Alma, NE, Zip 68920–0836, Mailing Address: P.O. Box 836, Zip 68920–0836; tel. 308/928–2151; Allen Van Driel, Administrator

KIOWA COUNTY MEMORIAL HOSPITAL, 501 South Walnut Street, Greensburg, KS, Zip 67054–1951; tel. 316/723–3341; Ronald J. Baker, Administrator

LANE COUNTY HOSPITAL, 243 South Second, Dighton, KS, Zip 67839, Mailing Address: P.O. Box 969, Zip 67839–0969; tel. 316/397–5321; Donna McGowan, R.N., Administrator

LINCOLN COUNTY HOSPITAL, 624 North Second Street, Lincoln, KS, Zip 67455–1738, Mailing Address: P.O. Box 406, Zip 67455–0406; tel. 913/524–4403; Jolene Yager, R.N., Administrator

MEDICINE LODGE MEMORIAL HOSPITAL, 710 North Walnut Street, Medicine Lodge, KS, Zip 67104–1019, Mailing Address: P.O. Drawer C., Zip 67104; tel. 316/886–3771; Kevin A. White, Administrator

MINNEOLA DISTRICT HOSPITAL, 212 Main Street, Minneola, KS, Zip 67865–8511; tel. 316/885–4264; Blaine K. Miller, Administrator

MITCHELL COUNTY HOSPITAL, 400 West Eighth, Beloit, KS, Zip 67420–1605, Mailing Address: P.O. Box 399, Zip 67420–0399; tel. 785/738–2266; John M. Osse, Administrator

OSBORNE COUNTY MEMORIAL HOSPITAL, 424 West New Hampshire Street, Osborne, KS, Zip 67473–0070, Mailing Address: P.O. Box 70, Zip 67473–0070; tel. 785/346–2121; Patricia Bernard, R.N., Administrator

OTTAWA COUNTY HEALTH CENTER, 215 East Eighth, Minneapolis, KS, Zip 67467–1999, Mailing Address: P.O. Box 209, Zip 67467–0209; tel. 785/392–2122; Joy Reed, R.N., Administrator

PHILLIPS COUNTY HOSPITAL, 1150 State Street, Phillipsburg, KS, Zip 67661–1799, Mailing Address: P.O. Box 607, Zip 67661–0607; tel. 913/543–5226; James L. Giedd, Administrator

RAWLINS COUNTY HEALTH CENTER, 707 Grant Street, Atwood, KS, Zip 67730–4700, Mailing Address: Box 47, Zip 67730–4700; tel. 785/626–3211; Donald J. Kessen, Administrator and Chief Executive Officer

REPUBLIC COUNTY HOSPITAL, 2420 G. Street, Belleville, KS, Zip 66935–2499; tel. 785/527–2255; Charles A. Westin, FACHE, Administrator

SABETHA COMMUNITY HOSPITAL, 14th and Oregon Streets, Sabetha, KS, Zip 66534, Mailing Address: P.O. Box 229, Zip 66534; tel. 785/284–2121; Rita K. Buurman, Chief Executive Officer

SALEM HOSPITAL, 701 South Main Street, Hillsboro, KS, Zip 67063–9981; tel. 316/947–3114; J. H. Seitz, Administrator

SATANTA DISTRICT HOSPITAL, 401 South Cheyenne Street, Satanta, KS, Zip 67870, Mailing Address: P.O. Box 159, Zip 67870–0159; tel. 316/649–2761; T. G. Lee, Administrator

SMITH COUNTY MEMORIAL HOSPITAL, 614 South Main Street, Smith Center, KS, Zip 66967–0349, Mailing Address: P.O. Box 349, Zip 66967–0349; tel. 785/282–6845; John Terrill, Administrator

TREGO COUNTY–LEMKE MEMORIAL HOSPITAL, 320 North 13th Street, Wakeeney, KS, Zip 67672–2099; tel. 785/743–2182; James Wahlmeier, Administrator

HAYS MEDICAL CENTER
201 East 7th Street, Hays, KS 67601; tel. 913/623–5116; Jodi Schmidt, Vice President–Regional Partnerships

CHEYENNE COUNTY HOSPITAL, 210 West First Street, Saint Francis, KS, Zip 67756, Mailing Address: P.O. Box 547, Zip 67756–0547; tel. 785/332–2104; Leslie Lacy, Administrator

DWIGHT D. EISENHOWER VETERANS AFFAIRS MEDICAL CENTER, 4101 South Fourth Street Trafficway, Leavenworth, KS, Zip 66048–5055; tel. 913/682–2000; Edgar L. Tucker, Director

GRISELL MEMORIAL HOSPITAL DISTRICT ONE, 210 South Vermont, Ransom, KS, Zip 67572–0268, Mailing Address: P.O. Box 268, Zip 67572–0268; tel. 785/731–2231; Kristine Ochs, R.N., Administrator

PHILLIPS COUNTY HOSPITAL, 1150 State Street, Phillipsburg, KS, Zip 67661–1799, Mailing Address: P.O. Box 607, Zip 67661–0607; tel. 913/543–5226; James L. Giedd, Administrator

RAWLINS COUNTY HEALTH CENTER, 707 Grant Street, Atwood, KS, Zip 67730–4700, Mailing Address: Box 47, Zip 67730–4700; tel. 785/626–3211; Donald J. Kessen, Administrator and Chief Executive Officer

SATANTA DISTRICT HOSPITAL, 401 South Cheyenne Street, Satanta, KS, Zip 67870, Mailing Address: P.O. Box 159, Zip 67870–0159; tel. 316/649–2761; T. G. Lee, Administrator

TREGO COUNTY–LEMKE MEMORIAL HOSPITAL, 320 North 13th Street, Wakeeney, KS, Zip 67672–2099; tel. 785/743–2182; James Wahlmeier, Administrator

HEART OF AMERICA NETWORK
929 North Saint Francis, Wichita, KS 67214; tel. 316/268–5000; Bruce Carmichael, Vice President Regional Development

RICE COUNTY HOSPITAL DISTRICT NUMBER ONE, 619 South Clark Street, Lyons, KS, Zip 67554–3003, Mailing Address: P.O. Box 828, Zip 67554–0828; tel. 316/257–5173; Robert L. Mullen, Administrator

ST. FRANCIS HOSPITAL AND MEDICAL CENTER, 1700 West Seventh Street, Topeka, KS, Zip 66606–1690; tel. 913/295–8000; Sister Loretto Marie Colwell, President

VIA CHRISTI REGIONAL MEDICAL CENTER, 929 North St. Francis Street, Wichita, KS, Zip 67214–3882; tel. 316/268–5000; Randall G. Nyp, President and Chief Executive Officer

JAYHAWK HEALTH ALLIANCE
20333 West 151st Street, Olathe, KS 66061; tel. 913/791–4200; Frank H. Devocelle, Network Contact

ANDERSON COUNTY HOSPITAL, 421 South Maple, Garnett, KS, Zip 66032–1334, Mailing Address: P.O. Box 309, Zip 66032–0309; tel. 913/448–3131; James K. Johnson, Senior Executive Officer

LAWRENCE MEMORIAL HOSPITAL, 325 Maine, Lawrence, KS, Zip 66044–1393; tel. 785/749–6100; Eugene W. Meyer, President and Chief Executive Officer

MIAMI COUNTY MEDICAL CENTER, 2100 Baptiste, Paola, KS, Zip 66071–0365, Mailing Address: P.O. Box 365, Zip 66071–0365; tel. 913/294–2327; Gerald Wiesner, Vice President and Chief Operating Officer

OLATHE MEDICAL CENTER, 20333 West 151st Street, Olathe, KS, Zip 66061–5352; tel. 913/791–4200; Frank H. Devocelle, President and Chief Executive Officer

PROVIDENCE MEDICAL CENTER, 8929 Parallel Parkway, Kansas City, KS, Zip 66112–1636; tel. 913/596–4000; Francis V. Creeden, Jr., President and Chief Executive Officer

SAINT JOHN HOSPITAL, 3500 South Fourth Street, Leavenworth, KS, Zip 66048–5092; tel. 913/680–6000; Francis V. Creeden, Jr., President and Chief Executive Officer

UNIVERSITY OF KANSAS MEDICAL CENTER, 3901 Rainbow Boulevard, Kansas City, KS, Zip 66160–7200; tel. 913/588–5000; Irene M. Cumming, Chief Executive Officer

MED–OP
202 Center Avenue, Oakley, KS 67748–1714; tel. 913/672–3540; Andrew Draper, Executive Director

CITIZENS MEDICAL CENTER, 100 East College Drive, Colby, KS, Zip 67701–3799; tel. 785/462–7511; Richard B. Gamel, Chief Executive Officer

DECATUR COUNTY HOSPITAL, 810 West Columbia Street, Oberlin, KS, Zip 67749–2450, Mailing Address: P.O. Box 268, Zip 67749–0268; tel. 785/475–2208; Asa B. Wilson, Administrator

GOODLAND REGIONAL MEDICAL CENTER, 220 West Second Street, Goodland, KS, Zip 67735–1602; tel. 785/899–3625; Jim Chaddic, Administrator and Chief Executive Officer

GOVE COUNTY MEDICAL CENTER, 520 West Fifth Street, Quinter, KS, Zip 67752, Mailing Address: P.O. Box 129, Zip 67752; tel. 785/754–3341; Paul Davis, Administrator

GRAHAM COUNTY HOSPITAL, 304 West Prout Street, Hill City, KS, Zip 67642–1435, Mailing Address: P.O. Box 339, Zip 67642–0339; tel. 785/421–2121; Fred J. Meis, Administrator and Chief Executive Officer

HAYS MEDICAL CENTER, 2220 Canterbury Road, Hays, KS, Zip 67601–2342, Mailing Address: P.O. Box 8100, Zip 67601–8100; tel. 785/623–5113; John H. Jeter, M.D., President and Chief Executive Officer

LOGAN COUNTY HOSPITAL, 211 Cherry Street, Oakley, KS, Zip 67748–1201; tel. 913/672–3211; Rodney Bates, Administrator

NESS COUNTY HOSPITAL NUMBER TWO, 312 East Custer Street, Ness City, KS, Zip 67560–1654; tel. 785/798–2291; Clyde T. McCracken, Administrator

NORTON COUNTY HOSPITAL, 102 East Holme, Norton, KS, Zip 67654–0250, Mailing Address: P.O. Box 250, Zip 67654–0250; tel. 785/877–3351; Richard Miller, Administrator and Chief Executive Officer

PLAINVILLE RURAL HOSPITAL DISTRICT NUMBER ONE, 304 South Colorado Avenue, Plainville, KS, Zip 67663–2505; tel. 785/434–4553; Leonard Hernandez, Administrator and Chief Executive Officer

RUSH COUNTY HEALTHCARE CENTER, 801 Locust Street, La Crosse, KS, Zip 67548–9673, Mailing Address: P.O. Box 520, Zip 67548–0520; tel. 785/222–2545; Donna L. Myers, Administrator and Chief Executive Officer

SCOTT COUNTY HOSPITAL, 310 East Third Street, Scott City, KS, Zip 67871–1299; tel. 316/872–5811; Greg Unruh, Chief Executive Officer

SHERIDAN COUNTY HOSPITAL, 826 18th Street, Hoxie, KS, Zip 67740–0167, Mailing Address: P.O. Box 167, Zip 67740–0167; tel. 785/675–3281; Brian Kirk, Chief Executive Officer

PIONEER NETWORK
P.O. Box 159, Santana, KS 67870; tel. 316/649–2761; Tom Lee, Administrator

SATANTA DISTRICT HOSPITAL, 401 South Cheyenne Street, Satanta, KS, Zip 67870, Mailing Address: P.O. Box 159, Zip 67870–0159; tel. 316/649–2761; T. G. Lee, Administrator

SUNFLOWER HEALTH NETWORK, INC.
P.O. Box 2568, Salina, KS 67402–2568; tel. 785/452–7028; Sheryl Dority, Director of Operations

CLAY COUNTY HOSPITAL, 617 Liberty Street, Clay Center, KS, Zip 67432–1599; tel. 913/632–2144; John F. Wiebe, Chief Executive Officer

CLOUD COUNTY HEALTH CENTER, 1100 Highland Drive, Concordia, KS, Zip 66901–3997; tel. 785/243–1234; Daniel R. Bartz, Chief Executive Officer

ELLSWORTH COUNTY HOSPITAL, 300 Kingsley Street, Ellsworth, KS, Zip 67439–0087, Mailing Address: P.O. Drawer 87, Zip 67439–0087; tel. 785/472–3111; Roger W. Pearson, Administrator

Section B

HERINGTON MUNICIPAL HOSPITAL, 100 East Helen Street, Herington, KS, Zip 67449–1697; tel. 913/258–2207; William D. Peterson, Administrator

JEWELL COUNTY HOSPITAL, 100 Crestvue Avenue, Mankato, KS, Zip 66956–2407, Mailing Address: P.O. Box 327, Zip 66956–0327; tel. 913/378–3137; Rodney Brockelman, Administrator

LINCOLN COUNTY HOSPITAL, 624 North Second Street, Lincoln, KS, Zip 67455–1738, Mailing Address: P.O. Box 406, Zip 67455–0406; tel. 913/524–4403; Jolene Yager, R.N., Administrator

LINDSBORG COMMUNITY HOSPITAL, 605 West Lincoln Street, Lindsborg, KS, Zip 67456–2399; tel. 785/227–3308; Greg Lundstrom, Administrator and Chief Executive Officer

MEMORIAL HOSPITAL, 511 N.E. Tenth Street, Abilene, KS, Zip 67410–2100, Mailing Address: P.O. Box 219, Zip 67410–0219; tel. 913/263–2100; Leon J. Boor, Chief Executive Officer

MEMORIAL HOSPITAL, 1000 Hospital Drive, McPherson, KS, Zip 67460–2321; tel. 316/241–2250; Stan Regehr, President and Chief Executive Officer

MITCHELL COUNTY HOSPITAL, 400 West Eighth, Beloit, KS, Zip 67420–1605, Mailing Address: P.O. Box 399, Zip 67420–0399; tel. 785/738–2266; John M. Osse, Administrator

OSBORNE COUNTY MEMORIAL HOSPITAL, 424 West New Hampshire Street, Osborne, KS, Zip 67473–0070, Mailing Address: P.O. Box 70, Zip 67473–0070; tel. 785/346–2121; Patricia Bernard, R.N., Administrator

OTTAWA COUNTY HEALTH CENTER, 215 East Eighth, Minneapolis, KS, Zip 67467–1999, Mailing Address: P.O. Box 209, Zip 67467–0209; tel. 785/392–2122; Joy Reed, R.N., Administrator

REPUBLIC COUNTY HOSPITAL, 2420 G. Street, Belleville, KS, Zip 66935–2499; tel. 785/527–2255; Charles A. Westin, FACHE, Administrator

RUSSELL REGIONAL HOSPITAL, 200 South Main Street, Russell, KS, Zip 67665–2997; tel. 913/483–3131; Talton L. Francis, FACHE, Administrator

SALINA REGIONAL HEALTH CENTER, 400 South Santa Fe Avenue, Salina, KS, Zip 67401–4198, Mailing Address: P.O. Box 5080, Zip 67401–5080; tel. 785/452–7000; Randy Peterson, President and Chief Executive Officer

SMITH COUNTY MEMORIAL HOSPITAL, 614 South Main Street, Smith Center, KS, Zip 66967–0349, Mailing Address: P.O. Box 349, Zip 66967–0349; tel. 785/282–6845; John Terrill, Administrator

VIA CHRISTI
929 N. St. Francis Avenue, Wichita, KS 67214; tel. 316/268–7000; Keith Lundquist, Vice President

VIA CHRISTI REGIONAL MEDICAL CENTER, 929 North St. Francis Street, Wichita, KS, Zip 67214–3882; tel. 316/268–5000; Randall G. Nyp, President and Chief Executive Officer

KENTUCKY

ALLIANT HEALTH SYSTEM
P.O. Box 35070, Louisville, KY 40232–5070; tel. 502/629–8000; Steven A. Williams, President/CEO

ALLIANT HOSPITALS, 200 East Chestnut Street, Louisville, KY, Zip 40202–1800, Mailing Address: P.O. Box 35070, Zip 40232–5070; tel. 502/629–8000; Stephen M. Tullman, Administrator

BAPTIST HEALTHCARE SYSTEM
4007 Kresge Way, Louisville, KY 40207; tel. 502/896–5000; Tom Smith, President & Chief Executive Officer

BAPTIST HOSPITAL EAST, 4000 Kresge Way, Louisville, KY, Zip 40207–4676; tel. 502/897–8100; Susan Stout Tamme, President

BAPTIST REGIONAL MEDICAL CENTER, 1 Trillium Way, Corbin, KY, Zip 40701–8420; tel. 606/528–1212; John S. Henson, President

CARITAS MEDICAL CENTER, 1850 Bluegrass Avenue, Louisville, KY, Zip 40215–1199; tel. 502/361–6000; Peter J. Bernard, President and Chief Executive Officer

CARITAS PEACE CENTER, 2020 Newburg Road, Louisville, KY, Zip 40205–1879; tel. 502/451–3330; Peter J. Bernard, President and Chief Executive Officer

CENTRAL BAPTIST HOSPITAL, 1740 Nicholasville Road, Lexington, KY, Zip 40503; tel. 606/275–6100; William G. Sisson, President

HARDIN MEMORIAL HOSPITAL, 913 North Dixie Avenue, Elizabethtown, KY, Zip 42701–2599; tel. 502/737–1212; David L. Gray, President

TRI COUNTY BAPTIST HOSPITAL, 1025 New Moody Lane, La Grange, KY, Zip 40031–0559; tel. 502/222–5388; Dennis B. Johnson, Administrator

WESTERN BAPTIST HOSPITAL, 2501 Kentucky Avenue, Paducah, KY, Zip 42003–3200; tel. 502/575–2100; Larry O. Barton, President

BLUE GRASS FAMILY HEALTH PLAN
651 Perimeter Park, Suite 2B, Lexington, KY 40517; tel. 606/269–4475; Katherine Schaefer, Network Coordinator

BAPTIST REGIONAL MEDICAL CENTER, 1 Trillium Way, Corbin, KY, Zip 40701–8420; tel. 606/528–1212; John S. Henson, President

BEREA HOSPITAL, 305 Estill Street, Berea, KY, Zip 40403–1909; tel. 606/986–3151; David E. Burgio, FACHE, President and Chief Executive Officer

BURBON COMMUNITY HOSPITAL, 9 Linville Drive, Paris, KY, Zip 40361–2196; tel. 606/987–1000; Bernie Mattingly, Chief Executive Officer

CENTRAL BAPTIST HOSPITAL, 1740 Nicholasville Road, Lexington, KY, Zip 40503; tel. 606/275–6100; William G. Sisson, President

CLARK REGIONAL MEDICAL CENTER, West Lexington Avenue, Winchester, KY, Zip 40391, Mailing Address: P.O. Box 630, Zip 40392–0630; tel. 606/745–3500; Robert D. Fraraccio, Administrator

FORT LOGAN HOSPITAL, 124 Portman Avenue, Stanford, KY, Zip 40484–1200; tel. 606/365–2187; Terry C. Powers, Administrator

FRANKFORT REGIONAL MEDICAL CENTER, 299 King's Daughters Drive, Frankfort, KY, Zip 40601–4186; tel. 502/875–5240; David P. Steitz, Chief Executive Officer

GARRARD COUNTY MEMORIAL HOSPITAL, 308 West Maple Avenue, Lancaster, KY, Zip 40444–1098; tel. 606/792–6844; John P. Rigsby, Administrator

GEORGETOWN COMMUNITY HOSPITAL, 1140 Lexington Road, Georgetown, KY, Zip 40324–9362; tel. 502/868–1100; Ronald T. Tyrer, Interim Chief Executive Officer

HARRISON MEMORIAL HOSPITAL, Millersburg Road, Cynthiana, KY, Zip 41031–0250, Mailing Address: P.O. Box 250, Zip 41031–0250; tel. 606/234–2300; Darwin E. Root, Administrator

KNOX COUNTY HOSPITAL, 321 High Street, Barbourville, KY, Zip 40906–1317, Mailing Address: P.O. Box 160, Zip 40906–0160; tel. 606/546–4175; Craig Morgan, Administrator

MARCUM AND WALLACE MEMORIAL HOSPITAL, 60 Mercy Court, Irvine, KY, Zip 40336–1331, Mailing Address: P.O. Box 928, Zip 40336–0928; tel. 606/723–2115; Christopher M. Goddard, Administrator

MARYMOUNT MEDICAL CENTER, 310 East Ninth Street, London, KY, Zip 40741–1299; tel. 606/878–6520; Lowell Jones, President

MEADOWVIEW REGIONAL MEDICAL CENTER, 989 Medical Park Drive, Maysville, KY, Zip 41056–8750; tel. 606/759–5311; Ronald T. Tyrer, Interim Chief Executive Officer

OWEN COUNTY MEMORIAL HOSPITAL, 330 Roland Avenue, Owenton, KY, Zip 40359–1502; tel. 502/484–3441; Richard D. McLeod, Administrator

PATTIE A. CLAY HOSPITAL, EKU By–Pass, Richmond, KY, Zip 40475, Mailing Address: P.O. Box 1600, Zip 40476–2603; tel. 606/625–3131; Richard M. Thomas, President

ST. JOSEPH HOSPITAL, One St. Joseph Drive, Lexington, KY, Zip 40504–3754; tel. 606/278–3436; Thomas J. Murray, President

THE JAMES B. HAGGIN MEMORIAL HOSPITAL, 464 Linden Avenue, Harrodsburg, KY, Zip 40330–1862; tel. 606/734–5441; Earl James Motzer, Ph.D., FACHE, Chief Executive Officer

WOODFORD HOSPITAL, 360 Amsden Avenue, Versailles, KY, Zip 40383–1286; tel. 606/873–3111; Nancy Littrell, Chief Executive Officer

CARITAS HEALTH SERVICES
1850 Bluegrass Avenue, Louisville, KY 40215–1199; tel. 502/361–6140; Conrad H. Thorne, Chief of Network Operations

CARITAS MEDICAL CENTER, 1850 Bluegrass Avenue, Louisville, KY, Zip 40215–1199; tel. 502/361–6000; Peter J. Bernard, President and Chief Executive Officer

CARITAS PEACE CENTER, 2020 Newburg Road, Louisville, KY, Zip 40205–1879; tel. 502/451–3330; Peter J. Bernard, President and Chief Executive Officer

CENTER CARE
1225 Fairway Street, Bowling Green, KY 42102–0148; tel. 502/745–1517; John M. Fones, Executive Director/Senior VP

BAPTIST HOSPITAL, 2000 Church Street, Nashville, TN, Zip 37236–0002; tel. 615/329–5555; C. David Stringfield, President and Chief Executive Officer

BAPTIST HOSPITAL EAST, 4000 Kresge Way, Louisville, KY, Zip 40207–4676; tel. 502/897–8100; Susan Stout Tamme, President

BAPTIST REGIONAL MEDICAL CENTER, 1 Trillium Way, Corbin, KY, Zip 40701–8420; tel. 606/528–1212; John S. Henson, President

BEDFORD COUNTY GENERAL HOSPITAL, 845 Union Street, Shelbyville, TN, Zip 37160–9971; tel. 931/685–5433; Richard L. Graham, Administrator

CAVERNA MEMORIAL HOSPITAL, 1501 South Dixie Street, Horse Cave, KY, Zip 42749–1477; tel. 502/786–2191; James J. Kerins, Sr., Administrator

CENTRAL BAPTIST HOSPITAL, 1740 Nicholasville Road, Lexington, KY, Zip 40503; tel. 606/275–6100; William G. Sisson, President

CHRIST HOSPITAL, 2139 Auburn Avenue, Cincinnati, OH, Zip 45219–2989; tel. 513/369–2000; Claus von Zychlin, Senior Executive Officer

CLARKSVILLE MEMORIAL HOSPITAL, 1771 Madison Street, Clarksville, TN, Zip 37043–4900, Mailing Address: P.O. Box 3160, Zip 37043–3160; tel. 931/552–6622; James Lee Decker, President and Chief Executive Officer

CLINTON COUNTY HOSPITAL, 723 Burkesville Road, Albany, KY, Zip 42602–1654; tel. 606/387–6421; Randel Flowers, Ph.D., Administrator

COFFEE MEDICAL CENTER, 1001 McArthur Drive, Manchester, TN, Zip 37355–2455, Mailing Address: P.O. Box 1079, Zip 37355–1079; tel. 931/728–3586; Edward A. Perdue, Administrator

COLUMBIA DOCTORS' HOSPITAL OF OPELOUSAS, 5101 Highway 167 South, Opelousas, LA, Zip 70570–8975; tel. 318/948–2100; Daryl J. Doise, Administrator

COOKEVILLE REGIONAL MEDICAL CENTER, 142 West Fifth Street, Cookeville, TN, Zip 38501–1760, Mailing Address: P.O. Box 340, Zip 38503–0340; tel. 931/528–2541; William M. Jennings, Administrator and Chief Operating Officer

CUMBERLAND COUNTY HOSPITAL, Highway 90 West, Burkesville, KY, Zip 42717–0280, Mailing Address: P.O. Box 280, Zip 42717–0280; tel. 502/864–2511; Mark E. Thompson, Chief Executive Officer

DAUTERIVE HOSPITAL, 600 North Lewis Street, New Iberia, LA, Zip 70560, Mailing Address: P.O. Box 11210, Zip 70562–1210; tel. 318/365–7311; Kyle J. Viator, Chief Executive Officer

FRANKLIN–SIMPSON MEMORIAL HOSPITAL, Brookhaven Road, Franklin, KY, Zip 42135–2929, Mailing Address: P.O. Box 2929, Zip 42135–2929; tel. 502/586–3253; William P. Macri, Chief Executive Officer

GOOD SAMARITAN HOSPITAL, 375 Dixmyth Avenue, Cincinnati, OH, Zip 45220–2489; tel. 513/872–1400; Sister Myra James Bradley, Chief Executive Officer

HARDIN MEMORIAL HOSPITAL, 913 North Dixie Avenue, Elizabethtown, KY, Zip 42701–2599; tel. 502/737–1212; David L. Gray, President

HARTON REGIONAL MEDICAL CENTER, 1801 North Jackson Street, Tullahoma, TN, Zip 37388–2201, Mailing Address: P.O. Box 460, Zip 37388–0460; tel. 931/393–3000; David C. Wilson, Chief Executive Officer

HENDERSONVILLE HOSPITAL, 355 New Shackle Island Road, Hendersonville, TN, Zip 37075–2393; tel. 615/264–4000; Robert Klein, Chief Executive Officer

JEWISH HOSPITAL, 217 East Chestnut Street, Louisville, KY, Zip 40202–1886; tel. 502/587–4011; Douglas E. Shaw, President

LAKEVIEW REHABILITATION HOSPITAL, 134 Heartland Drive, Elizabethtown, KY, Zip 42701–2778; tel. 502/769–3100; Kevin Stevenson, Chief Executive Officer

LOGAN MEMORIAL HOSPITAL, 1625 South Nashville Road, Russellville, KY, Zip 42276–8834, Mailing Address: P.O. Box 10, Zip 42276–0010; tel. 502/726–4011; Michael Clark, Chief Executive Officer

MACON COUNTY GENERAL HOSPITAL, 204 Medical Drive, Lafayette, TN, Zip 37083–1799, Mailing Address: P.O. Box 378, Zip 37083–0378; tel. 615/666–2147; Dennis A. Wolford, FACHE, Administrator

MEADOVIEW REGIONAL MEDICAL CENTER, 989 Medical Park Drive, Maysville, KY, Zip 41056–8750; tel. 606/759–5311; Ronald T. Tyrer, Interim Chief Executive Officer

MEDICAL CENTER AT SCOTTSVILLE, 456 Burnley Road, Scottsville, KY, Zip 42164–6355; tel. 502/622–2800; Sarah Moore, Vice President

MEDICAL CENTER OF MANCHESTER, 481 Interstate Drive, Manchester, TN, Zip 37355–3108, Mailing Address: P.O. Box 1409, Zip 37355–1409; tel. 931/728–6354; Margaret Hale, Chief Operating Officer

MEDICAL CENTER OF SOUTHWEST LOUISIANA, 2810 Ambassador Caffery Parkway, Lafayette, LA, Zip 70506–5900; tel. 318/981–2949; Madeleine L. Roberson, Chief Executive Officer

MONROE COUNTY MEDICAL CENTER, 529 Capp Harlan Road, Tompkinsville, KY, Zip 42167–1840; tel. 502/487–9231; Carolyn E. Riley, Chief Executive Officer

MUHLENBERG COMMUNITY HOSPITAL, 440 Hopkinsville Street, Greenville, KY, Zip 42345–1172, Mailing Address: P.O. Box 387, Zip 42345–0387; tel. 502/338–8000; Charles D. Lovell, Jr., Chief Executive Officer

NASHVILLE MEMORIAL HOSPITAL, 612 West Due West Avenue, Madison, TN, Zip 37115–4474; tel. 615/865–3511; Allyn R. Harris, Chief Executive Officer

NORTH OAKS MEDICAL CENTER, 15790 Medical Center Drive, Hammond, LA, Zip 70403–1436, Mailing Address: P.O. Box 2668, Zip 70404–2668; tel. 504/345–2700; James E. Cathey, Jr., Chief Executive Officer

OHIO COUNTY HOSPITAL, 1211 Main Street, Hartford, KY, Zip 42347–1619; tel. 502/298–7411; Blaine Pieper, Administrator

OWENSBORO MERCY HEALTH SYSTEM, 811 East Parrish Avenue, Owensboro, KY, Zip 42303–3268, Mailing Address: P.O. Box 20007, Zip 42303–0007; tel. 502/688–2000; Greg L. Carlson, President and Chief Executive Officer

PIKEVILLE UNITED METHODIST HOSPITAL OF KENTUCKY, 911 South Bypass, Pikeville, KY, Zip 41501–1595; tel. 606/437–3500; Martha O'Regan Chill, Administrator and Chief Executive Officer

PINELAKE REGIONAL HOSPITAL, 1099 Medical Center Circle, Mayfield, KY, Zip 42066–1179, Mailing Address: P.O. Box 1099, Zip 42066–1099; tel. 502/251–4100; Don A. Horstkotte, Chief Executive Officer

SOUTHERN TENNESSEE MEDICAL CENTER, 185 Hospital Road, Winchester, TN, Zip 37398–2468; tel. 931/967–8200; Michael W. Garfield, Administrator

ST. ELIZABETH MEDICAL CENTER–GRANT COUNTY, 238 Barnes Road, Williamstown, KY, Zip 41097–9460; tel. 606/824–2400; Chris Carle, Administrator

ST. ELIZABETH MEDICAL CENTER–NORTH, 401 East 20th Street, Covington, KY, Zip 41014–1585; tel. 606/292–4000; Joseph W. Gross, President and Chief Executive Officer

ST. JOSEPH HOSPITAL, One St. Joseph Drive, Lexington, KY, Zip 40504–3754; tel. 606/278–3436; Thomas J. Murray, President

ST. THOMAS HOSPITAL, 4220 Harding Road, Nashville, TN, Zip 37205–2095, Mailing Address: P.O. Box 380, Zip 37202–0380; tel. 615/222–2111; John F. Tighe, President and Chief Executive Officer

SUMNER REGIONAL MEDICAL CENTER, 555 Hartsville Pike, Gallatin, TN, Zip 37066–2449, Mailing Address: P.O. Box 1558, Zip 37066–1558; tel. 615/452–4210; William T. Sugg, President and Chief Executive Officer

T. J. SAMSON COMMUNITY HOSPITAL, 1301 North Race Street, Glasgow, KY, Zip 42141–3483; tel. 502/651–4444; H. Glenn Joiner, Chief Executive Officer

TAYLOR COUNTY HOSPITAL, 1700 Old Lebanon Road, Campbellsville, KY, Zip 42718–9600; tel. 502/465–3561; David R. Hayes, President

THE JAMES B. HAGGIN MEMORIAL HOSPITAL, 464 Linden Avenue, Harrodsburg, KY, Zip 40330–1862; tel. 606/734–5441; Earl James Motzer, Ph.D., FACHE, Chief Executive Officer

THE MEDICAL CENTER AT BOWLING GREEN, 250 Park Street, Bowling Green, KY, Zip 42101–1795, Mailing Address: P.O. Box 90010, Zip 42102–9010; tel. 502/745–1000; Connie Smith, Chief Executive Officer

TWIN LAKES REGIONAL MEDICAL CENTER, 910 Wallace Avenue, Leitchfield, KY, Zip 42754–1499; tel. 502/259–9400; Stephen L. Meredith, Chief Executive Officer

UNIVERSITY MEDICAL CENTER, 1411 Baddour Parkway, Lebanon, TN, Zip 37087–2573; tel. 615/444–8262; Larry W. Keller, Chief Executive Officer

WESTLAKE REGIONAL HOSPITAL, Westlake Drive, Columbia, KY, Zip 42728–1149, Mailing Address: P.O. Box 468, Zip 42728–0468; tel. 502/384–4753; Rex A. Tungate, Administrator

WILLIAMSON MEDICAL CENTER, 2021 Carothers Road, Franklin, TN, Zip 37067–5822, Mailing Address: P.O. Box 681600, Zip 37068–1600; tel. 615/791–0500; Ronald G. Joyner, Chief Executive Officer

WOMEN'S AND CHILDREN'S HOSPITAL, 4600 Ambassador Caffery Parkway, Lafayette, LA, Zip 70508–6923, Mailing Address: P.O. Box 88030, Zip 70598–8030; tel. 318/981–9100; Madeleine L. Roberson, Chief Executive Officer

CHA PROVIDER NETWORK, INC.
P.O. Box 24647, Lexington, KY 40522–2171; tel. 606/323–0285; Michael G. Strother, Director of Network

ARH REGIONAL MEDICAL CENTER, 100 Medical Center Drive, Hazard, KY, Zip 41701–1000; tel. 606/439–6610; Steven F. Ashcraft, Interim Administrator

BECKLEY APPALACHIAN REGIONAL HOSPITAL, 306 Stanaford Road, Beckley, WV, Zip 25801–3142; tel. 304/255–3000; David R. Lyon, Administrator

BEREA HOSPITAL, 305 Estill Street, Berea, KY, Zip 40403–1909; tel. 606/986–3151; David E. Burgio, FACHE, President and Chief Executive Officer

BOONE MEMORIAL HOSPITAL, 701 Madison Avenue, Madison, WV, Zip 25130–1699; tel. 304/369–1230; Tommy H. Mullins, Administrator

CABELL HUNTINGTON HOSPITAL, 1340 Hal Greer Boulevard, Huntington, WV, Zip 25701–0195; tel. 304/526–2000; W. Don Smith, II, President and Chief Executive Officer

CARDINAL HILL REHABILITATION HOSPITAL, 2050 Versailles Road, Lexington, KY, Zip 40504–1499; tel. 606/254–5701; Kerry G. Gillihan, President and Chief Executive Officer

CENTRAL BAPTIST HOSPITAL, 1740 Nicholasville Road, Lexington, KY, Zip 40503; tel. 606/275–6100; William G. Sisson, President

CHARTER RIDGE HOSPITAL, 3050 Rio Dosa Drive, Lexington, KY, Zip 40509–9990; tel. 606/269–2325; Ali A. Elhaj, Chief Executive Officer

CHRIST HOSPITAL, 2139 Auburn Avenue, Cincinnati, OH, Zip 45219–2989; tel. 513/369–2000; Claus von Zychlin, Senior Executive Officer

CLAIBORNE COUNTY HOSPITAL, 1850 Old Knoxville Road, Tazewell, TN, Zip 37879–3625, Mailing Address: P.O. Box 219, Zip 37879–0219; tel. 423/626–4211; Michael T. Hutchins, Administrator

CLARK REGIONAL MEDICAL CENTER, West Lexington Avenue, Winchester, KY, Zip 40391, Mailing Address: P.O. Box 630, Zip 40392–0630; tel. 606/745–3500; Robert D. Fraraccio, Administrator

EPHRAIM MCDOWELL REGIONAL MEDICAL CENTER, 217 South Third Street, Danville, KY, Zip 40422–9983; tel. 606/239–1000; Thomas W. Smith, President and Chief Executive Officer

FLEMING COUNTY HOSPITAL, 920 Elizaville Avenue, Flemingsburg, KY, Zip 41041, Mailing Address: P.O. Box 388, Zip 41041–0388; tel. 606/849–5000; Bobby B. Emmons, Administrator

FORT LOGAN HOSPITAL, 124 Portman Avenue, Stanford, KY, Zip 40484–1200; tel. 606/365–2187; Terry C. Powers, Administrator

FORT SANDERS LOUDON MEDICAL CENTER, 1125 Grove Street, Loudon, TN, Zip 37774–1512, Mailing Address: P.O. Box 217, Zip 37774–0217; tel. 423/458–8222; Ralph T. Williams, Administrator

FORT SANDERS REGIONAL MEDICAL CENTER, 1901 Clinch Avenue S.W., Knoxville, TN, Zip 37916–2394; tel. 423/541–1111; James R. Burkhart, FACHE, Administrator

FORT SANDERS–PARKWEST MEDICAL CENTER, 9352 Park West Boulevard, Knoxville, TN, Zip 37923–4387, Mailing Address: P.O. Box 22993, Zip 37933–0993; tel. 423/694–5700; James R. Burkhart, FACHE, Administrator

FORT SANDERS–SEVIER MEDICAL CENTER, 709 Middle Creek Road, Sevierville, TN, Zip 37862–5016, Mailing Address: P.O. Box 8005, Zip 37864–8005; tel. 423/429–6100; Ralph T. Williams, Administrator

GARRARD COUNTY MEMORIAL HOSPITAL, 308 West Maple Avenue, Lancaster, KY, Zip 40444–1098; tel. 606/792–6844; John P. Rigsby, Administrator

HARLAN ARH HOSPITAL, 81 Ball Park Road, Harlan, KY, Zip 40831–1792; tel. 606/573–8100; Daniel Fitzpatrick, Chief Executive Officer

HARRISON MEMORIAL HOSPITAL, Millersburg Road, Cynthiana, KY, Zip 41031–0250, Mailing Address: P.O. Box 250, Zip 41031–0250; tel. 606/234–2300; Darwin E. Root, Administrator

HEALTHSOUTH HUNTINGTON REHABILITATION HOSPITAL, 6900 West Country Club Drive, Huntington, WV, Zip 25705–2000; tel. 304/733–1060; Homer Fowler, Chief Operating Officer

HIGHLANDS REGIONAL MEDICAL CENTER, 5000 Kentucky Route 321, Prestonsburg, KY, Zip 41653, Mailing Address: P.O. Box 668, Zip 41653–0668; tel. 606/886–8511; Clarence Traum, President and Chief Executive Officer

JENKINS COMMUNITY HOSPITAL, Main Street, Jenkins, KY, Zip 41537–9614, Mailing Address: P.O. Box 472, Zip 41537–0472; tel. 606/832–2171; Sherrie Newcomb, Administrator

JEWISH HOSPITAL KENWOOD, 4777 East Galbraith Road, Cincinnati, OH, Zip 45236; tel. 513/745–2200; Warren C. Falberg, Senior Executive Officer

KNOX COUNTY HOSPITAL, 321 High Street, Barbourville, KY, Zip 40906–1317, Mailing Address: P.O. Box 160, Zip 40906–0160; tel. 606/546–4175; Craig Morgan, Administrator

LONESOME PINE HOSPITAL, 1990 Holton Avenue East, Big Stone Gap, VA, Zip 24219–0230; tel. 540/523–3111; Paul A. Bishop, Administrator

MAN ARH HOSPITAL, 700 East McDonald Avenue, Man, WV, Zip 25635–1011; tel. 304/583–8421; Louis G. Roe, Jr., Administrator

MARCUM AND WALLACE MEMORIAL HOSPITAL, 60 Mercy Court, Irvine, KY, Zip 40336–1331, Mailing Address: P.O. Box 928, Zip 40336–0928; tel. 606/723–2115; Christopher M. Goddard, Administrator

MARY BRECKINRIDGE HOSPITAL, Hospital Drive, Hyden, KY, Zip 41749–0000; tel. 606/672–2901; A. Ray Branaman, Administrator

MCDOWELL ARH HOSPITAL, Route 122, McDowell, KY, Zip 41647, Mailing Address: P.O. Box 247, Mc Dowell, Zip 41647–0247; tel. 606/377–3400; Dena C. Sparkman, Administrator

MEMORIAL HOSPITAL, 401 Memorial Drive, Manchester, KY, Zip 40962–9156; tel. 606/598–5104; Jimm Bunch, Chief Executive Officer

MIDDLESBORO APPALACHIAN REGIONAL HOSPITAL, 3600 West Cumberland Avenue, Middlesboro, KY, Zip 40965–2614, Mailing Address: P.O. Box 340, Zip 40965–0340; tel. 606/242–1101; Paul V. Miles, Administrator

MORGAN COUNTY APPALACHIAN REGIONAL HOSPITAL, 476 Liberty Road, West Liberty, KY, Zip 41472–2049, Mailing Address: P.O. Box 579, Zip 41472–0579; tel. 606/743–3186; Dennis R. Chaney, Administrator

NICHOLAS COUNTY HOSPITAL, 2323 Concrete Road, Carlisle, KY, Zip 40311–9721, Mailing Address: P.O. Box 232, Zip 40311–0232; tel. 606/289–7181; Doris Ecton, Administrator and Chief Executive Officer

OUR LADY OF BELLEFONTE HOSPITAL, St. Christopher Drive, Ashland, KY, Zip 41101, Mailing Address: P.O. Box 789, Zip 41105–0789; tel. 606/833–3333; Robert J. Maher, President

OUR LADY OF THE WAY HOSPITAL, 11022 Main Street, Martin, KY, Zip 41649–0910; tel. 606/285–5181; Lowell Jones, Chief Executive Officer

OWEN COUNTY MEMORIAL HOSPITAL, 330 Roland Avenue, Owenton, KY, Zip 40359–1502; tel. 502/484–3441; Richard D. McLeod, Administrator

PATTIE A. CLAY HOSPITAL, EKU By–Pass, Richmond, KY, Zip 40475, Mailing Address: P.O. Box 1600, Zip 40476–2603; tel. 606/625–3131; Richard M. Thomas, President

PENINSULA HOSPITAL, 2347 Jones Bend Road, Louisville, TN, Zip 37777–5213, Mailing Address: P.O. Box 2000, Zip 37777–2000; tel. 423/970–9800; David H. McReynolds, Chief Operating Officer and Administrator

PINEVILLE COMMUNITY HOSPITAL ASSOCIATION, Riverview Avenue, Pineville, KY, Zip 40977–0850; tel. 606/337–3051; J. Milton Brooks, III, Administrator

ROCKCASTLE HOSPITAL AND RESPIRATORY CARE CENTER, 145 Newcomb Avenue, Mount Vernon, KY, Zip 40456–2733, Mailing Address: P.O. Box 1310, Zip 40456–1310; tel. 606/256–2195; Lee D. Keene, Administrator

ST. CLAIRE MEDICAL CENTER, 222 Medical Circle, Morehead, KY, Zip 40351–1180; tel. 606/783–6500; Mark J. Neff, President and Chief Executive Officer

ST. LUKE HOSPITAL EAST, 85 North Grand Avenue, Fort Thomas, KY, Zip 41075–1796; tel. 606/572–3100; Daniel M. Vinson, CPA, Senior Executive Officer

ST. LUKE HOSPITAL WEST, 7380 Turfway Road, Florence, KY, Zip 41042–1337; tel. 606/525–5200; Daniel M. Vinson, CPA, Interim Administrator

ST. MARY'S HOSPITAL, 2900 First Avenue, Huntington, WV, Zip 25702–1272; tel. 304/526–1234; J. Thomas Jones, Executive Director

SUMMERS COUNTY APPALACHIAN REGIONAL HOSPITAL, Terrace Street, Hinton, WV, Zip 25951, Mailing Address: Drawer 940, Zip 25951–0940; tel. 304/466–1000; Clyde E. Bolton, Administrator

THE JAMES B. HAGGIN MEMORIAL HOSPITAL, 464 Linden Avenue, Harrodsburg, KY, Zip 40330–1862; tel. 606/734–5441; Earl James Motzer, Ph.D., FACHE, Chief Executive Officer

THREE RIVERS MEDICAL CENTER, Highway 644, Louisa, KY, Zip 41230, Mailing Address: P.O. Box 769, Zip 41230–0769; tel. 606/638–9451; Greg Kiser, Chief Executive Officer

UNIVERSITY HOSPITAL, 234 Goodman Street, Cincinnati, OH, Zip 45267–0700; tel. 513/558–1000; Elliot G. Cohen, Senior Executive Officer

UNIVERSITY OF KENTUCKY HOSPITAL, 800 Rose Street, Lexington, KY, Zip 40536–0084; tel. 606/323–5000; Frank Butler, Director

WELLMONT HOLSTON VALLEY MEDICAL CENTER, West Ravine Street, Kingsport, TN, Zip 37662–0224, Mailing Address: Box 238, Zip 37662–0224; tel. 423/224–4000; Louis H. Bremer, President and Chief Executive Officer

WHITESBURG APPALACHIAN REGIONAL HOSPITAL, 240 Hospital Road, Whitesburg, KY, Zip 41858–1254; tel. 606/633–3600; Nick Lewis, Administrator

WILLIAMSON ARH HOSPITAL, 260 Hospital Drive, South Williamson, KY, Zip 41503–4072; tel. 606/237–1700; John A. Grah, Administrator

WOODFORD HOSPITAL, 360 Amsden Avenue, Versailles, KY, Zip 40383–1286; tel. 606/873–3111; Nancy Littrell, Chief Executive Officer

COMMUNITY CARE NETWORK
1305 North Elm Street, Henderson, KY 42420; tel. 502/827–7380; LeaAnn H. Martin, Director of Marketing

CALDWELL COUNTY HOSPITAL, 101 Hospital Drive, Princeton, KY, Zip 42445–0410, Mailing Address: Box 410, Zip 42445–0410; tel. 502/365–0300; Marsha Woodall, Interim Chief Executive Officer

COMMUNITY METHODIST HOSPITAL, 1305 North Elm Street, Henderson, KY, Zip 42420–2775, Mailing Address: P.O. Box 48, Zip 42420–0048; tel. 502/827–7700; Bruce D. Begley, Executive Director

CRITTENDEN COUNTY HOSPITAL, Highway 60 South, Marion, KY, Zip 42064, Mailing Address: P.O. Box 386, Zip 42064–0386; tel. 502/965–5281; Rick Napper, Chief Executive Officer

FRANKLIN–SIMPSON MEMORIAL HOSPITAL, Brookhaven Road, Franklin, KY, Zip 42135–2929, Mailing Address: P.O. Box 2929, Zip 42135–2929; tel. 502/586–3253; William P. Macri, Chief Executive Officer

JENNIE STUART MEDICAL CENTER, 320 West 18th Street, Hopkinsville, KY, Zip 42241–2400, Mailing Address: P.O. Box 2400, Zip 42241–2400; tel. 502/887–0100; Lewis T. Peeples, Chief Executive Officer

LIVINGSTON HOSPITAL AND HEALTHCARE SERVICES, 131 Hospital Drive, Salem, KY, Zip 42078; tel. 502/988–2299; William C. Smith, Chief Executive Officer

MUHLENBERG COMMUNITY HOSPITAL, 440 Hopkinsville Street, Greenville, KY, Zip 42345–1172, Mailing Address: P.O. Box 387, Zip 42345–0387; tel. 502/338–8000; Charles D. Lovell, Jr., Chief Executive Officer

MURRAY–CALLOWAY COUNTY HOSPITAL, 803 Poplar Street, Murray, KY, Zip 42071–2432; tel. 502/762–1100; Stuart Poston, President

OWENSBORO MERCY HEALTH SYSTEM, 811 East Parrish Avenue, Owensboro, KY, Zip 42303–3268, Mailing Address: P.O. Box 20007, Zip 42303–0007; tel. 502/688–2000; Greg L. Carlson, President and Chief Executive Officer

REGIONAL MEDICAL CENTER OF HOPKINS COUNTY, 900 Hospital Drive, Madisonville, KY, Zip 42431–1694; tel. 502/825–5202; Bobby H. Dampier, Chief Executive Officer

UNION COUNTY METHODIST HOSPITAL, 4604 Highway 60 West, Morganfield, KY, Zip 42437–9570; tel. 502/389–3030; Patrick Donahue, Administrator

COMMUNITY HEALTH DELIVERY SYSTEM, INC.
2020 Newburg Road, Louisville, KY 40205; tel. 502/451–3330; Fran Dotson, Network Contact

ALLIANT HOSPITALS, 200 East Chestnut Street, Louisville, KY, Zip 40202–1800, Mailing Address: P.O. Box 35070, Zip 40232–5070; tel. 502/629–8000; Stephen M. Tullman, Administrator

BAPTIST HOSPITAL EAST, 4000 Kresge Way, Louisville, KY, Zip 40207–4676; tel. 502/897–8100; Susan Stout Tamme, President

BAPTIST REGIONAL MEDICAL CENTER, 1 Trillium Way, Corbin, KY, Zip 40701–8420; tel. 606/528–1212; John S. Henson, President

BRECKINRIDGE MEMORIAL HOSPITAL, 1011 Old Highway 60, Hardinsburg, KY, Zip 40143–2597; tel. 502/756–7000; George Walz, CHE, Chief Executive Officer

CALDWELL COUNTY HOSPITAL, 101 Hospital Drive, Princeton, KY, Zip 42445–0410, Mailing Address: Box 410, Zip 42445–0410; tel. 502/365–0300; Marsha Woodall, Interim Chief Executive Officer

CARITAS MEDICAL CENTER, 1850 Bluegrass Avenue, Louisville, KY, Zip 40215–1199; tel. 502/361–6000; Peter J. Bernard, President and Chief Executive Officer

CARITAS PEACE CENTER, 2020 Newburg Road, Louisville, KY, Zip 40205–1879; tel. 502/451–3330; Peter J. Bernard, President and Chief Executive Officer

CARROLL COUNTY HOSPITAL, 309 11th Street, Carrollton, KY, Zip 41008–1400; tel. 502/732–4321; Roger Williams, Chief Executive Officer

CAVERNA MEMORIAL HOSPITAL, 1501 South Dixie Street, Horse Cave, KY, Zip 42749–1477; tel. 502/786–2191; James J. Kerins, Sr., Administrator

CENTRAL BAPTIST HOSPITAL, 1740 Nicholasville Road, Lexington, KY, Zip 40503; tel. 606/275–6100; William G. Sisson, President

FLAGET MEMORIAL HOSPITAL, 201 Cathedral Manor, Bardstown, KY, Zip 40004–1299; tel. 502/348–3923; Suzanne Reasbeck, President and Chief Executive Officer

JANE TODD CRAWFORD HOSPITAL, 202–206 Milby Street, Greensburg, KY, Zip 42743–1100, Mailing Address: P.O. Box 220, Zip 42743–0220; tel. 502/932–4211; Larry Craig, Chief Executive Officer

MARYMOUNT MEDICAL CENTER, 310 East Ninth Street, London, KY, Zip 40741–1299; tel. 606/878–6520; Lowell Jones, President

ST. ELIZABETH MEDICAL CENTER–GRANT COUNTY, 238 Barnes Road, Williamstown, KY, Zip 41097–9460; tel. 606/824–2400; Chris Carle, Administrator

ST. ELIZABETH MEDICAL CENTER–NORTH, 401 East 20th Street, Covington, KY, Zip 41014–1585; tel. 606/292–4000; Joseph W. Gross, President and Chief Executive Officer

ST. JOSEPH HOSPITAL, One St. Joseph Drive, Lexington, KY, Zip 40504–3754; tel. 606/278–3436; Thomas J. Murray, President

TRI COUNTY BAPTIST HOSPITAL, 1025 New Moody Lane, La Grange, KY, Zip 40031–0559; tel. 502/222–5388; Dennis B. Johnson, Administrator

TRIGG COUNTY HOSPITAL, Highway 68 East, Cadiz, KY, Zip 42211, Mailing Address: P.O. Box 312, Zip 42211–0312; tel. 502/522–3215; Richard Chapman, Administrator

TWIN LAKES REGIONAL MEDICAL CENTER, 910 Wallace Avenue, Leitchfield, KY, Zip 42754–1499; tel. 502/259–9400; Stephen L. Meredith, Chief Executive Officer

WESTERN BAPTIST HOSPITAL, 2501 Kentucky Avenue, Paducah, KY, Zip 42003–3200; tel. 502/575–2100; Larry O. Barton, President

JEWISH HOSPITAL HEALTHCARE SERVICES
217 East Chestnut Street, Louisville, KY 40202; tel. 502/587–4011; Greg Pugh, Data Analyst

CLARK MEMORIAL HOSPITAL, 1220 Missouri Avenue, Jeffersonville, IN, Zip 47130–3743, Mailing Address: Box 69, Zip 47131–0069; tel. 812/282–6631; Merle E. Stepp, President and Chief Executive Officer

FRAZIER REHABILITATION CENTER, 220 Abraham Flexner Way, Louisville, KY, Zip 40202–1887; tel. 502/582–7400; Jason Roeback, President

HARDIN MEMORIAL HOSPITAL, 913 North Dixie Avenue, Elizabethtown, KY, Zip 42701–2599; tel. 502/737–1212; David L. Gray, President

JEWISH HOSPITAL, 217 East Chestnut Street, Louisville, KY, Zip 40202–1886; tel. 502/587–4011; Douglas E. Shaw, President

JEWISH HOSPITAL LEXINGTON, 150 North Eagle Creek Drive, Lexington, KY, Zip 40509–1807; tel. 606/268–4800; Rebecca Lewis, President

JEWISH HOSPITAL–SHELBYVILLE, 727 Hospital Drive, Shelbyville, KY, Zip 40065–1699; tel. 502/647–4000; Timothy L. Jarm, President

PATTIE A. CLAY HOSPITAL, EKU By–Pass, Richmond, KY, Zip 40475, Mailing Address: P.O. Box 1600, Zip 40476–2603; tel. 606/625–3131; Richard M. Thomas, President

SCOTT MEMORIAL HOSPITAL, 1415 North Gardner Street, Scottsburg, IN, Zip 47170–0456, Mailing Address: Box 430, Zip 47170–0430; tel. 812/752–8500; Clifford D. Nay, Executive Director

TAYLOR COUNTY HOSPITAL, 1700 Old Lebanon Road, Campbellsville, KY, Zip 42718–9600; tel. 502/465–3561; David R. Hayes, President

WASHINGTON COUNTY MEMORIAL HOSPITAL, 911 North Shelby Street, Salem, IN, Zip 47167; tel. 812/883–5881; Rodney M. Coats, President and Chief Executive Officer

SAINT ELIZABETH MEDICAL CENTER
1 Medical Village Drive, Covington, KY 41017; tel. 606/344–2000; Joseph W. Gross, President & Chief Executive Officer

ST. ELIZABETH MEDICAL CENTER–GRANT COUNTY, 238 Barnes Road, Williamstown, KY, Zip 41097–9460; tel. 606/824–2400; Chris Carle, Administrator

ST. ELIZABETH MEDICAL CENTER–NORTH, 401 East 20th Street, Covington, KY, Zip 41014–1585; tel. 606/292–4000; Joseph W. Gross, President and Chief Executive Officer

LOUISIANA

COLUMBIA LAKEVIEW REGIONAL MEDICAL CENTER
95 East Fairway Drive, Covington, LA 70433; tel. 504/867–3800; Scott Koenig, Chief Executive Officer

COLUMBIA LAKEVIEW REGIONAL MEDICAL CENTER, 95 East Fairway Drive, Covington, LA, Zip 70433–7507; tel. 504/876–3800; Scott Koenig, Chief Executive Officer

FRANCISCAN MISSIONARIES OF OUR LADY HEALTH NETWORK
4200 Essen Lane, Baton Rouge, LA 70809; tel. 504/923–2701; John Finan Jr., President/CEO

ABBEVILLE GENERAL HOSPITAL, 118 North Hospital Drive, Abbeville, LA, Zip 70510–4077, Mailing Address: P.O. Box 580, Zip 70511–0580; tel. 318/893–5466; Ray A. Landry, Administrator

ABROM KAPLAN MEMORIAL HOSPITAL, 1310 West Seventh Street, Kaplan, LA, Zip 70548–2998; tel. 318/643–8300; Lyman Trahan, Administrator

ACADIA–ST. LANDRY HOSPITAL, 810 South Broadway Street, Church Point, LA, Zip 70525–4497; tel. 318/684–5435; Alcus Trahan, Administrator

AMERICAN LEGION HOSPITAL, 1305 Crowley Rayne Highway, Crowley, LA, Zip 70526–9401; tel. 318/783–3222; Leonard J. Spears, Vice President and Chief Executive Officer

IBERIA GENERAL HOSPITAL AND MEDICAL CENTER, 2315 East Main Street, New Iberia, LA, Zip 70560–4031, Mailing Address: P.O. Box 13338, Zip 70562–3338; tel. 318/364–0441; Robert R. Stanley, Chief Executive Officer

JENNINGS AMERICAN LEGION HOSPITAL, 1634 Elton Road, Jennings, LA, Zip 70546–3614; tel. 318/821–4151; Terry J. Terrebonne, Administrator

OPELOUSAS GENERAL HOSPITAL, 520 Prudhomme Lane, Opelousas, LA, Zip 70570–6454, Mailing Address: P.O. Box 1208, Zip 70571–1208; tel. 318/948–3011; Patrick Brian Carrier, Administrator

OUR LADY OF LOURDES REGIONAL MEDICAL CENTER, 611 St. Landry Street, Lafayette, LA, Zip 70506–4697, Mailing Address: Box 4027, Zip 70502–4027; tel. 318/289–2000; Dudley Romero, President and Chief Executive Officer

OUR LADY OF THE LAKE REGIONAL MEDICAL CENTER, 5000 Hennessy Boulevard, Baton Rouge, LA, Zip 70808–4350; tel. 504/765–6565; Robert C. Davidge, President and Chief Executive Officer

ST. FRANCIS MEDICAL CENTER, 309 Jackson Street, Monroe, LA, Zip 71201–7498, Mailing Address: P.O. Box 1901, Zip 71210–1901; tel. 318/327–4000; H. Gerald Smith, President and Chief Executive Officer

VILLE PLATTE MEDICAL CENTER, 800 East Main Street, Ville Platte, LA, Zip 70586–4618, Mailing Address: P.O. Box 349, Zip 70586–0349; tel. 318/363–5684; Linda Deville, Chief Executive Officer

WEST FELICIANA PARISH HOSPITAL, Saint Francisville, LA, Mailing Address: Box 368, Zip 70775–0368; tel. 504/635–3811; John H. Green, Administrator

HEALTHCARE ADVANTAGE, INC.
829 Saint Charles Avenue, New Orleans, LA 70103; tel. 504/568–9009; Jane Cooper, President

DOCTORS HOSPITAL OF JEFFERSON, 4320 Houma Boulevard, Metairie, LA, Zip 70006–2973; tel. 504/456–5800; Gerald L. Parton, Chief Executive Officer

EAST JEFFERSON GENERAL HOSPITAL, 4200 Houma Boulevard, Metairie, LA, Zip 70006–2996; tel. 504/454–4000; Peter J. Betts, President and Chief Executive Officer

PENDLETON MEMORIAL METHODIST HOSPITAL, 5620 Read Boulevard, New Orleans, LA, Zip 70127–3154; tel. 504/244–5100; Frederick C. Young, Jr., President

WEST JEFFERSON MEDICAL CENTER, 1101 Medical Center Boulevard, Marrero, LA, Zip 70072–3191; tel. 504/347–5511; David M. Smith, FACHE, President and Chief Executive Officer

LOUISIANA HEALTH CARE AUTHORITY
8550 United Plaza Boulevard, Baton Rouge, LA 70809; tel. 504/342–2964; Carolyn Mattis, Director of Networks

E. A. CONWAY MEDICAL CENTER, 4864 Jackson Street, Monroe, LA, Zip 71202–6497, Mailing Address: P.O. Box 1881, Zip 71210–1881; tel. 318/330–7000; Roy D. Bostick, Director

EARL K. LONG MEDICAL CENTER, 5825 Airline Highway, Baton Rouge, LA, Zip 70805–2498; tel. 504/358–1000; Jonathan Roberts, Dr.PH, Chief Executive Officer

HUEY P. LONG MEDICAL CENTER, 352 Hospital Boulevard, Pineville, LA, Zip 71360, Mailing Address: P.O. Box 5352, Zip 71361–5352; tel. 318/448–0811; James E. Morgan, Director

LALLIE KEMP MEDICAL CENTER, 52579 Highway 51 South, Independence, LA, Zip 70443–2231; tel. 504/878–9421; LeVern Meades, Acting Administrator

LEONARD J. CHABERT MEDICAL CENTER, 1978 Industrial Boulevard, Houma, LA, Zip 70363–7094; tel. 504/873–2200; Stanley E. Hurstell, Administrator

MEDICAL CENTER OF LOUISIANA AT NEW ORLEANS, 2021 Perdido Street, New Orleans, LA, Zip 70112–1396; tel. 504/588–3000; John S. Berault, Chief Executive Officer

UNIVERSITY MEDICAL CENTER, 2390 West Congress Street, Lafayette, LA, Zip 70506–4298, Mailing Address: P.O. Box 69300, Zip 70596–9300; tel. 318/261–6004; Lawrence T. Dorsey, Administrator

WALTER OLIN MOSS REGIONAL MEDICAL CENTER, 1000 Walters Street, Lake Charles, LA, Zip 70605; tel. 318/475–8100; Patrick C. Robinson, M.D., Administrator

WASHINGTON–ST. TAMMANY REGIONAL MEDICAL CENTER, 400 Memphis Street, Bogalusa, LA, Zip 70427–0040, Mailing Address: Box 40, Zip 70429–0040; tel. 504/735–1322; Larry R. King, Administrator

OCHSNER/SISTERS OF CHARITY HEALTH NETWORK
One Galleria Boulevard, Suite 1224, New Orleans, LA 70001; tel. 504/836–8064; Jim Pittman, Director of Networks

BEAUREGARD MEMORIAL HOSPITAL, 600 South Pine Street, De Ridder, LA, Zip 70634–4998, Mailing Address: P.O. Box 730, Zip 70634–0730; tel. 318/462–7100; Theodore J. Badger, Jr., Chief Executive Officer

BUNKIE GENERAL HOSPITAL, Evergreen Highway, Bunkie, LA, Zip 71322, Mailing Address: P.O. Box 380, Zip 71322–0380; tel. 318/346–6681; Donald L. Kannady, Administrator

BYRD REGIONAL HOSPITAL, 1020 West Fertitta Boulevard, Leesville, LA, Zip 71446–4697; tel. 318/239–9041; Donald Henderson, Chief Executive Officer

COLUMBIA MEDICAL CENTER, 17000 Medical Center Drive, Baton Rouge, LA, Zip 70816–3224; tel. 504/755–4800; Joseph R. Dicapo, Chief Executive Officer

DE SOTO REGIONAL HEALTH SYSTEM, 207 Jefferson Street, Mansfield, LA, Zip 71052–2603, Mailing Address: P.O. Box 672, Zip 71052–0672; tel. 318/871–3101; William F. Barrow, President and Chief Executive Officer

HOMER MEMORIAL HOSPITAL, 620 East College Street, Homer, LA, Zip 71040–3202; tel. 318/927–2024; J. Larry Jordan, Administrator

JENNINGS AMERICAN LEGION HOSPITAL, 1634 Elton Road, Jennings, LA, Zip 70546–3614; tel. 318/821–4151; Terry J. Terrebonne, Administrator

LADY OF THE SEA GENERAL HOSPITAL, 200 West 134th Place, Cut Off, LA, Zip 70345–4145; tel. 504/632–6401; Lane M. Cheramie, Chief Executive Officer

LANE MEMORIAL HOSPITAL, 6300 Main Street, Zachary, LA, Zip 70791–9990; tel. 504/658–4000; David W. Fuller, Chief Executive Officer

MINDEN MEDICAL CENTER, 1 Medical Plaza, Minden, LA, Zip 71055–3330; tel. 318/377–2321; George E. French, III, Chief Executive Officer

Section B

NATCHITOCHES PARISH HOSPITAL, 501 Keyser Avenue, Natchitoches, LA, Zip 71457–6036, Mailing Address: P.O. Box 2009, Zip 71457–2009; tel. 318/352–1200; Eugene Spillman, Executive Director

NORTHSHORE REGIONAL MEDICAL CENTER, 100 Medical Center Drive, Slidell, LA, Zip 70461–8572; tel. 504/649–7070; George J. Saucier, Chief Executive Officer

OCHSNER FOUNDATION HOSPITAL, 1516 Jefferson Highway, New Orleans, LA, Zip 70121–2484; tel. 504/842–3000; Mary W. Brown, Executive Vice President and Director

PENDLETON MEMORIAL METHODIST HOSPITAL, 5620 Read Boulevard, New Orleans, LA, Zip 70127–3154; tel. 504/244–5100; Frederick C. Young, Jr., President

RIVER WEST MEDICAL CENTER, 59355 River West Drive, Plaquemine, LA, Zip 70764–9543; tel. 504/687–9222; Mark Nosacka, Chief Executive Officer

RIVERLAND MEDICAL CENTER, 1700 North E. 'E' Wallace Boulevard, Ferriday, LA, Zip 71334, Mailing Address: P.O. Box 111, Zip 71334–0111; tel. 318/757–6551; Vernon R. Stevens, Jr., Administrator

SABINE MEDICAL CENTER, 240 Highland Drive, Many, LA, Zip 71449–3718; tel. 318/256–5691; Karen Ford, Chief Executive Officer

SCHUMPERT MEDICAL CENTER, One St. Mary Place, Shreveport, LA, Zip 71101–4399, Mailing Address: P.O. Box 21976, Zip 71120–1076; tel. 318/681–4500; Arthur A. Gonzalez, Dr.PH, President and Chief Executive Officer

ST. ANNE GENERAL HOSPITAL, 4608 Highway 1, Raceland, LA, Zip 70394, Mailing Address: P.O. Box 440, Zip 70394–0440; tel. 504/537–6841; Milton D. Bourgeois, Jr., Administrator

ST. FRANCES CABRINI HOSPITAL, 3330 Masonic Drive, Alexandria, LA, Zip 71301–3899; tel. 318/487–1122; Sister Olive Bordelon, Chief Executive Officer

ST. PATRICK HOSPITAL OF LAKE CHARLES, 524 South Ryan Street, Lake Charles, LA, Zip 70601–5799, Mailing Address: P.O. Box 3401, Zip 70602–3401; tel. 318/436–2511; James E. Gardner, Jr., Chief Executive Officer

WEST CALCASIEU CAMERON HOSPITAL, 701 East Cypress Street, Sulphur, LA, Zip 70663–5000, Mailing Address: P.O. Box 2509, Zip 70664–2509; tel. 318/527–4240; Wayne A. Swiniarski, FACHE, Chief Executive Officer

WEST JEFFERSON MEDICAL CENTER, 1101 Medical Center Boulevard, Marrero, LA, Zip 70072–3191; tel. 504/347–5511; David M. Smith, FACHE, President and Chief Executive Officer

TENET HEALTH SYSTEM
111 Veterans Boulevard, Suite 1424, Metairie, LA 70005; tel. 504/833–1495; Reynold Jennings, Senior Vice President of Operations

DOCTORS HOSPITAL OF JEFFERSON, 4320 Houma Boulevard, Metairie, LA, Zip 70006–2973; tel. 504/456–5800; Gerald L. Parton, Chief Executive Officer

JO ELLEN SMITH MEDICAL CENTER, 4444 General Meyer Avenue, New Orleans, LA, Zip 70131–3595; tel. 504/363–7011; Rene Goux, Chief Executive Officer

KENNER REGIONAL MEDICAL CENTER, 180 West Esplanade Avenue, Kenner, LA, Zip 70065–6001; tel. 504/468–8600; Deborah C. Keel, Chief Executive Officer

MEADOWCREST HOSPITAL, 2500 Belle Chase Highway, Gretna, LA, Zip 70056–7196; tel. 504/392–3131; Jaime A. Wesolowski, Chief Executive Officer

MEDICAL CENTER OF LOUISIANA AT NEW ORLEANS, 2021 Perdido Street, New Orleans, LA, Zip 70112–1396; tel. 504/588–3000; John S. Berault, Chief Executive Officer

MEMORIAL MEDICAL CENTER–BAPTIST CAMPUS, New Orleans, LA, Randall L. Hoover, Chief Executive Officer

MEMORIAL MEDICAL CENTER–MERCY CAMPUS, 301 North Jefferson Davis Parkway, New Orleans, LA, Zip 70119–5397; tel. 504/483–5000; Randall L. Hoover, Chief Executive Officer

MINDEN MEDICAL CENTER, 1 Medical Plaza, Minden, LA, Zip 71055–3330; tel. 318/377–2321; George E. French, III, Chief Executive Officer

NORTH SHORE PSYCHIATRIC HOSPITAL, 104 Medical Center Drive, Slidell, LA, Zip 70461–7838; tel. 504/646–5500

NORTHSHORE REGIONAL MEDICAL CENTER, 100 Medical Center Drive, Slidell, LA, Zip 70461–8572; tel. 504/649–7070; George J. Saucier, Chief Executive Officer

ST. CHARLES GENERAL HOSPITAL, 3700 St. Charles Avenue, New Orleans, LA, Zip 70115–4680; tel. 504/899–7441; Lynn C. Orfgen, Chief Executive Officer

MAINE

BLUE HILL MEMORIAL HOSPITAL FOUNDATION
Water Street, Blue Hill, ME 04614; tel. 207/374–2836; Bruce D. Cummings, Chief Executive Officer

BLUE HILL MEMORIAL HOSPITAL, Water Street, Blue Hill, ME, Zip 04614–0823, Mailing Address: P.O. Box 823, Zip 04614–0823; tel. 207/374–2836; Bruce D. Cummings, Chief Executive Officer

CENTRAL MAINE HEALTHCARE CORP
304 Cambridge Road, Lewiston, ME 94240; tel. 207/795–2303; William W. Young, Jr., President & Chief Executive Officer

NORTHERN CUMBERLAND MEMORIAL HOSPITAL, South High Street, Bridgton, ME, Zip 04009, Mailing Address: P.O. Box 230, Zip 04009–0230; tel. 207/647–8841; Laird Covey, Interim President

RUMFORD COMMUNITY HOSPITAL, 420 Franklin Street, Rumford, ME, Zip 04276–2145, Mailing Address: P.O. Box 619, Zip 04276–0619; tel. 207/364–4581; John H. Welsh, Chief Executive Officer

STEPHENS MEMORIAL HOSPITAL, 181 Main Street, Norway, ME, Zip 04268–1297; tel. 207/743–5933; Timothy A. Churchill, President

HEALTH NET, INC.
One Merchants Plaza, 5th Floor, Bangor, ME 04401; tel. 207/942–2723; Paul Brough, Executive Director

ACADIA HOSPITAL, 268 Stillwater Avenue, Bangor, ME, Zip 04401–3945, Mailing Address: P.O. Box 422, Zip 04402–0422; tel. 207/973–6100; Dennis P. King, President

AROOSTOOK MEDICAL CENTER, 140 Academy Street, Presque Isle, ME, Zip 04769–3171, Mailing Address: P.O. Box 151, Zip 04769–0151; tel. 207/768–4000; David A. Peterson, President and Chief Executive Officer

BLUE HILL MEMORIAL HOSPITAL, Water Street, Blue Hill, ME, Zip 04614–0823, Mailing Address: P.O. Box 823, Zip 04614–0823; tel. 207/374–2836; Bruce D. Cummings, Chief Executive Officer

CHARLES A. DEAN MEMORIAL HOSPITAL, Pritham Avenue, Greenville, ME, Zip 04441–1395, Mailing Address: P.O. Box 1129, Zip 04441–1129; tel. 207/695–2223; Nancy Pelletier, Interim Administrator

EASTERN MAINE MEDICAL CENTER, 489 State Street, Bangor, ME, Zip 04401–6674, Mailing Address: P.O. Box 404, Zip 04402–0404; tel. 207/973–7000; Norman A. Ledwin, President and Chief Executive Officer

INLAND HOSPITAL, 200 Kennedy Memorial Drive, Waterville, ME, Zip 04901–4595; tel. 207/861–3000; Wilfred J. Addison, President and Chief Executive Officer

MILLINOCKET REGIONAL HOSPITAL, 200 Somerset Street, Millinocket, ME, Zip 04462–1298; tel. 207/723–5161; Craig A. Kantos, Chief Executive Officer

MOUNT DESERT ISLAND HOSPITAL, Wayman Lane, Bar Harbor, ME, Zip 04609–0008, Mailing Address: P.O. Box 8, Zip 04609–0008; tel. 207/288–5081; Leslie A. Hawkins, Chief Executive Officer

NORTHERN MAINE MEDICAL CENTER, 143 East Main Street, Fort Kent, ME, Zip 04743–1497; tel. 207/834–3155; Martin B. Bernstein, Chief Executive Officer

SEBASTICOOK VALLEY HOSPITAL, 99 Grove Street, Pittsfield, ME, Zip 04967–1199; tel. 207/487–5141; Ann Morrison, R.N., Chief Executive Officer

WALDO COUNTY GENERAL HOSPITAL, Northport Avenue, Belfast, ME, Zip 04915, Mailing Address: P.O. Box 287, Zip 04915–0287; tel. 207/338–2500; Mark A. Biscone, Executive Director

SYNERNET
222 Saint John Street, Suite 329, Portland, ME 04102; tel. 207/775–3415; Russ Peterson, Senior Vice President

BLUE HILL MEMORIAL HOSPITAL, Water Street, Blue Hill, ME, Zip 04614–0823, Mailing Address: P.O. Box 823, Zip 04614–0823; tel. 207/374–2836; Bruce D. Cummings, Chief Executive Officer

FRANKLIN MEMORIAL HOSPITAL, One Hospital Drive, Farmington, ME, Zip 04938–9990; tel. 207/778–6031; Richard A. Batt, President and Chief Executive Officer

HENRIETTA D. GOODALL HOSPITAL, 25 June Street, Sanford, ME, Zip 04073–2645; tel. 207/324–4310; Peter G. Booth, President

INLAND HOSPITAL, 200 Kennedy Memorial Drive, Waterville, ME, Zip 04901–4595; tel. 207/861–3000; Wilfred J. Addison, President and Chief Executive Officer

MERCY HOSPITAL PORTLAND, 144 State Street, Portland, ME, Zip 04101–3795; tel. 207/879–3000; Howard R. Buckley, President

MID COAST HOSPITAL, 1356 Washington Street, Bath, ME, Zip 04530–2897; tel. 207/443–5524; Herbert Paris, President

MILES MEMORIAL HOSPITAL, Bristol Road, Damariscotta, ME, Zip 04543, Mailing Address: Rural Route 2, Box 4500, Zip 04543–9767; tel. 207/563–1234; Judith Tarr, Chief Executive Officer

MOUNT DESERT ISLAND HOSPITAL, Wayman Lane, Bar Harbor, ME, Zip 04609–0008, Mailing Address: P.O. Box 8, Zip 04609–0008; tel. 207/288–5081; Leslie A. Hawkins, Chief Executive Officer

NORTHERN CUMBERLAND MEMORIAL HOSPITAL, South High Street, Bridgton, ME, Zip 04009, Mailing Address: P.O. Box 230, Zip 04009–0230; tel. 207/647–8841; Laird Covey, Interim President

NORTHERN MAINE MEDICAL CENTER, 143 East Main Street, Fort Kent, ME, Zip 04743–1497; tel. 207/834–3155; Martin B. Bernstein, Chief Executive Officer

PENOBSCOT BAY MEDICAL CENTER, 6 Glen Cove Drive, Rockport, ME, Zip 04856–4241; tel. 207/596–8000; Gary R. Daniels, President

REDINGTON–FAIRVIEW GENERAL HOSPITAL, Fairview Avenue, Skowhegan, ME, Zip 04976, Mailing Address: P.O. Box 468, Zip 04976–0468; tel. 207/474–5121; Richard Willett, Chief Executive Officer

RUMFORD COMMUNITY HOSPITAL, 420 Franklin Street, Rumford, ME, Zip 04276–2145, Mailing Address: P.O. Box 619, Zip 04276–0619; tel. 207/364–4581; John H. Welsh, Chief Executive Officer

SEBASTICOOK VALLEY HOSPITAL, 99 Grove Street, Pittsfield, ME, Zip 04967–1199; tel. 207/487–5141; Ann Morrison, R.N., Chief Executive Officer

SOUTHERN MAINE MEDICAL CENTER, One Medical Center Drive, Biddeford, ME, Zip 04005–9496, Mailing Address: P.O. Box 626, Zip 04005–0626; tel. 207/283–7000; Edward J. McGeachey, President and Chief Executive Officer

ST. JOSEPH HOSPITAL, 360 Broadway, Bangor, ME, Zip 04401–3897, Mailing Address: P.O. Box 403, Zip 04402–0403; tel. 207/262–1000; Sister Mary Norberta Malinowski, President

ST. MARY'S REGIONAL MEDICAL CENTER, 45 Golder Street, Lewiston, ME, Zip 04240–6033, Mailing Address: P.O. Box 291, Zip 04243–0291; tel. 207/777–8100; James E. Cassidy, President and Chief Executive Officer

STEPHENS MEMORIAL HOSPITAL, 181 Main Street, Norway, ME, Zip 04268–1297; tel. 207/743–5933; Timothy A. Churchill, President

WALDO COUNTY GENERAL HOSPITAL, Northport Avenue, Belfast, ME, Zip 04915, Mailing Address: P.O. Box 287, Zip 04915–0287; tel. 207/338–2500; Mark A. Biscone, Executive Director

WESTBROOK COMMUNITY HOSPITAL, 40 Park Road, Westbrook, ME, Zip 04092–3158; tel. 207/854–8464; Charlene Wallace, Interim President

YORK HOSPITAL, 15 Hospital Drive, York, ME, Zip 03909–1099; tel. 207/351–2395; Jud Knox, President

MARYLAND

DIMENSIONS HEALTHCARE SYSTEM
9200 Basil Court, Largo, MD 20785; tel. 301/925–7000; Winfield M. Kelly, Jr., President & Chief Executive Officer

LAUREL REGIONAL HOSPITAL, 7300 Van Dusen Road, Laurel, MD, Zip 20707–9266; tel. 301/725–4300; Patrick F. Mutch, President

PRINCE GEORGE'S HOSPITAL CENTER, 3001 Hospital Drive, Cheverly, MD, Zip 20785–1189; tel. 301/618–2000; Allan Earl Atzrott, President

HELIX HEALTH SYSTEM
2330 West Joppa Road, Suite 301, Lutherville, MD 21093; tel. 410/296–6050; Michael R. Merson, President & Chief Executive Officer

CHURCH HOSPITAL CORPORATION, 100 North Broadway, Baltimore, MD, Zip 21231–1593; tel. 410/522–8000; Ann C. Failing, President

FRANKLIN SQUARE HOSPITAL CENTER, 9000 Franklin Square Drive, Baltimore, MD, Zip 21237–3998; tel. 410/682–7000; Charles D. Mross, President and Chief Executive Officer

GOOD SAMARITAN HOSPITAL OF MARYLAND, 5601 Loch Raven Boulevard, Baltimore, MD, Zip 21239–2995; tel. 410/532–8000; Lawrence M. Beck, President

UNION MEMORIAL HOSPITAL, 201 East University Parkway, Baltimore, MD, Zip 21218–2391; tel. 410/554–2000; Kenneth R. Buser, President and Chief Executive Officer

JOHNS HOPKINS MEDICINE
600 North Wolfe Street, Baltimore, MD 21287; tel. 410/955–5000; Edward D. Miller, MD, President

JOHNS HOPKINS BAYVIEW MEDICAL CENTER, 4940 Eastern Avenue, Baltimore, MD, Zip 21224–2780; tel. 410/550–0100; Ronald R. Peterson, President

JOHNS HOPKINS HOSPITAL, 600 North Wolfe Street, Baltimore, MD, Zip 21287–0002; tel. 410/955–5000; Ronald R. Peterson, President

KENT & QUEEN ANNE'S HOSPITAL, 100 Brown Street, Chestertown, MD, Zip 21620–1499; tel. 410/778–3300; William R. Kirk, Jr., President and Chief Executive Officer

SUBURBAN HOSPITAL, 8600 Old Georgetown Road, Bethesda, MD, Zip 20814–1497; tel. 301/896–3100; Brian G. Grissler, President and Chief Executive Officer

MARYLAND HEALTH NETWORK
10440 Little Patuxent, Columbia, MD 21044; tel. 410/715–6601; Peter Clay, President

GREATER BALTIMORE MEDICAL CENTER, 6701 North Charles Street, Baltimore, MD, Zip 21204–6892; tel. 410/828–2000; Robert P. Kowal, President

HOLY CROSS HOSPITAL OF SILVER SPRING, 1500 Forest Glen Road, Silver Spring, MD, Zip 20910–1484; tel. 301/754–7000; Cornelius McKelvey, Interim Chief Executive Officer

MONTGOMERY GENERAL HOSPITAL, 18101 Prince Philip Drive, Olney, MD, Zip 20832–1512; tel. 301/774–8882; Peter W. Monge, President and Chief Executive Officer

NORTHWEST HOSPITAL CENTER, 5401 Old Court Road, Randallstown, MD, Zip 21133–5185; tel. 410/521–2200; Robert W. Fischer, President

ST. AGNES HEALTHCARE, 900 Caton Avenue, Baltimore, MD, Zip 21229–5299; tel. 410/368–6000; Robert E. Pezzoli, President and Chief Executive Officer

UNIVERSITY OF MARYLAND MEDICAL SYSTEM
22 South Greene Street, Baltimore, MD 21201; tel. 410/328–8667; Morton I. Rapoport, M.D., President & Chief Executive Officer

DEATON SPECIALTY HOSPITAL AND HOME, 611 South Charles Street, Baltimore, MD, Zip 21230–3898; tel. 410/547–8500; James E. Ross, FACHE, Chief Executive Officer

JAMES LAWRENCE KERNAN HOSPITAL, 2200 Kernan Drive, Baltimore, MD, Zip 21207–6697; tel. 410/448–2500; James E. Ross, FACHE, Chief Executive Officer

UNIVERSITY OF MARYLAND MEDICAL SYSTEM, 22 South Greene Street, Baltimore, MD, Zip 21201–1595; tel. 410/328–8667; Morton I. Rapoport, M.D., President and Chief Executive Officer

MASSACHUSETTS

BAYSTATE HEALTH SYSTEM
759 Chestnut Street, Springfield, MA 01199; tel. 413/784–3838; Donna J. Ross, VP Strategic & Program Planning

BAYSTATE MEDICAL CENTER, 759 Chestnut Street, Springfield, MA, Zip 01199–0001; tel. 413/794–0000; Mark R. Tolosky, Chief Executive Officer

FRANKLIN MEDICAL CENTER, 164 High Street, Greenfield, MA, Zip 01301–2613; tel. 413/773–0211; Harlan J. Smith, President

MARY LANE HOSPITAL, 85 South Street, Ware, MA, Zip 01082–1697; tel. 413/967–6211; Christine Shirtcliff, Executive Vice President

BERKSHIRE HEALTH SYSTEM
725 North Street, Pittsfield, MA 01201; tel. 413/447–2000; David Phelps, President

BERKSHIRE MEDICAL CENTER, 725 North Street, Pittsfield, MA, Zip 01201–4124; tel. 413/447–2000; Ruth P. Blodgett, Chief Operating Officer

FAIRVIEW HOSPITAL, 29 Lewis Avenue, Great Barrington, MA, Zip 01230–1713; tel. 413/528–0790; Claire L. Bowen, President

CAPE COD HEALTHCARE, INC.
88 Lewis Bay Road, Hyannisport, MA 02601; tel. 508/771–1800; Jim Lyons, Chief Executive Officer

CAPE COD HOSPITAL, 27 Park Street, Hyannis, MA, Zip 02601–5203; tel. 508/771–1800; Gail M. Frieswick, Ed.D., President and Chief Executive Officer

FALMOUTH HOSPITAL, 100 Ter Heun Drive, Falmouth, MA, Zip 02540–2599; tel. 508/457–3500; Gail Freiswick, President and Chief Executive Officer

CAREGROUP
375 Longwood Avenue, Boston, MA 02215; tel. 617/632–8011; Mitchell T. Rabkin, M.D., Chief Executive Officer

BETH ISRAEL DEACONESS MEDICAL CENTER, 330 Brookline Avenue, Boston, MA, Zip 02215–5491; tel. 617/667–2000; David Dolins, President

DEACONESS WALTHAM HOSPITAL, Hope Avenue, Waltham, MA, Zip 02254–9116; tel. 781/647–6000; Jeanette G. Clough, President and Chief Executive Officer

DEACONESS–GLOVER HOSPITAL CORPORATION, 148 Chestnut Street, Needham, MA, Zip 02192–2483; tel. 781/453–3000; John Dalton, President and Chief Executive Officer

DEACONESS–NASHOBA HOSPITAL, 200 Groton Road, Ayer, MA, Zip 01432–3300; tel. 978/784–9000; Jeffrey R. Kelly, President and Chief Executive Officer

MOUNT AUBURN HOSPITAL, 330 Mount Auburn Street, Cambridge, MA, Zip 02238; tel. 617/492–3500; Francis P. Lynch, President and Chief Executive Officer

NEW ENGLAND BAPTIST HOSPITAL, 125 Parker Hill Avenue, Boston, MA, Zip 02120–3297; tel. 617/754–5800; Alan H. Robbins, M.D., President

CARITAS CHRISTI HEALTH NETWORK
736 Cambridge Street, Boston, MA 02135; tel. 617/789–2500; Michael F. Collins, M.D., President & Chief Executive Officer

GOOD SAMARITAN MEDICAL CENTER, 235 North Pearl Street, Brockton, MA, Zip 02401–1794; tel. 508/427–3000; Frank J. Larkin, President and Chief Executive Officer

HOLY FAMILY HOSPITAL AND MEDICAL CENTER, 70 East Street, Methuen, MA, Zip 01844–4597; tel. 978/687–0151; William L. Lane, President

SAINT ANNE'S HOSPITAL, 795 Middle Street, Fall River, MA, Zip 02721–1798; tel. 508/674–5741; Michael W. Metzler, Acting President

ST. ELIZABETH'S MEDICAL CENTER OF BOSTON, 736 Cambridge Street, Boston, MA, Zip 02135–2997; tel. 617/789–3000; Michael F. Collins, M.D., President

ST. JOHN OF GOD HOSPITAL, 296 Allston Street, Brighton, MA, Zip 02146–1659; tel. 617/277–5750; William K. Brinkert, President

CHILDREN'S HOSPITAL
300 Longwood Avenue, Boston, MA 02115; tel. 617/355–7156; Deborah C. Jackson, Vice President of Network Development

CHILDREN'S HOSPITAL, 300 Longwood Avenue, Boston, MA, Zip 02115–5737; tel. 617/355–6000; David Stephen Weiner, President

CONTINUUM OF CARE NETWORK
57 Union Street, Marlborough, MA 01752; tel. 508/481–5000; Cheryl Herberg, Network Coordinator

MARLBOROUGH HOSPITAL, 57 Union Street, Marlborough, MA, Zip 01752–1297; tel. 508/481–5000; Anne Bourgeois, Interim Chief Executive Officer

FALLON HEALTHCARE SYSTEM
10 Chestnut Street, Worcester, MA 01608; tel. 508/799–2100; Margaret McKenna, Director of Provider Relations

ATHOL MEMORIAL HOSPITAL, 2033 Main Street, Athol, MA, Zip 01331–3598; tel. 978/249–3511; William DiFederico, President

BETH ISRAEL DEACONESS MEDICAL CENTER, 330 Brookline Avenue, Boston, MA, Zip 02215–5491; tel. 617/667–2000; David Dolins, President

BOSTON REGIONAL MEDICAL CENTER, 5 Woodland Road, Stoneham, MA, Zip 02180–1715, Mailing Address: P.O. Box 9102, Zip 02180–9102; tel. 781/979–7000; Charles S. Ricks, D.D.S., President and Chief Executive Officer

BRIGHAM AND WOMEN'S HOSPITAL, 75 Francis Street, Boston, MA, Zip 02115–6195; tel. 617/732–5500; Jeffrey Otten, President

CHILDREN'S HOSPITAL, 300 Longwood Avenue, Boston, MA, Zip 02115–5737; tel. 617/355–6000; David Stephen Weiner, President

CLINTON HOSPITAL, 201 Highland Street, Clinton, MA, Zip 01510–1096; tel. 978/368–3000; Thomas Devins, Chief Executive Officer

DANA–FARBER CANCER INSTITUTE, 44 Binney Street, Boston, MA, Zip 02115–6084; tel. 617/632–3000; David G. Nathan, M.D., President

DEACONESS WALTHAM HOSPITAL, Hope Avenue, Waltham, MA, Zip 02254–9116; tel. 781/647–6000; Jeanette G. Clough, President and Chief Executive Officer

DEACONESS–GLOVER HOSPITAL CORPORATION, 148 Chestnut Street, Needham, MA, Zip 02192–2483; tel. 781/453–3000; John Dalton, President and Chief Executive Officer

DEACONESS–NASHOBA HOSPITAL, 200 Groton Road, Ayer, MA, Zip 01432–3300; tel. 978/784–9000; Jeffrey R. Kelly, President and Chief Executive Officer

Section B

HARRINGTON MEMORIAL HOSPITAL, 100 South Street, Southbridge, MA, Zip 01550–4045; tel. 508/765–9771; Richard M. Mangion, President and Chief Executive Officer

HEALTH ALLIANCE HOSPITALS, 60 Hospital Road, Leominster, MA, Zip 01453–8004; tel. 978/466–2000; Douglas L. Fairfax, President and Chief Executive Officer

HOLY FAMILY HOSPITAL AND MEDICAL CENTER, 70 East Street, Methuen, MA, Zip 01844–4597; tel. 978/687–0151; William L. Lane, President

HUBBARD REGIONAL HOSPITAL, 340 Thompson Road, Webster, MA, Zip 01570–0608; tel. 508/943–2600; Gerald J. Barbini, Administrator and Chief Executive Officer

LAWRENCE GENERAL HOSPITAL, 1 General Street, Lawrence, MA, Zip 01842–0389, Mailing Address: P.O. Box 189, Zip 01842–0389; tel. 978/683–4000; Joseph S. McManus, President and Chief Executive Officer

MARLBOROUGH HOSPITAL, 57 Union Street, Marlborough, MA, Zip 01752–1297; tel. 508/481–5000; Anne Bourgeois, Interim Chief Executive Officer

MASSACHUSETTS GENERAL HOSPITAL, 55 Fruit Street, Boston, MA, Zip 02114–2696; tel. 617/726–2000; James J. Mongan, M.D., President

MILFORD–WHITINSVILLE REGIONAL HOSPITAL, 14 Prospect Street, Milford, MA, Zip 01757–3090; tel. 508/473–1190; Francis M. Saba, President and Chief Executive Officer

NEW ENGLAND BAPTIST HOSPITAL, 125 Parker Hill Avenue, Boston, MA, Zip 02120–3297; tel. 617/754–5800; Alan H. Robbins, M.D., President

SAINT VINCENT HOSPITAL, 25 Winthrop Street, Worcester, MA, Zip 01604–4593; tel. 508/798–1234; Robert E. Maher, Jr., President and Chief Executive Officer

SAINTS MEMORIAL MEDICAL CENTER, One Hospital Drive, Lowell, MA, Zip 01852–1389; tel. 978/458–1411; Thomas Clark, President and Chief Executive Officer

UNIVERSITY OF MASSACHUSETTS MEDICAL CENTER, 55 Lake Avenue North, Worcester, MA, Zip 01655–0002; tel. 508/856–0011; Lin C. Wilder, Dr.PH, R.N., Director

LAHEY NETWORK
41 Mall Road, Burlington, MA 01805;
tel. 617/273–8223; Bruce Steinhauer, M.D.,
President

ATLANTICARE MEDICAL CENTER, 500 Lynnfield Street, Lynn, MA, Zip 01904–1487; tel. 781/581–9200; Andrew J. Riddell, President and Chief Executive Officer

LAHEY CLINIC, 41 Mall Road, Burlington, MA, Zip 01805–0001; tel. 781/744–5100; John A. Libertino, M.D., Chief Executive Officer

MARY HITCHCOCK MEMORIAL HOSPITAL, One Medical Center Drive, Lebanon, NH, Zip 03756–0001; tel. 603/650–5000; James W. Varnum, President

SOUTHERN NEW HAMPSHIRE REGIONAL MEDICAL CENTER, 8 Prospect Street, Nashua, NH, Zip 03060–3925, Mailing Address: P.O. Box 2014, Zip 03061–2014; tel. 603/577–2000; Thomas E. Wilhelmsen, Jr., President

WING MEMORIAL HOSPITAL AND MEDICAL CENTERS, 40 Wright Street, Palmer, MA, Zip 01069–1138; tel. 413/283–7651; Richard H. Scheffer, President

NEW ENGLAND HEALTH PARTNERSHIP
34 Washington Street, Suite 320, Waltham, MA
02181–1903; tel. 617/431–0300; Dick
Lefebvre, President

BOSTON MEDICAL CENTER, One Boston Medical Center Place, Boston, MA, Zip 02118–2393; tel. 617/638–8000; Elaine S. Ullian, President and Chief Executive Officer

HALE HOSPITAL, 140 Lincoln Avenue, Haverhill, MA, Zip 01830–6798; tel. 978/374–2000; Robert J. Ingala, Chief Executive Officer

HUBBARD REGIONAL HOSPITAL, 340 Thompson Road, Webster, MA, Zip 01570–0608; tel. 508/943–2600; Gerald J. Barbini, Administrator and Chief Executive Officer

LAHEY CLINIC, 41 Mall Road, Burlington, MA, Zip 01805–0001; tel. 781/744–5100; John A. Libertino, M.D., Chief Executive Officer

QUINCY HOSPITAL, 114 Whitwell Street, Quincy, MA, Zip 02169–1899; tel. 617/773–6100; Jeffrey Doran, Chief Executive Officer

NORTHEAST HEALTH SYSTEMS
85 Herrick Street, Beverly, MA 01915;
tel. 978/922–3000; Elisabeth Babcock, Vice
President of Network Development

BEVERLY HOSPITAL, 85 Herrrick Street, Beverly, MA, Zip 01915–1777; tel. 978/922–3000; Robert R. Fanning, Jr., Chief Executive Officer

PARTNERS HEALTHCARE SYSTEM
32 Fruit Street, Boston, MA 02114;
tel. 617/732–5500; John McGonagle, Director
of Community Health Services

BRIGHAM AND WOMEN'S HOSPITAL, 75 Francis Street, Boston, MA, Zip 02115–6195; tel. 617/732–5500; Jeffrey Otten, President

MASSACHUSETTS GENERAL HOSPITAL, 55 Fruit Street, Boston, MA, Zip 02114–2696; tel. 617/726–2000; James J. Mongan, M.D., President

SALEM HOSPITAL, 81 Highland Avenue, Salem, MA, Zip 01970–2768; tel. 978/741–1200; Alexander Movahed, Acting President and Chief Executive Officer

SHAUGHNESSY–KAPLAN REHABILITATION HOSPITAL, Dove Avenue, Salem, MA, Zip 01970–2999; tel. 978/745–9000; Anthony Sciola, President and Chief Executive Officer

SISTERS OF PROVIDENCE HEALTH SYSTEM
146 Chestnut Street, Springfield, MA 01103;
tel. 413/731–5548; Bob Suchecki, Director of
Managed Care

MERCY HOSPITAL, 271 Carew Street, Springfield, MA, Zip 01104–2398, Mailing Address: P.O. Box 9012, Zip 01102–9012; tel. 413/748–9000; Vincent J. McCorkle, President

SOUTHCOAST HEALTH SYSTEM
101 Page Street, New Bedford, MA 02740;
tel. 508/679–7003; C. Tod Allen, Vice
President Planning

CHARLTON MEMORIAL HOSPITAL, 363 Highland Avenue, Fall River, MA, Zip 02720–3794; tel. 508/679–3131

ST. LUKE'S HOSPITAL OF NEW BEDFORD, 101 Page Street, New Bedford, MA, Zip 02740, Mailing Address: P.O. Box H–3000, Zip 02741–3000; tel. 508/997–1515

TOBEY HOSPITAL, 43 High Street, Wareham, MA, Zip 02571; tel. 508/295–0880

MICHIGAN

BATTLE CREEK HEALTH SYSTEM
300 North Avenue, Battle Creek, MI 49016;
tel. 616/966–8000; Stephen L. Abbott,
President & Chief Executive Officer

BATTLE CREEK HEALTH SYSTEM, 300 North Avenue, Battle Creek, MI, Zip 49016–3396; tel. 616/966–8000; Stephen L. Abbott, President and Chief Executive Officer

BORGESS HEALTH ALLIANCE
1521 Gull Road, Kalamazoo, MI 49001;
tel. 616/226–7000; Mike Alfred, Exec
Dir–Business Development & PR

BORGESS MEDICAL CENTER, 1521 Gull Road, Kalamazoo, MI, Zip 49001–1640; tel. 616/226–4800; Randall Stasik, President and Chief Executive Officer

COMMUNITY HEALTH CENTER OF BRANCH COUNTY, 274 East Chicago Street, Coldwater, MI, Zip 49036–2088; tel. 517/279–5489; Douglas L. Rahn, Chief Executive Officer

COMMUNITY HOSPITAL, Medical Park Drive, Watervliet, MI, Zip 49098–0158, Mailing Address: P.O. Box 158, Zip 49098–0158; tel. 616/463–3111; Dennis Turney, Chief Executive Officer

HILLSDALE COMMUNITY HEALTH CENTER, 168 South Howell Street, Hillsdale, MI, Zip 49242–2081; tel. 517/437–4451; Charles A. Bianchi, President

LEE MEMORIAL HOSPITAL, 420 West High Street, Dowagiac, MI, Zip 49047–1907; tel. 616/782–8681; Fritz Fahrenbacher, Chief Executive Officer

THREE RIVERS AREA HOSPITAL, 1111 West Broadway, Three Rivers, MI, Zip 49093–9362; tel. 616/278–1145; Matthew Chambers, Interim Chief Executive Officer

BUTTERWORTH HEALTH SYSTEM
100 Michigan Street, SouthEast, Grand
Rapids, MI 49503; tel. 616/776–2008; Carol
Sarosik, Regional Vice President

CARSON CITY HOSPITAL, 406 East Elm Street, Carson City, MI, Zip 48811–0879, Mailing Address: P.O. Box 879, Zip 48811–0879; tel. 517/584–3131; Bruce L. Traverse, President

GERBER MEMORIAL HOSPITAL, 212 South Sullivan Street, Fremont, MI, Zip 49412–1596; tel. 616/924–3300; Ned B. Hughes, Jr., President

METROPOLITAN HOSPITAL, 1919 Boston Street S.E., Grand Rapids, MI, Zip 49506–4199, Mailing Address: P.O. Box 158, Zip 49501–0158; tel. 616/247–7200; Michael D. Faas, President and Chief Executive Officer

PINE REST CHRISTIAN MENTAL HEALTH SERVICES, 300 68th Street S.E., Grand Rapids, MI, Zip 49501–0165, Mailing Address: P.O. Box 165, Zip 49501–0165; tel. 616/455–5000; Daniel L. Holwerda, President and Chief Executive Officer

SPECTRUM HEALTH–DOWNTOWN CAMPUS, 100 Michigan Street N.E., Grand Rapids, MI, Zip 49503–2551; tel. 616/391–1774; Philip H. McCorkle, Jr., Chief Executive Officer

UNITED MEMORIAL HOSPITAL ASSOCIATION, 615 South Bower Street, Greenville, MI, Zip 48838–2628; tel. 616/754–4691; Dennis G. Zielinski, Chief Executive Officer

ZEELAND COMMUNITY HOSPITAL, 100 South Pine Street, Zeeland, MI, Zip 49464–1619; tel. 616/772–4644; Henry A. Veenstra, President

DETROIT MEDICAL CENTER
4201 Saint Antoine Boulevard, Detroit, MI
48201; tel. 313/745–3605; Douglas Keegan,
Vice President Planning

CHILDREN'S HOSPITAL OF MICHIGAN, 3901 Beaubien Street, Detroit, MI, Zip 48201–9985; tel. 313/745–0073; Thomas M. Rozek, Senior Vice President

DETROIT RECEIVING HOSPITAL AND UNIVERSITY HEALTH CENTER, 4201 St. Antoine Boulevard, Detroit, MI, Zip 48201–2194; tel. 313/745–3605; Leslie C. Bowman, Regional Administrator, Ancillary Services and Site Administrator

GRACE HOSPITAL, 6071 West Outer Drive, Detroit, MI, Zip 48235–2679; tel. 313/966–3525; Anne M. Regling, Regional Executive

HARPER HOSPITAL, 3990 John R., Detroit, MI, Zip 48201–9027; tel. 313/745–8040; Paul L. Broughton, FACHE, Senior Vice President

HURON VALLEY–SINAI HOSPITAL, 1 William Carls Drive, Commerce Township, MI, Zip 48382–1272; tel. 248/360–3300; Paul L. Broughton, FACHE, Senior Vice President

HUTZEL HOSPITAL, 4707 St. Antoine Boulevard, Detroit, MI, Zip 48201–0154; tel. 313/745–7555; Phyllis Reynolds, R.N., Site Administrator

REHABILITATION INSTITUTE OF MICHIGAN, 261 Mack Boulevard, Detroit, MI, Zip 48201–2495; tel. 313/745–1203; Bruce M. Gans, M.D., Senior Vice President

DETROIT–MACOMB HOSPITAL CORP
12000 E. 12 Mile Road, Warren, MI
48093–3570; tel. 313/573–5914; Timothy J.
Ryan, President & Chief Executive Officer

DETROIT RIVERVIEW HOSPITAL, 7733 East Jefferson
Avenue, Detroit, MI, Zip 48214–2598;
tel. 313/499–4000; Richard T. Young, President

MACOMB HOSPITAL CENTER, 11800 East Twelve
Mile Road, Warren, MI, Zip 48093–3494;
tel. 810/573–5000; John E. Knox, President

FIRST CHOICE NETWORK
60 Kalamazoo Avenue, Southhaven, MI 49090;
tel. 616/637–1690; John P. Isaia, Executive
Director

COMMUNITY HOSPITAL, Medical Park Drive,
Watervliet, MI, Zip 49098–0158, Mailing
Address: P.O. Box 158, Zip 49098–0158;
tel. 616/463–3111; Dennis Turney, Chief
Executive Officer

LEE MEMORIAL HOSPITAL, 420 West High Street,
Dowagiac, MI, Zip 49047–1907;
tel. 616/782–8681; Fritz Fahrenbacher, Chief
Executive Officer

GREAT LAKES HEALTH NETWORK
P.O. Box 5153, Southfield, MI 48086;
tel. 810/356–3460; Barbara Potter, Network
Coordinator

BI–COUNTY COMMUNITY HOSPITAL, 13355 East Ten
Mile Road, Warren, MI, Zip 48089–2065;
tel. 810/759–7300; Gary W. Popiel, Executive
Vice President and Chief Executive Officer

BOTSFORD GENERAL HOSPITAL, 28050 Grand River
Avenue, Farmington Hills, MI, Zip 48336–5933;
tel. 248/471–8000; Gerson I. Cooper, President

GARDEN CITY HOSPITAL, 6245 North Inkster Road,
Garden City, MI, Zip 48135–4001;
tel. 734/421–3300; Gary R. Ley, President and
Chief Executive Officer

MOUNT CLEMENS GENERAL HOSPITAL, 1000
Harrington Boulevard, Mount Clemens, MI,
Zip 48043–2992; tel. 810/493–8000; Robert
Milewski, President and Chief Executive Officer

POH MEDICAL CENTER, 50 North Perry Street,
Pontiac, MI, Zip 48342–2253;
tel. 810/338–5000; Patrick Lamberti, Chief
Executive Officer

RIVERSIDE OSTEOPATHIC HOSPITAL, 150 Truax
Street, Trenton, MI, Zip 48183–2151;
tel. 313/676–4200; Dennis R. Lemanski, D.O.,
Vice President and Chief Administrative Officer

ST. JOHN HEALTH SYSTEM, OAKLAND HOSPITAL,
27351 Dequindre, Madison Heights, MI,
Zip 48071–3499; tel. 248/967–7000; Robert
Deputat, President

HENRY FORD HEALTH SYSTEM
1 Ford Place, Detroit, MI 48202;
tel. 313/874–2895; Gail Warden, President &
CEO

BI–COUNTY COMMUNITY HOSPITAL, 13355 East Ten
Mile Road, Warren, MI, Zip 48089–2065;
tel. 810/759–7300; Gary W. Popiel, Executive
Vice President and Chief Executive Officer

HENRY FORD COTTAGE HOSPITAL OF GROSSE
POINTE, 159 Kercheval Avenue, Grosse Pointe
Farms, MI, Zip 48236–3692;
tel. 313/640–1000; Martin Monastersky, Interim
Chief Executive Officer

HENRY FORD HOSPITAL, 2799 West Grand
Boulevard, Detroit, MI, Zip 48202–2689;
tel. 313/876–2600; Stephen H. Velick, Chief
Executive Officer

HENRY FORD WYANDOTTE HOSPITAL, 2333 Biddle
Avenue, Wyandotte, MI, Zip 48192–4693;
tel. 313/284–2400; William R. Alvin, President

KINGSWOOD HOSPITAL, 10300 West Eight Mile Road,
Ferndale, MI, Zip 48220–2198;
tel. 248/398–3200; Glenn Black, Associate Vice
President and Chief Operating Officer

MERCY HOSPITAL, 5555 Conner Avenue, Detroit, MI,
Zip 48213–3499; tel. 313/579–4000; David
Spivey, Interim Chief Executive Officer

RIVERSIDE OSTEOPATHIC HOSPITAL, 150 Truax
Street, Trenton, MI, Zip 48183–2151;
tel. 313/676–4200; Dennis R. Lemanski, D.O.,
Vice President and Chief Administrative Officer

ST. JOSEPH MERCY OAKLAND, 900 Woodward
Avenue, Pontiac, MI, Zip 48341–2985;
tel. 248/858–3000; Thomas L. Feurig, President
and Chief Executive Officer

ST. JOSEPH'S MERCY HOSPITALS AND HEALTH
SERVICES, Clinton Township, MI, Jack Weiner,
President and Chief Executive Officer

HOSPITAL NETWORK INC.
One Healthcare Plaza, Kalamazoo, MI 49007;
tel. 616/341–8888; Richard M. Fluke,
President & Chief Executive Officer

ALLEGAN GENERAL HOSPITAL, 555 Linn Street,
Allegan, MI, Zip 49010–1594;
tel. 616/673–8424; James A. Klun, President

BRONSON METHODIST HOSPITAL, 252 East Lovell
Street, Kalamazoo, MI, Zip 49007–5345;
tel. 616/341–6000; Frank J. Sardone, President
and Chief Executive Officer

BRONSON VICKSBURG HOSPITAL, 13326 North
Boulevard, Vicksburg, MI, Zip 49097–1099;
tel. 616/649–2321; Frank J. Sardone, President

OAKLAWN HOSPITAL, 200 North Madison Street,
Marshall, MI, Zip 49068–1199;
tel. 616/781–4271; Rob Covert, President and
Chief Executive Officer

STURGIS HOSPITAL, 916 Myrtle, Sturgis, MI,
Zip 49091–2001; tel. 616/651–7824; David
James, Chief Executive Officer

INGHAM REGIONAL MEDICAL CENTER
60 Kalamazoo, Lansing, MI 48910;
tel. 517/377–8757; Robert Heintz, Vice
President Network

INGHAM REGIONAL MEDICAL CENTER, 401 West
Greenlawn Avenue, Lansing, MI,
Zip 48910–2819; tel. 517/334–2121; Dennis
M. Litos, President and Chief Executive Officer

LAKELAND REGIONAL HEALTH SYSTEM
1234 Napier Avenue, St. Joseph, MI 49085;
tel. 616/927–5363; Sam Ocampo, Manager
Strategic Planning

BRONSON METHODIST HOSPITAL, 252 East Lovell
Street, Kalamazoo, MI, Zip 49007–5345;
tel. 616/341–6000; Frank J. Sardone, President
and Chief Executive Officer

LAKELAND MEDICAL CENTER, BERRIEN CENTER,
6418 Dean's Hill Road, Berrien Center, MI,
Zip 49102–9704; tel. 616/471–7761

LAKELAND MEDICAL CENTER–NILES, 31 North St.
Joseph Avenue, Niles, MI, Zip 49120–2287;
tel. 616/683–5510

LAKELAND MEDICAL CENTER–ST. JOSEPH, 1234
Napier Avenue, Saint Joseph, MI,
Zip 49085–2112; tel. 616/983–8300; Joseph
A. Wasserman, President and Chief Executive
Officer

SOUTH HAVEN COMMUNITY HOSPITAL, 955 South
Bailey Avenue, South Haven, MI,
Zip 49090–9797; tel. 616/637–5271; Craig J.
Marks, President and Chief Executive Officer

MERCY GENERAL HEALTH PARTNERS
1500 E. Sherman Boulevard, P.O. Box 358,
Muskegon, MI 49443; tel. 616/739–3901;
Roger Spoelman, President & Chief Executive
Officer

MERCY GENERAL HEALTH PARTNERS, 1500 East
Sherman Boulevard, Muskegon, MI, Zip 49443,
Mailing Address: P.O. Box 358,
Zip 49443–0358; tel. 616/739–3901; Roger
Spoelman, President and Chief Executive Officer

MERCY GENERAL HEALTH PARTNERS–OAK AVENUE
CAMPUS, 1700 Oak Avenue, Muskegon, MI,
Zip 49442–2407; tel. 616/773–3311; Roger
Spoelman, Chief Executive Officer

MERCY HEALTH SERVICES – MICHIGAN REGION
34605 Twelve Mile Road, Farmington Hills, MI
48331–3221; tel. 248/489–6783; Robert
Laverty, Executive VP System Integration

BATTLE CREEK HEALTH SYSTEM, 300 North Avenue,
Battle Creek, MI, Zip 49016–3396;
tel. 616/966–8000; Stephen L. Abbott,
President and Chief Executive Officer

MCPHERSON HOSPITAL, 620 Byron Road, Howell, MI,
Zip 48843–1093; tel. 517/545–6000; C. W.
Lauderbach, Jr., Chief Operating Officer

MERCY GENERAL HEALTH PARTNERS–OAK AVENUE
CAMPUS, 1700 Oak Avenue, Muskegon, MI,
Zip 49442–2407; tel. 616/773–3311; Roger
Spoelman, Chief Executive Officer

MERCY HEALTH SERVICES NORTH–GRAYLING, 1100
Michigan Avenue, Grayling, MI, Zip 49738–1398;
tel. 517/348–5461; Stephanie J.
Riemer-Matuzak, Chief Operating Officer

MERCY HEALTH SERVICES–NORTH, 400 Hobart
Street, Cadillac, MI, Zip 49601–9596;
tel. 616/876–7200; Michael J. Peterson, Interim
President and Chief Executive Officer

MERCY HOSPITAL, 5555 Conner Avenue, Detroit, MI,
Zip 48213–3499; tel. 313/579–4000; David
Spivey, Interim Chief Executive Officer

MERCY HOSPITAL, 2601 Electric Avenue, Port Huron,
MI, Zip 48060; tel. 810/985–1510; Mary R.
Trimmer, President and Chief Executive Officer

SAINT MARY'S HEALTH SERVICES, 200 Jefferson
Avenue S.E., Grand Rapids, MI,
Zip 49503–4598; tel. 616/752–6090; David J.
Ameen, President and Chief Executive Officer

SALINE COMMUNITY HOSPITAL, 400 West Russell
Street, Saline, MI, Zip 48176–1101;
tel. 734/429–1500; Garry C. Faja, President
and Chief Executive Officer

ST. JOSEPH MERCY OAKLAND, 900 Woodward
Avenue, Pontiac, MI, Zip 48341–2985;
tel. 248/858–3000; Thomas L. Feurig, President
and Chief Executive Officer

ST. JOSEPH'S MERCY HOSPITALS AND HEALTH
SERVICES, Clinton Township, MI, Jack Weiner,
President and Chief Executive Officer

MUNSON HEALTHCARE
1105 Sixth Street, Traverse City, MI 49684;
tel. 616/935–6000; John M. Rockwood,
President & Chief Executive Officer

KALKASKA MEMORIAL HEALTH CENTER, 419 South
Coral Street, Kalkaska, MI, Zip 49646–9438,
Mailing Address: P.O. Box 249,
Zip 49646–0249; tel. 616/258–7500; James D.
Austin, CHE, Administrator

LEELANAU MEMORIAL HEALTH CENTER, 215 South
High Street, Northport, MI, Zip 49670, Mailing
Address: P.O. Box 217, Zip 49670–0217;
tel. 616/386–0000; Jayne R. Bull, Administrator

PAUL OLIVER MEMORIAL HOSPITAL, 224 Park
Avenue, Frankfort, MI, Zip 49635–9658;
tel. 616/352–9621; James D. Austin, CHE,
Administrator

PORT HURON HOSPITAL/BLUE WATER HEALTH
SERVICES
1221 Pine Grove Avenue, Port Huron, MI
48060–5011; tel. 810/989–3708; Gary
LeRoy, Consultant

PORT HURON HOSPITAL, 1221 Pine Grove Avenue,
Port Huron, MI, Zip 48061–5011;
tel. 810/987–5000; Donald C. Fletcher,
President and Chief Executive Officer

RIVER DISTRICT HOSPITAL, 4100 South River Road,
East China, MI, Zip 48054; tel. 810/329–7111;
Frank W. Poma, President

SAINT JOHN HEALTH SYSTEM
22101 Moross Road, Detroit, MI 48236;
tel. 313/343–3201; Mark J. Brady, Senior
Planning Analyst

DETROIT RIVERVIEW HOSPITAL, 7733 East Jefferson
Avenue, Detroit, MI, Zip 48214–2598;
tel. 313/499–4000; Richard T. Young, President

HOLY CROSS HOSPITAL, 4777 East Outer Drive,
Detroit, MI, Zip 48234–0401;
tel. 313/369–9100; Michael F. Breen, President

MACOMB HOSPITAL CENTER, 11800 East Twelve
Mile Road, Warren, MI, Zip 48093–3494;
tel. 810/573–5000; John E. Knox, President

PORT HURON HOSPITAL, 1221 Pine Grove Avenue,
Port Huron, MI, Zip 48061–5011;
tel. 810/987–5000; Donald C. Fletcher,
President and Chief Executive Officer

RIVER DISTRICT HOSPITAL, 4100 South River Road,
East China, MI, Zip 48054; tel. 810/329–7111;
Frank W. Poma, President

ST. JOHN HEALTH SYSTEM, OAKLAND HOSPITAL,
27351 Dequindre, Madison Heights, MI,
Zip 48071–3499; tel. 248/967–7000; Robert
Deputat, President

ST. JOHN HEALTH SYSTEM–SARATOGA CAMPUS, 15000 Gratiot Avenue, Detroit, MI, Zip 48205–1999; tel. 313/245–1200; Michael F. Breen, President

ST. JOHN HOSPITAL–MACOMB CENTER, 26755 Ballard Road, Harrison Township, MI, Zip 48045–2458; tel. 810/465–5501; David Sessions, President

WILLIAM BEAUMONT HOSPITAL CORP
3601 West Thirteen Mile Road, Royal Oak, MI 48073; tel. 248/551–6405; Holic Zwar, Planning Assistant

ST. MARY HOSPITAL, 36475 West Five Mile Road, Livonia, MI, Zip 48154–1988; tel. 734/655–4800; Sister Mary Renetta Rumpz, FACHE, President and Chief Executive Officer

WILLIAM BEAUMONT HOSPITAL–ROYAL OAK, 3601 West Thirteen Mile Road, Royal Oak, MI, Zip 48073–6769; tel. 248/551–5000; John D. Labriola, Vice President and Director

WILLIAM BEAUMONT HOSPITAL–TROY, 44201 Dequindre Road, Troy, MI, Zip 48098–1198; tel. 248/828–5100; Eugene F. Michalski, Vice President and Director

MINNESOTA

AFFILIATED COMMUNITY HEALTH NETWORK, INC.
101 Wilmar Avenue, SouthWest, Willmar, MN 56201; tel. 612/231–6719; Burnell J. Mellema, M.D., President

MCKENNAN HOSPITAL, 800 East 21st Street, Sioux Falls, SD, Zip 57105–1096, Mailing Address: P.O. Box 5045, Zip 57117–5045; tel. 605/322–8000; Fredrick Slunecka, President and Chief Executive Officer

REDWOOD FALLS MUNICIPAL HOSPITAL, 100 Fallwood Road, Redwood Falls, MN, Zip 56283–1828; tel. 507/637–2907; James E. Schulte, Administrator

RICE MEMORIAL HOSPITAL, 301 Becker Avenue S.W., Willmar, MN, Zip 56201–3395; tel. 320/235–4543; Lawrence J. Massa, Chief Executive Officer

WEINER MEMORIAL MEDICAL CENTER, 300 South Bruce Street, Marshall, MN, Zip 56258–1934; tel. 507/532–9661; James F. Hanko, Administrator and Chief Executive Officer

WILLMAR REGIONAL TREATMENT CENTER, North Highway 71, Willmar, MN, Zip 56201–1128, Mailing Address: Box 1128, Zip 56201–1128; tel. 320/231–5100; Gregory G. Spartz, Chief Executive Officer

ALLINA HEALTH SYSTEM
5601 Smetana Drive, Minnetonka, MN 55343; tel. 612/992–3357; Mary Onstad, Network Contact

ABBOTT NORTHWESTERN HOSPITAL, 800 East 28th Street, Minneapolis, MN, Zip 55407–3799; tel. 612/863–4201; Mark Dixon, Administrator

BUFFALO HOSPITAL, 303 Catlin Street, Buffalo, MN, Zip 55313–1947, Mailing Address: P.O. Box 609, Zip 55313–0609; tel. 612/682–7180; Mary Ellen Wells, Administrator

CAMBRIDGE MEDICAL CENTER, 701 South Dellwood Street, Cambridge, MN, Zip 55008–1920; tel. 612/689–7700; Lenny Libis, Administrator

FAIRMONT COMMUNITY HOSPITAL, 835 Johnson Street, Fairmont, MN, Zip 56031, Mailing Address: P.O. Box 835, Zip 56031–0835; tel. 507/238–4254; Gerry Gilbertson, President

GRANITE FALLS MUNICIPAL HOSPITAL AND MANOR, 345 Tenth Avenue, Granite Falls, MN, Zip 56241–1499; tel. 320/564–3111; George Gerlach, President

HUTCHINSON AREA HEALTH CARE, 1095 Highway 15 South, Hutchinson, MN, Zip 55350–3182; tel. 320/234–5000; Philip G. Graves, President

LONG PRAIRIE MEMORIAL HOSPITAL AND HOME, 20 Ninth Street S.E., Long Prairie, MN, Zip 56347–1404; tel. 320/732–2141; Clayton R. Peterson, President

MILLE LACS HEALTH SYSTEM, 200 North Elm Street, Onamia, MN, Zip 56359–7978; tel. 320/532–3154; Randall A. Farrow, President

NEW ULM MEDICAL CENTER, 1324 Fifth Street North, New Ulm, MN, Zip 56073–1553, Mailing Address: P.O. Box 577, Zip 56073–0577; tel. 507/354–2111; David A. Grundstrom, President

NORTHFIELD HOSPITAL, 801 West First Street, Northfield, MN, Zip 55057–1697; tel. 507/645–6661; Kendall C. Bank, President

OWATONNA HOSPITAL, 903 Oak Street South, Owatonna, MN, Zip 55060–3234; tel. 507/451–3850; Richard G. Slieter, Administrator

PHILLIPS EYE INSTITUTE, 2215 Park Avenue, Minneapolis, MN, Zip 55404–3756; tel. 612/336–6000; Shari E. Levy, Administrator

RIVER FALLS AREA HOSPITAL, 1629 East Division Street, River Falls, WI, Zip 54022–1571; tel. 715/425–6155; Sharon Whelan, President

ST. FRANCIS REGIONAL MEDICAL CENTER, 1455 St. Francis Avenue, Shakopee, MN, Zip 55379–3380; tel. 612/403–3000; Venetia Kudrle, President

STEVENS COUNTY HOSPITAL, 1006 South Jackson Street, Hugoton, KS, Zip 67951–2842, Mailing Address: P.O. Box 10, Zip 67951–0010; tel. 316/544–8511; Ted Strote, Administrator

UNITED HOSPITAL, 333 North Smith Street, Saint Paul, MN, Zip 55102–2389; tel. 612/220–8000; M. Barbara Balik, R.N., Ed.D., Administrator

UNITED HOSPITAL DISTRICT, 515 South Moore Street, Blue Earth, MN, Zip 56013–2158, Mailing Address: P.O. Box 160, Zip 56013–0160; tel. 507/526–3273; Brian Kief, President

BENEDICTINE HEALTH SYSTEM
503 East Third Street, Duluth, MN 55805; tel. 218/720–2370; Barry J. Halm, President/CEO

ITASCA MEDICAL CENTER, 126 First Avenue S.E., Grand Rapids, MN, Zip 55744–3698; tel. 218/326–3401; Gary Kenner, President and Chief Executive Officer

PINE MEDICAL CENTER, 109 Court Avenue South, Sandstone, MN, Zip 55072–5120; tel. 612/245–2212; Michael Hedrix, Administrator

SOUTH SUBURBAN MEDICAL CENTER, 3410–213th Street West, Farmington, MN, Zip 55024–1197; tel. 612/463–7825; Lee Larson, Chief Executive Officer

ST. FRANCIS REGIONAL MEDICAL CENTER, 1455 St. Francis Avenue, Shakopee, MN, Zip 55379–3380; tel. 612/403–3000; Venetia Kudrle, President

ST. JOSEPH'S MEDICAL CENTER, 523 North Third Street, Brainerd, MN, Zip 56401–3098; tel. 218/829–2861; Thomas K. Prusak, President

ST. MARY'S HOSPITAL OF SUPERIOR, 3500 Tower Avenue, Superior, WI, Zip 54880–5395; tel. 715/392–8281; Terry Jacobson, Acting Administrator

ST. MARY'S MEDICAL CENTER, 407 East Third Street, Duluth, MN, Zip 55805–1984; tel. 218/726–4000; Sister Kathleen Hofer, President

ST. MARY'S REGIONAL HEALTH CENTER, 1027 Washington Avenue, Detroit Lakes, MN, Zip 56501–3598; tel. 218/847–5611; John H. Solheim, Chief Executive Officer

FAIRVIEW HEALTH SYSTEM
2450 Riverside Avenue, Minneapolis, MN 53454; tel. 612/672–6876; Barbara G. Nye, Vice President

FAIRVIEW NORTHLAND REGIONAL HEALTH CARE, 911 Northland Drive, Princeton, MN, Zip 55371–2173; tel. 612/389–6300; Jeanne Lally, Senior Vice President and Administrator

FAIRVIEW RIDGES HOSPITAL, 201 East Nicollet Boulevard, Burnsville, MN, Zip 55337–5799; tel. 612/892–2000; Mark M. Enger, Senior Vice President and Administrator

FAIRVIEW SOUTHDALE HOSPITAL, 6401 France Avenue South, Minneapolis, MN, Zip 55435–2199; tel. 612/924–5000; Mark M. Enger, Senior Vice President and Administrator

FAIRVIEW–UNIVERSITY MEDICAL CENTER, 2450 Riverside Avenue, Minneapolis, MN, Zip 55454–1400; tel. 612/626–6685; Pamela L. Tibbetts, Senior Vice President and Administrator

HEALTHEAST
1700 University Avenue, St. Paul, MN 55104; tel. 612/232–5615; Tim Hanson, President

HEALTHEAST BETHESDA LUTHERAN HOSPITAL AND REHABILITATION CENTER, 559 Capitol Boulevard, Saint Paul, MN, Zip 55103–2101; tel. 612/232–2133; Scott Batulis, Vice President and Administrator

HEALTHEAST ST. JOHN'S HOSPITAL, 1575 Beam Avenue, Maplewood, MN, Zip 55109; tel. 612/232–7000; William Knutson, Vice President and Administrator

HEALTHEAST ST. JOSEPH'S HOSPITAL, 69 West Exchange Street, Saint Paul, MN, Zip 55102–1053; tel. 612/232–3000; William Knutson, Vice President and Administrator

HEALTHPARTNERS
8100 34th Avenue South, Minneapolis, MN 55440; tel. 612/883–5585; George Halvorson, President

REGIONS HOSPITAL, 640 Jackson Street, Saint Paul, MN, Zip 55101–2595; tel. 612/221–3456; Terry S. Finzen, President

ITASCA PARTNERSHIP FOR QUALITY HEALTHCARE
126 1st Avenue Southeast, Grand Rapids, MN 55744; tel. 218/326–7513; Lee Jess, D.D.S., President

DEER RIVER HEALTHCARE CENTER, 1002 Comstock Drive, Deer River, MN, Zip 56636–9700; tel. 218/246–2900; Jeffrey Stampohar, Chief Executive Officer

ITASCA MEDICAL CENTER, 126 First Avenue S.E., Grand Rapids, MN, Zip 55744–3698; tel. 218/326–3401; Gary Kenner, President and Chief Executive Officer

NORTHERN ITASCA HEALTH CARE CENTER, 258 Pine Tree Drive, Bigfork, MN, Zip 56628, Mailing Address: P.O. Box 258, Zip 56628–0258; tel. 218/743–3177; Richard M. Ash, Chief Executive Officer

MAYO FOUNDATION
200 SouthWest First Street, Rochester, MN 55905; tel. 507/284–8860; Dave Sperling, President

LUTHER HOSPITAL, 1221 Whipple Street, Eau Claire, WI, Zip 54702–4105; tel. 715/838–3311; William Rupp, M.D., President and Chief Executive Officer

ROCHESTER METHODIST HOSPITAL, 201 West Center Street, Rochester, MN, Zip 55902–3084; tel. 507/266–7890; John M. Panicek, Administrator

SAINT MARYS HOSPITAL, 1216 Second Street S.W., Rochester, MN, Zip 55902–1970; tel. 507/255–5123; John M. Panicek, Administrator

MINNESOTA RURAL HEALTH COOPERATIVE
P.O. Box 104, Willmar, MN 56201; tel. 320/231–3849; Lyle Munneke, M.D., President & Chairperson

APPLETON MUNICIPAL HOSPITAL AND NURSING HOME, 30 South Behl Street, Appleton, MN, Zip 56208–1699; tel. 320/289–2422; Mark E. Paulson, Administrator

CANBY COMMUNITY HEALTH SERVICES, 112 St. Olaf Avenue South, Canby, MN, Zip 56220–1433; tel. 507/223–7277; Robert J. Salmon, Chief Executive Officer

CHIPPEWA COUNTY MONTEVIDEO HOSPITAL, 824 North 11th Street, Montevideo, MN, Zip 56265–1683; tel. 320/269–8877; Fred Knutson, Administrator

DIVINE PROVIDENCE HEALTH CENTER, 312 East George Street, Ivanhoe, MN, Zip 56142–0136, Mailing Address: P.O. Box G., Zip 56142–0136; tel. 507/694–1414; Patrick Branco, Administrator

GRACEVILLE HEALTH CENTER, 115 West Second Street, Graceville, MN, Zip 56240–0157, Mailing Address: P.O. Box 157, Zip 56240–0157; tel. 320/748–7223; Carollee Brinkman, Chief Executive Officer

GRANITE FALLS MUNICIPAL HOSPITAL AND MANOR, 345 Tenth Avenue, Granite Falls, MN, Zip 56241–1499; tel. 320/564–3111; George Gerlach, President

HENDRICKS COMMUNITY HOSPITAL, 503 East Lincoln Street, Hendricks, MN, Zip 56136–9598; tel. 507/275–3134; Kirk Stensrud, Administrator

JOHNSON MEMORIAL HEALTH SERVICES, 1282 Walnut Street, Dawson, MN, Zip 56232–2333; tel. 612/769–4323; Vern Silvernale, Administrator

MADISON HOSPITAL, 820 Third Avenue, Madison, MN, Zip 56256–1014, Mailing Address: P.O. Box 184, Zip 56256–0184; tel. 320/598–7556

ORTONVILLE AREA HEALTH SERVICES, 750 Eastvold Avenue, Ortonville, MN, Zip 56278–1133; tel. 320/839–2502; Michael R. Miller, Interim Administrator

REDWOOD FALLS MUNICIPAL HOSPITAL, 100 Fallwood Road, Redwood Falls, MN, Zip 56283–1828; tel. 507/637–2907; James E. Schulte, Administrator

RENVILLE COUNTY HOSPITAL, 611 East Fairview Avenue, Olivia, MN, Zip 56277–1397; tel. 320/523–1261; Dean G. Slagter, Administrator

RICE MEMORIAL HOSPITAL, 301 Becker Avenue S.W., Willmar, MN, Zip 56201–3395; tel. 320/235–4543; Lawrence J. Massa, Chief Executive Officer

SWIFT COUNTY–BENSON HOSPITAL, 1815 Wisconsin Avenue, Benson, MN, Zip 56215–1653; tel. 320/843–4232; Frank Lawatsch, Chief Executive Officer

TYLER HEALTHCARE CENTER, 240 Willow Street, Tyler, MN, Zip 56178–0280; tel. 507/247–5521; James G. Blum, Interim Administrator

WEINER MEMORIAL MEDICAL CENTER, 300 South Bruce Street, Marshall, MN, Zip 56258–1934; tel. 507/532–9661; James F. Hanko, Administrator and Chief Executive Officer

NORTHERN LAKES HEALTH CONSORTIUM
600 East Superior Street, Suite 404, Duluth, MN 55802; tel. 218/727–9393; Terry J. Hill, Executive Director

CLOQUET COMMUNITY MEMORIAL HOSPITAL, 512 Skyline Boulevard, Cloquet, MN, Zip 55720–1199; tel. 218/879–4641; James J. Carroll, Administrator

COMMUNITY MEMORIAL HOSPITAL AND NURSING HOME, 819 Ash Street, Spooner, WI, Zip 54801–1299; tel. 715/635–2111; Michael Schafer, Chief Executive Officer

COOK COUNTY NORTH SHORE HOSPITAL, Gunflint Trail, Grand Marais, MN, Zip 55604, Mailing Address: P.O. Box 10, Zip 55604–0010; tel. 218/387–3040; Diane Pearson, Administrator

COOK HOSPITAL AND CONVALESCENT NURSING CARE UNIT, 10 South Fifth Street East, Cook, MN, Zip 55723–9745; tel. 218/666–5945; Allen J. Vogt, Administrator

CUMBERLAND MEMORIAL HOSPITAL, 1110 Seventh Avenue, Cumberland, WI, Zip 54829, Mailing Address: P.O. Box 37, Zip 54829–0037; tel. 715/822–2741; James M. O'Keefe, Administrator

CUYUNA REGIONAL MEDICAL CENTER, 320 East Main Street, Crosby, MN, Zip 56441–1690; tel. 218/546–7000; Thomas F. Reek, Chief Executive Officer

DEER RIVER HEALTHCARE CENTER, 1002 Comstock Drive, Deer River, MN, Zip 56636–9700; tel. 218/246–2900; Jeffrey Stampohar, Chief Executive Officer

ELY–BLOOMENSON COMMUNITY HOSPITAL, 328 West Conan Street, Ely, MN, Zip 55731–1198; tel. 218/365–3271; John Fossum, Administrator

FALLS MEMORIAL HOSPITAL, 1400 Highway 71, International Falls, MN, Zip 56649–2189; tel. 218/283–4481; Mary Klimp, Administrator and Chief Executive Officer

FLAMBEAU HOSPITAL, 98 Sherry Avenue, Park Falls, WI, Zip 54552–1467, Mailing Address: P.O. Box 310, Zip 54552–0310; tel. 715/762–2484; Curtis A. Johnson, Administrator

GRAND VIEW HOSPITAL, N10561 Grand View Lane, Ironwood, MI, Zip 49938–9359; tel. 906/932–2525; Frederick Geissler, Chief Executive Officer

HAYWARD AREA MEMORIAL HOSPITAL AND NURSING HOME, Hayward, WI, Mailing Address: Route 3, Box 3999, Zip 54843–3999; tel. 715/634–8911; Barbara A. Peickert, R.N., Chief Executive Officer

ITASCA MEDICAL CENTER, 126 First Avenue S.E., Grand Rapids, MN, Zip 55744–3698; tel. 218/326–3401; Gary Kenner, President and Chief Executive Officer

LAKE VIEW MEMORIAL HOSPITAL, 325 11th Avenue, Two Harbors, MN, Zip 55616–1298; tel. 218/834–7300; Brian J. Carlson, President and Chief Executive Officer

LAKEVIEW MEDICAL CENTER, 1100 North Main Street, Rice Lake, WI, Zip 54868–1238; tel. 715/234–1515; Edward H. Wolf, Chief Executive Officer

MERCY HOSPITAL AND HEALTH CARE CENTER, 710 South Kenwood Avenue, Moose Lake, MN, Zip 55767–9405; tel. 218/485–4481; Dianne Mandernach, Chief Executive Officer

MILLE LACS HEALTH SYSTEM, 200 North Elm Street, Onamia, MN, Zip 56359–7978; tel. 320/532–3154; Randall A. Farrow, President

MILLER DWAN MEDICAL CENTER, 502 East Second Street, Duluth, MN, Zip 55805–1982; tel. 218/727–8762; William H. Palmer, President

NORTHERN ITASCA HEALTH CARE CENTER, 258 Pine Tree Drive, Bigfork, MN, Zip 56628, Mailing Address: P.O. Box 258, Zip 56628–0258; tel. 218/743–3177; Richard M. Ash, Chief Executive Officer

ONTONAGON MEMORIAL HOSPITAL, 601 Seventh Street, Ontonagon, MI, Zip 49953–1496; tel. 906/884–4134; Fred Nelson, Administrator

PINE MEDICAL CENTER, 109 Court Avenue South, Sandstone, MN, Zip 55072–5120; tel. 612/245–2212; Michael Hedrix, Administrator

RIVERWOOD HEALTH CARE CENTER, 301 Minnesota Avenue South, Aitkin, MN, Zip 56431–1626; tel. 218/927–2121; Debra Boardman, Chief Executive Officer

RUSH CITY HOSPITAL, 760 West Fourth Street, Rush City, MN, Zip 55069–9063; tel. 612/358–4708; Mark Lunseth, Administrator

ST. LUKE'S HOSPITAL, 915 East First Street, Duluth, MN, Zip 55805–2193; tel. 218/726–5555; John Strange, President and Chief Executive Officer

UNIVERSITY MEDICAL CENTER–MESABI, 750 East 34th Street, Hibbing, MN, Zip 55746–4600; tel. 218/262–4881; Richard W. Dinter, Chief Operating Officer

VIRGINIA REGIONAL MEDICAL CENTER, 901 Ninth Street North, Virginia, MN, Zip 55792–2398; tel. 218/741–3340; Kyle Hopstad, Administrator

WHITE COMMUNITY HOSPITAL, 5211 Highway 110, Aurora, MN, Zip 55705–1599; tel. 218/229–2211; Cheryl A. High, Administrator

QUALITY HEALTH ALLIANCE
501 Holly Lane – Sr. 11A, Mankato, MN 56001; tel. 507/389–4715; Todd Erik Henry, Executive Director

NEW ULM MEDICAL CENTER, 1324 Fifth Street North, New Ulm, MN, Zip 56073–1553, Mailing Address: P.O. Box 577, Zip 56073–0577; tel. 507/354–2111; David A. Grundstrom, President

SLEEPY EYE MUNICIPAL HOSPITAL, 400 Fourth Avenue N.W., Sleepy Eye, MN, Zip 56085–1109; tel. 507/794–3571; Chad Cooper, Administrator

SPRINGFIELD MEDICAL CENTER–MAYO HEALTH SYSTEM, 625 North Jackson Avenue, Springfield, MN, Zip 56087–1714, Mailing Address: P.O. Box 146, Zip 56087–0146; tel. 507/723–6201; Scott Thoreson, Administrator

ST. JAMES HEALTH SERVICES, 1207 Sixth Avenue South, Saint James, MN, Zip 56081–2415; tel. 507/375–3261; Lee Holter, Chief Executive Officer

ST. PETER REGIONAL TREATMENT CENTER, 100 Freeman Drive, Saint Peter, MN, Zip 56082–1599; tel. 507/931–7100; William L. Pedersen, Chief Executive Officer

UNITED HOSPITAL DISTRICT, 515 South Moore Street, Blue Earth, MN, Zip 56013–2158, Mailing Address: P.O. Box 160, Zip 56013–0160; tel. 507/526–3273; Brian Kief, President

WASECA AREA MEDICAL CENTER, 100 Fifth Avenue N.W., Waseca, MN, Zip 56093–2422; tel. 507/835–1210; Michael Milbrath, Administrator

SOUTHWEST MINNESOTA HEALTH ALLIANCE
305 East Luverne Street, Luverne, MN 56156; tel. 507/283–2775; Jeff Stevenson, President

CANBY COMMUNITY HEALTH SERVICES, 112 St. Olaf Avenue South, Canby, MN, Zip 56220–1433; tel. 507/223–7277; Robert J. Salmon, Chief Executive Officer

LUVERNE COMMUNITY HOSPITAL, 305 East Luverne Street, Luverne, MN, Zip 56156–2519, Mailing Address: P.O. Box 1019, Zip 56156–1019; tel. 507/283–2321; Gerald E. Carl, Administrator

MURRAY COUNTY MEMORIAL HOSPITAL, 2042 Juniper Avenue, Slayton, MN, Zip 56172–1016; tel. 507/836–6111; Jerry Bobeldyk, Administrator

TRACY AREA MEDICAL SERVICES, 251 Fifth Street East, Tracy, MN, Zip 56175–1536; tel. 507/629–3200; Thomas J. Quinlivan, Administrator

WINDOM AREA HOSPITAL, Highways 60 and 71 North, Windom, MN, Zip 56101, Mailing Address: P.O. Box 339, Zip 56101–0339; tel. 507/831–2400; J. Stephen Pautler, CHE, Administrator

WORTHINGTON REGIONAL HOSPITAL, 1018 Sixth Avenue, Worthington, MN, Zip 56187–2202, Mailing Address: P.O. Box 997, Zip 56187–0997; tel. 507/372–2941; Melvin J. Platt, Administrator

MISSISSIPPI

NORTH MISSISSIPPI HEALTH SERVICES
830 South Gloster Street, Tupelo, MS 38801; tel. 601/841–3000; Jeffrey B. Barber, Dr. P.H., President & Chief Executive Officer

CLAY COUNTY MEDICAL CENTER, 835 Medical Center Drive, West Point, MS, Zip 39773–9320; tel. 601/495–2300; David M. Reid, Administrator

IUKA HOSPITAL, 1777 Curtis Drive, Iuka, MS, Zip 38852–1001, Mailing Address: P.O. Box 860, Zip 38852–0860; tel. 601/423–6051; George Hand, Interim Administrator

NORTH MISSISSIPPI MEDICAL CENTER, 830 South Gloster Street, Tupelo, MS, Zip 38801–4934; tel. 601/841–3000; Jeffrey B. Barber, Dr.PH, President and Chief Executive Officer

PONTOTOC HOSPITAL AND EXTENDED CARE FACILITY, 176 South Main Street, Pontotoc, MS, Zip 38863–3311, Mailing Address: P.O. Box 790, Zip 38863–0790; tel. 601/489–5510; Fred B. Hood, Administrator

WEBSTER HEALTH SERVICES, 500 Highway 9 South, Eupora, MS, Zip 39744; tel. 601/258–6221; Harold H. Whitaker, Sr., Administrator

MISSOURI

BJC HEALTH SYSTEM
4444 Forest Park Avenue, Suite 500, St. Louis, MO 63108–2297; tel. 314/286–2000; Fred L. Brown, President & CEO

Section B

ALTON MEMORIAL HOSPITAL, One Memorial Drive, Alton, IL, Zip 62002–6722; tel. 618/463–7311; Ronald B. McMullen, President

BARNES–JEWISH HOSPITAL, One Barnes–Jewish Hospital Plaza, Saint Louis, MO, Zip 63110–1094; tel. 314/362–5400; Peter L. Slavin, M.D., President

BARNES–JEWISH ST. PETERS HOSPITAL, 10 Hospital Drive, Saint Peters, MO, Zip 63376–1659; tel. 314/916–9000; Carm Moceri, President

BARNES–JEWISH WEST COUNTY HOSPITAL, 12634 Olive Boulevard, Saint Louis, MO, Zip 63141–6354; tel. 314/996–8000; Gregory T. Wozniak, President

BOONE HOSPITAL CENTER, 1600 East Broadway, Columbia, MO, Zip 65201–5897; tel. 573/815–8000; Michael Shirk, President and Senior Executive Officer

CHRISTIAN HOSPITAL NORTHEAST–NORTHWEST, 11133 Dunn Road, Saint Louis, MO, Zip 63136–6192; tel. 314/653–5000; W. R. Van Bokkelen, President and Senior Executive Officer

CLAY COUNTY HOSPITAL, 700 North Mill Street, Flora, IL, Zip 62839–1823, Mailing Address: P.O. Box 280, Zip 62839–0280; tel. 618/662–2131; John E. Monnahan, President and Senior Executive Officer

FAYETTE COUNTY HOSPITAL AND LONG TERM CARE, Seventh and Taylor Streets, Vandalia, IL, Zip 62471–1296; tel. 618/283–1231; Daniel L. Gantz, President

MISSOURI BAPTIST HOSPITAL OF SULLIVAN, 751 Sappington Bridge Road, Sullivan, MO, Zip 63080–2354, Mailing Address: P.O. Box 190, Zip 63080–0190; tel. 573/468–4186; Davis D. Skinner, President

MISSOURI BAPTIST MEDICAL CENTER, 3015 North Ballas Road, Town and Country, MO, Zip 63131–2374; tel. 314/996–5000; Mark A. Eustis, President

PARKLAND HEALTH CENTER, 1101 West Liberty Street, Farmington, MO, Zip 63640–1997; tel. 573/756–6451; Richard L. Conklin, President

PUBLIC HOSPITAL OF THE TOWN OF SALEM, 1201 Ricker Drive, Salem, IL, Zip 62881–6250, Mailing Address: P.O. Box 1250, Zip 62881–1250; tel. 618/548–3194; Clarence E. Lay, Chief Executive Officer

ST. LOUIS CHILDREN'S HOSPITAL, One Children's Place, Saint Louis, MO, Zip 63110–1077; tel. 314/454–6000; Ted W. Frey, President

CARONDELET HEALTH
P.O. Box 8510, Kansas City, MO 64114; tel. 816/943–2673; Richard M. Abell, Chief Executive Officer

MCCUNE–BROOKS HOSPITAL, 627 West Centennial Avenue, Carthage, MO, Zip 64836–0677; tel. 417/358–8121; James W. McPheeters, III, Administrator

ST. JOHN'S REGIONAL MEDICAL CENTER, 2727 McClelland Boulevard, Joplin, MO, Zip 64804–1694; tel. 417/781–2727; Robert G. Brueckner, President and Chief Executive Officer

ST. JOSEPH HEALTH CENTER, 300 First Capitol Drive, Saint Charles, MO, Zip 63301–2835; tel. 314/947–5000; Kevin F. Kast, President

ST. MARY'S HOSPITAL OF BLUE SPRINGS, 201 West R. D. Mize Road, Blue Springs, MO, Zip 64014; tel. 816/228–5900; N. Gary Wages, President and Chief Executive Officer

HEALTH MIDWEST
2306 East Meyer Boulevard, B–11, Kansas City, MO 64132; tel. 816/276–9130; Richard W. Brown, President

ALLEN COUNTY HOSPITAL, 101 South First Street, Iola, KS, Zip 66749–3505, Mailing Address: P.O. Box 540, Zip 66749–0540; tel. 316/365–3131; Bill May, Chief Executive Officer

BAPTIST MEDICAL CENTER, 6601 Rockhill Road, Kansas City, MO, Zip 64131–1197; tel. 816/276–7000; Michael S. McCoy, Interim President and Chief Executive Officer

CASS MEDICAL CENTER, 1800 East Mechanic Street, Harrisonville, MO, Zip 64701–2099; tel. 816/884–3291; Alan Freeman, Administrator

HEDRICK MEDICAL CENTER, 100 Central Avenue, Chillicothe, MO, Zip 64601–1599; tel. 660/646–1480; R. Lynn Jackson, President and Chief Executive Officer

LAFAYETTE REGIONAL HEALTH CENTER, 1500 State Street, Lexington, MO, Zip 64067–1199; tel. 660/259–2203; Jeffrey S. Tarrant, Administrator

LEE'S SUMMIT HOSPITAL, 530 North Murray Road, Lees Summit, MO, Zip 64081–1497; tel. 816/251–7000; John L. Jacobson, President and Chief Executive Officer

MEDICAL CENTER OF INDEPENDENCE, 17203 East 23rd Street, Independence, MO, Zip 64057–1899; tel. 816/478–5000; Michael W. Chappelow, President and Chief Executive Officer

PARK LANE MEDICAL CENTER, 5151 Raytown Road, Kansas City, MO, Zip 64133–2199; tel. 816/358–8000; Derell Taloney, President and Chief Executive Officer

REHABILITATION INSTITUTE, 3011 Baltimore, Kansas City, MO, Zip 64108–3465; tel. 816/751–7900; Ronald L. Herrick, President

RESEARCH BELTON HOSPITAL, 17065 South 71 Highway, Belton, MO, Zip 64012–2165; tel. 816/348–1200; Daniel F. Sheehan, Administrator

RESEARCH MEDICAL CENTER, 2316 East Meyer Boulevard, Kansas City, MO, Zip 64132–1199; tel. 816/276–4000; Steven R. Newton, Interim President and Chief Executive Officer

RESEARCH PSYCHIATRIC CENTER, 2323 East 63rd Street, Kansas City, MO, Zip 64130–3495; tel. 816/444–8161; Todd Krass, Administrator and Chief Executive Officer

TRINITY LUTHERAN HOSPITAL, 3030 Baltimore Avenue, Kansas City, MO, Zip 64108–3404; tel. 816/751–4600; Ronald A. Ommen, President and Chief Executive Officer

NORTHWEST MISSOURI HEALTHCARE AGENDA
705 North College Avenue, Albany, MO 64402; tel. 816/726–3941; John Richmond, Chairman

HEARTLAND REGIONAL MEDICAL CENTER, 5325 Faraon Street, Saint Joseph, MO, Zip 64506–3398; tel. 816/271–6000; Lowell C. Kruse, Chief Executive Officer

SSM HEALTH CARE – SAINT LOUIS
1173 Corporate Lake Drive, St. Louis, MO 63132; tel. 314/989–2000; Stephanie McCutcheon, President & Chief Executive Officer

ARCADIA VALLEY HOSPITAL, Highway 21, Pilot Knob, MO, Zip 63663, Mailing Address: P.O. Box 548, Zip 63663–0548; tel. 573/546–3924; H. Clark Duncan, Administrator

CARDINAL GLENNON CHILDREN'S HOSPITAL, 1465 South Grand Boulevard, Saint Louis, MO, Zip 63104–1095; tel. 314/577–5600; Douglas A. Ries, President

DEPAUL HEALTH CENTER, 12303 DePaul Drive, Saint Louis, MO, Zip 63044–2588; tel. 314/344–6000; Robert G. Porter, President

PIKE COUNTY MEMORIAL HOSPITAL, 2305 West Georgia Street, Louisiana, MO, Zip 63353–0020; tel. 573/754–5531; Pamm Hancock, Interim Administrator

SSM REHAB, 6420 Clayton Road, Suite 600, Saint Louis, MO, Zip 63117–1861; tel. 314/768–5300; Melinda Clark, President

ST. JOSEPH HEALTH CENTER, 300 First Capitol Drive, Saint Charles, MO, Zip 63301–2835; tel. 314/947–5000; Kevin F. Kast, President

ST. JOSEPH HOSPITAL WEST, 100 Medical Plaza, Lake Saint Louis, MO, Zip 63367–1395; tel. 314/625–5200; Kevin F. Kast, President

ST. MARY'S HEALTH CENTER, 6420 Clayton Road, Saint Louis, MO, Zip 63117–1811; tel. 314/768–8000; Michael E. Zilm, President

ST. MARY'S HOSPITAL, 129 North Eighth Street, East St. Louis, IL, Zip 62201–2999; tel. 618/274–1900; Richard J. Mark, President and Chief Executive Officer

UNITY HEALTH SYSTEM
1650 Des Peres Road, Suite 301, St. Louis, MO 63131; tel. 314/909–3300; Jamer R. Hardman, V.P. Planning & Marketing

ALEXIAN BROTHERS HOSPITAL, 3933 South Broadway, Saint Louis, MO, Zip 63118–9984; tel. 314/865–3333; Glenn Appelbaum, Senior Vice President

COMMUNITY MEMORIAL HOSPITAL, 400 Caldwell Street, Staunton, IL, Zip 62088–1499; tel. 618/635–2200; Patrick B. Heise, Chief Executive Officer

ST. ANTHONY'S MEDICAL CENTER, 10010 Kennerly Road, Saint Louis, MO, Zip 63128–2185; tel. 314/525–1000; David P. Seifert, President

ST. CLEMENT HEALTH SERVICES, One St. Clement Boulevard, Red Bud, IL, Zip 62278–1194; tel. 618/282–3831; Michael Thomas McManus, President

ST. JOHN'S MERCY MEDICAL CENTER, 615 South New Ballas Road, Saint Louis, MO, Zip 63141–8277; tel. 314/569–6000; Mark Weber, FACHE, President

ST. JOSEPH'S HOSPITAL, 1515 Main Street, Highland, IL, Zip 62249–1656; tel. 618/654–7421; Anthony G. Mastrangelo, Executive Vice President and Chief Executive Officer

ST. LUKE'S HOSPITAL, 232 South Woods Mill Road, Chesterfield, MO, Zip 63017–3480; tel. 314/434–1500; George Tucker, M.D., President

MONTANA

MONTANA HEALTH NETWORK, INC.
11 South 7th Street, Suite 160, Miles City, MT 59301; tel. 406/232–1420; Janet Bastian, Chief Executive Officer

BEARTOOTH HOSPITAL AND HEALTH CENTER, 600 West 20th Street, Red Lodge, MT, Zip 59068, Mailing Address: P.O. Box 590, Zip 59068–0590; tel. 406/446–2345; Kelley Going, Administrator

CENTRAL MONTANA MEDICAL CENTER, 408 Wendell Avenue, Lewistown, MT, Zip 59457–2261, Mailing Address: P.O. Box 580, Zip 59457–0580; tel. 406/538–7711; David M. Faulkner, Chief Executive Officer and Administrator

DANIELS MEMORIAL HOSPITAL, 105 Fifth Avenue East, Scobey, MT, Zip 59263, Mailing Address: P.O. Box 400, Zip 59263–0400; tel. 406/487–2296; Glenn Haugo, Administrator

DEACONESS BILLINGS CLINIC, 2800 10th Avenue North, Billings, MT, Zip 59101–0799, Mailing Address: P.O. Box 37000, Zip 59107–7000; tel. 406/657–4000; Nicholas J. Wolter, M.D., Chief Executive Officer

FALLON MEDICAL COMPLEX, 202 South 4th Street West, Baker, MT, Zip 59313–0820, Mailing Address: P.O. Box 820, Zip 59313–0820; tel. 406/778–3331; David Espeland, Chief Executive Officer

FRANCES MAHON DEACONESS HOSPITAL, 621 Third Street South, Glasgow, MT, Zip 59230–2699; tel. 406/228–4351; Randall G. Holom, Chief Executive Officer

GLENDIVE MEDICAL CENTER, 202 Prospect Drive, Glendive, MT, Zip 59330–1999; tel. 406/365–3306; Paul Hanson, Chief Executive Officer

HOLY ROSARY HEALTH CENTER, 2600 Wilson Street, Miles City, MT, Zip 59301–5094; tel. 406/233–2600; H. Ray Gibbons, President and Chief Executive Officer

MCCONE COUNTY MEDICAL ASSISTANCE FACILITY, Circle, MT, Mailing Address: P.O. Box 48, Zip 59215–0048; tel. 406/485–3381; Mack N. Simpson, Administrator

NORTHEAST MONTANA HEALTH SERVICES, 315 Knapp Street, Wolf Point, MT, Zip 59201–1898; tel. 406/653–2110; Earl N. Sheehy, Chief Executive Officer

PHILLIPS COUNTY MEDICAL CENTER, 417 South Fourth East, Malta, MT, Zip 59538, Mailing Address: P.O. Box 640, Zip 59538–0640; tel. 406/654–1100; Larry E. Putnam, Administrator

ROOSEVELT MEMORIAL MEDICAL CENTER, 818 Second Avenue East, Culbertson, MT, Zip 59218, Mailing Address: P.O. Box 419, Zip 59218–0419; tel. 406/787–6281; Walter Busch, Administrator

ROUNDUP MEMORIAL HOSPITAL, 1202 Third Street West, Roundup, MT, Zip 59072–1816, Mailing Address: P.O. Box 40, Zip 59072–0040; tel. 406/323–2302; Dave McIvor, Administrator

SHERIDAN MEMORIAL HOSPITAL, 440 West Laurel Avenue, Plentywood, MT, Zip 59254–1596; tel. 406/765–1420; Ella Gutzke, Administrator

SIDNEY HEALTH CENTER, 216 14th Avenue S.W., Sidney, MT, Zip 59270–3586, Mailing Address: P.O. Box 1690, Zip 59270–1690; tel. 406/422–2100; Donald J. Rush, Chief Executive Officer

STILLWATER COMMUNITY HOSPITAL, 44 West Fourth Avenue North, Columbus, MT, Zip 59019, Mailing Address: P.O. Box 959, Zip 59019–0959; tel. 406/322–5316; Tim Russell, Administrator

NEBRASKA

ALEGENT HEALTH
1010 North 96th Street, Omaha, NE 68114; tel. 402/255–1661; Robert Azar, President of Public Health Information

ALEGENT HEALTH BERGAN MERCY MEDICAL CENTER, 7500 Mercy Road, Omaha, NE, Zip 68124; tel. 402/398–6060; Charles J. Marr, Chief Executive Officer

ALEGENT HEALTH COMMUNITY MEMORIAL HOSPITAL, 631 North Eighth Street, Missouri Valley, IA, Zip 51555–1199; tel. 712/642–2784; James A. Seymour, Regional Administrator

ALEGENT HEALTH IMMANUEL MEDICAL CENTER, 6901 North 72nd Street, Omaha, NE, Zip 68122–1799; tel. 402/572–2121; Charles J. Marr, Chief Executive Officer

ALEGENT HEALTH MERCY HOSPITAL, Rosary Drive, Corning, IA, Zip 50841, Mailing Address: P.O. Box 368, Zip 50841–0368; tel. 515/322–3121; James C. Ruppert, Regional Administrator

ALEGENT HEALTH MERCY HOSPITAL, 800 Mercy Drive, Council Bluffs, IA, Zip 51503–3128, Mailing Address: P.O. Box 1C, Zip 51502–3001; tel. 712/328–5000; Richard A. Hachten, II, Chief Executive Officer

ALEGENT HEALTH–MEMORIAL HOSPITAL, 104 West 17th Street, Schuyler, NE, Zip 68661–1396; tel. 402/352–2441; Al Klaasmeyer, Administrator

BLUE RIVER VALLEY HEALTH NETWORK
P.O. Box 156, Brainard, NE 68626; tel. 402/545–2728; JoEllen Urba, Network Coordinator

ANNIE JEFFREY MEMORIAL COUNTY HEALTH CENTER, 531 Beebe Street, Osceola, NE, Zip 68651, Mailing Address: P.O. Box 428, Zip 68651–0428; tel. 402/747–2031; Carol E. Jones, Administrator

BUTLER COUNTY HEALTH CARE CENTER, 372 South Ninth Street, David City, NE, Zip 68632–2199; tel. 402/367–3115; Roger Reamer, Administrator

CRETE MUNICIPAL HOSPITAL, 1540 Grove Street, Crete, NE, Zip 68333–0220, Mailing Address: P.O. Box 220, Zip 68333–0220; tel. 402/826–6800; Joe Lohrman, Administrator

HENDERSON HEALTH CARE SERVICES, 1621 Front Street, Henderson, NE, Zip 68371–0217, Mailing Address: P.O. Box 217, Zip 68371–0217; tel. 402/723–4512; Calvin C. Graber, Chief Executive Officer

MEMORIAL HEALTH CARE SYSTEMS, 300 North Columbia Avenue, Seward, NE, Zip 68434–9907; tel. 402/643–2971; Ronald D. Waltz, Chief Executive Officer

MEMORIAL HOSPITAL, 1423 Seventh Street, Aurora, NE, Zip 68818–1197; tel. 402/694–3171; Eldon A. Wall, Administrator

SAUNDERS COUNTY HEALTH SERVICE, 805 West Tenth Street, Wahoo, NE, Zip 68066–1102, Mailing Address: P.O. Box 185, Zip 68066–0185; tel. 402/443–4191; Michael Boyles, Administrator

WARREN MEMORIAL HOSPITAL, 905 Second Street, Friend, NE, Zip 68359–1198; tel. 402/947–2541; John Ramsay, Administrator

YORK GENERAL HOSPITAL, 2222 Lincoln Avenue, York, NE, Zip 68467–1095; tel. 402/362–0445; Charles K. Schulz, Chief Executive Officer

CENTRAL NEBRASKA PRIMARY CARE NETWORK
1518 J. Street, Ord, NE 68862; tel. 308/728–3011; Barbara Weems, Foundation President

BOONE COUNTY HEALTH CENTER, 723 West Fairview Street, Albion, NE, Zip 68620–1725, Mailing Address: P.O. Box 151, Zip 68620–0151; tel. 402/395–2191; Gayle E. Primrose, Administrator

VALLEY COUNTY HOSPITAL, 217 Westridge Drive, Ord, NE, Zip 68862–1675; tel. 308/728–3211; John E. Keelan, Chief Executive Officer and Administrator

HEARTLAND HEALTH ALLIANCE
1600 South 48th Street, Lincoln, NE 68506; tel. 402/483–3111; R. Lynn Wilson, President

BEATRICE COMMUNITY HOSPITAL AND HEALTH CENTER, 1110 North Tenth Street, Beatrice, NE, Zip 68310–2039, Mailing Address: P.O. Box 278, Zip 68310–0278; tel. 402/228–3344; Kenneth J. Zimmerman, Administrator

BOONE COUNTY HEALTH CENTER, 723 West Fairview Street, Albion, NE, Zip 68620–1725, Mailing Address: P.O. Box 151, Zip 68620–0151; tel. 402/395–2191; Gayle E. Primrose, Administrator

BRODSTONE MEMORIAL HOSPITAL, 520 East Tenth Street, Superior, NE, Zip 68978–1225, Mailing Address: P.O. Box 187, Zip 68978–0187; tel. 402/879–3281; Ronald D. Waggoner, Administrator and Chief Executive Officer

BRYAN MEMORIAL HOSPITAL, 1600 South 48th Street, Lincoln, NE, Zip 68506–1299; tel. 402/489–0200; R. Lynn Wilson, President

BUTLER COUNTY HEALTH CARE CENTER, 372 South Ninth Street, David City, NE, Zip 68632–2199; tel. 402/367–3115; Roger Reamer, Administrator

CHERRY COUNTY HOSPITAL, Highway 12 and Green Street, Valentine, NE, Zip 69201–0410; tel. 402/376–2525; Brent A. Peterson, Administrator

COMMUNITY HOSPITAL, 1301 East H. Street, McCook, NE, Zip 69001–1328, Mailing Address: P.O. Box 1328, Zip 69001–1328; tel. 308/345–2650; Gary Bieganski, President

COMMUNITY MEMORIAL HOSPITAL, 1579 Midland Street, Syracuse, NE, Zip 68446–9732, Mailing Address: P.O. Box N., Zip 68446; tel. 402/269–2011; Ron Anderson, Administrator

CRETE MUNICIPAL HOSPITAL, 1540 Grove Street, Crete, NE, Zip 68333–0220, Mailing Address: P.O. Box 220, Zip 68333–0220; tel. 402/826–6800; Joe Lohrman, Administrator

FRANKLIN COUNTY MEMORIAL HOSPITAL, 1406 Q. Street, Franklin, NE, Zip 68939–0315, Mailing Address: P.O. Box 315, Zip 68939–0315; tel. 308/425–6221; Jerrell F. Gerdes, Administrator

GOTHENBURG MEMORIAL HOSPITAL, 910 20th Street, Gothenburg, NE, Zip 69138–1237, Mailing Address: P.O. Box 469, Zip 69138–0469; tel. 308/537–3661; John H. Johnson, Chief Executive Officer

GREAT PLAINS REGIONAL MEDICAL CENTER, 601 West Leota Street, North Platte, NE, Zip 69101–6598, Mailing Address: P.O. Box 1167, Zip 69103–1167; tel. 308/534–9310; Lucinda A. Bradley, President

HARLAN COUNTY HOSPITAL, 717 North Brown Street, Alma, NE, Zip 68920–0836, Mailing Address: P.O. Box 836, Zip 68920–0836; tel. 308/928–2151; Allen Van Driel, Administrator

JEFFERSON COMMUNITY HEALTH CENTER, 2200 H. Street, Fairbury, NE, Zip 68352–1119, Mailing Address: P.O. Box 277, Zip 68352–0277; tel. 402/729–3351; Bill Welch, Administrator

JENNIE M. MELHAM MEMORIAL MEDICAL CENTER, 145 Memorial Drive, Broken Bow, NE, Zip 68822–1378, Mailing Address: P.O. Box 250, Zip 68822–0250; tel. 308/872–6891; Michael J. Steckler, Chief Executive Officer

JOHNSON COUNTY HOSPITAL, 202 High Street, Tecumseh, NE, Zip 68450–0599, Mailing Address: P.O. Box 599, Zip 68450–0599; tel. 402/335–3361; Lavonne M. Rowe, Administrator

MARY LANNING MEMORIAL HOSPITAL, 715 North St. Joseph Avenue, Hastings, NE, Zip 68901–4497; tel. 402/463–4521; W. Michael Kearney, President

MEMORIAL HEALTH CARE SYSTEMS, 300 North Columbia Avenue, Seward, NE, Zip 68434–9907; tel. 402/643–2971; Ronald D. Waltz, Chief Executive Officer

MEMORIAL HOSPITAL, 1423 Seventh Street, Aurora, NE, Zip 68818–1197; tel. 402/694–3171; Eldon A. Wall, Administrator

NEMAHA COUNTY HOSPITAL, 2022 13th Street, Auburn, NE, Zip 68305–1799; tel. 402/274–4366; Glen E. Krueger, Administrator

PHELPS MEMORIAL HEALTH CENTER, 1220 Miller Street, Holdrege, NE, Zip 68949–1200, Mailing Address: P.O. Box 828, Zip 68949–0828; tel. 308/995–2211; Jerome Seigfreid, Jr., Chief Executive Officer

TRI–COUNTY AREA HOSPITAL, 13th and Erie Streets, Lexington, NE, Zip 68850–0980, Mailing Address: P.O. Box 980, Zip 68850–0980; tel. 308/324–5651; Calvin A. Hiner, Administrator

TRI–VALLEY HEALTH SYSTEM, West Highway 6 and 34, Cambridge, NE, Zip 69022–0488, Mailing Address: P.O. Box 488, Zip 69022–0488; tel. 308/697–3329; Kristopher H. Marwin, CHE, Chief Executive Officer

WEBSTER COUNTY COMMUNITY HOSPITAL, Sixth Avenue and Franklin Street, Red Cloud, NE, Zip 68970–0465; tel. 402/746–2291; Terry L. Hoffart, Administrator

YORK GENERAL HOSPITAL, 2222 Lincoln Avenue, York, NE, Zip 68467–1095; tel. 402/362–0445; Charles K. Schulz, Chief Executive Officer

NORTH CENTRAL HOSPITAL NEBRASKA NETWORK
P.O. Box 429, Osmond, NE 68765; tel. 402/925–2811; Celine Mlady, President

ANTELOPE MEMORIAL HOSPITAL, 102 West Ninth Street, Neligh, NE, Zip 68756–0229, Mailing Address: P.O. Box 229, Zip 68756–0229; tel. 402/887–4151; Jack W. Green, Administrator

BROWN COUNTY HOSPITAL, 945 East Zero Street, Ainsworth, NE, Zip 69210–1547; tel. 402/387–2800; Colleen Chapp, Interim Administrator

LUTHERAN COMMUNITY HOSPITAL, 2700 Norfolk Avenue, Norfolk, NE, Zip 68701, Mailing Address: P.O. Box 869, Zip 68702–0869; tel. 402/371–4880

NIOBRARA VALLEY HOSPITAL, Lynch, NE, Mailing Address: P.O. Box 118, Zip 68746–0118; tel. 402/569–2451; E. R. Testerman, Administrator

OSMOND GENERAL HOSPITAL, 5th and Maple Street, Osmond, NE, Zip 68765–0429, Mailing Address: P.O. Box 429, Zip 68765–0429; tel. 402/748–3393; Celine Mlady, Chief Executive Officer

PLAINVIEW PUBLIC HOSPITAL, 705 North Third Street, Plainview, NE, Zip 68769, Mailing Address: P.O. Box 489, Zip 68769–0489; tel. 402/582–4245; Donald T. Naiberk, Administrator and Chief Executive Officer

ROCK COUNTY HOSPITAL, 102 East South Street, Bassett, NE, Zip 68714, Mailing Address: P.O. Box 100, Zip 68714–0100; tel. 402/684–3366; David Stephenson, Administrator

WEST HOLT MEMORIAL HOSPITAL, 406 Legion Street, Atkinson, NE, Zip 68713–0200, Mailing Address: Rural Route 1, Box 200, Zip 68713–0200; tel. 402/925–2811; Mel L. Snow, Administrator

RURAL HEALTH PARTNERS
513 North Grant Street, Suite 5, Lexington, NE 68850; tel. 308/324–3050; Sheila Rowe, Executive Director

BRODSTONE MEMORIAL HOSPITAL, 520 East Tenth Street, Superior, NE, Zip 68978–1225, Mailing Address: P.O. Box 187, Zip 68978–0187; tel. 402/879–3281; Ronald D. Waggoner, Administrator and Chief Executive Officer

COMMUNITY HOSPITAL, 1301 East H. Street, McCook, NE, Zip 69001–1328, Mailing Address: P.O. Box 1328, Zip 69001–1328; tel. 308/345–2650; Gary Bieganski, President

FRANKLIN COUNTY MEMORIAL HOSPITAL, 1406 Q. Street, Franklin, NE, Zip 68939–0315, Mailing Address: P.O. Box 315, Zip 68939–0315; tel. 308/425–6221; Jerrell F. Gerdes, Administrator

GOTHENBURG MEMORIAL HOSPITAL, 910 20th Street, Gothenburg, NE, Zip 69138–1237, Mailing Address: P.O. Box 469, Zip 69138–0469; tel. 308/537–3661; John H. Johnson, Chief Executive Officer

GREAT PLAINS REGIONAL MEDICAL CENTER, 601 West Leota Street, North Platte, NE, Zip 69101–6598, Mailing Address: P.O. Box 1167, Zip 69103–1167; tel. 308/534–9310; Lucinda A. Bradley, President

HARLAN COUNTY HOSPITAL, 717 North Brown Street, Alma, NE, Zip 68920–0836, Mailing Address: P.O. Box 836, Zip 68920–0836; tel. 308/928–2151; Allen Van Driel, Administrator

MARY LANNING MEMORIAL HOSPITAL, 715 North St. Joseph Avenue, Hastings, NE, Zip 68901–4497; tel. 402/463–4521; W. Michael Kearney, President

PHELPS MEMORIAL HEALTH CENTER, 1220 Miller Street, Holdrege, NE, Zip 68949–1200, Mailing Address: P.O. Box 828, Zip 68949–0828; tel. 308/995–2211; Jerome Seigfreid, Jr., Chief Executive Officer

TRI–COUNTY AREA HOSPITAL, 13th and Erie Streets, Lexington, NE, Zip 68850–0980, Mailing Address: P.O. Box 980, Zip 68850–0980; tel. 308/324–5651; Calvin A. Hiner, Administrator

TRI–VALLEY HEALTH SYSTEM, West Highway 6 and 34, Cambridge, NE, Zip 69022–0488, Mailing Address: P.O. Box 488, Zip 69022–0488; tel. 308/697–3329; Kristopher H. Marwin, CHE, Chief Executive Officer

WEBSTER COUNTY COMMUNITY HOSPITAL, Sixth Avenue and Franklin Street, Red Cloud, NE, Zip 68970–0465; tel. 402/746–2291; Terry L. Hoffart, Administrator

WESTERN NEBRASKA RURAL HEALTH CARE NETWORK
821 Morehead Street, Chadron, NE 69337; tel. 308/432–5586; Harold Krueger, Chief Executive Officer

BOX BUTTE GENERAL HOSPITAL, 2101 Box Butte Avenue, Alliance, NE, Zip 69301–0810, Mailing Address: P.O. Box 810, Zip 69301–0810; tel. 308/762–6660; Terrance J. Padden, Administrator

CHADRON COMMUNITY HOSPITAL, 821 Morehead Street, Chadron, NE, Zip 69337–2599; tel. 308/432–5586; Harold L. Krueger, Jr., Administrator

CHASE COUNTY COMMUNITY HOSPITAL, 600 West 12th Street, Imperial, NE, Zip 69033–0819, Mailing Address: P.O. Box 819, Zip 69033–0819; tel. 308/882–7111; James O'Neal, Administrator

GARDEN COUNTY HOSPITAL, 1100 West Second Street, Oshkosh, NE, Zip 69154, Mailing Address: P.O. Box 320, Zip 69154–0320; tel. 308/772–3283; Kelly Reece, Facility Manager

GORDON MEMORIAL HOSPITAL DISTRICT, 300 East Eighth Street, Gordon, NE, Zip 69343–9990; tel. 308/282–0401; Gladys Phemister, Administrator

KIMBALL COUNTY HOSPITAL, 505 South Burg Street, Kimball, NE, Zip 69145–1398; tel. 308/235–3621; Gerri Linn, Administrator

LEGEND BUTTES HEALTH SERVICES, 11 Paddock Street, Crawford, NE, Zip 69339–1143, Mailing Address: P.O. Box 272, Zip 69339–0272; tel. 308/665–1770; Kim Engel, Chief Executive Officer

MEMORIAL HEALTH CENTER, 645 Osage Street, Sidney, NE, Zip 69162–1799; tel. 308/254–5825; Rex D. Walk, Chief Executive Officer

MORRILL COUNTY COMMUNITY HOSPITAL, 1313 S. Street, Bridgeport, NE, Zip 69336–0579, Mailing Address: P.O. Box 579, Zip 69336–0579; tel. 308/262–1616; Julia Morrow, Administrator

REGIONAL WEST MEDICAL CENTER, 4021 Avenue B., Scottsbluff, NE, Zip 69361–4695; tel. 308/635–3711; David M. Nitschke, President and Chief Executive Officer

NEVADA

SAINT MARY'S HEALTH NETWORK
235 W. Sixth Street, Reno, NV 89520; tel. 702/323–2041; Tamara Bradshaw, Research Assistant

LASSEN COMMUNITY HOSPITAL, 560 Hospital Lane, Susanville, CA, Zip 96130–4809; tel. 530/257–5325; David S. Anderson, FACHE, Administrator

SAINT MARY'S REGIONAL MEDICAL CENTER, 235 West Sixth Street, Reno, NV, Zip 89520–0108; tel. 702/323–2041; Jeff K. Bills, Chief Executive Officer

NEW HAMPSHIRE

CARING COMMUNITY NETWORK OF THE TWIN RIVERS (CCNTR)
15 Aiken Avenue, Franklin, NH 03235; tel. 603/934–4616; Walter A. Strauch, Chairperson

FRANKLIN REGIONAL HOSPITAL, 15 Aiken Avenue, Franklin, NH, Zip 03235–1299; tel. 603/934–2060; Walter A. Strauch, Executive Director

HEALTHLINK
80 Highland Street, Laconia, NH 03246; tel. 603/527–2910; Sharon Swanson, Network Contact

CATHOLIC MEDICAL CENTER, 100 McGregor Street, Manchester, NH, Zip 03102–3770; tel. 603/668–3545; Peter B. Davis, Interim Chief Executive Officer

CONCORD HOSPITAL, 250 Pleasant Street, Concord, NH, Zip 03301–2598; tel. 603/225–2711; Michael B. Green, President

ELLIOT HOSPITAL, One Elliot Way, Manchester, NH, Zip 03103; tel. 603/669–5300; Peter B. Davis, Interim President and Chief Executive Officer

LAKES REGION GENERAL HOSPITAL, 80 Highland Street, Laconia, NH, Zip 03246–3298; tel. 603/524–3211; Thomas Clairmont, President

MARY HITCHCOCK MEMORIAL HOSPITAL, One Medical Center Drive, Lebanon, NH, Zip 03756–0001; tel. 603/650–5000; James W. Varnum, President

PARTNERS IN CARING
243 Elm Street, Claremont, NH 03743; tel. 603/542–7771; Joan Churchill, Chairperson

VALLEY REGIONAL HOSPITAL, 243 Elm Street, Claremont, NH, Zip 03743–2099; tel. 603/542–7771; Donald R. Holl, President

SAINT JOSEPH HEALTH CARE
172 Kinsley Street, Nashua, NH 03061; tel. 603/882–3000; Peter B. Davis, President

ST. JOSEPH HOSPITAL, 172 Kinsley Street, Nashua, NH, Zip 03061; tel. 603/882–3000; Kenneth R. Ferron, Senior Vice President and Chief Operating Officer

NEW JERSEY

ATLANTIC HEALTH SYSTEM
325 Columbia Turnpike, P.O. Box 959, Florham Park, NJ 07932; tel. 973/660–3100; Richard P. Oths, President & Chief Executive Officer

GENERAL HOSPITAL CENTER AT PASSAIC, 350 Boulevard, Passaic, NJ, Zip 07055–2800; tel. 973/365–4300; Marie Cassese, R.N., President

MORRISTOWN MEMORIAL HOSPITAL, 100 Madison Avenue, Morristown, NJ, Zip 07962–1956; tel. 973/971–5000; Jean M. McMahon, R.N., Vice President and General Manager

MOUNTAINSIDE HOSPITAL, Bay and Highland Avenues, Montclair, NJ, Zip 07042–4898; tel. 973/429–6000; Robert A. Silver, Senior Vice President and General Manager

OVERLOOK HOSPITAL, 99 Beauvoir Avenue, Summit, NJ, Zip 07902–0220; tel. 908/522–2000; David H. Freed, Vice President and General Manager

ATLANTICARE HEALTH SYSTEM
6725 Delilah Road, Egg Harbor Township, NJ 08234; tel. 609/272–6311; Dominic S. Moffa, Vice President–Administration

ATLANTIC CITY MEDICAL CENTER, 1925 Pacific Avenue, Atlantic City, NJ, Zip 08401–6713; tel. 609/345–4000; David P. Tilton, President and Chief Executive Officer

CAPE ADVANTAGE HEALTH ALLIANCE
Two Stone Harbor Boulevard, Cape May, NJ 08210; tel. 609/463–2480; Tom Scott, President & Chief Executive Officer

BURDETTE TOMLIN MEMORIAL HOSPITAL, 2 Stone Harbor Boulevard, Cape May Court House, NJ, Zip 08210–9990; tel. 609/463–2000; Thomas L. Scott, FACHE, President and Chief Executive Officer

CLARA MAASS HEALTH SYSTEM
One Franklin Avenue, Belleville, NJ 07109; tel. 201/450–2000; Robert S. Curtis, President

CLARA MAASS HEALTH SYSTEM, 1 Clara Maass Drive, Belleville, NJ, Zip 07109–3557; tel. 973/450–2000; Thomas A. Biga, Executive Director

COMMUNITY/KIMBALL HEALTH CARE SYSTEM
99 Highway 37 West, Toms River, NJ 08755; tel. 908/240–8000; Mark Pilla, President

COMMUNITY MEDICAL CENTER, 99 Route 37 West, Toms River, NJ, Zip 08755–6423; tel. 732/240–8000; Kevin R. Burchill, Executive Director

FIRST OPTION HEALTH PLAN
2 Bridge Street, Red Bank, NJ 07701; tel. 908/842–5000; Michele Severin, Director Network Development

MERCER MEDICAL CENTER, Trenton, NJ

BARNERT HOSPITAL, 680 Broadway Street, Paterson, NJ, Zip 07514–1472; tel. 973/977–6600; Fred L. Lang, President and Chief Executive Officer

BAYSHORE COMMUNITY HOSPITAL, 727 North Beers Street, Holmdel, NJ, Zip 07733–1598; tel. 732/739–5900; Thomas Goldman, President and Chief Executive Officer

BETH ISRAEL HOSPITAL, 70 Parker Avenue, Passaic, NJ, Zip 07055–7000; tel. 973/365–5000; Jeffrey S. Moll, President and Chief Executive Officer

BURDETTE TOMLIN MEMORIAL HOSPITAL, 2 Stone Harbor Boulevard, Cape May Court House, NJ, Zip 08210–9990; tel. 609/463–2000; Thomas L. Scott, FACHE, President and Chief Executive Officer

CENTRASTATE MEDICAL CENTER, 901 West Main Street, Freehold, NJ, Zip 07728–2549; tel. 732/431–2000; Thomas H. Litz, FACHE, President and Chief Executive Officer

CHILTON MEMORIAL HOSPITAL, 97 West Parkway, Pompton Plains, NJ, Zip 07444–1696; tel. 973/831–5000; James J. Doyle, Jr., President and Chief Executive Officer

Section B

CHRIST HOSPITAL, 176 Palisade Avenue, Jersey City, NJ, Zip 07306–1196, Mailing Address: P.O. Box J–1, Zip 07306–1196; tel. 201/795–8200; Daniel R. Connell, President

CLARA MAASS HEALTH SYSTEM, 1 Clara Maass Drive, Belleville, NJ, Zip 07109–3557; tel. 973/450–2000; Thomas A. Biga, Executive Director

COMMUNITY MEDICAL CENTER, 99 Route 37 West, Toms River, NJ, Zip 08755–6423; tel. 732/240–8000; Kevin R. Burchill, Executive Director

EAST ORANGE GENERAL HOSPITAL, 300 Central Avenue, East Orange, NJ, Zip 07019–2819; tel. 973/672–8400; Mark Chastang, President and Chief Executive Officer

ELIZABETH GENERAL MEDICAL CENTER, 925 East Jersey Street, Elizabeth, NJ, Zip 07201–2728; tel. 908/289–8600; David A. Fletcher, President and Chief Executive Officer

ENGLEWOOD HOSPITAL AND MEDICAL CENTER, 350 Engle Street, Englewood, NJ, Zip 07631–1898; tel. 201/894–3000; Daniel A. Kane, President and Chief Executive Officer

HACKETTSTOWN COMMUNITY HOSPITAL, 651 Willow Grove Street, Hackettstown, NJ, Zip 07840–1798; tel. 908/852–5100; Gene C. Milton, President and Chief Executive Officer

HOLY NAME HOSPITAL, 718 Teaneck Road, Teaneck, NJ, Zip 07666–4281; tel. 201/833–3000; Michael Maron, President and Chief Executive Officer

HUNTERDON MEDICAL CENTER, 2100 Wescott Drive, Flemington, NJ, Zip 08822–4604; tel. 908/788–6100; Robert P. Wise, President and Chief Executive Officer

IRVINGTON GENERAL HOSPITAL, 832 Chancellor Avenue, Irvington, NJ, Zip 07111–0709; tel. 973/399–6000; Paul A. Mertz, Executive Director

JFK MEDICAL CENTER, 65 James Street, Edison, NJ, Zip 08818–3947; tel. 732/321–7000; John P. McGee, President and Chief Executive Officer

KIMBALL MEDICAL CENTER, 600 River Avenue, Lakewood, NJ, Zip 08701–5281; tel. 732/363–1900; Joanne Carrocino, Executive Director

MEDICAL CENTER AT PRINCETON, 253 Witherspoon Street, Princeton, NJ, Zip 08540–3213; tel. 609/497–4000; Dennis W. Doody, President and Chief Executive Officer

MEMORIAL HOSPITAL OF BURLINGTON COUNTY, 175 Madison Avenue, Mount Holly, NJ, Zip 08060–2099; tel. 609/267–0700; Chester B. Kaletkowski, President and Chief Executive Officer

MONMOUTH MEDICAL CENTER, 300 Second Avenue, Long Branch, NJ, Zip 07740–6303; tel. 732/222–5200; Frank J. Vozos, M.D., FACS, Executive Director

MORRISTOWN MEMORIAL HOSPITAL, 100 Madison Avenue, Morristown, NJ, Zip 07962–1956; tel. 973/971–5000; Jean M. McMahon, R.N., Vice President and General Manager

MUHLENBERG REGIONAL MEDICAL CENTER, 1200 Park Avenue, Plainfield, NJ, Zip 07061; tel. 908/668–2000; John R. Kopicki, President and Chief Executive Officer

NEWARK BETH ISRAEL MEDICAL CENTER, 201 Lyons Avenue, Newark, NJ, Zip 07112–2027; tel. 973/926–7000; Paul A. Mertz, Executive Director

NEWTON MEMORIAL HOSPITAL, 175 High Street, Newton, NJ, Zip 07860–1004; tel. 973/383–2121; Dennis H. Collette, President and Chief Executive Officer

OUR LADY OF LOURDES MEDICAL CENTER, 1600 Haddon Avenue, Camden, NJ, Zip 08103–3117; tel. 609/757–3500; Alexander J. Hatala, President and Chief Executive Officer

PALISADES GENERAL HOSPITAL, 7600 River Road, North Bergen, NJ, Zip 07047–6217; tel. 201/854–5000; Bruce J. Markowitz, President and Chief Executive Officer

PASCACK VALLEY HOSPITAL, 250 Old Hook Road, Westwood, NJ, Zip 07675–3181; tel. 201/358–3000; Louis R. Ycre, Jr., FACHE, President and Chief Executive Officer

RIVERVIEW MEDICAL CENTER, 1 Riverview Plaza, Red Bank, NJ, Zip 07701–9982; tel. 908/741–2700; Paul S. Cohen, Executive Director and Chief Operating Officer

ROBERT WOOD JOHNSON UNIVERSITY HOSPITAL, 1 Robert Wood Johnson Place, New Brunswick, NJ, Zip 08903–2601; tel. 732/828–3000; Harvey A. Holzberg, President and Chief Executive Officer

SAINT BARNABAS MEDICAL CENTER, 94 Old Short Hills Road, Livingston, NJ, Zip 07039–5668; tel. 973/322–5000; Vincent D. Joseph, Executive Director

SHORE MEMORIAL HOSPITAL, 1 East New York Avenue, Somers Point, NJ, Zip 08244–2387; tel. 609/653–3500; Richard A. Pitman, President

SOMERSET MEDICAL CENTER, 110 Rehill Avenue, Somerville, NJ, Zip 08876–2598; tel. 908/685–2200; Michael A. Turner, President and Chief Executive Officer

SOUTH JERSEY HOSPITAL, 333 Irving Avenue, Bridgeton, NJ, Zip 08302–2100; tel. 609/451–6600; Paul S. Cooper, Chief Executive Officer

SOUTHERN OCEAN COUNTY HOSPITAL, 1140 Route 72 West, Manahawkin, NJ, Zip 08050–2499; tel. 609/978–8910; Steven G. Littleson, President and Chief Executive Officer

ST. FRANCIS MEDICAL CENTER, 601 Hamilton Avenue, Trenton, NJ, Zip 08629–1986; tel. 609/599–5000; Judith M. Persichilli, President and Chief Executive Officer

ST. JOSEPH'S HOSPITAL AND MEDICAL CENTER, 703 Main Street, Paterson, NJ, Zip 07503–2691; tel. 973/754–2000; Sister Jane Frances Brady, Chief Executive Officer

ST. PETER'S MEDICAL CENTER, 254 Easton Avenue, New Brunswick, NJ, Zip 08901–1780, Mailing Address: P.O. Box 591, Zip 08903–0591; tel. 732/745–8600; John E. Matuska, President and Chief Executive Officer

UNDERWOOD–MEMORIAL HOSPITAL, 509 North Broad Street, Woodbury, NJ, Zip 08096–1697, Mailing Address: P.O. Box 359, Zip 08096–0359; tel. 609/845–0100; Steven W. Jackmuff, President and Chief Executive Officer

UNION HOSPITAL, 1000 Galloping Hill Road, Union, NJ, Zip 07083–1652; tel. 908/687–1900; Kathryn W. Coyne, Executive Director and Chief Operating Officer

VALLEY HOSPITAL, 223 North Van Dien Avenue, Ridgewood, NJ, Zip 07450–9982; tel. 201/447–8000; Michael W. Azzara, President

WEST HUDSON HOSPITAL, 206 Bergen Avenue, Kearny, NJ, Zip 07032–3399; tel. 201/955–7051; Carmen Bruce Alecci, Executive Director

WEST JERSEY HOSPITAL–BERLIN, 100 Townsend Avenue, Berlin, NJ, Zip 08009–9035; tel. 609/322–3200; Ellen Guarnieri, Acting Executive Director

WEST JERSEY HOSPITAL–CAMDEN, 1000 Atlantic Avenue, Camden, NJ, Zip 08104–1595; tel. 609/246–3000; Frederick M. Carey, Executive Director

WEST JERSEY HOSPITAL–MARLTON, 90 Brick Road, Marlton, NJ, Zip 08053–9697; tel. 609/355–6000; Leroy J. Rosenberg, Executive Director

WEST JERSEY HOSPITAL–VOORHEES, 101 Carnie Boulevard, Voorhees, NJ, Zip 08043–1597; tel. 609/325–3000; Joan T. Meyers, R.N., Executive Director

WILLIAM B. KESSLER MEMORIAL HOSPITAL, 600 South White Horse Pike, Hammonton, NJ, Zip 08037–2099; tel. 609/561–6700; Warren E. Gager, Chief Executive Officer

QUALCARE PREFERRED PROVIDERS
242 Old Brunswick Road, Piscataway, NJ 08854; tel. 908/562–2800; Concetta Klucsik, Director of Marketing

HELENE FULD MEDICAL CENTER, 750 Brunswick Avenue, Trenton, NJ, Zip 08638–4174; tel. 609/394–6000

BAYONNE HOSPITAL, 29 East 29th Street, Bayonne, NJ, Zip 07002–4699; tel. 201/858–5000; Michael R. D'Agnes, President and Chief Executive Officer

BETH ISRAEL HOSPITAL, 70 Parker Avenue, Passaic, NJ, Zip 07055–7000; tel. 973/365–5000; Jeffrey S. Moll, President and Chief Executive Officer

CARRIER FOUNDATION, County Route 601, P.O. Box 147, Belle Mead, NJ, Zip 08502–0147; tel. 908/281–1000; C. Richard Sarle, President and Chief Executive Officer

CENTRASTATE MEDICAL CENTER, 901 West Main Street, Freehold, NJ, Zip 07728–2549; tel. 732/431–2000; Thomas H. Litz, FACHE, President and Chief Executive Officer

CHILDREN'S SPECIALIZED HOSPITAL, 150 New Providence Road, Mountainside, NJ, Zip 07091–2590; tel. 908/301–5431; Richard B. Ahlfeld, President

COLUMBUS HOSPITAL, 495 North 13th Street, Newark, NJ, Zip 07107–1397; tel. 973/268–1400; John G. Magliaro, President and Chief Executive Officer

COMMUNITY MEDICAL CENTER, 99 Route 37 West, Toms River, NJ, Zip 08755–6423; tel. 732/240–8000; Kevin R. Burchill, Director

ELIZABETH GENERAL MEDICAL CENTER, 925 East Jersey Street, Elizabeth, NJ, Zip 07201–2728; tel. 908/289–8600; David A. Fletcher, President and Chief Executive Officer

HACKENSACK UNIVERSITY MEDICAL CENTER, 30 Prospect Avenue, Hackensack, NJ, Zip 07601–1991; tel. 201/996–2000; John P. Ferguson, President and Chief Executive Officer

HOLY NAME HOSPITAL, 718 Teaneck Road, Teaneck, NJ, Zip 07666–4281; tel. 201/833–3000; Michael Maron, President and Chief Executive Officer

HOSPITAL CENTER AT ORANGE, 188 South Essex Avenue, Orange, NJ, Zip 07051; tel. 973/266–2200; James E. Romer, President and Chief Executive Officer

HUNTERDON MEDICAL CENTER, 2100 Wescott Drive, Flemington, NJ, Zip 08822–4604; tel. 908/788–6100; Robert P. Wise, President and Chief Executive Officer

IRVINGTON GENERAL HOSPITAL, 832 Chancellor Avenue, Irvington, NJ, Zip 07111–0709; tel. 973/399–6000; Paul A. Mertz, Director

KESSLER INSTITUTE FOR REHABILITATION, 1199 Pleasant Valley Way, West Orange, NJ, Zip 07052–1419; tel. 973/731–3600; Kenneth W. Aitchison, President and Chief Executive Officer

KIMBALL MEDICAL CENTER, 600 River Avenue, Lakewood, NJ, Zip 08701–5281; tel. 732/363–1900; Joanne Carrocino, Executive Director

MEDICAL CENTER OF OCEAN COUNTY, 2121 Edgewater Place, Point Pleasant, NJ, Zip 08742–2290; tel. 908/892–1100; John T. Gribbin, President and Chief Executive Officer

MEMORIAL HOSPITAL OF BURLINGTON COUNTY, 175 Madison Avenue, Mount Holly, NJ, Zip 08060–2099; tel. 609/267–0700; Chester B. Kaletkowski, President and Chief Executive Officer

MEMORIAL HOSPITAL OF SALEM COUNTY, 310 Woodstown Road, Salem, NJ, Zip 08079–2080; tel. 609/935–1000; Denise R. Williams, President and Chief Executive Officer

MERIDIAN HEALTH SYSTEM, 1945 State Highway 33, Neptune, NJ, Zip 07753; tel. 732/775–5500; John K. Lloyd, Chief Executive Officer

MONMOUTH MEDICAL CENTER, 300 Second Avenue, Long Branch, NJ, Zip 07740–6303; tel. 732/222–5200; Frank J. Vozos, M.D., FACS, Executive Director

MORRISTOWN MEMORIAL HOSPITAL, 100 Madison Avenue, Morristown, NJ, Zip 07962–1956; tel. 973/971–5000; Jean M. McMahon, R.N., Vice President and General Manager

MOUNTAINSIDE HOSPITAL, Bay and Highland Avenues, Montclair, NJ, Zip 07042–4898; tel. 973/429–6000; Robert A. Silver, Senior Vice President and General Manager

NEWARK BETH ISRAEL MEDICAL CENTER, 201 Lyons Avenue, Newark, NJ, Zip 07112–2027; tel. 973/926–7000; Paul A. Mertz, Executive Director

NORTHWEST COVENANT MEDICAL CENTER, 25 Pocono Road, Denville, NJ, Zip 07834–2995; tel. 973/625–6000; Kathryn J. McDonagh, President and Chief Executive Officer

OVERLOOK HOSPITAL, 99 Beauvoir Avenue, Summit, NJ, Zip 07902–0220; tel. 908/522–2000; David H. Freed, Vice President and General Manager

PALISADES GENERAL HOSPITAL, 7600 River Road, North Bergen, NJ, Zip 07047–6217; tel. 201/854–5000; Bruce J. Markowitz, President and Chief Executive Officer

PASCACK VALLEY HOSPITAL, 250 Old Hook Road, Westwood, NJ, Zip 07675–3181; tel. 201/358–3000; Louis R. Ycre, Jr., FACHE, President and Chief Executive Officer

RAHWAY HOSPITAL, 865 Stone Street, Rahway, NJ, Zip 07065–2797; tel. 732/381–4200; Kirk C. Tice, President and Chief Executive Officer

RARITAN BAY MEDICAL CENTER, 530 New Brunswick Avenue, Perth Amboy, NJ, Zip 08861–3685; tel. 732/442–3700; Keith H. McLaughlin, President and Chief Executive Officer

RIVERVIEW MEDICAL CENTER, 1 Riverview Plaza, Red Bank, NJ, Zip 07701–9982; tel. 908/741–2700; Paul S. Cohen, Executive Director and Chief Operating Officer

ROBERT WOOD JOHNSON UNIVERSITY HOSPITAL, 1 Robert Wood Johnson Place, New Brunswick, NJ, Zip 08903–2601; tel. 732/828–3000; Harvey A. Holzberg, President and Chief Executive Officer

ROBERT WOOD JOHNSON UNIVERSITY HOSPITAL AT HAMILTON, One Hamilton Health Place, Hamilton, NJ, Zip 08690–3599; tel. 609/586–7900; Christy Stephenson, Chief Administrative Officer

SAINT BARNABAS MEDICAL CENTER, 94 Old Short Hills Road, Livingston, NJ, Zip 07039–5668; tel. 973/322–5000; Vincent D. Joseph, Executive Director

SHORE MEMORIAL HOSPITAL, 1 East New York Avenue, Somers Point, NJ, Zip 08244–2387; tel. 609/653–3500; Richard A. Pitman, President

SOMERSET MEDICAL CENTER, 110 Rehill Avenue, Somerville, NJ, Zip 08876–2598; tel. 908/685–2200; Michael A. Turner, President and Chief Executive Officer

SOUTH JERSEY HOSPITAL, 333 Irving Avenue, Bridgeton, NJ, Zip 08302–2100; tel. 609/451–6600; Paul S. Cooper, Chief Executive Officer

SOUTHERN OCEAN COUNTY HOSPITAL, 1140 Route 72 West, Manahawkin, NJ, Zip 08050–2499; tel. 609/978–8910; Steven G. Littleson, President and Chief Executive Officer

ST. FRANCIS HOSPITAL, 25 McWilliams Place, Jersey City, NJ, Zip 07302–1698; tel. 201/418–1000; Robert S. Chaloner, President and Chief Executive Officer

ST. JOSEPH'S HOSPITAL AND MEDICAL CENTER, 703 Main Street, Paterson, NJ, Zip 07503–2691; tel. 973/754–2000; Sister Jane Frances Brady, Chief Executive Officer

ST. LAWRENCE REHABILITATION CENTER, 2381 Lawrenceville Road, Lawrenceville, NJ, Zip 08648; tel. 609/896–9500; Charles L. Brennan, Chief Executive Officer

ST. MARY HOSPITAL, 308 Willow Avenue, Hoboken, NJ, Zip 07030–3889; tel. 201/418–1000; Robert S. Chaloner, President and Chief Executive Officer

ST. PETER'S MEDICAL CENTER, 254 Easton Avenue, New Brunswick, NJ, Zip 08901–1780, Mailing Address: P.O. Box 591, Zip 08903–0591; tel. 732/745–8600; John E. Matuska, President and Chief Executive Officer

THE COOPER HEALTH SYSTEM, One Cooper Plaza, Camden, NJ, Zip 08103–1489; tel. 609/342–2000; Kevin G. Halpern, President and Chief Executive Officer

UNDERWOOD–MEMORIAL HOSPITAL, 509 North Broad Street, Woodbury, NJ, Zip 08096–1697, Mailing Address: P.O. Box 359, Zip 08096–0359; tel. 609/845–0100; Steven W. Jackmuff, President and Chief Executive Officer

UNION HOSPITAL, 1000 Galloping Hill Road, Union, NJ, Zip 07083–1652; tel. 908/687–1900; Kathryn W. Coyne, Executive Director and Chief Operating Officer

UNIVERSITY OF MEDICINE AND DENTISTRY OF NEW JERSEY–UNIVERSITY HOSPITAL, 150 Bergen Street, Newark, NJ, Zip 07103–2406; tel. 973/972–4300; William L. Vazquez, Vice President and Chief Executive Officer

WARREN HOSPITAL, 185 Roseberry Street, Phillipsburg, NJ, Zip 08865–9955; tel. 908/859–6700; Jeffrey C. Goodwin, President and Chief Executive Officer

WAYNE GENERAL HOSPITAL, 224 Hamburg Turnpike, Wayne, NJ, Zip 07470–2100; tel. 973/942–6900; Kenneth H. Kozloff, Executive Director

WEST JERSEY HOSPITAL–CAMDEN, 1000 Atlantic Avenue, Camden, NJ, Zip 08104–1595; tel. 609/246–3000; Frederick M. Carey, Executive Director

WEST JERSEY HOSPITAL–MARLTON, 90 Brick Road, Marlton, NJ, Zip 08053–9697; tel. 609/355–6000; Leroy J. Rosenberg, Executive Director

WEST JERSEY HOSPITAL–VOORHEES, 101 Carnie Boulevard, Voorhees, NJ, Zip 08043–1597; tel. 609/325–3000; Joan T. Meyers, R.N., Executive Director

SETON HEALTH NETWORK, INC.
703 Main Street, Paterson, NJ 07503; tel. 201/754–2790; Anthony Losardo, M.D., President

ST. JOSEPH'S HOSPITAL AND MEDICAL CENTER, 703 Main Street, Paterson, NJ, Zip 07503–2691; tel. 973/754–2000; Sister Jane Frances Brady, Chief Executive Officer

VIA CARITAS HEALTH SYSTEM, INC.
25 Pocono Road, Denville, NJ 07834; tel. 973/625–6681; Joseph A. Trunfio, Ph.D, President/CEO

NORTHWEST COVENANT MEDICAL CENTER, 25 Pocono Road, Denville, NJ, Zip 07834–2995; tel. 973/625–6000; Kathryn J. McDonagh, President and Chief Executive Officer

ST. JOSEPH'S HOSPITAL AND MEDICAL CENTER, 703 Main Street, Paterson, NJ, Zip 07503–2691; tel. 973/754–2000; Sister Jane Frances Brady, Chief Executive Officer

ST. MARY'S HOSPITAL, 211 Pennington Avenue, Passaic, NJ, Zip 07055–4698; tel. 973/470–3000; Patricia Peterson, President and Chief Executive Officer

NEW MEXICO

LOVELACE
5400 Gibson Boulevard, SouthEast, Albuquerque, NM 87108; tel. 505/262–7000; John Lucas, M.D., Chief Executive Officer

LOVELACE HEALTH SYSTEM, 5400 Gibson Boulevard S.E., Albuquerque, NM, Zip 87108–4763; tel. 505/262–7000; Martin Hickey, M.D., Chief Executive Officer

MEDICAL NETWORK OF NEW MEXICO
7850 Jefferson, Northeast, Albuquerque, NM 87109; tel. 505/727–8076; Marian Lowe, Executive Director

ST. JOSEPH MEDICAL CENTER, 601 Martin Luther King Drive N.E., Albuquerque, NM, Zip 87102, Mailing Address: P.O. Box 25555, Zip 87125–0555; tel. 505/727–8000; C. Vincent Townsend, Jr., Senior Vice President Hospital Group

ST. JOSEPH NORTHEAST HEIGHTS HOSPITAL, 4701 Montgomery Boulevard N.E., Albuquerque, NM, Zip 87109–1251, Mailing Address: P.O. Box 25555, Zip 87125–0555; tel. 505/727–7800; Tony Struthers, Administrator

ST. JOSEPH REHABILITATION HOSPITAL AND OUTPATIENT CENTER, 505 Elm Street N.E., Albuquerque, NM, Zip 87102–2500, Mailing Address: P.O. Box 25555, Zip 87125–5555; tel. 505/727–4700; Mary Lou Coors, Administrator

ST. JOSEPH WEST MESA HOSPITAL, 10501 Golf Course Road N.W., Albuquerque, NM, Zip 87114–5000, Mailing Address: P.O. Box 25555, Zip 87125–0555; tel. 505/727–2000; Mary Lou Coors, Administrator

PRESBYTERIAN HEALTHCARE SERVICES, INC.
P.O. Box 27489, Albuquerque, NM 87125–7489; tel. 505/923–5280; Kim Hedrick, Director–Network Provider Services

PRESBYTERIAN HEALTHCARE SERVICES, 1100 Central Avenue S.E., Albuquerque, NM, Zip 87106–4934, Mailing Address: P.O. Box 26666, Zip 87125–6666; tel. 505/260–6333; James M. Minton, President and Chief Executive Officer

PRESBYTERIAN KASEMAN HOSPITAL, 8300 Constitution Avenue N.E., Albuquerque, NM, Zip 87110–7624, Mailing Address: P.O. Box 26666, Zip 87125–6666; tel. 505/291–2000; Robert A. Garcia, Administrator

UNIVERSITY OF NEW MEXICO HEALTH SCIENCE CENTER
2211 Lomas Boulevard, NorthEast, Albuquerque, NM 87106; tel. 505/843–2121; William H. Johnson, Chief Executive

UNIVERSITY HOSPITAL, 2211 Lomas Boulevard N.E., Albuquerque, NM, Zip 87106–2745; tel. 505/272–2121; Stephen W. McKernan, Chief Executive Officer

UNIVERSITY OF NEW MEXICO MENTAL HEALTH CENTER, 2600 Marble N.E., Albuquerque, NM, Zip 87131–2600; tel. 505/272–2870; Christina B. Gunn, Chief Executive Officer

NEW YORK

ADIRONDACK RURAL HEALTH NETWORK
100 Park Street, Glens Falls, NY 12801; tel. 518/792–3151; David Kruczlnicki, President

GLENS FALLS HOSPITAL, 100 Park Street, Glens Falls, NY, Zip 12801–9898; tel. 518/792–3151; David G. Kruczlnicki, President and Chief Executive Officer

MOSES LUDINGTON HOSPITAL, Wicker Street, Ticonderoga, NY, Zip 12883–1097; tel. 518/585–2831; Diane M. Hart, Chief Executive Officer

ALLEGANY COUNTY HEALTH CARE NETWORK
191 North Main Street, Wellsville, NY 14895; tel. 716/593–1100; William M. DiBerardino, President & Chief Executive Officer

JONES MEMORIAL HOSPITAL, 191 North Main Street, Wellsville, NY, Zip 14895–1197, Mailing Address: P.O. Box 72, Zip 14895–0072; tel. 716/593–1100; William M. DiBerardino, FACHE, President and Chief Executive Officer

BASSETT HEALTHCARE
1 Atwell Road, Cooperstown, NY 13326; tel. 607/547–3100; William F. Streck, MD, VP External Affairs

BASSETT HOSPITAL OF SCHOHARIE COUNTY, 41 Grandview Drive, Cobleskill, NY, Zip 12043–1331; tel. 518/234–2511; Donald W. Massey, Administrator

MARY IMOGENE BASSETT HOSPITAL, One Atwell Road, Cooperstown, NY, Zip 13326–1394; tel. 607/547–3100; William F. Streck, M.D., President and Chief Executive Officer

BUFFALO GENERAL HEALTH SYSTEM
100 High Street, Buffalo, NY 14203; tel. 716/845–2732; John L. Friedlander, President & Chief Executive Officer

BUFFALO GENERAL HOSPITAL, 100 High Street, Buffalo, NY, Zip 14203–1154; tel. 716/845–5600; Carrie B. Frank, President and Chief Executive Officer

DE GRAFF MEMORIAL HOSPITAL, 445 Tremont Street, North Tonawanda, NY, Zip 14120–0750, Mailing Address: P.O. Box 0750, Zip 14120–0750; tel. 716/694–4500; Marcia B. Gutfeld, Vice President and Chief Operating Officer

TRI–COUNTY MEMORIAL HOSPITAL, 100 Memorial Drive, Gowanda, NY, Zip 14070–1194; tel. 716/532–3377; Diane J. Osika, Interim Chief Executive Officer

CHENANGO COUNTY RURAL HEALTH NETWORK
179 North Broad Street, Norwich, NY 13815; tel. 607/335–4111; Frank W. Mirabito, President

CHENANGO MEMORIAL HOSPITAL, 179 North Broad Street, Norwich, NY, Zip 13815–1097; tel. 607/337–4111; Frank W. Mirabito, President

COLUMBIA PRESBYTERIAN REGIONAL NETWORK
161 Fort Washington Avenue, 14th FL, New York, NY 10032–3784; tel. 212/305–2500; Marc H. Lory, Executive Vice President & COO

CORNWALL HOSPITAL, 33 Laurel Avenue, Cornwall, NY, Zip 12518–1499; tel. 914/534–7711; Val S. Gray, Executive Director

HELEN HAYES HOSPITAL, Route 9W, West Haverstraw, NY, Zip 10993–1195; tel. 914/947–3000; Magdalena Ramirez, Chief Executive Officer

HOLY NAME HOSPITAL, 718 Teaneck Road, Teaneck, NJ, Zip 07666–4281; tel. 201/833–3000; Michael Maron, President and Chief Executive Officer

HORTON MEDICAL CENTER, 60 Prospect Avenue, Middletown, NY, Zip 10940–4133; tel. 914/343–2424; Jeffrey D. Hirsch, Executive Vice President and Chief Operating Officer

LAWRENCE HOSPITAL, 55 Palmer Avenue, Bronxville, NY, Zip 10708–3491; tel. 914/787–1000; Roger G. Dvorak, President

NEW MILFORD HOSPITAL, 21 Elm Street, New Milford, CT, Zip 06776–2993; tel. 860/355–2611; Richard E. Pugh, President and Chief Executive Officer

NYACK HOSPITAL, North Midland Avenue, Nyack, NY, Zip 10960–1998; tel. 914/348–2000; Greger C. Anderson, President and Chief Executive Officer

PALISADES GENERAL HOSPITAL, 7600 River Road, North Bergen, NJ, Zip 07047–6217; tel. 201/854–5000; Bruce J. Markowitz, President and Chief Executive Officer

ST. FRANCIS HOSPITAL, 100 Port Washington Boulevard, Roslyn, NY, Zip 11576–1348; tel. 516/562–6000; Patrick J. Scollard, President and Chief Executive Officer

ST. LUKE'S HOSPITAL, 70 Dubois Street, Newburgh, NY, Zip 12550–4898, Mailing Address: P.O. Box 631, Zip 12550–0631; tel. 914/561–4400; Laurence E. Kelly, Executive Vice President and Administrator

VALLEY HOSPITAL, 223 North Van Dien Avenue, Ridgewood, NJ, Zip 07450–9982; tel. 201/447–8000; Michael W. Azzara, President

WHITE PLAINS HOSPITAL CENTER, Davis Avenue, White Plains, NY, Zip 10601–4699; tel. 914/681–0600; Jon B. Schandler, President and Chief Executive Officer

CONTINUUM HEALTH PARTNERS, INC.
555 West 57th Street, New York, NY 10019; tel. 212/523–8390; Robert G. Newman, M.D., President

BETH ISRAEL MEDICAL CENTER, 281 First Avenue, New York, NY, Zip 10003–3803; tel. 212/420–2000; Matthew E. Fink, M.D., President and Chief Executive Officer

BETH ISRAEL MEDICAL CENTER–KINGS HIGHWAY DIVISION, 3201 Kings Highway, Brooklyn, NY, Zip 11234; tel. 718/252–3000

CATHOLIC MEDICAL CENTER OF BROOKLYN AND QUEENS, 88–25 153rd Street, Jamaica, NY, Zip 11432–3731; tel. 718/558–6900; William D. McGuire, President and Chief Executive Officer

PENINSULA HOSPITAL CENTER, 51–15 Beach Channel Drive, Far Rockaway, NY, Zip 11691–1074; tel. 718/945–7100; Robert V. Levine, President and Chief Executive Officer

ST. LUKE'S–ROOSEVELT HOSPITAL CENTER, 1111 Amsterdam Avenue, New York, NY, Zip 10025; tel. 212/523–4295; Ronald C. Ablow, M.D., President and Chief Executive Officer

VICTORY MEMORIAL HOSPITAL, 9036 Seventh Avenue, Brooklyn, NY, Zip 11228–3625; tel. 718/630–1234; Krishin L. Bhatia, Administrator

CORTLAND AREA RURAL HEALTH NETWORK
134 Homer Avenue, Cortland, NY 13045; tel. 607/756–3500; Thomas H. Carman, President & Chief Executive Officer

CORTLAND MEMORIAL HOSPITAL, 134 Homer Avenue, Cortland, NY, Zip 13045–0960; tel. 607/756–3500; Thomas H. Carman, President and Chief Executive Officer

EASTERN ADIRONDACK HEALTH CARE NETWORK
P.O. Box 466, Westport, NY 12993; tel. 518/962–2313; Lynn Edmonds, Network Coordinator

CHAMPLAIN VALLEY PHYSICIANS HOSPITAL MEDICAL CENTER, 75 Beekman Street, Plattsburgh, NY, Zip 12901–1493; tel. 518/561–2000; Kevin J. Carroll, President

ELIZABETHTOWN COMMUNITY HOSPITAL, Park Street, Elizabethtown, NY, Zip 12932–0277; tel. 518/873–6377; Douglas G. Cushing, Administrator

EPISCOPAL HEALTH SERVICES, INC.
333 Earle Ovington Boulevard, Uniondale, NY 11787; tel. 516/228–6100; Jack Farrington, Ph.d, Executive Director

ST. JOHN'S EPISCOPAL HOSPITAL–SMITHTOWN, 50 Route 25–A, Smithtown, NY, Zip 11787–1398; tel. 516/862–3000; Laura Righter, Regional Administrator

ST. JOHN'S EPISCOPAL HOSPITAL–SOUTH SHORE, 327 Beach 19th Street, Far Rockaway, NY, Zip 11691–4424; tel. 718/869–7000; Paul J. Connor, III, Administrator

FIRST CHOICE NETWORK, INC.
288 Old Country Road, Mineola, NY 11501; tel. 516/663–8536; Paul E. Hacker, Marketing Director

EASTERN LONG ISLAND HOSPITAL, 201 Manor Place, Greenport, NY, Zip 11944–1298; tel. 516/477–1000; John M. Gwiazda, President and Chief Executive Officer

SOUTHAMPTON HOSPITAL, 240 Meeting House Lane, Southampton, NY, Zip 11968–5090; tel. 516/726–8555; John J. Ferry, Jr., M.D., President and Chief Executive Officer

SOUTHSIDE HOSPITAL, 301 East Main Street, Bay Shore, NY, Zip 11706–8458; tel. 516/968–3000; Theodore A. Jospe, President

ST. CHARLES HOSPITAL AND REHABILITATION CENTER, 200 Belle Terre Road, Port Jefferson, NY, Zip 11777; tel. 516/474–6000; Barry T. Zeman, President and Chief Executive Officer

ST. JOHN'S EPISCOPAL HOSPITAL–SMITHTOWN, 50 Route 25–A, Smithtown, NY, Zip 11787–1398; tel. 516/862–3000; Laura Righter, Regional Administrator

ST. JOHN'S EPISCOPAL HOSPITAL–SOUTH SHORE, 327 Beach 19th Street, Far Rockaway, NY, Zip 11691–4424; tel. 718/869–7000; Paul J. Connor, III, Administrator

WINTHROP–UNIVERSITY HOSPITAL, 259 First Street, Mineola, NY, Zip 11501; tel. 516/663–2200; Martin J. Delaney, President and Chief Executive Officer

FOUR LAKES RURAL HEALTH NETWORK
196 North Street, Geneva, NY 14456; tel. 315/787–4000; James J. Dooley, President & Chief Executive Officer

GENEVA GENERAL HOSPITAL, 196 North Street, Geneva, NY, Zip 14456–1694; tel. 315/787–4000; James J. Dooley, President

SOLDIERS AND SAILORS MEMORIAL HOSPITAL OF YATES COUNTY, 418 North Main Street, Penn Yan, NY, Zip 14527–1085; tel. 315/531–2000; James J. Dooley, President and Chief Executive Officer

GREENE COUNTY RURAL HEALTH NETWORK
71 Prospect Avenue, Catskill, NY 12534; tel. 518/828–7601; Andrew E. Toga, Acting Chief Executive Officer

ALBANY MEDICAL CENTER, 43 New Scotland Avenue, Albany, NY, Zip 12208–3478; tel. 518/262–3125; Thomas G. Foggo, Executive Vice President Care Delivery and General Director

COLUMBIA MEMORIAL HOSPITAL, 71 Prospect Avenue, Hudson, NY, Zip 12534–2900; tel. 518/828–8039; Jane Ehrlich, President and Chief Executive Officer

HAMILTON–BASSETT–CROUSE RURAL HEALTH NETWORK
150 Broad Street, Hamilton, NY 13346; tel. 315/824–6080; David W. Felton, Chief Executive Officer

COMMUNITY MEMORIAL HOSPITAL, Broad Street, Hamilton, NY, Zip 13346–9518; tel. 315/824–1100; David Felton, Administrator

CROUSE HOSPITAL, 736 Irving Avenue, Syracuse, NY, Zip 13210–1690; tel. 315/470–7111; Edward T. Wenzke, President and Chief Executive Officer

HEALTH FIRST
555 West 57th Street, Suite 1520, New York, NY 10019; tel. 212/801–1500; Paul Dickstein, Network Contact

BETH ISRAEL MEDICAL CENTER, 281 First Avenue, New York, NY, Zip 10003–3803; tel. 212/420–2000; Matthew E. Fink, M.D., President and Chief Executive Officer

BRONX–LEBANON HOSPITAL CENTER, 1276 Fulton Avenue, Bronx, NY, Zip 10456–3499; tel. 718/590–1800; Miguel A. Fuentes, President and Chief Executive Officer

BROOKLYN HOSPITAL CENTER, 121 DeKalb Avenue, Brooklyn, NY, Zip 11201–5493; tel. 718/250–8005; Frederick D. Alley, President and Chief Executive Officer

BRUNSWICK GENERAL HOSPITAL, 366 Broadway, Amityville, NY, Zip 11701–9820; tel. 516/789–7000; Benjamin M. Stein, M.D., President

INTERFAITH MEDICAL CENTER, 555 Prospect Place, Brooklyn, NY, Zip 11238–4299; tel. 718/935–7000; Corbett A. Price, Chief Executive Officer

JAMAICA HOSPITAL MEDICAL CENTER, 8900 Van Wyck Expressway, Jamaica, NY, Zip 11418–2832; tel. 718/206–6000; David P. Rosen, President

KINGSBROOK JEWISH MEDICAL CENTER, 585 Schenectady Avenue, Brooklyn, NY, Zip 11203–1891; tel. 718/604–5000; Milton M. Gutman, Chief Executive Officer

MAIMONIDES MEDICAL CENTER, 4802 Tenth Avenue, Brooklyn, NY, Zip 11219–2916; tel. 718/283–6000; Stanley Brezenoff, President

MONTEFIORE MEDICAL CENTER, 111 East 210th Street, Bronx, NY, Zip 10467–2490; tel. 718/920–4321; Spencer Foreman, M.D., President

MOUNT SINAI MEDICAL CENTER, One Gustave L. Levy Place, New York, NY, Zip 10029–6574; tel. 212/241–6500; John W. Rowe, M.D., President

NASSAU COUNTY MEDICAL CENTER, 2201 Hempstead Turnpike, East Meadow, NY, Zip 11554–1854; tel. 516/572–0123; Jerald C. Newman, Vice President

NEW YORK UNIVERSITY HOSPITALS CENTER, 550 First Avenue, New York, NY, Zip 10016–4576; tel. 212/263–7300; Theresa A. Bischoff, Deputy Provost and Executive Vice President

STATEN ISLAND UNIVERSITY HOSPITAL, 475 Seaview Avenue, Staten Island, NY, Zip 10305–9998; tel. 718/226–9000; Rick J. Varone, President

UNIVERSITY HOSPITAL, State University of New York, Stony Brook, NY, Zip 11794–8410; tel. 516/689–8333; Michael A. Maffetone, Director and Chief Executive Officer

UNIVERSITY HOSPITAL OF BROOKLYN–STATE UNIVERSITY OF NEW YORK HEALTH SCIENCE CENTER AT BROOKLYN, 445 Lenox Road, Brooklyn, NY, Zip 11203–2098; tel. 718/270–2404; Percy Allen, II, FACHE, Vice President Hospital Affairs and Chief Executive Officer

HEALTH STAR NETWORK
1 North Greenwich Road, Armonk, NY 10504; tel. 914/273–2850; Kevin G. Murphy, Vice President & Chief Financial Officer

LAWRENCE HOSPITAL, 55 Palmer Avenue, Bronxville, NY, Zip 10708–3491; tel. 914/787–1000; Roger G. Dvorak, President

NORTHERN WESTCHESTER HOSPITAL CENTER, 400 Main Street, Mount Kisco, NY, Zip 10549–3477; tel. 914/666–1200; Donald W. Davis, President

PHELPS MEMORIAL HOSPITAL CENTER, 701 North Broadway, Sleepy Hollow, NY, Zip 10591–1096; tel. 914/366–3000; Keith F. Safian, President and Chief Executive Officer

WHITE PLAINS HOSPITAL CENTER, Davis Avenue, White Plains, NY, Zip 10601–4699; tel. 914/681–0600; Jon B. Schandler, President and Chief Executive Officer

LAKE PLAINS COMMUNITY CARE NETWORK
426 Grider Street, Buffalo, NY 14215; tel. 716/898–5963; John N. Taylor, CEO

GENESEE MEMORIAL HOSPITAL, 127 North Street, Batavia, NY, Zip 14020–1697; tel. 716/343–6030; Douglas T. Jones, President and Chief Executive Officer

MEDINA MEMORIAL HOSPITAL, 200 Ohio Street, Medina, NY, Zip 14103–1095; tel. 716/798–2000; Walter S. Becker, Administrator

ST. JEROME HOSPITAL, 16 Bank Street, Batavia, NY, Zip 14020–2260; tel. 716/343–3131; Charles W. Smith, Jr., Chief Executive Officer

WYOMING COUNTY COMMUNITY HOSPITAL, 400 North Main Street, Warsaw, NY, Zip 14569–1097; tel. 716/786–2233; Lucille K. Sheedy, Administrator and Chief Executive Officer

MERCYCARE CORPORATION
315 South Manning Boulevard, Albany, NY 12208; tel. 518/454–1550; Steven P. Boyle, President

ST. PETER'S HOSPITAL, 315 South Manning Boulevard, Albany, NY, Zip 12208–1789; tel. 518/525–1550; Steven P. Boyle, President and Chief Executive Officer

MILLARD FILLMORE HEALTH SYSTEM
901 Washington Street, Buffalo, NY 14203; tel. 716/843–7308; Jan Fuller, Director of Planning

LAKE SHORE HOSPITAL, 845 Route 5 and 20, Irving, NY, Zip 14081–9716; tel. 716/934–2654; James B. Foster, Chief Executive Officer

MILLARD FILLMORE HEALTH SYSTEM, 3 Gates Circle, Buffalo, NY, Zip 14209–9986; tel. 716/887–4600; Carol M. Cassell, Executive Vice President and Chief Operating Officer

MOHAWK VALLEY NETWORK, INC.
P.O. Box 4308, Utica, NY 13504; tel. 315/798–2116; Fred Asforth, President

FAXTON HOSPITAL, 1676 Sunset Avenue, Utica, NY, Zip 13502–5475; tel. 315/738–6200; Andrew E. Peterson, President and Chief Executive Officer

LITTLE FALLS HOSPITAL, 140 Burwell Street, Little Falls, NY, Zip 13365–1725; tel. 315/823–1000; David S. Armstrong, Jr., Administrator

ST. LUKE'S MEMORIAL HOSPITAL CENTER, Utica, NY, Mailing Address: P.O. Box 479, Zip 13503–0479; tel. 315/798–6000; Andrew E. Peterson, President and Chief Executive Officer

NORTH SHORE REGIONAL HEALTH SYSTEMS
300 Community Drive, Manhasset, NY 11030; tel. 516/562–0100; John Gallagher, President

FRANKLIN HOSPITAL MEDICAL CENTER, 900 Franklin Avenue, Valley Stream, NY, Zip 11580–2190; tel. 516/256–6000; Albert Dicker, President and Chief Executive Officer

HUNTINGTON HOSPITAL, 270 Park Avenue, Huntington, NY, Zip 11743–2799; tel. 516/351–2200; J. Ronald Gaudreault, President and Chief Executive Officer

LONG ISLAND JEWISH MEDICAL CENTER, 270–05 76th Avenue, New Hyde Park, NY, Zip 11040–1496; tel. 718/470–7000; David R. Dantzker, M.D., President and Chief Executive Officer

NORTH SHORE UNIVERSITY HOSPITAL, 300 Community Drive, Manhasset, NY, Zip 11030–3876; tel. 516/562–0100; John S. T. Gallagher, President and Chief Executive Officer

NORTH SHORE UNIVERSITY HOSPITAL AT GLEN COVE, St. Andrews Lane, Glen Cove, NY, Zip 11542; tel. 516/674–7300; Mark R. Stenzler, Vice President Administration

NORTH SHORE UNIVERSITY HOSPITAL AT PLAINVIEW, 888 Old Country Road, Plainview, NY, Zip 11803–4978; tel. 516/719–3000; Glenn Hirsch, Executive Vice President, Administration

NORTH SHORE UNIVERSITY HOSPITAL AT SYOSSET, 221 Jericho Turnpike, Syosset, NY, Zip 11791–4567; tel. 516/496–6400; Deborah Tascone, R.N., Vice President for Administration

NORTH SHORE UNIVERSITY HOSPITAL—FOREST HILLS, Flushing, NY, Mailing Address: 102–01 66th Road, Zip 11375; tel. 718/830–4000; Andrew J. Mitchell, Vice President, Administration

SOUTHSIDE HOSPITAL, 301 East Main Street, Bay Shore, NY, Zip 11706–8458; tel. 516/968–3000; Theodore A. Jospe, President

STATEN ISLAND UNIVERSITY HOSPITAL, 475 Seaview Avenue, Staten Island, NY, Zip 10305–9998; tel. 718/226–9000; Rick J. Varone, President

NORTHERN NEW YORK RURAL HEALTH CARE ALLIANCE
200 Woolworth Building, Watertown, NY 13601; tel. 315/786–0565; Janice Charles, Chairman

CARTHAGE AREA HOSPITAL, 1001 West Street, Carthage, NY, Zip 13619–9703; tel. 315/493–1000; Kenn C. Rishel, Administrator and Chief Executive Officer

E. J. NOBLE HOSPITAL SAMARITAN, 19 Fuller Street, Alexandria Bay, NY, Zip 13607; tel. 315/482–2511; Richard A. Brooks, Administrator and Chief Operating Officer

EDWARD JOHN NOBLE HOSPITAL OF GOUVERNEUR, 77 West Barney Street, Gouverneur, NY, Zip 13642–1090; tel. 315/287–1000; Charles P. Conole, FACHE, Administrator

SAMARITAN HOSPITAL, 2215 Burdett Avenue, Troy, NY, Zip 12180–2475; tel. 518/271–3300; Paul A. Milton, Chief Operating Officer

NYU MEDICAL CENTER
550 First Avenue, New York, NY 10016; tel. 212/263–5500; John P. Harney, Senior Administrator, Hospital Operation

BROOKLYN HOSPITAL CENTER, 121 DeKalb Avenue, Brooklyn, NY, Zip 11201–5493; tel. 718/250–8005; Frederick D. Alley, President and Chief Executive Officer

HOSPITAL FOR JOINT DISEASES ORTHOPEDIC INSTITUTE, 301 East 17th Street, New York, NY, Zip 10003–3890; tel. 212/598–6000; Victor H. Frankel, M.D., President

JAMAICA HOSPITAL MEDICAL CENTER, 8900 Van Wyck Expressway, Jamaica, NY, Zip 11418–2832; tel. 718/206–6000; David P. Rosen, President

LENOX HILL HOSPITAL, 100 East 77th Street, New York, NY, Zip 10021–1883; tel. 212/434–2000; Gladys George, President and Chief Executive Officer

NEW YORK UNIVERSITY DOWNTOWN HOSPITAL, 170 William Street, New York, NY, Zip 10038–2649; tel. 212/312–5000; Leonard A. Aubrey, President and Chief Executive Officer

PREFERRED HEALTH NETWORK, INC.
45 Avenue & Parsons Boulevard, Flushing, NY 11355; tel. 718/963–7102; Charles J. Pandola, President

FLUSHING HOSPITAL MEDICAL CENTER, 45th Avenue at Parsons Boulevard, Flushing, NY, Zip 11355–2100; tel. 718/670–5000; Stephen S. Mills, President and Chief Executive Officer

WYCKOFF HEIGHTS MEDICAL CENTER, 374 Stockholm Street, Brooklyn, NY, Zip 11237–4099; tel. 718/963–7102; Dominick J. Gio, President and Chief Executive Officer

PREMIER PREFERRED CARE
441 Lexington Avenue, New York, NY 10017; tel. 908/205–0100; Jeff Nelson, President

MAIMONIDES MEDICAL CENTER, 4802 Tenth Avenue, Brooklyn, NY, Zip 11219–2916; tel. 718/283–6000; Stanley Brezenoff, President

QUEENS HEALTH NETWORK
79–01 Broadway, Elmhurst, NY 11373; tel. 718/334–4000; Pete Velez, Network Senior Vice President

ELMHURST HOSPITAL CENTER, 79–01 Broadway, Elmhurst, NY, Zip 11373; tel. 718/334–4000; Pete Velez, Executive Director

QUEENS HOSPITAL CENTER, 82–68 164th Street, Jamaica, NY, Zip 11432–1104; tel. 718/883–3000; Gladiola Sampson, Acting Executive Director

SETON HEALTH CARE SYSTEM
1300 Massachusetts Avenue, Troy, NY 12180; tel. 518/270–2520; Edward Murphy, President

SETON HEALTH SYSTEM, 1300 Massachusetts Avenue, Troy, NY, Zip 12180–1695; tel. 518/272–5000; Edward G. Murphy, M.D., President and Chief Executive Officer

SHARED HEALTH NETWORK, INC.
125 Wolf Road, Suite 404, Albany, NY 12205; tel. 518/458–8607; Eugene Stearns, Executive Director

ELLIS HOSPITAL, 1101 Nott Street, Schenectady, NY, Zip 12308–2487; tel. 518/243–4000; G. B. Serrill, President and Chief Executive Officer

GLENS FALLS HOSPITAL, 100 Park Street, Glens Falls, NY, Zip 12801–9898; tel. 518/792–3151; David G. Kruczlnicki, President and Chief Executive Officer

MEMORIAL HOSPITAL, 600 Northern Boulevard, Albany, NY, Zip 12204–1083; tel. 518/471–3221; Norman E. Dascher, Jr., Vice President and Chief Operating Officer

NATHAN LITTAUER HOSPITAL AND NURSING HOME, 99 East State Street, Gloversville, NY, Zip 12078–1293; tel. 518/725–8621; Thomas J. Dowd, President

SAMARITAN HOSPITAL, 2215 Burdett Avenue, Troy, NY, Zip 12180–2475; tel. 518/271–3300; Paul A. Milton, Chief Operating Officer

SARATOGA HOSPITAL, 211 Church Street, Saratoga Springs, NY, Zip 12866–1003; tel. 518/587–3222; David Andersen, President and Chief Executive Officer

SETON HEALTH SYSTEM, 1300 Massachusetts Avenue, Troy, NY, Zip 12180–1695; tel. 518/272–5000; Edward G. Murphy, M.D., President and Chief Executive Officer

ST. CLARE'S HOSPITAL OF SCHENECTADY, 600 McClellan Street, Schenectady, NY, Zip 12304–1090; tel. 518/382–2000; Paul J. Chodkowski, President and Chief Executive Officer

ST. MARY'S HOSPITAL, 427 Guy Park Avenue, Amsterdam, NY, Zip 12010–1095; tel. 518/842–1900; Peter E. Capobianco, President and Chief Executive Officer

ST. PETER'S HOSPITAL, 315 South Manning Boulevard, Albany, NY, Zip 12208–1789; tel. 518/525–1550; Steven P. Boyle, President and Chief Executive Officer

SUNNYVIEW HOSPITAL AND REHABILITATION CENTER, 1270 Belmont Avenue, Schenectady, NY, Zip 12308–2104; tel. 518/382–4500; Bradford M. Goodwin, President and Chief Executive Officer

SISTERS OF CHARITY HEALTH CARE SYSTEM
75 Vanderbilt Avenue, Staten Island, NY 10304; tel. 718/390–5080; John J. DePierro, President & Chief Executive Officer

ST VINCENT'S MEDICAL CENTER, 355 Bard Avenue, Staten Island, NY, Zip 10310–1699; tel. 718/876–1234

BAYLEY SETON CAMPUS, 75 Vanderbilt Avenue, Staten Island, NY, Zip 10304–3850; tel. 718/354–6000

SISTERS OF CHARITY HEALTHCARE
75 Vanderbilt Avenue, Staten Island, NY 10304; tel. 718/876–2820; Ray Pohlod, VP Corp. Comm.

ST VINCENT'S MEDICAL CENTER, 355 Bard Avenue, Staten Island, NY, Zip 10310–1699; tel. 718/876–1234

BAYLEY SETON CAMPUS, 75 Vanderbilt Avenue, Staten Island, NY, Zip 10304–3850; tel. 718/354–6000

CALVARY HOSPITAL, 1740 Eastchester Road, Bronx, NY, Zip 10461–2392; tel. 718/863–6900; Frank A. Calamari, President and Chief Executive Officer

OUR LADY OF MERCY MEDICAL CENTER, 600 East 233rd Street, Bronx, NY, Zip 10466–2697; tel. 718/920–9000; Gary S. Horan, FACHE, President and Chief Executive Officer

SAINT VINCENT'S HOSPITAL AND MEDICAL CENTER OF NEW YORK, 153 West 11th Street, New York, NY, Zip 10011–8397; tel. 212/604–7000; Karl P. Adler, M.D., President and Chief Executive Officer

ST. AGNES HOSPITAL, 305 North Street, White Plains, NY, Zip 10605–2299; tel. 914/681–4500; Gary S. Horan, FACHE, President and Chief Executive Officer

ST. CLARE'S HOSPITAL AND HEALTH CENTER, 415 West 51st Street, New York, NY, Zip 10019–6394; tel. 212/586–1500; James A. Rutherford, President and Chief Executive Officer

ST. JOSEPH'S MEDICAL CENTER, 127 South Broadway, Yonkers, NY, Zip 10701–4080; tel. 914/378–7000; Sister Mary Linehan, President

SULLIVAN COUNTY RURAL HEALTH NETWORK
Bushville Road, Harris, NY 12742; tel. 914/794–3300; Martin I. Richman, Executive Director

COMMUNITY GENERAL HOSPITAL OF SULLIVAN COUNTY, Bushville Road, Harris, NY, Zip 12742, Mailing Address: P.O. Box 800, Zip 12742–0800; tel. 914/794–3300; Martin I. Richman, Executive Director

THE BROOKLYN HEALTH NETWORK
121 DeKalb Avenue, Brooklyn, NY 11201; tel. 718/250–8000; Fred Alley, President & Chief Executive Officer

BROOKLYN HOSPITAL CENTER, 121 DeKalb Avenue, Brooklyn, NY, Zip 11201–5493; tel. 718/250–8005; Frederick D. Alley, President and Chief Executive Officer

INTERFAITH MEDICAL CENTER, 555 Prospect Place, Brooklyn, NY, Zip 11238–4299; tel. 718/935–7000; Corbett A. Price, Chief Executive Officer

KINGSBROOK JEWISH MEDICAL CENTER, 585 Schenectady Avenue, Brooklyn, NY, Zip 11203–1891; tel. 718/604–5000; Milton M. Gutman, Chief Executive Officer

VICTORY MEMORIAL HOSPITAL, 9036 Seventh Avenue, Brooklyn, NY, Zip 11228–3625; tel. 718/630–1234; Krishin L. Bhatia, Administrator

THE EXCELCARE SYSTEM, INC.
40 Palmer Avenue, Bronxville, NY 10708; tel. 914/337–6700; Donald S. Broas, President & Chief Executive Officer

HUDSON VALLEY HOSPITAL CENTER, 1980 Crompond Road, Peekskill, NY, Zip 10566–4182; tel. 914/737–9000; John C. Federspiel, President and Chief Executive Officer

LAWRENCE HOSPITAL, 55 Palmer Avenue, Bronxville, NY, Zip 10708–3491; tel. 914/787–1000; Roger G. Dvorak, President

PHELPS MEMORIAL HOSPITAL CENTER, 701 North Broadway, Sleepy Hollow, NY, Zip 10591–1096; tel. 914/366–3000; Keith F. Safian, President and Chief Executive Officer

ST. JOSEPH'S MEDICAL CENTER, 127 South Broadway, Yonkers, NY, Zip 10701–4080; tel. 914/378–7000; Sister Mary Linehan, President

UNITED HOSPITAL MEDICAL CENTER, 406 Boston Post Road, Port Chester, NY, Zip 10573–7300; tel. 914/934–3000; Kevin Dahill, President and Chief Executive Officer

THE MOUNT SINAI HEALTH SYSTEM
One Gustave L. Levy Place, New York, NY 10029; tel. 212/241–7597; Greg Banks, Senior Vice President

ARDEN HILL HOSPITAL, 4 Harriman Drive, Goshen, NY, Zip 10924–2499; tel. 914/294–5441; Wayne Becker, Interim Chief Executive Officer

BROOKDALE HOSPITAL MEDICAL CENTER, Linden Boulevard at Brookdale Plaza, Brooklyn, NY, Zip 11212–3198; tel. 718/240–5000; Frank J. Maddalena, President and Chief Executive Officer

CABRINI MEDICAL CENTER, 227 East 19th Street, New York, NY, Zip 10003–2600; tel. 212/995–6000; Jeffrey Frerichs, President and Chief Executive Officer

ELMHURST HOSPITAL CENTER, 79–01 Broadway, Elmhurst, NY, Zip 11373; tel. 718/334–4000; Pete Velez, Executive Director

ENGLEWOOD HOSPITAL AND MEDICAL CENTER, 350 Engle Street, Englewood, NJ, Zip 07631–1898; tel. 201/894–3000; Daniel A. Kane, President and Chief Executive Officer

GREENVILLE HOSPITAL, 1825 John F. Kennedy Boulevard, Jersey City, NJ, Zip 07305–2198; tel. 201/547–6100; Jonathan M. Metsch, Dr.PH, President and Chief Executive Officer

JERSEY CITY MEDICAL CENTER, 50 Baldwin Avenue, Jersey City, NJ, Zip 07304–3199; tel. 201/915–2000; Jonathan M. Metsch, Dr.PH, President and Chief Executive Officer

LONG BEACH MEDICAL CENTER, 455 East Bay Drive, Long Beach, NY, Zip 11561–2300, Mailing Address: P.O. Box 300, Zip 11561–2300; tel. 516/897–1200; Martin F. Nester, Jr., Chief Executive Officer

LONG ISLAND COLLEGE HOSPITAL, 339 Hicks Street, Brooklyn, NY, Zip 11201–5509; tel. 718/780–1000; Donald F. Snell, President and Chief Executive Officer

LUTHERAN MEDICAL CENTER, 150 55th Street, Brooklyn, NY, Zip 11220–2570; tel. 718/630–7000; Joseph P. Cerni, President and Chief Executive Officer

MAIMONIDES MEDICAL CENTER, 4802 Tenth Avenue, Brooklyn, NY, Zip 11219–2916; tel. 718/283–6000; Stanley Brezenoff, President

MEADOWLANDS HOSPITAL MEDICAL CENTER, Meadowland Parkway, Secaucus, NJ, Zip 07096–1580; tel. 201/392–3100; Paul V. Cavalli, M.D., President

MOUNT SINAI MEDICAL CENTER, One Gustave L. Levy Place, New York, NY, Zip 10029–6574; tel. 212/241–6500; John W. Rowe, M.D., President

PARKWAY HOSPITAL, Flushing, NY, Mailing Address: 70–35 113th Street, Zip 11375; tel. 718/990–4100; Paul E. Svensson, Chief Executive Officer

PHELPS MEMORIAL HOSPITAL CENTER, 701 North Broadway, Sleepy Hollow, NY, Zip 10591–1096; tel. 914/366–3000; Keith F. Safian, President and Chief Executive Officer

QUEENS HOSPITAL CENTER, 82–68 164th Street, Jamaica, NY, Zip 11432–1104; tel. 718/883–3000; Gladiola Sampson, Acting Executive Director

SAINT FRANCIS HOSPITAL, 35 North Road, Poughkeepsie, NY, Zip 12601–1399; tel. 914/471–2000; Sister M. Ann Elizabeth, President

ST. BARNABAS HOSPITAL, 183rd Street and Third Avenue, Bronx, NY, Zip 10457–9998; tel. 718/960–9000; Ronald Gade, M.D., President

ST. ELIZABETH HOSPITAL, 225 Williamson Street, Elizabeth, NJ, Zip 07202–3600; tel. 908/527–5000; Sister Elizabeth Ann Maloney, President and Chief Executive Officer

ST. JOHN'S EPISCOPAL HOSPITAL–SMITHTOWN, 50 Route 25–A, Smithtown, NY, Zip 11787–1398; tel. 516/862–3000; Laura Righter, Regional Administrator

ST. JOHN'S EPISCOPAL HOSPITAL–SOUTH SHORE, 327 Beach 19th Street, Far Rockaway, NY, Zip 11691–4424; tel. 718/869–7000; Paul J. Connor, III, Administrator

ST. JOSEPH'S HOSPITAL AND MEDICAL CENTER, 703 Main Street, Paterson, NJ, Zip 07503–2691; tel. 973/754–2000; Sister Jane Frances Brady, Chief Executive Officer

ST. MARY'S HOSPITAL, 901 45th Street, West Palm Beach, FL, Zip 33407–2495, Mailing Address: P.O. Box 24620, Zip 33416–4620; tel. 561/844–6300; Phillip C. Dutcher, President and Chief Executive Officer

STATEN ISLAND UNIVERSITY HOSPITAL, 475 Seaview Avenue, Staten Island, NY, Zip 10305–9998; tel. 718/226–9000; Rick J. Varone, President

VASSAR BROTHERS HOSPITAL, 45 Reade Place, Poughkeepsie, NY, Zip 12601–3990; tel. 914/454–8500; Ronald T. Mullahey, President

VETERANS AFFAIRS MEDICAL CENTER, 130 West Kingsbridge Road, Bronx, NY, Zip 10468–3992; tel. 718/584–9000; Maryann Musumeci, Director

WESTERN QUEENS COMMUNITY HOSPITAL, 25–10 30th Avenue, Astoria Station, Long Island City, NY, Zip 11102–2495; tel. 718/932–1000; Elliot J. Simon, FACHE, Chief Operating Officer

THE NEW YORK & PRESBYTERIAN HOSPITALS CARE NETWORK, INC.
525 East 68th Street, New York, NY 10021; tel. 212/746–4030; George A. Vecchione, President

FLUSHING HOSPITAL MEDICAL CENTER, 45th Avenue at Parsons Boulevard, Flushing, NY, Zip 11355–2100; tel. 718/670–5000; Stephen S. Mills, President and Chief Executive Officer

GRACIE SQUARE HOSPITAL, 420 East 76th Street, New York, NY, Zip 10021–3104; tel. 212/988–4400; Frank Bruno, Chief Executive Officer

HOSPITAL FOR SPECIAL SURGERY, 535 East 70th Street, New York, NY, Zip 10021–4898; tel. 212/606–1000; John R. Ahearn, Co–Chief Executive Officer

NEW YORK COMMUNITY HOSPITAL, 2525 Kings Highway, Brooklyn, NY, Zip 11229–1798; tel. 718/692–5300; Lin H. Mo, President and Chief Executive Officer

NEW YORK HOSPITAL MEDICAL CENTER OF QUEENS, 56–45 Main Street, Flushing, NY, Zip 11355–5000; tel. 718/670–1231; Stephen S. Mills, President and Chief Executive Officer

NEW YORK HOSPITAL, CORNELL UNIVERSITY MEDICAL CENTER, 525 East 68th Street, New York, NY, Zip 10021–4885; tel. 212/746–5454

NEW YORK METHODIST HOSPITAL, 506 Sixth Street, Brooklyn, NY, Zip 11215–3645; tel. 718/780–3000; Mark J. Mundy, President and Chief Executive Officer

PRESBYTERIAN HOSPITAL IN THE CITY OF NEW YORK, Columbia–Presbyterian Medical Center, New York, NY, Zip 10032–3784; tel. 212/305–2500

UNITED HOSPITAL MEDICAL CENTER, 406 Boston Post Road, Port Chester, NY, Zip 10573–7300; tel. 914/934–3000; Kevin Dahill, President and Chief Executive Officer

Section B

WYCKOFF HEIGHTS MEDICAL CENTER, 374 Stockholm Street, Brooklyn, NY, Zip 11237–4099; tel. 718/963–7102; Dominick J. Gio, President and Chief Executive Officer

TRI–STATE HEALTH SYSTEM
255 Lafayette Aven, Suffern, NY 10901; tel. 914/368–5000; James A. Martin, President

MERCY COMMUNITY HOSPITAL, 160 East Main Street, Port Jervis, NY, Zip 12771–2245, Mailing Address: P.O. Box 1014, Zip 12771–1014; tel. 914/856–5351; Marie T. Droege, Site Administrator

ST. ANTHONY COMMUNITY HOSPITAL, 15–19 Maple Avenue, Warwick, NY, Zip 10990–5180; tel. 914/986–2276; R. Andrew Brothers, President and Chief Executive Officer

UNITY HEALTH SYSTEM
89 Genesee Street, Rochester, NY 14611; tel. 716/464–3203; Timothy R. McCormick, President

PARK RIDGE HOSPITAL, 1555 Long Pond Road, Rochester, NY, Zip 14626–4182; tel. 716/723–7000; Martin E. Carlin, President

ST. MARY'S HOSPITAL, 89 Genesee Street, Rochester, NY, Zip 14611–3285; tel. 716/464–3000; Stewart Putnam, President

VIA HEALTH
1040 University Avenue, Rochester, NY 14607; tel. 716/756–4280; Roger S. Hunt, President & CEO

GENESEE HOSPITAL, 224 Alexander Street, Rochester, NY, Zip 14607–4055; tel. 716/263–6000; William R. Holman, President

NEWARK–WAYNE COMMUNITY HOSPITAL, Driving Park Avenue, Newark, NY, Zip 14513, Mailing Address: P.O. Box 111, Zip 14513–0111; tel. 315/332–2022; W. Neil Stroman, President

ROCHESTER GENERAL HOSPITAL, 1425 Portland Avenue, Rochester, NY, Zip 14621–3099; tel. 716/338–4000; Richard S. Constantino, M.D., President

WESTCHESTER HEALTH SERVICES NETWORK
116 Radio Circle Drive, Mt Kisco, NY 10549; tel. 914/244–1085; Frank Hemeon, President & Chief Executive Officer

GOOD SAMARITAN HOSPITAL, 255 Lafayette Avenue, Suffern, NY, Zip 10901–4869; tel. 914/368–5000; James A. Martin, Chief Executive Officer

HUDSON VALLEY HOSPITAL CENTER, 1980 Crompond Road, Peekskill, NY, Zip 10566–4182; tel. 914/737–9000; John C. Federspiel, President and Chief Executive Officer

NORTHERN WESTCHESTER HOSPITAL CENTER, 400 Main Street, Mount Kisco, NY, Zip 10549–3477; tel. 914/666–1200; Donald W. Davis, President

PUTNAM HOSPITAL CENTER, Stoneleigh Avenue, Carmel, NY, Zip 10512–9948; tel. 914/279–5711; Rodney N. Hubbers, President and Chief Executive Officer

SOUND SHORE MEDICAL CENTER OF WESTCHESTER, 16 Guion Place, New Rochelle, NY, Zip 10802; tel. 914/632–5000; John R. Spicer, President and Chief Executive Officer

ST. JOHN'S RIVERSIDE HOSPITAL, 967 North Broadway, Yonkers, NY, Zip 10701–1399; tel. 914/964–4444; James Foy, President and Chief Executive Officer

STAMFORD HOSPITAL, Shelburne Road and West Broad Street, Stamford, CT, Zip 06902–3696, Mailing Address: P.O. Box 9317, Zip 06904–9317; tel. 203/325–7000; Philip D. Cusano, President and Chief Executive Officer

WESTCHESTER MEDICAL CENTER, Valhalla Campus, Valhalla, NY, Zip 10595; tel. 914/493–7000; Edward A. Stolzenberg, President and Chief Executive Officer

WHITE PLAINS HOSPITAL CENTER, Davis Avenue, White Plains, NY, Zip 10601–4699; tel. 914/681–0600; Jon B. Schandler, President and Chief Executive Officer

NORTH CAROLINA

BLADEN COUNTY HOSPITAL
Clarkton Road, Elizabethtown, NC 28337; tel. 919/862–5100; Leo A. Petit, Jr., Chief Executive Officer

BLADEN COUNTY HOSPITAL, 501 South Poplar Street, Elizabethtown, NC, Zip 28337–0398, Mailing Address: P.O. Box 398, Zip 28337–0398; tel. 910/862–5100; Leo A. Petit, Jr., Chief Executive Officer

CAROLINAS HOSPITAL NETWORK
P.O. Box 32861, Charlotte, NC 28232–2861; tel. 704/355–8625; Austin Letson, President

ANSON COUNTY HOSPITAL AND SKILLED NURSING FACILITIES, 500 Morven Road, Wadesboro, NC, Zip 28170–2745; tel. 704/694–5131; Frederick G. Thompson, Ph.D., Administrator and Chief Executive Officer

CAROLINAS MEDICAL CENTER, 1000 Blythe Boulevard, Charlotte, NC, Zip 28203–5871, Mailing Address: P.O. Box 32861, Zip 28232–2861; tel. 704/355–2000; Paul S. Franz, President

CATAWBA MEMORIAL HOSPITAL, 810 Fairgrove Church Road S.E., Hickory, NC, Zip 28602–9643; tel. 704/326–3000; J. Anthony Rose, President and Chief Executive Officer

CHARLOTTE INSTITUTE OF REHABILITATION, 1100 Blythe Boulevard, Charlotte, NC, Zip 28203–5864; tel. 704/355–4300; Don Gabriel, Administrator

CHESTER COUNTY HOSPITAL AND NURSING CENTER, 1 Medical Park Drive, Chester, SC, Zip 29706–9799; tel. 803/581–9400; Robert E. Waters, Chief Executive Officer

CLEVELAND REGIONAL MEDICAL CENTER, 201 Grover Street, Shelby, NC, Zip 28150–3940; tel. 704/487–3000; John Young, President and Chief Executive Officer

CRAWLEY MEMORIAL HOSPITAL, 315 West College Avenue, Boiling Springs, NC, Zip 28017, Mailing Address: P.O. Box 996, Zip 28017–0996; tel. 704/434–9466; Daphne Bridges, President

IREDELL MEMORIAL HOSPITAL, 557 Brookdale Drive, Statesville, NC, Zip 28677–1828, Mailing Address: P.O. Box 1828, Zip 28687–1828; tel. 704/873–5661; S. Arnold Nunnery, President and Chief Executive Officer

KINGS MOUNTAIN HOSPITAL, 706 West King Street, Kings Mountain, NC, Zip 28086–2708, Mailing Address: P.O. Box 339, Zip 28086–0339; tel. 704/739–3601; Hank Neal, Administrator

LINCOLN MEDICAL CENTER, 200 Gamble Drive, Lincolnton, NC, Zip 28092–0677, Mailing Address: Box 677, Zip 28093–0677; tel. 704/735–3071; Peter W. Acker, President and Chief Executive Officer

MERCY HOSPITAL, 2001 Vail Avenue, Charlotte, NC, Zip 28207–1289; tel. 704/379–5000; C. Curtis Copenhaver, Chief Executive Officer

RICHMOND MEMORIAL HOSPITAL, 925 Long Drive, Rockingham, NC, Zip 28379–4815; tel. 910/417–3000; David G. Hohl, Chief Executive Officer

RUTHERFORD HOSPITAL, 288 South Ridgecrest Avenue, Rutherfordton, NC, Zip 28139–3097; tel. 704/286–5000; Robert D. Jones, President

SCOTLAND MEMORIAL HOSPITAL, 500 Lauchwood Drive, Laurinburg, NC, Zip 28352–5599; tel. 910/291–7000; Gregory C. Wood, Chief Executive Officer

STANLY MEMORIAL HOSPITAL, 301 Yadkin Street, Albemarle, NC, Zip 28001, Mailing Address: P.O. Box 1489, Zip 28002–1489; tel. 704/984–4000; Roy M. Hinson, CHE, President and Chief Executive Officer

UNION REGIONAL MEDICAL CENTER, 600 Hospital Drive, Monroe, NC, Zip 28112–6000, Mailing Address: P.O. Box 5003, Zip 28111–5003; tel. 704/283–3100; John W. Roberts, President and Chief Executive Officer

UNIVERSITY HOSPITAL, 8800 North Tryon Street, Charlotte, NC, Zip 28262–8415, Mailing Address: P.O. Box 560727, Zip 28256–0727; tel. 704/548–6000; W. Spencer Lilly, Administrator

VALDESE GENERAL HOSPITAL, Valdese, NC, Mailing Address: P.O. Box 700, Zip 28690–0700; tel. 704/874–2251; Lloyd E. Wallace, President and Chief Executive Officer

WATAUGA MEDICAL CENTER, Deerfield Road, Boone, NC, Zip 28607–2600, Mailing Address: P.O. Box 2600, Zip 28607–2600; tel. 704/262–4100; Richard G. Sparks, President

CENTRAL CAROLINA RURAL HOSPITAL ALLIANCE
P.O. Box 938, Albemarle, NC 28002; tel. 704/983–8955; Robert Smith, Executive Director

RICHMOND MEMORIAL HOSPITAL, 925 Long Drive, Rockingham, NC, Zip 28379–4815; tel. 910/417–3000; David G. Hohl, Chief Executive Officer

STANLY MEMORIAL HOSPITAL, 301 Yadkin Street, Albemarle, NC, Zip 28001, Mailing Address: P.O. Box 1489, Zip 28002–1489; tel. 704/984–4000; Roy M. Hinson, CHE, President and Chief Executive Officer

UNION REGIONAL MEDICAL CENTER, 600 Hospital Drive, Monroe, NC, Zip 28112–6000, Mailing Address: P.O. Box 5003, Zip 28111–5003; tel. 704/283–3100; John W. Roberts, President and Chief Executive Officer

DUKE HEALTH NETWORK
3100 Tower Building, Suite 600, Durham, NC 27707; tel. 919/419–5001; Paul Rosenberg, Chief Operating Officer

DUKE UNIVERSITY MEDICAL CENTER, Erwin Road, Durham, NC, Zip 27710, Mailing Address: P.O. Box 3708, Zip 27710–3708; tel. 919/684–8111; Michael D. Israel, Chief Executive Officer and Vice Chancellor

MARIA PARHAM HOSPITAL, 566 Ruin Creek Road, Henderson, NC, Zip 27536–2957; tel. 252/438–4143; Philip S. Lakernick, President and Chief Executive Officer

EASTERN CAROLINA HEALTH NETWORK
P.O. Box 8468, Greenville, NC 27835–8468; tel. 919/816–6750; Randall H.H. Madry, Chief Executive Officer

ALBEMARLE HOSPITAL, 1144 North Road Street, Elizabeth City, NC, Zip 27909, Mailing Address: P.O. Box 1587, Zip 27906–1587; tel. 252/335–0531; Philip D. Bagby, President and Chief Executive Officer

BEAUFORT COUNTY HOSPITAL, 628 East 12th Street, Washington, NC, Zip 27889–3498; tel. 919/975–4100; Kenneth E. Ragland, Administrator

BERTIE MEMORIAL HOSPITAL, 401 Sterlingworth Street, Windsor, NC, Zip 27983–1726, Mailing Address: P.O. Box 40, Zip 27983–1726; tel. 919/794–3141; Anthony F. Mullen, Administrator

CARTERET GENERAL HOSPITAL, 3500 Arendell Street, Morehead City, NC, Zip 28557–2901, Mailing Address: P.O. Box 1619, Zip 28557–1619; tel. 919/247–1616; F. A. Odell, III, FACHE, President

CHOWAN HOSPITAL, 211 Virginia Road, Edenton, NC, Zip 27932–0629, Mailing Address: P.O. Box 629, Zip 27932–0629; tel. 919/482–8451; Barbara R. Cale, Administrator

CRAVEN REGIONAL MEDICAL AUTHORITY, 2000 Neuse Boulevard, New Bern, NC, Zip 28560–3499, Mailing Address: P.O. Box 12157, Zip 28561–2157; tel. 252/633–8111; Raymond Budrys, Chief Executive Officer

DUPLIN GENERAL HOSPITAL, 401 North Main Street, Kenansville, NC, Zip 28349–9989, Mailing Address: P.O. Box 278, Zip 28349–0278; tel. 910/296–0941; Richard E. Harrell, President and Chief Executive Officer

HALIFAX REGIONAL MEDICAL CENTER, 250 Smith Church Road, Roanoke Rapids, NC, Zip 27870–4914, Mailing Address: P.O. Box 1089, Zip 27870–1089; tel. 919/535–8011; M. E. Gilstrap, President and Chief Executive Officer

HERITAGE HOSPITAL, 111 Hospital Drive, Tarboro, NC, Zip 27886–2011; tel. 919/641–7700; Janet Mullaney, Chief Executive Officer

LENOIR MEMORIAL HOSPITAL, 100 Airport Road, Kinston, NC, Zip 28501, Mailing Address: P.O. Box 1678, Zip 28503–1678; tel. 252/522–7171; Gary E. Black, President and Chief Executive Officer

MARTIN GENERAL HOSPITAL, 310 South McCaskey Road, Williamston, NC, Zip 27892–2150, Mailing Address: P.O. Box 1128, Zip 27892–1128; tel. 252/809–6121; George H. Brandt, Jr., Administrator

NASH HEALTH CARE SYSTEMS, 2460 Curtis Ellis Drive, Rocky Mount, NC, Zip 27804–2297; tel. 919/443–8000; Richard Kirk Toomey, President and Chief Executive Officer

ONSLOW MEMORIAL HOSPITAL, 317 Western Boulevard, Jacksonville, NC, Zip 28540, Mailing Address: P.O. Box 1358, Zip 28540–1358; tel. 910/577–2281; Douglas Kramer, Chief Executive Officer

PITT COUNTY MEMORIAL HOSPITAL–UNIVERSITY HEALTH SYSTEM OF EASTERN CAROLINA, 2100 Stantonsburg Road, Greenville, NC, Zip 27835–6028, Mailing Address: Box 6028, Zip 27835–6028; tel. 919/816–4451; Dave C. McRae, President and Chief Executive Officer

PUNGO DISTRICT HOSPITAL, 202 East Water Street, Belhaven, NC, Zip 27810–9998; tel. 919/943–2111; Thomas O. Miller, Administrator

ROANOKE–CHOWAN HOSPITAL, 500 South Academy Street, Ahoskie, NC, Zip 27910, Mailing Address: P.O. Box 1385, Zip 27910–1385; tel. 919/209–3000; Susan S. Lassiter, President and Chief Executive Officer

WASHINGTON COUNTY HOSPITAL, 958 U.S. Highway 64 East, Plymouth, NC, Zip 27962–9591; tel. 919/793–4135; Lawrence H. McAvoy, Administrator

WAYNE MEMORIAL HOSPITAL, 2700 Wayne Memorial Drive, Goldsboro, NC, Zip 27534–8001, Mailing Address: P.O. Box 8001, Zip 27533–8001; tel. 919/736–1110; James W. Hubbell, President and Chief Executive Officer

WILSON MEMORIAL HOSPITAL, 1705 South Tarboro Street, Wilson, NC, Zip 27893–3428; tel. 252/399–8040; Christopher T. Durrer, President and Chief Executive Officer

HOSPITAL ALLIANCE FOR COMMUNITY HEALTH
P.O. Box 14049, 10 Sunnybrook Road, Raleigh, NC 27620–4049; tel. 919/250–3813; Peter J. Morris, M.D., Secretary

RALEIGH COMMUNITY HOSPITAL, 3400 Wake Forest Road, Raleigh, NC, Zip 27609–7373, Mailing Address: P.O. Box 28280, Zip 27611–8280; tel. 919/954–3000; James E. Raynor, Chief Executive Officer

REX HEALTHCARE, 4420 Lake Boone Trail, Raleigh, NC, Zip 27607–6599; tel. 919/783–3100; James W. Albright, President and Chief Executive Officer

WAKE MEDICAL CENTER, 3000 New Bern Avenue, Raleigh, NC, Zip 27610–1295; tel. 919/250–8000; Raymond L. Champ, President

MISSION & SAINT JOSEPH HEALTH SYSTEM
509 Biltmore Avenue, Asheville, NC 28801; tel. 704/255–3100; Robert F. Burgin, President and Chief Executive Officer

MISSION HOSPITAL, 509 Biltmore Avenue, Asheville, NC, Zip 28801–4690; tel. 704/255–4000; Robert F. Burgin, President and Chief Executive Officer

ST. JOSEPH'S HOSPITAL, 428 Biltmore Avenue, Asheville, NC, Zip 28801–4502; tel. 704/255–3100; J. Lewis Daniels, President and Chief Executive Officer

NORTH CAROLINA HEALTH NETWORK
P.O. Box 668800, Charlotte, NC 28266–8800; tel. 704/529–3300; Rose Duncan, Interim Director

MOSES CONE HEALTH SYSTEM, 1200 North Elm Street, Greensboro, NC, Zip 27401–1020; tel. 336/832–1000; Dennis R. Barry, President

UNC HEALTH NETWORK
101 Manning Drive, Chapel Hill, NC 27514; tel. 919/966–3709; Carol Straight, Network Development Specialist

ALAMANCE REGIONAL MEDICAL CENTER, 1240 Huffman Mill Road, Burlington, NC, Zip 27216–0202, Mailing Address: P.O. Box 202, Zip 27216–0202; tel. 336/538–7000; Thomas E. Ryan, President

CHATHAM HOSPITAL, West Third Street and Ivy Avenue, Siler City, NC, Zip 27344–2343, Mailing Address: P.O. Box 649, Zip 27344; tel. 919/663–2113; Woodrow W. Hathaway, Jr., Chief Executive Officer

COLUMBUS COUNTY HOSPITAL, 500 Jefferson Street, Whiteville, NC, Zip 28472–9987; tel. 910/642–8011; William S. Clark, Chief Executive Officer

FIRSTHEALTH MOORE REGIONAL HOSPITAL, 35 Memorial Drive, Pinehurst, NC, Zip 28374, Mailing Address: P.O. Box 3000, Zip 28374–3000; tel. 910/215–1000; Charles T. Frock, President and Chief Executive Officer

GOOD HOPE HOSPITAL, 410 Denim Drive, Erwin, NC, Zip 28339–0668, Mailing Address: P.O. Box 668, Zip 28339–0668; tel. 910/897–6151; Donald E. Annis, Chief Executive Officer

GRANVILLE MEDICAL CENTER, 1010 College Street, Oxford, NC, Zip 27565–2507, Mailing Address: Box 947, Zip 27565–0947; tel. 919/690–3000; Andrew Mannich, Administrator

JOHNSTON MEMORIAL HOSPITAL, 509 North Bright Leaf Boulevard, Smithfield, NC, Zip 27577–1376, Mailing Address: P.O. Box 1376, Zip 27577–1376; tel. 919/934–8171; Leland E. Farnell, President

MARIA PARHAM HOSPITAL, 566 Ruin Creek Road, Henderson, NC, Zip 27536–2957; tel. 252/438–4143; Philip S. Lakernick, President and Chief Executive Officer

MOREHEAD MEMORIAL HOSPITAL, 117 East King's Highway, Eden, NC, Zip 27288–5299; tel. 336/623–9711; Robert Enders, President

NORTH CAROLINA BAPTIST HOSPITAL, Medical Center Boulevard, Winston–Salem, NC, Zip 27157; tel. 336/716–4745; Len B. Preslar, Jr., President and Chief Executive Officer

SAMPSON REGIONAL MEDICAL CENTER, 607 Beaman Street, Clinton, NC, Zip 28328–2697, Mailing Address: Drawer 258, Zip 28329–0258; tel. 910/592–8511; Lee Pridgen, Jr., Administrator

SCOTLAND MEMORIAL HOSPITAL, 500 Lauchwood Drive, Laurinburg, NC, Zip 28352–5599; tel. 910/291–7000; Gregory C. Wood, Chief Executive Officer

SOUTHEASTERN REGIONAL MEDICAL CENTER, 300 West 27th Street, Lumberton, NC, Zip 28358–3017, Mailing Address: P.O. Box 1408, Zip 28359–1408; tel. 910/671–5000; J. L. Welsh, Jr., President

UNIVERSITY OF NORTH CAROLINA HOSPITALS, 101 Manning Drive, Chapel Hill, NC, Zip 27514–4220; tel. 919/966–4131; Eric B. Munson, Executive Director

WAKE MEDICAL CENTER, 3000 New Bern Avenue, Raleigh, NC, Zip 27610–1295; tel. 919/250–8000; Raymond L. Champ, President

WAKE FOREST UNIVERSITY BAPTIST MEDICAL CENTER
Medical Center Boulevard, Winston–Salem, NC 27157; tel. 336/716–7846; Douglas Atkinson, Vice President of Networks

ALEXANDER COMMUNITY HOSPITAL, 326 Third Street S.W., Taylorsville, NC, Zip 28681–3096; tel. 828/632–4282; Joe W. Pollard, Jr., Administrator

ALLEGHANY MEMORIAL HOSPITAL, 233 Doctors Street, Sparta, NC, Zip 28675–0009, Mailing Address: P.O. Box 9, Zip 28675–0009; tel. 336/372–5511; James Yarborough, Chief Executive Officer

ANGEL MEDICAL CENTER, Riverview and White Oak Streets, Franklin, NC, Zip 28734, Mailing Address: P.O. Box 1209, Zip 28734–1209; tel. 704/524–8411; Michael E. Zuliani, Chief Executive Officer

ASHE MEMORIAL HOSPITAL, 200 Hospital Avenue, Jefferson, NC, Zip 28640; tel. 336/246–7101; R. D. Williams, Administrator and Chief Executive Officer

BLOWING ROCK HOSPITAL, Chestnut Street, Blowing Rock, NC, Zip 28605–0148, Mailing Address: Box 148, Zip 28605–0148; tel. 704/295–3136; Patricia Gray, Administrator and Chief Executive Officer

CALDWELL MEMORIAL HOSPITAL, 321 Mulberry Street S.W., Lenoir, NC, Zip 28645–5720, Mailing Address: P.O. Box 1890, Zip 28645–1890; tel. 704/757–5100; Frederick L. Soule, President and Chief Executive Officer

CATAWBA MEMORIAL HOSPITAL, 810 Fairgrove Church Road S.E., Hickory, NC, Zip 28602–9643; tel. 704/326–3000; J. Anthony Rose, President and Chief Executive Officer

HOOTS MEMORIAL HOSPITAL, 624 West Main Street, Yadkinville, NC, Zip 27055–7804, Mailing Address: P.O. Box 68, Zip 27055–0068; tel. 336/679–2041; Lance C. Labine, President

HUGH CHATHAM MEMORIAL HOSPITAL, Parkwood Drive, Elkin, NC, Zip 28621–0560, Mailing Address: P.O. Box 560, Zip 28621–0560; tel. 910/527–7000; Richard D. Osmus, Chief Executive Officer

LEXINGTON MEMORIAL HOSPITAL, 250 Hospital Drive, Lexington, NC, Zip 27292, Mailing Address: P.O. Box 1817, Zip 27293–1817; tel. 336/248–5161; John A. Cashion, FACHE, President

MEMORIAL HOSPITAL OF MARTINSVILLE AND HENRY COUNTY, 320 Hospital Drive, Martinsville, VA, Zip 24112–1981, Mailing Address: Box 4788, Zip 24115–4788; tel. 540/666–7200; Joseph Roach, Chief Executive Officer

MOREHEAD MEMORIAL HOSPITAL, 117 East King's Highway, Eden, NC, Zip 27288–5299; tel. 336/623–9711; Robert Enders, President

NORTH CAROLINA BAPTIST HOSPITAL, Medical Center Boulevard, Winston–Salem, NC, Zip 27157; tel. 336/716–4745; Len B. Preslar, Jr., President and Chief Executive Officer

NORTHERN HOSPITAL OF SURRY COUNTY, 830 Rockford Street, Mount Airy, NC, Zip 27030–5365, Mailing Address: P.O. Box 1101, Zip 27030–1101; tel. 910/719–7000; William B. James, Chief Executive Officer

PATRICK COUNTY MEMORIAL HOSPITAL, Stuart, VA, Mailing Address: Route 2, Box 71, Zip 24171–9512; tel. 540/694–3151; John M. Faulkner, FACHE, President and Chief Executive Officer

ROWAN REGIONAL MEDICAL CENTER, 612 Mocksville Avenue, Salisbury, NC, Zip 28144–2799; tel. 704/638–1000; James M. Freeman, Chief Executive Officer

RUTHERFORD HOSPITAL, 288 South Ridgecrest Avenue, Rutherfordton, NC, Zip 28139–3097; tel. 704/286–5000; Robert D. Jones, President

STOKES–REYNOLDS MEMORIAL HOSPITAL, Danbury, NC, Mailing Address: P.O. Box 10, Zip 27016–0010; tel. 336/593–2831; Sandra D. Priddy, President

TWIN COUNTY REGIONAL HOSPITAL, 200 Hospital Drive, Galax, VA, Zip 24333–2283; tel. 540/236–8181; Marcus G. Kuhn, President and Chief Executive Officer

UNIVERSITY OF NORTH CAROLINA HOSPITALS, 101 Manning Drive, Chapel Hill, NC, Zip 27514–4220; tel. 919/966–4131; Eric B. Munson, Executive Director

WILKES REGIONAL MEDICAL CENTER, 1370 West D. Street, North Wilkesboro, NC, Zip 28659–3506, Mailing Address: P.O. Box 609, Zip 28659–0609; tel. 336/651–8100; David L. Henson, Chief Executive Officer

WESTERN NORTH CAROLINA HEALTH NETWORK
509 Biltmore Avenue, Asheville, NC 28801; tel. 704/255–4495; MaryAnn Digman, Adminstrator of Regional Services

HARRIS REGIONAL HOSPITAL, 68 Hospital Road, Sylva, NC, Zip 28779–2795; tel. 828/586–7000

MARGARET R. PARDEE MEMORIAL HOSPITAL, 715 Fleming Street, Hendersonville, NC, Zip 28791–2563; tel. 828/696–1000; Frank J. Aaron, Jr., Chief Executive Officer

MCDOWELL HOSPITAL, 100 Rankin Drive, Marion, NC, Zip 28752–4989, Mailing Address: P.O. Box 730, Zip 28752–0730; tel. 828/659–5000; Jeffrey M. Judd, President and Chief Executive Officer

MISSION HOSPITAL, 509 Biltmore Avenue, Asheville, NC, Zip 28801–4690; tel. 704/255–4000; Robert F. Burgin, President and Chief Executive Officer

MURPHY MEDICAL CENTER, 4130 U.S. Highway 64 East, Murphy, NC, Zip 28906–7917; tel. 704/837–8161; Mike Stevenson, Administrator

RUTHERFORD HOSPITAL, 288 South Ridgecrest Avenue, Rutherfordton, NC, Zip 28139–3097; tel. 704/286–5000; Robert D. Jones, President

ST. JOSEPH'S HOSPITAL, 428 Biltmore Avenue, Asheville, NC, Zip 28801–4502; tel. 704/255–3100; J. Lewis Daniels, President and Chief Executive Officer

TRANSYLVANIA COMMUNITY HOSPITAL, Hospital Drive, Brevard, NC, Zip 28712–1116, Mailing Address: Box 1116, Zip 28712–1116; tel. 704/884–9111; Robert J. Bednarek, President and Chief Executive Officer

NORTH DAKOTA

HEARTLAND NETWORK, INC.
510 South 4th Street, Fargo, ND 58103; tel. 701/241–7077; Walter Rogers, President & Chief Executive Officer

DAKOTA HEARTLAND HEALTH SYSTEM, 1720 South Univeristy Drive, Fargo, ND, Zip 58103–4994; tel. 701/280–4100; Louis Kauffman, President and Chief Executive Officer

MEDCENTER ONE
300 North Seventh Street, Bismarck, ND 58506–5525; tel. 701/323–6000; Terrance G. Brosseau, President and Chief Executive Officer

JACOBSON MEMORIAL HOSPITAL CARE CENTER, 601 East Street North, Elgin, ND, Zip 58533–0376; tel. 701/584–2792; Jacqueline Seibel, Administrator

MCKENZIE COUNTY MEMORIAL HOSPITAL, 508 North Main Street, Watford City, ND, Zip 58854–7310, Mailing Address: P.O. Box 548, Zip 58854–0548; tel. 701/842–3000; Collette Anderson, Administrator

MEDCENTER ONE, 300 North Seventh Street, Bismarck, ND, Zip 58501–4439, Mailing Address: P.O. Box 5525, Zip 58506–5525; tel. 701/323–6000; Terrance G. Brosseau, President and Chief Executive Officer

RICHARDTON HEALTH CENTER, 212 Third Avenue West, Richardton, ND, Zip 58652–7103, Mailing Address: P.O. Box H., Zip 58652; tel. 701/974–3304; Arlene Mack, Administrator

MERITCARE HEALTH SYSTEM
720 Fourth Street, North, Fargo, ND 58122; tel. 701/234–6000; Roger Gilbertson, M.D., President

GRIGGS COUNTY HOSPITAL AND NURSING HOME, 1200 Roberts Avenue, Cooperstown, ND, Zip 58425, Mailing Address: P.O. Box 728, Zip 58425–0728; tel. 701/797–2221; Wayne Hendrickson, Interim Administrator

UNITED HOSPITAL
1200 South Columbia Road, Grand Forks, ND 58201; tel. 701/780–5000; Rosemary Jacobson, President & Chief Executive Officer

ALTRU HEALTH SYSTEM, 1000 South Columbia Road, Grand Forks, ND, Zip 58201; tel. 701/780–5000; Gregory Gerloff, Chief Executive Officer

OHIO

CLEVELAND HEALTH NETWORK
4700 Rockside Road, Suite 250, Independence, OH 44131; tel. 216/328–7550; Martin P. Hauser, President & CEO

ASHTABULA COUNTY MEDICAL CENTER, 2420 Lake Avenue, Ashtabula, OH, Zip 44004–4993; tel. 440/997–2262; R. D. Richardson, President and Chief Executive Officer

BARBERTON CITIZENS HOSPITAL, 155 Fifth Street N.E., Barberton, OH, Zip 44203–3398; tel. 330/745–1611; Ronald J. Elder, Chief Executive Officer

CHILDREN'S HOSPITAL MEDICAL CENTER OF AKRON, One Perkins Square, Akron, OH, Zip 44308–1062; tel. 330/379–8200; William H. Considine, President

CLEVELAND CLINIC HOSPITAL, 9500 Euclid Avenue, Cleveland, OH, Zip 44195–5108; tel. 216/444–2200; Frank L. Lordeman, Chief Operating Officer

DOCTORS HOSPITAL OF STARK COUNTY, 400 Austin Avenue N.W., Massillon, OH, Zip 44646–3554; tel. 330/837–7200; Thomas E. Cecconi, Chief Executive Officer

EMH AMHERST HOSPITAL, 254 Cleveland Avenue, Amherst, OH, Zip 44001–1699; tel. 440/988–6000; James L. Keegan, President and Chief Executive Officer

EMH REGIONAL MEDICAL CENTER, 630 East River Street, Elyria, OH, Zip 44035–5902; tel. 440/329–7500; Kevin C. Martin, Interim Chief Operating Officer

FAIRVIEW HOSPITAL, 18101 Lorain Avenue, Cleveland, OH, Zip 44111–5656; tel. 216/476–4040; Thomas M. LaMotte, President and Chief Executive Officer

FIRELANDS COMMUNITY HOSPITAL, 1101 Decatur Street, Sandusky, OH, Zip 44870–3335; tel. 419/626–7400; Dennis A. Sokol, President and Chief Executive Officer

FISHER–TITUS MEDICAL CENTER, 272 Benedict Avenue, Norwalk, OH, Zip 44857–2374; tel. 419/668–8101; Patrick J. Martin, President and Chief Executive Officer

HAMOT MEDICAL CENTER, 201 State Street, Erie, PA, Zip 16550–0002; tel. 814/877–6000; John T. Malone, President and Chief Executive Officer

LAKEWOOD HOSPITAL, 14519 Detroit Avenue, Lakewood, OH, Zip 44107–4383; tel. 216/521–4200; Revonda L. Shumaker, R.N., President and Chief Executive Officer

LUTHERAN HOSPITAL, 1730 West 25th Street, Cleveland, OH, Zip 44113; tel. 216/696–4300; Jack E. Bell, Chief Operating Officer

MARYMOUNT HOSPITAL, 12300 McCracken Road, Garfield Heights, OH, Zip 44125–2975; tel. 216/581–0500; Thomas J. Trudell, President and Chief Executive Officer

MERIDIA EUCLID HOSPITAL, 18901 Lake Shore Boulevard, Euclid, OH, Zip 44119–1090; tel. 216/531–9000; Denise Zeman, Chief Operating Officer

MERIDIA HILLCREST HOSPITAL, 6780 Mayfield Road, Cleveland, OH, Zip 44124–2202; tel. 216/449–4500; Catherine B. Leary, R.N., Chief Operating Officer

MERIDIA HURON HOSPITAL, 13951 Terrace Road, Cleveland, OH, Zip 44112–4399; tel. 216/761–3300; Beverly Lozar, Chief Operating Officer

METROHEALTH MEDICAL CENTER, 2500 MetroHealth Drive, Cleveland, OH, Zip 44109–1998; tel. 216/778–7800; Terry R. White, President and Chief Executive Officer

PARMA COMMUNITY GENERAL HOSPITAL, 7007 Powers Boulevard, Parma, OH, Zip 44129–5495; tel. 440/888–1800; Thomas A. Selden, President and Chief Executive Officer

ST. ELIZABETH HEALTH CENTER, 1044 Belmont Avenue, Youngstown, OH, Zip 44501, Mailing Address: P.O. Box 1790, Zip 44501–1790; tel. 330/746–7211; Norman F. Gruber, Chief Operating Officer

ST. JOSEPH HEALTH CENTER, 667 Eastland Avenue S.E., Warren, OH, Zip 44484–4531; tel. 330/841–4000; Robert W. Shroder, Chief Operating Officer

SUMMA HEALTH SYSTEM, Akron, OH, Albert F. Gilbert, Ph.D., President and Chief Executive Officer

WADSWORTH–RITTMAN HOSPITAL, 195 Wadsworth Road, Wadsworth, OH, Zip 44281–9505; tel. 330/334–1504; James W. Brumlow, Jr., President and Chief Executive Officer

COMMUNITY HOSPITALS OF OHIO
1320 West Main Street, Newark, OH 43055–3699; tel. 614/348–4000; William J. Andrews, President

ADENA HEALTH SYSTEM, 272 Hospital Road, Chillicothe, OH, Zip 45601–0708; tel. 740/779–7500; Allen V. Rupiper, President

BERGER HEALTH SYSTEM, 600 North Pickaway Street, Circleville, OH, Zip 43113–1499; tel. 740/474–2126; Brian R. Colfack, CHE, President and Chief Executive Officer

COSHOCTON COUNTY MEMORIAL HOSPITAL, 1460 Orange Street, Coshocton, OH, Zip 43812–6330, Mailing Address: P.O. Box 1330, Zip 43812–6330; tel. 614/622–6411; Gregory M. Nowak, Administrator

FORT HAMILTON–HUGHES MEMORIAL HOSPITAL, 630 Eaton Avenue, Hamilton, OH, Zip 45013–2770; tel. 513/867–2000; James A. Kingsbury, President and Chief Executive Officer

GENESIS HEALTHCARE SYSTEM, 800 Forest Avenue, Zanesville, OH, Zip 43701–2881; tel. 740/454–5000; Thomas L. Sieber, President and Chief Executive Officer

GRADY MEMORIAL HOSPITAL, 561 West Central Avenue, Delaware, OH, Zip 43015–1485; tel. 740/369–8711; Everett P. Weber, Jr., President and Chief Executive Officer

HOCKING VALLEY COMMUNITY HOSPITAL, Route 2, State Route 664, Logan, OH, Zip 43138–0966, Mailing Address: Box 966, Zip 43138–0966; tel. 740/385–5631; Larry Willard, Administrator

HOLZER MEDICAL CENTER, 100 Jackson Pike, Gallipolis, OH, Zip 45631–1563; tel. 740/446–5000; Charles I. Adkins, Jr., President

KNOX COMMUNITY HOSPITAL, 1330 Coshocton Road, Mount Vernon, OH, Zip 43050–1495; tel. 740/393–9000; Robert G. Polahar, Chief Executive Officer

LICKING MEMORIAL HOSPITAL, 1320 West Main Street, Newark, OH, Zip 43055–3699; tel. 740/348–4000; William J. Andrews, President

MARIETTA MEMORIAL HOSPITAL, 401 Matthew Street, Marietta, OH, Zip 45750–1699; tel. 740/374–1400; Larry J. Unroe, President

ST. RITA'S MEDICAL CENTER, 730 West Market Street, Lima, OH, Zip 45801–4670; tel. 419/227–3361; James P. Reber, President

COMPREHENSIVE HEALTHCARE OF OHIO, INC.
630 East River Street, Elyria, OH 44035; tel. 440/329–7591; Donald Miller, Vice President–Operations

EMH AMHERST HOSPITAL, 254 Cleveland Avenue, Amherst, OH, Zip 44001–1699; tel. 440/988–6000; James L. Keegan, President and Chief Executive Officer

EMH REGIONAL MEDICAL CENTER, 630 East River Street, Elyria, OH, Zip 44035–5902; tel. 440/329–7500; Kevin C. Martin, Interim Chief Operating Officer

FIRST INTERHEALTH NETWORK
3454 Oak Alley Court, Suite 510, Toledo, OH 43606; tel. 419/534–2000; Christine Pilliod, Director of Marketing

BETHESDA OAK HOSPITAL, 619 Oak Street, Cincinnati, OH, Zip 45206–1690; tel. 513/569–6111; Linda D. Schaffner, R.N., Vice President and Administrator

FLOWER HOSPITAL, 5200 Harroun Road, Sylvania, OH, Zip 43560–2196; tel. 419/824–1444; Randall Kelley, Senior Vice President and Chief Operating Officer

GOOD SAMARITAN HOSPITAL, 375 Dixmyth Avenue, Cincinnati, OH, Zip 45220–2489; tel. 513/872–1400; Sister Myra James Bradley, Chief Executive Officer

ST. CHARLES MERCY HOSPITAL, 2600 Navarre Avenue, Oregon, OH, Zip 43616–3297; tel. 419/698–7479; Cathleen K. Nelson, President and Chief Executive Officer

ST. LUKE'S HOSPITAL, 5901 Monclova Road, Maumee, OH, Zip 43537–1899; tel. 419/893–5911; Frank J. Bartell, III, President and Chief Executive Officer

ST. VINCENT MERCY MEDICAL CENTER, 2213 Cherry Street, Toledo, OH, Zip 43608–2691; tel. 419/251–3232; Steven L. Mickus, President and Chief Executive Officer

WOOD COUNTY HOSPITAL, 950 West Wooster Street, Bowling Green, OH, Zip 43402–2699; tel. 419/354–8900; Michael A. Miesle, Administrator

HEALTH CLEVELAND
18101 Lorain Avenue, Cleveland, OH 44111; tel. 216/476–7020; Kenneth Misener, Executive Vice President

FAIRVIEW HOSPITAL, 18101 Lorain Avenue, Cleveland, OH, Zip 44111–5656; tel. 216/476–4040; Thomas M. LaMotte, President and Chief Executive Officer

LUTHERAN HOSPITAL, 1730 West 25th Street, Cleveland, OH, Zip 44113; tel. 216/696–4300; Jack E. Bell, Chief Operating Officer

LAKE ERIE HEALTH ALLIANCE
2142 North Cove Boulevard, Toledo, OH 43606; tel. 419/471–3450; John E. Horns, President

BELLEVUE HOSPITAL, 811 Northwest Street, Bellevue, OH, Zip 44811, Mailing Address: P.O. Box 8004, Zip 44811–8004; tel. 419/483–4040; Michael K. Winthrop, President

CRESTLINE HOSPITAL, 700 Columbus Street, Crestline, OH, Zip 44827; tel. 419/683–1212; Susan Brown, Nursing Director and Site Administrator

DEFIANCE HOSPITAL, 1206 East Second Street, Defiance, OH, Zip 43512–2495; tel. 419/783–6955; Richard C. Sommer, Administrator

FIRELANDS COMMUNITY HOSPITAL, 1101 Decatur Street, Sandusky, OH, Zip 44870–3335; tel. 419/626–7400; Dennis A. Sokol, President and Chief Executive Officer

FISHER–TITUS MEDICAL CENTER, 272 Benedict Avenue, Norwalk, OH, Zip 44857–2374; tel. 419/668–8101; Patrick J. Martin, President and Chief Executive Officer

FLOWER HOSPITAL, 5200 Harroun Road, Sylvania, OH, Zip 43560–2196; tel. 419/824–1444; Randall Kelley, Senior Vice President and Chief Operating Officer

FULTON COUNTY HEALTH CENTER, 725 South Shoop Avenue, Wauseon, OH, Zip 43567–1701; tel. 419/335–2015; E. Dean Beck, Administrator

H. B. MAGRUDER MEMORIAL HOSPITAL, 615 Fulton Street, Port Clinton, OH, Zip 43452–2034; tel. 419/734–3131; David R. Norwine, President and Chief Executive Officer

HENRY COUNTY HOSPITAL, 11–600 State Road 424, Napoleon, OH, Zip 43545–9399; tel. 419/592–4015; Robert J. Coholich, Chief Executive Officer

LIMA MEMORIAL HOSPITAL, 1001 Bellefontaine Avenue, Lima, OH, Zip 45804–2894; tel. 419/228–3335; John B. White, President and Chief Executive Officer

MEDICAL COLLEGE OF OHIO HOSPITALS, 3000 Arlington Avenue, Toledo, OH, Zip 43614–5805; tel. 419/381–4172; Frank S. McCullough, M.D., President

MEMORIAL HOSPITAL, 715 South Taft Avenue, Fremont, OH, Zip 43420–3200; tel. 419/332–7321; John A. Gorman, Chief Executive Officer

MERCY HOSPITAL, 485 West Market Street, Tiffin, OH, Zip 44883–0727, Mailing Address: P.O. Box 727, Zip 44883–0727; tel. 419/447–3130; Mark Shugarman, President

MERCY MEMORIAL HOSPITAL, 740 North Macomb Street, Monroe, MI, Zip 48161–9974, Mailing Address: P.O. Box 67, Zip 48161–0067; tel. 734/241–1700; Richard S. Hiltz, President and Chief Executive Officer

ST. FRANCIS HEALTH CARE CENTRE, 401 North Broadway, Green Springs, OH, Zip 44836–9653; tel. 419/639–2626; Dan Schwanke, Chief Executive Officer

WOOD COUNTY HOSPITAL, 950 West Wooster Street, Bowling Green, OH, Zip 43402–2699; tel. 419/354–8900; Michael A. Miesle, Administrator

LAKE HOSPITAL SYSTEM, INC.
10 East Washington, Painesville, OH 44077; tel. 440/354–1642; Cynthia Moore–Hardy, President & Chief Executive Officer

LAKE HOSPITAL SYSTEM, 10 East Washington, Painesville, OH, Zip 44077–3472; tel. 216/354–2400; Cynthia Ann Moore–Hardy, President and Chief Executive Officer

MERCY REGIONAL HEALTH SYSTEM, GREATER CINCINNATI
4340 Glendale–Millford Road, Suite 100, Cincinnati, OH 45242; tel. 513/483–5200; Julie Hanser, President and Chief Executive Officer

CLERMONT MERCY HOSPITAL, 3000 Hospital Drive, Batavia, OH, Zip 45103–1998; tel. 513/732–8200; Karen S. Ehrat, Ph.D., President

MERCY HOSPITAL, 100 River Front Plaza, Hamilton, OH, Zip 45011–2780, Mailing Address: P.O. Box 418, Zip 45012–0418; tel. 513/870–7080; David A. Ferrell, President

MERCY HOSPITAL ANDERSON, 7500 State Road, Cincinnati, OH, Zip 45255–2492; tel. 513/624–4500; Karen S. Ehrat, Ph.D., President

MERIDA HEALTH SYSTEM
6700 Beta Drive, Suite 200, Mayfield Village, OH 44143; tel. 216/446–8000; Charles B. Miner, President & Chief Executive Officer

MERIDIA EUCLID HOSPITAL, 18901 Lake Shore Boulevard, Euclid, OH, Zip 44119–1090; tel. 216/531–9000; Denise Zeman, Chief Operating Officer

MERIDIA HILLCREST HOSPITAL, 6780 Mayfield Road, Cleveland, OH, Zip 44124–2202; tel. 216/449–4500; Catherine B. Leary, R.N., Chief Operating Officer

MERIDIA HURON HOSPITAL, 13951 Terrace Road, Cleveland, OH, Zip 44112–4399; tel. 216/761–3300; Beverly Lozar, Chief Operating Officer

MERIDIA SOUTH POINTE HOSPITAL, 4110 Warrensville Center Road, Warrensville Heights, OH, Zip 44122–7099; tel. 216/491–6000; Kathleen A. Rice, Chief Operating Officer

MOUNT CARMEL HEALTH SYSTEM
793 West State Street, Columbus, OH 43222; tel. 614/234–5000; Dale St. Arnold, President & Chief Executive Officer

ADENA HEALTH SYSTEM, 272 Hospital Road, Chillicothe, OH, Zip 45601–0708; tel. 740/779–7500; Allen V. Rupiper, President

BERGER HEALTH SYSTEM, 600 North Pickaway Street, Circleville, OH, Zip 43113–1499; tel. 740/474–2126; Brian R. Colfack, CHE, President and Chief Executive Officer

MOUNT CARMEL HEALTH SYSTEM, Columbus, OH, Mailing Address: 793 West State Street, Zip 43222–1551; tel. 614/234–5423; Joseph Calvaruso, Interim Chief Executive Officer

ST. ANN'S HOSPITAL, 500 South Cleveland Avenue, Westerville, OH, Zip 43081–8998; tel. 614/898–4000

NORTHEAST OHIO HEALTH NETWORK
400 Wabash Avenue, Akron, OH 44307; tel. 330/384–6781; David Kantor, Executive Director

AKRON GENERAL MEDICAL CENTER, 400 Wabash Avenue, Akron, OH, Zip 44307–2433; tel. 330/384–6000; Alan J. Bleyer, President

BARBERTON CITIZENS HOSPITAL, 155 Fifth Street N.E., Barberton, OH, Zip 44203–3398; tel. 330/745–1611; Ronald J. Elder, Chief Executive Officer

CHILDREN'S HOSPITAL MEDICAL CENTER OF AKRON, One Perkins Square, Akron, OH, Zip 44308–1062; tel. 330/379–8200; William H. Considine, President

CUYAHOGA FALLS GENERAL HOSPITAL, 1900 23rd Street, Cuyahoga Falls, OH, Zip 44223–1499; tel. 330/971–7000; Fred Anthony, President and Chief Executive Officer

MEDINA GENERAL HOSPITAL, 1000 East Washington Street, Medina, OH, Zip 44256–2170, Mailing Address: P.O. Box 427, Zip 44258–0427; tel. 330/725–1000; Gary D. Hallman, President and Chief Executive Officer

ROBINSON MEMORIAL HOSPITAL, 6847 North Chestnut Street, Ravenna, OH, Zip 44266–1204, Mailing Address: P.O. Box 1204, Zip 44266–1204; tel. 330/297–0811; Stephen Colecchi, President and Chief Executive Officer

OHIO STATE HEALTH NETWORK
1375 Perry Street 5th Floor Batelle, Columbus, OH 43201; tel. 614/293–3685; Ewing Crawfis, Board Chairman

ARTHUR G. JAMES CANCER HOSPITAL AND RESEARCH INSTITUTE, 300 West Tenth Avenue, Columbus, OH, Zip 43210–1240; tel. 614/293–5485; David E. Schuller, M.D., Chief Executive Officer

BARNESVILLE HOSPITAL ASSOCIATION, 639 West Main Street, Barnesville, OH, Zip 43713–1096, Mailing Address: P.O. Box 309, Zip 43713–0309; tel. 740/425–3941; Richard L. Doan, Chief Executive Officer

MARY RUTAN HOSPITAL, 205 Palmer Avenue, Bellefontaine, OH, Zip 43311–2298; tel. 937/592–4015; Ewing H. Crawfis, President

OHIO STATE UNIVERSITY MEDICAL CENTER, 410 West 10th Avenue, Columbus, OH, Zip 43210–1240; tel. 614/293–8000; R. Reed Fraley, Associate Vice President for Health Sciences and Chief Executive Officer

PIKE COMMUNITY HOSPITAL, 100 Dawn Lane, Waverly, OH, Zip 45690–9664; tel. 740/947–2186; Richard E. Sobota, President and Chief Executive Officer

RIVER VALLEY HEALTH SYSTEM, 2228 South Ninth Street, Ironton, OH, Zip 45638–2526; tel. 614/532–3231; Terry L. Vanderhoof, President and Chief Executive Officer

WYANDOT MEMORIAL HOSPITAL, 885 North Sandusky Avenue, Upper Sandusky, OH, Zip 43351–1098; tel. 419/294–4991; Joseph A. D'Ettorre, Chief Executive Officer

PROMEDICA HEALTH SYSTEM
2121 Hughes Drive, Toledo, OH 43606; tel. 419/291–3686; William Glover, President & CEO

FLOWER HOSPITAL, 5200 Harroun Road, Sylvania, OH, Zip 43560–2196; tel. 419/824–1444; Randall Kelley, Senior Vice President and Chief Operating Officer

THE TOLEDO HOSPITAL, 2142 North Cove Boulevard, Toledo, OH, Zip 43606–3896; tel. 419/471–4000; Barbara Steele, President

SAINT LUKES MEDICAL CENTER
11311 Shaker Boulevard, Cleveland, OH 44104; tel. 216/368–7354; James L. Heffernan, Senior Vice President

SAINT LUKE'S MEDICAL CENTER, 11311 Shaker Boulevard, Cleveland, OH, Zip 44104–3805; tel. 216/368–7000; Jeffrey S. Jeney, President and Chief Executive Officer

SUMMA HEALTH SYSTEM
525 East Market Street, Akron, OH 44309; tel. 330/375–3000; Albert Gilbert, Ph.d., President

SUMMA HEALTH SYSTEM, Akron, OH, Albert F. Gilbert, Ph.D., President and Chief Executive Officer

SUMMA HEALTH SYSTEM, Akron, OH, Albert F. Gilbert, Ph.D., President and Chief Executive Officer

THE HEALTHCARE ALLIANCE OF GREATER CINCINNATI
2060 Reading Road, Cincinnati, OH 45219; tel. 513/632–3700; Jack Cook, Chief Executive Officer

Section B

CHRIST HOSPITAL, 2139 Auburn Avenue, Cincinnati, OH, Zip 45219–2989; tel. 513/369–2000; Claus von Zychlin, Senior Executive Officer

JEWISH HOSPITAL KENWOOD, 4777 East Galbraith Road, Cincinnati, OH, Zip 45236; tel. 513/745–2200; Warren C. Falberg, Senior Executive Officer

ST. LUKE HOSPITAL EAST, 85 North Grand Avenue, Fort Thomas, KY, Zip 41075–1796; tel. 606/572–3100; Daniel M. Vinson, CPA, Senior Executive Officer

ST. LUKE HOSPITAL WEST, 7380 Turfway Road, Florence, KY, Zip 41042–1337; tel. 606/525–5200; Daniel M. Vinson, CPA, Interim Administrator

UNIVERSITY HOSPITAL, 234 Goodman Street, Cincinnati, OH, Zip 45267–0700; tel. 513/558–1000; Elliot G. Cohen, Senior Executive Officer

THE METROHEALTH SYSTEM
2500 MetroHealth Drive, Cleveland, OH 44109–1998; tel. 216/398–6000; Terry White, President & Chief Executive Officer

METROHEALTH MEDICAL CENTER, 2500 MetroHealth Drive, Cleveland, OH, Zip 44109–1998; tel. 216/778–7800; Terry R. White, President and Chief Executive Officer

THE MOUNT SINAI HEALTH CARE SYSTEM
One Mount Sinai Drive, Cleveland, OH 44106; tel. 216/421–4000; Robert Shakno, President & Chief Executive Officer

MT. SINAI MEDICAL CENTER, One Mt Sinai Drive, Cleveland, OH, Zip 44106–4198; tel. 216/421–3400; Geoffrey Moebivs, Chief Operating Officer

UHHS LAURELWOOD HOSPITAL, 35900 Euclid Avenue, Willoughby, OH, Zip 44094–4648; tel. 440/953–3000; Farshid Afsarifard, Executive Director

TRIHEALTH
375 Dixsmyth, Cincinnati, OH 45220; tel. 513/872–1828; John Prout, President & Chief Executive Officer

BETHESDA NORTH HOSPITAL, 10500 Montgomery Road, Cincinnati, OH, Zip 45242–4415; tel. 513/745–1111; John S. Prout, President and Chief Executive Officer

BETHESDA OAK HOSPITAL, 619 Oak Street, Cincinnati, OH, Zip 45206–1690; tel. 513/569–6111; Linda D. Schaffner, R.N., Vice President and Administrator

GOOD SAMARITAN HOSPITAL, 375 Dixmyth Avenue, Cincinnati, OH, Zip 45220–2489; tel. 513/872–1400; Sister Myra James Bradley, Chief Executive Officer

UNITED HEALTH PARTNERS
2213 Cherry Street, Toledo, OH 43608; tel. 419/321–3232; David Crane, Vice President of Marketing

BELLEVUE HOSPITAL, 811 Northwest Street, Bellevue, OH, Zip 44811, Mailing Address: P.O. Box 8004, Zip 44811–8004; tel. 419/483–4040; Michael K. Winthrop, President

DEFIANCE HOSPITAL, 1206 East Second Street, Defiance, OH, Zip 43512–2495; tel. 419/783–6955; Richard C. Sommer, Administrator

FISHER–TITUS MEDICAL CENTER, 272 Benedict Avenue, Norwalk, OH, Zip 44857–2374; tel. 419/668–8101; Patrick J. Martin, President and Chief Executive Officer

FOSTORIA COMMUNITY HOSPITAL, 501 Van Buren Street, Fostoria, OH, Zip 44830–0907, Mailing Address: P.O. Box 907, Zip 44830–0907; tel. 419/435–7734; Brad A. Higgins, President and Chief Executive Officer

FULTON COUNTY HEALTH CENTER, 725 South Shoop Avenue, Wauseon, OH, Zip 43567–1701; tel. 419/335–2015; E. Dean Beck, Administrator

MEMORIAL HOSPITAL, 715 South Taft Avenue, Fremont, OH, Zip 43420–3200; tel. 419/332–7321; John A. Gorman, Chief Executive Officer

MERCY HOSPITAL, 485 West Market Street, Tiffin, OH, Zip 44883–0727, Mailing Address: P.O. Box 727, Zip 44883–0727; tel. 419/447–3130; Mark Shugarman, President

MERCY HOSPITAL–WILLARD, 110 East Howard Street, Willard, OH, Zip 44890–1611; tel. 419/933–2931; James O. Detwiler, President

PROVIDENCE HOSPITAL, 1912 Hayes Avenue, Sandusky, OH, Zip 44870–4736; tel. 419/621–7000; Sister Nancy Linenkugel, FACHE, President and Chief Executive Officer

ST. VINCENT MERCY MEDICAL CENTER, 2213 Cherry Street, Toledo, OH, Zip 43608–2691; tel. 419/251–3232; Steven L. Mickus, President and Chief Executive Officer

WOOD COUNTY HOSPITAL, 950 West Wooster Street, Bowling Green, OH, Zip 43402–2699; tel. 419/354–8900; Michael A. Miesle, Administrator

UNIVERSITY HOSPITALS HEALTH SYSTEM
11100 Euclid Avenue, Cleveland, OH 44106; tel. 216/844–1000; James G. Lubetkin, Vice President Corporate Communications

UHHS BEDFORD MEDICAL CENTER, 44 Blaine Avenue, Bedford, OH, Zip 44146–2799; tel. 440/439–2000; Arlene A. Rak, R.N., President

UHHS GEAUGA REGIONAL HOSPITAL, 13207 Ravenna Road, Chardon, OH, Zip 44024–9012; tel. 440/269–6000; Richard J. Frenchie, President and Chief Executive Officer

UHHS–MEMORIAL HOSPITAL OF GENEVA, 870 West Main Street, Geneva, OH, Zip 44041–1295; tel. 440/466–1141; Gerard D. Klein, Chief Executive Officer

UNIVERSITY HOSPITALS OF CLEVELAND, 11100 Euclid Avenue, Cleveland, OH, Zip 44106–2602; tel. 216/844–1000; Farah M. Walters, President and Chief Executive Officer

UPPER VALLEY MEDICAL CENTERS, INC.
3130 North Dixie Highway, Troy, OH 45373; tel. 937/332–7858; Michele Elam, Financial Coordinator

WEST CENTRAL OHIO REGIONAL HEALTHCARE ALLIANCE, LTD.
730 West Market Street, Lima, OH 45801; tel. 419/226–9750; P. Anthony Long, Executive Director

JOINT TOWNSHIP DISTRICT MEMORIAL HOSPITAL, 200 St. Clair Street, Saint Marys, OH, Zip 45885–2400; tel. 419/394–3387; James R. Chick, President

MARY RUTAN HOSPITAL, 205 Palmer Avenue, Bellefontaine, OH, Zip 43311–2298; tel. 937/592–4015; Ewing H. Crawfis, President

MERCER COUNTY JOINT TOWNSHIP COMMUNITY HOSPITAL, 800 West Main Street, Coldwater, OH, Zip 45828–1698; tel. 419/678–2341; James W. Isaacs, Chief Executive Officer

ST. RITA'S MEDICAL CENTER, 730 West Market Street, Lima, OH, Zip 45801–4670; tel. 419/227–3361; James P. Reber, President

VAN WERT COUNTY HOSPITAL, 1250 South Washington Street, Van Wert, OH, Zip 45891–2599; tel. 419/238–2390; Mark J. Minick, President and Chief Executive Officer

OKLAHOMA

EASTERN OKLAHOMA HEALTH NETWORK
P.O. Box 14147, Tulsa, OK 74114; tel. 918/579–1000; Thomas P. Hadley, Executive Vice President

COLUMBIA DOCTORS HOSPITAL, 2323 South Harvard Avenue, Tulsa, OK, Zip 74114–3370; tel. 918/744–4000; Anthony R. Young, President and Chief Executive Officer

HILLCREST MEDICAL CENTER, 1120 South Utica, Tulsa, OK, Zip 74104–4090; tel. 918/579–1000; Donald A. Lorack, Jr., President and Chief Executive Officer

WAGONER COMMUNITY HOSPITAL, 1200 West Cherokee, Wagoner, OK, Zip 74467–4681, Mailing Address: Box 407, Zip 74477–0407; tel. 918/485–5514; John W. Crawford, Chief Executive Officer

FIRST HEALTH WEST
4411 West Gore Boulevard, Lawton, OK 73505; tel. 405/355–8620; Tanya Case, Director of Networks

CARNEGIE TRI–COUNTY MUNICIPAL HOSPITAL, 102 North Broadway, Carnegie, OK, Zip 73015, Mailing Address: P.O. Box 97, Zip 73015–0097; tel. 580/654–1050; Phil Hawkins, Administrator

COMANCHE COUNTY MEMORIAL HOSPITAL, 3401 Gore Boulevard, Lawton, OK, Zip 73505–0129, Mailing Address: Box 129, Zip 73502–0129; tel. 580/355–8620; Randall K. Segler, Chief Executive Officer

CORDELL MEMORIAL HOSPITAL, 1220 North Glenn English Street, Cordell, OK, Zip 73632–2099; tel. 580/832–3339; Charles H. Greene, Jr., Administrator

ELKVIEW GENERAL HOSPITAL, 429 West Elm Street, Hobart, OK, Zip 73651–1699; tel. 580/726–3324; J. W. Finch, Jr., Administrator

HARMON MEMORIAL HOSPITAL, 400 East Chestnut Street, Hollis, OK, Zip 73550–2030, Mailing Address: P.O. Box 791, Zip 73550–0791; tel. 580/688–3363; Al Allee, Administrator

JEFFERSON COUNTY HOSPITAL, Highway 70 and 81, Waurika, OK, Zip 73573, Mailing Address: P.O. Box 90, Zip 73573–0090; tel. 580/228–2344; Curtis R. Pryor, Administrator

SOUTHWESTERN MEMORIAL HOSPITAL, 215 North Kansas Street, Weatherford, OK, Zip 73096–5499; tel. 580/772–5551; Ronnie D. Walker, President

HILLCREST HEALTHCARE SYSTEM
1120 South Utica Avenue, Tulsa, OK 74104–4090; tel. 918/579–1000; Donald A. Lorack, Jr, President & Chief Executive Officer

CHILDREN'S MEDICAL CENTER, 5300 East Skelly Drive, Tulsa, OK, Zip 74135–6599, Mailing Address: Box 35648, Zip 74153–0648; tel. 918/664–6600; Gerard J. Rothlein, Jr., President and Chief Executive Officer

CUSHING REGIONAL HOSPITAL, 1027 East Cherry Street, Cushing, OK, Zip 74023–4101, Mailing Address: P.O. Box 1409, Zip 74023–1409; tel. 918/225–2915; Ron Cackler, President and Chief Executive Officer

EASTERN OKLAHOMA MEDICAL CENTER, 105 Wall Street, Poteau, OK, Zip 74953, Mailing Address: P.O. Box 1148, Zip 74953–1148; tel. 918/647–8161; Craig R. Cudworth, Chief Executive Officer

HILLCREST MEDICAL CENTER, 1120 South Utica, Tulsa, OK, Zip 74104–4090; tel. 918/579–1000; Donald A. Lorack, Jr., President and Chief Executive Officer

INTEGRIS HEALTH
3366 Northwest Expressway, Oklahoma City, OK 73112; tel. 405/949–6066; Stanley Hupfeld, President & Chief Executive Officer

BLACKWELL REGIONAL HOSPITAL, 710 South 13th Street, Blackwell, OK, Zip 74631–3700; tel. 580/363–2311; Greg Martin, Administrator and Chief Executive Officer

CHOCTAW MEMORIAL HOSPITAL, 1405 East Kirk Road, Hugo, OK, Zip 74743–3603; tel. 580/326–6414; Michael R. Morel, Administrator

DRUMRIGHT MEMORIAL HOSPITAL, 501 South Lou Allard Drive, Drumright, OK, Zip 74030–4899; tel. 918/352–2525; Jerry Jones, Administrator

INTEGRIS BAPTIST MEDICAL CENTER, 3300 N.W. Expressway, Oklahoma City, OK, Zip 73112–4481; tel. 405/949–3011; Thomas R. Rice, FACHE, President and Chief Operating Officer

INTEGRIS BAPTIST REGIONAL HEALTH CENTER, 200 Second Street S.W., Miami, OK, Zip 74354–6830, Mailing Address: P.O. Box 1207, Zip 74355–1207; tel. 918/540–7100; Steven G. Kelly, Consolidated Administrator

INTEGRIS BASS BAPTIST HEALTH CENTER, 600 South Monroe Street, Enid, OK, Zip 73701, Mailing Address: P.O. Box 3168, Zip 73702–3168; tel. 580/233–2300; Wayne A. Sensor, Administrator

INTEGRIS GROVE GENERAL HOSPITAL, 1310 South Main Street, Grove, OK, Zip 74344-1310; tel. 918/786-2243; Dee Renshaw, Administrator

INTEGRIS SOUTHWEST MEDICAL CENTER, 4401 South Western, Oklahoma City, OK, Zip 73109-3441; tel. 405/636-7000; Thomas R. Rice, FACHE, President and Chief Operating Officer

INTERGRIS CLINTON REGIONAL HOSPITAL, 100 North 30th Street, Clinton, OK, Zip 73601-3117, Mailing Address: P.O. Box 1569, Zip 73601-1569; tel. 580/323-2363; Jerry Jones, Administrator

MARSHALL MEMORIAL HOSPITAL, 1 Hospital Drive, Madill, OK, Zip 73446, Mailing Address: P.O. Box 827, Zip 73446-0827; tel. 405/795-3384; Norma Howard, Administrator

MAYES COUNTY MEDICAL CENTER, 129 North Kentucky Street, Pryor, OK, Zip 74361-4211, Mailing Address: P.O. Box 278, Zip 74362-0278; tel. 918/825-1600; W. Charles Jordan, Administrator

PAWNEE MUNICIPAL HOSPITAL, 1212 Fourth Street, Pawnee, OK, Zip 74058-4046, Mailing Address: P.O. Box 467, Zip 74058-0467; tel. 918/762-2577; John Ketring, Administrator

STROUD MUNICIPAL HOSPITAL, Highway 66 West, Stroud, OK, Zip 74079, Mailing Address: P.O. Box 530, Zip 74079-0530; tel. 918/968-3571; James D. Moore, Administrator

MERCY HEALTH SYSTEM
4300 West Memorial Road, Oklahoma City, OK 73120; tel. 405/752-3754; Bruce F. Buchanan, President & Chief Executive Officer

MERCY HEALTH CENTER, 4300 West Memorial Road, Oklahoma City, OK, Zip 73120-8362; tel. 405/755-1515; Bruce F. Buchanan, FACHE, President and Chief Executive Officer

MERCY MEMORIAL HEALTH CENTER, 1011 14th Street N.W., Ardmore, OK, Zip 73401-1889; tel. 405/223-5400; Bobby G. Thompson, President and Chief Executive Officer

ST. MARY'S MERCY HOSPITAL, 305 South Fifth Street, Enid, OK, Zip 73701-5899, Mailing Address: Box 232, Zip 73702-0232; tel. 580/233-6100; Frank Lopez, FACHE, President and Chief Executive Officer

UNIVERSITY HEALTH PARTNERS
6501 North Broadway, Oklahoma City, OK 73116; tel. 405/879-0999; David Dunlap, CEO

EDMOND MEDICAL CENTER, 1 South Bryant Street, Edmond, OK, Zip 73034-4798; tel. 405/359-5530; Stanley D. Tatum, Chief Executive Officer

PRESBYTERIAN HOSPITAL, 700 N.E. 13th Street, Oklahoma City, OK, Zip 73104-5070; tel. 405/271-5100; James O'Loughlin, Chief Executive Officer

SEMINOLE MUNICIPAL HOSPITAL, 606 West Evans Street, Seminole, OK, Zip 74868-3897, Mailing Address: P.O. Box 2130, Zip 74818-2130; tel. 405/382-0600; Stephen R. Schoaps, Chief Executive Officer

SOUTHWESTERN MEDICAL CENTER, 5602 S.W. Lee Boulevard, Lawton, OK, Zip 73505-9635, Mailing Address: P.O. Box 7290, Zip 73506-7290; tel. 580/531-4700; Thomas L. Rine, President and Chief Executive Officer

THE UNIVERSITY HOSPITALS, 920 N.E. 13th Street, Oklahoma City, OK, Zip 73104-5068, Mailing Address: P.O. Box 26307, Zip 73126-6307; tel. 405/271-5911; R. Timothy Coussons, M.D., President and Chief Executive Officer

UNIVERSITY HOSPITALS
P.O. Box 26307, Oklahoma City, OK 73126; tel. 405/271-5911; R. Tim Cousson, MD, Chief Executive Officer

THE UNIVERSITY HOSPITALS, 920 N.E. 13th Street, Oklahoma City, OK, Zip 73104-5068, Mailing Address: P.O. Box 26307, Zip 73126-6307; tel. 405/271-5911; R. Timothy Coussons, M.D., President and Chief Executive Officer

OREGON

CENTRAL OREGON HOSP NETWORK (CONET)
2500 NorthEast Neff Road, Bend, OR 97701; tel. 541/388-7702; James T. Lussier, Chief Executive Officer

BLUE MOUNTAIN HOSPITAL, 170 Ford Road, John Day, OR, Zip 97845; tel. 541/575-1311; David G. Triebes, Chief Executive Officer

CENTRAL OREGON DISTRICT HOSPITAL, 1253 North Canal Boulevard, Redmond, OR, Zip 97756-1395; tel. 541/548-8131; James A. Diegel, CHE, Executive Director

HARNEY DISTRICT HOSPITAL, 557 West Washington Street, Burns, OR, Zip 97720-1497; tel. 503/573-7281; David L. Harman, Administrator

LAKE DISTRICT HOSPITAL, 700 South J. Street, Lakeview, OR, Zip 97630-1679; tel. 503/947-2114; Richard T. Moore, Administrator

MOUNTAIN VIEW HOSPITAL DISTRICT, 470 N.E. A. Street, Madras, OR, Zip 97741; tel. 541/475-3882; Ronald W. Barnes, Executive Director

PIONEER MEMORIAL HOSPITAL, 1201 North Elm Street, Prineville, OR, Zip 97754; tel. 541/447-6254; Donald J. Wee, Executive Director

ST. CHARLES MEDICAL CENTER, 2500 N.E. Neff Road, Bend, OR, Zip 97701-6015; tel. 541/382-4321; James T. Lussier, President and Chief Executive Officer

HEALTH FUTURE, INC.
825 East Main Street, Suite D., Medford, OR 97504; tel. 503/772-3062; John Meenaghan, Executive Director

ALBANY GENERAL HOSPITAL, 1046 West Sixth Avenue, Albany, OR, Zip 97321-1999; tel. 541/812-4000; Richard J. Delano, President

ASHLAND COMMUNITY HOSPITAL, 280 Maple Street, Ashland, OR, Zip 97520, Mailing Address: P.O. Box 98, Zip 97520; tel. 541/482-2441; James R. Watson, Administrator

BAY AREA HOSPITAL, 1775 Thompson Road, Coos Bay, OR, Zip 97420-2198; tel. 541/269-8111; Dale Jessup, President and Chief Executive Officer

COLUMBIA MEMORIAL HOSPITAL, 2111 Exchange Street, Astoria, OR, Zip 97103; tel. 503/325-4321; Terry O. Finklein, Chief Executive Officer

DOUGLAS COMMUNITY MEDICAL CENTER, 738 West Harvard Avenue, Roseburg, OR, Zip 97470-2996; tel. 541/440-2800; Ronald E. Yates, Chief Executive Officer

GOOD SAMARITAN HOSPITAL CORVALLIS, 3600 N.W. Samaritan Drive, Corvallis, OR, Zip 97330, Mailing Address: P.O. Box 1068, Zip 97339; tel. 541/757-5111; Larry A. Mullins, President and Chief Executive Officer

GOOD SHEPHERD COMMUNITY HOSPITAL, 610 N.W. 11th Street, Hermiston, OR, Zip 97838-9696; tel. 541/567-6483; Dennis E. Burke, President

GRANDE RONDE HOSPITAL, 900 Sunset Drive, La Grande, OR, Zip 97850, Mailing Address: P.O. Box 3290, Zip 97850; tel. 541/963-8421; James A. Mattes, President

LEBANON COMMUNITY HOSPITAL, 525 North Santiam Highway, Lebanon, OR, Zip 97355, Mailing Address: P.O. Box 739, Zip 97355-0739; tel. 541/258-2101; Steven W. Jasperson, Executive Vice President Operations

MERCY MEDICAL CENTER, 2700 Stewart Parkway, Roseburg, OR, Zip 97470-1297; tel. 541/673-0611; Victor J. Fresolone, FACHE, President and Chief Executive Officer

MERLE WEST MEDICAL CENTER, 2865 Daggett Street, Klamath Falls, OR, Zip 97601-1180; tel. 541/882-6311; Paul R. Stewart, President and Chief Executive Officer

MID-COLUMBIA MEDICAL CENTER, 1700 East 19th Street, The Dalles, OR, Zip 97058-3316; tel. 541/296-1111; Mark D. Scott, President

OREGON HEALTH SCIENCES UNIVERSITY HOSPITAL, 3181 S.W. Sam Jackson Park Road, Portland, OR, Zip 97201-3098; tel. 503/494-8311; Roy G. Vinyard, Chief Administrative Officer

ROGUE VALLEY MEDICAL CENTER, 2825 East Barnett Road, Medford, OR, Zip 97504-8332; tel. 541/608-4900; Gary A. Sherwood, Executive Vice President

SILVERTON HOSPITAL, 342 Fairview Street, Silverton, OR, Zip 97381; tel. 503/873-1500; William E. Winter, Administrative Director

ST. CHARLES MEDICAL CENTER, 2500 N.E. Neff Road, Bend, OR, Zip 97701-6015; tel. 541/382-4321; James T. Lussier, President and Chief Executive Officer

THREE RIVERS COMMUNITY HOSPITAL AND HEALTH CENTER--DIMMICK, 715 N.W. Dimmick Street, Grants Pass, OR, Zip 97526-1596; tel. 541/476-6831; Mark W. Folger, Senior Vice President

INTER COMMUNITY HEALTH NETWORK
3600 North Samaritan Drive, Corvallis, OR 97339; tel. 503/757-5111; Larry Mullins, Chairman

ALBANY GENERAL HOSPITAL, 1046 West Sixth Avenue, Albany, OR, Zip 97321-1999; tel. 541/812-4000; Richard J. Delano, President

GOOD SAMARITAN HOSPITAL CORVALLIS, 3600 N.W. Samaritan Drive, Corvallis, OR, Zip 97330, Mailing Address: P.O. Box 1068, Zip 97339; tel. 541/757-5111; Larry A. Mullins, President and Chief Executive Officer

LEBANON COMMUNITY HOSPITAL, 525 North Santiam Highway, Lebanon, OR, Zip 97355, Mailing Address: P.O. Box 739, Zip 97355-0739; tel. 541/258-2101; Steven W. Jasperson, Executive Vice President Operations

LEGACY HEALTH SYSTEM
1919 NorthWest Lovejoy Street, Portland, OR 97209; tel. 503/415-8600; John G. King, President & Chief Executive Officer

LEGACY EMANUEL HOSPITAL AND HEALTH CENTER, 2801 North Gantenbein Avenue, Portland, OR, Zip 97227-1674; tel. 503/413-2200; Stephani White, Vice President and Site Administrator

LEGACY GOOD SAMARITAN HOSPITAL AND MEDICAL CENTER, 1015 N.W. 22nd Avenue, Portland, OR, Zip 97210; tel. 503/413-7711; John M. Mootry, Vice President and Site Administrator

LEGACY MERIDIAN PARK HOSPITAL, 19300 S.W. 65th Avenue, Tualatin, OR, Zip 97062-9741; tel. 503/692-1212; Jeff Cushing, Vice President and Site Administrator

LEGACY MOUNT HOOD MEDICAL CENTER, 24800 S.E. Stark, Gresham, OR, Zip 97030-0154; tel. 503/667-1122; Jane C. Cummins, Senior Vice President Clinical Operations

OREGON HEALTH SYSTEM IN COLLABORATION
4000 Kruse Way Place B2-100, Lake Oswego, OR 97035; tel. 503/636-2204; Kent Ballantyne, Project Coordinator

KAISER SUNNYSIDE MEDICAL CENTER, 10180 S.E. Sunnyside Road, Clackamas, OR, Zip 97015-9303; tel. 503/571-4002; Alide Chase, Administrator

LEGACY EMANUEL HOSPITAL AND HEALTH CENTER, 2801 North Gantenbein Avenue, Portland, OR, Zip 97227-1674; tel. 503/413-2200; Stephani White, Vice President and Site Administrator

LEGACY GOOD SAMARITAN HOSPITAL AND MEDICAL CENTER, 1015 N.W. 22nd Avenue, Portland, OR, Zip 97210; tel. 503/413-7711; John M. Mootry, Vice President and Site Administrator

LEGACY MERIDIAN PARK HOSPITAL, 19300 S.W. 65th Avenue, Tualatin, OR, Zip 97062-9741; tel. 503/692-1212; Jeff Cushing, Vice President and Site Administrator

LEGACY MOUNT HOOD MEDICAL CENTER, 24800 S.E. Stark, Gresham, OR, Zip 97030-0154; tel. 503/667-1122; Jane C. Cummins, Senior Vice President Clinical Operations

Section B

PROVIDENCE MEDFORD MEDICAL CENTER, 1111
Crater Lake Avenue, Medford, OR,
Zip 97504–6241; tel. 541/732–5000; Charles
T. Wright, Chief Executive, Southern Oregon
Service Area

PROVIDENCE MILWAUKIE HOSPITAL, 10150 S.E.
32nd Avenue, Milwaukie, OR, Zip 97222–6593;
tel. 503/513–8300; Janice Burger, Operations
Administrator

PROVIDENCE NEWBERG HOSPITAL, 501 Villa Road,
Newberg, OR, Zip 97132; tel. 503/537–1555;
Mark W. Meinert, CHE, Chief Executive, Yamhill
Service Area

PROVIDENCE PORTLAND MEDICAL CENTER, 4805
N.E. Glisan Street, Portland, OR,
Zip 97213–2967; tel. 503/215–1111; David T.
Underriner, Operations Administrator

PROVIDENCE SEASIDE HOSPITAL, 725 South
Wahanna Road, Seaside, OR, Zip 97138–7735;
tel. 503/717–7000; Ronald Swanson, Chief
Executive North Coast Service Area

PROVIDENCE ST. VINCENT MEDICAL CENTER, 9205
S.W. Barnes Road, Portland, OR,
Zip 97225–6661; tel. 503/216–1234; Donald
Elsom, Operations Administrator

PROVIDENCE HEALTH SYSTEM IN OREGON
1235 N.E. 47th Avenue, Portland, OR 97213;
tel. 503/215–4700; John Lee, Regional Vice
President

PROVIDENCE MEDFORD MEDICAL CENTER, 1111
Crater Lake Avenue, Medford, OR,
Zip 97504–6241; tel. 541/732–5000; Charles
T. Wright, Chief Executive, Southern Oregon
Service Area

PROVIDENCE MILWAUKIE HOSPITAL, 10150 S.E.
32nd Avenue, Milwaukie, OR, Zip 97222–6593;
tel. 503/513–8300; Janice Burger, Operations
Administrator

PROVIDENCE NEWBERG HOSPITAL, 501 Villa Road,
Newberg, OR, Zip 97132; tel. 503/537–1555;
Mark W. Meinert, CHE, Chief Executive, Yamhill
Service Area

PROVIDENCE PORTLAND MEDICAL CENTER, 4805
N.E. Glisan Street, Portland, OR,
Zip 97213–2967; tel. 503/215–1111; David T.
Underriner, Operations Administrator

PROVIDENCE SEASIDE HOSPITAL, 725 South
Wahanna Road, Seaside, OR, Zip 97138–7735;
tel. 503/717–7000; Ronald Swanson, Chief
Executive North Coast Service Area

PROVIDENCE ST. VINCENT MEDICAL CENTER, 9205
S.W. Barnes Road, Portland, OR,
Zip 97225–6661; tel. 503/216–1234; Donald
Elsom, Operations Administrator

PENNSYLVANIA

ALBERT EINSTEIN HEALTHCARE NETWORK
5501 Old York Road, Philadelphia, PA
19141–3098; tel. 215/456–7890; Martin
Goldsmith, President & Chief Executive Officer

ALBERT EINSTEIN MEDICAL CENTER, 5501 Old York
Road, Philadelphia, PA, Zip 19141–3098;
tel. 215/456–7890; Martin Goldsmith, President

BELMONT CENTER FOR COMPREHENSIVE
TREATMENT, 4200 Monument Road,
Philadelphia, PA, Zip 19131–1625;
tel. 215/877–2000; Jack H. Dembow, General
Director and Vice President

ALPHA HEALTH NETWORK
Foster Plaza, Pittsburgh, PA 15220;
tel. 412/937–1396; Rich Chiocchi, Network
Contact

ST. CLAIR MEMORIAL HOSPITAL, 1000 Bower Hill
Road, Pittsburgh, PA, Zip 15243–1899;
tel. 412/561–4900; Benjamin E. Snead,
President and Chief Executive Officer

COMMUNITY BENEFITS STRATEGY
P.O. Box 447, DuBois, PA 15801;
tel. 814/375–3495; Diane Skroba, Public
Relations Manager

DUBOIS REGIONAL MEDICAL CENTER, 100 Hospital
Avenue, Du Bois, PA, Zip 15801–1499, Mailing
Address: P.O. Box 447, Zip 15801–0447;
tel. 814/371–2200; Raymond A. Graeca,
President and Chief Executive Officer

COMMUNITY HEALTH NET
1202 State Street, Erie, PA 16501;
tel. 814/454–4530; Darleen Collen, Chief
Executive Officer

HAMOT MEDICAL CENTER, 201 State Street, Erie,
PA, Zip 16550–0002; tel. 814/877–6000; John
T. Malone, President and Chief Executive Officer

METRO HEALTH CENTER, 252 West 11th Street,
Erie, PA, Zip 16501–1798; tel. 814/870–3400;
Debra M. Dragovan, Chief Executive Officer

SAINT VINCENT HEALTH CENTER, 232 West 25th
Street, Erie, PA, Zip 16544–0001;
tel. 814/452–5000; Sister Catherine Manning,
President and Chief Executive Officer

CROZER–KEYSTONE HEALTH SYSTEM
100 W. Sproul Road, Springfield, PA 19064;
tel. 610/338–8203; John C. McMeekin,
President & Chief Executive Officer

CROZER–CHESTER MEDICAL CENTER, One Medical
Center Boulevard, Upland, PA, Zip 19013–3995;
tel. 610/447–2000; Joan K. Richards, President

DELAWARE COUNTY MEMORIAL HOSPITAL, 501
North Lansdowne Avenue, Drexel Hill, PA,
Zip 19026–1114; tel. 610/284–8100; Joan K.
Richards, President

SPRINGFIELD HOSPITAL, 190 West Sproul Road,
Springfield, PA, Zip 19064–2097;
tel. 610/328–8700; Gwendolyn A. Smith, R.N.,
Vice President

TAYLOR HOSPITAL, 175 East Chester Pike, Ridley
Park, PA, Zip 19078–2212; tel. 610/595–6000;
Diane C. Miller, President and Chief Operating
Officer

FIRST HEALTH ALLIANCE
10 Duff Road, Suite 211, Pittsburgh, PA
15235; tel. 412/243–2940; Don Hutchinson,
President

JEANNETTE DISTRICT MEMORIAL HOSPITAL, 600
Jefferson Avenue, Jeannette, PA,
Zip 15644–2504; tel. 724/527–3551; Robert J.
Bulger, President and Chief Executive Officer

FOX CHASE NETWORK
8 Huntingdon Pike, 3rd Floor, Rockledge, PA
19046; tel. 215/728–4773; Susan A. Higman,
Vice President

DELAWARE COUNTY MEMORIAL HOSPITAL, 501
North Lansdowne Avenue, Drexel Hill, PA,
Zip 19026–1114; tel. 610/284–8100; Joan K.
Richards, President

FOX CHASE CANCER CENTER–AMERICAN
ONCOLOGIC HOSPITAL, 7701 Burholme Avenue,
Philadelphia, PA, Zip 19111–2412;
tel. 215/728–6900; Robert C. Young, M.D.,
President

HUNTERDON MEDICAL CENTER, 2100 Wescott Drive,
Flemington, NJ, Zip 08822–4604;
tel. 908/788–6100; Robert P. Wise, President
and Chief Executive Officer

MONTGOMERY HOSPITAL, 1301 Powell Street,
Norristown, PA, Zip 19401, Mailing Address:
P.O. Box 992, Zip 19404–0992;
tel. 610/270–2000; Timothy M. Casey,
President and Chief Executive Officer

NORTH PENN HOSPITAL, 100 Medical Campus Drive,
Lansdale, PA, Zip 19446–1200;
tel. 215/368–2100; Robert H. McKay, President

PAOLI MEMORIAL HOSPITAL, 255 West Lancaster
Avenue, Paoli, PA, Zip 19301–1792;
tel. 610/648–1204; Kenneth Hanover, President
and Chief Executive Officer

PINNACLEHEALTH AT POLYCLINIC HOSPITAL, 2601
North Third Street, Harrisburg, PA,
Zip 17110–2098; tel. 717/782–4141; Susan A.
Edwards, Senior Vice President for Operations

READING HOSPITAL AND MEDICAL CENTER, Sixth
Avenue and Spruce Street, Reading, PA,
Zip 19611–1428, Mailing Address: P.O. Box
16052, Zip 19612–6052; tel. 610/378–6000;
Charles Sullivan, President and Chief Executive
Officer

RIVERVIEW MEDICAL CENTER, 1 Riverview Plaza, Red
Bank, NJ, Zip 07701–9982; tel. 908/741–2700;
Paul S. Cohen, Executive Director and Chief
Operating Officer

SHADYSIDE HOSPITAL, 5230 Centre Avenue,
Pittsburgh, PA, Zip 15232–1304;
tel. 412/623–2121; Henry A. Mordoh, President

SOUTH JERSEY HOSPITAL, 333 Irving Avenue,
Bridgeton, NJ, Zip 08302–2100;
tel. 609/451–6600; Paul S. Cooper, Chief
Executive Officer

ST. FRANCIS MEDICAL CENTER, 601 Hamilton
Avenue, Trenton, NJ, Zip 08629–1986;
tel. 609/599–5000; Judith M. Persichilli,
President and Chief Executive Officer

ST. MARY MEDICAL CENTER, Langhorne–Newtown
Road, Langhorne, PA, Zip 19047–1295;
tel. 215/750–2000; Sister Clare Carty,
President and Chief Executive Officer

GEISINGER HEALTH SYSTEM
100 North Academy Avenue, Danville, PA
17822; tel. 717/271–6211; Frank J.
Trembulak, Executive Vice President & COO

GEISINGER MEDICAL CENTER, 100 North Academy
Avenue, Danville, PA, Zip 17822–0150;
tel. 717/271–6211; Nancy Rizzo, Senior Vice
President, Operations

PENN STATE GEISINGER WYOMING VALLEY MEDICAL
CENTER, 1000 East Mountain Drive,
Wilkes–Barre, PA, Zip 18711–0027;
tel. 717/826–7300; Conrad W. Schintz, Senior
Vice President Operations

GREAT LAKES HEALTH NETWORK
201 State Street, Erie, PA 16550;
tel. 814/877–7053; Andrew J. Glass, CEO

ASHTABULA COUNTY MEDICAL CENTER, 2420 Lake
Avenue, Ashtabula, OH, Zip 44004–4993;
tel. 440/997–2262; R. D. Richardson, President
and Chief Executive Officer

BLANCHARD VALLEY HEALTH ASSOCIATION SYSTEM,
145 West Wallace Street, Findlay, OH,
Zip 45840–1299; tel. 419/423–4500; William
E. Ruse, FACHE, President and Chief Executive
Officer

BRADFORD REGIONAL MEDICAL CENTER, 116
Interstate Parkway, Bradford, PA,
Zip 16701–0218; tel. 814/368–4143; George
E. Leonhardt, President and Chief Executive
Officer

CORRY MEMORIAL HOSPITAL, 612 West Smith Street,
Corry, PA, Zip 16407–1152;
tel. 814/664–4641; Joseph T. Hodges,
President

HAMOT MEDICAL CENTER, 201 State Street, Erie,
PA, Zip 16550–0002; tel. 814/877–6000; John
T. Malone, President and Chief Executive Officer

ST. MARYS REGIONAL MEDICAL CENTER, 763
Johnsonburg Road, Saint Marys, PA,
Zip 15857–3417; tel. 814/781–7500; Paul A.
De Santis, President

UHHS BROWN MEMORIAL HOSPITAL, 158 West Main
Road, Conneaut, OH, Zip 44030–2039, Mailing
Address: P.O. Box 648, Zip 44030–0648;
tel. 440/593–1131; Carol Koellisch Drennen,
R.N., President and Chief Executive Officer

WOMAN'S CHRISTIAN ASSOCIATION HOSPITAL, 207
Foote Avenue, Jamestown, NY,
Zip 14702–9975; tel. 716/487–0141; Mark E.
Celmer, President and Chief Executive Officer

GUTHRIE HEALTHCARE SYSTEM
One Guthrie Square, Sayre, PA 18840;
tel. 717/882–6666; Antionette Arnold,
Adminstrative Resident

ROBERT PACKER HOSPITAL, 1 Guthrie Square, Sayre,
PA, Zip 18840–1698; tel. 717/888–6666;
William F. Vanaskie, President

TROY COMMUNITY HOSPITAL, 100 John Street, Troy,
PA, Zip 16947–1134; tel. 717/297–2121; Mark
A. Webster, President

HEALTH SHARE
111 South 11th Street, Philadelphia, PA
19107; tel. 215/955–6000; Carmhill Brown,
Associate Vice President of Marketing

THOMAS JEFFERSON UNIVERSITY HOSPITAL, 111
South 11th Street, Philadelphia, PA,
Zip 19107–5096; tel. 215/955–7022; Thomas
J. Lewis, President and Chief Executive Officer

JEFFERSON HEALTH SYSTEM
259 Radnor–Chestnut Road, Radnor, PA 19087; tel. 610/225–6200; Douglas S. Peters, President & Chief Executive Officer

ALBERT EINSTEIN MEDICAL CENTER, 5501 Old York Road, Philadelphia, PA, Zip 19141–3098; tel. 215/456–7890; Martin Goldsmith, President

ALFRED I.DUPONT HOSPITAL FOR CHILDREN, 1600 Rockland Road, Wilmington, DE, Zip 19803–3616, Mailing Address: Box 269, Zip 19899–0269; tel. 302/651–4000; Thomas P. Ferry, Administrator and Chief Executive

BRYN MAWR HOSPITAL, 130 South Bryn Mawr Avenue, Bryn Mawr, PA, Zip 19010–3160; tel. 610/526–3000; Kenneth Hanover, President and Chief Executive Officer

BRYN MAWR REHABILITATION HOSPITAL, 414 Paoli Pike, Malvern, PA, Zip 19355–3311, Mailing Address: P.O. Box 3007, Zip 19355–3300; tel. 610/251–5400; Barry S. Rabner, President

FRANKFORD HOSPITAL OF THE CITY OF PHILADELPHIA, Knights and Red Lion Roads, Philadelphia, PA, Zip 19114–1486; tel. 215/612–4000; Roy A. Powell, President

GERMANTOWN HOSPITAL AND MEDICAL CENTER, One Penn Boulevard, Philadelphia, PA, Zip 19144–1498; tel. 215/951–8000; David A. Ricci, President and Chief Executive Officer

LANKENAU HOSPITAL, 100 Lancaster Avenue West, Wynnewood, PA, Zip 19096–3411; tel. 610/645–2000; William McCune, Senior Vice President, Operations

MERCY HEALTH SYSTEM OF SOUTHEASTERN PENNSYLVANIA, One Bala Plaza, Suite 402, Bala Cynwyd, PA, Zip 19004–1401; tel. 610/660–7440; Plato A. Marinakos, President and Chief Executive Officer

METHODIST HOSPITAL, 2301 South Broad Street, Philadelphia, PA, Zip 19148; tel. 215/952–9000

OUR LADY OF LOURDES MEDICAL CENTER, 1600 Haddon Avenue, Camden, NJ, Zip 08103–3117; tel. 609/757–3500; Alexander J. Hatala, President and Chief Executive Officer

PAOLI MEMORIAL HOSPITAL, 255 West Lancaster Avenue, Paoli, PA, Zip 19301–1792; tel. 610/648–1204; Kenneth Hanover, President and Chief Executive Officer

POTTSTOWN MEMORIAL MEDICAL CENTER, 1600 East High Street, Pottstown, PA, Zip 19464–5008; tel. 610/327–7000; John J. Buckley, President and Chief Executive Officer

RIDDLE MEMORIAL HOSPITAL, 1068 West Baltimore Pike, Media, PA, Zip 19063–5177; tel. 610/566–9400; Donald L. Laughlin, President

THOMAS JEFFERSON UNIVERSITY HOSPITAL, 111 South 11th Street, Philadelphia, PA, Zip 19107–5096; tel. 215/955–7022; Thomas J. Lewis, President and Chief Executive Officer

UNDERWOOD–MEMORIAL HOSPITAL, 509 North Broad Street, Woodbury, NJ, Zip 08096–1697, Mailing Address: P.O. Box 359, Zip 08096–0359; tel. 609/845–0100; Steven W. Jackmuff, President and Chief Executive Officer

WILLS EYE HOSPITAL, 900 Walnut Street, Philadelphia, PA, Zip 19107–5598; tel. 215/928–3000; D. McWilliams Kessler, Executive Director

LAUREL HEALTH SYSTEM
15 Meade Street, Wellsboro, PA 16901–1813; tel. 717/723–0500; Ron Butler, President & Chief Executive Officer

SOLDIERS AND SAILORS MEMORIAL HOSPITAL, 32–36 Central Avenue, Wellsboro, PA, Zip 16901–1899; tel. 717/723–0100; Jan E. Fisher, R.N., Executive Director

PARTNERSHIP FOR COMMUNITY HEALTH–LEHIGH VALLEY
P.O. Box 689, Allentown, PA 18105; tel. 610/954–7550; Leo Conners, Chairman

SACRED HEART HOSPITAL, 421 Chew Street, Allentown, PA, Zip 18102–3490; tel. 610/776–4500; Joseph M. Cimerola, FACHE, President and Chief Executive Officer

PRIME CARE
2601 North 3rd Street, Harrisburg, PA 17110; tel. 717/782–4141; Alan Davidson, President

PINNACLEHEALTH AT POLYCLINIC HOSPITAL, 2601 North Third Street, Harrisburg, PA, Zip 17110–2098; tel. 717/782–4141; Susan A. Edwards, Senior Vice President for Operations

PROVIDENCE HEALTH SYSTEM
1100 Grampian Boulevard, Williamsport, PA 17701; tel. 717/326–8181; Anthony W. Deobil, President

MUNCY VALLEY HOSPITAL, 215 East Water Street, Muncy, PA, Zip 17756–8700; tel. 717/546–8282

SACRED HEART HEALTH CARE SYSTEM
421 Chew Street, Allentown, PA 18102; tel. 610/776–4500; Joseph M. Cimerola, FACHE

SACRED HEART HOSPITAL, 421 Chew Street, Allentown, PA, Zip 18102–3490; tel. 610/776–4500; Joseph M. Cimerola, FACHE, President and Chief Executive Officer

SAINT FRANCIS HEALTH SYSTEM
4410 Penn Avenue, Pittsburgh, PA 15224; tel. 412/622–4214; Sister M. Rosita Wellinger, President and Chief Executive Officer

ST. FRANCIS CENTRAL HOSPITAL, 1200 Centre Avenue, Pittsburgh, PA, Zip 15219–3594; tel. 412/562–3000; Robin Z. Mohr, Chief Executive Officer

ST. FRANCIS HOSPITAL OF NEW CASTLE, 1000 South Mercer Street, New Castle, PA, Zip 16101–4673; tel. 724/658–3511; Sister Donna Zwigart, FACHE, Chief Executive Officer

SAINT VINCENT HEALTH SYSTEM
232 West 25th Street, Erie, PA 16544; tel. 814/452–5000; Dorothy Law, Program Leader Mrktng & Communications

SAINT VINCENT HEALTH CENTER, 232 West 25th Street, Erie, PA, Zip 16544–0001; tel. 814/452–5000; Sister Catherine Manning, President and Chief Executive Officer

UNION CITY MEMORIAL HOSPITAL, 130 North Main Street, Union City, PA, Zip 16438–1094, Mailing Address: P.O. Box 111, Zip 16438–0111; tel. 814/438–1000; Thomas McLoughlin, President and Chief Executive Officer

SOUTHWEST INTEGRATED DELIVERY NETWORK
501 Holiday Drive, Pittsburgh, PA 15220; tel. 412/937–1396; Annette Fetchko, Vice President, Network Development

ALLEGHENY UNIVERSITY MEDICAL CENTER–ALLEGHENY VALLEY, 1301 Carlisle Street, Natrona Heights, PA, Zip 15065–1192; tel. 724/224–5100; John R. England, President and Chief Executive Officer

SEWICKLEY VALLEY HOSPITAL, (A DIVISION OF VALLEY MEDICAL FACILITIES), 720 Blackburn Road, Sewickley, PA, Zip 15143–1459; tel. 412/741–6600; James C. Cooper, Chief Executive Officer

ST. CLAIR MEMORIAL HOSPITAL, 1000 Bower Hill Road, Pittsburgh, PA, Zip 15243–1899; tel. 412/561–4900; Benjamin E. Snead, President and Chief Executive Officer

TEMPLE UNIVERSITY HEALTH NETWORK
3401 North Broad St., 1st FL Parkinson, Philadelphia, PA 19140; tel. 215/707–8000; Leon S. Malmud, M.D., President

JEANES HOSPITAL, 7600 Central Avenue, Philadelphia, PA, Zip 19111–2430; tel. 215/728–2000; G. Roger Martin, President and Chief Executive Officer

LOWER BUCKS HOSPITAL, 501 Bath Road, Bristol, PA, Zip 19007–3101; tel. 215/785–9200; Nathan Bosk, FACHE, Executive Director

NEUMANN MEDICAL CENTER, 1741 Frankford Avenue, Philadelphia, PA, Zip 19125–2495; tel. 215/291–2000; Joseph C. Hare, President and Chief Executive Officer

NORTHEASTERN HOSPITAL OF PHILADELPHIA, 2301 East Allegheny Avenue, Philadelphia, PA, Zip 19134–4499; tel. 215/291–3000; Jeffrey L. Susi, Executive Director and Chief Executive Officer

TEMPLE UNIVERSITY HOSPITAL, Broad and Ontario Streets, Philadelphia, PA, Zip 19140–5192; tel. 215/707–2000; Paul Boehringer, Executive Director

TRI–STATE NETWORK
81 Highland Avenue, Pittsburgh, PA 15213; tel. 412/692–7107; Nanci Case, Director of Planning/Marketing

CHILDREN'S HOSPITAL OF PITTSBURGH, 3705 Fifth Avenue at De Soto Street, Pittsburgh, PA, Zip 15213–2583; tel. 412/692–5325; Ronald L. Violi, President and Chief Executive Officer

MAGEE–WOMENS HOSPITAL, 300 Halket Street, Pittsburgh, PA, Zip 15213–3180; tel. 412/641–1000; Irma E. Goertzen, President and Chief Executive Officer

SOUTH HILLS HEALTH SYSTEM, 565 Coal Valley Road, Pittsburgh, PA, Zip 15236–0119, Mailing Address: Box 18119, Zip 15236–0119; tel. 412/469–5000; William R. Jennings, President and Chief Executive Officer

UPMC–PRESBYTERIAN, Pittsburgh, PA, Jeffrey A. Romoff, President

UPMC–ST. MARGARET, 815 Freeport Road, Pittsburgh, PA, Zip 15215–3399; tel. 412/784–4000; Stanley J. Kevish, President

UNIVERSITY OF PENNSYLVANIA HEALTH SYSTEM
21 Penn Tower, 399 South 34th Street, Philadelphia, PA 19104; tel. 215/898–5181; William N. Kelley, M.D., Chief Executive Officer

HOSPITAL OF THE UNIVERSITY OF PENNSYLVANIA, 3400 Spruce Street, Philadelphia, PA, Zip 19104–4204; tel. 215/662–4000; Thomas E. Beeman, Senior Vice President, Operations

PRESBYTERIAN MEDICAL CENTER OF THE UNIVERSITY OF PENNSYLVANIA HEALTH SYSTEM, 51 North 39th Street, Philadelphia, PA, Zip 19104–2640; tel. 215/662–8000; Michele M. Volpe, Executive Director

UNIVERSITY OF PITTSBURGH MEDICAL CENTER
3811 O'Hara Street, Pittsburgh, PA 15213; tel. 412/647–3000; Jeffrey Romoff, President

CHILDREN'S HOSPITAL OF PITTSBURGH, 3705 Fifth Avenue at De Soto Street, Pittsburgh, PA, Zip 15213–2583; tel. 412/692–5325; Ronald L. Violi, President and Chief Executive Officer

MAGEE–WOMENS HOSPITAL, 300 Halket Street, Pittsburgh, PA, Zip 15213–3180; tel. 412/641–1000; Irma E. Goertzen, President and Chief Executive Officer

UPMC–PRESBYTERIAN, Pittsburgh, PA, Jeffrey A. Romoff, President

UPMC–ST. MARGARET, 815 Freeport Road, Pittsburgh, PA, Zip 15215–3399; tel. 412/784–4000; Stanley J. Kevish, President

WASHINGTON HOSPITAL, 155 Wilson Avenue, Washington, PA, Zip 15301–3336; tel. 724/225–7000; Telford W. Thomas, President and Chief Executive Officer

VANTAGE HEALTH CARE NETWORK, INC.
265 Conneaut Lake Road, Meadville, PA 16335; tel. 814/337–0000; Gerald P. Alonge, Executive Director

HORIZON HOSPITAL SYSTEM, Greenville, PA, J. Larry Heinike, President and Chief Executive Officer

MEADVILLE MEDICAL CENTER, 751 Liberty Street, Meadville, PA, Zip 16335–2555; tel. 814/333–5000; Anthony J. DeFail, President and Chief Executive Officer

MILLCREEK COMMUNITY HOSPITAL, 5515 Peach Street, Erie, PA, Zip 16509–2603; tel. 814/864–4031; Mary L. Eckert, President and Chief Executive Officer

NORTHWEST MEDICAL CENTERS, 1 Spruce Street, Franklin, PA, Zip 16323–2544; tel. 814/437–7000; Neil E. Todhunter, Chief Executive Officer

SAINT VINCENT HEALTH CENTER, 232 West 25th Street, Erie, PA, Zip 16544–0001; tel. 814/452–5000; Sister Catherine Manning, President and Chief Executive Officer

TITUSVILLE AREA HOSPITAL, 406 West Oak Street, Titusville, PA, Zip 16354–1499; tel. 814/827–1851; Anthony J. Nasralla, FACHE, President and Chief Executive Officer

WARREN GENERAL HOSPITAL, 2 Crescent Park West, Warren, PA, Zip 16365–2111; tel. 814/723–3300; Alton M. Schadt, Executive Director

RHODE ISLAND

CARE NEW ENGLAND HEALTH SYSTEM
45 Willard Avenue, Providence, RI 02905; tel. 401/453–7900; John J. Hynes, Esq., President and Chief Executive Officer

BUTLER HOSPITAL, 345 Blackstone Boulevard, Providence, RI, Zip 02906–4829; tel. 401/455–6200; Frank A. Delmonico, President and Chief Executive Officer

KENT COUNTY MEMORIAL HOSPITAL, 455 Tollgate Road, Warwick, RI, Zip 02886–2770; tel. 401/737–7000; Robert E. Baute, M.D., President and Chief Executive Officer

WOMEN AND INFANTS HOSPITAL OF RHODE ISLAND, 101 Dudley Street, Providence, RI, Zip 02905–2499; tel. 401/274–1100; Thomas G. Parris, Jr., President

LIFESPAN
167 Point Street, Coro Building, Providence, RI 02903; tel. 401/444–3500; Jim Peters, Director/Communications

EMMA PENDLETON BRADLEY HOSPITAL, 1011 Veterans Memorial Parkway, East Providence, RI, Zip 02915–5099; tel. 401/434–3400; Daniel J. Wall, President and Chief Executive Officer

MIRIAM HOSPITAL, 164 Summit Avenue, Providence, RI, Zip 02906–2895; tel. 401/793–2000; Steven D. Baron, President

NEW ENGLAND MEDICAL CENTER, 750 Washington Street, Boston, MA, Zip 02111–1845; tel. 617/636–5000; Thomas F. O'Donnell, Jr., M.D., FACS, President and Chief Executive Officer

NEWPORT HOSPITAL, 11 Friendship Street, Newport, RI, Zip 02840–2299; tel. 401/846–6400; Arthur J. Sampson, President and Chief Executive Officer

RHODE ISLAND HOSPITAL, 593 Eddy Street, Providence, RI, Zip 02903–4900; tel. 401/444–4000; Steven D. Baron, President and Chief Executive Officer

SOUTH COUNTY HOSPITAL, 100 Kenyon Avenue, Wakefield, RI, Zip 02879–4299; tel. 401/782–8000; Patrick L. Muldoon, President and Chief Executive Officer

SAINT JOSEPH HOSPITAL
200 High Service Avenue, Providence, RI 02904; tel. 401/456–4419; Kathy Monteith, Network Coordinator

ST. JOSEPH HEALTH SERVICES OF RHODE ISLAND, 200 High Service Avenue, Providence, RI, Zip 02904–5199; tel. 401/456–3000; H. John Keimig, President and Chief Executive Officer

SOUTH CAROLINA

CAROLINA HEALTHCHOICE NETWORK
1718 Saint Julian Place, Columbia, SC 29204; tel. 803/988–8480; Suzanne H. Catalano, Executive Director

CLARENDON MEMORIAL HOSPITAL, 10 Hospital Street, Manning, SC, Zip 29102, Mailing Address: P.O. Box 550, Zip 29102–0550; tel. 803/435–8463; Edward R. Frye, Jr., Administrator

FAIRFIELD MEMORIAL HOSPITAL, 102 U.S. Highway 321 By-Pass North, Winnsboro, SC, Zip 29180, Mailing Address: P.O. Box 620, Zip 29180–0620; tel. 803/635–5548; Brent R. Lammers, Administrator

KERSHAW COUNTY MEDICAL CENTER, Haile and Roberts Streets, Camden, SC, Zip 29020–7003, Mailing Address: P.O. Box 7003, Zip 29020–7003; tel. 803/432–4311; Donnie J. Weeks, President and Chief Executive Officer

NEWBERRY COUNTY MEMORIAL HOSPITAL, 2669 Kinard Street, Newberry, SC, Zip 29108–0497, Mailing Address: P.O. Box 497, Zip 29108–0497; tel. 803/276–7570; Lynn W. Beasley, President and Chief Executive Officer

GREENVILLE HOSPITAL SYSTEM
701 Grove Road, Greenville, SC 29605; tel. 864/455–7000; Chris Sullivan, Director of Planning

ALLEN BENNETT HOSPITAL, 313 Memorial Drive, Greer, SC, Zip 29650–1521; tel. 864/848–8130; Michael W. Massey, Administrator

GREENVILLE MEMORIAL HOSPITAL, 701 Grove Road, Greenville, SC, Zip 29605–4295; tel. 864/455–7000; J. Bland Burkhardt, Jr., Senior Vice President and Administrator

HILLCREST HOSPITAL, 729 S.E. Main Street, Simpsonville, SC, Zip 29681–3280; tel. 864/967–6100; Mark Slyter, Administrator

MARSHALL I. PICKENS HOSPITAL, 701 Grove Road, Greenville, SC, Zip 29605–5601; tel. 864/455–7834; Jack W. Bonner, M.D., Administrator and Medical Director

ROGER C. PEACE REHABILITATION HOSPITAL, 701 Grove Road, Greenville, SC, Zip 29605–4295; tel. 864/455–7000; Dennis C. Hollins, M.D., Ph.D., Administrator and Medical Director

OPTIMUM HEALTH NETWORK
1 Saint Francis Drive, Greenville, SC 29601; tel. 803/220–4986; Paul D. Hovey, Vice President

CHARTER GREENVILLE BEHAVIORAL HEALTH SYSTEM, 2700 East Phillips Road, Greer, SC, Zip 29650–4816; tel. 864/968–6300; William L. Callison, Chief Executive Officer

MARY BLACK HEALTH SYSTEM, 1700 Skylyn Drive, Spartanburg, SC, Zip 29307–1061, Mailing Address: P.O. Box 3217, Zip 29304–3217; tel. 864/573–3000; William W. Fox, Chief Executive Officer

PALMETTO BAPTIST MEDICAL CENTER EASLEY, 200 Fleetwood Drive, Easley, SC, Zip 29640–2076, Mailing Address: P.O. Box 2129, Zip 29641–2129; tel. 864/855–7200; Roddey E. Gettys, III, Executive Vice President

ST. FRANCIS HEALTH SYSTEM, One St. Francis Drive, Greenville, SC, Zip 29601–3207; tel. 864/255–1000; Richard C. Neugent, President

PALMETTO COMMUNITY HEALTH NETWORK
900 C. Main Street, Conway, SC 29526; tel. 803/248–0342; Edward V. Schlaefer, FACHE, President

BYERLY HOSPITAL, 413 East Carolina Avenue, Hartsville, SC, Zip 29550–4309; tel. 843/339–2100; Page Vaughan, Executive Director

CHESTERFIELD GENERAL HOSPITAL, Highway 9 West, Cheraw, SC, Zip 29520, Mailing Address: P.O. Box 151, Zip 29520–0151; tel. 803/537–7881; Chris Wolf, Chief Executive Officer

CONWAY HOSPITAL, 300 Singleton Ridge Road, Conway, SC, Zip 29526, Mailing Address: P.O. Box 829, Zip 29528–0829; tel. 803/347–7111; Philip A. Clayton, President and Chief Executive Officer

HEALTHSOUTH REHABILITATION HOSPITAL, 900 East Cheves Street, Florence, SC, Zip 29506–2704; tel. 803/679–9000; Mark J. Stepanik, Interim Chief Executive Officer

LORIS COMMUNITY HOSPITAL, 3655 Mitchell Street, Loris, SC, Zip 29569–2827; tel. 803/716–7000; J. Timothy Browne, Chief Executive Officer

MARLBORO PARK HOSPITAL, 1138 Cheraw Highway, Bennettsville, SC, Zip 29512–0738, Mailing Address: P.O. Box 738, Zip 29512–0738; tel. 803/479–2881; Stephen Chapman, Chief Executive Officer

MCLEOD REGIONAL MEDICAL CENTER, 555 East Cheves Street, Florence, SC, Zip 29506–2617, Mailing Address: P.O. Box 100551, Zip 29501–0551; tel. 803/667–2000; J. Bruce Barragan, President and Chief Executive Officer

SAINT EUGENE MEDICAL CENTER, 301 East Jackson Street, Dillon, SC, Zip 29536–2509, Mailing Address: P.O. Box 1327, Zip 29536–1327; tel. 843/774–4111; Ronald W. Webb, President

PREMIER HEALTH SYSTEMS, INC.
P.O. Box 1640, Columbia, SC 29202; tel. 803/988–8999; C. Frank Riley, President

ABBEVILLE COUNTY MEMORIAL HOSPITAL, 901 West Greenwood Street, Abbeville, SC, Zip 29620–0887, Mailing Address: P.O. Box 887, Zip 29620–0887; tel. 864/459–5011; Bruce P. Bailey, Administrator

ALLEN BENNETT HOSPITAL, 313 Memorial Drive, Greer, SC, Zip 29650–1521; tel. 864/848–8130; Michael W. Massey, Administrator

ALLENDALE COUNTY HOSPITAL, Highway 278 West, Fairfax, SC, Zip 29827–0278, Mailing Address: Box 218, Zip 29827–0218; tel. 803/632–3311; M. K. Hiatt, Administrator

BAMBERG COUNTY MEMORIAL HOSPITAL AND NURSING CENTER, North and McGee Streets, Bamberg, SC, Zip 29003–0507, Mailing Address: P.O. Box 507, Zip 29003–0507; tel. 803/245–4321; Warren E. Hammett, Administrator

BARNWELL COUNTY HOSPITAL, 2501 Reynolds Road, Barnwell, SC, Zip 29812, Mailing Address: P.O. Box 588, Zip 29812–0588; tel. 803/259–1000; Tommy R. McDougal, Jr., Administrator and Chief Executive Officer

BON SECOURS–ST. FRANCIS XAVIER HOSPITAL, 2095 Henry Tecklenburg Drive, Charleston, SC, Zip 29414–0001, Mailing Address: P.O. Box 160001, Zip 29414–0001; tel. 803/402–1000; Allen P. Carroll, Chief Executive Officer

CANNON MEMORIAL HOSPITAL, 123 West G. Acker Drive, Pickens, SC, Zip 29671, Mailing Address: P.O. Box 188, Zip 29671–0188; tel. 864/878–4791; Norman G. Rentz, President and Chief Executive Officer

CAROLINAS HOSPITAL SYSTEM–LAKE CITY, 258 North Ron McNair Boulevard, Lake City, SC, Zip 29560–1029, Mailing Address: P.O. Box 1029, Zip 29560–1029; tel. 803/394–2036; Richard L. Gamber, Administrator

CHESTER COUNTY HOSPITAL AND NURSING CENTER, 1 Medical Park Drive, Chester, SC, Zip 29706–9799; tel. 803/581–9400; Robert E. Waters, Chief Executive Officer

CHESTERFIELD GENERAL HOSPITAL, Highway 9 West, Cheraw, SC, Zip 29520, Mailing Address: P.O. Box 151, Zip 29520–0151; tel. 803/537–7881; Chris Wolf, Chief Executive Officer

CLARENDON MEMORIAL HOSPITAL, 10 Hospital Street, Manning, SC, Zip 29102, Mailing Address: P.O. Box 550, Zip 29102–0550; tel. 803/435–8463; Edward R. Frye, Jr., Administrator

COLUMBIA PROVIDENCE HOSPITAL, 2435 Forest Drive, Columbia, SC, Zip 29204–2098; tel. 803/256–5300; Larry R. Ellis, Interim Chief Executive Officer

EAST COOPER REGIONAL MEDICAL CENTER, 1200 Johnnie Dodds Boulevard, Mount Pleasant, SC, Zip 29464–3294; tel. 803/881–0100; John F. Holland, President

EDGEFIELD COUNTY HOSPITAL, 300 Ridge Medical Plaza, Edgefield, SC, Zip 29824; tel. 803/637–3174; W. Joseph Seel, Administrator

FAIRFIELD MEMORIAL HOSPITAL, 102 U.S. Highway 321 By-Pass North, Winnsboro, SC, Zip 29180, Mailing Address: P.O. Box 620, Zip 29180–0620; tel. 803/635–5548; Brent R. Lammers, Administrator

GEORGETOWN MEMORIAL HOSPITAL, 606 Black River Road, Georgetown, SC, Zip 29440–3368, Mailing Address: Drawer 1718, Zip 29442–1718; tel. 803/527–7000; Paul D. Gatens, Sr., Administrator

GREENVILLE MEMORIAL HOSPITAL, 701 Grove Road, Greenville, SC, Zip 29605–4295; tel. 864/455–7000; J. Bland Burkhardt, Jr., Senior Vice President and Administrator

HEALTHSOUTH REHABILITATION HOSPITAL, 2935 Colonial Drive, Columbia, SC, Zip 29203–6811; tel. 803/254–7777; Debbie W. Johnston, Director Operations

HILLCREST HOSPITAL, 729 S.E. Main Street, Simpsonville, SC, Zip 29681–3280; tel. 864/967–6100; Mark Slyter, Administrator

HILTON HEAD MEDICAL CENTER AND CLINICS, 25 Hospital Center Boulevard, Hilton Head Island, SC, Zip 29926–2738, Mailing Address: P.O. Box 21117, Zip 29925–1117; tel. 803/681–6122; Dennis Ray Bruns, President and Chief Executive Officer

KERSHAW COUNTY MEDICAL CENTER, Haile and Roberts Streets, Camden, SC, Zip 29020–7003, Mailing Address: P.O. Box 7003, Zip 29020–7003; tel. 803/432–4311; Donnie J. Weeks, President and Chief Executive Officer

LAURENS COUNTY HEALTHCARE SYSTEM, Highway 76 West, Clinton, SC, Zip 29325, Mailing Address: P.O. Box 976, Zip 29325–0976; tel. 864/833–9100; Michael A. Kozar, Chief Executive Officer

LEXINGTON MEDICAL CENTER, 2720 Sunset Boulevard, West Columbia, SC, Zip 29169–4816; tel. 803/791–2000; Michael J. Biediger, President

MARLBORO PARK HOSPITAL, 1138 Cheraw Highway, Bennettsville, SC, Zip 29512–0738, Mailing Address: P.O. Box 738, Zip 29512–0738; tel. 803/479–2881; Stephen Chapman, Chief Executive Officer

MARSHALL I. PICKENS HOSPITAL, 701 Grove Road, Greenville, SC, Zip 29605–5601; tel. 864/455–7834; Jack W. Bonner, M.D., Administrator and Medical Director

MARY BLACK HEALTH SYSTEM, 1700 Skylyn Drive, Spartanburg, SC, Zip 29307–1061, Mailing Address: P.O. Box 3217, Zip 29304–3217; tel. 864/573–3000; William W. Fox, Chief Executive Officer

NEWBERRY COUNTY MEMORIAL HOSPITAL, 2669 Kinard Street, Newberry, SC, Zip 29108–0497, Mailing Address: P.O. Box 497, Zip 29108–0497; tel. 803/276–7570; Lynn W. Beasley, President and Chief Executive Officer

PALMETTO BAPTIST MEDICAL CENTER EASLEY, 200 Fleetwood Drive, Easley, SC, Zip 29640–2076, Mailing Address: P.O. Box 2129, Zip 29641–2129; tel. 864/855–7200; Roddey E. Gettys, III, Executive Vice President

PALMETTO BAPTIST MEDICAL CENTER/COLUMBIA, Taylor at Marion Street, Columbia, SC, Zip 29220; tel. 803/771–5010; James M. Bridges, Executive Vice President and Chief Operating Officer

ROGER C. PEACE REHABILITATION HOSPITAL, 701 Grove Road, Greenville, SC, Zip 29605–4295; tel. 864/455–7000; Dennis C. Hollins, M.D., Ph.D., Administrator and Medical Director

ROPER HOSPITAL, 316 Calhoun Street, Charleston, SC, Zip 29401–1125; tel. 803/724–2000; Edward L. Berdick, President and Chief Executive Officer

SELF MEMORIAL HOSPITAL, 1325 Spring Street, Greenwood, SC, Zip 29646–3860; tel. 864/227–4111; M. John Heydel, President and Chief Executive Officer

ST. JOSEPH'S HOSPITAL, 11705 Mercy Boulevard, Savannah, GA, Zip 31419–1791; tel. 912/927–5404; Paul P. Hinchey, President and Chief Executive Officer

UPSTATE CAROLINA MEDICAL CENTER, 1530 North Limestone Street, Gaffney, SC, Zip 29340–4738; tel. 864/487–1500; Nancy C. Fodi, Executive Director

WILLINGWAY HOSPITAL, 311 Jones Mill Road, Statesboro, GA, Zip 30458–4765; tel. 912/764–6236; Jimmy Mooney, Chief Executive Officer

RICHLAND COMMUNITY HEALTH PARTNERS
3 Richland Medical Park, Suite 100, Columbia, SC 29203; tel. 803/434–3100; Tom Brown, Director

PALMETTO RICHLAND MEMORIAL HOSPITAL, Columbia, SC, Mailing Address: P.O. Box 2266, Zip 29203–2266; tel. 803/434–7000; Kester S. Freeman, Jr., Chief Executive Officer

SAINT FRANCIS HEALTH SYSTEM
One Saint Francis Drive, Greenville, SC 29601; tel. 803/255–1000; Richard C. Neugent, Chief Executive Officer

ST. FRANCIS HEALTH SYSTEM, One St. Francis Drive, Greenville, SC, Zip 29601–3207; tel. 864/255–1000; Richard C. Neugent, President

SOUTH DAKOTA

BLACK HILLS HEALTHCARE NETWORK
930 10th Street, Spearfish, SD 57783; tel. 605/642–4641; Ellen D. Holley, Director of Marketing/Communications

LOOKOUT MEMORIAL HOSPITAL, 1440 North Main Street, Spearfish, SD, Zip 57783–1504; tel. 605/642–2617; Deb J. Krmpotic, R.N., Administrator

SOUTHERN HILLS GENERAL HOSPITAL, 209 North 16th Street, Hot Springs, SD, Zip 57747–1375; tel. 605/745–3159

STURGIS COMMUNITY HEALTH CARE CENTER, 949 Harmon Street, Sturgis, SD, Zip 57785–2452; tel. 605/347–2536; Deb J. Krmpotic, R.N., Administrator

MISSOURI VALLEY HEALTH NETWORK
1017 West 5th Street, Yankton, SD 57078; tel. 605/665–9005; Lanette Hinchly, Office Manager

COMMUNITY MEMORIAL HOSPITAL, Eighth and Jackson, Burke, SD, Zip 57523, Mailing Address: P.O. Box 319, Zip 57523–0319; tel. 605/775–2621; Carol A. Varland, Administrator

DOUGLAS COUNTY MEMORIAL HOSPITAL, 708 Eighth Street, Armour, SD, Zip 57313–2102; tel. 605/724–2159; Angelia K. Henry, Administrator

FREEMAN COMMUNITY HOSPITAL, 510 East Eighth Street, Freeman, SD, Zip 57029–0370, Mailing Address: P.O. Box 370, Zip 57029–0370; tel. 605/925–4231; James M. Krehbiel, Chief Executive Officer

GREGORY COMMUNITY HOSPITAL, 400 Park Street, Gregory, SD, Zip 57533–0400, Mailing Address: Box 408, Zip 57533–0408; tel. 605/835–8394; Carol A. Varland, Chief Executive Officer

LANDMANN–JUNGMAN MEMORIAL HOSPITAL, 600 Billars Street, Scotland, SD, Zip 57059–2026; tel. 605/583–2226; William H. Koellner, Administrator

PIONEER MEMORIAL HOSPITAL, 315 North Washington Street, Viborg, SD, Zip 57070, Mailing Address: P.O. Box 368, Zip 57070–0368; tel. 605/326–5161; Georgia Pokorney, Chief Executive Officer

PLATTE COMMUNITY MEMORIAL HOSPITAL, 609 East Seventh, Platte, SD, Zip 57369–2123, Mailing Address: P.O. Box 200, Zip 57369–0200; tel. 605/337–3364; Mark Burket, Chief Executive Officer

QUEEN OF PEACE HOSPITAL, 525 North Foster, Mitchell, SD, Zip 57301–2999; tel. 605/995–2000; Ronald L. Jacobson, President and Chief Executive Officer

SACRED HEART HEALTH SERVICES, 501 Summit Avenue, Yankton, SD, Zip 57078–3899; tel. 605/668–8000; Pamela J. Rezac, President and Chief Executive Officer

ST. BENEDICT HEALTH CENTER, Glynn Drive, Parkston, SD, Zip 57366, Mailing Address: P.O. Box B., Zip 57366; tel. 605/928–3311; Gale Walker, Administrator

ST. MICHAEL'S HOSPITAL, Douglas Street and Broadway, Tyndall, SD, Zip 57066, Mailing Address: P.O. Box 27, Zip 57066–0027; tel. 605/589–3341; Carol Deurmier, Chief Executive Officer

WAGNER COMMUNITY MEMORIAL HOSPITAL, Third and Walnut, Wagner, SD, Zip 57380, Mailing Address: P.O. Box 280, Zip 57380–0280; tel. 605/384–3611; Arlene C. Bich, Administrator

WINNER REGIONAL HEALTHCARE CENTER, 745 East Eighth Street, Winner, SD, Zip 57580–2677, Mailing Address: P.O. Box 745, Zip 57580–0745; tel. 605/842–7100; Robert Houser, Chief Executive Officer

RAPID CITY REGIONAL HOSPITAL SYSTEM OF CARE
353 Fairmont Boulevard, Rapid City, SD 57709; tel. 605/341–1000; Carolyn Helfenstein, Director of Marketing

CUSTER COMMUNITY HOSPITAL, 1039 Montgomery Street, Custer, SD, Zip 57730–1397; tel. 605/673–2229; Jason Petik, Administrator

FIVE COUNTIES HOSPITAL, 401 Sixth Avenue West, Lemmon, SD, Zip 57638–1318, Mailing Address: P.O. Box 479, Zip 57638–0479; tel. 605/374–3871; Helen S. Lindquist, Administrator

HANS P. PETERSON MEMORIAL HOSPITAL, 603 West Pine, Philip, SD, Zip 57567, Mailing Address: P.O. Box 790, Zip 57567–0790; tel. 605/859–2511; David Dick, Administrator

LEGEND BUTTES HEALTH SERVICES, 11 Paddock Street, Crawford, NE, Zip 69339–1143, Mailing Address: P.O. Box 272, Zip 69339–0272; tel. 308/665–1770; Kim Engel, Chief Executive Officer

NORTHERN HILLS GENERAL HOSPITAL, 61 Charles Street, Deadwood, SD, Zip 57732–1303; tel. 605/578–2313; Richard G. Soukup, Chief Executive Officer

RAPID CITY REGIONAL HOSPITAL SYSTEM OF CARE, 353 Fairmont Boulevard, Rapid City, SD, Zip 57701–7393, Mailing Address: P.O. Box 6000, Zip 57709–6000; tel. 605/341–1000; Adil M. Ameer, President and Chief Executive Officer

WESTON COUNTY HEALTH SERVICES, 1124 Washington Street, Newcastle, WY, Zip 82701–2996; tel. 307/746–4491; Jack Brinkers, CHE, Administrator

REGIONAL HOSPITAL HEALTHCARE NETWORK
61 Charles Street, Deadwood, SD 57732; tel. 605/578–2313; Wendall Rawling, Interim Chief Executive Officer

NORTHERN HILLS GENERAL HOSPITAL, 61 Charles Street, Deadwood, SD, Zip 57732–1303; tel. 605/578–2313; Richard G. Soukup, Chief Executive Officer

SIOUX VALLEY HEALTH SYSTEM
300 Main Street, Sioux Falls, SD 57117; tel. 605/333–1531; Tom Evans, Vice President of Rural Health

CANBY COMMUNITY HEALTH SERVICES, 112 St. Olaf Avenue South, Canby, MN, Zip 56220–1433; tel. 507/223–7277; Robert J. Salmon, Chief Executive Officer

CANTON–INWOOD MEMORIAL HOSPITAL, 440 North Hiawatha Drive, Canton, SD, Zip 57013–9404, Mailing Address: Rural Route 3, Box 7, Zip 57013–0007; tel. 605/987–2621; John Devick, Chief Executive Officer

MERRILL PIONEER COMMUNITY HOSPITAL, 801 South Greene Street, Rock Rapids, IA, Zip 51246–1998; tel. 712/472–2591; Gordon Smith, Administrator

MID DAKOTA HOSPITAL, 300 South Byron Boulevard, Chamberlain, SD, Zip 57325–9741; tel. 605/734–5511; Michael Penticoff, Administrator

MURRAY COUNTY MEMORIAL HOSPITAL, 2042 Juniper Avenue, Slayton, MN, Zip 56172–1016; tel. 507/836–6111; Jerry Bobeldyk, Administrator

NORTHWEST IOWA HEALTH CENTER, 118 North Seventh Avenue, Sheldon, IA, Zip 51201–1235; tel. 712/324–5041; Charles R. Miller, Chief Executive Officer

PIONEER MEMORIAL HOSPITAL, 315 North Washington Street, Viborg, SD, Zip 57070, Mailing Address: P.O. Box 368, Zip 57070–0368; tel. 605/326–5161; Georgia Pokorney, Chief Executive Officer

SIOUX VALLEY VERMILLION CAMPUS, 20 South Plum Street, Vermillion, SD, Zip 57069–3346; tel. 605/624–2611; Larry W. Veitz, Chief Executive Officer

TRACY AREA MEDICAL SERVICES, 251 Fifth Street East, Tracy, MN, Zip 56175–1536; tel. 507/629–3200; Thomas J. Quinlivan, Administrator

WESTBROOK HEALTH CENTER, 920 Bell Avenue, Westbrook, MN, Zip 56183–9636, Mailing Address: P.O. Box 188, Zip 56183–0188; tel. 507/274–6121; Thomas J. Quinlivan, Administrator

WINDOM AREA HOSPITAL, Highways 60 and 71 North, Windom, MN, Zip 56101, Mailing Address: P.O. Box 339, Zip 56101–0339; tel. 507/831–2400; J. Stephen Pautler, CHE, Administrator

TENNESSEE

CHATTANOOGA HEALTHCARE NETWORK
401 Chestnut Street, Suite 222, Chattanooga, TN 37402; tel. 423/266–5174; Judy Clay, Network Contact

ATHENS REGIONAL MEDICAL CENTER, 1114 West Madison Avenue, Athens, TN, Zip 37303–4150, Mailing Address: P.O. Box 250, Zip 37371–0250; tel. 423/745–1411; John R. Workman, Chief Executive Officer

COLUMBIA EAST RIDGE HOSPITAL, 941 Spring Creek Road, East Ridge, TN, Zip 37412, Mailing Address: P.O. Box 91229, Zip 37412–6229; tel. 423/894–7870; Brenda M. Waltz, CHE, Chief Executive Officer

COLUMBIA SOUTH PITTSBURG HOSPITAL, 210 West 12th Street, South Pittsburg, TN, Zip 37380, Mailing Address: P.O. Box 349, Zip 37380–0349; tel. 423/837–6781; Phil Rowland, Chief Executive Officer

COLUMBIA VALLEY HOSPITAL, 2200 Morris Hill Road, Chattanooga, TN, Zip 37421; tel. 423/894–4220

COLUMBIA HEALTHCARE NETWORK
Two Maryland Farms, Suite 300, Brentwood, TN 37027; tel. 615/661–7200; Luis A. Rosa, Chief Executive Officer

COLUMBIA CENTENNIAL MEDICAL CENTER AND PARTHENON PAVILION, 2300 Patterson Street, Nashville, TN, Zip 37203–1528; tel. 615/342–1000; Larry Kloess, President

COLUMBIA CHEATHAM MEDICAL CENTER, 313 North Main Street, Ashland City, TN, Zip 37015–1358; tel. 615/792–3030; Rick Wallace, FACHE, Chief Executive Officer and Administrator

COLUMBIA HORIZON MEDICAL CENTER, 111 Highway 70 East, Dickson, TN, Zip 37055–2033; tel. 615/441–2357; Rick Wallace, FACHE, Chief Executive Officer and Administrator

COLUMBIA SOUTHERN HILLS MEDICAL CENTER, 391 Wallace Road, Nashville, TN, Zip 37211–4859; tel. 615/781–4000; Jeffrey Whitehorn, Chief Executive Officer

COLUMBIA STONES RIVER HOSPITAL, 324 Doolittle Road, Woodbury, TN, Zip 37190–1139; tel. 615/563–4001; Bill Patterson, Interim Administrator

HENDERSONVILLE HOSPITAL, 355 New Shackle Island Road, Hendersonville, TN, Zip 37075–2393; tel. 615/264–4000; Robert Klein, Chief Executive Officer

NASHVILLE MEMORIAL HOSPITAL, 612 West Due West Avenue, Madison, TN, Zip 37115–4474; tel. 615/865–3511; Allyn R. Harris, Chief Executive Officer

NORTH CREST MEDICAL CENTER, 100 North Crest Drive, Springfield, TN, Zip 37172–2984; tel. 615/384–2411; William A. Kenley, President and Chief Executive Officer

PSYCHIATRIC HOSPITAL AT VANDERBILT, 1601 23rd Avenue South, Nashville, TN, Zip 37212–3198; tel. 615/320–7770; Richard A. Bangert, Chief Executive Officer and Administrator

RIVER PARK HOSPITAL, 1559 Sparta Road, McMinnville, TN, Zip 37110–1316; tel. 931/815–4000; Terry J. Gunn, Chief Executive Officer

SUMMIT MEDICAL CENTER, 5655 Frist Boulevard, Hermitage, TN, Zip 37076–2053; tel. 615/316–3000; Bryan K. Dearing, Chief Executive Officer

HIGHLANDS WELLMONT HEALTH NETWORK, INC.
1 Medical Park Boulevard, P.O. Box 989, Bristol, TN 37621–0989; tel. 423/844–4186; Dave Nowiski, Executive VP System Development

LONESOME PINE HOSPITAL, 1990 Holton Avenue East, Big Stone Gap, VA, Zip 24219–0230; tel. 540/523–3111; Paul A. Bishop, Administrator

NORTON COMMUNITY HOSPITAL, 100 15th Street N.W., Norton, VA, Zip 24273–1699; tel. 540/679–9700; Jerry Kincade, Chief Executive Officer

WELLMONT BRISTOL REGIONAL MEDICAL CENTER, 1 Medical Park Boulevard, Bristol, TN, Zip 37620–7430; tel. 423/844–4200; Randall M. Olson, Administrator

WELLMONT HOLSTON VALLEY MEDICAL CENTER, West Ravine Street, Kingsport, TN, Zip 37662–0224, Mailing Address: Box 238, Zip 37662–0224; tel. 423/224–4000; Louis H. Bremer, President and Chief Executive Officer

METHODIST HEALTH SYSTEMS, INC.
1211 Union Avenue, Memphis, TN 38104; tel. 901/726–8273; Maurice Elliott, President

METHODIST HEALTHCARE, 1850 Chadwick Drive, Jackson, MS, Zip 39204–3479, Mailing Address: P.O. Box 59001, Zip 39204–9001; tel. 601/376–1000; Cameron J. Welton, President and Chief Executive Officer

METHODIST HEALTHCARE – FAYETTE HOSPITAL, 214 Lakeview Drive, Somerville, TN, Zip 38068; tel. 901/465–0532; Michael Blome', Administrator

METHODIST HEALTHCARE MIDDLE MISSISSIPPI HOSPITAL, 239 Bowling Green Road, Lexington, MS, Zip 39095–9332; tel. 601/834–1321; James K. Greer, Administrator

METHODIST HOSPITAL OF DYERSBURG, 400 Tickle Street, Dyersburg, TN, Zip 38024–3182; tel. 901/285–2410; Richard McCormick, Administrator

METHODIST HOSPITAL OF LEXINGTON, 200 West Church Street, Lexington, TN, Zip 38351–2014; tel. 901/968–3646; Eugene Ragghianti, Administrator

METHODIST HOSPITAL OF MCKENZIE, 161 Hospital Drive, McKenzie, TN, Zip 38201–1636; tel. 901/352–4170; Randal E. Carson, Administrator

METHODIST HOSPITALS OF MEMPHIS, 1265 Union Avenue, Memphis, TN, Zip 38104–3499; tel. 901/726–7000; Gary S. Shorb, President

MIDDLE TENNESSEE HEALTHCARE NETWORK
3401 West End Avenue, Suite 120, Nashville, TN 37203; tel. 615/386–2680; Roy Wright, President & Chief Executive Officer

BAPTIST HOSPITAL, 2000 Church Street, Nashville, TN, Zip 37236–0002; tel. 615/329–5555; C. David Stringfield, President and Chief Executive Officer

BEDFORD COUNTY GENERAL HOSPITAL, 845 Union Street, Shelbyville, TN, Zip 37160–9971; tel. 931/685–5433; Richard L. Graham, Administrator

CARTHAGE GENERAL HOSPITAL, Highway 70 North, Carthage, TN, Zip 37030, Mailing Address: P.O. Box 319, Zip 37030–0319

CLARKSVILLE MEMORIAL HOSPITAL, 1771 Madison Street, Clarksville, TN, Zip 37043–4900, Mailing Address: P.O. Box 3160, Zip 37043–3160; tel. 931/552–6622; James Lee Decker, President and Chief Executive Officer

COOKEVILLE REGIONAL MEDICAL CENTER, 142 West Fifth Street, Cookeville, TN, Zip 38501–1760, Mailing Address: P.O. Box 340, Zip 38503–0340; tel. 931/528–2541; William M. Jennings, Administrator and Chief Operating Officer

CUMBERLAND MEDICAL CENTER, 421 South Main Street, Crossville, TN, Zip 38555–5031; tel. 931/484–9511; Edwin S. Anderson, President

MAURY REGIONAL HOSPITAL, 1224 Trotwood Avenue, Columbia, TN, Zip 38401–4823; tel. 931/381–1111; William R. Walter, Administrator

MIDDLE TENNESSEE MEDICAL CENTER, 400 North Highland Avenue, Murfreesboro, TN, Zip 37130–3854, Mailing Address: P.O. Box 1178, Zip 37133–1178; tel. 615/849–4100; Arthur W. Hastings, President and Chief Executive Officer

ST. THOMAS HOSPITAL, 4220 Harding Road, Nashville, TN, Zip 37205–2095, Mailing Address: P.O. Box 380, Zip 37202–0380; tel. 615/222–2111; John F. Tighe, President and Chief Executive Officer

SUMNER REGIONAL MEDICAL CENTER, 555 Hartsville Pike, Gallatin, TN, Zip 37066–2449, Mailing Address: P.O. Box 1558, Zip 37066–1558; tel. 615/452–4210; William T. Sugg, President and Chief Executive Officer

TENNESSEE CHRISTIAN MEDICAL CENTER, 500 Hospital Drive, Madison, TN, Zip 37115–5032; tel. 615/865–2373; Milton R. Siepman, Ph.D., President and Chief Executive Officer

VANDERBILT UNIVERSITY HOSPITAL, 1161 21st Avenue South, Nashville, TN, Zip 37232–2102; tel. 615/322–5000; Norman B. Urmy, Executive Director

WILLIAMSON MEDICAL CENTER, 2021 Carothers Road, Franklin, TN, Zip 37067–5822, Mailing Address: P.O. Box 681600, Zip 37068–1600; tel. 615/791–0500; Ronald G. Joyner, Chief Executive Officer

MOUNTAIN STATES HEALTHCARE NETWORK
400 North State of Franklin Road, Johnson City, TN 37604; tel. 423/431–6810; Patricia Holtsclaw, Executive Director

CHARLES A. CANNON JR. MEMORIAL HOSPITAL, 805 Shawneehaw Avenue, Banner Elk, NC, Zip 28604–9724, Mailing Address: P.O. Box 8, Zip 28604–0008; tel. 704/898–5111; Edward C. Greene, Jr., Administrator

COLUMBIA CLINCH VALLEY MEDICAL CENTER, 2949 West Front Street, Richlands, VA, Zip 24641–2099; tel. 540/596–6000; James W. Thweatt, Chief Executive Officer

INDIAN PATH PAVILION, 2300 Pavilion Drive, Kingsport, TN, Zip 37660–4672; tel. 423/378–7500

JOHNSON CITY MEDICAL CENTER HOSPITAL, 400 North State of Franklin Road, Johnson City, TN, Zip 37604–6094; tel. 423/431–6111; Dennis Vonderfecht, President and Chief Executive Officer

JOHNSTON MEMORIAL HOSPITAL, 351 North Court Street, Abingdon, VA, Zip 24210–2921; tel. 540/676–7000; Clark R. Beil, Chief Executive Officer

LAKEWAY REGIONAL HOSPITAL, 726 McFarland Street, Morristown, TN, Zip 37814–3990; tel. 423/586–2302; Robert B. Wampler, CPA, Chief Executive Officer

LEE COUNTY COMMUNITY HOSPITAL, West Morgan Avenue, Pennington Gap, VA, Zip 24277, Mailing Address: P.O. Box 70, Zip 24277–0070; tel. 540/546–1440; James L. Davis, Chief Executive Officer

MORRISTOWN–HAMBLEN HOSPITAL, 908 West Fourth North Street, Morristown, TN, Zip 37816; tel. 423/586–4231; Richard L. Clark, Administrator and Chief Executive Officer

SLOOP MEMORIAL HOSPITAL, One Crossnore Drive, Crossnore, NC, Zip 28616, Mailing Address: Drawer 470, Zip 28616; tel. 704/733–9231; Edward C. Greene, Jr., President

TAKOMA ADVENTIST HOSPITAL, 401 Takoma Avenue, Greeneville, TN, Zip 37743–4668; tel. 423/639–3151; Michael V. Gentry, President

UNICOI COUNTY MEMORIAL HOSPITAL, 100 Greenway Circle, Erwin, TN, Zip 37650–2196, Mailing Address: P.O. Box 802, Zip 37650–0802; tel. 423/743–3141; James L. McMackin, Chief Executive Officer

WOODRIDGE HOSPITAL, 403 State of Franklin Road, Johnson City, TN, Zip 37604–6009; tel. 423/928–7111; Thomas J. De Martini, Administrator

Section B

PREMIER HEALTH NETWORK
313 Princeton Road, Suite 7, Johnson City, TN 37601; tel. 615/844-4205; Eddie George, Chief Executive Officer

COLUMBIA NORTH SIDE HOSPITAL, 401 Princeton Road, Johnson City, TN, Zip 37601-2097, Mailing Address: P.O. Box 4900, Zip 37602-4900; tel. 423/854-5900; Eric Deaton, Chief Executive Officer

JOHNSON CITY SPECIALTY HOSPITAL, 203 East Watauga Avenue, Johnson City, TN, Zip 37601-4651; tel. 423/926-1111; Lori Caudell Fatherree, Chief Executive Officer

LAUGHLIN MEMORIAL HOSPITAL, 1420 Tusculum Boulevard, Greeneville, TN, Zip 37745; tel. 423/787-5000; Charles H. Whitfield, Jr., President and Chief Executive Officer

WELLMONT HOLSTON VALLEY MEDICAL CENTER, West Ravine Street, Kingsport, TN, Zip 37662-0224, Mailing Address: Box 238, Zip 37662-0224; tel. 423/224-4000; Louis H. Bremer, President and Chief Executive Officer

SAINT THOMAS HEALTH SERVICES
P.O. Box 380 – 4220 Harding Road, Nashville, TN 37202; tel. 615/222-6800; Susan R. Russell, Vice President of Community Relations

ST. THOMAS HOSPITAL, 4220 Harding Road, Nashville, TN, Zip 37205-2095, Mailing Address: P.O. Box 380, Zip 37202-0380; tel. 615/222-2111; John F. Tighe, President and Chief Executive Officer

VANDERBILT UNIVERSITY HOSPITAL, 1161 21st Avenue South, Nashville, TN, Zip 37232-2102; tel. 615/322-5000; Norman B. Urmy, Executive Director

WEST TENNESSEE HEALTHCARE, INC.
708 West Forest, Jackson, TN 38301; tel. 901/664-4254; Jim Moss, Chief Executive Officer

BOLIVAR GENERAL HOSPITAL, 650 Nuckolls Road, Bolivar, TN, Zip 38008-1500; tel. 901/658-3100; George L. Austin, Administrator

CAMDEN GENERAL HOSPITAL, 175 Hospital Drive, Camden, TN, Zip 38320-1617; tel. 901/584-6135; Billy Alred, Interim Administrator

DECATUR COUNTY GENERAL HOSPITAL, 969 Tennessee Avenue South, Parsons, TN, Zip 38363-0250, Mailing Address: Box 250, Zip 38363-0250; tel. 901/847-3031; Larry N. Lindsey, Administrator and Chief Executive Officer

GIBSON GENERAL HOSPITAL, 200 Hospital Drive, Trenton, TN, Zip 38382-3300; tel. 901/855-7900; Kelly R. Yenawine, Administrator

HARDIN COUNTY GENERAL HOSPITAL, 2006 Wayne Road, Savannah, TN, Zip 38372-2294; tel. 901/925-4954; Charlotte Burns, Administrator and Chief Executive Officer

HENRY COUNTY MEDICAL CENTER, 301 Tyson Avenue, Paris, TN, Zip 38242-4544, Mailing Address: Box 1030, Zip 38242-1030; tel. 901/644-8537; Thomas H. Gee, Administrator

HUMBOLDT GENERAL HOSPITAL, 3525 Chere Carol Road, Humboldt, TN, Zip 38343-3699; tel. 901/784-0301; Jeff Frieling, Administrator

JACKSON–MADISON COUNTY GENERAL HOSPITAL, 708 West Forest Avenue, Jackson, TN, Zip 38301-3855; tel. 901/425-5000; James T. Moss, President and Chief Executive Officer

MCNAIRY COUNTY GENERAL HOSPITAL, 705 East Poplar Avenue, Selmer, TN, Zip 38375-1748; tel. 901/645-3221; Rosamond M. Tyler, Administrator

MILAN GENERAL HOSPITAL, 4039 South Highland, Milan, TN, Zip 38358; tel. 901/686-1591; Alfred P. Taylor, Administrator and Chief Executive Officer

TEXAS

BAYLOR HEALTH CARE SYSTEM NETWORK
3600 Gaston Avenue, Suite 150, Dallas, TX 75246; tel. 214/820-2731; Boone Powell, Jr., President & Chief Executive Officer

BAYLOR CENTER FOR RESTORATIVE CARE, 3504 Swiss Avenue, Dallas, TX, Zip 75204-6224; tel. 214/820-9700; Gerry Brueckner, R.N., Executive Director

BAYLOR MEDICAL CENTER AT GARLAND, 2300 Marie Curie Boulevard, Garland, TX, Zip 75042-5706; tel. 972/487-5000; John B. McWhorter, III, Executive Director

BAYLOR MEDICAL CENTER AT GRAPEVINE, 1650 West College Street, Grapevine, TX, Zip 76051-1650; tel. 817/329-2500; Mark C. Hood, Executive Director

BAYLOR MEDICAL CENTER AT IRVING, 1901 North MacArthur Boulevard, Irving, TX, Zip 75061-2291; tel. 972/579-8100; H. J. Macfarland, FACHE, Executive Director

BAYLOR MEDICAL CENTER–ELLIS COUNTY, 1405 West Jefferson Street, Waxahachie, TX, Zip 75165-2275; tel. 972/923-7000; James Michael Lee, Executive Director

BAYLOR RICHARDSON MEDICAL CENTER, 401 West Campbell Road, Richardson, TX, Zip 75080-3499; tel. 972/498-4000; Ronald L. Boring, President and Chief Executive Officer

BAYLOR UNIVERSITY MEDICAL CENTER, 3500 Gaston Avenue, Dallas, TX, Zip 75246-2088; tel. 214/820-0111; M. Tim Parris, Executive Vice President and Chief Operating Officer

HOPKINS COUNTY MEMORIAL HOSPITAL, 115 Airport Road, Sulphur Springs, TX, Zip 75482-0115; tel. 903/885-7671; Richard L. Goddard, Chief Executive Officer

BRAZO'S VALLEY HEALTH NETWORK
3115 Pine Avenue, Waco, TX 76708; tel. 817/757-3882; Don Reeves, Executive Director

CEDARS HOSPITAL, 2000 North Old Hickory Trail, De Soto, TX, Zip 75115-2242; tel. 972/298-7323; Don Johnson, Administrator

CENTRAL TEXAS HOSPITAL, 806 North Crockett Avenue, Cameron, TX, Zip 76520-2599; tel. 254/697-6591; Louis West, President

FALLS COMMUNITY HOSPITAL AND CLINIC, 322 Coleman Street, Marlin, TX, Zip 76661-2358, Mailing Address: Box 60, Zip 76661-0060; tel. 254/803-3561; Willis L. Reese, Administrator

GOODALL–WITCHER HOSPITAL, 101 South Avenue T., Clifton, TX, Zip 76634-1897, Mailing Address: P.O. Box 549, Zip 76634-0549; tel. 254/675-8322; Jim B. Smith, President and Chief Executive Officer

HILL REGIONAL HOSPITAL, 101 Circle Drive, Hillsboro, TX, Zip 76645-2670; tel. 254/582-8425; Jan McClure, Chief Executive Officer

HILLCREST BAPTIST MEDICAL CENTER, 3000 Herring Avenue, Waco, TX, Zip 76708-3299, Mailing Address: Box 5100, Zip 76708-0100; tel. 254/202-2000; Richard E. Scott, President

KING'S DAUGHTERS HOSPITAL, 1901 S.W. H. K. Dodgen Loop, Temple, TX, Zip 76502-1896; tel. 254/771-8600; Tucker Bonner, President

LAKE WHITNEY MEDICAL CENTER, 200 North San Jacinto Street, Whitney, TX, Zip 76692-2388, Mailing Address: P.O. Box 458, Zip 76692-0458; tel. 254/694-3165; Ruth Ann Crow, Administrator

LIMESTONE MEDICAL CENTER, 701 McClintic Street, Groesbeck, TX, Zip 76642-2105; tel. 254/729-3281; Penny Gray, Administrator and Chief Executive Officer

MEDICAL CENTER OF MESQUITE, 1011 North Galloway Avenue, Mesquite, TX, Zip 75149-2433; tel. 214/320-7000; Terry J. Fontenot, Administrator

PARKVIEW REGIONAL HOSPITAL, 312 East Glendale Street, Mexia, TX, Zip 76667-3608; tel. 254/562-5332; William E. Price, Interim Administrator

WEST COMMUNITY HOSPITAL, 501 Meadow Drive, West, TX, Zip 76691-1018, Mailing Address: P.O. Box 478, Zip 76691-0478; tel. 817/826-7000; Betty York, Executive Director

CENTRAL TEXAS RURAL HEALTH NETWORK
503 East 4th Street, Harrietsville, TX 77964-2824; tel. 512/798-2302; Marcella V. Henke, Executive Director

CENTRAL TEXAS HOSPITAL, 806 North Crockett Avenue, Cameron, TX, Zip 76520-2599; tel. 254/697-6591; Louis West, President

FALLS COMMUNITY HOSPITAL AND CLINIC, 322 Coleman Street, Marlin, TX, Zip 76661-2358, Mailing Address: Box 60, Zip 76661-0060; tel. 254/803-3561; Willis L. Reese, Administrator

GOODALL–WITCHER HOSPITAL, 101 South Avenue T., Clifton, TX, Zip 76634-1897, Mailing Address: P.O. Box 549, Zip 76634-0549; tel. 254/675-8322; Jim B. Smith, President and Chief Executive Officer

HILL REGIONAL HOSPITAL, 101 Circle Drive, Hillsboro, TX, Zip 76645-2670; tel. 254/582-8425; Jan McClure, Chief Executive Officer

LAKE WHITNEY MEDICAL CENTER, 200 North San Jacinto Street, Whitney, TX, Zip 76692-2388, Mailing Address: P.O. Box 458, Zip 76692-0458; tel. 254/694-3165; Ruth Ann Crow, Administrator

LIMESTONE MEDICAL CENTER, 701 McClintic Street, Groesbeck, TX, Zip 76642-2105; tel. 254/729-3281; Penny Gray, Administrator and Chief Executive Officer

PARKVIEW REGIONAL HOSPITAL, 312 East Glendale Street, Mexia, TX, Zip 76667-3608; tel. 254/562-5332; William E. Price, Interim Administrator

WEST COMMUNITY HOSPITAL, 501 Meadow Drive, West, TX, Zip 76691-1018, Mailing Address: P.O. Box 478, Zip 76691-0478; tel. 817/826-7000; Betty York, Executive Director

COLUMBIA HEALTHCARE – SOUTH TEXAS DIVISION
6629 Wooldridge Road, Corpus Christi, TX 78414; tel. 512/985-5200; Donald Stewart, President

COLUMBIA ALICE PHYSICIANS AND SURGEONS HOSPITAL, 300 East Third Street, Alice, TX, Zip 78332-4794; tel. 512/664-4376; Abraham Martinez, Chief Executive Officer

COLUMBIA BAY AREA MEDICAL CENTER, 7101 South Padre Island Drive, Corpus Christi, TX, Zip 78412-4999; tel. 512/985-1200; Kirk G. Wilson, Chief Executive Officer

COLUMBIA BAYVIEW PSYCHIATRIC CENTER, 6226 Saratoga Boulevard, Corpus Christi, TX, Zip 78414-3421; tel. 512/993-9700; Janie L. Harwood, Chief Executive Officer

COLUMBIA DOCTORS HOSPITAL OF LAREDO, 500 East Mann Road, Laredo, TX, Zip 78041-2699; tel. 956/723-1131; Benjamin Everett, Chief Executive Officer

COLUMBIA DOCTORS REGIONAL MEDICAL CENTER, 3315 South Alameda Street, Corpus Christi, TX, Zip 78411-1883, Mailing Address: P.O. Box 3828, Zip 78463-3828; tel. 512/857-1501; Steven Woerner, Chief Executive Officer

COLUMBIA NORTH BAY HOSPITAL, 1711 West Wheeler Avenue, Aransas Pass, TX, Zip 78336-4536; tel. 512/758-8585; Steve Sutherlin, Chief Executive Officer

COLUMBIA NORTHWEST HOSPITAL, 13725 Farm to Market Road 624, Corpus Christi, TX, Zip 78410-5199; tel. 512/767-4500; Winston Borland, Chief Executive Officer

COLUMBIA REHABILITATION HOSPITAL, 6226 Saratoga Boulevard, Corpus Christi, TX, Zip 78414-3499; tel. 512/991-9690; John Krogness, Chief Executive Officer

COLUMBIA RIO GRANDE REGIONAL HOSPITAL, 101 East Ridge Road, McAllen, TX, Zip 78503-1299; tel. 956/632-6000; Randall M. Everts, Chief Executive Officer

VALLEY REGIONAL MEDICAL CENTER, 1 Ted Hunt Boulevard, Brownsville, TX, Zip 78521-7899, Mailing Address: P.O. Box 3710, Zip 78521-3710; tel. 956/831-9611; David Butler, Chief Executive Officer

Section B

COLUMBIA SAINT DAVID'S HEALTH NETWORK
98 San Jacinto Boulevard, Austin, TX 78731; tel. 512/482–4135; Sharon J. Alvis, Executive Director

COLUMBIA ST. DAVID'S SOUTH HOSPITAL, 901 West Ben White Boulevard, Austin, TX, Zip 78704–6903; tel. 512/447–2211; Richard W. Klusmann, Chief Executive Officer

ROUND ROCK HOSPITAL, 2400 Round Rock Avenue, Round Rock, TX, Zip 78681–4097; tel. 512/255–6066; Deborah L. Ryle, Chief Executive Officer

ST. DAVID'S MEDICAL CENTER, 919 East 32nd Street, Austin, TX, Zip 78705–2709, Mailing Address: P.O. Box 4039, Zip 78765–4039; tel. 512/476–7111; Cole C. Eslyn, Chief Executive Officer

ST. DAVID'S PAVILION, 1025 East 32nd Street, Austin, TX, Zip 78765; tel. 512/867–5800; Cole C. Eslyn, Chief Executive Officer

ST. DAVID'S REHABILITATION CENTER, 1005 East 32nd Street, Austin, TX, Zip 78705–2705, Mailing Address: P.O. Box 4270, Zip 78765–4270; tel. 512/867–5100; Cole C. Eslyn, Chief Executive Officer

GOOD SHEPERD HEALTH NETWORK
700 East Marshall, Longview, TX 75601–5571; tel. 903/236–2000; Dr. Rebecca Burrow, Executive Director

GOOD SHEPHERD MEDICAL CENTER, 700 East Marshall Avenue, Longview, TX, Zip 75601–5571; tel. 903/236–2000; Jerry D. Adair, President and Chief Executive Officer

GULF COAST PROVIDER NETWORK
2900 North Loop West, Suite 1230, Houston, TX 77092; tel. 713/956–4992; Susan D. Cowan, President

COLUMBIA BAYSHORE MEDICAL CENTER, 4000 Spencer Highway, Pasadena, TX, Zip 77504–1294; tel. 713/359–2000; Russell Meyers, Chief Executive Officer

COLUMBIA BELLAIRE MEDICAL CENTER, 5314 Dashwood Street, Houston, TX, Zip 77081–4689; tel. 713/512–1200; Walter Leleux, Chief Executive Officer

COLUMBIA CLEAR LAKE REGIONAL MEDICAL CENTER, 500 Medical Center Boulevard, Webster, TX, Zip 77598–4286; tel. 281/338–3110; Donald A. Shaffett, Chief Executive Officer

COLUMBIA ROSEWOOD MEDICAL CENTER, 9200 Westheimer Road, Houston, TX, Zip 77063–3599; tel. 713/780–7900; Pat Currie, Chief Executive Officer

COLUMBIA WEST HOUSTON MEDICAL CENTER, 12141 Richmond Avenue, Houston, TX, Zip 77082–2499; tel. 281/558–3444; Jeffrey S. Holland, Chief Executive Officer

CYPRESS FAIRBANKS MEDICAL CENTER, 10655 Steepletop Drive, Houston, TX, Zip 77065–4297; tel. 281/890–4285; Bill Klier, Chief Executive Officer

HERMANN HOSPITAL, 6411 Fannin, Houston, TX, Zip 77030–1501; tel. 713/704–4000; Lynn Walts, R.N., Dr.PH, President and Chief Executive Officer

HOUSTON NORTHWEST MEDICAL CENTER, 710 FM 1960 West, Houston, TX, Zip 77090–3496; tel. 281/440–1000; James Kelly, Chief Executive Officer

POLLY RYON MEMORIAL HOSPITAL, 1705 Jackson Street, Richmond, TX, Zip 77469–3289; tel. 281/341–3000; Sam L. Steffee, Executive Director and Chief Executive Officer

SAN JACINTO METHODIST HOSPITAL, 4401 Garth Road, Baytown, TX, Zip 77521–3160; tel. 281/420–8600; William Simmons, President and Chief Executive Officer

SPRING BRANCH MEDICAL CENTER, 8850 Long Point Road, Houston, TX, Zip 77055–3082; tel. 713/467–6555; Pat Currie, Chief Executive Officer

WOMAN'S HOSPITAL OF TEXAS, 7600 Fannin Street, Houston, TX, Zip 77054–1900; tel. 713/790–1234; Linda B. Russell, Chief Executive Officer

GULF HEALTH NETWORK
701 University Boulevard, Suite 229, Galveston, TX 77550; tel. 401/766–4235; Jim Shallock, President

UNIVERSITY OF TEXAS MEDICAL BRANCH HOSPITALS, 301 University Boulevard, Galveston, TX, Zip 77555–0138; tel. 409/772–1011; James F. Arens, M.D., Chief Executive Officer

HEALTHCARE PARTNERS OF EAST TEXAS, INC.
P.O. Box 6340, Tyler, TX 75711; tel. 903/533–0684; Cindy Martinez, Executive Director & President

COZBY–GERMANY HOSPITAL, 707 North Waldrip Street, Grand Saline, TX, Zip 75140–1555; tel. 903/962–4242; William Rowton, Chief Executive Officer

DOCTORS MEMORIAL HOSPITAL, 1400 West Southwest Loop 323, Tyler, TX, Zip 75701; tel. 903/561–3771; Olie E. Clem, Chief Executive Officer

EAST TEXAS MEDICAL CENTER ATHENS, 2000 South Palestine Street, Athens, TX, Zip 75751–5610; tel. 903/675–2216; Patrick L. Wallace, Administrator

EAST TEXAS MEDICAL CENTER CARTHAGE, 409 Cottage Road, Carthage, TX, Zip 75633–1466, Mailing Address: P.O. Box 549, Zip 75633–0549; tel. 903/693–3841; Gary Mikeal Hudson, Administrator

EAST TEXAS MEDICAL CENTER JACKSONVILLE, 501 South Ragsdale Street, Jacksonville, TX, Zip 75766–2413; tel. 903/586–3000; Steve Bowen, President

EAST TEXAS MEDICAL CENTER PITTSBURG, 414 Quitman Street, Pittsburg, TX, Zip 75686–1032; tel. 903/856–6663; W. Perry Henderson, Administrator

EAST TEXAS MEDICAL CENTER RUSK, 500 North Bonner Street, Rusk, TX, Zip 75785, Mailing Address: P.O. Box 317, Zip 75785–0317; tel. 903/683–2273; Brenda Copley, Acting Administrator

EAST TEXAS MEDICAL CENTER–MOUNT VERNON, Highway 37 South, Mount Vernon, TX, Zip 75457, Mailing Address: P.O. Box 477, Zip 75457–0477; tel. 903/537–4552; Jerry Edwards, CHE, Administrator

EAST TEXAS MEDICAL CENTER–WOOD COUNTY AT QUITMAN, 117 Winnsboro Street, Quitman, TX, Zip 75783–2144, Mailing Address: P.O. Box 1000, Zip 75783–1000; tel. 903/763–4505; Marion W. Stanberry, Administrator

FAIRFIELD MEMORIAL HOSPITAL, 125 Newman Street, Fairfield, TX, Zip 75840–1499; tel. 903/389–2121; Milton W. Meadows, Administrator

GOOD SHEPHERD MEDICAL CENTER, 700 East Marshall, Longview, TX, Zip 75601–5571; tel. 903/236–2000; Jerry D. Adair, President and Chief Executive Officer

HENDERSON MEMORIAL HOSPITAL, 300 Wilson Street, Henderson, TX, Zip 75652–5956; tel. 903/657–7541; George T. Roberts, Jr., Chief Executive Officer

HUNTSVILLE MEMORIAL HOSPITAL, 3000 I–45, Huntsville, TX, Zip 77340, Mailing Address: P.O. Box 4001, Zip 77342–4001; tel. 409/291–3411; Ralph E. Beaty, Administrator

LINDEN MUNICIPAL HOSPITAL, North Kaufman Street, Linden, TX, Zip 75563–5235, Mailing Address: P.O. Box 32, Zip 75563–0032; tel. 903/756–5561; C. Edward Anderson, Administrator

MEMORIAL HOSPITAL OF CENTER, 602 Hurst Street, Center, TX, Zip 75935–3414, Mailing Address: P.O. Box 1749, Zip 75935–1749; tel. 409/598–2781; Robert V. Deen, Chief Executive Officer

MEMORIAL MEDICAL CENTER–LIVINGSTON, 602 East Church Street, Livingston, TX, Zip 77351–1257, Mailing Address: P.O. Box 1257, Zip 77351–1257; tel. 409/327–4381; James C. Dickson, Administrator

MEMORIAL MEDICAL CENTER OF EAST TEXAS, 1201 West Frank Avenue, Lufkin, TX, Zip 75904–3357, Mailing Address: P.O. Box 1447, Zip 75902–1447; tel. 409/634–8111; Gary Lex Whatley, President and Chief Executive Officer

NACOGDOCHES MEMORIAL HOSPITAL, 1204 North Mound Street, Nacogdoches, TX, Zip 75961–4061; tel. 409/568–8521; Gary J. Blan, FACHE, President and Chief Executive Officer

PINELANDS HOSPITAL, 4632 Northeast Stallings Drive, Nacogdoches, TX, Zip 75961–1617, Mailing Address: P.O. Box 1004, Zip 79563–1004; tel. 409/560–5900; Steve Scott, Chief Operating Officer

PRESBYTERIAN HOSPITAL OF WINNSBORO, 719 West Coke Road, Winnsboro, TX, Zip 75494–3098, Mailing Address: P.O. Box 628, Zip 75494–0628; tel. 903/342–5227; Dan Noteware, Executive Director

ROY H. LAIRD MEMORIAL HOSPITAL, 1612 South Henderson Boulevard, Kilgore, TX, Zip 75662–3594; tel. 903/984–3505; Roderick G. La Grone, President

ST. MICHAEL HEALTH CARE CENTER, 2600 St. Michael Drive, Texarkana, TX, Zip 75503–2372; tel. 903/614–2009; Don A. Beeler, Chief Executive Officer

TITUS REGIONAL MEDICAL CENTER, 2001 North Jefferson Avenue, Mount Pleasant, TX, Zip 75455–2398; tel. 903/577–6000; Steven K. Jacobson, Chief Executive Officer

TRINITY VALLEY MEDICAL CENTER, 2900 South Loop 256, Palestine, TX, Zip 75801–6958; tel. 903/731–1000; Larry C. Bozeman, Chief Executive Officer

LUBBOCK METHODIST HOSPITAL SYSTEM
3615 19th Street, Lubbock, TX 79410; tel. 806/793–4217; William D. Pateet, III, President & Chief Executive Officer

ANSON GENERAL HOSPITAL, 101 Avenue J., Anson, TX, Zip 79501–2198; tel. 915/823–3231; Dudley R. White, Administrator

BROWNFIELD REGIONAL MEDICAL CENTER, 705 East Felt, Brownfield, TX, Zip 79316–3439; tel. 806/637–3551; Mike Click, Administrator

CAMPBELL HEALTH SYSTEM, 713 East Anderson Street, Weatherford, TX, Zip 76086–9971; tel. 817/596–8751; John B. Millstead, Chief Executive Officer

COCHRAN MEMORIAL HOSPITAL, 201 East Grant Street, Morton, TX, Zip 79346–3444; tel. 806/266–5565; Paul McKinney, Administrator

COMANCHE COMMUNITY HOSPITAL, 211 South Austin Street, Comanche, TX, Zip 76442–3224; tel. 915/356–5241; W. Evan Moore, Administrator

DE LEON HOSPITAL, 407 South Texas Avenue, De Leon, TX, Zip 76444–1947, Mailing Address: P.O. Box 319, Zip 76444–0319; tel. 254/893–2011; Michael K. Hare, Administrator

FISHER COUNTY HOSPITAL DISTRICT, Roby Highway, Rotan, TX, Zip 79546, Mailing Address: Drawer F., Zip 79546; tel. 915/735–2256; Ella Raye Helms, Administrator

HEREFORD REGIONAL MEDICAL CENTER, 801 East Third Street, Hereford, TX, Zip 79045–5727, Mailing Address: P.O. Box 1858, Zip 79045–1858; tel. 806/364–2141; George N. Parsley, Administrator

LAMB HEALTHCARE CENTER, 1500 South Sunset, Littlefield, TX, Zip 79339–4899; tel. 806/385–6411; Randall A. Young, Administrator

MEDICAL ARTS HOSPITAL, 1600 North Bryan Avenue, Lamesa, TX, Zip 79331; tel. 806/872–2183; Arla Jeffcoat, Administrator

MITCHELL COUNTY HOSPITAL, 1543 Chestnut Street, Colorado City, TX, Zip 79512–3998; tel. 915/728–3431; Roland K. Rickard, Administrator

MOORE COUNTY HOSPITAL DISTRICT, 224 East Second Street, Dumas, TX, Zip 79029–3808; tel. 806/935–7171; Scott R. Brown, Administrator and Chief Executive Officer

MULESHOE AREA MEDICAL CENTER, 708 South First Street, Muleshoe, TX, Zip 79347–3627; tel. 806/272–4524; Jim G. Bone, Interim Administrator

PECOS COUNTY GENERAL HOSPITAL, 305 West Fifth Street, Iraan, TX, Zip 79744, Mailing Address: P.O. Box 665, Zip 79744–2057; tel. 915/639–2871; David B. Shaw, Administrator and Chief Executive Officer

PECOS COUNTY MEMORIAL HOSPITAL, Sanderson Highway, Fort Stockton, TX, Zip 79735, Mailing Address: P.O. Box 1648, Zip 79735–1648; tel. 915/336–2241; David B. Shaw, Administrator and Chief Executive Officer

PERMIAN GENERAL HOSPITAL, Northeast By–Pass, Andrews, TX, Zip 79714, Mailing Address: P.O. Box 2108, Zip 79714–2108; tel. 915/523–2200; Randy R. Richards, Chief Executive Officer

MEMORIAL/SISTERS OF CHARITY HEALTH NETWORK
7737 SouthWest Freeway, Suite 200, Houston, TX 77074; tel. 713/776–6992; Dan Wilford, President

ANGLETON–DANBURY GENERAL HOSPITAL, 132 East Hospital Drive, Angleton, TX, Zip 77515–4197; tel. 409/849–7721; David A. Bleakney, Administrator

MEMORIAL HOSPITAL SOUTHWEST, 7600 Beechnut, Houston, TX, Zip 77074–1850; tel. 713/776–5000; James E. Eastham, Vice President and Chief Executive Officer

MEMORIAL HOSPITAL–MEMORIAL CITY, 920 Frostwood Drive, Houston, TX, Zip 77024–9173; tel. 713/932–3000; Jerel T. Humphrey, Vice President, Chief Executive Officer and Administrator

MEMORIAL HOSPITAL–THE WOODLANDS, 9250 Pinecroft Drive, The Woodlands, TX, Zip 77380–3225; tel. 281/364–2300; Steve Sanders, Vice President, Chief Executive Officer and Administrator

MEMORIAL SPRING SHADOWS GLEN, 2801 Gessner, Houston, TX, Zip 77080–2599; tel. 713/462–4000; G. Jerry Mueck, Vice President, Chief Executive Officer and Administrator

POLLY RYON MEMORIAL HOSPITAL, 1705 Jackson Street, Richmond, TX, Zip 77469–3289; tel. 281/341–3000; Sam L. Steffee, Executive Director and Chief Executive Officer

TOMBALL REGIONAL HOSPITAL, 605 Holderrieth Street, Tomball, TX, Zip 77375–0889, Mailing Address: Box 889, Zip 77377–0889; tel. 281/351–1623; Robert F. Schaper, President and Chief Executive Officer

VAL VERDE REGIONAL MEDICAL CENTER, 801 Bedell Avenue, Del Rio, TX, Zip 78840–4185, Mailing Address: P.O. Box 1527, Zip 78840–1527; tel. 830/775–8566; Don Griffin, Chief Executive Officer

METHODIST HEALTHCARE SYSTEM OF SAN ANTONIO, LTD.
7550 IH 10 West, Suite 1000, San Antonio, TX 78229; tel. 210/377–1647; John E. Hornbeak, President

METHODIST WOMEN'S AND CHILDREN'S HOSPITAL, 8109 Fredericksburg Road, San Antonio, TX, Zip 78229–3383; tel. 210/692–5000; Janet Porter, President and Chief Executive Officer

METROPOLITAN METHODIST HOSPITAL, 1310 McCullough Avenue, San Antonio, TX, Zip 78212–2617; tel. 210/208–2200; Mark L. Bernard, Chief Executive Officer

NORTHEAST METHODIST HOSPITAL, 12412 Judson Road, San Antonio, TX, Zip 78233–3272, Mailing Address: P.O. Box 659510, Zip 78265–9510; tel. 210/650–4949; Mark L. Bernard, Chief Executive Officer

SAN ANTONIO COMMUNITY HOSPITAL, 8026 Floyd Curl Drive, San Antonio, TX, Zip 78229–3915; tel. 210/692–8110; James C. Scoggin, Jr., Chief Executive Officer

SOUTHWEST TEXAS METHODIST HOSPITAL, 7700 Floyd Curl Drive, San Antonio, TX, Zip 78229–3993; tel. 210/575–4000; James C. Scoggin, Jr., Chief Executive Officer

METROPLEX HEALTH NETWORK
2201 South Cleer Creek Road, Kileen, TX 75642; tel. 817/519–8218; Vicki Carlson, Director of Managed Care

METROPLEX HOSPITAL, 2201 South Clear Creek Road, Killeen, TX, Zip 76542–9305; tel. 254/526–7523; Kenneth A. Finch, Chief Executive Officer

NORTH TEXAS HEALTH NETWORK
5601 MacArthur, Suite 300, Irving, TX 75038; tel. 214/751–0047; Charlie Coil, President

BAYLOR CENTER FOR RESTORATIVE CARE, 3504 Swiss Avenue, Dallas, TX, Zip 75204–6224; tel. 214/820–9700; Gerry Brueckner, R.N., Executive Director

BAYLOR INSTITUTE FOR REHABILITATION, 3505 Gaston Avenue, Dallas, TX, Zip 75246–2018; tel. 214/826–7030; Judith C. Waterston, Executive Director

BAYLOR MEDICAL CENTER AT GARLAND, 2300 Marie Curie Boulevard, Garland, TX, Zip 75042–5706; tel. 972/487–5000; John B. McWhorter, III, Executive Director

BAYLOR MEDICAL CENTER AT GRAPEVINE, 1650 West College Street, Grapevine, TX, Zip 76051–1650; tel. 817/329–2500; Mark C. Hood, Executive Director

BAYLOR UNIVERSITY MEDICAL CENTER, 3500 Gaston Avenue, Dallas, TX, Zip 75246–2088; tel. 214/820–0111; M. Tim Parris, Executive Vice President and Chief Operating Officer

MEDICAL CENTER AT TERRELL, 1551 Highway 34 South, Terrell, TX, Zip 75160–4833; tel. 972/563–7611; Ronald J. Ensor, Chief Executive Officer

PEDIATRIC CENTER FOR RESTORATIVE CARE, 3301 Swiss Avenue, Dallas, TX, Zip 75204–6219; tel. 214/828–4747; Geraldine Brueckner, Administrator

PRESBYTERIAN HOSPITAL OF PLANO, 6200 West Parker Road, Plano, TX, Zip 75093–7914; tel. 972/608–8000; Philip M. Wentworth, FACHE, Executive Director

NORTH TEXAS HEALTHCARE NETWORK
3333 Lee Parkway, Suite 900, Dallas, TX 75919; tel. 214/820–3425; Bill Cook, President

BAYLOR CENTER FOR RESTORATIVE CARE, 3504 Swiss Avenue, Dallas, TX, Zip 75204–6224; tel. 214/820–9700; Gerry Brueckner, R.N., Executive Director

BAYLOR INSTITUTE FOR REHABILITATION, 3505 Gaston Avenue, Dallas, TX, Zip 75246–2018; tel. 214/826–7030; Judith C. Waterston, Executive Director

BAYLOR MEDICAL CENTER AT GARLAND, 2300 Marie Curie Boulevard, Garland, TX, Zip 75042–5706; tel. 972/487–5000; John B. McWhorter, III, Executive Director

BAYLOR MEDICAL CENTER AT GRAPEVINE, 1650 West College Street, Grapevine, TX, Zip 76051–1650; tel. 817/329–2500; Mark C. Hood, Executive Director

BAYLOR MEDICAL CENTER–ELLIS COUNTY, 1405 West Jefferson Street, Waxahachie, TX, Zip 75165–2275; tel. 972/923–7000; James Michael Lee, Executive Director

BAYLOR RICHARDSON MEDICAL CENTER, 401 West Campbell Road, Richardson, TX, Zip 75080–3499; tel. 972/498–4000; Ronald L. Boring, President and Chief Executive Officer

BAYLOR UNIVERSITY MEDICAL CENTER, 3500 Gaston Avenue, Dallas, TX, Zip 75246–2088; tel. 214/820–0111; M. Tim Parris, Executive Vice President and Chief Operating Officer

HARRIS CONTINUED CARE HOSPITAL, 1301 Pennsylvania Avenue, 4th Floor, Fort Worth, TX, Zip 76104–2190, Mailing Address: P.O. Box 3471, Zip 76113–3471; tel. 817/878–5500; Larry Thompson, Administrator

HARRIS METHODIST FORT WORTH, 1301 Pennsylvania Avenue, Fort Worth, TX, Zip 76104–2895; tel. 817/882–2000; Barclay E. Berdan, Chief Executive Officer

HARRIS METHODIST NORTHWEST, 108 Denver Trail, Azle, TX, Zip 76020–3697; tel. 817/444–8600; Larry Thompson, Vice President and Administrator

HARRIS METHODIST SOUTHWEST, 6100 Harris Parkway, Fort Worth, TX, Zip 76132–4199; tel. 817/346–5050; David B. Rowe, Vice President and Administrator

HARRIS METHODIST–ERATH COUNTY, 411 North Belknap Street, Stephenville, TX, Zip 76401–3415, Mailing Address: P.O. Box 1399, Zip 76401–1399; tel. 254/965–1500; Ronald E. Dorris, Administrator

HARRIS METHODIST–HEB, 1600 Hospital Parkway, Bedford, TX, Zip 76022–6913, Mailing Address: P.O. Box 669, Zip 76095–0669; tel. 817/685–4000; Jack McCabe, Senior Vice President and Administrator

PRESBYTERIAN HOSPITAL OF DALLAS, 8200 Walnut Hill Lane, Dallas, TX, Zip 75231–4402; tel. 214/345–6789; Mark H. Merrill, Executive Director

PRESBYTERIAN HOSPITAL OF KAUFMAN, 850 Highway 243 West, Kaufman, TX, Zip 75142–9998, Mailing Address: P.O. Box 310, Zip 75142–0310; tel. 972/932–7200; Michael J. McBride, CHE, Executive Director

PRESBYTERIAN HOSPITAL OF PLANO, 6200 West Parker Road, Plano, TX, Zip 75093–7914; tel. 972/608–8000; Philip M. Wentworth, FACHE, Executive Director

PRESBYTERIAN HOSPITAL OF WINNSBORO, 719 West Coke Road, Winnsboro, TX, Zip 75494–3098, Mailing Address: P.O. Box 628, Zip 75494–0628; tel. 903/342–5227; Dan Noteware, Executive Director

WALLS REGIONAL HOSPITAL, 201 Walls Drive, Cleburne, TX, Zip 76031–1008; tel. 817/641–2551; Brent D. Magers, FACHE, Chief Executive Officer and Administrator

PERMIAN BASIN RURAL HEALTH NETWORK
P.O. Box 1648, Fort Stockton, TX 79735; tel. 915/336–2241; George Miller, Jr., President

BIG BEND REGIONAL MEDICAL CENTER, 801 East Brown Street, Alpine, TX, Zip 79830–3209; tel. 915/837–3447; Don Edd Green, Chief Executive Officer

BIG SPRING STATE HOSPITAL, Lamesa Highway, Big Spring, TX, Zip 79720, Mailing Address: P.O. Box 231, Zip 79721–0231; tel. 915/267–8216; Edward Moughon, Superintendent

CRANE MEMORIAL HOSPITAL, 1310 South Alford Street, Crane, TX, Zip 79731–3899; tel. 915/558–3555; Stan Wiley, Administrator

MARTIN COUNTY HOSPITAL DISTRICT, 610 North St. Peter Street, Stanton, TX, Zip 79782, Mailing Address: P.O. Box 640, Zip 79782–0640; tel. 915/756–3345; Rick Jacobus, Administrator

MCCAMEY HOSPITAL, Highway 305 South, McCamey, TX, Zip 79752, Mailing Address: P.O. Box 1200, Zip 79752–1200; tel. 915/652–8626; Bill Boswell, Chief Executive Officer

MEDICAL ARTS HOSPITAL, 1600 North Bryan Avenue, Lamesa, TX, Zip 79331; tel. 806/872–2183; Arla Jeffcoat, Administrator

MEDICAL CENTER HOSPITAL, 500 West Fourth Street, Odessa, TX, Zip 79761–5059, Mailing Address: P.O. Drawer 7239, Zip 79760–7239; tel. 915/640–4000; J. Michael Stephans, Administrator

MEMORIAL HOSPITAL, 821 Jeffee Drive, Kermit, TX, Zip 79745–4696, Mailing Address: Drawer H., Zip 79745–6008; tel. 915/586–5864; Judene Willhelm, Administrator

MEMORIAL HOSPITAL, 209 N.W. Eighth Street, Seminole, TX, Zip 79360–3447; tel. 915/758–5811; Steve Beck, Chief Executive Officer and Administrator

MEMORIAL HOSPITAL AND MEDICAL CENTER, 2200 West Illinois Avenue, Midland, TX, Zip 79701–6499; tel. 915/685–1111; Harold Rubin, President and Chief Executive Officer

PECOS COUNTY GENERAL HOSPITAL, 305 West Fifth Street, Iraan, TX, Zip 79744, Mailing Address: P.O. Box 665, Zip 79744–2057; tel. 915/639–2871; David B. Shaw, Administrator and Chief Executive Officer

Section B

PECOS COUNTY MEMORIAL HOSPITAL, Sanderson Highway, Fort Stockton, TX, Zip 79735, Mailing Address: P.O. Box 1648, Zip 79735–1648; tel. 915/336–2241; David B. Shaw, Administrator and Chief Executive Officer

PERMIAN GENERAL HOSPITAL, Northeast By–Pass, Andrews, TX, Zip 79714, Mailing Address: P.O. Box 2108, Zip 79714–2108; tel. 915/523–2200; Randy R. Richards, Chief Executive Officer

RANKIN HOSPITAL DISTRICT, 1105 Elizabeth Street, Rankin, TX, Zip 79778, Mailing Address: P.O. Box 327, Zip 79778–0327; tel. 915/693–2443; John Paul Loyless, Administrator

REAGAN MEMORIAL HOSPITAL, 805 North Main Street, Big Lake, TX, Zip 76932–3999; tel. 915/884–2561; Ron Galloway, Administrator

REEVES COUNTY HOSPITAL, 2323 Texas Street, Pecos, TX, Zip 79772–7338; tel. 915/447–3551; Charles N. Butts, Interim Chief Executive Officer

SCENIC MOUNTAIN MEDICAL CENTER, 1601 West 11th Place, Big Spring, TX, Zip 79720–4198; tel. 915/263–1211; Kenneth W. Randall, Chief Executive Officer

VETERANS AFFAIRS MEDICAL CENTER, 300 Veterans Boulevard, Big Spring, TX, Zip 79720–5500; tel. 915/263–7361; Cary D. Brown, Director

WARD MEMORIAL HOSPITAL, 406 South Gary Street, Monahans, TX, Zip 79756–4798; tel. 915/943–2511; Ray Mason, Interim Chief Executive Officer

PRESBYTERIAN HEALTHCARE SYSTEM
8200 Walnut Hill Lane, Dallas, TX 75231; tel. 214/345–8486; Douglas Hawthorne, President

HUNT MEMORIAL HOSPITAL DISTRICT, 4215 Joe Ramsey Boulevard East, Greenville, TX, Zip 75401–7899, Mailing Address: P.O. Drawer 1059, Zip 75403–1059; tel. 903/408–5000; Richard Carter, Chief Executive Officer

MCCUISTION REGIONAL MEDICAL CENTER, 865 Deshong Drive, Paris, TX, Zip 75462–2097, Mailing Address: P.O. Box 160, Zip 75461–0160; tel. 903/737–1111; Anthony A. Daigle, Executive Director

PRESBYTERIAN HOSPITAL OF DALLAS, 8200 Walnut Hill Lane, Dallas, TX, Zip 75231–4402; tel. 214/345–6789; Mark H. Merrill, Executive Director

PRESBYTERIAN HOSPITAL OF KAUFMAN, 850 Highway 243 West, Kaufman, TX, Zip 75142–9998, Mailing Address: P.O. Box 310, Zip 75142–0310; tel. 972/932–7200; Michael J. McBride, CHE, Executive Director

PRESBYTERIAN HOSPITAL OF PLANO, 6200 West Parker Road, Plano, TX, Zip 75093–7914; tel. 972/608–8000; Philip M. Wentworth, FACHE, Executive Director

PRESBYTERIAN HOSPITAL OF WINNSBORO, 719 West Coke Road, Winnsboro, TX, Zip 75494–3098, Mailing Address: P.O. Box 628, Zip 75494–0628; tel. 903/342–5227; Dan Noteware, Executive Director

PRIMARY CARENET OF TEXAS
6243 IH 10 West, Suite 1001, San Antonio, TX 78201; tel. 210/704–4800; Susan Ginnity, Vice President Marketing & Sales

SANTA ROSA HEALTH CARE CORPORATION, 519 West Houston Street, San Antonio, TX, Zip 78207–3108; tel. 210/704–2011; William C. Finlayson, President and Chief Executive Officer

REGIONAL HEALTHCARE ALLIANCE
110 N. College Suite 900, Tyler, TX 75701; tel. 903/531–4447; John Webb, President

ATLANTA MEMORIAL HOSPITAL, Highway 77 at South Williams, Atlanta, TX, Zip 75551, Mailing Address: P.O. Box 1049, Zip 75551–1049; tel. 903/799–3000; Tom Crow, Administrator

BAYLOR UNIVERSITY MEDICAL CENTER, 3500 Gaston Avenue, Dallas, TX, Zip 75246–2088; tel. 214/820–0111; M. Tim Parris, Executive Vice President and Chief Operating Officer

CHILDREN'S MEDICAL CENTER OF DALLAS, 1935 Motor Street, Dallas, TX, Zip 75235–7794; tel. 214/640–2000; George D. Farr, President and Chief Executive Officer

COZBY–GERMANY HOSPITAL, 707 North Waldrip Street, Grand Saline, TX, Zip 75140–1555; tel. 903/962–4242; William Rowton, Chief Executive Officer

EAST TEXAS MEDICAL CENTER CARTHAGE, 409 Cottage Road, Carthage, TX, Zip 75633–1466, Mailing Address: P.O. Box 549, Zip 75633–0549; tel. 903/693–3841; Gary Mikeal Hudson, Administrator

EAST TEXAS MEDICAL CENTER–WOOD COUNTY AT QUITMAN, 117 Winnsboro Street, Quitman, TX, Zip 75783–2144, Mailing Address: P.O. Box 1000, Zip 75783–1000; tel. 903/763–4505; Marion W. Stanberry, Administrator

FAIRFIELD MEMORIAL HOSPITAL, 125 Newman Street, Fairfield, TX, Zip 75840–1499; tel. 903/389–2121; Milton W. Meadows, Administrator

GOOD SHEPHERD MEDICAL CENTER, 700 East Marshall Avenue, Longview, TX, Zip 75601–5571; tel. 903/236–2000; Jerry D. Adair, President and Chief Executive Officer

HEALTHSOUTH REHABILITATION HOSPITAL–TYLER, 3131 Troup Highway, Tyler, TX, Zip 75701–8352; tel. 903/510–7000; Thomas J. Cook, Chief Executive Officer

HENDERSON MEMORIAL HOSPITAL, 300 Wilson Street, Henderson, TX, Zip 75652–5956; tel. 903/657–7541; George T. Roberts, Jr., Chief Executive Officer

HOPKINS COUNTY MEMORIAL HOSPITAL, 115 Airport Road, Sulphur Springs, TX, Zip 75482–0115; tel. 903/885–7671; Richard L. Goddard, Chief Executive Officer

LINDEN MUNICIPAL HOSPITAL, North Kaufman Street, Linden, TX, Zip 75563–5235, Mailing Address: P.O. Box 32, Zip 75563–0032; tel. 903/756–5561; C. Edward Anderson, Administrator

MARSHALL REGIONAL MEDICAL CENTER, 811 South Washington Avenue, Marshall, TX, Zip 75670–5336, Mailing Address: P.O. Box 1599, Zip 75671–1599; tel. 903/927–6000; Thomas N. Cammack, Jr., Chief Executive Officer

NACOGDOCHES MEDICAL CENTER, 4920 N.E. Stallings, Nacogdoches, TX, Zip 75961–1200, Mailing Address: P.O. Box 631604, Zip 75963–1604; tel. 409/568–3380; Glenn A. Robinson, Director

PINELANDS HOSPITAL, 4632 Northeast Stallings Drive, Nacogdoches, TX, Zip 75961–1617, Mailing Address: P.O. Box 1004, Zip 79563–1004; tel. 409/560–5900; Steve Scott, Chief Operating Officer

PRESBYTERIAN HOSPITAL OF DALLAS, 8200 Walnut Hill Lane, Dallas, TX, Zip 75231–4402; tel. 214/345–6789; Mark H. Merrill, Executive Director

PRESBYTERIAN HOSPITAL OF KAUFMAN, 850 Highway 243 West, Kaufman, TX, Zip 75142–9998, Mailing Address: P.O. Box 310, Zip 75142–0310; tel. 972/932–7200; Michael J. McBride, CHE, Executive Director

PRESBYTERIAN HOSPITAL OF WINNSBORO, 719 West Coke Road, Winnsboro, TX, Zip 75494–3098, Mailing Address: P.O. Box 628, Zip 75494–0628; tel. 903/342–5227; Dan Noteware, Executive Director

ROY H. LAIRD MEMORIAL HOSPITAL, 1612 South Henderson Boulevard, Kilgore, TX, Zip 75662–3594; tel. 903/984–3505; Roderick G. La Grone, President

SCHUMPERT MEDICAL CENTER, One St. Mary Place, Shreveport, LA, Zip 71101–4399, Mailing Address: P.O. Box 21976, Zip 71120–1076; tel. 318/681–4500; Arthur A. Gonzalez, Dr.PH, President and Chief Executive Officer

TITUS REGIONAL MEDICAL CENTER, 2001 North Jefferson Avenue, Mount Pleasant, TX, Zip 75455–2398; tel. 903/577–6000; Steven K. Jacobson, Chief Executive Officer

TRINITY MOTHER FRANCES HEALTH SYSTEM, 800 East Dawson, Tyler, TX, Zip 75701–2093; tel. 903/593–8441; J. Lindsey Bradley, Jr., FACHE, President and Chief Administrative Officer

UNIVERSITY OF TEXAS HEALTH CENTER AT TYLER, Gladewater Highway, Tyler, TX, Zip 75708, Mailing Address: P.O. Box 2003, Zip 75710–2003; tel. 903/877–3451; Ronald F. Garvey, M.D., Chief Administrative Officer and Director

WILLIS–KNIGHTON MEDICAL CENTER, 2600 Greenwood Road, Shreveport, LA, Zip 71103–2600, Mailing Address: P.O. Box 32600, Zip 71130–2600; tel. 318/632–4600; James K. Elrod, President

SAINT PAUL MEDICAL CENTER AFFILIATE NETWORK
5909 Harry Hines Boulevard, Dallas, TX 75235; tel. 214/879–3100; R. Chris Christy, Network Coordinator

CEDARS HOSPITAL, 2000 North Old Hickory Trail, De Soto, TX, Zip 75115–2242; tel. 972/298–7323; Don Johnson, Administrator

COLUMBIA MEDICAL CENTER–DALLAS SOUTHWEST, 2929 South Hampton Road, Dallas, TX, Zip 75224–3026; tel. 214/330–4611; James B. Warren, Chief Executive Officer

DALLAS–FORT WORTH MEDICAL CENTER, 2709 Hospital Boulevard, Grand Prairie, TX, Zip 75051–1083; tel. 972/641–5000; Robert A. Ficken, Chief Executive Officer

MEDICAL CENTER OF MESQUITE, 1011 North Galloway Avenue, Mesquite, TX, Zip 75149–2433; tel. 214/320–7000; Terry J. Fontenot, Administrator

SOUTHEAST TEXAS HOSPITAL SYSTEM
233 West 10th Street, Dallas, TX 75208; tel. 800/776–6959; Bob McElearney, Interim President

CITIZENS MEDICAL CENTER, 2701 Hospital Drive, Victoria, TX, Zip 77901–5749; tel. 512/572–5113; David P. Brown, Administrator

CUERO COMMUNITY HOSPITAL, 2550 North Esplanade Street, Cuero, TX, Zip 77954–4716; tel. 512/275–6191; James E. Buckner, Jr., Administrator

DRISCOLL CHILDREN'S HOSPITAL, 3533 South Alameda Street, Corpus Christi, TX, Zip 78411–1785, Mailing Address: P.O. Box 6530, Zip 78466–6530; tel. 512/694–5000; J. E. Ted Stibbards, Ph.D., President and Chief Executive Officer

EL CAMPO MEMORIAL HOSPITAL, 303 Sandy Corner Road, El Campo, TX, Zip 77437–9535; tel. 409/543–6251; Steve Gularte, Administrator

JACKSON COUNTY HOSPITAL, 1013 South Wells Street, Edna, TX, Zip 77957–4098; tel. 512/782–5241; Marcella V. Henke, Administrator and Chief Executive Officer

LAVACA MEDICAL CENTER, 1400 North Texana Street, Hallettsville, TX, Zip 77964–2099; tel. 512/798–3671; James Vanek, Administrator

MEMORIAL MEDICAL CENTER, 815 North Virginia Street, Port Lavaca, TX, Zip 77979–3025, Mailing Address: P.O. Box 25, Zip 77979–0025; tel. 512/552–6713; Bob L. Bybee, President and Chief Executive Officer

REFUGIO COUNTY MEMORIAL HOSPITAL, 107 Swift Street, Refugio, TX, Zip 78377–2425; tel. 512/526–2321; Bill Jones, Administrator

VICTORIA REGIONAL MEDICAL CENTER, 101 Medical Drive, Victoria, TX, Zip 77904–3198; tel. 512/573–6100; J. Michael Mastej, Chief Executive Officer and Managing Director

YOAKUM COMMUNITY HOSPITAL, 1200 Carl Ramert Drive, Yoakum, TX, Zip 77995–4198, Mailing Address: P.O. Box 753, Zip 77995–0753; tel. 512/293–2321; Elwood E. Currier, Jr., CHE, Administrator

SOUTHEAST TEXAS INTEGRATED COMMUNITY HEALTH NETWORK
2600 North Loop, Houston, TX 77092; tel. 713/681–8877; Stanley T. Urban, President & Chief Executive Officer

Section B

ST. ELIZABETH HOSPITAL, 2830 Calder Avenue, Beaumont, TX, Zip 77702, Mailing Address: P.O. Box 5405, Zip 77726–5405; tel. 409/892–7171; Sister Mary Fatima McCarthy, Administrator

ST. JOHN HOSPITAL, 18300 St. John Drive, Nassau Bay, TX, Zip 77058; tel. 281/333–5503; Thomas Permetti, Administrator

ST. JOSEPH HOSPITAL, 1919 LaBranch Street, Houston, TX, Zip 77002; tel. 713/757–1000; Sally E. Jeffcoat, Administrator

ST. MARY HOSPITAL, 3600 Gates Boulevard, Port Arthur, TX, Zip 77642–3601, Mailing Address: P.O. Box 3696, Zip 77643–3696; tel. 409/985–7431; Jeffrey Webster, Chief Executive Officer

SOUTHWEST PREFERRED NETWORK
14901 Quorum Drive, Suite 200, Dallas, TX 75240; tel. 214/866–7400; Ron Lutz, President & Chief Executive Officer

ARLINGTON MEMORIAL HOSPITAL, 800 West Randol Mill Road, Arlington, TX, Zip 76012–2503; tel. 817/548–6100; Wayne N. Clark, President and Chief Executive Officer

ST. JOSEPH'S HOSPITAL AND HEALTH CENTER, 820 Clarksville Street, Paris, TX, Zip 75460–9070, Mailing Address: P.O. Box 9070, Zip 75461–9070; tel. 903/785–4521; Monty E. McLaurin, President

SOUTHWEST TEXAS RURAL HEALTH ALLIANCE
900 Northeast Loop 410, Suite 500, San Antonio, TX 78209; tel. 210/829–0009; Kay Peck, President

CENTRAL TEXAS MEDICAL CENTER, 1301 Wonder World Drive, San Marcos, TX, Zip 78666–7544; tel. 512/353–8979; Kenneth Bacon, President and Chief Executive Officer

DIMMIT COUNTY MEMORIAL HOSPITAL, 704 Hospital Drive, Carrizo Springs, TX, Zip 78834–3836; tel. 210/876–2424; Ernest Flores, Jr., Administrator

EDGAR B. DAVIS MEMORIAL HOSPITAL, 130 Hays Street, Luling, TX, Zip 78648–3207, Mailing Address: P.O. Box 510, Zip 78648–0510; tel. 830/875–5643; Neal Kelley, Administrator

FRIO HOSPITAL, 320 Berry Ranch Road, Pearsall, TX, Zip 78061–3998; tel. 210/334–3617; Alan D. Holmes, Chief Executive Officer

GUADALUPE VALLEY HOSPITAL, 1215 East Court Street, Seguin, TX, Zip 78155–5189; tel. 830/379–2411; Don L. Richey, Administrator

HILL COUNTRY MEMORIAL HOSPITAL, 1020 Kerrville Road, Fredericksburg, TX, Zip 78624, Mailing Address: P.O. Box 835, Zip 78624–0835; tel. 830/997–4353; Jeff A. Bourgeois, Chief Executive Officer

KIMBLE HOSPITAL, 2101 Main Street, Junction, TX, Zip 76849–2101; tel. 915/446–3321; Jamie R. Jacoby, Administrator

MCKENNA MEMORIAL HOSPITAL, 600 North Union Avenue, New Braunfels, TX, Zip 78130; tel. 830/606–9111; M. Ray Harris, Jr., President and Chief Executive Officer

MEDINA COMMUNITY HOSPITAL, 3100 Avenue East, Hondo, TX, Zip 78861–3599; tel. 210/741–4677; Richard D. Arnold, Administrator

MEMORIAL HOSPITAL, Highway 90A By-Pass, Gonzales, TX, Zip 78629, Mailing Address: P.O. Box 587, Zip 78629–0587; tel. 830/672–7581; Douglas Langley, Administrator

OTTO KAISER MEMORIAL HOSPITAL, 3349 South Highway 181, Kenedy, TX, Zip 78119–5240; tel. 830/583–3401; Harold L. Boening, Administrator

SID PETERSON MEMORIAL HOSPITAL, 710 Water Street, Kerrville, TX, Zip 78028–5398; tel. 830/896–4200; Frederick W. Hall, Jr., Administrator

TRI–CITY COMMUNITY HOSPITAL, Highway 97 East, Jourdanton, TX, Zip 78026, Mailing Address: P.O. Box 189, Zip 78026–0189; tel. 512/769–3515; S. Allen Smith, Administrator

UVALDE COUNTY HOSPITAL AUTHORITY, 1025 Garner Field Road, Uvalde, TX, Zip 78801–1025; tel. 830/278–6251; Ben M. Durr, Administrator

VAL VERDE REGIONAL MEDICAL CENTER, 801 Bedell Avenue, Del Rio, TX, Zip 78840–4185, Mailing Address: P.O. Box 1527, Zip 78840–1527; tel. 830/775–8566; Don Griffin, Chief Executive Officer

WARM SPRINGS REHABILITATION HOSPITAL, Gonzales, TX, Mailing Address: P.O. Box 58, Zip 78629–0058; tel. 830/672–6592; John W. Davis, Administrator

WILSON MEMORIAL HOSPITAL, 1301 Hospital Boulevard, Floresville, TX, Zip 78114–2798; tel. 830/393–3122; Robert Duffield, Administrator

TEXOMA HEALTH NETWORK
1600 11th Street, Wichita Falls, TX 76301; tel. 817/872–1126; David Whitaker, Executive Director

BOWIE MEMORIAL HOSPITAL, 705 East Greenwood Avenue, Bowie, TX, Zip 76230–3199; tel. 940/872–1126; Joyce Crumpler, R.N., Administrator

CHILLICOTHE HOSPITAL DISTRICT, 303 Avenue I., Chillicothe, TX, Zip 79225, Mailing Address: P.O. Box 370, Zip 79225–0370; tel. 817/852–5131; Linda Hall, Administrator

CLAY COUNTY MEMORIAL HOSPITAL, 310 West South Street, Henrietta, TX, Zip 76365–3399; tel. 940/538–5621; Edward E. Browning, Chief Executive Officer and Administrator

ELECTRA MEMORIAL HOSPITAL, 1207 South Bailey Street, Electra, TX, Zip 76360–3221, Mailing Address: P.O. Box 1112, Zip 76360–1112; tel. 940/495–3981; Jan A. Reed, CPA, Administrator and Chief Executive Officer

FAITH COMMUNITY HOSPITAL, 717 Magnolia Street, Jacksboro, TX, Zip 76458–1111; tel. 940/567–6633; Don Hopkins, Administrator

HAMILTON HOSPITAL, 903 West Hamilton Street, Olney, TX, Zip 76374–1725, Mailing Address: P.O. Box 158, Zip 76374–0158; tel. 940/564–5521; William R. Smith, Administrator

HARDEMAN COUNTY MEMORIAL HOSPITAL, 402 Mercer Street, Quanah, TX, Zip 79252–4026, Mailing Address: P.O. Box 90, Zip 79252–0090; tel. 940/663–2795; Charles Hurt, Administrator

NOCONA GENERAL HOSPITAL, 100 Park Street, Nocona, TX, Zip 76255–3616; tel. 940/825–3235; Jamers Brasier, Administrator

SEYMOUR HOSPITAL, 200 Stadium Drive, Seymour, TX, Zip 76380–2344; tel. 940/888–5572; Charles Norris, Administrator

THROCKMORTON COUNTY MEMORIAL HOSPITAL, 802 North Minter Street, Throckmorton, TX, Zip 76483, Mailing Address: P.O. Box 729, Zip 76483–0729; tel. 940/849–2151; Charles Norris, Administrator

UNITED REGIONAL HEALTH CARE SYSTEM–ELEVENTH STREET CAMPUS, 1600 11th Street, Wichita Falls, TX, Zip 76301–9988; tel. 940/720–0055; David D. Whitaker, FACHE, President and Chief Operating Officer

THE HEART NETWORK OF TEXAS
511 East John Carpenter Freeway, Suite 440, Irving, TX '75062; tel. 972/409–9100; Daniel Hanzlik, Executive Director

BAYLOR UNIVERSITY MEDICAL CENTER, 3500 Gaston Avenue, Dallas, TX, Zip 75246–2088; tel. 214/820–0111; M. Tim Parris, Executive Vice President and Chief Operating Officer

HARRIS CONTINUED CARE HOSPITAL, 1301 Pennsylvania Avenue, 4th Floor, Fort Worth, TX, Zip 76104–2190, Mailing Address: P.O. Box 3471, Zip 76113–3471; tel. 817/878–5500; Larry Thompson, Administrator

HARRIS METHODIST FORT WORTH, 1301 Pennsylvania Avenue, Fort Worth, TX, Zip 76104–2895; tel. 817/882–2000; Barclay E. Berdan, Chief Executive Officer

HARRIS METHODIST NORTHWEST, 108 Denver Trail, Azle, TX, Zip 76020–3697; tel. 817/444–8600; Larry Thompson, Vice President and Administrator

HARRIS METHODIST SOUTHWEST, 6100 Harris Parkway, Fort Worth, TX, Zip 76132–4199; tel. 817/346–5050; David B. Rowe, Vice President and Administrator

HARRIS METHODIST–ERATH COUNTY, 411 North Belknap Street, Stephenville, TX, Zip 76401–3415, Mailing Address: P.O. Box 1399, Zip 76401–1399; tel. 254/965–1500; Ronald E. Dorris, Administrator

HARRIS METHODIST–HEB, 1600 Hospital Parkway, Bedford, TX, Zip 76022–6913, Mailing Address: P.O. Box 669, Zip 76095–0669; tel. 817/685–4000; Jack McCabe, Senior Vice President and Administrator

HENDRICK HEALTH SYSTEM, 1242 North 19th Street, Abilene, TX, Zip 79601–2316; tel. 915/670–2000; Michael C. Waters, FACHE, President

HILLCREST BAPTIST MEDICAL CENTER, 3000 Herring Avenue, Waco, TX, Zip 76708–3299, Mailing Address: Box 5100, Zip 76708–0100; tel. 254/202–2000; Richard E. Scott, President

TEXOMA HEALTHCARE SYSTEM, 1000 Memorial Drive, Denison, TX, Zip 75020–2035, Mailing Address: P.O. Box 890, Zip 75021–9988; tel. 903/416–4000; Arthur L. Hohenberger, FACHE, President and Chief Executive Officer

TRINITY MOTHER FRANCES HEALTH SYSTEM, 800 East Dawson, Tyler, TX, Zip 75701–2093; tel. 903/593–8441; J. Lindsey Bradley, Jr., FACHE, President and Chief Administrative Officer

UNITED REGIONAL HEALTH CARE SYSTEM–ELEVENTH STREET CAMPUS, 1600 11th Street, Wichita Falls, TX, Zip 76301–9988; tel. 940/720–0055; David D. Whitaker, FACHE, President and Chief Operating Officer

WADLEY REGIONAL MEDICAL CENTER, 1000 Pine Street, Texarkana, TX, Zip 75501–5170, Mailing Address: Box 1878, Zip 75504–1878; tel. 903/798–8000; Hugh R. Hallgren, President and Chief Executive Officer

WALLS REGIONAL HOSPITAL, 201 Walls Drive, Cleburne, TX, Zip 76031–1008; tel. 817/641–2551; Brent D. Magers, FACHE, Chief Executive Officer and Administrator

UTAH

INTERMOUNTAIN HEALTHCARE/AMERINET
36 South State Street, 22nd Floor, Salt Lake City, UT 84111; tel. 801/442–2000; Scott Parker, President

ALTA VIEW HOSPITAL, 9660 South 1300 East, Sandy, UT, Zip 84094–3793; tel. 801/576–2600; Wes Thompson, Administrator and Chief Executive Officer

AMERICAN FORK HOSPITAL, 170 North 1100 East, American Fork, UT, Zip 84003–9787; tel. 801/763–3300; Keith N. Alexander, Administrator and Chief Operating Officer

BEAR RIVER VALLEY HOSPITAL, 440 West 600 North, Tremonton, UT, Zip 84337–2497; tel. 801/257–7441; Robert F. Jex, Administrator

CASSIA REGIONAL MEDICAL CENTER, 1501 Hiland Avenue, Burley, ID, Zip 83318–2675; tel. 208/678–4444; Richard Packer, Administrator

COTTONWOOD HOSPITAL MEDICAL CENTER, 5770 South 300 East, Salt Lake City, UT, Zip 84107–6186; tel. 801/262–3461; Douglas R. Fonnesbeck, Administrator

DELTA COMMUNITY MEDICAL CENTER, 126 South White Sage Avenue, Delta, UT, Zip 84624–8937; tel. 801/864–5591; James E. Beckstrand, Administrator

DIXIE REGIONAL MEDICAL CENTER, 544 South 400 East, Saint George, UT, Zip 84770–3799; tel. 435/634–4000; L. Steven Wilson, Administrator

FILLMORE COMMUNITY MEDICAL CENTER, 674 South Highway 99, Fillmore, UT, Zip 84631–5013; tel. 801/743–5591; James E. Beckstrand, Administrator

GARFIELD MEMORIAL HOSPITAL AND CLINICS, 200 North 400 East, Panguitch, UT, Zip 84759, Mailing Address: P.O. Box 389, Zip 84759–0389; tel. 435/676–8811; Eric Packer, Administrator

MCKAY–DEE HOSPITAL CENTER, 3939 Harrison Boulevard, Ogden, UT, Zip 84409–2386, Mailing Address: Box 9370, Zip 84409–0370; tel. 801/398–2800; Thomas F. Hanrahan, Chief Executive Officer

OREM COMMUNITY HOSPITAL, 331 North 400 West, Orem, UT, Zip 84057–1999; tel. 801/224–4080; Kim Nielsen, Administrator and Chief Operating Officer

POCATELLO REGIONAL MEDICAL CENTER, 777 Hospital Way, Pocatello, ID, Zip 83201–2797; tel. 208/234–0777; Earl L. Christison, Administrator

PRIMARY CHILDREN'S MEDICAL CENTER, 100 North Medical Drive, Salt Lake City, UT, Zip 84113–1100; tel. 801/588–2000; Joseph R. Horton, Chief Executive Officer and Administrator

SANPETE VALLEY HOSPITAL, 1100 South Medical Drive, Mount Pleasant, UT, Zip 84647–2222; tel. 435/462–2441; George Winn, Administrator

SEVIER VALLEY HOSPITAL, 1100 North Main Street, Richfield, UT, Zip 84701–1843; tel. 435/896–8271; Gary E. Beck, Administrator

UTAH VALLEY REGIONAL MEDICAL CENTER, 1034 North 500 West, Provo, UT, Zip 84604–3337; tel. 801/373–7850; Chris Coons, Chief Operating Officer

VALLEY VIEW MEDICAL CENTER, 595 South 75 East, Cedar City, UT, Zip 84720–3462; tel. 435/586–6587; Craig M. Smedley, Administrator

WASATCH COUNTY HOSPITAL, 55 South 500 East, Heber City, UT, Zip 84032–1999; tel. 801/654–2500; Randall K. Probst, Administrator

VERMONT

FLETCHER ALLEN HEALTH CARE
111 Colchester Avenue, Burlington, VT 05401; tel. 802/865–5191; Jim Taylor, President

FLETCHER ALLEN HEALTH CARE, 111 Colchester Avenue, Burlington, VT, Zip 05401–1429; tel. 802/656–2345; William V. Boettcher, Chief Executive Officer

VIRGINIA

CARILION HEALTH SYSTEM
101 Elm Avenue, Roanoke, VA 24013; tel. 540/981–7900; Shirley Hollard, Vice President

CARILION BEDFORD MEMORIAL HOSPITAL, 1613 Oakwood Street, Bedford, VA, Zip 24523–0688, Mailing Address: P.O. Box 688, Zip 24523–0688; tel. 540/586–2441; Howard Ainsley, Director

CARILION FRANKLIN MEMORIAL HOSPITAL, 180 Floyd Avenue, Rocky Mount, VA, Zip 24151–1389; tel. 540/483–5277; Matthew J. Perry, Director

CARILION GILES MEMORIAL HOSPITAL, 1 Taylor Avenue, Pearisburg, VA, Zip 24134–1932; tel. 540/921–6000; Morris D. Reece, Administrator

CARILION MEDICAL CENTER, Belleview at Jefferson Street, Roanoke, VA, Zip 24014, Mailing Address: P.O. Box 13367, Zip 24033–3367; tel. 540/981–7000; Lucas A. Snipes, FACHE, Director

CARILION RADFORD COMMUNITY HOSPITAL, 700 Randolph Street, Radford, VA, Zip 24141–2430; tel. 540/731–2000; Virginia Ousley, Director

CARILION SAINT ALBANS HOSPITAL, Route 11, Lee Highway, Radford, VA, Zip 24143, Mailing Address: P.O. Box 3608, Zip 24143–3608; tel. 540/639–2481; Janet McKinney Crawford, Administrator

CENTRAL VIRGINIA HEALTH NETWORK
8100 Three Chopt Road, Suite 209, Richmond, VA 23229; tel. 804/673–2846; Michael B. Matthews, Chief Executive Officer

BON SECOURS ST. MARY'S HOSPITAL, 5801 Bremo Road, Richmond, VA, Zip 23226–1900; tel. 804/285–2011; Ann E. Honeycutt, Executive Vice President and Administrator

BON SECOURS–RICHMOND COMMUNITY HOSPITAL, 1500 North 28th Street, Richmond, VA, Zip 23223–5396, Mailing Address: Box 27184, Zip 23261–7184; tel. 804/225–1700; Samuel F. Lillard, Executive Vice President and Administrator

BON SECOURS–STUART CIRCLE, 413 Stuart Circle, Richmond, VA, Zip 23220–3799; tel. 804/358–7051; Edward Gerardo, Interim Executive Vice President and Administrator

COMMUNITY MEMORIAL HEALTHCENTER, 125 Buena Vista Circle, South Hill, VA, Zip 23970–0090, Mailing Address: P.O. Box 90, Zip 23970–0090; tel. 804/447–3151; R. Michael Berryman, President

MARY IMMACULATE HOSPITAL, 2 Bernardine Drive, Newport News, VA, Zip 23602–4499; tel. 757/886–6000; Cynthia B. Farrand, Executive Vice President

RAPPAHANNOCK GENERAL HOSPITAL, 101 Harris Drive, Kilmarnock, VA, Zip 22482, Mailing Address: P.O. Box 1449, Zip 22482–1449; tel. 804/435–8000; James M. Holmes, President and Chief Executive Officer

RICHMOND MEMORIAL HOSPITAL, 1300 Westwood Avenue, Richmond, VA, Zip 23227–4699, Mailing Address: P.O. Box 26783, Zip 23261–6783; tel. 804/254–6000; Michael Robinson, Executive Vice President and Administrator

SHELTERING ARMS REHABILITATION HOSPITAL, 1311 Palmyra Avenue, Richmond, VA, Zip 23227–4418; tel. 804/342–4100; Michael J. McDonnell, Interim Chief Executive Officer

SOUTHSIDE REGIONAL MEDICAL CENTER, 801 South Adams Street, Petersburg, VA, Zip 23803–5133; tel. 804/862–5000; David S. Dunham, President

UNIVERSITY OF VIRGINIA MEDICAL CENTER, Jefferson Park Avenue, Charlottesville, VA, Zip 22908, Mailing Address: P.O. Box 10050, Zip 22906–0050; tel. 804/924–0211; Michael J. Halseth, Executive Director

DEPAUL MEDICAL CENTER GROUP
150 Kingsley Lane, Norfolk, VA 23505; tel. 804/889–5000; Kevin P. Conlin, President & Chief Executive Officer

BON SECOURS–DEPAUL MEDICAL CENTER, 150 Kingsley Lane, Norfolk, VA, Zip 23505–4650; tel. 757/889–5000; David McCombs, Executive Vice President and Administrator

INOVA HEALTH SYSTEM
8001 Braddock Road, Springfield, VA 22151; tel. 703/321–4213; J. Knox Singleton, President & Chief Executive Officer

INOVA FAIR OAKS HOSPITAL, 3600 Joseph Siewick Drive, Fairfax, VA, Zip 22033–1709; tel. 703/391–3600; Steven E. Brown, Administrator

INOVA FAIRFAX HOSPITAL, 3300 Gallows Road, Falls Church, VA, Zip 22042–3300; tel. 703/698–1110; Jolene Tornabeni, Administrator

INOVA MOUNT VERNON HOSPITAL, 2501 Parker's Lane, Alexandria, VA, Zip 22306–3209; tel. 703/664–7000; Susan Herbert, Administrator

PREFERRED CARE OF RICHMOND
9100 Arboretum Parkway, Richmond, VA 23236; tel. 804/560–4160; Sheri Duff, Network Coordinator

CHIPPENHAM AND JOHNSTON–WILLIS HOSPITALS, 7101 Jahnke Road, Richmond, VA, Zip 23225–4044; tel. 804/320–3911; Marilyn B. Tavenner, Chief Executive Officer

HENRICO DOCTORS' HOSPITAL, 1602 Skipwith Road, Richmond, VA, Zip 23229–5298; tel. 804/289–4500; Patrick W. Farrell, Chief Executive Officer

JOHN RANDOLPH MEDICAL CENTER, 411 West Randolph Road, Hopewell, VA, Zip 23860, Mailing Address: P.O. Box 971, Zip 23860; tel. 804/541–1600; Daniel J. Wetta, Jr., Chief Executive Officer

POPLAR SPRINGS HOSPITAL, 350 Poplar Drive, Petersburg, VA, Zip 23805–4657; tel. 804/733–6874; Anthony J. Vadella, Chief Executive Officer

RETREAT HOSPITAL, 2621 Grove Avenue, Richmond, VA, Zip 23220–4308; tel. 804/254–5100; Paul L. Baldwin, Chief Operating Officer

SENTARA HEALTH SYSTEM
6015 Poplar Hall Drive, Suite 306, Norfolk, VA 23502; tel. 757/455–7170; David Bernd, CEO

SENTARA BAYSIDE HOSPITAL, 800 Independence Boulevard, Virginia Beach, VA, Zip 23455–6076; tel. 757/363–6100; Virginia Bogue, Site Administrator

SENTARA HAMPTON GENERAL HOSPITAL, 3120 Victoria Boulevard, Hampton, VA, Zip 23661–1585, Mailing Address: Drawer 640, Zip 23669–0640; tel. 757/727–7000; Russell Kenwood, Administrator

SENTARA LEIGH HOSPITAL, 830 Kempsville Road, Norfolk, VA, Zip 23502–3981; tel. 757/466–6000; Darleen S. Anderson, R.N., MSN, Site Administrator

SENTARA NORFOLK GENERAL HOSPITAL, 600 Gresham Drive, Norfolk, VA, Zip 23507–1999; tel. 757/668–3000; Mark R. Gavens, President

WILLIAMSBURG COMMUNITY HOSPITAL, 301 Monticello Avenue, Williamsburg, VA, Zip 23187–8700, Mailing Address: Box 8700, Zip 23187–8700; tel. 757/259–6000; Les A. Donahue, President and Chief Executive Officer

TIDEWATER HEALTH CARE
1080 First Colonial Road, Virginia Beach, VA 23454; tel. 804/496–6200; Douglas L. Johnson, Ph.D., President and Chief Executive Officer

VIRGINIA BEACH GENERAL HOSPITAL, 1060 First Colonial Road, Virginia Beach, VA, Zip 23454–9000; tel. 757/481–8000; Robert L. Graves, Administrator

VALLEY HEALTH SYSTEM
P.O. Box 3340, Winchester, VA 22604; tel. 540/722–8000; David W. Goff, Chief Executive Officer

WARREN MEMORIAL HOSPITAL, 1000 Shenandoah Avenue, Front Royal, VA, Zip 22630–3598; tel. 540/636–0300; Charlie M. Horton, President

WINCHESTER MEDICAL CENTER, 1840 Amherst Street, Winchester, VA, Zip 22601–2540, Mailing Address: P.O. Box 3340, Zip 22604–3340; tel. 540/722–8000; George B. Caley, President

VIRGINIA HEALTH NETWORK
7400 Beaufont Springs Drive, Suite 505, Richmond, VA 23225; tel. 804/320–3837; David Keplinger, Marketing Vice President

BON SECOURS ST. MARY'S HOSPITAL, 5801 Bremo Road, Richmond, VA, Zip 23226–1900; tel. 804/285–2011; Ann E. Honeycutt, Executive Vice President and Administrator

BON SECOURS–DEPAUL MEDICAL CENTER, 150 Kingsley Lane, Norfolk, VA, Zip 23505–4650; tel. 757/889–5000; David McCombs, Executive Vice President and Administrator

BON SECOURS–RICHMOND COMMUNITY HOSPITAL, 1500 North 28th Street, Richmond, VA, Zip 23223–5396, Mailing Address: Box 27184, Zip 23261–7184; tel. 804/225–1700; Samuel F. Lillard, Executive Vice President and Administrator

BON SECOURS–STUART CIRCLE, 413 Stuart Circle, Richmond, VA, Zip 23220–3799; tel. 804/358–7051; Edward Gerardo, Interim Executive Vice President and Administrator

CHARTER BEHAVIORAL HEALTH SYSTEM OF CHARLOTTESVILLE, 2101 Arlington Boulevard, Charlottesville, VA, Zip 22903–1593; tel. 804/977–1120; Wayne Adams, Chief Executive Officer

CHARTER WESTBROOK BEHAVIORAL HEALTH SYSTEM, 1500 Westbrook Avenue, Richmond, VA, Zip 23227–3399; tel. 804/266–9671; Stephen P. Fahey, Administrator

CHESAPEAKE GENERAL HOSPITAL, 736 Battlefield Boulevard North, Chesapeake, VA, Zip 23320–4941, Mailing Address: P.O. Box 2028, Zip 23327–2028; tel. 757/547–8121; Donald S. Buckley, FACHE, President

CHILDREN'S HOSPITAL OF THE KING'S DAUGHTERS, 601 Children's Lane, Norfolk, VA, Zip 23507–1971; tel. 757/668–7700; Robert I. Bonar, Jr., President and Chief Executive Officer

COMMUNITY MEMORIAL HEALTHCENTER, 125 Buena Vista Circle, South Hill, VA, Zip 23970–0090, Mailing Address: P.O. Box 90, Zip 23970–0090; tel. 804/447–3151; R. Michael Berryman, President

GREENSVILLE MEMORIAL HOSPITAL, 214 Weaver Avenue, Emporia, VA, Zip 23847–1482; tel. 804/348–2000; Rosemary C. Check, Chief Executive Officer

LOUISE OBICI MEMORIAL HOSPITAL, 1900 North Main Street, Suffolk, VA, Zip 23434–4323, Mailing Address: P.O. Box 1100, Zip 23439–1100; tel. 757/934–4000; William C. Giermak, President and Chief Executive Officer

MARTHA JEFFERSON HOSPITAL, 459 Locust Avenue, Charlottesville, VA, Zip 22902–9940; tel. 804/982–7000; James E. Haden, President and Chief Executive Officer

MARYVIEW HOSPITAL, 3636 High Street, Portsmouth, VA, Zip 23707–3236; tel. 757/398–2200; Wayne Jones, Executive Vice President and Administrator

MEDICAL COLLEGE OF VIRGINIA HOSPITALS, VIRGINIA COMMONWEALTH UNIVERSITY, 401 North 12th Street, Richmond, VA, Zip 23219, Mailing Address: P.O. Box 980510, Zip 23298–0510; tel. 804/828–9000; Carl R. Fischer, Associate Vice President and Chief Executive Officer

RICHMOND MEMORIAL HOSPITAL, 1300 Westwood Avenue, Richmond, VA, Zip 23227–4699, Mailing Address: P.O. Box 26783, Zip 23261–6783; tel. 804/254–6000; Michael Robinson, Executive Vice President and Administrator

RIVERSIDE REGIONAL MEDICAL CENTER, 500 J. Clyde Morris Boulevard, Newport News, VA, Zip 23601–1976; tel. 757/594–2000; Gerald R. Brink, President and Chief Executive Officer

RIVERSIDE TAPPAHANNOCK HOSPITAL, Tappahannock, VA, Mailing Address: Route 2, Box 612, Zip 22560; tel. 804/443–3311; Elizabeth J. Martin, Vice President and Administrator

RIVERSIDE WALTER REED HOSPITAL, 7519 Hospital Drive, Gloucester, VA, Zip 23061–4178, Mailing Address: P.O. Box 1130, Zip 23061–1130; tel. 804/693–8800; Grady W. Philips, III, Vice President and Administrator

SHELTERING ARMS REHABILITATION HOSPITAL, 1311 Palmyra Avenue, Richmond, VA, Zip 23227–4418; tel. 804/342–4100; Michael J. McDonnell, Interim Chief Executive Officer

SOUTHAMPTON MEMORIAL HOSPITAL, 100 Fairview Drive, Franklin, VA, Zip 23851–1206, Mailing Address: P.O. Box 817, Zip 23851–0817; tel. 757/569–6100; Edward J. Patnesky, President and Chief Executive Officer

VIRGINIA BEACH GENERAL HOSPITAL, 1060 First Colonial Road, Virginia Beach, VA, Zip 23454–9000; tel. 757/481–8000; Robert L. Graves, Administrator

WILLIAMSBURG COMMUNITY HOSPITAL, 301 Monticello Avenue, Williamsburg, VA, Zip 23187–8700, Mailing Address: Box 8700, Zip 23187–8700; tel. 757/259–6000; Les A. Donahue, President and Chief Executive Officer

WASHINGTON

COLUMBIAN BASIN HEALTH NETWORK
P.O. Box 185, Mead, WA 99021; tel. 509/238–2167; Jamie Norr, Network Contact

COLUMBIA BASIN HOSPITAL, 200 Southeast Boulevard, Ephrata, WA, Zip 98823–1997; tel. 509/754–4631; Allen L. Beach, Administrator

COULEE COMMUNITY HOSPITAL, 411 Fortuyn Road, Grand Coulee, WA, Zip 99133–8718; tel. 509/633–1753; Charlotte Lang, Administrator

EAST ADAMS RURAL HOSPITAL, 903 South Adams Street, Ritzville, WA, Zip 99169–2298; tel. 509/659–1200; James G. Parrish, Administrator

LINCOLN HOSPITAL, 10 Nichols Street, Davenport, WA, Zip 99122; tel. 509/725–7101; Victor Vander Does, Administrator

MID–VALLEY HOSPITAL, 810 Valley Way Road, Omak, WA, Zip 98841, Mailing Address: Box 793, Zip 98841; tel. 509/826–1760; Michael D. Billing, Administrator

OTHELLO COMMUNITY HOSPITAL, 315 North 14th Street, Othello, WA, Zip 99344; tel. 509/488–2636; Jerry Lane, Administrator

QUINCY VALLEY MEDICAL CENTER, 908 Tenth Avenue S.W., Quincy, WA, Zip 98848; tel. 509/787–3531; Arne Seim, Interim Administrator

SAMARITAN HEALTHCARE, 801 East Wheeler Road, Moses Lake, WA, Zip 98837–1899; tel. 509/765–5606; Keith J. Baldwin, Administrator

DOMINICAN NETWORK
5633 North Lidgerwood, Spokane, WA 99207; tel. 509/482–2458; Ron Schurra, President

DEER PARK HEALTH CENTER AND HOSPITAL, East 1015 D. Street, Deer Park, WA, Zip 99006, Mailing Address: P.O. Box 742, Zip 99006; tel. 509/276–5061; Cathy Simchuk, Chief Operating Officer

HOLY FAMILY HOSPITAL, North 5633 Lidgerwood Avenue, Spokane, WA, Zip 99207; tel. 509/482–0111; Ronald J. Schurra, Chief Executive Officer

MOUNT CARMEL HOSPITAL, 982 East Columbia Street, Colville, WA, Zip 99114–0351, Mailing Address: Box 351, Zip 99114–0351; tel. 509/684–2561; Gloria Cooper, Chief Executive Officer

ST. JOSEPH HOSPITAL, 2901 Squalicum Parkway, Bellingham, WA, Zip 98225–1898; tel. 360/734–5400; Nancy J. Bitting, Chief Executive Officer

GROUP HEALTH COOPERATIVE OF PUGET SOUND
521 Wall Street, Seattle, WA 98121; tel. 206/448–3000; Phil Nudelman, Ph.D, President & Chief Executive Officer

THE EASTSIDE HOSPITAL, 2700 152nd Avenue N.E., Redmond, WA, Zip 98052–5560; tel. 425/883–5151; Patricia Kennedy–Scott, Northern Region Vice President

HEALTH WASHINGTON
P.O. Box 14999, Seattle, WA 98104–5044; tel. 206/386–3462; Joe Leinonen, President & Chief Executive Officer

EVERGREEN COMMUNITY HEALTH CENTER, 12040 N.E. 128th Street, Kirkland, WA, Zip 98034; tel. 425/899–1000; Andrew Fallat, FACHE, Chief Executive Officer

MARY BRIDGE CHILDREN'S HOSPITAL AND HEALTH CENTER, 317 Martin Luther King Jr. Way, Tacoma, WA, Zip 98405–0299, Mailing Address: Box 5299, Zip 98405–0299; tel. 253/552–1400; William B. Connoley, President and Chief Executive Officer

STEVENS HEALTHCARE, 21601 76th Avenue West, Edmonds, WA, Zip 98026–7506; tel. 425/640–4000; Steve C. McCary, President and Chief Executive Officer

SWEDISH HEALTH SERVICES, 747 Broadway Avenue, Seattle, WA, Zip 98122–4307; tel. 206/386–6000; Richard H. Peterson, President and Chief Executive Officer

TACOMA GENERAL HOSPITAL, 315 Martin Luther King Jr. Way, Tacoma, WA, Zip 98405–0299, Mailing Address: P.O. Box 5299, Zip 98405–0299; tel. 253/552–1000; William B. Connoley, President and Chief Executive Officer

LINCOLN COUNTY PUBLIC HEALTH COALITION
22 Bramhall Street, Davenport, WA 99122; tel. 509/725–1001; Diane Martin, Administrator

LINCOLN HOSPITAL, 10 Nichols Street, Davenport, WA, Zip 99122; tel. 509/725–7101; Victor Vander Does, Administrator

ODESSA MEMORIAL HOSPITAL, 502 East Amende, Odessa, WA, Zip 99159, Mailing Address: P.O. Box 368, Zip 99159–0368; tel. 509/982–2611; Carol Schott, Administrator

MULTICARE HEALTH SYSTEM
P.O. Box 5299, Tacoma, WA 98405; tel. 206/552–1000; William B. Connoley, President & Chief Executive Officer

ALLENMORE HOSPITAL, South 19th and Union Avenue, Tacoma, WA, Zip 98405, Mailing Address: P.O. Box 11414, Zip 98411–0414; tel. 253/572–2323; Charles Hoffman, Vice President

MARY BRIDGE CHILDREN'S HOSPITAL AND HEALTH CENTER, 317 Martin Luther King Jr. Way, Tacoma, WA, Zip 98405–0299, Mailing Address: Box 5299, Zip 98405–0299; tel. 253/552–1400; William B. Connoley, President and Chief Executive Officer

TACOMA GENERAL HOSPITAL, 315 Martin Luther King Jr. Way, Tacoma, WA, Zip 98405–0299, Mailing Address: P.O. Box 5299, Zip 98405–0299; tel. 253/552–1000; William B. Connoley, President and Chief Executive Officer

PEACEHEALTH
15325 Southeast 30th Place, Suite 300, Bellevue, WA 98007; tel. 206/747–1711; Sister Monica Heeran, Chief Executive Officer

EVERGREEN COMMUNITY HEALTH CENTER, 12040 N.E. 128th Street, Kirkland, WA, Zip 98034; tel. 425/899–1000; Andrew Fallat, FACHE, Chief Executive Officer

KETCHIKAN GENERAL HOSPITAL, 3100 Tongass Avenue, Ketchikan, AK, Zip 99901–5746; tel. 907/225–5171; Edward F. Mahn, Chief Executive Officer

PEACE HARBOR HOSPITAL, 400 Ninth Street, Florence, OR, Zip 97439, Mailing Address: P.O. Box 580, Zip 97439; tel. 541/997–8412; James Barnhart, Administrator

SACRED HEART MEDICAL CENTER, 1255 Hilyard Street, Eugene, OR, Zip 97401, Mailing Address: P.O. Box 10905, Zip 97440; tel. 541/686–7300; Judy Hodgson, Administrator

ST. JOHN MEDICAL CENTER, 1614 East Kessler Boulevard, Longview, WA, Zip 98632, Mailing Address: P.O. Box 3002, Zip 98632–0302; tel. 360/423–1530; Doug Doorn, Chief Financial Officer

ST. JOSEPH HOSPITAL, 2901 Squalicum Parkway, Bellingham, WA, Zip 98225–1898; tel. 360/734–5400; Nancy J. Bitting, Chief Executive Officer

PROVIDENCE SERVICES
9 East 9th Avenue, Spokane, WA 99202; tel. 509/742–7337; Richard J. Umdenstock, President & Chief Executive Officer

BENEFIS HEALTH CARE, 500 15th Avenue South, Great Falls, MT, Zip 59403–4389; tel. 406/455–5000; Lloyd V. Smith, President and Chief Executive Officer

HOLY FAMILY HOSPITAL, North 5633 Lidgerwood Avenue, Spokane, WA, Zip 99207; tel. 509/482–0111; Ronald J. Schurra, Chief Executive Officer

MOUNT CARMEL HOSPITAL, 982 East Columbia Street, Colville, WA, Zip 99114–0351, Mailing Address: Box 351, Zip 99114–0351; tel. 509/684–2561; Gloria Cooper, Chief Executive Officer

SACRED HEART MEDICAL CENTER, West 101 Eighth Avenue, Spokane, WA, Zip 99220, Mailing Address: P.O. Box 2555, Zip 99220; tel. 509/455–3040; Ryland P. Davis, President

ST. JOSEPH HOSPITAL, Skyline Drive and 14th Avenue, Polson, MT, Zip 59860, Mailing Address: P.O. Box 1010, Zip 59860–1010; tel. 406/883–5377; John W. Glueckert, President

ST. JOSEPH'S HOSPITAL, 500 East Webster Street, Chewelah, WA, Zip 99109, Mailing Address: P.O. Box 197, Zip 99109; tel. 509/935–8211; Gary V. Peck, Chief Executive Officer

ST. MARY MEDICAL CENTER, 401 West Poplar Street, Walla Walla, WA, Zip 99362, Mailing Address: Box 1477, Zip 99362–0312; tel. 509/525–3320; John A. Isely, President

ST. PATRICK HOSPITAL, 500 West Broadway, Missoula, MT, Zip 59802–4096, Mailing Address: Box 4587, Zip 59806–4587; tel. 406/543–7271; Lawrence L. White, Jr., President

WEST VIRGINIA

EASTERN PANHANDLE INTEGRATED DELIVERY SYSTEM
P.O. Box 1019, Petersburg, WV 26847; tel. 304/257–1026; Robert L. Harman, Chairman

GRANT MEMORIAL HOSPITAL, Route 55 West, Petersburg, WV, Zip 26847, Mailing Address: P.O. Box 1019, Zip 26847–1019; tel. 304/257–1026; Robert L. Harman, Administrator

HEALTH PARTNERS NETWORK, INC.
1000 Technology Drive Suite 2320, Fairmont, WV 26554; tel. 304/368–2740; William G. Maclean, Executive Director

UNITED HOSPITAL CENTER, Route 19 South, Clarksburg, WV, Zip 26301, Mailing Address: P.O. Box 1680, Zip 26302–1680; tel. 304/624–2121; Bruce C. Carter, President

WEST VIRGINIA UNIVERSITY HOSPITALS, Medical Center Drive, Morgantown, WV, Zip 26506–4749; tel. 304/598–4000; Bruce McClymonds, President

INTEGRATED PROVIDER NETWORK
7000 Hampton Center, Suite F., Morgantown, WV 26505; tel. 304/598–3911; Brad Minton, Network Contact

UNITED HOSPITAL CENTER, Route 19 South, Clarksburg, WV, Zip 26301, Mailing Address: P.O. Box 1680, Zip 26302–1680; tel. 304/624–2121; Bruce C. Carter, President

WEST VIRGINIA UNIVERSITY HOSPITALS, Medical Center Drive, Morgantown, WV, Zip 26506–4749; tel. 304/598–4000; Bruce McClymonds, President

MID–OHIO VALLEY RURAL HEALTH NETWORK
P.O. Box 718, Parkersburg, WV 26102; tel. 304/424–2111; Iris McCrady, Network Contact

CAMDEN–CLARK MEMORIAL HOSPITAL, 800 Garfield Avenue, Parkersburg, WV, Zip 26101–5378, Mailing Address: P.O. Box 718, Zip 26102–0718; tel. 304/424–2111; Thomas J. Corder, President and Chief Executive Officer

SISTERSVILLE GENERAL HOSPITAL, 314 South Wells Street, Sistersville, WV, Zip 26175–1098; tel. 304/652–2611; Lynn McCormick, Administrator

PARTNERS IN HEALTH NETWORK, INC.
P.O. Box 1547, Charleston, WV 25326; tel. 304/348–3072; Scot Mitchell, Executive Director

BECKLEY APPALACHIAN REGIONAL HOSPITAL, 306 Stanaford Road, Beckley, WV, Zip 25801–3142; tel. 304/255–3000; David R. Lyon, Administrator

BOONE MEMORIAL HOSPITAL, 701 Madison Avenue, Madison, WV, Zip 25130–1699; tel. 304/369–1230; Tommy H. Mullins, Administrator

BRAXTON COUNTY MEMORIAL HOSPITAL, 100 Hoylman Drive, Gassaway, WV, Zip 26624–9308; tel. 304/364–5156; Tony E. Atkins, Administrator

CHARLESTON AREA MEDICAL CENTER, 501 Morris Street, Charleston, WV, Zip 25301–1300, Mailing Address: P.O. Box 1547, Zip 25326–1547; tel. 304/348–5432; Robert L. Savage, President and Chief Executive Officer

JACKSON GENERAL HOSPITAL, Pinnell Street, Ripley, WV, Zip 25271, Mailing Address: P.O. Box 720, Zip 25271–0720; tel. 304/372–2731; Richard L. Rohaley, President and Chief Executive Officer

MAN ARH HOSPITAL, 700 East McDonald Avenue, Man, WV, Zip 25635–1011; tel. 304/583–8421; Louis G. Roe, Jr., Administrator

MINNIE HAMILTON HEALTHCARE CENTER, High Street, Grantsville, WV, Zip 26147, Mailing Address: Route 1, Box 1A, Zip 26147; tel. 304/354–9244; Barbara Lay, Administrator

MONTGOMERY GENERAL HOSPITAL, 401 Sixth Avenue, Montgomery, WV, Zip 25136–0270, Mailing Address: P.O. Box 270, Zip 25136–0270; tel. 304/442–5151; William R. Laird, IV, President and Chief Executive Officer

PLATEAU MEDICAL CENTER, 430 Main Street, Oak Hill, WV, Zip 25901–3455; tel. 304/469–8600; David L. Brash, Administrator

RICHWOOD AREA COMMUNITY HOSPITAL, Riverside Addition, Richwood, WV, Zip 26261; tel. 304/846–2573; D. Parker Haddix, Chief Executive Officer

ROANE GENERAL HOSPITAL, 200 Hospital Drive, Spencer, WV, Zip 25276–1060; tel. 304/927–6200; Andrew Mazon, III, Administrator and Chief Executive Officer

SUMMERS COUNTY APPALACHIAN REGIONAL HOSPITAL, Terrace Street, Hinton, WV, Zip 25951, Mailing Address: Drawer 940, Zip 25951–0940; tel. 304/466–1000; Clyde E. Bolton, Administrator

WILLIAMSON ARH HOSPITAL, 260 Hospital Drive, South Williamson, KY, Zip 41503–4072; tel. 606/237–1700; John A. Grah, Administrator

SOUTHERN VIRGINIA RURAL HEALTH NETWORK
133 Morrison Drive, Princeton, WV 24740; tel. 540/322–5147; Jean Henshaw, Network Coordinator

BLUEFIELD REGIONAL MEDICAL CENTER, 500 Cherry Street, Bluefield, WV, Zip 24701–3390; tel. 304/327–1100; Eugene P. Pawlowski, President

PRINCETON COMMUNITY HOSPITAL, 12th Street, Princeton, WV, Zip 24740–1369, Mailing Address: P.O. Box 1369, Zip 24740–1369; tel. 304/487–7000; Daniel C. Dunmyer, Chief Executive Officer

TRI–STATE COMMUNITY CARE NETWORK
601 Colliers Way, Weirton, WV 26062; tel. 304/797–6413; Cynthia R. Nixon, Chief Financial Officer

WEIRTON MEDICAL CENTER, 601 Colliers Way, Weirton, WV, Zip 26062–5091; tel. 304/797–6000; Donald Muhlenthaler, FACHE, President and Chief Executive Officer

WEBSTER MEMORIAL/UNITED HOSPITAL CENTER EACH/RPCH NETWORK
324 Miller Mountain Drive, Webster Springs, WV 26288; tel. 304/847–5682; Steve Gavalchik, President

UNITED HOSPITAL CENTER, Route 19 South, Clarksburg, WV, Zip 26301, Mailing Address: P.O. Box 1680, Zip 26302–1680; tel. 304/624–2121; Bruce C. Carter, President

WEBSTER COUNTY MEMORIAL HOSPITAL, 324 Miller Mountain Drive, Webster Springs, WV, Zip 26288–1087; tel. 304/847–5682; Stephen M. Gavalchik, Administrator

WISCONSIN

AFFINITY HEALTH SYSTEM, INC.
631 Hazel Street, Oshkosh, WI 54902–5677; tel. 414/236–2010; Otto L. Cox, Chief Executive Officer

MERCY MEDICAL CENTER, 631 Hazel Street, Oshkosh, WI, Zip 54901–4680, Mailing Address: P.O. Box 1100, Zip 54902–1100; tel. 920/236–2000; Otto L. Cox, President and Chief Executive Officer

ST. ELIZABETH HOSPITAL, 1506 South Oneida Street, Appleton, WI, Zip 54915–1397; tel. 920/738–2000; Otto L. Cox, President and Chief Executive Officer

ALL SAINTS HEALTHCARE SYSTEM
3801 Spring Street, Racine, WI 53405; tel. 414/636–4860; Ed DeMeulenaere, President Chief Executive Officer

SAINT MARY'S MEDICAL CENTER, 3801 Spring Street, Racine, WI, Zip 53405–1690; tel. 414/636–4011; Edward P. Demeulenaere, President and Chief Executive Officer

ST. LUKE'S MEMORIAL HOSPITAL, 1320 Wisconsin Avenue, Racine, WI, Zip 53403–1987; tel. 414/636–2011; Edward P. Demeulenaere, President and Chief Executive Officer

AURORA HEALTH CARE
3000 West Montana Street, Milwaukee, WI 53215; tel. 414/647–3000; G. Edwin Howe, President

HARTFORD MEMORIAL HOSPITAL, 1032 East Sumner Street, Hartford, WI, Zip 53027–1698; tel. 414/673–2300; Mark Schwartz, Administrator

LAKELAND MEDICAL CENTER, West 3985 County Road NN, Elkhorn, WI, Zip 53121, Mailing Address: P.O. Box 1002, Zip 53121–1002; tel. 414/741–2000; Kathy Skowlund, Administrator

MEMORIAL HOSPITAL CORPORATION OF BURLINGTON, 252 McHenry Street, Burlington, WI, Zip 53105–1828; tel. 414/763–2411; Loren J. Anderson, President and Chief Executive Officer

MILWAUKEE PSYCHIATRIC HOSPITAL, 1220 Dewey Avenue, Wauwatosa, WI, Zip 53213–2598; tel. 414/454–6600; James A. Moore, Administrator

SHEBOYGAN MEMORIAL MEDICAL CENTER, 2629 North Seventh Street, Sheboygan, WI, Zip 53083–4998; tel. 920/451–5000; T. Gregg Watson, Administrator

SINAI SAMARITAN MEDICAL CENTER, 945 North 12th Street, Milwaukee, WI, Zip 53233–1337, Mailing Address: P.O. Box 342, Zip 53201–0342; tel. 414/219–2000; Leonard E. Wilk, Administrator

ST. LUKE'S MEDICAL CENTER, 2900 West Oklahoma Avenue, Milwaukee, WI, Zip 53215–4330, Mailing Address: P.O. Box 2901, Zip 53201–2901; tel. 414/649–6000; Mark S. Wiener, Administrator

ST. MARY'S KEWAUNEE AREA MEMORIAL HOSPITAL, 810 Lincoln Street, Kewaunee, WI, Zip 54216–1140, Mailing Address: P.O. Box 217, Zip 54216–0217; tel. 920/388–2210; Steven H. Spencer, Administrator

TWO RIVERS COMMUNITY HOSPITAL AND HAMILTON MEMORIAL HOME, 2500 Garfield Street, Two Rivers, WI, Zip 54241–2399; tel. 920/793–1178; Steven H. Spencer, Administrator

VALLEY VIEW MEDICAL CENTER, 901 Reed Street, Plymouth, WI, Zip 53073–2409; tel. 920/893–1771; T. Gregg Watson, Administrator

WEST ALLIS MEMORIAL HOSPITAL, 8901 West Lincoln Avenue, West Allis, WI, Zip 53227–0901, Mailing Address: P.O. Box 27901, Zip 53227–0901; tel. 414/328–6000; Richard A. Kellar, Administrator

COLUMBIA – ST. MARY'S, INC.
2025 East Newport Avenue, Milwaukee, WI 53211; tel. 414/961–3638; John Schuler, President & Chief Executive Officer

COLUMBIA HOSPITAL, 2025 East Newport Avenue, Milwaukee, WI, Zip 53211–2990; tel. 414/961–3300; Susan Henckel, Executive Vice President and Chief Executive Officer

SACRED HEART REHABILITATION INSTITUTE, 2350 North Lake Drive, Milwaukee, WI, Zip 53211–4507, Mailing Address: P.O. Box 392, Zip 53201–0392; tel. 414/298–6700; William H. Lange, Administrator and Senior Vice President

ST. MARY'S HOSPITAL, 2323 North Lake Drive, Milwaukee, WI, Zip 53211–9682, Mailing Address: P.O. Box 503, Zip 53201–0503; tel. 414/291–1000; Charles C. Lobeck, Chief Executive Officer

ST. MARY'S HOSPITAL OZAUKEE, 13111 North Port Washington Road, Mequon, WI, Zip 53097–2416; tel. 414/243–7300; Therese B. Pandl, Senior Vice President and Chief Operating Officer

COMMUNITY HEALTH CARE, INC.
425 Pine Ridge Boulevard, Wausau, WI 54401;
tel. 715/847-2121; L. J. Olkowski, Senior Vice
President

MEMORIAL HOSPITAL OF TAYLOR COUNTY, 135
South Gibson Street, Medford, WI,
Zip 54451-1696; tel. 715/748-8100; Greg
Roraff, President and Chief Executive Officer

WAUSAU HOSPITAL, 333 Pine Ridge Boulevard,
Wausau, WI, Zip 54401-4187, Mailing Address:
P.O. Box 1847, Zip 54402-1847;
tel. 715/847-2121; Paul A. Spaude, President
and Chief Executive Officer

COVENANT HEALTHCARE SYSTEM, INC.
1126 South 70th Street, Suite 306,
Milwaukee, WI 53214-0970;
tel. 414/456-2300; E. Thomas Sheahan,
President & Chief Executive Officer

ELMBROOK MEMORIAL HOSPITAL, 19333 West North
Avenue, Brookfield, WI, Zip 53045-4198;
tel. 414/785-2000; Kimry A. Johnsrud,
President

LAKEVIEW HOSPITAL, 10010 West Blue Mound Road,
Wauwatosa, WI, Zip 53226; tel. 414/259-7200;
J. E. Race, Administrator and Chief Executive
Officer

MARQUETTE GENERAL HOSPITAL, 420 West
Magnetic Street, Marquette, MI,
Zip 49855-2794; tel. 906/225-4774; William
Nemacheck, Chief Executive Officer

ST. FRANCIS HOSPITAL, 3237 South 16th Street,
Milwaukee, WI, Zip 53215-4592;
tel. 414/647-5000; Gregory A. Banaszynski,
President

ST. JOSEPH'S HOSPITAL, 5000 West Chambers
Street, Milwaukee, WI, Zip 53210-9988;
tel. 414/447-2000; Jon L. Wachs, President

ST. MICHAEL HOSPITAL, 2400 West Villard Avenue,
Milwaukee, WI, Zip 53209-4999;
tel. 414/527-8000; Jeffrey K. Jenkins,
President

ST. NICHOLAS HOSPITAL, 1601 North Taylor Drive,
Sheboygan, WI, Zip 53081-2496;
tel. 920/459-8300; Michael J. Stenger,
Executive Vice President and Administrator

FRANCISCAN SKEMP HEALTHCARE
700 West Avenue South, LaCrosse, WI 54601;
tel. 608/791-9703; Brian C. Campion, M.D.,
President & Chief Executive Officer

FRANCISCAN SKEMP HEALTHCARE–ARCADIA
CAMPUS, 464 South St. Joseph Avenue,
Arcadia, WI, Zip 54612-1401;
tel. 608/323-3341; Robert M. Tracey,
Administrator

FRANCISCAN SKEMP HEALTHCARE–LA CROSSE
CAMPUS, 700 West Avenue South, La Crosse,
WI, Zip 54601-4783; tel. 608/785-0940; Brian
C. Campion, M.D., Chief Executive Officer

FRANCISCAN SKEMP HEALTHCARE–SPARTA
CAMPUS, 310 West Main Street, Sparta, WI,
Zip 54656-2171; tel. 608/269-2132; William
P. Sexton, Administrator

HEALTH CARE NETWORK OF WISCONSIN (HCN)
250 Bishops Way, Suite 300, Brookfield, WI
53005-6222; tel. 414/784-0223; Jim
Wrocklage, Chief Executive Officer

AGNESIAN HEALTHCARE, 430 East Division Street,
Fond Du Lac, WI, Zip 54935-0385;
tel. 920/929-2300; Robert A. Fale, President

BURNETT MEDICAL CENTER, 257 West St. George
Avenue, Grantsburg, WI, Zip 54840-7827;
tel. 715/463-5353; Timothy J. Wick, Chief
Executive Officer

CHILDREN'S HOSPITAL OF WISCONSIN, 9000 West
Wisconsin Avenue, Milwaukee, WI,
Zip 53226-4810, Mailing Address: P.O. Box
1997, Zip 53201-1997; tel. 414/266-2000;
Jon E. Vice, President and Chief Executive
Officer

COLUMBIA HOSPITAL, 2025 East Newport Avenue,
Milwaukee, WI, Zip 53211-2990;
tel. 414/961-3300; Susan Henckel, Executive
Vice President and Chief Executive Officer

COMMUNITY MEMORIAL HOSPITAL, W180 N8085
Town Hall Road, Menomonee Falls, WI,
Zip 53051, Mailing Address: P.O. Box 408,
Zip 53052-0408; tel. 414/251-1000; Robert
Eugene Drisner, President and Chief Executive
Officer

COMMUNITY MEMORIAL HOSPITAL, 855 South Main
Street, Oconto Falls, WI, Zip 54154-1296;
tel. 920/846-3444; Jim Van Dornick,
Administrator

ELMBROOK MEMORIAL HOSPITAL, 19333 West North
Avenue, Brookfield, WI, Zip 53045-4198;
tel. 414/785-2000; Kimry A. Johnsrud,
President

FROEDTERT MEMORIAL LUTHERAN HOSPITAL, 9200
West Wisconsin Avenue, Milwaukee, WI,
Zip 53226-3596, Mailing Address: P.O. Box
26099, Zip 53226-3596; tel. 414/259-3000;
William D. Petasnick, President

HARTFORD MEMORIAL HOSPITAL, 1032 East Sumner
Street, Hartford, WI, Zip 53027-1698;
tel. 414/673-2300; Mark Schwartz,
Administrator

HUDSON MEDICAL CENTER, 400 Wisconsin Street,
Hudson, WI, Zip 54016-1600;
tel. 715/386-9321; John W. Marnell, Chief
Executive Officer

MEMORIAL HOSPITAL CORPORATION OF
BURLINGTON, 252 McHenry Street, Burlington,
WI, Zip 53105-1828; tel. 414/763-2411; Loren
J. Anderson, President and Chief Executive
Officer

OCONOMOWOC MEMORIAL HOSPITAL, 791 Summit
Avenue, Oconomowoc, WI, Zip 53066-3896;
tel. 414/569-9400; Douglas Guy, President and
Chief Executive Officer

SHEBOYGAN MEMORIAL MEDICAL CENTER, 2629
North Seventh Street, Sheboygan, WI,
Zip 53083-4998; tel. 920/451-5000; T. Gregg
Watson, Administrator

SINAI SAMARITAN MEDICAL CENTER, 945 North 12th
Street, Milwaukee, WI, Zip 53233-1337, Mailing
Address: P.O. Box 342, Zip 53201-0342;
tel. 414/219-2000; Leonard E. Wilk,
Administrator

ST. CATHERINE'S HOSPITAL, 3556 Seventh Avenue,
Kenosha, WI, Zip 53140-2595;
tel. 414/656-3011; Robert M. Lovell, Interim
Chief Executive Officer

ST. CLARE HOSPITAL AND HEALTH SERVICES, 707
14th Street, Baraboo, WI, Zip 53913-1597;
tel. 608/356-5561; David B. Jordahl, FACHE,
President

ST. CROIX VALLEY MEMORIAL HOSPITAL, 204 South
Adams Street, Saint Croix Falls, WI,
Zip 54024-9400; tel. 715/483-3261; Steve L.
Urosevich, Chief Executive Officer

ST. FRANCIS HOSPITAL, 3237 South 16th Street,
Milwaukee, WI, Zip 53215-4592;
tel. 414/647-5000; Gregory A. Banaszynski,
President

ST. JOSEPH'S COMMUNITY HOSPITAL OF WEST
BEND, 551 South Silverbrook Drive, West Bend,
WI, Zip 53095-3898; tel. 414/334-5533;
Gregory T. Burns, Executive Director

ST. JOSEPH'S HOSPITAL, 5000 West Chambers
Street, Milwaukee, WI, Zip 53210-9988;
tel. 414/447-2000; Jon L. Wachs, President

ST. LUKE'S MEDICAL CENTER, 2900 West Oklahoma
Avenue, Milwaukee, WI, Zip 53215-4330,
Mailing Address: P.O. Box 2901,
Zip 53201-2901; tel. 414/649-6000; Mark S.
Wiener, Administrator

ST. LUKE'S MEMORIAL HOSPITAL, 1320 Wisconsin
Avenue, Racine, WI, Zip 53403-1987;
tel. 414/636-2011; Edward P. Demeulenaere,
President and Chief Executive Officer

ST. MARY'S HOSPITAL, 2323 North Lake Drive,
Milwaukee, WI, Zip 53211-9682, Mailing
Address: P.O. Box 503, Zip 53201-0503;
tel. 414/291-1000; Charles C. Lobeck, Chief
Executive Officer

ST. MARY'S HOSPITAL OF SUPERIOR, 3500 Tower
Avenue, Superior, WI, Zip 54880-5395;
tel. 715/392-8281; Terry Jacobson, Acting
Administrator

ST. MARYS HOSPITAL MEDICAL CENTER, 707 South
Mills Street, Madison, WI, Zip 53715-0450;
tel. 608/251-6100; Gerald W. Lefert, President

ST. MICHAEL HOSPITAL, 2400 West Villard Avenue,
Milwaukee, WI, Zip 53209-4999;
tel. 414/527-8000; Jeffrey K. Jenkins,
President

VALLEY VIEW MEDICAL CENTER, 901 Reed Street,
Plymouth, WI, Zip 53073-2409;
tel. 920/893-1771; T. Gregg Watson,
Administrator

WAUKESHA MEMORIAL HOSPITAL, 725 American
Avenue, Waukesha, WI, Zip 53188-5099;
tel. 414/544-2011; Rexford W. Titus, III,
President and Chief Executive Officer

WAUPUN MEMORIAL HOSPITAL, 620 West Brown
Street, Waupun, WI, Zip 53963-1799;
tel. 920/324-5581; James E. Baer, FACHE,
President

WEST ALLIS MEMORIAL HOSPITAL, 8901 West
Lincoln Avenue, West Allis, WI, Zip 53227-0901,
Mailing Address: P.O. Box 27901,
Zip 53227-0901; tel. 414/328-6000; Richard
A. Kellar, Administrator

HORIZON HEALTHCARE, INC.
2300 North Mayfair Road, Suite 550,
Milwaukee, WI 53226; tel. 414/257-3888;
Kurt W. Metzner, President & Chief Executive
Officer

COLUMBIA HOSPITAL, 2025 East Newport Avenue,
Milwaukee, WI, Zip 53211-2990;
tel. 414/961-3300; Susan Henckel, Executive
Vice President and Chief Executive Officer

COMMUNITY MEMORIAL HOSPITAL, W180 N8085
Town Hall Road, Menomonee Falls, WI,
Zip 53051, Mailing Address: P.O. Box 408,
Zip 53052-0408; tel. 414/251-1000; Robert
Eugene Drisner, President and Chief Executive
Officer

FROEDTERT MEMORIAL LUTHERAN HOSPITAL, 9200
West Wisconsin Avenue, Milwaukee, WI,
Zip 53226-3596, Mailing Address: P.O. Box
26099, Zip 53226-3596; tel. 414/259-3000;
William D. Petasnick, President

KENOSHA HOSPITAL AND MEDICAL CENTER, 6308
Eighth Avenue, Kenosha, WI, Zip 53143-5082;
tel. 414/656-2011; Richard O. Schmidt, Jr.,
President, Chief Executive Officer and General
Counsel

OCONOMOWOC MEMORIAL HOSPITAL, 791 Summit
Avenue, Oconomowoc, WI, Zip 53066-3896;
tel. 414/569-9400; Douglas Guy, President and
Chief Executive Officer

ST. MARY'S HOSPITAL, 2323 North Lake Drive,
Milwaukee, WI, Zip 53211-9682, Mailing
Address: P.O. Box 503, Zip 53201-0503;
tel. 414/291-1000; Charles C. Lobeck, Chief
Executive Officer

ST. MARY'S HOSPITAL OZAUKEE, 13111 North Port
Washington Road, Mequon, WI,
Zip 53097-2416; tel. 414/243-7300; Therese
B. Pandl, Senior Vice President and Chief
Operating Officer

LUTHER/MIDELFORT/MAYO HEALTH SYSTEM
733 West Clairmont, Eau Claire, WI 54701;
tel. 715/838-6732; William C. Rupp,
President & Chief Executive Officer

BARRON MEMORIAL MEDICAL CENTER AND SKILLED
NURSING FACILITY, 1222 Woodland Avenue,
Barron, WI, Zip 54812-1798;
tel. 715/537-3186; Mark D. Wilson,
Administrator

BLOOMER COMMUNITY MEMORIAL HOSPITAL AND
THE MAPLEWOOD, 1501 Thompson Street,
Bloomer, WI, Zip 54724-1299;
tel. 715/568-2000; John Perushek,
Administrator

LUTHER HOSPITAL, 1221 Whipple Street, Eau Claire,
WI, Zip 54702-4105; tel. 715/838-3311;
William Rupp, M.D., President and Chief
Executive Officer

OSSEO AREA HOSPITAL AND NURSING HOME, 13025
Eighth Street, Osseo, WI, Zip 54758, Mailing
Address: P.O. Box 70, Zip 54758-0070;
tel. 715/597-3121; Bradley D. Groseth,
Administrator

LUTHERAN HEALTH SYSTEM
   1910 South Avenue, LaCrosse, WI 54601;
   tel. 608/785–0530; John Katrana, Chief
   Executive Officer

LUTHERAN HOSPITAL–LA CROSSE, 1910 South
   Avenue, La Crosse, WI, Zip 54601–9980;
   tel. 608/785–0530; John N. Katrana, Ph.D.,
   Chief Administrative Officer
TOMAH MEMORIAL HOSPITAL, 321 Butts Avenue,
   Tomah, WI, Zip 54660–1412;
   tel. 608/372–2181; Philip Stuart, Administrator
TRI–COUNTY MEMORIAL HOSPITAL, 18601 Lincoln
   Street, Whitehall, WI, Zip 54773–0065, Mailing
   Address: P.O. Box 65, Zip 54773–0065;
   tel. 715/538–4361; Ronald B. Fields, President

MARSHFIELD CLINIC'S REGIONAL SYSTEM
   1000 North Oak Avenue, Marshfield, WI
   54449; tel. 715/389–4884; John Smylie,
   Director of Regional Operations

FLAMBEAU HOSPITAL, 98 Sherry Avenue, Park Falls,
   WI, Zip 54552–1467, Mailing Address: P.O. Box
   310, Zip 54552–0310; tel. 715/762–2484;
   Curtis A. Johnson, Administrator

MISSISSIPPI VALLEY HEALTH PARTNERSHIP
   705 East Taylor Street, Prairie du Chien, WI
   53821; tel. 608/326–2431; Harold W. Brown,
   Chief Executive Officer

PRAIRIE DU CHIEN MEMORIAL HOSPITAL, 705 East
   Taylor Street, Prairie Du Chien, WI,
   Zip 53821–2196; tel. 608/326–2431; Harold
   W. Brown, Chief Executive Officer

PARTNERS HEALTH SYSTEM, INC.
   225 Memorial Drive, Berlin, WI 54923;
   tel. 414/361–5580; Craig W. C. Schmidt,
   Chairman & Chief Executive Officer

COMMUNITY HEALTH NETWORK, 225 Memorial Drive,
   Berlin, WI, Zip 54923–1295;
   tel. 920/361–1313; Craig W. C. Schmidt,
   President and Chief Executive Officer
WILD ROSE COMMUNITY MEMORIAL HOSPITAL, 601
   Grove Avenue, Wild Rose, WI, Zip 54984, Mailing
   Address: P.O. Box 243, Zip 54984–0243;
   tel. 414/622–3257; Donald Caves, President

SOUTHERN WISCONSIN HEALTH CARE SYSTEM
   1000 Mineral Point Avenue, Janesville, WI
   53545–5003; tel. 608/756–6625; Javon R.
   Bea, President & Chief Executive Officer

MERCY HEALTH SYSTEM, 1000 Mineral Point Avenue,
   Janesville, WI, Zip 53545–5003, Mailing
   Address: P.O. Box 5003, Zip 53547–5003;
   tel. 608/756–6000; Javon R. Bea, President and
   Chief Executive Officer

UNIVERSITY OF WISCONSIN HOSPITALS AND CLINICS
   600 Highland Avenue, Madison, WI 53792;
   tel. 608/263–6400; Gordon Derzon, Chief
   Executive Officer

UNIVERSITY OF WISCONSIN HOSPITAL AND CLINICS,
   600 Highland Avenue, Madison, WI,
   Zip 53792–0002; tel. 608/263–6400; Gordon
   M. Derzon, Chief Executive Officer

WAUKESHA HOSPITAL SYSTEM, INC.
   725 American Avenue, Waukesha, WI 53188;
   tel. 414/544–2011; Donald Fundingsland,
   President

WAUKESHA MEMORIAL HOSPITAL, 725 American
   Avenue, Waukesha, WI, Zip 53188–5099;
   tel. 414/544–2011; Rexford W. Titus, III,
   President and Chief Executive Officer

WYOMING

COMMUNITY HEALTH CARE NETWORK
   P.O. Box 428, Jackson, WY 83001;
   tel. 307/733–3636; Nancy Johnsen, Wellness
   Coordinator

ST. JOHN'S HOSPITAL AND LIVING CENTER, 625 East
   Broadway Street, Jackson, WY, Zip 83001,
   Mailing Address: P.O. Box 428,
   Zip 83001–0428; tel. 307/733–3636; John
   Valiante, Chief Executive Officer

WYOMING INTEGRATED NETWORK
   1233 East 2nd Street, Casper, WY 82601;
   tel. 307/577–2153; Fred Schroeder, Network
   Contact

IVINSON MEMORIAL HOSPITAL, 255 North 30th
   Street, Laramie, WY, Zip 82070–5195;
   tel. 307/742–2141; J. Michael Boyd, Chief
   Executive Officer
WYOMING MEDICAL CENTER, 1233 East Second
   Street, Casper, WY, Zip 82601–2988;
   tel. 307/577–7201; Michael E. Schrader,
   President and Chief Executive Officer

Statistics for Multihospital Health Care Systems and their Hospitals

The following tables describing multihospital health care systems refer to information in section B of the 1998/99 *AHA Guide*.

Table 1 shows the number of multihospital health care systems by type of control. Table 2 provides a breakdown of the number of systems that own, lease, sponsor or contract manage hospitals within each control category. Table 3 gives the number of hospitals and beds in each control category as well as total hospitals and beds. Finally, Table 4 shows the percentage of hospitals and beds in each control category.

For more information on multihospital health care systems, please write to the Section for Health Care Systems, One North Franklin, Chicago, Illinois 60606–3401 or call 312/422–3000.

Table 1. Multihospital Health Care Systems, by Type of Organizaton Control

Type of Control	Code	Number of Systems
Catholic (Roman) church–related	CC	45
Other church–related	CO	12
Subtotal, church–related		57
Other not–for–profit	NP	171
Subtotal, not–for–profit		228
Investor Owned	IO	39
Federal Government	FG	5
Total		272

Table 2. Multihospital Health Care Systems, by Type of Ownership and Control

Type of Ownership	Catholic Church–Related (CC)	Other Church–Related (CO)	Total Church–Related (CC + CO)	Other Not–for–Profit (NP)	Total Not–for–Profit (CC, CO, + NP)	Investor–Owned (IO)	Federal Government	All Systems
Systems that only own, lease or sponsor	35	8	43	139	182	32	5	219
Systems that only contract–manage	0	0	0	2	2	1	0	3
Systems that manage, own, lease, or sponsor	10	4	14	30	44	6	0	50
Total	45	12	57	171	228	39	5	272

Table 3. Hospitals and Beds in Multihospital Health Care Systems, by Type of Ownership and Control

Type of Ownership	Catholic Church–Related (CC) H	B	Other Church–Related (CO) H	B	Total Church–Related (CC + CO) H	B	Other Not–for–Profit (NP) H	B	Total Not–for–Profit (CC, CO, + NP) H	B	Investor–Owned (IO) H	B	Federal Government H	B	All Systems H	B
Owned, leased or sponsored	462	105,171	88	19,385	550	124,556	871	205,439	1,421	329,995	910	123,957	285	63,153	2,616	517,105
Contract–managed	45	2,637	6	610	51	3,247	120	12,174	171	15,421	295	28,570	0	0	466	43,991
Total	507	107,808	94	19,995	601	127,803	991	217,613	1,592	345,416	1,205	152,527	285	63,153	3,082	561,096

H = hospitals; B = beds.

Table 4. Hospitals and Beds in Multihospital Health Care Systems, by Type of Ownership and Control, as a Percentage of All Systems

Type of Ownership	Catholic Church–Related (CC) H	B	Other Church–Related (CO) H	B	Total Church–Related (CC + CO) H	B	Other Not–for–Profit (NP) H	B	Total Not–for–Profit (CC, CO, + NP) H	B	Investor–Owned (IO) H	B	Federal Government H	B	All Systems H	B
Owned, leased or sponsored	17.7	20.3	3.4	3.7	21.0	24.1	33.3	39.7	54.3	63.8	34.8	24.0	10.9	12.2	100.0	100.0
Contract–managed	9.7	6.0	1.3	1.4	10.9	7.4	25.8	27.7	36.7	35.1	63.3	64.9	0.0	0.0	100.0	100.0
Total	16.5	19.2	3.0	3.6	19.5	22.8	32.2	38.8	51.7	61.6	39.1	27.2	9.2	11.3	100.0	100.0

H = hospitals; B = beds.
*Please note that figures may not always equal the provided subtotal or total percentages due to rounding.

Section B

0071: ACCORD HEALTH CARE CORPORATION (IO)
3696 Ulmerton Road, Clearwater, FL Zip 34622;
tel. 813/573-1755; Stephen H. Noble, President

GEORGIA: STEWART–WEBSTER HOSPITAL (O, 25 beds) 300 Alston Street, Richland, GA Zip 31825-1406, Mailing Address: P.O. Box 190, Zip 31825-0190; tel. 912/887-3366; Jerry R. Wise, Administrator

WHEELER COUNTY HOSPITAL (O, 30 beds) Third Street, Glenwood, GA Zip 30428, Mailing Address: P.O. Box 398, Zip 30428-0398; tel. 912/523-5113; James L. Jarrett, Administrator

Owned, leased, sponsored:	2 hospitals	55 beds
Contract–managed:	0 hospitals	0 beds
Totals:	2 hospitals	55 beds

★0235: ADVENTIST HEALTH (CO)
2100 Douglas Boulevard, Roseville, CA Zip 95661-3898, Mailing Address: P.O. Box 619002, Zip 95661-9002; tel. 916/781-2000; Frank F. Dupper, President

CALIFORNIA: FEATHER RIVER HOSPITAL (O, 122 beds) 5974 Pentz Road, Paradise, CA Zip 95969-5593; tel. 530/877-9361; George Pifer, President

FRANK R. HOWARD MEMORIAL HOSPITAL (L, 28 beds) 1 Madrone Street, Willits, CA Zip 95490; tel. 707/459-6801; Kevin R. Erich, Administrator

GLENDALE ADVENTIST MEDICAL CENTER (O, 396 beds) 1509 Wilson Terrace, Glendale, CA Zip 91206-4007; tel. 818/409-8000; Robert G. Carmen, President and Chief Executive Officer

HANFORD COMMUNITY MEDICAL CENTER (O, 59 beds) 450 Greenfield Avenue, Hanford, CA Zip 93230-0240, Mailing Address: Box 240, Zip 93232-0240; tel. 209/582-9000; Darwin R. Remboldt, President and Chief Executive Officer

PARADISE VALLEY HOSPITAL (O, 130 beds) 2400 East Fourth Street, National City, CA Zip 91950; tel. 619/470-4321; Eric Martinsen, President

REDBUD COMMUNITY HOSPITAL (O, 34 beds) 18th Avenue and Highway 53, Clearlake, CA Zip 95422, Mailing Address: Box 6720, Zip 95422; tel. 707/994-6486; Michael Schultz, President

SAN JOAQUIN COMMUNITY HOSPITAL (O, 178 beds) 2615 Eye Street, Bakersfield, CA Zip 93301, Mailing Address: Box 2615, Zip 93303-2615; tel. 805/395-3000; Fred Manchur, President

SELMA DISTRICT HOSPITAL (C, 57 beds) 1141 Rose Avenue, Selma, CA Zip 93662-3293; tel. 209/891-2201; Terrence A. Curley, Executive Director

SIMI VALLEY HOSPITAL AND HEALTH CARE SERVICES (O, 225 beds) 2975 North Sycamore Drive, Simi Valley, CA Zip 93065-1277; tel. 805/527-2462; Alan J. Rice, President

SONORA COMMUNITY HOSPITAL (O, 113 beds) 1 South Forest Road, Sonora, CA Zip 95370; tel. 209/532-3161; Lary Davis, President

SOUTH COAST MEDICAL CENTER (O, 155 beds) 31872 Coast Highway, South Laguna, CA Zip 92677; tel. 714/499-1311; T. Michael Murray, President

ST. HELENA HOSPITAL (O, 168 beds) 650 Sanitarium Road, Deer Park, CA Zip 94576, Mailing Address: P.O. Box 250, Zip 94576; tel. 707/963-3611; JoAline Olson, R.N., President

UKIAH VALLEY MEDICAL CENTER (O, 101 beds) 275 Hospital Drive, Ukiah, CA Zip 95482; tel. 707/462-3111; ValGene Devitt, President and Chief Executive Officer

WHITE MEMORIAL MEDICAL CENTER (O, 354 beds) 1720 Cesar E. Chavez Avenue, Los Angeles, CA Zip 90033-2481; tel. 213/268-5000; Beth D. Zachary, Chief Operating Officer

HAWAII: CASTLE MEDICAL CENTER (O, 150 beds) 640 Ulukahiki Street, Kailua, HI Zip 96734-4498; tel. 808/263-5500; Robert J. Walker, President

OREGON: ADVENTIST MEDICAL CENTER (O, 278 beds) 10123 S.E. Market, Portland, OR Zip 97216-2599; tel. 503/257-2500; Larry D. Dodds, President

PIONEER MEMORIAL HOSPITAL (C, 41 beds) 564 East Pioneer Drive, Heppner, OR Zip 97836, Mailing Address: P.O. Box 9, Zip 97836; tel. 503/676-9133; Kenneth A. Schmidt, President

TILLAMOOK COUNTY GENERAL HOSPITAL (L, 30 beds) 1000 Third Street, Tillamook, OR Zip 97141-3430; tel. 503/842-4444; Wendell Hesseltine, President

WASHINGTON: WALLA WALLA GENERAL HOSPITAL (O, 72 beds) 1025 South Second Avenue, Walla Walla, WA Zip 99362, Mailing Address: Box 1398, Zip 99362; tel. 509/525-0480; Rodney T. Applegate, President

Owned, leased, sponsored:	17 hospitals	2593 beds
Contract–managed:	2 hospitals	98 beds
Totals:	19 hospitals	2691 beds

★4165: ADVENTIST HEALTH SYSTEM SUNBELT HEALTH CARE CORPORATION (CO)
111 North Orlando Avenue, Winter Park, FL Zip 32789-3675; tel. 407/975-1417; Mardian J. Blair, President

FLORIDA: EAST PASCO MEDICAL CENTER (O, 120 beds) 7050 Gall Boulevard, Zephyrhills, FL Zip 33541-1399; tel. 813/788-0411; Paul Michael Norman, President

FLORIDA HOSPITAL (O, 1354 beds) 601 East Rollins Street, Orlando, FL Zip 32803-1489; tel. 407/896-6611; Thomas L. Werner, President

FLORIDA HOSPITAL HEARTLAND DIVISION (O, 195 beds) 4200 Sun'n Lake Boulevard, Sebring, FL Zip 33872, Mailing Address: P.O. Box 9400, Zip 33872; tel. 941/314-4466; John R. Harding, President and Chief Executive Officer

FLORIDA HOSPITAL WATERMAN (O, 182 beds) 201 North Eustis Street, Eustis, FL Zip 32726-3488, Mailing Address: P.O. Box B., Zip 32727-0377; tel. 352/589-3333; Kenneth R. Mattison, President and Chief Executive Officer

GEORGIA: EMORY–ADVENTIST HOSPITAL (O, 54 beds) 3949 South Cobb Drive S.E., Smyrna, GA Zip 30080-6300; tel. 770/434-0710; Terry Owen, Chief Executive Officer

GORDON HOSPITAL (O, 54 beds) 1035 Red Bud Road, Calhoun, GA Zip 30701-2082, Mailing Address: P.O. Box 12938, Zip 30703-7013; tel. 706/629-2895; Dennis Kiley, President

ILLINOIS: GLENOAKS HOSPITAL (O, 116 beds) 701 Winthrop Avenue, Glendale Heights, IL Zip 60139-1403; tel. 630/545-8000; Jorge A. Heyde, CHE, Administrator

HINSDALE HOSPITAL (O, 344 beds) 120 North Oak Street, Hinsdale, IL Zip 60521-3890; tel. 630/856-9000; Ernie W. Sadau, President and Chief Executive Officer

KENTUCKY: MEMORIAL HOSPITAL (O, 61 beds) 401 Memorial Drive, Manchester, KY Zip 40962-9156; tel. 606/598-5104; Jimm Bunch, Chief Executive Officer

NORTH CAROLINA: PARK RIDGE HOSPITAL (O, 90 beds) Naples Road, Fletcher, NC Zip 28732, Mailing Address: P.O. Box 1569, Zip 28732-1569; tel. 704/684-8501; Michael V. Gentry, President

PUERTO RICO: BELLA VISTA HOSPITAL (C, 157 beds) State Road 349, Mayaguez, PR Zip 00680, Mailing Address: P.O. Box 1750, Zip 00681; tel. 787/834-6000; Samuel Leonor, Chief Executive Officer

TENNESSEE: JELLICO COMMUNITY HOSPITAL (L, 54 beds) 188 Hospital Lane, Jellico, TN Zip 37762-4400; tel. 423/784-7252; Jim Bunch, President and Chief Executive Officer

TAKOMA ADVENTIST HOSPITAL (O, 80 beds) 401 Takoma Avenue, Greeneville, TN Zip 37743-4668; tel. 423/639-3151; Michael V. Gentry, President

For explanation of codes following names, see page B2.
★ Indicates Type III membership in the American Hospital Association.

Section B

TENNESSEE CHRISTIAN MEDICAL CENTER (O, 281 beds) 500 Hospital Drive, Madison, TN Zip 37115–5032; tel. 615/865–2373; Milton R. Siepman, Ph.D., President and Chief Executive Officer

TEXAS: CENTRAL TEXAS MEDICAL CENTER (O, 109 beds) 1301 Wonder World Drive, San Marcos, TX Zip 78666–7544; tel. 512/353–8979; Kenneth Bacon, President and Chief Executive Officer

HUGULEY MEMORIAL MEDICAL CENTER (O, 169 beds) 11801 South Freeway, Burleson, TX Zip 76028, Mailing Address: P.O. Box 6337, Fort Worth, Zip 76115–6337; tel. 817/293–9110; Peter M. Weber, President and Chief Executive Officer

METROPLEX HOSPITAL (O, 213 beds) 2201 South Clear Creek Road, Killeen, TX Zip 76542–9305; tel. 254/526–7523; Kenneth A. Finch, Chief Executive Officer

WISCONSIN: CHIPPEWA VALLEY HOSPITAL AND OAKVIEW CARE CENTER (O, 81 beds) 1220 Third Avenue West, Durand, WI Zip 54736–1600, Mailing Address: P.O. Box 224, Zip 54736–0224; tel. 715/672–4211; Douglas R. Peterson, President and Chief Executive Officer

Owned, leased, sponsored:	17 hospitals	3557 beds
Contract–managed:	1 hospital	157 beds
Totals:	18 hospitals	3714 beds

★0064: ADVOCATE HEALTH CARE (NP)
2025 Windsor Drive, Oak Brook, IL Zip 60523; tel. 630/990–5003; Richard R. Risk, President and Chief Executive Officer

ILLINOIS: BETHANY HOSPITAL (O, 102 beds) 3435 West Van Buren Street, Chicago, IL Zip 60624–3399; tel. 773/265–7700; Lena L. Shields, Chief Executive

CHRIST HOSPITAL AND MEDICAL CENTER (O, 626 beds) 4440 West 95th Street, Oak Lawn, IL Zip 60453–2699; tel. 708/425–8000; Carol Schneider, Chief Executive

GOOD SAMARITAN HOSPITAL (O, 255 beds) 3815 Highland Avenue, Downers Grove, IL Zip 60515–1590; tel. 630/275–5900; David M. McConkey, Chief Executive

GOOD SHEPHERD HOSPITAL (O, 154 beds) 450 West Highway 22, Barrington, IL Zip 60010–1901; tel. 847/381–9600; Russell E. Feurer, Chief Executive

LUTHERAN GENERAL HOSPITAL (O, 545 beds) 1775 Dempster Street, Park Ridge, IL Zip 60068–1174; tel. 847/723–2210; Kenneth J. Rojek, Chief Executive

RAVENSWOOD HOSPITAL MEDICAL CENTER (O, 306 beds) 4550 North Winchester Avenue, Chicago, IL Zip 60640–5205; tel. 773/878–4300; John E. Blair, President and Chief Executive Officer

SOUTH SUBURBAN HOSPITAL (O, 191 beds) 17800 South Kedzie Avenue, Hazel Crest, IL Zip 60429–0989; tel. 708/799–8000; Robert Rutkowski, Chief Executive

TRINITY HOSPITAL (O, 218 beds) 2320 East 93rd Street, Chicago, IL Zip 60617–3982; tel. 773/978–2000; John N. Schwartz, Chief Executive Officer

Owned, leased, sponsored:	8 hospitals	2397 beds
Contract–managed:	0 hospitals	0 beds
Totals:	8 hospitals	2397 beds

0225: ALAMEDA COUNTY HEALTH CARE SERVICES AGENCY (NP)
1850 Fairway Drive, San Leandro, CA Zip 94577; tel. 510/351–1367; David J. Kears, Director

CALIFORNIA: ALAMEDA COUNTY MEDICAL CENTER (O, 193 beds) 15400 Foothill Boulevard, San Leandro, CA Zip 94578–1091; tel. 510/667–7920; Michael G. Smart, Administrator

ALAMEDA COUNTY MEDICAL CENTER–HIGHLAND CAMPUS (O, 247 beds) 1411 East 31st Street, Oakland, CA Zip 94602; tel. 510/437–5081; Michael Smart, Chief Executive Officer

Owned, leased, sponsored:	2 hospitals	440 beds
Contract–managed:	0 hospitals	0 beds
Totals:	2 hospitals	440 beds

1685: ALBERT EINSTEIN HEALTHCARE NETWORK (NP)
5501 Old York Road, Philadelphia, PA Zip 19141–3098; tel. 215/456–7890; Martin Goldsmith, President

PENNSYLVANIA: ALBERT EINSTEIN MEDICAL CENTER (O, 701 beds) 5501 Old York Road, Philadelphia, PA Zip 19141–3098; tel. 215/456–7890; Martin Goldsmith, President

BELMONT CENTER FOR COMPREHENSIVE TREATMENT (O, 146 beds) 4200 Monument Road, Philadelphia, PA Zip 19131–1625; tel. 215/877–2000; Jack H. Dembow, General Director and Vice President

Owned, leased, sponsored:	2 hospitals	847 beds
Contract–managed:	0 hospitals	0 beds
Totals:	2 hospitals	847 beds

0065: ALEXIAN BROTHERS HEALTH SYSTEM, INC. (CC)
600 Alexian Way, Elk Grove Village, IL Zip 60007–3395; tel. 847/640–7550; Brother Felix Bettendorf, President

CALIFORNIA: ALEXIAN BROTHERS HOSPITAL (O, 192 beds) 225 North Jackson Avenue, San Jose, CA Zip 95116–1691; tel. 408/259–5000; Steven R. Barron, President and Chief Executive Officer

ILLINOIS: ALEXIAN BROTHERS MEDICAL CENTER (O, 393 beds) 800 Biesterfield Road, Elk Grove Village, IL Zip 60007–3397; tel. 847/437–5500; Michael J. Schwartz, President

Owned, leased, sponsored:	2 hospitals	585 beds
Contract–managed:	0 hospitals	0 beds
Totals:	2 hospitals	585 beds

★2305: ALLEGHENY HEALTH, EDUCATION AND RESEARCH FOUNDATION (NP)
120 Fifth Avenue, Pittsburgh, PA Zip 15222–3009; tel. 412/359–8800; Anthony M. Sanzo, President and Chief Executive Officer

NEW JERSEY: ALLEGHENY UNIVERSITY HOSPITAL, RANCOCAS (O, 237 beds) 218–A Sunset Road, Willingboro, NJ Zip 08046–1162; tel. 609/835–2900; Joseph Flamini, President and Chief Executive Officer

OHIO: EAST OHIO REGIONAL HOSPITAL (C, 178 beds) 90 North Fourth Street, Martins Ferry, OH Zip 43935–1648; tel. 740/633–1100; Brian K. Felici, Vice President and Administrator

PENNSYLVANIA: ALLEGHENY UNIVERSITY HOSPITALS WEST–FORBES METROPOLITAN (O, 152 beds) 225 Penn Avenue, Pittsburgh, PA Zip 15221–2173; tel. 412/247–2424; April A. Stevens, R.N., Vice President and Administrator

ALLEGHENY UNIVERSITY HOSPITAL, BUCKS COUNTY (O, 135 beds) 225 Newtown Road, Warminster, PA Zip 18974–5221; tel. 215/441–6600; Margaret M. McGoldrick, President and Chief Executive Officer

ALLEGHENY UNIVERSITY HOSPITAL, CITY AVENUE (O, 195 beds) 4150 City Avenue, Philadelphia, PA Zip 19131–1610; tel. 215/871–1000; Melvyn E. Smith, President

ALLEGHENY UNIVERSITY HOSPITAL, ELKINS PARK (O, 151 beds) 60 East Township Line Road, Elkins Park, PA Zip 19027–2220; tel. 215/663–6000; Margaret M. McGoldrick, President and Chief Executive Officer

ALLEGHENY UNIVERSITY HOSPITAL, GRADUATE (O, 198 beds) One Graduate Plaza, Philadelphia, PA Zip 19146–1407; tel. 215/893–2000; Arnold Berman, M.D., President and Chief Executive Officer

ALLEGHENY UNIVERSITY HOSPITAL, MEDICAL COLLEGE OF PENNSYLVANIA (O, 401 beds) 3300 Henry Avenue, Philadelphia, PA Zip 19129–1121; tel. 215/842–6000; Margaret M. McGoldrick, President and Chief Executive Officer

ALLEGHENY UNIVERSITY HOSPITAL, PARKVIEW (O, 165 beds) 1331 East Wyoming Avenue, Philadelphia, PA Zip 19124–3895; tel. 215/537–7400; Margaret M. McGoldrick, President and Chief Executive Officer

Section B

For explanation of codes following names, see page B2.
★ Indicates Type III membership in the American Hospital Association.

ALLEGHENY UNIVERSITY HOSPITALS, ALLEGHENY GENERAL (O, 569 beds) 320 East North Avenue, Pittsburgh, PA Zip 15212–4756; tel. 412/359–3131; Anthony M. Sanzo, President and Chief Executive Officer

ALLEGHENY UNIVERSITY HOSPITALS, CANONSBURG (O, 120 beds) 100 Medical Boulevard, Canonsburg, PA Zip 15317–9762; tel. 724/745–6100; Barbara A. Bensaia, Chief Executive Officer

ALLEGHENY UNIVERSITY HOSPITALS, FORBES REGIONAL (O, 317 beds) 2570 Haymaker Road, Monroeville, PA Zip 15146–3592; tel. 412/858–2000; Dana W. Ramish, President and Chief Executive Officer

ALLEGHENY UNIVERSITY HOSPITALS, HAHNEMANN (O, 427 beds) Broad and Vine Streets, Philadelphia, PA Zip 19102–1192; tel. 215/762–7000; Margaret M. McGoldrick, President and Chief Executive Officer

ALLEGHENY UNIVERSITY MEDICAL CENTER–ALLEGHENY VALLEY (O, 268 beds) 1301 Carlisle Street, Natrona Heights, PA Zip 15065–1192; tel. 724/224–5100; John R. England, President and Chief Executive Officer

ST. CHRISTOPHER'S HOSPITAL FOR CHILDREN (O, 183 beds) Erie Avenue at Front Street, Philadelphia, PA Zip 19134–1095; tel. 215/427–5000; Calvin Bland, President and Chief Executive Officer

WEST VIRGINIA: OHIO VALLEY MEDICAL CENTER (C, 385 beds) 2000 Eoff Street, Wheeling, WV Zip 26003–3870; tel. 304/234–0123; Thomas P. Galinski, President and Chief Executive Officer

Owned, leased, sponsored:	14 hospitals	3518 beds
Contract–managed:	2 hospitals	563 beds
Totals:	16 hospitals	4081 beds

★2285: ALLIANT HEALTH SYSTEM (NP)
234 East Gray Street, Suite 225, Louisville, KY Zip 40202, Mailing Address: P.O. Box 35070, Zip 40232–5070; tel. 502/629–8025; Stephen A. Williams, President

ILLINOIS: FAIRFIELD MEMORIAL HOSPITAL (C, 185 beds) 303 N.W. 11th Street, Fairfield, IL Zip 62837–1203; tel. 618/842–2611; Jay Purvis, Acting Chief Executive Officer

MASSAC MEMORIAL HOSPITAL (C, 35 beds) 28 Chick Street, Metropolis, IL Zip 62960–2481, Mailing Address: P.O. Box 850, Zip 62960–0850; tel. 618/524–2176; Mark Edwards, Chief Executive Officer

PARIS COMMUNITY HOSPITAL (C, 49 beds) 721 East Court Street, Paris, IL Zip 61944–2420; tel. 217/465–4141; John M. Dillon, Chief Executive Officer

WABASH GENERAL HOSPITAL DISTRICT (C, 56 beds) 1418 College Drive, Mount Carmel, IL Zip 62863–2638; tel. 618/262–8621; James R. Farris, CHE, Chief Executive Officer

INDIANA: BLACKFORD COUNTY HOSPITAL (C, 36 beds) 503 East Van Cleve Street, Hartford City, IN Zip 47348–1897; tel. 765/348–0300; David Masterson, Chief Executive Officer

DECATUR COUNTY MEMORIAL HOSPITAL (C, 70 beds) 720 North Lincoln Street, Greensburg, IN Zip 47240–1398; tel. 812/663–4331; Charles Duffy, President

GIBSON GENERAL HOSPITAL (C, 109 beds) 1808 Sherman Drive, Princeton, IN Zip 47670–1043; tel. 812/385–3401; Michael J. Budnick, Administrator and Chief Executive Officer

HARRISON COUNTY HOSPITAL (C, 50 beds) 245 Atwood Street, Corydon, IN Zip 47112–1774; tel. 812/738–4251; Steven L. Taylor, Chief Executive Officer

PERRY COUNTY MEMORIAL HOSPITAL (C, 38 beds) 1 Hospital Road, Tell City, IN Zip 47586–0362; tel. 812/547–7011; Bradford W. Dykes, Chief Executive Officer

RANDOLPH COUNTY HOSPITAL AND HEALTH SERVICES (C, 27 beds) 325 South Oak Street, Winchester, IN Zip 47394–2235, Mailing Address: P.O. Box 407, Zip 47394–0407; tel. 765/584–9001; James M. Full, Chief Executive Officer

RUSH MEMORIAL HOSPITAL (C, 52 beds) 1300 North Main Street, Rushville, IN Zip 46173–1198; tel. 765/932–4111; H. William Hartley, Chief Executive Officer

KENTUCKY: ALLIANT HOSPITALS (O, 709 beds) 200 East Chestnut Street, Louisville, KY Zip 40202–1800, Mailing Address: P.O. Box 35070, Zip 40232–5070; tel. 502/629–8000; Stephen M. Tullman, Administrator

BRECKINRIDGE MEMORIAL HOSPITAL (C, 45 beds) 1011 Old Highway 60, Hardinsburg, KY Zip 40143–2597; tel. 502/756–7000; George Walz, CHE, Chief Executive Officer

CALDWELL COUNTY HOSPITAL (C, 50 beds) 101 Hospital Drive, Princeton, KY Zip 42445–0410, Mailing Address: Box 410, Zip 42445–0410; tel. 502/365–0300; Marsha Woodall, Interim Chief Executive Officer

CARROLL COUNTY HOSPITAL (L, 39 beds) 309 11th Street, Carrollton, KY Zip 41008–1400; tel. 502/732–4321; Roger Williams, Chief Executive Officer

CAVERNA MEMORIAL HOSPITAL (C, 28 beds) 1501 South Dixie Street, Horse Cave, KY Zip 42749–1477; tel. 502/786–2191; James J. Kerins Sr., Administrator

RUSSELL COUNTY HOSPITAL (C, 45 beds) Dowell Road, Russell Springs, KY Zip 42642, Mailing Address: P.O. Box 1610, Zip 42642–1610; tel. 502/866–4141; Richard Hacker, Interim Administrator

THE JAMES B. HAGGIN MEMORIAL HOSPITAL (C, 64 beds) 464 Linden Avenue, Harrodsburg, KY Zip 40330–1862; tel. 606/734–5441; Earl James Motzer, Ph.D., FACHE, Chief Executive Officer

TWIN LAKES REGIONAL MEDICAL CENTER (C, 75 beds) 910 Wallace Avenue, Leitchfield, KY Zip 42754–1499; tel. 502/259–9400; Stephen L. Meredith, Chief Executive Officer

Owned, leased, sponsored:	2 hospitals	748 beds
Contract–managed:	17 hospitals	1014 beds
Totals:	19 hospitals	1762 beds

★0041: ALLINA HEALTH SYSTEM (NP)
5601 Smetana Drive, Minneapolis, MN Zip 55343, Mailing Address: P.O. Box 9310, Zip 55440–9310; tel. 612/992–2000; Gordon M. Sprenger, Executive Officer

MINNESOTA: ABBOTT NORTHWESTERN HOSPITAL (O, 588 beds) 800 East 28th Street, Minneapolis, MN Zip 55407–3799; tel. 612/863–4201; Mark Dixon, Administrator

BUFFALO HOSPITAL (O, 20 beds) 303 Catlin Street, Buffalo, MN Zip 55313–1947, Mailing Address: P.O. Box 609, Zip 55313–0609; tel. 612/682–7180; Mary Ellen Wells, Administrator

CAMBRIDGE MEDICAL CENTER (O, 81 beds) 701 South Dellwood Street, Cambridge, MN Zip 55008–1920; tel. 612/689–7700; Lenny Libis, Administrator

COMMUNITY HOSPITAL AND HEALTH CARE CENTER (C, 118 beds) 618 West Broadway, Saint Peter, MN Zip 56082–1327; tel. 507/931–2200; Colleen A. Spike, Interim Administrator

GRANITE FALLS MUNICIPAL HOSPITAL AND MANOR (C, 94 beds) 345 Tenth Avenue, Granite Falls, MN Zip 56241–1499; tel. 320/564–3111; George Gerlach, President

HUTCHINSON AREA HEALTH CARE (C, 193 beds) 1095 Highway 15 South, Hutchinson, MN Zip 55350–3182; tel. 320/234–5000; Philip G. Graves, President

LONG PRAIRIE MEMORIAL HOSPITAL AND HOME (O, 141 beds) 20 Ninth Street S.E., Long Prairie, MN Zip 56347–1404; tel. 320/732–2141; Clayton R. Peterson, President

MERCY HOSPITAL (O, 192 beds) 4050 Coon Rapids Boulevard, Coon Rapids, MN Zip 55433–2586; tel. 612/421–8888

MILLE LACS HEALTH SYSTEM (C, 108 beds) 200 North Elm Street, Onamia, MN Zip 56359–7978; tel. 320/532–3154; Randall A. Farrow, President

NEW ULM MEDICAL CENTER (O, 47 beds) 1324 Fifth Street North, New Ulm, MN Zip 56073–1553, Mailing Address: P.O. Box 577, Zip 56073–0577; tel. 507/354–2111; David A. Grundstrom, President

NORTHFIELD HOSPITAL (C, 67 beds) 801 West First Street, Northfield, MN Zip 55057–1697; tel. 507/645–6661; Kendall C. Bank, President

OWATONNA HOSPITAL (O, 55 beds) 903 Oak Street South, Owatonna, MN Zip 55060–3234; tel. 507/451–3850; Richard G. Slieter, Administrator

PHILLIPS EYE INSTITUTE (O, 10 beds) 2215 Park Avenue, Minneapolis, MN Zip 55404–3756; tel. 612/336–6000; Shari E. Levy, Administrator

ST. FRANCIS REGIONAL MEDICAL CENTER (O, 63 beds) 1455 St. Francis Avenue, Shakopee, MN Zip 55379–3380; tel. 612/403–3000; Venetia Kudrle, President

---

For explanation of codes following names, see page B2.
★ Indicates Type III membership in the American Hospital Association.

STEVENS COMMUNITY MEDICAL CENTER (C, 39 beds) 400 East First Street, Morris, MN Zip 56267–1407, Mailing Address: P.O. Box 660, Zip 56267–0660; tel. 320/589–1313; John Rau, President

UNITED HOSPITAL (O, 407 beds) 333 North Smith Street, Saint Paul, MN Zip 55102–2389; tel. 612/220–8000; M. Barbara Balik, R.N., Ed.D., Administrator

UNITED HOSPITAL DISTRICT (C, 24 beds) 515 South Moore Street, Blue Earth, MN Zip 56013–2158, Mailing Address: P.O. Box 160, Zip 56013–0160; tel. 507/526–3273; Brian Kief, President

UNITY HOSPITAL (O, 219 beds) 550 Osborne Road N.E., Fridley, MN Zip 55432–2799; tel. 612/421–2222

WISCONSIN: RIVER FALLS AREA HOSPITAL (O, 36 beds) 1629 East Division Street, River Falls, WI Zip 54022–1571; tel. 715/425–6155; Sharon Whelan, President

Owned, leased, sponsored:	12 hospitals	1859 beds
Contract–managed:	7 hospitals	643 beds
Totals:	19 hospitals	2502 beds

0074: AMERICAN TRANSITIONAL HOSPITALS, INC. (IO)
112 Second Avenue North, Franklin, TN Zip 37064–2509; tel. 615/791–7099; T. Jerald Moore, President and Chief Executive Officer

TEXAS: ATH HEIGHTS HOSPITAL (O, 170 beds) 1917 Ashland Street, Houston, TX Zip 77008–3994; tel. 713/861–6161; Patrick W. Gandy, Chief Executive Officer

AMERICAN TRANSITIONAL HOSPITAL–DALLAS/FORT WORTH (O, 36 beds) 1745 West Irving Boulevard, Irving, TX Zip 75061–7111; tel. 972/488–9167; LouAnn O. Mathews, Administrator

BEVERLY SPECIALTY HOSPITALS–HMC (O, 58 beds) 6447 Main Street, Houston, TX Zip 77030, Mailing Address: 6500 Fannin Street, Suite 907, Zip 77030; tel. 713/791–9393; Connie Cowan, Administrator and Chief Executive Officer

Owned, leased, sponsored:	3 hospitals	264 beds
Contract–managed:	0 hospitals	0 beds
Totals:	3 hospitals	264 beds

★0135: ANCILLA SYSTEMS INC. (CC)
1000 South Lake Park Avenue, Hobart, IN Zip 46342–5970; tel. 219/947–8500; William D. Harkins, President and Chief Executive Officer

ILLINOIS: ST. ELIZABETH'S HOSPITAL (O, 240 beds) 1431 North Claremont Avenue, Chicago, IL Zip 60622–1791; tel. 773/278–2000; JoAnn Birdzell, President and Chief Executive Officer

ST. MARY'S HOSPITAL (O, 135 beds) 129 North Eighth Street, East St. Louis, IL Zip 62201–2999; tel. 618/274–1900; Richard J. Mark, President and Chief Executive Officer

INDIANA: COMMUNITY HOSPITAL OF BREMEN (C, 28 beds) 411 South Whitlock Street, Bremen, IN Zip 46506–1699; tel. 219/546–2211; Scott R. Graybill, Chief Executive Officer and Administrator

ST. CATHERINE HOSPITAL (O, 190 beds) 4321 Fir Street, East Chicago, IN Zip 46312–3097; tel. 219/392–7000; JoAnn Birdzell, President and Chief Executive Officer

ST. JOSEPH COMMUNITY HOSPITAL (O, 100 beds) 215 West Fourth Street, Mishawaka, IN Zip 46544–1999; tel. 219/259–2431; Stephen L. Crain, President and Chief Executive Officer

ST. JOSEPH MEDICAL CENTER OF FORT WAYNE (O, 175 beds) 700 Broadway, Fort Wayne, IN Zip 46802–1493; tel. 219/425–3000; John T. Farrell Sr., President and Chief Executive Officer

ST. MARY MEDICAL CENTER (O, 102 beds) 1500 South Lake Park Avenue, Hobart, IN Zip 46342–6699; tel. 219/942–0551; Milton Triana, President and Chief Executive Officer

Owned, leased, sponsored:	6 hospitals	942 beds
Contract–managed:	1 hospital	28 beds
Totals:	7 hospitals	970 beds

0145: APPALACHIAN REGIONAL HEALTHCARE (NP)
1220 Harrodsburg Road, Lexington, KY Zip 40504, Mailing Address: P.O. Box 8086, Zip 40533–8086; tel. 606/226–2440; Forrest Calico, M.D., President

KENTUCKY: ARH REGIONAL MEDICAL CENTER (O, 288 beds) 100 Medical Center Drive, Hazard, KY Zip 41701–1000; tel. 606/439–6610; Steven F. Ashcraft, Interim Administrator

HARLAN ARH HOSPITAL (O, 125 beds) 81 Ball Park Road, Harlan, KY Zip 40831–1792; tel. 606/573–8100; Daniel Fitzpatrick, Chief Executive Officer

MCDOWELL ARH HOSPITAL (O, 74 beds) Route 122, McDowell, KY Zip 41647, Mailing Address: P.O. Box 247, Mc Dowell, Zip 41647–0247; tel. 606/377–3400; Dena C. Sparkman, Administrator

MIDDLESBORO APPALACHIAN REGIONAL HOSPITAL (O, 96 beds) 3600 West Cumberland Avenue, Middlesboro, KY Zip 40965–2614, Mailing Address: P.O. Box 340, Zip 40965–0340; tel. 606/242–1101; Paul V. Miles, Administrator

MORGAN COUNTY APPALACHIAN REGIONAL HOSPITAL (L, 45 beds) 476 Liberty Road, West Liberty, KY Zip 41472–2049, Mailing Address: P.O. Box 579, Zip 41472–0579; tel. 606/743–3186; Dennis R. Chaney, Administrator

WHITESBURG APPALACHIAN REGIONAL HOSPITAL (O, 76 beds) 240 Hospital Road, Whitesburg, KY Zip 41858–1254; tel. 606/633–3600; Nick Lewis, Administrator

WILLIAMSON ARH HOSPITAL (O, 148 beds) 260 Hospital Drive, South Williamson, KY Zip 41503–4072; tel. 606/237–1700; John A. Grah, Administrator

WEST VIRGINIA: BECKLEY APPALACHIAN REGIONAL HOSPITAL (O, 173 beds) 306 Stanaford Road, Beckley, WV Zip 25801–3142; tel. 304/255–3000; David R. Lyon, Administrator

MAN ARH HOSPITAL (O, 42 beds) 700 East McDonald Avenue, Man, WV Zip 25635–1011; tel. 304/583–8421; Louis G. Roe Jr., Administrator

SUMMERS COUNTY APPALACHIAN REGIONAL HOSPITAL (L, 65 beds) Terrace Street, Hinton, WV Zip 25951, Mailing Address: Drawer 940, Zip 25951–0940; tel. 304/466–1000; Clyde E. Bolton, Administrator

Owned, leased, sponsored:	10 hospitals	1132 beds
Contract–managed:	0 hospitals	0 beds
Totals:	10 hospitals	1132 beds

0104: ARCHBOLD MEDICAL CENTER (NP)
910 South Broad Street, Thomasville, GA Zip 31792–6113; tel. 912/228–2739; Ken B. Beverly, President and Chief Executive Officer

GEORGIA: BROOKS COUNTY HOSPITAL (L, 35 beds) 903 North Court Street, Quitman, GA Zip 31643–1315, Mailing Address: P.O. Box 5000, Zip 31643–5000; tel. 912/263–4171; Andrew J. Finnegan, CHE, Administrator

EARLY MEMORIAL HOSPITAL (L, 176 beds) 630 Columbia Street, Blakely, GA Zip 31723–1798; tel. 912/723–4241; Rodney C. Watford, Administrator

GRADY GENERAL HOSPITAL (L, 45 beds) 1155 Fifth Street S.E., Cairo, GA Zip 31728–3142, Mailing Address: P.O. Box 360, Zip 31728–0360; tel. 912/377–1150; Glen C. Davis, Administrator

JOHN D. ARCHBOLD MEMORIAL HOSPITAL (O, 328 beds) Gordon Avenue at Mimosa Drive, Thomasville, GA Zip 31792–6113, Mailing Address: P.O. Box 1018, Zip 31799–1018; tel. 912/228–2000; Jason H. Moore, President and Chief Executive Officer

MITCHELL COUNTY HOSPITAL (L, 182 beds) 90 Stephens Street, Camilla, GA Zip 31730–1899, Mailing Address: P.O. Box 639, Zip 31730–0639; tel. 912/336–5284; Ronald M. Gilliard, FACHE, Administrator

Owned, leased, sponsored:	5 hospitals	766 beds
Contract–managed:	0 hospitals	0 beds
Totals:	5 hospitals	766 beds

★0094: ASANTE HEALTH SYSTEM (NP)
2650 Siskiyou Boulevard, Suite 200, Medford, OR Zip 97504–8389; tel. 541/608–4100; Jon K. Mitchell, FACHE, President and Chief Executive Officer

For explanation of codes following names, see page B2.
★ Indicates Type III membership in the American Hospital Association.

OREGON: ROGUE VALLEY MEDICAL CENTER (O, 249 beds) 2825 East Barnett Road, Medford, OR Zip 97504–8332; tel. 541/608–4900; Gary A. Sherwood, Executive Vice President

THREE RIVERS COMMUNITY HOSPITAL AND HEALTH CENTER–DIMMICK (O, 87 beds) 715 N.W. Dimmick Street, Grants Pass, OR Zip 97526–1596; tel. 541/476–6831; Mark W. Folger, Senior Vice President

Owned, leased, sponsored:	2 hospitals	336 beds
Contract–managed:	0 hospitals	0 beds
Totals:	2 hospitals	336 beds

★2215: AURORA HEALTH CARE (NP)
3000 West Montana, Milwaukee, WI Zip 53215–3268, Mailing Address: P.O. Box 343910, Zip 53234–3910; tel. 414/647–3000; G. Edwin Howe, President

WISCONSIN: HARTFORD MEMORIAL HOSPITAL (O, 71 beds) 1032 East Sumner Street, Hartford, WI Zip 53027–1698; tel. 414/673–2300; Mark Schwartz, Administrator

LAKELAND MEDICAL CENTER (O, 78 beds) West 3985 County Road NN, Elkhorn, WI Zip 53121, Mailing Address: P.O. Box 1002, Zip 53121–1002; tel. 414/741–2000; Kathy Skowlund, Administrator

MEMORIAL HOSPITAL CORPORATION OF BURLINGTON (O, 87 beds) 252 McHenry Street, Burlington, WI Zip 53105–1828; tel. 414/763–2411; Loren J. Anderson, President and Chief Executive Officer

MILWAUKEE PSYCHIATRIC HOSPITAL (O, 75 beds) 1220 Dewey Avenue, Wauwatosa, WI Zip 53213–2598; tel. 414/454–6600; James A. Moore, Administrator

SHEBOYGAN MEMORIAL MEDICAL CENTER (O, 138 beds) 2629 North Seventh Street, Sheboygan, WI Zip 53083–4998; tel. 920/451–5000; T. Gregg Watson, Administrator

SINAI SAMARITAN MEDICAL CENTER (O, 354 beds) 945 North 12th Street, Milwaukee, WI Zip 53233–1337, Mailing Address: P.O. Box 342, Zip 53201–0342; tel. 414/219–2000; Leonard E. Wilk, Administrator

ST. LUKE'S MEDICAL CENTER (O, 777 beds) 2900 West Oklahoma Avenue, Milwaukee, WI Zip 53215–4330, Mailing Address: P.O. Box 2901, Zip 53201–2901; tel. 414/649–6000; Mark S. Wiener, Administrator

ST. MARY'S KEWAUNEE AREA MEMORIAL HOSPITAL (O, 17 beds) 810 Lincoln Street, Kewaunee, WI Zip 54216–1140, Mailing Address: P.O. Box 217, Zip 54216–0217; tel. 920/388–2210; Steven H. Spencer, Administrator

TWO RIVERS COMMUNITY HOSPITAL AND HAMILTON MEMORIAL HOME (O, 138 beds) 2500 Garfield Street, Two Rivers, WI Zip 54241–2399; tel. 920/793–1178; Steven H. Spencer, Administrator

VALLEY VIEW MEDICAL CENTER (O, 98 beds) 901 Reed Street, Plymouth, WI Zip 53073–2409; tel. 920/893–1771; T. Gregg Watson, Administrator

WEST ALLIS MEMORIAL HOSPITAL (O, 199 beds) 8901 West Lincoln Avenue, West Allis, WI Zip 53227–0901, Mailing Address: P.O. Box 27901, Zip 53227–0901; tel. 414/328–6000; Richard A. Kellar, Administrator

Owned, leased, sponsored:	11 hospitals	2032 beds
Contract–managed:	0 hospitals	0 beds
Totals:	11 hospitals	2032 beds

★5255: AVERA HEALTH (CC)
610 West 23rd Street, Yankton, SD Zip 57078, Mailing Address: P.O. Box 38, Zip 57078–0038; tel. 605/322–7050; John T. Porter, President and Chief Executive Officer

IOWA: FLOYD VALLEY HOSPITAL (C, 22 beds) Highway 3 East, Le Mars, IA Zip 51031, Mailing Address: P.O. Box 10, Zip 51031–0010; tel. 712/546–7871; Michael Donlin, Chief Executive Officer

HEGG MEMORIAL HEALTH CENTER (C, 123 beds) 1202 21st Avenue, Rock Valley, IA Zip 51247–1497; tel. 712/476–5305; Chris Thomas, Administrator and Chief Executive Officer

HOLY FAMILY HEALTH SERVICES (O, 36 beds) 826 North Eighth Street, Estherville, IA Zip 51334–1598; tel. 712/362–2631; Thomas Nordwick, President and Chief Executive Officer

SIOUX CENTER COMMUNITY HOSPITAL AND HEALTH CENTER (C, 90 beds) 605 South Main Avenue, Sioux Center, IA Zip 51250–1398; tel. 712/722–1271; Marla Toering, Administrator

MINNESOTA: DIVINE PROVIDENCE HEALTH CENTER (C, 79 beds) 312 East George Street, Ivanhoe, MN Zip 56142–0136, Mailing Address: P.O. Box G., Zip 56142–0136; tel. 507/694–1414; Patrick Branco, Administrator

PIPESTONE COUNTY MEDICAL CENTER (C, 76 beds) 911 Fifth Avenue S.W., Pipestone, MN Zip 56164; tel. 507/825–6125; Carl P. Vaagenes, Administrator

TYLER HEALTHCARE CENTER (C, 49 beds) 240 Willow Street, Tyler, MN Zip 56178–0280; tel. 507/247–5521; James G. Blum, Interim Administrator

SOUTH DAKOTA: EUREKA COMMUNITY HOSPITAL (C, 9 beds) 410 Ninth Street, Eureka, SD Zip 57437–0517; tel. 605/284–2661; Robert A. Dockter, Administrator

FLANDREAU MUNICIPAL HOSPITAL (C, 18 beds) 214 North Prairie Avenue, Flandreau, SD Zip 57028–1243; tel. 605/997–2433; Paul Bergman, Administrator

HAND COUNTY MEMORIAL HOSPITAL (C, 23 beds) 300 West Fifth Street, Miller, SD Zip 57362–1238; tel. 605/853–2421; Clarence A. Lee, Administrator

MARSHALL COUNTY HEALTHCARE CENTER (C, 20 beds) 413 Ninth Street, Britton, SD Zip 57430–0230, Mailing Address: Box 230, Zip 57430–0230; tel. 605/448–2253; Stephanie Lulewicz, Administrator

MCKENNAN HOSPITAL (O, 521 beds) 800 East 21st Street, Sioux Falls, SD Zip 57105–1096, Mailing Address: P.O. Box 5045, Zip 57117–5045; tel. 605/322–8000; Fredrick Slunecka, President and Chief Executive Officer

PLATTE COMMUNITY MEMORIAL HOSPITAL (C, 63 beds) 609 East Seventh, Platte, SD Zip 57369–2123, Mailing Address: P.O. Box 200, Zip 57369–0200; tel. 605/337–3364; Mark Burket, Chief Executive Officer

QUEEN OF PEACE HOSPITAL (O, 183 beds) 525 North Foster, Mitchell, SD Zip 57301–2999; tel. 605/995–2000; Ronald L. Jacobson, President and Chief Executive Officer

SACRED HEART HEALTH SERVICES (C, 257 beds) 501 Summit Avenue, Yankton, SD Zip 57078–3899; tel. 605/668–8000; Pamela J. Rezac, President and Chief Executive Officer

ST. BENEDICT HEALTH CENTER (C, 105 beds) Glynn Drive, Parkston, SD Zip 57366, Mailing Address: P.O. Box B., Zip 57366; tel. 605/928–3311; Gale Walker, Administrator

ST. LUKE'S MIDLAND REGIONAL MEDICAL CENTER (O, 258 beds) 305 South State Street, Aberdeen, SD Zip 57402–4450; tel. 605/622–5000; Dale J. Stein, President and Chief Executive Officer

Owned, leased, sponsored:	4 hospitals	998 beds
Contract–managed:	13 hospitals	934 beds
Totals:	17 hospitals	1932 beds

★0355: BAPTIST HEALTH (NP)
9601 Interstate 630, Exit 7, Little Rock, AR Zip 72205–7299; tel. 501/202–2000; Russell D. Harrington Jr., President

ARKANSAS: BAPTIST MEDICAL CENTER (O, 621 beds) 9601 Interstate 630, Exit 7, Little Rock, AR Zip 72205–7299; tel. 501/202–2000; Steven Douglas Weeks, Senior Vice President and Administrator

BAPTIST MEDICAL CENTER ARKADELPHIA (L, 57 beds) 3050 Twin Rivers Drive, Arkadelphia, AR Zip 71923–4299; tel. 870/245–1100; Dan Gathright, Senior Vice President and Administrator

BAPTIST MEDICAL CENTER HEBER SPRINGS (L, 24 beds) 2319 Highway 110 West, Heber Springs, AR Zip 72543; tel. 501/206–3000; Dan Gathright, Vice President and Administrator

BAPTIST MEMORIAL MEDICAL CENTER (L, 200 beds) One Pershing Circle, North Little Rock, AR Zip 72114–1899; tel. 501/202–3000; Harrison M. Dean, Senior Vice President and Administrator

BAPTIST REHABILITATION INSTITUTE (O, 100 beds) 9601 Interstate 630, Exit 7, Little Rock, AR Zip 72205–7249; tel. 501/202–7000; Steven Douglas Weeks, Senior Vice President and Administrator

For explanation of codes following names, see page B2.
★ Indicates Type III membership in the American Hospital Association.

Owned, leased, sponsored:	5 hospitals	1002 beds
Contract–managed:	0 hospitals	0 beds
Totals:	5 hospitals	1002 beds

0185: BAPTIST HEALTH CARE CORPORATION (NP)
1717 North E. Street, Suite 320, Pensacola, FL Zip 32501–6335;
tel. 850/469–2337; James F. Vickery, President

ALABAMA: MIZELL MEMORIAL HOSPITAL (O, 57 beds) 702 Main Street, Opp,
AL Zip 36467–1626, Mailing Address: P.O. Box 1010, Zip 36467–1010;
tel. 334/493–3541; Allen Foster, Administrator

FLORIDA: BAPTIST HOSPITAL (O, 492 beds) 1000 West Moreno, Pensacola,
FL Zip 32501–2393, Mailing Address: P.O. Box 17500, Zip 32522–7500;
tel. 850/469–2313; Quinton Studer, President

GULF BREEZE HOSPITAL (O, 45 beds) 1110 Gulf Breeze Parkway, Gulf
Breeze, FL Zip 32561, Mailing Address: P.O. Box 159, Zip 32562;
tel. 850/934–2000; Richard C. Fulford, Administrator

JAY HOSPITAL (L, 47 beds) 221 South Alabama Street, Jay, FL
Zip 32565–1070, Mailing Address: P.O. Box 397, Zip 32565–0397;
tel. 850/675–8000; Robert E. Gowing, Administrator

Owned, leased, sponsored:	4 hospitals	641 beds
Contract–managed:	0 hospitals	0 beds
Totals:	4 hospitals	641 beds

0265: BAPTIST HEALTH SYSTEM (CO)
200 Concord Plaza, Suite 900, San Antonio, TX Zip 78216;
tel. 210/302–3000; Fred R. Mills, President and Chief Executive
Officer

TEXAS: BAPTIST MEDICAL CENTER (O, 480 beds) 111 Dallas Street, San
Antonio, TX Zip 78205–1230; tel. 210/297–7000; Fred R. Mills,
President and Chief Executive Officer

NORTH CENTRAL BAPTIST HOSPITAL (O, 88 beds) 520 Madison Oak Drive,
San Antonio, TX Zip 78258–3912; Dan Brown, Administrator

NORTHEAST BAPTIST HOSPITAL (O, 234 beds) 8811 Village Drive, San
Antonio, TX Zip 78217–5440; tel. 210/653–2330; Dan Brown, Administrator

SOUTHEAST BAPTIST HOSPITAL (O, 153 beds) 4214 East Southcross
Boulevard, San Antonio, TX Zip 78222–3740; tel. 210/297–3000; Kevin
Walters, Administrator

ST. LUKE'S BAPTIST HOSPITAL (O, 219 beds) 7930 Floyd Curl Drive, San
Antonio, TX Zip 78229–0100; tel. 210/692–8703; John Penn Krause,
Administrator

Owned, leased, sponsored:	5 hospitals	1174 beds
Contract–managed:	0 hospitals	0 beds
Totals:	5 hospitals	1174 beds

★0345: BAPTIST HEALTH SYSTEM (CO)
3500 Blue Lake Drive, Suite 100, Birmingham, AL Zip 35243, Mailing
Address: P.O. Box 830605, Zip 35283–0605; tel. 205/715–5319;
Dennis A. Hall, President

ALABAMA: BIRMINGHAM BAPTIST MEDICAL CENTER–MONTCLAIR CAMPUS
(O, 1023 beds) 800 Montclair Road, Birmingham, AL Zip 35213–1984;
tel. 205/592–1000; Dana S. Hensley, President

BIRMINGHAM BAPTIST MEDICAL CENTER–PRINCETON (O, 1033 beds) 701
Princeton Avenue S.W., Birmingham, AL Zip 35211–1305;
tel. 205/783–3000; Dana S. Hensley, President and Chief Executive Officer

CHEROKEE BAPTIST MEDICAL CENTER (O, 45 beds) 400 Northwood Drive,
Centre, AL Zip 35960–1023; tel. 205/927–5531; Barry S. Cochran,
President

CITIZENS BAPTIST MEDICAL CENTER (O, 97 beds) 604 Stone Avenue,
Talladega, AL Zip 35160–2217, Mailing Address: P.O. Box 978,
Zip 35161–0978; tel. 205/362–8111; Steven M. Johnson, President

COOSA VALLEY BAPTIST MEDICAL CENTER (O, 176 beds) 315 West Hickory
Street, Sylacauga, AL Zip 35150–2996; tel. 205/249–5000; Steven M.
Johnson, President

CULLMAN REGIONAL MEDICAL CENTER (O, 115 beds) 1912 Alabama
Highway 157, Cullman, AL Zip 35055, Mailing Address: P.O. Box 1108,
Zip 35056–1108; tel. 205/737–2000; Jesse O. Weatherly, President

DEKALB BAPTIST MEDICAL CENTER (O, 91 beds) 200 Medical Center Drive,
Fort Payne, AL Zip 35967, Mailing Address: P.O. Box 680778,
Zip 35968–0778; tel. 205/845–3150; Barry S. Cochran, President

LAWRENCE BAPTIST MEDICAL CENTER (L, 30 beds) 202 Hospital Street,
Moulton, AL Zip 35650–0039, Mailing Address: P.O. Box 39,
Zip 35650–0039; tel. 205/974–2200; Cheryl Hays, Administrator

MARION BAPTIST MEDICAL CENTER (L, 112 beds) 1256 Military Street
South, Hamilton, AL Zip 35570–5001; tel. 205/921–6200; Evan S. Dillard,
President

RANDOLPH COUNTY HOSPITAL (L, 66 beds) 59928 Highway 22, Roanoke,
AL Zip 36274, Mailing Address: P.O. Box 670, Zip 36274–0670;
tel. 334/863–4111; Moultrie D. Plowden, CHE, President

SHELBY BAPTIST MEDICAL CENTER (O, 228 beds) 1000 First Street North,
Alabaster, AL Zip 35007–0488, Mailing Address: Box 488, Zip 35007–0488;
tel. 205/620–8100; Charles C. Colvert, President

WALKER BAPTIST MEDICAL CENTER (O, 267 beds) 3400 Highway 78 East,
Jasper, AL Zip 35501–8956, Mailing Address: P.O. Box 3547,
Zip 35502–3547; tel. 205/387–4000; Jeff Brewer, President

WEDOWEE HOSPITAL (L, 34 beds) 290 North Main Street, Wedowee, AL
Zip 36278–5138, Mailing Address: P.O. Box 307, Zip 36278–0307;
tel. 205/357–2111; Karlene Mitchell, President

Owned, leased, sponsored:	13 hospitals	3317 beds
Contract–managed:	0 hospitals	0 beds
Totals:	13 hospitals	3317 beds

0122: BAPTIST HEALTH SYSTEM OF SOUTH FLORIDA (NP)
8900 North Kendall Drive, Miami, FL Zip 33176–2197;
tel. 305/596–1960; Brian E. Keeley, President and Chief Executive
Officer

FLORIDA: BAPTIST HOSPITAL OF MIAMI (O, 457 beds) 8900 North Kendall
Drive, Miami, FL Zip 33176–2197; tel. 305/596–6503; Fred M. Messing,
Chief Executive Officer

HOMESTEAD HOSPITAL (O, 105 beds) 160 N.W. 13th Street, Homestead, FL
Zip 33030–4299; tel. 305/248–3232; Bo Boulenger, Chief Executive Officer

MARINERS HOSPITAL (S, 31 beds) 50 High Point Road, Tavernier, FL
Zip 33070–2031; tel. 305/852–4418; Robert H. Luse, Chief Executive
Officer

SOUTH MIAMI HOSPITAL (O, 334 beds) 6200 S.W. 73rd Street, Miami, FL
Zip 33143–9990; tel. 305/661–4611; D. Wayne Brackin, Chief Executive
Officer

Owned, leased, sponsored:	4 hospitals	927 beds
Contract–managed:	0 hospitals	0 beds
Totals:	4 hospitals	927 beds

2155: BAPTIST HEALTH SYSTEM OF TENNESSEE (NP)
137 Blount Avenue S.E., Knoxville, TN Zip 37920–1643, Mailing
Address: P.O. Box 1788, Zip 37901–1788; tel. 615/632–5099;
Dale Collins, President and Chief Executive Officer

TENNESSEE: BAPTIST HOSPITAL OF COCKE COUNTY (O, 109 beds) 435
Second Street, Newport, TN Zip 37821–3799; tel. 423/625–2200;
Wayne Buckner, Administrator

BAPTIST HOSPITAL OF EAST TENNESSEE (O, 316 beds) 137 Blount Avenue
S.E., Knoxville, TN Zip 37920–1643, Mailing Address: P.O. Box 1788,
Zip 37901–1788; tel. 423/632–5011; Jon Foster, Executive Vice President
and Administrator

Owned, leased, sponsored:	2 hospitals	425 beds
Contract–managed:	0 hospitals	0 beds
Totals:	2 hospitals	425 beds

Section B

For explanation of codes following names, see page B2.
★ Indicates Type III membership in the American Hospital Association.

★0315: BAPTIST HEALTHCARE SYSTEM (CO)
4007 Kresge Way, Louisville, KY Zip 40207–4677;
tel. 502/896–5000; Tommy J. Smith, President and Chief Executive Officer

KENTUCKY: BAPTIST HOSPITAL EAST (O, 407 beds) 4000 Kresge Way, Louisville, KY Zip 40207–4676; tel. 502/897–8100; Susan Stout Tamme, President

BAPTIST REGIONAL MEDICAL CENTER (O, 255 beds) 1 Trillium Way, Corbin, KY Zip 40701–8420; tel. 606/528–1212; John S. Henson, President

CENTRAL BAPTIST HOSPITAL (O, 344 beds) 1740 Nicholasville Road, Lexington, KY Zip 40503; tel. 606/275–6100; William G. Sisson, President

HARDIN MEMORIAL HOSPITAL (C, 291 beds) 913 North Dixie Avenue, Elizabethtown, KY Zip 42701–2599; tel. 502/737–1212; David L. Gray, President

TRI COUNTY BAPTIST HOSPITAL (O, 95 beds) 1025 New Moody Lane, La Grange, KY Zip 40031–0559; tel. 502/222–5388; Dennis B. Johnson, Administrator

WESTERN BAPTIST HOSPITAL (O, 325 beds) 2501 Kentucky Avenue, Paducah, KY Zip 42003–3200; tel. 502/575–2100; Larry O. Barton, President

Owned, leased, sponsored:	5 hospitals	1426 beds
Contract–managed:	1 hospital	291 beds
Totals:	6 hospitals	1717 beds

★8810: BAPTIST HOSPITALS AND HEALTH SYSTEMS, INC. (NP)
2224 West Northern Avenue, Suite D–300, Phoenix, AZ Zip 85021–4987; tel. 602/864–1184; Gerald L. Wissink, President and Chief Executive Officer

ARIZONA: ARROWHEAD COMMUNITY HOSPITAL AND MEDICAL CENTER (O, 104 beds) 18701 North 67th Avenue, Glendale, AZ Zip 85308–5722; tel. 602/561–1000; Richard S. Alley, Regional Vice President and Administrator

LA PAZ REGIONAL HOSPITAL (O, 39 beds) 1200 Mohave Road, Parker, AZ Zip 85344–6349, Mailing Address: P.O. Box 1149, Zip 85344–1149; tel. 520/669–9201; William G. Coe, Executive Vice President and Chief Executive Officer

PHOENIX BAPTIST HOSPITAL AND MEDICAL CENTER (O, 201 beds) 2000 West Bethany Home Road, Phoenix, AZ Zip 85015–2110; tel. 602/249–0212; Richard S. Alley, Chief Executive Officer

WESTERN ARIZONA REGIONAL MEDICAL CENTER (O, 182 beds) 2735 Silver Creek Road, Bullhead City, AZ Zip 86442–8303; tel. 520/763–2273; Rita A. Campbell, Executive Vice President and Chief Executive Officer

Owned, leased, sponsored:	4 hospitals	526 beds
Contract–managed:	0 hospitals	0 beds
Totals:	4 hospitals	526 beds

★1625: BAPTIST MEMORIAL HEALTH CARE CORPORATION (NP)
899 Madison Avenue, Memphis, TN Zip 38146–0001; tel. 901/227–5117; Stephen Curtis Reynolds, President and Chief Executive Officer

ARKANSAS: BAPTIST MEMORIAL HOSPITAL–BLYTHEVILLE (L, 210 beds) 1520 North Division Street, Blytheville, AR Zip 72315, Mailing Address: P.O. Box 108, Zip 72316–0108; tel. 870/838–7300; Al Sypniewski, Administrator

BAPTIST MEMORIAL HOSPITAL–FORREST CITY (L, 86 beds) 1601 Newcastle Road, Forrest City, AR Zip 72335, Mailing Address: P.O. Box 667, Zip 72336–0667; tel. 870/633–2020; Charles R. Daugherty, Administrator

BAPTIST MEMORIAL HOSPITAL–OSCEOLA (L, 59 beds) 611 West Lee Avenue, Osceola, AR Zip 72370–3001, Mailing Address: P.O. Box 607, Zip 72370–0607; tel. 870/563–7000; Joel E. North, Administrator

MISSISSIPPI: BAPTIST MEMORIAL HOSPITAL–BOONEVILLE (L, 103 beds) 100 Hospital Street, Booneville, MS Zip 38829–3359; tel. 601/720–5000; Pamela W. Roberts, Administrator

BAPTIST MEMORIAL HOSPITAL–DESOTO (O, 230 beds) 7601 Southcrest Parkway, Southaven, MS Zip 38671–4742; tel. 601/349–4000; Melvin E. Walker, Administrator

BAPTIST MEMORIAL HOSPITAL–GOLDEN TRIANGLE (L, 328 beds) 2520 Fifth Street North, Columbus, MS Zip 39703–2095, Mailing Address: P.O. Box 1307, Zip 39701–1307; tel. 601/244–1000; J. Stuart Mitchell III, Administrator

BAPTIST MEMORIAL HOSPITAL–NORTH MISSISSIPPI (L, 158 beds) 2301 South Lamar Boulevard, Oxford, MS Zip 38655–5338, Mailing Address: P.O. Box 946, Zip 38655–0946; tel. 601/232–8100; James Hahn, Administrator

BAPTIST MEMORIAL HOSPITAL–UNION COUNTY (L, 153 beds) 200 Highway 30 West, New Albany, MS Zip 38652–3197; tel. 601/538–7631; John Tompkins, Administrator

TIPPAH COUNTY HOSPITAL (C, 110 beds) 1005 City Avenue North, Ripley, MS Zip 38663–0499; tel. 601/837–9221; Jerry Green, Administrator

TENNESSEE: BAPTIST MEMORIAL HOSPITAL (O, 1057 beds) 899 Madison Avenue, Memphis, TN Zip 38146–0001; tel. 901/227–2727; Stephen Curtis Reynolds, President and Chief Executive Officer

BAPTIST MEMORIAL HOSPITAL–HUNTINGDON (O, 70 beds) 631 R. B. Wilson Drive, Huntingdon, TN Zip 38344–1675; tel. 901/986–4461; Susan M. Breeden, Administrator

BAPTIST MEMORIAL HOSPITAL–LAUDERDALE (O, 70 beds) 326 Asbury Road, Ripley, TN Zip 38063–9701; tel. 901/635–1331; George S. Fray, Administrator

BAPTIST MEMORIAL HOSPITAL–TIPTON (O, 48 beds) 1995 Highway 51 South, Covington, TN Zip 38019–3635; tel. 901/476–2621; Glenn Baker, Administrator

BAPTIST MEMORIAL HOSPITAL–UNION CITY (O, 133 beds) 1201 Bishop Street, Union City, TN Zip 38261–5403, Mailing Address: P.O. Box 310, Zip 38281–0310; tel. 901/884–8601; Mike Perryman, Administrator

BAPTIST REHABILITATION–GERMANTOWN (O, 85 beds) 2100 Exeter Road, Germantown, TN Zip 38138; tel. 901/757–1350; Paula Gisler, Chief Executive Officer

ST. JOSEPH HOSPITAL AND HEALTH CENTERS (O, 295 beds) 220 Overton Avenue, Memphis, TN Zip 38105–2789; tel. 901/577–2700; Joan M. Carlson, Administrator

Owned, leased, sponsored:	15 hospitals	3085 beds
Contract–managed:	1 hospital	110 beds
Totals:	16 hospitals	3195 beds

★0107: BAYHEALTH MEDICAL CENTER (NP)
640 South State Street, Dover, DE Zip 19901, Mailing Address: 640 South State Street, Zip 19901; tel. 302/674–4700; Dennis E. Klima, President and Chief Executive Officer

DELAWARE: BAYHEALTH MEDICAL CENTER (O, 324 beds) 640 South State Street, Dover, DE Zip 19901–3597; tel. 302/674–4700; Dennis E. Klima, President and Chief Executive Officer

BAYHEALTH MEDICAL CENTER, MILFORD MEMORIAL CAMPUS (O, 130 beds) 21 West Clarke Avenue, Milford, DE Zip 19963–1840, Mailing Address: P.O. Box 199, Zip 19963–0199; tel. 302/424–5613; Joseph K. Whiting, Executive Vice President and Chief Operating Officer

Owned, leased, sponsored:	2 hospitals	454 beds
Contract–managed:	0 hospitals	0 beds
Totals:	2 hospitals	454 beds

★0095: BAYLOR HEALTH CARE SYSTEM (CO)
3500 Gaston Avenue, Dallas, TX Zip 75226–2088; tel. 214/820–0111; Boone Powell Jr., President

TEXAS: BAYLOR CENTER FOR RESTORATIVE CARE (O, 72 beds) 3504 Swiss Avenue, Dallas, TX Zip 75204–6224; tel. 214/820–9700; Gerry Brueckner, R.N., Executive Director

BAYLOR INSTITUTE FOR REHABILITATION (O, 92 beds) 3505 Gaston Avenue, Dallas, TX Zip 75246–2018; tel. 214/826–7030; Judith C. Waterston, Executive Director

For explanation of codes following names, see page B2.
★ Indicates Type III membership in the American Hospital Association.

BAYLOR MEDICAL CENTER AT GARLAND (O, 170 beds) 2300 Marie Curie Boulevard, Garland, TX Zip 75042–5706; tel. 972/487–5000; John B. McWhorter III, Executive Director

BAYLOR MEDICAL CENTER AT GRAPEVINE (O, 68 beds) 1650 West College Street, Grapevine, TX Zip 76051–1650; tel. 817/329–2500; Mark C. Hood, Executive Director

BAYLOR MEDICAL CENTER AT IRVING (L, 231 beds) 1901 North MacArthur Boulevard, Irving, TX Zip 75061–2291; tel. 972/579–8100; H. J. Macfarland, FACHE, Executive Director

BAYLOR MEDICAL CENTER–ELLIS COUNTY (O, 91 beds) 1405 West Jefferson Street, Waxahachie, TX Zip 75165–2275; tel. 972/923–7000; James Michael Lee, Executive Director

BAYLOR UNIVERSITY MEDICAL CENTER (O, 873 beds) 3500 Gaston Avenue, Dallas, TX Zip 75246–2088; tel. 214/820–0111; M. Tim Parris, Executive Vice President and Chief Operating Officer

Owned, leased, sponsored:	7 hospitals	1597 beds
Contract–managed:	0 hospitals	0 beds
Totals:	7 hospitals	1597 beds

★1095: **BAYSTATE HEALTH SYSTEM, INC.** (NP) 759 Chestnut Street, Springfield, MA Zip 01199–0001; tel. 413/789–0000; Michael J. Daly, President

MASSACHUSETTS: BAYSTATE MEDICAL CENTER (O, 685 beds) 759 Chestnut Street, Springfield, MA Zip 01199–0001; tel. 413/794–0000; Mark R. Tolosky, Chief Executive Officer

FRANKLIN MEDICAL CENTER (O, 112 beds) 164 High Street, Greenfield, MA Zip 01301–2613; tel. 413/773–0211; Harlan J. Smith, President

MARY LANE HOSPITAL (O, 34 beds) 85 South Street, Ware, MA Zip 01082–1697; tel. 413/967–6211; Christine Shirtcliff, Executive Vice President

Owned, leased, sponsored:	3 hospitals	831 beds
Contract–managed:	0 hospitals	0 beds
Totals:	3 hospitals	831 beds

0069: **BEHAVIORAL HEALTHCARE CORPORATION** (IO) 102 Woodmont Boulevard, Suite 800, Nashville, TN Zip 37205–2287; tel. 615/269–3492; Edward A. Stack, President and Chief Executive Officer

ARIZONA: BHC ASPEN HILL HOSPITAL (O, 26 beds) 305 West Forest Avenue, Flagstaff, AZ Zip 86001–1464; tel. 520/773–1060; Alan G. Chapman, Administrator and Chief Executive Officer

ARKANSAS: BHC PINNACLE POINTE HOSPITAL (O, 98 beds) 11501 Financial Center Parkway, Little Rock, AR Zip 72211–3715; tel. 501/223–3322; Joseph Fischer, Chief Executive Officer

CALIFORNIA: BHC ALHAMBRA HOSPITAL (O, 98 beds) 4619 North Rosemead Boulevard, Rosemead, CA Zip 91770–1498, Mailing Address: P.O. Box 369, Zip 91770; tel. 626/286–1191; Peggy Minnick, Administrator

BHC CANYON RIDGE HOSPITAL (O, 59 beds) 5353 G. Street, Chino, CA Zip 91710; tel. 909/590–3700; Diana L. Goulet, Chief Executive Officer

BHC CEDAR VISTA HOSPITAL (O, 61 beds) 7171 North Cedar Avenue, Fresno, CA Zip 93720; tel. 209/449–8000; Richard Adams, Ph.D., Administrator

BHC FREMONT HOSPITAL (O, 78 beds) 39001 Sundale Drive, Fremont, CA Zip 94538; tel. 510/796–1100; Ed Owen, Chief Executive Officer

BHC HERITAGE OAKS HOSPITAL (O, 76 beds) 4250 Auburn Boulevard, Sacramento, CA Zip 95841; tel. 916/489–3336; Ingrid L. Whipple, Chief Executive Officer

BHC ROSS HOSPITAL (O, 56 beds) 1111 Sir Francis Drake Boulevard, Kentfield, CA Zip 94904; tel. 415/258–6900; Judy G. House, Chief Executive Officer

BHC SAN LUIS REY HOSPITAL (O, 122 beds) 335 Saxony Road, Encinitas, CA Zip 92024–2723; tel. 619/753–1245; William T. Sparrow, Chief Executive Officer

BHC SIERRA VISTA HOSPITAL (O, 72 beds) 8001 Bruceville Road, Sacramento, CA Zip 95823; tel. 916/423–2000; Kenneth A. Meibert, Chief Executive Officer

BHC VISTA DEL MAR HOSPITAL (O, 87 beds) 801 Seneca Street, Ventura, CA Zip 93001; tel. 805/653–6434; Jerry Conway, Chief Executive Officer

BHC WALNUT CREEK HOSPITAL (O, 108 beds) 175 La Casa Via, Walnut Creek, CA Zip 94598; tel. 925/933–7990; Jay R. Kellison, Chief Executive Officer

FLORIDA: BHC FORT LAUDERDALE HOSPITAL (O, 100 beds) 1601 East Las Olas Boulevard, Fort Lauderdale, FL Zip 33301–2393; tel. 954/463–4321; Andrew Fuhrman, Chief Executive Officer

BHC ST. JOHNS RIVER HOSPITAL (O, 60 beds) 6300 Beach Boulevard, Jacksonville, FL Zip 32216–2782; tel. 904/724–9202; Patricia Vandergrift, Administrator

IDAHO: BHC INTERMOUNTAIN HOSPITAL (O, 75 beds) 303 North Allumbaugh Street, Boise, ID Zip 83704–9266; tel. 208/377–8400; Vernon G. Garrett, Chief Executive Officer

ILLINOIS: BHC STREAMWOOD HOSPITAL (O, 100 beds) 1400 East Irving Park Road, Streamwood, IL Zip 60107–3203; tel. 630/837–9000; Jeff Bergren, Chief Executive Officer and Administrator

INDIANA: BHC VALLE VISTA HOSPITAL (O, 96 beds) 898 East Main Street, Greenwood, IN Zip 46143–1400; tel. 317/887–1348; Sheila Mishler, Chief Executive Officer

BEHAVIORAL HEALTHCARE OF NORTHERN INDIANA (O, 80 beds) 1800 North Oak Road, Plymouth, IN Zip 46563–3492; tel. 219/936–3784; Wayne T. Miller, Administrator

BEHAVIORAL HEALTHCARE–COLUMBUS (O, 60 beds) 2223 Poshard Drive, Columbus, IN Zip 47203–1844; tel. 812/376–1711; Darla Derks, Administrator

KANSAS: BHC COLLEGE MEADOWS HOSPITAL (O, 120 beds) 14425 College Boulevard, Lenexa, KS Zip 66215; tel. 913/469–1100; James E. Ferguson, Chief Executive Officer

LOUISIANA: BHC EAST LAKE HOSPITAL (O, 36 beds) 5650 Read Boulevard, New Orleans, LA Zip 70127–3145; tel. 504/241–0888; Darlene Salvant, Chief Executive Officer

BHC MEADOW WOOD HOSPITAL (O, 55 beds) 9032 Perkins Road, Baton Rouge, LA Zip 70810–1507; tel. 504/766–8553; Ralph J. Waite III, Chief Executive Officer

DEPAUL/TULANE BEHAVIORAL HEALTH CENTER (O, 102 beds) 1040 Calhoun Street, New Orleans, LA Zip 70118–5999; tel. 504/899–8282; David Hoidel, Chief Executive Officer

MISSISSIPPI: BHC SAND HILL BEHAVIORAL HEALTHCARE (O, 60 beds) 11150 Highway 49 North, Gulfport, MS Zip 39503–4110; tel. 601/831–1700; David C. Bell, Chief Operating Officer

MISSOURI: BHC SPIRIT OF ST. LOUIS HOSPITAL (O, 75 beds) 5931 Highway 94 South, Saint Charles, MO Zip 63304–5601; tel. 314/441–7300; Gary L. Henry, Ph.D., Chief Executive Officer

NEVADA: BHC MONTEVISTA HOSPITAL (O, 80 beds) 5900 West Rochelle Avenue, Las Vegas, NV Zip 89103–3327; tel. 702/364–1111; Darryl S. Dubroca, Chief Executive Officer and Administrator

BHC WEST HILLS HOSPITAL (O, 95 beds) 1240 East Ninth Street, Reno, NV Zip 89512–2997, Mailing Address: P.O. Box 30012, Zip 89520–0012; tel. 702/323–0478; Pamela McCullough Broughton, Chief Executive Officer

BHC WILLOW SPRINGS RESIDENTIAL TREATMENT CENTER (O, 68 beds) 690 Edison Way, Reno, NV Zip 89502–4135; tel. 702/858–3303; Robert Bartlett, Administrator

NEW MEXICO: BHC MESILLA VALLEY HOSPITAL (O, 105 beds) 3751 Del Rey Boulevard, Las Cruces, NM Zip 88012–8526, Mailing Address: P.O. Box 429, Zip 88004–0429; tel. 505/382–3500; Alison Druck, R.N., Ed.D., Interim Chief Executive Officer

BHC PINON HILLS HOSPITAL (O, 34 beds) 313 Camino Alire, Santa Fe, NM Zip 87501–2319; tel. 505/988–8003; Jerry Smith, Chief Executive Officer

OHIO: BHC BELMONT PINES HOSPITAL (O, 77 beds) 615 Churchill–Hubbard Road, Youngstown, OH Zip 44505–1379; tel. 330/759–2700; Edward Nasca, Chief Executive Officer

For explanation of codes following names, see page B2.
★ Indicates Type III membership in the American Hospital Association.

Section B

BHC FOX RUN HOSPITAL (O, 65 beds) 67670 Traco Drive, Saint Clairsville, OH Zip 43950–9375; tel. 614/695–2131; J. Frank Gallagher III, Administrator

BHC WINDSOR HOSPITAL (O, 50 beds) 115 East Summit Street, Chagrin Falls, OH Zip 44022–2750; tel. 440/247–5300; Donald K. Sykes Jr., Chief Executive Officer

OREGON: PACIFIC GATEWAY HOSPITAL AND COUNSELING CENTER (O, 66 beds) 1345 S.E. Harney, Portland, OR Zip 97202; tel. 503/234–5353; George B. Rex, Chief Executive Officer

PUERTO RICO: BHC HOSPITAL SAN JUAN CAPESTRANO (O, 88 beds) San Juan, PR Mailing Address: Rural Route 2, Box 11, Zip 00926; tel. 787/760–0222; Laura Vargas, Administrator

TEXAS: BHC MILLWOOD HOSPITAL (O, 80 beds) 1011 North Cooper Street, Arlington, TX Zip 76011–5517; tel. 817/261–3121; Wayne Hallford, Chief Executive Officer

UTAH: BHC OLYMPUS VIEW HOSPITAL (O, 82 beds) 1430 East 4500 South, Salt Lake City, UT Zip 84117–4208; tel. 801/272–8000; Barry W. Woodward, Administrator

WASHINGTON: BHC FAIRFAX HOSPITAL (O, 133 beds) 10200 N.E. 132nd Street, Kirkland, WA Zip 98034; tel. 425/821–2000; Michelle Egerer, Chief Executive Officer

Owned, leased, sponsored:	38 hospitals	2983 beds
Contract–managed:	0 hospitals	0 beds
Totals:	38 hospitals	2983 beds

0515: BENEDICTINE HEALTH SYSTEM (CC)
503 East Third Street, Duluth, MN Zip 55805–1964; tel. 218/720–2370; Barry J. Halm, President and Chief Executive Officer

IDAHO: ST. MARY'S HOSPITAL (O, 28 beds) Lewiston and North Streets, Cottonwood, ID Zip 83522, Mailing Address: P.O. Box 137, Zip 83522–0137; tel. 208/962–3251; Casey Uhling, Administrator

MINNESOTA: ITASCA MEDICAL CENTER (L, 84 beds) 126 First Avenue S.E., Grand Rapids, MN Zip 55744–3698; tel. 218/326–3401; Gary Kenner, President and Chief Executive Officer

PINE MEDICAL CENTER (L, 91 beds) 109 Court Avenue South, Sandstone, MN Zip 55072–5120; tel. 612/245–2212; Michael Hedrix, Administrator

SOUTH SUBURBAN MEDICAL CENTER (O, 95 beds) 3410–213th Street West, Farmington, MN Zip 55024–1197; tel. 612/463–7825; Lee Larson, Chief Executive Officer

ST. JOSEPH'S MEDICAL CENTER (O, 162 beds) 523 North Third Street, Brainerd, MN Zip 56401–3098; tel. 218/829–2861; Thomas K. Prusak, President

ST. MARY'S MEDICAL CENTER (O, 286 beds) 407 East Third Street, Duluth, MN Zip 55805–1984; tel. 218/726–4000; Sister Kathleen Hofer, President

ST. MARY'S REGIONAL HEALTH CENTER (O, 163 beds) 1027 Washington Avenue, Detroit Lakes, MN Zip 56501–3598; tel. 218/847–5611; John H. Solheim, Chief Executive Officer

WISCONSIN: ST. MARY'S HOSPITAL OF SUPERIOR (O, 42 beds) 3500 Tower Avenue, Superior, WI Zip 54880–5395; tel. 715/392–8281; Terry Jacobson, Acting Administrator

Owned, leased, sponsored:	8 hospitals	951 beds
Contract–managed:	0 hospitals	0 beds
Totals:	8 hospitals	951 beds

0545: BENEDICTINE SISTERS OF THE ANNUNCIATION (CC)
7520 University Drive, Bismarck, ND Zip 58504–9653; tel. 701/255–1520; Sister Susan Berger, Prioress

NORTH DAKOTA: GARRISON MEMORIAL HOSPITAL (S, 54 beds) 407 Third Avenue S.E., Garrison, ND Zip 58540–0039; tel. 701/463–2275; Richard Spilovoy, Administrator

ST. ALEXIUS MEDICAL CENTER (S, 269 beds) 900 East Broadway, Bismarck, ND Zip 58501–4586, Mailing Address: P.O. Box 5510, Zip 58506–5510; tel. 701/224–7000; Richard A. Tschider, FACHE, Administrator and Chief Executive Officer

Owned, leased, sponsored:	2 hospitals	323 beds
Contract–managed:	0 hospitals	0 beds
Totals:	2 hospitals	323 beds

★2435: BERKSHIRE HEALTH SYSTEMS, INC. (NP)
725 North Street, Pittsfield, MA Zip 01201–4124; tel. 413/447–2743; David E. Phelps, President and Chief Executive Officer

MASSACHUSETTS: BERKSHIRE MEDICAL CENTER (O, 368 beds) 725 North Street, Pittsfield, MA Zip 01201–4124; tel. 413/447–2000; Ruth P. Blodgett, Chief Operating Officer

FAIRVIEW HOSPITAL (O, 21 beds) 29 Lewis Avenue, Great Barrington, MA Zip 01230–1713; tel. 413/528–0790; Claire L. Bowen, President

Owned, leased, sponsored:	2 hospitals	389 beds
Contract–managed:	0 hospitals	0 beds
Totals:	2 hospitals	389 beds

★0415: BETHESDA HOSPITAL, INC. (NP)
619 Oak Street, Cincinnati, OH Zip 45206–1690; tel. 513/569–6141; John S. Prout, President and Chief Executive Officer

OHIO: BETHESDA NORTH HOSPITAL (O, 361 beds) 10500 Montgomery Road, Cincinnati, OH Zip 45242–4415; tel. 513/745–1111; John S. Prout, President and Chief Executive Officer

BETHESDA OAK HOSPITAL (O, 361 beds) 619 Oak Street, Cincinnati, OH Zip 45206–1690; tel. 513/569–6111; Linda D. Schaffner, R.N., Vice President and Administrator

Owned, leased, sponsored:	2 hospitals	722 beds
Contract–managed:	0 hospitals	0 beds
Totals:	2 hospitals	722 beds

★0051: BJC HEALTH SYSTEM (NP)
4444 Forest Park Avenue, Saint Louis, MO Zip 63108–2259; tel. 314/286–2030; Fred L. Brown, President and Chief Executive Officer

ILLINOIS: ALTON MEMORIAL HOSPITAL (O, 224 beds) One Memorial Drive, Alton, IL Zip 62002–6722; tel. 618/463–7311; Ronald B. McMullen, President

CLAY COUNTY HOSPITAL (C, 31 beds) 700 North Mill Street, Flora, IL Zip 62839–1823, Mailing Address: P.O. Box 280, Zip 62839–0280; tel. 618/662–2131; John E. Monnahan, President and Senior Executive Officer

FAYETTE COUNTY HOSPITAL AND LONG TERM CARE (L, 142 beds) Seventh and Taylor Streets, Vandalia, IL Zip 62471–1296; tel. 618/283–1231; Daniel L. Gantz, President

MISSOURI: BARNES–JEWISH HOSPITAL (O, 974 beds) One Barnes–Jewish Hospital Plaza, Saint Louis, MO Zip 63110–1094; tel. 314/362–5400; Peter L. Slavin, M.D., President

BARNES–JEWISH ST. PETERS HOSPITAL (O, 91 beds) 10 Hospital Drive, Saint Peters, MO Zip 63376–1659; tel. 314/916–9000; Carm Moceri, President

BARNES–JEWISH WEST COUNTY HOSPITAL (O, 91 beds) 12634 Olive Boulevard, Saint Louis, MO Zip 63141–6354; tel. 314/996–8000; Gregory T. Wozniak, President

BOONE HOSPITAL CENTER (L, 313 beds) 1600 East Broadway, Columbia, MO Zip 65201–5897; tel. 573/815–8000; Michael Shirk, President and Senior Executive Officer

CHRISTIAN HOSPITAL NORTHEAST–NORTHWEST (O, 542 beds) 11133 Dunn Road, Saint Louis, MO Zip 63136–6192; tel. 314/653–5000; W. R. Van Bokkelen, President and Senior Executive Officer

MISSOURI BAPTIST HOSPITAL OF SULLIVAN (O, 60 beds) 751 Sappington Bridge Road, Sullivan, MO Zip 63080–2354, Mailing Address: P.O. Box 190, Zip 63080–0190; tel. 573/468–4186; Davis D. Skinner, President

For explanation of codes following names, see page B2.
★ Indicates Type III membership in the American Hospital Association.

MISSOURI BAPTIST MEDICAL CENTER (O, 360 beds) 3015 North Ballas Road, Town and Country, MO Zip 63131–2374; tel. 314/996–5000; Mark A. Eustis, President

PARKLAND HEALTH CENTER (O, 94 beds) 1101 West Liberty Street, Farmington, MO Zip 63640–1997; tel. 573/756–6451; Richard L. Conklin, President

ST. LOUIS CHILDREN'S HOSPITAL (O, 235 beds) One Children's Place, Saint Louis, MO Zip 63110–1077; tel. 314/454–6000; Ted W. Frey, President

Owned, leased, sponsored:	11 hospitals	3126 beds
Contract–managed:	1 hospital	31 beds
Totals:	12 hospitals	3157 beds

● ★0053: BLUE WATER HEALTH SERVICES CORPORATION (NP)

1221 Pine Grove Avenue, Port Huron, MI Zip 48060–3568; tel. 810/989–3717; Donald C. Fletcher, President and Chief Executive Officer

MICHIGAN: PORT HURON HOSPITAL (O, 175 beds) 1221 Pine Grove Avenue, Port Huron, MI Zip 48061–5011; tel. 810/987–5000; Donald C. Fletcher, President and Chief Executive Officer

Owned, leased, sponsored:	1 hospital	175 beds
Contract–managed:	0 hospitals	0 beds
Totals:	1 hospital	175 beds

★5085: BON SECOURS HEALTH SYSTEM, INC. (CC)

1505 Marriottsville Road, Marriottsville, MD Zip 21104–1399; tel. 410/442–5511; Christopher M. Carney, President and Chief Executive Officer

FLORIDA: BON SECOURS–ST. JOSEPH HOSPITAL (O, 316 beds) 2500 Harbor Boulevard, Port Charlotte, FL Zip 33952–5396; tel. 941/766–4122; Michael L. Harrington, Executive Vice President and Administrator

BON SECOURS–VENICE HOSPITAL (O, 209 beds) 540 The Rialto, Venice, FL Zip 34285–2900; tel. 941/485–7711; Roy E. Hess, Executive Vice President and Administrator

MARYLAND: BON SECOURS BALTIMORE HEALTH SYSTEM (O, 142 beds) 2000 West Baltimore Street, Baltimore, MD Zip 21223–1597; tel. 410/362–3000; Jane Durney Crowley, President and Chief Executive Officer

LIBERTY MEDICAL CENTER (O, 95 beds) 2600 Liberty Heights Avenue, Baltimore, MD Zip 21215–7892; tel. 410/383–4000; Jane Durney Crowley, Chief Executive Officer

MICHIGAN: BON SECOURS HOSPITAL (O, 435 beds) 468 Cadieux Road, Grosse Pointe, MI Zip 48230–1592; tel. 313/343–1000; Michael Serilla, Acting Executive Vice President and Administrator

PENNSYLVANIA: BON SECOURS–HOLY FAMILY REGIONAL HEALTH SYSTEM (O, 149 beds) 2500 Seventh Avenue, Altoona, PA Zip 16602–2099; tel. 814/944–1681; David McConnell, Interim Chief Executive Officer

SOUTH CAROLINA: BON SECOURS–ST. FRANCIS XAVIER HOSPITAL (O, 145 beds) 2095 Henry Tecklenburg Drive, Charleston, SC Zip 29414–0001, Mailing Address: P.O. Box 160001, Zip 29414–0001; tel. 803/402–1000; Allen P. Carroll, Chief Executive Officer

VIRGINIA: BON SECOURS ST. MARY'S HOSPITAL (O, 391 beds) 5801 Bremo Road, Richmond, VA Zip 23226–1900; tel. 804/285–2011; Ann E. Honeycutt, Executive Vice President and Administrator

BON SECOURS–DEPAUL MEDICAL CENTER (O, 202 beds) 150 Kingsley Lane, Norfolk, VA Zip 23505–4650; tel. 757/889–5000; David McCombs, Executive Vice President and Administrator

BON SECOURS–RICHMOND COMMUNITY HOSPITAL (O, 232 beds) 1500 North 28th Street, Richmond, VA Zip 23223–5396, Mailing Address: Box 27184, Zip 23261–7184; tel. 804/225–1700; Samuel F. Lillard, Executive Vice President and Administrator

BON SECOURS–STUART CIRCLE (O, 158 beds) 413 Stuart Circle, Richmond, VA Zip 23220–3799; tel. 804/358–7051; Edward Gerardo, Interim Executive Vice President and Administrator

MARY IMMACULATE HOSPITAL (O, 225 beds) 2 Bernardine Drive, Newport News, VA Zip 23602–4499; tel. 757/886–6000; Cynthia B. Farrand, Executive Vice President

MARYVIEW HOSPITAL (O, 321 beds) 3636 High Street, Portsmouth, VA Zip 23707–3236; tel. 757/398–2200; Wayne Jones, Executive Vice President and Administrator

MEMORIAL REGIONAL MEDICAL CENTER (O, 272 beds) 1300 Westwood Avenue, Richmond, VA Zip 23227–4699, Mailing Address: P.O. Box 26783, Zip 23261–6783; tel. 804/254–6000; Michael Robinson, Executive Vice President and Administrator

Owned, leased, sponsored:	14 hospitals	3292 beds
Contract–managed:	0 hospitals	0 beds
Totals:	14 hospitals	3292 beds

0073: BOWDON CORPORATE OFFICES (IO)

4250 Perimeter Park South, Suite 102, Atlanta, GA Zip 30341; tel. 770/452–1221; Bill E. Ehrhardt, Executive Director

GEORGIA: BOWDON AREA HOSPITAL (O, 41 beds) 501 Mitchell Avenue, Bowdon, GA Zip 30108–1499; tel. 770/258–7207; Yvonne Willis, Administrator

NEW MEXICO: ALLIANCE HOSPITAL OF SANTA TERESA (L, 72 beds) 100 Laura Court, Santa Teresa, NM Zip 88008, Mailing Address: P.O. Box 6, Las Cruces, Zip 88008–0006; tel. 505/589–0033; Michele Irwin, Administrator

Owned, leased, sponsored:	2 hospitals	113 beds
Contract–managed:	0 hospitals	0 beds
Totals:	2 hospitals	113 beds

2455: BRADFORD HEALTH SERVICES (IO)

2101 Magnolia Avenue South, Suite 518, Birmingham, AL Zip 35205; tel. 205/251–7753; Jerry W. Crowder, President and Chief Executive Officer

ALABAMA: BRADFORD HEALTH SERVICES AT HUNTSVILLE (O, 84 beds) 1600 Browns Ferry Road, Madison, AL Zip 35758–9769, Mailing Address: P.O. Box 176, Zip 35758–0176; tel. 205/461–7272; Bob Hinds, Executive Director

BRADFORD HEALTH SERVICES AT OAK MOUNTAIN (O, 84 beds) 2280 Highway 35, Pelham, AL Zip 35124–6120; tel. 205/664–3460; Jerry Caltrider, Administrator

Owned, leased, sponsored:	2 hospitals	168 beds
Contract–managed:	0 hospitals	0 beds
Totals:	2 hospitals	168 beds

★0585: BRIM, INC. (IO)

305 N.E. 102nd Avenue, Portland, OR Zip 97220–4199; tel. 503/256–2070; Jim McKinney, President

ARIZONA: COBRE VALLEY COMMUNITY HOSPITAL (C, 41 beds) One Hospital Drive, Claypool, AZ Zip 85532, Mailing Address: P.O. Box 3261, Zip 85532–3261; tel. 520/425–3261; Charles E. Bill, CHE, Chief Executive Officer

NAVAPACHE REGIONAL MEDICAL CENTER (C, 52 beds) 2200 Show Low Lake Road, Show Low, AZ Zip 85901–7800; tel. 520/537–4375; Leigh Cox, Administrator

NORTHERN COCHISE COMMUNITY HOSPITAL (C, 48 beds) 901 West Rex Allen Drive, Willcox, AZ Zip 85643–1009; tel. 520/384–3541; Chris Cronberg, Chief Executive Officer

CALIFORNIA: BEAR VALLEY COMMUNITY HOSPITAL (C, 30 beds) 41870 Garstin Road, Big Bear Lake, CA Zip 92315, Mailing Address: P.O. Box 1649, Zip 92315–1649; tel. 909/866–6501; James Sato, Chief Executive Officer

HAZEL HAWKINS MEMORIAL HOSPITAL (C, 86 beds) 911 Sunset Drive, Hollister, CA Zip 95023–5695; tel. 408/637–5711; Keith Mesmer, Interim Administrator

For explanation of codes following names, see page B2.
★ Indicates Type III membership in the American Hospital Association.
● Single hospital health care system

Section B

PIONEERS MEMORIAL HEALTHCARE DISTRICT (C, 80 beds) 207 West Legion Road, Brawley, CA Zip 92227–9699; tel. 760/351–3333; William W. Daniel, Chief Executive Officer

SAN GORGONIO MEMORIAL HOSPITAL (C, 68 beds) 600 North Highland Springs Avenue, Banning, CA Zip 92220; tel. 909/845–1121; Donald N. Larkin, Chief Executive Officer

IDAHO: CLEARWATER VALLEY HOSPITAL (L, 23 beds) 301 Cedar, Orofino, ID Zip 83544–9029; tel. 208/476–4555; Richard L. Wheat, Chief Financial Officer

ILLINOIS: HAMMOND–HENRY HOSPITAL (C, 105 beds) 210 West Elk Street, Geneseo, IL Zip 61254–1099; tel. 309/944–6431; Nathan C. Olson, President and Chief Executive Officer

HILLSBORO AREA HOSPITAL (C, 95 beds) 1200 East Tremont Street, Hillsboro, IL Zip 62049–1900; tel. 217/532–6111; Rex H. Brown, President

SPARTA COMMUNITY HOSPITAL (C, 39 beds) 818 East Broadway Street, Sparta, IL Zip 62286–0297, Mailing Address: P.O. Box 297, Zip 62286–0297; tel. 618/443–2177; Joann Emge, Chief Executive Officer

WOOD RIVER TOWNSHIP HOSPITAL (C, 113 beds) 101 East Edwardsville Road, Wood River, IL Zip 62095–1332; tel. 618/251–7103; Max L. Ludeke, FACHE, President and Chief Executive Officer

INDIANA: WIRTH REGIONAL HOSPITAL (C, 21 beds) Highway 64 West, Oakland City, IN Zip 47660–9379, Mailing Address: Rural Route 3, Box 14A, Zip 47660–9379; tel. 812/749–6111; Frank G. Fougerouse, President and Chief Executive Officer

IOWA: GUTTENBERG MUNICIPAL HOSPITAL (C, 21 beds) Second and Main Street, Guttenberg, IA Zip 52052–0550, Mailing Address: Box 550, Zip 52052–0550; tel. 319/252–1121; Roland D. Gee, Chief Executive Officer

LOUISIANA: LADY OF THE SEA GENERAL HOSPITAL (C, 55 beds) 200 West 134th Place, Cut Off, LA Zip 70345–4145; tel. 504/632–6401; Lane M. Cheramie, Chief Executive Officer

MINNESOTA: SWIFT COUNTY–BENSON HOSPITAL (C, 31 beds) 1815 Wisconsin Avenue, Benson, MN Zip 56215–1653; tel. 320/843–4232; Frank Lawatsch, Chief Executive Officer

MONTANA: BARRETT MEMORIAL HOSPITAL (C, 31 beds) 1260 South Atlantic Street, Dillon, MT Zip 59725–3597; tel. 406/683–3000; Jim D. Le Brun, Chief Executive Officer

BIG HORN COUNTY MEMORIAL HOSPITAL (C, 53 beds) 17 North Miles Avenue, Hardin, MT Zip 59034–0430, Mailing Address: P.O. Box 430, Zip 59034–0430; tel. 406/665–2310; Raymond T. Hino, Chief Executive Officer

COMMUNITY MEDICAL CENTER (C, 115 beds) 2827 Fort Missoula Road, Missoula, MT Zip 59801; tel. 406/728–4100; Grant M. Winn, President

MINERAL COMMUNITY HOSPITAL (C, 30 beds) Roosevelt and Brooklyn, Superior, MT Zip 59872, Mailing Address: P.O. Box 66, Zip 59872–0066; tel. 406/822–4841; Madelyn Faller, Chief Executive Officer

NORTHERN MONTANA HOSPITAL (C, 274 beds) 30 13th Street, Havre, MT Zip 59501–5222, Mailing Address: P.O. Box 1231, Zip 59501–1231; tel. 406/265–2211; David Henry, Chief Executive Officer

POWELL COUNTY MEMORIAL HOSPITAL (C, 35 beds) 1101 Texas Avenue, Deer Lodge, MT Zip 59722–1828; tel. 406/846–2212; Connie Huber, R.N., Chief Executive Officer

ROSEBUD HEALTH CARE CENTER (C, 75 beds) 383 North 17th Avenue, Forsyth, MT Zip 59327; tel. 406/356–2161; John M. Chioutsis, Chief Executive Officer

ROUNDUP MEMORIAL HOSPITAL (C, 54 beds) 1202 Third Street West, Roundup, MT Zip 59072–1816, Mailing Address: P.O. Box 40, Zip 59072–0040; tel. 406/323–2302; Dave McIvor, Administrator

ST. JOHN'S LUTHERAN HOSPITAL (C, 26 beds) 350 Louisiana Avenue, Libby, MT Zip 59923–2198; tel. 406/293–7761; Richard L. Palagi, Executive Director

NEBRASKA: TRI–VALLEY HEALTH SYSTEM (C, 56 beds) West Highway 6 and 34, Cambridge, NE Zip 69022–0488, Mailing Address: P.O. Box 488, Zip 69022–0488; tel. 308/697–3329; Kristopher H. Marwin, CHE, Chief Executive Officer

NEW MEXICO: NORTHEASTERN REGIONAL HOSPITAL (C, 56 beds) 1235 Eighth Street, Las Vegas, NM Zip 87701–4254, Mailing Address: P.O. Box 248, Zip 87701–0238; tel. 505/425–6751; Donna Beane, Interim Chief Executive Officer

UNION COUNTY GENERAL HOSPITAL (C, 30 beds) 301 Harding Street, Clayton, NM Zip 88415–3321, Mailing Address: P.O. Box 489, Zip 88415–0489; tel. 505/374–2585; W. C. McElhannon, Administrator

NEW YORK: ADIRONDACK MEDICAL CENTER (C, 100 beds) Lake Colby Drive, Saranac Lake, NY Zip 12983, Mailing Address: P.O. Box 471, Zip 12983–0471; tel. 518/891–4141; Chandler M. Ralph, Chief Executive Officer

LEWIS COUNTY GENERAL HOSPITAL (C, 214 beds) 7785 North State Street, Lowville, NY Zip 13367–1297; tel. 315/376–5200; Ernest R. McNeely Jr., Chief Executive Officer and Administrator

THE HOSPITAL (C, 87 beds) 43 Pearl Street West, Sidney, NY Zip 13838–1399; tel. 607/561–2153; Russell A. Test, Administrator and Chief Executive Officer

OKLAHOMA: MISSION HILL MEMORIAL HOSPITAL (C, 49 beds) 1900 South Gordon Cooper Drive, Shawnee, OK Zip 74801–8600; tel. 405/273–2240; Thomas G. Honaker III, Administrator

OREGON: BLUE MOUNTAIN HOSPITAL (C, 73 beds) 170 Ford Road, John Day, OR Zip 97845; tel. 541/575–1311; David G. Triebes, Chief Executive Officer

COTTAGE GROVE HEALTHCARE COMMUNITY (C, 67 beds) 1340 Birch Avenue, Cottage Grove, OR Zip 97424; tel. 541/942–0511; William N. Wilber, Administrator

MOUNTAIN VIEW HOSPITAL DISTRICT (C, 102 beds) 470 N.E. A. Street, Madras, OR Zip 97741; tel. 541/475–3882; Ronald W. Barnes, Executive Director

TEXAS: DE LEON HOSPITAL (C, 14 beds) 407 South Texas Avenue, De Leon, TX Zip 76444–1947, Mailing Address: P.O. Box 319, Zip 76444–0319; tel. 254/893–2011; Michael K. Hare, Administrator

WASHINGTON: COULEE COMMUNITY HOSPITAL (C, 48 beds) 411 Fortuyn Road, Grand Coulee, WA Zip 99133–8718; tel. 509/633–1753; Charlotte Lang, Administrator

PULLMAN MEMORIAL HOSPITAL (C, 36 beds) N.E. 1125 Washington Avenue, Pullman, WA Zip 99163–4742; tel. 509/332–2541; Scott K. Adams, Chief Executive Officer

SUNNYSIDE COMMUNITY HOSPITAL (C, 34 beds) 10th and Tacoma Avenue, Sunnyside, WA Zip 98944, Mailing Address: P.O. Box 719, Zip 98944–0719; tel. 509/837–1650; Jon D. Smiley, Chief Executive Officer

WISCONSIN: BURNETT MEDICAL CENTER (C, 70 beds) 257 West St. George Avenue, Grantsburg, WI Zip 54840–7827; tel. 715/463–5353; Timothy J. Wick, Chief Executive Officer

COMMUNITY MEMORIAL HOSPITAL AND NURSING HOME (C, 136 beds) 819 Ash Street, Spooner, WI Zip 54801–1299; tel. 715/635–2111; Michael Schafer, Chief Executive Officer

GRANT REGIONAL HEALTH CENTER (C, 28 beds) 507 South Monroe Street, Lancaster, WI Zip 53813–2099; tel. 608/723–2143; Larry D. Rentfro, FACHE, Chief Executive Officer

MEMORIAL COMMUNITY HOSPITAL (C, 115 beds) 313 Stoughton Road, Edgerton, WI Zip 53534–1198; tel. 608/884–3441; Charles E. Bruhn, Chief Executive Officer

MEMORIAL HOSPITAL OF IOWA COUNTY (C, 84 beds) 825 South Iowa Street, Dodgeville, WI Zip 53533–1999; tel. 608/935–2711; Ray Marmorstone, Administrator

RIPON MEDICAL CENTER (C, 29 beds) 933 Newbury Street, Ripon, WI Zip 54971–1798, Mailing Address: P.O. Box 390, Zip 54971–0390; tel. 920/748–3101; Jon W. Baker, Chief Executive Officer

SHAWANO MEDICAL CENTER (C, 46 beds) 309 North Bartlette Street, Shawano, WI Zip 54166–0477; tel. 715/526–2111; John J. Kestly, Administrator

SOUTHWEST HEALTH CENTER (C, 138 beds) 1100 Fifth Avenue, Platteville, WI Zip 53818–1299; tel. 608/348–2331; Anne K. Klawiter, President and Chief Executive Officer

ST. JOSEPH'S MEMORIAL HOSPITAL AND NURSING HOME (C, 85 beds) 400 Water Avenue, Hillsboro, WI Zip 54634–0527, Mailing Address: P.O. Box 527, Zip 54634–0527; tel. 608/489–2211; Nancy Bauman, Chief Executive Officer

For explanation of codes following names, see page B2.
★ Indicates Type III membership in the American Hospital Association.

WYOMING: POWELL HOSPITAL (C, 140 beds) 777 Avenue H., Powell, WY Zip 82435–2296; tel. 307/754–2267; Rod Barton, Chief Executive Officer

Owned, leased, sponsored:	1 hospital	23 beds
Contract–managed:	48 hospitals	3415 beds
Totals:	49 hospitals	3438 beds

★0595: BRONSON HEALTHCARE GROUP, INC. (NP)
One Healthcare Plaza, Kalamazoo, MI Zip 49007–5345; tel. 616/341–6000; Frank J. Sardone, President and Chief Executive Officer

MICHIGAN: BRONSON METHODIST HOSPITAL (O, 307 beds) 252 East Lovell Street, Kalamazoo, MI Zip 49007–5345; tel. 616/341–6000; Frank J. Sardone, President and Chief Executive Officer

BRONSON VICKSBURG HOSPITAL (O, 41 beds) 13326 North Boulevard, Vicksburg, MI Zip 49097–1099; tel. 616/649–2321; Frank J. Sardone, President

Owned, leased, sponsored:	2 hospitals	348 beds
Contract–managed:	0 hospitals	0 beds
Totals:	2 hospitals	348 beds

0077: CAMBRIDGE INTERNATIONAL, INC, (IO)
7505 Fannin, Suite 680, Houston, TX Zip 77225; tel. 713/790–1153; Timothy Sharma, M.D., President

TEXAS: FOREST SPRINGS HOSPITAL (O, 48 beds) 1120 Cypress Station, Houston, TX Zip 77090–3031; tel. 281/893–7200; Deo Shanker, CPA, Chief Executive Officer

INTRACARE MEDICAL CENTER HOSPITAL (O, 100 beds) 7601 Fannin Street, Houston, TX Zip 77054–1905; tel. 713/790–0949; Alice Hiniker, Ph.D., Administrator

Owned, leased, sponsored:	2 hospitals	148 beds
Contract–managed:	0 hospitals	0 beds
Totals:	2 hospitals	148 beds

★0955: CAMCARE, INC. (NP)
501 Morris Street, Charleston, WV Zip 25301–1300, Mailing Address: P.O. Box 1547, Zip 25326–1547; tel. 304/348–5432; Phillip H. Goodwin, President

WEST VIRGINIA: BRAXTON COUNTY MEMORIAL HOSPITAL (O, 30 beds) 100 Hoylman Drive, Gassaway, WV Zip 26624–9308; tel. 304/364–5156; Tony E. Atkins, Administrator

CHARLESTON AREA MEDICAL CENTER (O, 818 beds) 501 Morris Street, Charleston, WV Zip 25301–1300, Mailing Address: P.O. Box 1547, Zip 25326–1547; tel. 304/348–5432; Robert L. Savage, President and Chief Executive Officer

PLATEAU MEDICAL CENTER (O, 79 beds) 430 Main Street, Oak Hill, WV Zip 25901–3455; tel. 304/469–8600; David L. Brash, Administrator

Owned, leased, sponsored:	3 hospitals	927 beds
Contract–managed:	0 hospitals	0 beds
Totals:	3 hospitals	927 beds

0113: CANCER TREATMENT CENTERS OF AMERICA (IO)
3455 West Salt Creek Lane, Arlington Heights, IL Zip 60005–1080; tel. 847/342–7400; William A. Sanger, President and Chief Executive Officer

ILLINOIS: MIDWESTERN REGIONAL MEDICAL CENTER (O, 70 beds) 2520 Elisha Avenue, Zion, IL Zip 60099–2587; tel. 847/872–4561; Roger C. Cary, President and Chief Executive Officer

OKLAHOMA: MEMORIAL MEDICAL CENTER AND CANCER TREATMENT CENTER–TULSA (O, 72 beds) 2408 East 81st Street, Tulsa, OK Zip 74137–4210; tel. 918/496–5000; Sandra Jackson, President

Owned, leased, sponsored:	2 hospitals	142 beds
Contract–managed:	0 hospitals	0 beds
Totals:	2 hospitals	142 beds

0124: CAPE COD HEALTHCARE, INC. (NP)
88 Lewis Bay Road, Hyannis, MA Zip 02601–5210; tel. 508/862–5011; James F. Lyons, President and Chief Executive Officer

MASSACHUSETTS: CAPE COD HOSPITAL (O, 236 beds) 27 Park Street, Hyannis, MA Zip 02601–5203; tel. 508/771–1800; Gail M. Frieswick, Ed.D., President and Chief Executive Officer

FALMOUTH HOSPITAL (O, 83 beds) 100 Ter Heun Drive, Falmouth, MA Zip 02540–2599; tel. 508/457–3500; Gail Freiswick, President and Chief Executive Officer

Owned, leased, sponsored:	2 hospitals	319 beds
Contract–managed:	0 hospitals	0 beds
Totals:	2 hospitals	319 beds

★0099: CARE NEW ENGLAND HEALTH SYSTEM (NP)
45 Willard Avenue, Providence, RI Zip 02905–3218; tel. 401/453–7900; John J. Hynes, President and Chief Executive Officer

RHODE ISLAND: BUTLER HOSPITAL (O, 105 beds) 345 Blackstone Boulevard, Providence, RI Zip 02906–4829; tel. 401/455–6200; Frank A. Delmonico, President and Chief Executive Officer

KENT COUNTY MEMORIAL HOSPITAL (O, 317 beds) 455 Tollgate Road, Warwick, RI Zip 02886–2770; tel. 401/737–7000; Robert E. Baute, M.D., President and Chief Executive Officer

WOMEN AND INFANTS HOSPITAL OF RHODE ISLAND (O, 197 beds) 101 Dudley Street, Providence, RI Zip 02905–2499; tel. 401/274–1100; Thomas G. Parris Jr., President

Owned, leased, sponsored:	3 hospitals	619 beds
Contract–managed:	0 hospitals	0 beds
Totals:	3 hospitals	619 beds

★0096: CAREGROUP (NP)
375 Longwood Avenue, Boston, MA Zip 02215–5395; tel. 617/975–6060; James Reinertsen, M.D., Chief Executive Officer

MASSACHUSETTS: BETH ISRAEL DEACONESS MEDICAL CENTER (O, 656 beds) 330 Brookline Avenue, Boston, MA Zip 02215–5491; tel. 617/667–2000; David Dolins, President

DEACONESS WALTHAM HOSPITAL (O, 219 beds) Hope Avenue, Waltham, MA Zip 02254–9116; tel. 781/647–6000; Jeanette G. Clough, President and Chief Executive Officer

DEACONESS–GLOVER HOSPITAL CORPORATION (O, 41 beds) 148 Chestnut Street, Needham, MA Zip 02192–2483; tel. 781/453–3000; John Dalton, President and Chief Executive Officer

DEACONESS–NASHOBA HOSPITAL (O, 49 beds) 200 Groton Road, Ayer, MA Zip 01432–3300; tel. 978/784–9000; Jeffrey R. Kelly, President and Chief Executive Officer

MOUNT AUBURN HOSPITAL (O, 190 beds) 330 Mount Auburn Street, Cambridge, MA Zip 02238; tel. 617/492–3500; Francis P. Lynch, President and Chief Executive Officer

NEW ENGLAND BAPTIST HOSPITAL (O, 98 beds) 125 Parker Hill Avenue, Boston, MA Zip 02120–3297; tel. 617/754–5800; Alan H. Robbins, M.D., President

Owned, leased, sponsored:	6 hospitals	1253 beds
Contract–managed:	0 hospitals	0 beds
Totals:	6 hospitals	1253 beds

For explanation of codes following names, see page B2.
★ Indicates Type III membership in the American Hospital Association.

Networks, Health Care Systems and Alliances **B75**

★0070: CARILION HEALTH SYSTEM (NP)
1212 Third Street S.W., Roanoke, VA Zip 24016–4696, Mailing Address: P.O. Box 13727, Zip 24036–3727; tel. 540/981–7900; Thomas L. Robertson, President and Chief Executive Officer

VIRGINIA: CARILION BEDFORD MEMORIAL HOSPITAL (O, 161 beds) 1613 Oakwood Street, Bedford, VA Zip 24523–0688, Mailing Address: P.O. Box 688, Zip 24523–0688; tel. 540/586–2441; Howard Ainsley, Director

CARILION FRANKLIN MEMORIAL HOSPITAL (O, 37 beds) 180 Floyd Avenue, Rocky Mount, VA Zip 24151–1389; tel. 540/483–5277; Matthew J. Perry, Director

CARILION GILES MEMORIAL HOSPITAL (O, 53 beds) 1 Taylor Avenue, Pearisburg, VA Zip 24134–1932; tel. 540/921–6000; Morris D. Reece, Administrator

CARILION MEDICAL CENTER (O, 646 beds) Belleview at Jefferson Street, Roanoke, VA Zip 24014, Mailing Address: P.O. Box 13367, Zip 24033–3367; tel. 540/981–7000; Lucas A. Snipes, FACHE, Director

CARILION RADFORD COMMUNITY HOSPITAL (O, 122 beds) 700 Randolph Street, Radford, VA Zip 24141–2430; tel. 540/731–2000; Virginia Ousley, Director

CARILION SAINT ALBANS HOSPITAL (O, 66 beds) Route 11, Lee Highway, Radford, VA Zip 24143, Mailing Address: P.O. Box 3608, Zip 24143–3608; tel. 540/639–2481; Janet McKinney Crawford, Administrator

SOUTHSIDE COMMUNITY HOSPITAL (C, 88 beds) 800 Oak Street, Farmville, VA Zip 23901–1199; tel. 804/392–8811; John H. Greer, President

STONEWALL JACKSON HOSPITAL (C, 130 beds) 1 Health Circle, Lexington, VA Zip 24450–2492; tel. 540/462–1200; William Mahone V, Administrator

TAZEWELL COMMUNITY HOSPITAL (C, 42 beds) 141 Ben Bolt Avenue, Tazewell, VA Zip 24651–9700; tel. 540/988–2506; Craig B. James, Administrator

WYTHE COUNTY COMMUNITY HOSPITAL (C, 82 beds) 600 West Ridge Road, Wytheville, VA Zip 24382–1099; tel. 540/228–0200; Larry H. Chewning III, Chief Executive Officer

Owned, leased, sponsored:	6 hospitals	1085 beds
Contract–managed:	4 hospitals	342 beds
Totals:	10 hospitals	1427 beds

★0141: CARITAS CHRISTI HEALTH CARE (NP)
736 Cambridge Street, Boston, MA Zip 02135–2997; tel. 617/789–2500; Michael F. Collins, M.D., President

MASSACHUSETTS: CARITAS NORWOOD HOSPITAL (S, 179 beds) 800 Washington Street, Norwood, MA Zip 02062–3487; tel. 781/769–4000; Delia O'Connor, President

CARITAS SOUTHWOOD COMMUNITY HOSPITAL (S, 182 beds) 111 Dedham Street, Norfolk, MA Zip 02056–1664; tel. 508/668–0385; Delia O'Connor, President

CARNEY HOSPITAL (S, 216 beds) 2100 Dorchester Avenue, Boston, MA Zip 02124–5666; tel. 617/296–4000; Joyce A. Murphy, President

GOOD SAMARITAN MEDICAL CENTER (S, 223 beds) 235 North Pearl Street, Brockton, MA Zip 02401–1794; tel. 508/427–3000; Frank J. Larkin, President and Chief Executive Officer

HOLY FAMILY HOSPITAL AND MEDICAL CENTER (S, 265 beds) 70 East Street, Methuen, MA Zip 01844–4597; tel. 978/687–0151; William L. Lane, President

SAINT ANNE'S HOSPITAL (S, 165 beds) 795 Middle Street, Fall River, MA Zip 02721–1798; tel. 508/674–5741; Michael W. Metzler, Acting President

ST. ELIZABETH'S MEDICAL CENTER OF BOSTON (S, 238 beds) 736 Cambridge Street, Boston, MA Zip 02135–2997; tel. 617/789–3000; Michael F. Collins, M.D., President

ST. JOHN OF GOD HOSPITAL (S, 31 beds) 296 Allston Street, Brighton, MA Zip 02146–1659; tel. 617/277–5750; William K. Brinkert, President

Owned, leased, sponsored:	8 hospitals	1499 beds
Contract–managed:	0 hospitals	0 beds
Totals:	8 hospitals	1499 beds

0705: CAROLINAS HEALTHCARE SYSTEM (NP)
1000 Blythe Boulevard, Charlotte, NC Zip 28203–5871, Mailing Address: P.O. Box 32861, Zip 28232–2861; tel. 704/355–2000; Harry A. Nurkin, Ph.D., President and Chief Executive Officer

NORTH CAROLINA: CAROLINAS MEDICAL CENTER (O, 843 beds) 1000 Blythe Boulevard, Charlotte, NC Zip 28203–5871, Mailing Address: P.O. Box 32861, Zip 28232–2861; tel. 704/355–2000; Paul S. Franz, President

CHARLOTTE INSTITUTE OF REHABILITATION (O, 133 beds) 1100 Blythe Boulevard, Charlotte, NC Zip 28203–5864; tel. 704/355–4300; Don Gabriel, Administrator

CLEVELAND REGIONAL MEDICAL CENTER (C, 296 beds) 201 Grover Street, Shelby, NC Zip 28150–3940; tel. 704/487–3000; John Young, President and Chief Executive Officer

CRAWLEY MEMORIAL HOSPITAL (C, 51 beds) 315 West College Avenue, Boiling Springs, NC Zip 28017, Mailing Address: P.O. Box 996, Zip 28017–0996; tel. 704/434–9466; Daphne Bridges, President

KINGS MOUNTAIN HOSPITAL (O, 72 beds) 706 West King Street, Kings Mountain, NC Zip 28086–2708, Mailing Address: P.O. Box 339, Zip 28086–0339; tel. 704/739–3601; Hank Neal, Administrator

MERCY HOSPITAL (O, 244 beds) 2001 Vail Avenue, Charlotte, NC Zip 28207–1289; tel. 704/379–5000; C. Curtis Copenhaver, Chief Executive Officer

UNION REGIONAL MEDICAL CENTER (L, 207 beds) 600 Hospital Drive, Monroe, NC Zip 28112–6000, Mailing Address: P.O. Box 5003, Zip 28111–5003; tel. 704/283–3100; John W. Roberts, President and Chief Executive Officer

UNIVERSITY HOSPITAL (O, 115 beds) 8800 North Tryon Street, Charlotte, NC Zip 28262–8415, Mailing Address: P.O. Box 560727, Zip 28256–0727; tel. 704/548–6000; W. Spencer Lilly, Administrator

Owned, leased, sponsored:	6 hospitals	1614 beds
Contract–managed:	2 hospitals	347 beds
Totals:	8 hospitals	1961 beds

★5945: CARONDELET HEALTH SYSTEM (CC)
13801 Riverport Drive, Suite 300, Saint Louis, MO Zip 63043–4810; tel. 314/770–0333; Gary Christiansen, President and Chief Executive Officer

ARIZONA: CARONDELET HOLY CROSS HOSPITAL (O, 80 beds) 1171 Target Range Road, Nogales, AZ Zip 85621–2496; tel. 520/287–2771; Carol Field, Senior Corporate Director and Administrator

CARONDELET ST. JOSEPH'S HOSPITAL (O, 300 beds) 350 North Wilmot Road, Tucson, AZ Zip 85711–2678; tel. 520/296–3211; Sister St. Joan Willert, President and Chief Executive Officer

CARONDELET ST. MARY'S HOSPITAL (O, 354 beds) 1601 West St. Mary's Road, Tucson, AZ Zip 85745–2682; tel. 520/622–5833; Sister St. Joan Willert, President and Chief Executive Officer

CALIFORNIA: DANIEL FREEMAN MARINA HOSPITAL (O, 138 beds) 4650 Lincoln Boulevard, Venice, CA Zip 90291–6360; tel. 310/823–8911; Joseph W. Dunn, Ph.D., Chief Executive Officer

DANIEL FREEMAN MEMORIAL HOSPITAL (O, 365 beds) 333 North Prairie Avenue, Inglewood, CA Zip 90301–4514; tel. 310/674–7050; Joseph W. Dunn, Ph.D., Chief Executive Officer

SANTA MARTA HOSPITAL (O, 110 beds) 319 North Humphreys Avenue, Los Angeles, CA Zip 90022–1499; tel. 213/266–6500; Harry E. Whitney, Interim President and Chief Executive Officer

GEORGIA: ST. JOSEPH HOSPITAL (O, 143 beds) 2260 Wrightsboro Road, Augusta, GA Zip 30904–4726; tel. 706/481–7000; J. William Paugh, President and Chief Executive Officer

IDAHO: ST. JOSEPH REGIONAL MEDICAL CENTER (O, 156 beds) 415 Sixth Street, Lewiston, ID Zip 83501–0816; tel. 208/743–2511; Howard A. Hayes, President and Chief Executive Officer

MISSOURI: SAINT JOSEPH HEALTH CENTER (O, 257 beds) 1000 Carondelet Drive, Kansas City, MO Zip 64114–4673; tel. 816/942–4400; Richard M. Abell, President and Chief Executive Officer

---

For explanation of codes following names, see page B2.
★ Indicates Type III membership in the American Hospital Association.

Section B

ST. MARY'S HOSPITAL OF BLUE SPRINGS (O, 102 beds) 201 West R. D. Mize Road, Blue Springs, MO Zip 64014; tel. 816/228–5900; N. Gary Wages, President and Chief Executive Officer

NEW YORK: ST. JOSEPH'S HOSPITAL (O, 255 beds) 555 East Market Street, Elmira, NY Zip 14902–1512; tel. 607/733–6541; Sister Marie Castagnaro, President and Chief Executive Officer

ST. MARY'S HOSPITAL (O, 143 beds) 427 Guy Park Avenue, Amsterdam, NY Zip 12010–1095; tel. 518/842–1900; Peter E. Capobianco, President and Chief Executive Officer

WASHINGTON: LOURDES COUNSELING CENTER (O, 32 beds) 1175 Carondelet Drive, Richland, WA Zip 99352–1175; tel. 509/943–9104; Thomas Corley, Chief Executive Officer

LOURDES MEDICAL CENTER (O, 132 beds) 520 North Fourth Avenue, Pasco, WA Zip 99301, Mailing Address: P.O. Box 2568, Zip 99302; tel. 509/547–7704; Thomas Corley, Chief Executive Officer

Owned, leased, sponsored:	14 hospitals	2567 beds
Contract–managed:	0 hospitals	0 beds
Totals:	14 hospitals	2567 beds

0126: CARRAWAY METHODIST HEALTH SYSTEM (NP)

1600 Carraway Boulevard, Birmingham, AL Zip 35234–1990; tel. 205/502–6000; Robert M. Carraway, M.D., Chairman and Chief Executive Officer

ALABAMA: CARRAWAY BURDICK WEST MEDICAL CENTER (O, 36 beds) Highway 195 East, Haleyville, AL Zip 35565–9536, Mailing Address: P.O. Box 780, Zip 35565–0780; tel. 205/486–5213; Ronald L. Sparkman, Administrator

CARRAWAY METHODIST MEDICAL CENTER (O, 383 beds) 1600 Carraway Boulevard, Birmingham, AL Zip 35234–1990; tel. 205/502–6000; Cindy Williams, FACHE, Administrator

CARRAWAY NORTHWEST MEDICAL CENTER (O, 63 beds) Highway 78 West, Winfield, AL Zip 35594, Mailing Address: P.O. Box 130, Zip 35594–0130; tel. 205/487–4234; Robert E. Henger, Administrator

Owned, leased, sponsored:	3 hospitals	482 beds
Contract–managed:	0 hospitals	0 beds
Totals:	3 hospitals	482 beds

6545: CATHEDRAL HEALTHCARE SYSTEM, INC. (CC)

219 Chestnut Street, Newark, NJ Zip 07105–1558; tel. 201/690–3600; Frank L. Fumai, President and Chief Executive Officer

NEW JERSEY: SAINT JAMES HOSPITAL OF NEWARK (O, 189 beds) 155 Jefferson Street, Newark, NJ Zip 07105; tel. 973/589–1300; Ceu Cirne–Neves, Administrator

SAINT MICHAEL'S MEDICAL CENTER (O, 299 beds) 268 Dr. Martin Luther King Jr. Boulevard, Newark, NJ Zip 07102–2094; tel. 973/877–5000; Barbara Loughney, Acting Senior Vice President and Administrator

Owned, leased, sponsored:	2 hospitals	488 beds
Contract–managed:	0 hospitals	0 beds
Totals:	2 hospitals	488 beds

0136: CATHOLIC HEALTH EAST (CC)

3 Radnor Corp Center, Suite 220, Radnor, PA Zip 19087–4592; tel. 610/971–9770; Daniel F. Russell, President and Chief Executive Officer

ALABAMA: MERCY MEDICAL (O, 157 beds) 101 Villa Drive, Daphne, AL Zip 36526–4653, Mailing Address: P.O. Box 1090, Zip 36526–1090; tel. 334/626–2694; Sister Mary Eileen Wilhelm, President and Chief Executive Officer

FLORIDA: GOOD SAMARITAN MEDICAL CENTER (S, 341 beds) Flagler Drive at Palm Beach Lakes Boulevard, West Palm Beach, FL Zip 33401–3499; tel. 561/655–5511; Phillip C. Dutcher, Interim President

HOLY CROSS HOSPITAL (O, 437 beds) 4725 North Federal Highway, Fort Lauderdale, FL Zip 33308–4668, Mailing Address: P.O. Box 23460,

Zip 33307–3460; tel. 954/771–8000; John C. Johnson, Chief Executive Officer

ST. ANTHONY'S HOSPITAL (S, 329 beds) 1200 Seventh Avenue North, Saint Petersburg, FL Zip 33705–1388, Mailing Address: P.O. Box 12588, Zip 33733–2588; tel. 813/825–1100; Sue G. Brody, President and Chief Executive Officer

ST. JOSEPH'S HOSPITAL (S, 883 beds) 3001 West Martin Luther King Boulevard, Tampa, FL Zip 33607–6387, Mailing Address: P.O. Box 4227, Zip 33677–4227; tel. 813/870–4000; Isaac Mallah, President and Chief Executive Officer

ST. MARY'S HOSPITAL (S, 433 beds) 901 45th Street, West Palm Beach, FL Zip 33407–2495, Mailing Address: P.O. Box 24620, Zip 33416–4620; tel. 561/844–6300; Phillip C. Dutcher, President and Chief Executive Officer

GEORGIA: SAINT JOSEPH'S HOSPITAL OF ATLANTA (O, 346 beds) 5665 Peachtree Dunwoody Road N.E., Atlanta, GA Zip 30342–1764; tel. 404/851–7001; Brue Chandler, President and Chief Executive Officer

MAINE: MERCY HOSPITAL PORTLAND (O, 159 beds) 144 State Street, Portland, ME Zip 04101–3795; tel. 207/879–3000; Howard R. Buckley, President

MASSACHUSETTS: MERCY HOSPITAL (O, 228 beds) 271 Carew Street, Springfield, MA Zip 01104–2398, Mailing Address: P.O. Box 9012, Zip 01102–9012; tel. 413/748–9000; Vincent J. McCorkle, President

NEW JERSEY: OUR LADY OF LOURDES MEDICAL CENTER (O, 306 beds) 1600 Haddon Avenue, Camden, NJ Zip 08103–3117; tel. 609/757–3500; Alexander J. Hatala, President and Chief Executive Officer

NEW YORK: MERCY HOSPITAL (S, 290 beds) 565 Abbott Road, Buffalo, NY Zip 14220–2095; tel. 716/826–7000; James W. Connolly, President and Chief Executive Officer

ST. JAMES MERCY HOSPITAL (O, 200 beds) 411 Canisteo Street, Hornell, NY Zip 14843–2197; tel. 607/324–8000; Paul E. Shephard, President and Chief Executive Officer

ST. JOSEPH HOSPITAL (S, 184 beds) 2605 Harlem Road, Cheektowaga, NY Zip 14225–4097; tel. 716/891–2400; Patrick J. Wiles, Chief Executive Officer

ST. PETER'S HOSPITAL (O, 437 beds) 315 South Manning Boulevard, Albany, NY Zip 12208–1789; tel. 518/525–1550; Steven P. Boyle, President and Chief Executive Officer

PENNSYLVANIA: MERCY COMMUNITY HOSPITAL (S, 107 beds) 2000 Old West Chester Pike, Havertown, PA Zip 19083–2712; tel. 610/645–3600; Andrew E. Harris, Chief Executive Officer

MERCY HEALTH SYSTEM OF SOUTHEASTERN PENNSYLVANIA (S, 504 beds) One Bala Plaza, Suite 402, Bala Cynwyd, PA Zip 19004–1401; tel. 610/660–7440; Plato A. Marinakos, President and Chief Executive Officer

MERCY HOSPITAL OF PITTSBURGH (O, 493 beds) 1400 Locust Street, Pittsburgh, PA Zip 15219–5166; tel. 412/232–8111; Thomas J. Mattei, Chief Operating Officer

MERCY PROVIDENCE HOSPITAL (O, 146 beds) 1004 Arch Street, Pittsburgh, PA Zip 15212–5294; tel. 412/323–5600; Thomas J. Mattei, Chief Operating Officer

Owned, leased, sponsored:	18 hospitals	5980 beds
Contract–managed:	0 hospitals	0 beds
Totals:	18 hospitals	5980 beds

★0092: CATHOLIC HEALTH INITIATIVES (CC)

1999 Broadway, Suite 2605, Denver, CO Zip 80202–4004; tel. 303/298–9100; Patricia A. Cahill, President and Chief Executive Officer

ARKANSAS: ST. VINCENT INFIRMARY MEDICAL CENTER (O, 537 beds) Two St. Vincent Circle, Little Rock, AR Zip 72205–5499; tel. 501/660–3000; Diana T. Hueter, President and Chief Executive Officer

COLORADO: MERCY MEDICAL CENTER (O, 83 beds) 375 East Park Avenue, Durango, CO Zip 81301; tel. 970/247–4311; Renato V. Baciarelli, Administrator

PENROSE–ST. FRANCIS HEALTH SERVICES (S, 424 beds) Colorado Springs, CO Donna L. Bertram, R.N., Administrator

For explanation of codes following names, see page B2.
★ Indicates Type III membership in the American Hospital Association.

Section B

ST. ANTHONY CENTRAL HOSPITAL (S, 238 beds) 4231 West 16th Avenue, Denver, CO Zip 80204–4098; tel. 303/629–3511; Michael H. Erne, Senior Vice President and Administrator

ST. ANTHONY NORTH HOSPITAL (S, 110 beds) 2551 West 84th Avenue, Westminster, CO Zip 80030–3887; tel. 303/426–2151; Michael H. Erne, Chief Executive Officer

ST. MARY–CORWIN MEDICAL CENTER (S, 261 beds) 1008 Minnequa Avenue, Pueblo, CO Zip 81004–3798; tel. 719/560–4000; Walter Sackett, Senior Vice President and Administrator

ST. THOMAS MORE HOSPITAL AND PROGRESSIVE CARE CENTER (S, 218 beds) 1338 Phay Avenue, Canon City, CO Zip 81212–2221; tel. 719/269–2000; C. Ray Honaker, Administrator

DELAWARE: ST. FRANCIS HOSPITAL (S, 283 beds) Seventh and Clayton Streets, Wilmington, DE Zip 19805–0500, Mailing Address: P.O. Box 2500, Zip 19805–0500; tel. 302/421–4100; Daniel J. Sinnott, President and Chief Executive Officer

IDAHO: MERCY MEDICAL CENTER (S, 149 beds) 1512 12th Avenue Road, Nampa, ID Zip 83686–6008; tel. 208/467–1171; Joseph Messmer, President and Chief Executive Officer

IOWA: ALEGENT HEALTH MERCY HOSPITAL (S, 24 beds) Rosary Drive, Corning, IA Zip 50841, Mailing Address: P.O. Box 368, Zip 50841–0368; tel. 515/322–3121; James C. Ruppert, Regional Administrator

ALEGENT HEALTH MERCY HOSPITAL (S, 194 beds) 800 Mercy Drive, Council Bluffs, IA Zip 51503–3128, Mailing Address: P.O. Box 1C, Zip 51502–3001; tel. 712/328–5000; Richard A. Hachten II, Chief Executive Officer

MERCY HOSPITAL MEDICAL CENTER (S, 555 beds) 400 University Avenue, Des Moines, IA Zip 50314–3190; tel. 515/247–4278; Thomas A. Reitinger, President and Chief Executive Officer

ST. JOSEPH'S MERCY HOSPITAL (S, 58 beds) 1 St. Joseph's Drive, Centerville, IA Zip 52544; tel. 515/437–3411; William C. Assell, President and Chief Executive Officer

KANSAS: CENTRAL KANSAS MEDICAL CENTER (S, 175 beds) 3515 Broadway Street, Great Bend, KS Zip 67530–3691; tel. 316/792–2511; Gary L. Barnett, President and Chief Executive Officer

ST. CATHERINE HOSPITAL (S, 100 beds) 410 East Walnut, Garden City, KS Zip 67846–5672; tel. 316/272–2222; Gary L. Rowe, President and Chief Executive Officer

KENTUCKY: CARITAS MEDICAL CENTER (O, 213 beds) 1850 Bluegrass Avenue, Louisville, KY Zip 40215–1199; tel. 502/361–6000; Peter J. Bernard, President and Chief Executive Officer

CARITAS PEACE CENTER (O, 208 beds) 2020 Newburg Road, Louisville, KY Zip 40205–1879; tel. 502/451–3330; Peter J. Bernard, President and Chief Executive Officer

FLAGET MEMORIAL HOSPITAL (O, 36 beds) 201 Cathedral Manor, Bardstown, KY Zip 40004–1299; tel. 502/348–3923; Suzanne Reasbeck, President and Chief Executive Officer

MARYMOUNT MEDICAL CENTER (O, 70 beds) 310 East Ninth Street, London, KY Zip 40741–1299; tel. 606/878–6520; Lowell Jones, President

OUR LADY OF THE WAY HOSPITAL (S, 39 beds) 11022 Main Street, Martin, KY Zip 41649–0910; tel. 606/285–5181; Lowell Jones, Chief Executive Officer

ST. JOSEPH HOSPITAL (O, 468 beds) One St. Joseph Drive, Lexington, KY Zip 40504–3754; tel. 606/278–3436; Thomas J. Murray, President

MARYLAND: ST. JOSEPH MEDICAL CENTER (S, 460 beds) 7620 York Road, Towson, MD Zip 21204–7582; tel. 410/337–1000; Renee Kessler, Executive Vice President and Chief Operating Officer

MINNESOTA: ALBANY AREA HOSPITAL AND MEDICAL CENTER (S, 16 beds) 300 Third Avenue, Albany, MN Zip 56307–9363; tel. 320/845–2121; Ben Koppelman, Administrator

LAKEWOOD HEALTH CENTER (S, 64 beds) 600 South Main Avenue, Baudette, MN Zip 56623, Mailing Address: Route 1, Box 2120, Zip 56623–2120; tel. 218/634–2120; SharRay Palm, President and Chief Executive Officer

ST. FRANCIS MEDICAL CENTER (S, 171 beds) 415 Oak Street, Breckenridge, MN Zip 56520–1298; tel. 218/643–3000; David A. Nelson, President and Chief Executive Officer

ST. GABRIEL'S HOSPITAL (S, 205 beds) 815 Second Street S.E., Little Falls, MN Zip 56345–3596; tel. 320/632–5441; Larry A. Schulz, President and Chief Executive Officer

ST. JOSEPH'S AREA HEALTH SERVICES (S, 40 beds) 600 Pleasant Avenue, Park Rapids, MN Zip 56470–1432; tel. 218/732–3311; David R. Hove, President and Chief Executive Officer

MISSOURI: ST. JOHN'S REGIONAL MEDICAL CENTER (S, 367 beds) 2727 McClelland Boulevard, Joplin, MO Zip 64804–1694; tel. 417/781–2727; Robert G. Brueckner, President and Chief Executive Officer

NEBRASKA: ALEGENT HEALTH BERGAN MERCY MEDICAL CENTER (S, 646 beds) 7500 Mercy Road, Omaha, NE Zip 68124; tel. 402/398–6060; Charles J. Marr, Chief Executive Officer

GOOD SAMARITAN HEALTH SYSTEMS (S, 267 beds) 10 East 31st Street, Kearney, NE Zip 68847–2926, Mailing Address: P.O. Box 1990, Zip 68848–1990; tel. 308/865–7100; William Wilson Hendrickson, President and Chief Executive Officer

SAINT FRANCIS MEDICAL CENTER (S, 198 beds) 2620 West Faidley Avenue, Grand Island, NE Zip 68803–4297, Mailing Address: P.O. Box 9804, Zip 68802–9804; tel. 308/384–4600; Michael R. Gloor, FACHE, President and Chief Executive Officer

ST. ELIZABETH COMMUNITY HEALTH CENTER (S, 136 beds) 555 South 70th Street, Lincoln, NE Zip 68510–2494; tel. 402/489–7181; Robert J. Lanik, President

ST. MARY'S HOSPITAL (S, 28 beds) 1314 Third Avenue, Nebraska City, NE Zip 68410–1999; tel. 402/873–3321; Daniel J. Kelly, President and Chief Executive Officer

NEW JERSEY: ST. FRANCIS MEDICAL CENTER (S, 216 beds) 601 Hamilton Avenue, Trenton, NJ Zip 08629–1986; tel. 609/599–5000; Judith M. Persichilli, President and Chief Executive Officer

NEW MEXICO: ST. JOSEPH MEDICAL CENTER (S, 228 beds) 601 Martin Luther King Drive N.E., Albuquerque, NM Zip 87102, Mailing Address: P.O. Box 25555, Zip 87125–0555; tel. 505/727–8000; C. Vincent Townsend Jr., Senior Vice President Hospital Group

ST. JOSEPH NORTHEAST HEIGHTS HOSPITAL (S, 71 beds) 4701 Montgomery Boulevard N.E., Albuquerque, NM Zip 87109–1251, Mailing Address: P.O. Box 25555, Zip 87125–0555; tel. 505/727–7800; Tony Struthers, Administrator

ST. JOSEPH REHABILITATION HOSPITAL AND OUTPATIENT CENTER (S, 63 beds) 505 Elm Street N.E., Albuquerque, NM Zip 87102–2500, Mailing Address: P.O. Box 25555, Zip 87125–5555; tel. 505/727–4700; Mary Lou Coors, Administrator

ST. JOSEPH WEST MESA HOSPITAL (S, 92 beds) 10501 Golf Course Road N.W., Albuquerque, NM Zip 87114–5000, Mailing Address: P.O. Box 25555, Zip 87125–0555; tel. 505/727–2000; Mary Lou Coors, Administrator

NORTH DAKOTA: CARRINGTON HEALTH CENTER (S, 70 beds) 800 North Fourth Street, Carrington, ND Zip 58421–1217; tel. 701/652–3141; Brian J. McDermott, Administrator

MERCY HOSPITAL (S, 35 beds) 1031 Seventh Street, Devils Lake, ND Zip 58301–2798; tel. 701/662–2131; Marlene Krein, President and Chief Executive Officer

MERCY HOSPITAL (S, 50 beds) 570 Chautauqua Boulevard, Valley City, ND Zip 58072–3199; tel. 701/845–6400; Jane Bissel, President and Chief Executive Officer

MERCY MEDICAL CENTER (S, 105 beds) 1301 15th Avenue West, Williston, ND Zip 58801–3896; tel. 701/774–7400; Duane D. Jerde, President and Chief Executive Officer

ST. ANSGAR'S HEALTH CENTER (S, 20 beds) 115 Vivian Street, Park River, ND Zip 58270–0708; tel. 701/284–7500; Michael D. Mahrer, President

ST. JOSEPH'S HOSPITAL AND HEALTH CENTER (S, 90 beds) 30 Seventh Street West, Dickinson, ND Zip 58601–4399; tel. 701/225–7200; Greg Hanson, President and Chief Executive Officer

OHIO: GOOD SAMARITAN HOSPITAL (S, 401 beds) 375 Dixmyth Avenue, Cincinnati, OH Zip 45220–2489; tel. 513/872–1400; Sister Myra James Bradley, Chief Executive Officer

GOOD SAMARITAN HOSPITAL AND HEALTH CENTER (S, 428 beds) 2222 Philadelphia Drive, Dayton, OH Zip 45406–1813; tel. 937/278–2612; K. Douglas Deck, President and Chief Executive Officer

For explanation of codes following names, see page B2.
★ Indicates Type III membership in the American Hospital Association.

OREGON: HOLY ROSARY MEDICAL CENTER (S, 74 beds) 351 S.W. Ninth Street, Ontario, OR Zip 97914–2693; tel. 541/881–7000; Bruce Jensen, Chief Executive Officer and Team Leader

MERCY MEDICAL CENTER (S, 95 beds) 2700 Stewart Parkway, Roseburg, OR Zip 97470–1297; tel. 541/673–0611; Victor J. Fresolone, FACHE, President and Chief Executive Officer

ST. ANTHONY HOSPITAL (S, 49 beds) 1601 S.E. Court Avenue, Pendleton, OR Zip 97801–3297; tel. 541/276–5121; Jeffrey S. Drop, President and Chief Executive Officer

ST. ELIZABETH HEALTH SERVICES (S, 134 beds) 3325 Pocahontas Road, Baker City, OR Zip 97814; tel. 541/523–6461; Robert T. Mannix Jr., President and Chief Operations Officer

PENNSYLVANIA: NAZARETH HOSPITAL (S, 259 beds) 2601 Holme Avenue, Philadelphia, PA Zip 19152–2096; tel. 215/335–6000; Daniel J. Sinnott, President and Chief Executive Officer

ST. AGNES MEDICAL CENTER (S, 172 beds) 1900 South Broad Street, Philadelphia, PA Zip 19145–2304; tel. 215/339–4100; Daniel J. Sinnott, President and Chief Executive Officer

ST. JOSEPH HOSPITAL (S, 256 beds) 250 College Avenue, Lancaster, PA Zip 17604; tel. 717/291–8211; John Kerr Tolmie, President and Chief Executive Officer

ST. JOSEPH MEDICAL CENTER (O, 243 beds) Twelth and Walnut Streets, Reading, PA Zip 19603–0316, Mailing Address: P.O. Box 316, Zip 19603–0316; tel. 610/378–2000; Philip G. Dionne, President and Chief Executive Officer

ST. MARY MEDICAL CENTER (S, 270 beds) Langhorne–Newtown Road, Langhorne, PA Zip 19047–1295; tel. 215/750–2000; Sister Clare Carty, President and Chief Executive Officer

SOUTH DAKOTA: GETTYSBURG MEDICAL CENTER (S, 61 beds) 606 East Garfield, Gettysburg, SD Zip 57442–1398; tel. 605/765–2488; Mark Schmidt, Administrator

ST. MARY'S HOSPITAL (S, 191 beds) 800 East Dakota Avenue, Pierre, SD Zip 57501–3313; tel. 605/224–3100; James D. M. Russell, Chief Executive Officer

TENNESSEE: MEMORIAL HEALTH CARE SYSTEM (O, 299 beds) 2525 De Sales Avenue, Chattanooga, TN Zip 37404–3322; tel. 423/495–2525; L. Clark Taylor Jr., President and Chief Executive Officer

WASHINGTON: ST. CLARE HOSPITAL (S, 60 beds) 11315 Bridgeport Way S.W., Lakewood, WA Zip 98499–0998, Mailing Address: P.O. Box 99998, Zip 98499–0998; tel. 253/588–1711; Mike Fitzgerald, Chief Financial Officer

ST. FRANCIS HOSPITAL (S, 77 beds) 34515 Ninth Avenue South, Federal Way, WA Zip 98003–9710; tel. 253/927–9700; Mike Fitzgerald, Chief Financial Officer

ST. JOSEPH MEDICAL CENTER (S, 271 beds) 1717 South J. Street, Tacoma, WA Zip 98405, Mailing Address: P.O. Box 2197, Zip 98401–2197; tel. 253/627–4101; Joseph W. Wilczek, President and Chief Executive Officer

WISCONSIN: GOOD SAMARITAN HEALTH CENTER OF MERRILL (S, 63 beds) 601 Center Avenue South, Merrill, WI Zip 54452–3404; tel. 715/536–5511; Michael Hammer, President and Chief Executive Officer

Owned, leased, sponsored:	62 hospitals	11484 beds
Contract–managed:	0 hospitals	0 beds
Totals:	62 hospitals	11484 beds

★0079: CATHOLIC HEALTH PARTNERS (CC)
2913 North Commonwealth, Chicago, IL Zip 60657–6296; tel. 773/665–3170; Sister Theresa Peck, President and Chief Executive Officer

ILLINOIS: COLUMBUS HOSPITAL (O, 239 beds) 2520 North Lakeview Avenue, Chicago, IL Zip 60614–1895; tel. 773/388–7300; Sister Theresa Peck, President and Chief Executive Officer

SAINT ANTHONY HOSPITAL (O, 165 beds) 2875 West 19th Street, Chicago, IL Zip 60623–3596; tel. 773/521–1710; Sister Theresa Peck, President and Chief Executive Officer

ST. JOSEPH HOSPITAL (O, 335 beds) 2900 North Lake Shore Drive, Chicago, IL Zip 60657–6274; tel. 773/665–3000; Sister Theresa Peck, President and Chief Executive Officer

Owned, leased, sponsored:	3 hospitals	739 beds
Contract–managed:	0 hospitals	0 beds
Totals:	3 hospitals	739 beds

5155: CATHOLIC HEALTHCARE PARTNERS (CC)
2335 Grandview Avenue, 4th Floor, Cincinnati, OH Zip 45206–2280; tel. 513/221–2736; Michael D. Connelly, President and Chief Executive Officer

KENTUCKY: LOURDES HOSPITAL (S, 290 beds) 1530 Lone Oak Road, Paducah, KY Zip 42003, Mailing Address: P.O. Box 7100, Zip 42002–7100; tel. 502/444–2444; Robert P. Goodwin, President and Chief Executive Officer

MARCUM AND WALLACE MEMORIAL HOSPITAL (S, 16 beds) 60 Mercy Court, Irvine, KY Zip 40336–1331, Mailing Address: P.O. Box 928, Zip 40336–0928; tel. 606/723–2115; Christopher M. Goddard, Administrator

ST. ELIZABETH MEDICAL CENTER–GRANT COUNTY (O, 20 beds) 238 Barnes Road, Williamstown, KY Zip 41097–9460; tel. 606/824–2400; Chris Carle, Administrator

ST. ELIZABETH MEDICAL CENTER–NORTH (O, 466 beds) 401 East 20th Street, Covington, KY Zip 41014–1585; tel. 606/292–4000; Joseph W. Gross, President and Chief Executive Officer

OHIO: CLERMONT MERCY HOSPITAL (S, 133 beds) 3000 Hospital Drive, Batavia, OH Zip 45103–1998; tel. 513/732–8200; Karen S. Ehrat, Ph.D., President

LORAIN COMMUNITY/ST. JOSEPH REGIONAL HEALTH CENTER (S, 303 beds) 3700 Kolbe Road, Lorain, OH Zip 44053–1697; tel. 216/960–3000; Brian C. Lockwood, President and Chief Executive Officer

MERCY HOSPITAL (S, 248 beds) 100 River Front Plaza, Hamilton, OH Zip 45011–2780, Mailing Address: P.O. Box 418, Zip 45012–0418; tel. 513/870–7080; David A. Ferrell, President

MERCY HOSPITAL (S, 60 beds) 485 West Market Street, Tiffin, OH Zip 44883–0727, Mailing Address: P.O. Box 727, Zip 44883–0727; tel. 419/447–3130; Mark Shugarman, President

MERCY HOSPITAL ANDERSON (S, 156 beds) 7500 State Road, Cincinnati, OH Zip 45255–2492; tel. 513/624–4500; Karen S. Ehrat, Ph.D., President

MERCY HOSPITAL–WILLARD (S, 30 beds) 110 East Howard Street, Willard, OH Zip 44890–1611; tel. 419/933–2931; James O. Detwiler, President

MERCY MEDICAL CENTER (S, 218 beds) 1343 North Fountain Boulevard, Springfield, OH Zip 45501–1380; tel. 937/390–5000; Teresa Richle, Interim Senior Vice President Acute Care Operations

MERCY MEMORIAL HOSPITAL (S, 20 beds) 904 Scioto Street, Urbana, OH Zip 43078–2200; tel. 937/653–5231; Richard Rogers, Senior Vice President

RIVERSIDE MERCY HOSPITAL (S, 162 beds) 1600 North Superior Street, Toledo, OH Zip 43604–2199; tel. 419/729–6000; Scott E. Shook, President

ST. CHARLES MERCY HOSPITAL (S, 306 beds) 2600 Navarre Avenue, Oregon, OH Zip 43616–3297; tel. 419/698–7479; Cathleen K. Nelson, President and Chief Executive Officer

ST. ELIZABETH HEALTH CENTER (S, 318 beds) 1044 Belmont Avenue, Youngstown, OH Zip 44501, Mailing Address: P.O. Box 1790, Zip 44501–1790; tel. 330/746–7211; Norman F. Gruber, Chief Operating Officer

ST. JOSEPH HEALTH CENTER (S, 127 beds) 667 Eastland Avenue S.E., Warren, OH Zip 44484–4531; tel. 330/841–4000; Robert W. Shroder, Chief Operating Officer

ST. RITA'S MEDICAL CENTER (S, 312 beds) 730 West Market Street, Lima, OH Zip 45801–4670; tel. 419/227–3361; James P. Reber, President

ST. VINCENT MERCY MEDICAL CENTER (S, 457 beds) 2213 Cherry Street, Toledo, OH Zip 43608–2691; tel. 419/251–3232; Steven L. Mickus, President and Chief Executive Officer

PENNSYLVANIA: MERCY HOSPITAL OF SCRANTON (S, 285 beds) 746 Jefferson Avenue, Scranton, PA Zip 18501–1624; tel. 717/348–7100; John L. Nespoli, President and Chief Executive Officer

For explanation of codes following names, see page B2.
★ Indicates Type III membership in the American Hospital Association.

MERCY HOSPITAL OF WILKES–BARRE (S, 173 beds) 25 Church Street, Wilkes–Barre, PA Zip 18765–0999, Mailing Address: P.O. Box 658, Zip 18765–0658; tel. 717/826–3100; John L. Nespoli, President and Chief Executive Officer

MERCY SPECIAL CARE HOSPITAL (S, 38 beds) 128 West Washington Street, Nanticoke, PA Zip 18634–3198; tel. 717/735–5000; Robert D. Williams, Administrator

TENNESSEE: JEFFERSON MEMORIAL HOSPITAL (L, 51 beds) 1800 Bishop Avenue, Jefferson City, TN Zip 37760–1992, Mailing Address: P.O. Box 560, Zip 37760–0560; tel. 423/475–2091; Michael C. Hicks, President and Chief Executive Officer

ST. MARY'S HEALTH SYSTEM (S, 300 beds) 900 East Oak Hill Avenue, Knoxville, TN Zip 37917–4556; tel. 423/545–8000; Richard C. Williams, President and Chief Executive Officer

Owned, leased, sponsored:	23 hospitals	4489 beds
Contract–managed:	0 hospitals	0 beds
Totals:	23 hospitals	4489 beds

★5205: CATHOLIC HEALTHCARE WEST (CC)
1700 Montgomery Street, Suite 300, San Francisco, CA Zip 94111–9603; tel. 415/438–5500; Richard J. Kramer, President and Chief Executive Officer

ARIZONA: ST. JOSEPH'S HOSPITAL AND MEDICAL CENTER (S, 426 beds) 350 West Thomas Road, Phoenix, AZ Zip 85013–4496, Mailing Address: P.O. Box 2071, Zip 85001–2071; tel. 602/406–3100; Mary G. Yarbrough, President and Chief Executive Officer

CALIFORNIA: BAKERSFIELD MEMORIAL HOSPITAL (S, 293 beds) 420 34th Street, Bakersfield, CA Zip 93301, Mailing Address: P.O. Box 1888, Zip 93303–1888; tel. 805/327–1792; C. Larry Carr, President

DOMINICAN SANTA CRUZ HOSPITAL (S, 270 beds) 1555 Soquel Drive, Santa Cruz, CA Zip 95065–1794; tel. 408/462–7700; Sister Julie Hyer, President and Chief Executive Officer

MARIAN MEDICAL CENTER (O, 225 beds) 1400 East Church Street, Santa Maria, CA Zip 93454, Mailing Address: Box 1238, Zip 93456; tel. 805/739–3000; Charles J. Cova, Executive Vice President

MARK TWAIN ST. JOSEPH'S HOSPITAL (S, 33 beds) 768 Mountain Ranch Road, San Andreas, CA Zip 95249–9710; tel. 209/754–2515; Michael P. Lawson, Administrator

MERCY AMERICAN RIVER/MERCY SAN JUAN HOSPITAL (S, 352 beds) 6501 Coyle Avenue, Carmichael, CA Zip 95608, Mailing Address: P.O. Box 479, Zip 95608; tel. 916/537–5000; Sister Bridget McCarthy, President

MERCY GENERAL HOSPITAL (S, 405 beds) 4001 J. Street, Sacramento, CA Zip 95819; tel. 916/453–4950; Thomas A. Petersen, Vice President and Chief Operating Officer

MERCY HEALTHCARE–BAKERSFIELD (S, 261 beds) 2215 Truxtun Avenue, Bakersfield, CA Zip 93301, Mailing Address: Box 119, Zip 93302; tel. 805/632–5000; Bernard J. Herman, President and Chief Executive Officer

MERCY HOSPITAL AND HEALTH SERVICES (S, 101 beds) 2740 M. Street, Merced, CA Zip 95340–2880; tel. 209/384–6444; John Headding, Chief Administrative Officer

MERCY HOSPITAL OF FOLSOM (S, 66 beds) 1650 Creekside Drive, Folsom, CA Zip 95630–3405; tel. 916/983–7400; Donald C. Hudson, Vice President and Chief Operating Officer

MERCY MEDICAL CENTER (S, 220 beds) 2175 Rosaline Avenue, Redding, CA Zip 96001, Mailing Address: Box 496009, Zip 96049–6009; tel. 916/225–6000; George A. Govier, President and Chief Executive Officer

MERCY MEDICAL CENTER MOUNT SHASTA (S, 80 beds) 914 Pine Street, Mount Shasta, CA Zip 96067, Mailing Address: P.O. Box 239, Zip 96067–0239; tel. 530/926–6111; Rick J. Barnett, Executive Vice President and Chief Operating Officer

METHODIST HOSPITAL (S, 303 beds) 7500 Hospital Drive, Sacramento, CA Zip 95823–5477; tel. 916/423–3000; Stanley C. Oppegard, Vice President and Chief Operating Officer

O'CONNOR HOSPITAL (S, 257 beds) 2105 Forest Avenue, San Jose, CA Zip 95128–1471; tel. 408/947–2500; John G. Williams, President and Chief Executive Officer

ROBERT F. KENNEDY MEDICAL CENTER (S, 195 beds) 4500 West 116th Street, Hawthorne, CA Zip 90250; tel. 310/973–1711; Peter P. Aprato, Administrator and Chief Operating Officer

SAINT FRANCIS MEMORIAL HOSPITAL (S, 190 beds) 900 Hyde Street, San Francisco, CA Zip 94109, Mailing Address: Box 7726, Zip 94120–7726; tel. 415/353–6000; Cheryl A. Fama, Administrator, Vice President and Chief Operating Officer

SAINT LOUISE HOSPITAL (S, 55 beds) 18500 Saint Louise Drive, Morgan Hill, CA Zip 95037; tel. 408/779–1500; Joan A. Bero, Regional Vice President and Chief Operating Officer

SAINT MARY MEDICAL CENTER (S, 479 beds) 1050 Linden Avenue, Long Beach, CA Zip 90801, Mailing Address: P.O. Box 887, Zip 90801; tel. 562/491–9000; Tammie McMann Brailsford, Administrator

SEQUOIA HOSPITAL (S, 228 beds) 170 Alameda De Las Pulgas, Redwood City, CA Zip 94062–2799; tel. 650/369–5811; Glenna L. Vaskelis, Administrator

SETON MEDICAL CENTER (S, 273 beds) 1900 Sullivan Avenue, Daly City, CA Zip 94015; tel. 650/992–4000; Bernadette Smith, Chief Operating Officer

SETON MEDICAL CENTER COASTSIDE (S, 121 beds) 600 Marine Boulevard, Moss Beach, CA Zip 94038; tel. 650/728–5521; Bernadette Smith, Chief Operating Officer

SIERRA NEVADA MEMORIAL HOSPITAL (S, 111 beds) 155 Glasson Way, Grass Valley, CA Zip 95945–5792, Mailing Address: P.O. Box 1029, Zip 95945–5792; tel. 530/274–6000; C. Thomas Collier, President and Chief Executive Officer

ST. BERNARDINE MEDICAL CENTER (S, 323 beds) 2101 North Waterman Avenue, San Bernardino, CA Zip 92404; tel. 909/883–8711; Margo Walter, Administrator and Chief Operating Officer

ST. DOMINIC'S HOSPITAL (S, 63 beds) 1777 West Yosemite Avenue, Manteca, CA Zip 95337; tel. 209/825–3500; Richard Aldred, Chief Administrative Officer

ST. ELIZABETH COMMUNITY HOSPITAL (S, 53 beds) 2550 Sister Mary Columba Drive, Red Bluff, CA Zip 96080–4397; tel. 530/529–8005; Thomas Γ. Grimes III, Executive Vice President and Chief Operating Officer

ST. FRANCIS MEDICAL CENTER (S, 414 beds) 3630 East Imperial Highway, Lynwood, CA Zip 90262; tel. 310/603–6000; Gerald T. Kozai, Administrator and Chief Operating Officer

ST. FRANCIS MEDICAL CENTER OF SANTA BARBARA (O, 96 beds) 601 East Micheltorena Street, Santa Barbara, CA Zip 93103; tel. 805/568–5705; Ron Biscaro, Administrator

ST. JOHN'S PLEASANT VALLEY HOSPITAL (S, 110 beds) 2309 Antonio Avenue, Camarillo, CA Zip 93010–1459; tel. 805/389–5800; William J. Clearwater, Vice President and Administrator

ST. JOHN'S REGIONAL MEDICAL CENTER (S, 236 beds) 1600 North Rose Avenue, Oxnard, CA Zip 93030; tel. 805/988–2500; James R. Hoss, President and Chief Operating Officer

ST. JOSEPH'S BEHAVIORAL HEALTH CENTER (S, 35 beds) 2510 North California Street, Stockton, CA Zip 95204–5568; tel. 209/948–2100; James Sondecker, Administrator

ST. JOSEPH'S MEDICAL CENTER (S, 294 beds) 1800 North California Street, Stockton, CA Zip 95204–6088, Mailing Address: P.O. Box 213008, Zip 95213–9008; tel. 209/943–2000; Edward G. Schroeder, President and Chief Executive Officer

ST. MARY'S MEDICAL CENTER (S, 256 beds) 450 Stanyan Street, San Francisco, CA Zip 94117–1079; tel. 415/668–1000; John G. Williams, President

ST. VINCENT MEDICAL CENTER (S, 350 beds) 2131 West Third Street, Los Angeles, CA Zip 90057–0992, Mailing Address: P.O. Box 57992, Zip 90057; tel. 213/484–7111; Myda Magarian–Morse, Administrator and Chief Operating Officer

WOODLAND MEMORIAL HOSPITAL (S, 103 beds) 1325 Cottonwood Street, Woodland, CA Zip 95695–5199; tel. 916/662–3961; William Hunt, Chief Operating Officer

NEVADA: ST. ROSE DOMINICAN HOSPITAL (S, 135 beds) 102 Lake Mead Drive, Henderson, NV Zip 89015–5524; tel. 702/564–2622; Rod A. Davis, President and Chief Executive Officer

For explanation of codes following names, see page B2.
★ Indicates Type III membership in the American Hospital Association.

Section B

Owned, leased, sponsored:	35 hospitals	7412 beds
Contract–managed:	0 hospitals	0 beds
Totals:	35 hospitals	7412 beds

★2265: CENTRA HEALTH, INC. (NP)

1920 Atherholt Road, Lynchburg, VA Zip 24501–1104;
tel. 804/947–4700; George W. Dawson, President

VIRGINIA: LYNCHBURG GENERAL HOSPITAL (O, 350 beds) 1901 Tate
Springs Road, Lynchburg, VA Zip 24501–1167; tel. 804/947–3000; L.
Darrell Powers, Senior Vice President

VIRGINIA BAPTIST HOSPITAL (O, 326 beds) 3300 Rivermont Avenue,
Lynchburg, VA Zip 24503–9989; tel. 804/947–4000; Thomas C. Jividen,
Senior Vice President

Owned, leased, sponsored:	2 hospitals	676 beds
Contract–managed:	0 hospitals	0 beds
Totals:	2 hospitals	676 beds

0665: CENTURY HEALTHCARE CORPORATION (IO)

5555 East 71st Street, Suite 9220, Tulsa, OK Zip 74136–6540;
tel. 918/491–0780; Jerry D. Dillon, President and Chief Executive
Officer

ARIZONA: WESTBRIDGE TREATMENT CENTER (O, 78 beds) 1830 East
Roosevelt Street, Phoenix, AZ Zip 85006–3641; tel. 602/254–0884; Mike
Perry, Chief Executive Officer

OKLAHOMA: HIGH POINTE (O, 68 beds) 6501 N.E. 50th Street, Oklahoma
City, OK Zip 73141–9613; tel. 405/424–3383; Charlene Arnett, Chief
Executive Officer

Owned, leased, sponsored:	2 hospitals	146 beds
Contract–managed:	0 hospitals	0 beds
Totals:	2 hospitals	146 beds

0102: CGF HEALTH SYSTEM (NP)

300 Pearl Street, Suite 200, Buffalo, NY Zip 14202;
tel. 716/859–2732; John E. Friedlander, President and Chief
Executive Officer

NEW YORK: BUFFALO GENERAL HOSPITAL (O, 965 beds) 100 High Street,
Buffalo, NY Zip 14203–1154; tel. 716/845–5600; Carrie B. Frank,
President and Chief Executive Officer

CHILDREN'S HOSPITAL (O, 313 beds) 219 Bryant Street, Buffalo, NY
Zip 14222–2099; tel. 716/878–7000; Karen Blount, Vice President and Chief
Operating Officer

DE GRAFF MEMORIAL HOSPITAL (O, 210 beds) 445 Tremont Street, North
Tonawanda, NY Zip 14120–0750, Mailing Address: P.O. Box 0750,
Zip 14120–0750; tel. 716/694–4500; Marcia B. Gutfeld, Vice President and
Chief Operating Officer

MILLARD FILLMORE HEALTH SYSTEM (O, 588 beds) 3 Gates Circle, Buffalo,
NY Zip 14209–9986; tel. 716/887–4600; Carol M. Cassell, Executive Vice
President and Chief Operating Officer

Owned, leased, sponsored:	4 hospitals	2076 beds
Contract–managed:	0 hospitals	0 beds
Totals:	4 hospitals	2076 beds

0114: CHILDREN'S COMPREHENSIVE SERVICES, INC. (IO)

3401 West End Avenue, Suite 500, Nashville, TN Zip 37203–0376;
tel. 615/383–0376; H. Neil Campbell, Chief Executive Officer

ARKANSAS: RIVENDELL BEHAVIORAL HEALTH SERVICES (O, 77 beds) 100
Rivendell Drive, Benton, AR Zip 72015–9100; tel. 501/316–1255; Mark
E. Schneider, Chief Executive Officer

MICHIGAN: RIVENDELL OF MICHIGAN (O, 63 beds) 101 West Townsend
Road, Saint Johns, MI Zip 48879–9200; tel. 517/224–1177; Michael
Talmo, Chief Executive Officer

TEXAS: GULF PINES BEHAVIORAL HEALTH SERVICES (O, 140 beds) 205
Hollow Tree Lane, Houston, TX Zip 77090–2801; tel. 713/537–0700;
Lawrence Story, Chief Executive Officer and Administrator

RED RIVER HOSPITAL (O, 50 beds) 1505 Eighth Street, Wichita Falls, TX
Zip 76301–3106; tel. 940/322–3171; Ricky Powell, Chief Executive Officer

UTAH: COPPER HILLS YOUTH CENTER (O, 80 beds) 5899 West Rivendell
Drive, West Jordan, UT Zip 84088–5700, Mailing Address: P.O. Box 459,
Zip 84084–0459; tel. 801/561–3377; Sandy Podley, Chief Executive
Officer

Owned, leased, sponsored:	5 hospitals	410 beds
Contract–managed:	0 hospitals	0 beds
Totals:	5 hospitals	410 beds

★0131: CHRISTIANA CARE CORPORATION (NP)

501 West 14th Street, Wilmington, DE Zip 19899, Mailing Address:
P.O. Box 1668, Zip 19899; tel. 302/428–2570; Charles M. Smith,
M.D., President and Chief Executive Officer

DELAWARE: CHRISTIANA HOSPITAL (O, 737 beds) 4755 Ogletown–Stanton
Road, Newark, DE Zip 19718; tel. 302/733–1000; Charles M. Smith,
M.D., President and Chief Executive Officer

WILMINGTON HOSPITAL (O, 291 beds) 501 West 14th Street, Wilmington, DE
Zip 19801, Mailing Address: Box 1668, Zip 19899; tel. 302/428–2570;
Charles M. Smith, M.D., President and Chief Executive Officer

Owned, leased, sponsored:	2 hospitals	1028 beds
Contract–managed:	0 hospitals	0 beds
Totals:	2 hospitals	1028 beds

0101: CITRUS VALLEY HEALTH PARTNERS (NP)

210 West San Bernardino Road, Covina, CA Zip 91723;
tel. 626/938–7577; Peter E. Makowski, President and Chief
Executive Officer

CALIFORNIA: CITRUS VALLEY MEDICAL CENTER INTER–COMMUNITY
CAMPUS (O, 508 beds) 210 West San Bernardino Road, Covina, CA
Zip 91723–1901; tel. 626/331–7331; Warren J. Kirk, Administrator

CITRUS VALLEY MEDICAL CENTER–QUEEN OF THE VALLEY CAMPUS (O, 263
beds) 1115 South Sunset Avenue, West Covina, CA Zip 91790, Mailing
Address: Box 1980, Zip 91793; tel. 818/962–4011; Warren J. Kirk,
Administrator and Chief Operating Officer

FOOTHILL PRESBYTERIAN HOSPITAL–MORRIS L. JOHNSTON MEMORIAL (O,
106 beds) 250 South Grand Avenue, Glendora, CA Zip 91741;
tel. 626/963–8411; Bryan R. Rogers, President and Chief Executive Officer

Owned, leased, sponsored:	3 hospitals	877 beds
Contract–managed:	0 hospitals	0 beds
Totals:	3 hospitals	877 beds

0076: COLLEGE HEALTH ENTERPRISES (IO)

17100 Pioneer Boulevard, Suite 300, Cerritos, CA Zip 90701–2709;
tel. 562/467–5500; Elliot A. Sainer, President and Chief Executive
Officer

COLLEGE HOSPITAL (O, 125 beds) 10802 College Place, Cerritos, CA
Zip 90703–1579; tel. 562/924–9581; Stephen Witt, Chief Executive Officer

COLLEGE HOSPITAL COSTA MESA (O, 122 beds) 301 Victoria Street, Costa
Mesa, CA Zip 92627; tel. 714/642–2607; Susan Burden, Acting Chief
Executive Officer

Owned, leased, sponsored:	2 hospitals	247 beds
Contract–managed:	0 hospitals	0 beds
Totals:	2 hospitals	247 beds

★0048: COLUMBIA/HCA HEALTHCARE CORPORATION (IO)

One Park Plaza, Nashville, TN Zip 37203–1548; tel. 615/344–2003;
Jack O. Bovender Jr., President and Chief Operating Officer

For explanation of codes following names, see page B2.
★ Indicates Type III membership in the American Hospital Association.

Section B

ALABAMA: COLUMBIA ANDALUSIA HOSPITAL (O, 87 beds) 849 South Three Notch Street, Andalusia, AL Zip 36420–5325, Mailing Address: P.O. Box 760, Zip 36420–0760; tel. 334/222–8466; James L. Sample, Chief Executive Officer

COLUMBIA EAST MONTGOMERY MEDICAL CENTER (O, 150 beds) 400 Taylor Road, Montgomery, AL Zip 36117–3512, Mailing Address: P.O. Box 241267, Zip 36124–1267; tel. 334/277–8330; John W. Melton, Chief Executive Officer

COLUMBIA FOUR RIVERS MEDICAL CENTER (O, 150 beds) 1015 Medical Center Parkway, Selma, AL Zip 36701–6352; tel. 334/872–8461; John Anderson, Chief Executive Officer

COLUMBIA MEDICAL CENTER OF HUNTSVILLE (O, 120 beds) One Hospital Drive, Huntsville, AL Zip 35801–3403; tel. 256/882–3100; Thomas M. Weiss, Chief Executive Officer

COLUMBIA REGIONAL MEDICAL CENTER (O, 165 beds) 301 South Ripley Street, Montgomery, AL Zip 36104–4495; tel. 334/269–8000; Wayne S. Heatherly, Chief Executive Officer

FLORENCE HOSPITAL (O, 155 beds) 2111 Cloyd Boulevard, Florence, AL Zip 35630–1595, Mailing Address: P.O. Box 2010, Zip 35631–2010; tel. 205/767–8700; Doug Dailey, Chief Executive Officer

MEDICAL CENTER SHOALS (O, 128 beds) 201 Avalon Avenue, Muscle Shoals, AL Zip 35661–2805, Mailing Address: P.O. Box 3359, Zip 35662–3359; tel. 205/386–1600; Connie Hawthorne, Chief Executive Officer

NORTHRIDGE MEDICAL CENTER (O, 50 beds) 124 South Memorial Drive, Prattville, AL Zip 36067–3619, Mailing Address: P.O. Box 681630, Zip 36067–1638; tel. 334/365–0651; Duane Brookhart, Ph.D., President and Chief Executive Officer

NORTHWEST MEDICAL CENTER (O, 100 beds) Highway 43 By–Pass, Russellville, AL Zip 35653, Mailing Address: P.O. Box 1089, Zip 35653–1089; tel. 205/332–1611; Christine R. Stewart, President and Chief Executive Officer

ALASKA: ALASKA REGIONAL HOSPITAL (O, 189 beds) 2801 Debarr Road, Anchorage, AK Zip 99508, Mailing Address: P.O. Box 143889, Zip 99514–3889; tel. 907/276–1131; Ernie Meier, President and Chief Executive Officer

ARIZONA: COLUMBIA MEDICAL CENTER PHOENIX (O, 290 beds) 1947 East Thomas Road, Phoenix, AZ Zip 85016–7795; tel. 602/650–7600; Denny W. Powell, Chief Executive Officer

EL DORADO HOSPITAL (O, 166 beds) 1400 North Wilmot Road, Tucson, AZ Zip 85712–4498, Mailing Address: P.O. Box 13070, Zip 85732–3070; tel. 520/886–6361; Rhonda Dean, Chief Executive Officer

NORTHWEST MEDICAL CENTER (O, 152 beds) 6200 North La Cholla Boulevard, Tucson, AZ Zip 85741–3599; tel. 520/742–9000; W. Jefferson Comer, FACHE, Chief Executive Officer

PARADISE VALLEY HOSPITAL (O, 125 beds) 3929 East Bell Road, Phoenix, AZ Zip 85032–2196; tel. 602/867–1881; Rebecca C. Kuhn, R.N., President and Chief Executive Officer

ARKANSAS: COLUMBIA DE QUEEN REGIONAL MEDICAL CENTER (O, 75 beds) 1306 Collin Raye Drive, De Queen, AR Zip 71832–2198; tel. 501/584–4111; Charles H. Long, Chief Executive Officer

COLUMBIA DOCTORS HOSPITAL (O, 308 beds) 6101 West Capitol, Little Rock, AR Zip 72205–5331; tel. 501/661–4000; Maura Walsh, President and Chief Executive Officer

COLUMBIA MEDICAL PARK HOSPITAL (O, 75 beds) 2001 South Main Street, Hope, AR Zip 71801–8194; tel. 870/777–2323; Jimmy Leopard, Chief Executive Officer

MEDICAL CENTER OF SOUTH ARKANSAS (O, 195 beds) 700 West Grove Street, El Dorado, AR Zip 71730–4416, Mailing Address: P.O. Box 1998, Zip 71731–1998; tel. 870/864–3200; Luther J. Lewis, Chief Executive Officer

CALIFORNIA: CHINO VALLEY MEDICAL CENTER (O, 104 beds) 5451 Walnut Avenue, Chino, CA Zip 91710; tel. 909/464–8600; David Chu, Interim Chief Executive Officer

COLUMBIA HUNTINGTON BEACH HOSPITAL AND MEDICAL CENTER (O, 135 beds) 17772 Beach Boulevard, Huntington Beach, CA Zip 92647–9932; tel. 714/842–1473; Carol B. Freeman, Chief Executive Officer

COLUMBIA LOS ROBLES HOSPITAL AND MEDICAL CENTER (O, 236 beds) 215 West Janss Road, Thousand Oaks, CA Zip 91360–1899; tel. 805/497–2727; Robert C. Shaw, Administrator and Chief Executive Officer

COLUMBIA PALM DRIVE HOSPITAL (O, 48 beds) 501 Petaluma Avenue, Sebastopol, CA Zip 95472; tel. 707/823–8511; Jeff Frandsen, Chief Executive Officer

COLUMBIA SOUTH VALLEY HOSPITAL (O, 93 beds) 9400 No Name Uno, Gilroy, CA Zip 95020–2368; tel. 408/848–2000; Beverly Gilmore, Chief Executive Officer

COLUMBIA WEST HILLS MEDICAL CENTER (O, 236 beds) 7300 Medical Center Drive, Canoga Park, CA Zip 91307–9937, Mailing Address: P.O. Box 7937, West Hills, Zip 91309–7937; tel. 818/676–4000; Mark Meyers, President and Chief Executive Officer

GOOD SAMARITAN HOSPITAL (O, 388 beds) 2425 Samaritan Drive, San Jose, CA Zip 95124, Mailing Address: P.O. Box 240002, Zip 95154–2402; tel. 408/559–2011; William K. Piche, Chief Executive Officer

GOOD SAMARITAN HOSPITAL (O, 64 beds) 901 Olive Drive, Bakersfield, CA Zip 93308–4137; tel. 805/399–4461; Victor F. Brewer, Administrator

HEALDSBURG GENERAL HOSPITAL (O, 49 beds) 1375 University Avenue, Healdsburg, CA Zip 95448; tel. 707/431–6500; Mary Schwind, R.N., MS, Chief Executive Officer

LAS ENCINAS HOSPITAL (O, 138 beds) 2900 East Del Mar Boulevard, Pasadena, CA Zip 91107–4375; tel. 626/795–9901; Roland Metivier, Chief Executive Officer

MISSION BAY HOSPITAL (O, 108 beds) 3030 Bunker Hill Street, San Diego, CA Zip 92109–5780; tel. 619/274–7721; Deborah Brehe, Chief Executive Officer

SAN JOSE MEDICAL CENTER (O, 327 beds) 675 East Santa Clara Street, San Jose, CA Zip 95112, Mailing Address: P.O. Box 240003, Zip 95154–2403; tel. 408/998–3212; William L. Gilbert, Chief Executive Officer

SAN LEANDRO HOSPITAL (O, 136 beds) 13855 East 14th Street, San Leandro, CA Zip 94578–0398; tel. 510/667–4510; Kelly Mather, Chief Executive Officer

WEST ANAHEIM MEDICAL CENTER (O, 219 beds) 3033 West Orange Avenue, Anaheim, CA Zip 92804–3184; tel. 714/827–3000; David Culberson, Chief Executive Officer

COLORADO: COLUMBIA MEDICAL CENTER OF AURORA (O, 334 beds) 1501 South Potomac Street, Aurora, CO Zip 80012–5499; tel. 303/695–2600; Louis O. Garcia, President and Chief Executive Officer

COLUMBIA NORTH SUBURBAN MEDICAL CENTER (O, 125 beds) 9191 Grant Street, Thornton, CO Zip 80229–4341; tel. 303/451–7800; Margaret C. Cain, Chief Executive Officer

COLUMBIA PRESBYTERIAN–ST. LUKE'S MEDICAL CENTER (O, 461 beds) 1719 East 19th Avenue, Denver, CO Zip 80218–1281; tel. 303/839–6000; Kevin Gross, Chief Executive Officer

ROSE MEDICAL CENTER (O, 250 beds) 4567 East Ninth Avenue, Denver, CO Zip 80220–3941; tel. 303/320–2121; Kenneth H. Feiler, President and Chief Executive Officer

SPALDING REHABILITATION HOSPITAL (O, 176 beds) 900 Potomac Street, Aurora, CO Zip 80011–6716; tel. 303/367–1166; Lynn Dawson, Chief Executive Officer

SWEDISH MEDICAL CENTER (O, 335 beds) 501 East Hampden Avenue, Englewood, CO Zip 80110–0101; tel. 303/788–5000; Mary M. White, President and Chief Executive Officer

DELAWARE: ROCKFORD CENTER (O, 70 beds) 100 Rockford Drive, Newark, DE Zip 19713–2121; tel. 302/996–5480; Walter J. Yokobosky Jr., Chief Executive Officer

FLORIDA: ATLANTIC MEDICAL CENTER–DAYTONA (O, 214 beds) 400 North Clyde Morris Boulevard, Daytona Beach, FL Zip 32114–2770, Mailing Address: P.O. Box 9000, Zip 32120–9000; tel. 904/239–5000; Thomas R. Pentz, Chief Executive Officer

ATLANTIC MEDICAL CENTER–ORMOND (O, 119 beds) 264 South Atlantic Avenue, Ormond Beach, FL Zip 32176–8192; tel. 904/672–4161; Thomas R. Pentz, Chief Executive Officer

AVENTURA HOSPITAL AND MEDICAL CENTER (O, 407 beds) 20900 Biscayne Boulevard, Miami, FL Zip 33180–1407; tel. 305/682–7100; Davide M. Carbone, Chief Executive Officer

For explanation of codes following names, see page B2.
★ Indicates Type III membership in the American Hospital Association.

BARTOW MEMORIAL HOSPITAL (O, 56 beds) 1239 East Main Street, Bartow, FL Zip 33830–5005, Mailing Address: Box 1050, Zip 33830–1050; tel. 941/533–8111; Thomas C. Mathews, Administrator

BLAKE MEDICAL CENTER (O, 284 beds) 2020 59th Street West, Bradenton, FL Zip 34209–4669, Mailing Address: P.O. Box 25004, Zip 34206–5004; tel. 941/792–6611; Lindell W. Orr, Chief Executive Officer

BRANDON REGIONAL MEDICAL CENTER (O, 225 beds) 119 Oakfield Drive, Brandon, FL Zip 33511–5799; tel. 813/681–5551; Michael M. Fencel, Chief Executive Officer

CEDARS MEDICAL CENTER (O, 500 beds) 1400 N.W. 12th Avenue, Miami, FL Zip 33136–1003; tel. 305/325–5511; Ralph A. Aleman, Chief Executive Officer

CENTRAL FLORIDA REGIONAL HOSPITAL (O, 226 beds) 1401 West Seminole Boulevard, Sanford, FL Zip 32771–6764; tel. 407/321–4500; Doug Sills, President and Chief Executive Officer

CLEARWATER COMMUNITY HOSPITAL (O, 133 beds) 1521 Druid Road East, Clearwater, FL Zip 34616–6193, Mailing Address: P.O. Box 9068, Zip 34618–9068; tel. 813/447–4571; Betsy Bomar, Chief Executive Officer

COLUMBIA BEHAVIORAL HEALTH CENTER (O, 88 beds) 11100 N.W. 27th Street, Miami, FL Zip 33172–5000; tel. 305/591–3230; Cheryl Siegwald–Mays, Administrator

COLUMBIA HOSPITAL (O, 250 beds) 2201 45th Street, West Palm Beach, FL Zip 33407–2069; tel. 561/842–6141; Sharon L. Roush, Chief Executive Officer

COLUMBIA MEDICAL CENTER–PORT ST. LUCIE (O, 150 beds) 1800 S.E. Tiffany Avenue, Port St. Lucie, FL Zip 34952–7580; tel. 561/335–4000; Michael P. Joyce, President and Chief Executive Officer

COLUMBIA NORTHWEST MEDICAL CENTER (O, 150 beds) 2801 North State Road 7, Pompano Beach, FL Zip 33063–5727, Mailing Address: P.O. Box 639002, Margate, Zip 33063–9002; tel. 954/978–4000; Gina Melby, Chief Executive Officer

COMMUNITY HOSPITAL OF NEW PORT RICHEY (O, 414 beds) 5637 Marine Parkway, New Port Richey, FL Zip 34652–4331, Mailing Address: P.O. Box 996, Zip 34656–0996; tel. 813/848–1733; Andrew Oravec Jr., Administrator

DEERING HOSPITAL (O, 233 beds) 9333 S.W. 152nd Street, Miami, FL Zip 33157–1780; tel. 305/256–5100; Jude Torchia, Chief Executive Officer

DOCTORS HOSPITAL OF SARASOTA (O, 147 beds) 5731 Bee Ridge Road, Sarasota, FL Zip 34233–5056; tel. 941/342–1100; William C. Lievense, President and Chief Executive Officer

EAST POINTE HOSPITAL (O, 88 beds) 1500 Lee Boulevard, Lehigh Acres, FL Zip 33936–4897; tel. 941/369–2101; Valerie A. Jackson, Chief Executive Officer

EDWARD WHITE HOSPITAL (O, 135 beds) 2323 Ninth Avenue North, Saint Petersburg, FL Zip 33713–6898, Mailing Address: P.O. Box 12018, Zip 33733–2018; tel. 813/323–1111; Barry S. Stokes, President and Chief Executive Officer

ENGLEWOOD COMMUNITY HOSPITAL (O, 100 beds) 700 Medical Boulevard, Englewood, FL Zip 34223–3978; tel. 941/475–6571; Terry L. Moore, Chief Executive Officer

FAWCETT MEMORIAL HOSPITAL (O, 249 beds) 21298 Olean Boulevard, Port Charlotte, FL Zip 33952–6765, Mailing Address: P.O. Box 4028, Punta Gorda, Zip 33949–4028; tel. 941/629–1181; Steve Dobbs, Chief Executive Officer

FORT WALTON BEACH MEDICAL CENTER (O, 247 beds) 1000 Mar–Walt Drive, Fort Walton Beach, FL Zip 32547–6795; tel. 850/862–1111; Wayne Campbell, Chief Executive Officer

GULF COAST HOSPITAL (O, 120 beds) 13681 Doctors Way, Fort Myers, FL Zip 33912–4309; tel. 941/768–5000; Valerie A. Jackson, Chief Executive Officer

GULF COAST MEDICAL CENTER (O, 176 beds) 449 West 23rd Street, Panama City, FL Zip 32405–4593, Mailing Address: P.O. Box 15309, Zip 32406–5309; tel. 850/769–8341; Donald E. Butts, Chief Executive Officer

HAMILTON MEDICAL CENTER (O, 20 beds) 506 N.W. Fourth Street, Jasper, FL Zip 32052; tel. 904/792–7200; Amelia Tuten, R.N., Administrator

J. F. K. MEDICAL CENTER (O, 363 beds) 5301 South Congress Avenue, Atlantis, FL Zip 33462–1197; tel. 561/965–7300; Phillip D. Robinson, Chief Executive Officer

KENDALL MEDICAL CENTER (O, 235 beds) 11750 Bird Road, Miami, FL Zip 33175–3530; tel. 305/223–3000; Victor Maya, Chief Executive Officer

LAKE CITY MEDICAL CENTER (O, 75 beds) 1701 West U.S. Highway 90, Lake City, FL Zip 32055–3718; tel. 904/752–2922; Todd Gallati, Chief Executive Officer

LARGO MEDICAL CENTER (O, 243 beds) 201 14th Street S.W., Largo, FL Zip 33770–3133, Mailing Address: P.O. Box 2905, Zip 33779–2905; tel. 813/588–5200; Thomas L. Herron, FACHE, President and Chief Executive Officer

LAWNWOOD REGIONAL MEDICAL CENTER (O, 363 beds) 1700 South 23rd Street, Fort Pierce, FL Zip 34950–0188; tel. 561/461–4000; Gary Cantrell, President and Chief Executive Officer

LUCERNE MEDICAL CENTER (O, 267 beds) 818 Main Lane, Orlando, FL Zip 32801; tel. 407/649–6111; Rick O'Connell, Chief Executive Officer

MEMORIAL HOSPITAL OF JACKSONVILLE (O, 310 beds) 3625 University Boulevard South, Jacksonville, FL Zip 32216–4240, Mailing Address: P.O. Box 16325, Zip 32216–6325; tel. 904/399–6111; H. Rex Etheredge, President and Chief Executive Officer

MIAMI HEART INSTITUTE AND MEDICAL CENTER (O, 278 beds) 4701 Meridian Avenue, Miami, FL Zip 33140–2910; tel. 305/674–3114; Tim Parker, Chief Executive Officer

NORTH FLORIDA REGIONAL MEDICAL CENTER (O, 278 beds) 6500 Newberry Road, Gainesville, FL Zip 32605–4392, Mailing Address: P.O. Box 147006, Zip 32614–7006; tel. 352/333–4000; Brian C. Robinson, Chief Executive Officer

NORTHSIDE HOSPITAL AND HEART INSTITUTE (O, 301 beds) 6000 49th Street North, Saint Petersburg, FL Zip 33709–2145; tel. 813/521–4411; Bradley K. Grover Sr., FACHE, Chief Executive Officer

OAK HILL HOSPITAL (O, 204 beds) 11375 Cortez Boulevard, Spring Hill, FL Zip 34611, Mailing Address: P.O. Box 5300, Zip 34611–5300; tel. 352/596–6632; Jay Finnegan, Chief Executive Officer

OCALA REGIONAL MEDICAL CENTER (O, 216 beds) 1431 S.W. First Avenue, Ocala, FL Zip 34474–4058, Mailing Address: P.O. Box 2200, Zip 34478–2200; tel. 352/401–1000; Stephen Mahan, Chief Executive Officer

ORANGE PARK MEDICAL CENTER (O, 196 beds) 2001 Kingsley Avenue, Orange Park, FL Zip 32073–5156; tel. 904/276–8500; Robert M. Krieger, Chief Executive Officer

OSCEOLA MEDICAL CENTER (O, 156 beds) 700 West Oak Street, Kissimmee, FL Zip 34741–4996, Mailing Address: P.O. Box 422589, Zip 34742–2589; tel. 407/846–2266; E. Tim Cook, Chief Executive Officer

PALMS WEST HOSPITAL (O, 117 beds) 13001 Southern Boulevard, Loxahatchee, FL Zip 33470–1150; tel. 561/798–3300; Alex M. Marceline, Chief Executive Officer

PASCO COMMUNITY HOSPITAL (O, 120 beds) 13100 Fort King Road, Dade City, FL Zip 33525–5294; tel. 352/521–1100; Robert Meade, Chief Executive Officer

PLANTATION GENERAL HOSPITAL (O, 264 beds) 401 N.W. 42nd Avenue, Plantation, FL Zip 33317–2882; tel. 954/587–5010; Anthony M. Degina Jr., Chief Executive Officer

PUTNAM COMMUNITY MEDICAL CENTER (O, 161 beds) Highway 20 West, Palatka, FL Zip 32177, Mailing Address: P.O. Box 778, Zip 32178–0778; tel. 904/328–5711; David Whalen, President and Chief Executive Officer

RAULERSON HOSPITAL (O, 101 beds) 1796 Highway 441 North, Okeechobee, FL Zip 34972, Mailing Address: P.O. Box 1307, Zip 34973–1307; tel. 941/763–2151; Frank Irby, Chief Executive Officer

REGIONAL MEDICAL CENTER–BAYONET POINT (O, 256 beds) 14000 Fivay Road, Hudson, FL Zip 34667–7199; tel. 813/863–2411; Don Griffin, Ph.D., President and Chief Executive Officer

SOUTH BAY HOSPITAL (O, 112 beds) 4016 State Road 674, Sun City Center, FL Zip 33573–5298; tel. 813/634–3301; Hal Muetzel, Chief Executive Officer

SOUTHWEST FLORIDA REGIONAL MEDICAL CENTER (O, 330 beds) 2727 Winkler Avenue, Fort Myers, FL Zip 33901–9396; tel. 941/939–1147; Larry Pieretti, President and Chief Executive Officer

Section B

SPECIALTY HOSPITAL JACKSONVILLE (O, 61 beds) 4901 Richard Street, Jacksonville, FL Zip 32207; tel. 904/737–3120; W. Raymond C. Ford, Chief Executive Officer

ST. PETERSBURG MEDICAL CENTER (O, 199 beds) 6500 38th Avenue North, Saint Petersburg, FL Zip 33710–1629; tel. 813/384–1414; Bradley K. Grover Sr., FACHE, President and Chief Executive Officer

TALLAHASSEE COMMUNITY HOSPITAL (O, 180 beds) 2626 Capital Medical Boulevard, Tallahassee, FL Zip 32308–4499; tel. 850/656–5000; Thomas Paul Pemberton, Chief Executive Officer

TWIN CITIES HOSPITAL (O, 60 beds) 2190 Highway 85 North, Niceville, FL Zip 32578–1045; tel. 850/678–4131; David L. Blair, President

UNIVERSITY HOSPITAL AND MEDICAL CENTER (O, 211 beds) 7201 North University Drive, Tamarac, FL Zip 33321–2996; tel. 954/721–2200; James A. Cruickshank, Chief Executive Officer

WEST FLORIDA REGIONAL MEDICAL CENTER (O, 531 beds) 8383 North Davis Highway, Pensacola, FL Zip 32514–6088, Mailing Address: P.O. Box 18900, Zip 32523–8900; tel. 850/494–4000; Stephen Brandt, President and Chief Executive Officer

WESTSIDE REGIONAL MEDICAL CENTER (O, 204 beds) 8201 West Broward Boulevard, Plantation, FL Zip 33324–9937; tel. 954/473–6600; Michael G. Joseph, Chief Executive Officer

WINTER PARK MEMORIAL HOSPITAL (O, 339 beds) 200 North Lakemont Avenue, Winter Park, FL Zip 32792–3273; tel. 407/646–7000; Douglas P. DeGraaf, Chief Executive Officer

GEORGIA: BARROW MEDICAL CENTER (O, 56 beds) 316 North Broad Street, Winder, GA Zip 30680–2150, Mailing Address: P.O. Box 768, Zip 30680–0768; tel. 770/867–3400; Joe T. Hutchins, Chief Executive Officer

COLISEUM MEDICAL CENTERS (O, 188 beds) 350 Hospital Drive, Macon, GA Zip 31213; tel. 912/765–7000; Michael S. Boggs, Chief Executive Officer

COLUMBIA AUGUSTA MEDICAL CENTER (O, 245 beds) 3651 Wheeler Road, Augusta, GA Zip 30909–6426; tel. 706/651–3232; Michael K. Kerner, President and Chief Executive Officer

COLUMBIA CARTERSVILLE MEDICAL CENTER (O, 80 beds) 960 Joe Frank Harris Parkway, Cartersville, GA Zip 30120, Mailing Address: P.O. Box 200008, Zip 30120–9001; tel. 770/382–1530; Keith Sandlin, Chief Executive Officer

COLUMBIA COLISEUM PSYCHIATRIC HOSPITAL (O, 92 beds) 340 Hospital Drive, Macon, GA Zip 31201–8002; tel. 912/741–1355; Edward W. Ruffin, Administrator

COLUMBIA DOCTORS HOSPITAL (O, 100 beds) 616 19th Street, Columbus, GA Zip 31901–1528, Mailing Address: P.O. Box 2188, Zip 31902–2188; tel. 706/571–4262; Hugh D. Wilson, Chief Executive Officer

COLUMBIA EASTSIDE MEDICAL CENTER (O, 114 beds) 1700 Medical Way, Snellville, GA Zip 30078, Mailing Address: P.O. Box 587, Zip 30078–0587; tel. 770/979–0200; Les Beard, Chief Executive Officer

COLUMBIA FAIRVIEW PARK HOSPITAL (O, 190 beds) 200 Industrial Boulevard, Dublin, GA Zip 31021–2997, Mailing Address: P.O. Box 1408, Zip 31040–1408; tel. 912/275–2000; Richard P. Cook, Chief Executive Officer

COLUMBIA METROPOLITAN HOSPITAL (O, 64 beds) 3223 Howell Mill Road N.W., Atlanta, GA Zip 30327–4135; tel. 404/351–0500; Neil Heatherly, Chief Executive Officer

COLUMBIA PARKWAY MEDICAL CENTER (O, 233 beds) 1000 Thornton Road, Lithia Springs, GA Zip 30057, Mailing Address: P.O. Box 570, Zip 30057–0570; tel. 770/732–7777; Deborah S. Guthrie, Chief Executive Officer

COLUMBIA PEACHTREE REGIONAL HOSPITAL (O, 96 beds) 60 Hospital Road, Newnan, GA Zip 30264, Mailing Address: P.O. Box 2228, Zip 30264–2228; tel. 770/253–1912; Linda Jubinsky, Chief Executive Officer

DUNWOODY MEDICAL CENTER (O, 122 beds) 4575 North Shallowford Road, Atlanta, GA Zip 30338–6499; tel. 770/454–2000; Thomas D. Gilbert, President and Chief Executive Officer

HUGHSTON SPORTS MEDICINE HOSPITAL (O, 100 beds) 100 Frist Court, Columbus, GA Zip 31908–7188, Mailing Address: P.O. Box 7188, Zip 31908–7188; tel. 706/576–2100; Hugh D. Wilson, Chief Executive Officer

LANIER PARK HOSPITAL (O, 119 beds) 675 White Sulphur Road, Gainesville, GA Zip 30505, Mailing Address: P.O. Box 1354, Zip 30503–1354; tel. 770/503–3000; Jerry Fulks, Chief Executive Officer

MURRAY MEDICAL CENTER (O, 42 beds) 707 Old Ellijay Road, Chatsworth, GA Zip 30705–2060, Mailing Address: P.O. Box 1406, Zip 30705–1406; tel. 706/517–2031; Mickey Rabuka, Administrator

NORTHLAKE REGIONAL MEDICAL CENTER (O, 120 beds) 1455 Montreal Road, Atlanta, GA Zip 30084; tel. 770/270–3000; Michael R. Burroughs, President and Chief Executive Officer

PALMYRA MEDICAL CENTERS (O, 216 beds) 2000 Palmyra Road, Albany, GA Zip 31701–1528, Mailing Address: P.O. Box 1908, Zip 31702–1908; tel. 912/434–2000; Allen Golson, Chief Executive Officer

REDMOND REGIONAL MEDICAL CENTER (O, 199 beds) 501 Redmond Road, Rome, GA Zip 30165–7001, Mailing Address: Box 107001, Zip 30164–7001; tel. 706/291–0291; James R. Thomas, Chief Executive Officer

WEST PACES MEDICAL CENTER (O, 150 beds) 3200 Howell Mill Road N.W., Atlanta, GA Zip 30327–4101; tel. 404/351–0351; Charles H. Keaton, President and Chief Executive Officer

IDAHO: COLUMBIA EASTERN IDAHO REGIONAL MEDICAL CENTER (O, 286 beds) 3100 Channing Way, Idaho Falls, ID Zip 83404–7533, Mailing Address: P.O. Box 2077, Zip 83403–2077; tel. 208/529–6111; Ronald G. Butler, Chief Executive Officer

WEST VALLEY MEDICAL CENTER (O, 122 beds) 1717 Arlington, Caldwell, ID Zip 83605–4864; tel. 208/459–4641; Mark Adams, Chief Executive Officer

ILLINOIS: CHICAGO LAKESHORE HOSPITAL (O, 102 beds) 4840 North Marine Drive, Chicago, IL Zip 60640–4296; tel. 773/878–9700; Marcia S. Shapiro, Chief Executive Officer

COLUMBIA GRANT HOSPITAL (O, 242 beds) 550 Webster Avenue, Chicago, IL Zip 60614–9980; tel. 773/883–2000; Nancy R. Hellyer, R.N., Chief Executive Officer

COLUMBIA MICHAEL REESE HOSPITAL AND MEDICAL CENTER (O, 523 beds) 2929 South Ellis Avenue, Chicago, IL Zip 60616–3376; tel. 312/791–2000; F. Scott Winslow, President and Chief Executive Officer

COLUMBIA OLYMPIA FIELDS OSTEOPATHIC HOSPITAL AND MEDICAL CENTER (O, 174 beds) 20201 South Crawford Avenue, Olympia Fields, IL Zip 60461–1080; tel. 708/747–4000; Solon Boggus Jr., Interim Chief Executive Officer

COLUMBIA WOODLAND HOSPITAL (O, 94 beds) 1650 Moon Lake Boulevard, Hoffman Estates, IL Zip 60194–5000; tel. 847/882–1600; Carmen I. Fontanez, Chief Executive Officer

HOFFMAN ESTATES MEDICAL CENTER (O, 195 beds) 1555 North Barrington Road, Hoffman Estates, IL Zip 60194; tel. 847/843–2000; Edward M. Goldberg, President and Chief Executive Officer

LA GRANGE MEMORIAL HOSPITAL (O, 175 beds) 5101 South Willow Spring Road, La Grange, IL Zip 60525–2680; tel. 708/352–1200; Cathleen D. Biga, President and Chief Executive Officer

RIVEREDGE HOSPITAL (O, 100 beds) 8311 West Roosevelt Road, Forest Park, IL Zip 60130–2500; tel. 708/771–7000; Thomas J. Dattalo, Chief Executive Officer

INDIANA: COLUMBIA WOMEN'S HOSPITAL–INDIANAPOLIS (O, 132 beds) 8111 Township Line Road, Indianapolis, IN Zip 46260–8043; tel. 317/875–5994; Steven B. Reed, President and Chief Executive Officer

TERRE HAUTE REGIONAL HOSPITAL (O, 236 beds) 3901 South Seventh Street, Terre Haute, IN Zip 47802–4299; tel. 812/232–0021; Jerry Dooley, Chief Executive Officer

KANSAS: BETHANY MEDICAL CENTER (O, 240 beds) 51 North 12th Street, Kansas City, KS Zip 66102–9990; tel. 913/281–8400; Paul F. Herzog, President and Chief Executive Officer

HALSTEAD HOSPITAL (O, 140 beds) 328 Poplar Street, Halstead, KS Zip 67056–2099; tel. 316/835–2651; David Nevill, President and Chief Executive Officer

OVERLAND PARK REGIONAL MEDICAL CENTER (O, 262 beds) 10500 Quivira Road, Overland Park, KS Zip 66215–2373, Mailing Address: P.O. Box 15959, Shawnee Mission, Zip 66215–5959; tel. 913/541–5000; Kevin J. Hicks, Chief Executive Officer

For explanation of codes following names, see page B2.
★ Indicates Type III membership in the American Hospital Association.

WESLEY MEDICAL CENTER (O, 510 beds) 550 North Hillside Avenue, Wichita, KS Zip 67214–4976; tel. 316/688–2000; Carl W. Fitch Sr., President and Chief Executive Officer

WESTERN PLAINS REGIONAL HOSPITAL (O, 88 beds) 3001 Avenue A., Dodge City, KS Zip 67801–6508, Mailing Address: P.O. Box 1478, Zip 67801–1478; tel. 316/225–8401; Ken Hutchenrider, President and Chief Executive Officer

KENTUCKY: AUDUBON HOSPITAL (O, 421 beds) One Audubon Plaza Drive, Louisville, KY Zip 40217–1397, Mailing Address: P.O. Box 17550, Zip 40217–0550; tel. 502/636–7111; Stephen L. Newman, M.D., President and Chief Executive Officer

BURBON COMMUNITY HOSPITAL (O, 58 beds) 9 Linville Drive, Paris, KY Zip 40361–2196; tel. 606/987–1000; Bernie Mattingly, Chief Executive Officer

FRANKFORT REGIONAL MEDICAL CENTER (O, 147 beds) 299 King's Daughters Drive, Frankfort, KY Zip 40601–4186; tel. 502/875–5240; David P. Steitz, Chief Executive Officer

GEORGETOWN COMMUNITY HOSPITAL (O, 61 beds) 1140 Lexington Road, Georgetown, KY Zip 40324–9362; tel. 502/868–1100; Ronald T. Tyrer, Interim Chief Executive Officer

GREENVIEW REGIONAL HOSPITAL (O, 211 beds) 1801 Ashley Circle, Bowling Green, KY Zip 42104–3384, Mailing Address: P.O. Box 90024, Zip 42102–9024; tel. 502/793–1000; Philip A. Clendenin, Chief Executive Officer

LAKE CUMBERLAND REGIONAL HOSPITAL (O, 227 beds) 305 Langdon Street, Somerset, KY Zip 42501, Mailing Address: P.O. Box 620, Zip 42502–2750; tel. 606/679–7441; Jon C. O'Shaughnessy, President and Chief Executive Officer

LOGAN MEMORIAL HOSPITAL (O, 100 beds) 1625 South Nashville Road, Russellville, KY Zip 42276–8834, Mailing Address: P.O. Box 10, Zip 42276–0010; tel. 502/726–4011; Michael Clark, Chief Executive Officer

MEADOWVIEW REGIONAL MEDICAL CENTER (O, 87 beds) 989 Medical Park Drive, Maysville, KY Zip 41056–8750; tel. 606/759–5311; Ronald T. Tyrer, Interim Chief Executive Officer

PINELAKE REGIONAL HOSPITAL (O, 106 beds) 1099 Medical Center Circle, Mayfield, KY Zip 42066–1179, Mailing Address: P.O. Box 1099, Zip 42066–1099; tel. 502/251–4100; Don A. Horstkotte, Chief Executive Officer

SAMARITAN HOSPITAL (O, 219 beds) 310 South Limestone Street, Lexington, KY Zip 40508–3008; tel. 606/252–6612; Frank Beirne, Chief Executive Officer

SOUTHWEST HOSPITAL (O, 150 beds) 9820 Third Street Road, Louisville, KY Zip 40272–9984; tel. 502/933–8100; Cathryn A. Hibbs, Chief Executive Officer

SPRING VIEW HOSPITAL (O, 113 beds) 320 Loretto Road, Lebanon, KY Zip 40033–0320; tel. 502/692–3161; John D. Brock, Chief Executive Officer

SUBURBAN HOSPITAL (O, 380 beds) 4001 Dutchmans Lane, Louisville, KY Zip 40207–4799; tel. 502/893–1000; John A. Marshall, President and Chief Executive Officer

LOUISIANA: AVOYELLES HOSPITAL (O, 55 beds) 4231 Highway 1192, Marksville, LA Zip 71351, Mailing Address: P.O. Box 255, Zip 71351; tel. 318/253–8611; David M. Mitchel, Chief Executive Officer

COLUMBIA DOCTORS' HOSPITAL OF OPELOUSAS (O, 105 beds) 5101 Highway 167 South, Opelousas, LA Zip 70570–8975; tel. 318/948–2100; Daryl J. Doise, Administrator

COLUMBIA LAKEVIEW REGIONAL MEDICAL CENTER (O, 163 beds) 95 East Fairway Drive, Covington, LA Zip 70433–7507; tel. 504/876–3800; Scott Koenig, Chief Executive Officer

COLUMBIA MEDICAL CENTER (O, 183 beds) 17000 Medical Center Drive, Baton Rouge, LA Zip 70816–3224; tel. 504/755–4800; Joseph R. Dicapo, Chief Executive Officer

COLUMBIA RIVERVIEW MEDICAL CENTER (O, 104 beds) 1125 West Louisiana Highway 30, Gonzales, LA Zip 70737; tel. 504/647–5000; Kathy Bobbs, Chief Executive Officer

COLUMBIA SPRINGHILL MEDICAL CENTER (O, 86 beds) 2001 Doctors Drive, Springhill, LA Zip 71075, Mailing Address: P.O. Box 920, Zip 71075–0920; tel. 318/539–1000; James W. White, Chief Executive Officer

DAUTERIVE HOSPITAL (O, 92 beds) 600 North Lewis Street, New Iberia, LA Zip 70560, Mailing Address: P.O. Box 11210, Zip 70562–1210; tel. 318/365–7311; Kyle J. Viator, Chief Executive Officer

HIGHLAND HOSPITAL (O, 158 beds) 1453 East Bert Kouns Industrial Loop, Shreveport, LA Zip 71105–6050; tel. 318/798–4300; Anthony S. Sala Jr., Chief Executive Officer

LAKELAND MEDICAL CENTER (O, 140 beds) 6000 Bullard Avenue, New Orleans, LA Zip 70128; tel. 504/241–6335; Trudy Land, Chief Executive Officer

LAKESIDE HOSPITAL (O, 99 beds) 4700 I–10 Service Road, Metairie, LA Zip 70001–1269; tel. 504/885–3342; Gerald A. Fornoff, Chief Executive Officer

MEDICAL CENTER OF SOUTHWEST LOUISIANA (O, 107 beds) 2810 Ambassador Caffery Parkway, Lafayette, LA Zip 70506–5900; tel. 318/981–2949; Madeleine L. Roberson, Chief Executive Officer

NORTH MONROE HOSPITAL (O, 210 beds) 3421 Medical Park Drive, Monroe, LA Zip 71203–2399; tel. 318/388–1946; George E. Miller, Chief Executive Officer

OAKDALE COMMUNITY HOSPITAL (O, 60 beds) 130 North Hospital Drive, Oakdale, LA Zip 71463–4004, Mailing Address: P.O. Box 629, Zip 71463–0629; tel. 318/335–3700; LaQuita Johnson, Chief Executive Officer

RAPIDES REGIONAL MEDICAL CENTER (O, 359 beds) 211 Fourth Street, Alexandria, LA Zip 71301–8421, Mailing Address: Box 30101, Zip 71301–8421; tel. 318/473–3000; Lynn Truelove, President and Chief Executive Officer

SAVOY MEDICAL CENTER (O, 520 beds) 801 Poinciana Avenue, Mamou, LA Zip 70554–2298; tel. 318/468–5261; J. E. Richardson, Chief Executive Officer

TULANE UNIVERSITY HOSPITAL AND CLINIC (O, 259 beds) 1415 Tulane Avenue, New Orleans, LA Zip 70112–2632; tel. 504/588–5263; Shirley A. Stewart, President and Chief Executive Officer

WINN PARISH MEDICAL CENTER (O, 103 beds) 301 West Boundary Street, Winnfield, LA Zip 71483–3427, Mailing Address: P.O. Box 152, Zip 71483–0152; tel. 318/628–2721; Bobby Jordan, Chief Executive Officer

WOMEN AND CHILDREN'S HOSPITAL–LAKE CHARLES (O, 70 beds) 4200 Nelson Road, Lake Charles, LA Zip 70605–4118; tel. 318/474–6370; Alan E. McMillin, Chief Executive Officer

WOMEN'S AND CHILDREN'S HOSPITAL (O, 96 beds) 4600 Ambassador Caffery Parkway, Lafayette, LA Zip 70508–6923, Mailing Address: P.O. Box 88030, Zip 70598–8030; tel. 318/981–9100; Madeleine L. Roberson, Chief Executive Officer

MASSACHUSETTS: METROWEST MEDICAL CENTER (O, 398 beds) 115 Lincoln Street, Framingham, MA Zip 01702; tel. 508/383–1000; Thomas G. Hennessy, Chief Executive Officer

MISSISSIPPI: GARDEN PARK COMMUNITY HOSPITAL (O, 130 beds) 1520 Broad Avenue, Gulfport, MS Zip 39501, Mailing Address: P.O. Box 1240, Zip 39502–1240; tel. 228/864–4210; William E. Peaks, Chief Executive Officer

VICKSBURG MEDICAL CENTER (O, 154 beds) 1111 Frontage Road, Vicksburg, MS Zip 39181–5298; tel. 601/619–3800; Steve Roth, Chief Executive Officer

MISSOURI: COLUMBIA HOSPITAL NORTH AND SOUTH (O, 150 beds) 3535 South National Avenue, Springfield, MO Zip 65807–7399; tel. 417/882–4700; Michelle Fischer, Chief Executive Officer

INDEPENDENCE REGIONAL HEALTH CENTER (O, 329 beds) 1509 West Truman Road, Independence, MO Zip 64050–3498; tel. 816/836–8100; Darrell W. Moore, Chief Executive Officer

RESEARCH PSYCHIATRIC CENTER (O, 100 beds) 2323 East 63rd Street, Kansas City, MO Zip 64130–3495; tel. 816/444–8161; Todd Krass, Administrator and Chief Executive Officer

NEVADA: COLUMBIA SUNRISE HOSPITAL AND MEDICAL CENTER (O, 671 beds) 3186 Maryland Parkway, Las Vegas, NV Zip 89109–2306, Mailing Address: P.O. Box 98530, Zip 89193–8530; tel. 702/731–8000; Jerald F. Mitchell, President and Chief Executive Officer

COLUMBIA SUNRISE MOUNTAINVIEW HOSPITAL (O, 120 beds) 3100 North Tenaya Way, Las Vegas, NV Zip 89128; tel. 702/255–5000; Mark J. Howard, President and Chief Executive Officer

For explanation of codes following names, see page B2.
★ Indicates Type III membership in the American Hospital Association.

Section B

NEW HAMPSHIRE: PARKLAND MEDICAL CENTER (O, 77 beds) One Parkland Drive, Derry, NH Zip 03038–2750; tel. 603/432–1500; Scott W. Goodspeed, President and Chief Executive Officer

PORTSMOUTH REGIONAL HOSPITAL AND PAVILION (O, 179 beds) 333 Borthwick Avenue, Portsmouth, NH Zip 03801–7004; tel. 603/436–5110; William J. Schuler, Chief Executive Officer

NEW MEXICO: COLUMBIA LEA REGIONAL HOSPITAL (O, 250 beds) 5419 North Lovington Highway, Hobbs, NM Zip 88240–9125, Mailing Address: P.O. Box 3000, Zip 88240–3000; tel. 505/392–6581; Bill Gresco, Administrator

COLUMBIA MEDICAL CENTER OF CARLSBAD (O, 131 beds) 2430 West Pierce Street, Carlsbad, NM Zip 88220–3597; tel. 505/887–4100; Thomas McClintock, Chief Executive Officer

NORTH CAROLINA: CAPE FEAR MEMORIAL HOSPITAL (O, 109 beds) 5301 Wrightsville Avenue, Wilmington, NC Zip 28403–6599; tel. 910/452–8100; C. Mark Gregson, Chief Executive Officer

COLUMBIA BRUNSWICK HOSPITAL (O, 56 beds) 1 Medical Center Drive, Supply, NC Zip 28462–3350, Mailing Address: P.O. Box 139, Zip 28462–0139; tel. 910/755–8121; C. Mark Gregson, Chief Executive Officer

COLUMBIA DAVIS MEDICAL CENTER (O, 124 beds) 218 Old Mocksville Road, Statesville, NC Zip 28625, Mailing Address: P.O. Box 1823, Zip 28687–1823; tel. 704/873–0281; G. Phillip Lotti, Chief Executive Officer

HERITAGE HOSPITAL (O, 127 beds) 111 Hospital Drive, Tarboro, NC Zip 27886–2011; tel. 919/641–7700; Janet Mullaney, Chief Executive Officer

HIGHSMITH–RAINEY MEMORIAL HOSPITAL (O, 133 beds) 150 Robeson Street, Fayetteville, NC Zip 28301–5570; tel. 910/609–1000; Charles T. Adams, Interim Chief Executive Officer

HOLLY HILL CHARTER BEHAVIORAL HEALTH SYSTEM (O, 108 beds) 3019 Falstaff Road, Raleigh, NC Zip 27610–1812; tel. 919/250–7000; James B. Brawley, Chief Executive Officer

RALEIGH COMMUNITY HOSPITAL (O, 151 beds) 3400 Wake Forest Road, Raleigh, NC Zip 27609–7373, Mailing Address: P.O. Box 28280, Zip 27611–8280; tel. 919/954–3000; James E. Raynor, Chief Executive Officer

OHIO: MERCY MEDICAL CENTER (S, 376 beds) 1320 Mercy Drive N.W., Canton, OH Zip 44708–2641; tel. 330/489–1000; Jack W. Topoleski, President and Chief Executive Officer

SAINT LUKE'S MEDICAL CENTER (O, 161 beds) 11311 Shaker Boulevard, Cleveland, OH Zip 44104–3805; tel. 216/368–7000; Jeffrey S. Jeney, President and Chief Executive Officer

ST. JOHN WEST SHORE HOSPITAL (S, 183 beds) 29000 Center Ridge Road, Cleveland, OH Zip 44145–5219; tel. 440/835–8000; Fred M. DeGrandis, President and Chief Executive Officer

ST. VINCENT CHARITY HOSPITAL (S, 266 beds) 2351 East 22nd Street, Cleveland, OH Zip 44115–3111; tel. 216/861–6200; Alan H. Channing, Chief Executive Officer

OKLAHOMA: COLUMBIA CLAREMORE REGIONAL HOSPITAL (O, 79 beds) 1202 North Muskogee Place, Claremore, OK Zip 74017–3036; tel. 918/341–2556; Ken Seidel, Executive Director

COLUMBIA DOCTORS HOSPITAL (O, 121 beds) 2323 South Harvard Avenue, Tulsa, OK Zip 74114–3370; tel. 918/744–4000; Anthony R. Young, President and Chief Executive Officer

COLUMBIA SPECIALTY HOSPITAL OF TULSA (O, 45 beds) 2408 East 81st Street, 2500, Tulsa, OK Zip 74137–4210; tel. 918/491–2400; Kenneth Noteboom, Chief Executive Officer

EDMOND MEDICAL CENTER (O, 75 beds) 1 South Bryant Street, Edmond, OK Zip 73034–4798; tel. 405/359–5530; Stanley D. Tatum, Chief Executive Officer

PRESBYTERIAN HOSPITAL (O, 271 beds) 700 N.E. 13th Street, Oklahoma City, OK Zip 73104–5070; tel. 405/271–5100; James O'Loughlin, Chief Executive Officer

SOUTHWESTERN MEDICAL CENTER (O, 139 beds) 5602 S.W. Lee Boulevard, Lawton, OK Zip 73505–9635, Mailing Address: P.O. Box 7290, Zip 73506–7290; tel. 580/531–4700; Thomas L. Rine, President and Chief Executive Officer

TULSA REGIONAL MEDICAL CENTER (O, 255 beds) 744 West Ninth Street, Tulsa, OK Zip 74127–9990; tel. 918/599–5900; James M. MacCallum, President and Chief Executive Officer

WAGONER COMMUNITY HOSPITAL (O, 100 beds) 1200 West Cherokee, Wagoner, OK Zip 74467–4681, Mailing Address: Box 407, Zip 74477–0407; tel. 918/485–5514; John W. Crawford, Chief Executive Officer

OREGON: COLUMBIA WILLIAMETTE VALLEY MEDICAL CENTER (O, 67 beds) 2700 Three Mile Lane, McMinnville, OR Zip 97128–6498; tel. 503/472–6131; Rosemari Davis, Chief Executive Officer

DOUGLAS COMMUNITY MEDICAL CENTER (O, 88 beds) 738 West Harvard Avenue, Roseburg, OR Zip 97470–2996; tel. 541/440–2800; Ronald E. Yates, Chief Executive Officer

SOUTH CAROLINA: COLLETON MEDICAL CENTER (O, 131 beds) 501 Robertson Boulevard, Walterboro, SC Zip 29488–5714; tel. 803/549–2000; Rebecca T. Brewer, CHE, Chief Executive Officer

COLUMBIA GRAND STRAND REGIONAL MEDICAL CENTER (O, 205 beds) 809 82nd Parkway, Myrtle Beach, SC Zip 29572–1413; tel. 803/692–1100; Doug White, Chief Executive Officer

COLUMBIA PROVIDENCE HOSPITAL (S, 233 beds) 2435 Forest Drive, Columbia, SC Zip 29204–2098; tel. 803/256–5300; Larry R. Ellis, Interim Chief Executive Officer

COLUMBIA TRIDENT MEDICAL CENTER (O, 273 beds) 9330 Medical Plaza Drive, Charleston, SC Zip 29406–9195; tel. 803/797–7000; Gene B. Wright, President and Chief Executive Officer

SUMMERVILLE MEDICAL CENTER (O, 99 beds) 295 Midland Parkway, Summerville, SC Zip 29485–8104; tel. 843/875–3993; Ian W. Watson, Chief Executive Officer

TENNESSEE: ATHENS REGIONAL MEDICAL CENTER (O, 97 beds) 1114 West Madison Avenue, Athens, TN Zip 37303–4150, Mailing Address: P.O. Box 250, Zip 37371–0250; tel. 423/745–1411; John R. Workman, Chief Executive Officer

CENTENNIAL MEDICAL CENTER AND PARTHENON PAVILION (O, 680 beds) 2300 Patterson Street, Nashville, TN Zip 37203–1528; tel. 615/342–1000; Larry Kloess, President

COLUMBIA CHEATHAM MEDICAL CENTER (O, 29 beds) 313 North Main Street, Ashland City, TN Zip 37015–1358; tel. 615/792–3030; Rick Wallace, FACHE, Chief Executive Officer and Administrator

COLUMBIA HILLSIDE HOSPITAL (O, 80 beds) 1265 East College Street, Pulaski, TN Zip 38478–4541; tel. 931/363–7531; James H. Edmondson, Chief Executive Officer and Administrator

COLUMBIA HORIZON MEDICAL CENTER (O, 169 beds) 111 Highway 70 East, Dickson, TN Zip 37055–2033; tel. 615/441–2357; Rick Wallace, FACHE, Chief Executive Officer and Administrator

COLUMBIA INDIAN PATH MEDICAL CENTER (O, 220 beds) 2000 Brookside Drive, Kingsport, TN Zip 37660–4604; tel. 423/392–7000; Robert Bauer, Chief Executive Officer

COLUMBIA LIVINGSTON REGIONAL HOSPITAL (O, 88 beds) 315 Oak Street, Livingston, TN Zip 38570, Mailing Address: P.O. Box 550, Zip 38570–0550; tel. 931/823–5611; Timothy W. McGill, Chief Executive Officer

COLUMBIA NORTH SIDE HOSPITAL (O, 127 beds) 401 Princeton Road, Johnson City, TN Zip 37601–2097, Mailing Address: P.O. Box 4900, Zip 37602–4900; tel. 423/854–5900; Eric Deaton, Chief Executive Officer

COLUMBIA PARKRIDGE MEDICAL CENTER (O, 358 beds) 2333 McCallie Avenue, Chattanooga, TN Zip 37404–3285; tel. 423/698–6061; Christopher W. Dux, Chief Executive Officer

COLUMBIA REGIONAL HOSPITAL OF JACKSON (O, 104 beds) 367 Hospital Boulevard, Jackson, TN Zip 38305–4518, Mailing Address: P.O. Box 3310, Zip 38303–0310; tel. 901/661–2000; Tim Brady, Chief Executive Officer

COLUMBIA SOUTH PITTSBURG HOSPITAL (O, 47 beds) 210 West 12th Street, South Pittsburg, TN Zip 37380, Mailing Address: P.O. Box 349, Zip 37380–0349; tel. 423/837–6781; Phil Rowland, Chief Executive Officer

COLUMBIA SOUTHERN HILLS MEDICAL CENTER (O, 140 beds) 391 Wallace Road, Nashville, TN Zip 37211–4859; tel. 615/781–4000; Jeffrey Whitehorn, Chief Executive Officer

COLUMBIA STONES RIVER HOSPITAL (O, 55 beds) 324 Doolittle Road, Woodbury, TN Zip 37190–1139; tel. 615/563–4001; Bill Patterson, Interim Administrator

For explanation of codes following names, see page B2.
★ Indicates Type III membership in the American Hospital Association.

Section B

COLUMBIA SYCAMORE SHOALS HOSPITAL (O, 100 beds) 1501 West Elk Avenue, Elizabethton, TN Zip 37643–1368; tel. 423/542–1300; Larry R. Jeter, Chief Executive Officer

COLUMBIA TRINITY HOSPITAL (O, 31 beds) 353 Main Street, Erin, TN Zip 37061–0489, Mailing Address: P.O. Box 489, Zip 37061–0489; tel. 931/289–4211; Jay Woodall, Chief Executive Officer

CROCKETT HOSPITAL (O, 98 beds) U.S. Highway 43 South, Lawrenceburg, TN Zip 38464–0847, Mailing Address: P.O. Box 847, Zip 38464–0847; tel. 931/762–6571; Jack S. Buck, Chief Executive Officer

HENDERSONVILLE HOSPITAL (O, 67 beds) 355 New Shackle Island Road, Hendersonville, TN Zip 37075–2393; tel. 615/264–4000; Robert Klein, Chief Executive Officer

JOHNSON CITY SPECIALTY HOSPITAL (O, 49 beds) 203 East Watauga Avenue, Johnson City, TN Zip 37601–4651; tel. 423/926–1111; Lori Caudell Fatherree, Chief Executive Officer

NASHVILLE MEMORIAL HOSPITAL (O, 250 beds) 612 West Due West Avenue, Madison, TN Zip 37115–4474; tel. 615/865–3511; Allyn R. Harris, Chief Executive Officer

PSYCHIATRIC HOSPITAL AT VANDERBILT (O, 88 beds) 1601 23rd Avenue South, Nashville, TN Zip 37212–3198; tel. 615/320–7770; Richard A. Bangert, Chief Executive Officer and Administrator

RIVER PARK HOSPITAL (O, 86 beds) 1559 Sparta Road, McMinnville, TN Zip 37110–1316; tel. 931/815–4000; Terry J. Gunn, Chief Executive Officer

SMITH COUNTY MEMORIAL HOSPITAL (O, 53 beds) 158 Hospital Drive, Carthage, TN Zip 37030–1096; tel. 615/735–1560; Jerry H. Futrell, Chief Executive Officer

SOUTHERN TENNESSEE MEDICAL CENTER (O, 128 beds) 185 Hospital Road, Winchester, TN Zip 37398–2468; tel. 931/967–8200; Michael W. Garfield, Administrator

SUMMIT MEDICAL CENTER (O, 204 beds) 5655 Frist Boulevard, Hermitage, TN Zip 37076–2053; tel. 615/316–3000; Bryan K. Dearing, Chief Executive Officer

VOLUNTEER GENERAL HOSPITAL (O, 65 beds) 161 Mount Pelia Road, Martin, TN Zip 38237–0967, Mailing Address: P.O. Box 967, Zip 38237–0967; tel. 901/587–4261; R. Coleman Foss, Chief Executive Officer

TEXAS: AUSTIN DIAGNOSTIC MEDICAL CENTER (O, 141 beds) 12221 MoPac Expressway North, Austin, TX Zip 78758–2483; tel. 512/901–1000; Charles F. Sexton, Interim Chief Executive Officer

COLUMBIA ALICE PHYSICIANS AND SURGEONS HOSPITAL (O, 123 beds) 300 East Third Street, Alice, TX Zip 78332–4794; tel. 512/664–4376; Abraham Martinez, Chief Executive Officer

COLUMBIA ALVIN MEDICAL CENTER (O, 86 beds) 301 Medic Lane, Alvin, TX Zip 77511–5597; tel. 281/331–6141; Donald A. Shaffett, Chief Executive Officer

COLUMBIA BAY AREA MEDICAL CENTER (O, 149 beds) 7101 South Padre Island Drive, Corpus Christi, TX Zip 78412–4999; tel. 512/985–1200; Kirk G. Wilson, Chief Executive Officer

COLUMBIA BAYSHORE MEDICAL CENTER (O, 280 beds) 4000 Spencer Highway, Pasadena, TX Zip 77504–1294; tel. 713/359–2000; Russell Meyers, Chief Executive Officer

COLUMBIA BAYVIEW PSYCHIATRIC CENTER (O, 40 beds) 6226 Saratoga Boulevard, Corpus Christi, TX Zip 78414–3421; tel. 512/993–9700; Janie L. Harwood, Chief Executive Officer

COLUMBIA BEAUMONT MEDICAL CENTER (O, 364 beds) 3080 College, Beaumont, TX Zip 77701–4689, Mailing Address: P.O. Box 5817, Zip 77726–5817; tel. 409/833–1411; Luis G. Silva, Chief Executive Officer and Regional Administrator

COLUMBIA BEHAVIORAL CENTER (O, 25 beds) 1155 Idaho Street, El Paso, TX Zip 79902–1699; tel. 915/544–4000; Serena Pickman, Administrator

COLUMBIA BELLAIRE MEDICAL CENTER (O, 202 beds) 5314 Dashwood Street, Houston, TX Zip 77081–4689; tel. 713/512–1200; Walter Leleux, Chief Executive Officer

COLUMBIA BROWNWOOD REGIONAL MEDICAL CENTER (O, 164 beds) 1501 Burnet Drive, Brownwood, TX Zip 76801–5933, Mailing Address: P.O. Box 760, Zip 76804–0760; tel. 915/646–8541; Art Layne, Administrator and Chief Executive Officer

COLUMBIA CLEAR LAKE REGIONAL MEDICAL CENTER (O, 415 beds) 500 Medical Center Boulevard, Webster, TX Zip 77598–4286; tel. 281/338–3110; Donald A. Shaffett, Chief Executive Officer

COLUMBIA CONROE REGIONAL MEDICAL CENTER (O, 242 beds) 504 Medical Boulevard, Conroe, TX Zip 77304, Mailing Address: P.O. Box 1538, Zip 77305–1538; tel. 409/539–1111; Edward W. Myers, Chief Executive Officer

COLUMBIA DOCTORS HOSPITAL AIRLINE (O, 114 beds) 5815 Airline Drive, Houston, TX Zip 77076–4996; tel. 713/695–6041; Joe G. Baldwin, Chief Executive Officer

COLUMBIA DOCTORS HOSPITAL OF LAREDO (O, 107 beds) 500 East Mann Road, Laredo, TX Zip 78041–2699; tel. 956/723–1131; Benjamin Everett, Chief Executive Officer

COLUMBIA DOCTORS REGIONAL MEDICAL CENTER (O, 237 beds) 3315 South Alameda Street, Corpus Christi, TX Zip 78411–1883, Mailing Address: P.O. Box 3828, Zip 78463–3828; tel. 512/857–1501; Steven Woerner, Chief Executive Officer

COLUMBIA EAST HOUSTON MEDICAL CENTER (O, 179 beds) 13111 East Freeway, Houston, TX Zip 77015; tel. 713/455–6911; Merrily Walters, Administrator

COLUMBIA KINGWOOD MEDICAL CENTER (O, 152 beds) 22999 U.S. Highway 59, Kingwood, TX Zip 77339; tel. 281/359–7500; Charles D. Schuetz, Chief Executive Officer

COLUMBIA MAINLAND MEDICAL CENTER (O, 175 beds) 6801 E. F. Lowry Expressway, Texas City, TX Zip 77591; tel. 409/938–5000; Alice G. Adams, Administrator

COLUMBIA MEDICAL CENTER (O, 119 beds) 1604 Rock Prairie Road, College Station, TX Zip 77845–8345, Mailing Address: P.O. Box 10000, Zip 77842–3500; tel. 409/764–5100; Thomas W. Jackson, Chief Executive Officer

COLUMBIA MEDICAL CENTER AT LANCASTER (O, 74 beds) 2600 West Pleasant Run Road, Lancaster, TX Zip 75146–1199; tel. 972/223–9600; Ernest C. Lynch III, Chief Executive Officer

COLUMBIA MEDICAL CENTER OF ARLINGTON (O, 178 beds) 3301 Matlock Road, Arlington, TX Zip 76015–2998; tel. 817/465–3241; John A. Fromhold, Chief Executive Officer

COLUMBIA MEDICAL CENTER OF DENTON (O, 271 beds) 4405 North Interstate 35, Denton, TX Zip 76207–3499; tel. 940/566–4000; Bob J. Haley, Chief Executive Officer

COLUMBIA MEDICAL CENTER OF PAMPA (O, 107 beds) One Medical Plaza, Pampa, TX Zip 79065; tel. 806/665–3721; J. Phillip Young, President and Chief Executive Officer

COLUMBIA MEDICAL CENTER OF PLANO (O, 265 beds) 3901 West 15th Street, Plano, TX Zip 75075–7799; tel. 972/596–6800; Harvey L. Fishero, President and Chief Executive Officer

COLUMBIA MEDICAL CENTER OF SAN ANGELO (O, 143 beds) 3501 Knickerbocker Road, San Angelo, TX Zip 76904–7698; tel. 915/949–9511; Gregory R. Angle, President and Chief Executive Officer

COLUMBIA MEDICAL CENTER OF SHERMAN (O, 160 beds) 1111 Gallagher Road, Sherman, TX Zip 75090–1798; tel. 903/870–7000; John F. Adams, Chief Executive Officer

COLUMBIA MEDICAL CENTER–DALLAS SOUTHWEST (O, 104 beds) 2929 South Hampton Road, Dallas, TX Zip 75224–3026; tel. 214/330–4611; James B. Warren, Chief Executive Officer

COLUMBIA MEDICAL CENTER–EAST (O, 299 beds) 10301 Gateway West, El Paso, TX Zip 79925–7798; tel. 915/595–9000; Douglas A. Matney, Senior Vice President Operations

COLUMBIA MEDICAL CENTER–WEST (O, 221 beds) 1801 North Oregon Street, El Paso, TX Zip 79902–3591; tel. 915/521–1776; Hank Hernandez, Chief Executive Officer

COLUMBIA NORTH BAY HOSPITAL (O, 69 beds) 1711 West Wheeler Avenue, Aransas Pass, TX Zip 78336–4536; tel. 512/758–8585; Steve Sutherlin, Chief Executive Officer

COLUMBIA NORTH HILLS HOSPITAL (O, 133 beds) 4401 Booth Calloway Road, North Richland Hills, TX Zip 76180–7399; tel. 817/284–1431; Randy Moresi, Chief Executive Officer

For explanation of codes following names, see page B2.
★ Indicates Type III membership in the American Hospital Association.

COLUMBIA NORTH HOUSTON MEDICAL CENTER (O, 197 beds) 233 West Parker Road, Houston, TX Zip 77076–2999; tel. 713/697–2831; Joe G. Baldwin, Chief Executive Officer

COLUMBIA NORTHWEST HOSPITAL (O, 63 beds) 13725 Farm to Market Road 624, Corpus Christi, TX Zip 78410–5199; tel. 512/767–4500; Winston Borland, Chief Executive Officer

COLUMBIA REHABILITATION HOSPITAL (O, 40 beds) 300 Waymore Drive, El Paso, TX Zip 77902–1628; tel. 915/577–2600; Cristina Huerta, Administrative Director

COLUMBIA REHABILITATION HOSPITAL (O, 40 beds) 6226 Saratoga Boulevard, Corpus Christi, TX Zip 78414–3499; tel. 512/991–9690; John Krogness, Chief Executive Officer

COLUMBIA RIO GRANDE REGIONAL HOSPITAL (O, 267 beds) 101 East Ridge Road, McAllen, TX Zip 78503–1299; tel. 956/632–6000; Randall M. Everts, Chief Executive Officer

COLUMBIA ROSEWOOD MEDICAL CENTER (O, 184 beds) 9200 Westheimer Road, Houston, TX Zip 77063–3599; tel. 713/780–7900; Pat Currie, Chief Executive Officer

COLUMBIA SILSBEE DOCTORS HOSPITAL (O, 59 beds) Highway 418, Silsbee, TX Zip 77656, Mailing Address: P.O. Box 1208, Zip 77656–1208; tel. 409/385–5531; David Cottey, Chief Executive Officer

COLUMBIA ST. DAVID'S SOUTH HOSPITAL (O, 164 beds) 901 West Ben White Boulevard, Austin, TX Zip 78704–6903; tel. 512/447–2211; Richard W. Klusmann, Chief Executive Officer

COLUMBIA TEXAS ORTHOPEDIC HOSPITAL (O, 49 beds) 7401 South Main Street, Houston, TX Zip 77030–4509; tel. 713/799–8600; John J. Jackson, Chief Executive Officer

COLUMBIA WEST HOUSTON MEDICAL CENTER (O, 169 beds) 12141 Richmond Avenue, Houston, TX Zip 77082–2499; tel. 281/558–3444; Jeffrey S. Holland, Chief Executive Officer

COLUMBIA WOODLAND HEIGHTS MEDICAL CENTER (O, 110 beds) 500 Gaslight Boulevard, Lufkin, TX Zip 75901–3157, Mailing Address: P.O. Box 150610, Zip 75915–0610; tel. 409/634–8311; Don H. McBride, Chief Executive Officer

DETAR HOSPITAL (O, 217 beds) 506 East San Antonio Street, Victoria, TX Zip 77901–6060, Mailing Address: Box 2089, Zip 77902–2089; tel. 512/575–7441; William R. Blanchard, Chief Executive Officer

FORT BEND MEDICAL CENTER (O, 65 beds) 3803 FM 1092 at Highway 6, Missouri City, TX Zip 77459; tel. 281/403–4800; Jeffrey S. Holland, Chief Executive Officer

GULF COAST MEDICAL CENTER (O, 161 beds) 1400 Highway 59, Wharton, TX Zip 77488–3004, Mailing Address: P.O. Box 3004, Zip 77488–3004; tel. 409/532–2500; Michael D. Murphy, Chief Executive Officer

KATY MEDICAL CENTER (O, 73 beds) 5602 Medical Center Drive, Katy, TX Zip 77494–6399; tel. 281/392–1111; Brian S. Barbe, Chief Executive Officer

LONGVIEW REGIONAL MEDICAL CENTER (O, 164 beds) 2901 North Fourth Street, Longview, TX Zip 75605–5191, Mailing Address: P.O. Box 14000, Zip 75607–4000; tel. 903/758–1818; Velinda Stevens, Chief Executive Officer

MEDICAL ARTS HOSPITAL (O, 59 beds) 2501 College Drive, Texarkana, TX Zip 75501–2703, Mailing Address: P.O. Box 6045, Zip 75505–6045; tel. 903/798–5200; Jerry Kincade, Chief Executive Officer

MEDICAL CENTER AT TERRELL (O, 130 beds) 1551 Highway 34 South, Terrell, TX Zip 75160–4833; tel. 972/563–7611; Ronald J. Ensor, Chief Executive Officer

MEDICAL CENTER OF LEWISVILLE (O, 116 beds) 500 West Main, Lewisville, TX Zip 75057–3699; tel. 972/420–1000; Raymond M. Dunning Jr., Chief Executive Officer

MEDICAL CENTER OF MCKINNEY (O, 155 beds) 1800 North Graves Street, McKinney, TX Zip 75069–3499; tel. 972/548–3000; Dale Mulder, Chief Executive Officer

MEDICAL CITY DALLAS HOSPITAL (O, 511 beds) 7777 Forest Lane, Dallas, TX Zip 75230–2598; tel. 972/566–7000; Stephen Corbeil, President and Chief Executive Officer

METHODIST AMBULATORY SURGERY HOSPITAL (O, 37 beds) 9150 Huebner Road, San Antonio, TX Zip 78240–1545; tel. 210/691–0800; Elaine F. Morris, Administrator

METHODIST WOMEN'S AND CHILDREN'S HOSPITAL (O, 150 beds) 8109 Fredericksburg Road, San Antonio, TX Zip 78229–3383; tel. 210/692–5000; Janet Porter, President and Chief Executive Officer

METROPOLITAN METHODIST HOSPITAL (O, 237 beds) 1310 McCullough Avenue, San Antonio, TX Zip 78212–2617; tel. 210/208–2200; Mark L. Bernard, Chief Executive Officer

NAVARRO REGIONAL HOSPITAL (O, 144 beds) 3201 West Highway 22, Corsicana, TX Zip 75110; tel. 903/872–4861; Nancy A. Byrnes, President and Chief Executive Officer

NORTHEAST METHODIST HOSPITAL (O, 117 beds) 12412 Judson Road, San Antonio, TX Zip 78233–3272, Mailing Address: P.O. Box 659510, Zip 78265–9510; tel. 210/650–4949; Mark L. Bernard, Chief Executive Officer

PLAZA MEDICAL CENTER OF FORT WORTH (O, 306 beds) 900 Eighth Avenue, Fort Worth, TX Zip 76104–3986; tel. 817/336–2100; Stephen Bernstein, FACHE, Chief Executive Officer

ROUND ROCK HOSPITAL (O, 65 beds) 2400 Round Rock Avenue, Round Rock, TX Zip 78681–4097; tel. 512/255–6066; Deborah L. Ryle, Chief Executive Officer

SAN ANTONIO COMMUNITY HOSPITAL (O, 291 beds) 8026 Floyd Curl Drive, San Antonio, TX Zip 78229–3915; tel. 210/692–8110; James C. Scoggin Jr., Chief Executive Officer

SOUTHWEST TEXAS METHODIST HOSPITAL (O, 585 beds) 7700 Floyd Curl Drive, San Antonio, TX Zip 78229–3993; tel. 210/575–4000; James C. Scoggin Jr., Chief Executive Officer

SPRING BRANCH MEDICAL CENTER (O, 345 beds) 8850 Long Point Road, Houston, TX Zip 77055–3082; tel. 713/467–6555; Pat Currie, Chief Executive Officer

ST. DAVID'S MEDICAL CENTER (O, 296 beds) 919 East 32nd Street, Austin, TX Zip 78705–2709, Mailing Address: P.O. Box 4039, Zip 78765–4039; tel. 512/476–7111; Cole C. Eslyn, Chief Executive Officer

ST. DAVID'S PAVILION (O, 38 beds) 1025 East 32nd Street, Austin, TX Zip 78765; tel. 512/867–5800; Cole C. Eslyn, Chief Executive Officer

ST. DAVID'S REHABILITATION CENTER (O, 104 beds) 1005 East 32nd Street, Austin, TX Zip 78705–2705, Mailing Address: P.O. Box 4270, Zip 78765–4270; tel. 512/867–5100; Cole C. Eslyn, Chief Executive Officer

VALLEY REGIONAL MEDICAL CENTER (O, 183 beds) 1 Ted Hunt Boulevard, Brownsville, TX Zip 78521–7899, Mailing Address: P.O. Box 3710, Zip 78521–3710; tel. 956/831–9611; David Butler, Chief Executive Officer

WOMAN'S HOSPITAL OF TEXAS (O, 156 beds) 7600 Fannin Street, Houston, TX Zip 77054–1900; tel. 713/790–1234; Linda B. Russell, Chief Executive Officer

UTAH: BRIGHAM CITY COMMUNITY HOSPITAL (O, 21 beds) 950 South Medical Drive, Brigham City, UT Zip 84302–3090; tel. 435/734–4200; Tad A. Morley, Chief Executive Officer

CASTLEVIEW HOSPITAL (O, 84 beds) 300 North Hospital Drive, Price, UT Zip 84501–4200; tel. 801/637–4800; L. Allen Penry, Chief Executive Officer

COLUMBIA ASHLEY VALLEY MEDICAL CENTER (O, 29 beds) 151 West 200 North, Vernal, UT Zip 84078–1907; tel. 435/789–3342; Ronald J. Perry, Chief Executive Officer

COLUMBIA OGDEN REGIONAL MEDICAL CENTER (O, 179 beds) 5475 South 500 East, Ogden, UT Zip 84405–6978; tel. 801/479–2111; Steven B. Bateman, Chief Executive Officer

LAKEVIEW HOSPITAL (O, 128 beds) 630 East Medical Drive, Bountiful, UT Zip 84010–4996; tel. 801/292–6231; Craig Preston, Chief Executive Officer

MOUNTAIN VIEW HOSPITAL (O, 123 beds) 1000 East 100 North, Payson, UT Zip 84651–1690; tel. 801/465–9201; Kevin Johnson, Chief Executive Officer

ST. MARK'S HOSPITAL (O, 205 beds) 1200 East 3900 South, Salt Lake City, UT Zip 84124–1390; tel. 801/268–7111; John Hanshaw, Chief Executive Officer

VIRGINIA: CHIPPENHAM AND JOHNSTON–WILLIS HOSPITALS (O, 487 beds) 7101 Jahnke Road, Richmond, VA Zip 23225–4044; tel. 804/320–3911; Marilyn B. Tavenner, Chief Executive Officer

COLUMBIA ALLEGHANY REGIONAL HOSPITAL (O, 196 beds) One ARH Lane, Low Moor, VA Zip 24457, Mailing Address: P.O. Box 7, Zip 24457–0007; tel. 540/862–6200; Ward W. Stevens, CHE, Chief Executive Officer

For explanation of codes following names, see page B2.
★ Indicates Type III membership in the American Hospital Association.

COLUMBIA CLINCH VALLEY MEDICAL CENTER (O, 200 beds) 2949 West Front Street, Richlands, VA Zip 24641–2099; tel. 540/596–6000; James W. Thweatt, Chief Executive Officer

COLUMBIA PENTAGON CITY HOSPITAL (O, 102 beds) 2455 Army Navy Drive, Arlington, VA Zip 22206–2999; tel. 703/920–6700; Thomas Anderson, Chief Executive Officer

COLUMBIA RESTON HOSPITAL CENTER (O, 121 beds) 1850 Town Center Parkway, Reston, VA Zip 20190–3298; tel. 703/689–9023; William A. Adams, President and Chief Executive Officer

DOMINION HOSPITAL (O, 100 beds) 2960 Sleepy Hollow Road, Falls Church, VA Zip 22044–2001; tel. 703/536–2000; Barbara D. S. Hekimian, Chief Executive Officer

HENRICO DOCTORS' HOSPITAL (O, 340 beds) 1602 Skipwith Road, Richmond, VA Zip 23229–5298; tel. 804/289–4500; Patrick W. Farrell, Chief Executive Officer

JOHN RANDOLPH MEDICAL CENTER (O, 271 beds) 411 West Randolph Road, Hopewell, VA Zip 23860, Mailing Address: P.O. Box 971, Zip 23860; tel. 804/541–1600; Daniel J. Wetta Jr., Chief Executive Officer

LEWIS–GALE MEDICAL CENTER (O, 521 beds) 1900 Electric Road, Salem, VA Zip 24153–7494; tel. 540/776–4000; William B. Downey, Administrator

MONTGOMERY REGIONAL HOSPITAL (O, 105 beds) 3700 South Main Street, Blacksburg, VA Zip 24060–7081, Mailing Address: P.O. Box 90004, Zip 24062–9004; tel. 540/953–5101; David R. Williams, Chief Executive Officer

PENINSULA BEHAVIORAL CENTER (O, 90 beds) 2244 Executive Drive, Hampton, VA Zip 23666–2430; tel. 757/827–1001; Steuart A. Kimmeth, Chief Executive Officer

PULASKI COMMUNITY HOSPITAL (O, 62 beds) 2400 Lee Highway, Pulaski, VA Zip 24301–0759, Mailing Address: P.O. Box 759, Zip 24301–0759; tel. 540/994–8100; Jack Nunley, Chief Executive Officer

RETREAT HOSPITAL (O, 146 beds) 2621 Grove Avenue, Richmond, VA Zip 23220–4308; tel. 804/254–5100; Paul L. Baldwin, Chief Operating Officer

WASHINGTON: CAPITAL MEDICAL CENTER (O, 104 beds) 3900 Capital Mall Drive S.W., Olympia, WA Zip 98502–8654, Mailing Address: P.O. Box 19002, Zip 98507–0013; tel. 360/754–5858; Garry L. Gause, Chief Executive Officer

WEST VIRGINIA: BECKLEY HOSPITAL (O, 52 beds) 1007 South Oakwood Avenue, Beckley, WV Zip 25801–5999; tel. 304/256–1200; Albert M. Tieche Jr., Administrator

COLUMBIA RALEIGH GENERAL HOSPITAL (O, 275 beds) 1710 Harper Road, Beckley, WV Zip 25801–3397; tel. 304/256–4100; Brent A. Marsteller, Chief Executive Officer

COLUMBIA RIVER PARK HOSPITAL (O, 165 beds) 1230 Sixth Avenue, Huntington, WV Zip 25701–2312, Mailing Address: P.O. Box 1875, Zip 25719–1875; tel. 304/526–9111; Scott C. Stamm, Chief Executive Officer

COLUMBIA ST. LUKE'S HOSPITAL (O, 79 beds) 1333 Southview Drive, Bluefield, WV Zip 24701–4399, Mailing Address: P.O. Box 1190, Zip 24701–1190; tel. 304/327–2900; Barry A. Papania, President and Chief Executive Officer

GREENBRIER VALLEY MEDICAL CENTER (O, 122 beds) 202 Maplewood Avenue, Ronceverte, WV Zip 24970–0497, Mailing Address: P.O. Box 497, Zip 24970–0497; tel. 304/647–4411; James B. Wood, Chief Executive Officer

PUTNAM GENERAL HOSPITAL (O, 64 beds) 1400 Hospital Drive, Hurricane, WV Zip 25526–9210, Mailing Address: P.O. Box 900, Zip 25526–0900; tel. 304/757–1700; Patsy Hardy, Administrator

SAINT FRANCIS HOSPITAL (O, 155 beds) 333 Laidley Street, Charleston, WV Zip 25301–1628, Mailing Address: P.O. Box 471, Zip 25322–0471; tel. 304/347–6500; David R. Sirk, President and Chief Executive Officer

WYOMING: COLUMBIA RIVERTON MEMORIAL HOSPITAL (O, 59 beds) 2100 West Sunset Drive, Riverton, WY Zip 82501–2274; tel. 307/856–4161; Doug Crabtree, Chief Executive Officer

Owned, leased, sponsored:	320 hospitals	55617 beds
Contract–managed:	0 hospitals	0 beds
Totals:	320 hospitals	55617 beds

0215: COMMUNITY CARE SYSTEMS, INC. (IO)
15 Walnut Street, Wellesley Hills, MA Zip 02181–2101; tel. 781/304–3000; Frederick J. Thacher, Chairman

MAINE: JACKSON BROOK INSTITUTE (O, 106 beds) 175 Running Hill Road, South Portland, ME Zip 04106; tel. 207/761–2200; Steven E. Katz, M.D., President

MASSACHUSETTS: CHARLES RIVER HOSPITAL (O, 62 beds) 203 Grove Street, Wellesley, MA Zip 02181–7413; tel. 781/304–2800; Juliette Fay, President and Chief Executive Officer

Owned, leased, sponsored:	2 hospitals	168 beds
Contract–managed:	0 hospitals	0 beds
Totals:	2 hospitals	168 beds

★0080: COMMUNITY HEALTH SYSTEMS, INC. (IO)
155 Franklin Road, Suite 400, Brentwood, TN Zip 37027–4600, Mailing Address: P.O. Box 217, Zip 37024–0217; tel. 615/373–9600; Wayne T. Smith, President and Chief Executive Officer

ALABAMA: EDGE REGIONAL MEDICAL CENTER (O, 97 beds) 1330 Highway 231 South, Troy, AL Zip 36081–1224; tel. 334/670–5000; David E. Loving, Chief Executive Officer

HARTSELLE MEDICAL CENTER (O, 150 beds) 201 Pine Street N.W., Hartselle, AL Zip 35640–2309, Mailing Address: P.O. Box 969, Zip 35640–0969; tel. 205/773–6511; Mike H. McNair, Chief Executive Officer

L. V. STABLER MEMORIAL HOSPITAL (O, 74 beds) Highway 10 West, Greenville, AL Zip 36037–0915, Mailing Address: Box 1000, Zip 36037–0915; tel. 334/382–2676; Dwayne Moss, Administrator

PARKWAY MEDICAL CENTER HOSPITAL (O, 94 beds) 1874 Beltline Road S.W., Decatur, AL Zip 35601–5509, Mailing Address: P.O. Box 2211, Zip 35609–2211; tel. 205/350–2211; Philip J. Mazzuca, Executive Director

WOODLAND MEDICAL CENTER (O, 100 beds) 1910 Cherokee Avenue S.E., Cullman, AL Zip 35055–5599; tel. 205/739–3500; Lowell Benton, Executive Director

ARIZONA: PAYSON REGIONAL MEDICAL CENTER (O, 49 beds) 807 South Ponderosa Street, Payson, AZ Zip 85541–5599; tel. 520/474–3222; Duane H. Anderson, Chief Executive Officer

ARKANSAS: HARRIS HOSPITAL (O, 88 beds) 1205 McLain Street, Newport, AR Zip 72112–3533; tel. 870/523–8911; Robin E. Lake, Chief Executive Officer

RANDOLPH COUNTY MEDICAL CENTER (L, 50 beds) 2801 Medical Center Drive, Pocahontas, AR Zip 72455–9497; tel. 870/892–4511; Kenneth Breaux, Chief Executive Officer

CALIFORNIA: BARSTOW COMMUNITY HOSPITAL (L, 46 beds) 555 South Seventh Street, Barstow, CA Zip 92311; tel. 760/256–1761; Russell V. Judd, Chief Executive Officer

FLORIDA: DOCTORS MEMORIAL HOSPITAL (L, 34 beds) 401 East Byrd Avenue, Bonifay, FL Zip 32425–3007, Mailing Address: P.O. Box 188, Zip 32425–0188; tel. 850/547–1120; Dale Larson, Chief Executive Officer

NORTH OKALOOSA MEDICAL CENTER (O, 93 beds) 151 Redstone Avenue S.E., Crestview, FL Zip 32539–6026; tel. 850/689–8100; Roger L. Hall, Chief Executive Officer

GEORGIA: BERRIEN COUNTY HOSPITAL (O, 154 beds) 1221 East McPherson Street, Nashville, GA Zip 31639–2326, Mailing Address: P.O. Box 665, Zip 31639–0665; tel. 912/686–7471; James P. Seward Jr., Chief Executive Officer

FANNIN REGIONAL HOSPITAL (O, 46 beds) Highway 5 North, Blue Ridge, GA Zip 30513, Mailing Address: P.O. Box 1549, Zip 30513–1549; tel. 706/632–3711; Kent W. McMackin, Chief Executive Officer

Section B

ILLINOIS: CROSSROADS COMMUNITY HOSPITAL (O, 37 beds) 8 Doctors Park Road, Mount Vernon, IL Zip 62864–6224; tel. 618/244–5500; Donald J. Frederic, Chief Executive Officer

MARION MEMORIAL HOSPITAL (L, 84 beds) 917 West Main Street, Marion, IL Zip 62959–1836; tel. 618/997–5341; Ronald Seal, President and Chief Executive Officer

KENTUCKY: KENTUCKY RIVER MEDICAL CENTER (L, 55 beds) 540 Jett Drive, Jackson, KY Zip 41339–9620; tel. 606/666–6305; O. David Bevins, Chief Executive Officer

PARKWAY REGIONAL HOSPITAL (O, 70 beds) 2000 Holiday Lane, Fulton, KY Zip 42041; tel. 502/472–2522; Mary Jo Lewis, Chief Executive Officer

THREE RIVERS MEDICAL CENTER (O, 90 beds) Highway 644, Louisa, KY Zip 41230, Mailing Address: P.O. Box 769, Zip 41230–0769; tel. 606/638–9451; Greg Kiser, Chief Executive Officer

LOUISIANA: BYRD REGIONAL HOSPITAL (O, 59 beds) 1020 West Fertitta Boulevard, Leesville, LA Zip 71446–4697; tel. 318/239–9041; Donald Henderson, Chief Executive Officer

RIVER WEST MEDICAL CENTER (O, 60 beds) 59355 River West Drive, Plaquemine, LA Zip 70764–9543; tel. 504/687–9222; Mark Nosacka, Chief Executive Officer

SABINE MEDICAL CENTER (O, 48 beds) 240 Highland Drive, Many, LA Zip 71449–3718; tel. 318/256–5691; Karen Ford, Chief Executive Officer

MISSOURI: MOBERLY REGIONAL MEDICAL CENTER (O, 93 beds) 1515 Union Avenue, Moberly, MO Zip 65270–9449, Mailing Address: P.O. Box 3000, Zip 65270–3000; tel. 816/263–8400; Daniel E. McKay, Chief Executive Officer

NEW MEXICO: MIMBRES MEMORIAL HOSPITAL (O, 119 beds) 900 West Ash Street, Deming, NM Zip 88030–4098; tel. 505/546–2761; Timothy E. Schmidt, Chief Executive Officer

SOUTH CAROLINA: CHESTERFIELD GENERAL HOSPITAL (O, 72 beds) Highway 9 West, Cheraw, SC Zip 29520, Mailing Address: P.O. Box 151, Zip 29520–0151; tel. 803/537–7881; Chris Wolf, Chief Executive Officer

MARLBORO PARK HOSPITAL (O, 105 beds) 1138 Cheraw Highway, Bennettsville, SC Zip 29512–0738, Mailing Address: P.O. Box 738, Zip 29512–0738; tel. 803/479–2881; Stephen Chapman, Chief Executive Officer

SPRINGS MEMORIAL HOSPITAL (O, 137 beds) 800 West Meeting Street, Lancaster, SC Zip 29720–2298; tel. 803/286–1214; Robert M. Luther, Chief Executive Officer

TENNESSEE: CLEVELAND COMMUNITY HOSPITAL (O, 70 beds) 2800 Westside Drive N.W., Cleveland, TN Zip 37312–3599; tel. 423/339–4100; Phil Rowland, Chief Executive Officer

LAKEWAY REGIONAL HOSPITAL (O, 135 beds) 726 McFarland Street, Morristown, TN Zip 37814–3990; tel. 423/586–2302; Robert B. Wampler, CPA, Chief Executive Officer

SCOTT COUNTY HOSPITAL (L, 91 beds) 18797 Alberta Avenue, Oneida, TN Zip 37841–4939, Mailing Address: P.O. Box 4939, Zip 37841–4939; tel. 423/569–8521; Peter T. Petruzzi, Chief Executive Officer

WHITE COUNTY COMMUNITY HOSPITAL (O, 18 beds) 401 Sewell Road, Sparta, TN Zip 38583–1299; tel. 931/738–9211; Barry Keel, Chief Executive Officer

TEXAS: BIG BEND REGIONAL MEDICAL CENTER (O, 32 beds) 801 East Brown Street, Alpine, TX Zip 79830–3209; tel. 915/837–3447; Don Edd Green, Chief Executive Officer

CLEVELAND REGIONAL MEDICAL CENTER (O, 115 beds) 300 East Crockett Street, Cleveland, TX Zip 77327–4062, Mailing Address: P.O. Box 1688, Zip 77328–1688; tel. 281/593–1811; Don Willie, Chief Executive Officer

HIGHLAND MEDICAL CENTER (O, 76 beds) 2412 50th Street, Lubbock, TX Zip 79412–2494; tel. 806/788–4060; David Conejo, Chief Executive Officer

HILL REGIONAL HOSPITAL (O, 92 beds) 101 Circle Drive, Hillsboro, TX Zip 76645–2670; tel. 254/582–8425; Jan McClure, Chief Executive Officer

LAKE GRANBURY MEDICAL CENTER (L, 49 beds) 1310 Paluxy Road, Granbury, TX Zip 76048–5699; tel. 817/573–2683; John V. Villanueva, Chief Executive Officer

NORTHEAST MEDICAL CENTER (O, 48 beds) 504 Lipscomb Boulevard, Bonham, TX Zip 75418–4096, Mailing Address: P.O. Drawer C., Zip 75418–4096; tel. 903/583–8585; Glenn E. Lowery, Chief Executive Officer

SCENIC MOUNTAIN MEDICAL CENTER (O, 120 beds) 1601 West 11th Place, Big Spring, TX Zip 79720–4198; tel. 915/263–1211; Kenneth W. Randall, Chief Executive Officer

VIRGINIA: RUSSELL COUNTY MEDICAL CENTER (O, 78 beds) Carroll and Tate Streets, Lebanon, VA Zip 24266–4510; tel. 540/889–1224; Jerry E. Lowery, Executive Director

Owned, leased, sponsored:	38 hospitals	3028 beds
Contract–managed:	0 hospitals	0 beds
Totals:	38 hospitals	3028 beds

1085: COMMUNITY HOSPITALS OF CENTRAL CALIFORNIA (NP)
Fresno and R. Streets, Fresno, CA Zip 93721, Mailing Address: P.O. Box 1232, Zip 93721; tel. 209/442–6000; Philip Hinton, M.D., Chief Executive Officer

CALIFORNIA: CLOVIS COMMUNITY MEDICAL CENTER (O, 143 beds) 2755 Herndon Avenue, Clovis, CA Zip 93611; tel. 209/323–4060; Mike Barber, Facility Service Integrator

FRESNO COMMUNITY HOSPITAL AND MEDICAL CENTER (O, 375 beds) Fresno and R. Streets, Fresno, CA Zip 93721, Mailing Address: Box 1232, Zip 93715; tel. 209/442–6000; J. Philip Hinton, M.D., President and Chief Executive Officer

UNIVERSITY MEDICAL CENTER (O, 334 beds) 445 South Cedar Avenue, Fresno, CA Zip 93702–2907; tel. 209/453–4000; Terry Henry, Interim Administrator

Owned, leased, sponsored:	3 hospitals	852 beds
Contract–managed:	0 hospitals	0 beds
Totals:	3 hospitals	852 beds

0014: CONNECTICUT STATE DEPARTMENT OF MENTAL HEALTH (NP)
90 Washington Street, Hartford, CT Zip 06106–4415, Mailing Address: P.O. Box 341431, Zip 06134–1431; tel. 203/566–3650; Albert J. Solnit, M.D., Commissioner

CONNECTICUT: CEDARCREST HOSPITAL (O, 146 beds) 525 Russell Road, Newington, CT Zip 06111–1595; tel. 860/666–4613; Andrew J. Phillips, Ed.D., Superintendent

CONNECTICUT MENTAL HEALTH CENTER (O, 44 beds) 34 Park Street, New Haven, CT Zip 06519–1187, Mailing Address: P.O. Box 1842, Zip 06508–1842; tel. 203/789–7290; Selby Jacobs, M.D., M.P.H., Director

CONNECTICUT VALLEY HOSPITAL (O, 418 beds) Eastern Drive, Middletown, CT Zip 06457–7023, Mailing Address: P.O. Box 351, Zip 06457–7023; Garrell S. Mullaney, Superintendent

GREATER BRIDGEPORT COMMUNITY MENTAL HEALTH CENTER (O, 62 beds) 1635 Central Avenue, Bridgeport, CT Zip 06610–2700, Mailing Address: P.O. Box 5117, Zip 06610–5117; tel. 203/579–6646; James M. Lehane III, Director

Owned, leased, sponsored:	4 hospitals	670 beds
Contract–managed:	0 hospitals	0 beds
Totals:	4 hospitals	670 beds

●1715: CONTINENTAL MEDICAL SYSTEMS, INC. (IO)
600 Wilson Lane, Mechanicsburg, PA Zip 17055–0715, Mailing Address: P.O. Box 715, Zip 17055–0715; tel. 717/790–8300; Robert Ortenzio, President and Chief Executive Officer

CALIFORNIA: KENTFIELD REHABILITATION HOSPITAL (O, 60 beds) 1125 Sir Francis Drake Boulevard, Kentfield, CA Zip 94904, Mailing Address: P.O. Box 338, Zip 94914–0338; tel. 415/456–9680; John Behrmann, Administrator and Chief Executive Officer

Owned, leased, sponsored:	1 hospital	60 beds
Contract–managed:	0 hospitals	0 beds
Totals:	1 hospital	60 beds

For explanation of codes following names, see page B2.
★ Indicates Type III membership in the American Hospital Association.
● Single hospital health care system

● ★0098: CONTINUUM (NP)
951 East Hospital Drive, Kendallville, IN Zip 46755, Mailing Address: P.O. Box 249, Zip 46755–0249; tel. 219/347–6344; Jim Norris, Interim Chief Executive Officer

INDIANA: MCCRAY MEMORIAL HOSPITAL (O, 43 beds) 951 East Hospital Drive, Kendallville, IN Zip 46755–2293, Mailing Address: P.O. Box 249, Zip 46755–0249; tel. 219/347–1100; John Berhow, President

Owned, leased, sponsored:	1 hospital	43 beds
Contract–managed:	0 hospitals	0 beds
Totals:	1 hospital	43 beds

0127: CONTINUUM HEALTH PARTNERS (NP)
555 West 57th Street, New York, NY Zip 10019; tel. 212/420–2000; Robert G. Newman, M.D., Chief Executive Officer

NEW YORK: BETH ISRAEL MEDICAL CENTER (O, 1234 beds) 281 First Avenue, New York, NY Zip 10003–3803; tel. 212/420–2000; Matthew E. Fink, M.D., President and Chief Executive Officer

ST. LUKE'S–ROOSEVELT HOSPITAL CENTER (O, 729 beds) 1111 Amsterdam Avenue, New York, NY Zip 10025; tel. 212/523–4295; Ronald C. Ablow, M.D., President and Chief Executive Officer

Owned, leased, sponsored:	2 hospitals	1963 beds
Contract–managed:	0 hospitals	0 beds
Totals:	2 hospitals	1963 beds

0016: COOK COUNTY BUREAU OF HEALTH SERVICES (NP)
1835 West Harrison Street, Chicago, IL Zip 60612–3785; tel. 312/633–8533; Ruth M. Rothstein, Chief

ILLINOIS: COOK COUNTY HOSPITAL (O, 770 beds) 1835 West Harrison Street, Chicago, IL Zip 60612–3785; tel. 312/633–6000; Ruth M. Rothstein, Hospital Director

OAK FOREST HOSPITAL OF COOK COUNTY (O, 633 beds) 15900 South Cicero Avenue, Oak Forest, IL Zip 60452; tel. 708/687–7200; Cynthia T. Henderson, M.D., M.P.H., Hospital Director and Chief Operating Officer

PROVIDENT HOSPITAL OF COOK COUNTY (O, 110 beds) 500 East 51st Street, Chicago, IL Zip 60615–2494; tel. 312/572–2000; Stephanie Wright–Griggs, Chief Operating Officer

Owned, leased, sponsored:	3 hospitals	1513 beds
Contract–managed:	0 hospitals	0 beds
Totals:	3 hospitals	1513 beds

0103: COTTAGE HEALTH SYSTEM (NP)
Pueblo at Bath Streets, Santa Barbara, CA Zip 93102, Mailing Address: P.O. Box 689, Zip 93102; tel. 805/682–7111; James L. Ash, President and Chief Executive Officer

CALIFORNIA: GOLETA VALLEY COTTAGE HOSPITAL (O, 79 beds) 351 South Patterson Avenue, Santa Barbara, CA Zip 93111, Mailing Address: Box 6306, Zip 93160; tel. 805/967–3411; Diane Wisby, President and Chief Executive Officer

SANTA BARBARA COTTAGE HOSPITAL (O, 307 beds) Pueblo at Bath Streets, Santa Barbara, CA Zip 93105, Mailing Address: Box 689, Zip 93102; tel. 805/682–7111; James L. Ash, President and Chief Executive Officer

SANTA YNEZ VALLEY COTTAGE HOSPITAL (O, 20 beds) 700 Alamo Pintado Road, Solvang, CA Zip 93463; tel. 805/688–6431; James L. Ash, Chief Executive Officer

Owned, leased, sponsored:	3 hospitals	406 beds
Contract–managed:	0 hospitals	0 beds
Totals:	3 hospitals	406 beds

0123: COVENANT HEALTH (NP)
100 Fort Sanders West Boulevard, Nashville, TN Zip 37222; tel. 423/531–5555; Alan C. Guy, President and Chief Executive Officer

TENNESSEE: FORT SANDERS LOUDON MEDICAL CENTER (O, 30 beds) 1125 Grove Street, Loudon, TN Zip 37774–1512, Mailing Address: P.O. Box 217, Zip 37774–0217; tel. 423/458–8222; Ralph T. Williams, Administrator

FORT SANDERS REGIONAL MEDICAL CENTER (O, 410 beds) 1901 Clinch Avenue S.W., Knoxville, TN Zip 37916–2394; tel. 423/541–1111; James R. Burkhart, FACHE, Administrator

FORT SANDERS–PARKWEST MEDICAL CENTER (O, 281 beds) 9352 Park West Boulevard, Knoxville, TN Zip 37923–4387, Mailing Address: P.O. Box 22993, Zip 37933–0993; tel. 423/694–5700; James R. Burkhart, FACHE, Administrator

FORT SANDERS–SEVIER MEDICAL CENTER (O, 100 beds) 709 Middle Creek Road, Sevierville, TN Zip 37862–5016, Mailing Address: P.O. Box 8005, Zip 37864–8005; tel. 423/429–6100; Ralph T. Williams, Administrator

METHODIST MEDICAL CENTER OF OAK RIDGE (O, 250 beds) 990 Oak Ridge Turnpike, Oak Ridge, TN Zip 37830–6976, Mailing Address: P.O. Box 2529, Zip 37831–2529; tel. 423/481–1000; George A. Mathews, President and Chief Executive Officer

Owned, leased, sponsored:	5 hospitals	1071 beds
Contract–managed:	0 hospitals	0 beds
Totals:	5 hospitals	1071 beds

★5885: COVENANT HEALTH SYSTEMS, INC. (CC)
420 Bedford Street, Lexington, MA Zip 02173–1502; tel. 781/862–1634; David R. Lincoln, President and Chief Executive Officer

MAINE: ST. MARY'S REGIONAL MEDICAL CENTER (O, 187 beds) 45 Golder Street, Lewiston, ME Zip 04240–6033, Mailing Address: P.O. Box 291, Zip 04243–0291; tel. 207/777–8100; James E. Cassidy, President and Chief Executive Officer

MASSACHUSETTS: YOUVILLE LIFECARE (O, 286 beds) 1575 Cambridge Street, Cambridge, MA Zip 02138–4398; tel. 617/876–4344; T. Richard Quigley, President and Chief Executive Officer

NEW HAMPSHIRE: ST. JOSEPH HOSPITAL (O, 150 beds) 172 Kinsley Street, Nashua, NH Zip 03061; tel. 603/882–3000; Kenneth R. Ferron, Senior Vice President and Chief Operating Officer

Owned, leased, sponsored:	3 hospitals	623 beds
Contract–managed:	0 hospitals	0 beds
Totals:	3 hospitals	623 beds

0146: CROSS RIVER HEALTHCARE, INC. (NP)
Rhinebeck, NY Mailing Address: P.O. Box 288, Zip 12572; tel. 914/871–4343; Michael C. Mazzarella, Chief Executive Officer

NEW YORK: KINGSTON HOSPITAL (O, 140 beds) 396 Broadway, Kingston, NY Zip 12401–4692; tel. 914/331–3131; Anthony P. Marmo, Chief Executive Officer

NORTHERN DUTCHESS HOSPITAL (O, 68 beds) 10 Springbrook Avenue, Rhinebeck, NY Zip 12572–5002, Mailing Address: P.O. Box 5002, Zip 12572–5002; tel. 914/876–3001; Michael C. Mazzarella, Chief Executive Officer

Owned, leased, sponsored:	2 hospitals	208 beds
Contract–managed:	0 hospitals	0 beds
Totals:	2 hospitals	208 beds

★0008: CROZER–KEYSTONE HEALTH SYSTEM (NP)
100 West Sproul Road, Springfield, PA Zip 19064; tel. 610/338–8200; John C. McMeekin, President and Chief Executive Officer

PENNSYLVANIA: CROZER–CHESTER MEDICAL CENTER (O, 645 beds) One Medical Center Boulevard, Upland, PA Zip 19013–3995; tel. 610/447–2000; Joan K. Richards, President

DELAWARE COUNTY MEMORIAL HOSPITAL (O, 231 beds) 501 North Lansdowne Avenue, Drexel Hill, PA Zip 19026–1114; tel. 610/284–8100; Joan K. Richards, President

For explanation of codes following names, see page B2.
★ Indicates Type III membership in the American Hospital Association.
● Single hospital health care system

Section B

Owned, leased, sponsored:	2 hospitals	946 beds
Contract–managed:	0 hospitals	0 beds
Totals:	2 hospitals	946 beds

★**1855: DAUGHTERS OF CHARITY NATIONAL HEALTH SYSTEM** (CC)
4600 Edmundson Road, Saint Louis, MO Zip 63134–3806, Mailing Address: P.O. Box 45998, Zip 63145–5998; tel. 314/253–6700; Donald A. Brennan, President and Chief Executive Officer

ALABAMA: PROVIDENCE HOSPITAL (S, 349 beds) 6801 Airport Boulevard, Mobile, AL Zip 36608–3785, Mailing Address: P.O. Box 850429, Zip 36685–0429; tel. 334/633–1000; John R. Roeder, President

ST. VINCENT'S HOSPITAL (S, 338 beds) 810 St. Vincent's Drive, Birmingham, AL Zip 35205–1695, Mailing Address: P.O. Box 12407, Zip 35202–2407; tel. 205/939–7000; Vincent C. Caponi, President and Chief Executive Officer

CONNECTICUT: ST. VINCENT'S MEDICAL CENTER (S, 289 beds) 2800 Main Street, Bridgeport, CT Zip 06606–4292; tel. 203/576–6000; William J. Riordan, President and Chief Executive Officer

DISTRICT OF COLUMBIA: PROVIDENCE HOSPITAL (S, 556 beds) 1150 Varnum Street N.E., Washington, DC Zip 20017–2180; tel. 202/269–7000; Sister Carol Keehan, President

FLORIDA: BAPTIST MEDICAL CENTER (O, 501 beds) 800 Prudential Drive, Jacksonville, FL Zip 32207–8203; tel. 904/202–2000; A. Hugh Greene, Executive Vice President and Chief Operating Officer

BAPTIST MEDICAL CENTER–BEACHES (S, 80 beds) 1350 13th Avenue South, Jacksonville Beach, FL Zip 32250–3205; tel. 904/247–2900; Joseph Mitrick, Administrator

BAPTIST MEDICAL CENTER–NASSAU (S, 24 beds) 1250 South 18th Street, Fernandina Beach, FL Zip 32034–3098; tel. 904/321–3501; Jim L. Mayo, Administrator

SACRED HEART HOSPITAL OF PENSACOLA (S, 520 beds) 5151 North Ninth Avenue, Pensacola, FL Zip 32504–8795, Mailing Address: P.O. Box 2700, Zip 32513–2700; tel. 850/416–7000; Patrick J. Madden, President and Chief Executive Officer

ST. VINCENT'S MEDICAL CENTER (O, 768 beds) 1800 Barrs Street, Jacksonville, FL Zip 32204–2982, Mailing Address: P.O. Box 2982, Zip 32203–2982; tel. 904/308–7300; John W. Logue, Executive Vice President and Chief Operating Officer

INDIANA: SAINT JOSEPH HOSPITAL & HEALTH CENTER (S, 157 beds) 1907 West Sycamore Street, Kokomo, IN Zip 46904–9010, Mailing Address: P.O. Box 9010, Zip 46904–9010; tel. 765/452–5611; Kathleen M. Korbelak, President and Chief Executive Officer

ST. MARY'S HOSPITAL WARRICK (S, 30 beds) 1116 Millis Avenue, Boonville, IN Zip 47601–0629, Mailing Address: Box 629, Zip 47601–0629; tel. 812/897–4800; John D. O'Neil, Executive Vice President and Administrator

ST. MARY'S MEDICAL CENTER OF EVANSVILLE (S, 488 beds) 3700 Washington Avenue, Evansville, IN Zip 47750; tel. 812/485–4000; Richard C. Breon, President and Chief Executive Officer

ST. VINCENT HOSPITALS AND HEALTH SERVICES (S, 621 beds) 2001 West 86th Street, Indianapolis, IN Zip 46260–1991, Mailing Address: P.O. Box 40970, Zip 46240–0970; tel. 317/338–2345; Douglas D. French, President and Chief Executive Officer

ST. VINCENT MERCY HOSPITAL (O, 40 beds) 1331 South A. Street, Elwood, IN Zip 46036–1942; tel. 765/552–4600; Ann C. Parsons, Interim Administrator

ST. VINCENT WILLIAMSPORT HOSPITAL (O, 22 beds) 412 North Monroe Street, Williamsport, IN Zip 47993–0215; tel. 765/762–2496; Jane Craigin, Chief Executive Officer

MARYLAND: SACRED HEART HOSPITAL (S, 272 beds) 900 Seton Drive, Cumberland, MD Zip 21502–1874; tel. 301/759–4200; William T. Bradel, Executive Director

ST. AGNES HEALTHCARE (S, 565 beds) 900 Caton Avenue, Baltimore, MD Zip 21229–5299; tel. 410/368–6000; Robert E. Pezzoli, President and Chief Executive Officer

MICHIGAN: PROVIDENCE HOSPITAL AND MEDICAL CENTERS (S, 382 beds) 16001 West Nine Mile Road, Southfield, MI Zip 48075–4854, Mailing Address: Box 2043, Zip 48037–2043; tel. 248/424–3000; Brian M. Connolly, President and Chief Executive Officer

ST. MARY'S MEDICAL CENTER (S, 268 beds) 830 South Jefferson Avenue, Saginaw, MI Zip 48601–2594; tel. 517/776–8000; Frederic C. Fraizer, President and Chief Executive Officer

NEW YORK: MOUNT ST. MARY'S HOSPITAL OF NIAGARA FALLS (S, 159 beds) 5300 Military Road, Lewiston, NY Zip 14092–1997; tel. 716/297–4800; Angelo G. Calbone, President and Chief Executive Officer

OUR LADY OF LOURDES MEMORIAL HOSPITAL (S, 184 beds) 169 Riverside Drive, Binghamton, NY Zip 13905–4198; tel. 607/798–5328; Michael G. Guley, President and Chief Executive Officer

PARK RIDGE HOSPITAL (O, 259 beds) 1555 Long Pond Road, Rochester, NY Zip 14626–4182; tel. 716/723–7000; Martin E. Carlin, President

SETON HEALTH SYSTEM (S, 344 beds) 1300 Massachusetts Avenue, Troy, NY Zip 12180–1695; tel. 518/272–5000; Edward G. Murphy, M.D., President and Chief Executive Officer

SISTERS OF CHARITY HOSPITAL OF BUFFALO (S, 419 beds) 2157 Main Street, Buffalo, NY Zip 14214–2692; tel. 716/862–1000; Patrick J. Wiles, President and Chief Executive Officer

ST. MARY'S HOSPITAL (S, 218 beds) 89 Genesee Street, Rochester, NY Zip 14611–3285; tel. 716/464–3000; Stewart Putnam, President

PENNSYLVANIA: GOOD SAMARITAN REGIONAL MEDICAL CENTER (S, 221 beds) 700 East Norwegian Street, Pottsville, PA Zip 17901–2798; tel. 717/621–4000; Gino J. Pazzaglini, President and Chief Executive Officer

TENNESSEE: ST. THOMAS HOSPITAL (S, 516 beds) 4220 Harding Road, Nashville, TN Zip 37205–2095, Mailing Address: P.O. Box 380, Zip 37202–0380; tel. 615/222–2111; John F. Tighe, President and Chief Executive Officer

TEXAS: BRACKENRIDGE HOSPITAL (L, 291 beds) 601 East 15th Street, Austin, TX Zip 78701–1996; tel. 512/476–6461; John C. Brindley, Chief Executive Officer

PROVIDENCE HEALTH CENTER (S, 170 beds) 6901 Medical Parkway, Waco, TX Zip 76712–7998, Mailing Address: P.O. Box 2589, Zip 76702–2589; tel. 254/751–4000; Kent A. Keahey, President and Chief Executive Officer

SETON MEDICAL CENTER (S, 472 beds) 1201 West 38th Street, Austin, TX Zip 78705–1056; tel. 512/324–1000; John C. Brindley, Chief Executive Officer

SETON SHOAL CREEK HOSPITAL (O, 118 beds) 3501 Mills Avenue, Austin, TX Zip 78731–6391; tel. 512/452–0361; Gail M. Oberta, Administrator and Chief Executive Officer

WISCONSIN: SACRED HEART REHABILITATION INSTITUTE (S, 69 beds) 2350 North Lake Drive, Milwaukee, WI Zip 53211–4507, Mailing Address: P.O. Box 392, Zip 53201–0392; tel. 414/298–6700; William H. Lange, Administrator and Senior Vice President

ST. MARY'S HOSPITAL (S, 257 beds) 2323 North Lake Drive, Milwaukee, WI Zip 53211–9682, Mailing Address: P.O. Box 503, Zip 53201–0503; tel. 414/291–1000; Charles C. Lobeck, Chief Executive Officer

ST. MARY'S HOSPITAL OZAUKEE (S, 82 beds) 13111 North Port Washington Road, Mequon, WI Zip 53097–2416; tel. 414/243–7300; Therese B. Pandl, Senior Vice President and Chief Operating Officer

Owned, leased, sponsored:	34 hospitals	10049 beds
Contract–managed:	0 hospitals	0 beds
Totals:	34 hospitals	10049 beds

★**1825: DCH HEALTH SYSTEM** (NP)
809 University Boulevard East, Tuscaloosa, AL Zip 35401; tel. 205/759–7111; Bryan Kindred, Chief Executive Officer

ALABAMA: DCH REGIONAL MEDICAL CENTER (O, 457 beds) 809 University Boulevard East, Tuscaloosa, AL Zip 35401–9961; tel. 205/759–7111; Bryan N. Kindred, President and Chief Executive Officer

---

For explanation of codes following names, see page B2.
★ Indicates Type III membership in the American Hospital Association.

FAYETTE MEDICAL CENTER (L, 183 beds) 1653 Temple Avenue North, Fayette, AL Zip 35555–1314, Mailing Address: P.O. Drawer 878, Zip 35555–0878; tel. 205/932–5966; Harold Reed, Administrator

NORTHPORT HOSPITAL–DCH (O, 132 beds) 2700 Hospital Drive, Northport, AL Zip 35476–3380; tel. 205/333–4500; Charles L. Stewart, Administrator

Owned, leased, sponsored:	3 hospitals	772 beds
Contract–managed:	0 hospitals	0 beds
Totals:	3 hospitals	772 beds

9655: DEPARTMENT OF NAVY (FG)
Washington, DC Zip 20066

CALIFORNIA: NAVAL HOSPITAL (O, 21 beds) 930 Franklin Avenue, Lemoore, CA Zip 93246–5000; tel. 209/998–4201; Captain Steven Hart, Commanding Officer

NAVAL HOSPITAL (O, 209 beds) Camp Pendleton, CA Mailing Address: Box 555191, Zip 92055–5191; tel. 760/725–1288; Captain Thomas Burkhard, Commanding Officer

NAVAL HOSPITAL (O, 29 beds) Twentynine Palms, CA Mailing Address: Box 788250, MCAGCC, Zip 92278–8250; tel. 760/830–2492; Captain R. S. Kayler, MSC, USN, Commanding Officer

NAVAL MEDICAL CENTER (O, 342 beds) 34800 Bob Wilson Drive, San Diego, CA Zip 92134–5000; tel. 619/532–6400; Rear Admiral R. A. Nelson, MC, USN, Commander

FLORIDA: NAVAL HOSPITAL (O, 70 beds) 2080 Child Street, Jacksonville, FL Zip 32214–5000; tel. 904/777–7300; Captain M. J. Benson, MSC, USN, Commanding Officer

NAVAL HOSPITAL (O, 113 beds) 6000 West Highway 98, Pensacola, FL Zip 32512–0003; tel. 850/505–6413; Commander H. M. Chinnery, Director, Administration

GUAM: U. S. NAVAL HOSPITAL (O, 55 beds) Agana, GU Mailing Address: PSC 490, Box 7607, FPO, APZip 96538–1600; tel. 671/344–9340; Captain David Wheeler Sr., Chief Executive Officer

ILLINOIS: NAVAL HOSPITAL (O, 89 beds) 3001A Sixth Street, Great Lakes, IL Zip 60088–5230; tel. 847/688–4560; Captain R. William Holden, MC, USN, Commanding Officer

MARYLAND: NATIONAL NAVAL MEDICAL CENTER (O, 217 beds) 8901 Wisconsin Avenue, Bethesda, MD Zip 20889–5600; tel. 301/295–5800; Rear Admiral Richard T. Ridenour, MC, USN, Commander

NAVAL HOSPITAL (O, 5 beds) 47149 Buse Road, Patuxent River, MD Zip 20670–5370; tel. 301/342–1460; Captain Ralph A. Puckett, M.D., USN, Commanding Officer

NORTH CAROLINA: NAVAL HOSPITAL (O, 166 beds) Camp Lejeune, NC Mailing Address: P.O. Box 10100, Zip 28547–0100; tel. 910/451–4300; Captain Michael L. Cowan, MC, USN, Commanding Officer

NAVAL HOSPITAL (O, 23 beds) Cherry Point, NC Mailing Address: PSC Box 8023, Zip 28533–0023; tel. 919/466–0336; Captain Paul D. Garst, USN, Commanding Officer

PUERTO RICO: U. S. NAVAL HOSPITAL (O, 35 beds) Roosevelt Roads, PR Mailing Address: P.O. Box 3007, FPO, AAZip 34051–8100; tel. 787/865–5762; Captain G. R. Brown, Commanding Officer

SOUTH CAROLINA: NAVAL HOSPITAL (O, 43 beds) 1 Pinckney Boulevard, Beaufort, SC Zip 29902–6148; tel. 803/525–5301; Captain Clint E. Adams, MC, USN, Commanding Officer

NAVAL HOSPITAL (O, 32 beds) 3600 Rivers Avenue, North Charleston, SC Zip 29405; tel. 803/743–7000; Captain Kathleen L. Martin, Commanding Officer

TEXAS: NAVAL HOSPITAL (O, 25 beds) 10651 E. Street, Corpus Christi, TX Zip 78419–5131; tel. 512/961–2685; Captain N. J. Lescavage, Commanding Officer

VIRGINIA: NAVAL MEDICAL CENTER (O, 310 beds) 620 John Paul Jones Circle, Portsmouth, VA Zip 23708–2197; tel. 757/953–7424; Rear Admiral Marion Balsam, MC, USN, Commander

WASHINGTON: NAVAL HOSPITAL (O, 76 beds) Boone Road, Bremerton, WA Zip 98312–1898; tel. 360/475–4000; Captain Gregg S. Parker, Commanding Officer

NAVAL HOSPITAL (O, 25 beds) 3475 North Saratoga Street, Oak Harbor, WA Zip 98278–8800; tel. 360/257–9500; Captain Michael W. Benway, Commanding Officer

Owned, leased, sponsored:	19 hospitals	1885 beds
Contract–managed:	0 hospitals	0 beds
Totals:	19 hospitals	1885 beds

9495: DEPARTMENT OF THE AIR FORCE (FG)
110 Luke Avenue, Room 400, Bowling AFB, DC Zip 20332–7050; tel. 202/767–5066; Lieutenant General Charles H. Roadman II, Surgeon General

ALABAMA: MAXWELL HOSPITAL (O, 30 beds) 330 Kirkpatrick Avenue East, Montgomery, AL Zip 36112–6219; tel. 334/953–7801; Colonel Herman R. Greenberg, Administrator

ALASKA: U. S. AIR FORCE REGIONAL HOSPITAL (O, 50 beds) 24800 Hospital Drive, Elmendorf AFB, AK Zip 99506–3700; tel. 907/552–4033; Colonel Larry J. Sutterer, MSC, USAF, Administrator

ARIZONA: U. S. AIR FORCE HOSPITAL (O, 20 beds) 4175 South Alamo Avenue, Davis–Monthan AFB, AZ Zip 85707–4405; tel. 520/228–2930; Colonel Robert E. Edwards, Administrator and Deputy Commander

U. S. AIR FORCE HOSPITAL LUKE (O, 23 beds) Luke AFB, 7219 Litchfield Road, Glendale, AZ Zip 85309–1525; tel. 602/856–7501; Colonel Talbot N. Vivian, MSC, USAF, Administrator

ARKANSAS: U. S. AIR FORCE HOSPITAL LITTLE ROCK (O, 12 beds) Little Rock AFB, Jacksonville, AR Zip 72099–5057; tel. 501/987–7411; Colonel Norman L. Sims, MSC, USAF, Commander

CALIFORNIA: DAVID GRANT MEDICAL CENTER (O, 185 beds) 101 Bodin Circle, Travis AFB, CA Zip 94535–1800; tel. 707/423–7300; Lieutenant Colonel John Hill, MSC, USAF, FACHE, Administrator

U. S. AIR FORCE HOSPITAL (O, 8 beds) 338 South Dakota, Vandenberg AFB, CA Zip 93437–6307; tel. 805/734–8232; Colonel Donald T. Davis, Commander

U. S. AIR FORCE HOSPITAL (O, 6 beds) 15301 Warren Shingle Road, Beale AFB, CA Zip 95903–1907; tel. 530/634–4838; Lieutenant Colonel Robert G. Quinn, MSC, USAF, FACHE, Administrator

U. S. AIR FORCE HOSPITAL (O, 7 beds) 30 Hospital Road, Building 5500, Edwards AFB, CA Zip 93524–1730; tel. 805/277–2010; Lieutenant Colonel Greg Allen, MSC, USAF, Administrator

COLORADO: U. S. AIR FORCE ACADEMY HOSPITAL (O, 48 beds) 4102 Pinion Drive, USAF Academy, CO Zip 80840–4000; tel. 719/333–5102; Colonel David L. Hammer, USAF, MC, Commander

DELAWARE: U. S. AIR FORCE HOSPITAL DOVER (O, 16 beds) 260 Chad Street, Dover, DE Zip 19902–7260; tel. 302/677–2525; Major David M. Allen, MSC, Administrator

FLORIDA: U. S. AIR FORCE HOSPITAL (O, 15 beds) 1381 South Patrick Drive, Patrick AFB, FL Zip 32925–3606; tel. 407/494–8102; Colonel William Swindling, Commanding Officer

U. S. AIR FORCE HOSPITAL (O, 25 beds) Tyndall AFB, Panama City, FL Zip 32403–5300; tel. 850/283–7515; Colonel Harvey R. Crowder, Commander

U. S. AIR FORCE HOSPITAL (O, 50 beds) 8415 Bayshore Boulevard, MacDill AFB, FL Zip 33621–1607; tel. 813/828–3258; Colonel Roger H. Bower, MC, USAF, Commander

U. S. AIR FORCE REGIONAL HOSPITAL (O, 90 beds) 307 Boatner Road, Suite 114, Eglin AFB, FL Zip 32542–1282; tel. 850/883–8221; Colonel William C. Head, MSC, USAF, Administrator

GEORGIA: U. S. AIR FORCE HOSPITAL MOODY (O, 16 beds) 3278 Mitchell Boulevard, Moody AFB, GA Zip 31699–1500; tel. 912/257–3772; Colonel Stephan A. Giesecke, USAF, MSC, Commander

U. S. AIR FORCE HOSPITAL ROBINS (O, 32 beds) 655 Seventh Street, Robins AFB, GA Zip 31098–2227; tel. 912/327–7996; Lieutenant Colonel Carl M. Alley, USAF, MSC, Deputy Commander and Administrator

IDAHO: U. S. AIR FORCE HOSPITAL MOUNTAIN HOME (O, 29 beds) 90 Hope Drive, Mountain Home AFB, ID Zip 83648–5300; tel. 208/828–7600; Lieutenant Colonel Randall E. Fellman, MC, USAF, Commanding Officer

For explanation of codes following names, see page B2.
★ Indicates Type III membership in the American Hospital Association.

Section B

ILLINOIS: SCOTT MEDICAL CENTER (O, 59 beds) 310 West Losey Street, Scott AFB, IL Zip 62225–5252; tel. 618/256–7012; Colonel Stephen J. Pribyl, MSC, USAF, Administrator

LOUISIANA: U. S. AIR FORCE HOSPITAL (O, 25 beds) Barksdale AFB, Shreveport, LA Zip 71110–5300; tel. 318/456–6004; Colonel Dennis Marquardt, USAF, Commander

MARYLAND: MALCOLM GROW MEDICAL CENTER (O, 110 beds) 1050 West Perimeter, Andrews AFB, MD Zip 20762–6600, Mailing Address: 1050 West Perimeter, Suite A1–19, Zip 20762–6600; tel. 301/981–3002; Colonel Jeffrey L. Butler, Administrator

MISSISSIPPI: U. S. AIR FORCE HOSPITAL (O, 7 beds) 201 Independence, Suite 235, Columbus, MS Zip 39701–5300; tel. 601/434–2297; Lieutenant Colonel Karen A. Bradway, MSC, USAF, Administrator

U. S. AIR FORCE MEDICAL CENTER KEESLER (O, 135 beds) 301 Fisher Street, Room 1A132, Keesler AFB, MS Zip 39534–2519; tel. 228/377–6510; Colonel Paul Williamson, Administrator

MISSOURI: U. S. AIR FORCE CLINIC WHITEMAN (O, 20 beds) 331 Sijan Avenue, Whiteman AFB, MO Zip 65305–5001; tel. 660/687–1194; Lieutenant Colonel David Wilmot, USAF, MSC, Administrator

NEBRASKA: EHRLING BERGQUIST HOSPITAL (O, 45 beds) 2501 Capehart Road, Offutt AFB, NE Zip 68113–2160; tel. 402/294–7312; Colonel John R. Sheehan, USAF, MSC, Deputy Commander

NEVADA: MIKE O'CALLAGHAN FEDERAL HOSPITAL (O, 52 beds) 4700 Las Vegas Boulevard North, Suite 2419, Las Vegas, NV Zip 89191–6601; tel. 702/653–2000; Colonel Jack A. Gupton, MSC, USAF, Administrator

NEW MEXICO: U. S. AIR FORCE HOSPITAL (O, 7 beds) 280 First Street, Holloman AFB, NM Zip 88330–8273; tel. 505/475–5587; Colonel Bruce P. Heseltine, MSC, USAF, Commander

U. S. AIR FORCE HOSPITAL (O, 10 beds) 208 West Casablanca Avenue, Cannon AFB, NM Zip 88103–5300; tel. 505/784–6318; Major Douglas E. Anderson, MSC, USAF, Administrator

U. S. AIR FORCE HOSPITAL–KIRTLAND (O, 15 beds) 1951 Second Street S.E., Kirtland AFB, NM Zip 87117–5559; tel. 505/846–3547; Colonel Paul B. Christianson, USAF, Commander

NORTH CAROLINA: U. S. AIR FORCE HOSPITAL SEYMOUR JOHNSON (O, 41 beds) 1050 Jabara Avenue, Seymour Johnson AFB, NC Zip 27531–5300; tel. 919/736–5201; Colonel Michael Lischak, MC, USAF, Commander

NORTH DAKOTA: U. S. AIR FORCE HOSPITAL (O, 15 beds) Grand Forks SAC, Grand Forks AFB, ND Zip 58205–6332, Mailing Address: Grand Forks SAC, 220 G. Street, Zip 58205–6332; tel. 701/747–5391; Lieutenant Colonel Robert J. Rennie, Administrator

U. S. AIR FORCE REGIONAL HOSPITAL (O, 39 beds) 10 Missile Avenue, Minot, ND Zip 58705–5024; tel. 701/723–5103; Colonel Robert C. Tollefson, Commander

OHIO: U. S. AIR FORCE MEDICAL CENTER WRIGHT–PATTERSON (O, 135 beds) 4881 Sugar Maple Drive, Wright–Patterson AFB, OH Zip 45433–5529; tel. 937/257–0940; Brigadier General Earl W. Mabry II, Commander

OKLAHOMA: U. S. AIR FORCE HOSPITAL ALTUS (O, 23 beds) Altus AFB, Altus, OK Zip 73523–5005; tel. 580/481–5970; Colonel David L. Clark, USAF, Commander

U. S. AIR FORCE HOSPITAL TINKER (O, 25 beds) 5700 Arnold Street, Tinker AFB, OK Zip 73145; tel. 405/736–2237; Colonel David D. Bissell, MC, USAF, Commander

SOUTH CAROLINA: U. S. AIR FORCE HOSPITAL SHAW (O, 22 beds) 431 Meadowlark Street, Shaw AFB, SC Zip 29152–5300; tel. 803/668–2559; Lieutenant Colonel Donald Taylor, Administrator

SOUTH DAKOTA: U. S. AIR FORCE HOSPITAL (O, 31 beds) 2900 Doolittle Drive, Ellsworth AFB, SD Zip 57706; tel. 605/385–3201; Colonel Steven Sem, Commander

TEXAS: U. S. AIR FORCE HOSPITAL (O, 20 beds) 7th Medical Group, Dyess AFB, Abilene, TX Zip 79607–1367; tel. 915/696–5429; Major Robin M. King, Administrator

U. S. AIR FORCE REGIONAL HOSPITAL–SHEPPARD (O, 80 beds) 149 Hart Street, Suite 1, Sheppard AFB, TX Zip 76311–3478; tel. 940/676–2010; Colonel Richard D. Maddox, Administrator

WILFORD HALL MEDICAL CENTER (O, 715 beds) 2200 Bergquist Drive, Lackland AFB, TX Zip 78236–5300; tel. 210/292–7353; Colonel Arthur E. Aenchbacher Jr., Administrator

UTAH: U. S. AIR FORCE HOSPITAL (O, 15 beds) 7321 11th Street, Hill AFB, UT Zip 84056–5012; tel. 801/777–5457; Lieutenant Colonel Steven H. Regner, Commander

VIRGINIA: U. S. AIR FORCE HOSPITAL (O, 59 beds) 45 Pine Street, Hampton, VA Zip 23665–2080; tel. 757/764–6825; Colonel Glenn R. Willauer, Administrator

WASHINGTON: U. S. AIR FORCE HOSPITAL (O, 35 beds) 701 Hospital Loop, Fairchild AFB, WA Zip 99011–8701; tel. 509/247–5217; Major Stuart R. Cowles, MSC, Administrator

WYOMING: U. S. AIR FORCE HOSPITAL (O, 15 beds) 6900 Alden Drive, Cheyenne, WY Zip 82005–3913; tel. 307/773–2045; Major Angela D. Fowler, MSC, USAF, Administrator

Owned, leased, sponsored:	44 hospitals	2417 beds
Contract–managed:	0 hospitals	0 beds
Totals:	44 hospitals	2417 beds

9395: DEPARTMENT OF THE ARMY, OFFICE OF THE SURGEON GENERAL (FG)

5109 Leesburg Pike, Falls Church, VA Zip 22041; tel. 703/681–3114; Major Beverly Pritchett, Executive Officer

ALABAMA: FOX ARMY HEALTH CENTER (O, 22 beds) Redstone Arsenal, AL Zip 35809–7000; tel. 205/876–4147; Major Mark A. Miller, Deputy Commander

LYSTER U. S. ARMY COMMUNITY HOSPITAL (O, 42 beds) U.S. Army Aeromedical Center, Fort Rucker, AL Zip 36362–5333; tel. 334/255–7360; Lieutenant Colonel Melvin Leggett Jr., Deputy Commander, Administration

ALASKA: BASSETT ARMY COMMUNITY HOSPITAL (O, 55 beds) Fort Wainwright, Fort Wainwright, AK Zip 99703–7400; tel. 907/353–5108; Lieutenant Colonel Gordon Lewis, Deputy Commander for Administration

CALIFORNIA: WEED ARMY COMMUNITY HOSPITAL (O, 27 beds) Fort Irwin, CA Zip 92310–5065; tel. 760/380–3108; Colonel James Beson, Commander

COLORADO: EVANS U. S. ARMY COMMUNITY HOSPITAL (O, 103 beds) Fort Carson, CO Zip 80913–5101; tel. 719/526–7200; Colonel Kenneth W. Leisher, Deputy Commander, Administration

DISTRICT OF COLUMBIA: WALTER REED ARMY MEDICAL CENTER (O, 474 beds) 6825 16th Street N.W., Washington, DC Zip 20307–5001; tel. 202/782–6393; Colonel Robert James Heckert Jr., MSC, Chief of Staff

GEORGIA: DWIGHT DAVID EISENHOWER ARMY MEDICAL CENTER (O, 150 beds) Hospital Drive, Building 300, Fort Gordon, GA Zip 30905–5650; tel. 706/787–3253; Lieutenant Colonel David A. Rubenstein, Chief Operating Officer

MARTIN ARMY COMMUNITY HOSPITAL (O, 126 beds) Fort Benning, GA Mailing Address: P.O. Box 56100, Building 9200, Zip 31905–6100; tel. 706/544–2516; Colonel Joe W. Butler, Deputy Commander Administration

WINN ARMY COMMUNITY HOSPITAL (O, 100 beds) 1061 Harmon Avenue, Hinesville, GA Zip 31314–5611; tel. 912/370–6001; Colonel Donald J. Kasperik, Commander

HAWAII: TRIPLER ARMY MEDICAL CENTER (O, 298 beds) Honolulu, HI Zip 96859–5000; tel. 808/433–6661; Brigadier General Nancy R. Adams, Commander

KANSAS: IRWIN ARMY COMMUNITY HOSPITAL (O, 56 beds) Building 600, Fort Riley, KS Zip 66442; tel. 913/239–7000; Colonel J. Thomas Hardy, Commanding Officer

MUNSON ARMY HEALTH CENTER (O, 20 beds) 550 Pope Avenue, Fort Leavenworth, KS Zip 66027–2332; tel. 913/684–6420; Colonel Cloyd B. Gatrell, Commander

KENTUCKY: COLONEL FLORENCE A. BLANCHFIELD ARMY COMMUNITY HOSPITAL (O, 106 beds) 650 Joel Drive, Fort Campbell, KY Zip 42223–5349; tel. 502/798–8040; Colonel Lester Martinez–Lopez, Director Health Services

For explanation of codes following names, see page B2.
★ Indicates Type III membership in the American Hospital Association.

IRELAND ARMY COMMUNITY HOSPITAL (O, 54 beds) 851 Ireland Loop, Fort Knox, KY Zip 40121–5520; tel. 502/624–9020; Lieutenant Colonel Robert T. Foster, Deputy Commander for Administration

LOUISIANA: BAYNE–JONES ARMY COMMUNITY HOSPITAL (O, 58 beds) 1585 Third Street, Fort Polk, LA Zip 71459–5110; tel. 318/531–3928; Colonel Joe W. Butler, Deputy Commander and Administrator

MARSHALL ISLANDS: KWAJALEIN HOSPITAL (O, 14 beds) Kwajalein Island, MH Mailing Address: Box 1702, APO, APZip 96555–5000; tel. 805/355–2225; Mike Mathews, Administrator

MISSOURI: GENERAL LEONARD WOOD ARMY COMMUNITY HOSPITAL (O, 71 beds) 126 Missouri Avenue, Fort Leonard Wood, MO Zip 65473–8952; tel. 573/596–0414; Lieutenant Colonel Julie Martin, Administrator

NEW YORK: KELLER ARMY COMMUNITY HOSPITAL (O, 49 beds) U.S. Military Academy, West Point, NY Zip 10996–1197; tel. 914/938–3305; Colonel Joseph FitzHarris, Commander

NORTH CAROLINA: WOMACK ARMY MEDICAL CENTER (O, 173 beds) Normandy Drive, Fort Bragg, NC Zip 28307–5000; tel. 910/432–4802; Colonel Thomas H. Auer, Commander

OKLAHOMA: REYNOLDS ARMY COMMUNITY HOSPITAL (O, 116 beds) 4301 Mow–way Street, Fort Sill, OK Zip 73503–6300; tel. 580/458–3000; Colonel Gary Ripple, Commander

SOUTH CAROLINA: MONCRIEF ARMY COMMUNITY HOSPITAL (O, 69 beds) Fort Jackson, SC Mailing Address: P.O. Box 500, Zip 29207–5720; tel. 803/751–2284; Colonel Dale Carroll, Commander

TEXAS: BROOKE ARMY MEDICAL CENTER (O, 464 beds) Fort Sam Houston, San Antonio, TX Zip 78234–6200; tel. 210/916–4141; Colonel Joseph P. Gonzales, MS, USA, Chief of Staff

DARNALL ARMY COMMUNITY HOSPITAL (O, 117 beds) 36000 Darnall Loop, Fort Hood, TX Zip 76544–4752; tel. 254/288–8000; Colonel Kenneth L. Farmer Jr., Commander

WILLIAM BEAUMONT ARMY MEDICAL CENTER (O, 209 beds) 5005 North Piedras Street, El Paso, TX Zip 79920–5001; tel. 915/569–2121; Colonel Jimmy Sanders, Chief of Staff

VIRGINIA: DEWITT ARMY COMMUNITY HOSPITAL (O, 62 beds) 9501 Farrell Road, Fort Belvoir, VA Zip 22060–5901; tel. 703/805–0510; Colonel Stephen L. Jones, Commander

MCDONALD ARMY COMMUNITY HOSPITAL (O, 30 beds) Jefferson Avenue, Fort Eustis, Newport News, VA Zip 23604–5548; tel. 757/314–7501; Colonel George Weightman, Commander

WASHINGTON: MADIGAN ARMY MEDICAL CENTER (O, 181 beds) Tacoma, WA Zip 98431–5000; tel. 253/968–1110; Brigadier General George J. Brown, M.D., Commanding General

Owned, leased, sponsored:	27 hospitals	3246 beds
Contract–managed:	0 hospitals	0 beds
Totals:	27 hospitals	3246 beds

9295: DEPARTMENT OF VETERANS AFFAIRS (FG)
810 Vermont Avenue N.W., Washington, DC Zip 20420; tel. 202/273–5781; Kenneth W. Kizer, M.D., M.P.H., Under Secretary for Health

ALABAMA: CENTRAL ALABAMA VETERAN AFFAIRS HEALTH CARE SYSTEM (O, 499 beds) 215 Perry Hill Road, Montgomery, AL Zip 36109–3798; tel. 334/272–4670; James L. Clay, Director

VETERANS AFFAIRS MEDICAL CENTER (O, 156 beds) 700 South 19th Street, Birmingham, AL Zip 35233–1927; tel. 205/933–8101; Y. C. Parris, Director

VETERANS AFFAIRS MEDICAL CENTER (O, 307 beds) 3701 Loop Road, Tuscaloosa, AL Zip 35404–5015; tel. 205/554–2000; W. Kenneth Ruyle, Director

ARIZONA: CARL T. HAYDEN VETERANS AFFAIRS MEDICAL CENTER (O, 365 beds) 650 East Indian School Road, Phoenix, AZ Zip 85012–1894; tel. 602/277–5551; John R. Fears, Director

VETERANS AFFAIRS MEDICAL CENTER (O, 306 beds) 3601 South 6th Avenue, Tucson, AZ Zip 85723–0002; tel. 520/792–1450; Jonathan H. Gardner, Chief Executive Officer

VETERANS AFFAIRS MEDICAL CENTER (O, 235 beds) 500 Highway 89 North, Prescott, AZ Zip 86313–5000; tel. 520/445–4860; Patricia A. McKlem, Medical Center Director

ARKANSAS: VETERANS AFFAIRS MEDICAL CENTER (O, 51 beds) 1100 North College Avenue, Fayetteville, AR Zip 72703–6995; tel. 501/443–4301; Richard F. Robinson, Director

VETERANS AFFAIRS MEDICAL CENTER (O, 456 beds) 4300 West Seventh Street, Little Rock, AR Zip 72205–5484; tel. 501/661–1202; George H. Gray Jr., Director

CALIFORNIA: JERRY L. PETTIS MEMORIAL VETERANS MEDICAL CENTER (O, 231 beds) 11201 Benton Street, Loma Linda, CA Zip 92357; tel. 909/825–7084; Dean R. Stordahl, Director

VETERANS AFFAIRS MEDICAL CENTER (O, 135 beds) 2615 East Clinton Avenue, Fresno, CA Zip 93703; tel. 209/225–6100; Ada Neale, Acting Director

VETERANS AFFAIRS MEDICAL CENTER (O, 353 beds) 5901 East Seventh Street, Long Beach, CA Zip 90822–5201; tel. 562/494–5400; Lawrence C. Stewart, Director

VETERANS AFFAIRS MEDICAL CENTER (O, 238 beds) 3350 LaJolla Village Drive, San Diego, CA Zip 92161; tel. 619/552–8585; Gary J. Rossio, Acting Director

VETERANS AFFAIRS MEDICAL CENTER (O, 372 beds) 4150 Clement Street, San Francisco, CA Zip 94121–1598; tel. 415/750–2041; Sheila M. Cullen, Acting Director

VETERANS AFFAIRS MEDICAL CENTER–WEST LOS ANGELES (O, 1327 beds) 11301 Wilshire Boulevard, Los Angeles, CA Zip 90073–0275; tel. 310/268–3132; Kenneth J. Clark, Executive Director and Chief Executive Officer

VETERANS AFFAIRS PALO ALTO HEALTH CARE SYSTEM (O, 1009 beds) 3801 Miranda Avenue, Palo Alto, CA Zip 94304–1207; tel. 650/493–5000; James A. Goff, FACHE, Director

COLORADO: VETERANS AFFAIRS MEDICAL CENTER (O, 212 beds) 1055 Clermont Street, Denver, CO Zip 80220–3877; tel. 303/399–8020; Edgar Thorsland, Director

VETERANS AFFAIRS MEDICAL CENTER (O, 299 beds) Fort Lyon, CO Zip 81038; tel. 719/456–1260; W. David Smith, Director

VETERANS AFFAIRS MEDICAL CENTER (O, 73 beds) 2121 North Avenue, Grand Junction, CO Zip 81501–6499; tel. 970/242–0731; Kurt W. Schlegelmilch, M.D., Director

CONNECTICUT: VETERANS AFFAIRS CONNECTICUT HEALTHCARE SYSTEM–WEST HAVEN DIVISION (O, 208 beds) 950 Campbell Avenue, West Haven, CT Zip 06516; tel. 203/932–5711; Vincent Ng, Director

DELAWARE: VETERANS AFFAIRS MEDICAL CENTER (O, 160 beds) 1601 Kirkwood Highway, Wilmington, DE Zip 19805–4989; tel. 302/633–5201; Dexter D. Dix, Director

DISTRICT OF COLUMBIA: VETERANS AFFAIRS MEDICAL CENTER (O, 197 beds) 50 Irving Street N.W., Washington, DC Zip 20422–0002; tel. 202/745–8100; Sanford M. Garfunkel, Medical Center Director

FLORIDA: JAMES A. HALEY VETERANS HOSPITAL (O, 640 beds) 13000 Bruce B. Downs Boulevard, Tampa, FL Zip 33612–4798; tel. 813/972–2000; Richard A. Silver, Director

VETERANS AFFAIRS MEDICAL CENTER (O, 628 beds) Bay Pines & 100 Way, Bay Pines, FL Zip 33744, Mailing Address: P.O. Box 5005, Zip 33744–5005; tel. 813/398–6661; Thomas H. Weaver, FACHE, Director

VETERANS AFFAIRS MEDICAL CENTER (O, 233 beds) 7305 North Military Trail, West Palm Beach, FL Zip 33410–6400; tel. 561/882–8262; Lucille W. Swanson, Ph.D., Acting Director

VETERANS AFFAIRS MEDICAL CENTER (O, 669 beds) 1201 N.W. 16th Street, Miami, FL Zip 33125–1624; tel. 305/324–4455; Thomas C. Doherty, Medical Center Director

VETERANS AFFAIRS MEDICAL CENTER (O, 268 beds) 1601 S.W. Archer Road, Gainesville, FL Zip 32608–1197; tel. 352/376–1611; Malcom Randall, Director

VETERANS AFFAIRS MEDICAL CENTER (O, 350 beds) 801 South Marion Street, Lake City, FL Zip 32025–5898; tel. 904/755–3016; Marlis Meyer, Interim Director

Section B

Section B

GEORGIA: VETERANS AFFAIRS MEDICAL CENTER (O, 378 beds) 1670 Clairmont Road, Decatur, GA Zip 30033–4004; tel. 404/321–6111; Robert A. Perreault, Director

VETERANS AFFAIRS MEDICAL CENTER (O, 526 beds) 1 Freedom Way, Augusta, GA Zip 30904–6285; tel. 706/733–0188; Ralph R. Angelo, Acting Director

VETERANS AFFAIRS MEDICAL CENTER (O, 253 beds) 1826 Veterans Boulevard, Dublin, GA Zip 31021–3620; tel. 912/277–2701; James F. Trusley III, Director

IDAHO: VETERANS AFFAIRS MEDICAL CENTER (O, 176 beds) 500 West Fort Street, Boise, ID Zip 83702–4598; tel. 208/422–1100; Wayne C. Tippets, Director

ILLINOIS: VETERANS AFFAIRS CHICAGO HEALTH CARE SYSTEM–LAKESIDE DIVISION (O, 442 beds) 333 East Huron Street, Chicago, IL Zip 60611–3004; tel. 312/640–2100; Joseph L. Moore, Director

VETERANS AFFAIRS CHICAGO HEALTH CARE SYSTEM–WEST SIDE DIVISION (O, 323 beds) 820 South Damen Avenue, Chicago, IL Zip 60612–3776, Mailing Address: P.O. Box 8195, Zip 60680–8195; tel. 312/666–6500; Joseph L. Moore, Director

VETERANS AFFAIRS EDWARD HINES, JR. HOSPITAL (O, 957 beds) Fifth Avenue & Roosevelt Road, Hines, IL Zip 60141–5000, Mailing Address: P.O. Box 5000, Zip 60141–5000; tel. 708/343–7200; John J. DeNardo, Director

VETERANS AFFAIRS MEDICAL CENTER (O, 490 beds) 1900 East Main Street, Danville, IL Zip 61832–5198; tel. 217/442–8000; James S. Jones, Director

VETERANS AFFAIRS MEDICAL CENTER (O, 836 beds) 3001 Green Bay Road, North Chicago, IL Zip 60064–3049; tel. 847/688–1900; Alfred S. Pate, Director

VETERANS AFFAIRS MEDICAL CENTER (O, 97 beds) 2401 West Main Street, Marion, IL Zip 62959–1194; tel. 618/997–5311; Marilyn Small, Acting Site Executive Officer

INDIANA: RICHARD L. ROUDEBUSH VETERANS AFFAIRS MEDICAL CENTER (O, 176 beds) 1481 West Tenth Street, Indianapolis, IN Zip 46202–2884; tel. 317/554–0000; Alice Wood, Director

VETERANS AFFAIRS NORTHERN INDIANA HEALTH CARE SYSTEM (O, 731 beds) 2121 Lake Avenue, Fort Wayne, IN Zip 46805–5347; tel. 219/460–1310; Michael W. Murphy, Ph.D., Director

IOWA: VETERANS AFFAIRS CENTRAL IOWA HEALTH CARE SYSTEM (O, 523 beds) 3600 30th Street, Des Moines, IA Zip 50310–5774; tel. 515/699–5999; Ellen DeGeorge-Smith, Director

VETERANS AFFAIRS MEDICAL CENTER (O, 113 beds) Highway 6 West, Iowa City, IA Zip 52246–2208; tel. 319/338–0581; Gary L. Wilkinson, Director

KANSAS: COLMERY–O'NEIL VETERANS AFFAIRS MEDICAL CENTER (O, 218 beds) 2200 Gage Boulevard, Topeka, KS Zip 66622–0002; tel. 785/350–3111; Edgar Tucker, Director

DWIGHT D. EISENHOWER VETERANS AFFAIRS MEDICAL CENTER (O, 63 beds) 4101 South Fourth Street Trafficway, Leavenworth, KS Zip 66048–5055; tel. 913/682–2000; Edgar L. Tucker, Director

VETERANS AFFAIRS MEDICAL AND REGIONAL OFFICE CENTER (O, 83 beds) 5500 East Kellogg, Wichita, KS Zip 67218; tel. 316/685–2221; Kent D. Hill, Director

KENTUCKY: VETERANS AFFAIRS MEDICAL CENTER–LEXINGTON (O, 467 beds) 2250 Leestown Pike, Lexington, KY Zip 40511–1093; tel. 606/233–4511; Helen K. Cornish, Director

VETERANS AFFAIRS MEDICAL CENTER–LOUISVILLE (O, 168 beds) 800 Zorn Avenue, Louisville, KY Zip 40206–1499; tel. 502/895–3401; Larry J. Sander, FACHE, Director

LOUISIANA: OVERTON BROOKS VETERANS AFFAIRS MEDICAL CENTER (O, 123 beds) 510 East Stoner Avenue, Shreveport, LA Zip 71101–4295; tel. 318/221–8411; Billy M. Valentine, Director

VETERANS AFFAIRS MEDICAL CENTER (O, 308 beds) Shreveport Highway, Alexandria, LA Zip 71306–6002; tel. 318/473–0010; Allan S. Goss, Director

VETERANS AFFAIRS MEDICAL CENTER (O, 243 beds) 1601 Perdido Street, New Orleans, LA Zip 70146–1262; tel. 504/568–0811; John D. Church Jr., Director

MAINE: VETERANS AFFAIRS MEDICAL CENTER (O, 206 beds) 1 VA Center, Togus, ME Zip 04330; tel. 207/623–8411; John H. Sims Jr., Director

MARYLAND: VA MARYLAND HEALTH CARE SYSTEM–FORT HOWARD DIVISION (O, 245 beds) 9600 North Point Road, Fort Howard, MD Zip 21052–9989; tel. 410/477–1800; Dennis H. Smith, Director

VETERANS AFFAIRS MARYLAND HEALTH CARE SYSTEM–BALTIMORE DIVISION (O, 897 beds) 10 North Greene Street, Baltimore, MD Zip 21201–1524; tel. 410/605–7001; Dennis H. Smith, Director

VETERANS AFFAIRS MARYLAND HEALTH CARE SYSTEM–PERRY POINT DIVISION (O, 526 beds) Circle Drive, Perry Point, MD Zip 21902; tel. 410/642–2411; Dennis H. Smith, Director

MASSACHUSETTS: BROCKTON–WEST ROXBURY VETERANS AFFAIRS MEDICAL CENTER (O, 765 beds) 940 Belmont Street, Brockton, MA Zip 02401–5596; tel. 508/583–4500; Michael M. Lawson, Director

EDITH NOURSE ROGERS MEMORIAL VETERANS HOSPITAL (O, 608 beds) 200 Springs Road, Bedford, MA Zip 01730–1198; tel. 781/687–2000; William A. Conte, Director

VETERANS AFFAIRS MEDICAL CENTER (O, 324 beds) Boston, MA Mailing Address: 150 South Huntington Avenue, Jamaica Plain Station, Zip 02130–4820; tel. 617/232–9500; Elwood J. Headley, M.D., Director

VETERANS AFFAIRS MEDICAL CENTER (O, 167 beds) 421 North Main Street, Leeds, MA Zip 01053–9764; tel. 413/584–4040; Robert McNamara, Director

MICHIGAN: ALEDA E. LUTZ VETERANS AFFAIRS MEDICAL CENTER (O, 149 beds) 1500 Weiss Street, Saginaw, MI Zip 48602–5298; tel. 517/793–2340; Robert H. Sabin, Medical Center Director

JOHN D. DINGELL VETERANS AFFAIRS MEDICAL CENTER (O, 271 beds) 4646 John R. Street, Detroit, MI Zip 48201–1932; tel. 313/576–1000; Carlos B. Lott Jr., Director

VETERANS AFFAIRS MEDICAL CENTER (O, 203 beds) 2215 Fuller Road, Ann Arbor, MI Zip 48105–2399; tel. 734/769–7100; James W. Roseborough, CHE, Director

VETERANS AFFAIRS MEDICAL CENTER (O, 485 beds) 5500 Armstrong Road, Battle Creek, MI Zip 49016; tel. 616/966–5600; Michael K. Wheeler, Director

VETERANS AFFAIRS MEDICAL CENTER (O, 63 beds) 325 East H. Street, Iron Mountain, MI Zip 49801–4792; tel. 906/774–3300; Thomas B. Arnold, Director

MINNESOTA: VETERANS AFFAIRS MEDICAL CENTER (O, 471 beds) One Veterans Drive, Minneapolis, MN Zip 55417–2399; tel. 612/725–2000; Charles A. Milbrandt, Director

VETERANS AFFAIRS MEDICAL CENTER (O, 408 beds) 4801 Eighth Street North, Saint Cloud, MN Zip 56303–2099; tel. 320/252–1670; Barry I. Bahl, Associate Director

MISSISSIPPI: G.V. MONTGOMERY VETERANS AFFAIRS MEDICAL CENTER (O, 443 beds) 1500 East Woodrow Wilson Drive, Jackson, MS Zip 39216–5199; tel. 601/364–1201; Richard P. Miller, Director

VETERANS AFFAIRS MEDICAL CENTER (O, 510 beds) 400 Veterans Avenue, Biloxi, MS Zip 39531–2410; tel. 228/388–5541; Julie A. Catellier, Director

MISSOURI: HARRY S. TRUMAN MEMORIAL VETERANS HOSPITAL (O, 131 beds) 800 Hospital Drive, Columbia, MO Zip 65201–5297; tel. 573/814–6300; Gary L. Campbell, Director

JOHN J. PERSHING VETERANS AFFAIRS MEDICAL CENTER (O, 62 beds) 1500 North Westwood Boulevard, Poplar Bluff, MO Zip 63901–3318; tel. 573/686–4151; Nancy Arnold, Acting Director

VETERANS AFFAIRS MEDICAL CENTER (O, 383 beds) 1 Jefferson Barracks Drive, Saint Louis, MO Zip 63125–4199; tel. 314/652–4100; Linda Kurz, Acting Director

VETERANS AFFAIRS MEDICAL CENTER (O, 165 beds) 4801 Linwood Boulevard, Kansas City, MO Zip 64128–2295; tel. 816/861–4700; Hugh F. Doran, Director

MONTANA: VETERANS AFFAIRS HOSPITAL (O, 50 beds) Fort Harrison, MT Zip 59636; tel. 406/442–6410; Joseph Underkofler, Director

NEBRASKA: VETERANS AFFAIRS GREATER NEBRASKA HEALTH CARE SYSTEM (O, 147 beds) 600 South 70th Street, Lincoln, NE Zip 68510–2493; tel. 402/489–3802; David Asper, Director

VETERANS AFFAIRS MEDICAL CENTER (O, 122 beds) 4101 Woolworth Avenue, Omaha, NE Zip 68105–1873; tel. 402/449–0600; John J. Phillips, Director

For explanation of codes following names, see page B2.
★ Indicates Type III membership in the American Hospital Association.

NEVADA: IOANNIS A. LOUGARIS VETERANS AFFAIRS MEDICAL CENTER (O, 167 beds) 1000 Locust Street, Reno, NV Zip 89520–0111; tel. 702/786–7200; Gary R. Whitfield, Director

NEW HAMPSHIRE: VETERANS AFFAIRS MEDICAL CENTER (O, 157 beds) 718 Smyth Road, Manchester, NH Zip 03104–4098; tel. 603/624–4366; Paul J. McCool, Director

NEW JERSEY: VETERANS AFFAIRS NEW JERSEY HEALTH CARE SYSTEM (O, 1702 beds) 385 Tremont Avenue, East Orange, NJ Zip 07018–1095; tel. 973/676–1000; Kenneth H. Mizrach, Director

NEW MEXICO: VETERANS AFFAIRS MEDICAL CENTER (O, 261 beds) 1501 San Pedro S.E., Albuquerque, NM Zip 87108–5138; tel. 505/265–1711; Norman E. Browne, Director

NEW YORK: VETERAN AFFAIRS HUDSON VALLEY HEALTH CARE SYSTEM–CASTLE POINT DIVISION (O, 233 beds) Castle Point, NY Mailing Address: P.O. Box 100, Montrose, Zip 10548–0100; tel. 914/831–2000; William D. Montague, Acting Medical Center Director

VETERANS AFFAIRS HUDSON VALLEY HEALTH CARE SYSTEM–F.D. ROOSEVELT HOSPITAL (O, 550 beds) Montrose, NY Mailing Address: P.O. Box 100, Zip 10548–0100; tel. 914/737–4400; Michael A. Sabo, Director

VETERANS AFFAIRS MEDICAL CENTER (O, 154 beds) 113 Holland Avenue, Albany, NY Zip 12208–3473; tel. 518/462–3311; Lawrence H. Flesh, M.D., Director

VETERANS AFFAIRS MEDICAL CENTER (O, 615 beds) 76 Veterans Avenue, Bath, NY Zip 14810–0842; tel. 607/776–2111; Michael J. Sullivan, Director

VETERANS AFFAIRS MEDICAL CENTER (O, 496 beds) 800 Poly Place, Brooklyn, NY Zip 11209–7104; tel. 718/630–3500; Michael A. Sabo, Medical Director

VETERANS AFFAIRS MEDICAL CENTER (O, 488 beds) 400 Fort Hill Avenue, Canandaigua, NY Zip 14424–1197; tel. 716/396–3601; Stuart C. Collyer, Director

VETERANS AFFAIRS MEDICAL CENTER (O, 367 beds) 130 West Kingsbridge Road, Bronx, NY Zip 10468–3992; tel. 718/584–9000; Maryann Musumeci, Director

VETERANS AFFAIRS MEDICAL CENTER (O, 257 beds) 423 East 23rd Street, New York, NY Zip 10010–5050; tel. 212/686–7500; John J. Donnellan Jr., Director

VETERANS AFFAIRS MEDICAL CENTER (O, 489 beds) 79 Middleville Road, Northport, NY Zip 11768–2293; tel. 516/261–4400; Mary A. Dowling, Director

VETERANS AFFAIRS MEDICAL CENTER (O, 204 beds) 800 Irving Avenue, Syracuse, NY Zip 13210–2796; tel. 315/476–7461; Philip P. Thomas, Director

VETERANS AFFAIRS WESTERN NEW YORK HEALTHCARE SYSTEM–BATAVIA DIVISION (O, 158 beds) 222 Richmond Avenue, Batavia, NY Zip 14020–1288; tel. 716/343–7500; Richard S. Droske, Director

VETERANS AFFAIRS WESTERN NEW YORK HEALTHCARE SYSTEM–BUFFALO DIVISION (O, 388 beds) 3495 Bailey Avenue, Buffalo, NY Zip 14215–1129; tel. 716/834–9200; William F. Feeley, Acting Director

NORTH CAROLINA: VETERANS AFFAIRS MEDICAL CENTER (O, 330 beds) 508 Fulton Street, Durham, NC Zip 27705–3897; tel. 919/286–0411; Michael B. Phaup, Director

VETERANS AFFAIRS MEDICAL CENTER (O, 193 beds) 2300 Ramsey Street, Fayetteville, NC Zip 28301–3899; tel. 910/822–7059; Richard J. Baltz, Director

VETERANS AFFAIRS MEDICAL CENTER (O, 365 beds) 1100 Tunnel Road, Asheville, NC Zip 28805–2087; tel. 704/298–7911; James A. Christian, Director

VETERANS AFFAIRS MEDICAL CENTER (O, 612 beds) 1601 Brenner Avenue, Salisbury, NC Zip 28144–2559; tel. 704/638–9000; Betty Bolin Brown, Ed.D., Acting Director

NORTH DAKOTA: VETERANS AFFAIRS MEDICAL AND REGIONAL OFFICE CENTER (O, 125 beds) 2101 Elm Street, Fargo, ND Zip 58102–2498; tel. 701/232–3241; Douglas M. Kenyon, Director

OHIO: VETERANS AFFAIRS MEDICAL CENTER (O, 817 beds) 10701 East Boulevard, Cleveland, OH Zip 44106–1702; tel. 216/791–3800; Richard S. Citron, Acting Director

VETERANS AFFAIRS MEDICAL CENTER (O, 334 beds) 17273 State Route 104, Chillicothe, OH Zip 45601–0999; tel. 740/773–1141; Michael W. Walton, Director

VETERANS AFFAIRS MEDICAL CENTER (O, 250 beds) 3200 Vine Street, Cincinnati, OH Zip 45220–2288; tel. 513/475–6300; Gary N. Nugent, Medical Director

VETERANS AFFAIRS MEDICAL CENTER (O, 651 beds) 4100 West Third Street, Dayton, OH Zip 45428–1002; tel. 937/268–6511; Steven M. Cohen, M.D., Director

OKLAHOMA: VETERANS AFFAIRS MEDICAL CENTER (O, 99 beds) 1011 Honor Heights Drive, Muskogee, OK Zip 74401–1399; tel. 918/683–3261; Allen J. Colston, Acting Director

VETERANS AFFAIRS MEDICAL CENTER (O, 208 beds) 921 N.E. 13th Street, Oklahoma City, OK Zip 73104–5028; tel. 405/270–0501; Steven J. Gentling, Director

OREGON: VETERANS AFFAIRS MEDICAL CENTER (O, 314 beds) 3710 S.W. U.S. Veterans Hospital Road, Portland, OR Zip 97201; tel. 503/220–8262; Michael E. Bays, Acting Chief Executive Officer

VETERANS AFFAIRS ROSEBURG HEALTHCARE SYSTEM (O, 229 beds) 913 N.W. Garden Valley Boulevard, Roseburg, OR Zip 97470–6513; tel. 541/440–1000; Alan S. Perry, Director

PENNSYLVANIA: JAMES E. VAN ZANDT VETERANS AFFAIRS MEDICAL CENTER (O, 78 beds) 2907 Pleasant Valley Boulevard, Altoona, PA Zip 16602–4377; tel. 814/943–8164; Gerald L. Williams, Director and Chief Executive Officer

VETERANS AFFAIRS MEDICAL CENTER (O, 200 beds) 325 New Castle Road, Butler, PA Zip 16001–2480; tel. 724/287–4781; Michael E. Moreland, Director

VETERANS AFFAIRS MEDICAL CENTER (O, 710 beds) 1400 Black Horse Hill Road, Coatesville, PA Zip 19320–2097; tel. 610/384–7711; Gary W. Devansky, Chief Executive Officer

VETERANS AFFAIRS MEDICAL CENTER (O, 74 beds) 135 East 38th Street, Erie, PA Zip 16504–1559; tel. 814/868–6210; Stephen M. Lucas, Chief Executive Officer

VETERANS AFFAIRS MEDICAL CENTER (O, 369 beds) 1700 South Lincoln Avenue, Lebanon, PA Zip 17042–7529; tel. 717/272–6621; Leonard Washington Jr., Director

VETERANS AFFAIRS MEDICAL CENTER (O, 656 beds) University and Woodland Avenues, Philadelphia, PA Zip 19104–4594; tel. 215/823–5800; Earl F. Falast, Chief Executive Officer

VETERANS AFFAIRS MEDICAL CENTER (O, 315 beds) 1111 East End Boulevard, Wilkes–Barre, PA Zip 18711–0026; tel. 717/824–3521; Reedes Hurt, Chief Executive Officer

VETERANS AFFAIRS PITTSBURGH HEALTHCARE SYSTEM (O, 941 beds) Delafield Road, Pittsburgh, PA Zip 15240–1001; tel. 412/784–3900; Thomas A. Cappello, Director

PUERTO RICO: VETERANS AFFAIRS MEDICAL CENTER (O, 693 beds) One Veterans Plaza, San Juan, PR Zip 00927–5800; tel. 787/766–5665; James A. Palmer, Director

RHODE ISLAND: VETERANS AFFAIRS MEDICAL CENTER (O, 78 beds) 830 Chalkstone Avenue, Providence, RI Zip 02908–4799; tel. 401/457–3042; Edward H. Seiler, Director

SOUTH CAROLINA: VETERANS AFFAIRS MEDICAL CENTER (O, 105 beds) 109 Bee Street, Charleston, SC Zip 29401–5703; tel. 803/577–5011; Dean S. Billik, Director

WILLIAM JENNINGS BRYAN DORN VETERANS HOSPITAL (O, 342 beds) 6439 Garners Ferry Road, Columbia, SC Zip 29209–1639; tel. 803/776–4000; Brian Heckert, Director

SOUTH DAKOTA: ROYAL C. JOHNSON VETERANS MEMORIAL HOSPITAL (O, 131 beds) 2501 West 22nd Street, Sioux Falls, SD Zip 57105–1394, Mailing Address: P.O. Box 5046, Zip 57117–5046; tel. 605/336–3230; R. Vincent Crawford, Director

VETERANS AFFAIRS BLACK HILLS HEALTH CARE SYSTEM (O, 181 beds) 113 Comanche Road, Fort Meade, SD Zip 57741–1099; tel. 605/347–2511; Peter P. Henry, Director

TENNESSEE: ALVIN C. YORK VETERANS AFFAIRS MEDICAL CENTER (O, 503 beds) 3400 Lebanon Pike, Murfreesboro, TN Zip 37129–1236; tel. 615/893–1360; R. Eugene Konik, Director

For explanation of codes following names, see page B2.
★ Indicates Type III membership in the American Hospital Association.

JAMES H. QUILLEN VETERANS AFFAIRS MEDICAL CENTER (O, 388 beds) Mountain Home, TN Zip 37684–4000; tel. 423/926–1171; Carl J. Gerber, M.D., Ph.D., Director

VETERANS AFFAIRS MEDICAL CENTER (O, 376 beds) 1030 Jefferson Avenue, Memphis, TN Zip 38104–2193; tel. 901/523–8990; K. L. Mulholland Jr., Director

VETERANS AFFAIRS MEDICAL CENTER (O, 189 beds) 1310 24th Avenue South, Nashville, TN Zip 37212–2637; tel. 615/327–5332; William A. Mountcastle, Director

TEXAS: CENTRAL TEXAS VETERANS AFFAIRS HEALTHCARE SYSTEM (O, 1852 beds) 1901 South First Street, Temple, TX Zip 76504–7493; tel. 254/778–4811; Dean Billick, Director

SAM RAYBURN MEMORIAL VETERANS CENTER (O, 374 beds) 1201 East Ninth Street, Bonham, TX Zip 75418–4091; tel. 903/583–2111; Charles C. Freeman, Director

SOUTH TEXAS VETERANS HEALTH CARE SYSTEM (O, 1112 beds) 7400 Merton Minter Boulevard, San Antonio, TX Zip 78284–5799; tel. 210/617–5140; Jose R. Coronado, FACHE, Director

VETERANS AFFAIRS MEDICAL CENTER (O, 218 beds) 6010 Amarillo Boulevard West, Amarillo, TX Zip 79106–1992; tel. 806/354–7801; Wallace M. Hopkins, FACHE, Director

VETERANS AFFAIRS MEDICAL CENTER (O, 189 beds) 300 Veterans Boulevard, Big Spring, TX Zip 79720–5500; tel. 915/263–7361; Cary D. Brown, Director

VETERANS AFFAIRS MEDICAL CENTER (O, 859 beds) 2002 Holcombe Boulevard, Houston, TX Zip 77030–4298; tel. 713/791–1414; David Whatley, Director

VETERANS AFFAIRS NORTH TEXAS HEALTH CARE SYSTEM (O, 557 beds) 4500 South Lancaster Road, Dallas, TX Zip 75216–7167; tel. 214/376–5451; Alan G. Harper, Director

UTAH: VETERANS AFFAIRS MEDICAL CENTER (O, 180 beds) 500 Foothill Drive, Salt Lake City, UT Zip 84148–0002; tel. 801/582–1565; James R. Floyd, Medical Center Director

VERMONT: VETERANS AFFAIRS MEDICAL CENTER (O, 60 beds) North Hartland Road, White River Junction, VT Zip 05009–0001; tel. 802/295–9363; Gary M. De Gasta, Director

VIRGINIA: HUNTER HOLMES MCGUIRE VETERANS AFFAIRS MEDICAL CENTER (O, 616 beds) 1201 Broad Rock Boulevard, Richmond, VA Zip 23249–0002; tel. 804/675–5000; James W. Dudley, Director

VETERANS AFFAIRS MEDICAL CENTER (O, 670 beds) 100 Emancipation Drive, Hampton, VA Zip 23667–0001; tel. 757/722–9961; William G. Wright, Director

VETERANS AFFAIRS MEDICAL CENTER (O, 313 beds) 1970 Roanoke Boulevard, Salem, VA Zip 24153; tel. 540/982–2463; Stephen L. Lemons, Ed.D., Director

WASHINGTON: JONATHAN M. WAINWRIGHT MEMORIAL VETERANS AFFAIRS MEDICAL CENTER (O, 76 beds) 77 Wainwright Drive, Walla Walla, WA Zip 99362–3994; tel. 509/525–5200; George Marnell, Director

VETERANS AFFAIRS MEDICAL CENTER (O, 192 beds) North 4815 Assembly Street, Spokane, WA Zip 99205–6197; tel. 509/327–0200; Joseph M. Manley, Director

VETERANS AFFAIRS PUGET SOUND HEALTH CARE SYSTEM (O, 557 beds) 1660 South Columbian Way, Seattle, WA Zip 98108–1597; tel. 206/762–1010; Timothy B. Williams, Director

WEST VIRGINIA: LOUIS A. JOHNSON VETERANS AFFAIRS MEDICAL CENTER (O, 160 beds) 1 Medical Center Drive, Clarksburg, WV Zip 26301–4199; tel. 304/623–3461; Michael W. Neusch, FACHE, Director

VETERANS AFFAIRS MEDICAL CENTER (O, 112 beds) 200 Veterans Avenue, Beckley, WV Zip 25801–6499; tel. 304/255–2121; Gerard P. Husson, Director

VETERANS AFFAIRS MEDICAL CENTER (O, 170 beds) 1540 Spring Valley Drive, Huntington, WV Zip 25704–9300; tel. 304/429–6741; David N. Pennington, Chief Executive Officer

VETERANS AFFAIRS MEDICAL CENTER (O, 370 beds) Charles Town Road, Martinsburg, WV Zip 25401–0205; tel. 304/263–0811; Francis Citro Jr., M.D., Acting Director

WISCONSIN: CLEMENT J. ZABLOCKI VETERANS AFFAIRS MEDICAL CENTER (O, 566 beds) 5000 West National Avenue, Milwaukee, WI Zip 53295; tel. 414/384–2000; Glen W. Grippen, Director

VETERANS AFFAIRS MEDICAL CENTER (O, 569 beds) 500 East Veterans Street, Tomah, WI Zip 54660; tel. 608/372–3971; Stan Johnson, Medical Center Director

WILLIAM S. MIDDLETON MEMORIAL VETERANS HOSPITAL (O, 200 beds) 2500 Overlook Terrace, Madison, WI Zip 53705–2286; tel. 608/256–1901; Nathan L. Geraths, Director

WYOMING: VETERANS AFFAIRS MEDICAL CENTER (O, 125 beds) 2360 East Pershing Boulevard, Cheyenne, WY Zip 82001–5392; tel. 307/778–7550; Richard Fry, Acting Director

VETERANS AFFAIRS MEDICAL CENTER (O, 204 beds) 1898 Fort Road, Sheridan, WY Zip 82801–8320; tel. 307/672–3473; Maureen Humphrey, Director

Owned, leased, sponsored:	144 hospitals	53315 beds
Contract–managed:	0 hospitals	0 beds
Totals:	144 hospitals	53315 beds

★2145: DETROIT MEDICAL CENTER (NP)
3663 Woodward Avenue, Suite 200, Detroit, MI Zip 48201–2403; tel. 313/578–2020; David J. Campbell, President and Chief Executive Officer

MICHIGAN: CHILDREN'S HOSPITAL OF MICHIGAN (O, 245 beds) 3901 Beaubien Street, Detroit, MI Zip 48201–9985; tel. 313/745–0073; Thomas M. Rozek, Senior Vice President

DETROIT RECEIVING HOSPITAL AND UNIVERSITY HEALTH CENTER (O, 278 beds) 4201 St. Antoine Boulevard, Detroit, MI Zip 48201–2194; tel. 313/745–3605; Leslie C. Bowman, Regional Administrator, Ancillary Services and Site Administrator

GRACE HOSPITAL (O, 343 beds) 6071 West Outer Drive, Detroit, MI Zip 48235–2679; tel. 313/966–3525; Anne M. Regling, Regional Executive

HARPER HOSPITAL (O, 444 beds) 3990 John R., Detroit, MI Zip 48201–9027; tel. 313/745–8040; Paul L. Broughton, FACHE, Senior Vice President

HURON VALLEY–SINAI HOSPITAL (O, 140 beds) 1 William Carls Drive, Commerce Township, MI Zip 48382–1272; tel. 248/360–3300; Paul L. Broughton, FACHE, Senior Vice President

HUTZEL HOSPITAL (O, 243 beds) 4707 St. Antoine Boulevard, Detroit, MI Zip 48201–0154; tel. 313/745–7555; Phyllis Reynolds, R.N., Site Administrator

REHABILITATION INSTITUTE OF MICHIGAN (O, 96 beds) 261 Mack Boulevard, Detroit, MI Zip 48201–2495; tel. 313/745–1203; Bruce M. Gans, M.D., Senior Vice President

SINAI HOSPITAL (O, 446 beds) 6767 West Outer Drive, Detroit, MI Zip 48235–2899; tel. 313/493–6800; William Pinsky, M.D., Senior Vice President and Regional Executive

Owned, leased, sponsored:	8 hospitals	2235 beds
Contract–managed:	0 hospitals	0 beds
Totals:	8 hospitals	2235 beds

0845: DEVEREUX FOUNDATION (NP)
444 Deveraux Drive, Villanova, PA Zip 19085, Mailing Address: P.O. Box 400, Devon, Zip 19333–0400; tel. 610/520–3000; Ronald P. Burd, President and Chief Executive Officer

FLORIDA: DEVEREUX HOSPITAL AND CHILDREN'S CENTER OF FLORIDA (O, 100 beds) 8000 Devereux Drive, Melbourne, FL Zip 32940–7907; tel. 407/242–9100; James E. Colvin, Executive Director

GEORGIA: DEVEREUX GEORGIA TREATMENT NETWORK (O, 115 beds) 1291 Stanley Road N.W., Kennesaw, GA Zip 30152–4359; tel. 770/427–0147; Elizabeth M. Chadwick, JD, Executive Director

PENNSYLVANIA: DEVEREUX MAPLETON PSYCHIATRIC INSTITUTE–MAPLETON CENTER (O, 13 beds) 655 Sugartown Road, Malvern, PA Zip 19355–0297, Mailing Address: Box 297, Zip 19355–0297; tel. 610/296–6923; Richard Warden, Executive Director

For explanation of codes following names, see page B2.
★ Indicates Type III membership in the American Hospital Association.

Section B

TEXAS: DEVEREUX TEXAS TREATMENT NETWORK (O, 88 beds) 1150 Devereux Drive, League City, TX Zip 77573–2043; tel. 713/335–1000; L. Gail Atkinson, Executive Director

Owned, leased, sponsored:	4 hospitals	316 beds
Contract–managed:	0 hospitals	0 beds
Totals:	4 hospitals	316 beds

★**0029: DIMENSIONS HEALTH CORPORATION** (NP)
9200 Basil Court, Largo, MD Zip 20785; tel. 301/925–7000; Winfield M. Kelly Jr., President and Chief Executive Officer

MARYLAND: LAUREL REGIONAL HOSPITAL (O, 185 beds) 7300 Van Dusen Road, Laurel, MD Zip 20707–9266; tel. 301/725–4300; Patrick F. Mutch, President

PRINCE GEORGE'S HOSPITAL CENTER (O, 370 beds) 3001 Hospital Drive, Cheverly, MD Zip 20785–1189; tel. 301/618–2000; Allan Earl Atzrott, President

Owned, leased, sponsored:	2 hospitals	555 beds
Contract–managed:	0 hospitals	0 beds
Totals:	2 hospitals	555 beds

0010: DIVISION OF MENTAL HEALTH SERVICES, DEPARTMENT OF HUMAN SERVICES, STATE OF NEW JERSEY (NP)
Capital Center, P.O. Box 727, Trenton, NJ Zip 08625–0727; tel. 609/777–0702; Alan G. Kaufman, Director

NEW JERSEY: ANCORA PSYCHIATRIC HOSPITAL (O, 625 beds) 202 Spring Garden Road, Ancora, NJ Zip 08037–9699; tel. 609/561–1700; Yvonne A. Pressley, Chief Executive Officer

GREYSTONE PARK PSYCHIATRIC HOSPITAL (O, 605 beds) Central Avenue, Greystone Park, NJ Zip 07950, Mailing Address: P.O. Box A., Zip 07950; tel. 973/538–1800; Michael Greenstein, Chief Executive Officer

SENATOR GARRET T. W. HAGEDORN GERO PSYCHIATRIC HOSPITAL (O, 181 beds) 200 Sanitorium Road, Glen Gardner, NJ Zip 08826–9752; tel. 908/537–2141; Edna Volpe–Way, Chief Executive Officer

TRENTON PSYCHIATRIC HOSPITAL (O, 379 beds) Sullivan Way, Trenton, NJ Zip 08625, Mailing Address: P.O. Box 7500, West Trenton, Zip 08628–7500; tel. 609/633–1500; Joseph Jupin Jr., Chief Executive Officer

Owned, leased, sponsored:	4 hospitals	1790 beds
Contract–managed:	0 hospitals	0 beds
Totals:	4 hospitals	1790 beds

1045: DOCTORS HOSPITAL (NP)
1087 Dennison Avenue, Columbus, OH Zip 43201–3496; tel. 614/297–4000; Richard A. Vincent, President

OHIO: DOCTORS HOSPITAL (O, 337 beds) 1087 Dennison Avenue, Columbus, OH Zip 43201–3496; tel. 614/297–4000; Richard A. Vincent, President

DOCTORS HOSPITAL OF NELSONVILLE (O, 70 beds) 1950 Mount Saint Mary Drive, Nelsonville, OH Zip 45764–1193; tel. 614/753–1931; Mark R. Seckinger, Administrator

Owned, leased, sponsored:	2 hospitals	407 beds
Contract–managed:	0 hospitals	0 beds
Totals:	2 hospitals	407 beds

1895: EAST TEXAS MEDICAL CENTER REGIONAL HEALTHCARE SYSTEM (NP)
1000 South Beckham Street, Tyler, TX Zip 75701–1996, Mailing Address: P.O. Box 6400, Zip 75711–6400; tel. 903/535–6211; Elmer G. Ellis, President and Chief Executive Officer

TEXAS: EAST TEXAS MEDICAL CENTER ATHENS (L, 108 beds) 2000 South Palestine Street, Athens, TX Zip 75751–5610; tel. 903/675–2216; Patrick L. Wallace, Administrator

EAST TEXAS MEDICAL CENTER CROCKETT (L, 54 beds) 1100 Loop 304 East, Crockett, TX Zip 75835–1810; tel. 409/544–2002; Nelda K. Welch, Administrator

EAST TEXAS MEDICAL CENTER PITTSBURG (L, 43 beds) 414 Quitman Street, Pittsburg, TX Zip 75686–1032; tel. 903/856–6663; W. Perry Henderson, Administrator

EAST TEXAS MEDICAL CENTER REHABILITATION CENTER (O, 49 beds) 701 Olympic Plaza Circle, Tyler, TX Zip 75701–1996; tel. 903/596–3000; Eddie L. Howard, Vice President and Chief Operating Officer

EAST TEXAS MEDICAL CENTER RUSK (L, 25 beds) 500 North Bonner Street, Rusk, TX Zip 75785, Mailing Address: P.O. Box 317, Zip 75785–0317; tel. 903/683–2273; Brenda Copley, Acting Administrator

EAST TEXAS MEDICAL CENTER TYLER (O, 351 beds) 1000 South Beckham Street, Tyler, TX Zip 75701–1996, Mailing Address: Box 6400, Zip 75711–6400; tel. 903/597–0351

EAST TEXAS MEDICAL CENTER–CLARKSVILLE (L, 36 beds) Highway 82 West, Clarksville, TX Zip 75426, Mailing Address: P.O. Box 1270, Zip 75426–1270; tel. 903/427–3851; Terry Cutler, Executive Director

EAST TEXAS MEDICAL CENTER–MOUNT VERNON (L, 30 beds) Highway 37 South, Mount Vernon, TX Zip 75457, Mailing Address: P.O. Box 477, Zip 75457–0477; tel. 903/537–4552; Jerry Edwards, CHE, Administrator

Owned, leased, sponsored:	8 hospitals	696 beds
Contract–managed:	0 hospitals	0 beds
Totals:	8 hospitals	696 beds

★**0100: EASTERN HEALTH SYSTEM, INC.** (NP)
48 Medical Park East Drive, 450, Birmingham, AL Zip 35235; tel. 205/838–3999; Robert C. Chapman, FACHE, President and Chief Executive Officer

ALABAMA: BLOUNT MEMORIAL HOSPITAL (L, 57 beds) 1000 Lincoln Avenue, Oneonta, AL Zip 35121–2534, Mailing Address: P.O. Box 1000, Zip 35121–1000; tel. 205/625–3511; George McGowan, FACHE, Chief Executive Officer

MEDICAL CENTER EAST (O, 282 beds) 50 Medical Park East Drive, Birmingham, AL Zip 35235–9987; tel. 205/838–3000; David E. Crawford, FACHE, Executive Vice President and Chief Operating Officer

ST. CLAIR REGIONAL HOSPITAL (C, 51 beds) 2805 Hospital Drive, Pell City, AL Zip 35125–1499; tel. 205/338–3301; Douglas H. Beverly, CHE, Chief Operating Officer

Owned, leased, sponsored:	2 hospitals	339 beds
Contract–managed:	1 hospital	51 beds
Totals:	3 hospitals	390 beds

★**0555: EASTERN MAINE HEALTHCARE** (NP)
489 State Street, Bangor, ME Zip 04401–6674, Mailing Address: P.O. Box 404, Zip 04402–0404; tel. 207/973–7051; Norman A. Ledwin, President

MAINE: ACADIA HOSPITAL (O, 72 beds) 268 Stillwater Avenue, Bangor, ME Zip 04401–3945, Mailing Address: P.O. Box 422, Zip 04402–0422; tel. 207/973–6100; Dennis P. King, President

EASTERN MAINE MEDICAL CENTER (O, 344 beds) 489 State Street, Bangor, ME Zip 04401–6674, Mailing Address: P.O. Box 404, Zip 04402–0404; tel. 207/973–7000; Norman A. Ledwin, President and Chief Executive Officer

INLAND HOSPITAL (O, 44 beds) 200 Kennedy Memorial Drive, Waterville, ME Zip 04901–4595; tel. 207/861–3000; Wilfred J. Addison, President and Chief Executive Officer

Owned, leased, sponsored:	3 hospitals	460 beds
Contract–managed:	0 hospitals	0 beds
Totals:	3 hospitals	460 beds

0945: EMPIRE HEALTH SERVICES (NP)
West 800 Fifth Avenue, Spokane, WA Zip 99204, Mailing Address: P.O. Box 248, Zip 99210–0248; tel. 509/458–7960; Thomas M. White, President

WASHINGTON: DEACONESS MEDICAL CENTER–SPOKANE (O, 388 beds) 800 West Fifth Avenue, Spokane, WA Zip 99204, Mailing Address: P.O. Box 248, Zip 99210–0248; tel. 509/458–5800; Thomas J. Zellers, Chief Operating Officer

For explanation of codes following names, see page B2.
★ Indicates Type III membership in the American Hospital Association.

VALLEY HOSPITAL AND MEDICAL CENTER (O, 117 beds) 12606 East Mission Avenue, Spokane, WA Zip 99216–9969; tel. 509/924–6650; Michael T. Liepman, Chief Operating Officer

Owned, leased, sponsored:	2 hospitals	505 beds
Contract–managed:	0 hospitals	0 beds
Totals:	2 hospitals	505 beds

★0735: **EPISCOPAL HEALTH SERVICES INC.** (CO)
333 Earle Ovington Boulevard, Uniondale, NY Zip 11553–3645; tel. 516/228–6100; Jack N. Farrington, Ph.D., Executive Vice President

NEW YORK: ST. JOHN'S EPISCOPAL HOSPITAL–SMITHTOWN (O, 366 beds) 50 Route 25–A, Smithtown, NY Zip 11787–1398; tel. 516/862–3000; Laura Righter, Regional Administrator

ST. JOHN'S EPISCOPAL HOSPITAL–SOUTH SHORE (O, 314 beds) 327 Beach 19th Street, Far Rockaway, NY Zip 11691–4424; tel. 718/869–7000; Paul J. Connor III, Administrator

Owned, leased, sponsored:	2 hospitals	680 beds
Contract–managed:	0 hospitals	0 beds
Totals:	2 hospitals	680 beds

1255: **ESCAMBIA COUNTY HEALTH CARE AUTHORITY** (NP)
1301 Belleville Avenue, Brewton, AL Zip 36426; tel. 334/368–2500; Phillip L. Parker, Administrator

ALABAMA: ATMORE COMMUNITY HOSPITAL (O, 51 beds) 401 Medical Park Drive, Atmore, AL Zip 36502–3091; tel. 334/368–2500; Robert E. Gowing, Interim Administrator

D. W. MCMILLAN MEMORIAL HOSPITAL (O, 60 beds) 1301 Belleville Avenue, Brewton, AL Zip 36426–1306, Mailing Address: P.O. Box 908, Zip 36427–0908; tel. 334/867–8061; Phillip L. Parker, Administrator

Owned, leased, sponsored:	2 hospitals	111 beds
Contract–managed:	0 hospitals	0 beds
Totals:	2 hospitals	111 beds

★0134: **EXEMPLA HEALTHCARE, INC.** (NP)
600 Grant Street, Suite 700, Denver, CO Zip 80203; tel. 303/813–5000; Jeffrey D. Selberg, President and Chief Executive Officer

COLORADO: EXEMPLA LUTHERAN MEDICAL CENTER (O, 472 beds) 8300 West 38th Avenue, Wheat Ridge, CO Zip 80033–6005; tel. 303/425–4500; Jeffrey D. Selberg, President and Chief Executive Officer

EXEMPLA SAINT JOSEPH HOSPITAL (O, 394 beds) 1835 Franklin Street, Denver, CO Zip 80218–1191; tel. 303/837–7111; David Hamm, Interim Chief Executive Officer

Owned, leased, sponsored:	2 hospitals	866 beds
Contract–managed:	0 hospitals	0 beds
Totals:	2 hospitals	866 beds

★1325: **FAIRVIEW HOSPITAL AND HEALTHCARE SERVICES** (NP)
2450 Riverside Avenue, Minneapolis, MN Zip 55454–1400; tel. 612/672–6300; David R. Page, President and Chief Executive Officer

MINNESOTA: FAIRVIEW LAKES REGIONAL MEDICAL CENTER (O, 38 beds) 5200 Fairview Boulevard, Wyoming, MN Zip 55092–8013; tel. 612/982–7000; Daniel K. Anderson, Senior Vice President and Administrtor

FAIRVIEW NORTHLAND REGIONAL HEALTH CARE (O, 41 beds) 911 Northland Drive, Princeton, MN Zip 55371–2173; tel. 612/389–6300; Jeanne Lally, Senior Vice President and Administrator

FAIRVIEW RED WING HOSPITAL (O, 68 beds) 1407 West Fourth Street, Red Wing, MN Zip 55066–2198; tel. 612/388–6721; Craig Stockel, Interim Administrator

FAIRVIEW RIDGES HOSPITAL (O, 129 beds) 201 East Nicollet Boulevard, Burnsville, MN Zip 55337–5799; tel. 612/892–2000; Mark M. Enger, Senior Vice President and Administrator

FAIRVIEW SOUTHDALE HOSPITAL (O, 355 beds) 6401 France Avenue South, Minneapolis, MN Zip 55435–2199; tel. 612/924–5000; Mark M. Enger, Senior Vice President and Administrator

FAIRVIEW–UNIVERSITY MEDICAL CENTER (O, 1362 beds) 2450 Riverside Avenue, Minneapolis, MN Zip 55454–1400; tel. 612/626–6685; Pamela L. Tibbetts, Senior Vice President and Administrator

UNIVERSITY MEDICAL CENTER–MESABI (O, 126 beds) 750 East 34th Street, Hibbing, MN Zip 55746–4600; tel. 218/262–4881; Richard W. Dinter, Chief Operating Officer

Owned, leased, sponsored:	7 hospitals	2119 beds
Contract–managed:	0 hospitals	0 beds
Totals:	7 hospitals	2119 beds

2515: **FAIRVIEW HOSPITAL SYSTEM** (NP)
18101 Lorain Avenue, Cleveland, OH Zip 44111–5656; tel. 216/476–7000; Kenneth T. Misener, Vice President and Chief Operating Officer

OHIO: FAIRVIEW HOSPITAL (O, 397 beds) 18101 Lorain Avenue, Cleveland, OH Zip 44111–5656; tel. 216/476–4040; Thomas M. LaMotte, President and Chief Executive Officer

LUTHERAN HOSPITAL (O, 204 beds) 1730 West 25th Street, Cleveland, OH Zip 44113; tel. 216/696–4300; Jack E. Bell, Chief Operating Officer

Owned, leased, sponsored:	2 hospitals	601 beds
Contract–managed:	0 hospitals	0 beds
Totals:	2 hospitals	601 beds

2635: **FHC HEALTH SYSTEMS** (IO)
240 Corporate Boulevard, Norfolk, VA Zip 23502–4950; tel. 757/459–5100; Ronald I. Dozoretz, M.D., Chairman

PENNSYLVANIA: SOUTHWOOD PSYCHIATRIC HOSPITAL (O, 50 beds) 2575 Boyce Plaza Road, Pittsburgh, PA Zip 15241–3925; tel. 412/257–2290; Alan A. Axelson, M.D., Chief Executive Officer

PUERTO RICO: FIRST HOSPITAL PANAMERICANO (O, 165 beds) State Road 787 KM 1 5, Cidra, PR Zip 00739, Mailing Address: P.O. Box 1398, Zip 00739; tel. 787/739–5555; Jorge Torres, Executive Director

Owned, leased, sponsored:	2 hospitals	215 beds
Contract–managed:	0 hospitals	0 beds
Totals:	2 hospitals	215 beds

●1275: **FIRST HEALTH, INC.** (IO)
107 Public Square, Batesville, MS Zip 38606–2219; tel. 601/563–7676; Sandra Skinner, Chief Executive Officer

KENTUCKY: JENKINS COMMUNITY HOSPITAL (O, 60 beds) Main Street, Jenkins, KY Zip 41537–9614, Mailing Address: P.O. Box 472, Zip 41537–0472; tel. 606/832–2171; Sherrie Newcomb, Administrator

Owned, leased, sponsored:	1 hospital	60 beds
Contract–managed:	0 hospitals	0 beds
Totals:	1 hospital	60 beds

★1475: **FRANCISCAN MISSIONARIES OF OUR LADY HEALTH SYSTEM, INC.** (CC)
4200 Essen Lane, Baton Rouge, LA Zip 70809; tel. 504/923–2701; John J. Finan Jr., President and Chief Executive Officer

LOUISIANA: OUR LADY OF LOURDES REGIONAL MEDICAL CENTER (O, 280 beds) 611 St. Landry Street, Lafayette, LA Zip 70506–4697, Mailing Address: Box 4027, Zip 70502–4027; tel. 318/289–2000; Dudley Romero, President and Chief Executive Officer

OUR LADY OF THE LAKE REGIONAL MEDICAL CENTER (O, 660 beds) 5000 Hennessy Boulevard, Baton Rouge, LA Zip 70808–4350; tel. 504/765–6565; Robert C. Davidge, President and Chief Executive Officer

For explanation of codes following names, see page B2.
★ Indicates Type III membership in the American Hospital Association.
● Single hospital health care system

ST. FRANCIS MEDICAL CENTER (O, 372 beds) 309 Jackson Street, Monroe, LA Zip 71201–7498, Mailing Address: P.O. Box 1901, Zip 71210–1901; tel. 318/327–4000; H. Gerald Smith, President and Chief Executive Officer

Owned, leased, sponsored:	3 hospitals	1312 beds
Contract–managed:	0 hospitals	0 beds
Totals:	3 hospitals	1312 beds

★5375: FRANCISCAN SERVICES CORPORATION (CC)
6832 Convent Boulevard, Sylvania, OH Zip 43560–2897; tel. 419/882–8373; John W. O'Connell, President

OHIO: PROVIDENCE HOSPITAL (S, 180 beds) 1912 Hayes Avenue, Sandusky, OH Zip 44870–4736; tel. 419/621–7000; Sister Nancy Linenkugel, FACHE, President and Chief Executive Officer

TRINITY HEALTH SYSTEM (S, 347 beds) 380 Summit Avenue, Steubenville, OH Zip 43952–2699; tel. 740/283–7000; Fred B. Brower, President and Chief Executive Officer

TEXAS: BURLESON ST. JOSEPH HEALTH CENTER (S, 30 beds) 1101 Woodson Drive, Caldwell, TX Zip 77836–1052, Mailing Address: P.O. Drawer 360, Zip 77836–0360; tel. 409/567–3245; William H. Craig, President and Chief Executive Officer

MADISON ST. JOSEPH HEALTH CENTER (S, 35 beds) 100 West Cross Street, Madisonville, TX Zip 77864–0698, Mailing Address: Box 698, Zip 77864–0698; tel. 409/348–2631; James P. Gibson, President and Chief Executive Officer

ST. JOSEPH REGIONAL HEALTH CENTER (S, 237 beds) 2801 Franciscan Drive, Bryan, TX Zip 77802–2599; tel. 409/776–3777; Sister Gretchen Kunz, President and Chief Executive Officer

TRINITY COMMUNITY MEDICAL CENTER OF BRENHAM (S, 60 beds) 700 Medical Parkway, Brenham, TX Zip 77833–5498; tel. 409/836–6173; John L. Simms, President and Chief Executive Officer

Owned, leased, sponsored:	6 hospitals	889 beds
Contract–managed:	0 hospitals	0 beds
Totals:	6 hospitals	889 beds

★1455: FRANCISCAN SISTERS OF CHRISTIAN CHARITY HEALTHCARE MINISTRY, INC (CC)
1415 South Rapids Road, Manitowoc, WI Zip 54220–9302; tel. 920/684–7071; Sister Laura J. Wolf, President

NEBRASKA: ST. FRANCIS MEMORIAL HOSPITAL (O, 97 beds) 430 North Monitor Street, West Point, NE Zip 68788–1595; tel. 402/372–2404; Ronald O. Briggs, President

OHIO: GENESIS HEALTHCARE SYSTEM (O, 429 beds) 800 Forest Avenue, Zanesville, OH Zip 43701–2881; tel. 740/454–5000; Thomas L. Sieber, President and Chief Executive Officer

WISCONSIN: HOLY FAMILY MEMORIAL MEDICAL CENTER (O, 176 beds) 2300 Western Avenue, Manitowoc, WI Zip 54220, Mailing Address: P.O. Box 1450, Zip 54221–1450; tel. 920/684–2011; Daniel B. McGinty, President and Chief Executive Officer

Owned, leased, sponsored:	3 hospitals	702 beds
Contract–managed:	0 hospitals	0 beds
Totals:	3 hospitals	702 beds

★1485: FRANCISCAN SISTERS OF THE POOR HEALTH SYSTEM, INC. (CC)
8 Airport Park Boulevard, Latham, NY Zip 12110; tel. 518/783–5257; James H. Flynn Jr., President and Chief Executive Officer

KENTUCKY: OUR LADY OF BELLEFONTE HOSPITAL (S, 194 beds) St. Christopher Drive, Ashland, KY Zip 41101, Mailing Address: P.O. Box 789, Zip 41105–0789; tel. 606/833–3333; Robert J. Maher, President

NEW JERSEY: ST. FRANCIS HOSPITAL (S, 183 beds) 25 McWilliams Place, Jersey City, NJ Zip 07302–1698; tel. 201/418–1000; Robert S. Chaloner, President and Chief Executive Officer

ST. MARY HOSPITAL (S, 136 beds) 308 Willow Avenue, Hoboken, NJ Zip 07030–3889; tel. 201/418–1000; Robert S. Chaloner, President and Chief Executive Officer

NEW YORK: GOOD SAMARITAN HOSPITAL (S, 308 beds) 255 Lafayette Avenue, Suffern, NY Zip 10901–4869; tel. 914/368–5000; James A. Martin, Chief Executive Officer

MERCY COMMUNITY HOSPITAL (O, 187 beds) 160 East Main Street, Port Jervis, NY Zip 12771–2245, Mailing Address: P.O. Box 1014, Zip 12771–1014; tel. 914/856–5351; Marie T. Droege, Site Administrator

ST. ANTHONY COMMUNITY HOSPITAL (S, 73 beds) 15–19 Maple Avenue, Warwick, NY Zip 10990–5180; tel. 914/986–2276; R. Andrew Brothers, President and Chief Executive Officer

OHIO: FRANCISCAN HOSPITAL–MOUNT AIRY CAMPUS (S, 240 beds) 2446 Kipling Avenue, Cincinnati, OH Zip 45239–6650; tel. 513/853–5000; R. Christopher West, President

FRANCISCAN HOSPITAL–WESTERN HILLS CAMPUS (S, 226 beds) 3131 Queen City Avenue, Cincinnati, OH Zip 45238–2396; tel. 513/389–5000; R. Christopher West, President

FRANCISCAN MEDICAL CENTER–DAYTON CAMPUS (S, 357 beds) One Franciscan Way, Dayton, OH Zip 45408–1498; tel. 937/229–6000; Duane L. Erwin, Chief Executive Officer

Owned, leased, sponsored:	9 hospitals	1904 beds
Contract–managed:	0 hospitals	0 beds
Totals:	9 hospitals	1904 beds

★9650: FRANCISCAN SKEMP HEALTHCARE (CC)
700 West Avenue South, La Crosse, WI Zip 54601–4796; tel. 608/791–9710; Brian C. Campion, M.D., President and Chief Executive Officer

WISCONSIN: FRANCISCAN SKEMP HEALTHCARE–ARCADIA CAMPUS (O, 101 beds) 464 South St. Joseph Avenue, Arcadia, WI Zip 54612–1401; tel. 608/323–3341; Robert M. Tracey, Administrator

FRANCISCAN SKEMP HEALTHCARE–LA CROSSE CAMPUS (O, 213 beds) 700 West Avenue South, La Crosse, WI Zip 54601–4783; tel. 608/785–0940; Brian C. Campion, M.D., Chief Executive Officer

FRANCISCAN SKEMP HEALTHCARE–SPARTA CAMPUS (O, 60 beds) 310 West Main Street, Sparta, WI Zip 54656–2171; tel. 608/269–2132; William P. Sexton, Administrator

Owned, leased, sponsored:	3 hospitals	374 beds
Contract–managed:	0 hospitals	0 beds
Totals:	3 hospitals	374 beds

2115: FREMONT–RIDEOUT HEALTH GROUP (NP)
989 Plumas Street, Yuba City, CA Zip 95991; tel. 530/751–4010; Thomas P. Hayes, Chief Executive Officer

CALIFORNIA: FREMONT MEDICAL CENTER (O, 78 beds) 970 Plumas Street, Yuba City, CA Zip 95991; tel. 530/751–4000; Thomas P. Hayes, Chief Executive Officer

RIDEOUT MEMORIAL HOSPITAL (O, 97 beds) 726 Fourth Street, Marysville, CA Zip 95901–2128, Mailing Address: Box 2128, Zip 95901–2128; tel. 916/749–4300; Thomas P. Hayes, Chief Executive Officer

Owned, leased, sponsored:	2 hospitals	175 beds
Contract–managed:	0 hospitals	0 beds
Totals:	2 hospitals	175 beds

★0775: GENERAL HEALTH SYSTEM (NP)
3600 Florida Boulevard, Baton Rouge, LA Zip 70806–3854; tel. 504/387–7810; Chris W. Barnette, President and Chief Executive Officer

LOUISIANA: BATON ROUGE GENERAL HEALTH CENTER (O, 70 beds) 8585 Picardy Avenue, Baton Rouge, LA Zip 70809–3679, Mailing Address: P.O. Box 84330, Zip 70884–4330; tel. 504/763–4000; Linda Lee, Campus Administrator

For explanation of codes following names, see page B2.
★ Indicates Type III membership in the American Hospital Association.

BATON ROUGE GENERAL MEDICAL CENTER (O, 355 beds) 3600 Florida Street, Baton Rouge, LA Zip 70806–3889, Mailing Address: P.O. Box 2511, Zip 70821–2511; tel. 504/387–7770; Chris W. Barnette, President and Chief Executive Officer

VERMILION HOSPITAL (O, 54 beds) 2520 North University Avenue, Lafayette, LA Zip 70507–5306, Mailing Address: P.O. Box 91526, Zip 70509–1526; tel. 318/234–5614; John P. Patout, Administrator

Owned, leased, sponsored:	3 hospitals	479 beds
Contract–managed:	0 hospitals	0 beds
Totals:	3 hospitals	479 beds

★**0138: GEORGIA BAPTIST HEALTH CARE SYSTEM** (NP)
100 10th Street, Atlanta, GA Zip 30365; tel. 404/253–3011; David E. Harrell, Chief Executive Officer

GEORGIA: BAPTIST HOSPITAL, WORTH COUNTY (O, 50 beds) 807 South Isabella Street, Sylvester, GA Zip 31791–0545, Mailing Address: Box 545, Zip 31791–0545; tel. 912/776–6961; Billy Hayes, Administrator

BAPTIST MERIWETHER HOSPITAL (L, 105 beds) 5995 Spring Street, Warm Springs, GA Zip 31830, Mailing Address: P.O. Box 8, Zip 31830–0008; tel. 706/655–3331; William E. Daniel, Administrator

BAPTIST NORTH HOSPITAL (O, 30 beds) 133 Samaritan Drive, Cumming, GA Zip 30130, Mailing Address: P.O. Box 768, Zip 30130–0768; tel. 770/887–2355; John M. Herron, Administrator

DOOLY MEDICAL CENTER (L, 38 beds) 1300 Union Street, Vienna, GA Zip 31092–7541, Mailing Address: P.O. Box 278, Zip 31092–0278; tel. 912/268–4141; Kevin Paul, Administrator

Owned, leased, sponsored:	4 hospitals	223 beds
Contract–managed:	0 hospitals	0 beds
Totals:	4 hospitals	223 beds

★**1535: GREAT PLAINS HEALTH ALLIANCE, INC.** (NP)
625 Third Street, Phillipsburg, KS Zip 67661–2138, Mailing Address: P.O. Box 366, Zip 67661–0366; tel. 785/543–2111; Roger S. John, President and Chief Executive Officer

KANSAS: ASHLAND HEALTH CENTER (C, 48 beds) 709 Oak Street, Ashland, KS Zip 67831, Mailing Address: P.O. Box 188, Zip 67831; tel. 316/635–2241; Bryan Stacey, Administrator

CHEYENNE COUNTY HOSPITAL (L, 16 beds) 210 West First Street, Saint Francis, KS Zip 67756, Mailing Address: P.O. Box 547, Zip 67756–0547; tel. 785/332–2104; Leslie Lacy, Administrator

COMANCHE COUNTY HOSPITAL (C, 14 beds) Second and Frisco Streets, Coldwater, KS Zip 67029, Mailing Address: HC 65, Box 8A, Zip 67029; tel. 316/582–2144; Nancy Zimmerman, Administrator

ELLINWOOD DISTRICT HOSPITAL (L, 12 beds) 605 North Main Street, Ellinwood, KS Zip 67526–1440; tel. 316/564–2548; Marge Conell, R.N., Administrator

FREDONIA REGIONAL HOSPITAL (C, 42 beds) 1527 Madison Street, Fredonia, KS Zip 66736–1751, Mailing Address: P.O. Box 579, Zip 66736–0579; tel. 316/378–2121; Terry Deschaine, Chief Executive Officer

GREELEY COUNTY HOSPITAL (L, 50 beds) 506 Third Street, Tribune, KS Zip 67879, Mailing Address: P.O. Box 338, Zip 67879–0338; tel. 316/376–4221; Cynthia K. Schneider, Administrator

GRISELL MEMORIAL HOSPITAL DISTRICT ONE (C, 46 beds) 210 South Vermont, Ransom, KS Zip 67572–0268, Mailing Address: P.O. Box 268, Zip 67572–0268; tel. 785/731–2231; Kristine Ochs, R.N., Administrator

KIOWA COUNTY MEMORIAL HOSPITAL (L, 38 beds) 501 South Walnut Street, Greensburg, KS Zip 67054–1951; tel. 316/723–3341; Ronald J. Baker, Administrator

LANE COUNTY HOSPITAL (C, 31 beds) 243 South Second, Dighton, KS Zip 67839, Mailing Address: P.O. Box 969, Zip 67839–0969; tel. 316/397–5321; Donna McGowan, R.N., Administrator

LINCOLN COUNTY HOSPITAL (C, 34 beds) 624 North Second Street, Lincoln, KS Zip 67455–1738, Mailing Address: P.O. Box 406, Zip 67455–0406; tel. 913/524–4403; Jolene Yager, R.N., Administrator

MEDICINE LODGE MEMORIAL HOSPITAL (C, 42 beds) 710 North Walnut Street, Medicine Lodge, KS Zip 67104–1019, Mailing Address: P.O. Drawer C., Zip 67104; tel. 316/886–3771; Kevin A. White, Administrator

MINNEOLA DISTRICT HOSPITAL (C, 15 beds) 212 Main Street, Minneola, KS Zip 67865–8511; tel. 316/885–4264; Blaine K. Miller, Administrator

MITCHELL COUNTY HOSPITAL (L, 89 beds) 400 West Eighth, Beloit, KS Zip 67420–1605, Mailing Address: P.O. Box 399, Zip 67420–0399; tel. 785/738–2266; John M. Osse, Administrator

OSBORNE COUNTY MEMORIAL HOSPITAL (C, 29 beds) 424 West New Hampshire Street, Osborne, KS Zip 67473–0070, Mailing Address: P.O. Box 70, Zip 67473–0070; tel. 785/346–2121; Patricia Bernard, R.N., Administrator

OTTAWA COUNTY HEALTH CENTER (L, 53 beds) 215 East Eighth, Minneapolis, KS Zip 67467–1999, Mailing Address: P.O. Box 209, Zip 67467–0209; tel. 785/392–2122; Joy Reed, R.N., Administrator

PHILLIPS COUNTY HOSPITAL (L, 62 beds) 1150 State Street, Phillipsburg, KS Zip 67661–1799, Mailing Address: P.O. Box 607, Zip 67661–0607; tel. 913/543–5226; James L. Giedd, Administrator

RAWLINS COUNTY HEALTH CENTER (C, 24 beds) 707 Grant Street, Atwood, KS Zip 67730–4700, Mailing Address: Box 47, Zip 67730–4700; tel. 785/626–3211; Donald J. Kessen, Administrator and Chief Executive Officer

REPUBLIC COUNTY HOSPITAL (L, 86 beds) 2420 G. Street, Belleville, KS Zip 66935–2499; tel. 785/527–2255; Charles A. Westin, FACHE, Administrator

SABETHA COMMUNITY HOSPITAL (L, 27 beds) 14th and Oregon Streets, Sabetha, KS Zip 66534, Mailing Address: P.O. Box 229, Zip 66534; tel. 785/284–2121; Rita K. Buurman, Chief Executive Officer

SALEM HOSPITAL (C, 90 beds) 701 South Main Street, Hillsboro, KS Zip 67063–9981; tel. 316/947–3114; J. H. Seitz, Administrator

SATANTA DISTRICT HOSPITAL (C, 42 beds) 401 South Cheyenne Street, Satanta, KS Zip 67870, Mailing Address: P.O. Box 159, Zip 67870–0159; tel. 316/649–2761; T. G. Lee, Administrator

SMITH COUNTY MEMORIAL HOSPITAL (L, 54 beds) 614 South Main Street, Smith Center, KS Zip 66967–0349, Mailing Address: P.O. Box 349, Zip 66967–0349; tel. 785/282–6845; John Terrill, Administrator

TREGO COUNTY–LEMKE MEMORIAL HOSPITAL (C, 73 beds) 320 North 13th Street, Wakeeney, KS Zip 67672–2099; tel. 785/743–2182; James Wahlmeier, Administrator

NEBRASKA: COMMUNITY MEDICAL CENTER (C, 49 beds) 2307 Barada Street, Falls City, NE Zip 68355–1599; tel. 402/245–2428; Victor Lee, Chief Executive Officer and Administrator

HARLAN COUNTY HOSPITAL (C, 25 beds) 717 North Brown Street, Alma, NE Zip 68920–0836, Mailing Address: P.O. Box 836, Zip 68920–0836; tel. 308/928–2151; Allen Van Driel, Administrator

Owned, leased, sponsored:	10 hospitals	487 beds
Contract–managed:	15 hospitals	604 beds
Totals:	25 hospitals	1091 beds

0144: GREATER HUDSON VALLEY HEALTH SYSTEM (NP)
600A Stony Brook Court, Newburgh, NY Zip 12550; tel. 914/568–6050; Paul Dell Uomo, President and Chief Executive Officer

NEW YORK: CORNWALL HOSPITAL (O, 125 beds) 33 Laurel Avenue, Cornwall, NY Zip 12518–1499; tel. 914/534–7711; Val S. Gray, Executive Director

HORTON MEDICAL CENTER (O, 171 beds) 60 Prospect Avenue, Middletown, NY Zip 10940–4133; tel. 914/343–2424; Jeffrey D. Hirsch, Executive Vice President and Chief Operating Officer

ST. LUKE'S HOSPITAL (O, 184 beds) 70 Dubois Street, Newburgh, NY Zip 12550–4898, Mailing Address: P.O. Box 631, Zip 12550–0631; tel. 914/561–4400; Laurence E. Kelly, Executive Vice President and Administrator

For explanation of codes following names, see page B2.
★ Indicates Type III membership in the American Hospital Association.

Owned, leased, sponsored:	3 hospitals	480 beds
Contract–managed:	0 hospitals	0 beds
Totals:	3 hospitals	480 beds

★2015: GREATER SOUTHEAST HEALTHCARE SYSTEM (NP)
1310 Southern Avenue S.E., Washington, DC Zip 20032–4692;
tel. 202/574–6926; Dalton A. Tong, CPA, FACHE, President and
Chief Executive Officer

DISTRICT OF COLUMBIA: GREATER SOUTHEAST COMMUNITY HOSPITAL (O,
305 beds) 1310 Southern Avenue S.E., Washington, DC Zip 20032–4699;
tel. 202/574–6000; Robert C. Winfrey, President and Chief Operating
Officer

MARYLAND: FORT WASHINGTON HOSPITAL (O, 35 beds) 11711 Livingston
Road, Fort Washington, MD Zip 20744–5164; tel. 301/292–7000;
Theodore M. Lewis, President

Owned, leased, sponsored:	2 hospitals	340 beds
Contract–managed:	0 hospitals	0 beds
Totals:	2 hospitals	340 beds

1155: GREENLEAF HEALTH SYSTEMS, INC. (IO)
One Northgate Park, Chattanooga, TN Zip 37415;
tel. 423/870–5110; Dan B. Page, President

GEORGIA: GREENLEAF CENTER (C, 90 beds) 500 Greenleaf Circle, Fort
Oglethorpe, GA Zip 30742–3886; tel. 706/861–4357; R. Lindsay Shuff,
Administrator

GREENLEAF CENTER (O, 70 beds) 2209 Pineview Drive, Valdosta, GA
Zip 31602–7316; tel. 912/247–4357; Michael Lane, Administrator and Chief
Executive Officer

Owned, leased, sponsored:	1 hospital	70 beds
Contract–managed:	1 hospital	90 beds
Totals:	2 hospitals	160 beds

★1555: GREENVILLE HOSPITAL SYSTEM (NP)
701 Grove Road, Greenville, SC Zip 29605–4211;
tel. 864/455–7000; Frank D. Pinckney, President

SOUTH CAROLINA: ALLEN BENNETT HOSPITAL (O, 146 beds) 313 Memorial
Drive, Greer, SC Zip 29650–1521; tel. 864/848–8130; Michael W.
Massey, Administrator

GREENVILLE MEMORIAL HOSPITAL (O, 912 beds) 701 Grove Road,
Greenville, SC Zip 29605–4295; tel. 864/455–7000; J. Bland Burkhardt Jr.,
Senior Vice President and Administrator

HILLCREST HOSPITAL (O, 46 beds) 729 S.E. Main Street, Simpsonville, SC
Zip 29681–3280; tel. 864/967–6100; Mark Slyter, Administrator

MARSHALL I. PICKENS HOSPITAL (O, 106 beds) 701 Grove Road, Greenville,
SC Zip 29605–5601; tel. 864/455–7834; Jack W. Bonner, M.D.,
Administrator and Medical Director

ROGER C. PEACE REHABILITATION HOSPITAL (O, 50 beds) 701 Grove Road,
Greenville, SC Zip 29605–4295; tel. 864/455–7000; Dennis C. Hollins, M.D.,
Ph.D., Administrator and Medical Director

Owned, leased, sponsored:	5 hospitals	1260 beds
Contract–managed:	0 hospitals	0 beds
Totals:	5 hospitals	1260 beds

★0675: GUTHRIE HEALTHCARE SYSTEM (NP)
Guthrie Square, Sayre, PA Zip 18840; tel. 717/888–6666; Ralph H.
Meyer, FACHE, President and Chief Executive Officer

PENNSYLVANIA: ROBERT PACKER HOSPITAL (O, 243 beds) 1 Guthrie
Square, Sayre, PA Zip 18840–1698; tel. 717/888–6666; William F.
Vanaskie, President

TROY COMMUNITY HOSPITAL (O, 35 beds) 100 John Street, Troy, PA
Zip 16947–1134; tel. 717/297–2121; Mark A. Webster, President

Owned, leased, sponsored:	2 hospitals	278 beds
Contract–managed:	0 hospitals	0 beds
Totals:	2 hospitals	278 beds

★0082: HEALTH ALLIANCE OF GREATER CINCINNATI (NP)
2060 Reading Road, Suite 400, Cincinnati, OH Zip 45202–1456;
tel. 513/632–3700; Jack M. Cook, President and Chief Executive
Officer

KENTUCKY: ST. LUKE HOSPITAL EAST (O, 221 beds) 85 North Grand
Avenue, Fort Thomas, KY Zip 41075–1796; tel. 606/572–3100; Daniel
M. Vinson, CPA, Senior Executive Officer

ST. LUKE HOSPITAL WEST (O, 160 beds) 7380 Turfway Road, Florence, KY
Zip 41042–1337; tel. 606/525–5200; Daniel M. Vinson, CPA, Interim
Administrator

OHIO: CHRIST HOSPITAL (O, 459 beds) 2139 Auburn Avenue, Cincinnati, OH
Zip 45219–2989; tel. 513/369–2000; Claus von Zychlin, Senior
Executive Officer

JEWISH HOSPITAL KENWOOD (O, 437 beds) 4777 East Galbraith Road,
Cincinnati, OH Zip 45236; tel. 513/745–2200; Warren C. Falberg, Senior
Executive Officer

UNIVERSITY HOSPITAL (O, 418 beds) 234 Goodman Street, Cincinnati, OH
Zip 45267–0700; tel. 513/558–1000; Elliot G. Cohen, Senior Executive
Officer

Owned, leased, sponsored:	5 hospitals	1695 beds
Contract–managed:	0 hospitals	0 beds
Totals:	5 hospitals	1695 beds

1775: HEALTH MANAGEMENT ASSOCIATES (IO)
5811 Pelican Bay Boulevard, Suite 500, Naples, FL Zip 34108;
tel. 941/598–3175; William J. Schoen, Chairman and Chief Executive
Officer

ALABAMA: RIVERVIEW REGIONAL MEDICAL CENTER (O, 281 beds) 600 South
Third Street, Gadsden, AL Zip 35901–5399, Mailing Address: P.O. Box
268, Zip 35999–0268; tel. 205/543–5200; J. David McCormack,
Executive Director

STRINGFELLOW MEMORIAL HOSPITAL (L, 72 beds) 301 East 18th Street,
Anniston, AL Zip 36207–3999; tel. 205/235–8900; Vincent T. Cherry Jr.,
Administrator

ARKANSAS: CRAWFORD MEMORIAL HOSPITAL (L, 103 beds) East Main &
South 20th Streets, Van Buren, AR Zip 72956, Mailing Address: P.O. Box
409, Zip 72956–0409; tel. 501/474–3401; Richard Boone, Executive
Director

FLORIDA: CHARLOTTE REGIONAL MEDICAL CENTER (O, 148 beds) 809 East
Marion Avenue, Punta Gorda, FL Zip 33950–3898, Mailing Address: P.O.
Box 51–1328, Zip 33951–1328; tel. 941/639–3131; John D. Harryman,
Executive Director

FISHERMEN'S HOSPITAL (L, 58 beds) 3301 Overseas Highway, Marathon, FL
Zip 33050–0068; tel. 305/743–5533; Patrice L. Tavernier, Administrator

HEART OF FLORIDA BEHAVIORAL CENTER (O, 40 beds) 2510 North Florida
Avenue, Lakeland, FL Zip 33805–2298; tel. 941/682–6105; David M.
Polunas, Administrator and Chief Executive Officer

HEART OF FLORIDA REGIONAL MEDICAL CENTER (O, 51 beds) 1615 U.S.
Highway 27N, Davenport, FL Zip 33837, Mailing Address: P.O. Box 67,
Haines City, Zip 33844–0067; tel. 941/422–4971; Robert Mahaffey,
Administrator

HIGHLANDS REGIONAL MEDICAL CENTER (L, 126 beds) 3600 South
Highlands Avenue, Sebring, FL Zip 33870–5495, Mailing Address: Drawer
2066, Zip 33871–2066; tel. 941/385–6101; Micheal Terry, Executive
Director

SANDYPINES (O, 60 beds) 11301 S.E. Tequesta Terrace, Tequesta, FL
Zip 33469–8146; tel. 561/744–0211; David L. Beardsley, Administrator

SEBASTIAN RIVER MEDICAL CENTER (O, 133 beds) 13695 North U.S.
Highway 1, Sebastian, FL Zip 32958–3230, Mailing Address: Box 780838,
Zip 32978–0838; tel. 561/589–3186; Stephen L. Midkiff, Executive Director

For explanation of codes following names, see page B2.
★ Indicates Type III membership in the American Hospital Association.

Section B

UNIVERSITY BEHAVIORAL CENTER (O, 47 beds) 2500 Discovery Drive, Orlando, FL Zip 32826–3711; tel. 407/281–7000; David L. Beardsley, Administrator

GEORGIA: BULLOCH MEMORIAL HOSPITAL (O, 158 beds) 500 East Grady Street, Statesboro, GA Zip 30458–5105, Mailing Address: P.O. Box 1048, Zip 30459–1048; tel. 912/486–1000; C. Scott Campbell, Executive Director

KANSAS: PARKVIEW HOSPITAL OF TOPEKA (O, 80 beds) 3707 S.W. Sixth Street, Topeka, KS Zip 66606–2085; tel. 913/295–3000; Thomas G. Smith, Chief Executive Officer

KENTUCKY: PAUL B. HALL REGIONAL MEDICAL CENTER (O, 72 beds) 625 James S. Trimble Boulevard, Paintsville, KY Zip 41240–1055, Mailing Address: P.O. Box 1487, Zip 41240–1487; tel. 606/789–3511; Deborah C. Trimble, Administrator

MISSISSIPPI: BILOXI REGIONAL MEDICAL CENTER (L, 153 beds) 150 Reynoir Street, Biloxi, MS Zip 39530–4199, Mailing Address: P.O. Box 128, Zip 39533–0128; tel. 601/432–1571; Joseph J. Mullany, Executive Director

NATCHEZ COMMUNITY HOSPITAL (O, 101 beds) 129 Jefferson Davis Boulevard, Natchez, MS Zip 39120–5100, Mailing Address: P.O. Box 1203, Zip 39121–1203; tel. 601/445–6200; Raymond Bane, Executive Director

NORTHWEST MISSISSIPPI REGIONAL MEDICAL CENTER (L, 195 beds) 1970 Hospital Drive, Clarksdale, MS Zip 38614–7204, Mailing Address: P.O. Box 1218, Zip 38614–1218; tel. 601/624–3401; Roger C. LeDoux, Executive Director

RANKIN MEDICAL CENTER (L, 105 beds) 350 Crossgates Boulevard, Brandon, MS Zip 39042–2698; tel. 601/825–2811; Thomas Wiman, Executive Director

RILEY MEMORIAL HOSPITAL (O, 180 beds) 1102 21st Avenue, Meridian, MS Zip 39301–4096, Mailing Address: P.O. Box 1810, Zip 39302–1810; tel. 601/484–3590; Eric E. Weis, FACHE, Chief Executive Officer

RIVER OAKS EAST–WOMAN'S PAVILION (O, 76 beds) 1026 North Flowood Drive, Jackson, MS Zip 39208–9599, Mailing Address: P.O. Box 4546, Zip 39296–4546; tel. 601/932–1000; Carl Etter, Executive Director

RIVER OAKS HOSPITAL (O, 110 beds) 1030 River Oaks Drive, Jackson, MS Zip 39208–9729, Mailing Address: P.O. Box 5100, Zip 39296–5100; tel. 601/932–1030; John J. Cleary, President and Chief Executive Officer

NORTH CAROLINA: FRANKLIN REGIONAL MEDICAL CENTER (O, 85 beds) 100 Hospital Drive, Louisburg, NC Zip 27549–2256, Mailing Address: P.O. Box 609, Zip 27549–0609; tel. 919/496–5131; Thomas Hanenburg, Administrator

HAMLET HOSPITAL (O, 64 beds) Rice and Vance Streets, Hamlet, NC Zip 28345, Mailing Address: P.O. Box 1109, Zip 28345–1109; tel. 910/582–3611; Joe D. Howell, Executive Director

LAKE NORMAN REGIONAL MEDICAL CENTER (O, 100 beds) 610 East Center Avenue, Mooresville, NC Zip 28115, Mailing Address: P.O. Box 360, Zip 28115–0360; tel. 704/663–1113; P. Paul Smith Jr., Executive Director

OKLAHOMA: MEDICAL CENTER OF SOUTHEASTERN OKLAHOMA (O, 103 beds) 1800 University Boulevard, Durant, OK Zip 74701–3006, Mailing Address: P.O. Box 1207, Zip 74702–1207; tel. 580/924–3080; Joshua Putter, Executive Director

MIDWEST REGIONAL MEDICAL CENTER (L, 214 beds) 2825 Parklawn Drive, Midwest City, OK Zip 73110–4258; tel. 405/737–4411; Martin D. Smith, Chief Operating Officer

SOUTH CAROLINA: BYERLY HOSPITAL (L, 100 beds) 413 East Carolina Avenue, Hartsville, SC Zip 29550–4309; tel. 843/339–2100; Page Vaughan, Executive Director

UPSTATE CAROLINA MEDICAL CENTER (O, 125 beds) 1530 North Limestone Street, Gaffney, SC Zip 29340–4738; tel. 864/487–1500; Nancy C. Fodi, Executive Director

WEST VIRGINIA: WILLIAMSON MEMORIAL HOSPITAL (O, 76 beds) 859 Alderson Street, Williamson, WV Zip 25661–3215, Mailing Address: P.O. Box 1980, Zip 25661–1980; tel. 304/235–2500; James Arp, Administrator

Owned, leased, sponsored:	29 hospitals	3216 beds
Contract–managed:	0 hospitals	0 beds
Totals:	29 hospitals	3216 beds

★**8815: HEALTH MIDWEST** (NP)
2304 East Meyer Boulevard, Suite A–20, Kansas City, MO Zip 64132–4104; tel. 816/276–9181; Richard W. Brown, President and Chief Executive Officer

KANSAS: ALLEN COUNTY HOSPITAL (L, 41 beds) 101 South First Street, Iola, KS Zip 66749–3505, Mailing Address: P.O. Box 540, Zip 66749–0540; tel. 316/365–3131; Bill May, Chief Executive Officer

MENORAH MEDICAL CENTER (O, 109 beds) 5721 West 119th Street, Overland Park, KS Zip 66209; tel. 913/498–6000; Steven D. Wilkinson, President and Chief Executive Officer

MISSOURI: BAPTIST MEDICAL CENTER (O, 315 beds) 6601 Rockhill Road, Kansas City, MO Zip 64131–1197; tel. 816/276–7000; Michael S. McCoy, Interim President and Chief Executive Officer

CASS MEDICAL CENTER (C, 42 beds) 1800 East Mechanic Street, Harrisonville, MO Zip 64701–2099; tel. 816/884–3291; Alan Freeman, Administrator

LAFAYETTE REGIONAL HEALTH CENTER (L, 37 beds) 1500 State Street, Lexington, MO Zip 64067–1199; tel. 660/259–2203; Jeffrey S. Tarrant, Administrator

LEE'S SUMMIT HOSPITAL (O, 86 beds) 530 North Murray Road, Lees Summit, MO Zip 64081–1497; tel. 816/251–7000; John L. Jacobson, President and Chief Executive Officer

MEDICAL CENTER OF INDEPENDENCE (O, 123 beds) 17203 East 23rd Street, Independence, MO Zip 64057–1899; tel. 816/478–5000; Michael W. Chappelow, President and Chief Executive Officer

PARK LANE MEDICAL CENTER (O, 83 beds) 5151 Raytown Road, Kansas City, MO Zip 64133–2199; tel. 816/358–8000; Derell Taloney, President and Chief Executive Officer

REHABILITATION INSTITUTE (O, 36 beds) 3011 Baltimore, Kansas City, MO Zip 64108–3465; tel. 816/751–7900; Ronald L. Herrick, President

RESEARCH BELTON HOSPITAL (O, 47 beds) 17065 South 71 Highway, Belton, MO Zip 64012–2165; tel. 816/348–1200; Daniel F. Sheehan, Administrator

RESEARCH MEDICAL CENTER (O, 491 beds) 2316 East Meyer Boulevard, Kansas City, MO Zip 64132–1199; tel. 816/276–4000; Steven R. Newton, Interim President and Chief Executive Officer

TRINITY LUTHERAN HOSPITAL (O, 334 beds) 3030 Baltimore Avenue, Kansas City, MO Zip 64108–3404; tel. 816/751–4600; Ronald A. Ommen, President and Chief Executive Officer

Owned, leased, sponsored:	11 hospitals	1702 beds
Contract–managed:	1 hospital	42 beds
Totals:	12 hospitals	1744 beds

O395: HEALTHCARE AMERICA, INC. (IO)
1407 West Stassney Lane, Austin, TX Zip 78745–2998, Mailing Address: P.O. Box 4008, Zip 78765–4008; tel. 512/464–0200; John P. Harcourt Jr., President and Chief Executive Officer

COLORADO: CEDAR SPRINGS PSYCHIATRIC HOSPITAL (O, 100 beds) 2135 Southgate Road, Colorado Springs, CO Zip 80906–2693; tel. 719/633–4114; Connie Mull, Chief Executive Officer

OKLAHOMA: SHADOW MOUNTAIN HOSPITAL (O, 100 beds) 6262 South Sheridan Road, Tulsa, OK Zip 74133–4099; tel. 918/492–8200; Nancy J. Cranton, Chief Executive Officer

TEXAS: BROWN SCHOOLS REHABILITATION CENTER (O, 96 beds) 1106 West Dittmar, Austin, TX Zip 78745–9990, Mailing Address: P.O. Box 150459, Zip 78715–0459; tel. 512/444–4835; James G. Dalzell, Chief Executive Officer

CYPRESS CREEK HOSPITAL (O, 94 beds) 17750 Cali Drive, Houston, TX Zip 77090–2700; tel. 713/586–7600; Terry Scovill, Administrator

OAKS PSYCHIATRIC HEALTH SYSTEM (O, 118 beds) 1407 West Stassney Lane, Austin, TX Zip 78745–2998; tel. 512/464–0400; Mack Wigley, Chief Executive Officer

SAN MARCOS TREATMENT CENTER (O, 152 beds) Bert Brown Road, San Marcos, TX Zip 78667–0768, Mailing Address: P.O. Box 768, Zip 78667–0768; tel. 512/396–8500; Mack Wigley, Chief Executive Officer

For explanation of codes following names, see page B2.
★ Indicates Type III membership in the American Hospital Association.

Section B

WEST OAKS HOSPITAL (O, 144 beds) 6500 Hornwood Drive, Houston, TX Zip 77074–5095; tel. 713/995–0909; Terry Scovill, Chief Executive Officer

VIRGINIA: CUMBERLAND, A BROWN SCHOOLS HOSPITAL FOR CHILDREN AND ADOLESCENTS (O, 84 beds) 9407 Cumberland Road, New Kent, VA Zip 23124–2029; tel. 804/966–2242; Elizabeth B. Woodard, Chief Executive Officer

Owned, leased, sponsored:	8 hospitals	888 beds
Contract–managed:	0 hospitals	0 beds
Totals:	8 hospitals	888 beds

2795: HEALTHCORP OF TENNESSEE, INC. (IO)
735 Broad Street, Chattanooga, TN Zip 37402; tel. 615/267–8406; T. Farrell Hayes, President

ALABAMA: LAKESHORE COMMUNITY HOSPITAL (C, 28 beds) 201 Mariarden Road, Dadeville, AL Zip 36853, Mailing Address: P.O. Box 248, Zip 36853–0248; tel. 205/825–7821; Mavis B. Halko, Administrator

LAKEVIEW COMMUNITY HOSPITAL (C, 74 beds) 820 West Washington Street, Eufaula, AL Zip 36027–1899; tel. 205/687–5761; Carl D. Brown, Administrator

VAUGHAN CHILTON MEDICAL CENTER (L, 45 beds) 1010 Lay Dam Road, Clanton, AL Zip 35045; tel. 205/755–2500; Donald J. Jones, Administrator

ARKANSAS: DALLAS COUNTY HOSPITAL (O, 31 beds) 201 Clifton Street, Fordyce, AR Zip 71742–3099; tel. 501/352–3155; Greg R. McNeil, Administrator

TENNESSEE: MEMORIAL NORTH PARK HOSPITAL (C, 83 beds) 2051 Hamill Road, Chattanooga, TN Zip 37343–4096; tel. 423/870–6100; Sean S. McMurray, CHE, Administrator

Owned, leased, sponsored:	2 hospitals	76 beds
Contract–managed:	3 hospitals	185 beds
Totals:	5 hospitals	261 beds

★2185: HEALTHEAST (NP)
559 Capitol Boulevard, 6–South, Saint Paul, MN Zip 55103–0000; tel. 612/232–2300; Timothy H. Hanson, President and Chief Executive Officer

MINNESOTA: HEALTHEAST BETHESDA LUTHERAN HOSPITAL AND REHABILITATION CENTER (O, 127 beds) 559 Capitol Boulevard, Saint Paul, MN Zip 55103–2101; tel. 612/232–2133; Scott Batulis, Vice President and Administrator

HEALTHEAST ST. JOHN'S HOSPITAL (O, 163 beds) 1575 Beam Avenue, Maplewood, MN Zip 55109; tel. 612/232–7000; William Knutson, Vice President and Administrator

HEALTHEAST ST. JOSEPH'S HOSPITAL (O, 299 beds) 69 West Exchange Street, Saint Paul, MN Zip 55102–1053; tel. 612/232–3000; William Knutson, Vice President and Administrator

Owned, leased, sponsored:	3 hospitals	589 beds
Contract–managed:	0 hospitals	0 beds
Totals:	3 hospitals	589 beds

0023: HEALTHSOUTH CORPORATION (IO)
One Healthsouth Parkway, Birmingham, AL Zip 35243; tel. 205/967–7116; Anthony J. Tanner, Executive Vice President

ALABAMA: HEALTHSOUTH LAKESHORE REHABILITATION HOSPITAL (O, 100 beds) 3800 Ridgeway Drive, Birmingham, AL Zip 35209–5599; tel. 205/868–2000; Terry Brown, Administrator and Chief Executive Officer

HEALTHSOUTH MEDICAL CENTER (O, 201 beds) 1201 11th Avenue South, Birmingham, AL Zip 35205–5299; tel. 205/930–7000; Frank R. Gannon, Administrator and Regional Vice President

HEALTHSOUTH REHABILITATION HOSPITAL OF MONTGOMERY (O, 80 beds) 4465 Narrow Lane Road, Montgomery, AL Zip 36116–2900; tel. 334/284–7700; Arnold F. McRae, Administrator and Chief Executive Officer

HEALTHSOUTH REHABILITATION HOSPITAL OF NORTH ALABAMA (O, 50 beds) 107 Governors Drive S.W., Huntsville, AL Zip 35801–4329; tel. 205/535–2300; Rod Moss, Chief Executive Officer

ARIZONA: HEALTHSOUTH MERIDIAN POINT REHABILITATION HOSPITAL (O, 43 beds) 11250 North 92nd Street, Scottsdale, AZ Zip 85260–6148; tel. 602/860–0671; Michael S. Wallace, Chief Executive Officer

HEALTHSOUTH REHABILITATION INSTITUTE OF TUCSON (O, 80 beds) 2650 North Wyatt Drive, Tucson, AZ Zip 85712–6108; tel. 520/325–1300; Jay Underwood, Chief Executive Officer

HEALTHSOUTH VALLEY OF THE SUN REHABILITATION HOSPITAL (O, 42 beds) 13460 North 67th Avenue, Glendale, AZ Zip 85304–1042; tel. 602/878–8800; Michael S. Wallace, Director

ARKANSAS: HEALTHSOUTH REHABILITATION HOSPITAL (O, 60 beds) 153 East Monte Painter Drive, Fayetteville, AR Zip 72703–4002; tel. 501/444–2200; Dennis R. Shelby, Chief Executive Officer

HEALTHSOUTH REHABILITATION HOSPITAL OF FORT SMITH (O, 80 beds) 1401 South J. Street, Fort Smith, AR Zip 72901–5155; tel. 501/785–3300; Claudia A. Eisenmann, Director Operations

HEALTHSOUTH REHABILITATION HOSPITAL OF JONESBORO (O, 60 beds) 1201 Fleming Avenue, Jonesboro, AR Zip 72401–4311, Mailing Address: P.O. Box 1680, Zip 72403–1680; tel. 870/932–0440; Brenda Antwine, Administrator

ST. VINCENT–NORTH REHABILITATION HOSPITAL (O, 60 beds) 2201 Wildwood Avenue, Sherwood, AR Zip 72120–5074, Mailing Address: P.O. Box 6930, Zip 72124–6930; tel. 501/834–1800; Douglas W. Parker, Chief Executive Officer

CALIFORNIA: HEALTHSOUTH BAKERSFIELD REHABILITATION HOSPITAL (O, 60 beds) 5001 Commerce Drive, Bakersfield, CA Zip 93309; tel. 805/323–5500; Thomas J. Meagher, Chief Operating Officer

FLORIDA: HEALTHSOUTH DOCTORS' HOSPITAL (O, 157 beds) 5000 University Drive, Coral Gables, FL Zip 33146–2094; tel. 305/666–2111; Lincoln S. Mendez, Chief Executive Officer

HEALTHSOUTH REHABILITATION HOSPITAL (O, 60 beds) 901 North Clearwater–Largo Road, Largo, FL Zip 34640–1955; tel. 813/586–2999; Vincent O. Nico, Regional Vice President

HEALTHSOUTH REHABILITATION HOSPITAL (O, 45 beds) 20601 Old Cutler Road, Miami, FL Zip 33189–2400; tel. 305/251–3800; Nelson Lazo, Chief Executive Officer

HEALTHSOUTH REHABILITATION HOSPITAL OF SARASOTA (O, 60 beds) 3251 Proctor Road, Sarasota, FL Zip 34231–8538; tel. 941/921–8600; Jeff Garber, Administrator and Chief Executive Officer

HEALTHSOUTH REHABILITATION HOSPITAL OF TALLAHASSEE (O, 70 beds) 1675 Riggins Road, Tallahassee, FL Zip 32308–5315; tel. 850/656–4800; Mike Marshall, Chief Executive Officer

HEALTHSOUTH SEA PINES REHABILITATION HOSPITAL (O, 80 beds) 101 East Florida Avenue, Melbourne, FL Zip 32901–9966; tel. 407/984–4600; Henry J. Cranston, Chief Executive Officer

HEALTHSOUTH SUNRISE REHABILITATION HOSPITAL (O, 108 beds) 4399 Nob Hill Road, Fort Lauderdale, FL Zip 33351–5899; tel. 954/749–0300; Kevin R. Conn, Administrator

HEALTHSOUTH TREASURE COAST REHABILITATION HOSPITAL (O, 70 beds) 1600 37th Street, Vero Beach, FL Zip 32960–6549; tel. 561/778–2100; Denise B. McGrath, Chief Executive Officer

GEORGIA: HEALTHSOUTH CENTRAL GEORGIA REHABILITATION HOSPITAL (O, 50 beds) 3351 Northside Drive, Macon, GA Zip 31210–2591; tel. 912/471–3536; Elbert T. McQueen, Chief Executive Officer

INDIANA: HEALTHSOUTH TRI–STATE REHABILITATION HOSPITAL (O, 80 beds) 4100 Covert Avenue, Evansville, IN Zip 47714–5567, Mailing Address: P.O. Box 5349, Zip 47716–5349; tel. 812/476–9983; Gerald F. Vozel, Administrator and Chief Executive Officer

KOKOMO REHABILITATION HOSPITAL (O, 60 beds) 829 North Dixon Road, Kokomo, IN Zip 46901–7709; tel. 765/452–6700; David Bailey, Chief Executive Officer

KANSAS: MID–AMERICA REHABILITATION HOSPITAL (O, 75 beds) 5701 West 110th Street, Overland Park, KS Zip 66211; tel. 913/491–2400; Richard L. Allen, Chief Executive Officer

Section B

For explanation of codes following names, see page B2.
★ Indicates Type III membership in the American Hospital Association.

WESLEY REHABILITATION HOSPITAL (O, 65 beds) 8338 West 13th Street North, Wichita, KS Zip 67212–2984; tel. 316/729–9999; Lisa James, Administrator

KENTUCKY: HEALTHSOUTH NORTHERN KENTUCKY REHABILITATION HOSPITAL (O, 40 beds) 201 Medical Village Drive, Covington, KY Zip 41017–3407; tel. 606/341–2044; Ronald L. Bierman, Chief Executive Officer

LAKEVIEW REHABILITATION HOSPITAL (O, 40 beds) 134 Heartland Drive, Elizabethtown, KY Zip 42701–2778; tel. 502/769–3100; Kevin Stevenson, Chief Executive Officer

LOUISIANA: HEALTHSOUTH REHABILITATION HOSPITAL OF SOUTH LOUISIANA (O, 40 beds) 4040 North Boulevard, Baton Rouge, LA Zip 70806–3829; tel. 504/383–5055; Sharon S. Black, R.N., Administrator and Chief Operating Officer

NORTH LOUISIANA REHABILITATION HOSPITAL (O, 90 beds) 1401 Ezell Street, Ruston, LA Zip 71270–7221, Mailing Address: P.O. Box 490, Zip 71273–0490; tel. 318/251–5354; Alice M. Prophit, Chief Executive Officer

REHABILITATION HOSPITAL OF BATON ROUGE (O, 80 beds) 8595 United Plaza Boulevard, Baton Rouge, LA Zip 70809–2251; tel. 504/927–0567; Jay Pullman, Chief Executive Officer

MAINE: NEW ENGLAND REHABILITATION HOSPITAL OF PORTLAND (O, 76 beds) 335 Brighton Avenue, Portland, ME Zip 04102; tel. 207/775–4000; Patricia McMurry, Chief Executive Officer

MARYLAND: HEALTHSOUTH CHESAPEAKE REHABILITATION HOSPITAL (O, 44 beds) 220 Tilghman Road, Salisbury, MD Zip 21804–1921; tel. 410/546–4600; William Roth, Chief Executive Officer

MASSACHUSETTS: FAIRLAWN REHABILITATION HOSPITAL (O, 110 beds) 189 May Street, Worcester, MA Zip 01602–4399; tel. 508/791–6351; Peter M. Mantegazza, President and Chief Executive Officer

HEALTHSOUTH BRAINTREE REHABILITATION HOSPITAL (O, 187 beds) 250 Pond Street, Braintree, MA Zip 02185–5391; tel. 781/848–5353; Ernest J. Broadbent, President and Chief Executive Officer

HEALTHSOUTH NEW ENGLAND REHABILITATION HOSPITAL (O, 198 beds) Two Rehabilitation Way, Woburn, MA Zip 01801–6098; tel. 781/935–5050; Mary Moscato, Chief Executive Officer

HEALTHSOUTH REHABILITATION HOSPITAL OF WESTERN MASSACHUSETTS (O, 40 beds) 14 Chestnut Place, Ludlow, MA Zip 01056–3460; tel. 413/589–7581; Mark D. Kramer, Administrator

NEW HAMPSHIRE: HEALTHSOUTH REHABILITATION HOSPITAL (O, 50 beds) 254 Pleasant Street, Concord, NH Zip 03301–2508; tel. 603/226–9800; Anne M. Fugagli, Administrator

NEW JERSEY: HEALTHSOUTH REHABILITATION HOSPITAL OF NEW JERSEY (O, 155 beds) 14 Hospital Drive, Toms River, NJ Zip 08755–6470; tel. 732/244–3100; Patricia Ostaszewski, Chief Executive Officer and Administrator

NEW MEXICO: HEALTHSOUTH REHABILITATION CENTER (O, 60 beds) 7000 Jefferson N.E., Albuquerque, NM Zip 87109–4357; tel. 505/344–9478; Darby Brockette, Administrator

OKLAHOMA: HEALTHSOUTH REHABILITATION HOSPITAL (O, 46 beds) 700 N.W. Seventh Street, Oklahoma City, OK Zip 73102–1295; tel. 405/553–1192; Hank Ross, Chief Executive Officer

PENNSYLVANIA: HEALTHSOUTH GREAT LAKES REHABILITATION HOSPITAL (O, 108 beds) 143 East Second Street, Erie, PA Zip 16507–1595; tel. 814/878–1200; William R. Fox, Chief Executive Officer

HEALTHSOUTH GREATER PITTSBURGH REHABILITATION HOSPITAL (O, 89 beds) 2380 McGinley Road, Monroeville, PA Zip 15146–4400; tel. 412/856–2400; Faith A. Deigan, Administrator

HEALTHSOUTH HARMARVILLE REHABILITATION HOSPITAL (O, 202 beds) Guys Run Road, Pittsburgh, PA Zip 15238–0460, Mailing Address: Box 11460, Guys Run Road, Zip 15238–0460; tel. 412/781–5700; Frank G. DeLisi III, CHE, Chief Executive Officer and Director Operations

HEALTHSOUTH LAKE ERIE INSTITUTE OF REHABILITATION (O, 99 beds) 137 West Second Street, Erie, PA Zip 16507–1403; tel. 814/453–5602; Louis M. Condrasky, Chief Operating Officer

HEALTHSOUTH NITTANY VALLEY REHABILITATION HOSPITAL (O, 88 beds) 550 West College Avenue, Pleasant Gap, PA Zip 16823–8808; tel. 814/359–3421; Mary Jane Hawkins, Administrator and Chief Executive Officer

HEALTHSOUTH REHABILITATION HOSPITAL OF ALTOONA (O, 70 beds) 2005 Valley View Boulevard, Altoona, PA Zip 16602–4598; tel. 814/944–3535; Michael A. Fenello, Administrator

HEALTHSOUTH REHABILITATION HOSPITAL OF READING (O, 95 beds) 1623 Morgantown Road, Reading, PA Zip 19607–9455; tel. 610/796–6000; Teresa K. Stranko, Interim Administrator

HEALTHSOUTH REHABILITATION HOSPITAL OF YORK (O, 88 beds) 1850 Normandie Drive, York, PA Zip 17404–1534; tel. 717/767–6941; Cheryl Fleming, Chief Executive Officer

HEALTHSOUTH REHABILITATION OF MECHANICSBURG (O, 103 beds) 175 Lancaster Boulevard, Mechanicsburg, PA Zip 17055–2016, Mailing Address: P.O. Box 2016, Zip 17055–2016; tel. 717/691–3700; Melissa Kutz, Administrator and Chief Executive Officer

SOUTH CAROLINA: HEALTHSOUTH REHABILITATION HOSPITAL (O, 87 beds) 2935 Colonial Drive, Columbia, SC Zip 29203–6811; tel. 803/254–7777; Debbie W. Johnston, Director Operations

HEALTHSOUTH REHABILITATION HOSPITAL (O, 88 beds) 900 East Cheves Street, Florence, SC Zip 29506–2704; tel. 803/679–9000; Mark J. Stepanik, Interim Chief Executive Officer

TENNESSEE: HEALTHSOUTH CHATTANOOGA REHABILITATION HOSPITAL (O, 69 beds) 2412 McCallie Avenue, Chattanooga, TN Zip 37404–3398; tel. 423/698–0221; Susan Heath, Chief Executive Officer

HEALTHSOUTH REHABILITATION HOSPITAL (O, 50 beds) 113 Cassel Drive, Kingsport, TN Zip 37660–3775; tel. 423/246–7240; Terry R. Maxhimer, Regional Vice President

HEALTHSOUTH REHABILITATION HOSPITAL (O, 80 beds) 1282 Union Avenue, Memphis, TN Zip 38104–3414; tel. 901/722–2000; Jerry Gray, Administrator

TEXAS: HEALTHSOUTH HOUSTON REHABILITATION INSTITUTE (O, 80 beds) 17506 Red Oak Drive, Houston, TX Zip 77090–7721, Mailing Address: P.O. Box 73684, Zip 77273–3684; tel. 281/580–1212; Anne R. Leon, Chief Executive Officer

HEALTHSOUTH MEDICAL CENTER (O, 106 beds) 2124 Research Row, Dallas, TX Zip 75235–2504; tel. 214/904–6100; Robert M. Smart, Area Manager and Chief Executive Officer

HEALTHSOUTH REHABILITATION HOSPITAL (O, 58 beds) 19002 McKay Drive, Humble, TX Zip 77338–5701; tel. 281/446–6148; Darrell L. Pile, Administrator

HEALTHSOUTH REHABILITATION HOSPITAL OF ARLINGTON (O, 60 beds) 3200 Matlock Road, Arlington, TX Zip 76015–2911; tel. 817/468–4000; S. Denise Borroni, Administrator and Chief Executive Officer

HEALTHSOUTH REHABILITATION HOSPITAL OF AUSTIN (O, 80 beds) 1215 Red River Street, Austin, TX Zip 78701, Mailing Address: P.O. Box 13366, Zip 78711–3366; tel. 512/474–5700; William O. Mitchell Jr., Chief Executive Officer

HEALTHSOUTH REHABILITATION HOSPITAL OF BEAUMONT (O, 60 beds) 3340 Plaza 10 Boulevard, Beaumont, TX Zip 77707; tel. 409/835–0835; David J. Holly, Chief Executive Officer

HEALTHSOUTH REHABILITATION HOSPITAL OF FORT WORTH (O, 60 beds) 1212 West Lancaster Avenue, Fort Worth, TX Zip 76102–4510; tel. 817/870–2336; Laura J. Lycan, Administrator and Chief Executive Officer

HEALTHSOUTH REHABILITATION HOSPITAL OF TEXARKANA (O, 60 beds) 515 West 12th Street, Texarkana, TX Zip 75501–4416; tel. 903/793–0088; Jeffrey A. Livingston, Chief Executive Officer

HEALTHSOUTH REHABILITATION HOSPITAL–CITYVIEW (O, 62 beds) 6701 Oakmont Boulevard, Fort Worth, TX Zip 76132–2957; tel. 817/370–4700; Robert L. McNew, Chief Executive Officer

HEALTHSOUTH REHABILITATION HOSPITAL–PLANO (O, 62 beds) 2800 West 15th Street, Plano, TX Zip 75075–7526; tel. 972/612–9000; Laurence J. Frayne, Chief Executive Officer

HEALTHSOUTH REHABILITATION HOSPITAL–TYLER (O, 63 beds) 3131 Troup Highway, Tyler, TX Zip 75701–8352; tel. 903/510–7000; Thomas J. Cook, Chief Executive Officer

For explanation of codes following names, see page B2.
★ Indicates Type III membership in the American Hospital Association.

HEALTHSOUTH REHABILITATION INSTITUTE OF SAN ANTONIO (O, 108 beds) 9119 Cinnamon Hill, San Antonio, TX Zip 78240–5401; tel. 210/691–0737; Diane B. Lampe, Administrator and Chief Executive Officer

UTAH: HEALTHSOUTH REHABILITATION HOSPITAL OF UTAH (O, 73 beds) 8074 South 1300 East, Sandy, UT Zip 84094–0743; tel. 801/561–3400; Richard M. Richards, Administrator

VIRGINIA: HEALTHSOUTH MEDICAL CENTER (O, 147 beds) 7700 East Parham Road, Richmond, VA Zip 23294–4301; tel. 804/747–5600; Charles A. Stark, CHE, Administrator, Chief Executive and Regional Vice President

HEALTHSOUTH REHABILITATION HOSPITAL OF VIRGINIA (O, 40 beds) 5700 Fitzhugh Avenue, Richmond, VA Zip 23226–1800; tel. 804/288–5700; Jeff Ruskan, Administrator

WEST VIRGINIA: HEALTHSOUTH HUNTINGTON REHABILITATION HOSPITAL (O, 40 beds) 6900 West Country Club Drive, Huntington, WV Zip 25705–2000; tel. 304/733–1060; Homer Fowler, Chief Operating Officer

HEALTHSOUTH MOUNTAIN REGIONAL REHABILITATION HOSPITAL (O, 80 beds) 1160 Van Voorhis, Morgantown, WV Zip 26505–3435; tel. 304/598–1100; Sharon Nero, Chief Executive Officer

HEALTHSOUTH SOUTHERN HILLS REHABILITATION HOSPITAL (O, 40 beds) 120 Twelfth Street, Princeton, WV Zip 24740–2312; tel. 304/487–8000; Timothy Mitchell, Administrator

HEALTHSOUTH WESTERN HILLS REGIONAL REHABILITATION HOSPITAL (O, 40 beds) 3 Western Hills Drive, Parkersburg, WV Zip 26101–8122, Mailing Address: P.O. Box 1428, Zip 26102–1428; tel. 304/420–1300; Thomas Heller, Administrator

Owned, leased, sponsored:	73 hospitals	5787 beds
Contract–managed:	0 hospitals	0 beds
Totals:	73 hospitals	5787 beds

1985:   HEALTHSYSTEM MINNESOTA (NP)
6500 Excelsior Boulevard, Saint Louis Park, MN Zip 55426–4702; tel. 612/993–6400

MINNESOTA: GLENCOE AREA HEALTH CENTER (C, 149 beds) 705 East 18th Street, Glencoe, MN Zip 55336–1499; tel. 320/864–3121; Jon D. Braband, Chief Executive Officer

METHODIST HOSPITAL HEALTHSYSTEM MINNESOTA (O, 349 beds) 6500 Excelsior Boulevard, Saint Louis Park, MN Zip 55426–4702, Mailing Address: Box 650, Minneapolis, Zip 55440–0650; tel. 612/993–5000

Owned, leased, sponsored:	1 hospital	349 beds
Contract–managed:	1 hospital	149 beds
Totals:	2 hospitals	498 beds

★**2355:   HELIX HEALTH** (NP)
2330 West Joppa Road, Suite 301, Lutherville Timonium, MD Zip 21093–4635; tel. 410/847–6700; James A. Oakey, President and Chief Executive Officer

MARYLAND: CHURCH HOSPITAL CORPORATION (O, 151 beds) 100 North Broadway, Baltimore, MD Zip 21231–1593; tel. 410/522–8000; Ann C. Failing, President

FRANKLIN SQUARE HOSPITAL CENTER (O, 243 beds) 9000 Franklin Square Drive, Baltimore, MD Zip 21237–3998; tel. 410/682–7000; Charles D. Mross, President and Chief Executive Officer

GOOD SAMARITAN HOSPITAL OF MARYLAND (O, 274 beds) 5601 Loch Raven Boulevard, Baltimore, MD Zip 21239–2995; tel. 410/532–8000; Lawrence M. Beck, President

HARBOR HOSPITAL CENTER (O, 192 beds) 3001 South Hanover Street, Baltimore, MD Zip 21225–1290; tel. 410/347–3200; L. Barney Johnson, President and Chief Executive Officer

UNION MEMORIAL HOSPITAL (O, 378 beds) 201 East University Parkway, Baltimore, MD Zip 21218–2391; tel. 410/554–2000; Kenneth R. Buser, President and Chief Executive Officer

Owned, leased, sponsored:	5 hospitals	1238 beds
Contract–managed:	0 hospitals	0 beds
Totals:	5 hospitals	1238 beds

★**9505:   HENRY FORD HEALTH SYSTEM** (NP)
One Ford Place, Detroit, MI Zip 48202–3067; tel. 313/876–8715; Gail L. Warden, President and Chief Executive Officer

MICHIGAN: BI–COUNTY COMMUNITY HOSPITAL (O, 161 beds) 13355 East Ten Mile Road, Warren, MI Zip 48089–2065; tel. 810/759–7300; Gary W. Popiel, Executive Vice President and Chief Executive Officer

HENRY FORD COTTAGE HOSPITAL OF GROSSE POINTE (O, 144 beds) 159 Kercheval Avenue, Grosse Pointe Farms, MI Zip 48236–3692; tel. 313/640–1000; Martin Monastersky, Interim Chief Executive Officer

HENRY FORD HOSPITAL (O, 634 beds) 2799 West Grand Boulevard, Detroit, MI Zip 48202–2689; tel. 313/876–2600; Stephen H. Velick, Chief Executive Officer

HENRY FORD WYANDOTTE HOSPITAL (O, 355 beds) 2333 Biddle Avenue, Wyandotte, MI Zip 48192–4693; tel. 313/284–2400; William R. Alvin, President

KINGSWOOD HOSPITAL (O, 64 beds) 10300 West Eight Mile Road, Ferndale, MI Zip 48220–2198; tel. 248/398–3200; Glenn Black, Associate Vice President and Chief Operating Officer

RIVERSIDE OSTEOPATHIC HOSPITAL (O, 148 beds) 150 Truax Street, Trenton, MI Zip 48183–2151; tel. 313/676–4200; Dennis R. Lemanski, D.O., Vice President and Chief Administrative Officer

Owned, leased, sponsored:	6 hospitals	1506 beds
Contract–managed:	0 hospitals	0 beds
Totals:	6 hospitals	1506 beds

0130:   HILLCREST HEALTHCARE SYSTEM (NP)
1120 South Utica, Tulsa, OK Zip 74104–4090; tel. 918/579–1000; Donald A. Lorack Jr., President and Chief Executive Officer

OKLAHOMA: CHILDREN'S MEDICAL CENTER (C, 108 beds) 5300 East Skelly Drive, Tulsa, OK Zip 74135–6599, Mailing Address: Box 35648, Zip 74153–0648; tel. 918/664–6600; Gerard J. Rothlein Jr., President and Chief Executive Officer

CLEVELAND AREA HOSPITAL (L, 25 beds) 1401 West Pawnee Street, Cleveland, OK Zip 74020–3019; tel. 918/358–2501; Thomas Henton, President and Chief Executive Officer

HILLCREST MEDICAL CENTER (C, 365 beds) 1120 South Utica, Tulsa, OK Zip 74104–4090; tel. 918/579–1000; Donald A. Lorack Jr., President and Chief Executive Officer

Owned, leased, sponsored:	1 hospital	25 beds
Contract–managed:	2 hospitals	473 beds
Totals:	3 hospitals	498 beds

★**5585:   HOLY CROSS HEALTH SYSTEM CORPORATION** (CC)
3606 East Jefferson Boulevard, South Bend, IN Zip 46615–3097; tel. 219/233–8558; Sister Patricia Vandenberg, President and Chief Executive Officer

CALIFORNIA: SAINT AGNES MEDICAL CENTER (O, 326 beds) 1303 East Herndon Avenue, Fresno, CA Zip 93720–3397; tel. 209/449–3000; Sister Ruth Marie Nickerson, President and Chief Executive Officer

IDAHO: CASCADE MEDICAL CENTER (C, 10 beds) 402 Old State Highway, Cascade, ID Zip 83611, Mailing Address: P.O. Box 151, Zip 83611–0151; tel. 208/382–4242; Richard Holm, Administrator

ELMORE MEDICAL CENTER (C, 78 beds) 895 North Sixth East Street, Mountain Home, ID Zip 83647–2207, Mailing Address: P.O. Box 1270, Zip 83647–1270; tel. 208/587–8401; Gregory L. Maurer, Administrator

MCCALL MEMORIAL HOSPITAL (C, 15 beds) 1000 State Street, McCall, ID Zip 83638, Mailing Address: P.O. Box 906, Mc Call, Zip 83638–0906; tel. 208/634–2221; Karen J. Kellie, Administrator

SAINT ALPHONSUS REGIONAL MEDICAL CENTER (O, 280 beds) 1055 North Curtis Road, Boise, ID Zip 83706–1370; tel. 208/378–2121; Sandra B. Bruce, President and Chief Executive Officer

For explanation of codes following names, see page B2.
★ Indicates Type III membership in the American Hospital Association.

ST. BENEDICTS FAMILY MEDICAL CENTER (C, 65 beds) 709 North Lincoln Avenue, Jerome, ID Zip 83338–1851, Mailing Address: P.O. Box 586, Zip 83338–0586; tel. 208/324–4301; Michael C. Wiltermood, Administrator

INDIANA: SAINT JOHN'S HEALTH SYSTEM (O, 261 beds) 2015 Jackson Street, Anderson, IN Zip 46016–4339; tel. 765/649–2511; Jerry D. Brumitt, President and Chief Executive Officer

SAINT JOSEPH'S HOSPITAL OF MARSHALL COUNTY (O, 36 beds) 1915 Lake Avenue, Plymouth, IN Zip 46563–9905, Mailing Address: P.O. Box 670, Zip 46563–9905; tel. 219/936–3181; Brian E. Dietz, FACHE, Executive Vice President

ST. JOSEPH'S MEDICAL CENTER (O, 289 beds) 801 East LaSalle, South Bend, IN Zip 46617–2800, Mailing Address: P.O. Box 1935, Zip 46634–1935; tel. 219/237–7111; Robert L. Beyer, President and Chief Executive Officer

MARYLAND: HOLY CROSS HOSPITAL OF SILVER SPRING (O, 454 beds) 1500 Forest Glen Road, Silver Spring, MD Zip 20910–1484; tel. 301/754–7000; Cornelius McKelvey, Interim Chief Executive Officer

OHIO: MOUNT CARMEL HEALTH SYSTEM (O, 929 beds) Columbus, OH Mailing Address: 793 West State Street, Zip 43222–1551; tel. 614/234–5423; Joseph Calvaruso, Interim Chief Executive Officer

Owned, leased, sponsored:	7 hospitals	2575 beds
Contract–managed:	4 hospitals	168 beds
Totals:	11 hospitals	2743 beds

★0027: HORIZON HEALTHCARE, INC. (NP)
2300 North Mayfair Road, Suite 550, Milwaukee, WI Zip 53226–1508; tel. 414/257–3888; Sister Renee Rose, President and Chief Executive Officer

WISCONSIN: COLUMBIA HOSPITAL (C, 334 beds) 2025 East Newport Avenue, Milwaukee, WI Zip 53211–2990; tel. 414/961–3300; Susan Henckel, Executive Vice President and Chief Executive Officer

COMMUNITY MEMORIAL HOSPITAL (C, 142 beds) W180 N8085 Town Hall Road, Menomonee Falls, WI Zip 53051, Mailing Address: P.O. Box 408, Zip 53052–0408; tel. 414/251–1000; Robert Eugene Drisner, President and Chief Executive Officer

FROEDTERT MEMORIAL LUTHERAN HOSPITAL (C, 472 beds) 9200 West Wisconsin Avenue, Milwaukee, WI Zip 53226–3596, Mailing Address: P.O. Box 26099, Zip 53226–3596; tel. 414/259–3000; William D. Petasnick, President

KENOSHA HOSPITAL AND MEDICAL CENTER (C, 116 beds) 6308 Eighth Avenue, Kenosha, WI Zip 53143–5082; tel. 414/656–2011; Richard O. Schmidt Jr., President, Chief Executive Officer and General Counsel

OCONOMOWOC MEMORIAL HOSPITAL (C, 73 beds) 791 Summit Avenue, Oconomowoc, WI Zip 53066–3896; tel. 414/569–9400; Douglas Guy, President and Chief Executive Officer

Owned, leased, sponsored:	0 hospitals	0 beds
Contract–managed:	5 hospitals	1137 beds
Totals:	5 hospitals	1137 beds

0455: HOSPITAL GROUP OF AMERICA (IO)
1265 Drummers Lane, Suite 107, Wayne, PA Zip 19087; tel. 610/687–5151; Mark R. Russell, President and Chief Executive Officer

DELAWARE: MEADOW WOOD BEHAVIORAL HEALTH SYSTEM (O, 50 beds) 575 South Dupont Highway, New Castle, DE Zip 19720–4600; tel. 302/328–3330; Joseph Pyle, Administrator

ILLINOIS: HARTGROVE HOSPITAL (O, 119 beds) 520 North Ridgeway Avenue, Chicago, IL Zip 60624–1299; tel. 773/722–3113; Karen E. Johnson, Administrator

NEW JERSEY: HAMPTON HOSPITAL (O, 100 beds) Rancocas Road, Westampton Township, NJ Zip 08073, Mailing Address: P.O. Box 7000, Zip 08073; tel. 609/267–7000; Michael Terwilliger, Acting Chief Executive Officer

Owned, leased, sponsored:	3 hospitals	269 beds
Contract–managed:	0 hospitals	0 beds
Totals:	3 hospitals	269 beds

★5355: HOSPITAL SISTERS HEALTH SYSTEM (CC)
Springfield, IL Mailing Address: P.O. Box 19431, Zip 62794–9431; tel. 217/523–4747; Sister Jomary Trstensky, President

ILLINOIS: ST. ANTHONY'S MEMORIAL HOSPITAL (O, 146 beds) 503 North Maple Street, Effingham, IL Zip 62401–2099; tel. 217/347–1495; Anthony D. Pfitzer, Administrator

ST. ELIZABETH'S HOSPITAL (O, 289 beds) 211 South Third Street, Belleville, IL Zip 62222–0694; tel. 618/234–2120; Gerald M. Harman, Executive Vice President

ST. FRANCIS HOSPITAL (O, 97 beds) 1215 Franciscan Drive, Litchfield, IL Zip 62056, Mailing Address: P.O. Box 1215, Zip 62056–1215; tel. 217/324–2191; Michael Sipkoski, Executive Vice President and Chief Executive Officer

ST. JOHN'S HOSPITAL (O, 579 beds) 800 East Carpenter Street, Springfield, IL Zip 62769–0002; tel. 217/544–6464; Allison C. Laabs, Executive Vice President and Administrator

ST. JOSEPH'S HOSPITAL (O, 57 beds) 9515 Holy Cross Lane, Breese, IL Zip 62230–0099; tel. 618/526–4511; Jacolyn M. Schlautman, Executive Vice President

ST. JOSEPH'S HOSPITAL (O, 76 beds) 1515 Main Street, Highland, IL Zip 62249–1656; tel. 618/654–7421; Anthony G. Mastrangelo, Executive Vice President and Chief Executive Officer

ST. MARY'S HOSPITAL (O, 192 beds) 1800 East Lake Shore Drive, Decatur, IL Zip 62521–3883; tel. 217/464–2966; Keith L. Callahan, Executive Vice President and Administrator

ST. MARY'S HOSPITAL (O, 170 beds) 111 East Spring Street, Streator, IL Zip 61364–3399; tel. 815/673–2311; James F. Dover, Administrator and Executive Vice President

WISCONSIN: SACRED HEART HOSPITAL (O, 261 beds) 900 West Clairemont Avenue, Eau Claire, WI Zip 54701–5105; tel. 715/839–4121; Stephen F. Ronstrom, Executive Vice President

ST. JOSEPH'S HOSPITAL (O, 127 beds) 2661 County Highway I., Chippewa Falls, WI Zip 54729–1498; tel. 715/723–1811; David B. Fish, Executive Vice President

ST. MARY'S HOSPITAL MEDICAL CENTER (O, 119 beds) 1726 Shawano Avenue, Green Bay, WI Zip 54303–3282; tel. 920/498–4200; James G. Coller, Executive Vice President and Administrator

ST. NICHOLAS HOSPITAL (O, 185 beds) 1601 North Taylor Drive, Sheboygan, WI Zip 53081–2496; tel. 920/459–8300; Michael J. Stenger, Executive Vice President and Administrator

ST. VINCENT HOSPITAL (O, 298 beds) 835 South Van Buren Street, Green Bay, WI Zip 54307–3508, Mailing Address: P.O. Box 13508, Zip 54307–3508; tel. 920/433–0111; Joseph J. Neidenbach, Administrator and Executive Vice President

Owned, leased, sponsored:	13 hospitals	2596 beds
Contract–managed:	0 hospitals	0 beds
Totals:	13 hospitals	2596 beds

★5565: INCARNATE WORD HEALTH SERVICES (CC)
9311 San Pedro, Suite 1250, San Antonio, TX Zip 78216–4469; tel. 210/524–4100; Joseph Blasko Jr., President and Chief Executive Officer

TEXAS: SANTA ROSA HEALTH CARE CORPORATION (O, 608 beds) 519 West Houston Street, San Antonio, TX Zip 78207–3108; tel. 210/704–2011; William C. Finlayson, President and Chief Executive Officer

SPOHN HEALTH SYSTEM (O, 489 beds) 1702 Santa Fe, Corpus Christi, TX Zip 78404; tel. 512/881–3000; Jake Henry Jr., President

SPOHN KLEBERG MEMORIAL HOSPITAL (O, 100 beds) 1311 General Cavazos Boulevard, Kingsville, TX Zip 78363–1197, Mailing Address: P.O. Box 1197, Zip 78363–1197; tel. 512/595–1661; Ernesto M. Flores Jr., Administrator

For explanation of codes following names, see page B2.
★ *Indicates Type III membership in the American Hospital Association.*

© 1998 AHA Guide

ST. JOSEPH'S HOSPITAL AND HEALTH CENTER (O, 175 beds) 820 Clarksville Street, Paris, TX Zip 75460–9070, Mailing Address: P.O. Box 9070, Zip 75461–9070; tel. 903/785–4521; Monty E. McLaurin, President

Owned, leased, sponsored:	4 hospitals	1372 beds
Contract–managed:	0 hospitals	0 beds
Totals:	4 hospitals	1372 beds

2025: INFIRMARY HEALTH SYSTEM, INC. (NP)

3 Mobile Infirmary Circle, Mobile, AL Zip 36607–3520; tel. 334/431–5500; E. Chandler Bramlett Jr., President and Chief Executive Officer

ALABAMA: GROVE HILL MEMORIAL HOSPITAL (C, 46 beds) 295 South Jackson Street, Grove Hill, AL Zip 36451, Mailing Address: P.O. Box 935, Zip 36451; tel. 334/275–3191; Floyd N. Price, Administrator

MOBILE INFIRMARY MEDICAL CENTER (O, 511 beds) 5 Mobile Infirmary Drive North, Mobile, AL Zip 36601, Mailing Address: P.O. Box 2144, Zip 36652–2144; tel. 334/431–2400; E. Chandler Bramlett Jr., President and Chief Executive Officer

WASHINGTON COUNTY INFIRMARY AND NURSING HOME (C, 88 beds) St. Stephens Avenue, Chatom, AL Zip 36518, Mailing Address: P.O. Box 597, Zip 36518–0597; tel. 334/847–2223; Howard C. Holcomb, Administrator

Owned, leased, sponsored:	1 hospital	511 beds
Contract–managed:	2 hospitals	134 beds
Totals:	3 hospitals	645 beds

★1305: INOVA HEALTH SYSTEM (NP)

8001 Braddock Road, Springfield, VA Zip 22151–2150; tel. 703/321–4213; J. Knox Singleton, President

VIRGINIA: INOVA ALEXANDRIA HOSPITAL (O, 300 beds) 4320 Seminary Road, Alexandria, VA Zip 22304–1594; tel. 703/504–3000; H. Patrick Walters, President

INOVA FAIR OAKS HOSPITAL (O, 133 beds) 3600 Joseph Siewick Drive, Fairfax, VA Zip 22033–1709; tel. 703/391–3600; Steven E. Brown, Administrator

INOVA FAIRFAX HOSPITAL (O, 656 beds) 3300 Gallows Road, Falls Church, VA Zip 22042–3300; tel. 703/698–1110; Jolene Tornabeni, Administrator

INOVA MOUNT VERNON HOSPITAL (O, 229 beds) 2501 Parker's Lane, Alexandria, VA Zip 22306–3209; tel. 703/664–7000; Susan Herbert, Administrator

Owned, leased, sponsored:	4 hospitals	1318 beds
Contract–managed:	0 hospitals	0 beds
Totals:	4 hospitals	1318 beds

★0305: INTEGRIS HEALTH (NP)

3366 Northwest Expressway, Oklahoma City, OK Zip 73112–4416; tel. 405/949–6068; Stanley F. Hupfeld, President and Chief Executive Officer

OKLAHOMA: BLACKWELL REGIONAL HOSPITAL (L, 34 beds) 710 South 13th Street, Blackwell, OK Zip 74631–3700; tel. 580/363–2311; Greg Martin, Administrator and Chief Executive Officer

CHOCTAW MEMORIAL HOSPITAL (C, 38 beds) 1405 East Kirk Road, Hugo, OK Zip 74743–3603; tel. 580/326–6414; Michael R. Morel, Administrator

DRUMRIGHT MEMORIAL HOSPITAL (L, 15 beds) 501 South Lou Allard Drive, Drumright, OK Zip 74030–4899; tel. 918/352–2525; Jerry Jones, Administrator

INTEGRIS BAPTIST MEDICAL CENTER (O, 401 beds) 3300 N.W. Expressway, Oklahoma City, OK Zip 73112–4481; tel. 405/949–3011; Thomas R. Rice, FACHE, President and Chief Operating Officer

INTEGRIS BAPTIST REGIONAL HEALTH CENTER (O, 123 beds) 200 Second Street S.W., Miami, OK Zip 74354–6830, Mailing Address: P.O. Box 1207, Zip 74355–1207; tel. 918/540–7100; Steven G. Kelly, Consolidated Administrator

INTEGRIS BASS BAPTIST HEALTH CENTER (O, 140 beds) 600 South Monroe Street, Enid, OK Zip 73701, Mailing Address: P.O. Box 3168, Zip 73702–3168; tel. 580/233–2300; Wayne A. Sensor, Administrator

INTEGRIS GROVE GENERAL HOSPITAL (O, 72 beds) 1310 South Main Street, Grove, OK Zip 74344–1310; tel. 918/786–2243; Dee Renshaw, Administrator

INTEGRIS MENTAL HEALTH SYSTEM–WILLOW VIEW (O, 44 beds) 2601 North Spencer Road, Spencer, OK Zip 73084–3699, Mailing Address: P.O. Box 11137, Oklahoma City, Zip 73136–0137; tel. 405/427–2441; Murali Krishna, M.D., President and Chief Operating Officer

INTEGRIS SOUTHWEST MEDICAL CENTER (O, 343 beds) 4401 South Western, Oklahoma City, OK Zip 73109–3441; tel. 405/636–7000; Thomas R. Rice, FACHE, President and Chief Operating Officer

INTEGRIS BETHANY HOSPITAL (C, 70 beds) 7600 N.W. 23rd Street, Bethany, OK Zip 73008–4900; tel. 405/787–3450; David Lundquist, Chief Executive Officer

INTEGRIS CLINTON REGIONAL HOSPITAL (L, 49 beds) 100 North 30th Street, Clinton, OK Zip 73601–3117, Mailing Address: P.O. Box 1569, Zip 73601–1569; tel. 580/323–2363; Jerry Jones, Administrator

MARSHALL MEMORIAL HOSPITAL (C, 25 beds) 1 Hospital Drive, Madill, OK Zip 73446, Mailing Address: P.O. Box 827, Zip 73446–0827; tel. 405/795–3384; Norma Howard, Administrator

MAYES COUNTY MEDICAL CENTER (L, 34 beds) 129 North Kentucky Street, Pryor, OK Zip 74361–4211, Mailing Address: P.O. Box 278, Zip 74362–0278; tel. 918/825–1600; W. Charles Jordan, Administrator

PAWNEE MUNICIPAL HOSPITAL (L, 32 beds) 1212 Fourth Street, Pawnee, OK Zip 74058–4046, Mailing Address: P.O. Box 467, Zip 74058–0467; tel. 918/762–2577; John Ketring, Administrator

STROUD MUNICIPAL HOSPITAL (L, 20 beds) Highway 66 West, Stroud, OK Zip 74079, Mailing Address: P.O. Box 530, Zip 74079–0530; tel. 918/968–3571; James D. Moore, Administrator

Owned, leased, sponsored:	12 hospitals	1307 beds
Contract–managed:	3 hospitals	133 beds
Totals:	15 hospitals	1440 beds

★1815: INTERMOUNTAIN HEALTH CARE, INC. (NP)

36 South State Street, 22nd Floor, Salt Lake City, UT Zip 84111–1453; tel. 801/442–2000; Scott S. Parker, President

IDAHO: CASSIA REGIONAL MEDICAL CENTER (O, 38 beds) 1501 Hiland Avenue, Burley, ID Zip 83318–2675; tel. 208/678–4444; Richard Packer, Administrator

POCATELLO REGIONAL MEDICAL CENTER (O, 87 beds) 777 Hospital Way, Pocatello, ID Zip 83201–2797; tel. 208/234–0777; Earl L. Christison, Administrator

UTAH: ALTA VIEW HOSPITAL (O, 70 beds) 9660 South 1300 East, Sandy, UT Zip 84094–3793; tel. 801/576–2600; Wes Thompson, Administrator and Chief Executive Officer

AMERICAN FORK HOSPITAL (O, 66 beds) 170 North 1100 East, American Fork, UT Zip 84003–9787; tel. 801/763–3300; Keith N. Alexander, Administrator and Chief Operating Officer

BEAR RIVER VALLEY HOSPITAL (O, 58 beds) 440 West 600 North, Tremonton, UT Zip 84337–2497; tel. 801/257–7441; Robert F. Jex, Administrator

COTTONWOOD HOSPITAL MEDICAL CENTER (O, 148 beds) 5770 South 300 East, Salt Lake City, UT Zip 84107–6186; tel. 801/262–3461; Douglas R. Fonnesbeck, Administrator

DELTA COMMUNITY MEDICAL CENTER (O, 20 beds) 126 South White Sage Avenue, Delta, UT Zip 84624–8937; tel. 801/864–5591; James E. Beckstrand, Administrator

DIXIE REGIONAL MEDICAL CENTER (O, 149 beds) 544 South 400 East, Saint George, UT Zip 84770–3799; tel. 435/634–4000; L. Steven Wilson, Administrator

FILLMORE COMMUNITY MEDICAL CENTER (O, 20 beds) 674 South Highway 99, Fillmore, UT Zip 84631–5013; tel. 801/743–5591; James E. Beckstrand, Administrator

Section B

For explanation of codes following names, see page B2.
★ Indicates Type III membership in the American Hospital Association.

GARFIELD MEMORIAL HOSPITAL AND CLINICS (O, 44 beds) 200 North 400 East, Panguitch, UT Zip 84759, Mailing Address: P.O. Box 389, Zip 84759–0389; tel. 435/676–8811; Eric Packer, Administrator

LDS HOSPITAL (O, 412 beds) Eighth Avenue and C. Street, Salt Lake City, UT Zip 84143–0001; tel. 801/321–1100; Richard M. Cagen, Chief Executive Officer and Administrator

LOGAN REGIONAL HOSPITAL (O, 112 beds) 1400 North 500 East, Logan, UT Zip 84341–2455; tel. 435/752–2050; Richard Smith, Administrator

MCKAY–DEE HOSPITAL CENTER (O, 293 beds) 3939 Harrison Boulevard, Ogden, UT Zip 84409–2386, Mailing Address: Box 9370, Zip 84409–0370; tel. 801/398–2800; Thomas F. Hanrahan, Chief Executive Officer

OREM COMMUNITY HOSPITAL (O, 20 beds) 331 North 400 West, Orem, UT Zip 84057–1999; tel. 801/224–4080; Kim Nielsen, Administrator and Chief Operating Officer

PRIMARY CHILDREN'S MEDICAL CENTER (O, 183 beds) 100 North Medical Drive, Salt Lake City, UT Zip 84113–1100; tel. 801/588–2000; Joseph R. Horton, Chief Executive Officer and Administrator

SANPETE VALLEY HOSPITAL (O, 20 beds) 1100 South Medical Drive, Mount Pleasant, UT Zip 84647–2222; tel. 435/462–2441; George Winn, Administrator

SEVIER VALLEY HOSPITAL (O, 27 beds) 1100 North Main Street, Richfield, UT Zip 84701–1843; tel. 435/896–8271; Gary E. Beck, Administrator

UTAH VALLEY REGIONAL MEDICAL CENTER (O, 314 beds) 1034 North 500 West, Provo, UT Zip 84604–3337; tel. 801/373–7850; Chris Coons, Chief Operating Officer

VALLEY VIEW MEDICAL CENTER (O, 36 beds) 595 South 75 East, Cedar City, UT Zip 84720–3462; tel. 435/586–6587; Craig M. Smedley, Administrator

WASATCH COUNTY HOSPITAL (L, 20 beds) 55 South 500 East, Heber City, UT Zip 84032–1999; tel. 801/654–2500; Randall K. Probst, Administrator

WYOMING: EVANSTON REGIONAL HOSPITAL (O, 38 beds) 190 Arrowhead Drive, Evanston, WY Zip 82930–9266; tel. 307/789–3636; Robert W. Allen, Administrator

STAR VALLEY HOSPITAL (C, 39 beds) 110 Hospital Lane, Afton, WY Zip 83110, Mailing Address: P.O. Box 579, Zip 83110–0579; tel. 307/886–5800; Alberto Vasquez, Administrator

Owned, leased, sponsored:	21 hospitals	2175 beds
Contract–managed:	1 hospital	39 beds
Totals:	22 hospitals	2214 beds

★0061: IOWA HEALTH SYSTEM (NP)
1200 Pleasant Street, Des Moines, IA Zip 50309–1453; tel. 515/241–6161; Samuel T. Wallace, President

IOWA: ALLEN MEMORIAL HOSPITAL (O, 175 beds) 1825 Logan Avenue, Waterloo, IA Zip 50703–1916; tel. 319/235–3987; Richard A. Seidler, FACHE, Chief Executive Officer

ANAMOSA COMMUNITY HOSPITAL (L, 17 beds) 104 Broadway Place, Anamosa, IA Zip 52205–1100; tel. 319/462–6131; Margaret Robinson, Administrator

CLARKE COUNTY HOSPITAL (C, 48 beds) 800 South Fillmore Street, Osceola, IA Zip 50213; tel. 515/342–2184; David Stark, Interim Administrator

DALLAS COUNTY HOSPITAL (C, 49 beds) 610 10th Street, Perry, IA Zip 50220–2221, Mailing Address: P.O. Box 608, Zip 50220–0608; tel. 515/465–3547; Vernette Riley, Administrator and Chief Executive Officer

FINLEY HOSPITAL (O, 138 beds) 350 North Grandview Avenue, Dubuque, IA Zip 52001–6392; tel. 319/582–1881; Kevin L. Rogols, President and Chief Executive Officer

GRUNDY COUNTY MEMORIAL HOSPITAL (C, 71 beds) 201 East J. Avenue, Grundy Center, IA Zip 50638–2096; tel. 319/824–5421; James A. Faulwell, Administrator

IOWA LUTHERAN HOSPITAL (O, 770 beds) 700 East University Avenue, Des Moines, IA Zip 50316–2392; tel. 515/263–5612; James H. Skogsbergh, President

IOWA METHODIST MEDICAL CENTER (O, 770 beds) 1200 Pleasant Street, Des Moines, IA Zip 50309–9976; tel. 515/241–6212; James H. Skogsbergh, President

ST. LUKE'S HOSPITAL (O, 391 beds) 1026 A. Avenue N.E., Cedar Rapids, IA Zip 52402–3026, Mailing Address: P.O. Box 3026, Zip 52406–3026; tel. 319/369–7211; Stephen E. Vanourny, M.D., President and Chief Executive Officer

ST. LUKE'S REGIONAL MEDICAL CENTER (O, 187 beds) 2720 Stone Park Boulevard, Sioux City, IA Zip 51104–2000; tel. 712/279–3500; John D. Daniels, President and Chief Executive Officer

Owned, leased, sponsored:	7 hospitals	2448 beds
Contract–managed:	3 hospitals	168 beds
Totals:	10 hospitals	2616 beds

★7775: JEFFERSON HEALTH SYSTEM (NP)
259 Radnor–Chester Road, Suite 290, Wayne, PA Zip 19087–5288; tel. 610/225–6200; Douglas S. Peters, President and Chief Executive Officer

PENNSYLVANIA: BRYN MAWR HOSPITAL (O, 275 beds) 130 South Bryn Mawr Avenue, Bryn Mawr, PA Zip 19010–3160; tel. 610/526–3000; Kenneth Hanover, President and Chief Executive Officer

BRYN MAWR REHABILITATION HOSPITAL (O, 141 beds) 414 Paoli Pike, Malvern, PA Zip 19355–3311, Mailing Address: P.O. Box 3007, Zip 19355–3300; tel. 610/251–5400; Barry S. Rabner, President

LANKENAU HOSPITAL (O, 313 beds) 100 Lancaster Avenue West, Wynnewood, PA Zip 19096–3411; tel. 610/645–2000; William McCune, Senior Vice President, Operations

PAOLI MEMORIAL HOSPITAL (O, 137 beds) 255 West Lancaster Avenue, Paoli, PA Zip 19301–1792; tel. 610/648–1204; Kenneth Hanover, President and Chief Executive Officer

THOMAS JEFFERSON UNIVERSITY HOSPITAL (O, 686 beds) 111 South 11th Street, Philadelphia, PA Zip 19107–5096; tel. 215/955–7022; Thomas J. Lewis, President and Chief Executive Officer

Owned, leased, sponsored:	5 hospitals	1552 beds
Contract–managed:	0 hospitals	0 beds
Totals:	5 hospitals	1552 beds

★0052: JEWISH HOSPITAL HEALTHCARE SERVICES (NP)
217 East Chestnut Street, Louisville, KY Zip 40202–1886; tel. 502/587–4011; Henry C. Wagner, President

INDIANA: CLARK MEMORIAL HOSPITAL (C, 244 beds) 1220 Missouri Avenue, Jeffersonville, IN Zip 47130–3743, Mailing Address: Box 69, Zip 47131–0069; tel. 812/282–6631; Merle E. Stepp, President and Chief Executive Officer

SCOTT MEMORIAL HOSPITAL (C, 45 beds) 1415 North Gardner Street, Scottsburg, IN Zip 47170–0456, Mailing Address: Box 430, Zip 47170–0430; tel. 812/752–8500; Clifford D. Nay, Executive Director

SOUTHERN INDIANA REHABILITATION HOSPITAL (O, 60 beds) 3104 Blackiston Boulevard, New Albany, IN Zip 47150–9579; tel. 812/941–8300; Randy L. Napier, President and Chief Executive Officer

WASHINGTON COUNTY MEMORIAL HOSPITAL (C, 50 beds) 911 North Shelby Street, Salem, IN Zip 47167; tel. 812/883–5881; Rodney M. Coats, President and Chief Executive Officer

KENTUCKY: FRAZIER REHABILITATION CENTER (O, 95 beds) 220 Abraham Flexner Way, Louisville, KY Zip 40202–1887; tel. 502/582–7400; Jason Roeback, President

JEWISH HOSPITAL (O, 433 beds) 217 East Chestnut Street, Louisville, KY Zip 40202–1886; tel. 502/587–4011; Douglas E. Shaw, President

JEWISH HOSPITAL LEXINGTON (O, 174 beds) 150 North Eagle Creek Drive, Lexington, KY Zip 40509–1807; tel. 606/268–4800; Rebecca Lewis, President

JEWISH HOSPITAL–SHELBYVILLE (O, 58 beds) 727 Hospital Drive, Shelbyville, KY Zip 40065–1699; tel. 502/647–4000; Timothy L. Jarm, President

PATTIE A. CLAY HOSPITAL (C, 96 beds) EKU By–Pass, Richmond, KY Zip 40475, Mailing Address: P.O. Box 1600, Zip 40476–2603; tel. 606/625–3131; Richard M. Thomas, President

---

For explanation of codes following names, see page B2.
★ Indicates Type III membership in the American Hospital Association.

TAYLOR COUNTY HOSPITAL (C, 90 beds) 1700 Old Lebanon Road, Campbellsville, KY Zip 42718–9600; tel. 502/465–3561; David R. Hayes, President

UNIVERSITY OF LOUISVILLE HOSPITAL (C, 269 beds) 530 South Jackson Street, Louisville, KY Zip 40202–3611; tel. 502/562–3000; James H. Taylor, President and Chief Executive Officer

Owned, leased, sponsored:	5 hospitals	820 beds
Contract–managed:	6 hospitals	794 beds
Totals:	11 hospitals	1614 beds

★1015: JOHNS HOPKINS HEALTH SYSTEM (NP)
600 North Wolfe Street, Baltimore, MD Zip 21287–1193; tel. 410/955–9540; Ronald R. Peterson, President

MARYLAND: HOWARD COUNTY GENERAL HOSPITAL (O, 182 beds) 5755 Cedar Lane, Columbia, MD Zip 21044–2999; tel. 410/740–7890; Victor A. Broccolino, President and Chief Executive Officer

JOHNS HOPKINS BAYVIEW MEDICAL CENTER (O, 684 beds) 4940 Eastern Avenue, Baltimore, MD Zip 21224–2780; tel. 410/550–0100; Ronald R. Peterson, President

JOHNS HOPKINS HOSPITAL (O, 853 beds) 600 North Wolfe Street, Baltimore, MD Zip 21287–0002; tel. 410/955–5000; Ronald R. Peterson, President

Owned, leased, sponsored:	3 hospitals	1719 beds
Contract–managed:	0 hospitals	0 beds
Totals:	3 hospitals	1719 beds

★2105: KAISER FOUNDATION HOSPITALS (NP)
One Kaiser Plaza, Oakland, CA Zip 94612–3600; tel. 510/271–5910; David M. Lawrence, M.D., Chairman and Chief Executive Officer

CALIFORNIA: KAISER FOUNDATION HOSPITAL (O, 210 beds) 2425 Geary Boulevard, San Francisco, CA Zip 94115; tel. 415/202–2000; Richard R. Pettingill, Administrator

KAISER FOUNDATION HOSPITAL (O, 117 beds) 401 Bicentennial Way, Santa Rosa, CA Zip 95403; tel. 707/571–4000; Dorcas Walton, Administrator

KAISER FOUNDATION HOSPITAL (O, 384 beds) 4747 Sunset Boulevard, Los Angeles, CA Zip 90027–6072; tel. 213/783–4011; Joseph W. Hummel, Administrator

KAISER FOUNDATION HOSPITAL (O, 116 beds) 7300 North Fresno Street, Fresno, CA Zip 93720; tel. 209/448–4555; Edward S. Glavis, Administrator

KAISER FOUNDATION HOSPITAL (O, 264 beds) 280 West MacArthur Boulevard, Oakland, CA Zip 94611; tel. 510/987–1000; Bernard J. Tyson, Administrator

KAISER FOUNDATION HOSPITAL (O, 210 beds) 1425 South Main Street, Walnut Creek, CA Zip 94596; tel. 510/295–4000; Sandra Small, Administrator

KAISER FOUNDATION HOSPITAL (O, 150 beds) 441 North Lakeview Avenue, Anaheim, CA Zip 92807; tel. 714/279–4100; Gerald A. McCall, Administrator

KAISER FOUNDATION HOSPITAL (O, 241 beds) 9961 Sierra Avenue, Fontana, CA Zip 92335–6794; tel. 909/427–5000; Patricia Siegel, Senior Vice President and Area Manager

KAISER FOUNDATION HOSPITAL (O, 164 beds) 25825 South Vermont Avenue, Harbor City, CA Zip 90710; tel. 310/325–5111; Mary Ann Barnes, Administrator

KAISER FOUNDATION HOSPITAL (O, 190 beds) 27400 Hesperian Boulevard, Hayward, CA Zip 94545–4297; tel. 510/784–4313; Bernard J. Tyson, Administrator

KAISER FOUNDATION HOSPITAL (O, 277 beds) 4647 Zion Avenue, San Diego, CA Zip 92120; tel. 619/528–5000; Kenneth F. Colling, Senior Vice President and Area Manager

KAISER FOUNDATION HOSPITAL (O, 144 beds) 1150 Veterans Boulevard, Redwood City, CA Zip 94063–2087; tel. 650/299–2000; Helen Wilmot, Administrator

KAISER FOUNDATION HOSPITAL (O, 304 beds) 2025 Morse Avenue, Sacramento, CA Zip 95825–2115; tel. 916/973–5000; Sarah Krevans, Administrator

KAISER FOUNDATION HOSPITAL (O, 221 beds) 6600 Bruceville Road, Sacramento, CA Zip 95823; tel. 916/688–2430; Sarah Krevans, Administrator

KAISER FOUNDATION HOSPITAL (O, 119 beds) 99 Montecillo Road, San Rafael, CA Zip 94903–3397; tel. 415/444–2000; Richard R. Pettingill, Administrator

KAISER FOUNDATION HOSPITAL (O, 249 beds) 900 Kiely Boulevard, Santa Clara, CA Zip 95051–5386; tel. 408/236–6400; Helen Wilmot, Administrator

KAISER FOUNDATION HOSPITAL (O, 79 beds) 1200 El Camino Real, South San Francisco, CA Zip 94080–3299; tel. 650/742–2547; Richard R. Pettingill, Administrator

KAISER FOUNDATION HOSPITAL (O, 266 beds) 13652 Cantara Street, Panorama City, CA Zip 91402; tel. 818/375–2000; Dev Mahadevan, Administrator

KAISER FOUNDATION HOSPITAL (O, 139 beds) 5601 DeSoto Avenue, Woodland Hills, CA Zip 91365–4084; tel. 818/719–2000; James L. Breeden, Administrator

KAISER FOUNDATION HOSPITAL AND REHABILITATION CENTER (O, 219 beds) 975 Sereno Drive, Vallejo, CA Zip 94589; tel. 707/651–1000; Sandra Small, Administrator

KAISER FOUNDATION HOSPITAL–BELLFLOWER (O, 272 beds) 9400 East Rosecrans Avenue, Bellflower, CA Zip 90706–2246; tel. 562/461–3000; Timothy A. Reed, Administrator

KAISER FOUNDATION HOSPITAL–RIVERSIDE (O, 118 beds) 10800 Magnolia Avenue, Riverside, CA Zip 92505–3000; tel. 909/353–4600; Robert S. Lund, Administrator

KAISER FOUNDATION HOSPITAL–WEST LOS ANGELES (O, 161 beds) 6041 Cadillac Avenue, Los Angeles, CA Zip 90034; tel. 213/857–2201; Joseph W. Hummel, Administrator

SANTA TERESA COMMUNITY HOSPITAL (O, 178 beds) 250 Hospital Parkway, San Jose, CA Zip 95119; tel. 408/972–7000; Neil Humphrey, Administrator

HAWAII: KAISER FOUNDATION HOSPITAL (O, 188 beds) 3288 Moanalua Road, Honolulu, HI Zip 96819; tel. 808/834–5333; Bruce Behnke, Administrator

OREGON: KAISER SUNNYSIDE MEDICAL CENTER (O, 170 beds) 10180 S.E. Sunnyside Road, Clackamas, OR Zip 97015–9303; tel. 503/571–4002; Alide Chase, Administrator

Owned, leased, sponsored:	26 hospitals	5150 beds
Contract–managed:	0 hospitals	0 beds
Totals:	26 hospitals	5150 beds

★2755: LEGACY HEALTH SYSTEM (NP)
1919 N.W. Lovejoy Street, Portland, OR Zip 97209–1503; tel. 503/415–5600; John G. King, President and Chief Executive Officer

LEGACY EMANUEL HOSPITAL AND HEALTH CENTER (O, 350 beds) 2801 North Gantenbein Avenue, Portland, OR Zip 97227–1674; tel. 503/413–2200; Stephani White, Vice President and Site Administrator

LEGACY GOOD SAMARITAN HOSPITAL AND MEDICAL CENTER (O, 294 beds) 1015 N.W. 22nd Avenue, Portland, OR Zip 97210; tel. 503/413–7711; John M. Mootry, Vice President and Site Administrator

LEGACY MERIDIAN PARK HOSPITAL (O, 116 beds) 19300 S.W. 65th Avenue, Tualatin, OR Zip 97062–9741; tel. 503/692–1212; Jeff Cushing, Vice President and Site Administrator

LEGACY MOUNT HOOD MEDICAL CENTER (O, 86 beds) 24800 S.E. Stark, Gresham, OR Zip 97030–0154; tel. 503/667–1122; Jane C. Cummins, Senior Vice President Clinical Operations

Owned, leased, sponsored:	4 hospitals	846 beds
Contract–managed:	0 hospitals	0 beds
Totals:	4 hospitals	846 beds

★0060: LIFESPAN CORPORATION (NP)
167 Point Street, Providence, RI Zip 02903–4771; tel. 401/444–6699; William Kreykes, President and Chief Executive Officer

For explanation of codes following names, see page B2.
★ Indicates Type III membership in the American Hospital Association.

Section B

MASSACHUSETTS: NEW ENGLAND MEDICAL CENTER (O, 349 beds) 750 Washington Street, Boston, MA Zip 02111–1845; tel. 617/636–5000; Thomas F. O'Donnell Jr., M.D., FACS, President and Chief Executive Officer

RHODE ISLAND: EMMA PENDLETON BRADLEY HOSPITAL (O, 60 beds) 1011 Veterans Memorial Parkway, East Providence, RI Zip 02915–5099; tel. 401/434–3400; Daniel J. Wall, President and Chief Executive Officer

MIRIAM HOSPITAL (O, 216 beds) 164 Summit Avenue, Providence, RI Zip 02906–2895; tel. 401/793–2000; Steven D. Baron, President

NEWPORT HOSPITAL (O, 85 beds) 11 Friendship Street, Newport, RI Zip 02840–2299; tel. 401/846–6400; Arthur J. Sampson, President and Chief Executive Officer

RHODE ISLAND HOSPITAL (O, 677 beds) 593 Eddy Street, Providence, RI Zip 02903–4900; tel. 401/444–4000; Steven D. Baron, President and Chief Executive Officer

Owned, leased, sponsored:	5 hospitals	1387 beds
Contract–managed:	0 hospitals	0 beds
Totals:	5 hospitals	1387 beds

2295: LITTLE COMPANY OF MARY SISTERS HEALTHCARE SYSTEM (CC)
9350 South California Avenue, Evergreen Park, IL Zip 60805–2595; tel. 708/229–5491; Sister Carol Pacini, Provincialate Superior

CALIFORNIA: LITTLE COMPANY OF MARY HOSPITAL (O, 354 beds) 4101 Torrance Boulevard, Torrance, CA Zip 90503–4698; tel. 310/540–7676; Mark Costa, President

ILLINOIS: LITTLE COMPANY OF MARY HOSPITAL AND HEALTH CARE CENTERS (O, 326 beds) 2800 West 95th Street, Evergreen Park, IL Zip 60805–2795; tel. 708/422–6200; Sister Kathleen McIntyre, President

INDIANA: MEMORIAL HOSPITAL AND HEALTH CARE CENTER (O, 124 beds) 800 West Ninth Street, Jasper, IN Zip 47546–2516; tel. 812/482–2345; Sister M. Adrian Davis, Ph.D., President and Chief Executive Officer

Owned, leased, sponsored:	3 hospitals	804 beds
Contract–managed:	0 hospitals	0 beds
Totals:	3 hospitals	804 beds

2175: LOMA LINDA UNIVERSITY HEALTH SCIENCES CENTER (NP)
11161 Anderson Street, Loma Linda, CA Zip 92350; tel. 909/824–4540; B. Lyn Behrens, President

CALIFORNIA: LOMA LINDA UNIVERSITY BEHAVIORAL MEDICINE CENTER (O, 89 beds) 1710 Barton Road, Redlands, CA Zip 92373; tel. 909/793–9333; Alan Soderblom, Administrator

LOMA LINDA UNIVERSITY MEDICAL CENTER (O, 653 beds) 11234 Anderson Street, Loma Linda, CA Zip 92354–2870, Mailing Address: P.O. Box 2000, Zip 92354–0200; tel. 909/824–0800; J. David Moorhead, M.D., President

Owned, leased, sponsored:	2 hospitals	742 beds
Contract–managed:	0 hospitals	0 beds
Totals:	2 hospitals	742 beds

5755: LOS ANGELES COUNTY–DEPARTMENT OF HEALTH SERVICES (NP)
313 North Figueroa Street, Room 912, Los Angeles, CA Zip 90012–2691; tel. 213/240–8101; Mark Finucane, Director Health

LAC–HARBOR–UNIVERSITY OF CALIFORNIA AT LOS ANGELES MEDICAL CENTER (O, 336 beds) 1000 West Carson Street, Torrance, CA Zip 90509; tel. 310/222–2101; Tecla A. Mickoseff, Administrator

LAC–HIGH DESERT HOSPITAL (O, 76 beds) 44900 North 60th Street West, Lancaster, CA Zip 93536; tel. 805/945–8461; Mel Grussing, Administrator

LAC–KING–DREW MEDICAL CENTER (O, 240 beds) 12021 South Wilmington Avenue, Los Angeles, CA Zip 90059; tel. 310/668–4321; Randall S. Foster, Administrator and Chief Executive Officer

LAC–RANCHO LOS AMIGOS MEDICAL CENTER (O, 207 beds) 7601 East Imperial Highway, Downey, CA Zip 90242; tel. 562/401–7022; Consuelo C. Diaz, Chief Executive Officer

LAC–UNIVERSITY OF SOUTHERN CALIFORNIA MEDICAL CENTER (O, 1330 beds) 1200 North State Street, Los Angeles, CA Zip 90033–1084; tel. 213/226–2622; Douglas D. Bagley, Executive Director

OLIVE VIEW–UCLA MEDICAL CENTER (O, 219 beds) 14445 Olive View Drive, Sylmar, CA Zip 91342–1495; tel. 818/364–1555; Melinda Anderson, Administrator

Owned, leased, sponsored:	6 hospitals	2408 beds
Contract–managed:	0 hospitals	0 beds
Totals:	6 hospitals	2408 beds

0047: LOUISIANA STATE HOSPITALS (NP)
210 State Street, New Orleans, LA Zip 70118–5797; tel. 504/897–3400; M. E. Teague, Chief Executive Officer

LOUISIANA: CENTRAL LOUISIANA STATE HOSPITAL (O, 280 beds) 242 West Shamrock Avenue, Pineville, LA Zip 71360–6439, Mailing Address: P.O. Box 5031, Zip 71361–5031; tel. 318/484–6200; Gary S. Grand, Chief Executive Officer

EAST LOUISIANA STATE HOSPITAL (O, 452 beds) Jackson, LA Mailing Address: P.O. Box 498, Zip 70748–0498; tel. 504/634–0100; Warren T. Price Jr., Chief Executive Officer

GREENWELL SPRINGS HOSPITAL (O, 104 beds) 23260 Greenwell Springs Road, Greenwell Springs, LA Zip 70739–0999, Mailing Address: P.O. Box 549, Zip 70739–0549; tel. 504/261–2730; Warren T. Price Jr., Chief Executive Officer

NEW ORLEANS ADOLESCENT HOSPITAL (O, 95 beds) 210 State Street, New Orleans, LA Zip 70118–5797; tel. 504/897–3400; Walter W. Shervington, M.D., Chief Executive Officer

SOUTHEAST LOUISIANA HOSPITAL (O, 251 beds) Mandeville, LA Mailing Address: P.O. Box 3850, Zip 70470–3850; tel. 504/626–6300; Joseph C. Vinturella, Chief Executive Officer

Owned, leased, sponsored:	5 hospitals	1182 beds
Contract–managed:	0 hospitals	0 beds
Totals:	5 hospitals	1182 beds

★0715: LSU MEDICAL CENTER HEALTH CARE SERVICES DIVISION (NP)
8550 United Plaza Boulevard, 4th Floor, Baton Rouge, LA Zip 70809; tel. 504/922–0490; Cary M. Dougherty Jr., Chief Operating Officer

E. A. CONWAY MEDICAL CENTER (O, 187 beds) 4864 Jackson Street, Monroe, LA Zip 71202–6497, Mailing Address: P.O. Box 1881, Zip 71210–1881; tel. 318/330–7000; Roy D. Bostick, Director

EARL K. LONG MEDICAL CENTER (O, 204 beds) 5825 Airline Highway, Baton Rouge, LA Zip 70805–2498; tel. 504/358–1000; Jonathan Roberts, Dr.PH, Chief Executive Officer

HUEY P. LONG MEDICAL CENTER (O, 123 beds) 352 Hospital Boulevard, Pineville, LA Zip 71360, Mailing Address: P.O. Box 5352, Zip 71361–5352; tel. 318/448–0811; James E. Morgan, Director

LSU MEDICAL CENTER–UNIVERSITY HOSPITAL (O, 424 beds) 1541 Kings Highway, Shreveport, LA Zip 71130–4299, Mailing Address: P.O. Box 33932, Zip 71130–3932; tel. 318/675–5000; Ingo Angermeier, FACHE, Administrator and Chief Executive Officer

LALLIE KEMP MEDICAL CENTER (O, 68 beds) 52579 Highway 51 South, Independence, LA Zip 70443–2231; tel. 504/878–9421; LeVern Meades, Acting Administrator

LEONARD J. CHABERT MEDICAL CENTER (O, 133 beds) 1978 Industrial Boulevard, Houma, LA Zip 70363–7094; tel. 504/873–2200; Stanley E. Hurstell, Administrator

MEDICAL CENTER OF LOUISIANA AT NEW ORLEANS (O, 681 beds) 2021 Perdido Street, New Orleans, LA Zip 70112–1396; tel. 504/588–3000; John S. Berault, Chief Executive Officer

UNIVERSITY MEDICAL CENTER (O, 141 beds) 2390 West Congress Street, Lafayette, LA Zip 70506–4298, Mailing Address: P.O. Box 69300, Zip 70596–9300; tel. 318/261–6004; Lawrence T. Dorsey, Administrator

For explanation of codes following names, see page B2.
★ Indicates Type III membership in the American Hospital Association.

WALTER OLIN MOSS REGIONAL MEDICAL CENTER (O, 66 beds) 1000 Walters Street, Lake Charles, LA Zip 70605; tel. 318/475–8100; Patrick C. Robinson, M.D., Administrator

WASHINGTON–ST. TAMMANY REGIONAL MEDICAL CENTER (O, 55 beds) 400 Memphis Street, Bogalusa, LA Zip 70427–0040, Mailing Address: Box 40, Zip 70429–0040; tel. 504/735–1322; Larry R. King, Administrator

Owned, leased, sponsored:	10 hospitals	2082 beds
Contract–managed:	0 hospitals	0 beds
Totals:	10 hospitals	2082 beds

★**0036: LUBBOCK METHODIST HOSPITAL SYSTEM** (NP)
3615 19th Street, Lubbock, TX Zip 79410–1201; tel. 806/792–1011; George H. McCleskey, President and Chief Executive Officer

NEW MEXICO: NOR–LEA GENERAL HOSPITAL (C, 28 beds) 1600 North Main Avenue, Lovington, NM Zip 88260–2871; tel. 505/396–6611; David R. Jordan, Ph.D., Administrator and Chief Executive Officer

TEXAS: FISHER COUNTY HOSPITAL DISTRICT (C, 20 beds) Roby Highway, Rotan, TX Zip 79546, Mailing Address: Drawer F., Zip 79546; tel. 915/735–2256; Ella Raye Helms, Administrator

LAMB HEALTHCARE CENTER (C, 40 beds) 1500 South Sunset, Littlefield, TX Zip 79339–4899; tel. 806/385–6411; Randall A. Young, Administrator

METHODIST CHILDREN'S HOSPITAL (O, 65 beds) 3610 21st Street, Lubbock, TX Zip 79410–1218; tel. 806/784–5040; George H. McCleskey, President and Chief Executive Officer

METHODIST HOSPITAL (O, 520 beds) 3615 19th Street, Lubbock, TX Zip 79410–1201, Mailing Address: Box 1201, Zip 79408–1201; tel. 806/792–1011; George H. McCleskey, President and Chief Executive Officer

METHODIST HOSPITAL PLAINVIEW (L, 100 beds) 2601 Dimmitt Road, Plainview, TX Zip 79072–1833; tel. 806/296–5531; Joe S. Langford, Administrator

METHODIST HOSPITAL–LEVELLAND (L, 44 beds) 1900 South College Avenue, Levelland, TX Zip 79336–6508; tel. 806/894–4963; Jerry Osburn, Administrator

MITCHELL COUNTY HOSPITAL (C, 25 beds) 1543 Chestnut Street, Colorado City, TX Zip 79512–3998; tel. 915/728–3431; Roland K. Rickard, Administrator

MULESHOE AREA MEDICAL CENTER (C, 79 beds) 708 South First Street, Muleshoe, TX Zip 79347–3627; tel. 806/272–4524; Jim G. Bone, Interim Administrator

REEVES COUNTY HOSPITAL (C, 44 beds) 2323 Texas Street, Pecos, TX Zip 79772–7338; tel. 915/447–3551; Charles N. Butts, Interim Chief Executive Officer

Owned, leased, sponsored:	4 hospitals	729 beds
Contract–managed:	6 hospitals	236 beds
Totals:	10 hospitals	965 beds

★**2235: LUTHERAN HEALTH SYSTEMS** (NP)
4310 17th Avenue S.W., Fargo, ND Zip 58103–3339, Mailing Address: P.O. Box 6200, Zip 58106–6200; tel. 701/277–7500; Steven R. Orr, Chairman and Chief Executive Officer

ALASKA: FAIRBANKS MEMORIAL HOSPITAL (L, 200 beds) 1650 Cowles Street, Fairbanks, AK Zip 99701; tel. 907/452–8181; Michael K. Powers, Administrator

ARIZONA: MESA LUTHERAN HOSPITAL (O, 278 beds) 525 West Brown Road, Mesa, AZ Zip 85201–3299; tel. 602/834–1211; Robert A. Rundio, Executive Director of Hospital Operations

VALLEY LUTHERAN HOSPITAL (O, 231 beds) 6644 Baywood Avenue, Mesa, AZ Zip 85206–1797; tel. 602/981–2000; Robert A. Rundio, Executive Director of Hospital Operations

WICKENBURG REGIONAL HOSPITAL (L, 80 beds) 520 Rose Lane, Wickenburg, AZ Zip 85390–1447; tel. 520/684–5421; Carol Schmoyer, Administrator

CALIFORNIA: LASSEN COMMUNITY HOSPITAL (C, 59 beds) 560 Hospital Lane, Susanville, CA Zip 96130–4809; tel. 530/257–5325; David S. Anderson, FACHE, Administrator

COLORADO: EAST MORGAN COUNTY HOSPITAL (L, 29 beds) 2400 West Edison Street, Brush, CO Zip 80723–1640; tel. 970/842–5151; Anne Platt, Administrator

MCKEE MEDICAL CENTER (O, 109 beds) 2000 Boise Avenue, Loveland, CO Zip 80538–4281; tel. 970/669–4640; Charles F. Harms, Administrator

NORTH COLORADO MEDICAL CENTER (L, 262 beds) 1801 16th Street, Greeley, CO Zip 80631–5199; tel. 970/350–6000; Karl B. Gills, Administrator

STERLING REGIONAL MEDCENTER (O, 36 beds) 615 Fairhurst Street, Sterling, CO Zip 80751–4523, Mailing Address: P.O. Box 3500, Zip 80751–3500; tel. 970/522–0122; James O. Pernau, Administrator

KANSAS: DECATUR COUNTY HOSPITAL (L, 74 beds) 810 West Columbia Street, Oberlin, KS Zip 67749–2450, Mailing Address: P.O. Box 268, Zip 67749–0268; tel. 785/475–2208; Asa B. Wilson, Administrator

ST. LUKE HOSPITAL (L, 54 beds) 1014 East Melvin, Marion, KS Zip 66861–1299; tel. 316/382–2179; Craig Hanson, Administrator

NEBRASKA: OGALLALA COMMUNITY HOSPITAL (L, 29 beds) 300 East Tenth Street, Ogallala, NE Zip 69153–1509; tel. 308/284–4011; Linda Morris, Administrator

NEVADA: CHURCHILL COMMUNITY HOSPTIAL (O, 40 beds) 801 East Williams Avenue, Fallon, NV Zip 89406–3052; tel. 702/423–3151; Jeffrey Feike, Administrator

PERSHING GENERAL HOSPITAL (C, 34 beds) 855 Sixth Street, Lovelock, NV Zip 89419, Mailing Address: P.O. Box 661, Zip 89419–0661; tel. 702/273–2621; Helen Woolley, Administrator

NEW MEXICO: LOS ALAMOS MEDICAL CENTER (O, 47 beds) 3917 West Road, Los Alamos, NM Zip 87544–2293; tel. 505/662–4201; Paul J. Wilson, Administrator

NORTH DAKOTA: LISBON MEDICAL CENTER (O, 64 beds) 905 Main Street, Lisbon, ND Zip 58054–0353, Mailing Address: P.O. Box 353, Zip 58054–0353; tel. 701/683–5241; Jack Jacobs, Administrator

PEMBINA COUNTY MEMORIAL HOSPITAL AND WEDGEWOOD MANOR (L, 89 beds) 301 Mountain Street East, Cavalier, ND Zip 58220–4015; tel. 701/265–8461; George A. Rohrich, Administrator

OREGON: CENTRAL OREGON DISTRICT HOSPITAL (C, 48 beds) 1253 North Canal Boulevard, Redmond, OR Zip 97756–1395; tel. 541/548–8131; James A. Diegel, CHE, Executive Director

PIONEER MEMORIAL HOSPITAL (C, 30 beds) 1201 North Elm Street, Prineville, OR Zip 97754; tel. 541/447–6254; Donald J. Wee, Executive Director

SOUTH DAKOTA: GREGORY COMMUNITY HOSPITAL (O, 84 beds) 400 Park Street, Gregory, SD Zip 57533–0400, Mailing Address: Box 408, Zip 57533–0408; tel. 605/835–8394; Carol A. Varland, Chief Executive Officer

LOOKOUT MEMORIAL HOSPITAL (O, 32 beds) 1440 North Main Street, Spearfish, SD Zip 57783–1504; tel. 605/642–2617; Deb J. Krmpotic, R.N., Administrator

SOUTHERN HILLS GENERAL HOSPITAL (O, 60 beds) 209 North 16th Street, Hot Springs, SD Zip 57747–1375; tel. 605/745–3159; Eric Hanson, Administrator

STURGIS COMMUNITY HEALTH CARE CENTER (O, 114 beds) 949 Harmon Street, Sturgis, SD Zip 57785–2452; tel. 605/347–2536; Deb J. Krmpotic, R.N., Administrator

WYOMING: COMMUNITY HOSPITAL (O, 36 beds) 2000 Campbell Drive, Torrington, WY Zip 82240–1597; tel. 307/532–4181; Charles Myers, Administrator

PLATTE COUNTY MEMORIAL HOSPITAL (L, 86 beds) 201 14th Street, Wheatland, WY Zip 82201–3201, Mailing Address: P.O. Box 848, Zip 82201–0848; tel. 307/322–3636; Dana K. Barnett, Administrator

WASHAKIE MEMORIAL HOSPITAL (L, 30 beds) 400 South 15th Street, Worland, WY Zip 82401–3531, Mailing Address: P.O. Box 700, Zip 82401–0700; tel. 307/347–3221; James Kiser, Administrator

For explanation of codes following names, see page B2.
★ Indicates Type III membership in the American Hospital Association.

Owned, leased, sponsored:	22 hospitals	2064 beds
Contract–managed:	4 hospitals	171 beds
Totals:	26 hospitals	2235 beds

0695: MAGELLAN HEALTH SERVICES (IO)

3414 Peachtree Road N.E., Suite 1400, Atlanta, GA Zip 30326; tel. 404/841–9200; Henry Harbin, M.D., President and Chief Executive Officer

ALABAMA: CHARTER BEHAVIORAL HEALTH SYSTEM (O, 70 beds) 5800 Southland Drive, Mobile, AL Zip 36693–3396, Mailing Address: P.O. Box 991800, Zip 36691–1800; tel. 334/661–3001; Keith Cox, CHE, Chief Executive Officer

ALASKA: CHARTER NORTH STAR BEHAVIORAL HEALTH SYSTEM (O, 80 beds) 2530 DeBarr Road, Anchorage, AK Zip 99508; tel. 907/258–7575; Kathleen Cronen, Chief Executive Officer

CHARTER NORTH STAR HOSPITAL AND COUNSELING CENTER (O, 34 beds) 1650 South Bragaw, Anchorage, AK Zip 99508–3467; tel. 907/274–7313; Bob Marshall, Administrator

ARIZONA: CHARTER BEHAVIORAL HEALTH SYSTEM–EAST VALLEY (O, 80 beds) 2190 North Grace Boulevard, Chandler, AZ Zip 85224–7903; tel. 602/899–8989; Michael D. Todd, Chief Executive Officer

CHARTER BEHAVIORAL HEALTH SYSTEM–GLENDALE (O, 90 beds) 6015 West Peoria Avenue, Glendale, AZ Zip 85302–1201; tel. 602/878–7878; Kim Hall, Chief Executive Officer

ARKANSAS: CHARTER BEHAVIORAL HEALTH SYSTEM OF LITTLE ROCK (O, 60 beds) 1601 Murphy Drive, Maumelle, AR Zip 72113; tel. 501/851–8700; Lucinda DeBruce, Chief Executive Officer

CHARTER BEHAVIORAL HEALTH SYSTEM OF NORTHWEST ARKANSAS (O, 49 beds) 4253 North Crossover Road, Fayetteville, AR Zip 72703–4596; tel. 501/521–5731; Lucinda DeBruce, Administrator

CALIFORNIA: CHARTER BEHAVIORAL HEALTH SYSTEM OF SAN DIEGO (O, 80 beds) 11878 Avenue of Industry, San Diego, CA Zip 92128; tel. 619/487–3200; Lorraine Watson, Ph.D., Chief Executive Officer

CHARTER BEHAVIORAL HEALTH SYSTEM OF SOUTHERN CALIFORNIA–CHARTER OAK (O, 95 beds) 1161 East Covina Boulevard, Covina, CA Zip 91724–1161; tel. 626/966–1632; Todd A. Smith, Chief Executive Officer

CHARTER BEHAVIORAL HEALTH SYSTEM OF SOUTHERN CALIFORNIA–CORONA (O, 92 beds) 2055 Kellogg Avenue, Corona, CA Zip 91719; tel. 909/735–2910; Diana C. Hanyak, Chief Executive Officer

CHARTER BEHAVIORAL HEALTH SYSTEM OF SOUTHERN CALIFORNIA/MISSION VIEJO (O, 80 beds) 23228 Madero, Mission Viejo, CA Zip 92691; tel. 714/830–4800; Timothy Allen, Chief Executive Officer

CHARTER BEHAVIORAL HEALTH SYSTEM–PALM SPRINGS (O, 80 beds) 69–696 Ramon Road, Cathedral City, CA Zip 92234; tel. 619/321–2000; Robert Deney, Chief Executive Officer

COLORADO: CHARTER CENTENNIAL PEAKS BEHAVIORAL HEALTH SYSTEM (O, 72 beds) 2255 South 88th Street, Louisville, CO Zip 80027–9716; tel. 303/673–9990; Sharon Worsham, Administrator

CONNECTICUT: ELMCREST PSYCHIATRIC INSTITUTE (O, 92 beds) 25 Marlborough Street, Portland, CT Zip 06480–1829; tel. 860/342–0480; Anthony A. Ferrante, M.D., President and Chief Executive Officer

FLORIDA: CHARTER BEHAVIORAL HEALTH SYSTEM OF TAMPA BAY (O, 146 beds) 4004 North Riverside Drive, Tampa, FL Zip 33603–3212; tel. 813/238–8671; James C. Hill, Chief Executive Officer

CHARTER BEHAVIORAL HEALTH SYSTEM OF TAMPA BAY AT LARGO (O, 64 beds) 12891 Seminole Boulevard, Largo, FL Zip 33778; tel. 813/587–6000; Jim Hill, Chief Executive Officer

CHARTER BEHAVIORAL HEALTH SYSTEM–ORLANDO (O, 60 beds) 206 Park Place Drive, Kissimmee, FL Zip 34741–2356; tel. 407/846–0444; Daniel Kearney, Chief Executive Officer

CHARTER GLADE BEHAVIORAL HEALTH SYSTEM (O, 104 beds) 3550 Colonial Boulevard, Fort Myers, FL Zip 33912–1065, Mailing Address: P.O. Box 60120, Zip 33906–0120; tel. 941/939–0403; Martin Schappell, Chief Executive Officer

CHARTER HOSPITAL OF PASCO (O, 72 beds) 21808 State Road 54, Lutz, FL Zip 33549–6938; tel. 813/948–2441; Miriam K. Williams, Administrator

CHARTER SPRINGS HOSPITAL (O, 92 beds) 3130 S.W. 27th Avenue, Ocala, FL Zip 34474–4485, Mailing Address: P.O. Box 3338, Zip 34478–3338; tel. 352/237–7293; David C. Nissen, Chief Executive Officer

GEORGIA: CHARTER ANCHOR HOSPITAL (O, 84 beds) 5454 Yorktowne Drive, Atlanta, GA Zip 30349–5305; tel. 770/991–6044; Matthew Crouch, Chief Executive Officer

CHARTER BEHAVIORAL HEALTH SYSTEM OF ATLANTA (O, 40 beds) 811 Juniper Street N.E., Atlanta, GA Zip 30308–1398; tel. 404/881–5800; Dennis Workman, M.D., Medical Director

CHARTER BEHAVIORAL HEALTH SYSTEM OF ATLANTA AT PEACHFORD (O, 224 beds) 2151 Peachford Road, Atlanta, GA Zip 30338–6599; tel. 770/455–3200; Aleen S. Davis, Chief Executive Officer

CHARTER BEHAVIORAL HEALTH SYSTEM/CENTRAL GEORGIA (O, 118 beds) 3500 Riverside Drive, Macon, GA Zip 31210–2509; tel. 912/474–6200; Blair R. Johanson, Administrator

CHARTER SAVANNAH BEHAVIORAL HEALTH SYSTEM (O, 112 beds) 1150 Cornell Avenue, Savannah, GA Zip 31406–2797; tel. 912/354–3911; Thomas L. Ryba, Chief Executive Officer

CHARTER WINDS HOSPITAL (O, 80 beds) 240 Mitchell Bridge Road, Athens, GA Zip 30606–2043; tel. 706/546–7277; Susan Lister, Chief Executive Officer

CHARTER BY–THE–SEA BEHAVIORAL HEALTH SYSTEM (O, 101 beds) 2927 Demere Road, Saint Simons Island, GA Zip 31522–1620; tel. 912/638–1999; Wes Robbins, Chief Executive Officer

INDIANA: CHARTER BEACON (O, 97 beds) 1720 Beacon Street, Fort Wayne, IN Zip 46805–4700; tel. 219/423–3651; Robert Hails, Chief Executive Officer

CHARTER BEHAVIORAL HEALTH SYSTEM OF INDIANA AT JEFFERSON (O, 100 beds) 2700 River City Park Road, Jeffersonville, IN Zip 47130–5943; tel. 812/284–3400; James E. Ledbetter, Ph.D., Chief Executive Officer

CHARTER BEHAVIORAL HEALTH SYSTEM OF NORTHWEST INDIANA (O, 60 beds) 101 West 61st Avenue and State Road 51, Hobart, IN Zip 46342–6489; tel. 219/947–4464; Michael J. Perry, Chief Executive Officer

CHARTER BEHAVIORAL HEALTH SYSTEMS (O, 64 beds) 3700 Rome Drive, Lafayette, IN Zip 47905–4465, Mailing Address: P.O. Box 5969, Zip 47903–5969; tel. 765/448–6999; Mark Dooley, Chief Executive Officer

CHARTER INDIANAPOLIS BEHAVIORAL HEALTH SYSTEM (O, 80 beds) 5602 Caito Drive, Indianapolis, IN Zip 46226–1356; tel. 317/545–2111; Marina Cecchini, Chief Executive Officer

KENTUCKY: CHARTER BEHAVIORAL HEALTH SYSTEM OF PADUCAH (O, 56 beds) 435 Berger Road, Paducah, KY Zip 42003–4579, Mailing Address: P.O. Box 7609, Zip 42002–7609; tel. 502/444–0444; Pat Harrod, Chief Executive Officer

CHARTER RIDGE HOSPITAL (O, 110 beds) 3050 Rio Dosa Drive, Lexington, KY Zip 40509–9990; tel. 606/269–2325; Ali A. Elhaj, Chief Executive Officer

CHARTER LOUISVILLE BEHAVIORAL HEALTH SYSTEM (O, 66 beds) 1405 Browns Lane, Louisville, KY Zip 40207–4672; tel. 502/896–0495; Charles L. Webb Jr., Administrator

LOUISIANA: CHARTER CYPRESS BEHAVIORAL HEALTH SYSTEM (O, 70 beds) 302 Dulles Drive, Lafayette, LA Zip 70506–3099; tel. 318/233–9024; Denise Guthrie, Chief Executive Officer

CHARTER FOREST BEHAVIORAL HEALTH SYSTEM (O, 60 beds) 9320 Linwood Avenue, Shreveport, LA Zip 71106–7098, Mailing Address: P.O. Box 18130, Zip 71138–1130; tel. 318/688–3930; Randy J. Watson, Administrator

MARYLAND: CHARTER BEHAVIORAL HEALTH SYSTEM OF MARYLAND AT POTOMAC RIDGE (O, 140 beds) 14901 Broschart Road, Rockville, MD Zip 20850–3321; tel. 301/251–4500; Craig S. Juengling, Chief Executive Officer

MISSISSIPPI: CHARTER BEHAVIORAL HEALTH SYSTEM (O, 111 beds) 3531 Lakeland Drive, Jackson, MS Zip 39208–9794, Mailing Address: P.O. Box 4297, Zip 39296–4297; tel. 601/939–9030; Rick H. Gray, Ph.D., Chief Executive Officer

NEVADA: CHARTER BEHAVIORAL HEALTH SYSTEM OF NEVADA (O, 84 beds) 7000 West Spring Mountain Road, Las Vegas, NV Zip 89117–3816; tel. 702/876–4357; Lynn M. Rosenbach, Chief Executive Officer

For explanation of codes following names, see page B2.
★ Indicates Type III membership in the American Hospital Association.

NEW HAMPSHIRE: CHARTER BROOKSIDE BEHAVIORAL HEALTH SYSTEM OF NEW ENGLAND (O, 100 beds) 29 Northwest Boulevard, Nashua, NH Zip 03063–4005; tel. 603/886–5000; Spencer Moore, Chief Executive Officer

NEW JERSEY: CHARTER BEHAVIORAL HEALTH SYSTEM OF NEW JERSEY–SUMMIT (O, 90 beds) 19 Prospect Street, Summit, NJ Zip 07902–0100; tel. 908/522–7000; James Gallagner, Chief Executive Officer

NEW MEXICO: CHARTER HEIGHTS BEHAVIORAL HEALTH SYSTEM (O, 172 beds) 103 Hospital Loop N.E., Albuquerque, NM Zip 87109–2115; tel. 505/883–8777; Joel A. Hart, FACHE, Chief Executive Officer

NORTH CAROLINA: CHARTER ASHEVILLE BEHAVIORAL HEALTH SYSTEM (O, 139 beds) 60 Caledonia Road, Asheville, NC Zip 28803–2555, Mailing Address: P.O. Box 5534, Zip 28813–5534; tel. 704/253–3681; Tammy B. Wood, Chief Executive Officer

CHARTER GREENSBORO BEHAVIORAL HEALTH SYSTEM (O, 68 beds) 700 Walter Reed Drive, Greensboro, NC Zip 27403–1129, Mailing Address: P.O. Box 10399, Zip 27404–0399; tel. 336/852–4821; Nancy Reaves, Chief Executive Officer

CHARTER HOSPITAL OF WINSTON–SALEM (O, 99 beds) 3637 Old Vineyard Road, Winston–Salem, NC Zip 27104–4835; tel. 336/768–7710; Michael J. Carney, Chief Executive Officer

CHARTER PINES BEHAVIORAL HEALTH SYSTEM (O, 60 beds) 3621 Randolph Road, Charlotte, NC Zip 28211–1337, Mailing Address: P.O. Box 221709, Zip 28222–1709; tel. 704/365–5368; Bruce Chambers, Ph.D., Chief Executive Officer

OHIO: CHARTER HOSPITAL OF TOLEDO (O, 38 beds) 1725 Timber Line Road, Maumee, OH Zip 43537–4015; tel. 419/891–9333; Dennis J. Sajdak, Chief Executive Officer

PENNSYLVANIA: CHARTER BEHAVIORAL HEALTH SYSTEM AT COVE FORGE (O, 100 beds) New Beginnings Road, Williamsburg, PA Zip 16693; tel. 814/832–2121; Jonathan Wolf, Chief Executive Officer

CHARTER FAIRMOUNT INSTITUTE (O, 146 beds) 561 Fairthorne Avenue, Philadelphia, PA Zip 19128–2499; tel. 215/487–4000; Paul B. Henry, Administrator

SOUTH CAROLINA: CHARTER GREENVILLE BEHAVIORAL HEALTH SYSTEM (O, 66 beds) 2700 East Phillips Road, Greer, SC Zip 29650–4816; tel. 864/968–6300; William L. Callison, Chief Executive Officer

CHARTER HOSPITAL OF CHARLESTON (O, 70 beds) 2777 Speissegger Drive, Charleston, SC Zip 29405–8299; tel. 803/747–5830; Anne Battin, Administrator

CHARTER RIVERS BEHAVIORAL HEALTH SYSTEM (O, 80 beds) 2900 Sunset Boulevard, West Columbia, SC Zip 29169–3422; tel. 803/796–9911; Brooks Cagle, Chief Executive Officer

TENNESSEE: CHARTER LAKESIDE BEHAVIORAL HEALTH SYSTEM (O, 174 beds) 2911 Brunswick Road, Memphis, TN Zip 38133–4199, Mailing Address: P.O. Box 341308, Zip 38134–1308; tel. 901/377–4700; Rob S. Waggener, Chief Executive Officer

TEXAS: CHARTER BEHAVIORAL HEALTH SYSTEM (O, 80 beds) 2001 Ladbrook Drive, Kingwood, TX Zip 77339–3004; tel. 281/358–4501; Mark Micheletti, Chief Executive Officer

CHARTER BEHAVIORAL HEALTH SYSTEM OF AUSTIN (O, 40 beds) 8402 Cross Park Drive, Austin, TX Zip 78754–4588, Mailing Address: P.O. Box 140585, Zip 78714–0585; tel. 870/837–1800; Armin Steege, Chief Executive Officer

CHARTER BEHAVIORAL HEALTH SYSTEM–CORPUS CHRISTI (O, 80 beds) 3126 Rodd Field Road, Corpus Christi, TX Zip 78414–3901; tel. 512/993–8893; John S. Lacy, Chief Executive Officer

CHARTER GRAPEVINE BEHAVIORAL HEALTH SYSTEM (O, 80 beds) 2300 William D. Tate Avenue, Grapevine, TX Zip 76051–9964; tel. 817/481–1900; Michael V. Lee, Chief Executive Officer

CHARTER PALMS BEHAVIORAL HEALTH SYSTEM (O, 80 beds) 1421 East Jackson Avenue, McAllen, TX Zip 78501–1602, Mailing Address: P.O. Box 5239, Zip 78502–5239; tel. 956/631–5421; Leslie Bingham, Chief Executive Officer

CHARTER PLAINS BEHAVIORAL HEALTH SYSTEM (O, 80 beds) 801 North Quaker Avenue, Lubbock, TX Zip 79416–2408, Mailing Address: P.O. Box 10560, Zip 79408–0560; tel. 806/744–5505; Earl W. Balzen, R.N., Chief Executive Officer and Administrator

CHARTER REAL BEHAVIORAL HEALTH SYSTEM (O, 90 beds) 8550 Huebner Road, San Antonio, TX Zip 78240–1897, Mailing Address: P.O. Box 380157, Zip 78280–0157; tel. 210/699–8585; Robert Quintanilla, Chief Executive Officer

VIRGINIA: CHARTER BEHAVIORAL HEALTH SYSTEM AT SPRINGWOOD (O, 77 beds) 42009 Charter Springwood Lane, Leesburg, VA Zip 20176–6269; tel. 703/777–0800; Craig S. Juengling, Chief Executive Officer

CHARTER BEHAVIORAL HEALTH SYSTEM OF CHARLOTTESVILLE (O, 62 beds) 2101 Arlington Boulevard, Charlottesville, VA Zip 22903–1593; tel. 804/977–1120; Wayne Adams, Chief Executive Officer

CHARTER WESTBROOK BEHAVIORAL HEALTH SYSTEM (O, 210 beds) 1500 Westbrook Avenue, Richmond, VA Zip 23227–3399; tel. 804/266–9671; Stephen P. Fahey, Administrator

NORFOLK PSYCHIATRIC CENTER (O, 77 beds) 860 Kempsville Road, Norfolk, VA Zip 23502–3980; tel. 757/461–4565; Diane Carvalho, Administrator

WISCONSIN: CHARTER HOSPITAL OF MILWAUKEE (O, 80 beds) 11101 West Lincoln Avenue, Milwaukee, WI Zip 53227–1166; tel. 414/327–3000; Robert Kwech, Chief Executive Officer

Owned, leased, sponsored:	66 hospitals	5887 beds
Contract–managed:	0 hospitals	0 beds
Totals:	66 hospitals	5887 beds

★5305: MARIAN HEALTH SYSTEM (CC)
Tulsa, OK Mailing Address: P.O. Box 4753, Zip 74159–0753; tel. 918/742–9988; Sister M. Therese Gottschalk, President

CALIFORNIA: ST. ROSE HOSPITAL (O, 175 beds) 27200 Calaroga Avenue, Hayward, CA Zip 94545–4383; tel. 510/264–4000; Michael P. Mahoney, President and Chief Executive Officer

KANSAS: MOUNT CARMEL MEDICAL CENTER (O, 119 beds) 1102 East Centennial, Pittsburg, KS Zip 66762–6686; tel. 316/231–6100; John Daniel Lingor, President and Chief Executive Officer

VIA CHRISTI REGIONAL MEDICAL CENTER (O, 1009 beds) 929 North St. Francis Street, Wichita, KS Zip 67214–3882; tel. 316/268–5000; Randall G. Nyp, President and Chief Executive Officer

MINNESOTA: ST. ELIZABETH HOSPITAL (O, 160 beds) 1200 Fifth Grand Boulevard West, Wabasha, MN Zip 55981–1098; tel. 612/565–4531; Thomas Crowley, President

NEW JERSEY: NORTHWEST COVENANT MEDICAL CENTER (O, 644 beds) 25 Pocono Road, Denville, NJ Zip 07834–2995; tel. 973/625–6000; Kathryn J. McDonagh, President and Chief Executive Officer

ST. JOSEPH'S HOSPITAL AND MEDICAL CENTER (O, 651 beds) 703 Main Street, Paterson, NJ Zip 07503–2691; tel. 973/754–2000; Sister Jane Frances Brady, Chief Executive Officer

ST. MARY'S HOSPITAL (O, 229 beds) 211 Pennington Avenue, Passaic, NJ Zip 07055–4698; tel. 973/470–3000; Patricia Peterson, President and Chief Executive Officer

OKLAHOMA: ST. JOHN MEDICAL CENTER (O, 552 beds) 1923 South Utica Avenue, Tulsa, OK Zip 74104–5445; tel. 918/744–2345; Sister M. Therese Gottschalk, President

ST. JOSEPH REGIONAL MEDICAL CENTER OF NORTHERN OKLAHOMA (O, 88 beds) 14th Street and Hartford Avenue, Ponca City, OK Zip 74601–2035, Mailing Address: Box 1270, Zip 74602–1270; tel. 580/765–3321; Garry L. England, President and Chief Executive Officer

WISCONSIN: FLAMBEAU HOSPITAL (O, 42 beds) 98 Sherry Avenue, Park Falls, WI Zip 54552–1467, Mailing Address: P.O. Box 310, Zip 54552–0310; tel. 715/762–2484; Curtis A. Johnson, Administrator

MERCY MEDICAL CENTER (O, 221 beds) 631 Hazel Street, Oshkosh, WI Zip 54901–4680, Mailing Address: P.O. Box 1100, Zip 54902–1100; tel. 920/236–2000; Otto L. Cox, President and Chief Executive Officer

For explanation of codes following names, see page B2.
★ Indicates Type III membership in the American Hospital Association.

Section B

SACRED HEART–ST. MARY'S HOSPITALS (O, 47 beds) 1044 Kabel Avenue, Rhinelander, WI Zip 54501–3998, Mailing Address: P.O. Box 20, Zip 54501–0020; tel. 715/369–6600; Kevin J. O'Donnell, President and Chief Executive Officer

SAINT JOSEPH'S HOSPITAL (O, 524 beds) 611 St. Joseph Avenue, Marshfield, WI Zip 54449–1898; tel. 715/387–1713; Michael A. Schmidt, President and Chief Executive Officer

SAINT MICHAEL'S HOSPITAL (O, 104 beds) 900 Illinois Avenue, Stevens Point, WI Zip 54481–3196; tel. 715/346–5000; Jeffrey L. Martin, President and Chief Executive Officer

VICTORY MEDICAL CENTER (O, 127 beds) 230 East Fourth Avenue, Stanley, WI Zip 54768–1298; tel. 715/644–5571; Cynthia Eichman, Chief Executive Officer and Administrator

Owned, leased, sponsored:	15 hospitals	4692 beds
Contract–managed:	0 hospitals	0 beds
Totals:	15 hospitals	4692 beds

1975: MARSHALL COUNTY HEALTH CARE AUTHORITY (NP)
8000 Alabama Highway 69, Guntersville, AL Zip 35976; tel. 205/753–8000; Julian Sparks, Board Chairman

ALABAMA: MARSHALL MEDICAL CENTER NORTH (O, 90 beds) 8000 Alabama Highway 69, Guntersville, AL Zip 35976; tel. 205/753–8000; Gary R. Gore, Administrator

MARSHALL MEDICAL CENTER SOUTH (O, 102 beds) U.S. Highway 431 North, Boaz, AL Zip 35957–0999, Mailing Address: P.O. Box 758, Zip 35957–0758; tel. 256/593–8310; Marlin Hanson, Administrator

Owned, leased, sponsored:	2 hospitals	192 beds
Contract–managed:	0 hospitals	0 beds
Totals:	2 hospitals	192 beds

● **5395: MARYCREST HEALTH SYSTEM** (CC)
2861 West 52nd Avenue, Denver, CO Zip 80221–1259; tel. 303/458–8611; Dale G. Budde, President

NEBRASKA: ST. ANTHONY'S HOSPITAL (O, 29 beds) Second and Adams Streets, O'Neill, NE Zip 68763–1597; tel. 402/336–2611; Ronald J. Cork, President and Chief Executive Officer

Owned, leased, sponsored:	1 hospital	29 beds
Contract–managed:	0 hospitals	0 beds
Totals:	1 hospital	29 beds

0013: MASSACHUSETTS DEPARTMENT OF MENTAL HEALTH (NP)
25 Staniford Street, Boston, MA Zip 02114–2575; tel. 617/727–5600; Marylou Sudders, Commissioner

MASSACHUSETTS: LEMUEL SHATTUCK HOSPITAL (O, 230 beds) 170 Morton Street, Jamaica Plain, Boston, MA Zip 02130–3787; tel. 617/522–8110; Robert D. Wakefield Jr., Executive Director

MASSACHUSETTS MENTAL HEALTH CENTER (O, 27 beds) 74 Fenwood Road, Boston, MA Zip 02115–6196; tel. 617/734–1300; Jackie K. Moore, Ph.D., Chief Executive Officer

MEDFIELD STATE HOSPITAL (O, 212 beds) 45 Hospital Road, Medfield, MA Zip 02052–1099; tel. 508/359–7312; Theodore E. Kirousis, Area Director

TAUNTON STATE HOSPITAL (O, 188 beds) 60 Hodges Avenue Extension, Taunton, MA Zip 02780–3034, Mailing Address: P.O. Box 4007, Zip 02780–4007; tel. 508/824–7551; Katherine Chmiel, R.N., MSN, Administrator and Chief Operating Officer

TEWKSBURY HOSPITAL (O, 730 beds) 365 East Street, Tewksbury, MA Zip 01876–1998; tel. 978/851–7321; Raymond D. Sanzone, Executive Director

WESTBOROUGH STATE HOSPITAL (O, 220 beds) Lyman Street, Westborough, MA Zip 01581–0288, Mailing Address: P.O. Box 288, Zip 01581–0288; tel. 508/366–4401; Theodore E. Kirousis, Area Director

WORCESTER STATE HOSPITAL (O, 176 beds) 305 Belmont Street, Worcester, MA Zip 01604–1695; tel. 508/752–4681; Raymond Robinson, Chief Operating Officer

NEW YORK: KENMORE MERCY HOSPITAL (S, 184 beds) 2950 Elmwood Avenue, Kenmore, NY Zip 14217–1390; tel. 716/447–6100; Sister Mary Joel Schimscheiner, Chief Executive Officer

Owned, leased, sponsored:	8 hospitals	1967 beds
Contract–managed:	0 hospitals	0 beds
Totals:	8 hospitals	1967 beds

2505: MATAGORDA COUNTY HOSPITAL DISTRICT (NP)
1115 Avenue G., Bay City, TX Zip 77414–3544; tel. 409/245–6383; Wendell H. Baker Jr., District Administrator

TEXAS: MATAGORDA GENERAL HOSPITAL (O, 67 beds) 1115 Avenue G., Bay City, TX Zip 77414–3544; tel. 409/245–6383; Wendell H. Baker Jr., Chief Executive Officer

WAGNER GENERAL HOSPITAL (O, 6 beds) 310 Green Street, Palacios, TX Zip 77465–3214, Mailing Address: P.O. Box 859, Zip 77465–0859; tel. 512/972–2511; Kevin Hecht, Director

Owned, leased, sponsored:	2 hospitals	73 beds
Contract–managed:	0 hospitals	0 beds
Totals:	2 hospitals	73 beds

★**1875: MAYO FOUNDATION** (NP)
200 S.W. First Street, Rochester, MN Zip 55905–0002; tel. 507/284–2511; Robert R. Waller, M.D., President and Chief Executive Officer

FLORIDA: ST. LUKE'S HOSPITAL (O, 230 beds) 4201 Belfort Road, Jacksonville, FL Zip 32216–5898; tel. 904/296–3700; J. Larry Read, President

IOWA: FLOYD COUNTY MEMORIAL HOSPITAL (C, 29 beds) 800 Eleventh Street, Charles City, IA Zip 50616–3499; tel. 515/228–6830; Bill D. Faust, Administrator

MINNESOTA: ALBERT LEA MEDICAL CENTER (O, 72 beds) 404 West Fountain Street, Albert Lea, MN Zip 56007–2473; tel. 507/373–2384; Ronald A. Harmon, M.D., Chief Executive Officer

IMMANUEL/ST. JOSEPH'S–MAYO HEALTH SYSTEM (O, 147 beds) 1025 Marsh Street, Mankato, MN Zip 56001–4700, Mailing Address: P.O. Box 8673, Zip 56002–8673; tel. 507/625–4031; Douglas L. Wood, M.D., President

ROCHESTER METHODIST HOSPITAL (O, 335 beds) 201 West Center Street, Rochester, MN Zip 55902–3084; tel. 507/266–7890; John M. Panicek, Administrator

SAINT MARYS HOSPITAL (O, 797 beds) 1216 Second Street S.W., Rochester, MN Zip 55902–1970; tel. 507/255–5123; John M. Panicek, Administrator

WISCONSIN: BARRON MEMORIAL MEDICAL CENTER AND SKILLED NURSING FACILITY (C, 92 beds) 1222 Woodland Avenue, Barron, WI Zip 54812–1798; tel. 715/537–3186; Mark D. Wilson, Administrator

BLOOMER COMMUNITY MEMORIAL HOSPITAL AND THE MAPLEWOOD (C, 101 beds) 1501 Thompson Street, Bloomer, WI Zip 54724–1299; tel. 715/568–2000; John Perushek, Administrator

LUTHER HOSPITAL (O, 182 beds) 1221 Whipple Street, Eau Claire, WI Zip 54702–4105; tel. 715/838–3311; William Rupp, M.D., President and Chief Executive Officer

OSSEO AREA HOSPITAL AND NURSING HOME (C, 79 beds) 13025 Eighth Street, Osseo, WI Zip 54758, Mailing Address: P.O. Box 70, Zip 54758–0070; tel. 715/597–3121; Bradley D. Groseth, Administrator

Owned, leased, sponsored:	6 hospitals	1763 beds
Contract–managed:	4 hospitals	301 beds
Totals:	10 hospitals	2064 beds

★**6615: MEDLANTIC HEALTHCARE GROUP** (NP)
100 Irving Street N.W., Washington, DC Zip 20010–2975; tel. 202/877–6006; John P. McDaniel, Chief Executive Officer

---

For explanation of codes following names, see page B2.
★ Indicates Type III membership in the American Hospital Association.
● Single hospital health care system

DISTRICT OF COLUMBIA: NATIONAL REHABILITATION HOSPITAL (O, 160 beds) 102 Irving Street N.W., Washington, DC Zip 20010–2949; tel. 202/877–1000; Edward A. Eckenhoff, President and Chief Executive Officer

WASHINGTON HOSPITAL CENTER (O, 773 beds) 110 Irving Street N.W., Washington, DC Zip 20010–2975; tel. 202/877–7000; Kenneth A. Samet, President

Owned, leased, sponsored:	2 hospitals	933 beds
Contract–managed:	0 hospitals	0 beds
Totals:	2 hospitals	933 beds

0084: MEMORIAL HEALTH SERVICES (NP)
2801 Atlantic Avenue, Long Beach, CA Zip 90801, Mailing Address: P.O. Box 1428, Zip 90801–1428; tel. 562/933–2000; Thomas J. Collins, President and Chief Executive Officer

CALIFORNIA: ANAHEIM MEMORIAL MEDICAL CENTER (O, 192 beds) 1111 West La Palma Avenue, Anaheim, CA Zip 92801; tel. 714/774–1450; Michael C. Carter, Chief Executive Officer

LONG BEACH MEMORIAL MEDICAL CENTER (O, 726 beds) 2801 Atlantic Avenue, Long Beach, CA Zip 90806, Mailing Address: Box 1428, Zip 90801–1428; tel. 562/933–2000; Chris D. Van Gorder, Chief Executive Officer

ORANGE COAST MEMORIAL MEDICAL CENTER (O, 230 beds) 9920 Talbert Avenue, Fountain Valley, CA Zip 92708; tel. 714/378–7000; Barry Arbuckle, Ph.D., Chief Executive Officer

SADDLEBACK MEMORIAL MEDICAL CENTER (O, 220 beds) 24451 Health Center Drive, Laguna Hills, CA Zip 92653; tel. 714/837–4500; Barry Arbuckle, Ph.D., Chief Executive Officer

Owned, leased, sponsored:	4 hospitals	1368 beds
Contract–managed:	0 hospitals	0 beds
Totals:	4 hospitals	1368 beds

2335: MEMORIAL HEALTH SERVICES (IO)
706 North Parrish Avenue, Adel, GA Zip 31620–2064, Mailing Address: P.O. Box 677, Zip 31620–0677; tel. 912/896–2251; Wade E. Keck, Chief Executive Officer

GEORGIA: BLECKLEY MEMORIAL HOSPITAL (C, 45 beds) 408 Peacock Street, Cochran, GA Zip 31014–1559, Mailing Address: Box 536, Zip 31014–0536; tel. 912/934–6211; Henry T. Gibbs, Administrator

MEMORIAL HOSPITAL OF ADEL (C, 155 beds) 706 North Parrish Avenue, Adel, GA Zip 31620–0677, Mailing Address: Box 677, Zip 31620–0677; tel. 912/896–2251; Wade E. Keck, Chief Executive Officer

SMITH HOSPITAL (C, 71 beds) 117 East Main Street, Hahira, GA Zip 31632–1156, Mailing Address: P.O. Box 337, Zip 31632–0337; tel. 912/794–2502; Amanda M. Hall, Administrator

TELFAIR COUNTY HOSPITAL (C, 52 beds) U.S. 341 South, McRae, GA Zip 31055, Mailing Address: P.O. Box 150, Zip 31055–0150; tel. 912/868–5621; Gail B. Norris, Administrator

Owned, leased, sponsored:	0 hospitals	0 beds
Contract–managed:	4 hospitals	323 beds
Totals:	4 hospitals	323 beds

★0086: MEMORIAL HEALTH SYSTEM (NP)
800 North Rutledge Street, Springfield, IL Zip 62781–0001; tel. 217/788–3000; Robert T. Clarke, President and Chief Executive Officer

ILLINOIS: ABRAHAM LINCOLN MEMORIAL HOSPITAL (O, 45 beds) 315 8th Street, Lincoln, IL Zip 62656–2698; tel. 217/732–2161; Forrest G. Hester, President and Chief Executive Officer

MEMORIAL MEDICAL CENTER (O, 457 beds) 800 North Rutledge Street, Springfield, IL Zip 62781–0001; tel. 217/788–3000; Robert T. Clarke, President and Chief Executive Officer

ST. VINCENT MEMORIAL HOSPITAL (S, 151 beds) 201 East Pleasant Street, Taylorville, IL Zip 62568–1597; tel. 217/824–3331; Daniel J. Raab, President and Chief Executive Officer

Owned, leased, sponsored:	3 hospitals	653 beds
Contract–managed:	0 hospitals	0 beds
Totals:	3 hospitals	653 beds

★2615: MEMORIAL HEALTH SYSTEMS (NP)
875 Sterthaus Avenue, Ormond Beach, FL Zip 32174–5197; tel. 904/676–6114; Richard A. Lind, President and Chief Executive Officer

FLORIDA: MEMORIAL HOSPITAL–FLAGLER (O, 81 beds) Moody Boulevard, Bunnell, FL Zip 32110, Mailing Address: HCR1, Box 2, Zip 32110; tel. 904/437–2211; Clark P. Christianson, Senior Vice President and Administrator

MEMORIAL HOSPITAL–ORMOND BEACH (O, 205 beds) 875 Sterthaus Avenue, Ormond Beach, FL Zip 32174–5197; tel. 904/676–6000; Clark P. Christianson, Senior Vice President and Administrator

MEMORIAL HOSPITAL–WEST VOLUSIA (L, 156 beds) 701 West Plymouth Avenue, De Land, FL Zip 32720–3291, Mailing Address: P.O. Box 940, DeLand, Zip 32721–0509; tel. 904/734–3320; Johnette L. Vodenicker, Administrator

Owned, leased, sponsored:	3 hospitals	442 beds
Contract–managed:	0 hospitals	0 beds
Totals:	3 hospitals	442 beds

★0083: MEMORIAL HEALTHCARE SYSTEM (NP)
3501 Johnson Street, Hollywood, FL Zip 33021–5487; tel. 954/985–5805; Frank V. Sacco, FACHE, Chief Executive Officer

MEMORIAL HOSPITAL PEMBROKE (L, 190 beds) 2301 University Drive, Pembroke Pines, FL Zip 33024; tel. 954/962–9650; J. E. Piriz, Administrator

MEMORIAL HOSPITAL WEST (O, 110 beds) 703 North Flamingo Road, Pembroke Pines, FL Zip 33028; tel. 954/436–5000; Zeff Ross, Administrator

MEMORIAL REGIONAL HOSPITAL (O, 674 beds) 3501 Johnson Street, Hollywood, FL Zip 33021–5421; tel. 954/987–2000; C. Kennon Hetlage, Administrator

Owned, leased, sponsored:	3 hospitals	974 beds
Contract–managed:	0 hospitals	0 beds
Totals:	3 hospitals	974 beds

★2645: MEMORIAL HERMAN HEALTHCARE SYSTEM (NP)
7737 S.W. Freeway, Suite 200, Houston, TX Zip 77074–1800; tel. 713/776–6992; Dan S. Wilford, President

TEXAS: HERMANN HOSPITAL (O, 624 beds) 6411 Fannin, Houston, TX Zip 77030–1501; tel. 713/704–4000; Lynn Walts, R.N., Dr.PH, President and Chief Executive Officer

MEMORIAL HOSPITAL PASADENA (O, 173 beds) 906 East Southmore Avenue, Pasadena, TX Zip 77502–1124, Mailing Address: P.O. Box 1879, Zip 77502–1879; tel. 713/477–0411; Dennis M. Knox, Vice President and Chief Executive Officer

MEMORIAL HOSPITAL SOUTHWEST (O, 490 beds) 7600 Beechnut, Houston, TX Zip 77074–1850; tel. 713/776–5000; James E. Eastham, Vice President and Chief Executive Officer

MEMORIAL HOSPITAL–MEMORIAL CITY (L, 316 beds) 920 Frostwood Drive, Houston, TX Zip 77024–9173; tel. 713/932–3000; Jerel T. Humphrey, Vice President, Chief Executive Officer and Administrator

MEMORIAL HOSPITAL–THE WOODLANDS (O, 68 beds) 9250 Pinecroft Drive, The Woodlands, TX Zip 77380–3225; tel. 281/364–2300; Steve Sanders, Vice President, Chief Executive Officer and Administrator

MEMORIAL REHABILITATION HOSPITAL (L, 106 beds) 3043 Gessner Drive, Houston, TX Zip 77080–2597; tel. 713/462–2515; Roger Truskoloski, Administrator, Chief Executive Officer and Vice President

MEMORIAL SPRING SHADOWS GLEN (L, 108 beds) 2801 Gessner, Houston, TX Zip 77080–2599; tel. 713/462–4000; G. Jerry Mueck, Vice President, Chief Executive Officer and Administrator

For explanation of codes following names, see page B2.
★ Indicates Type III membership in the American Hospital Association.

Section B

Owned, leased, sponsored:	7 hospitals	1885 beds
Contract–managed:	0 hospitals	0 beds
Totals:	7 hospitals	1885 beds

★**5165: MERCY HEALTH SERVICES** (CC)
34605 Twelve Mile Road, Farmington Hills, MI Zip 48331–3221;
tel. 248/489–6000; Judith Pelham, President and Chief Executive
Officer

ILLINOIS: MORRISON COMMUNITY HOSPITAL (C, 60 beds) 303 North
Jackson Street, Morrison, IL Zip 61270–3042; tel. 815/772–4003; Mark
F. Fedyk, Administrator

IOWA: BAUM HARMON MEMORIAL HOSPITAL (C, 17 beds) 255 North Welch
Avenue, Primghar, IA Zip 51245–1034, Mailing Address: P.O. Box 528,
Zip 51245–0528; tel. 712/757–3905; Ronald Bender, Administrator

BELMOND COMMUNITY HOSPITAL (C, 22 beds) 403 First Street S.E.,
Belmond, IA Zip 50421–1201, Mailing Address: P.O. Box 326,
Zip 50421–0326; tel. 515/444–3223; Allan Atkinson, Administrator

ELDORA REGIONAL MEDICAL CENTER (C, 18 beds) 2413 Edgington Avenue,
Eldora, IA Zip 50627–1541; tel. 515/858–5416; Richard C. Hamilton,
Administrator

ELLSWORTH MUNICIPAL HOSPITAL (C, 40 beds) 110 Rocksylvania Avenue,
Iowa Falls, IA Zip 50126–2431; tel. 515/648–4631; John O'Brien,
Administrator

FRANKLIN GENERAL HOSPITAL (C, 82 beds) 1720 Central Avenue East,
Hampton, IA Zip 50441–1859; tel. 515/456–5000; Scott Wells, Interim Chief
Executive Officer

HANCOCK COUNTY MEMORIAL HOSPITAL (C, 26 beds) 531 First Street N.W.,
Britt, IA Zip 50423–0068, Mailing Address: P.O. Box 68, Zip 50423–0068;
tel. 515/843–3801; Harriet Thompson, Administrator

HAWARDEN COMMUNITY HOSPITAL (C, 17 beds) 1111 11th Street,
Hawarden, IA Zip 51023–1999; tel. 712/552–3100; Stuart A. Katz, FACHE,
Administrator

KOSSUTH REGIONAL HEALTH CENTER (C, 29 beds) 1515 South Phillips
Street, Algona, IA Zip 50511–3649; tel. 515/295–2451; James G.
Fitzpatrick, Administrator

MARIAN HEALTH CENTER (O, 284 beds) 801 Fifth Street, Sioux City, IA
Zip 51102, Mailing Address: P.O. Box 3168, Zip 51102–3168;
tel. 712/279–2010; Deborah VandenBroek, President and Chief Executive
Officer

MERCY HEALTH CENTER (O, 385 beds) 250 Mercy Drive, Dubuque, IA
Zip 52001–7360; tel. 319/589–8000; Russell M. Knight, President and Chief
Executive Officer

MITCHELL COUNTY REGIONAL HEALTH CENTER (C, 40 beds) 616 North
Eighth Street, Osage, IA Zip 50461–1498; tel. 515/732–3781; Kimberly J.
Miller, Administrator

NORTH IOWA MERCY HEALTH CENTER (O, 285 beds) 1000 Fourth Street
S.W., Mason City, IA Zip 50401–2800; tel. 515/422–7000; David H. Vellinga,
President and Chief Executive Officer

PALO ALTO COUNTY HOSPITAL (C, 54 beds) 3201 West First Street,
Emmetsburg, IA Zip 50536–2599; tel. 712/852–2434; Darrell E. Vondrak,
Administrator

REGIONAL HEALTH SERVICES OF HOWARD COUNTY (C, 32 beds) 235 Eighth
Avenue West, Cresco, IA Zip 52136–1098; tel. 319/547–2101; Elizabeth A.
Doty, Administrator

SAINT JOSEPH COMMUNITY HOSPITAL (O, 55 beds) 308 North Maple
Avenue, New Hampton, IA Zip 50659–1142; tel. 515/394–4121; Carolyn
Martin–Shaw, President

SAMARITAN HEALTH SYSTEM (O, 360 beds) 1410 North Fourth Street,
Clinton, IA Zip 52732–2999, Mailing Address: P.O. Box 2960,
Zip 52733–2960; tel. 319/244–5555; Thomas J. Hesselmann, President and
Chief Executive Officer

MICHIGAN: BATTLE CREEK HEALTH SYSTEM (O, 421 beds) 300 North
Avenue, Battle Creek, MI Zip 49016–3396; tel. 616/966–8000; Stephen
L. Abbott, President and Chief Executive Officer

DECKERVILLE COMMUNITY HOSPITAL (C, 17 beds) 3559 Pine Street,
Deckerville, MI Zip 48427–0126, Mailing Address: P.O. Box 126,
Zip 48427–0126; tel. 810/376–2835; Edward L. Gamache, Administrator

MCPHERSON HOSPITAL (O, 45 beds) 620 Byron Road, Howell, MI
Zip 48843–1093; tel. 517/545–6000; C. W. Lauderbach Jr., Chief Operating
Officer

MERCY GENERAL HEALTH PARTNERS (O, 175 beds) 1500 East Sherman
Boulevard, Muskegon, MI Zip 49443, Mailing Address: P.O. Box 358,
Zip 49443–0358; tel. 616/739–3901; Roger Spoelman, President and Chief
Executive Officer

MERCY HEALTH SERVICES NORTH–GRAYLING (O, 98 beds) 1100 Michigan
Avenue, Grayling, MI Zip 49738–1398; tel. 517/348–5461; Stephanie J.
Riemer–Matuzak, Chief Operating Officer

MERCY HEALTH SERVICES–NORTH (O, 79 beds) 400 Hobart Street, Cadillac,
MI Zip 49601–9596; tel. 616/876–7200; Michael J. Peterson, Interim
President and Chief Executive Officer

MERCY HOSPITAL (O, 248 beds) 5555 Conner Avenue, Detroit, MI
Zip 48213–3499; tel. 313/579–4000; David Spivey, Interim Chief Executive
Officer

MERCY HOSPITAL (O, 119 beds) 2601 Electric Avenue, Port Huron, MI
Zip 48060; tel. 810/985–1510; Mary R. Trimmer, President and Chief
Executive Officer

SAINT MARY'S HEALTH SERVICES (O, 287 beds) 200 Jefferson Avenue S.E.,
Grand Rapids, MI Zip 49503–4598; tel. 616/752–6090; David J. Ameen,
President and Chief Executive Officer

SALINE COMMUNITY HOSPITAL (O, 47 beds) 400 West Russell Street, Saline,
MI Zip 48176–1101; tel. 734/429–1500; Garry C. Faja, President and Chief
Executive Officer

ST. JOSEPH MERCY HEALTH SYSTEM (O, 482 beds) 5301 East Huron River
Drive, Ann Arbor, MI Zip 48106, Mailing Address: P.O. Box 995,
Zip 48106–0995; tel. 734/712–3456; Garry C. Faja, President and Chief
Executive Officer

ST. JOSEPH MERCY OAKLAND (O, 398 beds) 900 Woodward Avenue,
Pontiac, MI Zip 48341–2985; tel. 248/858–3000; Thomas L. Feurig,
President and Chief Executive Officer

ST. JOSEPH'S MERCY HOSPITALS AND HEALTH SERVICES (O, 298 beds)
Clinton Township, MI Jack Weiner, President and Chief Executive Officer

NEBRASKA: PENDER COMMUNITY HOSPITAL (C, 30 beds) 603 Earl Street,
Pender, NE Zip 68047–0100, Mailing Address: P.O. Box 100,
Zip 68047–0100; tel. 402/385–3083; Roger Mazour, Interim
Administrator

Owned, leased, sponsored:	17 hospitals	4066 beds
Contract–managed:	14 hospitals	484 beds
Totals:	31 hospitals	4550 beds

8835: MERIDIA HEALTH SYSTEM (NP)
6700 Beta Drive, Suite 200, Mayfield Village, OH Zip 44143;
tel. 216/446–8000; Charles B. Miner, President and Chief Executive
Officer

OHIO: MERIDIA EUCLID HOSPITAL (O, 209 beds) 18901 Lake Shore
Boulevard, Euclid, OH Zip 44119–1090; tel. 216/531–9000; Denise
Zeman, Chief Operating Officer

MERIDIA HILLCREST HOSPITAL (O, 263 beds) 6780 Mayfield Road, Cleveland,
OH Zip 44124–2202; tel. 216/449–4500; Catherine B. Leary, R.N., Chief
Operating Officer

MERIDIA HURON HOSPITAL (O, 471 beds) 13951 Terrace Road, Cleveland,
OH Zip 44112–4399; tel. 216/761–3300; Beverly Lozar, Chief Operating
Officer

MERIDIA SOUTH POINTE HOSPITAL (O, 178 beds) 4110 Warrensville Center
Road, Warrensville Heights, OH Zip 44122–7099; tel. 216/491–6000;
Kathleen A. Rice, Chief Operating Officer

Owned, leased, sponsored:	4 hospitals	1121 beds
Contract–managed:	0 hospitals	0 beds
Totals:	4 hospitals	1121 beds

For explanation of codes following names, see page B2.
★ Indicates Type III membership in the American Hospital Association.

Section B

★7235: **METHODIST HEALTH CARE SYSTEM** (CO)
6565 Fannin Street, D–200, Houston, TX Zip 77030–2707;
tel. 713/790–2221; Peter W. Butler, President and Chief Executive
Officer

TEXAS: DIAGNOSTIC CENTER HOSPITAL (O, 109 beds) 6447 Main Street,
Houston, TX Zip 77030–1595; tel. 713/790–0790; William A. Gregory,
Chief Executive Officer

SAN JACINTO METHODIST HOSPITAL (O, 231 beds) 4401 Garth Road,
Baytown, TX Zip 77521–3160; tel. 281/420–8600; William Simmons,
President and Chief Executive Officer

THE METHODIST HOSPITAL (O, 900 beds) 6565 Fannin Street, Houston, TX
Zip 77030–2707; tel. 713/790–3311; R. G. Girotto, Executive Vice President
and Chief Operating Officer

Owned, leased, sponsored:	3 hospitals	1240 beds
Contract–managed:	0 hospitals	0 beds
Totals:	3 hospitals	1240 beds

●2715: **METHODIST HEALTH SYSTEM** (CO)
580 West Eighth Street, Jacksonville, FL Zip 32209–6553;
tel. 904/798–8000; Marcus E. Drewa, President

FLORIDA: METHODIST MEDICAL CENTER (O, 204 beds) 580 West Eighth
Street, Jacksonville, FL Zip 32209–6553; tel. 904/798–8000; Marcus E.
Drewa, President and Chief Executive Officer

Owned, leased, sponsored:	1 hospital	204 beds
Contract–managed:	0 hospitals	0 beds
Totals:	1 hospital	204 beds

★9345: **METHODIST HEALTH SYSTEMS, INC.** (CO)
1211 Union Avenue, Suite 700, Memphis, TN Zip 38104–6600;
tel. 901/726–2300; Maurice W. Elliott, President

MISSISSIPPI: METHODIST HEALTHCARE (L, 319 beds) 1850 Chadwick Drive,
Jackson, MS Zip 39204–3479, Mailing Address: P.O. Box 59001,
Zip 39204–9001; tel. 601/376–1000; Cameron J. Welton, President and
Chief Executive Officer

METHODIST HEALTHCARE MIDDLE MISSISSIPPI HOSPITAL (O, 80 beds) 239
Bowling Green Road, Lexington, MS Zip 39095–9332; tel. 601/834–1321;
James K. Greer, Administrator

TENNESSEE: METHODIST HEALTHCARE – FAYETTE HOSPITAL (O, 38 beds)
214 Lakeview Drive, Somerville, TN Zip 38068; tel. 901/465–0532;
Michael Blome', Administrator

METHODIST HOSPITAL OF DYERSBURG (O, 105 beds) 400 Tickle Street,
Dyersburg, TN Zip 38024–3182; tel. 901/285–2410; Richard McCormick,
Administrator

METHODIST HOSPITAL OF LEXINGTON (O, 32 beds) 200 West Church Street,
Lexington, TN Zip 38351–2014; tel. 901/968–3646; Eugene Ragghianti,
Administrator

METHODIST HOSPITAL OF MCKENZIE (O, 27 beds) 161 Hospital Drive,
McKenzie, TN Zip 38201–1636; tel. 901/352–4170; Randal E. Carson,
Administrator

METHODIST HOSPITALS OF MEMPHIS (O, 1232 beds) 1265 Union Avenue,
Memphis, TN Zip 38104–3499; tel. 901/726–7000; Gary S. Shorb,
President

METHODIST–HAYWOOD PARK HOSPITAL (O, 44 beds) 2545 North
Washington Avenue, Brownsville, TN Zip 38012–1697; tel. 901/772–4110;
Sandra Bailey, Administrator

Owned, leased, sponsored:	8 hospitals	1877 beds
Contract–managed:	0 hospitals	0 beds
Totals:	8 hospitals	1877 beds

★2735: **METHODIST HOSPITALS OF DALLAS** (NP)
1441 North Beckley, Dallas, TX Zip 75203–1201, Mailing Address:
P.O. Box 655999, Zip 75265–5999; tel. 214/947–8181; Howard M.
Chase, FACHE, President and Chief Executive Officer

TEXAS: CHARLTON METHODIST HOSPITAL (O, 134 beds) 3500 West
Wheatland Road, Dallas, TX Zip 75222, Mailing Address: Box 225357,
Zip 75222–5357; tel. 214/947–7500; Kim N. Hollon, FACHE, Executive
Director

METHODIST MEDICAL CENTER (O, 375 beds) 1441 North Beckley Avenue,
Dallas, TX Zip 75203–1201, Mailing Address: Box 655999,
Zip 75265–5999; tel. 214/947–8181; John W. Carver, FACHE, Executive
Director

Owned, leased, sponsored:	2 hospitals	509 beds
Contract–managed:	0 hospitals	0 beds
Totals:	2 hospitals	509 beds

★0001: **MIDMICHIGAN HEALTH** (NP)
4005 Orchard Drive, Midland, MI Zip 48670–0001;
tel. 517/839–3000; Terence F. Moore, President

MICHIGAN: MIDMICHIGAN MEDICAL CENTER–CLARE (O, 64 beds) 104 West
Sixth Street, Clare, MI Zip 48617–1409; tel. 517/386–9951; Lawrence F.
Barco, President

MIDMICHIGAN MEDICAL CENTER–GLADWIN (O, 42 beds) 455 South Quarter
Street, Gladwin, MI Zip 48624–1918; tel. 517/426–9286; Mark E. Bush,
Executive Vice President

MIDMICHIGAN MEDICAL CENTER–MIDLAND (O, 221 beds) 4005 Orchard
Drive, Midland, MI Zip 48670; tel. 517/839–3000; David A. Reece, President

Owned, leased, sponsored:	3 hospitals	327 beds
Contract–managed:	0 hospitals	0 beds
Totals:	3 hospitals	327 beds

0143: **MISSION & ST. JOSEPH'S HEALTH SYSTEM** (CO)
509 Biltmore Avenue, Asheville, NC Zip 28801

NORTH CAROLINA: MISSION HOSPITAL (O, 436 beds) 509 Biltmore Avenue,
Asheville, NC Zip 28801–4690; tel. 704/255–4000; Robert F. Burgin,
President and Chief Executive Officer

ST. JOSEPH'S HOSPITAL (O, 275 beds) 428 Biltmore Avenue, Asheville, NC
Zip 28801–4502; tel. 704/255–3100; J. Lewis Daniels, President and Chief
Executive Officer

Owned, leased, sponsored:	2 hospitals	711 beds
Contract–managed:	0 hospitals	0 beds
Totals:	2 hospitals	711 beds

2855: **MISSIONARY BENEDICTINE SISTERS AMERICAN
PROVINCE** (CC)
300 North 18th Street, Norfolk, NE Zip 68701–3687;
tel. 402/371–3438; Sister M. Agnes Salber, Prioress

NEBRASKA: FAITH REGIONAL HEALTH SERVICES (O, 155 beds) 2700 Norfolk
Avenue, Norfolk, NE Zip 68702–0869, Mailing Address: P.O. BOX 869,
Zip 68702–0869; tel. 402/644–7201; Robert L. Driewer, Chief Executive
Officer

PROVIDENCE MEDICAL CENTER (O, 34 beds) 1200 Providence Road, Wayne,
NE Zip 68787–1299; tel. 402/375–3800; Marcile Thomas, Administrator

Owned, leased, sponsored:	2 hospitals	189 beds
Contract–managed:	0 hospitals	0 beds
Totals:	2 hospitals	189 beds

0017: **MISSISSIPPI STATE DEPARTMENT OF MENTAL
HEALTH** (NP)
1101 Robert E. Lee Building, Jackson, MS Zip 39201–1101;
tel. 601/359–1288; Roger McMurtry, Chief Mental Health Bureau

MISSISSIPPI: EAST MISSISSIPPI STATE HOSPITAL (O, 633 beds) 4555
Highland Park Drive, Meridian, MS Zip 39307–5498, Mailing Address: Box
4128, West Station, Zip 39304–4128; tel. 601/482–6186; Ramiro J.
Martinez, M.D., Director

MISSISSIPPI STATE HOSPITAL (O, 1297 beds) Whitfield, MS Mailing Address:
P.O. Box 157–A, Zip 39193–0157; tel. 601/351–8000; James G. Chastain,
Director

For explanation of codes following names, see page B2.
★ Indicates Type III membership in the American Hospital Association.
● Single hospital health care system

Section B

Owned, leased, sponsored:	2 hospitals	1930 beds
Contract–managed:	0 hospitals	0 beds
Totals:	2 hospitals	1930 beds

1335: MORTON PLANT MEASE HEALTH CARE (NP)

601 Main Street, Dunedin, FL Zip 34698, Mailing Address: P.O. Box 760, Zip 34697–0760; tel. 813/733–1111; Philip K. Beauchamp, FACHE, President and Chief Executive Officer

FLORIDA: MEASE COUNTRYSIDE HOSPITAL (O, 100 beds) 3231 McMullen–Booth Road, Safety Harbor, FL Zip 34695–1098, Mailing Address: P.O. 1098, Zip 34695–1098; tel. 813/725–6111; James A. Pfeiffer, Chief Administrative Officer

MEASE HOSPITAL DUNEDIN (O, 258 beds) 601 Main Street, Dunedin, FL Zip 34698–5891, Mailing Address: P.O. Box 760, Zip 34697–0760; tel. 813/733–1111; James A. Pfeiffer, Vice President and Chief Operating Officer

MORTON PLANT HOSPITAL (O, 742 beds) 323 Jeffords Street, Clearwater, FL Zip 34616–3892, Mailing Address: Box 210, Zip 34617–0210; tel. 813/462–7000; Frank V. Murphy III, President and Chief Executive Officer

Owned, leased, sponsored:	3 hospitals	1100 beds
Contract–managed:	0 hospitals	0 beds
Totals:	3 hospitals	1100 beds

6555: MULTICARE HEALTH SYSTEM (NP)

315 Martin Luther King Jr. Way, Tacoma, WA Zip 98405, Mailing Address: P.O. Box 5299, Zip 98405–0299; tel. 253/552–1000; William B. Connoley, President

WASHINGTON: ALLENMORE HOSPITAL (O, 72 beds) South 19th and Union Avenue, Tacoma, WA Zip 98405, Mailing Address: P.O. Box 11414, Zip 98411–0414; tel. 253/572–2323; Charles Hoffman, Vice President

MARY BRIDGE CHILDREN'S HOSPITAL AND HEALTH CENTER (O, 72 beds) 317 Martin Luther King Jr. Way, Tacoma, WA Zip 98405–0299, Mailing Address: Box 5299, Zip 98405–0299; tel. 253/552–1400; William B. Connoley, President and Chief Executive Officer

TACOMA GENERAL HOSPITAL (O, 282 beds) 315 Martin Luther King Jr. Way, Tacoma, WA Zip 98405–0299, Mailing Address: P.O. Box 5299, Zip 98405–0299; tel. 253/552–1000; William B. Connoley, President and Chief Executive Officer

Owned, leased, sponsored:	3 hospitals	426 beds
Contract–managed:	0 hospitals	0 beds
Totals:	3 hospitals	426 beds

★1465: MUNSON HEALTHCARE (NP)

1105 Sixth Street, Traverse City, MI Zip 49684–2386; tel. 616/935–6502; John M. Rockwood Jr., President

MICHIGAN: KALKASKA MEMORIAL HEALTH CENTER (C, 76 beds) 419 South Coral Street, Kalkaska, MI Zip 49646–9438, Mailing Address: P.O. Box 249, Zip 49646–0249; tel. 616/258–7500; James D. Austin, CHE, Administrator

LEELANAU MEMORIAL HEALTH CENTER (O, 91 beds) 215 South High Street, Northport, MI Zip 49670, Mailing Address: P.O. Box 217, Zip 49670–0217; tel. 616/386–0000; Jayne R. Bull, Administrator

MUNSON MEDICAL CENTER (O, 368 beds) 1105 Sixth Street, Traverse City, MI Zip 49684–2386; tel. 616/935–5000; Ralph J. Cerny, President and Chief Executive Officer

PAUL OLIVER MEMORIAL HOSPITAL (O, 48 beds) 224 Park Avenue, Frankfort, MI Zip 49635–9658; tel. 616/352–9621; James D. Austin, CHE, Administrator

Owned, leased, sponsored:	3 hospitals	507 beds
Contract–managed:	1 hospital	76 beds
Totals:	4 hospitals	583 beds

0116: NETCARE HEALTH SYSTEMS, INC. (IO)

424 Church Street, Suite 2100, Nashville, TN Zip 37219; tel. 615/742–8500; Michael A. Koban Jr., Chief Executive Officer

CALIFORNIA: SAN CLEMENTE HOSPITAL AND MEDICAL CENTER (O, 83 beds) 654 Camino De Los Mares, San Clemente, CA Zip 92673; tel. 714/496–1122; Karen Poole, Interim Chief Executive Officer

GEORGIA: CHATUGE REGIONAL HOSPITAL AND NURSING HOME (O, 39 beds) 110 Main Street, Hiawassee, GA Zip 30546, Mailing Address: P.O. Box 509, Zip 30546–0509; tel. 706/896–2222; Thomas I. Edwards, President and Chief Executive Officer

CHESTATEE REGIONAL HOSPITAL (O, 52 beds) 1111 Mountain Drive, Dahlonega, GA Zip 30533; tel. 706/864–6136; Stephen G. Widener, President and Chief Executive Officer

NORTH GEORGIA MEDICAL CENTER (O, 150 beds) 1362 South Main Street, Ellijay, GA Zip 30540–0346, Mailing Address: P.O. Box 2239, Zip 30540–0346; tel. 706/276–4741; Steve Grimm, Chief Executive Officer

MISSISSIPPI: MARSHALL COUNTY MEDICAL CENTER (O, 40 beds) 1430 East Salem, Holly Springs, MS Zip 38635, Mailing Address: P.O. Box 6000, Zip 38634–6000; tel. 601/252–1212; Bill Renick, Administrator

STONE COUNTY HOSPITAL (O, 50 beds) 1434 East Central Avenue, Wiggins, MS Zip 39577; tel. 601/928–6600; J. Clifton Quinn, Administrator

TRACE REGIONAL HOSPITAL (O, 84 beds) Highway 8 East, Houston, MS Zip 38851, Mailing Address: P.O. Box 626, Zip 38851–0626; tel. 601/456–3700; Bristol Messer, Chief Executive Officer

TEXAS: CENTRAL TEXAS HOSPITAL (O, 34 beds) 806 North Crockett Avenue, Cameron, TX Zip 76520–2599; tel. 254/697–6591; Louis West, President

DENTON COMMUNITY HOSPITAL (O, 110 beds) 207 North Bonnie Brae Street, Denton, TX Zip 76201–3798; tel. 940/898–7000; Timothy Charles, Chief Executive Officer

Owned, leased, sponsored:	9 hospitals	642 beds
Contract–managed:	0 hospitals	0 beds
Totals:	9 hospitals	642 beds

★0142: NEW YORK & PRESBYTERIAN HEALTHCARE (NP)

525 East 68th Street, New York, NY Zip 10021–4885; tel. 212/746–4000; David B. Skinner, M.D., President and Chief Executive Officer

NEW YORK: BROOKLYN HOSPITAL CENTER (O, 653 beds) 121 DeKalb Avenue, Brooklyn, NY Zip 11201–5493; tel. 718/250–8005; Frederick D. Alley, President and Chief Executive Officer

FLUSHING HOSPITAL MEDICAL CENTER (O, 321 beds) 45th Avenue at Parsons Boulevard, Flushing, NY Zip 11355–2100; tel. 718/670–5000; Stephen S. Mills, President and Chief Executive Officer

GRACIE SQUARE HOSPITAL (O, 100 beds) 420 East 76th Street, New York, NY Zip 10021–3104; tel. 212/988–4400; Frank Bruno, Chief Executive Officer

HOSPITAL FOR SPECIAL SURGERY (O, 138 beds) 535 East 70th Street, New York, NY Zip 10021–4898; tel. 212/606–1000; John R. Ahearn, Co–Chief Executive Officer

NEW YORK COMMUNITY HOSPITAL (O, 134 beds) 2525 Kings Highway, Brooklyn, NY Zip 11229–1798; tel. 718/692–5300; Lin H. Mo, President and Chief Executive Officer

NEW YORK HOSPITAL MEDICAL CENTER OF QUEENS (O, 449 beds) 56–45 Main Street, Flushing, NY Zip 11355–5000; tel. 718/670–1231; Stephen S. Mills, President and Chief Executive Officer

NEW YORK METHODIST HOSPITAL (O, 560 beds) 506 Sixth Street, Brooklyn, NY Zip 11215–3645; tel. 718/780–3000; Mark J. Mundy, President and Chief Executive Officer

NEW YORK AND PRESBYTERIAN HOSPITAL (O, 2038 beds) 525 East 68th Street, New York, NY Zip 10021–4885; tel. 212/746–5454; David B. Skinner, M.D., Vice Chairman and Chief Executive Officer

UNITED HOSPITAL MEDICAL CENTER (O, 191 beds) 406 Boston Post Road, Port Chester, NY Zip 10573–7300; tel. 914/934–3000; Kevin Dahill, President and Chief Executive Officer

For explanation of codes following names, see page B2.
★ Indicates Type III membership in the American Hospital Association.

WYCKOFF HEIGHTS MEDICAL CENTER (O, 299 beds) 374 Stockholm Street, Brooklyn, NY Zip 11237–4099; tel. 718/963–7102; Dominick J. Gio, President and Chief Executive Officer

Owned, leased, sponsored:	10 hospitals	4883 beds
Contract–managed:	0 hospitals	0 beds
Totals:	10 hospitals	4883 beds

3075: NEW YORK CITY HEALTH AND HOSPITALS CORPORATION (NP)

125 Worth Street, Room 514, New York, NY Zip 10013–4006; tel. 212/788–3321; Luis R. Marcos, M.D., President

BELLEVUE HOSPITAL CENTER (O, 888 beds) 462 First Avenue, New York, NY Zip 10016–9198; tel. 212/562–4141; Carlos Perez, Executive Director

COLER MEMORIAL HOSPITAL (O, 1025 beds) Roosevelt Island, New York, NY Zip 10044; tel. 212/848–6000; Samuel Lehrfeld, Executive Director

CONEY ISLAND HOSPITAL (O, 442 beds) 2601 Ocean Parkway, Brooklyn, NY Zip 11235–7795; tel. 718/616–3000; William Walsh, Executive Director

ELMHURST HOSPITAL CENTER (O, 498 beds) 79–01 Broadway, Elmhurst, NY Zip 11373; tel. 718/334–4000; Pete Velez, Executive Director

GOLDWATER MEMORIAL HOSPITAL (O, 986 beds) Franklin D. Roosevelt Island, New York, NY Zip 10044; tel. 212/318–8000; Samuel Lehrfeld, Executive Director

HARLEM HOSPITAL CENTER (O, 380 beds) 506 Lenox Avenue, New York, NY Zip 10037–1894; tel. 212/939–1340; Linnette Webb, Senior Vice President and Executive Director

JACOBI MEDICAL CENTER (O, 485 beds) Pelham Parkway South and Eastchester Road, Bronx, NY Zip 10461–1197; tel. 718/918–5000; Joseph S. Orlando, Executive Director

KINGS COUNTY HOSPITAL CENTER (O, 781 beds) 451 Clarkson Avenue, Brooklyn, NY Zip 11203–2097; tel. 718/245–3131; Jean G. Leon, R.N., Senior Vice President

LINCOLN MEDICAL AND MENTAL HEALTH CENTER (O, 440 beds) 234 East 149th Street, Bronx, NY Zip 10451–9998; tel. 718/579–5700; Lilliam Barrios–Paoli, Ph.D., Executive Director

METROPOLITAN HOSPITAL CENTER (O, 423 beds) 1901 First Avenue, New York, NY Zip 10029–7496; tel. 212/423–6262; Jose R. Sanchez, Executive Director

NORTH CENTRAL BRONX HOSPITAL (O, 268 beds) 3424 Kossuth Avenue, Bronx, NY Zip 10467–2489; tel. 718/519–3500; Arthur Wagner, Chief Operating Officer

QUEENS HOSPITAL CENTER (O, 292 beds) 82–68 164th Street, Jamaica, NY Zip 11432–1104; tel. 718/883–3000; Gladiola Sampson, Acting Executive Director

WOODHULL MEDICAL AND MENTAL HEALTH CENTER (O, 439 beds) 760 Broadway Street, Brooklyn, NY Zip 11206–5383; tel. 718/963–8000; Cynthia Carrington–Murray, Executive Director

Owned, leased, sponsored:	13 hospitals	7347 beds
Contract–managed:	0 hospitals	0 beds
Totals:	13 hospitals	7347 beds

0009: NEW YORK STATE DEPARTMENT OF MENTAL HEALTH (NP)

44 Holland Avenue, Albany, NY Zip 12229–3411; tel. 518/447–9611; Jesse Nixon Jr., Ph.D., Director

BINGHAMTON PSYCHIATRIC CENTER (O, 216 beds) 425 Robinson Street, Binghamton, NY Zip 13901–4198; tel. 607/724–1391; Margaret R. Dugan, Executive Director

BRONX CHILDREN'S PSYCHIATRIC CENTER (O, 75 beds) 1000 Waters Place, Bronx, NY Zip 10461–2799; tel. 718/892–0808; E. Richard Feinberg, M.D., Executive Director

BRONX PSYCHIATRIC CENTER (O, 658 beds) 1500 Waters Place, Bronx, NY Zip 10461–2796; tel. 718/931–0600; LeRoy Carmichael, Executive Director

BUFFALO PSYCHIATRIC CENTER (O, 260 beds) 400 Forest Avenue, Buffalo, NY Zip 14213–1298; tel. 716/885–2261; George Molnar, M.D., Executive Director

CAPITAL DISTRICT PSYCHIATRIC CENTER (O, 200 beds) 75 New Scotland Avenue, Albany, NY Zip 12208–3474; tel. 518/447–9611; Jesse Nixon Jr., Ph.D., Director

CREEDMOOR PSYCHIATRIC CENTER (O, 600 beds) Jamaica, NY Mailing Address: 80–45 Winchester Boulevard, Queens Village, Zip 11427–2199; tel. 718/264–3300; Charlotte Seltzer, Chief Executive Officer

ELMIRA PSYCHIATRIC CENTER (O, 130 beds) 100 Washington Street, Elmira, NY Zip 14901–2898; tel. 607/737–4739; Bert W. Pyle Jr., Director

HUDSON RIVER PSYCHIATRIC CENTER (O, 460 beds) Branch B., Poughkeepsie, NY Zip 12601–1197; tel. 914/452–8000; James Regan, Ph.D., Chief Executive Officer

KINGSBORO PSYCHIATRIC CENTER (O, 400 beds) 681 Clarkson Avenue, Brooklyn, NY Zip 11203–2199; tel. 718/221–7395; John Palmer, Ph.D., Director

MANHATTAN PSYCHIATRIC CENTER–WARD'S ISLAND (O, 745 beds) 600 East 125th Street, New York, NY Zip 10035–9998; tel. 212/369–0500; Horace Belton, Executive Director

MIDDLETOWN PSYCHIATRIC CENTER (O, 271 beds) 141 Monhagen Avenue, Middletown, NY Zip 10940–6198; tel. 914/342–5511; James H. Bopp, Executive Director

MOHAWK VALLEY PSYCHIATRIC CENTER (O, 614 beds) 1400 Noyes, Utica, NY Zip 13502–3803; tel. 315/797–6800; Sarah F. Rudes, Executive Director

NEW YORK STATE PSYCHIATRIC INSTITUTE (O, 58 beds) 722 West 168th Street, New York, NY Zip 10032–2695; tel. 212/543–5000; John M. Oldham, M.D., Director

PILGRIM PSYCHIATRIC CENTER (O, 744 beds) 998 Crooked Hill Road, Brentwood, NY Zip 11717–1087; tel. 516/761–3500; Kathleen Kelly, Chief Executive Officer

QUEENS CHILDREN'S PSYCHIATRIC CENTER (O, 106 beds) 74–03 Commonwealth Boulevard, Jamaica, NY Zip 11426–1890; tel. 718/264–4506; Gloria Faretra, M.D., Executive Director

RICHARD H. HUTCHINGS PSYCHIATRIC CENTER (O, 184 beds) 620 Madison Street, Syracuse, NY Zip 13210–2319; tel. 315/473–4980; Bryan F. Rudes, Executive Director

ROCHESTER PSYCHIATRIC CENTER (O, 267 beds) 1111 Elmwood Avenue, Rochester, NY Zip 14620–3005; tel. 716/473–3230; Martin H. Von Holden, Executive Director

ROCKLAND CHILDREN'S PSYCHIATRIC CENTER (O, 54 beds) 599 Convent Road, Orangeburg, NY Zip 10962; tel. 914/359–7400; Marcia Werby, Administrator

ROCKLAND PSYCHIATRIC CENTER (O, 525 beds) 140 Old Orangeburg Road, Orangeburg, NY Zip 10962–0071; tel. 914/359–1000; James H. Bopp, Executive Director

SAGAMORE CHILDREN'S PSYCHIATRIC CENTER (O, 69 beds) 197 Half Hollow Road, Huntington Station, NY Zip 11746; tel. 516/673–7700; Robert Schweitzer, Ed.D., Executive Director

SOUTH BEACH PSYCHIATRIC CENTER (O, 325 beds) 777 Seaview Avenue, Staten Island, NY Zip 10305–3499; tel. 718/667–2300; Lucy Sarkis, M.D., Executive Director

ST. LAWRENCE PSYCHIATRIC CENTER (O, 175 beds) 1 Chimney Point Drive, Ogdensburg, NY Zip 13669–2291; tel. 315/393–3000; John R. Scott, Director

WESTERN NEW YORK CHILDREN'S PSYCHIATRIC CENTER (O, 46 beds) 1010 East and West Road, Buffalo, NY Zip 14224–3698; tel. 716/674–9730; Jed M. Cohen, Acting Executive Director

Owned, leased, sponsored:	23 hospitals	7182 beds
Contract–managed:	0 hospitals	0 beds
Totals:	23 hospitals	7182 beds

★3115: NORTH BROWARD HOSPITAL DISTRICT (NP)

303 S.E. 17th Street, Fort Lauderdale, FL Zip 33316–2510; tel. 954/355–5100; G. Wil Trower, President and Chief Executive Officer

For explanation of codes following names, see page B2.
★ Indicates Type III membership in the American Hospital Association.

Section B

FLORIDA: BROWARD GENERAL MEDICAL CENTER (O, 548 beds) 1600 South Andrews Avenue, Fort Lauderdale, FL Zip 33316–2510; tel. 954/355–4400; Ruth A. Eldridge, R.N., Regional Vice President, Administration

CORAL SPRINGS MEDICAL CENTER (O, 167 beds) 3000 Coral Hills Drive, Coral Springs, FL Zip 33065; tel. 954/344–3000; A. Gary Muller, FACHE, Administrator and Regional Vice President

IMPERIAL POINT MEDICAL CENTER (O, 154 beds) 6401 North Federal Highway, Fort Lauderdale, FL Zip 33308–1495; tel. 954/776–8500; Dorothy J. Mancini, R.N., Regional Vice President Administration

NORTH BROWARD MEDICAL CENTER (O, 334 beds) 201 Sample Road, Pompano Beach, FL Zip 33064–3502; tel. 954/941–8300; James R. Chromik, Regional Vice President, Administration

Owned, leased, sponsored:	4 hospitals	1203 beds
Contract–managed:	0 hospitals	0 beds
Totals:	4 hospitals	1203 beds

0032: NORTH MISSISSIPPI HEALTH SERVICES, INC. (NP) 830 South Gloster Street, Tupelo, MS Zip 38801–4996; tel. 601/841–3136; Jeffrey B. Barber, Dr.PH, President and Chief Executive Officer

MISSISSIPPI: CLAY COUNTY MEDICAL CENTER (O, 60 beds) 835 Medical Center Drive, West Point, MS Zip 39773–9320; tel. 601/495–2300; David M. Reid, Administrator

IUKA HOSPITAL (O, 48 beds) 1777 Curtis Drive, Iuka, MS Zip 38852–1001, Mailing Address: P.O. Box 860, Zip 38852–0860; tel. 601/423–6051; George Hand, Interim Administrator

NORTH MISSISSIPPI MEDICAL CENTER (O, 721 beds) 830 South Gloster Street, Tupelo, MS Zip 38801–4934; tel. 601/841–3000; Jeffrey B. Barber, Dr.PH, President and Chief Executive Officer

PONTOTOC HOSPITAL AND EXTENDED CARE FACILITY (L, 71 beds) 176 South Main Street, Pontotoc, MS Zip 38863–3311, Mailing Address: P.O. Box 790, Zip 38863–0790; tel. 601/489–5510; Fred B. Hood, Administrator

WEBSTER HEALTH SERVICES (L, 76 beds) 500 Highway 9 South, Eupora, MS Zip 39744; tel. 601/258–6221; Harold H. Whitaker Sr., Administrator

Owned, leased, sponsored:	5 hospitals	976 beds
Contract–managed:	0 hospitals	0 beds
Totals:	5 hospitals	976 beds

★0062: NORTH SHORE– LONG ISLAND JEWISH HEALTH SYSTEM (NP) 300 Community Drive, Manhasset, NY Zip 11030–3876; tel. 516/562–4060; John S. T. Gallagher, Co–President and Chief Executive Officer

NEW YORK: FRANKLIN HOSPITAL MEDICAL CENTER (C, 441 beds) 900 Franklin Avenue, Valley Stream, NY Zip 11580–2190; tel. 516/256–6000; Albert Dicker, President and Chief Executive Officer

HUNTINGTON HOSPITAL (C, 269 beds) 270 Park Avenue, Huntington, NY Zip 11743–2799; tel. 516/351–2200; J. Ronald Gaudreault, President and Chief Executive Officer

LONG ISLAND JEWISH MEDICAL CENTER (O, 804 beds) 270–05 76th Avenue, New Hyde Park, NY Zip 11040–1496; tel. 718/470–7000; David R. Dantzker, M.D., President and Chief Executive Officer

NORTH SHORE UNIVERSITY HOSPITAL (O, 958 beds) 300 Community Drive, Manhasset, NY Zip 11030–3876; tel. 516/562–0100; John S. T. Gallagher, President and Chief Executive Officer

NORTH SHORE UNIVERSITY HOSPITAL AT GLEN COVE (O, 265 beds) St. Andrews Lane, Glen Cove, NY Zip 11542; tel. 516/674–7300; Mark R. Stenzler, Vice President Administration

NORTH SHORE UNIVERSITY HOSPITAL AT PLAINVIEW (O, 279 beds) 888 Old Country Road, Plainview, NY Zip 11803–4978; tel. 516/719–3000; Glenn Hirsch, Executive Vice President, Administration

NORTH SHORE UNIVERSITY HOSPITAL AT SYOSSET (O, 186 beds) 221 Jericho Turnpike, Syosset, NY Zip 11791–4567; tel. 516/496–6400; Deborah Tascone, R.N., Vice President for Administration

NORTH SHORE UNIVERSITY HOSPITAL–FOREST HILLS (O, 231 beds) Flushing, NY Mailing Address: 102–01 66th Road, Zip 11375; tel. 718/830–4000; Andrew J. Mitchell, Vice President, Administration

SOUTHSIDE HOSPITAL (C, 374 beds) 301 East Main Street, Bay Shore, NY Zip 11706–8458; tel. 516/968–3000; Theodore A. Jospe, President

STATEN ISLAND UNIVERSITY HOSPITAL (C, 617 beds) 475 Seaview Avenue, Staten Island, NY Zip 10305–9998; tel. 718/226–9000; Rick J. Varone, President

Owned, leased, sponsored:	6 hospitals	2723 beds
Contract–managed:	4 hospitals	1701 beds
Totals:	10 hospitals	4424 beds

★2075: NORTHBAY HEALTHCARE SYSTEM (NP) 1200 B. Gale Wilson Boulevard, Fairfield, CA Zip 94533–3587; tel. 707/429–3600; Gary J. Passama, President and Chief Executive Officer

CALIFORNIA: NORTHBAY MEDICAL CENTER (O, 121 beds) 1200 B. Gale Wilson Boulevard, Fairfield, CA Zip 94533–3587; tel. 707/429–3600; Deborah Sugiyama, President

VACAVALLEY HOSPITAL (O, 43 beds) 1000 Nut Tree Road, Vacaville, CA Zip 95687; tel. 707/429–7717; Deborah Sugiyama, President

Owned, leased, sponsored:	2 hospitals	164 beds
Contract–managed:	0 hospitals	0 beds
Totals:	2 hospitals	164 beds

0139: NOVANT HEALTH (NP) 3333 Silas Creek Parkway, Winston Salem, NC Zip 27103; tel. 336/718–5000; Paul M. Wiles, President

NORTH CAROLINA: COMMUNITY GENERAL HOSPITAL OF THOMASVILLE (O, 128 beds) 207 Old Lexington Road, Thomasville, NC Zip 27360, Mailing Address: P.O. Box 789, Zip 27361–0789; tel. 336/472–2000; Lynn Ingram Boggs, President and Chief Executive Officer

DAVIE COUNTY HOSPITAL (O, 30 beds) 223 Hospital Street, Mocksville, NC Zip 27028–2038, Mailing Address: P.O. Box 1209, Zip 27028–1209; tel. 336/751–8100; Mike Kimel, Administrator

FORSYTH MEMORIAL HOSPITAL (O, 747 beds) 3333 Silas Creek Parkway, Winston–Salem, NC Zip 27103–3090; tel. 336/718–5000; Gregory J. Beier, President

MEDICAL PARK HOSPITAL (O, 59 beds) 1950 South Hawthorne Road, Winston–Salem, NC Zip 27103–3993, Mailing Address: P.O. Box 24728, Zip 27114–4728; tel. 910/718–0600; Eduard R. Koehler, Administrator

PRESBYTERIAN HOSPITAL (O, 551 beds) 200 Hawthorne Lane, Charlotte, NC Zip 28204–2528, Mailing Address: P.O. Box 33549, Zip 28233–3549; tel. 704/384–4000; Thomas R. Revels, President and Chief Executive Officer

PRESBYTERIAN HOSPITAL–MATTHEWS (O, 82 beds) 1500 Matthews Township Parkway, Matthews, NC Zip 28105, Mailing Address: P.O. Box 3310, Zip 28106–3310; tel. 704/384–6500; Mark R. Farmer, Vice President and Administrator

PRESBYTERIAN SPECIALTY HOSPITAL (O, 15 beds) 1600 East Third Street, Charlotte, NC Zip 28204–3282, Mailing Address: P.O. Box 34425, Zip 28234–4425; tel. 704/384–6000; Chip Day, Acting Vice President

PRESBYTERIAN–ORTHOPAEDIC HOSPITAL (O, 166 beds) 1901 Randolph Road, Charlotte, NC Zip 28207–1195; tel. 704/370–1549; Paul M. Jenson, Chief Executive Officer

Owned, leased, sponsored:	8 hospitals	1778 beds
Contract–managed:	0 hospitals	0 beds
Totals:	8 hospitals	1778 beds

★1165: OAKWOOD HEALTHCARE SYSTEM (NP) One Parklane Boulevard, Suite 1000E, Dearborn, MI Zip 48126; tel. 313/253–6007; James L. Brexler, Chief Executive Officer

MICHIGAN: OAKWOOD HOSPITAL ANNAPOLIS CENTER (O, 219 beds) 33155 Annapolis Road, Wayne, MI Zip 48184–2493; tel. 313/467–4000; Mark Anthony, Vice President and Administrator

For explanation of codes following names, see page B2.
★ Indicates Type III membership in the American Hospital Association.

OAKWOOD HOSPITAL BEYER CENTER–YPSILANTI (O, 57 beds) 135 South Prospect Street, Ypsilanti, MI Zip 48198–5693; tel. 734/484–2200; Richard Hillbom, Administrator

OAKWOOD HOSPITAL SEAWAY CENTER (O, 89 beds) 5450 Fort Street, Trenton, MI Zip 48183–4625; tel. 734/671–3800; Brian Peltz, Site Leader

OAKWOOD HOSPITAL AND MEDICAL CENTER–DEARBORN (O, 548 beds) 18101 Oakwood Boulevard, Dearborn, MI Zip 48124–4093; Mailing Address: P.O. Box 2500, Zip 48123–2500; tel. 313/593–7000; Joseph Tasse, Administrator

OAKWOOD HOSPITAL–HERITAGE CENTER (O, 257 beds) 10000 Telegraph Road, Taylor, MI Zip 48180–3349; tel. 313/295–5000; Thomas E. Johnson, Vice President and Administrator

Owned, leased, sponsored:	5 hospitals	1170 beds
Contract–managed:	0 hospitals	0 beds
Totals:	5 hospitals	1170 beds

★9095: OHIOHEALTH (NP)
3555 Olentangy River Road, 4000, Columbus, OH Zip 43214–3900; tel. 614/566–5424; William W. Wilkins, President and Chief Executive Officer

OHIO: BUCYRUS COMMUNITY HOSPITAL (C, 47 beds) 629 North Sandusky Avenue, Bucyrus, OH Zip 44820–0627, Mailing Address: Box 627, Zip 44820–0627; tel. 419/562–4677; Mark E. Marley, Chief Executive Officer

GALION COMMUNITY HOSPITAL (C, 108 beds) 269 Portland Way South, Galion, OH Zip 44833–2399; tel. 419/468–4841; Mark E. Marley, President and Chief Executive Officer

GRANT/RIVERSIDE METHODIST HOSPITALS–GRANT CAMPUS (O, 470 beds) 111 South Grant Avenue, Columbus, OH Zip 43215–1898; tel. 614/566–9000; David P. Blom, President

GRANT/RIVERSIDE METHODIST HOSPITALS–RIVERSIDE CAMPUS (O, 775 beds) 3535 Olentangy River Road, Columbus, OH Zip 43214–3998; tel. 614/566–5000; David P. Blom, President

HARDIN MEMORIAL HOSPITAL (O, 51 beds) 921 East Franklin Street, Kenton, OH Zip 43326–2099, Mailing Address: P.O. Box 710, Zip 43326–0710; tel. 419/673–0761; Don J. Sabol, Chief Executive Officer

MARION GENERAL HOSPITAL (O, 148 beds) 1000 McKinley Park Drive, Marion, OH Zip 43302–6397; tel. 740/383–8400; Frank V. Swinehart, President and Chief Executive Officer

MORROW COUNTY HOSPITAL (C, 75 beds) 651 West Marion Road, Mount Gilead, OH Zip 43338–1096; tel. 419/946–5015; Alan C. Pauley, Administrator

SOUTHERN OHIO MEDICAL CENTER (O, 281 beds) 1805 27th Street, Portsmouth, OH Zip 45662–2400; tel. 740/354–5000; Randal M. Arnett, President and Chief Executive Officer

Owned, leased, sponsored:	5 hospitals	1725 beds
Contract–managed:	3 hospitals	230 beds
Totals:	8 hospitals	1955 beds

0018: OKLAHOMA STATE DEPARTMENT OF MENTAL HEALTH AND SUBSTANCE ABUSE SERVICES (NP)
1000 N.E. Tenth Street, Oklahoma City, OK Zip 73152, Mailing Address: P.O. Box 53277, Zip 73152–3277; tel. 405/271–6868; Jerry Nida, M.D., Commissioner of Health

OKLAHOMA: GRIFFIN MEMORIAL HOSPITAL (O, 182 beds) 900 East Main Street, Norman, OK Zip 73071–5305, Mailing Address: P.O. Box 151, Zip 73070–0151; tel. 405/321–4880; Dave Statton, Interim Superintendent

WESTERN STATE PSYCHIATRIC CENTER (O, 164 beds) Fort Supply, OK Mailing Address: P.O. Box 1, Zip 73841–0001; tel. 580/766–2311; Steve Norwood, Director

Owned, leased, sponsored:	2 hospitals	346 beds
Contract–managed:	0 hospitals	0 beds
Totals:	2 hospitals	346 beds

★3355: ORLANDO REGIONAL HEALTHCARE SYSTEM (NP)
1414 Kuhl Avenue, Orlando, FL Zip 32806–2093; tel. 407/841–5111; John Hillenmeyer, President and Chief Executive Officer

FLORIDA: ORLANDO REGIONAL MEDICAL CENTER (O, 904 beds) 1414 Kuhl Avenue, Orlando, FL Zip 32806–2093; tel. 407/841–5111; Abe Lopman, Executive Director

SOUTH LAKE HOSPITAL (O, 68 beds) 847 Eighth Street, Clermont, FL Zip 34711–2196; tel. 352/394–4071; Leslie Longacre, Executive Director and Chief Executive Officer

SOUTH SEMINOLE HOSPITAL (O, 206 beds) 555 West State Road 434, Longwood, FL Zip 32750–4999; tel. 407/767–1200; Sue Whelan–Williams, Site Administrator

ST. CLOUD HOSPITAL, A DIVISION OF ORLANDO REGIONAL HEALTHCARE SYSTEM (O, 68 beds) 2906 17th Street, Saint Cloud, FL Zip 34769–6099; tel. 407/892–2135; Jim Norris, Executive Director

Owned, leased, sponsored:	4 hospitals	1246 beds
Contract–managed:	0 hospitals	0 beds
Totals:	4 hospitals	1246 beds

★5335: OSF HEALTHCARE SYSTEM (CC)
800 N.E. Glen Oak Avenue, Peoria, IL Zip 61603–3200; tel. 309/655–2852; Sister Frances Marie Masching, President

ILLINOIS: SAINT ANTHONY MEDICAL CENTER (O, 210 beds) 5666 East State Street, Rockford, IL Zip 61108–2472; tel. 815/226–2000; David A. Schertz, Administrator

SAINT FRANCIS MEDICAL CENTER (O, 552 beds) 530 N.E. Glen Oak Avenue, Peoria, IL Zip 61637; tel. 309/655–2000; Sister M. Canisia, Administrator

SAINT JAMES HOSPITAL (O, 81 beds) 610 East Water Street, Pontiac, IL Zip 61764–2194; tel. 815/842–2828; David Ochs, Administrator

SAINT JOSEPH HOSPITAL (O, 58 beds) 1005 Julien Street, Belvidere, IL Zip 61008–9932; tel. 815/544–3411; David A. Schertz, Administrator

ST. JOSEPH MEDICAL CENTER (O, 154 beds) 2200 East Washington Street, Bloomington, IL Zip 61701–4323; tel. 309/662–3311; Kenneth J. Natzke, Administrator

ST. MARY MEDICAL CENTER (O, 141 beds) 3333 North Seminary Street, Galesburg, IL Zip 61401–1299; tel. 309/344–3161; Richard S. Kowalski, Administrator and Chief Executive Officer

MICHIGAN: ST. FRANCIS HOSPITAL (O, 66 beds) 3401 Ludington Street, Escanaba, MI Zip 49829–1377; tel. 906/786–3311; Roger M. Burgess, Administrator

Owned, leased, sponsored:	7 hospitals	1262 beds
Contract–managed:	0 hospitals	0 beds
Totals:	7 hospitals	1262 beds

0110: OUR LADY OF MERCY HEALTHCARE SYSTEM, INC. (CC)
600 East 233 Street, New York, NY Zip 10466–2697; tel. 718/920–9000; Gary S. Horan, FACHE, President and Chief Executive Officer

NEW YORK: OUR LADY OF MERCY MEDICAL CENTER (O, 508 beds) 600 East 233rd Street, Bronx, NY Zip 10466–2697; tel. 718/920–9000; Gary S. Horan, FACHE, President and Chief Executive Officer

ST. AGNES HOSPITAL (O, 184 beds) 305 North Street, White Plains, NY Zip 10605–2299; tel. 914/681–4500; Gary S. Horan, FACHE, President and Chief Executive Officer

Owned, leased, sponsored:	2 hospitals	692 beds
Contract–managed:	0 hospitals	0 beds
Totals:	2 hospitals	692 beds

0435: PACIFIC HEALTH CORPORATION (IO)
249 East Ocean Boulevard, Long Beach, CA Zip 90802; tel. 310/435–1300; Jens Mueller, Chairman

For explanation of codes following names, see page B2.
★ Indicates Type III membership in the American Hospital Association.

Networks, Health Care Systems and Alliances **B123**

Section B

CALIFORNIA: ANAHEIM GENERAL HOSPITAL (O, 88 beds) 3350 West Ball Road, Anaheim, CA Zip 92804–9998; tel. 714/827–6700; Reynold R. Welch, Chief Executive Officer

BELLFLOWER MEDICAL CENTER (O, 145 beds) 9542 East Artesia Boulevard, Bellflower, CA Zip 90706; tel. 310/925–8355; Stanley Otake, Chief Executive Officer

BUENA PARK MEDICAL CENTER (O, 58 beds) 5742 Beach Boulevard, Buena Park, CA Zip 90621; tel. 714/521–4770; Timothy L. Carda, Administrator and Chief Executive Officer

LOS ANGELES METROPOLITAN MEDICAL CENTER (O, 163 beds) 2231 South Western Avenue, Los Angeles, CA Zip 90018–1399; tel. 213/730–7342; Marc A. Furstman, Chief Executive Officer

Owned, leased, sponsored:	4 hospitals	454 beds
Contract–managed:	0 hospitals	0 beds
Totals:	4 hospitals	454 beds

★4155: PALMETTO HEALTH ALLIANCE (CO)
Taylor at Marion Street, Columbia, SC Zip 29220; tel. 803/771–5010; Charles D. Beaman Jr., President

SOUTH CAROLINA: PALMETTO BAPTIST MEDICAL CENTER EASLEY (O, 93 beds) 200 Fleetwood Drive, Easley, SC Zip 29640–2076, Mailing Address: P.O. Box 2129, Zip 29641–2129; tel. 864/855–7200; Roddey E. Gettys III, Executive Vice President

PALMETTO BAPTIST MEDICAL CENTER/COLUMBIA (O, 387 beds) Taylor at Marion Street, Columbia, SC Zip 29220; tel. 803/771–5010; James M. Bridges, Executive Vice President and Chief Operating Officer

Owned, leased, sponsored:	2 hospitals	480 beds
Contract–managed:	0 hospitals	0 beds
Totals:	2 hospitals	480 beds

★7555: PALOMAR POMERADO HEALTH SYSTEM (NP)
15255 Innovation Drive, Suite 204, San Diego, CA Zip 92128–3410; tel. 619/675–5100; Victoria M. Penland, President and Chief Executive Officer

CALIFORNIA: PALOMAR MEDICAL CENTER (O, 395 beds) 555 East Valley Parkway, Escondido, CA Zip 92025–3084; tel. 760/739–3000; Victoria M. Penland, Administrator and Chief Operating Officer

POMERADO HOSPITAL (O, 258 beds) 15615 Pomerado Road, Poway, CA Zip 92064; tel. 619/485–4600; Marvin W. Levenson, M.D., Administrator and Chief Operating Officer

Owned, leased, sponsored:	2 hospitals	653 beds
Contract–managed:	0 hospitals	0 beds
Totals:	2 hospitals	653 beds

5765: PARACELSUS HEALTHCARE CORPORATION (IO)
515 West Greens Road, Suite 800, Houston, TX Zip 77067–4511; tel. 281/774–5100; Charles R. Miller, President and Chief Operating Officer

BELLWOOD GENERAL HOSPITAL (O, 65 beds) 10250 East Artesia Boulevard, Bellflower, CA Zip 90706; tel. 562/866–9028; Michael Kerr, Administrator

CHICO COMMUNITY HOSPITAL (O, 109 beds) 560 Cohasset Road, Chico, CA Zip 95926; tel. 916/896–5000; John E. Fidler, FACHE, Chief Executive Officer

HOLLYWOOD COMMUNITY HOSPITAL OF HOLLYWOOD (O, 160 beds) 6245 De Longpre Avenue, Los Angeles, CA Zip 90028–9001; tel. 213/462–2271; Steven Courtier, Chief Executive Officer

LANCASTER COMMUNITY HOSPITAL (O, 123 beds) 43830 North Tenth Street West, Lancaster, CA Zip 93534; tel. 805/948–4781; Steve Schmidt, Administrator and Chief Executive Officer

LOS ANGELES COMMUNITY HOSPITAL (O, 186 beds) 4081 East Olympic Boulevard, Los Angeles, CA Zip 90023–3300; tel. 213/267–0477; Ted R. Estrada, Chief Executive Officer

MONROVIA COMMUNITY HOSPITAL (O, 49 beds) 323 South Heliotrope Avenue, Monrovia, CA Zip 91016, Mailing Address: Box 707, Zip 91017–0707; tel. 626/359–8341; Sheila M. Jordan, R.N., Administrator

ORANGE COUNTY COMMUNITY HOSPITAL OF BUENA PARK (O, 55 beds) 6850 Lincoln Avenue, Buena Park, CA Zip 90620–5703; tel. 562/827–1161; Joseph Sharp, Acting Administrator

FLORIDA: SANTA ROSA MEDICAL CENTER (O, 78 beds) 1450 Berryhill Road, Milton, FL Zip 32570–4028, Mailing Address: P.O. Box 648, Zip 32572–0648; tel. 850/626–7762; Renate Darby, Interim Chief Executive Officer

GEORGIA: FLINT RIVER COMMUNITY HOSPITAL (O, 50 beds) 509 Sumter Street, Montezuma, GA Zip 31063–0770, Mailing Address: P.O. Box 770, Zip 31063–0770; tel. 912/472–3100; James D. Tesar, Chief Executive Officer

MISSISSIPPI: SENATOBIA COMMUNITY HOSPITAL (O, 52 beds) 401 Getwell Drive, Senatobia, MS Zip 38668–2213, Mailing Address: P.O. Box 648, Zip 38668–0648; tel. 601/562–3100; Carol H. Hanes, Interim Chief Executive Officer

NORTH DAKOTA: DAKOTA HEARTLAND HEALTH SYSTEM (O, 203 beds) 1720 South Univeristy Drive, Fargo, ND Zip 58103–4994; tel. 701/280–4100; Louis Kauffman, President and Chief Executive Officer

TENNESSEE: BLEDSOE COUNTY GENERAL HOSPITAL (O, 26 beds) 128 Wheelertown Road, Pikeville, TN Zip 37367, Mailing Address: P.O. Box 699, Zip 37367–0699; tel. 423/447–2112; Gary Burton, Chief Executive Officer

CUMBERLAND RIVER HOSPITAL NORTH (O, 77 beds) 100 Old Jefferson Street, Celina, TN Zip 38551; tel. 931/243–3581; Patrick J. Gray, Chief Executive Officer

FENTRESS COUNTY GENERAL HOSPITAL (O, 73 beds) Highway 52 West, Jamestown, TN Zip 38556, Mailing Address: P.O. Box 1500, Zip 38556; tel. 615/879–8171; Curtis B. Courtney, Administrator

TEXAS: BAYCOAST MEDICAL CENTER (O, 191 beds) 1700 James Bowie Drive, Baytown, TX Zip 77520–3386, Mailing Address: P.O. Box 1451, Zip 77520–1451; tel. 713/420–6100; Frank T. Beirne, President and Chief Executive Officer

MEDICAL CENTER OF MESQUITE (O, 176 beds) 1011 North Galloway Avenue, Mesquite, TX Zip 75149–2433; tel. 214/320–7000; Terry J. Fontenot, Administrator

WESTWOOD MEDICAL CENTER (O, 80 beds) 4214 Andrews Highway, Midland, TX Zip 79703–4861; tel. 915/522–2273; Michael S. Potter, President and Chief Executive Officer

UTAH: DAVIS HOSPITAL AND MEDICAL CENTER (O, 126 beds) 1600 West Antelope Drive, Layton, UT Zip 84041–1142; tel. 801/825–9561; Bruce A. Baldwin, Chief Executive Officer

JORDAN VALLEY HOSPITAL (O, 50 beds) 3580 West 9000 South, West Jordan, UT Zip 84088–8811; tel. 801/561–8888; Jeffrey J. Manley, Chief Executive Officer

PIONEER VALLEY HOSPITAL (O, 104 beds) 3460 South Pioneer Parkway, Salt Lake City, UT Zip 84120–2648; tel. 801/964–3100; Brian Mottishaw, Chief Executive Officer

SALT LAKE REGIONAL MEDICAL CENTER (O, 200 beds) 1050 East South Temple, Salt Lake City, UT Zip 84102–1599; tel. 801/350–4111; Kay Matsumura, Chief Executive Officer

VIRGINIA: CAPITOL MEDICAL CENTER (O, 104 beds) 701 West Grace Street, Richmond, VA Zip 23220–4191; tel. 804/775–4100; Priscilla J. Shuler, Chief Executive Officer

Owned, leased, sponsored:	22 hospitals	2337 beds
Contract–managed:	0 hospitals	0 beds
Totals:	22 hospitals	2337 beds

0335: PARK HEALTHCARE COMPANY (IO)
149 Belle Forrest Circle, Nashville, TN Zip 37221; tel. 615/662–2577; Jerry E. Gilliland, President

KENTUCKY: LINCOLN TRAIL BEHAVIORAL HEALTH SYSTEM (O, 67 beds) 3909 South Wilson Road, Radcliff, KY Zip 40160–9714, Mailing Address: P.O. Box 369, Zip 40159–0369; tel. 502/351–9444; Melvin E. Modderman, Administrator

---

For explanation of codes following names, see page B2.
★ Indicates Type III membership in the American Hospital Association.

TEXAS: MEMORIAL HOSPITAL OF CENTER (O, 42 beds) 602 Hurst Street, Center, TX Zip 75935–3414, Mailing Address: P.O. Box 1749, Zip 75935–1749; tel. 409/598–2781; Robert V. Deen, Chief Executive Officer

Owned, leased, sponsored:	2 hospitals	109 beds
Contract–managed:	0 hospitals	0 beds
Totals:	2 hospitals	109 beds

★1785: PARTNERS HEALTHCARE SYSTEM, INC. (NP)
800 Boylston Street, Suite 1150, Boston, MA Zip 02199–8001; tel. 617/278–1004; Samuel O. Thier, M.D., President and Chief Executive Officer

MASSACHUSETTS: ATLANTICARE MEDICAL CENTER (O, 189 beds) 500 Lynnfield Street, Lynn, MA Zip 01904–1487; tel. 781/581–9200; Andrew J. Riddell, President and Chief Executive Officer

BRIGHAM AND WOMEN'S HOSPITAL (O, 617 beds) 75 Francis Street, Boston, MA Zip 02115–6195; tel. 617/732–5500; Jeffrey Otten, President

MASSACHUSETTS GENERAL HOSPITAL (O, 819 beds) 55 Fruit Street, Boston, MA Zip 02114–2696; tel. 617/726–2000; James J. Mongan, M.D., President

MCLEAN HOSPITAL (O, 161 beds) 115 Mill Street, Belmont, MA Zip 02178–9106; tel. 617/855–2000; Bruce M. Cohen, M.D., President and Psychiatrist–in–Chief

SALEM HOSPITAL (O, 255 beds) 81 Highland Avenue, Salem, MA Zip 01970–2768; tel. 978/741–1200; Alexander Movahed, Acting President and Chief Executive Officer

SHAUGHNESSY–KAPLAN REHABILITATION HOSPITAL (O, 160 beds) Dove Avenue, Salem, MA Zip 01970–2999; tel. 978/745–9000; Anthony Sciola, President and Chief Executive Officer

SPAULDING REHABILITATION HOSPITAL (O, 284 beds) 125 Nashua Street, Boston, MA Zip 02114–1198; tel. 617/573–7000; David E. Storto, Interim Chief Executive Officer

Owned, leased, sponsored:	7 hospitals	2485 beds
Contract–managed:	0 hospitals	0 beds
Totals:	7 hospitals	2485 beds

★5415: PEACEHEALTH (CC)
15325 S.E. 30th Place, Suite 300, Bellevue, WA Zip 98007; tel. 425/747–1711; John Hayward, President and Chief Executive Officer

ALASKA: KETCHIKAN GENERAL HOSPITAL (L, 65 beds) 3100 Tongass Avenue, Ketchikan, AK Zip 99901–5746; tel. 907/225–5171; Edward F. Mahn, Chief Executive Officer

OREGON: PEACE HARBOR HOSPITAL (O, 21 beds) 400 Ninth Street, Florence, OR Zip 97439, Mailing Address: P.O. Box 580, Zip 97439; tel. 541/997–8412; James Barnhart, Administrator

SACRED HEART MEDICAL CENTER (O, 390 beds) 1255 Hilyard Street, Eugene, OR Zip 97401, Mailing Address: P.O. Box 10905, Zip 97440; tel. 541/686–7300; Judy Hodgson, Administrator

WASHINGTON: ST. JOHN MEDICAL CENTER (O, 171 beds) 1614 East Kessler Boulevard, Longview, WA Zip 98632, Mailing Address: P.O. Box 3002, Zip 98632–0302; tel. 360/423–1530; Doug Doorn, Chief Financial Officer

ST. JOSEPH HOSPITAL (O, 206 beds) 2901 Squalicum Parkway, Bellingham, WA Zip 98225–1898; tel. 360/734–5400; Nancy J. Bitting, Chief Executive Officer

Owned, leased, sponsored:	5 hospitals	853 beds
Contract–managed:	0 hospitals	0 beds
Totals:	5 hospitals	853 beds

★5570: PENN STATE GEISINGER HEALTH SYSTEM (NP)
2601 Market Place, Suite 300, Harrisburg, PA Zip 17110–9368; tel. 717/214–2254; Stuart Heydt, M.D., Chief Executive Officer

PENNSYLVANIA: GEISINGER MEDICAL CENTER (O, 548 beds) 100 North Academy Avenue, Danville, PA Zip 17822–0150; tel. 717/271–6211; Nancy Rizzo, Senior Vice President, Operations

PENN STATE GEISINGER WYOMING VALLEY MEDICAL CENTER (O, 144 beds) 1000 East Mountain Drive, Wilkes–Barre, PA Zip 18711–0027; tel. 717/826–7300; Conrad W. Schintz, Senior Vice President Operations

PENN STATE GEISINGER–MILTON S. HERSHEY MEDICAL CENTER (O, 451 beds) 500 University Drive, Hershey, PA Zip 17033–0850, Mailing Address: P.O. Box 850, Zip 17033–0850; tel. 717/531–8521; Theodore E. Townsend, Senior Vice President, Operations

Owned, leased, sponsored:	3 hospitals	1143 beds
Contract–managed:	0 hospitals	0 beds
Totals:	3 hospitals	1143 beds

0091: PIONEER HEALTHCARE (IO)
200 Lake Street, Suite 102, Peabody, MA Zip 01960–4780; tel. 978/536–2777; Bruce A. Shear, President and Chief Executive Officer

MICHIGAN: HARBOR OAKS HOSPITAL (O, 64 beds) 35031 23 Mile Road, New Baltimore, MI Zip 48047–2097; tel. 810/725–5777; Gary J. LaHood, Administrator and Chief Executive Officer

UTAH: HIGHLAND RIDGE HOSPITAL (O, 34 beds) 4578 Highland Drive, Salt Lake City, UT Zip 84117–4200; tel. 801/272–9851; Robert H. Boswell, Administrator

VIRGINIA: MOUNT REGIS CENTER (O, 25 beds) 405 Kimball Avenue, Salem, VA Zip 24153–6299; tel. 703/389–4761; Gail S. Basham, Chief Operating Officer

Owned, leased, sponsored:	3 hospitals	123 beds
Contract–managed:	0 hospitals	0 beds
Totals:	3 hospitals	123 beds

● ★0034: PMH HEALTH RESOURCES, INC. (NP)
1201 South Seventh Avenue, Phoenix, AZ Zip 85007–3913, Mailing Address: P.O. Box 21207, Zip 85036–1207; tel. 602/824–3321; Reginald M. Ballantyne III, President

ARIZONA: PMH HEALTH SERVICES NETWORK (O, 183 beds) 1201 South Seventh Avenue, Phoenix, AZ Zip 85007–3995; tel. 602/258–5111; Jeffrey K. Norman, Chief Executive Officer

Owned, leased, sponsored:	1 hospital	183 beds
Contract–managed:	0 hospitals	0 beds
Totals:	1 hospital	183 beds

★3505: PRESBYTERIAN HEALTHCARE SERVICES (CO)
5901 Harper Drive N.E., Albuquerque, NM Zip 87109–3589, Mailing Address: P.O. Box 26666, Zip 87125–6666; tel. 505/260–6300; James H. Hinton, President and Chief Executive Officer

COLORADO: DELTA COUNTY MEMORIAL HOSPITAL (C, 44 beds) 100 Stafford Lane, Delta, CO Zip 81416–2297, Mailing Address: P.O. Box 10100, Zip 81416–5003; tel. 970/874–7681; Jerry Cantwell, Administrator

NEW MEXICO: ARTESIA GENERAL HOSPITAL (C, 20 beds) 702 North 13th Street, Artesia, NM Zip 88210–1199; tel. 505/748–3333; Anthony J. Plantier, Administrator

DR. DAN C. TRIGG MEMORIAL HOSPITAL (L, 37 beds) 301 East Miel De Luna Avenue, Tucumcari, NM Zip 88401–3810, Mailing Address: P.O. Box 608, Zip 88401–0608; tel. 505/461–0141; Dell Willis, Administrator

ESPANOLA HOSPITAL (O, 80 beds) 1010 Spruce Street, Espanola, NM Zip 87532–2746; tel. 505/753–7111; Marcella A. Romero, Administrator

LINCOLN COUNTY MEDICAL CENTER (L, 38 beds) 211 Sudderth Drive, Ruidoso, NM Zip 88345–6043, Mailing Address: P.O. Box 8000, Zip 88345–8000; tel. 505/257–7381; Valerie Miller, Administrator

PLAINS REGIONAL MEDICAL CENTER (O, 84 beds) 2100 North Thomas Street, Clovis, NM Zip 88101–9412, Mailing Address: P.O. Box 1688, Zip 88101–1688; tel. 505/769–2141; Dennis E. Headlee, Administrator

---

For explanation of codes following names, see page B2.
★ Indicates Type III membership in the American Hospital Association.
● Single hospital health care system

Section B

PRESBYTERIAN HEALTHCARE SERVICES (O, 344 beds) 1100 Central Avenue S.E., Albuquerque, NM Zip 87106–4934, Mailing Address: P.O. Box 26666, Zip 87125–6666; tel. 505/260–6333; James M. Minton, President and Chief Executive Officer

PRESBYTERIAN KASEMAN HOSPITAL (O, 120 beds) 8300 Constitution Avenue N.E., Albuquerque, NM Zip 87110–7624, Mailing Address: P.O. Box 26666, Zip 87125–6666; tel. 505/291–2000; Robert A. Garcia, Administrator

SOCORRO GENERAL HOSPITAL (O, 30 beds) 1202 Highway 60 West, Socorro, NM Zip 87801, Mailing Address: P.O. Box 1009, Zip 87801–1009; tel. 505/835–1140; Jeff Dye, Administrator

Owned, leased, sponsored:	7 hospitals	733 beds
Contract–managed:	2 hospitals	64 beds
Totals:	9 hospitals	797 beds

0147: PROMEDICA HEALTH SYSTEM (NP)
2121 Hughes Boulevard, Toledo, OH Zip 43606; tel. 419/291–7176; Alan W. Brass, FACHE, President and Chief Executive Officer

OHIO: FLOWER HOSPITAL (O, 472 beds) 5200 Harroun Road, Sylvania, OH Zip 43560–2196; tel. 419/824–1444; Randall Kelley, Senior Vice President and Chief Operating Officer

THE TOLEDO HOSPITAL (O, 673 beds) 2142 North Cove Boulevard, Toledo, OH Zip 43606–3896; tel. 419/471–4000; Barbara Steele, President

Owned, leased, sponsored:	2 hospitals	1145 beds
Contract–managed:	0 hospitals	0 beds
Totals:	2 hospitals	1145 beds

★0132: PROVENA HEALTH (NP)
9223 West St. Francis Road, Frankfort, IL Zip 60423–8334; tel. 815/469–4888; Gerald P. Pearson, President

ILLINOIS: PROVENA COVENANT MEDICAL CENTER (O, 258 beds) 1400 West Park Street, Urbana, IL Zip 61801–2396; tel. 217/337–2000; Diane Friedman, R.N., President and Chief Executive Officer

PROVENA MERCY CENTER (O, 245 beds) 1325 North Highland Avenue, Aurora, IL Zip 60506; tel. 630/859–2222; John K. Barto Jr., President and Chief Executive Officer

PROVENA SAINT JOSEPH HOSPITAL (O, 202 beds) 77 North Airlite Street, Elgin, IL Zip 60123–4912; tel. 847/695–3200; Larry Narum, President

PROVENA SAINT JOSEPH MEDICAL CENTER (O, 409 beds) 333 North Madison Street, Joliet, IL Zip 60435–6595; tel. 815/725–7133; David W. Benfer, President and Chief Executive Officer

PROVENA SAINT THERESE MEDICAL CENTER (O, 254 beds) 2615 Washington Street, Waukegan, IL Zip 60085–4988; tel. 847/249–3900; Timothy P. Selz, President and Chief Executive Officer

PROVENA ST. MARY'S HOSPITAL (O, 209 beds) 500 West Court Street, Kankakee, IL Zip 60901–3661; tel. 815/937–2400; Allan C. Sonduck, President and Chief Executive Officer

PROVENA UNITED SAMARITANS MEDICAL CENTER (O, 282 beds) 812 North Logan, Danville, IL Zip 61832–3788; tel. 217/442–6300; Dennis J. Doran, President and Chief Executive Officer

Owned, leased, sponsored:	7 hospitals	1859 beds
Contract–managed:	0 hospitals	0 beds
Totals:	7 hospitals	1859 beds

★5265: PROVIDENCE SERVICES (CC)
9 East Ninth Avenue, Spokane, WA Zip 99202; tel. 509/742–7337; Richard J. Umbdenstock, President and Chief Executive Officer

MONTANA: BENEFIS HEALTH CARE (S, 477 beds) 500 15th Avenue South, Great Falls, MT Zip 59403–4389; tel. 406/455–5000; Lloyd V. Smith, President and Chief Executive Officer

ST. JOSEPH HOSPITAL (S, 22 beds) Skyline Drive and 14th Avenue, Polson, MT Zip 59860, Mailing Address: P.O. Box 1010, Zip 59860–1010; tel. 406/883–5377; John W. Glueckert, President

ST. PATRICK HOSPITAL (S, 213 beds) 500 West Broadway, Missoula, MT Zip 59802–4096, Mailing Address: Box 4587, Zip 59806–4587; tel. 406/543–7271; Lawrence L. White Jr., President

WASHINGTON: DEER PARK HEALTH CENTER AND HOSPITAL (S, 26 beds) East 1015 D. Street, Deer Park, WA Zip 99006, Mailing Address: P.O. Box 742, Zip 99006; tel. 509/276–5061; Cathy Simchuk, Chief Operating Officer

HOLY FAMILY HOSPITAL (S, 206 beds) North 5633 Lidgerwood Avenue, Spokane, WA Zip 99207; tel. 509/482–0111; Ronald J. Schurra, Chief Executive Officer

MOUNT CARMEL HOSPITAL (S, 33 beds) 982 East Columbia Street, Colville, WA Zip 99114–0351, Mailing Address: Box 351, Zip 99114–0351; tel. 509/684–2561; Gloria Cooper, Chief Executive Officer

SACRED HEART MEDICAL CENTER (S, 607 beds) West 101 Eighth Avenue, Spokane, WA Zip 99220, Mailing Address: P.O. Box 2555, Zip 99220; tel. 509/455–3040; Ryland P. Davis, President

ST. JOSEPH'S HOSPITAL (S, 65 beds) 500 East Webster Street, Chewelah, WA Zip 99109, Mailing Address: P.O. Box 197, Zip 99109; tel. 509/935–8211; Gary V. Peck, Chief Executive Officer

ST. MARY MEDICAL CENTER (S, 134 beds) 401 West Poplar Street, Walla Walla, WA Zip 99362, Mailing Address: Box 1477, Zip 99362–0312; tel. 509/525–3320; John A. Isely, President

Owned, leased, sponsored:	9 hospitals	1783 beds
Contract–managed:	0 hospitals	0 beds
Totals:	9 hospitals	1783 beds

0108: PROVINCE HEALTHCARE CORPORATION (IO)
109 Westpark Drive, Suite 180, Brentwood, TN Zip 37026; tel. 615/370–1377; Marty Rash, President and Chief Executive Officer

CALIFORNIA: COLORADO RIVER MEDICAL CENTER (O, 39 beds) 1401 Bailey Avenue, Needles, CA Zip 92363; tel. 760/326–4531; Harley Smith, Chief Executive Officer

GENERAL HOSPITAL (O, 65 beds) 2200 Harrison Avenue, Eureka, CA Zip 95501; tel. 707/445–5111; David S. Wanger, Chief Executive Officer

OJAI VALLEY COMMUNITY HOSPITAL (O, 116 beds) 1306 Maricopa Highway, Ojai, CA Zip 93023–3180; tel. 805/646–1401; Mark Turner, Chief Executive Officer

COLORADO: COLORADO PLAINS MEDICAL CENTER (O, 40 beds) 1000 Lincoln Street, Fort Morgan, CO Zip 80701–3298; tel. 970/867–3391; Thomas Thomson, Administrator and Chief Executive Officer

INDIANA: STARKE MEMORIAL HOSPITAL (O, 35 beds) 102 East Culver Road, Knox, IN Zip 46534–2299; tel. 219/772–6231; Kathryn J. Norem, Executive Director

TEXAS: MEMORIAL MOTHER FRANCES HOSPITAL (O, 84 beds) 4000 South Loop 256, Palestine, TX Zip 75801–8467, Mailing Address: P.O. Box 4070, Zip 75802–4070; tel. 903/731–5000; Stephen M. Erixon, Chief Executive Officer

PARKVIEW REGIONAL HOSPITAL (O, 44 beds) 312 East Glendale Street, Mexia, TX Zip 76667–3608; tel. 254/562–5332; William E. Price, Interim Administrator

Owned, leased, sponsored:	7 hospitals	423 beds
Contract–managed:	0 hospitals	0 beds
Totals:	7 hospitals	423 beds

0011: PUERTO RICO DEPARTMENT OF HEALTH (NP)
Building A. – Medical Center, San Juan, PR Zip 00936, Mailing Address: Call Box 70184, Zip 00936; tel. 809/274–7676; Carmen Feliciano De Melecio, M.D., Secretary of Health

PUERTO RICO: AGUADILLA GENERAL HOSPITAL (O, 110 beds) Carr Aguadilla San Juan, Aguadilla, PR Zip 00605, Mailing Address: P.O. Box 4036, Zip 00605; tel. 787/891–3000; William Rodriguez Castro, Executive Director

ARECIBO REGIONAL HOSPITAL (O, 183 beds) 129 San Luis Avenue, Arecibo, PR Zip 00612, Mailing Address: P.O. Box 202, Zip 00613; tel. 787/878–7272; Samuel Monroig, Administrator

For explanation of codes following names, see page B2.
★ Indicates Type III membership in the American Hospital Association.

Section B

HOSPITAL UNIVERSITARIO DR. RAMON RUIZ ARNAU (O, 372 beds) Avenue Laurel, Santa Juanita, Bayamon, PR Zip 00956; tel. 787/787–5151; Iris J. Vazquez Rosario, Executive Director

PONCE REGIONAL HOSPITAL (O, 407 beds) 917 Tito Castro Avenue, Ponce, PR Zip 00731; tel. 787/844–2080; Julio Andino Rodriguez, Executive Director

STATE PSYCHIATRIC HOSPITAL (O, 425 beds) Monacillos Avenue, San Juan, PR Zip 00936, Mailing Address: Call Box 2100, Caparra Heights Station, Zip 00922–2100; tel. 787/766–4646; Guadalupe Alvarez, Administrator

UNIVERSITY HOSPITAL (O, 297 beds) Puerto Rico Medical Center, Rio Piedras Station, San Juan, PR Zip 00935; tel. 787/754–3654; Roberto Hernandez, Administrator

Owned, leased, sponsored:	6 hospitals	1794 beds
Contract–managed:	0 hospitals	0 beds
Totals:	6 hospitals	1794 beds

★0040: QUEEN'S HEALTH SYSTEMS (NP)
1099 Alakea Street, Suite 1100, Honolulu, HI Zip 96813; tel. 808/532–6100; Richard L. Griffith, President and Chief Executive Officer

HAWAII: MOLOKAI GENERAL HOSPITAL (O, 29 beds) Kaunakakai, HI Mailing Address: P.O. Box 408, Zip 96748–0408; tel. 808/553–5331; Phillip W. Reyes, M.D., Co–Medical Executive Director

QUEEN'S MEDICAL CENTER (O, 457 beds) 1301 Punchbowl Street, Honolulu, HI Zip 96813; tel. 808/538–9011; Arthur A. Ushijima, President and Chief Executive Officer

Owned, leased, sponsored:	2 hospitals	486 beds
Contract–managed:	0 hospitals	0 beds
Totals:	2 hospitals	486 beds

★0002: QUORUM HEALTH GROUP/QUORUM HEALTH RESOURCES, INC. (IO)
103 Continental Place, Brentwood, TN Zip 37027; tel. 615/371–7979; James E. Dalton Jr., President and Chief Executive Officer

ALABAMA: FLOWERS HOSPITAL (O, 215 beds) 4370 West Main Street, Dothan, AL Zip 36305, Mailing Address: P.O. Box 6907, Zip 36302–6907; tel. 334/793–5000; Keith Granger, President and Chief Executive Officer

GADSDEN REGIONAL MEDICAL CENTER (O, 257 beds) 1007 Goodyear Avenue, Gadsden, AL Zip 35999–1100; tel. 205/494–4000; William Russell Spray, Chief Executive Officer

JACKSONVILLE HOSPITAL (O, 56 beds) 1701 Pelham Road South, Jacksonville, AL Zip 36265–3399, Mailing Address: P.O. Box 999, Zip 36265–0999; tel. 205/435–4970; Charles Mitchener Jr., Chief Executive Officer

MEDICAL CENTER ENTERPRISE (O, 437 beds) 400 North Edwards Street, Enterprise, AL Zip 36330–9981; tel. 334/347–0584; Earl S. Whiteley, CHE, Chief Executive Officer

MONROE COUNTY HOSPITAL (C, 59 beds) 1901 South Alabama Avenue, Monroeville, AL Zip 36460, Mailing Address: P.O. Box 886, Zip 36461–0886; tel. 334/575–3111; Joe Zager, Chief Executive Officer

WIREGRASS HOSPITAL (C, 151 beds) 1200 West Maple Avenue, Geneva, AL Zip 36340–1694; tel. 334/684–3655; Mark LeNeave, Chief Executive Officer

ALASKA: BARTLETT REGIONAL HOSPITAL (C, 64 beds) 3260 Hospital Drive, Juneau, AK Zip 99801; tel. 907/586–2611; Robert F. Valliant, Administrator

ARIZONA: MARICOPA MEDICAL CENTER (C, 491 beds) 2601 East Roosevelt Street, Phoenix, AZ Zip 85008–4956, Mailing Address: P.O. Box 5099, Zip 85010–5099; tel. 602/267–5111; Frank D. Alvarez, Chief Executive Officer

ARKANSAS: CHICOT MEMORIAL HOSPITAL (C, 35 beds) 2729 Highway 65 and 82 South, Lake Village, AR Zip 71653, Mailing Address: P.O. Box 512, Zip 71653–0512; tel. 870/265–5351; Robert R. Reddish, Administrator and Chief Executive Officer

DELTA MEMORIAL HOSPITAL (C, 35 beds) 300 East Pickens Street, Dumas, AR Zip 71639–2710, Mailing Address: P.O. Box 887, Zip 71639–0887; tel. 870/382–4303; Rodney McPherson, Administrator

HELENA REGIONAL MEDICAL CENTER (C, 115 beds) 1801 Martin Luther king Drive, Helena, AR Zip 72342, Mailing Address: P.O. Box 788, Zip 72342–0788; tel. 870/338–5800; Steve Reeder, Chief Executive Officer

HOWARD MEMORIAL HOSPITAL (C, 50 beds) 800 West Leslie Street, Nashville, AR Zip 71852–0381, Mailing Address: Box 381, Zip 71852–0381; tel. 870/845–4400; Lynn Crowell, Chief Executive Officer

MENA MEDICAL CENTER (C, 48 beds) 311 North Morrow Street, Mena, AR Zip 71953–2516; tel. 501/394–6100; Albert Pilkington III, Administrator and Chief Executive Officer

NORTHWEST MEDICAL CENTER (C, 222 beds) 609 West Maple Avenue, Springdale, AR Zip 72764–5394, Mailing Address: P.O. Box 47, Zip 72765–0047; tel. 501/751–5711; Greg K. Stock, Chief Executive Officer

REBSAMEN REGIONAL MEDICAL CENTER (C, 113 beds) 1400 West Braden Street, Jacksonville, AR Zip 72076–3788; tel. 501/985–7000; Thomas R. Siemers, Chief Executive Officer

SALINE MEMORIAL HOSPITAL (C, 141 beds) 1 Medical Park Drive, Benton, AR Zip 72015–3354; tel. 501/776–6000; Roger D. Feldt, FACHE, President and Chief Executive Officer

SILOAM SPRING MEMORIAL HOSPITAL (C, 52 beds) 205 East Jefferson Street, Siloam Springs, AR Zip 72761–3697; tel. 501/524–4141; Donald E. Patterson, Administrator

CALIFORNIA: LOMPOC DISTRICT HOSPITAL (C, 170 beds) 508 East Hickory Street, Lompoc, CA Zip 93436, Mailing Address: Box 1058, Zip 93438; tel. 805/737–3300; Scott Rhine, Administrator and Chief Executive Officer

SANTA PAULA MEMORIAL HOSPITAL (C, 54 beds) 825 North Tenth Street, Santa Paula, CA Zip 93060–0270, Mailing Address: P.O. Box 270, Zip 93060–0270; tel. 805/525–7171; William M. Greene, FACHE, President

COLORADO: GRAND RIVER HOSPITAL DISTRICT (C, 75 beds) 701 East Fifth Street, Rifle, CO Zip 81650–2970, Mailing Address: P.O. Box 912, Zip 81650–0912; tel. 970/625–1510; Edwin A. Gast, Administrator

HEART OF THE ROCKIES REGIONAL MEDICAL CENTER (C, 33 beds) 448 East First Street, Salida, CO Zip 81201–0429, Mailing Address: P.O. Box 429, Zip 81201–0429; tel. 719/539–6661; Howard D. Turner, Chief Executive Officer

MEMORIAL HOSPITAL (C, 29 beds) 785 Russell Street, Craig, CO Zip 81625–9906; tel. 970/824–9411; M. Randell Phelps, Administrator

MONTROSE MEMORIAL HOSPITAL (C, 63 beds) 800 South Third Street, Montrose, CO Zip 81401–4291; tel. 970/249–2211; Tyler Erickson, Administrator

MOUNT SAN RAFAEL HOSPITAL (C, 31 beds) 410 Benedicta Avenue, Trinidad, CO Zip 81082–2093; tel. 719/846–9213; James P. D'Agostino, Executive Director

PARKVIEW MEDICAL CENTER (C, 260 beds) 400 West 16th Street, Pueblo, CO Zip 81003–2781; tel. 719/584–4000; C. W. Smith, President and Chief Executive Officer

PIONEERS HOSPITAL OF RIO BLANCO COUNTY (C, 46 beds) 345 Cleveland Street, Meeker, CO Zip 81641–0000; tel. 970/878–5047; Thomas E. Lake, Chief Executive Officer

PROWERS MEDICAL CENTER (C, 40 beds) 401 Kendall Drive, Lamar, CO Zip 81052–3993; tel. 719/336–4343; Earl J. Steinhoff, Chief Executive Officer

SOUTHWEST MEMORIAL HOSPITAL (C, 61 beds) 1311 North Mildred Road, Cortez, CO Zip 81321–2299; tel. 970/565–6666; Stephen R. Selzer, President and Chief Executive Officer

VALLEY VIEW HOSPITAL (C, 60 beds) 1906 Blake Avenue, Glenwood Springs, CO Zip 81601–4259, Mailing Address: P.O. Box 1970, Zip 81602–1970; tel. 970/945–6535; Gary L. Brewer, Chief Executive Officer

FLORIDA: BASCOM PALMER EYE INSTITUTE–ANNE BATES LEACH EYE HOSPITAL (C, 35 beds) 900 N.W. 17th Street, Miami, FL Zip 33136–1199, Mailing Address: Box 016880, Zip 33101–6880; tel. 305/326–6000; John Rossfeld, Administrator

BERT FISH MEDICAL CENTER (C, 85 beds) 401 Palmetto Street, New Smyrna Beach, FL Zip 32168–7399; tel. 904/424–5000; Kathy Leonard, Vice President and Administrator

Section B

BROOKSVILLE REGIONAL HOSPITAL (C, 91 beds) 55 Ponce De Leon Boulevard, Brooksville, FL Zip 34601–0037, Mailing Address: P.O. Box 37, Zip 34605–0037; tel. 352/796–5111; Robert Foreman, Associate Administrator

DESOTO MEMORIAL HOSPITAL (C, 62 beds) 900 North Robert Avenue, Arcadia, FL Zip 34266–8765, Mailing Address: P.O. Box 2180, Zip 34265–2180; tel. 941/494–3535; Gary M. Moore, President and Chief Executive Officer

GLADES GENERAL HOSPITAL (C, 47 beds) 1201 South Main Street, Belle Glade, FL Zip 33430–4911; tel. 561/996–6571; Gene Faile, Chief Executive Officer

HENDRY REGIONAL MEDICAL CENTER (C, 45 beds) 500 West Sugarland Highway, Clewiston, FL Zip 33440–3094; tel. 941/983–9121; J. Rudy Reinhardt, Administrator

JACKSON HOSPITAL (C, 84 beds) 4250 Hospital Drive, Marianna, FL Zip 32446–1939, Mailing Address: P.O. Box 1608, Zip 32447–1608; tel. 850/526–2200; Randy Smith, Interim Administrator

JUPITER MEDICAL CENTER (C, 156 beds) 1210 South Old Dixie Highway, Jupiter, FL Zip 33458–7299; tel. 561/747–2234; Hart Ransdell, Chief Executive Officer

SPRING HILL REGIONAL HOSPITAL (C, 75 beds) 10461 Quality Drive, Spring Hill, FL Zip 34609; tel. 352/688–8200; Sonia I. Gonzalez, R.N., Chief Operating Officer

SUN COAST HOSPITAL (C, 241 beds) 2025 Indian Rocks Road, Largo, FL Zip 34644, Mailing Address: P.O. Box 2025, Zip 34649–2025; tel. 813/581–9474; Jeffrey A. Collins, Chief Executive Officer

UNIVERSITY OF MIAMI HOSPITAL AND CLINICS (C, 40 beds) 1475 N.W. 12th Avenue, Miami, FL Zip 33136–1002; tel. 305/243–6418; John Rossfeld, Administrator

GEORGIA: CAMDEN MEDICAL CENTER (C, 40 beds) 2000 Dan Proctor Drive, Saint Marys, GA Zip 31558, Mailing Address: 2000 Dan Proctor Dirve, Zip 31558; tel. 912/576–4200; Warren Manley, Administrator

ELBERT MEMORIAL HOSPITAL (C, 52 beds) 4 Medical Drive, Elberton, GA Zip 30635–1897; tel. 706/283–3151; Ronald J. Vigus, Interim Chief Executive Officer

HABERSHAM COUNTY MEDICAL CENTER (C, 138 beds) Highway 441, Demorest, GA Zip 30535, Mailing Address: P.O. Box 37, Zip 30535–0037; tel. 706/754–2161; C. Richard Dwozan, President

HANCOCK MEMORIAL HOSPITAL (C, 35 beds) 453 Boland Street, Sparta, GA Zip 31087–1105, Mailing Address: P.O. Box 490, Zip 31087–0490; tel. 706/444–7006; Daniel D. Holtz, FACHE, Administrator and Chief Executive Officer

MACON NORTHSIDE HOSPITAL (O, 103 beds) 400 Charter Boulevard, Macon, GA Zip 31210–4853, Mailing Address: P.O. Box 4627, Zip 31208–4627; tel. 912/757–8200; Richard Gaston, Administrator

MCDUFFIE COUNTY HOSPITAL (C, 47 beds) 521 Hill Street S.W., Thomson, GA Zip 30824–2199; tel. 706/595–1411; Douglas C. Keir, Chief Executive Officer

MEMORIAL HEALTH SYSTEM (C, 373 beds) 4700 Waters Avenue, Savannah, GA Zip 31404–6283, Mailing Address: P.O. Box 23089, Zip 31403–3089; tel. 912/350–8000; Robert A. Colvin, President and Chief Executive Officer

MIDDLE GEORGIA HOSPITAL (O, 119 beds) 888 Pine Street, Macon, GA Zip 31201–2186, Mailing Address: P.O. Box 6278, Zip 31208–6278; tel. 912/751–1111; Richard L. McConahy, Chief Executive Officer

OCONEE REGIONAL MEDICAL CENTER (C, 145 beds) 821 North Cobb Street, Milledgeville, GA Zip 31061–2351, Mailing Address: P.O. Box 690, Zip 31061–0690; tel. 912/454–3500; Brian L. Riddle, Chief Executive Officer

RIDGECREST HOSPITAL (C, 45 beds) 393 Ridgecrest Circle, Clayton, GA Zip 30525; tel. 706/782–4297; Maryann J. Greenwell, Chief Executive Officer

SOUTHEAST GEORGIA REGIONAL MEDICAL CENTER (C, 341 beds) 3100 Kemble Avenue, Brunswick, GA Zip 31520–4252, Mailing Address: P.O. Box 1518, Zip 31521–1518; tel. 912/264–7000; E. Berton Whitaker, President and Chief Executive Officer

TANNER MEDICAL CENTER (C, 162 beds) 705 Dixie Street, Carrollton, GA Zip 30117–3818; tel. 770/836–9666; Loy M. Howard, Chief Executive Officer

TANNER MEDICAL CENTER–VILLA RICA (C, 45 beds) 601 Dallas Road, Villa Rica, GA Zip 30180–1202, Mailing Address: P.O. Box 638, Zip 30180–0638; tel. 770/459–7100; Larry N. Steed, Administrator

UPSON REGIONAL MEDICAL CENTER (C, 115 beds) 801 West Gordon Street, Thomaston, GA Zip 30286–2831, Mailing Address: P.O. Box 1059, Zip 30286–1059; tel. 706/647–8111; Samuel S. Gregory, Administrator

WALTON MEDICAL CENTER (C, 115 beds) 330 Alcovy Street, Monroe, GA Zip 30655–2140, Mailing Address: P.O. Box 1346, Zip 30655–1346; tel. 770/267–8461; Edgar L. Belcher, Administrator

WAYNE MEMORIAL HOSPITAL (C, 110 beds) 865 South First Street, Jesup, GA Zip 31598, Mailing Address: P.O. Box 408, Zip 31598–0408; tel. 912/427–6811; Charles R. Morgan, Administrator

WILLS MEMORIAL HOSPITAL (C, 50 beds) 120 Gordon Street, Washington, GA Zip 30673–1602, Mailing Address: P.O. Box 370, Zip 30673–0370; tel. 706/678–2151; Vincent DiFranco, Chief Executive Officer

WOODRIDGE HOSPITAL (C, 32 beds) 394 Ridgecrest Circle, Clayton, GA Zip 30525; tel. 706/782–3100; Maryann J. Greenwell, Chief Executive Officer

IDAHO: BINGHAM MEMORIAL HOSPITAL (C, 110 beds) 98 Poplar Street, Blackfoot, ID Zip 83221–1799; tel. 208/785–4100; Robert M. Peterson, Administrator

GRITMAN MEDICAL CENTER (C, 35 beds) 700 South Washington Street, Moscow, ID Zip 83843–3047; tel. 208/882–4511; Daniel R. Smigelski, Chief Executive Officer

ILLINOIS: COMMUNITY MEMORIAL HOSPITAL (C, 57 beds) 400 Caldwell Street, Staunton, IL Zip 62088–1499; tel. 618/635–2200; Patrick B. Heise, Chief Executive Officer

CRAWFORD MEMORIAL HOSPITAL (C, 102 beds) 1000 North Allen Street, Robinson, IL Zip 62454–1114, Mailing Address: P.O. Box 151, Zip 62454–0151; tel. 618/544–3131; Lesile P. Luke, Chief Executive Officer

GIBSON COMMUNITY HOSPITAL (C, 82 beds) 1120 North Melvin Street, Gibson City, IL Zip 60936–1066, Mailing Address: P.O. Box 429, Zip 60936–0429; tel. 217/784–4251; Craig A. Jesiolowski, Chief Executive Officer

ILLINI COMMUNITY HOSPITAL (C, 45 beds) 640 West Washington Street, Pittsfield, IL Zip 62363–1397; tel. 217/285–2113; Jete Edmisson, President and Chief Executive Officer

MEMORIAL HOSPITAL (C, 59 beds) South Adams Street, Carthage, IL Zip 62321, Mailing Address: P.O. Box 160, Zip 62321–0160; tel. 217/357–3131; Keith E. Heuser, Chief Executive Officer

MEMORIAL HOSPITAL (C, 47 beds) 1900 State Street, Chester, IL Zip 62233–0609, Mailing Address: P.O. Box 609, Zip 62233–0609; tel. 618/826–4581; Eric Freeburg, Administrator

THOMAS H. BOYD MEMORIAL HOSPITAL (C, 60 beds) 800 School Street, Carrollton, IL Zip 62016–1498; tel. 217/942–6946; Deborah Campbell, Administrator

INDIANA: CLINTON COUNTY HOSPITAL (O, 53 beds) 1300 South Jackson Street, Frankfort, IN Zip 46041–3394, Mailing Address: P.O. Box 669, Zip 46041–0669; tel. 765/659–4731; Brian R. Zeh, Executive Director

DAVIESS COUNTY HOSPITAL (C, 85 beds) 1314 Grand Avenue, Washington, IN Zip 47501–2198, Mailing Address: P.O. Box 760, Zip 47501–0760; tel. 812/254–2760; Marc Chircop, Chief Executive Officer

LUTHERAN HOSPITAL OF INDIANA (O, 341 beds) 7950 West Jefferson Boulevard, Fort Wayne, IN Zip 46804–1677; tel. 219/435–7001; Thomas D. Miller, Chief Executive Officer

MARY SHERMAN HOSPITAL (C, 53 beds) 320 North Section Street, Sullivan, IN Zip 47882–1239, Mailing Address: P.O. Box 10, Zip 47882–0010; tel. 812/268–4311; Thomas J. Hudgins, Administrator

IOWA: BOONE COUNTY HOSPITAL (C, 57 beds) 1015 Union Street, Boone, IA Zip 50036–4898; tel. 515/432–3140; Joseph S. Smith, Chief Executive Officer

DES MOINES GENERAL HOSPITAL (C, 174 beds) 603 East 12th Street, Des Moines, IA Zip 50309–5515; tel. 515/263–4200; Roy W. Wright, President and Chief Executive Officer

FORT MADISON COMMUNITY HOSPITAL (C, 50 beds) Highway 61 West, Fort Madison, IA Zip 52627–0174, Mailing Address: 5445 Avenue O, Box 174, Zip 52627–0174; tel. 319/372–6530; C. James Platt, Administrator

For explanation of codes following names, see page B2.
★ Indicates Type III membership in the American Hospital Association.

KNOXVILLE AREA COMMUNITY HOSPITAL (C, 52 beds) 1002 South Lincoln Street, Knoxville, IA Zip 50138–3121; tel. 515/842–2151; Jim Murphy, Chief Executive Officer

WASHINGTON COUNTY HOSPITAL (C, 83 beds) 400 East Polk Street, Washington, IA Zip 52353, Mailing Address: P.O. Box 909, Zip 52353; tel. 319/653–5481; Ronald D. Davis, Chief Executive Officer

KANSAS: BOB WILSON MEMORIAL GRANT COUNTY HOSPITAL (C, 42 beds) 415 North Main Street, Ulysses, KS Zip 67880–2196; tel. 316/356–1266; Steven G. Daniel, Administrator

COFFEYVILLE REGIONAL MEDICAL CENTER (C, 123 beds) 1400 West Fourth, Coffeyville, KS Zip 67337–3306; tel. 316/251–1200; Gerald Joseph Marquette Jr., Administrator

GREENWOOD COUNTY HOSPITAL (C, 46 beds) 100 West 16th Street, Eureka, KS Zip 67045–1096; tel. 316/583–7451; Emmett Schuster, Administrator and Chief Executive Officer

NEOSHO MEMORIAL REGIONAL MEDICAL CENTER (C, 60 beds) 629 South Plummer, Chanute, KS Zip 66720–1928; tel. 316/431–4000; Murray L. Brown, Administrator

NEWMAN MEMORIAL COUNTY HOSPITAL (C, 110 beds) 1201 West 12th Avenue, Emporia, KS Zip 66801–2597; tel. 316/343–6800; Terry R. Lambert, Chief Executive Officer

WILSON COUNTY HOSPITAL (C, 38 beds) 205 Mill Street, Neodesha, KS Zip 66757–1817, Mailing Address: P.O. Box 360, Zip 66757–0360; tel. 316/325–2611; Deanna Pittman, Administrator

KENTUCKY: CRITTENDEN COUNTY HOSPITAL (C, 67 beds) Highway 60 South, Marion, KY Zip 42064, Mailing Address: P.O. Box 386, Zip 42064–0386; tel. 502/965–5281; Rick Napper, Chief Executive Officer

CUMBERLAND COUNTY HOSPITAL (C, 31 beds) Highway 90 West, Burkesville, KY Zip 42717–0280, Mailing Address: P.O. Box 280, Zip 42717–0280; tel. 502/864–2511; Mark E. Thompson, Chief Executive Officer

FLEMING COUNTY HOSPITAL (C, 43 beds) 920 Elizaville Avenue, Flemingsburg, KY Zip 41041, Mailing Address: P.O. Box 388, Zip 41041–0388; tel. 606/849–5000; Bobby B. Emmons, Administrator

FRANKLIN–SIMPSON MEMORIAL HOSPITAL (C, 34 beds) Brookhaven Road, Franklin, KY Zip 42135–2929, Mailing Address: P.O. Box 2929, Zip 42135–2929; tel. 502/586–3253; William P. Macri, Chief Executive Officer

JENNIE STUART MEDICAL CENTER (C, 139 beds) 320 West 18th Street, Hopkinsville, KY Zip 42241–2400, Mailing Address: P.O. Box 2400, Zip 42241–2400; tel. 502/887–0100; Lewis T. Peeples, Chief Executive Officer

MARSHALL COUNTY HOSPITAL (C, 80 beds) 503 George McClain Drive, Benton, KY Zip 42025–1399, Mailing Address: P.O. Box 630, Zip 42025–0630; tel. 502/527–4800; David G. Fuqua, R.N., Chief Executive Officer

MONROE COUNTY MEDICAL CENTER (C, 49 beds) 529 Capp Harlan Road, Tompkinsville, KY Zip 42167–1840; tel. 502/487–9231; Carolyn E. Riley, Chief Executive Officer

MUHLENBERG COMMUNITY HOSPITAL (C, 135 beds) 440 Hopkinsville Street, Greenville, KY Zip 42345–1172, Mailing Address: P.O. Box 387, Zip 42345–0387; tel. 502/338–8000; Charles D. Lovell Jr., Chief Executive Officer

OHIO COUNTY HOSPITAL (C, 54 beds) 1211 Main Street, Hartford, KY Zip 42347–1619; tel. 502/298–7411; Blaine Pieper, Administrator

LOUISIANA: BOGALUSA COMMUNITY MEDICAL CENTER (C, 99 beds) 433 Plaza Street, Bogalusa, LA Zip 70429–0940; tel. 504/732–7122; Terry G. Whittington, Chief Executive Officer and Administrator

FRANKLIN FOUNDATION HOSPITAL (C, 60 beds) 1501 Hospital Avenue, Franklin, LA Zip 70538–3724, Mailing Address: P.O. Box 577, Zip 70538–0577; tel. 318/828–0760; Patricia Luker, Chief Executive Officer

LAKEWOOD MEDICAL CENTER (C, 122 beds) 1125 Marguerite Street, Morgan City, LA Zip 70380–1855, Mailing Address: Drawer 2308, Zip 70381–2308; tel. 504/384–2200; Joyce Grove Hein, Chief Executive Officer

LANE MEMORIAL HOSPITAL (C, 136 beds) 6300 Main Street, Zachary, LA Zip 70791–9990; tel. 504/658–4000; David W. Fuller, Chief Executive Officer

NORTH OAKS MEDICAL CENTER (C, 251 beds) 15790 Medical Center Drive, Hammond, LA Zip 70403–1436, Mailing Address: P.O. Box 2668, Zip 70404–2668; tel. 504/345–2700; James E. Cathey Jr., Chief Executive Officer

OPELOUSAS GENERAL HOSPITAL (C, 121 beds) 520 Prudhomme Lane, Opelousas, LA Zip 70570–6454, Mailing Address: P.O. Box 1208, Zip 70571–1208; tel. 318/948–3011; Patrick Brian Carrier, Administrator

ST. JAMES PARISH HOSPITAL (C, 26 beds) 2471 Louisiana Avenue, Lutcher, LA Zip 70071–5413; tel. 504/869–5512; Joan Murray, R.N., Administrator

THIBODAUX REGIONAL MEDICAL CENTER (C, 130 beds) 602 North Acadia Road, Thibodaux, LA Zip 70301–4847, Mailing Address: P.O. Box 1118, Zip 70302–1118; tel. 504/447–5500; Karen A. Fiducia, Interim Chief Executive Officer

MAINE: CALAIS REGIONAL HOSPITAL (C, 57 beds) 50 Franklin Street, Calais, ME Zip 04619–1398; tel. 207/454–7521; Ray H. Davis Jr., Chief Executive Officer

CARY MEDICAL CENTER (C, 64 beds) 163 Van Buren Road, Suite 1, Caribou, ME Zip 04736–2599; tel. 207/498–3111; Lee Ashjian, Chief Executive Officer

DOWN EAST COMMUNITY HOSPITAL (C, 38 beds) Upper Court Street, Machias, ME Zip 04654, Mailing Address: Rural Route 1, Box 11, Zip 04654–9702; tel. 207/255–3356; Richard Hanley, Chief Executive Officer

HOULTON REGIONAL HOSPITAL (C, 41 beds) 20 Hartford Street, Houlton, ME Zip 04730–9998; tel. 207/532–9471; Thomas J. Moakler, Chief Executive Officer

MAINE COAST MEMORIAL HOSPITAL (C, 48 beds) 50 Union Street, Ellsworth, ME Zip 04605–1599; tel. 207/667–5311; Paul R. Barrette, Chief Executive Officer

MAYO REGIONAL HOSPITAL (C, 46 beds) 75 West Main Street, Dover–Foxcroft, ME Zip 04426–1099; tel. 207/564–8401; Ralph Gabarro, Chief Executive Officer

MILLINOCKET REGIONAL HOSPITAL (C, 20 beds) 200 Somerset Street, Millinocket, ME Zip 04462–1298; tel. 207/723–5161; Craig A. Kantos, Chief Executive Officer

PENOBSCOT VALLEY HOSPITAL (C, 32 beds) Transalpine Road, Lincoln, ME Zip 04457–0368, Mailing Address: P.O. Box 368, Zip 04457–0368; tel. 207/794–3321; Ronald D. Victory, Administrator

MASSACHUSETTS: HALE HOSPITAL (C, 113 beds) 140 Lincoln Avenue, Haverhill, MA Zip 01830–6798; tel. 978/374–2000; Robert J. Ingala, Chief Executive Officer

HUBBARD REGIONAL HOSPITAL (C, 29 beds) 340 Thompson Road, Webster, MA Zip 01570–0608; tel. 508/943–2600; Gerald J. Barbini, Administrator and Chief Executive Officer

JORDAN HOSPITAL (C, 119 beds) 275 Sandwich Street, Plymouth, MA Zip 02360–2196; tel. 508/746–2001; Alan D. Knight, President and Chief Executive Officer

MASSACHUSETTS RESPIRATORY HOSPITAL (C, 110 beds) 2001 Washington Street, Braintree, MA Zip 02184–8664; tel. 781/848–2600; Jay Mitchell, Chief Executive Officer

QUINCY HOSPITAL (C, 186 beds) 114 Whitwell Street, Quincy, MA Zip 02169–1899; tel. 617/773–6100; Jeffrey Doran, Chief Executive Officer

MICHIGAN: ALLEGAN GENERAL HOSPITAL (C, 63 beds) 555 Linn Street, Allegan, MI Zip 49010–1594; tel. 616/673–8424; James A. Klun, President

COMMUNITY HEALTH CENTER OF BRANCH COUNTY (C, 96 beds) 274 East Chicago Street, Coldwater, MI Zip 49036–2088; tel. 517/279–5489; Douglas L. Rahn, Chief Executive Officer

COMMUNITY HOSPITAL (C, 54 beds) Medical Park Drive, Watervliet, MI Zip 49098–0158, Mailing Address: P.O. Box 158, Zip 49098–0158; tel. 616/463–3111; Dennis Turney, Chief Executive Officer

KELSEY MEMORIAL HOSPITAL (C, 66 beds) 418 Washington Avenue, Lakeview, MI Zip 48850; tel. 517/352–7211; Richard Waller, Chief Executive Officer

For explanation of codes following names, see page B2.
★ Indicates Type III membership in the American Hospital Association.

LAKEVIEW COMMUNITY HOSPITAL (C, 168 beds) 408 Hazen Street, Paw Paw, MI Zip 49079–1019, Mailing Address: P.O. Box 209, Zip 49079–0209; tel. 616/657–3141; Sue E. Johnson–Phillippe, Chief Executive Officer

MARLETTE COMMUNITY HOSPITAL (C, 91 beds) 2770 Main Street, Marlette, MI Zip 48453–0307, Mailing Address: P.O. Box 307, Zip 48453–0307; tel. 517/635–4000; David S. McEwen, Chief Executive Officer

MECOSTA COUNTY GENERAL HOSPITAL (C, 74 beds) 405 Winter Avenue, Big Rapids, MI Zip 49307–2099; tel. 616/796–8691; Thomas E. Daugherty, Chief Executive Officer

STURGIS HOSPITAL (C, 67 beds) 916 Myrtle, Sturgis, MI Zip 49091–2001; tel. 616/651–7824; David James, Chief Executive Officer

THREE RIVERS AREA HOSPITAL (C, 60 beds) 1111 West Broadway, Three Rivers, MI Zip 49093–9362; tel. 616/278–1145; Matthew Chambers, Interim Chief Executive Officer

MINNESOTA: FALLS MEMORIAL HOSPITAL (C, 35 beds) 1400 Highway 71, International Falls, MN Zip 56649–2189; tel. 218/283–4481; Mary Klimp, Administrator and Chief Executive Officer

VIRGINIA REGIONAL MEDICAL CENTER (C, 190 beds) 901 Ninth Street North, Virginia, MN Zip 55792–2398; tel. 218/741–3340; Kyle Hopstad, Administrator

MISSISSIPPI: BOLIVAR MEDICAL CENTER (C, 144 beds) Highway 8 East, Cleveland, MS Zip 38732–9722, Mailing Address: P.O. Box 1380, Zip 38732–1380; tel. 601/846–0061; Robert L. Hawley Jr., Chief Executive Officer

CROSBY MEMORIAL HOSPITAL (C, 71 beds) 801 Goodyear Boulevard, Picayune, MS Zip 39466–3221, Mailing Address: P.O. Box 909, Zip 39466–0909; tel. 601/798–4711; Calvin Green, Administrator

DELTA REGIONAL MEDICAL CENTER (C, 159 beds) 1400 East Union Street, Greenville, MS Zip 38703–3246, Mailing Address: P.O. Box 5247, Zip 38704–5247; tel. 601/378–3783; Barton A. Hove, Chief Executive Officer

FIELD MEMORIAL COMMUNITY HOSPITAL (C, 66 beds) 270 West Main Street, Centreville, MS Zip 39631, Mailing Address: P.O. Box 639, Zip 39631–0639; tel. 601/645–5221; Brock A. Slabach, Administrator

H. C. WATKINS MEMORIAL HOSPITAL (C, 43 beds) 605 South Archusa Avenue, Quitman, MS Zip 39355–2398; tel. 601/776–6925; Thomas G. Bartlett, President and Chief Executive Officer

HANCOCK MEDICAL CENTER (C, 66 beds) 149 Drinkwater Boulevard, Bay Saint Louis, MS Zip 39521–2790, Mailing Address: P.O. Box 2790, Zip 39521–2790; tel. 228/467–8600; Hal W. Leftwich, FACHE, Chief Executive Officer

KING'S DAUGHTERS HOSPITAL (C, 109 beds) 427 Highway 51 North, Brookhaven, MS Zip 39601–2600, Mailing Address: P.O. Box 948, Zip 39602–0948; tel. 601/833–6011; Phillip L. Grady, Chief Executive Officer

MAGNOLIA REGIONAL HEALTH CENTER (C, 163 beds) 611 Alcorn Drive, Corinth, MS Zip 38834–9368; tel. 601/293–1000; Douglas Garner, Chief Executive Officer

NATCHEZ REGIONAL MEDICAL CENTER (C, 121 beds) Seargent S. Prentiss Drive, Natchez, MS Zip 39120, Mailing Address: P.O. Box 1488, Zip 39121–1488; tel. 601/443–2100; David M. Snyder, Executive Director and Chief Executive Officer

NESHOBA COUNTY GENERAL HOSPITAL (C, 192 beds) 1001 Holland Avenue, Philadelphia, MS Zip 39350–2161, Mailing Address: P.O. Box 648, Zip 39350–0648; tel. 601/663–1200; Lawrence Graeber, Administrator

PARKVIEW REGIONAL MEDICAL CENTER (O, 183 beds) 100 McAuley Drive, Vicksburg, MS Zip 39180–2897, Mailing Address: P.O. Box 590, Zip 39181–0590; tel. 601/631–2131; Harry Alvis, Chief Executive Officer

UNIVERSITY HOSPITALS AND CLINICS, UNIVERSITY OF MISSISSIPPI MEDICAL CENTER (C, 576 beds) 2500 North State Street, Jackson, MS Zip 39216–4505; tel. 601/984–4100; Frederick Woodrell, Director

WESLEY MEDICAL CENTER (O, 211 beds) 5001 Hardy Street, Hattiesburg, MS Zip 39402, Mailing Address: P.O. Box 16509, Zip 39404–6509; tel. 601/268–8000; William K. Ray, President and Chief Executive Officer

MISSOURI: NEVADA REGIONAL MEDICAL CENTER (C, 97 beds) 800 South Ash Street, Nevada, MO Zip 64772–3223; tel. 417/667–3355; Michael L. Mullins, President

MONTANA: CENTRAL MONTANA MEDICAL CENTER (C, 124 beds) 408 Wendell Avenue, Lewistown, MT Zip 59457–2261, Mailing Address: P.O. Box 580, Zip 59457–0580; tel. 406/538–7711; David M. Faulkner, Chief Executive Officer and Administrator

COMMUNITY HOSPITAL OF ANACONDA (C, 101 beds) 401 West Pennsylvania Street, Anaconda, MT Zip 59711–1999; tel. 406/563–8500; Sam J. Allen, Administrator

GLACIER COUNTY MEDICAL CENTER (C, 59 beds) 802 Second Street S.E., Cut Bank, MT Zip 59427–3331; tel. 406/873–2251; Allison Harvie, Acting Administrator

NORTH VALLEY HOSPITAL (C, 99 beds) 6575 Highway 93 South, Whitefish, MT Zip 59937; tel. 406/863–2501; Kenneth E. S. Platou, Chief Executive Officer

WHEATLAND MEMORIAL HOSPITAL (C, 54 beds) 530 Third Street North, Harlowton, MT Zip 59036, Mailing Address: P.O. Box 287, Zip 59036–0287; tel. 406/632–4351; Craig E. Aasved, Administrator

NEBRASKA: GREAT PLAINS REGIONAL MEDICAL CENTER (C, 99 beds) 601 West Leota Street, North Platte, NE Zip 69101–6598, Mailing Address: P.O. Box 1167, Zip 69103–1167; tel. 308/534–9310; Lucinda A. Bradley, President

PHELPS MEMORIAL HEALTH CENTER (C, 55 beds) 1220 Miller Street, Holdrege, NE Zip 68949–1200, Mailing Address: P.O. Box 828, Zip 68949–0828; tel. 308/995–2211; Jerome Seigfreid Jr., Chief Executive Officer

NEW HAMPSHIRE: LITTLETON REGIONAL HOSPITAL (C, 49 beds) 262 Cottage Street, Littleton, NH Zip 03561–4101; tel. 603/444–7731; Robert S. Pearson, Administrator

NEW MEXICO: CIBOLA GENERAL HOSPITAL (C, 22 beds) 1212 Bonita Avenue, Grants, NM Zip 87020–2104; tel. 505/287–4446; Polly Pine, Administrator

GERALD CHAMPION MEMORIAL HOSPITAL (C, 73 beds) 1209 Ninth Street, Alamogordo, NM Zip 88310–0597, Mailing Address: P.O. Box 597, Zip 88311–0597; tel. 505/439–2100; Carl W. Mantey, Administrator

GILA REGIONAL MEDICAL CENTER (C, 68 beds) 1313 East 32nd Street, Silver City, NM Zip 88061; tel. 505/538–4000; Jeffrey Carey, Administrator

HOLY CROSS HOSPITAL (C, 42 beds) 630 Paseo De Pueblo Sur, Taos, NM Zip 87571, Mailing Address: P.O. Box DD, Zip 87571; tel. 505/758–8883; Warren K. Spellman, Administrator

NEW YORK: AMSTERDAM MEMORIAL HOSPITAL (C, 242 beds) 4988 State Highway 30, Amsterdam, NY Zip 12010–1699; tel. 518/842–3100; Cornelio R. Catena, President and Chief Executive Officer

AURELIA OSBORN FOX MEMORIAL HOSPITAL (C, 234 beds) 1 Norton Avenue, Oneonta, NY Zip 13820–2697; tel. 607/432–2000; John R. Remillard, President

ELLIS HOSPITAL (C, 434 beds) 1101 Nott Street, Schenectady, NY Zip 12308–2487; tel. 518/243–4000; G. B. Serrill, President and Chief Executive Officer

NORTH CAROLINA: ALEXANDER COMMUNITY HOSPITAL (C, 36 beds) 326 Third Street S.W., Taylorsville, NC Zip 28681–3096; tel. 828/632–4282; Joe W. Pollard Jr., Administrator

ALLEGHANY MEMORIAL HOSPITAL (C, 46 beds) 233 Doctors Street, Sparta, NC Zip 28675–0009, Mailing Address: P.O. Box 9, Zip 28675–0009; tel. 336/372–5511; James Yarborough, Chief Executive Officer

ANGEL MEDICAL CENTER (C, 59 beds) Riverview and White Oak Streets, Franklin, NC Zip 28734, Mailing Address: P.O. Box 1209, Zip 28734–1209; tel. 704/524–8411; Michael E. Zuliani, Chief Executive Officer

ASHE MEMORIAL HOSPITAL (C, 115 beds) 200 Hospital Avenue, Jefferson, NC Zip 28640; tel. 336/246–7101; R. D. Williams, Administrator and Chief Executive Officer

CHATHAM HOSPITAL (C, 35 beds) West Third Street and Ivy Avenue, Siler City, NC Zip 27344–2343, Mailing Address: P.O. Box 649, Zip 27344; tel. 919/663–2113; Woodrow W. Hathaway Jr., Chief Executive Officer

COLUMBUS COUNTY HOSPITAL (C, 117 beds) 500 Jefferson Street, Whiteville, NC Zip 28472–9987; tel. 910/642–8011; William S. Clark, Chief Executive Officer

GOOD HOPE HOSPITAL (C, 72 beds) 410 Denim Drive, Erwin, NC Zip 28339–0668, Mailing Address: P.O. Box 668, Zip 28339–0668; tel. 910/897–6151; Donald E. Annis, Chief Executive Officer

---

For explanation of codes following names, see page B2.
★ Indicates Type III membership in the American Hospital Association.

GRANVILLE MEDICAL CENTER (C, 146 beds) 1010 College Street, Oxford, NC Zip 27565–2507, Mailing Address: Box 947, Zip 27565–0947; tel. 919/690–3000; Andrew Mannich, Administrator

HUGH CHATHAM MEMORIAL HOSPITAL (C, 201 beds) Parkwood Drive, Elkin, NC Zip 28621–0560, Mailing Address: P.O. Box 560, Zip 28621–0560; tel. 910/527–7000; Richard D. Osmus, Chief Executive Officer

JOHNSTON MEMORIAL HOSPITAL (C, 127 beds) 509 North Bright Leaf Boulevard, Smithfield, NC Zip 27577–1376, Mailing Address: P.O. Box 1376, Zip 27577–1376; tel. 919/934–8171; Leland E. Farnell, President

MOREHEAD MEMORIAL HOSPITAL (C, 236 beds) 117 East King's Highway, Eden, NC Zip 27288–5299; tel. 336/623–9711; Robert Enders, President

NORTHERN HOSPITAL OF SURRY COUNTY (C, 115 beds) 830 Rockford Street, Mount Airy, NC Zip 27030–5365, Mailing Address: P.O. Box 1101, Zip 27030–1101; tel. 910/719–7000; William B. James, Chief Executive Officer

PENDER MEMORIAL HOSPITAL (C, 86 beds) 507 Freemont Street, Burgaw, NC Zip 28425; tel. 910/259–5451; J. Larry Bishop, Chief Executive Officer

RUTHERFORD HOSPITAL (C, 293 beds) 288 South Ridgecrest Avenue, Rutherfordton, NC Zip 28139–3097; tel. 704/286–5000; Robert D. Jones, President

WASHINGTON COUNTY HOSPITAL (C, 49 beds) 958 U.S. Highway 64 East, Plymouth, NC Zip 27962–9591; tel. 919/793–4135; Lawrence H. McAvoy, Administrator

NORTH DAKOTA: KENMARE COMMUNITY HOSPITAL (O, 42 beds) 317 First Avenue N.W., Kenmare, ND Zip 58746–7104, Mailing Address: P.O. Box 697, Zip 58746–0697; tel. 701/385–4296; Verlin Buechler, President and Chief Executive Officer

UNIMED MEDICAL CENTER (O, 160 beds) 407 3rd Street S.E., Minot, ND Zip 58702–5001; tel. 701/857–2000; James E. Richardson, FACHE, Interim Chief Executive Officer

OHIO: BARBERTON CITIZENS HOSPITAL (O, 272 beds) 155 Fifth Street N.E., Barberton, OH Zip 44203–3398; tel. 330/745–1611; Ronald Elder, Chief Executive Officer

BROWN COUNTY GENERAL HOSPITAL (C, 53 beds) 425 Home Street, Georgetown, OH Zip 45121–1407; tel. 937/378–6121; David T. Wallace, President and Chief Executive Officer

DEFIANCE HOSPITAL (C, 96 beds) 1206 East Second Street, Defiance, OH Zip 43512–2495; tel. 419/783–6955; Richard C. Sommer, Administrator

DOCTORS HOSPITAL OF STARK COUNTY (O, 166 beds) 400 Austin Avenue N.W., Massillon, OH Zip 44646–3554; tel. 330/837–7200; Thomas E. Cecconi, Chief Executive Officer

EAST LIVERPOOL CITY HOSPITAL (C, 198 beds) 425 West Fifth Street, East Liverpool, OH Zip 43920–2498; tel. 330/385–7200; Melvin R. Creeley, President

FAYETTE COUNTY MEMORIAL HOSPITAL (C, 48 beds) 1430 Columbus Avenue, Washington Court House, OH Zip 43160–1791; tel. 740/335–1210; Francis G. Albarano, Administrator

GREENFIELD AREA MEDICAL CENTER (C, 36 beds) 545 South Street, Greenfield, OH Zip 45123–1400; tel. 937/981–2116; Mark E. Marchetti, Chief Executive Officer

KNOX COMMUNITY HOSPITAL (C, 115 beds) 1330 Coshocton Road, Mount Vernon, OH Zip 43050–1495; tel. 740/393–9000; Robert G. Polahar, Chief Executive Officer

MEMORIAL HOSPITAL (C, 132 beds) 715 South Taft Avenue, Fremont, OH Zip 43420–3200; tel. 419/332–7321; John A. Gorman, Chief Executive Officer

PARK MEDICAL CENTER (O, 165 beds) 1492 East Broad Street, Columbus, OH Zip 43205–1546; tel. 614/251–3000; James L. Rieder, Chief Executive Officer

PAULDING COUNTY HOSPITAL (C, 51 beds) 11558 State Road 111, Paulding, OH Zip 45879–9220; tel. 419/399–4080; Joseph M. Dorko, Chief Executive Officer

SELBY GENERAL HOSPITAL (C, 44 beds) 1106 Colegate Drive, Marietta, OH Zip 45750–1323; tel. 740/373–0582; James J. Cliborne Jr., Chief Executive Officer

WOOSTER COMMUNITY HOSPITAL (C, 90 beds) 1761 Beall Avenue, Wooster, OH Zip 44691–2342; tel. 330/263–8100; William E. Sheron, Chief Executive Officer

OKLAHOMA: ATOKA MEMORIAL HOSPITAL (C, 25 beds) 1501 South Virginia Avenue, Atoka, OK Zip 74525–3298; tel. 580/889–3333; Bruce A. Bennett, Administrator and Chief Executive Officer

CUSHING REGIONAL HOSPITAL (L, 75 beds) 1027 East Cherry Street, Cushing, OK Zip 74023–4101, Mailing Address: P.O. Box 1409, Zip 74023–1409; tel. 918/225–2915; Ron Cackler, President and Chief Executive Officer

EASTERN OKLAHOMA MEDICAL CENTER (C, 72 beds) 105 Wall Street, Poteau, OK Zip 74953, Mailing Address: P.O. Box 1148, Zip 74953–1148; tel. 918/647–8161; Craig R. Cudworth, Chief Executive Officer

HENRYETTA MEDICAL CENTER (L, 52 beds) Dewey Bartlett and Main Streets, Henryetta, OK Zip 74437, Mailing Address: P.O. Box 1269, Zip 74437–1269; tel. 918/652–4463; James P. Bailey, President and Chief Executive Officer

HOLDENVILLE GENERAL HOSPITAL (C, 27 beds) 100 Crestview Drive, Holdenville, OK Zip 74848–9700; tel. 405/379–6631; Joseph J. Mitchell, Chief Executive Officer and Administrator

KINGFISHER REGIONAL HOSPITAL (C, 38 beds) 500 South Ninth Street, Kingfisher, OK Zip 73750–3528, Mailing Address: P.O. Box 59, Zip 73750–0059; tel. 405/375–3141; Daryle Voss, Chief Executive Officer

LOGAN HOSPITAL AND MEDICAL CENTER (C, 32 beds) Highway 33 West at Academy Road, Guthrie, OK Zip 73044, Mailing Address: P.O. Box 1017, Zip 73044–1017; tel. 405/282–6700; James R. Caton, Chief Executive Officer

MCCURTAIN MEMORIAL HOSPITAL (C, 89 beds) 1301 Lincoln Road, Idabel, OK Zip 74745–7341; tel. 405/286–7623; Ronald Campbell, Administrator

PERRY MEMORIAL HOSPITAL (C, 28 beds) 501 14th Street, Perry, OK Zip 73077–5099; tel. 580/336–3541; Judith K. Feuquay, Chief Executive Officer

PURCELL MUNICIPAL HOSPITAL (C, 16 beds) 1500 North Green Avenue, Purcell, OK Zip 73080–1699, Mailing Address: P.O. Box 511, Zip 73080–0511; tel. 405/527–6524; Curtis R. Pryor, Administrator

SAYRE MEMORIAL HOSPITAL (C, 46 beds) 501 East Washington Street, Sayre, OK Zip 73662, Mailing Address: P.O. Box 680, Zip 73662; tel. 405/928–5541; Larry Anderson, Administrator

SEMINOLE MUNICIPAL HOSPITAL (C, 39 beds) 606 West Evans Street, Seminole, OK Zip 74868–3897, Mailing Address: P.O. Box 2130, Zip 74818–2130; tel. 405/382–0600; Stephen R. Schoaps, Chief Executive Officer

SHARE MEDICAL CENTER (C, 117 beds) 800 Share Drive, Alva, OK Zip 73717–3699, Mailing Address: P.O. Box 727, Zip 73717–0727; tel. 580/327–2800; Barbara Oestmann, Chief Executive Officer

TAHLEQUAH CITY HOSPITAL (C, 74 beds) 1400 East Downing Street, Tahlequah, OK Zip 74464–3324, Mailing Address: P.O. Box 1008, Zip 74465–1008; tel. 918/456–0641; L. Gene Matthews, Chief Executive Officer

WATONGA MUNICIPAL HOSPITAL (C, 24 beds) 500 North Nash Boulevard, Watonga, OK Zip 73772–0370, Mailing Address: Box 370, Zip 73772–0370; tel. 580/623–7211; Terry Buckner, Administrator

WOODWARD HOSPITAL AND HEALTH CENTER (C, 68 beds) 900 17th Street, Woodward, OK Zip 73801–2423; tel. 580/256–5511; Joel A. Hart, Administrator

PENNSYLVANIA: BERWICK HOSPITAL CENTER (C, 340 beds) 701 East 16th Street, Berwick, PA Zip 18603–2316; tel. 717/759–5000; Thomas R. Sphatt, President and Chief Executive Officer

BROWNSVILLE GENERAL HOSPITAL (C, 115 beds) 125 Simpson Road, Brownsville, PA Zip 15417–9699; tel. 724/785–7200; Richard D. Constantine, Chief Executive Officer

CARLISLE HOSPITAL (C, 166 beds) 246 Parker Street, Carlisle, PA Zip 17013–3618; tel. 717/249–1212; Michael J. Halstead, President and Chief Executive Officer

CLARION HOSPITAL (C, 86 beds) One Hospital Drive, Clarion, PA Zip 16214–8599; tel. 814/226–9500; John J. Shepard, President and Chief Executive Officer

For explanation of codes following names, see page B2.
★ Indicates Type III membership in the American Hospital Association.

Section B

CORRY MEMORIAL HOSPITAL (C, 59 beds) 612 West Smith Street, Corry, PA Zip 16407–1152; tel. 814/664–4641; Joseph T. Hodges, President

GREENE COUNTY MEMORIAL HOSPITAL (C, 55 beds) Seventh Street and Bonar Avenue, Waynesburg, PA Zip 15370–1697; tel. 412/627–3101; Raoul Walsh, Chief Executive Officer

J. C. BLAIR MEMORIAL HOSPITAL (C, 104 beds) 1225 Warm Springs Avenue, Huntingdon, PA Zip 16652–2398; tel. 814/643–2290; Richard E. D'Alberto, Chief Executive Officer

JERSEY SHORE HOSPITAL (C, 49 beds) 1020 Thompson Street, Jersey Shore, PA Zip 17740–1729; tel. 717/398–0100; Louis A. Ditzel Jr., President and Chief Executive Officer

LOCK HAVEN HOSPITAL (C, 195 beds) 24 Cree Drive, Lock Haven, PA Zip 17745–2699; tel. 717/893–5000; Gary R. Rhoads, President and Chief Executive Officer

MEMORIAL HOSPITAL (C, 93 beds) One Hospital Drive, Towanda, PA Zip 18848–9702; tel. 717/265–2191; Gary A. Baker, President

METRO HEALTH CENTER (C, 112 beds) 252 West 11th Street, Erie, PA Zip 16501–1798; tel. 814/870–3400; Debra M. Dragovan, Chief Executive Officer

MINERS HOSPITAL NORTHERN CAMBRIA (C, 40 beds) 2205 Crawford Avenue, Spangler, PA Zip 15775, Mailing Address: P.O. Box 490, Zip 15775–0490; tel. 814/948–7171; Roger P. Winn, Chief Executive Officer

OHIO VALLEY GENERAL HOSPITAL (C, 103 beds) 25 Heckel Road, McKees Rocks, PA Zip 15136–1694; tel. 412/777–6161; William Provenzano, President

POTTSVILLE HOSPITAL AND WARNE CLINIC (C, 196 beds) 420 South Jackson Street, Pottsville, PA Zip 17901–3692; tel. 717/621–5000; Donald R. Gintzig, President and Chief Executive Officer

TYRONE HOSPITAL (C, 59 beds) One Hospital Drive, Tyrone, PA Zip 16686–1898; tel. 814/684–1255; Philip J. Stoner, Chief Executive Officer

SOUTH CAROLINA: ABBEVILLE COUNTY MEMORIAL HOSPITAL (C, 48 beds) 901 West Greenwood Street, Abbeville, SC Zip 29620–0887, Mailing Address: P.O. Box 887, Zip 29620–0887; tel. 864/459–5011; Bruce P. Bailey, Administrator

CAROLINAS HOSPITAL SYSTEM (O, 360 beds) 121 East Cedar Street, Florence, SC Zip 29501, Mailing Address: P.O. Box 100550, Zip 29501–0550; tel. 803/661–3000; David A. McClellan, Chief Executive Officer

CAROLINAS HOSPITAL SYSTEM–KINGSTREE (O, 47 beds) 500 Nelson Boulevard, Kingstree, SC Zip 29556–4027, Mailing Address: P.O. Drawer 568, Zip 29556–0568; tel. 803/354–9661; David T. Boucher, Chief Executive Officer

CAROLINAS HOSPITAL SYSTEM–LAKE CITY (O, 40 beds) 258 North Ron McNair Boulevard, Lake City, SC Zip 29560–1029, Mailing Address: P.O. Box 1029, Zip 29560–1029; tel. 803/394–2036; Richard L. Gamber, Administrator

GEORGETOWN MEMORIAL HOSPITAL (C, 131 beds) 606 Black River Road, Georgetown, SC Zip 29440–3368, Mailing Address: Drawer 1718, Zip 29442–1718; tel. 803/527–7000; Paul D. Gatens Sr., Administrator

LAURENS COUNTY HEALTHCARE SYSTEM (C, 216 beds) Highway 76 West, Clinton, SC Zip 29325, Mailing Address: P.O. Box 976, Zip 29325–0976; tel. 864/833–9100; Michael A. Kozar, Chief Executive Officer

MARY BLACK HEALTH SYSTEM (O, 212 beds) 1700 Skylyn Drive, Spartanburg, SC Zip 29307–1061, Mailing Address: P.O. Box 3217, Zip 29304–3217; tel. 864/573–3000; William W. Fox, Chief Executive Officer

NEWBERRY COUNTY MEMORIAL HOSPITAL (C, 75 beds) 2669 Kinard Street, Newberry, SC Zip 29108–0497, Mailing Address: P.O. Box 497, Zip 29108–0497; tel. 803/276–7570; Lynn W. Beasley, President and Chief Executive Officer

REGIONAL MEDICAL CENTER OF ORANGEBURG AND CALHOUN COUNTIES (C, 295 beds) 3000 St. Matthews Road, Orangeburg, SC Zip 29118–1470; tel. 803/533–2200; Thomas C. Dandridge, President

TUOMEY REGIONAL MEDICAL CENTER (C, 206 beds) 129 North Washington Street, Sumter, SC Zip 29150–4983; tel. 803/778–9000; Jay Cox, President and Chief Executive Officer

WALLACE THOMSON HOSPITAL (C, 215 beds) 322 West South Street, Union, SC Zip 29379–2857, Mailing Address: P.O. Box 789, Zip 29379–0789; tel. 864/429–2600; Harrell L. Connelly, Chief Executive Officer

SOUTH DAKOTA: HURON REGIONAL MEDICAL CENTER (C, 61 beds) 172 Fourth Street S.E., Huron, SD Zip 57350–2590; tel. 605/353–6200; John L. Single, Chief Executive Officer

TENNESSEE: LINCOLN COUNTY HEALTH FACILITIES (C, 51 beds) 700 West Maple Street, Fayetteville, TN Zip 37334–3202; tel. 931/438–1111; Gary G. Kendrick, Chief Executive Officer

MACON COUNTY GENERAL HOSPITAL (C, 43 beds) 204 Medical Drive, Lafayette, TN Zip 37083–1799, Mailing Address: P.O. Box 378, Zip 37083–0378; tel. 615/666–2147; Dennis A. Wolford, FACHE, Administrator

RHEA MEDICAL CENTER (C, 131 beds) 7900 Rhea County Highway, Dayton, TN Zip 37321–5912; tel. 423/775–1121; Kennedy L. Croom Jr., Administrator and Chief Executive Officer

WELLMONT BRISTOL REGIONAL MEDICAL CENTER (C, 339 beds) 1 Medical Park Boulevard, Bristol, TN Zip 37620–7430; tel. 423/844–4200; Randall M. Olson, Administrator

WELLMONT HOLSTON VALLEY MEDICAL CENTER (C, 384 beds) West Ravine Street, Kingsport, TN Zip 37662–0224, Mailing Address: Box 238, Zip 37662–0224; tel. 423/224–4000; Louis H. Bremer, President and Chief Executive Officer

TEXAS: ABILENE REGIONAL MEDICAL CENTER (O, 160 beds) 6250 Highway 83–84 at Antilley Road, Abilene, TX Zip 79606–5299; tel. 915/695–9900; Woody Gilliland, Chief Executive Officer

BRAZOSPORT MEMORIAL HOSPITAL (C, 156 beds) 100 Medical Drive, Lake Jackson, TX Zip 77566–9983; tel. 409/297–4411; Wesley W. Oswald, Chief Executive Officer

CAMPBELL HEALTH SYSTEM (C, 78 beds) 713 East Anderson Street, Weatherford, TX Zip 76086–9971; tel. 817/596–8751; John B. Millstead, Chief Executive Officer

DALLAS–FORT WORTH MEDICAL CENTER (C, 162 beds) 2709 Hospital Boulevard, Grand Prairie, TX Zip 75051–1083; tel. 972/641–5000; Robert A. Ficken, Chief Executive Officer

DOCTORS HOSPITAL (C, 78 beds) 5500 39th Street, Groves, TX Zip 77619–9805; tel. 409/962–5733; John Isbell, Chief Executive Officer

FORT DUNCAN MEDICAL CENTER (C, 69 beds) 350 South Adams Street, Eagle Pass, TX Zip 78852; tel. 830/757–7501; Don Spaulding, Administrator and Chief Executive Officer

HENDERSON MEMORIAL HOSPITAL (C, 96 beds) 300 Wilson Street, Henderson, TX Zip 75652–5956; tel. 903/657–7541; George T. Roberts Jr., Chief Executive Officer

HUNTSVILLE MEMORIAL HOSPITAL (C, 130 beds) 3000 I–45, Huntsville, TX Zip 77340, Mailing Address: P.O. Box 4001, Zip 77342–4001; tel. 409/291–3411; Ralph E. Beaty, Administrator

MISSION HOSPITAL (C, 110 beds) 900 South Bryan Road, Mission, TX Zip 78572–6613; tel. 956/580–9000; Paul H. Ballard, Chief Executive Officer

TITUS REGIONAL MEDICAL CENTER (C, 165 beds) 2001 North Jefferson Avenue, Mount Pleasant, TX Zip 75455–2398; tel. 903/577–6000; Steven K. Jacobson, Chief Executive Officer

VERMONT: NORTHEASTERN VERMONT REGIONAL HOSPITAL (C, 64 beds) Hospital Drive, Saint Johnsbury, VT Zip 05819–9962, Mailing Address: P.O. Box 905, Zip 05819–9962; tel. 802/748–8141; Paul R. Bengtson, Chief Executive Officer

NORTHWESTERN MEDICAL CENTER (C, 70 beds) 131 Fairfield Street, Saint Albans, VT Zip 05478–1734, Mailing Address: P.O. Box 1370, Zip 05478–1370; tel. 802/524–5911; Peter A. Hofstetter, Chief Executive Officer

VIRGINIA: BUCHANAN GENERAL HOSPITAL (C, 144 beds) Grundy, VA Mailing Address: Route 5, Box 20, Zip 24614–9611; tel. 540/935–1000; John West, Administrator

GREENSVILLE MEMORIAL HOSPITAL (C, 144 beds) 214 Weaver Avenue, Emporia, VA Zip 23847–1482; tel. 804/348–2000; Rosemary C. Check, Chief Executive Officer

Section B

HALIFAX REGIONAL HOSPITAL (C, 157 beds) 2204 Wilborn Avenue, South Boston, VA Zip 24592–1638; tel. 804/575–3100; Chris A. Lumsden, Administrator

LONESOME PINE HOSPITAL (C, 54 beds) 1990 Holton Avenue East, Big Stone Gap, VA Zip 24219–0230; tel. 540/523–3111; Paul A. Bishop, Administrator

MEMORIAL HOSPITAL OF MARTINSVILLE AND HENRY COUNTY (C, 152 beds) 320 Hospital Drive, Martinsville, VA Zip 24112–1981, Mailing Address: Box 4788, Zip 24115–4788; tel. 540/666–7200; Joseph Roach, Chief Executive Officer

RICHMOND EYE AND EAR HOSPITAL (C, 32 beds) 1001 East Marshall Street, Richmond, VA Zip 23219–1993; tel. 804/775–4500; William E. Holmes, Chief Executive Officer

SOUTHSIDE REGIONAL MEDICAL CENTER (C, 267 beds) 801 South Adams Street, Petersburg, VA Zip 23803–5133; tel. 804/862–5000; David S. Dunham, President

WASHINGTON: KADLEC MEDICAL CENTER (C, 124 beds) 888 Swift Boulevard, Richland, WA Zip 99352–9974; tel. 509/946–4611; Marcel Loh, President and Chief Executive Officer

KENNEWICK GENERAL HOSPITAL (C, 70 beds) 900 South Auburn Street, Kennewick, WA Zip 99336–0128, Mailing Address: Box 6128, Zip 99336; tel. 509/586–6111; Tom Nielsen, Administrator

WEST VIRGINIA: CITY HOSPITAL (C, 163 beds) Dry Run Road, Martinsburg, WV Zip 25401, Mailing Address: P.O. Box 1418, Zip 25402–1418; tel. 304/264–1000; Peter L. Mulford, Administrator

FAIRMONT GENERAL HOSPITAL (C, 224 beds) 1325 Locust Avenue, Fairmont, WV Zip 26554–1435; tel. 304/367–7100; Richard W. Graham, FACHE, President

MONONGALIA GENERAL HOSPITAL (C, 205 beds) 1200 J. D. Anderson Drive, Morgantown, WV Zip 26505–3486; tel. 304/598–1200; Robert P. Ritz, Chief Executive Officer

PRESTON MEMORIAL HOSPITAL (C, 60 beds) 300 South Price Street, Kingwood, WV Zip 26537–1495; tel. 304/329–1400; Charles Lonchar, President and Chief Executive Officer

WISCONSIN: APPLE RIVER HOSPITAL (C, 4 beds) 230 Deronda Street, Amery, WI Zip 54001–1407; tel. 715/268–7151; Michael Karuschak Jr., Administrator

RIVERSIDE MEDICAL CENTER (C, 36 beds) 800 Riverside Drive, Waupaca, WI Zip 54981–1999; tel. 715/258–1000; Jan V. Carrell, Chief Executive Officer

WYOMING: NIOBRARA COUNTY HOSPITAL DISTRICT (C, 46 beds) 939 Ballencee Avenue, Lusk, WY Zip 82225, Mailing Address: P.O. Box 780, Zip 82225–0780; tel. 307/334–2711; Gary W. Robertson, Administrator

WEST PARK HOSPITAL (C, 171 beds) 707 Sheridan Avenue, Cody, WY Zip 82414; tel. 307/527–7501; Douglas A. McMillan, Administrator and Chief Executive Officer

Owned, leased, sponsored:	22 hospitals	3726 beds
Contract–managed:	237 hospitals	24369 beds
Totals:	259 hospitals	28095 beds

0405: RAMSAY HEALTH CARE, INC. (IO)
1 Alhambra Plaza, Suite 750, Coral Gables, FL Zip 33134–5217; tel. 305/569–6993; Bert Cibran, President and Chief Operating Officer

ALABAMA: HILL CREST BEHAVIORAL HEALTH SERVICES (O, 100 beds) 6869 Fifth Avenue South, Birmingham, AL Zip 35212–1866; tel. 205/833–9000; Steve McCabe, Chief Executive Officer

ARIZONA: DESERT VISTA BEHAVIORAL HEALTH SERVICES (L, 119 beds) 570 West Brown Road, Mesa, AZ Zip 85201–3227; tel. 602/962–3900; Allen S. Nohre, Chief Executive Officer

FLORIDA: GULF COAST TREATMENT CENTER (O, 79 beds) 1015 Mar–Walt Drive, Fort Walton Beach, FL Zip 32547–6612; tel. 850/863–4160; Raul D. Ruelas, M.D., Administrator

LOUISIANA: BAYOU OAKS BEHAVIORAL HEALTH SYSTEM (L, 98 beds) 8134 Main Street, Houma, LA Zip 70360–3404, Mailing Address: P.O. Box 4374, Zip 70361–4374; tel. 504/876–2020; George H. Perry, Ph.D., Chief Executive Officer

GREENBRIER BEHAVIORAL HEALTH SYSTEM (O, 67 beds) 201 Greenbrier Boulevard, Covington, LA Zip 70433–9126; tel. 504/893–2970; Cheryl M. Schleuss, Chief Executive Officer

MICHIGAN: HAVENWYCK HOSPITAL (O, 120 beds) 1525 University Drive, Auburn Hills, MI Zip 48326–2675; tel. 810/373–9200; Robert A. Kercorian, Chief Executive Officer

MISSOURI: HEARTLAND BEHAVIORAL HEALTH SERVICES (O, 60 beds) 1500 West Ashland Street, Nevada, MO Zip 64772–1710; tel. 417/667–2666; Ed Goosman, Chief Executive Officer

NORTH CAROLINA: BRYNN MARR BEHAVIORAL HEALTHCARE SYSTEM (O, 76 beds) 192 Village Drive, Jacksonville, NC Zip 28546–7299; tel. 910/577–1400; Dale Armstrong, Chief Executive Officer

OKLAHOMA: INTEGRIS BASS BEHAVIORAL HEALTH SYSTEM (O, 50 beds) 2216 South Van Buren Street, Enid, OK Zip 73703–8299, Mailing Address: P.O. Box 5409, Zip 73702–5409; tel. 580/234–2220; James Hutchison, Director

SOUTH CAROLINA: COASTAL CAROLINA HOSPITAL (O, 48 beds) 152 Waccamaw Medical Park Drive, Conway, SC Zip 29526–8922; tel. 803/347–7156; Dale Armstrong, Chief Executive Officer

TEXAS: HAVEN HOSPITAL (O, 51 beds) 800 Kirnwood Drive, De Soto, TX Zip 75115–2092; tel. 972/709–3700; Sheila C. Kelly, R.N., MS, Chief Executive Officer

MISSION VISTA BEHAVIORAL HEALTH SYSTEM (L, 16 beds) 14747 Jones Maltsberger, San Antonio, TX Zip 78247–3713; tel. 210/490–0000; Holly Minis, Chief Executive Officer

UTAH: BENCHMARK BEHAVIORAL HEALTH SYSTEMS (O, 68 beds) 592 West 1350 South, Woods Cross, UT Zip 84087–1665; tel. 801/299–5300; Richard O. Hurt, Ph.D., Chief Executive Officer

WEST VIRGINIA: CHESTNUT RIDGE HOSPITAL (O, 70 beds) 930 Chestnut Ridge Road, Morgantown, WV Zip 26505–2854; tel. 304/293–4000; Lawrence J. Drake, Chief Executive Officer

Owned, leased, sponsored:	14 hospitals	1022 beds
Contract–managed:	0 hospitals	0 beds
Totals:	14 hospitals	1022 beds

4810: RIVERSIDE HEALTH SYSTEM (NP)
606 Denbigh Boulevard, Suite 601, Newport News, VA Zip 23608; tel. 757/875–7500; Nelson L. St. Clair, President

VIRGINIA: LAKE TAYLOR HOSPITAL (C, 330 beds) 1309 Kempsville Road, Norfolk, VA Zip 23502–2286; tel. 757/461–5001; David B. Tate Jr., President and Chief Executive Officer

RIVERSIDE REGIONAL MEDICAL CENTER (O, 576 beds) 500 J. Clyde Morris Boulevard, Newport News, VA Zip 23601–1976; tel. 757/594–2000; Gerald R. Brink, President and Chief Executive Officer

RIVERSIDE TAPPAHANNOCK HOSPITAL (O, 100 beds) Tappahannock, VA Mailing Address: Route 2, Box 612, Zip 22560; tel. 804/443–3311; Elizabeth J. Martin, Vice President and Administrator

RIVERSIDE WALTER REED HOSPITAL (O, 71 beds) 7519 Hospital Drive, Gloucester, VA Zip 23061–4178, Mailing Address: P.O. Box 1130, Zip 23061–1130; tel. 804/693–8800; Grady W. Philips III, Vice President and Administrator

Owned, leased, sponsored:	3 hospitals	747 beds
Contract–managed:	1 hospital	330 beds
Totals:	4 hospitals	1077 beds

★0109: RURAL HEALTH MANAGEMENT CORPORATION (NP)
549 North 400 East, Nephi, UT Zip 84648–1226; tel. 801/623–4924; Mark R. Stoddard, President

UTAH: ALLEN MEMORIAL HOSPITAL (L, 38 beds) 719 West 400 North Street, Moab, UT Zip 84532–2297, Mailing Address: P.O. Box 998, Zip 84532–0998; tel. 435/259–7191; Charles A. Davis, Administrator

CENTRAL VALLEY MEDICAL CENTER (L, 22 beds) 549 North 400 East, Nephi, UT Zip 84648–1226; tel. 801/623–1242; Mark R. Stoddard, President

For explanation of codes following names, see page B2.
★ Indicates Type III membership in the American Hospital Association.

Section B

GUNNISON VALLEY HOSPITAL (C, 21 beds) 64 East 100 North, Gunnison, UT Zip 84634, Mailing Address: P.O. Box 759, Zip 84634–0759; tel. 435/528–7246; Greg Rosenvall, Administrator

MILFORD VALLEY MEMORIAL HOSPITAL (C, 34 beds) 451 North Main Street, Milford, UT Zip 84751–0640, Mailing Address: P.O. Box 640, Zip 84751–0640; tel. 801/387–2411; John E. Gledhill, Administrator

TOOELE VALLEY REGIONAL MEDICAL CENTER (C, 122 beds) 211 South 100 East, Tooele, UT Zip 84074–2794; tel. 435/882–1697; Mark F. Dalley, Chief Executive Officer

Owned, leased, sponsored:	2 hospitals	60 beds
Contract–managed:	3 hospitals	177 beds
Totals:	5 hospitals	237 beds

★3855: RUSH–PRESBYTERIAN–ST. LUKE'S MEDICAL CENTER (NP)
1653 West Congress Parkway, Chicago, IL Zip 60612–3864; tel. 312/942–5000; Leo M. Henikoff, M.D., President

ILLINOIS: RUSH NORTH SHORE MEDICAL CENTER (O, 231 beds) 9600 Gross Point Road, Skokie, IL Zip 60076–1257; tel. 847/677–9600; John S. Frigo, President

RUSH–COPLEY MEMORIAL HOSPITAL (O, 142 beds) 2000 Ogden Avenue, Aurora, IL Zip 60504–4206; tel. 630/978–6200; Martin Losoff, President and Chief Operating Officer

RUSH–PRESBYTERIAN–ST. LUKE'S MEDICAL CENTER (O, 783 beds) 1653 West Congress Parkway, Chicago, IL Zip 60612–3833; tel. 312/942–5000; Leo M. Henikoff, M.D., President and Chief Executive Officer

Owned, leased, sponsored:	3 hospitals	1156 beds
Contract–managed:	0 hospitals	0 beds
Totals:	3 hospitals	1156 beds

★0118: SAINT BARNABAS HEALTH CARE SYSTEM (NP)
94 Old Short Hills Road, Livingston, NJ Zip 07039–5668; tel. 973/322–5000; Ronald Del Mauro, President and Chief Executive Officer

NEW JERSEY: CLARA MAASS HEALTH SYSTEM (O, 644 beds) 1 Clara Maass Drive, Belleville, NJ Zip 07109–3557; tel. 973/450–2000; Thomas A. Biga, Executive Director

COMMUNITY MEDICAL CENTER (O, 425 beds) 99 Route 37 West, Toms River, NJ Zip 08755–6423; tel. 732/240–8000; Kevin R. Burchill, Executive Director

IRVINGTON GENERAL HOSPITAL (O, 123 beds) 832 Chancellor Avenue, Irvington, NJ Zip 07111–0709; tel. 973/399–6000; Paul A. Mertz, Executive Director

KIMBALL MEDICAL CENTER (O, 248 beds) 600 River Avenue, Lakewood, NJ Zip 08701–5281; tel. 732/363–1900; Joanne Carrocino, Executive Director

MONMOUTH MEDICAL CENTER (O, 435 beds) 300 Second Avenue, Long Branch, NJ Zip 07740–6303; tel. 732/222–5200; Frank J. Vozos, M.D., FACS, Executive Director

NEWARK BETH ISRAEL MEDICAL CENTER (O, 451 beds) 201 Lyons Avenue, Newark, NJ Zip 07112–2027; tel. 973/926–7000; Paul A. Mertz, Executive Director

SAINT BARNABAS MEDICAL CENTER (O, 615 beds) 94 Old Short Hills Road, Livingston, NJ Zip 07039–5668; tel. 973/322–5000; Vincent D. Joseph, Executive Director

UNION HOSPITAL (O, 148 beds) 1000 Galloping Hill Road, Union, NJ Zip 07083–1652; tel. 908/687–1900; Kathryn W. Coyne, Executive Director and Chief Operating Officer

WAYNE GENERAL HOSPITAL (O, 146 beds) 224 Hamburg Turnpike, Wayne, NJ Zip 07470–2100; tel. 973/942–6900; Kenneth H. Kozloff, Executive Director

WEST HUDSON HOSPITAL (O, 217 beds) 206 Bergen Avenue, Kearny, NJ Zip 07032–3399; tel. 201/955–7051; Carmen Bruce Alecci, Executive Director

Owned, leased, sponsored:	10 hospitals	3452 beds
Contract–managed:	0 hospitals	0 beds
Totals:	10 hospitals	3452 beds

0120: SAINT LUKE'S SHAWNEE MISSION HEALTH SYSTEM (NP)
10920 Elm Avenue, Kansas City, MO Zip 64134–4108; tel. 816/932–3377; G. Richard Hastings, President and Chief Executive Officer

KANSAS: ANDERSON COUNTY HOSPITAL (O, 66 beds) 421 South Maple, Garnett, KS Zip 66032–1334, Mailing Address: P.O. Box 309, Zip 66032–0309; tel. 913/448–3131; James K. Johnson, Senior Executive Officer

SHAWNEE MISSION MEDICAL CENTER (O, 333 beds) 9100 West 74th Street, Shawnee Mission, KS Zip 66204–4019, Mailing Address: Box 2923, Zip 66201–1323; tel. 913/676–2000; William G. Robertson, Senior Executive Officer

MISSOURI: CRITTENTON (O, 110 beds) 10918 Elm Avenue, Kansas City, MO Zip 64134–4199; tel. 816/765–6600; Gary L. Watson, FACHE, Senior Executive Officer

SAINT LUKE'S HOSPITAL (O, 510 beds) 4400 Wornall Road, Kansas City, MO Zip 64111–3238; tel. 816/932–2000; James M. Brophy, Senior Executive Officer

SAINT LUKE'S NORTHLAND HOSPITAL (O, 58 beds) 5830 N.W. Barry Road, Kansas City, MO Zip 64154–9988; tel. 816/932–2199; James M. Brophy, FACHE, Senior Executive Officer

SAINT LUKE'S NORTHLAND HOSPITAL–SMITHVILLE CAMPUS (O, 50 beds) 601 South 169 Highway, Smithville, MO Zip 64089–9334; tel. 816/532–3700; Don Sipes, Senior Executive Officer

WRIGHT MEMORIAL HOSPITAL (O, 48 beds) 701 East First Street, Trenton, MO Zip 64683–0648, Mailing Address: P.O. Box 628, Zip 64683–0628; tel. 660/359–5621; Ralph G. Goodrich, Senior Executive Officer

Owned, leased, sponsored:	7 hospitals	1175 beds
Contract–managed:	0 hospitals	0 beds
Totals:	7 hospitals	1175 beds

★2535: SAMARITAN HEALTH SYSTEM (NP)
1441 North 12th Street, Phoenix, AZ Zip 85006–2666; tel. 602/495–4000; James C. Crews, President and Chief Executive Officer

ARIZONA: DESERT SAMARITAN MEDICAL CENTER (O, 511 beds) 1400 South Dobson Road, Mesa, AZ Zip 85202–9879; tel. 602/835–3000; Bruce E. Pearson, Vice President and Chief Executive Officer

GOOD SAMARITAN REGIONAL MEDICAL CENTER (O, 714 beds) 1111 East McDowell Road, Phoenix, AZ Zip 85006–2666, Mailing Address: P.O. Box 2989, Zip 85062–2989; tel. 602/239–2000; Steven L. Seiler, Senior Vice President and Chief Executive Officer

PAGE HOSPITAL (C, 25 beds) 501 North Navajo Drive, Page, AZ Zip 86040, Mailing Address: P.O. Box 1447, Zip 86040–1447; tel. 520/645–2424; Richard Polheber, Chief Executive Officer

SAMARITAN BEHAVIORAL HEALTH CENTER–SCOTTSDALE (O, 60 beds) 7575 East Earll Drive, Scottsdale, AZ Zip 85251–6998; tel. 602/941–7500; Robert F. Meyer, M.D., Chief Executive Officer

SAMARITAN–WENDY PAINE O'BRIEN TREATMENT CENTER (O, 88 beds) 5055 North 34th Street, Phoenix, AZ Zip 85018–1498; tel. 602/955–6200; Robert F. Meyer, M.D., Chief Executive Officer

THUNDERBIRD SAMARITAN MEDICAL CENTER (O, 220 beds) 5555 West Thunderbird Road, Glendale, AZ Zip 85306–4696; tel. 602/588–5555; Robert H. Curry, Senior Vice President and Chief Executive Officer

Owned, leased, sponsored:	5 hospitals	1593 beds
Contract–managed:	1 hospital	25 beds
Totals:	6 hospitals	1618 beds

For explanation of codes following names, see page B2.
★ Indicates Type III membership in the American Hospital Association.

★0037: SCOTTSDALE HEALTHCARE (NP)
3621 Wells Fargo Avenue, Scottsdale, AZ Zip 85251–5607;
tel. 602/481–4324; Max Poll, President and Chief Executive Officer

SCOTTSDALE HEALTHCARE–OSBORN (O, 328 beds) 7400 East Osborn
Road, Scottsdale, AZ Zip 85251–6403; tel. 602/675–4000; David R.
Carpenter, FACHE, Senior Vice President and Administrator

SCOTTSDALE HEALTHCARE–SHEA (O, 250 beds) 9003 East Shea Boulevard,
Scottsdale, AZ Zip 85260–6771; tel. 602/860–3000; Thomas J. Sadvary,
FACHE, Senior Vice President and Administrator

Owned, leased, sponsored:	2 hospitals	578 beds
Contract–managed:	0 hospitals	0 beds
Totals:	2 hospitals	578 beds

★1505: SCRIPPS HEALTH (NP)
4275 Campus Point Court, San Diego, CA Zip 92121, Mailing
Address: P.O. Box 28, La Jolla, Zip 92038; tel. 619/678–7472;
Sister Mary Jo Anderson, Senior Vice President, Hospital Operations

CALIFORNIA: GREEN HOSPITAL OF SCRIPPS CLINIC (O, 149 beds) 10666
North Torrey Pines Road, La Jolla, CA Zip 92037–1093;
tel. 619/455–9100; Linda L. Hodges, R.N., Associate Administrator

SCRIPPS HOSPITAL–CHULA VISTA (O, 159 beds) 435 H. Street, Chula Vista,
CA Zip 91912–1537, Mailing Address: P.O. Box 1537, Zip 91910–1537;
tel. 619/691–7000; Thomas A. Gammiere, Vice President and Administrator

SCRIPPS HOSPITAL–EAST COUNTY (O, 105 beds) 1688 East Main Street, El
Cajon, CA Zip 92021; tel. 619/593–5600; Deborah Dunne, Administrator

SCRIPPS MEMORIAL HOSPITAL–ENCINITAS (O, 145 beds) 354 Santa Fe
Drive, Encinitas, CA Zip 92024, Mailing Address: P.O. Box 230817,
Zip 92023; tel. 760/753–6501; Gerald E. Bracht, Vice President and
Administrator

SCRIPPS MEMORIAL HOSPITAL–LA JOLLA (O, 424 beds) 9888 Genesee
Avenue, La Jolla, CA Zip 92037–1276, Mailing Address: P.O. Box 28,
Zip 92038–0028; tel. 619/626–4123; Thomas C. Gagen, Administrator

SCRIPPS MERCY HOSPITAL (O, 417 beds) 4077 Fifth Avenue, San Diego, CA
Zip 92103–2180; tel. 619/260–7101; Nancy Wilson, Senior Vice President
and Regional Administrator

Owned, leased, sponsored:	6 hospitals	1399 beds
Contract–managed:	0 hospitals	0 beds
Totals:	6 hospitals	1399 beds

★2565: SENTARA HEALTH SYSTEM (NP)
6015 Poplar Hall Drive, Norfolk, VA Zip 23502–3800;
tel. 757/455–7000; David L. Bernd, President and Chief Executive
Officer

VIRGINIA: SENTARA BAYSIDE HOSPITAL (O, 116 beds) 800 Independence
Boulevard, Virginia Beach, VA Zip 23455–6076; tel. 757/363–6100;
Virginia Bogue, Site Administrator

SENTARA HAMPTON GENERAL HOSPITAL (O, 198 beds) 3120 Victoria
Boulevard, Hampton, VA Zip 23661–1585, Mailing Address: Drawer 640,
Zip 23669–0640; tel. 757/727–7000; Russell Kenwood, Administrator

SENTARA LEIGH HOSPITAL (O, 217 beds) 830 Kempsville Road, Norfolk, VA
Zip 23502–3981; tel. 757/466–6000; Darleen S. Anderson, R.N., MSN, Site
Administrator

SENTARA NORFOLK GENERAL HOSPITAL (O, 495 beds) 600 Gresham Drive,
Norfolk, VA Zip 23507–1999; tel. 757/668–3000; Mark R. Gavens, President

WILLIAMSBURG COMMUNITY HOSPITAL (C, 119 beds) 301 Monticello Avenue,
Williamsburg, VA Zip 23187–8700, Mailing Address: Box 8700,
Zip 23187–8700; tel. 757/259–6000; Les A. Donahue, President and Chief
Executive Officer

Owned, leased, sponsored:	4 hospitals	1026 beds
Contract–managed:	1 hospital	119 beds
Totals:	5 hospitals	1145 beds

★0111: SHANDS HEALTHCARE (NP)
1600 S.W. Archer Road, Gainesville, FL Zip 32610–0336;
tel. 352/395–0421; J. Richard Gaintner, M.D., Chief Executive
Officer

FLORIDA: SHANDS REHAB HOSPITAL (O, 40 beds) 8900 N.W. 39th Avenue,
Gainesville, FL Zip 32606–5625; tel. 352/338–0091; Cynthia M. Toth,
Administrator

SHANDS AT AGH (O, 267 beds) 801 S.W. Second Avenue, Gainesville, FL
Zip 32601–6289; tel. 352/372–4321; Robert B. Williams, Administrator

SHANDS AT LAKE SHORE (L, 128 beds) 560 East Franklin Street, Lake City,
FL Zip 32055–3047, Mailing Address: P.O. Box 1989, Zip 32056–1989;
tel. 904/754–8000; Linda A. McKnew, R.N., Administrator

SHANDS AT LIVE OAK (O, 20 beds) 1100 S.W. 11th Street, Live Oak, FL
Zip 32060–3608, Mailing Address: P.O. Drawer X., Zip 32060;
tel. 904/362–1413; Rhonda Sherrod, Administrator

SHANDS AT STARKE (O, 23 beds) 922 East Call Street, Starke, FL
Zip 32091–3699; tel. 904/964–6000; Jeannie Baker, Administrator

SHANDS AT THE UNIVERSITY OF FLORIDA (O, 564 beds) 1600 S.W. Archer
Road, Gainesville, FL Zip 32610–0326, Mailing Address: P.O. Box 100326,
Zip 32610–0326; tel. 352/395–0111; Jodi J. Mansfield, Senior Vice
President and Chief Operating Officer

Owned, leased, sponsored:	6 hospitals	1042 beds
Contract–managed:	0 hospitals	0 beds
Totals:	6 hospitals	1042 beds

★2065: SHARP HEALTHCARE (NP)
3131 Berger Avenue, San Diego, CA Zip 92123;
tel. 619/541–4000; Michael Murphy, President and Chief Executive
Officer

CALIFORNIA: GROSSMONT HOSPITAL (C, 444 beds) 5555 Grossmont Center
Drive, La Mesa, CA Zip 91942, Mailing Address: Box 158,
Zip 91944–0158; tel. 619/465–0711; Michele T. Tarbet, R.N., Chief
Executive Officer

SHARP CABRILLO HOSPITAL (O, 227 beds) 3475 Kenyon Street, San Diego,
CA Zip 92110–5067; tel. 619/221–3400; Randi Larsson, Chief Operating
Officer and Administrator

SHARP CHULA VISTA MEDICAL CENTER (O, 306 beds) 751 Medical Center
Court, Chula Vista, CA Zip 91911, Mailing Address: Box 1297, Zip 91912;
tel. 619/482–5800; Britt Berrett, Chief Executive Officer

SHARP CORONADO HOSPITAL (C, 195 beds) 250 Prospect Place, Coronado,
CA Zip 92118; tel. 619/522–3600; Marcia K. Hall, Chief Executive Officer

SHARP HEALTHCARE MURRIETA (O, 91 beds) 25500 Medical Center Drive,
Murrieta, CA Zip 92562–5966; tel. 909/696–6000; Juanice Lovett, Chief
Executive Officer

SHARP MEMORIAL HOSPITAL (O, 488 beds) 7901 Frost Street, San Diego,
CA Zip 92123–2788; tel. 619/541–3400; Dan Gross, Chief Executive Officer

Owned, leased, sponsored:	4 hospitals	1112 beds
Contract–managed:	2 hospitals	639 beds
Totals:	6 hospitals	1751 beds

★4125: SHRINERS HOSPITALS FOR CHILDREN (NP)
2900 Rocky Point Drive, Tampa, FL Zip 33607–1435, Mailing
Address: Box 31356, Zip 33631–3356; tel. 813/281–0300; Joseph
E. Melchiorre Jr., CHE, Executive Administrator

SHRINERS HOSPITALS FOR CHILDREN, LOS ANGELES (O, 60 beds) 3160
Geneva Street, Los Angeles, CA Zip 90020–1199; tel. 213/388–3151; Frank
LaBonte, FACHE, Administrator

SHRINERS HOSPITALS FOR CHILDREN, NORTHERN CALIFORNIA (O, 50 beds)
2425 Stockton Boulevard, Sacramento, CA 95817–2215;
tel. 916/453–2000; Margaret Bryan–Williams, Administrator

FLORIDA: SHRINERS HOSPITALS FOR CHILDREN, TAMPA (O, 60 beds) 12502
North Pine Drive, Tampa, FL Zip 33612–9499; tel. 813/972–2250; John
Holtz, Administrator

For explanation of codes following names, see page B2.
★ Indicates Type III membership in the American Hospital Association.

HAWAII: SHRINERS HOSPITALS FOR CHILDREN, HONOLULU (O, 40 beds) 1310 Punahou Street, Honolulu, HI Zip 96826–1099; tel. 808/941–4466; James B. Brasel, Administrator

ILLINOIS: SHRINERS HOSPITALS FOR CHILDREN–CHICAGO (O, 60 beds) 2211 North Oak Park Avenue, Chicago, IL Zip 60707; tel. 773/622–5400; A. James Spang, Administrator

KENTUCKY: SHRINERS HOSPITALS FOR CHILDREN–LEXINGTON UNIT (O, 50 beds) 1900 Richmond Road, Lexington, KY Zip 40502–1298; tel. 606/266–2101; Tony Lewgood, Administrator

LOUISIANA: SHRINERS HOSPITALS FOR CHILDREN, SHREVEPORT (O, 45 beds) 3100 Samford Avenue, Shreveport, LA Zip 71103–4289; tel. 318/222–5704; Thomas R. Schneider, Administrator

MASSACHUSETTS: SHRINERS HOSPITALS FOR CHILDREN, SHRINERS BURNS HOSPITAL–BOSTON (O, 30 beds) 51 Blossom Street, Boston, MA Zip 02114–2699; tel. 617/722–3000; Robert F. Bories Jr., FACHE, Administrator

SHRINERS HOSPITALS FOR CHILDREN, SPRINGFIELD (O, 40 beds) 516 Carew Street, Springfield, MA Zip 01104–2396; tel. 413/787–2000; Mark L. Niederpruem, Administrator

MINNESOTA: SHRINERS HOSPITALS FOR CHILDREN, TWIN CITIES (O, 40 beds) 2025 East River Parkway, Minneapolis, MN Zip 55414–3696; tel. 612/335–5300; Laurence E. Johnson, Administrator

MISSOURI: SHRINERS HOSPITALS FOR CHILDREN, ST. LOUIS (O, 80 beds) 2001 South Lindbergh Boulevard, Saint Louis, MO Zip 63131–3597; tel. 314/432–3600; Carolyn P. Golden, Administrator

OHIO: SHRINERS HOSPITALS FOR CHILDREN, SHRINERS BURNS HOSPITAL, CINCINNATI (O, 30 beds) 3229 Burnet Avenue, Cincinnati, OH Zip 45229–3095; tel. 513/872–6000; Ronald R. Hitzler, Administrator

OREGON: SHRINERS HOSPITALS FOR CHILDREN, PORTLAND (O, 25 beds) 3101 S.W. Sam Jackson Park Road, Portland, OR Zip 97201; tel. 503/241–5090; Nancy Jones, Administrator

PENNSYLVANIA: SHRINERS HOSPITALS FOR CHILDREN, ERIE (O, 30 beds) 1645 West 8th Street, Erie, PA Zip 16505–5007; tel. 814/875–8700; Richard W. Brzuz, Administrator

SHRINERS HOSPITALS FOR CHILDREN, PHILADELPHIA (O, 80 beds) 3551 North Broad Street, Philadelphia, PA Zip 19140; tel. 215/430–4000; Sharon J. Rajnic, Administrator

SOUTH CAROLINA: SHRINERS HOSPITALS FOR CHILDREN, GREENVILLE (O, 60 beds) 950 West Faris Road, Greenville, SC Zip 29605–4277; tel. 864/271–3444; Gary F. Fraley, Administrator

TEXAS: SHRINERS HOSPITALS FOR CHILDREN, GALVESTON BURNS INSTITUTE (O, 30 beds) 815 Market Street, Galveston, TX Zip 77550–2725; tel. 409/770–6600; John A. Swartwout, Administrator

SHRINERS HOSPITALS FOR CHILDREN, HOUSTON (O, 40 beds) 6977 Main Street, Houston, TX Zip 77030–3701; tel. 713/797–1616; Steven B. Reiter, Administrator

UTAH: SHRINERS HOSPITALS FOR CHILDREN–INTERMOUNTAIN (O, 40 beds) Fairfax Road and Virginia Street, Salt Lake City, UT Zip 84103–4399; tel. 801/536–3500; J. Craig Patchin, Administrator

WASHINGTON: SHRINERS HOSPITALS FOR CHILDREN–SPOKANE (O, 30 beds) 911 West Fifth Avenue, Spokane, WA Zip 99204–2901, Mailing Address: P.O. Box 2472, Zip 99210–2472; tel. 509/455–7844; Charles R. Young, Administrator

Owned, leased, sponsored:	20 hospitals	920 beds
Contract–managed:	0 hospitals	0 beds
Totals:	20 hospitals	920 beds

0067: SINGING RIVER HOSPITAL SYSTEM (NP)
2809 Denny Avenue, Pascagoula, MS Zip 39581–5301; tel. 228/938–5062; Robert L. Lingle, Executive Director

MISSISSIPPI: OCEAN SPRINGS HOSPITAL (O, 110 beds) 3109 Bienville Boulevard, Ocean Springs, MS Zip 39564–4361; tel. 228/818–1111; Dwight Rimes, Administrator

SINGING RIVER HOSPITAL (O, 297 beds) 2809 Denny Avenue, Pascagoula, MS Zip 39581–5301; tel. 228/938–5000; James S. Kaigler, FACHE, Administrator

Owned, leased, sponsored:	2 hospitals	407 beds
Contract–managed:	0 hospitals	0 beds
Totals:	2 hospitals	407 beds

★0078: SIOUX VALLEY HOSPITALS AND HEALTH SYSTEM (NP)
1100 South Euclid Avenue, Sioux Falls, SD Zip 57105–0496; tel. 605/333–1000; Kelby K. Krabbenhoft, President

IOWA: MERRILL PIONEER COMMUNITY HOSPITAL (L, 16 beds) 801 South Greene Street, Rock Rapids, IA Zip 51246–1998; tel. 712/472–2591; Gordon Smith, Administrator

NORTHWEST IOWA HEALTH CENTER (L, 95 beds) 118 North Seventh Avenue, Sheldon, IA Zip 51201–1235; tel. 712/324–5041; Charles R. Miller, Chief Executive Officer

ORANGE CITY MUNICIPAL HOSPITAL (C, 113 beds) 400 Central Avenue N.W., Orange City, IA Zip 51041–1398; tel. 712/737–4984; Martin W. Guthmiller, Administrator

SPENCER MUNICIPAL HOSPITAL (C, 86 beds) 1200 First Avenue East, Spencer, IA Zip 51301–4321; tel. 712/264–6198; Jerry Poehling, Interim Administrator

MINNESOTA: ARNOLD MEMORIAL HEALTH CARE CENTER (L, 50 beds) 601 Louisiana Avenue, Adrian, MN Zip 56110–0279, Mailing Address: Box 279, Zip 56110–0279; tel. 507/483–2668; Gerald E. Carl, Administrator

CANBY COMMUNITY HEALTH SERVICES (L, 102 beds) 112 St. Olaf Avenue South, Canby, MN Zip 56220–1433; tel. 507/223–7277; Robert J. Salmon, Chief Executive Officer

JACKSON MEDICAL CENTER (L, 41 beds) 1430 North Highway, Jackson, MN Zip 56143–1098; tel. 507/847–2420; Charlotte Heitkamp, Chief Executive Officer

LUVERNE COMMUNITY HOSPITAL (C, 38 beds) 305 East Luverne Street, Luverne, MN Zip 56156–2519, Mailing Address: P.O. Box 1019, Zip 56156–1019; tel. 507/283–2321; Gerald E. Carl, Administrator

MURRAY COUNTY MEMORIAL HOSPITAL (C, 30 beds) 2042 Juniper Avenue, Slayton, MN Zip 56172–1016; tel. 507/836–6111; Jerry Bobeldyk, Administrator

ORTONVILLE AREA HEALTH SERVICES (C, 105 beds) 750 Eastvold Avenue, Ortonville, MN Zip 56278–1133; tel. 320/839–2502; Michael R. Miller, Interim Administrator

TRACY AREA MEDICAL SERVICES (L, 24 beds) 251 Fifth Street East, Tracy, MN Zip 56175–1536; tel. 507/629–3200; Thomas J. Quinlivan, Administrator

WESTBROOK HEALTH CENTER (C, 8 beds) 920 Bell Avenue, Westbrook, MN Zip 56183–9636, Mailing Address: P.O. Box 188, Zip 56183–0188; tel. 507/274–6121; Thomas J. Quinlivan, Administrator

WINDOM AREA HOSPITAL (C, 27 beds) Highways 60 and 71 North, Windom, MN Zip 56101, Mailing Address: P.O. Box 339, Zip 56101–0339; tel. 507/831–2400; J. Stephen Pautler, CHE, Administrator

WORTHINGTON REGIONAL HOSPITAL (C, 66 beds) 1018 Sixth Avenue, Worthington, MN Zip 56187–2202, Mailing Address: P.O. Box 997, Zip 56187–0997; tel. 507/372–2941; Melvin J. Platt, Administrator

SOUTH DAKOTA: CANTON–INWOOD MEMORIAL HOSPITAL (L, 25 beds) 440 North Hiawatha Drive, Canton, SD Zip 57013–9404, Mailing Address: Rural Route 3, Box 7, Zip 57013–0007; tel. 605/987–2621; John Devick, Chief Executive Officer

DEUEL COUNTY MEMORIAL HOSPITAL (C, 16 beds) 701 Third Avenue South, Clear Lake, SD Zip 57226–1037, Mailing Address: P.O. Box 1037, Zip 57226–1037; tel. 605/874–2141; Robert J. Salmon, Interim Administrator

LAKE AREA HOSPITAL (C, 26 beds) North First Street, Webster, SD Zip 57274, Mailing Address: P.O. Box 489, Zip 57274–0489; tel. 605/345–3336; Donald J. Finn, Administrator

MID DAKOTA HOSPITAL (L, 54 beds) 300 South Byron Boulevard, Chamberlain, SD Zip 57325–9741; tel. 605/734–5511; Michael Penticoff, Administrator

PIONEER MEMORIAL HOSPITAL (C, 77 beds) 315 North Washington Street, Viborg, SD Zip 57070, Mailing Address: P.O. Box 368, Zip 57070–0368; tel. 605/326–5161; Georgia Pokorney, Chief Executive Officer

For explanation of codes following names, see page B2.
★ Indicates Type III membership in the American Hospital Association.

PRAIRIE LAKES HOSPITAL AND CARE CENTER (C, 122 beds) 400 Tenth Avenue N.W., Watertown, SD Zip 57201–1599, Mailing Address: P.O. Box 1210, Zip 57201–1210; tel. 605/882–7000; Edmond L. Weiland, President and Chief Executive Officer

SIOUX VALLEY HOSPITAL (O, 504 beds) 1100 South Euclid Avenue, Sioux Falls, SD Zip 57105–0496, Mailing Address: P.O. Box 5039, Zip 57117–5039; tel. 605/333–1000; Becky Nelson, President

SIOUX VALLEY VERMILLION CAMPUS (L, 95 beds) 20 South Plum Street, Vermillion, SD Zip 57069–3346; tel. 605/624–2611; Larry W. Veitz, Chief Executive Officer

WINNER REGIONAL HEALTHCARE CENTER (C, 116 beds) 745 East Eighth Street, Winner, SD Zip 57580–2677, Mailing Address: P.O. Box 745, Zip 57580–0745; tel. 605/842–7100; Robert Houser, Chief Executive Officer

Owned, leased, sponsored:	10 hospitals	1006 beds
Contract–managed:	13 hospitals	830 beds
Totals:	23 hospitals	1836 beds

5995: SISTERS OF CHARITY CENTER (CC)

Mount St. Vincent on Hudson, New York, NY Zip 10471–9930; tel. 718/549–9200; Sister Elizabeth A. Vermaelen, President

NEW YORK: SAINT VINCENT'S HOSPITAL AND MEDICAL CENTER OF NEW YORK (S, 622 beds) 153 West 11th Street, New York, NY Zip 10011–8397; tel. 212/604–7000; Karl P. Adler, M.D., President and Chief Executive Officer

ST. JOSEPH'S MEDICAL CENTER (S, 394 beds) 127 South Broadway, Yonkers, NY Zip 10701–4080; tel. 914/378–7000; Sister Mary Linehan, President

Owned, leased, sponsored:	2 hospitals	1016 beds
Contract–managed:	0 hospitals	0 beds
Totals:	2 hospitals	1016 beds

★5095: SISTERS OF CHARITY OF LEAVENWORTH HEALTH SERVICES CORPORATION (CC)

4200 South Fourth Street, Leavenworth, KS Zip 66048–5054; tel. 913/682–1338; Sister Marie Damian Glatt, President

CALIFORNIA: SAINT JOHN'S HOSPITAL AND HEALTH CENTER (O, 271 beds) 1328 22nd Street, Santa Monica, CA Zip 90404–2032; tel. 310/829–5511; Bruce Lamoureux, Chief Executive Officer

COLORADO: ST. MARY'S HOSPITAL AND MEDICAL CENTER (O, 250 beds) 2635 North 7th Street, Grand Junction, CO Zip 81501–8204, Mailing Address: P.O. Box 1628, Zip 81502–1628; tel. 970/244–2273; Sister Lynn Casey, President and Chief Executive Officer

KANSAS: PROVIDENCE MEDICAL CENTER (O, 219 beds) 8929 Parallel Parkway, Kansas City, KS Zip 66112–1636; tel. 913/596–4000; Francis V. Creeden Jr., President and Chief Executive Officer

SAINT JOHN HOSPITAL (O, 36 beds) 3500 South Fourth Street, Leavenworth, KS Zip 66048–5092; tel. 913/680–6000; Francis V. Creeden Jr., President and Chief Executive Officer

ST. FRANCIS HOSPITAL AND MEDICAL CENTER (O, 291 beds) 1700 West Seventh Street, Topeka, KS Zip 66606–1690; tel. 913/295–8000; Sister Loretto Marie Colwell, President

MONTANA: HOLY ROSARY HEALTH CENTER (O, 151 beds) 2600 Wilson Street, Miles City, MT Zip 59301–5094; tel. 406/233–2600; H. Ray Gibbons, President and Chief Executive Officer

SAINT VINCENT HOSPITAL AND HEALTH CENTER (O, 257 beds) 1233 North 30th Street, Billings, MT Zip 59101–0165, Mailing Address: P.O. Box 35200, Zip 59107–5200; tel. 406/657–7000; Patrick M. Hermanson, Senior Executive Officer

ST. JAMES COMMUNITY HOSPITAL (O, 103 beds) 400 South Clark Street, Butte, MT Zip 59701–2328, Mailing Address: P.O. Box 3300, Zip 59702–3300; tel. 406/723–2500; Robert Rodgers, Administrator and Senior Executive Officer

Owned, leased, sponsored:	8 hospitals	1578 beds
Contract–managed:	0 hospitals	0 beds
Totals:	8 hospitals	1578 beds

★0605: SISTERS OF CHARITY OF THE INCARNATE WORD HEALTHCARE SYSTEM (CC)

2600 North Loop West, Houston, TX Zip 77092–8999; tel. 713/681–8877; Sister Christina Murphy, President and Chief Executive Officer

ARKANSAS: MAGNOLIA HOSPITAL (C, 58 beds) 101 Hospital Drive, Magnolia, AR Zip 71753–2416, Mailing Address: Box 629, Zip 71753–0629; tel. 870/235–3000; Kirk Reamey, Administrator

LOUISIANA: NATCHITOCHES PARISH HOSPITAL (C, 175 beds) 501 Keyser Avenue, Natchitoches, LA Zip 71457–6036, Mailing Address: P.O. Box 2009, Zip 71457–2009; tel. 318/352–1200; Eugene Spillman, Executive Director

SCHUMPERT MEDICAL CENTER (O, 486 beds) One St. Mary Place, Shreveport, LA Zip 71101–4399, Mailing Address: P.O. Box 21976, Zip 71120–1076; tel. 318/681–4500; Arthur A. Gonzalez, Dr.PH, President and Chief Executive Officer

ST. FRANCES CABRINI HOSPITAL (O, 228 beds) 3330 Masonic Drive, Alexandria, LA Zip 71301–3899; tel. 318/487–1122; Sister Olive Bordelon, Chief Executive Officer

ST. PATRICK HOSPITAL OF LAKE CHARLES (O, 298 beds) 524 South Ryan Street, Lake Charles, LA Zip 70601–5799, Mailing Address: P.O. Box 3401, Zip 70602–3401; tel. 318/436–2511; James E. Gardner Jr., Chief Executive Officer

TEXAS: JASPER MEMORIAL HOSPITAL (L, 54 beds) 1275 Marvin Hancock Drive, Jasper, TX Zip 75951–4995; tel. 409/384–5461; George N. Miller Jr., Administrator

ST. ELIZABETH HOSPITAL (O, 468 beds) 2830 Calder Avenue, Beaumont, TX Zip 77702, Mailing Address: P.O. Box 5405, Zip 77726–5405; tel. 409/892–7171; Sister Mary Fatima McCarthy, Administrator

ST. JOHN HOSPITAL (O, 135 beds) 18300 St. John Drive, Nassau Bay, TX Zip 77058; tel. 281/333–5503; Thomas Permetti, Administrator

ST. JOSEPH HOSPITAL (O, 481 beds) 1919 LaBranch Street, Houston, TX Zip 77002; tel. 713/757–1000; Sally E. Jeffcoat, Administrator

ST. MARY HOSPITAL (O, 211 beds) 3600 Gates Boulevard, Port Arthur, TX Zip 77642–3601, Mailing Address: P.O. Box 3696, Zip 77643–3696; tel. 409/985–7431; Jeffrey Webster, Chief Executive Officer

ST. MICHAEL HEALTH CARE CENTER (O, 80 beds) 2600 St. Michael Drive, Texarkana, TX Zip 75503–2372; tel. 903/614–2009; Don A. Beeler, Chief Executive Officer

Owned, leased, sponsored:	9 hospitals	2441 beds
Contract–managed:	2 hospitals	233 beds
Totals:	11 hospitals	2674 beds

For explanation of codes following names, see page B2.
★ Indicates Type III membership in the American Hospital Association.

Section B

5805: SISTERS OF MARY OF THE PRESENTATION HEALTH CORPORATION (CC)

1102 Page Drive S.W., Fargo, ND Zip 58106–0007, Mailing Address: P.O. Box 10007, Zip 58106–0007; tel. 701/237–9290; Aaron Alton, President

ILLINOIS: ST. MARGARET'S HOSPITAL (O, 127 beds) 600 East First Street, Spring Valley, IL Zip 61362–2034; tel. 815/664–5311; Timothy Muntz, President

IOWA: VAN BUREN COUNTY HOSPITAL (C, 40 beds) Highway 1 North, Keosauqua, IA Zip 52565, Mailing Address: P.O. Box 70, Zip 52565–0070; tel. 319/293–3171; Lisa Wagner Schnedler, Administrator

NORTH DAKOTA: PRESENTATION MEDICAL CENTER (O, 102 beds) 213 Second Avenue N.E., Rolla, ND Zip 58367–7153, Mailing Address: P.O. Box 759, Zip 58367–0759; tel. 701/477–3161; Kimber Wraalstad, Chief Executive Officer

ST. ALOISIUS MEDICAL CENTER (O, 165 beds) 325 East Brewster Street, Harvey, ND Zip 58341–1605; tel. 701/324–4651; Ronald J. Volk, President

ST. ANDREW'S HEALTH CENTER (O, 67 beds) 316 Ohmer Street, Bottineau, ND Zip 58318–1018; tel. 701/228–2255; Keith Korman, President

Owned, leased, sponsored:	4 hospitals	461 beds
Contract–managed:	1 hospital	40 beds
Totals:	5 hospitals	501 beds

★5185: SISTERS OF MERCY HEALTH SYSTEM–ST. LOUIS (CC)

2039 North Geyer Road, Saint Louis, MO Zip 63131–0902, Mailing Address: P.O. Box 31902, Zip 63131–0902; tel. 314/965–6100; Sister Mary Roch Rocklage, President and Chief Executive Officer

ARKANSAS: CARROLL REGIONAL MEDICAL CENTER (O, 38 beds) 214 Carter Street, Berryville, AR Zip 72616–4303; tel. 870/423–3355; J. Rudy Darling, President and Chief Executive Officer

H.S.C. MEDICAL CENTER (O, 74 beds) 1001 Schneider Drive, Malvern, AR Zip 72104–4828; tel. 501/337–4911; Jeff Curtis, President and Chief Executive Officer

HARBOR VIEW MERCY HOSPITAL (O, 80 beds) 10301 Mayo Road, Fort Smith, AR Zip 72903–1631, Mailing Address: P.O. Box 17000, Zip 72917–7000; tel. 501/484–5550; Ron Summerhill, Administrator

MERCY HOSPITAL OF SCOTT COUNTY (O, 127 beds) Highways 71 and 80, Waldron, AR Zip 72958–9984, Mailing Address: Box 2230, Zip 72958–2230; tel. 501/637–4135; Sister Mary Alvera Simon, Administrator

MERCY HOSPITAL–TURNER MEMORIAL (O, 39 beds) 801 West River Street, Ozark, AR Zip 72949–3000; tel. 501/667–4138; John C. Neal, Administrator

NORTH LOGAN MERCY HOSPITAL (O, 16 beds) 500 East Academy, Paris, AR Zip 72855–4099; tel. 501/963–6101; Jim L. Maddox, Chief Administrative Officer

ST. EDWARD MERCY MEDICAL CENTER (O, 357 beds) 7301 Rogers Avenue, Fort Smith, AR Zip 72903–4189, Mailing Address: P.O. Box 17000, Zip 72917–7000; tel. 501/484–6000; Michael L. Morgan, President and Chief Executive Officer

ST. JOSEPH'S REGIONAL HEALTH CENTER (O, 278 beds) 300 Werner Street, Hot Springs, AR Zip 71913–6448; tel. 501/622–1000; Randall J. Fale, FACHE, President and Chief Executive Officer

ST. MARY–ROGERS MEMORIAL HOSPITAL (O, 102 beds) 1200 West Walnut Street, Rogers, AR Zip 72756–3599; tel. 501/636–0200; Michael J. Packnett, President and Chief Executive Officer

ILLINOIS: ST. CLEMENT HEALTH SERVICES (O, 105 beds) One St. Clement Boulevard, Red Bud, IL Zip 62278–1194; tel. 618/282–3831; Michael Thomas McManus, President

KANSAS: MERCY HEALTH SYSTEM OF KANSAS (O, 105 beds) 821 Burke Street, Fort Scott, KS Zip 66701–2497; tel. 316/223–2200; Susan Barrett, President and Chief Executive Officer

MERCY HOSPITALS OF KANSAS (O, 58 beds) 800 West Myrtle Street, Independence, KS Zip 67301–3240, Mailing Address: P.O. Box 388, Zip 67301–0388; tel. 316/331–2200; Susan Barrett, President and Chief Executive Officer

MISSOURI: ALEXIAN BROTHERS HOSPITAL (O, 203 beds) 3933 South Broadway, Saint Louis, MO Zip 63118–9984; tel. 314/865–3333; Glenn Appelbaum, Senior Vice President

BREECH MEDICAL CENTER (O, 35 beds) 325 Harwood Avenue, Lebanon, MO Zip 65536–2317, Mailing Address: P.O. Box N., Zip 65536–2317; tel. 417/532–2136; Gary W. Pulsipher, Chief Executive Officer

ST. ANTHONY'S MEDICAL CENTER (O, 674 beds) 10010 Kennerly Road, Saint Louis, MO Zip 63128–2185; tel. 314/525–1000; David P. Seifert, President

ST. JOHN'S MERCY MEDICAL CENTER (O, 913 beds) 615 South New Ballas Road, Saint Louis, MO Zip 63141–8277; tel. 314/569–6000; Mark Weber, FACHE, President

ST. JOHN'S REGIONAL HEALTH CENTER (O, 758 beds) 1235 East Cherokee Street, Springfield, MO Zip 65804–2263; tel. 417/885–2000; Allen L. Shockley, President and Chief Executive Officer

ST. LUKE'S HOSPITAL (O, 369 beds) 232 South Woods Mill Road, Chesterfield, MO Zip 63017–3480; tel. 314/434–1500; George Tucker, M.D., President

OKLAHOMA: MERCY HEALTH CENTER (O, 326 beds) 4300 West Memorial Road, Oklahoma City, OK Zip 73120–8362; tel. 405/755–1515; Bruce F. Buchanan, FACHE, President and Chief Executive Officer

MERCY MEMORIAL HEALTH CENTER (O, 199 beds) 1011 14th Street N.W., Ardmore, OK Zip 73401–1889; tel. 405/223–5400; Bobby G. Thompson, President and Chief Executive Officer

ST. MARY'S MERCY HOSPITAL (O, 137 beds) 305 South Fifth Street, Enid, OK Zip 73701–5899, Mailing Address: Box 232, Zip 73702–0232; tel. 580/233–6100; Frank Lopez, FACHE, President and Chief Executive Officer

TEXAS: MERCY REGIONAL MEDICAL CENTER (O, 320 beds) 1515 Logan Avenue, Laredo, TX Zip 78040–4617, Mailing Address: Drawer 2068, Zip 78044–2068; tel. 956/718–6222; Mark S. Stauder, President and Chief Executive Officer

Owned, leased, sponsored:	22 hospitals	5313 beds
Contract–managed:	0 hospitals	0 beds
Totals:	22 hospitals	5313 beds

6015: SISTERS OF MERCY OF THE AMERICAS–REGIONAL COMMUNITY OF BALTIMORE (CC)

1300 Northern Parkway, Baltimore, MD Zip 21239, Mailing Address: P.O. Box 11448, Zip 21239; tel. 410/435–4400; Sister Margaret Beatty, President

GEORGIA: ST. JOSEPH'S HOSPITAL (O, 305 beds) 11705 Mercy Boulevard, Savannah, GA Zip 31419–1791; tel. 912/927–5404; Paul P. Hinchey, President and Chief Executive Officer

MARYLAND: MERCY MEDICAL CENTER (O, 218 beds) 301 St. Paul Place, Baltimore, MD Zip 21202–2165; tel. 410/332–9000; Sister Helen Amos, President and Chief Executive Officer

Owned, leased, sponsored:	2 hospitals	523 beds
Contract–managed:	0 hospitals	0 beds
Totals:	2 hospitals	523 beds

★5275: SISTERS OF PROVIDENCE HEALTH SYSTEM (CC)

520 Pike Street, Seattle, WA Zip 98101, Mailing Address: P.O. Box 11038, Zip 98111–9038; tel. 206/464–3355; Henry G. Walker, President and Chief Executive Officer

ALASKA: PROVIDENCE ALASKA MEDICAL CENTER (O, 222 beds) 3200 Providence Drive, Anchorage, AK Zip 99508, Mailing Address: P.O. Box 196604, Zip 99519–6604; tel. 907/562–2211; Gene L. O'Hara, Administrator

PROVIDENCE KODIAK ISLAND MEDICAL CENTER (L, 44 beds) 1915 East Rezanof Drive, Kodiak, AK Zip 99615; tel. 907/486–3281; Phillip E. Cline, Administrator

PROVIDENCE SEWARD MEDICAL CENTER (L, 20 beds) 417 First Avenue, Seward, AK Zip 99664, Mailing Address: P.O. Box 365, Zip 99664–0365; tel. 907/224–5205; Gary Hughes, Administrator

For explanation of codes following names, see page B2.
★ Indicates Type III membership in the American Hospital Association.

CALIFORNIA: PROVIDENCE HOLY CROSS MEDICAL CENTER (O, 257 beds) 15031 Rinaldi Street, Mission Hills, CA Zip 91345–1285; tel. 818/365–8051; Michael J. Madden, Chief Executive Los Angeles Service Area

PROVIDENCE SAINT JOSEPH MEDICAL CENTER (O, 423 beds) 501 South Buena Vista Street, Burbank, CA Zip 91505–4866; tel. 818/843–5111; Michael J. Madden, Chief Executive Los Angeles Service Area

OREGON: PROVIDENCE MEDFORD MEDICAL CENTER (O, 140 beds) 1111 Crater Lake Avenue, Medford, OR Zip 97504–6241; tel. 541/732–5000; Charles T. Wright, Chief Executive, Southern Oregon Service Area

PROVIDENCE MILWAUKIE HOSPITAL (O, 56 beds) 10150 S.E. 32nd Avenue, Milwaukie, OR Zip 97222–6593; tel. 503/513–8300; Janice Burger, Operations Administrator

PROVIDENCE NEWBERG HOSPITAL (O, 35 beds) 501 Villa Road, Newberg, OR Zip 97132; tel. 503/537–1555; Mark W. Meinert, CHE, Chief Executive, Yamhill Service Area

PROVIDENCE PORTLAND MEDICAL CENTER (O, 380 beds) 4805 N.E. Glisan Street, Portland, OR Zip 97213–2967; tel. 503/215–1111; David T. Underriner, Operations Administrator

PROVIDENCE SEASIDE HOSPITAL (L, 26 beds) 725 South Wahanna Road, Seaside, OR Zip 97138–7735; tel. 503/717–7000; Ronald Swanson, Chief Executive North Coast Service Area

PROVIDENCE ST. VINCENT MEDICAL CENTER (O, 442 beds) 9205 S.W. Barnes Road, Portland, OR Zip 97225–6661; tel. 503/216–1234; Donald Elsom, Operations Administrator

WASHINGTON: MARK REED HOSPITAL (C, 7 beds) 322 South Birch Street, McCleary, WA Zip 98557; tel. 360/495–3244; Jean E. Roberts, Administrator

MORTON GENERAL HOSPITAL (C, 50 beds) 521 Adams Street, Morton, WA Zip 98356, Mailing Address: Drawer C., Zip 98356–0019; tel. 360/496–5112; Mike Lee, Superintendent

PROVIDENCE CENTRALIA HOSPITAL (O, 206 beds) 914 South Scheuber Road, Centralia, WA Zip 98531; tel. 360/736–2803; Mitzi VandeWege, Interim Administrator

PROVIDENCE GENERAL MEDICAL CENTER (O, 311 beds) 1321 Colby Street, Everett, WA Zip 98206, Mailing Address: P.O. Box 1067, Zip 98206–1067; tel. 425/261–2000; Mel Pyne, Administrator

PROVIDENCE SEATTLE MEDICAL CENTER (O, 334 beds) 500 17th Avenue, Seattle, WA Zip 98122, Mailing Address: P.O. Box 34008, Zip 98124–1008; tel. 206/320–2000; Nancy A. Giunto, Operations Administrator

PROVIDENCE ST. PETER HOSPITAL (O, 327 beds) 413 Lilly Road N.E., Olympia, WA Zip 98506–5116; tel. 360/491–9480; C. Scott Bond, Administrator

PROVIDENCE TOPPENISH HOSPITAL (O, 48 beds) 502 West Fourth Avenue, Toppenish, WA Zip 98948, Mailing Address: P.O. Box 672, Zip 98948–0672; tel. 509/865–3105; Steve Burdick, Administrator

PROVIDENCE YAKIMA MEDICAL CENTER (O, 190 beds) 110 South Ninth Avenue, Yakima, WA Zip 98902–3397; tel. 509/575–5000; Richard Brown, Operations Administrator

Owned, leased, sponsored:	17 hospitals	3461 beds
Contract–managed:	2 hospitals	57 beds
Totals:	19 hospitals	3518 beds

★5345: SISTERS OF ST. FRANCIS HEALTH SERVICES, INC. (CC)
1515 Dragoon Trail, Mishawaka, IN Zip 46546–1290, Mailing Address: P.O. Box 1290, Zip 46546–1290; tel. 219/256–3935; Kevin D. Leahy, President and Chief Executive Officer

ILLINOIS: ST. JAMES HOSPITAL AND HEALTH CENTERS (O, 332 beds) 1423 Chicago Road, Chicago Heights, IL Zip 60411–3483; tel. 708/756–1000; Peter J. Murphy, President and Chief Executive Officer

INDIANA: SAINT ANTHONY MEMORIAL HEALTH CENTERS (O, 162 beds) 301 West Homer Street, Michigan City, IN Zip 46360–4358; tel. 219/879–8511; Bruce E. Rampage, President and Chief Executive Officer

SAINT MARGARET MERCY HEALTHCARE CENTERS (O, 624 beds) 5454 Hohman Avenue, Hammond, IN Zip 46320–1999; tel. 219/933–2074; Eugene C. Diamond, President and Chief Executive Officer

ST. ELIZABETH MEDICAL CENTER (O, 205 beds) 1501 Hartford Street, Lafayette, IN Zip 47904–2126, Mailing Address: Box 7501, Zip 47903–7501; tel. 765/423–6011; Douglas W. Eberle, President and Chief Executive Officer

ST. FRANCIS HOSPITAL AND HEALTH CENTERS (O, 417 beds) 1600 Albany Street, Beech Grove, IN Zip 46107–1593; tel. 317/787–3311; Robert J. Brody, President and Chief Executive Officer

Owned, leased, sponsored:	5 hospitals	1740 beds
Contract–managed:	0 hospitals	0 beds
Totals:	5 hospitals	1740 beds

★0133: SISTERS OF ST. JOSEPH HEALTH SYSTEM (CC)
455 East Eisenhower Parkway, 300, Ann Arbor, MI Zip 48108–3324; tel. 313/741–1160; John S. Lore, President and Chief Executive Officer

MICHIGAN: BORGESS MEDICAL CENTER (O, 390 beds) 1521 Gull Road, Kalamazoo, MI Zip 49001–1640; tel. 616/226–4800; Randall Stasik, President and Chief Executive Officer

DETROIT RIVERVIEW HOSPITAL (O, 262 beds) 7733 East Jefferson Avenue, Detroit, MI Zip 48214–2598; tel. 313/499–4000; Richard T. Young, President

GENESYS REGIONAL MEDICAL CENTER (O, 386 beds) One Genesys Parkway, Grand Blanc, MI Zip 48439–8066; tel. 810/606–6600; Elliot Joseph, President and Chief Executive Officer

HOLY CROSS HOSPITAL (O, 161 beds) 4777 East Outer Drive, Detroit, MI Zip 48234–0401; tel. 313/369–9100; Michael F. Breen, President

LEE MEMORIAL HOSPITAL (O, 47 beds) 420 West High Street, Dowagiac, MI Zip 49047–1907; tel. 616/782–8681; Fritz Fahrenbacher, Chief Executive Officer

MACOMB HOSPITAL CENTER (O, 296 beds) 11800 East Twelve Mile Road, Warren, MI Zip 48093–3494; tel. 810/573–5000; John E. Knox, President

RIVER DISTRICT HOSPITAL (O, 68 beds) 4100 South River Road, East China, MI Zip 48054; tel. 810/329–7111; Frank W. Poma, President

ST. JOHN HOSPITAL AND MEDICAL CENTER (O, 662 beds) 22101 Moross Road, Detroit, MI Zip 48236–2172; tel. 313/343–4000; Timothy J. Grajewski, President and Chief Executive Officer

ST. JOHN HEALTH SYSTEM, OAKLAND HOSPITAL (O, 166 beds) 27351 Dequindre, Madison Heights, MI Zip 48071–3499; tel. 248/967–7000; Robert Deputat, President

ST. JOHN HEALTH SYSTEM–SARATOGA CAMPUS (O, 154 beds) 15000 Gratiot Avenue, Detroit, MI Zip 48205–1999; tel. 313/245–1200; Michael F. Breen, President

ST. JOSEPH HEALTH SYSTEM (O, 60 beds) 200 Hemlock Street, Tawas City, MI Zip 48763, Mailing Address: P.O. Box 659, Zip 48764–0659; tel. 517/362–3411; Paul R. Schmidt, CHE, President and Chief Executive Officer

Owned, leased, sponsored:	11 hospitals	2652 beds
Contract–managed:	0 hospitals	0 beds
Totals:	11 hospitals	2652 beds

5955: SISTERS OF THE 3RD FRANCISCAN ORDER (CC)
2500 Grant Boulevard, Syracuse, NY Zip 13208–1713; tel. 315/425–0115; Sister Grace Anne Dillenschneider, General Superior

HAWAII: ST. FRANCIS MEDICAL CENTER (O, 221 beds) 2230 Liliha Street, Honolulu, HI Zip 96817–9979, Mailing Address: P.O. Box 30100, Zip 96820–0100; tel. 808/547–6011; Cynthia Okinaka, Administrator

ST. FRANCIS MEDICAL CENTER–WEST (O, 100 beds) 91–2141 Fort Weaver Road, Ewa Beach, HI Zip 96706; tel. 808/678–7000; Sister Gretchen Gilroy, President and Chief Executive Officer

For explanation of codes following names, see page B2.
★ Indicates Type III membership in the American Hospital Association.

Section B

NEW YORK: ST. ELIZABETH MEDICAL CENTER (O, 176 beds) 2209 Genesee Street, Utica, NY Zip 13501–5999; tel. 315/798–8100; Sister Rose Vincent, President and Chief Executive Officer

ST. JOSEPH'S HOSPITAL HEALTH CENTER (O, 431 beds) 301 Prospect Avenue, Syracuse, NY Zip 13203–1895; tel. 315/448–5111; Theodore M. Pasinski, President

Owned, leased, sponsored:	4 hospitals	928 beds
Contract–managed:	0 hospitals	0 beds
Totals:	4 hospitals	928 beds

5575: SISTERS OF THE HOLY FAMILY OF NAZARETH–SACRED HEART PROVINCE (CC)

310 North River Road, Des Plaines, IL Zip 60016–1211; tel. 847/298–6760; Sister Marie Kielanowicz, Provincial Superior

ILLINOIS: HOLY FAMILY MEDICAL CENTER (O, 183 beds) 100 North River Road, Des Plaines, IL Zip 60016–1255; tel. 847/297–1800; Sister Patricia Ann Koschalke, President and Chief Executive Officer

SAINT MARY OF NAZARETH HOSPITAL CENTER (O, 325 beds) 2233 West Division Street, Chicago, IL Zip 60622–3086; tel. 312/770–2000; Sister Stella Louise, President and Chief Executive Officer

Owned, leased, sponsored:	2 hospitals	508 beds
Contract–managed:	0 hospitals	0 beds
Totals:	2 hospitals	508 beds

★8855: SOLARIS HEALTH SYSTEM (NP)

80 James Street, 2nd Floor, Edison, NJ Zip 08820–3998; tel. 732/632–1500; John P. McGee, President and Chief Executive Officer

NEW JERSEY: JFK JOHNSON REHABILITATION INSTITUTE (O, 92 beds) 65 James Street, Edison, NJ Zip 08818–3059; tel. 732/321–7050; Scott Gebhard, Senior Vice President Operations

JFK MEDICAL CENTER (O, 380 beds) 65 James Street, Edison, NJ Zip 08818–3947; tel. 732/321–7000; John P. McGee, President and Chief Executive Officer

MUHLENBERG REGIONAL MEDICAL CENTER (O, 314 beds) 1200 Park Avenue, Plainfield, NJ Zip 07061; tel. 908/668–2000; John R. Kopicki, President and Chief Executive Officer

Owned, leased, sponsored:	3 hospitals	786 beds
Contract–managed:	0 hospitals	0 beds
Totals:	3 hospitals	786 beds

★0106: SOUTHERN CALIFORNIA HEALTHCARE SYSTEMS (NP)

1300 East Green Street, Pasadena, CA Zip 91106; tel. 626/397–2900; Frederick C. Meyer, President and Chief Executive Officer

CALIFORNIA: BEVERLY HOSPITAL (O, 142 beds) 309 West Beverly Boulevard, Montebello, CA Zip 90640; tel. 213/726–1222; Matthew S. Gerlach, Chief Executive Officer and President

HUNTINGTON EAST VALLEY HOSPITAL (O, 128 beds) 150 West Alosta Avenue, Glendora, CA Zip 91740–4398; tel. 626/335–0231; James W. Maki, Chief Executive Officer

HUNTINGTON MEMORIAL HOSPITAL (O, 520 beds) 100 West California Boulevard, Pasadena, CA Zip 91105, Mailing Address: P.O. Box 7013, Zip 91109–7013; tel. 626/397–5000; Stephen A. Ralph, President and Chief Executive Officer

METHODIST HOSPITAL OF SOUTHERN CALIFORNIA (O, 304 beds) 300 West Huntington Drive, Arcadia, CA Zip 91007, Mailing Address: P.O. Box 60016, Zip 91066–6016; tel. 626/445–4441; Dennis M. Lee, President

VERDUGO HILLS HOSPITAL (O, 112 beds) 1812 Verdugo Boulevard, Glendale, CA Zip 91208; tel. 818/790–7100; Bernard Glossy, President

Owned, leased, sponsored:	5 hospitals	1206 beds
Contract–managed:	0 hospitals	0 beds
Totals:	5 hospitals	1206 beds

★4175: SOUTHERN ILLINOIS HOSPITAL SERVICES (NP)

608 East College Street, Carbondale, IL Zip 62901–3309, Mailing Address: P.O. Box 3988, Zip 62902–3988; tel. 618/457–5200; John J. Buckley Jr., President

ILLINOIS: FERRELL HOSPITAL (O, 51 beds) 1201 Pine Street, Eldorado, IL Zip 62930–1634; tel. 618/273–3361; E. T. Seely, Administrator

FRANKLIN HOSPITAL AND SKILLED NURSING CARE UNIT (L, 117 beds) 201 Bailey Lane, Benton, IL Zip 62812–1999; tel. 618/439–3161; Virgil Hannig, Senior Vice President and Administrator

HERRIN HOSPITAL (O, 80 beds) 201 South 14th Street, Herrin, IL Zip 62948–3631; tel. 618/942–2171; Virgil Hannig, Administrator

MEMORIAL HOSPITAL OF CARBONDALE (O, 132 beds) 405 West Jackson Street, Carbondale, IL Zip 62901–1467, Mailing Address: P.O. Box 10000, Zip 62902–9000; tel. 618/549–0721; George Maroney, Administrator

ST. JOSEPH MEMORIAL HOSPITAL (O, 59 beds) 2 South Hospital Drive, Murphysboro, IL Zip 62966–3333; tel. 618/684–3156; Betty Gaffney, Administrator

UNITED MINE WORKERS OF AMERICA UNION HOSPITAL (O, 32 beds) 507 West St. Louis Street, West Frankfort, IL Zip 62896–1999; tel. 618/932–2155; Virgil Hannig, Senior Vice President and Administrator

Owned, leased, sponsored:	6 hospitals	471 beds
Contract–managed:	0 hospitals	0 beds
Totals:	6 hospitals	471 beds

★4195: SPARTANBURG REGIONAL HEALTHCARE SYSTEM (NP)

101 East Wood Street, Spartanburg, SC Zip 29303–3016; tel. 864/560–6000; Joseph Michael Oddis, President

SOUTH CAROLINA: B.J. WORKMAN MEMORIAL HOSPITAL (O, 32 beds) 751 East Georgia Street, Woodruff, SC Zip 29388, Mailing Address: P.O. Box 699, Zip 29388–0699; tel. 864/476–8122; G. Curtis Walker, R.N., Administrator

SPARTANBURG REGIONAL MEDICAL CENTER (O, 471 beds) 101 East Wood Street, Spartanburg, SC Zip 29303–3016; tel. 864/560–6000; Joseph Michael Oddis, President

Owned, leased, sponsored:	2 hospitals	503 beds
Contract–managed:	0 hospitals	0 beds
Totals:	2 hospitals	503 beds

★5455: SSM HEALTH CARE SYSTEM (CC)

477 North Lindbergh Boulevard, Saint Louis, MO Zip 63141–7813; tel. 314/994–7800; Sister Mary Jean Ryan, President and Chief Executive Officer

ILLINOIS: GOOD SAMARITAN REGIONAL HEALTH CENTER (O, 127 beds) 605 North 12th Street, Mount Vernon, IL Zip 62864–2899; tel. 618/242–4600; Leo F. Childers Jr., FACHE, President

SAINT FRANCIS HOSPITAL AND HEALTH CENTER (O, 254 beds) 12935 South Gregory Street, Blue Island, IL Zip 60406–2470; tel. 708/597–2000; Jay E. Kreuzer, FACHE, President

ST. MARY'S HOSPITAL (C, 276 beds) 400 North Pleasant Avenue, Centralia, IL Zip 62801–3091; tel. 618/532–6731; James W. McDowell, President and Chief Executive Officer

WASHINGTON COUNTY HOSPITAL (C, 53 beds) 705 South Grand Street, Nashville, IL Zip 62263; tel. 618/327–8236; Michael P. Ellermann, Administrator

MISSOURI: ARCADIA VALLEY HOSPITAL (O, 50 beds) Highway 21, Pilot Knob, MO Zip 63663, Mailing Address: P.O. Box 548, Zip 63663–0548; tel. 573/546–3924; H. Clark Duncan, Administrator

For explanation of codes following names, see page B2.
★ Indicates Type III membership in the American Hospital Association.

CARDINAL GLENNON CHILDREN'S HOSPITAL (O, 172 beds) 1465 South Grand Boulevard, Saint Louis, MO Zip 63104–1095; tel. 314/577–5600; Douglas A. Ries, President

DEPAUL HEALTH CENTER (O, 282 beds) 12303 DePaul Drive, Saint Louis, MO Zip 63044–2588; tel. 314/344–6000; Robert G. Porter, President

PIKE COUNTY MEMORIAL HOSPITAL (C, 25 beds) 2305 West Georgia Street, Louisiana, MO Zip 63353–0020; tel. 573/754–5531; Pamm Hancock, Interim Administrator

SSM REHAB (O, 78 beds) 6420 Clayton Road, Suite 600, Saint Louis, MO Zip 63117–1861; tel. 314/768–5300; Melinda Clark, President

ST. FRANCIS HOSPITAL AND HEALTH SERVICES (O, 54 beds) 2016 South Main Street, Maryville, MO Zip 64468–2693; tel. 660/562–2600; Michael Baumgartner, President

ST. JOSEPH HEALTH CENTER (O, 176 beds) 300 First Capitol Drive, Saint Charles, MO Zip 63301–2835; tel. 314/947–5000; Kevin F. Kast, President

ST. JOSEPH HOSPITAL WEST (O, 100 beds) 100 Medical Plaza, Lake Saint Louis, MO Zip 63367–1395; tel. 314/625–5200; Kevin F. Kast, President

ST. JOSEPH HOSPITAL OF KIRKWOOD (O, 213 beds) 525 Couch Avenue, Saint Louis, MO Zip 63122–5594; tel. 314/966–1500; Carla S. Baum, President

ST. MARY'S HEALTH CENTER (O, 411 beds) 6420 Clayton Road, Saint Louis, MO Zip 63117–1811; tel. 314/768–8000; Michael E. Zilm, President

ST. MARYS HEALTH CENTER (O, 151 beds) 100 St. Marys Medical Plaza, Jefferson City, MO Zip 65101–1601; tel. 573/761–7000; John S. Dubis, President

OKLAHOMA: BONE AND JOINT HOSPITAL (O, 89 beds) 1111 North Dewey Avenue, Oklahoma City, OK Zip 73103–2615; tel. 405/552–9100; James A. Hyde, Administrator

HILLCREST HEALTH CENTER (O, 172 beds) 2129 S.W. 59th Street, Oklahoma City, OK Zip 73119–7001; tel. 405/685–6671; Ray Brazier, President

ST. ANTHONY HOSPITAL (O, 408 beds) 1000 North Lee Street, Oklahoma City, OK Zip 73102–1080, Mailing Address: P.O. Box 205, Zip 73101–0205; tel. 405/272–7000; Steven L. Hunter, President

WISCONSIN: ST. CLARE HOSPITAL AND HEALTH SERVICES (O, 76 beds) 707 14th Street, Baraboo, WI Zip 53913–1597; tel. 608/356–5561; David B. Jordahl, FACHE, President

ST. MARYS HOSPITAL MEDICAL CENTER (O, 332 beds) 707 South Mills Street, Madison, WI Zip 53715–0450; tel. 608/251–6100; Gerald W. Lefert, President

Owned, leased, sponsored:	17 hospitals	3145 beds
Contract–managed:	3 hospitals	354 beds
Totals:	20 hospitals	3499 beds

★2255: ST. FRANCIS HEALTH SYSTEM (NP)
4401 Penn Avenue, Pittsburgh, PA Zip 15224–1334; tel. 412/622–4214; Sister M. Rosita Wellinger, President and Chief Executive Officer

PENNSYLVANIA: ST. FRANCIS CENTRAL HOSPITAL (O, 134 beds) 1200 Centre Avenue, Pittsburgh, PA Zip 15219–3594; tel. 412/562–3000; Robin Z. Mohr, Chief Executive Officer

ST. FRANCIS HOSPITAL OF NEW CASTLE (O, 193 beds) 1000 South Mercer Street, New Castle, PA Zip 16101–4673; tel. 724/658–3511; Sister Donna Zwigart, FACHE, Chief Executive Officer

ST. FRANCIS MEDICAL CENTER (O, 885 beds) 400 45th Street, Pittsburgh, PA Zip 15201–1198; tel. 412/622–4343; Sister Florence Brandt, Chief Executive Officer

Owned, leased, sponsored:	3 hospitals	1212 beds
Contract–managed:	0 hospitals	0 beds
Totals:	3 hospitals	1212 beds

★5425: ST. JOSEPH HEALTH SYSTEM (CC)
440 South Batavia Street, Orange, CA Zip 92868–3995, Mailing Address: P.O. Box 14132, Zip 92613–1532; tel. 714/997–7690; Richard Statuto, Chief Executive Officer

CALIFORNIA: MISSION HOSPITAL REGIONAL MEDICAL CENTER (O, 234 beds) 27700 Medical Center Road, Mission Viejo, CA Zip 92691; tel. 714/364–1400; Peter F. Bastone, President and Chief Executive Officer

PETALUMA VALLEY HOSPITAL (L, 84 beds) 400 North McDowell Boulevard, Petaluma, CA Zip 94954–2339; tel. 707/778–1111; Alanna Brogan, Chief Operating Officer

QUEEN OF THE VALLEY HOSPITAL (O, 176 beds) 1000 Trancas Street, Napa, CA Zip 94558, Mailing Address: Box 2340, Zip 94558; tel. 707/252–4411; Dennis Sisto, Acting President and Chief Executive Officer

REDWOOD MEMORIAL HOSPITAL (O, 35 beds) 3300 Renner Drive, Fortuna, CA Zip 95540; tel. 707/725–3361; Neil Martin, President and Chief Executive Officer

SAINT JOSEPH HOSPITAL (O, 102 beds) 2700 Dolbeer Street, Eureka, CA Zip 95501; tel. 707/269–4223; Neil Martin, President and Chief Executive Officer

SANTA ROSA MEMORIAL HOSPITAL (O, 225 beds) 1165 Montgomery Drive, Santa Rosa, CA Zip 95405, Mailing Address: Box 522, Zip 95402; tel. 707/546–3210; Robert H. Fish, President and Chief Executive Officer

ST. MARY REGIONAL MEDICAL CENTER (O, 137 beds) 18300 Highway 18, Apple Valley, CA Zip 92307–0725, Mailing Address: Box 7025, Zip 92307–0725; tel. 760/242–2311; Catherine M. Pelley, President and Chief Executive Officer

ST. JOSEPH HOSPITAL (O, 367 beds) 1100 West Stewart Drive, Orange, CA Zip 92668, Mailing Address: P.O. Box 5600, Zip 92613–5600; tel. 714/633–9111; Larry K. Ainsworth, President and Chief Executive Officer

ST. JUDE MEDICAL CENTER (O, 347 beds) 101 East Valencia Mesa Drive, Fullerton, CA Zip 92635; tel. 714/992–3000; Robert J. Fraschetti, President and Chief Executive Officer

TEXAS: CROSBYTON CLINIC HOSPITAL (C, 35 beds) 710 West Main Street, Crosbyton, TX Zip 79322–2143; tel. 806/675–2382; Michael Johnson, Administrator and Chief Executive Officer

D. M. COGDELL MEMORIAL HOSPITAL (C, 72 beds) 1700 Cogdell Boulevard, Snyder, TX Zip 79549–6198; tel. 915/573–6374; Jeff Reecer, Chief Executive Officer

ST. MARY OF THE PLAINS HOSPITAL (O, 410 beds) 4000 24th Street, Lubbock, TX Zip 79410–1894; tel. 806/796–6000; Charley O. Trimble, President and Chief Executive Officer

SWISHER MEMORIAL HOSPITAL DISTRICT (C, 25 beds) 539 Southeast Second, Tulia, TX Zip 79088–2403, Mailing Address: P.O. Box 808, Zip 79088–0808; tel. 806/995–3581; Tony Staynings, Chief Executive Officer

YOAKUM COUNTY HOSPITAL (C, 24 beds) 412 Mustang Avenue, Denver City, TX Zip 79323–2750, Mailing Address: P.O. Drawer 1130, Zip 79323–1130; tel. 806/592–5484; Edward Rodgers, Chief Executive Officer

Owned, leased, sponsored:	10 hospitals	2117 beds
Contract–managed:	4 hospitals	156 beds
Totals:	14 hospitals	2273 beds

3555: STATE OF HAWAII, DEPARTMENT OF HEALTH (NP)
1250 Punchbowl Street, Honolulu, HI Zip 96813; tel. 808/586–4416; Bertrand Kobayashi, Deputy Director

HAWAII: HILO MEDICAL CENTER (O, 274 beds) 1190 Waianuenue Avenue, Hilo, HI Zip 96720–2095; tel. 808/974–4743; Robert Morris, M.D., Administrator

HONOKAA HOSPITAL (O, 50 beds) Honokaa, HI Mailing Address: P.O. Box 237, Zip 96727–0237; tel. 808/775–7211; Romel Dela Cruz, Administrator

KAU HOSPITAL (O, 21 beds) Pahala, HI Mailing Address: P.O. Box 40, Zip 96777–0040; tel. 808/928–8331; Dawn S. Pung, Administrator

KAUAI VETERANS MEMORIAL HOSPITAL (O, 49 beds) Waimea Canyon Road, Waimea, HI Zip 96796, Mailing Address: P.O. Box 337, Zip 96796–0337; tel. 808/338–9431; Orianna A. Skomoroch, Chief Executive Officer

KOHALA HOSPITAL (O, 26 beds) Kohala, HI Mailing Address: P.O. Box 10, Kapaau, Zip 96755–0010; tel. 808/889–6211; Herbert K. Yim, Administrator

---

For explanation of codes following names, see page B2.
★ Indicates Type III membership in the American Hospital Association.

KONA COMMUNITY HOSPITAL (O, 75 beds) Kealakekua, HI Mailing Address: P.O. Box 69, Zip 96750–0069; tel. 808/322–4429; Joseph C. Wall, Chief Executive Officer

KULA HOSPITAL (O, 105 beds) 204 Kula Highway, Kula, HI Zip 96790–9499; tel. 808/878–1221; Alan G. Lee, Administrator

LANAI COMMUNITY HOSPITAL (O, 14 beds) 628 Seventh Street, Lanai City, HI Zip 96763–0797, Mailing Address: P.O. Box 797, Zip 96763–0797; tel. 808/565–6411; John Schaumburg, Administrator

LEAHI HOSPITAL (O, 192 beds) 3675 Kilauea Avenue, Honolulu, HI Zip 96816; tel. 808/733–8000; Jerry Walker, Administrator

MAUI MEMORIAL HOSPITAL (O, 203 beds) 221 Mahalani Street, Wailuku, HI Zip 96793–2581; tel. 808/244–9056; David W. Patton, Chief Executive Officer

SAMUEL MAHELONA MEMORIAL HOSPITAL (O, 82 beds) 4800 Kawaihau Road, Kapaa, HI Zip 96746–1998; tel. 808/822–4961; Neva M. Olson, Chief Executive Officer

Owned, leased, sponsored:	11 hospitals	1091 beds
Contract–managed:	0 hospitals	0 beds
Totals:	11 hospitals	1091 beds

0805: STORMONT–VAIL HEALTHCARE (NP)
1500 Southwest Tenth Street, Topeka, KS Zip 66604–1353; tel. 785/354–6121; Maynard F. Oliverius, President and Chief Executive Officer

KANSAS: DECHAIRO HOSPITAL (O, 13 beds) First and North Streets, Westmoreland, KS Zip 66549; tel. 913/457–3311; Paula Lauer, Operations Manager

STORMONT–VAIL HEALTHCARE (O, 313 beds) 1500 S.W. Tenth Street, Topeka, KS Zip 66604–1353; tel. 785/354–6000; Maynard F. Oliverius, President and Chief Executive Officer

WAMEGO CITY HOSPITAL (C, 26 beds) 711 Genn Drive, Wamego, KS Zip 66547–1199; tel. 913/456–2295; Lisa J. Freeborn, R.N., Administrator

Owned, leased, sponsored:	2 hospitals	326 beds
Contract–managed:	1 hospital	26 beds
Totals:	3 hospitals	352 beds

●0905: SUMMIT HOSPITAL CORPORATION (IO)
5 Concourse Parkway, Suite 800, Atlanta, GA Zip 30328–6111; tel. 770/392–1454; Ken Couch, President

LOUISIANA: SUMMIT HOSPITAL OF NORTHWEST LOUISIANA (O, 54 beds) 4900 Medical Drive, Bossier City, LA Zip 71112–4596; tel. 318/747–9500; Louise Wiggins, Chief Executive Officer and Administrator

Owned, leased, sponsored:	1 hospital	54 beds
Contract–managed:	0 hospitals	0 beds
Totals:	1 hospital	54 beds

★0030: SUN HEALTH CORPORATION (NP)
13180 North 103rd Drive, Sun City, AZ Zip 85351–3038, Mailing Address: P.O. Box 1278, Zip 85372–1278; tel. 602/876–5301; Leland W. Peterson, President and Chief Executive Officer

ARIZONA: DEL E. WEBB MEMORIAL HOSPITAL (O, 177 beds) 14502 West Meeker Boulevard, Sun City West, AZ Zip 85375–5299, Mailing Address: P.O. Box 5169, Sun City, Zip 85375–5169; tel. 602/214–4000; Thomas C. Dickson, Executive Vice President and Chief Operating Officer

WALTER O. BOSWELL MEMORIAL HOSPITAL (O, 268 beds) 10401 West Thunderbird Boulevard, Sun City, AZ Zip 85351–3092, Mailing Address: P.O. Box 1690, Zip 85372–1690; tel. 602/876–5356; George Perez, Executive Vice President and Chief Operating Officer

Owned, leased, sponsored:	2 hospitals	445 beds
Contract–managed:	0 hospitals	0 beds
Totals:	2 hospitals	445 beds

★8795: SUTTER HEALTH (NP)
2800 L. Street, Sacramento, CA Zip 95816, Mailing Address: P.O. Box 160727, Zip 95816; tel. 916/733–8800; Van R. Johnson, President and Chief Executive Officer

CALIFORNIA: ALTA BATES MEDICAL CENTER–ASHBY CAMPUS (O, 555 beds) 2450 Ashby Avenue, Berkeley, CA Zip 94705; tel. 510/204–4444; George P. Caralis, President and Chief Executive Officer

CALIFORNIA PACIFIC MEDICAL CENTER (O, 520 beds) 2333 Buchanan Street, San Francisco, CA Zip 94115, Mailing Address: P.O. Box 7999, Zip 94120; tel. 415/563–4321; Martin Brotman, M.D., President and Chief Executive Officer

EDEN MEDICAL CENTER (O, 258 beds) 20103 Lake Chabot Road, Castro Valley, CA Zip 94546; tel. 510/537–1234; George Bischalaney, Interim President and Chief Executive Officer

MARIN GENERAL HOSPITAL (O, 110 beds) 250 Bon Air Road, Greenbrae, CA Zip 94904, Mailing Address: Box 8010, San Rafael, Zip 94912–8010; tel. 415/925–7000; Henry J. Buhrmann, President and Chief Executive Officer

MEMORIAL HOSPITALS ASSOCIATION (O, 373 beds) Modesto, CA Mailing Address: P.O. Box 942, Zip 95353; tel. 209/526–4500; David P. Benn, President and Chief Executive Officer

MILLS–PENINSULA HEALTH SERVICES (O, 414 beds) 1783 El Camino Real, Burlingame, CA Zip 94010–3205; tel. 650/696–5400; Robert W. Merwin, Chief Executive Officer

NOVATO COMMUNITY HOSPITAL (O, 28 beds) 1625 Hill Road, Novato, CA Zip 94947, Mailing Address: P.O. Box 1108, Zip 94948; tel. 415/897–3111; Anne Hosfeld, Chief Administrative Officer

SUTTER AMADOR HOSPITAL (O, 85 beds) 810 Court Street, Jackson, CA Zip 95642–2379; tel. 209/223–7500; Scott Stenberg, Chief Executive Officer

SUTTER AUBURN FAITH COMMUNITY HOSPITAL (O, 105 beds) 11815 Education Street, Auburn, CA Zip 95604, Mailing Address: Box 8992, Zip 95604–8992; tel. 916/888–4518; Joel E. Grey, Administrator

SUTTER CENTER FOR PSYCHIATRY (O, 69 beds) 7700 Folsom Boulevard, Sacramento, CA Zip 95826–2608; tel. 916/386–3000; Diane Gail Stewart, Administrator

SUTTER COAST HOSPITAL (O, 47 beds) 800 East Washington Boulevard, Crescent City, CA Zip 95531; tel. 707/464–8511; John E. Menaugh, Chief Executive Officer

SUTTER COMMUNITY HOSPITALS (O, 497 beds) 5151 F. Street, Sacramento, CA Zip 95819–3295; tel. 916/454–3333; Lou Lazatin, Chief Executive Officer

SUTTER DAVIS HOSPITAL (O, 48 beds) 2000 Sutter Place, Davis, CA Zip 95616, Mailing Address: P.O. Box 1617, Zip 95617; tel. 530/756–6440; Lawrence A. Maas, Administrator

SUTTER DELTA MEDICAL CENTER (O, 80 beds) 3901 Lone Tree Way, Antioch, CA Zip 94509; tel. 925/779–7200; Linda Horn, Administrator

SUTTER LAKESIDE HOSPITAL (O, 54 beds) 5176 Hill Road East, Lakeport, CA Zip 95453–6111; tel. 707/262–5001; Paul J. Hensler, Chief Executive Officer

SUTTER MATERNITY AND SURGERY CENTER OF SANTA CRUZ (O, 30 beds) 2900 Chanticleer Avenue, Santa Cruz, CA Zip 95065–1816; tel. 408/477–2200; Iris C. Frank, Administrator

SUTTER MEDICAL CENTER, SANTA ROSA (O, 128 beds) 3325 Chanate Road, Santa Rosa, CA Zip 95404; tel. 707/576–4000; Cliff Coates, Chief Executive Officer

SUTTER MERCED MEDICAL CENTER (O, 180 beds) 301 East 13th Street, Merced, CA Zip 95340–6211; tel. 209/385–7000; Brian S. Bentley, Administrator

SUTTER ROSEVILLE MEDICAL CENTER (O, 183 beds) One Medical Plaza, Roseville, CA Zip 95661–3477; tel. 916/781–1000; Joel E. Grey, Chief Executive Officer

SUTTER SOLANO MEDICAL CENTER (O, 55 beds) 300 Hospital Drive, Vallejo, CA Zip 94589–2517, Mailing Address: P.O. Box 3189, Zip 94589; tel. 707/554–4444; Patrick R. Brady, Administrator

For explanation of codes following names, see page B2.
★ Indicates Type III membership in the American Hospital Association.
● Single hospital health care system

Section B

SUTTER TRACY COMMUNITY HOSPITAL (O, 80 beds) 1420 North Tracy Boulevard, Tracy, CA Zip 95376–3497; tel. 209/835–1500; Gary D. Rapaport, Chief Executive Officer

HAWAII: KAHI MOHALA (O, 88 beds) 91–2301 Fort Weaver Road, Ewa Beach, HI Zip 96706; tel. 808/671–8511; Margi Drue, Administrator

Owned, leased, sponsored:	22 hospitals	3987 beds
Contract–managed:	0 hospitals	0 beds
Totals:	22 hospitals	3987 beds

0039: TARRANT COUNTY HOSPITAL DISTRICT (NP)
1500 South Main Street, Fort Worth, TX Zip 76104–4941; tel. 817/927–1230; Anthony J. Alcini, President and Chief Executive Officer

TEXAS: TARRANT COUNTY HOSPITAL DISTRICT (O, 375 beds) 1500 South Main Street, Fort Worth, TX Zip 76104–4941; tel. 817/921–3431; Anthony J. Alcini, President and Chief Executive Officer

TRINITY SPRINGS PAVILION–EAST (O, 34 beds) 1500 South Main Street, Fort Worth, TX Zip 76104–4917; tel. 817/927–3636; Robert N. Bourassa, Executive Director

Owned, leased, sponsored:	2 hospitals	409 beds
Contract–managed:	0 hospitals	0 beds
Totals:	2 hospitals	409 beds

★0063: TENET HEALTHCARE CORPORATION (IO)
3820 State Street, Santa Barbara, CA Zip 93105, Mailing Address: P.O. Box 31907, Zip 93130; tel. 805/563–7000; Jeffrey Barbakow, Chairman and Chief Executive Officer

ALABAMA: BROOKWOOD MEDICAL CENTER (O, 501 beds) 2010 Brookwood Medical Center Drive, Birmingham, AL Zip 35209; tel. 205/877–1000; Gregory H. Burfitt, President and Chief Executive Officer

LLOYD NOLAND HOSPITAL AND HEALTH SYSTEM (O, 222 beds) 701 Lloyd Noland Parkway, Fairfield, AL Zip 35064–2699; tel. 205/783–5106; Gary M. Glasscock, Administrator

ARIZONA: COMMUNITY HOSPITAL MEDICAL CENTER (O, 59 beds) 6501 North 19th Avenue, Phoenix, AZ Zip 85015–1690; tel. 602/249–3434; Patrick Walz, Chief Executive Officer

MESA GENERAL HOSPITAL MEDICAL CENTER (L, 125 beds) 515 North Mesa Drive, Mesa, AZ Zip 85201–5989; tel. 602/969–9111; J. O. Lewis, Chief Executive Officer

ST. LUKE'S BEHAVIORAL HEALTH CENTER (O, 70 beds) 1800 East Van Buren, Phoenix, AZ Zip 85006–3742; tel. 602/251–8484; Patrick D. Waugh, Chief Executive Officer

ST. LUKE'S MEDICAL CENTER (L, 296 beds) 1800 East Van Buren Street, Phoenix, AZ Zip 85006–3742; tel. 602/251–8100; William W. Webster, Chief Executive Officer

TEMPE ST. LUKE'S HOSPITAL (L, 110 beds) 1500 South Mill Avenue, Tempe, AZ Zip 85281–6699; tel. 602/784–5510; Mary Jo Gregory, Chief Executive Officer

TUCSON GENERAL HOSPITAL (O, 80 beds) 3838 North Campbell Avenue, Tucson, AZ Zip 85719–1497; tel. 520/318–6300; Allan Harrington Jr., Chief Executive Officer

ARKANSAS: CENTRAL ARKANSAS HOSPITAL (O, 173 beds) 1200 South Main Street, Searcy, AR Zip 72143–7397; tel. 501/278–3131; David C. Laffoon, CHE, Chief Executive Officer

METHODIST HOSPITAL OF JONESBORO (O, 104 beds) 3024 Stadium Boulevard, Jonesboro, AR Zip 72401–7493; tel. 870/972–7000; Philip H. Walkley Jr., Chief Executive Officer

NATIONAL PARK MEDICAL CENTER (O, 166 beds) 1910 Malvern Avenue, Hot Springs, AR Zip 71901–7799; tel. 501/321–1000; Jerry D. Mabry, Executive Director

SAINT MARY'S REGIONAL MEDICAL CENTER (O, 151 beds) 1808 West Main Street, Russellville, AR Zip 72801–2724; tel. 501/968–2841; Mike McCoy, Chief Executive Officer

CALIFORNIA: ALVARADO HOSPITAL MEDICAL CENTER (O, 144 beds) 6655 Alvarado Road, San Diego, CA Zip 92120–5298; tel. 619/287–3270; Barry G. Weinbaum, Chief Executive Officer

BROTMAN MEDICAL CENTER (O, 240 beds) 3828 Delmas Terrace, Culver City, CA Zip 90231–2459, Mailing Address: Box 2459, Zip 90231–2459; tel. 310/836–7000; John V. Fenton, Chief Executive Officer

CENTINELA HOSPITAL MEDICAL CENTER (O, 375 beds) 555 East Hardy Street, Inglewood, CA Zip 90301–4073, Mailing Address: Box 720, Zip 90307–0720; tel. 310/673–4660; John Smithhisler, CHE, Chief Executive Officer

CENTURY CITY HOSPITAL (L, 156 beds) 2070 Century Park East, Los Angeles, CA Zip 90067; tel. 310/553–6211; John R. Nickens III, Chief Executive Officer

CHAPMAN MEDICAL CENTER (L, 40 beds) 2601 East Chapman Avenue, Orange, CA Zip 92869; tel. 714/633–0011; Maxine T. Cooper, Chief Executive Officer

COASTAL COMMUNITIES HOSPITAL (O, 177 beds) 2701 South Bristol Street, Santa Ana, CA Zip 92704–9911, Mailing Address: P.O. Box 5240, Zip 92704–0240; tel. 714/754–5454; Kent G. Clayton, Chief Executive Officer

COMMUNITY HOSPITAL OF HUNTINGTON PARK (L, 226 beds) 2623 East Slauson Avenue, Huntington Park, CA Zip 90255; tel. 213/583–1931; Charles Martinez, Ph.D., Chief Executive Officer

COMMUNITY HOSPITAL OF LOS GATOS (L, 153 beds) 815 Pollard Road, Los Gatos, CA Zip 95030; tel. 408/378–6131; Truman L. Gates, Chief Executive Officer

DESERT REGIONAL MEDICAL CENTER (L, 348 beds) 1150 North Indian Canyon Drive, Palm Springs, CA Zip 92262, Mailing Address: Box 2739, Zip 92263; tel. 760/323–6511; Robert A. Minkin, CHE, President and Chief Executive Officer

DOCTORS HOSPITAL OF MANTECA (O, 73 beds) 1205 East North Street, Manteca, CA Zip 95336, Mailing Address: Box 191, Zip 95336; tel. 209/823–3111; Patrick W. Rafferty, Administrator

DOCTORS MEDICAL CENTER (O, 368 beds) 1441 Florida Avenue, Modesto, CA Zip 95350–4418, Mailing Address: P.O. Box 4138, Zip 95352–4138; tel. 209/578–1211; Chris DiCicco, Chief Executive Officer

DOCTORS MEDICAL CENTER–PINOLE CAMPUS (L, 137 beds) 2151 Appian Way, Pinole, CA Zip 94564; tel. 510/724–5000; Gary Sloan, Chief Executive Officer

DOCTORS MEDICAL CENTER–SAN PABLO CAMPUS (L, 286 beds) 2000 Vale Road, San Pablo, CA Zip 94806; tel. 510/235–7000; Gary Sloan, Chief Executive Officer

ENCINO–TARZANA REGIONAL MEDICAL CENTER ENCINO CAMPUS (L, 165 beds) 16237 Ventura Boulevard, Encino, CA Zip 91436–2201; tel. 818/995–5000

FOUNTAIN VALLEY REGIONAL HOSPITAL AND MEDICAL CENTER (O, 396 beds) 17100 Euclid at Warner, Fountain Valley, CA Zip 92708; tel. 714/966–7200; Timothy Smith, President and Chief Executive Officer

GARDEN GROVE HOSPITAL AND MEDICAL CENTER (O, 167 beds) 12601 Garden Grove Boulevard, Garden Grove, CA Zip 92843–1959; tel. 714/741–2700; Timothy Smith, President and Chief Executive Officer

GARFIELD MEDICAL CENTER (O, 207 beds) 525 North Garfield Avenue, Monterey Park, CA Zip 91754; tel. 626/573–2222; Philip A. Cohen, Chief Executive Officer

GREATER EL MONTE COMMUNITY HOSPITAL (O, 113 beds) 1701 South Santa Anita Avenue, South El Monte, CA Zip 91733–9918; tel. 626/579–7777; Elizabeth A. Primeaux, Chief Executive Officer

IRVINE MEDICAL CENTER (L, 153 beds) 16200 Sand Canyon Avenue, Irvine, CA Zip 92618–3714; tel. 714/753–2000; Richard H. Robinson, Chief Executive Officer

JOHN F. KENNEDY MEMORIAL HOSPITAL (O, 130 beds) 47–111 Monroe Street, Indio, CA Zip 92201, Mailing Address: P.O. Drawer LLLL, Zip 92202–2558; tel. 760/347–6191; Michael A. Rembis, FACHE, Chief Executive Officer

LAKEWOOD REGIONAL MEDICAL CENTER (O, 148 beds) 3700 East South Street, Lakewood, CA Zip 90712; tel. 562/531–2550; Gustavo A. Valdespino, Chief Executive Officer

---

For explanation of codes following names, see page B2.
★ Indicates Type III membership in the American Hospital Association.

LOS ALAMITOS MEDICAL CENTER (O, 173 beds) 3751 Katella Avenue, Los Alamitos, CA Zip 90720; tel. 562/598-1311; Gustavo A. Valdespino, Chief Executive Officer

MIDWAY HOSPITAL MEDICAL CENTER (O, 141 beds) 5925 San Vicente Boulevard, Los Angeles, CA Zip 90019-6696; tel. 213/938-3161; John V. Fenton, Chief Executive Officer

MONTEREY PARK HOSPITAL (O, 93 beds) 900 South Atlantic Boulevard, Monterey Park, CA Zip 91754; tel. 626/570-9000; Dan F. Ausman, Chief Executive Officer

NORTH HOLLYWOOD MEDICAL CENTER (O, 150 beds) 12629 Riverside Drive, North Hollywood, CA Zip 91607-3495; tel. 818/980-9200; Sonja Hagel, Chief Executive Officer

PLACENTIA-LINDA HOSPITAL (O, 114 beds) 1301 Rose Drive, Placentia, CA Zip 92870; tel. 714/993-2000; Maxine T. Cooper, Chief Executive Officer

REDDING MEDICAL CENTER (O, 162 beds) 1100 Butte Street, Redding, CA Zip 96001-0853, Mailing Address: Box 496072, Zip 96049-6072; tel. 530/244-5454; Steve Schmidt, Chief Executive Officer

SAN DIMAS COMMUNITY HOSPITAL (O, 93 beds) 1350 West Covina Boulevard, San Dimas, CA Zip 91773-0308; tel. 909/599-6811; Patrick A. Petre, Chief Executive Officer

SAN RAMON REGIONAL MEDICAL CENTER (O, 95 beds) 6001 Norris Canyon Road, San Ramon, CA Zip 94583; tel. 925/275-9200; Philip P. Gustafson, Administrator

SANTA ANA HOSPITAL MEDICAL CENTER (L, 69 beds) 1901 North Fairview Street, Santa Ana, CA Zip 92706; tel. 714/554-1653; Kent G. Clayton, Chief Executive Officer

SIERRA VISTA REGIONAL MEDICAL CENTER (O, 117 beds) 1010 Murray Street, San Luis Obispo, CA Zip 93405, Mailing Address: Box 1367, Zip 93406-1367; tel. 805/546-7600; Harold E. Chilton, Chief Executive Officer

ST. LUKE MEDICAL CENTER (O, 120 beds) 2632 East Washington Boulevard, Pasadena, CA Zip 91107-1994; tel. 626/797-1141; Mark H. Uffer, Chief Executive Officer

SUBURBAN MEDICAL CENTER (L, 130 beds) 16453 South Colorado Avenue, Paramount, CA Zip 90723; tel. 562/531-3110; Gustavo Valdespino, Chief Executive Officer

TWIN CITIES COMMUNITY HOSPITAL (O, 84 beds) 1100 Las Tablas Road, Templeton, CA Zip 93465; tel. 805/434-3500; Harold E. Chilton, Chief Executive Officer

USC UNIVERSITY HOSPITAL (L, 247 beds) 1500 San Pablo Street, Los Angeles, CA Zip 90033-4585; tel. 213/342-8482; Lee Domanico, Chief Executive Officer

UNIVERSITY OF SOUTHERN CALIFORNIA-KENNETH NORRIS JR. CANCER HOSPITAL (O, 60 beds) 1441 Eastlake Avenue, Los Angeles, CA Zip 90033-1085, Mailing Address: P.O. Box 33804, Zip 90033-3804; tel. 213/764-3000; Adrianne Black Bass, Administrator

VALLEY COMMUNITY HOSPITAL (L, 70 beds) 505 East Plaza Drive, Santa Maria, CA Zip 93454-9943; tel. 805/925-0935; William C. Rasmussen, Administrator

WESTERN MEDICAL CENTER HOSPITAL ANAHEIM (O, 171 beds) 1025 South Anaheim Boulevard, Anaheim, CA Zip 92805; tel. 714/533-6220; Doug Norris, Chief Operating Officer

WESTERN MEDICAL CENTER-SANTA ANA (O, 288 beds) 1001 North Tustin Avenue, Santa Ana, CA Zip 92705-3502; tel. 714/835-3555; Richard E. Butler, Chief Executive Officer

WHITTIER HOSPITAL MEDICAL CENTER (O, 172 beds) 9080 Colima Road, Whittier, CA Zip 90605; tel. 562/907-1541; Sandra M. Chester, Chief Executive Officer

FLORIDA: CORAL GABLES HOSPITAL (O, 205 beds) 3100 Douglas Road, Coral Gables, FL Zip 33134-6990; tel. 305/445-8461; Martha Garcia, Chief Executive Officer

DELRAY MEDICAL CENTER (O, 224 beds) 5352 Linton Boulevard, Delray Beach, FL Zip 33484-6580; tel. 561/498-4440; Mitchell S. Feldman, Chief Executive Officer

FAIR OAKS HOSPITAL (O, 102 beds) 5440 Linton Boulevard, Delray Beach, FL Zip 33484-6578; tel. 561/495-1000; Bill Russell, Chief Operating Officer and Administrator

FLORIDA MEDICAL CENTER HOSPITAL (O, 459 beds) 5000 West Oakland Park Boulevard, Fort Lauderdale, FL Zip 33313-1585; tel. 954/735-6000; Denny De Narvaez, Chief Executive Officer

HIALEAH HOSPITAL (O, 256 beds) 651 East 25th Street, Hialeah, FL Zip 33013-3878; tel. 305/693-6100; Clifford J. Bauer, Chief Executive Officer

HOLLYWOOD MEDICAL CENTER (O, 238 beds) 3600 Washington Street, Hollywood, FL Zip 33021-8216; tel. 954/966-4500; Holly Lerner, Chief Executive Officer

MEMORIAL HOSPITAL OF TAMPA (O, 138 beds) 2901 Swann Avenue, Tampa, FL Zip 33609-4057; tel. 813/873-6400; Charles F. Scott, President and Chief Executive Officer

NORTH BAY MEDICAL CENTER (O, 122 beds) 6600 Madison Street, New Port Richey, FL Zip 34652-1900; tel. 813/842-8468; Dennis A. Taylor, Administrator

NORTH RIDGE MEDICAL CENTER (O, 391 beds) 5757 North Dixie Highway, Fort Lauderdale, FL Zip 33334-4182, Mailing Address: P.O. Box 23160, Zip 33307; tel. 954/776-6000; Emil P. Miller, Chief Executive Officer

NORTH SHORE MEDICAL CENTER (O, 320 beds) 1100 N.W. 95th Street, Miami, FL Zip 33150-2098; tel. 305/835-6000; Steven M. Klein, President and Chief Executive Officer

PALM BEACH GARDENS MEDICAL CENTER (L, 204 beds) 3360 Burns Road, Palm Beach Gardens, FL Zip 33410-4304; tel. 561/622-1411; Clint Matthews, Chief Executive Officer

PALMETTO GENERAL HOSPITAL (O, 360 beds) 2001 West 68th Street, Hialeah, FL Zip 33016-1898; tel. 305/823-5000; Ron Stern, Chief Executive Officer

PALMS OF PASADENA HOSPITAL (O, 267 beds) 1501 Pasadena Avenue South, Saint Petersburg, FL Zip 33707-3798; tel. 813/381-1000; John D. Bartlett, Chief Executive Officer

PARKWAY REGIONAL MEDICAL CENTER (O, 392 beds) 160 N.W. 170th Street, North Miami Beach, FL Zip 33169-5576; tel. 305/654-5050; Stephen M. Patz, Chief Executive Officer

PINECREST REHABILITATION HOSPITAL (O, 90 beds) 5360 Linton Boulevard, Delray Beach, FL Zip 33484-6538; tel. 561/495-0400; Paul D. Echelard, Administrator

SEVEN RIVERS COMMUNITY HOSPITAL (O, 128 beds) 6201 North Suncoast Boulevard, Crystal River, FL Zip 34428-6712; tel. 352/795-6560; Michael L. Collins, Chief Executive Officer

TOWN AND COUNTRY HOSPITAL (O, 148 beds) 6001 Webb Road, Tampa, FL Zip 33615-3291; tel. 813/885-6666; Charles F. Scott, President

WEST BOCA MEDICAL CENTER (O, 150 beds) 21644 State Road 7, Boca Raton, FL Zip 33428-1899; tel. 561/488-8000; Richard Gold, Chief Executive Officer

GEORGIA: GEORGIA BAPTIST MEDICAL CENTER (O, 450 beds) 303 Parkway Drive N.E., Atlanta, GA Zip 30312-1239; tel. 404/265-4000; James E. Lathren, President and Chief Executive Officer

NORTH FULTON REGIONAL HOSPITAL (L, 167 beds) 3000 Hospital Boulevard, Roswell, GA Zip 30076-9930; tel. 770/751-2500; Frederick R. Bailey, Chief Executive Officer

SPALDING REGIONAL HOSPITAL (O, 160 beds) 601 South Eighth Street, Griffin, GA Zip 30224-4294, Mailing Address: P.O. Drawer V., Zip 30224-1168; tel. 770/228-2721; Phil Shaw, Executive Director

SYLVAN GROVE HOSPITAL (L, 28 beds) 1050 McDonough Road, Jackson, GA Zip 30233-1599; tel. 770/775-7861; Mike Patterson, Administrator

INDIANA: CULVER UNION HOSPITAL (O, 98 beds) 1710 Lafayette Road, Crawfordsville, IN Zip 47933-1099; tel. 765/362-2800; Gregory D. Starnes, Chief Executive Officer

WINONA MEMORIAL HOSPITAL (O, 159 beds) 3232 North Meridian Street, Indianapolis, IN Zip 46208-4693; tel. 317/924-3392; Keith R. King, Chief Executive Officer

LOUISIANA: DOCTORS HOSPITAL OF JEFFERSON (L, 138 beds) 4320 Houma Boulevard, Metairie, LA Zip 70006-2973; tel. 504/456-5800; Gerald L. Parton, Chief Executive Officer

For explanation of codes following names, see page B2.
★ Indicates Type III membership in the American Hospital Association.

Section B

JO ELLEN SMITH MEDICAL CENTER (O, 186 beds) 4444 General Meyer Avenue, New Orleans, LA Zip 70131–3595; tel. 504/363–7011; Rene Goux, Chief Executive Officer

KENNER REGIONAL MEDICAL CENTER (O, 213 beds) 180 West Esplanade Avenue, Kenner, LA Zip 70065–6001; tel. 504/468–8600; Deborah C. Keel, Chief Executive Officer

MEADOWCREST HOSPITAL (O, 181 beds) 2500 Belle Chase Highway, Gretna, LA Zip 70056–7196; tel. 504/392–3131; Jaime A. Wesolowski, Chief Executive Officer

MEMORIAL MEDICAL CENTER–BAPTIST CAMPUS (O, 634 beds) New Orleans, LA Randall L. Hoover, Chief Executive Officer

MEMORIAL MEDICAL CENTER–MERCY CAMPUS (O, 272 beds) 301 North Jefferson Davis Parkway, New Orleans, LA Zip 70119–5397; tel. 504/483–5000; Randall L. Hoover, Chief Executive Officer

MINDEN MEDICAL CENTER (O, 121 beds) 1 Medical Plaza, Minden, LA Zip 71055–3330; tel. 318/377–2321; George E. French III, Chief Executive Officer

NORTH SHORE PSYCHIATRIC HOSPITAL (O, 58 beds) 104 Medical Center Drive, Slidell, LA Zip 70461–7838; tel. 504/646–5500

NORTHSHORE REGIONAL MEDICAL CENTER (L, 147 beds) 100 Medical Center Drive, Slidell, LA Zip 70461–8572; tel. 504/649–7070; George J. Saucier, Chief Executive Officer

ST. CHARLES GENERAL HOSPITAL (O, 173 beds) 3700 St. Charles Avenue, New Orleans, LA Zip 70115–4680; tel. 504/899–7441; Lynn C. Orfgen, Chief Executive Officer

MASSACHUSETTS: SAINT VINCENT HOSPITAL (O, 369 beds) 25 Winthrop Street, Worcester, MA Zip 01604–4593; tel. 508/798–1234; Robert E. Maher Jr., President and Chief Executive Officer

MISSISSIPPI: GULF COAST MEDICAL CENTER (O, 189 beds) 180–A Debuys Road, Biloxi, MS Zip 39531–4405; tel. 228/388–6711; Gary L. Stokes, Chief Executive Officer

MISSOURI: COLUMBIA REGIONAL HOSPITAL (O, 265 beds) 404 Keene Street, Columbia, MO Zip 65201–6698; tel. 573/875–9000; Bruce Eady, Chief Executive Officer

DEACONESS CENTRAL HOSPITAL (O, 324 beds) 6150 Oakland Avenue, Saint Louis, MO Zip 63139–3297; tel. 314/768–3000; Glennon K. McFadden, Chief Executive Officer

DEACONESS WEST HOSPITAL (O, 96 beds) 2345 Dougherty Ferry Road, Saint Louis, MO Zip 63122–3313; tel. 314/768–3000; Joan D'Ambrose, Chief Executive Officer

LAFAYETTE–GRAND HOSPITAL (O, 214 beds) 3545 Lafayette Avenue, Saint Louis, MO Zip 63104–9984; tel. 314/865–6500; Doug Doris, President and Chief Executive Officer

LUCY LEE HOSPITAL (L, 185 beds) 2620 North Westwood Boulevard, Poplar Bluff, MO Zip 63901–2341, Mailing Address: P.O. Box 88, Zip 63901–2341; tel. 573/785–7721; Brian T. Flynn, Chief Executive Officer

LUTHERAN MEDICAL CENTER (O, 243 beds) 2639 Miami Street, Saint Louis, MO Zip 63118–3999; tel. 314/772–1456; Clifford A. Yeager, Chief Executive Officer

SAINT LOUIS UNIVERSITY HOSPITAL (O, 303 beds) 3635 Vista at Grand Boulevard, Saint Louis, MO Zip 63110–0250, Mailing Address: P.O. Box 15250, Zip 63110–0250; tel. 314/577–8000; James Kimmey, M.D., M.P.H., Chairman and Chief Executive Officer

TWIN RIVERS REGIONAL MEDICAL CENTER (O, 118 beds) 1301 First Street, Kennett, MO Zip 63857–2508; tel. 573/888–4522; John W. Sanders, Chief Executive Officer

NEBRASKA: ST. JOSEPH CENTER FOR MENTAL HEALTH (O, 70 beds) 819 Dorcas Street, Omaha, NE Zip 68108–1198; tel. 402/449–4000; Robert C. Caldwell, Chief Operating Officer

ST. JOSEPH HOSPITAL (O, 282 beds) 601 North 30th Street, Omaha, NE Zip 68131–2197; tel. 402/449–5021; J. Richard Stanko, President and Chief Executive Officer

NEVADA: LAKE MEAD HOSPITAL MEDICAL CENTER (O, 184 beds) 1409 East Lake Mead Boulevard, North Las Vegas, NV Zip 89030–7197; tel. 702/649–7711; Ernest Libman, Chief Executive Officer

NORTH CAROLINA: CENTRAL CAROLINA HOSPITAL (O, 137 beds) 1135 Carthage Street, Sanford, NC Zip 27330; tel. 919/774–2100; L. Glenn Davis, Executive Director

FRYE REGIONAL MEDICAL CENTER (L, 355 beds) 420 North Center Street, Hickory, NC Zip 28601–5049; tel. 704/322–6070; Dennis Phillips, Chief Executive Officer

SOUTH CAROLINA: EAST COOPER REGIONAL MEDICAL CENTER (O, 112 beds) 1200 Johnnie Dodds Boulevard, Mount Pleasant, SC Zip 29464–3294; tel. 803/881–0100; John F. Holland, President

HILTON HEAD MEDICAL CENTER AND CLINICS (O, 79 beds) 25 Hospital Center Boulevard, Hilton Head Island, SC Zip 29926–2738, Mailing Address: P.O. Box 21117, Zip 29925–1117; tel. 803/681–6122; Dennis Ray Bruns, President and Chief Executive Officer

PIEDMONT HEALTHCARE SYSTEM (O, 276 beds) 222 Herlong Avenue, Rock Hill, SC Zip 29732–1952; tel. 803/329–1234; Paul A. Walker, President

TENNESSEE: HARTON REGIONAL MEDICAL CENTER (O, 137 beds) 1801 North Jackson Street, Tullahoma, TN Zip 37388–2201, Mailing Address: P.O. Box 460, Zip 37388–0460; tel. 931/393–3000; David C. Wilson, Chief Executive Officer

MEDICAL CENTER OF MANCHESTER (L, 49 beds) 481 Interstate Drive, Manchester, TN Zip 37355–3108, Mailing Address: P.O. Box 1409, Zip 37355–1409; tel. 931/728–6354; Margaret Hale, Chief Operating Officer

SAINT FRANCIS HOSPITAL (O, 506 beds) 5959 Park Avenue, Memphis, TN Zip 38119–5198, Mailing Address: P.O. Box 171808, Zip 38187–1808; tel. 901/765–1000; David L. Archer, Chief Executive Officer

UNIVERSITY MEDICAL CENTER (O, 225 beds) 1411 Baddour Parkway, Lebanon, TN Zip 37087–2573; tel. 615/444–8262; Larry W. Keller, Chief Executive Officer

TEXAS: BROWNSVILLE MEDICAL CENTER (O, 196 beds) 1040 West Jefferson Street, Brownsville, TX Zip 78520–5829, Mailing Address: Box 3590, Zip 78523–3590; tel. 956/544–1400; Tim A. Joslin, Chief Executive Officer

CYPRESS FAIRBANKS MEDICAL CENTER (O, 133 beds) 10655 Steepletop Drive, Houston, TX Zip 77065–4297; tel. 281/890–4285; Bill Klier, Chief Executive Officer

DOCTORS HOSPITAL OF DALLAS (O, 197 beds) 9440 Poppy Drive, Dallas, TX Zip 75218–3694; tel. 214/324–6100; Robert S. Freymuller, Chief Executive Officer

GARLAND COMMUNITY HOSPITAL (O, 113 beds) 2696 West Walnut Street, Garland, TX Zip 75042–6499; tel. 972/276–7116; K. Dwayne Ray, Administrator and Chief Executive Officer

HOUSTON NORTHWEST MEDICAL CENTER (O, 383 beds) 710 FM 1960 West, Houston, TX Zip 77090–3496; tel. 281/440–1000; James Kelly, Chief Executive Officer

LAKE POINTE MEDICAL CENTER (O, 88 beds) 6800 Scenic Drive, Rowlett, TX Zip 75088, Mailing Address: P.O. Box 1550, Zip 75030–1550; tel. 972/412–2273; Kenneth R. Teel, Administrator

MID–JEFFERSON HOSPITAL (O, 138 beds) Highway 365 and 27th Street, Nederland, TX Zip 77627–6288, Mailing Address: P.O. Box 1917, Zip 77627–1917; tel. 409/727–2321; Wilson J. Weber, Chief Executive Officer

NACOGDOCHES MEDICAL CENTER (O, 113 beds) 4920 N.E. Stallings, Nacogdoches, TX Zip 75961–1200, Mailing Address: P.O. Box 631604, Zip 75963–1604; tel. 409/568–3380; Glenn A. Robinson, Director

ODESSA REGIONAL HOSPITAL (O, 100 beds) 520 East Sixth Street, Odessa, TX Zip 79761–4565, Mailing Address: P.O. Box 4859, Zip 79760–4859; tel. 915/334–8200; Lex A. Guinn, Chief Executive Officer

PARK PLACE MEDICAL CENTER (O, 219 beds) 3050 39th Street, Port Arthur, TX Zip 77642–5535, Mailing Address: P.O. Box 1648, Zip 77641–1648; tel. 409/983–4951; Wilson J. Weber, Chief Executive Officer

PARK PLAZA HOSPITAL (O, 370 beds) 1313 Hermann Drive, Houston, TX Zip 77004–7092; tel. 713/527–5000; Robert L. Quist, Chief Executive Officer

PROVIDENCE MEMORIAL HOSPITAL (O, 378 beds) 2001 North Oregon Street, El Paso, TX Zip 79902–3368; tel. 915/577–6011; L. Marcus Fry Jr., Chief Executive Officer

For explanation of codes following names, see page B2.
★ Indicates Type III membership in the American Hospital Association.

RHD MEMORIAL MEDICAL CENTER (L, 150 beds) Seven Medical Parkway, Dallas, TX Zip 75381, Mailing Address: P.O. Box 819094, Zip 75381–9094; tel. 972/247–1000; Craig E. Sims, President and Chief Executive Officer

RIO VISTA PHYSICAL REHABILITATION HOSPITAL (O, 100 beds) 1740 Curie Drive, El Paso, TX Zip 79902–2900; tel. 915/544–3399; Patsy A. Parker, Administrator and Chief Executive Officer

SHARPSTOWN GENERAL HOSPITAL (O, 120 beds) 6700 Bellaire at Tarnef, Houston, TX Zip 77074–4999, Mailing Address: P.O. Box 740389, Zip 77274–0389; tel. 713/774–7611; Steve Altmiller, Chief Executive Officer

SIERRA MEDICAL CENTER (O, 328 beds) 1625 Medical Center Drive, El Paso, TX Zip 79902–5044; tel. 915/747–4000; L. Marcus Fry Jr., Chief Executive Officer

SOUTHWEST GENERAL HOSPITAL (O, 223 beds) 7400 Barlite Boulevard, San Antonio, TX Zip 78224–1399; tel. 210/921–2000; Keith Swinney, Chief Executive Officer

TRINITY MEDICAL CENTER (L, 149 beds) 4343 North Josey Lane, Carrollton, TX Zip 75010–4691; tel. 972/492–1010; Craig E. Sims, President

TRINITY VALLEY MEDICAL CENTER (O, 150 beds) 2900 South Loop 256, Palestine, TX Zip 75801–6958; tel. 903/731–1000; Larry C. Bozeman, Chief Executive Officer

TWELVE OAKS HOSPITAL (O, 213 beds) 4200 Portsmouth Street, Houston, TX Zip 77027–6899; tel. 713/623–2500; Steve Altmiller, Chief Executive Officer

Owned, leased, sponsored:	129 hospitals	24915 beds
Contract–managed:	0 hospitals	0 beds
Totals:	129 hospitals	24915 beds

0020: TEXAS DEPARTMENT OF HEALTH (NP)
1100 West 49th Street, Austin, TX Zip 78756–3199; tel. 512/458–7111; William R. Archer III, M.D., Commissioner

SOUTH TEXAS HOSPITAL (O, 84 beds) 1301 Rangerville Road, Harlingen, TX Zip 78552–7609, Mailing Address: P.O. Box 592, Zip 78551–0592; tel. 956/423–3420; James N. Elkins, FACHE, Director

TEXAS CENTER FOR INFECTIOUS DISEASE (O, 109 beds) 2303 S.E. Military Drive, San Antonio, TX Zip 78223–3597; tel. 210/534–8857; James N. Elkins, FACHE, Director

Owned, leased, sponsored:	2 hospitals	193 beds
Contract–managed:	0 hospitals	0 beds
Totals:	2 hospitals	193 beds

★0129: TEXAS HEALTH RESOURCES (NP)
600 East Las Colinas Boulevard, Suite 1550, Irving, TX Zip 75039, Mailing Address: 600 East Las Colinas Boulevard, 1550, Zip 75039; tel. 214/818–4500; Douglas D. Hawthorne, President and Chief Executive Officer

ARLINGTON MEMORIAL HOSPITAL (O, 375 beds) 800 West Randol Mill Road, Arlington, TX Zip 76012–2503; tel. 817/548–6100; Wayne N. Clark, President and Chief Executive Officer

HARRIS CONTINUED CARE HOSPITAL (O, 10 beds) 1301 Pennsylvania Avenue, 4th Floor, Fort Worth, TX Zip 76104–2190, Mailing Address: P.O. Box 3471, Zip 76113–3471; tel. 817/878–5500; Larry Thompson, Administrator

HARRIS METHODIST FORT WORTH (O, 511 beds) 1301 Pennsylvania Avenue, Fort Worth, TX Zip 76104–2895; tel. 817/882–2000; Barclay E. Berdan, Chief Executive Officer

HARRIS METHODIST NORTHWEST (O, 44 beds) 108 Denver Trail, Azle, TX Zip 76020–3697; tel. 817/444–8600; Larry Thompson, Vice President and Administrator

HARRIS METHODIST SOUTHWEST (O, 75 beds) 6100 Harris Parkway, Fort Worth, TX Zip 76132–4199; tel. 817/346–5050; David B. Rowe, Vice President and Administrator

HARRIS METHODIST–ERATH COUNTY (O, 75 beds) 411 North Belknap Street, Stephenville, TX Zip 76401–3415, Mailing Address: P.O. Box 1399, Zip 76401–1399; tel. 254/965–1500; Ronald E. Dorris, Administrator

HARRIS METHODIST–HEB (O, 177 beds) 1600 Hospital Parkway, Bedford, TX Zip 76022–6913, Mailing Address: P.O. Box 669, Zip 76095–0669; tel. 817/685–4000; Jack McCabe, Senior Vice President and Administrator

MCCUISTION REGIONAL MEDICAL CENTER (O, 158 beds) 865 Deshong Drive, Paris, TX Zip 75462–2097, Mailing Address: P.O. Box 160, Zip 75461–0160; tel. 903/737–1111; Anthony A. Daigle, Executive Director

PRESBYTERIAN HOSPITAL OF DALLAS (O, 655 beds) 8200 Walnut Hill Lane, Dallas, TX Zip 75231–4402; tel. 214/345–6789; Mark H. Merrill, Executive Director

PRESBYTERIAN HOSPITAL OF KAUFMAN (O, 68 beds) 850 Highway 243 West, Kaufman, TX Zip 75142–9998, Mailing Address: P.O. Box 310, Zip 75142–0310; tel. 972/932–7200; Michael J. McBride, CHE, Executive Director

PRESBYTERIAN HOSPITAL OF PLANO (O, 91 beds) 6200 West Parker Road, Plano, TX Zip 75093–7914; tel. 972/608–8000; Philip M. Wentworth, FACHE, Executive Director

PRESBYTERIAN HOSPITAL OF WINNSBORO (O, 50 beds) 719 West Coke Road, Winnsboro, TX Zip 75494–3098, Mailing Address: P.O. Box 628, Zip 75494–0628; tel. 903/342–5227; Dan Noteware, Executive Director

ST. PAUL MEDICAL CENTER (O, 308 beds) 5909 Harry Hines Boulevard, Dallas, TX Zip 75235–6285; tel. 214/879–1000; Frank Tiedemann, President and Chief Executive Officer

WALLS REGIONAL HOSPITAL (O, 112 beds) 201 Walls Drive, Cleburne, TX Zip 76031–1008; tel. 817/641–2551; Brent D. Magers, FACHE, Chief Executive Officer and Administrator

Owned, leased, sponsored:	14 hospitals	2709 beds
Contract–managed:	0 hospitals	0 beds
Totals:	14 hospitals	2709 beds

0093: TRANSITIONAL HOSPITALS CORPORATION (IO)
5110 West Sahara Avenue, Las Vegas, NV Zip 89102–3465; tel. 702/257–4000; Richard L. Conte, Chief Executive Officer and Chairman of the Board

FLORIDA: VENCOR HOSPITAL – CENTRAL TAMPA (O, 102 beds) 4801 North Howard Avenue, Tampa, FL Zip 33603–1484; tel. 813/874–7575; Ken Stone, Administrator

ILLINOIS: VENCOR HOSPITAL–CHICAGO CENTRAL (O, 81 beds) 4058 West Melrose Street, Chicago, IL Zip 60641–4797; tel. 773/736–7000; Richard Cerceo, Administrator

LOUISIANA: VENCOR HOSPITAL – NEW ORLEANS (O, 78 beds) 3601 Coliseum Street, New Orleans, LA Zip 70115–3606; tel. 504/899–1555; John R. Watkins, Chief Executive Officer

NEVADA: THC LAS VEGAS HOSPITAL (O, 52 beds) 5100 West Sahara Avenue, Las Vegas, NV Zip 89102–3436; tel. 702/871–1418; Dale A. Kirby, Chief Executive Officer

NEW MEXICO: VENCOR HOSPITAL – ALBUQUERQUE (O, 61 beds) 700 High Street N.E., Albuquerque, NM Zip 87102–2565; tel. 505/242–4444; Jean Koester, Chief Executive Officer

TEXAS: VENCOR ARLINGTON, TEXAS (O, 75 beds) 1000 North Cooper Street, Arlington, TX Zip 76011–5540; tel. 817/543–0200; A. C. Buchanan, Administrator

VENCOR HOSPITAL–FORT WORTH SOUTHWEST (O, 80 beds) 7800 Oakmont Boulevard, Fort Worth, TX Zip 76132–4299; tel. 817/346–0094; Barbara Schmidt, Administrator

WISCONSIN: THC–MILWAUKEE (O, 34 beds) 5017 South 110th Street, Greenfield, WI Zip 53228; tel. 414/427–8282; Lee Jaeger, Chief Executive Officer

Owned, leased, sponsored:	8 hospitals	563 beds
Contract–managed:	0 hospitals	0 beds
Totals:	8 hospitals	563 beds

★9255: TRUMAN MEDICAL CENTER (NP)
2301 Holmes Street, Kansas City, MO Zip 64108–2677; tel. 816/556–3000; E. Ratcliffe Anderson Jr., M.D., Executive Director

For explanation of codes following names, see page B2.
★ Indicates Type III membership in the American Hospital Association.

MISSOURI: TRUMAN MEDICAL CENTER–EAST (C, 302 beds) 7900 Lee's Summit Road, Kansas City, MO Zip 64139–1241; tel. 816/373–4415; Donald R. Smithburg, Administrator

TRUMAN MEDICAL CENTER–WEST (C, 237 beds) 2301 Holmes Street, Kansas City, MO Zip 64108–2677; tel. 816/556–3000; Rosa L. Miller, R.N., Administrator

Owned, leased, sponsored:	0 hospitals	0 beds
Contract–managed:	2 hospitals	539 beds
Totals:	2 hospitals	539 beds

9195: U. S. PUBLIC HEALTH SERVICE INDIAN HEALTH SERVICE (FG)
5600 Fishers Lane, Rockville, MD Zip 20857; tel. 301/443–1083; Michael Trujillo, M.D., M.P.H., Director

ALASKA: KANAKANAK HOSPITAL (O, 16 beds) Dillingham, AK Mailing Address: P.O. Box 130, Zip 99576; tel. 907/842–5201; Darrel C. Richardson, Chief Operating Officer

MANIILAQ HEALTH CENTER (O, 17 beds) Kotzebue, AK Zip 99752–0043; tel. 907/442–3321; Clinton Gray Jr., Administrator

NORTON SOUND REGIONAL HOSPITAL (O, 34 beds) Bering Straits, Nome, AK Zip 99762, Mailing Address: P.O. Box 966, Zip 99762–0966; tel. 907/443–3311; Charles Fagerstrom, Vice President

SAMUEL SIMMONDS MEMORIAL HOSPITAL (O, 15 beds) 1296 Agvik Street, Barrow, AK Zip 99723, Mailing Address: P.O. Box 29, Zip 99723; tel. 907/852–4611; Michael S. Herring, Administrator

SEARHC MT. EDGECUMBE HOSPITAL (O, 62 beds) 222 Tongass Drive, Sitka, AK Zip 99835–9416; tel. 907/966–2411; Arthur C. Willman, Vice President Operations

U. S. PUBLIC HEALTH SERVICE ALASKA NATIVE MEDICAL CENTER (O, 150 beds) 4315 Diplomacy Drive, Anchorage, AK Zip 99508; tel. 907/563–2662; Richard Mandsager, M.D., Director

YUKON–KUSKOKWIM DELTA REGIONAL HOSPITAL (O, 50 beds) Bethel, AK Mailing Address: P.O. Box 528, Zip 99559–3000; tel. 907/543–6300; Edwin L. Hansen, Vice President

ARIZONA: CHINLE COMPREHENSIVE HEALTH CARE FACILITY (O, 60 beds) Highway 191, Chinle, AZ Zip 86503, Mailing Address: P.O. Drawer PH, Zip 86503; tel. 520/674–7011; Ronald Tso, Chief Executive Officer

FORT DEFIANCE INDIAN HEALTH SERVICE HOSPITAL (O, 49 beds) Fort Defiance, AZ Mailing Address: P.O. Box 649, Zip 86504–0649; tel. 520/729–3223; Franklin Freeland, Ed.D., Chief Executive Officer

HUHUKAM MEMORIAL HOSPITAL (O, 10 beds) Seed Farm & Skill Center Road, Sacaton, AZ Zip 85247–0038, Mailing Address: P.O. Box 38, Zip 85247–0038; tel. 602/562–3321; Viola L. Johnson, Chief Executive Officer

TUBA CITY INDIAN MEDICAL CENTER (O, 69 beds) Main Street, Tuba City, AZ Zip 86045–6211, Mailing Address: P.O. Box 600, Zip 86045–6211; tel. 520/283–2827; Susie John, M.D., Chief Executive Officer

U. S. PUBLIC HEALTH SERVICE INDIAN HOSPITAL (O, 18 beds) Parker, AZ Mailing Address: Route 1, Box 12, Zip 85344; tel. 520/669–2137; Gary Davis, Service Unit Director

U. S. PUBLIC HEALTH SERVICE INDIAN HOSPITAL (O, 34 beds) Sells, AZ Mailing Address: P.O. Box 548, Zip 85634–0548; tel. 520/383–7251; Darrell Rumley, Service Unit Director and Chief Executive Officer

U. S. PUBLIC HEALTH SERVICE INDIAN HOSPITAL (O, 28 beds) San Carlos, AZ Mailing Address: P.O. Box 208, Zip 85550–0208; tel. 520/475–2371; Nella Ben, Chief Executive Officer

U. S. PUBLIC HEALTH SERVICE INDIAN HOSPITAL (O, 45 beds) State Route 73, Box 860, Whiteriver, AZ Zip 85941–0860; tel. 520/338–4911; Carla Alchesay–Nachu, Service Unit Director

U. S. PUBLIC HEALTH SERVICE PHOENIX INDIAN MEDICAL CENTER (O, 137 beds) 4212 North 16th Street, Phoenix, AZ Zip 85016–5389; tel. 602/263–1200; Anna Albert, Chief Executive Officer

U. S. PUBLIC HEALTH SERVICES INDIAN HOSPITAL (O, 17 beds) Keams Canyon, AZ Mailing Address: P.O. Box 98, Zip 86034–0098; tel. 520/738–2211; Taylor Satala, Service Unit Director

CALIFORNIA: U. S. PUBLIC HEALTH SERVICE INDIAN HOSPITAL (O, 34 beds) Winterhaven, CA Mailing Address: P.O. Box 1368, Yuma, AZ Zip 85366–1368; tel. 760/572–0217; Hortense Miguel, R.N., Service Unit Director

MARYLAND: WARREN G. MAGNUSON CLINICAL CENTER, NATIONAL INSTITUTES OF HEALTH (O, 314 beds) 9000 Rockville Pike, Bethesda, MD Zip 20892–1504; tel. 301/496–4114; John I. Gallin, M.D., Director

MINNESOTA: U. S. PUBLIC HEALTH SERVICE INDIAN HOSPITAL (O, 13 beds) 7th Street and Grant Utley Avenue N.W.

U.S. PUBLIC HEALTH SERVICE INDIAN HOSPITAL (O, 23 beds) Highway 1, Redlake, MN Zip 56671; tel. 218/679–3912; Essimae Stevens, Service Unit Director

MISSISSIPPI: CHOCTAW HEALTH CENTER (O, 35 beds) Highway 16 West, Philadelphia, MS Zip 39350, Mailing Address: Route 7, Box R–50, Zip 39350; tel. 601/656–2211; Jim Wallace, Executive Director

MONTANA: U. S. PUBLIC HEALTH SERVICE BLACKFEET COMMUNITY HOSPITAL (O, 25 beds) Browning, MT Mailing Address: P.O. Box 760, Zip 59417–0760; tel. 406/338–6100; Reese Fisher, Service Unit Director

U. S. PUBLIC HEALTH SERVICE INDIAN HOSPITAL (O, 24 beds) Crow Agency, MT Mailing Address: P.O. Box 9, Zip 59022–0009; tel. 406/638–2626; Tennyson Doney, Service Unit Director

U. S. PUBLIC HEALTH SERVICE INDIAN HOSPITAL (O, 12 beds) Rural Route 1, Box 67, Harlem, MT Zip 59526; tel. 406/353–3191; Charles D. Plumage, Director

NEBRASKA: U. S. PUBLIC HEALTH SERVICE INDIAN HOSPITAL (O, 30 beds) Highway 7577, Winnebago, NE Zip 68071; tel. 402/878–2231; Donald Lee, Service Unit Director

NEVADA: U. S. PUBLIC HEALTH SERVICE OWYHEE COMMUNITY HEALTH FACILITY (O, 15 beds) Owyhee, NV Mailing Address: P.O. Box 130, Zip 89832–0130; tel. 702/757–2415; Walden Townsend, Service Unit Director

NEW MEXICO: ACOMA–CANONCITO–LAGUNA HOSPITAL (O, 15 beds) San Fidel, NM Mailing Address: P.O. Box 130, Zip 87049–0130; tel. 505/552–6634; Richard L. Zephier, Ph.D., Service Unit Director

GALLUP INDIAN MEDICAL CENTER (O, 99 beds) 516 East Nizhoni Boulevard, Gallup, NM Zip 87301–5748, Mailing Address: P.O. Box 1337, Zip 87305–1337; tel. 505/722–1000; Timothy G. Fleming, M.D., Chief Executive Officer

NORTHERN NAVAJO MEDICAL CENTER (O, 59 beds) Shiprock, NM Mailing Address: P.O. Box 160, Zip 87420–0160; tel. 505/368–6001; Dee Hutchison, Chief Executive Officer

PHS SANTA FE INDIAN HOSPITAL (O, 39 beds) 1700 Cerrillos Road, Santa Fe, NM Zip 87505–3554; tel. 505/988–9821; Lawrence A. Jordan, Director

PUBLIC HEALTH SERVICE INDIAN HOSPITAL (O, 28 beds) 801 Vassar Drive N.E., Albuquerque, NM Zip 87106–2799; tel. 505/256–4000; Cheri Lyon, Service Unit Director

U. S. PUBLIC HEALTH SERVICE INDIAN HOSPITAL (O, 32 beds) Crownpoint, NM Mailing Address: P.O. Box 358, Zip 87313–0358; tel. 505/786–5291; Anita Muneta, Chief Executive Officer

U. S. PUBLIC HEALTH SERVICE INDIAN HOSPITAL (O, 13 beds) Mescalero, NM Mailing Address: Box 210, Zip 88340–0210; tel. 505/671–4441; Joe Wahnee Jr., Service Unit Director

U. S. PUBLIC HEALTH SERVICE INDIAN HOSPITAL (O, 37 beds) Zuni, NM Mailing Address: P.O. Box 467, Zip 87327–0467; tel. 505/782–4431; Jean Othole, Service Unit Director

NORTH CAROLINA: U. S. PUBLIC HEALTH SERVICE INDIAN HOSPITAL (O, 28 beds) Hospital Road, Cherokee, NC Zip 28719; tel. 704/497–9163; Janet Belcourt, Administrator

NORTH DAKOTA: U. S. PUBLIC HEALTH SERVICE INDIAN HOSPITAL (O, 42 beds) Belcourt, ND Mailing Address: P.O. Box 160, Zip 58316–0130; tel. 701/477–6111; Ray Grandbois, M.P.H., Service Unit Director

U. S. PUBLIC HEALTH SERVICE INDIAN HOSPITAL (O, 14 beds) Fort Yates, ND Mailing Address: P.O. Box J., Zip 58538; tel. 701/854–3831; Terry Pourier, Service Unit Director

OHIO: PHS MT. SINAI MEDICAL CENTER EAST (O, 98 beds) 27100 Chardon Road, Richmond Heights, OH Zip 44143–1198; tel. 440/585–6500; Keith J. Petersen, Chief Executive Officer

For explanation of codes following names, see page B2.
★ Indicates Type III membership in the American Hospital Association.

Networks, Health Care Systems and Alliances **B147**

Section B

OKLAHOMA: CARL ALBERT INDIAN HEALTH FACILITY (O, 53 beds) 1001 North Country Club Road, Ada, OK Zip 74820–2847; tel. 580/436–3980; Kenneth R. Ross, Administrator

CHOCTAW NATION INDIAN HOSPITAL (O, 44 beds) Rural Route 2, Box 1725, Talihina, OK Zip 74571–9517; tel. 918/567–2211; Rosemary Hooser, Administrator

CREEK NATION COMMUNITY HOSPITAL (O, 34 beds) 309 North 14th Street, Okemah, OK Zip 74859–2099; tel. 918/623–1424; Bert Robison, Chief Executive Officer

U. S. PUBLIC HEALTH SERVICE COMPREHENSIVE INDIAN HEALTH FACILITY (O, 46 beds) 101 South Moore Avenue, Claremore, OK Zip 74017–5091; tel. 918/342–6434; John Daugherty Jr., Service Unit Director

U. S. PUBLIC HEALTH SERVICE INDIAN HOSPITAL (O, 11 beds) Clinton, OK Mailing Address: Route 1, Box 3060, Zip 73601–9303; tel. 580/323–2884; Thedis V. Mitchell, Director

U. S. PUBLIC HEALTH SERVICE INDIAN HOSPITAL (O, 44 beds) 1515 Lawrie Tatum Road, Lawton, OK Zip 73507–3099; tel. 580/353–0350; George E. Howell, Service Unit Director

WILLIAM W. HASTINGS INDIAN HOSPITAL (O, 60 beds) 100 South Bliss Avenue, Tahlequah, OK Zip 74464–3399; tel. 918/458–3100; Hickory Starr Jr., Administrator

SOUTH DAKOTA: INDIAN HEALTH SERVICE HOSPITAL (O, 32 beds) 3200 Canyon Lake Drive, Rapid City, SD Zip 57702–8197; tel. 605/355–2280; James Cournoyer, Director

U. S. PUBLIC HEALTH SERVICE INDIAN HOSPITAL (O, 27 beds) Eagle Butte, SD Mailing Address: P.O. Box 1012, Zip 57625–1012; tel. 605/964–3001; Orville Night Pipe, Service Unit Director

U. S. PUBLIC HEALTH SERVICE INDIAN HOSPITAL (O, 46 beds) Pine Ridge, SD Mailing Address: P.O. Box 1201, Zip 57770–1201; tel. 605/867–5131; Vern F. Donnell, Service Unit Director

U. S. PUBLIC HEALTH SERVICE INDIAN HOSPITAL (O, 35 beds) Highway 18, Soldier Creek Road, Rosebud, SD Zip 57570; tel. 605/747–2231; Gayla J. Twiss, Service Unit Director

U. S. PUBLIC HEALTH SERVICE INDIAN HOSPITAL (O, 18 beds) Chestnut Street, Sisseton, SD Zip 57262, Mailing Address: P.O. Box 189, Zip 57262–0189; tel. 605/698–7606; Richard Huff, Administrator

Owned, leased, sponsored:	51 hospitals	2290 beds
Contract–managed:	0 hospitals	0 beds
Totals:	51 hospitals	2290 beds

★2315: UNIHEALTH (NP)
3400 Riverside Drive, Burbank, CA Zip 91505; tel. 818/238–6000; James T. Yoshioka, President

CALIFORNIA: CALIFORNIA HOSPITAL MEDICAL CENTER (O, 309 beds) 1401 South Grand Avenue, Los Angeles, CA Zip 90015–3063; tel. 213/748–2411; Melinda D. Beswick, President and Chief Executive Officer

GLENDALE MEMORIAL HOSPITAL AND HEALTH CENTER (O, 275 beds) 1420 South Central Avenue, Glendale, CA Zip 91204–2594; tel. 818/502–1900; Arnold R. Schaffer, President and Chief Executive Officer

LA PALMA INTERCOMMUNITY HOSPITAL (O, 139 beds) 7901 Walker Street, La Palma, CA Zip 90623–5850, Mailing Address: P.O. Box 5850, Buena Park, Zip 90622; tel. 714/670–7400; Stephen E. Dixon, President and Chief Executive Officer

LONG BEACH COMMUNITY MEDICAL CENTER (O, 278 beds) 1720 Termino Avenue, Long Beach, CA Zip 90804; tel. 562/498–1000; Makoto Nakayama, President and Chief Executive Officer

MARTIN LUTHER HOSPITAL (O, 205 beds) 1830 West Romneya Drive, Anaheim, CA Zip 92801–1854; tel. 714/491–5200; Stephen E. Dixon, President and Chief Executive Officer

NORTHRIDGE HOSPITAL MEDICAL CENTER–ROSCOE BOULEVARD CAMPUS (O, 404 beds) 18300 Roscoe Boulevard, Northridge, CA Zip 91328; tel. 818/885–8500; Roger E. Seaver, President and Chief Executive Officer

NORTHRIDGE HOSPITAL AND MEDICAL CENTER, SHERMAN WAY CAMPUS (O, 211 beds) 14500 Sherman Circle, Van Nuys, CA Zip 91405; tel. 818/997–0101; Richard D. Lyons, President and Chief Executive Officer

SAN GABRIEL VALLEY MEDICAL CENTER (O, 273 beds) 438 West Las Tunas Drive, San Gabriel, CA Zip 91776, Mailing Address: P.O. Box 1507, Zip 91778–1507; tel. 626/289–5454; Thomas D. Mone, President and Chief Executive Officer

Owned, leased, sponsored:	8 hospitals	2094 beds
Contract–managed:	0 hospitals	0 beds
Totals:	8 hospitals	2094 beds

★2445: UNITED HEALTH GROUP (NP)
Five Innovation Court, Appleton, WI Zip 54914–1663, Mailing Address: P.O. Box 8025, Zip 54913–8025; tel. 920/730–0330; James Edward Raney, President and Chief Executive Officer

WISCONSIN: APPLETON MEDICAL CENTER (O, 146 beds) 1818 North Meade Street, Appleton, WI Zip 54911–3496; tel. 920/731–4101; Paul E. Macek, Senior Vice President

THEDA CLARK MEDICAL CENTER (O, 216 beds) 130 Second Street, Neenah, WI Zip 54956–2883, Mailing Address: P.O. Box 2021, Zip 54957–2021; tel. 920/729–3100; Paul E. Macek, Senior Vice President

Owned, leased, sponsored:	2 hospitals	362 beds
Contract–managed:	0 hospitals	0 beds
Totals:	2 hospitals	362 beds

1765: UNITED HOSPITAL CORPORATION (IO)
6189 East Shelby Drive, Memphis, TN Zip 38115; tel. 901/794–8440; James C. Henson, President

ALABAMA: FLORALA MEMORIAL HOSPITAL (O, 23 beds) 515 East Fifth Avenue, Florala, AL Zip 36442–0189, Mailing Address: P.O. Box 189, Zip 36442–0189; tel. 334/858–3287; Blair W. Henson, Administrator

ARKANSAS: VAN BUREN COUNTY MEMORIAL HOSPITAL (C, 144 beds) Highway 65 South, Clinton, AR Zip 72031, Mailing Address: P.O. Box 206, Zip 72031–0206; tel. 501/745–2401; Barry Brady, Administrator

Owned, leased, sponsored:	1 hospital	23 beds
Contract–managed:	1 hospital	144 beds
Totals:	2 hospitals	167 beds

9605: UNITED MEDICAL CORPORATION (IO)
603 Main Street, Windermere, FL Zip 34786–3548, Mailing Address: P.O. Box 1100, Zip 34786–1100; tel. 407/876–2200; Donald R. Dizney, Chairman

KENTUCKY: TEN BROECK HOSPITAL (O, 94 beds) 8521 Old LaGrange Road, Louisville, KY Zip 40242–3800; tel. 502/426–6380; Pat Hammer, Chief Executive Officer

LOUISIANA: ST. CLAUDE MEDICAL CENTER (O, 136 beds) 3419 St. Claude Avenue, New Orleans, LA Zip 70117–6198; tel. 504/948–8200; Joseph R. Tucker, President

PUERTO RICO: DOCTORS GUBERN'S HOSPITAL (O, 51 beds) 110 Antonio R. Barcelo, Fajardo, PR Zip 00738, Mailing Address: P.O. Box 846, Zip 00738–0846; tel. 787/863–0669; Edwin Sueiro, Executive Director

HATO REY COMMUNITY HOSPITAL (O, 105 beds) San Juan, PR Mailing Address: 435 Ponce De Leon, Hato Rey, Zip 00917; tel. 787/754–0909; Jorge De Jesus, Executive Director

HOSPITAL PAVIA (O, 183 beds) 1462 Asia Street, San Juan, PR Zip 00909, Mailing Address: Box 11137, Santurce Station, Zip 00910; tel. 787/727–6060; Jorge De Jesus, Executive Director

HOSPITAL PEREA (O, 82 beds) 15 Basora Street, Mayaguez, PR Zip 00681, Mailing Address: P.O. Box 170, Zip 00681; tel. 787/834–0101; Ramon Lopez, Administrator

SAN JORGE CHILDREN'S HOSPITAL (O, 85 beds) 258 San Jorge Avenue, San Juan, PR Zip 00912; tel. 787/727–1000; Domingo Cruz Vivaldi, Administrator

Owned, leased, sponsored:	7 hospitals	736 beds
Contract–managed:	0 hospitals	0 beds
Totals:	7 hospitals	736 beds

For explanation of codes following names, see page B2.
★ Indicates Type III membership in the American Hospital Association.

9555: UNIVERSAL HEALTH SERVICES, INC. (IO)
367 South Gulph Road, King of Prussia, PA Zip 19406–0958; tel. 610/768–3300; Alan B. Miller, President and Chief Executive Officer

ARKANSAS: BRIDGEWAY (L, 70 beds) 21 Bridgeway Road, North Little Rock, AR Zip 72113; tel. 501/771–1500; Barry Pipkin, Chief Executive Officer and Managing Director

CALIFORNIA: DEL AMO HOSPITAL (O, 166 beds) 23700 Camino Del Sol, Torrance, CA Zip 90505; tel. 310/530–1151; E. Daniel Thomas, Administrator and Chief Executive Officer

INLAND VALLEY REGIONAL MEDICAL CENTER (L, 80 beds) 36485 Inland Valley Drive, Wildomar, CA Zip 92595; tel. 909/677–1111; Christopher L. Boyd, Chief Executive Officer and Managing Director

DISTRICT OF COLUMBIA: GEORGE WASHINGTON UNIVERSITY HOSPITAL (O, 295 beds) 901 23rd Street N.W., Washington, DC Zip 20037–2377; tel. 202/994–1000; Phillip S. Schaengold, JD, Chief Executive Officer

FLORIDA: MANATEE MEMORIAL HOSPITAL (O, 512 beds) 206 Second Street East, Bradenton, FL Zip 34208–1000; tel. 941/746–5111; Michael Marquez, Chief Executive Officer

WELLINGTON REGIONAL MEDICAL CENTER (L, 93 beds) 10101 Forest Hill Boulevard, West Palm Beach, FL Zip 33414–6199; tel. 561/798–8500; Gregory E. Boyer, Chief Executive Officer

GEORGIA: TURNING POINT HOSPITAL (O, 59 beds) 319 East By–Pass, Moultrie, GA Zip 31776, Mailing Address: P.O. Box 1177, Zip 31768–1177; tel. 912/985–4815; Ben Marion, Chief Executive Officer

ILLINOIS: THE PAVILION (O, 46 beds) 809 West Church Street, Champaign, IL Zip 61820; tel. 217/373–1700; Nina W. Eisner, Chief Executive Officer

LOUISIANA: CHALMETTE MEDICAL CENTER (L, 196 beds) 9001 Patricia Street, Chalmette, LA Zip 70043–1799; tel. 504/277–8011; Larry M. Graham, Chief Executive Officer

DOCTORS' HOSPITAL OF SHREVEPORT (L, 118 beds) 1130 Louisiana Avenue, Shreveport, LA Zip 71101–3998, Mailing Address: P.O. Box 1526, Zip 71165–1526; tel. 318/227–1211; Charles E. Boyd, Administrator

RIVER OAKS HOSPITAL (O, 56 beds) 1525 River Oaks Road West, New Orleans, LA Zip 70123–2199; tel. 504/734–1740; Daryl Sue White, R.N., Managing Director

RIVER PARISHES HOSPITAL (O, 54 beds) 500 Rue De Sante, La Place, LA Zip 70068–5418; tel. 504/652–7000; B. Ann Kuss, Chief Executive Officer and Managing Director

MASSACHUSETTS: ARBOUR HOSPITAL (O, 118 beds) 49 Robinwood Avenue, Boston, MA Zip 02130–2156, Mailing Address: P.O. Box 9, Zip 02130; tel. 617/522–4400; Roy A. Ettlinger, Chief Executive Officer

FULLER MEMORIAL HOSPITAL (O, 46 beds) 200 May Street, South Attleboro, MA Zip 02703–5599; tel. 508/761–8500; Landon Kite, President

H. R. I. HOSPITAL (O, 51 beds) 227 Babcock Street, Brookline, MA Zip 02146; tel. 617/731–3200; Roy A. Ettlinger, Chief Executive Officer

MICHIGAN: FOREST VIEW HOSPITAL (O, 62 beds) 1055 Medical Park Drive S.E., Grand Rapids, MI Zip 49546–3671; tel. 616/942–9610; John F. Kuhn, Chief Executive Officer

MISSOURI: TWO RIVERS PSYCHIATRIC HOSPITAL (O, 80 beds) 5121 Raytown Road, Kansas City, MO Zip 64133–2141; tel. 816/356–5688; Richard Failla, Chief Executive Officer

NEVADA: DESERT SPRINGS HOSPITAL (O, 225 beds) 2075 East Flamingo Road, Las Vegas, NV Zip 89119–5121, Mailing Address: P.O. Box 19204, Zip 89132–9204; tel. 702/733–8800; Thomas L. Koenig, Chief Executive Officer

NORTHERN NEVADA MEDICAL CENTER (O, 100 beds) 2375 East Prater Way, Sparks, NV Zip 89434–9645; tel. 702/331–7000; James R. Pagels, Chief Executive Officer and Managing Director

VALLEY HOSPITAL MEDICAL CENTER (O, 365 beds) 620 Shadow Lane, Las Vegas, NV Zip 89106–4194; tel. 702/388–4000; Roger Collins, Chief Executive Officer and Managing Director

PENNSYLVANIA: CLARION PSYCHIATRIC CENTER (O, 52 beds) 2 Hospital Drive, Clarion, PA Zip 16214, Mailing Address: Rural Delivery 3, Box 188, Zip 16214; tel. 814/226–9545; Michael R. Keefer, CHE, Administrator and Chief Executive Officer

HORSHAM CLINIC (O, 138 beds) 722 East Butler Pike, Ambler, PA Zip 19002–2398; tel. 215/643–7800; David A. Baron, D.O., Medical Director

KEYSTONE CENTER (O, 76 beds) 2001 Providence Avenue, Chester, PA Zip 19013–5504; tel. 610/876–9000; Jimmy Patton, Chief Executive Officer and Managing Director

MEADOWS PSYCHIATRIC CENTER (O, 101 beds) Centre Hall, PA Mailing Address: Rural Delivery 1, Box 259, Zip 16828–9798; tel. 814/364–2161; Joseph Barszczewski, Chief Executive Officer

PUERTO RICO: DR. JOSE RAMOS LEBRON HOSPITAL (O, 180 beds) General Valero Avenue, #194, Fajardo, PR Zip 00738, Mailing Address: P.O. Box 1283, Zip 00738–1283; tel. 787/863–0505; Victor R. Marrero, Executive Administrator

HOSPITAL SAN FRANCISCO (O, 160 beds) 371 De Diego Avenue, San Juan, PR Zip 00923, Mailing Address: P.O. Box 29025, Zip 00929–0025; tel. 787/767–2528; Domingo Nevarez, Executive Director

HOSPITAL SAN PABLO (O, 362 beds) Calle San Cruz 70, Bayamon, PR Zip 00961, Mailing Address: P.O. Box 236, Zip 00960; tel. 787/740–4747; Jorge De Jesus, Executive Director

SOUTH CAROLINA: AIKEN REGIONAL MEDICAL CENTER (O, 269 beds) 202 University Parkway, Aiken, SC Zip 29801–2757, Mailing Address: P.O. Box 1117, Zip 29802–1117; tel. 803/641–5000; Richard H. Satcher, Chief Executive Officer

TEXAS: EDINBURG HOSPITAL (O, 139 beds) 333 West Freddy Gonzalez Drive, Edinburg, TX Zip 78539–6199; tel. 956/383–6211; Leon J. Belila, Administrator

GLEN OAKS HOSPITAL (O, 54 beds) 301 East Division, Greenville, TX Zip 75401–4199; tel. 903/454–6000; Thomas E. Rourke, Administrator

MCALLEN MEDICAL CENTER (L, 451 beds) 301 West Expressway 83, McAllen, TX Zip 78503; tel. 956/632–4000; Daniel P. McLean, Executive Director

MERIDELL ACHIEVEMENT CENTER (L, 78 beds) 12550 West Highway 29, Liberty Hill, TX Zip 78642, Mailing Address: P.O. Box 87, Zip 78642–0087; tel. 800/366–8656; Scott McAvoy, Managing Director

NORTHWEST TEXAS HEALTHCARE SYSTEM (O, 334 beds) 1501 South Coulter Avenue, Amarillo, TX Zip 79106–1790, Mailing Address: P.O. Box 1110, Zip 79175–1110; tel. 806/354–1000; Michael A. Callahan, Chief Executive Officer

RIVER CREST HOSPITAL (O, 80 beds) 1636 Hunters Glen Road, San Angelo, TX Zip 76901–5016; tel. 915/949–5722; Larry Grimes, Managing Director

TIMBERLAWN MENTAL HEALTH SYSTEM (O, 124 beds) 4600 Samuell Boulevard, Dallas, TX Zip 75228–6800, Mailing Address: P.O. Box 151489, Zip 75315–1489; tel. 214/381–7181; Debra S. Lowrance, R.N., Chief Executive Officer and Managing Director

VICTORIA REGIONAL MEDICAL CENTER (O, 156 beds) 101 Medical Drive, Victoria, TX Zip 77904–3198; tel. 512/573–6100; J. Michael Mastej, Chief Executive Officer and Managing Director

WASHINGTON: AUBURN REGIONAL MEDICAL CENTER (O, 100 beds) 202 North Division, Plaza One, Auburn, WA Zip 98001–4908; tel. 253/833–7711; Michael M. Gherardini, Chief Executive Officer and Managing Director

Owned, leased, sponsored:	37 hospitals	5646 beds
Contract–managed:	0 hospitals	0 beds
Totals:	37 hospitals	5646 beds

0112: UNIVERSITY HOSPITALS HEALTH SYSTEM (NP)
11100 Euclid Avenue, Cleveland, OH Zip 44106–5000; tel. 216/844–1000; Farah M. Walters, President and Chief Executive Officer

OHIO: UHHS BEDFORD MEDICAL CENTER (O, 110 beds) 44 Blaine Avenue, Bedford, OH Zip 44146–2799; tel. 440/439–2000; Arlene A. Rak, R.N., President

UHHS BROWN MEMORIAL HOSPITAL (O, 51 beds) 158 West Main Road, Conneaut, OH Zip 44030–2039, Mailing Address: P.O. Box 648, Zip 44030–0648; tel. 440/593–1131; Carol Koellisch Drennen, R.N., President and Chief Executive Officer

For explanation of codes following names, see page B2.
★ Indicates Type III membership in the American Hospital Association.

UHHS GEAUGA REGIONAL HOSPITAL (O, 122 beds) 13207 Ravenna Road, Chardon, OH Zip 44024–9012; tel. 440/269–6000; Richard J. Frenchie, President and Chief Executive Officer

UHHS LAURELWOOD HOSPITAL (O, 160 beds) 35900 Euclid Avenue, Willoughby, OH Zip 44094–4648; tel. 440/953–3000; Farshid Afsarifard, Executive Director

UHHS–MEMORIAL HOSPITAL OF GENEVA (O, 35 beds) 870 West Main Street, Geneva, OH Zip 44041–1295; tel. 440/466–1141; Gerard D. Klein, Chief Executive Officer

UNIVERSITY HOSPITALS OF CLEVELAND (O, 752 beds) 11100 Euclid Avenue, Cleveland, OH Zip 44106–2602; tel. 216/844–1000; Farah M. Walters, President and Chief Executive Officer

Owned, leased, sponsored:	6 hospitals	1230 beds
Contract–managed:	0 hospitals	0 beds
Totals:	6 hospitals	1230 beds

6405: UNIVERSITY OF CALIFORNIA–SYSTEMWIDE ADMINISTRATION (NP)
300 Lakeside Drive, 18th Floor, Oakland, CA Zip 94612–3550; tel. 510/987–9701; Cornelius L. Hopper, M.D., Vice President Health Affairs

CALIFORNIA: SANTA MONICA–UCLA MEDICAL CENTER (O, 221 beds) 1250 16th Street, Santa Monica, CA Zip 90404–1200; tel. 310/319–4000; William D. Parente, Director and Chief Executive Officer

UNIVERSITY OF CALIFORNIA LOS ANGELES MEDICAL CENTER (L, 610 beds) 10833 Le Conte Avenue, Los Angeles, CA Zip 90095–1730; tel. 310/825–9111; Michael Karpf, M.D., Vice Provost Hospital System and Director Medical Center

UNIVERSITY OF CALIFORNIA LOS ANGELES NEUROPSYCHIATRIC HOSPITAL (O, 117 beds) 760 Westwood Plaza, Los Angeles, CA Zip 90095; tel. 310/825–0511; Fawzy I. Fawzy, M.D., Medical Director

UNIVERSITY OF CALIFORNIA SAN DIEGO MEDICAL CENTER (O, 413 beds) 200 West Arbor Drive, San Diego, CA Zip 92103–8970; tel. 619/543–6222; Sumiyo E. Kastelic, Director

UNIVERSITY OF CALIFORNIA SAN FRANCISCO MEDICAL CENTER (O, 663 beds) 500 Parnassus, San Francisco, CA Zip 94143–0296; tel. 415/476–1000; Bruce Schroffel, Chief Operating Officer

UNIVERSITY OF CALIFORNIA, DAVIS MEDICAL CENTER (O, 446 beds) 2315 Stockton Boulevard, Sacramento, CA Zip 95817–2282; tel. 916/734–2011; Frank J. Loge, Director

UNIVERSITY OF CALIFORNIA, IRVINE MEDICAL CENTER (O, 383 beds) 101 The City Drive, Orange, CA Zip 92668–3298; tel. 714/456–7890; Mark R. Laret, Executive Director

Owned, leased, sponsored:	7 hospitals	2853 beds
Contract–managed:	0 hospitals	0 beds
Totals:	7 hospitals	2853 beds

★0058: UNIVERSITY OF CHICAGO HEALTH SYSTEM (NP)
322 South Green Street, Suite 500, Chicago, IL Zip 60607; tel. 312/697–8403; Ralph W. Muller, Chief Executive Officer

ILLINOIS: LOUIS A. WEISS MEMORIAL HOSPITAL (O, 200 beds) 4646 North Marine Drive, Chicago, IL Zip 60640–1501; tel. 773/878–8700; Gregory A. Cierlik, President and Chief Executive Officer

UNIVERSITY OF CHICAGO HOSPITALS (O, 514 beds) 5841 South Maryland Avenue, Chicago, IL Zip 60637–1470; tel. 773/702–1000; Steven Lipstein, President and Chief Operating Officer

Owned, leased, sponsored:	2 hospitals	714 beds
Contract–managed:	0 hospitals	0 beds
Totals:	2 hospitals	714 beds

0021: UNIVERSITY OF NEW MEXICO (NP)
915 Camino De Salud, Albuquerque, NM Zip 87131–0001; tel. 505/272–5849; Jane E. Henney, M.D., Vice President Health Sciences

NEW MEXICO: CARRIE TINGLEY HOSPITAL (O, 18 beds) 1127 University Boulevard N.E., Albuquerque, NM Zip 87102–1715; tel. 505/272–5200; Robert T. Maruca, Administrator

UNIVERSITY HOSPITAL (O, 263 beds) 2211 Lomas Boulevard N.E., Albuquerque, NM Zip 87106–2745; tel. 505/272–2121; Stephen W. McKernan, Chief Executive Officer

UNIVERSITY OF NEW MEXICO CHILDREN'S PSYCHIATRIC HOSPITAL (O, 53 beds) 1001 Yale Boulevard N.E., Albuquerque, NM Zip 87131–3830; tel. 505/272–2945; Christina B. Gunn, Chief Executive Officer

UNIVERSITY OF NEW MEXICO MENTAL HEALTH CENTER (O, 60 beds) 2600 Marble N.E., Albuquerque, NM Zip 87131–2600; tel. 505/272–2870; Christina B. Gunn, Chief Executive Officer

Owned, leased, sponsored:	4 hospitals	394 beds
Contract–managed:	0 hospitals	0 beds
Totals:	4 hospitals	394 beds

0057: UNIVERSITY OF SOUTH ALABAMA HOSPITALS (NP)
2451 Fillingim Street, Mobile, AL Zip 36617–2293; tel. 334/471–7000; Stephen H. Simmons, Senior Administrator

ALABAMA: USA CHILDREN'S AND WOMEN'S HOSPITAL (O, 131 beds) 1700 Center Street, Mobile, AL Zip 36604–3391; tel. 334/415–1000; Stanley K. Hammack, Administrator

UNIVERSITY OF SOUTH ALABAMA KNOLLWOOD PARK HOSPITAL (O, 150 beds) 5600 Girby Road, Mobile, AL Zip 36693–3398; tel. 334/660–5120; Thomas J. Gibson, Administrator

UNIVERSITY OF SOUTH ALABAMA MEDICAL CENTER (O, 316 beds) 2451 Fillingim Street, Mobile, AL Zip 36617–2293; tel. 334/471–7000; Stephen H. Simmons, Administrator

Owned, leased, sponsored:	3 hospitals	597 beds
Contract–managed:	0 hospitals	0 beds
Totals:	3 hospitals	597 beds

0033: UNIVERSITY OF TEXAS SYSTEM (NP)
601 Colorado Street, Austin, TX Zip 78701–2982; tel. 512/499–4224; Charles B. Mullins, Executive Vice Chancellor

TEXAS: HARRIS COUNTY PSYCHIATRIC CENTER (O, 250 beds) 2800 South MacGregor Way, Houston, TX Zip 77021–1000, Mailing Address: P.O. Box 20249, Zip 77225–0249; tel. 713/741–5000; Robert W. Guynn, M.D., Executive Director

UNIVERSITY OF TEXAS HEALTH CENTER AT TYLER (O, 167 beds) Gladewater Highway, Tyler, TX Zip 75708, Mailing Address: P.O. Box 2003, Zip 75710–2003; tel. 903/877–3451; Ronald F. Garvey, M.D., Chief Administrative Officer and Director

UNIVERSITY OF TEXAS M. D. ANDERSON CANCER CENTER (O, 417 beds) 1515 Holcombe Boulevard, Box 506, Houston, TX Zip 77030–4009; tel. 713/792–6000; John Mendelsohn, M.D., President

UNIVERSITY OF TEXAS MEDICAL BRANCH HOSPITALS (O, 884 beds) 301 University Boulevard, Galveston, TX Zip 77555–0138; tel. 409/772–1011; James F. Arens, M.D., Chief Executive Officer

Owned, leased, sponsored:	4 hospitals	1718 beds
Contract–managed:	0 hospitals	0 beds
Totals:	4 hospitals	1718 beds

0137: UPMC HEALTH SYSTEM (NP)
200 Lothrop, Pittsburgh, PA Zip 15213; tel. 412/647–2345; Jeffrey A. Romoff, President

PENNSYLVANIA: LEE HOSPITAL (O, 224 beds) 320 Main Street, Johnstown, PA Zip 15901–1694; tel. 814/533–0123; David R. Davis, President and Chief Executive Officer

MCKEESPORT HOSPITAL (O, 281 beds) 1500 Fifth Avenue, McKeesport, PA Zip 15132–2482; tel. 412/664–2000; Ronald H. Ott, President and Chief Executive Officer

SHADYSIDE HOSPITAL (O, 631 beds) 5230 Centre Avenue, Pittsburgh, PA Zip 15232–1304; tel. 412/623–2121; Henry A. Mordoh, President

For explanation of codes following names, see page B2.
★ Indicates Type III membership in the American Hospital Association.

UPMC BEAVER VALLEY (O, 148 beds) 2500 Hospital Drive, Aliquippa, PA Zip 15001–2123; tel. 724/857–1212; Thomas P. Timcho, President

UPMC BEDFORD MEMORIAL (O, 59 beds) 10455 Lincoln Highway, Everett, PA Zip 15537–4076; tel. 814/623–6161; James C. Vreeland, FACHE, President and Chief Executive Officer

UPMC BRADDOCK (O, 227 beds) 400 Holland Avenue, Braddock, PA Zip 15104–1599; tel. 412/636–5000; Richard Wilson Benfer, President

UPMC SOUTH SIDE (O, 140 beds) 2000 Mary Street, Pittsburgh, PA Zip 15203–2095; tel. 412/488–5550; George J. Korbakes, President

UPMC–PRESBYTERIAN (O, 840 beds) Pittsburgh, PA Jeffrey A. Romoff, President

UPMC–ST. MARGARET (O, 223 beds) 815 Freeport Road, Pittsburgh, PA Zip 15215–3399; tel. 412/784–4000; Stanley J. Kevish, President

UNIVERSITY OF PITTSBURGH MEDICAL CENTER–PASSAVANT (O, 292 beds) 9100 Babcock Boulevard, Pittsburgh, PA Zip 15237–5842; tel. 412/367–6700; Ralph T. DeStefano, President and Chief Executive Officer

Owned, leased, sponsored:	10 hospitals	3065 beds
Contract–managed:	0 hospitals	0 beds
Totals:	10 hospitals	3065 beds

★0038: **UPPER CHESAPEAKE HEALTH SYSTEM** (NP)
1916 Belair Road, Fallston, MD Zip 21047–2797; tel. 410/893–0322; Lyle Ernest Sheldon, President and Chief Executive Officer

MARYLAND: FALLSTON GENERAL HOSPITAL (O, 115 beds) 200 Milton Avenue, Fallston, MD Zip 21047–2777; tel. 410/877–3700; Lyle Ernest Sheldon, Executive Vice President and Chief Operating Officer

HARFORD MEMORIAL HOSPITAL (O, 168 beds) 501 South Union Avenue, Havre De Grace, MD Zip 21078–3493; tel. 410/939–2400; Lyle Ernest Sheldon, President and Chief Executive Officer

Owned, leased, sponsored:	2 hospitals	283 beds
Contract–managed:	0 hospitals	0 beds
Totals:	2 hospitals	283 beds

★0043: **VALLEY HEALTH SYSTEM** (NP)
1117 East Devonshire Avenue, Hemet, CA Zip 92543; tel. 909/652–2811; John Ruffner, Interim Chief Executive Officer

CALIFORNIA: HEMET VALLEY MEDICAL CENTER (O, 285 beds) 1117 East Devonshire Avenue, Hemet, CA Zip 92543; tel. 909/652–2811; John Ruffner, Administrator

MENIFEE VALLEY MEDICAL CENTER (O, 84 beds) 28400 McCall Boulevard, Sun City, CA Zip 92585–9537; tel. 909/679–8888; Susan Ballard, Administrator

MORENO VALLEY COMMUNITY HOSPITAL (O, 73 beds) 27300 Iris Avenue, Moreno Valley, CA Zip 92555; tel. 909/243–0811; Janice Ziomek, Administrator

Owned, leased, sponsored:	3 hospitals	442 beds
Contract–managed:	0 hospitals	0 beds
Totals:	3 hospitals	442 beds

0128: **VALLEY HEALTH SYSTEM** (IO)
1830 Amherst Street, Winchester, VA Zip 22604, Mailing Address: P.O. Box 1334, Zip 22604–1334; tel. 540/722–8024; David W. Goff, President and Chief Executive Officer

VIRGINIA: WARREN MEMORIAL HOSPITAL (O, 95 beds) 1000 Shenandoah Avenue, Front Royal, VA Zip 22630–3598; tel. 540/636–0300; Charlie M. Horton, President

WINCHESTER MEDICAL CENTER (O, 392 beds) 1840 Amherst Street, Winchester, VA Zip 22601–2540, Mailing Address: P.O. Box 3340, Zip 22604–3340; tel. 540/722–8000; George B. Caley, President

WEST VIRGINIA: MORGAN COUNTY WAR MEMORIAL HOSPITAL (C, 44 beds) 1124 Fairfax Street, Berkeley Springs, WV Zip 25411–1718; tel. 304/258–1234; David A. Sweeney, FACHE, Administrator

Owned, leased, sponsored:	2 hospitals	487 beds
Contract–managed:	1 hospital	44 beds
Totals:	3 hospitals	531 beds

0097: **VALLEYCARE HEALTH SYSTEM** (NP)
5575 West Las Positas Boulevard, 300, Pleasanton, CA Zip 94588; tel. 925/447–7000; Marcy Feit, Chief Executive Officer

CALIFORNIA: VALLEY MEMORIAL HOSPITAL (O, 110 beds) 1111 East Stanley Boulevard, Livermore, CA Zip 94550; tel. 510/447–7000; Marcelina Feit, President and Chief Executive Officer

VALLEYCARE MEDICAL CENTER (O, 68 beds) 5555 West Los Positas Boulevard, Pleasanton, CA Zip 94588; tel. 510/847–3000; Marcy Feit, Chief Executive Officer

Owned, leased, sponsored:	2 hospitals	178 beds
Contract–managed:	0 hospitals	0 beds
Totals:	2 hospitals	178 beds

0081: **VALUEMARK HEALTHCARE SYSTEMS, INC.** (IO)
300 Galleria Parkway, Suite 650, Atlanta, GA Zip 30339; tel. 770/933–5500; James T. McAfee Jr., Chairman, President and Chief Executive Officer

VALUEMARK PINE GROVE BEHAVIORAL HEALTHCARE SYSTEM (O, 62 beds) 7011 Shoup Avenue, Canoga Park, CA Zip 91307; tel. 818/348–0500; Diane Sharpe, Chief Executive Officer

FLORIDA: VALUEMARK BEHAVIORAL HEALTHCARE SYSTEM OF FLORIDA (O, 48 beds) 6601 Central Florida Parkway, Orlando, FL Zip 32821–8091; tel. 407/345–5000; Robert Berteau, Chief Executive Officer

GEORGIA: VALUEMARK–BRAWNER BEHAVIORAL HEALTHACARE SYSTEM–NORTH (O, 108 beds) 3180 Atlanta Street S.E., Smyrna, GA Zip 30080–8256; tel. 404/436–0081; Edward J. Osborne, Chief Executive Officer

MISSOURI: VALUEMARK BEHAVIORAL HEALTHCARE SYSTEM OF KANSAS CITY (O, 72 beds) 4800 N.W. 88th Street, Kansas City, MO Zip 64154–2757; tel. 816/436–3900; John Hunter, Chief Executive Officer

VIRGINIA: VALUEMARK WEST END BEHAVIORAL HEALTHCARE SYSTEM (O, 84 beds) 12800 West Creek Parkway, Richmond, VA Zip 23238–1116; tel. 804/784–2200; James D. McBeath, Chief Executive Officer

Owned, leased, sponsored:	5 hospitals	374 beds
Contract–managed:	0 hospitals	0 beds
Totals:	5 hospitals	374 beds

0026: **VENCOR, INCORPORATED** (IO)
400 West Market Street, Suite 3300, Louisville, KY Zip 40202–3360; tel. 502/596–7300; W. Bruce Lunsford, Board Chairman, President and Chief Executive Officer

ARIZONA: VENCOR HOSPITAL – TUCSON (O, 51 beds) 355 North Wilmot Road, Tucson, AZ Zip 85711–2635; tel. 520/747–8200; Kevin Christiansen, Chief Executive Officer

VENCOR HOSPITAL–PHOENIX (O, 58 beds) 40 East Indianola Avenue, Phoenix, AZ Zip 85012–2059; tel. 602/280–7000; John L. Harrington Jr., FACHE, Administrator

CALIFORNIA: VENCOR HOSPITAL–BREA (O, 48 beds) 875 Brea Boulevard, Brea, CA Zip 92821; tel. 714/529–6842; Mindy S. Moore, Administrator

VENCOR HOSPITAL–LOS ANGELES (O, 81 beds) 5525 West Slauson Avenue, Los Angeles, CA Zip 90056; tel. 310/642–0325; Michael F. Hunn, Chief Executive Officer

VENCOR HOSPITAL–ONTARIO (O, 100 beds) 550 North Monterey, Ontario, CA Zip 91764; tel. 909/391–0333; Virgis Narbutas, Administrator

VENCOR HOSPITAL–SACRAMENTO (O, 32 beds) 223 Fargo Way, Folsom, CA Zip 95630; tel. 916/351–9151; Meredith Taylor, Administrator

VENCOR HOSPITAL–SAN DIEGO (O, 70 beds) 1940 El Cajon Boulevard, San Diego, CA Zip 92104; tel. 619/543–4500; Michael D. Cress, Administrator

For explanation of codes following names, see page B2.
★ Indicates Type III membership in the American Hospital Association.

VENCOR HOSPITAL–SAN LEANDRO (O, 42 beds) 2800 Benedict Drive, San Leandro, CA Zip 94577; tel. 510/357–8300; Wayne M. Lingenfelter, Ed.D., Administrator and Chief Executive Officer

FLORIDA: VENCOR HOSPITAL–CORAL GABLES (O, 53 beds) 5190 S.W. Eighth Street, Coral Gables, FL Zip 33134–2495; tel. 305/445–1364; Theodore Welding, Chief Executive Officer

VENCOR HOSPITAL–FORT LAUDERDALE (O, 64 beds) 1516 East Las Olas Boulevard, Fort Lauderdale, FL Zip 33301–2399; tel. 954/764–8900; Lewis A. Ransdell, Administrator

VENCOR HOSPITAL–ST PETERSBURG (O, 60 beds) 3030 Sixth Street South, Saint Petersburg, FL Zip 33705–3720; tel. 813/894–8719; Pamela M. Riter, R.N., Administrator

VENCOR HOSPITAL–TAMPA (O, 73 beds) 4555 South Manhattan Avenue, Tampa, FL Zip 33611–2397; tel. 813/839–6341; Theresa Hunkins, Administrator

VENCOR–NORTH FLORIDA (O, 48 beds) 801 Oak Street, Green Cove Springs, FL Zip 32043–4317; tel. 904/284–9230; Tim Simpson, Administrator

GEORGIA: VENCOR HOSPITAL–ATLANTA (O, 66 beds) 705 Juniper Street N.E., Atlanta, GA Zip 30365–2500; tel. 404/873–2871; Skip Wright, Administrator

ILLINOIS: VENCOR HOSPITAL–CHICAGO NORTH (O, 111 beds) 2544 West Montrose Avenue, Chicago, IL Zip 60618–1589; tel. 773/267–2622; Steven A. Matarelli, Administrator

VENCOR HOSPITAL–SYCAMORE (O, 50 beds) 225 Edward Street, Sycamore, IL Zip 60178–2197; tel. 815/895–2144; Betty Walker, Administrator

INDIANA: VENCOR HOSPITAL–LAGRANGE (O, 57 beds) 207 North Townline Road, LaGrange, IN Zip 46761–1325; tel. 219/463–2143; Joe Murrell, Administrator

KENTUCKY: VENCOR HOSPITAL–LOUISVILLE (O, 156 beds) 1313 St. Anthony Place, Louisville, KY Zip 40204–1765; tel. 502/627–1102; James H. Wesp, Administrator

MASSACHUSETTS: VENCOR HOSPITAL NORTH SHORE (O, 59 beds) 15 King Street, Peabody, MA Zip 01960–4268; tel. 978/531–2900; Della Underwood, Chief Executive Officer

VENCOR HOSPITAL–BOSTON (O, 59 beds) 1515 Commonwealth Avenue, Boston, MA Zip 02135–3696; tel. 617/254–1100; Steven E. Levitsky, Administrator

MICHIGAN: VENCOR HOSPITAL–DETROIT (O, 114 beds) 26400 West Outer Drive, Lincoln Park, MI Zip 48146–2088; tel. 313/594–6000; Deborah A. Sopo, Administrator

MINNESOTA: VENCOR HOSPITAL–MINNEAPOLIS (O, 111 beds) 4101 Golden Valley Road, Golden Valley, MN Zip 55422; tel. 612/588–2750; Patrick A. Auman, Ph.D., Chief Executive Officer

MISSOURI: VENCOR HOSPITAL–KANSAS CITY (O, 110 beds) 8701 Troost Avenue, Kansas City, MO Zip 64131–3495; tel. 816/995–2000; Suzanne R. Wilsey, Administrator

NORTH CAROLINA: VENCOR HOSPITAL–GREENSBORO (O, 125 beds) 2401 Southside Boulevard, Greensboro, NC Zip 27406–3311; tel. 336/271–2800; Leanne Fiorentino, Chief Executive Officer

PENNSYLVANIA: VENCOR HOSPITAL–PHILADELPHIA (O, 52 beds) 6129 Palmetto Street, Philadelphia, PA Zip 19111–5729; tel. 215/722–8555; Debra Condon, Administrator

VENCOR HOSPITAL–PITTSBURGH (O, 63 beds) 7777 Steubenville Pike, Oakdale, PA Zip 15071–3409; tel. 412/494–5500; Patricia B. Speak, Administrator

TENNESSEE: VENCOR HOSPITAL–CHATTANOOGA (O, 43 beds) 709 Walnut Street, Chattanooga, TN Zip 37402–1961; tel. 423/266–7721; Steven E. McGraw, Administrator

TEXAS: VENCOR HOSPITAL–DALLAS (O, 51 beds) 1600 Abrams Road, Dallas, TX Zip 75214–4499; tel. 214/818–2400; Dorothy J. Elford, Executive Director and Chief Executive Officer

VENCOR HOSPITAL–FORT WORTH SOUTH (O, 67 beds) 1802 Highway 157 North, Mansfield, TX Zip 76063–9555; tel. 817/473–6101; Bill Grey, Administrator

VENCOR HOSPITAL–HOUSTON (O, 96 beds) 6441 Main Street, Houston, TX Zip 77030–1596; tel. 713/790–0500; Bob Stein, Executive Director

VIRGINIA: VENCOR HOSPITAL–ARLINGTON (O, 206 beds) 601 South Carlin Springs Road, Arlington, VA Zip 22204–1096; tel. 703/671–1200; Robert S. Davis III, CHE, Administrator

WASHINGTON: VENCOR SEATTLE HOSPITAL (O, 30 beds) 10560 Fifth Avenue N.E., Seattle, WA Zip 98125–0977; tel. 206/364–2050; Deborah L. Abrams, Chief Executive Officer

WISCONSIN: VENCOR HOSPITAL–MILWAUKEE (O, 51 beds) 5700 West Layton Avenue, Milwaukee, WI Zip 53202; tel. 414/325–5900; E. Kay Gray, Interim Administrator

Owned, leased, sponsored:	33 hospitals	2457 beds
Contract–managed:	0 hospitals	0 beds
Totals:	33 hospitals	2457 beds

●5435: VIA CHRISTI HEALTH SYSTEM (CC)
929 North St. Francis, Wichita, KS Zip 67214–3882; tel. 316/268–5000; LeRoy E. Rheault, President and Chief Executive Officer

KANSAS: MERCY HEALTH CENTER OF MANHATTAN (O, 99 beds) Manhattan, KS Mailing Address: 1823 College Avenue, Zip 66502–3381; E. Michael Nunamaker, President and Chief Executive Officer

Owned, leased, sponsored:	1 hospital	99 beds
Contract–managed:	0 hospitals	0 beds
Totals:	1 hospital	99 beds

★0046: VIA HEALTH (NP)
1040 University Avenue, Rochester, NY Zip 14607–1239; tel. 716/756–4280; Roger S. Hunt, President and Chief Executive Officer

NEW YORK: GENESEE HOSPITAL (O, 305 beds) 224 Alexander Street, Rochester, NY Zip 14607–4055; tel. 716/263–6000; William R. Holman, President

NEWARK–WAYNE COMMUNITY HOSPITAL (O, 241 beds) Driving Park Avenue, Newark, NY Zip 14513, Mailing Address: P.O. Box 111, Zip 14513–0111; tel. 315/332–2022; W. Neil Stroman, President

ROCHESTER GENERAL HOSPITAL (O, 526 beds) 1425 Portland Avenue, Rochester, NY Zip 14621–3099; tel. 716/338–4000; Richard S. Constantino, M.D., President

Owned, leased, sponsored:	3 hospitals	1072 beds
Contract–managed:	0 hospitals	0 beds
Totals:	3 hospitals	1072 beds

0012: VIRGINIA DEPARTMENT OF MENTAL HEALTH (NP)
109 Governor Street, Richmond, VA Zip 23219–3623, Mailing Address: P.O. Box 1797, Zip 23218–1797; tel. 804/786–3921; Richard E. Kellogg, Acting Commissioner

VIRGINIA: CENTRAL VIRGINIA TRAINING CENTER (O, 1112 beds) 210 East Colony Road, Madison Heights, VA Zip 24572–2005, Mailing Address: P.O. Box 1098, Lynchburg, Zip 24505–1098; tel. 804/947–6326; Judy Dudley, Director

DE JARNETTE CENTER (O, 60 beds) 1355 Richmond Road, Staunton, VA Zip 24401–1091, Mailing Address: Box 2309, Zip 24402–2309; tel. 540/332–2100; Andrea C. Newsome, FACHE, Director

EASTERN STATE HOSPITAL (O, 727 beds) Williamsburg, VA Mailing Address: P.O. Box 8791, Zip 23187–8791; tel. 757/253–5161; John M. Favret, Director

NORTHERN VIRGINIA MENTAL HEALTH INSTITUTE (O, 62 beds) 3302 Gallows Road, Falls Church, VA Zip 22042–3398; tel. 703/207–7111; John Russotto, Facility Director

PIEDMONT GERIATRIC HOSPITAL (O, 210 beds) Burkeville, VA Mailing Address: P.O. Box 427, Zip 23922–0427; tel. 804/767–4401; Willard R. Pierce Jr., Director

SOUTHERN VIRGINIA MENTAL HEALTH INSTITUTE (O, 96 beds) 382 Taylor Drive, Danville, VA Zip 24541–4023; tel. 804/799–6220; Constance N. Fletcher, Ph.D., Director

---

For explanation of codes following names, see page B2.
★ Indicates Type III membership in the American Hospital Association.
● Single hospital health care system

SOUTHWESTERN VIRGINIA MENTAL HEALTH INSTITUTE (O, 266 beds) 502 East Main Street, Marion, VA Zip 24354–3390; tel. 540/783–1200; Gerald E. Deans, Director

WESTERN STATE HOSPITAL (O, 432 beds) 1301 Richmond Avenue, Staunton, VA Zip 24401–9146, Mailing Address: P.O. Box 2500, Zip 24402–2500; tel. 540/332–8000; Lynwood F. Harding, Director

Owned, leased, sponsored:	8 hospitals	2965 beds
Contract–managed:	0 hospitals	0 beds
Totals:	8 hospitals	2965 beds

★**0995: WELLSTAR HEALTH SYSTEM** (NP)
1791 Mulkey Road, Suite 102, Austell, GA Zip 30106–1124; tel. 770/732–5517; Thomas E. Hill, Chief Executive Officer

GEORGIA: WELLSTAR COBB HOSPITAL (O, 311 beds) 3950 Austell Road, Austell, GA Zip 30106–1121; tel. 770/732–4000; Thomas E. Hill, Chief Executive Officer

WELLSTAR DOUGLAS HOSPITAL (O, 79 beds) 8954 Hospital Drive, Douglasville, GA Zip 30134–2282; tel. 770/949–1500; Thomas E. Hill, Chief Executive Officer

WELLSTAR KENNESTONE HOSPITAL (O, 415 beds) 677 Church Street, Marietta, GA Zip 30060–1148; tel. 770/793–5000; Thomas E. Hill, Chief Executive Officer

WELLSTAR PAULDING HOSPITAL (O, 212 beds) 600 West Memorial Drive, Dallas, GA Zip 30132–1335; tel. 770/445–4411; Thomas E. Hill, Chief Executive Officer

WELLSTAR WINDY HILL HOSPITAL (O, 60 beds) 2540 Windy Hill Road, Marietta, GA Zip 30067–8632; tel. 770/644–1000; Thomas E. Hill, Chief Executive Officer

Owned, leased, sponsored:	5 hospitals	1077 beds
Contract–managed:	0 hospitals	0 beds
Totals:	5 hospitals	1077 beds

★**6725: WEST JERSEY HEALTH SYSTEM** (NP)
1000 Atlantic Avenue, Camden, NJ Zip 08104–1595; tel. 609/246–3604; Richard P. Miller, President and Chief Executive Officer

NEW JERSEY: WEST JERSEY HOSPITAL–BERLIN (O, 79 beds) 100 Townsend Avenue, Berlin, NJ Zip 08009–9035; tel. 609/322–3200; Ellen Guarnieri, Acting Executive Director

WEST JERSEY HOSPITAL–CAMDEN (O, 117 beds) 1000 Atlantic Avenue, Camden, NJ Zip 08104–1595; tel. 609/246–3000; Frederick M. Carey, Executive Director

WEST JERSEY HOSPITAL–MARLTON (O, 163 beds) 90 Brick Road, Marlton, NJ Zip 08053–9697; tel. 609/355–6000; Leroy J. Rosenberg, Executive Director

WEST JERSEY HOSPITAL–VOORHEES (O, 244 beds) 101 Carnie Boulevard, Voorhees, NJ Zip 08043–1597; tel. 609/325–3000; Joan T. Meyers, R.N., Executive Director

Owned, leased, sponsored:	4 hospitals	603 beds
Contract–managed:	0 hospitals	0 beds
Totals:	4 hospitals	603 beds

★**0004: WEST TENNESSEE HEALTHCARE.** (NP)
708 West Forest Avenue, Jackson, TN Zip 38301–3901; tel. 901/425–5000; James T. Moss, President

TENNESSEE: BOLIVAR GENERAL HOSPITAL (O, 47 beds) 650 Nuckolls Road, Bolivar, TN Zip 38008–1500; tel. 901/658–3100; George L. Austin, Administrator

CAMDEN GENERAL HOSPITAL (O, 40 beds) 175 Hospital Drive, Camden, TN Zip 38320–1617; tel. 901/584–6135; Billy Alred, Interim Administrator

GIBSON GENERAL HOSPITAL (O, 42 beds) 200 Hospital Drive, Trenton, TN Zip 38382–3300; tel. 901/855–7900; Kelly R. Yenawine, Administrator

HUMBOLDT GENERAL HOSPITAL (O, 44 beds) 3525 Chere Carol Road, Humboldt, TN Zip 38343–3699; tel. 901/784–0301; Jeff Frieling, Administrator

JACKSON–MADISON COUNTY GENERAL HOSPITAL (O, 660 beds) 708 West Forest Avenue, Jackson, TN Zip 38301–3855; tel. 901/425–5000; James T. Moss, President and Chief Executive Officer

MILAN GENERAL HOSPITAL (O, 62 beds) 4039 South Highland, Milan, TN Zip 38358; tel. 901/686–1591; Alfred P. Taylor, Administrator and Chief Executive Officer

PATHWAYS OF TENNESSEE (O, 47 beds) 238 Summar Drive, Jackson, TN Zip 38301–3982; tel. 901/935–8200; John D. Rudnick Jr., FACHE, Executive Director

Owned, leased, sponsored:	7 hospitals	942 beds
Contract–managed:	0 hospitals	0 beds
Totals:	7 hospitals	942 beds

0119: WEST VIRGINIA UNITED HEALTH SYSTEM (NP)
1000 Technology Drive, Suite 2320, Fairmont, WV Zip 26554; tel. 304/368–2700; Bernard G. Westfall, President and Chief Executive Officer

WEST VIRGINIA: UNITED HOSPITAL CENTER (O, 309 beds) Route 19 South, Clarksburg, WV Zip 26301, Mailing Address: P.O. Box 1680, Zip 26302–1680; tel. 304/624–2121; Bruce C. Carter, President

WEST VIRGINIA UNIVERSITY HOSPITALS (O, 331 beds) Medical Center Drive, Morgantown, WV Zip 26506–4749; tel. 304/598–4000; Bruce McClymonds, President

Owned, leased, sponsored:	2 hospitals	640 beds
Contract–managed:	0 hospitals	0 beds
Totals:	2 hospitals	640 beds

★**6745: WHEATON FRANCISCAN SERVICES, INC.** (CC)
26W171 Roosevelt Road, Wheaton, IL Zip 60189–0667, Mailing Address: P.O. Box 667, Zip 60189–0667; tel. 630/462–9271; Wilfred F. Loebig Jr., President and Chief Executive Officer

ILLINOIS: MARIANJOY REHABILITATION HOSPITAL AND CLINICS (O, 107 beds) 26 West 171 Roosevelt Road, Wheaton, IL Zip 60187–0795, Mailing Address: P.O. Box 795, Zip 60189–0795; tel. 630/462–4000; Bruce A. Schurman, President

OAK PARK HOSPITAL (O, 176 beds) 520 South Maple Avenue, Oak Park, IL Zip 60304–1097; tel. 708/383–9300; Bruce M. Elegant, President and Chief Executive Officer

IOWA: COVENANT MEDICAL CENTER (O, 293 beds) 3421 West Ninth Street, Waterloo, IA Zip 50702–5499; tel. 319/272–8000; Raymond F. Burfeind, President

MERCY HOSPITAL OF FRANCISCAN SISTERS (O, 64 beds) 201 Eighth Avenue S.E., Oelwein, IA Zip 50662–2447; tel. 319/283–6000; Richard Schrupp, President and Chief Executive Officer

WISCONSIN: ELMBROOK MEMORIAL HOSPITAL (O, 136 beds) 19333 West North Avenue, Brookfield, WI Zip 53045–4198; tel. 414/785–2000; Kimry A. Johnsrud, President

SAINT MARY'S MEDICAL CENTER (O, 196 beds) 3801 Spring Street, Racine, WI Zip 53405–1690; tel. 414/636–4011; Edward P. Demeulenaere, President and Chief Executive Officer

ST. CATHERINE'S HOSPITAL (S, 148 beds) 3556 Seventh Avenue, Kenosha, WI Zip 53140–2595; tel. 414/656–3011; Robert M. Lovell, Interim Chief Executive Officer

ST. ELIZABETH HOSPITAL (O, 166 beds) 1506 South Oneida Street, Appleton, WI Zip 54915–1397; tel. 920/738–2000; Otto L. Cox, President and Chief Executive Officer

ST. FRANCIS HOSPITAL (S, 265 beds) 3237 South 16th Street, Milwaukee, WI Zip 53215–4592; tel. 414/647–5000; Gregory A. Banaszynski, President

ST. JOSEPH'S HOSPITAL (O, 595 beds) 5000 West Chambers Street, Milwaukee, WI Zip 53210–9988; tel. 414/447–2000; Jon L. Wachs, President

---

For explanation of codes following names, see page B2.
★ Indicates Type III membership in the American Hospital Association.

ST. LUKE'S MEMORIAL HOSPITAL (C, 183 beds) 1320 Wisconsin Avenue, Racine, WI Zip 53403–1987; tel. 414/636–2011; Edward P. Demeulenaere, President and Chief Executive Officer

ST. MICHAEL HOSPITAL (O, 155 beds) 2400 West Villard Avenue, Milwaukee, WI Zip 53209–4999; tel. 414/527–8000; Jeffrey K. Jenkins, President

Owned, leased, sponsored:	11 hospitals	2301 beds
Contract–managed:	1 hospital	183 beds
Totals:	12 hospitals	2484 beds

★9575: WILLIAM BEAUMONT HOSPITAL CORPORATION (NP) 3601 West Thirteen Mile Road, Royal Oak, MI Zip 48073–6769; tel. 248/551–5000; Ted D. Wasson, President and Chief Executive Officer

MICHIGAN: WILLIAM BEAUMONT HOSPITAL–ROYAL OAK (O, 859 beds) 3601 West Thirteen Mile Road, Royal Oak, MI Zip 48073–6769; tel. 248/551–5000; John D. Labriola, Vice President and Director

WILLIAM BEAUMONT HOSPITAL–TROY (O, 189 beds) 44201 Dequindre Road, Troy, MI Zip 48098–1198; tel. 248/828–5100; Eugene F. Michalski, Vice President and Director

Owned, leased, sponsored:	2 hospitals	1048 beds
Contract–managed:	0 hospitals	0 beds
Totals:	2 hospitals	1048 beds

● ★0068: YORK HEALTH SYSTEM (NP) 1001 South George Street, York, PA Zip 17405–3645; tel. 717/851–2121; Bruce M. Bartels, President

PENNSYLVANIA: YORK HOSPITAL (O, 430 beds) 1001 South George Street, York, PA Zip 17405–3645; tel. 717/851–2345; Bruce M. Bartels, President

Owned, leased, sponsored:	1 hospital	430 beds
Contract–managed:	0 hospitals	0 beds
Totals:	1 hospital	430 beds

Geographically

United States

ALABAMA

Birmingham: 0345 ★ BAPTIST HEALTH SYSTEM 3500 Blue Lake Drive, Suite 100, Zip 35243, Mailing Address: P.O. Box 830605, Zip 35283-0605; tel. 205/715-5319; Dennis A. Hall, President, p. B69

2455 BRADFORD HEALTH SERVICES 2101 Magnolia Avenue South, Suite 518, Zip 35205; tel. 205/251-7753; Jerry W. Crowder, President and Chief Executive Officer, p. B73

0126 CARRAWAY METHODIST HEALTH SYSTEM 1600 Carraway Boulevard, Zip 35234-1990; tel. 205/502-6000; Robert M. Carraway, M.D., Chairman and Chief Executive Officer, p. B77

0100 ★ EASTERN HEALTH SYSTEM, INC. 48 Medical Park East Drive, 450, Zip 35235; tel. 205/838-3999; Robert C. Chapman, FACHE, President and Chief Executive Officer, p. B99

0023 HEALTHSOUTH CORPORATION One Healthsouth Parkway, Zip 35243; tel. 205/967-7116; Anthony J. Tanner, Executive Vice President, p. B105

Brewton: 1255 ESCAMBIA COUNTY HEALTH CARE AUTHORITY 1301 Belleville Avenue, Zip 36426; tel. 334/368-2500; Phillip L. Parker, Administrator, p. B100

Guntersville: 1975 MARSHALL COUNTY HEALTH CARE AUTHORITY 8000 Alabama Highway 69, Zip 35976; tel. 205/753-8000; Julian Sparks, Board Chairman, p. B116

Mobile: 2025 INFIRMARY HEALTH SYSTEM, INC. 3 Mobile Infirmary Circle, Zip 36607-3520; tel. 334/431-5500; E. Chandler Bramlett Jr., President and Chief Executive Officer, p. B109

0057 UNIVERSITY OF SOUTH ALABAMA HOSPITALS 2451 Fillingim Street, Zip 36617-2293; tel. 334/471-7000; Stephen H. Simmons, Senior Administrator, p. B150

Tuscaloosa: 1825 ★ DCH HEALTH SYSTEM 809 University Boulevard East, Zip 35401; tel. 205/759-7111; Bryan Kindred, Chief Executive Officer, p. B92

ARIZONA

Phoenix: 8810 ★ BAPTIST HOSPITALS AND HEALTH SYSTEMS, INC. 2224 West Northern Avenue, Suite D-300, Zip 85021-4987; tel. 602/864-1184; Gerald L. Wissink, President and Chief Executive Officer, p. B70

0034 ★ PMH HEALTH RESOURCES, INC. 1201 South Seventh Avenue, Zip 85007-3913, Mailing Address: P.O. Box 21207, Zip 85036-1207; tel. 602/824-3321; Reginald M. Ballantyne III, President, p. B125

2535 ★ SAMARITAN HEALTH SYSTEM 1441 North 12th Street, Zip 85006-2666; tel. 602/495-4000; James C. Crews, President and Chief Executive Officer, p. B134

Scottsdale: 0037 ★ SCOTTSDALE HEALTHCARE 3621 Wells Fargo Avenue, Zip 85251-5607; tel. 602/481-4324; Max Poll, President and Chief Executive Officer, p. B135

Sun City: 0030 ★ SUN HEALTH CORPORATION 13180 North 103rd Drive, Zip 85351-3038, Mailing Address: P.O. Box 1278, Zip 85372-1278; tel. 602/876-5301; Leland W. Peterson, President and Chief Executive Officer, p. B142

ARKANSAS

Little Rock: 0355 ★ BAPTIST HEALTH 9601 Interstate 630, Exit 7, Zip 72205-7299; tel. 501/202-2000; Russell D. Harrington Jr., President, p. B68

CALIFORNIA

Burbank: 2315 ★ UNIHEALTH 3400 Riverside Drive, Zip 91505; tel. 818/238-6000; James T. Yoshioka, President, p. B148

Cerritos: 0076 COLLEGE HEALTH ENTERPRISES 17100 Pioneer Boulevard, Suite 300, Zip 90701-2709; tel. 562/467-5500; Elliot A. Sainer, President and Chief Executive Officer, p. B81

Covina: 0101 CITRUS VALLEY HEALTH PARTNERS 210 West San Bernardino Road, Zip 91723; tel. 626/938-7577; Peter E. Makowski, President and Chief Executive Officer, p. B81

Fairfield: 2075 ★ NORTHBAY HEALTHCARE SYSTEM 1200 B. Gale Wilson Boulevard, Zip 94533-3587; tel. 707/429-3600; Gary J. Passama, President and Chief Executive Officer, p. B122

Fresno: 1085 COMMUNITY HOSPITALS OF CENTRAL CALIFORNIA Fresno and R. Streets, Zip 93721, Mailing Address: P.O. Box 1232, Zip 93721; tel. 209/442-6000; Philip Hinton, M.D., Chief Executive Officer, p. B90

Hemet: 0043 ★ VALLEY HEALTH SYSTEM 1117 East Devonshire Avenue, Zip 92543; tel. 909/652-2811; John Ruffner, Interim Chief Executive Officer, p. B151

Loma Linda: 2175 LOMA LINDA UNIVERSITY HEALTH SCIENCES CENTER 11161 Anderson Street, Zip 92350; tel. 909/824-4540; B. Lyn Behrens, President, p. B112

Long Beach: 0084 MEMORIAL HEALTH SERVICES 2801 Atlantic Avenue, Zip 90801, Mailing Address: P.O. Box 1428, Zip 90801-1428; tel. 562/933-2000; Thomas J. Collins, President and Chief Executive Officer, p. B117

0435 PACIFIC HEALTH CORPORATION 249 East Ocean Boulevard, Zip 90802; tel. 310/435-1300; Jens Mueller, Chairman, p. B123

Los Angeles: 5755 LOS ANGELES COUNTY-DEPARTMENT OF HEALTH SERVICES 313 North Figueroa Street, Room 912, Zip 90012-2691; tel. 213/240-8101; Mark Finucane, Director Health, p. B112

Oakland: 2105 ★ KAISER FOUNDATION HOSPITALS One Kaiser Plaza, Zip 94612-3600; tel. 510/271-5910; David M. Lawrence, M.D., Chairman and Chief Executive Officer, p. B111

6405 UNIVERSITY OF CALIFORNIA-SYSTEMWIDE ADMINISTRATION 300 Lakeside Drive, 18th Floor, Zip 94612-3550; tel. 510/987-9701; Cornelius L. Hopper, M.D., Vice President Health Affairs, p. B150

Orange: 5425 ★ ST. JOSEPH HEALTH SYSTEM 440 South Batavia Street, Zip 92868-3995, Mailing Address: P.O. Box 14132, Zip 92613-1532; tel. 714/997-7690; Richard Statuto, Chief Executive Officer, p. B141

Pasadena: 0106 ★ SOUTHERN CALIFORNIA HEALTHCARE SYSTEMS 1300 East Green Street, Zip 91106; tel. 626/397-2900; Frederick C. Meyer, President and Chief Executive Officer, p. B140

Pleasanton: 0097 VALLEYCARE HEALTH SYSTEM 5575 West Las Positas Boulevard, 300, Zip 94588; tel. 925/447-7000; Marcy Feit, Chief Executive Officer, p. B151

Roseville: 0235 ★ ADVENTIST HEALTH 2100 Douglas Boulevard, Zip 95661-3898, Mailing Address: P.O. Box 619002, Zip 95661-9002; tel. 916/781-2000; Frank F. Dupper, President, p. B64

Sacramento: 8795 ★ SUTTER HEALTH 2800 L. Street, Zip 95816, Mailing Address: P.O. Box 160727, Zip 95816; tel. 916/733-8800; Van R. Johnson, President and Chief Executive Officer, p. B142

San Diego: 7555 ★ PALOMAR POMERADO HEALTH SYSTEM 15255 Innovation Drive, Suite 204, Zip 92128-3410; tel. 619/675-5100; Victoria M. Penland, President and Chief Executive Officer, p. B124

1505 ★ SCRIPPS HEALTH 4275 Campus Point Court, Zip 92121, Mailing Address: P.O. Box 28, La Jolla, Zip 92038; tel. 619/678-7472; Sister Mary Jo Anderson, Senior Vice President, Hospital Operations, p. B135

2065 ★ SHARP HEALTHCARE 3131 Berger Avenue, Zip 92123; tel. 619/541-4000; Michael Murphy, President and Chief Executive Officer, p. B135

San Francisco: 5205 ★ CATHOLIC HEALTHCARE WEST 1700 Montgomery Street, Suite 300, Zip 94111-9603; tel. 415/438-5500; Richard J. Kramer, President and Chief Executive Officer, p. B80

San Leandro: 0225 ALAMEDA COUNTY HEALTH CARE SERVICES AGENCY 1850 Fairway Drive, Zip 94577; tel. 510/351-1367; David J. Kears, Director, p. B65

Santa Barbara: 0103 COTTAGE HEALTH SYSTEM Pueblo at Bath Streets, Zip 93102, Mailing Address: P.O. Box 689, Zip 93102; tel. 805/682-7111; James L. Ash, President and Chief Executive Officer, p. B91

0063 ★ TENET HEALTHCARE CORPORATION 3820 State Street, Zip 93105, Mailing Address: P.O. Box 31907, Zip 93130; tel. 805/563-7000; Jeffrey Barbakow, Chairman and Chief Executive Officer, p. B143

Yuba City: 2115 FREMONT-RIDEOUT HEALTH GROUP 989 Plumas Street, Zip 95991; tel. 530/751-4010; Thomas P. Hayes, Chief Executive Officer, p. B101

COLORADO

Denver: 0092 ★ CATHOLIC HEALTH INITIATIVES 1999 Broadway, Suite 2605, Zip 80202-4004; tel. 303/298-9100; Patricia A. Cahill, President and Chief Executive Officer, p. B77

0134 ★ EXEMPLA HEALTHCARE, INC. 600 Grant Street, Suite 700, Zip 80203; tel. 303/813-5000; Jeffrey D. Selberg, President and Chief Executive Officer, p. B100

5395 MARYCREST HEALTH SYSTEM 2861 West 52nd Avenue, Zip 80221-1259; tel. 303/458-8611; Dale G. Budde, President, p. B116

CONNECTICUT

Hartford: 0014 CONNECTICUT STATE DEPARTMENT OF MENTAL HEALTH 90 Washington Street, Zip 06106-4415, Mailing Address: P.O. Box 341431, Zip 06134-1431; tel. 203/566-3650; Albert J. Solnit, M.D., Commissioner, p. B90

DELAWARE

Dover: 0107 ★ BAYHEALTH MEDICAL CENTER 640 South State Street, Zip 19901, Mailing Address: 640 South State Street, Zip 19901; tel. 302/674-4700; Dennis E. Klima, President and Chief Executive Officer, p. B70

Wilmington: 0131 ★ CHRISTIANA CARE CORPORATION 501 West 14th Street, Zip 19899, Mailing Address: P.O. Box 1668, Zip 19899; tel. 302/428-2570; Charles M. Smith, M.D., President and Chief Executive Officer, p. B81

DISTRICT OF COLUMBIA

Bowling AFB: 9495 DEPARTMENT OF THE AIR FORCE 110 Luke Avenue, Room 400, Zip 20332-7050; tel. 202/767-5066; Lieutenant General Charles H. Roadman II, Surgeon General, p. B93

Washington: 9655 DEPARTMENT OF NAVY Zip 20066, p. B93

9295 DEPARTMENT OF VETERANS AFFAIRS 810 Vermont Avenue N.W., Zip 20420; tel. 202/273-5781; Kenneth W. Kizer, M.D., M.P.H., Under Secretary for Health, p. B95

2015 ★ GREATER SOUTHEAST HEALTHCARE SYSTEM 1310 Southern Avenue S.E., Zip 20032-4692; tel. 202/574-6926; Dalton A. Tong, CPA, FACHE, President and Chief Executive Officer, p. B103

6615 ★ MEDLANTIC HEALTHCARE GROUP 100 Irving Street N.W., Zip 20010-2975; tel. 202/877-6006; John P. McDaniel, Chief Executive Officer, p. B116

FLORIDA

Clearwater: 0071 ACCORD HEALTH CARE CORPORATION 3696 Ulmerton Road, Zip 34622; tel. 813/573-1755; Stephen H. Noble, President, p. B64

Coral Gables: 0405 RAMSAY HEALTH CARE, INC. 1 Alhambra Plaza, Suite 750, Zip 33134-5217; tel. 305/569-6993; Bert Cibran, President and Chief Operating Officer, p. B133

Dunedin: 1335 MORTON PLANT MEASE HEALTH CARE 601 Main Street, Zip 34698, Mailing Address: P.O. Box 760, Zip 34697-0760; tel. 813/733-1111; Philip K. Beauchamp, FACHE, President and Chief Executive Officer, p. B120

Fort Lauderdale: 3115 ★ NORTH BROWARD HOSPITAL DISTRICT 303 S.E. 17th Street, Zip 33316-2510; tel. 954/355-5100; G. Wil Trower, President and Chief Executive Officer, p. B121

Gainesville: 0111 ★ SHANDS HEALTHCARE 1600 S.W. Archer Road, Zip 32610-0336; tel. 352/395-0421; J. Richard Gaintner, M.D., Chief Executive Officer, p. B135

Hollywood: 0083 ★ MEMORIAL HEALTHCARE SYSTEM 3501 Johnson Street, Zip 33021-5487; tel. 954/985-5805; Frank V. Sacco, FACHE, Chief Executive Officer, p. B117

Jacksonville: 2715 METHODIST HEALTH SYSTEM 580 West Eighth Street, Zip 32209-6553; tel. 904/798-8000; Marcus E. Drewa, President, p. B119

Miami: 0122 BAPTIST HEALTH SYSTEM OF SOUTH FLORIDA 8900 North Kendall Drive, Zip 33176-2197; tel. 305/596-1960; Brian E. Keeley, President and Chief Executive Officer, p. B69

Naples: 1775 HEALTH MANAGEMENT ASSOCIATES 5811 Pelican Bay Boulevard, Suite 500, Zip 34108; tel. 941/598-3175; William J. Schoen, Chairman and Chief Executive Officer, p. B103

Orlando: 3355 ★ ORLANDO REGIONAL HEALTHCARE SYSTEM 1414 Kuhl Avenue, Zip 32806-2093; tel. 407/841-5111; John Hillenmeyer, President and Chief Executive Officer, p. B123

Ormond Beach: 2615 ★ MEMORIAL HEALTH SYSTEMS 875 Sterthaus Avenue, Zip 32174-5197; tel. 904/676-6114; Richard A. Lind, President and Chief Executive Officer, p. B117

Pensacola: 0185 BAPTIST HEALTH CARE CORPORATION 1717 North E. Street, Suite 320, Zip 32501-6335; tel. 850/469-2337; James F. Vickery, President, p. B69

Tampa: 4125 ★ SHRINERS HOSPITALS FOR CHILDREN 2900 Rocky Point Drive, Zip 33607-1435, Mailing Address: Box 31356, Zip 33631-3356; tel. 813/281-0300; Joseph E. Melchiorre Jr., CHE, Executive Administrator, p. B135

Windermere: 9605 UNITED MEDICAL CORPORATION 603 Main Street, Zip 34786-3548, Mailing Address: P.O. Box 1100, Zip 34786-1100; tel. 407/876-2200; Donald R. Dizney, Chairman, p. B148

Winter Park: 4165 ★ ADVENTIST HEALTH SYSTEM SUNBELT HEALTH CARE CORPORATION 111 North Orlando Avenue, Zip 32789-3675; tel. 407/975-1417; Mardian J. Blair, President, p. B64

GEORGIA

Adel: 2335 MEMORIAL HEALTH SERVICES 706 North Parrish Avenue, Zip 31620-2064, Mailing Address: P.O. Box 677, Zip 31620-0677; tel. 912/896-2251; Wade E. Keck, Chief Executive Officer, p. B117

Atlanta: 0073 BOWDON CORPORATE OFFICES 4250 Perimeter Park South, Suite 102, Zip 30341; tel. 770/452-1221; Bill E. Ehrhardt, Executive Director, p. B73

0138 ★ GEORGIA BAPTIST HEALTH CARE SYSTEM 100 10th Street, Zip 30365; tel. 404/253-3011; David E. Harrell, Chief Executive Officer, p. B102

0695 MAGELLAN HEALTH SERVICES 3414 Peachtree Road N.E., Suite 1400, Zip 30326; tel. 404/841-9200; Henry Harbin, M.D., President and Chief Executive Officer, p. B114

0905 SUMMIT HOSPITAL CORPORATION 5 Concourse Parkway, Suite 800, Zip 30328-6111; tel. 770/392-1454; Ken Couch, President, p. B142

0081 VALUEMARK HEALTHCARE SYSTEMS, INC. 300 Galleria Parkway, Suite 650, Zip 30339; tel. 770/933-5500; James T. McAfee Jr., Chairman, President and Chief Executive Officer, p. B151

Austell: 0995 ★ WELLSTAR HEALTH SYSTEM 1791 Mulkey Road, Suite 102, Zip 30106-1124; tel. 770/732-5517; Thomas E. Hill, Chief Executive Officer, p. B153

Thomasville: 0104 ARCHBOLD MEDICAL CENTER 910 South Broad Street, Zip 31792-6113; tel. 912/228-2739; Ken B. Beverly, President and Chief Executive Officer, p. B67

HAWAII

Honolulu: 0040 ★ QUEEN'S HEALTH SYSTEMS 1099 Alakea Street, Suite 1100, Zip 96813; tel. 808/532-6100; Richard L. Griffith, President and Chief Executive Officer, p. B127

3555 STATE OF HAWAII, DEPARTMENT OF HEALTH 1250 Punchbowl Street, Zip 96813; tel. 808/586-4416; Bertrand Kobayashi, Deputy Director, p. B141

ILLINOIS

Arlington Heights: 0113 CANCER TREATMENT CENTERS OF AMERICA 3455 West Salt Creek Lane, Zip 60005-1080; tel. 847/342-7400; William A. Sanger, President and Chief Executive Officer, p. B75

Carbondale: 4175 ★ SOUTHERN ILLINOIS HOSPITAL SERVICES 608 East College Street, Zip 62901-3309, Mailing Address: P.O. Box 3988, Zip 62902-3988; tel. 618/457-5200; John J. Buckley Jr., President, p. B140

Chicago: 0079 ★ CATHOLIC HEALTH PARTNERS 2913 North Commonwealth, Zip 60657-6296; tel. 773/665-3170; Sister Theresa Peck, President and Chief Executive Officer, p. B79

0016 COOK COUNTY BUREAU OF HEALTH SERVICES 1835 West Harrison Street, Zip 60612-3785; tel. 312/633-8533; Ruth M. Rothstein, Chief, p. B91

3855 ★ RUSH-PRESBYTERIAN-ST. LUKE'S MEDICAL CENTER 1653 West Congress Parkway, Zip 60612-3864; tel. 312/942-5000; Leo M. Henikoff, M.D., President, p. B134

0058 ★ UNIVERSITY OF CHICAGO HEALTH SYSTEM 322 South Green Street, Suite 500, Zip 60607; tel. 312/697-8403; Ralph W. Muller, Chief Executive Officer, p. B150

Des Plaines: 5575 SISTERS OF THE HOLY FAMILY OF NAZARETH-SACRED HEART PROVINCE 310 North River Road, Zip 60016-1211; tel. 847/298-6760; Sister Marie Kielanowicz, Provincial Superior, p. B140

Elk Grove Village: 0065 ALEXIAN BROTHERS HEALTH SYSTEM, INC. 600 Alexian Way, Zip 60007–3395; tel. 847/640–7550; Brother Felix Bettendorf, President, p. B65

Evergreen Park: 2295 LITTLE COMPANY OF MARY SISTERS HEALTHCARE SYSTEM 9350 South California Avenue, Zip 60805–2595; tel. 708/229–5491; Sister Carol Pacini, Provincialate Superior, p. B112

Frankfort: 0132 ★ PROVENA HEALTH 9223 West St. Francis Road, Zip 60423–8334; tel. 815/469–4888; Gerald P. Pearson, President, p. B126

Oak Brook: 0064 ★ ADVOCATE HEALTH CARE 2025 Windsor Drive, Zip 60523; tel. 630/990–5003; Richard R. Risk, President and Chief Executive Officer, p. B65

Peoria: 5335 ★ OSF HEALTHCARE SYSTEM 800 N.E. Glen Oak Avenue, Zip 61603–3200; tel. 309/655–2852; Sister Frances Marie Masching, President, p. B123

Springfield: 5355 ★ HOSPITAL SISTERS HEALTH SYSTEM Mailing Address: P.O. Box 19431, Zip 62794–9431; tel. 217/523–4747; Sister Jomary Trstensky, President, p. B108

0086 ★ MEMORIAL HEALTH SYSTEM 800 North Rutledge Street, Zip 62781–0001; tel. 217/788–3000; Robert T. Clarke, President and Chief Executive Officer, p. B117

Wheaton: 6745 ★ WHEATON FRANCISCAN SERVICES, INC. 26W171 Roosevelt Road, Zip 60189–0667, Mailing Address: P.O. Box 667, Zip 60189–0667; tel. 630/462–9271; Wilfred F. Loebig Jr., President and Chief Executive Officer, p. B153

INDIANA

Hobart: 0135 ★ ANCILLA SYSTEMS INC. 1000 South Lake Park Avenue, Zip 46342–5970; tel. 219/947–8500; William D. Harkins, President and Chief Executive Officer, p. B67

Kendallville: 0098 ★ CONTINUUM 951 East Hospital Drive, Zip 46755, Mailing Address: P.O. Box 249, Zip 46755–0249; tel. 219/347–6344, p. B91

Mishawaka: 5345 ★ SISTERS OF ST. FRANCIS HEALTH SERVICES, INC. 1515 Dragoon Trail, Zip 46546–1290, Mailing Address: P.O. Box 1290, Zip 46546–1290; tel. 219/256–3935; Kevin D. Leahy, President and Chief Executive Officer, p. B139

South Bend: 5585 ★ HOLY CROSS HEALTH SYSTEM CORPORATION 3606 East Jefferson Boulevard, Zip 46615–3097; tel. 219/233–8558; Sister Patricia Vandenberg, President and Chief Executive Officer, p. B107

IOWA

Des Moines: 0061 ★ IOWA HEALTH SYSTEM 1200 Pleasant Street, Zip 50309–1453; tel. 515/241–6161; Samuel T. Wallace, President, p. B110

KANSAS

Leavenworth: 5095 ★ SISTERS OF CHARITY OF LEAVENWORTH HEALTH SERVICES CORPORATION 4200 South Fourth Street, Zip 66048–5054; tel. 913/682–1338; Sister Marie Damian Glatt, President, p. B137

Phillipsburg: 1535 ★ GREAT PLAINS HEALTH ALLIANCE, INC. 625 Third Street, Zip 67661–2138, Mailing Address: P.O. Box 366, Zip 67661–0366; tel. 785/543–2111; Roger S. John, President and Chief Executive Officer, p. B102

Topeka: 0805 STORMONT–VAIL HEALTHCARE 1500 Southwest Tenth Street, Zip 66604–1353; tel. 785/354–6121; Maynard F. Oliverius, President and Chief Executive Officer, p. B142

Wichita: 5435 VIA CHRISTI HEALTH SYSTEM 929 North St. Francis, Zip 67214–3882; tel. 316/268–5000; LeRoy E. Rheault, President and Chief Executive Officer, p. B152

KENTUCKY

Lexington: 0145 APPALACHIAN REGIONAL HEALTHCARE 1220 Harrodsburg Road, Zip 40504, Mailing Address: P.O. Box 8086, Zip 40533–8086; tel. 606/226–2440; Forrest Calico, M.D., President, p. B67

Louisville: 2285 ★ ALLIANT HEALTH SYSTEM 234 East Gray Street, Suite 225, Zip 40202, Mailing Address: P.O. Box 35070, Zip 40232–5070; tel. 502/629–8025; Stephen A. Williams, President, p. B66

0315 ★ BAPTIST HEALTHCARE SYSTEM 4007 Kresge Way, Zip 40207–4677; tel. 502/896–5000; Tommy J. Smith, President and Chief Executive Officer, p. B70

0052 ★ JEWISH HOSPITAL HEALTHCARE SERVICES 217 East Chestnut Street, Zip 40202–1886; tel. 502/587–4011; Henry C. Wagner, President, p. B110

0026 VENCOR, INCORPORATED 400 West Market Street, Suite 3300, Zip 40202–3360; tel. 502/596–7300; W. Bruce Lunsford, Board Chairman, President and Chief Executive Officer, p. B151

LOUISIANA

Baton Rouge: 1475 ★ FRANCISCAN MISSIONARIES OF OUR LADY HEALTH SYSTEM, INC. 4200 Essen Lane, Zip 70809; tel. 504/923–2701; John J. Finan Jr., President and Chief Executive Officer, p. B100

0775 ★ GENERAL HEALTH SYSTEM 3600 Florida Boulevard, Zip 70806–3854; tel. 504/387–7810; Chris W. Barnette, President and Chief Executive Officer, p. B101

0715 ★ LSU MEDICAL CENTER HEALTH CARE SERVICES DIVISION 8550 United Plaza Boulevard, 4th Floor, Zip 70809; tel. 504/922–0490; Cary M. Dougherty Jr., Chief Operating Officer, p. B112

New Orleans: 0047 LOUISIANA STATE HOSPITALS 210 State Street, Zip 70118–5797; tel. 504/897–3400; M. E. Teague, Chief Executive Officer, p. B112

MAINE

Bangor: 0555 ★ EASTERN MAINE HEALTHCARE 489 State Street, Zip 04401–6674, Mailing Address: P.O. Box 404, Zip 04402–0404; tel. 207/973–7051; Norman A. Ledwin, President, p. B99

MARYLAND

Baltimore: 1015 ★ JOHNS HOPKINS HEALTH SYSTEM 600 North Wolfe Street, Zip 21287–1193; tel. 410/955–9540; Ronald R. Peterson, President, p. B111

6015 SISTERS OF MERCY OF THE AMERICAS–REGIONAL COMMUNITY OF BALTIMORE 1300 Northern Parkway, Zip 21239, Mailing Address: P.O. Box 11448, Zip 21239; tel. 410/435–4400; Sister Margaret Beatty, President, p. B138

Fallston: 0038 ★ UPPER CHESAPEAKE HEALTH SYSTEM 1916 Belair Road, Zip 21047–2797; tel. 410/893–0322; Lyle Ernest Sheldon, President and Chief Executive Officer, p. B151

Largo: 0029 ★ DIMENSIONS HEALTH CORPORATION 9200 Basil Court, Zip 20785; tel. 301/925–7000; Winfield M. Kelly Jr., President and Chief Executive Officer, p. B99

Lutherville Timonium: 2355 ★ HELIX HEALTH 2330 West Joppa Road, Suite 301, Zip 21093–4635; tel. 410/847–6700; James A. Oakey, President and Chief Executive Officer, p. B107

Marriottsville: 5085 ★ BON SECOURS HEALTH SYSTEM, INC. 1505 Marriottsville Road, Zip 21104–1399; tel. 410/442–5511; Christopher M. Carney, President and Chief Executive Officer, p. B73

Rockville: 9195 U. S. PUBLIC HEALTH SERVICE INDIAN HEALTH SERVICE 5600 Fishers Lane, Zip 20857; tel. 301/443–1083; Michael Trujillo, M.D., M.P.H., Director, p. B147

MASSACHUSETTS

Boston: 0096 ★ CAREGROUP 375 Longwood Avenue, Zip 02215–5395; tel. 617/975–6060; James Reinertsen, M.D., Chief Executive Officer, p. B75

0141 ★ CARITAS CHRISTI HEALTH CARE 736 Cambridge Street, Zip 02135–2997; tel. 617/789–2500; Michael F. Collins, M.D., President, p. B76

0013 MASSACHUSETTS DEPARTMENT OF MENTAL HEALTH 25 Staniford Street, Zip 02114–2575; tel. 617/727–5600; Marylou Sudders, Commissioner, p. B116

1785 ★ PARTNERS HEALTHCARE SYSTEM, INC. 800 Boylston Street, Suite 1150, Zip 02199–8001; tel. 617/278–1004; Samuel O. Thier, M.D., President and Chief Executive Officer, p. B125

Hyannis: 0124 CAPE COD HEALTHCARE, INC. 88 Lewis Bay Road, Zip 02601–5210; tel. 508/862–5011; James F. Lyons, President and Chief Executive Officer, p. B75

Lexington: 5885 ★ COVENANT HEALTH SYSTEMS, INC. 420 Bedford Street, Zip 02173–1502; tel. 781/862–1634; David R. Lincoln, President and Chief Executive Officer, p. B91

Peabody: 0091 PIONEER HEALTHCARE 200 Lake Street, Suite 102, Zip 01960–4780; tel. 978/536–2777; Bruce A. Shear, President and Chief Executive Officer, p. B125

Pittsfield: 2435 ★ BERKSHIRE HEALTH SYSTEMS, INC. 725 North Street, Zip 01201–4124; tel. 413/447–2743; David E. Phelps, President and Chief Executive Officer, p. B72

Springfield: 1095 ★ BAYSTATE HEALTH SYSTEM, INC. 759 Chestnut Street, Zip 01199–0001; tel. 413/789–0000; Michael J. Daly, President, p. B71

Wellesley Hills: 0215 COMMUNITY CARE SYSTEMS, INC. 15 Walnut Street, Zip 02181–2101; tel. 781/304–3000; Frederick J. Thacher, Chairman, p. B89

Section B Index

MICHIGAN

Ann Arbor: 0133 ★ SISTERS OF ST. JOSEPH HEALTH SYSTEM 455 East Eisenhower Parkway, 300, Zip 48108–3324; tel. 313/741–1160; John S. Lore, President and Chief Executive Officer, p. B139

Dearborn: 1165 ★ OAKWOOD HEALTHCARE SYSTEM One Parklane Boulevard, Suite 1000E, Zip 48126; tel. 313/253–6007; James L. Brexler, Chief Executive Officer, p. B122

Detroit: 2145 ★ DETROIT MEDICAL CENTER 3663 Woodward Avenue, Suite 200, Zip 48201–2403; tel. 313/578–2020; David J. Campbell, President and Chief Executive Officer, p. B98

9505 ★ HENRY FORD HEALTH SYSTEM One Ford Place, Zip 48202–3067; tel. 313/876–8715; Gail L. Warden, President and Chief Executive Officer, p. B107

Farmington Hills: 5165 ★ MERCY HEALTH SERVICES 34605 Twelve Mile Road, Zip 48331–3221; tel. 248/489–6000; Judith Pelham, President and Chief Executive Officer, p. B118

Kalamazoo: 0595 ★ BRONSON HEALTHCARE GROUP, INC. One Healthcare Plaza, Zip 49007–5345; tel. 616/341–6000; Frank J. Sardone, President and Chief Executive Officer, p. B75

Midland: 0001 ★ MIDMICHIGAN HEALTH 4005 Orchard Drive, Zip 48670–0001; tel. 517/839–3000; Terence F. Moore, President, p. B119

Port Huron: 0053 ★ BLUE WATER HEALTH SERVICES CORPORATION 1221 Pine Grove Avenue, Zip 48060–3568; tel. 810/989–3717; Donald C. Fletcher, President and Chief Executive Officer, p. B73

Royal Oak: 9575 ★ WILLIAM BEAUMONT HOSPITAL CORPORATION 3601 West Thirteen Mile Road, Zip 48073–6769; tel. 248/551–5000; Ted D. Wasson, President and Chief Executive Officer, p. B154

Traverse City: 1465 ★ MUNSON HEALTHCARE 1105 Sixth Street, Zip 49684–2386; tel. 616/935–6502; John M. Rockwood Jr., President, p. B120

MINNESOTA

Duluth: 0515 BENEDICTINE HEALTH SYSTEM 503 East Third Street, Zip 55805–1964; tel. 218/720–2370; Barry J. Halm, President and Chief Executive Officer, p. B72

Minneapolis: 0041 ★ ALLINA HEALTH SYSTEM 5601 Smetana Drive, Zip 55343, Mailing Address: P.O. Box 9310, Zip 55440–9310; tel. 612/992–2000; Gordon M. Sprenger, Executive Officer, p. B66

1325 ★ FAIRVIEW HOSPITAL AND HEALTHCARE SERVICES 2450 Riverside Avenue, Zip 55454–1400; tel. 612/672–6300; David R. Page, President and Chief Executive Officer, p. B100

Rochester: 1875 ★ MAYO FOUNDATION 200 S.W. First Street, Zip 55905–0002; tel. 507/284–2511; Robert R. Waller, M.D., President and Chief Executive Officer, p. B116

Saint Louis Park: 1985 HEALTHSYSTEM MINNESOTA 6500 Excelsior Boulevard, Zip 55426–4702; tel. 612/993–6400, p. B107

Saint Paul: 2185 ★ HEALTHEAST 559 Capitol Boulevard, 6–South, Zip 55103–0000; tel. 612/232–2300; Timothy H. Hanson, President and Chief Executive Officer, p. B105

MISSISSIPPI

Batesville: 1275 FIRST HEALTH, INC. 107 Public Square, Zip 38606–2219; tel. 601/563–7676; Sandra Skinner, Chief Executive Officer, p. B100

Jackson: 0017 MISSISSIPPI STATE DEPARTMENT OF MENTAL HEALTH 1101 Robert E. Lee Building, Zip 39201–1101; tel. 601/359–1288; Roger McMurtry, Chief Mental Health Bureau, p. B119

Pascagoula: 0067 SINGING RIVER HOSPITAL SYSTEM 2809 Denny Avenue, Zip 39581–5301; tel. 228/938–5062; Robert L. Lingle, Executive Director, p. B136

Tupelo: 0032 NORTH MISSISSIPPI HEALTH SERVICES, INC. 830 South Gloster Street, Zip 38801–4996; tel. 601/841–3136; Jeffrey B. Barber, Dr.PH, President and Chief Executive Officer, p. B122

MISSOURI

Kansas City: 8815 ★ HEALTH MIDWEST 2304 East Meyer Boulevard, Suite A–20, Zip 64132–4104; tel. 816/276–9181; Richard W. Brown, President and Chief Executive Officer, p. B104

0120 SAINT LUKE'S SHAWNEE MISSION HEALTH SYSTEM 10920 Elm Avenue, Zip 64134–4108; tel. 816/932–3377; G. Richard Hastings, President and Chief Executive Officer, p. B134

9255 ★ TRUMAN MEDICAL CENTER 2301 Holmes Street, Zip 64108–2677; tel. 816/556–3000; E. Ratcliffe Anderson Jr., M.D., Executive Director, p. B146

Saint Louis: 0051 ★ BJC HEALTH SYSTEM 4444 Forest Park Avenue, Zip 63108–2259; tel. 314/286–2030; Fred L. Brown, President and Chief Executive Officer, p. B72

5945 ★ CARONDELET HEALTH SYSTEM 13801 Riverport Drive, Suite 300, Zip 63043–4810; tel. 314/770–0333; Gary Christiansen, President and Chief Executive Officer, p. B76

1855 ★ DAUGHTERS OF CHARITY NATIONAL HEALTH SYSTEM 4600 Edmundson Road, Zip 63134–3806, Mailing Address: P.O. Box 45998, Zip 63145–5998; tel. 314/253–6700; Donald A. Brennan, President and Chief Executive Officer, p. B92

5185 ★ SISTERS OF MERCY HEALTH SYSTEM–ST. LOUIS 2039 North Geyer Road, Zip 63131–0902, Mailing Address: P.O. Box 31902, Zip 63131–0902; tel. 314/965–6100; Sister Mary Roch Rocklage, President and Chief Executive Officer, p. B138

5455 ★ SSM HEALTH CARE SYSTEM 477 North Lindbergh Boulevard, Zip 63141–7813; tel. 314/994–7800; Sister Mary Jean Ryan, President and Chief Executive Officer, p. B140

NEBRASKA

Norfolk: 2855 MISSIONARY BENEDICTINE SISTERS AMERICAN PROVINCE 300 North 18th Street, Zip 68701–3687; tel. 402/371–3438; Sister M. Agnes Salber, Prioress, p. B119

NEVADA

Las Vegas: 0093 TRANSITIONAL HOSPITALS CORPORATION 5110 West Sahara Avenue, Zip 89102–3465; tel. 702/257–4000; Richard L. Conte, Chief Executive Officer and Chairman of the Board, p. B146

NEW JERSEY

Camden: 6725 ★ WEST JERSEY HEALTH SYSTEM 1000 Atlantic Avenue, Zip 08104–1595; tel. 609/246–3604; Richard P. Miller, President and Chief Executive Officer, p. B153

Edison: 8855 ★ SOLARIS HEALTH SYSTEM 80 James Street, 2nd Floor, Zip 08820–3998; tel. 732/632–1500; John P. McGee, President and Chief Executive Officer, p. B140

Livingston: 0118 ★ SAINT BARNABAS HEALTH CARE SYSTEM 94 Old Short Hills Road, Zip 07039–5668; tel. 973/322–5000; Ronald Del Mauro, President and Chief Executive Officer, p. B134

Newark: 6545 CATHEDRAL HEALTHCARE SYSTEM, INC. 219 Chestnut Street, Zip 07105–1558; tel. 201/690–3600; Frank L. Fumai, President and Chief Executive Officer, p. B77

Trenton: 0010 DIVISION OF MENTAL HEALTH SERVICES, DEPARTMENT OF HUMAN SERVICES, STATE OF NEW JERSEY Capital Center, P.O. Box 727, Zip 08625–0727; tel. 609/777–0702; Alan G. Kaufman, Director, p. B99

NEW MEXICO

Albuquerque: 3505 ★ PRESBYTERIAN HEALTHCARE SERVICES 5901 Harper Drive N.E., Zip 87109–3589, Mailing Address: P.O. Box 26666, Zip 87125–6666; tel. 505/260–6300; James H. Hinton, President and Chief Executive Officer, p. B125

0021 UNIVERSITY OF NEW MEXICO 915 Camino De Salud, Zip 87131–0001; tel. 505/272–5849; Jane E. Henney, M.D., Vice President Health Sciences, p. B150

NEW YORK

Albany: 0009 NEW YORK STATE DEPARTMENT OF MENTAL HEALTH 44 Holland Avenue, Zip 12229–3411; tel. 518/447–9611; Jesse Nixon Jr., Ph.D., Director, p. B121

Buffalo: 0102 CGF HEALTH SYSTEM 300 Pearl Street, Suite 200, Zip 14202; tel. 716/859–2732; John E. Friedlander, President and Chief Executive Officer, p. B81

Latham: 1485 ★ FRANCISCAN SISTERS OF THE POOR HEALTH SYSTEM, INC. 8 Airport Park Boulevard, Zip 12110; tel. 518/783–5257; James H. Flynn Jr., President and Chief Executive Officer, p. B101

Manhasset: 0062 ★ NORTH SHORE– LONG ISLAND JEWISH HEALTH SYSTEM 300 Community Drive, Zip 11030–3876; tel. 516/562–4060; John S. T. Gallagher, Co–President and Chief Executive Officer, p. B122

New York: 0127 CONTINUUM HEALTH PARTNERS 555 West 57th Street, Zip 10019; tel. 212/420–2000; Robert G. Newman, M.D., Chief Executive Officer, p. B91

0142 ★ NEW YORK & PRESBYTERIAN HEALTHCARE 525 East 68th Street, Zip 10021–4885; tel. 212/746–4000; David B. Skinner, M.D., President and Chief Executive Officer, p. B120

3075 NEW YORK CITY HEALTH AND HOSPITALS CORPORATION 125 Worth Street, Room 514, Zip 10013–4006; tel. 212/788–3321; Luis R. Marcos, M.D., President, p. B121

0110 OUR LADY OF MERCY HEALTHCARE SYSTEM, INC. 600 East 233 Street, Zip 10466–2697; tel. 718/920–9000; Gary S. Horan, FACHE, President and Chief Executive Officer, p. B123

5995 SISTERS OF CHARITY CENTER Mount St. Vincent on Hudson, Zip 10471–9930; tel. 718/549–9200; Sister Elizabeth A. Vermaelen, President, p. B137

Newburgh: 0144 GREATER HUDSON VALLEY HEALTH SYSTEM 600A Stony Brook Court, Zip 12550; tel. 914/568–6050; Paul Dell Uomo, President and Chief Executive Officer, p. B102

Rhinebeck: 0146 CROSS RIVER HEALTHCARE, INC. Mailing Address: P.O. Box 288, Zip 12572; tel. 914/871–4343; Michael C. Mazzarella, Chief Executive Officer, p. B91

Rochester: 0046 ★ VIA HEALTH 1040 University Avenue, Zip 14607–1239; tel. 716/756–4280; Roger S. Hunt, President and Chief Executive Officer, p. B152

Syracuse: 5955 SISTERS OF THE 3RD FRANCISCAN ORDER 2500 Grant Boulevard, Zip 13208–1713; tel. 315/425–0115; Sister Grace Anne Dillenschneider, General Superior, p. B139

Uniondale: 0735 ★ EPISCOPAL HEALTH SERVICES INC. 333 Earle Ovington Boulevard, Zip 11553–3645; tel. 516/228–6100; Jack N. Farrington, Ph.D., Executive Vice President, p. B100

NORTH CAROLINA

Asheville: 0143 MISSION & ST. JOSEPH'S HEALTH SYSTEM 509 Biltmore Avenue, Zip 28801, p. B119

Charlotte: 0705 CAROLINAS HEALTHCARE SYSTEM 1000 Blythe Boulevard, Zip 28203–5871, Mailing Address: P.O. Box 32861, Zip 28232–2861; tel. 704/355–2000; Harry A. Nurkin, Ph.D., President and Chief Executive Officer, p. B76

Winston Salem: 0139 NOVANT HEALTH 3333 Silas Creek Parkway, Zip 27103; tel. 336/718–5000; Paul M. Wiles, President, p. B122

NORTH DAKOTA

Bismarck: 0545 BENEDICTINE SISTERS OF THE ANNUNCIATION 7520 University Drive, Zip 58504–9653; tel. 701/255–1520; Sister Susan Berger, Prioress, p. B72

Fargo: 2235 ★ LUTHERAN HEALTH SYSTEMS 4310 17th Avenue S.W., Zip 58103–3339, Mailing Address: P.O. Box 6200, Zip 58106–6200; tel. 701/277–7500; Steven R. Orr, Chairman and Chief Executive Officer, p. B113

5805 SISTERS OF MARY OF THE PRESENTATION HEALTH CORPORATION 1102 Page Drive S.W., Zip 58106–0007, Mailing Address: P.O. Box 10007, Zip 58106–0007; tel. 701/237–9290; Aaron Alton, President, p. B138

OHIO

Cincinnati: 0415 ★ BETHESDA HOSPITAL, INC. 619 Oak Street, Zip 45206–1690; tel. 513/569–6141; John S. Prout, President and Chief Executive Officer, p. B72

5155 CATHOLIC HEALTHCARE PARTNERS 2335 Grandview Avenue, 4th Floor, Zip 45206–2280; tel. 513/221–2736; Michael D. Connelly, President and Chief Executive Officer, p. B79

0082 ★ HEALTH ALLIANCE OF GREATER CINCINNATI 2060 Reading Road, Suite 400, Zip 45202–1456; tel. 513/632–3700; Jack M. Cook, President and Chief Executive Officer, p. B103

Cleveland: 2515 FAIRVIEW HOSPITAL SYSTEM 18101 Lorain Avenue, Zip 44111–5656; tel. 216/476–7000; Kenneth T. Misener, Vice President and Chief Operating Officer, p. B100

0112 UNIVERSITY HOSPITALS HEALTH SYSTEM 11100 Euclid Avenue, Zip 44106–5000; tel. 216/844–1000; Farah M. Walters, President and Chief Executive Officer, p. B149

Columbus: 1045 DOCTORS HOSPITAL 1087 Dennison Avenue, Zip 43201–3496; tel. 614/297–4000; Richard A. Vincent, President, p. B99

9095 ★ OHIOHEALTH 3555 Olentangy River Road, 4000, Zip 43214–3900; tel. 614/566–5424; William W. Wilkins, President and Chief Executive Officer, p. B123

Mayfield Village: 8835 MERIDIA HEALTH SYSTEM 6700 Beta Drive, Suite 200, Zip 44143; tel. 216/446–8000; Charles B. Miner, President and Chief Executive Officer, p. B118

Sylvania: 5375 ★ FRANCISCAN SERVICES CORPORATION 6832 Convent Boulevard, Zip 43560–2897; tel. 419/882–8373; John W. O'Connell, President, p. B101

Toledo: 0147 PROMEDICA HEALTH SYSTEM 2121 Hughes Boulevard, Zip 43606; tel. 419/291–7176; Alan W. Brass, FACHE, President and Chief Executive Officer, p. B126

OKLAHOMA

Oklahoma City: 0305 ★ INTEGRIS HEALTH 3366 Northwest Expressway, Zip 73112–4416; tel. 405/949–6068; Stanley F. Hupfeld, President and Chief Executive Officer, p. B109

0018 OKLAHOMA STATE DEPARTMENT OF MENTAL HEALTH AND SUBSTANCE ABUSE SERVICES 1000 N.E. Tenth Street, Zip 73152, Mailing Address: P.O. Box 53277, Zip 73152–3277; tel. 405/271–6868; Jerry Nida, M.D., Commissioner of Health, p. B123

Tulsa: 0665 CENTURY HEALTHCARE CORPORATION 5555 East 71st Street, Suite 9220, Zip 74136–6540; tel. 918/491–0780; Jerry D. Dillon, President and Chief Executive Officer, p. B81

0130 HILLCREST HEALTHCARE SYSTEM 1120 South Utica, Zip 74104–4090; tel. 918/579–1000; Donald A. Lorack Jr., President and Chief Executive Officer, p. B107

5305 ★ MARIAN HEALTH SYSTEM Mailing Address: P.O. Box 4753, Zip 74159–0753; tel. 918/742–9988; Sister M. Therese Gottschalk, President, p. B115

OREGON

Medford: 0094 ★ ASANTE HEALTH SYSTEM 2650 Siskiyou Boulevard, Suite 200, Zip 97504–8389; tel. 541/608–4100; Jon K. Mitchell, FACHE, President and Chief Executive Officer, p. B67

Portland: 0585 ★ BRIM, INC. 305 N.E. 102nd Avenue, Zip 97220–4199; tel. 503/256–2070; Jim McKinney, President, p. B73

2755 ★ LEGACY HEALTH SYSTEM 1919 N.W. Lovejoy Street, Zip 97209–1503; tel. 503/415–5600; John G. King, President and Chief Executive Officer, p. B111

PENNSYLVANIA

Harrisburg: 5570 ★ PENN STATE GEISINGER HEALTH SYSTEM 2601 Market Place, Suite 300, Zip 17110–9368; tel. 717/214–2254; Stuart Heydt, M.D., Chief Executive Officer, p. B125

King of Prussia: 9555 UNIVERSAL HEALTH SERVICES, INC. 367 South Gulph Road, Zip 19406–0958; tel. 610/768–3300; Alan B. Miller, President and Chief Executive Officer, p. B149

Mechanicsburg: 1715 CONTINENTAL MEDICAL SYSTEMS, INC. 600 Wilson Lane, Zip 17055–0715, Mailing Address: P.O. Box 715, Zip 17055–0715; tel. 717/790–8300; Robert Ortenzio, President and Chief Executive Officer, p. B90

Philadelphia: 1685 ALBERT EINSTEIN HEALTHCARE NETWORK 5501 Old York Road, Zip 19141–3098; tel. 215/456–7890; Martin Goldsmith, President, p. B65

Pittsburgh: 2305 ★ ALLEGHENY HEALTH, EDUCATION AND RESEARCH FOUNDATION 120 Fifth Avenue, Zip 15222–3009; tel. 412/359–8800; Anthony M. Sanzo, President and Chief Executive Officer, p. B65

2255 ★ ST. FRANCIS HEALTH SYSTEM 4401 Penn Avenue, Zip 15224–1334; tel. 412/622–4214; Sister M. Rosita Wellinger, President and Chief Executive Officer, p. B141

0137 UPMC HEALTH SYSTEM 200 Lothrop, Zip 15213; tel. 412/647–2345; Jeffrey A. Romoff, President, p. B150

Radnor: 0136 CATHOLIC HEALTH EAST 3 Radnor Corp Center, Suite 220, Zip 19087–4592; tel. 610/971–9770; Daniel F. Russell, President and Chief Executive Officer, p. B77

Sayre: 0675 ★ GUTHRIE HEALTHCARE SYSTEM Guthrie Square, Zip 18840; tel. 717/888–6666; Ralph H. Meyer, FACHE, President and Chief Executive Officer, p. B103

Springfield: 0008 ★ CROZER–KEYSTONE HEALTH SYSTEM 100 West Sproul Road, Zip 19064; tel. 610/338–8200; John C. McMeekin, President and Chief Executive Officer, p. B91

Villanova: 0845 DEVEREUX FOUNDATION 444 Deveraux Drive, Zip 19085, Mailing Address: P.O. Box 400, Devon, Zip 19333–0400; tel. 610/520–3000; Ronald P. Burd, President and Chief Executive Officer, p. B98

Wayne: 0455 HOSPITAL GROUP OF AMERICA 1265 Drummers Lane, Suite 107, Zip 19087; tel. 610/687–5151; Mark R. Russell, President and Chief Executive Officer, p. B108

7775 ★ JEFFERSON HEALTH SYSTEM 259 Radnor–Chester Road, Suite 290, Zip 19087–5288; tel. 610/225–6200; Douglas S. Peters, President and Chief Executive Officer, p. B110

York: 0068 ★ YORK HEALTH SYSTEM 1001 South George Street, Zip 17405–3645; tel. 717/851–2121; Bruce M. Bartels, President, p. B154

PUERTO RICO

San Juan: 0011 PUERTO RICO DEPARTMENT OF HEALTH Building A. – Medical Center, Zip 00936, Mailing Address: Call Box 70184, Zip 00936; tel. 809/274–7676; Carmen Feliciano De Melecio, M.D., Secretary of Health, p. B126

RHODE ISLAND

Providence: 0099 ★ CARE NEW ENGLAND HEALTH SYSTEM 45 Willard Avenue, Zip 02905–3218; tel. 401/453–7900; John J. Hynes, President and Chief Executive Officer, p. B75

0060 ★ LIFESPAN CORPORATION 167 Point Street, Zip 02903–4771; tel. 401/444–6699; William Kreykes, President and Chief Executive Officer, p. B111

SOUTH CAROLINA

Columbia: 4155 ★ PALMETTO HEALTH ALLIANCE Taylor at Marion Street, Zip 29220; tel. 803/771–5010; Charles D. Beaman Jr., President, p. B124

Greenville: 1555 ★ GREENVILLE HOSPITAL SYSTEM 701 Grove Road, Zip 29605–4211; tel. 864/455–7000; Frank D. Pinckney, President, p. B103

Spartanburg: 4195 ★ SPARTANBURG REGIONAL HEALTHCARE SYSTEM 101 East Wood Street, Zip 29303–3016; tel. 864/560–6000; Joseph Michael Oddis, President, p. B140

SOUTH DAKOTA

Sioux Falls: 0078 ★ SIOUX VALLEY HOSPITALS AND HEALTH SYSTEM 1100 South Euclid Avenue, Zip 57105–0496; tel. 605/333–1000; Kelby K. Krabbenhoft, President, p. B136

Yankton: 5255 ★ AVERA HEALTH 610 West 23rd Street, Zip 57078, Mailing Address: P.O. Box 38, Zip 57078–0038; tel. 605/322–7050; John T. Porter, President and Chief Executive Officer, p. B68

TENNESSEE

Brentwood: 0080 ★ COMMUNITY HEALTH SYSTEMS, INC. 155 Franklin Road, Suite 400, Zip 37027–4600, Mailing Address: P.O. Box 217, Zip 37024–0217; tel. 615/373–9600; Wayne T. Smith, President and Chief Executive Officer, p. B89

0108 PROVINCE HEALTHCARE CORPORATION 109 Westpark Drive, Suite 180, Zip 37026; tel. 615/370–1377; Marty Rash, President and Chief Executive Officer, p. B126

0002 ★ QUORUM HEALTH GROUP/QUORUM HEALTH RESOURCES, INC. 103 Continental Place, Zip 37027; tel. 615/371–7979; James E. Dalton Jr., President and Chief Executive Officer, p. B127

Chattanooga: 1155 GREENLEAF HEALTH SYSTEMS, INC. One Northgate Park, Zip 37415; tel. 423/870–5110; Dan B. Page, President, p. B103

2795 HEALTHCORP OF TENNESSEE, INC. 735 Broad Street, Zip 37402; tel. 615/267–8406; T. Farrell Hayes, President, p. B105

Franklin: 0074 AMERICAN TRANSITIONAL HOSPITALS, INC. 112 Second Avenue North, Zip 37064–2509; tel. 615/791–7099; T. Jerald Moore, President and Chief Executive Officer, p. B67

Jackson: 0004 ★ WEST TENNESSEE HEALTHCARE. 708 West Forest Avenue, Zip 38301–3901; tel. 901/425–5000; James T. Moss, President, p. B153

Knoxville: 2155 BAPTIST HEALTH SYSTEM OF TENNESSEE 137 Blount Avenue S.E., Zip 37920–1643, Mailing Address: P.O. Box 1788, Zip 37901–1788; tel. 615/632–5099; Dale Collins, President and Chief Executive Officer, p. B69

Memphis: 1625 ★ BAPTIST MEMORIAL HEALTH CARE CORPORATION 899 Madison Avenue, Zip 38146–0001; tel. 901/227–5117; Stephen Curtis Reynolds, President and Chief Executive Officer, p. B70

9345 ★ METHODIST HEALTH SYSTEMS, INC. 1211 Union Avenue, Suite 700, Zip 38104–6600; tel. 901/726–2300; Maurice W. Elliott, President, p. B119

1765 UNITED HOSPITAL CORPORATION 6189 East Shelby Drive, Zip 38115; tel. 901/794–8440; James C. Henson, President, p. B148

Nashville: 0069 BEHAVIORAL HEALTHCARE CORPORATION 102 Woodmont Boulevard, Suite 800, Zip 37205–2287; tel. 615/269–3492; Edward A. Stack, President and Chief Executive Officer, p. B71

0114 CHILDREN'S COMPREHENSIVE SERVICES, INC. 3401 West End Avenue, Suite 500, Zip 37203–0376; tel. 615/383–0376; H. Neil Campbell, Chief Executive Officer, p. B81

0048 ★ COLUMBIA/HCA HEALTHCARE CORPORATION One Park Plaza, Zip 37203–1548; tel. 615/344–2003; Jack O. Bovender Jr., President and Chief Operating Officer, p. B81

0123 COVENANT HEALTH 100 Fort Sanders West Boulevard, Zip 37222; tel. 423/531–5555; Alan C. Guy, President and Chief Executive Officer, p. B91

0116 NETCARE HEALTH SYSTEMS, INC. 424 Church Street, Suite 2100, Zip 37219; tel. 615/742–8500; Michael A. Koban Jr., Chief Executive Officer, p. B120

0335 PARK HEALTHCARE COMPANY 149 Belle Forrest Circle, Zip 37221; tel. 615/662–2577; Jerry E. Gilliland, President, p. B124

TEXAS

Austin: 0395 HEALTHCARE AMERICA, INC. 1407 West Stassney Lane, Zip 78745–2998, Mailing Address: P.O. Box 4008, Zip 78765–4008; tel. 512/464–0200; John P. Harcourt Jr., President and Chief Executive Officer, p. B104

0020 TEXAS DEPARTMENT OF HEALTH 1100 West 49th Street, Zip 78756–3199; tel. 512/458–7111; William R. Archer III, M.D., Commissioner, p. B146

0033 UNIVERSITY OF TEXAS SYSTEM 601 Colorado Street, Zip 78701–2982; tel. 512/499–4224; Charles B. Mullins, Executive Vice Chancellor, p. B150

Bay City: 2505 MATAGORDA COUNTY HOSPITAL DISTRICT 1115 Avenue G., Zip 77414–3544; tel. 409/245–6383; Wendell H. Baker Jr., District Administrator, p. B116

Dallas: 0095 ★ BAYLOR HEALTH CARE SYSTEM 3500 Gaston Avenue, Zip 75226–2088; tel. 214/820–0111; Boone Powell Jr., President, p. B70

2735 ★ METHODIST HOSPITALS OF DALLAS 1441 North Beckley, Zip 75203–1201, Mailing Address: P.O. Box 655999, Zip 75265–5999; tel. 214/947–8181; Howard M. Chase, FACHE, President and Chief Executive Officer, p. B119

Fort Worth: 0039 TARRANT COUNTY HOSPITAL DISTRICT 1500 South Main Street, Zip 76104–4941; tel. 817/927–1230; Anthony J. Alcini, President and Chief Executive Officer, p. B143

Houston: 0077 CAMBRIDGE INTERNATIONAL, INC, 7505 Fannin, Suite 680, Zip 77225; tel. 713/790–1153; Timothy Sharma, M.D., President, p. B75

2645 ★ MEMORIAL HERMAN HEALTHCARE SYSTEM 7737 S.W. Freeway, Suite 200, Zip 77074–1800; tel. 713/776–6992; Dan S. Wilford, President, p. B117

7235 ★ METHODIST HEALTH CARE SYSTEM 6565 Fannin Street, D–200, Zip 77030–2707; tel. 713/790–2221; Peter W. Butler, President and Chief Executive Officer, p. B119

5765 PARACELSUS HEALTHCARE CORPORATION 515 West Greens Road, Suite 800, Zip 77067–4511; tel. 281/774–5100; Charles R. Miller, President and Chief Operating Officer, p. B124

0605 ★ SISTERS OF CHARITY OF THE INCARNATE WORD HEALTHCARE SYSTEM 2600 North Loop West, Zip 77092–8999; tel. 713/681–8877; Sister Christina Murphy, President and Chief Executive Officer, p. B137

Irving: 0129 ★ TEXAS HEALTH RESOURCES 600 East Las Colinas Boulevard, Suite 1550, Zip 75039, Mailing Address: 600 East Las Colinas Boulevard, 1550, Zip 75039; tel. 214/818–4500; Douglas D. Hawthorne, President and Chief Executive Officer, p. B146

Lubbock: 0036 ★ LUBBOCK METHODIST HOSPITAL SYSTEM 3615 19th Street, Zip 79410–1201; tel. 806/792–1011; George H. McCleskey, President and Chief Executive Officer, p. B113

San Antonio: 0265 BAPTIST HEALTH SYSTEM 200 Concord Plaza, Suite 900, Zip 78216; tel. 210/302–3000; Fred R. Mills, President and Chief Executive Officer, p. B69

5565 ★ INCARNATE WORD HEALTH SERVICES 9311 San Pedro, Suite 1250, Zip 78216–4469; tel. 210/524–4100; Joseph Blasko Jr., President and Chief Executive Officer, p. B108

Tyler: 1895 EAST TEXAS MEDICAL CENTER REGIONAL HEALTHCARE SYSTEM 1000 South Beckham Street, Zip 75701–1996, Mailing Address: P.O. Box 6400, Zip 75711–6400; tel. 903/535–6211; Elmer G. Ellis, President and Chief Executive Officer, p. B99

UTAH

Nephi: 0109 ★ RURAL HEALTH MANAGEMENT CORPORATION 549 North 400 East, Zip 84648–1226; tel. 801/623–4924; Mark R. Stoddard, President, p. B133

Salt Lake City: 1815 ★ INTERMOUNTAIN HEALTH CARE, INC. 36 South State Street, 22nd Floor, Zip 84111–1453; tel. 801/442–2000; Scott S. Parker, President, p. B109

VIRGINIA

Falls Church: 9395 DEPARTMENT OF THE ARMY, OFFICE OF THE SURGEON GENERAL 5109 Leesburg Pike, Zip 22041; tel. 703/681–3114; Major Beverly Pritchett, Executive Officer, p. B94

Lynchburg: 2265 ★ CENTRA HEALTH, INC. 1920 Atherholt Road, Zip 24501–1104; tel. 804/947–4700; George W. Dawson, President, p. B81

Newport News: 4810 RIVERSIDE HEALTH SYSTEM 606 Denbigh Boulevard, Suite 601, Zip 23608; tel. 757/875–7500; Nelson L. St. Clair, President, p. B133

Norfolk: 2635 FHC HEALTH SYSTEMS 240 Corporate Boulevard, Zip 23502–4950; tel. 757/459–5100; Ronald I. Dozoretz, M.D., Chairman, p. B100

2565 ★ SENTARA HEALTH SYSTEM 6015 Poplar Hall Drive, Zip 23502–3800; tel. 757/455–7000; David L. Bernd, President and Chief Executive Officer, p. B135

Richmond: 0012 VIRGINIA DEPARTMENT OF MENTAL HEALTH 109 Governor Street, Zip 23219–3623, Mailing Address: P.O. Box 1797, Zip 23218–1797; tel. 804/786–3921; Richard E. Kellogg, Acting Commissioner, p. B152

Roanoke: 0070 ★ CARILION HEALTH SYSTEM 1212 Third Street S.W., Zip 24016–4696, Mailing Address: P.O. Box 13727, Zip 24036–3727; tel. 540/981–7900; Thomas L. Robertson, President and Chief Executive Officer, p. B76

Springfield: 1305 ★ INOVA HEALTH SYSTEM 8001 Braddock Road, Zip 22151–2150; tel. 703/321–4213; J. Knox Singleton, President, p. B109

Winchester: 0128 VALLEY HEALTH SYSTEM 1830 Amherst Street, Zip 22604, Mailing Address: P.O. Box 1334, Zip 22604–1334; tel. 540/722–8024; David W. Goff, President and Chief Executive Officer, p. B151

WASHINGTON

Bellevue: 5415 ★ PEACEHEALTH 15325 S.E. 30th Place, Suite 300, Zip 98007; tel. 425/747–1711; John Hayward, President and Chief Executive Officer, p. B125

Seattle: 5275 ★ SISTERS OF PROVIDENCE HEALTH SYSTEM 520 Pike Street, Zip 98101, Mailing Address: P.O. Box 11038, Zip 98111–9038; tel. 206/464–3355; Henry G. Walker, President and Chief Executive Officer, p. B138

Spokane: 0945 EMPIRE HEALTH SERVICES West 800 Fifth Avenue, Zip 99204, Mailing Address: P.O. Box 248, Zip 99210–0248; tel. 509/458–7960; Thomas M. White, President, p. B99

5265 ★ PROVIDENCE SERVICES 9 East Ninth Avenue, Zip 99202; tel. 509/742–7337; Richard J. Umbdenstock, President and Chief Executive Officer, p. B126

Tacoma: 6555 MULTICARE HEALTH SYSTEM 315 Martin Luther King Jr. Way, Zip 98405, Mailing Address: P.O. Box 5299, Zip 98405–0299; tel. 253/552–1000; William B. Connoley, President, p. B120

WEST VIRGINIA

Charleston: 0955 ★ CAMCARE, INC. 501 Morris Street, Zip 25301–1300, Mailing Address: P.O. Box 1547, Zip 25326–1547; tel. 304/348–5432; Phillip H. Goodwin, President, p. B75

Fairmont: 0119 WEST VIRGINIA UNITED HEALTH SYSTEM 1000 Technology Drive, Suite 2320, Zip 26554; tel. 304/368–2700; Bernard G. Westfall, President and Chief Executive Officer, p. B153

WISCONSIN

Appleton: 2445 ★ UNITED HEALTH GROUP Five Innovation Court, Zip 54914–1663, Mailing Address: P.O. Box 8025, Zip 54913–8025; tel. 920/730–0330; James Edward Raney, President and Chief Executive Officer, p. B148

La Crosse: 9650 ★ FRANCISCAN SKEMP HEALTHCARE 700 West Avenue South, Zip 54601–4796; tel. 608/791–9710; Brian C. Campion, M.D., President and Chief Executive Officer, p. B101

Manitowoc: 1455 ★ FRANCISCAN SISTERS OF CHRISTIAN CHARITY HEALTHCARE MINISTRY, INC 1415 South Rapids Road, Zip 54220–9302; tel. 920/684–7071; Sister Laura J. Wolf, President, p. B101

Milwaukee: 2215 ★ AURORA HEALTH CARE 3000 West Montana, Zip 53215–3268, Mailing Address: P.O. Box 343910, Zip 53234–3910; tel. 414/647–3000; G. Edwin Howe, President, p. B68

0027 ★ HORIZON HEALTHCARE, INC. 2300 North Mayfair Road, Suite 550, Zip 53226–1508; tel. 414/257–3888; Sister Renee Rose, President and Chief Executive Officer, p. B108

Alliances

ALLIANCE OF INDEPENDENT ACADEMIC MEDICAL CENTERS

435 N Michigan Ave, Ste 2700, Chicago, IL Zip 60611; tel. 312/923–9770; Ms Nancie Noie, Managing Director

ARIZONA
Phoenix
Member
Good Samaritan Regional Medical Center
Maricopa Medical Center
St. Joseph's Hospital and Medical Center

CALIFORNIA
Long Beach
Member
Long Beach Memorial Medical Center

Los Angeles
Member
Cedars–Sinai Medical Center

Oakland
Member
Kaiser Foundation Hospital

CONNECTICUT
Hartford
Member
Hartford Hospital
Saint Francis Hospital and Medical Center

DELAWARE
Newark
Member
Christiana Hospital

DISTRICT OF COLUMBIA
Washington
Member
Washington Hospital Center

FLORIDA
Miami Beach
Member
Mount Sinai Medical Center

Orlando
Member
Orlando Regional Medical Center

ILLINOIS
Berwyn
Member
MacNeal Hospital

Chicago
Shareholder
Illinois Masonic Medical Center

Park Ridge
Member
Lutheran General Hospital

INDIANA
Indianapolis
St. Vincent Hospitals and Health Services

LOUISIANA
New Orleans
Member
Ochsner Foundation Hospital

MAINE
Portland
Member
Maine Medical Center

MARYLAND
Lutherville Timonium
Member
Helix Health

MASSACHUSETTS
Springfield
Member
Baystate Medical Center

MICHIGAN
Detroit
Member
Henry Ford Health System

Royal Oak
Member
William Beaumont Hospital–Royal Oak

MISSOURI
Kansas City
Member
Saint Luke's Hospital

Saint Louis
St. John's Mercy Medical Center

NEW JERSEY
Livingston
Member
Saint Barnabas Medical Center

Long Branch
Member
Monmouth Medical Center

Paterson
Member
St. Joseph's Hospital and Medical Center

NEW YORK
Bronx
Member
Bronx–Lebanon Hospital Center

Brooklyn
Member
Maimonides Medical Center

Jamaica
Member
Catholic Medical Center of Brooklyn and Queens

Mineola
Member
Winthrop–University Hospital

New Hyde Park
Member
Long Island Jewish Medical Center

NORTH CAROLINA
Charlotte
Member
Carolinas Medical Center

OHIO
Akron
Member
Akron General Medical Center
Summa Health System

Columbus
Member
Grant/Riverside Methodist Hospitals–Riverside Campus

PENNSYLVANIA
Allentown
Member
Lehigh Valley Hospital

Philadelphia
Member
Albert Einstein Medical Center

Pittsburgh
Member
Mercy Hospital of Pittsburgh
Shadyside Hospital
Western Pennsylvania Hospital

SOUTH CAROLINA
Columbia
Member
Palmetto Richland Memorial Hospital

Greenville
Member
Greenville Hospital System

TEXAS
Dallas
Member
Baylor University Medical Center

ASSOCIATION OF INDEPENDENT HOSPITALS

8300 Troost, Kansas City, MO Zip 64131; tel. 816/276–7580; Mr Jeff Tindle, President and Chief Executive Officer

KANSAS
Council Grove
Member
Morris County Hospital

Garnett
Member
Anderson County Hospital

Girard
Member
Crawford County Hospital District One

Hiawatha
Member
Hiawatha Community Hospital

Holton
Member
Holton Community Hospital

Horton
Member
Horton Health Foundation

Iola
Member
Allen County Hospital

Junction City
Member
Geary Community Hospital

Kansas City
Member
University of Kansas Medical Center

Lawrence
Member
Lawrence Memorial Hospital

Manhattan
Member
Mercy Health Center of Manhattan

Marysville
Member
Community Memorial Hospital

Onaga
Member
Community Hospital Onaga

Ottawa
Member
Ransom Memorial Hospital

Overland Park
Member
Menorah Medical Center

Pittsburg
Member
Mount Carmel Medical Center

Seneca
Member
Nemaha Valley Community Hospital

Topeka
Member
C. F. Menninger Memorial Hospital
St. Francis Hospital and Medical Center

MISSOURI
Albany
Member
Gentry County Memorial Hospital

Belton
Member
Research Belton Hospital

Bethany
Member
Harrison County Community Hospital

Boonville
Member
Cooper County Memorial Hospital

Brookfield
Member
General John J. Pershing Memorial Hospital

Carrollton
Member
Carroll County Memorial Hospital

Carthage
Member
McCune–Brooks Hospital

Chillicothe
Member
Hedrick Medical Center

Clinton
Member
Golden Valley Memorial Hospital

Columbia
Member
University Hospitals and Clinics

Excelsior Springs
Member
Excelsior Springs Medical Center

Fairfax
Member
Community Hospital Association

Farmington
Member
Mineral Area Regional Medical Center

Fulton
Member
Callaway Community Hospital

Hannibal
Member
Hannibal Regional Hospital

Harrisonville
Member
Cass Medical Center

Hermann
Member
Hermann Area District Hospital

Independence
Member
Medical Center of Independence

Jefferson City
Member
Capital Region Medical Center–Southwest

Joplin
Member
St. John's Regional Medical Center

Kansas City
Member
Baptist Medical Center
Park Lane Medical Center
Research Medical Center
Trinity Lutheran Hospital

Kirksville
Member
Northeast Regional Medical Center–Jefferson Campus

Lees Summit
Member
Lee's Summit Hospital

Lexington
Member
Lafayette Regional Health Center

Macon
Member
Samaritan Memorial Hospital

Memphis
Member
Scotland County Memorial Hospital

Mexico
Member
Audrain Medical Center

Milan
Member
Sullivan County Memorial Hospital

Moberly
Member
Moberly Regional Medical Center

North Kansas City
Member
North Kansas City Hospital

Osceola
Member
Sac–Osage Hospital

Richmond
Member
Ray County Memorial Hospital

Saint Joseph
Member
Heartland Regional Medical Center

Sedalia
Member
Bothwell Regional Health Center

Warrensburg
Member
Western Missouri Medical Center

CHILD HEALTH CORPORATION OF AMERICA
6803 West 64th Street, Ste 208, Shawnee Mission, KS Zip 66202; tel. 913/262–1436; Mr Don C Black, President and Chief Executive Officer

ALABAMA
Birmingham
Member
Children's Hospital of Alabama

ARKANSAS
Little Rock
Member
Arkansas Children's Hospital

CALIFORNIA
Fresno
Member
Valley Children's Hospital

Los Angeles
Member
Childrens Hospital of Los Angeles

Oakland
Member
Children's Hospital Oakland

Orange
Member
Children's Hospital of Orange County

Palo Alto
Member
Lucile Salter Packard Children's Hospital at Stanford

San Diego
Member
Children's Hospital and Health Center

COLORADO
Denver
Member
Children's Hospital

DISTRICT OF COLUMBIA
Washington
Member
Children's National Medical Center

FLORIDA
Miami
Member
Miami Children's Hospital

Saint Petersburg
Member
All Children's Hospital

GEORGIA
Atlanta
Member
Egleston Children's Hospital at Emory University

ILLINOIS
Chicago
Member
Children's Memorial Hospital

LOUISIANA
New Orleans
Member
Children's Hospital

MASSACHUSETTS
Boston
Member
Children's Hospital

MICHIGAN
Detroit
Member
Children's Hospital of Michigan

MINNESOTA
Minneapolis
Member
Children's Hospitals and Clinics, Minneapolis

MISSOURI
Kansas City
Member
Children's Mercy Hospital

Saint Louis
Member
St. Louis Children's Hospital

NEBRASKA
Omaha
Member
Children's Hospital

NEW YORK
Buffalo
Member
Children's Hospital

OHIO
Akron
Member
Children's Hospital Medical Center of Akron

Cincinnati
Member
Children's Hospital Medical Center

Columbus
Member
Children's Hospital

Dayton
Member
Children's Medical Center

PENNSYLVANIA
Philadelphia
Member
Children's Hospital of Philadelphia

Pittsburgh
Member
Children's Hospital of Pittsburgh

TENNESSEE
Memphis
Member
Le Bonheur Children's Medical Center

TEXAS
Corpus Christi
Member
Driscoll Children's Hospital

Dallas
Member
Children's Medical Center of Dallas

Fort Worth
Member
Cook Children's Medical Center

Houston
Member
Texas Children's Hospital

VIRGINIA
Norfolk
Member
Children's Hospital of the King's Daughters

WASHINGTON
Seattle
Member
  Children's Hospital and Regional Medical Center

WISCONSIN
Milwaukee
Member
  Children's Hospital of Wisconsin

CONSOLIDATED CATHOLIC HEALTH CARE
  1301 W 22nd Street, Suite 202, Oak Brook, IL Zip 60521–2011; tel. 708/990–2242; Mr Roger N Butler, Executive Director

CALIFORNIA
Orange
Member
  St. Joseph Health System

COLORADO
Denver
Member
  Catholic Health Initiatives

ILLINOIS
Frankfort
Member
  Provena Health

INDIANA
Mishawaka
Member
  Sisters of St. Francis Health Services, Inc.

South Bend
Member
  Holy Cross Health System Corporation

KANSAS
Leavenworth
Member
  Sisters of Charity of Leavenworth Health Services Corporation

Wichita
Member
  Via Christi Health System

MARYLAND
Marriottsville
Member
  Bon Secours Health System, Inc.

MICHIGAN
Ann Arbor
Member
  Sisters of St. Joseph Health System

Farmington Hills
Member
  Mercy Health Services

MISSOURI
Saint Louis
Member
  Carondelet Health System
  Daughters of Charity National Health System

NEW YORK
Latham
Member
  Franciscan Sisters of the Poor Health System, Inc.

OHIO
Cincinnati
Member
  Catholic Healthcare Partners

Sylvania
Member
  Franciscan Services Corporation

PENNSYLVANIA
Radnor
Member
  Catholic Health East

TEXAS
San Antonio
Member
  Incarnate Word Health Services

WASHINGTON
Seattle
Member
  Sisters of Providence Health System

HOSPITAL NETWORK, INC.
  One Healthcare Plaza, Kalamazoo, MI Zip 49007; tel. 616/341–8888; Mr Richard Fluke, President and Chief Executive Officer

MICHIGAN
Allegan
Member
  Allegan General Hospital

Hastings
Member
  Pennock Hospital

Kalamazoo
Member
  Bronson Healthcare Group, Inc.
  Bronson Methodist Hospital

Marshall
Member
  Oaklawn Hospital

Sturgis
Member
  Sturgis Hospital

Vicksburg
Member
  Bronson Vicksburg Hospital

PREMIER, INC.
  3 Westbrook Corporate Center, 9th Floor, Westchester, IL Zip 60154–5735; tel. 708/409–4100; Mr Alan Weinstein, President

ALABAMA
Birmingham
Member
  Children's Hospital of Alabama
  Eye Foundation Hospital

Dadeville
Member
  Lakeshore Community Hospital

Daphne
Member
  Mercy Medical

Dothan
Member
  Flowers Hospital
  Southeast Alabama Medical Center

Enterprise
Member
  Medical Center Enterprise

Gadsden
Member
  Gadsden Regional Medical Center

Geneva
Member
  Wiregrass Hospital

Jacksonville
Member
  Jacksonville Hospital

Monroeville
Member
  Monroe County Hospital

Opelika
Member
  East Alabama Medical Center

Valley
Member
  George H. Lanier Memorial Hospital and Health Services

ALASKA
Anchorage
Member
  Providence Alaska Medical Center

Fairbanks
Member
  Fairbanks Memorial Hospital

Homer
Member
  South Peninsula Hospital

Juneau
Member
  Bartlett Regional Hospital

Ketchikan
Member
  Ketchikan General Hospital

Kodiak
Member
  Providence Kodiak Island Medical Center

Palmer
Member
  Valley Hospital

Seward
Member
  Providence Seward Medical Center

Soldotna
Member
  Central Peninsula General Hospital

Valdez
Member
  Valdez Community Hospital

Wrangell
Member
  Wrangell General Hospital and Long Term Care Facility

ARIZONA
Bullhead City
Member
  Western Arizona Regional Medical Center

Casa Grande
Member
  Casa Grande Regional Medical Center

Ganado
Member
  Sage Memorial Hospital

Glendale
Member
  Arrowhead Community Hospital and Medical Center

Mesa
Member
  Mesa Lutheran Hospital
  Valley Lutheran Hospital

Phoenix
Member
  Baptist Hospitals and Health Systems, Inc.
  Maricopa Medical Center
  Maryvale Samaritan Medical Center
  Phoenix Baptist Hospital and Medical Center

Prescott
Member
  Yavapai Regional Medical Center

ARKANSAS
Ashdown
Member
  Little River Memorial Hospital

Batesville
Shareholder
  White River Medical Center

Benton
Member
  Saline Memorial Hospital

Camden
Member
  Ouachita Medical Center

Crossett
Shareholder
  Ashley County Medical Center

Danville
Shareholder
  Chambers Memorial Hospital

Dardanelle
Shareholder
  Dardanelle Hospital

De Witt
Shareholder
DeWitt City Hospital

Dumas
Member
Delta Memorial Hospital

Gravette
Shareholder
Gravette Medical Center Hospital

Harrison
Shareholder
North Arkansas Regional Medical Center

Hot Springs National Park
Shareholder
Levi Hospital

Jacksonville
Member
Rebsamen Regional Medical Center

Lake Village
Member
Chicot Memorial Hospital

Little Rock
Shareholder
Arkansas Children's Hospital

Magnolia
Shareholder
Magnolia Hospital

McGehee
Shareholder
McGehee–Desha County Hospital

Mena
Member
Mena Medical Center

Monticello
Shareholder
Drew Memorial Hospital

Nashville
Member
Howard Memorial Hospital

Paragould
Shareholder
Arkansas Methodist Hospital

Pine Bluff
Shareholder
Jefferson Regional Medical Center

Siloam Springs
Member
Siloam Spring Memorial Hospital

Springdale
Shareholder
Northwest Medical Center

Warren
Shareholder
Bradley County Medical Center

West Memphis
Shareholder
Crittenden Memorial Hospital

CALIFORNIA

Alhambra
Member
Alhambra Hospital

Anaheim
Member
Martin Luther Hospital

Apple Valley
Member
St. Mary Regional Medical Center

Arroyo Grande
Member
Arroyo Grande Community Hospital

Bakersfield
Member
Kern Medical Center
San Joaquin Community Hospital

Burbank
Member
Providence Saint Joseph Medical Center
UniHealth

Chula Vista
Member
Sharp Chula Vista Medical Center

Clearlake
Member
Redbud Community Hospital

Corona
Member
Corona Regional Medical Center

Coronado
Member
Sharp Coronado Hospital

Deer Park
Member
St. Helena Hospital

Delano
Member
Delano Regional Medical Center

Escondido
Member
Palomar Medical Center

Eureka
Member
Saint Joseph Hospital

Fortuna
Member
Redwood Memorial Hospital

Fresno
Member
Valley Children's Hospital

Fullerton
Member
St. Jude Medical Center

Glendale
Member
Glendale Adventist Medical Center
Glendale Memorial Hospital and Health Center

Hanford
Member
Hanford Community Medical Center

Harbor City
Member
Bay Harbor Hospital

La Mesa
Member
Grossmont Hospital

La Palma
Member
La Palma Intercommunity Hospital

Lompoc
Member
Lompoc District Hospital

Long Beach
Member
Long Beach Community Medical Center

Los Angeles
Member
California Hospital Medical Center
Childrens Hospital of Los Angeles
White Memorial Medical Center

Mission Hills
Member
Providence Holy Cross Medical Center

Mission Viejo
Member
Mission Hospital Regional Medical Center

Murrieta
Member
Sharp Healthcare Murrieta

Napa
Member
Queen of the Valley Hospital

National City
Member
Paradise Valley Hospital

Northridge
Member
Northridge Hospital Medical Center–Roscoe Boulevard
Campus

Oakland
Member
Children's Hospital Oakland
Summit Medical Center

Orange
Member
St. Joseph Health System
St. Joseph Hospital

Palo Alto
Member
Lucile Salter Packard Children's Hospital at Stanford

Paradise
Member
Feather River Hospital

Petaluma
Member
Petaluma Valley Hospital

Poway
Member
Pomerado Hospital

Rancho Mirage
Member
Eisenhower Memorial Hospital and Betty Ford Center
at Eisenhower

Roseville
Member
Adventist Health

San Diego
Member
Children's Hospital and Health Center
Mesa Vista Hospital
Palomar Pomerado Health System
Sharp Cabrillo Hospital
Sharp Healthcare
Sharp Memorial Hospital

San Francisco
Member
Davies Medical Center

San Gabriel
Member
San Gabriel Valley Medical Center

San Luis Obispo
Member
French Hospital Medical Center

San Pedro
Member
San Pedro Peninsula Hospital

Santa Paula
Member
Santa Paula Memorial Hospital

Santa Rosa
Member
Santa Rosa Memorial Hospital

Selma
Member
Selma District Hospital

Simi Valley
Member
Simi Valley Hospital and Health Care Services

Sonora
Member
Sonora Community Hospital

South Laguna
Member
South Coast Medical Center

Ukiah
Member
Ukiah Valley Medical Center

Van Nuys
Member
Northridge Hospital and Medical Center, Sherman
Way Campus

Victorville
Member
Victor Valley Community Hospital

Willits
Member
Frank R. Howard Memorial Hospital

COLORADO

Brush
Member
East Morgan County Hospital

Cortez
Member
Southwest Memorial Hospital

Craig
Member
Memorial Hospital

Delta
Member
Delta County Memorial Hospital

Denver
Member
Children's Hospital

Glenwood Springs
Member
Valley View Hospital

Greeley
Member
North Colorado Medical Center

Lamar
Member
Prowers Medical Center

Loveland
Member
McKee Medical Center

Meeker
Member
Pioneers Hospital of Rio Blanco County

Montrose
Member
Montrose Memorial Hospital

Rifle
Member
Grand River Hospital District

Salida
Member
Heart of the Rockies Regional Medical Center

Sterling
Member
Sterling Regional Medcenter

Trinidad
Member
Mount San Rafael Hospital

Yuma
Affiliate
Yuma District Hospital

CONNECTICUT

Bristol
Member
Bristol Hospital

Hartford
Member
Saint Francis Hospital and Medical Center

New Haven
Member
Hospital of Saint Raphael

Stafford Springs
Member
Johnson Memorial Hospital

DELAWARE

Dover
Member
Bayhealth Medical Center

Lewes
Member
Beebe Medical Center

Newark
Member
Christiana Hospital

Seaford
Member
Nanticoke Memorial Hospital

Wilmington
Member
Alfred I.duPont Hospital for Children
Christiana Care Corporation
Eugene Dupont Preventive Medicine and Rehabilitation
Institute
Wilmington Hospital

DISTRICT OF COLUMBIA

Washington
Member
Children's National Medical Center
Columbia Hospital for Women Medical Center
George Washington University Hospital
Sibley Memorial Hospital

FLORIDA

Altamonte Springs
Member
Florida Hospital–Altamonte

Apopka
Member
Florida Hospital–Apopka

Arcadia
Member
DeSoto Memorial Hospital

Belle Glade
Member
Glades General Hospital

Brooksville
Member
Brooksville Regional Hospital

Bunnell
Member
Memorial Hospital–Flagler

Clearwater
Member
Accord Health Care Corporation

Clewiston
Member
Hendry Regional Medical Center

Coral Springs
Member
Coral Springs Medical Center

De Land
Member
Memorial Hospital–West Volusia

Dunedin
Member
Mease Hospital Dunedin
Morton Plant Mease Health Care

Eustis
Member
Florida Hospital Waterman

Fernandina Beach
Member
Baptist Medical Center–Nassau

Fort Lauderdale
Member
Broward General Medical Center
Cleveland Clinic Hospital
Holy Cross Hospital
Imperial Point Medical Center
North Broward Hospital District

Gainesville
Member
AvMed–Santa Fe

Hollywood
Member
Memorial Regional Hospital

Homestead
Member
Homestead Hospital

Jacksonville
Member
St. Vincent's Medical Center

Jacksonville Beach
Member
Baptist Medical Center–Beaches

Jupiter
Member
Jupiter Medical Center

Kissimmee
Member
Florida Hospital Kissimmee

Lake City
Member
Shands at Lake Shore

Lake Wales
Member
Lake Wales Medical Centers

Largo
Member
Sun Coast Hospital

Marianna
Member
Jackson Hospital

Miami
Member
Baptist Hospital of Miami
Bascom Palmer Eye Institute–Anne Bates Leach Eye
Hospital
Miami Children's Hospital
Pan American Hospital
South Miami Hospital

Miami Beach
Member
Mount Sinai Medical Center

Naples
Member
Naples Community Hospital

New Port Richey
Member
North Bay Medical Center

New Smyrna Beach
Member
Bert Fish Medical Center

Orange City
Member
Florida Hospital Fish Memorial

Orlando
Member
Florida Hospital

Ormond Beach
Member
Memorial Health Systems
Memorial Hospital–Ormond Beach

Pembroke Pines
Member
Memorial Hospital Pembroke
Memorial Hospital West

Plant City
Member
South Florida Baptist Hospital

Pompano Beach
Member
North Broward Medical Center

Port Charlotte
Member
Bon Secours–St. Joseph Hospital

Rockledge
Member
Wuesthoff Hospital

Safety Harbor
Member
Mease Countryside Hospital

Saint Petersburg
Member
All Children's Hospital
Bayfront Medical Center
St. Anthony's Hospital

Sebring
Member
Florida Hospital Heartland Division

Spring Hill
Member
Spring Hill Regional Hospital

Tampa
Member
H. Lee Moffitt Cancer Center and Research Institute
St. Joseph's Hospital
Tampa Children's Hospital at St. Joseph's, St.
Joseph's Women's Hospital – Tampa

Tarpon Springs
Member
  Helen Ellis Memorial Hospital

Tavernier
Member
  Mariners Hospital

Titusville
Member
  Parrish Medical Center

Venice
Member
  Bon Secours–Venice Hospital

Vero Beach
Member
  Indian River Memorial Hospital

Winter Haven
Member
  Winter Haven Hospital

Winter Park
Member
  Adventist Health System Sunbelt Health Care
    Corporation

Zephyrhills
Member
  East Pasco Medical Center

GEORGIA

Athens
Member
  St. Mary's Hospital

Atlanta
Member
  Egleston Children's Hospital at Emory University
  Georgia Baptist Medical Center
  Northside Hospital
  Saint Joseph's Hospital of Atlanta

Augusta
Member
  University Hospital
  Walton Rehabilitation Hospital

Blairsville
Member
  Union General Hospital

Bremen
Member
  Higgins General Hospital

Brunswick
Member
  Southeast Georgia Regional Medical Center

Calhoun
Member
  Gordon Hospital

Carrollton
Member
  Tanner Medical Center

Columbus
Member
  St. Francis Hospital

Cumming
Member
  Baptist North Hospital

Demorest
Member
  Habersham County Medical Center

Elberton
Member
  Elbert Memorial Hospital

Fort Oglethorpe
Member
  Hutcheson Medical Center

Glenwood
Member
  Wheeler County Hospital

Greensboro
Member
  Minnie G. Boswell Memorial Hospital

Hiawassee
Member
  Chatuge Regional Hospital and Nursing Home

Jesup
Member
  Wayne Memorial Hospital

La Grange
Member
  West Georgia Health System

Macon
Member
  Macon Northside Hospital
  Middle Georgia Hospital

Milledgeville
Member
  Oconee Regional Medical Center

Monroe
Member
  Walton Medical Center

Richland
Member
  Stewart–Webster Hospital

Saint Marys
Member
  Camden Medical Center

Savannah
Member
  Candler Hospital
  Memorial Health System
  St. Joseph's Hospital

Smyrna
Member
  Emory–Adventist Hospital

Sparta
Member
  Hancock Memorial Hospital

Sylvania
Member
  Screven County Hospital

Sylvester
Member
  Baptist Hospital, Worth County

Thomaston
Member
  Upson Regional Medical Center

Tifton
Member
  Tift General Hospital

Vienna
Member
  Dooly Medical Center

Warm Springs
Member
  Baptist Meriwether Hospital

Washington
Member
  Wills Memorial Hospital

HAWAII

Honolulu
Member
  Kuakini Medical Center

Kailua
Member
  Castle Medical Center

IDAHO

Blackfoot
Member
  Bingham Memorial Hospital

Moscow
Member
  Gritman Medical Center

ILLINOIS

Aurora
Member
  Provena Mercy Center

Barrington
Member
  Good Shepherd Hospital

Blue Island
Member
  Saint Francis Hospital and Health Center

Canton
Member
  Graham Hospital

Carmi
Member
  White County Medical Center

Carrollton
Member
  Thomas H. Boyd Memorial Hospital

Carthage
Member
  Memorial Hospital

Centralia
Member
  St. Mary's Hospital

Chicago
Member
  Bethany Hospital
  Children's Memorial Hospital
  Mercy Hospital and Medical Center
  Mount Sinai Hospital Medical Center of Chicago
  Our Lady of the Resurrection Medical Center
  Ravenswood Hospital Medical Center
  Resurrection Medical Center
  Thorek Hospital and Medical Center
  Trinity Hospital

Downers Grove
Member
  Good Samaritan Hospital

Elk Grove Village
Member
  Alexian Brothers Medical Center

Galesburg
Member
  Galesburg Cottage Hospital

Geneva
Member
  Delnor–Community Hospital

Gibson City
Member
  Gibson Community Hospital

Glendale Heights
Member
  GlenOaks Hospital

Hazel Crest
Member
  South Suburban Hospital

Hinsdale
Member
  Hinsdale Hospital

Hoopeston
Member
  Hoopeston Community Memorial Hospital

Melrose Park
Member
  Gottlieb Memorial Hospital

Metropolis
Member
  Massac Memorial Hospital

Morrison
Member
  Morrison Community Hospital

Mount Carmel
Member
  Wabash General Hospital District

Mount Vernon
Member
  Good Samaritan Regional Health Center

Nashville
Member
  Washington County Hospital

Oak Brook
Member
  Advocate Health Care

Oak Lawn
Member
  Christ Hospital and Medical Center

Ottawa
Member
  Community Hospital of Ottawa

Paris
Member
  Paris Community Hospital

Park Ridge
Member
  Lutheran General Hospital

Peoria
Member
  Methodist Health Services Corporation
  Methodist Medical Center of Illinois

Pinckneyville
Member
  Pinckneyville Community Hospital

Pittsfield
Member
  Illini Community Hospital

Robinson
Member
  Crawford Memorial Hospital

Staunton
Member
  Community Memorial Hospital

Urbana
Member
  Carle Foundation Hospital

Winfield
Member
  Central DuPage Hospital

INDIANA

Bluffton
Member
  Caylor–Nickel Medical Center

Brazil
Member
  Clay County Hospital

Charlestown
Member
  Medical Center of Southern Indiana

Evansville
Member
  Welborn Memorial Baptist Hospital

Frankfort
Member
  Clinton County Hospital

Gary
Member
  Methodist Hospitals

Greensburg
Member
  Decatur County Memorial Hospital

Hartford City
Member
  Blackford County Hospital

Jeffersonville
Member
  Clark Memorial Hospital

North Vernon
Member
  Jennings Community Hospital

Princeton
Member
  Gibson General Hospital

Rushville
Member
  Rush Memorial Hospital

Salem
Member
  Washington County Memorial Hospital

Scottsburg
Member
  Scott Memorial Hospital

Sullivan
Member
  Mary Sherman Hospital

Tell City
Member
  Perry County Memorial Hospital

Wabash
Member
  Wabash County Hospital

Washington
Member
  Daviess County Hospital

Winchester
Member
  Randolph County Hospital and Health Services

IOWA

Algona
Member
  Kossuth Regional Health Center

Ames
Member
  Mary Greeley Medical Center

Anamosa
Member
  Anamosa Community Hospital

Belmond
Member
  Belmond Community Hospital

Boone
Member
  Boone County Hospital

Britt
Member
  Hancock County Memorial Hospital

Burlington
Member
  Burlington Medical Center

Cedar Rapids
Member
  Mercy Medical Center
  St. Luke's Hospital

Chariton
Member
  Lucas County Health Center

Charles City
Member
  Floyd County Memorial Hospital

Clarion
Member
  Community Memorial Hospital

Clinton
Member
  Samaritan Health System

Corning
Member
  Alegent Health Mercy Hospital

Council Bluffs
Member
  Alegent Health Mercy Hospital

Cresco
Member
  Regional Health Services of Howard County

Davenport
Member
  Genesis Medical Center

De Witt
Member
  DeWitt Community Hospital

Des Moines
Member
  Harrison Treat and Rehabilitation Center
  Iowa Health System
  Iowa Lutheran Hospital
  Iowa Methodist Medical Center

Dubuque
Member
  Finley Hospital
  Mercy Health Center

Dyersville
Member
  Mercy Health Center–St. Mary's Unit

Eldora
Member
  Eldora Regional Medical Center

Elkader
Member
  Central Community Hospital

Emmetsburg
Member
  Palo Alto County Hospital

Estherville
Member
  Holy Family Health Services

Fairfield
Member
  Jefferson County Hospital

Fort Dodge
Member
  Trinity Regional Hospital

Fort Madison
Member
  Fort Madison Community Hospital

Grinnell
Member
  Grinnell Regional Medical Center

Hampton
Member
  Franklin General Hospital

Hawarden
Member
  Hawarden Community Hospital

Humboldt
Member
  Humboldt County Memorial Hospital

Iowa City
Member
  Mercy Hospital

Iowa Falls
Member
  Ellsworth Municipal Hospital

Knoxville
Member
  Knoxville Area Community Hospital

Manchester
Member
  Delaware County Memorial Hospital

Maquoketa
Member
  Jackson County Public Hospital

Marengo
Member
  Marengo Memorial Hospital

Marshalltown
Member
  Marshalltown Medical and Surgical Center

Mason City
Member
  North Iowa Mercy Health Center

Missouri Valley
Member
  Alegent Health Community Memorial Hospital

New Hampton
Member
  Saint Joseph Community Hospital

Newton
Member
  Skiff Medical Center

Osage
Member
  Mitchell County Regional Health Center

Osceola
Member
  Clarke County Hospital

Oskaloosa
Member
  Mahaska County Hospital

Ottumwa
Member
  Ottumwa Regional Health Center

Pella
Member
  Pella Regional Health Center

Pocahontas
Member
  Pocahontas Community Hospital

Primghar
Member
  Baum Harmon Memorial Hospital

Rock Valley
Member
  Hegg Memorial Health Center

Sac City
Member
  Loring Hospital

Shenandoah
Member
  Shenandoah Memorial Hospital

Sibley
Member
  Osceola Community Hospital

Sioux City
Member
  Marian Health Center
  St. Luke's Regional Medical Center

Spencer
Member
  Spencer Municipal Hospital

Storm Lake
Member
  Buena Vista County Hospital

Washington
Member
  Washington County Hospital

Waterloo
Member
  Allen Memorial Hospital

Winterset
Member
  Madison County Memorial Hospital

KANSAS
Chanute
Member
  Neosho Memorial Regional Medical Center

Coffeyville
Member
  Coffeyville Regional Medical Center

Emporia
Member
  Newman Memorial County Hospital

Iola
Member
  Allen County Hospital

Lawrence
Member
  Lawrence Memorial Hospital

Marion
Member
  St. Luke Hospital

Neodesha
Member
  Wilson County Hospital

Oberlin
Member
  Decatur County Hospital

Overland Park
Member
  Menorah Medical Center

Ulysses
Member
  Bob Wilson Memorial Grant County Hospital

KENTUCKY
Benton
Member
  Marshall County Hospital

Berea
Member
  Berea Hospital

Bowling Green
Member
  The Medical Center at Bowling Green

Burkesville
Member
  Cumberland County Hospital

Cadiz
Member
  Trigg County Hospital

Campbellsville
Member
  Taylor County Hospital

Carrollton
Member
  Carroll County Hospital

Corbin
Member
  Baptist Regional Medical Center

Elizabethtown
Member
  Hardin Memorial Hospital

Flemingsburg
Member
  Fleming County Hospital

Franklin
Member
  Franklin–Simpson Memorial Hospital

Glasgow
Member
  T. J. Samson Community Hospital

Greensburg
Member
  Jane Todd Crawford Hospital

Greenville
Member
  Muhlenberg Community Hospital

Hardinsburg
Member
  Breckinridge Memorial Hospital

Harrodsburg
Member
  The James B. Haggin Memorial Hospital

Henderson
Member
  Community Methodist Hospital

Horse Cave
Member
  Caverna Memorial Hospital

Irvine
Member
  Marcum and Wallace Memorial Hospital

La Grange
Member
  Tri County Baptist Hospital

Lancaster
Member
  Garrard County Memorial Hospital

Leitchfield
Member
  Twin Lakes Regional Medical Center

Lexington
Member
  Central Baptist Hospital
  Jewish Hospital Lexington

Louisville
  Charter louisville Behavioral Health System
Member
  Alliant Health System
  Alliant Hospitals
  Baptist Healthcare System
  Baptist Hospital East
  Caritas Medical Center
  Caritas Peace Center
  Jewish Hospital
  Jewish Hospital HealthCare Services
  Kosair Children's Hospital
  Norton Hospital
  University of Louisville Hospital

Manchester
Member
  Memorial Hospital

Morganfield
Member
  Union County Methodist Hospital

Mount Sterling
Member
  Mary Chiles Hospital Extended Care Facility

Mount Vernon
Member
  Rockcastle Hospital and Respiratory Care Center

Murray
Member
  Murray–Calloway County Hospital

Paducah
Member
  Lourdes Hospital
  Western Baptist Hospital

Pikeville
Member
  Pikeville United Methodist Hospital of Kentucky

Pineville
Member
  Pineville Community Hospital Association

Princeton
Member
  Caldwell County Hospital

Richmond
Member
  Pattie A. Clay Hospital

Russell Springs
Member
  Russell County Hospital

Salem
Member
  Livingston Hospital and Healthcare Services

Scottsville
Member
  Medical Center at Scottsville

Shelbyville
Member
  Jewish Hospital–Shelbyville

Stanford
Member
  Fort Logan Hospital

Versailles
Member
  Woodford Hospital

Winchester
Member
  Clark Regional Medical Center

LOUISIANA
Alexandria
Member
  St. Frances Cabrini Hospital

Baton Rouge
Member
  Baton Rouge General Health Center
  Baton Rouge General Medical Center
  General Health System
  Woman's Hospital

Bossier City
Member
  Bossier Medical Center

Farmerville
Member
  Union General Hospital

Franklin
Member
  Franklin Foundation Hospital

Hammond
Member
  North Oaks Medical Center

Homer
Member
  Homer Memorial Hospital

Houma
Member
  Terrebonne General Medical Center

Jena
Member
  La Salle General Hospital

Kaplan
Member
  Abrom Kaplan Memorial Hospital

Alliances

Lafayette
Member
 Lafayette General Medical Center

Lake Charles
Member
 St. Patrick Hospital of Lake Charles

Lutcher
Member
 St. James Parish Hospital

Marrero
Member
 West Jefferson Medical Center

Morgan City
Member
 Lakewood Medical Center

Natchitoches
Member
 Natchitoches Parish Hospital

New Orleans
Member
 Touro Infirmary

Opelousas
Member
 Opelousas General Hospital

Raceland
Member
 St. Anne General Hospital

Shreveport
Member
 Schumpert Medical Center

Sterlington
Member
 Sterlington Hospital

Tallulah
Member
 Madison Parish Hospital

Thibodaux
Member
 Thibodaux Regional Medical Center

West Monroe
Member
 Glenwood Regional Medical Center

MAINE

Blue Hill
Member
 Blue Hill Memorial Hospital

Brunswick
Member
 Parkview Hospital

Calais
Member
 Calais Regional Hospital

Caribou
Member
 Cary Medical Center

Dover–Foxcroft
Member
 Mayo Regional Hospital

Ellsworth
Member
 Maine Coast Memorial Hospital

Houlton
Member
 Houlton Regional Hospital

Lewiston
Member
 St. Mary's Regional Medical Center

Lincoln
Member
 Penobscot Valley Hospital

Machias
Member
 Down East Community Hospital

Millinocket
Member
 Millinocket Regional Hospital

Portland
Member
 Mercy Hospital Portland

MARYLAND

Annapolis
Member
 Anne Arundel Medical Center

Baltimore
Member
 Bon Secours Baltimore Health System
 Church Hospital Corporation
 Franklin Square Hospital Center
 Good Samaritan Hospital of Maryland
 Harbor Hospital Center
 Liberty Medical Center
 Mercy Medical Center
 Mt. Washington Pediatric Hospital
 Sinai Hospital of Baltimore
 The New Children's Hospital
 Union Memorial Hospital

Berlin
Member
 Atlantic General Hospital

Bethesda
Member
 Suburban Hospital

Cheverly
Member
 Prince George's Hospital Center

Columbia
Member
 Howard County General Hospital

Cumberland
Member
 Memorial Hospital and Medical Center of Cumberland
 Sacred Heart Hospital

Elkton
Member
 Union Hospital

Frederick
Member
 Frederick Memorial Hospital

Hagerstown
Member
 Washington County Hospital Association

Lanham
Member
 Doctors Community Hospital

Laurel
Member
 Laurel Regional Hospital

Lutherville Timonium
Member
 Helix Health

Marriottsville
Member
 Bon Secours Health System, Inc.

Olney
Member
 Montgomery General Hospital

Randallstown
Member
 Northwest Hospital Center

Rockville
Member
 Shady Grove Adventist Hospital

Salisbury
Member
 Peninsula Regional Medical Center

Takoma Park
Member
 Washington Adventist Hospital

Westminster
Member
 Carroll County General Hospital

MASSACHUSETTS

Attleboro
Member
 Sturdy Memorial Hospital

Ayer
Member
 Deaconess–Nashoba Hospital

Boston
Member
 Beth Israel Deaconess Medical Center
 Boston Medical Center
 Children's Hospital
 New England Baptist Hospital
 Vencor Hospital–Boston

Braintree
Member
 Massachusetts Respiratory Hospital

Brockton
Member
 Brockton Hospital
 Good Samaritan Medical Center

Cambridge
Member
 Youville Lifecare

Great Barrington
Member
 Fairview Hospital

Greenfield
Member
 Franklin Medical Center

Haverhill
Member
 Hale Hospital

Lowell
Member
 Saints Memorial Medical Center

Needham
Member
 Deaconess–Glover Hospital Corporation

Palmer
Member
 Wing Memorial Hospital and Medical Centers

Pittsfield
Member
 Berkshire Medical Center

Plymouth
Member
 Jordan Hospital

Quincy
Member
 Quincy Hospital

Springfield
Member
 Baystate Health System, Inc.
 Baystate Medical Center

Stoneham
Member
 Boston Regional Medical Center

Waltham
Member
 Deaconess Waltham Hospital

Ware
Member
 Mary Lane Hospital

Webster
Member
 Hubbard Regional Hospital

Winchester
Member
 Winchester Hospital

Worcester
Member
 Memorial Hospital

MICHIGAN

Allegan
Member
 Allegan General Hospital

Alma
Member
 Gratiot Community Hospital

Ann Arbor
Member
 St. Joseph Mercy Health System

Battle Creek
Member
 Battle Creek Health System

Big Rapids
Member
Mecosta County General Hospital

Cadillac
Member
Mercy Health Services–North

Carson City
Member
Carson City Hospital

Chelsea
Member
Chelsea Community Hospital

Clinton Township
Member
St. Joseph's Mercy Hospitals and Health Services

Commerce Township
Member
Huron Valley–Sinai Hospital

Detroit
Member
Detroit Medical Center
Detroit Receiving Hospital and University Health
Center
Detroit Riverview Hospital
Grace Hospital
Harper Hospital
Henry Ford Health System
Henry Ford Hospital
Hutzel Hospital
Mercy Hospital
Sinai Hospital

Dowagiac
Member
Lee Memorial Hospital

Farmington Hills
Member
Botsford General Hospital
Mercy Health Services

Flint
Member
McLaren Regional Medical Center

Frankfort
Member
Paul Oliver Memorial Hospital

Garden City
Member
Garden City Hospital

Grand Rapids
Spectrum Health–East Campus
Member
Metropolitan Hospital
Saint Mary's Health Services

Grayling
Member
Mercy Health Services North–Grayling

Grosse Pointe
Member
Bon Secours Hospital

Grosse Pointe Farms
Member
Henry Ford Cottage Hospital of Grosse Pointe

Jackson
Member
Doctors Hospital of Jackson
W. A. Foote Memorial Hospital

Kalamazoo
Member
Borgess Medical Center

Kalkaska
Member
Kalkaska Memorial Health Center

Lansing
Member
Ingham Regional Medical Center
Sparrow Health System

Lapeer
Member
Lapeer Regional Hospital

Madison Heights
Member
Madison Community Hospital
St. John Health System, Oakland Hospital

Marlette
Member
Marlette Community Hospital

Marshall
Member
Oaklawn Hospital

Monroe
Member
Mercy Memorial Hospital

Mount Clemens
Member
Mount Clemens General Hospital

Mount Pleasant
Member
Central Michigan Community Hospital

Muskegon
Member
Mercy General Health Partners
Mercy General Health Partners–Oak Avenue Campus

Northport
Member
Leelanau Memorial Health Center

Paw Paw
Member
LakeView Community Hospital

Pontiac
Member
POH Medical Center
St. Joseph Mercy Oakland

Port Huron
Member
Mercy Hospital

Rochester
Member
Crittenton Hospital

Romeo
Member
St. Joseph's Mercy–North

Saginaw
Member
HealthSource Saginaw

Saint Johns
Member
Clinton Memorial Hospital

Saline
Member
Saline Community Hospital

Southfield
Member
Straith Hospital for Special Surgery

Sturgis
Member
Sturgis Hospital

Tecumseh
Member
Herrick Memorial Hospital

Three Rivers
Member
Three Rivers Area Hospital

Traverse City
Member
Munson Medical Center

Trenton
Member
Riverside Osteopathic Hospital

Warren
Member
Bi–County Community Hospital
Macomb Hospital Center

Watervliet
Member
Community Hospital

Wyandotte
Member
Henry Ford Wyandotte Hospital

MINNESOTA

Aitkin
Member
Riverwood Health Care Center

Alexandria
Member
Douglas County Hospital

Austin
Member
Austin Medical Center

Burnsville
Member
Fairview Ridges Hospital

Cloquet
Member
Cloquet Community Memorial Hospital

Cook
Member
Cook Hospital and Convalescent Nursing Care Unit

Crosby
Member
Cuyuna Regional Medical Center

Duluth
Member
Miller Dwan Medical Center

Ely
Member
Ely–Bloomenson Community Hospital

Fairmont
Member
Fairmont Community Hospital

Faribault
Member
District One Hospital

Glencoe
Member
Glencoe Area Health Center

Hastings
Member
Regina Medical Center

Hibbing
Member
University Medical Center–Mesabi

International Falls
Member
Falls Memorial Hospital

Litchfield
Member
Meeker County Memorial Hospital

Madison
Member
Madison Hospital

Minneapolis
Member
Fairview Hospital and Healthcare Services
Fairview Southdale Hospital
Fairview–University Medical Center

Monticello
Member
Monticello Big Lake Hospital

Moose Lake
Member
Mercy Hospital and Health Care Center

Mora
Member
Kanabec Hospital

New Prague
Member
Queen of Peace Hospital

Northfield
Member
Northfield Hospital

Ortonville
Member
Ortonville Area Health Services

Pipestone
Member
Pipestone County Medical Center

Princeton
Member
Fairview Northland Regional Health Care

Red Wing
Member
  Fairview Red Wing Hospital

Robbinsdale
Member
  North Memorial Medical Center

Rochester
Member
  Olmsted Medical Center

Saint Louis Park
Member
  HealthSystem Minnesota

Sandstone
Member
  Pine Medical Center

Staples
Member
  Lakewood Health System

Stillwater
Member
  Lakeview Hospital

Thief River Falls
Member
  Northwest Medical Center

Tyler
Member
  Tyler Healthcare Center

Virginia
Member
  Virginia Regional Medical Center

Wadena
Member
  Tri–County Hospital

Winona
Member
  Community Memorial Hospital and Convalescent and
    Rehabilitation Unit

Wyoming
Member
  Fairview Lakes Regional Medical Center

MISSISSIPPI

Amory
Member
  Gilmore Memorial Hospital

Bay Saint Louis
Member
  Hancock Medical Center

Bay Springs
Member
  Jasper General Hospital

Brookhaven
Member
  King's Daughters Hospital

Centreville
Member
  Field Memorial Community Hospital

Columbia
Member
  Marion General Hospital

Corinth
Member
  Magnolia Regional Health Center

Durant
Member
  University Hospital and Clinics–Durant

Greenville
Member
  Delta Regional Medical Center
  King's Daughters Hospital

Grenada
Member
  Grenada Lake Medical Center

Hattiesburg
Member
  Wesley Medical Center

Jackson
Member
  Methodist Healthcare
  Mississippi Baptist Medical Center
  University Hospitals and Clinics, University of
    Mississippi Medical Center

Laurel
Member
  South Central Regional Medical Center

Lexington
Member
  Methodist Healthcare Middle Mississippi Hospital

Louisville
Member
  Winston Medical Center

Magee
Member
  Magee General Hospital

Meridian
Member
  Rush Foundation Hospital

Natchez
Member
  Natchez Regional Medical Center

Philadelphia
Member
  Neshoba County General Hospital

Picayune
Member
  Crosby Memorial Hospital

Prentiss
Member
  Prentiss Regional Hospital and Extended Care
    Facilities

Union
Member
  Laird Hospital

Vicksburg
Member
  Parkview Regional Medical Center

Yazoo City
Member
  King's Daughters Hospital

MISSOURI

Albany
Member
  Gentry County Memorial Hospital

Belton
Member
  Research Belton Hospital

Bridgeton
Member
  DePaul Hospital

Carrollton
Member
  Carroll County Memorial Hospital

Farmington
Member
  Mineral Area Regional Medical Center

Harrisonville
Member
  Cass Medical Center

Independence
Member
  Medical Center of Independence

Jefferson City
Member
  St. Marys Health Center

Kansas City
Member
  Baptist Medical Center
  Children's Mercy Hospital
  Health Midwest
  Park Lane Medical Center
  Research Medical Center
  Trinity Lutheran Hospital

Lake Saint Louis
Member
  St. Joseph Hospital West

Lees Summit
Member
  Lee's Summit Hospital

Lexington
Member
  Lafayette Regional Health Center

Louisiana
Member
  Pike County Memorial Hospital

Maryville
Member
  St. Francis Hospital and Health Services

Mexico
Member
  Audrain Medical Center

Nevada
Member
  Nevada Regional Medical Center

Pilot Knob
Member
  Arcadia Valley Hospital

Rolla
Member
  Phelps County Regional Medical Center

Saint Charles
Member
  St. Joseph Health Center

Saint Joseph
Member
  Heartland Regional Medical Center

Saint Louis
Member
  Cardinal Glennon Children's Hospital
  SSM Health Care System
  St. Joseph Hospital of Kirkwood
  St. Mary's Health Center

West Plains
Member
  Ozarks Medical Center

MONTANA

Anaconda
Member
  Community Hospital of Anaconda

Cut Bank
Member
  Glacier County Medical Center

Great Falls
Member
  Benefis Health Care–West Campus

Harlowton
Member
  Wheatland Memorial Hospital

Lewistown
Member
  Central Montana Medical Center

Missoula
Member
  St. Patrick Hospital

Plains
Member
  Clark Fork Valley Hospital

Polson
Member
  St. Joseph Hospital

Whitefish
Member
  North Valley Hospital

NEBRASKA

Ainsworth
Member
  Brown County Hospital

Albion
Member
  Boone County Health Center

Atkinson
Member
  West Holt Memorial Hospital

Auburn
Member
  Nemaha County Hospital

Aurora
Member
  Memorial Hospital

Bassett
Member
  Rock County Hospital

Central City
Member
  Litzenberg Memorial County Hospital

Chadron
Member
  Chadron Community Hospital

Cozad
Member
  Cozad Community Hospital

Crawford
Member
  Legend Buttes Health Services

Creighton
Member
  Creighton Area Health Services

Fairbury
Member
  Jefferson Community Health Center

Fremont
Member
  Fremont Area Medical Center

Geneva
Member
  Fillmore County Hospital

Genoa
Member
  Genoa Community Hospital

Gordon
Member
  Gordon Memorial Hospital District

Gothenburg
Member
  Gothenburg Memorial Hospital

Hebron
Member
  Thayer County Health Services

Henderson
Member
  Henderson Health Care Services

Holdrege
Member
  Phelps Memorial Health Center

Humboldt
Member
  Community Memorial Hospital

Imperial
Member
  Chase County Community Hospital

Lincoln
Member
  Lincoln General Hospital

Lynch
Member
  Niobrara Valley Hospital

North Platte
Member
  Great Plains Regional Medical Center

Oakland
Member
  Oakland Memorial Hospital

Ogallala
Member
  Ogallala Community Hospital

Omaha
Member
  Alegent Health Bergan Mercy Medical Center
  Alegent Health Immanuel Medical Center
  Boys Town National Research Hospital
  Nebraska Health System
  Veterans Affairs Medical Center

Ord
Member
  Valley County Hospital

Osceola
Member
  Annie Jeffrey Memorial County Health Center

Papillion
Member
  Midlands Community Hospital

Pawnee City
Member
  Pawnee County Memorial Hospital

Pender
Member
  Pender Community Hospital

Red Cloud
Member
  Webster County Community Hospital

Saint Paul
Member
  Howard County Community Hospital

Schuyler
Member
  Alegent Health–Memorial Hospital

Seward
Member
  Memorial Health Care Systems

Superior
Member
  Brodstone Memorial Hospital

Syracuse
Member
  Community Memorial Hospital

Tecumseh
Member
  Johnson County Hospital

Valentine
Member
  Cherry County Hospital

Wahoo
Member
  Saunders County Health Service

Wayne
Member
  Providence Medical Center

West Point
Member
  St. Francis Memorial Hospital

NEVADA
Fallon
Member
  Churchill Community Hosptial

Las Vegas
Member
  Desert Springs Hospital

Lovelock
Member
  Pershing General Hospital

NEW HAMPSHIRE
Exeter
Member
  Exeter Hospital

Littleton
Member
  Littleton Regional Hospital

Manchester
Member
  Elliot Hospital

Nashua
Member
  St. Joseph Hospital

NEW JERSEY
Belleville
Member
  Clara Maass Health System

Edison
Member
  JFK Medical Center
  Solaris Health System

Englewood
Member
  Englewood Hospital and Medical Center

Freehold
Member
  Centrastate Medical Center

Hackensack
Member
  Hackensack University Medical Center

Hackettstown
Member
  Hackettstown Community Hospital

Holmdel
Member
  Bayshore Community Hospital

Irvington
Member
  Irvington General Hospital

Jersey City
Member
  Greenville Hospital
  Jersey City Medical Center

Kearny
Member
  West Hudson Hospital

Lakewood
Member
  Kimball Medical Center

Livingston
Member
  Saint Barnabas Health Care System
  Saint Barnabas Medical Center

Long Branch
Member
  Monmouth Medical Center

Manahawkin
Member
  Southern Ocean County Hospital

Newark
Member
  Newark Beth Israel Medical Center

Passaic
Member
  Beth Israel Hospital

Paterson
Member
  Barnert Hospital
  St. Joseph's Hospital and Medical Center

Salem
Member
  Memorial Hospital of Salem County

Secaucus
Member
  Meadowlands Hospital Medical Center

Toms River
Member
  Community Medical Center

Union
Member
  Union Hospital

Wayne
Member
  Wayne General Hospital

NEW MEXICO
Alamogordo
Member
  Gerald Champion Memorial Hospital

Albuquerque
Member
  Presbyterian Healthcare Services
  Presbyterian Healthcare Services
  Presbyterian Kaseman Hospital

Artesia
Member
  Artesia General Hospital

Clovis
Member
  Plains Regional Medical Center

Espanola
Member
  Espanola Hospital

Los Alamos
Member
  Los Alamos Medical Center

Section B

Ruidoso
Member
  Lincoln County Medical Center

Socorro
Member
  Socorro General Hospital

Taos
Member
  Holy Cross Hospital

Truth or Consequences
Member
  Sierra Vista Hospital

Tucumcari
Member
  Dr. Dan C. Trigg Memorial Hospital

NEW YORK
Member
  St. John's Queens Hospital

Albany
Member
  Albany Medical Center
  St. Peter's Hospital

Amityville
Affiliate
  South Oaks Hospital

Amsterdam
Member
  Amsterdam Memorial Hospital

Batavia
Member
  Genesee Memorial Hospital
  St. Jerome Hospital

Bath
Member
  Ira Davenport Memorial Hospital

Bayside
Member
  St. Mary's Hospital for Children

Beacon
Member
  Saint Francis Hospital–Beacon

Bethpage
Member
  Mid–Island Hospital

Brockport
Member
  Lakeside Memorial Hospital

Bronx
Member
  Bronx–Lebanon Hospital Center
  Calvary Hospital
  Fulton Division
  Jewish Home and Hospital for Aged
  Montefiore Medical Center
  Our Lady of Mercy Healthcare System, Inc.
  Our Lady of Mercy Medical Center
  St. Barnabas Hospital
  Union Hospital of the Bronx

Brooklyn
Member
  Brookdale Hospital Medical Center
  Interfaith Medical Center
  Kingsbrook Jewish Medical Center
  Long Island College Hospital
  Lutheran Medical Center
  Maimonides Medical Center
  New York Methodist Hospital
  St. Mary's Hospital of Brooklyn
  University Hospital of Brooklyn–State University of
    New York Health Science Center at Brooklyn
  Victory Memorial Hospital

Buffalo
Member
  Brylin Hospitals
  Children's Hospital
  Mercy Hospital
  Millard Fillmore Health System
  Sheehan Memorial Hospital

Canandaigua
Member
  F. F. Thompson Health System

Cheektowaga
Member
  St. Joseph Hospital

Clifton Springs
Member
  Clifton Springs Hospital and Clinic

Corning
Member
  Corning Hospital

Dansville
Member
  Nicholas H. Noyes Memorial Hospital

Dobbs Ferry
Member
  Community Hospital at Dobbs Ferry

Elizabethtown
Member
  Elizabethtown Community Hospital

Elmira
Member
  Arnot Ogden Medical Center
  St. Joseph's Hospital

Far Rockaway
Member
  Peninsula Hospital Center
  St. John's Episcopal Hospital–South Shore

Flushing
Member
  Parkway Hospital
  St. Joseph's Hospital

Glen Oaks
Member
  Hillside Hospital

Glens Falls
Member
  Glens Falls Hospital

Hornell
Member
  St. James Mercy Hospital

Irving
Member
  Lake Shore Hospital

Jamaica
Member
  Catholic Medical Center of Brooklyn and Queens
  Jamaica Hospital Medical Center

Kenmore
Member
  Kenmore Mercy Hospital

Lackawanna
Member
  Our Lady of Victory Hospital

Long Beach
Member
  Long Beach Medical Center

Long Island City
Member
  Western Queens Community Hospital

Medina
Member
  Medina Memorial Hospital

Mineola
Member
  Winthrop–University Hospital

Montour Falls
Member
  Schuyler Hospital

Mount Vernon
Member
  Mount Vernon Hospital

New Hyde Park
Member
  Long Island Jewish Medical Center
  Schneider Children's Hospital

New York
Member
  Cabrini Medical Center
  Greater New York Hospital Association
  Hospital for Special Surgery
  Lenox Hill Hospital
  Manhattan Eye, Ear and Throat Hospital
  Mount Sinai Medical Center
  New York Eye and Ear Infirmary
  North General Hospital
  Saint Vincent's Hospital and Medical Center of New
    York
  St. Clare's Hospital and Health Center
  St. Luke's–Roosevelt Hospital Center

Newark
Member
  Newark–Wayne Community Hospital

Newfane
Member
  Inter–Community Memorial Hospital

Oceanside
Member
  South Nassau Communities Hospital

Oneonta
Member
  Aurelia Osborn Fox Memorial Hospital

Patchogue
Member
  Brookhaven Memorial Hospital Medical Center

Peekskill
Member
  Hudson Valley Hospital Center

Penn Yan
Member
  Soldiers and Sailors Memorial Hospital of Yates
    County

Plattsburgh
Member
  Champlain Valley Physicians Hospital Medical Center

Port Jefferson
Member
  John T. Mather Memorial Hospital
  St. Charles Hospital and Rehabilitation Center

Poughkeepsie
Member
  Saint Francis Hospital
  Vassar Brothers Hospital

Rochester
Member
  Genesee Hospital
  Monroe Community Hospital
  Rochester General Hospital

Rockville Centre
Member
  Mercy Medical Center

Roslyn
Member
  St. Francis Hospital

Schenectady
Member
  Ellis Hospital

Seaford
Member
  Massapequa General Hospital

Smithtown
Member
  St. John's Episcopal Hospital–Smithtown
  St. John's Episcopal Medical Healthcare Center

Sodus
Member
  Myers Community Hospital

Staten Island
Member
  Doctors' Hospital of Staten Island
  Sisters of Charity Healthcare
  Sisters of Charity Medical Center
  Staten Island University Hospital

Syracuse
Member
  University Hospital–SUNY Health Science Center at
    Syracuse

Troy
Member
Samaritan Hospital

Uniondale
Member
Episcopal Health Services Inc.

Valhalla
Member
Blythedale Children's Hospital
Westchester Medical Center

Warsaw
Member
Wyoming County Community Hospital

West Islip
Member
Good Samaritan Hospital Medical Center

Westfield
Member
Westfield Memorial Hospital

Williamsville
Member
Millard Fillmore Suburban Hospital

Yonkers
Member
St. John's Riverside Hospital
Yonkers General Hospital

NORTH CAROLINA

Albemarle
Member
Stanly Memorial Hospital

Asheboro
Member
Randolph Hospital

Asheville
Member
Mission Hospital
St. Joseph's Hospital
Thoms Rehabilitation Hospital

Banner Elk
Member
Charles A. Cannon Jr. Memorial Hospital

Blowing Rock
Member
Blowing Rock Hospital

Boiling Springs
Member
Crawley Memorial Hospital

Boone
Member
Watauga Medical Center

Brevard
Member
Transylvania Community Hospital

Bryson City
Member
Swain County Hospital

Burgaw
Member
Pender Memorial Hospital

Burlington
Member
Alamance Regional Medical Center

Charlotte
Member
Presbyterian Specialty Hospital

Clinton
Member
Sampson Regional Medical Center

Clyde
Member
Haywood Regional Medical Center

Crossnore
Member
Sloop Memorial Hospital

Danbury
Member
Stokes-Reynolds Memorial Hospital

Durham
Member
Durham Regional Hospital

Eden
Member
Morehead Memorial Hospital

Edenton
Member
Chowan Hospital

Elizabethtown
Member
Bladen County Hospital

Elkin
Member
Hugh Chatham Memorial Hospital

Erwin
Member
Good Hope Hospital

Fayetteville
Member
Cape Fear Valley Health System
Cumberland Hospital

Fletcher
Member
Park Ridge Hospital

Franklin
Member
Angel Medical Center

Gastonia
Member
Gaston Memorial Hospital

Goldsboro
Member
Wayne Memorial Hospital

Henderson
Member
Maria Parham Hospital

Hendersonville
Member
Margaret R. Pardee Memorial Hospital

Hickory
Member
Catawba Memorial Hospital

Highlands
Member
Highlands-Cashiers Hospital

Jefferson
Member
Ashe Memorial Hospital

Kenansville
Member
Duplin General Hospital

Kinston
Member
Lenoir Memorial Hospital

Laurinburg
Member
Scotland Memorial Hospital

Lenoir
Member
Caldwell Memorial Hospital

Lexington
Member
Lexington Memorial Hospital

Lumberton
Member
Southeastern Regional Medical Center

Marion
Member
McDowell Hospital

Matthews
Member
Presbyterian Hospital-Matthews

Morganton
Member
Grace Hospital

Mount Airy
Member
Northern Hospital of Surry County

Murphy
Member
Murphy Medical Center

North Wilkesboro
Member
Wilkes Regional Medical Center

Oxford
Member
Granville Medical Center

Pinehurst
Member
FirstHealth Moore Regional Hospital

Plymouth
Member
Washington County Hospital

Roanoke Rapids
Member
Halifax Regional Medical Center

Roxboro
Member
Person County Memorial Hospital

Shelby
Member
Cleveland Regional Medical Center

Siler City
Member
Chatham Hospital

Smithfield
Member
Johnston Memorial Hospital

Sparta
Member
Alleghany Memorial Hospital

Spruce Pine
Member
Spruce Pine Community Hospital

Statesville
Member
Iredell Memorial Hospital

Sylva
Member
Harris Regional Hospital

Taylorsville
Member
Alexander Community Hospital

Troy
Member
FirstHealth Montgomery Memorial Hospital

Whiteville
Member
Columbus County Hospital

Williamston
Member
Martin General Hospital

Wilmington
Member
New Hanover Regional Medical Center

Wilson
Member
Wilson Memorial Hospital

Winston-Salem
Member
North Carolina Baptist Hospital

Yadkinville
Member
Hoots Memorial Hospital

NORTH DAKOTA

Cavalier
Member
Pembina County Memorial Hospital and Wedgewood
Manor

Fargo
Member
Lutheran Health Systems

Kenmare
Member
Kenmare Community Hospital

Lisbon
Member
Lisbon Medical Center

Minot
Member
   UniMed Medical Center

OHIO
Akron
Member
   Akron City Hospital
   Children's Hospital Medical Center of Akron
   Edwin Shaw Hospital for Rehabilitation
   Saint Thomas Hospital
   Summa Health System

Alliance
Member
   Alliance Community Hospital

Amherst
Member
   EMH Amherst Hospital

Ashtabula
Member
   Ashtabula County Medical Center

Barberton
Member
   Barberton Citizens Hospital

Batavia
Member
   Clermont Mercy Hospital

Cincinnati
Member
   Bethesda North Hospital
   Bethesda Oak Hospital
   Catholic Healthcare Partners
   Children's Hospital Medical Center
   Mercy Hospital Anderson

Cleveland
Member
   Cleveland Clinic Hospital
   Fairview Hospital
   Fairview Hospital System
   Grace Hospital
   Health Hill Hospital for Children
   Lutheran Hospital
   Meridia Hillcrest Hospital
   Meridia Huron Hospital
   MetroHealth Medical Center

Columbus
Member
   Children's Hospital
   Ohio State University Medical Center
   Park Medical Center

Dayton
Member
   Good Samaritan Hospital and Health Center

Defiance
Member
   Defiance Hospital

Dennison
Member
   Twin City Hospital

East Liverpool
Member
   East Liverpool City Hospital

Elyria
Member
   EMH Regional Medical Center

Euclid
Member
   Meridia Euclid Hospital

Fremont
Member
   Memorial Hospital

Garfield Heights
Member
   Marymount Hospital

Georgetown
Member
   Brown County General Hospital

Green Springs
Member
   St. Francis Health Care Centre

Greenfield
Member
   Greenfield Area Medical Center

Hamilton
Member
   Mercy Hospital

Kettering
Member
   Kettering Medical Center

Lakewood
Member
   Lakewood Hospital

Lima
Member
   St. Rita's Medical Center

Lodi
Member
   Lodi Community Hospital

Lorain
Member
   Lorain Community/St. Joseph Regional Health Center

Marietta
Member
   Selby General Hospital

Marysville
Member
   Memorial Hospital

Massillon
Member
   Doctors Hospital of Stark County
   Massillon Community Hospital

Mayfield Village
Member
   Meridia Health System

Middleburg Heights
Member
   Southwest General Health Center

Mount Vernon
Member
   Knox Community Hospital

Oberlin
Member
   Allen Memorial Hospital

Oregon
Member
   St. Charles Mercy Hospital

Parma
Member
   Parma Community General Hospital

Paulding
Member
   Paulding County Hospital

Sandusky
Member
   Providence Hospital

Springfield
Member
   Mercy Medical Center

Tiffin
Member
   Mercy Hospital

Toledo
Member
   Riverside Mercy Hospital
   St. Vincent Mercy Medical Center

Urbana
Member
   Mercy Memorial Hospital

Van Wert
Member
   Van Wert County Hospital

Wadsworth
Member
   Wadsworth–Rittman Hospital

Warren
Member
   Hillside Rehabilitation Hospital
   St. Joseph Health Center

Warrensville Heights
Member
   Meridia South Pointe Hospital

Washington Court House
Member
   Fayette County Memorial Hospital

Willard
Member
   Mercy Hospital–Willard

Wooster
Member
   Wooster Community Hospital

Youngstown
Member
   St. Elizabeth Health Center
   Youngstown Osteopathic Hospital

OKLAHOMA
Alva
Member
   Share Medical Center

Atoka
Member
   Atoka Memorial Hospital

Cordell
Member
   Cordell Memorial Hospital

Cushing
Member
   Cushing Regional Hospital

Frederick
Member
   Memorial Hospital

Guthrie
Member
   Logan Hospital and Medical Center

Henryetta
Member
   Henryetta Medical Center

Holdenville
Member
   Holdenville General Hospital

Idabel
Member
   McCurtain Memorial Hospital

Kingfisher
Member
   Kingfisher Regional Hospital

Lawton
Member
   Comanche County Memorial Hospital

Mangum
Member
   Mangum City Hospital

Oklahoma City
Member
   Bone and Joint Hospital
   Hillcrest Health Center
   St. Anthony Hospital

Okmulgee
Affiliate
   OMH Medical Center
Member
   Okmulgee Memorial Hospital Authority

Perry
Member
   Perry Memorial Hospital

Purcell
Member
   Purcell Municipal Hospital

Sayre
Member
   Sayre Memorial Hospital

Seiling
Member
   Seiling Hospital

Seminole
Member
   Seminole Municipal Hospital

Tahlequah
Member
   Tahlequah City Hospital

Tulsa
Member
Laureate Psychiatric Clinic and Hospital
Saint Francis Hospital

Watonga
Member
Watonga Municipal Hospital

Woodward
Member
Woodward Hospital and Health Center

OREGON

Cottage Grove
Member
Cottage Grove Healthcare Community

Dallas
Member
Valley Community Hospital

Eugene
Member
Sacred Heart Medical Center

Florence
Member
Peace Harbor Hospital

Gold Beach
Member
Curry General Hospital

Gresham
Member
Legacy Mount Hood Medical Center

Heppner
Member
Pioneer Memorial Hospital

Lakeview
Member
Lake District Hospital

Lebanon
Member
Lebanon Community Hospital

Lincoln City
Member
North Lincoln Hospital

Medford
Providence Medford Medical Center

Milwaukie
Member
Providence Milwaukie Hospital

Newport
Member
Pacific Communities Health District

Portland
Member
Adventist Medical Center
Colonial Manor Sanitarium
Legacy Good Samaritan Hospital and Medical Center
Legacy Health System
Providence St. Vincent Medical Center

Prineville
Member
Pioneer Memorial Hospital

Salem
Member
Salem Hospital

Seaside
Member
Providence Seaside Hospital

Springfield
Member
McKenzie–Willamette Hospital

Stayton
Member
Santiam Memorial Hospital

Tillamook
Member
Tillamook County General Hospital

Tualatin
Member
Legacy Meridian Park Hospital

PENNSYLVANIA

Altoona
Member
Bon Secours–Holy Family Regional Health System

Berwick
Member
Berwick Hospital Center

Bethlehem
Member
St. Luke's Hospital

Brownsville
Member
Brownsville General Hospital

Bryn Mawr
Member
Bryn Mawr Hospital
Bryn Mawr Hospital

Carlisle
Member
Carlisle Hospital

Clarion
Member
Clarion Hospital

Coaldale
Member
Miner's Memorial Medical Center

Danville
Member
Geisinger Medical Center

Darby
Member
Mercy Fitzgerald Hospital

Easton
Member
Easton Hospital

Erie
Member
Millcreek Community Hospital
Saint Vincent Health Center

Harrisburg
Member
Penn State Geisinger Health System

Havertown
Member
Mercy Community Hospital

Hazleton
Member
Hazleton–St. Joseph Medical Center

Hershey
Member
Penn State Geisinger–Milton S. Hershey Medical Center

Huntingdon
Member
J. C. Blair Memorial Hospital

Jersey Shore
Member
Jersey Shore Hospital

Kane
Member
Kane Community Hospital

Lock Haven
Member
Lock Haven Hospital

Malvern
Member
Bryn Mawr Rehabilitation Hospital

McKees Rocks
Member
Ohio Valley General Hospital

Meadville
Member
Meadville Medical Center

Media
Member
Riddle Memorial Hospital

Monroeville
Member
Allegheny University Hospitals, Forbes Regional

Nanticoke
Member
Mercy Special Care Hospital

Palmerton
Member
Palmerton Hospital

Paoli
Member
Paoli Memorial Hospital

Philadelphia
Member
Albert Einstein Healthcare Network
Albert Einstein Medical Center
Belmont Center for Comprehensive Treatment
Germantown Hospital and Medical Center
Mercy Hospital of Philadelphia
Methodist Hospital
Thomas Jefferson University Hospital
Wills Eye Hospital

Pittsburgh
Member
Allegheny University Hospitals West–Forbes
Metropolitan
Mercy Hospital of Pittsburgh
Mercy Providence Hospital
Suburban General Hospital
Western Pennsylvania Hospital

Pottsville
Member
Pottsville Hospital and Warne Clinic

Quakertown
Member
St. Luke's Quakertown Hospital

Radnor
Member
Catholic Health East

Ridley Park
Member
Taylor Hospital

Scranton
Member
Mercy Hospital of Scranton

Spangler
Member
Miners Hospital Northern Cambria

Titusville
Member
Titusville Area Hospital

Towanda
Member
Memorial Hospital

Tyrone
Member
Tyrone Hospital

Union City
Member
Union City Memorial Hospital

Warren
Member
Warren General Hospital

Wayne
Member
Jefferson Health System

Waynesburg
Member
Greene County Memorial Hospital

West Grove
Member
Southern Chester County Medical Center

Wilkes–Barre
Member
Mercy Hospital of Wilkes–Barre
Penn State Geisinger Wyoming Valley Medical Center

Wynnewood
Member
Lankenau Hospital

York
Member
Memorial Hospital

PUERTO RICO

Mayaguez
Member
Bella Vista Hospital

Ponce
Member
Hospital De Damas

RHODE ISLAND

Providence
Member
Roger Williams Medical Center

SOUTH CAROLINA

Abbeville
Member
Abbeville County Memorial Hospital

Anderson
Member
Anderson Area Medical Center

Beaufort
Member
Beaufort Memorial Hospital

Camden
Member
Kershaw County Medical Center

Charleston
Member
Bon Secours–St. Francis Xavier Hospital
Roper Hospital
Roper Hospital North

Clinton
Member
Laurens County Healthcare System

Columbia
Member
Palmetto Richland Memorial Hospital

Conway
Member
Conway Hospital

Dillon
Member
Saint Eugene Medical Center

Edgefield
Member
Edgefield County Hospital

Florence
Member
Carolinas Hospital System
McLeod Regional Medical Center

Georgetown
Member
Georgetown Memorial Hospital

Greenville
Member
Greenville Hospital System
Greenville Memorial Hospital
Shriners Hospitals for Children, Greenville

Greenwood
Member
Self Memorial Hospital

Greer
Member
Allen Bennett Hospital

Lake City
Member
Carolinas Hospital System–Lake City

Lexington
Member
Keisler Nursing Home

Loris
Member
Loris Community Hospital

Orangeburg
Member
Regional Medical Center of Orangeburg and Calhoun
Counties

Pickens
Member
Cannon Memorial Hospital

Simpsonville
Member
Hillcrest Hospital

Spartanburg
Member
Mary Black Health System
Spartanburg Regional Medical Center

Sumter
Member
Tuomey Regional Medical Center

Union
Member
Wallace Thomson Hospital

West Columbia
Member
Lexington Medical Center

Winnsboro
Member
Fairfield Memorial Hospital

Woodruff
Member
B.J. Workman Memorial Hospital

SOUTH DAKOTA

Aberdeen
Member
St. Luke's Midland Regional Medical Center

Armour
Member
Douglas County Memorial Hospital

Britton
Member
Marshall County Healthcare Center

Burke
Member
Community Memorial Hospital

Custer
Member
Custer Community Hospital

Deadwood
Member
Northern Hills General Hospital

Dell Rapids
Member
Dell Rapids Community Hospital

Eureka
Member
Eureka Community Hospital

Faulkton
Member
Faulk County Memorial Hospital

Flandreau
Member
Flandreau Municipal Hospital

Gettysburg
Member
Gettysburg Medical Center

Gregory
Member
Gregory Community Hospital

Hot Springs
Member
Southern Hills General Hospital

Hoven
Member
Holy Infant Hospital

Martin
Member
Bennett County Community Hospital

Milbank
Member
St. Bernard's Providence Hospital

Miller
Member
Hand County Memorial Hospital

Mitchell
Member
Queen of Peace Hospital

Parkston
Member
St. Benedict Health Center

Platte
Member
Platte Community Memorial Hospital

Rapid City
Member
Rapid City Regional Hospital System of Care

Redfield
Member
Community Memorial Hospital

Scotland
Member
Landmann–Jungman Memorial Hospital

Sioux Falls
Member
McKennan Hospital

Spearfish
Member
Lookout Memorial Hospital

Sturgis
Member
Sturgis Community Health Care Center

Tyndall
Member
St. Michael's Hospital

Wagner
Member
Wagner Community Memorial Hospital

Watertown
Member
Prairie Lakes Hospital and Care Center

Wessington Springs
Member
Weskota Memorial Medical Center

Yankton
Member
Avera Health
Sacred Heart Health Services

TENNESSEE

Brentwood
Shareholder
Quorum Health Group/Quorum Health Resources, Inc.

Bristol
Member
Wellmont Bristol Regional Medical Center

Brownsville
Member
Haywood County Memorial Hospital

Chattanooga
Member
Siskin Hospital for Physical Rehabilitation

Cleveland
Member
Bradley Memorial Hospital

Copperhill
Member
Copper Basin Medical Center

Crossville
Member
Cumberland Medical Center

Dayton
Member
Rhea Medical Center

Dyersburg
Member
Methodist Hospital of Dyersburg

Erwin
Member
Unicoi County Memorial Hospital

Etowah
Member
Woods Memorial Hospital District

Fayetteville
Member
Lincoln County Health Facilities

Gallatin
Member
Sumner Regional Medical Center

Greeneville
Member
Takoma Adventist Hospital

Jackson
Member
Jackson–Madison County General Hospital

Jefferson City
Member
Jefferson Memorial Hospital

Jellico
Member
Jellico Community Hospital

Johnson City
Member
Johnson City Medical Center Hospital

Kingsport
Member
Wellmont Holston Valley Medical Center

Knoxville
Member
Baptist Hospital of East Tennessee
St. Mary's Health System

La Follette
Member
La Follette Medical Center

Lafayette
Member
Macon County General Hospital

Lexington
Member
Methodist Hospital of Lexington

Madison
Member
Tennessee Christian Medical Center

Maryville
Member
Blount Memorial Hospital

McKenzie
Member
Methodist Hospital of McKenzie

Memphis
Member
Extendicare of Memphis
Methodist Health Systems, Inc.
Methodist Hospitals of Memphis
Regional Medical Center at Memphis
St. Jude Children's Research Hospital

Morristown
Member
Morristown–Hamblen Hospital

Nashville
Member
Vanderbilt University Hospital

Newport
Member
Baptist Hospital of Cocke County

Rockwood
Member
Baptist Urgent Care

Rogersville
Member
Hawkins County Memorial Hospital

Somerville
Member
Methodist Healthcare – Fayette Hospital

Sweetwater
Member
Sweetwater Hospital

Tazewell
Member
Claiborne County Hospital

TEXAS
Abilene
Member
Abilene Regional Medical Center
Hendrick Health System

Anahuac
Member
Bayside Community Hospital

Anson
Member
Anson General Hospital

Aspermont
Member
Stonewall Memorial Hospital

Azle
Member
Harris Methodist Northwest

Ballinger
Member
Ballinger Memorial Hospital

Bay City
Member
Matagorda General Hospital

Beaumont
Member
St. Elizabeth Hospital

Bedford
Member
Harris Methodist–HEB

Big Lake
Member
Reagan Memorial Hospital

Bowie
Member
Bowie Memorial Hospital

Brady
Member
Heart of Texas Memorial Hospital

Breckenridge
Member
Stephens Memorial Hospital

Brenham
Member
Trinity Community Medical Center of Brenham

Bryan
Member
St. Joseph Regional Health Center

Burleson
Member
Huguley Memorial Medical Center

Burnet
Member
Seton Highland Lakes

Caldwell
Member
Burleson St. Joseph Health Center

Canadian
Member
Hemphill County Hospital

Canyon
Member
Palo Duro Hospital

Carrizo Springs
Member
Dimmit County Memorial Hospital

Childress
Member
Childress Regional Medical Center

Chillicothe
Member
Chillicothe Hospital District

Cleburne
Member
Walls Regional Hospital

Clifton
Member
Goodall–Witcher Hospital

Coleman
Member
Coleman County Medical Center

Columbus
Member
Columbus Community Hospital

Comanche
Member
Comanche Community Hospital

Commerce
Member
Presbyterian Hospital of Commerce

Corpus Christi
Member
Driscoll Children's Hospital

Crane
Member
Crane Memorial Hospital

Crosbyton
Member
Crosbyton Clinic Hospital

Dallas
Member
Charlton Methodist Hospital
Children's Medical Center of Dallas
Methodist Hospitals of Dallas
Methodist Medical Center
Presbyterian Hospital of Dallas
St. Paul Medical Center

Decatur
Member
Decatur Community Hospital

Denison
Member
Texoma Medical Center Restorative Care Hospital

Denver City
Member
Yoakum County Hospital

Dimmitt
Member
Plains Memorial Hospital

Eagle Lake
Member
Rice Medical Center

Eagle Pass
Member
Fort Duncan Medical Center

Eastland
Member
Eastland Memorial Hospital

Eden
Member
Concho County Hospital

Edna
Member
Jackson County Hospital

El Campo
Member
El Campo Memorial Hospital

El Paso
Member
R. E. Thomason General Hospital

Eldorado
Member
Schleicher County Medical Center

Fort Stockton
Member
Pecos County Memorial Hospital

Fort Worth
Member
Cook Children's Medical Center
Harris Methodist Fort Worth
Harris Methodist Health System
Harris Methodist Southwest
Osteopathic Medical Center of Texas

Fredericksburg
Member
Hill Country Memorial Hospital

Friona
Member
Parmer County Community Hospital

Galveston
Member
University of Texas Medical Branch Hospitals

Graham
Member
Graham General Hospital

Grand Prairie
Member
  Dallas–Fort Worth Medical Center

Greenville
Member
  Presbyterian Hospital of Greenville

Groves
Member
  Doctors Hospital

Hale Center
Member
  Hi–Plains Hospital

Hallettsville
Member
  Lavaca Medical Center

Hamilton
Member
  Hamilton General Hospital

Hamlin
Member
  Hamlin Memorial Hospital

Haskell
Member
  Haskell Memorial Hospital

Henderson
Member
  Henderson Memorial Hospital

Hondo
Member
  Medina Community Hospital

Houston
Member
  Methodist Health Care System
  St. Joseph Hospital
  St. Luke's Episcopal Hospital
  The Methodist Hospital
  University of Texas M. D. Anderson Cancer Center

Junction
Member
  Kimble Hospital

Kaufman
Member
  Presbyterian Hospital of Kaufman

Kenedy
Member
  Otto Kaiser Memorial Hospital

Kermit
Member
  Memorial Hospital

Killeen
Member
  Metroplex Hospital

Knox City
Member
  Knox County Hospital

Lamesa
Member
  Medical Arts Hospital

Livingston
Member
  Memorial Medical Center–Livingston

Lockney
Member
  W. J. Mangold Memorial Hospital

Lubbock
Member
  St. Mary of the Plains Hospital
  University Medical Center

Lufkin
Member
  Memorial Medical Center of East Texas

Luling
Member
  Edgar B. Davis Memorial Hospital

Madisonville
Member
  Madison St. Joseph Health Center

McAllen
Member
  McAllen Medical Center

Midland
Member
  Westwood Medical Center

Mineral Wells
Member
  Palo Pinto General Hospital

Mission
Member
  Mission Hospital

Monahans
Member
  Ward Memorial Hospital

Morton
Member
  Cochran Memorial Hospital

Mount Pleasant
Member
  Titus Regional Medical Center

Muleshoe
Member
  Muleshoe Area Medical Center

Nacogdoches
Member
  Nacogdoches Memorial Hospital

Navasota
Member
  Grimes St. Joseph Health Center

Nocona
Member
  Nocona General Hospital

Olney
Member
  Hamilton Hospital

Paris
Member
  McCuistion Regional Medical Center

Pecos
Member
  Reeves County Hospital

Plano
Member
  Presbyterian Hospital of Plano

Port Arthur
Member
  St. Mary Hospital

Quanah
Member
  Hardeman County Memorial Hospital

Rockdale
Member
  Richards Memorial Hospital

Rotan
Member
  Fisher County Hospital District

San Augustine
Member
  Memorial Medical Center of San Augustine

San Marcos
Member
  Central Texas Medical Center

Seminole
Member
  Memorial Hospital

Seymour
Member
  Seymour Hospital

Shamrock
Member
  Shamrock General Hospital

Snyder
Member
  D. M. Cogdell Memorial Hospital

Sonora
Member
  Lillian M. Hudspeth Memorial Hospital

Spearman
Member
  Hansford Hospital

Stamford
Member
  Stamford Memorial Hospital

Stanton
Member
  Martin County Hospital District

Stephenville
Member
  Harris Methodist–Erath County

Sweetwater
Member
  Rolling Plains Memorial Hospital

Tahoka
Member
  Lynn County Hospital District

Texarkana
Member
  St. Michael Health Care Center

Throckmorton
Member
  Throckmorton County Memorial Hospital

Tulia
Member
  Swisher Memorial Hospital District

Van Horn
Member
  Culberson Hospital District

Wellington
Member
  Collingsworth General Hospital

Weslaco
Member
  Knapp Medical Center

Whitney
Member
  Lake Whitney Medical Center

Winnsboro
Member
  Presbyterian Hospital of Winnsboro

Winters
Member
  North Runnels Hospital

Woodville
Member
  Tyler County Hospital

UTAH
Monticello
Member
  San Juan Hospital

VERMONT
Saint Albans
Member
  Northwestern Medical Center

Saint Johnsbury
Member
  Northeastern Vermont Regional Hospital

VIRGINIA
Abingdon
Member
  Johnston Memorial Hospital

Alexandria
Member
  Inova Mount Vernon Hospital

Bedford
Member
  Carilion Bedford Memorial Hospital

Big Stone Gap
Member
  Lonesome Pine Hospital

Chesapeake
Member
  Chesapeake General Hospital

Culpeper
Member
  Culpeper Memorial Hospital

Danville
Member
  Danville Regional Medical Center

Fairfax
Member
Inova Fair Oaks Hospital

Falls Church
Member
Inova Fairfax Hospital

Farmville
Member
Southside Community Hospital

Front Royal
Member
Warren Memorial Hospital

Galax
Member
Twin County Regional Hospital

Gloucester
Member
Riverside Walter Reed Hospital

Grundy
Member
Buchanan General Hospital

Kilmarnock
Member
Rappahannock General Hospital

Leesburg
Member
Loudoun Hospital Center

Lexington
Member
Stonewall Jackson Hospital

Luray
Member
Page Memorial Hospital

Manassas
Member
Prince William Hospital

Marion
Member
Smyth County Community Hospital

Martinsville
Member
Memorial Hospital of Martinsville and Henry County

Nassawadox
Member
Shore Memorial Hospital

Newport News
Member
Mary Immaculate Hospital
Riverside Health System
Riverside Regional Medical Center
Riverside Rehabilitation Institute

Norfolk
Member
Bon Secours–DePaul Medical Center

Norton
Member
Norton Community Hospital

Pearisburg
Member
Carilion Giles Memorial Hospital

Pennington Gap
Member
Lee County Community Hospital

Petersburg
Member
Southside Regional Medical Center

Portsmouth
Member
Maryview Hospital
Portsmouth General Hospital

Radford
Member
Carilion Radford Community Hospital

Richmond
Member
Bon Secours St. Mary's Hospital
Bon Secours–Richmond Community Hospital
Bon Secours–Stuart Circle
Children's Hospital
Richmond Eye and Ear Hospital
Richmond Memorial Hospital

Roanoke
Member
Carilion Health System
Carilion Medical Center

Rocky Mount
Member
Carilion Franklin Memorial Hospital

South Boston
Member
Halifax Regional Hospital

South Hill
Member
Community Memorial Healthcenter

Springfield
Member
Inova Health System

Stuart
Member
Patrick County Memorial Hospital

Suffolk
Member
Louise Obici Memorial Hospital

Tappahannock
Member
Riverside Tappahannock Hospital

Virginia Beach
Member
Tidewater Health Care, Inc.
Virginia Beach General Hospital

Warrenton
Member
Fauquier Hospital

Winchester
Member
Valley Health System
Winchester Medical Center

Woodbridge
Member
Potomac Hospital

Woodstock
Member
Shenandoah Memorial Hospital

Wytheville
Member
Wythe County Community Hospital

WASHINGTON

Aberdeen
Member
Grays Harbor Community Hospital

Bellevue
Member
Overlake Hospital Medical Center
PeaceHealth

Bellingham
Member
St. Joseph Hospital

Brewster
Member
Okanogan–Douglas County Hospital

Centralia
Member
Providence Centralia Hospital

Chelan
Member
Lake Chelan Community Hospital

Chewelah
Member
St. Joseph's Hospital

Clarkston
Member
Tri–State Memorial Hospital

Colfax
Member
Whitman Hospital and Medical Center

Colville
Member
Mount Carmel Hospital

Coupeville
Member
Whidbey General Hospital

Davenport
Member
Lincoln Hospital

Deer Park
Member
Deer Park Health Center and Hospital

Edmonds
Member
Stevens Healthcare

Ephrata
Member
Columbia Basin Hospital

Everett
Member
Providence General Medical Center

Grand Coulee
Member
Coulee Community Hospital

Kirkland
Member
Evergreen Community Health Center

Longview
Member
St. John Medical Center

Morton
Member
Morton General Hospital

Moses Lake
Member
Samaritan Healthcare

Newport
Member
Newport Community Hospital

Odessa
Member
Odessa Memorial Hospital

Olympia
Member
Providence St. Peter Hospital

Omak
Member
Mid–Valley Hospital

Othello
Member
Othello Community Hospital

Prosser
Member
Prosser Memorial Hospital

Pullman
Member
Pullman Memorial Hospital

Puyallup
Member
Good Samaritan Community Healthcare

Quincy
Member
Quincy Valley Medical Center

Redmond
Member
The Eastside Hospital

Renton
Member
Valley Medical Center

Republic
Member
Ferry County Memorial Hospital

Richland
Member
Kadlec Medical Center

Ritzville
Member
East Adams Rural Hospital

Seattle
Member
Children's Hospital and Regional Medical Center
Northwest Hospital
Providence Seattle Medical Center
Sisters of Providence Health System

Shelton
Member
  Mason General Hospital

Spokane
Member
  Deaconess Medical Center–Spokane
  Empire Health Services
  Holy Family Hospital
  Providence Services
  Sacred Heart Medical Center
  Shriners Hospitals for Children–Spokane
  St. Lukes Rehabilitation Institute
  Valley Hospital and Medical Center

Tonasket
Member
  North Valley Hospital

Toppenish
Member
  Providence Toppenish Hospital

Vancouver
Member
  Southwest Washington Medical Center
  Woodside Hospital

Walla Walla
Member
  St. Mary Medical Center
  Walla Walla General Hospital

Wenatchee
Member
  Central Washington Hospital

WEST VIRGINIA
Berkeley Springs
Member
  Morgan County War Memorial Hospital

Bluefield
Member
  Bluefield Regional Medical Center

Buckhannon
Member
  St. Joseph's Hospital

Clarksburg
Member
  United Hospital Center

Elkins
Member
  Davis Memorial Hospital

Fairmont
Member
  Fairmont General Hospital

Huntington
Member
  St. Mary's Hospital

Keyser
Member
  Potomac Valley Hospital

Kingwood
Member
  Preston Memorial Hospital

Martinsburg
Member
  City Hospital

Morgantown
Member
  Monongalia General Hospital

Parkersburg
Member
  Camden–Clark Memorial Hospital

Petersburg
Member
  Grant Memorial Hospital

Philippi
Member
  Broaddus Hospital

Point Pleasant
Member
  Pleasant Valley Hospital

Ranson
Member
  Jefferson Memorial Hospital

Romney
Member
  Hampshire Memorial Hospital

Sistersville
Member
  Sistersville General Hospital

South Charleston
Member
  Thomas Memorial Hospital

Summersville
Member
  Summersville Memorial Hospital

Weirton
Member
  Weirton Medical Center

Weston
Member
  Stonewall Jackson Memorial Hospital

WISCONSIN
Amery
Member
  Apple River Hospital

Baldwin
Member
  Baldwin Hospital

Baraboo
Member
  St. Clare Hospital and Health Services

Barron
Member
  Barron Memorial Medical Center and Skilled Nursing
    Facility

Berlin
Member
  Community Health Network

Burlington
Member
  Memorial Hospital Corporation of Burlington

Cumberland
Member
  Cumberland Memorial Hospital

Durand
Member
  Chippewa Valley Hospital and Oakview Care Center

Elkhorn
Member
  Lakeland Medical Center

Green Bay
Member
  Bellin Hospital

Hartford
Member
  Hartford Memorial Hospital

Janesville
Member
  Mercy Health System

Kewaunee
Member
  St. Mary's Kewaunee Area Memorial Hospital

Madison
Member
  St. Marys Hospital Medical Center

Marinette
Member
  Bay Area Medical Center

Milwaukee
Member
  Children's Hospital of Wisconsin
  Sinai Samaritan Medical Center
  St. Luke's Medical Center

Monroe
Member
  The Monroe Clinic

Osceola
Member
  Osceola Medical Center

Plymouth
Member
  Valley View Medical Center

Sheboygan
Member
  Sheboygan Memorial Medical Center

Two Rivers
Member
  Two Rivers Community Hospital and Hamilton
    Memorial Home

Viroqua
Member
  Vernon County Hospital

West Allis
Member
  West Allis Memorial Hospital

WYOMING
Buffalo
Member
  Johnson County Memorial Hospital

Cody
Member
  West Park Hospital

Gillette
Member
  Campbell County Memorial Hospital

Jackson
Member
  St. John's Hospital and Living Center

Lusk
Member
  Niobrara County Hospital District

Newcastle
Member
  Weston County Health Services

Sundance
Member
  Crook County Medical Services District

Torrington
Member
  Community Hospital

Wheatland
Member
  Platte County Memorial Hospital Nursing Home

Worland
Member
  Washakie Memorial Hospital

SYNERNET, INC.
  222 St John Street, Portland, ME
  Zip 04102; tel. 207/775–6081; Mr Paul I
  Davis, III, President

MAINE
Bangor
Member
  St. Joseph Hospital

Bar Harbor
Member
  Mount Desert Island Hospital

Bath
Member
  Mid Coast Hospital

Belfast
Member
  Waldo County General Hospital

Biddeford
Member
  Southern Maine Medical Center

Blue Hill
Member
  Blue Hill Memorial Hospital

Bridgton
Member
  Northern Cumberland Memorial Hospital

Damariscotta
Member
  Miles Memorial Hospital

Farmington
Member
  Franklin Memorial Hospital

Section B

Fort Kent
Member
Northern Maine Medical Center

Lewiston
Member
St. Mary's Regional Medical Center

Norway
Member
Stephens Memorial Hospital

Pittsfield
Member
Sebasticook Valley Hospital

Portland
Member
Mercy Hospital Portland

Rockport
Member
Penobscot Bay Medical Center

Rumford
Member
Rumford Community Hospital

Sanford
Member
Henrietta D. Goodall Hospital

Skowhegan
Member
Redington–Fairview General Hospital

Waterville
Member
Inland Hospital

Westbrook
Member
Westbrook Community Hospital

York
Member
York Hospital

UNIVERSITY HEALTH SYSTEM OF NEW JERSEY
154 West State Street, Trenton, NJ
Zip 08608; tel. 609/656–9600; Dr
Thomas E Terrill , Ph.D., President

NEW JERSEY
Camden
Member
Our Lady of Lourdes Medical Center
The Cooper Health System

Flemington
Member
Hunterdon Medical Center

Florham Park
Member
Atlantic Health System

Hackensack
Member
Hackensack University Medical Center

Hamilton
Member
Robert Wood Johnson University Hospital at Hamilton

New Brunswick
Member
Robert Wood Johnson University Hospital

Newark
Member
Saint Michael's Medical Center
University of Medicine and Dentistry of New
Jersey–University Hospital

Paramus
Member
Bergen Regional Medical Center

Phillipsburg
Member
Warren Hospital

Somerville
Member
Somerset Medical Center

Trenton
Member
Capital Health System at Mercer

West Orange
Member
Kessler Institute for Rehabilitation

UNIVERSITY HEALTHSYSTEM CONSORTIUM, INC.
2001 Spring Road, Suite 700, Oak Brook,
IL Zip 60523; tel. 630/954–1700; Mr
Robert J Baker, President and Chief
Executive Officer

ALABAMA
Birmingham
Member
University of Alabama Hospital

Mobile
Associate
University of South Alabama Knollwood Park Hospital
Member
University of South Alabama Medical Center

ARIZONA
Tucson
Member
University Medical Center

ARKANSAS
Little Rock
Member
University Hospital of Arkansas

CALIFORNIA
Downey
Associate
LAC–Rancho Los Amigos Medical Center

Lancaster
Associate
LAC–High Desert Hospital

Los Angeles
Member
LAC–King–Drew Medical Center
LAC–University of Southern California Medical Center
University of California Los Angeles Medical Center

Martinez
Associate
Contra Costa Regional Medical Center

Moreno Valley
Associate
Riverside County Regional Medical Center

Orange
Member
University of California, Irvine Medical Center

Sacramento
Member
University of California, Davis Medical Center

San Diego
Member
University of California San Diego Medical Center

San Francisco
Associate
University of California–San Francisco Mount Zion
Medical Center
Member
San Francisco General Hospital Medical Center

San Jose
Associate
Santa Clara Valley Medical Center

San Leandro
Associate
Alameda County Medical Center

Santa Monica
Associate
Santa Monica–UCLA Medical Center

Stanford
Member
Stanford University Hospital

Sylmar
Associate
Olive View–UCLA Medical Center

Torrance
Member
LAC–Harbor–University of California at Los Angeles
Medical Center

Valencia
Associate
Henry Mayo Newhall Memorial Hospital

COLORADO
Denver
Associate
National Jewish Medical and Research Center
Member
Denver Health Medical Center
University of Colorado Hospital

CONNECTICUT
Farmington
Member
University of Connecticut Health Center, John
Dempsey Hospital

New Haven
Member
Yale–New Haven Hospital

DISTRICT OF COLUMBIA
Washington
Member
Georgetown University Hospital
Howard University Hospital

FLORIDA
Gainesville
Associate
Shands at AGH
Member
Shands at the University of Florida

Jacksonville
Associate
University Medical Center

Lake City
Associate
Shands at Lake Shore

Live Oak
Affiliate
Shands at Live Oak

Orlando
Associate
Princeton Hospital

Starke
Associate
Shands at Starke

Tampa
Member
Tampa General Healthcare

GEORGIA
Atlanta
Member
Crawford Long Hospital of Emory University
Emory University Hospital

Augusta
Member
Medical College of Georgia Hospital and Clinics

ILLINOIS
Chicago
Associate
Cook County Hospital
Louis A. Weiss Memorial Hospital
Member
University of Chicago Hospitals
University of Illinois at Chicago Medical Center

Maywood
Member
Loyola University Medical Center

INDIANA
Indianapolis
Member
Clarian Health Partners
Wishard Health Services

IOWA
Iowa City
Member
University of Iowa Hospitals and Clinics

KANSAS
Kansas City
Member
University of Kansas Medical Center

KENTUCKY
Lexington
Member
  University of Kentucky Hospital

LOUISIANA
Shreveport
Member
  LSU Medical Center–University Hospital

MARYLAND
Baltimore
Associate
  James Lawrence Kernan Hospital
Member
  University of Maryland Medical System

MASSACHUSETTS
Boston
Member
  Brigham and Women's Hospital
  Massachusetts General Hospital

Clinton
Associate
  Clinton Hospital

Marlborough
Associate
  Marlborough Hospital

Worcester
Member
  University of Massachusetts Medical Center

MICHIGAN
Ann Arbor
Member
  University of Michigan Hospitals and Health Centers

MINNESOTA
Minneapolis
Associate
  Hennepin County Medical Center

MISSOURI
Columbia
Member
  University Hospitals and Clinics

Jefferson City
Associate
  Capital Region Medical Center–Madison

NEBRASKA
Omaha
Member
  Nebraska Health System

NEVADA
Las Vegas
Associate
  University Medical Center

NEW JERSEY
Neptune
Associate
  Meridian Health System

New Brunswick
Member
  Robert Wood Johnson University Hospital

Newark
Member
  University of Medicine and Dentistry of New Jersey–University Hospital

NEW YORK
Albany
Member
  Albany Medical Center

Brooklyn
Member
  University Hospital of Brooklyn–State University of New York Health Science Center at Brooklyn

New York
Affiliate
  New York University Hospitals Center

Stony Brook
Member
  University Hospital

Syracuse
Member
  University Hospital–SUNY Health Science Center at Syracuse

NORTH CAROLINA
Ahoskie
Associate
  Roanoke–Chowan Hospital

Chapel Hill
Member
  University of North Carolina Hospitals

Greenville
Member
  Pitt County Memorial Hospital–University Health System of Eastern Carolina

Windsor
Associate
  Bertie Memorial Hospital

Winston–Salem
Member
  North Carolina Baptist Hospital

OHIO
Bedford
Associate
  UHHS Bedford Medical Center

Chardon
Associate
  UHHS Geauga Regional Hospital

Cincinnati
Member
  University Hospital

Cleveland
Member
  University Hospitals of Cleveland

Columbus
Member
  Ohio State University Medical Center

Conneaut
Associate
  UHHS Brown Memorial Hospital

Geneva
Associate
  UHHS–Memorial Hospital of Geneva

Ironton
Associate
  River Valley Health System

Toledo
Member
  Medical College of Ohio Hospitals

Waverly
Associate
  Pike Community Hospital

Willoughby
Associate
  UHHS Laurelwood Hospital

OREGON
Portland
Member
  Oregon Health Sciences University Hospital

PENNSYLVANIA
Allentown
Associate
  Lehigh Valley Hospital

Philadelphia
Associate
  Friends Hospital
  Presbyterian Medical Center of the University of Pennsylvania Health System
  Thomas Jefferson University Hospital
Member
  Allegheny University Hospitals, Hahnemann
  Hospital of the University of Pennsylvania

Phoenixville
Associate
  Phoenixville Hospital

Pittsburgh
Member
  UPMC–Presbyterian

SOUTH CAROLINA
Charleston
Associate
  Charleston Memorial Hospital
Member
  MUSC Medical Center of Medical University of South Carolina

TENNESSEE
Knoxville
Member
  University of Tennessee Memorial Hospital

Memphis
Member
  University of Tennessee Bowld Hospital

Nashville
Member
  Vanderbilt University Hospital

TEXAS
Dallas
Member
  Zale Lipshy University Hospital

Galveston
Member
  University of Texas Medical Branch Hospitals

Houston
Member
  Hermann Hospital

Tyler
Associate
  University of Texas Health Center at Tyler

UTAH
Salt Lake City
Member
  University of Utah Hospitals and Clinics

VIRGINIA
Charlottesville
Member
  University of Virginia Medical Center

Richmond
Member
  Medical College of Virginia Hospitals, Virginia Commonwealth University

WASHINGTON
Seattle
Member
  Harborview Medical Center
  University of Washington Medical Center

WEST VIRGINIA
Morgantown
Member
  West Virginia University Hospitals

WISCONSIN
Antigo
Associate
  Langlade Memorial Hospital

Madison
Member
  University of Wisconsin Hospital and Clinics

Medford
Associate
  Memorial Hospital of Taylor County

Merrill
Associate
  Good Samaritan Health Center of Merrill

Milwaukee
Member
  Froedtert Memorial Lutheran Hospital

Wausau
Associate
  Wausau Hospital

VHA, INC.
220 East Las Colinas Boulevard, Irving, TX Zip 75039–5500; tel. 972/830–0000; Mr C Thomas Smith, President and Chief Executive Officer

ALABAMA

Anniston
Partner
Northeast Alabama Regional Medical Center

Athens
Partner
Athens–Limestone Hospital

Birmingham
Shareholder
Baptist Health System

Cullman
Partner
Cullman Regional Medical Center

Decatur
Partner
Decatur General Hospital

Florence
Partner
Eliza Coffee Memorial Hospital

Guntersville
Partner
Marshall County Health Care Authority

Jackson
Partner
Vaughn Jackson Medical Center

Mobile
Shareholder
Infirmary Health System, Inc.

Montgomery
Shareholder
Baptist Medical Center

Scottsboro
Partner
Jackson County Hospital

Tuscaloosa
Partner
DCH Health System

ARIZONA

Phoenix
Shareholder
Samaritan Health System

Tucson
Shareholder
Health Partners of Southern Arizona

ARKANSAS

Fayetteville
Partner
Washington Regional Medical Center

Fort Smith
Shareholder
Sparks Regional Medical Center

Jonesboro
Partner
St. Bernards Regional Medical Center

Little Rock
Shareholder
Baptist Health

CALIFORNIA

Anaheim
Partner
Anaheim Memorial Medical Center

Covina
Partner
Citrus Valley Health Partners

Fresno
Shareholder
Community Hospitals of Central California

La Jolla
Shareholder
Scripps Memorial Hospital–La Jolla

Lancaster
Partner
Antelope Valley Hospital

Long Beach
Shareholder
Memorial Health Services

Los Angeles
Shareholder
Cedars–Sinai Medical Center

Modesto
Partner
Memorial Hospitals Association

Newport Beach
Shareholder
Hoag Memorial Hospital Presbyterian

Pasadena
Partner
Southern California Healthcare Systems

Pomona
Partner
Pomona Valley Hospital Medical Center

Riverside
Partner
Riverside Community Hospital

Sacramento
Shareholder
Sutter Health

San Francisco
Shareholder
California Pacific Medical Center

Santa Barbara
Partner
Santa Barbara Cottage Hospital

Stockton
Partner
St. Joseph's Regional Health System

Torrance
Partner
Torrance Memorial Medical Center

Turlock
Partner
Emanuel Medical Center

Valencia
Partner
Santa Clarita Health Care Association

Van Nuys
Partner
Valley Presbyterian Hospital

Walnut Creek
Partner
John Muir Medical Center

Whittier
Partner
Presbyterian Intercommunity Hospital

COLORADO

Alamosa
Partner
San Luis Valley Regional Medical Center

Aspen
Partner
Aspen Valley Hospital District

Boulder
Partner
Boulder Community Hospital

Colorado Springs
Partner
Memorial Hospital

Englewood
Shareholder
HealthONE Healthcare System

Fort Collins
Partner
Poudre Valley Hospital

Grand Junction
Partner
Community Hospital

La Junta
Partner
Arkansas Valley Regional Medical Center

Longmont
Partner
Longmont United Hospital

Steamboat Springs
Partner
Routt Memorial Hospital

Vail
Shareholder
Vail Valley Medical Center

Wheat Ridge
Shareholder
Exempla Lutheran Medical Center

CONNECTICUT

Danbury
Partner
Danbury Hospital

Greenwich
Partner
Greenwich Hospital

Hartford
Shareholder
Hartford Hospital

Meriden
Partner
Veterans Memorial Medical Center

Middletown
Partner
Middlesex Hospital

Stamford
Partner
Stamford Hospital

Torrington
Partner
Charlotte Hungerford Hospital

DELAWARE

Milford
Partner
Bayhealth Medical Center, Milford Memorial Campus

DISTRICT OF COLUMBIA

Washington
Shareholder
Medlantic Healthcare Group

FLORIDA

Boca Raton
Partner
Boca Raton Community Hospital

Boynton Beach
Partner
Bethesda Memorial Hospital

Daytona Beach
Shareholder
Halifax Community Health System

Fort Myers
Partner
Lee Memorial Health System

Inverness
Partner
Citrus Memorial Hospital

Jacksonville
Partner
Methodist Medical Center
St. Luke's Hospital

Lakeland
Shareholder
Lakeland Regional Medical Center

Melbourne
Shareholder
Holmes Regional Medical Center

Miami
Partner
South Miami Hospital

Ocala
Partner
Munroe Regional Medical Center

Orlando
Shareholder
Orlando Regional Healthcare System

Panama City
Partner
Bay Medical Center

Pensacola
Shareholder
Baptist Health Care Corporation

Section B

Saint Petersburg
Partner
Bayfront Medical Center

Sarasota
Partner
Sarasota Memorial Hospital

Stuart
Partner
Martin Memorial Health Systems

Tallahassee
Shareholder
Tallahassee Memorial Regional Medical Center

Tampa
Partner
University Community Hospital

West Palm Beach
Partner
Good Samaritan Medical Center

GEORGIA

Albany
Partner
Phoebe Putney Memorial Hospital

Athens
Partner
Athens Regional Medical Center

Atlanta
Partner
Northside Hospital
Shareholder
Piedmont Hospital

Columbus
Partner
Columbus Regional Health Care System, Inc

Dalton
Partner
Hamilton Medical Center

Decatur
Partner
DeKalb Medical Center

East Point
Partner
South Fulton Medical Center

Gainesville
Partner
Northeast Georgia Health Services

Lawrenceville
Partner
Promina Gwinnett Hospital System

Macon
Partner
Medical Center of Central Georgia

Marietta
Partner
WellStar Kennestone Hospital

Riverdale
Partner
Southern Regional Medical Center

Rome
Partner
Floyd Medical Center

Royston
Partner
Cobb Memorial Hospital

Savannah
Partner
Candler Hospital

Thomasville
Partner
Archbold Medical Center
John D. Archbold Memorial Hospital

Valdosta
Partner
South Georgia Medical Center

HAWAII

Honolulu
Shareholder
Queen's Medical Center

IDAHO

Boise
Shareholder
St. Luke's Regional Medical Center

Coeur D'Alene
Partner
Kootenai Medical Center

Pocatello
Partner
Bannock Regional Medical Center

Twin Falls
Partner
Magic Valley Regional Medical Center

ILLINOIS

Arlington Heights
Partner
Northwest Community Healthcare

Berwyn
Partner
MacNeal Hospital

Carbondale
Partner
Southern Illinois Hospital Services

Chicago
Shareholder
Northwestern Memorial Hospital
Rush–Presbyterian–St. Luke's Medical Center

De Kalb
Partner
Kishwaukee Community Hospital

Decatur
Shareholder
Decatur Memorial Hospital

Dixon
Partner
Katherine Shaw Bethea Hospital

Elgin
Partner
Sherman Hospital

Elmhurst
Partner
Elmhurst Memorial Hospital

Evanston
Shareholder
Evanston Hospital

Evergreen Park
Partner
Little Company of Mary Hospital and Health Care
Centers

Freeport
Partner
Freeport Memorial Hospital

Harvey
Shareholder
Ingalls Health System
Ingalls Hospital

Highland Park
Partner
Highland Park Hospital

Jacksonville
Partner
Passavant Area Hospital

Joliet
Partner
Silver Cross Hospital

Kankakee
Partner
Riverside Medical Center

Macomb
Partner
McDonough District Hospital

Maryville
Partner
Anderson Hospital

Mattoon
Partner
Sarah Bush Lincoln Health System

Normal
Partner
BroMenn Healthcare

Oak Brook
Shareholder
Advocate Health Care

Quincy
Partner
Blessing Hospital

Rock Island
Partner
Trinity Medical Center–West Campus

Rockford
Partner
Rockford Memorial Hospital

Springfield
Shareholder
Memorial Medical Center
Memorial Medical Center System

INDIANA

Bloomington
Partner
Bloomington Hospital

Columbus
Partner
Columbus Regional Hospital

Danville
Partner
Hendricks Community Hospital

Elkhart
Partner
Elkhart General Hospital

Evansville
Shareholder
Deaconess Hospital

Fort Wayne
Partner
Parkview Hospital

Indianapolis
Shareholder
Clarian Health Partners
Community Hospitals Indianapolis

La Porte
Partner
La Porte Hospital and Health Services

Madison
Partner
King's Daughters' Hospital

Marion
Partner
Marion General Hospital

Muncie
Shareholder
Ball Memorial Hospital

New Albany
Partner
Floyd Memorial Hospital and Health Services

Noblesville
Partner
Riverview Hospital

Richmond
Partner
Reid Hospital and Health Care Services

South Bend
Shareholder
Memorial Health System, Inc.

Terre Haute
Partner
Union Hospital

Valparaiso
Partner
Porter Memorial Hospital

Vincennes
Partner
Good Samaritan Hospital

IOWA

Atlantic
Shareholder
Cass County Memorial Hospital

Council Bluffs
Shareholder
Jennie Edmundson Memorial Hospital

Keokuk
Shareholder
Keokuk Area Hospital

Red Oak
Shareholder
Montgomery County Memorial Hospital

Sioux City
Shareholder
St. Luke's Regional Medical Center

KANSAS
Atchison
Shareholder
Atchison Hospital

Colby
Shareholder
Citizens Medical Center

Hays
Shareholder
Hays Medical Center

Hutchinson
Shareholder
Hutchinson Hospital Corporation

Kansas City
Shareholder
Bethany Medical Center

Liberal
Shareholder
Southwest Medical Center

Phillipsburg
Shareholder
Great Plains Health Alliance, Inc.

Pratt
Shareholder
Pratt Regional Medical Center

Salina
Partner
Salina Regional Health Center

Shawnee Mission
Shareholder
Shawnee Mission Medical Center

Topeka
Partner
St. Francis Hospital and Medical Center
Shareholder
Stormont–Vail HealthCare

Wichita
Partner
Via Christi Health System

KENTUCKY
Fort Thomas
Partner
St. Luke Hospital East

Madisonville
Partner
Regional Medical Center of Hopkins County

Owensboro
Partner
Owensboro–Daviess County Hospital

LOUISIANA
Baton Rouge
Member
Our Lady of the Lake Regional Medical Center
Partner
Woman's Hospital

Crowley
Partner
American Legion Hospital

De Ridder
Partner
Beauregard Memorial Hospital

Lafayette
Partner
Our Lady of Lourdes Regional Medical Center

Lake Charles
Partner
Lake Charles Memorial Hospital

Monroe
Partner
St. Francis Medical Center

New Orleans
Partner
Pendleton Memorial Methodist Hospital
Shareholder
Ochsner Foundation Hospital

Ruston
Partner
Lincoln General Hospital

Shreveport
Shareholder
Willis–Knighton Medical Center

MAINE
Bangor
Partner
Eastern Maine Healthcare

Biddeford
Shareholder
Southern Maine Medical Center

Lewiston
Shareholder
Central Maine Medical Center

Portland
Shareholder
Maine Medical Center

Waterville
Shareholder
MaineGeneral Medical Center–Waterville Campus

MARYLAND
Easton
Partner
Memorial Hospital at Easton Maryland

Fallston
Partner
Upper Chesapeake Health System

MASSACHUSETTS
Beverly
Partner
Beverly Hospital

Boston
Partner
Massachusetts Eye and Ear Infirmary
Shareholder
New England Medical Center
Partners HealthCare System, Inc.

Cambridge
Partner
Mount Auburn Hospital

Concord
Partner
Emerson Hospital

Fall River
Member
Southcoast Hospitals Group

Hyannis
Partner
Cape Cod Hospital

Lawrence
Owner
Lawrence General Hospital

Leominster
Partner
Health Alliance Hospitals

Lowell
Partner
Lowell General Hospital

Melrose
Partner
Melrose–Wakefield Hospital

Newton
Partner
Newell Home Health Service

South Weymouth
Partner
South Shore Health & Education Corporation

Southbridge
Partner
Harrington Memorial Hospital

Worcester
Partner
Saint Vincent Hospital

MICHIGAN
Bay City
Partner
Bay Medical Center

Dearborn
Member
Oakwood Healthcare System

Detroit
Partner
St. John Hospital and Medical Center

Flint
Partner
Genesys Health System

Grand Rapids
Shareholder
Spectrum Health–Downtown Campus

Holland
Partner
Holland Community Hospital

Kalamazoo
Partner
Bronson Healthcare Group, Inc.

Lansing
Partner
Michigan Capital Healthcare

Monroe
Partner
Mercy Memorial Hospital

Petoskey
Partner
Healthshare Group

Port Huron
Partner
Blue Water Health Services Corporation

Royal Oak
Shareholder
William Beaumont Hospital–Royal Oak

Saginaw
Partner
Saginaw General Hospital

MINNESOTA
Bemidji
Partner
North Country Regional Hospital

Duluth
Partner
St. Luke's Hospital

Fergus Falls
Partner
Lake Region Healthcare Corporation

Mankato
Partner
Immanuel/St. Joseph's–Mayo Health System

Minneapolis
Shareholder
Allina Health System

Saint Cloud
Partner
St. Cloud Hospital

Saint Paul
Shareholder
HealthEast

Waconia
Partner
Ridgeview Medical Center

Willmar
Partner
Rice Memorial Hospital

MISSISSIPPI
Greenwood
Partner
Greenwood Leflore Hospital

Gulfport
Partner
  Memorial Hospital at Gulfport

Hattiesburg
Partner
  Forrest General Hospital

Jackson
Partner
  St. Dominic–Jackson Memorial Hospital

McComb
Partner
  Southwest Mississippi Regional Medical Center

Meridian
Partner
  Jeff Anderson Regional Medical Center

Pascagoula
Partner
  Singing River Hospital System

Tupelo
Shareholder
  North Mississippi Health Services, Inc.

MISSOURI

Bolivar
Partner
  Citizens Memorial Hospital

Branson
Partner
  Skaggs Community Health Center

Cameron
Partner
  Cameron Community Hospital

Cape Girardeau
Partner
  Saint Francis Medical Center
  Southeast Missouri Hospital

Carthage
Partner
  McCune–Brooks Hospital

Joplin
Partner
  Freeman Health System
  Freeman Hospital West

Kansas City
Shareholder
  Saint Luke's Hospital
  Saint Luke's Shawnee Mission Health System

Liberty
Partner
  Liberty Hospital

Saint Louis
Shareholder
  BJC Health System

Springfield
Shareholder
  Cox Health Systems

West Plains
Partner
  Ozarks Medical Center

MONTANA

Billings
Partner
  Deaconess Billings Clinic

Bozeman
Partner
  Bozeman Deaconess Hospital

Great Falls
Partner
  Benefis Health Care–East Campus

Helena
Partner
  St. Peter's Community Hospital

NEBRASKA

Aurora
Partner
  Memorial Hospital

Beatrice
Partner
  Beatrice Community Hospital and Health Center

Columbus
Partner
  Columbus Community Hospital

Hastings
Partner
  Mary Lanning Memorial Hospital

Lincoln
Partner
  Bryan Memorial Hospital

Norfolk
Partner
  Faith Regional Health Services

Omaha
Partner
  Children's Hospital
Shareholder
  Nebraska Methodist Hospital

Scottsbluff
Partner
  Regional West Medical Center

NEW HAMPSHIRE

Concord
Partner
  Capital Region Family Health Center

Dover
Partner
  Wentworth–Douglass Hospital

Keene
Partner
  Cheshire Medical Center

Nashua
Partner
  Southern New Hampshire Regional Medical Center

Rochester
Partner
  Frisbie Memorial Hospital

NEW JERSEY

Belleville
Shareholder
  Clara Maass Health System

Camden
Partner
  Our Lady of Lourdes Medical Center

Elizabeth
Partner
  Elizabeth General Medical Center

Flemington
Partner
  Hunterdon Medical Center

Florham Park
Shareholder
  Atlantic Health System

Hackettstown
Partner
  Hackettstown Community Hospital

Hammonton
Partner
  William B. Kessler Memorial Hospital

Jersey City
Partner
  Christ Hospital

Mount Holly
Shareholder
  Memorial Hospital of Burlington County

Newton
Partner
  Newton Memorial Hospital

Phillipsburg
Partner
  Warren Hospital

Plainfield
Partner
  Muhlenberg Regional Medical Center

Pompton Plains
Partner
  Chilton Memorial Hospital

Rahway
Partner
  Rahway Hospital

Somers Point
Partner
  Shore Memorial Hospital

Toms River
Shareholder
  Community Medical Center

Trenton
Partner
  Capital Health System

Woodbury
Partner
  Underwood–Memorial Hospital

NEW MEXICO

Albuquerque
Partner
  University Hospital

Farmington
Partner
  San Juan Regional Medical Center

Gallup
Partner
  Rehoboth McKinley Christian Hospital

Las Cruces
Partner
  Memorial Medical Center

Roswell
Partner
  Eastern New Mexico Medical Center

NEW YORK

Binghamton
Shareholder
  United Health Services Hospitals–Binghamton

Brooklyn
Partner
  Brooklyn Hospital Center

Cobleskill
Partner
  Bassett Hospital of Schoharie County

Geneva
Partner
  Geneva General Hospital

Ithaca
Partner
  Cayuga Medical Center at Ithaca

Jamestown
Partner
  Woman's Christian Association Hospital

Manhasset
Partner
  North Shore– Long Island Jewish Health System

Mount Kisco
Partner
  Northern Westchester Hospital Center

New Rochelle
Partner
  Sound Shore Medical Center of Westchester

New York
Partner
  Lenox Hill Hospital
  New York University Hospitals Center
  St. Luke's–Roosevelt Hospital Center

North Tonawanda
Partner
  De Graff Memorial Hospital

Plattsburgh
Partner
  Champlain Valley Physicians Hospital Medical Center

Rochester
Partner
  Highland Hospital of Rochester
  Park Ridge Health System

Rockville Centre
Partner
  Mercy Medical Center

Southampton
Partner
  Southampton Hospital

Suffern
Partner
Good Samaritan Hospital

Syracuse
Partner
Crouse Hospital

Troy
Partner
Samaritan Hospital

Utica
Partner
Mohawk Valley Psychiatric Center

White Plains
Partner
White Plains Hospital Center

Yonkers
Partner
St. John's Riverside Hospital

NORTH CAROLINA

Charlotte
Shareholder
Carolinas HealthCare System

Raleigh
Partner
Wake Medical Center

Rocky Mount
Partner
Nash Health Care Systems

Thomasville
Partner
Community General Hospital of Thomasville

Winston–Salem
Shareholder
Carolina Medicorp, Inc.

NORTH DAKOTA

Bismarck
Partner
MedCenter One

Fargo
Shareholder
MeritCare Health System

Grand Forks
Partner
Altru Health System

Jamestown
Partner
Jamestown Hospital

Minot
Partner
Trinity Medical Center

OHIO

Akron
Shareholder
Akron General Medical Center

Ashtabula
Partner
Ashtabula County Medical Center

Cincinnati
Partner
Bethesda Corporate Health Services
Shareholder
Christ Hospital

Columbus
Shareholder
OhioHealth

Dover
Partner
Union Hospital

Elyria
Partner
EMH Regional Medical Center

Fremont
Partner
Memorial Hospital

Garfield Heights
Partner
Marymount Hospital

Hamilton
Partner
Fort Hamilton–Hughes Memorial Hospital

Lima
Partner
Lima Memorial Hospital

Mansfield
Partner
Mansfield Hospital

Maumee
Partner
St. Luke's Hospital

Middletown
Partner
Middletown Regional Hospital

Painesville
Partner
Lake Hospital System

Springfield
Partner
Community Hospital

Steubenville
Partner
Trinity Health System

Toledo
Shareholder
The Toledo Hospital

Troy
Partner
Upper Valley Medical Center

Xenia
Partner
Greene Memorial Hospital

Zanesville
Partner
Genesis HealthCare System

OKLAHOMA

Ada
Partner
Valley View Regional Hospital

Altus
Partner
Jackson County Memorial Hospital

Ardmore
Partner
Mercy Memorial Health Center

Chickasha
Partner
Grady Memorial Hospital

Duncan
Partner
Duncan Regional Hospital

McAlester
Partner
McAlester Regional Health Center

Midwest City
Partner
Midwest Regional Medical Center

Muskogee
Partner
Muskogee Regional Medical Center

Norman
Partner
Norman Regional Hospital

Oklahoma City
Partner
Deaconess Hospital
Shareholder
Oklahoma Health System

Poteau
Partner
Eastern Oklahoma Medical Center

Stillwater
Partner
Stillwater Medical Center

Tulsa
Shareholder
Hillcrest Medical Center

OREGON

Hillsboro
Partner
Tuality Healthcare

PENNSYLVANIA

Allentown
Shareholder
Lehigh Valley Hospital

Altoona
Partner
Altoona Hospital

Beaver
Partner
The Medical Center, Beaver

Bristol
Partner
Lower Bucks Hospital

Butler
Partner
Butler Health System

Erie
Shareholder
Hamot Health Systems

Johnstown
Partner
Conemaugh Valley Memorial Hospital

Kingston
Partner
Wyoming Valley Health Care System

Lancaster
Partner
Lancaster General Hospital

Latrobe
Partner
Latrobe Area Hospital

Natrona Heights
Partner
Allegheny University Medical Center–Allegheny Valley

Norristown
Partner
Montgomery Hospital

Philadelphia
Partner
Chestnut Hill HealthCare
Episcopal Hospital
Frankford Hospital of the City of Philadelphia
Jeanes Health System
Shareholder
Pennsylvania Hospital

Pittsburgh
Partner
Shadyside Hospital
St. Clair Memorial Hospital
UPMC–St. Margaret
Shareholder
Allegheny Health, Education and Research Foundation

Pottstown
Partner
Pottstown Memorial Medical Center

Reading
Partner
Reading Hospital and Medical Center

Sayre
Shareholder
Guthrie Healthcare System

Scranton
Partner
Community Medical Center

Sellersville
Partner
Grand View Hospital

Sewickley
Partner
Sewickley Valley Hospital, (A Division of Valley Medical Facilities)

Springfield
Shareholder
Crozer–Keystone Health System

Uniontown
Partner
Uniontown Hospital

Washington
Partner
Washington Hospital

West Chester
Partner
Chester County Hospital

Williamsport
Partner
Susquehanna Health System

York
Partner
York Health System

RHODE ISLAND
Providence
Shareholder
Lifespan Corporation
Rhode Island Hospital

SOUTH CAROLINA
Columbia
Shareholder
Palmetto Health Alliance

SOUTH DAKOTA
Sioux Falls
Shareholder
Sioux Valley Hospital

TENNESSEE
Jackson
Shareholder
West Tennessee Healthcare.

Knoxville
Shareholder
Fort Sanders Alliance

Memphis
Shareholder
Baptist Memorial Hospital

Nashville
Shareholder
Baptist Hospital

Oak Ridge
Partner
Methodist Medical Center of Oak Ridge

TEXAS
Amarillo
Partner
Baptist St. Anthony Health System

Arlington
Partner
Arlington Memorial Hospital

Austin
Partner
St. David's Medical Center

Beaumont
Partner
Baptist Hospital of Southeast Texas

Dallas
Shareholder
Baylor Health Care System

El Paso
Partner
Providence Memorial Hospital

Fort Worth
Shareholder
All Saints Episcopal Hospital of Fort Worth

Grapevine
Partner
Baylor Medical Center at Grapevine

Harlingen
Partner
Valley Baptist Medical Center

Houston
Shareholder
Memorial Hospital Southwest

Irving
Partner
Baylor Medical Center at Irving

Lubbock
Shareholder
Lubbock Methodist Hospital System

Marshall
Partner
Marshall Regional Medical Center

Midland
Partner
Memorial Hospital and Medical Center

San Antonio
Partner
Baptist Health System

Sherman
Partner
Wilson N. Jones Regional Health System

Temple
Partner
King's Daughters Hospital

Texarkana
Partner
Wadley Regional Medical Center

Waco
Partner
Hillcrest Baptist Medical Center

Wichita Falls
Partner
United Regional Health Care System

VERMONT
Barre
Partner
Central Vermont Medical Center

Burlington
Shareholder
Fletcher Allen Health Care

Rutland
Partner
Rutland Regional Medical Center

VIRGINIA
Alexandria
Partner
Inova Alexandria Hospital

Arlington
Partner
Arlington Hospital

Charlottesville
Partner
Martha Jefferson Hospital

Franklin
Partner
Southampton Memorial Hospital

Fredericksburg
Partner
MWH Medicorp

Harrisonburg
Partner
Rockingham Memorial Hospital

Lynchburg
Partner
Centra Health, Inc.

Norfolk
Shareholder
Sentara Health System

Richmond
Partner
Children's Hospital

Warrenton
Partner
Fauquier Hospital

WASHINGTON
Tacoma
Shareholder
MultiCare Health System

WEST VIRGINIA
Charleston
Shareholder
Camcare, Inc.

Glen Dale
Partner
Reynolds Memorial Hospital

Huntington
Partner
Cabell Huntington Hospital

Morgantown
Partner
West Virginia University Hospitals

Parkersburg
Owner
St. Joseph's Hospital

Princeton
Partner
Princeton Community Hospital

Wheeling
Partner
Wheeling Hospital

WISCONSIN
Appleton
Shareholder
United Health Group

Beaver Dam
Partner
Beaver Dam Community Hospitals

Eau Claire
Partner
Luther Hospital

Green Bay
Partner
Bellin Hospital

Kenosha
Partner
Kenosha Hospital and Medical Center

La Crosse
Shareholder
Lutheran Hospital–La Crosse

Madison
Shareholder
Meriter Hospital

Menomonee Falls
Partner
Community Memorial Hospital

Milwaukee
Partner
Columbia Hospital
Froedtert Memorial Lutheran Hospital
Horizon Healthcare, Inc.

Rice Lake
Partner
Lakeview Medical Center

Watertown
Partner
Watertown Memorial Hospital

Waukesha
Partner
Waukesha Health System, Inc.

West Bend
Owner
St. Joseph's Community Hospital of West Bend

WYOMING
Casper
Partner
Wyoming Medical Center

Cheyenne
Partner
United Medical Center

Laramie
Partner
Ivinson Memorial Hospital

Sheridan
Partner
Memorial Hospital of Sheridan County

VANTAGE HEALTH GROUP
265 Conneaut Lake Road, Meadville, PA
Zip 16335; tel. 814/337-0000; Mr David
C Petno, Vice President Business
Development

PENNSYLVANIA

Erie
Member
  Millcreek Community Hospital
  Saint Vincent Health Center

Franklin
Member
  Northwest Medical Centers

Greenville
Member
  Horizon Hospital System

Meadville
Member
  Meadville Medical Center

Titusville
Member
  Titusville Area Hospital

Warren
Member
  Warren General Hospital

YANKEE ALLIANCE
  300 Brickstone Square, 5th Floor,
  Andover, MA Zip 01810–1429;
  tel. 978/475–2000; Mr R Paul O'Neill,
  President

CONNECTICUT

New Haven
Member
  Hospital of Saint Raphael

MAINE

Blue Hill
Affiliate
  Blue Hill Memorial Hospital

Lewiston
Member
  St. Mary's Regional Medical Center

MASSACHUSETTS

Attleboro
Affiliate
  Sturdy Memorial Hospital

Boston
Member
  Boston Medical Center

Cambridge
Member
  Youville Lifecare

Fall River
Member
  Southcoast Hospitals Group

Great Barrington
Member
  Fairview Hospital

Lexington
Member
  Covenant Health Systems, Inc.

Lowell
Member
  Saints Memorial Medical Center

North Adams
Affiliate
  North Adams Regional Hospital

Pittsfield
Member
  Berkshire Health Systems, Inc.
  Berkshire Medical Center

Winchester
Member
  Winchester Hospital

NEW HAMPSHIRE

Manchester
Affiliate
  Catholic Medical Center
  Elliot Hospital

Nashua
Member
  St. Joseph Hospital

NEW YORK

Albany
Member
  Albany Medical Center

Elizabethtown
Affiliate
  Elizabethtown Community Hospital

Glens Falls
Member
  Glens Falls Hospital

Plattsburgh
Affiliate
  Champlain Valley Physicians Hospital Medical Center

Troy
Member
  Samaritan Hospital

Section B

†List supplied by the Joint Commission on
Accreditation of Healthcare Organizations

For more information on membership contact:
Manager, Department of Membership
American Hospital Association
One North Franklin
Chicago, Illinois 60606-3401

Section C

Description of Lists

This section was compiled to provide a directory of information useful to the health care field.

National and International Organizations

The national and international lists include many types of voluntary organizations concerned with matters of interest to the health care field. The organizational information includes address, telephone number, FAX number, and the contact person. For organizations that maintain permanent offices, office addresses and telephone numbers are given. For organizations not maintaining offices, the addresses and telephone numbers given are those of their corresponding secretaries. The information was obtained directly from the organizations.

National Organizations are listed alphabetically by their full names. International Organizations are grouped alphabetically by country.

Also included is the Healthfinder listings. The Healthfinder is composed of two listing types: toll–free numbers for health information and federal health information centers and clearinghouses. Organizations are listed alphabetically by topic area.

We present this list simply as a convenient directory. Inclusion or omission of any organization's name indicates neither approval nor disapproval by Healthcare InfoSource, Inc., a subsidiary of the American Hospital Association.

United States Government Agencies

National agencies concerned with health–related matters are listed by the major department of government under which the different functions fall.

State and Local Organizations and Agencies

The lists of organizations in states, associated areas, and provinces include Blue Cross and Blue Shield plans, health systems agencies, hospital associations and councils, hospital licensure agencies, medical and nursing licensure agencies, peer review organizations, state health planning and development agencies, and statewide health coordinating councils.

There are many active local organizations that do not fall within these categories. Contact the hospital association of the state or province for information about such additional groups. The hospital association and councils listed have offices with full-time executives.

The selected state and provincial government agencies include those within state departments of health and welfare, and other agencies, such as comprehensive health planning, crippled children's services, maternal and child health, mental health, and vocational rehabilitation.

Health Care Providers

Lists of JCAHO Accredited Freestanding Long–Term Care Organizations, Health Maintenance Organizations, Freestanding Ambulatory Surgery Centers, Freestanding Hospices, JCAHO Accredited Freestanding Substance Abuse Organizations, JCAHO Accredited Freestanding Mental Health Care Organizations are provided in this section. The lists were developed from information supplied by the providers themselves.

As with the lists of National and International Organizations, these lists are provided simply as a convenient directory. Inclusion or omission of any organization's name indicates neither approval nor disapproval by Healthcare InfoSource, Inc.

A

ADARA: Professionals Networking for Excellence in Service Delivery, with Individuals Who are Deaf or Hard of Hearing, P.O. Box 6956, San Mateo, CA 94403–6956; tel. 650/372–0620; FAX. 650/372–0661; Elizabeth Charlson, Ph.D.

AVSC International, 79 Madison Avenue, Seventh Floor, New York, NY 10016; tel. 212/561–8065; Bob Geisler, Director, Information Services

Academy for Implants and Transplants, P.O. Box 223, Springfield, VA 22150; tel. 703/451–0001; FAX. 703/451–0004; Anthony J. Viscido, D.D.S., Secretary–Treasurer

Academy of Dentistry for Persons with Disabilities, 211 East Chicago Avenue, Suite 948, Chicago, IL 60611; tel. 312/440–2660; FAX. 312/440–2824; John S. Rutkauskas, M.S., D.D.S., Executive Director

Academy of General Dentistry, 211 East Chicago Avenue, Suite 1200, Chicago, IL 60611–2670; tel. 312/440–4300; FAX. 312/440–0559; Harold E. Donnell, Jr., Executive Director

Academy of Oral Dynamics, 1590 West Street Road, Warminster, PA 18974; tel. 215/957–0700; Dr. William J. Crielly, Treasurer

Academy of Oral Dynamics, 8919 Sudley Road, Manassas, VA 22110; tel. 703/330–0195; Dr. E. Paul Byrne, Secretary

Academy of Organizational and Occupational Psychiatry, 6728 Old McLean Village Drive, McLean, VA 22101; tel. 703/556–9222; George K. Degnon, Executive Director

Accreditation Association for Ambulatory Health Care, 9933 Lawler Avenue, Skokie, IL 60077–3708; tel. 847/676–9610; FAX. 847/676–9628; John E. Burke, Ph. D., Executive Director

Aerospace Medical Association, 320 South Henry Street, Alexandria, VA 22314–3579; tel. 703/739–2240 ext. 103; FAX. 703/739–9652; Russell B. Rayman, M.D., Executive Director

Alexander Graham Bell Association for the Deaf, Inc., 3417 Volta Place, N.W., Washington, DC 20007; tel. 202/337–5220; Donna McCord Dickman, Ph.D., Executive Director

Allergy Associates, 2004 Grand Avenue, Baldwin, NY 11510; tel. 516/223–7656; FAX. 516/223–0583; Joseph D'Amore, M.D.

Alzheimer's Association, (Alzheimer's Disease and Related Disorders Association, Inc.), 919 North Michigan Avenue, Suite 1000, Chicago, IL 60611; tel. 312/335–8700; FAX. 312/335–1110; Thomas Kirk, Vice President, Patient, Family and Education Services

Ambulatory Pediatric Association, 6728 Old McLean Village Drive, McLean, VA 22101; tel. 703/556–9222; FAX. 703/556–8729; Marge Degnon, Executive Secretary

America's Blood Centers, 725 15th Street, N.W., Suite 700, Washington, DC 20005–2109; tel. 202/393–5725; FAX. 202/393–1282; Jim MacPherson, Executive Director

American Academy for Cerebral Palsy and Developmental Medicine, 6300 North River Road, Suite 727, Rosemont, IL 60018–4226; tel. 847/698–1635; FAX. 847/823–0536; Sheril King, Executive Director

American Academy of Allergy, Asthma and Immunology, 611 East Wells Street, Milwaukee, WI 53202; tel. 414/272–6071; FAX. 414/272–6070; Rick Iber, Executive Vice President

American Academy of Child and Adolescent Psychiatry, 3615 Wisconsin Avenue, N.W., Washington, DC 20016; tel. 202/966–7300; FAX. 202/966–2891; Virginia Q. Anthony, Executive Director

American Academy of Dental Electrosurgery, Planetarium Station, P.O. Box 374, New York, NY 10024; tel. 212/595–1925; Maurice J. Oringer, D.D.S., Executive Secretary

American Academy of Dental Practice Administration, 1063 Whippoorwill Lane, Palatine, IL 60067; tel. 847/934–4404; Kathleen Uebel, Executive Director

American Academy of Dermatology, P.O. Box 4014, Schaumburg, IL 60168–4014; tel. 847/330–0230; FAX. 847/330–0050; Bradford W. Claxton, Executive Director

American Academy of Environmental Medicine, 4510 West 89th Street, Suite 110, Prairie Village, KS 66207–2282; tel. 913/642–6062; FAX. 913/341–6912; Matt Tidwell, Executive Director

American Academy of Facial Plastic and Reconstructive Surgery, Inc., 1110 Vermont Avenue, N.W., Suite 220, Washington, DC 20005; tel. 202/842–4500; FAX. 202/371–1514; Stephen C. Duffy, Executive Vice President

American Academy of Family Physicians, 8880 Ward Parkway, Kansas City, MO 64114; tel. 816/333–9700 ext. 5100; FAX. 816/333–2237; Robert Graham, M.D., Executive Vice President

American Academy of Implant Dentistry, 6900 Grove Road, Thorofare, NJ 08086; tel. 609/848–7027; FAX. 609/853–5991; Christine Malin, Executive Secretary

American Academy of Insurance Medicine, P.O. Box 59811, Potomac, MD 20859–9811; tel. 301/365–3572; FAX. 301/365–7705; Russell E. Barker, C.A.E., Executive Vice President

American Academy of Medical Administrators, 30555 Southfield Road, Suite 150, Southfield, MI 48076–7747; tel. 248/540–4310; FAX. 248/645–0590; Thomas R. O'Donovan, Ph.D., FAAMA, President

American Academy of Neurology, 1080 Montreal Avenue, St. Paul, MN 55116–2325; tel. 612/695–1940; FAX. 612/695–2791; Jan W. Kolehmainen, Executive Director

American Academy of Ophthalmology, 655 Beach Street, P.O. Box 7424, San Francisco, CA 94120; tel. 415/561–8500; FAX. 415/561–8533; H. Dunbar Hoskins, Jr., M.D., Executive Vice President

American Academy of Optometry, 6110 Executive Boulevard, Suite 506, Rockville, MD 20852, USA; tel. 301/984–1441; FAX. 301/984–4737; Lois Schoenbrun, CAE, Executive Director

American Academy of Oral Medicine, 2910 Lightfoot Drive, Baltimore, MD 21209–1452; tel. 410/602–8585; FAX. 410/602–8585; Mrs. Joyce Caplan, Executive Secretary

American Academy of Orthopaedic Surgeons, 6300 North River Road, Rosemont, IL 60018–4262; tel. 847/823–7186; FAX. 847/823–8125; William W. Tipton, Jr., M.D., Executive Vice President

American Academy of Otolaryngic Allergy, 8455 Colesville Road, Suite 745, Silver Spring, MD 20910; tel. 301/588–1800; FAX. 301/588–2454; Jami Lucas, Executive Director

American Academy of Otolaryngology–Head and Neck Surgery, Inc., One Prince Street, Alexandria, VA 22314; tel. 703/836–4444; FAX. 703/683–5100; Michael D. Maves, M.D., M.B.A., Executive Vice President

American Academy of Pain Management, 13947 Mono Way, Suite A, Sonora, CA 95370–2807; tel. 209/533–9744; FAX. 209/533–9750; Richard S. Weiner, Ph.D., Executive Director

American Academy of Pediatric Dentistry, 211 East Chicago Avenue, Suite 700, Chicago, IL 60611; tel. 312/337–2169; FAX. 312/337–6329; Dr. John A. Bogert, Executive Director

American Academy of Pediatrics, 141 Northwest Point Boulevard, P.O. Box 927, Elk Grove Village, IL 60009–0927; tel. 847/228–5005; FAX. 847/228–5097; Joe M. Sanders, Jr., M.D., Executive Director

American Academy of Physical Medicine and Rehabilitation, One IBM Plaza, Suite 2500, Chicago, IL 60611–3604; tel. 312/464–9700; FAX. 312/464–0227; Ronald A. Henrichs, CAE, Executive Director

American Academy of Physician Assistants, 950 North Washington Street, Alexandria, VA 22314; tel. 703/836–2272; FAX. 703/684–1924; Stephen C. Crane, Ph.D., M.P.H., Executive Vice President

American Academy of Physiologic Dentistry, 567 South Washington Street, Naperville, IL 60540; tel. 630/355–2625; Dr. William Kopperud, Secretary

American Academy of Psychoanalysis, 47 East 19th Street, Sixth Floor, New York, NY 10003; tel. 212/475–7980; FAX. 212/475–8101; James J. D. Tendean–Luce, Executive Director

American Academy of Restorative Dentistry, 1235 Lake Plaza Drive, Suite 251, Colorado Springs, CO 80906; tel. 719/576–8840; Donald H. Downs, D.D.S., Secretary–Treasurer

American Aging Association, The Sally Balin Medical Center, 110 Chesley Drive, Media, PA 19063; tel. 610/627–2626; FAX. 610/565–9747; Arthur K. Balin, M.D., Ph.D., Executive Director

American Alliance for Health, Physical Education, Recreation, and Dance, 1900 Association Drive, Reston, VA 22091; tel. 703/476–3400; FAX. 703/476–9527; Michael G. Davis, Executive Vice President

American Ambulance Association, 3800 Auburn Boulevard, Suite C, Sacramento, CA 95821; tel. 916/483–3827; FAX. 916/482–5473; David A. Nevins, Executive Vice President

American Art Therapy Association, 1202 Allanson Road, Mundelein, IL 60060; tel. 847/949–6064; FAX. 847/566–4580; Edward J. Stygar, Jr., Executive Director

American Assembly for Men in Nursing, 437 Twin Bay Drive, Pensacola, FL 32534–1350; tel. 904/474–0144; FAX. 904/484–8762; Robert T. Rupp, Executive Director

American Association for Adult and Continuing Education, 1200 19th Street, N.W., Suite 300, Washington, DC 20036; tel. 202/429–5131; FAX. 202/223–4579; Dr. Drew Allbritten, Executive Director

American Association for Clinical Chemistry, Inc., 2101 L Street, N.W., Suite 202, Washington, DC 20037; tel. 202/857–0717; FAX. 202/887–5093; Richard Flaherty, Executive Vice President

American Association for Dental Research, 1619 Duke Street, Alexandria, VA 22314–3406; tel. 703/548–0066; FAX. 703/548–1883; John J. Clarkson, BDS, Ph.D., Executive Director

American Association for Laboratory Animal Science, 70 Timber Creek Drive, Cordova, TN 38018; tel. 901/754–8620; FAX. 901/753–0046; Michael R. Sondag, Executive Director

American Association for Respiratory Care, 11030 Ables Lane, Dallas, TX 75229; tel. 214/243–2272; FAX. 214/484–2720; Sam P. Giordano, Executive Director

American Association for the Advancement of Science, 1200 New York Avenue, N.W., Washington, DC 20005; tel. 202/326–6400; FAX. 202/321–5526; Richard S. Nicholson, Executive Officer

American Association for the Study of Headache, 19 Mantua Road, Mt. Royal, NJ 08096; tel. 609/423–0043; FAX. 609/423–0082; Linda McGillicuddy, Executive Director

American Association for the Surgery of Trauma, Department of Surgery, UCLA Medical Center, Room 21–178 CHS, 10833 LeConte Avenue, Los Angeles, CA 90024; tel. 310/825–5981; FAX. 310/206–2472; H. Gill Cryer, M.D.

American Association of Ambulatory Surgery Centers, 401 North Michigan Avenue, Chicago, IL 60611–4267; tel. 800/237–3768; FAX. 312/527–6636; Kari Dabrowski, Account Coordinator

American Association of Anatomists, Department of Anatomy, Tulane Medical School, 1430 Tulane Avenue, New Orleans, LA 70112; tel. 504/584–1687; Robert Yates, Secretary–Treasurer

American Association of Bioanalysts, 917 Locust Street, Suite 1100, St. Louis, MO 63101–1413; tel. 314/241–1445; FAX. 314/241–1449; Mark S. Birenbaum, Ph.D., Administrator

American Association of Certified Orthoptists, 501 Hill Street, Waycross, GA 31501; tel. 912/285-2020; FAX. 912/285-8112; Jill Clark, President

American Association of Colleges of Nursing, One Dupont Circle, N.W., Suite 530, Washington, DC 20036; tel. 202/463-6930; FAX. 202/785-8320; Geraldine Bednash, Ph.D., RN, FAAN, Executive Director

American Association of Colleges of Pharmacy, 1426 Prince Street, Alexandria, VA 22314-2841; tel. 703/739-2330; FAX. 703/836-8982; Richard P. Penna, Pharm.D., Executive Vice President

American Association of Colleges of Podiatric Medicine, 1350 Piccard Drive, Suite 322, Rockville, MD 20850-4307; tel. 301/990-7400; FAX. 301/990-2807; Anthony J. McNevin, CAE, President

American Association of Critical-Care Nurses, 101 Columbia, Suite 200, Aliso Viejo, CA 92656-1491; tel. 714/362-2000ext201; FAX. 714/362-2020; Sarah J. Sanford, RN, M.A., CNAA, FAAN, Chief Executive Officer

American Association of Dental Consultants, Inc., P.O. Box 3345, Lawrence, KS 66046; tel. 785/749-2727; FAX. 785/749-1140; Ed Schooley, D.D.S., Secretary-Treasurer

American Association of Dental Schools, 1625 Massachusetts Avenue, N.W., Washington, DC 20036; tel. 202/667-9433; FAX. 202/667-0642; Richard W. Valachonic, D.M.D., Executive Director

American Association of Endodontists, 211 East Chicago Avenue, Suite 1100, Chicago, IL 60611; tel. 312/266-7255; FAX. 312/266-9867; Irma S. Kudo, Executive Director

American Association of Fund-Raising Counsel, Inc., 25 West 43rd Street, Suite 820, New York, NY 10036; tel. 212/354-5799; FAX. 212/768-1795; Ann Kaplan, Research Director

American Association of Health Plans, (AAHP), 1129 20th Street, N.W., Suite 600, Washington, DC 20036-3421; tel. 202/778-3200; FAX. 202/778-8486; Charles W. Stellar, Executive Vice President

American Association of Healthcare Administrative Management, (Formerly The American Guild of Patient Account Management), 1200 19th Street, N.W., Suite 300, Washington, DC 20036; tel. 202/857-1179; FAX. 202/223-4579; Dennis E. Smeage, Executive Director

American Association of Healthcare Consultants, 11208 Waples Mill Road, Suite 109, Fairfax, VA 22030; tel. 800/362-4674; FAX. 703/691-2247; Vaughan A. Smith, President, Chief Executive Officer

American Association of Homes and Services for the Aging, 901 E Street, N.W., Suite 500, Washington, DC 20004-2037; tel. 202/783-2242; FAX. 202/783-2255; Sheldon L. Goldberg, President

American Association of Hospital Dentists, Inc., 211 East Chicago Avenue, Suite 948, Chicago, IL 60611; tel. 312/440-2661; FAX. 312/440-2824; John S. Rutkauskas, M.S., D.D.S., Executive Director

American Association of Kidney Patients, 100 South Ashley Drive, Suite 280, Tampa, FL 33602; tel. 800/749-2257; FAX. 813/223-0001; Kris Robinson, Executive Director

American Association of Medical Assistants, 20 North Wacker Drive, Suite 1575, Chicago, IL 60606-2903; tel. 312/899-1500; FAX. 312/899-1259; Donald A. Balasa, J.D., M.B.A., Executive Director, Legal Counsel

American Association of Neuroscience Nurses, 224 North DesPlaines, Suite 601, Chicago, IL 60661; tel. 312/993-0043; FAX. 312/993-0362; Shelly A. Johnson, Executive Director

American Association of Nurse Anesthetists, 222 South Prospect Avenue, Park Ridge, IL 60068-4001; tel. 847/692-7050, ext. 302; FAX. 847/692-6968; John F. Garde, CRNA, M.S., FAAN, Executive Director

American Association of Nutritional Consultants, 880 Canarios Court, Suite 210, Chula Vista, CA 91910; tel. 619/482-8533; FAX. 619/482-0938; Lenda Summerfield, Administrator

American Association of Occupational Health Nurses, Inc., 2920 Brandywine Road, Suite 100, Atlanta, GA 30341-4146; tel. 770/455-7757; FAX. 770/455-7271; Ann R. Cox, CAE, Executive Director

American Association of Oral and Maxillofacial Surgeons, 9700 West Bryn Mawr Avenue, Rosemont, IL 60018-5701; tel. 847/678-6200; FAX. 847/678-6286; Robert C. Rinadi, Ph.D., Executive Director

American Association of Orthodontists, 401 North Lindbergh Boulevard, St. Louis, MO 63141-7816; tel. 314/993-1700; FAX. 314/997-1745; Ronald S. Moen, Executive Director

American Association of Pastoral Counselors, 9504A Lee Highway, Fairfax, VA 22031-2303; tel. 703/385-6967; FAX. 703/352-7725; C. Roy Woodruff, Ph.D., Executive Director

American Association of Physicists in Medicine, One Physics Ellipse, College Park, MD 20740-3846; tel. 301/209-3350; FAX. 301/209-0862; Salvatore Trofi, Jr., Executive Director

American Association of Plastic Surgeons, 2317 Seminole Road, Atlantic Beach, FL 32233; tel. 904/359-3759; FAX. 904/359-3789; Francis A. Harris, Executive Secretary

American Association of Poison Control Centers, 3201 New Mexico Avenue, N.W., Suite 310, Washington, DC 20016; tel. 202/362-7217; Rose Ann Soloway, RN, MSED, ABAT

American Association of Preferred Provider Organizations, 601 13th Street, N.W., 370 South, Washington, DC 20005; tel. 202/347-7600; FAX. 202/347-7601; Gordon Wheeler, President, Chief Operating Officer

American Association of Psychiatric Technicians, Inc., A.A.P.T., 2059 South 3rd Street, Niles, MI 49120; tel. 616/684-3164; FAX. 616/683-0032; George Blake, Ph.D., Director, President

American Association of Public Health Dentistry, A.A.P.H.D. National Office, 10619 Jousting Lane, Richmond, VA 23235-3838; tel. 804/272-8344; FAX. 804/272-0802; B. Alexander White, D.D.S., Dr.P.H.

American Association of Public Health Physicians, 515 North State Street, 14th Floor, Chicago, IL 60610; tel. 312/464-4299; FAX. 312/464-5993; David Cloud, Executive Manager

American Association on Mental Retardation, 444 North Capitol Street, N.W., Suite 846, Washington, DC 20001-1512; tel. 202/387-1968; FAX. 202/387-2193; M. Doreen Croser, Executive Director

American Baptist Homes and Hospitals Association, P.O. Box 851, Valley Forge, PA 19482-0851; tel. 610/768-2411; FAX. 610/768-2470; Kenneth A. Fennal, Acting Director

American Board of Allergy and Immunology, A Conjoint Board of the American Board of Internal Medicine and the American Board of Pediatrics, 510 Walnut Street, Suite 1701, Philadelphia, PA 19106-3699; tel. 215/592-9466; FAX. 215/592-9411; John W. Yunginger, M.D., Executive Secretary

American Board of Anesthesiology, 4101 Lake Boone Trail, Suite 510, Raleigh, NC 27607-7506; tel. 919/881-2570; FAX. 919/881-2575; Francis M. James III, M.D., Secretary – Treasurer

American Board of Cardiovascular Perfusion, 207 North 25th Avenue, Hattiesburg, MS 39401; tel. 601/582-3309; Beth A. Richmond, Ph.D., Mark G. Richmond, Ed.D., Co-Executive Directors

American Board of Colon and Rectal Surgery, 20600 Eureka Road, Suite 713, Taylor, MI 48180; tel. 734/282-9400; FAX. 734/282-9402; Herand Abcarian, M.D., Executive Director

American Board of Dermatology, Inc., Henry Ford Hospital, One Ford Place, Detroit, MI 48202-3450; tel. 313/874-1088; FAX. 313/872-3221; Harry J. Hurley, M.D., Executive Director

American Board of Emergency Medicine, 3000 Coolidge Road, East Lansing, MI 48823; tel. 517/332-4800; FAX. 517/332-2234; Benson S. Munger, Ph.D., Executive Director

American Board of Family Practice, Inc., 2228 Young Drive, Lexington, KY 40505; tel. 606/269-5626; FAX. 606/335-7501; Robert F. Avant, M.D., Executive Director

American Board of Internal Medicine, 510 Walnut Street, Suite 1700, Philadelphia, PA 19106-3699; tel. 215/446-3500; FAX. 215/446-3473; Harry R. Kimball, M.D., President

American Board of Medical Management, 4890 West Kennedy Boulevard, Suite 200, Tampa, FL 33609-2575; tel. 813/287-2815; FAX. 813/287-8993; Roger S. Schenke, Executive Vice President

American Board of Medical Specialties, 1007 Church Street, Suite 404, Evanston, IL 60201-5913; tel. 847/491-9091; FAX. 847/328-3596; J. Lee Dockery, M.D., Executive Vice President

American Board of Neurological Surgery, 6550 Fannin Street, Suite 2139, Houston, TX 77030; tel. 713/790-6015; Mary Louise Sanderson, Administrator

American Board of Nuclear Medicine, 900 Veteran Avenue, Los Angeles, CA 90024; tel. 310/825-6787; FAX. 310/825-9433; Joseph F. Ross, M.D., President

American Board of Ophthalmology, 111 Presidential Boulevard, Suite 241, Bala Cynwyd, PA 19004; tel. 610/664-1175; Denis M. O'Day, M.D., Executive Director

American Board of Oral and Maxillofacial Surgery, 625 North Michigan Avenue, Suite 1820, Chicago, IL 60611; tel. 312/642-0070; FAX. 312/642-8584; Cheryl E. Mounts, Executive Secretary

American Board of Orthopedic Surgery, Inc., 400 Silver Cedar Court, Chapel Hill, NC 27514; tel. 919/929-7103; FAX. 919/942-8988; G. Paul De Rosa, M.D., Executive Director

American Board of Otolaryngology, 5615 Kirby Drive, Suite 936, Houston, TX 77005-2452; tel. 713/528-6200; FAX. 713/528-1171; Robert W. Cantrell, M.D., Executive Vice President

American Board of Pathology, One Urban Centre, 4830 West Kennedy Boulevard, P.O. Box 25915, Tampa, FL 33622-5915; tel. 813/286-2444; FAX. 813/289-5279; William H. Hartmann, M.D., Executive Vice President

American Board of Pediatric Dentistry, 1193 Woodgate Drive, Carmel, IN 46033-9232; tel. 317/573-0877; FAX. 317/846-7235; James R. Roche, D.D.S., Executive Secretary-Treasurer

American Board of Pediatrics, Inc., 111 Silver Cedar Court, Chapel Hill, NC 27514; tel. 919/929-0461; FAX. 919/929-9255; James A. Stockman III, M.D., President

American Board of Physical Medicine and Rehabilitation, Norwest Center, Suite 674, 21 First Street, S.W., Rochester, MN 55902; tel. 507/282-1776; FAX. 507/282-9242; Mark R. Raymond, Ph.D., Executive Director

American Board of Podiatric Orthopedics and Primary Podiatric Medicine, 401 North Michigan Avenue, Suite 2400, P.O. Box 39, Chicago, IL 60611-4267; tel. 312/321-5139; FAX. 312/881-1815; Jeffrey P. Knezovich, Executive Director

American Board of Podiatric Surgery, 1601 Dolores Street, San Francisco, CA 94110-4906; tel. 415/826-3200; FAX. 415/826-4640; James A. Lamb, Executive Director

American Board of Preventive Medicine, Inc., 9950 West Lawrence Avenue, Suite 106, Schiller Park, IL 60176; tel. 847/671-1750; FAX. 847/671-1751; James M. Vanderploeg, M.D., MPH, Executive Director

American Board of Prosthodontics, P.O. Box 8437, Atlanta, GA 31106; tel. 404/876-2625; FAX. 404/872-8804; William D. Culpepper, D.D.S., M.S.D., Executive Director

American Board of Psychiatry and Neurology, Inc., 500 Lake Cook Road, Suite 335, Deerfield, IL 60015; tel. 847/945-7900; FAX. 847/945-1146; Stephen C. Scheiber, M.D., Executive Vice President

American Board of Quality Assurance and Utilization Review Physicians, 4890 West Kennedy Boulevard, Suite 260, Tampa, FL 33609; tel. 813/286-4411; FAX. 813/286-4387; H.E. Hartsell, Chief Operating Officer

American Board of Radiology, 5255 East Williams Circle, Suite 3200, Tucson, AZ 85711; tel. 520/790-2900; FAX. 520/790-3200; M. Paul Capp, M.D., Executive Director

American Board of Surgery, Inc., 1617 John F. Kennedy Boulevard, Suite 860, Philadelphia, PA 19103; tel. 215/568–4000; FAX. 215/563–5718; Wallace P. Ritchie, Jr., M.D., Executive Director

American Board of Thoracic Surgery, One Rotary Center, Suite 803, Evanston, IL 60201; tel. 847/475–1520; FAX. 847/475–6240; Richard J. Cleveland, M.D., Secretary–Treasurer

American Broncho–Esophagological Association, Vanderbilt University Medical Center, Department of Otolaryngology, S–2100 MCN, Nashville, TN 37232–2559; tel. 615/322–7267; FAX. 615/343–7604; James A. Duncavage, M.D., Secretary

American Burn Association, Department of Surgery, 625 North Michigan Avenue, Suite 1530, Chicago, IL 60611; tel. 312/642–9260; fax 312/642–9130; John Krichbaum, Executive Director

American Cancer Society, 1599 Clifton Road, N.E., Atlanta, GA 30329; tel. 404/320–3333; Gerald P. Murphy, M.D., Senior Vice President, Medical Affairs

American Center for the Alexander Technique, Inc., 129 West 67th Street, New York, NY 10023; tel. 212/799–0468; Jane Tomkiewiez, Executive Director

American Chiropractic Association, 1701 Clarendon Boulevard, Arlington, VA 22209; tel. 703/276–8800; FAX. 703/243–2593; Garrett F. Cuaco, Executive Vice President

American Cleft Palate–Craniofacial Association, 1829 E. Franklin Street, Suite 1022, Chapel Hill, NC 27514; tel. 919/933–9044; FAX. 919/933–9604; Nancy C. Smythe, Executive Director

American Clinical Neurophysiology Society, (formerly the American Electroencephalographic Society), One Regency Drive, P.O. Box 30, Bloomfield, CT 06002; tel. 203/243–3977; FAX. 203/286–0787; Jacquelyn T. Coleman, Executive Director

American College Health Association, P.O. Box 28937, Baltimore, MD 21240–8937; tel. 410/859–1500; FAX. 410/859–1510; Charles H. Hartman, Ed.D, CAE, Executive Director

American College of Allergy, Asthma and Immunology, 85 West Algonquin Road, Suite 550, Arlington Heights, IL 60005; tel. 847/427–1200; FAX. 847/427–1294; James R. Slawny, Executive Director

American College of Apothecaries, P.O. Box 341266, Bartlett, TN 38184; tel. 901/383–8119; FAX. 901/383–8882; D. C. Huffman, Jr., Ph.D., Executive Vice President

American College of Cardiology, 9111 Old Georgetown Road, Bethesda, MD 20814; tel. 800/253–4636; FAX. 301/897–9745; Penny S. Mills, Associate Executive Vice President

American College of Cardiovascular Administrators, 30555 Southfield Road, Suite 150, Southfield, MI 48076–7747; tel. 810/540–4598; FAX. 810/645–0590; Michael Flaherty, FAAMA, FACCA

American College of Chest Physicians, 3300 Dundee Road, Northbrook, IL 60062–2348; tel. 847/498–1400; FAX. 847/498–5460; Alvin Lever, Executive Vice President, Chief Executive Officer

American College of Dentists, 839 Quince Orchard Boulevard, Suite J, Gaithersburg, MD 20878–1603; tel. 301/977–3223; FAX. 301/977–3330; Sherry Keramidas, Ph.D., CAE

American College of Emergency Physicians, P.O. Box 619911, Dallas, TX 75261–9911; tel. 972/550–0911; FAX. 972/580–2816; Colin C. Rorrie, Jr., Ph.D., CAE, Executive Director

American College of Foot and Ankle Orthopedics and Medicine (ACFAOM), 4603 Highway 95 South, P.O. Box 39, Cocolalla, ID 83813–0039; tel. 208/683–3900; FAX. 208/683–3700; Judith A. Baerg, Executive Director

American College of Foot and Ankle Surgeons, 515 Busse Highway, Park Ridge, IL 60068–3150; tel. 847/292–2237; FAX. 847/292–2022; Thomas R. Schedler, CAE, Executive Director

American College of Health Care Administrators, 325 South Patrick Street, Alexandria, VA 22314; tel. 703/739–7900; FAX. 703/739–7901; Karen S. Tucker, CAE, President/Chief Exective Officer

American College of Healthcare Executives, One North Franklin, Suite 1700, Chicago, IL 60606–3491; tel. 312/424–2800; FAX. 312/424–0023; Thomas C. Dolan, Ph.D., FACHE, CAE, President/Chief Executive Officer

American College of Healthcare Information Administrators, 30555 Southfield Road, Suite 150, Southfield, MI 48076–7747; tel. 810/540–4310; FAX. 810/645–0590; Robert J. Berger, Ph.D., President

American College of Legal Medicine, 611 East Wells Street, Milwaukee, WI 53202; tel. 800/433–9137; FAX. 414/276–3349; Janet Haynes, Director, Administration

American College of MOHS Micrographic Surgery and Cutaneous Oncology, 930 North Meacham, Schaumburg, IL 60173–4965; tel. 847/330–9830; FAX. 847/330–0050; Christina Achziger, Executive Director

American College of Managed Care Administrators, 30555 Southfield Road, Suite 150, Southfield, MI 48076–7747; tel. 810/540–4310; FAX. 810/645–0590; Eugene Migilaccio, Dr.P.H., Chairman

American College of Medical Staff Development, 6855 Jimmy Carger Blvd., Suite 2100, Norcross, GA 30044; tel. 770/734–9940; FAX. 770/734–9709; Kristi Warren, Administration

American College of Nurse–Midwives, 818 Connecticut Avenue, N.W., Suite 900, Washington, DC 20006; tel. 202/728–9860; FAX. 202/728–9897; Deanne Williams, Executive Director

American College of Obstetricians and Gynecologists, 409 12th Street, S.W., Washington, DC 20024–2188; tel. 202/638–5577; FAX. 202/484–5107; Ralph W. Hale, M.D., Executive Director

American College of Occupational and Environmental Medicine, (Includes ACOEM Research and Education Fund, and Occupational Physicians Scholarship Fund OPSF), 55 West Seegers, Arlington Heights, IL 60005; tel. 847/228–6850; FAX. 847/228–1856; Donald L. Hoops, Ph.D., Executive Vice President

American College of Oncology Administrators, 30555 Southfield Road, Suite 150, Southfield, MI 48076–7747; tel. 810/540–4310; FAX. 810/645–0590; Jeanne M. Walter, RN, M.S., OCN, President

American College of Osteopathic Pediatricians, 5301 Wisconsin Avenue, NW, Suite 630, Washington, DC 20015; tel. 202/362–3229; FAX. 202/537–1362; David Kushner, Executive Director

American College of Physician Executives, 4890 West Kennedy Boulevard, Suite 200, Tampa, FL 33609–2575; tel. 813/287–2000; FAX. 813/287–8993; Roger S. Schenke, Executive Vice President

American College of Physicians, Independence Mall West, Sixth Street at Race, Philadelphia, PA 19106; tel. 215/351–2800; FAX. 215/351–2829; Walter J. McDonald, M.D., FACP, Executive Vice President

American College of Preventive Medicine, 1660 L Street, N.W., Washington, DC 20036; tel. 202/466–2044; FAX. 202/466–2662; Hazel K. Keimowitz, M.A., Executive Director

American College of Radiology, 1891 Preston White Drive, Reston, VA 20191–4397; tel. 703/648–8900; FAX. 703/648–9176; John J. Curry, Executive Director

American College of Rheumatology, 60 Executive Park South, Suite 150, Atlanta, GA 30329; tel. 404/633–3777; FAX. 404/633–1870; Lynn Bonfiglio, Director, Membership

American College of Sports Medicine, P.O. Box 1440, Indianapolis, IN 46206–1440; tel. 317/637–9200; FAX. 317/634–7817; James R. Whitehead, Executive Vice President

American College of Surgeons, 633 N. Saint Clair Street, Chicago, IL 60611; tel. 312/202–5000; FAX. 312/202–5023; Samuel A. Wells, Jr., M.D., Director

American Congress of Rehabilitation Medicine, 4700 West Lake Avenue, Glenview, IL 60025; tel. 847/375–4725; FAX. 847/375–4777; Diane Burgher, Executive Director

American Council on Pharmaceutical Education, Inc., 311 West Superior Street, Suite 512, Chicago, IL 60610; tel. 312/664–3575; FAX. 312/664–4652; Daniel A. Nona, Ph.D., Executive Director

American Dental Assistants Association, 203 North LaSalle, Suite 1320, Chicago, IL 60601; tel. 312/541–1550, ext. 204; FAX. 312/541–1496; Lawrence H. Sepin, Executive Director

American Dental Association, 211 East Chicago Avenue, Chicago, IL 60611; tel. 312/440–2500; FAX. 312/440–7494; John S. Zapp, D.D.S., Executive Director

American Dental Society of Anesthesiology, Inc., 211 East Chicago Avenue, Suite 780, Chicago, IL 60611; tel. 312/664–8270; FAX. 312/642–9713; R. Knight Charlton, Director of Programs and Communication

American Diabetes Association, Inc., 1660 Duke Street, Alexandria, VA 22314; tel. 703/549–1500; FAX. 703/836–7439; John H. Graham IV, Chief Executive Officer

American Dietetic Association, 216 West Jackson Boulevard, Suite 800, Chicago, IL 60606–6995; tel. 312/899–0040, ext. 4889; FAX. 312/899–1758; Beverly Bajus, Chief Operating Officer

American Federation for Medical Research, 1200 19th Street, N.W., Suite 300, Washington, DC 20036–2422; tel. 202/429–5161; FAX. 202/223–4579; Susan Eisenberg, Executive Director

American Foundation for Aging Research, North Carolina State University, Biochemistry Department, P.O. Box 7622, Raleigh, NC 27695–7622; tel. 919/515–5679; FAX. 919/515–2047; Paul F. Agris, President

American Foundation for Aids Research, 733 Third Avenue, 12th Floor, New York, NY 10017; tel. 212/682–7440; Mathilde Krim, Ph.D., Founding Co–Chair

American Foundation for the Blind, Inc., 11 Penn Plaza, Suite 300, New York, NY 10001; tel. 212/502–7600; FAX. 212/502–7770; Liz Greco, Vice President, Communications

American Fracture Association, 2406 East Washington Street, Bloomington, IL 61704; tel. 309/663–6272; Sarah Olson, Executive Secretary

American Geriatrics Society, 770 Lexington Avenue, Suite 300, New York, NY 10021; tel. 212/308–1414; FAX. 212/832–8646; Linda Hiddemen Barondess, Executive Vice President

American Group Psychotherapy Association, Inc., 25 East 21st Street, Sixth Floor, New York, NY 10010; tel. 212/477–2677; FAX. 212/979–6627; Marsha S. Block, CAE, Chief Executive Officer

American Health Care Association, 1201 L Street, N.W., Washington, DC 20005; tel. 202/842–4444; FAX. 202/842–3860; Paul R. Willging, Ph.D., Executive Vice President

American Health Foundation, One Dana Road, Valhalla, NY 10595; tel. 914/789–7122; FAX. 914/592–6317; Ernst L. Wynder, M.D., President

American Health Information Management Association, 919 North Michigan Avenue, Suite 1400, Chicago, IL 60611; tel. 312/787–2672; FAX. 312/787–9793; Linda Kloss, R.R.A., Executive Director

American Health Lawyers Association, 1120 Connecticut Avenue, N.W., Suite 950, Washington, DC 20036; tel. 202/833–1100; FAX. 202/833–1105; Marilou M. King, Esq., Executive Vice President, Chief Executive Officer

American Health Planning Association, 7245 Arlington Boulevard, Suite 300, Falls Church, VA 22042; tel. 703/573–3103; FAX. 703/573–1276; Dean Montgomery

American Healthcare Radiology Administrators, P.O. Box 334, Sudbury, MA 01776; tel. 978/443–7591; FAX. 978/443–8046; Mary Reitter, Executive Director

American Heart Association, Inc., Office of Scientific Affairs, 7320 Greenville Avenue, Dallas, TX 75231; tel. 214/706–1446; Mary Jane Jesse, M.D., Senior Vice President

American Hospital Association, One North Franklin, Chicago, IL 60606–3491; tel. 312/422–3000, Office of the President: 325 Seventh Street, N.W., Washington, DC 20004; tel. 202/638–1100; FAX. 202/626–2345; Richard J. Davidson, President

Health Organizations, Agencies, and Providers **C5**

American Hospital Association, National Grassroots/Political Project Director, 3405 22nd Street, Boulder, CO 80304; tel. 800/999–1462; FAX. 303/442–7158; Mary Lynne Shickich, National Grassroots/Political Project Director

American Hospital Association, Washington Office, 325 Seventh Street, N.W., Suite 700, Washington, DC 20004; tel. 202/638–1100; FAX. 202/626–2345; Richard Pollack, Executive Vice President, Government and Public Affairs

American Institute of Architects, Committee on Architecture for Health, 1735 New York Avenue, N.W., Washington, DC 20006; tel. 202/626–7366; FAX. 206/626–7518; Todd S. Phillips, Ph.D., Director

American Juvenile Arthritis Organization,a Council of the Arthritis Foundation, 1330 West Peachtree Street, Atlanta, GA 30309; tel. 404/872–7100, ext. 6271; FAX. 404/872–9559; Janet S. Austin, Ph.D., Vice President

American Laryngological Association, 300 Longwood Avenue, Fegan 9, Boston, MA 02115; tel. 617/335–6417; FAX. 617/355–8041; G. B. Healy, M.D., Secretary

American Laryngological, Rhinological, and Otological Society, Inc., (The Triological Society), 10 South Broadway, Suite 1401, St. Louis, MO 63102–1741; tel. 314/621–6550; FAX. 314/621–6688; Daniel Henroid, Sr., Executive Director

American Library Association, 50 East Huron Street, Chicago, IL 60611; tel. 312/280–3215; FAX. 312/944–3897; William R. Gordon, Executive Director

American Lung Association, 1740 Broadway, New York, NY 10019–4374; tel. 212/315–8700, ext. 701; FAX. 212/765–7876; John R. Garrison, Managing Director

American Lung Association of Ohio, Dayton Office, 7560 McEwen Road, Dayton, OH 45459; tel. 937/291–0451; FAX. 937/291–0453; Roberta M. Taylor, Director

American Medical Association, 515 North State Street, Chicago, IL 60610; tel. 312/464–5000; FAX. 312/464–4184; Lynn E. Jensen, Ph. D., Interim Executive V.P.

American Medical Association Alliance, 515 North State Street, Chicago, IL 60610; tel. 312/464–4470; FAX. 312/464–5020; Hazel J. Lewis, Executive Director

American Medical Group Association, Inc., 1422 Duke Street, Alexandria, VA 22314–3430; tel. 703/838–0033; FAX. 703/548–1890; Donald W. Fisher, Ph.D., Chief Executive Officer

American Medical Student Association/Foundation, 1902 Association Drive, Reston, VA 22091; tel. 703/620–6600; FAX. 703/620–5873; Paul R. Wright, Executive Director

American Medical Technologists, 710 Higgins Road, Park Ridge, IL 60068; tel. 847/823–5169; FAX. 847/823–0458; Gerard P. Boe, Ph.D., Executive Director

American Medical Women's Association, Inc., 800 North Fairfax Street, Suite 400, Alexandria, VA 22314; tel. 703/838–0500; FAX. 703/549–3864; Eileen McGrath, J.D., CAE, Executive Director

American Medical Writers Association, 9650 Rockville Pike, Bethesda, MD 20814–3998; tel. 301/493–0003; FAX. 301/493–6384; Lillian Sablack, Executive Director

American Music Therapy Association, (Formerly The National Association for Music Therapy), 8455 Colesville Road, Suite 1000, Silver Spring, MD 20910–3392; tel. 301/589–3300; FAX. 301/589–5175; Andrea Farbman, Ed.D., Executive Director

American National Standards Institute, 11 West 42nd Street, New York, NY 10036; tel. 212/642–4900; FAX. 212/398–0023; Sergio Mazza, President

American Nephrology Nurses' Association, East Holly Avenue, P.O. Box 56, Pitman, NJ 08071; tel. 609/256–2320; FAX. 609/589–7463; T.B.D., Executive Director

American Neurological Association, 5841 Cedar Lake Road, Suite 108, Minneapolis, MN 55416; tel. 612/545–6284; FAX. 612/545–6073; Linda Wilkerson, Executive Director

American Nurses' Association, 600 Maryland Avenue, S.W., Suite 100 W, Washington, DC 20024–2571; tel. 202/651–7012; FAX. 202/651–7001; Argene Carswell, J.D., R.N., Interim Executive Director

American Occupational Therapy Association, Inc., 4720 Montgomery Lane, P.O. Box 31220, Bethesda, MD 20824–1220; tel. 301/652–2682, ext. 2101; FAX. 301/652–7711; Jeanette Bair,M.B.A.,O.T.,F.A.O.T.A.

American Ophthalmological Society, P.O. Box 193940, San Francisco, CA 94119–3940; tel. 415/561–8578; FAX. 415/561–8569; W. Banks Anderson, Jr., M.D., Secretary–Treasurer

American Optometric Association, 243 North Lindbergh Boulevard, St. Louis, MO 63141; tel. 314/991–4100; FAX. 314/991–4101; Jeffrey G. Mays, Executive Director

American Organization of Nurse Executives (AONE), One North Franklin, 34th Floor, Chicago, IL 60606; tel. 312/422–2800; FAX. 312/422–4503; Marjorie Beyers, RN, Ph.D., FAAN

American Orthopsychiatric Association, 330 Seventh Avenue, 18th Floor, New York, NY 10001; tel. 212/564–5930; FAX. 212/564–6180; Gale Siegel, M.S.W., Executive Director

American Orthoptic Council, 3914 Nakoma Road, Madison, WI 53711; tel. 608/233–5383; FAX. 608/263–4247; Leslie France, Administrator

American Osteopathic Academy of Addiction Medicine, 5301 Wisconsin Avenue, N.W., Suite 630, Washington, DC 20015; tel. 202/966–7732; FAX. 202/537–1362; David Kushner, Executive Director

American Osteopathic Association, 142 East Ontario Street, Chicago, IL 60611; tel. 312/202–8000; FAX. 312/202–8212; Ann M. Wittner, Director, Department of Administration

American Osteopathic Healthcare Association, 5301 Wisconsin Avenue, N.W., Suite 630, Washington, DC 20015; tel. 202/686–1700; FAX. 202/686–7615; David Kushner, President and Chief Executive Officer

American Otological Society, Inc., Loyola University Medical Center, 2160 South First Avenue, Building 105, Number 1870, Maywood, IL 60153; tel. 708/216–8526; FAX. 708/216–4834; Gregory J. Matz, M.D., Secretary–Treasurer

American Parkinson Disease Association, Inc., 1250 Hylan Boulevard, Suite 4B, Staten Island, NY 10305; tel. 800/223–2732; FAX. 718/981–4399; G. Maestrone, D.V.M., Scientific and Medical Affairs Director

American Pediatric Society, Inc., 3400 Research Forest Drive, Suite B7, The Woodlands, TX 77381; tel. 281/296–0244; FAX. 281/296–0255; Kathy Cannon, Associate Executive Director

American Pharmaceutical Association, 2215 Constitution Avenue, N.W., Washington, DC 20037; tel. 202/628–4410; FAX. 202/783–2351; John A. Gans, Pharm.D., Executive Vice President

American Physical Therapy Association, 1111 North Fairfax Street, Alexandria, VA 22314; tel. 703/684–2782; FAX. 703/684–7343; Francis J. Mallon, Esq., Chief Executive Officer

American Physiological Society, 9650 Rockville Pike, Bethesda, MD 20814–3991; tel. 301/530–7118; FAX. 301/571–8305; Martin Frank, Ph.D., Executive Director

American Podiatric Medical Association, 9312 Old Georgetown Road, Bethesda, MD 20814–1698; tel. 301/571–9200; FAX. 301/530–2752; Glenn B. Gastwirth, DPM, Executive Director

American Psychiatric Association, 1400 K Street, N.W., Washington, DC 20005; tel. 202/682–6000; FAX. 202/682–6114; Steven M. Mirin, M.D., Medical Director

American Psychoanalytic Association, 309 East 49th Street, New York, NY 10017; tel. 212/752–0450; FAX. 212/593–0571; Ellen B. Fertig, Administrative Director

American Psychological Association, 750 First Street, N.E., Washington, DC 20002–4242; tel. 202/336–5500; FAX. 202/336–6069; Russ Newman, Ph.D., J.D., Executive Director, Professional Practice

American Psychosomatic Society, 6728 Old McLean Village Drive, McLean, VA 22101; tel. 703/556–9222; George K. Degnon, Executive Director

American Public Health Association, 1015 15th Street, N.W., Suite 300, Washington, DC 20005; tel. 202/789–5600; FAX. 202/789–5661; Mohammed N. Akhter, N.D., MPH, Executive Vice President

American Public Welfare Association, 810 First Street, N.E., Suite 500, Washington, DC 20002; tel. 202/682–0100; FAX. 202/289–6555; Sidney Johnson III, Executive Director

American Red Cross, National Headquarters, 8111 Gatehouse Road, Falls Church, VA 22042; tel. 703/206–7764; FAX. 703/206–7765; Susan M. Livingstone, Vice President, Health and Safety Services

American Registry of Medical Assistants, 69 Southwick Road, Suite A, Westfield, MA 01085–4729; tel. 800/527–2762; Annette H. Heyman, R.M.A., Director

American Registry of Radiologic Technologists, 1255 Northland Drive, St. Paul, MN 55120; tel. 612/687–0048; Jerry B. Reid, Ph.D., Executive Director

American Rhinologic Society, Department of Otolaryngology, LSU Medical Center, 1501 Kings Highway, Shreveport, LA 71130; tel. 888/520–9585; FAX. 318/675–6260; Fred J. Stucker, M.D., Secretary

American Roentgen Ray Society, 1891 Preston White Drive, Reston, VA 22091; tel. 703/648–8992; FAX. 703/264–8863; Paul R. Fullagar, Executive Director

American School Health Association, 7263 S.R. 43, P.O. Box 708, Kent, OH 44240–0708; tel. 330/678–1601; FAX. 330/678–4526; Thomas M. Reed, Acting Executive Director

American Society for Adolescent Psychiatry, 4340 East West Highway, Suite 401, Bethesda, MD 20814; tel. 301/718–6502; FAX. 301/656–0989; Ann T. Loew, Ed.M.

American Society for Biochemistry and Molecular Biology, Inc., 9650 Rockville Pike, Bethesda, MD 20814–3996; tel. 301/530–7145; FAX. 301/571–1824; Charles C. Hancock, Executive Officer

American Society for Clinical Laboratory Science, 7910 Woodmont Avenue, Suite 530, Bethesda, MD 20814; tel. 301/657–2768; FAX. 301/657–2909; Elissa Passiment, Executive Director

American Society for Clinical Pharmacology and Therapeutics, 1718 Gallagher Road, Norristown, PA 19401–2800; tel. 610/825–3838; FAX. 610/834–8652; Elaine Galasso, Executive Director

American Society for Cytotechnology, 4101 Lake Boone Trail, Suite 2A, Raleigh, NC 27607; tel. 919/787–5181; FAX. 919/787–4916; Pamela Sproul, Executive Director

American Society for Head and Neck Surgery, 203 Lithrop Street, Suite 519, Pittsburgh, PA 15213; tel. 414/647–2227; FAX. 412/647–8944; Jonas T. Johnson, M.D., Secretary

American Society for Healthcare Central Service Professionals (AHA), One North Franklin, 30th Floor, Chicago, IL 60606; tel. 312/422–3570; FAX. 312/422–4573; Kathy Svedman, Executive Director

American Society for Healthcare Engineering (AHA), One North Franklin, Chicago, IL 60606; tel. 312/422–3800; FAX. 312/422–4571; Joseph Martori, Executive Director

American Society for Healthcare Food Service Administrators (AHA), One North Franklin, Chicago, IL 60606; tel. 312/422–3870; FAX. 312/422–4581; Patricia Burton, Executive Director

American Society for Healthcare Human Resources Administration (AHA), One North Franklin, 31st Floor, Chicago, IL 60606; tel. 312/422–3720; FAX. 312/422–4579; Mary Anne Kelly, Executive Director

American Society for Healthcare Materials Management (AHA), One North Franklin, Chicago, IL 60606–3491; tel. 312/422–3840; FAX. 312/422–4573; Albert J. Sunseri, Ph.D, Executive Director

American Society for Healthcare Risk Management (AHA), One North Franklin, Chicago, IL 60606; tel. 312/422–3980; FAX. 312/422–4580; Christy Kessler, Executive Director

American Society for Investigative Pathology, 9650 Rockville Pike, Bethesda, MD 20814–3993; tel. 301/530–7130; FAX. 301/571–1879; Frances A. Pitlick, Ph.D., Executive Officer

American Society for Laser Medicine and Surgery, Inc., 2404 Stewart Square, Wausau, WI 54401; tel. 715/845–9283; FAX. 715/848–2493; Richard O. Gregory, M.D., Secretary

American Society for Microbiology, 1325 Massachusetts Avenue, N.W., Washington, DC 20005; tel. 202/924–9265; FAX. 202/942–9333; Michael I. Goldberg, Ph.D., Executive Director

American Society for Pharmacology and Experimental Therapeutics, Inc., 9650 Rockville Pike, Bethesda, MD 20814–3995; tel. 301/530–7060; FAX. 301/530–7061; Christine K. Carrico, Ph. D., Executive Officer

American Society for Public Administration, 1120 G Street, N.W., Suite 700, Washington, DC 20005; tel. 202/393–7878; FAX. 202/638–4952; Mary Hamilton, Executive Director

American Society for Reproductive Medicine, (formerly The American Fertility Society), 1209 Montgomery Highway, Birmingham, AL 35216–2809; tel. 205/978–5000 ext. 114; FAX. 205/978–5005; J. Benjamin Younger, M.D., Executive Director

American Society for Therapeutic Radiology and Oncology, 1891 Preston White Drive, Reston, VA 22091; tel. 800/962–7876; FAX. 703/476–8167; Gregg Robinson, Chief Operating Officer

American Society for the Advancement of Anesthesia in Dentistry, Six East Union Avenue, P.O. Box 551, Bound Brook, NJ 08805; tel. 201/469–9050; David Crystal, D.D.S., Executive Secretary

American Society of Anesthesiologists, 520 North Northwest Highway, Park Ridge, IL 60068; tel. 847/825–5586; FAX. 847/825–1692; Glenn W. Johnson, Executive Director

American Society of Cardiovascular Professionals, Society for Cardiovascular Management ASCP/SCM, 910 Charles Street, Fredericksburg, VA 22401; tel. 540/370–0102; FAX. 540/370–0015; Peggy McElgunn, Executive Director

American Society of Clinical Oncology, 435 North Michigan Avenue, Suite 1717, Chicago, IL 60611–4067; tel. 312/644–0828; FAX. 312/644–8557; Robert E. Becker, J.D., CAE, Executive Director

American Society of Clinical Pathologists., (Includes Board of Registry), 2100 West Harrison Street, Chicago, IL 60612–3798; tel. 312/738–1336; FAX. 312/738–9798; Robert C. Rock, M.D., Senior Vice President

American Society of Colon and Rectal Surgeons, 85 West Algonquin Road, Suite 550, Arlington Heights, IL 60005; tel. 847/290–9184; FAX. 847/290–9203; James Slawny, Executive Director

American Society of Consultant Pharmacists, 1321 Duke Street, Alexandria, VA 22314–3563; tel. 703/739–1300; FAX. 703/739–1321; R. Timothy Webster, Executive Director

American Society of Contemporary Medicine and Surgery, 4711 Golf Road, Suite 408, Skokie, IL 60076; tel. 800/621–4002; FAX. 847/568–1527; Randall T. Bellows, M.D., Director

American Society of Contemporary Ophthalmology, 4711 Golf Road, Suite 408, Skokie, IL 60076; tel. 800/621–4002; FAX. 847/568–1527; Randall T. Bellows, M.D., Director

American Society of Cytopathology, 400 West Ninth Street, Suite 201, Wilmington, DE 19801; tel. 302/429–8802; FAX. 302/429–8807; Petrina M. Smith, RN, M.B.A., Executive Secretary

American Society of Dentistry for Children, John Hancock Center, 875 North Michigan Avenue, Suite 4040, Chicago, IL 60611; tel. 312/943–1244; FAX. 312/943–5341; Dr. Peter Fos, Interim Executive Director

American Society of Directors of Volunteer Services (AHA), One North Franklin, Chicago, IL 60606; tel. 312/422–3938; FAX. 312/422–4575; Nancy A. Brown, Executive Secretary

American Society of Electroneurodiagnostic Technologists, Inc., 204 West Seventh Street, Carroll, IA 51401–2317; tel. 712/792–2978; FAX. 712/792–6962; M. Fran Pedelty, Executive Director

American Society of Extra–Corporeal Technology, Inc., 11480 Sunset Hills Road, Suite 210E, Reston, VA 20190–5208; tel. 703/435–8556; FAX. 703/435–0056; George M. Cate, Executive Director

American Society of Group Psychodrama and Psychotherapy, 6728 Old McLean Village Drive, McLean, VA 22101; tel. 703/556–9222; George K. Degnon, Executive Director

American Society of Health–System Pharmacists, 7272 Wisconsin Avenue, Bethesda, MD 20814; tel. 301/657–3000; FAX. 301/652–8278; Henri R. Manasse, Jr., Executive Vice President, Chief Executive Officer

American Society of Internal Medicine, 2011 Pennsylvania Avenue, N.W., Suite 800, Washington, DC 20006–1808; tel. 202/835–2746; FAX. 202/835–0443; Alan R. Nelson, M.D., Executive Vice President

American Society of Law, Medicine & Ethics, 765 Commonwealth Avenue, 16th Floor, Boston, MA 02215; tel. 617/262–4990ext13; FAX. 617/437–7596; Michael Vasko, M.A., Associate Director

American Society of Maxillofacial Surgeons, 444 East Algonquin Road, Arlington Height, IL 60005; tel. 847/228–8375; FAX. 847/228–6509; Gina Cappellania, Administrative Coordinator

American Society of Neuroimaging, 5841 Cedar Lake Road, Suite 108, Minneapolis, MN 55416; tel. 612/545–6204; FAX. 612/545–6073; Linda Wilkerson, Executive Director

American Society of Plastic and Reconstructive Surgeons, 444 East Algonquin Road, Arlington Height, IL 60005; tel. 847/228–9900; FAX. 847/228–9131; Dave Fellers, CAE, Executive Director

American Society of Radiologic Technologists, 15000 Central Avenue, S.E., Albuquerque, NM 87123–3917; tel. 505/298–4500; FAX. 505/298–5063; Joan L. Parsons, Executive Vice President, Operations

American Speech–Language–Hearing Association, 10801 Rockville Pike, Rockville, MD 20852; tel. 301/897–5700; FAX. 301/571–0457; Frederick T. Spahr, Ph.D., Executive Director

American Surgical Association, 13 Elm Street, Manchester, MA 01944; tel. 978/526–8330; FAX. 978/526–4018; John L. Cameron, M.D., Secretary

American Thoracic Society, 1740 Broadway, New York, NY 10019–4374; tel. 212/315–8700, ext. 778; FAX. 212/315–6498; Marilyn Hansen, Executive Director

American Thyroid Association, Inc., Montefiore Medical Center, 111 East 210th Street, Room 311, Bronx, NY 10467; tel. 718/882–6047; FAX. 718/882–6085; Martin I. Surks, M.D., Secretary

American Trauma Society, 8903 Presidential Parkway, Suite 512, Upper Marlboro, MD 20772–2656; tel. 800/556–7890; FAX. 301/420–0617; Harry Teter, Executive Director

American Urological Association, Inc., 1120 North Charles Street, Baltimore, MD 21201; tel. 410/223–4300; FAX. 410/223–4370; G. James Gallagher, Executive Director

Arthritis Foundation, 1330 West Peachtree Street, Atlanta, GA 30309; tel. 404/872–7100, ext. 6200; FAX. 404/872–0457; Don L. Riggin, President, Chief Executive Officer

Association for Applied Psychophysiology and Biofeedback, 10200 West 44th Avenue, Suite 304, Wheat Ridge, CO 80033; tel. 303/422–8436; FAX. 303/422–8894; Francine Butler, Ph.D.

Association for Clinical Pastoral Education, Inc., 1549 Clairmont Road, Suite 103, Decatur, GA 30033; tel. 404/320–1472; FAX. 404/320–0849; Russell H. Davis, Executive Director

Association for Healthcare Philanthropy, 313 Park Avenue, Suite 400, Falls Church, VA 22046; tel. 703/532–6243; FAX. 703/532–7170; Dr. William C. McGinly, CAE, President, Chief Executive Officer

Association for Hospital Medical Education, 1200 19th Street, N.W., Suite 300, Washington, DC 20036–2401; tel. 202/857–1196; FAX. 202/223–4579; Dennis Smeage, Executive Director

Association for Professionals in Infection Control and Epidemiology, Inc., 1016 16th Street, Sixth Floor, Washington, DC 20036; tel. 202/296–2742; FAX. 202/296–5645; Christopher E. Laxton, Executive Director

Association for Quality HealthCare, Inc., P.O. Box 670, Columbus, GA 31902; tel. 404/571–2122; FAX. 404/571–2650; L. B. Skip Teaster, Executive Director

Association for Volunteer Administration, 10565 Lee Highway, Suite 104, Fairfax, VA 22030; tel. 703/352–6222; FAX. 703/352–6767; Joan Shephard, Executive Director

Association for the Advancement of Automotive Medicine, 2340 DesPlaines Avenue, Suite 106, Des Plaines, IL 60018; tel. 847/390–8927; FAX. 847/390–9962; Elaine Petrucelli, Executive Director

Association for the Advancement of Medical Instrumentation, 3330 Washington Boulevard, Suite 400, Arlington, VA 22201–4598; tel. 703/525–4890; FAX. 703/276–0793; Michael J. Miller, J.D., President

Association for the Care of Children's Health (ACCH), 7910 Woodmont Avenue, Suite 300, Bethesda, MD 20814; tel. 301/654–6549; FAX. 301/986–4553; Heather Bennett McCabe, Ph.D., Executive Director

Association of American Medical Colleges, 2450 N Street, N.W., Washington, DC 20037–1127; tel. 202/828–0400; FAX. 202/828–1125; Jordan J. Cohen, M.D., President

Association of American Physicians, Krannert Institute of Cardiology, Indiana University School of Medicine, 1111 West 10th Street, Indianapolis, IN 46202–4800; tel. 317/630–7712; FAX. 317/274–9697; David R. Hathaway, M.D., Secretary

Association of American Physicians and Surgeons, Inc., 1601 North Tucson Boulevard, Suite Nine, Tucson, AZ 85716; tel. 520/327–4885; FAX. 520/325–4230; Jane M. Orient, M.D., Executive Director

Association of Birth Defect Children, 827 Irma Avenue, Orlando, FL 32803; tel. 407/245–7035; FAX. 407/245–7087; Betty Mekdeci, Executive Director

Association of Community Cancer Centers, 11600 Nebel Street, Suite 201, Rockville, MD 20852; tel. 301/984–9496; FAX. 301/770–1949; Lee E. Mortenson, DPA, Executive Director

Association of Mental Health Administrators, 60 Revere Drive, Suite 500, Northbrook, IL 60062; tel. 847/480–9626; FAX. 847/480–9282; Alison C. Brown, Executive Director

Association of Military Surgeons of the U.S., 9320 Old Georgetown Road, Bethesda, MD 20814; tel. 301/897–8800; FAX. 301/530–5446; Rear Admiral Frederic G. Sanford, MC, MSN Ret., Executive Director

Association of Operating Room Nurses, Inc., 2170 South Parker Road, Suite 300, Denver, CO 80231–5711; tel. 303/755–6300; FAX. 303/750–2927; Lola M. Fehr, RN, M.S., CAE, FAAN, Executive Director

Association of Osteopathic Directors and Medical Educators, 5301 Wisconsin Avenue, N.W., Suite 630, Washington, DC 20015; tel. 202/537–1021; FAX. 202/537–1362; David Kushner, Executive Director

Association of Professional Chaplains, 1701 East Woodfield Road, Suite 311, Schaumburg, IL 60173–5191; tel. 847/240–1014; FAX. 847/240–1015; Jo Schrader, Administrative Director

Association of Schools of Allied Health Professions, 1730 M Street, N.W., Suite 500, Washington, DC 20036; tel. 202/293–4848; FAX. 202/293–4852; Thomas W. Elwood, Dr. P.H., Executive Director

Association of Schools of Public Health, Inc., 1660 L Street, N.W., Suite 204, Washington, DC 20036; tel. 202/296–1099; FAX. 202/296–1252; Michael K. Gemmell, CAE, Executive Director

Association of Specialized and Cooperative Library Agencies, 50 East Huron Street, Chicago, IL 60611; tel. 312/280-4399; FAX. 312/944-8085; Cathleen Bourdon, ASCLA, Executive Director

Association of State and Territorial Health Officials, 1275 K Street,NW, Suite 800, Washington, DC 20005-4006; tel. 202/371-9090; FAX. 202/371-9797; Cheryl A. Beversdorf, RN, M.H.S., CAE, Executive Vice President

Association of Surgical Technologists, Inc., 7108-C South Alton Way, Englewood, CO 80112-2106; tel. 303/694-9130; FAX. 303/694-9169; William J. Teutsch, Executive Director

Association of University Anesthesiologists, 2033 Sixth Avenue, Suite 804, Seattle, WA 98121-2586; tel. 206/441-6020; FAX. 206/441-8262; Shirley Bishop

Association of University Programs in Health Administration, 1110 Vermont Avenue, NW, Suite 220, Washington, DC 20005-3500; tel. 202/822-8550, ext. 112; FAX. 202/822-8555; Henry A. Fernandez, J.D., President, Chief Executive Officer

Asthma Foundation of Southern Arizona, P.O. Box 30069, Tucson, AZ 85751-0069; tel. 602/323-6046; FAX. 602/324-1137; Lynn Krust, Executive Director

Asthma and Allergy Foundation of America, 1125 15th Street, N.W., Suite 502, Washington, DC 20005; tel. 202/466-7643; FAX. 202/466-8940; Mary E. Worstell, M.P.H., Executive Director

B

BCS Financial Corporation, 676 North St. Clair, Chicago, IL 60611; tel. 312/951-7700; FAX. 312/951-7777; Edward J. Baran, Chairman, Chief Executive Officer

Bereavement Services/RTS, Gundersen Lutheran Medical Center, 1910 South Avenue, La Crosse, WI 54601; tel. 800/362-9567, ext. 4747; FAX. 608/791-5137; Fran Rybarik, Director

Biological Photographic Association, Inc., 1819 Peachtree Road, N.E., Suite 620, Atlanta, GA 30309; tel. 404/351-6300; FAX. 404/351-3348; William Just, Executive Director

Biological Stain Commission, Inc., University of Rochester, Department Pathology, Box 626, Rochester, NY 14642-0001; tel. 716/275-6335; FAX. 716/442-8993; David P. Penney, Ph.D., Treasurer

Blinded Veterans Association, 477 H Street, N.W., Washington, DC 20001; tel. 800/669-7079; FAX. 202/371-8258; Thomas H. Miller, Executive Director

Blue Cross and Blue Shield Association, 225 N. Michigan Avenue, Chicago, IL 60601; tel. 312/297-6010; FAX. 312/297-6120; Patrick G. Hays, President, Chief Executive Officer

C

Catholic Health Association of the United States, 4455 Woodson Road, St. Louis, MO 63134-3797; tel. 314/427-2500; FAX. 314/427-0029; Rev. Michael D. Place, STD, President and Chief Executive Officer

Catholic Medical Association, 850 Elm Grove Road, Elm Grove, WI 53122; tel. 414/784-3435; FAX. 414/782-8788; Michael J. Herzog, Executive Director

Center for Health Administration Studies, University of Chicago, 969 East 60th Street, Chicago, IL 60637; tel. 773/702-7104; FAX. 773/702-7222; Edward F. Lawlor, Ph.D., Director

Central Neuropsychiatric Association, 128 East Milltown Road, Wooster, OH 44691; tel. 330/345-6555; FAX. 330/345-6648; Dennis O. Helmuth, M.D., Secretary-Treasurer

Central Society for Clinical Research, Inc., 1228 West Nelson Street, Chicago, IL 60657; tel. 312/871-1618; Morton F. Arnsdorf, M.D., Secretary-Treasurer

Central Surgical Association, Northwestern University Medical School, Department of Surgery, 250 East Superior Street, Suite 201, Chicago, IL 60611-2950; tel. 312/908-8060; FAX. 312/908-7404; David L. Nahrwold, M.D., Secretary

Children's Rights Council (CRC), a/k/a National Council for Children's Rights, 300 Eye Street, N.E., Suite 401, Washington, DC 20002; tel. 202/547-6227; FAX. 202/546-4272; David E. Levy,Esq.,President,Chief Executive Officer

Christian Record Services, Inc., 4444 South 52nd Street, Lincoln, NE 68516; tel. 402/488-0981; FAX. 402/488-7582; Ron Bowes, Public Relations Director

College of American Pathologists, 325 Waukegan Road, Northfield, IL 60093-2750; tel. 847/832-7000; FAX. 847/832-8151; Lee VanBremen, Ph.D., Executive Vice President

College of Osteopathic Healthcare Executives, 5301 Wisconsin Avenue, N.W., Suite 630, Washington, DC 20015; tel. 202/686-1700; FAX. 202/686-7615; David Kushner, President

Commission on Accreditation of Rehabilitation Facilities, 4891 East Grant Road, Tucson, AZ 85712; tel. 520/325-1044; FAX. 520/318-1129; Donald E. Galvin, Ph.D., President, Chief Executive Officer

Commission on Recognition of Postsecondary Accreditation, Inc., One Dupont Circle, N.W., Suite 305, Washington, DC 20036; tel. 202/452-1433; FAX. 202/331-9571; Dorothy Fenwick, Ph.D., Executive Director

Committee of Interns and Residents, 386 Park Avenue, S., New York, NY 10016; tel. 212/725-5500; FAX. 212/779-2413; John Ronches, Executive Director

Cooley's Anemia Foundation, Inc., 129-09 26th Avenue, Suite 203, Flushing, NY 11354; tel. 800/522-7222; FAX. 718/321-3340; Gina Cioffi, Esq. National Executive Director

Corporate Angel Network, Inc., CAN (Arranges Free Air Transportation for Cancer Patients), Westchester County Airport, One Loop Road, White Plains, NY 10604; tel. 914/328-1313; FAX. 914/328-4226; Laura Adler, Administrator

Council of Jewish Federations, Inc., 730 Broadway, New York, NY 10003; tel. 212/475-5000; FAX. 212/529-5842; Martin S. Kraar, Executive Vice President

Council of Medical Specialty Societies, 51 Sherwood Terrace, Suite Y, Lake Bluff, IL 60044; tel. 847/295-3456; FAX. 847/295-3759; Rebecca R. Gschwend, M.A., M.B.A., Executive Vice President

Council of State Administrators of Vocational Rehabilitation, P.O. Box 3776, Washington, DC 20007; tel. 202/638-4634; Jack G. Duncan, General Counsel, Rehabilitation Policy

Council on Education for Public Health, 1015 Fifteenth Street, N.W., Washington, DC 20005; tel. 202/789-1050; FAX. 202/789-1895; Patricia P. Evans, Executive Director

Council on Social Work Education, 1600 Duke Street, Alexandria, VA 22314; tel. 703/683-8080; FAX. 703/683-8099; Donald W. Beless, Ph.D., Executive Director

Crohn's and Colitis Foundation of America, Inc., 386 Park Avenue, S., 17th Floor, New York, NY 10016-8804; tel. 800/932-2423; FAX. 212/779-4098; James V. Romano, Ph. D., President and Chief Executive Officer

Cystic Fibrosis Foundation, 6931 Arlington Road, Bethesda, MD 20814; tel. 301/951-4422; FAX. 301/951-6378; Robert J. Beall, Ph.D., President/Chief Executive Officer

D

Damien Dutton Society for Leprosy Aid, Inc., 616 Bedford Avenue, Bellmore, NY 11710; tel. 516/221-5829; FAX. 516/221-5909; Howard E. Crouch, President

Delta Dental Plans Association, 211 East Chicago Avenue, Suite 800, Chicago, IL 60611; tel. 312/337-4707; FAX. 312/337-7991; James Bonk, President

Dermatology Foundation, 1560 Sherman Avenue, Evanston, IL 60201-4802; tel. 847/328-2256; FAX. 847/328-0509; Sandra Rahn Goldman, Executive Director

Dietary Managers Association, 406 Surrey Woods Drive, St. Charles, IL 60174; tel. 630/587-6336; FAX. 630/587-6308; William St. John, President

Dysautonomia Foundation, Inc., 20 East 46th Street, Suite 302, New York, NY 10017; tel. 212/949-6644; FAX. 212/682-7625; Lenore F. Roseman, Executive Director

E

ECRI, 5200 Butler Pike, Plymouth Meeting, PA 19462; tel. 610/825-6000; FAX. 610/834-1275; Joel J. Nobel, M.D., President

Eastern Orthopaedic Association, Inc., Pier Five North, Suite 5D, Seven North Columbus Boulevard, Philadelphia, PA 19106-1486; tel. 215/351-4110; FAX. 215/351-1825; Elizabeth F. Capella, Executive Director

Educational Commission for Foreign Medical Graduates, 3624 Market Street, Philadelphia, PA 19104-2685; tel. 215/386-5900; FAX. 215/387-9963; Nancy E. Gary, M.D., President, Chief Executive Officer

Ehlers-Danlos National Foundation, P.O. Box 13157, Richmond, VA 23225; tel. 804/320-8192; FAX. 804/320-8192; Susan L. Stephenson, Vice President, Patient Advocate

Emergency Nurses Association, 216 Higgins Road, Park Ridge, IL 60068-5736; tel. 847/698-9400; FAX. 847/698-9406

Environmental Management Association, 4350 Dipaolo Center, Suite C, Glenview, IL 60025; tel. 847/699-6362; FAX. 847/699-6369; Carl Wangman, President

Epilepsy Foundation of America, 4351 Garden City Drive, Landover, MD 20785-2267; tel. 301/459-3700; FAX. 301/577-2684; Paulette V. Maehara, Chief Executive Officer

Epilepsy Foundation of Connecticut, 1800 Silas Deane Highway, Suite 168, Rocky Hill, CT 06067; tel. 860/721-9226; Linda Wallace

F

Family Service America, Inc., 11700 West Lake Park Drive, Milwaukee, WI 53224; tel. 414/359-1040; FAX. 414/359-1074; Peter B. Goldberg, President, Chief Executive Officer

Federation of American Health Systems, 1111 19th Street, N.W., Suite 402, Washington, DC 20036; tel. 202/833-3090; FAX. 202/861-0063; Lauren Maddox, Vice President, Communications

Federation of State Medical Boards of the United States, Inc., 400 Fuller Wiser Road, Suite 300, Euless, TX 76039-3855; tel. 817/868-4000; FAX. 817/868-4099; James R. Winn, M.D., Executive Vice President

Financial Accounting Standards Board, 401 Merritt 7, P.O. Box 5116, Norwalk, CT 06856-5116; tel. 203/847-0700ext250, ext. 250; FAX. 203/849-9714; Timothy S. Lucas, Director, Research, Technical Activities

Foundation for Chiropractic Education and Research, 1330 Beacon Street, Suite 315, Brookline, MA 02146-3202; tel. 617/734-3397; FAX. 617/734-0989; Anthony L. Rosner, Ph.D., Director of Research and Education

Foundation for Osteopathic Health Services, 5301 Wisconsin Avenue, N.W., Suite 630, Washington, DC 20015; tel. 202/686-1700; FAX. 202/686-7615; David Kushner, President

G

Gerontological Society of America, 1275 K Street, N.W., Suite 350, Washington, DC 20005-4006; tel. 202/842-1275; FAX. 202/842-1150; Carol A. Schutz, Executive Director

Great Plains Health Alliance, Inc., 625 Third Street, Box 366, Phillipsburg, KS 67661; tel. 913/543-2111; FAX. 913/543-5098; Roger S. John, President, Chief Executive Officer

Greater Flint Area Hospital Assembly, 702 South Ballenger Highway, Flint, MI 48532-3803; tel. 810/766-8898; FAX. 810/766-6422; Marlene Soderstrom, Executive Director

Guide Dog Users, Inc., 57 Grandview Avenue, Watertown, MA 02172; tel. 617/926-9198; Kim Charlson, Editor

H

HEAR Center, 301 East Del Mar Boulevard, Pasadena, CA 91101; tel. 626/796-2016; FAX. 626/796-2320; Josephine Wilson, Executive Director

Health Industry Distributors Association, 66 Canal Center Plaza, Suite 520, Alexandria, VA 22314; tel. 703/549-4432; FAX. 703/549-6495; Edward Wissing, Chairman

Health Industry Manufacturers Association, 1200 G Street, N.W., Suite 400, Washington, DC 20005; tel. 202/783-8700; FAX. 202/783-8750; Alan H. Magazine, President

Health Insurance Association of America, 1025 Connecticut Avenue, N.W., Washington, DC 20036-3998; tel. 202/223-7780; FAX. 202/223-7897; Gloria Tibby, Administrative Assistant

Healthcare Financial Management Association, Two Westbrook Corporate Center, Suite 700, Westchester, IL 60154; tel. 708/531-9600; FAX. 708/531-0032; Richard L. Clarke, F.H.F.M.A., President

Healthcare Information and Management Systems Society (HIMSS), 230 East Ohio Street, Suite 500, Chicago, IL 60611-3201; tel. 312/664-4467; FAX. 312/664-6143; John A. Page, Executive Director

Hispanic American Geriatrics Society, One Cutts Road, Durham, NH 03824-3102; tel. 603/868-5757; Eugene E. Tillock, Ed.D., President

Histochemical Society, Inc., 4 Barlows Landing Road, Suite Eight, Pocasset, MA 02559; tel. 508/563-1155; FAX. 508/563-1211

Hospital Research and Educational Trust, One North Franklin, Chicago, IL 60606; tel. 312/422-2624; FAX. 312/422-4568; Mary Pittman, President

Huntington's Disease Society of America, Inc., 140 West 22nd Street, Sixth floor, New York, NY 10011-2420; tel. 212/242-1968; FAX. 212/243-2443; Barbara T. Boyle, National Executive Director

I

Institutes for the Achievement of Human Potential, 8801 Stenton Avenue, Philadelphia, PA 19118; tel. 215/233-2050; FAX. 215/233-3940; Roselise H. Wilkinson, M.D., Medical Director

InterHealth, P.O. Box 10624, White Bear Lake, MN 55110; tel. 612/407-7075; FAX. 612/407-7077; Thomas LaMotte, Chairman of the Board

International Childbirth Education Association, Inc., P.O. Box 20048, Minneapolis, MN 55420-0048; tel. 612/854-8660; FAX. 612/854-8772; Doris Olson, Administrator

International College of Surgeons/United States Section, 1516 North Lake Shore Drive, Chicago, IL 60610-1694; tel. 312/787-6274; FAX. 312/787-9289; Susan Zelner, Meeting and Convention Manager

International Council for Health, Physical Education, Recreation, Sport and Dance, 1900 Association Drive, Reston, VA 20191; tel. 703/476-3486; FAX. 703/476-9527; Dr. Dong Ja Yang, Secretary General

International Society for Clinical Laboratory Technology, 818 Olive Street, Suite 918, St. Louis, MO 63101-1598; tel. 314/241-1445; FAX. 314/241-1449; Mark S. Birenbaum, Ph.D., Administrator

Intravenous Nurses Society, Inc., 10 Fawcett Street, Fresh Pond Square, Cambridge, MA 02138; tel. 617/441-3008; FAX. 617/576-5452; Mary Alexander, Chief Executive Officer

J

J. S. Anesthesia Consultants, P.O. Box 232, Jersey Shore, PA 17740; tel. 717/769-7735; John A. Hunter, D.D.S., Secretary

John Milton Society for the Blind, 475 Riverside Drive, Suite 455, New York, NY 10115; tel. 212/870-3335; FAX. 212/870-3229; Darcy Quigley, Executive Director

Joint Commission on Accreditation of Healthcare Organizations, One Renaissance Boulevard, Oakbrook Terrace, IL 60181; tel. 630/792-5000; FAX. 630/792-5005; Dennis S. O'Leary, M.D., President

Juvenile Diabetes Foundation International, 432 Park Avenue, S., New York, NY 10016; tel. 212/889-7575; Gloria Pennington, Executive Director

L

LHS, Inc./ Lutheran Health Systems, Box 6200, 4310 17th Avenue, S.W., Fargo, ND 58106-6200; tel. 701/277-7629; FAX. 701/277-7636; Steven R. Orr, Chairman, Chief Executive Officer

Lamaze International, Inc., (formerly ASPO/LAMAZE), 1200 19th Street, N.W., Suite 300, Washington, DC 20036; tel. 202/857-1128; FAX. 202/223-4579; Linda L. Harmon, Executive Director

Leukemia Society of America, Inc., 600 Third Avenue, New York, NY 10016; tel. 212/573-8484; FAX. 212/338-0323; Dwayne Howell, President and Chief Executive Officer

Long Term Acute Care Hospital Association of America, 1301 K Street, N.W., Suite 1100 East Tower, Washington, DC 20005-3317; tel. 202/296-4446; FAX. 202/414-9299; James T. Marrinan, Executive Director

Lupus Foundation of America, Inc., 1300 Piccard Drive, Suite 200, Rockville, MD 20850; tel. 301/670-9292; FAX. 301/670-9486; K. Hurley, Director, Information Services

M

March of Dimes Birth Defects Foundation, 1275 Mamaroneck Avenue, White Plains, NY 10605; tel. 914/428-7100; FAX. 914/428-8203; Jennifer L. Howse, Ph.D., President

Maternity Center Association, 48 East 92nd Street, New York, NY 10128; tel. 212/369-7300; FAX. 212/369-8747; Maureen P. Corry, M.P.H., General Director

Medic Alert, 2323 Colorado Avenue, Turlock, CA 95382; tel. 800/825-3785; FAX. 209/668-8752; David Roth, Public Relations

Medical Group Management Association, 104 Inverness Terrace, E., Englewood, CO 80112-5306; tel. 888/608-5601; FAX. 303/643-4427; Thomas L. Adams, CAE, Chief Executive Officer

Medical Library Association, Six North Michigan Avenue, Suite 300, Chicago, IL 60602-4805; tel. 312/419-9094; FAX. 312/419-8950; Carla J. Funk, Executive Director

Medical Staff Recruitment Certification Program, 3150 Holcomb Road, Suite 205, Norcross, GA 30071; tel. 800/258-4081; FAX. 404/417-2176; Susan Woodbury

Mended Hearts, Inc., 7272 Greenville Avenue, Dallas, TX 75231; tel. 214/706-1442; FAX. 214/987-4334; Darla Bonham, Executive Director

Minnesota Healthcare Conference, 2221 University Avenue, S.E., Suite 425, Minneapolis, MN 55414; tel. 612/331-5571; FAX. 612/331-1001; Peggy Westby, Manager

Muscular Dystrophy Association, 3300 East Sunrise Drive, Tucson, AZ 85718; tel. 602/529-2000; FAX. 602/529-5300; Robert Ross, Senior Vice President and Executive Director

N

NSF International, 3475 Plymouth Road, P.O. Box 130140, Ann Arbor, MI 48113-0140; tel. 313/769-8010; FAX. 313/769-0109; Dennis R. Mangino, Ph. D., President, Chief Executive Officer

National Academy of Sciences, National Research Council/Commission on Life Sciences, 2101 Constitution Avenue, N.W., NAS 343, Washington, DC 20418; tel. 202/334-2500; FAX. 202/334-1639; Paul Gilman, Ph.D., Executive Director

National Accreditation Council for Agencies Serving the Blind and Visually Handicapped, 260 Northland Blvd., Suite 233, Cincinnati, OH 45246; tel. 513/772-8449; FAX. 513/772-8854; Ruth Westman, Executive Director

National Accrediting Agency for Clinical Laboratory Sciences, 8410 West Bryn Mawr, Suite 670, Chicago, IL 60631-3415; tel. 773/714-8880; FAX. 773/714-8886; Olive M. Kimball, Executive Director

National Alliance for the Mentally Ill, 200 N. Glebe Road, Suite 1015, Arlington, VA 22203-3754; tel. 703/524-7600; FAX. 703/524-9094; Laurie Flynn, Executive Director

National Assembly on School Based Health Care, 1522 K Street NW, Suite 600, Washington, DC 20005; tel. 202/289-5400; FAX. 202/289-0776; Jennifer Fincken, Membership Manager

National Association Medical Staff Services, 631 East Butterfield, Suite 311, Lombard, IL 60148; tel. 630/271-9814; FAX. 630/271-0295; Robert A. Dengler, CAE, CMP, Executive Director

National Association for Home Care, 228 Seventh Street, S.E., Washington, DC 20003; tel. 202/547-7424; FAX. 202/547-3540; Val J. Halamandaris, President

National Association for Medical Equipment Services (NAMES), 625 Slaters Lane, Suite 200, Alexandria, VA 22314-1171; tel. 703/836-6263; FAX. 703/836-6730; Steve Haracznak, Vice President, Communications and Member Relation

National Association for Practical Nurse Education and Service, Inc. (NAP, 1400 Spring Street, Suite 330, Silver Spring, MD 20910; tel. 301/588-2491; FAX. 301/588-2839; John H. Word, LPN, Executive Director

National Association of Boards of Pharmacy, 700 Busse Highway, Park Ridge, IL 60068; tel. 847/698-6227; FAX. 847/698-0124; Carmen A. Catizone, R.Ph., M.S., Executive Director, Secretary

National Association of Children's Hospitals and Related Institutions, In, 401 Wythe Street, Alexandria, VA 22314; tel. 703/684–1355; FAX. 703/684–1589; Lawrence A. McAndrews, President, Chief Executive Officer

National Association of Dental Assistants, 900 South Washington, Suite G13, Falls Church, VA 22046; tel. 703/237–8616; S. Young, Director

National Association of Dental Laboratories, (Includes National Board for Certification in Dental Laboratory Technology), 555 East Braddock Road, Alexandria, VA 22314–2199; tel. 703/683–5263; FAX. 703/549–4788; Robert W. Stanley, Executive Director

National Association of Health Services Executives, 8630 Fenton Street, Suite 126, Silver Spring, MD 20910; tel. 202/628–3953; FAX. 301/588–0011; Ozzie Jenkins, CMP, Executive Director

National Association of Hospital Hospitality Houses, Inc., 4915 Auburn Avenue, Suite 303, Bethesda, MD 20814; tel. 800/542–9730; FAX. 301/961–3094; Sherrie L. Williams, Manager of Admin.

National Association of Institutional Laundry Managers, 781 Twin Oaks Avenue, Chula Vista, CA 92010; tel. 619/420–1396; FAX. 619/420–1396; Betty Conard, Executive Secretary

National Association of Psychiatric Health Systems, 1317 F Street, N.W., Suite 301, Washington, DC 20004; tel. 202/393–6700, ext. 16; FAX. 202/783–6041; Mark J. Covall, Executive Director

National Association of Social Workers, Inc., 750 First Street, N.E., Suite 700, Washington, DC 20002; tel. 202/408–8600, ext. 233; FAX. 202/336–8311; Senior Staff Associate, Health, Mental

National Association of State Mental Health Program Directors, 66 Canal Center Plaza, Suite 302, Alexandria, VA 22314; tel. 703/739–9333; FAX. 703/548–9517; Robert W. Glover, Ph.D., Executive Director

National Board of Anesthesiology, Inc. 308 Main Street, Lawrence, KS 66044; tel. 785/842–7067; FAX. 785/842–7088; Thomas Nique, M.D., D.D.S., President

National Board for Respiratory Care, 8310 Nieman Road, Lenexa, KS 66214; tel. 913/599–4200; FAX. 913/541–0156; Steven K. Bryant, Executive Director

National Board of Medical Examiners, 3750 Market Street, Philadelphia, PA 19104; tel. 215/590–9500; FAX. 215/590–9755; L. Thompson Bowles, M.D., Ph.D., President

National Children's Eye Care Foundation, P.O. Box 795069, Dallas, TX 75379–5069; tel. 972/407–0404; FAX. 972/407–0616; Suzanne C. Beauchamp, Administrator

National Commission on Certification of Physician Assistants, 2845 Henderson Mill Road, N.E., Atlanta, GA 30341; tel. 404/493–9100; FAX. 404/493–7316; David L. Glazer, Executive Vice President, Managing Director

National Council on Alcoholism and Drug Dependence, Inc., 12 West 21st Street, New York, NY 10010; tel. 212/206–6770; FAX. 212/645–1690; Jeffrey Hon, Director, Public Information

National Council on Radiation Protection and Measurements, 7910 Woodmont Avenue, Suite 800, Bethesda, MD 20814; tel. 301/657–2652; FAX. 301/907–8768; William M. Beckner, Executive Director

National Council on the Aging, Inc., 409 Third Street, S.W., Suite 200, Washington, DC 20024; tel. 202/479–1200; FAX. 202/479–0735; James Firman, President

National Dental Association, 5506 Connecticut Avenue, N.W., Suite 24–25, Washington, DC 20015; tel. 202/244–7555; FAX. 202/244–5992; Robert S. Johns, Executive Director

National Depressive and Manic–Depressive Association, 730 North Franklin Street, Suite 501, Chicago, IL 60610; tel. 312/642–0049; FAX. 312/642–7243; Donna DePaul-Kelly, Acting Executive Director

National Easter Seal Society, 230 West Monroe Street, Suite 1800, Chicago, IL 60606–4802; tel. 312/726–6200; FAX. 312/726–1494; James E. Williams, Jr., President

National Environmental Health Association, 720 South Colorado Boulevard, South Tower, Suite 970, Denver, CO 80222; tel. 303/756–9090; FAX. 303/691–9490; Nelson Fabian, Executive Director

National Federation of Licensed Practical Nurses, 1418 Aversboro Road, Garner, NC 27529; tel. 919/779–0046; FAX. 919/779–5642; Charlene Barbour, Administrator

National Fire Protection Association, P.O. Box 9101, One Batterymarck Park, Quincy, MA 02269–9101; tel. 617/770–3000; FAX. 617/770–7110; Burton R. Klein, Health Care Fire Protection Engineer

National Gaucher Foundation, 11140 Rockville Pike, Suite 350, Rockville, MD 20852; tel. 301/816–1515; FAX. 301/816–1516; Rhonda Buyers, Executive Director

National Headache Foundation, 428 West St. James Place, Second Floor, Chicago, IL 60614–2750; tel. 800/843–2256; FAX. 773/525–7357; Suzanne Simons, Executive Director

National Health Council, Inc., 1730 M Street, N.W., Suite 500, Washington, DC 20036; tel. 202/785–3910; FAX. 202/785–5923; Myrl Weinberg, CAE, President

National Hemophilia Foundation, 110 Greene Street, Suite 303, New York, NY 10012; tel. 212/219–8180, ext. 3020; FAX. 212/966–9247; Stephen E. Bajard, Executive Director

National Institute for Jewish Hospice, Central Telephone Network, P.O. Box 48025, Los Angeles, CA 90048; tel. 800/446–4448; Levana Lev, Executive Director, or Shirley Lam, Executive Vice President

National Kidney Foundation, Inc. 30 East 33rd Street, New York, NY 10016; tel. 800/622–9010; FAX. 212/779–0068; John Davis, Executive Director

National League for Nursing, 350 Hudson Street, New York, NY 10014; tel. 212/989–9393ext100; FAX. 212/989–9256; Ruth D. Corcorau, EdD, R.N., Chief Executive Officer

National Medical Association, 1012 10th Street, N.W., Washington, DC 20001; tel. 202/347–1895; FAX. 202/842–3293; Lorraine Cole, Ph.D., Executive Director

National Mental Health Association, 1021 Prince Street, Alexandria, VA 22314–2971; tel. 703/684–7722; FAX. 703/684–5968; Michael M. Faenza, President, Chief Executive Officer

National Multiple Sclerosis Society, 733 Third Avenue, New York, NY 10017; tel. 212/986–3240; FAX. 212/986–7981; Dwayne Howell, Executive Vice President

National Nutrition Consortium, Inc., 24 Third Street, N.E., Suite 200, Washington, DC 20002; tel. 202/547–4819; Betty B. Blouin, Executive Director

National Osteopathic Women Physicians Association, 5301 Wisconsin Avenue, N.W., Suite 630, Washington, DC 20015; tel. 202/686–1700; FAX. 202/537–1362; David Kushner, Executive Director

National Parkinson Foundation, Inc., 1501 Northwest Ninth Avenue, Miami, FL 33136–1494; tel. 305/547–6666; FAX. 305/548–4403; Brian Morton, Controller

National Perinatal Association, 3500 East Fletcher Avenue, Suite 209, Tampa, FL 33613–4712; tel. 813/971–1008; FAX. 813/971–9306; Julie Leachman, Executive Director

National Recreation and Park Association, 22377 Belmont Ridge Road, Ashburn, VA 20148; tel. 703/858–0784; FAX. 703/858–0794; R. Dean Tice, Executive Director

National Registry in Clinical Chemistry, 815 15th Street, N.W., Suite 630, Washington, DC 20005; tel. 202/393–7140; FAX. 202/393–4059; Gilbert E. Smith, Ph.D, Executive Director

National Registry of Emergency Medical Technicians, 6610 Busch Boulevard, P.O. Box 29233, Columbus, OH 43229; tel. 614/888–4484; William E. Brown, Jr., Executive Director

National Rehabilitation Association, (Includes Nine National Associations and 58 Affiliate Chapters), 633 South Washington Street, Alexandria, VA 22314; tel. 703/836–0850; FAX. 703/836–0848; Michelle A. Vaughan, Executive Director

National Resident Matching Program, 2450 N Street, N.W., Suite 201, Washington, DC 20037–1141; tel. 202/828–0676; FAX. 202/828–1121; Robert L. Beran, Ph. D., Deputy Executive Director

National Rural Health Association, 1320 19th Street, N.W., Suite 350, Washington, DC 20036; tel. 202/232–6200; FAX. 202/232–1133; Darin F. Johnson, Government Affairs Director

National Safety Council, 1121 Spring Lake Drive, Itasca, IL 60143–3201, P.O. Box 558, Itasca, IL 60143–0558; tel. 800/621–7619; FAX. 630/285–0797; Kimberly D. Spoolstra, Customer Service

National Spinal Cord Injury Association, 545 Concord Avenue, Suite 29, Cambridge, MA 02138; tel. 617/441–8500; FAX. 617/441–3449; Dianne M. Barry, Executive Director

National Student Nurses' Association, Inc., 555 West 57th Street, Suite 1327, New York, NY 10019; tel. 212/581–2211; FAX. 212/581–2368; Diane J. Mancino, Ed.D., RN, CAE, Executive Director

National Tay–Sachs and Allied Diseases Association, 2001 Beacon Street, Brookline, MA 02146; tel. 617/277–4463; FAX. 617/277–0134; Debi Gutter, Executive Director

Neurosurgical Society of America, UCLA Division of Neurosurgery, 10833 Le Conte Avenue, Los Angeles, CA 90024; tel. 310/825–3998; FAX. 310/794–2147; Donald P. Becker, M.D., President

Neurotics Anonymous, 11140 Bainbridge Drive, Little Rock, AR 72212; tel. 501/221–2809; FAX. 501/221–2809; Grover Boydston, Chairman

New England Gerontological Association, One Cutts Road, Durham, NH 03824–3102; tel. 603/868–5757; Eugene E. Tillock, Ed.D., Executive Director

New England Healthcare Assembly, Inc., 500 Spaulding Turnpike, Suite W–310, Portsmouth, NH 03802–7100; tel. 603/422–6100; FAX. 603/422–6101; James S. Dolph, President

O

Osteogenesis Imperfecta Foundation, Inc., 804 West Diamond Avenue, Suite 210, Gaithersburg, MD 20878; tel. 301/947–0083; FAX. 301/947–0456; Heller An Shapiro, Executive Director

Otosclerosis Study Group, 6465 Yale, Tulsa, OK 74136; Roger E. Wehrs, M.D., Secretary–Treasurer

P

Pan American Health Organization, 525 23rd Street, N.W., Washington, DC 20037; tel. 202/861–3200; Jose M. Paganini, Director HSS

Pathology Practice Association, 1225 Eighth Street, Suite 590, Sacramento, CA 95814; tel. 916/446–2651; J. Michael Allen, Executive Secretary

Physician Executive Management Center, 4014 Gunn Highway, Suite 160, Tampa, FL 33624–4787; tel. 813/963–1800; FAX. 813/264–2207; David R. Kirschman, President

Pilot Dogs, Inc., 625 West Town Street, Columbus, OH 43215; tel. 614/221–6367; FAX. 614/221–1577; J. Jay Gray, Executive Director

Prevent Blindness America, 500 East Remington Road, Schaumburg, IL 60173–4557; tel. 847/843–2020; FAX. 847/843–8458; Richard T. Hellner, President

Public Relations Society of America, 33 Irving Place, New York, NY 10003–2376; tel. 212/995–2230; FAX. 212/995–0757; Ray Gaulke, Chief Operating Officer

R

Radiological Society of North America, Inc., 2021 Spring Road, Suite 600, Oak Brook, IL 60523; tel. 630/571–2670; FAX. 630/571–7837; Delmar J. Stauffer, Executive Director

Recording for the Blind and Dyslexic, 20 Roszel Road, Princeton, NJ 08540; tel. 609/452–0606; FAX. 609/520–7990; Ritchie L. Geisel, President, Chief Executive Officer

Renal Physicians Association, 2011 Pennsylvania Avenue, N.W., Suite 800, Washington, DC 20006–1808; tel. 202/835–0436; FAX. 202/835–0443; Dale Singer, MHA, Executive Director

Robert Wood Johnson Foundation, P.O. Box 2316, Route One and College Road East, Princeton, NJ 08543–2316; tel. 609/452–8701; FAX. 609/987–8845; Richard J. Toth, Proposal Manager

S

Shriners Hospitals for Children, P.O. Box 31356, Tampa, FL 33631–3356; tel. 813/281–0300, ext. 8163; FAX. 813/281–8113; Lee M. Woodfin, Executive Secretary

Sickle Cell Disease Foundation of Greater New York, 127 West 127th Street, Suite 421, New York, NY 10027; tel. 212/865–1500; FAX. 212/865–0917; Beryl Murray, Executive Director

Society for Academic Emergency Medicine, 901 North Washington Avenue, Lansing, MI 48906; tel. 517/485–5484; FAX. 517/485–0801; Mary Ann Schropp, Executive Director

Society for Adolescent Medicine, Inc., 1916 Northwest Copper Oaks Circle, Blue Springs, MO 64015; tel. 816/224–8010; FAX. 816/224–8009; Edie Moore, Administrative Director

Society for Healthcare Consumer Advocacy, One North Franklin, Chicago, IL 60606; tel. 312/422–3774; FAX. 312/422–4580; Eleanore Kirsch, Executive Director

Society for Healthcare Strategy and Market Development, of the American Hospital Association, One North Franklin, 31st Floor, Chicago, IL 60606; tel. 312/422–3888; FAX. 312/422–4579; Lauren A. Barnett, Executive Director

Society for Occupational and Environmental Health, 6728 Old McLean Village Drive, McLean, VA 22101; tel. 703/556–9222; FAX. 703/556–8729; Juliet Mason, Account Manager

Society for Pediatric Pathology, 6728 Old McLean Village Drive, McLean, VA 22101; tel. 703/556–9222; FAX. 703/556–8729; Johanna O'Toole, Account Manager

Society for Social Work Administrators in Health Care, One North Franklin, Chicago, IL 60606–3401; tel. 312/422–3774; FAX. 312/422–4580; Eleanore Kirsch, Executive Director

Society of Critical Care Medicine, 8101 East Kaiser Boulevard, Anaheim, CA 92808–2214; tel. 714/282–6000; FAX. 714/282–6050; Norma J. Shoemaker, M.N., Executive Director

Society of Neurological Surgeons, New England Medical Center, Department of Neurosurgery, 750 Washington Street, P.O. Box 178, Boston, MA 02111; tel. 617/636–5858; William Shucart, M.D., Secretary

Society of Nuclear Medicine, 1850 Samuel Morse Drive, Reston, VA 22090; tel. 703/708–9000ext246; FAX. 703/708–9777; c/o Administrator

Society of University Otolaryngologists–Head and Neck Surgeons, Joint Center for Otolaryngology, Harvard Medical School, 333 Longwood Avenue, Boston, MA 02115; tel. 617/732–7003; FAX. 617/217–1372; Marvin Fried, M.D., Secretary–Treasurer

Southeastern Healthcare Association, 1345 Carmichael Way, P.O. Box 11126, Montgomery, AL 36111–0126; tel. 334/260–8600; FAX. 205/260–0023; Tommy R. McDougal, FACHE, President

T

Technologist Section, Society of Nuclear Medicine, 1850 Samuel Morse Drive, Reston, VA 22090; tel. 703/708–9000, ext. 241; FAX. 703/708–9015; Virginia M. Pappas, Administrator

The Alliance For Healthcare Strategy And Marketing, 11 South LaSalle, Suite 2300, Chicago, IL 60603; tel. 312/704–9700; FAX. 312/704–9709; Carla Windhorst, President

The American Association of Immunologists, 9650 Rockville Pike, Bethesda, MD 20814; tel. 301/530–7178; FAX. 301/571–1816; M. Michele Hogan, Ph.D., Executive Director

The American Board of Obstetrics and Gynecology, Inc., 2915 Vine Street, Dallas, TX 75204–1069; tel. 214/871–1619; FAX. 214/871–1943; Dr. Norman F. Gant, Executive Director

The American Board of Plastic Surgery, Inc., Seven Penn Center, Suite 400, 1635 Market Street, Philadelphia, PA 19103–2204; tel. 215/587–9322; Gwen A. Hanuscin, Administrative Assistant

The American Board of Professional Disability Consultants, 1350 Beverly Road, Suite 115–327, McLean, VA 22101; tel. 703/790–8644; Taras J. Cerkevitch, Ph.D., Director, Operations

The American Board of Urology, Inc., 2216 Ivy Road, Suite 210, Charlottesville, VA 22903; tel. 804/979–0059; FAX. 804/979–0266; Stuart S. Howards, M.D., Executive Secretary

The American Orthopaedic Association, 6300 North River Road, Suite 300, Rosemont, IL 60018–4263; tel. 847/318–7330; FAX. 847/318–7339; Hildegard A. Weiler, Executive Director

The Arc of the United States, Formerly Association for Retarded Citizens, 500 East Border Street, Suite 300, Arlington, TX 76011; tel. 817/640–0204; FAX. 817/277–3491; Alan Abeson, Ed.D., Executive Director

The Association for Research in Vision and Ophthalmology, 9650 Rockville Pike, Suite 1500, Bethesda, MD 20814–3998; tel. 301/571–1844; FAX. 301/571–8311; Joanne G. Angle, Executive Director

The Association of Medical Illustrators, 1819 Peachtree Street, N.E., Suite 712, Atlanta, GA 30309; tel. 404/350–7900; FAX. 404/351–3348; William H. Just, Executive Director

The Association of Women's Health, Obstetric, and Neonatal Nurses, 700 14th Street, N.W., Suite 600, Washington, DC 20005–2019; tel. 202/662–1600, ext. 1608; FAX. 202/737–0575; Gail G. Kincaide, Executive Director

The Duke Endowment, 100 North Tryon Street, Suite 3500, Charlotte, NC 28202; tel. 704/376–0291; FAX. 704/376–9336; Elizabeth H. Locke, President

The Endocrine Society, 4350 East West Highway, Suite 500, Bethesda, MD 20814–4410; tel. 301/941–0200; FAX. 301/941–0259; David Thomas, Director, Public Affairs

The Foundation Fighting Blindness, Executive Plaza I, Suite 800, 11350 McCormick Road, Hunt Valley, MD 21031–1014; tel. 888/374–3937; FAX. 410/771–9470;

The Foundation for Ichthyosis and Related Skin Types, Inc., (F.I.R.S.T.), P.O. Box 20921, Raleigh, NC 27619–0921; tel. 919/782–5728; FAX. 919/781–0679; Nicholas Gattuccio, Executive Director

The Healthcare Forum, 425 Market Street, 16th Floor, San Francisco, CA 94105; tel. 415/356–4300; FAX. 415/356–9300; Kathryn E. Johnson, President, Chief Executive Officer

The Institute for Rehabilitation and Research, Administration, 1333 Moursund, Houston, TX 77030; tel. 713/799–5000; FAX. 713/799–7095; Louisa Adelung, Chief Executive Officer

The International Dyslexia Association, (Formerly The Orton Dyslexia Society), Chester Building, Suite 382, 8600 LaSalle Road, Baltimore, MD 21286; tel. 410/296–0232; FAX. 410/321–5069; Susan Brickley, Director, Marketing and Public Relations

The Points of Light Foundation, 1737 H Street, N.W., Washington, DC 20006; tel. 202/223–9186 ext. 209; FAX. 202/223–9256; Yael Israel, Customer Information Coordinator

The Salvation Army National Corporation, 615 Slaters Lane, P.O. Box 269, Alexandria, VA 22313; tel. 703/684–5500; FAX. 703/684–3478; Commissioner Robert A. Watson, National Commander

The Seeing Eye, Inc., Washington Valley Road, Box 375, Morristown, NJ 07963–0375; tel. 973/539–4425; FAX. 973/539–0922; Kenneth Rosenthal, President

The Southwestern Surgical Congress, 401 North Michigan Avenue, Chicago, IL 60611–4267; tel. 312/527–6667; FAX. 312/321–6869; Thomas E. Stautzenbach, Executive Director

U

USP, 12601 Twinbrook Parkway, Rockville, MD 20852; tel. 301/881–0666; FAX. 301/816–8299; Jerome A. Halperin, Executive Vice President, Chief Executive Offic

United Cerebral Palsy Associations, Inc., 1660 L Street, N.W., Suite 700, Washington, DC 20036; tel. 800/872–5827; Michael Morris, Executive Director

United Methodist Association of Health and Welfare Ministries, 601 West Riverview Avenue, Dayton, OH 45406–5543; tel. 937/227–9494; FAX. 937/222–7364; Dean W. Pulliam, President, Chief Executive Officer

United Ostomy Association, Inc., 36 Executive Park, Suite 120, Irvine, CA 92714; tel. 800/826–0826; FAX. 714/660–9262; Darlene A. Smith, Executive Director

United Parkinson Foundation, 833 West Washington Boulevard, Chicago, IL 60607; tel. 312/733–1893; FAX. 312/733–1896; Judy Rosner, Executive Director

United Way of America, 701 North Fairfax Street, Alexandria, VA 22314–2045; tel. 703/836–7100; FAX. 703/683–7840; Betty Stanley Beene, President

W

W. K. Kellogg Foundation, One Michigan Avenue East, Battle Creek, MI 49017–4058; tel. 616/968–1611; FAX. 616/968–0413; Robert A. DeVries, Program Director

Western Orthopaedic Association, 1834 First Street, Suite 3, Napa, CA 94559–2353; tel. 707/259–9481; FAX. 707/259–9486; Susan Hanf, Executive Director

Western Surgical Association, Mayo Clinic, 200 First Street, S.W., Rochester, MN 55905; Jon A. VanHeerden, M.D., Secretary

Section C

Healthfinder

The healthfinder is composed of two listing types: toll–free numbers for health information and federal health information centers and clearinghouses. Toll–free numbers are denoted with the letter A and federal numbers are denoted with the letter B. Toll–free numbers are listed first, followed by the federal numbers.

This file was released in 1998. This document is revised annually.

This Federal document is in the public domain, but is distributed subject to two conditions: 1) Any person or organization posting and/or distributing this document in electronic or paper form MUST respect the integrity of the document and post or distribute it ONLY in its entirety, including this paragraph, and without any change whatsoever; and 2) Any person or organization either posting or distributing this document MUST agree to post and/or distribute future editions of the document in the same manner as this edition to ensure that the most current information is made available to those parties who received the earlier version.

If you would like more information, contact the National Health Information Center at 800/336–4797 or through the internet at nhic–nt:health.org.

TOLL–FREE NUMBERS FOR HEALTH INFORMATION

This Healthfinder™ lists selected toll–free numbers and describes organizations that provide health–related information. The organizations do not diagnose or recommend treatment for any disease. Some offer recorded information; others provide personalized counseling, referrals, and/or written materials. Unless otherwise stated, numbers can be reached within the continental United States Monday through Friday, and hours of operation are Eastern time. Numbers that operate 24 hours a day can be reached 7 days a week unless otherwise noted.

This Healthfinder™ is one in a series of publications, on a variety of topics, prepared by the National Health Information Center (NHIC). NHIC is a service of the Office of Disease Prevention and Health Promotion, Public Health Service, U.S. Department of Health and Human Services. The information contained on the following pages in no way should be construed as an endorsement, real or implied, by the U.S. Department of Health and Human Services.

ADOPTION

A–1. Bethany Christian Services
(800)238–4269
Services for women considering adoption as an option. Free counseling. Housing is available. 8 a.m.–12 midnight, every day. (See also B–24)

A–2. National Adoption Center
(800)TO–ADOPT
(215)735–9988
Expands adoption opportunities throughout the United States, particularly for children with special needs. Links all State adoption agencies through a telecommunication network. Addresses adoption and child welfare issues. 9 a.m.–5 p.m.

AGING

American Health Assistance Foundation
(800)437–2423
Funds scientific research on age–related and degenerative diseases, educates the public about these diseases and provides emergency financial assistance to Alzheimer's patients and their caregivers.

Eldercare Locator
(800)677–1116
Provides referrals to local resources nationwide. 9 a.m. 11 p.m. (Eastern)

A–3. National Institute on Aging Information Center
(800)222–2225
(800)222–4225 (TTY)
(301)589–3014 (Fax)
Provides publications on health topics of interest to older adults, to the public, and to doctors, nurses, social activities directors, and health educators. 8:30 a.m.–5 p.m. (See also A–16, A–17, A–18, A–81, B–1)

AIDS/HIV

A–4. AIDS Clinical Trials Information Service
(800)874–2572
(800)243–7012 (TTY/TDD)
(301)217–0023
(301)738–6616 (Fax)
Sponsored by the Centers for Disease Control and Prevention, the Food and Drug Administration, the National Institute of Allergy and Infectious Diseases, and the National Library of Medicine. Provides current information on federally and privately sponsored clinical trials for AIDS patients and others with HIV infection and on the drugs used in those trials. All calls are confidential. Spanish–speaking operators available. 9 a.m.–7 p.m.

A–5. CDC National AIDS Clearinghouse
(800)458–5231
(800)243–7012 (TDD)
(301)217–0023
(301)738–6616 (Fax)
(800)458–5231 (NAC Fax–Back Service)
aidsinfo@cdcnac.aspensys.com (E–Mail)
Sponsored by the Centers for Disease Control and Prevention. A national reference, referral, and distribution service for HIV/AIDS–related information. Answers questions and provides technical assistance; distributes published HIV–related materials including current information on scientific findings, CDC guidelines, and trends in the HIV epidemic; and provides specific information on AIDS–related organizations, educational materials, funding opportunities, and other topics. Services include a 24–hour fax–back service for HIV/AIDS–related information and the Business and Labor Resource Service for resources, technical assistance, publications, and referrals concerning managing AIDS in the workplace. Provides information and publications in English and Spanish. 9 a.m.–7 p.m. (See also B–3)

A–6. CDC National AIDS Hotline
(800)342–2437 (English)
(800)344–7432 (Spanish)
(800)243–7889 (TDD)
Sponsored by the Centers for Disease Control and Prevention. Provides information to the public on the prevention and spread of HIV/AIDS. The first toll–free number provides 24–hour service; the second number provides service in Spanish 8 a.m.–2 a.m., everyday except holidays. The third toll–free number is available 10 a.m.–10 p.m., Monday–Friday.

HIV/AIDS Treatment Information Service
(800)HIV–0440
(800)243–7012 (TDD)
(301)217–0023
(301)738–6616 (Fax)
Sponsored by the CDC National AIDS Clearinghouse. Provides timely, accurate treatment information on HIV and AIDS. Answers questions about treatment of HIV disease; distributes copies of federally approved HIV/AIDS treatment guidelines and information; provides services in Spanish and English. 9 a.m. 7 p.m. All calls are confidential.

A–8. Project Inform HIV/AIDS Treatment Hotline
(800)822–7422
(415)558–9051
Provides treatment information and referral for HIV–infected individuals. Information on clinical trials. No diagnosis. 10 a.m.–4 p.m., Monday–Saturday (Pacific).

ALCOHOL ABUSE

See also DRUG ABUSE

A–9. ADCARE Hospital Helpline
(800)ALCOHOL
Provides information and referral for alcohol and other drug concerns. Operates 24 hours.

A–10. Al–Anon Family Group Headquarters
(800)356–9996
Al–Anon and Alateen provide help for families and friends of alcoholics. The headquarters provides literature and refers people who need assistance to local meetings. 9 a.m.–4:30 p.m.

A–11. Alcohol and Drug Helpline
(800)821–4357
(801)272–4357
Sponsored by Pioneer Health Care. Provides referrals to local facilities where adolescents and adults can seek help. Operates 24 hours.

A–12. American Council on Alcoholism
(800)527–5344
(410)889–0297 (Fax)
Offers information and sources for alcoholism treatment to callers concerned about excessive drinking of someone close to them. 9 a.m.–5 p.m.

Calix Society
(800)398–0524
Catholic alcoholics who maintain their sobriety through participation in Alcoholics Anonymous while they work at regaining their spiritual lives through Calix. Both non–Catholics and non–alcoholics are welcome to join.

Children of Alcoholics Foundation
(800)359–COAF
Serves and educates young and adult children from alcoholic families, informs the public about children of alcoholics, stimulates interest in seeking solutions to their problems and promotes research on alcoholism and its effect on children of alcoholics.

A–13. National Clearinghouse for Alcohol and Drug Information
(800)729–6686
(301)468–2600
(800)487–4889 (TTY/TDD)
(301)230–2867 (TTY/TDD)
(301)468–6433 (Fax)
Sponsored by the Center for Substance Abuse Prevention, Substance Abuse and Mental Health Services Administration. Gathers and disseminates information on alcohol and other drug–related subjects, including tobacco. Distributes publications. Services include subject searches and provision of statistics and other information. Operates the Regional Alcohol and Drug Awareness Resource Network, a nationwide linkage of alcohol and other drug information centers. Maintains a library open to the public. 8 a.m.–7 p.m.

A-15. National Council on Alcoholism and Drug Dependence, Inc.
(800)622-2255
(212)206-6770
(212)645-1690 (Fax)
Refers to local affiliates for counseling and provides written information on alcoholism and drug dependence. The toll-free number operates 24 hours; the other number is staffed 9 a.m.–5 p.m.

National Woman's Christian Temperance Union
(800)755-1321
Founded to build public sentiment for sobriety. Educational activities are directed at teaching the scientific facts about the effects of alcohol and other narcotics on the body and on society.

ALLERGY/ASTHMA

See LUNG DISEASE/ASTHMA/ALLERGY

ALZHEIMER'S DISEASE

See also AGING

A-16. Alzheimer's Association
(800)272-3900
(312)335-8882 (TDD)
(312)335-1110 (Fax)
http://www.alz.org (World Wide Web)
Refers to local chapters and support groups. Offers basic information about Alzheimer's disease and related disorders including research, drug treatments and clinical trials, warning signs of the disease, and caregiving information. Printed materials are available in English and Spanish. Spanish-speaking operators are available. The information and referral line is available 24 hours; operators staff the line 8:30 a.m.–5 p.m. Central, M–F. Leave message after hours.

A-17. Alzheimer's Disease Education and Referral Center
(800)438-4380
(301)495-3334 (Fax)
adear@alzheimers.org (E-mail)
Sponsored by the National Institute on Aging. Provides information and publications on Alzheimer's disease. 8:30 a.m.–5 p.m.

ARTHRITIS

American Juvenile Arthritis Organization
(800)283-7800
Offers information about childhood rheumatic diseases to patients, their families and health professionals.

A-18. Arthritis Foundation Information Line
(800)283-7800
Provides information about arthritis and referrals to local chapters. 24 hours. (See also B-7)

Lyme Disease Foundation, Inc.
(800)886-5963
Services include public education; supporting research relating to the condition; guiding and supporting self-help groups; and providing medical referrals. Distributes brochures on Lyme disease and reprints of scientific articles.

AUDIOVISUALS

See LIBRARY SERVICES

AUTISM

See CHILD DEVELOPMENT

AUTOIMMUNE DISEASES

American Autoimmune Related Diseases Association, Inc.
(800)598-4668
Professional and consumer inquiries on research, education, detection and support services for autoimmune related diseases are addressed.

BONE MARROW

See CANCER

CANCER

A-19. American Cancer Society Response Line
(800)227-2345 (Voice/TDD/TT)
Provides information and publications about cancer and pain management. Offers support services to cancer patients. Through the One-Day Memorial Response Service, donors can make contributions, during or after hours, in memory of a friend or loved one to help American Cancer Society Programs. 8:30 a.m. 4:30 p.m.

A-20. Cancer Information Service
(800)422-6237
Provides information about cancer and cancer-related resources to patients, the public, and health professionals. Inquiries are handled by trained information specialists. Spanish-speaking staff members are available. Distributes free publications from the National Cancer Institute. Operates 9 a.m.–7 p.m.

Candlelighters Childhood Cancer Foundation
(800)366-2223
Provides support, information and referrals to families of children with cancer and to professionals who work with them.

Chemocare
(800)55-CHEMO
Offers personal one-on-one support for people undergoing chemotherapy and/or radiation treatment. Support is provided by over 300 trained and certified volunteers who have themselves survived treatment. The service is free and confidential.

National Alliance of Breast Cancer Organizations
(800)719-9154
Provides information, assistance and referral to anyone with questions about breast cancer. It is made up of a network of 375 breast cancer organizations.

National Bone Marrow Transplant Link
(800)LINK-BMT
Alleviates some of the psychological, financial and physical burdens of bone marrow transplant patients through education, support and resource referrals.

National Kidney Cancer Association
(800)850-9132
Works to improve care and increase survival of kidney cancer patients through information, research and patient advocacy. Local meetings are held for patients, but there are no organized local chapters.

A-21. National Marrow Donor Program
(800)MARROW-2
Sponsored by the National Heart, Lung, and Blood Institute and the Department of the Navy. Provides multilingual information on donating marrow and the transplant process. Also provides information on donor centers in the caller's area. Professional staff answer questions from 8 a.m.–6 p.m. (Central); recorded message at all other times. (See also A-117)

Susan G. Komen Breast Cancer Foundation
(800)IM-AWARE
Organizes breast health seminars throughout the country and provides education material about breast cancer, mammo-graphy, and breast self-examination.

Reach to Recovery Program
(800)227-2345
A one-on-one visitation program for women who have a personal concern about breast cancer. Information and support is provided by a volunteer who has had breast cancer.

US Too International
(800)808-7866
Founded to provide support group services and information to patients and families affected by prostate cancer.

A-22. Y-Me National Breast Cancer Organization
(800)221-2141
(312)986-8228
Provides breast cancer patients with presurgery counseling, treatment information/peer support, self-help counseling, and patient literature. Also provides information to any and all women concerned about breast health and breast cancer. Y-ME has a matching caller program for men whose partners have been diagnosed with breast cancer. 9 a.m.–5 p.m. (Central). Local number operates 24 hours.

CEREBRAL PALSY

See RARE DISORDERS

CHEMICAL PRODUCTS/PESTICIDES

See also HOUSING

A-23. Chemtrec Non-Emergency Services Hotline
(800)262-8200
Provides nonemergency referrals to companies that manufacture chemicals and to Federal and State agencies for health and safety information and information regarding chemical regulations. 9 a.m.–6 p.m.

A-24. National Pesticide Telecommunications Network
(800)858-7378
Sponsored by the U.S. Environmental Protection Agency and Oregon State University. Provides information about a variety of pesticide-related subjects, including: pesticide product information; information on the recognition and management of pesticide poisonings; toxicology; environmental chemistry; referrals for laboratory analyses, investigation of pesticide incidents, and emergency treatment information; safety information; health and environmental effects; clean-up and disposal procedures. TDD capability. 6:30 a.m.–4:30 p.m. (Pacific); voice mail provided for off-hours calls. (See also B-23)

CHILD ABUSE/MISSING CHILDREN/MENTAL HEALTH

A-25. Boys Town National Hotline
(800)448-3000
(800)448-1833 (TDD)
Provides short-term intervention and counseling and refers callers to local community resources. Counsels on parent-child conflicts, family issues, suicide, pregnancy, runaway youth, physical and sexual abuse, and other issues that impact children and families. Spanish-speaking operators are available. TDD capability. Operates 24 hours.

A-26. Child Find of America, Inc.
(800)426-5678 (I-AM-LOST)
Searches for missing children under age 18 who are victims of parental abduction, stranger abduction, or who have run away. Provides safety prevention information. Operates 24 hours.

(800)292-9688 (A-WAY-OUT)
Provides unique crisis mediation program for parents contemplating abduction of their children, or who have already abducted their children and want to use Child Find Volunteer Family Mediators to resolve their custody dispute. Operates 24 hours.

A-27. CHILDHELP/IOF Foresters National Child Abuse Hotline
(800)4-A-CHILD
(800)2-A-CHILD (TDD)
Provides multilingual crisis intervention and professional counseling on child abuse and domestic violence issues. Gives referrals to local agencies offering counseling and other services related to child abuse, adult survivor issues, and domestic violence. Provides literature on child abuse in English and Spanish. Operates 24 hours.

A-28. Covenant House Nineline
(800)999-9999
Crisis line for youth, teens, and families. Locally based referrals throughout the United States. Help for youth and parents regarding drugs, abuse, homelessness, runaway children, and message relays. Operates 24 hours.

The Danny Foundation
(800)83-DANNY
Educates the public about crib dangers and attempts to eliminate unsafe cribs currently in use or in storage.

The Magic Foundation for Children's Growth
(800)3-MAGIC-3
Assists the families of children whose physical growth is affected by a medical problem and creates public education in the area of children's growth. Provides a variety of informational, educational and support services to professionals and consumers.

A–31. National Center for Missing and Exploited Children
(800)843–5678
(703)235–3900
(800)826–7653 (TDD)
(703)235–4067 (Fax)
Operates a hotline for reporting missing children and sightings of missing children. Offers assistance and training to law enforcement agents. Takes reports of sexually exploited children. Serves as the National Child Porn TipLine. Provides books and other publications on prevention and issues related to missing and sexually exploited children. Ability to serve callers in over 140 languages. Operates 24 hours.

A–29. National Child Safety Council Childwatch
(800)222–1464
Answers questions and distributes literature on safety, including drug abuse, household dangers, and electricity. Provides safety information to local police departments. Sponsor of the missing kids milk carton program. Operates 24 hours.

A–30. National Clearinghouse on Child Abuse and Neglect Information
(800)394–3366
(703)385–7565
(703)385–3206 (Fax)
nccanch@clark.net (E–mail)
Serves as a national resource for the acquisition and dissemination of child abuse and neglect materials and distributes a free publications catalog upon request. Maintains bibliographic databases of documents, audiovisuals, and national organizations. Services include searches of databases and annotated bibliographies on frequently requested topics. CD–ROM containing Clearinghouse databases is available free to qualified institutions. 8:30 a.m.–5 p.m. (See also B–11, B–12)

National Lekotek Center
(800)366–PLAY
(800)573–4446 (Voice and TTY)
Leads the way for accessible play for children with disabilities. Maintains a nationwide network of play–centered programs including play sessions, toy lending libraries and assistive technology classes.

National Program for Playground Safety
(800)554–PLAY
Sponsored by the University of Northern Iowa, under a grant from the Centers for Disease Control and Prevention. Established to address the growing concerns for playground safety in this country. Through its efforts, parents, educators and administrators responsible for playground construction and maintenance, will have access to the latest information on playground safety and injury prevention.

Public Information and Communications Branch, National Institute of Child Health and Human Development
(800)505–CRIB (SIDS Information Line)
A component of the National Institute of Child Health and Human Development, National Institutes of Health, Department of Health and Human Services. Provides information on sudden infant death syndrome.

A–33. National Runaway Switchboard
(800)621–4000
(800)621–0394 (TDD)
(312)929–5150 (Fax)
Provides crisis intervention and travel assistance information to runaways. Gives referrals to shelters nationwide. Also relays messages to, or sets up conference calls with, parents at the request of the child. Has access to AT&T Language Line. Operates 24 hours.

A–34. National Youth Crisis Hotline
(800)448–4663
Provides counseling and referrals to local drug treatment centers, shelters, and counseling services. Responds to youth dealing with pregnancy, molestation, suicide, and child abuse. Operates 24 hours.

Pediatric Projects, Inc.
(800)947–0947
Advocates for quality mental health care for chronically ill, disabled or hospitalized children and their families. Focuses on supporting parents and promoting better understanding of procedures, and helping children cope with stressful medical or surgical events.

Safe Sitter
(800)255–4089
Medically oriented instructional program for teenagers aged 11–13. The goal of the program is to reduce the number of preventable and accidental deaths among children under the care of baby–sitters. There is a $10 to $40 fee for the program. Scholarships are available for those unable to pay.

Starlight Foundation International
(800)274–7827
Enhances the lives of over 42,000 seriously ill children each month through wish–granting, entertainment and recreational activities for pediatric projects.

CHILD DEVELOPMENT

Association for the Care of Children's Health
(800)808–2224
Committed to improving the quality of care for children and their families through education, dissemination of resources, research and advocacy.

Association of Birth Defect Children
(800)313–ABCD
Sponsors the National Birth Defects Registry hotline that contains demographic data and medical histories from member families in the United States and Canada, and matches families of children with similar disabilities.

Autism Society of America
(800)3AUTISM
(301)657–0869 (Fax)
Educates parents, professionals, and the public regarding autism; improves the welfare of people with autism; supports research regarding autism; and oversees over 200 local chapters nationwide.

National Organization on Fetal Alcohol Syndrome
(800)66–NOFAS
Raises public awareness about fetal alcohol syndrome, the leading known cause of mental retardation.

Zero to Three: National Center for Infants, Toddlers and Families
(800)899–4301
Advances the healthy development of America's babies and young children. Works to strengthen the roles of professionals, policymakers and parents in the first 3 years of life, because this is the time of greatest human development. This toll–free number is for ordering publications.

CHILD EDUCATION

A–37. National Association for the Education of Young Children
(800)424–2460
(202)232–8777
(202)328–1846 (Fax)
The National Association for the Education of Young Children is neither a helpline nor hotline. The association publishes books, posters, and brochures for teachers and parents of young children, birth through age 8. Sponsors conferences and public awareness activities concerning quality programs for the education of young children. 9 a.m.–5 p.m.

CLEFT PALATE

See RARE DISORDERS

CYSTIC FIBROSIS

See RARE DISORDERS

DIABETES/DIGESTIVE DISEASES

American Association of Diabetes Educators
(800)TEAM–UP 4
Individuals with diabetes can call this number to obtain a referral to a diabetes educator in their area.

A–38. American Diabetes Association
(800)232–3472
(703)549–1500
(703)549–6995 (Fax, Customer Service)
(800)ADA ORDER (Fax, Order Fulfillment)
Offers patient assistance in many areas, including general information about diabetes, nutrition, exercise, treatment, and referrals to diabetes medical professionals. For people with diabetes facing discrimination, the association offers referrals from a nationwide attorney's network and information on how to influence public leaders. The association also conducts a variety of patient activities, including educational seminars and workshops, culturally diverse programs, support groups, and youth programs. Spanish–speaking operators available. 8:30 a.m.–5 p.m. (See also B–16)

A–39. Crohn's and Colitis Foundation of America, Inc.
(800)932–2423
(800)343–3637 (Warehouse)
Provides educational materials on Crohn's disease and ulcerative colitis. Refers to local support groups and physicians. 9 a.m.–5 p.m. Recording after hours. Warehouse is open 8 a.m.–5 p.m.

A–40. Juvenile Diabetes Foundation International Hotline
(800)223–1138
(212)785–9500
Answers questions and provides brochures on diabetes. Refers to local chapters, physicians, and clinics. Chapters located worldwide. 9 a.m.–5 p.m.

DISABLING CONDITIONS

See also HEARING AND SPEECH

The Access Group
(800)821–8580
Serves children with disabilities born to Vietnam veterans and youth and adults who have any disability. Provides information on technology that can help people perform daily tasks more independently.

Americans with Disabilities Act Hotline
(800)514–0301
(800)514–0383 (TTY)
(202)514–6193 (Electronic Bulletin Board)
Sponsored by the U.S. Department of Justice. Provides a 24–hour recording of information on the Americans with Disabilities Act. The recording also allows callers to request publications. ADA Specialists available 10 a.m. 6 p.m. on Monday, Tuesday, Wednesday, and Friday and 1 p.m. 6 p.m. on Thursday.

ADA Technical Assistance Hotline
(800)466–4232
Maintained by the Disability Rights Education and Defense Fund, Inc. Provides technical assistance on protecting and advancing the civil rights of people with disabilities.

Children's Craniofacial Association
(800)535–3643
Addresses the medical, financial, psychosocial, emotional and educational concerns relating to craniofacial conditions. Services include information, support, physician referral, free patient clinics, public awareness and a family retreat.

Faces: The National Craniofacial Association
(800)332–2373
Assists individuals with facial disfigurements and their families by maintaining a registry of centers offering corrective surgery and providing financial assistance to qualified applicants.

Families of Spinal Muscular Atrophy
(800)886–1762
Founded to support families of those suffering from spinal muscular atrophy, a group of neuromuscular diseases that affects all age groups. Promotes research into treatments for the disease.

Family Resource Center on Disabilities
(800)952–4199
Provides assistance to parents of children with disabilities in order to ensure that these children have access to the full range of services and benefits available to them. Conducts training sessions and workshops and publishes a variety of fact sheets.

A–43. Job Accommodation Network
(800)ADA–Work (Voice/TDD)
(800)526–7234 (Voice/TDD)
(800)526–2262 (in Canada)
(800)DIAL–JAN (Electronic Bulletin Board)
(304)293–5407 (Fax)
Sponsored by the President's Commission on the Employment of People with Disabilities. Offers ideas for accommodating disabled persons in the workplace and information on the availability of accommodation aids and procedures. Services available in English, Spanish, and French. 8 a.m.–8 p.m., Monday–Thursday; 8 a.m.–5 p.m., Friday.

A–44. Medical Rehabilitation Education Foundation
(800)438–7342
Provides medical rehabilitation information and a referral service for help in locating rehabilitation facilities throughout the country. 8 a.m.–5 p.m.

A–47. National Easter Seal Society
(800)221–6827
(312)726–6200
(312)726–1494 (Fax)
(312)726–4258 (TDD)
Through its 160 affiliates nationwide, provides rehabilitative and other support services to assist children and adults with disabilities to achieve their maximum independence. 8:30 a.m.–5 p.m. (Central).

A–48. National Information Center for Children and Youth with Disabilities
(800)695–0285 (Voice/TT)
(202)884–8200 (Voice/TT)
(202)884–8441 (Fax)
nichcy@capcon.net (Internet)
Sponsored by the U.S. Department of Education. Information and referral service dedicated to disabled children. 9 a.m.–5 p.m. or leave recorded message after hours.

A–51. National Rehabilitation Information Center (NARIC)
(800)346–2742 (Voice/TDD)
(301)588–9284 (Voice/TDD)
(301)587–1967 (Fax)
Sponsored by the National Institute on Disability and Rehabilitation Research. Collects and disseminates the results of federally funded research projects. The collection includes commercially published books, journal articles, and audiovisuals. Spanish–speaking operators available. 8 a.m.–6 p.m. (See also B–49)

Scoliosis Association
(800)800–0669
(407)994–4435 (Fax)
Provides information on scoliosis and related spinal deformities. [new entry 8/16 SM]

DOWN SYNDROME

See RARE DISORDERS

DRINKING WATER SAFETY

A–52. Safe Drinking Water Hotline
(800)426–4791
(202)260–8072 (Fax)
sdwa@epamail.epa.gov (E–mail)
Sponsored by the U.S. Environmental Protection Agency. Provides general and technical information on the Federal drinking water program and referrals to other organizations when appropriate. Does not provide site–specific information on local water quality, bottled water, or home water treatment units. Has the ability to communicate in English, Spanish, French, Lebanese, and Persian. 9 a.m.–5:30 p.m., weekdays, except Federal holidays.

Water Quality Association
(800)749–0234 (Consumer Information)
Facilitates the exchange of information, offers training programs, develops voluntary product standards, conducts research, publishes water treatment information and provides this toll–free consumer information line on water quality issues.

DRUG ABUSE

See also ALCOHOL ABUSE and SUBSTANCE ABUSE

A–53. CSAP Workplace Helpline
(800)843–4971
Sponsored by the Center for Substance Abuse Prevention, Substance Abuse and Mental Health Services Administration. Offers information, publications, and referrals to corporations, businesses, industry, and national organizations on assessing drug abuse within an organization and developing and implementing drug abuse policy and programs. 9 a.m.–8 p.m.

A–54. Housing and Urban Development Drug Information and Strategy Clearinghouse
(800)578–3472
Promotes strategies for eradicating drugs and drug trafficking from public housing. Provides housing officials, residents, and community leaders a source for information and assistance on drug abuse prevention and trafficking control techniques. Maintains a database system consisting of national and community program descriptions, publications, research, and news articles. Provides resource lists. 8 a.m.–5 p.m. (See also B–21)

A–55. "Just Say No" International
(800)258–2766
(510)451–6666
Thirteen thousand clubs. Founded in 1985. Provides materials, technical assistance, and training to help children and teenagers lead healthy, productive, drug–free lives. The New Youth Power program builds on young people's resiliency, drawing on and encouraging the skills and attributes that allow young people to cope with challenges and adversity. Youth Power empowers youth to discover and hone their assets to succeed in all areas of their lives. 7 a.m.–5 p.m. (Pacific).

National Parents Resource Institute For Drug Education
(800)279–6361
(800)677–7433 (Taped Drug Information)
Serves parents, educators and others interested in adolescent drug abuse. Provides a broad range of materials on drug–related health issues, technical assistance to those who wish to begin parent and youth groups and referrals to local centers nationwide.

National Substance Abuse Helplines
(800)DRUG HELP
(800)COCAINE
(212)496–6035 (Fax)
Sponsored by the Phoenix House Foundation. Answers questions on cocaine, alcohol, and other drugs from users, their friends, and families. Provides referrals to drug rehabilitation centers. Operates 24 hours.

DWARFISM

Human Growth Foundation
(800)451–6434
(703)883–1773
Provides parent education and mutual support, funds research, and promotes public awareness of the physical and emotional problems of short–statured people. Offers brochures on child growth abnormalities. 8:30 a.m.–5 p.m.

Little People of America
(800)243–9273
Provides information on dwarfism, local support groups, and membership. Literature, physician and medical referrals are also provided.

DYSLEXIA

See LEARNING DISORDERS

ENDOMETRIOSIS

See WOMEN

ENVIRONMENT

Environmental Health Clearinghouse, NIEHS
(800)643–4794
Sponsored by the National Institute of Environmental Health Sciences, the clearinghouse is operated from 9:00 a.m. until 8:00 p.m., EST, and offers free information on the environmental health effects of lead, radon, ozone, electromagnetic fields, and hazardous waste sites. Environmental justice issues and multiple chemical sensitivities are also addressed. Database searches and referrals are offered when appropriate.

A–58. Indoor Air Quality Information Clearinghouse
(800)438–4318
Provides information on indoor air quality, including the health effects of passive smoke, formaldehyde, and various indoor air pollutants. 9 a.m.–5 p.m. (See also B–23, B–35)

U.S. Environmental Protection Agency
(800)962–6215
Information is provided on the agency, its programs and activities, and when appropriate, refers inquirers to proper technical or regional offices. Materials are available on all major environmental topics. Hours of operation are 10:00 a.m. to 4:00 p.m., Monday through Friday, excluding Federal holidays.

EPILEPSY

See RARE DISORDERS

ETHICS

A–59. Joseph and Rose Kennedy Institute of Ethics National Reference Center for Bioethics Literature Georgetown University
(800)633–3849
(202)687–3885
(202)687–6770 (Fax)
medeth@guvm.ccf.georgetown.edu (E–mail)
Provides reference assistance and conducts free searches on bioethical topics. Produces a variety of publications, as well as the BIOETHICSLINE database on the MEDLARS information system. 9 a.m.–5 p.m., Monday, Wednesday, Thursday, Friday; 9 a.m.–9 p.m., Tuesday; 10 a.m.–3 p.m., Saturday, except summers and holidays.

FIRE PREVENTION

A–60. National Fire Protection Association
(800)344–3555 (Customer Service)
(617)770–3000
(617)984–7880 (TDD)
(617)770–0200 (Fax)
Develops fire protection codes and standards, fire safety education materials, and provides technical information on fire prevention, firefighting procedures, and the fire loss experience. 8:30 a.m.–5 p.m.

FITNESS

A–61. Aerobics and Fitness Foundation of America
(800)446–2322 (For Professionals)
(800)YOUR–BODY (Consumer Hotline)
Answers questions regarding safe and effective exercise programs and practices. Written health and fitness guidelines also available (shipping and handling charges may apply). 7:30 a.m.–5:30 p.m. (Pacific).

American Running and Fitness Association
(800)776–2732
Provides information and support programs for people interested in exercise and promotes running and other aerobic sports as a practical way of achieving physical fitness.

Consumer Fitness Hotline
(800)529–8227
Sponsored by the American Council on Exercise. Provides information on health and fitness, including information on how to start an exercise program. Answers specific questions concerning a variety of fitness topics. 8 a.m. 5 p.m. (Pacific)

The Weight Control Information Network, NIDDK
(800)WIN–8098
Established by the National Institutes of Health's National Institute of Diabetes and Digestive and Kidney Diseases. A national source of information on weight control, obesity and weight–related nutritional disorders for health professionals and the public. Produces and disseminates educational materials and will provide literature searches on request.

Tops Club, Inc.
(800)932–8677
Focuses on weight reduction through sensible dieting, regular exercise and group support. This toll–free number is a chapter locator.

A–62. YMCA of the USA
(800)872–9622
(312)977–9063 (Fax)
Provides information about YMCA services and locations of Ys in residential areas. 8 a.m.–5 p.m. (Central).

Section C

FOOD SAFETY

A–63. Food Labeling Hotline Meat and Poultry Hotline
(800)535–4555
Sponsored by the U.S. Department of Agriculture. Provides information on safe handling, preparation, and storage of meat, poultry, and eggs. Also provides tips on buying a turkey, holiday food safety, and understanding labels on meat and poultry. 10 a.m.–4 p.m. (See also B–26)

A–64. Seafood Hotline
(800)FDA–4010
(202)205–4314
http://vm.cfsan.fda.gov/list.html (WWW)
Sponsored by the Food and Drug Administration. Provides information on seafood buying, handling, and storage for home consumption. Also provides seafood publications and prerecorded seafood safety messages. Information available on food safety, chemicals and contaminants, food and color additives, biotechnology, food labeling, nutrition, health and disease, and women's health. Messages and publications available in Spanish. Staff are available for assistance 12 p.m.–4 p.m. (Eastern). Automated Hotline operates 24 hours.

FOOT HEALTH

American Podiatric Medical Association, Inc.
(800)FOOTCARE
(301)571–9200
(301)530–2752 (Fax)
Provides a variety of patient education literature on topics including specific foot problems and diseases, sports and fitness activities, and systemic disease manifestations in the foot and ankle. Operates 24 hours.

GAMBLING ADDICTION

NATIONAL COUNCIL ON PROBLEM GAMBLING
(800)522–4700
Disseminates information on compulsive gambling as an illness and a public health problem. Strives to stimulate the concern of the medical profession, educators, legislators and the criminal justice system to provide community services and medical treatment for compulsive gamblers and their families.

GENERAL HEALTH

A–65. Agency for Health Care Policy and Research Clearinghouse
(800)358–9295
(301)495–3453
Distributes lay and scientific publications produced by the agency, including clinical practice guidelines on a variety of topics, reports from the National Medical Expenditure Survey, and health care technology assessment reports. 9 a.m.–5 p.m. (See also B–28)

Air Lifeline
(800)446–1231
Uses volunteer pilots to provide assistance to patients getting to and from medical appointments. Patients must be able to walk on their own and be in financial need.

American Chiropractic Association
(800)986–4636
Encourages and supports standards of education, ethics and professional competency for the practice of chiropractic. Disseminates information on chiropractic to the media, government, industries, labor and insurance companies.

American Osteopathic Association
(800)621–1773
Provides materials on osteopathic medicine and patient education materials. Directories of osteopathic physicians and specialists are also available.

Family Caregiver Alliance
(800)445–8106
Provides information, education and assistance in long–term care planning for adults with cognitive impairments such as Alzheimer's disease, stroke, Parkinson's disease, Huntington's disease, amyotrophic lateral sclerosis and brain injury. Information may be accessed by calling or by contacting the group's website.

A–66. MedicAlert Foundation
(800)432–5378
(800)344–3226
(209)669–2495 (Fax)
Provides emergency service for people who cannot speak for themselves by means of a unique member number on a Medic–Alert bracelet or necklace. Operates 24 hours.

Mercy Medical Airlift
(800)296–1191
Acts on the local, State and national level. Its purpose, as a charitable air medical transportation program, is to ensure that no one is denied access to medical treatment, rehabilitation or recovery. Populations served typically include the medically indigent requiring air travel to distant cities for medical treatment.

National Health Service Corps
(800)221–9393 (Recruitment/Loans)
(800)638–0824 (Medical Scholarship Programs)
Sponsored by the Bureau of Primary Health Care. Health professionals with service obligations under the NHSC Scholarship Program and NHSC Loan Repayment Program and volunteers are sent to communities with health professional shortages.

A–67. National Health Information Center
(800)336–4797
(301)565–4167
(301)984–4256 (Fax)
nhicinfo@health.org (E–Mail)
http://nhic–nt.health.org (World Wide Web)
Helps the public and health professionals locate health information through identification of health information resources, an information and referral system, and publications. Uses a database containing descriptions of health–related organizations to refer inquirers to the most appropriate resources. Does not diagnose medical conditions or give medical advice. Prepares and distributes publications and directories on health promotion and disease prevention topics.

Office for Civil Rights
(800)368–1019
(800)527–7697 (TDD)
Through prevention and elimination of unlawful discrimination, helps the Department of Health and Human Services carry out its overall mission of improving the health and well–being of all people affected by its many programs.

GRIEF

A–68. Grief Recovery Helpline
(800)445–4808
Provides educational services on recovering from loss. 9 a.m.–5 p.m., Monday– Friday (Pacific).

HEADACHE/HEAD INJURY

American Council for Headache Education
(800)255–ACHE
Helps headache sufferers find effective treatment while educating non–sufferers about this illness.

A–70. Brain Injury Association, Inc.
(800)444–6443 (Family Helpline)
(202)296–6443 (Business office)
(202)296–8850 (Fax)
Formerly the National Head Injury Foundation. Dedicated to improving the quality of life of people with brain injuries and promoting prevention of brain injury. Provides information and resources for people with brain injury, their families, and professionals. Offers educational materials on the impact of brain injury, location of rehabilitative facilities, and availability of community services. 9 a.m.–5 p.m. (Eastern).

A–69. National Headache Foundation
(800)843–2256
(312)907–6278 (Fax)
Disseminates free information on headache causes and treatments, funds research, and sponsors public and professional education programs nationwide. Offers audio and videotapes, brochures, and other helpful materials for purchase. Organized a nationwide network of local support groups. 9 a.m.–5 p.m. (Central) Monday–Friday.

HEARING AND SPEECH

American Society for Deaf Children
(800)942–2732
Provides information about deafness to parents and the general public and refers parents to local contacts when appropriate.

A–71. American Speech–Language–Hearing Association
(800)638–8255
(301)897–5700
Offers information on speech, language, and hearing disabilities. Also provides referrals to speech language pathologists and audiologists certified by the American Speech–Language–Hearing Association. 8:30 a.m.–5 p.m.

DB–Link
(800)438–9376
Identifies, coordinates and disseminates information on children and youth who are deaf–blind. It is a collaborative effort of the American Association of the Deaf–Blind, Helen Keller National Center, and the Perkins School for the Blind and Teaching Research.

A–72. Deafness Research Foundation
(800)535–3323
(212)684–6556 (Voice/TDD)
(212)779–2125 (Fax)
Funds research into causes, treatment, and prevention of hearing loss and other ear disorders. Also offers resource and referral information on ear–related problems. 9 a.m.–5 p.m. (Eastern).

A–73. Dial A Hearing Screening Test
(800)222–3277 (Voice/TDD)
(610)543–2802 (Fax)
Sponsored by Occupational Hearing Services. Answers questions on hearing problems and makes referrals to local numbers for a 2–minute telephone hearing screening test, as well as for ear, nose, and throat specialists. Also makes referrals to organizations that have information on ear–related problems, including broken earing aids. 9 a.m.–5 p.m. (Eastern).

A–74. The Ear Foundation at Baptist Hospital
(800)545–4327
(615)329–7849
(615)329–7935 (Fax)
Committed to integration of hearing and balance impaired people into the mainstream of society through public awareness and medical education. Includes the Meniere's Network and Young EAR's Program. Provides brochure about Meniere's disease and other literature, including newsletters. 8:30 a.m.–4:30 p.m. (Central) or leave recorded message after hours.

A–75. Hear Now
(800)648–4327 (Voice/TDD)
(303)695–7797 (Voice/TDD)
(303)695–7789 (Fax)
Provides hearing aids and cochlear implants for deaf and hard of hearing individuals with limited financial resources. Collects used hearing aids. Applications for assistance available. 8 a.m.–4 p.m. (Mountain).

A–78. International Hearing Society
(800)521–5247
(810)478–4520 (Fax)
Provides general information on hearing aids and a listing of local hearing aid specialists. 9 a.m.–5 p.m.

A–77. John Tracy Clinic
(800)522–4582 (Voice/TTY)
(213)749–1651 (Fax)
Provides free diagnostic, habilitative, and educational services to preschool deaf children and their families through onsite services and to the preschool deaf and deaf–blind children through worldwide correspondence courses in Spanish and English. 8 a.m.–4 p.m. (Pacific). Leave recorded message after hours.

National Family Association for Deaf–Blind
(800)255–0411, ext. 275
Provides information and resources; facilitates family organizations in each state; and develops family/professional partnerships to benefit people with deaf–blindness.

A–79. National Institute on Deafness and Other Communication Disorders Information Clearinghouse
(800)241–1044
(800)241–1055 (TT)
Collects and disseminates information on hearing, balance, smell, taste, voice, speech, and language for health professionals, patients, people in industry, and the public. Maintains a database of references to brochures, books, articles, fact sheets, organizations, and educational materials, which is a subfile on the Combined Health Information Database (CHID). Develops publications. 8:30 a.m.–5 p.m.

Lead Line
(800)352–8888 (Voice/TDD in the U.S.)
(800)287–4763 (California)
(818)972–2090 (Fax)
tripodla@aol (E–Mail)
Offers information on deafness, including raising and educating a deaf child. Refers callers to parents, professionals, and other resources in their own communities nationwide. 8 a.m.–5 p.m. (Pacific) or leave recorded message after hours.

Vestibular Disorders Association
(800)837–8428
Provides a support network for people coping with dizziness and balance disorders and provides publications.

HEART DISEASE

A–81. American Heart Association
(800)242–8721
Provides English and Spanish publications and information about heart and blood vessel diseases, exercise, nutrition, and smoking cessation. Additional information is available for minority and senior citizen audiences. Callers are routed to local AHA offices for additional local information. 9 a.m.–5 p.m.

The Coronary Club, Inc.
(800)478–4255
Provides patients and their families with information on preventing heart attacks. Subscribers receive reports on coronary care and treatment, diet and exercise, stress management, surgery and medications.

Heart Information Service
(800)292–2221
A program of the Texas Heart Institute. Designed to answer questions from the public on diagnosis, treatment and prevention of cardiovascular disease.

National Heart, Lung, and Blood Institute's High Blood Pressure Program
(800)575–WELL
Provides a 24–hour recording of information on high blood pressure and high blood cholesterol in English and Spanish.

HISTIOCYTOSIS

See RARE DISORDERS

HOMELESSNESS

A–82. National Resource Center on Homelessness and Mental Illness
(800)444–7415
Sponsored by the Center for Mental Health Services, Substance Abuse and Mental Health Services Administration. Provides technical assistance and information about services and housing for the homeless and mentally ill population. 8 a.m.–5 p.m.

HORMONAL DISORDERS

Thyroid Foundation of America, Inc.
(800)832–8321
Provides health education and support for thyroid patients and health professionals. Responds to inquiries on all aspects of thyroid dysfunction. Provides information on genetically related autoimmune diseases including vitiligo, diabetes mellitus, and pernicious anemia.

The Thyroid Society for Education and Research
(800)THYROID
Provides health education for thyroid patients and health professionals. Pursues prevention, treatment and cure of thyroid disease.

HOSPITAL/HOSPICE CARE

A–83. Children's Hospice International
(800)242–4453
(703)684–0330
Provides support system and information for health care professionals, families, and the network of organizations that offer hospice care to terminally ill children. Distributes educational materials. 9:30 a.m.–5:30 p.m. [rev 8/14 SM]

A–84. Hill–Burton Hospital Free Care
(800)638–0742
(800)492–0359 (in MD)
Sponsored by the Bureau of Health Resources Development, Health Resources and Services Administration. Provides information on hospitals and other health facilities participating in the Hill–Burton Hospital Free Care Program. 9:30 a.m.–5:30 p.m. or leave recorded message after hours.

A–85. Hospice Education Institute "Hospice Link"
(800)331–1620
(860)767–2746 (Fax)
Offers information and advice about hospice and palliative care, makes referrals to local hospice and palliative care programs nationwide, and offers information and advice on grief support programs. Maintains a current database of hospices and palliative care units, publishes books and pamphlets, offers continuing education. No medical advice or psychological counseling offered, but "sympathetic listening" is available to patients and families coping with advanced illness and loss. 9 a.m.–4 p.m.

National Association of Hospitality Houses, Inc.
(800)542–9730
Assists in the creation and development of places to stay for families when medical referral is made away from home communities and to give information about such places when needed.

National Hospice Organization
(800)658–8898
Advocates for the rights of the terminally ill. Provides informational and educational materials to members and information and referrals to the public.

A–86. Shriners Hospital Referral Line
(800)237–5055
Gives information on free hospital care available to children under 18 who need orthopedic care or burn treatment. Sends application forms to requesters who meet eligibility requirements for treatment provided by 22 Shriners Hospitals in the United States, Mexico, and Canada. 8 a.m.–5 p.m.

HOUSING

See also CHEMICAL PRODUCTS/PESTICIDES, LEAD

A–87. Housing and Urban Development User
(800)245–2691
Disseminates publications for U.S. Department of Housing and Urban Development's Office of Policy Development and Research. Offers database searches on housing research. Provides reports on housing safety, housing for elderly and handicapped persons, and lead–based paint. 8:30 a.m.–5:15 p.m. (See also B–34)

HUNTINGTON'S DISEASE

See RARE DISORDERS

IMMUNIZATION

CDC Immunization Hotline
(800)232–SHOT
Provides information on childhood immunizations and specific vaccinations.

IMPOTENCE

A–88. Impotence Information Center
(800)843–4315
(800)543–9632
Provides free information to prospective patients regarding the causes of and treatments for impotence. Provides referrals to local physicians. 8:30 a.m.–5 p.m. (Central) or leave recorded message after hours.

INSURANCE/MEDICARE/MEDICAID

A–90. DHHS Inspector General's Hotline
(800)HHS–TIPS
Handles complaints regarding fraud, employee misconduct, and waste and abuse of U.S. Department of Health and Human Services' funds, including medicare, and medicaid. 9 a.m.–8 p.m.

A–91. Medicare Issues Hotline
(800)638–6833
(800)820–1202 (TDD/TTY)
Sponsored by the Health Care Financing Administration. Gives information on medicare/ medigap insurance and policies, answers general questions on medicare problems, and sends free medicare publications. Publications include: Your Medicare Handbook, The Guide to Health Insurance for People with Medicare, and publications related to Mammograms, HMOs, Low Income Beneficiaries, Hospice Benefits, and Nursing Homes. 8 a.m.–8 p.m.

Health Insurance Association of America Consumer Helpline
(800)942–4242
Provides general information and answers questions regarding life, health, and home and automobile insurance. Free consumer publications available. Spanish–speaking operators available. 8 a.m.–8 p.m.

Pension Benefit Guaranty Corporation
(800)400–PBGC
Protects the retirement incomes of more than 42 million American workers in defined benefit pension plans. It is financed through premiums collected from companies that sponsor insured pension plans, investment returns on PBGC assets and recoveries from employers responsible for underfunded, terminated plans.

Social Security Administration
(800)772–1213
Provides public information materials about the Social Security and supplemental security income (SSI) programs, as well as information on entitlement to Medicare. Free pamphlets on Social Security benefits, disability benefits, and supplemental security income are available.

JUSTICE

A–93. National Criminal Justice Reference Service (NCJRS)
(800)851–3420
(301)738–8895 (Electronic Bulletin Board)
Provides criminal justice research findings and documents from bureaus within the Office of Justice Programs, U.S. Department of Justice. The NCJRS library collection contains more than 130,000 documents and is accessible online. Clearinghouse resources and activities also can be accessed via the NCJRS electronic bulletin board. 8:30 a.m.–7 p.m. Leave recorded message after hours.

KIDNEY DISEASE

See UROLOGICAL DISORDERS

LEAD

See also HOUSING

A–94. National Lead Information Hotline
(800)LEAD–FYI (Hotline)
(800)424–LEAD (Clearinghouse)
(800)526–5456 (TDD)
EHC@cais.com (E–mail)
cais.com (Internet gopher)
Hotline supplies a basic information packet to the public in English or Spanish on lead poisoning and prevention through a 24–hour automated response system. Clearinghouse provides technical information and answers in English or Spanish to specific lead–related questions for private citizens and professionals. 8:30 a.m.–5 p.m. (See also B–34)

LEARNING DISORDERS

See also HANDICAPPING CONDITIONS

Children and Adults with Attention Deficit Disorders (CH.A.D.D.)
(800)233–4050
Provides an information packet on attention deficit disorders and information on joining CH.A.D.D.

A–95. The Orton Dyslexia Society
(800)222–3123
(410)296–0232
Clearinghouse that provides information on testing; tutoring; and computers used to aid people with dyslexia and related disorders and general information. Operates 24 hours a day.

Section C

LIBRARY SERVICES

See also HANDICAPPING CONDITIONS

A–96. Modern Talking Picture Service, Inc. Captioned Films/Videos
(800)237–6213 (Voice/TDD)
(800)538–5636 (Fax)
Provides free loan of captioned films and videos for deaf and hearing impaired people. 9 a.m.–5 p.m.

A–99. National Library Service for the Blind and Physically Handicapped
(800)424–8567
(202)707–5100
(202)707–0744 (TDD)
(202)707–0712 (Fax)
A total of over 140 network libraries that work in cooperation with the Library of Congress to provide free library service to anyone who is unable to read standard print because of visual or physical impairment. Provides both audio and braille formats through a network of regional libraries. 8 a.m.–4:30 p.m.

A–100. Recording for the Blind and Dyslexic
(800)221–4792
Serves people who cannot read standard print because of a visual, perceptual or other physical disability. Service includes free lending library of academic textbooks on audio cassette and sale of books on computer diskette and specially adapted tape players and recorders. Provides information on becoming a registered borrower.

LIVER DISEASES

A–101. American Liver Foundation
(800)223–0179
(201)256–2550
Provides information, including fact sheets, and makes physician and support group referrals. Liver disease information brochures and information sheets available upon request. 9 a.m.–5 p.m.

Hepatitis Foundation International
(800)891–0707
(201)857–5044 (Fax)
Educates the public about the prevention, diagnosis and treatment of viral hepatitis. Disseminates a variety of materials on viral hepatitis.

LUNG DISEASE/ASTHMA/ALLERGY

American Lung Association
(800)586–4872
Provides information on such topics as air pollution, smoking, tuberculosis, lung hazards on the job, marijuana, asthma, emphysema, and other lung diseases. Some materials are available in Spanish.

A–102. Asthma and Allergy Foundation of America
(800) 7–ASTHMA (727–8462)
Provides a 24–hour recording for callers to request general information, publications and videotapes.

A–103. Asthma Information Line
(800)822–2762
(414)276–3349 (Fax)
Sponsored by the American Academy of Allergy, Asthma, and Immunology. Provides written materials on asthma and allergies and offers a printed listing of physician referrals. Operates 24 hours.

A–104. Lung Line National Jewish Center for Immuno–logy and Respiratory Medicine
(800)222–5864
(303)355–5864
(800)552–LUNG (LUNG FACTS)
(303)270–2150 (Fax)
http://www.njc.org (Internet)
Answers questions about asthma, emphysema, chronic bronchitis, allergies, juvenile rheumatoid arthritis, smoking, and other respiratory and immune system disorders. Questions answered by registered nurses. 8 a.m.–5 p.m. (Mountain). LUNG FACTS, a companion to LUNG LINE, is a 24–hour, 7–days–a–week automated information service. Using a touch–tone telephone, callers can choose among a selection of recorded topics on lung disease and immunological disorders.

THE FOOD ALLERGY NETWORK
(800)929–4040
Increases public awareness about food allergies and anaphylaxis, a life–threatening allergic reaction, and provides education and emotional support to individuals with food allergies.

ORAL HEALTH

American Dental Association
(800)947–4746
Distributes educational materials on dental health topics such as dentures, tooth decay, smoking, diet, oral care, and fluoridation.

MATERNAL AND INFANT HEALTH

Alliance of Genetic Support Groups
(800)336–4363
Provides support group referrals, genetic counseling, and other services for individuals with genetic disorders.

A–105. La Leche League International
800)LA–LECHE
(708)519–7730
(708)519–0035 (Fax)
Provides breastfeeding information and mother–to–mother support for women who wish to breastfeed. Distributes and sells a wide variety of materials on breastfeeding and parenting. Also organizes training for health professionals and provides a reliable source for current breastfeeding research information through the Center for Breastfeeding Information. Catalogue free of charge upon request. 9 a.m.–5 p.m. (Central).

National Fragile X Foundation
(800)688–8765
Dedicated to education and research concerning children and families with X–linked mental retardation.

National Life Center
(800)848–5683
Organized to provide assistance to woman and girls with unplanned pregnancies. Assistance includes anonymous pregnancy tests, education guidance, shelter homes, community resource information, maternity clothes, layettes, medical care, legal advice and referrals for professional counseling or adoption information.

Pregnancy/Environmental Hotline, The Genesis Fund/National Birth Defects Center
(800)322–5014
Provides information regarding exposure to environmental factors during pregnancy and the effects on the developing fetus.

Prenatal Care Hotline
(800)311–BABY (English)
(800)504–7081 (Spanish)
Sponsored by the Health Resources and Services Administration and its Maternal and Child Health Bureau. Links national 800 number hotlines, the State maternal and child health offices and Healthy Start projects, making local health resources and clinics easily available to callers needing prenatal care.

MEDICARE/MEDICAID

See INSURANCE/MEDICARE/MEDICAID

MENTAL HEALTH

See also CHILD ABUSE/MISSING CHILDREN/ MENTAL HEALTH

American Academy of Child and Adolescent Psychiatry
(800)333–7636
Distributes fact sheets on mental illnesses affecting youngsters.

Anxiety Disorders Information, NIMH
(888)8–ANXIETY
Sponsored by the National Institute of Mental Health, National Institutes of Health, Department of Health and Human Services. Provides information on anxiety disorders, depression and panic disorders.

A–106. Depression Awareness, Recognition, and Treatment (D/ART)
(800)421–4211
Sponsored by the National Institute of Mental Health. Provides a 24 hour recording for callers to request free brochures on clinical depression. Foreign language materials available upon request.

National Alliance for the Mentally Ill
(800)950–6264
Provides information on severe mental illness and its effects on families, support for the rights of patients and families, and help in starting local groups.

A–107. National Clearinghouse on Family Support and Children's Mental Health
(800)628–1696
(503)725–4040
(503)725–4165 (TTD)
(503)725–4180 (Fax)
Sponsored by the National Institute on Disability and Rehabilitation Research, U.S. Department of Education, and the Center for Mental Health Services, U.S. Department of Health and Human Services. Provides publications on parent/family support groups, financing, early intervention, various mental disorders, and other topics concerning children's mental health. Also offers a computerized databank and a State by State resource file. Recording operates 24 hours a day.

A–108. National Foundation for Depressive Illness
(800)248–4344
(212)268–4434 (Fax)
NAFDI@pipeline.com (E–mail)
A 24–hour recorded message describes symptoms of depression and manic depression and gives an address for more information and physician and support group referrals by State.

National Gaucher Foundation
(800)925–8885
Founded to help find a cure and viable treatment program for Gaucher's disease. Attempts to increase public awareness of this genetic lipid metabolism disorder and provides medical referrals to affected individuals and families.

National Institute for Mental Health Information Line
(800)64–PANIC
Sponsored by the National Institute of Mental Health. Provides educational materials on panic disorder symptoms, diagnosis, referral, and treatment to health care and mental health professionals and the public. Also disseminates lists of additional resource materials and organizations that can help callers locate a treatment professional. Spanish–speaking operators available. Operates 24 hours.

A–109. National Mental Health Association
(800)969–6642
(703)684–5968 (Fax)
Provides public education, direct services and advocacy for mental health and mental illness concerns in communities across the nation. Distributes information on various mental health topics and provides referrals to other organizations.

National Mental Health Services, Knowledge Exchange Network
(800)790–2647
Provides referrals to individuals requesting mental health services within their communities. 9 a.m. 5:30 p.m. (Pacific)

The Arc of the United States
(800)433–5255
Devoted to improving the welfare of people with mental retardation. Publishes a variety of informative and educational pamphlets, guides and brochures as well as a newspaper.

See HOMELESSNESS

MINORITY HEALTH

A–112. Office of Minority Health Resource Center
(800)444–6472
Responds to consumer and professional inquiries on minority health–related topics by distributing materials, providing referrals, and identifying sources of technical assistance. Spanish– and Asian–speaking operators available. 9 a.m.–5 p.m. (See also B–42)

NUTRITION

A–113. American Dietetic Association's Consumer Nutrition Hotline
(800)366–1655
Provides consumers with direct and immediate access to reliable food and nutrition information. Callers may listen to recorded nutrition messages in English or Spanish, 8 a.m.–8 p.m. (Central). Registered dietitians (RDs) answer food and nutrition questions and provide referrals to RDs in the caller's area 9 a.m.–4 p.m. (Central). TDD available. (See also B–27)

Section C

A–114. American Institute for Cancer Research
(800)843–8114
Provides free educational publications about diet, nutrition, and cancer prevention, as well as a Nutrition Hotline staffed by registered dietitians. 9 a.m.–5 p.m.

A–115. National Dairy Council
(800)426–8271
(800)974–6455 (Fax)
(708)803–2077 (Fax)
Develops and provides educational materials on nutrition. 8:30 a.m.–4:30 p.m. (Central).

ORGAN DONATION

See also VISION and UROLOGICAL DISORDERS

Barbara Anne Deboer Foundation
(800)895–8478
Assists those in need of organ transplants and other life–saving procedures, particularly those procedures not covered by insurance. Provides outreach, support and advocacy services and answers inquiries from patients and professionals.

A–116. The Living Bank
(800)528–2971
(713)961–0979 (Fax)
The Living Bank is a nonprofit organization established in 1969 to promote organ, tissue, and body donations through public education and registration of donors. Assistance is available in English and Spanish. Operates 24 hours.

A–117. National Marrow Donor Program

(800)MARROW–2

See CANCER

A–118. United Network for Organ Sharing
(800)243–6667
(804)330–8507 (Fax)
http://www.infi.net/shreorg/unos.html (World–Wide Web)
Offers information and referrals for organ donation and transplantation. Answers requests for organ donor cards. Operates 24 hours.

PARALYSIS AND SPINAL CORD INJURY

See also HANDICAPPING CONDITIONS, STROKE

A–119. American Paralysis Association
(800)225–0292
(201)912–9433 (Fax)
Raises money to fund world–wide research to find a cure for paralysis caused by spinal injuries and other central nervous system disorders. Provide information about spinal cord research. 9 a.m.–5 p.m.

A–120. National Rehabilitation Information Center
(800)346–2742 (Voice/TDD)
(301)588–9284 (Voice/TDD)
(301)587–1967 (Fax)
Provides research referrals and information on rehabilitation issues and concerns. Spanish–speaking interpreters available upon request. 8 a.m.–6 p.m.

A–121. National Spinal Cord Injury Association
(800)962–9629 (Members and individuals with spinal cord injuries; no vendors)
(617)441–8500 (Nonmembers, public, professionals)
Provides peer counseling to those with spinal cord injuries through local chapters and organizations. Provides information and referral service. 9 a.m.–5 p.m.

A–122. National Spinal Cord Injury Hotline
(800)526–3456
(410)366–2325 (Fax)
Financially supported by the Paralyzed Veterans of America. Offers information on spinal cord injuries and peer support to those with spinal cord injuries and their families. 24–hour answering service will page for emergency. 9 a.m.–5 p.m.

A–123. National Stroke Association
(800)STROKES
(303)771–1700
(303)771–1887 (TDD)
Provides both written and referral information to individuals, including stroke survivors, families, and health care providers on prevention, treatment, and rehabilitation. 8 a.m.–4:30 p.m., Monday–Thursday; 8 a.m.–4 p.m., Friday (Mountain).

Paralyzed Veterans of America
(800)424–8200
(800)795–4327 (TDD)
An organization for veterans of the armed forces who have experienced spinal cord injury or dysfunction. Advocates for quality health care and civil rights and opportunities for its members. Conducts research and disseminates information addressing spinal cord injury and dysfunction.

PARKINSON'S DISEASE

A–124. American Parkinson's Disease Association
(800)223–2732
(718)981–4399 (Fax)
Operates 51 information and referral centers throughout the United States. Raises funds for Parkinson's disease research and education. Provides information and referrals to patients and families. Multilingual educational literature available. 9 a.m.–5 p.m. (Eastern). Leave recorded message after hours.

A–125. National Parkinson Foundation, Inc.
(800)327–4545
(800)433–7022 (in FL)
(305)548–4403 (Fax)
A worldwide research, clinical, and therapeutic organization. Also provides physician references, support group systems, and educational materials in both English and Spanish. Professional staff answer questions about the disease from 9 a.m.–5 p.m., Monday–Friday; recorded messages at all other times.

Parkinson's Disease Foundation
(800)457–6676
Dedicated to research into the cause, prevention, treatment and cure of Parkinson's disease and related conditions, and serves as a source of information to patients and physicians in all aspects of Parkinson's disease.

PESTICIDES

See CHEMICAL PRODUCTS/PESTICIDES

PRACTITIONER REPORTING

A–128. USP Practitioners Reporting Network
(800)4–USP–PRN (487–7776)
(800)23–ERROR (Medication error)
Offers a service for health professionals to report problems with drugs, medical devices, radiopharmaceuticals, animal drugs, and actual or potential medication errors. Recording operates 24 hours a day; staff available 9 a.m.–4:30 p.m., Monday–Friday. Medication error telephone number records information 24 hours a day.

PREGNANCY/MISCARRIAGE

A–129. American Academy of Husband–Coached Childbirth
(800)4–ABIRTH
Provides free listing of teachers of the Bradley Method, including package of information and referral for local classes in natural childbirth. Books and videotapes may be ordered also. 9 a.m. 5 p.m. (Pacific). Leave recorded message after hours.

A–130. ASPO/Lamaze (American Society for Psychoprophylaxis in Obstetrics)
(800)368–4404
(202)857–1128
(202)223–4579 (Fax)
MThompso@SBA.Com (E–mail)
Operates a toll–free telephone service to provide consumers with information about prepared childbirth and how to locate a local ASPO–Certified Childbirth Educator. 9 a.m.–5 p.m. (Eastern).

DES Action USA
(800)DES–9288
Provides information on the consequences of the use of diethylstilbestrol (DES) for women who have taken it and the children born to them. Publishes educational material, provides a list of gynecologists familiar with the potential medical complications of DES use and has 32 local chapters to provide education, information and support.

A–131. International Childbirth Education Association
(800)624–4934 (Book Center orders)
(612)854–8660 (General information)
Provides referrals to local chapters and support groups, membership information, certification, and mail–order service. 7 a.m.–4:30 p.m. (Central).

A–132. Liberty Godparent Home
800)542–4453
Provides a residential program for unwed mothers. Provides counseling referrals to local and national organizations and distributes brochures on request. An adoption agency is also on site. Operates 24 hours. [rev. 7/25/95 SR unsure re. wording for adoption agency]

National Abortion Federation
(800)772–9100
Offers information on abortion issues and provides referral services.

RADIATION

National Association of Radiation Survivors
(800)798–5102
Promotes education of the public on the long–term health effects of radioactive substances and responds to inquiries regarding radiogenic illnesses and birth defects.

RADON

A–133. Radon Hotline
(800)SOS–RADON
(800)526–5456 (TDD)
Operated by the National Safety Council. Provides a 24–hour recording for callers to request a brochure on reducing radon risks in the home and a listing of local contacts. (See also B–23, B–34)

RARE DISORDERS*

*A rare disorder is defined as a disorder that affects less than 1 percent of the population at any given time.

American Behcet's Disease Association
(800)723–4238
Gathers and disseminates information about Behcet's Disease, an inflammatory and ulcerative condition, to the public and health professionals.

American Cleft Palate–Cranio–Facial Association/ Cleft Palate Foundation
(800)242–5338
(412)481–1376
(412)481–0847 (Fax)
Provides information and referral to individuals and families affected by cleft lip, cleft palate, or other craniofacial birth defects. Referrals are made to local cleft palate/craniofacial teams for treatment and to parent/patient support groups. Free information on various aspects of clefting is available; some available in Spanish. CLEFTLINE operates 24 hours. Spanish–speaking operators available 8:30 a.m.–4:30 p.m., Monday–Friday.

A–134. American Leprosy Missions (Hansen's Disease)
(800)543–3131
(803)271–7040
(803)271–7062 (Fax)
Answers questions and distributes materials on the disease. Also assists in raising funds for people with this disease. 8 a.m.–5 p.m.

A–136. American SIDS Institute
(800)232–7437
(800)847–7437 (in GA)
Answers inquiries from families and physicians, distributes literature, and makes referrals to other organizations. 8 a.m. 5 p.m. Leave recorded message after hours.

American Syringomyelia Alliance Project
(800)ASAP–282
Support network and information clearinghouse for people who have the rare spinal cord disorder, syringomyelia. Also a source of information, support and research for chiari malformations.

A–137. Amyotrophic Lateral Sclerosis Association (ALS, Lou Gehrig's Disease)
(800)782–4747
(818)340–2060 (Fax)
Provides names of support groups and locations of clinics and distributes literature. 8 a.m.–5 p.m. (Pacific). Leave recorded message after hours.

A–138. Batten's Disease Support and Research Association
(800)448–4570
Provides a 24 hour recording for callers to request information on Batten's Disease.

Beckwith–Wiedemann Support Network
(800)837–2976
Provides information and peer support to families and individuals affected by Beckwith–Wiedemann Syndrome, a congenital growth–related disorder.

Charcot–Marie–Tooth Association
(800)606–2682
Devoted to the Charcot–Marie–Tooth community and the clinical and research communities that serve them. Its programs include patient and professional education and support. Charcot–Marie–Tooth disease is an inherited neurological disorder.

The CFIDS Association of America
(800)442–3437
Provides information on chronic Epstein–Barr Virus, myalgic encephalomyelitis, HBLV, and related disorders, such as interstitial cystitis, mitral valve prolapse, and vestibular problems.

A–140. Cooley's Anemia Foundation
(800)522–7222
(718)321–CURE
(718)321–3340 (Fax)
Provides information on patient care, research, fundraising, patient–support groups, and research grants. Makes referrals to local chapters and screening centers. 9 a.m.–5 p.m.

A–141. Cornelia de Lange Syndrome Foundation, Inc.
(800)223–8355
(800)753–2357
(203)693–0159
(203)693–6819 (Fax)
Promotes research and provides a variety of materials for families, friends, and professionals about this syndrome. Services include an international professional network, a newsletter, Family Support Program, and a Scientific Advisory Committee. 9 a.m.–4:30 p.m. (Eastern) Leave recorded message after hours.

A–143. Cystic Fibrosis Foundation
(800)344–4823
(301)951–6378 (Fax)
Responds to patient and family questions, offers literature, and provides referrals to local clinics. 8:30 a.m.–5:30 p.m.

A–144. Epilepsy Foundation of America
(800)332–1000
(800)213–5821 (Publications)
(301)459–3700
(301)577–2684 or 4941 (Fax)
Provides information on epilepsy and makes referrals to local chapters. Spanish–speaking operators available. 9 a.m.–5 p.m.

Epilepsy Information Service
(800)642–0500
Provides general information on epilepsy. Distributes pamphlets on epilepsy free of charge. 8 a.m. 5 p.m. (Eastern)

Fibromyalgia Network
(800)853–2929
(520)290–5550 (Fax)
Provides information on Fibromyalgia, Chronic Fatigue Syndrome, and Myofascial Pain Syndrome. Maintains state–by–state listings for support group and health professional referrals. 8 a.m. 5 p.m. (Mountain)

Gillis W. Long Hansen's Disease Center
(800)642–2477
Offers information for the public and for health professionals on research and treatment of Hansen's disease, also known as leprosy.

A–145. Histiocytosis Association
(800)548–2758
(609)589–6614 (Fax)
Provides patient and family support to those affected with any of the histiocytoses. Quarterly newsletter, information, brochures, networking directory, regional meetings, and funds research. Operates 8:30 a.m.–4 p.m., Monday–Friday. Voice mail at all other times.

A–146. Huntington's Disease Society of America, Inc.
(800)345–4372
(212)242–1968
(212)243–2443 (Fax)
Provides written and audiovisual materials pertaining to all aspects of Huntington's Disease; information and referral to local support groups, chapter social workers, physicians, nursing homes and a variety of other resources via local representatives; and support for research into the causes, treatment and cure of Huntington's Disease.

Les Turner Amyotrophic Lateral Sclerosis Foundation, Ltd.
(888)ALS–1107
Offers support to patients and families living with the difficulties associated with amyotrophic lateral sclerosis, also known as Lou Gehrig's disease. Services include an out–patient clinic, visiting nurse program, equipment and communication system banks, educational materials, programs and support groups.

A–148. Meniere's Network
(800)545–4327
(see the Ear Foundation at Baptist Hospital, HEARING AND SPEECH)

Multiple Sclerosis Association of America
(800)LEARN–MS
Dedicated to enhancing, through patient care services and expanding public awareness and support, the quality of life for those affected by multiple sclerosis.

Multiple Sclerosis Foundation
(800)441–7055
Provides information, referral and support services to professionals, those diagnosed with multiple sclerosis, family members and friends. Supports conventional, alternative and complementary healing to treat multiple sclerosis, and aids research into the prevention, treatment and cure of multiple sclerosis.

Muscular Dystrophy Association
(800)572–1717
(520)529–5300 (Fax)
Provides information on 40 neuromuscular diseases, including the muscular dystrophies, motor neuron diseases, inflammatory myopathies, diseases of the neuromuscular junction, diseases of the peripheral nerve, metabolic diseases of the muscles, myopathies due to endocrine abnormalities, and certain other myopathies.

A–149. Myasthenia Gravis Foundation
(800)541–5454
(312)258–0461 (Fax)
Provides information regarding services for myasthenia patients, and patient and medical literature. Promotes public awareness. Funds research. 8:45 a.m.–4:45 p.m. (Central).

A–150. National Down Syndrome Congress
(800)232–6372
(404)633–2817 (Fax)
ndsc@charitiesusa.com (E–mail)
Responds to questions concerning all aspects of Down syndrome. Refers to local organizations. Information available in Spanish. 9 a.m.–5 p.m. (Eastern). Recording after hours.

A–151. National Down Syndrome Society Hotline
(800)221–4602
(212)460–9330
Sponsors internationally renowned scientific symposia. Advocates on behalf of families and individuals affected by this condition. Provides information and referral services through its toll–free hotline staffed by English and Spanish speakers. Develops educational materials, many of which are distributed free of charge.

National Hemophilia Foundation
(888)INFO–NHF
Serves hemophiliacs and their families through its local chapters. Patient services include scholarships, patient education, blood drives, emergency financial assistance and referrals.

National Leigh's Disease Foundation
(800)819–2551
Founded to raise funds for medical research on Leigh's disease, to share contact information on physicians and to share names and addresses of individuals affected by Leigh's disease to others who are searching for support and information.

A–153. National Lymphedema Network
(800)541–3259
Provides information on the prevention and management of primary and secondary lymphedema to the general public as well as health care professionals. Offers referrals to health care professionals and treatment centers, local support groups, and exercise programs. Provides a quarterly newsletter, resource guide, and information on support groups, conferences, and professional training courses. Leave recorded message.

National Marfan Foundation
(800)8–MARFAN
Educates the public, patients and physicians about Marfan Syndrome, a genetic disease of the connective tissue. Provides support to patients and families, and fosters research.

A–154. National Multiple Sclerosis Society
(800)FIGHT–MS
(212)986–7981 (Fax)
Offers a 24–hour telephone message line. Staff members available to answer questions 11 a.m.–5 p.m., Monday–Thursday.

A–155. National Neurofibromatosis Foundation
(800)323–7938
(212)344–6633
(212)747–0004 (Fax)
Responds to inquiries from health professionals and patients and families. Makes referrals to physicians on clinical advisory board. 9 a.m.–5 p.m.

National Organization for Albinism and Hypopigmentation
(800)473–2310
Founded to provide information and support to individuals and families with albinism and hypopigmentation. Promotes public and professional education and encourages research that will lead to improved diagnosis and treatment.

A–156. National Organization for Rare Disorders
(800)999–6673
(203)746–6518
(203)746–6481 (Fax)
(203)746–6927 (TDD)
A clearinghouse for information on over 3,000 rare diseases, offers networking programs linking patients and family members together, and administers several medication assistance programs for indigent patients. Fees charged for some services. 9 a.m.–5 p.m. (Eastern) Monday–Friday. Leave recorded message after hours.

A–157. National Reye's Syndrome Foundation
(800)233–7393
(419)636–2679
(419)636–3366 (Fax)
Provides awareness materials to the public and medical community, raises funds for research, and offers guidance and counseling to victims. 8 a.m.–5 p.m. Leave recorded message after hours.

A–159. National Sarcoidosis Foundation
(800)223–6429
Provides a 24 hour recording for callers to request information on sarcoidosis.

National Sjogren's Syndrome Association
(800)395–6772
Provides emotional support to Sjogren's Syndrome patients and their families and educational information to patients and health care professionals worldwide.

National Spasmodic Torticollis Association
(800)487–8385
Serves the needs of patients with spasmodic torticollis. Works to further research into this condition, caused by a dysfunction in the brain. Has an outreach program designed to bring patients together and increase awareness among the public and health professionals.

A–158. National Tuberous Sclerosis Association
(800)225–6872
(301)459–9888
(301)459–0394 (Fax)
ntsa@aol.com (Internet)
Answers questions about the disease and makes parent–to–parent contact referrals. Literature is provided to families and professionals. 8:30 a.m.–5 p.m.

Office of Orphan Products Development (Food and Drug Administration)
(800)300–7469
Disseminates information on orphan drugs and rare diseases; responds to inquiries from patients, health professionals, and pharmaceutical manufacturers, as well as the general public.

Osteogenesis Imperfecta Foundation
(800)981–BONE
Disseminates information on osteogenesis imperfecta, a genetic bone disease, to patients, their families and health professionals, and initiates and supports research in this field.

Oxalosis and Hyperoxaluria Foundation
(888)712–2432 X5392
Provides research and support to physicians and patients affected by these conditions.

The Paget Foundation for Paget's Disease of Bone and Related Disorders
(800)23–PAGET
(212)229–1582
(212)229–1502 (Fax)
Provides educational literature on Paget's disease of bone, primary hyperparathyroidism and other disorders to patients and the medical community. Gives physician referrals. 9 a.m.–5 p.m. (Eastern).

Prader–Willi Syndrome Association
(800)926–4797
Provides a forum for the exchange of ideas and experiences for parents and professionals interested in children affected by Prader–Willi Syndrome.

International Rett Syndrome Association
(800)818–7388
Provides support to parents and encourages research in the prevention, treatment and eradication of Rett Syndrome, a brain disorder that affects only female infants.

Scleroderma Federation, Inc.
(800)422–1113
Worldwide affiliation of scleroderma support groups helps in the formation of new groups. Programs include public education, a telephone helpline, fundraising and development of support service programs. Involved with the support of scleroderma–related research.

A–167. Scleroderma Foundation, United
(800)722–HOPE
(408)728–2202
(408)728–3328 (Fax)
outreach@scleroderma.com (E–Mail)
Develops chapter and support groups, distributes printed materials, and provides patient support and information and medical reference lists. 8 a.m.–5 p.m. (Pacific).

A–160. Sickle Cell Disease Association of America, Inc.
(800)421–8453
Offers educational materials, referrals for client services, research support, and public awareness. 8:30 a.m.–5 p.m. (Pacific). Recording after hours and weekends.

A–161. SIDS Alliance
(800)221–SIDS (7437)
(410)653–8226
(410)653–8709 (Fax)
Hotline is available for parents who wish to discuss their concerns with a SIDS counselor, request additional information, and/or be connected to the local SIDS Affiliate for support services in their area. 9 a.m.–5 p.m. (Eastern). Phone line available 24 hours. (See also B–52)

Sjogren's Syndrome Foundation, Inc.
(800)475–6473
Provides information, support and limited physician referrals to patients with Sjogren's Syndrome. Educational materials may be ordered through this toll–free number.

A–162. Spina Bifida Association of America
(800)621–3141
(202)944–3285
(202)944–3295 (Fax)
Provides information to consumers and health professionals and referrals to local chapters. 9 a.m.–5 p.m.

A–163. Spondylitis Association of America (formerly the Ankylosing Spondylitis Association)
(800)777–8189
(818)981–1616
(818)981–9826 (Fax)
Provides information on ankylosing spondylitis, psoriatic arthritis, and Reiter's syndrome. 9 a.m.–5 p.m. (Pacific). Leave recorded message after hours.

A–164. Sturge–Weber Foundation
(800)627–5482
Provides list of publications, long–distance support groups, and referrals for families, friends, and professionals. 9 a.m.–3 p.m., Monday–Friday.

Sudden Infant Death Syndrome Network
(800)560–1454
Dedicated to eliminating sudden infant death syndrome (SIDS) through research, providing support for those who have been touched by the tragedy of SIDS and raising awareness of SIDS through education. Provides counseling services and up–to–date medical information about SIDS.

Support Organization for Trisomy 18, 13 and Related Disorders
(800)716–SOFT
Families and professionals dedicated to providing support and understanding to families involved in the issues surrounding these and related chromosomal disorders.

A–165. Tourette Syndrome Association, Inc.
(800)237–0717
(718)224–2999
(718)279–9596 (Fax)
Provides a 24–hour recording for callers to request information and leave name and address. To speak with a staff member, call the local number between 9 a.m.–5 p.m.

Treacher Collins Foundation
(800)TCF–2055
Serves the needs of families and individuals affected by Treacher Collins Syndrome, a rare facial deformity. Links together affected people and families for support and provides information and referral. Services are free.

Turner's Syndrome Society of the United States
(800)365–9944
Provides individuals and families affected by Turner's Syndrome with knowledge, understanding and practical information on how to face challenges throughout their lifetime. Services are available for information on medical care, insurance, physician referrals and support groups.

A–166. United Cerebral Palsy Association
(800)872–5827
(202)776–0406
(202)776–0414 (Fax)
Provides literature about cerebral palsy and related disorders. Responds to inquiries from people with cerebral palsy and related disorders, their families, and the public. Makes referrals to local affiliates. 8:30 a.m.–5:30 p.m.

United Leukodystrophy Foundation
(800)728–5483
Dedicated to providing patients and their families with information about leukodystrophy, a group of genetic nervous system disorders, and to providing assistance in identifying sources of medical care, social services and genetic counseling. Promotes and supports research into the causes, treatment and prevention of the leukodystrophies.

Wegener's Granulomatosis Support Group, Inc.
(800)277–9474
Provides access to clinical information concerning this disease, assists survivors and families in coping with and understanding the disease and informs the general public about Wegener's Granulomatosis.

Wilson's Disease Association
(800)399–0266
Gives aid and support to victims of Wilson's disease, a rare, genetic disorder of copper metabolism. Puts affected families in contact with one another for support, disseminates information and supports research on this disease and the orphan drugs used to treat it.

REHABILITATION

See DISABLING CONDITIONS, PARALYSIS AND SPINAL CORD INJURY

Abledata
(800)227–0216
Funded by the National Institute on Disability and Rehabilitation Research, U.S. Department of Education. Provides information on disability–related products. Staff are available from 8:00 a.m. to 5:30 p.m., EST, Monday through Friday.

National Institute for Rehabilitation Engineering
(800)736–2216
Provides custom–made devices, training and on–site services for severely and multiply handicapped individuals. Services are offered with a sliding fee scale. No one is denied service based on inability to pay.

Phoenix Society for Burn Survivors
(800)888–2876
Attempts to ease the psychosocial adjustment of severely burned and disfigured persons and to facilitate their return to normal lives.

United Ostomy Association
(800)826–0826
Formed to help ostomy patients return to normal living through moral support and education in proper ostomy care and management. Trained members often visit ostomy patients in hospitals and in their homes to offer moral support and assistance.

RETINITIS PIGMENTOSA

See VISION

RURAL

A–168. Rural Information Center Health Service (RICHS)
(800)633–7701
(301)504–5547
(301)504–6856 (TTY/TDD)
(301)504–5181 (Fax)
ric@nalusda.gov (E–mail)
gopher://gopher.nalusda.gov (Internet)
Provides information and referrals to the public and to professionals on rural health issues. Performs brief, complimentary literature searches. 8 a.m.–4:30 p.m. (See also B–50)

SAFETY

See also CHEMICAL PRODUCTS/PESTICIDES

A–169. National Child Safety Council Childwatch
(800)222–1464
(see CHILD ABUSE/MISSING CHILDREN/MENTAL HEALTH)

A–170. National Highway Traffic Safety Administration Auto Safety Hotline
(800)424–9393
(202)366–0123
Provides information and referral on the effectiveness of occupant protection, such as safety belt use, child safety seats, and automobile recalls. Gives referrals to other Government agencies for consumer questions on warranties, service, automobile safety regulations, and reporting safety problems. 8 a.m.–4 p.m. (See also B–32)

A–171. Clearinghouse for Occupational Safety and Health Information, National Institute for Occupational Safety and Health
(800)356–4674
(513)538–8588 (Fax)
Provides information on chemical and physical hazards in the workplace, training courses, publications, and the health hazard evaluation program. 9 a.m.–4 p.m. (See also B–36, B–44, B–48)

National Safety Council
(800)621–7615
Offers a safety training institute, a child safety club, home study courses in safety, and traffic and transportation safety services. Provides materials on all aspects of safety accident prevention, and prevention of occupational illnesses.

A–172. Office of Navigation Safety and Waterway Services U.S. Coast Guard Customer Infoline
(800)368–5647
(202)267–0780
(800)689–0816 (TDD/TT)
(202)267–6707 (TDD/TT)
Modem #703313591 (Navigation Center Bulletin Board)
http://www.dot.gov/affairs/index.htm (Internet)
Provides information on boating safety, including a kit for consumers, recalls on boating products, makes referrals to other organizations, and other Coast Guard missions. 8 a.m.–4 p.m.

Section C

A–173. U.S. Consumer Product Safety Commission Hotline
(800)638–2772
(800)638–8270 (TDD)
info@cpsc.gov (Internet)
Provides 24–hour messages on consumer product safety, including product hazards and product recalls. Covers only products used in and around the home, excluding automobiles, child safety seats, health care products, warranties, foods, drugs, cosmetics, boats, and firearms. (See also B–36, B–48)

SEXUAL EDUCATION

A–174. Planned Parenthood Federation of America, Inc.
(800)669–0156
Provides family planning, reproductive, and sexual health care information.
(800)230–PLAN
Callers will reach the nearest Planned Parenthood center for clinical appointments or education staff. (See also B–24)
(800)230–PLAN
Callers will reach the nearest Planned Parenthood center for clinical appointments or education staff.

SEXUALLY TRANSMITTED DISEASES

A–175. Centers for Disease Control and Prevention National STD Hotline
(800)227–8922
Information regarding all sexually transmitted diseases. Referral to community clinics offering free or low–cost examination and treatment. 8 a.m.–11 p.m. Free written information available.

Herpes Resource Center
(800)230–6039
(800)478–3227 (Canada)
Provides information and support services to persons who suffer from herpes. Sponsors local support groups nationwide, telephone counseling services, information, research and education projects. 9 a.m. 7 p.m.

National STD Hotline
(800)227–8922
Sponsored by the American Social Health Association. Provides patients with linkages to 5,000 local clinics throughout the United States.

SKIN DISEASE

Foundation for Ichthyosis and Related Skin Types, Inc.
(800)545–3286
Raises funds to promote research on the congenital skin disease, ichthyosis. Provides advice, guidance and support among sufferers and distributes educational material to the public and medical professionals.

National Psoriasis Foundation
(800)723–9166
Provides support and information to psoriasis patients, attempts to increase public awareness, funds research, answers inquiries, disseminates publications and coordinates a hotline and pen pal clubs for patients of all ages.

SPINAL CORD INJURY

See PARALYSIS AND SPINAL CORD INJURY

SMOKING

Office on Smoking and Health
(800)CDC–1311
A division of the Centers for Disease Control and Prevention's National Center for Chronic Disease Prevention and Health Promotion. Develops and distributes the annual *Surgeon General's Report on Smoking and Health*, coordinates a national public information and education program on tobacco use and health and coordinates tobacco education and research efforts within the Department of Health and Human Services and throughout both Federal and State governments. Materials can be requested through this toll–free hotline.

STROKE

See also PARALYSIS AND SPINAL CORD INJURY

A–176. American Heart Association Stroke Connection
(800)553–6321
(214)696–5211 (Fax)
Maintains a listing of more than 1000 groups across the Nation for referral to stroke survivors, their families, care givers, and interested professionals. Publishes Stroke Connection magazine, a forum for stroke survivors and their families to share information about coping with stroke. Provides information and referral and carries stroke–related books, videotapes, and literature available for purchase. 8:30 a.m.–5 p.m. (Central).

National Institute of Neurological Disorders and Stroke
(800)352–9424
Conducts and supports research on the causes, prevention, diagnosis, and treatment of neurological disorders and stroke. Consumer publications are available on the brain and nervous system and a variety of neurological disorders.

STUTTERING

A–177. National Center for Stuttering
(800)221–2483
Provides treatment for older children (age 7 and above) and adults, training for professionals, and information for parents with young children (below age 7). 9 a.m.–6 p.m.

A–178. Stuttering Foundation of America
(800)992–9392
(901)452–7343
(901)452–3931 (Fax)
stuttersfa@aol.com (E–mail)
Provides materials and makes referrals to speech–language pathologists. 9 a.m.–5 p.m.

SUBSTANCE ABUSE

See also ALCOHOL ABUSE and DRUG ABUSE

National Inhalent Prevention Coalition
(800)269–4237
Provides a free information packet on inhalent abuse. Distributes videotapes and posters on inhalent abuse (a fee is charged for this material when sent to States other than Texas).

SUDDEN INFANT DEATH SYNDROME

See RARE DISORDERS

SURGERY/FACIAL PLASTIC SURGERY

A–179. American Society for Dermatologic Surgery, Inc.
(800)441–2737
Provides information about various dermatologic surgical procedures, as well as referrals to dermatologic surgeons in local areas. 8:30 a.m.–5 p.m. (Central).

A–180. American Society of Plastic and Reconstructive Surgeons, Inc.
(800)635–0635
Provides referrals to board–certified plastic surgeons nationwide and in Canada. 8:30 a.m.–4:30 p.m. (Central). Leave recorded message after hours.

A–181. Facial Plastic Surgery Information Service
(800)332–3223
(202)842–4500
Provides physician referral list and brochures. 24 hours.

TRAUMA

A–182. American Trauma Society (ATS)
(800)556–7890
(301)420–4189
(301)420–0617 (Fax)
Offers information to health professionals and the public; answers questions about trauma prevention and trauma systems. 9 a.m.–5 p.m.

UROLOGICAL DISORDERS

A–183. American Association of Kidney Patients
(800)749–2257
(813)223–0001 (Fax)
Helps renal patients and their families to deal with the physical and emotional impact of kidney disease. Supplies information on renal conditions. 9 a.m.–5 p.m.

A–184. American Foundation for Urologic Disease
(800)242–2383
(410)528–0550 (Fax)
Provides a 24 hour recording for callers seeking patient information on urologic diseases and dysfunctions. (See also B–37)

A–185. American Kidney Fund
(800)638–8299
Offers financial assistance to kidney patients who are unable to pay treatment–related costs. Also provides information on organ donations and kidney–related diseases. 8 a.m.–5 p.m.

Incontinence Information Center
(800)843–4315
(800)543–9632
Provides free information to prospective patients regarding the causes and treatments for incontinence. Provides referrals to local physicians. 8:30 a.m.–5 p.m. (Central) or leave recorded message after hours.

National Association for Continence
(800)252–3337
Dedicated to improving the quality of life for people with incontinence through education, advocacy and support.

A–186. National Kidney Foundation
(800)622–9010
(212)689–9261 (Fax)
Provides information and referrals to the public and health professionals regarding kidney disorders. 9 a.m.–5 p.m.

Polycystic Kidney Research Foundation
(800)753–2873
Devoted entirely to research into the cause, treatment and cure of polycystic kidney disease, an inherited kidney condition. Works to educate the public and professionals and assists patients in finding mutual support groups.

A–187. The Simon Foundation for Continence
(800)237–4666 (Patient information)
(708)864–3913
(708)864–9758 (Fax)
Provides information on continence and ordering a quarterly newsletter and other publications. Also has a community–based education program/self–help group and informational videotape. Toll–free number operates 24 hours; second number is staffed 9 a.m.–5 p.m. (Central).

VENEREAL DISEASES

See SEXUALLY TRANSMITTED DISEASES

VETERANS

Persian Gulf Veterans Information Helpline
(800)PGW–VETS
Sponsored by the Department of Veterans Affairs. Offers Persian Gulf veterans special examinations and priority follow–up care. This number is to inform these veterans of the program and their benefits.

Vietnam Veterans Agent Orange Victims
(800)521–0198
Supports and informs those who were exposed to the defoliant Agent Orange, or dioxin, while serving in Vietnam. Distributes a medical information package to health professionals and a set of medical records request forms to veterans.

VISION

See also LIBRARY SERVICES

A–188. American Council of the Blind
(800)424–8666 (Live operators available 3p.m.–5:30 p.m. Eastern)
(202)467–5081 (9 a.m.–5:30 Eastern)
(202)467–5085 (Fax)
(202)331–1058 (Electronic Bulletin Board)
hcraff@ACCESS.DIGEX.NET (E–mail)
Offers information on blindness and referrals to rehabilitation organizations, research centers, and chapters. Publishes resource lists. Leave recorded message after hours.

American Foundation for the Blind
(800)AFB–LINE
Improves services for people who are blind or visually impaired by conducting research and informing the public about issues relating to blindness.

Section C

Better Vision Institute
(800)424–8422
Dedicated to informing the public about the importance of vision care. Organizes informative television, radio and print media announcements and offers informative brochures.

Braille Institute
(800)272–4553
Refers callers nationwide to organizations serving the blind in their areas, as well as providing information on its services, which include production of more than 5 million Braille pages yearly.

A–189. Blind Childrens Center
(800)222–3566
(800)222–3567
(213)665–3828 (Fax)
info@blindcntr.org (E–mail)
http://www.blindcntr.org/bcc (World Wide Web)
Nonprofit early intervention program and educational preschool. Family support services. Information and referral line. Educational booklets for parents, educators, and specialists. 7:30 a.m.–5 p.m. (Pacific).

DB–Link
(800)438–9376
Identifies, coordinates and disseminates information on children and youth who are deaf–blind. It is a collaborative effort of the American Association of the Deaf–Blind, Helen Keller National Center, and the Perkins School for the Blind and Teaching Research.

A–199. The Foundation Fighting Blindness
(800)683–5555
(800)683–5551 (TDD)
(410)771–9470 (Fax)
Funds medical research and provides information on retinitis pigmentosa and other inherited retinal degenerations. Scope of information includes current research, genetics, retina donor program, and practical resources available throughout the United States. 8:30 a.m.–5 p.m.

A–190. Guide Dog Foundation for the Blind, Inc.
(800)548–4337
(516)265–2121
(516)361–5192 (Fax)
(516)366–4462 (Electronic Bulletin Board)
School for blind individuals requiring guide dogs. Operates a computer bulletin board system. Operates 24 hours.

Guide Dogs for the Blind
(800)295–4050
Provides trained guide dogs to legally blind persons 16 years of age and older and also provides training in the use of guide dogs. The group does not charge the blind for its services.

A–191. The Lighthouse National Center for Education
(800)334–5497
(212)821–9200
(212)821–9705 (Fax)
(212)821–9713 (TDD)
Provides educational materials and information on vision and child development and age–related vision loss to professionals and consumers. Provides information nationwide on local resources such as low vision centers, support groups, and vision rehabilitation agencies. Some materials in Spanish. 9 a.m.–5 p.m. Leave recorded message after hours.

A–192. Louisiana Center for the Blind
(800)234–4166
(318)251–2891
(318)251–0109 (Fax)
Private, residential training program for legally blind adults and children. 8 a.m.–5 p.m. (Central).

National Alliance of Blind Students
(800)424–8666
Provides a forum for blind and visually impaired students and promotes progress toward full accessibility to colleges and universities for persons with disabilities.

A–193. National Association for Parents of the Visually Impaired
(800)562–6265
(617)972–7444 (Fax)
Provides support and information to parents of visually impaired, blind, deaf–blind, and blind multi–handicapped children. 9 a.m.–5 p.m. (Central).

A–194. National Eye Care Project Helpline
(800)222–EYES (3937)
Provides medical and surgical eye care to disadvantaged elderly people who can no longer access the ophthalmologists they have visited in the past. 8 a.m.–4 p.m. (Pacific).

A–195. National Eye Research Foundation
(800)621–2258
(708)564–4652
(708)564–0807 (Fax)
Recording provides patient and membership information. Publishes the Green Directory, an international listing of member optometrists for patient referrals. 8:30 a.m.–5 p.m. Leave recorded message after hours.

A–196. The National Eye Research Foundation's Memorial Eye Clinic
(800)621–2258
Provides low–vision care, orthokeratology, and problem contact lens care. 9 a.m. 5 p.m., Monday, Tuesday, Wednesday; 9 a.m.–2 p.m., Friday. Leave recorded message after hours.

National Family Association for Deaf–Blind
(800)255–0411, ext. 275
See HEARING AND SPEECH

A–198. Prevent Blindness Center for Sight
(800)331–2020
Sponsored by Prevent Blindness America. Provides information on a broad range of eye health and safety topics. 8 a.m.–5 p.m. (Central).

VIOLENCE

National Domestic Violence Hotline
(800)787–3224 (TDD)
(800)799–SAFE
Sponsored by the Texas Council on Family Violence and the Department of Health and Human Services. Committed to making sure that information about temporary shelters and legal services are made available to women and families who are victims of domestic violence.

National Organization for Victim Assistance
(800)TRY–NOVA
Serves as a national forum for victim advocacy and serves individual victims and witnesses of crime. Supports local victim assistance programs and sponsors conferences and forums on these issues. Operated 24 hours a day and is intended for use by victims and survivors.

Rape, Abuse, and Incest National Network
(800)656–4673
Connects caller to the nearest counseling center which provides counseling for rape, abuse, and incest victims.

WOMEN

A–201. Endometriosis Association
(800)992–3636
(414)355–6065 (Fax)
Provides a 24–hour recording for callers to request information and leave name and address.

National Osteoporosis Foundation
(800)464–6700
(202)223–2237 (Fax)
Provides women with information on bone density testing, advice on how to talk to physicians about osteoporosis, and location of bone density testing facilities.

A–202. PMS Access
(800)222–4767
(608)833–7412 (Fax)
Sponsored by Madison Pharmacy Associates, Inc. Provides information, literature, and counseling on premenstrual syndrome (PMS). Gives referrals to physicians and clinics in the caller's area. 9 a.m.–5 p.m. (Central).

A–203. Women's Sports Foundation
(800)227–3988
(516)542–4716 (Fax)
A national, nonprofit, educational organization that promotes and enhances sports and fitness opportunities for all girls and women.

Women's Health America Group
(800)558–7046
(888)898–7412 (Fax)
Encourages and enables women to make sound decisions concerning their health by providing current, accurate health information and quality products and services.

GUIDE TO FEDERAL HEALTH INFORMATION CLEARINGHOUSES

The Federal Government operates many clearinghouses and information centers that focus on specific topics. Their services include distributing publications, providing referrals, and answering inquiries. Many offer toll–free numbers. Unless otherwise stated, numbers can be reached within the continental United States Monday through Friday, during normal business hours, and hours of operation are eastern time. The clearinghouses are listed below by keyword.

National ADOPTION Information Clearinghouse
(215)735–9988
(703)246–9095 (703)385–3206 (FAX)
naic@calib.com (E–Mail) http://www.calib.com/naic
Provides professionals and the general public with easily accessible information on all aspects of adoption, including infant and intercountry adoption and the adoption of children with special needs. NAIC maintains an adoption literature database, a database of adoption experts, listings of adoption agencies, crisis pregnancy centers, and other adoption–related services, as well as excerpts of State and Federal laws on adoption. Ultimately, NAIC's goal is to strengthen adoptive family life. NAIC does not place children for adoption or provide counseling. It does however, make referrals for such services. NAIC is funded by the Children's Bureau, Administration for Children and Families, U.S. Department of Health and Human Services.

National AGING Information Center
U.S. Administration on Aging
330 Independence Avenue SW.
Room 4656
Washington, DC 20201
(800)411–2112
(202)554–9800
(202)554–0571 (TDD)
(202)554–0695 (Fax)
naic@ageinfo.org (E–Mail)
http://www.aoa.dhhs.gov/naic/
Central source for a wide variety of program– and policy–related materials, demographic, and other statistical data on health, economic, and social status of older Americans. NAIC develops special reports on key aging issues for publication and dissemination to the aging community; produces statistical reports and data tables; and compiles an annual compendium of Title IV products.

B–1. National Institute on AGING Information Center
P.O. Box 8057
Gaithersburg, MD 20898–8057
(800)222–2225 (Voice/TTY)
(301)587–2528
(800)222–4225 (TDD)
(301)589–3014 (Fax)
niainfo@access.digex.net (E–Mail)
http://www.nih.gov/nia/
Provides publications on health topics of interest to older adults, to the public, and to doctors, nurses, social activities directors, and health educators.

B–2. U.S. Department of AGRICULTURE Extension Service
See the listing in the Government section of your telephone book for your local extension office. Provides information on health, nutrition, fitness, and family well–being.

Section C

B–3. CDC National AIDS Clearinghouse
P.O. Box 6003
Rockville, MD 20849–6003
(800)458–5231
(800)243–7012 (TDD)
(800)874–2572 AIDS Clinical Trials
(800)458–5231 (NAC Fax–Back Service)
(800)448–0440 HIV/AIDS Treatment
(301)217–0023 (International)
(301)738–6616 (Fax)
aidsinfo@cdcnac.aspensys.com (E–Mail)
http://www.cdcnac.org
Sponsored by the Centers for Disease Control and
Prevention. A national reference, referral, and
distribution service for HIV/AIDS–related information.
Answers questions and provides technical
assistance; distributes published HIV–related
materials including current information on scientific
findings, CDC guidelines, and trends in the HIV
epidemic; and provides specific information on
AIDS–related organizations, educational materials,
funding opportunities, and other topics. Services
include a 24–hour fax–back service for HIV/
AIDS–related information and the Business and
Labor Resource Service for resources, technical
assistance, publications, and referrals concerning
managing AIDS in the workplace. Provides
information and publications in English and Spanish.
9 a.m.–7 p.m.

**B–4. National Clearinghouse for ALCOHOL and
DRUG Information**
P.O. Box 2345
Rockville, MD 20847–2345
(800)729–6686
(301)468–2600
(800)487–4889 (TTY/TDD)
(301)230–2867 (TTY/TDD)
(301)468–6433 (Fax)
info@health.org (E–Mail)
http://www.health.org
Sponsored by the Center for Substance Abuse
Prevention, Substance Abuse and Mental Health
Services Administration. Gathers and disseminates
information on alcohol and other drug–related
subjects, including tobacco. Distributes publications.
Services include subject searches and provision of
statistics and other information. Operates the
Regional Alcohol and Drug Awareness Resource
Network, a nationwide linkage of alcohol and other
drug information centers. Maintains a library open to
the public. 8 a.m.–7 p.m.

**B–5. National Institute of ALLERGY and
INFECTIOUS DISEASES**
Office of Communications
Building 31, Room 7A50
9000 Rockville Pike
Bethesda, MD 20892
(301)496–5717
niaidoc@flash.niaid.nih.gov (E–Mail)
http://www.niaid.nih.gov/
Distributes publications to the public and to doctors,
nurses, and researchers.

Office of ALTERNATIVE MEDICINE Clearinghouse
P.O. Box 8218
Silver Spring, Maryland 20907–8218
(888)644–6226 (Voice – Toll–free)
(888)644–6226 (Voice – TTY)
(301)495–4957 (FAX)
(800)531–1794 (FAXBACK)
http://altmed.od.nih.gov/oam/clearinghouse/
Develops and disseminates fact sheets, information
packages, and publications to enhance public
understanding about complementary and alternative
medicine research supported by the NIH. OAM
public information is currently free of charge;
however, due to printing and duplication costs, only
a limited number of copies can be requested.
Information Specialists can answer inquiries in both
English or Spanish. Monday through Friday, 8:30
a.m. – 5:00 p.m. Eastern Time. After normal
business hours, callers have the option of receiving
fact sheets and other information by fax.

**B–6. ALZHEIMER'S DISEASE Education and
Referral Center**
P.O. Box 8250
Silver Spring, MD 20907–8250
(800)438–4380
(301)495–3311
(301)495–3334 (Fax)
adear@alzheimers.org (E–mail)
http://www.cais.com/adear/
Sponsored by the National Institute on Aging.
Provides information and publications on Alzheimer's
disease to health and service professionals, patients
and their families, caregivers, and the public.

**B–7. National ARTHRITIS and Musculoskeletal
and Skin Diseases Information Clearinghouse**
1 AMS Circle
Bethesda, MD 20892–3675
(301)495–4484
(301)587–4352 (Fax)
http://www.nih.gov/niams/
Identifies educational materials about arthritis and
musculoskeletal and skin diseases and serves as an
information exchange for individuals and
organizations involved in public, professional, and
patient education. Conducts subject searches and
makes resource referrals.

**B–9. National Library Service for the BLIND and
Physically Handicapped**
Library of Congress
1291 Taylor Street NW.
Washington, DC 20542
(800)424–8567
(202)707–5100
(202)707–0744 (TDD)
(202)707–0712 (Fax)
nls@loc.gov (E–Mail)
http://lcweb.loc.gov/nls/
A network of 56 regional and 87 local libraries that
work in cooperation with the Library of Congress to
provide free library service to anyone who is unable
to read standard print due to visual or physical
disabilities. Delivers recorded and Braille books and
magazines to eligible readers. Specially designed
phonographs and cassette players also are loaned.
A list of participating local and regional libraries is
available.

U.S. Coast Guard Office of BOATING SAFETY
2100 Second Street SW.
Washington, DC 20593–0001
(800)368–5647 (Customer InfoLine)
(202)267–1077
(800)689–0816 (TDD/TT)
(703)313–5910 (BBS)
http://www.uscgboating.org/
Provides safety information to recreational boaters;
assists the public in finding boating education
classes; answers technical questions; and
distributes literature on boating safety, Federal laws,
and the prevention of recreational boating
casualties.

B–10. CANCER Information Service
Office of Cancer Communications
National Cancer Institute
Building 31, Room 10A16
9000 Rockville Pike
Bethesda, MD 20892
(800)4–CANCER (422–6237)
(301)496–5583
(301)402–2594 (Fax)
cancernet@icicb.nci.nih.gov (E–Mail)
http://rex.nci.nih.gov
Provides information about cancer and
cancer–related resources to patients, the public,
and health professionals. Inquiries are handled by
trained information specialists. Spanish–speaking
staff members are available. Distributes free
publications from the National Cancer Institute.
Operates 9 a.m.–7 p.m.

**B–11. National Clearinghouse on CHILD ABUSE
and Neglect Information**
P.O. Box 1182
Washington, DC 20013–1182
(800)FYI–3366
(703)385–7565
(703)385–3206 (Fax)
nccanch@clark.net (E–mail)
http://www.calib.com/nccanch
Serves as a national resource for the acquisition and
dissemination of child abuse and neglect materials
and distributes a free publications catalog upon
request. Maintains bibliographic databases of
documents, audiovisuals, and national organizations.
Services include searches of databases and
annotated bibliographies on frequently requested
topics.

National CHILD CARE Information Center
301 Maple Avenue West
Suite 602
Vienna, VA 22180
(800)516–2242 (Voice – TTY)
(800)616–2242 (Voice)
(800)716–2242 (Fax)
agoldstein@acf.dhhs.gov (E–Mail)
http://ericps.crc.uiuc.edu/nccic/nccichome.html
Disseminates child care information; reaches out to
ACF child care grantees and broader child care
community via toll–free 800 number, and by fax,
mail and electronic media; and publication of the
Child Care Bulletin; supports the Child Care Bureau
in the collection and analysis of child care data; and
maintains the database of information reported by
State, Tribal and Territorial Grantees. The
information Center assists the Child Care Bureau
with its analysis of programmatic and expenditure
data. Information and resources are available on–line
through the Internet.

**B–12. National Clearinghouse on Family Support
and CHILDREN'S MENTAL HEALTH**
Portland State University
P.O. Box 751
Portland, OR 97207–0751
(800)628–1696
(503)725–4040
(503)725–4165 (TTD)
(503)725–4180 (Fax)
Sponsored by the National Institute on Disability and
Rehabilitation Research, U.S. Department of
Education, and the Center for Mental Health
Services, U.S. Department of Health and Human
Services. Provides publications on parent/family
support groups, financing, early intervention, various
mental disorders, and other topics concerning
children's mental health. Also offers a computerized
databank and a State–by– State resource file.
Recording operates 24 hours a day.

NIH CONSENSUS Program Clearinghouse
P.O. Box 2577
Kensington, MD 20891
(800)644–6627
(301)816–9840 (Electronic Bulletin Board)
(301)816–2494 (Fax)
http://odp.od.nih.gov/consensus/
A service of the Office of Medical Applications of
Research (OMAR), National Institutes of Health.
Provides up–to–date information on biomedical
technologies to all health care providers. Offers a
24–hour voice mail service to order consensus
statements produced by non–Federal panels of
experts that evaluate scientific information on
biomedical technologies. Information Specialists
available between 8:30 a.m. and 5 p.m. (Eastern).
Consensus statements can also be ordered by mail,
fax, and electronic bulletin board.

B–14. CONSUMER INFORMATION Center
Pueblo, CO 81009
(719)948–4000
catalog.pueblo@gsa.gov (E–Mail)
http://www.pueblo.gsa.gov/
Distributes Federal agency publications. Publishes
quarterly catalog of Federal publications of
consumer interest.

B-15. National Institute on DEAFNESS and Other Communication Disorders Information Clearinghouse
1 Communication Avenue
Bethesda, MD 20892-3456
(800)241-1044
(800)241-1055 (TT)
(301)907-8830 (Fax)
nidcd@aerie.com (E-Mail)
http://www.nih.gov/nidcd
Collects and disseminates information on hearing, balance, smell, taste, voice, speech, and language for health professionals, patients, people in industry, and the public. Maintains a database of references to brochures, books, articles, fact sheets, organizations, and educational materials, which is a subfile on CHID. Develops publications, including directories, fact sheets, brochures, information packets, and newsletters.

B-16. National DIABETES Information Clearinghouse
1 Information Way
Bethesda, MD 20892-3560
(301)654-3327
(301)907-8906 (Fax)
NDIC@aerie.com (E-mail)
http://www.niddk.nih.gov/Brochures/NDIC.htm
The National Diabetes Information Clearinghouse (NDIC) is an information and referral service of the National Institute of Diabetes and Digestive and Kidney Diseases, one of the National Institutes of Health. The clearinghouse responds to written inquires, develops and distributes publications about diabetes, and provides referrals to diabetes organizations, including support groups. The NDIC maintains a database of patient and professional education materials, from which literature searches are generated.

B-17. National DIGESTIVE DISEASES Information Clearinghouse
2 Information Way
Bethesda, MD 20892-3570
(301)654-3810
(301)907-8906 (Fax)
NDDIC@aerie.com (E-mail)
http://www.niddk.nih.gov/Brochures/NDDIC.htm
The National Digestive Diseases Information Clearinghouse (NDDIC) is an information and referral service of the National Institute of Diabetes and Digestive and Kidney Diseases, one of the National Institutes of Health. A central information resource on the prevention and management of digestive diseases, the clearinghouse responds to written inquires, develops and distributes publications about digestive diseases, and provides referrals to digestive disease organizations, including support groups. The NDDIC maintains a database of patient and professional education materials, from which literature searches are generated.

B-18. National Information Center for Children and Youth with DISABILITIES
P.O. Box 1492
Washington, DC 20013-1492
(800)695-0285 (Voice/TT)
(202)884-8200 (Voice/TT)
(202)884-8441 (Fax)
nichcy@capcon.net (E-mail)
http://www.nichcy.org
Sponsored by the U.S. Department of Education. Assists individuals by providing information on disabilities and disability-related issues, with a special focus on children and youth with disabilities (birth to age 22). Services include responses to questions, referrals, and technical assistance to parents, educators, caregivers, and advocates. Develops and distributes fact sheets on disability and general information on parent support groups and public advocacy. All information and services are provided free of charge.

B-19. Clearinghouse on DISABILITY INFORMATION
Office of Special Education and Rehabilitative Services
U.S. Department of Education
330 C Street SW.
Switzer Building, Room 3132
Washington, DC 20202-2524
(202)205-8241
(202)205-9252 (Fax)
http://www.ed.gov/offices/OSERS/
Responds to inquiries on a wide range of topics, especially in the areas of Federal funding, legislation, and programs benefiting people with disabling conditions. Provides referrals.

B-20. National Center for Chronic DISEASE PREVENTION and Health Promotion (NCCDPHP)
Technical Information Services Branch enters for Disease Control and Prevention
4770 Buford Highway, MS K13
Atlanta, GA 30341-3724
(770)488-5080
(770)488-5969 (Fax)
http://www.cdc.gov/nccdphp/nccdhome.htm
Provides information and referrals to the public and to professionals. Gathers information on chronic disease prevention and health promotion. Develops the following bibliographic databases focusing on health promotion program information: Health Promotion and Education, Cancer Prevention and Control, Comprehensive School Health with an AIDS school health component, Prenatal Smoking Cessation, and Epilepsy Education and Prevention Activities. Produces bibliographies on topics of interest in chronic disease prevention and health promotion. The NCCDPHP Information Center collections include approximately 400 periodical subscriptions, 4,000 books, and 400 reference books. Visitors may use the collection by appointment. Produces the CDP File CD-ROM, which includes the above databases and the Chronic Disease Prevention Directory, a listing of key contacts in public health.

B-21. Housing and Urban Development DRUG INFORMATION and Strategy Clearinghouse
P.O. Box 6424
Rockville, MD 20850
(800)955-2232
(301)519-6655 (FAX)
http://www.hud.gov
Sponsored by the U.S. Department of Housing and Urban Development. Promotes strategies for eradicating drugs and drug trafficking from public housing. Provides housing officials, residents, and community leaders a source for information and assistance on drug abuse prevention and trafficking control techniques. Maintains an automated database system consisting of national and community program descriptions, publications, research, and news articles. Provides resource lists.

DRUGS and CRIME Data Center and Clearinghouse
1600 Research Boulevard
Rockville, MD 20850
(800)666-3332
A service of the Bureau of Justice Statistics (BJS), Office of Justice Programs, U.S. Department of Justice. Responds to policy makers' need for the most current data about illegal drugs, drug law violations, drug-related crime, drug-using offenders in the criminal justice system, and the impact of drugs on criminal justice administration. The Data Center prepares special reports on drugs and crime; analyzes and evaluates existing drug data; prepares annotated bibliographies of drugs-and-crime reports; and responds to request for drug and crime information. The Clearinghouse disseminates BJS and other Department of Justice publications relating to drugs and crime; distributes information on specific drugs-and-crime topics; maintains a data base of reports, books, and articles on crime; and maintains a reading room where visitors can use the Clearinghouse collection. 8:30 a.m.–5:15 p.m. (Eastern). Leave recorded message after hours.

B-22. ERIC Clearinghouse on Teaching and Teacher EDUCATION
One Dupont Circle NW.
Suite 610
Washington, DC 20036-1186
(202)293-2450
(202)457-8095 (Fax)
ericsp@inet.ed.gov (E-Mail)
http://www.aspensys.com/eric/
Sponsored by the U.S. Department of Education. Acquires, evaluates, abstracts, and indexes literature on the preparation and development of education personnel and on selected aspects of health and physical education, recreation, and dance. Publishes monographs, trends and issues papers, ERIC Digests and ERIC Recent Resources (annotated bibliographies from the ERIC database). Performs computer searches of the ERIC database and sponsors work-shops on searching the ERIC database.

B-23. U.S. ENVIRONMENTAL PROTECTION Agency Public Information Center
401 M Street S.W., 3404
Washington, DC 20460
(202)260-2080
(202)260-6257 (Fax)
public-access@epamail.epa.gov (E-Mail)
http://www.epa.gov
Offers general information about the Agency and nontechnical publications on various environmental topics, such as air quality, pesticides, radon, indoor air, drinking water, water quality, and Superfund. Refers inquiries for technical information to the appropriate regional or program office. The public may visit the PIC Visitor Center between the hours of 10 a.m. and 4 p.m., Monday–Friday, except Federal holidays.

National Clearinghouse on FAMILIES AND YOUTH
P.O. Box 13505
Silver Spring, MD 20911
(301)608-8098
(301)608-8721 (FAX)
info@ncfy.com (E-Mail)
http://www.acf.dhhs.gov/programs/fysb/programs/ncfy.htm
Links those interested in youth issues with the resources they need to serve young people, families, and communities better. Offers services that can assist in locating answers to questions or in making valuable contacts with other programs.

FEDERAL INFORMATION Center (FIC) Program
(800)688-9889
(800)326-2996 (TDD/TTY)
http://fic.info.gov
Provides information about the Federal Government's agencies, programs, and services. Information specialists use an automated database, printed reference materials, and other resources to provide answers to inquiries or accurate referrals. Callers who speak Spanish will be assisted. A descriptive brochure on the FIC program is available free from Department 584B at the Consumer Information Center (see listing in this publication). 9 a.m. Eastern–5 p.m. Pacific Monday–Friday except Federal holidays.

B-26. FOOD AND DRUG Administration
Office of Consumer Affairs
5600 Fishers Lane, HFE-88
Rockville, MD 20857
(301)443-3170
(301)443-9767 (Fax)
http://www.fda.gov/fdahomepage.html
Responds to consumer requests for information and publications on foods, drugs, cosmetics, medical devices, radiation-emitting products, and veterinary products. 1 p.m.–3:30 p.m.

B-27. FOOD AND NUTRITION Information Center
National Agricultural Library/FNIC
U.S. Department of Agriculture, ARS
10301 Baltimore Boulevard Room 304
Beltsville, MD 20705-2351
(301)504-5719
(301)504-6409 (Fax)
fnic@nalusda.gov (E-Mail)
http://www.nal.usda.gov/fnic/
Provides information on human nutrition, food service management, and food technology. Acquires and lends books and audiovisual materials. Offers database searching and access through electronic mail.

Section C

B–28. Agency for HEALTH CARE POLICY and Research Clearinghouse
P.O. Box 8547
Silver Spring, MD 20907–8547
(800)358–9295
(301)495–3453
http://www.ahcpr.gov
Distributes lay and scientific publications produced by the agency, including clinical practice guidelines on a variety of topics, reports from the National Medical Expenditure Survey, and health care technology assessment reports.

B–29. National HEALTH INFORMATION Center
P.O. Box 1133
Washington, DC 20013–1133
(800)336–4797
(301)565–4167
(301)984–4256 (Fax)
nhicinfo@health.org (E–Mail)
http://nhic–nt.health.org (World Wide Web)
Helps the public and health professionals locate health information through identification of health information resources, an information and referral system, and publications. Uses a data–base containing descriptions of health–related organizations to refer inquirers to the most appropriate resources. Does not diagnose medical conditions or give medical advice. Prepares and distributes publications and directories on health promotion and disease prevention topics.

B–30. National Center for HEALTH STATISTICS
Data Dissemination Branch
6525 Belcrest Road, Room 1064
Hyattsville, MD 20782
(301)436–8500
nchsquery@cdc.gov (E–Mail)
http://www.cdc.gov/nchshome.htm (World Wide Web)
The Data Dissemination Branch of the National Center for Health Statistics answers requests for catalogs of publications and electronic data products; single copies of publications, such as Advance Data reports; ordering information for publications and electronic products sold through the Government Printing Office and National Technical Information Service; adding addresses to the mailing list for new publications; and specific statistical data collected by the National Center for Health Statistics.

Hereditary HEARING Impairment Resource Registry
555 North 30th Street
Omaha, NE 68131–9909
(800)320–1171
(402)498–6331 (FAX)
Disseminates and collects information, and matches families with scientists. Demographic information is collected from hearing–impaired individuals via a survey found in the HHIRR brochure (the demographic survey is also on–line). The brochure describes the mission and function of the HHIRR. Detailed enrolling information is collected via a 12–page registration questionnaire. Scientists wishing to access HHIRR families must submit a written research collaboration application. This request is reviewed by the HHIRR's National Advisory Committee. Information about the research project is given to appropriate HHIRR families, who then decide whether or not to participate.

B–31. National HEART, LUNG, AND BLOOD Institute (NHLBI)
Information Center
P.O. Box 30105
Bethesda, MD 20824–0105
(301)251–1222
(301)251–1223 (Fax)
nhlbiic@dgs.dgsys.com (E–Mail)
http://www.nhlbi.nih.gov/nhlbi/infcntr/infocent.htm
NHLBI serves as a source of information and materials on risk factors for cardiovascular disease. Services include dissemination of public education materials, programmatic and scientific information for health professionals, and materials on worksite health, as well as responses to information requests. Materials on cardiovascular health are available to consumers and professionals.

B–32. National HIGHWAY TRAFFIC SAFETY Administration
U.S. Department of Transportation
400 Seventh Street, SW.
Washington, DC 20590
(800)424–9393 (Hotline)
(202)366–0123 (Hotline)
(202)366–5962 (Fax)
http://www.nhtsa.dot.gov/
Provides information and referral on the effectiveness of occupant protection, such as safety belt use, child safety seats, and automobile recalls. Gives referrals to other Government agencies for consumer questions on warranties, service, automobile safety regulations, and reporting safety problems. Works with private organizations to promote safety programs. Provides technical and financial assistance to state and local governments and awards grants for highway safety.

B–33. The National Resource Center on HOMELESSNESS and Mental Illness
262 Delaware Avenue
Delmar, NY 12054
(800)444–7415
(518)439–7415
(518)439–7612 (Fax)
nrc@prainc.com. (E–Mail)
http://www.samhsa.gov/cmhs/cmhs.htm
Collects, synthesizes, and disseminates information on the services, supports, and housing needs of homeless people with serious mental illnesses. Maintains extensive database of published and unpublished materials, prepares customized database searches, holds workshops and national conferences, provides technical assistance.

B–34. HOUSING AND URBAN DEVELOPMENT (HUD) User
P.O. Box 6091
Rockville, MD 20850
(800)245–2691
(301)251–5154
(800)483–2209 (TDD)
http://www.hud.gov
Disseminates publications for U.S. Department of Housing and Urban Development's Office of Policy Development and Research. Offers database searches on housing research. Provides reports on housing safety, housing for elderly and handicapped persons and lead–based paint. (See also A–87, A–94, A–133)

B–35. INDOOR AIR Quality Information Clearinghouse
P.O. Box 37133
Washington, DC 20013–7133
(800)438–4318
Information specialists provide information, referrals, publications, and database searches on indoor air quality. Information is provided about pollutants and sources, health effects, control methods, commercial building operations and maintenance, standards and guidelines, and Federal and State legislation.

B–36. National INJURY Information Clearinghouse
U.S. Consumer Product Safety Commission
4330 East West Highway
Bethesda, MD 20814
(301)504–0424
(301)504–0124 (Fax)
info@cpsc.gov (E–Mail)
http://www.cpsc.gov/
Sponsored by the U.S. Consumer Product Safety Commission (CPSC). The clearinghouse collects and disseminates information on the causes and prevention of death, injury, and illness associated with consumer products. Compiles data obtained from accident reports, consumer complaints, death certificates, news clips, and the National Electronic Injury Surveillance System operated by the CPSC. Publications include statistical analyses of data and hazard and accident patterns.

B–37. National KIDNEY AND UROLOGIC Diseases Information Clearinghouse
3 Information Way
Bethesda, MD 20892–3580
(301)654–4415
(301)907–8906 (Fax)
NKUDIC@aerie.com
http://www.niddk.nih.gov/Brochures/NKUDIC.htm
The National Kidney and Urologic Diseases Information Clearinghouse (NKUDIC) is an information and referral service of the National Institute of Diabetes and Digestive and Kidney Diseases, one of the National Institutes of Health. The clearinghouse responds to written inquires, develops and distributes publications about kidney and urologic diseases, and provides referrals to digestive disease organizations, including support groups. The NKUDIC maintains a database of patient and professional education materials, from which literature searches are generated.

B–38. National LEAD Information Center
1019 19th Street, NW.
Suite 401
Washington, DC 20036–5015
(800)424–LEAD (Clearinghouse)
(800)LEAD–FYI (Hotline)
(800)526–5456 (TDD)
(202)659–1192 (Fax)
leadctr@nsc.org (E–Mail)
http://www.nsc.org/ehc/lead.htm
Sponsored by the National Safety Council. Responds to inquiries regarding lead and lead poisoning. Provides information on lead poisoning and children, lead–based paint, a list of local and State contacts who can help, and other lead–related questions. (See also A–87, A–94)

B–39. National Center for Education in MATERNAL AND CHILD HEALTH
2000 15th Street, North
Suite 701
Arlington, VA 22201–2617
(703)524–7802
(703)524–9335 (Fax)
ncemch@gumedlib.dml.georgetown.edu (E–mail)
http://www.ncemch.org
Sponsored by the Maternal and Child Health Bureau, Health Resources and Services Administration. Provides information to health professionals and the public, develops educational and reference materials, and provides technical assistance in program development. Subjects covered are women's health including pregnancy and childbirth; infant, child, and adolescent health; nutrition; children with special health needs; injury and violence prevention; health and safety in day care; and maternal and child health programs and services. Types of materials include professional literature, curricula, patient education materials, audiovisuals, and information about organizations and programs. Appointment preferred for on–site visits. Participates in the following electronic services: the Combined Health Information Database (CHID), National Library of Medicine's DIRLINE, and MCH–NetLink.

B–40. National MATERNAL AND CHILD HEALTH Clearinghouse
8201 Greensboro Drive
Suite 600
McLean, VA 22102
(703)821–8955, ext. 254 or 265
(703)821–2098 (Fax)
nmchc@circsol.com (E–Mail)
http://www.circsol.com/mch/
Sponsored by the Maternal and Child Health Bureau, Health Resources and Services Administration. Centralized source of materials and information in the areas of human genetics and maternal and child health. Distributes publications and provides referrals.

Section C

B–41. National Institute of MENTAL HEALTH
Information Resources and Inquiries Branch
5600 Fishers Lane
Room 7C–02
Rockville, MD 20857
(301)443–4513
(301)443–8431 (TDD)
(301)443–0008 (Fax)
(301)443–5158 (MENTAL HEALTH FAX4U   Fax Information System)
(800)64–PANIC (PANIC DISORDER Information)
(800)421–4211 (Depression/Awareness, Recognition, and Treatment Information)
nimhpubs@nih.gov (E–Mail)
nimhinfo@nih.gov (E–Mail)
http://www.nimh.nih.gov
Responds to information requests from the public, clinicians, and the scientific community, with a variety of printed materials on such subjects as children's mental disorders, schizophrenia, oppression, bipolar disorder, seasonal affective disorder, anxiety and panic disorders, obsessive–compulsive disorder, eating disorders, learning disabilities, and Alzheimer's disease. Information and publications on the Depression/ Awareness, Recognition, and Treatment Program (D/ART) and on the Panic Disorder Education Program, NIMH–sponsored educational programs on depressive and panic disorders, their symptoms and treatment, are distributed. Single copies of publications are free of charge. A list of NIMH publications, including several in Spanish, is available upon request.

B–42. Office of MINORITY HEALTH Resource Center
P.O. Box 37337
Washington, DC 20013–7337
(800)444–6472
(301)565–5112 (Fax)
info@omhrc.gov (E–Mail)
http://www.omhrc.gov/
Responds to information requests from health professionals and consumers on minority health issues and locates sources of technical assistance. Provides referrals to relevant organizations and distributes materials. Spanish– and Asian–speaking operators are available. (See also A–112)

B–44. Clearinghouse for OCCUPATIONAL SAFETY AND HEALTH INFORMATION
4676 Columbia Parkway
Cincinnati, OH 45226–1998
(800)35–NIOSH
(513)533–8326
(513)533–8573 (Fax)
pubstaff@cdc.gov (E–Mail)
http://www.cdc.gov/niosh/homepage.html
Provides technical information support for National Institute for Occupational Safety and Health (NIOSH) research programs and disseminates information to others on request. Services include reference and referral, and information about NIOSH studies. Distributes a publications list of NIOSH materials. Maintains automated database covering the field of occupational safety and health.

B–24. OPA Clearinghouse
P.O. Box 30686
Bethesda, MD 20824–0686
(301)654–6190
(301)907–9655 (Fax)
opa@osophs.dhhs.gov (E–Mail)
http://www.hhs.gov/progorg/opa/clearing.html
Sponsored by the Office of Population Affairs. Provides information and distributes publications to health professionals and the public in the areas of family planning, adolescent pregnancy, and adoption. Makes referrals to other information centers in related subject areas.

National ORAL HEALTH Information Clearinghouse
1 NOHIC Way
Bethesda MD 20892–3500
(301)403–7364
(301)907–8830 (Fax)
nidr@aerie.com (E–Mail)
http://www.nidr.nih.gov
A service of the National Institute of Dental Research (NIDR). Focuses on the oral health concerns of special care patients, including: people with genetic disorders or systemic diseases that compromise oral health, people whose medical treatment causes oral problems, and people with mental or physical disabilities that make good oral hygiene practices and dental care difficult. Develops and distributes information and educational materials on special care topics, maintains a bibliographic database on oral health information and materials, and provides information services with trained staff to respond to specific interests and questions.

OSTEOPOROSIS and Related Bone Diseases
National Resource Center
1150 17th Street NW., Suite 500
Washington, DC 20036
(800)624–BONE
(202)223–0344
(202)466–4315 (TDD)
(202)223–2237 (Fax)
orbdnrc@nof.org (E–Mail)
http://www.osteo.org/
Sponsored by the National Institute of Arthritis and Musculoskeletal and Skin Diseases. Provides patients, health professionals, and the public with resources and information on metabolic bone diseases such as osteo–porosis, Paget's disease of the bone, osteogenesis imper–fecta, and primary hyperparathyroidism. Specific populations include the elderly, men, women, and adolescents.

B–45. President's Council on PHYSICAL FITNESS and Sports
701 Pennsylvania Avenue NW.
Suite 250
Washington, DC 20004
(202)272–3421
(202)504–2064 (Fax)
http://www.whitehouse.gov/WH/PCPFS/html/fitnet.html
Conducts a public service advertising program, prepares educational materials, and works to promote the development of physical fitness leadership, facilities, and programs. Helps schools, clubs, recreation agencies, employers, and Federal agencies design and implement programs. Offers a variety of testing, recognition, and incentive programs for individuals, institutions, and organizations. Materials on exercise and physical fitness for all ages are available.

B–46. POLICY Information Center
Office of the Assistant Secretary for Planning and Evaluation
U.S. Department of Health and Human Services
Hubert H. Humphrey Building
Room 438F
200 Independence Avenue SW.
Washington, DC 20201
(202)690–6445
(202)690–6518 (Fax)
http://www.os.dhhs.gov (World Wide Web)
http://www.whitehouse.gov/WH/PCPFS/html/fitnet.html
A centralized repository of evaluations, short–term evaluative research reports and program inspections/audits relevant to the Department's operations, programs, and policies. It also includes relevant reports from the General Accounting Office (GAO), Congressional Budget Office (CBO), Office of Technology Assessment (OTA), and the Institute of Medicine and the National Research Council's Committee on National Statistics, both part of the National Academy of Sciences, Departments of Agriculture, Labor, and Education, as well as from the private sector. Final reports and executive summaries are available for review at the facility, or final reports may be purchased from the National Technical Information Service (NTIS). In addition, the PIC online database of evaluation abstracts are accessible on Internet through HHS HomePage, http://www.os.dhhs.gov or gopher.os.dhhs.gov. The database includes over 6,000 project descriptions of both in–process and completed studies. PIC Highlights, a quarterly publication, features articles of recently completed studies.

B–47. National Clearinghouse for PRIMARY CARE Information
Ticon Courthouse
2070 Chain Bridge Road
Suite 450
Vienna, VA 22182
(703)821–8955, ext. 245
(703)556–4831 (TTY/TDD)
(703)821–2098 (Fax)
http://www.bphc.hrsa.dhhs.gov
Sponsored by the Bureau of Primary Health Care (BPHC), Health Resources and Services Administration. Provides information services to support the planning, development, and delivery of ambulatory health care to urban and rural areas that have shortages of medical personnel and services. A primary role of the clearinghouse is to identify, obtain, and disseminate information to community and migrant health centers. Distributes publications focusing on ambulatory care, financial management, primary health care, and health services administration of special interest to professionals working in primary care centers funded by BPHC. Materials are available on health education, governing boards, financial management, administrative management, and clinical care. Bilingual medical phrase books, a directory of federally funded health centers, and an annotated bibliography are available also.

B–48. U.S. Consumer PRODUCT SAFETY Commission Hotline
Washington, DC 20207
(800)638–2772
(800)638–8270 (TT)
(301)504–0580
(301)504–0399 (Fax)
http://www.cpsc.gov
Maintains the National Injury Information Clearinghouse, conducts investigations of alleged unsafe/defective products, and establishes product safety standards. Assists consumers in evaluating the comparative safety of products and conducts education programs to increase consumer awareness. Operates the National Electronic Injury Surveillance System, which monitors a statistical sample of hospital emergency rooms for injuries associated with consumer products. Maintains free hotline to provide information about recalls and to receive reports on unsafe products and product–related injuries. Publications describe hazards associated with electrical products and children's toys. Spanish–speaking operator available through the toll–free number listed above.

Section C

B–49. National REHABILITATION Information Center
8455 Colesville Road
Suite 935
Silver Spring, MD 20910
(800)346–2742 (Voice/TT)
(301)588–9284 (Voice/TT)
(301)587–1967 (Fax)
http://www.naric.com/naric
The National Rehabilitation Center (NARIC) is a library and information center on disability and rehabilitation. Funded by the National Institute on Disability and Rehabilitation Research, NARIC collects and disseminates the results of federally funded research projects. The collection, which also includes commercially published books, journal articles, and audiovisuals, grows at a rate of about 300 documents per month.

B–50. RURAL Information Center Health Service (RICHS)
National Agricultural Library
Room 304
10301 Baltimore Boulevard
Beltsville, MD 20705–2351
(800)633–7701
(301)504–5547
(301)504–6856 (TDD)
(301)504–5181 (Fax)
ric@nalusda.gov (E–mail)
http://www.nal.usda.gov/ric/richs
Disseminates information on a variety of rural health issues including health professions, health care financing, special populations and the delivery of health care services. Provides information, referrals, publications, brief complimentary literature searches and access to an electronic bulletin board to professionals and the public. Posts rural health information on the Internet. RICHS is funded by the Federal Office of Rural Health Policy, DHHS and is part of the USDA Rural Information Center, which provides information on rural issues such as economic development, local government viability and community well–being. (See also A–168)

National Center on SLEEP DISORDERS Research
2 Rockledge Center
6701 Rockledge Drive
MSC 7920
Bethesda, MD 20892–7920
(301)435–0199
(301)480–3451 (FAX)
http://www.nhlbi.nih.gov/nhlbi/nhlbi.htm
Promotes basic, clinical and applied research on sleep and sleep disorders by strengthening existing sleep research programs, training new investigators, and creating new programs aimed at addressing important gaps and opportunities in sleep and sleep disorders.

B–51. Office on SMOKING and Health Centers for Disease Control and Prevention
National Center for Chronic Disease Prevention and Health Promotion
Mailstop K–50
4770 Buford Highway, N.E.
Atlanta, GA 30341–3724
(800)CDC–1311
(770)488–5705
(770)488–5939 (Fax)
ccdinfo@ccdod1.em.cdc.gov (E–Mail)
http://www.cdc.gov/nccdphp/osh/tobacco.htm
Develops and distributes the annual Surgeon General's report on smoking and health, coordinates a national public information and education program on tobacco use and health, and coordinates tobacco education and research efforts within the Department of Health and Human Services and throughout both federal and state governments. Maintains the Smoking and Health database, consisting of approximately 60,000 records available on CD–ROM (CDP File) through the Government Printing Office (Superintendent of Documents, Government Printing Office, Washington, D.C. 20402.) Provides information on smoking cessation, ETS/passive smoking, pregnancy/infants, professional/technical information, and a publications list upon request. Provides specific promotional campaign materials through its toll–free hotline.

B–52. National SUDDEN INFANT DEATH SYNDROME Resource Center
2070 Chan Bridge Road
Vienna, VA 22182
(703)821–8955
(703)821–2098 (Fax)
sids@circsol.com (E–Mail)
http://www.circsol.com/SIDS
Sponsored by the Maternal and Child Health Bureau, Health Resources and Services Administration. Provides information and educational materials on sudden infant death syndrome (SIDS), apnea, and other related issues. Responds to information requests from professionals and from the public. Maintains a library of standard reference materials on topics related to SIDS. Maintains and updates mailing lists of State programs, groups, and individuals concerned with SIDS. Also develops fact sheets, catalogs, and bibliographies on areas of special interest to the community. Conducts customized searches of database on SIDS and SIDS–related materials.

National TECHNICAL INFORMATION Service
U.S. Department of Commerce
Springfield, VA 22161
(703)487–4650
(703)321–8547 (Fax)
http://www.fedworld.gov/ntis/ntishome.html
Sells more than 9,000 federally produced audiovisual programs. Provides catalogs at no cost. Several catalogs cover health–related topics, including alcohol and other drug abuse, emergency fire services, industrial safety, and occupational health.

National Clearinghouse for Worker Safety and Health Training for HAZARDOUS MATERIALS, WASTE OPERATIONS, and EMERGENCY RESPONSE
c/o The George Meany Center for Labor Studies
10000 New Hampshire Avenue
Silver Spring, MD 20903
(301)431–5425
(301)434–0371 (Fax)
chouse@dgsys.com (E–mail)
http://www.niehs.nih.gov/wetp/clear.htm
The Clearinghouse is supported by the Superfund Worker Training Program of the National institute of Environmental Health Sciences (NIEHS) to provide information and support services to NIEHS–funded hazardous materials, waste operations, and emergency response worker training programs. Disseminates related information and materials to the general public.

International Organizations

ARGENTINA

Argentinan Association of Dermatology, Asociacion Argentina De Dermatolo, Mexico 1720, 1100 Buenos Aires, Argentina; tel. 381–2737; FAX. 381–2737; Dra. Lidia Ester Valle, Chairman

AUSTRALIA

Australian Healthcare Association, P.O. Box 54, Deakin West, ACT, 2600, Australia; tel. +612 62851488; FAX. +612 62822395; Tracey Turner, Office Manager

BELGIUM

International Federation of Oto–Rhino–Laryngological Societies, IFOS–MISA–NKO Oosterveldlaan 24, 2610 WILRIJK, Belgium; tel. 3 4433611; Ms. Gadeyne, Administrator, Publication Manager

Verbond der Verzorgingsinstellingen V.Z.W., 1, Guimardstraat, Brussels 1040, Belgium; tel. 2 5118008; FAX. 2 5135269; Mrs. C. Boonen, M.D., General Director

BRAZIL

Fraternidade Crista De Doentes E Deficientes, Cap. Correa Pacheco 134, Americana, SP, 13470, Brazil; tel. 0 194 619754; Celso Zoppi

CANADA

Association des Medecins de langue francaise du Canada, 8355 St. Laurent Boulevard, Montreal, PQ H2P 2Z6, Canada; tel. 514/388–2228; FAX. 514/388–5335; Andre' de Seve, General Director

Canadian Anaesthetists' Society, One Eglinton Avenue East, Suite 208, Toronto, ON M4P 3A1, Canada; tel. 416/480–0602; FAX. 416/480–0320; Ann Andrews, CAE, Executive Director

Canadian Association of Medical Radiation Technologists, 280 Metcalfe Street, Suite 410, Ottawa, ON K2P 1R7, Canada; tel. 613/234–0012; FAX. 613/234–1097; Earl P. Rooney, Executive Director

Canadian Association of Pathologists, Office of the Secretariat, 774 Echo Drive, Ottawa, ON K1S 5N8, Canada; tel. 613–730–6230; FAX. 613/730–0260; Dr. Rosemary Henderson, Secretary–Treasurer

Canadian Association of Social Workers, 383 Parkdale Avenue, Suite 402, Ottawa, ON K1Y 4R4, Canada; tel. 613/729–6668; FAX. 613/729–9608; Eugenia Repetur Moreno, Executive Director

Canadian Cancer Society, 10 Alcorn Avenue, Suite 200, Toronto, ON M4V 3B1, Canada; tel. 416/961–7223; FAX. 416/961–4189; Dorothy Lamont, Chief Executive Officer

Canadian Cardiovascular Society, 222 Queen Street, Suite 1403, Ottawa, On K1P SV9, Canada; tel. 613/569–3407; FAX. 613/569–6574; Charles Shields, Jr., Executive Director

Canadian College of Health Record Administrators, Canadian Health Record Association, 1090 Don Mills Road, Suite 501, Don Mills, ON M3C 3G8, Canada; tel. 416/447–4900; FAX. 416/447–4598; Deborah Del Duca, Executive Director

Canadian Council of the Blind, 396 Cooper Street, Suite 405, Ottawa, ON K2P 2H7, Canada; tel. 613/567–0311; FAX. 613/567–2728; Mary Lee Moran, Executive Director

Canadian Council on Social Development, 441 Maclaren, Fourth Floor, Ottawa, ON K2P 2H3, Canada; tel. 613/236–8977; FAX. 613/236–2750; Nancy Perkins, Communications Coordinator

Canadian Dental Association, 1815 Alta Vista Drive, Ottawa, ON K1G 3Y6, Canada; tel. 613/523–1770; FAX. 613/523–7736; Jardine Neilson, Executive Director

Canadian Healthcare Association, Association Canadienne des soins de sante, 17 York Street, Suite 100, Ottawa, ON K1N 9J6, Canada; tel. 613/241–8005; FAX. 613/241–5055; Sharon Sholzberg–Gray, President

Canadian Medical Engineering Consultants, 594 Bush Street, Belfountain, ON L0N 1B0, Canada; tel. 519/927–3286; FAX. 519/927–9440; A. M. Dolan, President

Canadian Mental Health Association, 2160 Yonge Street, Toronto, ON M4S 2Z3, Canada; tel. 416/484–7750; FAX. 416/484–4617; Edward J. Pennington, General Director

Canadian National Institute for the Blind, 320 McLeod Street, Ottawa, ON K2P1A3, Canada; tel. 613/563–4021; FAX. 416/480–7677; Angelo Nikias, National Director, Gov't Relations

Canadian Nurses Association, 50 Driveway, Ottawa, ON K2P 1E2, Canada; tel. 613/237–2133; FAX. 613/237–3520; Mary Ellen Jeans, RN, Ph.D., Executive Director

Canadian Orthopaedic Association, 1440 Ste. Catherine Street, W., Suite 421, Montreal, PQ H3G 1R8, Canada; tel. 514/874–9003; FAX. 514/874–0464; Dr. David Petrie, President (as of 6/23/98)

Canadian Pharmacists Association, 1785 Alta Vista Drive, Ottawa, ON K1G 3Y6, Canada; tel. 613/523–7877; FAX. 613/523–0445; Leroy C. Fevang, Executive Director

Canadian Physiotherapy Association, National Office, 2345 Yonge Street, Suite 410, Toronto, ON M4P 2E5, Canada; tel. 416/932–1888; FAX. 416/932–9708; Dan Stapleton, Chief Executive Officer

Canadian Psychiatric Association, 441 MacLaren Street, Suite 260, Ottawa, ON K2P2H3, Canada; tel. 613/234–2815; FAX. 613/234–9857, ext. 36; Alex Saunders, Chief Executive Officer

Canadian Public Health Association, 1565 Carling Avenue, Suite 400, Ottawa, ON K1Z 8R1, Canada; tel. 613/725–3769; FAX. 613/725–9826; Gerald H. Dafoe, M.H.A., Chief Executive Officer

Canadian Rehabilitation Council for the Disabled, 45 Sheppard Avenue, E., Suite 801, Toronto, ON M2N 5W9, Canada; tel. 416/250–7490; FAX. 416/229–1371; Henry Botchford, National Executive Director

Canadian Society for Medical Laboratory Science, Box 2830, LCD 1, Hamilton, ON L8N 3N8, Canada; tel. 905/528–8642; FAX. 905/528–4968; E. Valerie Booth, Executive Director

Canadian Society of Hospital Pharmacists, 1145 Hunt Club Road, Suite 350, Ottawa, ON K1V 0Y3, Canada; tel. 613/736–9733; FAX. 613/736–5660; Bill Leslie, Executive Director

Catholic Health Association of Canada, 1247 Kilborn Place, Ottawa, ON K1H 6K9, Canada; tel. 613/731–7148; FAX. 613/731–7797; Richard Haughian, President

College des medecins du Quebec, 2170, boul. Rene–Levesque Quest, Montreal, PQ H3H 2T8, Canada; tel. 514/933–4441; FAX. 514/993–3112; Joelle Lescop, MD, Secretary General

College of Family Physicians of Canada, 2630 Skymark Avenue, Mississauga, ON L4W 5A4, Canada; tel. 905/629–0900; FAX. 905/629–0893; Dr. Claude A. Renaud, Director, Professional Affairs

College of Physicians and Surgeons of New Brunswick, One Hampton Road, Suite 300, Rothesay, NB E2E 5K8, Canada; tel. 506/849–5050; FAX. 506/849–5069; Ed Schollenberg, M.D., Registrar

Dietitions of Canada, 480 University Avenue, Suite 604, Toronto, ON M5G 1V2, Canada; tel. 416/596–0857; FAX. 416/596–0603; Marsha Sharp, Chief Executive Officer

National Cancer Institute of Canada, 10 Alcorn Avenue, Suite 200, Toronto, ON M4V 3B1, Canada; tel. 416/961–7223; FAX. 416/961–4189; Robert A. Phillips, Ph. D., Executive Director

The Canadian Hearing Society, 271 Spadina Road, Toronto, ON M5R 2V3, Canada; tel. 416/964–9595; FAX. 416/928–2506; David Allen, Executive Director

The Canadian Medical Association, Box 8650, Ottawa, ON K1G 0G8, Canada; tel. 613/731–9331; FAX. 613/731–7314; Leo–Paul Landry, M.D., Secretary General

The Canadian Red Cross Society, National Office, 1800 Alta Vista Drive, Ottawa, ON K1G 4J5, Canada; tel. 613/739–2220; FAX. 613/739–2505; Claude Houde, National Director, Blood Services

The Royal College of Physicians and Surgeons of Canada, 774 Echo Drive, Ottawa, ON K1S 5N8, Canada; tel. 613/730–6201; FAX. 613/730–2410; Mrs. Pierrette Leonard, APR, Head Communications Section

World Federation of Hemophilia, 1310 Greene Ave., Suite 500, Montreal, PQ H3Z 2B2, Canada; tel. 514/933–7944; FAX. 514/933–8916; Mrs. Line Robillard, Executive Director

DENMARK

Amtsradsforeningen, Dampfaergevej 22, Postboks 2593, DK–2100 Copenhagen 0, Denmark; tel. +45 35 29 81 00; FAX. +45 35 29 83 00; Ida Sofie Jensen, Assistant Director

Danish Dental Association, Amaliegade 17, Postboks 143, DK–1004, Copenhagen, Denmark; tel. 45 33157711; FAX. 45 33151637; Karsten Thuen, Chief Executive Director

National Committee for Danish Hospitals, Amtsradsforeningen, Dampfaergevej 2, Postboks 2593, DK–2100 Copenhagen 0, Denmark; tel. +45 35 29 81 00; FAX. +45 35 29 83 00; Ida Sofie Jensen, Assistant Director

ENGLAND

British Medical Association, B.M.A. House Tavistock Square, London, WCH1 9JP, England; tel. 0171/387–4499; FAX. 0171/383–6400; Dr. E.M. Armstrong, B. Sc., LFRCP(Glas),FRCGP,LFRCP ED., Secretary

European Association of Poisons/Centres and Clinical Toxicologists (EAPCCT), City Hospital, Birmingham, B187QH, England; tel. (44) 121 507 4123; FAX. (44) 121 507 5580; Dr. Allister Vale, President

Institute of Health Services Management (United Kingdom and International), 7–10 Chandos Street, London,WIM,9DE, England; tel. 0171/460–7654; FAX. 0171/460–7655; Suzanne Tyler, Deputy Director

International Hospital Federation, Four Abbots Place, London, NW6 4NP, England; tel. 44/171 372 7181; FAX. 44/171 328 7433; Professor Per–Gunnar Svensson, Director General

King's Fund, 11–13 Cavendish Square, London, W1M 0AN, England; tel. 0171/307–2400; FAX. 0171/307–2801; R. J. Maxwell, Chief Executive Officer, Secretary

Nuffield Trust, 59 New Cavendish Street, London W1M 7RD, England; tel. 0171/631–8450; FAX. 0171/631–8451; John Owen, Secretary

FRANCE

World Medical Association, 28 Avenue des Alpes, B.P. 63, 01212 Ferney–Voltaire, Cedex, France; tel. 450 407575; FAX. 450 405937; Dr. Delon Human, Secretary General

GERMANY

Deutsche Krankenhausgesellschaft, (German Hospital Association), Tersteegenstrasse 9, D40474, Dusseldorf, Germany; tel. 211 454730; FAX. 211 4547361; Jorg Robbers, Director General

International Academy of Cytology, Universitaets–Frauenklinik, Hugstetterstrausse 55, D–79106 Freiburg i. Br., Germany; tel. 761 2703012; FAX. 761 2703112; Manuel Hilgarth, M.D., F.I.A.C.

HUNGARY

Magyar Korhazszovetseg, Furedi utca 9/c. VIII.34., 1144 Hungary, Budapest, Hungary; tel. (36–1) 163–52–73; FAX. (36–1) 163–52–73; Dr. I. Mikola, President

KOREA

Korean Hospital Association, (Mapo Hyun Dai Building), 35–1 Mapo–dong, Mapo–g, Seoul 121–050, Korea; tel. 2 7187521; FAX. 2 7187522; Ho Uk Ha, Ph.D., Vice President

MEXICO

Federacion Latinoamericana de Hospitales, Apartado Postal 107–076, C.P. 06741, Mexico D.F., Mexico; tel. 5 482650; Dr. Guillermo Fajardo, Representative

NETHERLANDS

Federation of Health Care Organizations in the Netherlands, Postbus 9696, NL–3506 GR Utrecht, Netherlands; tel. 30 739911; FAX. 30 739438

PERU

Peruvian Hospital Association, Av. Dos De Mayo 8502 Of. 203, San Isidro, Lima 27, Peru; tel. 14 419546; Arturo Vasi Paez, President

PHILIPPINES

Philippine Hospital Association, 14 Kamias Rd., Quezon City–1102 Metro M, Philippines; tel. 2 9227674/75; Thelma Navarrete–Clemente, M.D., M.H.A., President

Health Organizations, Agencies, and Providers **C29**

SOUTH AFRICA

Provincial Administration, Health Services Branch, P.O. Box 517, Bloemfontein 9300, South Africa, South Africa; tel. 051/4055818; FAX. 051/304958; Dr. J. H. Kotze

SWITZERLAND

H+ Die Spitaler der Schweiz, (Swiss Hospital Association), Rain 32, CH–5001, Aarau, Switzerland; tel. 62 824 1222; FAX. 62 822 33 35; Mr. Christof Haudenschild, Director

World Health Organization, 20 Avenue Appia, CH–1211 Geneva 27, Switzerland; tel. 22 791 21 11; FAX. 22 791 07 46; Hiroshi Nakajima, M.D., Ph.D., Director–General

UNITED STATES

American College of Gastroenterology, 4900B South 31st Street, Arlington, VA 22206, United State; tel. 703/820–7400; FAX. 703/931–4520; Thomas F. Fise, Executive Director

American Society for Testing and Materials, 100 Barr Harbor Drive, West Conshohocken, PA 19428–2959, United State; tel. 610/832–9672; FAX. 610/832–9666; Kenneth C. Pearson, Vice President

Association for Assessment and Accreditation of Laboratory Animal Care International, 11300 Rockville Pike, Suite 1211, Rockville, MD 20852–3035, United State; tel. 301/231–5353; FAX. 301/231–8282; Dr. John G. Miller, Executive Director

Association for Volunteer Administration, P.O. Box 32092, Richmond, VA 23294, United State; tel. 804/346–2266; FAX. 804/346–3318; Katherine H. Campbell, Executive Director

International Academy of Podiatric Medicine (IAPM), 4603 Highway 95 South, P.O. Box 39, Cocolalla, ID 83813–0039, United State; tel. 208/683–3900; FAX. 208/683–3700; Judith A. Baerg, Executive Director

International Aid, Inc., 17011 West Hickory, Spring Lake, MI 49456–9712, United State; tel. 616/846–7490; FAX. 616/846–3842; Warren L. Prelesnik, FACHE, Director, Medical Procurement

International Association for Dental Research, 1619 Duke Street, Alexandria, VA 22314–3406, United State; tel. 703/548–0066; FAX. 703/548–1883; John J. Clarkson, BDS, Ph.D., Executive Director

International Association of Ocular Surgeons, 4711 Golf Road, Suite 408, Skokie, IL 60076, United State; tel. 847/568–1500; FAX. 847/568–1527; Randall T. Bellows, M.D., Director

International Association of Pediatric Laboratory Medicine, 6728 Old McLean Village Drive, McLean, VA 22101, United State; tel. 703/556–9222; FAX. 703/556–8729; George K. Degnon, Executive Director

International Council on Social Welfare/U.S. Committee, 750 First Street, N.E., Washington, DC 20002, United State; tel. 202/336–8274; FAX. 202/336–8311; Toshio Tatara, Chair

International Executive Housekeepers Association, Inc., 1001 Eastwind Drive, Suite 301, Westerville, OH 43081–3361, United State; tel. 800/200–6342; FAX. 614/895–1248; Beth Risinger, Chief Executive Officer, Executive Director

International Tremor Foundation, 7046 W. 105th Street, Overland Park, KS 66212–1803, United State; tel. 913/341–3880; FAX. 913/341–1296; Catherine S. Rice, Executive Director

Rehabilitation International, 25 East 21st Street, New York, NY 10010, United State; tel. 212/420–1500; FAX. 212/505–0871; John Stott, President

Sigma Theta Tau International Honor Society of Nursing, 550 West North Street, Indianapolis, IN 46202, United State; tel. 317/634–8171; FAX. 317/634–8188; Nancy A. Dickenson–Hazard, Executive Officer

World Federation of Public Health Associations, c/o APHA, 1015 15th Street, N., Washington, DC 20005, United State; tel. 202/789–5696; FAX. 202/789–5681; Diane Kuntz, M.P.H., Executive Secretary

VENEZUELA

Latin American Association for the Study of the Liver (LAASL), P.O. Box 51890, Sabana Grande, Caracas, 1050–A, Venezuela; tel. 58–2–9799380; FAX. 58–2–9799380; Dr. Miguel A. Garassini, President

U. S. GOVERNMENT AGENCIES

The following information is based on data available as of March 1998.
For more information about U.S. government agencies, consult the U.S. Government Manual, available from the Office of the Federal Register, *National Archives and Records Service, Washington, DC 20408. A telephone directory of the U.S. Department of Health and Human Services is available from the Superintendent of Documents, Government Printing Office, Washington, DC 20402. Additional assistance may be obtained by contacting the American Hospital Association's Washington office, 325 Seventh Street, N.W., Washington, DC 20004.*

Executive Office of the President
tel. 202/456-1414

Counsel to the President: Charles Ruff; 202/456-2632

Chief of Staff: Erskine Dowles; 202/456-6797

Assistant to the President for Economic Policy: Gene B. Sperling; 202/456-5808

Assistant to the President for Domestic Policy: Bruce Reed; 202/456-2216

Assistant to the President and Director of Public Liaison: Maria Echaveste; 202/456-2930

COUNCIL OF ECONOMIC ADVISORS
Chairman: Dr. Janet Yellen

OFFICE OF MANAGEMENT AND BUDGET
Director: Franklin D. Raines; 202/395-3080

Department of Agriculture
tel. 202/720-8732

Secretary: Dan Glickman; 202/720-3631

Department of Commerce
tel. 202/482-2000

Secretary: William M. Daley; 202/482-2112
BUREAU OF ECONOMIC ANALYSIS
Director: Steven Landefeld; 202/606-9900
ECONOMIC DEVELOPMENT ADMINISTRATION
Assistant Secretary: Phillip Singerman; 202/482-5112
NATIONAL INSTITUTE OF STANDARDS AND TECHNOLOGY
Director: Raymond Krammer; 301/975-3058

Department of Defense
tel. 703/545-6700

Secretary: William S. Cohen; 703/695-5261

Assistant Secretary of Defense (Health Affairs): VACANT
CIVILIAN HEALTH AND MEDICAL PROGRAMS OF THE UNIFORMED SERVICES (OCHAMPUS) (Denver, CO)
Director: Seileen Mullen; 303/361-1313
UNIFORMED SERVICES UNIVERSITY OF THE HEALTH SCIENCES
President: James A. Zimble; 301/295-3030
DEPARTMENT OF THE AIR FORCE
Surgeon General: Charles H. Roadman II; 202/767-4343
DEPARTMENT OF THE ARMY
Surgeon General: Lt. Gen. Ronald R. Blanck; 703/681-3000
DEPARTMENT OF THE NAVY
Surgeon General of the Navy: V.A.D.M. Harold M. Koenig; 202/762-3701

Department of Education
tel. 202/401-2000

Secretary: Richard W. Riley; 202/401-3000

Department of Health and Human Services
tel. 202/619-0257

Secretary: Donna E. Shalala; 202/690-7000
General Counsel: Harriet Rabb; 202/690-7741
MANAGEMENT AND BUDGET
Assistant Secretary: John J. Callahan, Ph.D.; 202/690-6396
HEALTH
Acting Assistant Secretary: Jo Ivey Boufford; 202/690-7694
ADMINISTRATION FOR CHILDREN AND FAMILIES
Assistant Secretary: Olivia A. Golden; 202/401-2337
LEGISLATION
Assistant Secretary/Designate: Richard J. Tarplin; 202/690-7627
PLANNING AND EVALUATION
Principal deputy Association Secretary: David Garrison; 202/690-7858
PUBLIC AFFAIRS
Assistant Secretary: Melissa Skolfield; 202/690-7850
PUBLIC HEALTH SERVICE
Surgeon General: David Satcher, M.D.; 301/443-4000
Center for Disease Control, Atlanta 30333
Deputy Director: Dr. Claire V. Broome; 404/639-7000
Food and Drug Administration, Rockville, MD 20857
Commissioner: VACANT
Health Resources and Services Administration, Hyattsville, MD 20782
Administrator: Ciro Sumaya, M.D.; 301/443-2216
Rockville, MD 20857
Administrator: Claude E. Fox, M.D. (Acting)
National Institutes of Health, Bethesda, MD 20892
Director: Harold Varmus, M.D.; 301/496-2433
Substance Abuse and Mental Health Services Administration, Rockville, MD
Administrator: Nelba Chavez, Ph.D.; 301/443-4795
HEALTH CARE FINANCING ADMINISTRATION
Administrator: Nancy-Ann Min De Parle; 202/690-6726
SOCIAL SECURITY ADMINISTRATION: Baltimore, MD 21235
Commissioner: John W. Callahan; 410/965-7700
Regional Commissioners telephone: 800/772-1213
(1) Boston
Manny Vaz
(2) New York
Beatrice M. Disman
(3) Philadelphia
Larry G. Massanari
(4) Atlanta
Gordon M. Sherman
(5) Chicago
Myrtle S. Habersham
(6) Dallas
Horace L. Dickerson
(7) Kansas City
Michael Grochowski
(8) Denver
Horace L. Dickerson
(9) San Francisco
Linda S. McMahon
(10) Seattle
Marty Baer

Department of Housing and Urban Development
tel. 202/708-1112

Secretary: Andrew Cuomo; 202/708-0417

Department of Justice
tel. 202/514-2000

Attorney General: Janet Reno; 202/514-2000

DRUG ENFORCEMENT ADMINISTRATION
Administrator: Thomas A. Constantine; 202/307-8000

Department of Labor
tel. 202/219-5000

Secretary: Alexis M. Herman; 202/219-8271

BUREAU OF LABOR STATISTICS
Commissioner: Katharine G. Abraham; 202/606-7800

EMPLOYMENT AND TRAINING ADMINISTRATION
Acting Assistant Secretary: Ray Uhalde; 202/219-6050

OCCUPATIONAL SAFETY AND HEALTH ADMINISTRATION
Acting Assistant Secretary: Greg Watchman; 202/219-7162

Department of State
tel. 202/647-4000

Secretary: Madeleine Albright; 202/647-6575

AGENCY FOR INTERNATIONAL DEVELOPMENT
Administrator: J. Brian Atwood; 202/647-9620

Independent Agencies

U.S. COMMISSION ON CIVIL RIGHTS
Chairperson: Mary Frances Berry; 202/376-7572

CONSUMER PRODUCT SAFETY COMMISSION
Chairperson: Ann Brown; 301/504-0213

ENVIRONMENTAL PROTECTION AGENCY
Administrator: Carol M. Browner; 202/260-4700

EQUAL EMPLOYMENT OPPORTUNITY COMMISSION
Chairman: Gilbert Casellas; 202/663-4001

FEDERAL EMERGENCY MANAGEMENT AGENCY
Director: James Lee Witt; 202/646-3923

Government-Related Groups *Federally aided corporations and quasi-official agencies, such as American Red Cross, National Academy of Sciences and World Health Organization, are listed with International, National, and Regional Organizations beginning on page C3.*

State and Local Organizations and Agencies

Blue Cross–Blue Shield Plans

The following list of Blue Cross and Blue Shield Plans is based on the Winter 1997 edition of the Directory Blue Cross and Blue Shield Plans, obtained from Blue Cross and Blue Shield Association, 225 N. Michigan Ave., Chicago, IL 60601; tel. 312/297–6000. When addressing mail to a plan, use the post office box number.

United States

ALABAMA: Blue Cross and Blue Shield of Alabama, 450 Riverchase Parkway, E., P.O. Box 995, Birmingham, AL 35298; tel. 205/988–2200; FAX. 205/988–2949; E. Gene Thrasher, Chief Executive Officer

ALASKA: Blue Cross of Washington and Alaska, Blue Cross and Blue Shield of Alaska, 7001 220th Street, S.W., Mountlake Terrace, WA 9804, P.O. Box 327, Seattle, WA 98111–0327; tel. 206/670–5900; FAX. 206/670–4900; Betty Woods, President, Chief Executive Officer

ARIZONA: Blue Cross and Blue Shield of Arizona, Inc., 2444 West Las Palmaritas Drive, Phoenix, AZ 85021, P.O. Box 13466, Phoenix, AZ 85002–3466; tel. 602/864–4100; FAX. 602/864–4242; Robert B. Bulla, President, Chief Executive Officer

ARKANSAS: Arkansas Blue Cross and Blue Shield, a Mutual Insurance Company, 601 Gaines Street, Little Rock, AR 72201, P.O. Box 2181, Little Rock, AR 72203; tel. 501/378–2010; FAX. 501/378–2037; Robert L. Shoptaw, President, Chief Executive Officer

CALIFORNIA: Blue Cross of California, CaliforniaCare Health Plans, 21555 Oxnard Street, Woodland Hills, CA 91367, P.O. Box 70000, Van Nuys, CA 91470; tel. 818/703–2345; FAX. 818/703–2848; Leonard D. Schaeffer, Chairman, Chief Executive Office

Blue Shield of California, California Physicians' Service Corporation, P.O. Box 7168, San Francisco, CA 94120; tel. 415/229–5000; FAX. 415/229–5056; Wayne R. Moon, Chairman, Chief Executive Officer

COLORADO: Blue Cross and Blue Shield of Colorado, Rocky Mountain Hospital and Medical Service, 700 Broadway, Denver, CO 80273–0002; tel. 303/831–2131; FAX. 303/830–0887; C. David Kikumoto, President, Chief Executive Officer

CONNECTICUT: Anthem Blue Cross and Blue Shield of Connecticut, Inc., 370 Bassett Road, P.O. Box 504, North Haven, CT 06473; tel. 203/239–4911; FAX. 203/239–7742; Harry J. Torello, President, Chief Executive Officer

DELAWARE: Blue Cross and Blue Shield of Delaware, Blue Cross and Blue Shield of Delaware, Inc., One Brandywine Gateway, P.O. Box 1991, Wilmington, DE 19899; tel. 302/429–0260; FAX. 302/421–2089; Robert C. Cole, Jr., President, Chief Executive Officer

DISTRICT OF COLUMBIA: Blue Cross and Blue Shield of the National Capital Area, 550 12th Street, S.W., Washington, DC 20065; tel. 202/479–8000; FAX. 202/479–3520; Larry C. Glasscock, President, Chief Executive Officer

FLORIDA: Blue Cross and Blue Shield of Florida, Inc., 532 Riverside Avenue, Jacksonville, FL 32202, P.O. Box 1798, Jacksonville, FL 32231–0014; tel. 904/791–6111; FAX. 904/791–8081; William E. Flaherty, Chairman, Chief Executive Officer

GEORGIA: Blue Cross and Blue Shield of Georgia, Inc., Capital City Plaza, 3350 Peachtree Road, N.E., Atlanta, GA 30326, P.O. Box 4445, Atlanta, GA 30302–4445; tel. 404/842–8000; FAX. 404/842–8010; Richard D. Shirk, President, Chief Executive Officer

HAWAII: Blue Cross and Blue Shield of Hawaii, Hawaii Medical Service Association, 818 Keeaumoku Street, Honolulu, HI 96814, P.O. Box 860, Honolulu, HI 96808–0860; tel. 808/948–5517; FAX. 808/948–5999; Robert P. Hiam, President

IDAHO: Blue Cross of Idaho Health Service, Inc., 3000 East Pine Avenue, Meridian, ID 83642; tel. 208/345–4550; FAX. 208/331–7311; David L. Barnett, President, Chief Executive Officer

Regence Blue Shield of Idaho, 1602 21st Avenue, P.O. Box 1106, Lewiston, ID 83501; tel. 208/798–2102; FAX. 208/798–2085; John Ruch, President, Chief Executive Officer

ILLINOIS: Blue Cross and Blue Shield of Illinois, Health Care Service Corporation, a Mutual Legal Reserve C, 300 East Randolph Street, P.O. Box 1364, Chicago, IL 60690; tel. 312/653–7500; FAX. 312/819–1220; Raymond F. McCaskey, President, Chief Executive Office

INDIANA: Anthem Blue Cross and Blue Shield, Anthem Insurance Companies, Inc., 120 Monument Circle, Indianapolis, IN 46204; tel. 317/488–6489; FAX. 317/488–6477; L. Ben Lytle, President, Chief Executive Officer

IOWA: Wellmark Inc., Blue Cross and Blue Shield of Iowa, 636 Grand Avenue, Des Moines, IA 50309; tel. 515/245–4545; FAX. 515/245–5090; John D. Forsyth, President, Chief Executive Officer

KANSAS: Blue Cross and Blue Shield of Kansas, Inc., 1133 Topeka Boulevard, Topeka, KS 66629–0001, P.O. Box 239, Topeka, KS 66601–0239; tel. 800/432–3990; FAX. 913/291–8997; John W. Knack, President, Chief Executive Officer

KENTUCKY: Anthem Blue Cross and Blue Shield, Anthem Insurance Companies, Inc., 9901 Linn Station Road, Louisville, KY 40223; tel. 502/423–2011; FAX. 502/339–5483; Jim LeMaster, President

LOUISIANA: Blue Cross and Blue Shield of Louisiana, Louisiana Health Service and Indemnity Company, 5525 Reitz Avenue, Baton Rouge, LA 70809–3802, P.O. Box 98029, Baton Rouge, LA 70898–9029; tel. 504/295–2511; FAX. 504/295–2506; P. J. Mills, President, Chief Executive Officer

MAINE: Blue Cross Blue Shield of Maine, Associated Hospital Service of Maine, Two Gannett Drive, South Portland, ME 04106–6911; tel. 207/822–7000; FAX. 207/822–7350; Andrew W. Greene, President, Chief Executive Officer

MARYLAND: Blue Cross and Blue Shield of Maryland, Inc., 10455 Mill Run Circle, P.O. Box 1010, Owings Mills, MD 21117; tel. 800/524–4555; FAX. 410/998–5576; William L. Jews, President, Chief Executive Officer

MASSACHUSETTS: Blue Cross and Blue Shield of Massachusetts, Inc., 100 Summer Street, Boston, MA 02110; tel. 617/832–3300; FAX. 617/832–3353; William C. Van Faasen, President, Chief Executive Officer

MICHIGAN: Blue Cross and Blue Shield of Michigan, 600 Lafayette East, Detroit, MI 48226–2998; tel. 313/225–8000; FAX. 313/225–6239; Richard E. Whitmer, President, Chief Executive Officer

MINNESOTA: Blue Cross and Blue Shield of Minnesota, BCBSM, Inc., 3535 Blue Cross Road, St. Paul, MN 55122, P.O. Box 64560, St. Paul, MN 55164; tel. 612/456–5040; FAX. 612/456–1657; Andrew P. Czajkowski, President, Chief Executive Officer

MISSISSIPPI: Blue Cross & Blue Shield of Mississippi, a Mutual Insurance Company, 3545 Lakeland Drive, Jackson, MS 39208–9799, P.O. Box 1043, Jackson, MS 39215–1043; tel. 601/932–3704; FAX. 601/939–7035; Richard J. Hale, President, Chief Executive Officer

MISSOURI: Alliance Blue Cross Blue Shield, 1831 Chestnut Street, St. Louis, MO 63103–2275; tel. 314/923–4444; FAX. 314/923–4809; John A. O'Rourke, Chairman, President & Chief Executive Officer

Blue Cross and Blue Shield of Kansas City, 2301 Main, Kansas City, MO 64108, P.O. Box 419169, Kansas City, MO 64141–6169; tel. 816/395–2222; FAX. 816/395–2035; Richard P. Krecker, President, Chief Executive Officer

MONTANA: Blue Cross Blue Shield of Montana, Inc., 560 North Park Avenue, Helena, MT 59601, P.O. Box 4309, Helena, MT 59604–4309; tel. 406/444–8200; FAX. 406/442–6946; Alan F. Cain, President, Chief Executive Officer

NEBRASKA: Blue Cross and Blue Shield of Nebraska, 7261 Mercy Road, P.O. Box 3248 Main P.O. Station, Omaha, NE 68180–0001; tel. 402/390–1800; FAX. 402/392–2141; Richard L. Guffey, Chairman of the Board, Chief Executive Officer

NEVADA: Blue Cross and Blue Shield of Nevada, 5250 South Virginia Street, Reno, NV 89502, P.O. Box 10330, Reno, NV 89520–0330; tel. 702/829–4040; FAX. 702/829–4101; C. David Kikumoto, President, Chief Executive Officer

NEW HAMPSHIRE: Blue Cross and Blue Shield of New Hampshire, New Hampshire–Vermont Health Service, 3000 Goffs Falls Road, Manchester, NH 03111–0001; tel. 603/695–7064; FAX. 603/695–7304; David Jensen, President, Chief Executive Officer

NEW JERSEY: Blue Cross and Blue Shield of New Jersey, Inc., Three Penn Plaza East, P.O. Box 420, Newark, NJ 07105–2200; tel. 201/466–4000; FAX. 201/466–8762; William J. Marino, President, Chief Executive Officer

NEW MEXICO: Blue Cross and Blue Shield of New Mexico, New Mexico Blue Cross and Blue Shield, Inc., 12800 Indian School Road, N.E., Albuquerque, NM 87112, P.O. Box 27630, Albuquerque, NM 87125–7630; tel. 505/291–3500; FAX. 505/237–5324; Norman P. Becker, President, Chief Operating Officer

NEW YORK: Blue Cross and Blue Shield of Central New York, Inc., Excellus Health Plan, Inc., 344 South Warren Street, Syracuse, NY 13202, P.O. Box 4809, Syracuse, NY 13221–4809; tel. 315/448–3902; FAX. 315/448–6763; Albert F. Antonini, President, Chief Executive Officer

Blue Cross and Blue Shield of Western New York, Inc., 1901 Main Street, Buffalo, NY 14208, P.O. Box 80, Buffalo, NY 14240–0080; tel. 716/884–2911; FAX. 716/887–8981; Thomas P. Hartnett, Ph.D., President

Empire Blue Cross and Blue Shield, 622 Third Avenue, New York, NY 10017–6758, P.O. Box 345, New York, NY 10163–0345; tel. 800/261–5962; FAX. 212/983–7615; Michael A. Stocker, M.D., President, Chief Executive Officer

Finger Lakes Blue Cross and Blue Shield, Finger Lakes Medical Insurance Company, Inc., 150 East Main Street, Rochester, NY 14647; tel. 716/454–1700; FAX. 716/238–4400; David Klein, President, Chief Operating Officer

Utica–Watertown Health Insurance Company, Inc., d/b/a Blue Cross and Blue Shield of Utica–Watertown and H, Utica Business Park, 12 Rhoads Drive, Utica, NY 13502–6398; tel. 315/798–4200; FAX. 315/797–5254; Christopher D. Berna, President and Chief Executive Officer

NORTH CAROLINA: Blue Cross and Blue Shield of North Carolina, 5901 Chapel Hill Road, Durham, NC 27707–0718, P.O. Box 2291, Durham, NC 27702; tel. 919/498–7431; FAX. 919/765–7105; Kenneth C. Otis II, President

NORTH DAKOTA: Blue Cross Blue Shield of North Dakota, 4510 13th Avenue, S.W., Fargo, ND 58121–0001; tel. 800/342–4718; FAX. 701/282–1866; Michael B. Unhjem, President, Chief Executive Officer

OHIO: Anthem Blue Cross and Blue Shield, Community Insurance Company, Anthem Insurance Companies, Inc., 1351 William Howard Taft Road, Cincinnati, OH 45206; tel. 513/977–8811; FAX. 513/977–8812; Dwane R. Houser, Chairman of the Board, Chief Executive Officer

Blue Cross and Blue Shield of Ohio, Blue Cross and Blue Shield Mutual of Ohio, 2060 East Ninth Street, Cleveland, OH 44115–1355; tel. 216/687–7000; FAX. 216/687–6044; John Burry, Jr., Chairman, Chief Executive Officer

OKLAHOMA: Blue Cross and Blue Shield of Oklahoma, (Group Health Service of Oklahoma, Inc.), 1215 South Boulder Avenue, Tulsa, OK 74119–2800, P.O. Box 3283, Tulsa, OK 74102–3283; tel. 918/560–3500; FAX. 918/560–2095; Ronald F. King, Chief Executive Officer

OREGON: Blue Cross and Blue Shield of Oregon, 100 Southwest Market Street, Portland, OR 97201, P.O. Box 1271, Portland, OR 97207; tel. 800/452–7390; FAX. 503/225–5232; Richard L. Woolworth, President, Chief Executive Officer

PENNSYLVANIA: Blue Cross of Northeastern Pennsylvania, Hospital Service Association of Northeastern Pennsylvania, 70 North Main Street, Wilkes Barre, PA 18711; tel. 717/831–3676; FAX. 717/831–3670; Thomas J. Ward, President, Chief Executive Officer

Capital Blue Cross, 2500 Elmerton Avenue, Harrisburg, PA 17177–1032; tel. 717/541–7000; FAX. 717/541–6072; James M. Mead, President, Chief Executive Officer

Highmark Blue Cross Blue Shield, 120 Fifth Avenue, Pittsburgh, PA 15222–3099; tel. 412/255–7000; FAX. 412/255–8158; William M. Lowry, President, Chief Executive Officer

Independence Blue Cross, 1901 Market Street, Philadelphia, PA 19103; tel. 800/358–0050; FAX. 215/241–3824; G. Fred DiBona, Jr., President, Chief Executive Officer

Pennsylvania Blue Shield, Medical Service Association of Pennsylvania, 1800 Center Street, Camp Hill, PA 17011, P.O.Box 890089, Camp Hill, PA 17089–0089; tel. 800/637–3493; FAX. 717/763–3544; John S. Brouse, President & Chief Executive Officer

RHODE ISLAND: Blue Cross & Blue Shield of Rhode Island, 444 Westminster Street, Providence, RI 02903–3279; tel. 401/459–1200; FAX. 401/459–1290; Douglas J. McIntosh, President

SOUTH CAROLINA: Blue Cross and Blue Shield of South Carolina, I–20 East at Alpine Road, Columbia, SC 29219; tel. 803/788–3860; FAX. 803/736–3420; M. Edward Sellers, President, Chief Executive Officer

SOUTH DAKOTA: Blue Cross and Blue Shield of South Dakota, Wellmark of South Dakota, Inc., 1601 West Madison Street, Sioux Falls, SD 57104; tel. 605/361–5981; FAX. 605/361–5898; F. Joseph DuBray, President, Chief Executive Officer

TENNESSEE: Blue Cross Blue Shield of Tennessee, 801 Pine Street, Chattanooga, TN 37402; tel. 423/755–5600; FAX. 423/755–2178; Thomas Kinser, Chief Executive Officer

Blue Cross Blue Shield of Tennessee–Memphis, Memphis Hospital Service and Surgical Association, Inc., 85 North Danny Thomas Boulevard, Memphis, TN 38103, P.O. Box 98, Memphis, TN 38101; tel. 901/544–2111; FAX. 901/544–2440; Gene Holcomb, President

TEXAS: Blue Cross and Blue Shield of Texas, Inc., 901 South Central Expressway, Richardson, TX 75080, P.O. Box 655730, Dallas, TX 75265–5730; tel. 972/766–6900; FAX. 972/766–8586; Rogers K. Coleman, M.D., President, Chief Executive Officer

UTAH: Regence Blue Cross Blue Shield of Utah, 2890 East Cottonwood Parkway, Salt Lake Cit, UT 84121; tel. 801/481–6198; FAX. 801/481–6994; Jed H. Pitcher, Chairman, President, Chief Executive Officer

VERMONT: Blue Cross and Blue Shield of Vermont, One East Road, Berlin, VT 05602, P.O. Box 186, Montpelier, VT 05601; tel. 802/223–6131; FAX. 802/229–0511; Preston Jordan, President, Chief Executive Officer

VIRGINIA: Trigon Blue Cross Blue Shield, Blue Cross and Blue Shield of Virginia, 2015 Staples Mill Road, Richmond, VA 23230, P.O. Box 27401, Richmond, VA 23279; tel. 804/354–7173; FAX. 804/354–7044; Norwood H. Davis, Jr., Chairman, Chief Executive Officer

WASHINGTON: Blue Cross Blue Shield of Alaska, Blue Cross of Washington and Alaska, Blue Shield in North Central Washington, 7001 220th Street, S.W., Mountlake Terrace, WA 98043–2124, P.O. Box 327, Seattle, WA 98111–0327; tel. 425/670–5900; FAX. 425/670–4900; Betty Woods, President, Chief Executive Officer

King County Medical Blue Shield, 1800 Ninth Avenue, Seattle, WA 98101–1322, P.O. Box 21267, Seattle, WA 98111–3267; tel. 206/464–3600; FAX. 206/389–6778; Dale M. Francis, President, Chief Executive Officer

Medical Service Corporation of Eastern Washington, 3900 East Sprague Avenue, Spokane, WA 99202, P.O. Box 3048, Spokane, WA 99220–3048; tel. 509/536–4500; FAX. 509/536–4770; Henry F. Keaton, President

Pierce County Medical Bureau, Inc., 1501 Market Street, Tacoma, WA 98402, P.O. Box 2354, Tacoma, WA 98401–2354; tel. 206/597–6557; FAX. 206/597–7475; Rich Nelson, President

Skagit County Medical Bureau, P.O. Box 699, Mount Vernon, WA 98273; tel. 360/336–9660; FAX. 360/336–2028; Karen Larson, President and Chief Executive Officer

Whatcom Medical Bureau, 3000 Northwest Avenue, Bellingham, WA 98225, P.O. Box 9753, Bellingham, WA 98227–9753; tel. 360/734–8000; FAX. 360/734–6676; Bela M. Biro, Chief Financial Officer

WEST VIRGINIA: Mountain State Blue Cross & Blue Shield, Inc., 700 Market Square, Parkersburg, WV 26101, P.O. Box 1948, Parkersburg, WV 26102; tel. 304/424–7732; FAX. 304/424–7789; Gregory K. Smith, President, Chief Executive Officer

WISCONSIN: Blue Cross and Blue Shield United of Wisconsin, 401 West Michigan Street, Milwaukee, WI 53203, P.O. Box 2025, Milwaukee, WI 53201; tel. 414/224–6100; FAX. 414/226–5488; Thomas R. Hefty, Chairman, Chief Executive Officer

WYOMING: Blue Cross and Blue Shield of Wyoming, 4000 House Avenue, Cheyenne, WY 82001–2266, P.O. Box 2266, Cheyenne, WY 82003–2266; tel. 307/634–1393; FAX. 307/778–8582; C. E. Chapman, President

U. S. Associated Areas

JAMAICA: Blue Cross of Jamaica, 85 Hope Road, Kingston 6, JA, West Indies; tel. 809/927–9821, ext. 224; FAX. 809/927–9817; Henry Lowe, Ph.D., C.D., J.P., President, Chief Executive Officer

PUERTO RICO: La Cruz Azul de Puerto Rico, Blue Cross of Puerto Rico, Carretera Estatal 1, K.M. 17.3–Rio Piedras, PR 00927, P.O. Box 366068, San Juan, PR 00936–6068; tel. 787/272–9898; FAX. 787/272–7867; Jose Julian Alvarez, Executive President

Triple–S, Inc., P.O. Box 363628, San Juan, PR 00936–3628; tel. 809/749–4114; FAX. 809/749–4191; Miguel A. Vazquez–Deynes, President

Canada

ALBERTA: Alberta Blue Cross Plan, 10009–108th Street, Edmonton, AB T5J 3C5, CANADA; tel. 403/498–8000; FAX. 403/425–4627; V. George Ward, President, Chief Executive Officer

BRITISH COLUMBIA: Pacific Blue Cross, 2025 West Broadway, P.O. Box 9300, Vancouver, BC V6B 5M1, CANADA; tel. 604/737–5700; FAX. 604/737–5781; John D. Seney, President, Chief Executive Officer

MANITOBA: Manitoba Blue Cross, United Health Services Corporation, 100A Polo Park Centre, 1485 Portage Avenue, Winnipeg, MB R3G OW, 4 P.O. Box 1046, Winnipeg, MB R3C 2X7, CANADA; tel. 204/775–0151; FAX. 204/774–1761; Kerry V. Bittner, President

NEW BRUNSWICK: Blue Cross of Atlantic Canada, 644 Main Street, Moncton, NB E1C 1E2, P.O. Box 220, Moncton, NB E1C 8L3, CANADA; tel. 506/853–1811; FAX. 506/853–4651; Leon R. Furlong, President, Chief Executive Officer

NEWFOUNDLAND: Blue Cross in Ontario, (Moncton Office), 644 Main Street, Moncton, NB E1C 1E2, P.O. Box 220, Moncton, NB E1C 8L3; tel. 506/853–1811; FAX. 506/867–4646; Pierre–Yves Julien, President, Chief Executive Officer

NOVA SCOTIA: Blue Cross of Atlantic Canada, 644 Main Street, Moncton, NB E1C 1E2, P.O. Box 220, Moncton, NB E1C 8L3; tel. 506/853–1811; FAX. 506/867–4651; Leon R. Furlong, President, Chief Executive Officer

ONTARIO: Blue Cross in Ontario, (Ontario Office), 185 The West Mall, Suite 600, P.O. Box 2000, Etobicoke, ON M9C 5P1; tel. 416/626–1688; FAX. 416/626–0997; Andrew Yorke, Chief Operating Officer

QUEBEC: Quebec Blue Cross Quebec Hospital Service Association, 550 Sherbrooke Street, W., Suite 160, Montreal, PQ H3A 1B9, CANADA; tel. 514/286–8482; FAX. 514/286–8475; Claude Bolvin,CA, President, Chief Executive Officer

SASKATCHEWAN: Group Medical Services, 1992 Hamilton Street, Regina, SK S4P 2C6, CANADA; tel. 306/352–7638; FAX. 306/525–3825; Ms. Shirley Raab, President and Chief Executive Office

Saskatchewan Blue Cross, 516 Second Avenue, N., Saskatoon, SK S7K 2C5, P.O. Box 4030, Saskatoon, SK S7K 3T2, CANADA; tel. 306/244–1192; FAX. 306/664–1945; Terry R. Brash, President, Chief Executive Officer

Section C

The following is a list of federally funded Health Systems Agencies. The information was obtained from the National Directory of Health Planning Policy and Regulatory Agencies, published by the Missouri Department of Health, Certificate of Need Program and the agencies themselves. For information about other local agencies and organizations that fulfill similar functions, contact the state or metropolitan hospital associations; see also the list of State Health Planning and Development Agencies in section C.

United States

FLORIDA: Big Bend Health Council, Inc. (District Two), 2629 West 10th Street, Panama City, FL 32401; tel. 904/872–4128; FAX. 904/872–4131; David W. Carter, Executive Director

Broward Regional Health Planning Council (District 10), 915 Middle River Drive, Suite 521, Fort Lauderdale, FL 33304; tel. 954/561–9681; FAX. 954/561–9685; John H. Werner, Executive Director

Health Council of South Florida, Inc., 5757 Blue Lagoon Drive, Suite 170, Miami, FL 33126; tel. 305/263–9020; FAX. 305/262–9905; Sonya Albury, Executive Director

Health Council of West Central Florida (District Six), 9721 Executive Center Drive, N., Suite 114, St. Petersburg, FL 33702–2438; tel. 813/576–7772; FAX. 813/570–3033; Elizabeth Rugg, Director

Health Planning Council of Northeast Florida, Inc., 900 University Blvd. N, Suite 202, Jacksonville, FL 32211; tel. 904/745–3050; FAX. 904/745–3054; Lori A. Bilello, Executive Director

Health Planning Council of Southwest Florida, Inc., 9250 College Parkway, Suite Three, Fort Myers, FL 33919; tel. 941/433–4600; FAX. 941/433–6703; Mary W. Schulthess, Executive Director

North Central Florida Health Planning Council, 11 West University Avenue, Suite Seven, Gainesville, FL 32601; tel. 904/955–2264; FAX. 904/955–3109; Carol J. Gormley, Executive Director

Northwest Florida Health Council, Inc. (District One), 2629 West 10th Street, Panama City, FL 32401; tel. 904/872–4128; FAX. 904/872–4131; David W. Carter, Executive Director

Suncoast Health Council, Inc. (District Five), 9721 Executive Center Drive, N., Suite 114, St. Petersburg, FL 33702–2451; tel. 813/576–7772; FAX. 813/570–3033; Elizabeth Rugg, Executive Director

The Local Health Council of East Central Florida Inc. (District Seven), 1155 South Semoran Boulevard, Suite 1111, Winter Park, FL 32792–5505; tel. 407/671–2005; Steve Windham, Chief Executive Officer

Treasure Coast Health Council, Inc. (District Nine), 4152 W. Blue Heron Blvd, Suite 229, Riviera Beach, FL 33404; tel. 561/844–4220; FAX. 516/844–3310; Barbara H. Jacobowitz, Executive Director

MARYLAND: Chesapeake Health Planning System, Inc., P.O. Box 773, Cambridge, MD 21613; tel. 410/221–0907; FAX. 410/221–2605; John Bennett, President

MINNESOTA: Region 1 (Northwest MN) and Region II (Northeast MN), Regional Coordinating Boards, Minnesota Department of Health, P.O. Box 64975, St. Paul, MN 55164–0975; tel. 612/282–5644; FAX. 612/282–5628; Michele Holten

Region III (Central MN) and Region IV (Twin City Metro), Minnesota Department of Health, P.O. Box 64975, St. Paul, MN 55164–0975; tel. 612/282–6330; Kristin Pederson

Region V (Southwest MN) and Region VI (Southeast MN), Minnesota Department of Heatlh, CHS Division, Suite 4, P.O. Box 64975, St. Paul, MN 55164–0975; tel. 612/282–6328; FAX. 612/282–5628; Kay Markling

NEW JERSEY: Essex and Union Advisory Board for Health Planning, Inc., 14 South Orange Avenue, South Orange, NJ 07079; tel. 201/761–6969; FAX. 201/761–7401; Sharon Postel, Executive Director

Fairleigh Dickinson University, Region Two Health Planning Advisory Board, 1000 River Road, Teaneck, NJ 07666; tel. 201/692–7180; FAX. 201/692–7189; Thomas Pavlak, Ph.D., Executive Director

Health Visions, Inc., 6981 North Park Drive, East Building, Suite 307, Pennsauken, NJ 08109; tel. 609/662–2050; FAX. 609/662–2261; Charles Daly, Vice President, Health Planning

Mid–State Health Advisory Corporation–Rider University, Rider University, 2083 Lawrenceville Ro, Lawrenceville, NJ 08648; tel. 609/219–2121; FAX. 609/219–2120; Bernadette West, Executive Director

New Health Initiatives, Inc., 205 West Main Street, Somerville, NJ 08876; tel. 908/722–4600; FAX. 908/722–4702; Robert Schermer, Executive Director

South Central Health Planning Council, Inc., Local Advisory Board 3, 515 Route 70, Suite 208, Brick, NJ 08723; tel. 732/262–9047; FAX. 732/262–9049; Eleanor Jaeger, Executive Director

NEW YORK: Central New York Health Systems Agency, Inc., 101 Intrepid Lane, Syracuse, NY 13205; tel. 315/492–8557; FAX. 315/492–8563; Timothy J. Bobo, Executive Director

Finger Lakes Health Systems Agency, 1150 University Avenue, Rochester, NY 14607; tel. 716/461–3520; FAX. 716/461–0997; Martha P. Bond, Executive Director

Health Systems Agency of New York City, 450 Seventh Avenue, 13th Floor, New York, NY 10001; tel. 212/244–8100; FAX. 212/244–8120; Robert D. Gumbs, Executive Director

Health Systems Agency of Northeastern New York, Pine West Plaza, One United Way, Washington Avenue Extension, Albany, NY 12205–5558; tel. 518/452–3300; FAX. 518/452–5943; Bruce R. Stanley, Executive Director

Health Systems Agency of Western New York, 2070 Sheridan Drive, Buffalo, NY 14223; tel. 716/876–7131; FAX. 716/876–4968; Brian G. McBride, Ph.D., Executive Director

Hudson Valley Health Systems Agency, P.O. Box 696, Tuxedo, NY 10987; tel. 914/351–5146; Regina M. Kelly, Executive Director

NY Penn Health Systems Agency, 84 Court Street, Suite 300, Binghamton, NY 13901; tel. 607/772–0336; FAX. 607/772–0158; Denise Murray, Executive Director

Nassau–Suffolk Health Systems Agency, 1537 Old Country Road, Plainview, NY 11803; tel. 516/293–5740; FAX. 516/293–6288; Renee Pekmezaris, Ph.D., Executive Director

OHIO: Health Planning and Resource Development Association of Central Ohio River Valley, 35 East Seventh Street, Suite 311, Cincinnati, OH 45202; tel. 513/621–2434; FAX. 513/621–4307; James F. Sandmann, President

Health Systems Agency, 415 Bulkley Building, 1501 Euclid Avenue, Cleveland, OH 44115; tel. 216/771–6814; FAX. 216/771–2939; Nancy J. Roth, Executive Director

Lake to River Health Care Coalition, 106 Robbins Avenue, Niles, OH 44446–1768; tel. 330/652–8111; FAX. 330/652–0003; Thomas J. Flynn, Executive Director

Miami Valley Health Improvement Council, 7039 Taylorsville Road, Huber Heights, OH 45424–3103; tel. 937/236–5358; FAX. 937/237–9750; Robert P. Thimmes, President, Chief Executive

Northwest Ohio Health Planning, Inc., 635 North Erie Street, Toledo, OH 43624; tel. 419/255–1190; FAX. 419/255–2900; David G. Pollick, Executive Director

Scioto Valley Health Systems Agency (SVHSA), 600 West Spring Street, Columbus, OH 43215–2327; tel. 614/645–7438; FAX. 614/645–7637; Franklin Hirsch, Executive Director

VIRGINIA: Central Virginia Health Planning Agency, Inc., P.O. Box 24287, Richmond, VA 23224; tel. 804/233–6206; FAX. 804/233–8834; Karen L. Cameron, Executive Director

Eastern Virginia Health Systems Agency, Inc., The Koger Center, Suite 232, Norfolk, VA 23502; tel. 757/461–4834; FAX. 757/461–3255; Paul M. Boynton, Executive Director

Health Systems Agency of Northern Virginia, 7245 Arlington Boulevard, Suite 300, Falls Church, VA 22042; tel. 703/573–3100; FAX. 703/573–1276; Dean Montgomery, Executive Director

Northwestern Virginia Health Systems Agency, 1924 Arlington Boulevard, Suite 211, Charlottesville, VA 22903; tel. 804/977–6010; FAX. 804/977–0748; Margaret P. King, Executive Director

Southwest Virginia Health Systems Agency, Inc., 3100–A Peters Creek Road, N.W., Roanoke, VA 24019; tel. 540/362–9528; FAX. 540/362–9676; Pamela P. Clark, MPA, Executive Director

The following list of state and metropolitan hospital associations is derived from the American Hospital Association's 1998 Directory of Hospital and Health System Associations.

United States

ALABAMA: Alabama Hospital Association, 500 North East Boulevard, Zip 36117, P.O. Box 210759, Montgomery, AL 36121–0759; tel. 334/272–8781; FAX. 334/270–9527; J. Michael Horsley, President, Chief Executive Officer

ALASKA: Alaska State Hospital and Nursing Home Association, 426 Main Street, Juneau, AK 99801; tel. 907/586–1790; FAX. 907/463–3573; Laraine Derr, President, Chief Executive Officer

ARIZONA: Arizona Hospital and Healthcare Association, 1501 West Fountainhead Parkway, Suite 650, Tempe, AZ 85282; tel. 602/968–1083; FAX. 602/967–2029; John R. Rivers, President, Chief Executive Officer

ARKANSAS: Arkansas Hospital Association, 419 Natural Resources Drive, Little Rock, AR 72205–1539; tel. 501/224–7878; FAX. 501/224–0519; James R. Teeter, President, Chief Executive Officer

CALIFORNIA: California Healthcare Association, 1201 K Street, Suite 800, Sacramento, CA 95814, P.O. Box 1100, Sacramento, CA 95812–1100; tel. 916/443–7401; FAX. 916/552–7596; C. Duane Dauner, President

Healthcare Association of San Diego and Imperial Counties, 402 West Broadway, 22nd Floor, San Diego, CA 92101–3542; tel. 619/544–0777; FAX. 619/544–0888; Gary R. Stephany, President, Chief Executive Officer

Healthcare Association of Southern California, 515 South Figueroa Street, Suite 1300, Los Angeles, CA 90071–3322; tel. 213/538–0700; FAX. 213/629–4272; James D. Barber, President, Chief Executive Officer

Hospital Council of Northern and Central California, 7901 Stoneridge Drive, Suite 500, Pleasanton, CA 94588; tel. 510/460–5444, ext. 304; FAX. 510/460–5457; Gregg Schnepple, President, Chief Executive Officer

COLORADO: Colorado Health and Hospital Association, 2140 South Holly Street, Denver, CO 80222–5607; tel. 303/758–1630; FAX. 303/758–0047; Larry Wall, President

CONNECTICUT: Connecticut Hospital Association, 110 Barnes Road, P.O. Box 90, Wallingford, CT 06492–0090; tel. 203/265–7611; FAX. 203/284–9318; Dennis P. May, President

DELAWARE: Delaware Healthcare Association, 1280 South Governors Avenue, Dover, DE 19901–4802; tel. 302/674–2853; FAX. 302/734–2731; Joseph M. Letnaunchyn, President

DISTRICT OF COLUMBIA: District of Columbia Hospital Association, 1250 Eye Street, N.W., Suite 700, Washington, DC 20005–3930; tel. 202/682–1581; FAX. 202/682–1581; Robert A. Malson, President, Chief Executive Officer

FLORIDA: Florida Hospital Association, 307 Park Lake Circle, P.O. Box 531107, Orlando, FL 32853–1107; tel. 407/841–6230; FAX. 407/422–5948; Charles F. Pierce, Jr., President

South Florida Hospital and Healthcare Association, Inc., 6363 Taft Street, Suite 200, Hollywood, FL 33024; tel. 954/964–1660; FAX. 954/962–1260; Linda S. Quick, President

The Tampa Bay Hospital Association, Inc., P.O. Box 1003, Tampa, FL 33601–1003; tel. 813/223–0806; FAX. 813/223–0012; Sharon E. Schur, President

GEORGIA: GHA: An Association of Hospitals and Health Systems, 1675 Terrell Mill Road, Marietta, GA 30067; tel. 770/955–0324; FAX. 770/955–5801; Joseph A. Parker, President

HAWAII: Healthcare Association of Hawaii, 932 Ward Avenue, suite 430, Honolulu, HI 96814–2126; tel. 808/521–8961; FAX. 808/599–2879; Richard E. Meiers, President, Chief Executive Officer

IDAHO: Idaho Hospital Association, 802 West Bannock Street, Suite 500, P.O. Box 1278, Boise, ID 83701–1278; tel. 208/338–5100; FAX. 208/338–7800; Steven A. Millard, President

ILLINOIS: Illinois Hospital and HealthSystems Association, 1151 East Warrenville Road, P.O. Box 3015, Naperville, IL 60566–7015; tel. 630/505–7777; FAX. 630/505–4237; Kenneth C.Robbins, President

Metropolitan Chicago Healthcare Council, 222 South Riverside Plaza, 19th Floor, Chicago, IL 60606; tel. 312/906–6000; FAX. 312/993–0779; Earl C. Bird, President

INDIANA: Indiana Hospital&Health Association, One American Square, P.O. Box 82063, Indianapolis, IN 46282; tel. 317/633–4870; FAX. 317/633–4875; Kenneth G. Stella, President

IOWA: The Association of Iowa Hospitals and Health Systems, 100 East Grand Avenue, Suite 100, Des Moines, IA 50309; tel. 515/288–1955; FAX. 515/283–9366; Stephen F. Brenton, President

KANSAS: Kansas Hospital Association, Post Office Box 2308, Topeka, KS 66601–2308; tel. 785/233–7436; FAX. 785/233–6955; Donald A. Wilson, President

KENTUCKY: KHA: An Association of Kentucky Hospitals and Health Systems, 1302 Clear Spring Trace, P.O. Box 24163, Louisville, KY 40224; tel. 502/426–6220; FAX. 502/426–6226; Michael T. Rust, President

LOUISIANA: Louisiana Hospital Association, 9521 Brookline Avenue, Baton Rouge, LA 70809, P.O. Box 80720, Baton Rouge, LA 70898–0720; tel. 504/928–0026; FAX. 504/923–1004; Robert D. Merkel, President

Metropolitan Hospital Council of New Orleans, 2450 Severn Avenue, Suite 210, Metairie, LA 70001; tel. 504/837–1171; FAX. 504/837–1174; John J. Finn, Ph.D., President

MAINE: MHA . . . An Association of Maine Hospitals and Healthcare Organizations, 150 Capitol Street, Augusta, ME 04330; tel. 207/622–4794; FAX. 207/622–3073; Bruce J. Rueben, President

MARYLAND: MHA: The Association of Maryland Hospitals Health Systems, 1301 York Road, Suite 800, Lutherville, MD 21093–6087; tel. 410/321–6200; FAX. 410/321–6268; Calvin M. Pierson, President

Healthcare Council of the National Capital Area, 8201 Corporate Drive, Suite 410, Landover, MD 20785–2229; tel. 301/731–4700; FAX. 301/731–8286; Joseph P. Burns, President, Chief Executive Officer

MASSACHUSETTS: Massachusetts Hospital Association, Five New England Executive Park, Burlington, MA 01803; tel. 781/272–8000; FAX. 781/272–0466, ext. 111; Ronald M. Hollander, President

MICHIGAN: Michigan Health & Hospital Association, 6215 West St. Joseph Highway, Lansing, MI 48917; tel. 517/323–3443; FAX. 517/323–0946; Spencer C. Johnson, President

Center for Health Affairs, 3075 Charlevoix Drive, S.E., Grand Rapids, MI 49546; tel. 616/940–3337; FAX. 616/940–0723; Edward A. Rode, President

Healthcare Council of MidMichigan, 3927 Beecher Road, Flint, MI 48532–3803; tel. 810/766–8898; FAX. 810/762–4108; Marlene Soderstrom, President

Hospital Council of East Central Michigan, 141 Harrow Lane, Suite 11, Saginaw, MI 48603; tel. 517/792–1725; FAX. 517/792–3099; Randolph K. Flechsig, President

North Central Council of MHA, 114 North Court Street, Gaylord, MI 49735; tel. 517/732–7002; FAX. 517/732–3059; Mary E. Fox, Executive Director

Southeast Michigan Health and Hospital Council, 24725 West Twelve Mile Road, Suite 104A, Southfield, MI 48034; tel. 248/358–2950; FAX. 248/358–1098; Donald P. Potter, President

Southwest Michigan Hospital Council, 6215 West St. Joseph Highway, Lansing, MI 48917; tel. 517/323–3443; FAX. 517/323–0946; Clark R. Ballard, President

MINNESOTA: Minnesota Hospital and Healthcare Partnership, 2550 University Avenue, W., Suite 350S, St. Paul, MN 55114–1900; tel. 612/641–1121; FAX. 612/659–1477; Stephen Rogness, President

MISSISSIPPI: Mississippi Hospital Association, 6425 Lakeover Road, Jackson, MS 39213, P.O. Box 16444, Jackson, MS 39236–6444; tel. 601/982–3251; FAX. 601/368–3224; Sam W. Cameron, President

MISSOURI: Missouri Hospital Association, 4712 Country Club Drive, Jefferson City, MO 65109–4544, P.O. Box 60, Jefferson City, MO 65102–0060; tel. 573/893–3700; FAX. 573/893–2809; Marc D. Smith, President

Greater Kansas City Health Council, 10401 Holmes Road, Suite 280, Kansas City, MO 64131–3368; tel. 816/941–3800; FAX. 816/941–0818; Sheryl Jacobs, Senior Vice President

MONTANA: MHA... An Association of Health Care Providers, 1720 Ninth Avenue, Helena, MT 59601, P.O. Box 5119, Helena, MT 59604; tel. 406/442–1911; FAX. 406/443–3894; James F. Ahrens, President

NEBRASKA: Nebraska Association of Hospitals and Health Systems, 1640 L Street, Suite D, Lincoln, NE 68508–2509; tel. 402/458–4900; FAX. 402/476–3776; Harlan M. Heald, Ph.D., President

NEVADA: Nevada Association of Hospitals and Health Systems, 4600 Kietzke Lane, Suite A–108, Reno, NV 89502; tel. 702/827–0184; FAX. 702/827–0190; Jeanette Belz, President, Chief Executive Officer

NEW HAMPSHIRE: New Hampshire Hospital Association, 125 Airport Road, Concord, NH 03301–5388; tel. 603/225–0900; FAX. 603/225–4346; Michael J. Hill, President

NEW JERSEY: New Jersey Hospital Association, P.O. Box One, 760 Alexander Road, CN–1, Princeton, NJ 08543–0001; tel. 609/275–4000; FAX. 609/275–8097; Gary S. Carter, FACHE, President, Chief Executive Officer

NEW MEXICO: New Mexico Hospitals and Health Systems Association, 2121 Osuna Road, N.E., Albuquerque, NM 87113; tel. 505/343–0010; FAX. 505/343–0012; Maureen L. Boshier, Chief Executive Officer, President

NEW YORK: Healthcare Association of New York State, 74 North Pearl Street, Albany, NY 12207; tel. 518/431–7600; FAX. 518/431–7915; Daniel Sisto, President

Greater New York Hospital Association, Subsidiaries, and Affiliates, 555 West 57th Street, 15th Floor, New York, NY 10019; tel. 212/246–7100, ext. 401; FAX. 212/262–6350; Kenneth E. Raske, President

Iroquois Healthcare Alliance, 17 Halfmoon Executive Park Drive, Clifton Park, NY 12065; tel. 518/383–5060; FAX. 518/383–2616; 5740 Commons Park; East Syracuse, NY 13057; tel. 315/445–1851; FAX. 315/445–2293; Gary J. Fitzgerald, President

Nassau–Suffolk Hospital Council, Inc., 888 Veterans Highway, Hauppauge, NY 11788; tel. 516/435–3000; FAX. 516/435–2343; Peter M. Sullivan, Executive Vice President, Chief Executive Officer

Northern Metropolitan Hospital Association, 400 Stony Brook Court, Newburgh, NY 12550; tel. 914/562–7520; FAX. 914/562–0187; Arthur E. Weintraub, President

Rochester Regional Healthcare Association, 3445 Winton Place, Rochester, NY 14623; tel. 716/273–8180; FAX. 716/273–8189; Robert M. Swinnerton, President, Chief Executive Officer

Western New York Healthcare Association, 1876 Niagara Falls Boulevard, Tonawanda, NY 14150–6439; tel. 716/695–0843; FAX. 716/695–0073, ext. 208; William D. Pike, President

NORTH CAROLINA: NCHA, P.O. Box 80428, Raleigh, NC 27623–0428; tel. 919/677–2400; FAX. 919/677–4200; C. Edward McCauley, President

NORTH DAKOTA: North Dakota Healthcare Association, 1120 College Drive, P.O. Box 7340, Bismarck, ND 58507–7340; tel. 701/224–9732; FAX. 701/224–9529; Arnold R. Thomas, President

OHIO: OHA: The Association for Hospitals and Health Systems, 155 East Broad Street, Columbus, OH 43215; tel. 614/221–7614; FAX. 614/221–4771; James R. Castle, President

Akron Regional Hospital Association, 326 Locust Street, Akron, OH 44302–1801; tel. 330/379–8989; FAX. 330/379–8189; Marianne G. Lorini, President

Greater Cincinnati Health Council, 2100 Sherman Avenue, Suite 100, Cincinnati, OH 45212–2775; tel. 513/531–0200; FAX. 513/531–0278; Lynn R. Olman, President

Greater Dayton Area Hospital Association, 32 North Main Street, Suite 1441, Key Bank Building, Dayton, OH 45402; tel. 937/228–1000; FAX. 937/228–1035; Joseph M. Krella, President

Hospital Council of Northwest Ohio, 5515 Southwyck Boulevard, Suite 203, Toledo, OH 43614; tel. 419/865–1274; FAX. 419/867–4425; W. Scott Fry, President, Chief Executive Officer

The Center for Health Affairs, 1226 Huron Road, Cleveland, OH 44115; tel. 216/696–6900; FAX. 216/696–1837; C. Wayne Rice, Ph.D., President, Chief Executive Officer

OKLAHOMA: Oklahoma Hospital Association, 4000 Lincoln Boulevard, Oklahoma City, OK 73105; tel. 405/427–9537; FAX. 405/424–4507; John C. Coffey, FACHE, President

Greater Oklahoma City Hospital Council, 4000 Lincoln Boulevard, Oklahoma City, OK 73105; tel. 405/427–9537; FAX. 405/424–4507; Bruce Buchanan, Chairman

OREGON: Oregon Association of Hospitals and Health Systems, 4000 Kruse Way Place, Building 2, Suite 100, Lake Oswego, OR 97035–2543; tel. 503/636–2204; FAX. 503/636–8310; Kenneth M. Rutledge, President

PENNSYLVANIA: The Hospital & Healthsystem Association of Pennsylvania, 4750 Lindle Road, P.O. Box 8600, Harrisburg, PA 17105–8600; tel. 717/564–9200; FAX. 717/561–5334; Carolyn F. Scanlan, President, Chief Executive Officer

Hospital Council of Western Pennsylvania, 500 Commonwealth Drive, Warrendale, PA 15086; tel. 412/776–6400; FAX. 412/776–6969; Ian G. Rawson, Ph.D., President

The Delaware Valley Healthcare Council of HAP, 121 South Broad Street, Philadelphia, PA 19107; tel. 215/735–9695; FAX. 215/790–1267; Andrew B. Wigglesworth, President

RHODE ISLAND: Hospital Association of Rhode Island, 880 Butler Drive, Suite One, Providence, RI 02906; tel. 401/453–8400; FAX. 401/453–8411; Gerald G. McClure, President

SOUTH CAROLINA: South Carolina Health Alliance, 101 Medical Circle, P.O. Box 6009, West Columbia, SC 29171–6009; tel. 803/796–3080; FAX. 803/796–2938; Ken A. Shull, FACHE, President

SOUTH DAKOTA: South Dakota Association of Healthcare Organizations, 3708 Brooks Place, Suite 1, Sioux Falls, SD 57106; tel. 605/361–2281; FAX. 605/361–5175; David R. Hewitt, President/Chief Executive Officer

TENNESSEE: THA: An Association of Hospitals and Health Systems, 500 Interstate Boulevard, S., Nashville, TN 37210–4634; tel. 615/256–8240; FAX. 615/242–4803; Craig A. Becker, President

TEXAS: THA—The Association of Texas Hospitals and Health Care Organizations, 6225 U.S. Highway 290, E., P.O. Box 15587, Austin, TX 78761–5587; tel. 512/465–1000; FAX. 512/465–1090; Terry Townsend, FACHE, CAE, President, Chief Executive Officer

Dallas–Fort Worth Hospital Council, 250 Decker Court, Irving, TX 75062; tel. 972/719–4900; FAX. 972/719–4009; John C. Gavras, President

Greater San Antonio Hospital Council, 8620 North New Braunfels, Suite 420, San Antonio, TX 78217; tel. 210/820–3500; FAX. 210/820–3888; William Dean Rasco, FACHE, President, Chief Executive Officer

UTAH: UHA, Utah Hospitals and Health Systems Association, 2180 South 1300 East, Suite 440, Salt Lake City, UT 84106–2843; tel. 801/486–9915; FAX. 801/486–0882; Richard B. Kinnersley, President

VERMONT: Vermont Association of Hospitals and Health Systems, 148 Main Street, Montpelier, VT 05602; tel. 802/223–3461; FAX. 802/223–0364; Norman E. Wright, President

VIRGINIA: Virginia Hospital & Healthcare Association, 4200 Innslake Drive, Glen Allen, VA 23060, P.O. Box 31394, Richmond, VA 23294; tel. 804/747–8600; FAX. 804/965–0475; Laurens Sartoris, President

WASHINGTON: Washington State Hospital Association, 300 Elliott Avenue, W., Suite 300, Seattle, WA 98119–4118; tel. 206/281–7211; FAX. 206/283–6122; Leo F. Greenawalt, President, Chief Executive Officer

WEST VIRGINIA: West Virginia Hospital Association, 100 Association Drive, Charleston, WV 25311; tel. 304/344–9744; FAX. 304/344–9745; Steven J. Summer, President

WISCONSIN: Wisconsin Health & Hospital Association, 5721 Odana Road, Madison, WI 53719–1289; tel. 608/274–1820; FAX. 608/274–8554; Robert C. Taylor, President, Chief Executive Officer

WYOMING: Wyoming Hospital Association, 2005 Warren Avenue, Cheyenne, WY 82001, P.O. Box 5539, Cheyenne, WY 82003; tel. 307/632–9344; FAX. 307/632–9347; Robert C. Kidd II, President

---

U. S. Associated Areas

PUERTO RICO: Puerto Rico Hospital Association, Officina 101–103, Villa Nevarez Professional Center, Centro Commercial Villa Nevarez, San Juan, PR 00927; tel. 787/764–0290; FAX. 787/753–9748; Juan Rivera, Executive Vice President

---

Canada

ALBERTA: Provincial Health Authorities of Alberta, 200–44 Capital Boulevard, 10044–108 Street, N.W., Edmonton, AB T5J 3S7; tel. 403/426–8500; FAX. 403/424–4309; E. Michael Higgins, Executive Director

NEW BRUNSWICK: New Brunswick Healthcare Association, 861 Woodstock Road, Fredericton, NB E3B 7R7; tel. 506/451–0750; FAX. 506/451–0760; Michel J. Poirier, Executive Director

NEWFOUNDLAND: Newfoundland Hospital and Nursing Home Association, P.O. Box 8234, St. John's, NF A1B 3N5; tel. 867/873–9253; FAX. 867/873–9254; John F. Peddle, Executive Director

NORTHWEST TERRITORY: Northwest Territories Health Care Association, P.O. Box 1709, Yellowknife, NT X1A 2P3; tel. 867/873–9253; FAX. 867/873–9254; Norman M. Hatlevik, Executive Director

NOVA SCOTIA: Nova Scotia Association of Health Organizations, Bedford Professional Centre, 2 Dartmouth Road, Bedford, NS B4A 2K7; tel. 902/832–8500; FAX. 902/832–8505; Robert A. Cook, President, Chief Executive Officer

ONTARIO: Ontario Hospital Association, 200 Front Street, W., Suite 2000, Toronto, ON M5V 3L1; tel. 416/205–1300; FAX. 416/205–1360; David MacKinnon, President

Catholic Health Association of Canada, 1247 Kilborn Place, Ottawa, ON K1H 6K9; tel. 613/731–7148; FAX. 613/731–7797; Richard Haughian, D.Th., President

PRINCE EDWARD ISLAND: Health Association of Prince Edward Island, Inc., 10 Pownal Street, P.O. Box 490, Charlottetown, PEI C1A 3V6; tel. 902/368–3901; FAX. 902/368–3231; Carol Gabanna, Executive Director

QUEBEC: Quebec Hospital Association, 505 boulevard de Maisonneuve, W., Suite 400, Montreal, PQ H3A 3C2; tel. 514/842–4861; FAX. 514/282–4271; Yvon Marcoux, Executive Vice President

SASKATCHEWAN: Saskatchewan Association of Health Organizations, 1445 Park Street, Regina, SK S4N 4C5; tel. 306/347–5500; FAX. 306/347–5500; Arliss Wright, President, Chief Executive Officer

Hospital Licensure Agencies

Information for the following list of state hospital licensure agencies was obtained directly from the agencies.

United States

ALABAMA: Alabama Department of Public Health, Division of Health Care Facilities, The RSA Tower, Suite 600, 201 Monroe Street, P.O. Box 303017, Montgomery, AL 36130–3017; tel. 334/206–5077; FAX. 334/206–5088; Elva Goldman, Director

ALASKA: Health Facilities Licensing and Certification, 4730 Business Park Boulevard, Building H, Suite 18, Anchorage, AK 99503–7137; tel. 907/561–8081; FAX. 907/561–3011; Shelbert Larsen, Administrator

ARIZONA: Arizona Department of Health Services, Office of Health Care Facilities Licensure, Medical Facilities Section, 1647 East Morten Avenue, Suite 160, Phoenix, AZ 85020; tel. 602/255–1144; FAX. 602/395–8913; Catherine Rosenthal, Program Manager

ARKANSAS: Division of Health Facility Services, Arkansas Department of Health, 5800 West 10th Street, Suite 400, Little Rock, AR 72204–9916; tel. 501/661–2201; FAX. 501/661–2468; Valetta M. Buck, Director

CALIFORNIA: Licensing and Certification, Department of Health Services, 1800 Third Street, Suite 2195814, P.O. Box 942732, Sacramento, CA 94234–7320; tel. 916/445–2070; FAX. 916/445–6979; Brenda G. Klutz, Deputy Director

COLORADO: Health Facilities Division, Colorado Department of Public Health and Environment, 4300 Cherry Creek Drive, S., Denver, CO 80222–1530; tel. 303/692–2800; FAX. 303/782–4883; Janell Little, Deputy Director

CONNECTICUT: Department of Public Health and Addiction Service, Connecticut State Department of Health Services, 150 Washington Street, Hartford, CT 06106; tel. 203/566–1073; FAX. 203/566–1097; Elizabeth M. Burns, RN, M.S., Director

DELAWARE: Office of Health Facilities Licensing and Certification, Department of Health and Social Services, Three Mill Road, Suite 308, Wilmington, DE 19806; tel. 302/577–6666; FAX. 302/577–6672; Ellen T. Reap, Director

DISTRICT OF COLUMBIA: Licensing Regulation Administration, 614 H Street, N.W., Suite 1003, Washington, DC 20001; tel. 202/727–7190; FAX. 202/727–7780; Geraldine K. Sykes

FLORIDA: Division of Health Quality Assurance, Hospital and Outpatient Services Unit, Agency for Health Care Administration, 2727 Mahan Drive, Tallahassee, FL 32308; tel. 850/487–2717; FAX. 850/487–6240; Daryl Barowicz, Unit Manager

GEORGIA: Health Care Section, Office of Regulatory Services, Department of Human Resources, Two Peachtree Street, N.W., Suite 33.250, Atlanta, GA 30303–3167; tel. 404/657–5550; FAX. 404/657–8934; Susie M. Woods, Director

HAWAII: Hawaii Department of Health, Hospital and Medical Facilities Branch, P.O. Box 3378, Honolulu, HI 96801; tel. 808/586–4080; FAX. 808/586–4747; Helen K. Yoshimi, B.S.N., M.P.H., Chief, HMFB

IDAHO: Bureau of Facility Standards, Department of Health and Welfare, P.O. Box 83720, Boise, ID 83720–0036; tel. 208/334–6626; FAX. 208/332–7204; Sylvia Creswell, Supervisor, Non–Long Term Care

ILLINOIS: Division of Health Care Facilities and Programs, Illinois Department of Public Health, 525 West Jefferson Street, Springfield, IL 62761; tel. 217/782–7412; FAX. 217/782–0382; Michelle Gentry–Wiseman, Chief

INDIANA: Division of Acute Care, Indiana State Department of Health, Two North Meridian Street, Indianapolis, IN 46204; tel. 317/233–7472; FAX. 317/233–7157; John A. Braeckel, Director

IOWA: Division of Health Facilities, Iowa State Department of Inspections and Appeals, Lucas State Office Building, Des Moines, IA 50319; tel. 515/281–4115; FAX. 515/242–5022

KANSAS: Kansas Department of Health and Environment, Bureau of Adult and Child Care, 900 Southwest Jackson, Suite 1001, Topeka, KS 66612–1290; tel. 785/296–1280; FAX. 785/296–1266; George A. Dugger, Medical Facilities Certification Administrator

KENTUCKY: Division of Licensing and Regulation, Cabinet for Health Services, 275 East Main Street, 4E–A, Frankfort, KY 40621; tel. 502/564–2800; FAX. 502/564–6546; Rebecca J. Cecil, R.Ph., Director

LOUISIANA: Health Standards Section, Louisiana Department of Health and Hospitals, P.O. Box 3767, Baton Rouge, LA 70821; tel. 504/342–5782; FAX. 504/342–5292; Lily W. McAlister, RN, Manager

MAINE: Division of Licensing and Certification, Department of Human Services, State House, Station 11, Augusta, ME 04333; tel. 207/624–5443; FAX. 207/624–5378; Louis Dorogi, Director

MARYLAND: Department of Health and Mental Hygiene, Licensing and Certification Administration, 4201 Patterson Avenue, Baltimore, MD 21215; tel. 410/764–4970; FAX. 410/358–0750; James L. Ralls, Assistant Director

MASSACHUSETTS: Massachusetts Department of Public Health, Division of Health Care Quality, 10 West Street, Fifth Floor, Boston, MA 02111; tel. 617/753–8000; FAX. 617/753–8125; Paul I. Dreyer, Ph.D., Director

MICHIGAN: Bureau of Health Systems, Michigan Department of Consumer and Industry Services, 525 West Ottawa, P.O. Box 30664, Lansing, MI 48909; tel. 517/241–2626; FAX. 517/241–2635; Walter S. Wheeler III, Director

MINNESOTA: Facility and Provider Compliance Division, Minnesota Department of Health, 393 North Dunlap Street, P.O. Box 64900, St. Paul, MN 55164–0900; tel. 612/643–2100; FAX. 612/643–2593; Linda G. Sutherland, Director

MISSISSIPPI: Division of Health Facilities Licensure and Certification, Mississippi State Department of Health, P.O. Box 1700, Jackson, MS 39215; tel. 601/354–7300; FAX. 601/354–7230; Vanessa Phipps, Director

MISSOURI: Bureau of Hospital Licensing and Certification, Missouri Department of Health, P.O. Box 570, Jefferson City, MO 65102; tel. 314/751–6302; FAX. 314/526–3621; Darrell Hendrickson, Administrator

MONTANA: Division of Quality Assurance, Department of Public Health and Human Services, Cogswell Building, 1400 Broadway, Helena, MT 59620; tel. 406/444–2037; FAX. 406/444–1742; Denzel Davis, Administrator

NEBRASKA: Nebraska Department of Regulation and Licensure, Credentialing Division, 301 Centennial Mall, S., P.O. Box 95007, Lincoln, NE 68509–5007; tel. 402/471–2946; FAX. 402/471–0555; Helen Meeks, Director

NEVADA: Bureau of Licensure and Certification, Nevada Health Division, 1550 East College Parkway, Suite 158, Carson City, NV 89706–7921; tel. 702/687–4475; FAX. 702/687–6588; Richard J. Panelli, Chief

NEW HAMPSHIRE: Bureau of Health Facilities Administration, Office of Program Support, Licensure and Regulation, Health and Human Services Building, Six Hazen Drive, Concord, NH 03301; tel. 603/271–4966; FAX. 603/271–4968; Raymond Rusim, Bureau Chief

NEW JERSEY: Certificate of Need and Acute Care Licensing, N.J. Department of Health and Senior Services, P.O. Box 360, Trenton, NJ 08625–0360; tel. 609/292–8772; FAX. 609/292–3780; John Calabria, Acting Director

NEW MEXICO: Department of Health, Health Facility Licensing & Certification Bureau Medical Care Program, 525 Camino de los Marquez, Suite Two, Santa Fe, NM 87501; tel. 505/827–4200; FAX. 505/827–4203; Matthew Gervase, Bureau Chief

NEW YORK: New York State Department of Health, Bureau of Hospital and Primary Care Services, Hedley Park Place, Suite 303, 433 River Street, Troy, NY 12180–2299; tel. 518/402–1003; FAX. 518/402–1010; Frederick J. Heigel, Director

NORTH CAROLINA: Division of Facility Services, Department of Human Resources, 701 Barbour Drive, P.O. Box 29530, Raleigh, NC 27626–0530; tel. 919/733–1610; FAX. 919/733–3207; Steve White, Chief, Licensure and Certification

NORTH DAKOTA: Health Resources Section, State Department of Health, 600 East Boulevard Avenue, Bismarck, ND 58505–0200; tel. 701/328–2352; FAX. 701/328–4727; Fred Gladden, Chief

OHIO: Bureau of Quality Assessment and Improvement, Department of Health, P.O. Box 118, Columbus, OH 43266–0118; tel. 614/466–3325; FAX. 614/644–8661; Louis Pomerantz, Chief, Bureau of Quality Assessment a

OKLAHOMA: State Department of Health, 1000 Northeast 10th, Oklahoma City, OK 73117; tel. 405/271–4200; FAX. 405/271–3431; Jerry R. Nida, M.D., Commissioner, Health

OREGON: Health Care Licensure and Certification, Oregon Health Division, P.O. Box 14450, Portland, OR 97214–0450; tel. 503/731–4013; FAX. 503/731–4080; Kathleen Smail, Director

PENNSYLVANIA: Division of Acute and Ambulatory Care Facilities, Bureau of Quality Assurance, Health and Welfare Building, S, Harrisburg, PA 17120; tel. 717/783–8980; FAX. 717/772–2163; William White, Director

RHODE ISLAND: Rhode Island Department of Health, Division of Facilities Regulation, Three Capitol Hill, Providence, RI 02908–5097; tel. 401//222–2566; FAX. 401/222–3999; Wayne I. Farrington, Chief Division, Facilities Regulation

SOUTH CAROLINA: Department of Health and Environmental Control, Division of Health Licensing, 2600 Bull Street, Columbia, SC 29201; tel. 803/737–7370; FAX. 803/737–7212; Jerry Paul, Director

SOUTH DAKOTA: Office of Health Care Facilities Licensure and Certification, State Department of Health, Health Lab, 615 E. 4th Street, Pierre, SD 57501–1700; tel. 605/773–3356; FAX. 605/773–6667; Joan Bachman, Administrator

TENNESSEE: Tennessee Department of Health, Division of Health Care Facilities, 425 5th Avenue North, 1st Floor, Cordell Hull B, Nashville, TN 37247–0508; tel. 615/741–7294; FAX. 615/741–7051; Marie Fitzgerald, Director

TEXAS: Health Facility Certification Division, Texas Department of Health, 1100 West 49th Street, Austin, TX 78756–3199; tel. 512/834–6650; Nance Stearman, Division Director

UTAH: Utah State Department of Health, Bureau of Licensing, Box 142003, Salt Lake Cit, UT 84114–2003; tel. 801/538–6152; FAX. 801/538–6325; Debra Wynkoop–Green, Director

VERMONT: Health Improvement, Vermont Department of Health, 108 Cherry Street, P.O. Box 70, Burlington, VT 05402; tel. 802/863–7606; FAX. 802/651–1634; Ellen B. Thompson, Planning Chief

VIRGINIA: Center for Quality Health Care Services and Consumer Protection, Virginia Department of Health, 3600 Centre, Suite 216, 3600 West Broad Street, Richmond, VA 23230–4920; tel. 804/367–2102; FAX. 804/367–2149; Nancy R. Hofheimer, Director

WASHINGTON: Acute Care and In–Home Services, Washington Department of Health, Target Plaza, Suite 500, 2725 Harrison Avenue,, P.O. Box 47852, Olympia, WA 98504–7852; tel. 360/705–6612; FAX. 360/705–6654; Byron Plan, Manager

WEST VIRGINIA: Office of Health Facility Licensure and Certification, West Virginia Division of Health, State Capitol Complex, Building Three, Suite 550, Charleston, WV 25305; tel. 304/558–0050; FAX. 304/558–2515; John Wilkinson, Director

WISCONSIN: Bureau of Quality Assurance, Division of Supportive Living, Department of Health and Family Services, One West Wilson Street, P.O. Box 309, Madison, WI 53701; tel. 608/267–7185; FAX. 608/267–0352; Judy Fryback, Director, Bureau of Quality Assurance

WYOMING: Office of Health Quality, Health Facilities Licensing, First Bank Building, Eighth Floor, Cheyenne, WY 82002; tel. 307/777–7123; FAX. 307/777–5970; Jane Y. Taylor, Program Manager

Section C

Medical and Nursing Licensure Agencies

Information for the following list of state medical licensure agencies was obtained from the Federation of State Medical Board and nursing licensure agencies was obtained from the National League for Nursing.

United States

ALABAMA
Alabama Board of Nursing, RSA Plaza, Suite 250, 770 Washington Avenue, Montgomery, AL 36130–3900; tel. 334/242–4060; FAX. 334/242–4360; Judi Crume, Executive Officer
Alabama State Board of Medical Examiners, 848 Washington Avenue, Zip 36104, P.O. Box 946, Montgomery, AL 36101–0946; tel. 334/242–4116; FAX. 334/242–4155; Larry D. Dixon, Executive Director

ALASKA
Alaska Board of Nursing, Division of Occupational Licensing, 3601 C Street, Suite 722, Anchorage, AK 99503; tel. 907/269–8161; FAX. 907/269–8156; Dorothy Fulton, Executive Secretary
Alaska State Medical Board, Division of Occupational Licensing, 3601 C Street, Suite 722, Anchorage, AK 99503; tel. 907/269–8163; FAX. 907/269–8156; Leslie G. Abel, Executive Administrator

ARIZONA
Arizona Board of Osteopathic Examiners in Medicine and Surgery, AZ Osteopathic Examiners in Medicine and Surgery, 9535 E. Doubletree Ranch Road, Scottsdale, AZ 85258; tel. 602/657–7703; FAX. 602/657–7715; Ann Marie Berger, Executive Director
Arizona State Board of Medical Examiners, 1651 East Morton, Suite 210, Phoenix, AZ 85020; tel. 602/255–3751; FAX. 602/255–1848; Mark R. Speicher, Executive Director
Arizona State Board of Nursing, 1651 East Morten, Suite 150, Phoenix, AZ 85020; tel. 602/331–8111; FAX. 602/906–9365; Joey Ridenour, RN, M.N., Executive Director

ARKANSAS
Arkansas State Board of Nursing, University Tower Building, Suite 800, 1123 South University Avenue, Little Rock, AR 72204; tel. 501/686–2700; FAX. 501/686–2714; Faith A. Fields, M.S.N., RN, Executive Director
Arkansas State Medical Board, 2100 Riverfront Drive, Suite 200, Little Rock, AR 72202; tel. 501/296–1802; FAX. 501/296–1805; Peggy P. Cryer, Executive Secretary

CALIFORNIA
California Board of Registered Nursing, 400 R Street, Suite 4030, Zip 95814, P.O. Box 944210, Sacramento, CA 94244–2100; tel. 916/322–3350; FAX. 916/227–4402; Ruth Ann Terry, RN, M.P.H., Executive Officer
Medical Board of California, 1426 Howe Avenue, Suite 54, Sacramento, CA 95825; tel. 916/263–2344; FAX. 916/263–2487; Neil Fippin, Program Manager
Osteopathic Medical Board of California, 444 North Third Street, Suite A–200, Sacramento, CA 95814; tel. 916/322–4306; FAX. 916/327–6119; Linda J. Bergmann, Executive Director

COLORADO
Colorado State Board of Medical Examiners, 1560 Broadway, Suite 1300, Denver, CO 80202–5140; tel. 303/894–7690; FAX. 303/894–7692; Susan Miller, Program Administrator
Colorado State Board of Nursing, 1560 Broadway, Suite 670, Denver, CO 80202; tel. 303/894–2430; Karen Brumley, Program Administrator

CONNECTICUT
Connecticut Board of Examiners for Nursing, Department of Public Health, 410 Capitol Avenue, MS #12 HSR, P.O. Box 340308, Hartford, CT 06134–0308; tel. 860/509–7624; FAX. 860/509–7286; Wendy H. Furniss, R.N.C., M.S., Health Services Supervisor
Connecticut Department of Public Health, 410 Capitol Avenue, MS #12 APP, P.O. Box 340308, Hartford, CT 06134–0308; tel. 860/509–7563; FAX. 860/509–8247; Debra L. Johnson, Health Program Associate

DELAWARE
Delaware Board of Medical Practice, Cannon Building, 861 Silver Lake Boulevard, Suite 203, Dover, DE 19901; tel. 302/739–4522 ext. 229; FAX. 302/739–2711; Brenda D. Petty–Ball, Executive Director
Delaware Board of Nursing, Cannon Building, 861 Silver Lake Boulevard, Suite 203, Dover, DE 19904; tel. 302/739–4522 ext. 215, 216, 217; FAX. 302/739–2711; Iva J. Boardman, RN, M.S.N., Executive Director

DISTRICT OF COLUMBIA
District of Columbia Board of Medicine, 614 H Street, N.W., Room 108, Washington, DC 20001; tel. 202/727–5365; FAX. 202/727–4087; James R. Granger, Jr., Executive Director
District of Columbia Board of Nursing, 614 H Street, N.W., Washington, DC 20001; tel. 202/727–7461; FAX. 202/727–8030; Barbara Hatcher, Chairperson

FLORIDA
Florida Board of Medicine, 1940 North Monroe Street, Northwood Centre, Suite 60, Tallahassee, FL 32399–0750; tel. 904/488–0595; FAX. 904/922–3040; Marm M. Harris, Executive Director
Florida Board of Osteopathic Medicine, 1940 North Monroe Street, Northwood Centre, Suite 60, Tallahassee, FL 32399–0757; tel. 850/488–0595; FAX. 904/921–6184; Pamela King
Florida State Board of Nursing, 4080 Woodcock Drive, Suite 202, Jacksonville, FL 32207; tel. 904/858–6940; FAX. 904/858–6964; Marilyn A. Bloss, RNC, M.S.N., Executive Director

GEORGIA
Georgia Board of Nursing, 166 Pryor Street, S.W., Atlanta, GA 30303; tel. 404/656–3943; FAX. 404/657–7489; Shirley A. Camp, RN, JD, Executive Director
Georgia Composite State Board of Medical Examiners, 166 Pryor Street, S.W., Atlanta, GA 30303; tel. 404/656–3913; FAX. 404/656–9723; Greg W. Schader, Acting Executive Director

HAWAII
Hawaii Board of Medical Examiners, Department of Commerce and Consumer Affairs, 1010 Richards Street, Zip 96813, P.O. Box 3469, Honolulu, HI 96801; tel. 808/586–2708; Constance Cabral–Makanani, Executive Officer
Hawaii Board of Nursing, P.O. Box 3469, Honolulu, HI 96801; tel. 808/586–2695; FAX. 808/586–2689; Kathy Yokouchi, Executive Officer

IDAHO
Idaho State Board of Medicine, State House Mail, 280 North Eighth, Suite 202, P.O. Box 83720, Boise, ID 83720–0058; tel. 208/334–2822; FAX. 203/334–2801; Darleen Thorsted, Executive Director
Idaho State Board of Nursing, 280 North Eighth Street, Suite 210, P.O. Box 83720, Boise, ID 83720–0061; tel. 208/334–3110; FAX. 208/334–3262; Sandra Evans, Executive Director

ILLINOIS
Illinois Department of Professional Regulation, 320 West Washington Street, Springfield, IL 62786; tel. 217/782–0458; FAX. 217/782–7645; Tony Sanders, Public Information Officer
Illinois Department of Professional Regulation, James R. Thompson Center, 100 West Randolph Street, Suite 9–300, Chicago, IL 60601; tel. 312/814–4500; FAX. 312/814–1837; Nikki M. Zollar, Director

INDIANA
Indiana Health Professions Bureau, Medical Licensing Board of Indiana, 402 West Washington, Room 041, Indianapolis, IN 46204; tel. 317/233–4401; FAX. 317/233–4236; Laura Langford, Executive Director
Indiana State Board of Nursing, Health Professions Bureau, 402 West Washington, Suite 041, Indianapolis, IN 46204; tel. 317/233–4405; FAX. 317/233–4236; Gina Voorhies, Board Administrator

IOWA
Iowa Board of Nursing, State Capitol Complex, 1223 East Court Avenue, Des Moines, IA 50319; tel. 515/281–3255; FAX. 515/281–4825; Lorinda K. Inman, RN, M.S.N., Executive Director
Iowa State Board of Medical Examiners, Executive Hills West, 1209 East Court Avenue, Des Moines, IA 50319–0180; tel. 515/281–5171; FAX. 515/242–5908; Ann M. Martino, Ph.D., Executive Director

KANSAS
Kansas State Board of Healing Arts, 235 Southwest Topeka Boulevard, Topeka, KS 66603–3068; tel. 913/296–7413; FAX. 913/296–0852; Lawrence T. Buening, Jr., J.D., Executive Director
Kansas State Board of Nursing, Landon State Office Building, 900 Southwest Jackson, Suite 551–S, Topeka, KS 66612–1230; tel. 785/296–4929; FAX. 785/296–3929; Patsy Johnson, RN, M.N., Executive Administrator

KENTUCKY
Kentucky Board of Medical Licensure, The Hurstbourne Office Park, 310 Whittington Parkway, Suite 1B, Louisville, KY 40222; tel. 502/429–8046; FAX. 502/429–9923; C. William Schmidt, Executive Director
Kentucky Board of Nursing, 312 Whittington Parkway, Suite 300, Louisville, KY 40222; tel. 502/329–7000; FAX. 502/329–7011; Sharon M. Weisenbeck, M.S., RN, Executive Director

LOUISIANA
Louisiana State Board of Medical Examiners, P.O. Box 30250, New Orleans, LA 70190–0250; tel. 504/524–6763; FAX. 504/568–8893; Mrs. Delmar Rorison, Executive Director
Louisiana State Board of Nursing, 912 Pere Marquette Building, New Orleans, LA 70112; tel. 504/568–5464; FAX. 504/568–5467; Barbara L. Morvant, RN, M.N., Executive Director

MAINE
Maine Board of Licensure in Medicine, Two Bangor Street, 137 State House Station, Augusta, ME 04333–0137; tel. 207/287–3601; FAX. 207/287–6590; Randal C. Manning, Executive Director
Maine Board of Osteopathic Licensure, 142 State House Station, Two Bangor Street, Augusta, ME 04333–0142; tel. 207/287–2480; FAX. 207/287–2480; Susan E. Stout, Executive Secretary
Maine State Board of Nursing, 24 Stone Street, 158 State House Station, Augusta, ME 04333; tel. 207/287–1133; FAX. 207/287–1149; Myra A. Broadway, RN, Executive Director

MARYLAND
Maryland Board of Nursing, 4140 Patterson Avenue, Baltimore, MD 21215; tel. 410/764–5124; FAX. 410/358–3530; Donna M. Dorsey, RN, M.S., Executive Director
Maryland Board of Physician Quality Assurance, 4201 Patterson Avenue, Third Floor, P.O. Box 2571, Baltimore, MD 21215–0095; tel. 800/492–6836; FAX. 410/358–2252; J. Michael Compton, Executive Director

MASSACHUSETTS
Massachusetts Board of Registration in Medicine, 10 West Street, Third Floor, Boston, MA 02111; tel. 617/727–3086; FAX. 617/451–9568; Alexander F. Fleming, J.D., Executive Director
Massachusetts Board of Registration in Nursing, 100 Cambridge Street, Suite 1519, Boston, MA 02202; tel. 617/727–9961; FAX. 617/727–9961; Theresa M. Bonanno, M.S.N., RN, Executive Director

MICHIGAN
Michigan Board of Medicine, 611 West Ottawa Street, Fourth Floor, Box 30192, Lansing, MI 48909; tel. 517/335–0918; FAX. 517/373–2179; Brenda Rogers, Assistant Administrator
Michigan Board of Nursing, Department of Consumer and Industry Service, 611 West Ottawa Street, P.O. Box 30670, Lansing, MI 48909; tel. 517/335–0918; FAX. 517/373–2179; Brenda Rogers, Assistant Administrator

Michigan Board of Osteopathic Medicine and Surgery, 611 West Ottawa Street, Fourth Floor, P.O. Box 30670, Lansing, MI 48909; tel. 517/335–0918; FAX. 517/373–2179; Brenda Rogers, Assistant Administrator

MINNESOTA
Minnesota Board of Medical Practice, 2829 University Avenue, S.E., Suite 400, Minneapolis, MN 55414–3246; tel. 612/617–2130; FAX. 612/617–2166; Robert A. Leach, Executive Director
Minnesota Board of Nursing, 2829 University Avenue, S.E., Suite 500, Minneapolis, MN 55414–3253; tel. 612/617–2270; FAX. 612/617–2190; Joyce M. Schowalter, Executive Director

MISSISSIPPI
Mississippi Board of Nursing, 239 North Lamar Street, Suite 401, Jackson, MS 39201–1397; tel. 601/359–6170; FAX. 601/359–6185; Marcia M. Rachel, Ph.D., RN, Executive Director
Mississippi State Board of Medical Licensure, 2600 Insurance Center Drive, Suite 200–B, Jackson, MS 39216; tel. 601/354–6645; FAX. 601/987–4159; Thomas E. Stevens, M.D., Executive Officer

MISSOURI
Missouri State Board of Nursing, 3605 Missouri Boulevard, P.O. Box 656, Jefferson Cit, MO 65102; tel. 573/751–0681; FAX. 573/751–0075; JoAnn Hanley, Executive Assistant
Missouri State Board of Registration for the Healing Arts, 3605 Missouri Boulevard, Zip 65109, P.O. Box Four, Jefferson Cit, MO 65102; tel. 314/751–0098; FAX. 314/751–3166; Tina M. Steinman, Executive Director

MONTANA
Montana Board of Medical Examiners, 111 North Jackson, P.O. Box 200513, Helena, MT 59620–0513; tel. 406/444–4284; FAX. 406/444–9396; Patricia I. England, J.D., Executive Secretary
Montana State Board of Nursing, 111 North Jackson–4C, P.O. Box 200513, Arcade Building, Helena, MT 59620–0513; tel. 406/444–2071; FAX. 406/444–7759; Dianne Wickham, RN, M.N., Executive Director

NEBRASKA
Nebraska State Board of Examiners in Medicine and Surgery, 301 Centennial Mall, S., P.O. Box 94986, Lincoln, NE 68509–4986; tel. 402/471–2118; FAX. 402/471–3577; Katherine A. Brown, Executive Secretary

NEVADA
Nevada State Board of Medical Examiners, 1105 Terminal Way, Suite 301, Zip 89502, P.O. Box 7238, Reno, NV 89510; tel. 702/688–2559; FAX. 702/688–2321; Larry D. Lessly, Executive Director
Nevada State Board of Nursing, 4335 South Industrial Road, Suite 420, Las Vegas, NV 89103; tel. 702/739–1575; FAX. 702/739–0298; Kathy Apple, Executive Director
Nevada State Board of Osteopathic Medicine, 2950 East Flamingo Road, Suite E–3, Las Vegas, NV 89121; tel. 702/732–2147; FAX. 702/732–2079; Larry J. Tarno, D.O., Executive Director

NEW HAMPSHIRE
New Hampshire Board of Medicine, Two Industrial Park Drive, Suite 8, Concord, NH 03301; tel. 603/271–1203; FAX. 603/271–6702; Karen Lamoureux, Administrator
New Hampshire State Board of Nursing, Six Hazen Drive, Concord, NH 03301; tel. 603/271–2323; FAX. 603/271–6605; Doris G. Nuttelman, RN, Ed.D., Executive Director

NEW JERSEY
New Jersey Board of Nursing, 124 Halsey Street, Newark, NJ 07102; P.O. Box 45010, Newark, NJ 07101; tel. 201/504–6430; FAX. 201/648–3481; Patricia A. Polansky, Executive Director
New Jersey State Board of Medical Examiners, 140 East Front Street, Second Floor, Trenton, NJ 08608; tel. 609/826–7100; FAX. 609/984–3930; Kevin B. Earle, Executive Director

NEW MEXICO
New Mexico Board of Osteopathic Medical Examiners, 725 St. Michael's Drive, Santa Fe, NM 87501, P.O. Box 25101, Santa Fe, NM 87504; tel. 505/827–7171; FAX. 505/827–7095; Liz Z. Montoya, Executive Director

New Mexico State Board of Medical Examiners, 491 Old Santa Fe Trail, Lamy Building, Second Floor, Santa Fe, NM 87501; tel. 505/827–5022; FAX. 505/827–7377; Kristen A. Hedrick, Executive Secretary
State of New Mexico, Board of Nursing, 4206 Louisiana, N.E., Suite A, Albuquerque, NM 87109; tel. 505/841–8340; FAX. 505/841–8347; Nancy L. Twigg, Executive Director

NEW YORK
New York Board for Professional Medical Conduct, State Department of Health, 433 River Street, Suite 303, Troy, NY 12180–2299; tel. 518/402–0855; FAX. 518/402–0866; Anne F. Saile, Director
New York State Board for Nursing, State Education Department, The Cultural Center, Suite 3023, Albany, NY 12230; tel. 518/474–3845; FAX. 518/473–0578; Milene A. Megel, RN, Ph.D., Executive Secretary
New York State Division of Professional Licensing Services, Cultural Education Center, Suite 3021, Empire State Plaza, Albany, NY 12230; tel. 518/474–3817; FAX. 518/473–0578; Robert G. Bentley, Director, Professional Licensing

NORTH CAROLINA
North Carolina Board of Nursing, P.O. Box 2129, Raleigh, NC 27602–2129; tel. 919/782–3211; FAX. 919/781–9461; Mary P. 'Polly' Johnson, RN, MSN, Executive Director
North Carolina Medical Board, P.O. Box 20007, Raleigh, NC 27619; tel. 919/828–1212, ext. 21; FAX. 919/828–1295; Andrew W. Watry, Executive Director

NORTH DAKOTA
North Dakota Board of Nursing, 919 South Seventh Street, Suite 504, Bismarck, ND 58504–5881; tel. 701/328–9777; FAX. 701/328–9785; Ida H. Rigley, RN, Executive Director
North Dakota State Board of Medical Examiners, City Center Plaza, Suite 12, 418 East Broadway Avenue, Bismarck, ND 58501; tel. 701/328–6500; FAX. 701/328–6505; Rolf P. Sletten, Executive Secretary–Treasurer

OHIO
Ohio Board of Nursing, 77 South High Street, 17th Floor, Columbus, OH 43266–0316; tel. 614/466–3947; Dorothy Fiorino, RN, Executive Director
State Medical Board of Ohio, 77 South High Street, 17th Floor, Columbus, OH 43266–0315; tel. 614/466–3934; FAX. 614/728–5946; Ray Q. Bumgarner, Executive Director

OKLAHOMA
Oklahoma Board of Nursing, 2915 North Classen Boulevard, Suite 524, Oklahoma City, OK 73106; tel. 405/962–1800; FAX. 405/962–1821; Sulinda Moffett, M.S.N., RN, Executive Director
Oklahoma State Board of Osteopathic Examiners, 4848 North Lincoln Boulevard, Suite 100, Oklahoma City, OK 73105–3321; tel. 405/528–8625; FAX. 405/557–0653; Gary R. Clark, Executive Director
Oklahoma State Board of Medical Licensure and Supervision, 5104 North Francis, Suite C, Oklahoma City, OK 73118, P.O. Box 18256, Oklahoma City, OK 73154–0256; tel. 405/848–6841; FAX. 405/848–8240; Lyle Kelsey, Executive Director

OREGON
Oregon Board of Medical Examiners, 620 Crown Plaza, 1500 Southwest First Avenue, Portland, OR 97201–5826; tel. 503/229–5770; FAX. 503/229–6543; Kathleen Haley, J.D., Executive Director
Oregon State Board of Nursing, 800 Northeast Oregon Street, Suite 465, Portland, OR 97232–2162; tel. 503/731–4745; FAX. 503/731–4755; Joan C. Bouchard, Executive Director

PENNSYLVANIA
Pennsylvania State Board of Medicine, P.O. Box 2649, Harrisburg, PA 17105–2649; tel. 717/783–1400; FAX. 717/787–7769; Cindy L. Warner, Administrative Officer
Pennsylvania State Board of Nursing, Department of State, P.O. Box 2649, Harrisburg, PA 17105–2649; tel. 717/783–7142; FAX. 717/783–0822; Miriam H. Limo, Executive Secretary
Pennsylvania State Board of Osteopathic Medicine, P.O. Box 2649, Harrisburg, PA 17105–2649; tel. 717/783–4858; Gina Bittner, Administrative Assistant

RHODE ISLAND
Board of Nursing Education and Nurse Registration, Three Capitol Hill, Room 104, Providence, RI 02908–5097; tel. 401/277–2827; FAX. 401/277–1272; Carol Lietar, RN, M.S.N., Director
Rhode Island Board of Medical Licensure and Discipline, Rhode Island Department of Health, Room 205, 3 Capitol Hill, Providence, RI 02908–5097; tel. 401/222–3855; FAX. 401/222–2158; Milton W. Hamolsky, M.D., Chief Administrative Officer

SOUTH CAROLINA
Department of Labor, Licensing and Regulation, State Board of Nursing for South Carolina, P.O. Box 12367, Columbia, SC 29211; tel. 803/896–4550; FAX. 803/896–4525; Brenda Shaw, Secretary
South Carolina Department of Labor, Licensing and Regulation, Board of Medical Examiners, 110 Centerview Drive, Suite 202, Columbia, S.C. 29210, P.O. Box 11289, Columbia, SC 29211–1289; tel. 803/896–4500; FAX. 803/896–4515; Aaron Kozloski, J.D., Board Administrator

SOUTH DAKOTA
South Dakota Board of Nursing, 4300 South Louise Avenue, Sioux Falls, SD 57106; tel. 605/362–2760; FAX. 605/362–2768; Diana Vander Woude, Executive Secretary
South Dakota State Board of Medical and Osteopathic Examiners, 1323 South Minnesota Avenue, Sioux Falls, SD 57105; tel. 605/336–1965; FAX. 605/336–0270; Robert D. Johnson, Executive Secretary

TENNESSEE
Tennessee Board of Nursing, 283 Plus Park Boulevard, Nashville, TN 37217; tel. 615/367–6232; FAX. 615/367–6397; Elizabeth J. Lund, RN, Executive Director
Tennessee State Board of Medical Examiners, First Floor, Cordell Hull Building, 425 Fifth Avenue, N. 1st Floor, Nashville, TN 37247–1010; tel. 888/310–4650; FAX. 615/532–5369; Linda Hudgins, Administrator
Tennessee State Board of Osteopathic Examination, First Floor, Cordell Hull Building, 425 Fifth Avenue, N., Nashville, TN 37247–1010; tel. 615/532–5080; FAX. 615/532–5369; Judy Hartman, Administrator

TEXAS
Texas Board of Nurse Examiners, P.O. Box 430, Austin, TX 78767–0430; tel. 512/305–7400; Katherine Thomas, MN, RN
Texas State Board of Medical Examiners, 333 Guadalupe, Tower Three, Suite 610, Austin, TX 7, P.O. Box 2018, Austin, TX 78768–7008; tel. 512/305–7010; FAX. 512/305–7008; Bruce A. Levy, M.D., J.D., Executive Director

UTAH
Utah Physicians Licensing Board, Division of Occupational and Professional L, Heber M. Wells Building, Fourth Floor, 160 East 300 South, Salt Lake City, UT 84111, P.O. Box 146741, Salt Lake City, UT 84114–6741; tel. 801/530–6628; FAX. 801/530–6511; Karen Reimherr, Bureau Manager
Utah State Board of Nursing, 160 East 300 South, Box 146741, Salt Lake Cit, UT 84114–6741; tel. 801/530–6628; FAX. 801/530–6511; Laura Poe, Executive Administrator

VERMONT
Vermont Board of Medical Practice, 109 State Street, Montpelier, VT 05609–1106; tel. 802/828–2673; FAX. 802/828–5450; Barbara Neuman, J.D., Executive Director
Vermont Board of Nursing Licensure and Regulation Division, 109 State Street, Montpelier, VT 05609–1106; tel. 802/828–2396; FAX. 802/828–2484; Anita Ristau, RN, M.S., Executive Director
Vermont Board of Osteopathic Physicians and Surgeons, 109 State Street, Montpelier, VT 05609–1106; tel. 802/828–2373; FAX. 802/828–2465; Peggy Atkins, Staff Assistant

VIRGINIA
Virginia Board of Medicine, 6606 West Broad Street, Fourth Floor, Richmond, VA 23230–1717; tel. 804/662–9908; FAX. 804/662–9943; Warren W. Koontz, Jr., M.D., Executive Director
Virginia Board of Nursing, 6606 West Broad Street, Fourth Floor, Richmond, VA 23230; tel. 804/662–9909; FAX. 804/662–9512; Nancy K. Durrett, RN, Executive Director

WASHINGTON

Washington State Board of Osteopathic Medicine and Surgery, Department of Health, 1300 Southeast Quince Street, P.O. Box 47870, Olympia, WA 98504–7870; tel. 360/586–5962; FAX. 360/586–0745; Ericka Newton, Administrative Assistant

Washington State Medical Quality Assurance Commision, 1300 Southeast Quince Street, P.O. Box 47866, Olympia, WA 98504–7866; tel. 360/753–2287; FAX. 360/586–4573; Bonnie L. King, Executive Director

Washington State Nursing Care Quality Assurance Commission, Department of Health, 1300 Southeast Quince Street, P.O. Box 47864, Olympia, WA 98504–7864; tel. 360/664–4100; FAX. 360/586–5935; Patty L. Hayes, RN, M.N., Executive Director

WEST VIRGINIA

West Virginia Board of Examiners for Registered Professional Nurses, 101 Dee Drive, Charleston, WV 25311–1620; tel. 304/558–3596; FAX. 304/558–3666; Laura S. Rhodes, RN, M.S.N., Executive Secretary

West Virginia Board of Medicine, 101 Dee Drive, Charleston, WV 25311; tel. 304/558–2921; FAX. 304/558–2084; Ronald D. Walton, Executive Director

West Virginia Board of Osteopathy, 334 Penco Road, Weirton, WV 26062; tel. 304/723–4638; FAX. 304/723–2877; Cheryl D. Schreiber, Executive Secretary

WISCONSIN

Division of Health Professions and Services Licensing, 1400 East Washington Avenue, Room 178, P.O. Box 8935, Madison, WI 53708–8935; tel. 608/266–5432; FAX. 608/267–0644; Deanna Zychowski, Administrative Assistant

Wisconsin Medical Examining Board, 1400 East Washington Avenue, Zip 53702, P.O. Box 8935, Madison, WI 53708; tel. 608/266–2811; FAX. 608/267–0644; Patrick D. Braatz, Bureau Director

WYOMING

Wyoming Board of Medicine, The Colony Building, 211 West 19th Street, Second Floor, Cheyenne, WY 82002; tel. 307/778–7053; FAX. 307/778–2069; Carole Shotwell, Executive Secretary

Wyoming State Board of Nursing, 2020 Carey Avenue, Suite 110, Cheyenne, WY 82002; tel. 307/777–7601; FAX. 307/777–3519; Toma A. Nisbet, RN, M.S., Executive Director

U. S. Associated Areas

AMERICAN SAMOA–GUAM

American Samoa Health Services Regulatory Board, LBJ Tropical Medical Center, Pago Pago, AS 96799; tel. 684/633–5995; FAX. 684/633–1869; Etenauga L. Lutu, RN, Executive Secretary

GUAM

Guam Board of Medical Examiners, 1304 East Sunset Boulevard, Barrigada, GU 96913; tel. 671/475–0251; FAX. 671/477–4733; Teofila P. Cruz, Administrator Health Professional Licensing Office

Guam Board of Nurse Examiners, Department of Public Health and Social Services, 1304 East Sunset Boulevard, Barrigada (Tiyan), Guam, P.O. Box 2816, Agana, GU 96910; tel. 671/475–0251; FAX. 671/477–4733; Teofila P. Cruz, RN, M.S., Administrator

PUERTO RICO

Council on Higher Education of Puerto Rico, UPR Station, P.O. Box 23305, San Juan, PR 00931–3305; tel. 809/758–3356; Madeline Quilichini Paz, Director, Office of Licensing and Accreditation

Puerto Rico Board of Medical Examiners, Kennedy Avenue, ILA Building, Hogar del Obrero Portuario, Piso 8, Puerto Nuevo,, Call Box 13969, San Juan, PR 00908; tel. 787/793–1333; FAX. 787/782–8733; Lorenne E. Montalvo Garcia, Esq., Executive Director

VIRGIN ISLANDS

Virgin Islands Board of Medical Examiners, Virgin Islands Department of Health, 48 Sugar Estate, St. Thomas, VI 00802; tel. 809/774–0117; FAX. 809/777–4001; Lydia T. Scott, Executive Assistant to the Boards

Virgin Islands Board of Nursing Licensure, P.O. Box 4247, St. Thomas, VI 00803; tel. 809/776–7397; FAX. 809/777–4003; Winifred L. Garfield, CRNA, Executive Secretary

Canada

ALBERTA

College of Physicians and Surgeons of Alberta, 900 Manulife Place, 10180–101 Street, Edmonton, AB T5J 4P8; tel. 403/423–4764; FAX. 403/420–0651; Dr. L.R. Ohlhauser, Registrar

MANITOBA

College of Physicians and Surgeons of Manitoba, 494 St. James Street, Winnipeg, MB R3G 3J4; tel. 204/774–4344; FAX. 204/774–0750; Kenneth R. Brown, M.D., Registrar

NEW BRUNSWICK

College of Physicians and Surgeons of New Brunswick, One Hampton Road, Suite 300, Rothesay, NB E2E 5K8; tel. 506/849–5050; FAX. 506/849–5069; Dr. Ed Schollenberg, Registrar

NOVA SCOTIA

College of Physicians and Surgeons of Nova Scotia, Office of the Registrar, 5248 Morris Street, Halifax, NS B3J 1B4; tel. 902/422–5823; FAX. 902/422–5035; Dr. Cameron Little, Registrar

PRINCE EDWARD ISLAND

College of Physicians and Surgeons of Prince Edward Island, 199 Grafton Street, Charlottetown, PE C1A 1L2; tel. 902/566–3861; FAX. 902/566–3861; H. E. Ross, M.D., Registrar

QUEBEC

College des medecins du Quebec, 2170, boul. Rene–Levesque Quest, Montreal, PQ H3H 2T8; tel. 514/933–4441ext244; FAX. 514/933–3112; Joelle Lescop, M.D., Secretary General

SASKATCHEWAN

College of Physicians and Surgeons of Saskatchewan, 211 Fourth Avenue, S., Saskatoon, SK S7K 1N1; tel. 306/244–7355; FAX. 306/244–0090; D. A. Kendel, M.D., Registrar

Section C

Peer Review Organizations

The following list of PROs was obtained from the Office of Medical Review, Division of Program Operation, HCFA. For more information, contact the office at 410/786–8781.

United States

ALABAMA: Alabama Quality Assurance Foundation, One Perimeter Park, S., Suite 200 North, Birmingham, AL 35243–2354; tel. 205/970–1600; FAX. 205/970–1616; H. Terrell Lindsey, President, Chief Executive Officer

ALASKA: PRO–WEST, 10700 Meridian Avenue, N., Suite 100, Seattle, WA 98133–9075; tel. 206/364–9700; FAX. 206/368–2419; John W. Daise, Chief Executive Officer

ARIZONA: Health Services Advisory Group, Inc., 301 East Bethany Home Road, Suite B–157, Phoenix, AZ 85012; tel. 602/264–6382; FAX. 602/241–0757; Lawrence J. Shapiro, M.D., President, Chief Executive Officer

ARKANSAS: Arkansas Foundation for Medical Care, Inc., 809 Garrision Avenue, P.O. Box 2424, Fort Smith, AR 72902; tel. 501/785–2471; FAX. 501/785–3460; Russell G. Brasher, Ph.D., Chief Executive Officer

CALIFORNIA: California Medical Review, Inc., 60 Spear Street, Suite 400, San Francisco, CA 94105; tel. 415/882–5800; FAX. 415/882–5995; Jo Ellen H. Ross, Chief Executive Officer

COLORADO: Colorado Foundation for Medical Care, 2851 South Parker Road, Suite 200, Aurora, CO 80014–2713; tel. 303/695–3300, ext. 3032; FAX. 303/695–3350; Arja P. Adair, Jr., Executive Director

CONNECTICUT: Connecticut Peer Review Organization, Inc., 100 Roscommon Drive, Suite 200, Middletown, CT 06457; tel. 860/632–2008; FAX. 860/632–5865; Marcia K. Petrillo, Chief Executive Officer

DELAWARE: West Virginia Medical Institute, Inc., 3001 Chesterfield Place, Charleston, WV 25304; tel. 304/346–9864, ext. 269; FAX. 304/346–9863; Mabel M. Stevenson, M.D., President

DISTRICT OF COLUMBIA: Delmarva Foundation for Medical Care, Inc., 9240 Centreville Road, Easton, MD 21601; tel. 410/822–0697; FAX. 410/822–9572; Thomas J. Schaefer, Chief Executive Officer

FLORIDA: Florida Medical Quality Assurance, Inc., 4350 West Cypress Street, Suite 900, Tampa, FL 33607; tel. 813/354–9111; FAX. 813/354–0737; Jennifer Barnett, President, Chief Executive Officer

GEORGIA: Georgia Medical Care Foundation, 57 Executive Park, S., Suite 200, Atlanta, GA 30329; tel. 404/982–0411; FAX. 404/982–7584; Tom W. Williams, Chief Executive Officer

HAWAII: Mountain–Pacific Quality Health Foundation, 1360 South Beretania, Suite 400, Honolulu, HI 96814; tel. 808/545–2550; FAX. 808/599–2875; Dee Dee Nelson, Director of Hawaii Office

IDAHO: PRO–WEST, 10700 Meridian Avenue, N., Suite 100, Seattle, WA 98133–9075; tel. 206/364–9700; FAX. 206/368–2419; John W. Daise, Chief Executive Officer

ILLINOIS: Iowa Foundation for Medical Care/The Sunderbruch Corporation/, Illinois Foundation for Quality Health, 6000 Westown Parkway, Suite 350E, West Des Moines, IA 50266–7771; tel. 515/223–2900; FAX. 515/222–2407; Rebecca Hemann, VP Government Quality Improvement Program

INDIANA: Health Care Excel, Incorporated, 2901 Ohio Boulevard, P.O. Box 3713, Terre Haute, IN 47803; tel. 812/234–1499; FAX. 812/232–6167; Philip L. Morphew, Chief Executive Officer

IOWA: Iowa Foundation for Medical Care/The Sunderbruch Corporation/, Illinois Foundation for Quality Health, 6000 Westown Parkway, Suite 350E, West Des Moines, IA 50266–7771; tel. 515/223–2900; FAX. 515/222–2407; Fred A. Ferree, Executive Vice President

KANSAS: The Kansas Foundation for Medical Care, Inc., 2947 Southwest Wanamaker Drive, Topeka, KS 66614; tel. 913/273–2552, ext. 363; FAX. 913/273–5130; Larry Pitman, President and Chief Executive Officer

KENTUCKY: Health Care Excel, Incorporated, 9502 Williamsburg Plaza, Suite 102, P.O. Box 23540, Louisville, KY 40222; tel. 502/339–7442; FAX. 502/339–8641; Philip L. Morphew, Chief Executive Director

LOUISIANA: Louisiana Health Care Review, Inc., 8591 United Plaza Boulevard, Suite 270, Baton Rouge, LA 70809; tel. 504/926–6353; FAX. 504/923–0957; Leo Stanley, Chief Executive Officer

MAINE: Northeast Health Care Quality Foundation, 15 Old Rollinsford Road, Suite 302, Dover, NH 03820; tel. 603/749–1641; FAX. 603/749–1195; Robert A. Aurilio, Chief Executive Officer

MARYLAND: Delmarva Foundation for Medical Care, Inc., 9240 Centreville Road, Easton, MD 21601; tel. 410/822–0697; FAX. 410/822–9572; Thomas J. Schaefer, Chief Executive Officer

MASSACHUSETTS: Massachusetts Peer Review Organization, Inc., 235 Wyman Street, Waltham, MA 02154–1231; tel. 781/890–0011; FAX. 781/487–0083; Kathleen E. McCarthy, President and Chief Executive Officer

MICHIGAN: Michigan Peer Review Organization, 40600 Ann Arbor Road, Suite 200, Plymouth, MI 48170–4495; tel. 313/459–0900; FAX. 313/454–7301; Sheryl L. Stogis, Chief Executive Officer

MINNESOTA: Stratis Health, 2901 Metro Drive, Suite 400, Bloomington, MN 55425; tel. 612/854–3306; FAX. 612/853–8503; David M. Ziegenhagen, Chief Executive Officer

MISSISSIPPI: Mississippi Foundation for Medical Care, Inc., 735 Riverside Drive, P.O. Box 4665, Jackson, MS 39296–4665; tel. 601/948–8894; FAX. 601/948–8917; James McIlwain, M.D.

MISSOURI: Missouri Patient Care Review Foundation, 505 Hobbs Road, Suite 100, Jefferson City, MO 65109; tel. 573/893–7900; FAX. 573/893–5827; Dan Jaco, Chief Executive Officer

MONTANA: Mountain Pacific Quality Health Foundation, 400 North Park Avenue, Second Floor, Helena, MT 59601; tel. 406/443–4020; FAX. 406/443–4585; Janice Connors, Executive Director

NEBRASKA: Iowa Foundation for Medical Care/The Sunderbruch Corporation/, Illinois Foundation for Quality Health, 6000 Westown Parkway, Suite 350E, West Des Moines, IA 50266–7771; tel. 515/223–2900; FAX. 515/222–2407; Fred Ferree, Executive Vice President

NEVADA: HealthInsight, 675 East 2100 South, Suite 270, Salt Lake City, UT 84106–1864; tel. 702/385–9933; FAX. 702/385–4586; James Q. Cannon, Chief Executive Officer

NEW HAMPSHIRE: Northeast Health Care Quality Foundation, 15 Old Rollinsford Road, Suite 302, Dover, NH 03820–2830; tel. 603/749–1641; FAX. 603/749–1195; Robert A. Aurilio, Chief Executive Officer

NEW JERSEY: The Peer Review Organization of New Jersey, Inc., Central Division, Brier Hill Court, Building J, East Brunswick, NJ 08816; tel. 732/238–5570; FAX. 732/238–7766; Martin P. Margolies, Chief Executive Officer

NEW MEXICO: NMMRA, (New Mexico Medical Review Association, 2340 Menaul Blvd.,NE,Suite 300, P.O. Box 3200, Albuquerque, NM 87190–3200; tel. 505/998–9898; FAX. 505/998–9899; Gary Horvat, Chief Executive Officer

NEW YORK: IPRO, 1979 Marcus Avenue, First Floor, Lake Success, NY 11042–1002; tel. 516/326–7767, ext. 540; FAX. 516/328–2310; Theodore O. Will, Executive Vice President

NORTH CAROLINA: Medical Review of North Carolina, Inc., 5625 Dillard Drive, Suite 203, Cary, NC 27511–9227; tel. 919/851–2955; FAX. 919/851–8457; Charles Riddick, Executive Director

NORTH DAKOTA: North Dakota Health Care Review Inc., 800 31st Avenue S.W., Minot, ND 58701; tel. 701/852–4231; FAX. 701/838–6009; David Remillard, Chief Executive Officer

OHIO: Peer Review Systems, Inc., 757 Brooksedge Plaza Drive, Westerville, OH 43081–4913; tel. 614/895–9900; FAX. 614/895–6784; Gregory J. Dykes, Chief Executive Officer

OKLAHOMA: Oklahoma Foundation for Medical Quality, Inc., The Paragon Building, 5801 Broadway Extension, Suite 400, Oklahoma City, OK 73118–7489; tel. 405/840–2891; FAX. 405/840–1343; Jim L. Williams, President, Chief Executive Officer

OREGON: Oregon Medical Professional Review Organization, 2020 S.W. 4th Avenue, Suite 520, Portland, OR 97201–4960; tel. 503/279–0100; FAX. 503/279–0190; Robert S. Kinoshita, President

PENNSYLVANIA: Keystone Peer Review Organization, Inc., 777 East Park Drive, P.O. Box 8310, Harrisburg, PA 17105–8310; tel. 717/564–8288; FAX. 717/564–4188; John DiNardi III, Executive Director

RHODE ISLAND: Rhode Island Quality Partners, Inc. (C/O CT PRO), 100 Roscommon Drive, Suite 200, Middletown, CT 06457; tel. 860/632–2008; FAX. 860/632–5865; Marcia K. Petrillo, Chief Executive Officer

SOUTH CAROLINA: Carolina Medical Review, 250 Berryhill Road, Suite 101, Columbia, SC 29210; tel. 803/731–8225; FAX. 803/731–8229; Blake Williams, Director of Operations

SOUTH DAKOTA: South Dakota Foundation for Medical Care, 1323 South Minnesota Avenue, Sioux Falls, SD 57105; tel. 605/336–3505; FAX. 605/336–0270; Robert D. Johnson, Chief Executive Officer

TENNESSEE: Mid–South Foundation for Medical Care, Inc., 6401 Poplar Avenue, Suite 400, Memphis, TN 38119; tel. 901/682–0381; FAX. 901/761–3786; Logan Malone, Chief Executive Officer

TEXAS: Texas Medical Foundation, Barton Oaks Plaza Two, Suite 200, 901 Mopac Expressway, S., Austin, TX 78746–5799; tel. 512/329–6610; FAX. 512/327–7159; Phillip K. Dunne, Chief Executive Officer

UTAH: HealthInsight, 675 East 2100 South, Suite 270, Salt Lake City, UT 84106–1864; tel. 801/487–2290; FAX. 801/487–2296; James Q. Cannon, President, Chief Executive Officer

VERMONT: Northeast Health Care Quality Foundation, 15 Old Rollinsford Road, Suite 302, Dover, NH 03820–2830; tel. 603/749–1641; FAX. 603/749–1195; Robert A. Aurilio, Chief Executive Officer

VIRGINIA: Virginia Health Quality Center, 1604 Santa Rosa Road, Suite 200, Richmond, VA 23229–5008, P.O. Box K–70, Richmond, VA 23288–0070; tel. 804/289–5320; FAX. 804/289–5324; Joy Hogan Rozman, Executive Director

WASHINGTON: PRO–WEST, 10700 Meridian Avenue, N., Suite 100, Seattle, WA 98133–9075; tel. 206/364–9700; FAX. 206/368–2419; John W. Daise, Chief Executive Officer

WEST VIRGINIA: West Virginia Medical Institute, Inc., 3001 Chesterfield Place, Charleston, WV 25304; tel. 304/346–9864, ext. 269; FAX. 304/346–9863; Mabel M. Stevenson, M.D., President

WISCONSIN: Meta Star, 2909 Landmark Place, Madison, WI 53713; tel. 608/274–1940; FAX. 608/274–5008; Greg E. Simmons, President, Chief Executive Officer

**WYOMING: Mountain–Pacific Quality Health
Foundation,** 400 North Park Avenue, Second Floor,
Helena, MT 59601; tel. 406/443–4020; FAX.
406/443–4585; Janice Connors, Executive Director

U. S. Associated Areas

**PUERTO RICO: Quality Improvement Professional
Research Organization,** Mercantile Plaza Building,
Suite 605, Hato Rey, PR 00918; tel.
787/753–6705; FAX. 787/753–6885; Jose
Robles, Chief Executive Officer

**VIRGIN ISLANDS: Virgin Islands Medical Institute,
Inc.,** 1AD Estate Diamond Ruby, P.O. Box 5989,
Sunny Isle, St. Croix, U.S., VI 00823–5989; tel.
340/712–2400; FAX. 340/778–6801; Denyce E.
Singleton, Chief Executive Officer

Section C

State Health Planning and Development Agencies

The following is a list of state health planning and development agencies. The information was obtained from the Missouri Department of Health, Certificate of Need Program and the agencies themselves. For information about other state agencies and organizations that fulfill many of the same functions, contact the state or metropolitan hospital associations.

United States

ALABAMA: State Health Planning and Development Agency, 100 North Union Street, Suite 870, Montgomery, AL 36104; tel. 334/242–4103; FAX. 334/242–4113; J. Elbert Peters, Executive Director

ALASKA: Facilities and Planning Section, Department of Health and Social Services, P.O. Box 110650, Juneau, AK 99811–0650; tel. 907/465–3015; FAX. 907/465–2499; Larry J. Streuber, Section Chief

ARIZONA: Office of Health Planning, Evaluation and Statistics, 1740 West Adams, Room 301, Phoenix, AZ 85007; tel. 602/542–1216; FAX. 602/542–1244; Merle Lustig, Chief

CALIFORNIA: Office of Statewide Health Planning and Development, 1600 Ninth Street, Suite 440, Sacramento, CA 95814; tel. 916/654–2087; FAX. 916/654–3138; Priscilla Gonzalez–Leiva, RN, Deputy Director, Primary Care Resources

COLORADO: Department of Health, Office of Health, 4300 Cherry Creek Drive, S., Denver, CO 80222–1530; tel. 303/692–2478; FAX. 303/782–5576; Susan Rehak, Deputy Director

CONNECTICUT: Connecticut Department of Public Health and Addiction, Office of Policy, Planning and Evaluation, 410 Capitol Avenue, MS# 13PPE, Box 340308, Hartford, CT 06134–0308; tel. 860/509–7123; FAX. 860/509–7160; Donald Iodice, Health Program Associate

DELAWARE: Bureau of Health Planning and Resources Management, Department of Health and Social Services, P.O. Box 637, Dover, DE 19903; tel. 302/739–4776; FAX. 302/739–3008; Robert I. Welch, Director

DISTRICT OF COLUMBIA: Plan Development and Implementation Division, 800 Ninth Street, S.W., Third Floor, Washington, DC 20024; tel. 202/645–5525; FAX. 202/645–0526; Gail Smith, Chief

FLORIDA: Agency for Health Care Administration, Medicaid Program Development, 2727 Mahan Drive, Tallahassee, FL 32308–5403; tel. 904/488–9347; FAX. 904/414–6236; H. Robert Sharpe, Chief

GEORGIA: State Health Planning Agency, Planning and Implementation Division, Four Executive Park Drive, N.E., Suite 2100, Atlanta, GA 30329; tel. 404/679–4821; FAX. 404/679–4914; Karen Butler–Decker, Director, Division of Planning and Implementation

HAWAII: State Health Planning and Development Agency, 1177 Alaska Street, Suite 402, Honolulu, HI 96813; tel. 808/587–0788; FAX. 808/587–0783; Marilyn A. Matsunaga, Administrator

IDAHO: Center for Vital Statistics and Health Policy, Division of Health, Idaho Department of Health and Welfare, 450 West State Street, First Floor, P.O. Box 83720, Boise, ID 83720–0036; tel. 208/334–5976; FAX. 208/334–0685; Jane Smith, Chief

ILLINOIS: Illinois Department of Public Health, Division of Health Policy, 525 West Jefferson, Springfield, IL 62761; tel. 217/782–6235; FAX. 217/785–4308; Angela Oldfield, M.S.W., L.S.W., Chief

INDIANA: Indiana State Department of Health, Local Liaison Office, Two North Meridian Street, Suite Eight–B, Indianapolis, IN 46204–3003; tel. 317/233–7846; FAX. 317/233–7761; Randall Ritter, M.P.A.

IOWA: Department of Public Health, Division of Substance Abuse and Health Promotion, Lucas State Office Building, Des Moines, IA 50319; tel. 515/281–5914; FAX. 515/281–4535; Ronald Eckoff, Medical Director

KANSAS: Health Care Commission, 900 Southwest Jackson, Ninth Floor, Landon State Office B, Topeka, KS 66612; tel. 913/296–7488; FAX. 913/296–2664; Steve Ashley

MAINE: Division of Health Planning and State Health Planning, 35 Anthony Ave., SHS #11, Augusta, ME 04330–0011; tel. 207/624–5424; FAX. 207/624–5431; Helen Zidowecki, Director

MARYLAND: Maryland Health Resources Planning Commission, 4201 Patterson Avenue, Baltimore, MD 21215–2299; tel. 410/764–3255; FAX. 410/358–1311; James Stanton, Executive Director

MICHIGAN: Division of Community Health Services, Health Systems and Special Populations, Metro Square Building, 121 East Seventh Place, Suite 460, P.O. Box 64975, St. Paul, MN 55164–0975; tel. 612/296–9720; FAX. 612/296–9362; Ryan Church, Director

MISSISSIPPI: Mississippi State Department of Health, Health Planning and Resource Development Division, 2423 North State Street, P.O. Box 1700, Jackson, MS 39215–1700; tel. 601/960–7874; FAX. 601/354–6123; Harold B. Armstrong, Chief

MISSOURI: Missouri Department of Health, Office of Planning, 1738 East Elm Street, P.O. Box 570, Jefferson Cit, MO 65102; tel. 314/751–6005; FAX. 314/751–6041; Linda Hillemann, Chief

MONTANA: Health Policy and Services Division, Department of Public Health and Human Services, Cogswell Building, P.O. Box 202951, Helena, MT 59620–2951; tel. 406/444–4473; FAX. 406/444–1861; Walter Timmerman, Health Care Needs Analyst

NEBRASKA: Nebraska Health and Human Services, Regulation and Lic, Performance Accountability Division, Nebraska State Office Building–3rd Fl, 301 Centennial Mall South, Lincoln, NE 68509; tel. 402/471–9513; FAX. 402/471–7049; Davina Shutzer, Division Administrator

NEVADA: State Health Division, Bureau of Health Planning and Statistics, 505 East King Street, Suite 102, Carson City, NV 89701–4749; tel. 702/687–4720; FAX. 702/687–6151; Emil DeJan, Chief

NEW HAMPSHIRE: Office of Health Services Planning and Review, Six Hazen Drive, Concord, NH 03301–6527; tel. 603/271–4606; FAX. 603/271–4141; William Bolton, Chief

NEW JERSEY: Certificate of Need and Acute Care Licensure Program, New Jersey Department of Health, CN 360, John Fitch Plaza, Trenton, NJ 08625–0360; tel. 609/292–8773; FAX. 609/984–3165; Darcy Saunders, Director

NEW MEXICO: New Mexico Health Policy Commission, 435 St. Michael's Drive, Suite A–202, Santa Fe, NM 87505; tel. 505/827–7500; FAX. 505/827–7506; Katherine Ganz, M.D., Director

NEW YORK: New York State Department of Health, Division of Planning, Policy and Resource Development, Corning Tower, Suite 1495, Empire State Plaza, Albany, NY 12237; tel. 518/474–0180; FAX. 518/474–5450; Judith Arnold, Deputy Commissioner

NORTH CAROLINA: State Medical Facilities Planning Section, P.O. Box 29530, Raleigh, NC 27626–0530; tel. 919/733–2342; FAX. 919/715–4413; Robert J. Fitzgerald, Deputy Director, Division of Facility Services

NORTH DAKOTA: Division of Health Information Systems, North Dakota Department of Health, 600 East Boulevard Avenue, Bismarck, ND 58505–0200; tel. 701/328–2894; FAX. 701/328–4727; Fred Larson, Project Review Administrator

OHIO: Ohio Department of Health, Health Systems Planning, Primary Care and Rural Health, 246 North High Street, P.O. Box 118, Columbus, OH 43266–0118; tel. 614/466–3325; FAX. 614/644–8661; Louis Pomerantz, Chief, Health Systems Planning, Primary Care, Rural Health

OKLAHOMA: Oklahoma State Department of Health, Health Promotion and Policy Analysis, 1000 Northeast 10th Street, Oklahoma City, OK 73117–1299; tel. 405/271–1110; FAX. 405/271–1225; Jerry Prilliman, Director Planning

PENNSYLVANIA: Bureau of Health Planning, Pennsylvania Department of Health, Health and Welfare Building, Room 709, P.O. Box 90, Harrisburg, PA 17108; tel. 717/772–5298; FAX. 717/783–3794; Joseph B. May, Director

RHODE ISLAND: Rhode Island Department of Health, Cannon Building, Three Capitol Hill, Suite 401, Providence, RI 02908; tel. 401/277–2231; FAX. 401/277–6548; William J. Waters, Jr., Ph.D., Deputy Director

SOUTH CAROLINA: DHEC, Division of Planning and Certificate of Need, 2600 Bull Street, Columbia, SC 29201; tel. 803/737–7200; FAX. 803/737–7579; Albert Whiteside, Director

SOUTH DAKOTA: South Dakota Department of Health, Office of Administrative Services, 445 East Capitol Avenue, Pierre, SD 57501–3185; tel. 605/773–3361; FAX. 605/773–5683; Joan Adam, Director, Office of Administrative Services

TENNESSEE: Assessment and Planning, Tennessee Department of Health, Cordell Hull Building, Fourth Floor, 426 Fifth Avenue, Nashville, TN 37247–5261; tel. 615/741–0244; FAX. 615/532–7904; Arthur Mader, Health Planner

TEXAS: Bureau of State Health Data and Policy Analysis, Texas Department of Health, 1100 West 49th Street, Austin, TX 78756; tel. 512/458–7261; FAX. 512/458–7344; Rick A. Danko, Planning Director

UTAH: Executive Management Team, Utah Department of Health / Policy Support, P.O. Box 144102, Salt Lake Cit, UT 84114–4102; tel. 801/538–6352; FAX. 801/538–9338; Laverne Snow, Senior Health Policy Consultant

VERMONT: Division of Health Care Administration, Department of Banking Insurance, Securities, and Health Care Adm, 89 Main Street, Drawer 20, Montpelier, VT 05620–3601; tel. 802/828–2900; FAX. 802/828–2949; Stan Lane, Policy Analyst

VIRGINIA: Virginia Department of Health, Division of Certificate of Public Need, 3600 West Broad Street, Suite 216, Richmond, VA 23220; tel. 804/367–2126; FAX. 804/367–2006; Paul E. Parker, Director

WASHINGTON: Washington State Board of Health, 1102 SE Quince Street, P.O. Box 47990, Olympia, WA 98504–7990; tel. 360/586–0399; FAX. 360/586–6033; Sylvia I. Beck, M.P.A., Executive Director

WEST VIRGINIA: West Virginia Health Care Cost Review Authority, 100 Dee Drive, Charleston, WV 25311; tel. 304/558–7000; FAX. 304/558–7001; D. Parker Haddix

WYOMING: Department of Health, 117 Hathaway Building, Cheyenne, WY 82002; tel. 307/777–7656; FAX. 307/777–7439; Douglas Thiede, Data and Communications Manager

State and Provincial Government Agencies

The following list includes state departments of health and welfare, and their subagencies as well as such independent agencies as those for crippled children's services, maternal and child health, mental health, and vocational rehabilitation. The information was obtained directly from the agencies.

United States

ALABAMA
The Honorable Fob James, Jr., Governor, 334/242-7100

Health

Department of Public Health, 201 Monroe Street, P.O. Box 303017, Montgomery, AL 36130-3017; tel. 334/206-5200; FAX. 334/206-2008; Donald E. Williamson, M.D., State Health Officer

Family

Alabama Department of Public Health, Bureau of Family Health Services, The RSA Tower, P.O. Box 303017, Montgomery, AL 36130-3017; tel. 334/206-2940; FAX. 334/206-2950; Thomas M. Miller, M.D., M.P.H., Director

Licensing

Alabama Department of Public Health, Division of Licensure and Certification, The RSA Tower, P.O. Box 303017, Montgomery, AL 36130-3017; tel. 334/206-5078; FAX. 334/240-3147; Rick Harris, Director

Welfare

Department of Human Resources, Gordon Persons Building, 50 Ripley Street, Montgomery, AL 36130; tel. 334/242-1160; FAX. 334/242-0198; Tony Petelos, Commissioner

Medical Services

Alabama Medicaid Agency, 501 Dexter Avenue, P.O. Box 5624, Montgomery, AL 36103-5624; tel. 334/242-5600; FAX. 334/242-5097; Gwendolyn H. Williams, Commissioner

Insurance

Department of Insurance, 201 Monroe Street, Suite 1700, Montgomery, AL 36130; tel. 334/241-4101; FAX. 334/241-4192; Richard H. Cater, Commissioner

Other

Education

State Department of Education, Gordon Persons Building, Suite 5114, P.O. Box 302101, Montgomery, AL 36130-2101; tel. 334/242-9700; FAX. 334/242-9708; Ed Richardson, Superintendent

Mental Health

State Department of Mental Health and Mental Retardation, RSA Union, 100 North Union Street, P.O. Box 301410, Montgomery, AL 36130-1410; tel. 334/242-3107; FAX. 334/242-0684; Virginia A. Rogers, Commissioner

Nursing

Alabama Board of Nursing, RSA Plaza, 770 Washington Avenue, Suite 250, Montgomery, AL 36130; tel. 334/242-4060; FAX. 334/242-4360; Judi Crume, RN, M.S.N., Executive Officer

Rehabilitation

Department of Rehabilitation Services, 2129 East South Boulevard, Montgomery, AL 36116; tel. 800/441-7607; FAX. 334/281-1973; Lamona H. Lucas, Commissioner

ALASKA
The Honorable Tony Knowles, Governor, 907/465-3500

Health

Department of Health and Social Services, 350 Main Street, Room 229, P.O. Box 110601, Juneau, AK 99811-0601; tel. 907/465-3030; FAX. 907/465-3068; Jay A. Livey, Acting Commissioner

Family

Division of Family and Youth Services, P.O. Box 110630, Juneau, AK 99811; tel. 907/465-3191; FAX. 907/465-3397; Theresa Tanoury, Family Services Administrator

Finance

Division of Administrative Services, Department of Health and Social Services, P.O. Box 110650, Juneau, AK 99811-0650; tel. 907/465-3082; FAX. 907/465-2499; Janet E. Clarke, Director

Assistance

State of Alaska, Division of Medical Assistance, P.O. 110660, Juneau, AK 99811-0640; tel. 907/465-3355; FAX. 907/465-2204; Bob Labbe, Director

Licensing

Health Facilities Licensing and Certification, 4730 Business Park Boulevard, Suite 18, Building H, Anchorage, AK 99503-7137; tel. 907/561-8081; FAX. 907/561-3011; Shelbert Larsen, Administrator

Mental Health

Division of Mental Health and Developmental Disabilities, P.O. Box 110620, Juneau, AK 99811-0620; tel. 907/465-3370; FAX. 907/465-2668; Karl Brimner, Director

Substance Abuse

Mental Health and Substance Abuse Services, P.O. Box 110607, Juneau, AK 99811-0607; tel. 907/465-2071; FAX. 907/465-2185; Loren A. Jones, Director

Other

State of Alaska, Department of Health and Social Services, 350 Main Street, Room 229, P.O. Box 110601, Juneau, AK 99811-0601; tel. 907/465-3030; FAX. 907/465-3068; Jay A. Livey, Deputy Commissioner

Other

Education

Department of Education, 801 West 10th Street, Suite 200, Juneau, AK 99801-1894; tel. 907/465-2887; FAX. 907/465-2713; Beth Shober, Health Promotion Specialist

Licensing

Department of Commerce and Economic Development, Division of Occupational Licensing, State Medical Board, 3601 C Street, Suite 722, Anchorage, AK 99503; tel. 907/269-8163; FAX. 907/269-8156; Leslie G. Abel, Executive Administrator

Nursing

Alaska Board of Nursing, 3601 C Street, Suite 722, Anchorage, AK 99503; tel. 907/269-8160; FAX. 907/269-8156; Dorothy P. Fulton, RN, M.A., Executive Administrator

Rehabilitation

Division of Vocational Rehabilitation, 801 West 10th Street, Suite 200, Juneau, AK 99801-1894; tel. 907/465-2814; FAX. 907/465-2856; Duane M. French, Director

ARIZONA
The Honorable Jane Dee Hull, Governor, 602/542-4331

Health

Arizona Department of Health Services, 1740 West Adams Street, Suite 407, Phoenix, AZ 85007; tel. 602/542-1025; FAX. 602/542-1062; James R. Allen, M.D., M.P.H., Director

Environment

Arizona Department of Environmental Quality, 3033 North Central Avenue, Phoenix, AZ 85012; tel. 602/207-2300; FAX. 602/207-2218, ext. 2200; Russell F. Rhoades, Director

Family

Community and Family Health Services, 1740 West Adams Street, Suite 307, Phoenix, AZ 85007; tel. 602/542-1223; FAX. 602/542-1265; W. Sundin Applegate, M.D., Acting Bureau Chief

Health

Behavioral Health Services, Arizona Department of Health Services, 2122 East Highland, Suite 100, Phoenix, AZ 85016; tel. 602/381-8999; FAX. 602/553-9140; Rhonda Baldwin, Assistant Director

Licensing

Arizona Department of Health Services, Division of Health and Child Care Review Services, Office of Health Care Licensure, 1647 East Morten, Phoenix, AZ 85020; tel. 602/255-1197; FAX. 602/255-1135; John Zemaitis, Assistant Director

Prevention

Arizona Department of Health Services, Division of Public Health Services, Bureau of Epidemiology and Disease Control Services, 3815 North Black Canyon Highway, Phoenix, AZ 85015; tel. 602/230-5808; FAX. 602/230-5959; Norman J. Petersen, Bureau Chief

Children

Office for Children with Special Health Care Needs, Administrative Offices, 1740 West Adams Street, Suite 200, Phoenix, AZ 85007; tel. 602/542-1860; FAX. 602/542-2589; Susan Burke, Chief

Welfare

Department of Economic Security, Site Code 010A, P.O. Box 6123, Phoenix, AZ 85005; tel. 602/542-5678; FAX. 602/542-5339; Linda J. Blessing, Director

Rehabilitation

Rehabilition Services Administration (930A), 1789 West Jefferson, Second Floor Northwest, Phoenix, AZ 85007; tel. 602/542-3332; FAX. 602/542-3778; Roger J. Hodges, Administrator

Insurance

Department of Insurance, 3030 North Third Street, Suite 1100, Phoenix, AZ 85012; tel. 602/255-5400; FAX. 602/255-5316

Other

Medical Examiners

Arizona Board of Medical Examiners, 1651 East Morten, Suite 210, Phoenix, AZ 85020; tel. 602/255-3751; FAX. 602/255-1848; Donna Nemer, Acting Deputy Director

Nursing

Arizona State Board of Nursing, 1651 East Morten, Suite 150, Phoenix, AZ 85020; tel. 602/331-8111; FAX. 602/9069365

ARKANSAS
The Honorable Mike Huckabee, Governor, 501/682-2345

Health

Arkansas Department of Health, 4815 West Markham Street, Slot 39, Little Rock, AR 72205-3867; tel. 501/661-2111; FAX. 501/671-1450; Sandra B. Nichols, M.D., Director

Community

Arkansas Department of Health, Bureau of Community Health Services, 4815 West Markham Street, Slot 2, Little Rock, AR 72205-3867; tel. 501/661-2167; FAX. 501/661-2601; Jim Mills, Director

Facilities

Division of Health Facility Services, 5800 West 10th Street, Suite 400, Little Rock, AR 72204; tel. 501/661-2201; FAX. 501/661-2165; Valetta M. Buck, Director

Health

Bureau of Public Health Programs, Arkansas Department of Health, 4815 West Markham Street, Slot 41, Little Rock, AR 72205-3867; tel. 501/661-2243; FAX. 501/661-2055; Martha Hiett, Director

Planning

Arkansas Department of Health, Planning and Policy Development, 4815 West Markham, Slot 55, Little Rock, AR 72205; tel. 501/661-2238; FAX. 501/661-2414; Nancy Kirsch, Deputy Director

Administration

Bureau of Administrative Support, State Health Building, Little Rock, AR 72205-3867; tel. 501/661-2252; Tom Butler, Director

Resources

Bureau of Health Resources, Arkansas Department of Health, 4815 West Markham Street, Slot 21, Little Rock, AR 72205-3867; tel. 501/661-2831; FAX. 501/661-2544; C. Lewis Leslie, Director

Welfare

Arkansas Department of Human Services, P.O. Box 1437, Little Rock, AR 72203-1437; tel. 501/682-8650; FAX. 501/682-6836; Lee Frazier, Director

Aging

Division of Aging and Adult Services, P.O. Box 1437, Slot 1412, Little Rock, AR 72203-1437; tel. 501/682-2441; FAX. 501/682-8155; Herb Sanderson, Director

Long Term Care

Office of Long-Term Care, Lafayette Building, Sixth and Louisiana Streets, P.O. Box 8059, Slot 400, Little Rock, AR 72203-8059; tel. 501/682-8487; FAX. 501/682-6955; Shirley Gamble, Director

Medical Services

Division of Medical Services, Donaghey Building, Seventh and Main Streets, P.O. Box 1437, Slot 1100, Little Rock, AR 72203; tel. 501/682-8292; FAX. 501/682-1197; Ray Hanley, Director

Mental Health

Division of Mental Health Services, Arkansas State Hospital, 4313 West Markham, Little Rock, AR 72205-4096; tel. 501/686-9000; FAX. 501/686-9182; John Selig, Director

Rehabilitation

Arkansas Rehabilitation Services, 1616 Brookwood, P.O. Box 3781, Little Rock, AR 72203; tel. 501/296-1616; FAX. 501/296-1675; Bobby C. Simpson, Commissioner

Substance Abuse

Bureau of Alcohol & Drug Abuse Prevention, Freeway Medical Center, Suite 907, 5800 West 10th Street, Little Rock, AR 72204; tel. 501/280-4501; FAX. 501/280-4532; Joe M. Hill, Director

Children

Children's Medical Service, Donaghey Plaza South, Seventh and Main Streets, P.O. Box 1437, Slot 526, Little Rock, AR 72203; tel. 501/682-8202; FAX. 501/682-8247; G. A. Buchanan, M.D., Medical Director

Insurance

Arkansas Insurance Department, 1200 W. 3rd Street, Little Rock, AR 72201; tel. 501/371-2600; FAX. 501/371-2626; Mike Pickens, Commissioner

Other

Nursing

Arkansas State Board of Nursing, University Tower Building, Suite 800, 1123 South University, Little Rock, AR 72204; tel. 501/686-2700; FAX. 501/686-2714; Faith A. Fields, M.S.N., RN, Executive Director

CALIFORNIA

The Honorable Pete Wilson, Governor, 916/445-2864

Health

Department of Health Services, 714 P Street, Suite 1253, Sacramento, CA 95814; tel. 916/657-1425; FAX. 916/657-1156; S. Kimberly Belshe, Director

Welfare

Health and Welfare Agency, Office of the Secretary, 1600 Ninth Street, Suite 460, Sacramento, CA 95814; tel. 916/654-3454; FAX. 916/654-3343; Garry Morck, Manager, Administrative Services

Developmental Disabilities

Department of Developmental Services, 1600 Ninth Street, Suite 240, Sacramento, CA 95814; tel. 916/654-1897; FAX. 916/654-2167; Cliff Allenby, Director

Mental Health

Department of Mental Health, 1600 Ninth Street, Room 151, Sacramento, CA 95814; tel. 916/654-2309; FAX. 916/654-3198; Stephen W. Mayberg, Ph.D., Director

Rehabilitation

Department of Rehabilitation, 830 K Street Mall, Sacramento, CA 95814; tel. 916/445-8638;

Social Services

Department of Social Services, 744 P Street, Sacramento, CA 95814; tel. 916/657-3661; FAX. 916/654-2049; Eloise Anderson, Director

Substance Abuse

Department of Alcohol and Drug Programs, 1700 K Street, Sacramento, CA 95814; tel. 916/445-1943; FAX. 916/323-5873; Andrew M. Mecca, Dr.P.H., Director

Community

Community Resources Development Section, California Department of Rehabilitation, 830 K Street Mall, Sacramento, CA 95814; tel. 916/323-0390; FAX. 916/322-0503; Sig Brivkalns, Chief

Other

Nurse Examiners

Board of Vocational Nursing and Psychiatric Technicians, 2535 Capitol Oaks Drive, Suite 205, Sacramento, CA 95833; tel. 916/263-7800; FAX. 916/263-7859; Teresa Bello-Jones, J.D., M.S.N., RN, Executive Officer

Nursing

Board of Registered Nursing, 400 R Street, Suite 4030, P.O. Box 944210, Sacramento, CA 94244-2100; tel. 916/322-3350; FAX. 916/327-4402; Ruth Ann Terry, M.P.H., R.N., Executive Officer

Quality Assurance

Medical Board of California, 1426 Howe Avenue, Suite 54, Sacramento, CA 95825-3236; tel. 916/263-2389; FAX. 916/263-2387; Ron Joseph, Executive Director

Other

Department of Corporations, Health Care Division, 3700 Wilshire Boulevard, Suite 600, Los Angeles, CA 90010-3001; tel. 213/736-2776; Gary G. Hagen, Assistant Commissioner

COLORADO

The Honorable Roy Romer, Governor, 303/866-2471

Health

Colorado Department of Public Health and Environment, 4300 Cherry Creek Drive, S., Denver, CO 80222-1530; tel. 303/692-2100; FAX. 303/691-7702; Patti Shwayder, Executive Director

Facilities

Colorado Department of Public Health and Environment, Health Facilities Division, 4300 Cherry Creek Drive S., Denver, CO 80246-1530; tel. 303/692-2800; FAX. 303/782-4883; Janell Little, Deputy Director

Family

Family and Community Health Services Division, Colorado Department of Public Health and Environment, 4300 Cherry Creek Drive South, Denver, CO 80246-1530; tel. 303/692-2302; FAX. 303/753-9249; Merril Stern, Director

Substance Abuse

Alcohol and Drug Abuse Division, Colorado Department of Human Services, 4300 Cherry Creek Drive South, Denver, CO 80222; tel. 303/692-2930; FAX. 303/753-9775; Robert Aukerman, Director

Welfare

State Department of Health Care Policy and Financing, 1575 Sherman Street, Fourth Floor, Denver, CO 80203; tel. 303/866-2859; FAX. 303/866-2803; Richard Allen, Manager, Medical Assistance

Aging

Division of Aging and Adult Services, Colorado Department of Human Services, 110 16th Street, Second Floor, Denver, CO 80202; tel. 303/620-4127; FAX. 303/620-4191; Rita A. Barreras, Director

Rehabilitation

State Department of Health Care Policy and Financing, 1575 Sherman Street, 10th Floor, Denver, CO 80203-1714; tel. 303/866-2993; FAX. 303/866-4411; Barbara McDonnell, Acting Director

Other

Division of Insurance, 1560 Broadway, Suite 850, Denver, CO 80202; tel. 303/894-7499; FAX. 303/894-7455; Jack Ehnes, Commissioner

Medical Examiners

Colorado Board of Medical Examiners, 1560 Broadway, Suite 1300, Denver, CO 80202-5140; tel. 303/894-7690; FAX. 303/894-7692; Susan Miller, Program Administrator

Mental Health

Mental Health Services, 3824 West Princeton Circle, Denver, CO 80236; tel. 303/866-7400; FAX. 303/866-7428; Thomas J. Barrett, Ph.D., Director

Regulatory

Department of Regulatory Agencies, 1560 Broadway, Suite 1550, Denver, CO 80202; tel. 303/894-7855; FAX. 303/894-7885; Joseph A. Garcia, Executive Director

Other

Department of Human Services, 1575 Sherman Street, Eighth Floor, Denver, CO 80203; tel. 303/866-5096; FAX. 303/866-4740; Barbara McDonnell, Executive Director

CONNECTICUT

The Honorable John G. Rowland, Governor, 203/566-4840

Health

Department of Health Services, 150 Washington Street, Hartford, CT 06106; tel. 203/566-2038; Frederick G. Adams, D.D.S., M.P.H., Commissioner

Health

Connecticut Department of Public Health and Addiction Services, Bureau of Health Promotion, 150 Washington Street, Hartford, CT 06106; tel. 203/566-5475; FAX. 203/566-1400; Peter Galbraith, D.M.D., Bureau Chief

Quality

Department of Public Health, 410 Capitol Avenue, Mail Stop 12APP, P.O. Box 340308, Hartford, CT 06134-0308; tel. 860/509-7579; FAX. 860/509-8457; Cynthia Denne, Director

Regulation

Department of Public Health, 410 Capitol Avenue, P.O. Box 340308, Hartford, CT 06134-0308; tel. 860/509-7101; FAX. 860/509-7111; Stephen A. Harriman, Commissioner

Other

Department of Public Health, Division of Health Systems Regulation, 410 Capitol Avenue, Mail Stop 12 HSR, Hartford, CT 06134-0308; tel. 860/509-7407; FAX. 860/509-7539; Cynthia Denne, RN, M.P.A., Director

Welfare

Department of Social Services, 25 Sigourney Street, Hartford, CT 06106; tel. 203/424-5008; Patricia Giardi, Commissioner

Insurance

Department of Insurance, P.O. Box 816, Hartford, CT 06142-0816; tel. 860/297-3862; FAX. 860/297-3941; Mary Ellen Breault, Director, Life and Health Division

Other

Education

Department of Education, 165 Capitol Avenue, Hartford, CT 06145; tel. 203/566-5061; FAX. 203/566-8964

Aging

Elderly Services Division, Department of Social Services, 25 Sigourney Street, Hartford, CT 06106-5033; tel. 203/424-5274; FAX. 203/424-4966; Christine M. Lewis, Director of Elder Rights and Community Services

Mental Health

State Department of Mental Health and Addiction Services, 410 Capitol Avenue, P.O. Box 341431, Hartford, CT 06134; tel. 860/418-7000; FAX. 860/418-6691; Albert J. Solnit, M.D., Commissioner

Nurse Examiners

Connecticut Board of Examiners for Nursing, Department of Public Health - MS#13ADJ, 410 Capital Avenue, P.O. Box 340308, Hartford, CT 06134-0308; tel. 860/509-7624; FAX. 860/509-7286; Wendy H. Furniss, RNC, MS, Health Services Supervisor

Rehabilitation

Department of Social Services, Bureau of Rehabilitation Services, Division of Organizational Support, 10 Griffin Road, N., Windsor, CT 06095; tel. 203/298-2032; FAX. 203/298-9590; John J. Galiette, Chief

DELAWARE

The Honorable Thomas R. Carper, Governor, 302/739-4101

Health

Department of Health and Social Services, 1901 North DuPont Highway, Main Administration Building, New Castle, DE 19720; tel. 302/577-4500; FAX. 302/577-4510

Aging

Division of Services for Aging and Adults with Physical Disabilities, 1901 North DuPont Highway, New Castle, DE 19720; tel. 302/577-4791; FAX. 302/577-4793; Eleanor L. Cain, Director

Children

Community Health Care Access, Jesse Cooper Building, P.O. Box 637, Dover, DE 19901; tel. 302/739-4768; FAX. 302/739-6617; Prudence Kobasa

Division of Public Health, P.O. Box 637, Dover, DE 19903; tel. 302/739-4700; FAX. 302/739-6659; Steven F. Boedigheimer, Deputy Director, Division of Public Health

Laboratories

Delaware Public Health Laboratory, 30 Sunnyside Road, P.O. Box 1047, Smyrna, DE 19977-1047; tel. 302/653-2870; FAX. 302/653-2877; Christopher K. Zimmerman, M.A., Acting Director

Licensing

Office of Health Facilities Licensing and Certification, Department of Health and Social Services, Three Mill Road, Suite 308, Wilmington, DE 19806; tel. 302/577-6666; FAX. 302/577-6672; Ellen Reap, Director

Medical Assistance

Division of Social Services, P.O. Box 906, New Castle, DE 19720; tel. 302/577-4400; FAX. 302/577-4405; Elaine Archangelo, Director

Medical Services

Emergency Medical Services, Blue Hen Corporate Center, 655 South Bay Road, Suite 4H, Dover, DE 19901; tel. 302/739-4710; FAX. 302/739-2352; Bill Stevenson, EMS Director

Children

Division of Public Health, Community Health Care Access Section, Jesse S. Cooper Building, Federal Street, P.O. Box 637, Dover, DE 19903; tel. 302/739-4785; FAX. 302/739-6617

Maternal and Child Health, Division of Public Health, P.O. Box 637, Dover, DE 19903; tel. 302/739-3111; FAX. 302/739-6653; Joan Powell, MPA, Director

Other

Medicine

Delaware Board of Medical Practice, Cannon Building, Suite 203, 861 Silver Lake Boulevard, Dover, DE 19901; tel. 302/739-4522, ext. 229; FAX. 302/739-2711; Brenda D. Petty-Ball, Executive Director

Nursing

Delaware Board of Nursing, Cannon Building, Suite 203, 861 Silver Lake Boulevard, Dover, DE 19904; tel. 302/739-4522, ext. 216; FAX. 302/739-2711; Iva J. Boardman, RN, M.S.N., Executive Director

Rehabilitation

Department of Labor, Division of Vocational Rehabilitation, 4425 North Market Street, Wilmington, DE 19802; tel. 302/761-8275; FAX. 302/761-6611; Michelle P. Pointer, Director

Substance Abuse

Delaware State Hospital, Division of Alcoholism, Drug Abuse and Mental Health, 1901 North DuPont Highway, New Castle, DE 19720; tel. 302/577-4000; FAX. 302/577-4359; Charles H. Debnam, Interim Director

DISTRICT OF COLUMBIA

Government Switchboard, 202/727-1000

Health

D.C. Department of Public Health, 800 Ninth Street, S.W., Washington, DC 20024; tel. 202/645-5556; FAX. 202/645-0526; Allan S. Noonan, M.D., M.P.H., Director

Long-Term Care

Long-Term Care Administration, 1660 L Street, N.W., 10th Floor, Washington, DC 20036; tel. 202/673-3597; A. Sue Brown, Administrator

Prevention

Department of Health, Preventive Health Services Administration, 800 Ninth Street, S.W., Third Floor, Washington, DC 20024; tel. 202/645-5550; FAX. 202/645-0454

Rehabilitation

Rehabilitation Services Administration, 800 Ninth Street, S.W., Fourth Floor, Washington, DC 20024; tel. 202/645-5703; FAX. 202/645-0840

Substance Abuse

Alcohol and Drug Abuse Services Administration, 1300 1st Street, N.E., Washington, DC 20002; tel. 202/727-1762, ext. 223; FAX. 202/535-2028;

Children

Bureau of Maternal and Child Health Services, Dept. of Health, Office of Maternal and Child Health, 800 Ninth Street, S.W., 3rd Floor, Washington, DC 20024; tel. 202/645-5620; Michelle S. Davis, M.S.P.H., Interim Chief

Welfare

Social Services

Commission on Social Services, 609 H Street, N.E., Fifth Floor, Washington, DC 20002; tel. 202/727-5930; FAX. 202//727-6529, ext. 1687; A. Sue Brown, Acting Commissioner of Social Services

Consumer

Department of Consumer and Regulatory Affairs, 614 H Street, N.W., Suite 1120, Washington, DC 20001; tel. 202/727-7120; FAX. 202/727-7842; W. David Watts, Director

Facility

Department of Consumer and Regulatory Affairs, Service Facility Regulation Administration, 614 H Street, N.W., Suite 1003, Washington, DC 20001; tel. 202/727-7190; FAX. 202/727-7780; Geraldine K. Sykes, Administrator

Licensing

Occupational and Professional Licensing Administration, Department of Consumer and Regulatory Affairs, 614 H Street, N.W., Suite 903, Washington, DC 20001; tel. 202/727-7480; FAX. 202/727-7662; Winnie R. Huston, Administrator

Mental Health

Commission on Mental Health Services, Office of the Receiver, 4301 Conn. Avenue, N.W., Suite 310, Washington, DC 20008; tel. 202/364-3422; FAX. 202/364-4886; Dr. Scott H. Nelson, Receiver

FLORIDA

The Honorable Lawton Chiles, Governor, 850/488-2272

Health

Department of Health, Secretary's Office, 1317 Winewood Boulevard, Building Six, Room 306, Tallahassee, FL 32399-0700; tel. 904/487-2945; FAX. 904/487-3729; James T. Howell, M.D., M.P.H., Secretary

Welfare

Health

Department of Health, Secretary's Office, Building 6, Room 306, 1317 Winewood Boulevard, Tallahassee, FL 32399-0700; tel. 904/487-2945; FAX. 904/487-3729; James T. Howell, M.D., M.P.H., Secretary

Aging

Adult Services, 1317 Winewood Boulevard, Building 8, Room 327, Tallahassee, FL 32399-0700; tel. 904/488-8922; Ms. Nancy Fulton, Director, Adult Services

Facilities

Certificate of Need/Budget Review Office, Agency for Health Care Administration, 2727 Mahan Drive, Tallahassee, FL 32308; tel. 850/488-8673; FAX. 850/922-6964; Elfie Stamm, Chief

Licensing

Division of Health Quality Assurance, 2727 Mahan Drive, Tallahassee, FL 32308; tel. 850/487-2528; FAX. 850/487-6240; Marshall E. Kelley, Director

Rehabilitation

Department of Health and Rehabilitative Services, Alcohol, Drug Abuse and Mental Health Program Office, 1317 Winewood Boulevard, Tallahassee, FL 32399-0700; tel. 904/488-8304; FAX. 904/487-2239

Children

Children's Medical Services, 1317 Winewood Boulevard, Tallahassee, FL 32399-0700; tel. 904/487-2690; FAX. 904/488-3813; Eric G. Handler, M.D., M.P.H., Director, CMS

Insurance

Department of Insurance, Bureau of Specialty Insurers, 200 East Gaines Street, Tallahassee, FL 32399; tel. 904/488-6766; FAX. 904/488-0313; Al Willis, Chief

Other

Medicine

Florida Board of Medicine, 1940 North Monroe Street, Tallahassee, FL 32399-0750; tel. 904/488-0595; Marm M. Harris, Executive Director

Rehabilitation

Division of Vocational Rehabilitation, 2002 Old St. Augustine Road, Building A, Tallahassee, FL 32399-0696; tel. 850/488-6210; FAX. 850/921-7215; Tamara Allen Bibb, Director

Other

Department of Labor and Employment Security, 2012 Capital Circle, S.E., 303 Hartman Building, Tallahassee, FL 32399-2152; tel. 904/922-7021; FAX. 904/488-8930; Doug Jamerson, Secretary

GEORGIA

The Honorable Zell Miller, Governor, 404/656-1776

Health

Department of Human Resources, Two Peachtree N.W., Suite 29.250, Atlanta, GA 30303-3142; tel. 404/656-5680; FAX. 404/651-8669; Tommy C. Olmstead, Commissioner

Health

Division of Public Health, Two Peachtree Street, S.W., Suite 7-300, Atlanta, GA 30303; tel. 404/657-2700; FAX. 404/657-2715; Patrick Meehan, M.D., Director

Laboratories

Diagnostic Services Unit, Health Care Section, Office of Regulatory Services, Two Peachtree Street, N.W., 33rd Floor, Room 250, Atlanta, GA 30303-3142; tel. 404/657-5447; FAX. 404/657-8934; Betty J. Logan, Regional Director, Diagnostic Services Unit

Licensing

Child Care Licensing Section, Two Peachtree Street, N.W., 32-458, Atlanta, GA 30303; tel. 404/657-5562; FAX. 404/657-8936; Jo Cato, Director

Department of Human Resources, Office of Regulatory Services, Health Care Section, Two Peachtree Street, N.W., Suite 33.250, Atlanta, GA 30303-3167; tel. 404/657-5550; FAX. 404/657-8934; Susie M. Woods, Director of the HCS

Mental Health

Division of Mental Health, Mental Retardation and Substance Abuse, Two Peachtree Street, Fourth Floor, Atlanta, GA 30303; tel. 404/657-2252; FAX. 404/657-1137; Carl E. Roland, Jr., Director

Radiology

Diagnostic Services Unit, 878 Peachtree Street, N.E., Suite 719, Atlanta, GA 30309-3997; tel. 404/894-4747; FAX. 404/894-2185; Betty Logan, Director

Regulation

Office of Regulatory Services, Georgia Department of Human Resources, Two Peachtree Street, N.W., Room 32-415, Atlanta, GA 30303-3142; tel. 404/657-5700; FAX. 404/657-5708; Martin J. Rotter, Director

Rehabilitation

Division of Rehabilitation Services, Two Peachtree Street, N.W., 35th Floor, Atlanta, GA 30303-3142; tel. 404/657-3000; FAX. 404/657-3079; Peggy Rosser, Director

Other

Personal Care Home Program, Office of Regulatory Services, Two Peachtree Street, 31st Floor, Atlanta, GA 30303-3167; tel. 404/657-4076; FAX. 404/657-3655; Victoria L. Flynn, Director

Insurance

Office of Commissioner of Insurance, Two Martin Luther King, Jr. Drive, Seventh Floor, West Tower, Floyd Build, Atlanta, GA 30334; tel. 404/656-2056; FAX. 404/656-4030; John W. Oxendine, Commissioner of Insurance

Other

Medical Examiners

Composite State Board of Medical Examiners, 166 Pryor Street, S.W., Atlanta, GA 30303; tel. 404/656-3913; FAX. 404/656-9723; Gregg W. Scheder, Acting Executive Director

Nursing

Georgia Board of Nursing, 166 Pryor Street, S.W., Atlanta, GA 30303; tel. 404/656-3943; FAX. 404/657-7489; Shirley A. Camp, Executive Director

Planning

State Health Planning Agency, Four Executive Park Drive, N.E., Suite 2100, Atlanta, GA 30329; tel. 404/679-4821; FAX. 404/679-4914; Pamela S. Stephenson, Esq., Executive Director

HAWAII

The Honorable Benjamin J. Cayetano, Governor, 808/586-0034

Health

Hawaii Department of Health, P.O. Box 3378, Honolulu, HI 96801; tel. 808/586-4410; FAX. 808/586-4444; Lawrence Miike, Director

Dental

Dental Health Division, 1700 Lanakila Avenue, Suite 203, Honolulu, HI 96817-2199; tel. 808/832-5700; FAX. 808/832-5722; Mark H.K. Greer, D.M.D., M.P.H., Chief

Environment

Environmental Health, P.O. Box 3378, Honolulu, HI 96801; Shinji Soneda, Chief

Family

Family Health Services Division, Hawaii State Department of Health, 1250 Punchbowl Street, Room 216, Honolulu, HI 96813; tel. 808/586-4122; FAX. 808/586-9303; Nancy L. Kuntz, M.D, Chief, Family Health Services Division

Licensing

Department of Health/Hospital and Medical Facilities, Licensing and Certification, P.O. Box 3378, Honolulu, HI 96801; tel. 808/586-4080; FAX. 808/586-4747; Helen K. Yoshimi, B.S.N., M.P.H., Chief, H.M.F.B.

Mental Health

Adult Mental Health Division, P.O. Box 3378, Honolulu, HI 96801-9984; tel. 808/586-4686; FAX. 808/586-4745; Linda Fox, Ph.D.

Planning

State Health Planning and Development Agency, 335 Merchant Street, Suite 214 E, Honolulu, HI 96813; tel. 808/587-0788; FAX. 808/587-0783; Patrick J. Boland, Administrator

Substance Abuse

Alcohol and Drug Abuse Division, 1270 Queen Emma Street, Suite 305, Honolulu, HI 96813; tel. 808/586-3961; FAX. 808/586-4016; Elaine Wilson, Chief

Chronic Disease

Communicable Disease Division, P.O. Box 3378, Honolulu, HI 96801; tel. 808/586-4580; FAX. 808/586-4595; Richard L. Vogt, M.D., State Epidemiologist

Welfare

Medical Services

Department of Human Services, Med-QUEST Division, 820 Mililani Street, Suite 606, Box 339, Honolulu, HI 96813; tel. 808/586-5391; FAX. 808/586-5389; Charles C. Duarte, Med-QUEST Administrator

Rehabilitation

Vocational Rehabilitation, 1000 Bishop Street, Suite 605, Honolulu, HI 96813; tel. 808/586-5355; FAX. 808/586-5377; Neil Shim, Administrator

Other

Disability

Department of Labor and Industrial Relations, Disability Compensation Division, P.O. Box 3769, Honolulu, HI 96812; tel. 808/586-9151; FAX. 808/586-9219; Gary S. Hamada, Administrator

Medical Examiners

Department of Commerce and Consumer Affairs, Board of Medical Examiners, P.O. Box 3469, Honolulu, HI 96801; tel. 808/586-2708; Constance Cabral-Makanani, Executive Officer

IDAHO

The Honorable Philip E. Batt, Governor, 208/334-2100

Health

Department of Health and Welfare, Division of Health, 450 West State, Fourth Floor, P.O. Box 83720, Boise, ID 83720-0036; tel. 208/334-5945; FAX. 208/334-6581; Richard H. Schultz, Administrator

Laboratories

Bureau of Laboratories, 2220 Old Penitentiary Road, Boise, ID 83712; tel. 208/334-2235; FAX. 208/334-2382; Richard F. Hudson, Ph.D., Chief

Licensing

Bureau of Facility Standards, Department of Health and Welfare, P.O. Box 83720, Boise, ID 83720-0036; tel. 208/334-6626; FAX. 208/332-7204; Sylvia Creswell, Supervisor-Non LTC

Medical Services

Bureau of Emergency Medical Services, P.O. Box 83720, Boise, ID 83720-0036; tel. 208/334-4000; FAX. 208/334-4015; Dia Gainor, Bureau Chief

Statistics

Center for Vital Statistics and Health Policy, 450 West State, First Floor, P.O. Box 83720, Boise, ID 83720-0036; tel. 208/334-5976; FAX. 208/334-0685; Jane S. Smith, State Registrar, Chief

Substance Abuse

Division of Family and Community Services, Bureau of Mental Health and Substance Abuse, P.O. Box 83720, Boise, ID 83720-0036; tel. 208/334-5935; FAX. 208/334-6664; Tina Klamt, Substance Abuse Project Manager

Children

Bureau of Clinical and Preventive Services, P.O. Box 83720, Boise, ID 83720-0036; tel. 208/334-5930; FAX. 208/332-7346; Roger Perotto, Chief

Insurance

Department of Insurance, 700 West State Street, Third Floor, P.O. Box 83720, Boise, ID 83720-0043; tel. 208/334-4250; FAX. 208/334-4398; James M. Alcorn, Director

Other

Medicine

Idaho State Board of Medicine, 280 North Eighth Street, Suite 202, P.O. Box 83720, Boise, ID 83720-0058; tel. 208/334-2822; FAX. 208/334-2801; Darleene Thorsted, Executive Director

Nursing

Idaho State Board of Nursing, 280 North Eighth Street, Suite 210, P.O. Box 83720, Boise, ID 83720-0061; tel. 208/334-3110; FAX. 208/334-3262; Sandra Evans, MA.Ed., RN, Executive Director

Rehabilitation

Vocational Rehabilitation, 650 West State, P.O. Box 83720, Len B. Jordan Building, Suite 1, Boise, ID 83720-0096; tel. 208/334-3390; FAX. 208/334-5305; F. Pat Young, Interim Administrator

ILLINOIS

The Honorable Jim Edgar, Governor, 217/782-6830

Health

Illinois Department of Public Health, Office of Epidemeliology and Health Systems Development, 535 West Jefferson Street, Springfield, IL 62761; tel. 217/782-4977; FAX. 217/782-3987; John R. Lumpkin, M.D., M.P.H., Director

Facilities

Illinois Department of Public Health, Office of Health Care Regulation, Bureau of Hospitals and Ambulatory Services, 525 West Jefferson Street, Fourth Floor, Springfield, IL 62761; tel. 217/782-7412; FAX. 217/782-0382; Catherine M. Stokes, Assistant Deputy Director

Health

Illinois Department of Public Health, Office of Health Protection, 525 West Jefferson Street, Springfield, IL 62761; tel. 217/782-3984; FAX. 217/524-0802; Dave King, Deputy Director

Laboratories

Illinois Department of Public Health Laboratories, 825 North Rutledge Street, P.O. Box 19435, Springfield, IL 62794-9435; tel. 217/782-6562; FAX. 217/524-7924; David Carpenter, Ph.D., State Laboratory Director

Medical Services

Illinois Department of Public Health, 535 West Jefferson Street, Springfield, IL 62761; tel. 217/785-0245; FAX. 217/524-2491; James R. Nelson, Deputy Director, Community Health

Policy

Illinois Department of Public Health, 525 West Jefferson Street, Springfield, IL 62761; tel. 217/785-2040; FAX. 217/785-4308; Laura B. Landrum, Deputy Director

Administration

Office of Finance and Administration, 535 West Jefferson Street, Springfield, IL 62761; tel. 217/785-2033; FAX. 217/782-3987; Gary Robinson, Deputy Director

Regulation

Illinois Department of Public Health, Office of Health Care Regulation, 525 West Jefferson Street, Springfield, IL 62761; tel. 217/782-2913; FAX. 217/524-6292; William A. Bell, Deputy Director

Welfare

Department of Public Aid, 201 South Grand Avenue, E., Springfield, IL 62763; tel. 217/782-1200; FAX. 217/524-7979; Joan Walters, Director

Insurance

Department of Insurance, 320 West Washington Street, Fourth Floor, Springfield, IL 62767; tel. 217/782-4515; FAX. 217/782-5020; Arnold Dutcher, Acting Director

Other

Illinois Department of Human Services, 100 South Grand Avenue East, Springfield, IL 62762; tel. 217/557-1601; FAX. 217/557-1647; Howard A. Peters III, Secretary

Regulatory

Illinois Department of Professional Regulation, James R. Thompson Center, 100 West Randolph, Suite 9-300, Chicago, IL 60601; tel. 312/814-4500; FAX. 312/814-1837; Nikki M. Zollar, Director

Rehabilitation

Illinois Department of Human Services,Division of Disability and Behavioral Health, Office of Rehabilitation Services Home Services Program, 623 East Adams Street, P.O. Box 19509, Springfield, IL 62794-9509; tel. 217/782-2722; FAX. 217/557-0142; Sharon Banks, Field Operations Manager, Home Service Program

Children

Division of Specialized Care for Children, University of Illinois at Chicago, (Illinois' Title V Program for Children with Special Health Care Needs), 2815 West Washington, Suite 300, Springfield, IL 62794-9481; tel. 217/793-2350; FAX. 217/793-0773; Charles N. Onufer, M.D., Interim Director

INDIANA

The Honorable Frank O'Bannon, Governor, 317/232-4567

Health

Indiana State Department of Health, Two North Meridian Street, Indianapolis, IN 46204; tel. 317/233-7400; FAX. 317/233-7387; Richard D. Feldman, M.D., State Health Commissioner

Facilities

Division of Long Term Care, Two North Meridian Street, Fourth Floor, Indianapolis, IN 46204; tel. 317/233-7442; FAX. 317/233-7322; Suzanne Hornstein, Director

Children

Maternal and Child Health Services, Indiana State Department of Health, Two North Meridian Street, Suite 700, Indianapolis, IN 46204; tel. 317/233-1262; FAX. 317/233-1299; Judith A. Ganser, M.D., M.P.H., Medical Director

Other

Indiana State Department of Health, Division of Acute Care, Two North Meridian Street, Indianapolis, IN 46204; tel. 317/233-7474; FAX. 317/233-7157; Tom Iozzo, H.F.A., Director

Welfare

Indiana Family and Social Services Administration, Office of Medicaid Policy and Planning, Indiana Government Center-South, 402 West Washington, Room W 382, Indianapolis, IN 46204-2739; tel. 317/233-4455; FAX. 317/232-7382; Kathleen D. Gifford, Assistant Secretary

Children

Children's Special Health Care Services, Indiana State Department of Health, Two North Meridian Street, Section 7B, Indianapolis, IN 46204; tel. 317/233-5578; FAX. 317/233-5609; Wendy S. Gettelfinger, Director

Insurance

Department of Insurance, 311 West Washington Street, Suite 300, Indianapolis, IN 46204; tel. 317/232-2387; FAX. 317/232-5251; Liz Carroll, Chief Deputy Commissioner

Other

Human Services

Indiana Family and Social Services Administration, 402 West Washington Street, P.O. Box 7083, Indianapolis, IN 46207-7083; tel. 317/233-4452; FAX. 317/233-4693; Katherine L. Davis, Secretary

Licensing

Medical Licensing Board of Indiana, Health Professions Bureau, 402 West Washington, Suite 041, Indianapolis, IN 46204; tel. 317/232-2960; FAX. 317/233-4236;

Mental Health

Indiana Family and Social Services Administration, Division of Mental Health, Indiana Government Center-South, W353, 402 West Washington Street, Indianapolis, IN 46204; tel. 317/232-7800; FAX. 317/233-3472; Patrick Sullivan, Ph.D., Director

Nursing

Indiana State Board of Nursing, Health Professions Bureau, 402 West Washington Street, Room 041, Indianapolis, IN 46204; tel. 317/232-1105; FAX. 317/233-4236; Barbara Powers, Director

IOWA

The Honorable Terry E. Branstad, Governor, 515/281-5211

Health

Department of Public Health, Lucas State Office Building, 1st, 3rd and 4th Floors, Des Moines, IA 50319-0075; tel. 515/281-5605; FAX. 515/281-4958; Christopher G. Atchison, Director

Section C

Planning
Center for Health Policy, Iowa Department of Public Health, Lucas State Office Building, Fourth Floor, Des Moines, IA 50319; tel. 515/281-4346; FAX. 515/281-4958; Gerd Clabaugh, Director

Prevention
Division of Health Protection, Iowa Department of Public Health, Lucas State Office Building, First Floor, Des Moines, IA 50319; tel. 515/281-7785; FAX. 515/281-4529; John R. Kelly, Director

Substance Abuse
Division of Substance Abuse and Health Promotion, Iowa Department of Public Health, Lucas State Office Building, 321 East 12th Street, Des Moines, IA 50319-0075; tel. 515/281-3641; FAX. 515/281-4535; Janet Zwick, Director

Governor's Alliance on Substance Abuse, Lucas State Office Building, Des Moines, IA 50319; tel. 515/281-4518; FAX. 515/242-6390; Dale Woolery, Administrator

Welfare
Department of Human Services, Hoover State Office Building, Des Moines, IA 50319; tel. 515/281-5452; FAX. 515/281-4597; Charles M. Palmer, Director

Mental Health
Division of Mental Health/Developmental Disabilities, Hoover State Office Building, Des Moines, IA 50319-0114; tel. 515/281-5874; FAX. 515/281-4597; Division Administrator

Insurance
Division of Insurance, 330 E. Maple, Des Moines, IA 50319-0065; tel. 515/281-5705; FAX. 515/281-3059; Therese M. Vaughan, Commissioner

Other

Aging
Iowa Department of Elder Affairs, 236 Jewett Building, 914 Grand Avenue, Des Moines, IA 50309-2801; tel. 515/281-5187; FAX. 515/281-4036; Betty L. Grandquist, Executive Director

Facility
Department of Inspection and Appeals, Division of Health Facilities, Lucas State Office Building, Des Moines, IA 50319; tel. 515/281-4115; FAX. 515/242-5022; J. B. Bennett, Administrator

Medical Examiners
Iowa State Board of Medical Examiners, State Capitol Complex, Executive Hills West, Des Moines, IA 50319; tel. 515/281-5171; FAX. 515/242-5908; Ann M. Martino, Ph.D., Executive Director

Nursing
Iowa Board of Nursing, State Capitol Complex, 1223 East Court Avenue, Des Moines, IA 50319; tel. 515/281-3255; FAX. 515/281-4825; Lorinda K. Inman, RN, M.S.N., Executive Director

Rehabilitation
Department of Education, Division of Vocational Rehabilitation Services, 510 East 12th Street, Des Moines, IA 50319; tel. 515/281-4311; Marge Knudsen, Administrator

Children
Child Health Specialty Clinics, 247 Hospital School, University of Iowa, Iowa City, IA 52242-1011; tel. 319/356-1469; FAX. 319/356-3715; Jeffrey G. Lobas, M.D., Director

KANSAS
The Honorable Bill Graves, Governor, 913/296-3232

Health
Kansas Department of Health and Environment, Landon State Office Building, 900 Southwest Jackson, Suite 620, Topeka, KS 66612-1290; tel. 913/296-0461; FAX. 913/368-6368; Gary R. Mitchell, Secretary, Kansas Health and Environment

Children
Hospital and Medical Programs, Kansas Department of Health and Environment, Bureau of Adult and Child Care Facilities, 900 Southwest Jackson, Suite 1001, Topeka, KS 66612-1290; tel. 913/296-3362; FAX. 913/296-1266; Greg L. Reser, Director, Hospital and Medical Programs

Welfare
State Department of Social and Rehabilitation Services, Docking State Office Building, Suite 681-W, Topeka, KS 66612; tel. 913/296-6750; FAX. 913/296-6960; Candy Shively, Commissioner

Medical Services
Adult and Medical Services, Docking State Office Building, 915 Southwest Harrison, Room 628-S, Topeka, KS 66612; tel. 913/296-3981; FAX. 913/296-4813; Ann E. Koci, Commissioner

Mental Health
Mental Health and Developmental Disabilities, Docking State Office Building, Fifth Floor-N, Topeka, KS 66612; tel. 913/296-3773; FAX. 913/296-6142; Connie Hubbell, Commissioner

Rehabilitation
Rehabilitation Services, 3640 SW Topeka Blvd., Suite 150, Topeka, KS 66611-2373; tel. 785/267-5301; Joyce A. Cussimanio, Commissioner

Insurance
Kansas Insurance Department, 420 Southwest Ninth, Topeka, KS 66612; tel. 913/296-3071; FAX. 913/296-2283; Kathleen Sebelius, Commissioner, Insurance

Health
Kansas Insurance Department, Accident and Health Division, 420 Southwest Ninth, Topeka, KS 66612; tel. 913/296-7850; FAX. 913/296-2283; Richard G. Huncker, Supervisor

Other

Nursing
Kansas State Board of Nursing, Landon State Office Building, 900 Southwest Jackson, Suite 55, Topeka, KS 66612-1230; tel. 913/296-4929; FAX. 913/296-3929; Patsy Johnson, RN, M.N., Executive Administrator

Other
Kansas State Board of Healing Arts, 235 South Topeka Boulevard, Topeka, KS 66603-3068; tel. 913/296-7413; FAX. 913/296-0852; Lawrence T. Buening, Jr., Executive Director

KENTUCKY
The Honorable Paul E. Patton, Governor, 502/564-2611

Health
Department for Public Health, Cabinet for Health Services, 275 East Main Street, Frankfort, KY 40621; tel. 502/564-3970; FAX. 502/564-6533; Rice C. Leach, M.D., MSHSA, Commissioner

Licensing
Division of Licensing and Regulation, Cabinet for Health Services, C.H.R. Building, Fourth Floor, E., 275 East Main Street, Frankfort, KY 40621; tel. 502/564-2800; FAX. 502/565-6546; Rebecca J. Cecil, R.Ph., Director

Policy
Health Data Branch, 275 East Main Street, HSIE-C, Frankfort, KY 40621; tel. 502/564-2757; FAX. 502/564-6533; George Robertson, Manager

Welfare
Department for Social Insurance, 275 East Main Street, Frankfort, KY 40621; tel. 502/564-3703; FAX. 502/564-6907; Dietra Paris, Interim Commissioner

Insurance
Department of Insurance, Life and Health Division, 215 West Main Street, P.O. Box 517, Frankfort, KY 40602; tel. 502/564-6088; FAX. 502/564-6090; Paula Isaacs, Program Manager, Health Care

Other

Medical Services
Department for Medicaid Services, 275 East Main Street, Frankfort, KY 40621; tel. 502/564-4321; FAX. 502/564-6917; John Morse, Commissioner

Mental Health
Department For Mental Health/Mental Retardation Services, 100 Fair Oaks Lane, Frankfort, KY 40621-0001; tel. 502/564-4527; FAX. 502/564-5478; Elizabeth Rehm Wachtel, Ph.D., Commissioner

Nursing
Kentucky Board of Nursing, 312 Whittington Parkway, Suite 300, Louisville, KY 40222-5172; tel. 502/329-7000, ext. 226; FAX. 502/329-7011; Sharon M. Weisenbeck, M.S., RN, Executive Director

Rehabilitation
Department of Vocational Rehabilitation, 209 St. Clair Street, Frankfort, KY 40601; tel. 502/564-4440; FAX. 502/564-6745; Sam Srralgio, Commissioner

Children
Commission for Children with Special Health Care Needs, 982 Eastern Parkway, Louisville, KY 40217; tel. 502/595-4459, ext. 267; FAX. 502/595-4673; Denzle L. Hill, Executive Director

Other
Commission for Health Economics Control, 275 East Main Street, Frankfort, KY 40621; tel. 502/564-6620; W. R. Hourigan, Ph.D., Chairman

LOUISIANA
The Honorable Mike Foster, Governor, 504/342-7015

Health
Louisiana Department of Health and Hospitals, P.O. Box 629 Bin 2, Baton Rouge, LA 70821; tel. 504/342-9509; FAX. 504/342-9508; Rose V. Forrest, Secretary

Louisiana State University Medical Center, Health Care Services Division, 2021 Perdido Street, New Orleans, LA 70112-1352; tel. 504/588-3332; FAX. 504/588-3580; John S. Berault, MSPH, Chief Executive Officer

Louisiana State University Medical Center, Health Care Services Division, 8550 United Plaza Boulevard, Fourth Floor, Baton Rouge, LA 70809; tel. 504/922-0490; FAX. 504/922-2259; Cary M. Dougherty, Jr., Chief Operating Officer

Family
Office of Family Support, P.O. Box 94065, Baton Rouge, LA 70804-4065; tel. 504/342-3950; Vera W. Blakes, Assistant Secretary

Finance
Office of The Secretary, P.O. Box 629 Bin 2, Baton Rouge, LA 70821; tel. 504/342-9500; FAX. 504/342-9508; David W. Hood, Secretary

Licensing
Department of Health and Hospitals, Bureau of Health Services Financing, Health Standards Section, Box 3767, Baton Rouge, LA 70821; tel. 504/342-0138; FAX. 504/342-5292; Lily W. McAlister, RN, Manager, Health Standards Section

Substance Abuse
Office of Alcohol and Drug Abuse, P.O. Box 2790, Bin 18, Baton Rouge, LA 70821-2790; tel. 504/342-6717; FAX. 504/342-3875; Alton E. Hadley, Assistant Secretary

Office of Community Services, P.O. Box 3318, Baton Rouge, LA 70821; tel. 504/342-2297; FAX. 504/342-2268; Shirley Goodwin, Assistant Secretary

Insurance
Department of Insurance, P.O. Box 94214, Baton Rouge, LA 70804; tel. 504/342-0860; FAX. 504/342-3078; James H. Brown, Commissioner

Other

Medical Examiners
Louisiana State Board of Medical Examiners, 630 Camp Street, Zip 70130, P.O. Box 30250, New Orleans, LA 70190-0250; tel. 504/524-6763, ext. 222; FAX. 504/568-8893; Paula M. Mensen, Administrative Manager II

Nurse Examiners
Louisiana State Board of Practical Nurse Examiners, 3421 North Causeway Boulevard, Suite 203, Metairie, LA 70002; tel. 504/838-5791; FAX. 504/838-5279; Dennis S. Mann, Esq., Executive Director

Nursing
Louisiana State Board of Nursing, 150 Baronne Street, 912 Pere Marquette Building, New Orleans, LA 70112; tel. 504/568-5464; Barbara L. Movant, RN, M.N.

MAINE
The Honorable Angus S. King, Jr., Governor, 207/287-3531

Health
Maine Department of Human Services, State House, Station 11, Augusta, ME 04333; tel. 207/287-2736; FAX. 207/287-3005; Kevin W. Concannon, Commissioner

Aging
Bureau of Elder and Adult Services, State House, Station 11, Augusta, ME 04333; tel. 207/624-5335; FAX. 207/624-5361; Christine Gianopoulos, Director

Health
Bureau of Health, Department of Human Services, 11 State House Station, Augusta, ME 04333; tel. 207/287-8016; FAX. 207/287-9058; Dora Anne Mills, M.D., M.P.H., Director

Section C

Licensing

Division of Licensing and Certification, Department of Human Services, 35 Anthony Avenue, Station 11, Augusta, ME 04333; tel. 207/624-5443; FAX. 207/624-5378; Louis Dorogi, Director

Medical Services

Department of Human Services, Bureau of Medical Services, State House, Station 11, Augusta, ME 04333; tel. 207/287-2674; FAX. 207/287-2675; Frances T. Finnegan, Jr., Director

Children

Division of Community and Family Health, 151 Capitol Street, 11 State House Station, Augusta, ME 04333-0011; tel. 207/287-3311; FAX. 207/287-4631; Valerie Ricker, MSN, MS, NP

Insurance

Bureau of Insurance, Department of Professional and Financial Regulation, 34 State House Station, Augusta, ME 04333; tel. 207/624-8475; FAX. 207/624-8599; David Stetson, Supervisor, Life and Health Division

Financial

Department of Professional and Financial Regulation, 35 State House Station, Augusta, ME 04333; tel. 207/624-8511; FAX. 207/624-8595; S. Catherine Longley, Commissioner

Other

Medicine

Board of Licensure in Medicine, Two Bangor Street, 137 State House Station, Augusta, ME 04333; tel. 207/287-3601; FAX. 207/287-6590; Randal C. Manning, Executive Director

Mental Health

Department of Mental Health, Mental Retardation and Substance Abuse Services, State House Station 40, Augusta, ME 04333; tel. 207/287-4220; FAX. 207/287-4268; Andrea Blanch, Associate Commissioner, Programs

Mental Retardation

Department of Mental Health, Mental Retardation and Substance Abuse Services, 40 State House Station, Augusta, ME 04333-0040; tel. 207/287-4223; FAX. 207/287-4268; Melodie J. Peet, Commissioner

Nursing

Maine State Board of Nursing, 24 Stone Street, 158 State House Station, Augusta, ME 04333; tel. 207/287-1133; FAX. 207/287-1149; Myra A. Broadway, RN, Executive Director

Rehabilitation

Bureau of Rehabilitation Services, 35 Anthony Avenue, Augusta, ME 04333-0150; tel. 207/624-5323; FAX. 207/624-5302; Margaret Brewster, Director

Other

Bureau of Rehabilitation Services, Division of Deafness, 35 Anthony Avenue, Augusta, ME 04333-0150; tel. 207/624-5318; FAX. 207/624-5302; Alice C. Johnson, State Coordinator

Division for the Blind and Visually Impaired, 150 State House Station, Augusta, ME 04333-0150; tel. 207/624-5323; FAX. 207/624-5302; Harold Lewis, Director

MARYLAND
The Honorable Parris N. Glendening, Governor, 410/974-3901

Health

Department of Health and Mental Hygiene, 201 West Preston Street, Baltimore, MD 21201; tel. 410/767-6500; FAX. 410/767-6489; Martin P. Wasserman, M.D., J.D., Secretary

Developmental Disabilities

Developmental Disabilities Administration, 201 West Preston Street., Baltimore, MD 21201; tel. 410/767-5600; FAX. 410/767-5850; Diane K. Coughlin, Director

Environment

Maryland Department of the Environment, Office of Environmental Health Coordination, 2500 Broening Highway, Baltimore, MD 21224; tel. 410/631-3851; FAX. 410/631-4112; Tom Allen, Director

Family

Local and Family Health Administration, 201 West Preston Street, Baltimore, MD 21201; tel. 410/767-5300; FAX. 410/333-7106; Carlessia A. Hussein, Dr.P.H., Director

Health

Local and Family Health Administration, 201 West Preston Street, Baltimore, MD 21201; tel. 410/225-5300; FAX. 410/333-7106; Alan Baker, Interim Director

Laboratories

Laboratories Administration, 201 West Preston Street, Baltimore, MD 21201; tel. 410/767-6100; FAX. 410/333-5403; J. Mehsen Joseph, Ph.D., Director

Licensing

Licensing and Certification Administration, 4201 West Patterson Avenue, Baltimore, MD 21215; tel. 410/764-2750; FAX. 410/764-5969; Carol Benner, Director

Mental Health

Mental Hygiene Administration, 201 West Preston Street, Baltimore, MD 21201; tel. 410/767-6611; FAX. 410/333-5402; Oscar L. Morgan, Director

Planning

Office of Planning and Capital Financing, 201 West Preston Street, Baltimore, MD 21201; tel. 410/767-6816; FAX. 410/333-7525; Elizabeth G. Barnard, Director

Policy

Department of Health and Mental Hygene, 201 West Preston Street, Room 500, Baltimore, MD 21201; tel. 410/767-6500; FAX. 410/767-6489; Martin P. Wasserman, M.D., J.D., Secretary

Substance Abuse

Alcohol and Drug Abuse Administration, 201 West Preston Street, Baltimore, MD 21201; tel. 410/767-6925; FAX. 410/333-7206; Thomas Davis, Director, Alcohol and Drug Abuse Administration

Welfare

Social Services Administration, 311 West Saratoga Street, Fifth Floor, Baltimore, MD 21201; tel. 410/767-7216; FAX. 410/333-0127; Linda D. Ellard, Executive Director

Insurance

Maryland Insurance Administration, 501 St. Paul Place, Baltimore, MD 21202; tel. 410/333-2521; FAX. 410/333-6650; Dwight K. Bartlett III, Insurance Commissioner

Other

Education

Maryland State Department of Education, 200 West Baltimore Street, Baltimore, MD 21201-1595; tel. 410/767-0100; FAX. 410/333-6033; Nancy S. Grasmick, State Superintendent of Schools

Medical Examiners

Board of Physician Quality Assurance, 4201 Patterson Avenue, Baltimore, MD 21215; tel. 800/492-6836; FAX. 410/358-2252; J. Michael Compton, Executive Director

Nursing

Maryland Board of Nursing, 4140 Patterson Avenue, Baltimore, MD 21215-2254; tel. 410/764-5124; FAX. 410/358-3530; Donna M. Dorsey, RN, M.S., Executive Director

Rehabilitation

Division of Rehabilitation Services, 2301 Argonne Drive, Baltimore, MD 21218-1696; tel. 410/554-9385; FAX. 410/554-9412; Robert A. Burns, Assistant State Superintendent

MASSACHUSETTS
The Honorable Argeo Paul Cellucci, Governor, 617/727-9173

Health

Massachusetts Department of Public Health, 150 Tremont Street, 10th Floor, Boston, MA 02111; tel. 617/727-2700; FAX. 617/727-2559; David H. Mulligan, Commissioner

Environment

Bureau of Environmental Health Assessment, 250 Washington Street, Seventh Floor, Boston, MA 02108; tel. 617/624-5757; FAX. 617/624-5777; Suzanne K. Condon, Director

Medical Services

Office of Emergency Medical Services, 470 Atlantic Avenue, Second Floor, Boston, MA 02210-2208; tel. 617/753-8300; FAX. 617/753-8350; Louise Goyette, Director

Quality

Division of Health Care Quality, 10 West Street, Fifth Floor, Boston, MA 02111; tel. 617/753-8100; FAX. 617/753-8125; Paul I. Dreyer, Ph.D., Director

Statistics

Bureau of Health Statistics, Research and Evaluation, Massachusetts Department of Public Health, 250 Washington Street, Sixth Floor, Boston, MA 02108-4619; tel. 617/624-5613; FAX. 617/624-5698; Daniel J. Friedman, Ph.D., Assistant Commissioner

Systems

Bureau of Health Quality Management, Massachusetts Department of Public Health, 250 Washington Street, Boston, MA 02108-4619; tel. 617/624-5280; FAX. 617/624-5046; Nancy Ridley, Assistant Commissioner

Welfare

Department of Transitional Assistance, 600 Washington Street, Boston, MA 02111; tel. 617/348-8402; FAX. 617/348-8575; Claire McIntire, Commissioner

Insurance

Division of Insurance, 470 Atlantic Avenue, Boston, MA 02210-2223; tel. 617/521-7794; FAX. 617/521-7770; Linda Ruthardt, Commissioner

Other

Medicine

Board of Registration in Medicine, Commonwealth of Massachusetts, Ten West Street, Boston, MA 02111; tel. 617/727-3086; FAX. 617/451-9568, ext. 321; Alexander F. Fleming, Executive Director

Mental Health

Massachusetts Department of Mental Health, Central Office, 25 Staniford Street, Boston, MA 02114; tel. 617/727-5500, ext. 448; FAX. 617/727-4350; Marylou Sudders, Commissioner

Nursing

Massachusetts Board of Registration in Nursing, 100 Cambridge Street, Suite 1519, Boston, MA 02202; tel. 617/727-9961; FAX. 617/727-9961; Theresa M. Bonanno, M.S.N., RN, Executive Director

Blind

Commission for the Blind, 88 Kingston Street, Boston, MA 02111; tel. 617/727-5550; FAX. 617/727-5960; Charles Crawford, Commissioner

Rehabilitation

Massachusetts Rehabilitation Commission, Fort Point Place, 27-43 Wormwood Street, Boston, MA 02210-1606; tel. 617/727-2172; FAX. 617/727-1354; Elmer C. Bartels, Commissioner

Substance Abuse

Massachusetts Department of Public Health, Bureau of Substance Abuse, 250 Washington Street, Third Floor, Boston, MA 02108-4619; tel. 617/624-5111; FAX. 617/624-5185; Mayra Rodriguez-Howard, Director

MICHIGAN
The Honorable John Engler, Governor, 517/373-3400

Health

Michigan Department of Community Health, Community Public Health Agency, 3423 North Martin Luther King, Jr. Boulevard, P.O. Box 30195, Lansing, MI 48909; tel. 517/335-8024; FAX. 517/335-9476; James K. Haveman, Jr., Director, MDCH

Community

Michigan Department of Community Health, Health Legislation and Policy Development, 320 S. Walnut Street, Lewis Cass Building, 6th Floor, Lansing, MI 48913; tel. 517/373-2559; FAX. 517/241-1200; Carol L. Isaacs, Director

Environment

Michigan Department of Environmental Quality,Drinking Water and Radiological Protection, Medical Waste Regulatory Program, 3423 North Martin Luther King Jr. Boulevard, P.O. Box 30630, Lansing, MI 48909; tel. 517/335-8637; FAX. 517/335-9033; John N. Gohlke, R.S., M.S.A., Program Chief

Facilities

Bureau of Health Systems, Michigan Department of Consumer and Industry Services, 525 West Ottawa, P.O. Box 30664, Lansing, MI 48909; tel. 517/241-2626; FAX. 517/241-2635; Walter S. Wheeler III, Director

Health

Division of Chronic Disease and Injury Control, 3423 North Martin Luther King, Jr. Boulevard, P.O. Box 30195, Lansing, MI 48909; tel. 517/335-8368; FAX. 517/335-8593; Jean Chabut, Chief

Laboratories

Michigan Department of Consumer and Industry Services,Laboratory Improvement Section, Division of Health Facility Licensing & Certification, Bureau of Health Systems, P.O. Box 30664, Lansing, MI 48909; tel. 517/241-2645; FAX. 517/241-2635; Jeffrey P. Massey, Dr.P.H., Chief

Licensing

Division of Licensing and Certification, 3500 North Logan Street, Lansing, MI 48909; tel. 517/335-8505; Nancy Graham, Supervisor

Medical Services

Managed Care Quality Assessment and Improvement Division, Michigan Department of Community Health, P.O. Box 30195, Lansing, MI 48909; tel. 517/335-8551; FAX. 517/335-9239; Janet D. Olszewski, Director Quality Improvement and Eligibility Services

Substance Abuse

Bureau of Substance Abuse Services, Michigan Department of Community Health, 320 S. Walnut Street, Lewis Cass Building, Lansing, MI 48913; tel. 517/335-0278; FAX. 517/241-2611

Welfare

Family Independence Agency, 235 South Grand Avenue, P.O. Box 30037, Lansing, MI 48909; tel. 517/373-2035; FAX. 517/373-8471; Mark Murray, Acting Director

Medical Services

Medical Services Administration, 400 South Pine, P.O. Box 30037, Lansing, MI 48909; tel. 517/335-5000; FAX. 517/335-5007; Robert M. Smedes, Chief Executive Officer

Insurance

Department of Consumer and Industry Services, Michigan Insurance Bureau, 611 West Ottawa, Second Floor, P.O. Box 30220, Lansing, MI 48909-7720; tel. 517/373-9273; FAX. 517/335-4978; D.A. D'Annunzio, Acting Commissioner

Other

Education

Department of Education, Box 30008, Lansing, MI 48909; tel. 517/373-7247; FAX. 517/373-1233; Patricia Nichols, Supervisor, School Health Programs Unit

Aging

Office of Services to the Aging, P.O. Box 30026, Lansing, MI 48909; tel. 517/373-8230; FAX. 517/373-4092; Carol Parr, Acting Director

Licensing

Office of Health Services, Department of Consumer and Industry Services, P.O. Box 30670, Lansing, MI 48909; tel. 517/373-8068; FAX. 517/373-2179; Thomas C. Lindsay II, Director

Licensing

Michigan Department of Consumer and Industry Services, Office of Health Services, Box 30670, Lansing, MI 48909; tel. 517/373-8068; FAX. 517/373-2179; Thomas C. Lindsay II, Director

Medicine

Michigan Board of Medicine, 611 West Ottawa Street, Box 30670, Lansing, MI 48909; tel. 517/373-6873; FAX. 517/373-2179; Carole Hakala Engle, Director, Licensing

Mental Health

Michigan Department of Community Health, Lewis Cass Building, 320 South Walnut, Lansing, MI 48913; tel. 517/373-3500; FAX. 517/335-3090; James K. Haveman, Jr., Director

Nursing

Michigan Board of Nursing, 611 West Ottawa Street, Box 30670, Lansing, MI 48909; tel. 517/335-0918; FAX. 517/373-2179; Doris Foley, Licensing Administrator

Rehabilitation

Bureau of Rehabilitation and Disability Determination, Box 30010, Lansing, MI 48909; tel. 517/373-3390; Ivan L. Cotman, Associate Superintendent

Other

Office of Health and Human Services, Michigan Department of Management and Budget, Lewis Cass Building, Box 30026, Lansing, MI 48909; tel. 517/373-1076; FAX. 517/373-3624; Paul Reinhart, Director

MINNESOTA
The Honorable Arne H. Carlson, Governor, 612/296-3391

Health

Minnesota Department of Health, 121 East 7th Place, Suite 450, St. Paul, MN 55101; tel. 612/215-5813; FAX. 612/215-5801; Anne M. Barry, Commissioner

Community

Minnesota Department of Health, Division of Community Health Services, Metro Square Building, Suite 460, 121 East Seventh Place, Zip 55101, P.O. Box 64975, St. Paul, MN 55164-0975; tel. 612/296-9720; FAX. 612/296-9362; Ryan Church, Director

Environment

Division of Environmental Health, 121 East Seventh Place, P.O. Box 64975, St. Paul, MN 55164-0975; tel. 612/215-0700; FAX. 612/215-0979; Patricia A. Bloomgren, Director

Laboratories

Public Health Laboratory Division, 717 Southeast Delaware Street, P.O. Box 9441, Minneapolis, MN 55440; tel. 612/623-5331; FAX. 612/623-5514; Pauline Bouchard, J.D., Director

Prevention

Minnesota Department of Health, Division of Disease Prevention and Control, 717 Southeast Delaware Street, P.O. Box 9441, Minneapolis, MN 55440-9441; tel. 612/623-5363; FAX. 612/623-5743; Agnes T. Leitheiser, Director

Administration

Minnesota Department of Health, Division of Finance and Administration, 717 Southeast Delaware Street, P.O. Box 9441, Minneapolis, MN 55440; tel. 612/623-5465; Christine Everson, Director

Resources

Facility and Provider Compliance Division, Minnesota Department of Health, 393 North Dunlap Street, P.O. Box 64900, St. Paul, MN 55164-0900; tel. 612/643-2100; FAX. 612/643-2593; Linda G. Sutherland, Director

Systems

Minnesota Department of Health, Office of Regulatory Reform, 121 East Seventh Place, P.O. Box 64975, St. Paul, MN 55164-0975; tel. 612/282-5627; FAX. 612/282-3839; Nanette M. Schroeder, Director

Children

Minnesota Department of Health, Division of Family Health, 717 Southeast Delaware Street, P.O. Box 9441, Minneapolis, MN 55440; tel. 612/623-5167; FAX. 612/623-5442; Norbert Hirschhorn, M.D., Director

Licensing

Licensing and Certification, 393 North Dunlap Street, P.O. Box 64900, St. Paul, MN 55164-0900; tel. 612/643-2130; FAX. 612/643-3534; Carol Hirschfeld, Supervisor, Program Assurance Unit

Welfare

Minnesota Department of Human Services, 444 Lafayette Road, N., St. Paul, MN 55155-3815; tel. 612/296-6117; FAX. 612/296-6244; David S. Doth, Commissioner

Other

Medical Examiners

Minnesota Board of Medical Practice, 2829 University Avenue, S.E., Suite 400, Minneapolis, MN 55414-3246; tel. 612/617-2130; FAX. 612/617-2166; Robert A. Leach, Executive Director

Nursing

Minnesota Board of Nursing, 2829 University Avenue, S.E., Suite 500, Minneapolis, MN 55414-3253; tel. 612/617-2270; FAX. 612/617-2190; Joyce M. Schowalter, Executive Director

Rehabilitation

Rehabilitation Services Branch, 390 North Robert Street, Fifth Floor, St. Paul, MN 55101; tel. 612/296-1822; FAX. 612/296-0994; Michael T. Coleman, Assistant Commissioner

Other

Department of Commerce, 133 East Seventh Street, St. Paul, MN 55101; tel. 612/296-4026; FAX. 612/296-4328; David B. Gruenes

MISSISSIPPI
The Honorable Kirk Fordice, Governor, 601/359-3150

Health

Department of Health, Felix J. Underwood State Board of Health Building, P.O. Box 1700, Jackson, MS 32915-1700; tel. 601/960-7634; FAX. 601/960-7931; F.E. Thompson, Jr., M.D., M.P.H., State Health Officer

Environment

Bureau of Environmental Health, Mississippi State Department of Health, Felix J. Underwood State Board of Health Building, P.O. Box 1700, Jackson, MS 32915-1700; tel. 601/960-7680; FAX. 601/354-6794; Ricky Boggan, Director

Health

Bureau of Health Services, Felix J. Underwood State Board of Health Building An, P.O. Box 1700, Jackson, MS 32915; tel. 601/960-7472; FAX. 601/960-7480; Michael J. Gandy, Ed.D., Bureau Director, Deputy

Licensing

Division of Health Facilities Licensure and Certification, P.O. Box 1700, Jackson, MS 39215; tel. 601/354-7300; FAX. 601/354-7230; Vanessa Phipps, Director

Medical Services

Mississippi State Department of Health, Felix J. Underwood State Board of Health Building, P.O. Box 1700, Jackson, MS 32915-1700; tel. 601/960-7634; Betty Jane Phillips, Dr.P.H. Deputy State Health Officer

Planning

Health Planning and Resources Development Division, Mississippi State Department of Health, Felix J. Underwood State Board of Health Building, 2423 North State Street, P.O. Box 1700, Jackson, MS 39215-1700; tel. 601/960-7874; FAX. 601/354-6123; Harold B. Armstrong, Chief

Statistics

Public Health Statistics, Mississippi State Department of Health, Bureau of Health Statistics, Box 1700, Jackson, MS 39215-1700; tel. 601/960-7960; FAX. 601/354-6174; Nita C. Gunter, Director

Children

Children's Medical Program, 421 Stadium Circle, P.O. Box 1700, Jackson, MS 39215-1700; tel. 601/987-3965; FAX. 601/987-5560; Mike Gallarno, Director

Other

State Epidemiologist, Underwood Annex, P.O Box 1700, Jackson, MS 32915-1700; tel. 601/960-7725; FAX. 601/354-6061; Mary Currier, M.D., M.P.H.

Welfare

Mississippi Department of Human Services, 750 North State Street, Jackson, MS 39202; tel. 601/359-4480; FAX. 601/359-4477; Donald R. Taylor, Executive Director

Other

Mental Health

Department of Mental Health, 1101 Robert E. Lee Building, Jackson, MS 39201; tel. 601/359-1288; FAX. 601/359-6295; Randy Hendrix, Ph.D., Director

Nursing

Mississippi Board of Nursing, 239 North Lamar Street, Suite 401, Jackson, MS 39201-1397; tel. 601/359-6170; FAX. 601/359-6185; Marcia M. Rachel, Ph.D., RN, M.S.N., Executive Director

Rehabilitation

State Department of Rehabilitation Services, P.O. Box 1698, Jackson, MS 39215-1698; tel. 601/853-5100; FAX. 601/853-5205; Pery Winegarden, Interim Director

MISSOURI
The Honorable Mel Carnahan, Governor, 573/751-3222

Health

Department of Health, Box 570, Jefferson City, MO 65102; tel. 314/751-6001; FAX. 314/751-6041; Maureen E. Dempsey, M.D., Director

Licensing

Bureau of Hospital Licensing and Certification, Missouri Department of Health, Box 570, Jefferson City, MO 65102; tel. 314/751-6302; FAX. 314/526-3621; Darrell Hendrickson, Administrator

Resources

Center for Health Information Management and Epidemiology (CHIME), Box 570, Jefferson City, MO 65102; tel. 573/751-6272; FAX. 573/526-4102; Garland H. Land, Director

Insurance

Department of Insurance, P.O. Box 690, Jefferson City, MO 65102; tel. 314/751-4126; FAX. 314/751-1165; Jay Angoff, Director

Health

Life and Health Section, Missouri Department of Insurance, P.O. Box 690, Jefferson City, MO 65102; tel. 573/751-4363; FAX. 573/526-6075; James W. Casey, Supervisor

Other

Education

Department of Elementary and Secondary Education, 205 Jefferson, P.O. Box 480, Jefferson City, MO 65102; tel. 573/751-4446; FAX. 573/751-1179; Dr. Robert E. Bartman, Commissioner of Education

Mental Health

Department of Mental Health, 1706 East Elm Street, P.O. Box 687, Jefferson City, MO 65102; tel. 573/751-4122; FAX. 573/751-8224; Roy C. Wilson, M.D., Director

Rehabilitation

Missouri Division of Vocational Rehabilitation, 3024 West Truman Boulevard, Jefferson City, MO 65109-0525; tel. 573/751-3251; FAX. 314/751-1441; Ronald W. Vessell, Assistant Commissioner

Children

Division of Maternal, Child and Family Health, 930 Wildwood Drive, Box 570, Jefferson City, MO 65109; tel. 314/526-5520; FAX. 314/526-5348; Gretchen C. Wartmen, Director

Other

Bureau of Special Health Care Needs, 930 Wildwood Drive, P.O. Box 570, Jefferson City, MO 65109; tel. 314/751-6246; FAX. 314/751-6237; Richard Brown, Chief

Missouri State Board of Registration for the Healing Arts, 3605 Missouri Boulevard, Zip 65109, P.O. Box 4, Jefferson City, MO 65102; tel. 314/751-0098; FAX. 314/751-3166; Tina Steinman, Executive Director

MONTANA

The Honorable Marc Racicot, Governor, 406/444-3111

Health

Montana Department of Public Health and Human Services, 111 North Sanders, P.O. Box 4210, Helena, MT 59604; tel. 406/444-5622; FAX. 406/444-1970; Laurie Ekanger, Director

Family

Family/Maternal and Child Health Services Bureau, W. F. Cogswell Building, Helena, MT 59620; tel. 406/444-4740; FAX. 406/444-2606; JoAnn Walsh Dotson, RN MSN, Bureau Chief

Licensing

Quality Assurance Division, Department of Public Health and Human Services, Certification Bureau, Cogswell Building, 1400 Broadway, P.O. Box 202951, Helena, MT 59620-2951; tel. 406/444-2099; FAX. 406/444-3456; Linda Sandman, Chief

Medical Services

Health Policy and Services Division, Montana Department of Public Health and Human Services, 1400 Broadway, P.O. Box 202951, Helena, MT 59620-2951; tel. 406/444-4540; FAX. 406/444-1861; Nancy Ellery, Administrator

Welfare

Department of Public Health and Human Services, 111 North Sanders Street, Box 4210, Helena, MT 59604-4210; tel. 406/444-5622; FAX. 406/444-1970; Laurie Ekanger, Director

Aging

Aging Services, Senior and Long Term Care Division, Department of Public Health and Human Services, 111 Sanders, P.O. Box 4210, Helena, MT 59604; tel. 406/444-7785; FAX. 406/444-7743; Robert E. Bartholomew, State Long Term Care Ombudsman

Rehabilitation

Division of Disability Services, P.O. Box 4210, Helena, MT 59604; tel. 406/444-2590; FAX. 406/444-3632; Joe A. Mathews, Administrator

Community

Child and Family Services Division, P.O. Box 8005, Helena, MT 59604-8005; tel. 406/444-5902; FAX. 406/444-5956; Hank Hudson, Administrator

Other

Department of Commerce, Montana State Board of Nursing, Arcade Building - 4-C, 111 North Jackson, P.O. Box 200513, Helena, MT 59620-0513; tel. 406/444-2071; FAX. 406/444-7759; Joan Bowers, Administrative Assistant

NEBRASKA

The Honorable E. Benjamin Nelson, 402/471-2244

Health

State Department of Health, 301 Centennial Mall South, Lincoln, NE 68509; tel. 402/471-2133; FAX. 402/471-0383; Mark B. Horton, M.D., M.S.P.H., Director of Health

Facilities

Nebraska Department of Health, Certificate of Need Program, P.O. Box 95007, Lincoln, NE 68509-5007; tel. 402/471-2105; FAX. 402/471-0180; Charlene Gondring, Program Manager

Health

Nebraska Department of Health and Human Services, 301 Centennial Mall, S., P.O. Box 95044, Lincoln, NE 68509; tel. 402/471-0191; FAX. 402/471-8259; Sue Medinger, Nutrition Consultant

Licensing

Nebraska Department of Regulation and Licensure, Credentialing Division, 301 Centennial Mall, S., P.O. Box 95007, Lincoln, NE 68509-5007; tel. 402/471-2946; FAX. 402/471-0555; Helen Meeks, Director

Policy

Division of Health Policy and Planning, 301 Centennial Mall, S., P.O. Box 95007, Lincoln, NE 68509; tel. 402/471-2337; David Palm, Ph.D., Director

Radiology

Nebraska Department of Health, Division of Radiological Health, 301 Centennial Mall, S., P.O. Box 95007, Lincoln, NE 68509; tel. 402/471-2168; FAX. 402/471-0169; Harold Borchert, Director

Children

Division of Family Health, Nebraska Department of Health and Human Services, 301 Centennial Mall South, P.O. Box 95044, Lincoln, NE 68509-5044; tel. 402/471-3980; FAX. 402/471-7049; Paula Eurek, R.D., Division Administrator

Welfare

Nebraska Health and Human Services System, 301 Centennial Mall, S., P.O. Box 95026, Lincoln, NE 68509-5026; tel. 402/471-3121; FAX. 401/471-9449; Deb Thomas, Policy Secretary

Medical Services

Nebraska Department of Social Services, Medical Services Division, 301 Centennial Mall, S., P.O. Box 95026, Lincoln, NE 68509; tel. 402/471-9147; FAX. 402/471-9092; Ric Compton, Administrator

Children

Nebraska Department of Health and Human Services, Special Services for Children and Adults, 301 Centennial Mall, S., P.O. Box 95044, Lincoln, NE 68509-5044; tel. 402/471-9345; FAX. 402/471-9455; Mary Jo Iwan, Administrator

Insurance

Department of Insurance, 941 O Street, Suite 400, Lincoln, NE 68508; tel. 402/471-2201; FAX. 402/471-4610; Timothy J. Hall, Director

Other

Rehabilitation

Department of Education, Vocational Rehabilitation, 301 Centennial Mall, S., P.O. Box 94987, Lincoln, NE 68509; tel. 402/471-3644; Frank Lloyd, Director

Other

HHS R&L Credentialing Division, 301 Centennial Mall, S., Box 94986, Lincoln, NE 68509-4986; tel. 402/471-2115; FAX. 402/471-3577; Helen L. Meeks, Director

NEVADA

The Honorable Bob Miller, Governor, 702/687-5670

Health

Department of Human Resources, Kinkead Building, 505 East King, Suite 600, Carson City, NV 89710; tel. 702/687-4400; FAX. 702/687-4733; Charlotte Crawford, Director

Community

Nevada State Health Division, Bureau of Community Health Services, 3656 Research Way, Suite 32, Carson City, NV 89706; tel. 702/687-6944; FAX. 702/687-7693; Mary D. Sassi, Bureau Chief

Health

Nevada Division of Health, Kinkead Building, 505 East King Street, Room 201, Carson City, NV 89701-4761; tel. 702/687-3786; FAX. 702/687-3859; Yvonne Sylva, Administrator

Laboratories

Nevada State Health Laboratory, 1660 North Virginia Street, Reno, NV 89503; tel. 702/688-1335; FAX. 702/688-1460; Arthur F. DiSalvo, M.D., Director

Medical Services

Division of Health Care Financing and Policy-Medicaid, 2527 North Carson Street, Carson City, NV 89710; tel. 702/687-4775; FAX. 702/687-5080; April Townley, Deputy Administrator

Mental Health

Division of Mental Health and Mental Retardation, Kinkead Building, Suite 602, 505 East King Street, Carson City, NV 89701-3790; tel. 702/687-5943; FAX. 702/687-4773; Carlos Brandenburg, Ph.D., Administrator

Regulation

Bureau of Licensure and Certification, Nevada Health Division, 1550 College Parkway, Capitol Complex, Suite 158, Carson City, NV 89706-7921; tel. 702/687-4475; FAX. 702/687-6588; Richard J. Panelli, Chief

Rehabilitation

Rehabilitation Division, Kinkead Building, 505 East King, Suite 502, Carson City, NV 89710; tel. 702/687-4440; FAX. 702/687-5980; Maynard R. Yasmer, Administrator

Resources

Bureau of Health Planning and Statistics, Nevada State Health Division, 505 East King Street, Room 102, Carson City, NV 89701-4761; tel. 702/687-4720; FAX. 702/687-6151; Emil DeJan, Chief

Children

Children With Special Health Care Needs Program, Nevada State Health Division, Kinkead Building, 505 East King, Suite 205, Carson City, NV 89710; tel. 702/687-4885; FAX. 702/687-1383; Gloria Deyhle, MCH Nurse Consultant

Other

Welfare Division, 2527 North Carson Street, Carson City, NV 89710; tel. 702/687-4770; FAX. 702/687-5080; Myla C. Florence, Administrator

Insurance

Nevada Department of Business and Industry, Director's Office, 555 East Washington, Suite 4900, Las Vegas, NV 89101; tel. 702/486-2750; FAX. 702/486-2758; Claudia Cormier, Director

Insurance

Division of Insurance, Capitol Complex, 1665 Hot Springs Road, Suite 152, Carson City, NV 89710; tel. 702/687-4270; FAX. 702/687-3937; Alice A. Molasky-Arman, Commissioner

Other

Medical Examiners

Nevada State Board of Medical Examiners, 1105 Terminal Way, Suite 301, Zip 89502, P.O. Box 7238, Reno, NV 89510; tel. 702/688-2559; FAX. 702/688-2321; Larry D. Lessly, Executive Director

Nursing

Nevada State Board of Nursing, 2755 East Plumb Lane, Suite 260, Reno, NV 89502; tel. 702/786-2778; FAX. 702/322-6993; Kathy Apple, M.S., RN, Executive Director

NEW HAMPSHIRE

The Honorable Jeanne Shaheen, Governor, 603/271-2121

Health

Department of Health and Human Services, Six Hazen Drive, Concord, NH 03301; tel. 603/271-4334; FAX. 603/271-4232; Kathleen G. Sgambati, Deputy Commissioner

Community

Division of Public Health Services, Office of Family and Community Health, Health and Welfare Building, Six Hazen Drive, Concord, NH 03301; tel. 603/271-4726; FAX. 603/271-4779; Roger Taillefer, Assistant Director

Facilities

Office of Program Support, Licensing and Regulation, Health Facilities Administration, Six Hazen Drive, Concord, NH 03301; tel. 603/271-4966; FAX. 603/271-4968; Raymond Rusin, Chief

Health

Department of Health and Human Services, Six Hazen Drive, Concord, NH 03301-6527; tel. 603/271-4372; FAX. 603/271-4727; Charles E. Danielson, M.D., M.P.H., State Medical Director

Mental Health

Office of Community Supports and Long Term Care, State Office Park, S., 105 Pleasant Street, Concord, NH 03301; tel. 603/271-5007; FAX. 603/271-5058; Paul G. Gorman, Ed.D., Director

Prevention

New Hampshire Department of Health and Human Services, Office of Health Management, Six Hazen Drive, Concord, NH 03301; tel. 603/271-4496; FAX. 603/271-4933; Richard DiPentima, Program Chief

Welfare

Department of Health and Human Services, Office of Family Services, Six Hazen Drive, Concord, NH 03301-6521; tel. 603/271-4321; FAX. 603/271-4727; Richard A. Chevrefils, Assistant Commissioner

Health

Department of Health and Human Services, Office of Health Management, Six Hazen Drive, Concord, NH 03301-6527; tel. 603/271-4726; FAX. 603/271-4779; Roger Taillefer, Assistant Director, Family and Community Health

Insurance

Department of Insurance, 169 Manchester Street, Concord, NH 03301; tel. 603/271-2661; FAX. 603/271-1406; Sylvio L. Dupuis, O.D., Commissioner

Other

Examination Division, 169 Manchester Street, Concord, NH 03301; tel. 603/271-2241; FAX. 603/271-1406; Thomas S. Burke, Director

Other

Education

State Department of Education, 101 Pleasant Street, State Office Park, S., Concord, NH 03301; tel. 603/271-3494; FAX. 603/271-1953; Elizabeth M. Twomey, Commissioner

Environment

Department of Environmental Services, Six Hazen Drive, Concord, NH 03301; tel. 603/271-3503; FAX. 603/271-2867; Robert W. Varney, Commissioner

Medicine

New Hampshire Board of Medicine, Board of Medicine, Two Industrial Park Drive, Suite Eight, Concord, NH 03301; tel. 603/271-1203; FAX. 603/271-6702; Karen Lamoureux, Administrator

Nursing

New Hampshire Board of Nursing, 78 Regional Drive, Concord, NH 0330; tel. 603/271-2323; Doris G. Nuttelman, RN, Ed.D., Executive Director

Rehabilitation

Vocational Rehabilitation Division, 78 Regional Drive, Concord, NH 03301; tel. 603/271-3471; Bruce A. Archambault, Director

NEW JERSEY
The Honorable Christine T. Whitman, Governor, 609/292-6000

Health

New Jersey Department of Health and Senior Services, Office of the Commissioner, P.O. Box 360, Trenton, NJ 08625-0360; tel. 609/292-7837; FAX. 609/984-5474; Len Fishman, State Commissioner of Health and Senior Services

Facilities

Health Facilities Construction Service, CN-367, 300 Whitehead Road, Trenton, NJ 08625; tel. 609/588-7731; FAX. 609/588-7823; Kenneth A. Hess, Director

N.J. Department of Health and Senior Services, Office of the Commissioner, CN-360, Trenton, NJ 08625; tel. 609/292-7874; FAX. 609/984-5474; Susan C. Reinhard, RN, Ph.D., Deputy Commissioner Senior Services

Family

Division of Family Health Services, 50 East State Street, CN-364, Trenton, NJ 08625; tel. 609/292-4043; FAX. 609/292-9599; Henry Spring, M.D., Esq.

Licensing

New Jersey Department of Health and Senior Services, Certificate of Need and Acute Care Licensing, P.O. Box 360, Trenton, NJ 08625-0360; tel. 609/292-8773; FAX. 609/292-3780; Darcy Saunders, Director

Planning

Division of Health Care Systems Analysis, CN-360, Trenton, NJ 08625; tel. 609/292-8772; FAX. 609/984-3165; Maria Morgan, Assistant Commissioner

Systems

Office of Managed Care, New Jersey State Department of Health, P.O. Box 360, Trenton, NJ 08625; tel. 609/633-0660; FAX. 609/633-0807; Edwin V. Kelleher, Chief

Children

Maternal Child Health and Regional Services, New Jersey Department of Health and Senior Services, 50 East State Street, CN 364, Trenton, NJ 08625-0364; tel. 609/292-5656; FAX. 609/292-3580

Welfare

Division of Family Development, CN-716, Hamilton Township, NJ 08625; tel. 609/588-2000; FAX. 609/588-3369; Karen D. Highsmith, Director

Other

Medical Examiners

State Board of Medical Examiners, 140 East Front Street, Second Floor, Trenton, NJ 08608; tel. 609/826-7100; FAX. 609/984-3930; Kevin B. Earle, Executive Director

Nursing

New Jersey Board of Nursing, P.O. Box 45010, Newark, NJ 07101; tel. 201/504-6430; FAX. 201/648-3481; Patricia Polansky, Executive Director

Other

Department of Law and Public Safety, CN080, Trenton, NJ 08625; tel. 609/292-4925; FAX. 609/292-3508; Peter Verniero, Attorney General

Division of Consumer Affairs, 124 Halsey Street, P.O. Box 45027, Newark, NJ 07101; tel. 201/504-6534; FAX. 201/648-3538; Mark S. Herr, Director

NEW MEXICO
The Honorable Gary E. Johnson, Governor, 505/827-3000

Health

Department of Health, P.O. Box 26110, Santa Fe, NM 87502-6110; tel. 505/827-2613; FAX. 505/827-2530; J. Alex Valdez, Secretary

Health

Public Health Division, Department of Health, P.O. Box 26110, Santa Fe, NM 87502-6110; tel. 505/827-2389; FAX. 505/827-2329; William H. Wiese, Director

Other

Health Facility Licensing and Certification Bureau, Long Term Care Program, 525 Camino de los Marquez, Suite Two, Santa Fe, NM 87501; tel. 505/827-4200; FAX. 505/827-4203; Matthew M. Gervase, Bureau Chief

Welfare

Human Services Department, P.O. Box 2348, Santa Fe, NM 87504-2348; tel. 505/827-7750; FAX. 505/827-6286; Duke Rodriguez, Secretary

Social Services

Social Services Division, P.O. Box 2348, Santa Fe, NM 87504-2348; tel. 505/827-4439; Jack Callaghan, Ph.D., Director

Other

Income Support Division, P.O. Box 2348, Santa Fe, NM 87504-2348; tel. 505/827-7252; FAX. 505/827-7203

Insurance

New Mexico Department of Insurance, P.O. Drawer 1269, Santa Fe, NM 87504-1269; tel. 505/827-4601; FAX. 505/827-4734; Helen Hordes, Manager, Life and Health Forms Division

Other

State Corporation Commission, P.O. Drawer 1269, Santa Fe, NM 87504; tel. 505/827-4529; Eric P. Serna, Chairman

Other

Education

State Department of Education, Education Building, 300 Don Gaspar, Santa Fe, NM 87501-2786; tel. 505/827-6516; FAX. 505/827-6696; Michael J. Davis, State Superintendent of Public Instruction

Medical Examiners

New Mexico Board of Medical Examiners, 491 Old Santa Fe Trail, Lamy Building, Second Floor, Santa Fe, NM 87501; tel. 505/827-5022; FAX. 505/827-7377; Kristen A. Hedrick, Executive Secretary

Nursing

State of New Mexico, Board of Nursing, 4206 Louisiana, N.E., Suite A, Albuquerque, NM 87109; tel. 505/841-8340; FAX. 505/841-8340; Debra Brady, Executive Director

Rehabilitation

Division of Vocational Rehabilitation, 435 St. Michaels Drive, Building D, Santa Fe, NM 87505; tel. 505/954-8511; FAX. 505/954-8562; Terry Brigance, Director

NEW YORK
The Honorable George E. Pataki, Governor, 518/474-7516

Health

State Department of Health, Tower Building, Empire State Plaza, Albany, NY 12237; tel. 518/474-2011; FAX. 518/474-5450; Barbara A. DeBuono, M.D., M.P.H., Commissioner

Health

Bureau of Home Health Care Services, New York State Department of Health, Frear Building, 2 Third Street, Troy, NY 12180; tel. 518/271-2741; FAX. 518/271-2771; Dr. Nancy Barhydt, Director

New York State Department of Health, Tower Building, Empire State Plaza, Room 1482, Albany, NY 12237; tel. 518/474-6462; FAX. 518/473-3824

Laboratories

Wadsworth Center for Laboratories and Research, Clinical Lab Evaluation, P.O. Box 509, Empire State Plaza, Albany, NY 12201-0509; tel. 518/474-7592; Dr. Herbert W. Dickerman, M.D., Ph.D., Director

Systems

New York State Department of Health, Office of Managed Care, Bureau of Managed Care Certification and Surveillance, 1911 Corning Tower Building, Empire State Plaza, Albany, NY 12237; tel. 518/473-4842; FAX. 518/473-3583; Vallencia Lloyd, Director

Office of Health Systems Management, Tower Building, Empire State Plaza, Room 1441, Albany, NY 12237-0701; tel. 518/474-7028; FAX. 518/486-2564;

Other

Bureau of Project Management, New York State Department of Health, 433 River Street, Suite 303, Troy, NY 12180-2299; tel. 518/402-0911; FAX. 518/402-0975; Robert J. Stackrow, Director

Welfare

New York State Department of Social Services, 40 North Pearl Street, Albany, NY 12243; tel. 518/474-9003; FAX. 518/474-9004; Brian J. Wing, Acting Commissioner

Other

Education

New York State Education Department, Main Education Building, Room 111, 89 Washington Avenue, Albany, NY 12234; tel. 518/474-5844; FAX. 518/473-4909;

Medicine

New York State Board for Medicine, Cultural Education Center, Albany, NY 12230; tel. 518/474-3841; FAX. 518/473-6995; Thomas J. Monahan, Executive Secretary

Mental Health

New York State Office of Mental Health, 44 Holland Avenue, Albany, NY 12229; tel. 518/474-4403; FAX. 518/474-2149; James L. Stone, M.S.W., Commissioner

Mental Retardation

Office of Mental Retardation and Developmental Disabilities, 44 Holland Avenue, Albany, NY 12229; tel. 518/473-1997; FAX. 518/473-1271; Thomas A. Maul, Commissioner

Nursing

State Board for Nursing, New York State Education Department, Cultural Education Center, Room 3023, Albany, NY 12230; tel. 518/474-3843; FAX. 518/473-0578; Milene A. Sower, Ph.D., RN, Executive Secretary

Section C

Rehabilitation
New York State Education Department, Vocational and Educational Services for Individuals with Disabilities, One Commerce Plaza, Suite 1606, Albany, NY 12234; tel. 518/474-2714; Lawrence C. Gloeckler, Deputy Commissioner

Substance Abuse
New York State Office of Alcoholism and Substance Abuse Services, 1450 Western Avenue, Albany, NY 12203; tel. 518/457-2061; FAX. 518/457-5474; Jean Somers Miller, Commissioner

NORTH CAROLINA
The Honorable James B. Hunt, Jr., Governor, 919/733-4240

Health
Department of Human Resources, 101 Blair Drive, Raleigh, NC 27603; tel. 919/733-4534; FAX. 919/715-4645; C. Robin Britt, Sr., Secretary

Facilities
Department of Health and Human Services, Division of Facility Services, 701 Barbour Drive, Raleigh, NC 27603; tel. 919/733-2342; FAX. 919/733-2757; Lynda D. McDaniel, Director

Health
Department of Health and Human Services, P.O. Box 29526, Raleigh, NC 27626-0526; tel. 919/715-4126; FAX. 919/715-4685; Ronald H. Levine, M.D., M.P.H., Deputy Secretary

Mental Health
Division of Mental Health, Developmental Disabilities and Substance Abuse Services, 325 North Salisbury Street, Raleigh, NC 27603; tel. 919/733-7011; FAX. 919/733-9455; John F. Baggett, Ph. D., Director

Rehabilitation
Division of Vocational Rehabilitation Services, 805 Ruggles Drive, P.O. Box 26053, Raleigh, NC 27611; tel. 919/733-3364; FAX. 919/733-7968; Bob H.. Philbeck, Director

Welfare

Medical Assistance
Division of Medical Assistance, 1985 Umstead Drive, P.O. Box 29529, Raleigh, NC 27626-0529; tel. 919/857-4011; FAX. 919/733-6608; Paul R. Perruzzi, Director

Insurance
Department of Insurance, P.O. Box 26387, Raleigh, NC 27611; tel. 919/733-7343; FAX. 919/733-6495; James E. Long, Commissioner

Other

Medical Examiners
North Carolina Medical Board, P.O. Box 20007, Raleigh, NC 27619; tel. 919/828-1212; FAX. 919/828-1295; Andrew W. Watry, Executive Director

Nursing
North Carolina Board of Nursing, P.O. Box 2129, Raleigh, NC 27602; tel. 919/782-3211; FAX. 919/781-9461; Mary P. Johnson, RN, MSN, Executive Director

NORTH DAKOTA
The Honorable Edward T. Schafer, Governor, 701/328-2200

Health
State Department of Health, 600 East Boulevard Avenue, Bismarck, ND 58505-0200; tel. 701/328-2372; FAX. 701/328-4727; Londa Rodahl, Administrative Assistant

Facilities
Division of Health Facilities, North Dakota Department of Health, 600 East Boulevard Avenue, Bismarck, ND 58505-0200; tel. 701/328-2352; FAX. 701/328-1890; Fred Gladden, Director

Resources
Health Resources Section, North Dakota Department of Health, 600 East Boulevard Avenue, Bismarck, ND 58505-0200; tel. 701/328-2352; FAX. 701/328-1890; Fred Gladden, Chief

Children
Division of Maternal and Child Health, North Dakota Department of Health, State Capitol, 600 East Boulevard Avenue, Bismarck, ND 58505-0200; tel. 701/328-2493; FAX. 701/328-1412; Sandra Anseth, Director

Welfare

Developmental Disabilities
Developmental Disabilities Unit, Disability Services Division, Department of Human Services, 600 South Second Street, Suite 1A, Bismarck, ND 58504-5729; tel. 701/328-8930; FAX. 701/328-8969; Gene Hysjulien, Director

Medical Services
Medical Services Division, North Dakota Department of Human Services, 600 East Boulevard Avenue, Bismarck, ND 58505-0261; tel. 701/328-2321; FAX. 701/328-1544; David J. Zentner, Director

Mental Health
Division of Mental Health and Substance Abuse Services, 600 S. 2nd Street, Suite 1E, Bismarck, ND 58504-5729; tel. 701/328-8920; FAX. 701/328-8969; Karen Larson, Director

Rehabilitation
Office of Vocational Rehabilitation, Department of Human Services, 400 East Broadway Avenue, Suite 303, Bismarck, ND 58501-4038; tel. 701/328-3999; FAX. 701/328-3976; Gene Hysjulien, Director

Substance Abuse
Division of Alcoholism and Drug Abuse, 600 South Second Street, Suite 1E, Bismarck, ND 58504-5729; tel. 701/328-8920; FAX. 701/328-8969; Karen Larson, Director

Children
Children's Special Health Services, Department of Human Services, State Capitol, 600 East Boulevard Avenue, Bismarck, ND 58505-0269; tel. 701/328-2436; FAX. 701/328-2359; Robert W. Nelson, Director

Other
Office of Economic Assistance, North Dakota Department of Human Services, 600 East Boulevard Avenue, Bismarck, ND 58505-0250; tel. 701/328-4060; FAX. 701/328-1545; Wayne J. Anderson, Deputy Director
Program and Policy, State Capitol, 600 East Boulevard Avenue, Bismarck, ND 58505-0265; tel. 701/328-2310; FAX. 701/328-2359; Carol K. Olson, Executive Director

Insurance
North Dakota Department of Insurance, State Capitol, 600 East Boulevard, Bismarck, ND 58505-0320; tel. 701/328-2440; FAX. 701/328-4880; Glenn Pomeroy, Commissioner

Other

Medical Examiners
North Dakota State Board of Medical Examiners, City Center Plaza, 418 East Broadway Avenue, Suite 12, Bismarck, ND 58501; tel. 701/328-6500; FAX. 701/328-6505; Rolf P. Sletten, Executive Secretary, Treasurer

Nursing
North Dakota Board of Nursing, 919 South Seventh Street, Suite 504, Bismarck, ND 58504-5881; tel. 701/328-9777; FAX. 701/328-9785; Ida H. Rigley, RN, Executive Director

Other
Facility Management Division, Office of Management and Budget, 600 East Boulevard, State Capitol, Bismarck, ND 58505; tel. 701/328-2471; Greg Larson, Director, Facility Management

OHIO
The Honorable George V. Voinovich, Governor, 614/466-3555

Health
Ohio Department of Health, 246 North High Street, Columbus, OH 43266-0588; tel. 614/466-2253; FAX. 614/644-0085; William Ryan, Director

Licensing
Division of Quality Assurance, Ohio Department of Health, 246 North High Street, Columbus, OH 43266-0588; tel. 614/466-8739; FAX. 614/644-0208; Rebecca S. Maust, Chief

Nursing
Ohio Department of Health, Bureau of Local Services, 246 North High Street, Columbus, OH 43266-0118; tel. 614/466-0666; FAX. 614/752-4157; John Wanchick, M.P.A., R.S., Chief

Resources
Ohio Department of Health, Bureau of Quality Assessment and Improvement, 246 North High Street, P.O. Box 118, Columbus, OH 43266-0118; tel. 614/466-3325; FAX. 614/644-8661; Louis Pomerantz, Chief, Bureau of Quality Assessment and Improvement

Substance Abuse
Ohio Department of Alcohol and Drug Addiction Services, Two Nationwide Plaza, 280 North High Street, 12th Floor, Columbus, OH 43215-2537; tel. 614/466-3445; FAX. 614/752-8645; Luceille Fleming, Director

Children
Division of Family and Community Health Services, 246 North High Street, P.O. Box 118, Columbus, OH 43266-0118; tel. 614/466-3263; FAX. 614/728-3616; Kathryn K. Peppe, RN, M.S., Chief

Welfare
Ohio Department of Human Services, 30 East Broad Street, 32nd Floor, Columbus, OH 43266-0423; tel. 614/466-6282; FAX. 614/466-2815; Arnold R. Tompkins, Director

Medical Assistance
Bureau of Medical Assistance, 30 East Broad Street, 31st Floor, Columbus, OH 43266-0423; tel. 614/466-2365; John J. Nichols, Chief

Medical Services
Ohio Department of Human Services, Office of Medicaid, 30 East Broad Street, 31st Floor, Columbus, OH 43266-0423; tel. 614/466-4443; FAX. 614/752-3986; Barbara Coulter Edwards, Deputy Director

Insurance
Department of Insurance, 2100 Stella Court, Columbus, OH 43215-1067; tel. 614/644-2658; FAX. 614/644-3743; Harold T. Duryee, Director

Other
Managed Care Division, 2100 Stella Court, Columbus, OH 43215-1067; tel. 614/644-2661; FAX. 614/644-3741; Teresa Reedus, Senior Contract Analyst

Other

Disability
Bureau of Disability Determination, P.O. Box 359001, Columbus, OH 43235-9001; tel. 614/438-1500; FAX. 614/438-1504; Linda Krauss, Director

Medicine
State Medical Board of Ohio, 77 South High Street, 17th floor, Columbus, OH 43266-0315; tel. 614/466-3934; FAX. 614/728-5946; Ray Q. Bumgarner, Executive Director

Mental Health
Department of Mental Health, 30 East Broad Street, Eighth Floor, Columbus, OH 43266-0414; tel. 614/466-2596; FAX. 614/752-9453; Michael F. Hogan, Ph.D. Director

Mental Retardation
Department of Mental Retardation and Developmental Disabilities, 30 East Broad Street, Suite 1280, Columbus, OH 43266-0415; tel. 614/466-5214; FAX. 614/644-5013; Jerome C. Manuel, Director

Nursing
Ohio Board of Nursing, 77 South High Street, 17th Floor, Columbus, OH 43266-0316; tel. 614/466-3947; Dorothy Fiorino, RN, M.S., Executive Director

Rehabilitation
Ohio Rehabilitation Services Commission, Bureau of Vocational Rehabilitation, 400 East Campus View Boulevard (SW3), Columbus, OH 43235-4604; tel. 614/438-1250; FAX. 614/438-1257; June K. Gutterman, Ed.D., Director

Other
Ohio Rehabilitation Services Commission, Bureau of Services for the Visually Impaired, 400 East Campus View Boulevard, Columbus, OH 43235-4604; tel. 614/438-1255; FAX. 614/438-1257; William A. Casto II, Director

OKLAHOMA
The Honorable Frank Keating, Governor, 405/521-2342

Health

Licensing
Oklahoma State Board of Medical Licensure and Supervision, P.O. Box 18256, Oklahoma City, OK 73154-0256; tel. 405/848-6841; FAX. 405/848-8240; Jan Ewing, Deputy Director

Health
State Department of Health, 1000 Northeast 10th, Oklahoma City, OK 73117-1299; tel. 405/271-4200; FAX. 405/271-3431; Jerry R. Nida, M.D., Commissioner of Health

Dental
State Department of Health, Dental Services, 1000 Northeast 10th Street, Oklahoma City, OK 73117-1299; tel. 405/271-5502; FAX. 405/271-6199; Michael L. Morgan, D.D.S., Chief

Facilities
Special Health Services, 1000 Northeast 10th, Oklahoma City, OK 73117; tel. 405/271-6576; FAX. 405/271-1308; Gary Glover, Chief, Medical Facilities

Health
State Department of Health, Special Health Services, 1000 Northeast 10th, Oklahoma City, OK 73117-1299; tel. 405/271-4200; FAX. 405/271-3431; Brent E. VanMeter, Deputy Commissioner

Laboratories
Public Health Laboratory Services, 1000 Northeast 10th, Oklahoma City, OK 73117-1299; tel. 405/271-5070; FAX. 405/271-4850; Garry McKee, Ph.D., Chief

Nursing
State Department of Health, Nursing Service, 1000 Northeast 10th, Oklahoma City, OK 73117-1299; tel. 405/271-5183; FAX. 405/271-1897; Toni Frioux, M.S., RN, C.N.S.

Children
Maternal and Child Health Service, 1000 Northeast 10th Street, Oklahoma City, OK 73117-1299; tel. 405/271-4477; FAX. 405/271-1011; Edd D. Rhoades, M.D., M.P.H., Chief

Maternal and Infant Health Service, 1000 Northeast 10th Street, Oklahoma City, OK 73117-1299; tel. 405/271-4476; FAX. 405/271-6199; Shari Kinney, RN, M.S., Acting Assistant Chief

Welfare
Oklahoma Health Care Authority, 4545 North Lincoln, Suite 124, Oklahoma City, OK 73105; tel. 405/530-3439; FAX. 405/530-3471; Garth L. Splinter, M.D., M.B.A., Chief Executive Officer

Aging
Aging Services Division, 312 Northeast 28th, Oklahoma City, OK 73105; tel. 405/521-2327; FAX. 405/521-2086; Roy R. Keen, Division Administrator

Children
Oklahoma Health Care Authority, 4545 North Lincoln Boulevard, Suite 124, Oklahoma City, OK 73105; tel. 405/530-3373; FAX. 405/530-3478; Mike Fogarty, State Medicaid Director

Rehabilitation
Rehabilitation Services, 3535 Northwest 58th Street, Suite 500, Oklahoma City, OK 73112-4815; tel. 405/951-3400; FAX. 405/951-3529; Linda Parker, Director

Children
Oklahoma Health Care Authority, Medical Authorization Unit, 4545 North Lincoln Boulevard, Suite 124, Oklahoma City, OK 73105; tel. 405/530-3400; FAX. 405/530-3215; Peggy Davis, Supervisor, Medical Authorization Unit

Other
Mental Health
Department of Mental Health and Substance Abuse Services, P.O. Box 53277, Oklahoma City, OK 73152; tel. 405/522-3877; FAX. 405/522-0637; Sharron D. Boehler, Commissioner

Nursing
Oklahoma Board of Nursing, 2915 North Classen Boulevard, Suite 524, Oklahoma City, OK 73106; tel. 405/962-1800; FAX. 405/962-1821; Sulinda Moffett, RN, Executive Director

OREGON
The Honorable John A. Kitzhaber, Governor, 503/378-3111
Health
Oregon Health Division, 800 Oregon Street, Suite 925, Portland, OR 97232; tel. 503/731-4000; FAX. 503/731-4078; Elinor Hall, M.P.H., Administrator

Facilities
Oregon Health Division, Health Care Licensure and Certification, P.O. Box 14450, Portland, OR 97214-0450; tel. 503/731-4013; FAX. 503/731-4080; Kathleen Smail, Manager

Laboratories
Oregon State Public Health Laboratory, P.O. Box 275, Portland, OR 97207-0275; tel. 503/229-5882; FAX. 503/229-5682; Michael R. Skeels, Ph.D., M.P.H.

Welfare
Family
Adult and Family Services Division, 500 Summer Street, N.E., Salem, OR 97310-1013; tel. 503/945-5601; Sandie Hoback, Administrator

Insurance
Department of Consumer and Business Services, 350 Winter Street, N.E., Salem, OR 97310; tel. 503/947-7200; FAX. 503/378-4351; Nancy Ellison

Other
Mental Health
Mental Health and Developmental Disability Services Division, 2575 Bittern Street, N.E., Salem, OR 97310; tel. 503/945-9449; FAX. 503/378-3796; Barry S. Kast, M.S.W., Administrator

Nursing
Oregon State Board of Nursing, 800 Northeast Oregon Street, Suite 465, Portland, OR 97232-2162; tel. 503/731-4745; FAX. 503/731-4755; Joan C. Bouchard, RN, M.N., Executive Director

Rehabilitation
Vocational Rehabilitation Division, Human Resources Building, 500 Summer Street N.E., Salem, OR 97310-1018; tel. 503/945-5880; FAX. 503/378-3318; Mr. Joil A. Southwell, Administrator

Substance Abuse
Office of Alcohol and Drug Abuse Programs, 500 Summer Street, N.E., Salem, OR 97310-1016; tel. 503/945-5763; FAX. 503/378-8467

Children
Child Development and Rehabilitation Center, Oregon Health Sciences University, Box 574, Portland, OR 97207; tel. 503/494-8362; FAX. 503/494-6868; Clifford J. Sells, M.D., Director

PENNSYLVANIA
The Honorable Tom Ridge, Governor, 717/787-2500
Health
Pennsylvania Department of Health, Health and Welfare Building, Suite 802, Harrisburg, PA 17120; tel. 717/787-6436; FAX. 717/787-0191; Daniel F. Hoffmann, Secretary

Health
Pennsylvania Department of Health, Division of Home Health, 132 Kline Plaza, Suite A, Harrisburg, PA 17104; tel. 717/783-1379; FAX. 717/783-3188; Robert Bastian, Director

Pennsylvania Department of Health, Public Health Programs, 809 Health and Welfare Building, Harrisburg, PA 17120; tel. 717/787-9857; FAX. 717/772-6959; Gary L. Gurian, Deputy Secretary

Laboratories
Department of Health, Bureau of Laboratories, P.O. Box 500, Exton, PA 19341-0500; tel. 610/363-8500; FAX. 610/436-3346; Dr. Bruce Kleger, Director

Planning
Pennsylvania Department of Health, Quality Assurance, Health and Welfare Building, Room 805, P.O. Box 90, Harrisburg, PA 17108; tel. 717/783-1078; FAX. 717/772-6959; Molly Raphael, Deputy Secretary

Quality
Bureau of Facility Licensure and Certification, Health and Welfare Building, Room 930, Harrisburg, PA 17120; tel. 717/787-8015; FAX. 717/787-1491; John C. Hair, Acting Director

Substance Abuse
Pennsylvania Department of Health, Bureau of Drug and Alcohol Programs, Health and Welfare Building, P.O. Box 90, Harrisburg, PA 17108; tel. 717/783-8200, ext.301; FAX. 717/787-6285; Gene R. Boyle, Director

Other
Division of Acute and Ambulatory Care, Health and Welfare Building, Room 532, Harrisburg, PA 17120; tel. 717/783-8980; Jack W. Means Jr., Director

Welfare
Medical Assistance
Pennsylvania Department of Public Welfare, Office of Medical Assistance Programs, Health and Welfare Building, Harrisburg, PA 17120; tel. 717/787-1870; FAX. 717/787-4639; Robert S. Zimmerman, Jr., Deputy Secretary

Family
Office of Children, Youth, and Families, Department of Public Welfare, P.O. Box 2675, Harrisburg, PA 17105-2675; tel. 717/787-4756; FAX. 717/787-0414; Jo Ann R. Lawer, Deputy Secretary

Mental Health
Mental Health and Substance Abuse Services, Health and Welfare Building, Room 502, P.O. Box 2675, Harrisburg, PA 17120; tel. 717/787-6443; FAX. 717/787-5394; Charles G. Curie, Deputy Secretary, Mental Health and Substance Abuse

Other
Office of Income Maintenance, Health and Welfare Building, Room 432, Harrisburg, PA, Street Zip 17120; P.O. Box 2675, Harrisburg, PA 17105; tel. 717/783-3063; FAX. 717/787-6765; Sherri Z. Heller, Deputy Secretary

Insurance
Department of Insurance, 1326 Strawberry Square, Harrisburg, PA 17120; tel. 717/783-0442; FAX. 717/772-1969; M. Diane Koken, Insurance Commissioner

Business Regulation
Pennsylvania Insurance Department, Office of Rate and Policy Regulation, 1311 Strawberry Square, Harrisburg, PA 17120; tel. 717/783-5079; FAX. 717/787-8555; Gregory Martino, Deputy Insurance Commissioner

Other
Laboratories
Division of Laboratory Improvement, Bureau of Laboratories, P.O. Box 500, Exton, PA 19341-0500; tel. 610/363-8500; FAX. 610/436-3346; Joseph W. Gasiewski, Director

Medicine
State Board of Medicine, P.O. Box 2649, Harrisburg, PA 17105-2649; tel. 717/783-1400; FAX. 717/787-7769; Cindy L. Warner, Administrative Offices

Nursing
Pennsylvania State Board of Nursing, Department of State, P.O. Box 2649, Harrisburg, PA 17105-2649; tel. 717/783-7142; FAX. 717/783-0822; Miriam H. Limo, Executive Secretary

Rehabilitation
Office of Vocational Rehabilitation, Labor and Industry Building, Room 1300, Seventh and Forster Streets, Harrisburg, PA 17120; tel. 717/787-5244; FAX. 717/783-5221; Susan L. Aldrete, Executive Director

RHODE ISLAND
The Honorable Lincoln Almond, Governor, 401/277-2080
Health
Department of Health, Three Capitol Hill, Providence, RI 02908-5097; tel. 401/277-2231; FAX. 401/277-6548; Barbara A. DeBuono, M.D., M.P.H., Director, Health

Facilities
Rhode Island Department of Health, Division of Facilities Regulation, Three Capitol Hill, Providence, RI 02908-5097; tel. 401/277-2566; FAX. 401/277-3999; Wayne I. Farrington, Chief

Family
Rhode Island Department of Health, Division of Family Health, Three Capitol Hill, Room 302, Providence, RI 02908-5097; tel. 401/277-1185, ext. 142; FAX. 401/277-1442; William H. Hollinshead, M.D., M.P.H., Medical Director

Mental Health
Rhode Island Department of Mental Health, Retardation and Hospitals, Aime J. Forand Building, 600 New London Avenue, Cranston, RI 02920; tel. 401/464-3201; FAX. 401/464-3204; A. Kathryn Power, Director

Policy
Rhode Island Department of Health, Three Capitol Hill, Providence, RI 02908-5097; tel. 401/222-2231; FAX. 401/222-6548; William J. Waters, Jr., Ph.D., Deputy Director

Regulation
Division of Professional Regulation, Three Capitol Hill, Suite 104, Providence, RI 02908-5097; tel. 401/222-2827; FAX. 401/222-1272; Russell J. Spaight, Administrator

Systems
Rhode Island Department of Health, Office of Health Systems Development, Three Capitol Hill, Providence, RI 02908-5097; tel. 401/222-2788; FAX. 401/273-4350; John X. Donahue, Chief

Section C

Insurance

Division of Insurance, 233 Richmond Street, Suite 233, Providence, RI 02903-4233; tel. 401/277-2223; FAX. 401/751-4887; Charles P. Kwolek, Jr, CPA, Associate Director, Superintendent of Insurance

Business Regulation

Department of Business Regulation, 233 Richmond Street, Suite 237, Providence, RI 02903-4237; tel. 401/222-2246; FAX. 401/222-6098; Barry G. Hittner, Director

Other

Human Services

Department of Human Services, 600 New London Avenue, Cranston, RI 02920; tel. 401/464-3575; FAX. 401/464-2174; John Young, Associate Director, Division of Medical Services

Rehabilitation

Office of Rehabilitation Services, 40 Fountain Street, Providence, RI 02903; tel. 401/421-7005, ext. 301; FAX. 401/421-9259; Raymond A. Carroll, Administrator

Other

Division of Medical Services, 600 New London Avenue, Cranston, RI 02920; tel. 401/464-5274; John Young, Associate Director

SOUTH CAROLINA
The Honorable David M. Beasley, Governor, 803/734-9818

Health

Department of Health and Environmental Control, 2600 Bull Street, Columbia, SC 29201; tel. 803/734-4880; FAX. 803/734-4620; Douglas E. Bryant, Commissioner

Environment

Division of Environmental Health, 2600 Bull Street, Columbia, SC 29201; tel. 803/935-7945; FAX. 803/935-7825; Jack H. Vaughan, Jr., Chief

Laboratories

Bureau of Laboratories, P.O. Box 2202, Columbia, SC 29202; tel. 803/935-7045; FAX. 803/935-7357; Sarah J. Robinson, Acting Chief

Licensing

Department of Health and Environmental Control, Division of Health Licensing, 2600 Bull Street, Columbia, SC 29201; tel. 803/737-7370; FAX. 803/737-7212; Jerry Paul, Director

Long Term Care

South Carolina Department of Health and Environmental Control, Bureau of Home Health Services and Long Term Care, 2600 Bull Street, Columbia, SC 29201; tel. 803/737-3955; FAX. 803/734-3352; Michael Byrd, Chief

Prevention

Division of Preventive and Personal Health, South Carolina Department of Health and Environmental Control, 2600 Bull Street, Columbia, SC 29201; tel. 803/737-4040; FAX. 803/737-4036; Mick Henry, Division Chief

Substance Abuse

Bureau of Drug Control, South Carolina Department of Health and Environmental Control, 2600 Bull Street, Columbia, SC 29201; tel. 803/935-7817; FAX. 803/935-7820; Wilbur L. Harling, Director

Children

Bureau of Maternal and Child Health, South Carolina Department of Health and Environmental Control, Robert Mills Complex, P.O. Box 101106, Columbia, SC 29211; tel. 803/737-4190; FAX. 803/734-4442; Marie Meglen, M.S., C.N.M., Bureau Director

Welfare

South Carolina Department of Social Services, P.O. Box 1520, Columbia, SC 29202; tel. 803/734-5760; FAX. 803/734-5597; James T. Clark, State Director

Other

Aging

South Carolina Department of Health and Human Services - Office on Aging, 1801 Main Street, P.O. Box 8206, Columbia, SC 29202-8206; tel. 803/253-6100; FAX. 803/253-4137; Constance C. Rinehart, M.S.W., Deputy Director - Office on Aging

Medical Examiners

South Carolina Department of Labor, Licensing and Regulation, Board of Medical Examiners, 110 Centerview Drive, Suite 202, Columbia, SC, 29210, P.O. Box 11289, Columbia, SC 29211-1289; tel. 803/896-4500; FAX. 803/896-4515; Aaron Kozloski, Board Administrator

Mental Health

State Department of Mental Health, 2414 Bull Street, P.O. Box 485, Columbia, SC 29202; tel. 803/734-7780; FAX. 803/734-7879

Mental Retardation

South Carolina Department of Disabilities and Special Needs, 3440 Harden Street Extension, P.O. Box 4706, Columbia, SC 29240; tel. 803/737-6444; FAX. 803/737-6323; Philip S. Massey, Ph.D, State Director

Nursing

Department of Labor, Licensing and Regulation, Board of Nursing, 110 Centerview Drive, Columbia, SC 29210; tel. 803/896-4550; FAX. 803/896-4515; Patricia Durgin, RN, Nursing Board Administrator

Blind

South Carolina Commission for the Blind, 1430 Confederate Avenue, Columbia, SC 29201; tel. 803/734-7522; FAX. 803/734-7885; Donald Gist, Commissioner

Rehabilitation

Vocational Rehabilitation Department, 1410 Boston Avenue, P.O. Box 15, West Columbia, SC 29171-0015; tel. 803/896-6500; P. Charles LaRosa, Jr., Commissioner

Services

Department of Health and Human Services, 1801 Main Street, P.O. Box 8206, Columbia, SC 29202-8206; tel. 803/253-6100; FAX. 803/253-4137; Gwen Power, Director

Substance Abuse

South Carolina Department of Alcohol and Other Drug Abuse Services, 3700 Forest Drive, Suite 300, Columbia, SC 29204; tel. 803/734-9520; FAX. 803/734-9663; Beverly G. Hamilton, Director

SOUTH DAKOTA
The Honorable William J. Janklow, Governor, 605/773-3212

Health

South Dakota Department of Health, 600 East Capitol, Pierre, SD 57501-2536; tel. 605/773-3361; FAX. 605/773-5683; Doneen B. Hollingsworth, Secretary of Health

Health

Division of Health Systems Development and Regulation, South Dakota Department of Health, Health Building, 600 East Capitol, Pierre, SD 57501; tel. 605/773-3364; FAX. 605/773-5904; Kevin Forsch, Division Director

Licensing

Office of Health Care Facilities Licensure and Certification, State Department of Health, Anderson Building, 445 East Capitol, Pierre, SD 57501; tel. 605/773-3356; FAX. 605/773-6667; Joan Bachman, Administrator

Medical Services

Division of Health, Medical and Laboratory Services, 615 East Fourth Street, Pierre, SD 57501; tel. 605/773-3737; FAX. 605/773-5509; Rex VanDenBerg, Director

Policy

Division of Administration Services, South Dakota Department of Health, 600 East Capitol Avenue, Pierre, SD 57501-2536; tel. 605/773-3361; FAX. 605/773-5683; Joan Adam, Director

Substance Abuse

Division of Alcohol and Drug Abuse, 3800 East Highway 34, Hillsview Plaza, c/o 500 East Capitol, Pierre, SD 57501; tel. 605/773-3123; FAX. 605/773-5483; Gilbert Sudbeck, Director

Welfare

Developmental Disabilities

Division of Developmental Disabilities, Hillsview Plaza, E. Highway 34, c/o 500 East Capitol, Pierre, SD 57501-5070; tel. 605/773-3438; FAX. 605/773-5483; Kim Malsam-Rysdon, Director

Medical Services

Office of Medical Services, 700 Governor's Drive, Pierre, SD 57501-2291; tel. 605/773-3495; FAX. 605/773-4855; David Christensen, Administrator

Social Services

Department of Social Services, 700 Governors Drive, Pierre, SD 57501-2291; tel. 605/773-3165; FAX. 605/773-4855; James W. Ellenbecker, Secretary

Other

Medical Examiners

State Board of Medical and Osteopathic Examiners, 1323 South Minnesota Avenue, Sioux Falls, SD 57105; tel. 605/336-1965; FAX. 605/336-0270; Robert D. Johnson, Executive Secretary

Rehabilitation

Department of Human Services, East Highway 34, Hillsview Plaza, c/o 500 East Capitol, Pierre, SD 57501; tel. 605/773-5990; FAX. 605/773-5483; John N. Jones, Secretary

TENNESSEE
The Honorable Don Sundquist, Governor, 615/741-2001

Health

Department of Health, Cordell Hull Building, 425 Fifth Avenue, N., Third Floor, Nashville, TN 37247-0101; tel. 615/741-5949; FAX. 615/741-0544; Fredia Wadley, State Health Officer

Environment

Bureau of Environment, L & C Tower-21st Floor, 401 Church Street, Nashville, TN 37243-1530; tel. 615/532-0220; FAX. 615/532-0120; Wayne K. Scharber, Assistant Commissioner

Facilities

Department of Health, Office of Health Licensure and Regulation, Cordell Hull Building, 425 Fifth Avenue, N., First Floor, Nashville, TN 37247-0501; tel. 615/741-8402; FAX. 615/741-5542; Judy Eads, Assistant Commissioner

Division of Health Care Facilities, Cordell Hull Building, 426 Fifth Avenue, N., Nashville, TN 37247-0508; tel. 615/741-7221; FAX. 615/741-7051; Marie Fitzgerald, Director

Health

Tennessee Department of Health, Commissioner's Office, Cordell Hull Building, 425 Fifth Avenue,N., Third Floor, Nashville, TN 37217-1010; tel. 615/741-5949; FAX. 615/741-0544; Denise Lewis, Executive Secretary

Laboratories

Tennessee Medical Laboratory Board, Cordell Hull Building, 425 Fifth Avenue,N., First Floor, Nashville, TN 37247-1010; tel. 615/532-5080; FAX. 615/532-5369; Lynda England, BSMT(ASCP), Administrator

Licensing

Board for Licensing Health Care Facilities, Cordell Hull Building, 425 Fifth Avenue, N., Nashville, TN 37247-0530; tel. 615/741-7221; FAX. 615/741-7051; Melanie Hill, Director

Medical Services

Medicaid/TennCare, 729 Church Street, Nashville, TN 37247-6501; tel. 615/741-0213; FAX. 615/741-0882; Theresa Clarke, Assistant Commissioner

Administration

Bureau of Administrative Services, Tennessee Department of Health, Andrew Johnson Tower, Tenth Floor, Nashville, TN 37247-0301; tel. 615/741-3824; FAX. 615/532-9952; Donna Dickens, Director

Welfare

Tennessee Department of Human Services, 400 Deaderick Street, Nashville, TN 37248; tel. 615/741-3241; FAX. 615/741-4165; Robert A. Grunow, Commissioner

Family

Family Assistance, 400 Deaderick Street, Nashville, TN 37248-0070; tel. 615/313-4712; FAX. 615/741-4165; Michael O'Hara, Assistant Commissioner

Rehabilitation

Division of Rehabilitation Services, Citizens Plaza State Office Building, 15th Floor, 400 Deaderick Street, Nashville, TN 37248-0060; tel. 615/313-4714; FAX. 615/741-4165; Jack Van Hooser, Assistant Commissioner

Tennessee Rehabilitation Center, 460 Ninth Avenue, Smyrna, TN 37167; tel. 615/741-4921; FAX. 615/355-1373; H. Key Dillard, Superintendent

Social Services

Department of Children's Services, Program Operations which includes Departmental Services, Regional Services and Resource, Cordell Hull Building, 436 Sixth Avenue, N., Seventh Floor, Nashville, TN 37243-1290; tel. 615/532-1102; FAX. 615/532-6495; Cathy Rogers Smith, Assistant Commissioner, Department Children's

Section C

Other

Aging
Tennessee Commission on Aging, 500 Deaderick Street, Ninth Floor, Nashville, TN 37243-0860; tel. 615/741-2056; FAX. 615/741-3309; James S. Whaley, Executive Director

Medical Examiners
Tennessee Board of Medical Examiners, Cordell Hull Building, 425 Fifth Avenue,N., First Floor, Nashville, TN 37247-1010; tel. 615/532-4384; Jerry Kosten, Administrator

Mental Health
Tennessee Department of Mental Health and Mental Retardation, 710 James Robertson Parkway, Nashville, TN 37243-0675; tel. 615/532-6500; FAX. 615/532-6514; Ben Dishman, Acting Commissioner

Nursing
Tennessee Board of Nursing, Cordell Hull Building, 1st Floor, 425 Fifth Avenue, Nashville, TN 37217-1010; tel. 615/532-5166; Elizabeth J. Lund, RN, Executive Director

Substance Abuse
Bureau of Alcohol and Drug Abuse Services, Cordell Hull Building, 425 Fifth Avenue, Third Floor, Nashville, TN 37247-4401; tel. 615/741-1921; FAX. 615/532-2419; Stephanie W. Perry, M.D., Assistant Commissioner

TEXAS
The Honorable George W. Bush, Governor, 512/463-2000

Health
Texas Department of Health, 1100 West 49th Street, Austin, TX 78756; tel. 512/458-7111, ext. 7375; William R. Archer III, M.D., Commissioner

Data Analysis
Texas Department of Health, Bureau of State Health Data and Policy Analysis, 1100 West 49th Street, Austin, TX 78756; tel. 512/458-7261; FAX. 512/458-7344; Ann Henry, Data Division Director

Licensing
Bureau of Licensing and Certification, Texas Department of Health, 1100 West 49th Street, Austin, TX 78756-3199; tel. 512/834-6645; FAX. 512/834-6653; Maurice B. Shaw, Chief

Health Facility Compliance Division, 1100 West 49th Street, Austin, TX 78756; tel. 512/834-6650; FAX. 512/834-6653; Nance Stearman, RN, M.S.N., Director

Children
Bureau of Children's Health, (Texas Department of Health), 1100 West 49th Street, Austin, TX 78756; tel. 512/458-7700; FAX. 512/458-7203; Jack Baum, D.D.S., Chief

Texas Department of Health, Centers for Minority Health Initiatives and Cultural Competency, 1100 West 49th Street, Suite M543, Austin, TX 78756; tel. 512/458-7555, ext. 3005; FAX. 512/458-7713; John E. Evans, Executive Director

Welfare
Texas Department of Health, 1100 West 49th Street, Austin, TX 78756-3167; tel. 512/338-6501; FAX. 512/338-6945; Randy P. Washington, Deputy Commissioner, Health Care Financing

Insurance
Texas Department of Insurance, P.O. Box 149104, Mail Code 106-1A, Austin, TX 78714-9104; tel. 512/322-3401; FAX. 512/322-3552; Kimberly Stokes, Deputy Commissioner, Life/Health Group

Other

Mental Health
Texas Department of Mental Health and Mental Retardation, 909 West 45th Street, P.O. Box 12668, Capitol Station, Austin, TX 78711-2668; tel. 512/454-3761; FAX. 512/206-4560; Tex Killion, Deputy Medical Director for Administration

Nurse Examiners
Board of Nurse Examiners for the State of Texas, P.O. Box 430, Austin, TX 78767-0430; tel. 512/305-7400; FAX. 512/305-7401; Katherine A. Thomas, M.N., RN, Executive Director

Board of Vocational Nurse Examiners, William P. Hobby Building, 333 Guadalupe Street, Suite 3-400, Austin, TX 78701; tel. 512/305-8100, ext. 205; FAX. 512/305-8101; Marjorie Bronk, Executive Director

UTAH
The Honorable Michael O. Leavitt, Governor, 801/538-1500

Health
Utah Department of Health, 288 North 1460 West, Salt Lake City, UT 84116; tel. 801/538-6111; FAX. 801/538-6306; Rod L. Betit, Executive Director

Environment
Department of Environmental Quality, 168 No 1950 West, Salt Lake City, UT 84116; tel. 801/536-4404; FAX. 801/538-0061; Dianne R. Nielson, Ph.D., Executive Director

Family
Utah Department of Health, Community and Family Health Services Division, P.O. Box 142001, Salt Lake City, UT 84114-2001; tel. 801/538-6901; FAX. 801/538-6510; George Delavan, M.D., Director

Finance
Division of Health Care Financing (Utah Medicaid), P.O. Box 143101, Salt Lake City, UT 84114-3101; tel. 801/538-6406; FAX. 801/538-6099; Michael J. Deily, Director

Health
Utah Department of Health, Bureau of Primary Care and Rural Health Systems, Box 142005, Salt Lake City, UT 84114-2005; tel. 801/538-6113; FAX. 801/538-6387; Robert W. Sherwood, Jr., Bureau Director

Laboratories
Utah Department of Health, Division of Epidemiology and Laboratory Services, 46 North Medical Drive, Salt Lake City, UT 84113; tel. 801/584-8400; FAX. 801/584-8486; Charles D. Brokopp, Dr.P.H., Director

Licensing
Utah Department of Health, Bureau of Licensing, Box 142003, Salt Lake City, UT 84114-2003; tel. 801/538-6152; FAX. 801/538-6325; Debra Wynkoop-Green, Director

Medical Examiner
Office of The Medical Examiners, State of Utah, 48 North Medical Drive, Salt Lake City, UT 84113; tel. 801/584-8410; FAX. 801/584-8435; Todd C. Grey, M.D., Director

Insurance
Insurance Department, State Office Building, Suite 3110, Salt Lake City, UT 84114; tel. 801/538-3800; FAX. 801/538-3829; Merwin U. Stewart

Other

Education
State Office of Education, 250 East 500 South, Salt Lake City, UT 84111; tel. 801/538-7500; FAX. 801/538-7521; Scott W. Bean, Superintendent

Aging
Division of Aging and Adult Services, 120 North 200 West, Room 401, Salt Lake City, UT 84103; tel. 801/538-3910; FAX. 801/538-4395; Helen Goddard, Director

Family
Division of Child and Family Services, P.O. Box 45500, Salt Lake City, UT 84145-0500; tel. 801/538-4100; FAX. 801/538-3993; Mary T. Noonan, Director

Licensing
Division of Occupational and Professional Licensing, Heber M. Wells Building, 160 East 300 South, Box 146741, Salt Lake City, UT 84114-6741; tel. 801/530-6628; FAX. 801/530-6511; J. Craig Jackson, Director

Mental Health
Mental Health, P.O. Box 45500, Salt Lake City, UT 84145-0500; tel. 801/538-4270; Paul Thorpe, Director

Rehabilitation
Utah State Office of Rehabilitation, 250 East 500 South, Salt Lake City, UT 84111; tel. 801/538-7530; FAX. 801/538-7522; Blaine Petersen, Ed.D., Executive Director

Services
Department of Human Services, 120 North 200 West, P.O. Box 45500, Salt Lake City, UT 84145-0500; tel. 801/538-4001; FAX. 801/538-4016; Robin Arnold-Williams, Executive Director

Division of Services for People With Disabilities, 120 North 200 West, Suite 411, Salt Lake City, UT 84103; tel. 801/538-4200; FAX. 801/538-4279; Sue Geary, Ph.D., Director

Substance Abuse
Division of Substance Abuse, 120 North 200 West, Room 201, Salt Lake City, UT 84145; tel. 801/538-3939; FAX. 801/538-4696; F. Leon PoVey, Director

Children
Youth Corrections, P.O. Box 45500, Salt Lake City, UT 84145-0500; tel. 801/538-4330; FAX. 801/538-4334; Gary K. Dalton, Director

VERMONT
The Honorable Howard Dean, M.D., Governor, 802/828-3333

Health
Vermont Department of Health, 108 Cherry Street, P.O. Box 70, Burlington, VT 05402; tel. 802/863-7280; FAX. 802/863-7425; Jan K. Carney, M.D., M.P.H., Commissioner

Environment
Environmental Health Division, 108 Cherry Street, P.O. Box 70, Burlington, VT 05402; tel. 802/863-7220; FAX. 802/863-7425; William C. Bress, Ph. D., Director

Laboratories
Vermont Department of Health Laboratory, 195 Colchester Avenue, P.O. Box 1125, Burlington, VT 05402-1125; tel. 802/863-7335; FAX. 802/863-7632; Burton W. Wilcke,Jr.,Ph.D, Director, Division of Health Surveillance

Licensing
Licensing and Protection, Ladd Hall, 103 South Main Street, Waterbury, VT 05671-2306; tel. 802/241-2345; FAX. 802/241-2358; Laine Lucenti, Director

Medical Services
Vermont Department of Health, Division of Community Public Health, P.O. Box 70, Burlington, VT 05402-0070; tel. 802/863-7347; FAX. 802/863-7229; Patricia Berry, Director

Regulation
Vermont Department of Aging and Disabilities, Division of Licensing and Protection, Ladd Hall, 103 South Main Street, Waterbury, VT 05671-2306; tel. 802/241-2345; FAX. 802/241-2358; Robert Aiken, Director

Statistics
Vermont Department of Health, Division of Health Surveillance, Public Health Statistics, 108 Cherry Street, P.O. Box 70, Burlington, VT 05402-0070; tel. 802/863-7300; FAX. 802/865-7701; Karen Baron, Statistical Consultant

Other
Vermont Department of Health Infectious Disease Epidemioology, 108 Cherry Street, P.O. Box 70, Burlington, VT 05402; tel. 802/863-7240; FAX. 802/865-7701; Peter Galbraith, State Epidemiologist

Welfare
Agency of Human Services, 103 South Main Street, Waterbury, VT 05676; tel. 802/241-2220; FAX. 802/241-2979; Cornelius Hogan, Secretary

Department of Social Welfare, 103 South Main Street, Waterbury, VT 05671-1201; tel. 802/241-2853; FAX. 802/241-2830; M. Jane Kitchel, Commissioner

Medical Services
Office of Vermont Health Access/Medicaid, 103 South Main Street, Waterbury, VT 05671-1201; tel. 802/241-2880; FAX. 802/241-2974; Paul Wallace-Brodeur, Acting Director

Mental Health
Department of Developmental and Mental Health Services, Weeks Building, 103 South Main Street, Waterbury, VT 05671-1601; tel. 802/241-2610; FAX. 802/241-1129; Rodney E. Copeland, Ph.D., Commissioner

Rehabilitation
Department of Social and Rehabilitation Services, 103 South Main Street, Waterbury, VT 05671-2401; tel. 802/241-2100; FAX. 802/241-2980; William M. Young, Commissioner

Vocational Rehabilitation Division, 103 South Main Street, Osgood Building, Waterbury, VT 05671-2303; tel. 802/241-2186; FAX. 802/241-3359; Diane P. Dalmasse, Director

Substance Abuse
Office of Alcohol and Drug Abuse Programs, 108 Cherry Street, Burlington, VT 05401; tel. 802/651-1550; FAX. 802/651-1573; Thomas E. Perras, Director

Section C

Insurance

Department of Banking, Insurance, Securities and Health Care Administration, 89 Main Street, Drawer 20, Montpelier, VT 05620-3101; tel. 802/828-3301; FAX. 802/828-3306; Elizabeth R. Costle, Commissioner

Other

Nursing

Vermont State Board of Nursing, 109 State Street, Montpelier, VT 05609-1106; tel. 802/828-2396; FAX. 802/828-2484; Anita Ristau, RN, M.S., Executive Director

VIRGINIA
The Honorable James S. Gilmore III, Governor, 804/786-2211

Health

State Department of Health, Main Street Station, P.O. Box 2448, Richmond, VA 23218; tel. 804/786-3561; FAX. 804/786-4616; Randolph L. Gordon, M.D., M.P.H., Commissioner

Licensing

Center for Quality Health Care Services and Consumer Protection, Virginia Department of Health, 3600 Centre, Suite 216, 3600 West Broad Street, Richmond, VA 23230-4920; tel.804/367-2102; FAX. 804/367-2149; Nancy R. Hofheimer, Director

Children

Division of Children's Specialty Services, Virginia Department of Health, P.O. Box 2448, Room 135, Richmond, VA 23218; tel. 804/786-3691; FAX. 804/225-3307; Nancy R. Bullock, RN, M.P.H., Director

Division of Women's and Infants' Health, 1500 East Main Street, Suite 135, P.O. Box 2448, Richmond, VA 23218-2448; tel. 804/786-5916; FAX. 804/371-6032; Carolyn L. Beverly, M.D., M.P.H., Director

Welfare

Virginia Department of Social Services, 730 East Broad Street, Richmond, VA 23219-1949; tel. 804/692-1900; FAX. 804/692-1849; Carol A. Brunty, Commissioner

Insurance

State Corporation Commission-Bureau of Insurance, P.O. Box 1157, Richmond, VA 23218; tel. 804/371-9869; FAX. 804/371-9511; Douglas C. Stolte, Deputy Insurance Commissioner

Insurance

Bureau of Insurance, Virginia State Corporation Commission, P.O. Box 1157, Richmond, VA 23218; tel. 804/371-9691; FAX. 804/371-9944; Life and Health Consumer Services Section

Business Regulation

State Corporation Commission Bureau of Insurance, Company Licensing and Regulatory Compliance Section, P.O. Box 1157, Richmond, VA 23209; tel. 904/371-9636; FAX. 904/371-9396; Andy Delbridge, Supervisor

Other

Aging

Department for the Aging, 1600 Forest Avenue, Suite 102, Richmond, VA 23229; tel. 804/662-9333; FAX. 804/662-9354; Dr. Ann Y McGee, Commissioner

Medical Assistance

Department of Medical Assistance Services, 600 East Broad Street, Suite 1300, Richmond, VA 23219; tel. 804/786-8099; FAX. 804/371-4981; Robert W. Lauterberg, Acting Director

Medicine

Virginia State Board of Medicine, 6606 West Board Street, Fourth Floor, Richmond, VA 23230-1717; tel. 804/662-9908; FAX. 804/662-9943; Warren W. Koontz, Jr., M.D., Executive Director

Mental Health

Department of Mental Health, Mental Retardation and Substance Abuse Services, P.O. Box 1797, Richmond, VA 23214; tel. 804/786-3921; FAX. 804/371-6638; Richard E. Kellogg, Acting Commissioner

Rehabilitation

Department of Rehabilitative Services, 8004 Franklin Farms Drive, Richmond, VA 23288; tel. 804/662-7000; FAX. 804/662-9532; John Vaughan, Commissioner

WASHINGTON
The Honorable Gary Locke, Governor, 360/753-6780

Health

State Department of Social and Health Services, P.O. Box 45080, Olympia, WA 98504-5080; tel. 206/753-1777; FAX. 206/586-5874; Jane Beyer, Assistant Secretary, Medical Assistance, Administration

Health

Department of Health, Facilities and Services Licensing, P.O. Box 47852, Olympia, WA 98504-7852; tel. 206/705-6652; FAX. 206/705-6654; Kathy Stout, Director

Department of Health, Office of Emergency Medical and Trauma Prevention, P.O. Box 47853, Olympia, WA 98504-7853; tel. 360/705-6700; FAX. 360/705-6706; Janet Griffith, Director

Medical Assistance

Medical Assistance Administration, P.O. Box 45080, Olympia, WA 98504-5080; tel. 360/902-7807; FAX. 360/902-7855; Jane Beyer, Assistant Secretary

Policy

Medical Assistance Administration, P.O. Box 45506, Olympia, WA 98504-5506; tel. 360/664-9419; FAX. 360/664-3884; Nancy L. Fisher, RN, MD, MPH, Medical Director

Rehabilitation

Division of Vocational Rehabilitation, P.O. Box 45340, Olympia, WA 98504-5340; tel. 206/438-8000; FAX. 206/438-8007; Jeanne Munro, Director

Substance Abuse

Division of Alcohol and Substance Abuse, P.O. Box 45330, Mail Stop 5330, Olympia, WA 98504-5330; tel. 206/438-8200; FAX. 206/438-8078; Ken Stark, Director

Other

Washington State Department of Health, P.O. Box 47812, Mail Stop 7812, Olympia, WA 98504-7812; tel. 206/705-6060; FAX. 206/705-6043; Dan Rubin, Director, Special Projects Office

Insurance

Office of the Insurance Commissioner, Insurance Building, P.O. Box 40255, Olympia, WA 98504-0255; tel. 206/753-7300; FAX. 206/586-3535; Deborah Senn, Insurance Commissioner

Other

Licensing

Health Systems Quality Assurance, Department of Health, 1112 Quince, Mail Stop 7850, Olympia, WA 98504-7850; tel. 360/753-2241; FAX. 360/664-0398; Sherman Cox, Assistant Secretary

Nursing

Washington State Nursing Care Quality Assurance Commission, 1300 Southeast Quince Street, P.O. Box 47864, Olympia, WA 98504-7864; tel. 206/664-4100; FAX. 206/586-5935; Patty L. Hayes, RN, M.N., Interim Executive Director

WEST VIRGINIA
The Honorable Cecil H. Underwood, Governor, 304/558-2000

Health

Bureau for Public Health, Building Three, Room 518, State Capitol Complex, Charleston, WV 25305; tel. 304/558-2971; FAX. 304/558-1035; Henry G. Taylor, M.D., M.P.H., Commissioner

Community

Office of Community and Rural Health Services, Bureau for Public Health, 1411 Virginia Street, E., Charleston, WV 25301-3013; tel. 304/558-0580; FAX. 304/558-1437

Environment

Office of Environmental Health Services, Morrison Building, 815 Quarrier Street, Suite 418, Charleston, WV 25301-2616; tel. 304/558-2981; FAX. 304/558-1291; C. Russell Rader, P.E., Director

Licensing

Office of Health Facility Licensure and Certification, West Virginia Division of Health, Capitol Complex, 1900 Kanawha Boulevard, E., Building Three, Suite 550, Charleston, WV 25305; tel. 304/558-0050; FAX. 304/558-2515; John Wilkinson, Director

Medical Examiner

Office of Chief Medical Examiner, State of West Virginia, 701 Jefferson Road, South Charleston, WV 25309; tel. 304/558-3920; FAX. 304/558-7886; James A. Kaplan, M.D., Chief Medical Examiner

Substance Abuse

Division on Alcoholism and Drug Abuse, Capitol Complex, Building Six, Room B-738, Charleston, WV 25305; tel. 304/558-2276; FAX. 304/558-1008; DeDe Serverino, Acting Director

Other

West Virginia Department of Health and Human Resources, Division of Primary Care and Recruitment, 1411 Virginia Street, E., Charleston, WV 25301; tel. 304/558-4007; FAX. 304/558-1437; Frances L. Jackson, Director

Welfare

Department of Health and Human Resources, Capitol Complex, Building Three, Room 206, Charleston, WV 25305; tel. 304/558-0684; FAX. 304/558-1130; Joan E. Ohl, Secretary

Children

Children with Special Health Care Needs, 1116 Quarrier Street, Charleston, WV 25301; tel. 304/558-3071; FAX. 304/558-2866; Patricia Kent, MSW, Administrative Director

Other

Division of Medical Care, Department of Human Services, 1900 Washington Street, E., Charleston, WV 25305; tel. 304/348-8990; Helen Condry, Director

Insurance

Insurance Commissioners Office, P.O. Box 50540, Charleston, WV 25305-0540; tel. 304/558-3354; FAX. 304/558-0412; Hanley C. Clark, Commissioner

Financial

Office of the West Virginia Insurance Commissioner, 1124 Smith Street, Charleston, WV 25301; tel. 304/558-2100; FAX. 304/558-1365; Jeffrey W. VanGilder, Director, Chief Examiner

Other

Education

West Virginia Department of Education, Division of Technical and Adult Education Services, 1900 Kanawha Boulevard, E, Bldg. 6 Room B221, Charleston, WV 25305-0330; tel. 304/558-2346, ext. 523; FAX. 304/558-3946; Adam Sponaugle, Assistant State Superintendent

Medicine

West Virginia Board of Medicine, 101 Dee Drive, Charleston, WV 25311; tel. 304/558-2921; FAX. 304/558-2084; Ronald D. Walton, Executive Director

Nurse Examiners

West Virginia Board of Examiners for Registered Professional Nurses, 101 Dee Drive, Charleston, WV 25311-1620; tel. 304/558-3596; FAX. 304/558-3666; Laura S. Rhodes, M.S.N., RN, Executive Secretary

Rehabilitation

Division of Rehabilitation Services, P.O. Box 50890, State Capitol Complex, Charleston, WV 25305-0890; tel. 304/766-4601; FAX. 304/766-4905; James S. Jeffers, Director

WISCONSIN
The Honorable Tommy G. Thompson, Governor, 608/266-1212

Health

Department of Health and Family Services, P.O. Box 7850, Madison, WI 53707-7850; tel. 608/266-9622; FAX. 608/266-7882; Joe Leean, Secretary

Bureau of Public Health, P.O. Box 309, Madison, WI 53701; tel. 608/266-1704; FAX. 608/267-4853

Finance

Bureau of Health Care Financing (Wisconsin Medicaid), One West Wilson Street, Suite 250, P.O. Box 309, Madison, WI 53701-0309; tel. 608/266-2522; FAX. 608/266-1096; Peggy L. Bartels, Director

Health

Bureau of Health Services, P.O. Box 7925, Madison, WI 53707-7925; tel. 608/267-1720; FAX. 608/261-7103; Sharon Zunker, Director

State Division of Health, One West Wilson Street, Room 218, P.O. Box 309, Madison, WI 53701-0309; tel. 608/266-1511; FAX. 608/267-2832; John D. Chapin, Administrator

Prevention

Bureau of Public Health, 1414 East Washington Avenue, Room 233, Madison, WI 53703-3044; tel. 608/266-1251; FAX. 608/264-6078; Kenneth Baldwin, Director

Quality

Bureau of Quality Assurance, Division of Supportive Living, Department of Health and Family Services, P.O. Box 309, Madison, WI 53701; tel. 608/267-7185; FAX. 608/267-0352; Judy Fryback, Director, Bureau of Quality Assurance

Rehabilitation

Division of Vocational Rehabilitation, Box 7852, Madison, WI 53707-7852; tel. 608/243-5600; FAX. 608/243-5680; Judy Norman-Nunnery, Administrator

Statistics

Center for Health Statistics, P.O. Box 309, Madison, WI 53701-0309; tel. 608/266-1334; FAX. 608/261-6380; James John Vaura, Director

Insurance

Office of the Commissioner of Insurance, 121 East Wilson Street, P.O. Box 7873, Madison, WI 53707-7873; tel. 608/266-3585; FAX. 608/266-9935; Linda Keegan, Public Information Officer

Other

Medical Examiners

Wisconsin Medical Examining Board, 1400 East Washington Avenue, P.O. Box 8935, Madison, WI 53708; tel. 608/266-2811; FAX. 608/267-0644; Patrick D. Braatz, Bureau Director

Professions

Department of Regulation and Licensing, 1400 East Washington Avenue, Room 173, P.O. Box 8935, Madison, WI 53708-8935; tel. 608/266-8609; FAX. 608/267-0644; Grace Schwingel, Secretary

Regulatory

State of Wisconsin, Department of Regulation and Licensing, 1400 East Washington Avenue, Suite 173, P.O. Box 8935, Madison, WI 53708-8935; tel. 608/266-8609; FAX. 608/267-0644; Marlene A. Cummings, Secretary

Children

Division for Learning Support: Equity and Advocacy, 125 South Webster Street, P.O. Box 7841, Madison, WI 53707-7841; tel. 608/266-8960; FAX. 608/267-3746; Michael J. Thompson, Student Services, Prevention and Wellness

Other

State Department of Public Instruction, 125 South Webster Street, P.O. Box 7841, Madison, WI 53707-7841; tel. 608/266-1771; FAX. 608/267-1052; John T. Benson, State Superintendent

WYOMING
The Honorable Jim Geringer, Governor, **307/777-7434**

Health

Department of Health, 117 Hathaway Building, Cheyenne, WY 82002; tel. 307/777-7656; FAX. 307/777-7439;

Facilities

Health Facilities Licensing, Department of Health, Metropolitan Bank Building, Eighth Floor, Cheyenne, WY 82002; tel. 307/777-7123; FAX. 307/777-5970; Charlie Simineo, Program Manager

Medical Assistance

Division of Health Care Financing, 6101 Yellowstone Road, Room 259B, Cheyenne, WY 82002; tel. 307/777-7531; FAX. 307/777-6964; James D. Shepard, Administrator

Medical Services

Department of Health, 117 Hathaway Building, Cheyenne, WY 82002; tel. 307/777-7656; FAX. 307/777-7439;

Prevention

Preventive Medicine, Hathaway Building, 2300 Capitol Avenue, Cheyenne, WY 82002; tel. 307/777-6004; FAX. 307/777-3617;

Children

Childrens Health Service, Department of Health, Hathaway Building, Fourth Floor, Cheyenne, WY 82002; tel. 307/777-7941; FAX. 307/777-5402; Cathy Parish, Program Manager

Welfare

Department of Family Services, Hathaway Building, Third Floor, 2300 Capitol Avenue, Cheyenne, WY 82002-0490; tel. 307/777-7561; FAX. 307/777-7747; Shirley R. Carson, Director

Other

Aging

Wyoming Department of Health, Division on Aging, 139 Hathaway Building, Cheyenne, WY 82002; tel. 800/442-2766; FAX. 307/777-5340; Wayne A. Milton, Administrator

Medical Examiners

Wyoming Board of Medicine, The Colony Building, Second Floor, 211 West 19th Street, Cheyenne, WY 82002; tel. 307/778-7053; FAX. 307/778-2069; Carole Shotwell, Executive Secretary

Nursing

Wyoming State Board of Nursing, 2020 Carey Avenue, Suite 110, Cheyenne, WY 82002; tel. 307/777-7601; FAX. 307/777-3519; Toma A. Nisbet, RN, M.S., Executive Director

Rehabilitation

Division of Vocational Rehabilitation, Herschler Building, Room 1128, Cheyenne, WY 82002; tel. 307/777-7385; FAX. 307/777-5939; Gary W. Child, Administrator

Community

Division of Behavioral Health, 447 Hathaway Building, Cheyenne, WY 82002-0480; tel. 307/777-7094; FAX. 307/777-5580; Pablo Hernandez, M.D., Administrator

U. S. Associated Areas

GUAM

Health

Department of Public Health and Social Services, Box 2816, Agana, GU 96932; tel. 671/735-7102; FAX. 671/734-5910; Dennis G. Rodriguez, Director

Planning

Guam Health Planning and Development Agency, P.O. Box 2950, Agana, GU 96910; tel. 671/477-3920; FAX. 671/477-3956; Helen B. Ripple, Director

Welfare

Division of Public Welfare, Box 2816, Agana, GU 96910; tel. 671/735-7274; FAX. 671/734-7015; Adoracion A. Solidum, Acting Chief Human Services Administrator

Other

Rehabilitation

Department of Vocational Rehabilitation, Government of Guam, 122 Harmon Plaza, Suite B201, Harmon Industrial Pa, GU 96911; tel. 671/646-9468; FAX. 671/649-7672; Albert San Agustin, Acting Director

PUERTO RICO

Health

Puerto Rico Department of Health, Building A-Medical Center, Call Box 70184, San Juan, PR 00936; tel. 809/766-1616; FAX. 809/766-2240; Carmen A. Feliciano-De-Melecio, Secretary, Health

Dental

Dental Health, Building A-Medical Center, Call Box 70184, San Juan, PR 00936; tel. 809/751-4750; FAX. 809/765-5675; Wanda Urbiztondo, D.M.D., Oral Health Coordinator

Environment

Environmental Health, Department of Health, Building A, Psiq Hospital, Box 70184, San Juan, PR 00936-0184; tel. 787/274-7798; FAX. 787/758-6285; Hernan Horta, Assistant Secretary, Environmental Health

Mental Health

Mental Health and Anti-Addiction Services Administration, P.O. Box 21414, San Juan, PR 00928-1414; tel. 809/764-3670; FAX. 809/765-5895; Jose Acevedo, Administrator

Prevention

Department of Health, Secretaryship for Preventive Medicine and Family Health, Building E-Medical Center, Call Box 70184, San Juan, PR 00936; tel. 809/765-0482; FAX. 809/765-5675; Dr. Raul G. Castellanos Bran, Director, Division of Family Health

Administration

Administration, Building A-Medical Center, Call Box 70184, San Juan, PR 00936; tel. 809/765-1616; FAX. 809/250-6547; Antonia Pizarrro Lago, Assistant Secretary for Administration

Other

Legal Services, Building A-Medical Center, Call Box 70184, San Juan, PR 00936; tel. 809/766-1616; FAX. 809/766-2240; J. Gerardo Cruz-Arroyo, Esq. General Counsel

Welfare

Department of Family, Call Box 11398, San Juan, PR 00910; tel. 809/721-4624; FAX. 809/723-1223; Carmen L. Rodriguez de Rivera, Secretary

Other

Rehabilitation

Vocational Rehabilitation Program, Department of Social Services, Apartado 191118, San Juan, PR 00919-1118; tel. 809/725-1792; FAX. 809/721-6286; Sr. Francisco Vallejo, Assistant Secretary

VIRGIN ISLANDS

Health

Virgin Islands Department of Health, St. Thomas Hospital, 48 Sugar Estate, St. Thomas, VI 00802; tel. 809/774-0117; FAX. 809/777-4001; Ralph A. de Chabert, M.D., Acting Commissioner

Environment

Division of Environmental Health, Old Hospital Complex, Charlotte Amalie, St. Thomas, VI 00802; tel. 809/774-9000, ext. 4644; FAX. 809/776-7899; Laura A. Hassell, Director

Medical Services

Division of Hospitals and Medical Services, Roy Lester Schneider Hospital, 9048 Sugar Estate, St. Thomas, VI 00802; tel. 809/776-3687; FAX. 809/777-8421; Bruce Goldman, Chief Executive Officer

Mental Health

Division of Mental Health, Alcoholism, and Drug Dependency Services, Barbel Plaza South, St. Thomas, VI 00802; tel. 340/774-4888; FAX. 340/774-4701; Mr. Carlos Ortiz, Director

Prevention

Prevention, Health, Promotion and Protection, Department of Health, Charles Harwood Hospital, 3500 Richmond Christiansted, St. Croix, VI 00820-4300; tel. 809/773-1311; FAX. 809/772-5895; Olaf G. Hendricks, M.D., Assistant Commissioner

Children

Division of Maternal and Child Health Services, Virgin Islands Department of Health, Nisky Center Suite 210, St. Thomas, VI 00801; tel. 809/776-3580; FAX. 809/774-8633; Dr. Mavis Matthew, Director

Other

Department of Health, Division of Financial Services, Knud Hansen Complex, St. Thomas, VI 00802; tel. 809/774-3171; FAX. 809/777-5120; Alphonse J. Stalliard, Deputy Commissioner

Welfare

Virgin Islands Department of Human Services, Knud Hansen Complex, Building A, 1303 Hospital Ground, St. Thomas, VI 00802; tel. 340/774-1166; FAX. 340/774-3466; Sedonie Halbert, Acting Commissioner

Other

Rehabilitation

Disabilities and Rehabilitation Services, Department of Human Services, Knud Hansen Complex-Building A, 1303 Hospital Ground, St. Thomas, VI 00802; tel. 809/774-0930; FAX. 809/774-3466; Sedonie Halbert, Administrator

Canada

ALBERTA

Health

Department of Family and Social Services, 109 Street and 97 Avenue, 104 Legislature Building, Edmonton, AB T5K 2B6; tel. 403/427-2606; FAX. 403/427-0954; Dr. Lyle Oberg, Minister

BRITISH COLUMBIA

Health

Ministry of Health, Parliament Building, Room 306, Victoria, BC V8V 1X4; tel. 604/387-5394; FAX. 604/387-3696; The Honorable Joy K. MacPhail

MANITOBA

Health

Department of Health, 302 Legislative Building, Winnipeg, MB R3C 0V8; tel. 204/945-3731; FAX. 204/945-0441; The Honorable Darren Praznik, Minister

Other

Community

Department of Manitoba Family Services, 450 Broadway, Room 357, Legislative Building, Winnipeg, MB R3C 0V8; tel. 204/945-4173; FAX. 204/945-5149; The Honorable Bonnie Mitchelson, Minister

NEW BRUNSWICK

Health

Department of Health and Community Services, Box 5100, Fredericton, NB E3B 5G8; tel. 506/453-2581; FAX. 506/453-5243; The Honorable Russell H. T. King, M.D.

NEWFOUNDLAND

Health

Department of Health, Confederation Building, P.O. Box 8700, St. John's, NF A1B 4J6; tel. 709/729-3124; FAX. 709/729-0121; Joan Marie Alyward, Minister, Health and Community Services

NOVA SCOTIA

Health

Department of Health, P.O. Box 488, Halifax, NS B3J 2R8; tel. 902/424-5818; FAX. 902/424-0559; The Honorable James Smith, M.D.

PRINCE EDWARD ISLAND

Health

Department of Health and Social Services, Sullivan Building, Second Floor, P.O. Box 2000, Charlottetown, PE C1A 7N8; tel. 902/368-4930; FAX. 902/368-4969; The Honorable Walter A. McEwen, Q.C./Minister

QUEBEC

Health

Ministry of Health and Social Services, Ministere de la Sante et des Services Sociaux, 1075 Chemin Ste-Foy, 15e Etage, Quebec, PQ G1S 2M1; tel. 418/643-3160; FAX. 418/644-4534; Jean Rochon, Minister

SASKATCHEWAN

Health

Department of Health, 3475 Albert Street, Third Floor, Regina, SK S4S 6X6; tel. 306/787-3168; FAX. 306/787-8677; The Honorable, Clay Serby, Minister

Health Care Providers

Health Maintenance Organizations

The following is a list of Health Maintenance Organizations developed with the assistance of state government agencies and the individual facilities listed.

We present this list simply as a convenient directory. Inclusion or omission of any organization indicates neither approval nor disapproval by Healthcare InfoSource, Inc., a subsidiary of the American Hospital Association.

United States

ALABAMA

Apex Healthcare of Alabama, Inc., 104 Inverness Center Parkway, Suite 230, Birmingham, AL 35243; tel. 334/279-5000; Stan Sherlin, Executive Director

CACH HMO, Inc., 1600 7th Avenue South, Birmingham, AL 35233; tel. 205/939-6905; Mike Burgess, CEO

CIGNA Healthcare of Georgia, Inc., 31 Inverness Center Parkway, Suite 340, Birmingham, AL 35242; tel. 205/991-1005; David Figliuzzi, Operations Manager

Complete Health, Inc., 2160 Highland Avenue, Birmingham, AL 35205; tel. 205/933-7661; FAX. 205/933-0083; William W. Featheringill, President, Chief Executive Officer

DirectCare, Inc., 629 Interstate Park Drive, Montgomery, AL 36109; tel. 334/277-6670; T. David Lewis, President & CEO

Foundation Health Plan, 1900 International Park Drive, Suite 200, Birmingham, AL 35243; tel. 205/298-0679; Michael Newman, Acting Executive Director

Health Advantage Plans, Inc., 140 Riverchase Parkway, E., Birmingham, AL 35244; tel. 205/982-8400; FAX. 205/982-8411; James Denman, Chief Executive Officer

Health Maintenance Group of Birmingham, 936 19th Street South, Birmingham, AL 35205; tel. 205/988-2537; Joe Bolen, Director

Health Options, Inc., 532 Riverside Avenue, Jacksonville, FL 32203; tel. 904/791-6086; Harvey Matoren, President

Health Partners of Alabama, Inc., Two Perimeter Park South, Suite 200W, Birmingham, AL 35243; tel. 205/991-6000; Carl Sather, President & CEO

Healthcare USA-Alabama, Inc., 1855 Data Drive, Suite 250, Birmingham, AL 35244; tel. 205/988-9400; Christopher T. Fey, President

Humana Health Plan of Alabama, Inc., 303 Williams Avenue, S.W., Suite 121, Huntsville, AL 35801; tel. 205/532-2000; FAX. 205/532-2025; Rene Moret, Executive Director

PCA Health Plans of Alabama, Inc., 104 Inverness Parkway W., Suite 280, Birmingham, AL 35242; tel. 205/991-6000; Bill Whitaker, President, Chief Operating Officer

PrimeHealth of Alabama, 1400 South University Boulevard, Mobile, AL 36609; tel. 334/342-0022; FAX. 334/342-6428; Becky S. Tate, Director

Primehealth of Alabama, Inc., 1400 South University Boulevard, Suite M, Mobile, AL 36609; tel. 334/342-0022; Becky S. Holliman, President

Principal Health Care of Florida, Inc., 7282 Plantation Road, Suite 200, Pensacola, FL 32504; tel. 904/484-4000; Rebecca McQueen, Executive Director

United Healthcare of Alabama, Inc., 3700 Colonnade Parkway, Birmingham, AL 35243; tel. 205/977-6300; Charles Pitts, President & CEO

Viva Health, Inc., 1401 South 21st Street, Birmingham, AL 35205; tel. 205/939-1718; John Davis, Interim President

ARIZONA

Aetna Health Plan of Arizona, Inc., 7878 North 16th Street, Suite 210, Phoenix, AZ 85020; tel. 602/395-8800; FAX. 602/395-8813; James W. Jones, Acting Vice President, Market Manager

CIGNA HealthCare of Arizona, Inc., 11001 North Black Canyon Highway, Suite 400, Phoenix, AZ 85029; tel. 602/942-4462; FAX. 602/371-2625; Clyde Wright, M.D., President, General Manager

FHP Inc., 410 North 44th Street, P.O. Box 52078, Phoenix, AZ 85072-2078; tel. 602/244-8200; FAX. 602/681-7680; Clifford Klima, President, Arizona Region

First Health of Arizona, Inc., 10448 West Coggins Drive, Sun City, AZ 85351; tel. 602/933-1344; FAX. 602/977-8808; Glenn D. Jones, Administrative Director

HMO Arizona, 2444 West Las Palmaritas, P.O. Box 13466, Phoenix, AZ 85002-3466; tel. 602/864-4250; FAX. 602/864-4035; Deborah Marshall, Director

HealthPartners Health Plans, Inc., (formerly Partners Health Plan of Arizona, Inc.), 333 East Wetmore, Tucson, AZ 85705; tel. 520/696-8020; Jeannie M. Byrne, Administrative Secretary

Humana Health Plan, Inc., Anchor Centre III, 2231 East Camelback Road, Suite 208, Phoenix, AZ 85016; tel. 602/381-4300; FAX. 602/381-4381; Elizabeth Kelly, Associate Executive Director

Intergroup Prepaid Health Plan of Arizona, Inc., 1010 North Finance Center Drive, Suite 100, Tucson, AZ 85710; tel. 602/290-7350; FAX. 602/290-7389; Edward J. Munno, Jr., President, Chief Operating Officer

Premier Healthcare, Inc., d/b/a Premier Healthcare of Arizona, 100 East Clarendon, Suite 400, Phoenix, AZ 85013; tel. 602/248-0404; FAX. 602/248-7771; David K. Stewart, Vice President, Marketing, Sales

United Healthcare of Arizona, Inc., (formerly MetraHealth Care Plan of Arizona, Inc.), 3020 East Camelback, Suite 100, Phoenix, AZ 85016; tel. 602/553-1300; FAX. 602/553-1331; Kathleen Garast, President, Chief Executive Officer

University Physicians Health Maintenance Organization, Inc., 575 East River Road, Tucson, AZ 85704-5822; tel. 520/795-3500

ARKANSAS

American Dental Providers, Inc., 614 Center Street, P.O. Box 34045, Little Rock, AR 72203-4045; tel. 501/376-0544; FAX. 501/371-3820; Robert E. Iriana

American Health Care Providers, Inc., 900 S. Shackleford, #3 Financial Centre, Little Rock, AR 72211; tel. 501/221-3534; Asif Sayeed, President

DentiCare of Arkansas, Inc., Regional Administration Office, 7112 South Mingo, Suite 108, Tulsa, OK 74133; tel. 918/254-9055; FAX. 918/254-9076; John K. Wright, Secretary

HMO Partners, Inc., d/b/a HEALTH ADVANTAGE & HMO Arkansas, 10816 Executive Centre Drive, Suite 300, Little Rock, AR 72211; tel. 501/221-1800; FAX. 501/954-5481; Jack L. Blackshear, M.D., FACP, Chief Medical Officer

Healthsource Arkansas, Inc., 333 Executive Court, Little Rock, AR 72205-4548; tel. 501/227-7222; Donald T. Jack

Healthwise of Arkansas, Ltd., Three Financial Centre, 900 South Shackleford, Suite 400, Little Rock, AR 72211; tel. 501/228-9473; FAX. 501/221-0974; Caralee Pruitt

Mercy Health Plans of Missouri, Inc., 12935 North Outer 40 Drive, St. Louis, MO 63141-8636; tel. 314/214-8100; FAX. 314/214-8101; Thomas L. Kelly, President

Prudential Health Care Plan Inc., d/b/a Prucare of Arkansas, 10800 Financial Centre Parkway, Suite 499, Little Rock, AR 72211-3525; tel. 501/227-7776; Norine Yukon

QCA Health Plan, Inc., 10800 Financial Centre Parkway, Suite 540, Little Rock, AR 72211; tel. 501/954-9595; FAX. 501/228-0135; James M. Stewart, President, Chief Executive Officer

United HealthCare of Arkansas, Inc., 415 North McKinley Street, Plaza West Building, Suite 820, Little Rock, AR 72205; tel. 501/664-7700; FAX. 501/664-7768; V. Rob Herndon III

CALIFORNIA

Access Dental Plan, Inc., 555 University Avenue, Suite 182, Sacramento, CA 95825; tel. 916/922-5000, ext. 310; FAX. 916/646-9000; Reza Abbaszaden, D.D.S., Chief Executive Officer

Advanced Dental Systems, Inc., 3162 Newberry Drive, San Jose, CA 95118; tel. 800/448-1942; FAX. 408/448-5418; Germaine Anderson, Vice President

Aetna Dental Care of California, Inc., 201 North Civic Drive, Suite 300, Walnut Creek, CA 94596; tel. 510/977-7865; FAX. 510/746-6560; Bryan J. Geremia, Chief Executive Officer

Aetna Health Plans of California, Inc., 201 North Civic Drive, Suite 300, Walnut Creek, CA 94596; tel. 909/386-3145; FAX. 909/386-3330; Michael Dobbs, Market Vice President

Almeda Alliance for Health, 1850 Fairway Drive, San Leandro, CA 94577; tel. 510/895-4500; FAX. 510/483-6038; David J. Kears, President, Chief Executive Officer

Alternative Dental Care of California, Inc., 21700 Oxnard Street, Suite 500, Woodland Hills, CA 91367; tel. 818/710-9400, ext. 421; FAX. 818/704-9817; Sargis Khaziran, Chief Finance Officer

American Chiropractic Network Health Plan, Inc., 8989 Rio San Diego Drive, Suite 250, San Diego, CA 92108; tel. 619/297-8100; FAX. 619/297-8189; George DeVries, President

American Healthguard Corporation, Centaguard Dental Plan, 485 E. 17th Street, Suite 604, Costa Mesa, CA 92627; tel. 714/574-8874; David Kutner, M.D., President

Ameritas Managed Dental Plan, 151 Kalmus Drive, Suite B-250, Costa Mesa, CA 92626; tel. 714/437-5966; FAX. 714/437-5967; Karin Truxillo, President

Baycare Health Plan, 122 Saratoga Avenue, Suite B, Santa Clara, CA 95051; tel. 408/441-9340; Tracy K. Heeter, D.D.S., President

Blue Cross of California/Wellpoint Health Network Inc./, CaliforniaCare Health Plans, 21555 Oxnard Street, Woodland Hills, CA 91367; tel. 818/703-2412; Thomas Geiser, Executive Vice President/Counsel

CIGNA Dental Health of California, Inc., 5990 Sepulveda Boulevard, Suite 500, Van Nuys, CA 91411; tel. 818/756-2900; FAX. 818/756-2997; Claire Marie Burchill, President, Chief Executive Officer

CMG Behavioral Health of California, Inc., 865 South Figueroa Street, Suite 1450, Los Angeles, CA 90017; tel. 213/312-9400; FAX. 213/312-9413; Michael L. Jospe, Ph.D., Executive Director

California Benefits Dental Plan, 4911 Warner Avenue, Suite 208, Huntington Beach, CA 92649; tel. 714/840-2852; FAX. 714/840-3213; Robert F. Gosin, D.D.S., President

California Dental Health Plan, 14471 Chambers Road, 92680, P.O. Box 899, Tustin, CA 92681-0899; tel. 714/731-4751; FAX. 714/731-2049; James R. Lindsey, President

California Pacific Medical Group, d/b/a Brown and Toland Medical Group, 1388 Sutter Street, Suite 400, P.O. Box 640469, San Francisco, CA 94109; tel. 415/776-5140; Michael Abel, M.D., President

California Physicians' Service, Blue Shield of California, 50 Beale Street, 22nd Floor, San Francisco, CA 94105; tel. 415/229-5195; Patricia Ernsberger, Associate General Counsel

Care 1st Health Plan, 6255 Sunset Boulevard, Suite 1700, Los Angeles, CA 90028; tel. 213/957-4310; Bill Gil, President, Chief Executive Officer

CareAmerica, 6300 Canoga Avenue, Woodland Hills, CA 91367; tel. 818/228-2207; FAX. 818/228-5117; Robert P. White, President, Chief Executive Officer

Chinese Community Health Plan, 170 Columbus Avenue, Suite 210, San Francisco, CA 94133; tel. 415/397-3190; FAX. 415/397-6140; Kwong (K.C.) Wong, Administrator

Chrioserve, Inc., 3833 Atlantic Avenue, Long Beach, CA 90808; tel. 310/595-8164; Rodney Shelley, President, Chief Executive Officer

Cigna Dental Health of California, Inc., 5990 Sepulveda Blvd., Suite 500, Van Nuys, CA 91411; tel. 954/423–5674; Ann Fulks, Director of Compliance

Cohen Medical Corporation, d/b/a Tower Health Service, 200 Ocean Gate, Sixth Floor, Long Beach, CA 90802; tel. 310/435–2676; Robert Cohen, M.D., Vice President

Community Dental Services, Smilecare, 18101 Von Karman Avenue, Irvine, CA 92715; tel. 714/756–1111; M. E. Hardin, President, Chief Executive Officer

Community Health Group, 740 Bay Boulevard, Chula Vista, CA 91910; tel. 619/422–0422; FAX. 619/422–5930; Gabriel Arce, Chief Executive Officer

Concentrated Care, 450 East Romie Lane, Salinas, CA 92660; tel. 714/752–8522; Dennis Fratt, Acting President

ConsumerHealth, Inc., d/b/a Newport Dental Plan, 1401 Dove Street, Suite 290, Newport Beach, CA 92660; tel. 714/752–8522, ext. 220; FAX. 714/833–9172; Dennis Fratt, Acting President

Continental Dental Plan, 300 Corporate Pointe, Suite 385, Culver City, CA 90230; tel. 310/216–1154; James M. Hubbard, President

Contra Costa Health Plan, 595 Center Avenue, Suite 100, Martinez, CA 94553; tel. 510/313–6000; FAX. 510/313–6002; Milton Camhi, Executive Director

County of Los Angeles, Department of Health Services, d/b/a Community Health Plan, 313 North Figueroa Street, Los Angeles, CA 90012; tel. 213/240–7775; Steven A. Escoboza, Interim Director

County of Ventura, Ventura County Health Care Plan, 133 West Santa Clara Street, Ventura, CA 93001; tel. 805/648–9562; FAX. 805/648–9593; Patricia S. Neumann, Insurance Administrator

Dedicated Dental Systems, Inc., 3990 Ming Avenue, Bakersfield, CA 93309; tel. 805/397–5513; FAX. 805/397–2888; Robert J. Newman, Vice President

Delta Dental Plan of California, 100 First Street, San Francisco, CA 94105; tel. 415/972–8312; Carl W. Ludwig, Director, Northern California Sales

Dental Benefit Providers of California, Inc., 311 California Street, Suite 550, San Francisco, CA 94104; tel. 415/391–1211; Jill Schultze Evans, Accting COO

Dental Health Services, 3833 Atlantic Avenue, Long Beach, CA 90807–3505; tel. 310/595–6000; FAX. 310/424–0150; Godfrey Pernell, D.D.S., President, Chief Executive Officer

Denticare of California, Inc., 28202 Cabot Road, Suite 600, Zip 92677, P.O. Box 30019, Laguna Niguel, CA 92607–0019; tel. 714/365–8010, ext. 215; FAX. 714/347–7612; Robert E. Wergin, President

Dr. Leventhal's Vision Care Centers of America, 3680 Rosecrans Street, Zip 92110, P.O. Box 87808, San Diego, CA 92138; tel. 619/223–5656; FAX. 619/223–2318; Debra Brant, Chief Operating Officer

Eyecare Service Plan, Inc., 9090 Burton Way, Beverly Hills, CA 90211; tel. 310/271–0145; FAX. 310/271–0784; Matthew Rips, Vice President

Eyexam 2000 of California, Inc., 170 Newport Center Drive, Suite 130, Newport Beach, CA 92661; tel. 513/583–6373; Keith Borders, Attorney

FHP, Inc., 18000 Studebaker Road, Suite 750, Cerritos, CA 90701; tel. 213/809–5399; FAX. 714/968–7159; Stuart Byer, Associate Vice President, Consumer, Government Affairs

For Eyes Vision Plan, Inc., 2104 Shattuck Avenue, Berkeley, CA 94704; tel. 510/843–0787; Robert Schoen, President

Foundation Health, a California Health Plan, 3400 Data Drive, Rancho Cordova, CA 95670; tel. 916/631–5299; FAX. 916/631–5294; Marshall Bentley, Vice President, Counsel

Foundation Health Psychcare Services, Inc., d/b/a Occupational Health Services (OHS), 1600 Los Gamos Drive, Suite 300, San Rafael, CA 94903; tel. 415/491–7232; Nancy B. Diamond, Director of Admin. Reg. Compl.

Foundation Health Vision Services, Vision Plans, 125 Technology, PO Box 57074, Irvine, CA 92619–7074; tel. 800/999–2848, ext. 215; Robert E. Wergin, President

Golden West Dental and Vision Plan, 888 West Ventura Boulevard, Camarillo, CA 93010; tel. 805/987–8941, ext. 138; Karl H. Lehmann, President

Great American Health Plan, 2525 Camino Del Rio, S., Suite 350, San Diego, CA 92108; tel. 619/574–6600; Riley McWilliams, Chief Executive Officer

Greater California Dental Plan, Smilesaver, Signature Dental Plan, 22144 Clarendon Street, First Floor, P.O. Box 4281, Woodland Hills, CA 91365–4281; tel. 818/348–1500; FAX. 818/348–2942; Mark Johnson, President

Greater Pacific HMO, Inc., 9267 Haven Avenue, Suite 210, Rancho Cucamonga, CA 91730; tel. 909/483–9595; Lee Reynolds, President

HMO California, d/b/a healthmax America, 17922 Fitch, Irvine, CA 92614; tel. 714/756–5555; Peter Young, Chief Financial Officer

Health & Human Resource Center, 9370 Sky Park Court, Suite 140, San Diego, CA 92123; tel. 619/571–1698; Stephen H. Heidel, MD, President & CEO

Health Benefits, Inc., H.B.I. Prepaid Dental Plans, 1776 West March Lane, Suite 140, Stockton, CA 92507; tel. 209/472–2000; R. Dennis Spain, President

Health Net, 21600 Oxnard Street, Woodland Hills, CA 91367, P.O. Box 9103, Van Nuys, CA 91409–9103; tel. 818/719–6800; FAX. 818/719–5450; Arthur Southam, M.D., Chief Executive Officer

Health Plan of the Redwoods, 3033 Cleveland Avenue, Santa Rosa, CA 95403; tel. 707/525–4231; FAX. 707/547–4101; William D. Hughes, Chief Executive Officer

Health and Human Resource Center, 7798 Starling Drive, San Diego, CA 92123; tel. 619/571–1698; FAX. 619/571–1868; Stephen H. Heidel, M.D., President, Chief Executive Officer

Healthdent of California, Inc., 2848 Arden Way, Suite 100, Sacramento, CA 95825; tel. 916/486–0749; FAX. 916/486–3642; Edward L. Cruchley, D.D.S., President

Holman Professional Counseling Centers, 21050 Van Owen Street, Canoga Park, CA 91303; tel. 818/704–1444, ext. 235; FAX. 818/704–9339; Ron Holman, Ph.D., President

Human Affairs International of California, 300 North Continental Boulevard, Suite 200, El Segundo, CA 90245; tel. 310/414–0066; FAX. 310/414–9282; Jonathan Wormhoudt, Ph.D., Chief Executive Officer

Ideal Dental Health Plan, 1720 South San Gabriel Boulevard, Suite 102, San Gabriel, CA 91776; tel. 818/288–2203; Richard Sun, D.D.S., President

Inland Empire Health Plan, 303 East Vanderbilt Way, Suite 400, San Bernardino, CA 92408; tel. 909/430–2700; FAX. 909/430–2703; Richard Bruno, Chief Executive Officer

Inter Valley Health Plan, 300 South Park Avenue, Suite 300, Pomona, CA 91766; tel. 909/623–6333; FAX. 909/622–2907; Mark C. Covington, President, Chief Executive Officer

Kaiser Foundation Health Plan, Inc., 1800 Harrison Street, 8th Floor, Oakland, CA 94612; tel. 510/987–2146; Renee Kullick, Director, H.P. Licensing

Kern Health Systems, 1600 Norris Road, Bakersfield, CA 93380; tel. 805/391–4000; FAX. 805/391–4097; Carol L. Sorrell, RN, Chief Executive Officer

Kern Health Systems, 1600 Norris Road, Bakersfield, CA 93380; tel. 805/931–4000; Carol L. Sorrell, RN, CEO

Key Health Plan, Inc., 5959 South Mooney Boulevard, Visalia, CA 93277–9329; tel. 209/730–4175; Dean K. Ward, Chief Executive Officer

Key Health Plan, Inc., d/b/a Key Health Plan of CA, KEY HMO, Key Choice, 5959 South Mooney Blvd., Visalia, CA 93277–3929; tel. 209/730–4100; Sheri A. Shannon, Acting CEO

Landmark Healthplan of California, Inc., 1750 Howe Avenue, Suite 400, Sacramento, CA 95825–3369; tel. 916/569–3300; Marla Jane Orth, CEO

Laurel Dental Plan, Inc., 5451 Laurel Canyon Boulevard, Suite 209, North Hollywood, CA 91607; tel. 818/980–0929; FAX. 818/980–4668; Dr. Victor Sands, President

Lifeguard, Inc., 1851 McCarthy Boulevard, Milpitas, CA 95035; tel. 408/943–9400; FAX. 408/383–4259; Mark G. Hyde, President, Chief Executive Officer

Local Initiative Health Authority for LA Co., 3530 Wilshire Blvd., Suite 704, Los Angeles, CA 90010; tel. 213/251–8300; Anthony D. Rodgers, CEO

MAXICARE, 1149 South Broadway Street, Los Angeles, CA 90015; tel. 213/765–2000, ext. 2101; FAX. 213/765–2694; Peter J. Ratican, Chairman, President, Chief Executive Officer

MCC Behavioral Care of California, Inc., 801 North Brand Boulevard, Suite 1150, Glendale, CA 91203; tel. 818/551–2200; Bernhild E. Quintero, Vice President

MCC Behavioral Care of California, Inc., 801 North Brand Blvd., #1150, Glendale, CA 91203; tel. 800/433–5768; Susan Speltz Feltus, VP, Counsel

Managed Dental Care of California, 6200 Canoga Avenue, Suite 100, Woodland Hills, CA 91367; tel. 800/273–3330; FAX. 818/347–7302; Michael Gould, President, Chief Executive Officer

Managed Health Network, Inc., 5100 West Goldleaf Circle, Suite 300, Los Angeles, CA 90056; tel. 213/299–0999; FAX. 213/298–2765; Alethea Caldwell, President

Maxicare, 1149 South Broadway Street, Suite 819, Los Angeles, CA 90015; tel. 213/365–3451; Warren D. Foon, Vice President, General Manager

Merit Behavioral Care of California, Inc., 400 Oyster Point Boulevard, Suite 306, South San Francisco, CA 94080; tel. 415/742–0980; FAX. 415/742–0988; Douglas Studebaker, President

Molina Medical Centers, One Golden Shore, Long Beach, CA 90802; tel. 310/435–3666; John Molina, J.D., Vice President

Monarch Plan, Inc., 201 North Salsipuedes, Suite 206, Santa Barbara, CA 93103–3256; tel. 805/963–0566; FAX. 805/564–4167; Peter J. Leeson, D.O., Chief Executive Officer

National Health Plans, 1005 West Orangeburg Avenue, Suite B, Modesto, CA 95350–4163; tel. 209/527–3350; FAX. 209/527–6773; Mike Sheley, President & Chief Executive Officer

Omni Healthcare, 2450 Venture Oaks Way, Suite 300, Sacramento, CA 95833–3292; tel. 916/921–4000; FAX. 916/921–4100; Robert E. Edmonson, President, Chief Executive Officer

One Health Plan of California, Inc., 1740 Technology Drive, Suite 530, San Jose, CA 95110; tel. 408/437–4100; FAX. 408/437–0253; Jackie L. James, President

Oral Health Services, Inc., Mida Dental Plan, 21700 Oxnard Street, Suite 500, Woodland Hills, CA 91367; tel. 818/710–9400, ext. 421; FAX. 818/710–9400; Sargis Khaziran, Chief Financial Officer

PacifiCare Behavioral Health of California, 23046 Avenida de la Carlota, Suite 700, Laguna Hills, CA 92653; tel. 714/859–7971; Heidi Prescott, National Sales Manager

PacifiCare of California, Secure Horizons, 5995 Plaza Drive, P.O. Box 6006, Cypress, CA 90630–6006; tel. 714/236–5674; FAX. 714/236–7887; Nancy J. Monk, Regulatory Affairs, VP

Pacific Union Dental, Inc., 1300 Clay Street, Suite 550, Oakland, CA 94612; tel. 510/271–0600; John Gaebel, President

Pearle Vision Care, Inc., 6480 Weathers Place, Suite 225, San Diego, CA 92121; tel. 619/625–9173; Debbie Hyde–Duby, President

Pioneer Provider Network, Inc., 5000 Airport Plaza Drive, Long Beach, CA 90815; tel. 310/627–6019; David Maggenti, Chief Operating Officer

Preferred Health Plan, Inc., Personal Dental Services, 4002 Park Boulevard, Suite B, San Diego, CA 92103; tel. 619/297–6670; FAX. 619/297–0317; Joan Contratti, Secretary/Treasurer

Preventive Dental Systems, Inc., 801 Broadway, Sacramento, CA 95818; tel. 916/448–2994; FAX. 916/448–2997; Gregory Thomas, Interim CEO

Priority Health Services, Central Valley Health Plan, Inc., P.O. Box 25790, Fresno, CA 93729–5790; tel. 209/446–6810; FAX. 209/435–7693; John M. Cronin, President, Chief Executive Officer

Private Medical–Care, Inc., PMI, 12898 Towne Center Drive, Cerritos, CA 90701; tel. 310/924–8311; FAX. 310/924–8039; Robert B. Elliott, President

Prudential Health Care Plan of California, Inc., 5800 Canoga Avenue, Woodland Hills, CA 91367; tel. 818/712–5705; FAX. 818/992–2474; Cora M. Tellez, President

Regents of the University of California, 1899 McKee Street, San Diego, CA 92101; tel. 619/294–3743; Nancy White, RN, MPH, CEO, COO

Ross–Loos Health Plan of California, Inc., d/b/a CIGNA HealthCare of California, 505 North Brand Boulevard, P.O. Box 2125, Glendale, CA 91203; tel. 818/500–6726; FAX. 818/500–6831; Leslie A. Margolin, Chief Counsel

SCAN Health Plan, 3780 Kilroy Airport Way, Suite 600, P.O. Box 22616, Zip 90801–5616, Long Beach, CA 90806–2460; tel. 310/989–5100; FAX. 310/989–5200; Sam L. Ervin, President, Chief Executive Officer

Safeguard Health Plans, 505 North Euclid Street, P.O. Box 3210, Anaheim, CA 92803–3210; tel. 714/778–1005; FAX. 714/778–4383; Ronald I. Brendzel, Senior Vice President

San Francisco Health Plan, 568 Howard Street, Fifth Floor, San Francisco, CA 94105; tel. 415/547–7800; FAX. 415/547–7824; Shahnaz Nikpay, Ph.D., Chief Executive Officer

San Joaquin County Health Commission, d/b/a The Health Plan of San Joaquin, 1550 West Fremont Street, Suite 200, Stockton, CA 95203–2643; tel. 209/939–3500; FAX. 209/939–3535; Mr. Terry G. Mack, Acting CEO

San Joaquin Valley Dental Plan, Inc., 2000 Fresno Street, Suite 100, Fresno, CA 93721; tel. 209/442–1111; John Howard Thomas, Vice President, Operations

Santa Clara Health Authority, d/b/a Santa Clara Family Health Plan, 4050 Moorpark Avenue, San Jose, CA 95117; tel. 408/260–4490; Ronald Wojtaszek, Interim CEO

Santa Clara Valley Medical Center, Valley Health Plan, 750 South Bascom Avenue, San Jose, CA 95l28; tel. 408/885–5704; FAX. 408/885–4050; Roger Wells, Executive Director

Sharp Health Plan, 9325 Sky Park Court, Suite 300, San Diego, CA 92123; tel. 619/637–6530; FAX. 619/637–6504; Kathlyn Mead, President, Chief Executive Officer

U.S. Behavioral Health Plan, California, 425 Market Street, 27th Floor, San Francisco, CA 94105–2426; tel. 415/547–5203; FAX. 415/547–5512; Joseph Cronin, Jr., Executive Director

UDC Dental California, Inc., (formerly The Dental Advantage/National Dental Health), 3111 Camino Del Rio North, Suite 1000, San Diego, CA 92108; tel. 800/288–9992; FAX. 619/283–9437; Keith C. Macumber, Senior Vice President, Western Regional Manager

United Healthcare of California, Inc., d/b/a MetraHealth Care Plan, UHC Healthcare, 4500 East Pacific Coast Highway, Suite 120, Long Beach, CA 90804–6441; tel. 310/498–5106; FAX. 310/498–5137; George S. Goldstein, Ph.D., Chief Executive Officer

Universal Care, 1600 East Hill Street, Signal Hill, CA 90806; tel. 562/424–6200; FAX. 562/427–4634; Jay Davis, Vice President

Value Behavioral Health of California, Inc., (formerly American Psychmanagement of California, Inc.), 340 Golden Shore, Long Beach, CA 90802; tel. 562/590–9004; FAX. 562/951–6130; Tim Kotas, Acting Executive Director

Value Healthplan of California, Inc., 5251 Viewridge Court, San Diego, CA 92123; tel. 619/278–2273; Lory Wallach, Vice President, Chief Operating Officer

Vision First Eye care, Inc., 1937–A Tully Road, San Jose, CA 95122; tel. 408/923–0400; James K. Eu, O.D., Ph.D., President

Vision Plan of America, 8111 Beverly Boulevard, Suite 306, Los Angeles, CA 90048; tel. 213/658–6113; FAX. 213/658–8611; Dr. Stuart Needleman

Vision Service Plan, 3333 Quality Drive, Rancho Cordova, CA 95670; tel. 800/852–7600; Al Schubert, Vice President, Managed Care

Visioncare of California, d/b/a Sterling Visioncare, 6540 Lusk Boulevard, Suite 234, San Diego, CA 92121; tel. 619/458–9983; Martin J. Shomank, President

Vista Behavioral Health Plans, 2355 Northside Drive, 3rd floor, San Diego, CA 92108; tel. 619/521–4440; FAX. 619/497–5244; Erik Bradbury, Chief Executive Officer

VivaHealth, Inc., d/b/a BPS HMO, 888 South Figueroa Street, Suite 1400, San Francisco, CA 90017; tel. 213/489–2694; Barbara Rodin, Ph.D., President

Watts Health Foundation, Inc., United Health Plan, 3405 W. Imperial Highway, Inglewood, CA 90303; tel. 310/412–3569; FAX. 310/412–4198; ALma Graham, VP and General Counsel

Wellpoint Dental Plan, 21555 Oxnard Street, Woodland Hills, CA 91367; tel. 818/703–2412; Thomas C. Geiser, Senior Vice President, General Counsel

Wellpoint Health Networks, Inc., 21555 Oxnard Street, Woodland Hills, CA 91367; tel. 818/703–2412; FAX. 818/703–4406; Thomas Geiser, Executive Vice President, General Counsel

Wellpoint Pharmacy Plan, 27001 Agoura Road, Suite 325, Calabasas Hills, CA 91301–5339; tel. 818/878–2675; FAX. 818/880–4981; Richard C. Bleil, General Manager

Western Dental Services, Inc., Western Dental Plan, 300 Plaza Alicante, Suite 800, Garden Grove, CA 92640; tel. 714/938–1600; FAX. 714/938–1611; Robert C. Schur, President

Western Health Advantage, 1331 Garden Highway, Suite 100, Sacramento, CA 95833; tel. 916/563–3184; Garry Maisel, COO

COLORADO

Antero Healthplans, 600 Grant Street, Suite 900, Denver, CO 80203; tel. 303/830–3150; FAX. 303/830–2392; Charlie Stark, President, Chief Executive Officer

CIGNA HealthCare of Colorado, Inc., 3900 East Mexico Avenue, Suite 1100, Denver, CO 80210–3946; tel. 303/782–1500; FAX. 303/782–1577; Dennis Mouras, General Manager

Colorado Access, 501 South Cherry Street, Suite 700, Denver, CO 80222; tel. 303/355–6707; Judith M. Fenhart, Health Plan Director

Community Health Plan of the Rockies, Inc., 400 South Colorado Boulevard, Suite 300, Denver, CO 80222; tel. 303/355–3220; Laura Barribo, Human Resources

Denver Health Medical Plan, Inc., 777 Bannock Street, Denver, CO 80204–4507; tel. 303/436–6000

FHP of Colorado, Inc., 6455 South Yosemite Street, Englewood, CO 80111; tel. 303/220–5800; FAX. 303/714–3999; James J. Swayze, Vice President, Sales and Marketing

Foundation Health, a Colorado Health Plan, Inc., P.O. Box 958, Pueblo, CO 81002; tel. 719/583–7500

Frontier Community Health Plans, Inc., 6312 South Fiddler's Green Circle, Suite 260–N, Englewood, CO 80111; tel. 303/771–7200; FAX. 303/771–0366; Dr. Thomas J. Hazy

HMO Colorado, Inc., d/b/a HMO Blue, 700 Broadway, Suite 612, Denver, CO 80273; tel. 303/831–2131

HMO Health Plans, Inc., d/b/a San Luis Valley HMO, Inc., 95 West First Avenue, Monte Vista, CO 81144; tel. 719/852–4055; FAX. 719/852–3481; Douglas Johnson, Executive Director, Chief Executive Officer

HSI Health Plans, Inc., P.O. Box 1668, Fort Collins, CO 80522; tel. 970/482–8403; FAX. 970/482–8911; Karen Morgan, Vice President, Group and Member Services

Health Network of Colorado Springs, Inc., 555 East Pikes Peaks Avenue, Suite 108, Colorado Springs, CO 80903; tel. 719/365–5025; FAX. 719/365–5004; Ron Burnside, Chief Executive Officer

Humana Health Plan, Inc., P.O. Box 740036, Louisville, KY 40201–7436; tel. 502/580–5804; Craig Drablos, Executive Director

Kaiser Foundation Health Plan of Colorado, 2500 S. Havana Street, Aurora, CO 80014–1622; tel. 303/338–3000; Kathryn A. Paul, President

One Health Plan of Colorado, Inc., 8505 East Orchard Road, Englewood, CO 80111; tel. 303/804–6800

Prudential Health Care Plan, Inc., d/b/a Prudential HealthCare HMO, 4643 South Ulster Street, Suite 1000, Denver, CO 80237; tel. 303/796–6161; FAX. 303/796–6183; Denise Saabye, Communication Manager

Qual–Med Plans for Health of Colorado, Inc., P.O. Box 1986, Pueblo, CO 81002–1986; tel. 719/542–0500; FAX. 719/542–4921; Malik Hasan, M.D., Chairman, President

Rocky Mountain Health Maintenance Organization, d/b/a Rocky Mountain HMO, P.O. Box 10600, Grand Junction, CO 81502–5500; tel. 303/244–7760; FAX. 303/244–7880; Michael J. Weber, Executive Director

Sloans Lake Health Plan, Inc., 1355 South Colorado Boulevard, Suite 902, Denver, CO 80222; tel. 303/691–2200

Unicare, 1840 West Mountain View Avenue, Suite Four, Longmont, CO 80501; tel. 303/678–4035; FAX. 303/678–5588; Rick Spears, Chief Executive Officer

United Healthcare of Colorado, Inc., 6251 Greenwood Plaza Boulevard, Englewood, CO 80111; tel. 303/694–9336

CONNECTICUT

Aetna Health Plans of Southern New England, 80 Lamberton Road, Conveyor LB2B, Windsor, CT 06095; tel. 203/298–4000; Craig W. Gage, M.D., Vice President, Health Services Management

Blue Care Health Plan, 370 Bassett Road, North Haven, CT 06473; tel. 203/239–8483; FAX. 203/234–8573; Robert Scalettar, M.D., M.P.H., Vice President, Medical Policy

CIGNA HealthCare of Connecticut, Inc., 900 Cottage Grove Road, A–118, Hartford, CT 06152–1118; tel. 860/769–2300; FAX. 860/769–2399; Donald S. Grossman, M.D., Medical Director

ConnectiCare, Inc., 30 Batterson Park Road, Farmington, CT 06032–3006; tel. 203/674–5700; FAX. 203/674–5728; Marcel Gamache, President, Chief Executive Officer

Healthsource Connecticut, Inc., 40 Stanford Drive, Farmington, CT 06032; tel. 860/674–9922; FAX. 860/674–9924; Steven T. Burnett, Chief Executive Officer

Kaiser Foundation Health Plan, 76 Batterson Park Road, P.O. Box 4011, Farmington, CT 06034–4011; tel. 203/678–6178; FAX. 203/678–6160; Pat Parkerton, Area Operations Manager

M.D. Health Plan, Six Devine Street, North Haven, CT 06473; tel. 800/772–5869; FAX. 203/407–2899; Barbara G. Bradow, President

MedSpan, Inc., 55 Farmington Avenue, Hartford, CT 06105; tel. 860/541–6789; Kevin W. Kelly, President, Chief Executive Officer

NYLCare Health Plans of Connecticut, Inc., Four Armstrong Road, Shelton, CT 06484; tel. 203/944–1900; Theresa Atwood, Regional Vice President

Oxford Health Plans, 800 Connecticut Avenue, Norwalk, CT 06854; tel. 800/444–6222; Julie Summers, Marketing Associate

Physicians Health Services, Inc., 120 Hawley Lane, Trumbull, CT 06611–5343; tel. 800/848–4747, ext. 5642; FAX. 203/381–7665; Sharon Williams, Director, Marketing Administration

Prudential Health Care of Connecticut, Inc., 101 Merritt Seven, Norwalk, CT 06851; tel. 203/849–1800; FAX. 203/849–8387; Lewis E. Devendorf, Executive Director

Suburban Health Plan, Inc., 680 Bridgeport Avenue, Shelton, CT 06484; tel. 203/926–8882; FAX. 203/925–1202; Tim Pusch, Manager, Sales, Marketing

U.S. Healthcare, Inc., 1000 Middle Street, Middletown, CT 06457; tel. 860/636–8300; Leonard Abramson, President

Wellcare of Connecticut, Inc., 1781 Highland Avenue, Cheshire, CT 06410; tel. 203/250–9355; FAX. 203/699–8593; G. William Strein, President

Yale Preferred Health, Inc., 23 Maiden Lane, North Haven, CT 06473; tel. 203/239–7444; FAX. 203/239–5308; Sylvia B. Kelly, Operations Director

DELAWARE

Aetna Health/U.S. Healthcare, Rockwood Office Park, 501 Carr Road, Third Floor, Wilmington, DE 19809; tel. 800/231–8430; Cynthia Mazer, Manager

Amerihealth HMO, Inc., 919 North Market Street, Suite 1200, Wilmington, DE 19801–3021; Alfred F. Meyer, Executive Director

CIGNA HealthCare of Pennsylvania, New Jersey and Delaware, One Beaver Valley Road, Suite CHP, Wilmington, DE 19803; tel. 302/477–3000, ext. 3725; FAX. 302/477–3707; Norman Scott, M.D., Medical Director

CareLink, Georgetown Professional Park, Route 113 North, Suite 109, Georgetown, DE 19947; tel. 302/856–3100; FAX. 302/856–3999; Craig Gieseman, Vice President, Managed Care Services

Delaware network Health Plan, 121 South Front Street, Seaford, DE 19973; tel. 302/629–6611; Donald Pinner, Vice President

Delmarva Health Plan, Inc., 106 Marlboro Road, Easton, MD 21601; tel. 410/822–7223; Richard Moore, Chief Executive Officer

HMO of Delaware, Inc., The Health Care Center at Christiana, 200 Hygeia Drive, P.O. Box 6008, Newark, DE 19714; tel. 302/421–2466; FAX. 302/421–2577; Robert Tremain, President

Healthcare Delaware, Inc., Seventh and Clayton Streets, P.O. Box 7498, Wilmington, DE 19803; tel. 302/652–8038, ext. 4799; FAX. 215/358–5238; James J. Thomas III, Senior Vice President

Optimum Choice Inc./MDIPA, Inc./Alliance PPO, Inc., Four Taft Court, Rockville, MD 20850; tel. 301/762–8205, ext. 3994; Gloria Stem, Human Resource, Senior Director

Section C

Principal Health Care of Delaware, Inc., 1 Corporate Commons, 100 West Commons Blvd, Suite 300, New Castle, DE 19720; tel. 302/322–4700; FAX. 302/633–4044; Max Kenyon, Executive Director

Total Health, Inc., One Brandywine Gateway, P.O. Box 8792, Wilmington, DE 19899; tel. 302/421–3034; FAX. 302/421–2577; Robert C. Cole, Jr., President

U.S. Healthcare, Inc., 980 Jolly Road, P.O. Box 1109, Blue Bell, PA 19422; tel. 215/628–4800; Leonard Abramson, President

DISTRICT OF COLUMBIA

Aetna Health Plans of the Mid–Atlantic, Inc., 7799 Leesburgh Pike South, Suite 1100, Falls Church, VA 22045; tel. 703/903–7100; Russ Dickhart, Executive Director

CIGNA HealthCare Mid–Atlantic, Inc., 9700 Patuxent Woods Drive, Columbia, MD 21046; tel. 410/720–5800; Linda Hacker

CapitalCare, Inc., 550 12th Street, S.W., Washington, DC 20065–0001; tel. 202/479–3678; FAX. 202/479–3660; M. Bruce Edwards, President

D.C. Chartered Health Plan, Inc., 820 First Street, N.E., Suite LL100, Washington, DC 20002–4205; tel. 202/408–4710; Robert L. Bowles, Jr., DBA, Chairman, President and Chief Executive Officer

George Washington University Health Plan, Inc., 4550 Montgomery Avenue, Suite 800, Bethesda, MD 20814; tel. 301/941–2000, ext. 2100; FAX. 301/941–2005; Dr. John E. Ott, Executive Director, Chief Executive Officer

HealthPlus, Inc., NYLCare Health Plans of the Mid–Atlantic, Inc., 7601 Ora Glen Drive, Suite 200, Greenbelt, MD 20770–3641; tel. 301/441–1600, ext. 3308; FAX. 301/489–5282; Jeff D. Emerson, President, Chief Executive Officer

Humana Group Health Association, Inc., 430l Connecticut Avenue, N.W., Washington, DC 20008; tel. 202/364–2000; FAX. 202/364–7418; Robert Pfotenhauer, President, Chief Executive Officer

Kaiser Foundation Health Plan of the Mid–Atlantic States, 2101 East Jefferson Street, Box 6611, Rockville, MD 20849–6611; tel. 301/468–6000; FAX. 301/816–7465; Robert A. Essink, Acting President

M.D. Individual Practive Association, Inc., Four Taft Court, Rockville, MD 20850; tel. 800/544–2853; Susan Goff, President

Optimum Choice, MAMSI, Four Taft Court, Rockville, MD 20850; tel. 301/294–5100; FAX. 301/309–1709; George Jochum, President

Physicians Health Plan, Inc./Physicians Care, d/b/a Health Keepers, 2111 Wilson Boulevard, Suite 11510, Arlington, VA 22201; tel. 703/525–0602; Wyndahm Kidd

Prudential Health Care Plan, 2800 North Charles Street, Baltimore, MD 21218; tel. 410/554–7222

United Mine Workers of America, 4455 Connecticut Avenue, N.W., Washington, DC 20008; tel. 202/895–3960; Robert Condra

FLORIDA

AHL Select HMO, Inc., 1776 American Heritage Life Drive, Jacksonville, FL 32224; tel. 904/992–2529; FAX. 904/992–2658; James H. Baum, Administrator

Aetna US Healthcare, Inc., 4890 West Kennedy, Suite 545, Tampa, FL 33609; tel. 800/232–2385; FAX. 813/286–3041; J. Scott Murphy, Administrator

AmeriCan Medical Plans of Missouri, Inc., 1 Southeast Third Avenue, Suite 2900, Miami, FL 33131; tel. 800/552–7733

American Medical Healthcare, 1900 Summit Tower Boulevard, Suite 700, Orlando, FL 32810; tel. 407/660–1611; FAX. 407/660–0203; Sandra K. Johnson, President, Chief Executive Officer

Anthem Health Plan of Florida, Inc., 10151 Deerwood Park Blvd., Bldg. 200, Suite 400, Jacksonville, FL 32256; tel. 800/274–5466; FAX. 904/998–5402; Rose M. Mullins, Administrator

AvMed Health Plan, P.O. Box 749, Gainesville, FL 32606–0749; tel. 904/372–8400; FAX. 904/372–5155; Edward C. Peddie, President, Chief Executive Officer

Beacon Health Plans, Inc., 2511 Ponce de Leon Boulevard, Coral Gables, FL 33134; tel. 305/930–8181; FAX. 305/445–4614; Raymond Noonan, Administrator

CIGNA HealthCare of Florida, Inc., 5404 Cypress Center Drive, P.O. Box 24203, Tampa, FL 33623; tel. 813/281–1000; FAX. 813/282–0356; Betty Kimmel, President, General Manager

Capital Group Health Services of Florida, Inc., 2140 Centerville Place, P.O. Box 13267, Tallahassee, FL 32317; tel. 904/386–3161; FAX. 904/385–3193; John Hogan, Administrator

Champion Healthcare, 7406 Fullerton Street, Suite 200, Jacksonville, FL 32256; tel. 904/519–0900; FAX. 904/519–0838; Richard C. Powell, President, Chief Executive Officer

Community Health Care Systems, Inc., 2301 Lucien Way, Suite 440, Maitland, FL 32751; tel. 800/635–4345; FAX. 407/481–7190; Karl W. Hodges, Administrator

DentiCare, Inc., 8130 Baymeadows Way West, Suite 200, Jacksonville, FL 32256; tel. 904/731–1870; Glenn Kollen

Florida Health Care Plan, Inc., 1340 Ridgewood Avenue, Holly Hill, FL 32117; tel. 904/676–7193; FAX. 904/676–7196; Edward F. Simpson, Jr., President, Chief Executive Officer

Florida Ist Health Plan, Inc., 3425 Lake Alfred Road, P.O. Box 9126, Winter Haven, FL 33883–9126; tel. 813/293–0785, ext. 5125; FAX. 813/297–9095; John J. Torti, President

Foundation Health, a Florida Health Plan, Inc., 1340 Concord Terrace, Sunrise, FL 33323; tel. 954/858–3000; FAX. 954/846–0331; Steven Griffin, Adminstrator

Foundation Health, a South Florida Health Plan, Inc., 7950 Northwest 53rd Street, Miami, FL 33166; tel. 305/591–3311

HIP Health Plan of Florida, Inc., 200 South Park Road, Hollywood, FL 333021; tel. 954/962–3008, ext. 4100; FAX. 954/985–4379; Steven M. Cohen, President, Chief Executive Officer

HIP Health Plan of Florida, Inc., formerly: HIP Network of FLorida, Inc., 300 South Park Road, Hollywood, FL 33021; tel. 800/385–4447; FAX. 305/493–9587; Steven M. Cohen, Administrator

Health First HMO, 8247 Devereux Drive, Suite 103, Melbourne, FL 32940–7955; tel. 407/953–5600; FAX. 407/752–1129; Jerry Seme, President, Chief Executive ˈOfficer

Health Options, Inc., 532 Riverside Avenue, P.O. Box 60729, Jacksonville, FL 32202; tel. 800/457–4713; FAX. 904/791–6054; Robert I. Lufrano, Administrator

Healthcare USA, Inc., 8705 Perimeter Park Boulevard, Suite Three, Jacksonville, FL 32216; tel. 904/565–2950; FAX. 904/646–9238; Christopher Fey, President, Chief Executive Officer

Healthplan Southeast, Inc., 3520 Thomasville Road, Suite 200, Tallahassee, FL 32308; tel. 800/833–2169; FAX. 904/668–3133; C. Marion Butler, Jr., Administrator

Healthplans of America, Inc., 2605 Maitland Center Parkway, Suite 300, Maitland, FL 32751; tel. 800/769–2848; FAX. 407/875–9581; Robert Flanagan, Administrator

Healthy Palm Beaches, inc., 324 Datura Street, Suite 401, West Palm Beach, FL 33401; tel. 561/659–1270; FAX. 561/833–9489; Dwight Chenette, Administrator

Humana Medical Plan, Inc., 3400 Lakeside Drive, Miramar, FL 33027; tel. 305/626–5619; FAX. 305/626–5297; Joe Berding, Vice President, South Florida Market Operations

Mayo Health Plans, Inc., 4168 Southpoint Parkway, Suite 102, Jacksonville, FL 32216; tel. 888/279–2646; FAX. 904/279–9777; Patrick Healy, Administrator

Neighborhood Health Partnership, Inc., 7600 Corporate Center Drive, Miami, FL 33126; tel. 800/354–0222; FAX. 305/260–4308; William H. Mauk, Jr., Administrator

PCA Family Health Plan, Inc., d/b/a Century Medical Health Plan, Inc., 5959 Blue Lagoon Drive, Miami, FL 33126; tel. 800/562–9262; FAX. 605/267–6290; Elias Hourani, Administrator

Physicians Healthcare Plans, Inc., One Harbour Place, 777 South Harbor Island Boulevard, Tampa, FL 33602; tel. 813/229–5300; FAX. 813/229–5301; Miguel B. Fernandez, Chief Executive Officer

Preferred Choice, HMO of Florida Health Choice, Inc., 5300 West Atlantic Avenue, Suite 302, Delray Beach, FL 33484–8190; tel. 800/233–0505; FAX. 407/496–0513; Jeff Keiser, Administrator

Preferred Medical Plan, Inc., 6090 SW 40th St., Miami, FL 33155; tel. 305/669–1501; FAX. 305/669–4121; Sylvia Urlich, President

Principal Health Care of Florida, Inc., 1200 Riverplace Boulevard, Suite 500, Jacksonville, FL 32207; tel. 800/358–6205, ext. 200; FAX. 301/231–1033; Kenneth S. Bryant, Administrator

Prudential Health Care Plan, Inc., d/b/a PruCare, 2301 Lucien Way, Suite 230, Maitland, FL 32751–7086; tel. 800/628–3801; FAX. 201/716–2193; John Hogan, Administrator

Riscorp Health Plan, Inc., 1390 Main Street, Zip 34236, P.O. Box 1598, Sarasota, FL 34230–1598; tel. 800/226–9899; FAX. 813/954–4611; Rich Fogle, Administrator

St. Augustine Health Care, Inc., 1511 N. Westshore Blvd., 7th floor, Tampa, FL 33607; tel. 813/288–7600; FAX. 813/288–7664; Dennis Mihale, MD, Administrator

Sunrise Healthcare Plan, Inc., 500 West Cypress Creek Road, Suite 740, Suite 740, Fort Lauderdale, FL 33309; tel. 954/492–4243; FAX. 954/267–9673; Sheila D. Williams, Executive Administrator

Sunstar Health Plan, Inc., formerly: Boro Medical Corporation, 521 East State Road 434, Longwood, FL 32750; tel. 407/339–4997; FAX. 407/339–4151; Warren Stowell, Administrator

Tampa General Healthplan, Inc., 100 South Ashley Drive, Suite 300, Tampa, FL 33602; tel. 813/276–5047; FAX. 813/276–5040; Julia Smith, Administrator

The Public Health Trust of Dade County, 1500 Northwest 12th Avenue, JMT, Suite West 1001, Miami, FL 33136; tel. 305/585–7120; FAX. 305/545–5212; Joseph Rogers, Administrator

Total Health Choice, Inc., formerly: Pacificare of Florida, Inc., One Alhambra Plaza, Suite 1000, Coral Gables, FL 33134; tel. 800/887–6888; FAX. 305/443–5445; Kenneth G. Rimmer, Administrator

Ultramedix Health Care Systems, Inc., 3450 West Buschwood Park Drive, Suite 245, Tampa, FL 33618; tel. 813/933–6200; FAX. 813/930–2949; John S. Zaleskie, Chief Executive Officer

United Healthcare of Florida, Inc., 800 N. Magnolia Avenue, Orlando, FL 32803; tel. 800/543–3145; FAX. 305/447–3292; Frederick C. Dunlap, Administrator

Vantage Health Plan, Inc., 4250 Lakeside Drive, Suite 210, Jacksonville, FL 32210; tel. 904/387–4451; FAX. 904/387–0338; James Burt, MD, Administrator

Well Care HMO, Inc., 11016 North Dale Mabry, Suite 301, Tampa, FL 33618; tel. 813/963–6128; FAX. 813/960–1623; Pradip C. Patel, Administrator

GEORGIA

AETNA Health Plans of Georgia, Inc., 11675 Great Oaks Way, Alpharetta, GA 30022; tel. 404/814–4300; FAX. 404/814–4294; Joseph Wild, General Manager

American Dental Plan of North Carolina, Inc., 100 Mansell Court East, Suite 400, Roswell, GA 30076; tel. 770/998–8936; John Gasiorowski

American Medical Plans of Georgia, Inc., 1355 Peachtree Street, N.E., Suite 1500, Atlanta, GA 30309; tel. 404/347–8005; Tom Stockdale, Executive Director

Anthem Health Plan of Georgia, Inc., 1117 Perimeter Center West, Suite E–402, Atlanta, GA 30338; tel. 770/668–0187; Jerry Wehmhoefer, Executive Director

Athens Area Health Plan Select, Inc., 1199 Prince Avenue, Athens, GA 30606; tel. 706/549–0549; W.Larry Webb, Executive Director

CIGNA HealthCare of Georgia, Inc., 100 Peachtree Street, N.E., Suite 700, Equitable Building, Atlanta, GA 30301; tel. 404/681–7000; FAX. 404/898–4701; Heywood Donigan, President

Complete Health of Georgia, Inc., 2970 Clairmont Road, N.E., Atlanta, GA 30329; tel. 404/698–8600; Gail Smallridge, Executive Director

FamilyPlus Health Plans of Georgia, Inc., Two Decatur Town Center, 125 Clairemont Road, Suite 360, Decatur, GA 30030; tel. 404/235–1010; FAX. 404/248–3858; Michael Brohm, President

Grady Healthcare, Inc., 100 Edgewood Avenue, Atlanta, GA 30303; tel. 404/616–4307; Alma Roberts, President

HMO Georgia, Inc., 3350 Peachtree Road, N.E., P.O. Box 3417, Atlanta, GA 30326; tel. 404/842–8422; FAX. 404/842–8451; John Harris, President

HPC Health Plans of Georgia, Inc., Two Midtown Plaza, Suite 1000, 1349 West Peachtree Street, NE, Atlanta, GA 30309; tel. 404/815–7160; Mark Mixer, President

Healthsource Georgia, Inc., 7130 Hodgson Memorial Drive, Suite 4000, Savannah, GA 31406; tel. 912/351–2140; FAX. 912/351–2416; James L. Boone, Executive Director

Healthsource Georgia, Inc., 1000 Parkwood Circle, Suite 700, Atlanta, GA 30339–2175; tel. 770/303–1900; Heywood Donigan, Executive Director

Humana Employers Health Plan of Georgia, Inc., 115 Perimeter Center Place, N.E., Suite 540, Atlanta, GA 30346; tel. 770/399-5916; Gregory H. Wolf, Executive Director

John Deere Health Plan of Georgia, Inc., Building 200, 2743 Perimeter Parkway, Suite 105, Augusta, GA 30909; tel. 706/860-6776; Dean Anderson, Executive Director

Kaiser Foundation Health Plan of Georgia, Inc., 3495 Piedmont Road, N.E., Building Nine, Atlanta, GA 30305-1736; tel. 404/364-7000; Christopher L. Binkley, Executive Director

Master Health Plan, Inc., 3652 J. Dewey Gray Circle, Augusta, GA 30909; tel. 706/863-5955; Libby Young, Executive Director

Metrahealth Care Plan of Georgia, Inc., 1130 Northchase Parkway, Suite 250, Marietta, GA 30067; tel. 404/980-0740; Thomas David, Administrator

One Health Plan of Georgia, Inc., 400 Perimeter Center Terrace, Suite 300, Atlanta, GA 30306; tel. 770/901-9937; Dan Anderson, Executive Director

PCA Health Plans of Georgia, Inc., Two Midtown Plaza, 1349 West Peachtree Street, N.E., Suite 1000, Atlanta, GA 30309; tel. 404/815-7160; Rodney Spencer, Acting President

Principal Health Care of Georgia, Inc., 3715 Northside Parkway, 400 Northcreek, Suite 4-300, Atlanta, GA 30327; tel. 404/231-9911; Kenneth J. Linde, Presdient

Promina Health Plan, Inc., 2000 South Park Place, Suite 100, Atlanta, GA 30339-2049; tel. 770/956-6940; Bonnie Phipps, Executive Director

Prudential Health Care Plan of Georgia, Inc., Prudential Health Care, 2839 Paces Ferry Road, Suite 1000, Atlanta, GA 30339; tel. 770/955-8010; FAX. 770/433-0616; Richard F. Rivers, Executive Director

U.S. Healthcare of Georgia, Inc., 115 Perimeter Center Place, Suite 777, South Terraces, Atlanta, GA 30346; tel. 770/481-0100; FAX. 770/481-0800; J. Scott Murphy, Senior Vice President

United Healthcare of Georgia, Inc., 2970 Clairmont Road, Atlanta, GA 30329; tel. 404/364-8800; FAX. 404/364-8818; A. Kelly Atkinson, Executive Director

HAWAII

HMO Hawaii (HMSA), 818 Keeaumoko Street, P.O. Box 860, Honolulu, HI 96808; tel. 808/948-5408; FAX. 808/948-5999; Robert C. Nickel, Vice President

Health Plan Hawaii (HMSA), 818 Keeaumoku Street, P.O. Box 860, Honolulu, HI 96814; tel. 808/948-5408; FAX. 808/948-5063; Robert C. Nickel, Vice President

Health Plan Partners, d/b/a Kapi'olani HealthHawai'i, 677 Ala Moana Boulevard, Suite 602, Honolulu, HI 96813; tel. 808/522-5107; FAX. 808/522-6137; Kevin Somerfield, Vice President, Managed Care Systems

Island Care (HMO), Queen's Hawaii Care (HMO), Two Waterfront Plaza, Suite 200, 500 Ala Moana Boulevard, Honolulu, HI 96813; tel. 808/532-4114; FAX. 808/532-7996; Nate Nygaard, Vice President, Director, Tricare

Kaiser Foundation Health Plan, Inc., 711 Kapiolani Boulevard, Honolulu, HI 96813; tel. 808/834-5333; FAX. 808/529-5495; Cora M. Tellez, Vice President, Regional Manager

Pacific Health Care, 1946 Young Street, Suite 450, Honolulu, HI 96826; tel. 808/973-3000; FAX. 808/949-3259; John Kim, M.D., President, Medical Director

Straub Plan, 888 South King Street, Honolulu, HI 96813; tel. 808/522-4540; FAX. 808/522-4544; Karen Lennox, Executive Director

IDAHO

Group Health Northwest, West 5615 Sunset Highway, Spokane, WA 99204; tel. 509/838-9100; FAX. 509/458-0368; Henry S. Berman, M.D., President, Chief Executive Officer

HealthSense, 1602 21st Avenue, Lewiston, ID 83501; tel. 208/746-2671; FAX. 208/746-1030; Carolyn Steinbrecher-Loera, Manager, Managed Care Programs

Healthplus, P.O. Box 2113, Seattle, WA 98111-2113; tel. 206/670-4700; FAX. 206/670-4505; Gary Meade, President, Chief Executive Officer

IHC Health Plans, Inc., 36 South State Street, 15th Floor, Salt Lake City, UT 84111; tel. 801/442-5000; Sid Paulson, Chief Operating Officer

Primary Health Network, Inc., 800 Park Boulevard, Suite 760, Boise, ID 83712; tel. 208/344-1811; FAX. 208/344-4262; Elden Mitchell, President, Chief Executive Officer

QualMed Washington Health Plan, Inc., West 508 Sixth Avenue, Suite 700, P.O. Box 2470, Spokane, WA 99210-2470; tel. 509/459-6690, ext. 469; FAX. 509/459-9299; Nicolette Crowley, Provider Services Manager

ILLINOIS

Access HMO, Inc., d/b/a Unity HMO of Illinois, 150 South Wacker Drive, Suite 2100, Chicago, IL 60606; tel. 312/251-0955; FAX. 312/251-0294; Robert Currie, President & CEO

Aetna U.S. Healthcare of Illinois, Inc., 100 North Riverside Plaza, 20th Floor, Chicago, IL 60606; tel. 860/273-0123; FAX. 312/441-3067; Ken Malcolmson, President

Americaid Community Care, Americaid Illinois, Inc., 4425 Corporation Lane, Suite 100, Virginia Beach, VA 23462; tel. 804/490-6900; Michael L. Cotton, President & CEO

American Health Care Providers, Inc., 142 Towncenter Road, Matteson, IL 60443; tel. 708/503-5000; FAX. 708/503-5001; Asif A. Sayeed, President

BCI HMO, Inc., 300 East Randolph Street, 21st floor, Chicago, IL 60601-5090; tel. 312/653-6699; Eileen Holderbaum, Executive Director

Benchmark Health Insurance Company, 2550 Charles Street, Rockford, IL 61108; tel. 815/391-7000; FAX. 815/966-2089; Michael J. Gallagher

CIGNA HealthCare of Illinois, Inc., 525 West Monroe, Suite 1800, Chicago, IL 60661; tel. 312/496-5366; Bert B. Wagener, General Manager

Cigna HealthCare of St. Louis, Inc., 8182 Maryland Avenue, Suite 900, St. Louis, MO 63105; tel. 314/726-7841; FAX. 314/726-7819; James A. Young, General Manager

Community Health Choice, 650 South Clark, Suite 400, Chicago, IL 60605; tel. 312/922-4501; FAX. 312/922-6358; Patsy K. Crawford, CEO

Community Health Plan of Sarah Bush Lincoln, 1000 Health Center Drive, P.O. Box 372, Mattoon, IL 61938-0372; tel. 217/258-2572; Eugene A. Leblond, FACHE, President and Chief Executive Officer

Compass Health Care Plans, 310 South Michigan Avenue, Chicago, IL 60604; tel. 312/294-0200; FAX. 312/294-5826; Aldo Giacchino, Chief Executive Officer

Country Medical Plans, d/b/a Country Care HMO, PO BOx 2000, Bloomington, IL 61702-2000; tel. 309/557-5464; Terry Uppinghouse, Manager

Dreyer Health Plans, 1877 West Downer Place, Aurora, IL 60506; tel. 630/859-1100, ext. 5501; FAX. 630/906-5100; Richard A. Lutz, President

Exclusive Healthcare, Inc., Mutual of Omaha Plaza, Omaha, NE 68175; tel. 402/342-7600; David Creamer, Senior Managed Care Development Specialist

FHP of Illinois, Inc., One Lincoln Centre, Suite 700, Oakbrook Terrace, IL 60181-4260; tel. 630/916-8400; FAX. 630/916-4275; Gary M. Cole, President

Gencare Health Systems, Inc., P.O. Box 419079, St. Louis, MO 63141-9079; tel. 314/434-6114

Group Health Plan, 940 Westport Plaza, Suite 300, St. Louis, MO 63146; tel. 314/453-1700; FAX. 314/453-1958; Jerry Hansen, CEO

HMO Illinois a product of Health Care Services Corporation, 300 East Randolph Street, Chicago, IL 60601-5099; tel. 312/653-0000; Ray McCaskey, President

HMO Missouri (Blue Choice), 1831 Chestnut Street, P.O. Box 66828, St. Louis, MO 63166-6828; tel. 314/923-8623; FAX. 314/923-8958; Ken Evelyn, President, Chief Operating Officer

Harmony Health Plan of Illinois, Inc., 125 South Wacker Drive, Suite 2900, Chicago, IL 60606; tel. 312/630-2025; Keri Rosenbloom, Operations

Health Alliance Medical Plans, Inc., d/b/a Health Alliance HMO, 102 East Main, Suite 200, P.O. Box 6003, Urbana, IL 61801; tel. 217/337-8010; FAX. 217/337-8093; Jeffrey Ingram, CEO

Health Alliance Midwest, Inc., P.O. Box 6003, Urbana, IL 61801; tel. 217/337-8000; Jeffrey Ingram, CEO

Health Direct Insurance, Inc., 1011 East Touhy Avenue, Suite 500, Des Plaines, IL 60018-2808; tel. 847/391-9590; Jennifer L. Cline, CEO

Healthlink HMO, Inc., 777 Craig Road, PO BOx 410289, St. Louis, MO 63141; tel. 314/569-7200; FAX. 314/569-3268; Dennis McCart, Executive Director

Heritage National Healthplan of Tennessee, Inc., 1515 Fifth Avenue, Suite 200, Moline, IL 61265; tel. 309/765-1200; G. Michael Hammes, President

Heritage National Healthplan, Inc., 1300 River Drive0, Moline, IL 61265-1368; tel. 309/765-1200; FAX. 309/765-1322; G. Michael Hammes, President

Humana Health Chicago, Inc., P.O. Box 740036, Louisville, KY 40201-7436; tel. 312/441-9111; Barry Averill, Vice President

Humana Health Plan, Inc., 30 South Wacker Drive, Suite 3100, CHicago, IL 60606; tel. 312/441-5350; Barry Averill, Vice President

Illinois Healthcare Insurance Co., 303 E. Washington, Bloomington, IL 61701; tel. 309/829-1061; Thomas J. Pliura, MD, JD, President

Illinois Masonic Community Health Plan, 836 West Wellington, Room 1707, Chicago, IL 60657; tel. 312/975-1600; Dana Gilbert, Administrative Director

John Deere Family Healthplan, Inc., 1300 River Drive, Moline, IL 61265-1368; tel. 309/765-1600; G. Michael Hammes, President

Maxicare Health Plans of the Midwest, Inc., 111 East Wacker Drive, Suite 1500, Chicago, IL 60601; tel. 312/616-4700; FAX. 312/616-4998; Mark Hanrahan, Vice President, General Manager

Medical Associates Health Plan, Inc., One CyCare Plaza, Suite 230, PO Box 5002, Dubuque, IA 52004-5002; tel. 319/556-8070; FAX. 319/556-5134; Lawrence E. Cremer, Executive Director

Medical Center Health Plan, d/b/a Partners HMO, One City Place Drive, Suite 670, St. Louis, MO 63141; tel. 314/567-6660; Delbert E. Snoberger, Chief Executive Officer

Mercy Care Corporation, 2600 South Michigan Avenue, Chicago, IL 60616-2477; tel. 312/567-5649; FAX. 312/567-2786; Ramesh Joshi, Director

Mercy Health Plans of Missouri, Inc., 12935 North Outer 40 Drive, St. Louis, MO 63141-8636; tel. 314/214-8100; FAX. 314/214-8101; Thomas L. Kelly, President

NYLCare Health Plans of the Midwest, Inc., 111 West 22nd Street, 8th floor, Oak Brook, IL 60521; tel. 630/368-1800; FAX. 630/368-1802; William P. Donahue, President

OSF Health Plans, Inc., 300 S.W. Jefferson Street, Peoria, IL 61602-1413; tel. 309/677-8207; FAX. 309/677-8330; William F. Pierce, Jr., President

One Health Plan of Illinois, Inc., 6250 River Road, Suite 10-100, Rosemont, IL 60018; tel. 708/292-0024; Patricia Ann Moldovan, President

Oxford Health Plans, Inc., 9801 West Higgins, Suite 720, Rosemont, IL 60018-4701; tel. 847/685-2273; Aldo Giacchio, President

Personal Care Insurance of Illinois, Inc., 510 Devonshire Drive, Suite G, Champaign, IL 61820; tel. 217/366-1226; FAX. 217/366-5571; Kenneth W. Mooney, President/Chief

Principal Health Care of Illinois, Inc., One Lincoln Center, Suite 1040, Oakbrook Terrace, IL 60181-4267; tel. 630/916-6622; FAX. 630/916-9595, ext. 200; Lee Green, Executive Director

Principal Health Care of St. Louis, Inc., 12312 Olive Boulevard, Suite 150, St. Louis, MO 63141; tel. 314/434-6990; FAX. 314/434-7540; Barbara C. Buenemann, Executive Director

Rockford Health Plans, 3401 North Perryville Road, Rockford, IL 61114; tel. 815/654-3600; FAX. 815/654-5186; John W. Zilavy, Executive DIrector

Rush Prudential Health Plans, 233 South Wacker Drive, Suite 3900, Chicago, IL 60605-6309; tel. 312/234-7000; FAX. 312/986-4859; Scott Serota, President/CEO

UIHMO, Inc., 2023 West Ogden Avenue, Suite 205, M/C 692, Chicago, IL 60612-3741; tel. 312/996-3553; FAX. 312/413-7872; Anthony A. Ferrara, President

Union Health Service, 1634 West Polk, Chicago, IL 60612; tel. 312/829-4224; FAX. 312/829-8241; Helen M. Hrynkiw, Executive Director

United HealthCare of Illinois, Inc., d/b/a Chicago HMO, Ltd., One South Wacker Drive, P.O. Box 909714, Chicago, IL 60609-9714; tel. 312/424-4460; FAX. 312/424-4448; Marshall Rozzi, President, Chief Executive Officer

Wellmark Health Plan of Northern Ilinois, Inc., 1420 Kensington Road, Suite 203, Oak Brook, IL 60521-2106; tel. 800/345-7848

INDIANA

Aetna Health Plans of Ohio, Inc., 3690 Orange Place, Suite 200, Cleveland, OH 44122; tel. 203/636–9279

Alternative Dental Care of Indiana, Inc., One Penmark, Suite 200, 11595 Meridian Street, Carmel, IN 46032; tel. 800/237–7727; David P. McSweeney, President

Alternative Health Delivery Systems, Inc., 1901 Campus Place, Louisville, KY 40299; tel. 502/261–2176; FAX. 502/261–2255; Carol H. Muldoon, Vice President, Chief Operating Officer

American Health Care Providers, Inc., 4801 Southwick Drive, Matteson, IL 60443; tel. 708/503–5000; Asif Sayeed, President

Anthem Health Plan, d/b/a Key Health Plan, 120 Monument Circle, Indianapolis, IN 46204; tel. 317/488–6000; FAX. 317/290–5695; Dijuana Lewis, Vice President, Health Care Management

Arnett HMO, Inc., 3768 Rome Drive, Lafayette, IN 47905; tel. 317/448–8200; FAX. 317/448–8660; James A. Brunnemer, Executive Director

BCI HMO, Inc., (formerly HMO Illinois, Inc.), 233 North Michigan Avenue, Chicago, IL 60601; tel. 312/938–6347; FAX. 312/819–1220; Simeon Martin Hickman, President

Benefit Directions, Inc., 3901 West 86th Street, Suite 230, Indianapolis, IN 46268; tel. 317/872–2202

CIGNA Healthplan of Illinois, Inc., 1700 Higgins, Suite 600, Des Plaines, IL 60018; tel. 708/699–5600; FAX. 708/699–5675; John W. Rohfritch, Senior Vice President

ChoiceCare Health Plans, Inc., 655 Eden Park Drive, Cincinnati, OH 45202; tel. 513/784–5200; FAX. 513/784–5300; Daniel A. Gregorie, M.D., Chief Executive Officer

CompDent Corporation, 1930 Bishop Lane, 16th Floor, Louisville, KY 40218; tel. 800/456–5500, ext. 201; FAX. 502/456–2772; Allan Brockway Morris, President, Chief Executive Officer

Coordinated Care Corporation Indiana, Inc., d/b/a Managed Health Services, 8688 Broadway, Merrillville, IN 46410; tel. 219/756–7134

Delta Dental Plan of Indiana, Inc., 5875 Castle Creek Parkway, North Drive, Indianapolis, IN 46250; tel. 317/842–4022

Dental Care Plus, Inc., 4500 Lake Forest Drive, Suite 512, Cincinnati, OH 45242; tel. 513/554–1100; FAX. 513/554–3187; Dennis K. Coleman, President, Chief Executive Officer

FHP of Illinois, 747 East 22nd Street, Suite 100, Lombard, IL 60148; tel. 708/916–8400

Family Health Plan of Indiana, Inc., 3510 Park Place West, Mishawaka, IN 46545; tel. 219/271–8901; FAX. 219/271–8911; Larry L. Donaldson, Chief Executive Officer

First Commonwealth, Inc., 444 North Wells, Suite 600, Chicago, IL 60610; tel. 312/644–1800, ext. 8638; FAX. 312/644–1822; Mark R. Lundberg, Vice President, Sales

HMO Kentucky, Inc., 9901 Linn Station Road, Louisville, KY 40223; tel. 502/423–2282; FAX. 502/423–6979; G. Douglas Sutherland, President

HMPK, Inc., P.O. Box 740036, Louisville, KY 40201–7436; tel. 502/580–5804; Craig Drablos, Executive Director

HPlan, Inc., 101 East Main Street, 12th Floor, Louisville, KY 40204; tel. 800/245–4446; FAX. 502/580–5044

Health Resources, Inc., 314 Southeast Riverside Drive, P.O. Box 3607, Evansville, IN 47735–3607; tel. 812/424–1444; FAX. 812/424–2096; Edward L. Fritz, D.D.S., President

Healthpoint, LLC, 8900 Keystone Crossing, Suite 500, Indianapolis, IN 46240; tel. 317/574–8181; FAX. 317/574–8182; L. Denise Smith, Administrative Assistant

Healthsource Indiana Managed Care Plan, Inc., 225 South East Street, Suite 240, Indianapolis, IN 46206; tel. 800/933–3466; FAX. 317/687–8500; David H. Smith, Chief Executive Officer

Humana Health Plan, Inc., 500 West Main Street, Louisville, KY 40202; tel. 502/580–1860; FAX. 502/580–3127; Greg Donaldson, Director, Corporate Communications

Humana HealthChicago, Inc., 500 West Main Street, P.O. Box 1438, Louisville, KY 40201–1438; tel. 502/580–1000; Norman J. Beles, President

Indiana Vision Services, Inc., 115 West Washington Street, Suite 1370, Indianapolis, IN 46204; tel. 317/687–1066

M Plan, Inc., 8802 North Meridian Street, Suite 100, Indianapolis, IN 46260; tel. 317/571–5300; FAX. 317/571–5306; Alex Slabosky, President

MIDA Dental Plans, Inc., 2000 Town Center, Suite 2200, Southfield, MI 48075; tel. 810/353–6410; Walter Knysz, Jr., D.D.S., President

Maxicare Health Plans of the Midwest, Maxicare Illinois, 111 East Wacker Dr., Suite 1500, Chicago, IL 60601; tel. 312/616–4700

Maxicare Indiana, Inc., 9480 Priority Way, West Drive, Indianapolis, IN 46240–3899; tel. 317/844–5775; FAX. 317/574–0713; Vicki F. Perry, Vice President, General Manager

Metrahealth Care Plan of Illinois, Inc., 1900 East Golf Road, Suite 501, Schaumburg, IL 60173; tel. 708/619–2222

Metrahealth Care Plan of Kentucky, Inc., Northmark Business Center III, 4501 Erskin, Suite 100, Cincinnati, OH 45242–4713; tel. 513/745–9700; Charles Stark, President

National Foot Care Program, Inc., Pinewood Plaza, 22255 Greenfield, Suite 550, Southfield, MI 48075; tel. 313/559–2579

Partners National Health Plans of Indiana, Inc., One Michiana Square, 100 East Wayne, Suite 502, South Bend, IN 46601; tel. 219/233–4899; FAX. 219/234–7484; Richard C. Born, Senior Vice President Finance, Operations

Physicians Health Network, Inc., One Riverfront Place, Suite 400, P.O. Box 3357, Evansville, IN 47732; tel. 812/465–6000; FAX. 812/465–6014; Kevin M. Clancy, Chairman, President, Chief Executive Officer

Physicians Health Plan of Northern Indiana, Inc., 8101 West Jefferson Boulevard, Fort Wayne, IN 46804; tel. 219/432–6690; FAX. 219/432–0493; John P. Smith, M.D., President

Physicians Health Plan of Northern Indiana, Inc., 8101 West Jefferson Boulevard, Fort Wayne, IN 46804–4163; tel. 800/982–6257; FAX. 219/432–0493

Principal Health Care of Indiana, Inc., One North Pennsylvania, Suite 1100, Indianapolis, IN 46204; tel. 317/263–0920; FAX. 317/972–8249; Douglas Stratton, Executive Director

Prudential Health Care Plan, Inc., PruCare, 24 Greenway Plaza, Suite 500, Houston, TX 77046; tel. 201/716–8174

Riverside Dental Care of Indiana, Inc., 1100 Dennison Avenue, Columbus, OH 43201; tel. 614/297–4870; Richard A. Mitchell, President

Rush Prudential HMO, Inc., 233 South Wacker Drive, Suite 3900, Chicago, IL 60606; tel. 312/234–7000; FAX. 312/234–8555; Carmeline Esposito, Public Relations Manager

Sagamore Health Network, Inc., 11555 North Meridian, Suite 400, Carmel, IN 46032; tel. 317/573–2904; FAX. 317/580–8488; Malinda Hinkle, Vice President, Marketing

Southeastern Indiana Health Organization, Inc. (SIHO), 432 Washington Street, P.O. Box l787, Columbus, IN 47202–1787; tel. 812/378–7000; FAX. 812/378–7048; Roy H. Flaherty, President, Chief Executive Officer

SpecialMed of Indiana, Inc., 120 Monument Circle, Indianapolis, IN 46204–4903; tel. 317/488–6128; Mike Hostetter, M.D., President

The Dental Concern, Ltd., 222 North LaSalle Street, Suite 2140, Chicago, IL 60601; tel. 312/201–1260; Polly Reese, D.D.S., Dental Director

United Dental Care of Indiana, Inc., 50 South Meridian, Suite 700, Indianapolis, IN 46204–3542; tel. 800/262–5388

Universal Health Services, Inc., 403 West 14th Street, Chicago Heights, IL 60411–2498; tel. 708/755–2462; Ralph R. Crescenzo, President

Welborn Clinic/Welborn HMO, Welborn Health Options, 421 Chestnut Street, Evansville, IN 47713; tel. 812/425–3939; David Christeson, M.D., Medical Director

IOWA

Care Choices HMO, 600 Fourth Street, Terra Centre, Suite 401, Sioux City, IA 51101; tel. 712/252–2344; FAX. 712/233–3684; Bill Windsor, Executive Director

Exclusive Healthcare, Mutual of Omaha Plaza, Omaha, NE 68175; tel. 402/978–2700; FAX. 402/978–2999; Dick L. Easley, President

HMO Nebraska, Inc., 10040 Regency Circle, Suite 300, Omaha, NE 68114; tel. 402/392–2800; Richard L. Guffey, President

Health Alliance Midwest, Inc., 102 East Main Street, Suite 200, P.O. Box 6003, Urbana, IL 61801; tel. 217/337–8000; Robert C. Parker, M.D., President

Heritage National Healthplan, 1300 River Drive, Suite 200, Moline, IL 61265; tel. 309/765–1200; G. Michael Hammes, President

John Deere Family Health Plan, 1300 River Drive, Suite 200, Moline, IL 61265–1368; tel. 309/765–1200; Richard Van Belle, President

Medical Associates Health Plan, Inc., One CyCare Plaza, Suite 230, Dubuque, IA 52001; tel. 319/556–8070; FAX. 319/556–5134; Lawrence Cremer, Chief Executive Officer

Mercy Alternative HMO – IA, (d/b/a Care Choices), 600 4th St., Sioux City, IA 51101–1744; tel. 712/252–2344

Nevada Care, d/b/a Iowa Health Solutions, 300 N. W. Bank Tower, Spruce Hills Drive at Middle Road, Bettendorf, IA 52722; tel. 319/359–8999; James Dyer, Chairman & CEO

Principal Health Care of Iowa, Inc., 4600 Westown Parkway, Suite 301, West Des Moines, IA 50266–1099; tel. 515/225–1234; FAX. 515/223–0097; Louis Garcia, Executive Director

Principal Health Care of Nebraska, Inc., 330 N. 117th Street, PO Box 541210, Omaha, NE 68154–9210; tel. 800/288–3343; FAX. 402/333–1116; Kenneth Klaasmeyer, Executive Director

United HealthCare of Midlands, Inc., 2717 North 118th Circle, Omaha, NE 68164; tel. 402/445–5600; FAX. 402/445–5572; John Michael Braasch, President

Wellmark Health Plan of Iowa, 636 Grand Avenue, Des Moines, IA 50309; tel. 800/355–2031; Thomas E. Press, President

KANSAS

BMA Selectcare, Inc., One Penn Valley Park, Zip 64108, P.O. Box 419458, Kansas City, MO 64141; tel. 816/753–8000, ext. 5309; FAX. 816/751–5571; John R. Barton, President

Blue–Care, Inc., 2301 Main, Zip 64108–2428, P.O. Box 413163, Kansas City, MO 64141–6163; tel. 816/395–2222; Larry K. Chastain, President

CIGNA HealthCare of Ohio, Inc., 3700 Corporate Drive, Suite 200, Business Campus N.E. # Five, Columbus, OH 43231; tel. 614/823–7500; FAX. 614/823–7519; Elmond A. Kenyon, President

Community Health Plan, 5301 Faraon, St. Joseph, MO 64506; tel. 816/271–1247; Joan Copeland, President

Community Health Plans of KS Inc., 900 Mass., Suite 602, Lawrence, KS 66044; tel. 913/749–6100; Mike Herbert

Exclusive Healthcare, Inc., 7300 College Boulevard, Suite 208, Overland Park, KS 66210; tel. 913/451–1777; FAX. 913/451–7742; Kim Daniels, Executive Director

FirstGuard Health Plan, Inc., 3801 Blue Parkway, Kansas City, MO 64130; tel. 816/922–7645; Mark Bryant

GenCare Health Systems, Inc., 969 Executive Parkway, Suite 100, P.O. Box 27379, St. Louis, MO 63141–6301; tel. 314/434–6114; FAX. 314/434–6328; Tom Zorumski, President, Chief Executive Officer

HMO Kansas, Inc., 419 West 29th Street, Topeka, KS 66601–0110; tel. 913/291–8600; Thomas Miller, President

HealthNet, Inc., Two Pershing Square, 2300 Main Street, Suite 700, Kansas City, MO 64108; tel. 816/221–8400; FAX. 816/221–7709; Andrew Dahl, Sc.D., Chief Executive Officer

Healthcare America Plans, Inc., 453 South Webb Road, Wichita, KS 67207–1309; tel. 316/262–7400; FAX. 316/262–1395; Stan Vaughn

Horizon Health Plan, Inc., 623 Southwest 10th Avenue, Suite 300, Topeka, KS 66612–1627; tel. 913/235–0402; Bruce M. Gosser, President

Humana Health Plan, Inc., 10450 Holmes, Suite 330, Kansas City, MO 64131–1471; tel. 816/941–8900; FAX. 816/941–8630; David Fields, Executive Director

Humana Kansas City, Inc., 10405 Holmes, Second Floor, Kansas City, MO 64131–3471; tel. 816/941–8900; Gregory D. Wolf, President

Kaiser Foundation Health Plan of Kansas City, Inc., 10561 Barkley, Suite 200, Overland Park, KS 66212–1886; tel. 913/967–4600; FAX. 913/642–0209; Kathryn Paul, President, Regional Manager

Lawrence Community Health Plan, Inc., 1112 West Sixth, Suite 210, Lawrence, KS 66044; tel. 913/832–6850; FAX. 913/832–6875; Michael J. Herbert, Chief Operating Officer

MetraHealth Care Plan of Kansas City, Inc., (a wholly owned subsidiary of United HealthCare of the Midwest, Inc.), 9300 West 110th Street, Suite 350A, Overland Park, KS 66210; tel. 913/451–5656; FAX. 913/451–0492; Robert S. Bonney, Vice President

Preferred Plus of Kansas, Inc., 345 Riverview, Suite 103, P.O. Box 49288, Wichita, KS 67203; tel. 316/268–0390; Marlon Dauner, President

Premier Health, Inc., d/b/a Premier Blue, 1133 Topeka Avenue, Topeka, KS 66629–0001; tel. 913/291–7000; John W. Knack, Jr., President

Principal Health Care of Kansas City, Inc., 1001 East 101st Terrace, Suite 230, Kansas City, MO 64131; tel. 816/941–3030; FAX. 816/941–8516; Kenneth J. Linde, President

Prudential Health Care Plan, Inc., 4600 Madison Avenue, Suite 300, Kansas City, MO 64112; tel. 816/756–5588; FAX. 816/756–5667; David W. Dingley, Executive Director

Total Health Care, 2301 Main Street, 64108–2428, P.O. Box 413613, Kansas City, MO 64141–6163; tel. 816/395–2222; Larry K. Chastain, President

TriSource HealthCare, Inc., d/b/a Blue Advantage, 2301 Main Street, P.O. Box 419130, Kansas City, MO 64141–6130; tel. 816/395–3636; FAX. 816/395–3811; Larry K. Chastain, President, Chief Executive Officer

Trucare, Inc., 2301 Holmes, Kansas City, MO 64108; tel. 816/556–3186; Joseph Cecil, President

KENTUCKY

Advantage Care, Inc., 120 Prosperous Place, Suite 100, Lexington, KY 40509; tel. 606/264–4600; Jeffrey P. Johnson, Chief Executive Officer

Aetna U.S. Healthcare, 3690 Orange Place, Suite 200, Cleveland, OH 44122; tel. 216/486–8979; David K. Ellwanger, Administrator

Alternative Health Delivery Systems, 1901 Campus Place, 1st Floor, Louisville, KY 40299; tel. 502/261–2100; Thomas J. Schifano, Administrator

American Health Network of Kentucky, Inc., 300 West Main, Suite 100, Louisville, KY 40202; tel. 502/681–0960; Denise Schifano, Regional Director, Operations

Anthem Blue Cross Blue Shield, 9901 Linn Station Road, Louisville, KY 40223; tel. 502/423–2277; FAX. 502/423–2729; Robert McIntire, Vice President

Anthem Blue Cross and Blue Shield, 9901 Linn Station Road, Louisville, KY 40223; tel. 502/423–2373; FAX. 502/423–6974; George L. Walker, Chief Operating Officer

Bluegrass Family Health, Inc., 651 Perimeter Drive, Suite Two B, Lexington, KY 40517; tel. 606/269–4475; Katherine Schaefer

CHA Health, 220 Canary Road (Street Zip Code 40503–3382), P.O. Box 23468, Lexington, KY 40523–3468; tel. 606/257–8074; Robert K. Davy, Chief Executive Officer

ChoiceCare, 655 Eden Park Drive, Cincinnati, OH 45202; tel. 513/784–5200; FAX. 513/784–5300; Robert W. Quirk, Dir. of Legislative & Regulatory Affairs

FHP Health Care, 11260 Chester Road, Suite 800, Cincinnati, OH 45246; tel. 513/772–7325; John Davren

HMPK, 500 West Main Street, P.O. Box 1438, Louisville, KY 40201–1438; tel. 502/580–1854; FAX. 502/580–5044; Heidi Margulis, Director, Government Programs

HPLAN, Inc., 500 West Main Street, P.O. Box 1438, Louisville, KY 40201–1438; tel. 502/580–1854; Heidi Margulis, Director, Government Programs

Healthsource Kentucky, Inc., 100 Mallard Creek Road, Suite 300, Louisville, KY 40207; tel. 502/899–7500; Paul E. Stamp, Interim Executive Director

Healthwise of Kentucky, Ltd., 2409 Harrodsburg Road, Lexington, KY 40504; tel. 606/296–6100; FAX. 606/255–9134; Harold Bischoff, Executive Director

Heritage National Healthplan, Inc., 909 River Drive, Moline, IL 61265; tel. 309/765–7660; Douglas R. Niska, Director

Humana Health Plan, Inc., 500 West Main Street, P.O. Box 1438, Louisville, KY 40201–1438; tel. 502/580–1854; FAX. 502/580–5018; Heidi Margulis, Director, Government Programs

MetraHealth Care Plan of Kentucky, 4501 Erskine Road, Suite 150, Cincinnati, OH 45242; tel. 502/339–8481; Charles Stark, Administrator

Owensboro Community Health Plan, 2211 Mayfair Avenue, Suite 205, Owensboro, KY 42301; tel. 502/686–6368; Ronald T. Derstadt, Executive Director

Prudential HealthCare, 312 Elm Street, Suite 1400, Cincinnati, OH 45202; tel. 513/784–7559; FAX. 513/784–7020; Lynn Gross, Manager, Health Care Services

United Health Care of Kentucky, 2409 Harrodsburg Road, Lexington, KY 40504; tel. 606/296–6100; Budd Fisher, Chief Executive Officer

LOUISIANA

Advantage Health Plan, Inc., 829 St. Charles Avenue, New Orleans, LA 70130; tel. 504/568–9009; FAX. 504/568–0301; Jane Cooper, President, Chief Executive Officer

Aetna Health Plans of Louisiana, Inc., 3900 North Causeway Boulevard, Suite 410, Metairie, LA 70002–7283; tel. 504/830–5600; FAX. 504/837–6571; Michael L. Rogers, President

Apex Healthcare of Louisiana, Inc., 639 Loyola Avenue, Suite 1725, New Orleans, LA 70113; tel. 504/585–0508; Warwick D. Syphers

CIGNA HealthCare of Louisiana, Inc., 4354 South Sherwood Forest Boulevard, Suite 240, Baton Rouge, LA 70816; tel. 504/295–2800; FAX. 504/295–2888; Nancy T. Horstmann, Executive Director

CIGNA HealthCare of North Louisiana, Inc., 4354 South Sherwood Forest Boulevard, Suite 240, Baton Rouge, LA 70816; tel. 504/295–2800; FAX. 504/295–2888; Nancy T. Horstmann, Executive Director

Capitol Health Network, Inc., 4700 Wichers Drive, Suite 300, Marrero, LA 70072; tel. 504/347–4515; John Sudderth, Chief Executive Officer

Community Health Network of Louisiana, 2431 South Acadian Thruway, Suite 350, P.O. Box 80159, Baton Rouge, LA 70898–0159; tel. 504/237–2106; FAX. 504/237–2222; Glen J. Golemi, President, Chief Executive Officer

Foundation Health, Louisiana Health Plan, Inc., 5353 Essen Lane, Suite 450, Baton Rouge, LA 70809; tel. 504/763–5300; Joseph Klinger

Futurecare Health Plans of Louisiana, Inc., 3029 South Sherwood Forest Boulevard, Suite 300, Baton Rouge, LA 70816; tel. 800/764–5201; David P. Giles

Gulf South Health Plans, Inc., 5615 Corporate Boulevard, Suite Three, P.O. Box 80339, Baton Rouge, LA 70898–0339; tel. 504/237–1700; FAX. 504/237–1939; Jack W. Walker, President

HMO of Louisiana, Inc., P.O. Box 98029, Baton Rouge, LA 70898–8024; tel. 504/295–2383; FAX. 504/295–2491; Michael A. Hayes, Executive Director

Health Plus of Louisiana, Inc., 2600 Greenwood Road, Shreveport, LA 71103; tel. 318/632–4590; FAX. 318/632–4463; Peter J. Babin, President

Humana Health Plan of Louisiana, Inc., 500 West Main Street, P.O. Box 740036, Louisville, KY 40201–7436; tel. 502/580–1000; James E. Murray, Vice President, Finance

Life Net Health Plans HMO, Inc., 9100 Bluebonnet Centre Boulevard, Suite 200, Baton Rouge, LA 70809; tel. 504/295–7000; Robert Jackson

Maxicare Louisiana, Inc., 3850 North Causeway Boulevard, Suite 990, Metairie, LA 70002; tel. 504/836–2022; FAX. 504/835–0493; Alan M. Preston, Vice President, General Manager

Medfirst Health Plans of Louisiana, Inc., 3500 North Causeway Boulevard, Suite 520, Metairie, LA 70002; tel. 504/837–4000; FAX. 504/831–1107; Carol A. Solomon, President

MetraHealth Corporation, 3900 North Causeway Boulevard, Suite 860, Metairie, LA 70002; tel. 504/832–7655; FAX. 504/836–5506; Susan Sharkey, Vice President, Executive Director

NYLCare Health Plans of Louisiana, Inc., 2014 West Pinhook Road, Suite 200, Lafayette, LA 70508; tel. 800/825–0568; FAX. 318/237–1703; Burley J. Pellerin II, Director, Operations

Ochsner Health Plan, Inc. (HMO), One Galleria Boulevard, Suite 1224, Metairie, LA 70001; tel. 504/836–6600; FAX. 504/836–6566; R. Lyle Luman, President, Chief Executive Officer

OmniCare Health Plan of Louisiana, Inc., 400 Poydras Street, Suite 2400, New Orleans, LA 70130; tel. 504/523–9751; FAX. 504/523–2638; Joan G. Savoy, Director, Operations

Principal Health Care of Louisiana, 3421 North Causeway Boulevard, Suite 600, Metairie, LA 70002; tel. 504/834–0840; FAX. 504/834–2694; Erin R. Glynn, Executive Director

SMA HMO, Inc., 111 Veteran's Memorial Boulevard, Heritage Plaza, Suite 500, Metairie, LA 70005; tel. 504/837–7374; FAX. 504/837–7366; Barbara B. Louviere, President

Sunbelt Health Plan of Louisiana, Inc., 3434 South Causeway Boulevard, Suite 901, Metairie, LA 70001; tel. 504/922–9142; John F. Ales

Vantage Health Plan, Inc., 909 North 18th Street, Suite 201, Monroe, LA 71201; tel. 318/323–2269; Angela Olden, Executive Director

MAINE

AssureCare of Maine, Inc., 2367 Congress Street, Portland, ME 04102; tel. 800/600–5905; Courtney Hudson, Vice President

Blue Cross and Blue Shield of Maine, Two Gannett Drive, South Portland, ME 04106; tel. 800/527–7706; Nancy Hutchings, Director, Customer Service

Harvard Community Health Plan, Inc., 10 Brookline Place West, Brookline, MA 02146; tel. 617/421–6400; Laura Peabody, Assistant General Counsel

Health Plans, Inc., 202 US Route One, P.O. Box 165, Falmouth, ME 04105; tel. 207/781–9890; FAX. 207/828–2408; Jeffrey W. Kirby, Controller

Healthsource Maine, Inc., Two Stonewood Drive, P.O. Box 447, Freeport, ME 04032–0447; tel. 207/865–5000, ext. 5201; FAX. 207/865–5632; Richard White, Chief Executive Officer

Healthsource New Hampshire, Donovan Street Extension, P.O. Box 2041, Concord, NH 03302; tel. 603/225–5077; FAX. 603/225–7621; Susan Berry, Director, Marketing

NYLCare of Maine Health Plans, Inc., One Monument Square, Portland, ME 04102; tel. 207/791–7916; Charlotte Pease, Manager

Tufts Health Plan of New England, Inc., 333 Wyman Street, Waltham, MA 02254–9112; tel. 617/466–9055; Theresa Gallinaro, Manager

MARYLAND

Aetna Health Plans of the Mid–Atlantic, Inc., 7600 A Leesburg Pike, Falls Church, VA 22043; tel. 703/903–7100; Jon Glaudemans, Vice President, Health Services

CIGNA Healthplan of the MidAtlantic, Inc., 9700 Patuxent Woods Drive, Columbia, MD 21046; tel. 410/720–5800; FAX. 410/720–5860

Capital Care, Inc., 550 12th Street, S.W., Washington, DC 20065; tel. 202/479–3678; FAX. 202/479–3660; M. Bruce Edwards, President

Chesapeake Health Plan, Inc., Executive Office, 814 Light Street, Baltimore, MD 21230; tel. 410/539–8622; FAX. 410/752–0271; Leon Kaplan, President, Chief Executive Officer

Columbia Medical Plan, Inc., Two Knoll North Drive, Columbia, MD 21045; tel. 410/997–8500; FAX. 410/964–4563; Marilyn M. Levinson, Director, Patient Services

Delmarva Health Care Plan, 106 Marlboro Road, P.O. Box 2410, Easton, MD 21601; tel. 410/822–7223; FAX. 410/822–8152; Richard Moore, President

Free State Health Plan, Inc., 100 South Charles Street, Tower II, Baltimore, MD 21201; tel. 410/528–7000

George Washington University Health Plan, Inc., 4550 Montgomery Avenue, Suite 800, Bethesda, MD 20814; tel. 301/941–2000; FAX. 301/941–2005; Lawrence E. Berman, Director, Government Relations and Legal Affairs

Healthcare Corporation of Mid–Atlantic, 100 South Charles Street, Baltimore, MD 21201; tel. 301/828–7000; David D. Wolf, Chief Executive Officer

Healthcare Corporation of the Potomac, Inc., Care First–Free State Potomac, Equitable Bank Center's Tower–II, 100 South Charles Street, Baltimore, MD 21201; tel. 410/528–7025; FAX. 410/528–7013; David Wolf, President

Humana Group Health Association, Inc., 4301 Connecticut Avenue, N.W., Washington, DC 20008; tel. 202/364–2000; FAX. 202/364–7418; Robert P. Pfotenhauer, President, Chief Executive Officer

Kaiser Foundation Health Plan of the Mid–Atlantic States, Inc., 2101 East Jefferson Street, Rockville, MD 20852; tel. 301/816–6420; FAX. 301/816–7478; Cleve Killingsworth, President

MD Individual Practice Association, MDIPA/Optimum, Four Taft Court, Rockville, MD 20850; tel. 301/762–8205; FAX. 301/762–2479; Steve B. Griffin, President

NYL Care Health Plans of the Mid–Atlantic, Inc., 7601 Ora Glen Drive, Suite 200, Greenbelt, MD 20770; tel. 301/982–0098, ext. 3308; FAX. 301/489–5282; Jeff D. Emerson, President, Chief Executive Officer

Optimum Choice, Inc., Four Taft Court, Rockville, MD 20850; tel. 301/762–8205

PHN–HMO, Inc., 5700 Executive Drive, Suite 104, Baltimore, MD 21228–1798; tel. 410/747–9060; FAX. 410/788–7543; L. David Taylor, President, Chief Executive Officer

Physicians Health Plan, Inc., 2111 Wilson Boulevard, Suite 1150, Arlington, VA 22201; tel. 703/525-0602; FAX. 703/243-3066; Suellen Rainey, Executive Director

Primehealth Corporation, 9602 C Martin Luther King Jr. Highway, Lanham, MD 20706; Edward L. Mosley, Jr., President

Principal Health Care Plan of the Mid-Atlantic, Inc., 1801 Rockville Pike, Suite 110, Rockville, MD 20852; tel. 301/881-4903; FAX. 301/881-9808; Julia Campion, Executive Director

Principal Health Care of Delaware, Inc., One Corporate Commons, 100 West Commons Boulevard, Suite 300, New Castle, DE 19720; tel. 302/322-4700

Prudential Health Care Plan, Inc., Seton Court, 2800 North Charles Street, Baltimore, MD 21218; tel. 410/554-7000; FAX. 410/554-7070

Total Health Care, Inc., 2305 North Charles Street, Baltimore, MD 21218; tel. 410/383-8300; FAX. 410/554-9012; Edwin R. Golden, President

U.S. Healthcare, 980 Jolly Road, Blue Bell, PA 19422; tel. 215/628-4800; FAX. 215/283-6858

MASSACHUSETTS

Aetna U.S. Healthcare Inc., 3 Burlington Woods Drive, Burlington, MA 01803; tel. 800/233-3105

CIGNA HealthCare of Massachusetts, Inc., Three Newton Executive Park, 2223 Washington Street, Suite 200, Newton, MA 02162; tel. 800/345-9458

Central Massachusetts Health Care, Mechanics Tower, 100 Front Street, Suite 300, Worcester, MA 01608; tel. 508/798-8667; FAX. 508/798-4197, ext. 4201; Brian D. Wells, Chief Executive Officer

Community Health Plan, One CHP Plaza, Latham, NY 12110-1080; tel. 800/638-0668; Fred H. Hooven, Regional Administrator

ConnectiCare of Massachusetts, Inc., P.O. Box 522, Farmington, CT 06032-0522; tel. 800/474-1466

Coordinated Health Partners, Inc., d/b/a Blue Chip/Coordinated Health Partners, Inc., 15 LaSalle Square, Providence, RI 02903; tel. 800/528-4141; James E. Bobbitt, Chief Operating Officer

Fallon Community Health Plan, One Chestnut Place, 10 Chestnut Street, Worcester, MA 01608; tel. 508/799-2100; FAX. 508/831-0921; Gary J. Zelch, Executive Director

HMO Blue, 100 Summer Street, Boston, MA 02110; tel. 617/832-7797; FAX. 617/832-7973; Maureen Coneys, Executive Director

Harvard Community Health Plan, 10 Brookline Place West, Brookline, MA 02146; tel. 617/731-8240; FAX. 617/730-4695; Manuel M. Ferris, President, Chief Executive Officer

Harvard Pilgrim Health Care, 10 Brookline Place West, Brookline, MA 02146; tel. 617/745-1000; FAX. 617/982-9668; Allan Greenberg, Chief Executive Officer

Harvard Pilgrim Health Care of New England, One Hoppin Street, Providence, RI 02903-4199; tel. 401/331-3000; FAX. 401/331-0496; Stephen Schoenbaum, M.D., Medical Director

Health New England, One Monarch Place, Springfield, MA 01144; tel. 413/787-4000; FAX. 413/734-3356; Phil M. Pin, Interim President

Healthsource Massachusetts, (d/b/a Healthsource CMHC), 100 Front Street, Worcester, MA 01608-1449; tel. 800/922-8380

Healthsource New Hampshire, 54 Regional Drive, P.O. Box 2041, Concord, NH 03302-2041; tel. 603/225-5077; FAX. 603/229-2983; Donna K. Lencki, Chief Executive Officer

Kaiser Foundation Health Plan, 170 University Drive, P.O. Box 862, Amherst, MA 01002; tel. 413/256-0151, ext. 5162; FAX. 413/549-1601; Linda Todaro, Massachusetts Area Administrator

Neighborhood Health Plan, 253 Summer Street, Boston, MA 02210; tel. 617/772-5500; FAX. 617/772-5513; James Hooley, Chief Executive Officer

One Health Plan of Massachusetts, Inc., One University Office Park, 29 Sawyer Road, 3rd Floor, Waltham, MA 02154; tel. 800/725-0748

Pilgrim Health Care Inc., 1200 Crown Colony Drive, Quincy, MA 02169; tel. 800/742-8326

Prudential HealthCare of New England, 10 New England Business Center, Suite 200, P.O. Box 1827, Andover, MA 01810; tel. 508/681-4723; FAX. 508/659-4198; Larry L. Hsu, M.D., Executive Director

Tufts Health Plan, 333 Wyman Street, P.O. Box 9112, Waltham, MA 02254-9112; tel. 617/466-9400; FAX. 617/466-9430; Harris A. Berman, M.D., President, Chief Executive Officer

Tufts Health Plan of New England, Inc., 333 Wyman Street, P.O. Box 9112, Walthma, MA 02254-9112; tel. 800/442-0422

U.S. Healthcare, Inc., Three Burlington Woods Drive, Burlington, MA 01803; tel. 617/273-5600; Robert Roy, M.D., Medical Director

United Health Plans of NE, Inc., 475 Kilvert Street, Warwick, RI 02886-1392; tel. 800/447-1245; FAX. 401/732-7208; Robert K. Winston, Director, Corporate Communications

MICHIGAN

Apex Healthcare, Inc., 104 Inverness Center Parkway, Suite 320, Birmingham, AL 35242; tel. 205/991-3233

Blue Care Network of East Michigan, 4200 Fashion Square Boulevard, Saginaw, MI 48603; tel. 517/249-3200; FAX. 517/249-3730; Arnold C. DuFort, President, Chief Executive Officer

Blue Care Network of Southeast Michigan, 25925 Telegraph, P.O. Box 5043, Southfield, MI 48086-5043; tel. 313/354-7450; FAX. 313/799-6970; David H. Smith, President, Chief Executive Officer

Blue Care Network–Great Lakes, 1769 South Garfield Avenue, Suite B, Traverse City, MI 49684; tel. 616/941-6000, ext. 6030; FAX. 616/941-6012; Sharon Carlin, Regional Director

Blue Care Network–Great Lakes, 3624 South Westnedge, Kalamazoo, MI 49008; tel. 616/388-9500; FAX. 616/388-5156; Marcia Lallaman, Regional Manager

Blue Care Network–Great Lakes, 611 Cascade West Parkway, S.E., Grand Rapids, MI 49546; tel. 616/957-5057; FAX. 616/956-5866; Sharon Carlin, President, Chief Executive Officer

Blue Care Network–Great Lakes, 3375 Merriam Avenue, Muskegon Heights, MI 49444-3173; tel. 616/739-6600; FAX. 616/739-6670; Barbara Carlson, Regional Manager

Blue Care Network–Health Central, 1403 South Creyts Road, Lansing, MI 48917; tel. 517/322-8000; FAX. 517/322-8015; Arnold C. DuFort, President, Chief Executive Officer

Care Choices HMO, Mercy Health Plans, 34605 Twelve Mile Road, Farmington Hills, MI 48331; tel. 313/489-6203; FAX. 810/489-6278; Robert J. Flanagan, Ph.D., President, Chief Executive Officer

Care Choices–Brighton, 7990 West Grand River, Brighton, MI 48116; tel. 810/229-6866; FAX. 810/229-6811; Louise Zackmann

Care Choices–Eastern Michigan, South East Region–Michigan, 2000 Hogback Road, Suite 15, Ann Arbor, MI 48105; tel. 313/971-7667; FAX. 313/971-7455; Dennis Angellis, M.D., Medical Director, South East Region

Care Choices–Grand Rapids, 1500 East Beltline S.E., Suite 300, Grand Rapids, MI 49506; tel. 616/285-3801; FAX. 616/285-3810; Janie Begeman, Site Manager

Care Choices–Lansing, 2111 University Park, Suite 100, Okemos, MI 48864; tel. 517/349-2111; FAX. 517/349-6449; Jeffrey Ash, Executive Director

Care Choices–Muskegon, 950 West Norton Avenue, Suite 500, Muskegon, MI 49441; tel. 616/737-0307; FAX. 616/733-6352; Molly McCarthy, Site Director

Family Health Plan of Michigan, 901 North Macomb, Monroe, MI 48162-3048; tel. 313/457-5370; FAX. 313/457-5506; Robert Campbell, Executive Vice President

Grand Valley Health Plan, 829 Forest Hill Avenue, S.E., Grand Rapids, MI 49546; tel. 616/949-2410; FAX. 616/949-4978; Roland Palmer, President

Great Lakes Health Plan, Inc., 17117 West Nine Mile Road, Suite 1600, Southfield, MI 48075; tel. 810/559-5656; FAX. 810/559-4640; Donald A. Zinner, President

Health Alliance Plan, 2850 West Grand Boulevard, Detroit, MI 48202; tel. 313/874-8310; FAX. 313/874-8301; Joseph E. Schmitt, Chief Financial Officer

HealthPlus of Michigan, 2050 South Linden Road, P.O. Box 1700, Flint, MI 48501-1700; tel. 810/230-2000; FAX. 810/230-2208; Paul A. Fuhs, Ph.D., President, Chief Executive Officer

HealthPlus of Michigan–Saginaw, 5560 Gratiot Avenue, Saginaw, MI 48603; tel. 517/797-4000; FAX. 517/799-6471; Bruce Hill, Regional Vice President

M-Care, 2301 Commonwealth Boulevard, Ann Arbor, MI 48105-1573; tel. 313/747-8700; FAX. 313/747-7152; Peter W. Roberts, President

NorthMed HMO, 109 East Front Street, Suite 204, Traverse City, MI 49684; tel. 616/935-0500; FAX. 616/935-0505; Walter J. Hooper III, President

OmniCare Health Plan, 1155 Brewery Park, Suite 250, Detroit, MI 48207-2602; tel. 313/259-4000, ext. 4570; FAX. 313/393-7944; Ronald R. Dobbins, President, Chief Executive Officer

PHP-Kalamazoo, 106 Farmers Alley, P.O. Box 50271, Kalamazoo, MI 49005; tel. 616/349-6692; FAX. 616/349-1476; Michael Koehler, Executive Director

Parmount Care of Michigan, Inc., 1339 North Telegraph Road, Monroe, MI 48162; tel. 313/241-5604; FAX. 313/241-5998; Robert J. Kolodgy, Vice President, Finance

Physicians Health Plan, P.O. Box 30377, Lansing, MI 48909-7877; tel. 517/349-2101; FAX. 517/347-9460; John G. Ruther, President, Chief Executive Officer

Physicians Health Plan–Jackson, 209 East Washington Avenue, Suite 315 E, Jackson, MI 49201; tel. 517/782-7154; FAX. 517/782-4512; Susan K. Sharkey, Chief Executive Officer

Physicians Health Plan–Muskegon, Terrace Plaza, 250 Morris Avenue, Suite 550, Muskegon, MI 49440-1143; tel. 616/728-3900; FAX. 616/728-5189; Ronald Franzese, Chief Executive Officer

Priority Health, 1231 East Beltline, Suite 300, Grand Rapids, MI 49505; tel. 616/942-0954; FAX. 616/942-0145; Vic Turvey, President, Chief Executive Officer

Priority Health Managed Benefits, Inc., 1231 East Beltline, N.E., Grand Rapids, MI 49503; tel. 800/942-0954; FAX. 616/942-5651; Kimberly K. Horn, Chief Executive Officer

SelectCare HMO, Inc., 2401 West Big Beaver Road, Suite 700, Troy, MI 48084; tel. 810/637-5300, ext. 5571; FAX. 810/637-6710; Roman T. Kulich, President, Chief Executive Officer

The Wellness Plan, Comprehensive Health Services, Inc., 6500 John C. Lodge, Detroit, MI 48202; tel. 313/875-6960; FAX. 313/875-7416; Sharon P. Matthews, Regional Administrator

The Wellness Plan, 1060 West Norton Avenue, Suite Four B, Muskegon, MI 49442; tel. 616/780-4722; FAX. 616/780-3557; Evangeline Zimmerman, Health Systems Manager

The Wellness Plan, One East First Street, Genesse Tower, Suite 1620, Flint, MI 48502; tel. 810/767-7400; FAX. 810/767-6338; Sharon P. Matthews, Regional Administrator

The Wellness Plan, 320 North Washington Square, Lansing, MI 48933; tel. 517/484-1400; FAX. 517/484-8801; Mary Anne Sesti, Health Systems Manager

Total Health Care, Inc., 1600 Fisher Building, Detroit, MI 48202; tel. 313/871-7800; FAX. 313/871-0196; Kenneth G. Rimmer, Executive Director

MINNESOTA

Blue Plus, P.O. Box 64179, St. Paul, MN 55164; tel. 612/456-8438; FAX. 612/456-6768; Mark Banks, M.D., President, Chief Executive Officer

First Plan HMO, 1010 Fourth Street, Two Harbors, MN 55616; tel. 218/834-7210; John Bjorum, Executive Director

HealthPartners, 8100-34th Avenue South, P.O. Box 1309, Minneapolis, MN 55440-1309; tel. 612/883-5382; FAX. 612/883-5120; George Halvorson, President, Chief Executive Director

HealthPartners, 8100-34th Avenue South, P.O. Box 1309, Minneapolis, MN 55440-1309; tel. 612/883-7000; George Halvorson, President, Chief Executive Officer

Mayo Health Plan, 21 First Street S.W., Suite 401, Rochester, MN 55902; tel. 507/284-5811; FAX. 507/284-0528; Shirley A. Weis, Executive Director

Medica Choice, 5601 Smetana Drive, Minneapolis, MN 55440-7001; tel. 612/992-5450; James Ehlen, M.D., Chief Executive Officer

Medica Health Plans, 5601 Smetana Drive, P.O. Box 9310, Minneapolis, MN 55440-9310; tel. 612/992-3952; FAX. 612/992-3998; David Strand, President

Metropolitan Health Plan, 822 South Third Street, Suite 140, Minneapolis, MN 55415; tel. 612/347-2340; FAX. 612/904-4214; John Bluford, Executive Director

Northern Plains Health Plan, 1000 South Columbia Road, Grand Forks, ND 58201; tel. 800/675-2467; FAX. 701/780-1683; Tim Sayler, Executive Director

UCARE Minnesota, 2550 University Avenue, W., Suite 201 S, St. Paul, MN 55114; tel. 612/647-2630; FAX. 612/603-0650; Nancy Feldman, Chief Executive Officer

MISSISSIPPI

AmeriCan Medical Plans of Mississippi, Inc., 633 North State Street, Suite 211, Jackson, MS 39202; tel. 601/968–9000; FAX. 601/968–9800; Rissa P. Richardson, Director, Provider Relations

Apex Healthcare of Mississippi, Inc., 405 Briarwood Drive, Suite 104A, Jackson, MS 39206; tel. 601/991–0505

Canton Management Group, Inc., 3330 South Liberty Street, Suite 300, Canton, MS 39046; tel. 601/859–4450

Cigna Healthcare of Tennessee, Inc., 6555 Quince Road, Suite 215, Memphis, TN 38119; tel. 901/755–7411; David O. Hollis, M.D., Medical Director

Family Healthcare Plus, 118 Service Drive, Suite 10, Brandon, MS 39042; tel. 601/825–7280

HMO of Mississippi, Inc., 3545 Lakeland Drive, Jackson, MS 39208; tel. 601/932–3704; Thomas C. Fenter, M.D., Executive Director

Health Link, Inc., 830 South Gloster Street, Tupelo, MS 38801; tel. 800/453–7536; FAX. 800/453–0648; Pamela J. Hansen, Director

Integrity Health Plan of Mississippi, Inc., 6360 I–55 North, Suite 460, Jackson, MS 39211; tel. 601/977–0010; FAX. 601/977–0019; Robert S. Parenteau, Director, Marketing

Mississippi Managed Care Network, Inc., 713 South Pear Orchard Road, Suite B–102, Ridgeland, MS 39157; tel. 601/977–9834; FAX. 601/977–9553; Jesse Buie, President

Phoenix Healthcare of Mississippi, Inc., 795 Woodlands Parkway, Suite 200, Ridgeland, MS 39157; tel. 601/956–2706; FAX. 601/957–0847; Stephen G. Braden, Executive Director

PrimeHealth of Alabama, Inc., 1400 University Boulevard, South, Mobile, AL 36609; tel. 334/342–0022

Prudential Health Care Plan, Inc., One Prudential Circle, Sugar Land, TX 77478–3833; tel. 713/276–3940

South East Managed Care Organization, Inc., (SEMCOs Magnolia Health Plan), 713 South Pear Orchard Road, Suite 404, Ridgeland, MS 39157; tel. 601/977–7557, ext. 9001; Elizabeth M. Mitchell, President, Chief Executive Officer

United HealthCare of Mississippi, Inc., 713 South Pear Orchard Road, Suite 205, Ridgeland, MS 39157; tel. 601/956–8030; FAX. 601/957–1306; Charles C. Pitts, Chief Executive Officer

MISSOURI

Alliance for Community Health, Inc., d/b/a A Healthcare Partnership, 5615 Pershing, Suite 29, St. Louis, MO 63112; tel. 314/454–0055, ext. 234; FAX. 314/454–9595; James D. Sweat, Chief Executive Officer

BMA Selectcare, Inc., One Penn Valley Park, P.O. Box 419458, Kansas City, MO 64141; tel. 816/751–5336; FAX. 816/751–5571; Sara L. Adams, Vice President

CIGNA HealthCare of Ohio, Inc.,, dba CIGNA Healthcare of Kansas/Missouri, Inc., 7400 West 110th Street, Suite 600, Overland Park, KS 66210; tel. 913/339–4700; FAX. 913/451–0974; Cynthia Finter, President, General Manager

CIGNA HealthCare of St. Louis, Inc., 8182 Maryland Avenue, Suite 900, St. Louis, MO 63105–3721; tel. 314/726–7860; FAX. 314/726–7819; Jim Young, General Manager, President

Childrens Mercy Family Plan, 2401 Gilham Road, Kansas City, MO 64108

Childrens Mercy Hospital/Truman Medical Center Family Health Partners, Inc., d/b/a Family Health Partners, 215 West Pershing, Suite 310, Kansas City, MO 64141; tel. 816/855–1881

Citizens Advantage, P.O. Box 479, 1500 North Oakland, Bolivar, MO 65613; tel. 417/777–6000

Community Health Plan, 801 Faraon, St. Joseph, MO 64501; tel. 816/271–1247; FAX. 816/271–1248; Joan E. Copeland, Executive Vice President, Chief Operating Officer

Cox–Freeman Community HealthPlans, Inc., 2202 West 32nd Street, Joplin, MO 64804–3599; tel. 417/269–2900

Cox–Freeman HealthPlans, Inc., 1443 North Robberson, #700, Springfield, MO 65802; tel. 800/800–2901

Exclusive Healthcare, Inc., Mutual of Omaha Plaza, Omaha, NE 68175; tel. 402/978–2869; FAX. 402/978–2999; Kurt Irlbeck, Administrative Services Coordinator

FirstGuard Health Plan, Inc., 3801 Blue Parkway, Kansas City, MO 64130; tel. 816/922–7250; FAX. 816/922–7251; Joy Haug, Executive Director, Chief Operating Officer

Gencare Health Systems, Inc., d/b/a Sanus Health Plan, Inc., P.O.Box 27379, St. Louis, MO 63141–6301; tel. 800/627–0687, ext. 3307; FAX. 314/469–9854; Thomas Zorumski, Chief Executive Officer

Good Health HMO, Inc., d/b/a Blue–Care, Inc., One Pershing Square, 2301 Main Street, Kansas City, MO 64108; tel. 816/395–2222; FAX. 816/395–3811; Larry K. Chastain, President, Chief Operating Officer

Group Health Plan, Inc., 940 West Port Plaza, Suite 300, St. Louis, MO 63146; tel. 314/453–1700; FAX. 314/453–0375; Richard H. Jones, President, Chief Executive Officer

HMO Missouri, Inc., d/b/a BlueChoice, 4444 Forest Park, St. Louis, MO 63108–2292; tel. 314/658–4444; FAX. 314/289–6239; Seymour Kaplan, President, Chief Executive Officer

HealthCare American Plans, Inc., P.O. Box 780467, Wichita, KS 67278–0467

HealthFirst Health Management Organization, 1102 West 32nd Street, Joplin, MO 64804–3599

HealthLink HMO, Inc., d/b/a HealthLink HMO, 777 Craig Road, Suite 110, Creve Coeur, MO 63141; tel. 314/569–7200; FAX. 314/569–3268; Dennis McCart, Executive Director

HealthNet, Inc., 2300 Main Street, Suite 700, Kansas City, MO 64108–2415; tel. 816/221–8400; FAX. 816/221–7709; Beth Johnson, Executive Assistant

Healthcare USA of Missouri LLC, 100 South Fourth Street, Suite 1100, St. Louis, MO 63102; tel. 800/213–7792; FAX. 314/241–8010; Davina Lane, President, Chief Executive Officer

Humana Kansas City, Inc., 10450 Holmes Road, Kansas City, MO 64131–3471; tel. 816/941–8900; FAX. 816/941–3910; David W. Fields, Executive Director

Kaiser Foundation Health Plan of Kansas City, Inc., 10561 Barkley, Suite 200, Overland Park, KS 66212–1886; tel. 913/967–4600; Robert Biblo, Regional Manager

Medical Center Health Plan, d/b/a Partners HMO, One City Place Drive, Suite 670, St. Louis, MO 63141; tel. 314/567–6660; FAX. 314/567–3627; Del Snoberger, Executive Director

Mercy Health Plans of Missouri, Inc., d/b/a Premier Health Plans, 12935 North Outer Forty Drive, Suite 200, St. Louis, MO 63141–8636; tel. 314/214–8100; FAX. 314/214–8101; Thomas L. Kelly, President

MetraHealth Care Plan of Kansas City, Inc., (a wholly owned subsidiary of United HealthCare of the Midwest, Inc.), 9300 West 110th Street, Suite 350A, Building 55, Overland Park, KS 66210; tel. 913/451–5656; Robert S. Bonney, Vice President

Missouri Advantage LLC, 428 East Capital Avenue, 3rd Floor, Jefferson City, MO 65101; tel. 573/659–5200; Kevin G. McRoberts, Executive Director

Missouri Care, LC, 2404 Forum Blvd., Columbia, MO 65203; tel. 573/441–2100

Physicians Health Plan of Greater St. Louis, Inc., 77 West Port Plaza, Suite 500, St. Louis, MO 63146; tel. 314/275–7000; FAX. 314/542–1155; Thomas Zorumski, President, Chief Executive Officer

Physicians Health Plan of Midwest, Inc., 77 Westport Plaza, Suite 500, St. Louis, MO 63146; tel. 314/275–7000; FAX. 314/542–1155

Principal Health Care Plan of St. Louis, Inc., 12312 Olive Boulevard, Suite 150, Creve Coeur, MO 63141; tel. 314/434–6990; FAX. 314/434–7540; Barbara C. Buenemann, Executive Director

Principal Health Care of Kansas City, Inc., 101 East 101st Terrace, Suite 300, Kansas City, MO 64131; tel. 816/941–3030; FAX. 816/941–8516; Jan Stallmeyer, Executive Director

Prudential Health Care Plan, Inc., 12312 Olive Boulevard, Suite 500, St. Louis, MO 63141; tel. 314/567–1100; Gary C. Hawkins, Executive Director

TriSource HealthCare, Inc., d/b/a Blue Advantage HMO, P.O. Box 419169, 2301 Main St., Kansas City, MO 64141–6169; tel. 800/892–6408; FAX. 816/395–3325; Tom Bowser, Chief Operating Officer, HMO Programs

Truman Medical Center, Inc., 2301 Holmes Street, Kansas City, MO 64108; tel. 816/556–3094; James J. Mongan, M.D., Executive Director

United Health Care of the Midwest, Inc. (FKA Gencare), 76 West Port Plaza, Suite 500, St. Louis, MO 63145; tel. 314/275–6999; Thomas Zorumski, President

United Healthcare of the Midwest, Inc., 77 West Port Plaza, Suite 500, St. Louis, MO 63141; tel. 800/535–9291; FAX. 314/542–1157; Vic Turvey, President & CEO

MONTANA

Glacier Community Health Plan, 1297 Burns Way, Suite Three, Kalispell, MT 59901; tel. 406/758–6900; FAX. 406/758–6907; Patsy Stinger, Administrative Assistant

HMO Montana, 404 Fuller Avenue, Helena, MT 59604; tel. 406/447–8753; Carol Wood, Manager

Yellowstone Community Health Plan, 1222 North 27th Street, Suite 201, Billings, MT 59101; tel. 406/238–6868; FAX. 406/238–6898; Jennifer A. Parise, Director, Marketing

NEBRASKA

Care Choices HMO, 34605 Twelve Mile Road, Farmington Hills, MI 48331; tel. 810/489–6200

Exclusive Healthcare, Inc., Mutual of Omaha Plaza, Omaha, NE 68175; tel. 402/978–2700; Dick L. Easley, President

HMO Nebraska, Inc., 10040 Regency Circle, Suite 300, Omaha, NE 68114–3734; tel. 402/392–2800; FAX. 402/392–2761; Maxine E. Crossley, Executive Vice President, Chief Operating Officer

Humana Health Plan, Inc., 101 East Main Street, Louisville, KY 40202; tel. 502/580–5005

Mutual of Omaha Health Plans of Lincoln, Inc., 220 South 17th Street, Lincoln, NE 68508; tel. 402/475–7000; FAX. 402/475–6005; Steve Burnham, Chief Operating Officer

Principal Health Care of Nebraska, Inc., 330 North 117th Street, Omaha, NE 68154–2595; tel. 402/333–1720; FAX. 402/333–1116; Ken Klaasmeyer, Executive Director

United Health Care of Midlands, Inc., d/b/a Share Health Plan of Nebraska, Inc., 2717 North 118 Circle, Omaha, NE 68164; tel. 402/445–5000; Sara Hemenway, Marketing Communications Manager

NEVADA

Amil International of Nevada, 1050 East Flamingo Road, Suite E–120, Las Vegas, NV 89119; tel. 702/693–5250; FAX. 702/693–5399; Jeff Allen, Director, Provider Relations Director

Exclusive Healthcare, Inc., Mutual of Omaha Plaza, Omaha, NE 68175

FHP Health Care, Inc., 2300 West Sahara, Suite 700, Box 14, Las Vegas, NV 89102; tel. 702/222–4641; FAX. 702/222–4705; R. Lyle Luman, President, Nevada Region

HMO Colorado, Inc., d/b/a HMO Nevada, 6900 Westcliff Drive, Suite 600, Las Vegas, NV 89128; tel. 702/228–2583; Norman P. Becker, CLU, Regional Vice President

Health Plan of Nevada, Inc., 2720 North Tenaya Way, Mailing Address: P.O. Box 15645, Las Vegas, NV 89114–5645; tel. 702/242–7300; Jon Bunker, President

Hometown Health Plan, Inc., 400 South Wells Avenue, Reno, NV 89502; tel. 702/325–3000; FAX. 702/325–3220; Ed Holme, Executive Director

Humana Health Plan, Inc., 3107 South Maryland Parkway, Las Vegas, NV 89109; tel. 702/737–7211; FAX. 702/791–5826; Craig A. Drablos, Executive Director

John Alden Nevadaplus Health Plan, 7300 Corporate Center Drive, Miami, FL 33126

Med One Health Plan, 2085 East Sahara Avenue, Las Vegas, NV 89104; tel. 702/650–4000; FAX. 702/650–4030; Joy McClenahan, Vice President, Administration

Nevadacare, Inc., 85 Washington Street, Reno, NV 89503

Silmo Healthcare Services, Inc., 6655 West Sahara Avenue, Las Vegas, NV 89102–0846

St. Mary's HealthFirst, 5290 Neil Road, Reno, NV 89502; tel. 702/829–6000; FAX. 702/829–6010; Lin Howland, Executive Director

NEW HAMPSHIRE

HMO Blue, c/o Blue Cross Blue Shield of New Hampshire, 3000 Goffs Falls Road, Manchester, NH 03111–0001; tel. 603/621–3724

Harvard Community Health Plan of New England, Inc., 10 Brookline Place, W., Brookline, MA 02146; tel. 617/731–8250

Healthsource New Hampshire, Inc., Donovan Street Extension, P.O. Box 2041, Concord, NH 03302–2041; tel. 603/225–5077; FAX. 603/225–7621; Sally Crawford, Chief Executive Officer

Section C

Matthew Thornton Health Plan, 43 Constitution Drive, Bedford, NH 03110–6020; tel. 603/695–1100; FAX. 603/695–1157; Everett Page, President

Oxford Health Plans, 10 Tara Boulevard, Nashua, NH 03062; tel. 603/891–7000; FAX. 603/891–7015; Craig Tobin, Regional Chief Executive Officer

Tufts Associated Health Maintenance Organization, Inc., 333 Wyman Street, P.O. Box 9112, Waltham, MA 02254–9112; tel. 617/466–9400

U.S. Healthcare New Hampshire, Inc., U.S. Healthcare Massachusetts, Inc., Three Burlington Woods Drive, Burlington, MA 01803; tel. 617/273–5600; FAX. 617/238–8999; James J. Broderick, General Manager

NEW JERSEY

Aetna Health Plans of New Jersey, 8000 Midlantic Drive, Suite 100 North, Mount Laurel, NJ 08054; tel. 609/866–7880; Dennis Allen, Medical Director

AltantiCare Health Plans, 6727 Delilah Road, Egg Harbor Township, NJ 08234; tel. 609/272–6330; FAX. 609/407–7770; Patricia Koelling, Chief Operating Officer

Americaid, Inc., 550 Broad Street, 11th Floor, Newark, NJ 07102; tel. 201/242–8840; Gerry McNair, Chief Executive Officer

American Preferred Provider Plan, Inc., 810 Broad Street, Newark, NJ 07102; tel. 201/799–0900; FAX. 201/799–0911; Harold E. Smith, President, Chief Executive Officer

Amerihealth HMO, Inc., 8000 Midlantic Drive, Suite 333, Mount Laurel, NJ 08054; tel. 609/778–6500; FAX. 609/778–6550; Leo Carey, Chief Executive Director

CIGNA Health Plan of Southern New Jersey, CIGNA HealthCare of PA, NJ & DE, One Beaver Valley Road, Suite CHP, Wilmington, DE 19803; tel. 302/477–3700; FAX. 302/477–3707; Norman Scott, M.D.

CIGNA of Northern New Jersey, Inc., Three Stewart Court, Denville, NJ 07834–1028; tel. 201/262–7700; FAX. 201/262–9135; Diane Foy–Noa, Vice President, General Manager

Chubbhealth, Inc., 380 Madison Avenue, 20th Floor, New York, NY 10017; tel. 212/880–5455; Keith Collins, M.D., President

Community Healthcare Plan, 309 Market Street, Camden, NJ 08102; tel. 609/541–7526; FAX. 609/635–9328; Mark R. Bryant, President

First Option Health Plan, The Galleria, Two Bridge Avenue, Building Six, Second Floor, Red Bank, NJ 07701–1106; tel. 908/842–5000; Donald Parisi, Senior Vice President, Secretary, General Counsel

Garden State Health Plan, CN–712, Trenton, NJ 08625–0712; tel. 800/525–0047; FAX. 609/588–4643; Beverly Blacher, EIDG, Chief Executive Officer

HIP Health Plan of New Jersey, One HIP Plaza, North Brunswick, NJ 08902; tel. 908/937–7600; FAX. 908/937–7870; Victoria A. Wicks, President, Chief Executive Officer

HMO Blue, Three Penn Plaza East, Newark, NJ 07105–2000; tel. 201/466–8120; FAX. 201/466–6745; Donna M. Celestini, Acting President, Chief Operating Officer

HMO New Jersey, U.S. HealthCare, 55 Lane Road, Fairfield, NJ 07004; tel. 201/575–5600; Andrew Schuyler, M.D., Medical Director

Harmony Health Plan, 200 Executive Drive, Suite 230, West Orange, NJ 07052; tel. 201/669–2900; FAX. 201/669–4666; Stephan N. Yelenik, President, Chief Executive Officer

Liberty Health Plan, 115 Christopher Columbus Drive, Jersey City, NJ 07302; tel. 201/946–6800; FAX. 201/946–1740; Donald L. Picuri, Senior Vice President, Chief Operating Officer

Managed Health Care Systems of New Jersey, Inc., One Gateway Center, Newark, NJ 07102; tel. 201/645–0800; Tony Welters, Chief Executive Officer

MetraHealth Care Plan of New Jersey, 485 B. Route One, Suite 150, Iselin, NJ 08830; tel. 908/602–6500; FAX. 908/602–6519; William Lamoreaux, Director

Metrahealth Care Plan of Upstate New York, Two Penn Plaza, Suite 700, New York, NY 10121; tel. 212/216–6591; James T. Kerr, Chief Executive Officer

NYLCare Health Plans of New Jersey, Inc., 530 East Swedesford Road, Suite 201, Wayne, PA 19087; tel. 610/971–0404; FAX. 610/971–0159; Peter Linder, Executive Director

Oxford Health Plans, Inc., 800 Connecticut Avenue, Norwalk, CT 06854; tel. 800/889–7546; Stephen Wiggins, Chief Executive Officer

Physician Health Services of New Jersey, Inc., Mack Centre IV, South 61 Paramus Road, Paramus, NJ 07652; tel. 201/291–9300; Ronald L. Hjelm, Executive Director

Physician Healthcare Plan of New Jersey, 1009 Lenox Drive, Building Four East, Lawrenceville, NJ 08648; tel. 609/896–1233; FAX. 609/896–3041; Joseph D. Billotti, M.D., Chairman

PruCare of New Jersey, (Northern Division), 200 Wood Avenue, S., Iselin, NJ 08830; tel. 908/632–7333; FAX. 908/494–8207; Paul Conlin, Vice President, Group Operations

QualMed Plans for Health, Inc., 1835 Market Street, Ninth Floor, Philadelphia, PA 19103; tel. 215/209–6704; FAX. 215/209–6708, ext. 6701; Kenneth B. Allen, Director, Legal Services

University Health Plans, Inc., 60 Park Place, 15th Floor, Newark, NJ 07102; tel. 201/623–8700; FAX. 201/623–3635; Steven Marcus, Chief Executive Officer

NEW MEXICO

Cimarron HMO, 2801 East Missouri, Suite 15, Las Cruces, NM 88011; tel. 505/521–1234; FAX. 505/521–1262; Garrey Carruthers, President, Chief Executive Officer

FHP of New Mexico, Inc., 4300 San Mateo, N.E., Albuquerque, NM 87110; tel. 505/881–7900; FAX. 505/883–0102; John Tallent, President

HMO New Mexico, 12800 Indian School Road, N.E., Zip 87112, P.O. Box 11968, Albuquerque, NM 87192; tel. 505/271–4441; FAX. 505/237–5324; Blair Christensen, President

Lovelace, Inc., P.O. Box 27107, Albuquerque, NM 87125–7107; tel. 505/262–7363; Derick Pasternak, M.D., President

Presbyterian Health Plan, 7500 Jefferson, N.E., Building Two, Albuquerque, NM 87109; tel. 505/823–0700; FAX. 505/823–0718; Robert L. Simmons, President

Qual–Med, Inc.–New Mexico Health Plan, 6100 Uptown Boulevard, N.E., Suite 400, Albuquerque, NM 87110; tel. 505/889–8800; FAX. 505/889–8819; Michael J. Mayer, President

NEW YORK

Aetna Health Plans of New York, Inc., 2700 Westchester Avenue, Purchase, NY 10577; tel. 914/251–0600; FAX. 914/251–0260; Paula Adderson, President

Better Health Plan, Inc., 120 Pineview Drive, Amherst, NY 14228; tel. 518/482–1200; Daniel Tillotson, Chief Executive Officer

Blue Cross and Blue Shield of Western New York, Community Blue, 1901 Main Street, P.O. Box 159, Buffalo, NY 14240–0159; tel. 716/887–8874; FAX. 716/887–7911; Nora K. McGuire, Executive Director

Bronx Health Plan, One Fordham Plaza, Bronx, NY 10458; tel. 718/733–4747; Maura Bluestone, Chief Executive Officer

CIGNA HealthCare of New York, Inc., 195 Broadway, Eighth Floor, New York, NY 10007; tel. 212/618–4200; FAX. 212/618–4258; Tom Garvey, Assistant Vice President, Network Management

Capital Area Community Health Plan, Inc., 1201 Troy–Schenectady Road, Latham, NY 12110; tel. 518/783–1864, ext. 4216; FAX. 518/783–0234; John Baackes, President, Chief Executive Officer

Capital District Physicians' Health Plan, 17 Columbia Circle, Albany, NY 12203; tel. 518/862–3700; FAX. 518/452–0003; Diane E. Bergman, President

CarePlus, 350 Fifth Avenue, Suite 5119, New York, NY 10118; tel. 212/563–5570; Robert Porper, M.D., Chief Executive Officer

Catholic Health Services of Brooklyn/Queens, 26 Court Street, Brooklyn, NY 11242; tel. 718/935–1164; Father Patrick Frawley, Chief Executive Officer

CenterCare, Inc., 555 West 57th Street, 18th Floor, New York, NY 10019–2925; tel. 212/293–9200; FAX. 212/293–9298; Paul Accardi, Executive Vice President

ChubbHealth, Inc., 380 Madison Avenue, 20th Floor, New York, NY 10017; tel. 212/880–5400; FAX. 212/880–5454; Keith Collins, M.D., President, Chief Executive Officer

Community Choice Health Plan of Westchester, Inc., 35 East Grassy Sprain Road, Suite 300, Yonkers, NY 10710; tel. 914/337–6908; FAX. 914/337–6919; Kristen M. Johnson, Chief Executive Officer

Community Premier Plus, Inc., 161 Fort Washington Avenue, Suite AP1220, New York, NY 10032; tel. 212/305–7040; FAX. 212/305–3301; Harris Lampert, M.D., President, Medical Director

Compre–Care, Inc., Two Broad Street Plaza, P.O. Box 222, Glens Falls, NY 12801; tel. 518/798–3555; John Rugge, M.D., Chief Executive Officer

Elderplan, Inc., 6323 Seventh Avenue, Brooklyn, NY 11220; tel. 718/921–7990; FAX. 718/921–7962; Eli S. Feldman, Executive Vice President, Chief Executive Officer

Empire Blue Cross and Blue Shield Healthnet/Blue Choice, Three Park Avenue, New York, NY 10016; tel. 212/251–2623; FAX. 212/779–7876; Victor Botnick, Vice President, Managed Care

Empire Health Choice, Inc., 622 Third Avenue, New York, NY 10017–6758; tel. 800/453–0113; Michael Stocker, M.D., Chief Executive Officer

Finger Lakes Blue Cross/Blue Shield, Blue Choice, 150 East Main Street, Rochester, NY 14647; tel. 716/454–1700; FAX. 716/238–4526; Richard D. Dent, M.D., Senior Vice President, Managed Care

GENESIS Healthplan, Inc., One Executive Boulevard, Second Floor, Yonkers, NY 10701; tel. 914/476–6000; Ms. M. A. Chagnon, President

HMO–CNY, Inc., 344 South Warren Street, P.O. Box 4809, Syracuse, NY 13221; tel. 315/448–4931; FAX. 315/448–6802; Ralph Carelli, Jr., Senior Vice President

HUM HealthCare Systems, Inc., d/b/a Partner's Health Plans, Two Broad Street Plaza, P.O. Box 140, Glens Falls, NY 12801; tel. 518/745–0903; FAX. 518/745–1099; Richard Sanford, Chief Executive Officer

Health Care Plan, Inc., 900 Guaranty Building, Buffalo, NY 14202; tel. 716/847–1480; FAX. 716/847–1817; Arthur R. Goshin, M.D., Plan President, Chief Executive Officer

Health Insurance Plan of Greater New York (HIP), Seven West 34th Street, New York, NY lOOOl; tel. 212/630–5110; FAX. 212/630–5078; Anthony Watson, President

Health Services Medical Corporation of Central New York, Inc., a/k/a Prepaid Health Plan (PHP) in Syracuse, NY, PHP/SDMN in Utica, NY, 8278 Willett Parkway, Baldwinsville, NY 13027; tel. 315/638–2133; FAX. 315/638–0985; Frederick F. Yanni, Jr., President, Chief Executive Officer

HealthFirst PHSP, Inc., 25 Broadway, Ninth Floor, New York, NY 10004; tel. 212/801–6000; FAX. 212/801–1799; Paul Dickstein, Chief Executive Officer

HealthPlus, Inc., 5800 Third Avenue, Brooklyn, NY 11220; tel. 718/745–0030; Thomas Early, Chief Executive Officer

Healthsource HMO of New York, Inc., P.O. Box 1498, Syracuse, NY 132011498; tel. 315/449–1100; FAX. 315/449–2200; Ron Harms, Chief Executive Officer

Independent Health Association, Inc., 511 Farber Lakes Drive, Buffalo, NY 14221; tel. 716/631–3001; FAX. 716/635–3838; Frank Colantuono, President, Chief Executive Officer

Institute for Urban Family Health, Inc., d/b/a ABC Health Plan, 16 East 16th Street, New York, NY 10003; tel. 212/633–0800; FAX. 212/691–4610; Neil Calman, M.D., Chief Executive Officer

Kaiser Foundation Health Plan of New York, 210 Westchester Avenue, White Plains, NY lO604; tel. 914/682–6401; FAX. 914/682–6403; Maura Carley, New York Area Operations Manager

MD:LI, 275 Broad Hollow Road, Melville, NY 11747; tel. 516/454–1900; Richard Ridoccia, Chief Executive Officer

MVP Health Plan, Inc., 111 Liberty Street, Schenectady, NY 12305; tel. 518/370–4793; FAX. 518/370–0852; David W. Oliker, President, Chief Executive Officer

MagnaHealth, 100 Garden City Plaza, Garden City, NY 11530; tel. 516/294–0700; Anthony Bacchi, Chief Executive Officer

Managed Health, Inc., 162 EAB Plaza, Uniondale, NY 11556–0162; tel. 516/683–1010; FAX. 516/683–1034; James Molbihill, M.D., President

Managed Healthcare Systems of New York, Inc., Seven Hanover Square, Fifth Floor, New York, NY 10004; tel. 212/509–5999; FAX. 212/509–2151; Karen Clark, Chief Executive Officer

MetraHealth Care Plan of Upstate NY, Inc., 5015 CampusWood Drive, Suite 303, East Syracuse, NY 13057; tel. 315/433–5851; David Barker, Chief Executive Officer

Metroplus Health Plan, 11 West 42nd Street, Second Floor, New York, NY 10036; tel. 212/597–8600; FAX. 212/597–8666; Denice F. Davis, J.D., Executive Director

Mohawk Valley Physicians Health Plan, 111 Liberty Street, Schenectady, NY 12305; tel. 518/370–4793; David Oliker, Chief Executive Officer

NYLCare Health Plans of New York, Inc., 75–20 Astoria Boulevard, Jackson Heights, NY 11370; tel. 718/899–5200; Arthur J. Drechsler, Executive Director

Neighborhood Health Providers, 630 Third Avenue, New York, NY 10017; tel. 212/808–4775; Steven Bory, Chief Executive Officer

New York Hospital Community Health Plan, 333 East 38th Street, New York, NY 10016; tel. 212/297–5547; FAX. 212/297–5923; Rosaire McDonald, Chief Executive Officer

North American HealthCare, Inc., 300 Corporate Parkway, Amherst, NY 14226; tel. 716/446–5500; Ronald Zoeller, Chief Executive Officer

North Medical Community Health Plan, Inc., 5112 West Taft Road, Suite R, Liverpool, NY 13088; tel. 315/452–2500; James Butler, Chief Executive Officer

OLM/Soundview, 190 East 162nd Street, Bronx, NY 10451; tel. 718/681–5070; FAX. 718/681–5281; John Connors, Chief Executive Officer

Oxford Health Plans of New York, 521 Fifth Avenue, 15th Floor, New York, NY 10175; tel. 212/599–2266; FAX. 212/599–3552; Stephen F. Wiggins, Chief Executive Officer

Physicians Health Services of New York, Inc., Crosswest Office Center, 399 Knollwood Road, Suite 212, White Plains, NY 10603; tel. 914/682–8006; FAX. 914/682–5692; Ronald L. Hjelm, Executive Director

PruCare of New York, Tri–State Health Care Management, The Office Center at Monticello, 400 Rella Boulevard, Suffern, NY 10901; tel. 914/368–4497

Rochester Area HMO, Inc., d/b/a Preferred Care, 259 Monroe Avenue, Suite A, Rochester, NY 14607; tel. 716/325–3920; FAX. 716/325–3122; John Urban, President

SCHC Total Care, Inc., 819 South Salina Street, Syracuse, NY 13202; tel. 315/476–7921; Rueben Cowart, D.D.S., Chief Executive Officer

St. Barnabas Community Health Plan, 183rd Street and Third Avenue, Bronx, NY 10457; tel. 718/960–6232; Steven Anderman, Chief Executive Officer

Suffolk County Department of Health Services, 225 Rabro Drive, E., Happauge, NY 11788–4290; tel. 516/342–0063; Mary Hibberd, M.D., Chief Executive Officer

U.S. Healthcare, Inc., Nassau Omni West, 333 Earle Ovington Boulevard, Suite 502, Uniondale, NY 11553; tel. 516/794–6565; Michael A. Stocker, M.D., President

United HealthCare Plan of NY, Inc., United HealthCare Plan of NJ, Two Penn Plaza, Suite 700, New York, NY 10121; tel. 212/216–6401; FAX. 212/216–6595; R. Channing Wheeler, Chief Executive Officer

Utica–Watertown Health Insurance Co., Inc., The Utica Business Park, 12 Rhoads Drive, Utica, NY 13502; tel. 315/798–4358; FAX. 315/797–4298; Thomas Flannery, M.D.

Vytra Healthcare, Corporate Center, 395 North Service Road, Melville, NY 11747–3127; tel. 516/694–4000; FAX. 516/694–5780; David S. Reynolds, Ph.D., President

WellCare of New York, Inc., P.O. Box 4059, Park West/Hurley Avenue Ext., Kingston, NY 12402; tel. 914/334–7185; FAX. 914/338–0566; Robert Goff, Chief Executive Officer

Westchester Prepaid Health Services Plan, Inc., d/b/a HealthSource, 303 South Broadway, Suite 321, Tarrytown, NY 10591; tel. 914/631–1611; FAX. 914/631–1615; Georganne Chapin, Chief Executive Officer

NORTH CAROLINA

Aetna Health Plans of the Carolinas, Inc., 1010 Charlotte Plaza, Charlotte, NC 28244; tel. 704/353–7799; FAX. 704/353–7180; Patrick W. Dowd

Association of Eye Care Centers Total Vision Health Plan, Inc., P.O. Box 7185, 110 Zebulon Court, Rocky Mount, NC 27804; tel. 919/937–6650; FAX. 919/451–2182; Samuel B. Petteway, Jr., President

Atlantic Health Plan, Inc., 7415 Pineville–Matthews Road, Suite 200, Charlotte, NC 28226; tel. 704/544–1075; Wallace Hilliard

Blue Cross Blue Shield of North Carolina, P.O. Box 2291, Durham, NC 27702; tel. 919/765–2400; FAX. 919/765–7105; Ken Otis II, President

CIGNA Dental Health of North Carolina, Inc., P.O. Box 189060, Plantation, FL 33318–9060; tel. 305/423–5800; David O. Cannady, President

CIGNA Health Plan of North Carolina, Inc., P.O. Box 470068, Charlotte, NC 28247; tel. 704/544–4350; FAX. 704/544–4375; Joseph L. Murgo

Carolina Summit Healthcare, Inc., 2100 Stantonsburg Rd., Greenville, NC 27835; tel. 919/816–6751; William Bull

Community Choice of North Carolina, Inc., 100 North Green Street, Greensboro, NC 27401; tel. 910/691–3001; Randolph Ferguson

Doctors Health Plan of North Carolina, Inc., 2828 Croasdaile Drive, P.O. Box 15309, Durham, NC 27704; tel. 919/383–4175, ext. 6124; FAX. 919/383–3286; Richard A. Felice, President

Generations Family Health Plan, Inc., 6330 Quadrangle Dr., Suite 100, Chapel Hill, NC 27514; tel. 919/490–0102; Raymond L. Champ

Health Maintenance Organization of North Carolina, Inc., P.O. Box 2291, Durham, NC 27702; tel. 919/489–7431; FAX. 919/419–1338; Ken Otis

Healthsource North Carolina, Inc., 701 Corporate Center Drive, Raleigh, NC 27607; tel. 919/854–7000, ext. 7700; FAX. 919/854–7102; Robert J. Greczyn, Jr., President, Chief Executive Officer

Kaiser Foundation Health Plan of North Carolina, 3120 Highwoods Boulevard, Suite 300, Raleigh, NC 27604–1038; tel. 919/981–6000; FAX. 919/878–5835; Ted Carpenter, Vice President, Regional Manager

Kanawha HealthCare, Inc., 4609 Old Course Drive, Charlotte, NC 28277; tel. 704/333–8810; James L. Tillotson

Maxicare North Carolina, Inc., 5550 77 Center Drive, Suite 380, Charlotte, NC 28217–0710; tel. 704/525–0880, ext. 6451; FAX. 704/529–0382; Peter J. Ratican

Optimum Choice of the Carolinas, Inc., Crabtree Center, 4600 Marriott Drive, Suite 300, Raleigh, NC 27612; tel. 919/881–8481; George T. Jochum

PARTNERS National Health Plans of North Carolina, Inc., P.O. Box 24907, Winston–Salem, NC 27114–4907; tel. 910/760–4822; FAX. 910/659–2950; John W. Jones, President

Personal Care Plan of North Carolina, Inc., P.O. Box 2291, Durham, NC 27702; tel. 919/489–7431; Kenneth C. Otis II

Principal Health Care of the Carolinas, Inc., 2300 Yorkmont Road, Suite 710, Charlotte, NC 28217; tel. 919/357–1421; Kenneth J. Linde, President

Provident Health Care Plan, Inc. of North Carolina, 701 Corporate Center Dr., Raleigh, NC 27604; tel. 919/460–1610; Barry Martins

Prudential Health Care Plan, Inc., 2701 Coltsgate Road, Suite 300, Charlotte, NC 28211; tel. 704/365–6070; FAX. 704/365–9959; Jim Ebitt, Vice President

QualChoice of North Carolina, Inc., 2000 West First Street, Suite 210, Winston–Salem, NC 27104; tel. 919/716–0907; FAX. 910/716–0920; Douglas Cueny, President

Spectera Dental Services, Inc., (formerly United Dental Services), 2811 Lord Baltimore Drive, Baltimore, MD 21244–2644; tel. 410/265–6033; Oscar B. Camp, President

The Wellness Plan of North Carolina, Inc., 4601 Park Road, Suite 550, Charlotte, NC 28209–3239; tel. 704/679–3700; FAX. 704/679–3706; Timothy O'Brien, Chief Executive Officer

U. S. Healthcare of the Carolinas, Inc., 205 Regency Executive Park, Suite 410, Charlotte, NC 28217; tel. 704/672–2700; Amy N. Williams, General Manager

United Health Care of North Carolina, Northwestern Plaza, 2307 West Cone Boulevard, Greensboro, NC 27408; tel. 910/282–0900; FAX. 910/545–5099; Frank R. Mascia, President, Chief Executive Officer

Wellpath Select, Inc., 6330 Quadrangle Drive, Suite 500, Chapel Hill, NC 27514; tel. 919/493–1210; Anna Lore

NORTH DAKOTA

Heart of America HMO, 802 South Main, Rugby, ND 58368; tel. 701/776–5848; FAX. 701/776–5425; Mary Ann Jaeger, Executive Director

Northern Plains Health Plan, 1000 South Columbia Road, Grand Forks, ND 58201; tel. 701/780–1600; Raymond Kuntz

OHIO

Aetna U.S. Healthcare, Inc., 4059 Kinross Lakes Parkway, Richfield, OH 44286–5009; tel. 800/537–5312; FAX. 216/464–2723; David K. Ellwanger, Executive Director

Aultcare HMO, 2600 Sixth Street, S.W., Canton, OH 44710; tel. 216/438–6360; Rick L. Haines, Vice President, Managed Care

Bethesda Managed Care, Inc., 619 Oak Street, Cincinnati, OH 45206; tel. 513/569–6490; FAX. 513/569–6233; Robert Smith, M.D., Medical Director

Butler Health Plan, 111 Buckeye Street, Suite 107, Hamilton, OH 45011; tel. 800/872–9093; FAX. 513/863–6437; Pamela A. Poland, Executive Director

ChoiceCare, 655 Eden Park Drive, Suite 400, Cincinnati, OH 45202; tel. 513/784–5200; FAX. 513/784–5300; Daniel A. Gregorie, M.D., Chief Executive Officer

Cigna Healthcare of Ohio, Inc., 3700 Corporate Drive, Suite 200, Business Campus, N.E., Columbus, OH 43231–4963; tel. 614/823–7500; FAX. 614/823–7775; James Massie, General Manager

Community Health Plan of Ohio, 1915 Tamarack Road, Newark, OH 43055–3699; tel. 614/348–4901; FAX. 614/348–4909; Robert R. Kamps, M.D., President, Chief Executive Officer

Day–Med Health Maintenance Plan, 9797 Springboro Pike, Suite 200, Miamisburg, OH 45342; tel. 937/847–5646, ext. 120; FAX. 513/847–5620; Jeanette Prear, President, Chief Executive Officer

Dayton Area Health Plan, One Dayton Centre, One South Main Street, Suite 440, Dayton, OH 45402–9794; tel. 937/224–3300; FAX. 937/224–2272, ext. 2200; Pamela B. Morris, President, Chief Executive Officer

Emerald HMO, Inc., Diamond Building, 100 Superior Avenue, 16th Floor, Cleveland, OH 44114–2591; tel. 216/241–4133; FAX. 216/241–4158; Randolph C. Hoffman, President

FHP of Ohio, Inc., Spectrum Office Tower, 11260 Chester Road, Suite 800, Cincinnati, OH 45246–9928; tel. 513/772–9191; FAX. 513/772–1466; John Davren, M.D., Plan Director

Family Health Plan, Inc., 2200 Jefferson Ave., 6th Floor, Toledo, OH 43264; tel. 419/241–6501; FAX. 419/241–5441; Robert Campbell, Executive Vice President

Genesis Health Plan of Ohio, Inc., Two Summit Park Drive, Suite 340, Cleveland, OH 44131; tel. 216/642–3344; FAX. 216/642–3345; Karl Rajani, President

HMO Health Ohio, 2060 East Ninth Street, Cleveland, OH 44115–1355; tel. 216/522–8622; Gerry P. Long, Director, ADS Products

Health Guard, d/b/a Advantage Health Plan, 3000 Guernsey Street, Bellaire, OH 43906–1598; tel. 614/676–4623; Daniel Splain, President

Health Maintenance Plan, 221 East 4th Street, Suite 2600, Cincinnati, OH 45202; tel. 513/247–6688; FAX. 513/247–6789; Bradford A. Buxton, Executive Director

Health Power HMO, Inc., 560 East Town Street, Columbus, OH 43215–0346; tel. 614/461–9900; FAX. 614/461–0960; Thomas Beaty, Jr., President

HealthFirst, 278 Barks Road West, Marion, OH 43301–1820; tel. 614/387–6355; FAX. 614/387–0665; N. Robert Jones, President, Chief Executive Officer

HealthPledge, a product of U.S. Health HMO, 300 East Wilson Bridge Road, Suite 200, Worthington, OH 43085–2339; tel. 614/566–0111; FAX. 614/566–0403; Colleen M. Tincher, Director, Operations

Healthassurance HMO, 2601 Market Place, Harrisburg, PA 17110–9339; tel. 412/577–4340; FAX. 412/497–5880; Deborah Zuroski, Senior Compliance Analyst

Healthsource Ohio, Inc., 580 Lincoln Park Blvd., Suite 100, Kettering, OH 45429; tel. 937/296–7460; David Smith, Chief Executive Officer

HomeTown Hospital Health Plan, 100 Lillian Gish Boulevard, Suite 301, Massillon, OH 44647; tel. 216/837–6880; FAX. 216/837–6869; William C. Epling, Vice President, Chief Operating Officer

Humana Health Plan of Ohio, Inc., 8044 Montgomery Road, Suite 460, Cincinnati, OH 45236; tel. 513/792–0511; FAX. 513/792–0520; Bill Wakefield, Executive Director

InHealth, Inc., 200 East Campus View Boulevard, Worthington, OH 43235; tel. 614/888–2223; Jeralyn Green, President

John Alden Health Systems, Inc., 5500 Glendon Court, Dublin, OH 43017; tel. 614/798–2930; William F. Sterling, Vice President, Senior Associate Counsel

Section C

Kaiser Permanente, North Point Tower, 1001 Lakeside Avenue, Suite 1200, Cleveland, OH 44114–1153; tel. 216/621–5600, ext. 5296; FAX. 216/623–8776; Jeffrey Werner, Vice President, Marketing

Medical Value Plan, 405 Madison Avenue, P.O. Box 2147, Toledo, OH 43604; tel. 419/245–5165; Hal A. White, M.D., Medical Director

Mount Carmel Health Plan, Inc., 495 Cooper Road, Suite 300, Westerville, OH 43081; tel. 614/898–8951

Mutual of Omaha Health Plans of Ohio, Inc., Rockside Square I, 6155 Rockside Road, Suite 201, Independence, OH 44131; tel. 216/524–3555; FAX. 216/524–5035; Susan Mego, Executive Director

Nationwide Health Plans, Inc., 5525 Parkcenter Circle, Dublin, OH 43017–3584; tel. 614/888–2223

OhioHealth Group HMO, Inc., 300 East Wilson Bridge Road, Suite 200, Worthington, OH 43085–2339; tel. 614/566–0111

PacifiCare/FHP of Ohio, Spectrum Office Tower, 11260 Chester Road, #800, Cincinnati, OH 45246–9928; tel. 513/772–7325

Pacificare of Ohio, Inc., 11260 Chester Road, Suite 800, Cincinnati, OH 45246; tel. 513/772–7325; Brenda A. Pettit, Supervisor, Compliance

Paramount Health Care, 1715 Indian Wood Circle, Suite 200, P.O. Box 928, Toledo, OH 43697–0928; tel. 419/891–2500; FAX. 419/891–2530; John C. Randolph, President

Personal Physician Care, Inc., Sterling Building, 1255 Euclid Avenue, Suite 500, Cleveland, OH 44115–1807; tel. 216/687–0015; FAX. 216/687–9484; Wilton A. Savage, Executive Director

PrimeTime Health Plan, 6th St. SW, Canton, OH 44710; tel. 330/438–6360

Prudential Health Care Plan, Inc., PruCare of Central Ohio, 485 Metro Place S., Suite 450, Dublin, OH 43017; tel. 614/761–0002; FAX. 614/761–1757; Budd Fisher, Director, Group Operations

QualChoice Health Plan, 6000 Parkland Boulevard, Cleveland, OH 44124; tel. 216/460–4010; FAX. 216/460–4000; Ray S. Herschman, Chief Financial Officer

SummaCare, Inc., 400 West Market Street, P.O. Box 3620, Akron, OH 44309–3620; tel. 330/996–8410; FAX. 330/996–8415; Martin P. Hauser, President

Super Med HMO, 2060 East Ninth Street, Cleveland, OH 44115; tel. 216/522–8622; Gerry Long, Director, ADS Products

The Health Plan, 52160 National Road, East, St. Clairsville, OH 43950–9365; tel. 614/695–3585; Philip D. Wright, President, Chief Operating Officer

Total Health Care Plan, Inc., 12800 Shaker Boulevard, Cleveland, OH 44120; tel. 216/991–3000, ext. 2221; FAX. 222/991–3011; James G. Turner, President, Chief Executive Officer

USHC, 375 Carriage Lane, Canfield, OH 44406; tel. 215/283–6656; FAX. 215/654–6078; Jean Moriarity

United HealthCare of Ohio, Inc., 3650 Olentangy River Road, P.O. Box 1138, Columbus, OH 43216–1138; tel. 614/442–7100; Robert J. Sheehy, President

OKLAHOMA

CIGNA HealthCare of Oklahoma, Inc., Cigna Center, 5100 North Brookline, Ninth Floor, Oklahoma City, OK 73112; tel. 405/943–7711; FAX. 405/946–9568; Cynthia A. Finter, General Manager

Comanche County Hospital Authority, d/b/a Prime Advantage Health Plan, 4411 West Gore Boulevard, Suite B4, Lawton, OK 73505; tel. 405/357–6684; FAX. 405/357–9064; Tanya Case, Director

Community Care HMO, Inc., 4720 South Harvard, Suite 202, Tulsa, OK 74135; tel. 918/749–1171; FAX. 918/749–7970; David J. Pynn, President

Foundation Health, An Oklahoma Health Plan, Inc., 5810 East Skelly Drive, Suite 1100, Tulsa, OK 74135; tel. 918/621–5900; Richard McCutchen, Senior Vice President, Executive Officer

GHS Health Maintenance Organization, Inc., d/b/a BlueLincs HMO, 1400 South Boston, Tulsa, OK 74119–3630; tel. 918/592–9414; FAX. 918/592–0611; Robert D. Peacry, Group Vice President

Healthcare Oklahoma, Inc., 3030 Northwest Expressway, Suite 140, Oklahoma City, OK 73112–4481; tel. 405/951–4700; FAX. 405/951–4701; Jon H. Friesen, President, Chief Executive Officer

PROklahoma Care, Inc., 5005 North Lincoln, P.O. Box 25127, Oklahoma City, OK 73126; tel. 405/521–8253; Joe Crosthwait, M.D., Vice President, Medical Director

PacifiCare of Oklahoma, 7666 East 61st Street, Tulsa, OK 74133–1112; tel. 918/459–1100; FAX. 918/459–1451; Chris Whitty, Vice President, General Manager

Prudential Health Care Plan, Inc., d/b/a Prudential Health Care HMO, 7912 East 31st Court, Tulsa, OK 74145; tel. 918/624–4600; FAX. 918/627–9759; Ann Paul, Executive Director

Prudential HealthCare Plan, Inc., 4005 Northwest Expressway, Suite 300, Oklahoma City, OK 73116; tel. 405/879–1780; James K. McNaughton, Executive Director

OREGON

HMO Oregon, Inc., P.O. Box 12625, Salem, OR 97309; tel. 503/364–4868; FAX. 503/588–4350; Roger B. Lyman, President

Health Maintenance of Oregon, Inc., P.O. Box 139, Portland, OR 97207–0139; tel. 503/274–0755; FAX. 501/223–5993; Richard Woolworth, President, Chief Executive Officer

Health Masters of Oregon, Inc., 201 High Street, S.E., Salem, OR 97301; tel. 503/779–9468; FAX. 503/779–3238; Jud Holtey, Chief Operating Officer, Southern Regional Office, BCBSO

HealthGuard Services, Inc., d/b/a SelectCare, 600 Country Club Road, Zip 97401, P.O. Box 10106, Eugene, OR 97440; tel. 541/686–3948; FAX. 541/984–4030; Larry Abramson, President

Kaiser Foundation Health Plan of the Northwest, 500 Northeast Multnomah Street, Suite 100, Portland, OR 97232–2099; tel. 503/813–2800; Michael H. Katcher, President

Liberty Health Plan, Inc., 825 Northeast Multnomah Street, Suite 1600, Portland, OR 97232; tel. 503/234–5345; FAX. 503/234–5381; Kristen A. Fassenfelt, Vice President

PACC, P.O. Box 286, Clackamas, OR 97015–0286; tel. 503/659–4212; FAX. 503/794–3409; Martin A. Preizler, President, Chief Executive Officer

Pacificare of Oregon, Inc., Five Centerpointe Drive, Suite 600, Lake Oswego, OR 97035–8650; tel. 503/620–9324; FAX. 503/603–7377; Mary O. McWilliams, President

Providence Health Plans, 1235 Northeast 47th Avenue, Suite 220, Portland, OR 97213; tel. 503/215–2981; FAX. 503/215–7655; Jack Friedman, Executive Director

QualMed Oregon Health Plan, Inc., 4800 Southwest Macadam, Suite 400, Portland, OR 97201; tel. 503/222–5217; FAX. 503/796–6366; Chris du Laney, Executive Director

PENNSYLVANIA

Aetna Health Plans of Central and Eastern Pennsylvania, Inc., 955 Chesterbrook Boulevard, Suite 200, Wayne, PA 19087; tel. 610/644–3800; FAX. 610/251–6441; Anthony Buividas, Chief Executive Officer

Alliance Health Network, 1700 Peach Street, Suite 244, Erie, PA 16501; tel. 814/878–1700; FAX. 814/452–4358; James R. Smith, President, Chief Executive Officer

Best Health Care of Western Pennsylvania, Towne Centre Offices, P.O. Box 8440, Pittsburgh, PA 15218–0440; tel. 800/699–3527

Central Medical Health Plan, d/b/a Advantage Health, 121 Seventh Avenue, Suite 500, Pittsburgh, PA 15222–3408; tel. 412/391–9300, ext. 509; FAX. 412/391–0457; Elizabeth Stolkowski, Executive Vice President, Chief Operating Officer

Cigna Health Plan of Pennsylvania, Inc., One Beaver Valley Road, Suite CHP, Wilmington, DE 19803; tel. 302/477–3700

Geisinger Health Plan, Geisinger Office Building, 100 North Academy Avenue, Danville, PA 17822–3020; tel. 717/271–8760; FAX. 717/271–5268; Howard G. Hughes, M.D., Senior Vice President Health Plans

HIP of Pennsylvania, d/b/a HIP Health Plan, Six Neshaminy Interplex, Suite 600, Trevose, PA 19053; tel. 215/633–7780

HMO of Northeastern Pennsylvania, d/b/a First Priority Health, 70 North Main Street, Wilkes–Barre, PA 18711; tel. 717/829–6044; FAX. 717/830–6319; Denise S. Cesare, Executive Vice President, Chief Operating Officer

Health Partners of Philadelphia, 4700 Wissachickon Avenue, Suite 118, Philadelphia, PA 19144–4283; tel. 215/849–9606

HealthAmerica of Pennsylvania, Inc., Five Gateway Center, Pittsburgh, PA 15222; tel. 412/553–7300; FAX. 412/553–7384; Mike Blackwood, Chief Executive Officer

HealthGuard of Lancaster, Inc., 280 Granite Run Drive, Suite 105, Lancaster, PA 17601–6810; tel. 717/560–9049; FAX. 717/581–4580; James R. Godfrey, President

Healthcare Management Alternatives, Inc., 5070 Parkside Avenue, Suite 6200, Philadelphia, PA 19131; tel. 215/473–7511; FAX. 215/473–0446; Dr. Denise Ross, Chief Executive Officer

Healthcentral, Inc., 2605 Interstate Drive, Suite 140, Harrisburg, PA 17110; tel. 717/540–0033; Martin R. Miracle, President, Chief Executive Officer

Keystone Health Plan Central, Inc., 300 Corporate Center Drive, P.O. Box 898812, Camp Hill, PA 17089–8812; tel. 717/763–3458; FAX. 717/975–6895; Joseph M. Pfister, President, Chief Executive Officer

Keystone Health Plan East, Inc., 1901 Market Street, Philadelphia, PA 19101–7516; tel. 215/241–2001; John Daddis, Executive Vice President, Chief Operating Officer

Keystone Health Plan West, Inc., Fifth Avenue Place, 120 Fifth Avenue, Suite 3116, Pittsburgh, PA 15222; tel. 412/255–7245; FAX. 412/255–7583; Kenneth R. Melani, M.D., President

Medigroup HMO, Inc., 1700 Market Street, Suite 1050, Philadelphia, PA 19103; tel. 215/575–0530

Optimum Choice, Inc. of Pennsylvania, 1755 Oregon Pike, First Floor, Lancaster, PA 17601; tel. 800/474–6647; FAX. 717/569–7820; J. Steve DuFresne, President

Oxford Health Plans, The Curtis Center, 601 Walnut Street, Suite 900E, Philadelphia, PA 19106; tel. 215/625–8800; FAX. 215/625–5601; Michael C. Gaffney, Chief Executive Officer

Philcare Health Systems, Inc., 2005 Market Street, Commerce Square, PA 19103; tel. 215/564–4050

Prudential Health Care Plan, Inc., Prudential HealthCare, 220 Gibraltar Road, Suite 200, P.O. Box 901, Horsham, PA 19044–0901; tel. 215/672–1944; FAX. 215/442–2946; Brian J. Keane, Senior Director, Network Management, Operations

QualMed Plans for Health of Pennsylvania, Inc., 1835 Market Street, Ninth Floor, Philadelphia, PA 19103; tel. 215/209–6300; FAX. 215/209–6561; Diane C. Chiponis, Chief Financial Officer

Qualmed Plans for Health, Inc., (formerly Greater Atlantic Health Service, Inc.), 3550 Market Street, Philadelphia, PA 19104; tel. 215/823–8600; Ernest Monfiletto, President, Chief Executive Officer

Three Rivers Health Plans, Inc., 300 Oxford Drive, Monroeville, PA 15146; tel. 412/858–4000; FAX. 412/858–4060; Warren Carmichael, Chairman, Chief Executive Officer

United States Health Care Systems, Inc., d/b/a The Health Maintenance Organization of Pennsylvania, 980 Jolly Road, P.O. Box 1109, Blue Bell, PA 19422; tel. 215/628–4800; Leonard Abramson, President

RHODE ISLAND

Blue Cross & Blue Shield of Rhode Island, 444 Westminster Street, Providence, RI 02903; tel. 401/459–1000; Douglas J. McIntosh, President

Coordinated Health Partners, Inc., 30 Chestnut Street, Providence, RI 02903; tel. 401/274–6644; FAX. 401/453–5586; Paula Nordhoff, Executive Vice President

Delta Dental of Rhode Island, 50 Park Row West, Providence, RI 02903–1143; tel. 401/453–0800; Colin MacGillvary

Harvard Pilgrim Health Care of New England, One Hoppin Street, Providence, RI 02903; tel. 401/331–3000; FAX. 401/331–0496; Stephen Schoenbaum, M.D., Medical Director

Neighborhood Health Plan of Rhode Island, Inc., 32 Branch Avenue, Providence, RI 02904; tel. 401/459–6000; Chris Schneider

Pilgrim Health Care, 10 Accord Executive Drive, P.O. Box 200, Norwell, MA 02061; tel. 617/871–3950; FAX. 617/982–9668; Allan Greenberg, Executive Vice President

U. S. Healthcare, Inc., 980 Jolly Road, P.O. Box 1109, Blue Bell, PA 19422; tel. 215/283–6656; Timothy Nolan, President

United Health Plans of New England, Inc., 475 Kilvert Street, Suite 310, Warwick, RI 02886–1392; tel. 401/737–6900; FAX. 401/737–6957; Max Powell, Chief Executive Officer

SOUTH CAROLINA

Aetna Health Plans of the Carolinas, Inc., 1010 Charlotte Plaza, Suite 1010, Charlotte, NC 28244; tel. 704/353–7201

American Medical Plans of South Carolina, Inc., 246 Stoneridge Drive, Suite 101, Columbia, SC 29210; tel. 803/748–7395; FAX. 803/748–9597; George A. Schneider, Chief Executive Officer

Carolina Care Health Plan, Inc., 111 Stonemark Lane, Suite 202, Columbia, SC 29210; tel. 800/641–5584; FAX. 813/265–6213; Laurie Burrell, Chief Operating Officer

Companion HealthCare Corporation, I–20 at Alpine Road, Columbia, SC 29219–2401; tel. 803/786–8466; FAX. 803/699–2374; Harvey L. Galloway, Executive Vice President, Chief Operating Officer

Doctors Health Plan, Inc., 2828 Croasdaile Drive, Durham, NC 27705; tel. 919/383–4173; FAX. 919/383–4175; Richard Allan Felice, President

Health First, Inc., 255 Enterprise Boulevard, Suite 200, Greenville, SC 29615; tel. 864/455–4098; FAX. 864/455–1120; R. Wesley Champion, Chief Financial Officer

Healthsource South Carolina, Inc., 215 East Bay Street, Suite 401, Charleston, SC 29401; tel. 803/723–5520; FAX. 803/723–7715; Michael V. Clark, President, Chief Executive Officer

Heritage National Healthplan, Inc., 1515 Fifth Avenue, Suite 200, Moline, IL 61265–1368; tel. 309/765–1200; G. Michael Hammes, President

Kaiser Foundation Health Plan of North Carolina, 3120 Highwoods Boulevard, Raleigh, NC 27604; tel. 704/551–1986; William Dewey Brown, Jr.

Maxicare North Carolina, Inc., 5550 77 Center Drive, Suite 380, Charlotte, NC 28210; tel. 704/525–0880; FAX. 704/529–0382; Richard T. Hedlund, Vice President, General Manager

Optimum Choice of the Carolinas, Inc., 4600 Marriott Drive, Suite 300, Raleigh, NC 27612; tel. 800/373–5879; Jim Bendel, Sales Director

Partners National Health Plans of NC, Inc., 2085 Frontis Plaza Boulevard, Winston–Salem, NC 27103; tel. 910/760–4822; FAX. 910/760–6218; Cosby M. Davis, III, Chief Financial Officer

Physicians Health Plan of South Carolina, Inc., 110 Centerview Drive, Suite 301, Columbia, SC 29210–8438; tel. 803/750–7400, ext. 4; FAX. 803/750–7474; William E. Martin, Chief Executive Officer

Preferred Health Systems, Inc., I–20 at Alpine Road, Columbus, SC 29219; tel. 803/788–0222; FAX. 803/736–2851; Gail Bragg, Senior Director

Principal Health Care of the Carolinas, Inc., One Coliseum Center, 2300 Yorkmont Road, Suite 710, Charlotte, NC 28217; tel. 704/357–1421; FAX. 704/357–3164; Chuck Trinchitella, Executive Director

Provident Health Care Plan, Inc. of South Carolina, 201 Brookfield Parkway, Suite 100, Greenville, SC 29607; tel. 803/987–3100; James D. Kollefrath

Select Health of South Carolina, Inc., 7410 Northside Drive, Suite 208, North Charleston, SC 29420; tel. 803/569–1759; FAX. 803/569–0702; Michael Jernigan, President, Chief Executive Officer

U. S. Healthcare of the Carolinas, Inc., 205 Regency Executive Park Drive, Charlotte, NC 28217; tel. 800/278–0122; Vaughn Delk

WellPath Select, Inc., 6330 Quadrangle Drive, Suite 500, Chapel Hill, NC 27514; tel. 919/493–1210; FAX. 919/419–3872; Anna M. Lore, President, Chief Executive Officer

SOUTH DAKOTA

Mutual of Omaha of South Dakota and Community Health Plus HMO, Inc., 3904 Technology Circle, Sioux Falls, SD 57106; tel. 605/361–9591; FAX. 605/361–9593; William P. Jetter, Executive Director

Sioux Valley Health Plan, 1100 S. Euclid Ave., Sioux Falls, SD 57117–5039; tel. 605/333–1000

South Dakota State Medical Holding Company, Inc., d/b/a Dakota Care, 1323 South Minnesota Avenue, Sioux Falls, SD 57105; tel. 605/334–4000; FAX. 605/336–0270; Robert D. Johnson, Chief Executive Officer

TENNESSEE

Aetna Health Plans of Tennessee, 1801 West End Avenue, Suite 500, Nashville, TN 37203; tel. 615/322–1600; FAX. 615/322–1217; David R. Field, President

American Medical Security Health Plan, Inc., 22 North Front Street, Suite 960, Memphis, TN 38103; tel. 901/523–2672; Eric B. Taylor, President

CIGNA HealthCare of Tennessee, Inc., Palmer Plaza, Suite 800, 1801 West End Avenue, Nashville, TN 37203; tel. 615/340–3059; FAX. 615/340–3590; Sherri A. Silvas, Administrative Assistant

Community Health Plan of Chattanooga, Inc., d/b/a Wellport Health Plan, Franklin Building, Suite 101, Chattanooga, TN 37411; tel. 423/490–1120; Brian E. Dalbey, President

Erlanger Health Plan Trust, 979 East Third Street, Chattanooga, TN 37403; tel. 423/778–8255; John Barnes, President

Health 123, Inc., 706 Church Street, Suite 500, Nashville, TN 37203; tel. 615/782–7811; FAX. 615/782–7812; Thomas J. Nagle, President, Chief Executive Officer

HealthNet HMO, Inc., 44 Vantage Way, Suite 300, Nashville, TN 37228; tel. 800/881–9466; Gary Brukardt, President

HealthWise of Tennessee, Inc., 404 BNA Drive, Suite 204, Nashville, TN 37217; tel. 615/366–6010; FAX. 615/367–5008; Len Cantrell, Chief Executive Officer

Healthsource Tennessee, Inc., 5409 Maryland Way, Suite 300, Brentwood, TN 37027; tel. 615/373–6995; FAX. 615/370–9396; Steve White, Chief Executive Officer

Humana Health Plan, Inc., P.O. Box 740036, Louisville, KY 40201–7436; tel. 502/580–5804; Craig Drablos, Executive Director

Mid–South Health Plan, Inc., 889 Ridge Lake Boulevard, Suite 111, Memphis, TN 38120; tel. 901/766–7500; William C. Stewart, Jr., Chief Executive Director, Medical Director

PHP Health Plans, Inc., 1420 Centrerpoint Boulevard, Knoxville, TN 37932; tel. 423/470–7470; Jerry M. Marsh, CPA, Director, Finance

Phoenix Healthcare of Tennessee, Inc., 3401 West End Avenue, Suite 470, Nashville, TN 37203; tel. 615/298–3666, ext. 260; FAX. 615/297–2036; Samuel H. Howard, Chairman

Provident Health Care Plan, Inc. of Tennessee, Two Northgate Park, Chattanooga, TN 37415

Prudential Health Care Plan, Inc., 227 French Landing Drive, Suite 200, Nashville, TN 37228

Southern Health Plan, Inc., 600 Jefferson, Memphis, TN 38105; tel. 901/544–2336; FAX. 901/544–2220; Bill Graham, Executive Director

Tennessee Health Care Network, Inc., P.O. Box 1407, Chattanooga, TN 37401–1407; tel. 423/755–2033; FAX. 615/755–5630; Robert M. Fox, President

TriPoint Health Plan, Inc., 706 Church Street, Suite 500, Nashville, TN 37203–3511; tel. 800/557–4874; Barbara Bennett, General Counsel

Tripoint Health Plan, Inc., 706 Church Street, Suite 500, Nashville, TN 37203–3511; tel. 800/557–4874

Vanderbilt Health Plans, Inc., 706 Church Street Building, Suite 500, Nashville, TN 37203; tel. 615/343–2670; FAX. 615/343–2823; Randal B. Farr, Executive Vice President

TEXAS

AECC Total Vision Health Plan of Texas, Inc., 3010 LBJ Freeway, Suite 240, Dallas, TX 75234; tel. 800/268–8847; Samuel Petteway, Jr., President

Aetna Dental Care of Texas, Inc., 2777 Stemmons Freeway, Suite 300, Dallas, TX 75207; tel. 214/470–7990; Jackie Eveslage, Chief Operating Officer

Aetna Health Plans of Texas, Inc., 2900 North Loop West, Suite 200, Houston, TX 77092; tel. 713/683–7500; FAX. 713/683–5819; Joseph T. Blanford III, General Manager

Aetna U.S. Healthcare of North Texas, Inc., P.O. Box 569440, 2777 Stemmons Freeway, Suite 400, Dallas, TX 75356–9440; tel. 214/401–8610; John Coyle, President

Alpha Dental Programs, Inc., d/b/a Delta Care, 1431 Greenway Drive, Suite 230, Irving, TX 75038; tel. 972/580–1616; FAX. 972/580–1333; Lee Schneider, Vice President, Marketing, Western Region

Alternative Dental Care of Texas, Inc., 2023 South Gessner K–3, Houston, TX 77063; tel. 713/781–6607; Thomas Anthony Dzuryachko, President

AmeriHealth HMO of Texas, Inc., 770 South Post Oak Lane, Houston, TX 77056; tel. 215/241–2432

Americaid Texas, Inc., d/b/a Americaid Community Care, 617 Seventh Avenue, Second Floor, Fort Worth, TX 76104; tel. 817/870–1281; James Donovan, Jr., President

Anthem Health Plan of Texas, Inc., 5055 Keller Springs Road, Dallas, TX 75243; tel. 972/732–2000; FAX. 972/732–2043; Joseph W. Hrbek, President

Block Vision of Texas, Inc., 14228 Midway Road, Suite 213, Dallas, TX 75244; tel. 800/914–9795; FAX. 972/991–4704; Andrew Alcorn, President

CIGNA Dental Health of Texas, Inc., d/b/a CIGNA Dental Health, 600 East Las Colinas Boulevard, Suite 1000, Irving, TX 75039; tel. 800/367–1037; Brent Martin, D.D.S., M.B.A., Chief Executive Officer, Regional Vice Pres.

CIGNA HealthCare of Texas, Inc., d/b/a CIGNA HealthCare for Seniors, 600 East Las Colinas Boulevard, Suite II00, Irving, TX 75039; tel. 214/401–5200; FAX. 214/401–5209; Vernon W. Walters, M.D., Vice President, Medical Director

Certus Healthcare, L.L.C., 1300 North 10th Street, Suite 450, McAllen, TX 78501; tel. 210/630–1956, ext. 106; FAX. 210/630–1957; David Rodriguez, President

Community First Health Plans, Inc., P.O. Box 7548, San Antonio, TX 78207–0548; tel. 210/227–2347; FAX. 210/244–3014; Charles L. Knight, President, Chief Executive Officer

Community Health Choice, Inc., 2525 Holly Hall, Houston, TX 77054; tel. 713/746–6790

Comprehensive Heatlh Services of Texas, Inc., 100 Northeast Loop 410, Suite 675, San Antonio, TX 78217; tel. 210/321–4050; Thomas C. Jackson, Chief Executive Officer

Dental Benefits, Inc., d/b/a Bluecare Dental HMO, 12170 Abrams Road, Dallas, TX 75081; tel. 972/644–5066; Doyle C. Williams, President

Denticare, Inc., d/b/a CompDent, 2929 Briarpark Drive, Suite 314, Houston, TX 77042–3709; tel. 713/784–7011; Henry New, President

Dorsey Dental Plans of America, Inc., 1177 West Loop South, Suite 725, Houston, TX 77027; tel. 713/621–6050; Michael P. Stern, President, Chief Executive Officer

ECCA Managed Vision Care, Inc., 11103 West Avenue, San Antonio, TX 78213–1392; tel. 800/340–0129; FAX. 210/524–6587; Melissa Kazen, Director

Exclusive Healthcare, Inc., Park Central IX, 12790 Merit Drive, Suite 714, Dallas, TX 75251; tel. 214/450–4500; Robert Robidou, Plan Manager

FHP of New Mexico, d/b/a FHP of El Paso, 4300 San Mateo Boulevard, N.E., Albuquerque, NM 87110; tel. 505/881–7900; FAX. 505/875–3305; Mark Zobel, Regional Compliance Officer

FHP of Texas, Inc., 12 Greenway Plaza, Suite 500, Houston, TX 77046–1201; tel. 800/455–4156; FAX. 713/621–9647; Patrick Stewart, President

First American Dental Benefits, Inc., 14800 Landmark Boulevard, Suite 700, Dallas, TX 75240; tel. 214/661–5848; Jim Davenport, President, Acting Chief Executive Officer

Foundation Health, a Texas Health Plan, Inc., 110 Wild Basin Road, Suite 230, Austin, TX 78746; tel. 512/314–8436; Penny Zagroba, Operations Manager

HMO Texas, L.C., P.O. Box 42416, Houston, TX 77242–2416; tel. 713/952–6868; FAX. 713/974–1650; John Micale, President

Harris Health Plan, Inc., d/b/a Harris Methodist Health Plan, 611 Ryan Plaza Drive, Suite 900, Arlington, TX 76011–4009; tel. 817/570–8044; Donna A. Goldin, Chief Operating Officer

Harris Methodist Texas Health Plan, Inc., d/b/a Harris Methodist Health Plan, 611 Ryan Plaza Drive, Suite 900, Arlington, TX 76011–4009; tel. 817/462–7000; FAX. 817/462–7235; Tom Keenan, Chief Operating Officer

Healthcare Partner HMO, 821 ESE, Loop 323, Two American Center, Zip 75701, P.O. Box 130187, Zip 75713, Tyler, TX 75701; tel. 903/581–2600; Tom Slack, Chief Executive Officer

Healthplan of Texas, Inc., 110 North College Ave., Suite 900, Tyler, TX 75702; tel. 903/531–4447; Edwin McClusky, M.D., Chief Executive Officer

Healthsource North Texas, Inc., 1612 Summit Avenue, Suite 300, Fort Worth, TX 76102; tel. 817/336–1044; FAX. 817/332–2330; David Mier, Manager, Provider Relations

Healthsource Texas, Inc., d/b/a Healthsource, 1701 Directors Blvd., Suite 110, Austin, TX 78744; tel. 512/440–5030; Terry Steven Shilling, President, Chief Executive Officer

Humana Health Plan of Texas, Inc., d/b/a Humana Health Plan of San Antonio, 8431 Fredericksburg Road, Suite 570, San Antonio, TX 78229; tel. 210/617–1000; FAX. 210/617–1704; Michael A. Seltzer, Director, Texas Operations

Humana Health Plan of Texas, Inc., d/b/a Humana Health Plan of Dallas, 8431 Fredericksburg Road, San Antonio, TX 78229; tel. 512/617–1000; Brenda Luckett, Executive Director

Kaiser Foundation Health Plan of Texas, 12720 Hillcrest Road, Suite 600, Dallas, TX 75230; tel. 972/458–5000; FAX. 972/458–5173; William A. Gillespie, M.D., President

Memorial Sisters of Charity HMO, LLC, d/b/a MSCH HMO/d/b/a MSCH, 9494 Southwest Freeway, Suite 300, Houston, TX 77074; tel. 713/776–2885; Brigid Pace, President, Chief Executive Officer

Mercy Health Plans of Missouri, Inc., 5901 McPherson, Suites 1 & 2B, Centre Plaza, Laredo, TX 78041; tel. 210/723–7667; Ernesto Seguna, Vice President

MethodistCare, 6560 Fannin, Suite 734, Houston, TX 77030; tel. 713/790–2221; James Henderson, President, Chief Executive Officer

Metrowest Health Plan, Inc., 1500 South Main Street, 3rd Floor, Fort Worth, TX 76104; tel. 817/927–3999

Mid–Con Health Plans, L.C., d/b/a HMO Blue, SouthWest Texas, 500 Chestnut Street, Suite 1699, Abilene, TX 79602; tel. 915/695–6191; Harold Rubin, President

NYLCare Dental Plan of the Southwest, Inc., 4500 Fuller Drive, Irving, TX 75038; tel. 972/650–5500; FAX. 972/650–5707; Steve Yerxa, Chief Executive Officer, Executive Director

NYLCare Health Plan of the Southwest, 4500 Fuller Drive, Irving, TX 75038; tel. 972/650–5500; FAX. 972/650–5703; Steve Yerxa

NYLCare Health Plans of the Gulf Coast, 2425 West Loop South, Suite 1000, Houston, TX 77027; tel. 713/624–5000; FAX. 713/963–9417; Thomas S. Lucksinger, President, Chief Executive Officer

One Health Plan of Texas, Inc., 10000 North Central Expressway, Suite 900, Lock Box 46, Dallas, TX 75231; tel. 800/866–3136; Jim White, President

Orthopedic Healthcare of Texas, Inc., 729 Bedford–Euless Road, W., Suite 100, Hurst, TX 76053; tel. 817/282–6905; Edward William Smith, D.O., President

PCA Health Plans of Texas, Inc., 8303 MoPac, Suite 450, Austin, TX 78759; tel. 512/338–6100; FAX. 512/338–6137; Donald Gessler, M.D., President, Chief Executive Officer

Pacificare of Texas, Inc., San Antonio Region, 8200 I.H. 10 West, Suite 1000, San Antonio, TX 78230; tel. 210/524–9800; Patrick Feyen, President

Parkland Community Health Plan, Inc., 7920 Elmbrook, Suite 120, Dallas, TX 75247; tel. 214/590–2800; Ron J. Anderson, President

Parliament Dental Plans, Inc., 2909 Hillcroft, Suite 515, Houston, TX 77057; tel. 713/784–6262; FAX. 713/784–0488; Paul H. Michael, President

Physicians Care HMO, Inc., 2777 Stemmons Freeway, Suite 957, Stemmons Place, Dallas, TX 75207; tel. 214/631–0221; Amanullah Khan, President

Principal Health Care of Texas, Inc., 555 North Caracahua, Suite 500, Corpus Christi, TX 78478; tel. 512/887–0101; Diana Tchida, Executive Director

Prudential Dental Maintenance Organization, Inc., Stop 206, One Prudential Circle, Sugar Land, TX 77478–3833; tel. 713/494–6000; FAX. 713/276–3752; Royce Rosemond, Executive Director

Prudential Health Care Plan, Inc., Stop 204, One Prudential Circle, Sugar Land, TX 77478; tel. 713/276–3850; FAX. 713/276–8254; Dennis Edmonds, Executive Director

Rio Grande HMO, Inc., d/b/a HMO Blue, 4150 Pinnacle, Suite 203, El Paso, TX 79902; tel. 800/831–0576; Anne McDow, Vice President, Operations

Safeguard Health Plans, Inc., 14800 Landmark Blvd., 7th Floor, Dallas, TX 75240; tel. 214/265–7041; FAX. 214/265–7702; David Branstetter, Executive Director

Scott & White Health Plan, 2401 South 31st Street, Temple, TX 76508; tel. 817/742–3030; FAX. 817/742–3011; Deny Radefeld, Executive Director

Seton Health Plan, Inc., 1201 West 38th Street, Austin, TX 78705; tel. 800/749–7404; FAX. 512/323–1952; John H. Evler III, President, Chief Operating Officer

Sha, L.L.C., d/b/a Firstcare, 3310 Danvers, Amarillo, TX 79109; tel. 806/356–5151; Dale Bowerman, President and Chief Executive Officer

Spectera Dental, Inc., (formerly United Healthcare Dental, Inc.), 1445 North Loop West, Suite 1000, Houston, TX 77008; tel. 713/861–3231; Arlene Sheldon, Executive Director

Superior Healthplan, L.P., 816 Congress Ave., Suite 1100, Austin, TX 78701; tel. 512/480–2206; Jose Comacho, Executive Director

Texas Children's Health Plan, Inc., 1919 South Braeswood Boulevard, P.O. Box 301011, Houston, TX 77230–1011; tel. 713/770–2600; FAX. 713/770–2686; Christopher Born, President

Texas Universities Health Plan, Inc., d/b/a TUHP, 700 University Blvd., Galveston, TX 77550; tel. 409/747–5430

USABLE HMO, Inc., d/b/a USABLE Health Advantage, 1406 College Drive, Suite A, Texarkana, TX 75503; tel. 800/844–6047

Unicare of Texas Health Plans, Inc., (formerly Affiliated Health Plans, Inc.), 11200 Westheimer, Suite 700, Houston, TX 77042; tel. 713/782–4555; Sam John Nicholson II, President

United Dental Care of Texas, Inc., 14755 Preston Road, Suite 300, Dallas, TX 75240; tel. 214/458–7474; James B. Kingston, President

United Healthcare of Texas, Inc., (formerly Metrahealth Care Plan of Texas, Inc.), 1250 Capital of Texas, Highway South, Building One, Suite 400, Austin, TX 78746; tel. 800/424–6480; FAX. 512/338–6812; Karen England, Director, Network Operations

United Healthcare of Texas, Inc., Dallas/Fort Worth Division, 4835 LBJ Freeway, Suite 1100, Dallas, TX 75244; tel. 214/866–6000; FAX. 214/866–6018; Richard Cook, Chief Executive Officer

Universal HealthPlan, Inc., 2900 Elgin, Houston, TX 77004; tel. 713/526–2441

VHP Dental, Inc., P.O. Box 15800, 7801 North IH 35, Austin, TX 78761; tel. 512/433–1000

Vista Health Plan, Inc., (formerly The Wellness Health Plan of Texas, Inc.), 7801 North IH–35, Austin, TX 78753; tel. 512/433–1000; Paul Tovar, President

West Texas Health Plans, d/b/a HMO Blue, West Texas, Sentry Plaza II, 5225 South Loop 289, Suite 207, Lubbock, TX 79424; tel. 806/798–6362; Michael A. Huesman, President

UTAH

American Family Care of Utah, Inc., 3098 South Highland Drive, Suite 335, Salt Lake City, UT 84106; tel. 801/486–1664; Jose Fernandez, President

Benchoice, Inc., 310 East 4500 South, Suite 550, Murray, UT 84157–0906; tel. 801/262–2999; Talmage Pond, President

CIGNA Health Plan of Utah, Inc., 5295 South 320 West, Suite 280, Salt Lake City, UT 84107; tel. 801/265–2777, ext. 7501; FAX. 801/261–5349; Robert Immitt, President

Delta Care Dental Plan, Inc., 257 East 200 South, Suite 375, Salt Lake City, UT 84111; tel. 801/575–5168

Educators Health Care, 852 East Arrowhead Lane, Murray, UT 84107–5298; tel. 801/262–7476; FAX. 801/269–9734; Andy I. Galano, Ph.D., President

Employees Choice Health Option, 35 West Broadway, Salt Lake City, UT 84101; tel. 801/355–1234; Larry Bridge, President

FHP of Utah, Inc., 35 West Broadway, Salt Lake City, UT 84101; tel. 801/355–1234, ext. 3500; FAX. 801/531–9003; Larry Bridge, President

HealthWise, 2455 Parley's Way, P.O. Box 30270, Salt Lake City, UT 84130–0270; tel. 801/481–6184; FAX. 801/481–6994; Jed H. Pitcher, Chairman

Humana Health Plan of Utah, Inc., 500 West Main Street, 20th Floor, Louisville, KY 40201; tel. 502/580–1000

IHC Care, Inc., 36 South State Street, 15th Floor, Salt Lake City, UT 84111; tel. 801/442–5000; FAX. 801/538–5003; Sid Paulson, Chief Operating Officer

IHC Group, Inc., 36 South State Street, 15th Floor, Salt Lake City, UT 84111; tel. 801/442–5000; Sid Paulson, Chief Operating Officer

IHC Health Plans, Inc., 36 South State Street, 15th Floor, Salt Lake City, UT 84111; tel. 801/442–5000; Sid Paulson, Chief Operating Officer

Intergroup Healthcare Corporation of Utah, 127 South 500 East, Suite 410, Salt Lake City, UT 84102; tel. 801/532–7665; FAX. 801/297–4585; Elden Mitchell, President

Opticare of Utah, 159 1/2 South Main Street, Salt Lake City, UT 84111; tel. 801/363–0950; Stephen H. Schubach, President

Safeguard Health Plans, Inc., P.O. Box 3210, Anaheim, CA 92803–3210; tel. 714/778–1005; Steven J. Baileys, D.D.S., President

U. S. Dental Plan, Inc., 4001 South 700 East, Suite 300, Salt Lake City, UT 84107; tel. 801/263–8884; Christopher A. Jehle, President

United HealthCare of Utah, 7910 South 3500 East, Salt Lake City, UT 84121; tel. 801/942–6200; FAX. 801/944–0940; Colin Gardner, Chief Executive Officer

Utah Community Health Plan, 36 South State Street, Suite 1020, Salt Lake City, UT 84111–1418; tel. 801/442–3780; FAX. 801/442–3791; William K. Willson, Executive Director

VERMONT

Capital District Physicians Health Plan, 17 Columbia Circle, Albany, NY 12203; tel. 518/862–3923; FAX. 518/452–3767; Ellen M. Pierce, Director, Accounting

Community Health Plan (CHP), 1201 Troy–Schenectady Road, Latham, NY 12110; tel. 518/783–1864; FAX. 518/783–0234; John Baackes, President, Chief Executive Officer

Harvard Community Health Plan, 10 Brookline Place West, Brookline, MA 02146; tel. 617/731–8240

MVP Health Plan, 111 Liberty Street, P.O. Box 2207, Schenectady, NY 12301–2207; tel. 518/370–4793; David W. Oliker, President

Matthew Thornton Health Plan, 43 Constitution Drive, Bedford, NH 03110–6020; tel. 603/695–1100; FAX. 603/695–1157; Everett Page, President

VIRGINIA

Aetna Health Plans of the Mid–Atlantic, Inc., 7799 Leesburg Pike, Suite 1100 South, Falls Church, VA 22043; tel. 703/903–7100; FAX. 703/903–0316; Russell R. Dickhart, President, Executive Director

CIGNA HealthCare of Virginia, Inc., 4050 Innslake Drive, Glen Allen, VA 23060; tel. 804/273–1100; John E. Sharp, Vice President, Executive Director

CIGNA Healthplan Mid–Atlantic, Inc., 9700 Patuxent Woods Drive, Columbia, MD 21046; tel. 301/720–5800; Timothy P. Fitzgerald, President

CapitalCare, Inc., Tysons International Plaza, 550 12th Street, S.W., Suite 2, Washington, DC 20065–0001; tel. 703/761–5400; FAX. 703/761–5576; David L. Ward, President, Chief Executive Officer

Chesapeake Health Plan, Inc., 814 Light Street, Baltimore, MD 21230; tel. 410/539–8622

George Washington University Health Plan, Inc., 4550 Montgomery Avenue, Suite 800, Bethesda, MD 20814; tel. 301/941–2000; FAX. 301/941–2005; Dr. Kenneth A. Tannenbaum, Chief Executive Officer

Group Health Association, Inc., 4301 Connecticut Avenue, N.W., Washington, DC 20008; tel. 202/364–7523

HMO Virginia, Inc., Health Keepers, 2220 Edward Holland Drive, Richmond, VA 23230; tel. 804/354–7961; FAX. 804/354–3554; Sam Weidman, Vice President, Finance

Health First, Inc., 621 Lynnhaven Parkway, Suite 450, Virginia Beach, VA 23452–7330; tel. 804/431–5298; Russell F. Mohawk, President

HealthKeepers, Inc., 2220 Edward Holland Drive, P.O. Box 26623, Richmond, VA 23230; tel. 804/354–7961; FAX. 804/354–3554; Sam Weidman, Vice President, Finance

Heritage National Healthplan, Inc., 1515 Fifth Avenue, Suite 200, Moline, IL 61265–1358; tel. 309/765–1203

Humana Group Health Plan, Inc., 4301 Connecticut Avenue, N.W., Washington, DC 20008; tel. 202/364–2000; FAX. 202/364–7418; Ted W. LaBedz

Kaiser Foundation Health Plan of the Mid–Atlantic States, Inc., 2101 East Jefferson Street, Rockville, MD 20852; tel. 301/816–2424; FAX. 301/816–7478; Alan J. Silverstone, President

MD–Individual Practice Association, Inc., Four Taft Court, Rockville, MD 20850; tel. 301/294–5100; FAX. 301/309–1709; Susan Goff, President

NYLCare Health Plans of Mid–Atlantic, Inc., 7601 Ora Glen Drive, Suite 200, Greenbelt, MD 20770; tel. 301/982–0098, ext. 3308; FAX. 301/489–5282; Jeff D. Emerson, President, Chief Executive Officer

National Capital Health Plan, Inc., 5850 Versar Center, Suite 420, Springfield, VA 22151; tel. 703/914–5650

Optimum Choice, Inc., Four Taft Court, Rockville, MD 20850; tel. 301/738–7920; FAX. 301/309–3782; George T. Jochum, President, Chief Executive Officer

Partners National Health Plans of NC, Inc., 2000 Frontis Plaza Boulevard, P.O. Box 24907, Winton–Salem, NC 27114–4907; tel. 910/760–4822

Peninsula Health Care, Inc., 606 Denbigh Boulevard, Suite 500, Newport News, VA 23608; tel. 757/875–5760; FAX. 757/875–5785; C. Burke King, President

Physicians Health Plan, Inc., Health Keepers, 2220 Edward Holland Drive, Richmond, VA 23230; tel. 804/354–7961; FAX. 804/354–3554; Sam Weidman, Vice President, Finance

Principal Health Care, Inc., 1801 Rockville Pike, Suite 601, Rockville, MD 20852; tel. 301/881–1033, ext. 2211; FAX. 301/881–5403; Kenneth J. Linde, President

Priority Health Plan, Inc., 621 Lynnhaven Parkway, Suite 450, Virginia Beach, VA 23452–7330; tel. 804/463–4600; Russell F. Mohawk, President

Prudential Health Care Plan, Inc., d/b/a PruCare and Prudential Health Care Plan of the Mid–Atlantic, 1000 Boulders Parkway, Richmond, VA 23225; tel. 804/323–0900; William Patrick Link, President

QualChoice of VA Health Plan, Inc., 1807 Seminole Trail, Suite 201, Charlottesville, VA 22901; tel. 804/975–1212; FAX. 804/975–1414; Jay V. Garriss, President, Chief Executive Officer

Sentara Health Plans, Inc., d/b/a Sentara Health Plan, 4417 Corporation Lane, Virginia Beach, VA 23462; tel. 804/552–7100; FAX. 804/552–7396; John E. McNamara III, President

Southern Health Services, 9881 Mayland Drive, P.O. Box 85603, Richmond, VA 23285–5603; tel. 804/747–3700; FAX. 804/747–8723; James L. Gore, President

U. S. Healthcare, Inc., 980 Jolly Road, P.O. Box 1109, Blue Bell, PA 19422; tel. 215/628–4800

United Optical, d/b/a Spectera, 2811 Lord Baltimore Drive, Baltimore, MD 21244; tel. 410/265–6033; FAX. 410/594–9862; Dave Hall, Vice President, Marketing

VA Chartered Health Plan, Inc., 4701 Cox Road, Glen Allen, VA 23060; tel. 804/967–0747; Sheila Blackman, Chief Operating Officer

WASHINGTON

Good Health Plan of Washington, Century Square, 1501 Fourth Avenue, Suite 500, Seattle, WA 98101; tel. 206/622–6111; FAX. 206/346–0969; Lee Hooks, Executive Director

Group Health Cooperative of Puget Sound, Administration and Conference Center, 521 Wall Street, Seattle, WA 98121–1535; tel. 206/448–6460; FAX. 206/448–6080; Phil Nudelman, Ph.D., President, Chief Executive Officer

Group Health Northwest, 5615 West Sunset Highway, Spokane, WA 99204; tel. 509/838–9100; FAX. 509/838–3823; Henry S. Berman, M.D., President, Chief Executive Officer

HMO Washington, 1800 Ninth Avenue, P.O. Box 2088, Seattle, WA 98111–2088; tel. 206/389–6721; FAX. 206/389–6719; Bryan Heinrich, Executive Director

Health Maintenance of Oregon, Inc., 1800 First Avenue, Suite 505, P.O. Box 139, Portland, OR 97201; tel. 503/274–0755; FAX. 503/225–5431; Eric Bush

HealthFirst Partners, Inc., 601 Union Street, Suite 700, Seattle, WA 98101; tel. 206/667–8070; FAX. 206/667–8060; Eileen Duncan

HealthGuard Services, Inc., d/b/a SelectCare, 600 Country Club Road, P.O. Box 10106, Eugene, OR 97401–2240; tel. 541/485–1850; FAX. 503/686–2504; David L. Slade, President

HealthPlus, P.O. Box 2113, Seattle, WA 98111–2113; tel. 206/670–4700; FAX. 206/670–4766; Gary L. Meade, President, Chief Executive Officer

Humana Health Plan of Washington, Inc., P.O. Box 1438, Louisville, KY 40201–1438; tel. 502/580–3620; FAX. 502/580–3942; Sandra Lewis, Director, Government Compliance

Kaiser Foundation Health Plan of the Northwest, 500 Northeast Multnomah, Suite 100, Portland, OR 97232–2099; tel. 503/813–2800; FAX. 503/813–2283; Denise L. Honzel, Vice President

PACC, d/b/a PACC Health Plans of Washington, 12901 Southeast 97th Avenue, P.O. Box 286, Clackamas, OR 97015–0286; tel. 503/659–4212; FAX. 503/786–5319; Ron Morgan

PacifiCare of Oregon, Inc., Five Centerpointe Drive, Suite 600, Lake Oswego, OR 97035; tel. 503/620–9324; Patrick Feyen, President

PacificCare of Washington, 600 University Street, Suite 700, Seattle, WA 98101; tel. 206/326–4645; FAX. 206/442–5399; Brad Bowlus, President, Chief Executive Officer

QualMed Washington Health Plan, Inc, d/b/a Qual–Med Health Plan, 2331 130th Avenue, N.E., Suite 200, Zip 98009, P.O. Box 3387, Bellevue, WA 98009–3387; tel. 206/869–3500; FAX. 206/869–3568; C.F. du Laney, President

Sisters of Providence, Good Health Plan of Oregon, Inc., 1235 Northeast 47th Avenue, Suite 220, Portland, OR 97213; tel. 503/249–2981; Jack Friedman, Executive Director

Unified Physicians of Washington, Inc., 33301 Ninth Avenue, S., Suite 200, Federal Way, WA 98003–6394; tel. 206/815–1888; FAX. 206/815–0486; Dodie Wine, Associate Director, Communications

Virginia Mason Health Plan, Inc., Metropolitan Park West, 1100 Olive Way, Suite 1580, Seattle, WA 98101–1828; tel. 206/223–8844; FAX. 206/223–7506; John Clarke, Director, Operations

WEST VIRGINIA

Anthem Health Plan of West Virginia, Inc., d/b/a PrimeONE, 602 Virginia Street, East, Charleston, WV 25301; tel. 304/353–8728; FAX. 304/353–8732; A. Paul Holdren, President, Chief Executive Officer

Carelink Health Plans, 141 Summers Square, P.O. Box 1711, Charleston, WV 25326–1711; tel. 304/348–2901; FAX. 304/348–2948; Alan L. Mytty, President

Coventry Health Plan of West Virginia, Inc., (Health Assurance HMO), 887 National Road, Wheeling, WV 26003; tel. 304/234–5100; FAX. 304/234–5119; Marilyn White, Manager

Health Guard, Inc., d/b/a Advantage Health Plan, Inc., 300 Guernsey Street, Bellaire, OH 43906; tel. 614/676–4623; Dan Splain

Optimum Choice, 3025 Hamaker Court, Suite 301, Fairfax, VA 22031; tel. 703/207–6570; Susan Hrubes, Senior Director

The Health Plan of the Upper Ohio Valley, 52160 National Road, E., St. Clairsville, OH 43950; tel. 614/695–3585; Philip D. Wright, President

WISCONSIN

Atrium Health Plan, Inc., 2215 Vine Street, Suite E, Hudson, WI 54016–5802; tel. 800/535–4041; FAX. 715/386–8326; Michael L. Christensen, Director of Operations

Compcare Health Services Insurance Corp., 401 West Michigan Street, P.O. Box 2947, Milwaukee, WI 53201–2025; tel. 414/226–6171; FAX. 414/226–6229; Jeffrey J. Nohl, President, Chief Operating Officer

Dean Health Plan, Inc., P.O. Box 56099, Madison, WI 53705–9399; tel. 608/836–1400; FAX. 608/836–9620; John A. Turcott, President, Chief Executive Officer

Emphesys Wisconsin Insurance Company, 1100 Employers Boulevard, DePere, WI 54115; tel. 800/558–4444; Mark R. Minsloff, Executive Director

Family Health Plan Cooperative, 11524 West Theo Trecker Way, Milwaukee, WI 53214–7260; tel. 414/256–0006; FAX. 414/256–5681; Conrad Sobczak, Executive Director

Genesis Health Plan Insurance Corporation, P.O. Box 20007, Greenfield, WI 53220–0007; tel. 414/425–3323; FAX. 414/425–3034; Karl Rajani, Chief Executive Officer

Greater La Crosse Health Plans, Inc., 1285 Rudy Street, Onalaska, WI 54650; tel. 608/782–2638; FAX. 608/781–8862; Steven M. Kunes, Plan Administrator

Group Health Cooperative of Eau Claire, P.O. Box 3217, Eau Claire, WI 54702–3217; tel. 715/836–8552; FAX. 715/836–7683; Claire W. Johnson, General Manager

Group Health Cooperative of South Central Wisconsin, 8202 Excelsior Drive, P.O. Box 44971, Madison, WI 53744–4971; tel. 608/251–4156; FAX. 608/257–3842; Lawrence Zanoni, Executive Director

Gundersen Lutheran Health Plan, Inc., 1836 South Avenue, LaCrosse, WI 54601; tel. 608/798–8020; FAX. 608/791–8042; Jeff Treasure, Chief Executive Officer

Humana Wisconsin Health Organization Insurance Corporation, 111 West Pleasant Street, P.O.Box 12359, Milwaukee, WI 53212–0359; tel. 414/223–3300; FAX. 414/223–7777; William L. Carr, Executive Director

Managed Health Services, 10607 West Oklahoma Avenue, Milwaukee, WI 53227; tel. 414/328–5005; FAX. 414/321–9724; Michael F. Neidorff, President, Chief Executive Officer

Maxicare Health Insurance Company, 790 North Milwaukee Street, Milwaukee, WI 53202; tel. 414/271–6371; John F. Southworth, Administrator

Medica Health Plans of Wisconsin, Inc., 5901 Smetana Drive, P.O. Box 9310, Minneapolis, MN 55440–9310; tel. 612/992–2000

Medical Associates Clinic Health Plan of Wisconsin, 700 Locust Street, Suite 230, Dubuque, IA 52001–6800; tel. 319/556–8070; FAX. 319/556–5134; Ross A. Madden, Chairman of the Board, Director

MercyCare Health Plan, Inc., One Parker Place, Suite 750, Janesville, WI 53545; tel. 608/752–3431; FAX. 608/752–3751; Don Schreiner, Senior Vice President

Network Health Plan of Wisconsin, Inc., 1165 Appleton Road, P.O. Box 120, Menasha, WI 54952–0120; tel. 414/727–0100; FAX. 414/727–5634; Michael D. Wolff, President, Chief Executive Officer

North Central Health Protection Plan, 2000 Westwood Drive, Zip 54401, P.O. Box 969, Wausau, WI 54402–0969; tel. 715/847–8866; Larry A. Baker, Administrator

Physicians Plus Insurance Corporation, 340 West Washington Avenue, P.O. Box 2078, Madison, WI 53703; tel. 608/282–8900; FAX. 608/282–8944; Thomas R. Sobocinski, President, Chief Executive Officer

Premier Medical Insurance Group, Inc., 2711 Allen Boulevard, Middleton, WI 53562; tel. 608/836–1400; Daniel E. Edge, CEO

PrimeCare Health Plan, Inc., 10701 West Research Drive, Milwaukee, WI 53226–0649; tel. 414/443–4000; FAX. 414/443–4750; James Schultz, Administrator

Security Health Plan of Wisconsin, Inc., 1000 North Oak Avenue, Marshfield, WI 54449; tel. 715/387–5534; FAX. 715/387–5240; Richard A. Leer, President

United Health of Wisconsin Insurance Company, Inc., P.O. Box 507, Appleton, WI 54912–0507; tel. 414/735–6440; FAX. 414/731–7232; Jay Fulkerson, Chief Executive Officer

Unity Health Plans Insurance Corp., 840 Carolina Street, Sauk City, WI 53583; tel. 800/362–3308; FAX. 608/643–2564; Mary Traver, Interim President

Valley Health Plan, 2270 East Ridge Center, P.O. Box 3128, Eau Claire, WI 54702–3128; tel. 715/832–3235; FAX. 715/836–1298; Kathryn R. Teeters, Director

WYOMING

IHC Health Plans, Inc., 36 South State Street, Salt Lake City, UT 84111; tel. 801/442–5000; FAX. 801/442–5003; Martin Byrnes, Compliance Supervisor

WINhealth Partners, 2600 East 18th Street, Cheyenne, WY 82001; tel. 307/633–7051; FAX. 307/633–7053; Beth Wasson, Executive Director

---

U. S. Associated Areas

GUAM

F.H.P., Inc., P.O. Box 6578, Tamunig, GU 96911; tel. 671/646–5824; FAX. 671/646–6923; Edward English, Associate Regional Vice President

Guam Memorial Health Plan, 142 West Seaton Boulevard, Agana, GU 96910; tel. 671/472–4647; FAX. 671/477–1784; James W. Gillan, Chief Operating Officer

PUERTO RICO

First Medical Comprehensive Health Care, Inc., (Antes Plan Comprensivo de Salud, Inc.), Apartado 40954, Estacion Minillas, Santurce, PR 00940; tel. 809/723–6016; FAX. 809/723–6014; J. A. Soler, President

Golden Cross HMO Health Plan Corporation, Antes HMO Medical System Corporation, Apartado 1727, Estacion Viejo San Juan, San Juan, PR 00902; tel. 809/721–0427; FAX. 809/724–7249; Maria J. Gonzalez

Medical One, Inc., (Antes Plan Medico Doctor Gubern, Inc.), Miramar Plaza, Ave. Ponce de Leon 954, Suite 102A, Santurce, PR 00907; tel. 809/289–6969; Montserrat G. de Garcia, Chief Executive Officer

Mennonite General Hospital, Inc., Calle Jose C. Vazquez, Apartado 1379, Aibonito, PR 00705; tel. 809/735–8001; FAX. 809/735–8073; Domingo Torres Zayas, Chief Executive Officer

PCA Health Plans, 383 F. D. Roosevelt Avenue, San Juan, PR 00918–2131; tel. 809/282–7900; FAX. 809/793–1450; Jose A. Cuevas, President, Chief Executive Officer

Section C

Plan Medico U.T.I. de Puerto Rico, Inc., Apartado 23316–Estacion U.P.R., Rio Piedras, PR 00924; tel. 809/758–1500; FAX. 809/758–3210; David Munoz, President

Plan de Salud Hospital de la Concepcion, Inc., Calle Luna 41, Apartado 285, San German, PR 00683; tel. 809/892–1860; Ivonne Montaluo, Executive Director

Plan de Salud U.I.A., Inc., Calle Mayaguez #49, San Juan, PR 00917; tel. 787/763–4004; FAX. 787/763–7095; Jose E. Sanchez, Consultant

Plan de Salud de la Federacion de Maestros, de Puerto Rico, Inc., P.O. Box 71336, San Juan, PR 00936–8436; tel. 787/758–5610; FAX. 787/281–7392; Eugenio Aponte, Executive Director

Ryder Health Plan, Inc., Call Box 859, Humacao, PR 00792; tel. 809/852–0846; FAX. 809/850–4863; Juan L. De Le Rosa, Director

Servi Medical, Inc., Avenida Munoz Rivera 402, Parada 31, Hato Rey, PR 00917; tel. 809/758–5555; FAX. 809/250–1425; Lexie Gomez

Servicios de Salud Bella Vista, Bella Vista Gardens Numero 43, Carr. 349–Cerro Las Mesas, Mayaguez, PR 00680; tel. 787/833–8070; FAX. 787/832–5400; Victor Prosper–Rios, President

United Healthcare Plans of Puerto Rico, Inc., (Antes Group Sales and Service of Puerto Rico, Inc.), Rexco Office Park, Apartado 364864, San Juan, PR 00936–4864; tel. 809/782–7005; FAX. 809/782–5269; Luis A. Salgado Munoz, Executive Vice President

Information for the following list was obtained directly from the agencies.

State Government Agencies for HMO's

United States

ALABAMA: Department of Insurance, 201 Monroe Street, Suite 1700, Montgomery, AL 36130–3351; tel. 334/269–3550; FAX. 334/241–4192; Richard H. Cater, Commissioner of Insurance

ALASKA: Alaska Division of Insurance, P.O. Box 110805, Juneau, AK 99811–0805; tel. 907/465–2596; FAX. 907/465–3422; Marianne K. Burke, Director

ARIZONA: Department of Insurance, 2910 North 44th Street, Suite 210, Phoenix, AZ 85018; tel. 602/912–8443; FAX. 602/912–8453; Mary Butterfield, Assistant Director, Life and Health Division

ARKANSAS: Arkansas Insurance Department, 1200 West Third Street, Little Rock, AR 72201–1904; tel. 501/371–2600; FAX. 501/371–2629; Mike Pickens, Insurance Commissioner

CALIFORNIA: Department of Corporations, Health Care Service Plan Division, 3700 Wilshire Boulevard, Los Angeles, CA 90010; tel. 213/736–2776; Gary G. Hagen, Assistant Commissioner, Health Care Division

COLORADO: Department of Regulatory Agencies, Colorado Division of Insurance, 1560 Broadway, Suite 850, Denver, CO 80202; tel. 303/894–7499, ext. 322; FAX. 303/894–7455, ext. 322; Nancy Litwinski, Assistant Commissioner of Financial Regulation

CONNECTICUT: Department of Insurance, P.O. Box 816, Hartford, CT 06142–0816; tel. 203/297–3800; FAX. 203/566–7410; Mary Ellen Breault, Director, Life and Health Division

DELAWARE: Department of Health and Social Services, Office of Health Facilities Licensure and Certification, Three Mill Road, Suite 308, Wilmington, DE 19806; tel. 302/577–6666; FAX. 302/577–6672; Ellen T. Reap, Director

DISTRICT OF COLUMBIA: District of Columbia Department of Insurance and Securities Regulation, 441 Fourth Street, N.W., Suite 870 North, Washington, DC 20001; tel. 202/727–8000, ext. 3031; FAX. 202/727–8055; Herman Hunter, Chief Consumer Services Branch

FLORIDA: Florida Department of Insurance, Bureau of Life and Health Insurer Solvency and Market Conduct, 200 East Gaines, Larson Building, Tallahassee, FL 32399–0327; tel. 850/922–3153, ext. 2471; FAX. 904/413–9019; Mark Shealy, Administrator

GEORGIA: Department of Insurance, 604 West Tower, Floyd Building, Two Martin Luther King Jr. Drive, Atlanta, GA 30334; tel. 404/656–2074; FAX. 404/657–7743; John Oxendine, Commissioner

HAWAII: State of Hawaii Department of Labor and Industrial Relations, Disability Compensation Division, P.O. Box 3769, Honolulu, HI 96812; tel. 808/586–9151; Gary S. Hamada, Administrator

IDAHO: Department of Insurance, 700 West State Street, Third Floor, P.O. Box 83720, Boise, ID 83720–0043; tel. 208/334–4250; FAX. 208/334–4398; Joan Krosch, Health Insurance Coordinator

ILLINOIS: Department of Insurance, 320 West Washington Street, Fourth Floor, Springfield, IL 62767–0001; tel. 217/782–6369; FAX. 217/524–2122; David E. Grant, Health Care Coordinator

INDIANA: Department of Insurance, 311 West Washington Street, Suite 300, Indianapolis, IN 46204; tel. 317/232–5695; FAX. 317/232–5251; Jim Fuller, Health Deputy

IOWA: Iowa Department of Commerce, Division of Insurance, 330 Maple, Des Moines, IA 50319–0065; tel. 515/281–5705; FAX. 515/281–3059; Therese M. Vaughan, Commissioner

KANSAS: Kansas Insurance Department, 420 Southwest Ninth Street, Topeka, KS 66612; tel. 785/296–3071; FAX. 785/296–2283; Kathleen Sebelius, Commissioner

KENTUCKY: Department of Insurance, Life and Health Division, 215 West Main Street, P.O. Box 517, Frankfort, KY 40602; tel. 502/564–6088; FAX. 502/564–6090; Janie Miller, Director

LOUISIANA: Department of Insurance, Attn: Company Licensing Division, P.O. Box 94214, Baton Rouge, LA 70804; tel. 504/342–1216; FAX. 504/342–3078; Mike Boutwell, Assistant Director of Licensing

MAINE: Department of Professional and Financial Regulation, Bureau of Insurance, 34 State House Station, Augusta, ME 04333; tel. 207/624–8416; FAX. 207/624–8599; Michael F. McGonigle, Senior Insurance Analyst

MARYLAND: Department of Health and Mental Hygiene, Insurance Division, 201 West Preston Street, Baltimore, MD 21201–2399; tel. 410/225–6860; Martin P. Wasserman, M.D., J.D., Secretary

MASSACHUSETTS: Division of Insurance, 470 Atlantic Avenue, Boston, MA 02210–2223; tel. 617/521–7794; FAX. 617/521–7770; Robert Dynan, Company Licensing

MICHIGAN: Department of Community Health, Managed Care Quality Assessment and Improvement Division, 3423 North Logan/Martin Luther King Boulevard, P.O. Box 30195, Lansing, MI 48909; tel. 517/335–8515; FAX. 517/335–9239; Janet Olszewski, Director

MINNESOTA: Department of Health, Health Systems Development Division, 121 East Seventh Place, Suite 450, P.O. Box 64975, St. Paul, MN 55164–0975; tel. 612/282–5600; Brenda Holden, Director

MISSISSIPPI: Mississippi Department of Insurance, P.O. Box 79, Jackson, MS 39205; tel. 601/359–3577; FAX. 601/359–2474; J. Mark Haire, Special Assistant Attorney General

MISSOURI: Department of Insurance, Division of Company Regulation Life and Health Section, P.O. Box 690, Jefferson City, MO 65102; tel. 573/751–4363; FAX. 573/526–6075; Wendy Taparanskas

MONTANA: Montana State Auditor, Insurance Department, Insurance Examinations Division, Mitchell Building, Room 270, 126 North Sanders, P.O. Box 4009, Helena, MT 59604–4009; tel. 406/444–4372; FAX. 406/444–3497; James Borchardt, Chief Examiner, Montana Insurance Department

NEBRASKA: Department of Insurance, 941 O Street, Suite 400, Lincoln, NE 68508; tel. 402/471–2201; FAX. 402/471–4610; Timothy J. Hall, Director

NEVADA: Nevada Division of Insurance, Capitol Complex, 1665 Hot Springs Road, Suite 152, Carson City, NV 89710; tel. 702/687–4270; FAX. 702/687–3937; Alice A. Molasky, Esq., Commissioner

NEW HAMPSHIRE: Department of Health and Human Services, Office of Health Management, Medicaid Administration Bureau, 6 Hazen Drive, Concord, NH 03301–6521; tel. 603/271–4365; FAX. 603/271–4376; Diane Kemp, Supervisor IV

NEW JERSEY: Office of Managed Care, Department of Health, P.O. Box 300, Trenton, NJ 08625; tel. 609/588–2510; FAX. 609/588–7823; Edwin V. Kelleher, Chief

NEW MEXICO: State Corporation Commission, Department of Insurance, P.O. Drawer 1269, Santa Fe, NM 87504; tel. 505/827–4601; FAX. 505/827–4734; Helen S. Hordes, Manager, Life and Health Forms Division

NEW YORK: The Bureau of Managed Care Certification and Surveillance, Empire State Plaza, Corning Tower Building, Albany, NY 12237; tel. 518/474–5515; Valencia Lloyd, Director

NORTH CAROLINA: Department of Insurance, Financial Evaluation Division, P.O. Box 26387, Raleigh, NC 27611; tel. 919/733–5633; Jackie Obusek, Financial Analyst

NORTH DAKOTA: North Dakota Department of Insurance, State Capitol, 600 East Boulevard, Bismarck, ND 58505–0320; tel. 701/328–2440; FAX. 701/328–4880; Glenn Pomeroy, Commissioner

OHIO: Department of Insurance, Managed Care Division, 2100 Stella Court, Columbus, OH 43215–1067; tel. 614/644–3348; FAX. 614/644–3741; Phil Bisesi, Assistant Director

OKLAHOMA: Oklahoma State Department of Health, 1000 Northeast 10th Street, Oklahoma City, OK 73117–1299; tel. 405/271–6868; FAX. 405/271–3442; Lajuana Wire, Director, Managed Care Systems

OREGON: Department of Consumer and Business Services, Insurance Division, 350 Winter St. NE #440, Salem, OR 97310; tel. 503/947–7980; FAX. 503/378–4351

PENNSYLVANIA: Pennsylvania Insurance Department, Company Licensing Division, 1345 Strawberry Square, Harrisburg, PA 17120; tel. 717/787–2735; FAX. 717/787–8557; Steven Harman, Chief

RHODE ISLAND: Department of Business Regulation, Division of Insurance, 233 Richmond Street, Suite 233, Providence, RI 02903–4233; tel. 401/277–2223; FAX. 401/751–4887; Alfonso E. Mastrostefano, Associate Director, Superintendent, Insurance

SOUTH CAROLINA: Office of Insuracne LIcensing and Solvency Services, 1612 Marion Street, Columbia, SC 29201; tel. 803/737–6221; Timothy W. Campbell, Director Financial Analyst

SOUTH DAKOTA: Division of Administration, South Dakota Department of Health, 600 East Capitol Avenue, Pierre, SD 57501–2536; tel. 605/773–3361; FAX. 605/773–5683; Joan Adam, Division Director

TENNESSEE: Department of Commerce and Insurance, 500 James Robertson Parkway, Nashville, TN 37243–1135; tel. 615/741–6796; Don Spann, Chief Financial Executive, Insurance Examiner

TEXAS: Texas Department of Insurance, Mail Code 103–6A, P.O. Box 149104, Austin, TX 78714–9104; tel. 512/322–4266; Leah Rummel, Deputy Commissioner, HMO/URA/QA

UTAH: Utah Insurance Department, State Office Building, Room 3110, Salt Lake City, UT 84114; tel. 801/538–3800; FAX. 801/538–3829; Tilane Whitby, Information Specialist

VERMONT: Department of Banking, Insurance and Securities, 89 Main Street, Drawer 20, Montpelier, VT 05620–3101; tel. 802/828–2900; FAX. 802/828–3306; Theresa Alberghini, Deputy Commissioner

VIRGINIA: State Corporation Commission, Bureau of Insurance, P.O. Box 1157, Richmond, VA 23219; tel. 804/371–9637; FAX. 804/371–9511; Laura Lee Viergever, Senior Insurance Examiner

WASHINGTON: Office of the Insurance Commissioner, Insurance Building, P.O. Box 40255, Olympia, WA 98504–0255; tel. 360/664–8002; FAX. 360/586–3535; Chris Daugherty, Manager, Health Care Contracts

WEST VIRGINIA: Insurance Commissioner's Office, Financial Conditions Division, 1124 Smith Street, Charleston, WV 25301; tel. 304/558–2100; FAX. 304/558–1365; Jeffrey W. Van Gilder, Director, Chief Examiner

WISCONSIN: Office of the Commissioner of Insurance, P.O. Box 7873, Madison, WI 53707–7873; tel. 608/266–3585; FAX. 608/266–9935; Randy Blumer, Acting Commissioner

Section C

WYOMING: Department of Insurance, Herschler Building, Third Floor East, 122 West 25th Street, Cheyenne, WY 82002; tel. 307/777–6807; FAX. 307/777–5895; Lloyd Wilder, Insurance Standards Consultant

U. S. Associated Areas

GUAM: Department of Public Health and Social Services, Government of Guam, P.O. Box 2816, Agana, GU 96932; tel. 671/735–7102; FAX. 671/734–5910; Dennis G. Rodriguez, Director

PUERTO RICO: Aurea Lopez, Chief Examiner, Office of the Commissioner of Insurance, P.O. Box 8330, Fernandez Juncos Station, Santurce, PR 00910–8330; tel. 787/722–8686, ext. 2212; FAX. 809/722–4400; Aurea Lopez, Chief Examiner

Section C

Freestanding Ambulatory Surgery Centers

The following list of freestanding ambulatory surgery centers was developed with the assistance of state government agencies and the individual facilities listed.

The AHA Guide contains two types of ambulatory surgery center listings; those that are hospital based and those that are freestanding. Hospital based ambulatory surgery centers are listed in section A of the AHA Guide and are identified by Facility Code F44. Please refer to that section for information on the over 5,000 hospital based ambulatory surgery centers.

We present this list simply as a convenient directory. Inclusion or omission of any organization's name indicates neither approval nor disapproval by Healthcare InfoSource, Inc., a subsidiary of the American Hospital Association.

United States

ALABAMA

American Surgery Centers of Alabama, d/b/a American Surgery Center, 2802 Ross Clark Circle, S.W., Dothan, AL 36301; tel. 334/793-3411; FAX. 334/712-0227; Carlotta McCallister, Administrator

Baptist Surgery Center, 2035 East South Boulevard, Montgomery, AL 36111-0000; tel. 334/286-3180; FAX. 334/286-3381; Faye Wimberly, RN, Administrator

Birmingham Endoscopy Center, Inc., 2621 19th Street, South, Homewood, AL 35209; tel. 205/271-8200; Leonard Ou-Tim, M.D., Administrator

Birmingham Outpatient Surgery Center, Ltd., d/b/a Columbia Outpatient CareCenter, 2720 University Boulevard, Birmingham, AL 35233; tel. 205/933-0050; FAX. 205/933-8212; Jackie Harrison, RN, Administrator

Cleburne Center for Healthcare Ambulatory Surgical Center, 150 Tompkins Street, Heflin, AL 36264; tel. 205/463-8900; Victoria Minter, Administrator

Columbia Surgicare of Mobile, 2890 Dauphin Street, Mobile, AL 36606; tel. 334/473-2020; FAX. 334/478-6737; Sandy Bunch, Administrator

Dauphin West Surgery Center, 3701 Dauphin Street, Mobile, AL 36608; tel. 334/341-3405; FAX. 334/341-3404; James L. Spires, Executive Director

Decatur Ambulatory Surgery Center, 2828 Highway 31, S., Decatur, AL 35603; tel. 205/340-1212; FAX. 205/340-0252; Andrew Hetrick, Administrator

Dothan Surgery Center, 1450 Ross Clark Circle, S.E., Dothan, AL 36301; tel. 334/793-3442; FAX. 334/793-3318; Denise Harrington, Facility Administrator

Florence Surgery Center, 103 Helton Court, Florence, AL 35630; tel. 205/760-0672; FAX. 205/766-4547; Pam Watson, Administrator

Gadsden Surgery Center, 418 South Fifth Street, Gadsden, AL 35901; tel. 205/543-1253; FAX. 205/543-1260; Bobo Martin, RN, Administrator

Healthsouth Surgical Center of Tuscaloosa, 1400 McFarland Boulevard, N., Tuscaloosa, AL 35406; tel. 205/345-5500; Jeff Hayes, Administrator

Huntsville Endoscopy Center, Inc., 119 Longwood Drive, Huntsville, AL 35801; tel. 205/533-6488; FAX. 205/533-6495; Michael W. Brown, M.D.

Medplex Outpatient Medical Centers, Inc., 4511 Southlake Parkway, Birmingham, AL 35422; tel. 205/985-4398; FAX. 205/985-4486; Dawn Ousley, RN, Administrator

Mobile Surgery Center, 1721 Springhill Avenue, Mobile, AL 36608; tel. 334/438-3614; Julie Saucier, RN, B.S.N., Facility Administrator

Montgomery Eye Surgery Center, 2752 Zelda Road, Montgomery, AL 36106; tel. 334/271-3804; Chris Green, Administrator

Montgomery Surgical Center, 855 East South Boulevard, Montgomery, AL 36116; tel. 334/284-9600; FAX. 334/284-4233; Susan N. Lamar, Administrator

Outpatient Services East, Inc., 52 Medical Park Drive, E., Suite 401, Birmingham, AL 35235; tel. 205/838-3888, ext. 211; FAX. 205/838-3875; James E. Stidham, Chief Executive Officer, President

The Kirklin Clinic Ambulatory Surgical Center, 2000 Sixth Avenue, S., Birmingham, AL 35233; tel. 205/801-8000; Steven C. Schultz, Executive Vice President

The Surgery Center of Huntsville, 721 Madison Street, Huntsville, AL 35801; tel. 205/533-4888; FAX. 205/532-9510; William Sammons, Chief Executive Officer

Tuscaloosa Endoscopy Center, 100 Rice Mine Road, N.E., Suite E, Tuscaloosa, AL 35406; tel. 205/345-0010; FAX. 205/752-1175; A. B. Reddy, M.D., Medical Director

ALASKA

Alaska Surgery Center, 4001 Laurel Street, Anchorage, AK 99508; tel. 907/563-3327, ext. 226; FAX. 907/562-7042; Louise M. Bjornstad, Executive Director

Alaska Women's Health Services, Inc., 4115 Lake Otis Drive, Anchorage, AK 99508; tel. 907/563-7228; FAX. 907/563-6278; Ellen Cowgill, Administrator

Geneva Woods Surgical Center, 3730 Rhone Circle, Suite 100, Anchorage, AK 99508; tel. 907/562-4764; FAX. 907/561-8519; Theresa Thurston, Administrator

Pacific Cataract & Laser Institute, 1600 'A' Street, Suite 200, Anchorage, AK 99501; tel. 907/272-2423; Hans Kell, O.D., Administrator

Susitna Surgery Center, 950 East Bogard Road, Wasilla, AK 99645, P.O. Box 1687, Palmer, AK 99645; tel. 907/746-8625; Patsy Crofford, RN, Chief Clinical Officer

ARIZONA

A.I.M.S. Outpatient Surgery, 3636 Stockton Hill Road, Kingman, AZ 86401; tel. 602/757-3636; FAX. 602/757-7224; Bill Margita

Adobe Plastic Surgery, 2585 North Wyatt Drive, Tucson, AZ 85712; tel. 602/322-5295; FAX. 602/325-7763; Lucricia Banks, Administrative Assistant

Aesthetic Reconstructive Associates, P.C., 4222 East Camelback, Suite H-150, Phoenix, AZ 85018; tel. 602/952-8100; FAX. 602/952-9519; Martin L. Johnson, M.D.

Ambulatory Surgicenter, Inc., 1940 East Southern Avenue, Tempe, AZ 85282; tel. 602/820-7101; FAX. 602/820-9291; H. William Reese, D.P.M., Medical Director

Arizona Diagnostic and Surgical Center, 545 North Mesa Drive, Mesa, AZ 85201; tel. 602/461-4407; FAX. 602/461-4401; Lynnette King, RN, Administrator

Arizona Foot Institute, P.C., 1901 West Glendale Avenue, Phoenix, AZ 85021; tel. 602/246-0816; FAX. 602/433-2257; Barry Kaplan

Arizona Medical Clinic, Ltd., 13640 North Plaza Del Rio Boulevard, Peoria, AZ 85381; tel. 602/876-3800; Jan Kaplan, Director, Operations

Arizona Surgical Arts, Inc., 1245 North Wilmot Road, Tucson, AZ 85712; tel. 520/296-7550; Marilyn C. Mazeika, Administrator

Barnet Dulaney Eye Center, 9425 West Bell Road, Sun City, AZ 85351; tel. 602/974-1000; FAX. 602/933-5462; David D. Dulaney, Executive Director

Barnet Dulaney Eye Center, 13760 North 93rd Avenue, Peoria, AZ 85381; tel. 602/977-4291; Ronald W. Barnet, M.D.

Barnet Dulaney Eye Center, 1375 West 16th Street, Yuma, AZ 85364; tel. 602/955-1000; Imelda Kelly, Administrator

Barnet Dulaney Eye Center-Phoenix, 3333 East Camelback Road, Suite 122, Phoenix, AZ 85018; tel. 602/955-1000; FAX. 602/957-9202; Ronald W. Barnet, M.D.

Barnet Eye Center-Mesa, 6335 East Main Street, Mesa, AZ 85205; tel. 602/981-1000; FAX. 602/981-0467; Carolyn Miller, Administrator

Boswell Eye Institute, 10541 West Thunderbird Boulevard, Sun City, AZ 85351; tel. 602/933-3402; FAX. 602/972-5014; Jan Zellmann, Administrator

CIGNA Healthplan of Arizona, Outpatient Surgery, 755 East McDowell Road, Phoenix, AZ 85006; tel. 602/371-2500; Clifton Worsham, M.D., Administrator

Carriker Eye Center, 6425 North 16th Street, Phoenix, AZ 85016; tel. 602/274-1703; FAX. 602/274-3216; Richard G. Carriker, M.D.

Casa Blanca Clinic I.P.L.L.C., 4001 East Baseline Road, Gilbert, AZ 85234; tel. 602/926-6200; FAX. 602/926-6202; Stanley W. Decker, Executive Director

Cataract Surgery Clinic, 215 South Power Road, Suite 112, Mesa, AZ 85206; tel. 602/981-1345; Robert P. Calderone, M.D., Administrator

Cochise Eye and Laser, PC, 2445 East Wilcox Drive, Sierra Vista, AZ 85635; tel. 520/458-8131; FAX. 520/458-0422; Douglas R. Knolles, Administrator

Cottonwood Day Surgery Center, Inc., 55 South Sixth Street, P.O. Box 400, Cottonwood, AZ 86326; tel. 602/634-2444; Linda Davis, Administrator

Desert Mountain Surgicenter, Ltd., 7776 Pointe Parkway West, Suite 135, Phoenix, AZ 85044; tel. 602/431-8500; FAX. 602/431-1677; David M. Creech, M.D.

Desert Samaritan Surgicenter, 1500 South Dobson Road, Suite 101, Mesa, AZ 85202; tel. 602/835-3590; FAX. 602/890-4675; Brenda Hollander, Administrator

Dooley Outpatient Surgery Center, 151 Riviera Drive, Lake Havasu City, AZ 86403; tel. 602/855-9477; FAX. 602/855-2983; William J. Dooley, Jr., M.D., Medical Director

East Valley Surgical Associates, Ltd., 6424 East Broadway Road, Suite 102, Mesa, AZ 85206; tel. 602/833-2216; Manuel J. Chee

FH-Arizona Surgery Centers, Inc., 750 North Alvernon Way, Tucson, AZ 85711; tel. 602/322-8440; FAX. 602/322-2653; Vicki Gagnier, RN, Manager

Fifty-Ninth Avenue Surgical Facility, Ltd., 8608 North 59th Avenue, Glendale, AZ 85302; tel. 602/934-0272; FAX. 602/930-1891; Mark Gorman, Administrator

Fishkind and Bakewell Eye Care and Surgery Center, 5599 North Oracle Road, Tucson, AZ 85704; tel. 602/293-6740; FAX. 602/293-6771; Kathleen A. Brown, Surgery Center Supervisor

Flagstaff Outpatient Surgery Center, 77 West Forest Avenue, Suite 306, Flagstaff, AZ 86001; tel. 520/773-2597; FAX. 520/773-2327; Jackie Mosier, RN, Administrator

Footcare Surgi Center, 10249 West Thunderbird, Suite 100, Sun City, AZ 85351; tel. 602/979-4466; FAX. 602/933-8354; Gary N. Friedlander, D.P.M.

Footcare Surgi Center of Northern Arizona, 10 West Columbus Avenue, Flagstaff, AZ 86001; tel. 602/774-4191; Dr. Edward L. Wiebe

Gary Hall Eye Surgery Institute, 2501 North 32nd Street, Phoenix, AZ 85008; tel. 602/957-6799; FAX. 602/957-0172; Gary W. Hall, M.D., President

Glendale Surgicenter, 5757 West Thunderbird Road, Suite E-150, Glendale, AZ 85306; tel. 602/843-1900; FAX. 602/843-5607; Douglas G. Merrill, M.D., Medical Director

Good Samaritan Surgicenter, 1111 B East McDowell Road, Phoenix, AZ 85006; tel. 602/239-2776; FAX. 602/239-5352; Brenda Hollander, Administrator

Greenbaum Outpatient Surgery and Recovery Care Center, 3624 Wells Fargo Avenue, Scottsdale, AZ 85251; tel. 602/481-4958; Craig Stout, Administrator

Grimm Eye Clinic and Cataract Institute, P.C., 1502 North Tucson Boulevard, Tucson, AZ 85716; tel. 602/326-4321; Stephen F. Grimm, M.D.; Eleanor M. Grimm, M.D.

Havasu Arthritis and Sports Medicine Institute, 1840 Mesquite Avenue, Suite G, Lake Havasu, AZ 86403; tel. 602/453–2663; Marc H. Zimmerman, M.D., Administrator

Havasu Foot and Ankle Surgi–Center, 90 Riviera Drive, Lake Havasu, AZ 86403; tel. 520/855–7800; FAX. 520/855–5392; Robert Novack, D.P.M., Director

HealthSouth Surgery Center of Tucson, 310 North Wilmot Road, Suite 309, Tucson, AZ 85711; tel. 520/296–7080; FAX. 520/886–6518; Aaron Chatterson, Administrator

Lear Surgery Clinic–Scottsdale, 7351 East Osborn Road, Suite 104, Scottsdale, AZ 85251–6452; tel. 602/990–9400; FAX. 602/990–2664; David E. Marine, Executive Director

Lear Surgery Clinic–Sun City, 10615 West Thunderbird, Suite A–100, Sun City, AZ 85351; tel. 602/974–9375; FAX. 602/977–2598; David E. Marine, Executive Director

Mayo Clinic Scottsdale Ambulatory Surgery Center, 13400 East Shea Boulevard, Scottsdale, AZ 85259; tel. 602/301–8188; FAX. 602/301–8367; Karen A. Biel, Administrator

McCready Eye Surgery Center, 310 North Wilmot Road, Suite 106, Tucson, AZ 85711; tel. 520/885–6783; FAX. 520/885–5366; Joseph L. McCready, M.D., Administrator

Medivision of Tucson, Inc./Columbia HCA, 5632 East Fifth Street, Tucson, AZ 85711; tel. 602/790–8888; FAX. 602/790–1427; Clara Dupnik

Metro Ambulatory Surgery, Inc., a/k/a Metro Recovery Care Center, 3131 West Peoria Avenue, Phoenix, AZ 85029; tel. 602/375–1083; FAX. 602/789–6833; Jody M. Jones, RN, Chief Executive Officer

Mohave Surgery Center, Inc., 1919 Florence Avenue, Kingman, AZ 86401; tel. 520/753–5454; FAX. 520/753–7790, ext. 11; Frank Brown, Administrator

Moon Valley Surgery Center, Inc., 14045 North Seventh Street, Suite Two, Phoenix, AZ 85022; tel. 602/942–3966; Andrew E. Lowy

Nogales Medical Clinic Outpatient Surgery, 480 North Morley Avenue, Nogales, AZ 85621; tel. 520/287–2726; Imogene A. Bell, Administrator

Osborn Ambulatory Surgical Center, 3330 North Second Street, Suite 300, Phoenix, AZ 85012; tel. 602/265–0113; FAX. 602/277–8580; Donna -Klamm, RN, Administrator

Outpatient Surgical Care, Ltd., 1530 West Glendale, Suite 105, Phoenix, AZ 85021; tel. 602/995–3395; FAX. 602/995–1853; James Kennedy, M.D., Medical Director

Outpatient Surgical Center, 456 North Mesa Drive, Mesa, AZ 85201; tel. 602/464–8000; FAX. 602/969–7107; Maddie Dauernheim, Administrator

Phoenix Center for Outpatient Surgery, 1950 West Heatherbrae Drive, Suite Seven, Phoenix, AZ 85015; tel. 602/230–0437; Eric Reints, Administrator

Porter, Michael, D.P.M., 3620 East Campbell, Suite B, Phoenix, AZ 85018; tel. 602/954–6224; Michael Porter

Prescott Outpatient Surgery Center, Inc., 815 Ainsworth Drive, Prescott, AZ 86301; tel. 602/778–9770; Gail Reidhead, Administrative Director

Prescott Urocenter, Ltd., 811 Ainsworth, Suite 101, Prescott, AZ 86301; tel. 520/771–5282; FAX. 520/771–5283; Gregory Oldani

Romania Eye Care, P.C., 2820 North Glassford Hill Road, Suite 106, Prescott Valley, AZ 86314; tel. 520/775–5606; FAX. 520/772–4999; Linda Talerico, Administrator

Safford Surgi–Care, 825 20th Avenue, Safford, AZ 85546; tel. 602/428–6930; FAX. 602/428–7272; James Holder, O.D.

Santa Cruz Ambulatory Surgical Center, 699 West Ajo Way, Tucson, AZ 85713; tel. 602/746–1711; Richard Edward Quint, Administrator

Scottsdale Eye Surgery Center, P.C., 3320 North Miller Road, Scottsdale, AZ 85251; tel. 602/949–1208; FAX. 602/994–3316; Karen Borowiak, Administrator

Southwestern Eye Center–Casa Grande, 1919 North Trekell Road, Casa Grande, AZ 85222; tel. 520/426–9224; FAX. 520/426–1554; Lothaire Bluth, Administrator

Southwestern Eye Center–Yuma, 2179 West 24th Street, Yuma, AZ 85364; tel. 520/726–4120; FAX. 520/341–0315; Lance K. Wozniak, M.D.

Southwestern Eye Surgi Center–Falcon Field, 4760 Falcon Drive, Mesa, AZ 85205; tel. 602/985–7400; Karen Buck, Administrator

Southwestern Eye Surgicenter–Dobson Ranch, 2150 South Dobson Road, Mesa, AZ 85202; tel. 602/839–1717; FAX. 602/839–2862; Pat Bray, RN, CRNO, Director, Surgical and Medical Services

Southwestern Eye Surgicenter–Flagstaff, 1355 North Beaver, Suite 140, Flagstaff, AZ 86001; tel. 520/773–1184; FAX. 520/773–1815; Suzi Jensen, Surgical Services

Southwestern Eye Surgicenter–Nogales, 1815 North Mastick Way, Nogales, AZ 85621; tel. 520/281–0160; Pat Bray, Administrator

Sun City Endoscopy Center, Inc., 13203 North 103rd Avenue, Suite C 3, Sun City, AZ 85351; tel. 602/972–2116; John E. Phelps, M.D., Medical Director

Sun City Surgical Center, 13260 North 94th Drive, Suite 300, Peoria, AZ 85381; tel. 602/277–0619; FAX. 602/933–5787; H. William Reese, D.P.M., Director

Surgi–Care, 5115 North Central Avenue, Suite B, Phoenix, AZ 85012; tel. 602/264–1818; FAX. 602/264–2172; Ellison F. Herro M.D., Administrator

Surgi–Tech Centers, 3271 North Civic Center Plaza, Suite Three, Scottsdale, AZ 85251; tel. 602/994–5978; FAX. 602/990–9397; Richard Jacoby, D.P.M., President

SurgiCenter, 1040 East McDowell Road, Phoenix, AZ 85006; tel. 602/258–1521; FAX. 602/340–0889; Sharon Shafer, RN, Administrator

Surgical Eye Center of Arizona, Inc., 5133 North Central Avenue, Suite 100, Phoenix, AZ 85012; tel. 602/277–7997; Robert Lorenzen, Administrator

Surginet of Arizona, Ltd., 7725 North 43rd Avenue, Suite 510, Phoenix, AZ 85051; tel. 602/931–9400; FAX. 602/930–9884; Steve McLaughlin, Administrator

Swagel Wootton Eye Center, 220 South 63rd Street, Mesa, AZ 85206; tel. 602/641–3937; FAX. 602/924–5096; S. Joyce Graham

T.A.S.I. Surgery Center, 5585 North Oracle Road, Suite B, Tucson, AZ 85704; tel. 602/293–4730; John A. Pierce, M.D., Medical Director

Tempe Surgical Center, Inc., 2000 East Southern Avenue, Suite 106, Tempe, AZ 85282; tel. 602/838–9313; Richard F. Pavese, M.D.

Thunderbird Samaritan Surgicenter, 5555 B West Thunderbird Road, Glendale, AZ 85306–4622; tel. 602/588–5475; FAX. 602/588–5472; Diane Elmore, RN, Administrator

Valley Outpatient Surgery Center, 160 West University Drive, Mesa, AZ 85201; tel. 602/835–7373; FAX. 602/969–7981; Craig R. Cassidy, D.O., President

Warner Medical Park Outpatient Surgery, Inc., 604 West Warner Road, Building A, Chandler, AZ 85224; tel. 602/899–2571; FAX. 602/899–4263; Robert Thunberg, Managing Director

White Mountain Ambulatory Surgery Center, 2650 East Show Low Lake Road, Suite Two, Show Low, AZ 85901; tel. 602/537–4240; William J. Waldo

Yuma Outpatient Surgery Center, L.P., 2475 Avenue A, Suite B, Yuma, AZ 85364; tel. 520/726–6910; FAX. 520/726–7423; Cairne–Lee Larson, RN, Facility Manager

ARKANSAS

Ambulatory Surgical Center, Inc., d/b/a Fort Smith Surgi–Center, 7306A Rogers Avenue, Fort Smith, AR 72903; tel. 501/452–7333; Reem Zofari, Administrator

Arkansas Endoscopy Center, P.A., 9501 Lile Drive, Suite 100, Little Rock, AR 72205; tel. 501/224–9100; FAX. 501/224–0420; Ronald D. Hardin, M.D.

Arkansas Otolaryngology Ambulatory Surgery Center, 1200 Medical Towers Building, 9601 Lile Drive, Little Rock, AR 72205; tel. 501/227–5050; Joseph R. Phillips, RN, Administrator

Arkansas Surgery Center, 10 Hospital Circle, Batesville, AR 72501; tel. 501/793–4040; Fredric J. Sloan, M.D., Administrator

Arkansas Surgery Center of Fayetteville, 3873 North Parkview Drive, Suite One, Fayetteville, AR 72703; tel. 501/582–3200; FAX. 501/582–1338; Russ Greene, Administrator

Arkansas Surgery and Endoscopy Center, L.L.C., 4800 Hazel Street, Pine Bluff, AR 71603; tel. 501/536–4800; Mazahir Husain, Administrator

BEC Surgery Center, One Mercy Lane, Suite 201, P.O. Box 6409, Hot Springs, AR 71902; tel. 501/623–0755; Terry D. Brown

Boozman–Hof Eye Surgery and Laser Center, 3737 West Walnut Street, P.O. Box 1353, Rogers, AR 72757–1353; tel. 501/636–7506; Michael D. Malone, Administrator

Cooper Clinic Ambulatory Surgery Center, 6801 Rogers Avenue, P.O. Box 3528, Fort Smith, AR 72903; tel. 501/452–2077; FAX. 501/484–4611; Jerry Stewart, M.D., Administrator

Dempsey–McKee, Inc., d/b/a McKee Outpatient Surgery Center, 601 East Matthews, Jonesboro, AR 72401; tel. 501/935–6396; FAX. 501/935–4063; Terry V. DePriest, Administrator

Doctors Surgery Center, 303 West Polk Street, Suite B, West Memphis, AR 72301; tel. 501/732–2100; Doris Davis, Administrator

Gastroenterology and Surgery Center Of Arkansas, P.A., 8908 Kanis Road, Little Rock, AR 72205; tel. 501/227–7688; FAX. 501/225–2930; Alonzo D. Williams, M.D., Medical Director

H. Lewis Pearson Eye Institute, 3211 Surger Hill Road, Texarkana, AR 71854–9265; tel. 501/772–4440; FAX. 501/772–7190; F. Douglas Kesner, Administrator

Holt–Krock Clinic, 1500 Dodson Avenue, Fort Smith, AR 72901; tel. 501/788–4000; Harold H. Mings, M.D., Chief Executive Officer

Hot Springs Outpatient Surgery, 100 Ridgeway Boulevard, Suite Seven, Hot Springs, AR 71901; tel. 501/624–4464; FAX. 501/624–4602; Edwin L. Harper, M.D., Administrator

James Trice, M.D., P.A., d/b/a Digestive Disease Center, 7005 South Hazel Street, Pine Bluff, AR 71603; tel. 501/536–3070; Louis Triace, Administrator

Little Rock Diagnostic Clinic ASC, 10001 Lile Drive, Little Rock, AR 72205; tel. 501/227–8000, ext. 845; Roger J. St. Onge, Administrator

Little Rock Pain Clinic, Two Lile Court, Suite 100, Little Rock, AR 72205; tel. 501/224–7246; FAX. 501/224–7644; Virginia Johnson, Administrator

Little Rock Surgery Center, 8820 Knoedl Court, Little Rock, AR 72205; tel. 501/224–6767; FAX. 501/224–8203; Pamela J. Hooper, Administrator

Lowery Medical/Surgical Eye Center, P.A., 105 Central Avenue, Searcy, AR 72143; tel. 501/268–7154; FAX. 501/268–9071; Benjamin R. Lowery, M.D., Administrator

North Hills Gastroenterology Endoscopy Center, Inc., 3344 North Futrall Drive, Fayetteville, AR 72703; tel. 501/582–7280; William C. Martin, M.D.

Northeast Arkansas Surgery Center, Inc., 505 East Matthews, Jonesboro, AR 72401; tel. 501/972–1723; FAX. 501/972–5941; Carol D. Crawford, Administrator

Ozark Eye Center, 360 Highway Five North, Mountain Home, AR 72653; tel. 501/425–2277; Rick Galkoski, Administrator

Physicians Day Surgery Center, 3805 West 28th, Pine Bluff, AR 71603; tel. 501/536–4100; FAX. 501/536–3100; Joan Fletcher, Administrator

Russellville Surgery Center, L.L.C., 2205 West Main Street, P.O. Box 2654, Russellville, AR 72801; tel. 501/890–2654; FAX. 501/890–5101; James Kennedy, Administrator

South Arkansas Surgery Center, 4310 South Mulberry, Pine Bluff, AR 71603; tel. 501/535–5719; Tammy L. Studdard, Administrator

The Center for Day Surgery, 4200 Jenny Lind, Suite A, Fort Smith, AR 72901; tel. 501/648–9496; Monte Winn, Administrator

The Endoscopy Center of Hot Springs, 151 McGowan Court, Hot Springs, AR 71913; tel. 501/623–4101; FAX. 501/623–0103; Rebecca Bates, Administrator

The Gastro–Intestinal Center, 405 North University, Little Rock, AR 72205; tel. 501/663–1074; James G. Dunlap, Administrator

The Physicians Surgery Center of Arkansas, Inc., d/b/a Physicians Surgery Center, 1024 North University Avenue, Little Rock, AR 72207; tel. 501/663–0158; FAX. 501/663–4652; Martha Plant, Administrator

CALIFORNIA

Advanced Surgery Center, 5771 North Fresno Street, Suite 101, Fresno, CA 93710; tel. 209/448–9900; David B. Singh, Administrator

Aesthetic Facial Surgery Center of Menlo Park, 2200 Sand Hill Road, Suite 130, Menlo Park, CA 94025; tel. 415/854–6444; Dr. Harry Mittelman

Aestheticare Outpatient Surgery Center, 30260 Rancho Viejo Road, San Juan Capistrano, CA 92675; tel. 714/661–1700; FAX. 714/661–4913; Ronald E. Moser, M.D.

Alvarado Family Surgery Center, 215 West Madison Avenue, El Cajon, CA 92020; tel. 619/593–2110; Noreen K. Valentine, R.N., Administrator

Ambulatory Surgical Center of Chico, 1950 East 20th Street, Suite 102, Chico, CA 95928; tel. 916/343–1674; Robert G. Basinger, D.P.M.

Ambulatory Surgical Center of Southern California, 880 South Atlantic Boulevard, Monterey Park, CA 91754; tel. 213/483–9080; Marco Sprintis, M.D.

Ambulatory Surgical Center of the Zeiter Eye, 117 North San Joaquin Street, Stockton, CA 95202; tel. 209/466–5566; FAX. 209/466–0535; Donna M. Tschirky

Ambulatory Surgical Center, Inc., 14400 Bear Valley Road, Victorville, CA 92392; tel. 916/951–5162; FAX. 818/368–2290; Garey L. Weber, D.P.M., Administrator

Ambulatory Surgical Centers, Inc., 18952 Mac Arthur Boulevard, Suite 102, Irvine, CA 92612; tel. 714/833–3406; FAX. 818/368–2290; Garey L. Weber, D.P.M., Administrator

Anaheim Surgical Center, 1324 South Euclid Street, Anaheim, CA 92802; tel. 714/533–9880; FAX. 714/533–1802; Debra Berntsen, RN, Charge Nurse

Antelope Valley Surgery Center, 44301 North Lorimer Avenue, Lancaster, CA 93534; tel. 805/940–1112; FAX. 805/940–6856; Yolanda Gomez

Apple Valley Surgery Center, 18122 Outer Highway 18, Apple Valley, CA 92307; tel. 619/946–1170; FAX. 619/946–2646; Virginia Budington, Administrator

Arlington Podiatry Surgery Center, 7310 Magnolia Avenue, Riverside, CA 92504; tel. 909/354–8787; FAX. 909/354–0350; James A. De Silva, Administrator

Aspen Outpatient Center, 2750 North Sycamore Drive, Simi Valley, CA 93065; tel. 805/583–5923; FAX. 805/583–0952; Jay Evans, Administrator

Associates Outpatient Surgery Center, 2128 Eureka Way, Redding, CA 96001; tel. 916/246–9737; FAX. 916/246–4052; Reed Lockwood, M.D., Administrator

Atherton Plastic Surgery Center, 3351 El Camino Real, Suite 201, Atherton, CA 94027; tel. 415/363–0300; FAX. 415/363–0302; David Apfelberg

Auburn Surgery Center, 3123 Professional Drive, Suite 100, Auburn, CA 95603; tel. 916/888–8899; FAX. 916/888–1464; Charles Smith, Administrator

Bakersfield Endoscopy Center, 1902 B Street, Bakersfield, CA 93301; tel. 805/327–4455; Ramesh Gupta, M.D., Medical Director

Bakersfield Surgery Center, 2120 19th Street, Bakersfield, CA 93301; tel. 805/323–2020; FAX. 805/323–6552; Kathleen Allman, Administrator

Beverly Hills Ambulatory Surgery Center, Inc., 9201 Sunset Boulevard, Suite 405, Los Angeles, CA 90069; tel. 310/887–1730; Sandra Cericola, Administrator

Beverly Hills Outpatient Surgery Center, 250 North Robertson Boulevard, Suite 104, Los Angeles, CA 90211; tel. 310/273–9255; FAX. 310/273–6167; Peter Golden, M.D., Medical Director

Beverly Surgical Center, 105 West Beverly Boulevard, Montebello, CA 90640–4375; tel. 213/728–5400; FAX. 213/887–0058; James G. Ovieda, Administrator

Blackhawk Surgery Center, Inc., 4165 Blackhawk Plaza Circle, Suite 195, Danville, CA 94506; tel. 510/736–7881; Molly Healy, Administrator

Bolsa Out–Patient Surgery Center, 10362 Bolsa Avenue, Westminster, CA 92683; tel. 714/531–2091; D. L. Pham, M.D., Medical Director

Bonaventure Surgery Center, 221 North Jackson Avenue, San Jose, CA 95116; tel. 408/729–2848; FAX. 408/729–2880; Virginia Field, RN, M.B.A., Director

Brawley Endoscopy and Surgery Center, 205 West Legion Road, Brawley, CA 92227; tel. 619/351–3655; FAX. 619/351–3675; Mahomed Suliman, M.D., Administrator

Brockton Surgical Center, 5905 Brockton Avenue, Suite B, Riverside, CA 92506; tel. 909/686–5373; FAX. 909/778–9064; Michael N. Durrant, D.P.M., M.P.H.

Bruce A. Kaplan, M.D., 39000 Bob Hope Drive, Wright Building, Suite 209, Rancho Mirage, CA 92270; tel. 619/346–5603; FAX. 619/346–5604; Jessie Schumaker

California Eye Clinic, 3747 Sunset Lane, Suite A, Antioch, CA 94509; tel. 510/754–2300; Jean Kemp, Administrator

Camden Surgery Center of Beverly Hills, 414 North. Camden Drive, Suite 800, Beverly Hills, CA 90210; tel. 310/859–3991; FAX. 310/859–7126; Yasmin Sibulo, Administrator

Capistrano Surgicenter, Inc., 30280 Rancho Viejo Road, San Juan Capistrano, CA 92675; tel. 714/248–5757; FAX. 714/248–9339; Jeffrey A. Klein, President

Cedars–Sinai, Saint John's, Daniel Freeman SurgiCenter, 9675 Brighton Way, Suite 100, Beverly Hills, CA 90210; tel. 310/205–6080; FAX. 310/205–6090; Diane Tharp, Program Coordinator

Center for Ambulatory Medicine and Surgery, 111 East Noble Avenue, Visalia, CA 93277; tel. 209/739–8383; FAX. 209/739–7929; James J. Shea, M.D., Administrator

Central Coast Surgery Center, 1941 Johnson Avenue, Suite 103, San Luis Obispo, CA 93406; tel. 805/546–9999; FAX. 804/546–8904; Helen Swanagon, Nurse Administrator

Channel Islands Surgicenter, 2300 Wankel Way, Oxnard, CA 93030; tel. 805/485–1908; FAX. 805/485–5767; Mary K. Fish, Administrator

Children's Surgery Center, 744 Fifty–Second Street, Oakland, CA 94609; tel. 510/428–3133; FAX. 510/450–5606; Terry Hawes, Administrator

Columbia Arcadia Outpatient Surgery, Inc., 614 West Duarte Road, Arcadia, CA 91006; tel. 818/445–4714; Sandy Lazare, Administrator

Columbia Los Gatos Surgical Center, 15195 National Avenue, Los Gatos, CA 95032; tel. 408/356–0454; FAX. 408/358–3924; Martha Ponce, Administrator

Columbia North Coast Surgery Center, 3903 Waring Road, Oceanside, CA 92056; tel. 619/940–0997; FAX. 619/940–0407; Donna Danley, Administrator

Columbia Saddleback Valley Outpatient Surgery, 24302 Paseo De Valencia, Laguna Hills, CA 92653; tel. 714/472–0244; FAX. 714/472–0380; Brian FitzGerald, Administrator

Columbia Sereno Surgery Center, 14601 South Bascom Avenue, Suite 100, Los Gatos, CA 95032–2043; tel. 408/358–2727; FAX. 408/358–2950; Martha Ponce, Administrator

Columbia Southwest Surgical Clinic, Inc., 4201 Torrance Boulevard, Suite 240, Torrance, CA 90503; tel. 310/540–7803; FAX. 310/316–3903; Otto Munchow, M.D., Director

Columbia Surgicenter of South Bay, 23500 Madison Street, Torrance, CA 90505; tel. 310/539–5120; Debra Saxton

Columbia West Hills Surgical Center, 7240 Medical Center Drive, West Hills, CA 91307; tel. 818/226–6170; Carol Valeri, R.N., Administrator

Columbia/Woodward Park Surgicenter, 7055 North Fresno Street, Suite 100, Fresno, CA 93720; tel. 209/449–9977; FAX. 209/449–9350; Lori Ruffner, RN, Administrator

Community Surgery Centre, 17190 Bernado Center Drive, Suite 100, San Diego, CA 92128; tel. 619/675–3270; FAX. 619/675–3260; Regina S. Boore, B.S.N., M.S.

Corona Del Mar Plastic Surgery, 1101 Bayside Drive, Suite 100, Corona Del Mar, CA 92625; tel. 714/644–5000; W. Graham Wood, M.D.

Crown Valley Surgicenter, 26921 Crown Valley Parkway, Suite 110, Mission Viejo, CA 92691; tel. 714/348–7252; FAX. 714/348–7246; Maurice Chammas, M.D., Administrator

Cypress Outpatient Surgical Center, Inc., 1665 Dominican Way, Suite 120, Santa Cruz, CA 95065; tel. 408/476–6943; FAX. 408/476–1473; Sandra Warren, Administrator

Cypress Surgery Center, 842 South Akers Road, Visalia, CA 93277; tel. 209/740–4094; FAX. 209/740–4100; Jack K. Waller

Del Rey Surgery Center, 4640 Admiralty Way, Suite 1020, Marina Del Rey, CA 90292; tel. 310/305–7570; Lee Estes, Administrator

Digestive Disease Center, 24411 Health Center Drive, Suite 450, Laguna Hills, CA 92653; tel. 714/586–9386; FAX. 714/586–0864; Crisynda Buss, RN

Doctors Surgery Center of Whittier, 8135 South Painter Avenue, Suite 103, Whittier, CA 90602; tel. 310/945–8961; FAX. 310/698–3578; Veronica Coughenour, RN

Doctors Surgical Center, Inc., 9461 Grindlay Street, Suite 102, Cypress, CA 90630; tel. 714/995–3001; R. Wayne Ives, Administrator

Doctors' Surgery Center, 1441 Liberty Street, Suite 104, Redding, CA 96001; tel. 916/244–6300; FAX. 916/246–2051; Charles Kassis, Administrator

Downey Surgery Center, 8555 East Florence Avenue, Downey, CA 90240; tel. 310/923–9784; Marisol Magana, Administrator

E. N. T. Facial Surgery Center, 1351 East Spruce, Fresno, CA 93720; tel. 209/432–3724; FAX. 209/432–8579; JoAnn LoForti, RN, Division of Nursing

East Bay Medical Surgical Center, 20998 Redwood Road, Castro Valley, CA 94546; tel. 510/538–2828; FAX. 510/538–2508; Yoshitsugu Teramoto, M.D., Administrator

El Camino Surgery Center, 2480 Grant Road, Mountain View, CA 94040–4300; tel. 415/961–1200; FAX. 415/960–7041; Nancy Kessler

El Mirador Surgical Center, 1180 North Indian Canyon Drive, Palm Springs, CA 92263; tel. 619/416–4600; Marilyn M. Perkins, Nurse Administrator

Endoscopy Center of Chula Vista, 681 Third Avenue, Suite B, Chula Vista, CA 91910; tel. 619/425–2150; Robert Penner, M.D., Administrator

Endoscopy Center of Southern California, 2336 Santa Monica Boulevard, Suite 204, Santa Monica, CA 90404; tel. 310/453–4477; FAX. 310/453–4811; Parviz D. Afshani

Endoscopy Center of the Central Coast, 77 Casa Street, Suite 106, San Luis Obispo, CA 93405; tel. 805/541–1021; FAX. 805/541–3142; Judy Grossi, Clinical Director

Escondido Surgery Center, 343 East Second Avenue, Escondido, CA 92025; tel. 619/480–6606; FAX. 619/480–6671; Marvin W. Levenson, M.D., Managing Medical Director

Eye Center of Northern California Surgicenter, 6500 Fairmount Avenue, Suite Two, El Cerrito, CA 94530; tel. 510/525–2600; FAX. 510/524–1887; William Ellis

Eye Life Institute, 6283 Clark Road, Suite Seven, Paradise, CA 95969; tel. 916/877–2020; FAX. 916/877–4641; Almary Hivale, RN, Administrator

Eye Surgery Center of Southern California, Inc./Med. Group, 2023 West Vista Way, Suite E, Vista, CA 92083; tel. 619/941–8152; FAX. 619/726–4822; Regg V. Antle, M.D., Medical Director

Eye Surgery Center of the Desert, 39700 Bob Hope Drive, Suite 111, Rancho Mirage, CA 92270; tel. 619/340–3937; FAX. 619/340–1940; Albert T. Milauskas, Administrator

Feather River Surgery Center, 370 Del Norte Avenue, Yuba City, CA 95991; tel. 916/751–4800; FAX. 916/751–4884; Elizabeth LaBouyer, RN, CNOR, Perioperative Coordinator

Fig Garden Surgi–Med Center, 1332 West Herndon Avenue, Suite 102, Fresno, CA 93711–0431; tel. 209/439–3100

Foothill Ambulatory Surgery Center, 1030 East Foothill Boulevard, Suite 101B, Upland, CA 91786; tel. 909/981–5859; FAX. 909/981–8293; Montra M. Kanok, M.D.

Fort Sutter Surgery Center, 2801 K Street, Suite 525, Sacramento, CA 95816; tel. 916/733–5017; FAX. 916/733–8738; Bill Davis, Administrator

Fountain Valley Outpatient Surgical Center, 11160 Warner Avenue, Suite 421, Fountain Valley, CA 92708; tel. 714/751–5621; Eugene Elliott, M.D.

Four Thirty–Six North Bedford Surgicenter, Inc., 436 North Bedford, Suite 101, Beverly Hills, CA 90210; tel. 310/278–0188; FAX. 310/278–1791; Robert Kotler, M.D.

Fritch Eye Care Medical Center, 2525 Eye Street, Suite A and B, Bakersfield, CA 93301; tel. 805/327–8511; FAX. 805/327–9809; Charles D. Fritch, M.D.

Frost Street Outpatient Surgical Center, Inc., 8008 Frost Street, Suite 200, San Diego, CA 92123; tel. 619/576–8320; FAX. 619/576–8568; Jacqueline McWilliams

GastroDiagnostics, A Medical Group, 1140 West La Veta, Suite 550, Orange, CA 92868; tel. 714/835–5100; FAX. 714/835–5567; Stephanie Quinn, Administrator

Glendale Eye Surgery Center, 607 North Central, Suite 103, Glendale, CA 91203; tel. 818/956–1010; FAX. 818/543–6083; James M. McCaffery, M.D.

Glenwood Surgical Center, L.P., 8945 Magnolia Avenue, Suite 200, Riverside, CA 92503; tel. 909/688–7270; Calvin Nash

Golden Empire Surgical Center, 1519 Graces Highway, Suite 103, Delano, CA 93215; tel. 805/721–7900; Lucy Lara

Golden Triangle Surgicenter, 25405 Hancock Avenue, Suite 103, Murrieta, CA 92562; tel. 909/698–4670; FAX. 909/698–4675; Ella Stockstill, Administrator

Golden West Pain Therapy Center, 25405 Hancock Avenue, Suite 110, Murrieta, CA 92562–5964; tel. 909/698–4710; FAX. 909/698–4715; Richard Harris, Administrator

Greater Long Beach Endoscopy Center, 2880 Atlantic Avenue, Suite 180, Long Beach, CA 90806; tel. 310/426–2606; FAX. 310/426–5866; Andrea Campbell, Business Office Manager

Greater Sacramento Surgery Center, 2288 Auburn Boulevard, Suite 201, Sacramento, CA 95821; tel. 916/929–7229; FAX. 916/929–2590; Susan Brunone, MHS, Administrator

Grossmont Plaza Surgery Center, 5525 Grossmont Center Drive, La Mesa, CA 91942; tel. 619/644–4561; Lois Hoke, Administrator

Grossmont Surgery Center, 8881 Fletcher Parkway, Suite 100, La Mesa, CA 91942; tel. 619/698–0930; FAX. 619/698–3093; Mary Ribulotta, Administrator

Halcyon Laser and Surgery Center, Inc., 303 South Halcyon Road, Arroyo Grande, CA 93420; tel. 805/489–8254; Sanja Batista, Administrator

Harbor–UCLA Medical Foundation, Inc., Ambulatory Surgery Center, 21840 South Normandie Avenue, Suite 700, Torrance, CA 90502; tel. 310/222–5189; Lee Scher, R.N., Administrator

HealthSouth Center for Surgery of Encinitas, 477 North El Camino Real, Suite C–100, Encinitas, CA 92024; tel. 619/942–8800; FAX. 619/942–0106; John Cashman, Co–Administrator

HealthSouth Forest Surgery Center, 2110 Forest Avenue, San Jose, CA 95128; tel. 408/297–3432; FAX. 408/298–3338; Helen Maloney, RN, Administrator

HealthSouth South Bay Ambulatory Surgical Center, 251 Landis Street, Chula Vista, CA 91910; tel. 619/585–1020; FAX. 619/585–0247; Arthur E. Casey, Administrator

HealthSouth Surgery Center of San Luis Obispo, 1304–C Ella Street, San Luis Obispo, CA 93401; tel. 805/544–7874; FAX. 805/544–6057; Linda M. Harris, RN, M.S.N, Administrator

HealthSouth Surgery Center–J Street, 3810 J Street, Sacramento, CA 95816; tel. 916/929–9431; FAX. 916/929–0132; Charlene Nakayama, Administrator

HealthSouth Surgery Center–Scripps, 75 Scripps Drive, Sacramento, CA 95825; tel. 916/929–9431; FAX. 916/929–0132; Charlene Nakayama, Administrator

HealthSouth Surgery Center–Solano, 991 Nut Tree Road, Suite 100, Vacaville, CA 95687; tel. 707/447–5400; FAX. 707/447–2356; Bill Davis, Administrator

Heart Institute of the Desert, 39–600 Bob Hope Drive, Rancho Mirage, CA 92270; tel. 619/324–3278; Jack J. Sternlieb, Administrator

Hemet Cataract Surgery Clinic, 162 North Santa Fe, Hemet, CA 92343; tel. 714/929–3200; Stephen K. Schaller, M.D., Administrator

Hemet Endoscopy Center, 2390 East Florida Avenue, Suite 101, Hemet, CA 92544; tel. 909/652–2252; FAX. 909/925–9252; Milan S. Chakrabarty, M.D.

Hemet Healthcare Surgicenter, 301 North San Jacinto Avenue, Hemet, CA 92543; tel. 909/765–1717; FAX. 909/765–1716; Kali Chaudhuri, M.D.

Henry Tahl, M.D., 790 East Latham, Hemet, CA 92343; tel. 714/658–3224

Hesperia Podiatry Surgery Center, 14661 Main Street, Hesperia, CA 92345; tel. 619/244–0222; FAX. 619/244–1242; William S. Beal

Hi–Desert Surgery Center, 18002 Outer Highway 18, Apple Valley, CA 92307; tel. 619/242–5505; FAX. 619/242–3502; Venkat R. Vangala, M.D.

High Desert Endoscopy, 18523 Corwin Road, Suite H2, Apple Valley, CA 92307; tel. 619/242–3000; FAX. 619/262–1802; Raman S. Poola, M.D., Administrator

Hospitality Surgery Center, 275 West Hospitality Lane, Suite 106, San Bernardino, CA 92408; tel. 909/885–0180; Milton A. Miller, M.D., Administrator

Huntington Outpatient Surgery Center, 797 South Fair Oaks Avenue, Pasadena, CA 91105; tel. 818/397–3173; FAX. 818/397–8003; Sandra Bidlack, Administrator

Imperial Valley Surgery Center, 608 G Street, Brawley, CA 92227; tel. 619/344–II0I; FAX. 619/344–4985; Vida C. Baron, M.D., Administrator

Inland Endoscopy Center, Inc., d/b/a Mountain View Surgery Center, 10408 Industrial Circle, Redlands, CA 92374; tel. 909/796–0363; FAX. 909/796–0614; Khushal Stanisai

Inland Eye Surgicenter, 361 North San Jacinto, Hemet, CA 92543; tel. 909/652–4343; R. Michael Duffin, M.D., Medical Director

Inland Surgery Center, 1620 Laurel Avenue, Redlands, CA 92373; tel. 909/793–4701; FAX. 909/792–6397; Rodger Slininger, Facility Administrator

Irvine Multi–Specialty Surgical Care, 4900 Barranca Parkway, Suite 104, Irvine, CA 92604–8603; tel. 714/726–0677; FAX. 714/726–0678; Carol R. Stevenson, RN, Administrator

John Muir/Mt. Diablo HealthCare System, Inc., d/b/a Diablo Valley Surgery Center, 2222 East Street, Suite 200, Concord, CA 94520; tel. 510/671–2222; FAX. 510/671–2672; Virginia Goodrich, Administrator

Kaiser Ambulatory Surgical Center, 2025 Morse Avenue, Sacramento, CA 95825; tel. 916/973–7675; FAX. 916/973–7786; Richard R. Stading, RN, Team Facilitator

Kaiser Ambulatory Surgical Center, 10725 International Drive, Rancho Cordova, CA 95670; tel. 916/973–7675; FAX. 916/631–2013; Angela Hardiman, RN, M.S., Manager

Kaiser Permanente Medical Facility–Stockton, 7373 West Lane, Stockton, CA 95210; tel. 209/476–3300; Jose R. Rivera, Administrator

Klaus Kuehn, M.D., Inc.–Eye Center, 1900 North Waterman Avenue, San Bernardino, CA 92404; tel. 909/882–3728; FAX. 909/881–2078; Klaus Kuehn, M.D., Director

La Jolla Gastroenterology Medical Group, Inc., Endoscopy Center, 9850 Genesee Avenue, Suite 980, La Jolla, CA 92037; tel. 619/453–5200; FAX. 619/453–5753; Otto T. Nebel, M.D., Medical Director

La Veta Surgical Center, 725 West La Veta, Suite 270, Orange, CA 92668; tel. 714/744–0900; Joyce Hall, Administrator

Laser Surgery Center, LTD., 2021 Ygnacio Valley Road, Building H–102, Walnut Creek, CA 94598; tel. 510/944–9400; FAX. 510/947–2160; Lori Fried, Administrator

Laser and Skin Surgery Center of La Jolla, 9850 Genesee Avenue, Suite 480, La Jolla, CA 92037; tel. 619/558–2424; Nancy Fritzenkotter

Lassen Surgery Center, 103 Fair Drive, P.O. Box 1150, Susanville, CA 96130; tel. 916/257–7773; FAX. 916/257–2939; Deborah L. Sutton, Medical Staff Secretary

Lodi Outpatient Surgical Center, 521 South Ham Lane, Suite F, Lodi, CA 95242; tel. 209/333–0905; FAX. 209/333–0219; Marklin E. Brown, Administrator

Loma Linda Foot and Ankle Center, Ambulatory Surgical Center, 11332 Mountain View Avenue, Suite A, Loma Linda, CA 92354; tel. 909/796–3707; FAX. 909/796–3709; Sheldon Collis, D.P.M., Administrator

Los Robles Surgicenter, 2190 Lynn Road, Suite 100, Thousand Oaks, CA 91360; tel. 805/497–3737; FAX. 805/373–8878; Le Anne Schai, Administrative Director

M/S Surgery Center, 3510 Martin Luther King Boulevard, Lynwood, CA 90262; tel. 310/635–7550; FAX. 310/603–8749; John H. Shammas, M.D., Medical Director

Madera Ambulatory Endoscopy Center, 1015 West Yosemite Avenue, Suite 101, Madera, CA 93637; tel. 209/673–4000; FAX. 209/673–1430; Naeem M. Akhtar, M.D.

Madison Park Surgery and Laser Center, 3445 Pacific Coast Highway, Suite 250, Torrance, CA 90505; tel. 310/530–2900; FAX. 310/891–0367; Lawrence Saks, M.D., Administrator

Magnolia Outpatient Surgery Center, 14571 Magnolia Street, Suite 107, Westminster, CA 92683; tel. 714/898–6448; FAX. 714/893–1681; Cynthia Begg, Administrator

Magnolia Plastic Surgery Center, 10694 Magnolia Avenue, Riverside, CA 92505; tel. 909/358–1445; FAX. 909/688–2803; Alexander Carli

Marin Opthalmic Ambulatory Surgi Clinic, 901 E Street, Suite 270, San Rafael, CA 94901; tel. 415/454–2112; FAX. 415/454–6542; Audrey M. DeMars, Administrator

Mariners Bay Surgical Medical Center, 318 South Lincoln Boulevard, Suite 100, Venice, CA 90291; tel. 310/314–2191; FAX. 310/392–8020; Gregory Panos II, Administrator

Martel Eye Surgical Center, 11216 Trinity River, Suite G, Rancho Cordova, CA 95670; tel. 916/635–6161; FAX. 916/635–5145; Joseph Martel, M.D.

McHenry Surgery Center, 1524 McHenry Street, Suite 240, Modesto, CA 95350; tel. 209/576–2900; FAX. 209/575–5815; Syd Fuentes, RN, Director

Medical Arts Ambulatory Surgery Center, 205 South West Street, Suite B, Visalia, CA 93291; tel. 209/625–9601; FAX. 209/625–3124; Thomas F. Mitts, M.D., Administrator

Medical Plaza Orthopedic Surgery Center, 1301 20th Street, Suite 140, Santa Monica, CA 90404; tel. 310/315–0333; FAX. 310/315–0341; Carolyn A. Hankinson, RN, Director, Nursing

Merced Ambulatory Endoscopy Center, 750 West Olive Avenue, Suite 107A, Merced, CA 95348; tel. 209/384–3116; Monika Grasley, Administrator

Mercy Surgical and Diagnostic Center, 3303 North M Street, Merced, CA 95348; tel. 209/384–3533; FAX. 209/383–5047; Lynda Pitts, Administrator

Mirage Center Outpatient Surgery, 39–935 Vista Del Sol, P.O. Box 6000, Rancho Mirage, CA 92270; tel. 619/779–9951; Dr. Peter Scheer

Mission Ambulatory Surgicenter, Ltd., 26730 Crown Valley Parkway, First Floor, Mission Viejo, CA 92691; tel. 714/364–2201; FAX. 714/364–5372; Thomas H. Catlett, Administrator

Mission Valley Surgery Centre, 39263 Mission Boulevard, Fremont, CA 94539; tel. 510/796–4500; FAX. 510/796–4573; Sarb S. Hundal, M.D.

Mittleman/Moran Reconstructive Surgery, 2200 Sandhill Road, Suite 130, Menlo Park, CA 94025; tel. 415/854–2000; Mary Lynn Moran, M.D., Administrator

Modesto Surgery Center, Inc., 400 East Orangeburg Avenue, Suite One, Modesto, CA 95350; tel. 209/526–3000; Dr. Greg Teslue, Administrator

Monterey Bay Endoscopy Center, 833 Cass Street, Suite B, Monterey, CA 93940; tel. 408/375–3598; FAX. 408/375–1478; James Farrow, Administrator

Monterey Peninsula Surgery Center, Inc., 966 Cass Street, Suite 210, Monterey, CA 93940; tel. 408/372–2169; FAX. 408/372–6323; William McAfee, M.D., Chairman

Moreno Valley Ambulatory Surgery Center, 24384 Sunnymead Boulevard, Moreno Valley, CA 92388; tel. 714/247–8080; FAX. 714/247–9381; John E. Bohn, Administrator

Napa Surgery Center, 3444 Valle Verde Drive, Napa, CA 94558; tel. 707/252–9660; Eric Grigsby, M.D., Medical Director

Newport Beach Orange Coast Endoscopy Center, 1525 Superior Avenue, Suite 114, Newport Beach, CA 92663; tel. 714/646–6999; FAX. 714/646–9699; Donald Abrahm

Newport Beach Surgery Center, 361 Hospital Road, Suite 124, Newport Beach, CA 92663; tel. 714/631–0988, ext. 3002; FAX. 714/631–2036; Eric Reints, Administrator

Newport Surgery Institute, 360 San Miguel Drive, Suite 406, Newport Beach, CA 92660; tel. 714/759–0995; Linda Shelman, Office Manager

North Anaheim Surgicenter, 1154 North Euclid, Anaheim, CA 92801; tel. 714/635–6272; FAX. 714/635–0943; Monica Briton, Administrator

North County Outpatient Surgery Center, 1101 Las Tablas Road, P.O. Box 147, Templeton, CA 93465; tel. 805/434–I333; FAX. 805/434–3171; Carolyn Lash, RN, Surgery Center Manager

Northern California Kidney Stone Center, 15195 National Avenue, Suite 204, Los Gatos, CA 95032; tel. 408/358–2111; FAX. 408/356–2359; John Kersten Kraft, Medical Director

Northern California Plastic Surgery Medical Group, 2650 Edith Avenue, Redding, CA 96001; tel. 916/241–2028

Northridge Maxillofacial Surgery Center, 18546 Roscoe Boulevard, Suite 120, Northridge, CA 91324; tel. 818/349–8851; Robert G. Hale, D.D.S., Administrator

Northridge Surgery Center, 8327 Reseda Boulevard, Northridge, CA 91324; tel. 818/993–3131; FAX. 818/993–3347; Robert Vassey, Administrator

Optima Ophthalmic Medical Associates, Inc., 1237 B Street, Hayward, CA 94541–2977; tel. 510/886–3937; FAX. 510/886–4465; Nora J. McQuinn, Administrative Director

Orange County Institute of Gastroenterology and Endoscopy, 26732 Crown Valley Parkway, Suite 241, Mission Viejo, CA 92691; tel. 714/364–2611; FAX. 714/364–0226; Ahmad M. Shaban, M.D., Medical Director

Orange County Litho Center, Inc., 12555 Garden Grove Boulevard, Suite 200, Garden Grove, CA 92843; tel. 714/530–6000; Guy A. Biagiotti, M.D.

Orange Surgical Services, 302 West La Veta Avenue, Suite 100, Orange, CA 92866; tel. 714/771-3432; FAX. 714/741-7606; Elizabeth E. Grant, RN, M.S.

Out-Patient Surgery Center, 17752 Beach Boulevard, Huntington Beach, CA 92647; tel. 714/842-1426; FAX. 714/847-1503; Madelyn Tinkler, Administrator

Outpatient Care Surgery Center South, 5225 Kearny Villa Way, Suite 110, San Diego, CA 92123; tel. 619/278-1611; FAX. 619/278-5853; Ronald Gertsch, M.D.

PFC Surgicenter, 3445 Pacific Court Highway, Suite 110, Torrance, CA 90505; tel. 213/539-9100; Rifaat Salem, M.D., Ph.D.

Pacific Dental Surgery Center, 820 34th Street, Suite 201, Bakersfield, CA 93301; tel. 805/327-7878; Charles Nicholson III, Administrator

Pacific Eye Institute, 555 North 13th Avenue, Upland, CA 91786; tel. 909/982-8846; FAX. 909/949-3967; Robert Fabricant, M.D., FACS, Medical Director

Pacific Hills Surgery Center, Inc., 24022 Calle De La Plata, Suite 180, Laguna Hills, CA 92653; tel. 714/951-9470; FAX. 714/951-9478; Norman D. Peterson, M.D., Medical Director

Pacific Surgicenter, Inc., 1301 20th Street, Suite 470, Santa Monica, CA 90404; tel. 310/315-0222; FAX. 310/828-8852; Jocelyne Rosenthal, RN, Administrator

Palm Desert Ambulatory Surgery Center, 73-345 Highway 111, Palm Desert, CA 92260; tel. 619/346-4780; FAX. 619/340-4650; S. C. Shah, M.D., Administrator

Paul L. Archambeau, M.D., Inc., Ambulatory Surgery Center, 380 Tesconi Court, Santa Rosa, CA 95401; tel. 707/544-3375; FAX. 707/544-0808; Paul L. Archambeau, M.D., Administrator

Petaluma Surgicenter, 1400 Professional Drive, Suite 102, Petaluma, CA 94954; tel. 707/769-8481; FAX. 707/769-0751; Ronald M. La Vigna, D.P.M.

Physician's Surgery Center, 901 Campus Drive, Suite 102, Daly City, CA 94015; tel. 415/991-2000; FAX. 415/755-8638; Kathleen O'Riordan

Physicians Plaza Surgical Center, 6000 Physicians Boulevard, Vista Road, CA 93301; tel. 805/322-4744, ext. 26; FAX. 805/322-2938; Michael G. Clark, Administrator

Physicians Resource Group, d/b/a Barr Eye Surgery Center, 1805 North California Street, Stockton, CA 95204; tel. 209/948-3241; FAX. 209/948-9321; Susan Ford, Administrator

Plastic Surgery Center, 1515 El Camino Real, Palo Alto, CA 94304; tel. 415/322-2723; FAX. 415/322-3260; Julia Solinger, Administrator

Plastic and Reconstructive Surgery Center, 1387 Santa Rita Road, Pleasanton, CA 94566; tel. 510/462-3700; FAX. 510/462-4681; Ronald Iverson, Administrator

Plaza Surgical Center, Inc., 168 North Brent Street, Suite 403B, Ventura, CA 93003; tel. 805/643-5438; FAX. 805/643-1625; Dale P. Armstrong, M.D.

Podiatric Surgery Center, 255 North Gilbert, Suite B, Hemet, CA 92543; tel. 909/925-2186; FAX. 909/925-4947; Robert Drake, D.P.M., Administrator

Point Loma Surgical Center, 3434 Midway Drive, Suite 1006, San Diego, CA 92110; tel. 619/223-0910; David M. Kupfer, M.D., Medical Director

Porterville Surgical Center, 577 West Putnam Avenue, Porterville, CA 93257; tel. 209/788-6400; Lucy Lara, Administrator

Premier Endoscopy Center of the Desert, 1100 North Palm Canyon Drive, Suite 209, Palm Springs, CA 92262; tel. 619/776-7580; Phillip R. Roy, Administrator

Premier Surgery of Palm Desert, 73-180 El Paseo, Palm Desert, CA 92660; tel. 619/776-7580; Phillip R. Roy

Premiere Surgery Center, Inc., 700 West El Norte Parkway, Escondido, CA 92026; tel. 619/738-7830; FAX. 619/738-7841; R. K. Massengill, M.D., Medical Director

Providence Ambulatory Surgical Center, 1310 West Stewart Drive, Suite 310, Orange, CA 92668; tel. 714/771-6363; FAX. 714/771-0754; Harrell E. Robinson, M.D., President

Providence Holy Cross Surgery Center, 11550 Indian Hills Road, Suite 160, Mission Hills, CA 91345; tel. 818/898-1061; FAX. 818/898-3866; Laura Moore, Administrator

Pueblo Nuevo Aesthetic and Reconstructive Surgery, 1334 Nelson Avenue, Modesto, CA 95350; tel. 209/524-9904; FAX. 209/524-4101; Diane Payne, Administrator

Redlands Dental Surgery Center, 1180 Nevada Street, Suite 100, Redlands, CA 92374; tel. 909/335-0474; Russell O. Seheult, D.D.S.

Richburg Valley Eye Institute Ambulatory Surgical Center, 1680 East Herndon Avenue, Fresno, CA 93710-1234; tel. 209/432-4200; FAX. 209/432-0147; Frederick Richburg, M.D., Administrator

Riverside Community Surgi-Center, 3980 14th Street, Riverside, CA 92501; tel. 909/787-0580; FAX. 909/787-8201; Pat Finley, Administrator

Riverside Eye, Ear, Nose and Throat Institute Surgery Center, 4500 Brockton Avenue, Suite 105, Riverside, CA 92501; tel. 714/788-2788; FAX. 909/788-4374; B. G. Smith, M.D., Medical Director

Riverside Medical Clinic Surgery Center, 7160 Brockton Avenue, Riverside, CA 92506; tel. 714/782-3801; FAX. 909/782-3861; Jan Gough, RN, Office Manager

Rose Eye Cataract Surgical Center, 3325 North Broadway, Los Angeles, CA 90031; tel. 213/221-6121; Michael R. Rose, Administrator

Ross Valley Medical Group, 1350 So Eliseo Drive, Greenbrae, CA 94904; tel. 415/461-1350; Edward J. Boland, Administrator

Sacramento Eye Surgicenter, 3150 J Street, Sacramento, CA 95816; tel. 916/446-2020; Jill Quinn, RN

Sacramento Midtown Endoscopy Center, 3941 J Street, Suite 460, Sacramento, CA 95819; tel. 916/733-6940; FAX. 916/733-6934; Tommy Poirier, M.D.

Saddleback Eye Center, 23161 Moulton Parkway, Laguna Hills, CA 92653; tel. 714/951-4641; FAX. 714/951-4601; Linda Riley, Administrator

Salinas Surgery Center, 955-A Blanco Circle, Salinas, CA 93901; tel. 408/753-5800; FAX. 408/753-5808; Christine Gallagher, Administrator

Samaritan Pain Management Center, 2520 Samaritan Drive, San Jose, CA 95124; tel. 408/356-2731; FAX. 408/356-6366; Ilka E. McAlister, Administrator

San Buenaventura Surgery Center, A Partnership, 3525 Loma Vista Road, Ventura, CA 93003; tel. 805/641-6434; FAX. 805/641-6437; M. P. Bacon, Medical Director

San Diego Endoscopy Center, A Partnership, 4033 Third Avenue, Suite 106, San Diego, CA 92103; tel. 619/291-6064; FAX. 619/291-3078; John D. Goodman, M.D.

San Diego Outpatient Surgical Center, 770 Washington Street, Suite 101, San Diego, CA 92103; tel. 619/299-9530; FAX. 619/296-5386; Carla G. Ramirez, Administrator

San Francisco Surgi Center, 1635 Divisidero Street, Suite 200, San Francisco, CA 94115; tel. 415/346-1218; FAX. 415/346-1819; Peggy Wellman, Administrator

San Gabriel Valley Surgical Center, 1250 South Sunset Avenue, Suite 100, West Covina, CA 91790; tel. 818/960-6623; FAX. 818/962-4341; Susan Raub, Administrator

San Jose Eye Ambulatory Surgicenter, Inc., 4585 Stevens Creek Boulevard, Suite 500, Santa Clara, CA 95051; tel. 408/247-2706; FAX. 408/296-2020; Lolita Ancheta, Clinical Coordinator

San Leandro Surgery Center, 15035 East 14th Street, San Leandro, CA 94578; tel. 510/276-2800; FAX. 510/276-2890; Sheila L. Cook, Executive Director

Sani Eye Surgery Center, 1315 Las Tablas Road, Templeton, CA 93465; tel. 805/434-2533; FAX. 805/434-3037

Santa Cruz Surgery Center, 3003 Paul Sweet Road, Santa Cruz, CA 95065; tel. 408/462-5512; FAX. 408/462-2451; Donald S. Harner, M.D.

Santa Monica Surgery and Laser Center, 2001 Santa Monica Boulevard, Suite 1288W, Santa Monica, CA 90404; tel. 310/829-2005; FAX. 310/453-9201; Cindy Schlaak, RN, Administrator

Scoffield Foot Care Center, 3796 North Fresno Street, Suite 103, Fresno, CA 93726; tel. 209/228-1475; Mark H. Scoffield, Administrator

Sebastopol Ambulatory Surgery Center, 6880 Palm Avenue, Sebastopol, CA 95472; tel. 707/823-7628; FAX. 707/823-1521; Edward J. Boland, Administrator

Sequoia Endoscopy Center, 2900 Whipple Avenue, Suite 100, Redwood City, CA 94062; tel. 415/363-5200; FAX. 415/369-4609; Stuart Weisman, Administrator

Shepard Eye Center Medical Group, 1414 East Main Street, Santa Maria, CA 93454-4806; tel. 805/925-2637; FAX. 809/928-2067; Dennis D. Shepard, M.D.

Sierra Plastic Surgery Center, 6153 North Thesta, Fresno, CA 93710; tel. 209/432-5156; FAX. 209/432-2247; Terry A. Gillian, M.D., Medical Director

Sierra Vista Medical Pavilion Ambulatory Surgery, 77 Casa Street, Suite 203, San Luis Obispo, CA 93405; tel. 805/544-6471; James W. Thornton, M.D., Administrator

Simi Health Center, 1350 Los Angeles Avenue, Simi Valley, CA 93065; tel. 805/522-3782; FAX. 805/522-1283; Lorna Holland, Administrator

Solis Surgical Arts Center, 4940 Van Nuys Boulevard, Suite 105, Sherman Oaks, CA 91403; tel. 818/787-1144; Dr. H. William Gottschalk, Administrator

Sonora Eye Surgery Center, 940 Sylva Lane, Suite G, Sonora, CA 95370; tel. 209/532-2020; FAX. 209/532-1687; Pamela Donaldson

South Area Procedure Center, 8120 Timberlake Way, Suite 103, Sacramento, CA 95823; tel. 916/854-4400; Debra Quast, Administrator

South Bay Endoscopy Center, 256 Landis Avenue, Suite 100, Chula Vista, CA 91910; tel. 619/420-6864; FAX. 619/420-0477; Janet Lemon, Director

South Coast Eye Institute, A Medical Clinic, 3420 Bristol Street, Suite 701, Costa Mesa, CA 92626; tel. 714/957-0272; FAX. 714/641-2020; Michael R. Rose, M.D., Medical Director

Southern California Surgery Center, 7305 Pacific Boulevard, Huntington Park, CA 90255; tel. 213/584-8222; Amgad A. Awad, Administrator

Southland Endoscopy Center, 949 East Calhoun Place, Suite B, Hemet, CA 92543; tel. 909/929-1177; FAX. 909/765-9111; Sreenivasa R. Nakka, M.D., F.A.C.P.

Southwest Surgical Center, 201 New Stine Road, Suite 130, Bakersfield, CA 93309; tel. 805/396-8900; FAX. 805/397-2929; Mark Miller, M.D., Administrator

St. Joseph Surgery and Laser Center, Inc., 436 South Glassell Street, Orange, CA 92666; tel. 714/633-9566; FAX. 714/633-5193

Stanislaus Surgery Center, 1421 Oakdale Road, Modesto, CA 95355; tel. 209/572-2700; Michael Lipomi, Administrator

Stevenson Surgery Center, 2675 Stevenson Boulevard, Fremont, CA 94538; tel. 510/793-4987; FAX. 510/745-0136; Margaret Holmes, Director, Nursing

Stockton Eye Surgery Center, 36 West Yokuts Avenue, Stockton, CA 95207; tel. 209/473-2940; FAX. 209/474-1181

Surgecenter of Palo Alto, 400 Forest Avenue, Palo Alto, CA 94301; tel. 415/324-1832; FAX. 415/324-2282; Rose Parkes, Chief Executive Officer

Surgery Center of Corona, 1124 South Main Street, Suite 102, Corona, CA 91720; tel. 909/737-9091; FAX. 909/737-9093; Teri Ransbury, Administrator

Surgery Center of Northern California, 950 Butte Street, Redding, CA 96001; tel. 916/241-4044; FAX. 916/241-1408; Keveta Andersen, RN, Director

Surgery Center of San Bernardino, 2150 North Sierra Way, San Bernardino, CA 92405; tel. 909/881-2595; FAX. 909/881-1146; Patricia Bishop, RN, Administrator

Surgery Center of Santa Monica, 2121 Wilshire Boulevard, Santa Monica, CA 90403; tel. 310/260-5577; Carolyn G. Catton

Surgery Centers of the Desert, 1180 North Palm Canyon, Palm Springs, CA 92262; tel. 619/320-7600; FAX. 619/320-1694; Rosemary Coombs, Executive Director

Surgery Centers of the Desert, 39700 Bob Hope Drive, Suite 301, Rancho Mirage, CA 92270; tel. 619/346-7696; FAX. 619/776-1069; Marilee Kyler, Administrator

Surgical Eye Care Center, 655 Laguna Drive, Carlsbad, CA 92008; tel. 619/729-7101; Ellen Powers, Administrator

Surgitek Outpatient Center, Inc., 460 North Greenfield Avenue, Suite Eight, Hanford, CA 93230; tel. 209/582-0238; Wiley Elick, Owner, Administrator

Sutter Alhambra Surgery Center, 1201 Alhambra Boulevard, Sacramento, CA 95816; tel. 916/733-8222; FAX. 916/733-8224; Bill Davis, Administrator

Section C

Sutter North Procedure Center, 550 B Street, Yuba City, CA 95991; tel. 916/749-3650; Brenda Nakayama, Manager

Sutter Street Surgery Center, 450 Sutter Street, San Francisco, CA 94108; tel. 415/981-1666; Jack K. Waller, Administrator

The Beverly Hills Center for Special Surgery, 1125 South Beverly Drive, Suite 505, Los Angeles, CA 90035; tel. 310/277-6780; Alina Pnini, Administrator

The Center for Endoscopy, 3921 Waring Road, Suite B, Oceanside, CA 92056; tel. 619/940-6300; FAX. 619/940-8074; Barbara Bockover, RN, Administrator

The Centre for Plastic Surgery, 401 East Highland Avenue, Suite 352, San Bernardino, CA 92404; tel. 909/883-8686; FAX. 909/881-6537; Dennis K. Anderson, Administrator

The Darr Eye Clinic Surgical Medical Group, Inc., 44139 Monterey Avenue, Suite A, Palm Desert, CA 92260; tel. 619/773-3099; FAX. 619/341-6863; Joseph L. Darr, M.D., Administrator

The Endoscopy Center, 870 Shasta Street, Suite 100, Yuba City, CA 95991; tel. 916/671-3636; FAX. 916/671-4099; Floyd V. Burton, M.D.

The Endoscopy Center of the South Bay, 23560 Madison Street, Suite 109, Torrance, CA 90505; tel. 310/325-6331; FAX. 310/325-6335; Norman M. Panitch, M.D.

The Eye Surgery Center (Colton), 1900 East Washington, Colton, CA 92324; tel. 909/825-8002; FAX. 909/422-8930; Sally Chalk, RN, Operating Room Manager

The Eye Surgery Center of Northern California, 5959 Greenback Lane, Citrus Heights, CA 95621; tel. 916/723-7400; Shari Sloan, Administrator

The Eye Surgery Center of Riverside, 8990 Garfield, Suite One, Riverside, CA 92503; tel. 909/785-5421; FAX. 909/785-0130

The Montebello Surgery Center, 229 East Beverly Boulevard, Montebello, CA 90640; tel. 213/728-7998; Clifton M. Baker, Administrator

The Palos Verdes Ambulatory Surgery Medical Center, 3400 West Lomita Boulevard, Suite 307A, Torrance, CA 90505; tel. 310/517-8689; FAX. 310/517-9916; Christine Petti, M.D., Administrator

The Plastic Surgery Center Medical Group, Inc., 95 Scripps Drive, Sacramento, CA 95825; tel. 916/929-1833; FAX. 916/929-6730; Mark L. Ross, Administrator

The Sinskey Eye Institute, 2232 Santa Monica Boulevard, Santa Monica, CA 90411; tel. 310/453-8911; FAX. 310/453-2519; Sherry Bennett, Administrator

The Specialists Surgery Center, 2450 Martin Road, Fairfield, CA 94533; tel. 707/422-2325; FAX. 707/429-6088; Ronald D. Fike, Jr.

The Surgery Center, 1111 Sonoma Avenue, Santa Rosa, CA 95405; tel. 707/578-4100; Ken Alban, Administrator

The Surgery Center, 6840 Sepulveda Boulevard, Van Nuys, CA 91405-4401; tel. 818/785-6840; FAX. 818/785-3931; Gail Morales, RN, Nurse Manager

The Surgery Center, A HealthSouth Surgery Center, 3875 Telegraph Avenue, Oakland, CA 94609; tel. 510/547-2244; Peggy S. Wellman, Director, Operations

The Valley Endoscopy Center, 18425 Burbank Boulevard, Suite 525, Tarzana, CA 91356; tel. 818/708-6050; FAX. 818/708-6009; Betty Asato, RN, Clinical Director

Third Street Surgery Center, 420 East Third Street, Suite 604, Los Angeles, CA 90013; tel. 213/680-1551

Thousand Oaks Endoscopy Center, 227 West Janss Road, Suite 240, Thousand Oaks, CA 91360; tel. 805/371-0455; FAX. 805/371-0455; Hector Caballero, M.D., Administrator

Time Surgical Facility, 720 North Tustin Avenue, Suite 202, Santa Ana, CA 92705; tel. 714/972-1811; Denise Reale, Administrator

Torrance Surgicenter, 22410 Hawthorne Boulevard, Suite Three, Torrance, CA 90505; tel. 310/373-2238; FAX. 310/373-8238; Lindon KenKawahara, M.D., Medical Director

Tri-Valley Surgery Center, 4487 Stoneridge Drive, Pleasanton, CA 94588; tel. 510/484-3100; FAX. 510/484-3113; Karen Stevens, RN, CNOR, Administrator

Truxtun Surgery Center, Inc., 4260 Truxtun Avenue, Suite 120, Bakersfield, CA 93309; tel. 805/327-3636; Velma Reed, Administrator

Twin Cities Surgicenter, Inc., 812 Fourth Street, Suite A, Marysville, CA 95901; tel. 916/741-3937; FAX. 916/743-0427; Bonnie Archuleta, Administrator

UTC Surgicenter, 8929 University Center Lane, Suite 103, San Diego, CA 92122; tel. 619/554-0220; FAX. 619/554-0458; Dawn Ainsworth, RN, Administrator

University Surgi-Center Medical Group, 23961 Calle De La Magdalena, Suite 430, Laguna Hills, CA 92653; tel. 714/830-5500; Bernard Berry, M.D., Administrator

Upland Outpatient Surgical Center, Inc., 1330 San Bernardino Road, Upland, CA 91786; tel. 909/981-8755; FAX. 909/981-9462; Roger E. Murken, M.D., President

Valencia Outpatient Surgical Center, L.P., d/b/a Valencia Surgical Center, 24355 Lyons Avenue, Suite 120, Santa Clarita, CA 91321; tel. 805/255-6644; FAX. 805/255-6717; Nina Turner, Administrative Director

Valley Surgical Center, 5555 West Las Positas Boulevard, Pleasanton, CA 94566; tel. 510/734-3360; FAX. 510/734-3358; Beth Combs, RN, Director, Nursing

Ventura Out-Patient Surgery, Inc., 3555 Loma Vista Road, Suite 204, Ventura, CA 93003; tel. 805/653-5460; FAX. 805/653-1470; Brian D. Brantner, M.D.

Victorville Ambulatory Surgery Center, 15030 Seventh Street, Victorville, CA 92392; tel. 619/241-2273; FAX. 619/245-6798; John D. Amar, M.D., Medical Director

Vision Care Surgery Center, 1045 S Street, Fresno, CA 93721; tel. 209/486-2000; Lynn Horton, Executive Director

Walnut Creek Ambulatory Surgery Center, 112 La Casa Via, Suite 300, Walnut Creek, CA 94598; tel. 510/933-0290; Catherine Nichol, Administrator

Wardlow Surgery Center, 200 West Wardlow Road, Long Beach, CA 90806; tel. 310/424-3574; FAX. 310/490-0329; Marisol Magana, Administrator

Washington Outpatient Surgery Center, 2299 Mowry Avenue, First Floor, Fremont, CA 94538; tel. 510/791-5374; FAX. 510/790-8916; Gerald G. Pousho, M.D.

West Olympic Surgery Center and Laser Institute, 11570 West Olympic Boulevard, Los Angeles, CA 90064; tel. 310/479-4211; FAX. 310/473-6069; Chris Klimaszewski, Operating Room Supervisor

West Valley Surgery Center, 3803 South Bascom Avenue, Suite 106, Campbell, CA 95008; tel. 408/559-4886; FAX. 408/559-4908; Annette Wunderlich, RN, Administrator

Westlake Eye Surgery Center, 2900 Townsgate Road, Suite 201, Westlake Village, CA 91361; tel. 805/496-6789; FAX. 805/494-8392; Don Hirschman, M.H.A., Administrator

Westwood Surgery Center, 11819 Wilshire Boulevard, Suite 214, Los Angeles, CA 90025; tel. 310/575-1616; FAX. 310/575-1622; Thomas Cloud, M.D., Administrator

Women's Health Care and Cosmetic Surgical Center, 15306 Devonshire Street, Mission Hills, CA 91311; tel. 818/893-4044; Martha P. Nazemi, Administrator

Woodland Surgery Center, 1321 Cottonwood Street, Woodland, CA 95695; tel. 916/662-9112; FAX. 916/668-5783; Donna Fields, Manager

COLORADO

Ambulatory Surgery, Ltd., 320 East Fontanero, Colorado Springs, CO 80907; tel. 719/634-8878; Dana Alexander, Vice President, Clinical Operations

Aurora Outpatient Surgery, 2900 South Peoria Street, Suite D, Aurora, CO 80014; tel. 303/752-2496; FAX. 303/752-2577; L. F. Peede, Jr., M.D., Administrator

Aurora Outpatient Surgery, 2900 S. Peoria St., #D, Aurora, CO 80014; tel. 303/752-2496; Randolph Robinson, Administrator

Aurora Surgery Center LTD, 13701 E. Mississippi, #200, Aurora, CO 80012; tel. 303/363-8646; Beverly Kirchner, RN, Administrator

Aurora Surgery Center, Ltd., 13701 Mississippi Avenue, Suite 200, Aurora, CO 80012; tel. 303/363-8646; FAX. 303/363-8689; Beverly Kirchner, RN, Administrator

Avista Surgery Center, 2525 Fourth Street, Lower Level, Boulder, CO 80304; tel. 303/443-3672; John Sackett, Administrator

Avista Surgery Center, 2525 4th Street, Lower Level, BOulder, CO 80304; tel. 303/443-3672; John Sackett, Administrator

Boulder Medical Center, P C, 2750 Broadway, Boulder, CO 80304; tel. 303/440-3000; Mr. Bradford McKane, Administrator

Boulder Medical Center, P.C., 2750 Broadway, Boulder, CO 80304; tel. 303/440-3000; Bradford B. McKane

Centennial Healthcare Plaza, a Division of Healthone/Columbia, 14200 East Arapahoe Road, Englewood, CO 80112; tel. 303/699-3000; FAX. 303/699-3182; Ginger McNally, Administrator

Center for Reproductive Surgery, 799 East Hampden Avenue, Suite 300, Englewood, CO 80110; tel. 303/788-8309; FAX. 303/788-8310; Dr. William Schoolcraft, Administrator

Centura Health-Summit Surgery Center, Highway Nine at School Road, P.O. Box 4460, Frisco, CO 80443; tel. 303/668-1458; FAX. 970/668-1703; Carol Turrin, Administrator

Centura Health-Surgery LTD, 320 E. Fontanero #101, Pavilion Blvd, Colorado Springs, CO 80907; tel. 719/634-8878; Carol Jackson, Administrator

Cherry Creek Eye Surgery Center, (Rose Medical Center), 4999 East Kentucky Avenue, Denver, CO 80222; tel. 303/692-0903; Jeffrey Dorsey, Administrator

Colorado Outpatient Eye Surgical Center, 2480 South Downing, Suite G-20, Denver, CO 80210; tel. 303/777-3882; FAX. 300/778-0738; Thomas P. Larkin, M.D.

Colorado Outpatient Eye Surgical Center, 2480 S. Downing, Denver, CO 80210; tel. 303/777-3852; Thomas Larkin, Administrator

Colorado Springs Eye Surgery Center, 2920 North Cascade Avenue, Colorado Springs, CO 80907; tel. 719/636-5054; FAX. 719/520-3576; Paul Angotti, Administrator

Colorado Springs Health Partners Ambulatory Surgery Unit, 209 South Nevada Avenue, Colorado Springs, CO 80903; tel. 719/475-7700; FAX. 719/475-1241; Ms. Joan Compton, Administrator

Columbia Centrum Surgical Center, 8200 East Belleview, Suite 300, East Tower, Englewood, CO 80111; tel. 303/290-0600; FAX. 303/290-6359; Jane Klinglesmith, Administrator

Denver Eye Surgery Center, Inc., 13772 Denver West Parkway, Building 55, Golden, CO 80401; tel. 303/273-8770; Larry W. Kreider, M.D., Administrator

Denver Midtown Surgery Center, 1919 East 18th Avenue, Denver, CO 80206; tel. 303/322-3993; Connie Holtz, Administrator

Durango Surgicenter, 316 Sawyer Drive, Durango, CO 81301; tel. 970/259-3818; D.J. Winder, MD, Administrator

ENT Surgicenter, Inc., 1032 Luke, Fort Collins, CO 80524; tel. 970/484-8686; FAX. 970/484-1064; Debbie Brown, Manager

Eye Center of Northern Colorado Surgery Center, 1725 E. Prospect Ave., Fort Collins, CO 80525; tel. 970/484-5322; Carol Wittmer, Administrator

Eye Surgery Center of Colorado, 8403 Bryant Street, Westminster, CO 80030; tel. 303/426-4810; FAX. 303/426-8708; William G. Self, Jr., M.D., Administrator

Foot Surgery Center of Northern Colorado, 1355 Riverside Ave., #B, Fort Collins, CO 80524; tel. 970/484-4620; Adriann Anderson, Administrator

HealthSouth Denver West Surgery Center, 13952 Denver West Parkway, Building 53, Suite 100, Golden, CO 80401; tel. 303/271-1112; FAX. 303/271-1117; Ms. Susan Byers, Administrator

HealthSouth Pueblo Ambulatory Surgery Center, 25 Montebello Road, Pueblo, CO 81001; tel. 719/544-1600; FAX. 719/544-2599; Marlene Keithley, Administrator

HealthSouth Surgery Center of Colorado Springs, 1615 Medical Center Point, Colorado Springs, CO 80907; tel. 719/635-7740; FAX. 719/635-7750; B. J. Schott, Administrator

HealthSouth Surgery Center of Fort Collins, 1100 East Prospect Road, Fort Collins, CO 80525; tel. 970/493-7200; FAX. 970/493-2380; Alice Fischer, Administrator

Kaiser Permanente Ambulatory Surgery Center, 2045 Franklin Street, Denver, CO 80205; tel. 303/764-4444; Rosemarie Polemi, Director

Lakewood Surgical Center, 2201 Wadsworth Boulevard, Lakewood, CO 80215; tel. 303/234-0445; FAX. 303/232-7182; Connie Holtz, Administrator

Laser Institute of the Rockies, 8400 East Prentice Avenue, Suite 1200, Englewood, CO 80111; tel. 303/793-3000; Jon Dishler, M.D., President

Littleton Day Surgery Center, 8381 South Park Lane, Littleton, CO 80120; tel. 303/795-2244; FAX. 303/795-5965; Keith A. Chambers, Administrator

Mountain View Surgery Center, 1850 N. Boise Ave., P.O. Box 887, Loveland, CO 80538; tel. 970/622-1999; Charles Harms, Administrator

North Denver Surgical Center, Ltd., 10001 North Washington, Thornton, CO 80229; tel. 303/252–0083; FAX. 303/252–9095; Charlotte Santoro, Administrator

Orthopaedic Center of the Rockies Ambulatory Surgery Center, 2500 East Prospect Road, Fort Collins, CO 80525; tel. 303/493–4010; FAX. 303/493–0521; Scott M. Thomas, Executive Director

Pain Management Center, 455 E. Pikes Peak Ave., #201, Colorado Springs, CO 80903; tel. 719/442–0777; Sue Hayes Golden, Administrator

Pikes Peak Endoscopy & Surgery Center, 1699 Medical Center Pt., #100, Colorado Springs, CO 80907; tel. 719/632–7101; Karen Parks, Administrator

Rocky Mountain Surgery Center, LTD., 2405 Broadway, Boulder, CO 80304–4108; tel. 303/449–2020; FAX. 303/440–6893; James R. Schubert, Executive Director

South Denver Endoscopy Center, Inc., 499 East Hampden Avenue, Suite 430, Englewood, CO 80110; tel. 303/788–8888; Dr. Pete Baker, Administrator

Southern Colorado Center for Endoscopy and Surgery, 2002 Lake Avenue, Pueblo, CO 81004; tel. 719/560–7111; FAX. 719/564–0122; Dr. Andrew Perry, Administrator

Spring Creek Surgery Center, Spring Creek Medical Park, 2001 South Shields Street, Building H, Suite 100, Fort Collins, CO 80526; tel. 970/221–9363; FAX. 970/221–9636; Natalie Coubrough, Facility Administrator

Springs Pain Research & Surgery Facility, 1625 MEdical Center Point, #240, Colorado Springs, CO 80907; tel. 719/577–9063; Charles Ripp, MD, Administrator

Springs Pain Research and Surgery Facility, 1625 Medical Center Point, Suite 240, Colorado Springs, CO 80907; tel. 719/577–9063; FAX. 719/577–9124; Charles Ripp, Administrator

Sterling Eye Surgery Center, 1410 S. 7th Ave., P.O. Box 951, Sterling, CO 80751; tel. 970/522–1833; Rashell Fritzler, Administrator

Sterling Eye Surgical Center, 1410 South Seventh Avenue, Sterling, CO 80751; tel. 303/522–1833; FAX. 970/522–3677; Inez C. Plank, General Manager

Surgicenter of the San Luis Valley Medical, P.C., 2115 Stuart, Alamosa, CO 81101; tel. 719/589–8010; FAX. 719/589–8112; Lauriann Blakeman, RN, Supervisor

Western Rockies Surgery Center, Inc., 1000 Wellington Avenue, Grand Junction, CO 81501; tel. 970/243–9000; FAX. 970/245–4936; Marilyn M. Smith, RN, Surgery Center Administrator

Western Rockies Surgery Center, Inc., 1000 Wellington Ave., Grand Junction CO 81501; tel. 970/243–9000; Marilyn Smith, Administrator

CONNECTICUT

Bridgeport Surgical Center, 4920 Main Street, Bridgeport, CT 06606; tel. 203/374–1515; FAX. 203/374–4702; Anthony German, Administrative Director

Connecticut Foot Surgery Center, 318 New Haven Avenue, Milford, CT 06460; tel. 203/882–0065; Martin Pressman, D.P.M., Administrator

Connecticut Surgical Center, 81 Gillett Street, Hartford, CT 06105; tel. 203/247–5555; FAX. 203/249–5860; Margaret Rubino, President

Danbury Surgical Center, 73 Sandpit Road, Suite 101, Danbury, CT 06810; tel. 203/743–2400; Bernard A. Kershner, President

Hartford Surgical Center, 100 Retreat Avenue, Hartford, CT 06106; tel. 860/549–7970; FAX. 860/247–4121; Christine M. Quallen, Administrative Director

Johnson Surgery Center, 148 Hazard Avenue, P.O. Box 909, Enfield, CT 06083; tel. 860/763–7650; FAX. 860/763–7675; Anthony T. Valente, Vice President, Chief Operating Officer

Middlesex Surgical Center, 530 Saybrook Road, Middletown, CT 06457; tel. 203/343–0400; FAX. 203/343–0396; Louise DeChesser, RN, CNOR, M.S.

Naugatuck Valley Surgical Center, Ltd., 160 Robbins Street, Waterbury, CT 06708; tel. 203/755–6663; FAX. 203/756–9645; Bernard A. Kershner, President

Stamford Surgical Center, 1290 Summer Street, Stamford, CT 06905; tel. 203/961–1345; FAX. 213/324–1470; Charles Tienken, Administrative Director

Waterbury Outpatient Surgical Center, 87 Grandview Avenue, Waterbury, CT 06708; tel. 203/574–2020; Nancy Noll, Administrator

Woman's Surgical Center, 40 Temple Street, New Haven, CT 06510; tel. 203/624–3080; Bruce I. Fisher, Administrator

Yale–New Haven Ambulatory Services Corporation, d/b/a Temple Surgical Center, 60 Temple Street, New Haven, CT 06510; tel. 203/624–6008; Alvin D. Greenberg, M.D., Administrator

DELAWARE

Bayview Endoscopy Center, Inc., 1539 Savannah Road, Lewes, DE 19958; tel. 302/644–0455; FAX. 302/645–9325; Harry J. Anagnostakos, D.O., President

Central Delaware Endoscopy Unit, 644 South Queen Street, Suite 105, Dover, DE 19904; tel. 302/672–1617; William M. Kaplan, M.D., Medical Director

Central Delaware Surgery Center, 100 Scull Terrace, Dover, DE 19901; tel. 302/735–8290; Paul Fransisco, Administrator

Endoscopy Center of Delaware, Inc., 1090 Old Churchman's Road, Newark, DE 19713; tel. 302/892–2710; FAX. 302/892–2715; Jean–Marie M. Taylor, Administrator

Eye Care of Delaware Cataract and Laser Center, 4201 Ogletown Road, Suite 1, Newark, DE 19713; tel. 302/454–8802

Glasgow Medical Center, L.L.C., 2400 Summit Bridge Road, Newark, DE 19702–4777; tel. 302/536–8350; Joseph M. Rule, Ph.D., Administrator

Limestone Medical Center, Inc., 1941 Limestone Road, Suite 113, Wilmington, DE 19808; tel. 302/633–9873; Thomas Mulhern, Chief Financial Officer

DISTRICT OF COLUMBIA

Capitol Women's Center, 1339 22nd Street, N.W., Washington, DC 20037; tel. 202/338–2772; Kelly Turner–Minor, Administrator

Hillcrest Northwest, 7603 Georgia Avenue, N.W., Washington, DC 20012; tel. 202/829–5620; FAX. 202/882–8387; Alice Harper, Administrator

Hillcrest Women's Surgi–Center, 3233 Pennsylvania Avenue, S.E., Washington, DC 20020; tel. 202/584–6500; Ms. Caridad V. Wright, Administrator

Medlantic Center for Ambulatory Surgery, Inc., 1145 19th Street, N.W., Suite 850, Washington, DC 20036; tel. 202/223–9040; FAX. 202/223–9047; Marcia F. Zensinger, President

New Summit Medical Center II, Inc., 1630 Euclid Street, N.W., Suite 130, Washington, DC 20037; tel. 202/337–7200; Johnette Anderson, RNC, Administrator

Planned Parenthood of Metropolitan Washington, D.C., Schumacher Center, 1108 16th Street, N.W., Washington, DC 20036; tel. 202/483–3999; FAX. 202/347–0281; Claudia Allers, Center Manager

Premier Ambulatory Center, 6323 Georgia Avenue, N.W., Washington, DC 20011; tel. 202/291–0036; Gwen S. Robinson–Terry, Chief Operating Officer

The Endoscopy Center of Washington, DC, L.P., 2021 K Street, N.W., Suite T–115, Washington, DC 20006; tel. 202/775–8692; FAX. 202/296–9122; Phyllis J. Krchma, Administrator

Washington Surgi–Clinic, 1018 22nd Street, N.W., Washington, DC 20037; tel. 202/659–9403; FAX. 202/467–0056; Maria Barrera, Administrator

FLORIDA

Aker–Kasten Cataract and Laser Institute, 1445 Northwest Boca Raton Boulevard, Boca Raton, FL 33432; tel. 407/338–7722, ext. 238; FAX. 407/338–7785; Kim Harrington, Administrator

Alpha Ambulatory Surgery, Inc., 2160 Capital Circle, N.E., Tallahassee, FL 32308; tel. 904/385–0013; FAX. 904/422–0201; Gloria Jeter, Office Manager

Ambulatory Ankle and Foot Center of Florida, 1509 South Orange Avenue, P.O. Box 536951, Orlando, FL 32853; tel. 407/895–2432; Craig C. Maguire, D.P.M.

Ambulatory Surgery Center of Brevard, 719 East New Haven Avenue, Melbourne, FL 32901; tel. 407/726–4106; Dwight Miller, General Manager

Ambulatory Surgery Center of Naples, 1351 Pine Street, Naples, FL 34104; tel. 941/793–0664; FAX. 941/793–4318; Christian Mogelvang, M.D., Medical Director

Ambulatory Surgery Center/Bradenton, 5817 21st Avenue, W., Bradenton, FL 34209; tel. 813/794–0379; J. Leikensohn, M.D. Medical Director

Ambulatory Surgical Care, 1045 North Courtenay Parkway, Merritt Island, FL 32953; tel. 407/452–4448; FAX. 407/452–5404; John L. Stellner, MHA, Administrative Director

Ambulatory Surgical Center of Central Florida, Inc., 801 North Stone Street, Deland, FL 32720; tel. 904/734–4431; FAX. 904/738–1045; Albert C. Neumann, M.D., Medical Director

Ambulatory Surgical Center of Lake County, Inc., 803 East Dixie Avenue, Leesburg, FL 32748; tel. 904/787–6656; FAX. 904/787–9008; Patricia R. Hux, RN, Business Manager

Ambulatory Surgical Centre, 8700 North Kendall Drive, Suite 100, Miami, FL 33176; tel. 305/595–9511; FAX. 305/271–0383; Gail Tauriello, Administrator

Ambulatory Surgical Facility of South Florida, LTD–East, 4470 Sheridan Street, Hollywood, FL 33021; tel. 305/962–3210; FAX. 305/962–3466; Ross S. Ackerman, Executive Director, Administrator

American Surgery Center of Tallahassee, 3411 Capital Medical Boulevard, P.O. Box 13675, Tallahassee, FL 32317–3675; tel. 904/878–4830; FAX. 904/656–1692; Brenda J. Fletcher, Surgical Coordinator

American Surgery Centers of Coral Gables, Inc., 1097 Le Jeune Road, Miami, FL 33134

Atlantic Surgery Center, 541 Health Boulevard, Daytona Beach, FL 32114; tel. 904/239–0021

Atlantic Surgery Center, A HealthSouth Facility, 1707 South 25th Street, Fort Pierce, FL 34947; tel. 561/464–8900; FAX. 561/879–4416; Roni Brockington, Business Office Coordinator

Atlantic Surgical Center, 150 Southwest 12th Avenue, Suite 450, Pompano Beach, FL 33069; tel. 305/941–3369; Ruben Paradela, Chief Executive Officer

Ayers Surgery Center, 720 Southwest Second Avenue, Suite 101, Gainesville, FL 32601; tel. 904/338–7100; FAX. 904/338–7102; Barbara Hyder, RN, Nurse Manager

Barkley Surgicenter, 63 Barkley Circle, Suite 104, Fort Myers, FL 33907; tel. 813/275–8452; Kerri Gantt, Administrative Director

Bay Med Surgery, 1936 Jenks Avenue, Panama City, FL 32405; tel. 904/763–6700; FAX. 904/763–5779; Riyad Albibi, M.D., Director

Bayfront Medical Plaza Same Day Surgery, 603 Seventh Street South, St. Petersburg, FL 33701; tel. 813/553–7906; FAX. 813/553–7992; Gail A. Cook, RN, Assistant Nurse Manager

Beraja Clinics Laser and Surgery Center, 2550 Douglas Road, Suite 301, Coral Gables, FL 33134

Bethesda Health City Same Day Surgery, 10301 Hagen Ranch Road, Boynton Beach, FL 33437; tel. 561/374–5400; FAX. 561/374–5405; Constance Hillman, Clinical Coordinator

Boca Raton Outpatient Surgery and Laser Center, 501 Glades Road, Boca Raton, FL 33432; tel. 561/362–4400; FAX. 561/362–4440; Karen Raiano, Administrator

Bon Secours–Venice HealthPark, 1283 Jacaranda Boulevard, Venice, FL 34292; tel. 941/497–5660; FAX. 941/492–3942; Kermit Knight, Administrator

Bonita Bay Surgery Center, 26711 Tamiami Trail South, Bonita Springs, FL 33923

Brevard Surgery Center, 665 Apollo Boulevard, Melbourne, FL 32901; tel. 407/984–0300; FAX. 407/984–0032; Narda Cotman, Surgical Director

Cape Coral Endoscopy and Surgery Center, 1413 Viscaya Parkway, Cape Coral, FL 33990; tel. 941/772–0404; Nancy Rhodes, Administrator

Cape Surgery Center, 1941 Waldemere Street, Sarasota, FL 34239–3555; tel. 941/917–1900; FAX. 941/917–2356; Sharon Tolhurst, RN, M.B.A., Director

Capital Eye Surgery Center, 2535 Capital Medical Boulevard, Tallahassee, FL 32308; tel. 904/942–3937; FAX. 904/942–6279

Center for Advanced Eye Surgery, L.P., 3920 Bee Ridge Road Building, Suite C, Sarasota, FL 34233; tel. 941/925–0000; FAX. 941/927–2726; E. Helen Smith, RN, Nurse Manager

Central Florida Eye Institute, 3133 Southwest 32nd Avenue, Ocala, FL 34474; tel. 904/237–8400; Thomas L. Croley, M.D.

Clearwater Endoscopy Center, 401 Corbett Street, Suite 220, Clearwater, FL 34616; tel. 813/443–0100; Roberta Hayer, RN, Clinical Director

Cleveland Clinic Florida, 3000 West Cypress Creek Road, Fort Lauderdale, FL 33309

Section C

Columbia Ambulatory Surgery Center, 4500 East Fletcher Avenue, Tampa, FL 33613; tel. 813/977-8550; FAX. 813/977-7941; Carole Cornell, Administrator

Columbia Belleair Surgery Center, 1130 Ponce de Leon Boulevard, Clearwater, FL 34616; tel. 813/581-4800; FAX. 813/585-0319; Margie Maddock, Administrator

Columbia Brandon Surgery Center, 711 South Parsons, Brandon, FL 33511; tel. 813/654-7771, ext. 29; FAX. 813/654-3347; Charlene Harrell, RN, Administrator

Columbia Cape Coral Surgery Center, 2721 Del Prado Boulevard, S., Suite 100, Cape Coral, FL 33904; tel. 941/458-9000; Barry Kandell, Administrator

Columbia Center for Special Surgery, 4650 Fourth Street, N., St. Petersburg, FL 33703; tel. 813/527-1919; FAX. 813/527-0714; Paula Russo, RN, CNOR, Administrator

Columbia Central Florida SurgiCenter, 814 Griffin Road and 900 Griffin Road, Lakeland, FL 33805; tel. 941/686-1010; FAX. 941/686-1711; Jan Townsend, Administrator

Columbia Countryside Surgery Center, 3291 North McMullen Booth Road, Clearwater, FL 34621; tel. 813/725-5800; FAX. 813/797-4002; Sandra McFarland, Administrator

Columbia DeLand Surgery Center, 651 West Plymouth Avenue, Deland, FL 32720; tel. 904/738-6811; FAX. 904/822-4316; Reid Anderson, Administrator

Columbia Florida Surgery Center, 180 Boston Avenue, Altamonte Springs, FL 32701; tel. 407/830-0573; FAX. 407/830-4373; Paige L. Adams, Administrator

Columbia Gulf Coast Surgery Center, 411 Second Street, E., Bradenton, FL 34208; tel. 941/746-1121; FAX. 941/746-7816; Carlene Bailey, RN, Administrator

Columbia Kissimmee Surgery Center, 2275 North Central Avenue, Kissimmee, FL 34741; tel. 407/870-0573; FAX. 407/870-1859; Lou Warmijak, Administrator

Columbia New Port Richey Surgery Center, 5415 Gulf Drive, New Port Richey, FL 34652; tel. 813/848-0446; FAX. 813/842-3166; Sandra McFarland, RN, Administrator

Columbia North County Surgicenter, 4000 Burns Road, Palm Beach Gardens, FL 33410; tel. 407/626-6446; Theresa Vasquez, Business Manager

Columbia Outpatient Surgical Services, Ltd., 301 Northwest 82nd Avenue, Plantation, FL 33324; tel. 954/424-1766; FAX. 954/424-1966; Debbie Haga-Cofu, Controller

Columbia Parkside Surgery Center, 2731 Park Street, Jacksonville, FL 32205; tel. 904/389-1077; FAX. 904/389-9959; Chris Edmond, Administrator

Columbia Plaza Surgery Center, 3901 Beach Boulevard South, Jacksonville, FL 32216; tel. 904/448-1948; Debbie Overton-Raines, Administrator

Columbia Surgery Center Merritt Island, 270 North Sykes Creek Parkway, Merritt Island, FL 32953; tel. 407/459-0015; Cynthia Johnson, Administrator

Columbia Surgery Center at Coral Springs, 967 University Drive, Coral Springs, FL 33071; tel. 954/975-4166; FAX. 954/344-7054

Columbia Surgery Center at St. Andrews, Inc., 1350 East Venice Avenue, Venice, FL 34292; tel. 941/488-2030; FAX. 941/484-2010; Judy Miller, Business Office Manager

Columbia Surgery Center of Stuart, 2096 Southeast Ocean Boulevard, Stuart, FL 34996; tel. 561/223-0174; FAX. 561/223-0946; Jill Logan, Administrator

Coral View Surgery Center, 8390 West Flager, Suite 216, Miami, FL 33144; tel. 305/226-5574; Victor Suarez, M.D., President

Cordova Ambulatory Surgical Center, 545 Brent Lane, Pensacola, FL 32503; tel. 904/477-5437; Cynthia Blake, Assistant Administrator

Cortez Foot Surgery Center, PA, 1800 Cortez Road, W., Suite B, Bradenton, FL 34207; tel. 941/758-4608, ext. 27; FAX. 941/755-2901; Margaret Provencher, Administrator

Day Surgery, Inc., 1715 Southeast Tiffany Avenue, Port St. Lucie, FL 34952; tel. 407/335-7005; Mary Holobaugh, RN, Administrator

Dermatologic and Cosmetic Surgery Center, 2668 Swamp Cabbage Court, Fort Myers, FL 33901; tel. 813/275-7546; FAX. 813/275-5074; Charles Eby, M.D.

Diagnostic Clinic Center for Outpatient Surgery, 1401 West Bay Drive, Largo, FL 34640; tel. 813/581-8767; FAX. 813/584-1938; Robert R. Dippong, Administrator, Chief Executive Officer

Doctors Surgery Center, 921 North Main Street, Kissimmee, FL 34744; tel. 407/933-7800

East Lake Outpatient Center, 3890 Tampa Road, Palm Harbor, FL 34684

Endoscopy Associates of Citrus, 6412 West Gulf to Lake Highway, Crystal River, FL 34429

Endoscopy Center of Ocala, Inc., 1160 Southeast 18th Place, Ocala, FL 34471; tel. 352/732-8679, ext. 203; FAX. 352/732-2440; Linda L. Brooks, RN, Nurse Manager

Endoscopy Center of Sarasota, 1435 Osprey Avenue, Suite 100, Sarasota, FL 34239; tel. 941/366-4475; FAX. 941/366-4390; Susan M. Brongel, RN, Administrator

Eye Care and Surgery Center of Ft. Lauderdale, 2540 Northeast Ninth Street, Ft. Lauderdale, FL 33304; tel. 305/561-3533; FAX. 305/565-9706; Michael Goldstone, Administrator

Eye Surgery Facility, P.A., 2808 West Martin Luther King Boulevard, Tampa, FL 33607; tel. 813/876-1331; FAX. 813/872-0647; Phyllis S. Chisholm, RN, M.A., Executive Director

Eye Surgery and Laser Center, 4120 Del Prado Boulevard, Cape Coral, FL 33904; tel. 813/542-2020; FAX. 813/542-0704; Louise Bennett, RN, Administrator

Eye Surgery and Laser Center of Mid-Florida, Inc., 409 Avenue K, S.E., Winter Haven, FL 33880; tel. 941/294-3504, ext. 303; FAX. 941/294-8305; Sue Koha, ASC Supervisor

Eye Surgicenter, 2521 Northwest 41st Street, Gainesville, FL 32606; tel. 904/377-7733; William A. Newsome, M.D.

Faculty Clinic, Inc., 653 West Eighth Street, Jacksonville, FL 32209; tel. 904/350-6708

Family Medical Center, 100 Commercial Drive, Keystone Heights, FL 32656; tel. 352/473-6595; FAX. 352/473-6597; Sue Russell, Office Manager

Florida Eye Clinic Ambulatory Surgical Center, 160 Boston Avenue, Altamonte Springs, FL 32701; tel. 407/834-7776; FAX. 407/831-8607; Genevieve Parm, Chief Executive Officer

Florida Eye Institute Surgicenter, Inc., 2750 Indian River Boulevard, Vero Beach, FL 32960; tel. 407/569-9500; FAX. 407/569-9507; Mary Lynne Schlitt, Administrator

Florida Medical Clinic Special Procedures Center, 38135 Market Square, Zephyrhills, FL 33540

Forest Oaks Ambulatory Surgical Center, Inc., 7320 Forest Oaks Boulevard, Spring Hill, FL 34606; tel. 904/683-5666; Thomas D. Stelnicki, D.P.M.

Foundation for Advanced Eye Care, 3737 Pine Island Road, Sunrise, FL 33351; tel. 305/572-5888; FAX. 305/572-5994; Andrea B. Lettman, Administrator

Gaskins Eye Care and Surgery Center, 2335 Ninth Street, N., Suite 304, Naples, FL 34103; tel. 941/263-7750; FAX. 941/263-1754; Cindy Gaskins, RN, M.S.N., R.M.

Gulf Coast Endoscopy Center, Inc., 665 Del Prado Boulevard, Cape Coral, FL 33990; tel. 813/772-3800; FAX. 813/772-5073; Mrs. Lee Caruso, Administrator

Gulfshore Endoscopy Center, 1064 Goodletter Road, Naples, FL 33940

Harborside Surgery Center, 610 East Olympia Avenue, Punta Gorda, FL 33950

HealthSouth Central Florida Outpatient Surgery Center, 11140 West Colonial Drive, Suite Three, Ocoee, FL 34761; tel. 407/656-2700; FAX. 407/877-9432; Antonio Caos, M.D., Medical Director

HealthSouth Citrus Surgery Center, 110 North Lecanto Highway, Lecanto, FL 34461; tel. 352/527-1825; FAX. 352/527-1827; Douglas Vybiral, Facility Administrator

HealthSouth Collier Surgery Center, 800 Goodlette Road, N., Suite 120, Naples, FL 33940; tel. 813/262-5757; FAX. 813/262-6073; Donna Rae Malone, Administrator

HealthSouth Emerald Coast Surgery Center, 995 Northwest Mar Walt Drive, Fort Walton Beach, FL 32547; tel. 904/863-7887; FAX. 904/863-4955; Teresa French, Facility Administrator

HealthSouth Indian River Surgery Center, 1200 37th Street, Vero Beach, FL 32960; tel. 407/770-5600; FAX. 407/770-1793; Regina Ludicke, Clinical Administrator

HealthSouth Melbourne Surgery Center, 624 East Hibiscus Boulevard, Suite 101, Melbourne, FL 32901; tel. 407/729-9493; FAX. 407/768-6043; Robert C. Miner, Administrator

HealthSouth Oakwater Surgical Center, 3885 Oakwater Circle, Suite B, Orlando, FL 32806; tel. 407/438-9533; FAX. 407/438-9542; Doug Oakley, Business Office Manager

HealthSouth Orlando Center for Outpatient Surgery, 1405 South Orange Avenue, Suite 400, Orlando, FL 32806; tel. 407/426-8331; FAX. 407/425-9582

Hialeah Ambulatory Care Center, 445 East 25th Street, Hialeah, FL 33176; tel. 305/691-4450; FAX. 305/693-0823; Jose Kone, Administrative Director

Highlands Surgery Center, 7200 South George Boulevard, Sebring, FL 33872; tel. 941/471-6336; FAX. 941/471-6654; Mary Roger, Administrator

Institute for Plastic and Reconstructive Surgery, 820 Arthur Godfrey Road, Third Floor, Miami Beach, FL 33140; tel. 305/673-6164; FAX. 305/534-9759; Lawrence B. Robbins, M.D.

Jacksonville Surgery Center, 4253 Salisbury Road, Jacksonville, FL 32216; tel. 904/281-0021; FAX. 904/281-0988; Katherine Anderson, RN, B.S.N., Center Director

Johnson Eye Institute Surgery Center, Inc., 5923 Seventh Street, Zephyrhills, FL 33539; tel. 813/788-7656; FAX. 813/788-6011; Jane Dempsey, RN, Surgery Services Coordinator

Kimmel Outpatient Surgical Center, 903 45th Street, West Palm Beach, FL 33407; tel. 407/845-8343; FAX. 407/840-8970; Pamela V. Burgering, Administrator

Lake Surgery and Endoscopy Center, 8100 CR 44A, Leesburg, FL 34788

Lazenby Eye Care Center, 1109 U.S. Highway 19, Suite B, Holiday, FL 34691; tel. 813/934-5705; Laverne Peyton, Administrator

Lee County Center for Foot and Ankle Surgery, Inc., 12734 Kenwood Lane, Suite 44, Fort Myers, FL 33907; tel. 941/936-2454; FAX. 941/936-1974; Steve Ostendorf, D.P.M.

Leesburg Regional Day Surgery Center, 601 East Dixie Avenue, Plaza 501, Leesburg, FL 34748; tel. 904/365-0700; FAX. 904/365-0758; Renae Vaughn, RN, B.S.N., CNOR, Clinical Director

Lowrey Eye Clinic, 1840 North Highland Avenue, Clearwater, FL 34615-1915; tel. 813/442-4147; FAX. 813/446-9297; Miquel E. Mulet, Jr., M.D.

Manatee Endoscopy Center, Inc., 6010 Pointe West Boulevard, Bradenton, FL 34209; tel. 813/792-4239

Martin Memorial SurgiCenter, 509 Riverside Drive, Suite 100, Stuart, FL 34994; tel. 407/223-5920; FAX. 407/288-1821

Martin Memorial Surgicenter at St. Lucie West, 1095 Northwest St. Lucie West Boulevard, Port St. Lucie, FL 34986; tel. 561/223-5945, ext. 6678; FAX. 561/223-6862; Charles S. Immordino, RN, Director, Clinical Operations

Mayo Clinic Jacksonville Ambulatory Surgery Center for G.I., 4500 San Pablo Road, Jacksonville, FL 32224; tel. 904/223-2000; Evelyn Leddy, ASC for GI Coordinator

Mayo Outpatient Surgery Center, 4500 San Pablo Road, Jacksonville, FL 32224

Mease Countryside Ambulatory Care Center, 1880 Mease Drive, Safety Harbor, FL 34695; tel. 813/726-2873; FAX. 813/791-4317; William G. Harger, Administrator

Medical Development Corporation of Pasco County, 7315 Hudson Avenue, Hudson, FL 34667; tel. 813/868-9563, ext. 251; FAX. 813/869-6918; Dawn M. Ernst, Director, Nursing

Medical Partners Surgery Center, 4545 Emerson Expressway, Jacksonville, FL 32207; tel. 904/399-2600; Kim Chitty, Director

Medivision of Northern Palm Beach County, 2889 10th Avenue, N., Suite 201, Lake Worth, FL 33461; tel. 407/969-0139; FAX. 407/642-1167; Denise Brower, Administrator

Medivision of Orange County, 116 West Sturtevant Street, Orlando, FL 32806; tel. 407/423-4090; Margie Brill, Administrator

Miami Eye Center, 619 Northwest 12th Avenue, Miami, FL 33136; tel. 305/326-0260; FAX. 305/326-1907; Edward C. Gelber, M.D., F.A.C.S.

Mid Florida Surgery Center, 17564 West Highway 441, Mt. Dora, FL 32757; tel. 904/735-4100; FAX. 904/735-2444; Patsy Lentz, RN, Administrative Director

Montgomery Eye Center, 700 Neapolitan Way, Naples, FL 33940; tel. 813/261–8383; FAX. 813/261–8448; Mary Lee Montgomery, Administrator

Mullis Eye Institute, Inc., 1600 Jenks Avenue, Panama City, FL 32405; tel. 904/763–6666; FAX. 904/763–6665; O. Lee Mullis, M.D., Administrator

Naples Day Surgery, 790 Fourth Avenue, N., Naples, FL 33940; tel. 813/263–3863; FAX. 813/263–7429; Sara May McCallum, Executive Director

Naples Day Surgery North, 11161 Health Park Boulevard, Naples, FL 34110; tel. 813/598–3111; FAX. 813/598–1707; Sara May McCallum, Executive Director

New Smyrna Beach Ambulatory Care Center, Inc., 612 Palmetto Street, New Smyrna Beach, FL 32168; tel. 904/423–5500

Newgate Surgery Center, Inc., 5200 Tamiami Trail, Suite 202, Naples, FL 34103; tel. 941/263–6766; FAX. 941/263–3320; Dr. R. Crane

North Florida Eye Clinic Surgicenter, 590 Dundas Drive, Jacksonville, FL 32218; tel. 904/751–3600; FAX. 904/757–8922; Mary Miller, RN, Director Surgical Services

North Florida Surgery Center, 4600 North Davis, Pensacola, FL 32503; tel. 904/494–0048; FAX. 904/494–0065; D. M. Whitehead, Administrator, Chief Executive Officer

North Florida Surgery Center, 2745 South First Street, Lake City, FL 32025; tel. 904/758–8937; Angela Kohlhepp, Administrator

North Florida Surgical Pavilion, 6705 Northwest 10th Place, Gainesville, FL 32605; tel. 352/333–4555; FAX. 352/333–4569; Becky Hite, Administrative Director

North Ridge Surgery Center, 4650 North Dixie Highway, Fort Lauderdale, FL 33334; tel. 305/772–7995

Northwest Florida Gastroenterology Center, Inc., 202 Doctors Drive, Panama City, FL 32405; tel. 904/769–7599; FAX. 904/769–7389

Northwest Florida Surgery Center, 767 Airport Road, Panama City, FL 32405; tel. 904/747–0400; FAX. 904/913–9744; Ron Samuelian, Chief Executive Officer

Oak Hill Ambulatory Surgery and Endoscopy Center, 11377 Cortez Boulevard, Spring Hill, FL 34613; tel. 904/597–3060; FAX. 904/597–3077

Orange Park Surgery Center, 2050 Professional Center Drive, Orange Park, FL 32073; tel. 904/272–2550; FAX. 904/272–7911; Michele K. Cook, RN, Administrator, Nursing Director

Orlando Surgery Center, LTD., 2000 North Orange Avenue, Orlando, FL 32804; tel. 407/894–5808; FAX. 407/894–7802; Pat Churchwell, Administrator

Ormond Eye Surgi Center, 26 North Beach Street, Suite A, Ormond Beach, FL 32174; tel. 904/673–3344; FAX. 904/672–1854; Karen S. LaMotte, RN, Assistant Administrator

Pal–Med Same Day Surgery, 6950 West 20th Avenue, Hialeah, FL 33016; tel. 305/821–0079, ext. 321; FAX. 305/558–7494; Mario Machado, RN, Director

Palm Beach Endoscopy Center, 2015 North Flagler Drive, West Palm Beach, FL 33407; tel. 407/659–6543; FAX. 407/659–3533

Palm Beach Eye Clinic, 130 Butler Street, West Palm Beach, FL 33407; tel. 407/832–6113; FAX. 407/833–3003; Andre J. Golino, M.D.

Palm Beach Lakes Surgery Center, 2047 Palm Beach Lakes Boulevard, West Palm Beach, FL 33409; tel. 561/684–1375; FAX. 561/683–0332; Marjorie F. Konigsberg, Administrator

Parikh Volusia Ambulatory Surgery Center, 598 Sterthaus Avenue, Ormond Beach, FL 32174; tel. 904/673–2262; FAX. 904/677–3808; Robin Hess, Administrator

Physician's Surgical Care Center, 2056 Aloma Avenue, Winter Park, FL 32792; tel. 407/647–5100; FAX. 407/647–1966

Physicians Ambulatory Surgery Center, 300 Clyde Morris Boulevard, Suite B, Ormond Beach, FL 32174; tel. 904/672–1080; FAX. 904/672–8628

Physicians Surgery Center, Ltd., 4035 Evans Avenue, Fort Myers, FL 33901; tel. 941/939–7375; FAX. 941/275–5248; Caryl A. Serbin, RN, Administrator

Pinebrook Surgery Center, 14540 Cortez Boulevard, Brooksville, FL 34613; tel. 904/596–1130, ext. 7260; FAX. 904/596–1063

Premier Medical Group, P.A., Surgical Center of Florida, 1799 Woolbright Road, Boynton Beach, FL 33426; tel. 407/737–5500; FAX. 407/737–7055; Lily Lee, Administrator

Premier Surgery Center of Zephyrhills, 37834 Medical Arts Court, Zephyrhills, FL 33541; tel. 813/782–8778; FAX. 813/782–2811; Debra Fortenberry, RN, Director, Nursing

Presidential Surgicenter, Inc., 1501 Presidential Way, Suite Nine, West Palm Beach, FL 33401; tel. 407/689–7255; FAX. 407/683–7342; Steve S. Spector, M.D.

Rand Surgical Pavillion Corp., Five West Sample Road, Pompano Beach, FL 33064; tel. 800/782–1711; FAX. 954/782–7490; Deborah Rand, Administrator

Reed Centre for Ambulatory Urological Surgery, 1111 Kane Concourse, Suite 311, Bay Harbor, FL 33154; tel. 305/865–2000

Riverside Park Surgicenter, 2001 College Street, Jacksonville, FL 32204; tel. 904/355–9800; Janice Carter, RN, Director, Nursing

Same–Day Surgicenter of Orlando, Ltd., 88 West Kaley Street, Orlando, FL 32806; tel. 407/423–0573; Barbara Starr, Administrator

Samuel Wells Surgicenter, Inc., 3599 University Boulevard, S., Suite 604, Jacksonville, FL 32216; tel. 904/399–0905; FAX. 904/346–0757; Faye T. Evans, Administrator

San Pablo Surgery Center, 14444 Beach Boulevard, Suite 50, Jacksonville, FL 32250; tel. 904/223–7800; FAX. 904/223–0081; Kim Chitty, Director

Santa Lucia Surgical Center Inc., 2441 Southwest 37th Avenue, Miami, FL 33145; tel. 305/442–0066; FAX. 305/445–6896

Sarasota Surgery Center, 983 South Beneva Road, Sarasota, FL 34232; tel. 813/365–5355; FAX. 813/953–7080; Margo Post, Administrator

Seven Springs Surgery Center, Inc., 2024 Seven Springs Boulevard, New Port Richey, FL 34655; tel. 813/376–7000; Barbara Perich, Administrator

Southwest Florida Endoscopy Center, 5050 Mason Corbin Court, Ft. Myers, FL 33907; tel. 813/275–6678; FAX. 813/275–1785; Nancy Rhodes, Administrator

Southwest Florida Institute of Ambulatory Surgery, 3700 Central Avenue, Suite Two, Ft. Myers, FL 33901; tel. 941/275–0665; Susan Hanzevack, Executive Director

St. Augustine Endoscopy Center, 212 South Park Circle, E., St. Augustine, FL 32086; tel. 904/824–6108; Michael D. Schiff, M.D., President

St. John's Surgery Center, Inc., Conference Drive, Southpointe Commercial Park, Fort Myers, FL 33919; tel. 941/481–8833; FAX. 941/481–7898

St. Joseph's Same Day Surgery Center, 3003 West Martin Luther King Boulevard, Tampa, FL 33607; tel. 813/870–4711; FAX. 813/870–4907; Paula McGuiness, Executive Director

St. Lucy's Outpatient Surgery Center, 21275 Olean Boulevard, Port Charlotte, FL 33952; tel. 813/625–1325; FAX. 813/625–6482; Anthony Limoncelli, M.D.

St. Luke's Surgical Center, 43309 U.S. Highway 19, N., P.O. Box 5000, Tarpon Springs, FL 34688–5000; tel. 813/938–2020; FAX. 813/938–5606; Glenn S. Wolfson, M.D., Medical Director

St. Petersburg Medical Clinic P.A., Ambulatory Surgery Center, 1099 Fifth Avenue, N., St. Petersburg, FL 33705–1419; tel. 813/821–1221, ext. 8740; FAX. 813/892–8770; Iverson Pace, RN, Facility Manager, Director of Nursing, SPMC

St. Petersburg Surgery Center, 539 Pasadena Avenue, S., St. Petersburg, FL 33707; tel. 813/345–8337; FAX. 813/347–4675; Patty Grover, Administrator

Suburban Medical Ambulatory Surgical Center, 17615 Southwest 97th Avenue, Miami, FL 33157; tel. 305/255–3950; FAX. 305/233–2503; Jules G. Minkes, D.O., Administrator

Suncoast Endoscopy Center, 601 Seventh Street, S., St. Petersburg, FL 33701; tel. 813/824–7116; FAX. 813/824–7177; Denise Epstein, RN, Director, Nursing

Suncoast Eye Center, Eye Surgery Institute, 14003 Lakeshore Boulevard, Hudson, FL 34667; tel. 813/868–9442; FAX. 813/862–6210; Lawrence A. Seigel, M.D., P.A., Medical Director

Suncoast Skin Surgery Clinic, 4519 U.S. Highway 19, New Port Richey, FL 34652; tel. 813/849–8922; FAX. 813/841–7553; Bethany Carvallo, Administrator

Suncoast Surgery Center of Hernando, Inc., 5060 Commercial Way, Spring Hill, FL 34606; tel. 904/596–3696; FAX. 904/596–2707; Bethany Carvallo, Administrator

Sunrise Surgical Center, 110 Yorktowne Drive, Daytona Beach, FL 32119; tel. 904/788–6696

Surgery Center of Jupiter, Inc., 102 Coastal Way, Jupiter, FL 33477; tel. 407/747–1111; FAX. 407/747–4151; Jane MacDonald, Administrator

Surgery Center of North Florida, Inc., 6520 Northwest Ninth Boulevard, Gainsville, FL 32615; tel. 352/331–7987; FAX. 352/331–2787; Joy Ingram, Administrator

Surgery Center of Ocala, 3241 Southwest 34th Avenue, Ocala, FL 34474; tel. 352/237–5906; FAX. 352/237–5785; Verla Heffrin, Administrator

Surgical Center of Central Florida, 3601 South Highlands Avenue, Sebring, FL 33870; tel. 813/382–7500; FAX. 813/385–7332; Sharon Keiber, RN, Administrator

Surgical Licensed Ward, 110 West Underwood Street, Suite B, Orlando, FL 32806; tel. 407/648–9151; FAX. 407/426–7017; Cheryl Modica, RN, Administrator

Surgical Park Center, Ltd., 9100 Southwest 87th Avenue, Miami, FL 33176; tel. 305/271–9100; FAX. 305/270–8527; Deborah O'Connor, Administrator

Surgicare Center, 4101 Evans Avenue, Ft. Myers, FL 33901; tel. 813/939–3456; FAX. 813/939–1164; Robin Fox, Administrative Coordinator

Surgicare Center of Venice, 950 Cooper Street, Venice, FL 34285; tel. 813/485–4868; FAX. 813/484–4084; Cherie Mooney, Administrator

Tallahassee Endoscopy Center, 2400 Miccosukee Road, Tallahassee, FL 32308; tel. 904/877–2105; FAX. 904/942–1761; Noel Withers, Administrator

Tallahassee Outpatient Surgery Center, Inc., 3334 Capital Medical Boulevard, Suite 500, Tallahassee, FL 32308; tel. 904/877–4688; FAX. 904/877–0368; Martin Shipman, Administrator

Tallahassee Single Day Surgery, 1661 Phillips Road, Tallahassee, FL 32308; tel. 904/878–5165; FAX. 904/942–9711; Susan Kizirian, Executive Director

Tampa Bay Surgery Center, Inc., 11811 North Dale Mabry, Tampa, FL 33618; tel. 813/961–8500; FAX. 813/968–6818; Jay L. Rosen, M.D., Executive Director

Tampa Eye Surgery Center, 4302 North Gomez, Tampa, FL 33607; tel. 813/870–6330; FAX. 813/871–3956; Margie Brill, Administrator

Tampa Outpatient Surgical Facility, 5013 North Armenia Avenue, Tampa, FL 33603; tel. 813/875–0562; FAX. 813/875–1983; Dianne Pugh, Facility Administrator

The Aesthetic Plastic Surgery Center, 135 San Marco Drive, Venice, FL 34285; tel. 941/484–6836; Claudell Crowe, Administrative Director

The Center for Digestive Health, 12700 Creekside Lane, Suite 202, P.O. Box 60157, Fort Myers, FL 33919; tel. 941/489–4454; FAX. 941/489–2114

The Endoscopy Center of Naples, 150 Tamiami Trail, N., Suite One, Naples, FL 34102; tel. 941/262–6665; Marjorie Rogers, Office Manager

The Endoscopy Center of Pensacola, Inc., 4810 North Davis Highway, Pensacola, FL 32503; tel. 904/474–8988; FAX. 904/478–9903; Alice Cartee, Administrator

The Endoscopy Center, Inc., 5101 Southwest Eighth Street, Miami, FL 33134

The Eye Associates Surgery Center, 6002 Pointe West Boulevard, Bradenton, FL 34209; tel. 941/792–2020; FAX. 941/792–2832; Linda Colson, RN, Director

The Gastrointestinal Center of Hialeah, 135 West 49th Street, Hialeah, FL 33012; tel. 305/825–0500; FAX. 305/826–6910; Darlene Boytell, M.S.N, ARNP

The Ocala Eye Surgery Center, 3330 Southwest 33rd Street, Ocala, FL 34474; Carol Hiatt, RN, Nurse Administrator

The Sheridan Surgery Center, 95 Bulldog Boulevard, Melbourne, FL 32901; tel. 407/952–9800; FAX. 407/952–7889; Patrice Curtis, RN, Clinical Director

The Treasure Coast Cosmetic Surgery Center, 1901 Port St. Lucie Boulevard, Port St. Lucie, FL 34952; tel. 407/335–3954; Donato A. Viggiano, M.D.

Total Surgery Center, 130 Tamiami Trail, Suite 210, Naples, FL 33940; tel. 941/434–4118; FAX. 941/434–6343; Elizabeth Ross, Administrator

Treasure Coast Center for Surgery, 1411 East Ocean Boulevard, Stuart, FL 34996; tel. 561/286–8028; FAX. 561/283–6628; Andrea Scoville, Business Office Manager

Trinity Outpatient Center, 2101 Trinity Oaks Boulevard, New Port Richey, FL 34655; tel. 813/372–4000; FAX. 813/372–4082; Nancy Burden, Director

United Surgical Center, 2589 North State Road Seven, Lauderhill, FL 33313

University Surgical Center, Inc., 7251 University Boulevard, Suite 100, Winter Park, FL 32792; tel. 407/677–0066; FAX. 407/677–4199; Laura Hofma, RRA, Director, Operations

Urological Ambulatory Surgery Center, Inc., 1812 North Mills Avenue, Orlando, FL 32803; tel. 407/897–5499; FAX. 407/894–8746; Susan A. Wuerz, Administrator

Urology Center of Florida, Inc., 3201 Southwest 34th Street, Ocala, FL 34474; tel. 904/237–8100; FAX. 904/237–5684; Christopher S. Hill, Administrator

Urology Health Center, 5652 Meadow Lane, New Port Richey, FL 34652; tel. 813/842–9561; FAX. 813/848–7270; Greg Toney, Administrator

Venture Ambulatory Surgery Center, Inc., 16853 Northeast Second Avenue, Suite 400, North Miami Beach, FL 33162; tel. 305/652–2999; FAX. 305/652–8156; Claire D. Maze, RN, B.S.N., Clinical Director

Vero Eye Center, 70 Royal Palm Boulevard, Vero Beach, FL 32960; tel. 407/569–6600

Volusia Endoscopy & Surgery Center, Inc., 550 Memorial Circle, Suite G, Ormond Beach, FL 32174; tel. 904/672–0017; FAX. 904/676–0506

Winter Park Ambulatory Surgical Center, 1000 South Orlando Avenue, Winter Park, FL 32789; tel. 407/629–1500; FAX. 407/629–1741; Linda Dingman, Administrator

GEORGIA

Advanced Aesthetics Plastic Surgery Center, 499 Arrowhead Boulevard, Jonesboro, GA 30236; tel. 770/603–6000; FAX. 770/603–7064; Paul D. Feldman, President

Advanced Surgery Center of Georgia, 220 Hospital Road, Canton, GA 30114; tel. 770/479–2202; FAX. 770/479–6666; Debbie Moore, Administrator

Aesthetic Laser & Surgery Facility, 416 Gordon Ave., Thomasville, GA 31792–6644; tel. 912/228–7200; Judy Warmack, Administrator

Aesthetica, P.C., 975 Johnson Ferry Road, Suite 500, Atlanta, GA 30342; tel. 404/256–1311; FAX. 404/705–2774; G. Marshall Franklin, Jr., Administrator

Affinity Outpatient Services, 712 East 18 Street, Tifton, GA 31794; tel. 912/382–3814; Barry L. Cutts, Administrator

Albany Ambulatory Surgery Center, 531 Seventh Avenue, Albany, GA 31701; tel. 912/883–3535; FAX. 912/888–1079; J. Kenneth Durham, Medical Director

Ambulatory Foot and Leg Surgical Center, 1650 Mulkey Road, Austell, GA 30001; tel. 404/941–3633; Alan Shaw, D.P.M., Chief Executive Officer

Ambulatory Laser and Surgery Center, 425 Forest Parkway, Suite 103, Forest Park, GA 30050; tel. 404/363–1087; FAX. 404/363–9951; Dr. Paul A. Colon, Administrator

Ambulatory Surgical Facility of Brunswick, Eight Tower Medical Park, 3215 Shrine Road, Brunswick, GA 31520; tel. 912/264–4882; Jimmy L. Dixon, Administrator

Athens Plastic Surgery Clinic, 2325 Prince Avenue, Athens, GA 30606; tel. 706/546–0280; FAX. 404/548–0258; James C. Moore, M.D., Administrator

Atlanta Aesthetic Surgery Center, Inc., 4200 Northside Parkway, Building Eight, Atlanta, GA 30327; tel. 404/233–3833; Debbie Clotfelter, Administrator

Atlanta Endoscopy Center, LTD, 2665 North Decatur Road, Suite 545, Decatur, GA 30033; tel. 404/297–5000; FAX. 404/296–9890; Ronda L. Knapp, RN, Clinical Coordinator

Atlanta Eye Surgery Center, P.C., 3200 Downwood Circle, NW, Suite 200, Atlanta, GA 30327; tel. 404/355–8721; Robert J. Allen, Administrator

Atlanta Outpatient Peachtree Dunwoody Center, 5505 Peachtree–Dunwoody Road, Suite 150, Atlanta, GA 30342; tel. 404/847–0893; FAX. 404/843–8664; Janie Ellison, Administrator

Atlanta Outpatient Surgery Center, 993 Johnson Ferry Road, Suite 300, Atlanta, GA 30342; tel. 404/252–3074; FAX. 404/843–2089; Marjane Ellison, Administrator

Atlanta Surgi–Center, Inc., 1113 Spring Street, Atlanta, GA 30309; tel. 404/892–8608; FAX. 404/892–8143; Elizabeth Petzelt, Administrator

Atlanta Women's Medical Center, Inc., 235 West Wieuca Road, Atlanta, GA 30342; tel. 404/257–0057; FAX. 404/257–1245; Ann Garzia, Administrator

Augusta Plastic Surgery Center, Inc., 811 13th Street, Suite 28, Richmond, GA 30901–2772; tel. 706/724–5611; Pat McBride, Administrator

Augusta Surgical Center, 915 Russell Street, Augusta, GA 30904–4115; tel. 404/738–4925; Beryl Barrett, Administrator

Brunswick Endoscopy Center, 3217 4th Street, Brunswick, GA 31520–3759; tel. 912/267–0445; Rita Warren, Administrator

Center for Plastic Surgery, Inc., 365 East Paces Ferry Road, Atlanta, GA 30305; tel. 404/814–0868; Dr. Vincent Zubowicz, Medical Director

Center for Reconstructive Surgery, 5335 Old National Highway, College Park, GA 30349; tel. 404/768–3668; FAX. 404/763–2929; Gregory Alvarez, D.P.M.

Clayton Outpatient Surgical Center, Inc., 6911 Tara Boulevard, Jonesboro, GA 30236; tel. 770/477–9535; FAX. 770/471–7826; Yvonne Guettler, Operating Room Supervisor

Cobb Foot and Leg Surgery Center, 792 Church Street, Suite Two, Marietta, GA 30060; tel. 404/422–9864; FAX. 404/984–0303; Glya Lewis, Administrator

Coliseum Same Day Surgery, 310 Hospital Drive, P.O. Box 6154, Macon, GA 31208; tel. 912/742–1403; FAX. 912/742–1671; Michael Boggs, Chief Executive Officer, Executive Director

Columbia Augusta Surgical Center, 915 Russell Street, Augusta, GA 30904; tel. 706/738–4925; FAX. 706/738–7224; Beryl Barrett, RN, Administrator

Columbia County Medical Plaza–Surgery, 635 Washington West, Evans, GA 30809; tel. 706/868–1050; Jeff Simless, Assistant Vice President, Finance

Columbus Ambulatory Surgery Center, 725–22nd Street, Columbus, GA 31904–8845; tel. 706/322–6335; Freda R. Stewart, Administrator

Columbus Women's Health Organization, Inc., 3850 Rosemont Drive, Columbus, GA 31901; tel. 404/323–8363

DeKalb Endoscopy Center, 2675 North Decatur Road, Suite 506, Decatur, GA 30033; tel. 404/299–1679; FAX. 404/501–7558; Peter Leff, M.D.

Decatur Urological Clinic–Ambulatory Surgery Center, Inc., 428 Winn Court, Decatur, GA 30030; tel. 404/292–3727; FAX. 404/294–9674; Diane Moore, RN, M.B.A., Administrator

Dennis Surgery Center, Inc., 3193 Howell Mill Road, Suite 215, Atlanta, GA 30327; tel. 404/355–1312; Valerie Garrett, Administrator

Dunwoody Outpatient Surgicenter, Inc., 4553 North Shallowford Road, Suite 6, Atlanta, GA 30338; tel. 770/457–6303; FAX. 770/457–2823; Maureen Little, Administrator

Endoscopy Center of Columbus, 1041 Talbotton Road, Columbus, GA 31904–8745; tel. 706/327–0700; Jean Patterson,R.N., Administrator

Endoscopy Center of Southeast Georgia, Inc., 200 Maple Drive, P.O. Box 1367, Vidalia, GA 30475; tel. 912/537–9851; Dixie Calhoun, RN, Administrator

Feminist Women's Health Center, 580 14th Street, N.W., Atlanta, GA 30318; tel. 404/874–7551; FAX. 404/875–7644; Jan Lockridge, Administrator

Friedrich Surgical Center, 2916 Glynn Avenue, Brunswick, GA 31530; tel. 912/265–3210; Ann Friedrich, Administrator

G.I. Endoscopy Center, 6555 Professional Place, Suite B, Riverdale, GA 30274; tel. 404/996–8830; FAX. 404/991–1596; Aruna Jaya Prakash, Administrator

Gainesville Surgery Center, 1945 Beverly Road, Gainesville, GA 30501–2034; tel. 770/287–1500; Mary W. Hoffman, Administrator

Gastrointestinal Endoscopy of Gwinnett, 600 Professional Drive, Suite 130, Lawrenceville, GA 30245; tel. 770/995–7989; FAX. 770/339–8646; Elizabeth Bonner, Office Manager

Georgia Lithotripsy Center, 120 Trinity Place, Athens, GA 30607; tel. 404/543–2718; David C. Allen, M.D., Administrator

Georgia Surgical Centers – South, 541 Forest parkway, Suite 14, Forest Park, GA 30297–6110; tel. 404/366–5652; Trudy Hunley, Administrator

Gwinnet Endoscopy Center, 575 Professional Drive, Suite 150, Lawrenceville, GA 30245; tel. 770/822–5560; FAX. 770/822–4989; Kerry H. King, M.D., President

HealthSouth Surgery Center of Atlanta, 1140 Hammond Drive, Building F, Suite 6100, Atlanta, GA 30328; tel. 770/551–9944; FAX. 770/551–8826; Nichole Busch, Administrator

HealthSouth Surgery Center of Gwinnett, 2131 Fountain Drive, Snellville, GA 30278; tel. 770/979–8200; FAX. 770/979–1327; Dianne Barrow, RN, Administrator

Hollis Eye Surgery Center, Inc., 7351 Old Moon Road, Columbus, GA 31909; tel. 706/323–8127; Kenneth Hopkins, Administrator

Marietta Surgical Center, Ambulatory Surgery Division, Columbia Healthcare Corporation, 796 Church Street, Marietta, GA 30060; tel. 770/422–1579; FAX. 770/422–1057; Charlotte Bellantoni, Administrator

Medical Eye Associates, Inc., 1429 Oglethorpe Street, Macon, GA 31201; tel. 912/743–7061; FAX. 912/743–6296; Susan Branand, Office Manager

Midtown Urology Surgical Center, 128 North Avenue, N.E., Suite 100, Atlanta, GA 30308; tel. 404/881–0966; FAX. 404/874–5902; Jenelle E. Foote, M.D., Administrator

North Atlanta Endoscopy Center, 5555 Peachtree–Dunwoody Road, Suite G70, Atlanta, GA 30342–1703; tel. 404/843–0500; Phyllis Pritchett, Administrator

North Atlanta Endoscopy Center, L.P., 5555 Peachtree–Dunwoody Road, Suite G–70, Atlanta, GA 30342; tel. 404/843–0500; FAX. 404/843–0675; Laura Dixon, Clinical Supervisor

North Atlanta Head and Neck Surgery Center, 980 Johnson Ferry Road, Northside Doctors Building, Suite 110, Atlanta, GA 30342; tel. 404/256–5428; Ramon S. Franco, M.D.

North Fulton Diagnostic Gastrointestinal, 2500 Hospital Boulevard, Suite 480, Roswell, GA 30076; tel. 770/475–3085; David A. Atefi, M.D.

North Georgia Endoscopy Center, Inc., 320 Hospital Road, Canton, GA 30114; tel. 770/479–5535; FAX. 770/479–8821; Florene Brookshire, Administrator

North Georgia Outpatient Surgery Center, 795 Red Bud Road, Calhoun, GA 30701; tel. 706/629–1852; Herbert E. Kosmahl, President

North Oak Ambulatory Surgical Center, 2718 North Oak Street, Valdosta, GA 31602; tel. 912/242–3668; FAX. 912/242–9905; A. R. Pitts, Jr., D.P.M.

Northeast Georgia Plastic Surgery Center, 1296 Sims Street, Gainesville, GA 30501; tel. 404/534–1856; FAX. 404/531–0355; Sam Richwine, Medical Director

Northlake Ambulatory Surgical Center, 2193 Northlake Parkway, Building 12, Suite 114, Tucker, GA 30084–4113; tel. 770/938–4860; Winfield Butlin, Administrator

Northlake Endoscopy Center, 1459 Montreal Road, Suite 204, Tucker, GA 30084; tel. 770/939–4721; FAX. 770/939–1187; Gayle Carter, Administrator

Northlake–Tucker Ambulatory Surgery Center, 1491 Montreal Road, Tucker, GA 30084; tel. 404/934–1984; FAX. 404/493–4900; Doris Boye–Mintz

Northside Foot and Ankle Outpatient Surgical Center, 3415 Holcomb Bridge Road, Norcross, GA 30092; tel. 770/449–1122; FAX. 770/242–8709; Steven T. Arminio, Administrator

Northside Hospital Outpatient Surgical Center, 3400–A State Bridge Road, Suite 240, Alpharetta, GA 30202; tel. 404/667–4060; Sidney Kirscher, Administrator

Northside Surgery Center, Inc., 5505 Peachtree–Dunwoody Road, Suite 115, Atlanta, GA 30358–2091; tel. 404/843–1008; Irving Miller, Administrator

Northside Women's Clinic, Inc., 3543 Chamblee–Dunwoody Road, Atlanta, GA 30341; tel. 404/455–4210; FAX. 404/451–9529; James W. Gay, M.D., Administrator

Outpatient Center for Foot Surgery, 730 South Eighth Street, Griffin, GA 30224; tel. 770/228–6644; FAX. 770/228–5769; Janice Parker, Administrator

Paces Plastic Surgery Center, Inc., 3200 Downwood Circle, Suite 640, Atlanta, GA 30327; tel. 404/351–0051; FAX. 404/351–0632; Robert Cole, Administrator

Parkwood Ambulatory Surgical Center, 2605 Parkwood Drive, Brunswick, GA 31520; tel. 912/265–4766; FAX. 912/267–9857; Betty Bauer, RN

Piedmont Surgery Center, 4660 Riverside Park Boulevard, Macon, GA 31210; tel. 912/471–6300; Mikell Peed, Administrator

Planned Parenthood of East Central Georgia, 1289 Broad Street, Augusta, GA 30911; tel. 706/724–5557; FAX. 706/724–5293; Mary Beth Peirucci, Administrator

Podiatric Surgi Center, 215 Clairemont Avenue, Decatur, GA 30030; tel. 404/373-2529; FAX. 404/370-1688; Jerald N. Kramer, President

Pulliam Ambulatory Surgical Center, 4167 Hospital Drive, Covington, GA 30209, P.O. Box 469, Covington, GA 30210; tel. 404/786-1234; M.M. Pulliam, P.C., Medical Director

Resurgens Surgical Center, 5671 Peachtree Dunwoody Road, Suite 800, Atlanta, GA 30342; tel. 404/847-9999; Kay F. Elliott, RN

Roswell Ambulatory Surgery Center, 1240 Upper Hembree Road, Roswell, GA 30076; tel. 770/663-8011

Savannah Medical Clinic, 120 East 34th Street, Savannah, GA 31401; tel. 912/236-1603; FAX. 912/236-1605; William Knorr, M.D., Administrator

Savannah Outpatient Foot Surgery Center, 310 Eisenhower Drive, Suite Seven, Savannah, GA 31406; tel. 912/355-6503; Dr. Kalman Baruch, President

Savannah Plastic Surgicenter, 4750 Waters Avenue, Suite 505, Savannah, GA 31404; tel. 912/351-5050; Dr. E. D. Deloach

Southeastern Fertility Institute Surgical Associates, 5505 Peachtree Dunwood Road, Suite 400, Atlanta, GA 30342; tel. 404/257-1900; FAX. 404/256-1528; Ron Davidson, Administrator

Southlake Ambulatory Surgery Center, 4000 Corporate Center Drive, Suite 100, Morrow, GA 30260-1407; tel. 770/960-2701; Robert Rhymer, Administrator

Statesboro Ambulatory Surgery Center, 95 Bel-Air Drive, Statesboro, GA 30461-6879; tel. 912/489-6519; FAX. 912/764-7882; Dianne Collins, Office Manager

Surgery Center of Rome, 16 John Maddox Drive, Rome, GA 30161; tel. 404/234-0315; Jan Routledge, Director

The Cosmetic and Plastic Surgicenter of South Atlanta, 6524 Professional Place, Riverdale, GA 30274; tel. 770/991-1733; FAX. 770/997-7204; Nabil Elsahy, M.D.

The Emory Clinic Ambulatory Surgery Center, 1365 Clifton Road, N.E., Atlanta, GA 30322; tel. 404/778-5000; W. Mike Mason, Administrator

The Foot Surgery Center, 2520 Windy Hill Road, Suite 105, Marietta, GA 30067; tel. 770/952-0868; L. Susan Rothstein, Administrator

The Rome Endoscopy Center, Inc., 16 John Maddox Drive, Rome, GA 30165; tel. 706/295-3992; FAX. 706/290-5384; Connie Barris, Administrator

Tifton Endoscopy Center, Inc., 1111 E. 20th Street, Tifton, GA 31794-3668; tel. 912/382-9338; Sharon M. Brogdon, Administrator

HAWAII

Aloha Eye Clinic and Surgical Center Ltd., 239 East Wakea Avenue, Kahului, HI 96732; tel. 808/877-3984; FAX. 808/871-6498; Russell T. Stodd, M.D., Administrator

Cataract and Retina Center of Hawaii, 1712 Liliha Street, Suite 400, Honolulu, HI 96817; Worldster Lee, M.D., Administrator

Hawaiian Eye Surgicenter, 606 Kilani Avenue, Wahiawa, HI 96786; tel. 808/621-8448; FAX. 808/621-2082; John M. Corboy, M.D., Surgeon, Director

Kaiser Honolulu Clinic, 1010 Pensacola Street, Honolulu, HI 96814; tel. 808/593-2950; Jonathan Gans, Administrator

Kaiser Wailuku Clinic, 80 Mahalani Street, Wailuku, HI 96793; tel. 808/243-6000; FAX. 808/243-6009; Mary Hew, Clinics Manager

Surgical Suites at Thomas Square, 1100 Ward Avenue, Suite 1001, Honolulu, HI 96814; tel. 808/521-2305; FAX. 808/599-4818; Gerald D. Faulkner, M.D., President

Surgicare of Hawaii, Inc., 550 South Beretania Street, Honolulu, HI 96813; tel. 808/528-2511; FAX. 808/526-0651; Eileen M. Peyton, Facility Manager

The Endoscopy Center, 134 Pu'uhou Way, Hilo, HI 96720; tel. 808/969-3979; FAX. 808/935-7657; Jody Montell, Administrator

IDAHO

Boise Center for Foot Surgery, 1400 West Bannock, Boise, ID 83702; tel. 208/345-1871; FAX. 208/368-9707; Marshall D. Ogden, D.P.M., Medical Director

Boise Gastroenterology Associates, P.A., Idaho Endoscopy Center, 5680 West Gage, Boise, ID 83706; tel. 208/378-2894; Samuel S. Gibson, M.D., President

Coeur D'Alene Foot and Ankle Surgery Center, 101 Ironwood Drive, Suite 131, Coeur D'Alene, ID 83814; tel. 208/666-0814; Stephen A. Isham, D.P.M., Chairman, Board of Directors

Coeur d'Alene Surgery Center, 2121 Ironwood Center Drive, Coeur d'Alene, ID 83814; tel. 208/765-9059; FAX. 208/664-9998; Peter C. Jones, M.D., President

Emerald Surgical Center, 811 North Liberty, Boise, ID 83704; tel. 208/323-4522; FAX. 208/376-5258; Stanley B. Leis, D.P.M., Medical Director

Idaho Ambucare Center, Inc., 211 West Iowa, Nampa, ID 83686; tel. 208/467-4222; FAX. 208/466-0328; Gary Botimer, Administrator

Idaho Eye Surgicenter, 2025 East 17th Street, Idaho Falls, ID 83404; tel. 208/524-2025; FAX. 208/529-1924; Kenneth W. Turley, M.D., Medical Director

Idaho Falls Surgical Center, 1945 East 17th Street, Idaho Falls, ID 83404; tel. 208/529-1945; James A. Haney, M.D., Medical Director

Idaho Foot Surgery Center, 782 South Woodruff, Idaho Falls, ID 83401; tel. 208/529-8393; FAX. 208/529-8078; Bruce G. Tolman, D.P.M., Facility Director

Jefferson Day Surgery Center, 220 West Jefferson, Boise, ID 83702; tel. 208/343-3802; William Stano, President

Lake City Surgery Center, 2201 Ironwood Place, Suite B, Coeur d'Alene, ID 83814; tel. 208/667-9362; FAX. 208/765-1310; Rachel Muthersbaugh, Director

North Idaho Cataract and Laser Center, Inc., 1814 Lincoln Way, Coeur d'Alene, ID 83814; tel. 208/667-2531; Paul Wail, Administrator

North Idaho Day Surgery and Laser Center, Inc., 2205 North Ironwood Place, Coeur d'Alene, ID 83814; tel. 208/664-0543; FAX. 208/765-2867; Michael P. Christensen, M.D., President

Pacific Cataract and Laser Institute, 250 Bobwhite Court, Suite 100, Boise, ID 83706-3983; tel. 208/385-7576; Debbie Eldredge, Vice President, Chief Operating Officer

Rock Creek Endoscopy Center, 284 Martin Street, Suite Two, Twin Falls, ID 83301; tel. 208/734-1266; FAX. 208/736-0390; Arlene Hansen, Administrator

South Idaho Surgery Center, 191 Addison Avenue, Twin Falls, ID 83301; tel. 208/734-5993; David A. Blackmer, D.P.M., President

Surgicare Center of Idaho, L.C., 360 East Mallard Drive, Suite 125, Boise, ID 83706; tel. 208/336-8700; W. Andrew Lyle, M.D., Medical Director

The Surgery Center, 115 Falls Avenue, W., P.O. Box 1864, Twin Falls, ID 83303-1864; tel. 208/733-1662; FAX. 208/734-3632; Larry Maxwell, M.D., Administrator

ILLINOIS

25 East Same Day Surgery, 25 East Washington, Chicago, IL 60602; tel. 312/726-3329; FAX. 312/726-3823; Tom Mallon, Administrator

A.C.T. Medical Center, 5714 West Division Street, Chicago, IL 60651; tel. 312/921-4300; Anthony Centrachio, Administrator

A.C.U. Health Center, LTD., 736 York Road, Hinsdale, IL 60521; tel. 630/794-0645; Lisa Shyne, Administrator

Able Health Center, Ltd., 1640 Arlington Heights Road, Suite 110, Arlington Heights, IL 60004; tel. 847/255-7400

Access Health Center, Ltd., 1700 75th Street, Downers Grove, IL 60516; tel. 630/964-0000; FAX. 630/964-0047; Diane L. Duddles, R.N., Administrator

Advantage Health Care, LTD., 203 E. Irving Park Road, Wood Dale, IL 60191; tel. 630/595-1515; Lynn Pfingsten, Administrator

Albany Medical Surgical Center, 5086 North Elston, Chicago, IL 60630; tel. 312/725-0200; FAX. 312/725-6152; Diana Lammon, Administrator

Alton Surgical and Imaging Center L.L.C., 4325 Alby, P.O. Box 3195, Alton, IL 62002; tel. 618/474-8000, ext. 8052; FAX. 618/474-8054; Bruce T. Vest, Jr., M.D., Director, Surgery

AmSurg/Columbia HCA, 330 North Madison Street, Joliet, IL 60435; tel. 815/744-3000; FAX. 815/744-7916; Anne M. Cole, Administrator

Ambulatory Surgicenter of Downers Grove, Ltd., 4333 Main Street, Downers Grove, IL 60515; tel. 630/810-0212; Inga Ferdkoff, M.D., Administrator

American Women's Medical Center, 2744 North Western, Chicago, IL 60647; tel. 773/772-7726; FAX. 773/772-3696; Jan Barton, M.D., Administrator

Arlington Health Center, Ltd., 1640 Arlington Heights Road, Suite 210, Arlington Heights, IL 60004; tel. 847/255-7474

Bel-Clair Ambulatory Surgical Treatment Center, 325 West Lincoln, Belleville, IL 62220; tel. 618/235-2299; FAX. 618/235-2556; David Horace, Administrator

Bio Enterprises, Ltd., P.O. Box 56069, Chicago, IL 60656-0069; tel. 312/266-1235; Laura Palomino

CMP Surgicenter, 3412 West Fullerton Avenue, Chicago, IL 60647; tel. 773/235-8000; FAX. 773/235-7018; Carlos G. Baldoceda, M.D., Medical Director

Carbondale Clinic Ambulatory Surgical Treatment Center, 2601 West Main Street, Carbondale, IL 62901; tel. 618/549-5361, ext. 218; FAX. 618/549-5128; William R. Hamilton, M.D., Chief Executive Officer, Medical Director

Carle Clinic Association, 1702 South Mattis Avenue, Champaign, IL 61821; tel. 217/326-2030; Julie Root, RN, Administrator

Center for Reconstructive Surgery, 6309 West 95th Street, Oak Lawn, IL 60453; tel. 708/499-3355; FAX. 708/423-2305; Lori Brown, Administrator

Chang's Medical Arts Surgicenter, Apple Tree Health Care, 2809 North Center Street, Maryville, IL 62062; tel. 618/288-1882; FAX. 618/288-3575; Donna Evans, RN

Children's Outpatient Services at Westchester, 2301 Enterprise Drive, Westchester, IL 60154; tel. 708/947-4000; FAX. 708/947-4044; Jan Jennings, Administrator

Columbia Surgery Center of Southern Illinois, New Route 13 West, P.O. Box 1729, Marion, IL 62959; tel. 618/993-2113; FAX. 618/993-2041; Linda Bickers, RN, Administrator

Columbia Surgicare–North Michigan Avenue, L.P., 60 East Delaware, 15th Floor, Chicago, IL 60611; tel. 312/440-5100; FAX. 312/440-5114; Barbara Villa, Administrator

Columbia–Northwest Surgicare, 1100 West Central Road, Arlington Heights, IL 60005; tel. 847/259-3080; FAX. 847/259-3190; Barbara Cerwin, RN, Administrator

Community Health and Emergency Services, R.R. 1, Box 11, P.O. Box 233, Cairo, IL 62914; tel. 618/734-4400, ext. 303; FAX. 618/734-2884; Frederick L. Bernstein, Executive Director

Concord Medical Center, 17 West Grand, Chicago, IL 60610; tel. 312/467-6555; FAX. 312/467-9683; Elizabeth Reiker, Administrator

Concord West Medical Center, Ltd., 530 North Cass Avenue, Westmont, IL 60559; tel. 630/963-2500; Faramarz Farahati, Managing Director

Day SurgiCenters, Inc., 18 South Michigan Avenue, Suite 700, Chicago, IL 60603; tel. 312/726-2000; FAX. 312/726-3921; Andy Andrikos, Regional Vice President

Day Surgicenters, Inc., One South 224 Summit Avenue, Suite 201, Oakbrook Terrace, IL 60181; tel. 630/916-7008; Andrew Andrikos, Administrator

Dimensions Medical Center, Ltd., 1455 East Golf Road, Suite 108, Des Plaines, IL 60016; tel. 847/390-9300; FAX. 847/390-0035; Vera Schmidt, Administrator

Doctors Surgicenter, Ltd., 1045 Martin Luther King Jr. Drive, Centralia, IL 62801; tel. 618/532-3110; FAX. 618/532-7226; Charles K. Fischer, M.D., Medical Director

Dreyer Ambulatory Surgery Center, 1221 North Highland Avenue, Aurora, IL 60506; tel. 630/264-8400; James Kuyper, R.N., Administrator

Eastland Medical Plaza SurgiCenter, 1505 Eastland Drive, Bloomington, IL 61701; tel. 309/662-2500, ext. 1284; FAX. 309/662-7143; Marsha Reeves, Administrator

Edwardsville Ambulatory Surgical Center, LLC, 12, Ginger Creek Parkway, Glen Carbon, IL 62034; tel. 618/656-8200; FAX. 618/656-8204; Maxine Johnson, Interm Administrator

Effingham Ambulatory Surgical Treatment Center, LTD., 904 West Temple Street, Effingham, IL 62401; tel. 217/342-1234; FAX. 217/342-1230; Leanne Fish, RN, CNOR, Administrator

Foot and Ankle Surgical Center, Ltd., 1455 Golf Road, Suite 134, Des Plaines, IL 60016; tel. 847/390-7666; Lowell S. Weil, DPM, FACFS, Administrator

Golf Surgical Center, 8901 Golf Road, Des Plaines, IL 60016; tel. 847/299-2273; FAX. 847/299-2297; Bernard Abrams, M.D., Administrator

Hauser-Ross Surgicenter, Inc., 2240 Gateway Drive, Sycamore, IL 60178; tel. 815/756-8571; FAX. 815/756-1226; Barbara Lauger, Administrator

HealthSouth Surgery Center of Hawthorn, 1900 Hollister Drive, Suite 100, Libertyville, IL 60048; tel. 847/367–8100; FAX. 847/367–8335; James Kartsimas, Administrator

Hinsdale Surgical Center, Inc., 908 North Elm Street, Suite 401, Hinsdale, IL 60521; tel. 630/325–5035; FAX. 630/325–5134; Shirley E. Zemansky, RN, Administrator

Hope Clinic for Women, Ltd., 1602 21st Street, Granite City, IL 62040; tel. 618/451–5722; Sally Burgess–Griffin, Director

Horizons Ambulatory Surgery Center, 630 Locust Street, Carthage, IL 62321; tel. 217/357–2173; James E. Coeur, M.D., Administrator

Hugar Surgery Center, 1614 North Harlem Avenue, Elmwood Park, IL 60635; tel. 708/452–6102; FAX. 708/452–1614; Frank A. Salvino, FACHA, Administrator

Illinois Eye Surgeons Cataract Surgery, 3990 North Illinois Street, Belleville, IL 62221; tel. 618/235–3100; Cathy Vieluf, Administrator

Ingalls Same Day Surgery, 6701 West 159th Street, Tinley Park, IL 60477; tel. 708/429–0222; FAX. 708/429–0293; Jeffry A. Peters, Administrator

LP Central Community Halth Centre, 355 East Fifth Ave., P.O. Box 68, Clifton, IL 60927; tel. 815/694–2392; Steve Wilder, Administrator

Lakeshore Physicians and Surgery Center, 7200 North Western Avenue, Chicago, IL 60645; tel. 312/743–6700; FAX. 312/761–9226; Phyllis J. Allen, RN, Administrator

Magna Surgical Center, 9831 South Western Avenue, Chicago, IL 60643; tel. 312/445–9696; FAX. 312/445–9590; Terrence Longo, Administrator

Midwest Ambulatory Surgicenter, 7340 West College Drive, Palos Heights, IL 60463; tel. 708/361–3233; FAX. 708/361–4876; Thomas A. Evans, Administrator

Midwest Center for Day Surgery, 3811 Highland Avenue, Downers Grove, IL 60515; tel. 630/852–9300; FAX. 630/852–7773; Ronald P. Ladniak, Administrator

Midwest Eye Center, S.C., 1700 East West Road, Calumet City, IL 60409; tel. 708/891–3330; FAX. 708/891–0904; Afzal Ahmad, MD, Administrator

Naperville Surgical Centre, 1263 Rickert Drive, Naperville, IL 60540; tel. 630/305–3300; FAX. 630/305–3301; Ronald P. Ladniak

National Health Care Services of Peoria, Inc., 7501 N. University Road, Suite 200, Peoria, IL 61614; tel. 309/691–9073; Margaret A. Vanduyn

North Shore Endoscopy Center, 101 South Waukegan Road, Suite 980, Lake Bluff, IL 60044; tel. 847/604–8700; FAX. 847/604–8711; Everett P. Kirch, M.D., Administrator

North Shore Outpatient Surgicenter, L.P., 815 Howard Street, Evanston, IL 60202; tel. 847/869–8500; FAX. 847/869–0028; Edward Atkins, M.D., Medical Director

Northern Illinois Surgery Center, 1620 Sauk Road, Dixon, IL 61021; tel. 815/288–7722; James R. Zeman, Administrator

Northern Illinois Women's Center, Ltd., 1400 Broadway Street, Suite 201, Rockford, IL 61104; tel. 815/963–4101; FAX. 815/963–6122; Deborah D. Demars, Administrator

Northwest Community Day Surgery Center, 675 West Kirchoff Road, Arlington Heights, IL 60005; tel. 847/506–4361; FAX. 847/577–4001; Meaghan Reshoft, Administrator

Notre Dame Hills Surgical Center, 28 North 64th Street, Belleville, IL 62223; tel. 618/398–5705; FAX. 618/398–5764; Kathleen Claunch, RN, Administrator

Nova Med Eye Surgery Center of Maryville, L.L.C., 12 Maryville Professional Center, Maryville, IL 62062; tel. 618/288–7483; Adrienne Forsythe, Administrator

NovaMed Eye Surgery Center River Forest, 7427 Lake Street, River Forest, IL 60305; tel. 708/771–3334; FAX. 708/771–0841; John G. Yeatman, Administrator

NovaMed Eye Surgery Center–Northshore, 3034 West Peterson Avenue, Chicago, IL 60659; tel. 312/973–7432; FAX. 312/973–1119; Susan Vaughn, Administrator

Oak Brook Surgical Centre, Inc., 2425 West 22nd Street, Oak Brook, IL 60521; tel. 630/990–2212; FAX. 630/990–3130; George H. Olsen, Administrator

Oak Park Eye Center, S.C., 7055–61 West North Avenue, Oak Park, IL 60302; tel. 708/848–1182; FAX. 708/848–5033; James L. McCarthy, M.D., Administrator

One Day Surgery Center, 4211 North Cicero Avenue, Chicago, IL 60641–1699; tel. 773/794–1000, ext. 228; FAX. 773/794–9738; Christopher Lloyd, Administrator

Orthopedic Institute of Illinois Ambulatory Surgery Center, 303 North Kumpf Boulevard, Peoria, IL 61605; tel. 309/676–5559; FAX. 309/676–5045; Donna Adair, Administrator

Paulina Surgi–Center, Inc., 7616 North Paulina, Chicago, IL 60626; tel. 312/761–0500; Sheldon Schecter, Administrator

Peoria Ambulatory Surgery Center, 4909 North Glen Park Place, Peoria, IL 61614; tel. 309/691–9069; FAX. 309/691–9286; Carl W. Soderstrom, MD, Administrator

Peoria Day Surgery Center, 7309 North Knoxville, Peoria, IL 61614; tel. 309/692–9210; FAX. 309/692–9055; Wanda Spacht, RN, CNOR, Nursing Administrator

Physicians' Surgical Center, Ltd., 311 West Lincoln, Suite 300, Belleville, IL 62220; tel. 618/233–7077; FAX. 618/234–5650; Cindy Chapman, RN, Administrator

Planned Parenthood of East Central Illinois, 302 East Stoughton Street, Champaign, IL 61820; tel. 217/359–4768; FAX. 217/359–2683; Terri Giesing, Administrator

Poplar Creek Surgical Center, 1800 McDonough Road, Hoffman Estates, IL 60192; tel. 847/742–7272; FAX. 847/697–3210; JoAnn Uteg, Administrative Director

Quad City Ambulatory Surgery Center, 520 Valley View Drive, Moline, IL 61265; tel. 309/762–1952; FAX. 309/762–3642; Vicki Sullivan, RN, CNOR, Director, Surgical Services

Quad City Endoscopy, 2525 24th Street, Rock Island, IL 61201; tel. 309/788–5624; FAX. 309/788–5668; Najwa Bayrakdar, Administrator

Regional Surgicenter, Ltd., 545 Valley View Drive, Moline, IL 61265; tel. 309/762–5560; FAX. 309/762–7351; Patt Hunter, Administrator

Resurrection Health Care Surgery Center, 3101 North Harlem Avenue, Chicago, IL 60634; tel. 773/282–9700, ext. 304; FAX. 312/745–5522; Sandra Ankebrant, Executive Director

River North Same Day Surgery, One East Erie, Suite 115, Chicago, IL 60611; tel. 312/649–3939; FAX. 312/649–5747; Patricia Wamsley, Administrator

Rockford Ambulatory Surgery Center, 1016 Featherstone Drive, Rockford, IL 61107; tel. 815/226–3300; FAX. 815/226–9990; Dr. Steven Gunderson, Administrator

Rockford Endoscopy Center, 401 Roxbury Road, Rockford, IL 61107; tel. 815/397–7340; FAX. 815/397–7388; Nancy Norman, Administrator

South Shore Surgicenter, Inc., 8300 South Brandon Avenue, Chicago, IL 60617; tel. 312/721–6000; FAX. 312/721–9861; Lucy Morales, RN, Administrator

Spiritus Dei Eye Surgery Center, 7600 West College Drive, Palos Heights, IL 60463; tel. 708/361–0010; Audrey Schmidt–Annerino, Administrator

Springfield Clinic Ambulatory Surgical Treatment Center, Inc., 1025 South Seventh Street, Springfield, IL 62794–9248; tel. 217/528–7541; Michael Maynard

Springfield Clinic Ambulatory Surgical Treatment Center, Inc., 1025 S. Seventh Street, Springfield, IL 62794–7541; tel. 217/528–7541; J. Michael Maynard, Administrator

Suburban Otolaryngology SurgiCenter, 3340 South Oak Park Avenue, Berwyn, IL 60402; tel. 708/749–3070; FAX. 708/749–3410; Edward A. Razim, M.D., Administrator

Surgicare Center, Inc., 333 Dixie Highway, Chicago Heights, IL 60411; tel. 708/754–4890; FAX. 708/756–1149; Paul Katz, Administrator

Surgicore, Inc., 10547 South Ewing Avenue, Chicago, IL 60617; tel. 773/221–1690; William Wood, DPM, Medical Director

The Center for Orthopedic Medicine, LLC, 2502–B East Empire, Bloomington, IL 61704; tel. 309/662–6120; FAX. 309/663–8972; Tracy J. Silver, RN, Administrator

The Center for Surgery, 475 East Diehl Road, Naperville, IL 60563–1253; tel. 630/505–7733; FAX. 630/505–0656; Eric Myers, Administrator

Valley Ambulatory Surgery Center, 2210 Dean Street, St. Charles, IL 60175; tel. 630/584–9800; FAX. 630/584–9805; Mark Mayo, Facility Director

Watertower Surgicenter Corp., 845 North Michigan Avenue, Suite 994–W, Chicago, IL 60611; tel. 312/944–2929; FAX. 312/944–7769; John M. Sevcik, President, Chief Executive Officer

Women's Aid Clinic, 4751 West Touhy Avenue, Lincolnwood, IL 60646; tel. 847/676–2428; Iris Schneider

INDIANA

Aesthetic Surgery Center, 13590 N. Meridian, Carmel, IN 46032; tel. 317/846–0846; FAX. 317/846–0722; William H. Beeson, MD, Medical Director

Akin Medical Center, 2019 State Street, New Albany, IN 47150–4963; tel. 812/945–3557; FAX. 812/949–3469; Karyn Cureton, RN, Director, Surgery

Broadwest Surgical Center, 315 W. 89th Ave., Merrillville, IN 46410–2904; tel. 219/757–5275; FAX. 219/757–5290; Lisa M. Goranovich, Administrator

Calumet Surgery Center, 7847 Calumet Avenue, Munster, IN 46321–1296; tel. 219/836–5102; FAX. 219/836–2249; Gloria J. Portney, RN, Chief Administrative Officer

Central Indiana Surgery Center, 9002 North Meridian, Lower Level, Indianapolis, IN 46260; tel. 317/846–9906; FAX. 317/846–9949; William E. Whitson, M.D., Medical Director

Columbia Physiciancare Outpatient Surgery Center, L.L.P., 7460 North Shadeland, Indianapolis, IN 46250; tel. 317/577–7450; FAX. 317/577–7462; Maureen Chernoff, RN, Administrator

Columbus Surgery Center, 940 North Marr Road, Suite B, Columbus, IN 47201; tel. 812/372–1370; Colleen M. North, Executive Director

Digestive Health Center, 1120 AAA Way, Suite A, Carmel, IN 46032–3210; tel. 317/848–5494; FAX. 317/575–0392; Daniel J. Stout, M.D., President

Dupont Ambulatory Surgery Center, 2510 East Dupont Road, Suite 130, Fort Wayne, IN 46825; tel. 219/489–8785; FAX. 219/489–2148; Rick C. Trego, Administrator

Evansville Surgery Center, 1212 Lincoln Ave., Evansville, IN 47714–1076; tel. 812/428–0810; FAX. 812/421–6070; Cathy Head, RN, Facility Manager

Foot and Ankle Surgery Center, Inc., 1950 West 86th Street, Suite 105, Indianapolis, IN 46260; tel. 317/334–0232; FAX. 317/334–0268; Anthony E. Miller, D.P.M., Administrator

Fort Wayne Cardiology Outpatient Catheterization Laboratory, 1819 Carew Street, Fort Wayne, IN 46805; tel. 219/481–4896; FAX. 219/481–4814; Douglas W. Martin, Director, Clinical Operations

Fort Wayne Ophthalmic Surgical Center, 321 East Wayne Street, Ft. Wayne, IN 46802–2713; tel. 219/422–5976; FAX. 219/424–4511; J. Rex Parent, M.D., Chief Executive Officer

Fort Wayne Orthopaedics LLC Surgicenter, 7601 West Jefferson Boulevard, P.O. Box 2526, Fort Wayne, IN 46801–2526; tel. 219/436–8383; FAX. 219/436–8585; Ronald W. Cousino, Jr., Administrator

Gastrointestinal Endoscopy Center, 801 St. Mary's Drive, Suite 110 West, Evansville, IN 47714; tel. 812/477–6103; FAX. 812/477–4897; Christine Wittman, Administrator

Grand Park Surgical Center, 1479 East 84th Place, Merrillville, IN 46410; tel. 219/738–2828; FAX. 219/756–3349; Chris Macarthy, Administrator

Grossnickle Eye Surgery Center, Inc., 2251 DuBois Drive, Warsaw, IN 46580–3292; tel. 219/269–3777; FAX. 219/269–9828; Shirley Rhodes, RN, Administrative Director

IMA Endoscopy Surgicenter, P.C., 8895 Broadway, Merrillville, IN 46411; tel. 219/738–2081; FAX. 219/736–4658; Dawn Graham, Administrator

Illiana Surgery Center, 701 Superior Avenue, Munster, IN 46321; tel. 219/924–1300; FAX. 219/922–4856; Virgil Villaflor, Executive Director

Indiana Eye Clinic, 30 North Emerson Avenue, Greenwood, IN 46143–9760; tel. 317/881–3931; FAX. 317/887–4008; Charles O. McComnick, M.D., Administrator

Indiana Surgery Center, 8040 Clearvista Parkway, Indianapolis, IN 46256–1695; tel. 317/841–2000; FAX. 317/841–2005; Amy Glover, Administrator

Indiana Surgery Center – North Campus, 8040 Clearvista Parkway, Indianapolis, IN 46256; tel. 317/841–2000; FAX. 317/841–2005; Amy D. Glover, RN, BSN, Administrator

Indiana Surgery Center, South Campus, 1550 East County Line Road, Suite 100, Indianapolis, IN 46227; tel. 317/887–7600; FAX. 317/887–7687; Peggy Davidson, Administrator

Indianapolis Endoscopy Center, 7353 East 21st Street, Indianapolis, IN 46219; tel. 317/353–2232; FAX. 317/353–2522; David Hollander, M.D.

Section C

Lafayette Ambulatory Surgery Center, 3733 Rome Drive, Box 6477, Lafayette, IN 47905–6477; tel. 765/449–5272; FAX. 765/449–5856; Dale T. Krynak, Executive Director

MHC Surgical Center Associates, Inc., d/b/a Broadwest Surgical Center, 315 West 89th Avenue, Merrillville, IN 46410–2904; tel. 219/757–5275; FAX. 219/757–5290; Lisa M. Goranovich, Administrator

Medivision, 1305 Wall Street, Suite 101, Jeffersonville, IN 47130–3898; tel. 812/288–9674; FAX. 812/283–6955; Marsha Parker, Administrator

Meridian Endoscopy Center, 1801 North Senate, Suite 400, Indianapolis, IN 46202; tel. 317/929–5660; FAX. 317/929–2346; Robert J. Whitmore, Executive Director

Meridian Plastic Surgery Center, 170 West 106th Street, Indianapolis, IN 46290–1004; tel. 317/575–0110; FAX. 317/846–5719; Sally Gentner, Director

Michiana Endoscopy Center, LLC, 53822 Generation Drive, South Bend, IN 46635; tel. 219/234–2024; John G. Mathis, MD, CEO

Midwest Surgery Centers, Inc., 650 Surgery Center Drive, Terre Haute, IN 47802; tel. 812/232–8325; FAX. 812/234–8385; Terry Havens, RN, Administrator

Muncie Ambulatory Surgicenter, LLC, 200 North Tillotson Avenue, Muncie, IN 47304–3988; tel. 765/286–8888; FAX. 765/747–7962; L. Marshall Roch, M.D., Medical Director

Munster Same Day Surgery Center, 761 Forty Fifth Avenue, Suite 116, Munster, IN 46321; tel. 219/924–3090; FAX. 219/924–2161; Edward Atkins, President

Nasser Smith and Pinkerton Cardiac Cath Lab, 8333 Naab Road, Suite 400, Indianapolis, IN 46260; tel. 317/338–6094; FAX. 317/338–6066; Stephen A. McAdams, M.D., CEO

North Indianapolis Surgery Center, 8651 North Township Line Road, Indianapolis, IN 46260–1578; tel. 317/876–2090; FAX. 317/876–2097; Dean E. Lehmkuhler, Facility Administrator

North Meridian Surgery Center, 10601 North Meridian, Indianapolis, IN 46290; tel. 317/574–5400; FAX. 317/575–2713; Susan Mantouk, Director

Northeast Indiana Endoscopy Center, 7900 West Jefferson Boulevard, Fort Wayne, IN 46804; tel. 219/436–6213; FAX. 219/432–6388; Jerry Steele, Administrator

Northside Cardiac Cath Lab, 8333 Naab Road, Suite 180, Indianapolis, IN 46260; tel. 317/338–9001; FAX. 317/338–9045; Mary Ellen Boyd, RN, MSN, Clinical Manager

NovaMed Eyecare Management, L.L.C., d/b/a NovaMed Eye Surgery Center–Hammond, 6836 Hohman Avenue, Hammond, IN 46324; tel. 219/937–5063; FAX. 219/937–5068; Renee Peters, Administrator

NovaMed Eyecare Management, L.L.C., 8514 Broadway, Merrillville, IN 46410; tel. 219/756–5010; FAX. 219/736–2222; Joan Klug, Administrator

Oakview Surgical Center, Inc., 120 E. 18th St., Rochester, IN 66975; tel. 219/224–7500; Laurence C. Rogers, D.P.M., Administrator

Outpatient Surgery Center of Indiana, Inc., 711 Gardner Drive, Marion, IN 46952; tel. 317/664–2000; FAX. 317/668–6797; Sheryl Miller, RN, Director

Richmond Surgery Center, 1900 Chester Boulevard, Richmond, IN 47374; tel. 317/966–1776; FAX. 317/962–1191; Debra Day, Director

Riverpointe Surgery Center, 500 Arcade Avenue, Elkhart, IN 46514–2459; tel. 219/523–3475; Robert Scheller, Administrator

Sagamore Surgical Services, Inc., 2320 Concord Road, Suite B, Lafayette, IN 47905; tel. 317/474–7838; FAX. 317/474–7853; Carol Blanar, Administrator

South Bend Clinic Surgicenter, 211 North Eddy Street, P.O. Box 4061, South Bend, IN 46634–4061; tel. 219/237–9366; FAX. 219/237–9363; Kevin R. Boyer, Administrator

Southern Indiana Surgery Center, 2800 Rex Grossman Boulevard, Bloomington, IN 47403; tel. 812/333–8969; FAX. 812/335–2309; Miriam Malone, RN, B.S.N., Executive Director

Surgery Center Plus, 7430 North Shadeland Avenue, Suite 100, Indianapolis, IN 46250–2025; tel. 317/841–8005; FAX. 317/577–7538; James Hansen, Administrator

Surgery Center of Eye Specialists, 1901 North Meridian Street, Indianapolis, IN 46202; tel. 317/925–2200; FAX. 317/921–6614; Dan Bradford, Administrator

Surgery Center of Fort Wayne, L. P., d/b/a Premier Ambulatory Surgery Center, 1333 Maycrest Drive, Fort Wayne, IN 46805–5478; tel. 219/423–3339; FAX. 219/423–6344; Mary Schafer, Administrator

Surgery Center of Southeastern Indiana, Inc., 999 N. Michigan Ave., Greensburg, IN 47240; tel. 812/663–3222; FAX. 812/663–3622; Charlotte Boden, BSN, RN

Surgery One, 5052 North Clinton, Fort Wayne, IN 46825–5822; tel. 219/482–5194; FAX. 219/482–5686; Rich Hively, Administrator

Surgical Care Center, Inc., 8103 Clearvista Parkway, Indianapolis, IN 46256–4600; tel. 317/842–5173; FAX. 317/576–9644; Larry Gardner, Executive Director

Surgical Center of New Albany, 2201 Green Valley Road, New Albany, IN 47150–4648; tel. 812/949–1223; FAX. 812/945–4765; Tamara E. Jones, BSN, Administrator

Surgicare, 2907 McIntire Drive, Bloomington, IN 47403; tel. 812/332–8765; FAX. 812/336–3425; Sonya M. Zeller, Administrator

Talley Cataract and Laser Institute, Inc., 220 East Virginia, Evansville, IN 47711; tel. 812/435–1600; FAX. 812/435–1603; Patricia S. Fisher, Facility Manager

The Ambulatory Care Center, 1125 Professional Boulevard, Evansville, IN 47714; tel. 812/475–1000; FAX. 812/475–1001; Diana McDaniel, Clinical Administrator

The Center for Specialty Surgery of Fort Wayne, Inc., 2730 East State Boulevard, Fort Wayne, IN 46805–4731; tel. 219/483–2540; FAX. 219/483–3097, ext. 2; Andrea Kelley, RN, Director, Nursing

The Endoscopy Center, 8051 South Emerson, Suite 150, Indianapolis, IN 46237; tel. 317/865–2950; FAX. 317/865–2952; Robert Intress, Ph.D., Administrator

The Heart Group Outpatient Cath Lab, 415 West Columbia Street, Evansville, IN 47710; tel. 812/464–9133; FAX. 812/426–6023; Lisa Attebery, Director, Ancillary Services

The Indiana Hand Surgery Center, 8501 Harcourt Road, P.O. Box 80434, Indianapolis, IN 46260–0434; tel. 317/875–9105; FAX. 317/875–8638; Mark S. Fritz, Chief Executive Officer

Unity Surgery Center, 1011 West Second Street, Bloomington, IN 47403–2216; tel. 812/334–1213, ext. 250; FAX. 812/333–5039; Michael D. Bishop, MD, CEO

Valparaiso Physician and Surgery Center, 1700 Pointe Drive, Valparaiso, IN 46383; tel. 219/531–5000; FAX. 219/531–5010; Lilly Veljovic, RN, Manager

Welborn Clinic Surgery Center, 421 Chestnut Street, Evansville, IN 47713; tel. 812/426–9412; Claudia R. Earnest, Administrator

Zollman Surgery Center, Inc., 7439 Woodland Drive, Indianapolis, IN 46268; tel. 317/328–1100; FAX. 317/328–6948; Julie Berzins, RN, Administrator

IOWA

Center for Day Surgery, 931 13th Ave., North, Clinton, IA 52733–0608; tel. 319/242–3937; Patricia McCeachron, Administrator

Iowa Endoscopy Center, 2600 Grand Avenue, Suite 418, Des Moines, IA 50312; tel. 515/288–3342; Gloria Dayton, Administrator

Iowa Eye Institute, 1721 West 18th Street, Spencer, IA 51301; tel. 712/262–8878; FAX. 712/262–8807; Dennis D. Gordy, M.D., Administrator

Jones Eye Clinic, 4405 Hamilton Boulevard, Sioux City, IA 51104; tel. 712/239–3937; Charles E. Jones, M.D., Medical Director

Land–Barowsky Ambulatory Surgery Center, Center for Sight, Iowa/Illinois, 931 13th Avenue, N., P.O. Box 608, Clinton, IA 52733–0608; tel. 319/242–3937; FAX. 319/242–3845; Renelda Ebensberger, Supervisor

Mississippi Valley Surgery Center, L.C., 3400 Dexter Court, Suite 200, Davenport, IA 52807; tel. 319/344–6600; FAX. 319/344–6699; John B. Dooley, Administrator

Surgery Center of Des Moines, 1301 Penn Avenue, Suite 100, Des Moines, IA 50312; tel. 515/266–3140; FAX. 515/266–3073; Kathleen Supplee, RN, Administrator

Tower Surgical Center, 3200 Grand Avenue, Des Moines, IA 50312; tel. 515/271–1735; FAX. 515/271–1726; Karen Stewart, Administrator

Uro Surgery Center, 3319 Spring Street, Suite 202–A, Davenport, IA 52807; tel. 319/355–6236; Paul Rohlf, M.D., Administrator

KANSAS

College Park Family Care Center, 11725 West 112th Street, Overland Park, KS 66210–2761; tel. 913/469–5579; Chuck Chambers, Administrator

Columbia Mt. Oread Surgery Centre, 3500 Clinton Parkway Place, Lawrence, KS 66047–1985; tel. 913/843–9300; FAX. 913/843–9301; Nancy Sturgeon, Administrator

Columbia Surgicenter of Johnson County, 8800 Ballentine Street, Overland Park, KS 66214–1985; tel. 913/894–4050; FAX. 913/894–0384; Nancy E. Sturgeon, Administrator

Comprehensive Health for Women, 4401 West 109th Street, Overland Park, KS 66211–1303; tel. 913/345–1400; Sheila Kostas, Director, Human Resources

Cotton–O'Neil Clinic Endoscopy Center, 823 Southwest Mulvane Street, Suite 375, Topeka, KS 66606–1679; tel. 913/354–0538; FAX. 913/368–0735; Irene Hasenbank, RN, Administrator

Emporia Ambulatory Surgery Center, 2528 West 15th Avenue, Emporia, KS 66801–6102; tel. 316/343–2233; J. E. Bosiljevac, M.D., Administrator

Endoscopic Services, P.A., 1431 South Bluffview Street, Suite 215, Wichita, KS 67218–3000; tel. 316/687–0234; FAX. 316/687–0360; Jace Hyder, M.D.

Endoscopy and Surgery Center of Topeka, L.P., 2200 Southwest Sixth Avenue, Suite 103, Topeka, KS 66606–1707; tel. 913/354–1254; FAX. 913/354–1255; Ashraf M. Sufi, M.D., Medical Director

EyeSurg of Kansas City, 5520 College Boulevard, Overland Park, KS 66211–1600; tel. 913/491–3757; FAX. 913/469–6686; Phillip Hoopes, M.D., Medical Administrator

Great Plains Clinic, 201 East Seventh, Hays, KS 67601; tel. 913/628–8251; William Norris, Administrator

Hutchinson Clinic Ambulatory Surgery Center, 2101 North Waldron, Hutchinson, KS 67502; tel. 316/669–2500; Murray Holcomb, Administrator

Kansas Ambulatory Surgery Center, 7015 East Central Street, Wichita, KS 67206–1940; tel. 316/684–9300; FAX. 316/652–7618; Robert G. Clark, M.D., Medical Director

Laser Center, 1518A East Iron Avenue, Salina, KS 67401–3236; tel. 913/825–6016; Brian E. Conner, M.D., Administrator

Laser Center–Russell, 222 South Kansas, Suite A, Russell, KS 67665–3029; tel. 913/825–6016; Brian Conner, Administrator

Microsurgery, Inc., 920 Southwest Washburn Avenue, Topeka, KS 66606–1527; tel. 913/233–3939; Adrienne V. Prokop, Administrator

Newman–Young Clinic–A.S.C., 710 West Eighth Street, Fort Scott, KS 66701–2404; tel. 316/223–3100; FAX. 316/223–5390; Thomas W. Smith, Administrator

Newton Surgery Centre, 215 South Pine Street, Newton, KS 67114–3761; tel. 316/283–4400; Sondra L. Leatherman, Administrator

Ochsner Eye Medical/Associated Eye Surgical Center, 1100 North Topeka Street, Wichita, KS 67214–2810; tel. 316/263–6273; FAX. 316/263–5568; Bruce B. Ochsner, Medical Director

South Pointe Surgery Center, 151 West 151st Street, Suite 200, Olathe, KS 66061–5351; tel. 913/782–3631; FAX. 913/782–2606; Katherine Thon, RN, Administrator

Surgery Center of Kansas, Inc., 1507 West 21st Street, Wichita, KS 67203–2449; tel. 316/838–8388; FAX. 316/838–2999; Karen Gabbert, RN, B.S.N., Administrator

Surgicare of Wichita, Inc., 810 North Lorraine, Wichita, KS 67214–4841; tel. 316/685–2207; FAX. 316/685–2861; Carolyn J. Exley, Administrator

Team Vision Surgery Center East, 6100 East Central Street, Suite Six, Wichita, KS 67208–4237; tel. 316/684–8013; Linda S. Buettner, Vice President

Team Vision Surgery Center West, 834 North Socora, Suite One, Wichita, KS 67212–3238; tel. 316/681–2020; Linda Buettner, Administrator

Section C

The Center for Same Day Surgery, 818 North Emporia Street, Suite 108, Wichita, KS 67214–3725; tel. 316/262–7263; FAX. 316/262–6253; Michele LeGate, RN, B.S., Administrator

The Headache and Pain Center, 11111 Nall Avenue, Suite 222, Leawood, KS 66211–1625; tel. 913/491–3999; FAX. 913/491–6453; Steven D. Waldman, Administrator

The Wichita Clinic DaySurgery, 3311 East Murdock Street, Wichita, KS 67208–3054; tel. 316/689–9349; James A. Greer, Jr., Administrator

Topeka Single Day Surgery, 823 Southwest Mulvane Street, Suite 101, Topeka, KS 66606–1679; tel. 913/354–8737; FAX. 913/354–1440; Linda Daniel, Executive Director

KENTUCKY

Ambulatory Surgery Center, 2831 Lone Oak Road, Paducah, KY 42003; tel. 502/554–8373; FAX. 502/554–8987; Laxmaiah Manchikanti, M.D.

Caritas Surgical Center, 4414 Churchman Avenue, Louisville, KY 40215; tel. 502/366–9525; Danny Cain

Center For Surgical Care, 7575 U.S. 42, Florence, KY 41042; tel. 606/283–9100; FAX. 606/283–6046; Thomas Mayer, M.D., Medical Director

Columbia Owensboro Surgery Center, 1100 Walnut Street, Suite 13, Owensboro, KY 42301; tel. 502/683–2751; FAX. 502/926–1618; Donna R. Norton, Administrator

Dupont Surgery Center, 4004 Dupont Circle, Louisville, KY 40207; tel. 502/896–6428; FAX. 502/895–6787; Vicki Lococo, Nurse Manager

E.M.W. Women's Surgical Center, 138 West Market Street, Louisville, KY 40202; tel. 502/589–2124; FAX. 502/589–1588; Dona F. Wells, Administrator

East Bernstadt Outpatient Surgery Center, 2737 North U.S. Highway 25, East Bernstadt, KY 40729; tel. 606/843–6100; Darby Radmanedsh, Administrator

HEALTHSOUTH Surge Center of Louisville, 4005 DuPont Circle, Louisville, KY 40207; tel. 502/897–7401; FAX. 502/897–5652; Sheila S. Boros, Administrator

Lexington Clinic, 1221 South Broadway, Lexington, KY 40504; tel. 606/258–4000; FAX. 606/258–4795; Thomas Holets, Executive Director

Lexington Surgery Center, 1725 Harrodsburg Road, Lexington, KY 40504; tel. 606/276–2525; FAX. 606/277–6497; Bemedji Asher, Administrator

Louisville Surgery Center, 614 East Chestnut Street, Louisville, KY 40202; tel. 502/589–9488; FAX. 502/589–9928; Jane E. Burbank, Administrator

McPeak Center For Eye Care, 1507 Bravo Boulevard, Glasgow, KY 42141; tel. 502/651–2181; FAX. 502/651–2183; Nancy McPeak, Administrator

Medical Heights Surgery Center, 2374 Nicholasville Road, Lexington, KY 40503; tel. 606/278–1460; FAX. 606/278–0115; John Johnson, Facility Director

Outpatient Care Center at Jewish Hospital, 225 Abraham Flexner Way, Louisville, KY 40202; tel. 502/587–4709; FAX. 502/587–4323; Kim Tharp–Barrie, Administrator

Pikeville United Methodist Hospital of Kentucky, Inc., 911 South By-Pass Road, Pikeville, KY 41501; tel. 606/437–3500; FAX. 606/432–9479; Martha O'Regan Chill, Administrator, Chief Executive Officer

Somerset Surgery Center, 353 Bogle Street, Suite 101, Somerset, KY 42501; tel. 606/679–9322; FAX. 606/678–2666; Kathy Turner, Administrator

Stone Road Surgery Center, 280 Pasadena Drive, Lexington, KY 40503; tel. 606/278–1316; FAX. 606/276–3847; Ballard Wright, President

Surgical Center of Elizabethtown, 708 Westport Road, Elizabethtown, KY 42701; tel. 502/737–5200; FAX. 502/765–5362; Suzanne Broadwater, Administrator

The Eye Surgery Center of Paducah, 100 Medical Center Drive, P.O. Box 8269, Paducah, KY 42002–8269; tel. 502/442–1024; FAX. 502/442–1001; Kelly Harris, RN, Administrator

Tri–State Digestive Disorder Center Ambulatory Surgery Center, 196 Barnwood Drive, Edgewood, KY 41017; tel. 606/341–3575; Stephen W. Hiltz, M.D.

LOUISIANA

Acadiana Endoscopy Center, 113 St. Louis Street, Lafayette, LA 70506; tel. 318/269–1126; FAX. 318/269–0553; Stephen M. Person, M.D., Administrator

Acadiana Surgery Center, Inc., 1100 Andre Street, Suite 300, New Iberia, LA 70560; tel. 318/364–9680; FAX. 318/364–9689

Alexandria Laser and Surgery Center, 4100 Parliment Drive, Alexandria, LA 71303; tel. 318/487–8342, ext. 318; FAX. 318/487–9942; M. L. Revelett, Administrator

Ambulatory Eye Surgery Center of Louisiana, 3900 Veterans Boulevard, Suite 100, Metairie, LA 70002; tel. 504/455–1550; FAX. 504/455–2011; Mark Brown, Administrator

Baton Rouge Ambulatory Surgicare Services, 5328 Didesse Drive, Baton Rouge, LA 70808; tel. 504/766–1718; FAX. 504/767–3034; Laura B. Cronin, Administrator

Broussard Surgery Institute, 1250 Pecanland Road, Suite E–1, Monroe, LA 71203; tel. 318/387–2015; FAX. 318/387–2097; Gerald Broussard, M.D., Administrator

Browne–McHardy Outpatient Surgery Center, 4315 Houma Boulevard, Metairie, LA 70006–2981; tel. 504/889–5218; FAX. 504/889–5224; Robert L. Goldstein, Chief Administrative Officer

Central Louisiana Ambulatory Surgical Center, 720 Madison Street, P.O. Box 8646, Alexandria, LA 71301; tel. 318/443–3511; Louise Barker, RN, Administrator

Colonnade Surgery, 555 South Ryan Street, Lake Charles, LA 70601; tel. 318/439–6226; FAX. 312/436–6223; Pam Ragusa, Administrator

Columbia Greater New Orleans Surgery Center, 3434 Houma Boulevard, Metairie, LA 70006; tel. 504/888–7100; Claire G. Manuel, RN, Administrator

Columbia Surgicare of Lake Charles, 214 South Ryan Street, Lake Charles, LA 70601; tel. 318/436–6941; FAX. 318/439–3384; Debbie Boudreaux, Administrator

Eye Care and Surgery Center, 10423 Old Hammond Highway, Baton Rouge, LA 70816; tel. 504/923–0960; FAX. 504/923–2419; M. Brian Roper

Foot Surgery Center of Shreveport, 9308 Mansfield Road, Suite 300, Shreveport, LA 71118; tel. 318/686–9622; Arnold M. Castellano, Administrator

Gamble Ambulatory Surgery Center, 2601 Line Avenue, Suite B, Shreveport, LA 71104; tel. 318/424–3291; Michael Drews, D.P.M., Administrator

Green Clinic Surgery Center, 1200 South Farmerville Street, Ruston, LA 71270; tel. 318/255–3690; FAX. 318/251–6116; Glenn Scott, Executive Director

Hedgewood Surgical Center, 2427 St. Charles Avenue, New Orleans, LA 70130; tel. 504/895–7642; FAX. 504/895–0728; Sally Carpenter, RN

Houma Outpatient Surgery Center, Ltd., 3800 Houma Boulevard, Suite 250, Metairie, LA 70006; tel. 504/456–1515; Jay Weil III, President, Chief Executive Officer

Houma Surgi Center, Inc., 1020 School Street, Houma, LA 70360; tel. 504/868–4320; FAX. 504/868–3617; Robert M. Alexander, M.D., Administrator

LSU Eye Surgery Center, 2020 Gravier Street, Suite B, New Orleans, LA 70112; tel. 504/568–6700; W. L. Blackwell, Chief Executive Officer

LaHaye Center for Advanced Care, 201 Rue Iberville, Lafayette, LA 70508; tel. 318/235–2149; Darryl Wagley

LaHaye Eye and Ambulatory Surgical Center, 100 Harry Guilbeau Road, Opelousas, LA 70570; tel. 318/942–2024; FAX. 318/948–8869; Dana Cockran, Administrator

Lake Forest Surgical Center, 10545 Lake Forest Boulevard, New Orleans, LA 70127; tel. 504/244–3000; FAX. 504/246–2600; Nina Ory, RN, Facility Manager

Lakeview Surgery and Diagnostic Center, Inc., 800 Heavens Drive, Mandeville, LA 70471; tel. 504/845–7100; FAX. 504/845–7596; Glenda P. Escudero–Dobson, Administrator

Laser and Surgery Center of Acadiana, 514 St. Landry Street, Lafayette, LA 70506; tel. 318/234–2020; FAX. 318/234–8230; Barbara L. Azar, Administrator

Laser and Surgery Center of the South, 1101 Audubon Avenue, Suite S–Four, Thibodaux, LA 70301; tel. 504/447–7258; FAX. 504/448–1521; M. L. Revelett, Administrator

Louisiana Endoscopy Center, Inc., 8150 Jefferson Highway, Baton Rouge, LA 70809; tel. 504/927–0970; FAX. 504/927–0988; Lorrie Rogerson, Administrator

Louisville Plaza Surgery Center, 3101 Kilpatrick Boulevard, Suite B, Monroe, LA 71201; tel. 318/322–5916; FAX. 318/322–5916; Frank Wilderman, D.P.M., Administrator

MGA GI Diagnostic and Therapeutic Center, 1111 Medical Center Boulevard, Suite 310, Marrero, LA 70072; tel. 504/349–6401; FAX. 504/349–6444; Thomas D. McCaffery, Jr., President

MGA GI Diagnostic and Therapeutic Center, 2633 Napolean Avenue, Suite 707, New Orleans, LA 70115; tel. 504/349–6401; FAX. 504/349–6444; Thomas D. McCaffery, Jr., Administrator

Magnolia Surgical Facility, 3939 Houma Boulevard, Suite 216, Metairie, LA 70006; tel. 504/455–7771; FAX. 504/885–5063; Hamid Massiha, M.D., Administrator

Marrero SurgiCenter, Inc., 4511 Westbank Expressway, Suite B, Marrero, LA 70072; tel. 504/340–1993; John Schiro, M.D., Administrator

Ochsner Clinic–Center for Cosmetic Surgery, 1514 Jefferson Highway, Fifth Floor, New Orleans, LA 70121; tel. 504/842–3950; FAX. 504/842–5003; Rachel Franz, RN, B.S.N., Manager

Omega Ambulatory Surgical Institute, One Galleria Boulevard, Suite 810, Metairie, LA 70001; tel. 504/832–4200; Rene Rosenson, Administrator

Outpatient Eye Surgery Center, 4324 Veterans Boulevard, Metairie, LA 70006; tel. 504/455–4046; FAX. 504/455–9890; Cheryl Crouse, RN, Administrator

Outpatient Surgery Center for Sight, 550 Connell's Park Lane, Baton Rouge, LA 70809; tel. 504/924–2020; Alan DeCorte, Administrator

Physicians Surgery Center, 106 Corporate Drive, Houma, LA 70360; tel. 504/853–1390; FAX. 504/853–1470; Connie K. Martin, Administrator

Prytania Surgery, Inc., 3525 Prytania Street, New Orleans, LA 70115; tel. 504/897–8880; Jay Weil III, Administrator

Saints Streets ASC Endoscopy Center, Inc., 201 St. Patrick Street, Suite 202, Lafayette, LA 70506; tel. 318/232–6697; FAX. 318/233–8065; Stephen G. Abshire, M.D., Administrator

Shreveport Endoscopy Center, A.M.C., 3217 Mabel Street, P.O. Box 37045, Shreveport, LA 71133–7045; tel. 318/631–0072; FAX. 318/631–9688; Linda Sibley, Administrator

Shreveport Surgery Center, 745 Olive Street, Suite 100, Shreveport, LA 71104; tel. 318/227–1163; FAX. 318/227–0413; Mary Jones, Administrator

St. Charles Avenue Surgical Facility, Inc., 3600 St. Charles Avenue, New Orleans, LA 70115; tel. 504/897–2237; George W. Hoffman, Administrator

St. Francis P and S Surgery Center, 312 Grammont Street, P.O. Box 3187, Monroe, LA 71201–3187; tel. 318/388–4040; FAX. 318/388–4099; Keith Kelley, Administrator

Surgery Center, Inc., 1101 South College Road, Suite 100, Lafayette, LA 70503; tel. 318/233–8603; FAX. 318/234–0341; Russell J. Arceneaux, Administrator

Surgi–Center of Baton Rouge, 5222 Brittany Drive, Baton Rouge, LA 70809; tel. 504/767–5636; FAX. 504/769–9107; Celeste M. Wiggins, Administrator

Surginet of Louisiana, LTD, 101 La Rue France, Suite 400, Lafayette, LA 70508; tel. 318/269–9828; FAX. 318/269–9823; August J. Rantz III, Administrator

Surgiunit, Inc., 4204 Teuton Street, Metairie, LA 70006; tel. 504/888–3836; Gustavo A. Colon, M.D., Administrator

The Endoscopy Center of Monroe, 316 South Sixth Street, Monroe, LA 71201; tel. 318/325–2649; FAX. 318/325–0717; Andy W. Waldo, Administrator

The Endoscopy Clinic of Lake Charles Medical and Surgical Clinic, 501 South Ryan, Lake Charles, LA 70601; tel. 318/433–8400; Robert Oates, Administrator

The Outpatient Surgery Center of Baton Rouge, 505 East Airport Drive, Baton Rouge, LA 70806; tel. 504/925–2031; FAX. 504/924–2809; Lorraine Caraway, Administrator

The Plastic Surgery Center, Inc., 4224 Houma Boulevard, Suite 430, Metairie, LA 70006; tel. 504/456–5150; FAX. 504/456–5055; James B. Johnson, M.D., Administrator

The Surgery Suite, 103 Medical Center Drive, Slidell, LA 70461; tel. 504/646–4466; FAX. 504/646–4485; Allison F. Maestri, RN, Administrator

Urology Specialty and Surgery Center, 234 South Ryan Street, Lake Charles, LA 70601; tel. 318/433–5282; FAX. 318/433–1159; Charles Enright, Administrator

West Monroe Endoscopy Center, 102 Thomas Road, Suite 506, West Monroe, LA 71291; tel. 318/388-8878; Fred W. Ortmann III, Administrator

Westbank Medical Clinic Surgical Facility, Inc., 4700 Wichers Drive, Suite 200, Marrero, LA 70072; Robert L. Sudderth, Administrator

Young Eye Surgery Center, Inc., 204 North Magdalen Square, Abbeville, LA 70510; tel. 318/893-4452; FAX. 318/893-7870; Virginia Y. Hebert, Administrator

MAINE

Acadia Medical Arts Ambulatory Surgical Suite, 404 State Street, Bangor, ME 04401; tel. 207/990-0928; Jordan J. Shubert, M.D., President

Aroostook County Regional Ophthalmology Center, 148 Academy Street, Presque Isle, ME 04769; tel. 207/764-0376; FAX. 207/764-7612; Craig W. Young, M.D., Director

Eye Care and Surgery Center of Maine, P.A., 53 Sewall Street, Portland, ME 04102; tel. 207/773-6336; FAX. 207/773-7034; William S. Holt, M.D., President

Maine Cataract and Eye Center, 386 Bridgton Road, Route 302, Westbrook, ME 04092; tel. 207/797-9214; FAX. 207/797-8236; Elliot Schweid, D.O., Director

Maine Eye Center, P.A., 15 Lowell Street, Portland, ME 04102; tel. 207/774-8277; FAX. 207/871-1415; Frank Read, M.D., Director

Northern Maine Ambulatory Endoscopy Center, 11 Martin Street, P.O. Box 748, Presque Isle, ME 04769-0151; tel. 207/764-2482; FAX. 207/764-1569; Shelley Kenney, RN, Nurse Manager

Orthopaedic Surgery Center, 33 Sewall Street, Portland, ME 04102; tel. 207/828-2130; FAX. 207/828-2190; Linda M. Ruterbories, Medical Director

Portland Endoscopy Center, 131 Chadwick Street, Portland, ME 04102-3266; tel. 207/773-7964; FAX. 207/773-9073; Michael Roy, M.D., President

Western Avenue Day Surgery Center, a/k/a Plastic and Hand Surgical Associates, P.A., 244 Western Avenue, South Portland, ME 04106; tel. 207/775-3446; FAX. 207/879-1646; Jean J. Labelle, M.D., President

MARYLAND

Albert Shoumer, D.P.M., Dundalk Professional Center, 40 South Dundalk Avenue, Dundalk, MD 21222; tel. 410/282-6434; FAX. 410/284-4636; Darleen Grupp, Office Manager

Albert Shoumer, D.P.M., 1645 Liberty Road, Eldersburg, MD 21784; tel. 310/795-2889

Amber Meadows Ambulatory Care Center, Inc., 198 Thomas Johnson Drive, Suite Three, Frederick, MD 21702; tel. 301/695-9669; FAX. 301/695-0346

Amber Ridge Operating Room Center, 1475 Taney Avenue, Suite 101, Frederick, MD 21702; tel. 301/694-5656; FAX. 301/846-4117; Lorin F. Busselberg, M.D., Director

Ambulatory Foot Surgery Center of Burtonsville, Inc., 15300 Spencerville Court, Suite 101, Burtonsville, MD 20866; tel. 301/421-4286; Dr. Kressin, President

Ambulatory Plastic Surgery–Robert Conrad, M.D., 9715 Medical Center Drive, Rockville, MD 20850; tel. 301/948-5670; FAX. 301/948-5598; Linda Quesenberry, Assistant Office Manager

American Podiatric Surgery, 10236 River Road, Potomac, MD 20854; tel. 301/983-9873; FAX. 301/299-3985; Amy Meehan, Administrator

Annapolis Plastic Surgery Center, 1300 Ritchie Highway, Arnold, MD 21012; tel. 410/544-0707; FAX. 410/544-0724; Jack Frost, M.D., President

Anne Arundel Gastroenterology Endoscopy Center, 703 Giddings Avenue, Suite M, Annapolis, MD 21401; tel. 410/224-2116; Cheryl L. Smith, Office Manager

Armiger, William G., M.D., P.A., d/b/a Chesapeake Plastic Surgery Associates, 1421 South Caton Avenue, Suite 203, Baltimore, MD 21227; tel. 410/646-3226; FAX. 410/644-2134; Sandra Pappas, Administrator

Arundel Ambulatory Center for Endoscopy, 621 Ridgley Avenue, Suite 101, Annapolis, MD 21401; tel. 410/224-3636; FAX. 410/224-6971; Jeff Hazel, Practice Administrator

Ashok K. Narang, M.D., P.A., Two North Avenue, Suite 102, Belair, MD 21014; tel. 410/877-7595

Baltimore Ambulatory Center for Endoscopy, 19 Fontana Lane, Suite 104, Baltimore, MD 21237; tel. 410/574-7776; FAX. 410/574-9038; Dr. V. Sivan, Medical Director

Baltimore County Out-Patient Plastic Surgery Center, 1205 York Road, Suite 36, Lutherville, MD 21093; tel. 410/828-9570; FAX. 410/583-9120; Bernard McGibbon, M.D.

Baltimore Podiatry Group, 5205 East Drive, Suite I, Arbutus, MD 21227; tel. 410/247-5333; FAX. 410/242-5449; Neil Scheffler, D.P.M., President

Baltimore Washington Eye Center, 200 Hospital Drive, Suite 600, Glen Burnie, MD 21061; tel. 410/761-1267; FAX. 410/761-4386; Phillip L. Harrington, Administrator

Bayside Foot and Ankle Center, 8023 Ritchie Highway, Pasadena, MD 21122; tel. 410/761-4190; Sheila Freeze, Office Manager

Beitler, Samuel D., D.P.M. Ambulatory Surgery Center, 795 Aquahart Road, Suite 125, Glen Burnie, MD 21061; tel. 410/768-0702; Samuel D. Beitler, D.P.M.

Benson Surgery Center, Inc., 3421 Benson Avenue, Baltimore, MD 21227; tel. 410/644-3311; FAX. 410/247-9446; Ann Rogowski, Assistant Administrator

Bethesda Ambulatory Surgical Center, 8000 Old Georgetown Road, Bethesda, MD 20814; tel. 301/652-2248; FAX. 301/654-1150; John Lydon, D.P.M., Administrator

Bowie Health Center, 15001 Health Center Drive, Bowie, MD 20716; tel. 301/262-5511; FAX. 301/464-3572

Breschi, Sclama and Hoofnagle (Drs.), 6830 Hospital Drive, Suite 204, Baltimore, MD 21237; tel. 410/391-6131; FAX. 410/391-6144; Anthony O. Sclama, M.D., President

Carroll Medicine, d/b/a Steven Shaffer, M.D., 211 Hanover Pike, Hampstead, MD 21074; tel. 410/239-7073

Center for Eye Surgery P.C., 5550 Friendship Boulevard, Suite 270, Chevy Chase, MD 20815; tel. 301/215-7347; FAX. 301/215-7345; Leila Cabrera-Reid, RN, Administrator

Center for Plastic Surgery, 5550 Friendship Boulevard, Suite 130, Chevy Chase, MD 20815; tel. 301/652-7700; Jean, Administrator

Chesapeake Ambulatory Surgery Center, 8028 Governor Ritchie Highway, Suite 100, Pasadena, MD 21122; tel. 410/768-5800; FAX. 410/768-5806; Ira J. Gottlieb, D.P.M., Owner, Administrator

Clinical Associates, 515 Fairmont Avenue, Suite 500, Towson, MD 21286; tel. 410/494-1335

Columbia Surgery Center, Inc., 1105 Little Patuxent Parkway, Columbia, MD 21044; tel. 410/730-6673; Paul Valvoe, Administrator

De Leonibus and Palmer, L.L.C., A.S.C., MedSurg Foot Center, 2086 Generals Highway, Suite 101, Annapolis, MD 21401; tel. 410/266-7666; FAX. 410/266-7703

Digestive Disease Consultant of Frederick, 915 Toll House Avenue, Suite 201, Frederick, MD 21701; tel. 301/662-7822; James A. Frizzell, M.D.

Dr. Gary Lieberman, P.A., A.S.C., d/b/a Four Corners Ambulatory Surgical Center, 10101 Lorain Avenue, Silver Spring, MD 20901; tel. 301/681-8400

Dr. Michael K. Schwartz, D.D.S., P.A., 723 South Charles Street, Baltimore, MD 21230; tel. 410/727-4886

Dr. W. Alan Hopson, P.A., 560 Riverside Drive, Suite A-101, Salisbury, MD 21801; tel. 410/749-0121; FAX. 410/749-6807; Pat Timmons, Office Manager

Drs. Abelson and Cameron, P.A., ASC, 1212 York Road, Suite A201, Lutherville, MD 21093; tel. 410/337-7755; FAX. 410/337-7922; Laurie Kolmer, Office Manager

Drs. Smith and Schwartz, D.D.S., P.A., 10 Warren Road, Suite 330, Cockeysville, MD 21030; tel. 410/666-5225; FAX. 410/666-7220; Mary Thompson, Office Manager

Dulaney Eye Institute, 901 Dulaney Valley Road, Towson, MD 21204; tel. 410/583-1000; Andrea Hyatt, Administrator

Dundalk Ambulatory Surgery Center, 1123 Merritt Boulevard, Baltimore, MD 21222; tel. 410/282-6666

Easton Foot Center, 8579 Commerce Drive, Suite 100A, Easton, MD 21601; tel. 410/822-0645

Endocenter of Baltimore, 7211 Park Heights Avenue, Baltimore, MD 21208; tel. 410/764-6107; FAX. 410/358-4167

Eye Surgery Center at Greenspring Station of Ophthalmology Associates, L.L.C., 10755 Falls Road, Suite 110B, Lutherville, MD 21093; tel. 410/583-2810; FAX. 410/583-2807; Shalini Pahuja, Operations Manager

Eye Surgical Center Associates of Baltimore, 1122 Kenilworth Drive, Suite 18, Towson, MD 21204; tel. 410/321-4400; FAX. 410/321-4909; Terry Lewis, Administrator

Facial Plastic Surgicenter, Ltd., 21 Crossroads Drive, Suite 310, Owings Mills, MD 21117; tel. 410/356-1100; Ira D. Papel, M.D., President

Family Foot Health Specialists, P.C., 339 East Antietam Street, Hagerstown, MD 21740; tel. 301/797-7272; Judy Cline, Office Manager

Flaum, Martin/Rockville Podiatry Center, 50 West Edmonston Drive, Suite 306, Rockville, MD 20852; tel. 301/340-8666; Martin C. Flaum, Owner

Foot Care Associates Ambulatory Care Center at Hamilton Foot Care, 5508 Harford Road, Baltimore, MD 21214; tel. 410/426-5508

Foot Care Associates Ambulatory Care Center at Joppa Foot Care, 2316 East Joppa Road, Baltimore, MD 21234; tel. 410/882-5100

Foot and Ankle Surgical Center, 2415 Musgrove Road, Suite 103, Silver Spring, MD 20904; tel. 301/384-6500

Footer, Ronald, D.P.M., P.A., 16220 Frederick Avenue, Suite 200, Gaithersburg, MD 20877; tel. 301/948-2995; FAX. 301/948-6056; Maryrose Hanks, Office Manager

Frederick Surgical Center, 915 Toll House Avenue, Suite 103, Frederick, MD 21701; tel. 301/694-3400; FAX. 301/694-3620; Barbara Smith, Administrator

Gastrointestinal Diagnostic Center, 4660 Wilkens Avenue, Suite 302, Baltimore, MD 21229; tel. 410/242-3636; FAX. 410/242-4404; Mary c. Harrison, Business Manager

Gaurdino and Glubo, P.A., 4660 Wilkens Avenue, Baltimore, MD 21229; tel. 410/242-7066; FAX. 410/242-4126; Eileen Giardina, RN

Gehris, Heroy and Associates of Lutherville, 1212 York Road, Suite 201B, Lutherville, MD 21093; tel. 410/821-6130; James H. Heroy III, Administrator

Gynemed Surgi-Center, 17 Fontana Lane, Suite 201, Baltimore, MD 21237; tel. 410/686-8220; FAX. 410/391-0943; David O'Neil, M.D.

HEALTHSOUTH Central Maryland Surgery, 1500 Joh Avenue, Baltimore, MD 21227; tel. 410/536-0012; FAX. 410/536-0016; Thelma Hoerl, RN, Facility Manager

Johns Hopkins Plastic Surgery Associates, JHOC 8, 601 North Caroline Street, Baltimore, MD 21287; tel. 410/955-6897; FAX. 410/614-1296

Kaiser-Permanente-Kensington, 10810 Connecticut Avenue, Kensington, MD 20895; tel. 301/929-7100; FAX. 301/929-7433; Kathleen Owens, RN, M.S.N., Director, Surgical Services

Kenneth Margolis, M.D., P.A., Ambulatory Endoscopy Surgical Center, 9101 Franklin Square Drive, Suite 213, Baltimore, MD 21237; tel. 410/687-0202; FAX. 410/687-0985; Jo Ann Smith, Office Manager

Klatsky Plastic Surgery Facility, 122 Slade Avenue, Pikesville, MD 21208; tel. 410/484-0400; FAX. 410/484-2993; Stanley A. Klatsky, M.D., Director

Lake Forest Ambulatory Surgical Center, 702 Russell Avenue, Gaithersburg, MD 20877; tel. 301/948-3668; FAX. 301/926-7787

Laser Surgery Center, 484A Ritchie Highway, Severna Park, MD 21146; tel. 410/544-4600; Stan Karloff, Office Manager

Laurel Foot and Ankle Center, 14440 Cherry Lane Court, Suite 104, Laurel, MD 20707; tel. 301/953-3668; Dr. Frank Smith, Administrator

Maclean, Kishel, Applestein, M.D., A.S.C., 11085 Little Patuxent Parkway, Columbia, MD 21044; tel. 410/997-1930

Maple Springs Ambulatory Surgery Center, 10810 Darnstown Road, Suite 101, Gaithersburg, MD 20878; tel. 301/762-3338; FAX. 301/762-1585

Maryland Digestive Disease Center, 7350 Van Ducen Road, Suite 230, Laurel, MD 20707; tel. 301/498-5500

Maryland Ear, Nose and Throat Group, P.A., 2112 Bell Air Road, Suite Three, Fallston, MD 21047; tel. 410/879-7049; Barbara Huckeba, Corporate Secretary

Maryland Endoscopy Center, L.L.C., 100 West Road, Suite 115, Towson, MD 21204; tel. 410/494-0144; FAX. 410/494-0147; Gretchen Caron, RN, Administrator

Maryland Kidney Stone Center, 6115 Falls Road, Baltimore, MD 21209; tel. 410/377-2622; FAX. 410/377-4410; Walter Weinstein, General Manager

Maryland Outpatient Foot Surgery Center, Dennis M. Weber D.P.M., 4701 Randolph Road, Suite 115, Rockville, MD 20852; tel. 301/770-5741; FAX. 301/468-1093; Dennis M. Weber, D.P.M., Director

Section C

McCone, Jonathan, Jr., M.D., 6196 Oxon Hill Road, Suite 640, Oxon Hill, MD 20745; tel. 301/567-2400

Metropolitan Ambulatory Urologic Institute Inc., 7753 Belle Point Drive, Greenbelt, MD 20770; tel. 301/474-5583; FAX. 301/513-5087; Amy Boone, Manager

Michetti, Michael, Dr. of District Heights, 6400 Marlboro Pike, District Heights, MD 20747; tel. 301/736-6900

Mid Shore Surgical Eye Center, 8420 Ocean Gateway, Suite One, Easton, MD 21601; tel. 410/822-0424; FAX. 410/822-2283; Adrienne Welch, RN

Mid-Atlantic Surgery Center, 1120 Professional Court, Hagerstown, MD 21740; tel. 301/739-7900

Montgomery Endoscopy Center, Montgomery Gastroenterology P.A., 12012 Veirs Mill Road, Wheaton, MD 20906; tel. 301/942-3550; FAX. 301/933-3621; Howard Goldberg, M.D., A.S.C Director

Montgomery Surgical Center, 46 West Gude Drive, Rockville, MD 20850; tel. 301/424-6901; FAX. 301/294-7847; Jeannie M. Lohmeyer, RN, CNOR, Administrative Director

Moulsdale, Murphy, Siegelbaum and Lerner, 7505 Osler Drive, Suite 508, Towson, MD 21204; tel. 410/296-0166; FAX. 410/828-7275

Neil J. Napora, D.P.M., 7809 Wise Avenue, Baltimore, MD 21222; tel. 410/285-0310; FAX. 410/288-1569; Neil J. Napora, D.P.M.

North Arundel Plastic Surgery Specialists, 203 Hospital Drive, Suite 308, Glen Burnie, MD 21061; tel. 410/841-5355; FAX. 410/766-7145; Ajia S. Layman, Administrator

Parris-Castro Eye Association, Six North Boulton Street, Bel Air, MD 21014; tel. 410/836-7010; Michael Grasham, Administrator

Peninsula Obstetrics and Gynecology, 314 West Carroll Street, Salisbury, MD 21801; tel. 410/546-3125; FAX. 410/546-3128

Peninsula Surgery Center, P.A., 145 East Carroll Street, Salisbury, MD 21801; tel. 410/548-1108; FAX. 410/546-8338; Joseph G. Walters, PA-C Administrative Director

Plastic Surgery Specialists, 2448 Holly Avenue, Suite 400, Annapolis, MD 21401; tel. 410/841-5355; FAX. 410/841-6589; Ajia S. Layman, Administrator

Plastic and Aesthetic, Surgical Center of Maryland, Orchard Square, 1212 York Road, Suite B101, Lutherville, MD 21093; tel. 410/337-2551; FAX. 410/321-1550; Oscar M. Ramirez, M.D., Medical Director

Plaza Podiatry, 6568 Reisterstown Road, Suite 501, Baltimore, MD 21215; tel. 410/764-7044; Brian Kashan, Administrator

Podiatry Associates of Hagerstown, A.S.C, 12821 Oak Hill Avenue, Hagerstown, MD 21742; tel. 301/739-1575; FAX. 301/739-1578; Crystal Shockey, Office Manager

Podiatry Associates, P.A., 9712 Bel Air Road, Baltimore, MD 21236; tel. 410/574-6060; FAX. 410/256-2727; Stanley Book

Podiatry Associates, P.A., One North Main Street, Bel Air, MD 21014; tel. 410/879-1212; FAX. 410/893-1081

Podiatry Associates, P.A., 10840 Little Patuxent Parkway, Columbia, MD 21044; tel. 410/730-0970; FAX. 410/730-0161; Dr. Cappello, Podiatrist

Podiatry Associates, P.A., 6569 North Charles Street, Suite 702, Towson, MD 21204; tel. 410/828-5420; Nancy L. Patterson, Billing Manager

Podiatry Associates, P.A., 9101 Franklin Square Drive, Baltimore, MD 21237; tel. 410/574-3900; FAX. 410/574-3902; Vincent J. Martorana, D.P.M.

Podiatry Group, P.A. of Annapolis, 139 Old Solomons Island Road, Suite C, Annapolis, MD 21401; tel. 410/224-4448; FAX. 410/841-5200; Kate Pearson, Administrator

Podiatry Group, P.A. of Laurel, Ambulatory Surgery Center, 1433 Laurel-Bowie Road, Suite 205, Laurel, MD 20708; tel. 301/725-5650; Bruce A. Wenzel, Administrator

Prince George's Ambulatory Care Center/Endoscopy Suites, Inc., 6001 Landover Road, Suite One, Cheverly, MD 20785; tel. 301/773-1111; Jeannette Figueroa, Administrator

Prince George's Multi-Specialty Surgery Centre, Inc., 8700 Central Avenue, Suite 106, Landover, MD 20785; tel. 301/808-9298; FAX. 301/499-1266; Banner E. Williams, Administrator

Professional Village Surgical Center, 356 Mill Street, Hagerstown, MD 21740; tel. 301/791-1800

Queen Anne Plastic, L.L.C., 2110 Red Apple Plaza, Chester, MD 2161; tel. 410/643-7207; FAX. 410/643-6945

Queen Anne Podiatry Center, 2108 DiDonato Drive, Chester, MD 21619; tel. 410/643-7207; FAX. 410/643-9274; Grace LeSage, Administrator

Rafiq Patel, M.D., Ambulatory Surgery Center, 1952 Pulaski Highway, Edgewood, MD 21040; tel. 410/679-5800

River Reach Outpatient Surgery Center, 790 Governor Ritchie Highway, Suite E-35, Severna Park, MD 21146; tel. 410/544-2487

Rivertowne Surgery Center, 6196 Oxon Hill Road, Suite 650, Oxon Hill, MD 20745; tel. 301/839-7499; FAX. 301/839-8726; Beth Smith, Manager

Robinwood Surgery, 11110 Medical Campus Road, Hagerstown, MD 21742; tel. 301/714-4300; FAX. 301/714-4324; Niki Showe, Office Supervisor

Roger J. Oldham, M.D., Ambulatory Surgery Center, 10215 Fernwood Road, Suite 412, Bethesda, MD 20817; tel. 301/530-6100; Nancy Aprill, RN

Rotunda Ambulatory Surgery Center, 711 West 40th Street, Suite 410, Baltimore, MD 21211; tel. 410/889-4885

Sagoskin and Levy, M.D., 9707 Medical Center Drive, Suite 230, Rockville, MD 20850; tel. 301/340-1188; Arthur Sagoskin, M.D., Administrator

Saint Mary's Ambulatory Foot Surgery Center, Route 235 and Chancellors Run Road, Suite 15, California, MD 20619; tel. 301/862-3338; Douglas H. Hallgren, D.P.M., Administrator

Siegel and Langer (Drs.), P.A., Ambulatory Surgery Center, 1001 Pine Heights Avenue, Suite 104, Baltimore, MD 21229; tel. 410/644-0929; Narang Ashok, Administrator

Silver Spring Ambulatory Surgical Center, Inc., 1104 Spring Street, Suite T110, Silver Spring, MD 20910; tel. 301/589-7664; FAX. 301/589-3410; Todd A. Nitkin, D.P.M., President

Silverman, David H., M.D., 6490 Landover Road, Suite D, Cleverly, MD 20785; tel. 301/322-5885

Smith and Harne, M.D., P.A., 2007 Rock Spring Road, Forest Hill, MD 21050; tel. 410/879-4879; FAX. 410/893-4763; Louise Pollard, Office Manager

Smith, Schwartz and Hyatt, D.D.S., P.A. of Owings Mills, 25 Crossroads Drive, Owings Mills, MD 21117; tel. 410/363-7780; Michael K. Schwartz, D.D.S., Administrator

Spector, Adam, D.P.M., Ambulatory Surgery Center, 1111 Spring Street, Silver Spring, MD 20910; tel. 301/589-8886; FAX. 301/589-8889; Adam Spector, D.P.M., Administrator

St. Agnes Surgery Center of Ellicott City, 2850 North Ridge Road, Ellicott City, MD 21043; tel. 410/461-1600; FAX. 410/750-7615

Suburban Endoscopy Center, L.L.C., 10215 Fernwood Road, Suite 206, Bethesda, MD 20817; tel. 301/530-2800

Sugar, Mark, D.P.M., A.S.C., 6505 Belcrest Road, Suite One, Hyattsville, MD 20782; tel. 301/699-5900; FAX. 301/699-9297; Mark H. Sugar, D.P.M.

Suhayl Kalash, Ambulatory Surgery Center, 3455 Wilkens Avenue, Suite 203, Baltimore, MD 21229; tel. 410/646-0330; Bridget Vracar, Accounts Coordinator

SurgiCenter of Baltimore, Formerly Health Specialists, P.A., 23 Crossroads Drive, Suite 100, Owings Mills, MD 21117; tel. 410/356-0300; FAX. 410/356-7507, ext. 101; Jerry W. Henderson, Executive Director, Chief Operating Officer

Surgical Center of Greater Annapolis, Inc., 83 Church Road, Arnold, MD 21012; tel. 410/757-5018; FAX. 410/757-0632; LoRain Potter, RN, Administrator

The Ambulatory Urosurgical Center, 401 East Jefferson Street, Suite 105, Rockville, MD 20850; tel. 301/309-8219; FAX. 301/309-9370; Jacqueline Hillman, RN, B.S.N., M.S., Director, Nursing

The Endoscopy Center, 7402 York Road, Suite 101, Towson, MD 21204; tel. 410/494-0156; FAX. 410/828-1706; Dianne M. Johnson, General Manager

Total Foot Care Surgery Center, Inc., 7525 Greenway Center Drive, Suite 112, Greenbelt, MD 20770; tel. 301/345-4087; FAX. 301/345-0482; Dale Scoville, Office Manager

Towson Ambulatory Surgical Center, 912 A Tower Avenue, Towson, MD 21204; tel. 410/583-8637; FAX. 410/583-8691

Tri County Endoscopy, Shanti Medical Center, P.O. Box 664, Leonardstown, MD 20650; tel. 301/475-5579; Dr. A. Shah

Tri County Endoscopy, Charlotte Hall, Route Five, Charlotte Hall, MD 20622; tel. 301/884-7322; Dr. Shah

Tri County Endoscopy, Calvert Medical Office Building, Suite 303, 110 Hospital Road, Prince Frederick, MD 20678; tel. 410/535-4333; Dr. A. Shah

United Foot Care Center, 420 South Crain Highway, Glen Burnie, MD 21061; tel. 410/766-7500; Steven Brownstein, Administrator

Urology Center, 120 Sister Pierre Drive, Towson, MD 21204; tel. 410/494-1396; Dr. Schonwald, Administrator

Urology Center at Charles North, 1104 Kenilworth Avenue, Suite 300, Towson, MD 21204; tel. 410/823-1565

Urology Center at Glen Burnie, 203 Hospital Drive, Glen Burnie, MD 21162; tel. 410/582-4002; Robert B. Goldstein, M.D., Administrator

Urology Center at Security, 7000 Security Boulevard, Baltimore, MD 21207; tel. 410/281-1892; Mary Hall, Administrator

Urology Center at White Marsh, 8114 Sandpiper Court, Suite 215, Baltimore, MD 21236; tel. 410/931-3229; Michael J. McCormick, Administrator

Vahos Aesthetic Plastic Surgery Institute, 1001 Pine Heights Avenue, Suite 100, Baltimore, MD 21229; tel. 410/644-4877; FAX. 410/525-1346; Mario Vahos, M.D., Director

Waldorf Endoscopy Center Inc., 11340 Pembrooke Square, Suite 202, Waldorf, MD 20603; tel. 301/645-7220; FAX. 301/843-5184; Mary Lou Champney, Office Manager

Washington Surgi Center, 6228 Oxon Hill Road, Oxon Hill, MD 20745; tel. 301/839-0770; FAX. 301/839-1350

Western Maryland Eye Surgical Center, 1003 West Seventh Street, Suite 400, Frederick, MD 21701; tel. 301/662-3721; FAX. 301/698-8164

MASSACHUSETTS

Advanced Pain Management Center, Three Woodland Road, Suite 206, Stoneham, MA 02180; tel. 617/662-2243; FAX. 617/662-4878

Andover Surgical Day Care Clinic, 138 Haverhill Street, Andover, MA 01810; tel. 508/475-2880; FAX. 508/475-9562; Edward G. George, Administrator

Boston Center for Ambulatory Surgery, Inc., 170 Commonwealth Avenue, Boston, MA 02116; tel. 617/267-0701; FAX. 617/236-8704

Boston Eye Surgery & Laser Center, P.C., 50 Staniford Street, Boston, MA 02114; tel. 617/723-2015; FAX. 617/723-7787; Sheila M. Harney, Business Manager

Cataract and Laser Center West, P.C., 171 Interstate Drive, West Springfield, MA 01089; tel. 413/732-2333; FAX. 413/732-3514; John Dunne, Administrator

Cataract and Laser Center, Inc., 333 Elm Street, Dedham, MA 02026; tel. 617/326-3800; John Dunne, Administrator

Cosmetic Surgery Center, 68 Camp Street, Hyannis, MA 02601; tel. 508/775-7026; FAX. 508/778-6327; Laura Norkatis, Office Manager

Eye Institute of the Merrimack Valley, 280 Haverhill Street, Lawrence, MA 01840; tel. 508/685-5366

Goddard Medical Association Outpatient Surgery, One Pearl Street, Caputo Building First Floor, Brockton, MA 02401; tel. 508/586-3600

Greater New Bedford Surgicare, Inc., 540 Hawthorne Street, North Dartmouth, MA 02747; tel. 508/997-1271; FAX. 508/992-7701; George A. Picord, Administrator

HealthSouth Maple Surgery Center, 298 Carew Street, Springfield, MA 01104; tel. 413/739-9668; FAX. 413/781-3652; Kathleen S. Loomis, RN, Facility Administrator

McGowan Eye Care Center, 297 Union Avenue, Framingham, MA 01701; tel. 800/873-4590; FAX. 508/872-0038; Bernard L. McGowan, M.D., Director

New England Eye Surgery Center, 696 Main Street, Weymouth, MA 02190; tel. 617/331-3820; FAX. 617/331-1076; Kenneth Camerota

New England Surgicare, One Brookline Place, Suite 201, Brookline, MA 02146; tel. 617/730-9650; Gratia S. Chase, RN, Administrator

Plymouth Laser and Surgical Center, 40 Industrial Park Road, Plymouth, MA 02360; tel. 508/746-8600; FAX. 508/747-0824; Kathleen Murphy, Administrator

Same Day SurgiClinic, 272 Stanley Street, Fall River, MA 02720; tel. 508/672-2290; FAX. 508/679-3766; John Harries, M.D., Chief Executive Officer

Surgery Center of Waltham, 40 Second Avenue, Suite 200, Waltham, MA 02154

The Eye Center, 15 Florence Street, Route 128, Danvers, MA 01923; tel. 508/774-2040; FAX. 508/750-4463

University Eye Associates, Inc., 90 New State Highway, Raynham, MA 02767; tel. 508/822-8839; FAX. 508/880-3616; Judith A. Orsie, RN, Nurse Manager

Worcester Surgical Center, Inc., 300 Grove Street, Worcester, MA 01650; tel. 508/754-0700; FAX. 508/831-9989; Andy H. Poritz, M.D., Professional Services Director

MICHIGAN

Balian Eye Center, 432 West University Drive, Rochester, MI 48307; tel. 313/651-6122; John V. Balian, M.D.

Birth Control Center, Inc., 2783 Fourteen Mile Road, Sterling Height, MI 48310; tel. 810/939-4000; Armen Vartanian, Administrator

Blodgett Memorial Medical Center, 1000 East Paris S.E., Suite 100, Grand Rapids, MI 49506; Lori Streeter, Office Manager

Borgess at Woodbridge Hills Outpatient Surgery, 7901 Angling Road, Portage, MI 49024; tel. 616/324-8406; FAX. 616/324-8476; Renee Langeland, Administrator

Bronson Outpatient Surgery–Crosstown Center, 150 East Crosstown Parkway, Suite One, Kalamazoo, MI 49007; tel. 616/341-6166; Frank Sardone, Administrator

Castleman Eye Center, 14050 Dix–Toledo Road, Southgate, MI 48195; tel. 313/283-0500; FAX. 313/283-2720

Centre for Plastic Surgery, 426 Michigan Street, N.E., Suite 300, Grand Rapids, MI 49503; tel. 616/454-1256; FAX. 616/454-0308; Daniel Reeder, Administrator

Community Surgical Center, 30671 Stephenson Highway, Madison Heights, MI 48071; tel. 810/588-8000; FAX. 810/588-9140; C. J. Yanos, Administrator

Detroit Medical Center Surgery Center, 27207 Lahser Road, Suite 100, Southfield, MI 48034; tel. 810/357-0880; FAX. 810/357-1738; Patrick Voight, Administrative Manager

East Michigan Eye Surgery Center, 701 South Ballenger, Flint, MI 48532; tel. 810/238-3603; FAX. 810/767-5194; Judith A. Kirby, RN, Administrative Director

Eastside Endoscopy Center, 28963 Little Mack, Suite 103, St. Clair Shores, MI 48081; tel. 810/447-5110; FAX. 810/774-6091; Beth Miller, Administrator

Feminine Health Care Clinic of Flint, 2032 South Saginaw Street, Flint, MI 48503; tel. 800/323-6205; FAX. 313/232-8071; Dawn LoRec, Director

Glascco Ambulatory Surgery Center, 1707 West Lake Lansing Road, Lansing, MI 48912; tel. 517/267-0033; FAX. 517/267-0430; Jane Beshore, Administrator

Hemmorrhoid Clinics of America, 22000 Greenfield Road, Oak Park, MI 48237; tel. 810/967-4140; FAX. 810/967-0745; Max Ali, M.D., President

Henry Ford Hospital Fairlane Center, 19401 Hubbard Drive, Dearborn, MI 48126; tel. 313/593-8100; Jay Zerwekh, Administrator

Henry Ford Medical Center–Lakeside Ambulatory Surgery, 14500 Hall Road, Sterling Heights, MI 48313; tel. 810/247-2680; FAX. 810/247-2682; Paul Szilagyi, Administrator

Henry Ford Medical Center–West Bloomfield, Ambulatory Surgery Center, 6777 West Maple Road, West Bloomfield, MI 48033; tel. 810/663-4100; FAX. 810/661-6494; Linda Messina, Administrator

Holland Eye Clinic, 999 South Washington, Holland, MI 49423; tel. 616/396-2316; FAX. 616/396-0085; Kristine Curtis, Assistant Administrator

Hutzel Health Center, 4050 East 12 Mile Road, Warren, MI 48092; tel. 810/573-3140

John Michael Garrett, P.C., 1301 Carpenter Avenue, Iron Mountain, MI 49801; tel. 906/774-1404; FAX. 906/774-8132; Cathy Hartwig, RN, Supervisor

M.D. Surgicenter, 375 Barclay Circle, Rochester Hills, MI 48307; tel. 810/852-3636; FAX. 810/852-3631; Robert Swartz, Administrator

Metropolitan Eye Center, 21711 Greater Mack, St. Clair Shores, MI 48080; tel. 313/774-6820; FAX. 313/777-2214; Richard C. Mertz, Jr., M.D., Director

Michigan Center for Outpatient Ocular Surgery, 33080 Utica Road, P.O. Box 26010, Fraser, MI 48026; tel. 810/296-7250; FAX. 810/296-0276; Norbert P. Czajkowski, M.D., Director

Midwest Health Center, 5050 Schaefer Avenue, Dearborn, MI 48126; tel. 313/581-2600, ext. 286; FAX. 313/581-6013; Mark B. Saffer, M.D., President, Chief Executive Officer

Oakland Surgi Center, 2820 Crooks Road, Rochester Hills, MI 48309; tel. 810/852-7484; Ravindranath Kambhampati, M.D., Administrator

Oakwood Healthcare Center–Dearborn, 10151 Michigan Avenue, Dearborn, MI 48126; tel. 313/436-2430; FAX. 313/436-2411; Dan West, Regional Director, Ambulatory Services

Park Eye and Surgicenter, 5014 Villa Linde Parkway, Flint, MI 48532

Planned Parenthood League, Inc., 25932 Dequindre, Warren, MI 48091; tel. 810/758-2100; FAX. 810/758-2104; Carrie Haneckow, Administrator

Planned Parenthood of Mid–Michigan, 3100 Professional Drive, P.O. Box 3673, Ann Arbor, MI 48106-3673; tel. 313/973-0710, ext. 131; FAX. 313/973-0595; Cindy Bourland, Clinic Manager

Planned Parenthood of South Central Michigan, 4201 West Michigan Avenue, Kalamazoo, MI 49006-5833; tel. 616/372-1205; FAX. 616/372-1279; Louise D. Safron, Executive Director

Port Huron Eye Surgery Center, 1131 Erie Street, Port Huron, MI 48060; tel. 810/984-2681; FAX. 810/984-1024; Richard Engle, Administrator

Providence Hospital Ambulatory Surgery Center, 47601 Grand River, Novi, MI 48374; tel. 810/380-4170; Brian Connolly, Administrator

Providence Surgical Center, 29877 Telegraph Road, Suite 200, Southfield, MI 48034

Reconstructive Surgery Center, 125 West Walnut, Kalamazoo, MI 49007; tel. 616/343-1381; Frank J. Newman, M.D., Medical Director

Saginaw General North, 5400 Mackinaw, Saginaw, MI 48603; tel. 517/797-5000

Sinai Surgery Center, 28500 Orchard Lake Road, Farmington Hills, MI 48334; tel. 810/851-9215; FAX. 810/851-2077; Michael K. Rosenberg, M.D., Medical Director

Somerset Troy Surgical Center, 1565 West Big Beaver Road, Building F, Troy, MI 48084; tel. 810/643-7775; FAX. 810/643-0999; Reza S. Mohajer, M.D., Administrator

St. John Surgery Center, 21000 12 Mile Road, St. Clair Shore, MI 48081; tel. 810/447-5015; FAX. 810/447-5012; Cheri Dendy, Administrator

St. Mary's Ambulatory Care Center, 4599 Towne Centre, Saginaw, MI 48604; tel. 517/797-3000; FAX. 517/797-3010; Donna Juhala, Director

Superior Endoscopy Center/U P Digestive Disease Associates, P.C., 1414 West Fair Avenue, Suite 135, Marquette, MI 49855; tel. 906/226-6025; Jeffrey P. Shaffer, Administrator

Surgery Center of Michigan, 44650 Delco Boulevard, Sterling Height, MI 48313; tel. 810/254-3391; Jay Novetsky, Administrator

Surgical Care Center of Michigan, 750 East Beltline, N.E., Grand Rapids, MI 49505; tel. 616/940-3600; FAX. 616/954-0216; Kris Kilgore, RN, B.S.N, Administrative Director

Troy Bloomfield Surgery Center, 2515 North Woodward Avenue, Bloomfield Hill, MI 48304; tel. 810/332-3332; Joseph Posch, Administrator

University of Michigan Surgery Center, 19900 Haggerty Road, Livonia, MI 48152; tel. 313/462-1888; FAX. 313/462-1944; Pamela Cittan, Administrator

Upper Peninsula Surgery Center, 1414 West Fair Avenue, Suite 232, Marquette, MI 49855; tel. 906/225-7547; FAX. 906/225-7548; Sally J. Achatz, R.N., Administrator

Waterford Ambulatory Surgi–Center, 1305 North Oakland Boulevard, Waterford, MI 48327; tel. 810/666-5519; FAX. 810/666-5550; Sandra K. Parrott, General Manager

MINNESOTA

Centennial Lakes Same Day Surgery Center, 7373 France Avenue, S., Suite 404, Edina, MN 55435; tel. 612/921-0100; FAX. 612/921-0999; Kathleen L. Whatley, Administrator

Children's Health Care–West, 6050 Clearwater Drive, Minnetonka, MN 55343; tel. 612/930-8600; FAX. 612/930-8650; Jane Price, Director

Columbia St. Cloud Surgical Center, 1526 Northway Drive, St. Cloud, MN 56303; tel. 320/251-8385; FAX. 320/251-1267; Jeanette I. Stack, Administrator

Dakota Clinic, Ltd., 125 East Frazee Street, Detroit Lakes, MN 56501; tel. 218/847-3181; FAX. 218/847-2795; Linda L. Walz, Division Manager

First Eye Care Center, Inc., 9117 Lyndale Avenue, S., Bloomington, MN 55420; tel. 612/884-7568; FAX. 612/884-2656; Barbara McGovern, Administrator

Healtheast Maplewood Surgery Center, 1655 Beam Avenue, Maplewood, MN 55109; tel. 612/232-7780; FAX. 612/232-7786; Sandra Todd, Director

Healtheast St. Paul Endoscopy Center, 17 West Exchange Street, Suite 215, St. Paul, MN 55102; tel. 612/224-9677; FAX. 612/223-5683; Glenda Tims, RN, Clinical Manager

Landmark Surgical Center, 17 West Exchange Street, Suite 307, St. Paul, MN 55102; tel. 612/223-7400; FAX. 612/223-5903; Peg Olin, Administrator

Maplewood Surgery Center, 1655 Beam Ave., Maplewood, MN 55109; tel. 612/232-7780; Sandra Todd, Administrator

Midwest Surgicenter, d/b/a Midwest Eye and Ear Institute, 393 North Dunlap Street, Suite 900, St. Paul, MN 55104; tel. 612/642-1106; FAX. 612/645-3346; H. Joseph Drannen, Administrator

Park Nicollet Clinic Health System Minnesota, 3800 Park Nicollet Boulevard, St. Louis Park, MN 55416; tel. 612/993-1953; FAX. 612/993-9250; Kathy Beckman, RN, Manager

WestHealth, Inc., 2855 Campus Drive, Plymouth, MN 55441; tel. 612/577-7120, ext. 7123; FAX. 612/577-7130; Paula Green, Administrator

Willmar Surgery Center, 1320 South First Street, P.O. Box 773, Willmar, MN 56201; tel. 320/235-6506; John Seifert, Administrator

MISSISSIPPI

Ambu–Care Outpatient Surgery Center, 6204 North State Street, Jackson, MS 39213; tel. 601/956-3251; FAX. 601/957-8456; Frank McCune, M.D., Administrator

Better Living Clinic Endoscopy Center, 3000 Halls Ferry Road, Vicksburg, MS 39180; tel. 601/638-9800; Linda Antoine, Administrative Assistant

Biloxi Outpatient Surgery and Endoscopy Center, Inc., 111 Lameuse Street, Suite 104, Biloxi, MS 39530; tel. 601/374-2130; FAX. 601/374-0938; Michael T. Gossman, Administrator

Columbia Mississippi Surgical Center, 1421 North State Street, Jackson, MS 39202; tel. 601/353-8000; Virginia Brown, Administrator

ENT and Facial Plastic Surgery, 107 Millsaps Drive, P.O. Box 17829, Hattiesburg, MS 39402; tel. 601/268-5131; FAX. 601/268-5138; Pam Carter, Office Manager

Gastroenterology Clinic of Laurel, P.A., 1020 Adams Street, Laurel, MS 39440; tel. 601/649-0633

Gulf South Outpatient Center, 1206 31st Avenue, P.O. Box 1778, Gulfport, MS 39501; tel. 601/864-0008; FAX. 601/863-1747; Jason V. Smith, M.D., President

Gulfport Outpatient Surgical Center, 1240 Broad Avenue, Gulfport, MS 39501; tel. 601/868-1120; William Peaks, Administrator

Lowery A. Woodall Outpatient Surgery Facility, 105 South 28th Avenue, Hattiesburg, MS 39401; tel. 601/288-1072; FAX. 601/288-3111; Marshall H. Tucker, FACHE, Administrator

North Mississippi Surgery Center, 500 West Eason Boulevard, Tupelo, MS 38801; tel. 601/841-4700; FAX. 601/841-3101; Beth Taylor, RN, Director

Southern Eye Center of Excellence, 1420 South 28th Avenue, Hattiesburg, MS 39402; tel. 601/264-3937; Lynn McMahan, M.D., Medical Director

Southwest Mississippi Ambulatory Surgery Center, 215 Marion Avenue, McComb, MS 39648; tel. 601/249-1477; FAX. 601/249-1375; Norman M. Price, Administrator

Surgicare of Jackson, 766 Lakeland Drive, Jackson, MS 39216; tel. 601/362-8700; FAX. 601/362-6439; Sheila Grillis, RN, Administrator

MISSOURI

Arnold Eye Surgery Center, Inc., 1265 East Primrose, Springfield, MO 65804; tel. 417/886-3937; FAX. 417/886-1285; Stephen C. Sheppard, Administrator

Section C

Associated Plastic Surgeons Ambulatory Surgical Center, 6420 Prospect, Suite 115, Kansas City, MO 64132; tel. 816/333–5524; Joni Reist, RN

BarnesCare, 401 Pine Street, St. Louis, MO 63102; tel. 314/331–3000; FAX. 314/331–3012; Gary Payne, Vice President, BJC Corporate Health

CMMP Surgical Center, 1705 Christy Drive, Jefferson City, MO 65101; tel. 573/635–7022; FAX. 573/635–7029; Angela R. Sumner–Hahn, Business Director

Cape Girardeau Outpatient Surgery Center, 1429 Mount Auburn Road, Cape Girardeau, MO 63701; tel. 573/334–5895; FAX. 573/335–2392; Katherine Bloodworth, RN, Administrator

Cataract Surgery Center of St. Louis, Inc., 900 North Highway 67 (Lindbergh), Florissant, MO 63031; tel. 314/838–0321; FAX. 314/838–4682; Karen E. Wilson, RN, Nurse Manager

Cataract Surgery Center of Young Eye Clinic, Inc., 3201 Ashland Avenue, St. Joseph, MO 64506; tel. 816/279–0079; FAX. 816/364–1100; Judy Watowa, RN, B.S.N., Administrator

Cataract and Glaucoma Outpatient Surgicenter, 7220 Watson Road, St. Louis, MO 63119; tel. 314/352–5515; Stanley C. Becker, M.D.

Center for Eye Surgery, 6650 Troost, Suite 305, Kansas City, MO 64131; tel. 816/276–7757; FAX. 816/926–2231; Connie B. Watson, Administrator

Creekwood Surgery Center, 211 Northeast 54th Street, Suite 100, Kansas City, MO 64118; tel. 816/455–4214; FAX. 816/455–4216; Carol Ohmes, Administrator

Creve Coeur Surgery Center, 633 Emerson, Creve Coeur, MO 63141; tel. 314/872–7100; Judy Henderson, Nursing Administrator

Doctors' Park Surgery, Inc., 30 Doctors' Park, Cape Girardeau, MO 63701; tel. 314/334–9606; FAX. 314/334–9608; Ronald G. Wittmer, President

ENT/Urology Surgical Care, Inc., 5301 Faraon Street, St. Joseph, MO 64506; tel. 816/364–2772; Sidney G. Christiansen, M.D.

Eye Surgery Center–The Cliffs, 4801 Cliff Avenue, Suite 100, Independence, MO 64055; tel. 816/478–4400; FAX. 816/478–8240; Patricia Thomas, RN, Director, Nursing

G.I. Diagnostics, Inc., 4321 Washington, Suite 5700, Kansas City, MO 64111; tel. 816/561–2000; FAX. 816/931–7559; Craig B. Reeves, Administrator

HealthSouth Surgery Center of West County, 1130 Town and Country Commons, Chesterfield, MO 63017; tel. 314/394–0698; FAX. 314/394–7493; Sherry Mohr, Administrator

Hunkeler Eye Surgery Center, Inc., 4321 Washington, Suite 6000, Kansas City, MO 64111; tel. 816/753–6511; FAX. 816/931–9498; Deborah M. Highfill, R.N.

Kansas City Surgicenter, Ltd., 1800 East Meyer Boulevard, Kansas City, MO 64132; tel. 816/523–0100; FAX. 816/523–6241; Barbara Klein, RN, Administrator

Laser Surgery Center North, 7700 South Florissant Road, St. Louis, MO 63122; tel. 314/261–2020; FAX. 314/821–4080; Irvin C. Hoffman, Administrator

Laser Surgery Center West, 1028 South Kirkwood, St. Louis, MO 63122; tel. 314/984–0080; FAX. 314/821–4080; Irvin C. Hoffman, Administrator

Midwest Eye Institute, 5139 Mattis Road, St. Louis, MO 63128; tel. 314/849–8400; Anwar Shah, M.D.

Missouri Surgery Center, Inc., 300 South Mount Auburn Road, Suite 200, Cape Girardeau, MO 63701; tel. 314/339–7575; FAX. 314/339–7887; Steve Telford, Administrator

North County Surgery Center, One Village Square, Hazelwood, MO 63042; tel. 314/895–4001; FAX. 314/895–1791; Connie Moore, Administrator

Outpatient Surgery Center, 450 North New Ballas Road, Suite 103, St. Louis, MO 63141; tel. 314/991–0776; FAX. 314/991–3076; Karen Barrow, Administrator

Regional Surgery Center, P.C., 1531 West 32nd Street, Suite 107, Joplin, MO 64804; tel. 417/781–9595; FAX. 417/781–9814; Cynthia Shofner, Administrator

South County Outpatient Surgery Center, 13303 Tesson Ferry Road, St. Louis, MO 63128; tel. 314/842–3200; Stephen L. Partridge, Administrator

St. Charles County Surgery Center, Inc., 4203 South Cloverleaf Drive, St. Peters, MO 63376; tel. 314/928–0087; FAX. 314/928–1242; Sandi Baber, Administrator

Surgery Center of Springfield, L.P., 1350 East Woodhurst Drive, Springfield, MO 65804; tel. 417/887–5243; FAX. 417/887–6507; Celine Snyder, RN, Administrator

Surgi–Care Center of Independence, 2311 Redwood Avenue, Independence, MO 64057; tel. 816/373–7995; FAX. 816/373–8580; Dolores Sabia, Administrator

The Ambulatory Head and Neck Surgical Center, 1965 South Fremont, Suite 1940, Springfield, MO 65804; tel. 417/887–5750; FAX. 417/887–6612; Charles R. Taylor, Administrator

The Endoscopy Center, 3800 South Whitney, Independence, MO 64055; tel. 816/478–6868; John A. Woltjen, M.D.

The Endoscopy Center II, 5330 North Oak Trafficway, Suite 100, Kansas City, MO 64118; tel. 816/836–1616; Jean Thompson, Public Relations, Marketing

The Surgery Center, 802 North Riverside Road, St. Joseph, MO 64507; tel. 816/364–5030; FAX. 816/364–5810; Nancy Moore, RN

The Tobin Eye Institute, 3902 Sherman Avenue, St. Joseph, MO 64506; tel. 816/279–1363; FAX. 816/233–8936; Linda S. Wildhagen, Administrator

Tri County Surgery Center, 1111 East Sixth Street, Washington, MO 63090; tel. 314/239–I766; FAX. 314/239–2964; Sharry Mohr, RN, Administrator

MONTANA

Billings Cataract and Laser Surgicenter, 1221 North 26th Street, Billings, MT 59101; tel. 406/252–5681

Eye Microsurgery Center, Inc., 1232 North 30th Street, Billings, MT 59101; tel. 406/256–9006; Nancy Oliphant, Office Manager

Flathead Outpatient Surgical Center, 66 Claremont Street, Kalispell, MT 59901; tel. 406/752–8484; FAX. 406/756–8008; Victoria L. Johnson, RN, Facility Manager

Great Falls Eye Surgery Center, Inc., 1717 Fourth Street South, Great Falls, MT 59405; tel. 406/727–9920; FAX. 406/727–9904

Montana Surgical Center, Inc., 840 South Montana, Butte, MT 59701; tel. 406/782–2391; Charles Harris, Manager

Northern Rockies Surgicenter, Inc., 1020 North 27th Street, Suite 100, Billings, MT 59101; tel. 406/248–7186; FAX. 406/248–6889; Sharon McLeod, RN, OR Supervisor

Rocky Mountain Eye Surgery Center, 700 West Kent, Missoula, MT 59801; tel. 406/543–8179; Darlene Timmerhoff, Administrator

Same Day Surgery Center, Inc., 300 North Willson, Suite 600F, Bozeman, MT 59715; tel. 406/586–1956; Ann Guenther, Supervisor

The Eye Surgicenter, 2475 Village Lane, Billings, MT 59102; tel. 406/252–6608; FAX. 406/252–6600; Sara Coleman, Supervisor

NEBRASKA

Aesthetic Surgical Images, P.C., 8900 West Dodge Road, Omaha, NE 68114; tel. 402/390–0100; FAX. 402/390–2711; Rita Petersen, Administrator

Anis Eye Institute, P.C., d/b/a The Nebraska Eye Surgical Center, 1500 South 48th Street, Suite 612, Lincoln, NE 68506; tel. 402/483–4448; FAX. 402/483–4750; Dr. Aziz Y. Anis

Bergan Mercy Surgical Center, 11704 West Center Road, Omaha, NE 68124; tel. 402/333–3111; Richard A. Hachten III

Clarkson Hospital Outpatient Surgery, 4353 Dodge Street, Omaha, NE 68131; tel. 402/552–6065; Dr. Louis Burgher, Administrator

Clarkson West Emergicare, 2727 S. 144th Street, Omaha, NE 68144; tel. 402/334–1243; Cindy Alloway, Director

Jones Eye Clinic, 825 North 90th Street, Omaha, NE 68114; tel. 402/397–2010; Craig Borsdorf, Administrator

Lincoln Surgery Center, 1710 South 70th, Suite 200, Lincoln, NE 68506; tel. 402/483–1550; FAX. 402/483–0476; Robin Linnafelter, Administrator

Omaha Surgical Center, 8051 West Center Road, Omaha, NE 68124; tel. 402/391–3333; James Quinn, M.D., Administrator

The Nebraska Eye Surgical Center, 1500 S. 48th Street, Suite 610, Lincoln, NE 68506; tel. 402/483–4448; Aziz Anis, MD, Administrator

The Omaha Eye Institute Surgery Center, 11606 Nicholas Street, Suite 200, Omaha, NE 68154; tel. 402/493–2020; FAX. 402/493–8987; Dr. Robert S. Vandervort, Administrator

The Urology Center, P.C., 111 1/2 South 90th Street, Omaha, NE 68114; tel. 402/397–9800; Laura Forehead, Administrator

Tobin Eye Institute, 4151 E Street, Omaha, NE 68107; tel. 402/731–1363; Dr. Robert Livingston, Administrator

NEVADA

Aesthetic Associates Day Surgery Center, 1580 East Desert Inn Road, Las Vegas, NV 89109; tel. 702/735–6755; FAX. 702/733–8221; Charles A. Vinnik, M.D., Administrator

Ambulatory Surgery Center of Nevada, 4631 E. Charleston Blvd., Las Vegas, NV 89104; tel. 702/438–8417; Neal A. Marek, Administrator

Carson Ambulatory Surgery Center, Inc., 1299 Mountain Street, Carson City, NV 89703; tel. 702/883–1700; FAX. 702/883–8905; Joan P. Lapham, RN, Executive Director

Carson Endoscopy Center, 707 North Minnesota, Carson City, NV 89703; tel. 702/884–4567; Jay M. Coller, Administrator

Carson Valley Ambulatory Surgery Center, 1107 Highway 395, Gardnerville, NV 89410; tel. 702/782–1595; Richard L. Davis, Administrator

Center for Outpatient Surgery, 343 Elm Street, Suite 100, Reno, NV 89503; tel. 702/789–6500; FAX. 702/789–6535; Christine Balascoe, Executive Director

Columbia Reno Medical Plaza, 2005 Silverada Boulevard, Suite 100, Reno, NV 89512; tel. 702/359–0212; FAX. 702/359–0645; Sandra Walker–Wright, Director, Operations

Columbia Sunrise Flamingo Surgery Center, 2565 East Flamingo Road, Las Vegas, NV 89121; tel. 702/697–7900; FAX. 702/697–5383; Carolyn C. Weaver, Administrator

Columbia Sunrise Surgical Center–Sahara, 2401 Paseo Del Prado, Las Vegas, NV 89102; tel. 702/362–7874; FAX. 702/362–3567; Stephanie Finkelstein, Administrator

Desert Surgery Center, 1569 East Flamingo Road, Suite B, Las Vegas, NV 89119; tel. 702/735–5177; FAX. 702/735–3140; Steven C. Wilson, Administrator

Diagnostic Imaging of South Nevada, ASC, 1661 East Flamingo Road, Las Vegas, NV 89119; tel. 702/791–0380; Judith L. Atwell, Administrator

Digestive Disease Center, 2136 East Desert Inn Road, Suite B, Las Vegas, NV 89109; tel. 702/734–0075; Osama Haikal, M.D., Administrator

Digestive Health Center, 5250 Kietzke Lane, Reno, NV 89511; tel. 702/829–8855; FAX. 702/829–3757; Kenneth A. Griggs, Jr., Administrator

Endoscopic Institute of Nevada, 3777 Pecos–McLeod, Suite 102, Las Vegas, NV 89121; tel. 702/433–5686; Vicki A. Montijo, Administrator

Endoscopy Center of Nevada, LTD, 700 Shadow Lane, Suite 165B, Las Vegas, NV 89106; tel. 702/382–8101; Dipak K. Desai, Administrator

Eye Surgery Center of Nevada, 3839 North Carson Street, Carson City, NV 89706; tel. 702/882–3950; FAX. 708/882–1726; Michael J. Fischer, M.D., Administrator

Foot Surgery Center of Northern Nevada, 1300 East Plumb Lane, Suite A, Reno, NV 89502; tel. 702/829–8066; FAX. 702/829–8069; Dr. Frank M. Davis, Jr., Administrator

Ford Center for Foot Surgery, 2321 Pyramid Way, Sparks, NV 89431; tel. 702/331–1919; FAX. 702/331–2008; Dr. L. Bruce Ford, Administrator

Gastrointestinal Diagnostic Clinic, 3196 South Maryland Parkway, Suite 207, Las Vegas, NV 89109; tel. 702/369–3400; Nourollah Gharhreman, MD, Administrator

Goldring Surgical Center, 2020 Goldring, Suite 300, Las Vegas, NV 89106; tel. 817/922–9042; Texas Gustavson, Administrator

Institute for Pain Surgery, 630 South Rancho Drive, Suite A, Las Vegas, NV 89106; tel. 702/870–1111; FAX. 702/870–7121; Carl R. Noback, Administrator

La Tourette Surgical Center, 2300 South Rancho Drive, Suite 216, Las Vegas, NV 89102; tel. 702/386–6979; FAX. 702/386–8700; Gary J. La Tourette, Administrator

Las Vegas Surgicare, Ltd., 870 South Rancho Drive, Las Vegas, NV 89106; tel. 702/870–2090; FAX. 702/870–5468; Stephanie Finkelstein, Administrator

NMC–Red Rock Surgical Center, 5701 West Charleston Boulevard, Suite 102, Las Vegas, NV 89102; tel. 702/870–3443; FAX. 702/258–8238; Diane McNamee, Administrator

Nevada Institute of Ambulatory Surgery, 2316 West Charleston, Suite 120, Las Vegas, NV 89102; tel. 702/878–5668; FAX. 702/878–0265; Lois M. Webb, RN, Administrator

Nevada Surgery Center, 4187 Pecos Road, Las Vegas, NV 89121; tel. 702/458–2522; Lyndell Kewley, Administrator

Northern Nevada Plastic Surgery Associates, 932 Ryland Street, Reno, NV 89502; tel. 702/322–3446; FAX. 702/322–4529; Averill M. Moser, RN, Administrator

Reno Endoscopy Center, Inc., 753 Ryland Street, Reno, NV 89502; tel. 702/329–1009; FAX. 702/329–4992; Jay M. Collier, Administrator

Reno Outpatient Surgery Center, LTD., 350 West Sixth Street, Reno, NV 89503; tel. 702/334–4888; Sandra Walker–Wright, Administrator

SMA Surgery Center, 2450 West Charleston, Las Vegas, NV 89106; tel. 702/877–8660; FAX. 702/877–5180; Steve Evans, M.D., Medical Director

Sahara–Lindell Surgery Center, 2575 Lindell Road, Las Vegas, NV 89102; tel. 702/362–3937; FAX. 702/362–7935; Elizabeth Sayers, Administrator

Shepherd Eye Surgicenter, 3575 Pecos McLeod, Las Vegas, NV 89121; tel. 702/731–2088; FAX. 702/734–7836; Leslie E. Soper, Administrator

Sierra Center for Foot Surgery, 1801 North Carson, Suite B, Carson City, NV 89701; tel. 702/882–1441; FAX. 702/882–6844; H. Kim Bean, MD, Administrator

Valley View Surgery Center, 1330 Valley View Boulevard, Las Vegas, NV 89102; tel. 702/870–7101; FAX. 702/870–7118; Steven C. Wilson, Administrator

NEW HAMPSHIRE

Ambulatory Surgery Center, 100 Hitchcock Way, Manchester, NH 03104; tel. 603/695–2500; Deborah A. Andriski, Administrator

Bedford Ambulatory Surgical Center, 11 Washington Place, Bedford, NH 03110; tel. 603/622–3670; FAX. 603/626–9750; Linda Dwyer, RN, B.S.N., Director

Clinic Surgery Center (The), 253 Pleasant Street, Concord, NH 03301; tel. 603/226–2200; Kevin Appleton, Administrator

Day Surgery, 590 Court Street, Keene, NH 03431; tel. 603/357–3411; Michael Chelstowski, Director

Dunning Street Ambulatory Care Center, Seven Dunning Street, Claremont, NH 03743; tel. 603/543–3501; Jyl Bradley, Administrator

Elliot One Day Surgery Center, 445 Cypress Street, Manchester, NH 03103; tel. 603/627–4889; FAX. 603/626–4300; Donna Quinn, RN, B.S.N., M.B.A., Director

Nashua Eye Surgery Center, Inc., Five Coliseum Avenue, Nashua, NH 03063; tel. 603/882–9800; FAX. 603/882–0556; Paul O'Leary, Administrator

New Hampshire Eye Surgicenter, 19 Riverway Place, Bedford Commons, Building One, Bedford, NH 03110; tel. 603/627–9540; FAX. 603/668–7952; Paul Pender, M.D.

Northeast Pain Consultation and Management PC, 255 State Route 16, Somersworth, NH 03878; tel. 603/692–3166; FAX. 603/692–3168; Michael J. O'Connell, M.D., M.H.A., Director

Nutfield Surgicenter, Inc., 44 Birch Street, Suite 304, Derry, NH 03038; tel. 603/898–3610; Claire Teneglia, Administrator

Orthopeadic Surgery Center, 264 Pleasant Street, Concord, NH 03301; tel. 603/228–7211; FAX. 603/228–7192; Gail McNulty, Administrator

Salem Surgery Center, 32 Stiles Road, Salem, NH 03079; tel. 603/898–3610; FAX. 603/890–3313; Deborah M. Baker, Administrator

Seacoast Outpatient Surgical Center, 200 Route 108, Somersworth, NH 03878; tel. 603/749–4327; FAX. 603/749–5379; David M. Laplante, Executive Director

The Clinic Surgery Center, 253 Pleasant Street, Concord, NH 03301; tel. 603/226–2200; Kevin Appleton, Administrator

NEW JERSEY

A Center for Advanced Surgery, Three Winslow Place, Paramus, NJ 07652; tel. 201/843–9390; FAX. 201/843–0591; Marc L. Reichman, Director of Administration

Affiliated Ambulatory Surgery PA, 182 South Street, Suite One, Morristown, NJ 07960; tel. 201/267–0300; FAX. 201/984–2670; Sylvia Wexler, Administrator

Allan H. Schoenfeld, M.D., PA, 501 Lakehurst Road, Toms River, NJ 08753

Arthur W. Perry, MD, FACS Plastic Surgery Center, 3055 Route 27, Franklin Park, NJ 08823; tel. 908/422–9600; FAX. 908/422–9606; Arthur W. Perry, Director

Associated Surgeon of Northern New Jersey, 25 Rockwood Place, Englewood, NJ 07631; tel. 201/567–3999; FAX. 201/567–9288

Atlantic Eye Physicians, P.A., d/b/a Monmouth Opthalmic Associates, P.A., 279 Third Avenue, Suite 204, Long Branch, NJ 07740; tel. 908/222–7373; FAX. 908/229–1556; Daniel B. Goldberg, M.D., President

Atrium Surgery Center, Inc., 195 Route 46, Suite 202, Mine Hill, NJ 07803; tel. 201/989–5185; FAX. 201/328–4097; Jennifer Rand, RN, CNOR, President

Bergen Gastroenterology, 466 Old Hook Road, Suite One, Emerson, NJ 07630; tel. 201/967–8221; FAX. 201/967–0340; Robert Ein, M.D., President

Bergen Surgical Center, One West Ridgewood Avenue, Paramus, NJ 07652; tel. 201/444–7666; Ralph Perricelli, Administrator

Burlington County Internal Medicine, 651 John F Kennedy Way, Willingboro, NJ 08046

Campus Eye Group, 1700 Whitehorse Hamilton Square Road, Suite A, Hamilton Square, NJ 08690

Cataract Surgery and Laser Center, Inc., 19 21 Fair Lawn Avenue, Fair Lawn, NJ 07410

Cataract and Laser Institute, PA, 101 Prospect Street, Suite 102, Lakewood, NJ 08701; tel. 908/367–0699; FAX. 908/367–0937

Center for Special Surgery, 104 Lincoln Avenue, Hawthorne, NJ 07506; tel. 201/427–6800; FAX. 201/427–9602; John Tauber, Business Administrator

Clifton Surgery Center, 1117 Route 46 East Suite 303, Clifton, NJ 07013; tel. 201/779–7210; FAX. 201/779–7387; Ramon Silen, M.D., President, Medical Director

Drs. Scherl Scherl Chessler and Zingler, P.A., 1555 Center Avenue, Fort Lee, NJ 07024; tel. 201/945–6564; FAX. 201/461–9038; Dorothy Hoffmann–Freeman, Office Manager

Eichler Surgeye Center, 50 Newark Avenue, Belleville, NJ 07109; tel. 201/751–6060; FAX. 201/450–1464; Eileen Beltramba, Administrator

Endo–Surgi Center, 1201 Morris Avenue, Union, NJ 07083; tel. 908/686–0066; Sharon DeMato, Administrator

Endo/Surgical Center of New Jersey, 925 Clifton Avenue, Clifton, NJ 07013; tel. 201/777–3938; FAX. 201/777–6738; Pauline Perrino, RN, CGRN, Director of Nursing

Englewood Endoscopic Associates, 420 Grand Avenue, Englewood, NJ 07631

Enrico Monti and Murphy, PA, 715 Broadway, Second Floor, Paterson, NJ 07514

Essex Eye Surgery and Laser Center, 1460 Broad Street, Bloomfield, NJ 07003; tel. 201/338–5566; FAX. 201/338–0753

Eye Physician of Sussex County Surgical Center, 183 High Street, Newton, NJ 07860; tel. 201/383–6345; FAX. 201/383–0032; Patricia Fowler, RN

Eye Surgery Princeton, 419 North Harrison Street, Princeton, NJ 08540; tel. 609/921–9437; FAX. 609/921–0277; Richard H. Wong, M.D., Medical Director

Freehold Ent, d/b/a Face to Face, Patriots Park, 222 Schanck Road, Freehold, NJ 07728; tel. 908/431–1666; FAX. 908/431–1665

Garden State Ambulatory Surgical Center, One Plaza Drive, Suite 20–21, Toms River, NJ 08757; tel. 908/341–7010; FAX. 908/341–5066; Moshe Rothkopf, M.D., FACS

Garden State Surgi–Center, 550 Newark Avenue, Jersey City, NJ 07306; tel. 201/795–0646; FAX. 201/795–0744; Gary P. Pard, Executive Director

Gastroenterology Diag Northern New Jersey, 205 Browertown Road, West Paterson, NJ 07424; Barbara Wattenberg, Administrative Director

Hackensack Surgery Center, 321 Essex Street, Hackensack, NJ 07601

Hand Surgery and Rehabilitation Center of New Jersey, P.A., 5000 Sagemore Drive, Suite 103, Marlton, NJ 08053; tel. 609/983–4263; FAX. 609/983–9362

HealthSouth Surgical Center of South Jersey, 130 Gaither Drive, Suite 160, Mount Laurel, NJ 08054; tel. 609/722–7000; FAX. 609/722–8962; Eleanor O. Peschko, Administrator

Horizon Laser and Eye Surgery Center, 9701 Ventnor Avenue, Suite 301, Margate City, NJ 08402; tel. 609/822–7171; FAX. 609/822–3211; Suzanne D. Bruno, Administrator

Hunterdon Center for Surgery, 121 Highway 31, Flemington, NJ 08822; tel. 908/806–7017; David I. Rosen, M.D., Medical Director

James Street Surgical Suite, 261 James Street, Morristown, NJ 07960

Mediplex Surgery Center, 98 James Street, Suite 108, Edison, NJ 08820–3998; tel. 908/632–1600; FAX. 908/632–1678; Ruth Mosher, Administrator

Metropolitan Surgical Association, 40 Eagle Street, Englewood, NJ 07631

Mid Atlantic Eye Center, 70 East Front Street, Red Bank, NJ 07701; tel. 908/741–0858; FAX. 908/219–0180; Walter J. Kahn, M.D.

Middlesex Same Day Surgical Center, 561 Cranbury Road, East Brunswick, NJ 08816; tel. 908/390–4300; FAX. 908/390–4405; Evelyn Tornquist, Office Manager

Monmouth Surgi Center, Inc., 370 State Highway 35, Middletown, NJ 07748

Newark Mini–Surgi Site, Inc., 145 Roseville Avenue, Newark, NJ 07107; tel. 201/485–3300; FAX. 201/485–2404; Monica Chomsky

North Jersey Center for Surgery, 39 Newton Sparta Road, Newton, NJ 07860; tel. 201/383–0153; FAX. 201/383–3201; Bruno J. Casatelli, D.P.M., Administrator

North Jersey Women's Medical Center, Inc., 6000 Kennedy Boulevard, West New York, NJ 07093; tel. 201/869–9293; Saul Luchs, M.D.

Northern New Jersey Eye Institute, 71 Second Street, South Orange, NJ 07079; tel. 201/763–2203; FAX. 201/762–9449; Shirley Vitale, Medical, Business Director

Northwest Jersey Ambulatory Surgery Center, 350 Sparta Avenue, Sparta, NJ 07871; tel. 201/729–8580; FAX. 201/729–8185; Sharon L. Marquardt, RN, Operating Room Coordinator

Ocean County Eye Associates, P.C., 18 Mule Road, Toms River, NJ 08755

Ocean Surgical Pavilion, Inc., 1907 Highway 35, Suite Nine, Oakhurst, NJ 07755; tel. 908/517–8885; FAX. 908/517–8589; Marie T. Scoles, RN, Administrator

Ophthalmic Physicians of Monmouth, 733 North Beers Street, Holmdel, NJ 07733; tel. 908/739–0707; FAX. 908/739–6722; Beverly Savlov, Office Manager

Pavonia Surgery Center, Inc., 600 Pavonia Avenue, Fourth Floor, Jersey City, NJ 07306; tel. 201/216–1700; FAX. 201/216–1800; William H. Constad, M.D., President

Princeton Ambulatory Surgery Center, Inc., 281 Witherspoon Street, Third Floor, Princeton, NJ 08542; tel. 609/497–4380; FAX. 609/497–4986; Dennis Doody, President

Princeton Orthopedic Association, 727 State Road, Princeton, NJ 08540; tel. 609/924–8131; William G. Hyncik, Jr., Executive Director

Retina Consultants Surgery Center, 39 Sycamore Avenue, Little Silver, NJ 07739

Ridgedale Surgery Center, 14 Ridgedale Avenue, Suite 120, Cedar Knolls, NJ 07927; tel. 201/605–5151; FAX. 201/605–1208; Enza Guagenti, Administrator

Ridgewood Ambulatory Surgery Center, 1200 Ridgewood Avenue, Ridgewood, NJ 07450; tel. 201/444–4499; FAX. 201/612–8114

Roseland Surgery Center, 556 Eagle Rock Avenue, Roseland, NJ 07068; tel. 201/226–1717; FAX. 201/403–9034; Joseph Brandspiegel, Executive Director

Saddle Brook Surgicenter, Inc., 289 Market Street, Saddle Brook, NJ 07663; tel. 201/843–4444; FAX. 201/368–2817

Seashore Surgery Center, 1907 New Road, Northfield, NJ 08225; tel. 609/646–2323; FAX. 609/645–9780; Michael J. Lahoud, Administrator

Shore Surgery Center, 142 Route 35, Eatontown, NJ 07724; tel. 908/542–9666; FAX. 908/542–9393; Simone Bendary, Manager

Somerset Eye Institute, P.C., 562 Easton Avenue, Somerset, NJ 08873

Somerset Surgical Center, P.A., 1081 Route 22 West, Bridgewater, NJ 08807

South Jersey Endoscopy Center, 17 West Red Bank Avenue, Suite 302, Woodbury, NJ 08096; tel. 609/848–4464; FAX. 609/848–8706; Sue Lampman, Billing Manager

South Jersey Surgicenter, 2835 South Delsea Drive, Vineland, NJ 08360; tel. 609/696–0020; FAX. 609/794–9799; James Yondura, RN, Administrator

Springfield Eye Surgery Laser Center, 105 Morris Avenue, Springfield, NJ 07081; tel. 201/376–3113; FAX. 201/376–1378; Dr. Christine Zolli

St. Barnabas Outpatient Centers, Same Day Surgery Center, 101 Old Short Hills Road, West Orange, NJ 07052; tel. 201/325–6565; FAX. 201/325–6551; Veronica Rose, RN, Acting Administrative Director

Summit Eye Group T/A Suburban Eye Institute, 369 Springfield Avenue, Berkeley Heights, NJ 07922; tel. 908/464–4600; FAX. 908/464–4737; Patricia K. Ketcham, RN, Administrator

Section C

Summit Surgical and Endoscopy Center, 110 Carnie Boulevard, Voorhees, NJ 08043; tel. 609/770–5813; FAX. 609/751–8960; Maureen Miller, Executive Director

Surgery Center of Cherry Hill, 408 Route 70 East, Cherry Hill, NJ 08034; tel. 609/354–1600; FAX. 609/429–7555; Yvonne M. Bley, Director of Nursing

Surgicare Surgical Associates, PC, 15 01 Broadway, Route 4 West, Suite One and Three, Fairlawn, NJ 07410; tel. 201/791–6585; John H. Haffar, M.D., Medical Director

Surgicare of Central Jersey, Inc., 40 Stirling Road, Watchung, NJ 07060; tel. 908/769–8000; FAX. 908/668–3139; Jacqueline Jerko, Executive Director

Teaneck Gastroenterology and Endoscopy Center, 1086 Teaneck Road, Suite Three B, Teaneck, NJ 07666; tel. 201/837–9636; FAX. 201/837–9544

The Endoscopy Center of Red Bank, 365 Broad Street, Red Bank, NJ 07701; tel. 908/842–4294; FAX. 908/842–3854; Elizabeth Boyle, Provider Relations

The Endoscopy Center of South Jersey, 2791 South Delsea Drive, South Vineland, NJ 08360; tel. 609/691–1400; FAX. 609/691–7117; Richard Wagar, Assistant Director

The Eye Care Center, 500 West Main Street, Freehold, NJ 07728; tel. 908/462–8707; FAX. 908/462–1296; Dale A. Ingram, Administrator

The Hernia Center, 222 Schanck Road, Suite 100, Freehold, NJ 07728; tel. 908/462–2999; FAX. 908/462–7760; Jackie Porter, RN

The New Jersey Eye Center, 21 West Main Street, Bergenfield, NJ 07621; tel. 201/384–7333; FAX. 201/385–3881; Joyce Katzman, Administrator

The Peck Center Incorporated, 1200 Route 46, Clifton, NJ 07013; tel. 201/471–3906; FAX. 201/471–7048; George C. Peck, Jr., M.D.

The Surgical Center at South Jersey Eye Physicians, P.A., 509 South Lenola Road, Building 11, Moorestown, NJ 08057; tel. 609/727–9333; FAX. 609/727–0064; Janet Daniels, RN, ASC Nurse Manager

Trocki Plastic Surgery Center, PA, 635 Tilton Road, Northfield, NJ 08225

United Hospital Community Health Center, 194 Clinton Avenue, Newark, NJ 07108; tel. 201/242–2300; Delores Henderson

NEW MEXICO

Alamogordo Eye Clinic and Surgical Center, 1124 10th Street, Alamogordo, NM 88310; tel. 505/434–1200; FAX. 505/437–3947; Donald J. Ham, Administrator

Eastern New Mexico Eye Clinic, 1820 West 21st Street, Clovis, NM 88101; tel. 505/762–2207; Dik S. Cheung, M.D.

HealthSouth Albuquerque Surgery Center, 1720 Wyoming Boulevard, N.E., Albuquerque, NM 87112; tel. 505/292–9200; FAX. 505/292–1398; Sharon Prudhomme, Administrator

Lazaro Eye Surgical Center, 1131 Mall Drive, Las Cruces, NM 88011; tel. 505/522–7676; Corine B. Lazaro, M.D., Administrator

Northside Presbyterian, P.O. Box 26666, 5901 Harper Drive, NE, Albuquerque, NM 87125; tel. 505/823–8500; FAX. 505/823–8088; Robert Garcia, Administrator

Presbyterian Family Healthcare, 4100 High Resort Boulevard, Rio Rancho, NM 87124; tel. 505/823–8804; Andrew Scianimanico, Administrator

The Endoscopy Center of Santa Fe, 1650 Hospital Drive, Suite 900, Santa Fe, NM 87505; tel. 505/988–3373; FAX. 505/984–1858; Jim Howlett, Administrator

Valley Eye Surgery Center, 110 North Coronado Avenue, Espanola, NM 87532; tel. 505/753–7391; FAX. 505/753–2749; Dr. Gary Puro

NEW YORK

Ambulatory Surgery Center of Brooklyn, 313 43rd Street, Brooklyn, NY 11232; tel. 718/369–1900; FAX. 718/965–4157; Michael M. Levi, M.D., Ph.D., Governing Authority

Ambulatory Surgery Center of Greater New York, Inc., 1101 Pelham Parkway, N., Bronx, NY 10469; tel. 718/515–3500; FAX. 718/655–1795, ext. 3204; Joanne McLaughlin, Administrator

Brook Plaza Ambulatory Surgical Center, 1901 Utica Avenue, Brooklyn, NY 11234; tel. 718/968–8700; Sharron Resnick, Office Manager

Brooklyn Eye Surgery Center, 1301–1311 Avenue J, Brooklyn, NY 11230; tel. 718/645–0600; FAX. 718/692–4456; Rosalind A. Kochman, Administrator

Buffalo Ambulatory Services, Inc., 3095 Harlem Road, Cheektowaga, NY 14225; tel. 716/896–7234

Central New York Eye Center, 22 Green Street, Poughkeepsie, NY 12601; tel. 914/471–3720; Maureen Lashway

Day–Op Center of Long Island, Inc., 110 Willis Avenue, Mineola, NY 11501; tel. 516/294–0030; FAX. 516/294–0228; Robin Fishman, Executive Director

Fifth Avenue Surgery Center, 1049 Fifth Avenue, New York, NY 10028; tel. 212/772–6667; Francois Simon, Vice President

Harrison Center Outpatient Surgery, Inc., 550 Harrison Street, Suite 230, Syracuse, NY 13202; tel. 315/472–4424; FAX. 315/475–8056; Margaret M. Alteri, Administrator, Chief Executive Officer

Hurley Avenue Surgical Center, Inc., 40 Hurley Avenue, Kingston, NY 12401; tel. 914/338–4777; FAX. 914/339–7339; Steven L. Kelley, Administrator

Lattimore Community Surgicenter, 125 Lattimore Road, Rochester, NY 14620; tel. 716/473–9000; FAX. 716/473–9018; John J. Goehle, CPA, Administrator

Long Island Eye Surgery Center, 601 Suffolk Avenue, Brentwood, NY 11717; tel. 516/231–4455

Long Island Surgi–Center, 1895 Walt Whitman Road, Melville, NY 11747; tel. 516/293–9700; FAX. 516/293–1018; Howard Leemon, D.D.S.

Mackool Eye Institute, 31–27 41st Street, Astoria, NY 11103; tel. 718/728–3400; Jeanne Mackool, Administrator

Millard Fillmore Ambulatory Surgery Center, 215 Klein Road, Williamsville, NY 14221; tel. 716/689–2300; FAX. 716/689–2385; Gary Schultz, Fiscal Officer

Nassau Center for Ambulatory Surgery, Inc., 400 Endo Boulevard, Garden City, NY 11530; tel. 516/832–8504; FAX. 516/832–1085; Miriam DeJesus, RN, Operating Room Supervisor

New York Institute for Same Day Surgery, Inc., 99 Dutch Hill Plaza, Orangeburg, NY 10962; tel. 914/359–9000; FAX. 914/359–1495; Richard Sherman, CPA, Director of Finance and Business Development

North Shore Surgi Center, Inc., 989 Jericho Turnpike, Smithtown, NY 11787; tel. 516/864–7100; FAX. 516/864–7129; Gerald Mazzola, Administrator

Our Lady of Victory Surgery Center, 6300 Powers Road, Orchard Park, NY 14127; tel. 716/667–3222; FAX. 716/667–3120; Dana M. Mata, Administrative Director

Queens Surgi–Center, 83–40 Woodhaven Boulevard, Glendale, NY 11385; tel. 718/849–8700; FAX. 718/849–6523; Stanley H. Kornhauser, Ph.D., Chief Operating Officer

Queens Surgical Community Center, 46–04 31st Avenue, Long Island City, NY 11103; tel. 718/545–5050; FAX. 718/721–8709; Mr. Misk, Partner

Same Day Surgery of Latham, Inc., Seven Century Hill Drive, Latham, NY 12110; tel. 518/785–5741; FAX. 518/785–5741; Bruce Woods, Administrator

Westfall Surgery Center, LLP, 919 Westfall Road, Rochester, NY 14618; tel. 716/256–1330; FAX. 716/256–3823; Gary J. Scott, Administrative Director

NORTH CAROLINA

Asheboro Endoscopy Center, 700 Sunset Avenue, P.O. Box 4830, Asheboro, NC 27203; tel. 910/626–4328; FAX. 910/625–9941; Trudy Hogan, RN, Clinical Director

Asheville Hand Ambulatory Surgery Center, 34 Granby Street, P.O. Box 1980, Asheville, NC 28802; tel. 704/258–0847; FAX. 704/258–0374; E. Brown Crosby, M.D., Executive Officer

Blue Ridge Day Surgery Center, 2308 Wesvill Court, Raleigh, NC 27607; tel. 919/781–4311; FAX. 919/781–0625; Susan S. Swift, Facility Manager

Carteret Surgery Center, 3714 Guardian Avenue, Morehead City, NC 28557; tel. 919/247–2101; Frances Meyer, Administrator

Chapel Hill Surgical Center, 109 Conner Drive, Suite 1201, Chapel Hill, NC 27514; tel. 919/968–0611; FAX. 919/967–8637; Gary S. Berger, M.D., President

Charlotte Surgery and Laser Center, 2825 Randolph Road, Charlotte, NC 28211; tel. 704/377–1647; FAX. 704/358–8267; Margaret Slattery, Manager

Christenbury Ambulatory Surgical Center, 449 North Wendover Road Park Place, Charlotte, NC 28211; tel. 704/332–9365; Brenda Haughney, Administrator

Cleveland Ambulatory Services, 1100 North Lafayette Street, Shelby, NC 28150; tel. 704/482–1331; Thomas D. Bailey, M.D., Medical Director

Columbia MediVision of Hickory, 27 13th Avenue, N.E., Hickory, NC 28601; tel. 704/328–1493; FAX. 704/322–6097; Marie Hudson,RN, BSN, Administrator

Columbia Medivision Inc., 2200 East Seventh Street, Charlotte, NC 28204; tel. 704/334–4317; FAX. 704/377–1830; Dian H. Matthews, Administrator

Durham Ambulatory Surgical Center, 120 Carver Street, P.O. Box 15727, Durham, NC 27704; tel. 919/477–9677; FAX. 919/479–6755; Joseph T. Jordan, Director

Eye Surgery Center of Shelby, 1622 East Marion Street, Shelby, NC 28150; tel. 704/482–2020; FAX. 704/482–7707; Frank T. Hannah, Administrator

Eye Surgery and Laser Clinic, 500 Lake Concord Road, N.E., Concord, NC 28025; tel. 704/782–1127; FAX. 704/782–1207; David K. Harper, Administrator

Fayetteville Ambulatory Surgery Center, 1781 Metromedical Drive, Fayetteville, NC 28304; tel. 910/323–1647; FAX. 910/323–4142; John T. Henley, Jr., M.D., Director

FemCare, 62 Orange Street, Asheville, NC 28801; tel. 704/255–8400; Philip J. Kittner, M.D., Executive Director

Gaston Ambulatory Surgery, 2545 Court Drive, Gastonia, NC 28054; tel. 704/834–2086; FAX. 704/834–2085; James R. Parks, II, Administrator

Goldsboro Endoscopy Center, Inc., 2705 Medical Office Place, Goldsboro, NC 27534; tel. 919/580–9111; FAX. 919/580–0988; Venkata C. Motaparthy, M.D., Chief Executive Officer

Greensboro Center for Digestive Diseases, 520 North Elam Avenue, P.O. Box 10829, Greensboro, NC 27403; tel. 910/547–1718; FAX. 910/547–1711; Paul Green, Clinical Operations Director

Greensboro Specialty Surgical Center, 522 North Elam Avenue, Greensboro, NC 27403; tel. 910/294–1833; FAX. 910/294–8831; Ken Overbey, Administrator

Hawthorne Surgical Center, 1999 South Hawthorne Road, Winston–Salem, NC 27103; tel. 910/718–6800; FAX. 910/718–6847; Teresa L. Carter, Facility Director

HealthSouth Blue Ridge Surgery Center, 2308 Wesvill Court, Raleigh, NC 27607; tel. 919/781–4311; Susan Swift, Administrator

HealthSouth Surgery Center of Charlotte, 2825 Randolph Rd., Charlotte, NC 28211; tel. 704/377–1647; Margaret L. Slattery, Administrator

HealthSouth Surgicenter of Wilson, 1709 Medical Park Drive, Wilson, NC 27893; tel. 919/237–5649; Phyllis S. Renfrow, Administrator

High Point Endoscopy Center, Inc., 624 Quaker Lane, Suite C–106, High Point, NC 27262; tel. 910/885–1400; Lester E. Hurrelbrink, Administrator

High Point Surgery Center, 600 Lindsay Street, P.O. Box 2476, High Point, NC 27261; tel. 910/884–6068; FAX. 910/888–6111; Joan Gayle, Administrator

Iredell Head, Neck and Ear Ambulatory Surgery Center, Inc., 707 Bryant Street, Statesville, NC 28677; tel. 704/873–5224; FAX. 704/873–5984; Scott Seagle, Administrator

Iredell Surgical Center, 1720 Davie Avenue, Statesville, NC 28677; tel. 704/871–0081; Kimberly J. Ericson, Administrator

Lexington Ambulatory Surgery, Inc., Seven Medical Park Drive, Lexington, NC 27292; tel. 910/243–2431; FAX. 910/243–2359; Kathy R. Anderson, Administrator

MediVision, Inc., 3312 Battleground Avenue, Greensboro, NC 27410; tel. 919/282–8330; Jeanne Whitley, Administrator

MediVision, Inc., 2170 Midland Road, P.O. Box 1938, Southern Pines, NC 28387; tel. 910/295–1221; FAX. 910/295–0512; Kathy Stout, RN, Administrator

New Bern Outpatient Surgery Center, 801 College Court, P.O. Box 12446, New Bern, NC 28561; tel. 919/633–2000; FAX. 919/633–0096; Lila Cotten, Business Manager

Section C

Piedmont Gastroenterology Center, Inc., 1901 South Hawthorne Road, Suite 308, Winston–Salem, NC 27103; tel. 910/760–4340; FAX. 919/765–2869; Charles H. Hauser, Administrator

Plastic Surgery Center of North Carolina, Inc., 2901 Maplewood Avenue, Winston–Salem, NC 27103; tel. 910/768–6210; FAX. 910/768–6236; Melba Edwards, Administrator

Quandrangle Endoscopy Center, 620 South Memorial Drive, Greenville, NC 27834; tel. 919/752–6101; Mark Dellasega

RMS Surgery Center, 5200 North Croatan Highway, Kitty Hawk, NC 27949; tel. 919/261–9009; FAX. 919/261–4329; Dougleas L. Fairfax, FACHE, Administrator

Raleigh Endoscopy Center, 3320 Wake Forest Road, Raleigh, NC 27609; tel. 919/878–1151; Robert N. Harper, Jr., Medical Director

Raleigh Plastic Surgery Center, Inc., 1112 Dresser Court, Raleigh, NC 27609; tel. 919/872–2616; FAX. 919/872–2771; Kelly Hodges, Administrator

Raleigh Women's Health Organization, Inc., 3613 Haworth Drive, Raleigh, NC 27609; tel. 919/783–0444; FAX. 919/781–8432; Susan Hill, Vice President

SameDay Surgery Center at Presbyterian, 1800 East Fourth Street, P.O. Box 34425, Charlotte, NC 28234; tel. 704/384–4200; Chip Day, Administrator

Southern Eye Associates, P.A., Ophthalmic Surgery Center, 2801 Blue Ridge Road, Suite 200, Raleigh, NC 27607; tel. 919/571–0081; Philip L. Martin, Administrator

Surgery Center of Morganton Eye Physicians, P.A., 335 East Parker Road, Morganton, NC 28655; tel. 704/433–6225; L. A. Raynor, M.D., Medical Director

SurgiCenter of Wilson, 209 Richards Street, Wilson, NC 27893; tel. 919/237–5649; FAX. 919/237–4977; Phyllis Renfrow, President

Surgical Center of Greensboro, Inc., 1211 Virginia Street, P.O. Box 29347, Greensboro, NC 27429; tel. 919/272–0012; FAX. 919/272–4063; Ken Overbey, Administrator

Surgicenter Services of Pitt, Inc., 102 Bethesda Drive, Greenville, NC 27834; tel. 919/816–7700; FAX. 919/816–7733; Anna M. Weaver, Administrator

The Endoscopy Center, 191 Biltmore Avenue, Asheville, NC 28801; tel. 704/254–0881; Michael Grier, M.D.

The Surgery Center, 166 Memorial Court, Jacksonville, NC 28546; tel. 910/353–9565; FAX. 919/353–5497; Takey Crist, M.D., President

WHA Medical Center, PLLC, 1202 Medical Center Drive, Wilmington, NC 28401; tel. 910/341–3433; Diane A. Atkinson, Executive Director

Wilmington SurgCare, Inc., 1801 South 17th Street, Wilmington, NC 28401; tel. 910/763–4555; FAX. 910/763–9044; Catherine Peterman, President, Chief Executive Officer

Wilson OB–GYN, 2500 Horton Boulevard, Zip 27893, P.O. Box 7639, Wilson, NC 27895; tel. 919/206–1000; FAX. 919/237–0704; Daniel P. Michalak, M.D., Administrator

Woman Care and Carolina Birth Center, 712 North Elm Street, High Point, NC 27262; tel. 910/889–3646; Robert C. Crawford, M.D., Chief Executive Officer

NORTH DAKOTA

Centennial Medical Center, 1500 24th Avenue, S.W., Minot, ND 58702; tel. 701/852–0777; Dr. Manuel Neto, Administrator

Dakota Day Surgery, 1717 South University Drive, P.O. Box 6014, Fargo, ND 58103; tel. 701/280–4700; FAX. 701/280–4703; Vicki Beaton, Administrator

Day Surgery–Wahpeton, 275 South 11th Street, Wahpeton, ND 58075; tel. 701/642–2000; FAX. 701/671–4153; Keith Robberstad, Administrator

Grand Forks Clinic Ltd., ASC, 1000 South Columbia Road, Grand Forks, ND 58201; tel. 701/780–6000; Wayne K. Larson, Associate Administrator

Great Plains Clinic Surgery Center, 33 Ninth Street, W., Dickinson, ND 58601; tel. 701/225–6017; FAX. 701/225–5018; Joel Frey, Administrator

Medical Arts, ASC, Inc., 400 East Burdick Expressway, Minot, ND 58702; tel. 701/857–7000; Phil Gorby, Administrator

North Dakota Surgery Center, 3035 Demers Ave., Grand Forks, ND 58201; tel. 701/775–3151; Ross J. Gonitzke, Administrator

Western Dakota Medical Group, 1102 Main, Williston, ND 58801; tel. 701/572–7711; FAX. 701/572–2283; Jeff Neuberger, Administrator

OHIO

Advanced Cosmetic and Laser Surgery Center, Inc., 2200 Philadelphia Drive, Suite 651, Dayton, OH 45406; tel. 513/278–0809

Amend Center for Eye Surgery, 5939 Colerain Avenue, Cincinnati, OH 45239; tel. 513/923–3900; FAX. 513/923–3012

Aultman Center for One Day Surgery, 4715 Whipple Avenue, N.W., Canton, OH 44718; tel. 216/492–3050; Eric Draime, Administrator

Austintown Ambulatory Healthcare Center, 45 North Canfield–Niles Road, Youngstown, OH 44515; tel. 216/792–2722; FAX. 216/793–4883; James M. Conti, President, Chief Executive Officer

Big Run Surgery Center, 950 Georgesville Road, Columbus, OH 43228; tel. 614/234–2144

Bloomberg Eye Center, 1651 West Main Street, Newark, OH 43055; tel. 614/522–3937; FAX. 614/522–6766; John E. Reid, Executive Director

Carnegie Surgery Center, 10681 Carnegie Avenue, Cleveland, OH 44106; tel. 216/231–5566; FAX. 216/231–1441; K. L. Rosacco, RN, CNOR, Nurse Administrator

Central Ohio Eye Surgery Center, 210 Sharon Road, Suite B, Circleville, OH 43113; tel. 614/477–7200; FAX. 614/477–8349; Debbie Neal, RN, B.S.N.

Cincinnati Eye Institute and Outpatient Eye Surgery Center, 10494 Montgomery Road, Cincinnati, OH 45242; tel. 513/984–5133; FAX. 513/984–4240; Doris Holton, Administrator

Cincinnati Foot Clinic, Inc., 9600 Colerain Avenue, Suite 400, Cincinnati, OH 45239; tel. 513/385–6946; Robert Hayman, M.D., President

Columbia The Surgery Center, 19250 East Bagley Road, Middleburg Heights, OH 44130; tel. 216/826–3240; FAX. 216/826–3250

Columbus Eye Surgery Center, 5965 East Broad Street, Suite 460, Columbus, OH 43213; tel. 614/751–4080; FAX. 614/751–4092; Terri Gatton, RN, CNOR, Director Surgery

Consultants in Gastroenterology, Inc., 29001 Cedar Road, Suite 110, Lyndhurst, OH 44124; tel. 216/461–2550; FAX. 216/461–5319; Gloria Bradshaw, Office Manager

Crystal Clinic Surgery Center, 3975 Embassy Parkway, Akron, OH 44313; tel. 216/668–4085; Katherine L. McNeal, RN, Administrator

Dayton Ear, Nose and Throat Surgeons, Inc., 7076 Corporate Way, Centerville, OH 45459; tel. 937/434–0555; FAX. 937/434–7413; K. Jean Christian, Administrator

Digestivecare Endoscopy Unit, 75 Sylvania Drive, Beavercreek, OH 45440; tel. 513/325–5065; FAX. 513/325–5060; Patty Mannix, RN, CGRN Endoscopy Coordinator

Endoscopy Center West, 3654 Werk Road, Cincinnati, OH 45248; tel. 513/451–6001; FAX. 513/451–7310

Endoscopy Center of Dayton LTD, 4200 Indian Ripple Road, Beaver Creek, OH 45440; tel. 937/427–1680; FAX. 937/427–9496; Christy L. McBride, Office Manager

Eye Care Center of Cincinnati, 5300 Cornell Road, Cincinnati, OH 45242; tel. 513/489–6161; FAX. 513/489–6442; Amy D. Riegler, Coordinator

Eye Institute of Northwestern Ohio, Inc., 5555 Airport Highway, Suite 110, Toledo, OH 43615; tel. 419/865–3866; FAX. 419/865–3451; Carol R. Kollarits, M.D., President

Eye Surgery Center of Wooster, 3519 Friendsville Road, Wooster, OH 44691; tel. 330/345–6371; FAX. 330/345–8029; Michelle Morrison, Director

Facial Surgery Center, 1130 Congress Avenue, Glendale, OH 45246; tel. 513/772–2442; FAX. 513/772–2844; Joseph J. Moravec, M.D., Medical Director

Firas Atassi, M.D. Outpatient Surgery Center, 34500 Center Ridge Road, North Ridgeville, OH 33039; tel. 216/327–2414

Gastroenterology Associates of Cleveland, 6801 Mayfield Road, Suite 142, Mayfield Heights, OH 44124; tel. 216/461–8800; James Andrassy, Administrator

Gastroenterology Associates, Inc., 4665 Belpar Street, NW, P.O. Box 36329, Canton, OH 44735; tel. 216/493–1480; FAX. 216/493–6805

Gastroenterology Specialists, Inc., 2732 Fulton Drive, N.W., Canton, OH 44718; tel. 330/455–5011; FAX. 330/588–7127; Melissa Smith, RN, C.G.C.

Halpin–Poweleit Eye Surgery Center, (Division of Tri–State Eye Care), 8044 Montgomery Road, Suite 155, Cincinnati, OH 45236; tel. 513/791–3937; FAX. 513/791–1473

Heritage Surgical Associates of Cincinnati, d/b/a Healthsouth Surgery Center of Cincinnati, 2925 Vernon Place, Suite 101, Cincinnati, OH 45219; tel. 513/872–4541; FAX. 513/872–4558; Patti Murphy, RN, Director

Innova Surgery Center East, d/b/a Eastside Surgical Center, 3755 Orange Place, Beachwood, OH 44122; tel. 216/464–7300; FAX. 216/467–3050; Nancy Halkerston, RN, Director Clinical Services

Kahn and Diehl Center for Progressive Eye Care, 2740 Navarre Avenue, Oregon, OH 43616; tel. 419/697–3658; FAX. 419/697–2149; Karen R. Hess, RN, C.O.T., O.R. Supervisor

Kunesh Eye Surgery Center, 2601 Far Hills Avenue, Dayton, OH 45419–1665; tel. 937/298–1093; FAX. 937/298–6344; Lucy Helmers, Administrator

Mercy Ambulatory Surgery Center, 2990 Mack Road, Fairfield, OH 45014; tel. 513/874–6440; FAX. 513/874–6005; Patricia Ann Clark, RN, M.S., Administrator

Mid–Ohio Outpatient Surgery Center, 245 Taylor Station Road, Columbus, OH 43213; tel. 614/861–0448; FAX. 614/861–7717; Dr. Grace Z. Kim, Director

MidWest Eye Center, 119 West Kemper Road, Cincinnati, OH 45246; tel. 513/671–6112; FAX. 513/671–6386; Lorrie Walters, Business Office Supervisor

North Coast Endoscopy, Inc., 9500 Mentor Avenue, Suite 380, Mentor, OH 44060; tel. 216/352–9400; FAX. 216/352–9407; Ahmad Ascha, M.D.

Northshore Endoscopy Center, 850 Columbia Road, Suite 201, Westlake, OH 44145; tel. 216/808–1212

Northwest Ohio Urologic, A.S.C., P.O. Box 351837, Toledo, OH 43635–6254; tel. 419/535–1837; FAX. 419/535–6254; Carl V. Dreyer, M.D., President

Ohio Eye Associates Eye Surgery Center, 466 South Trimble Road, Mansfield, OH 44906; tel. 419/756–8000; FAX. 419/756–7100; John L. Marquardt, M.D.

Ohio Gastroenterology Group, Inc., Endoscopy Center, 777 West State Street, Suite 402, Columbus, OH 43222; tel. 614/221–8368; FAX. 614/341–2408; Jean Yarletts, RN, B.S.N.

Parkside Women's Center, Inc., 1011 Boardman–Canfield Road, Boardman, OH 44512; tel. 216/758–0975; FAX. 216/758–8453

Parkway Urology Center, Inc., 3500 Executive Parkway, Toledo, OH 43606; tel. 419/531–8349; FAX. 419/534–5337; Gregor K. Emmert, Sr., M.D., Chief Executive Officer

Ram Bandi M.D. A.S.C., 1037 North Main Street, Suite B, Akron, OH 44310; tel. 330/923–0094; FAX. 330/923–0193; Ann Marie Faber, RN

Restorative Vision Center, 4452 Eastgate Boulevard, Suite 305, Cincinnati, OH 45245; tel. 513/752–5700; FAX. 513/752–5716; Holly Schwab, RN, Surgery Manager

Richfield Surgery Center, Inc., 3030 Streetsboro Road, Richfield, OH 44286; tel. 216/659–4790; FAX. 216/659–3355; Carol A. Westfall, Vice President

Rockside Surgery Center, 6701 Rockside Road, Suite 101, Independence, OH 44131; tel. 216/520–3030; FAX. 216/520–3068; Elizabeth A. Bus, Administrator

Ross Park Surgical Services, One Ross Park, Steubenville, OH 43952; tel. 614/282–4790; Kathy Lemasters, RN, Manager

Sandusky Surgeons, Inc., 1221 Hayes Avenue, Sandusky, OH 44870; tel. 419/625–1374; Donald Lenhart, M.D., President

Sidney Foot and Ankle Surgical Center, 1000 Michigan, Sidney, OH 45365; tel. 513/492–1211; FAX. 513/492–6557; Micki Heater, Administrative Director

South Dayton Urological Associates, Inc., 10 Southmoor Circle, N.W., Kettering, OH 45429; tel. 513/294–1489; FAX. 513/294–7999; Donald Bailey, Practice Administrator

Stoneridge Endoscopy Center, 3900 Stoneridge Lane, Dublin, OH 43017; tel. 614/889–5001, ext. 1236; FAX. 614/889–5913; Cheryl Miller, Clinic Manager

Surgery Alliance Ltd., 975 Sawburg Avenue, Alliance, OH 44601; tel. 216/821–7997; Hazel Thomas, Administrator

Surgery Center At Southwoods, 7525 California Avenue, Youngstown, OH 44513; tel. 330/758–1954

Section C

Surgery Center West, 850 Columbia Road, Westlake, OH 44145; tel. 216/808–4000; FAX. 216/808–4010; Michelle Padden, RN, Administrator

Surgiplex, 950 Clague Road, Westlake, OH 44145; tel. 216/333–1020; FAX. 216/333–3278

Taylor Station Surgery Center, 275 Taylor Station Road, Columbus, OH 43213; tel. 614/751–4466; FAX. 614/751–4475; Bridget A. Huston, Manager

The Endoscopy Center, 3439 Granite Circle, Toledo, OH 43617; tel. 419/843–7993; FAX. 419/841–7789; Myung S. Lee, RN, Nurse Manager

The LCA Center for Surgery, 7840 Montgomery Road, Cincinnati, OH 45236; tel. 513/792–9099; FAX. 513/792–5634; Rene Fischer, President, Chief Executive Officer

The Surgical Center of East Liverpool, 16480 St. Clair Avenue, P.O. Box 2640, East Liverpool, OH 43920; tel. 216/386–9000; FAX. 216/386–1255; Robin Menchen, Chief Executive Officer

The Zeeba Clinic, A Meridia Outpatient and Laser Surgery Center, 29017 Cedar Road, Lyndhurst, OH 44124; tel. 216/461–7774; FAX. 216/461–5401; Sharon Luke, RN, B.S.N., Clinical Manager

Tippecanoe Endoscopy, Inc., 1210 Boardman Canfield Road, Youngstown, OH 44512; tel. 330/726–0132; FAX. 330/726–0571; Mary Amorn, RN, Administrator

Toledo Clinic, Inc., 4235 Secor Road, Toledo, OH 43623; tel. 419/473–3561; FAX. 419/472–0838; David J. Sobczak, Senior Vice President, Chief Financial Officer

Toledo Community Lithotripter Center, 3158 West Central Avenue, Toledo, OH 43606; tel. 419/531–3538

Toledo Plastic Surgeons Center, 2865 North Reynolds Road, Toledo, OH 43615; tel. 419/534–3330; FAX. 419/534–5716; Charles E. Jaeger, General Manager, Chief Executive Officer

Wedgewood Surgery Center, 10330 Sawmill Parkway, Powell, OH 43065; tel. 614/234–0500; FAX. 614/234–0540; Kim Heimlich, RN, Nurse Manager

Western Reserve Surgery Center, LP, 1930 State Route 59, Kent, OH 44240; tel. 216/677–3292; FAX. 330/677–3624; Laurie Simon, Office Manager

Wilson Eye Clinic Surgicenter, 300 West National Road, Vandalia, OH 45377; tel. 513/890–8992

Wright Surgery Center, 1611 South Green Road, Suite 124, South Euclid, OH 44121; tel. 216/382–1868; Barbara McCann, Director of Marketing and Communications

OKLAHOMA

A.M. Surgery, Inc., d/b/a Lawton Physician's Surgery Center, 3617 West Gore Boulevard, Suite D, Lawton, OK 73505; tel. 405/357–1900; FAX. 405/357–1775; Roxanne H. Gibson, Administrator

Ambulatory Surgery Associates, 6160 South Yale Avenue, Tulsa, OK 74136; tel. 918/495–2625; FAX. 918/495–2601; Jaquelyn S. Moore, RN, Director

Center for Plastic Surgery, P.C., 1826 East 15th Street, Tulsa, OK 74104; tel. 918/749–7177; Mark L. Mathers, D.O., Administrator

Central Oklahoma Ambulatory Surgical Center, Inc., 3301 Northwest 63rd Street, Oklahoma City, OK 73116; tel. 405/842–9732; FAX. 405/842–9771; Paul Silverstein, M.D., Administrator

Columbia Oklahoma Surgicare, 13313 North Meridian, Suite B, Oklahoma City, OK 73120; tel. 405/755–6240; FAX. 405/752–1819; Lindie Slater, Administrator

Columbia Surgicare of Tulsa, 4415 South Harvard Avenue, Suite 100, Tulsa, OK 74135; tel. 918/742–2502; FAX. 918/745–9750; Dirk Foxworthy, Administrator

Columbia Surgicare–Midtown, 1000 North Lincoln, Suite 150, Oklahoma City, OK 73104; tel. 405/232–8696; FAX. 405/232–6002; Connie M. Belding, RN, Administrator

Digestive Disease Specialists, Inc., 3366 Northwest Expressway, Suite 400, P.O. Box 99521, Oklahoma City, OK 73199; tel. 405/943–2001; FAX. 405/947–1966; Larry A. Bookman, M.D.

Eastern Oklahoma Surgery Center, L. L. C., 5020 East 68th Street, Tulsa, OK 74136; tel. 918/492–1539, ext. 138; FAX. 918/494–8683; Bobbie Huff, RN, Director

Grisham Eye Surgery Center, P.O. Box 1437, Bartlesville, OK 74005; tel. 918/333–1990, ext. 119; Dennis McKinley

Heritage Eye Surgicenter of Oklahoma, Heritage Building, 6922 South Western, Suite 104, Oklahoma City, OK 73139; tel. 405/636–1508; Edward D. Glinski, D.O., Administrator

Medical Plaza Endoscopy Unit, 1125 North Porter, Suite 304, Norman, OK 73071; tel. 405/360–2799; FAX. 405/447–0321; Philip C. Bird, M.D.

Oklahoma Ambulatory Surgery Center, 6908–B East Reno, Midwest City, OK 73110; tel. 405/737–6900; FAX. 405/732–0885; A.C. Vyas, M.D., Administrator

Oklahoma City Clinic, 701 Northwest 10th Street, Oklahoma City, OK 73104; tel. 405/280–5700; FAX. 405/280–5200; Mike Klein, Executive Director

Orthopedic Associates Ambulatory Surgery Center, Inc., 3301 Northwest 50th Street, P.O. Box 57027, Oklahoma City, OK 73157–7027; tel. 405/947–5610; FAX. 405/947–1341; Thomas H. Flesher, President

Outpatient Surgical Center of Ponca City, 400 Fairview, Ponca City, OK 74601; tel. 405/762–0695; FAX. 405/765–9406; Peggy Maples, RN, Executive Director

Physicians Surgical Center, 805 East Robinson, Norman, OK 73071–6610; tel. 405/364–9789; FAX. 405/366–8081; Ruth Beller, RN, Director

Southern Oklahoma Surgical Center, Inc., 2412 North Commerce, Ardmore, OK 73401; tel. 405/226–5000; Ann Willis, RN, Administrator

Southern Plains Ambulatory Surgery Center, 2222 Iowa Avenue, P.O. Box 1069, Chickasha, OK 73023; tel. 405/224–8111; FAX. 405/222–9557; H. Wayne Delony, Executive Director

Southwest Orthopedic Ambulatory Surgery Center, Inc., 8125 South Walker Avenue, Oklahoma City, OK 73139; tel. 405/631–1014; Anthony L. Cruse, D.O., President

Surgery Center of Edmond, 1700 South State Street, Edmon, OK 73013; tel. 405/330–1003; FAX. 405/330–1087; Timothy A. Gee, Administrator

Surgery Center of Enid, Inc., 1133 West Willow Road, Enid, OK 73703, P.O. Box 5069, Enid, OK 73702; tel. 405/233–6680; Tina C. Brooks, Administrator

Surgery Center of Midwest City, 8121 National Avenue, Suite 108, Midwest City, OK 73110; tel. 405/732–7905; FAX. 405/732–3561; Jackie Reed, Administrator

Surgery Center of Oklahoma, 815 Northwest 12th Street, Oklahoma City, OK 73106; tel. 405/235–4525; Olivia Dick, RN, Administrator

Surgery Center of South Oklahoma City, 100 Southeast 59th Street, Oklahoma City, OK 73109; tel. 405/634–9300; FAX. 405/634–8300; Larry Smith, Administrator

The Cataract Center of Lawton, 4214 Southwest Lee Boulevard, Lawton, OK 73505; tel. 405/353–5860; Stephen W. Gilkeson, Executive Administrator

Three Rivers Surgery Center, 3800 West Okmulgee, Muskogee, OK 74401; tel. 918/682–9899; FAX. 918/687–0786; Doug Blessen, Chief Executive Officer

Tower Day Surgery, 1044 Southwest 44th Street, Suite 100, Oklahoma City, OK 73109; tel. 405/636–1701; FAX. 405/636–4314; Marie Smith, RN, Director

Triad Eye Medical Clinic and Cataract Institute, 6140 South Memorial, Tulsa, OK 74133; tel. 918/252–2020; FAX. 918/252–7466; Marc L. Abel, D.O., Medical Director

Wilson Surgery Center, 5404 West Lee Boulevard, Lawton, OK 73505; tel. 405/357–2020; Gary Wilson, M.D., Administrator

OREGON

Aesthetic Breast Care Center, 10201 Southeast Main, Suite 20, Portland, OR 97216; tel. 503/253–3458; FAX. 503/253–0856; Mary K. Barnhart, M.D., Administrator

Center for Cosmetic and Plastic Surgery, 1353 East McAndrews Road, Medford, OR 97504; tel. 503/770–6776; FAX. 503/770–5791; Robert M. Jensen, M.D., Administrator

Eye Surgery Center, 2925 Siskiyou Boulevard, Medford, OR 97504; tel. 541/779–2020; FAX. 541/770–6838; Loren R. Barrus, M.D., Administrator

Eye Surgery Institute, The, 813 S.W. Highland Ave., Redmond, OR 97756; tel. 541/548–7170; FAX. 541/548–3842; Kathleen Peterson, RN, Administrator

Futures Outpatient Surgical Center, Inc., 1849 Northwest Kearney, Suite 302, Portland, OR 97209; tel. 503/224–0723; FAX. 503/224–0722; Bryce E. Potter, M.D.

GI Endoscopy Center, 2560 N.W. Medical Park Drive, Roseburg, OR 97470; tel. 541/673–2044; FAX. 541/673–0454; Ruth E. Harpole, RN, Administrator

Lawrence W. O'Dell, d/b/a Northwest Eye Center, 9975 Southwest Nimbus Avenue, Beaverton, OR 97005; tel. 503/646–7644; Jim Heath, Administrator

Lovejoy Surgicenter, Inc., 933 Northwest 25th Avenue, Portland, OR 97210; tel. 503/221–1870; FAX. 503/221–1488; Allene M. Klass, Administrator

McKenzie Surgery Center, 940 Country Club Road, Eugene, OR 97401; tel. 541/344–2600; FAX. 541/344–3317; Lynn M. Staples, RN, Administrator

Medford Clinic, P.C., 555 Black Oak Drive, Medford, OR 97504; tel. 541/734–3520; FAX. 541/734–3597; Jon D. Ness, Chief Executive Officer

Medford Plastic Surgeons, 1690 East McAndrews Road, Medford, OR 97504; tel. 541/779–5655; FAX. 541/770–6943; R. Kenneth Pons, M.D., Administrator

North Bend Medical Center, Inc., 1900 Woodland Drive, Coos Bay, OR 97420; tel. 503/267–5151, ext. 298; FAX. 503/269–0797; J. Peter Johnson, Administrator

Northbank Surgical Center, 700 Bellevue Street, S., Suite 300, Salem, OR 97301; tel. 503/364–3704; Peggy Seidler, Administrator

Northwest Eye Center, 1700 Valley River Drive, Eugene, OR 97401; tel. 503/343–3900; FAX. 503/343–2313; Carol L. Hernandez, RN, Administrator

Ontario Surgery Center, 251 S.W. 19th Street, Ontario, OR 97914; tel. 541/889–3198; FAX. 541/889–3904; Jeffrey C. Pitts, M.D., Administrator

Oregon Cataract and Laser Institute, 2700 Southeast 14th Avenue, Albany, OR 97321; tel. 503/928–1666; Darrell Genstler, M.D., Administrator

Oregon Eye Surgery Center, Inc., 1550 Oak Street, Eugene, OR 97401; tel. 541/484–4988; FAX. 541/344–1692; Virginia Pecora, RN, Administrator

Roseburg Surgicenter, LTD., 631 West Stanton, Roseburg, OR 97470; tel. 503/440–6311; FAX. 503/440–6394; William I Calhoun, M.D., Executive Officer

The Gastroenterology Endoscopy Center, Inc., 6464 Southwest Borland Road, Suite D–4, Tualatin, OR 97062; tel. 503/692–4537; FAX. 503/691–2324; Gale R. Dupek, M.B.A., Administrator

The Oregon Clinic Gastroenterology Division Gresham Office, 24900 Southeast Stark, Suite 205, Gresham, OR 97030; tel. 503/661–2000; FAX. 503/661–2001; Jeffrey S. Albaugh, M.D., Administrator

The Portland Clinic Surgical Center, 800 Southwest 13th Avenue, Portland, OR 97205; tel. 503/221–0161; FAX. 503/274–1697; J. Michael Schwab, Administrator

Tigard Surgery Center, 13240 Southwest Pacific Highway, Suite 200, Tigard, OR 97223; tel. 503/639–6571; FAX. 503/624–6037; Ivan L. Bakos, M.D., Administrator

Willamette Valley Eye SurgiCenter, 2001 Commercial Street, S.E., Salem, OR 97302; tel. 503/363–1500; FAX. 503/588–2028; Gordon Miller, M.D., Administrator

PENNSYLVANIA

Abington Surgical Center, 2701 Blair Mill Road, Suite 35, Willow Grove, PA 19090; tel. 215/443–8505; FAX. 215/957–0565; Deborah S. Kitz, Ph.D., Executive Director

Aesthetic and Reconstructive Surgery, 816 Belvedere Street, Carlisle, PA 17013

Aestique Ambulatory Surgical Center, One Aesthetic Way, Greensburg, PA 15601; tel. 412/832–7555; FAX. 412/832–7568; Theordore A. Lazzaro, M.D., Medical Director

Apple Hill Surgical Center, 25 Monument Road, Suite 270, York, PA 17403; tel. 717/741–8250; FAX. 717/741–8254; Gwendolyn J. Grothouse, RN, Administrative Director

Delaware Valley Laser Surgery Institute, Two Bala Plaza, Pl 33, Bala Cynwd, PA 19004; tel. 215/668–2847; FAX. 215/668–1509; Herbert J. Nevyas, M.D., Medical Director

Dermatologic Surgery Center, P.C., 6415 Bustleton Avenue, Philadelphia, PA 19149

Dermatologic SurgiCenter, 1200 Locust Street, Philadelphia, PA 19107; tel. 215/546-3666; FAX. 215/546-6060; Anthony V. Benedetto, D.O., FACP, Medical Director

Dermatologic SurgiCenter, 2221 Garrett Road, Drexel Hill, PA 19026; tel. 610/623-5885; FAX. 610/623-7276; Anthony V. Benedetto, D.O. Medical Director

Digestive Disease Institute, 897 Poplar Church Road, Camp Hill, PA 17011; tel. 717/763-1239; FAX. 717/763-9854; Iris Garman, Administrator

Eye Clinic Ambulatory Surgical Center, Inc., 601 Wyoming Avenue, Kingston, PA 18704; tel. 717/288-7405; Mark Kelly, Administrator

Fairgrounds Surgical Center, 400 North 17th Street, Suite 300, Allentown, PA 18104; tel. 610/821-2020; FAX. 610/821-2016; Darlene G. Hinkle, Administrative Director

Fort Washington Surgery Center, 467 Pennsylvania Avenue, Fort Washington, PA 19034; tel. 215/628-4300; FAX. 215/628-4253; Elizabeth Brennan, Administrator

Grandview Surgery & Laser Center, 205 Grandview Avenue, Camp Hill, PA 17011; tel. 717/731-5444; FAX. 717/731-0415; Sherry L. Rhodes, RN, Administrative Director

Hanover Surgicenter, 3130 Grandview Road, Building B, Hanover, PA 17331; tel. 717/633-1600; FAX. 717/633-6556; Melvin L. Brooks, Jr., CRNA, Administrator

HealthSouth Scranton Surgery and Laser Center, 425 Adams Street, Scranton, PA 18510; tel. 717/348-1114; FAX. 717/347-4351; Nancy A. Nealon, RN, B.S.N., Administrative Director

HealthSouth Surgery Center of Lancaster, 217 Harrisburg Avenue, Suite 103, Lancaster, PA 17603; tel. 717/295-2500; FAX. 717/295-4898; Debra K. Sanders, RN, Administrative Director

Healthsouth Mt. Pleasant Surgery Center, 200 Bessemer Road, Mt. Pleasant, PA 15666; tel. 412/547-5432; FAX. 412/547-2435; Brian Kowleczny, Administrative Director

Jefferson Surgery Center, Coal Valley Road, P.O. Box 18420, Pittsburgh, PA 15236; tel. 412/469-6060; FAX. 412/469-7322; Sheran Sullivan, Manager

John A. Zitelli, M.D., P.C., Ambulatory Surgery Facility, 5200 Centre Avenue, Suite 303, Pittsburgh, PA 15232; tel. 412/681-9400; FAX. 412/681-5240; John A. Zitelli, M.D.

Kremer Laser Eye Center, 200 Mall Boulevard, King of Prussia, PA 19406; tel. 610/337-1580; FAX. 610/337-1815; Tara Hopewell, RN

Lebanon Outpatient Surgical Center, L.P., 830 Tuck Street, Lebanon, PA 17042; tel. 717/228-1620; FAX. 717/228-1642; Anita Gingrich Fuhrman, Manager

Lowry SurgiCenter, 1115 Lowry Avenue, Jeannette, PA 15644; tel. 412/527-2885; FAX. 412/527-6885; K. Diddle, M.D., Medical Director

Mt. Lebanon Surgical Center, Professional Office Building, 1050 Bower Hill Road, Suite 102, Pittsburgh, PA 15243; tel. 412/563-6808; FAX. 412/563-6857; Patricia Strosnider, Director, Nursing

N.E.I. Ambulatory Surgery, Inc., 204 Mifflin Avenue, Scranton, PA 18503; tel. 717/342-3145, ext. 2400; FAX. 717/342-3136

North Shore Surgi-Center, Two Allegheny Center, Suite 530, Pittsburgh, PA 15212-5493; tel. 412/231-0200; FAX. 412/231-0613; Jack Demos, M.D., FACS

Northwood Surgery Center, 3729 Easton-Nazareth Highway, Easton, PA 18045; tel. 610/559-7110; FAX. 610/559-7317; Pankesh Kadam, Administrator

Ophthalmology Laser and Surgery Center, Inc., 92 Tuscarora Street, Harrisburg, PA 17104; tel. 717/233-2020; FAX. 717/232-3294; Jeanne Megella, RN, Director, Nursing

Paoli Surgery Center, One Industrial Boulevard, Paoli, PA 19301; tel. 610/408-0822; FAX. 610/408-9933; Marcia L. Collymore, Facility Manager

Pennsylvania Eye Surgery Center, 4100 Linglestown Road, Harrisburg, PA 17112; tel. 717/657-2020; FAX. 717/657-2071; Sandra Benner, RN, Director, Surgical Services

Pocono Ambulatory Surgery Center, One Veterans Place, Stroudsburg, PA 18360; tel. 717/421-4978; Mary P. Hayden RN, B.S., A.S.C. Coordinator

Ridgeway Esper Medical Center Ambulatory Surgical Center, 5050 West Ridge Road, Erie, PA 16506-1298; tel. 814/833-8800; FAX. 814/833-2079; Deborah Hartmann, RN, Director, Nursing

Sewickley Surgical Center at Edgeworth Commons, 301 Ohio River Boulevard, Edgeworth, Suite 100, Sewickley, PA 15143; tel. 412/741-5866; FAX. 412/741-5884; Carol Figas, RN, CNOR, Supervisor

Shadyside Surgi-Center, Inc., 5727 Centre Avenue, Pittsburgh, PA 15206; tel. 412/363-6626; FAX. 412/363-7008; Susan M. Katch, RN, Director

Southwestern Ambulatory Surgery Center, 500 Lewis Run Road, Pittsburgh, PA 15236; tel. 412/469-6964; FAX. 412/469-6948; Pamela Wrobleski, CRNA, M.P.M., Director

Southwestern Pennsylvania Eye Surgery Center, 750 East Beau Street, Washington, PA 15301; tel. 412/228-7477; FAX. 412/228-8117; Karen A. Dynice, Clinical Director

Specialists Health Care Clinic of Monroeville, 125 Daugherty Drive, Monroeville, PA 15146-2749; tel. 412/374-9385, ext. 224; FAX. 412/374-9490; Carol Fiske, CMSC, Administrative Assistant, Medical Staff Manager

St. Francis Surgery Center North, One St. Francis Way, Cranberry Township, PA 16066; tel. 412/772-5360; FAX. 412/772-4644; Gerry Matt, RN, M.Ed., Director

Surgery Center of Bucks County, 401 North York Road, Warminster, PA 18974; tel. 215/443-3022; FAX. 215/443-5859; JoAnn Quinn, Director, Nursing

Surgical Center of York, 1750 Fifth Avenue, P.O. Box 290, York, PA 17405; tel. 717/843-7613; Thomas R. Harlow, Administrative Director

Surgical Eye Institute of Western Pennsylvania, 618 Monongahela Avenue, Glassport, PA 15045; tel. 412/664-7874; FAX. 412/673-5720; Shirley A. Smith, RN

The Surgery Center of Chester County, 460 Creamery Way, Oaklands Corporate Center, Exton, PA 19341-2500; tel. 610/594-8900; FAX. 215/594-8907; Stephen P. Barainyak, Executive Director

The SurgiCenter at Ligonier, 221 West Main Street, Ligonier, PA 15658; tel. 412/238-9573; FAX. 412/238-4709; Kim Kenney-Ciarimboli, Supervisor

West Shore Endoscopy Center, 423 North 21st Street, Camp Hill, PA 17011; tel. 717/975-2430; Marilee Ball, RN, Director

Wills Eye Surgery Center of the Northeast, 1815 Cottman Avenue, Philadelphia, PA 19111; tel. 215/722-2505; FAX. 215/742-6386; Lawrence S. Schaffzin, M.D., Medical Director

Wyoming Valley Surgery Center, 1130 Highway 315, Wilkes-Barre, PA 18702; tel. 717/821-2830; FAX. 717/825-7962; David N. Culp, Chief Executive Officer

RHODE ISLAND

Bayside Endoscopy Center, 120 Dudley Street, Suite 103, Providence, RI 02905; tel. 401/274-1810; FAX. 401/273-9689; Nicholas Califano, M.D., Administrator

Blackstone Valley Surgicare, Inc., 333 School Street, Pawtucket, RI 02860; tel. 401/728-3800; FAX. 401/723-2440; Ann Dugan, Administrator

Koch Eye Surgi Center, Inc., 566 Tollgate Road, Warwick, RI 02886; tel. 401/738-4800; FAX. 401/738-8153; Paul S. Koch, M.D., Administrator

Ocean State Endoscopy, 100 Highland Avenue, Providence, RI 02906; tel. 401/421-6306; Joel Spellun, M.D.

Planned Parenthood of Rhode Island, 111 Point Street, Providence, RI 02903; tel. 401/421-9620; FAX. 401/621-6250; Miriam Inocencio, President, Chief Executive Officer

Wayland Square Surgicare, 17 Seekonk Street, Providence, RI 02906; tel. 401/453-3311; FAX. 401/351-1280; Ann Dugan, Administrator

Women's Medical Center, 1725 Broad Street, Cranston, RI 02905; tel. 401/467-9111; FAX. 401/461-1390; Carol Belding, Administrator

SOUTH CAROLINA

Ambulatory Eye Surgery and Laser Center, Inc., 9297 Medical Plaza Drive, Charleston, SC 29406; tel. 803/572-2888; Margaret A. Thompson

Bay Microsurgical Unit, Inc., 400 Marina Drive, P.O. Drawer L, Georgetown, SC 29442; tel. 803/546-8421; FAX. 803/546-1173; Rebecca Lammonds, Administrator, Director, Nursing

Bearwood Ambulatory Surgery Center, 3031 Highway 81, N., Anderson, SC 29621; tel. 864/226-0837; FAX. 864/226-8367; Patricia P. Smith, Administrator

Bishopville Ambulatory Surgical Center, 800 West Church Street, Bishopville, SC 29010; tel. 803/484-6976; Carolyn Sellers, Administrator

Carolina Eye Ambulatory Surgery Center, 210 University Parkway, Suite 1500 B, Aiken, SC 29801; tel. 803/649-3953; FAX. 803/641-3801; Stephen K. VanDerVliet, M.D.

Carolina Regional Surgery Center, Ltd., 900 Medical Circle, Myrtle Beach, SC 29572; tel. 803/449-7885; FAX. 803/497-5137; Mary Garvey, RN, Administrator

Carolina Surgical Center, 198 South Herlong Avenue, Rock Hill, SC 29732; tel. 803/327-4664; Jackie Ridley, Administrator

Charleston Plastic Surgery Center, Inc., 159 Rutledge Avenue, Charleston, SC 29403; tel. 803/722-1985; FAX. 803/722-4840; Anna Lambert, Office Manager

Columbia Ambulatory Plastic Surgery Center, Inc., 338 Harbison Boulevard, Columbia, SC 29212; tel. 803/732-6655; FAX. 803/732-6644; Vickie H. Ott, Administrator

Columbia Eye Surgery Center, Inc., 1920 Pickens Street, P.O. Box 1754, Columbia, SC 29202; tel. 803/254-7732; FAX. 803/748-7199; Kenneth W. Gibbons, Administrator

Columbia Gastrointestinal Endoscopy Center, 2739 Laurel Street, Suite One-B, Columbia, SC 29240; tel. 803/254-9588; FAX. 803/252-0052; Frederick F. DuRant III, Administrator

Cross Creek Surgery Center of Greenville Hospital System, Nine Doctors Drive, Crosscreek Medical Park, Greenville, SC 29605; tel. 803/455-8400; Greg Rusnak, Administrator

Greenville Endoscopy Center, Inc., 317 St. Francis Drive, Suite 150, Greenville, SC 29601; tel. 803/232-7338; Rebecca K. Swoyer, Administrator

HealthSouth Surgery Center of Charleston, 2690 Lake Park Drive, North Charleston, SC 29406; tel. 803/764-0992; FAX. 803/764-3187; Donna Padgette, RN, M.S.N., Facility Manager

Healthsouth Surgery Center of Greenville, Five Memorial Medical Court, Greenville, SC 29605; tel. 864/295-3067; FAX. 864/295-3096; Vickie Waters, Facility Manager

Outpatient Surgery Center of Lexington Medical Center in Irmo, 7035 Saint Andrews Road, Columbia, SC 29212; tel. 803/749-0924; Barbara Willm, Administrator

Pee Dee Ambulatory Surgery Center, 602 Cheves, P.O. Box F-17, Florence, SC 29506; tel. 803/669-3822; Joseph J. McEvoy, Administrator

Roper West Ashley Surgery Center, 18 Farmfield Avenue, Charleston, SC 29407; tel. 803/763-3763; FAX. 803/763-3881; Maria I. Sample, Administrator

Same Day Surgery East, 10 Enterprise Boulevard, Suite 104, Greenville, SC 29615; tel. 803/458-7141; FAX. 803/676-9116; Mary Jane Knottek, RN, B.S.N., CNOR, Clinical Nurse Manager

Spartanburg Urology Surgicenter, 391 Serpentine Drive, Suite 330, Spartanburg, SC 29303; tel. 864/585-2002; FAX. 864/585-3300; Anita Womick, RN, OR Director

The Greenwood Endoscopy Center, 103 Liner Drive, Greenwood, SC 29646; tel. 803/227-3838; FAX. 803/227-6116; A. A. Ramage, M.D., Administrator

The Microsurgery Center, Inc., 1655 East Greenville Street, P.O. Box 1886, Anderson, SC 29622-1886; tel. 864/225-1933; FAX. 864/225-9035; Ann Geier, Director, Clinical Services

Trident Surgery Center, 9313 Medical Plaze Drive, Suite 102, Charleston, SC 29406; tel. 803/797-8992; FAX. 803/797-4094; Leah J. Dawson, Administrator

SOUTH DAKOTA

Aberdeen Surgical Center, 1200 South Main, Box 1150, Aberdeen, SD 57401-1150; tel. 605/225-2466; Scott H. Berry, M.D., Administrator

Black Hills Regional Eye Surgery Center, 2800 Third Street, Rapid City, SD 57701-7394; tel. 605/341-4100; FAX. 605/341-0278; Richard B. Hanafin, Executive Director

Jones Eye Clinic, 3801 South Elmwood Avenue, Sioux Falls, SD 57105-6565; tel. 605/336-3142; FAX. 605/334-0737; Charles E. Jones, M.D.

Mallard Pointe Surgical Center, 1201 Mickelson Drive, Watertown, SD 57201-7100; tel. 605/882-4743; FAX. 605/882-6064; James Arlt, Operations Director

Medical Associates Surgi Center, 772 East Dakota, Pierre, SD 57501-3399; tel. 605/224-5901; Michael Pfeifer, Administrator

Sioux Falls Surgical Center, 910 East 20th Street, Sioux Falls, SD 57105–1012; tel. 605/334–6730; Donald A. Schellpfeffer, M.D., Ph.D., Medical Director

Spearfish Surgery Center, Inc., 1316 10th Street, Spearfish, SD 57783–1530; tel. 605/642–3113; FAX. 605/642–3117; Linda Redding, Administrator

SurgiClinic, 1010 Ninth Street, Rapid City, SD 57701–3599; tel. 605/348–7607; FAX. 605/342–1359; Ray G. Burnett, M.D., Medical Director

Women's Health Clinic, 909 South Miller, Mitchell, SD 57301; tel. 605/995–5560; Donna Gerlach, RN, Clinic Director

Yankton Medical Clinic P.C., 1104 West Eighth Street, Yankton, SD 57078–3306; tel. 605/665–7841; FAX. 605/665–0546; Don P. Lake, Administrator

TENNESSEE

Appalachian Ambulatory Surgical Center, Medical Arts Building, 106 Rogosin Drive, Elizabethton, TN 37643; tel. 615/543–5888

Arrowsmith Eye Surgery Center, Parkview Tower, Suite 900, 210 25th Avenue, N., Nashville, TN 37203; tel. 615/327–2244; FAX. 615/321–3175; Cyndi Hamill, RN, Operating Room Supervisor

Atrium Memorial Surgical Center, 1949 Gunbarrel Road, Suite 290, Chattanooga, TN 37421; tel. 615/495–3550; FAX. 615/495–3580; Sandy Proctor, Administrator

Baptist Physicians Pavilion Surgery Center, 360 Wallace Road, Nashville, TN 37211; tel. 615/781–9020; FAX. 615/781–9944; Sandra Holshouser, Administrator

Bristol Surgery Center, 350 Blountville Highway, Suite 108, Bristol, TN 37620; tel. 423/844–6120; FAX. 423/844–6126; David Paul Gross, Administrator

Cataract Surgery Center, 5406 Knight Arnold Road, Memphis, TN 38115; tel. 901/360–8081; FAX. 901/368–3822

Centennial Surgery Center, 340 23rd Avenue, N., Nashville, TN 37203; tel. 615/327–1123; FAX. 615/327–0261; Cynthia S. Duvall, RN, B.S., Administrator

Chattanooga Surgery Center, 400 North Holtzclaw Avenue, Chattanooga, TN 37404; tel. 615/698–6871; Becky Myers, Administrator

Clarksville Encoscopy Center, 132 Hillcrest Drive, Clarksville, TN 37043; tel. 615/552–0180; FAX. 615/572–0915

Cleveland Surgery Center, L.P., 137 25th Street, N.E., Cleveland, TN 37311; tel. 423/472–7874; R. Scott Peterson, Executive Director

Columbia Endoscopy Center, Inc., 1510 1/2 Hatcher Lane, Columbia, TN 38401; tel. 615/381–7818; FAX. 615/381–5625; Dianne Roberts, RN, Head Nurse

Columbia Outpatient Surgery, Inc., 1405 Hatcher Lane, Columbia, TN 38401; tel. 615/381–3700; Deborah Woodard, Administrator

Columbia Sullins Surgery Center, 2761 Sullins Street, Knoxville, TN 37919; tel. 423/522–2949; FAX. 423/637–3259; Tina Shelby–Kahl, Assistant Administrator

D D C Surgery Center, Nine Physicians Drive, Jackson, TN 38305; tel. 901/661–0086; Regina Phelps, Billing Manager

Digestive Disease Endoscopy Center, 2021 Church Street, Suite 303, Nashville, TN 37203; tel. 615/340–4625; FAX. 615/340–4628

East Memphis Surgery Center, 80 Humphreys Center Drive, Suite 101, Memphis, TN 38120; tel. 901/747–3233; FAX. 901/747–3230

Endoscopy Center of Kingsport, 2204 Pavilion Drive, Kingsport, TN 37660; tel. 423/392–6100; FAX. 423/392–6159; Barbara Light, Office Manager

Endoscopy Center of Northeast Tennessee, 310 State of Franklin Road, Suite 202, Johnson City, TN 37604; tel. 615/929–7111

Eye Surgery Center of East Tennessee, 1124 Weisgarber Road, Suite 110, Knoxville, TN 37909; tel. 423/588–1037, ext. 108; FAX. 423/909–9104; Donna Chambless, RN

Fort Sanders West Outpatient Surgery Center, Ltd., 210 Fort Sanders West Boulevard, Knoxville, TN 37922; tel. 615/531–5222; FAX. 615/531–5043; Leslie Irwin, Administrator

Franklin Surgery Center at MedCore, 2105 Edward Curd Lane, Franklin, TN 37067; tel. 615/794–7320

G. Baker Hubbard Ambulatory Surgery Center, 616 West Forest Avenue, Jackson, TN 38301; tel. 901/422–0330

G. I. Diagnostic and Therapeutic Center, 1068 Cresthaven Road, Suite 300, Memphis, TN 38119; tel. 901/682–6700; FAX. 901/683–3046; Randolph M. McCloy, M.D., Medical Director

Germantown Ambulatory Surgical Center, Inc., 7499 Old Poplar Pike, Germantown, TN 38138; tel. 901/755–6465; FAX. 901/757–5543; Carol Harper, Facility Manager

Health South Surgery Center of Clarksville, 121 Hillcrest Drive, Clarksville, TN 37043; tel. 615/552–9992

HealthSouth Nashville Surgery Center, 1717 Patterson Street, Nashville, TN 37203; tel. 615/329–1888; FAX. 615/329–0179; Patricia Middleton, Facility Manager

HealthSouth Surgery Center of Chattanooga, 924 Spring Creek Road, Chattanooga, TN 37412; tel. 423/899–1600; FAX. 423/899–2171; Melissa Powers, Administrator

Kingsport Bronchoscopy Center, Inc., 135 West Ravine Road, Suite Eight–A, Kingsport, TN 37660; tel. 615/247–5197; FAX. 615/247–5254; Shirley Hawkins, Administrator

Kingsport Endoscopy Corporation, 135 West Ravine Street, Suite 7A, Kingsport, TN 37660; tel. 423/246–6077; Bettye Reed, Administrator

Knoxville Center for Reproductive Health, 1547 West Clinch Avenue, Knoxville, TN 37916; tel. 423/637–3861; Bernadette McNabb, Executive Director

Knoxville Surgery Center, 9300 Park West Boulevard, Knoxville, TN 37923; tel. 615/691–2725; FAX. 615/691–3090; Ranae Thompson, RN, Facility Administrator

LeBonheur East Surgery Center, L.P., 786 Estate Place, Memphis, TN 38120; tel. 901/681–4100; FAX. 901/681–4140; Diane Swain, Director

Lebanon Surgery Center, Inc., 1414 Baddour Parkway, P.O. Box 549, Lebanon, TN 37088; tel. 615/444–8944; Sheena Sloan, Administrator

Maternity Center of East Tennessee, 1925–B Ailor Avenue, Knoxville, TN 37921; tel. 615/524–4422

Medical Center Endoscopy Group, 930 Madison, Suite 870, Memphis, TN 38103; tel. 901/578–2538; FAX. 901/578–2572; John W. Flowers, Business Manager

Memphis Area Medical Center for Women, 29 South Bellevue Boulevard, Memphis, TN 38104; tel. 901/722–8050

Memphis Center for Reproductive Health, 1462 Poplar Avenue, Memphis, TN 38104; tel. 901/274–3550

Memphis Eye and Cataract Ambulatory Surgery Center, 6485 Poplar Avenue, Memphis, TN 38119; tel. 901/767–3937

Memphis Gastroenterology Group, 80 Humphrey's Blvd., Suite 220, Memphis, TN 38120; tel. 901/747–3630; FAX. 901/747–4039; Sylvia Hawkins, RN, Nurse Manager

Memphis Planned Parenthood, Inc., 1407 Union Avenue, Third Floor, Memphis, TN 38104; tel. 901/725–1717

Memphis Regional Gamma Knife Center, 1265 Union Avenue, Memphis, TN 38104; tel. 901/726–6444

Memphis Surgery Center, 1044 Cresthaven Road, Memphis, TN 38119; tel. 901/682–1516; FAX. 901/682–1545; Barbara Hopper, RN, B.S., CNOR, Facility Manager

Mid–State Endoscopy Center, 2010 Church Street, Suite 420, Nashville, TN 37203; tel. 615/329–2141; FAX. 615/321–0522; Allan H. Bailey, M.D., Medical Director

Nashville Endoscopy Center, 300 20th N., Eighth Floor, Nashville, TN 37203; tel. 615/284–1335; FAX. 615/284–1316; Margaret Sullivan, RN

Nashville Gastrointestinal Endoscopy Center, 4230 Harding Road, Suite 309, Nashville, TN 37205; tel. 615/383–0165; FAX. 615/292–4657; Ron E. Pruitt, M.D.

Ophthalmic Ambulatory Surgery Center, P.C., 342 22nd Street, Nashville, TN 37203; tel. 615/327–2001; FAX. 615/327–2069; Alec Dryden, Administrator

Oral Facial Surgery Center, 322 22nd Avenue, N., Nashville, TN 37203; tel. 615/321–6160; FAX. 615/327–9612; Kelly Ingle, Administrator

PRISM Aesthetic Surgery Center, 80 Humphreys Center, Suite 310, Memphis, TN 38120; tel. 901/747–0446; FAX. 901/747–4406; Judy Sharp, Director, PRISM ASC

Physicians Surgery Center, 207 Stonebridge, Jackson, TN 38305; tel. 901/661–6340; FAX. 901/661–6363; Judy Haskins, RN, Manager

Planned Parenthood Association of Nashville, 412 D.B. Todd Boulevard, Nashville, TN 37203; tel. 615/321–7216

Ridge Lake Ambulatory Surgery Center, 825 Ridge Lake Boulevard, Memphis, TN 38119; tel. 901/685–0777

Rivergate Surgery Center, 647 Myatt Drive, Madison, TN 37115; tel. 615/868–8942; FAX. 615/860–3820; Brenda Cruse, Director

Shea Clinic, 6133 Poplar Pike, Memphis, TN 38119; tel. 901/761–9720; FAX. 901/683–8440

Southern Endoscopy Center, 397 Wallace Road, Suite 407, Nashville, TN 37211; tel. 615/832–5530; FAX. 615/832–5713; Robert W. Herring, Jr., M.D., Medical Director

St. Thomas Medical Group Endoscopy Center, 4230 Harding Road, Suite 400, Nashville, TN 37205; tel. 615/297–2700

Surgical Services, P.C., 604 South Main Street, Sweetwater, TN 37874; tel. 423/337–4508; FAX. 423/337–4588

Surgicenter Of Murfreesboro Medical Clinic, P.A., 1004 North Highland Avenue, Murfreesboro, TN 37130; tel. 615/893–4480, ext. 351; FAX. 615/895–6212

Tennessee Endoscopy Center, 1706 East Lamar Alexander Parkway, Maryville, TN 37804; tel. 615/983–0073; FAX. 615/984–1731; Craig Jarvis, M.D., Administrator

The Cookeville Surgery Center, 100 West Fourth Street, Suite 100, Cookeville, TN 38501; tel. 615/528–6115; FAX. 615/526–2962; Diana Welch, RN, Administrator

The Endoscopy Center, 801 Weisgarber Road, Suite 100, Knoxville, TN 37909, P.O. Box 59002, Knoxville, TN 37950–9002; tel. 615/588–5121; Gayle Mahan, Office Manager

The Endoscopy Center of Centennial, L.P., 2400 Patterson Street, Suite 515, Nashville, TN 37203; tel. 615/327–2111; FAX. 615/327–9292; Dawn Lynn Gray, RN, B.S., Endoscopy Administrator

The Eye Surgery Center Oak Ridge, 90 Vermont Avenue, Oak Ridge, TN 37830; tel. 423/482–8894; Sally Jones

The Pain Clinic and Rehabilitation Center, 55 Humphreys Center Drive, Suite 200, Memphis, TN 38120; tel. 901/747–0040; FAX. 901/747–3424; Lori Parris, RN, Administrator

Tullahoma Outpatient Surgery Center, 1918 North Jackson, Tullahoma, TN 37388; tel. 615/455–2006

Urology Surgery Center, Inc., 2011 Church Street, Sixth Floor, Nashville, TN 37203; tel. 615/329–7700; Robert B. Barnett, M.D., Medical Director

Van Dyke Ambulatory Surgery Center, 1024 Kelley Drive, Paris, TN 38242; tel. 901/642–5003; FAX. 901/642–8756; John T. VanDyck III, M.D., Owner

Volunteer Medical Clinic, 313 Concord Street, Knoxville, TN 37919; tel. 423/522–5173; FAX. 423/522–9907

Wesberry Surgery Center, 2900 South Perkins Road, Memphis, TN 38118–3237; tel. 901/362–3100; FAX. 901/362–3372; Jess Wesberry, Jr., M.D., President

Wesley Ophthalmic Plastic Surgery Center, 250 25th Avenue North, Suite 213, Nashville, TN 37203; tel. 615/329–3624

Women's Wellness and Maternity Center, Inc., 3459 Highway 68, Madisonville, TN 37354; tel. 423/442–6624; FAX. 423/442–5746; Betti Wilson, Administrator

TEXAS

AHCA–Mainland Outpatient Surgery Center, 3810 Hughes Court, Dickinson, TX 77539; tel. 713/337–7001; FAX. 713/337–7091; Terry R. Williams, Administrator

Abilene Cataract and Refractive Surgery Center, 2120 Antilley Road, Abilene, TX 79606; tel. 915/695–2020; FAX. 915/695–2326; Robert W. Cameron, M.D., Medical Director

Abilene Endoscopy Center, 1249 Ambler Avenue, Abilene, TX 79601; tel. 915/695–2020; Royce Harrell

Amarillo Cataract and Eye Surgery Center, Inc., 7310 Fleming Avenue, Amarillo, TX 79106; tel. 806/354–8891; FAX. 806/354–2591; Carol A. Pearson, Director

Ambulatory Urological Surgery Center, Inc., 1149 Ambler, Abilene, TX 79601; tel. 915/676–3557; FAX. 915/673–2143; Angela X. Young, RN, Manager

American Surgery Centers of South Texas, LTD, 7810 Louis Pasteur, Suite 101, San Antonio, TX 78229; tel. 210/692–0218; Britt F. Mitchell, C.O.T., Director, Operations

Bailey Square Surgical Center, Ltd., 1111 West 34th Street, Austin, TX 78705; tel. 512/454-6753; FAX. 512/454-4314; Katherine S. Wilson, RN, M.H.A., Administrator

Barbara Jean Bartlett Memorial Surgery Center, 4200 Andrews Highway, Midland, TX 79707; tel. 915/520-5888; Sylvan Bartlett, M.D., Administrator

Bay Area Endoscopy Center, 444 FM 1959, Houston, TX 77034; tel. 281/481-9400; FAX. 281/481-9490; N. S. Bala, Medical Director

Bay Area Surgery, 7101 South Padre Island Drive, Corpus Christi, TX 78412; tel. 512/985-3500; FAX. 512/985-3754; Gene Hybner, Administrator

Bay Area Surgicare Center, Inc., 502 Medical Center Boulevard, P.O. Box 57767, Webster, TX 77598; tel. 713/332-2433; FAX. 713/332-0619; Mary P. Colombo, Administrator

Baylor SurgiCare, 3920 Worth Street, Dallas, TX 75246; tel. 214/820-2581; FAX. 214/820-7484; Patty Crabb, Administrative Director

Bellaire Surgicare, Inc., 6699 Chimney Rock, Suite 200, Houston, TX 77081; tel. 713/665-1406; FAX. 713/665-8262; Sheila M. Liccketto, Administrator

Brazosport Eye Institute, 103 Parking Way, P.O. Box 369, Lake Jackson, TX 77566; tel. 409/297-2961; FAX. 409/297-2395; Frank J. Grady, M.D., Ph.D., FACS, Director

Brownsville Surgicare, 1024 Los Ebanos Boulevard, Brownsville, TX 78520; tel. 210/548-0101; FAX. 210/541-3752; Norberto J. Sanchez, Administrator

Central Texas Day Surgery Center, L.P., 1817 Southwest Dodgen, Loop, Temple, TX 76502; tel. 817/773-7785; FAX. 817/773-9333; Debby Meyer, Director

Coastal Bend Ambulatory Surgical Center, 900 Morgan, Corpus Christi, TX 78404; tel. 512/888-4288; FAX. 512/888-4786; Barbara VandenBout

Columbia Endoscopy Center of Dallas, 6390 LBJ Freeway, Suite 200, Dallas, TX 75240; tel. 972/934-3691; Jeane Suggs, Administrator

Columbia North Texas Surgi-Center, 917 Midwestern Parkway, E., Wichita Falls, TX 76302; tel. 817/767-7273; FAX. 817/723-9059; Barbara Dawson, Administrator

Columbia Physicians Daysurgery Center, 3930 Crutcher Street, Dallas, TX 75246; tel. 214/827-0760; FAX. 214/827-0944; Vickie Roberts, RN, Administrator

Columbia Surgery Center at Park Central, 12200 Park Central Drive, Third Floor, Dallas, TX 75251; tel. 972/661-0505; FAX. 972/661-0505; Molly Paulose, Administrator

Columbia Surgery Center of Las Colinas, 4255 North Macarthur Boulevard, Irving, TX 75038; tel. 214/257-0144; FAX. 214/258-0436; Bill Beaman, Administrator

Columbia Surgery Center of Sherman, 3400 North Calais Drive, Sherman, TX 75090; tel. 903/813-3377; FAX. 903/870-7617; Brian Roland, Business Office Manager

Columbia Surgical Center, 2800 East 29th Street, Bryan, TX 77802, P.O. Box 2700, Bryan, TX 77805; tel. 409/776-4300; FAX. 409/774-7149; Joan Dougan, Interim Chief Operating Officer

Columbia Surgical Center of Southeast Texas, 3127 College Street, Beaumont, TX 77701; tel. 409/835-2607; Jim Hoeks, Administrator

Columbia Surgicare Outpatient Center of Victoria, 1903 East Sabine, Victoria, TX 77901; tel. 512/576-4105; FAX. 512/576-9830; Margaret Coleman, RN, Administrator

Columbia West Houston Surgicare, 970 Campbell Road, Houston, TX 77024-2804; tel. 713/461-3547; FAX. 713/722-8921; Penny A. Menge, RN, M.S.N., Administrator

Columbia/Waco Medical Group Surgery Center, 2911 Herring, Waco, TX 76708; tel. 817/755-4430; FAX. 817/755-4590; Kay H. O'Leary, RN, Administrator

Crystal Outpatient Surgery Center, Inc., 215 Oak Drive, S., Suite J, Lake Jackson, TX 77566; tel. 409/299-6118; FAX. 409/299-1007; R. Scott Yarish, M.D., Administrator

Cy-Fair Surgery Center, 11250 Fallbrook Drive, Houston, TX 77065; tel. 713/955-7194; FAX. 713/890-0895; Scott Washko, Administrator

Dallas Day Surgery Center, Inc., 411 North Washington, Suite 5400, Dallas, TX 75246; tel. 214/821-8613; Henry S. Byrd, President

Dallas Eye Surgicenter, Inc., 720 South Cedar Ridge Road, Duncanville, TX 75137; tel. 214/296-6634; William Hamilton, Administrator

Dallas Opthalmology Center, Inc., 2811 Lemmon Avenue E., Suite 102, Dallas, TX 75204; tel. 214/520-7600; FAX. 214/528-6522; Jean Vining, RN, Administrator

Dallas Surgi Center, 8230 Walnut Hill Lane, Suite 808, Dallas, TX 75231; tel. 214/696-8828; FAX. 214/696-1444

DeHaven Surgical Center, Inc., 1424 East Front Street, Tyler, TX 75702; tel. 903/595-4168; FAX. 903/595-6821; Barbara Shamburger, RN, Administrator

Diagnostic Clinic of San Antonio Ambulatory Surgical Center, 4647 Medical Drive, P.O. Box 29249, San Antonio, TX 78224-3100; tel. 210/692-3382; FAX. 512/692-3397; Nancy Nixon, RN, ASC Supervisor

Doctors Surgery Center, Inc., 5300 North Street, Nacogdoches, TX 75961; tel. 409/569-8278; Robert P. Lehmann, M.D., Director

Duncanville Surgery Center, (an affiliate of ASC Network Corporation), 1018 East Wheatland Road, Duncanville, TX 75116; tel. 214/296-6912; Michael Kincaid, Vice President

East El Paso Surgery Center, 7835 Corral Drive, El Paso, TX 79915; tel. 915/595-3353; FAX. 915/595-6796; Ruth Robertson, Administrator

East Side Surgery Center, Inc., 10918 East Freeway, Houston, TX 77029; tel. 713/451-4299; FAX. 713/451-4383; Clifford E. Kirby, Administrator

East Texas Eye Associates Surgery Center, 1306 Frank Avenue, Lufkin, TX 75901; tel. 409/634-8381; Jo Ann O'Neill, C.O.T., Administrator

El Paso Institute of Eye Surgery, Inc., 1717 North Brown Street, Building Three, El Paso, TX 79902; tel. 915/544-0526; FAX. 915/544-2877; Esthern A. Calderon, Administrator

Elm Place Ambulatory Surgical Center, 2217 South Danville Drive, Abilene, TX 79605; tel. 915/695-0600; FAX. 915/695-3908; Susan King, RN, Director

Eye Surgery Center, 2001 Ed Carey Drive, Suite Three, Harlingen, TX 78550; tel. 210/423-2100; Michael Laney, C.O.M.T., Administrator

Facial Plastic and Cosmetic Surgical Center, 6300 Humana Plaza, Suite 475, Abilene, TX 79606; tel. 915/695-3630; FAX. 915/695-3633; Howard A. Tobin, M.D., FACS, Medical Director

Forest Park Surgery Pavilion, 5920 Forest Park Road, Suite 700, Dallas, TX 75235; tel. 214/350-2400; FAX. 214/352-3853; Mark Turner, Administrator

Fort Worth Endoscopy Center, 1201 Summit Avenue, Suite 400, Fort Worth, TX 76102; tel. 817/332-6500; Donna Drerup, RN, M.S.N., Administrator

Garland Surgery Center L.P., 777 Walter Reed Boulevard, Suite 105, Garland, TX 75042; tel. 214/494-2400; FAX. 214/494-3873; Dan Nicholson, President

Gastroenterology Consultants Outpatient Surgical Center, 8214 Wurzbach, San Antonio, TX 78229; tel. 210/614-1234; FAX. 210/614-7749; Bonnie Draude, B.S.N., RN, C.G.R.N., Clinical Manager

Gastrointestinal Endoscopy Center Number Two, LTD, 1600 Coit Road, Suite 401A, Plano, TX 75075; tel. 214/867-0019; Brian Cooley, M.D., Administrator

Gonzaba Surgical Center, 720 Pleasanton Road, San Antonio, TX 78214; tel. 210/921-3826; FAX. 210/921-3825; William Gonzaba, M.D., Chief Executive Officer

Gramercy Outpatient Surgery Center, LTD, 2727 Gramercy, Houston, TX 77025; tel. 713/660-6900; FAX. 713/660-0704; Elaine Hand, RN, CNOR, Clinical Director

HEALTHSOUTH Surgery Center of Beaumont, 3050 Liberty, Beaumont, TX 77702; tel. 409/835-3535; FAX. 409/835-6005; Tammie Clodfelter, Administrator

HEALTHSOUTH Surgery Center of Conroe, 233 Interstate 45 N., P.O. Box 3091, Conroe, TX 77304; tel. 409/760-3443; FAX. 409/760-1322; Kathy Schutz, RN, B.S.N., Facility Administrator

HEALTHSOUTH Surgery Center of Dallas, 7150 Greenville Avenue, Suite 200, Dallas, TX 75231; tel. 214/891-0466; FAX. 214/739-4702; Vicki V. Schultz, RN, Administrator

HealthSouth Surgery Center of Southwest Houston, 8111 Southwest Freeway, Houston, TX 77074; tel. 713/988-7600; FAX. 713/988-4070; Karen Whigham, Administrator

Healthsouth Arlington Day Surgery, 918 North Davis Street, Arlington, TX 76012; tel. 817/860-9933; FAX. 817/860-2314; Diane Wood, RN, Administrator

Healthsouth Outpatient Surgery Center, 7515 South Main Street, Suite 800, Houston, TX 77030; tel. 713/796-9666; FAX. 713/796-9660; Joan M. Culberson, RN, Administrator

Heart of Texas Outpatient Cataract Center, 100 South Park Drive, Brownwood, TX 76801; tel. 915/643-3561; FAX. 915/646-0670; Larry Smith, CRNA, Administrator

Heritage Surgery Center, 1501 Redbud, McKinney, TX 75069; tel. 214/548-0771; FAX. 214/562-2300; Rudolf Churner, M.D., Administrator

Houston Eye Clinic Partnership, 1200 Binz, Suite 1000, Houston, TX 77004; tel. 713/526-1600; FAX. 713/529-5254; Darcy Falbey, Director, Nursing

Howerton Eye and Laser Surgical Center, 2610 I.H. 35 South, Austin, TX 78704-5703; tel. 512/443-9715; FAX. 512/443-9845; Ernest E. Howerton, M.D., Administrator

Key Whitman Surgery Center, 2801 Lemmon Avenue, Suite 400, Dallas, TX 75204; tel. 214/754-0000; FAX. 214/754-0079; Jeffrey Whitman, M.D.

Knolle Ocular Surgery Center, 4126 Southwest Freeway, Suite 108, Houston, TX 77027; tel. 713/621-3920; FAX. 713/621-7217; Guy E. Knolle, Jr., M.D., Administrator

Lipsky Sight Center, 1060 Hercules, Houston, TX 77058; tel. 713/488-7213; Ed Bercier, Administrator

Longview Ambulatory Surgical Center, 703 East Marshall Avenue, Suite 2000, Longview, TX 75601-5563; tel. 903/236-2111; FAX. 903/236-2479; Jerry D. Adair, President, Chief Executive Officer

Lubbock Surgi Center, LLP, 3610 34th Street, Suite D, Lubbock, TX 79410; tel. 806/793-0255; Robert M. Brodkin, D.P.M., Administrator

Lufkin Endoscopy Center, 317 Gaslight Boulevard, Lufkin, TX 75901; tel. 409/634-3713; FAX. 409/634-8136; Bhagvan R. Malladi, M.D., Administrator

MSCH Health Center, 1211 Highway Six, Suite One, Sugarland, TX 77478; tel. 713/242-7200; John Araiza, Administrator

Maddox Outpatient Eye Surgery Center, 1755 Curie Drive, El Paso, TX 79902; tel. 915/544-9597; FAX. 915/533-3460; Robert M. Maddox, M.D., Administrator

Mann Cataract Surgery Center, 18850 South Memorial Boulevard, Humble, TX 77338; tel. 713/446-9164; Elpidio Fahel, Administrator

Medical City Dallas Ambulatory Surgery Center, 7777 Forest Lane, Suite C-150, Dallas, TX 75230; tel. 214/661-7000; FAX. 214/788-6181; Michael D. Pugh, President, Chief Executive Officer

Medical Mall Surgery Center, Inc., 1665 Antilley Road, Suite 170, Abilene, TX 79606; tel. 915/692-6694; FAX. 915/691-1568; Melissa Boyd, RN

Methodist Ambulatory Surgery Center–Central San Antonio, 1008 Brooklyn Avenue, San Antonio, TX 78215-1600; tel. 210/225-0496; FAX. 210/225-8462; Carl J. Collazo, Administrator

Methodist Malone and Hogan–Texas Surgery, 1501 West 11th Place, Suite A, Big Spring, TX 79720-4199; tel. 915/267-1623; FAX. 915/267-1137; Penny Phillips, Administrator

Metroplex Ambulatory Surgical Center, 2717 Osler Drive, Suite 102, Grand Prairie, TX 75051; tel. 214/647-6272; FAX. 214/660-1822; Glenda Daniels, RN, Director

Metroplex Surgicare, 1600 Central Drive, Suite 180, Bedford, TX 76022; tel. 817/571-1999; FAX. 817/571-1220; Julie Walker, Administrator

Mid-Cities Surgi-Center, 2012 Plaza Drive, Bedford, TX 76021; tel. 817/283-5994; Melany Pierson

Mid-Town Surgical Center, Inc., 2105 Jackson Street, Suite 200, Houston, TX 77003; tel. 713/659-3050; FAX. 713/659-3037; Glory Gee, Administrator

North Carrier Surgicenter, 517 North Carrier Parkway, Suite A, Grand Prairie, TX 75050-5494; tel. 214/264-0533; FAX. 214/262-5974; Abraham F. Syrquin, M.D., Medical Director

North Dallas Surgicare, 375 Municipal Drive, Suite 214, Richardson, TX 75080; tel. 214/918-9400; FAX. 214/918-9749; Bill MacKnight, Administrator

Northeast Surgery Center, 18929 Highway 59, Humble, TX 77338; tel. 713/446-4053; Harold Taylor

Northeast Texas Surgical Center, 1801 Galleria Oaks Drive, Texarkana, TX 75503; tel. 903/792-2108; FAX. 903/792-0606; Ruby Bearden, Business Manager

Northwest Ambulatory Surgery Center, 2833 Babcock Road, San Antonio, TX 78229; tel. 210/705-5100; FAX. 210/705-5025; Jim Brown, Administrator

Outpatient Surgical Center, 2507 Medical Row, Suite 101, Grand Prairie, TX 75051; tel. 214/647-8520; Jack Gray, Administrator

Outpatient Surgisite, 401-A East Pinecrest Drive, Marshall, TX 75670; tel. 903/938-3110; Carol C. Hall

Piney Point Ambulatory Surgery Center, 2500 Fondren, Suite 350, Houston, TX 77063; tel. 713/782-8279; FAX. 713/782-3139

Plano Ambulatory Surgery Associates, L.P., d/b/a Columbia Surgery Center of Plano, 1620 Coit Road, Plano, TX 75075-7799; tel. 972/519-1100; Dolores Holland

Plastic and Reconstructive Surgery Centre of the SW, 461 Westpark Way, Euless, TX 76040; tel. 817/540-1755; Catherine Lugger, Director

Plaza Day Surgery, 909 Ninth Avenue, Fort Worth, TX 76104-3986; tel. 817/336-6060; Nancy Kilekas, RN, B.S., CNOR, Administrator

Port Arthur Day Surgery Center, 3449 Gates Boulevard, Port Arthur, TX 77642; tel. 409/983-6144; Vicki Clark, Administrative Director

Premier Ambulatory Surgery of Austin, 4207 James Casey, Suite 203, Austin, TX 78745; tel. 512/440-7894; FAX. 512/440-1932; Patricia Philbin, Executive Director

Regional Eye Surgery Center, 107 West 30th Street, Pampa, TX 79065; tel. 806/665-0051; FAX. 806/665-0640; George R. Walters, M.D., President

Rio Grande Surgery Center, 1809 South Cynthia, McAllen, TX 78503; tel. 512/618-4402; FAX. 210/618-4174; Janet R. West, Director

San Antonio Digestive Disease Endoscopy Center, 1804 Northeast Loop 410, Suite 101, San Antonio, TX 78217; tel. 210/828-8400; FAX. 210/828-8648

San Antonio Eye Surgicenter, 800 McCullough, San Antonio, TX 78215; tel. 210/226-6169; FAX. 210/226-6383; Carol Harris, Administrator

San Antonio Gastroenterology Endoscopy Center, 520 Euclid Avenue, San Antonio, TX 78212; tel. 210/271-0606; FAX. 210/271-0180; Ernesto Guerra, M.D.

San Antonio Surgery Center, Inc., 5290 Medical Drive, San Antonio, TX 78229; tel. 210/614-0187; FAX. 210/692-7757; Ann Finney, RN, Facility Administrator

Santa Rosa Diagnostic and Surgical Center, 315 North San Saba, San Antonio, TX 78207; tel. 210/704-4000; FAX. 210/704-4014; Julie Meador, Clinical Manager

South Plains Endoscopy Center, 3610 24th Street, Lubbock, TX 79410; tel. 806/797-1015; Pat S. Wheeler, Administrator

South Texas Eye Surgicenter, Inc., 4406 North Laurent, Victoria, TX 77901; tel. 800/352-5928; Robert T. McMahon, M.D., Chief Executive Officer

South Texas Outpatient Surgical Center, Inc., 4025 East Southcross Boulevard, Building Three, Suite 15, San Antonio, TX 78222; tel. 210/333-0633; FAX. 210/333-0671; Michael P. Lewis, Administrator

South West Surgery Center, 1717 Precinct Line Road, Suite 101, Hurst, TX 76054; tel. 817/498-0525; FAX. 817/656-1490; Kim Gustin, Office Manager

Southwest Endoscopy Center, 11803 South Freeway, Suite 115, Fort Worth, TX 76115; tel. 817/293-9292; FAX. 817/551-0616; Pamela Payne, RN

St. Mary Surgicenter, Ltd., 2301 Quaker Avenue, Lubbock, TX 79410; tel. 806/793-8801; David S. Weil, Executive Director

SurgEyeCare, Inc., 5421 La Sierra Drive, Dallas, TX 75231; tel. 214/361-1443; FAX. 214/691-3299; Sandra J. Yankee, Administrator

Surgery Center Southwest, 8230 Walnut Hill Lane, Suite 102, Dallas, TX 75231; tel. 214/345-4076; FAX. 214/345-4055; Tom Blair, Director, PHS

Surgery Center of Fort Worth, 2001 West Rosedale, Fort Worth, TX 76104; tel. 817/877-4777; Debra Delain, RN, Administrator

Surgi-Care Center of Midland, Inc., 3001 West Illinois, Suite Five-A, Midland, TX 79701; tel. 915/697-1067; FAX. 915/697-8802; Michelle Edelbrock, RN, B.S.N., Director

SurgiSystems, Inc., 427 West 20th Street, Houston, TX 77008; tel. 713/868-3641; FAX. 713/865-5460; Jo McBeth, RN

Surgical Center of El Paso, 1815 North Stanton, El Paso, TX 79902; tel. 915/533-8412; FAX. 915/542-0367; Thomas Reynolds, Managing Director

Surgical and Diagnostic Center, Inc., 729 Bedford Euless Road West 100, Hurst, TX 76053; tel. 817/282-6905; FAX. 817/285-8114; Edward William Smith, D.O., Medical Director

Surgicare of Travis Centre, Inc., 6655 Travis, Suite 200, Houston, TX 77030; tel. 713/526-5100; Carol Simons, Administrator

Surgicare, Ltd., 3534 Vista, Pasadena, TX 77504; tel. 713/947-0330; Evelyn Grimes, Administrator

Surgicenter of San Antonio, L.P., 7902 Ewing Halsell Drive, San Antonio, TX 78229; tel. 210/614-7372; FAX. 210/614-7362; Russell Furth, Executive Director

Texarkana Surgery Center, 5404 Summerhill Road, Texarkana, TX 75503; tel. 903/792-7151; Karen Stephens, Director

Texas Ambulatory Surgical Center, Inc., 2505 North Shepherd, Houston, TX 77008; tel. 713/880-3940; FAX. 713/880-1923; Kwang S. Park, Administrator

Texas Institute of Surgery, 12700 North Featherwood Drive, Suite 100, Houston, TX 77034; tel. 713/481-9303; FAX. 713/481-4263; Glenn Rodriguez, Administrator

Texoma Outpatient Surgery Center, Inc., 1712 Eleventh Street, Wichita Falls, TX 76301; tel. 817/723-1274; Tracy Youngblood, Administrator

The Birth Center of Southeast Texas, Inc., 2400 Highway 96 S., Lumberton, TX 77656; tel. 409/755-0252; Dennis D. Riston, M.D., Administrator

The Cataract Center of East Texas, P.A., 802 Turtle Creek Drive, Tyler, TX 75701; tel. 903/595-4333; FAX. 903/535-9845; Connie Bryan, RN

The Center for Sight, P.A., Two Medical Center Boulevard, Lufkin, TX 75904-3175; tel. 409/634-8434; FAX. 409/639-2581; Richard J. Ruckman, M.D.

The Endoscopy Center of Southeast Texas, 950 North 11th Street, Beaumont, TX 77702; tel. 409/833-5555; FAX. 409/833-9911; Royce D. Harrell

The Eye Surgery Center of the Rio Grande Valley, 1402 East Sixth Street, Weslaco, TX 78596; tel. 210/968-6155; FAX. 210/968-8291; Linda Funston, Administrator

The Ocular Surgery Center, Inc., 1100 North Main Avenue, San Antonio, TX 78212; tel. 210/222-2154; FAX. 512/222-0706; Jane Wilson, Administrator

The Surgery Center of Mesquite, 2690 North Galloway Avenue, Mesquite, TX 75150; tel. 972/279-8100; FAX. 972/279-3300; Jeffrey S. Houston, Administrator

The Surgery Center of Texas, 155 East Loop 338, Suite 500, Odessa, TX 79762; tel. 915/367-3906; FAX. 915/367-3895; Ann Wilson, Interim Administrator

The Surgery Center of the Woodlands, 1441 Woodstead Court, Suite 100, The Woodlands, TX 77380; tel. 281/363-0058; FAX. 281/363-0450; Kathy Budd, Administrator

Thorstenson Eye Clinic Surgery Center, 3302 Northeast Stallings Drive, Nacogdoches, TX 75963-2020; tel. 409/564-2411; FAX. 409/564-1280; Lyle S. Thorstenson, M.D., FACS, Administrator

University Surgery Center, Inc., 311 University Drive, Fort Worth, TX 76107; tel. 817/877-1002; FAX. 817/877-1006; Lori Schooler, Administrator

Urological Surgery Center of Fort Worth, 418 South Henderson, Fort Worth, TX 76104; tel. 817/338-4637; Charles Bamberger, M.D.

Valley Endoscopy Center, LLP, 3101 South Sunshine Strip, Harlingen, TX 78550; tel. 210/421-2324; FAX. 210/428-2561; Noel B. Searle, MD

Valley Eye Surgery Center, 1515 North Ed Carey Drive, Harlingen, TX 78550; tel. 210/423-2773; FAX. 210/423-5618; Michael D. Laney, Administrator

Valley View Surgery Center, 5744 LBJ Freeway, Suite 200, Dallas, TX 75240; tel. 972/490-4333; FAX. 972/490-3408; Ronald W. Disney, Chief Executive Officer

Vista Healthcare, Inc., 4301 Vista, Pasadena, TX 77504; tel. 713/947-0891; FAX. 713/947-1377; Chiu M. Chan, Administrator

WestPark Surgery Center, 130 South Central Expressway, McKinney, TX 75070; tel. 214/542-9382; FAX. 214/548-5303; Debbie Taylor

Westside Surgery Center, Ltd., 16100 Cairnway, Houston, TX 77084; tel. 713/550-5556; FAX. 713/550-7888; Harold F. Taylor, President, Chief Executive Officer

Wilson Surgicenter, 4315 28th Street, Lubbock, TX 79410; tel. 806/792-2104; Bill W. Wilson, M.D., Chief Executive Officer

UTAH

Central Utah Surgical Center, 1067 North 500 West, Provo, UT 84604; tel. 801/374-0354; FAX. 801/374-2615; Jill Andrews, RN, Administrator

Institute of Facial and Cosmetic Surgery, 5929 Fashion Boulevard, Murray, UT 84107; tel. 801/261-3637; FAX. 801/261-4096; Dr. Brent D. Kennedy, Administrator

Intermountain Surgical Center, 359 Eighth Avenue, Salt Lake City, UT 84103; tel. 801/321-3200; FAX. 801/321-3035; Joan W. Lelis, Administrative Director

McKay-Dee Surgical Center, 3903 Harrison Boulevard, Suite 100, Ogden, UT 84403; tel. 801/625-2809; FAX. 801/629-5938; Suzanne Richins, Administrator

Provo Surgical Center, 585 North 500 West, Provo, UT 84601; tel. 801/375-0983; Brent K. Ashby, Administrator

Salt Lake Endoscopy Center, 24 South 1100 East, Salt Lake City, UT 84102; tel. 801/355-2987; FAX. 801/531-9704; Clifford G. Harmon, M.D., Administrator

Salt Lake Surgical Center, 617 East 3900 South, Salt Lake City, UT 84107; tel. 801/261-3141; FAX. 801/268-2599; Jay T. Lighthall, Administrator

St. George Surgical Center, 676 South Bluff Street, St. George, UT 84770; tel. 801/673-8080; FAX. 801/673-0096; Terrill Dick, Administrator

St. Mark's Outpatient Surgery Center, 1250 East 3900 South, Suite 100, Salt Lake City, UT 84124; tel. 801/262-0358; FAX. 801/262-0901; Marjorie Kimes, Administrator

The SurgiCare Center of Utah, 755 East 3900 South, Salt Lake City, UT 84107; tel. 801/266-2283; FAX. 801/268-6151; Andrew Lyle, M.D., Administrator

Wasatch Endoscopy, 1220 East 3900 South, Suite 1B, Salt Lake City, UT 84124; tel. 801/281-3657; Marjorie Kimes, R.N., Administrator

Wasatch Surgery Center, 555 South Foothill Boulevard, Salt Lake City, UT 84112; tel. 801/585-3088; FAX. 801/581-8962; Patricia Carroll, Administrator, Manager

Western Surgery Center, Inc., 850 East 1200 North, Logan, UT 84341; tel. 801/797-3670; FAX. 801/797-3848; Barbara Smehland, Administrator

VERMONT

David S. Chase, M.D., Ambulatory Surgical Center, 183 St. Paul Street, Burlington, VT 05401; tel. 802/864-0381; David S. Chase, M.D., Administrator

VIRGINIA

Ambulatory Surgery Center, 844 Kempsville Road, Norfolk, VA 23502; tel. 804/466-6900; FAX. 804/461-6796; Darleen S. Anderson, Site Administrator

Cataract and Refractive Surgery Center, 2010 Bremo Road, Suite 128, Richmond, VA 23226; tel. 804/285-0680; FAX. 804/282-6365; Jeffry A. Staples, Administrator

Columbia Fairfax Surgical Center, 10730 Main Street, Fairfax, VA 22030; tel. 703/691-0670; Sharon B. Johnson, Chief Executive Officer

CountrySide Ambulatory Surgery Center, Four Pidgeon Hill Drive, Sterling, VA 20165; tel. 703/444-6060; FAX. 703/444-2278; Deborah F. Arminio, RN, Director

Fredericksburg Ambulatory Surgery Center, Inc., 2216 Princess Anne Street, Fredericksburg, VA 22401; tel. 540/899-3403; FAX. 540/899-6893; Jeane Bullock, Administrator

Kaiser Permanente Falls Church Medical Center Ambulatory Surgery Center, 201 North Washington Street, Falls Church, VA 22046; tel. 703/237-4046; FAX. 703/536-1400; Debbie Bland, Director, Surgical Services

Lakeview Medical Center, Inc., 2000 Meade Parkway, Suffolk, VA 23424; tel. 804/539-0251; FAX. 804/934-2620; Michael B. Stout, Administrator

Lewis–Gale Clinic, Inc., Same Day Surgery, 1802 Braeburn Drive, Salem, VA 24153; tel. 703/772–3673; FAX. 703/989–0879; Lyndell B. Brooks, President

Piedmont Day Surgery Center, Inc., 1040 Main Street, P.O. Box 1360, Danville, VA 24543–1360; tel. 804/792–1433, ext. 258; FAX. 804/797–1398; Aaron Lieberman, Chief Operating Officer

Retreat Regional Medical Center, 7016 Lee Park Road, Mechanicsville, VA 23111; tel. 804/730–9000; FAX. 804/730–1460; Timothy E. Wildt, Administrator

Riverside Surgery Center–Warwick, 12420 Warwick Boulevard, Building Three, Suite C, Newport News, VA 23606; tel. 804/594–2796; FAX. 804/594–3911; M. Caroline Martin, Executive Vice President

Sentara Care Plex, 3000 Coliseum Drive, Hampton, VA 23666; tel. 804/827–2000; FAX. 804/827–6748; Jeri Eastridge, Director

Surgi Center of Central Virginia, Inc., 223 Willow Street, Fredericksburg, VA 22405; tel. 703/371–5349; FAX. 703/373–1745; Janet P. O'Keefe, Facility Administrator

Surgi–Center of Winchester, Inc., 1860 Amherst Street, P.O. Box 2660, Winchester, VA 22604; tel. 703/722–8934; FAX. 703/722–8936; H. Emerson Poling, M.D., Administrator

Tuckahoe Surgery Center, Inc., 8919 Three Chopt Road, Richmond, VA 23229; tel. 804/285–4763; FAX. 804/288–2850; Charles A. Stark, CHE, Administrator

Urosurgical Center of Richmond, 5224 Monument Avenue, Richmond, VA 23226; tel. 804/288–4137; FAX. 804/288–3529; Terry W. Coffey, Administrator

Urosurgical Center of Richmond–North, 8228 Meadowbridge Road, Mechanicsville, VA 23111; tel. 804/730–5023; FAX. 804/746–4015; Terry W. Coffey, Administrator

Urosurgical Center of Richmond–South, 7001 Jahnke Road, Richmond, VA 23225; tel. 804/560–4483; FAX. 804/272–1178; Terry W. Coffey, Administrator

Virginia Ambulatory Surgery Center, 337–15th Street, S.W., Charlottesville, VA 22903; tel. 804/295–4800; FAX. 804/977–0544; Gerry Dobrasz, Administrator

Virginia Beach Ambulatory Surgery Center, 1700 Will–o–Wisp Drive, Virginia Beach, VA 23454; tel. 804/496–6400; FAX. 804/496–3137; Brian Murray, M.D., Administrator

Virginia Eye Institute/Eye Surgeons of Richmond, Inc., 400 Westhampton Station, Richmond, VA 23226; tel. 804/282–3931; FAX. 804/287–4256; Kenneth J. Newell, Administrator

Virginia Heart Institute, LTD., 205 North Hamilton Street, Richmond, VA 23221; tel. 804/359–9265; Charles L. Baird, Jr., M.D., Director

Woodburn Surgery Center, 3289 Woodburn Road, Suite 100, Annandale, VA 22003; tel. 703/207–7520; Jolene Tornabeni, Senior Vice President, Administrator

WASHINGTON

AEsteem Outpatient Surgery Center, 1200 North Northgate Way, Seattle, WA 98133–8916; tel. 206/522–0200; FAX. 206/522–7019; Peter R. N. Chatard, Jr., M.D., Medical Director

Aesthetic Eye Associates, P.S., 1810 116th Avenue, N.E., Suite B, Bellevue, WA 98004; tel. 206/462–0400; FAX. 206/454–1085; Janet Jordan, Business Manager

Bel–Red Ambulatory Surgical Facility, 1370 116th Avenue, N.E., Suite 209, Bellevue, WA 98004; tel. 206/455–7225; FAX. 206/455–0045

Bellingham Surgery Center, 2980 Squalicum Parkway, Bellingham, WA 98225; tel. 206/671–6933; Richard Brumenschenkel, Managing Agent

Boyd Davis Eye Center, 1051 116th Avenue, N.E., Bellevue, WA 98004; tel. 206/454–2018; Herschell H. Boyd, M.D.

Cascade Ambulatory Surgery Center, 407 Northeast 87th Street, Vancouver, WA 98664; tel. 360/253–9201; Joseph R. McFarland, M.D.

Cascade Regional Eye Surgery Center, 16404 Smokey Point Boulevard, Suite 111, Arlington, WA 98223; tel. 206/653–4000; FAX. 206/658–1266; Smokey Simons, Director

Central Washington Cataract Surgery, 1450 North 16th Avenue, Building J, Yakima, WA 98902; tel. 509/457–5000; FAX. 509/457–6498; Paul Almeida, CRNA

Central Washington Surgicare, 307 South 12th Avenue, Suite Nine, Yakima, WA 98902; tel. 509/248–4900; FAX. 509/248–0609

Covington Day Surgery Center, 17700 Southeast 272nd Street, Kent, WA 98042; tel. 206/639–8302; FAX. 206/639–8301; Victoria Fitzpatrick, B.S.N., Director

Dietrich Von Feldmann, M.D., Inc., 16259 Sylvester S.W., Suite 401, Seattle, WA 98166; tel. 206/244–5335; FAX. 206/244–4147; Dietrich Von Feldmann, M.D.

Ear, Nose, Throat and Plastic Surgery, 101 Second Street, N.E., Auburn, WA 98002; tel. 206/833–6241; FAX. 206/833–4113; William Portuese, M.D., Medical Director

Eastside Podiatry Ambulatory Surgery Center, 15617 Bel–Red Road, Bellevue, WA 98008; tel. 206/881–5592; G. Curda, D.P.M.

Edmonds Surgery Center, 21229 84th Avenue W., Edmonds, WA 98026; tel. 206/775–1505; FAX. 206/775–9078; Mark A. Kuzel, D.P.M.

Everett Surgical Center, Inc., 3025 Rucker Avenue, Everett, WA 98201; tel. 206/339–2464; FAX. 206/252–4700; Rita Sweeney, RNFA, CNOR, Administrator

Evergreen Endoscopy Center, 13030 121st Way, N.E., Suite 101, Kirkland, WA 98034; tel. 206/899–4600; Lynn Bookkeeper

Evergreen Eye Surgery Center, 34719 Sixth Avenue South, Federal Way, WA 98003; tel. 206/874–3969; Richard A. Boudreau, Administrator

Evergreen Surgical Center, 12034 Northeast 130th Lane, Kirkland, WA 98034; tel. 206/821–3131; Ronald E. Abrams, M.D.

Good Samaritan Surgery Center, 1322 Third Street S.E., Suite 100, Puyallup, WA 98372; tel. 206/840–2200; FAX. 206/840–2352; Roger D. Robinett, M.D., Medical Director

Health South, Green River Surgical Center, 126 Auburn Avenue, Suite 200, Auburn, WA 98002; tel. 206/735–0500; FAX. 206/939–8526; Gail A. Okon, Facility Manager

Hernia Treatment Center, NW, 205 Lilly Road, NE, Suite D, Olympia, WA 98506; tel. 360/491–8667; Robert Kugel, M.D., Director

Inland Empire Endoscopy Center, South 820 McClellan, Suite 314, Spokane, WA 99204; tel. 509/747–0143; J. D. Fitterer, M.D.

Inland Eye Center, South 842 Cowley, Spokane, WA 99202; tel. 509/624–5300; FAX. 509/747–1348; Michael H. Cunningham, M.D., President

Kruger Clinic Day Surgery, 21600 Highway 99, Suite 150, Edmonds, WA 98026; tel. 206/774–2636

Laboratory for Reproductive Health, 1370 116th Avenue, N.E., Suite 100, Bellevue, WA 98004; tel. 206/462–6100

Lomas Surgery Center, 17800 Talbot Road, S., Renton, WA 98055; tel. 425/255–0986; FAX. 425/271–5703; Inese A. Lomas, Administrator

Madrona Medical Group, ASC, 4370 Cordata Parkway, Bellingham, WA 98226; tel. 360/676–1712

McIntyre Eye Surgical Center, 1920 116th Avenue, N.E., Bellevue, WA 98004; tel. 206/454–3937; FAX. 206/646–5914; David McIntyre, M.D., FACS

Mid–Columbia Surgical Suite, Inc., 471 Williams Boulevard, Suite Four, Richland, WA 99352; tel. 509/943–1134; Robert C. Luckey, M.D., Medical Director

Minor & James Medical, PLLC, 515 Minor Avenue, Suite 200, Seattle, WA 98104; tel. 206/386–9500; FAX. 206/386–9605; Sylvia Croy, RN, ASC Coordinator

Monroe Foot Care Associates Ambulatory Surgery Center, 14692 179th Avenue, S.E., Suite 300, Monroe, WA 98272; tel. 206/794–1266; Dr. Brunsman, Medical Director

Moses Lake Surgery Center, 840 East Hill Avenue, Moses Lake, WA 98837; tel. 509/765–0216; John Rodriguez, ASC Manager

NW Aesthetic Surgery Center, 550 16th Avenue, Suite 404, Seattle, WA 98122; tel. 206/328–2250; Mary Ann Beberman, Administrator

NW Center for Corrective Jaw Surgery, 550 16th Avenue, Seattle, WA 98122; tel. 206/324–6570; FAX. 206/324–9936; Carolyn Conroy, Office Administrator

North Cascade ENT Facial Plastic Surgery, 20302 77th Avenue, N.E., Arlington, WA 98223; tel. 360/435–6300; FAX. 360/435–8381; Alex O'Dell

North Cascade ENT and Facial Plastic Surgery, 111 South 13th Street, Mount Vernon, WA 98273; tel. 206/336–2178

North Kitsap Ambulatory Surgical Center, 20696 Bond Road, N.E., Poulsbo, WA 98370; tel. 360/779–6527; FAX. 360/697–2743; Susan Chu, RN

Northwest Center for Plastic and Reconstructive Surgery, 16259 Sylvester Road, S.W., Suite 302, Seattle, WA 98166; tel. 206/241–5400; FAX. 206/241–8591; Sindi Miller, Office Manager

Northwest Eye Surgery, P.C., N1120 Pines Road, Spokane, WA 99206; tel. 509/927–0700

Northwest Gastroenterology, d/b/a Northwest Endoscopy, 2930 Squalicum, Suite 202, Bellingham, WA 98225; tel. 360/733–3231; FAX. 360/734–8748; Kathy Bruns, Manager

Northwest Nasal Sinus Center, 10330 Meridan Avenue, N., Suite 240, Seattle, WA 98133; tel. 206/525–2525; FAX. 206/525–0346

Northwest Surgery Center, 1920 100th Street, S.E., Everett, WA 98208; tel. 206/316–3700; Chris Vance, President

Northwest Surgery Center, Inc., West 123 Francis, Spokane, WA 99205; tel. 509/483–9363; FAX. 509/483–0355; Douglas P. Romney

Northwest Surgical Center, 3120 Squalicum Parkway, Bellingham, WA 98225; tel. 360/647–0557; FAX. 360/733–2892; Marianne Karuza, A.R.T.

Olympic Ambulatory Surgery Center, Inc., 2601 Cherry Avenue, Suite 115, Bremerton, WA 98310; tel. 206/479–5990; FAX. 360/377–5731; Audrey E. Harris, RN

Olympic Plastic Surgery Suite, 2600 Cherry Avenue, Suite 201, Bremerton, WA 98310; tel. 206/479–4370

Pacific Cataract and Laser Institute, 2517 Northeast Kresky, Chehalis, WA 98532; tel. 206/748–8632; Debbie Eldredge, Vice President, Chief Operating Officer

Pacific Cataract and Laser Institute, 10500 Northeast Eighth Street, Suite 1650, Bellevue, WA 98004–4332; tel. 206/462–7664; FAX. 206/462–6429; Maynard Pohl, O.D., Clinical Director

Pacific Cataract and Laser Institute, 8200 West Grandridge, Kennewick, WA 99336

Pacific Medical Center, 1200 12th Avenue, S., Seventh Floor, Seattle, WA 98144; tel. 206/326–4000, ext. 2469; Carolyn Bodeen, RN, Clinic Director

Pacific NW Facial Plastic Ambulatory Surgery Center, 600 Broadway, Suite 280, Seattle, WA 98122; tel. 206/386–3550; FAX. 206/386–3553

Parkway Surgical Center, 2940 Squalicum Parkway, Suite 204, Bellingham, WA 98225; tel. 206/676–8350; FAX. 206/676–8351; Orville Vandergriend, M.D., Administrator

Physicians Eye Surgical Center, 3930 Hoyt Avenue, Everett, WA 98201; tel. 206/259–2020; Carol Schoenfelder, Administrator

Plastic Surgery Center, 1017 South 40th Avenue, Yakima, WA 98904; tel. 509/966–6000; FAX. 509/966–6565; Julie Marquis, RN, Quality Assurance Manager

Plastic Surgicenter of Olympia, 400 Lilly Road, N.E., Building Four, Olympia, WA 98506; tel. 360/456–4400; FAX. 360/491–7619; Wayne L. Dickason, M.D.

Plastic and Reconstructive Surgeons, 17930 Talbot Road, S., Renton, WA 98055; tel. 206/228–3187; Mack D. Richey, M.D.

Professional Surgical Specialists, 1609 Meridian South, Puyallup, WA 98371; tel. 206/841–1331

Redmond Foot Care Associates, ASC, 16146 Cleveland Street, Redmond, WA 98052; tel. 206/885–7004

Rockwood Clinic, d/b/a Gastrointestinal Endoscopy Unit, Sacred Heart Building, West 105 Eighth Avenue, Suite 7050, Spokane, WA 99204; tel. 509/838–2531; FAX. 509/459–1527; Stephen Burgert, M.D., Administrator

Rockwood Clinic, PS, East 400 Fifth Avenue, Spokane, WA 99202; tel. 509/838–2531; FAX. 509/455–5315; William R. Poppy, Chief Executive Officer, Administrator

Seattle Endoscopy Center, 11027 Meridian Avenue, N., Suite 100, Seattle, WA 98133; tel. 206/363–8502; FAX. 206/365–3456; Patty Carroll, CGRN, Manager

Seattle Eye Plastic Surgery Center, 1229 Madison Street, Suite 1190, Seattle, WA 98104; tel. 206/621–0800; FAX. 206/621–7023; R. Toby Sutcliffe, M.D.

Seattle Hand Surgery Group, P.C., 600 Broadway, Suite 440, Seattle, WA 98122; tel. 206/292–6252; FAX. 206/292–7893; Suzann H. Demianew, Administrator

Seattle Head and Neck Office Surgery, 515 Minor Avenue, Suite 130, Seattle, WA 98104; tel. 206/682–6103; Adrienne C. Peach, RN, Director

Seattle Microsurgical Eyecare Center, 5300 17th Avenue, N.W., Seattle, WA 98107; tel. 206/783–3929; Jack C. Bunn, M.D., Medical Director

Seattle Plastic Surgery Center, 600 Broadway, Suite 320, Seattle, WA 98122; tel. 206/324–1120; FAX. 206/720–0800; Wendy Discher, Manager

Seattle Surgery Center, Columbus Pavilion, 900 Terry Avenue, Fourth Floor, Seattle, WA 98104–1240; tel. 206/382–1021; FAX. 206/382–1026; Naya Kehayes, M.P.H., Administrator

Sequim Same Day Surgery, 777 North Fifth Avenue, Sequim, WA 98382; tel. 360/681–0358; Tammy Paolini, Surgical Technician

South Hill Ambulatory Surgical Center, South 3028 Grand Boulevard, Spokane, WA 99203; tel. 509/747–0279; FAX. 509/747–3220

Southwest Washington Ambulatory Surgery Center, Inc., 416 Northeast 87th Avenue, Vancouver, WA 98664; tel. 206/696–4000; FAX. 206/696–4287

Southwest Washington Ambulatory Surgery Center, Inc., 102 West Fourth Plain Boulevard, Vancouver, WA 98666; tel. 206/696–4400; Kim Fehly

Spokane Digestive Disease Center, 105 West Eighth Avenue, Suite 6010, Spokane, WA 99204–2318; tel. 509/838–5950; FAX. 509/838–5961; Margie Troske–Johnson, RN, B.S.N., Director

Spokane Eye Surgery Center, West 208 Fifth Street, Spokane, WA 99204; tel. 509/456–8150; FAX. 509/455–9887; Donald Ellingsen, M.D.

Spokane Foot and Ankle Surgery Center, 9405 East Sprague Avenue, Spokane, WA 99206; tel. 509/922–3199; Rita Kinney, RN

Spokane Surgery Center, North 1120 Pines Road, Spokane, WA 99206; tel. 509/924–3235; Stewart P. Brim, D.P.M.

St. Mark's Micro Surgical Center, Inc., 502 South M Street, Tacoma, WA 98405; tel. 206/627–8266; Roy Baker, Chief Executive Officer

Stanley M. Jackson, M.D., Plastic and Reconstructive Surgery, 105 27th Avenue, S.E., Puyallup, WA 98374; tel. 206/848–8110; FAX. 206/845–3561; Karen Smith, RN

TLC Northwest Eye, Inc., 10330 Meridian Avenue N., Suite 370, Seattle, WA 98133–9451; tel. 206/528–6000, ext. 114; FAX. 206/528–0014; Wendy R. Williams, Marketing Director

Tacoma Ambulatory Surgery Center, 1112 Sixth Avenue, Suite 100, Tacoma, WA 98405; tel. 206/272–3916, ext. 324; FAX. 206/627–1713; Joan Hoover, Administrator

Tacoma Endoscopy Center, 1112 Sixth Avenue, Suite 200, Tacoma, WA 98405; tel. 206/272–8664; FAX. 206/627–7880; Richard Baerg, M.D., Medical Director

Tacoma Speciality ASU, 209 Martin Luther King Jr. Way, Tacoma, WA 98405; tel. 206/596–3590; Linda Bradley, Manager

The Eastside Endoscopy Center, P.L.L.C., 1700 116th Avenue, N.E., Suite 100, Bellevue, WA 98004–3049; tel. 206/451–7335; FAX. 206/451–7335; Bunny McCormack, RN, Director, Nursing

The Plastic SurgiCentre, Inc., 535 South Pine Street, Spokane, WA 99202; tel. 509/623–2160; FAX. 509/623–1135; Pamala Silvers, RN, Manager

The Polyclinic, Inc., 1145 Broadway, Seattle, WA 98122; tel. 206/329–1760; Lloyd David, Chief Executive Officer

Trenton J. Spolar, 505 Northeast 87th Avenue, Suite 203, Vancouver, WA 98664; tel. 206/254–8596

Valley Outpatient Surgery Center, North 1414 Houk Road, Suite 204, Spokane, WA 99216; tel. 509/922–0362; FAX. 509/927–8316; Dr. Douglas Norquist, President

Valley Surgi Centre, Five South 14th Avenue, Yakima, WA 98902; tel. 509/248–6813; FAX. 509/457–9691

Virginia Mason Clinic South, 33501 First Way South, Federal Way, WA 98003; tel. 206/874–1635; Steve Alley

Virginia Mason–Issaquah, 100 Northeast Gilman Boulevard, Issaquah, WA 98027; tel. 206/557–8000; Bobbie Eatmon, Manager

Washington Orthopaedic Center, Inc., PS, 1900 Cooks Hill Road, Centralia, WA 98531; tel. 360/736–2889, ext. 400; JoAnn Wilkey, Director

Wenatchee Surgical Center, 600 Orondo Avenue, Wenatchee, WA 98807; tel. 509/662–8956; Shirley DeWitz, RN, Manager

Wenatchee Valley Clinic/Cascade Surgery Center, 820 North Chelan, Wenatchee, WA 98801; tel. 509/663–8711; FAX. 509/665–2309; Dr. Don Paugh, Chief, Cascade Surgery Center

Westlake Surgical Center, 509 Olive Way, Third Floor, Seattle, WA 98101; tel. 206/623–4755; Maria T. Burrows, Administrative Assistant

Whidbey SurgiCare, 31775–SR 20, Suite A Two, Oak Harbor, WA 98277–2334; tel. 360/679–3117; FAX. 360/679–3118

Whitehorse Surgical Center, 875 Wesley Street, Suite 160, Arlington, WA 98223; tel. 360/435–6969; FAX. 360/435–1068

WEST VIRGINIA

Anwar Eye Center, 1500 Lafayette Avenue, Moundsville, WV 26041; tel. 304/845–0908; M. F. Anwar, M.D.

Cabell Huntington Surgery Center, 1201 Hal Greer Boulevard, Huntington, WV 25701; tel. 304/523–1885; FAX. 304/523–8942; John Stone, Facility Administrator

Cook Eye Surgery Center, 1300 Third Avenue, Huntington, WV 25701; tel. 304/522–1802; FAX. 304/529–6752; David W. Cook, M.D., President

Jerry N. Black, M.D., Surgical Suite, 10 Amalia Drive, Buckhannon, WV 26201; tel. 304/472–2100; Jerry N. Black, M.D., Medical Director

Kanawha Valley Surgi–Center, 4803 MacCorkle Avenue, S.E., Charleston, WV 25304; tel. 304/925–6390; Gorli Harish, M.D., Medical Director

Lee's Surgi–Center, 415 Morris Street, Suite 200, Charleston, WV 25301; tel. 304/342–1113; FAX. 304/346–2271; Hans Lee, M.D., President

SurgiCare, 3200 MacCorkle Avenue, S.E., Charleston, WV 25304; tel. 304/348–9556; Robert L. Savage, President

West Virginia Surgery Center, Inc., 425 Greenway Avenue, South Charleston, WV 25309; tel. 304/768–7310; FAX. 304/768–8211; Nancy Jo Vinson, Administrator

WISCONSIN

Aurora Health Center, 10400 75th Street, Kenosha, WI 53142; tel. 414/697–6901; FAX. 414/697–3022; Carol Ragalie, Administrator

Bay Lake Surgery Outpatient Surgery Center, Inc., 1843 Michigan Street, P.O. Box 678, Sturgeon Bay, WI 54235; tel. 414/746–1070; FAX. 414/746–1072; Michael Herlache, Administrator

Baycare Surgery Center, 2253 West Mason, P.O. Box 33227, Green Bay, WI 54303–0102; tel. 414/592–9100; FAX. 414/497–6830; Jeff Mason, Administrator

Center for Digestive Health, 2901 West Kinnickinnic River Parkway, Suite 560, Milwaukee, WI 53215; tel. 414/649–3522; FAX. 414/649–5454; Robert Chang, Administrator

Davis Duehr Day Surgery, 1025 Regent Street, Madison, WI 53715; tel. 608/282–2050; Rodney Sturm, M.D., President

Dean St. Mary's Surgery Center, 800 South Brooks Street, Madison, WI 53715; tel. 608/259–3510; FAX. 608/255–1272; Patricia Klitzman, Director

Eau Claire Surgery Center, 950 West Clairemont Avenue, Eau Claire, WI 54701; tel. 715/839–9339; FAX. 715/839–9033; Kathryn Hentz, RN, Facility Manager

Green Bay Surgical Center, Ltd., 704 South Webster Avenue, Green Bay, WI 54301; tel. 414/432–7433; FAX. 414/432–6313; Herbert F. Sandmire, M.D., Medical Director, Administrator

HealthSouth Surgery Center of Wausau, 2809 Westhill Drive, Wausau, WI 54401; tel. 715/842–4490; FAX. 715/842–4645; Kathy Eisenschink, RN, Facility Administrator

Kenosha Surgical Center, Inc., 3505 30th Avenue, Kenosha, WI 53142; tel. 414/656–8638; FAX. 414/656–8631; David Bittner, Business Manager

LaSalle Surgery Center, 1550 Midway Place, Menasha, WI 54952; tel. 414/727–8200; FAX. 414/727–8203; Laura Ruys, Manager

Marshfield Clinic Ambulatory Surgery Center, 1000 North Oak Avenue, Marshfield, WI 54449; tel. 715/387–5315; FAX. 715/387–5240; Robert J. DeVita, Executive Director

Menomonee Falls Ambulatory Surgery Center, W180 N8045 Town Hall Road, Menomonee Falls, WI 53051; tel. 414/250–0950; FAX. 414/250–0955; Robert W. Scheller Jr, CPA, Business Director

Mercy Walworth, ASC, N2950 State Road 67, Lake Geneva, WI 53147; tel. 414/245–0535; Cynthia Job, Administrator

Meriter Ambulatory Surgery Center, 20 South Park Street, Madison, WI 53715; tel. 608/267–6479; FAX. 608/267–6370; Robert L. Coats, President, Chief Operating Officer

North Shore Surgical Center, 7007 North Range Line Road, Milwaukee, WI 53209; tel. 414/352–3341; FAX. 414/352–3218; Robert Lonergan, Executive Director

Northlake Surgery Center, 2110 Medical Drive, Box 636, Menomonee, WI 54751; tel. 715/235–8884; Douglas Carson

Northwest Surgery Center, 2300 North Mayfair Road, Wauwatosa, WI 53226; tel. 414/257–3322; Nancy Jones, Administrator

Oshkosh Surgery Center, 1925 Surgery Center Drive, Oshkosh, WI 54901; tel. 414/233–1233; FAX. 414/233–2101; Jean Cox, Administrator

Riverview Surgery Center, 616 North Washington Street, Janesville, WI 53545; tel. 608/758–7300; FAX. 608/758–1050; Cheryl A. Wilson, Director

Surgery Center of Wisconsin, 10401 West Lincoln Avenue, Suite 201, West Allis, WI 53227; tel. 414/321–7850; Penny Leinbeck, Administrator

Surgicenter of Greater Milwaukee, 3223 South 103rd Street, Milwaukee, WI 53227; tel. 414/328–5800; Raymond E. Grundman, General Manager

Surgicenter of Racine, Ltd., 5802 Washington Avenue, Racine, WI 53406; tel. 414/886–9100; Dennis J. Kontra, Administrator

Wauwatosa Surgery Center, d/b/a HealthSouth Surgery Center of Wauwatosa, 10900 West Potter Road, Wauwatosa, WI 53226–3424; tel. 414/774–9227; FAX. 414/774–0957; Carol Leitinger, RN, B.S.N., CNOR, Administrator

WYOMING

Casper Endoscopy Center, 167 South Conwell, Suite Seven, Casper, WY 82601; tel. 307/262–3896; Robert A. Schlidt, M.D., Administrator

Gem City Bone and Joint Surgery Center, 1909 Vista Drive, Laramie, WY 82070; tel. 307/745–8851; FAX. 307/742–8851; Linda Simpson, Director

Wyoming Endoscopy Center, 1200 East 20th Street, Cheyenne, WY 82001; tel. 307/635–5439; John W. Beckman, M.D., Administrator

Wyoming Outpatient Services, 5050 Powderhouse Road, Cheyenne, WY 82009; tel. 307/634–1311; FAX. 307/638–6820; Robin Brown, Director

Yellowstone Surgery Center, Ltd., 5201 Yellowstone Road, Cheyenne, WY 82009; tel. 307/635–7070; FAX. 307/632–9920; Linnea McNair, RN, B.S.N., Director

---

U. S. Associated Areas

PUERTO RICO

ASC Centro Inst de Gastroenterologia y Endoscopia Las Americas, Suite 206, Hato Rey, PR 00919; tel. 787/764–8787

ASC Espanola Clinic, Box 490, La Quinta, Mayaguez, PR 00681; tel. 787/832–2094

ASC Hato Rey Comm., 435 Ponce de Leon Avenue, Hato Rey, PR 00919; tel. 787/754–0909; FAX. 787/753–1625

ASC Mimiya, P.O. Box 41245, 303 De Diego Avenue, Santurce, PR 00940; tel. 809/721–2590

Arecibo Medical Center, Carr. 2 Km 80.1, Call Box AMC, Arecibo, PR 00613; tel. 809/878–3185

Cirugia Ambulatoria y Centro de Diagnostico y Tratamiento de San Sebastian, Box 486, San Sebastian, PR 00755; tel. 809/896–1850

Clinica de Cirugia Ambulatoria de Puerto Rico, Box 3748, Marina Station, Mayaguez, PR 00681; tel. 787/833–4400; Roberto Ruiz, Asencio, Administrator

Clinica del Turabo, P.O. Box 1900, Caguas, PR 00626; tel. 787/746–8899; FAX. 787/258–1776; Loda A. M. Negron, M.H.S.A.

Instituto Cirugia, Plastica del Oeste, 165 Este Mendez Virgo Street, Mayaguez, PR 00680; tel. 787/833–3248; FAX. 787/831–4400; Mrs. Leonor M. Jaume, Executive Director

Instituto Quirurgico De Un Dia – Dr. Pila, P.O. Box 1910, Ponce, PR 00733; tel. 809/844–5600

Instituto de Ojos y Piel, Carr Three, Km 12.3, Carolina, PR 00985; tel. 809/769–2477

Las Americas Ambulatory Surgical Center, P.O. Box 194236, San Juan, PR 00919–4236; tel. 787/756–8418; FAX. 787/250–8597; Carmen Martin, MHSA, Administrator

OJOS, Inc., Calle Hipodromo, Esquina Las Palmas, Pda. 20, Santurce, PR 00908; tel. 787/721–8330; FAX. 787/722–3222; Maria Delos A. Tirado, Administrator

San Juan Health Centre, 150 De Diego Avenue, Esquina Baldorioty, San Juan, PR 00911; tel. 809/725–0202

Sothern SurgiCenter, Edificio Parra, Ofic. 201, Ponce By Pass, Ponce, PR 00731; tel. 787/841–0303; FAX. 787/841–0387; Roberta Rentas

Section C

State Government Agencies for FASC's

United States

ALABAMA
Alabama Department of Public Health, Division of Licensure and Certification, 434 Monroe Street, Montgomery, AL 36130–1701; tel. 334/240–3503; FAX. 334/240–3147; L. O'Neal Green, Director

ALASKA
Health Facilities Licensing and Certification, 4730 Business Park Boulevard, Suite 18, Anchorage, AK 99503–7137; tel. 907/561–8081; FAX. 907/561–3011; Shelbert Larsen, Administrator

ARIZONA
Arizona Department of Health Services, Health and Child Care Review Services, 1647 East Morten, Suite 220, Phoenix, AZ 85020; tel. 602/255–1221; FAX. 602/255–1108; John Zemaitis, Assistant Director

ARKANSAS
Department of Health, Division of Health Facility Services, 5800 West 10th Street, Suite 400, Little Rock, AR 72204–9916; tel. 501/661–2201; FAX. 501/661–2165; Valetta Buck, Director

CALIFORNIA
Department of Health Services, Licensing and Certification Division, 1800 Third Street, Suite 210, P.O. Box 942732, Sacramento, CA 94234–7320; tel. 916/445–2070; FAX. 916/445–6979; Michael Rodrian, Branch Manager

COLORADO
Department of Health, Division of Health Facilities, 4210 East 11th Avenue, Denver, CO 80220; tel. 303/331–6600; FAX. 303/331–6559; Diane Carter, Deputy, Director

CONNECTICUT
Department of Health and Addiction Services, Hospital and Medical Care Division, 150 Washington Street, Hartford, CT 06106; tel. 203/566–1073; FAX. 203/566–1097; Elizabeth M. Burns, RN, M.S., Director

DELAWARE
Department of Health and Social Services, Licensing and Certification, Office of Health Facilities, 3000 Newport Gap Pike, Wilmington, DE 19808; tel. 302/995–6674; FAX. 302/995–8332; Ellen T. Reap, Director

DISTRICT OF COLUMBIA
Department of Health, Licensing Regulation Administration, 614 H Street, N.W., Suite 1003, Washington, DC 20001; tel. 202/727–7190; FAX. 202/727–7780; Geraldine K. Sykes

FLORIDA
Division of Health Quality Assurance, Agency for Health Care Administration, Fort Knox Executive Office Center, 2727 Mahan Drive, Suite 214, Tallahassee, FL 32308–5407; tel. 904/487–2527; FAX. 904/487–6240; Gloria Crawford–Henderson, Director

GEORGIA
Health Care Section, Office of Regulatory Services, Department of Human Resources, Two Peachtree Street, N.W., Suite 19.204, Atlanta, GA 30303–3167; tel. 404/657–5550; FAX. 404/657–8934; Susie M. Woods, Director

HAWAII
Hawaii Department of Health, Hospital and Medical Facilities Branch, P.O. Box 3378, Honolulu, HI 96801; tel. 808/586–4080; FAX. 808/586–4747; Helen K. Yoshimi, B.S.N., M.P.H., Chief, HMFB

IDAHO
Bureau of Facility Standards, Department of Health and Welfare, P.O. Box 83720, Boise, ID 83720–0036; tel. 208/334–6626; FAX. 208/332–7204; Sylvia Creswell, Supervisor–Non Long Term Care

ILLINOIS
Department of Public Health, Division of Health Care Facilities and Programs, 525 West Jefferson Street, Springfield, IL 62761; tel. 217/782–7412; FAX. 217/782–0382; Michelle Gentry–Wiseman, Chief

INDIANA
Indiana State Department of Health, Division of Acute Care, Two North Meridian Street, 4/A, Indianapolis, IN 46204; tel. 317/233–7472; FAX. 317/233–7157; Tom Iozzo, H.F.A.

IOWA
Department of Inspection and Appeals, Division of Health Facilities, Lucas State Office Building, Des Moines, IA 50319; tel. 515/281–4115; FAX. 515/242–5022; J. Bennett, Administrator

KANSAS
Kansas Department of Health and Environment, Bureau of Adult and Child Care, 900 Southwest Jackson, Suite 1001, Topeka, KS 66612–1290; tel. 785/296–1280; FAX. 785/296–1266; George A. Dugger, Medical Facilities Certification Administrator

KENTUCKY
Cabinet for Health Services, Division of Licensing and Regulation, 275 East Main Street, 4E–A, Frankfort, KY 40621; tel. 502/564–2800; FAX. 502/564–6546; Rebecca J. Cecil, R.Ph., Director

LOUISIANA
Department of Health and Hospitals, Bureau of Health Services Financing–Health Standards Section, P.O. Box 3767, Baton Rouge, LA 70821; tel. 504/342–0138; FAX. 504/342–5292; Lily W. McAlister, RN, Manager

MAINE
Division of Licensing and Certification, Department of Human Services, 35 Anthony Avenue, Station 11, Augusta, ME 04333; tel. 207/624–5443; FAX. 207/624–5378; Louis Dorogi, Director

MARYLAND
Department of Health and Mental Hygiene, Office of Licensing and Certification, 4201 Patterson Avenue, Baltimore, MD 21215; tel. 410/764–4980; FAX. 410/764–5969

MASSACHUSETTS
Department of Public Health, Division of Health Care Quality, 80 Boylston Street, Suite 1100, Boston, MA 02116; tel. 617/727–5860; Irene McManus, Director

MICHIGAN
Department of Public Health, Division of Licensing and Certification, 3500 North Logan, Lansing, MI 48909; tel. 517/335–8505; Pauline DeRose

MINNESOTA
Department of Health, Facility and Provider Compliance Division, Licensing and Certification Section, 393 North Dunlap Street, P.O. Box 64900, St. Paul, MN 55164–0900; tel. 612/643–2130; FAX. 612/643–3534; Carol Hirschfeld, Supervisor, Records and Information Unit

MISSISSIPPI
Department of Health, Division of Health Facilities Licensure and Certification, P.O. Box 1700, Jackson, MS 39215; tel. 601/354–7300; FAX. 601/354–7230; Vanessa Phipps, Director

MISSOURI
Missouri Department of Health, Bureau of Hospital Licensing and Certification, P.O. Box 570, Jefferson City, MO 65102; tel. 573/751–6302; FAX. 573/526–3621; Darrell Hendrickson, Administrator

MONTANA
Health Facilities Division, Department of Health and Environmental Sciences, Cogswell Building, Helena, MT 59620; tel. 406/444–2037; FAX. 406/444–1742; Denzel C. Davis, Division Administrator

NEBRASKA
Credentialing Division, Nebraska Department of Health and Human Servies Regulation & Licensure, 301 Centennial Mall, S., P.O. Box 94986, Lincoln, NE 68509–4986; tel. 402/471–2116; FAX. 402/471–0555; Helen L. Meeks, Director

NEVADA
Bureau of Licensure & Certification, Nevada Health Divison, 1550 E. College Parkway, Suite 158, Carson City, NV 89706–7921; tel. 702/687–4475; FAX. 702/687–6588; Richard J. Panelli, Chief

NEW HAMPSHIRE
Office of Program Support, Licensing and Regulation, Six Hazen Drive, Concord, NH 03301; tel. 603/271–4592; FAX. 603/271–3745

NEW JERSEY
Division of Health Systems Analysis, Certificate of Need and Acute Licensing, CN–360, Trenton, NJ 08625; tel. 609/292–5960; FAX. 609/588–7823; Darcy Saunders, Esq., Director

NEW MEXICO
Department of Health and Environment, Health Facility Licensing and Certification Bureau, 525 Camino de los Marquez, Suite Two, Santa Fe, NM 87501; tel. 505/827–4200; FAX. 505/827–4203; Matthew M. Gervase, Chief, Licensing and Certification Bureau

NEW YORK
Health Education Services, P.O. Box 7126, Albany, NY 12224; tel. 518/439–7286; FAX. 518/439–7286

NORTH CAROLINA
Department of Human Resources, Division of Facility Services, 701 Barbour Drive, P.O. Box 29530, Raleigh, NC 27626–0530; tel. 919/733–7451; FAX. 919/733–8274; Steve White, Chief, Licensure and Certification

NORTH DAKOTA
North Dakota Department of Health, Health Resources Section, 600 East Boulevard Avenue, Bismarck, ND 58505–0200; tel. 701/328–2352; FAX. 701/328–4727; Fred Gladden, Chief

OHIO
Division of Quality Assurance, Ohio Department of Health, 246 North High Street, Columbus, OH 43266–0588; tel. 614/466–7857; FAX. 614/644–0208; Rebecca Maust, Chief

OKLAHOMA
Department of Health, Special Health Services, 1000 Northeast 10th Street, P.O. Box 53551, Oklahoma City, OK 73152; tel. 405/271–6576; FAX. 405/271–3442; Gary Glover, Chief, Medical Facilities

OREGON
Health Care Licensure and Certification, Oregon Health Division, 800 Northeast Oregon Street, Suite 640, # 21, Portland, OR 97232; tel. 503/731–4013; FAX. 503/731–4080; Kathleen Smail, Manager

PENNSYLVANIA
Bureau of Quality Assurance, Division of Acute and Ambulatory Care Facilities, Health and Welfare Building, Room 532, Harrisburg, PA 17120; tel. 717/783–8980; FAX. 717/772–2163; Jack W. Means, Jr., Director

RHODE ISLAND
Rhode Island Department of Health, Division of Facilities Regulation, Three Capitol Hill, Providence, RI 02908–5097; tel. 401/277–2566; FAX. 401/277–3999; Wayne I. Farrington, Chief

SOUTH CAROLINA
Department of Health and Environmental Control, Division of Health Licensing, 2600 Bull Street, Columbia, SC 29201; tel. 803/737–7202; FAX. 803/737–7212; Alan Samuels, Director

SOUTH DAKOTA
 Department of Health, Office of Health Care Facilities, Licensure and Certification, 615 East 4th Street, Pierre, SD 57501; tel. 605/773–3356; FAX. 605/773–6667; Joan Bachman, Administrator

TENNESSEE
 Department of Health, Division of Health Care Facilities, Cordell Hull Building, First Floor, 426 Fifth Avenue, N., Nashville, TN 37247–0508; tel. 615/741–7221; Marie Fitzgerald, Director

TEXAS
 Department of Health, Health Facility Licensure and Certification Division, 8407 Wall Street, Zip 78754, 1100 West 49th Street, Austin, TX 78756; tel. 512/834–6650; FAX. 512/834–6653; Nance Stearman, RN, M.S.N., Director

UTAH
 Utah Department of Health, Bureau of Facility Licensing, P.O. Box 142003, Salt Lake City, UT 84114–2003; tel. 801/538–6152; FAX. 801/538–6325; Debra Wynkoop–Green, Director

VERMONT
 Department of Aging and Disability, 103 South Main Street, Waterbury, VT 05671; tel. 802/241–2345; Dave Yacovone, Commissioner

VIRGINIA
 Virginia Department of Health, Center for Quality Health Care Services and Consumer Protection, 3600 Centre, Suite 216, 3600 West Broad Street, Richmond, VA 23230; tel. 804/367–2102; FAX. 804/367–2149; Nancy R. Hofheimer, Director

WASHINGTON
 Washington Department of Health, Facilities and Services Licensing, Target Plaza, Suite 500, 2725 Harrison Avenue N.W., P.O. Box 47852, Olympia, WA 98504–7852; tel. 360/705–6780; FAX. 360/705–6654; Byron R. Plan, Manager

WEST VIRGINIA
 Office of Health Facility Licensure and Certification, West Virginia Division of Health, 1900 Kanawha Boulevard, E., Charleston, WV 25305; tel. 304/558–0050; FAX. 304/588–2515; Jeannie Miller, Program Administrator

WISCONSIN
 Bureau of Quality Assurance, Division of Supportive Living, Department of Health and Family Services, P.O. Box 309, Madison, WI 53701–0309; tel. 608/266–8481; FAX. 608/267–0352; Judy Fryback, Director, Bureau of Quality Assurance

WYOMING
 Wyoming Department of Health, Health Facilities Licensing, U.S. Bank Building, Eighth Floor, Cheyenne, WY 82001; tel. 307/777–7123; FAX. 307/777–5970; Jane Taylor, Program Manager

U. S. Associated Areas

PUERTO RICO
 Department of Health, P. O. Box 70184, San Juan, PR 00936; tel. 809/766–1616; FAX. 809/766–2240; Carmen Feliciano de Melecio, M.D., Secretary of Health

Section C

The following list of freestanding hospices was developed with the assistance of state government agencies and the individual facilities listed. For a complete list of hospital based hospice programs please refer to Section A. In Section A, hospice programs are identified by Facility Code F33.

We present this list simply as a convenient directory. Inclusion or omission of any organization's name indicates neither approval nor disapproval by Healthcare InfoSource, Inc., a subsidiary of the American Hospital Association.

United States

ALABAMA

Alacare Hospice, 2790 Hoover Road, Birmingham, AL 35226; tel. 205/981–8000; FAX. 205/981–8021; Jackie Lawrence, Director, Hospice, Palliative Care

BHS Hospice–Walker, Medical Arts Tower, Suite 215, Jasper, AL 35502; tel. 205/387–4514; FAX. 205/387–4888; Dawn Young, Administrator

Baptist Hospice, 301 Brown Springgs Road, P.O. Box 11010, Montgomery, AL 36111; tel. 334/273–4262; Lynne Parker, Rn, MSN, Administrator

Birmingham Area Hospice, 1400 Sixth Avenue, S., P.O. Box 2648, Birmingham, AL 35233; tel. 205/930–1330; FAX. 205/930–1390; Flora Y. Blackledge, Director

Brookwood Hospice, 2010 Brookwood Medical Center Drive, Birmingham, AL 35209; tel. 205/877–2140; Sue Esleck, Administrator

Caring Hands Hospice, Inc., 225 University Blvd., E., Suite 203, Tuscaloosa, AL 35401; tel. 205/349–3065; Toni D. Welbourne, Administrator

Chattahoochee Hospice, Inc., #6 Medical Park, North, Valley, AL 36854; tel. 334/756–8043; FAX. 334/756–8059; Judy Guin, RN, Administrator

Columbia Community Hospice, 209 Dunson Street, Andalusia, AL 36420; tel. 334/222–7048; Charlotte Parker

Community Hospice of Baldwin County, 1113B North McKenzie Street, Foley, AL 36535; tel. 334/943–5015; Matthew Bowdoin, Administrator

Community Hospice of Escambia County, 1023 Douglas Avenue, Suite F–2, Brewton, AL 36427; tel. 334/867–6993; Daniel M. Scarbrough, M.D., Administrator

Health Services East, Inc., Hospice Care, 7916 Second Avenue, S., Birmingham, AL 35206; tel. 205/838–5730; FAX. 205/838–5757; Lizabeth B. Harvey, RNC, Administrator

Hospice Care, Division of St. Clair Care, A Hospice, Inc., 17 Lake Plaza, P.O. Box 544, Pell City, AL 35125; tel. 205/884–1111; FAX. 205/884–1114; Nancy Odom, Director

Hospice South, Inc., Of Livingston, 112 Lafayette Street, Livingston, AL 35470; tel. 205/652–2451; David Looney, Administrator

Hospice of Blount County, Inc., 204 Washington Avenue, E., Oneonta, AL 35121; tel. 205/274–0549; FAX. 205/274–0550; Debbie Hyde

Hospice of Cullman County, Inc., 402 Fourth Avenue, N.E., P.O. Box 1227, Cullman, AL 35055; tel. 205/739–5185; Roger Hood, Administrator

Hospice of EAMC, 459 North Dean Road, Auburn, AL 36830; tel. 334/826–1899; Nancy A. Penaskovic

Hospice of East Alabama, Inc., 825 Keith Avenue, Anniston, AL 36207; tel. 205/236–5334; FAX. 205/231–4558; Pamela Harvey, Administrator

Hospice of Limestone County, 405 South Marion Street, P.O. Box 626, Athens, AL 35612; tel. 205/232–5017; FAX. 205/230–0085; Patricia P. Jackson, Administrator

Hospice of Marshall County, 8787 U.S. Highway 431, Albertville, AL 35950; tel. 205/891–7724; FAX. 205/891–7754; Rhonda Floyd, RN, B.S.N., OCN, CRNH, Executive Director

Hospice of Montgomery, 1111 Holloway Park, Montgomery, AL 36117; tel. 334/279–6677; FAX. 334/277–2223; Clare W. Lacey, Executive Director

Hospice of Northeast Alabama, a Member of the Baptist Health System, 112 College Street, P.O. Box 981, Scottsboro, AL 35768; tel. 205/574–4622; FAX. 205/259–3772; Virginia Stone, Director

Hospice of Northwest Alabama, 40 First Avenue East, P.O. Box 1216, Winfield, AL 35594; tel. 205/487–8140; FAX. 205/487–8740; Linda Martin Sewell, Executive Director

Hospice of West Alabama, 1800 McFarland Boulevard, N., Suite 310, Tuscaloosa, AL 35406; tel. 205/345–0067; FAX. 205/345–9806; Julie Sittason, Executive Director

Hospice of the Shoals, Inc., 1106 Bradshaw Drive, P.O. Box 307, Florence, AL 35630–0000; tel. 205/767–6699; FAX. 205/767–3116; Blake Edwards, Executive Director

Hospice of the Valley, Inc., 216 Johnston Street, S.E., P.O. Box 2745, Decatur, AL 35602; tel. 205/350–5585; FAX. 205/350–5567; Carolyn Dobson, Executive Director

Huntsville Hospice Cares, Inc., 2225 Drake Avenue, S.W., Suite 14, Huntsville, AL 35805; tel. 205/880–9898; FAX. 205/880–2929

Infirmary Hospice Care, Inc., 28260 Highway 98, Suite 2, Daphne, AL 36526; tel. 334/625–3333; Andrew McDonald, Administrator

Lakeview Hospice, 820 West Washington Street, Eufaula, AL 36027; tel. 334/687–5761; Sherrie Mills, Administrator

Mercy Hospice, 101 Villa Drive, P.O. Box 1090, Daphne, AL 36526; tel. 334/626–2694; Sister Mary Eileen Wilhelm

Providence Hospice, 1141 Montlimar Drive, Mobile, AL 36609; tel. 334/344–2234; FAX. 334/344–4642; Frances Glenn, Administrator

Saad's Hospice Services, Inc., 3725 Airport Boulevard, Suite 180, Mobile, AL 36608; tel. 334/343–9600; FAX. 334/380–3328; Barbara S. Fulgham

St. Vincent's Hospice, 2145 Highland Ave., Suite 110, Birmingham, AL 35205; tel. 205/939–8797; Dibbie Cox, Administrator

Wiregrass Hospice, Inc., 1211 West Main Street, Dothan, AL 36301; tel. 334/792–1101; FAX. 334/792–0009; Ray L. Shrout, Administrator

Wiregrass Hospice, Inc., 557 Colony Square, Suite Seven and Eight, Glover Avenue, Enterprise, AL 36330; tel. 205/347–3353; Ray Shrout, Administrator

ALASKA

Alaska Home Health Care Agency, Inc., 1200 Airport Heights, Suite 170, Anchorage, AK 99508; tel. 907/272–0018; FAX. 907/272–0014; Lawrence Smith, Title Company President

Hospice of Anchorage, 3305 Arctic Road, Suite 105, Anchorage, AK 99503; tel. 907/561–5322; FAX. 907/561–0334; Paula McCarron

Hospice of Mat–Su, 950 East Bogard Road, Suite 133, Wasilla, AK 99654; tel. 907/352–2845; FAX. 907/352–2844; Donna J. Harding, Director

ARIZONA

Community Hospice, 4330 North Campbell Avenue, Suite 256, Tucson, AZ 85718; tel. 520/544–2273; FAX. 520/577–8862; Bonnie Lindstrom

Community Hospice, 340 East Palm Lane, Suite 150, Phoenix, AZ 85004; tel. 602/252–2273; FAX. 602/254–6166; Dan Johnson, Interim Executive Director

Dignita Home Hospice, 202 East Earll Drive, Suite 478, Phoenix, AZ 85012; tel. 602/279–0677; FAX. 602/279–1085; Gary Polsky

FHP Hospice, 540 West Iron, Suite 110, Mesa, AZ 85210; tel. 602/244–8200; Donna O'Brien

Hospice Family Care, 3443 East Fort Lowell Road, Tucson, AZ 85716; tel. 520/323–3288; FAX. 520/323–6557; Dan Johnson

Hospice Family Care Inpatient Unit, 5037 East Broadway Road, Mesa, AZ 85206; tel. 602/807–2655; FAX. 602/807–2660; Donna Jazz

Hospice Family Care Inpatient Unit–Santa Rita, 150 North La Canada Drive, Green Valley, AZ 85614; tel. 520/648–3099; Nancy Smith

Hospice Family Care Inpatient Unit–Sonora, 1920 West Rudasill, Tucson, AZ 85704; tel. 602/797–3442; Nancy Smith

Hospice Family Care, Inc., 7330 North 16th Street, Suite A100, Phoenix, AZ 85020; tel. 602/331–9200; FAX. 602/331–9222; Vicki Moscow, Regional Public Relations Coordinator

Hospice Family Care, Inc., 10240 West Bell Road, Suite E, Sun City, AZ 85351; tel. 602/876–9100; Vicki Mascaro, Regional Public Relations Coordinator

Hospice Family Care, Inc., 1125 East Southern Avenue, Suite 202, Mesa, AZ 85204; tel. 602/926–6089; Don Johnson

Hospice Family Care, Inc. Green Valley Program, 210 West Continental Road, Suite 134, Green Valley, AZ 85614; tel. 520/648–6166; FAX. 520/648–6165; Karen Hoefle

Hospice Family Care–Greenfield Inpatient Unit, 13617 North 55th Avenue, Glendale, AZ 85304; tel. 602/547–9939; Mike Reimann

Hospice of Arizona, 7600 North 15th Street, Suite 165, Phoenix, AZ 85020; tel. 602/678–1313; FAX. 602/678–5220; Jerene Maierle

Hospice of Havasu, Inc., 1685 Mesquite Avenue, Suite I, Lake Havasu City, AZ 86403; tel. 520/453–2111; FAX. 520/453–3003; Nancy Iannone, Administrator

Hospice of Yuma, 1824 South Eighth Avenue, Yuma, AZ 85364; tel. 602/343–2222; FAX. 602/343–0688; Phyllis K. Swanson, Executive Director

Hospice of the Valley, 1510 East Flower Street, Phoenix, AZ 85014; tel. 602/530–6900; FAX. 602/530–6901; Susan Goldwater, Executive Director

Hospice of the Valley Gardiner Hospice Home, 1522 West Myrtle Avenue, Phoenix, AZ 85021; tel. 602/995–9323; Susan Goldwater, Executive Director

In Home Health Hospice, 4600 South Mill Avenue, Suite 170, Tempe, AZ 85282; tel. 602/839–5686; FAX. 602/839–3872; Walter Bendick, Director

Jacob C. Fruchthendler Jewish Community Hospice, 5100 East Grant Road, P.O. Box 13090, Tucson, AZ 85732–3090; tel. 520/881–5300; FAX. 520/322–3620; Jo Turnbull, RN, B.S.

LHS Home and Community Care–Hospice, 325 East Elliot Road, Suite 27, Chandler, AZ 85225; tel. 602/497–5535; FAX. 602/497–8250; Jennifer P. Huppenthal, Executive Director

Mt. Graham Community Hospital–Hospice Services, 1600 20th Avenue, Building E, Safford, AZ 85546; tel. 520/348–4045; FAX. 520/428–3868; Carol Bradford, Clinical Coordinator

Northern Arizona/Cottonwood, 203 South Candy Lane, Suite Two–B, Cottonwood, AZ 86326; tel. 520/634–2251; Renate Atkins

Northland Hospice, 702 North Beaver, P.O. Box 997, Flagstaff, AZ 86001; tel. 520/779–1227; FAX. 520/779–5884; Marilyn J. Pate, Executive Director

Olsten Kimberly Qualitycare Hospice, 711 East Missouri, Suite 140, Phoenix, AZ 85014; tel. 602/279–9898; FAX. 602/279–2019

RTA Hospice, 107 East Frontier, Payson, AZ 85541; tel. 602/472–6340, ext. 12; FAX. 602/472–6464; Vicki Dietz, RN, B.S.N., Executive Director

RTA Hospice, Inc., 177 West Cottonwood Lane, Suite 10, Casa Grande, AZ 85222; tel. 520/421–7143; FAX. 520/421–7315; Hope A. Hood, Patient Care Administrator

Samaritan Hospice, 2222 South Dobson Road, Suite 401, Mesa, AZ 85202; tel. 602/835–0711; FAX. 602/730–6078; Sandra Rose Simmons

Special Care Hospice, 1514 C Gold Rush Road, Suite 236, Bullhead City, AZ 86442; tel. 602/758–3800; FAX. 602/758–4403; Jayne Knox, Director

Sun Health Hospice, 13101 North 103rd Avenue, Sun City, AZ 85351; tel. 602/974–7819; FAX. 602/974–7894; Marlene Stolz, Acting Director

Vista Hospice Care, Inc., 6991 East Camelback Road, Suite C–250, Scottsdale, AZ 85251; tel. 602/945–2200; Roseanne Berry

ARKANSAS

Area Agency of Aging Hospice of West Central Arkansas, 103 West Parkway Drive, Suite Two A, Russellville, AR 72801; tel. 501/967–9300; Oren Yates, Program Administrator

Area Agency on Aging Hospice of Western Arkansas, 524 Garrison Avenue, P.O. Box 1724, Fort Smith, AR 72902; tel. 501/783–4500; FAX. 501/783–0029; Jim Medley, Executive Director CEO

Area Agency on Aging of Southeast Arkansas Hospice Two, 529 West Trotter, P.O. Box 722, Monticello, AR 71655; tel. 501/367–9873; Betty Bradshaw, Administrator

Area Agency on Aging of Southeast Arkansas, Inc. Hospice, 709 East Eighth Avenue, P.O. Box 8569, Pine Bluff, AR 71611; tel. 501/534–3268; Betty Bradshaw, President, Chief Executive Officer

Area Agency on Aging of Western Arkansas, Inc., Mena Hospice, 600 Seventh Street, Mena, AR 71953; tel. 501/394–5458; FAX. 501/394–7675; Mary Keith, RNC, Vice President

Area Agency on Aging of Western Arkansas, Inc., d/b/a Visiting Nurses Agency of Western Arkansas, Inc., 389 School Street, Winslow, AR 72959; tel. 501/634–3812; Jim Medley, Executive Director

Area Three Hospice, Faulkner County Health Unit, 811 North Creek Drive, P.O. Box 1726, Conway, AR 72033; tel. 501/450–4941; FAX. 501/450–4946; Elese Brown, Administrator

Ark La Tex Visiting Nurses, Inc., d/b/a Ark La Tex Home Health and Hospice Care, 421 Hickory Street, Texarkana, AR 71854; tel. 501/772–0958; Debbie Turner, Director of Nursing

Arkansas Department of Health Hospice 10, 40 Allen Chapel Road, P.O. Box 4267, Batesville, AR 72503; tel. 870/251–2848; FAX. 870/251–3449; Susan Coleman, Hospice Specialist

Arkansas Department of Health Hospice Five, Miller County Health Unit, 503 Walnut, Texarkana, AR 71852; tel. 870/773–2108; Mary Johnson, Administrator

Arkansas Department of Health Hospice Four, 301 East McNeil, Benton, AR 72015; tel. 501/776–1606; FAX. 501/776–5654; John Selig, Administrator

Arkansas Department of Health Hospice Nine West, Monroe County Health Unit, 306 West King Drive, Brinkley, AR 72021; tel. 501/734–1461; FAX. 501/734–1024; John Selig, Administrator

Arkansas Department of Health Hospice Six, Area Six Office, Highway 167 South, P.O. Box 630, Hampton, AR 71744; tel. 870/798–3113; Nealia Neal, Administrator

Arkansas Department of Health–Hospice Area Nine, Crittenden County Health Unit, 901 North Seventh, West Memphis, AR 72301; tel. 501/735–4334; FAX. 501/735–1393; John Selig, Administrator

Baptist Health, d/b/a Baptist Hospice, 11900 Colonel Glenn Road, Suite 2300, Little Rock, AR 72210; tel. 501/223–7494; FAX. 501/223–7443; Becky Pryor, Administrator

Baptist Memorial Regional Home Health Care, d/b/a Arkansas Home Health and Hospice, 824 North Washington, P.O. Box 90, Forrest City, AR 72335; tel. 501/633–6184; Gary Hughes, Administrator

Baptist Memorial Regional Home Health Care, Inc., d/b/a Arkansas Home Health and Hospice–West Memphis, 310 Mid–Continent Building, Suite 400, P.O. Box 2013, West Memphis, AR 72303; tel. 870/735–0363; FAX. 870/735–7156; Gary Hughes, Administrator

Best Care Hospice Services, 4425 Jefferson, Suite 115, Texarkana, AR 71854; tel. 501/773–4671; Patricia Stevens, Administrator

CareNetwork, Inc., d/b/a CareNetwork Hospice of Rogers, 1227 West Walnut, Rogers, AR 72756; tel. 501/636–1700; Barry Solomon, Administrator

CareNetwork, Inc., d/b/a CareNetwork of Hot Springs Hospice, 2212 Malvern, Suite 3, Hot Springs, AR 71901; tel. 501/623–5656; Cheryl Drake, Director, Hospice Services

CareNetwork, Inc., d/b/a CareNetwork Hospice of Little Rock, 9712 West Markham, Little Rock, AR 72205; tel. 501/223–3333; FAX. 501/228–0252; Barry Solomon, Administrator

CareNetwork, Inc., d/b/a CareNetwork Hospice of Fort Smith, Central Mall, Suite 600, Fort Smith, AR 72903; tel. 501/484–7273; Barny Solomon, Administrator

Central Arkansas Area Agency on Aging, d/b/a Hospice of Central Arkansas, 706 West Fourth Street, P.O. Box 5988, North Little Rock, AR 72119; tel. 501/372–5300, ext. 223; FAX. 501/688–7443; Elaine Eubank, Director

County Medical Services of Arkansas, Inc., d/b/a Eastern Ozarks Home Health and Hospice, Route Two, Box 79, Hardy, AR 72542; tel. 501/856–3241; Norman Steinig, Administrator

Hospice Care for Southeast Arkansas, Inc., d/b/a Hospice Care Services, 2214 South Blake, Pine Bluff, AR 71603; tel. 501/534–4847; Bud Millenbaugh

Hospice Home Care, Inc., Prospect Building, 1501 North University Avenue, Suite 340, Little Rock, AR 72207; tel. 501/666–9697; FAX. 501/666–4616; Cecilia Troppoli, Administrator

Hospice of Cherokee Village, Inc., 13 Minentonka, P.O. Box 986, Cherokee Village, AR 72525; tel. 501/257–3108; Sally Lindemood, Administrator

Hospice of Preferred Choice, Inc., d/b/a Fort Smith Community Hospice, 1115 South Waldron, Suite 108, Fort Smith, AR 72903; tel. 501/478–3200; Jim Petrus, Administrator

Hospice of St. Michael Health Care Center, 300 East Fifth Street, Texarkana, AR 75502; tel. 501/779–2720; Steven F. Wright, Administrator

Hospice of Texarkana, 122 East Broad Street, Suite 207, P.O. Box 2341, Texarkana, AR 75502; tel. 501/773–1899; Cynthia L. Marsh, Administrator

Jonesboro Health Services, L.L.C., d/b/a Methodist Hospital of Jonesboro Hospice, Forrest City, 815 North Washington, P.O. Box 1388, Forrest City, AR 72335; tel. 501/633–8977; Phillip H. Walkley Jr., FACHE, Chief Executive Officer

Leo N. Levi National Arthritis Hospital Hospice, 300 Prospect Avenue, Hot Springs AR 71901, P.O. Box 850, Hot Springs, AR 71902; tel. 501/624–1281, ext. 416; FAX. 501/622–3500; Patrick G. McCabe, Jr., Administrator

Northwest Health System, Inc., Circle of Life Hospice, 205 Northwest A Street, P.O. Box 1169, Bentonville, AR 72712; tel. 501/273–3658; FAX. 501/273–9080; Gail Hubbell, Hospice Manager

Share Foundation, d/b/a Community Hospice, 516 West Faulkner, El Dorado, AR 71730; tel. 501/862–0337; FAX. 501/862–0727; Linda D. Stringfellow, Administrator

Texarkana Memorial Hospital, Inc., d/b/a Wadley Care Source Hospice, 718 East Fifth Street, Texarkana, AR 71854; tel. 903/798–7660; FAX. 903/798–7667; Hugh R. Hallgren, President, Chief Executive Officer

Visiting Nurses Agency of Western Arkansas, Inc., 207 College Avenue, Clarksville, AR 72830; tel. 501/754–8280; Lois Phillips, RNC, Regional Nursing Supervisor

Washington Regional Medical Center Hospice, 4209 Frontage Road, Fayetteville, AR 72703; tel. 501/442–1000; Patrick D. Flynn, Administrator

CALIFORNIA

AIDS Hospice Foundation, 1300 Scott Boulevard, Los Angeles, CA 90026; tel. 213/482–2500; FAX. 213/962–8513; Tay Aston, Cesar Mier, Admissions Officers

All Nations Hospice, Inc., 3325 Wilshire Boulevard, Los Angeles, CA 90010; tel. 213/738–9741; Ugochi Obuge, Chief Executive Officer

Allied Home Health and Hospice, 1916 Orange Tree Lane, Suite 450–E, Redlands, CA 92374; tel. 909/798–8006; Ruth R. Jackson

Alternative Health Care Inc., Home Health and Hospice, 21601 Devonshire Street, Suite 215, Chatsworth, CA 91311; tel. 818/998–0525; FAX. 818/998–2529; John Teige

American Home Health Hospice, 1950 E. 17th Street, Santa Ana, CA 92705; tel. 714/550–0800; FAX. 714/550–0521; Marylyn A. Hagerty, Chief Executive Officer

American Home Health Hospice, 245 East Main Street, Suite 118, Alhambra, CA 91801; tel. 818/457–9825; Kim Loan To

Assisted Home Hospice, 16909 Parthenia Street, Suite 201, North Hills, CA 91343; tel. 818/894–8117; FAX. 818/894–8707; Sherry Netherland, M.A., Executive Director, Hospice

Avalon Home Health Services, Inc., 9608 Van Nuys Boulevard, Suite 209, Panorama, CA 91046; tel. 818/830–5898; Anatoly Smolyansky

Care One Health Center, 1252 Turley Street, Riverside, CA 92501; tel. 909/780–5455; Viola Delphine Donton

Carl Bean House, 2146 West Adams Boulevard, Los Angeles, CA 90018; tel. 213/766–2326; FAX. 213/730–8244; Roland Palencia, Executive Director

Casa Encino, 4600 Woodley Avenue, Encino, CA 91316; tel. 818/905–8625; Ronald Morgan

Children's Homecare–Hospice, 9550 Chesapeake Drive, Suite 201, San Diego, CA 92123; tel. 619/495–4941; James Rodisch, Director

Community Home Care Services/Hospice, 1925 East Dakota, Suite 208, Fresno, CA 93726; tel. 209/221–5615; FAX. 209/221–5798; Jami L. de Santigo, Service Integrator

Community Hospice Care–Orange County, 333 South Anita Drive, Suite 950, Orange, CA 92668; tel. 714/921–2273

Community Hospice of the Bay Area, d/b/a Hospice by the Bay, 1540 Market Street, Suite 350, San Francisco, CA 94102–6035; tel. 415/626–5900; FAX. 415/626–7800; Constance L. Borden, Executive Director

Community Hospice, Inc., 601 McHenry Avenue, Modesto, CA 95350; tel. 209/577–0615; FAX. 209/577–0738; Harold A. Peterson III, Executive Director

Community Hospice–San Diego, 8880 Rio San Diego Drive, Suite 950, San Diego, CA 92108; tel. 619/280–2273; Catherine Estherheld, RN

Companion Hospice, 12072 Trask Avenue, Suite 100, Garden Grove, CA 92643; tel. 714/741–0953; FAX. 714/534–0998; Michael Uranga, Administrator

Compassionate Care Hospice of San Francisco, L.P., 785 Market Street, Suite 850, San Francisco, CA 94103; tel. 415/979–0925; Victoria A. Condon

Coordinated Hospice, 13800 Arizona Street, Suite 202, Westminster, CA 92683; tel. 714/898–7106; FAX. 714/898–0407; Kay Donald, Hospice Manager

Covina Health Care Center, 5109 North Greer, Covina, CA 91724; tel. 818/339–9460; Rajinder Kutty

Crossroads Home Health Care and Hospice, Inc., 320 Judah Street, Suite Seven, San Francisco, CA 94122; tel. 415/682–2111; Virginia A. Kahn

Elizabeth Hospice, 1845 East Valley Parkway, Escondido, CA 92027; tel. 619/737–2050; FAX. 619/737–2088; Laura Miller, Executive Director

Fremont–Rideout Home Health Valley Hospice, 16911 Willow Glen Road, Brownsville, CA 95919; tel. 916/692–1410; Cindy White, RN, Supervisor, Patient Care Coordinator

Garden Grove Hospice, 12882 Shackelford Lane, Garden Grove, CA 92841; tel. 714/638–9470; Rosa Valdivia

Gran Care Hospice, 19682 Hesperian Boulevard, Suite 200, Hayward, CA 94541; tel. 510/887–1622; Virginia Bartow

Group One, 14520 Hesby Street, Sherman Oaks, CA 91403; tel. 818/906–7825; FAX. 818/906–7151; Elizabeth Dean

Group One Health, Inc.–Erwin, 13634 Erwin Street, Van Nuys, CA 91401; tel. 818/906–7825; Elizabeth Dean

Harmony Hospice, 888 Prospect Street, Suite 201, LaJolla, CA 92037; tel. 619/456–9703; Robert Cohn, Administrator

Helping Hands–Hospice, 1310 South Imperial Avenue, El Centro, CA 92243; tel. 619/352–7100; FAX. 619/352–7448; Suzi Jacobson, Executive Director

Hinds Hospice Services, 1616 West Shaw Avenue, Suite B–Six, Fresno, CA 93711; tel. 209/226–5683; FAX. 209/226–1028; Nancy Hinds, Administrator, Director of Nursing

Hoffman Hospice of the Valley, Inc., 3550 Q Street, Suite 204, Bakersfield, CA 93301; tel. 805/833–3900; M. Earl Ward, Director

Home Health Plus, 2005 De La Cruz Boulevard, Suite 221, Santa Clara, CA 95050; tel. 408/986–1801; Anne Mason

Home Health Plus, 2511 Garden Road, Suite B–200, Monterey, CA 93940; tel. 408/373–8442; Anne Mason

Home Health Plus, 1200 Concord Avenue, Suite 150, Concord, CA 94520; tel. 510/674–8610; Marie Wisniewski, Hospice Supervisor

Home Health Plus, 2334 Merced Street, San Leandro, CA 94577; tel. 510/357–5852; Anne Mason

Home Health Plus, 411 Borel Avenue, San Mateo, CA 94402; tel. 510/357–5852; Michelle V. Gillmore

Home Health Plus–Hospice, 3558 Round Barn Boulevard, Suite 212, Santa Rosa, CA 95403; tel. 707/523–0111; Suzanne Chevalier

Home Health Plus/Hospice, 1770 Iowa Avenue, Suite 500, Riverside, CA 92507; tel. 909/369–8054; Judith K. Kafantaris

Section C

Home Health/Hospice of San Luis Obispo, 285 South Street, Suite J, P.O. Box 1489, San Luis Obispo, CA 93406; tel. 805/781-4141; FAX. 805/781-1236; Michele S. Groff, Administrator

Hope Hospice, 6500 Dublin Boulevard, Suite 100, Dublin, CA 94568-3151; tel. 510/829-8770; FAX. 510/829-0868; Joanne Howard, Executive Director

Horizon Hospice, 12709 Poway Road, Suite E-Two, Poway, CA 92064; tel. 619/748-3030; Thomas Dusmu-Johnson

Hospice Care of California, 377 East Chapman Avenue, Suite 280, Placentia, CA 92670; tel. 714/577-9656; FAX. 714/577-9679; Ann Hablitzel, Executive Director

Hospice Care of California, 1340 East Alosta, Suite 200-J, Glendora, CA 91740; tel. 818/335-1399; Ann Hablitzel

Hospice Cheer, 4032 Wilshire Boulevard, Suite 305, Los Angeles, CA 90010; tel. 213/383-9905; FAX. 213/383-9908; Bonnie Farwell, RN, B.S.N.

Hospice Family Care, Inc., 17291 Irvine Boulevard, Suite 412, Tustin, CA 92680; tel. 714/730-1114; FAX. 714/730-9236; Sandy Dunn, General Manager

Hospice Preferred Choice, Inc., d/b/a HPC-Concord, 1470 Enea Circle, Suite 1710, Concord, CA 94520; tel. 510/798-1014; Victoria Condon, Executive Director

Hospice Services of California, 11266 Washington Place, Culver City, CA 90230; tel. 310/636-8484; FAX. 310/636-8480; Fred Jackson, Executive Director

Hospice Services of Lake County, 1717 South Main Street, Lakeport, CA 95453; tel. 707/263-6222; FAX. 707/263-6045; Michael Brooks

Hospice Services of Santa Barbara, a Division of the Santa Barbara Visiting Nurse Association, 222 East Canon Perdido, Santa Barbara, CA 93101; tel. 805/963-6794; Carol Brainerd, RN, M.N., Vice President, Professional Services

Hospice by the Sea, 312 South Cedros Street, Suite 205, Solana Beach, CA 92075; tel. 619/794-0195; FAX. 619/794-0147; Kathie Jackson, Administrator

Hospice of Amador, 839 North Highway 49/88, Suite F, P.O. Box 595, Jackson, CA 95642; tel. 209/223-5500; FAX. 209/223-4964; Hazel Joyce, Executive Director

Hospice of Contra Costa, 2051 Harrison Street, Concord, CA 94520; tel. 510/609-1830; FAX. 510/609-1841; Cindy Siljestrom, Executive Director

Hospice of Emanuel, 2101 Geer Road, Suite 120, Turlock, CA 95382; tel. 209/667-4663; Renette Bronken

Hospice of Humboldt, Inc., 2010 Myrtle Avenue, Eureka, CA 95501; tel. 707/445-8443; FAX. 707/445-2209; Jacqueline Berry, Executive Director

Hospice of Madera County, 115 North P Street, P.O. Box 1325, Madera, CA 93639; tel. 209/674-0407; Nancy Hinds, Administrator

Hospice of Marin, 150 Nellen Avenue, Corte Madera, CA 94925; tel. 415/927-2273; FAX. 415/927-2284; Mary Tavema, President

Hospice of Merced, 149 16th Street, Suite A, P.O. Box 763, Merced, CA 95341; tel. 209/383-3123; FAX. 209/383-5308; Nancy Hinds, RN, Administrator

Hospice of Napa Valley, Five Financial Plaza, Suite 201, Napa, CA 94558; tel. 707/258-9080; FAX. 707/258-9088; Judy Garrison, Executive Director

Hospice of Saddleback Valley, 24022 Calle De La Plata, Suite 200, Laguna Hills, CA 92653; tel. 714/458-8551; Ann Buchanan, Administrator

Hospice of San Joaquin, 2609 East Hammer Lane, Stockton, CA 95210; tel. 209/957-3888; FAX. 209/957-3986; Barbara Tognoli, Administrator

Hospice of Tulare County, Inc., 332 North Johnson, Visalia, CA 93291; tel. 209/733-0642; FAX. 209/733-0658; Debbie Westfall

Hospice of the Canyon, 5045 Parkway Calabasas, Calabasas, CA 91302; tel. 818/591-1459; FAX. 815/591-1486; David Bernstein, D.D.S., Executive Director

Hospice of the Central Coast/Adobe Home Health, 100 Barnet Segal Lane, Monterey, CA 93940; tel. 408/648-7744; FAX. 408/648-7746; Patricia Cincone

Hospice of the East San Gabriel Valley, d/b/a Home Care Advantage, 820 North Phillips Avenue, West Covina, CA 91791; tel. 818/859-2263; FAX. 818/859-2272

Hospice of the North Coast, 4002 Vista Way, Oceanside, CA 92056; tel. 619/724-8411; John P. Lauri, President, Chief Executive Officer

Hospice of the Sierra, 20100 Cedar Road North, Sonora, CA 95370; tel. 209/532-7166; Judy Villalobos, Administrator

Hospice of the Valley, 1150 South Bascom Avenue, Suite Seven A, San Jose, CA 95128; tel. 408/947-1233; FAX. 408/288-4172; Barbara Noggle

Hospital Home Health Care-Hospice, 2601 Airport Drive, Suite 110, Torrance, CA 90505; tel. 310/530-3800; FAX. 310/534-1754; Kaye Daniels, President

Inland Valley Hospice, 7710 Limonite Avenue, Suite E, Riverside, CA 92509; tel. 909/360-5848; Katherine L. Allen

Kern Hospice, 4300 Stine Road, Suite 720, Bakersfield, CA 93313; tel. 805/327-1012; David Christen, Vice President, General Manager

Lifecare Hospice, 1588 West 48th Street, Los Angeles, CA 90062; tel. 213/734-3945; James A. Miller

Livingston Memorial VNA and Hospice, 1996 Eastman Avenue, Suite 101, Ventura, CA 93003; tel. 805/642-0239; FAX. 805/642-2320; Deborah Roberts, RN, B.S.N., Ph.D., President, Chief Executive Officer

Madrone Hospice, Inc., 107 South Broadway, P.O. Box 1193, Yreka, CA 96097; tel. 916/842-3160; FAX. 916/842-4025; Audrey Flower, Executive Director

Marian Hospital Homecare and Hospice, 1300 East Cypress, Suite G, Santa Maria, CA 93454; tel. 805/922-9609; FAX. 805/349-9229; Marie Whitford, Vice President, Alternate Care Services

Matched Caregivers Home Health and Hospice, 211 Town and Country Village, Palo Alto, CA 94301; tel. 415/321-2273; FAX. 415/321-2352; Darrell Owens, M.S., CRNH, Vice President

Memorial Hospice Program, 3711 Long Beach Boulevard, Suite 621, Long Beach, CA 90807; tel. 213/595-2000

Metropolitan Hospice, 4904 Crenshaw Boulevard, Los Angeles, CA 90043; tel. 213/293-6163; FAX. 213/296-3913; Kathleen I. Jones, RN, B.S., Director

Midpeninsula HomeCare and Hospice, 201 San Antonio Circle, Suite 135, Mountain View, CA 94040; tel. 415/949-3029; FAX. 415/949-4317; John D. Hart, Executive Director

Mission Hospice, Inc. of San Mateo County, 1515 Trousdale Drive, Suite 109, Burlingame, CA 94010; tel. 415/692-3080; Carol L. Gray, RN, Administrator

Mountain Home Health Services, Inc., 35680 Wish-i-ah Road, Auberry, CA 93602; tel. 209/855-2200; FAX. 209/855-2284; Lori M. Harshman

My Father's House-Hospice, 2429 Leeward Circle, Westlake Village, CA 91361; tel. 805/495-7368; FAX. 805/495-6466; May Isobel Oxx

Nations Healthcare, Inc.-Hospice, 9823 Pacific Heights Boulevard, Suite N, San Diego, CA 92121; tel. 619/546-3834; FAX. 619/546-0701; David Golman, Administrator

Orangegrove Hospice, 12332 Garden Grove Boulevard, Garden Grove, CA 92843; tel. 714/534-1041; FAX. 714/534-7921; Maria Aguilar, Director, Hospice Services

Pacific Home Health Group, 106 East Manchester, Inglewood, CA 90301; tel. 310/677-4574; Evadne Wright

Pacific Home Health and Hospice, 1168 Park Avenue, San Jose, CA 95126-2913; tel. 408/971-4151; Lemuel F. Ignacio, M.S.W., Administrator

Pathways to Care, Hospice, 1650 Iowa Avenue, Suite 220, Riverside, CA 92507; tel. 909/320-7070; FAX. 909/320-7060; Ed Gardner, President

Quality Continuum Hospice, 5505 Garden Grove Boulevard, Westminster, CA 92683; tel. 800/797-2686; FAX. 714/379-7910; Janet Horn, Administrator

Ramona Care Center Hospice, 11900 Ramona Boulevard, El Monte, CA 91732; tel. 818/442-5721

San Diego Hospice Corporation, 4311 Third Avenue, San Diego, CA 92103; tel. 619/688-1600; FAX. 619/688-9665; Jan Cetti, President, Chief Executive Officer

San Pedro Peninsula Home Care/Hospice, 1386 B West Seventh Street, San Pedro, CA 90732; tel. 310/548-4106; FAX. 310/514-5328; Susan Nowinski, M.S.N., Executive Director

Self-Help HomeCare and Hospice, 407 Sansome Street, Suite 300, San Francisco, CA 94111; tel. 415/982-9171; FAX. 415/398-5903; Nellie Kwan, RN

Spectrum Health Services, Home Health and Hospice, 2421 Mendocino Avenue, Suite 150, Santa Rosa, CA 95403; tel. 707/528-4663, ext. 365; FAX. 707/528-2301; Charmaine Noon, RN, Intake/Referral and Triage

St. Ambrose Hospice Care, 15022 Pacific Street, Suite #A, Midway City, CA 92655; tel. 714/379-6738; FAX. 714/379-6740; Mike Peiton, Director, Operations

St. Joseph Health System Home Care Services-Hospice, 1845 West Orangewood Avenue, Suite 100 A, Orange, CA 92868; tel. 714/712-9559; FAX. 714/712-9529; June van den Noort, Hospice Director

St. Joseph Medical Center Home Hospice, 2101 West Alameda Avenue, Burbank, CA 91506; tel. 818/843-5111, ext. 7051; Roosevelt Travis, Jr., Manager, Home Hospice

Tender Loving Care Home Hospice, 2139 Tapo Street, Suite 205, Simi Valley, CA 93063; tel. 805/520-3166; FAX. 805/520-3167; Shelley Hurt, Administrator

Tendercare Hospice and Home Health, 10882 Kyle Street, Suite A, Los Alamitos, CA 90720; tel. 310/596-5033; Susan Falkner

The Miller Project, 970 North Van Ness, Fresno, CA 93728; tel. 209/264-0061

Tri-Med Hospice, 534 West Manchester Boulevard, Inglewood, CA 90301; tel. 310/419-4836; Margaret R. Lanam

VNA Home Health Systems-Hospice, 1337 Braden Court, Orange, CA 92668; tel. 714/288-4500; Mavis Scott, Director of Hospice

VNA and Home Hospice, 1110 North Dutton Avenue, Santa Rosa, CA 95401-4606; tel. 707/542-5045; FAX. 707/542-6731; Rebecca LaLonde, Regional Director

Verdugo Hills VNA Hospice in the Home, 1101 East Broadway, Suite 201, Glendale, CA 91205-1386; tel. 818/956-1860; FAX. 818/956-1881; Marie Reynolds, RN, Executive Director

Visiting Nurse Association Los Angeles, Inc., 2461 208th Street, Torrance, CA 90501; tel. 310/782-8886; FAX. 310/782-9172; Judy Regotti, PHN

Visiting Nurse Association and Hospice of Northern California, 1900 Powell Street, Suite 300, Emeryville, CA 94608; tel. 510/450-8596; FAX. 510/450-8532; Pat Sussman, Director

Visiting Nurse Association and Hospice of Pomona/San Bernardino, Inc., 150 West First Street, P.O. Box 908, Claremont, CA 91711; tel. 714/624-3574; FAX. 714/624-8904; Karen H. Green, President

Visiting Nurse Association of Long Beach-Hospice, 3295 Pacific Avenue, Long Beach, CA 90807; tel. 310/426-8856; FAX. 310/988-9474; Jean Lawrence, Director, Agency Operations

Visiting Nurse Association of Los Angeles and Yvette Luque Hospice, 520 South Lafayette Park Place, Suite 500, Los Angeles, CA 90057; tel. 213/386-7200; FAX. 213/386-4227; June Simmons, Chief Executive Officer

Visiting Nurse Service Hospice, Serving Santa Barbara County and San Luis Obispo County, 521 East Chapel Street, P.O. Box 1029, Santa Maria, CA 93454; tel. 805/925-8694; FAX. 805/925-1387; John W. Puryear, Executive Director

West Healthcare Hospice Services, 180 Otay Lakes Road, Suite 100, Bonita, CA 91902; tel. 619/472-7500; FAX. 619/472-1534; Suzanne L. Purdy

Wilcare Hospice and Home Health, 2001 Gateway Place, Suite 150, San Jose, CA 95110; tel. 408/467-0777; FAX. 408/467-0770; Sandra K. Rohlfing, Administrator

COLORADO

Angel of Shavano Hospice, 543 East First Street, Salida, CO 81201; tel. 719/539-7638; FAX. 719/539-3699; Claudia Dixon

Arkansas Valley Hospice, 118 West Fourth Street, Box 1067, LaJunta, CO 81050; tel. 719/384-8827; FAX. 719/384-2045; Erma J. Isaac, Executive Director

Baca County Hospice, 204 East 10th Avenue, Springfield, CO 81073; tel. 719/523-4851; FAX. 719/523-4763; Annie Dukes, Administrator

Boulder County Hospice, Inc., 2825 Marine Street, Boulder, CO 80303; tel. 303/449-7740; FAX. 303/449-6961; Constance Holden, Director

Bristlecone Home Care and Hospice, Inc., 416 Main Street, Suite Six, P.O. Box 1327, Frisco, CO 80443; tel. 970/668–5604; FAX. 970/668–3189; Ms. Grace Rome–Kuhn, Administrator

Caring Unlimited Hospice Services, Inc., 4490 Bent Bros Boulevard, Colorado City, CO 81019; tel. 719/676–3637; FAX. 719/676–3695; Karen Clouse, RN

Colorado Palliative Care Hospice, 1425 Senter Street, Burlington, CO 80807; tel. 719/346–7700; FAX. 719/346–7754; Nancy Hendricks

Colorado Palliative Care Hospice, 559 East Pikes Peak, #300, Colorado Springs, CO 80903; tel. 719/447–1511; Mary Hahns, RN

Colorado Palliative Care Hospice, 6795 East Tennessee, Suite 250, Denver, CO 80224; tel. 303/355–5890; Mr. Brent Baker, Administrator

Grand Valley Hospice, Inc., d/b/a Hospice of the Grand Valley, 2784 Compass Drive, Suite 377, Grand Junction, CO 81506; tel. 970/241–2212; FAX. 970/257–2400; Christy Whitney, Executive Director

Hospice Associates of America, 2223 S. Monaco, #A–Z, Denver, CO 80222; tel. 303/753–0421; Mr. Edward Lowe, Administrator

Hospice Del Valle, Inc., 231 State Avenue, P.O. Box 1554, Alamosa, CO 81101; tel. 719/589–9019; FAX. 719/589–5094; Ms. Mindy Montague, Administrator

Hospice Services of Northwest Colorado, 135 Sixth Street, P.O. Box 775816, Steamboat Springs, CO 80477; tel. 970/879–9218; FAX. 970/870–1326; Janet Fritz, Executive Director

Hospice of Custer County, 5th & Rosita, P.O. Box 120, Westcliffe, CO 81252; tel. 719/783–2380; Dr. Robert Bliss, Administrator

Hospice of Estes Valley, 555 Prospect, P.O. Box 2740, Estes Park, CO 80517–2740; tel. 970/586–2273; Kay Rosenthal, Acting Director

Hospice of Larimer County, 7604 Colland Drive, Fort Collins, CO 80525; tel. 970/663–3500; FAX. 970/663–1180; Brian Hoag, Executive Director

Hospice of Mercy, 3801 N. Main Street, Durango, CO 81301; tel. 970/382–2000; Ms. Michelle Appenzeller, Administrator

Hospice of Metro Denver, Inc., 425 South Cherry Street, Suite 700, Denver, CO 80222–1234; tel. 303/321–2828; FAX. 303/321–7171; Jacob S. Blass, President, Chief Executive Officer

Hospice of Montezuma, 44 North Ash, Cortez, CO 81321; tel. 970/565–4400; FAX. 970/565–9543; Claudia Poynter, Administrator

Hospice of Northern Colorado, 2726 11th Street Road, Greeley, CO 80631; tel. 970/352–8487; FAX. 970/352–6685; Jane M. Schnell, RN, Executive Director

Hospice of Peace, 1601 A Lowell Boulevard, Denver, CO 80204–1545; tel. 303/575–8393; FAX. 303/575–8390; Ann Luke, Supervisor

Hospice of St. John, 1320 Everett Court, Lakewood, CO 80215; tel. 303/232–7900; FAX. 303/232–3614; Ms. Cindy Morrison, Administrator

Hospice of the Comforter, 2790 N. Academy Blvd., Suite 100, Colorado Springs, CO 80917; tel. 719/573–4166; FAX. 719/573–4164; Ronald Coffin, Ph.D., M.B.A., Executive Director

Hospice of the Gunnison Valley, 1500 West Tomichi Avenue, Gunnison, CO 81230; tel. 970/641–0704; FAX. 970/641–5593; Robert Patterson, Administrator

Hospice of the Plains, Inc., 240 Brich, P.O. Box 231, Wray, CO 80758; tel. 970/332–4116; Ms. Sandra Crossland, Manager

Hospice of the Rockies, 826 1/2 Grand Avenue, P.O. Box 1025, Glenwood Springs, CO 81601; tel. 970/928–8796; FAX. 970/945–8661; Mr. Dennis McWorter, Administrator

LHS Home & Community Care Hospice, 615 Fairhurst Street, Sterling, CO 80751; tel. 970/521–3126; James Pernau, Administrator

Lamar Area Hospice Association, Inc., 1001 South Main, P.O. Box 843, Lamar, CO 81052; tel. 719/336–2100; Linda Earl, Executive Director

Life Source Services, Inc., 245 S. Benton Street, Suite 205, Lakewood, CO 80226; tel. 303/237–4673; Janet Bezuidenhout, Executive Director

Lutheran Homecare and Hospice, 3964 Youngfield, Wheat Ridge, CO 80033; tel. 303/467–4700; FAX. 303/424–5260; Ms. Kim Hegemann, Administrator

Mount Evans Hospice, 3721 Evergreen Parkway, P.O. Box 2770, Evergreen, CO 80439; tel. 303/674–6400; Louisa B. Walthers, Executive Director

Pikes Peak Hospice, Inc., 3630 Sinton Road, Suite 302, Colorado Springs, CO 80907; tel. 719/633–3400; FAX. 719/633–1150; Martha Barton, RN, Chief Executive Officer

PorterCare Hospice, 2465 South Downing Street, Suite 202, Denver, CO 80210; tel. 303/871–0835; FAX. 303/778–5859; Terri Walter, Director

Prospect Home Care Hospice, Inc., 321 West Henrietta Avenue, Suite E, P.O. Box 6278, Woodland Park, CO 80866; tel. 719/687–0549; FAX. 719/687–8558; Joleen Bailey, Executive Director

Roaring Fork Hospice, 410 20th Street, #203, Glenwood Spring, CO 81601; tel. 970/928–0601; Susan Jones, Administrator

Sangre de Cristo Hospice, 704 Elmhurst Place, Pueblo, CO 81004; tel. 719/542–0032; FAX. 719/542–1413; Joni Fair, President, Chief Executive Officer

Vail Valley Home Health, and Maintenance Hospice, 0101 Eagle Road, Avon, CO 81620; tel. 970/845–9155; Ray McMahan, Administrator

Visiting Nurse Association Hospice at Home, 3801 East Florida, Suite 800, Denver, CO 80210; tel. 303/757–6363, ext. 413; FAX. 303/782–2573; Judith Sutherland, President

CONNECTICUT

Bristol Hospital Home Care Agency, Seven North Washington Street, Plainville, CT 06062; tel. 860/585–4752; FAX. 860/747–6719; Mary C. Smith, RN, Administrator

East Hartford Visiting Nurse Association, Inc., 60 Hartland Street, East Hartford, CT 06108–3213; tel. 860/528–2273; FAX. 860/920–6777; Karen Stone, RN, President

Foothills Visiting Nurse & Home Care, Inc., 32 Union Street, Winsted, CT 06098; tel. 860/379–8561; FAX. 860/738–7479; Jeannette Jakubiak, RN, Administrator

Home and Community Health Services, Inc., The Nirenberg Medical Center, 140 Hazard Avenue, P.O. Box 1199, Enfield, CT 06083; tel. 860/763–7600; FAX. 860/763–7613; Kathryn D. Roby, RN, B.S.N., Administrator

Hospice Care, Inc., 461 Atlantic Street, Stamford, CT 06902; tel. 203/324–2592; Janice Casey, RN

Hospice at Home, a program of Visiting Nurse Services of Connecticut, Inc., 765 Fairfield Avenue, Bridgeport, CT 06606; tel. 203/366–3821, ext. 310; FAX. 203/334–0543; Lois Ravage – Mass, RN, M.S.N, Director, Hospice

Hospice of Eastern Connecticut, a Program at Visiting Nurse and Community Health of Eastern Connecticut, Inc., 34 Ledgebrook Drive, P.O. Box 716, Mansfield Center, CT 06250; tel. 860/456–7288; FAX. 860/456–4267; Susan Lund, Hospice Director

Hospice of Northeastern Connecticut, 13 Railroad Street, P.O. Box 203, Pomfret Center, CT 06259; tel. 860/928–0422; FAX. 860/928–4545

Hospice of Southeastern Connecticut, Inc., 179 Gallivan Lane, P.O. Box 902, Uncasville, CT 06382–0902; tel. 860/848–5699; FAX. 860/848–6898

McLean Community and Home Services, 75 Great Pond Road, Simsbury, CT 06070; tel. 860/658–3950; FAX. 860/408–1319; Nancy E. Ryan, RN, Administrator

Mid–Fairfield Hospice, Inc., 112 Main Street, Norwalk, CT 06851; tel. 203/847–7646; FAX. 203/847–8394; Carol Yoder, RN, M.S.N., Administrator, Supervisor

Middlesex Visiting Nurse and Home Health Services, Inc., 51 Broad Street, Middletown, CT 06457; tel. 860/704–5600; Janine Fay, Administrator

New Milford Visiting Nurse Association, Inc., 68 Park Lane Road, New Milford, CT 06776; tel. 860/354–2216; FAX. 860/350–2852; Andrea Wilson, B.S., M.P.A., Executive Director

Project Care, Inc., Home and Hospice Services, 51 Depot Street, Suite 203, Watertown, CT 06795; tel. 860/274–9239; FAX. 860/945–3625; Joel Schlank, Administrator

Regional Hospice of Western Connecticut, Inc., 30 West Street, Danbury, CT 06810; tel. 203/797–1685; Patricia Coyle, RN, Administrator, Supervisor

Salisbury Public Health Nursing Association, Inc., 30 Salmon Kill Road, Salisbury, CT 06068; tel. 203/435–0816; Marilyn Joseph, RN, Administrator, Supervisor

Southington Visiting Nurse Association, Inc., 80 Meriden Avenue, Southington, CT 06489; tel. 203/621–0157; Mary Jane Corn, RN, Administrator

The Connecticut Hospice, Inc., 61 Burban Drive, Branford, CT 06405; tel. 203/481–6231; FAX. 203/483–9539; Rosemary J. Hurzeler, President, Chief Executive Officer

The Greater Bristol VNA, Inc., 10 Maltby Street, P.O. Box 2826, Bristol, CT 06011–2826; tel. 860/583–1644; FAX. 860/584–2100; Anita Baldwin, Hospice Coordinator

United Home Care, Inc., United Home Hospice, 1931 Black Rock Turnpike, Fairfield, CT 06430; tel. 203/330–9198; Karen Speer, RN, B.S.N, Hospice Administrator

VNA Health at Home, Inc., 27 Princeton Road, Watertown, CT 06795; tel. 860/274–7531; FAX. 860/274–8492; W. Rennard Wieland, President

VNA Hospice, Inc., 103 Woodland Street, Hartford, CT 06105; tel. 860/525–7001; FAX. 860/278–0581; Judith Milewsky Bigler, Executive Director

VNA Valley Care, Inc., Eight Old Mill Lane, Simsbury, CT 06070–1932; tel. 860/651–3539; FAX. 860/651–5082; Incy Severance, RN, M.P.A., Executive Director

Visiting Nurse Association and Hospice, of Pioneer Valley, Inc., 701 Enfield Street, Enfield, CT 06082; tel. 203/253–5316; Kimberly A. Barbaro, RN, M.B.A., Administrator

Visiting Nurse Association of Central Connecticut, Inc., 205 West Main Street, P.O. Box 1327, New Britain, CT 06050; tel. 860/224–7131; FAX. 860/224–8303; Mary Jane Corn, B.S.N., R.N., President, Chief Executive Officer

Visiting Nurse and Community Care, Inc., Eight Keynote Drive, Vernon, CT 06066; tel. 860/872–9163; FAX. 860/872–3030; Rafael Sciullo, Administrator

Visiting Nurse and Home Care Northwest, Inc., Four Old Middle Street, P.O. Box 266, Goshen, CT 06756; tel. 860/491–3740; FAX. 860/491–8635; Pamela Duchaine, Hospice Coordinator

Visiting Nurse and Home Care of Manchester, Inc., 545 North Main Street, Manchester, CT 06040; tel. 860/647–1481; FAX. 860/643–4942; Mary Lavery, Hospice Supervisor

DELAWARE

Compassionate Care Hospice of Delaware, 256 Chapman Road, Suite 201–A, Newark, DE 19702; tel. 302/454–7002; FAX. 302/454–7003; Cathy Stauffer Kimble, M.P.H., Regional Director

Delaware Hospice – Northern Division, 100 Clayton Building, 3515 Silverside Road, Wilmington, DE 19810; tel. 302/478–5707; FAX. 302/479–2586; Susan D. Lloyd, RN, M.S.N., Executive Director

Delaware Hospice, Inc.–Southern Division, 600 DuPont Highway, Suite 107, Georgetown Professional Park, Georgetown, DE 19947; tel. 302/856–7717; Susan D. Lloyd, RN, M.S.N., Executive Director

Delaware Hospice–Central Division, Lotus Plaza, 911 South DuPont Highway, Dover, DE 19901; tel. 302/734–4700; FAX. 302/678–4451; Susan D. Lloyd, R.N., MSN, Executive Director

First State Hospice, 5165 West Woodmill Drive, Suite 12, Wilmington, DE 19808; tel. 302/995–2273; FAX. 302/995–2280; Terry L. Hastings, RN, Executive Director

DISTRICT OF COLUMBIA

American Home Health Care/Hospice, 6856 Eastern Avenue, N.W., Washington, DC 20012; tel. 202/541–0810; Hakim Abduliah Alkalim

Americare InHome Nursing, 5203 Leesburg Pike, Suite 705, Falls Church, VA 22041; tel. 703/931–9002; FAX. 703/826–0076; Mary L. Tatum

Health Cap Medical Service, 3332 Georgia Avenue, N.W., Washington, DC 20010; tel. 202/882–0112; Terrance Monkou

Home Health Partners NCA, 1234 Massachusetts Avenue, N.W., Washington, DC 20005; tel. 202/638–2382; Margaret Terry

Hospice Care of the District of Columbia, 1325 Massachusetts Avenue, N.W., Suite 606, Washington, DC 20005–4171; tel. 202/347–1700; FAX. 202/347–4285; Darla Schueth, Executive Director

Hospice of Washington, 3720 Upton Street, N.W., Washington, DC 20016; tel. 202/966–3720; FAX. 202/895–0177; Mary Ann Griffin, Vice President Hospice

Housecall Hospice, 801 Pennsylvania Avenue, S.E., Washington, DC 20003; tel. 202/546–6764; Karlene Conrad, Regional Manager

Inova Health Care–District of Columbia Branch, 1331 Pennsylvania Avenue, N.W., S–500, Washington, DC 20005; tel. 202/638–5828; Regina Silver

Section C

Interim HealthCare Inc., 8401 Colesville Road, Silver Spring, MD 20910; tel. 301/587-3136; FAX. 301/587-3478; Arlene Berger, RN, B.S.N., Executive Director

Jewish Social Service Home Health Association, 6123 Montrose Road, Rockville, MD 20852; tel. 301/881-3700; Laura Freiden

Optimum Home Health Care, 1050 17th Street, N.W., Washington, DC 20036; tel. 202/496-1289; FAX. 202/296-2854; Patricia Austin

Personal Touch, 4400 Jenifer Street, N.W., Washington, DC 20015; tel. 202/537-7200; Mary Ellen Conway

Potomac Home Health Care, 6001 Montrose Road, Rockville, MD 20852; tel. 301/896-6999; Lauren Simpson, Chief Executive Officer

Urgent Home Health Care, 1535 P Street, N.W., Washington, DC 20005; tel. 202/483-3355; Pauline NGO Bapack

Visiting Nurses Association, 5151 Wisconsin Avenue, N.W., Washington, DC 20016; tel. 202/686-2862; Susan Walker, Hospice Director

FLORIDA

Big Bend Hospice, Inc., 1723 Mahan Center Boulevard, Tallahassee, FL 32308-5428; tel. 904/878-5310; FAX. 904/309-1638; Elaine C. Bartelt, M.S., Executive Director

Bon Secours Hospice, 21234 Olean Boulevard, Suite Four, Port Charlotte, FL 33952; tel. 813/764-8204; FAX. 813/764-6494; Jackie Homes, Team Manager

Brevard Hospice, 8060 Spyglass Rd., Veira, FL 32940; tel. 407/253-2222; FAX. 407/253-2238; Cynthia P. Harris Panning, RN, B.B.A., Executive Director

Catholic Hospice, Inc., 14100 Palmetto Frontage Road, Suite 370, Miami, FL 33016; tel. 305/822-2380; FAX. 305/824-0665; Janet L. Jones, President, Chief Executive Officer

Good Shepherd Hospice of Mid-Florida, Inc., 247 South Commerce Avenue, Sebring, FL 33870; tel. 941/471-3700; FAX. 941/471-9452; Ruth Angus, RN, Director Highlands/Hardee

Good Shepherd Hospice of Mid-Florida/Winter Haven, Inc., 105 Arneson Avenue, Auburndale, FL 33823; tel. 813/297-1880; FAX. 813/965-5601; Mary Ellen Poe, Administrator

Hernando-Pasco Hospice, Inc., 12107 Majestic Boulevard, Hudson, FL 34667; tel. 813/863-7971; FAX. 813/868-9261; Rodney Taylor, Executive Director

Holmes Regional Hospice, Inc., 1900 Dairy Road, West Melbourne, FL 32904; tel. 407/952-0494; FAX. 407/952-0382; Roberta Van Dusen, Director

Hope Hospice of Lee County, Inc., 9470 Health Park Circle, Ft. Myers, FL 33908; tel. 941/482-4673; FAX. 941/482-2488; Samira K. Beckwith, President, Chief Executive Officer

Hospice Care of Broward County, Inc., 309 Southeast 18th Street, Ft. Lauderdale, FL 33316; tel. 954/467-7423; FAX. 954/524-6067; Susan G. Telli, Executive Director

Hospice Care of South Florida, 7270 Northwest 12th Street, Penthouse Six, Miami, FL 33126; tel. 305/591-1606; FAX. 305/591-1618; Rose Marie R. Marty, Executive Director

Hospice by the Sea, Inc., 1531 West Palmetto Park Road, Boca Raton, FL 33486-3395; tel. 561/395-5031; FAX. 561/393-7137; Trudi Webb, Executive Director

Hospice of Citrus County, Inc., 3350 West Audubon Park Path, Lecanto, FL 34461-8450; tel. 904/527-2020; FAX. 904/527-0386; William J. Murphy, Executive Director

Hospice of Hillsborough, Inc., 3010 West Azeele Street, Tampa, FL 33609-3139; tel. 813/877-2200; FAX. 813/872-7037

Hospice of Lake and Sumter, Inc., 12300 Lane Park Road, Taveres, FL 32778-9660; tel. 904/343-1341; FAX. 904/343-6115; Rebecca A. McDonald, Chief Executive Officer

Hospice of Naples, Inc., 1095 Whippoorwill Lane, Naples, FL 34105; tel. 941/261-4404; FAX. 941/261-3278; Diane S. Cox, Executive Director

Hospice of Northeast Florida, Inc., 4266 Sunbeam Road, The Earl Hadlow Center for Caring, Jacksonville, FL 32257; tel. 904/268-5200; FAX. 904/268-9674; Susan Ponder-Stansel, President, Chief Executive Officer

Hospice of Northwest Florida, Inc., 2001 North Palafox Street, Pensacola, FL 32501; tel. 904/433-2155; FAX. 904/433-7212; Dale O. Knee, President, Chief Executive Officer

Hospice of Okeechobee, Inc., 411 Southeast Fourth Street, Okeechobee, FL 34973; tel. 813/467-2321; FAX. 813/467-8330; Pat Ballengee, Executive Director

Hospice of Palm Beach County, Inc., 5300 East Avenue, West Palm Beach, FL 33407; tel. 561/848-5200; FAX. 561/863-2955; Deborah S. Dailey, M.B.A., President, Chief Executive Officer

Hospice of Pasco, Inc., 6224-6230 Lafayette Street, New Port Richey, FL 34652-2626; tel. 813/845-5707; Michael Wilson, Executive Director

Hospice of St. Francis, Inc., 6770 South U.S. Highway 1, P.O. Box 5563, Titusville, FL 32783-5563; tel. 407/269-4240; FAX. 407/269-5428; Cheryl M. Parker, Executive Director

Hospice of Treasure Coast, Inc., 805 Virginia Avenue, P.O. Box 1748, Ft. Pierce, FL 34982-1748; tel. 407/465-0504; FAX. 407/465-6309; Sharon A. Rivers, President, Chief Executive Officer

Hospice of Volusia and Flagler, 3800 Woodbriar Trail, Port Orange, FL 32119; tel. 904/322-4701; FAX. 904/322-4702; Debbie Harley, Director

Hospice of the Comforter, 595 Montgomery Road, Altamonte Springs, FL 32714; tel. 407/682-0808; FAX. 407/682-5787; Robert G. Wilson, President, Director

Hospice of the Florida Keys, 1319 William Street, Key West, FL 33040; tel. 305/294-8812; FAX. 305/292-9466; Liz Kern, Chief Executive Officer

Hospice of the Florida Suncoast, Inc., 300 East Bay Drive, Largo, FL 33770; tel. 813/586-4432; FAX. 813/581-5846; Mary Labyak, M.S.S.W., L.C.S.W., President

Hospice of the Gold Coast H.H.S., 911 East Atlantic Boulevard, Suite 200, Pompano Beach, FL 33060; tel. 305/785-2990; FAX. 305/785-2993; Lynda Friedman, Administrator

The Hospice of Martin & St. Lucie, Inc., 2030 Southeast Ocean Boulevard, Stuart, FL 34996; tel. 561/287-7860; FAX. 561/287-7982; Mary C. Knox, Executive Director

The Hospice of North Central Florida, 4200 Northwest 90th Blvd., Gainesville, FL 32606; tel. 352/378-2121; FAX. 352/378-4111; Patrice Moore, Administrator

VITAS Healthcare Corporation of Central Florida, Inc., 2500 Maitland Center Parkway, Suite 300, Maitland, FL 32751; tel. 407/875-0028; FAX. 407/875-2074; Brenda K. Horne, General Manager

VNA Hospice of Indian River County, 1111 36th Street, Vero Beach, FL 32960; tel. 407/567-5551; FAX. 407/567-9308; Sharon L. Kennedy, President, Chief Executive Officer

Vitas Healthcare Corporation of Florida, 3323 West Commercial Boulevard, Suite 200, Ft. Lauderdale, FL 33309; tel. 305/486-4085; FAX. 305/777-5328; Deirdre Lawe, Regional Vice President

Vitas Healthcare Corporation of Florida, 3700 Executive Way, Miramar, FL 33025; tel. 954/437-5433; FAX. 954/704-2797; Barbara Gray, General Manager

GEORGIA

Albany Community Hospice, 416 Fifth Avenue, P.O. Box 1828, Albany, GA 31701; tel. 912/889-7050; FAX. 912/889-7447; Tricia Helmls, Executive Director

American HospiceCare, 32 Medical Arts, Savannah, GA 31405-4415; tel. 912/356-9090; Mr. Neil Bennett, Administrator

Atlanta Hospice International L.L.C., 236 Forsyth Street, Suite 405, Atlanta, GA 30303; tel. 404/681-1212; Renee M. Folsom

Avondale Hospice Services, Inc., 3500 Kensington Road, Decatus, GA 30032-1328; tel. 404/299-6111; Rachel Waldemar, Administrator

Blue-Gray Community Hospice, Perry House Road, P.O. Box 1349, Fitzgerald, GA 31750-1447; tel. 912/424-7152; Lenora Kirby, RN, Executive Director

Columbus Hospice, Inc., 1315 Delauney Ave., Suite 104, Columbus, GA 31901; tel. 706/327-5153; Mike Smajd, Executive Director

Community Hospice Care, 1207 Martha Berry Blvd., Rome, GA 30165; tel. 706/295-9731; Joy Jones, Director

Elysium House, 6490 West Fayetteville Road, Riverdale, GA 30296; tel. 404/997-0889; FAX. 404/997-8559; Juanita Little, Administrator

Georgia Baptist Hospice, 1895 Phoenix Blvd, One Crown Center, Suite 400, College Park, GA 30349; tel. 404/909-1000; FAX. 770/265-1414; Myra J. Downs, Administrator

Georgia Mountain Hospice, Inc., 1476 East Church Street, P.O. Box 881, Jasper, GA 30143; tel. 706/692-3491; FAX. 706/692-4300; Lynn Corliss, Executive Director

Hamilton Medical Center-Hospice, P.O. Box 1168, 1200 Memorial Drive, Dalton, GA 30720-1168; tel. 706/278-2848; Judy Hannah, Administrator

Hand In Hand Hospice, 2150 Limestone Parkway, Gainesville, GA 30501; tel. 404/536-0497; FAX. 404/536-0157; Gregory N. Robinson, Administrator

Haven House at Midtown, Inc., 250 14th Street, Atlanta, GA 30309; tel. 404/874-8313; FAX. 404/875-4363; Clyde W. Johnson, Jr., President, Chief Executive Officer

Healthfield Hospice Services, Inc., 2045 Peachtree Road, N.E., Suite 210, Atlanta, GA 30309-1414; tel. 404/355-3134; Richard Stroder, RN Director

Hospice Atlanta, 1244 Park Vista Drive, Atlanta, GA 30319; tel. 404/869-3000; FAX. 404/869-3099; Pamela Melbourne, Administrator

Hospice Care of Carroll County, Inc., 906 South Park Street, Carrollton, GA 30117; tel. 770/214-2355; FAX. 770/214-8301; Pat Alfrey, Administrator

Hospice Care, Inc., 1310 13th Avenue, Suite 200, P.O. Box 9401, Columbus, GA 31901; tel. 706/660-8899; FAX. 706/660-8899; Mr. Adeleye Tokes, Ph.D., Administrator

Hospice Satilla of Memorial Hospital, Inc., 1906 Tebeau Street, Waycross, GA 31501; tel. 912/287-2664; FAX. 912/283-0200; Rai B. Duane, Director

Hospice Savannah, Inc., 1352 Eisenhower Drive, P.O. Box 13190, Savannah, GA 31406; tel. 912/355-2289; FAX. 912/355-2376; Judith B. Brunger, Executive Director

Hospice of Americus and Sumter County, 121 Brannan Street, P.O. Box 1434, Americus, GA 31709; tel. 912/928-4000; FAX. 912/928-1322; Debra Hackett, Executive Director

Hospice of Baldwin, Inc., 811 North Cobb Street, Milledgeville, GA 31061; tel. 912/453-8432; FAX. 912/453-8432; Jeannie Sweeney, Administrator

Hospice of Central Georgia, 3920 Arkwright Rd., Macon, GA 31210; tel. 912/477-0335; FAX. 912/477-0690; Connie McCracken, Director

Hospice of Chattanooga, Inc., 165 Hamm Road, Chattanooga, TN 37405; tel. 615/267-6828; Viston Taylor III, Executive Director

Hospice of Georgia, Inc., 3450 New High Shoals Road, P.O. Box 10, High Shoals, GA 30645; tel. 706/769-8835; FAX. 706/769-5944; Fran Keisel, Administrator

Hospice of Houston Co., Inc., 2066 Watson Boulevard, P.O. Box 1023, Warner Robins, GA 31093; tel. 912/922-1777; FAX. 912/922-9433; Jackie Connors, Administrator

Hospice of Laurens County, 1103 Bellevue Avenue, P.O. Box 1344, Suite 100, Dublin, GA 31021; tel. 912/272-8333; Kaye Bracewell, Executive Director

Hospice of Northeast Georgia, Inc., Highway 76 West, P.O. Box 586, Clayton, GA 30525; tel. 706/782-7505; FAX. 404/782-3343; Dan Pumphrey, Executive Director

Hospice of South Georgia, 205 Woodrow Wilson Drive, P.O. Box 1727, Valdosta, GA 31602; tel. 912/333-1661; FAX. 912/249-4102; Frances Rowell, Director

Hospice of Southeast Georgia, Inc., 333 South Ashley Street, P.O. Box 1077, Kingsland, GA 31548; tel. 912/673-7000; Chuck Chapman, President

Hospice of Southwest Georgia, 818 Gordon Avenue, Thomasville, GA 31792; tel. 912/227-5520; FAX. 912/227-5526; Patricia Whetsell, Administrator

Hospice of Tift Area, 802 East 20th Street, P.O. Drawer 747, Tifton, GA 31794-3645; tel. 912/382-5030; Ruth L. Lee, Director

Hospice of Wilkinson County, Inc., Mission Road, P.O. Box 720, Gordon, GA 31031; tel. 912/628-5655; Edwin Lavender, Administrator

Hospice of the Golden Isles, Inc., 1692 Glynco Parkway, Brunswick, GA 31525; tel. 912/265-4735; Cheryl Johns, RN, Executive Director

House Call Hospice, Inc., Executive Business Park, 6025 Lee Highway, Suite 415, Chattanooga, TN 37421; tel. 615/892-2561; Caroline McBrayer

Northside Hospice, 5825 Glenridge Drive, Building Four, Atlanta, GA 30328-5544; tel. 404/851-6300; Margot Marcus, Manager

Ogeechee Area Hospice, 209 B South Zetterower Avenue, P.O. Box 531, Statesboro, GA 30458; tel. 912/764-8441; FAX. 912/489-8247; Nancy Bryant, RN

Olsten Kimberly Quality Care Hospice, 1395 South Marietta Parkway, Suite 222, Marietta, GA 30061; tel. 770/422–5741; FAX. 770/425–3516; Joan Richters, RN, M.N.

Peachtree Hospice, 3600 Dekalb Technology Parkway, P.O. 942029, Altanta, GA 30340; tel. 404/451–1903; Curtis Stubblefield, Executive Director

Pormina Northwest Hospice, 55 S. Medical Dr., Suite 340, Marietta, GA 30060–1161; tel. 404/793–7370; Sharon Smith, Administrator

Portsbridge, Inc., 4598 Barclay Drive, Dunwoody, GA 30338–5883; tel. 404/936–9546, ext. 12; FAX. 770/936–9547; T.M. Mahone, Administrator

Samaritan Care Hospice of Georgia, 705 Red Bud Rd., Suite B, Calhoun, GA 30701–1966; tel. 706/629–2722; Cynthia Brown, Administrator

Shepherd's Gate Hospice, 2149 Pace Street, Covington, GA 30014–6652; tel. 706/787–6975; FAX. 706/784–7650; John J. McBride, Executive Director

Southwest Christian Hospice, 7225 Lester Road, Union City, GA 30291; tel. 404/969–8354; FAX. 404/969–1940; Mike Sorrow, Executive Director

United Hospice of Calhoun, 1195 Curtis Parkway, Calhoun, GA 30701; tel. 706/602–9546; William Wells, Administrator

United Hospice of Macon, Inc., 2484 Ingleside Avenue, Building B, Macon, GA 31204; tel. 912/477–9713; FAX. 912/745–9321; Scott Schull

United Hospice, Inc., 3945 Lawrenceville Highway, Lilburn, GA 30047; tel. 800/544–4788; FAX. 770/925–4619; Elaine Hagley, Administrator

Vencare Hospice–Atlanta, 1190 Winchester Parkway, Suite 200, Smyrna, GA 30080–6544; tel. 770/803–0881; Douglas J. Thompson, Administrator

Vencare Hospice–Columbus, 3646 Edgewood Road, Columbus, GA 31907; tel. 706/569–0200; Margarita Jara, Administrator

Vencare Hospice–Macon, 750 Baconsfield Drive, Suite 115, Macon, GA 31211; tel. 912/750–9777; Jaquita White, Administrator

West Georgia Hospice, 1510 Vernon Road, Lagrange, GA 30240–4130; tel. 706/845–3905; Charles Foster, Administrator

Willow Way Hospice, 6000 Lake Forrest Drive, Suite 400, Atlanta, GA 30328; tel. 404/255–4015; FAX. 404/255–8340; Maxine McCullar

Wiregrass Hospice, Inc., 1211 W. Main Street, Dothan, AL 36301; tel. 334/792–1101; FAX. 334/794–0009; Ray L. Shrout, Administrator

Wiregrass Hospice, Inc., 430 E. Shotwell Street, Bainbridge, GA 31717–4058; tel. 912/246–6330; Ray L. Shrout, Administrator

HAWAII

Hospice Hawaii, 445 Seaside Avenue, Suite 604, Honolulu, HI 96815; tel. 808/924–9255; FAX. 808/922–9161; Stephen A. Kula, President, Chief Professional Officer

Hospice Maui, 400 Mahalani Street, Wailuku, HI 96793; tel. 808/244–5555; FAX. 808/244–5557; Dr. Gregory LaGoy, Executive Director

Hospice of Hilo, 1266 Waianuenue Avenue, Hilo, HI 96720; tel. 808/969–1733; FAX. 808/969–4863; Brenda Ho, Executive Director

Hospice of Kona, 74–5094 Palani Road, Kailua–Kona, HI 96740; tel. 808/334–0334; FAX. 808/334–0365; David Kula, Administrator

Kauai Hospice, 3175 Elua Street, P.O. Box 3286, Lihue, HI 96766; tel. 808/245–7277; FAX. 808/245–5006; Kathleen Boyle

North Hawaii Hospice, Inc., P.O. Box 1236, Kamuela, HI 96743; tel. 808/885–7547; FAX. 808/885–5592; Nancy Bouvet, Executive Director

St. Francis Hospice, 24 Puiwa Road, Honolulu, HI 96817; tel. 808/595–7566; FAX. 808/595–6996; Sister Francine Gries, Administrator

IDAHO

Blackfoot Medical Clinic, Home Care & Hospice, Inc., 625 West Pacific, Blackfoot, ID 83221; tel. 208/785–2600; James Marriott, Administrator

Crest Hospice Care, 1009 Highway Two West, Suite E, Sandpoint, ID 83864; tel. 208/265–9200; FAX. 208/265–0622; Lorraine P. Gruner, Administrator

Good Samaritan Community Hospice, 840 East Elva, Idaho Falls, ID 83401; tel. 208/529–8326; FAX. 208/522–7473; Carol Ord, RN, B.S.N., Director

Horizon Hospice, Inc., 1406 East First Street, Suite 107, Meridan, ID 83642; tel. 208/884–5051; FAX. 208/884–5054; Marcella Little, President

Hospice Visions, Inc., 1300 Kimberly Road, Suite 11, Twin Falls, ID 83301; tel. 208/326–4068; Tamala Klinsky, Director

Hospice of Idaho, 812 East Clark, Pocatello, ID 83201; tel. 208/232–0088; FAX. 208/232–7941; Debbie Osborn, Administrator

Hospice of North Idaho, West 280 Prairie Avenue, Coeur d'Alene, ID 83814; tel. 208/772–7994; John Nugent, Administrator

Hospice of the Palouse, P.O. Box 9461, Moscow, ID 83843; tel. 208/882–1228; FAX. 208/883–2239; Norman Bowers, Administrator

Latah Health Home Care & Hospice, 510 West Palouse River Drive, Moscow, ID 83843; tel. 208/882–4802; FAX. 208/882–1819; Irma Laskowski, RNC, Hospice Director

Life's Doors Hospice, Inc., 1111 South Orchard, Suite 400, P.O. Box 5754, Boise, ID 83705; tel. 208/344–6500; FAX. 208/344–6590; Mary L. Langenfeld, Chief Executive Officer

MSTI – Hospice of Boise, 151 East Bannock, Boise, ID 83712; tel. 208/386–2711; Nan Hart, Administrator

Magic Valley Staffing Service, Inc., 200 Second Avenue, N., Twin Falls, ID 83301; tel. 208/734–0600; FAX. 208/733–5980; Debbie Osborn, Administrator

Mercy Hospice, 111 Third Street, S., Nampa, ID 83651; tel. 208/465–5235; Robert A. Fale, Chief Executive Officer

Southeastern District Hospice, 465 Memorial Drive, Pocatello, ID 83201; tel. 208/239–5240; FAX. 208/234–7169; Judy Moyer, Administrator

The Oaks Hospice, 316 West Washington, Boise, ID 83702; tel. 208/343–7755; Shelley Greget, Vice President

XL Hospice, Inc., 1401 North Whitley Drive, Suite 16, Fruitland, ID 83619; tel. 208/452–5911; FAX. 208/452–4090; Leon C. Felder, President

ILLINOIS

Advocate Hospice, 1441 Branding Avenue, Suite 240, Downers Grove, IL 60515; tel. 630/963–6800; FAX. 630/963–6877; Nancy Kitts–Woodworth, Director

All Care, Inc., 900 Jorie Blvd., Suite 220, Oak Brook, IL 60523; tel. 630/346–2575; Robert M. Wesolowski

Ariston Hospice Service, 3051 Oak Grove Road, Downers Grove, IL 60515; tel. 630/435–2111; Lynn MacMillan, Administrator

Beacon of Hope Hospice, Inc., 615 35th Ave., Moline, IL 61265; tel. 309/757–0579; Darren Chrisop

Beloit Hospice, Inc., 5512 Elevator Road, Roscoe, IL 61073; tel. 608/365–7421; Virginia Burton, Administrator

Bro–Menn Hospice, 1322 S. Main Street, Normal, IL 61761; tel. 309/838–0930; Mary Nugent, Administrator

Bureau Valley Area Hospice, 530 Park Avenue, E., Princeton, IL 61356; tel. 815/875–2811; Janice Shue, Administrator

Carle Hospice, 2011 Round Barn Road, Champagne, IL 61821; tel. 217/383–3151; Sheryl Imlay, Administrator

Cass–Schuyler Area Hospice, 331 South Main Street, Virginia, IL 62691; tel. 217/452–3057; FAX. 217/452–7245; Virginia Hertweck, Administrator

Community Hospices of America Northwest Illinois, 256 South Soangetaha Road, Suite 103, Galesburg, IL 61401–5586; tel. 309/342–3007; FAX. 309/342–6973; Susan Myer, Program Director

Covenant Hospice Care Program, 1400 West Park, Urbana, IL 61801; tel. 217/337–2470; Ruth Madawick

DeKalb County Hospice, 213 E. Locust Street, DeKalb, IL 60115; tel. 815/756–3000; Karen Hagen, RN, M.S., Executive Director

Evanston–Glenbrook Hospitals Home Services, 5215 Old Orchard, Suite 700, Skokie, IL 60077; tel. 847/581–1717; FAX. 847/581–1919; Janet Sullivan, Administrator

Family Hospice of Belleville Area, 11B Park Place, Professional Center, Swansea, IL 62221; tel. 618/277–1800; FAX. 618/277–1074; Diane Smith, Administrator

Fox Valley Hospice, 200 Whitfield Drive, P.O. Box 707, Geneva, IL 60134; tel. 630/232–2233; FAX. 630/232–0023; Vivian J. Nimmo, Executive Director

Franciscan Hospice of Central Illinois, 301 W. Washington Street, Pontiac, IL 61764; tel. 815/844–6982; Donna O'Shaughnessy, Administrator

Genesis Hospice Care, 1705 Second Avenue, Rock Island, IL 61201; tel. 309/794–1626; Sharon Meister, Administrator

Grundy Community Hospice, 1802 North Division Street, Suite 307, Morris, IL 60450; tel. 815/942–8525; Joan Sereno

Harbor Light Hospice, 800 Roosevelt Road, Building C, Suite 206, Glen Ellyn, IL 60137; tel. 800/419–0542; FAX. 630/942–0118; Dorothy M. Stahl, Administrator

Home Health Plus Hospice Program, 2215 Enterprise Drive, Suite 1512, Westchester, IL 60154; tel. 708/531–9339; Mary Shafer, Administrator

Home Health Plus Hospice Program, 333 Salem Place, Suite 165, Fairview Heights, IL 62208; tel. 618/632–0304; Robin Carnett, Administrator

Horizon Hospice, Inc., 833 West Chicago Avenue, Chicago, IL 60622; tel. 312/733–2233; FAX. 312/733–8931; Kathryn A. Meshenberg, President, Chief Executive Officer

Hospice Alliance, Inc., 3452 North Sheridan Road, Zion, IL 60099; tel. 847/263–1180; Connie Matter, Administrator

Hospice Care, 319 East Madison, Suite Three J, Springfield, IL 62701; tel. 217/789–6506; FAX. 217/525–3739; Janet Thomson

Hospice Care of Illinois, Visiting Nurse Association of Central Illinois, 720 North Bond Street, Springfield, IL 62702; tel. 217/757–7322; Barbara Sullivan, Administrator

Hospice Suburban South, 78 Cherry Street, Park Forest, IL 60466; tel. 708/481–2104; Maureen Rinella, Executive Director

Hospice of Bond County, 305 West Franklin, Greenville, IL 62246; tel. 618/664–9701; Elnora Hamel, Administrator

Hospice of Dubuque, 50 Sinsinawa, P.O. Box 236, East Dubuque, IL 61025; tel. 815/747–3622; Barbara Zoeller, Administrator

Hospice of DuPage, Inc., 690 East North Avenue, Carol Stream, IL 60188; tel. 630/690–9000; Kimberly Jensen, Administrator

Hospice of Kankakee Valley, Inc., 1015 North Fifth Avenue, Suite Five, Kankakee, IL 60901; tel. 815/939–4141; FAX. 815/939–1501; Dorothea MacDonald–Lagesse, Executive Director

Hospice of Lincolnland, 75 Professional Plaza, Mattoon, IL 61938; tel. 217/234–4044; FAX. 217/345–3261; Connie R. Oetinger, President, Chief Executive Officer

Hospice of Madison County, 1909 Edison Ave., Granite City, IL 62040; tel. 618/798–3399; Denise Saksa, Administrator

Hospice of Northeastern Illinois, Inc., 410 South Hager Avenue, Barrington, IL 60010; tel. 847/381–5599; FAX. 847/381–5713; Jane Bilyeu, Executive Director

Hospice of Northwest Illinois, Inc., 155 West Front Street, P.O. Box 185, Stockton, IL 61085–0185; tel. 815/947–3260; FAX. 815/947–3257; Deann Anderson, Administrator

Hospice of Southeastern Illinois, 800 East Locust Street, Olney, IL 62450; tel. 618/395–7340; Harvey H. Pettry, Administrator

Hospice of Southern Illinois, Inc., 305 South Illinois Street, Belleville, IL 62220; tel. 618/235–1703; FAX. 618/235–2828; Merle L. Aukamp, President, Chief Executive Officer

Hospice of the Calumet Area, Inc., 3224 Ridge Road, Suite 202 and 203, Lansing, IL 60438; tel. 708/895–8332; FAX. 219/922–1947; Adrianne May, Administrator

Hospice of the Good Samaritan, 605 N. 12th Street, Mt. Vernon, IL 62864; tel. 618/242–4600; Christina Adams, Administrator

Hospice of the Great Lakes, 3130 Commercial Avenue, Northbrook, IL 60062; tel. 847/559–8999; FAX. 847/559–9005; Mary Jo Fox, Administrator

Hospice of the North Shore, A Division of Palliative Care Center of the North Shore, 2821 Central Street, Evanston, IL 60201; tel. 847/467–7423; FAX. 847/866–6023; Dorothy L. Pitner, RN, B.S.N., MM, President

Hospice of the Rock River Valley, 264 Illinois, Route 2, Dixon, IL 61021; tel. 815/626–9242; FAX. 815/626–7438; Cheryl Price, Administrator

Illinois Valley Hospice, 1701 Fourth Street, Peru, IL 61354; tel. 815/224–1307; Peggy A. Sebastian, Administrator

Ingalls Home Hospice, One Ingalls Drive, Harvey, IL 60426; tel. 708/331–0226; Jeane Laroche, Administrator

Joliet Area Community Hospice, Inc., 335 West Jefferson Street, Joliet, IL 60435; tel. 815/740–4104; FAX. 815/740–4107; Duane A. Krieger, Executive Director

Section C

Lourdes Hospice, 600 Market Street, Metropolis, IL 62960; tel. 618/524–3647; FAX. 618/524–3920; Donna Stewart, Director

Monroe Clinic Hospice, 1301 South Kiwanis Drive, Freeport, IL 61032; tel. 815/235–1406; Carla Stadel, Administrator

Northern Illinois Hospice Association, 4215 Newburg Road, Rockford, IL 61108; tel. 815/398–0500; FAX. 815/398–0588; Judith A. Engblom, Executive Director

Ogle County Hospice Association, 421 Pines Road, P.O. Box 462, Oregon, IL 61061; tel. 815/732–2499; Lorrie Bearrows, RN, Executive Director

Provena Hospice – Waukegan, 2615 Washington Street, Waukegan, IL 60085; tel. 847/360–2220; Nancy Delaney, Administrator

QLS Community Home Health Based Hospice, 353 South Lewis Lane, Carbondale, IL 62901; tel. 618/529–2262; FAX. 618/457–8599; Monica J. Brahler, Administrator

QV, Inc., 322 South Green Street, Suite 500, Chicago, IL 60607–3599; tel. 312/736–8622; Dan Woods, Administrator

Rainbow Hospice, Inc., 1550 North Northwest Highway, Suite 220, Park Ridge, IL 60068–1427; tel. 847/699–2000; FAX. 847/699–2047; Betty Pasternak, Administrator

Rockford VNA, 4223 East State Street, Rockford, IL 61108; tel. 815/229–1100; FAX. 815/229–2226; Susan Schreier, Administrator

Rush Hospice Partners, 1035 Madison Street, Oak Park, IL 60302; tel. 708/386–9191; FAX. 708/386–9933; Kathleen Nash

Saint Francis Hospice, 355 Ridge Ave., Evanston, IL 60202; tel. 847/316–7114; Virginia G. Niemann, Administrator

Samaritan Hospice, 102 E. Washington, Mount Carroll, IL 60153; tel. 319/244–3666; Joan Noe, Administrator

Seasons Hospice, 1600 W. Dempster, Park Ridge, IL 60068; tel. 847/759–9449; Marcia Norman, Administrator

St. Margaret's Hospice, 600 East First Street, Spring Valley, IL 61362; tel. 815/664–1132; Carol Stevenson, Administrator

St. Thomas Hospice, Inc., Seven Salt Creek Lane, Suite 101, Hinsdale, IL 60521; tel. 630/850–3990; FAX. 630/850–3969; Marilyn Retter, Administrator

Staff Builders Services, Inc., Eight Cottonwood Road, Suite One, Edwardsville, IL 62034; tel. 618/288–8000; FAX. 618/288–8099; Linda Linkes, Administrator

The Blessing Hospice, Broadway at 14th, P.O. Box 7005, Quincy, IL 62305; tel. 217/223–1200; Ann Abrams

Tip Hospice Program, Four Executive Woods Court, Belleville, IL 62226; tel. 618/257–2184; FAX. 618/997–0922; Becky Ashton, Administrator

Unity Hospice, 439 East 31st Street, Suite 213, Chicago, IL 60616; tel. 312/949–1188; FAX. 312/949–0158; Michael Klein, President

VNA Hospice, 3122 Brettwood Circle, Decatur, IL 62526; tel. 217/877–1222; Karen Adell, Administrator

VNA Hospice Care of Central Illinois, 720 North Bond Street, Springfield, IL 62702; tel. 217/523–4113; Barbara Sullivan, Administrator

VNA Lincolnland, Inc., 100 Professional Plaza, Mattoon, IL 61938; tel. 217/234–4044; Connie R. Oetinger, Administrator

VNA of Fox Valley Hospice, 1245 Corporate Boulevard, Aurora, IL 60504; tel. 630/978–2532; FAX. 630/978–1129; Janet S. Craft, President, Chief Executive Officer

VNA of Illinois Hospice, 1809 West McCord, Centralia, IL 62801; tel. 618/533–2781; FAX. 618/533–3265; Celeste Krahl, Administrator

VNHA of Rock Island County Pathway Hospice, 500 42nd Street, Rock Island, IL 61201; tel. 309/788–0600; Mary Oelschlaeger, Administrator

Visiting Nurse Association Hospice, 1300 U.S. 45 North, Eldorado, IL 62930; tel. 618/273–9305; FAX. 618/273–2469; Cissy Kraft, Administrator

Vitas Corporation, 100 West 22nd Street, Suite 101, Lombard, IL 60148; tel. 630/495–8484; David Fielding, Administrator

Vitas Corporation, 5215 Old Orchard Road, Suite 800, Skokie, IL 60077; tel. 847/470–9193; Brian D. Wohl, Administrator

Vitas Corporation, 1055 West 175th Street, Suite One, Homewood, IL 60430; tel. 708/957–8777; Jay Koeper, Administrator

Vitas Corporation, 1424 East 53rd Street, Suite 201, Chicago, IL 60615; tel. 312/643–6222; Anna Chavez–Schaider, Administrator

Woodhaven Hospice and Special Support Services, 800 Hoagland Boulevard, Jacksonville, IL 62650; tel. 217/245–0838; Bette Jackson, Administrator

INDIANA

A Priority Hospice, 761 – 45th Street, Munster, IN 46321; tel. 219/922–8695; Barbara Hoyer, Administrator

Americare Home Health and Hospice Services, 49 East Monroe, Franklin, IN 46131; tel. 317/736–6005; Kim Weddle, Administrator

Cameron Home Health Care & Hospice, 416 East Maumee Street, Angola, IN 46703; tel. 219/665–2141; Pat Grosenbacher, Administrator

Care at Home Hospice Services, 1721 South Main Street, Goshen, IN 46527; tel. 219/535–2700; Nancy Buss

Clarian Hospice, Clarian Health Partners, Inc., 2039 North Capitol Avenue, Indianapolis, IN 46202; tel. 317/929–4663; FAX. 317/929–3815; William Loveday, Administrator

Comprecare Home Health and Hospice, 1607 East Dowling Street, P.O. Box 517, Kendallville, IN 46755–0517; tel. 800/824–5860; Marilyn Alligood, Administrator

Deaconess Ohio Valley Hospice, 600 Mary Street, Evansville, IN 47747; tel. 812/426–3169; Rosemary Knight, Administrator

Dekalb Memorial Hospice, 221 N. Main Street, Auburn, IN 46706; tel. 219/927–1640; Annette Vincent, Administrator

Elkhart Community Hospice, Inc., 600 E. Boulevard, Elkhart, IN 46514; tel. 219/294–2621; Janice M. Yoder, Administrator

Family Hospice of Indiana, LLC, 1710 East 10th L–185, Jeffersonville, IN 47130; tel. 812/284–0455

Family Hospice of Northeast Indiana, 1521 W. Main Street, Berne, IN 46711; tel. 219/589–8598; Rbernhard P. Wiebe, Administrator

Good Samaritan Lincoln Trail, 520 South Seventh Street, Vincennes, IN 47591; tel. 812/885–8035; Vonetta Vories, Administrator

Grancare Hospice Services, 945 Veterans Dr., P.O. Box 909, North Vernon, IN 47265; tel. 812/346–8774; Vivian B. Filosa, Administrator

Hancock Memorial Hospice, 801 North State Street, Greenfield, IN 46140; tel. 317/462–0522; Robert Keen, Administrator

Harbor Light Hospice, 500 West Lincoln Highway, Suite F, Merrillville, IN 46410; tel. 219/793–1200; FAX. 219/793–9292; Stephanie Mayercik, Director

Heartland Hospice, 1315 Directors Row, Suite 206, Fort Wayne, IN 46808; tel. 219/484–7622; FAX. 219/484–5662; Tim Booth, Administrator

Heartland Hospice, 412 West State Street, Princeton, IN 47670; tel. 812/385–2550; Kim Ross, Administrator

Helping Hearts Hospice, 1314 Grand Ave., Washington, IN 47501; tel. 812/254–2760; Diane Shepard, Administrator

Home Health Care/Hospice Services, 902 Provident Drive, Warsaw, IN 46580; tel. 219/267–3683; Colleen A. Nettleton, Administrator

Home Hospital Home Health Care, 2500 Ferry Street, Lafayette, IN 47904; tel. 765/449–5046; Cheryl Ransom, Administrator

Hoosier Uplands Hospice, 1500 West Main Street, P.O. Box Nine, Mitchell, IN 47446; tel. 812/849–4447; FAX. 812/849–3068; Allen Burris, Director

Hoosier Uplands Hospice, 1500 West Main Street, P.O. Box 9, Mitchell, IN 47446; tel. 812/849–4447; Allen Burris, Administrator

Hope Hospice, Inc., 100 West 9th Street, Rochester, IN 46975; tel. 219/224–4673; Rev. Ronald C. Purkey

Hospice Preferred Choice, 9302 North Meridian, Suite 251, Indianapolis, IN 46260; tel. 317/575–8590; FAX. 317/575–8698; Sharon O'Morrow

Hospice of BAM Health Associates, Inc., 9223 Broadway, Suite A, Merrillville, IN 46410; tel. 219/738–5230

Hospice of Bloomington, 619 W. First Street, Bloomington, IN 47402; tel. 812/336–9818; Carole Ebeling

Hospice of Margaret Mary Community, 321 Mitchell Avenue, Batesville, IN 47006; tel. 812/934–6624; John L. Amos, Administrator

Hospice of South Central Indiana, Inc., 2400 East 17th Street, Columbus, IN 47201–5351; tel. 812/376–5813; FAX. 812/376–5929; Sandra Carmichael, Executive Director

Hospice of Southeastern Indiana, 606 Wilson Creek Road, Suite 430, Lawrenceburg, IN 47025; tel. 812/537–8192; Sally Kinghorn, Administrator

Hospice of Southern Indiana, 624 East Market Street, P.O. Box 17, New Albany, IN 47150–4621; tel. 812/945–4596; FAX. 812/945–4733; Patricia Payne, Administrator

Hospice of St. Joseph County, Inc., 111 North Sunnybrook Court, South Bend, IN 46637; tel. 219/243–3100; FAX. 219/243–0349; Thomas Burzynski, Executive Director

Hospice of Wabash Valley, 600 South 1st Street, Terre Haute, IN 47807; tel. 812/234–2515; FAX. 812/232–2047; Jacquelyn Fox, Administrator

Hospice of the Calumet Area, Inc., 600 Superior Avenue, Munster, IN 46321–4032; tel. 219/922–2732; FAX. 219/922–1947; Adrianne May, Administrator

Hospice of the Miami Valley, 706 Eads Parkway, Lawrenceburg, IN 47025; tel. 812/537–5976; Rebecca Hight, Administrator

Hospicecare, Inc., 11555 North Meridian, Suite 190, Carmel, IN 46032; tel. 317/580–9336; Anthony Chase, Administrator

Oakwood Hospice, 1000 N. 16th Street, New Castle, IN 47362; tel. 765/521–1420; Colleen Fedders, Administrator

Odyssey HealthCare of Central Indiana, Inc., 8765 Guion Road, Indianapolis, IN 46268; tel. 317/334–9302; Joseph D. Lingengelter

Parkview Home Health and Hospice, 105 N. Madison, Columbia City, IN 46725; tel. 219/244–6191; Bridget Dolohanty–Johns

Parkview Home Health and Hospice, 2270 Lake Ave., Suite 200, Fort Wayne, IN 46805; tel. 219/484–6636; Frank D. Byrne

Parkview Home Heath & Hospice, 240 South Jefferson Street, Huntington, IN 46750; tel. 219/356–3000; L.K. McCoy, Administrator

Premier Hospice, Inc., 5490 Broadway, Merrillville, IN 46410; tel. 219/985–0160; Donna S. Huddleston, Adminstrator

Saint Joseph at Home Hospice Services, 400 North Main, Kokomo, IN 46903; tel. 317/452–6066; FAX. 317/457–4817; Darcy Herr, RN, Director

St. Francis Hospice, 438 South Emerson, Greenwood, IN 46143; tel. 317/865–2095; Pamela Franklin, Administrator

The Community Hospice of VNA of NCI, 1354 South B Street, Elwood, IN 46036; tel. 317/552–3393; FAX. 317/552–3994; Jessie A. Westlund

VNA Home Care Services Hospice, Inc., 901 South Woodland Avenue, Michigan City, IN 46360–5672; tel. 219/877–2070; FAX. 219/877–2089; Mary Craymer, Chief Executive Officer

VNA Hospice Home Care, 501 Marquette Street, Valparaiso, IN 46383–2058; tel. 219/462–5195; FAX. 219/462–6020; Laura Harting, Administrator

VNA Hospice of Southeastern Indiana, 1806 East 10th Street, Jeffersonville, IN 47130; tel. 812/288–0700; FAX. 812/285–8111; Nanci Brill, Hospice Director

Vencare Hospice of Indiana, 2601 Fortune Circle East Drive, Suite 105B, Indianapolis, IN 46241; tel. 317/484–9400; FAX. 317/484–9500; Marita Barthuly, Administrator

Visiting Nurse Association Hospice, 610 East Walnut Street, P.O. Box 3487, Evansville, IN 47734–3487; tel. 800/326–4862; FAX. 812/463–4300; Carole Mattingly, Client Services Supervisor

Visiting Nurse Association of Northwest Indiana, Inc., 201 West 89th Avenue, Merrillville, IN 46410–6283; tel. 219/769–3644; FAX. 219/756–7372; Susan Rehrer, Executive Director

Visiting Nurse Hospice, 2323 Shoshone Court, Lafayette, IN 47905; tel. 317/474–7677; FAX. 317/474–72; John Ammerman, Administrator

Visiting Nurse Service Hospice of Central Indiana, 4701 North Keystone Avenue, Indianapolis, IN 46205; tel. 317/722–8200; FAX. 317/722–8223; Scott A. Himelstein, Administrator

Visiting Nurse Service and Hospice, Inc., 3015 South Wayne Avenue, Fort Wayne, IN 46807; tel. 219/456–9888, ext. 232; FAX. 219/458–3089; Karen Gardner, President

Vitas Healthcare Corporation, 5240 Fountain Drive, Suite E, Crown Point, IN 46307; tel. 219/736–8921; FAX. 219/736–0972; Jay Koeper, General Manager

IOWA

Beacon of Hope Hospice Inc., 3906 Lillie, Suite Six, Davenport, IA 52806; tel. 319/391–6933; FAX. 319/391–5104; Edward Lowe, Administrator

Bremer–Butler Hospice, 406 West Bremer Avenue, Suites C and D, Waverly, IA 50677; tel. 319/352–1274; FAX. 319/352–9001; Rod Meyer, Administrator

Calhoun County HHA/Hospice, 515 Court Street, P.O. Box 71, Rockwell City, IA 50579; tel. 712/297–8323; FAX. 712/297–5309; Jane E. Condon, Administrator

Cedar Valley Hospice, 2101 Kimball Avenue, Suite 401, Waterloo, IA 50702; tel. 319/292–1450; FAX. 319/292–1256; Cheryl A. Hoerner, Executive Director

Community Hospice of Iowa, 508 East Broadway, Council Bluffs, IA 51503; tel. 712/325–1751; FAX. 712/325–1895; Barbara Coppa, Administrator

Hamilton County PHNS–Hospice Division, 821 Seneca Street, Webster City, IA 50595; tel. 515/832–9565; FAX. 515/832–9554; Jacqueline Butler, Administrator

Heartland Hospice, 2301 Eastern Ave., Red Oak, IA 51566; tel. 712/623–7227; Rick J. Leinen, Administrator

Homeward Hospice, 1506 South Duff, Ames, IA 50010; tel. 515/233–1960; FAX. 515/233–7556; Kimberly Russell, Administrator

Hospice of Cass County, 1501 East Tenth Street, Atlantic, IA 50022; tel. 712/243–3250; Patricia A. Markham, Administrator

Hospice of Central Iowa, 3619 1/2 Douglas Avenue, Des Moines, IA 50310; tel. 515/274–3400; FAX. 515/271–1302; William P. Havekost, President, Chief Executive Officer

Hospice of Comfort, 709 West Main Street, Manchester, IA 52057; tel. 319/927–7303; Lon D. Butikoker, Administrator

Hospice of Compassion, 406 Court, P.O. Box 1034, Williamsburg, IA 52361–1034; tel. 319/668–2262; FAX. 319/668–1656; Carole Moore, Executive Director

Hospice of Dubuque, 3448 Hillcrest Road, Dubuque, IA 52002; tel. 319/582–1220; FAX. 319/582–8089; Barbara Zoeller, Director

Hospice of Grinnell, 210 Fourth Ave., Grinnell, IA 50112; tel. 515/236–7511; Todd C. Linden, Administrator

Hospice of Lee County, Lee County Health Department–Community Nursing, 2218 Avenue H, Fort Madison, IA 52627; tel. 319/372–5225; FAX. 319/372–4374; M. Therese O'Brien, Administrator

Hospice of Mahaska County, 1229 C Avenue, E., Oskaloosa, IA 52577; tel. 515/672–3100; David E. Rutter, Administrator

Hospice of North Iowa, 232 Second Street, S.E., Mason City, IA 50401; tel. 515/423–3508; FAX. 515/423–5250; Ann MacGregor, Administrator

Hospice of Northwest Iowa, 1200 First Avenue East, Spencer, IA 51301; tel. 712/264–6380; FAX. 712/264–6470; Sheryl Thu, Director

Hospice of Pella, 404 Jefferson Street, Pella, IA 50219; tel. 515/628–6644; Robert D. Kroese, Administrator

Hospice of Siouxland, 224 Fourth Street, Sioux City, IA 51101; tel. 712/233–1298; FAX. 712/233–1123; Linda Todd, Hospice Director

Hospice of VNA, 242 North Bluff Boulevard, Clinton, IA 52732; tel. 319/242–7165; FAX. 319/242–7197; Laurie Engleking, Administrator

Hospice of Wapello County, 312 East Alta Vista, Ottumwa, IA 52501; tel. 515/682–0684; FAX. 515/684–9209; Cindy Donohue, RN, B.S.N., Director

Hospice of the Midlands, 800 Mercy Drive, Council Bluffs, IA 51502; tel. 515/328–5106; Denise McNitt, Administrator

Humboldt County PHNS and Hospice, Home Care Connection, Courthouse, Dakota City, IA 50529; tel. 515/332–2492; FAX. 515/332–4756; Janna Emick, Administrator

Iowa City Hospice, Inc., 613 Bloomington Street, Iowa City, IA 52245; tel. 319/351–5665; FAX. 319/351–5729; Maggie Elliott, Executive Director

Iowa River Hospice, Inc., 206 West Church Street, Marshalltown, IA 50158; tel. 515/753–7704; FAX. 515/753–0379; Brent D. Blackwell, Executive Director

Mercy Hospice, 1055 Sixth Avenue, Suite 105, Des Moines, IA 50314; tel. 515/247–8383

Wings of Hope Hospice, Northwest Iowa Home Health Care and Hospice, 160 South Hayes Avenue, Primghar, IA 51245; tel. 712/757–0060; FAX. 712/757–0060; Beverly Van Beek, Executive Director

KANSAS

Central Homecare and Hospice, Inc., 427 S.E. Second, P.O. Box 645, Newton, KS 67114; tel. 316/283–8220; FAX. 316/283–8576; Robert E. Carlton, Executive Director

Community Hospice, 100 West Eighth Street, Onaga, KS 66521; tel. 913/889–7200; FAX. 913/889–4808; Mary Abitz, Director

Community Hospice of Kansas, 1650 South Georgetown, Suite 160, Wichita, KS 67218; tel. 316/686–5999; FAX. 316/686–5634; Karen Everhart, M.Ed., Director

Homecare and Hospice, Inc., 323 Poyntz Avenue, Suite A, Manhattan, KS 66502; tel. 913/537–0688; FAX. 913/537–1309; Pam Oehme, Director, Health Services

Hospice Care in Douglas County, 336 Missouri, Lower Level, Lawrence, KS 66044; tel. 913/749–5006; FAX. 913/843–0757; L. Kay Metzger, Director

Hospice Inc., 313 South Market, P.O. Box 3267, Wichita, KS 67202–3267; tel. 316/265–9441; FAX. 316/265–6066; John G. Carney, President

Hospice Services, Inc., 424 Eighth Street, P.O. Box 116, Phillipsburg, KS 67661; tel. 913/543–2900; FAX. 913/543–5688; Sandy Kuhlman

Hospice of Golden Belt HHS, 3623 Broadway, Great Bend, KS 67530; tel. 316/792–8171; Gayle Edwards

Hospice of Jefferson County, 1212 Walnut, Highway 59, P.O. Box 324, Oskaloosa, KS 66066–0275; tel. 913/863–2447; FAX. 913/863–2652; Marilyn Zieg, RN, Hospice Coordinator

Hospice of NE Kansas Multi–County, 326 East Ninth Street, Holton, KS 66436; tel. 913/364–4921; FAX. 913/364–3001; Patricia Scott, RN

Hospice of Reno County, Inc., Three Compound Drive, Hutchinson, KS 67502; tel. 316/665–2473; FAX. 316/669–5959; Carolyn Carter, RN, M.N., Executive Director

Hospice of Salina, Inc., 333 South Santa Fe, P.O. Box 2238, Salina, KS 67402–2238; tel. 913/825–1717; FAX. 913/825–4949; Kim Fair, Executive Director

Hospice of the Flint Hills, 527 Commercial, Suite 501, P.O. Box 102, Emporia, KS 66801; tel. 316/342–6640; FAX. 316/342–9424; Jay O'Daniel, Interim Director

Hospice of the Heartland, Inc., 400 West Eighth, Suite 207, P.O. Box 21, Beloit, KS 67420; tel. 913/738–9227; FAX. 913/738–9227; Robert Monty, Executive Director

Hospice of the Prairie, Inc., 2010 A First Avenue, P.O. Box 1294, Dodge City, KS 67801–2623; tel. 316/227–7209; FAX. 316/227–7429; Jeannie Reinert–Schuette, Executive Director

Leavenworth County Hospice, 920 Sixth Avenue, Leavenworth, KS 66048; tel. 913/684–1305; Charles L. Rogers

Midland Hospice Care, Inc., 200 Southwest Frazier Circle, Topeka, KS 66606–2800; tel. 913/232–2044; FAX. 913/232–5567; Karren Weichert, Executive Director

Ottawa County Home Health/Hospice Agency, 307 North Concord, Suite 200, Minneapolis, KS 67467; tel. 913/392–2822; June Clark, RN

SCCS Home Health and Hospice, P.A., 1410 North Woodlawn, Suite D, Derby, KS 67037; tel. 316/788–7626; FAX. 316/788–7072; Cheryl Pelaccio, RN, Administrator

South Wind Hospice, Inc., 337 North Pine, P.O. Box 862, Pratt, KS 67124; tel. 316/672–7553; FAX. 316/672–7554; Diane L. Johnson, Director

Southwest Homecare and Hospice, 103 East 11th Street, Liberal, KS 67901; tel. 316/629–2456; FAX. 316/629–2453, ext. 509; Ida Rodkey, Administrator

KENTUCKY

Community Hospice, 1538 Carter Avenue, Ashland, KY 41101; tel. 606/329–1890; FAX. 606/329–0018; Susan Hunt, Administrator

Cumberland Valley District Health Department Hospice, 102 South Court Street, Manchester, KY 40962; tel. 606/287–8437; Dottie Dunsil, RN, Nursing Supervisor

Green River Hospice, P.O. Box 449, Calhoun, KY 42327; tel. 502/273–3486; FAX. 502/273–9794; Jeana Bamberger, Patient Care Coordinator

Heritage Hospice, 337 West Broadway, P.O. Box 1213, Danville, KY 40422; tel. 606/236–2425; FAX. 606/236–6152; Janelle Lane, Executive Director

Hospice Association, Inc., 2225 Frederica Street, P.O. Box 1403, Owensboro, KY 42301; tel. 502/926–7565; FAX. 502/926–1223; Linda Domerese, Ph.D., Executive Director

Hospice East, 24 West Lexington Avenue, P.O. Box 115, Winchester, KY 40392; tel. 606/744–9866; FAX. 606/744–1971; Carol Richardson, Director

Hospice of Big Sandy, 236 College Street, Paintsville, KY 41240–1747; tel. 606/789–3841; FAX. 667/789–1527; Claire Arsenault, Executive Director

Hospice of Central Kentucky, 105 Diecks Drive, P.O. Box 2149, Elizabethtown, KY 42701–2444; tel. 502/737–6300; FAX. 502/737–4053; Stephen Connor, Ph.D., Director

Hospice of Hope, One West McDonald Parkway, Maysville, KY 41056; tel. 606/564–4848; FAX. 606/564–7615; Norman McRae, Chief Executive Officer

Hospice of Lake Cumberland, 108 College Street, P.O. Box 651, Somerset, KY 42502; tel. 606/679–4389; FAX. 606/678–0191; Jeanne Travis, Executive Director

Hospice of Louisville, 3532 Ephraim McDowell Drive, Louisville, KY 40205–3224; tel. 502/456–6200; FAX. 502/456–6655; Helen Donaldson, Executive Director

Hospice of Nelson County, 111 N. Third, Bardstown, KY 40004; tel. 502/348–3660; FAX. 502/349–1292; Sharon Bade, Administrator

Hospice of Pike County, 229 College Street, Pikeville, KY 41501; tel. 606/432–2112; FAX. 606/432–4631; Sharon Branham, President, Chief Executive Officer

Hospice of Southern Kentucky, 1027 Broadway, Bowling Green, KY 42104; tel. 502/782–3402; FAX. 502/782–3496; Connie Jones, Director of Program Development and Volunteers

Hospice of the Bluegrass, 2312 Alexandria Drive, Lexington, KY 40504; tel. 606/276–5344; FAX. 606/223–0490; Gretchen M. Brown, President, Chief Executive Officer

Hospice of the Kentucky River, Inc., 210 St. George Street, Richmond, KY 40475–2376; tel. 606/624–8820; FAX. 606/624–9230; Gail McGillis, M.S.N., Chief Executive Officer

Jessamine County Hospice, 109 Shannon Parkway, P.O. Box 873, Nicholasville, KY 40356; tel. 606/887–2696; FAX. 606/885–1474; Susan G. Swinford, M.S.W., Executive Director

Lourdes Hospice, 2855 Jackson Street, Paducah, KY 42001; tel. 502/444–2262; FAX. 502/444–2380; Donna Stewart, Administrator

Mountain Community Hospice, P.O. Box 1234, Hazard, KY 41702; tel. 606/439–2111; FAX. 606/439–4198; Amy Asher, RN, Director

Mountain Heritage Hospice, Inc., 163 Belkway, Village Center, Building Two, P.O. Box 189, Harlan, KY 40831–0189; tel. 606/573–6111; FAX. 606/573–7964; Bernice Reynolds, Administrator

Pennyroyal Hospice, Inc., 1821 East Ninth Street, Suite A, Hopkinsville, KY 42240; tel. 502/885–6428; FAX. 502/889–5005; Hanna Sabel, Executive Director

St. Anthony's Hospice, Inc., 2410 South Green Street, P.O. Box 351, Henderson, KY 42420; tel. 502/826–2326; FAX. 502/831–2169; Rebecca S. Curry, Administrator

Tri County Hospice, P.O. Box 395, London, KY 40741; tel. 606/877–3950; Ed Valentine

LOUISIANA

Alternative Care Hospice, P.O. Box 691, Coushatta, LA 71019; tel. 318/932–8855; Faye Ross, Director

Alternative Hospice Care, Inc., 4560 North Boulevard, Suite 103, Baton Rouge, LA 70806; tel. 504/926–1550; Glenn Adams

American Hospice of Louisiana, Inc., 3340 Severn Avenue, Suite 215, Metairie, LA 70002; tel. 504/887–8128; FAX. 504/887–8206; Pat McCue, General Manager

Community Hospice of Bossier Medical Center, 2285 Benton Road, Suite 201D, Bossier City, LA 71111; tel. 318/741–6032; FAX. 318/747–0142; Linda McMillan, Director

Community Hospice of Louisiana, Inc., 5647 Superior Drive, Baton Rouge, LA 70816; tel. 504/293–1948; Frank Reuter, Program Director

Friendship Hospice of New Orleans, Inc., 1406 Esplanade Avenue, New Orleans, LA 70116; tel. 504/522–3183; Valarie Davis, Administrator

Golden Age Hospice, 5627 South Sherwood Forest Boulevard, Baton Rouge, LA 70816; tel. 504/292–2000; Martha C. Sewell

Good Shepherd in Hospice, Inc., 327 North Canal Boulevard, P.O. Box 1223, Thibodaux, LA 70302–1223; tel. 504/448–2200; Barbara Lofton

Hancock Hospice, P.O. Box 329, Tallulah, LA 71282–0329; tel. 318/574–2240; Ronald Hancock

Hospice Home Care of Lake Charles Memorial Hospital, 3050 Aster Street, Lake Charles, LA 70601; tel. 318/494–6444; FAX. 318/494–6451; Cyntia Clark, Administrator

Hospice Managed Care, Inc., 1423 Peterman Drive, Alexandria, LA 71301; tel. 318/442–5002; FAX. 318/442–5009; Susan Stephens, Administrator

Hospice of Acadiana, Inc., 125 South Buchanan, P.O. Box 3467, Lafayette, LA 70501; tel. 318/232-1234; FAX. 318/232-1297; Nelson Waguespack, Jr., Executive Director

Hospice of Greater Baton Rouge, 8322 One Calais Avenue, Suite A, Baton Rouge, LA 70809-3412; tel. 504/767-4673; FAX. 504/769-8113; Kathryn Grigsby, Executive Director

Hospice of Greater New Orleans, 3616 South I-10 Service Road, Suite 109, New Orleans, LA 70001; tel. 504/838-8944; FAX. 504/838-9034; Jo-Ann Mueller, Chief Executive Officer

Hospice of Jefferson, 3715 Williams Blvd., Suite 240, Kenner, LA 70062; tel. 504/464-7357; FAX. 504/466-9482; Tracy McCann, Administrator

Hospice of Louisiana, 2915 Missouri Avenue, Shreveport, LA 71109; tel. 318/632-4697; FAX. 318/632-2382; Peggy Gavin, Hospice Administrative Representative

Hospice of Saint Landry, P.O. Box 488, Palmetto, LA 71358; tel. 318/623-3404; FAX. 318/623-3414; Dorothy Rabalais, RN, Director, Patient Services

Hospice of Shreveport/Bossier, 910 Pierremont, Suite 107, Shreveport, LA 71106; tel. 318/865-7177; Susan P. Stephens

Hospice of South Louisiana, 210 Mystic Boulevard, Houma, LA 70360; tel. 504/851-4273; FAX. 504/872-6543; Dottie Landry, RN, Administration

Hospice of Southwest Louisiana, 1000 South Huntington, Suite C, Sulphur, LA 70663; tel. 318/528-3011; FAX. 318/528-3035; Gail Hale, RN

Hospice of St. Jude, 615 Baronne Street, Suite 300 A, New Orleans, LA 70113; tel. 504/522-7108; Charles C. Harding

Hospice of St. Luke, 237 North Second Street, Eunice, LA 70535; tel. 800/869-2067; Willadean McWhorter, Administrator

Metro Hospice Care, Inc., 714 St. John, Monroe, LA 71201; tel. 318/361-9000; FAX. 318/361-9047; Deeni Shannon, Administrator

North Shore Regional Medical Center Hospice, 104 Smart Place, Slidell, LA 70458; tel. 504/641-7373; FAX. 504/641-4772; Aubrey Price, Director

Peoples Hospice, 1743 Stumpf Boulevard, Gretna, LA 70056; tel. 504/364-1494; FAX. 504/362-1056; Maggie Faucheux, RN, Administrator

Red River Hospice, Inc., 5501 John Eskew Drive, Alexandria, LA 71303; tel. 318/443-5694; E. W. Parker, Administrator

Samaritan Care Hospice of Louisiana, 3000 Knight Street, Suite 3000, Shreveport, LA 71105; tel. 318/869-2722; FAX. 318/869-2744; Toni Camp, Administrator

MAINE

Androscoggin Home Health Services, 15 Strawberry Avenue, P.O. Box 819, Lewiston, ME 04243-0819; tel. 207/777-7740; Richard C. Stephenson, M.D., Medical Director

Community Health And Nursing Services, d/b/a CHANS Hospice Care, 50 Baribeau Drive, Brunswick, ME 04011; tel. 207/729-6782; FAX. 207/725-5640; Julianna L'Heureux, Executive Director

Community Health Services, Inc., 901 Washington Avenue, Suite 104, Portland, ME 04103; tel. 207/775-7231; FAX. 207/775-5520; Robert P. Liversidge, Jr., President, Chief Executive Officer

HealthReach Hospice, Eight Highwood Street, P.O. Box 1568, Waterville, ME 04903-1568; tel. 207/873-1127; FAX. 207/873-2059; Rebecca K. Colwell, Vice President, Home Care

Hospice Volunteers of Kennebec Valley, 150 Dresden Avenue, (First floor, KVMC), Gardiner, ME 04345; tel. 207/626-1779; FAX. 207/626-1798; Barbara Bell, Director

Hospice Volunteers of Waldo County, 118 Northport Avenue, P.O. Box 772, Belfast, ME 04915; tel. 207/338-2268, ext. 119; Michael L. Weaver, RN, Volunteer Coordinator

Hospice Volunteers of Waterville Area, 76 Silver Street, Waterville, ME 04901; tel. 207/873-3615; Susan Hermann-McMorrow, Program Coordinator

Hospice of Aroostook, Route 89 Access Highway, P.O. Box 688, Caribou, ME 04736; tel. 207/498-2578; FAX. 207/493-3111; Saundra Scott-Adams, Executive Director

Hospice of Hancock County, 29 Union Street, P.O. Box 224, Ellsworth, ME 04605; tel. 207/667-2531; FAX. 207/667-9406; Vesta Kowalski, Administrative Director

Hospice of Maine, 693 Rear Congress Street, Portland, ME 04102-3303; tel. 207/774-4417; Martha Wooten, Acting Executive Director

Hospice of Mid Coast Maine, 29 Parkview Circle, Brunswick, ME 04011-0741; tel. 207/729-3602; Gary Araujo, Executive Director

Kno-Wal-Lin Coastal Family Hospice, 170 Pleasant Street, Rockland, ME 04841; tel. 207/594-9561; FAX. 207/594-2527; Kathleen Deupree, RN, Patient Care Coordinator

Miles Home Health Hospice Division, R.R. Two, P.O. Box 4500, Damariscotta, ME 04543-8903; tel. 207/563-4592; FAX. 207/563-8652; Carol Knipping, Executive Director

New Hope Hospice, Inc., Route 46, Eddington, ME 04429; tel. 207/843-7521; Nancy S. Burgess, Director

Pine Tree Hospice, 65 West Main Street, Dover-Foxcroft, ME 04426; tel. 207/564-8401, ext. 346; Theresa Boettner, Program Coordinator

Southern Maine Health and Homecare Services, Route One South, P.O. Box 739, Kennebunk, ME 04043; tel. 207/985-4767; FAX. 207/985-6715; Elaine Brady, Executive Director

Tri-Area Visiting Nurse Association, Inc., 301 High Street, Somersworth, NH 03878-1800; tel. 603/692-2112; FAX. 603/692-9940; Susan Karmeris, President/Chief Executive Officer

Visiting Nurse Association and Hospice, 50 Foden Road, South Portland, ME 04106; tel. 207/780-8624; FAX. 207/756-8676; Delthia Vilasuso, Executive Director

Visiting Nurse Service of Southern Maine, 15 Industrial Park Road, Saco, ME 04072; tel. 207/284-4566; FAX. 207/282-4148; Maryanna Arsenault, Chief Executive Officer

MARYLAND

Bay Area Hospice, Inc., 410 West Lombard Street, Suite 602, Baltimore, MD 21201; tel. 410/328-1160; FAX. 410/328-1165; Karen L. Holland, Director

Bon Secours Home Health/Hospice, 1502 Joh Avenue, Suite 190, Baltimore, MD 21227; tel. 410/837-8500; FAX. 410/536-9739; Vic Ribaudo, Acting Executive Director

Calvert Hospice, 238 Merrimac Court, P.O. Box 838, Prince Frederick, MD 20678; tel. 410/535-0892; FAX. 301/855-1226; Carolyn S. Lewis, Executive Director

Caroline County Home Health/Hospice, 601 North Sixth Street, P.O. Box 10, Denton, MD 21629; tel. 410/479-3500; FAX. 410/479-3425; L. Carol Smith, Administrator

Carroll Hospice, 95 Carroll Street, Westminster, MD 21157; tel. 410/857-1838; Marie Bossie, Executive Director

Children's Hospice Services, 111 Michigan Avenue, N.W., Washington, DC 20010; tel. 202/884-4663; FAX. 202/884-6950

Coastal Hospice, Inc., 2604 Old Ocean City Road, P.O. Box 1733, Salisbury, MD 21802-1733; tel. 410/742-6044; FAX. 410/548-5669; Marion F. Keenan, President

Dorchester County Home Health Hospice, 751 Woods Road, Cambridge, MD 21613; tel. 410/228-5860; FAX. 410/228-4475; Joyce T. Hyde, RN, M.S., Director

Harford Hospice, Inc., 56 East Bel Air Avenue, Aberdeen, MD 21001-3759; tel. 410/272-2266; FAX. 410/272-8413; Barry E. Yingling, President, Chief Executive Officer

Holy Cross Home Care and Hospice, 9805 Dameron Drive, Silver Spring, MD 20902; tel. 301/754-7740; FAX. 301/754-7743; Margaret Hadley, Assistant Director

Hospice Caring, Inc., Volunteer Hospice, 707 Conservation Lane, Suite 100, Gaithersburg, MD 20878; tel. 301/869-4673; FAX. 301/869-4673; Carol Sheehan, Executive Director

Hospice Services of Howard County, 5537 Twin Knoll Road, Suite 433, Columbia, MD 21045; tel. 410/730-5072; FAX. 410/730-5284; Nancy Weber

Hospice of Baltimore, Gilchrist Center for Hospice Care, 6601 North Charles Street, Baltimore, MD 21204; tel. 410/512-8200; FAX. 410/512-8284; Regina Bodnar, Director, Clinical Services

Hospice of Charles County, 105 La Grange Avenue, P.O. Box 1703, LaPlata, MD 20646; tel. 301/934-1268; FAX. 301/934-6437; Geri Firosz, President

Hospice of Frederick County, 1730 North Market Street, P.O. Box 1799, Frederick, MD 21702; tel. 301/694-6444; FAX. 301/694-9012; Laurel A. Cucchi, Executive Director

Hospice of Garrett County, 2008 Maryland Highway, P.O. Box 271, Mountain Lake Park, MD 21550; tel. 301/334-5151; FAX. 301/334-5800; Brenda Butscher, Executive Director

Hospice of Prince George's County, 96 Harry Truman Drive, Largo, MD 20774; tel. 301/499-0550; FAX. 301/350-7844; Lois Kimber, Director, Nursing Services

Hospice of Queen Anne's, Inc., 206 North Commerce Street, P.O. Box 179, Centreville, MD 21617; tel. 410/758-3043; FAX. 410/758-2838; Mildred H. Barnette, Director

Hospice of St. Mary's, Inc., 100 Courthouse Drive, Leonardtown, MD 20650; tel. 301/475-2023; FAX. 301/475-3497; Dana McGarity, Executive Director

Hospice of Washington County, 101 East Baltimore Street, Hagerstown, MD 21740; tel. 301/791-6360; FAX. 301/791-6579; Robert Rauch, Executive Director

Hospice of the Chesapeake, Inc., 8424 Veterans Highway, Millersville, MD 21108; tel. 410/987-2003; FAX. 410/987-3961; Erwin E. Abrams, President

Jewish Social Service Agency, 22 C Montgomery Village Avenue, Gaithersburg, MD 20879; tel. 301/990-6880; Joanne Nattrass, Director

Joseph Richey Hospice, 828 North Eutaw Street, Baltimore, MD 21201; tel. 410/523-2150; FAX. 410/523-1146; Suzanne Hetzer, RN, Director, Patient Services

Kent Home Health/Hospice, 125 South Lynchburg Street, P.O. Box 359, Chestertown, MD 21620; tel. 410/778-1050; FAX. 410/778-7399; Karen Russum, RN, Director

Mid-Atlantic Hospice Care, 4805 Benson Avenue, Baltimore, MD 21227; tel. 410/247-2900; FAX. 410/247-2581; Darlene Tamburri

Montgomery Hospice Society, 1450 Research Boulevard, Suite 310, Rockville, MD 20850; tel. 301/279-2566; Ann Mitchell, Executive Director

Northern Chesapeake Hospice, Inc., 239 South Bridge Street, Suite Two, Elkton, MD 21921; tel. 410/392-4742; FAX. 410/392-6448; Cathy Stauffer Kimble, Executive Director

Stella Maris Hospice Care Program, 2300 Dulaney Valley Road, Towson, MD 21204; tel. 410/252-4500; FAX. 410/560-9675; Sister Karen McNally, R.S.M., Chief Operating Officer

Talbot County Home Health/Hospice, 100 South Hanson Street, Easton, MD 21601; tel. 410/822-3855; FAX. 410/822-2583; Gloria W. Dill, RN, MS, Nurse Manager

Tri-Home Health Care and Services, 2000 Rock Springs Road, P.O. Box 240, Forest Hills, MD 21050; tel. 410/893-0544; Susan Parks, RN, Hospice Coordinator

VNA Hospice of Maryland L.L.C., 6000 Metro Drive, Suite 101, Baltimore, MD 21215; tel. 410/358-7300; FAX. 410/358-7326; Janet Melancon, RN, Hospice Director

MASSACHUSETTS

Bay State Health Care Center South Shore, 780 Main Street, South Weymouth, MA 02190

Cranberry Area Hospice, Inc., 161 Summer Street, Kingston, MA 02364-1224; tel. 617/585-1881; FAX. 617/585-1898; John A. Brennan, Executive Director

Diversified VNA Hospice, 316 Nichols Road, Fitchburg, MA 01420; tel. 508/342-6013; FAX. 508/343-5629; Noreen Basque, Administrator

Good Samaritan Hospice, Inc., 310 Allston Street, Brighton, MA 02146; tel. 617/566-6242; FAX. 617/566-3055; Leo P. Smith, Executive Director

Hampshire County Hospice, Inc., Seven Denniston Place, P.O. Box 1087, Northampton, MA 01061; tel. 413/586-8288; FAX. 413/584-9615; Joan Keochakian, Executive Director

HealthCare Dimensions, 254 South Street, Waltham, MA 02154-2707; tel. 617/894-1100; FAX. 617/736-0908; Patricia A. Field, Executive Director

Hospice Care of Greater Taunton, One Taunton Green, Taunton, MA 02780; tel. 508/822-1447; Joanne Smith, Vice President, Clinical Services

Hospice Care, Inc., 41 Montvale Avenue, Stoneham, MA 02180; tel. 781/279-4100; FAX. 781/279-4677; Kathleen Colburn, Interim Executive Director

Hospice Community Care, 495 Pleasant Street, Winthrop, MA 02152

Hospice Life Care, P.O. Box 10428, Holyoke, MA 01041; tel. 413/533-3923; FAX. 413/536-4513; Patricia Cavanaugh, Director

Hospice Outreach, Inc., 243 Forest Street, Fall River, MA 02721; tel. 508/673-1589; FAX. 508/677-3144; Linda Valley, Executive Director

Hospice of Boston and Hospice of Greater Brockton, 500 Belmont Street, Suite 215, Brockton, MA 02401; tel. 508/583-0383; FAX. 508/583-1193; Ruth Capernaros, Executive Director

Hospice of Cape Cod, Inc., 923 Route 6A, Yarmouthport, MA 02675; tel. 508/362-1103; FAX. 508/362-6885; Marilyn Hannus, RN, Director

Hospice of Central Massachusetts, Inc., 120 Thomas Street, Worcester, MA 01608; tel. 508/756-7176

Hospice of Community Health Services, 423 Main Street, Athol, MA 01331; tel. 508/249-5366

Hospice of Community Nurse Association, 40 Centre Street, P.O. Box 831, Fairhaven, MA 02719; tel. 508/999-3400; FAX. 508/999-6401; Brenda M. Van Laarhoven, RN, Supervisor

Hospice of Community Visiting Nurse Agency, 141 Park Street, Attleboro, MA 02703; tel. 800/220-0110; FAX. 508/226-8939; Kathleen M. Trier, Executive Director

Hospice of Greater Milford, 391 South Main Street, P.O. Box 122, Hopedale, MA 01747; tel. 508/634-8382; FAX. 508/634-8738; Renee Merolli, RN, M.A., Director

Hospice of Northern Berkshire, Inc. at CompCare, 46 Howland Avenue, Adams, MA 01220; tel. 413/743-2960; FAX. 413/743-1515; Camille Richards, Executive Director

Hospice of the Good Shepherd, 2042 Beacon Street, Waban, MA 02168; tel. 617/969-6130; FAX. 617/928-1450; Ellen Rudikoff, Ph.D., Executive Director

Hospice of the North Shore, Inc., 10 Elm Street, Danvers, MA 01923; tel. 508/774-7566; FAX. 508/774-4389; Diane Stringer, Executive Director

Hospice of the South Shore, P.O. Box 334, 100 Bay State Drive, Braintree, MA 02184

HospiceCare of the Berkshires, Inc., 235 East Street, Pittsfield, MA 01201; tel. 413/443-2994; FAX. 413/433-7814; Peter Briguglio, Executive Director

Lighthouse Hospice Association, Inc., 166 Main Street, P.O. Box 448, Wareham, MA 02571-0448; tel. 508/295-8544; FAX. 508/295-0930; Phyllis G. Pheeney, Executive Director

Merrimack Valley Hospice, Inc., One Water Street, Haverhill, MA 01830; tel. 508/470-1615; FAX. 508/470-4690; Raymond Brockill, Director

Neponset Valley Hospice, Inc., Three Edgewater Drive, Norwood, MA 02062; tel. 617/769-8282; FAX. 617/762-0718; Susan DiBona, Hospice Manager

Old Colony Hospice, Inc., 14 Page Terrace, Stoughton, MA 02072; tel. 617/341-4145; FAX. 617/297-7345; Analee Wulfhuhle, Executive Director

Staff Builders Hospice Program, 529 Main Street, Suite 1M07, Boston, MA 02129; tel. 617/242-4872; FAX. 617/241-2880; Victoria Gunfolino, Director

Trinity Hospice of Greater Boston, Inc., 111 Cypress Street, Brookline, MA 02146

VNA Care Choices, Inc., 245 Winter Street, Suite 110, Waltham, MA 02154; tel. 617/890-2931; FAX. 617/890-6627; Patricia O'Brien, M.S., RN, Executive Director, VNA Care Choices, Inc.

VNA of Greater Gardner Hospice, 34 Pearly Lane, Gardner, MA 01440; tel. 508/632-1230; FAX. 508/632-4513; Tina Griffin, Director

Visiting Nurse Association and Hospice of Pioneer Valley, Inc., 50 Maple Street, P.O. Box 9058, Springfield, MA 01102-9058; tel. 413/781-5070; FAX. 413/781-3342; Maureen Skipper, President

Visiting Nurse Association of Greater Lowell Hospice, 336 Central Street, P.O. Box 1965, Lowell, MA 01853-1965; tel. 508/459-9343; FAX. 508/459-0981; Nancy L. Pettinelli, Executive Director

Visiting Nurse Association of Middlesex-East and Affiliated Visiting Nurse Hospice, 12 Beacon Street, Stoneham, MA 02180; tel. 617/438-3770; FAX. 617/438-7994; Jacquelyn Galluzzi, Chief Executive Officer

Wayside Hospice/Parmenter Health Services, 266 Cochituate Road, Wayland, MA 01778; tel. 508/358-3000; FAX. 508/358-3005; Edith L. Murray, Director

Westhills Home Health and Hospice, Inc., 77 Mill Street, Suite 207, Westfield, MA 01085; tel. 413/562-7049; FAX. 413/568-9434; Jacqueline Schmitz, RNC, Hospice Director

MICHIGAN

Allen Hospice–Southfield, 26300 Telegraph Road, Suite 102, Southfield, MI 48034; tel. 810/948-1019; Annette F. Sherry, Executive Director

Andy Scholett Memorial, 12426 State Street, P.O. Box 587, Atlanta, MI 49709-0587; tel. 517/785-3134; FAX. 517/785-2834; Shirley Burnham, Executive Director

Angela Hospice Home Care, Inc. and Care Center, 14100 Newburgh Road, Livonia, MI 48154-5010; tel. 313/464-7810; FAX. 313/464-6930; Mary Giovanni, Administrator

Arbor Hospice, Home Care and Care-ousel, 7445 Allen Road, Suite 230, Allen Park, MI 48101; tel. 313/383-8800; FAX. 313/383-0115; Mary Lindquist, Administrator

Arcadia Hospice, Inc., 340 East Big Beaver, Suite 250, Troy, MI 48083; tel. 810/740-1400; FAX. 810/740-8726; Kristen Olson, Administrator

Baraga County Hospice, Inc., 913 Meador Street, L'Anse, MI 49946; tel. 906/524-5168

Barry Community Hospice, A Division of Good Samaritan Hospice Care, Inc., 450 Meadow Run Drive, Suite 200, P.O. Box 308, Hastings, MI 49058; tel. 616/948-8452; FAX. 616/948-9545; Kay Rowley, Patient Care Coordinator

Barry–Eaton District Health Department – Hospice Program, 528 Beech Street, Charlotte, MI 48813; tel. 517/543-2430; FAX. 517/541-2612; Penny Pierce, RN, Director

Blue Water Hospices, Inc., 1422 Lyon Street, Port Huron, MI 48060; tel. 313/982-8809; FAX. 313/984-1612; Brenda K. Clark, Vice President, Operations

Branch–Hillsdale–St. Joseph District, Health Department Hospice, 809 Marshall Road, Coldwater, MI 49036; tel. 517/279-5961; FAX. 517/278-2923; Helen Jakstas, RN, B.S.N., M.P.H., Director

Branch–Hillside–St. Joseph DHD, 600 South Lakeview, Sturgis, MI 49091; tel. 616/659-4013; Duke Anderson

Cass Branch Hospice Program, 201 M–62 North, Cassopolis, MI 49031; tel. 616/445-2296; Jill Eldred

Cass County Hospice, Inc., 58253 M52, Cassopolis, MI 49031; tel. 616/782-5078; Jean Maile, Administrator

Charlevoix County Hospice, 601 Bridge Street, East Jordan, MI 49727; tel. 616/536-2842; FAX. 616/536-7150; Margaret Lasater

Citizens for Hospice, 27 East Chicago Street, Coldwater, MI 49028; tel. 517/278-5903; Sara Semmelroth

Community Home Health and Hospice, G–5095 West Bristol Road, Flint, MI 48507; tel. 810/733-7250; FAX. 810/733-8424; Donna Lloyd, Executive Director

Community Hospice Services, Inc., 32932 Warren Road, Suite 100, Westland, MI 48185; tel. 313/522-4244; FAX. 313/522-2099; Maureen Butrico, Executive Director

Cranbrook Hospice Care, 281 Enterprise Court, Suite 300, Bloomfield, MI 48302-0313; tel. 810/334-6700; FAX. 810/334-7064; Brian Hansen, Director

Dickinson–Iron DHD, 818 Pyle Drive, Kingsford, MI 49801; tel. 906/774-1868; FAX. 906/265-2950; Linda Piper, RNC, M.P.H.

District Health Department, #3, 220 West Garfield Street, Charleviox, MI 49720; tel. 616/547-6523; FAX. 616/547-1164; Gerald Chase, Administrator

Downriver Hospice, Inc., 1545 Kingsway Court, Trenton, MI 48183; tel. 313/671-6343

Genesys Hospice, 7280 South State Road, Goodrich, MI 48438; tel. 810/762-7500; FAX. 810/762-0027; Sandra Lammy, Administrator

Good Samaritan Hospice Care, Inc., 166 East Goodale Avenue, Battle Creek, MI 49017-2728; tel. 561/666-0360, ext. 0; Mary Cunningham, Executive Director

Grancare Hospice Services, 38935 Ann Arbor Road, Livonia, MI 48150; tel. 313/467-8209; FAX. 313/467-7244; Michelle Strait, Administrator

Grand Traverse Area Hospice, 1105 Sixth Street, Traverse City, MI 49684; tel. 616/935-6520; FAX. 616/935-7270; Kay Benisek, Manager

Heartland Hospice, 814 Adams, Suite 109, Bay City, MI 48708; tel. 517/892-0355; FAX. 517/892-0896; Christine Satkowiak, RN, Administrator

Heartland Hospice, 700 West Ash Street, Suite Three–A, Mason, MI 48854; Lynn Howes

Heartland Hospice, 6504 28th Street, S.E., Suite T, Grand Rapids, MI 49546; tel. 616/942-7733

Helping Hands Hospice, 545 Apple Tree Drive, Ionia, MI 48846; tel. 616/527-5550; FAX. 616/527-5683; Becky Mason, RN, Administrator

Henry Ford Hospice–West Bloomfield, 6020 West Maple Road, Suite 500, West Bloomfield, MI 48322; tel. 810/539-0660; FAX. 810/539-8868; Laura Zeile, RN, B.S.N., Manager

Home Health Plus Hospice, 26211 Central Park Boulevard, Suite 110, Southfield, MI 48076; tel. 313/357-3650; Sharon Kohlitz, RN, B.S., Director, Operations

Home Hospice, Inc., 315 Ives, Big Rapids, MI 49307; tel. 616/796-7371; FAX. 616/796-4841; Kathy Shefferly, RN, Director

Hospice Care, Inc., 110 South Clay, Sturgis, MI 49091; tel. 616/651-6255

Hospice at Home, Inc., 2618 West John Beers Road, Stevensville, MI 49127; tel. 616/429-7100; FAX. 616/428-3499; Helen Parrott, Administrator

Hospice for Presque Isle County, 658 South Bradley, Rogers City, MI 49779; tel. 517/734-7200; FAX. 517/734-2059

Hospice of Bay Area, 1460 West Center Avenue, Essexville, MI 48732; tel. 517/895-4750; FAX. 517/895-4701; Christine Chesny

Hospice of Bay Area, 150 Millwood, Caro, MI 48723; tel. 517/672-2094; Christine Chesny

Hospice of Central Michigan, Inc., 210 North Court Street, Suite C, Mt. Pleasant, MI 48858; tel. 517/773-6137; FAX. 517/773-1072; Mary Grenier, Administrator

Hospice of Chippewa County/Chippewa County Health Department, 140 W. Spruce Street, Sault Ste. Marie, MI 49783; tel. 906/635-1568; FAX. 906/635-1701; Rosemary Blashill, Administrator

Hospice of Clinton Memorial and Sparrow, 304 Brush Street, St. Johns, MI 48879; tel. 517/224-5650; FAX. 517/224-1501, ext. 330; Michelle Wiseman, Director

Hospice of Crawford County, P.O. Box Two, Grayling, MI 49738; tel. 517/348-5461

Hospice of Gladwin Area, Inc., 612 North M–18, P.O. Box 557, Gladwin, MI 48624; tel. 517/426-4464; FAX. 517/426-3057; Georgann Schuster, Executive Director

Hospice of Greater Grand Rapids, 1260 Ekhart, N.E., Grand Rapids, MI 49503; tel. 616/454-1426; David G. Zwicky, Program Director

Hospice of Greater Kalamazoo, Inc., 301 West Cedar Street, Kalamazoo, MI 49007-5106; tel. 616/345-0273; FAX. 616/345-8522; Jean Maile, Administrator

Hospice of Helping Hands, Inc., 801 East Houghton Avenue, P.O. Box 71, West Branch, MI 48661; tel. 517/345-4700; FAX. 517/345-2991; Christopher Lauckner, Director

Hospice of Hillsdale County, 111 South Howell Street, Suite B, Hillsdale, MI 49242; tel. 517/437-5252; FAX. 517/437-5253; Kathryn Aemisegger

Hospice of Holland Home, 2100 Raybrook, S.E., Grand Rapids, MI 49546; tel. 616/285-8020; FAX. 616/235-5111; Karen Bacon Washburn, Director

Hospice of Holland, Inc., 270 Hoover Boulevard, Holland, MI 49423; tel. 616/396-2972; FAX. 616/396-2808; Judith A. Zylman, RN, Executive Director

Hospice of Ionia, 117 North Depot Street, Ionia, MI 48846; tel. 616/527-0681; Bernice Falsetta

Hospice of Jackson, 915 Airport Road, Jackson, MI 49202; tel. 517/783-2648; FAX. 517/783-2674; Michael L. Freytag, M.A., L.P.C., Executive Director

Hospice of Lake County, 4967 Michigan Ave., Baldwin, MI 49304; tel. 616/745-6161; FAX. 616/745-7676; Thomas Nobel, Administrator

Hospice of Lansing, Inc., 6035 Executive Drive, Suite 103, Lansing, MI 48911; tel. 517/882-4500; FAX. 517/882-3010; Barbara A. Kowalski, M.P.A., Executive Director

Hospice of Lenawee, 415 Mill Road, Adrian, MI 49221; tel. 517/263-2323; FAX. 517/263-1279; Susan Engle, Administrator

Hospice of Little Traverse Bay, 416 Connable Avenue, Petoskey, MI 49770; tel. 616/347-9700; FAX. 616/348-4228; Barbara Terry, Administrator

Hospice of Mason County, Inc., 10 Atkinson Drive, Suite Three, Ludington, MI 49431; tel. 616/845-0321; Kathleen Babbin, Administrator

Hospice of Michigan, Crossroads Building, 16250 Northland Drive, Suite 212, Southfield, MI 48075-5200; tel. 810/559-9200; FAX. 810/559-6489; Carolyn Fitzpatrick, Adminstrator

Hospice of Michigan–Roscommon, 107 South Main, P.O. Box 532, Roscommon, MI 48653; tel. 517/275-8967; FAX. 517/275-6130; Sheila Simpson, Program Director

Section C

Hospice of Monroe, 502 West Elm Street, Monroe, MI 48161; tel. 313/457-3220; FAX. 313/457-5060; Paul Doerfler, Administrator

Hospice of Muskegon–Oceana, 1095 Third Street, Suite 209, Muskegon, MI 49441; tel. 616/728-3442; FAX. 616/722-0708; Mary Anne Gorman, Executive Director

Hospice of Muskegon–Oceana, 339B Dewey, Shelby, MI 49455; tel. 616/861-4761; FAX. 616/722-0708

Hospice of Newaygo County, A division of Hospice of Michigan, Inc., 819 West Main Street, Fremont, MI 49412; tel. 616/924-6123; FAX. 616/924-8028; Marie Malone, RN, B.S.N., Hospice Director

Hospice of North Ottawa Community, Inc., 1515 South Despelder, Grand Haven, MI 49417; tel. 616/846-2015; FAX. 616/846-7227; Carolyn K. Howes, Executive Director

Hospice of Northeastern Michigan, Inc., 112 West Chisholm, Alpena, MI 49707; tel. 517/354-5258; Jeraldyne Habermehl, Executive Director

Hospice of Southeast Michigan/Detroit, 2990 West Grand Boulevard, Suite 402, Detroit, MI 48202; tel. 313/874-2000; June William

Hospice of Southeast Michigan/Franklin, 12900 West Chicago Boulevard, Detroit, MI 48228; tel. 313/491-0022; Carolyn Fitzgerald

Hospice of Southeastern Michigan – North Oakland, 530 West Huron, Pontiac, MI 48341; tel. 810/253-2580; FAX. 810/253-2599; Rita Ann Mahon, RN, Director

Hospice of Southeastern Michigan–St. Clair Shores, 22811 Greater Mack Avenue, St. Clair Shore, MI 48080; tel. 313/559-9209; Carolyn Fitzgerald

Hospice of Sturgis, 600 South Lakeview Avenue, Sturgis, MI 49091; Pamela Pope

Hospice of Van Buren County/Greater Kalamazoo, 404 North Hazen Street, Paw Paw, MI 49079; tel. 616/657-7769; FAX. 616/657-7225; Carolyn Stephenson, Administrator

Hospice of Washtenaw, 806 Airport Boulevard, Ann Arbor, MI 48108; tel. 313/741-5777; FAX. 313/741-5757; Teri Turner, Administrator

Hospice of Wexford–Missaukee, A Program of Hospice of Michigan, 932 North Mitchell Street, Cadillac, MI 49601; tel. 616/779-9570; FAX. 616/779-0717; Pat Spragg, RN, Director

Hospice of the North, Inc., 110 South Elm Street, Gaylord, MI 49735; tel. 517/732-3722

Hospice of the Straits/Vital Care, 761 Lafayette, Cheboygan, MI 49721; tel. 616/627-4774; FAX. 616/627-4416; Fran Hilal, Manager

Hospice of the VNA of Southeastern Michigan, 7700 Second Avenue, Detroit, MI 48202; tel. 313/876-8550; FAX. 313/876-8518; Charlene T. Coting, RN

Hospice of the VNA of Southeastern Michigan–East, 26000 Hoover, Warren, MI 48089; tel. 810/756-9000; Charlene T. Cotting, RN

Hospice of the VNA of Southeastern Michigan–Oakland, 26200 Lahser Road, Suite 204, Southfield, MI 48034; tel. 810/354-5250; Charlene T. Cotting, RN

Hospice of the VNA of Southeastern Michigan–West, 8600 Silvery Lane, Dearborn Height, MI 48127; tel. 313/730-8020; Charlene T. Cotting, RN

Hospice's of Henry Ford Health System, 23000 Mack Avenue, Suite 500, St. Clair Shore, MI 48080; tel. 810/774-4141; FAX. 810/774-0515; Sondra Seely, Administrator

Hospice–Partners in Caring, Division of VNA of Saginaw, 500 South Hamilton, Saginaw, MI 48602; tel. 517/799-6020; FAX. 517/799-6062; S. J. Schultz, B.S.N., M.S., President, Chief Executive Officer

Individualized Hospice, 3003 Washtenaw Avenue, Suite Two, Ann Arbor, MI 48104; tel. 313/971-0444; FAX. 313/971-1980; Patricia Love, Clinical Director

International Pediatric Hospice, 2300 Buhl Building, Detroit, MI 48226; tel. 313/965-6100; Paul Manion

Kaleidoscope Kids, 1 Ford Place, 2–A, Detroit, MI 48202; tel. 313/972-1980; Sondra Seely

Karmanos Cancer Institute–Hospice Program, 24601 Northwestern Highway, Southfield, MI 48075; tel. 810/827-1592; FAX. 810/827-0972; Shelia A. Sperti, MSN, RN, Administrator

Keweenaw Home Nursing and Hospice, 311 Sixth Street, Calumet, MI 49913; tel. 906/487-9305; FAX. 906/337-9929; Wanda Kolb, Administrator

LMAS DHD Hospice, 200 Hamilton Lake Road, Newberry, MI 49868; tel. 906/293-5107; FAX. 906/293-5453; Rosemary Blashill, Administrator

LMAS DHD Hospice/St. Ignace, 749 Hombach Street, St. Ignace, MI 49781; tel. 906/643-7700; FAX. 906/643-7719; Judy Misner, Home Health Nursing Supervisor

Lake Superior Hospice Association, 148 West Washington, Marquette, MI 49855; tel. 906/226-2646; FAX. 906/226-7735; Jill Baker, Executive Director

Lake Superior Hospice Association, 502 North Main Street, L'Anse, MI 49946; tel. 906/524-4477; Jill Baker

MI Home Health Care/Terminal Care, 955 East Commerce Drive, Traverse City, MI 49684; tel. 616/943-8451; FAX. 616/943-4515; Lilo Hoelzel–Seipp

Manistee Area Volunteer Hospice, Inc., P.O. Box 293, Manistee, MI 49660; tel. 616/723-6064; Diane Cameron, President

Marinette–Menominee County Hospice, 3133 Carney Avenue, Marinette, WI 54143; tel. 906/863-6331

McLaren Hospice Service, Inc., 237 Davis Lake Road, Lapeer, MI 48446; tel. 810/667-0042; Terry Morgan, President

Memorial Hospice, 1320 South Carpenter Street, Iron Mountain, MI 48901; tel. 906/774-5589

Mid Michigan VNA Hospice/Clare, 1438 North McEwan, Clare, MI 48617; tel. 517/539-5320; FAX. 517/839-1773; Sandra Simmons, Administrator

MidMichigan Visiting Nurses Association and Hospice, 3007 North Saginaw Road, Midland, MI 48640; tel. 517/839-1770; FAX. 517/839-1749; Miriam Markowitz, Hospice Director

Montcalm Area Hospice, 302 1/2 East Main, Stanton, MI 48888; tel. 517/831-5045; Carol Goffnett

North County Hospice, Inc., 301 South Cedar, Kalkaska, MI 49646; tel. 616/258-5286

North Woods Home Nursing and Hospice, 226 South Cedar, P.O. Box 307, Manistique, MI 49854; tel. 906/341-6963; FAX. 906/341-2490; Susan Bjorne, Administrator

Northwest Ohio Hospice Association, 3930 Sunforest Court, Suite 200, Toledo, OH 43624; tel. 419/479-3115; Virginia Clifford

Otsego Area Hospice, a program of Hospice of Michigan, 810 North Otsego, Suite 111, Gaylord, MI 49735; tel. 517/732-2151; FAX. 517/731-2897; Sheila Simpson, Area Director

Samaritan Care, Inc., 24445 Northwestern Highway, Suite 105, Southfield, MI 48075; tel. 800/397-9360; FAX. 810/355-5705; Margaret Karvala, Administrator

South Haven Area Hospice, 05055 Blue Star Highway, P.O. Box 990, South Haven, MI 49090-0990; tel. 616/637-3825; FAX. 616/637-6777; Barbara Reicherts, Executive Director

St. Joseph Huron Home Health and Hospice, Inc., 516 Oak Street, Tawas City, MI 48763; tel. 517/362-4611; FAX. 517/362-8771; Ann Balfour, Administrator

St. Joseph's Hospice/Affiliate of Henry Ford Cottage Hospice, 43411 Garfield Boulevard, Building Two, Suite B, Clinton Township, MI 48038; tel. 810/263-2840; FAX. 810/263-2895; Patti Ciechanovski, CRNH, Manager

United Home Hospice, Inc., 2401 20th Street, Detroit, MI 48216; tel. 313/964-1133; Alice Okwu, Director, Nursing

United Hospice Service, Six Eastgate Plaza, Sandusky, MI 48471; tel. 800/635-7490

Upper Peninsula Home Nursing/Hospice, 1414 West Fair, Suite 44, Marquette, MI 49855; tel. 906/225-4544; FAX. 906/225-4545; Cynthia A. Nyquist, RN, B.S.N., Administrator, Chief Executive Officer

VNA Home Care Services Hospice, Inc., 901 South Woodland Avenue, Michigan City, IN 46360-5672; tel. 219/877-2070; FAX. 219/877-2089; Mary Craymer, Chief Executive Officer

VNA of Southwest Michigan Hospice, County Road #681, Suite D, Hartford, MI 49057; tel. 616/621-3154; Jill Eldred

VNA of Southwest Michigan–Hospice Program, 348 North Burdick Street, Kalamazoo, MI 49007-3843; tel. 616/343-1396; FAX. 616/382-8686; Jill Eldred

Visiting Nurse Hospice, 4801 Willoughby, Suite Seven, Holt, MI 48842; tel. 517/694-8300; FAX. 517/694-4968; Jeanne Zabihaylo, Admissions Coordinator

Visiting Nurse Service of Western Michigan Hospice Program, 1401 Cedar, N.E., Grand Rapids, MI 49503; tel. 616/774-2702; FAX. 616/774-7017; Laurie Sefton, RN, M.S.N., Hospice Program Director

West Bloomfield Hospice, 6020 West Maple Road, Suite 500, West Bloomfield, MI 48322; tel. 810/884-8600; Sondra Seely

Wings of Hope Hospice, Inc. of Allegan County, 663 North 10th Street, Plainwell, MI 49080; tel. 616/685-1645; FAX. 616/685-2105; Marie Tucker, Executive Director

MINNESOTA

Community Hospice, 323 South Minnesota, Crookston, MN 56716; tel. 218/281-9478; Thomas C. Lenertz, Administrator

Coram Hospice, 1355 Mendota Heights Road, Suite 240, Mendota Heights, MN 55120; tel. 612/452-5600; Deborah Meyer, Administrator

Crossroads Community Hospice, 404 Fountain Street, Albert Lea, MN 56007; tel. 507/377-6385; Shelley Doran, Administrator

Douglas County PHNS Hospice, 725 Elm Street, Suite 1200, Alexandria, MN 56308; tel. 320/763-6018; FAX. 320/763-4127; Mark Lundin, RN

Faibault Area Hospice, 631 Southeast First Street, Faribault, MN 55021; tel. 507/334-6451; James N. Wolf, Administrator

Fairview Hospice, 2450 26th Avenue South, Minneapolis, MN 55406; tel. 612/728-2380; Mark Enger

Faribault County Area Hospice, 519 S. Galbraith St., Box 160, Blue Earth, MN 56013; tel. 507/526-3273, ext. 345; FAX. 507/526-3621; Janet Johansen, Administrator

First Care Hospice, 900 Hilligoss Blvd, Southeast, Fosston, MN 56542; tel. 218/435-1133; David S. Hubbard, Administrator

Good Shepherd Hospice, 503 East Lincoln Street, Hendricks, MN 56136; tel. 507/275-3134; Kirk Strensrud, Administrator

HealthSpan Home Care and Hospice, 2750 Arthur Street, Roseville, MN 55113; tel. 612/628-4200; FAX. 612/628-9074; Cletis Hoffer, Acting Administrator

Healtheast Hospice, 69 West Exchange Street, St. Paul, MN 55102; tel. 612/232-3312; Kathleen M. Lucas, Administrator

Homecaring Hospice, 11685 Lake Boulevard North, Chisago City, MN 55013; tel. 612/257-8402; Scott Wordelman, Administrator

Homehealth Partnership, 320 E. Main Street, Crosby, MN 56441; tel. 218/546-2311; Thomas F. Reek, Administrator

Hospice Partners, Inc., 6750 France Ave. South, Suite 290, Edina, MN 55435; tel. 612/920-0035; Roberta S. Cline, Chief Executive Officer, President

Hospice of Luverne Community Hospital, 305 East Luverne Street, P.O. Box 1019, Luverne, MN 56156; tel. 507/283-2321; Gerald E. Curl, Administrator

Hospice of Murray County, 2129 Broadway, Slayton, MN 56172; tel. 507/836-8114; Holly Miller, Administrator

Hospice of the Lakes, 8100 34th Avenue, S., P.O. Box 1309, Minneapolis, MN 55440-1309; tel. 612/883-6877; FAX. 612/883-6883; Paul Brat, Administrator

Hospice of the Twin Cities Inc., 7100 Northland Circle, Suite 205, Brooklyn Park, MN 55428; tel. 612/531-2424; FAX. 612/531-2422; Lisa Abicht-Swensen, Administrator

Immanuel St. Joseph's Hospice, 501 Holly Lane, Suite 10, Mankato, MN 56601; tel. 507/345-2618; Jerome Crest, Administrator

Lake City Area Hospice, 904 South Lakeshore Drive, Lake City, MN 55041; tel. 612/345-3321; Mark Rinehardt, Administrator

Lakeland Hospice, Inc., 715 S. Pebble Lake Road, P.O. Box 824, Fergus Falls, MN 56538; tel. 218/736-7885; FAX. 218/736-2231; Delores Peterson, Director

Litchfield Area Hospice, 218 N. Holcombe, Litchfield, MN 55355; tel. 320/693-7367; Michael P. Boyle, Administrator

Long Prairie Memorial Hospice, 20 Ninth Street Southeast, Long Prairie, MN 56347; tel. 320/732-7287; Rona Bleess, Administrator

Mayo Hospice Program, 200 First Street, S.W., Rochester, MN 55905; tel. 507/284-4002; FAX. 507/284-0161; Margaret Gillard, RN, Program Coordinator

North Country Hospice, 3525 Pine Ridge Avenue, NW, Bemidji, MN 56601; tel. 218/759-5665; Jessica Conrad, Administrator

North Memorial Medical Center Hospice, 3500 France Avenue North, Suite 101, Robbinsdale, MN 55422; tel. 612/520–3900; FAX. 612/520–3920; Rosemary Moneta, Administrator

Northern Communities Hospice, 715 Delmore Drive, Roseau, MN 56751; tel. 218/463–3211; David Hagen, Administrator

Northfield Hospice, 801 W. First Street, Northfield, MN 55057; tel. 507/645–3386; Kendall C. Bank, Administrator

Owatonna Area Hospice, 903 South Oak Ave., Owatonna, MN 55060; tel. 507/455–7628; Marlene H. Breckner, Administrator

Pine to Prairie Hospice Inc., 201 Hillestad Avenue North, Fosston, MN 56542; tel. 218/435–2017; FAX. 218/435–6909; Bev Leier, Administrator

Pope County Hospice, 10 Fourth Avenue, Southeast, Glenwood, MN 56334; tel. 320/634–4521; Douglas Reker, Administrator

Prairie Home Hospice, 300 South Bruce, Marshall, MN 56258; tel. 507/537–9247; Lynn Yueill, Administrator

Prairie Home Hospice, Inc., 300 South Bruce, Marshall, MN 56258; tel. 507/537–9247; FAX. 507/537–9258; Lynn Yueill, Administrative Director

Red Wing Hospice, 434 West Fourth Street, Suite 200, Red Wing, MN 55066; tel. 612/385–3410; FAX. 612/385–3414; Beth Krehbiel, Administrator

Renville County Hospice, 611 East Fairview Ave., Olivia, MN 56277; tel. 320/523–3427; Dean Slagter, Administrator

Rice Hospice Program, 301 Becker Ave., SW, Willmar, MN 56201; tel. 320/231–4450; Margaret Sietsema, Administrator

Ridgeview Hospice, 240 Willow Street, Tyler, MN 56178; tel. 507/247–5521; James A. Rotert, Administrator

Seasons Hospice, 5650 Weatherhill Rd, SW, Rochester, MN 55902; tel. 507/281–3029; Doris Oehlke, Administrator

Shamrock Seasons Hospice, 1242 Whitewater Avenue, St. Charles, MN 55972; tel. 507/932–3949; FAX. 507/932–5125; Doris Oehlke, Director

St. Cloud Hospital Hospice, 48 North 29 Avenue, Suite 15, St. Cloud, MN 56303; tel. 320/259–9375; FAX. 320/240–3266; Kathleen Murphy, Care Center Director

St. Joseph's Home Care and Hospice, 303 Kingwood Street, Brainerd, MN 56401; tel. 218/828–7444; FAX. 218/828–7579; Jani Wiebolt, Administrator

St. Luke's Hospice Duluth, 915 East First Street, Duluth, MN 55805; tel. 218/722–6220; Lynette Rauscher, Administrator

St. Mary's Medical Center Hospice, 404 East Fourth Street, Duluth, MN 55805; tel. 218/726–4020; Joanne Hagen, Administrator

St. Michael's Hospice, 425 North Elm Street, Sauk Centre, MN 56378; tel. 320/352–2221; Karen Rau, Administrator

The Hospice of Morrison County, 815 Southeast Second Street, Little Falls, MN 56345; tel. 320/632–1144; Dianne Jackson, Administrator

Waseca Area Hospice, Inc., 204 Second Street, N.W., P.O. Box 94, Waseca, MN 56093; tel. 507/835–8983; FAX. 507/835–8737; Linda Grant, Director

Winona Area Hospice Services, 825 Mankato Avenue, Suite 111, Winona, MN 55987; tel. 507/457–4468; Charles R. Haugh, Administrator

Zumbrota Area Hospice Program, 383 West Fifth Street, Zumbrota, MN 55992; tel. 507/732–5131; Daniel E. Will, Administrator

MISSISSIPPI

Appletree Hospice, Inc., 521 Main Street, Suite U–Four, P.O. Box 299, Natchez, MS 39121; tel. 601/446–8000; Linda L. Carlton, Administrator

Baptist Memorial Regional Home Health Care, Inc., Magnolia Health Services and Hospice North, 396 Southcrest Court Five, Southhaven, MS 38671; tel. 601/349–1394; Bill Caldwell, Administrator

Community Hospice of Mississippi, Inc., d/b/a Gulf Coast, 154 Porter Avenue, Biloxi, MS 39530; tel. 601/435–1948; L. Jim Anthis, Ph.D, Administrator

DHS HospiceCare, 862 Goodman Road East, P.O. Box 744, Southaven, MS 38671; tel. 601/349–6711; FAX. 601/349–8826; Linda Crum, Administrator

Delta Area Hospice Care, Ltd., 522 Arnold Avenue, P.O. Box 5915, Greenville, MS 38704–5915; tel. 601/335–7040; FAX. 601/335–7048; Gloria Blakely, Administrator

Friendship Hospice of Natchez, Inc., 133 Jeff Davis Boulevard, Natchez, MS 39120; tel. 601/445–0307; Cynthia Paul, Administrator

Hospice Care, 202 South Washington Avenue, Greenville, MS 38701; tel. 601/335–4298; FAX. 601/335–4292; Emry Oxford, Administrator

Hospice Care Foundation, Inc., P.O. Box 2056, Vicksburg, MS 39181; tel. 800/380–3070; FAX. 601/634–6010; Rachel Y. Goodman, RN, Coordinator

Hospice Care Foundation, Inc., 317–B Highland Avenue, Natchez, MS 39120; tel. 601/442–3070; Janie Calloway, Office Manager

Hospice South, Inc., 112 Lafayette Street, P.O. Box 219, Livingston, AL 35470; tel. 205/652–2451; FAX. 205/652–5212; Bobby T. Williams, Ph.D., Chief Executive Officer

Hospice South, Inc., 1448 22nd Avenue, Tuscaloosa, AL 35401; tel. 205/366–9681; Dr. Bobby T. Williams, Chief Executive Officer

Hospice of Central Mississippi, Inc., 2600 Insurance Center Drive, Suite B–120, Jackson, MS 39216–4911; tel. 601/366–9881; FAX. 601/981–0150; John Fletcher, Executive Director

Hospice of Central Mississippi, Inc., 224 South First Street, Brookhaven, MS 39601; tel. 601/835–1020; FAX. 601/835–1063; Jean Berch, Branch Director

Hospice of Light, 4341 Gautier & Vancleave Road, Suite Four, Gautier, MS 39553; tel. 208/497–2400; FAX. 208/497–9035; Laurie H. Grady, Nurse Coordinator

Hospice of North Mississippi Clarksdale, 130 Desota Avenue, P.O. Box 1490, Clarksdale, MS 38614; tel. 601/624–8144; Jessie Rudd, RN, Patient Care Coordinator

Hospice of North Mississippi Olive Branch, 6920 Oak Forrest Drive, Suite B, Olive Branch, MS 38654; tel. 601/893–8900; FAX. 601/893–8905; Kim M. Ross, RN, Patient Care Coordinator

Hospice of North Mississippi, Inc., 619 East Lee Street, Sardis, MS 38666; tel. 601/487–1827; FAX. 601/487–1060; Renee Wright, Administrator

Hospice–North Mississippi Medical Center, 600 West Main, Tupelo, MS 38801; tel. 601/841–3612; Laura Kelley, Administrator

Magnolia Health Service and Hospice, 2130 Jackson Avenue West, Oxford, MS 38655; tel. 601/234–8553; FAX. 601/236–1459; Susan Eftink, L.M.S.W., Hospice Coordinator

Methodist Alliance Hospice, 930 South White Station Road, Suite 100, Memphis, TN 38117; tel. 901/680–0169; FAX. 901/537–2109; Caby E. Byrne, Administrator

Quality Hospice of Gulf Coast, Inc., P.O. Box 549, Biloxi, MS 39533; tel. 601/374–4434; FAX. 601/436–3679; Patricia Hiers, Administrator

Rush Hospital Hospice, Highway 15, Route Nine, Box 28, Philadelphia, MS 39350; tel. 601/656–8388; Ken Boyette, Patient Care Coordinator, Supervisor

Sta–Home Hospice, 105 North Van Buren, Carthage, MS 39051; tel. 800/898–1159; Claudette Hathcock, Administrator

Sta–Home Hospice, 1620 24th Avenue, Meridan, MS 39305; tel. 601/485–8489; FAX. 601/693–7457; Edwina White, Patient Care Coordinator

Whispering Pines Hospice, 1480 Raymond Road, Jackson, MS 39204; tel. 601/373–2472; Jeanne H. Jones, Consulting Administrator

MISSOURI

American Heartland Hospice, 7555 South Lindbergh Boulevard, St. Louis, MO 63125; tel. 314/894–8189; FAX. 314/894–7334; Susan O'Kane, Administrator

Barnes Jewish Hospice, 9890 Clayton Road, Ladue, MO 63124; tel. 314/993–4600; Ruth Sedano, Administrator

Barr Hospice and Palliative Care, 2701 Rockcreek Parkway, Suite 200, Kansas City, MO 64117; tel. 816/471–2218; FAX. 816/471–2434; Linda Ault, Administrator

Bates County Hospice, 501 North Orange, Butler, MO 64730; tel. 816/679–6108; George Taylor, Administrator

Beacon of Hope Hospice, Inc., 4191 Crescent Drive, Suite A, St. Louis, MO 63129; tel. 314/894–1000; FAX. 314/894–8389; Dawn Counts, Executive Director

Community Hospice of America–Central, 3600 I–70 Drive, S.E., Suite H, Columbia, MO 65201; tel. 314/443–8360; FAX. 314/499–4601; Tom Howard, RN, Patient Care Supervisor

Community Hospice of America–South Central, 101 East Second Street, Mountain Grove, MO 65711; tel. 417/926–4146; FAX. 417/926–6123; Virginia Holtmann, Administrator

Community Hospice of America–Tri Lakes, 1756 Bee Creek Road, Suite G, Branson, MO 65616; tel. 417/335–2004; FAX. 417/335–2012; Janet Gard, Program Director

Comprehealth, Inc., Hospice Services Division, 2001 South Hanley Road, Suite 450, St. Louis, MO 63144; tel. 314/781–2800; FAX. 314/781–4844; Carolynn Ingerson–Hoffman, Administrator

Hands of Hope Hospice, 801 Faraon Street, St. Joseph, MO 64501; tel. 816/271–7190; FAX. 816/271–7191; Jim Pierce, Director

Harrison County Hospice, Highway 136 West, P.O. Box 425, Bethany, MO 64424; tel. 816/425–6324; FAX. 816/425–7642; Nola Martz, RN, B.S.N., Administrator

Hartline Hospice, Inc., Serving Southern Missouri, 3322 South Campbell, Suite T, Springfield, MO 65807; tel. 800/241–3798; FAX. 417/886–0082; Denise Stroud, B.S.N., Patient Care Administrator

HealthCor, Inc., 3215 LeMone Industrial Boulevard, Suite 100, Columbia, MO 65201–8245; tel. 314/449–0206; Rebecca Rastkar, RN, Administrator

Heart of America Hospice, L.C., 9229 Ward Parkway, Suite 350, Kansas City, MO 64114; tel. 816/333–1980; FAX. 816/333–2421; Jacquelin Tuohig, Executive Director

HomeCare of Mid–Missouri Hospice, 102 West Reed Street, Moberly, MO 65270; tel. 816/263–1517; Marsha Ideus Cooper, Administrator

Hospice 2000, Inc., 406 South Fourth, Kirksville, MO 63501; tel. 816/627–9711; FAX. 816/627–7005; Ron McCullough, Administrator

Hospice Care of Mid–America, 3100 Broadway, Suite 300, Kansas City, MO 64111–2415; tel. 816/931–4276; FAX. 816/931–9147; Patricia Walters, Interim Director

Hospice Preferred Choice of Kansas City and Kansas, 1170 West 152 Highway 152, Suite R–Two, Liberty, MO 64068; tel. 816/792–8700; FAX. 816/792–8701; Charlene Jaeger, RN, Executive Director

Hospice of Southwest Missouri, Inc., 3653 South Avenue, Springfield, MO 65807; tel. 417/882–0453; FAX. 417/882–1245; Richard Williams, President, Chief Executive Officer

HospiceCare of Visiting Nurse Association, 531 B South Union, Springfield, MO 65802; tel. 417/866–4374; FAX. 417/866–0233; Suzanne Dollar, Administrator

HospiceCare, Inc., P.O. Box 1000, Mineral Area College, North College Center, Park Hills, MO 63601; tel. 573/431–0162; Fred McDaniel, Administrator

Howard County Home Health and Hospice, 104 East Davis, Fayette, MO 65248; tel. 816/248–1780; FAX. 816/248–3347; Serese M. Wiehardt, Administrator

Kansas City Hospice, 1625 West 92nd Street, Kansas City, MO 64114; tel. 816/363–2600; FAX. 816/523–0068; Elaine McIntosh, President

Kendallwood Hospice, 10015 North Executive Hills Boulevard, Kansas City, MO 64153; tel. 816/891–7766; FAX. 816/891–7748; Charlotte Bruyn, Administrator

Lake Ozark Area Home Health and Hospice, A Department of Pulaski County Health Department, 602 Commercial Street, P.O. Box 498, Crocker, MO 65452; tel. 314/736–2219; FAX. 314/736–5847; Beth Hutton, Administrator

Meramec Hospice, 200 North Main, Rolla, MO 65401; tel. 314/364–2425; FAX. 314/364–1575; Shirley Rutz, Administrator

Missouri River Hospice, 1440 Aaron Court, Jefferson City, MO 65101; tel. 314/635–5643; FAX. 314/635–6552; Marge Borst, Administrator

Pershing Hospice, 225 West Hayden, Marceline, MO 64658; tel. 816/376–2222; FAX. 816/376–2432; Rose Ayers, Director

Pike County Home Health Agency and Hospice, 19 North Main Cross, Bowling Green, MO 63334; tel. 573/324–2111; FAX. 573/324–5517; Lisa Pitzer, RN, Patient Care Coordinator

Providence Hospice Group, Inc., 510 North Main, Sikeston, MO 63801; tel. 314/472–4041; FAX. 314/472–4043; Matthew Brauss, Administrator

Randolph County Health Department, Home Care and Hospice, 425 East Logan, P.O. Box 488, Moberly, MO 65270; tel. 816/263–6643; FAX. 816/263–0333; Mary D. Wolf, M.S.N., RNC, Patient Care Coordinator

Riverways Hospice of Ozarks Medical Center, 114 East Main, West Plains, MO 65775; tel. 417/256–3133; FAX. 417/256–5961; Mary Dyck, Administrator

Samaritan Care Hospice of Missouri, 10910 Kennerly Road, St. Louis, MO 63128; tel. 314/849–3324; FAX. 314/842–9077; Betty Richards, Administrator

St. Clair County Hospice, 101 Hospital Drive, Osceola, MO 64776; tel. 417/646–8157; FAX. 417/646–8159; Candice J. Baker, Administrator

Twin Lakes Hospice, Inc., 304 Main, P.O. Box 211, Warsaw, MO 65355; tel. 816/438–9700; FAX. 816/438–6404; Sandra Spooner, Administrator

VNA of Southeast Missouri Hospice, 100 East Harrison, Kennett, MO 63857; tel. 573/888–5892; FAX. 573/888–0538; Teresa McCulloch, Administrator

Visiting Nurse Association Hospice Care, 1260 Andes Boulevard, St. Louis, MO 63132; tel. 314/993–6800; Susan Pettit, Administrator

Visiting Nurses Association of Central Missouri, 1809 Vandiver Drive, Columbia, MO 65202; tel. 314/474–6000; FAX. 314/474–6400; Ron Barnes, Administrator

MONTANA

Anaconda Pintler Hospice of Community Hospital of Anaconda, 112 Oak Street, P.O. Box 596, Anaconda, MT 59711; tel. 406/563–5422; FAX. 406/563–5427; Alice Cortright, Director

Big Sky Hospice, 3021 Sixth Avenue, N., Suite 205, P.O. Box 1049, Billings, MT 59103–1049; tel. 406/248–7442; FAX. 406/248–2572; Bernice Bjertness, RN, M.N., Director

Highlands Hospice, 507 Centennial Avenue, Butte, MT 59701; tel. 406/723–5780; FAX. 406/723–9595; Virginia Mick, Director

Hospice of Powell County, 310 Milwaukee Avenue, P.O. Box 808, Deer Lodge, MT 59722; tel. 406/846–3975; Nora E. Meier, Office Manager

Kootenai Volunteer Hospice, P.O. Box 781, Libby, MT 59923; tel. 406/293–3923; Theresa Schneider, Director

Lake County Home Health Hospice, 107 6th Ave SW, Ronan, MT 59864

Partners in Home Care Home Health & Hospice, Inc.–Hospice, 500 North Higgins, Suite 201, Missoula, MT 59801; tel. 406/728–8848; Teresa Smith, RN, Patient Care Coordinator

Partners in Home Care, Inc. (Residential Hospice), 10450 West Mullan Road, Missoula, MT 59802; tel. 406/542–1478; FAX. 406/721–0256; Teresa Smith, Clinical Manager

Peace Hospice of Montana, 125 Northwest Bypass H, P.O. Box 5013, Great Falls, MT 59404; tel. 406/727–6161; FAX. 406/727–9758; Mary Gray, RNCS, Director

Pondera Hospice, 300 North Virginia, Suite 305, Conrad, MT 59425; tel. 406/278–5566; FAX. 406/278–5569

Stillwater Big Sky Hospice Team, 350 West Pike Avenue, P.O. Box 1109, Columbus, MT 59019; tel. 406/322–5100; FAX. 406/322–5737; Sharon Marten, Chairperson

Westmont Home Health Services Inc Hospice, 2525 Colonial Drive, Helena, MT 59601; tel. 406/443–4140; Lynn Zavalney, RN, M.A., Hospice Coordinator

NEBRASKA

Alegent Health Home Care, 10802 Farnam Dr., Suite 150, Omaha, NE 68154; tel. 402/334–0456; Carolyn Geiger, Administrator

Central Plains Hospice, 300 E. 12th Street, P.O. Box 108, Cozad, NE 69130; tel. 308/784–4630; Rita Johnson, R.N., Administrator

Chadron Community Hospital Hospice, 821 Morehead Street, Chadron, NE 69337; tel. 308/432–5586; Harold Krueger, Jr., Administrator

Custer County Hospice, 145 Memorial Dr., P.O. Box 250, Broken Bow, NE 68822–0250; tel. 308/872–6891; Michael Steckler, Administrator

Faith Regional Hospice Care, 1500 Koenigstein, Norfolk, NE 68701; tel. 402/371–4880; Robert Driewer, Administrator

Fremont Area Medical Center Hospice, 450 East 23rd, Fremont, NE 68025; tel. 402/727–3373; Vincent O'Connor, Jr., Administrator

Hospice Care of Nebraska LLC, 1600 South 70th Street, Suite 201, Lincoln, NE 68506; tel. 402/488–1363; FAX. 402/488–5976; Marcia Cederdahl, RN, CRNH, B.S.Ed.

Hospice Preferred Choice, 407 South 27th Ave., Suite 200, Omaha, NE 68131; tel. 402/346–2273; Barbara Coppa, Administrator

Hospice of Tabitha, 4720 Randolph Street, Lincoln, NE 68510; tel. 402/483–7671; Roberta Daughterty, R.N., Administrator

Mary Lanning Memorial Hospice, 715 North St. Joseph Ave., Hastings, NE 68901; tel. 402/461–5161; W. Michael Kearney, Administrator

Memorial Health Center Hospice, 1103 Illinois, Sidney, NE 69162; tel. 308/256–5825; Susan Peters, Administrator

St. Elizabeth Heartland Hospice, 245 South 84, Suite 111, Lincoln, NE 68510; tel. 402/486–7043; Phyllis Rizzo, Administrator

St. Francis Hospice, 430 N. Monitor Street, West Point, NE 68788–1595; tel. 402/372–2404; Ronald Briggs, Administrator

St. Joe Ville Homecare and Hospice, 2305 South Tenth Street, Omaha, NE 68108–1154; tel. 402/345–3333; FAX. 402/345–3826; Michael Van Meter, Administrator

Syracuse Hospice, 1527 Midland Street, Syracuse, NE 68446; tel. 402/269–2011; Ron Anderson, Administrator

Visiting Nurse Association of the Midlands, 8710 F Street, Omaha, NE 68127; tel. 402/342–2566; FAX. 402/342–2587; Janice Treml, Administrator

NEVADA

Family Home Hospice, 1701 West Charleston, Suite 150, Zip 89102, P.O. Box 15645, Las Vegas, NV 89114–5645; tel. 702/383–0887; FAX. 702/383–1173; Jerilyn D. Hudgens, Administrator

Hospice of Northern Nevada, 1155 West Fourth Street, Suite 122, Reno, NV 89503; tel. 702/789–3081; FAX. 702/789–3909; Marva Slight, Director

Hospice of Northern Nevada–Carson City, 809 North Plaza, Carson City, NV 89701; tel. 702/884–8900; FAX. 702/884–8909; Elissa DeWolfe, Administrator

Margaret Rose Home Hospice, 1500 East Tropicana Avenue, Las Vegas, NV 89119; tel. 702/626–1966; Jackie Crawley

Nathan Adelson Hospice, 4141 South Swenson Street, Las Vegas, NV 89119; tel. 702/733–0320; FAX. 702/796–3195; Betsy Peirson–Gornet, Chief Executive Officer

PRN Home Hospice, 3022 West Post Road, Las Vegas, NV 89118; tel. 702/361–6801; Marti Norris, Administrator

Proper Care Hospice, 3601 West Sahara, Las Vegas, NV 89102; tel. 702/248–4119; Marlen P. Spagnol, Administrator

Safe Harbor Hospice, Inc., 3910 Pecos McLeod Building, Las Vegas, NV 89121; tel. 702/435–7660; Kristy Thompson, Executive Director

Special Care Hospice, 1514 C Gold Rush Road, Suite 236, Bullhead City, AZ 86442; tel. 520/758–3800; Dianne H. Butler, B.S.N., RNC, Administrator

Vista Care, Inc., 1830 East Sahara Avenue, Suite 102, Las Vegas, NV 89104; tel. 702/734–0307; FAX. 702/734–0310; Diana Hopkins–Weiss, Administrator

Washoe Home Connection, 1000 Ryland, Suite 410, Reno, NV 89502; tel. 702/328–5790; FAX. 702/328–5795; Michael Girard, Administrator

NEW HAMPSHIRE

Community Health and Hospice, Inc., 780 North Main Street, P.O. Box 578, Laconia, NH 03247–0578; tel. 603/524–8444; FAX. 603/524–8217; Charlotte Leavitt, Administrator

Concord Regional VNA–Hospice, 250 Pleasant Street, P.O. Box 1797, Concord, NH 03302; tel. 603/224–4093; FAX. 603/224–4093; Mary B. DeVeau, Administrator

Connecticut Valley Home Care Inc., 958 John Stark Highway, Newport, NH 03773; tel. 603/543–0164; Lynn Holland, RN

Elliot Home Care and Hospice, 25 South Maple Street, Manchester, NH 03103; tel. 603/628–4430; FAX. 603/622–4800; Diane LaBossiere, M.S.W.

Heritage Home Health, Inc., 169 Daniel Webster Highway, Suite Seven, Meredith, NH 03253; tel. 603/279–4700; FAX. 603/279–1370; Carolyn Virtue, Administrator

Hillsborough Hospice, 400 Mast Road, Goffstown, NH 03045; tel. 603/627–5540; Sandra Kinsey, RN, Hospice Administrator

Home Health and Hospice Care, 22 Prospect Street, Nashua, NH 03060; tel. 603/882–2941; FAX. 603/883–1515; Gail Spera, Administrator

Home Healthcare, Hospice and Community Services, Inc., 69L Island Street, P.O. Box 564, Keene, NH 03431; tel. 603/352–2253; FAX. 603/358–3904; Lois Hopkins, Hospice Program Coordinator

Hospice America of New Hampshire, Inc., 169 D W Highway, Suite 1, Meredith, NH 03253; tel. 603/279–9800; Nancy Wiggin, Administrator

Hospice at HCS, 69L Island Street, P.O. Box 564, Keene, NH 03431; tel. 603/352–2253; Lois Hopkins, Administrator

Hospice of VNH, 20 South Main Street, White River Junction, VT 05001; tel. 802/295–2604; FAX. 802/295–3163; Marie Kirn, Executive Director

Lake Sunapee Home Care and Hospice, 290 County Road, P.O. Box 2209, New London, NH 03257; tel. 603/526–4077; FAX. 603/526–4272; Barbara Boulton, RN, Hospice Patient Care Coordinator

Merrimack Valley Hospice, Inc., One Union Street, Andover, MA 01810; tel. 508/623–3100; FAX. 508/470–4690; Diane Bergeron, Administrator

North Country Home Health Agency, 536 Cottage Street, Littleton, NH 03561; tel. 603/444–5317; FAX. 603/444–0980; Sharon E. Covill, Administrator

Optima Health Visiting Nurse Services, VNA Hospice, 1850 Elm Street, Manchester, NH 03104; tel. 603/622–3781; FAX. 603/641–4074; Jane Clough, Director, Hospice

Pemi–Baker Home Health Agency, 258 Highland Street, Plymouth, NH 03264; tel. 603/536–2232; Elaine Vieira, Administrator

Portsmouth Regional Visiting Nurses Association and Hospice, 127 Parrott Avenue, Portsmouth, NH 03801; tel. 603/436–0815; FAX. 603/431–5457; Joan P. Nickell, President

Rochester Visiting Nurse Association, Inc., 89 Charles Street, Rochester, NH 03867; tel. 603/332–1133; FAX. 603/332–9223; Marianne Gagne, Hospice Coordinator

Rockingham VNA and Hospice, 137 Epping Road, Exeter, NH 03833; tel. 603/772–2981; Ann Blair, Administrator

Rural District VNA Inc., 36 Charles Street, Farmington, NH 03835; tel. 603/755–2202; FAX. 603/755–3760; Sue Houle, Administrator

Seacoast Hospice, 10 Hampton Road, Exeter, NH 03833; tel. 603/778–7391; FAX. 603/772–7692; Susan Cole, Admnistrator

Souhegan Nursing Association Inc., 24 North River Road, Milford, NH 03055; tel. 603/673–3460; FAX. 603/673–0159; Suzanne Frederick, Administrator

Squamscott Visiting Nurse and Hospice Care, 113 New Rochester Rd., Suite 4, Dover, NH 03820; tel. 603/742–7921; FAX. 603/742–3835; Mary Jo Sceggell, Administrator

Tri–Area VNA Hospice, 301 High Street, Somersworth, NH 03878; tel. 603/692–2112; FAX. 603/692–9940; Maxine Lacy, Clinical Services Coordinator

VNA – Hospice of Southern Carroll County and Vicinity, South Main Street, Wolfeboro, NH 03894; tel. 603/569–2729; FAX. 603/569–2409; Carol C. Tubman, RN, CRNH

Visiting Nurse and Hospice Care of Northern Carroll County, Route 16, P.O. Box 432, North Conway, NH 03818; tel. 603/447–6766; FAX. 603/447–6370; Kathleen T. Sheehan, Administrator

NEW JERSEY

Atlantic City Medical Center Hospice, 1406 Doughty Road, Pleasantville, NJ 08232; tel. 609/272–2424; FAX. 609/272–2414; Diana Ciurczak, Director

Atlantic Home Care and Hospice, 33 Bleeker Street, Millburn, NJ 07041

Barbara E. Cheung Memorial Hospice at Roosevelt Hospital, P.O. Box 151, CN4003 and Parsonage Road, Metuchen, NJ 08840–0151; tel. 908/321–9334; FAX. 908/321–9044; Enory Coughlin, RN, Supervisor

Center for Hope Hospice, Inc., 176 Hussa Street, Linden, NJ 07036; tel. 908/486–0700; FAX. 908/486–2450; Margaret J. Coloney, President

Compassionate Care Hospice, 1373 Broad Street, Suite 304, Clifton, NJ 07013; tel. 201/916–1400; FAX. 201/916–0066; Judith Grey, M.P.H., RNC, Director

Garden State Hospice, 256 Columbia Turnpike, Suite 100 N, Florham Park, NJ 07932; tel. 201/660–9400; FAX. 201/660–1122; Elise Power–Crystal, Chief Executive Officer, Marketing Director

Greater Monmouth VNA Hospice, 111 Union Avenue, Long Branch, NJ 07740; tel. 908/229–0816; FAX. 908/229–0561; Debra Cox, RN, Hospice Supervisor

Holy Redeemer Hospice, 1801 Route Nine North, P.O. Box 280A, Swainton, NJ 08210; tel. 609/465–2082; FAX. 609/465–6185; Arleen Moffitt, ACSW

Home Care Resources Hospice, 615 Hope Road, Building Three, First Floor, Eatontown, NJ 07724; tel. 908/935–1797; FAX. 908/935–0949; Kerri A. Johnston, Hospice Administrator

Hospice Program of Bayonne VNA, 325 Broadway, Bayonne, NJ 07002; tel. 201/339–2500; FAX. 201/339–1255; Barbara Halosz, RN, B.S.N., Coordinator

Hospice at Bergen Community Health Care, 400 Old Hook Road, Westwood, NJ 07675–3131; tel. 201/358–2900; FAX. 201/358–0836; Patricia Hutzelman, RN, Hospice Coordinator

Hospice of Delaware Valley, Inc., 2564 Route 1, Lawrenceville, NJ 08648; tel. 609/695–3461, ext. 2222; FAX. 695/771–8010; Sister Katheleen Manning, RN, M.S.N., ONCSC, Director of Hospice

Hospice of New Jersey, 400 Broadacres Drive, Fourth Floor, Bloomfield, NJ 07003; tel. 973/893–0818; FAX. 973/893–0828; Michelle Steganelli, Administrator

Hospice of VNA of Northern New Jersey, 38 Elm Street, Morristown, NJ 07960

HospiceCare of South Jersey, Inc., 2848 South Delsea Drive, Vineland, NJ 08360; tel. 609/794–1515; FAX. 609/691–7660; Yvonne Crouch, Executive Director

Jerseycare Hospice, 50 Newark Avenue, Suite 101, Belleville, NJ 07109

Karen Ann Quinlan Center of Hope Hospice, 99 Sparta Avenue, Newton, NJ 07860; tel. 201/383–0115; FAX. 201/383–6889; Jackie Petrazzelli, Executive Director

Passaic Valley Hospice, VHS of New Jersey, Inc., 783 Riverview Drive, Totowa, NJ 07511; tel. 201/785–7457; FAX. 201/256–6778; Nancy Jacoby, Associate Director

Samaritan Hospice, 214 West Second Street, Moorestown, NJ 08057; tel. 800/229–8183; FAX. 609/778–0237; Ritamarie A. Frey, President, Chief Executive Officer

Somerset Valley Visiting Nurse Association Hospice, 586 East Main Street, Bridgewater, NJ 08807; tel. 908/725–9355; FAX. 908/725–1033; Anita G. Busch, B.S.N., CRNH, Hospice Manager

The Center for Hospice Care, Inc., Three High Street, Glen Ridge, NJ 07028–2306; tel. 201/429–0300; FAX. 201/429–9274; Lorraine M. Sciara, President, Chief Executive Officer

Trinity Hospice, 150 Ninth Street, Runnemede, NJ 08078; tel. 609/939–9000, ext. 7166; FAX. 609/939–9010; Barbara Billington, Director

Unity Hospice, 17 Academy Street, Newark, NJ 07102; tel. 201/596–9661; FAX. 201/596–9664; Terry M. Copeland, Administrator

VNA of Central Jersey Hospice, 1100 Wayside Road, Asbury Park, NJ 07712; tel. 908/493–2220; FAX. 908/493–4256; Barbara Buczny, Director of Hospice

Valley Hospice, a Division of Valley Home Care, Inc., 505 Goffle Road, Ridgewood, NJ 07450; tel. 201/447–8822; FAX. 201/447–0105; Roberta White, Director

Visiting Nurse Association Somerset Hills Hospice, 12 Olcott Avenue, Bernardsville, NJ 07924; tel. 908/766–0180; FAX. 908/766–2268; Barbara Fox, Hospice Coordinator

Visiting Nurse and Health Services Hospice, 354 Union Avenue, P.O. Box 170, Elizabeth, NJ 07208; tel. 908/352–5694, ext. 302; FAX. 908/352–9216; Shirley Altman, Hospice Administrator

Vitas Health Care Corporation of Penn, Two Executive Campus, Route 70 and Cuthbert Road, Cherry Hill, NJ 08002; tel. 609/661–5600; FAX. 609/661–5650; Emily Fedullo, Director, Operations

West Essex Hospice, 799 Bloomfield Avenue, Verona, NJ 07044; tel. 973/857–7300; FAX. 973/857–3433; Thomas Koester, President, Chief Executive Officer

NEW MEXICO

Alamogordo Home Care–Hospice, 505 11th Street, Alamogordo, NM 88310; tel. 800/617–3555; FAX. 505/437–2399; Pat Raub, Administrator

Alternative Home Health Care Hospice, 1118 National Avenue, Las Vegas, NM 87701; tel. 800/296–1538; FAX. 505/425–7682; Maxine E.Gonzales, Administrator

Caring Unlimited Hospice Services, 200 South Third, Raton, NM 87740; tel. 505/445–5113; Jo Ellen Ferguson, Administrator

Carlsbad Hospice, Inc., 1003 West Riverside Drive, P.O. Drawer PP, Carlsbad, NM 88220; tel. 505/885–8257; Nancy Flanagan, Administrator

Esperanza Home Health Care Hospice, Inc., Highway 518 Buena Vista, P.O. Box 270, Mora, NM 87732; tel. 505/387–2215; Josephine P. Garcia

Helping Hand Hospice, 615 South Second, Tucumcari, NM 88401; tel. 505/461–0099; Diana Beck, Administrator

Hospice Services, Inc., 90I East Bender, P.O. Box 249, Hobbs, NM 88241; tel. 800/658–6844; FAX. 505/393–3985; Brenda Chambers

Hospice Services, Inc. – Eddy, 1031 North Thomas, P.O. Box 280, Carlsbad, NM 88220; tel. 505/887–1835; FAX. 505/887–6967; Jan Shields, RN, Branch Manager

Hospice at VNS, 2960 Rodeo Park Drive, W., Santa Fe, NM 87505; tel. 505/984–2571; FAX. 505/984–2571; Janet Rose, Chief Executive Officer

Hospice of Artesia, 702 North 13th, Artesia, NM 88210; tel. 505/748–3333, ext. 604; FAX. 505/746–8918, ext. 424; Beverly Morehead, RN, Director

Los Alamos Visiting Nurse Service Hospice, 901 18th Street, Suite 203, Los Alamos, NM 87544; tel. 505/662–2525; FAX. 505/662–7093; Deborah Simon, Director

Mesilla Valley Hospice, Inc., 299 East Montana Avenue, Las Cruces, NM 88005; tel. 505/523–4700; FAX. 505/527–2204; Patti Lyman, RN, Executive Director

Mountain Home Health Hospice, 630 Paseo del Pueblo Sur, Suite 180, Taos, NM 87571; tel. 505/758–4786; Patricia Heinen, Administrator

New Hope Hospice of New Mexico, 4153 Montgomery Boulevard, N.E., Albuquerque, NM 87109; tel. 505/881–7336; Michael Garcia, Administrator

Northwest New Mexico Hospice, 608 Reilly Avenue, P.O. Box 3336, Farmington, NM 87499; tel. 505/327–0301; FAX. 505/325–2477; Lizette Vannest, Program Coordinator

Presbyterian Hospice, 4545 McLeod N.E., Suite G, Albuquerque, NM 87109; tel. 505/888–5656; June Vermillion

Professional Home Health Care, Inc., 1345 Pacheco Street, Santa Fe, NM 87505; tel. 505/982–8581; FAX. 505/982–0457; Debbie Conway

Quality Continuum Hospice, 5608 Zuni, S.E., Albuquerque, NM 87108; tel. 505/256–8360; Kathleen M. Hart, Administrator

Roswell Hospice Home Care, 600 North Richardson, Roswell, NM 88201; tel. 505/623–5887; FAX. 505/624–8566; Nancy Smith, Program Director

Sandia Hospice, 5740 Osuna, N.E., Albuquerque, NM 87109; tel. 505/888–0095; FAX. 505/888–2025; Catherine A. Esterheld, Executive Director

St. Anthony's Hospice, 1008 Douglas Avenue, P.O. Box 1170, Las Vegas, NM 87701; tel. 505/425–3353; Beatrice R. Velasquez, Administrator

Staff Builders Services, Inc., 826 Camino De Monte Rey, P.O. Box 23448, Santa Fe, NM 87502; tel. 505/983–5408; Pamela Brunsell, RN, Administrator

The Hospice Center, 1422 Paseo De Peralta, Santa Fe, NM 87501; tel. 505/988–2211; FAX. 505/986–1833; Barbara Elder Owas, RN, Executive Director

VNS Health Services, Inc., 706 La Joya, N.E., Espanola, NM 87532; tel. 505/753–2284; FAX. 505/756–2179; Beatrice Sceery, Manager, Home Health, Hospice

Victory Home Health Hospice, 624 University, P.O. Box 670, Las Vegas, NM 87701; tel. 505/454–0499; FAX. 505/425–9105; Maria Luisa Padilla, Administrator

NEW YORK

Capital District Hospice, Inc., a/k/a Hospice of Schenectady, Hospice of Saratoga, Hospice of Amsterdam, Hospice of Warren County, 1411 Union Street, Schenectady, NY 12308; tel. 518/377–8846; FAX. 518/377–8868; Philip G. Di Sorbo, Executive Director

Caring Community Hospice of Cortland, 4281 North Homer Avenue, Cortland, NY 13045; tel. 607/753–9105; Mary Beach, Administrator, Patient Care Coordinator

Catskill Area Hospice, Inc., 542 Main Street, Oneonta, NY 13820; tel. 607/432–6773; FAX. 607/432–7741; Lesley Deleski, Executive Director

Christian Nursing Hospice, Inc., d/b/a CNR Hospice, 110 Lake Avenue South, Suite 33, Nesconset, NY 11767; tel. 516/265–5300; FAX. 516/265–5789; Camille Harlow, Executive Director

Comstock Hospice Care Network, 1225 West State Street, Olean, NY 14760; tel. 716/372–2106; FAX. 716/372–4635; Kathleen Mack, Hospice Director

East End Hospice, Inc., 1111 Riverhead Road, P.O. Box 1048, Westhampton Beach, NY 11978; tel. 516/288–8400; FAX. 512/288–8492; Priscilla Ruffin, Executive Director

Herkimer County Hospice, 267 North Main Street, Herkimer, NY 13350; tel. 315/867–1317; FAX. 315/867–1371; Sue Campagna, Administrator

High Peaks Hospice, Inc., P.O. Box 840, Trudeau Road, Saranac Lake, NY 12983; tel. 518/891–0606; FAX. 518/891–0657; Maureen Sayles, Executive Director

Hospicare of Tompkins County, Inc., 172 East King Road, Ithaca, NY 14850; tel. 607/272–0212; FAX. 607/272–0237; Nina K. Miller, Executive Director

Hospice Buffalo, Inc., 225 Como Park Boulevard, Cheektowaga, NY 14227–1480; tel. 716/686–8060; FAX. 716/686–8128; J. Donald Schumacher, Psy.D., President, Chief Executive Officer

Hospice Care Network, 900 Ellison Avenue, Westbury, NY 11590; tel. 516/832–7100; FAX. 516/832–7160; Maureen Hinkleman, Chief Executive Officer

Hospice Care, Inc., 4277 Middlesettlement Road, New Hartford, NY 13413; tel. 315/735–6484; FAX. 315/735–8545; Wes Case, Executive Director

Hospice Chautauqua County, Inc., Nine Park Street, P.O. Box 503, Sinclairville, NY 14782–0503; tel. 716/962–2010; FAX. 716/962–2020; Susan Schwartz, M.P.A., Executive Director

Hospice Family Care, 550 East Main Street, Batavia, NY 14020; tel. 716/343–7596; FAX. 716/343–7629; Deborah Schafer, Operating Director

Hospice VNSW/WPHC, Inc., d/b/a Hospice of Westchester, 95 South Broadway, White Plains, NY 10601; tel. 914/682–1484; FAX. 914/682–9425; Emily R. Giannattasio, Executive Director

Hospice of Central New York, 990 7th North Street, Liverpool, NY 13088; tel. 315/634–1100; FAX. 315/634–5559; Peter Moberg-Sarver, President, Chief Executive Officer

Hospice of Chenango County, Inc., 21 Hayes Street, Norwich, NY 13815; tel. 607/334–3556; FAX. 607/334–3688; Laurie Vogel, Executive Director

Hospice of Dutchess County, 70 South Hamilton Street, Poughkeepsie, NY 12601; tel. 914/485–2273; Wayne Herron, Chief Executive Officer

Hospice of Jefferson County, Inc., 425 Washington Street, Watertown, NY 13601; tel. 315/788–7323; FAX. 315/785–9932; Frances Calabrese, Executive Director

Hospice of North Country, 386 Rugar Street, Plattsburgh, NY 12901–2306; tel. 518/561–8465; FAX. 518/561–3182; Sarah Anderson, Executive Director

Hospice of Northern Westchester and Putnam, Inc., an Affiliate of VNA of Hudson Valley, 43 Kensico Drive, Mount Kisco, NY 10549; tel. 914/666–4228; FAX. 914/666–0378; Cornelia Schimert, Director

Hospice of Orange in Hudson Valley, Inc., Hospice of Sullivan County, 70 Dubois Street, Newburgh, NY 12550; tel. 914/561–6111; FAX. 914/561–2179; Daniel Grady, Executive Director

Hospice of Orleans County, 13996 Route 31 West, Albion, NY 14411; tel. 716/589–0809; Mary Ann Fisher, Executive Director

Hospice of Rochester and Hospice of Wayne and Seneca Counties, 49 Stone Street, Rochester, NY 14604; tel. 716/325–1880, ext. 1155; FAX. 716/325–7678; Sue Greer, RN, B.S.N., Vice President, Hospice Services

Hospice of St. Lawrence Valley, Inc., 6439 State Highway 56, P.O. Box 469, Potsdam, NY 13676; tel. 315/265–3105; FAX. 315/265–0323; Brian Gardam, Executive Director

Hospice of the Finger Lakes, 25 William Street, Auburn, NY 13021; tel. 315/255–2733; FAX. 315/252–9080; Theresa Kenny Kline, Executive Director

Jansen Memorial Hospice/Home Nursing Association of Westchester, 69 Main Street, Tuckahoe, NY 10707; tel. 914/961–2818, ext. 307; FAX. 914/961–8654; Lucille D. Winton, Director

Livingston County Hospice, Two Livingston County Campus, Mount Morris, NY 14510; tel. 716/243–7290; FAX. 716/243–7287; Cheryl Pletcher, Administrator

Mercy Hospice, St. Pius X Service Center, 1220 Front Street, Uniondale, NY 11553; tel. 516/485–3060; FAX. 516/485–1007; Sister Dolores Castellano, Executive Director

Section C

Mountain Valley Hospice, 73 North Main Street, Gloversville, NY 12078; tel. 518/725–4545; FAX. 518/725–8066; Nancy Dowd, Executive Director

Niagara Hospice, Inc., 4675 Sunset Drive, Lockport, NY 14094; tel. 716/439–4417; FAX. 716/439–6035; Carol E. Gettings, M.S., Executive Director

Ontario–Yates Hospice, 756 Pre–Emption Road, Geneva, NY 14456; tel. 315/781–0071; Bonnie Hollenbeck, Administrator

Oswego County Hospice, Oswego County Health Department, 70 Bunner Street, Oswego, NY 13126; tel. 315/349–8259; FAX. 315/349–8269; Steven D. Rose, Administrator

Pax Christi Hospice, 355 Bard Avenue, Staten Island, NY 10310; tel. 718/876–1022; Patricia Farrington, Executive Director

Southern Tier Hospice, Inc., 244 West Water Street, Elmira, NY 14901; tel. 607/734–1570; FAX. 607/734–1902; Mary Ann Starbuck, Executive Director

The Brooklyn Hospice, 6323 Seventh Avenue, Brooklyn, NY 11220; tel. 718/921–7900; FAX. 718/921–0752; Abby Gordon, Administrator

Tioga County Hospice, 231 Main Street, Owego, NY 13827; tel. 607/687–0682; FAX. 607/684–6041; Janette Swindell, Administrator

United Hospice of Rockland, 18 Thiells–Mount Ivy Road, Pomona, NY 10970; tel. 914/354–5100; FAX. 914/354–2128; Amy Stern, Executive Director

VNS Hospice of Suffolk, 505 Main Street, Northport, NY 11768; tel. 516/261–7200; FAX. 516/261–1985; Virginia Stein, RN, M.S., Director, Patient Services

VNSNY Hospice Care, 1250 Broadway, New York, NY 10001; tel. 212/290–3888; FAX. 212/290–3933; Eileen Hanley, RN, M.B.A., Administrator

Visiting Nurse Hospice, 2180 Empire Boulevard, Webster, NY 14580; tel. 716/787–8315; FAX. 716/787–9726; Dorothy Chilton, Administrator

NORTH CAROLINA

Albemarle Home Care, 103 Charles Street, P.O. Box 189, Hertford, NC 27907; tel. 919/426–5488; Paula Vanhorn, Administrator

Albemarle Home Care, County Office Building, P.O. Box 189, Edenton, NC 27907; tel. 919/482–7001; Angie Layden, Administrator

Albemarle Home Care, Highway 168, P.O. Box 189, Currituck, NC 27907; tel. 919/232–2026; Victoria Rentrop, Administrator

Albemarle Home Care, South 343, Courthouse Complex, P.O. Box 189, Elizabeth City, NC 27907–0189; tel. 800/478–0477; FAX. 919/338–4364; Kay Cherry, Director

Albemarle Home Care and Hospice, 400 South Road Street, P.O. Box 189, Elizabeth City, NC 27907–0189; tel. 919/338–4066; FAX. 919/338–4069; Beth Ehrhardt, M.S.W., Hospice Program Coordinator

Angel Home Health Agency, 268 Highway 19S, Suite Three, P.O. Box 389, Bryson City, NC 28713; tel. 704/488–3877; Sandy Smith, Administrator

Caldwell County Hospice, Inc., 902 Kirkwood Street, N.W., Lenoir, NC 28645; tel. 704/754–0101; FAX. 704/757–3335; Cathy S. Simmons, Executive Director

Cape Fear Valley Home Health and Hospice, 3357 Village Drive, Fayetteville, NC 28304

Cashiers Home Health, Highway 107 South, 59 Hospital Road, Sylva, NC 28779; tel. 704/586–7410

Center of Living Home Health and Hospice, d/b/a Center of Living Healthcare, 416 Vision Drive, Zip 27203, P.O. Box 9, Asheboro, NC 27204–0009; tel. 910/672–9300, ext. 263; FAX. 910/672–0868; Billie Vuncannon, Chief Executive Officer, President

Community Home Care and Hospice, 516 Owen Drive, Fayetteville, NC 28304; tel. 910/323–9816; FAX. 910/484–6724; Brinda L. Williams, Business Office Manager

Comprehensive Home Health Care, 3840 Henderson Drive, Jacksonville, NC 28456; tel. 910/346–4800; Linda Powers, Patient Care Manager

Comprehensive Home Health Care, 819 Jefferson Street, P.O. Box 366, Whiteville, NC 28472; tel. 910/642–5808; FAX. 910/640–1374; Sheila Faulk, Director

Comprehensive Home Health Care, 1120 Ocean Highway W, P.O. Box 200, Supply, NC 28462; tel. 910/754–8133, ext. 212; FAX. 910/754–2096; Crystal Floyd, RN, Director

Comprehensive Home Health Care and Comprehensive Hospice, Inc., 101 South Craig Street, P.O. Drawer 2540, Elizabethtown, NC 28337; tel. 910/862–8538; Sherry Hester, Director, Office Operations

Comprehensive Home Health Care–Hospice, 3311 Burnt Mill Drive, Wilmington, NC 28403; tel. 910/251–8111; FAX. 910/343–1218; Debra Nixion Jones, Patient Case Manager

Comprehensive Home Health Care/Comprehensive Hospice, 1800 Skibo Road, Suite 228, Fayetteville, NC 28303; tel. 910/864–8411; Gwendolynn Harrell, Regional Director

Craven County Home Health–Hospice Agency, 2818 Neuse Boulevard, P.O. Drawer 12610, New Bern, NC 28561; tel. 919/636–4930; FAX. 919/636–5301

Dare Hospice, Villa Dunes Road T1, Nags Head, NC 2795927948; tel. 919/441–6242; Mary A. Burrus, Executive Director

Davie County Health Department, and Home Health, Hospice of Davie County, 210 Hospital Street, P.O. Box 848, Mocksville, NC 27028; tel. 704/634–8770; FAX. 704/634–0335; Dennis E. Harrington, M.P.H. Health Director

Duplin Home Care and Hospice Inc., 234 Smith Chapel Road, Mt. Olive, NC 28365; tel. 910/296–0819; FAX. 910/296–0482; Rhonda Lucus, RN, Hospice Coordinator

Duplin Home Care and Hospice, Inc., 101 East Main Street, Wallace, NC 28466; tel. 919/285–1100, ext. 6637; FAX. 910/285–1172; Glenda Kenan, RN, Home Health Coordinator

Duplin Home Care and Hospice, Inc., 238 Smith Chapel Road, Mount Olive, NC 28365

Edgecombe County HomeCare and Hospice, 2909 North Main Street, Tarboro, NC 27886; tel. 919/641–7558; FAX. 919/641–7004; Jessie Worthington, Hospice Program Director

Four Seasons Hospice, 802 Old Spartanburg Highway, P.O. Box 2395, Hendersonville, NC 28739; tel. 704/692–6178; FAX. 704/692–2365; Barbara W. Stewart, Executive Director

Good Shepherd Home Health and Hospice Agency, Inc., P.O. Box 465, Hayesville, NC 28904; tel. 704/389–6311; Ruth Kraushaar, RN, Hospice Coordinator

Good Shepherd Home Health and Hospice Agency, Inc., Main and May Streets, Hayesville, NC 28904

Good Shepherd Home Health and Hospice Agency, Inc., P.O. Box 465, Hayesville, NC 28904; tel. 704/389–6311; FAX. 704/389–9584; Ruth Onsum, Hospice Coordinator

Home Health Agency of Chapel Hill, Inc., 1101 Weaver Dairy Road, P.O. Box 4126, Chapel Hill, NC 27514; tel. 919/929–7149; Paula Balber, Hospice Coordinator

Home Health and Hospice Care, Inc., 1004 Jenkins Avenue, P.O. Box 190, Maysville, NC 28555; tel. 919/743–2800; Janet Haddow–Green, Administrator

Home Health and Hospice Care, Inc., 1023 Beaman Street, P.O. Box 852, Clinton, NC 28328; tel. 800/695–4442; FAX. 910/592–7392; Richard Stone, Administrator

Home Health and Hospice Care, Inc., d/b/a Kitty Askins Hospice Center, 107 Handley Park Court, Goldsboro, NC 27534; tel. 800/260–4442; FAX. 919/735–8460; Donna Boren, RN

Home Health and Hospice Care, Inc., 2305 Wellington Drive, Suite G, P.O. Box 3673, Wilson, NC 27835–3673; tel. 919/291–4400; Deede Morgan, Hospice Director

Home Health and Hospice Care, Inc., 15 Noble Street, P.O. Box 1524, Smithfield, NC 27577–9300; tel. 919/934–0664; FAX. 919/934–9046; Phil Adams Administrator

Home Health and Hospice Care, Inc., 2419 East Ash Street, Suite Four and Five, Goldsboro, NC 27532; tel. 919/735–1386; FAX. 919/731–4985; Jim Wall, Administrator

Home Health and Hospice Care, Inc., 907A Southeast Second Street, Snow Hill, NC 28580

Home Health and Hospice Care, Inc., 702 BWH Smith Boulevard, Greenville, NC 27834

Home Health and Hospice Care, Inc., 102 North Carolina Highway 55 West, Mount Olive, NC 28365

Home Health and Hospice of Halifax, 1229 Julian R. Allsbrook Road, Roanoke Rapids, NC 27870; tel. 919/308–0700; FAX. 919/537–1872; Sheila Alford, RN, Home Care Director

Home Health and Hospice of Person County, 325 South Morgan Street, Roxboro, NC 27573; tel. 910/597–2542; FAX. 910/597–3367; Joyce Franke, Administrator

Home Technology Health Care–Hospice of Tar Heel, U.S. Highway 11 South and Chapman Road, P.O. Box 1645, Greenville, NC 27835; tel. 919/758–4622; FAX. 919/758–7006; Patti Lotts, Executive Director

HomeHealth and Hospice Care Inc., 744 Airport Road, P.O. Box 1396, Kinston, NC 28503; tel. 919/527–9561; Ann Harrison, Clinical Director

Hometown Hospice, Inc., 2404 South Charles Street, Suite E, Greenville, NC 27835

Hospice Home, 918 Chapel Hill Road, Burlington, NC 27215; tel. 910/513–4460; FAX. 910/513–4471; Judy Bowman, Manager

Hospice at Charlotte, Inc., 1420 East Seventh Street, Charlotte, NC 28204; tel. 704/375–0100; FAX. 704/375–8623; Janet Fortner, President

Hospice at Greensboro–Beacon Place, 2500 Summit Avenue, Greensboro, NC 27405; tel. 910/621–2500; FAX. 910/621–4516; Pamela Barrett, Executive Director

Hospice at Greensboro–Beacon Place, 2502 Summit Avenue, Greensboro, NC 27405

Hospice of Alamance–Caswell, 730 Hermitage Road, P.O. Box 2122, Burlington, NC 27216; tel. 910/538–8040; FAX. 910/538–8049; Peter Barcus, Executive Director

Hospice of Alexander County, Inc., 412 Third Street, S.W., Taylorsville, NC 28681; tel. 704/632–5026; FAX. 704/632–3707; Donna W. AuBuchon, Executive Director

Hospice of Alleghany, P.O. Box 1278, Sparta, NC 28675; tel. 910/373–8018; Wanda Branch, Administrator

Hospice of Ashe, 392 Highway 88 East, P.O. Box 421, Jefferson City, NC 28640; tel. 704/265–3926; FAX. 704/264–2125; Wanda Branch, Administrator

Hospice of Avery County, Inc., 351 West Mitchell Street, P.O. Box 1357, Newland, NC 28657; tel. 704/733–0663; FAX. 704/733–0375; Sharon Cole, RN, Patient Care Coordinator

Hospice of Burke County, Inc., 402 Main Street, Valdese, NC 28690; tel. 704/879–1601; FAX. 704/879–3500; A. Malanie Price, Executive Director

Hospice of Cabarrus County, Inc., 1060 Diploma Place, S.W., P.O. Box 1235, Concord, NC 28025–1235; tel. 704/788–9434; FAX. 704/788–6013; Shirley McDowell, Executive Director

Hospice of Carteret County, Inc., P.O. Box 1818, Morehead City, NC 28557; tel. 919/247–2808; Ruth Yearick–Jones, Administrator

Hospice of Catawba Valley, Inc., 263 Third Avenue, N.W., Hickory, NC 28601; tel. 704/328–4200; FAX. 704/328–3031; Julie Packer, Interim Executive Director

Hospice of Chatham County, Inc., 200 East Street, P.O. Box 1077, Pittsboro, NC 27312; tel. 919/542–5545; FAX. 919/542–6232; Susan H. Balfour, RN, Executive Director

Hospice of Cleveland County, Inc., 951 Wendover Heights Drive, Shelby, NC 28150; tel. 704/487–4677; FAX. 704/481–8050; Myra McGinnis Hamrick, Executive Director

Hospice of Cumberland County, 711 Executive Place, Suite 207, P.O. Box 53324, Fayetteville, NC 28305; tel. 910/484–1776; FAX. 910/484–6294; Melissa Harris, Hospice Coordinator

Hospice of Davidson County, Inc., 524 South State Street, P.O. Box 1941, Lexington, NC 27293–1941; tel. 910/248–6185; FAX. 910/248–4574; Gary Drake, Executive Director

Hospice of Gaston County, Inc., d/b/a Gaston Hospice, 717 North New Hope Road, P.O. Box 3984, Gastonia, NC 28054; tel. 704/861–8405; FAX. 704/865–0590; Lee Bucci, Executive Director

Hospice of Harnett County, Inc., 111A North Ellis Avenue, Dunn, NC 28339; tel. 910/892–1213; FAX. 910/892–1229; Grace E. Tart, Administrator

Hospice of Iredell County, Inc., 2347 Simonton Road, P.O. Box 822, Statesville, NC 28677; tel. 704/873–4719; FAX. 888/464–4673; Ron D. Thompson, Executive Director

Hospice of Iredell County, Inc., 153 North Main Street, Suite One, Mooresville, NC 28115; tel. 704/663–0051; FAX. 704/872–1810; Judy Snowden, Executive Director

Hospice of Lee County, Inc., P.O. Box 1181, Sanford, NC 27331–1181; tel. 919/774–4169; FAX. 919/774–6348; Janet MacLaren Scovil, Executive Director

Hospice of Lincoln County, Inc., 107 North Cedar Street, P.O. Box 1526, Lincolnton, NC 28093–1526; tel. 704/732–6146; FAX. 704/732–9808; Gregory Urban, Executive Director

Hospice of Macon County, Inc., 30 Roller Mill Road, P.O. Box 1594, Franklin, NC 28734; tel. 704/369-6641; Suzanne A. Owens, Executive Director

Hospice of McDowell County, Inc., 116 North Logan Street, P.O. Box 1072, Marion, NC 28752; tel. 704/652-1318; FAX. 704/659-1631

Hospice of Mitchell County, 188 C Highway 226 South, Bakersville, NC 28705; tel. 704/688-4090; FAX. 704/688-3566; Clarice Turner, Executive Director

Hospice of Pamlico County, Inc., 13628 North Carolina Highway 55, Alliance, NC 28509; tel. 919/745-5171; Diane McDaniel, Executive Director

Hospice of Rockingham County, Inc., 2150 North Carolina 65, P.O. Box 281, Wentworth, NC 27375; tel. 910/427-9022; FAX. 919/427-9030; Fran Hughes, Director

Hospice of Rutherford County, Inc., 374 Hudlow Road, P.O. Box 336, Forest City, NC 28043; tel. 704/245-0095; FAX. 704/248-1035; Rita Burch, Executive Director

Hospice of Scotland County, 600 South Main Street, Suite F, P.O. Box 1033, Laurinburg, NC 28353; tel. 910/276-7176; FAX. 910/277-1941; Linda McQueen, RN, Executive Director

Hospice of Stanly County, Inc., 960 North First Street, Albemarle, NC 28001-3350; tel. 704/983-4216; FAX. 704/983-6662; Elvin T. Henry, Executive Director

Hospice of Stokes County, Highway 8 and 89, P.O. Box 10, Danbury, NC 27016; tel. 910/593-5309; FAX. 910/593-5354; Margaret Arey, Executive Director

Hospice of Surry County, Inc., 1326 North Main Street, Mount Airy, NC 27030; tel. 910/789-2922; FAX. 910/789-0856; Laney Johnson, Director

Hospice of Surry County, Inc., 688 N. North Bridge Street, Elkin, NC 28621; tel. 910/526-2650; FAX. 910/526-2383; Laney Johnson, Executive Director

Hospice of Union County, Inc., 700 West Roosevelt Boulevard, Monroe, NC 28110; tel. 704/292-2100; FAX. 704/292-2190; Charlene C. Broome, Executive Director

Hospice of Wake County, Inc., 4513 Creedmoor Road, Suite 400, Raleigh, NC 27612; tel. 919/782-3959; FAX. 919/782-3598; Karolyn H. Kaye, Executive Director

Hospice of Watauga, 136 Furman Road, Route Five, Box 199, Boone, NC 28607; tel. 704/265-3926; Wanda Branch, Administrator

Hospice of Winston-Salem/Forsyth County, Inc., 1100 South Stratford Road, Building C, Winston-Salem, NC 27103-3212; tel. 910/768-3972; FAX. 910/659-0461; Jo Ann Davis, Chief Executive Officer

Hospice of Yancey County, 314 West Main Street, P.O. Box 471, Burnsville, NC 28714; tel. 704/682-9675; FAX. 704/682-4713; Donna Messenger, Executive Director

Hospice of the Carolina Foothills, Inc., 421 North Tryon Street, Tryon, NC 28782; tel. 704/859-2270; FAX. 704/859-2731; Jean H. Eckert, Executive Director

Hospice of the Piedmont/Care Connection, 1801 Westchester Drive, High Point, NC 27262; tel. 910/889-8446; FAX. 910/889-3450; Leslie Kalinowski, President

Lower Cape Fear Hospice, Inc., 810 Princess Street, Wilmington, NC 28401; tel. 910/762-0200; FAX. 910/762-9146; Eloise Thomas, Executive Director

Lower Cape Fear Hospice, Inc., 121 West Main Street, P.O. Box 636, Whiteville, NC 28472; tel. 919/642-9051; Barbara Godwin, RN, BSN, Patient Care Coordinator

Lower Cape Fear Hospice, Inc., 2507-B North Marine Boulevard, Jacksonville, NC 28546; tel. 919/347-6266; FAX. 910/347-9279; Lori Griffin, Patient Care Coordinator

Lower Cape Fear Hospice, Inc., 112 Pine Street, P.O. Box 1926, Shallotte, NC 28459; tel. 910/754-5356; FAX. 910/754-5351; Jeff Hickey, Director, Operations

Lower Cape Fear Hospice, Inc., 103 North Morehead Street, Elizabethtown, NC 28337

Madison Home Care and Hospice, P.O. Box 909, 170 Carl Eller Road, Mars Hill, NC 28754; tel. 704/689-3491; FAX. 704/689-3496; John H. Estes, Executive Director

Mountain Area Hospice, Inc., 85 Zillicoa Street, P.O. Box 16, Asheville, NC 28802; tel. 704/255-0231; FAX. 704/255-2880; Kit Cosgrove, Associate Director

Northern Hospital Home Care and Hospice, 933 Old Rockford Street, P.O. Box 1605, Mount Airy, NC 27030; tel. 910/719-7434; FAX. 910/719-7435; Mary Alice Culler, Administrator

Onslow Home Health and Hospice, 612 College Street, Jacksonville, NC 28540; tel. 910/577-6660; FAX. 910/577-6636; Shirley P. Moore, RN, Director

Pemberton Hospice, 106 North Main Street, P.O. Box 3069, Pembroke, NC 28372; tel. 910/521-5550; FAX. 910/521-3335

Richmond County Hospice, Inc., 230 South Lawrence Street, Rockingham, NC 28379, P.O. Box 2136, Rockingham, NC 28380; tel. 910/997-4464; FAX. 910/997-4484; Lydia P. Talbert,CRNH, Patient Care Coordinator

Roanoke Home Care, 210 West Liberty Street, Williamston, NC 27892; tel. 919/792-5899; Barbara Owens, Nursing Director

Roanoke Home Care-Hospice, 408 Bridge Street, P.O. Box 238, Columbia, NC 27925; tel. 919/796-2681; FAX. 919/796-0818; Barbara Owens, RN, Director, Nursing

Roanoke Home Care-Hospice, 198 North Carolina Highway 45 North, Plymouth, NC 27962; tel. 800/842-8275; FAX. 919/793-3417; Phyllis McCombs, Referrals and Intake

Roanoke-Chowan Hospice, Inc., 521 Myers Street, P.O. Box 272, Ahoskie, NC 27910; tel. 919/332-3392; FAX. 919/332-5705; Brenda Hoggard, Director

Sandhills Hospice, Inc., Inverness Park, Five Aviemore Drive, P.O. Box 1956, Pinehurst, NC 28374; tel. 910/295-2220; FAX. 910/295-3720; Carole White, RN, Executive Director

St. Joseph of the Pines Home Health Agency, 117 Wortham Street, P.O. Box 974, Wadesboro, NC 28170; tel. 704/694-5992; Kathy Appenzeller, Director, Daily Operations

St. Joseph of the Pines Home Health Agency, 404 North Main Street, Troy, NC 27371; tel. 910/572-4962; FAX. 910/572-5010; Barbara Smith, CRNH Coordinator

St. Joseph of the Pines Home Health Agency, 336 South Main Street, P.O. Box 879, Raeford, NC 28376; tel. 910/875-8198; FAX. 910/875-8862; Ronda Pickler, Administrator

Staff Builders, 112 Broad Street, Oxford, NC 27565

Staff Builders/MedVisit Home Health and Hospice, 1924 Ruin Creek Road, Suite 207, Henderson, NC 27536; tel. 919/492-6046; FAX. 919/492-9967; Dorothy Forrest, Administrator

Staff Builders/MedVisit Home Health and Hospice, Highway 39 North, Route Three, Box 48, Louisburg, NC 27549; tel. 919/496-1900; FAX. 919/496-7052; Sherry Watson, Administrator

Swain County Home Health Agency, Main Street, Robbinsville, NC 28771; tel. 704/479-2110; FAX. 704/479-3848; Betty DeHart, RN

Triangle Hospice at the Meadowlands, 1001 Corporate Drive, Hillsborough, NC 27278; tel. 919/644-0764; FAX. 919/644-0932; Jerome Schiro, RN, M.N., Director

Triangle Hospice, Inc., 1804 Martin Luther King, Jr. Parkway, Suite 112, Durham, NC 27707; tel. 919/490-8480; FAX. 919/493-0242; Lucy Worth, Executive Director

Wendover, 953 Wendover Heights Drive, Shelby, NC 28150; tel. 704/487-7018; FAX. 704/487-7028; Myra McGinnis Hamrick, Executive Director

Wilson Home Care, Inc. d/b/a Hometown Hospice, 1705 South Tarboro Street, P.O. Box 2303, Wilson, NC 27894; tel. 919/237-4333; FAX. 919/237-1125; Gail Brewer, RN, M.P.H., Home Care Manager

Yadkin County Home Health/Hospice Agency, 217 East Willow Street, P.O. Box 457, Yadkinville, NC 27055; tel. 910/679-4207; FAX. 910/679-6358; Jackie Harrell, Nursing Supervisor

NORTH DAKOTA

Heart of America Hospice, 800 S. Main, Rugby, ND 58368; tel. 701/776-5261; FAX. 701/776-5448; Duane Jerde, Administrator

Heartland Hospice, 30 W. 7th Street, Dickinson, ND 58601; tel. 701/225-7251; FAX. 701/227-3803; Bruce Hopkins, Administrator

Hospice of the Red River Valley, 702 28th Avenue, N., Fargo, ND 58102; tel. 701/237-4629; FAX. 701/280-9069; Susan J. Fuglie, Executive Director

Mercy Hospice, 1031 7th Street, Devils Lake, ND 58301; tel. 701/662-2131; FAX. 701/662-4862; Marlene Krein, Administrator

Riveredge Hospice of St. Francis, 415 Oak Street, Breckenridge, ND 56520; tel. 218/643-7594; FAX. 218/643-7502; Cindy Splichal, Director

St. Alexius Hospice, 1120 E. Main Street, Bismarck, ND 58501; tel. 701/224-7888; FAX. 701/224-7811; Barbara Schweitzer, Administrator

Trinity Hospice, 1015 South Broadway, Minot, ND 58701; tel. 701/857-5083; FAX. 701/857-5079; Marilyn Bader, Administrator

United Community Hospice, 216 South Broadway, Minot, ND 58701; tel. 701/857-2499; FAX. 701/857-2565; Sister Lona Thorson, Administrator

OHIO

Allen Hospice, 5700 Southwyck Boulevard, Suite 111, Toledo, OH 43614; tel. 419/867-4655; FAX. 419/865-1601; Jane Wilcox, RN, Executive Director

Aultman Hospice Program, 4510 Dressler Road, N.W., Canton, OH 44718; tel. 216/493-3344; FAX. 330/493-8637; Kathy Cummings, RN, Program Coordinator

Bridge Home Health and Hospice, 1900 South Main Street, Findlay, OH 45840; tel. 419/423-5351; FAX. 419/423-8967; Karen Mallett, Vice President, Home Care Services

CHWC-Hospice Care, 909 Snyder Avenue, Montpelier, OH 43543; tel. 419/485-3154

Columbia Mercy Medical Center Hospice, 1445 Harrison Avenue, N.W., Suite 201, Canton, OH 44708; tel. 330/489-6855; FAX. 330/489-6868; Ken Wasiniak, L.I.S.W., Hospice Manager

Community Hospice, 2609 Franklin Boulevard, Cleveland, OH 44113; tel. 216/363-2397; FAX. 216/363-2284; Cheryl Carrino, Patient Care Coordinator

Community Hospice Care, 182 St. Francis Avenue, Rear Suite, Tiffin, OH 44883; tel. 419/447-4040; FAX. 419/447-4657; Rebecca S. Shank, Executive Director

Crawford County Hospice, 1810 East Mansfield Street, Bucyrus, OH 44820; tel. 419/562-2001; FAX. 419/562-2803; Bert Maglott, RN, Executive Director

Geauga County Visiting Nurse Service and Hospice, 13221 Ravenna Road, Chardon, OH 44024; tel. 216/286-9461; Patricia Huels, RN, Director, Patient Services

Holmes County Hospice, 931 Wooster Road, Millersburg, OH 44654; tel. 330/674-5035; FAX. 330/674-2528; Diana L. Henry, RN, B.S.N., Director

Home Nursing Service and Hospice, 900 Third Street, Marietta, OH 45750; tel. 614/373-8549; FAX. 614/373-3995; Pamela Parr, Director

Hospice Care of Williams Co., Inc., 127 West Butler Street, Bryan, OH 43506; tel. 419/636-8034; FAX. 419/636-8221

Hospice Homecare, 92 Northwoods Boulevard, #A, Columbus, OH 43235; tel. 614/781-1444; FAX. 614/781-1450; Belinda R. Shaw, RN, Clinical Manager

Hospice Service of Licking County, Inc., d/b/a Hospice of Central Ohio, Homecare of Central Ohio, 1435 B West Main Street, Newark, OH 43055; tel. 614/344-0311; FAX. 614/344-6577; Michele McMahon, Executive Director

Hospice and Health Services of Fairfield County, 1111 East Main Street, Lancaster, OH 43130; tel. 614/654-7077; FAX. 614/654-6321; Donna J. Householder, Executive Director

Hospice of Alliance VNA, 2367 West State Street, Alliance, OH 44601; tel. 330/821-7055; Lin Severs, M.S.N., Executive Director

Hospice of Appalachia, 282 East State Street, P.O. Box 768, Athens, OH 45701; tel. 614/592-3493; FAX. 614/594-5591; Carol May, Director

Hospice of Care Corporation, 831 South Street, Chardon, OH 44024; tel. 216/338-6628; FAX. 216/286-7662; Elizabeth A. Petersen, RN, Vice President, Operations

Hospice of Cincinnati, Inc., 4310 Cooper Road, Cincinnati, OH 45242; tel. 513/891-7700; Leigh Gerdsen, RN, Director

Hospice of Columbus, 181 South Washington Boulevard, Columbus, OH 43215; tel. 614/645-6471; FAX. 614/645-5895; Larry L. Miracle, Director

Hospice of Coshocton County, Inc., 230 South Fourth, P.O. Box 1284, Coshocton, OH 43812; tel. 614/622-7311; FAX. 614/622-7310; Barbara Brooks-Emmons, Director

Hospice of Darke County, Inc., 122 West Martz Street, Greenville, OH 45331; tel. 937/548-2999; FAX. 937/548-7144; Joy Marchal, Executive Director

Hospice of Dayton, Inc., 324 Wilmington Avenue, Dayton, OH 45420; tel. 513/256-4490; Betty Schmoll, President

Hospice of Guernsey, Inc., 1300 Clark Street, P.O. Box 1537, Cambridge, OH 43725; tel. 614/432–7440; Patricia Howell, RN, Administrator

Hospice of Henry County, 104 East Washington, Suite 302, Napoleon, OH 43545; tel. 419/599–5545; FAX. 419/599–1714

Hospice of Knox County, 302 East High Street, Mount Vernon, OH 43050; tel. 614/397–5188; FAX. 614/397–5189; Linda M. Bales, Interim Executive Director

Hospice of Medina County, 797 North Court Street, Medina, OH 44256; tel. 330/722–4771; FAX. 330/722–5266; Patricia M. Stropko–O'Leary, Executive Director

Hospice of Miami County, Inc., P.O. Box 502, Troy, OH 45373; tel. 937/335–5191; FAX. 937/335–8841; Sidney J. Pinkus, Chief Executive Officer

Hospice of Morrow County, P.O. Box 272, 851 West Marion Road, Mount Gilead, OH 43338; tel. 419/946–9822; FAX. 419/946–9971; Frances Turner, RN, Executive Director

Hospice of North Central Ohio, Inc., 1605 County Road 1095, Ashland, OH 44805; tel. 419/281–7107; FAX. 419/281–8427; Ruth A. Lindsey, Executive Director

Hospice of Northwest Ohio, 30000 East River Road, Perrysburg, OH 43551; tel. 419/661–4001; FAX. 419/661–4015; Virginia Clifford, Executive Director

Hospice of Pickaway County, 702 Pickaway Street, Circleville, OH 43113; tel. 614/474–3525; FAX. 614/474–1832

Hospice of Tuscarawas County, Inc., 201 West Third Street, Dover, OH 44622; tel. 330/343–7605; FAX. 330/343–3542; Janie Jones, Administrator

Hospice of V.N.A., 1195–C Professional Drive, Van Wert, OH 45891; tel. 419/238–9223; FAX. 419/238–9391; Donna Grimm, President, Chief Executive Officer

Hospice of Visiting Nurse Service, 3358 Ridgewood Road, Akron, OH 44333; tel. 800/335–1455; FAX. 216/668–4680; Patricia Waickman, M.S.N., RN, Vice President, Hospice

Hospice of Wayne County, Ohio, 2330 Cleveland Road, Wooster, OH 44691; tel. 330/264–4899; FAX. 330/264–4874; Mary Ellen Walsh, Executive Director

Hospice of Wyandot County, 320 West Maple Street, Suite C, Upper Sandusky, OH 43351; tel. 419/294–5787; FAX. 419/294–4721; Susan Barth, RN, Interim Director

Hospice of the Miami Valley, Inc., 930 Laurel Avenue, Hamilton, OH 45015; tel. 513/863–3433; FAX. 513/867–7444; Rebecca Hight, RN, President, Chief Executive Officer

Hospice of the Valley, Inc., 5190 Market Street, Youngstown, OH 44512; tel. 330/788–1992; FAX. 330/788–1998; Kenneth O. Drees, Executive Director

Hospice of the Western Reserve, 300 East 185th Street, Cleveland, OH 44119; tel. 216/383–2222; FAX. 216/383–3750; David A. Simpson, Executive Director

Hospice, The Caring Way of Defiance County, 197–C Island Park Avenue, Defiance, OH 43512; tel. 419/784–3818; FAX. 419/782–4979; Ruthann Czartoski, Hospice Coordinator

Loving Care Hospice, Inc., 106 West High Street, P.O. Box 445, London, OH 43140; tel. 614/852–7755

M J Nursing Registry, 2534 Victory Parkway, Cincinnati, OH 45206; tel. 513/961–1000; FAX. 513/872–7550; Jan Brown, RN, Assistant Administrator, Home Care

Madison County Home Health Hospice Inc., 212 North Main Street, London, OH 43140; tel. 614/852–3915; FAX. 614/852–5125; Barbara C. Anderson, Executive Director

Mercy Hospice, 7010 Rowan Hill Drive, Cincinnati, OH 45227; tel. 513/271–1440; FAX. 513/271–2405

Mount Carmel Hospice, 1144 Dublin Road, Columbus, OH 43215; tel. 614/234–0200; FAX. 614/234–0201; Mary Ann Gill, Director

NCJW/Montefiore Hospice, One David N. Myers Parkway, Beachwood, OH 44122; tel. 216/360–9080, ext. 338; FAX. 216/360–9697; Jennifer Hooks, Hospice Director

New Life–Choices in LifeCare, 5255 North Abbe Road, Elyria, OH 44035; tel. 216/934–1458; FAX. 216/934–1567; Micki M. Tubbs, President, Chief Executive Officer

Ohio's Integrated Hospice, 2365 Lakeview Drive, Suite B, Beavercreek, OH 45431; tel. 513/427–3074; Patricia B. Kehl, M.A., RN, Administrator

Stein Hospice Services, Inc., 1200 Sycamore Line, Sandusky, OH 44870; tel. 800/625–5269; FAX. 419/625–5761; Rosalie A. Perry, Executive Director

The Hospice of Staff Builders, 6100 Rockside Woods Boulevard, Suite 100, Independence, OH 44131; tel. 216/642–0202; FAX. 216/642–3273; Marion Keathley, Intake Coordinator

The VNA of North Central Ohio Hospice, 188 West Third Street, P.O. Box 1322, Mansfield, OH 44901–1322; tel. 419/524–4663; FAX. 419/524–4862

Tri County Hospice, Inc., One Park Centre, Suite 209, Wadsworth, OH 44281; tel. 210/336–6595

Tricare Hospice, 701 Park Road, Bellefontaine, OH 43311; tel. 800/886–5936; FAX. 513/593–9783; Jim Hoffman, Director

VNA of Cleveland Hospice, 2500 East 22nd Street, Cleveland, OH 44115; tel. 216/931–1450; FAX. 216/694–6355; Roberta Laurie, Executive Director, Hospice

Valley Hospice, Inc., One Ross Park, Steubenville, OH 43952; tel. 614/283–7487; FAX. 614/283–7507; Karen Nichols, RN, B.S.N., Executive Director

Vencare Hospice, 2055 Reading Road, Suite 240, Cincinnati, OH 45202; tel. 513/241–9209; FAX. 513/241–4012; Rebecca Wright, RN, CRNH, Administrator

Visiting Nurse Hospice and Health Care, 383 West Dussel Drive, Maumee, OH 43537; tel. 419/897–2803; FAX. 419/897–2810; Nancy Host, Executive Director

Vitas Health Care Corporation of Ohio, 4700 Smith Road, Suite M, Cincinnati, OH 45212; tel. 513/531–6317; FAX. 513/531–7551; Gay Haggard, General Manager

OKLAHOMA

Blaine County Hospice, 401 North Clarence Nash, P.O. Box 567, Watonga, OK 73772; tel. 405/623–7414; FAX. 405/623–7412; Lisa Watson, RN

Carter Hospice Care, 1235 Sovereign Row, Suite C–5, Oklahoma City, OK 73108; tel. 405/942–1161; FAX. 405/947–2718; Kathi Egan, RN, Executive Director

Carter Hospice Care, 828 North Porter, Norman, OK 73069; tel. 405/942–1161; Stanley F. Carter, Administrator

Carter Hospice Care, Inc., 9916A East 43rd Street, S., Tulsa, OK 74146; tel. 405/942–1161; FAX. 405/947–2718; Stanley F. Carter, Administrator

Columbia Hospice Oklahoma, 7508 North Broadway Extension, Suite 110, Oklahoma City, OK 73112; tel. 800/243–7776; FAX. 405/848–5135; Sharon Collins, RN, CRNH, Hospice Director

Community Hospice, Inc., 1400 South Broadway, Edmond, OK 73034; tel. 405/359–1948; FAX. 405/359–4913; L. Jim Anthis, Ph.D., President, Chief Executive Officer

Crossroads Hospice of Oklahoma, L.L.C., 10810 East 45th Street, Suite 310, Tulsa, OK 74146; tel. 918/663–3234; FAX. 918/663–3334; G. Perry Farmer, Jr., Executive Director

Eastern Oklahoma Hospice, 1301 Reynolds, Poteau, OK 74953; tel. 918/647–8235; Jody L. Shepherd, RN, Agency Director

Family Hospice of Greater Oklahoma City, 4900 Richmond Square, Suite 203, Oklahoma City, OK 73118; tel. 405/843–4097; FAX. 405/843–5629; Steven L. Edwards, Executive Director

Family Hospice of Tulsa, 4325 E. 51st Street, Suite 103, Tulsa, OK 74135; tel. 918/488–9477; FAX. 918/488–9506; Robert D. Lane, ARNP, L.C.S.W., Executive Director

Four Square Hospice, 223 Plaza, P.O. Box 827, Madill, OK 73446; tel. 405/795–3384; Norma Howard

Good Shepherd Hospice, 1300 Sovereign Row, Oklahoma City, OK 73108; tel. 405/943–0903; FAX. 405/943–0950; Don Greiner, Executive Director

Hospice Care of Oklahoma, 5901 North Western, Suite 101, Oklahoma City, OK 73118; tel. 405/848–2324; Jean Calder, CRNH

Hospice Circle of Love, 605 South Monroe, Enid, OK 73701; tel. 405/234–2273; FAX. 405/234–1990; Cathy Graber, Director

Hospice of Central Oklahoma, 4549 Northwest 36th Street, Oklahoma City, OK 73122; tel. 405/491–0828; Sharon Holland, President

Hospice of Green Country, Inc., 3010 South Harvard, Suite 110, Tulsa, OK 74114–6136; tel. 918/747–2273; FAX. 918/747–2573; Sue Mosher, M.S., Executive Director

Hospice of Lawton Area, Inc., 1930 Northwest Ferris Avenue, Suite 10, Lawton, OK 73505; tel. 405/248–5885; FAX. 405/355–2446; Lee Young, Executive Director

Hospice of McAlester, First National Center, Suite 112, McAlester, OK 74501; tel. 918/423–3911; FAX. 918/426–6335; Vicki Schaff, Executive Director

Hospice of Oklahoma County, Inc., 4334 Northwest Expressway, Suite 106, Oklahoma City, OK 73116–1515; tel. 405/848–8884; FAX. 405/841–4899; Douglas M. Gibson, Executive Director

Hospice of Ponca City, 1904 North Union, Suite 103, Ponca City, OK 74601; tel. 405/762–9102; FAX. 405/762–9111; Melody Lahann, Director

Hospice of the Heartland, 1002 South College, Tahlequah, OK 74464; tel. 918/458–3011; FAX. 918/458–3067; Deborah Huggins, Administrator

Judith Karman Hospice, Inc., 824 South Main Street, P.O. Box 818, Stillwater, OK 74076; tel. 405/377–8012; FAX. 405/624–9007; Mary Lee Warren, Executive Director

Lawton Community Hospice, Inc., 4645 West Gore Boulevard, Lawton, OK 73505; tel. 405/250–0440; FAX. 405/250–0489; Jerry W. Black, Program Director

Mid–Lakes Hospice Care, 500 East Main Street, P.O. Box 728, Stigler, OK 74462; tel. 918/967–8499; FAX. 918/967–2584; John C. Neal, Administrator

Mission Hospice, Inc., 7301 North Broadway, Suite 225, Oklahoma City, OK 73116; tel. 405/848–3779; FAX. 405/848–8481; Susan Osborne, RN, Administrator

New Hope Hospice of Oklahoma, Inc., 5460 South Garnett, Suite H, Tulsa, OK 74146; tel. 918/622–7744; Tonia Caselman, L.S.W., Executive Director

Norman Community Hospice, 2424 Springer, Suite 105, Norman, OK 73069; tel. 405/360–4884; FAX. 405/360–4913; Debbie Standefer, RN, PCC

Preferred Hospice, 1200 North Walker, Suite 200, Oklahoma City, OK 73103; tel. 405/235–7674; FAX. 405/235–5478; Dean A. Deason, M.D., Director, Operations

Russell–Murray Hospice, Inc., 221 South Bickford, P.O. Box 1423, El Reno, OK 73036; tel. 405/262–3088; FAX. 405/262–3082; Cathie Sales, Administrator

The Hospice, 2023 West Broadway, Muskogee, OK 74401; tel. 918/683–1192; FAX. 918/687–0750; Jamie Bridgewater, Executive Director

Visiting Nurses Agency of Eastern Oklahoma Hospice, 220 South Main Street, Spiro, OK 74959; tel. 918/962–9491; Jim Medley, Chief Executive Officer

Visiting Nurses Agency of Eastern Oklahoma, Inc., Two Eastern Heights Shopping Center, P.O. Box 1647, Muldrow, OK 74948; tel. 918/427–1010; Mary Keith, RNC, Vice President

OREGON

Benton Hospice Service, Inc., 917 Northwest Grant Street, P.O. Box 100, Corvallis, OR 97333; tel. 541/757–9616; FAX. 541/757–1760; Judy List, Executive Director

Curry County Home/Health Hospice, 29984 Ellensburg, P.O. Box 746, Gold Beach, OR 97444; tel. 541/247–7084; FAX. 541/247–2117; Lori Kent, RN

Harney County Home Health/Hospice, 420 North Fairview, Burns, OR 97720; tel. 541/573–8360; FAX. 541/573–8389; Angela Ivey, Director

Hospice of Bend, 1303 Northwest Galveston, Bend, OR 97701; tel. 541/383–3910; FAX. 541/388–4221

Hospice of Redmond and Sisters, P.O. Box 1092, Redmond, OR 97756; tel. 541/548–7483; FAX. 541/548–1507; Ellen Garcia, Executive Director

Hospice of St. Vincent, 9340 Southwest Barnes Road, Suite M, Portland, OR 97225; tel. 503/297–6109; Jerry Hunter

Hospice of the Gorge, Inc., 114 Cascade Street, P.O. Box 36, Hood River, OR 97031; tel. 503/387–6449; FAX. 503/386–6700; Ina Holman, Executive Director

Kaiser Permanente, Home Health/Hospice, 2701 Northwest Vaughn Street, Suite 140, Portland, OR 97210; tel. 503/499–5200; FAX. 503/499–5200; Linda Van Buren, RN, Administrator

Klamath Hospice, Inc., 437 Main Street, Klamath Falls, OR 97601; tel. 541/882–2902; FAX. 541/883–1992; Teresa C. Pastorius

Legacy VNA Hospice, 2701 Northwest Vaughn, Suite 720, P.O. Box 3426, Portland, OR 97208; tel. 503/225–6370; FAX. 503/225–6398; Linda Downey, Director

Lovejoy Hospice, Inc., 132 Northeast B Street, Suite 23, P.O. Box 356, Grants Pass, OR 97526; tel. 503/474–1193; FAX. 503/474–3035; Charlotte Carroll, RN, P.H.N., Executive Director

Lower Umpqua Hospice, 600 Ranch Road, Reedsport, OR 97467; tel. 541/271–2171, ext. 229; FAX. 541/271–1108; Geraldine Simms, RN, Manager

Mid–Willamette Valley Hospice, 1467 13th Street, S.E., Salem, OR 97302; tel. 503/588–3600; FAX. 503/363–3891; Simon B. Paquette, M.S.W., Administrator

Mt. Hood Hospice, 17270 Southeast Bluff Road, P.O. Box 835, Sandy, OR 97055; tel. 503/668–5545; FAX. 503/668–7951; Lindy Blaesing, Executive Director

Pathway Hospice, Inc., 323 West Idaho Avenue, Ontario, OR 97914; tel. 541/889–0847; FAX. 541/889–0849; Betty Cooper, RN

Providence Home Services Hospice, 1235 Northeast 47th, Suite 215, 4805 Northeast Glisan (Mailing Address), Portland, OR 97213; tel. 503/331–4601; FAX. 503/215–4624; Karen Bell, Director

South Coast Hospice, 371 West Anderson, Suite 218, Coos Bay, OR 97420; tel. 503/269–2986; FAX. 503/267–0458; Linda J. Furman, Administrator

Washington County Hospice, Inc., 427 Southeast Eighth Avenue, Hillsboro, OR 97123–4519; tel. 503/648–9565; FAX. 503/648–1282; Christine Larch, Administrator

Willamette Falls Hospice, 1678 Beavercreek Road, Suite K, Oregon City, OR 97045; tel. 503/655–0550; FAX. 503/655–7585; Robert Steed, Administrator

XL Hospice of Lakeview, 100 North D Street, Suite Three, P.O. Box 337, Lakeview, OR 97630; tel. 541/947–5122; FAX. 541/947–2253; Dian Jepson, RN, Patient Care Coordinator

PENNSYLVANIA

Abington Memorial Hospital Home Care and Hospice Program, 2510 Maryland Road, Suite 250, Willow Grove, PA 19090–0520; tel. 215/881–5800; FAX. 215/881–5850; Marilyn D. Harris, Administrator

Albert Gallatin Hospice Program, 20 Highland Park Drive, Suite 203, Uniontown, PA 15401; tel. 412/438–6660; FAX. 412/438–4468; Chris Constantine, RN, Administrator

All Care Hospice, 472 1/2 South Poplar Street, Hazelton, PA 18201; tel. 717/459–2004; Mary Ann Barletta, RN, Administrator

Berks Visiting Nurse Association, Inc., 1170 Berkshire Boulevard, Wyomissing, PA 19610; tel. 610/378–0481; FAX. 610/378–9762; Lucille D. Gough, RN, President, Chief Executive Officer

Brandywine Hospice, 1219 East Lincoln Highway, Coatesville, PA 19320; tel. 610/384–4200; FAX. 610/384–6871; Margaret Zazo, RN, M.S.N., CS

Brookline Home Care & Hospice, 3901 South Atherton Street, State College, PA 16801; tel. 814/238–2121; FAX. 814/466–4806; Diane Good, Administrator

Centre Hospice, A Program of Centre HomeCare, Inc., 221 West High Street, Bellefonte, PA 16823–1385; tel. 814/355–2273; FAX. 814/353–9292; Molly Schwantz, Executive Director

Chandler Hall Hospice, 99 Barclay Street, Newtown, PA 18940; tel. 215/860–4000; FAX. 215/860–3458; Jane W. Fox, Executive Director

Clarion Forest VNA Hospice, R.D. 3, Box 186, Clarion, PA 16214; tel. 814/226–1140; FAX. 814/226–1143; Deborah J. Kelly, Director, Hospice

Cohhcare's Home Hospice Care, 10 Duff Road, Suite 213, Pittsburgh, PA 15235; tel. 412/247–5606; Carole K. Rimer

Columbia–Montour Home Hospice, Locust Court, 599 East Seventh Street, Suite One, Bloomsburg, PA 17815; tel. 717/784–1723; FAX. 717/784–8512; Jane Gittler, Chief Executive Officer

Comfort Care Hospice, 205 Grandview Corporate Place, Camp Hill, PA 17011; tel. 800/255–3300; FAX. 717/766–5037; Linda L. Smith, RN, Director

Community Nurses Professional Health Services/Hospice, 99 Erie Avenue, St. Marys, PA 15857; tel. 814/781–1415; FAX. 814/781–6987; Elizabeth A. Roberts, RN, Executive Director

Community Nursing Hospice, 1425 Scalp Avenue, Johnstown, PA 15904; tel. 814/262–0246; FAX. 814/262–9616; Gayle Petrunak, Patient Care Coordinator

Compassionate Care Hospice, 100 Granite Drive, Suite 200, Media, PA 19063; tel. 610/892–7741; FAX. 610/892–7721; Catherine A. Stevens, Administrator

Compassionate Care of Gwynedd, Inc., 716 Bethlehem Pike, Suite 100, Lower Gwynedd, PA 19002; tel. 215/540–1244; FAX. 215/540–9849; Christine M. Coletta, RNC, B.S.N., CRNH, Program Director

Crozer Hospice, One Medical Center Boulevard, Upland, PA 19013; tel. 610/447–6141; FAX. 215/447–6027; Maryann Dreisbach, RN, Director

Ephrata Community Home Care's Hospice Program, 169 Martin Avenue, Box 1002, Ephrata, PA 17522–1002; tel. 717/738–6599; FAX. 717/738–6343; Susan Auxier, RN, Clinical Supervisor

Family Hospice of Indiana County, a division of the V.N.A. of Indiana County, 119 Professional Center, 1265 Wayne Avenue, Indiana, PA 15701; tel. 412/463–8711; FAX. 412/463–8907; Linda E. Lutz, B.S.N., RN, Director, Special Care Services, Hospice

Family Hospice, Inc., 250 Mount Lebanon Blvd., Suite 203, Pittsburgh, PA 15234; tel. 412/572–8800; FAX. 412/572–8827; Judy Palbert, Executive Director

Forbes Hospice–Forbes Health System, 6655 Frankstown Avenue, Pittsburgh, PA 15206; tel. 412/665–3301; FAX. 412/665–3234; Maryanne Fello, RN, Manager

General Care Services, d/b/a Hospice of Warren County, Two Crescent Park, W., P.O. Box 68, Warren, PA 16365; tel. 814/723–2455; FAX. 814/723–1177; Elsa L. Redding, Director

Great Lakes Hospice, 300 State Street, Suite 301–H, Erie, PA 16507; tel. 814/877–6120; Debbie Burbules, Director

Guthrie Hospice, R.R. One, P.O. Box 154, Towanda, PA 18848; tel. 800/598–6155; FAX. 717/265–3570; Jocelyn O'Donnell, Administrator

Healthreach Home Care and Hospice, 409 South Second Street, Harrisburg, PA 17104; tel. 717/231–6363; Janet T. Foreman, RN

Holy Family Home Health and Hospice Care, 900 West Market Street, Owigsburg, PA 17961; tel. 717/366–0990; FAX. 717/366–3735; Arlene L. Mongrain, RN, B.S., Executive Director

Holy Redeemer, Nazarath and St. Home Health Services, 12265 Townsend Road, Philadelphia, PA 19154; tel. 215/671–9200; FAX. 215/671–1950; Jerold S. Cohen, President

Home Hospice Agency of St. Francis, 131 Columbus Innerbelt, New Castle, PA 16101; tel. 412/652–8847; FAX. 412/656–0876; Susan N. Ludu, Executive Director

Home Nursing Agency/VNA Hospice Program, 201 Chestnut Avenue, P.O. Box 352, Altoona, PA 16603–0352; tel. 814/946–5411; FAX. 814/941–2482; Sylvia H. Schraff, RN, Chief Executive Officer

Hospice Care of the VNA, 400 Third Avenue, Suite 100, Kingston, PA 18704; tel. 717/287–4402; FAX. 717/287–4809; Mary Ann Keirans, Administrator

Hospice Community Care, Inc., 385 Wyoming Avenue, Kingston, PA 18704; tel. 717/288–2288; FAX. 717/288–7424; Philip Decker, President

Hospice Preferred Choice, Inc., 2400 Ardmore Boulevard, Suite 302, Pittsburgh, PA 15221; tel. 412/271–2273; FAX. 412/271–3361; Christean Dugan, Administrator

Hospice Program/VNA of Hanover and Spring Grove, 440 North Madison Street, Hanover, PA 17331; tel. 717/637–1227; FAX. 717/637–9772; Sandra L. Wojtkowiak, RN, MSN, Administrator

Hospice Saint John, 665 Carey Avenue, Wilkes–Barre, PA 18702; tel. 717/823–2114; FAX. 717/823–6438; W. David Keating, Administrator

Hospice Services of the VNA of York County, 218 East Market Street, York, PA 17403; tel. 717/846–9900; FAX. 717/846–1933; Marie V. Fraser, President, Chief Executive Officer

Hospice of Central Pennsylvania, 98 South Enola Drive, P.O. Box 266, Enola, PA 17025–0266; tel. 717/732–1000; FAX. 717/732–5348; Karen M. Paris, Chief Executive Officer

Hospice of Community and Home Health Services, 117 North Hanover Street, Carlisle, PA 17013; tel. 717/245–5600; FAX. 717/249–9346; Elizabeth Hain, RN, Administrator

Hospice of Crawford County, Inc., 448 Pine Street, Meadville, PA 16335; tel. 814/333–5403; FAX. 814/333–5407; John E. Brown, Chief Executive Officer

Hospice of Lancaster County, 685 Good Drive, P.O. Box 4125, Lancaster, PA 17604–4125; tel. 717/295–3900; FAX. 717/391–9582; Mary Graner, President, Executive Director

Hospice of North Penn Visiting Nurse Association, 51 Medical Campus Drive, Lansdale, PA 19446; tel. 215/855–8297; FAX. 215/855–1305; Jane Spizzirri, Hospice Coordinator

Hospice of the Delaware Valley, 527 Plymouth Road, Suite 417, Plymouth Meeting, PA 19462; tel. 610/941–6700; FAX. 610/941–6440; Marcia M. Cook, Administrator

Hospice of the VNA of Bethlehem and Vicinity, 1510 Valley Center Parkway, Suite 200, Bethlehem, PA 18017; tel. 215/691–1100; FAX. 610/691–2271; Jean Fiore, RN, Administrator

Hospice of the VNA of Greater Philadelphia, One Winding Way, Philadelphia, PA 19131; tel. 215/581–2046; FAX. 215/473–5047; Beverly Pauktis, Administrator

Hospice–The Bridge, Lewistown Hospital, 1126 West Fourth Street, Lewistown, PA 17044–1909; tel. 717/242–5000; FAX. 717/242–5009; Shirley McNeal, RN, CRNH, Manager

HospiceCare of Pittsburgh, 11 Parkway Center, Suite 275, Pittsburgh, PA 15220; tel. 412/937–8088; FAX. 412/922–9609; Fran Romito, RN, Administrator

In Home Health, Inc., 750 Holiday Drive, Foster Plaza Nine, Suite 110, Pittsburgh, PA 15220; tel. 412/928–2126; Margaret Timm, Director, Operations

Jefferson Hospice–Main Line, Gerhard Building, 130 South Bryn Mawr Avenue, Bryn Mawr, PA 19018; tel. 610/526–3265; Timothy P. Cousounis, Executive Director

Keystone Hospice, 275 Commerce Drive, Suite 314, Fort Washington, PA 19034; tel. 215/628–8592; FAX. 215/628–8491; Gail A. Inoerwies, Director

Lehigh Valley Hospice, 2166 South 12th Street, Allentown, PA 18103; tel. 610/402–7400; FAX. 610/402–7382; William V. Dunstan, Administrator

Lutheran Home Health Care Services/Hospice, 2700 Luther Drive, Chambersburg, PA 17201; tel. 717/264–8178; FAX. 717/264–6347; Diane M. Howell, Executive Director

McKean County VNA Hospice, 20 School Street, P.O. Box 465, Bradford, PA 16701–0465; tel. 814/362–7466; FAX. 814/362–2916; Elizabeth M. Costello, Administrator

Mercy Health Hospice Program, 1500 Lansdowne Avenue, Darby, PA 19023; tel. 610/237–5010; FAX. 610/237–4689; Cathy Franklin

Montgomery Hospital Hospice Program, 25 West Fornance Street, Norristown, PA 19401; tel. 610/272–1080; Elise N. Lamarra, B.S.N.

Neighborhood Visiting Nurse Association, 795 East Marshall Street, West Chester, PA 19380; tel. 610/696–6511; FAX. 610/344–7064; Mahlon R. Fiscel, Chief Executive Officer

North Chester County Community Nursing Service Hospice, 301 Gay Street, Phoenixville, PA 19460; tel. 215/933–1263; Thomasina A. Chamberlain, Administrator

North Penn HH Agency/Hospice Program, 520 Ruah Street, P.O. Box Eight, Blossburg, PA 16912; tel. 717/638–2141, ext. 700; FAX. 717/638–2163; Wilma Hall, Program Director

Northeast Health and Hospice Care, Inc., 38 North Main Street, Pittston, PA 18640; tel. 717/654–0220; FAX. 717/654–0360; Stephan Hannon, Administrator

Odyssey Health Care of Pennsylvania, Park West One, Suite 500, Cliff Mine Road, Pittsburgh, PA 15275; tel. 412/494–0870; Deborah Yakunich

Olsten Kimberly Quality Care Hospice, 4811 Jonestown Road, Suite 235, Harrisburg, PA 17109; tel. 717/541–4466; Susan Gearhart, RN

Olsten Kimberly QualityCare Hospice, 749 Northern Boulevard, Clarks Summit, PA 18411; tel. 800/870–0085; Peggy Durkin, Administrator

Palliative Care Services, Fox Chase Cancer Center, 500 Township Line Road, Cheltenham, PA 19012; tel. 215/728–3011; FAX. 215/728–5270; Susanne Seeber, RN, MSN

Penn Care at Home, 51 North 39th Street, Philadelphia, PA 19104; tel. 215/662–8996; Rita P. Rebman, RN, MSN

Professional Hospice Care, 3605 Vartan Way, Harrisburg, PA 17110; tel. 717/671–3700; FAX. 717/671–3713; Denise K. Harris, M.S.W., Director

Ridgway Community Nurse Service, Inc., Hospice, 20 North Broad Street, P.O. Box 179, Ridgway, PA 15853; tel. 814/773–5705; FAX. 814/776–6246; Catherine M. Grove, RN, Executive Director

SUN Home Hospice, 61 Duke Street, Northumberland, PA 17857; tel. 717/473–8320; FAX. 717/473–3070; Patricia Campbell, Director

Samaritan Care Hospice of Pennsylvania, 6198 Butler Pike, Suite 275, Blue Bell, PA 19422; tel. 215/653–7310; FAX. 215/653–7340; Peggy Bertels

Sivitz Jewish Hospice, 1620 Murry Avenue, Pittsburgh, PA 15217; tel. 412/422–5700; Deborah Shtulman, Executive Director

St. Gregory's Hospice, Inc., 359 Steubenville Pike, Burgettstown, PA 15021; tel. 412/729–3051; FAX. 412/729–3820; Patricia Murphy, RN, M.S.N., Director

Susquehanna Regional Home Health Services and Hospice, 1201 Grampian Boulevard, Suite Three A, Williamsport, PA 17701–1967; tel. 717/323–9891; FAX. 717/323–0716; Pamela B. McCowan, RN, Director, Hospice

Three Rivers Family Hospice, Inc., 3025 Jacks Run Road, White Oak, PA 15131; tel. 412/672–6737; FAX. 412/672–5823; Jan Diehl, RN, M.S.N., Executive Director

Ultimate Home Health and Hospice Care, 212 North Second Street, Girardville, PA 17935; tel. 717/276–1148; Barbara McDonald, Administrator

Unlimited Home Care, Inc., Hospice, P.O. Box 1070, Uniontown, PA 15401; tel. 412/439–1610; FAX. 412/430–6891; Diane Sanner Crossan, Director

Upper Bucks Hospice, a Division of Life Quest Home Care, 2075 Quaker Pointe Drive, Quakertown, PA 18951; tel. 215/529–6100; FAX. 215/529–6253; Beth Gotwals, RN, M.S.N., Hospice Manager

VNA Community Services Hospice, 354 North Prince Street, P.O. Box 4304, Lancaster, PA 17604–4304; tel. 717/397–8251, ext. 1270; FAX. 717/397–8666; Cynthia Theurer, Hospice Director

VNA Health Care Services, 1789 South Braddock Avenue, Pittsburgh, PA 15218; tel. 412/256–6800; Andrew R. Peacock

VNA Hospice, 334 Jefferson Avenue, Scranton, PA 18501; tel. 717/341–6840; Nancy S. Menapace, RN, M.A., Administrator

VNA Hospice Services of Erie County, 1305 Peach Street, Erie, PA 16501; tel. 814/454–2831; Mary Frances Bauman, Administrator

VNA Hospice, Western Pennsylvania, 154 Hindman Road, Butler, PA 16001; tel. 412/282–6806; FAX. 412/282–7517; Liz Powell, RN, M.N., CRNP, Vice President

VNA of Easton Hospice, 3421 Nightingale Drive, Easton, PA 18045; tel. 215/258–7189; Theresa P. Onorata

VNA of Harrisburg, Inc. Hospice, 118 Washington Street, Harrisburg, PA 17104; tel. 717/233–1035; FAX. 717/233–2759; Thomas Tarasewich, Chief Executive Officer

VNA of Pottstown and Vicinity Comprehensive Hospice Program, 1963 East High Street, Pottstown, PA 19464; tel. 610/327–5700; FAX. 610/327–5701; Sandra Levengood, Executive Director

VNA/Hospice of Monroe County, Inc., R.R. Two, P.O. Box 2159A, East Stroudsburg, PA l8360; tel. 7l7/421–5390; FAX. 717/421–7423; Mark Hodgson, Administrator

Visiting Nurse Association of Northumberland County, 101 South Market Street, Shamokin, PA 17872; tel. 800/232–2486; FAX. 717/648–9590; Joseph L. Scopelliti, Jr., Executive Director

Visiting Nurses Association of the Lehigh Valley, Inc., 1710 Union Boulevard, Allentown, PA 18103; tel. 610/434–6134, ext. 177; FAX. 610/821–1982; Patricia Frenduto, President, Chief Executive Officer

Vitas Health Care Corporation, 805 East Germantown Pike, Suite 805, Norristown, PA 19401; tel. 215/275–2370; Emily B. Fedullo, RN, Director, Development

White Rose Hospice, 2870 Eastern Boulevard, York, PA 17402; tel. 717/849–5642; FAX. 717/849–5630; Karen Hook, B.S., Manager

Wissahickon Hospice, 8835 Germantown Avenue, Philadelphia, PA 19118; tel. 215/247–0277; FAX. 215/248–3253; Priscilla D. Kissick, RN, M.N., Executive Director

RHODE ISLAND

Hospice Care of Rhode Island, 169 George Street, Pawtucket, RI 02860–3868; tel. 401/727–7070; FAX. 401/727–7080; David Rehm, Executive Director

Hospice Care of the Visiting Nurse Service of Greater Woonsocket, Marquette Plaza, Woonsocket, RI 02895; tel. 401/769–5670; FAX. 401/762–2966; Elaine D. Bartro, RN, M.P.H., Chief Executive Officer

Hospice of Nursing Placement, 339 Angell Street, P.O. Box 603337, Providence, RI 02906; tel. 401/453–4544; Marcia Bigney, Administrator

Kent County Visiting Nurse Association Hospice, 51 Health Lane, Warwick, RI 02886; tel. 401/737–6050; FAX. 401/738–0247; Nancy Roberts, RN, M.S.N., Chief Executive Director

Northwest Home Care (Hospice), 185 Putnam Pike, P.O. Box 423, Harmony, RI 02829; tel. 401/949–2600; FAX. 401/949–5115; Beverly McGuire, President

VNA of Rhode Island, 157 Waterman Avenue, Providence, RI 02906; tel. 401/444–9400; FAX. 401/444–9430; Sandra L. Hooper, RN, M.B.A., CNAA, Director, Adult Services

VNS Hospice, 14 Woodruff Avenue, Narragansett, RI 02882–3467; tel. 401/788–2000; FAX. 401/788–2064; Lyle Mook, Director, Hospice Services

Valley Hospice–VNS of Pawtucket, Central Falls, Lincoln and Cumberland, 172 Armistice Boulevard, Pawtucket, RI 02860; tel. 401/725–3414; FAX. 401/728–4999; Christopher L. Boys, Chief Executive Officer

Visiting Nurse Health Services Hospice, 1184 East Main Road, P.O. Box 690, Portsmouth, RI 02871; tel. 401/682–2100; FAX. 401/682–2112; Jean Anderson, RN, M.S., Acting Chief Executive Officer

SOUTH CAROLINA

Hitchcock Rehabilitation Center Home Health and Hospice, 721 Richland Avenue, Aiken, SC 29801; tel. 803/643–0001, ext. 226; FAX. 803/649–0490; Gayle Jones, Director, Home Health, Hospice

Hospice Care of Tri–County, 111 Executive Pointe Boulevard, Columbia, SC 29212; tel. 803/750–8690; FAX. 803/750–8695; Edna McClain, RN, M.N., Administrator

Hospice Care of the Low Country, Hospice Care of the Low Country Home Health, 20 Palmetto Parkway, Hilton Head Island, SC 29926; tel. 803/681–7814; FAX. 803/681–7821; Carole B. Klein, Administrator

Hospice Care of the Piedmont, 303 West Alexander Street, Greenwood, SC 29646; tel. 864/227–9393; FAX. 864/227–9377; Nancy B. Corley, Director

Hospice Community Care, (Serving York, Chester, Lancaster, Cherokee, Union and Fairfield Counties), 325 South Oakland Avenue, Rock Hill, SC 29730; tel. 803/329–4663; FAX. 803/329–5935; Janet Dudek, Executive Director

Hospice Health Services, One Carriage Lane, Suite F1, Charleston, SC 29407; tel. 803/852–2177; FAX. 803/769–0148; Sylvia Barnes Green, RN, Executive Director

Hospice of Charleston, Inc., 3896 Leeds Avenue, North Charleston, SC 29405; tel. 803/529–3100; FAX. 803/529–3111; Carol Younker, Executive Director

Hospice of Chesterfield County, Inc., 140 South Page Street, P.O. Box 293, Chesterfield, SC 29709; tel. 803/623–9155; FAX. 803/623–3833; Monnie W. Bittle, Executive Director

Hospice of Colleton County, Inc., 214 Wichman Street, Walterboro, SC 29488; tel. 803/549–5948; FAX. 803/549–1451; Alfred S. Givens, Administrator

Hospice of Georgetown County, Inc., 1018 Huger Drive, P.O. Box 1436, Georgetown, SC 29442; tel. 803/546–3410; FAX. 803/527–6964; Brenda Stroup, RN, Executive Director

Hospice of Laurens County, 16 Peachtree Street, P.O. Box 178, Clinton, SC 29325; tel. 803/833–6287; FAX. 803/833–0556; Martha Ficklin, RN, Executive Director

Hospice of Marlboro County, Inc., P.O. Box 474, Bennettsville, SC 29512; tel. 803/479–5979; FAX. 803/479–3711; Kevin Long, Administrator

Hospice of Polk County, Inc., 423 North Trade Street, Tryon, NC 28782; tel. 803/859–2270; Jean H. Eckert, Administrator

Hospice of the Upstate, Inc., 506 Summit Avenue, Anderson, SC 29621; tel. 803/261–1594; FAX. 803/261–1523; Nancy Garrett–Boyle, Administrator

Interim HealthCare Hospice, 775 Spartan Boulevard, P.O. Box 9199, Greenville, SC 29604; tel. 864/587–6129; Nancy A. Dereng

Island Hospice, 94–C Main Street, Hilton Head Island, SC 29926; tel. 803/681–7035; FAX. 803/681–8506; Pamela D. Walker, Administrator

Lutheran Hospice Ministry, Lowman Home–Bolick Building, P.O. Box 444, White Rock, SC 29177; tel. 803/732–8756; Jean Tilley, Administrator

Mercy Hospice of Horry County, Columbus Plaza, 131 Wesley Street, P.O. Box 1409, Myrtle Beach, SC 29578; tel. 803/347–2282; FAX. 803/236–4306; Connie Fahey, FSM, Executive Director

Saint Francis Hospital Home Care–Hospice Services, 414 Pettigru Street, P.O. Box 9312, Greenville, SC 29601; tel. 864/233–5300; FAX. 864/233–4873; James A. Rogers

United Hospice, Inc., 6300 St. Andrews Road, Columbia, SC 29212; tel. 803/798–6605; FAX. 803/798–3001; Tamra N. West, Administrator

SOUTH DAKOTA

Ellen Stephen Hospice, P.O. Box 1805, Pine Ridge, SD 57770; tel. 605/455–1217; FAX. 605/455–1218; Susan Kay, Administrator

Hospice of the Hills, 1011 11th Street, Rapid City, SD 57701; tel. 605/341–7118; FAX. 605/399–7820; Dorothy Brown, Administrator

Lyon County Hospice, 803 South Greene Street, Rock Rapids, IA 51246; tel. 712/472–3618; FAX. 712/472–3616; Marge Smith, RN

Tekawitha Nursing Home, Sisseton, SD 57262; tel. 605/886–8491; Charleen Thompson, RN

TENNESSEE

A Plus Hospice, Inc., 116 Wilson Pike Circle, Suite 103, Brentwood, TN 37027; tel. 615/377–6276; FAX. 615/377–6287; Barbara Brown, Director

Advanced Home Care and Hospice, Inc., 507 A Hill Street, Springfield, TN 37172; tel. 615/384–0962

Alive Hospice, Inc., 1718 Patterson Road, Nashville, TN 37203; tel. 615/327–1085; FAX. 615/963–4700; Dick Hamilton, Interim Executive Director

Baptist Community Home Care and Hospice, 139 East Swan Street, Centerville, TN 37033; tel. 615/729–4500; FAX. 615/729–9000

Baptist Homecare Hospice Division, 1988 Rivermont Manor, 433 Sevier Avenue, Knoxville, TN 37901; tel. 615/632–5711

Buckeye Quality HHA, Inc. Hospice, Highway 52W, P.O. Box 697, Jamestown, TN 38556; tel. 615/879–9928; Sandra Hall, RN, Director, Patient Services

Columbia Homecare, 404 F East College, Dickson, TN 37055; tel. 615/441–1365; FAX. 615/446–8109; Susan Brink, RN, Acting Administrator

Columbia Homecare Hospice, 1084 Bradford Hicks Drive, Livingston, TN 38570; tel. 615/823–2050; FAX. 615/823–7982; Denise Elder, RN, Hospice Director

Community Health Services, Inc., 3918 Dickerson Road, Nashville, TN 37207

Comprehensive HHC Hospice Services, Inc., 1720 Church Street, Suite Two, Tazewell, TN 37879; tel. 423/626–0388; FAX. 423/626–0300; Patricia Brooks, Administrator, Coordinator

Country Hospice, 72 Stonebridge, Suite Three, Jackson, TN 38305; tel. 901/661–0800; Andy Gardner, RN, CRNH, Regional Hospice Director

Country Hospice, Highway 45 South, Route Two Box 23A, Selmer, TN 38375; tel. 901/645–6475; Andy Gardner, RN, CRNH, Regional Hospice Director

Country Hospice, 224 Memorial Drive, Paris, TN 38242; tel. 901/644–9200; Andy Gardner, RN, CRNH, Regional Hospice Director

Elk Valley Hospice Services, 303 South Morgan Avenue, Fayetteville, TN 37334; tel. 615/433–7026

Friendship Hospice of Nashville, Inc., 1326 Eighth Avenue, N., Nashville, TN 37203; tel. 615/327–3950; Andre L. Lee, DPA, Chairman of the Board

Home Health Care of East Tennessee, Inc., 1796 Mount Vernon Drive, N.W., Cleveland, TN 37311; tel. 423/479–4581; FAX. 423/479–5422; Annette Green, DOPC

Home–Bound Medical Care, 4355 Highway 58, Suite 101, Chattanooga, TN 37416; tel. 423/855–9128

Home–Bound Medical Care, Inc., 2165 Spicer Cove, Suite One, Memphis, TN 38134; tel. 901/386–5061

Homecare Hospice Services, 115 Vicksburg Avenue, Camden, TN 38320; tel. 901/584–1927; FAX. 901/584–0401

Hospice of Chattanooga, Inc., 165 Hamm Road, Chattanooga, TN 37405; tel. 423/267–6828; FAX. 423/756–4765; Viston Taylor III, Executive Director

Hospice of Cumberland County, Inc., 140 North Maine, Crossville, TN 38555; tel. 615/484–4748; Shirley Freeman, Executive Director

Hospice of Murfreesboro, 417 North University Street, Murfreesboro, TN 37130; tel. 615/896–4663

Hospice of Tennessee, 521 West Main Street, Lebanon, TN 37087; tel. 800/889–4673; FAX. 615/444–2547

Hospice of Tennessee Nursing Services, 900 East Hill Avenue, Suite 270, Knoxville, TN 37915; tel. 423/524–2138

Hospice of Tennessee, Inc., 112 Louise Avenue, Nashville, TN 37203; tel. 800/252–7442; FAX. 615/773–3033; Debbie Baumgart, RN, Regional Director

Hospice of Tennessee, Inc.–Franklin, 415 Williamson Square, Franklin, TN 37064

Hospice of West Tennessee, 1804 Highway 45 Bypass, West Tennessee Healthcare, Jackson, TN 38305; tel. 901/664–4220; FAX. 901/664–4231; Shirley Rowe, RN, Director

Housecall Hospice, 117 Center Park Drive, Suite 201, Knoxville, TN 37922; tel. 423/693–2474; FAX. 423/693–4031; Pamela Winch–Matayoshi, Vice President, Palliative Services

Housecall Hospice, 100 Rogosin Drive, Suite B, Elizabethton, TN 37643; tel. 615/547–0852; FAX. 615/543–6449; Rachel Vollman, Hospice Administrator

Housecall Hospice, 6025 Lee Highway, Executive Business Park, Chattanooga, TN 37421; tel. 615/892–2561; Caroline McBrayer

Housecall Hospice, 5350 Poplar Avenue, Suite 118A, Memphis, TN 38119; tel. 901/685–5300; FAX. 901/761–4321; Lynn Thomasson, Hospice Administrator

Housecall Hospice, 3343 Perimeter Hill Drive, Suite 102, Nashville, TN 37211; tel. 615/333–3994

JEM Health Care Inc., 315 10th Avenue, N., Suite 109, Nashville, TN 37207; tel. 615/726–8668; FAX. 615/726–8665; Marilyn McClain, Administrator

Lazarus House Hospice, Inc., 260 West Fifth Street, Cookeville, TN 38501; tel. 615/528–5133; J. Steve Mathias, Executive Director

Methodist Home Care Services, 1716 Parr Avenue, Dyersburg, TN 38024; tel. 901/287–2307; FAX. 901/287–2174

Methodist Hospice and Health Care Services, Inc., d/b/a Methodist Alliance Hospice, 930 South White Station Road, Suite 100, Memphis, TN 38117; tel. 901/680–0169; FAX. 901/537–2109; Caby Byrne, Director

Procare Support Services, Inc., 111 West Main, Jackson, TN 38301; tel. 800/211–7573; FAX. 901/427–1234; Elaine Kirk, Administrator

Robert Ramsey Memorial Hospice, 317 Steam Plant Road, Gallatin, TN 37066

Smoky Mountain Hospice, Inc., 324 West Broadway, Newport, TN 37821

St. Mary's Hospice, 900 Hill Avenue, Suite 120, Knoxville, TN 37915

TLC Hospice, 1200 Mountain Creek Road, Suite 440, Chattanooga, TN 37405; tel. 423/877–0983; FAX. 423/877–4944; Gloria J. Dodds, RN, B.S.N., Administrator

Tennessee Nursing Services of Knoxville, 1530 West Andrew Johnson Highway, Morristown, TN 37816; tel. 615/586–6808

Tennessee Nursing Services of Morristown, Coldwell Bank Building, 415 North Fairmont, Morristown, TN 37816; tel. 423/581–7690; FAX. 423/581–8164; Glena Duffield, Director, Hospice

Tri County Quality Homecare and Hospice, 20 Lee Avenue, Box 308, McKenzie, TN 38201; tel. 901/352–2240; FAX. 901/352–0320; Kay Taylor, RN, Patient Care Coordinator

Trinity Hospice, 1640 Cresthaven Road, Memphis, TN 38119; tel. 901/767–6767; FAX. 901/767–4627; Bradford A. Austin, RN, Hospice Director

University Home Health and Hospice, Inc., 135 Kennedy Drive, Martin, TN 38237; tel. 901/587–2996; FAX. 800/627–3228; Kellie Sims, B.S.W., Hospice Director

Willowbrook Hospice, Inc., 220 Second Avenue South, Franklin, TN 37064; tel. 800/790–8499; June Baldini, RN, Director

TEXAS

AIM Hospice, 703 East Concho, P.O. Box 2300, Rockport, TX 78381–2300; tel. 512/729–0507; FAX. 512/790–0243; Judith Johnson, RN, Ph.D., Administrator

Abacus Home Health Care, Inc., 3626 North Hall Street, Suite 818, Dallas, TX 75219

Absolute Home Care, Inc., 723 North Upper Broadway, Suite 610, Corpus Christi, TX 78401

Advantage Healthcare Services, 800 North Industrial Boulevard, Suite 102, Euless, TX 76039; tel. 817/545–5215; FAX. 817/545–0533; Carla S. Johnston, Administrator

American Home Health and Hospice, 315 South Oak, Pecos, TX 79772

American Hospice, Inc., 1349 Empire Central, Suite 707, Dallas, TX 75247; tel. 214/689–1010; Danny Walker, Administrator

Ann's Haven/VNA, 216 West Mulberry Street, Denton, TX 76201; tel. 817/566–6550; FAX. 817/383–4000; Karen Pemberton, RN, B.S.N.

Ark–La–Tex Health and Hospice Care, 6500 Summerhill Road, Suite 1–D, Texarkana, TX 75503; tel. 903/792–6430; FAX. 903/792–5537; Doyle Land, Chief Financial Officer

Burton Hospice Care, Inc., 6640 Eastex Freeway, Suite 140, Beaumont, TX 77708; tel. 409/892–7476; FAX. 409/892–7740; Vergie A. Burton, Administrator

Care United Hospice, 801 West Freeway, Suite 500, Grand Prairie, TX 75051

Center for Hospice Care, 1101 Decker Drive, Baytown, TX 77520

Christian Hospice Services, 215 Dalton Drive, Suite B, Desoto, TX 76115

Circle of Hope Hospice of VNA, 2211 East Missouri, Suite 220, El Paso, TX 79923; tel. 915/543–6201; Tom Meagher, Vice President, Hospice

Circle of Life Hospice, 2512 A Grandview, Odesa, TX 79761; tel. 915/367–7771; FAX. 915/367–2932; Jo Cheryl Miller, Administrator

Columbia Hospice Gulf Coast, 1102 North Mechanic, El Campo, TX 77437; tel. 409/543–9487; FAX. 409/543–9426; Ruth Kainer, RN, Director

Community Care Services, Inc., 403 East Blackjack, Dublin, TX 76446; tel. 817/445–4675; Bobbie Nichols, Administrator

Community Hospice of St. Joseph, 1000 Summit, Fort Worth, TX 76102

Community Hospice of Waco, 3215 Pine Avenue, Waco, TX 76708; tel. 817/756–6911; FAX. 817/756–0029; Richard E. Scott, President

Comprehensive Home Health Services, 901 North Galloway Avenue, Suite 101, Mesquite, TX 75149; tel. 972/285–3713; FAX. 972/285–3699; Julie Francis, Director

Country Nurses, Inc. Hospice and Home Care, 608 A North Rockwall Street, Terrell, TX 75160; tel. 972/563–2415; FAX. 972/563–4042; Carla Menasco, RN, B.S.N., Owner, Administrator

Crawford Hospice Services, Inc., 709 West 34th Street, Suite B, Austin, TX 78705; tel. 800/909–5543; FAX. 512/450–1281; Barbara Powell, Administrator

Cross Timbers Hospice, 103 East Frey, Stephenville, TX 76401; tel. 817/968–6142; FAX. 817/965–2388; Jan Hoover, RN, Administrator

Crown of Texas Hospice, 1000 South Jefferson, Amarillo, TX 79101; tel. 806/372–7696; FAX. 806/372–2825; Sharla Roselius, B.S.N., CRNH, RN, President

Crown of Texas Hospice, 100 I–45 North, Suite 240, Box 103, Conroe, TX 77301; tel. 409/788–7707; FAX. 409/788–7708; Marsha J. Irwin, RN, Ph.D., Director

Cypress Basin Hospice, Inc., 1805 North Jefferson, P.O. Box 544, Mount Pleasant, TX 75455; tel. 903/577–1510; FAX. 903/577–9377; Edd C. Hess, Executive Director

DNS Hospice, 2101 Kemp Boulevard, Wichita Falls, TX 76309; tel. 817/723–2771; FAX. 817/322–1754; Helen Dipprey, Chief Operating Officer

Denson Community Hospice, 1100 Gulf Freeway, N., Suite 122, League City, TX 77573; tel. 713/332–4970; FAX. 713/338–1766; Suzanne Denson, Administrator

East Harris County Hospice Services, Inc., Holland Avenue Medical Center, 1313 Holland Avenue, Building B, Houston, TX 77029; tel. 713/450–4500; FAX. 281/450–4006; Ipe Mathai, Executive Director

Family Hospice, 8701 Shoal Creek Boulevard, Suite 104, Austin, TX 78757; tel. 800/444–2405; FAX. 512/453–4165; Annette McDonald, Executive Director

Family Hospice of Dallas, 1140 Empire Central, Suite 235, Dallas, TX 75247; tel. 214/631–7273; FAX. 214/630–4032; Jim Grant, RN, B.S.N., M.S., Executive Director

Family Hospice of Fort Worth, 4040 Fossil Creek Boulevard, Suite 204, Fort Worth, TX 76137; tel. 817/232–3492; FAX. 817/232–3499; Sally Day, RN, B.S.N., Executive Director

Family Hospice of San Antonio, 6800 Park Ten Boulevard, Suite 110 North, San Antonio, TX 78213–4201; tel. 210/738–8141; FAX. 210/738–3507; Berdie Dailey, Executive Director

Family Hospice, Inc., 819 South Fifth Street, Temple, TX 76504; tel. 800/643–3139; FAX. 817/742–2023; Carrie Carson, Administrator

Family Service, Inc., 1424 Hemphill Street, Fort Worth, TX 76104–4790; tel. 817/927–8884, ext. 311; FAX. 817/926–0701; Oliver W. Gerland, Jr., President

First Community Homecare, 9323 Garland Road, Suite 308, Dallas, TX 75218

Genesis Hospice Care, 6724 South Broadway, Tyler, TX 75703; tel. 903/581–8700; FAX. 903/509–0138; Betty Johnson, RN

Golden Acres Hospice, 2525 Centerville Road, Dallas, TX 75228–2693; tel. 214/327–4503; FAX. 214/320–2683; Robert J. Watson, Director

Harris Hospice, 6000 Western Place, Suite 118, Fort Worth, TX 76107; tel. 817/570–8200; Barbara Hunt, Director

Heart of West Texas Hospice, 1927 Hickory, Colorado City, TX 79512

Heart of the Valley Hospice, 320 North Williams Road, San Benito, TX 78586; tel. 800/333–6131; FAX. 210/399–3553; Rebecca Hernandez, RN, Administrator

Heritage Health Care, 606 Avenue K, Cisco, TX 76437

Home Health Plus, 8122 Datapoint Drive, Suite 200, San Antonio, TX 78229–3264

Home Health Plus, 1900 West Loop South, Suite 150, Houston, TX 77027; tel. 713/622–9050; Mary James, RN

Home Health Plus, 5080 Spectrum Drive, Suite 105 West, Dallas, TX 75248–4641; tel. 800/925–1155; Ruby Marrero, RN

Home Health Services of Dallas, Inc., 2929 Carlisle Street, Suite 375, Dallas, TX 75204–1050

Home Health Specialists, Inc., 813 North Palestine, Athens, TX 75751; tel. 800/801–8126; FAX. 903/657–9513; Linda Johnson, RN, Administrator

Home Hospice, Grayson County Office, 505 West Center Street, P.O. Box 2306, Sherman, TX 75091; tel. 903/868–9315; FAX. 903/893–2772; Marty Barr, Executive Director

Home Hospice, 516 N. Texas, Odessa, TX 79761; tel. 915/580–4333; FAX. 915/580–2442; Hilton Chancellor, Director

Horizon Hospice Care, Inc., 9535 Forest Lane, Suite 126, Dallas, TX 75243; tel. 972/690–6632; FAX. 972/690–0834; Debbie Hoffpauir, National Director, Hospice Operations

Hospice Austin, 3710 Cedar Street, Suite 299, Austin, TX 78705; tel. 512/458–3261; FAX. 512/467–0767; Marjorie D. Mulanax, Executive Director

Hospice Brazos Valley, Inc., 2729 A East 29th Street, Bryan, TX 77802; tel. 409/776–0793; FAX. 409/774–0041; John Foster, B.S., M.S., CPM, Executive Director

Hospice Family Care, Inc., 1408 19th Street, Lubbock, TX 79401; tel. 806/765–6111; FAX. 806/762–0828; Connie Nutt, Administrator

Hospice Highland Lakes, 2001 South Water Street, Burnet, TX 78611; tel. 512/756–8003; FAX. 512/756–8046; Mary Kay Stephens, RNC, CRNH, Acting Director

Hospice Home Care, 10221 Desert Sands, Suite 108, San Antonio, TX 78216; tel. 210/377–1033; FAX. 210/377–2560; Al Hafer, Business Administrator

Hospice Longview, Inc., 802 Medical Circle, Suite C, Longview, TX 75601; tel. 903/753–7870; Ed Arneson, Executive Director

Hospice New Braunfels, 613 North Walnut, New Braunfels, TX 78130; tel. 210/625–7500; FAX. 210/625–0773; Opal Umpierre, Interim Administrator

Hospice Preferred Choice, 8203 Willow Place South, Suite 530, Houston, TX 77070; tel. 713/469–7990; FAX. 713/894–1294; Diane A. Incognito, Executive Director

Section C

Hospice Preferred Choice, 427 West 20th, Suite 603, Houston, TX 77008; tel. 713/864–2626; FAX. 713/864–9476; Diane Incognito, Administrator

Hospice Preferred Choice–DFW, 4425 West Airport Freeway, Suite 450, Irving, TX 75062; tel. 972/256–1881; FAX. 972/257–3740; Serene Smith, Administrator

Hospice Uvalde Area, (a program of Hospice San Antonio), P.O. Box 5280, Uvalde, TX 78802–5280; tel. 210/278–6691; FAX. 210/278–8925; Edwin Sasek, Bereavement Coordinator

Hospice in the Pines, 116 South Raguet, Lufkin, TX 75904; tel. 800/324–8557; FAX. 409/632–1352; Sherri D. Flynt, L.S.W., Social Services

Hospice in the Pines, 1300 South Frazier, Suite 315, Conroe, TX 77301; tel. 888/539–5252; FAX. 409/539–5272; Sheryl Wallace, Executive Director

Hospice of Abilene, Inc., 1682 Hickory, Abilene, TX 79602; tel. 915/677–8516; FAX. 915/675–5031; Lana Cunningham, RN, M.S.N., Clinical Director

Hospice of Cedar Lake, 409 North Third Street, Mabank, TX 75147–8614; tel. 903/887–3772; FAX. 903/887–3700; Karen Gilmore, Director

Hospice of Central Texas, 2007 B Medical Parkway, San Marcos, TX 78666; tel. 512/753–3584; FAX. 512/353–6573; Dawn O'Donnell, RNC, M.A., Administrator

Hospice of East Texas, 3800 Paluxy, Suite 560, Tyler, TX 75703; tel. 903/581–5585; FAX. 903/581–5293; Michael C. Couch, Executive Director

Hospice of El Paso, Inc., 3901 North Mesa, Suite 400, El Paso, TX 79902; tel. 915/532–5699; FAX. 915/532–7822; Charles E. Roark, Ed.D. FACHE

Hospice of Galveston County, Inc., 1708 Amburn Road, Suite C, Texas City, TX 77591; tel. 409/938–0070; FAX. 409/938–1509; Sue Mistretta, Executive Director

Hospice of Lubbock, Inc., 4314 South Loop 289, Zip 79413, P.O. Box 53276, Lubbock, TX 79453; tel. 806/795–2751; FAX. 806/795–8464; Linda McMurry, RN, B.S.N.

Hospice of Mercy, 500 West Third Avenue, Suite Two, Corsicana, TX 75110; tel. 903/872–4430; FAX. 903/872–4499; Ann Massey, Administrator

Hospice of Midland, Inc., 911 West Texas, Midland, TX 79701; tel. 915/682–2855; FAX. 915/682–2989; Carol Armstrong, Executive Director

Hospice of North Texas, Inc., 1420 Pioneer Road, Suite A, Mesquite, TX 75149; tel. 888/285–8081; FAX. 972/288–0742; Angela Herrin, Director

Hospice of Northeast Texas, 51 North Side Square, Cooper, TX 75432; tel. 903/395–2811; FAX. 903/395–2766; Nicki J. Beeler, Director

Hospice of San Angelo, Inc., 36 East Beauregard, Suite 1100, P.O. Box 471, San Angelo, TX 76902; tel. 915/658–6524; David McBride, Executive Director

Hospice of South Texas, 2004 Fagan Circle, Victoria, TX 77901; tel. 512/572–4300; FAX. 512/572–4532; Doug Eaves, Executive Director

Hospice of St. Michael Hospital of Texarkana, 1400 College Drive, Texarkana, TX 75501; tel. 903/794–1206; FAX. 903/735–5390; Tommy McGee, Administrator

Hospice of Texarkana, Inc., 803 Spruce Street, Texarkana, TX 75501; tel. 903/794–4263; FAX. 501/744–1108; Cynthia L. Marsh, Administrator

Hospice of V.N.A., 2905 Sackett, Houston, TX 77098; tel. 713/520–8115; FAX. 713/520–6054; Maggie Kao, Dr.P.H., Chief Executive Officer

Hospice of Wichita Falls, 4909 Johnson Road, Wichita Falls, TX 76310; tel. 817/691–0982; FAX. 817/691–1608; Jan Banta, Executive Director

Hospice of the Big Bend, 611 East Avenue E, Alpine, TX 79830–4817; tel. 915/837–7286; FAX. 915/837–1132; Marvie Burton, RN, Patient Care Coordinator, Executive Director

Hospice of the Big Country, Inc., 3113 Oldham Lane, Abilene, TX 79602; tel. 915/677–1191; FAX. 915/677–1808; Danna L. Clouse, Administrator

Hospice of the Gulf Coast, Inc., 17041 El Camino Real, Suite 102, Houston, TX 77058; tel. 281/282–0116; FAX. 281/282–0122

Hospice of the Heart, 305 North Brazos, Suite 10, P.O. Box 2180, Whitney, TX 76962; tel. 817/694–6009; FAX. 817/694–9926

Hospice of the Panhandle, 800 North Sumner, P.O. Box 2795, 79066–2795, Pampa, TX 79065; tel. 806/665–6677; Sherry McCavit, Executive Director

Hospice of the Plains, Inc., 7109 Olton Road, Plainview, TX 79072; tel. 806/293–5127; FAX. 806/293–5902; Roxey Williams, Executive Director

Hospice of the Southwest, Inc., 3800 East 42nd Street, Suite 500, P.O. Box 14710, Odessa, TX 79768–4710; tel. 915/362–1431; FAX. 915/362–1468; Connie Brinker, Executive Director

Hospice of the Three Rivers, 51 North 11th Street, Beaumont, TX 77702–2224; tel. 800/946–7742; Andi Whitmer, Administrator

Houston Hospice, 8811 Gaylord, Suite 100, Houston, TX 77024; tel. 713/468–2441; FAX. 713/468–0879; Margaret Caddy, RN, Executive Director

Huguley Hospice Care, 11801 South Freeway, Ft. Worth, TX 76115; tel. 817/551–2545; FAX. 817/568–3294; Donna Reddell, RN, Director

La Mariposa Hospice, 2001 North Oregon, El Paso, TX 79902; tel. 915/452–6802; Frances Witt, Director

Lakes Area Hospice, 254 Ethel Street, Jasper, TX 75951; tel. 409/384–5995; FAX. 409/384–9655; Jeanette Coffield, Executive Director

Lion Health Services, Inc., 800 West Airport Freeway, Suite 1100, Irving, TX 75062; tel. 972/445–4105; FAX. 972/445–4104; Susan Cerroni, RN, Director, Patient Services

Lone Star Hospice, 1212 Palm Valley Boulevard, Round Rock, TX 78664; tel. 512/467–7423; FAX. 512/218–9288; Janet A. Baker, Executive Director

Managed Home Health Care, 2211 Calder Avenue, Beaumont, TX 77707; tel. 409/832–4164; FAX. 409/832–4182; Charles Bray, C.E.D.

Nurses Hospice, Inc., 1330 East Eighth, Suite 323, Odessa, TX 79762; tel. 915/550–5066; Patsy Gerron, Administrator

Nurses In Touch Community Hospice, 7410 Blanco Road, Suite 450, San Antonio, TX 78216; tel. 210/979–9771; FAX. 210/979–6644; Mary Helen Tieken, RN, B.S.N., Administrator

Pacesetter Hospice, Inc., 6800 Manhattan, Suite 401, Fort Worth, TX 76120

Personal Touch Hospice of Texas, Inc., 8200 Brookriver Drive, Suite N109, Dallas, TX 75247; tel. 214/638–0357, ext. 305; FAX. 214/905–8687; Roy W. Terry, RN, Director

Rhodes Home Health Care, Inc., 3224 I–30 East, Suite 132, Mesquite, TX 75150; tel. 972/613–9772; Cherie Rhodes Cunigan

Robinson Creek Home Care, Inc., 1000 Westbank Drive, Suite 6B201, Austin, TX 78746; tel. 512/328–7606; Vanessa Nunnelly, Administrator

Rural Hospice, Inc., 501 South Alford, Crane, TX 79731; tel. 888/558–2300; FAX. 915/558–2335; Pam Ross, RN, Director

Samaritan Care Hospice of Texas, 17103 Preston Road, Suite 200, Dallas, TX 75248; tel. 800/669–3695; FAX. 972/407–5021; Martha Schueler, M.S., CRNH, Director Clinical Services

San Juan Home Health and Hospice, 300 North Nebraska Avenue, San Juan, TX 78589; tel. 210/782–0333; FAX. 210/782–0335; Tony Cortez, Director

Spohn Hospice, 600 Elizabeth Street, Corpus Christi, TX 78404; tel. 512/881–3159; FAX. 512/888–7405; Rita Mueller, RN, Director

St. Anthony's Hospice and Life Enrichment Program, 600 North Tyler, Zip 79107, P.O. Box 950, Amarillo, TX 79176–0001; tel. 806/378–6777; FAX. 806/378–5031; Lezlie Roberson, Executive Director

St. Joseph Hospice Houston, 1404 Calhoun Cullen Family Building, Houston, TX 77002; tel. 713/757–7488; FAX. 713/756–5127; Maresa Henry, Associate Director

St. Paul Hospice, 7920 Elmbrook Drive, Suite 116, Dallas, TX 75247; tel. 214/637–7474; Gwendolyn Pipkins, Director

Stephen's Hospice, 925 A North Graham, Stephenville, TX 76401–4216; tel. 817/965–7119; FAX. 817/965–3228; Kim Davis, Administrator

Taras Prime Home Health Care, Inc., 2765 East Trinity Mills, Suite 400, Carrollton, TX 75006

Tender Loving Care Home Health Hospice Agency, 5787 South Hampton Road, Suite 295, Dallas, TX 75232

Texas Health Staffing Services, Inc., 1115 Chihuahua Street, Suite B, Laredo, TX 78040; tel. 210/791–3012; Maria Elena Montemayor, Administrator

Texoma Community Hospice, 3821 Wilbarger Street, Vernon, TX 76384; tel. 800/658–6330; FAX. 817/552–2305; Jean Tucker, Administrator

The Hospice at the Texas Medical Center, 1905 Holcombe Boulevard, Houston, TX 77030; tel. 713/467–7423; FAX. 713/799–9227; Randal A. Condit, Vice President, Operations

The Southeast Texas Hospice, Inc., 912 West Cherry, P.O. Box 2385, Orange, TX 77630; tel. 409/886–0622; FAX. 409/886–0623; Mary McKenna, Administrator

Thee Hospice, Robinson Creek Center, 3100 I–45, Suite 10, Huntsville, TX 77342–6548; tel. 409/291–8439; FAX. 409/295–8582; Mollie Martin, RN, Patient Care Coordinator

Tomlinson Health Services, Hospice Program, 1300 West Mockingbird, Suite 160, Dallas, TX 75247; tel. 214/630–8847; FAX. 817/573–3160; Reba Tomlinson, Chief Executive Officer

Tyler Hospice, 423 South Beckham Avenue, Tyler, TX 75701; tel. 903/592–9703; FAX. 903/593–0639; Sandra L. Bunch, Administrator

Ultimate Hospice Care, 2300 Highway 365, Suite 440, Nederland, TX 77627; tel. 409/722–4993; FAX. 409/721–4930; Lewanna D. Jones, Administrator

Ultra Home Health Care, Inc., 8303 Southwest Freeway, Suite 410, Houston, TX 77074; tel. 713/988–5872; FAX. 713/271–1002; Mr. Tracy Potts, General Manager

VNA and Hospice of South Texas, 8207 Callaghan, Suite 355, San Antonio, TX 78230; tel. 210/377–3882; FAX. 210/349–4896; Frederick W. Hines, President

VNA and Hospice of the Texas Gulf Coast, P.O. Box 1777, Angleton, TX 77516–1777; tel. 409/849–6476; FAX. 409/849–0343; Jenny Carswell, Administrator

Visiting Nurse Association Hospice, 212 Brown Street, Brownwood, TX 76801–2915; tel. 915/646–6500; FAX. 915/646–6412; Mary Suther, President, Chief Executive Officer

Visiting Nurse Association of Texas Hospice, 1440 West Mockingbird Lane, Suite 500, Dallas, TX 75247–4929; tel. 214/689–0000; FAX. 214/689–0010; Shiela Jacobs

Vitas Healthcare Corporation, 5001 LBJ Freeway, Suite 1050, Dallas, TX 75244; tel. 214/661–2004; FAX. 214/661–3474; David C. Gasmire, General Manager

Vitas Healthcare Corporation, 4828 Loop Central Drive, Suite 890, Houston, TX 77081; tel. 713/663–7777; FAX. 713/663–4990, ext. 4912; Diane Incognito, General Manager

Vitas Healthcare Corporation, 801 West Freeway, Suite 620, Grand Prairie, TX 75051; tel. 972/269–4200; Chuck Dowling, Regional Vice President

Vitas Healthcare Corporation, 4241 Piedras Drive East, Suite 111, San Antonio, TX 78228; tel. 210/731–4300; FAX. 210/731–4380; Ruth R. Castillo, Administrator

Vitas Healthcare Corporation, 211 East Parkwood, Suite 211, Friendswood, TX 77546; tel. 713/996–4400; Ruth Castillo, General Manager

Wadley Care Source Hospice, 1001 Main Street, Suite 107, Texarkana, TX 75501; tel. 903/798–7640; FAX. 903/798–7647; Sheri Milam, RN, OCN, Manager

UTAH

CNS Community Hospice, 2970 South Main, Suite 300, Salt Lake City, UT 84115; tel. 801/461–9500; FAX. 801/486–2193; Grant C. Howarth, President, Chief Executive Officer

Castle Country Hospice, 11 West Main Street, Suite 100, Price, UT 84501; tel. 801/637–8070; Lavina Kirkwood, Administrator

Creative Health Services, Inc. Hospice Care, 6777 South 1560 East, Salt Lake City, UT 84121; tel. 801/943–8374; FAX. 801/942–2949; Joyce L. Smith, Administrator

Creekside Hospice Care, 1935 East Vine Street, Suite 350, Salt Lake City, UT 84121; tel. 801/272–8617; FAX. 801/277–3790; Maryann Pales, Administrator

Dixie Regional Home Health Hospice, 354 East 600 South, Suite 304, St. George, UT 84770; tel. 801/634–4567; FAX. 801/634–4564; Kathy Andrus, RN, Administrator

East Lake Home Health Hospice/Family Hospice Care, 668 West 980 North, Provo, UT 84601; tel. 801/374–9986; Kory Coleman, Director

Family Hospice Care, 404 East 5600 South, Murray, UT 84107; tel. 801/268–8083; FAX. 801/268–8096; Pat Burns, Director, Home Care Services

Hospice of Cache Valley, 1400 North 500 East, Logan, UT 84341; tel. 801/750–5477; FAX. 801/750–5361; Neil C. Perkes, RN, M.B.A., Administrator

Hospice of Northern Utah Vista Hospice Care, 2404 Washington Boulevard, Suite 304, Ogden, UT 84401; tel. 801/399-5232; FAX. 801/399-2742; Alan Green, Administrator

IHC Home Health Agency–Hospice of IHC, 2250 South 1300 West, Suite A, Salt Lake City, UT 84119; tel. 801/977-9900; FAX. 801/977-9956; Shauna Einerson, Administrator

Paracelsus Hospice, 404 East 4500 South, Salt Lake City UT 84107; tel. 801/288-1900; FAX. 801/288-2939; James C. Summerfelt

Premier Hospice Care, 4885 South 900 East, Suite 207, Salt Lake City, UT 84117; tel. 801/288-1619; David West, R.N., Administrator

Rocky Mountain Hospice, 315 East 400 South, Bountiful, UT 84010; tel. 801/397-4900; Carol Holmes

Uintah Basin Hospice, 26 West 200 North 78–15, Roosevelt, UT 84066; tel. 801/722-2418; Jan L. Roberts, Administrator

Vista Hospice Care of Utah, 204 East 860 South, Orem, UT 84058; tel. 801/224-2999; Alan Green, Administrator

VERMONT

Addison County Hospice, Inc., P.O. Box 772, Middlebury, VT 05753; tel. 802/388-4111; Catherine Studley, Executive Director

Brattleboro Area Hospice, 31 South Main Street, P.O. Box 1053, Brattleboro, VT 05302-1053; tel. 802/257-0775; Susan Parris, Administrator

Caledonia Home Health Care–Hospice, Sherman Drive, P.O. Box 383, St. Johnsbury, VT 05819; tel. 802/748-8116; FAX. 802/748-4628; Brenda B. Smith, Director, Home Care, Hospice

Central Vermont Home Health and Hospice, Inc., R.R. 3, Box 6694, Barre, VT 05641; tel. 802/223-1878; FAX. 802/223-6835, ext. 249; Diana Peirce, RN, CRNH, Director, Hospice Services

Franklin County Home Health and Hospice, Three Home Health Circle, St. Albans, VT 05478; tel. 802/527-7531; FAX. 802/527-7533; Janet McCarthy, Executive Director

Hospice of Bennington County, Inc., P.O. Box 1231, Bennington, VT 05201; tel. 802/447-0307; Amy Barber–Thomas, Executive Director

Hospice of Champlain Valley, 25 Prim Road, Colchester, VT 05446; tel. 802/860-4410; FAX. 802/860-6149; Barbara Segal, RN, M.S., Program Director

Lamoille Home Health and Hospice, R.R. 3, Box 790, Farr Avenue, Morrisville, VT 05661; tel. 802/888-4651; FAX. 802/888-7822; Linda Taft, Clinical Director

Orleans Essex VNA and Hospice, Inc., Three Lakemont Road, Newport, VT 05855-1550; tel. 802/334-5213, ext. 19; FAX. 802/334-8822, ext. 45; Diana Hamilton, RN, Director, Hospice

Randolph Area Hospice, 36 South Main Street, Randolph, VT 05060; tel. 802/728-6100, ext. 2273

Rutland Area Visiting Nurse Association, Seven Albert Cree Drive, Rutland, VT 05701; tel. 802/775-0568; FAX. 802/775-2304; Sally Tobin, Associate Director, Community Health Programs

Southern Vermont Home Health Agency, Three Holstein Place, Brattleboro, VT 05301; tel. 802/257-4390; FAX. 802/257-2188; Ellen Bristol, M.S.N., CRNH

Springfield Area Hospice, Inc., 366 River Street, Springfield, VT 05156; tel. 802/886-2525; Marisa Bolognese, Volunteer Coordinator

Visiting Nurse Alliance of Vermont and New Hampshire, 20 South Main Street, Old Court House, White River Junction, VT 05001; tel. 802/295-2604; FAX. 802/295-3163; Betsy Davis, Chief Executive Officer

VIRGINIA

At Home Care Hospice, 3386 Holland Road, Suite 102, Virginia Beach, VA 23452; tel. 757/427-0099; FAX. 757/427-0505; Judy Ray, Program Supervisor

Blue Ridge Hospice, Inc., 333 West Cork Street, Winchester, VA 22601; tel. 540/665-5210; FAX. 540/678-0584; Terrie Stevens, Executive Director

Cana Hospice, Route 1, Highway 52 North, P.O. Box Nine, Cana, VA 24317; tel. 800/719-7434; William B. James, Chief Executive Officer

Columbia Hospice and Family Care, 1405 Johnston–Willis Drive, Richmond, VA 23235; tel. 804/330-2300; FAX. 804/330-2280; Robert S. Dendy, Jr., Director

Commonwealth Home Nursing and Hospice, Inc., 990 Main Street, Suite 104, Danville, VA 24541; tel. 804/792-4663; FAX. 804/793-7429; Janet R. Hamilton, Executive Director

Community Hospices of America, Inc., 540 West Main Street, Wytheville, VA 24382; tel. 703/228-5424; FAX. 703/228-9225; Rita C. Cobbs, Program Director

Crater Community Hospice, Inc., 4233 Crossings Boulevard, Prince George, VA 23875; tel. 804/458-4300; FAX. 804/458-9417; Sparky Clark, Executive Director

Edmarc Hospice for Children, 1131 Crawford Parkway, P.O. Box 7188, Portsmouth, VA 23707; tel. 804/397-0432; FAX. 804/397-5827; Julie S. Sligh, Executive Director

Family Care Home Care and Hospice Care, 610 Laurel Street, P.O. Box 592, Culpeper, VA 22701; tel. 540/829-5760; FAX. 540/829-5761; Lee Kirk, President

First Choice Home Services, Inc., 915 Central Avenue, P.O. Box 1146, Harrisonburg, VA 22801; tel. 703/434-3916; Diana Berkshire, Administrator

Gentle Shepherd Hospice, Inc., 4040 Franklin Road, S.W., Roanoke, VA 24014; tel. 540/989-6265; FAX. 540/989-1547; Donald A. Eckenroth III, Administrator

Good Samaritan Hospice, Inc., 3528 Electric Road, Suite A, Roanoke, VA 24018; tel. 540/776-0198; FAX. 540/776-0841; Sue Moore, President

Homedco, Inc., 8210 Cinderked Road, Norton, VA 22079; Elaine Jakubowski, Administrator

Hospice Care of the Eastern Shore, Inc., 20154 Market Street, Onancock, VA 23417; tel. 757/789-5153; Patricia Seekings, RN, CRNH, Director

Hospice Choice, Highway 235, Big Stone Gap, VA 24219; tel. 703/523-7208; Victoria Daniels Smith, Administrator

Hospice Choice, Inc., 444 Orby Cantrell Highway, South, P.O. Box 359, Big Stone Gap, VA 24219; tel. 703/523-7208; FAX. 703/523-1103; Bonnie Elosser, Hospice Director

Hospice of Central Virginia, 5540 Falmouth Street, Suite 307, Richmond, VA 23230; tel. 804/281-0541; FAX. 804/281-0954; Brenda Clarkson, Administrator

Hospice of Northern Virginia, 13168 Centerpointe Way, Suite 201–202, Woodbridge, VA 22193; tel. 703/670-5080; Marjorie Shipley, Regional Vice President

Hospice of Northern Virginia, Inc., 6400 Arlington Boulevard, Suite 1000, Falls Church, VA 22042; tel. 703/534-7070; FAX. 703/538-2163; David J. English, President, Chief Executive Officer

Hospice of Northern Virginia, Inc., 11166 Main Street, Suite 405, Fairfax, VA 22030; tel. 703/352-7115; FAX. 703/591-2376; Jacqueline Wright, Regional Vice President

Hospice of Northern Virginia, Inc., 885 Harrison Street, S.E., Leesburg, VA 21075; tel. 703/777-7866; FAX. 703/771-8904; Jackie Wright, Regional Vice President

Hospice of the Piedmont, Inc., 1290 Seminole Trail, Charlottesville, VA 22901; tel. 804/975-5500; FAX. 804/975-4040; Victoria Todd, Executive Director

Hospice of the Rapidan, Inc., 1200 Sunset Lane, Suite 2320, Culpeper, VA 22701; tel. 703/825-4840; FAX. 703/825-7752; Patricia Tuffy, Executive Director

House Call Hospice, 603–605 King Street, Fourth Floor, Alexandria, VA 22314; tel. 703/548-2197; Ray Evans, President

Housecall Hospice, Two Main Street, P.O. Box 850, Jonesville, VA 24263; tel. 703/346-1095; Ethel Combs, Administrator

Housecall Hospice, 2167 Apperson Drive, Salem, VA 24153; tel. 540/776-3207; FAX. 540/776-3215; Sara Brown, RN, LCSW, Administrator

Housecall Hospice, Route 8, Box 335, Martinsville, VA 24112; tel. 540/632-9611; Ellen Boone, Administrator

In Home Health, 5040 Corporate Woods Drive, Virginia Beach, VA 23462; tel. 757/490-9323; FAX. 757/490-8711; Rita E. Wool, Director, Operations

In Home Health and Hospice, 542 East Constance Road, Suffolk, VA 23430; tel. 757/934-7935; FAX. 757/934-7940; Rita E. Wool, Director, Operations

Jewish Family Service, 7300 Newport Avenue, P.O. Box 9503, Norfolk, VA 23505; tel. 804/489-3111; Harry Graber, Executive Director

Mary Washington Hospice, 406 Chatham Square Office Park, 312 Butler Road, Falmouth, VA 22405; tel. 540/899-6433; FAX. 540/899-6328; Dianne Tracy, Administrator

Maryview Wellspring Hospice, 485 Rodman Avenue, Portsmouth, VA 23707; tel. 804/398-2338; Marie F. Biggers-Gray, Director

Mountain Regional Hospice, 1533 Ingalls Street, P.O. Box 53, Clifton Forge, VA 24422; tel. 540/863-3333; FAX. 540/863-5353; Glenn Perry, Executive Director

New River Valley Hospice, Inc., 111 West Main Street, Christiansburg, VA 24073; tel. 703/381-5001; FAX. 703/381-5008; Bhanu Iyengar, Executive Director

Personal Touch Hospice of Virginia, Inc., 18 Koger Center, Suite 205, Norfolk, VA 23502; tel. 757/459-2523; FAX. 757/459-2615; Dawn Barnes, RNC, B.S.N., Administrator

Rockbridge Area Hospice, Inc., 129 South Randolph Street, P.O. Box 948, Lexington, VA 24450; tel. 540/463-1848; FAX. 540/463-5219; Susan Hogg, Executive Director

Sentara Hospice, Eight Koger Executive Building, Suite 210, Norfolk, VA 23502; tel. 804/628-3602; Dorothy Weeks, Manager

Twin County Hospice, 605 Glendale Road, Galax, VA 24333; tel. 540/236-7935; Patty S. Cooke, Administrator

VNA Community Hospice, 2775 South Quincy Street, Suite 260, Arlington, VA 22206; tel. 703/824-5200; FAX. 703/824-5228; Eileen L. Dohmann, Executive Director

WASHINGTON

Associated Health Services, P.O. Box 5200, Tacoma, WA 98415-0200; tel. 206/552-1825; FAX. 206/552-1838; Beverly Hatter, Director Grief, Loss and Transitional Care

Assured Home Health and Hospice, 1817 South Market Boulevard, Chehalis, WA 98532; tel. 360/748-0151; FAX. 360/748-0518; Wilma Wayson, RN, B.S.N., Director

Central Basin Home Health and Hospice, 410 West Third Avenue, Moses Lake, WA 98837; tel. 509/765-1856; FAX. 509/765-3323; Patti A. Weaver, Administrator

Community Home Health and Hospice, 1035 11th Avenue, P.O. Box 2067, Longview, WA 98632-8189; tel. 360/425-8510; FAX. 360/425-4667; Lorraine Berndt, Executive Director

Community Hospice of the Northwest, 5610 Kitsap Way, Suite 301, Bremerton, WA 98312; tel. 360/373-5280; FAX. 360/373-5398; Karen Williams, Executive Director

Evergreen Community Home Health and Hospice, 12822 – 124th Lane, N.E., Kirkland, WA 98034; tel. 206/899-1040; FAX. 206/899-1033; Ben Lindekugel, Assistant Administrator

Group Health Cooperative Hospice Program, 83 South King Street, Suite 515, Seattle, WA 98104-2848; tel. 425/882-2022; FAX. 425/881-7147; Barbara Boyd, Administrator, Home and Community Services

Harbors Home Health and Hospice, 201 Seventh Street, Hoquiam, WA 98550; tel. 360/532-5454; DeLila Thorp, Administrator

Highline Home Care Services, 2801 South 128th, Tukwila, WA 98168; tel. 206/439-9095; FAX. 206/433-1031

Home Health Plus Hospice, 13810 Southeast Eastgate Way, Suite 100, Bellevue, WA 98005; tel. 206/644-3027; FAX. 206/644-3286; Carrie Malmberg, RN

Home Health and Hospice of Southeastern Washington, South 106 Mill Street, Colfax, WA 99111; tel. 509/334-6016; FAX. 509/397-4650; Monica Diteman, Chief Executive Officer

Hospice of Kitsap County, 1007 Scott Avenue, Suite D, Bremerton, WA 98310; tel. 360/479-1749; FAX. 360/479-5800; M. Beth Duchaine, Executive Director

Hospice of Snohomish County, 2731 Wetmore Avenue, Suite 520, Everett, WA 98201-3581; tel. 206/261-4800; FAX. 206/258-1097; Mary L. Brueggeman, Executive Director

Hospice of Spokane, West 1325 First Avenue, Suite 200, P.O. Box 2215, Spokane, WA 99210; tel. 509/456-0438; FAX. 509/458-0359; Anne Koepsell, Executive Director

Hospice of the Palouse, 700 South Main Street, P.O. Box 9461, Moscow, ID 83843-0119; tel. 208/882-1228; FAX. 208/883-2239; Norman Bowers, Administrator

Kaiser Permanente Home Health/Hospice, 2701 Northwest Vaughn Street, Suite 140, Portland, OR 97210-5398; tel. 503/499-5200; FAX. 503/499-5213; Linda Van Buren, Administrator

Lower Valley Hospice, 526 South 11th, Sunnyside, WA 98944; tel. 509/837-1676; FAX. 509/837-8622; Vicki Meyer, Executive Director

Section C

Okanogan Regional Home Health Care Agency, 217 Second Avenue, S., P.O. Box 1248, Okanogan, WA 98840; tel. 509/422–6721; Bernice Hartzell, Executive Director

Providence Homecare/Hospice of Seattle, 425 Pontius Avenue, N., Suite 300, Seattle, WA 98109; tel. 206/320–4000; FAX. 206/320–3804; Robert Anderson, Administrator, Home Services

Providence SoundHome Care and Hospice, 3706 Griffin Lane, S.E., Olympia, WA 98501; tel. 360/459–8311; FAX. 360/493–4657; Alice G. Armstrong, Chief Executive Officer

Swedish Home Health and Hospice and Infusion, 5701 Sixth Avenue, S., Suite 504, Seattle, WA 98108–2522; tel. 206/386–6602; FAX. 206/386–6613; Betty Jorgensen, Hospice Director

Tri-Cities Chaplaincy/Hospice and Counseling, 2108 West Entiat Avenue, Kennewick, WA 99336; tel. 509/783–7416; FAX. 509/735–7850; Thomas H. Halazon, Executive Director

VNS Hospice, 400 North 34th Street, Suite 202, Seattle, WA 98103–8600; tel. 206/548–2344; FAX. 206/547–6182; Don W. Tarbutton, MHA, Hospice Program Administrator

Walla Walla Community Hospice, P.O. Box 2026, 35 Jade Street, Walla Walla, WA 99362; tel. 509/525–5561; FAX. 509/525–3517; Marlow B. Wootton, Executive Director

Whatcom Hospice, 600 Birchwood Avenue, Bellingham, WA 98225; tel. 360/733–5877; FAX. 360/734–9621; Marsha J. Johnson

WEST VIRGINIA

Albert Gallatin Hospice, 3280 University Avenue, Morgantown, WV 25605; tel. 304/598–0226; Christine Constantine, Administrator

Community Home Care and Hospice, 1209 Warwood Avenue, Wheeling, WV 26003; tel. 304/277–1500; FAX. 304/277–1507; Ruth Prosser, M.S.N., RN, Administrator

Community Hospices of America – The Virginias, RR 2 Box 380, Bluefield, WV 24701; tel. 304/325–7220; FAX. 304/325–9384; Vicki Webb, Program Director

Dignity Hospice, P.O. Box 4455, Chapmanville, WV 25508; tel. 304/855–7104; Regina Bias, RN, M.S.N., OCN, Director

Extend–A–Care Hospice, 103 Guyandotte Avenue, Mullens, WV 25882; tel. 304/294–4732; FAX. 304/294–4735; Violet A. Burdette, Administrator

Greenbrier Valley Hospice, Inc., 540 North Jefferson Street, Box 5, Lewisburg, WV 24901; tel. 304/645–2700; FAX. 304/645–3188; Deb Cashdollar, Executive Director

Hospice Care Corporation, 202 Tunnelton Street, Suite 321, Garden Towers, Kingwood, WV 26537; tel. 304/329–1161; FAX. 304/329–3285; Malene J. Davis, RN, Executive Director

Hospice of Huntington, 1101 Sixth Avenue, P.O. Box 464, Huntington, WV 25709; tel. 304/529–4217; FAX. 304/523–6051; Charlene Farrell, Executive Director

Hospice of Marion County, P.O. Box 1112, Fairmont, WV 26555–1112; tel. 304/366–0700, ext. 8725; FAX. 304/366–9529; Joe Licata, M.S.W., Hospice Director

Hospice of South West Virginia, 105 South Eisenhower Drive, P.O. Box 1472, Beckley, WV 25802; tel. 304/255–6404; FAX. 304/255–6494; Thomas A. Williams, Executive Director

Hospice of the Panhandle, Inc., 2015 Boyd Orchard Court, Martinsburg, WV 25401; tel. 304/264–0406; FAX. 304/264–0409; Margaret Cogswell, RN, Executive Director

Housecalls Home Health and Hospice, Inc., 914 Market Street, Suite 301, Parkersburg, WV 26101; tel. 304/485–1410; FAX. 304/422–7902; Teresa Roby, Director

Journey Hospice, 314 South Wells Street, Sisterville, WV 26175; tel. 304/652–2611; FAX. 304/652–1440; Lynn L. McCormick, Administrator

Kanawha Hospice Care, Inc., 1143 Dunbar Avenue, Dunbar, WV 25064; tel. 304/768–8523; FAX. 304/768–8627; Shirley Hyatt, Director of Patient Services

Lewis County Home Health and Hospice Care, P.O. Box 1750, Weston, WV 26452; tel. 304/269–6432; FAX. 304/269–8220; Nancy Hosey, RN, Patient Care Coordinator

Monongalia County Health Department Hospice, 453 Van Voorhis Road, Morgantown, WV 26505–3408; tel. 304/598–5500; FAX. 304/598–5167; Vicky Kennedy, Hospice Supervisor, Patient Care Coordinator

Morgantown Hospice, 1159 Van Voorhis Road, Suite B, P.O. Box 4222, Morgantown, WV 26505; tel. 304/285–2777; FAX. 304/285–2787; Margaret M. Kearney, Director, Home Health and Hospice

Mountain Hospice, Inc., P.O. Box 661, Philippi, WV 26416; tel. 304/457–2180, ext. 323; FAX. 304/457–2267; Patricia Arnett, Director

People's Hospice, United Hospital Center, P.O. Box 1680, Clarksburg, WV 26302–1680; tel. 304/623–0524; FAX. 304/623–3399; Janice Chapman, Director

St. Gregory's Hospice, Inc., 836 Charles Street, Wellsburg, WV 26070; tel. 800/252–7290; FAX. 304/737–0871; Patricia Murphy, RN, M.S.N., Director

St. Joseph's Hospice, 92 West Main Street, Buckannon, WV 26201; tel. 304/472–6846; Sandra Knotts, Director

Valley Hospice, One Ross Park, Steubenville, OH 43952; tel. 614/264–7161; Karen Nichols, Executive Director

WISCONSIN

All Saints VNA–Hospice/Racine, 4000 Spring Street, P.O. Box 4045, Racine, WI 53404; tel. 414/635–7580; FAX. 414/633–7332; Debra Ostroski, Administrator

Beloit Hospice, Inc., 2958 Prairie Avenue, Beloit, WI 53511; tel. 608/363–7421; FAX. 608/363–7426; Virginia Young, Administrator

Community Home Hospice, 3149 Saemann Avenue, Sheboygan, WI 53081; tel. 414/457–5770; Bobbi Illig

Community Hospice–VNA, 811 Monitor Street, Suite 101, LaCrosse, WI 54603; tel. 608/796–1666; Margaret Mossholder

Crossroads Hospice, 125 Fowler Street, Oconomowoc, WI 53066; tel. 414/569–8711; FAX. 414/569–8744; Barb Lemke, Intake

Dr. Kate–Lakeland Hospice, P.O. Box 770, Woodruff, WI 54568; tel. 715/356–8805; FAX. 715/358–7299; Helen Mozuch, RN, Director, Operations

Fox Cities Community Hospice, 820 Association Drive, Appleton, WI 54914; tel. 414/733–8562; Susan Kostka, Hospice Director

Franciscan Skemp Healthcare Hospice, 212 South 11th Street, LaCrosse, WI 54601; tel. 608/791–9790; FAX. 608/791–9548; Marilyn Viehl, Administrator

Grancare Hospice, N56W 13365 Silver Spring Drive, Menomonee Falls, WI 53051; tel. 414/252–5303; FAX. 414/252–3974; Phyllis Locicero, Administrator

Grant County Hospice, 111 South Jefferson Street, Lancaster, WI 53813; tel. 608/723–6416; FAX. 608/723–6501; Linda S. Adrian, Director, Health Officer

Heartland Hospice, 455 Davis Street, P.O. Box 487, Hammond, WI 54015; tel. 715/796–2223; Mary Troftgruben, Administrator

Hillside Homecare/Hospice, 709 South University Avenue, Beaver Dam, WI 53916; tel. 414/887–4050, ext. 4181; FAX. 414/887–6815; Marla Noordhof, Director

Home Health United Hospice, 520 South Boulevard, P.O. Box 527, Baraboo, WI 53913; tel. 608/356–2288; FAX. 608/356–2290; Thomas H. Brown, President

HomeCaring and Hospice, 11685 Lake Boulevard, N., Chisago City, MN 55013; tel. 612/257–8850; FAX. 612/257–8852; Karen Brohaugh, Manager

Hope Hospice, Inc., 709 McComb Avenue, P.O. Box 237, Rib Lake, WI 54470; tel. 715/427–3532; FAX. 715/427–3537; Barbara Meyer, Director

Horizon Home Care and Hospice, Inc., 8949 Deebrook Trail, Brown Deer, WI 53223; tel. 414/365–8300; FAX. 414/351–8338; Beth Huetting, Hospice Executive Director

Hospice Alliance, Inc., 6334 8th Ave., Kenosha, WI 53143; tel. 414/942–1630; Connie Matler, Director, Clinical Services

Hospice Preferred Choice, 3118 South 27th Street, Milwaukee, WI 53215; tel. 414/649–8302; FAX. 414/649–8441; Cathy Ott, Executive Director

Hospice Program of Waupaca County, 811 Harding Street, Waupaca, WI 54981; tel. 715/258–6323; Barbara J. Black

Hospice of Portage County, Inc., 2232 Prais, P.O. Box 1017, Stevens Point, WI 54481–8217; tel. 715/346–5355; FAX. 715/345–1304; Judy N. Mason

Hospice of the Twin Cities, Inc., d/b/a Hospice of the Valley, 7100 Northland Circle, Suite 205, Minneapolis, MN 55428; tel. 800/364–2478; FAX. 612/531–2422; Lisa Abicht Swensen, Administrator

HospiceCare, Inc., 2802 Coho Street, Suite 100, Madison, WI 53713–4521; tel. 608/276–4660; FAX. 608/276–4672; Susan Phillips, Executive Director

Jefferson Home Health and Hospice, 1007 Washington Street, P.O. Box 117, Baraboo, WI 53913; tel. 608/356–7570; FAX. 608/356–2629; William J. Hamilton, Jr., Managing Director

Lafayette County Hospice, 740 East Street, P.O. Box 118, Darlington, WI 53530; tel. 608/776–4895; FAX. 608/776–4885; Kristie Lueck, RN, Coordinator

Lakeview Hospice, 927 West Churchill Street, Stillwater, MN 55082; tel. 612/430–3320; Geri Wagner

Manitowoc County Community Hospice, 1004 Washington Street, Manitowoc, WI 54220; tel. 414/684–7155; FAX. 414/684–8653; Lynn Seidl–Babcock, RN, B.S.N., Administrator

Marquette General Home Health and Hospice, Doctors Park, Suite 105, Escanaba, MI 49829; tel. 906/789–1305; FAX. 906/789–9144; Linda S. Lewandowski, Director, Hospice

Mayo Hospice Program, 200 First Street, S.W., Rochester, MN 55905; tel. 507/284–4002; FAX. 507/284–0161; Ann Bartlett, RN, Coordinator

Milwaukee Hospice Home Care and Residence, 4067 North 92nd Street, Wauwatosa, WI 53222; tel. 414/438–8000; FAX. 414/438–8010; James Ewens, Mary New, Co–Directors

Northwest Wisconsin HomeCare/Hospice, 2321 East Clairemont Parkway, P.O. Box 2060, Eau Claire, WI 54702–2060; tel. 715/831–0100; FAX. 715/831–0108; Jill Hurlburt, RN, B.S.N., Director, Clinical Services

Rainbow Hospice Care, LLC, 147 West Rockwell Street, Jefferson, WI 53549; tel. 414/674–6255; FAX. 414/674–5288; Zelpha Pease, Patient Care Coordinator

Red Wing Hospice, 434 West Fourth, Suite 200, Red Wing, MN 55066; tel. 612/385–3410; FAX. 612/385–3414; Beth Krehbiel, Director

Regional Hospice, 2101 Beaser Avenue, Ashland, WI 54806; tel. 715/682–8677; FAX. 715/682–6404; Phil Garrison, Executive Director

Rolland Nelson Memorial Home Hospice, 419 Frederick Street, Waukesha, WI 53186; tel. 414/542–0724; FAX. 414/542–0608; Jacalyn Burdick, Program Manager

UPC Health Network–Hospice Services, 3724 West Wisconsin Avenue, Milwaukee, WI 53208; tel. 414/342–9292, ext. 449; FAX. 414/342–8721; Walter Orzechowski, National Director, Hospice Services

Unity Hospice, P.O. Box 22395, Green Bay, WI 54305–2395; tel. 414/433–7470; FAX. 414/437–1934; Donald W. Seibel, Director

V.N.A. Home Care and Hospice, 201 East Bell Street, Neenah, WI 54956; tel. 414/727–5555; FAX. 414/727–5552; Judith Eberhardy, President, Chief Executive Officer

VNA Community Hospice, 11333 West National Avenue, Milwaukee, WI 53227; tel. 414/327–2295; FAX. 414/328–4499; Mary Runge, Chief Operating Officer

Visiting Nurse Association Comfortcare Hospice, 3306 Superior Avenue, Sheboygan, WI 53081; tel. 414/458–4314; FAX. 414/458–1819; Robert W. Walters, Vice President, Regional Operations

Visiting Nurse Health Care Services, 901 Mineral Point Avenue, Janesville, WI 53545; tel. 608/754–2201; FAX. 608/754–1147; Caryn Oleston, Executive Director

Vitas Healthcare, 450 North Sunny Slope Road, Brookfield, WI 53005; tel. 414/821–6500; FAX. 414/821–6533; Jay Koeper, Administrator

WYOMING

Central Wyoming Hospice Program, 319 South Wilson Street, Casper, WY 82601; tel. 307/577–4832; FAX. 307/577–4841; Janace Chapman, RN, Director

Columbia Little Wind Hospice, 2300 Rose Lane, Riverton, WY 82501; tel. 307/857–3708; FAX. 307/856–4129; Shirley Abraham, Director

Hospice of Laramie, 710 East Garfield, Suite 114, Laramie, WY 82070; tel. 307/745–9254; FAX. 307/742–5967; Connie M. Coca, M.S.W., Director

Hospice of Sweetwater County, 809 Thompson, Suite D, Rock Springs, WY 82901; tel. 307/362–1990; FAX. 307/352–6769; Pamela L. Jelaca, Executive Director

Hospice of the Big Horns, 1401 West 5th Street, Sheridan, WY 82801; tel. 307/672–7633; FAX. 307/672–2585; T. Marvin Goldman, Administrator

Hospice of the Tetons, 555 East Broadway, P.O. Box 428, Jackson, WY 83001; tel. 307/739–7465; FAX. 307/739–7645; Kathryn Baldwin, Director

Northeast Wyoming Hospice, 400 S. Kendrick, #301, P.O. Box 3259, Gillette, WY 82717–3259; tel. 307/682–6570; FAX. 307/682–2781; Ann M. Herman, R.N., Administrator

Spirit Mountain Hospice, 707 Sheridan Ave., Cody, WY 82414; tel. 307/578–2413; FAX. 307/578–2270; Fred Whitmore, Administrator

Susie Bowling Lawrence Hospice, 497 West Lott, Buffalo, WY 82834; tel. 307/684–5521; FAX. 307/684–5385; Kent Ward, Administrator

U. S. Associated Areas

PUERTO RICO

Caribbean Hospice, 153 Winston Churchill Avenue, Rio Piedras, PR 00926; tel. 809/764–6565; Adalberto Sandoval

Community Hospice, Inc., Avenue Hipodromo #756, Doctors Medical Building, Santurce, PR 00910; tel. 809/723–4177; FAX. 809/722–4243; Edna Vazquez

Condado Hospice, P.O. Box 5417, Station Hato Rey, PR 00919–5417; tel. 809/758–2325; Manuel de Leon

Condado Hospice, Avenue Laurel Z–U–6, Bayamon, PR 00956; tel. 809/269–0175; Carmen L. Rosa

Divina Presencia Hospice, 52 Se St 1228, Reparto Metropolitano, Rio Piedras, PR 00921; tel. 809/767–5124; Norma Williams, M.D., Medical Director

Emmanuel Hospice Care, Bo Lares Cruce Mijan, Lares, PR 00661; tel. 809/897–7040; Moises Rivera

Font Martelo Hospice, Avenue Munoz Marin, P.O. Box 8924, Humacao, PR 00791; tel. 809/852–3685; Martin Lopez Cosme

Guaynabo Hospice, Nine Jose Julian Acosta Street, Guaynabo, PR 00969; tel. 809/789–7878; Ricardo Larin, President

Hospicio Atencion Medica en el Hogar, Cipres K 1A Turabo, Caguas, PR; tel. 809/743–1121; Sandra Torres

Hospicio Del Oeste, Dr Veve 84, San German, PR 00683; tel. 809/892–1820; Anibal Velez Rodriguez

Hospicio El Nuevo Amanecer, Calle Garcia De La, Noceda 38, Rio Grande, PR 00745; tel. 809/888–8885; Melvin Acosta Roman

Hospicio Fe y Esperanza, P.O. Box 1834, Manati, PR 00674; tel. 809/854–4971; Eduardo Alvarez

Hospicio Font Martelo, Calle Calimano 121 Norte, P.O. box 910, Guayama, PR 00784; tel. 787/866–1925; Ana R. Caraballo

Hospicio La Caridad, Calle Cipres, Villa Turabo, Caguas, PR 00725; tel. 787/286–8745; FAX. 787/746–5750; Glorivette Seneriz

Hospicio La Montana, Road 152 Km 12.4, Cedro Arriba P.O. Box 515, Naranjito, PR 00719; tel. 809/869–5500; Hector A. Rodriguez Ortiz

Hospicio La Paz, Calle Jose Rodriguez, Irizarry 152, Arecibo, PR 00612; tel. 809/879–4733; Luis Monrouzeau

Hospicio Luzamor, P.O. Box 1312, Calle Patron, #11, Morovis, PR 00687; tel. 809/862–0608; Ms. Brunilda Otero Declet, Executive Director

Hospicio Nuestra Sra. de la Guadalupe, P.O. Box 7699, Ponce, PR 00732; tel. 787/259–8210; FAX. 787/259–0206; Lucy Gonzalez, Administrator

Hospicio Santa Rita, La Paz Street, Box 1143, Aguada, PR 00602; tel. 787/868–2945; FAX. 787/868–0010; Licedia Rosado

Hospicio Servicios Suplementarios, Roosevelt Avenue 114, Hato Rey, PR 00919; tel. 809/759–7036; Carmen Martino

Hospicio de Esperanza, Avenue General Valero 267, Fajardo, PR 00738; tel. 809/863–0924; Luis Vazquez

Hospital Sin Paredes, P.O. Box 2015, Hato Rey, PR 00919; tel. 809/767–8959; Luis Serrano

La Piedad Hospice, 626 Escorial Hospice, San Juan, PR 00920; tel. 809/792–2411; Antonio Bisono

La Providencia Hospice, 36 Munoz Street, P.O. Box 10447, Ponce, PR 00731; tel. 787/843–2364; FAX. 787/841–2940; Eyleen Rodriguez Lugo

Monserrate Hospice Care, Inc., P.O. Box 366148, San Juan, PR 00936–6148; tel. 809/754–0449; Luis Class

Programa de Servicios de Adjuntas, Inc., Rius Rivera 18, P.O. Box 993, Adjuntas, PR 00601; tel. 787/829–2953; Abraham Gonzalez

Providencia Hospice, Beleares 354 Puerto, Nuevo, PR 00920; tel. 809/793–7535; Eyleen Rodriguez Lugo

San Francisco Asis Hospice, P.O. Box 877, Aguada, PR 00602; tel. 787/868–2920; FAX. 787/252–0211; Dilia Dajer, Executive Director

Santa Rita Hospice, Inc., Condominio Medical Center Plaza, Box 1143, Aguada, PR 00602; tel. 787/831–7225; Licedia Rosado

Sendero de Luz, Inc., 11 Georgetti Street, P.O. Box 875, Comerio, PR 00782; tel. 787/875–5701; FAX. 787/875–0887; Juan C. Santiago, Executive Director

St. Lukes Hospice, Ponce, Urb. Industrial, Reparada, Edif. A–B, Ponce, PR 00732; tel. 809/843–4185; Annie Grave

Un Toque de Amor Hospice, Marginal A–2 Urb, San Salvador, Manati, PR 00674; tel. 809/884–3326; Jenny Olivo

Vista Bahia Hospice, Barrio Magas, Guayanilla, PR 00656; tel. 809/836–3314; Luisa I. Carrasquillo

State Government Agencies for Freestanding Hospices

United States

ALABAMA
Alabama Department of Public Health, Division of Licensure and Certification, 434 Monroe Street, Montgomery, AL 36130-1701; tel. 334/240-3503; FAX. 334/240-3147; Rick Harris, Director

ALASKA
Division of Medical Assistance, Health Facilities Licensing and Certification Section, 4501 Business Park Blvd., Suite 24, Anchorage, AK 99503; tel. 907/561-2171; FAX. 907/561-1684; Karen Martz, Superior

ARIZONA
Arizona Department of Health Services, Health Care Facilities, 1647 East Morten, Phoenix, AZ 85020; tel. 602/674-4200; FAX. 602/255-1108; Linda Palmer, Assistant Director

ARKANSAS
Department of Health, Division of Health Facility Services, 5800 West 10th, Suite 400, Little Rock, AR 72204-9916; tel. 501/661-2201; FAX. 501/661-2165; Valetta M. Buck, Director

CALIFORNIA
Department of Health Services, Licensing and Certification Program, 1800 Third Street, Suite 210, P.O. Box 942732, Sacramento, CA 94234-7320; tel. 916/324-8628; FAX. 916/445-6979; Marilyn Pearman, Chief, Policy Section

COLORADO
Colorado Department of Public Health and Environment, Health Facilities Division A–Two, 4300 Cherry Creek Drive, S., Denver, CO 80222-1530; tel. 303/692-2800; FAX. 303/782-4883; Peggy Waldon, RN, Program Administrator

CONNECTICUT
Department of Public Health and Addiction Services, Hospital and Medical Care Division, 150 Washington Street, Hartford, CT 06106; tel. 860/566-1073; FAX. 860/566-1097; Elizabeth M. Burns, RN, M.S., Director

DELAWARE
Department of Health and Social Services, Office of Health Facilities Licensing and Certification, Three Mill Road, Suite 308, Wilmington, DE 19806; tel. 302/577-6666; FAX. 302/577-6672; Ellen T. Reap, Director

DISTRICT OF COLUMBIA
Department of Consumer and Regulatory Affairs, Service Facility Regulation Administration, 614 H Street, N.W., Suite 1003, Washington, DC 20001; tel. 202/727-7190; FAX. 202/727-7780; Geraldine Sykes, Administrator

FLORIDA
Agency for HealthCare Administration, Division of Health Quality Assurance, Long Term Care Unit, Fort Knox Executive Center, 2727 Mahan Drive, Tallahassee, FL 32308-5407; tel. 850/922-8540; FAX. 850/487-6240; Patricia Hall, Unit Manager

GEORGIA
Health Care Section, Office of Regulatory Services, Two Peachtree Street, N.W., Suite 33-250, Atlanta, GA 30303-3147; tel. 404/657-5550; FAX. 404/657-8934; Susie M. Woods, Director

HAWAII
Department of Health, Licensing and Certification, Hospital and Medical Facilities Branch, P.O. Box 3378, Honolulu, HI 96801; tel. 808/586-4080; FAX. 808/586-4747; Helen K. Yoshimi, B.S.N., M.P.H., HMF Branch, Chief

IDAHO
Bureau of Facility Standards, Department of Health and Welfare, P.O. Box 83720, Boise, ID 83720-0036; tel. 208/334-6626; FAX. 208/334-0657; Silva Cresell, Supervisor

ILLINOIS
Department of Public Health, Office of Health Care Regulation, Bureau of Hospitals and Ambulatory Services, 525 West Jefferson Street, Fourth Floor, Springfield, IL 62761; tel. 217/782-7412; FAX. 217/782-0382; Catherine M. Stokes, Assistant Deputy Director

INDIANA
Indiana State Department of Health, Division of Acute Care, Two North Meridian Street, Indianapolis, IN 46204; tel. 317/233-7472; FAX. 317/233-7157; Tom Iozzo, Director

IOWA
Department of Inspection and Appeals, Division of Health Facilities, Lucas State Office Building, Des Moines, IA 50319; tel. 515/281-4115; FAX. 515/242-5022; J.B. Bennett, Administrator

KANSAS
Department of Health and Environment, Bureau of Adult and Child Care, 900 Southwest Jackson, Suite 1001, Topeka, KS 66612-0001; tel. 785/296-1280; FAX. 785/296-1266; George A. Dugger, Medical Facilities Certification Administrator

KENTUCKY
Cabinet for Human Resources, Division of Licensing and Regulation, C.H.R. Building, 275 East Main Street, Fourth Floor, East, Frankfort, KY 40621; tel. 502/564-2800; FAX. 502/564-6546; Rebecca J. Cecil, Director

LOUISIANA
Department of Health and Hospitals, Bureau of Health Services Financing, Health Standards Section Licensing Unit, P.O. Box 3767, Baton Rouge, LA 70821; tel. 504/342-0138; FAX. 504/342-5292; Lily W. McAlister, RN, Manager

MAINE
Division of Licensing and Certification, Department of Human Services, State House, Station 11, Augusta, ME 04333; tel. 207/624-5443; FAX. 207/624-5378; Louis Dorogi, Director

MARYLAND
Department of Health and Mental Hygiene, Office of Licensing and Certification Administration, 4201 Patterson Avenue, Baltimore, MD 21215; tel. 410/764-4980; FAX. 410/358-0750; James Ralls, Assistant Director

MASSACHUSETTS
Massachusetts Department of Public Health, Division of Health Care Quality, 10 West Street, 5th Floor, Boston, MA 02111; tel. 617/727-5860; Dr. Howard Kyongju Koh New, Commissioner

MICHIGAN
Department of Consumer and Industry Services, Division of Licensing and Certification, G. Mennen Williams Building, 525 W. Ottawa, Lansing, MI 48909; tel. 517/241-2626; Dr. Gladys Thomas, Director

MINNESOTA
Department of Health, Facility and Provider Compliance Division, Licensing and Certification Section, 393 North Dunlap Street, P.O. Box 64900, St. Paul, MN 55164-0900; tel. 612/643-2130; FAX. 612/643-3534; Carol Hirschfeld, Supervisor, Records Information Unit

MISSISSIPPI
Department of Health, Division of Health Facilities, Licensure and Certification, P.O. Box 1700, Jackson, MS 39215; tel. 601/354-7300; FAX. 601/354-7230; Vanessa Phipps, Director

MISSOURI
Department of Health, Bureau of Home Health Licensing and Certification, P.O. Box 570, Jefferson City, MO 65102; tel. 573/751-6336; FAX. 573/751-6315; Carol Gourd, RN, Administrator

MONTANA
Department of Public Health and Human Services, Quality Assurance Division, Licensure Bureau, Cogswell Building, 1400 Broadway, P.O. Box 202951, Helena, MT 59620-2951; tel. 406/444-2676; FAX. 406/444-1742; Roy P. Kemp, Chief

NEBRASKA
Nebraska Department of Health, Health Facility Licensure and Inspection Section, 301 Centennial Mall, S., P.O. Box 95007, Lincoln, NE 68509-5007; tel. 402/471-2946; FAX. 402/471-0555; Helen Meeks, Section Administrator

NEVADA
Nevada State Health Division, Bureau of Licensure and Certification, 1550 East College Parkway, Suite 158, Carson City, NV 89706-7921; tel. 702/687-4475; FAX. 702/687-6588; Richard J. Panelli, Chief

NEW HAMPSHIRE
Office of Program Support, Licensing and Regulation, Six Hazen Drive, 2nd Floor, West Wing, Concord, NH 03301; tel. 603/271-4592; FAX. 603/271-4968; Raymond Rusin, Bureau Chief

NEW JERSEY
New Jersey Department of Health and Senior Services, Division of Health Care Systems Analysis, Certificate of Need and Acute Care Licensure, Inspections, Compliance and Enforcement, John Fitchway, Market and Warren Streets, CN-360, Trenton, NJ 08625-0360; tel. 609/292-8773; FAX. 609/984-3165; John Caiabira, Acting Dir. of Certificate of NAAC Licensure Program

NEW MEXICO
Department of Health, Health Facility Licensing and Certification Bureau, 525 Camino de los Marquez, Suite Two, Santa Fe, NM 87501; tel. 505/827-4200; FAX. 505/827-4222; Mathew Gervase, Bureau Chief

NEW YORK
Bureau of Home Health Care Services, Department of Health, Frear Building, Two Third Street, Suite 401, Troy, NY 12180-3298; tel. 518/271-2741; FAX. 518/271-2771; Dr. Nancy Barhydt, Director

NORTH CAROLINA
Department of Human Resources, Division of Facility Services, 701 Barbour Drive, Raleigh, NC 27626-0530; tel. 919/733-1610; FAX. 919/733-3207; Steve White, Chief, Licensure and Certification

NORTH DAKOTA
Department of Health, Health Resources Section, 600 East Boulevard Avenue, Bismarck, ND 58505; tel. 701/328-2352; FAX. 701/328-4727; Darleen Bartz, Acting Dir., Division of Health Facilities

OHIO
Division of Quality Assurance, Ohio Department of Health, 246 North High Street, Columbus, OH 43266-0588; tel. 614/466-7857; FAX. 614/644-0208; Rebecca Maust, Chief

OKLAHOMA
Department of Health, Special Health Services, 1000 Northeast 10th Street, Oklahoma City, OK 73117; tel. 405/271–6576; FAX. 405/271–1308; Gary Glover, Chief, Medical Facilities

OREGON
Health Care Licensing and Certification, Oregon Health Division, 800 Northeast Oregon Street, # 21, Suite 640, Portland, OR 97232; tel. 503/731–4013; FAX. 503/731–4080; Kathleen Smail, Manager

PENNSYLVANIA
Department of Health, Division of Primary Care and Home Health, 132 Kline Plaza, Suite A, Harrisburg, PA 17104; tel. 717/783–1379; FAX. 717/787–3188; Robert Bastian, Director

RHODE ISLAND
Rhode Island Department of Health, Division of Facilities Regulation, Three Capitol Hill, Providence, RI 02908–5097; tel. 401/277–2566; FAX. 401/277–3999; Wayne I. Farrington, Chief

SOUTH CAROLINA
Department of Health and Environmental Control, Division of Certification, 2600 Bull Street, Columbia, SC 29201; tel. 803/737–7205; FAX. 803/737–7292; Arthur I. Starnes, Division Director

SOUTH DAKOTA
Department of Health, Office of Health Care Facilities Licensure and Certification, 615 East 4th Street, Pierre, SD 57501–1700; tel. 605/773–3356; FAX. 605/773–6667; Joan Bachman, Administrator

TENNESSEE
Department of Health, Division of Health Care Facilities, Cordell Hull Building, 425 5th Ave. North, 1st Floor, Nashville, TN 37247–0508; tel. 615/741–7603; FAX. 615/367–6397; Evelyn Foust

TEXAS
Department of Health, Health Facility Licensure and Certification Division, 8407 Wall Street, Zip 78754, 1100 West 49th Street, Austin, TX 78756; tel. 512/834–6647; FAX. 512/834–6653; Nance Stearman, RN, M.S.N., Director

UTAH
Utah Department of Health, Bureau of Health Facility Licensure, Box 142003, Salt Lake City, UT 84114–2003; tel. 801/538–6152; FAX. 801/538–6325; Debra Wynkoop–Green, Director

VERMONT
Hospice Council of Vermont, 10 Maine Street, Montpelier, VT 05602; tel. 802/223–6218; FAX. 802/229–0579; Virginia L. Fry, Director

VIRGINIA
Virginia Department of Health, Office of Health Facilities Regulation, 3600 Centre, Suite 216, 3600 West Broad Street, Richmond, VA 23230; tel. 804/367–2102; FAX. 804/367–2149; Nancy R. Hofheimer, Director

WASHINGTON
Washington Department of Health, Facilities and Services Licensing, Target Plaza, Suite 500, 2725 Harrison Avenue, N.W., P.O. Box 47852, Olympia, WA 98504–7852; tel. 360/705–6611; FAX. 360/705–6654; Fern Bettridge, Manager

WEST VIRGINIA
Office of Health Facility Licensure and Certification, West Virginia Division of Health, 1900 Kanawha Boulevard, E., Building Three, Suite 550, Charleston, WV 25305; tel. 304/558–0050; FAX. 304/558–2515; Robert P. Brauner, R.Ph., D.P.M., Program Administrator

WISCONSIN
Bureau of Quality Assurance, Division of Supportive Living, P.O. Box 309, Madison, WI 53701–0309; tel. 608/267–7185; FAX. 608/267–0352; Judy Fryback, Director, Bureau of Quality Assurance

WYOMING
Department of Health, Office of Health Quality, 2020 Carey Avenue, 8th Floor, Cheyenne, WY 82002; tel. 307/777–7123; FAX. 307/777–7127; Gerald E. Bronnenberg, Administrator

U. S. Associated Areas

PUERTO RICO
Puerto Rico Department of Health, Call Box 70184, San Juan, PR 00936; tel. 787/274–7602; FAX. 787/250–6547; Carmen Feliciano de Melecio, M.D., Secretary of Health

Section C

JCAHO Accredited Freestanding Long–Term Care Organizations

The accredited freestanding long–term care organizations listed have been accredited as of April, 1998 by the Joint Commission on Accreditation of Healthcare Organizations by decision of the Accreditation Committee of the Board of Commissioners.

The organizations listed here have been found to be in compliance with the Joint Commission standards for long–term care organizations, as found in the Comprehensive Accreditation Manual for the Long–Term Care Organizations.

Please refer to section A of the AHA Guide for information on hospitals with Long–Term Care services. These hospitals are identified by Facility Code 64. In section A, those hospitals identified by Approval Code 1 are JCAHO accredited.

We present this list simply as a convenient directory. Inclusion or omission of any organization's name indicates neither approval nor disapproval by Healthcare InfoSource, Inc., a subsidiary of the American Hospital Association.

United States

ALABAMA
Canterbury Health Facility, 1720 Knowles Road, Phenix City, AL 36869; tel. 334/291–0485; FAX. 334/297–5816; Charles Birkett, MD, MBA

Cedar Crest, 4490 Virginia Loop Road, Montgomery, AL 36116; tel. 334/281–6826; Greg Wooten

Dauphin Health Care Facility, 3717 Dauphin Street, Mobile, AL 36608; tel. 334/343–0909; FAX. 334/344–0953; Sheila McArdle, Chief Executive Officer

Integrated Health Services at Briarcliff, 850 Northwest Ninth Street, Alabaster, AL 35007; tel. 205/663–3859; FAX. 205/663–9791; Andy Clements, Administrator

Integrated Health Services at Hanover, 39 Hanover Circle, Birmingham, AL 35205; tel. 205/933–1828; FAX. 205/933–0900; Vicki Worley, Chief Executive Officer

Northside Health Care, 700 Hutchins Avenue, Gadsden, AL 35901; tel. 205/543–7101; FAX. 205/546–3924; Treieva Ridgeway, Administrator

Tyson Manor Healthcare Facility, 2020 North Country Club Drive, Montgomery, AL 36106; tel. 334/263–1643; FAX. 205/263–1645; Suzanne Sherlock

Westside Health Care Center, 4320 Judith Lane, Huntsville, AL 35805; tel. 205/837–1730; FAX. 205/430–3287; Donna Guyton

Windsor House Nursing Home, 441 McAllister Drive, Huntsville, AL 35805; tel. 205/837–8585; FAX. 205/837–2214; Charles Birkett

ARIZONA
Casa Delmar Nursing and Rehabilitation Center, 3333 North Civic Center Plaza, Scottsdale, AZ 85251; tel. 602/994–1333; FAX. 602/990–3895; Patricia A. Phillips

Catalina Care Center, 2611 North Warren, Tucson, AZ 85719; tel. 520/795–9574; FAX. 520/321–4983; James K. Kinsey, Administrator

Citadel Care Center, 5121 East Broadway Road, Mesa, AZ 85206; tel. 602/832–5555; David Hendry

Coronado Care Center, 11411 North 19th Avenue, Phoenix, AZ 85029; tel. 602/256–7500; FAX. 602/943–7697; Jacqueline Lanter, Administrator

Desert Cove Nursing Center, 1750 West Frye Road, Chandler, AZ 85224; tel. 602/899–0641; Melanie S. Seamans

Desert Samaritan Care Center, 2145 West Southern Avenue, Mesa, AZ 85202; tel. 602/890–4800; FAX. 602/890–4829; Steven D. Bakken, Administrator

Desert Sky Health and Rehabilitation Center, 5125 North 58th Ave., Glendale, AZ 85301; tel. 602/931–5800; Steven Flynt

East Mesa Care Center, 51 South 48th Street, Mesa, AZ 83956; tel. 602/832–8333; FAX. 602/830–2466; W. H. Syckes, Administrator

East Valley Health Care Center, 420 West 10th Place, Mesa, AZ 85201; tel. 602/833–4226; Andy Shane

Glendale Care Center, 4704 West Diana Ave., Glendale, AZ 85302; tel. 602/247–3949; Frances Crockett, RN

Good Samaritan Care Center, 901 East Willetta Street, Phoenix, AZ 85006; tel. 602/223–3000; FAX. 602/223–3197; Michael J. Oliver, Administrator

GranCare Health Care Center, 16640 North 38th Street, Phoenix, AZ 85032; tel. 602/482–6671; Sandy Tolle

Heritage Health Care Center, P.O. Box 391, Globe, AZ 85502; tel. 520/425–3118; Greg LeCheminant

Kachina Point Health Care and Rehab Center, 505 Jacks Canyon Road, Sedona, AZ 86351; tel. 520/284–1000; Christine Walker

La Canada Care Center, 7970 North La Canada Drive, Tucson, AZ 85704; tel. 520/797–1191; John P. O'Brien, Jr.

La Mesa Rehabilitation and Care Center, 2470 South Arizona Avenue, Yuma, AZ 85364; tel. 520/344–8541; FAX. 520/344–0823; John E. Bowman, Executive Director

Life Care Center at South Mountain, 8008 South Jesse Owens Parkway, Phoenix, AZ 85040; tel. 602/243–2780; Carolyn Wild

Life Care Center of North Glendale, 13620 North 55th Ave., Glendale, AZ 85304; tel. 602/843–8433; Gary Davis

Life Care Center of Paradise Valley, 4065 East Bell Road, Phoenix, AZ 85032; tel. 602/867–0212; Domenic Todarello

Life Care Center of Scottsdale, 9494 East Becker Lane, Scottsdale, AZ 85260; tel. 602/860–6396; Linda L. Villa

Life Care Center of Sierra Vista, 2305 East Wilcox, Sierra Vista, AZ 85635; tel. 520/458–1050; Arloa Johnson

Life Care Center of Tucson, 6211 West LaCholla Blvd., Tucson, AZ 85741; tel. 520/575–0900; Betsy Maier

Life Care Center of Yuma, 2450 South 19th Ave., Yuma, AZ 85364; tel. 520/344–0425; Robert Frechette

ManorCare Health Services, 3705 North Swan, Tucson, AZ 85718; tel. 520/299–7088; FAX. 520/529–0038; Richard Park, Administrator

Mi Casa Nursing Center, 330 South Pinnule Circle, Mesa, AZ 85206; tel. 602/981–0687; Rosemary Anderson

Payson Care Center, 107 East Lone Pine Drive, Payson, AZ 85541; tel. 520/474–6896; Todd L. Corless

Pecos Nursing and Rehabilitation Center, 1980 West Pecos Road, Chandler, AZ 85224; tel. 602/821–1268; Donald D. Abdouch

Scottsdale Heritage Court, 3339 N. Civic Center Blvd., Scottsdale, AZ 85251; tel. 602/949–5400; Carolyn S. Wild

Scottsdale Village Square, 2620 North 68th Street, Scottsdale, AZ 85257; tel. 602/946–6571; FAX. 602/946–0082; Colleen Sweet

Sonoran Rehabilitation and Care Center, 4202 North 20th Avenue, Phoenix, AZ 85015; tel. 602/264–3824; David Brown

Sun Health Care Center, 10601 West Santa Fe Drive, Sun City, AZ 85372; tel. 602/974–7000; Genny Rose

The Village Green HealthCare Center, 2932 North 14th Street, Phoenix, AZ 85014; tel. 602/264–5274; FAX. 602/277–8455; Gayle Stocking, Executive Director

Villa Campana Healthcare Center, 6651 East Carondelet Drive, Tucson, AZ 85710; tel. 520/296–6100; FAX. 602/721–3601; Robin Gwozdz

ARKANSAS
Grant County Nursing Home, Route 2, Box 100BB, Sheridan, AR 72150; tel. 501/942–2183; Boyd Wright

Pocahontas Nursing and Rehabilitation Center, 105 Country Club Road, Pocahontas, AR 72455; tel. 501/892–2523; Shelba Doan

CALIFORNIA
Akin's Post Acute Rehabilitation Hospital, 2750 Atlantic Ave., Long Beach, CA 90806; tel. 310/424–8101; Ronald M. Akin

Alamaden Care and Rehab Center, 2065 Los Gatos Almaden Road, San Jose, CA 95124; tel. 408/377–9275; Debbie Cota

Alamitos Belmont Rehabilitation Hospital, 3901 East Fourth Street, Long Beach, CA 90814; tel. 562/434–8421; FAX. 562/433–6732; Alan Anderson, President, Chief Executive Officer

Anaheim Terrace Care Center, 141 South Knott Ave., Anaheim, CA 92804; tel. 714/821–7310; David G. Schumacher

Autumn Hills Health Care Center, 430 North Glendale Ave., Glendale, CA 91206; tel. 818/246–5677; Jenik Akopian

Bayside Nursing and Rehabilitation Center, 1251 South Eliseo Drive, Kentfield, CA 94904; tel. 415/461–1900; FAX. 415/461–2736; Carol Walker

Beverly Manor Nursing and Rehabilitation Center, 1041 South Main Street, Burbank, CA 91506; tel. 818/843–2330; Terri S. Sweeney

Beverly Manor Nursing and Rehabilitation Center, 6700 Sepulveda Blvd., Van Nuys, CA 91411; tel. 818/988–7501; Cathy Davis

Brier Oak Terrace Care Center, 5154 Sunset Blvd., Los Angeles, CA 90027; tel. 213/663–3951; Sheila Snukal

Brittany Healthcare Center, Inc., 3900 Garfield Avenue, Carmichael, CA 95608; tel. 916/481–6455; FAX. 916/481–6489; Diane Hoyt, Administrator

Brookside Skilled Nursing Hospital, 2620 Flores Street, San Mateo, CA 94403; tel. 415/349–2161; FAX. 415/345–3955; Stan Coppel

Burlingame Nursing and Rehabilitation Center, 1100 Trousdale Drive, Burlingame, CA 94010; tel. 415/692–3758; FAX. 415/692–5190; Martin S. Gittleman

California Nursing and Rehabilitation Center of Palm Springs, 2299 North Indian Canyon Drive, Palm Springs, CA 92262; tel. 619/325–2937; FAX. 619/322–7250; Linda Jackson, Administrator

California Special Care Center, Inc., 8787 Center Drive, La Mesa, CA 91942; tel. 619/460–4444; FAX. 619/460–6341; Ed Long

Calistoga Nursing and Rehabilitation Center, 1715 Washington Street, Calistoga, CA 94515; tel. 707/942–6253; FAX. 707/942–6288; Cindy Reed

Canyonwood Nursing and Rehabilitation Center, 2120 Benton Drive, Redding, CA 96003; tel. 916/243–6317; FAX. 916/243–4646; JoAnn Steinmetz, CAC, CEAP

Care West Arizona Nursing and Rehabilitation Center, 1330 17th Street, Santa Monica, CA 90404; tel. 310/829–5411; Sherri Silverberg

Care West–Anza Nursing and Rehabilitation Center, 622 South Anza Street, El Cajon, CA 92020; tel. 619/442–0544; FAX. 619/442–6177; John Jimenez

Carmichael Convalescent Hospital, 8336 Fair Oaks Boulevard, Carmichael, CA 95608; tel. 916/944–3100; FAX. 916/944–4202; Rick Matros, Administrator

Casa Colina Peninsula Rehabilitation Center, 26303 Western Avenue, Lomita, CA 90717; tel. 310/325–3202; FAX. 310/534–2782; Terry Banta Winkowski, Administrator

Casa Palmera Care Center, 14750 El Camino Real, Del Mar, CA 92014; tel. 619/481–4411; FAX. 619/792–7356; Lee Johnson, Administrator

Chapman Harbor Skilled Nursing Facility, 12232 West Chapman Avenue, Garden Grove, CA 92640; tel. 714/971–5517; FAX. 714/748–7851; Patricia Smith, Administrator

Clear View Sanitarium and Convalescent Center, 15823 South Western Avenue, Gardena, CA 90247–3788; tel. 310/538–2323; FAX. 310/538–3509; W. Lee Towns, President

Country Villa Nursing and Rehabilitation Center, 340 South Alvarado Street, Los Angeles, CA 90057; tel. 213/484–9730; FAX. 213/484–9507; Jose Lynch

Country Villa Sheraton Nursing and Rehabilitation Center, 9655 Sepulveda Boulevard, North Hills, CA 91343; tel. 818/892–8665; FAX. 818/891–1208; Steve Reissman

Country Villa South, 3515 Overland Avenue, Los Angeles, CA 90034; tel. 310/839–5201; FAX. 310/839–4763; Cvia Rosen

Country Villa Westwood Nursing Center, 12121 Santa Monica Boulevard, Los Angeles, CA 90025; tel. 310/826–0821; FAX. 310/826–2768; Jane Corr

Courtyard Care Center, 1625 Denton Avenue, Hayward, CA 94545; tel. 510/782–2133; FAX. 510/783–3659; Nathaniel Fripp

Covina Rehabilitation Center, 261 West Badillo, Covina, CA 91723; tel. 813/967–3874; FAX. 813/332–6532; Sheryl Baykman, Administrator

Creekside HealthCare Center, 1900 Church Lane, San Pablo, CA 94806; tel. 510/235–5514; George H. Eslinger

Devonshire Care Center, 1350 East Devonshire Avenue, Hemet, CA 92544; tel. 909/925–2571; FAX. 909/929–5469; Jacqueline Arcara

Driftwood Health Care Center, 4109 Emerald Street, Torrance, CA 90503; tel. 310/371–4628; FAX. 310/214–1882; Gary Yoshida

Driftwood Health Care Center, 19700 Hesperian Blvd., Hayward, CA 94541; tel. 510/785–2880; Michael Walsh

Driftwood Healthcare Center, 675 24th Street, Santa Cruz, CA 95062; tel. 408/475–6323; Elizabeth P. Byrne

Earlwood Care Center, 20820 Earl Street, Torrance, CA 90503; tel. 310/371–1228; William C. Scott

Eastwood Convalescent Hospital, 4029 East Anaheim Street, Long Beach, CA 90804; tel. 310/494–4421; Ronald M. Akin, Jr.

Edgewater Convalescent Hospital, 2625 East 4th Street, Long Beach, CA 90814; tel. 562/434–0974; Debbie Kremel

El Encanto Healthcare and Habilitation Center, 555 South El Encanto Road, Hacienda Heights, CA 91745; tel. 818/336–1274; Steve Blackwell

Elmcrest Convalescent Hospital, 3111 Santa Anita Ave., El Monte, CA 91733; tel. 818/443–0218; Sheila Snukal

English Oaks Convalescent and Rehabilitation Hospital, 2633 West Rumble Road, Modesto, CA 95350; tel. 209/577–1001, ext. 7601; FAX. 209/577–0366; Jerry Holloway, RN, NHA

Escondido Nursing Center, 201 North Fig Street, Escondido, CA 92025; tel. 619/746–0303; Richard Matros

Eskaton Manzanita Manor, 5318 Manzanita Ave., Carmichael, CA 95608; tel. 916/331–8513; John Breaux

Eskaton Village, 3939 Walnut Ave., Carmichael, CA 95608; tel. 916/974–2000; John Breaux

Evergreen Convalescent Hospital and Rehabilitation Center, 2030 Evergreen Avenue, Modesto, CA 95350; tel. 209/577–1055; FAX. 209/526–6961; Daniel J. Cipponeri, Vice President

Excell Health Care Center, 3025 High Street, Oakland, CA 94619; tel. 510/261–5200; FAX. 510/261–1012; Carol Shields

FHP Westminster, 206 Hospital Circle, Westminster, CA 92683; tel. 714/891–2769; Kim Phan

Fairfield Health Care Center, 1255 Travis Boulevard, Fairfield, CA 94533; tel. 707/425–0623; FAX. 707/425–0704; Diane Hinkle, Administrator

Flagship Healthcare Center, 466 Flagship Road, Newport Beach, CA 92663; tel. 714/642–8044; Gene Burleson

Florin Health Care Center, 7400 24th Street, Sacramento, CA 95822; tel. 916/422–4825; Brigitte Coleman

Fountain Care Center, 1835 West LaVeta Ave., Orange, CA 92668; tel. 714/978–6800; William Scott

Fremont Health Center, 39022 Presidio Way, Fremont, CA 94538; tel. 510/792–3743; FAX. 510/792–1966; Lisa Walke, Executive Director

Fruitvale Health Care Center, 3020 East 15th Street, Oakland, CA 94601; tel. 510/261–5613; Remedios B. Tibayan

Gateway, 26660 Patrick Avenue, Hayward, CA 94544; tel. 510/782–1845; FAX. 510/782–9913; Andrea B. Dapper, Director, Nursing

Glendora Rehabilitation Center, 435 East Gladstone, Glendora, CA 91740; tel. 818/963–5955; FAX. 818/963–8683; Barbara Dube, Administrator

Grand Terrace Convalescent Hospital, 12000 Mt. Vernon Avenue, Grand Terrace, CA 92313; tel. 909/825–5221; FAX. 909/783–4811; Richard K. Matros, Administrator

Greenhaven Country Place, 455 Florin Road, Sacramento, CA 95831; tel. 916/393–2550; John Breaux

Guardian Ygnacio, 1449 Ygnacio Valley Road, Walnut Creek, CA 94598; tel. 510/939–5820; FAX. 510/939–0231; Robert Pierce

Hanford Nursing and Rehabilitation Hospital, 1007 West Lacey Boulevard, Hanford, CA 92319; tel. 209/582–2871; FAX. 209/582–5853; Mark Fisher

Hayward Hills Convalescent Center, 1768 B Street, Hayward, CA 94541; tel. 510/538–4424; FAX. 510/538–9221; Terry McGregor

Heritage Paradise, 8777 Skyway Street, Paradise, CA 95969; tel. 916/872–3200; FAX. 916/872–5318; Barbara Wright

Heritage Rehabilitation Center, 21414 South Vermont Avenue, Torrance, CA 90502; tel. 310/320–8714; FAX. 310/320–1809; Doug Nelson, Administrator

Huntington Beach Convalescent Hospital, 18811 Florida Street, Huntington Beach, CA 92648; tel. 714/847–3515; FAX. 714/847–2852; Michael Williams, Administrator

Huntington Drive Skilled Nursing Facility, 400 West Huntington Drive, Arcadia, CA 91007; tel. 818/445–2421; FAX. 818/821–5916; Terry S. Sweeney, Executive Director

Huntington Valley Nursing Center, 8382 Newman Avenue, Huntington Beach, CA 92648; tel. 714/842–5551; FAX. 714/848–5359; Jill Greene, Director, Nursing

Imperial Convalescent Center, 11926 S. La Mirada Blvd., La Mirada, CA 90638; tel. 310/943–7156; Stephen L. Ramsdell

Inglewood Healthcare Center, 100 South Hillcrest Blvd., Inglewood, CA 90301; tel. 310/677–9114; Shirley B. Schouleman, MHA

Integrated Health Services at Orange Hills, 5017 East Chapman Avenue, Orange, CA 92669; tel. 714/997–7090; FAX. 714/997–4631; William Hibbard

Integrated Health Services at Park Regency, 1770 West La Habra Boulevard, La Habra, CA 90631; tel. 310/691–8810; FAX. 310/697–8478; Phyllis Debelak, Administrator

John Douglas French Center for Alzheimer's Disease, 3951 Katella Avenue, Los Alamitos, CA 90720; tel. 562/493–1555; FAX. 562/596–7526; Ferri Kidane, Executive Director

Julia Healthcare Center, 276 Sierra Vista Ave., Mountain View, CA 94043; tel. 415/967–5714; Terry Campbell

La Mariposa Nursing and Rehabilitation Center, 1244 Travis Boulevard, Fairfield, CA 94533; tel. 707/422–7750; FAX. 707/422–8102; Lisa Churches, Administrator

La Palma Nursing Center, 1130 West La Palma Avenue, Anaheim, CA 92801; tel. 714/772–7480; FAX. 714/776–1841; Patricia Smith, Administrator

La Salette Health and Rehabilitation Center, 538 East Fulton Street, Stockton, CA 95204; tel. 209/466–2066; Jeanne Wright

Lancaster Health Care Center, 1642 West Avenue J, Lancaster, CA 93534; tel. 805/942–8463; FAX. 805/948–5133; Jeri–Anne I. Shelton, Executive Director

Laurelwood Health Care Center, 13000 Victory Boulevard, North Hollywood, CA 91606; tel. 818/985–5990; FAX. 818/505–1947; Scott Herzig, Executive Director

Leisure Court Nursing Center, 1135 North Leisure Court, Anaheim, CA 92801; tel. 714/722–1353; Patricia Smith

Magnolia Gardens Care Center, 1609 Trousdale Dr., Burlingame, CA 94010; tel. 650/697–1865; C. David Wilcox

Magnolia Special Care Center, 635 South Magnolia, El Cajon, CA 92020; tel. 619/442–8826; FAX. 619/442–0288; Harriet Haugen, Administrator

Manor Care Nursing and Rehabilitation Center, 11680 Warneer Avenue, Fountain Valley, CA 92708; tel. 714/241–9800; FAX. 714/966–1654; Christine Davis

ManorCare Health Services, 1150 Tilton Drive, Sunnyvale, CA 94087; tel. 408/735–7200; FAX. 408/736–8619; Jennifer Oldfather, Administrator

Manteca Nursing and Rehabilitation Center, 410 Eastwood Avenue, Manteca, CA 95336; tel. 209/239–1222; FAX. 209/239–9101; Maxine Niel

Marlora Post Acute Rehabilitation Hospital, 3801 East Anaheim Street, Long Beach, CA 90804; tel. 310/494–3311; Marilyn A. Hauser

McClure Convalescent Hospital and Rehabilitation Center, 2910 McClure Street, Oakland, CA 94609; tel. 510/836–3677; FAX. 510/836–1938; Daniel Alger, Administrator

Mission Terrace Convalescent Hospital, 623 West Junipero Street, Santa Barbara, CA 93105; tel. 805/682–7443; FAX. 805/682–5311; Evelina Murphy, Administrator

Nob Hill Healthcare Center, 1359 Pine Street, San Francisco, CA 94109; tel. 415/673–8405; Paul D. Tunnell

Nursing Inn of Menlo Park, 16 Coleman Place, Menlo Park, CA 94025; tel. 415/326–0802; FAX. 415/326–4145; Daniel Alger, Administrator

Orinda Rehabilitation and Convalescent Hospital, 11 Altarinda Road, Orinda, CA 94563; tel. 510/254–6500; FAX. 510/254–9063; David Cronin, Administrator

Pacific Coast Manor, 1935 Wharf Road, Capitola, CA 95010; tel. 408/476–0770; FAX. 408/476–0737; Charles H. Bruffey, Administrator

Pacific Hills Manor, 370 Noble Court, Morgan Hill, CA 95037; tel. 408/779–7346; FAX. 408/779–9435; Laurie Behrend, Administrator

Pacific Regency/Bakersfield, 6212 Tudor Way, Bakersfield, CA 93306; tel. 805/871–3133; Deana Shannon

Pacifica Nursing and Rehabilitation Center, 385 Esplanade, Pacifica, CA 94044; tel. 650/993–5576; FAX. 650/359–9388; William Connell, Administrator

Palm Grove Care Center, 13075 Blackbird Street, Garden Grove, CA 92843; tel. 714/530–6322; Tony Ricci

Park Central Nursing and Rehabilitation Center, 2100 Parkside Drive, Fremont, CA 94536; tel. 510/797–5300; FAX. 510/797–2159; Donna Jeffares, PhD

Park Tustin Rehabilitation and Healthcare Center, 2210 East First Street, Santa Ana, CA 92705; tel. 714/547–7091; FAX. 714/547–4516; Mark Schroepfer, Administrator

Parkmont Rehabilitation and Nursing Care Center, 2400 Parkside Drive, Fremont, CA 94536; tel. 510/793–7222; FAX. 510/793–4361; Tom Konig

Parkview Health Care Center, 27350 Tampa Avenue, Hayward, CA 90115; tel. 510/783–8150; FAX. 510/783–8161; Jeff Lambkin, Executive Director

Petaluma Nursing and Rehabilitation Center, 1115 B Street, Petaluma, CA 94952; tel. 707/765–3030; Sean Wood

Santa Monica Nursing Center, 1321 Franklin Street, Santa Monica, CA 90404; tel. 310/828–5596; Richard Matros

Scripps Memorial Ocean View Convalescent Hospital, 900 Santa Fe Drive, Encinitas, CA 92024; tel. 619/753–6423; FAX. 619/753–4979; Pamela I. Turner, Administrator

Scripps Memorial Torrey Pines Convalescent Hospital, 2552 Torrey Pines Road, La Jolla, CA 92037; tel. 619/453–5810; FAX. 619/452–4301; Elena M. Gulla, Administrator

Simi Valley Rehabilitation and Nursing Center, 5270 Los Angeles Avenue, Simi Valley, CA 93063; tel. 805/527–6204; FAX. 805/527–2082; Janiece Lackey

Skyline Convalescent Hospital, 2065 Forest Ave., San Jose, CA 95128; tel. 408/298–3950; W. M. Nicholson, Jr.

Subacute Saratoga Hospital, 13425 Sousa Lane, Saratoga, CA 95070; tel. 408/378–8875; FAX. 408/866–8144; Alton King, President

SunRise Care Center for San Dimas, 1033 East Arrow Highway, Glendora, CA 91740; tel. 818/963–7531; Sandra Fahey

Tarzana Rehabilitation Center, 5650 Reseda Boulevard, Tarzana, CA 91356; tel. 818/881–4261; FAX. 818/343–7451; Gene Burleson

The Cloisters of La Jolla, 7160 Fay Ave., La Jolla, CA 92037; tel. 619/459–4361; Cheryl M. Thompson

The Cloisters of Mission Hills, 3680 Reynard Way, San Diego, CA 92103; tel. 619/297–4484; Scott M. Harmon

The Homestead of Fair Oaks, 11300 Fair Oaks Blvd., Fair Oaks, CA 90456; tel. 916/965–4663; John Breaux

Thousand Oaks Health Care Center, 93 West Avenida de Los Arboles, Thousand Oaks, CA 91360; tel. 805/492–2444; FAX. 805/493–1643; Cynthia Poulsen, Administrator

Tulare Convalescent Hospital, 680 East Merritt Avenue, Tulare, CA 93274; tel. 209/686–8581; FAX. 209/686–5393; Mark Fisher, Administrator

Vale Care Center, 13484 San Pablo Ave., San Pablo, CA 94806; tel. 510/232–5945; Tim Neal

Valley Manor Rehabilitation Care Center, 3806 Clayton Road, Concord, CA 94521; tel. 510/689–2266; FAX. 510/689–0509; Robert Elkin, MD

Villa Maria Care Center, 425 East Barcellus Avenue, Santa Maria, CA 93454; tel. 805/922–3558; FAX. 805/349–8443; Laurie Smith, Administrator

Village Square Nursing and Rehabilitation Center, 1586 West San Marcos Boulevard, San Marcos, CA 92069; tel. 619/471–2986; FAX. 619/471–5176; Gary Leiderman, Administrator

Western Medical Center Bartlett, 600 East Washington Avenue, Santa Ana, CA 92701; tel. 714/973–1656, ext. 408; FAX. 714/836–4349; Page Van Hoy, Chief Executive Officer

Woodland Care Center, 7120 Corbin Ave., Reseda, CA 91335; tel. 818/881–4540; Jane Anderson

Woodland Nursing Inn, 3721 Mount Diablo Boulevard, Lafayette, CA 94549; tel. 510/284–5544; FAX. 510/284–5673; Daniel Alger

COLORADO

Alpine Living Center, 501 East Thornton Parkway, Thornton, CO 80229; tel. 303/452–6101; FAX. 303/452–4330; Bruce Odenthal

Applewood Living Center, 1800 Stroh Place, Longmont, CO 80501; tel. 303/776–6081; Cheryl P. Nelson

Arvado Health Center, 6121 West 60th Ave., Arvada, CO 80003; tel. 303/420–4550; Holly Raymer

Bear Creek Nursing Center, P.O. Box 117, Morrison, CO 80465; tel. 303/697–8181; Bruce Busby

Bethany Healthplex, 5301 W. First Avenue, Lakewood, CO 80226; tel. 812/422–7774; Joan M. Dugan

Bonell Good Samaritan Center, 708 22nd Street, P.O. Box 1508, Greeley, CO 80632–1508; tel. 970/352–6082; FAX. 970/356–7970; Art Hess, Administrator

Boulder Manor, 4685 East Baseline Road, Boulder, CO 80303; tel. 303/494–0535; FAX. 303/494–0162; Sherry Thompson, Administrator

Camellia Health Care Center, 500 Geneva Street, Aurora, CO 75705; tel. 303/364–9311; Patsy M. Bagully

Castle Garden Care Center, 401 Malley Drive, Northglenn, CO 80233; tel. 303/452–4700; Bruce Busby

Cedars Health Care Center, 1599 Ingalls Street, Lakewood, CO 80214; tel. 303/232–3551; FAX. 303/232–8992; Terrance Sharron

Cherrelyn Health Care Center, 5555 South Eldti Street, Littleton, CO 80120; tel. 303/798–8686; FAX. 303/798–0145; Lori Moore

Cherry Hills Health Care Center, 3575 South Washington Street, Englewood, CO 80110; tel. 303/789–2276; Bruce Busby

Community Care at Canon City, 515 Fairview, Canon City, CO 81212; tel. 719/275–0665; Larry Lavelle

Garden Terrace Alzheimer's Center of Excellence, 1600 South Potomac Street, Aurora, CO 80012; tel. 303/750–8418; Jennifer D. Marcols

Hallmark Nursing Center, 3701 West Radcliff Ave., Denver, CO 80236; tel. 303/794–6484; Kevin Fletcher

IHS of Colorado at Cherry Creek, 14699 East Hampden Ave., Aurora, CO 80014; tel. 303/693–0111; Ann Kokish

Integrated Health Services of Colorado Springs, 3625 Parkmoor Village Drive, Colorado Springs, CO 80917; tel. 719/550–0200; FAX. 719/637–0756; Rick Haskell

Julia Temple Center, 3401 South Lafayette Street, Englewood, CO 80110; tel. 303/761–0075; Nancy K. Schwalm

Kenton Manor Living Center, 850 27th Avenue, Greeley, CO 80631; tel. 970/353–1018; FAX. 970/353–2476; Sieglinde Donohue, Administrator

Life Care Center of Aurora, 14101 East Evans Ave., Aurora, CO 80014; tel. 303/751–2000; Donna Ulrich

Life Care Center of Evergreen, 2987 Evergreen Parkway, Evergreen, CO 80439; tel. 303/674–4500; Dawn Visscher

Manor Care Nursing Center, Medbridge Medical and Physical Rehabilitation Center, 290 South Monaco Parkway, Denver, CO 80224; tel. 303/355–2525; FAX. 303/333–6960; Nancy Schwalm, Executive Director

Manor Care Nursing and Rehabilitation Center, 2800 Palo Parkway, Boulder, CO 80301; tel. 303/440–9100; Marilyn Israel

Mariner Health of Denver, 895 South Monaco Parkway, Denver, CO 80224; tel. 303/321–3110; Palma Chambers

Mariner Health of Greenwood Village, 6005 South Holly Street, Littleton, CO 80121; tel. 303/773–1000; FAX. 303/773–0024; Tracy Scruggs

Red Rocks HealthCare Center, 4450 East Jewell, Denver, CO 80222; tel. 303/757–7438; Steven Flynt

San Juan Living Center, 1043 Ridge, Montrose, CO 81401; tel. 970/249–9683; Dale D. Pelton

Spring Creek Health Care Center, 1000 East Stuart, Fort Collins, CO 80525; tel. 970/482–5712; FAX. 970/493–8376; Dennis Ziefel

Terrace Gardens Health Care Center, 2438 East Fountain Boulevard, Colorado Springs, CO 80910; tel. 719/473–8000; FAX. 719/473–7370; John Bowman

Vista Grande Rehabilitation and Care Center, P.O. Box 1718, Cortez, CO 81321; tel. 970/565–0386; Jo Ann Aldrich

CONNECTICUT

Aaron Manor Health Care Facility, P.O. Box 336, Chester, CT 06412; tel. 860/526–5316; Robert Sbriglio, LPN

Abbott Terrace Health Center, 44 Abbott Terrace, Waterbury, CT 06702–1499; tel. 203/755–4870; FAX. 203/755–9016; Diane MacSweeney

Adams House Healthcare, 80 Fern Drive, Torrington, CT 06790; tel. 860/482–7668; FAX. 203/496–7815; Dawn Dempsey, Administrator

Alexandria Manor, 55 Tunxis Ave., Bloomfield, CT 06002; tel. 860/242–0703; Benjamin Fischman

Ashlar of Newtown, Toddy Hill Road, P.O. Box 5505, Newtown, CT 06470; tel. 203/426–5847; FAX. 203/270–0695; Thomas Gutner, President

Astoria Park, 725 Park Avenue, Bridgeport, CT 06604; tel. 203/366–3653; FAX. 203/333–6974; Donald Franco

Avery Heights, 705 New Britain Avenue, Hartford, CT 06106; tel. 860/527–9126; FAX. 860/525–2090; Mariam Parker, MD

Avon Convalescent Home, Inc., d/b/a Avon Health Center, 652 West Avon Road, Avon, CT 06001; tel. 860/673–2521; FAX. 860/675–1587; Laura L. Nelson, Administrator

Bayview Health Care Center, Inc., 301 Rope Ferry Road, Waterford, CT 06385; tel. 203/444–1175; FAX. 203/437–2173; Michelle Willis, NHA, MS

Beacon Brook Health Center, 89 Weid Drive, Naugatuck, CT 06770; tel. 203/729–9889; FAX. 203/729–9889; Marion Najamy

Beechwood Rehabilitation and Nursing Center, 31 Vauxhall Street, P.O. Box 308, New London, CT 06320; tel. 860/442–4363; FAX. 860/447–3749; William G. White

Bel–Air Manor Nursing and Rehabilitation Center, 256 New Britain Ave., Newington, CT 06111; tel. 860/666–5689; Martin Sbriglio

Bethel Health Care Center, 13 Parklawn Drive, Bethel, CT 06801; tel. 203/830–4180; FAX. 203/830–4185; Roland Butler

Bishop Wicke Health and Rehabilitation Center, Inc., 584 Long Hill Ave., Shelton, CT 06484; tel. 203/929–5321; Robert Clapp

Blair Manor, 612 Hazard Ave., Enfield, CT 06082; tel. 860/749–8388; Joel Carmichael

Bloomfield Health Care Center, 355 Park Avenue, Bloomfield, CT 06002; tel. 860/242–8595; Marvin Ostreicher

Branford Hills Health Care Center, 189 Alps Road, Branford, CT 06405; tel. 203/481–6221; FAX. 203/483–1893; Charles F. Shelton, Administrator

Brightview Nursing & Retirement Center, 220 Scoville Road, Avon, CT 06001; tel. 860/673–3265; FAX. 860/673–4883; Peggy Coburn

Brittany Farms Health Center, 400 Brittany Farms Road, New Britain, CT 06053; tel. 860/224–3111; FAX. 860/229–0066; Thomas Tolisano

Brook Hollow Health Care Center, 55 Kondracki Lane, Wallingford, CT 06492; tel. 203/265–6771; FAX. 203/284–3883; Pamela R. Miller, Administrator

Brookview Health Care Facility, 130 Loomis Drive, West Hartford, CT 06107; tel. 860/521–8700; FAX. 203/521–7452; Clifton P. Mix, Administrator

Carolton Chronic and Convalescent Hospital, Inc., 400 Mill Plain Road, Fairfield, CT 06430; tel. 203/255–3573; Carmen A. Tortora

Cedar Lane Rehabilitation and Health Care Center, 128 Cedar Avenue, Waterbury, CT 06705; tel. 203/757–9271; FAX. 203/757–2988; Joan P. Lyke

Center for Optimum Care Windham, 595 Valley Street, Willimantic, CT 06226; tel. 203/423–2597; FAX. 203/450–7070; Richard Kase

Cherry Brook Health Care Center, 102 Dyer Avenue, Collinsville, CT 06022; tel. 203/693–7777; FAX. 203/693–7779; David Bordonaro

Cheshire Convalescent Center, 745 Highland Avenue, Cheshire, CT 06410; tel. 203/272–7285; FAX. 203/250–6066; William Thompson, Administrator

Chestelm Health Care, 534 Town Street, P.O. Box 719, Moodus, CT 06469; tel. 203/873–1455; FAX. 203/873–2307; Brenda Epright

Chesterfields Health Care Center, 132 Main Street, Chester, CT 06412; tel. 860/526–5363; Peter W. Allen

Clifton House Rehabilitation Center, 181 Clifton Street, New Haven, CT 06513; tel. 203/467–1666; FAX. 203/469–7213; Earle R. Hollings, Administrator

Coccomo Memorial Health Care Center, 33 Cone Ave., Meriden, CT 06450; tel. 203/238–1606; Brian Foley

Colchester Nursing and Rehabilitation Center, 59 Harrington Court, Colchester, CT 06415; tel. 860/537–2339; FAX. 860/537–4747; Moshael Straus

Cook Willow Health Center, 81 Hillside Avenue, Plymouth, CT 06782; tel. 860/283–8208; FAX. 860/283–6667; Susan MacDonald

County Manor Health Care Center, P.O. Box 7060, Prospect, CT 06712; tel. 203/758–4431; Jack Freidler

Crescent Manor, 1243 West Main Street, Waterbury, CT 06708; tel. 203/757–0561; George Giblin

Crestfield Rehabilitation Center and Fenwood Manor, 565 Vernon Street, Manchester, CT 06040; tel. 860/643–5151; FAX. 860/643–5203; Rolland Castleman

Derby Nursing Center, 210 Chatfield Street, Derby, CT 06418; tel. 203/735–7401; FAX. 203/736–0898; Albert Saunders

Evergreen Health Care Center, P.O. Box 549, Stafford Springs, CT 06076; tel. 860/684–6341; David T. Panteleakos

Fairview, Starr Hill Road, P.O. Box 7218, Groton, CT 06340; tel. 860/445–7478; FAX. 860/445–9575; Jack Van Verdeghem, Administrator

Filosa Convalescent Home, Inc., 13 Hakim Street, Danbury, CT 06810; tel. 203/744–3366; Frank D. Malone, PhD.

Fowler Nursing Center, Inc., 10 Boston Post Road, Guilford, CT 06437; tel. 203/453–3725; Mary Filloramo

Geer Nursing and Rehabilitation Center, 99 South Canaan Road, P.O. Box 819, Canaan, CT 06018; tel. 203/824–5137; FAX. 203/824–1474; Anthony Nania

Gladeview Health Care Center, 60 Boston Post Road, Old Saybrook, CT 06475; tel. 203/388–6696; FAX. 203/395–0093; Jeannette Terragna

Glastonbury Health Care Center, 969 Hebron Avenue, 1175 Hebron Avenue, Glastonbury, CT 06033; tel. 203/659–1905; FAX. 203/652–3055; Thomas C. Gaccione, Administrator

Glen Hill Convalescent Center, One Glen Hill Road, Danbury, CT 06811; tel. 203/744–2840; FAX. 203/792–1521; James Malloy, Administrator

Golden Heights Health Center, 62 Coleman Street, Bridgeport, CT 06604; tel. 203/367–8444; Louis P. Affinito

Grant Street Health and Rehabilitation Center, 425 Grant Street, Bridgeport, CT 06610; tel. 203/366–5255; Donna M. Deitch

Greenery Extended Care Center at Cheshire, 50 Hazel Drive, Cheshire, CT 06410; tel. 203/272–7204; FAX. 203/272–4607; Denis Twigg, Administrator

Greenery Rehabilitation Center at Waterbury, 177 Whitewood Road, Waterbury, CT 06708; tel. 203/757–9491; FAX. 203/575–1714; Mark Finkelstein, Administrator

Grove Manor Nursing Home, Inc., 145 Grove Street, Waterbury, CT 06710; tel. 203/753–7205; Rose J. Schaefer

Hamilton Rehabilitation and Healthcare Center, 50 Palmer Street, Norwich, CT 06360; tel. 860/889–8358; Joseph Bontempo

Harbor Hill Care Center, Inc., 111 Church Street, Middletown, CT 06457; tel. 860/347–7286; FAX. 860/346–5589; Lewis Abramson, Administrator

Harbor View Manor, 308 Savin Ave, West Haven, CT 06516; tel. 203/932–6411; Andrew S. Krochko

Harborside Healthcare–Willows, 225 Amity Road, Woodbridge, CT 06525; tel. 203/387–0076; Harold J. Moffie

Harborside Healthcare Arden House, 850 Mix Avenue, Hamden, CT 06514; tel. 203/282–3500; FAX. 203/287–9534; Harold Moffie

Hebrew Home and Hospital, Inc., One Abrahms Boulevard, West Hartford, CT 06117–1525; tel. 860/523–3800; FAX. 203/523–3949; Irving Kronenberg

Heritage Heights Care Center, 22 Hospital Avenue, Danbury, CT 06810; tel. 203/744–3700; FAX. 203/798–8322; Susan Jodoin, Administrator

High View Health Care Center, 600 Highland Ave., Middletown, CT 06457; tel. 860/347–3315; Frank Fiore

Hill Crest Health Care Center, Five Richard Brown Drive, Uncasville, CT 06382; tel. 860/848–8466; FAX. 860/848–7456; Judith Hilburger

Honey Hill Care Center, 34 Midrocks Drive, Norwalk, CT 06851; tel. 203/847–9686; FAX. 203/840–1584; David W. Osborne

Ingraham Manor, 400 North Main Street, Bristol, CT 06010; tel. 203/584–3400; FAX. 203/589–8686; Linda A. Urbanski, Administrator

Jerome Home, 975 Corbin Ave., New Britain, CT 06052; tel. 860/229–3707; John A. Kelly

Jewish Home for the Elderly of Fairfield County, 175 Jefferson Street, Fairfield, CT 06432; tel. 203/374–9461; FAX. 203/374–8082; Dennis J. Magid

Kettle Brook Nonprofit Healthcare Center, 96 Prospect Hill Road, East Windsor, CT 06088; tel. 860/623–9846; Daniel S. O'Brien

Kimberly Hall South, One Emerson Drive, Windsor, CT 06095; tel. 860/688–6443; Allan DeBlasio

Laurel Woods, 451 North High Street, East Haven, CT 06512; tel. 203/466–6850; FAX. 203/466–6852; Herman Dostie

Laurelwood Rehabilitation and Skilled Nursing Center, 642 Danbury Road, Ridgefield, CT 06877; tel. 203/438–8226; FAX. 203/438–8378; Joanne Maccione, Administrator

Liberty Specialty Care Center, Inc., 36 Broadway, Colchester, CT 06415; tel. 860/537–4606; Mary Filloramo

Litchfield Woods Health Care Center, 255 Roberts Street, Torrington, CT 06790; tel. 860/489–5801; FAX. 860/489–6102; Gene Heavens, Administrator

Lord Chamberlain Nursing Facility Rehabilitation Center, 7003 Main Street, Stratford, CT 06497; tel. 203/375–5894; FAX. 203/375–1199; Martin Sbriglio, RN, Licensed Administrator, Chief Executive Officer

Maefair Health Care Center, 21 Maefair Court, Trumbull, CT 06611; tel. 203/459–5152; FAX. 203/549–5156; Margaret Crescione, Administrator

Manchester Manor Health Care Center, 385 West Center Street, Manchester, CT 06040; tel. 860/646–0129; FAX. 860/645–0841; Stephen Surprenant, Administrator

Mansfield Center for Nursing and Rehabilitation, 100 Warren Circle, Storrs, CT 06268; tel. 860/487–2300; FAX. 203/487–2312; Kathleen Sutherland

Maple View Manor, Inc., 856 Maple Street, Rocky Hill, CT 06067; tel. 860/563–2861; Thomas E. Harris

Mariner Health Care at Bride Brook, 23 Liberty Way, Niantic, CT 06357; tel. 860/739–4007; FAX. 860/739–3880; John D. Hooker, Administrator

Mariner Health of Pendleton, 44 Maritime Drive, Mystic, CT 06355; tel. 203/572–1700; FAX. 203/527–7830; Susan D. Peglow, MPA

Mariner Health of Southern Connecticut, 126 Ford Street, Ansonia, CT 06401; tel. 203/736–1100; Heidi Gil

Marlborough Health Care Center, Inc., 85 Stage Harbor Road, P.O. Box 476, Marlborough, CT 06447; tel. 203/295–9531; FAX. 203/295–6232; Marianne Harold, Administrator

Mary Elizabeth Nursing Center, P.O. Box 98, Mystic, CT 06355; tel. 860/536–9655; Eleanaor R. Bond

McLean Home and Home Care Services, 75 Great Pond Road, Simsbury, CT 06070; tel. 860/658–3700; FAX. 860/651–1247; David R. Bailey

Meadowbrook of Granby, 350 Salmon Brook Street, Granby, CT 06035; tel. 203/653–9888; FAX. 203/653–8938; Samuel Paul

Mediplex Rehabilitation and Skilled Nursing Center of Southern Connecticut, 2028 Bridgeport Avenue, P.O. Box 109, Milford, CT 06460; tel. 203/877–0371; FAX. 203/877–6185; Mary Grabell, Executive Director

Mediplex Rehabilitation and Skilled Nursing Center of Central Connecticut, 261 Summit Street, Plantsville, CT 06479; tel. 860/628–0364; FAX. 860/628–9166; Raymond C. DeBlasio, Administrator

Mediplex of Danbury, 107 Osborne Street, Danbury, CT 06810; tel. 203/792–8102; FAX. 203/731–5306; John Kolanda

Mediplex of Darien Rehabilitation Center, 599 Boston Post Road, Darien, CT 06820; tel. 203/655–7727, ext. 202; FAX. 203/655–6718; Lisa J. Jaser

Mediplex of Greater Hartford, 160 Coventry Street, Bloomfield, CT 06002; tel. 860/243–2995; FAX. 860/243–1902; William B. Pond, Administrator

Mediplex of Milford, 245 Orange Avenue, Milford, CT 06460; tel. 203/876–5123; FAX. 203/876–5129; Donna C. Stango, Administrator

Mediplex of Newington, 240 Church Street, Newington, CT 06111; tel. 203/667–2256; FAX. 203/667–6367; Patricia Salisbury, Administrator

Mediplex of Southbury, 162 South Britain Road, Southbury, CT 06488; tel. 203/264–9600; FAX. 203/264–9603; Ann M. Rogers, Administrator

Mediplex of Stamford, 710 Long Ridge Road, Stamford, CT 06902; tel. 203/379–4026; Andrew Turner

Mediplex of Westport, One Burr Road, Westport, CT 06880; tel. 203/226–4201; FAX. 203/221–4766; Dorothy H. Feigin, Administrator

Mediplex of Wethersfield, 341 Jordan Lane, Wethersfield, CT 06109; tel. 860/563–0101; FAX. 860/257–6107; J. Kevin Prisco, Administrator

MercyKnoll, Inc., 243 Steele Road, W. Hartford, CT 06117; tel. 860/236–3503; Irene Holowesko, RSM

Meriden Nursing and Rehabilitation Center, 845 Paddock Avenue, Meriden, CT 06450; tel. 203/238–2645; FAX. 203/238–7376; Carolyn M. Fields

Meridian Manor Corporation, 1132 Meridien Road, Waterbury, CT 06705; tel. 203/757–1228; James E. Cleary

Middlesex Convalescent Center, 100 Randolph Road, Middletown, CT 06457; tel. 860/344–0353; FAX. 860/346–1932; Robert Shepard, Administrator

Milford Health Care Center, Inc., 195 Platt Street, Milford, CT 06460; tel. 203/878–5958; FAX. 203/878–4299; Brian J. Dickstein

Miller Memorial Community, 360 Broad Street, Meriden, CT 06450; tel. 203/237–8815; FAX. 203/630–3714; Sister Ann Noonan, R.S.M., Administrator, Chief Operating Officer

Montowese Health and Rehabilitation Center, Inc., 163 Quinnipiac Avenue, North Haven, CT 06473; tel. 203/624–3303; FAX. 203/787–9243; Farooq H. Khan

New London Rehabilitation and Care Center, 88 Clark Lane, Waterford, CT 06385; tel. 860/442–0471; Kenneth J. Kallan

Noble Horizons, 17 Cobble Road, Salisbury, CT 06068; tel. 860/435–9851; FAX. 860/435–0636; Norman E. Harper

Northbridge Health Care Center, 2875 Main Street, Bridgeport, CT 06606; tel. 203/336–0232; Kathy Pajor, ADM

Norwichtown Rehabilitation and Care Center, 93 West Town Street, Norwichtown, CT 06360; tel. 860/889–2614; Rosemary Clark

Notre Dame Convalescent Home, Inc., 76 West Rocks Road, Norwalk, CT 06851; tel. 203/847–5893; John J. Farling

Parkway Pavilion Healthcare, 1157 Enfield Street, Enfield, CT 06082; tel. 860/745–1641; Terrance Kuzman

Plainville Health Care Center, 269 Farmington Avenue, Plainville, CT 06062; tel. 860/747–1637; FAX. 860/747–9757; Terri Golec

Pope John Paul II Center for Health Care, 33 Lincoln Ave., Danbury, CT 06810; tel. 203/797–9300; Diane A. Pimentel

Portland Care and Rehabilitation Centre, Inc., 333 Main Street, Portland, CT 06480; tel. 860/342–0370; Gregory A. Yuska

Regency House of Wallingford, 181 East Main Street, Wallingford, CT 06492; tel. 203/265–1661; FAX. 203/265–7842; Nancy K. Wright

Rehabilitation and Healthcare Center of Litchfield, 225 Wyoming Avenue, Torrington, CT 06790; tel. 203/482–8563; Sheila Murray

Ridgeview Health Care Center, 156 Berlin Road, Cromwell, CT 06416; tel. 860/635–1010; Ken Lewis

Riverside Health Care Center, Inc., 745 Main Street, East Hartford, CT 06108; tel. 860/289–2791; FAX. 860/289–7713; Karen Chadderton, Administrator

Rose Haven, Ltd., 33 North Street, P.O. Box 157, Litchfield, CT 06759; tel. 860/567–9475; FAX. 860/567–8132; Elsie Kenney

Saint Mary Home, Inc., 2021 Albany Ave., W. Hartford, CT 03416; tel. 860/236–1924; Maureen Kolaczenko

Saint Regis Health Center, Inc., 1354 Chapel Street, New Haven, CT 06511; tel. 203/867–8300; FAX. 203/867–8370; Sister Anne Virginia

Salmon Brook Nursing and Rehabilitation Center, 72 Salmon Brook Drive, Glastonbury, CT 06033; tel. 203/633–5244; FAX. 203/657–2360; Michael Strauss

Seabury Retirement Community, 200 Seabury Drive, Bloomfield, CT 06002; tel. 860/286–0243; John S. Mobley

Shady Knoll Health Center, Inc., 41 Skokorat Street, Seymour, CT 06483; tel. 203/881–2555; FAX. 203/881–0853; Robert Fritz, Administrator

Sharon Health Care Center, 27 Hospital Hill Road, P.O. Box 1268, Sharon, CT 06069; tel. 203/364–1002; FAX. 203/364–0237; Sally Erdman, Administrator

Sheriden Woods Health Care Center, 321 Stonecrest Drive, Bristol, CT 06010–5300; tel. 203/583–1827; FAX. 203/589–1976; Dorothy Rossetti

Skyview Nursing and Rehabilitation Center, 35 Marc Drive, Wallingford, CT 06492; tel. 203/265–0981; FAX. 203/284–1759; Robert Guastella, Executive Director

Southington Care Center, 45 Meriden Avenue, Southington, CT 06489; tel. 203/621–9559; FAX. 203/628–9366; Patricia Walden, Executive Director

Southport Manor Convalescent Center, Inc., 930 Mill Hill Terrace, Southport, CT 06490; tel. 203/259–7894; FAX. 203/254–3720; Albert A. Garofalo, Administrator

St. Joseph Living Center, Inc., 14 Club Road, Windham, CT 06280; tel. 860/456–1107; FAX. 860/450–7114; Patricia Hamill, Nursing Home Administrator

St. Joseph's Manor, 6448 Main Street, Trumball, CT 04533; tel. 203/268–6204; Michelle Anne Reho

Sterling Manor, Inc., 870 Burnside Avenue, East Hartford, CT 06108; tel. 203/289–9571; FAX. 203/289–8348; Thomas Blonski, Administrator

Subacute Center of Bristol, 23 Fair Street, Forestville, CT 06010; tel. 860/589–2923; FAX. 860/589–3148; Linda Bradigo, Administrator

Sylvan Manor Healthcare Center, 1037 Sylvan Avenue, Bridgeport, CT 06606; tel. 203/372–3508; Kenneth S. Kopchik

Talmadge Park Health Care, 38 Talmadge Avenue, East Haven, CT 06512; tel. 203/469–2316; FAX. 203/467–5582; Donald Franco

The Center for Optimum Care of Danielson, 111 Westcott Road, Danielson, CT 06239; tel. 203/774–9540; FAX. 203/774–9703; Judy Ann Johnson, Executive Director

The Center for Optimum Care–New Haven, 915 Ella T. Grasso Blvd., New Haven, CT 06519; tel. 203/865–5155; Denis Twig

The Center for Optimum Care–Sound View, One Care Lane, West Haven, CT 06516; tel. 203/934–7955; FAX. 203/934–1038; Jonathan Sherwin

The Center for Optimum Care–Waterford, 171 Rope Ferry Road, Waterford, CT 06385; tel. 860/443–8357; FAX. 860/447–8351; Peter Madden

The Curtis Home, 380 Crown Street, Meriden, CT 06450; tel. 203/237–4338; Steven M. Jackson

The Elim Park Baptist Home, Inc., 140 Cook Hill Road, Cheshire, CT 06410; tel. 203/272–3547; FAX. 203/250–6282; David MacNeill, President

The Glendale Center, 4 Hazel Ave., Naugatuck, CT 06770; tel. 203/723–1456; Patricia S. Worhunsky–Hamm

The Kent Specialty Care Center, 46 Maple Street, P.O. Box 340, Kent, CT 06757; tel. 860/927-5368; FAX. 860/927-1594; Judy Begley

The Madison House, 34 Wildwood Avenue, Madison, CT 06443; tel. 203/245-8008; FAX. 203/245-2107; Kathleen Dess

The Reservoir, One Emily Way, West Hartford, CT 06107; tel. 203/521-7022; FAX. 203/521-7023; Harold Moffie

The Suffield House, One Canal Road, Suffield, CT 06078; tel. 860/668-6111; FAX. 860/668-0061; Harold Moffie

The William and Sally Tandet Center for Continuing Care, 146 West Broad Street, Stamford, CT 06902; tel. 203/964-8500; FAX. 203/356-9925; Daniel Katz

Valerie Manor, Inc., 1360 Torringford Street, Route 183, Torrington, CT 06790; tel. 203/489-1008; FAX. 203/496-9252; Ann Wallace, Administrator

Vernon Manor Health Care Center, 180 Regan Road, Vernon, CT 06066-2818; tel. 860/871-0385; FAX. 860/871-9098; Kate Shepard, Administrator

Village Manor Health Care, 16 Windsor Ave., Plainfield, CT 06374; tel. 860/564-4081; Stanley Rodowicz, Jr.

Wadsworth Glen Health Care and Rehabilitation Center, 30 Boston Road, Middletown, CT 06457; tel. 860/346-9299; FAX. 860/343-5030; Elaine Madden, Administrator

Walnut Hill Convalescent Home, 55 Grand Street, New Britain, CT 06052; tel. 860/223-3617; Donald J. Griggs

Waterbury Extended Care Facility, 35 Bunker Hill Road, Watertown, CT 06795; tel. 203/274-5428; FAX. 203/945-3736; Timothy L. Curran, Jr.

Watrous Nursing Center, Nine Neck Road, Madison, CT 06443; tel. 203/245-9483; FAX. 203/245-4668; John Sweeney, Administrator

Waveny Care Center, Three Farm Road, New Canaan, CT 06840; tel. 203/966-8725; FAX. 203/966-1641; Jeremy Vickers, Executive Director

Westfield Care and Rehabilitation Center, 65 Westfield Road, Meriden, CT 06450; tel. 203/238-1291; FAX. 203/238-7763; Jane DeVries

Westview Nursing Care and Rehabilitation Center, Inc., 150 Ware Road, P.O. Box 428, Dayville, CT 06241; tel. 860/774-8574; FAX. 860/779-5425; Eileen Panteleakos, Chief Executive Officer, Administrator

Wintonbury Healthcare Center, 140 Park Avenue, Bloomfield, CT 06002; tel. 860/243-9591; FAX. 860/286-0161; William E. Stafford

Wolcott Hall Nursing Center, 215 Forest Street, Torrington, CT 06790; tel. 860/482-8554; Judy Begley

Wolcott View Manor, Inc., 50 Beach Road, P.O. Box 6192, Wolcott, CT 06716; tel. 203/879-8066; FAX. 203/879-8072; Dennis Cleary, RN, Administrator

Woodlake at Tolland, 26 Shenipsit Lake Road, Tolland, CT 06084; tel. 203/872-2999; FAX. 203/872-1848; Martha Dale

DELAWARE

Arbors at New Castle Subacute and Rehabilitation, 32 Buena Vista Drive, New Castle, DE 19720; tel. 614/791-2920; Robert Reed

Franciscan Care Center at Brackenville, 100 St. Claire Drive, Hockessin, DE 19707; tel. 302/234-5420; Ruth G. Murphy

ManorCare Health Services–Wilmington, 5651 Limestone Road, Wilmington, DE 19808; tel. 302/239-8583; FAX. 302/239-4523; John Fredericks

Methodist Country House, 4830 Kennett Pike, Wilmington, DE 19807; tel. 302/654-5101; FAX. 302/426-8108; William H. James, Jr., Executive Director

Silver Lake Center – Genesis Health Care Network, 1080 Silver Lake Blvd., Dover, DE 19904; tel. 302/734-5990; Vickie Cox

DISTRICT OF COLUMBIA

Benjamin King Health Center, U.S. Soldiers' and Airmen's Home, 3700 North Capitol Street, N.W., Washington, DC 10319; tel. 202/722-3324; FAX. 202/722-3570; Paul D. Gleason, M.D., Associate Director, Health Care Services

Center for Aging Health Care Institute, 1380 Southern Avenue, S.E., Washington, DC 20032; tel. 202/279-5880; FAX. 202/574-0192; Vanessa Mattox, Administrator

FLORIDA

Arbor at Jacksonville, 4101 Southpoint Drive East, Jacksonville, FL 32216; tel. 813/555-5555; Terry Carpenter

Arbors at Bayonet Point/Hudson, 8132 Hudson Avenue, Hudson, FL 34667; tel. 813/863-3100; FAX. 813/862-0941; Stephen Jones, Administrator

Arbors at Brandon, 701 Victoria Street, Brandon, FL 33510; tel. 813/681-4220; FAX. 813/791-2930; Terry L. Hilker, Executive Director

Arbors at Lakeland, 2020 West Lake Parker Drive, Lakeland, FL 33805; tel. 941/682-7580; FAX. 941/683-9564; Kathryn Smith, NHA

Arbors at Melbourne, 3033 Serno Blvd., Melbourne, FL 32934; tel. 813/555-5555; Greg Roberts

Arbors at Orange Park Nursing and Rehabilitation Center, 1215 Kingsley Avenue, Orange Park, FL 32073; tel. 904/269-8922; FAX. 904/264-2253; Terry Carpenter, Executive Director

Arbors at Orlando Subacute and Rehabilitation Center, 1099 West Town Parkway, Altamonte Springs, FL 32714; tel. 407/865-8000; FAX. 407/865-7288; Mr. Pier Borra

Arbors at Safety Harbor, 1410 4th Street North, Safety Harbor, FL 34695; tel. 813/555-5555; Stefanie Englebrecht

Arbors at St. Petersburg, 9393 Park Blvd., Seminole, FL 34642; tel. 813/555-5555; Gail Ward

Arbors at Tallahassee Subacute and Rehabilitation Center, 1650 Phillips Road, Tallahassee, FL 32308; tel. 904/942-9868; FAX. 904/942-1074; Joseph M. Jicha, Administrator

Arbors at Tampa, 2811 Campus Hill Dr., Tampa, FL 33612; tel. 813/555-5555, ext. 5; Rich Kase

Atlantis Center, 6026 Old Congress Road, Lantana, FL 33462; tel. 407/774-8700; FAX. 407/641-9711; Lawrence Militello

Bay Pointe Nursing Pavilion, 4201 31st Street South, St. Petersburg, FL 33712; tel. 813/867-1104; David Boyer

BayShore Convalescent Center, 16650 West Dixie Highway, North Miami Beach, FL 33160; tel. 305/945-7447; Terry Delia

Beverly Health and Rehabilitation Center, 600 Business Parkway, Royal Palm Beach, FL 33411; tel. 407/798-3700; FAX. 407/795-3583; Lisa Ryman-Porelli

Beverly Manor of Margate, 5951 Colonial Drive, Margate, FL 33063; tel. 954/979-6401; Jean Kuhlman

Boca Raton Rehabilitation Center, 755 Meadows Road, Boca Raton, FL 33486; tel. 561/391-5200; FAX. 561/391-5487; W. Bruce Lunsford

Bowman's Health Care Center, 350 South Ridgewood Avenue, Ormond Beach, FL 32174; tel. 904/677-4545; FAX. 904/677-3445; Merle Zinck, Administrator

Brandywyne Health Care Center, 1801 North Lake Mariam Drive, Winter Haven, FL 33884; tel. 813/293-1989; FAX. 813/299-6427; Kathryn Smith

Cedar Hills Nursing Center, 2061 Hyde Park Road, Jacksonville, FL 32210; tel. 904/786-7331; Billy F. Miles

Colonial Care Center, 6300 46th Avenue North, St. Petersbury, FL 33709; tel. 813/544-1444; James Mason

Coquina Center, 170 North Center Street, Ormond Beach, FL 32174; tel. 904/672-7113; Pat Freeman

Cross Creek Health Care Center, 10040 Hillview Road, Pensacola, FL 32514; tel. 904/474-0570; Debra Lawrence

Darcy Hall of Life Care, 2170 Palm Beach Lakes Blvd., West Palm Beach, FL 33409; tel. 407/683-3333; Eugenia C. DePonte

Deltona Healthcare Rehabilitation Center, 1851 Elkcam Blvd., Deltona, FL 32725; tel. 904/789-3769; Renee Rizzuti

Desoto Manor Nursing Home, 1002 North Brevard Ave., Arcadia, FL 33821; tel. 941/494-5766; Dennis Ramsey

Drew Village Rehabilitation and Nursing Center, 401 Fairwood Ave., Clearwater, FL 34619; tel. 813/797-6313; Michael Panarese

Fairway Oaks, 13806 North 46th Street, Tampa, FL 33613; tel. 813/977-4514; Jim Fielding

First Coast Health and Rehab Center, 7723 Jasper Ave., Jacksonville, FL 32211; tel. 904/725-8044; Guy Smith

Golfcrest Nursing Home, 600 North 17th Avenue, Hollywood, FL 33020; tel. 305/927-2531; FAX. 305/927-0425; Janet L. Horton

Golfview Nursing Home, 3636 10th Avenue, N., Saint Petersburg, FL 33713; tel. 813/323-3611; FAX. 813/327-5802; Linda Howard, NHA

Good Samaritan Nursing Home, 3127 57th Avenue, N., Saint Petersburg, FL 33714; tel. 813/527-2171; FAX. 813/522-8929; Lorraine Sedlock

Greenbriar Rehabilitation and Nursing Center, 210 21st Avenue West, Bradenton, FL 34205; tel. 941/747-3786; Gerald P. Dahill

Greenbrook Nursing and Rehab Center, 1000 24th Street North, St. Petersburg, FL 33713; tel. 813/323-4711; Sandra Ryczek

Greynolds Park Manor Rehabilitation Center, 17400 West Dixie Highway, North Miami Beach, FL 33160; tel. 305/944-2361; FAX. 305/949-9464; Martin E. Casper, Executive Director

Hallandale Rehabilitation Center, 2400 E. Hallandale Beach Blvd., Hallandale, FL 33009; tel. 954/457-9717; George I. Pollack

Harborside Healthcare – Clearwater, 1980 Sunset Point Road, Clearwater, FL 34625; tel. 813/443-1588; Robert C. Lauer, Sr.

Harborside Healthcare – Gulf Coast, 4927 Voorhees Road, New Port Richey, FL 34653; tel. 813/848-3578; Marie Panapolis

Harborside Healthcare – Naples, 2900 12th Street North, Naples, FL 34103; tel. 941/261-2554; Pam Cox

Harborside Healthcare – Ocala, 1501 Southeast 24th Road, Ocala, FL 34471; tel. 352/629-8900; Steve Watson

Harborside Healthcare Tampa Bay Rehabilitation and Nursing Center, 3865 Tampa Road, Oldsmar, FL 34677; tel. 813/855-4661; FAX. 813/854-2129; Michele Forney

Harborside Healthcare–Palm Harbor, 2600 Highlands Boulevard, N., Palm Harbor, FL 34684; tel. 813/785-5671; FAX. 813/787-5486; Sharon Harris, Administrator

Harborside Healthcare–Sarasota, 4602 Northgate Court, Sarasota, FL 34234; tel. 813/355-2913; FAX. 813/355-4259; Stephen Buillard

Hardee Manor Care Center, 401 Orange Place, Wauchula, FL 33873; tel. 813/773-3231; FAX. 813/773-0959; Mary Love, Administrator

HealthPark Care Center, 16131 Rose Rush Court, Fort Meyers, FL 33908; tel. 813/433-4647; FAX. 813/432-3456; Spring Rosen

Heartland Health Care Center – Fort Myers, 1600 Matthew Drive, Fort Myers, FL 33907; tel. 941/275-6067; Nancy Zant

Heartland Health Care Center – Kendall, 9400 Southwest 137th Avenue, Kendall, FL 33186; tel. 305/385-8290; Mavis Matthews

Heartland Health Care Center Miami Lakes, 5725 Northwest 186th Street, Hialeah, FL 33015; tel. 305/625-9857; FAX. 305/621-3682; Reid Aaron, FACHE, Administrator

Heartland Health Care Center–Jacksonville, 8495 Normandy Boulevard, Jacksonville, FL 32221; tel. 904/783-3749; FAX. 904/693-9137; Ron Ferro

Heartland Health Care Center–Sunrise, 9711 West Oakland Park Boulevard, Sunrise, FL 33351; tel. 305/572-4000; FAX. 305/749-4927; Joylin Nation

Heartland Health Care and Rehabilitaiton Center, 5401 Sawyer Road, Sarasota, FL 34233; tel. 941/925-3427; FAX. 941/925-8469; Teresa Martin

Heartland Health Care and Rehabilitation Center, 7225 Boca Del Mar Drive, Boca Raton, FL 33433-5517; tel. 407/362-9644; FAX. 407/362-9641; Jerry Labouene, Chief Executive Officer

Heartland Healthcare Center – Boynton Beach, 3600 Old Boynton Road, Boynton Beach, FL 33436; tel. 561/736-9992; Jeff Yankow

Heartland Healthcare Center – Prosperity Oaks, 11375 Prosperity Farms Road, Palm Beach Garden, FL 33410; tel. 407/626-9702; Sally Gates

Heartland Healthcare Convalescent Center, 3600 Boynton Road, Boynton Beach, FL 33436; tel. 561/736-9992; FAX. 561/369-0019; Jeff Yankow

Heartland Healthcare of Lauderhill, 2599 Northwest 55th Ave., Lauderhill, FL 33313; tel. 305/485-8873; David Chamberlain

Heartland of Tamarac, 5901 Northwest 79th Avenue, Tamarac, FL 33321; tel. 954/722-7001; FAX. 954/720-5419; John Wall

Heartland of Zephyrhills, 38220 Henry Drive, Zephyrhills, FL 33540; tel. 813/788-7114; FAX. 813/788-0758; Dixie Goodell

Heritage Health Care Center, 1815 Ginger Drive, Tallahassee, FL 32308; tel. 904/877–2177; Chuck Cascio

Heritage Park Specialty Care Center, 37135 Coleman Ave., Dade City, FL 33525; tel. 352/567–8615; Carrie M. Lund

Highlands Lake Center, 4240 Lakeland Highlands Road, Lakeland, FL 33813; tel. 941/646–8699; Tom Glass

Horizon Specialty and Rehab Center, 221 Park Place Blvd., Kissimmee, FL 34741; tel. 407/935–0200; Jennifer Searl

IHS at Avenel, 7751 West Broward Boulevard, Plantation, FL 33324; tel. 954/473–8040; FAX. 954/473–0897; William D. Savett

IHS at Central Park Village, 9309 South Orange Blossom Trail, Orlando, FL 32837; tel. 407/859–7990; FAX. 407/850–2470; Suyrea Reynolds

IHS at Green Briar (Integrated Health Services), 9820 North Kendall Drive, Miami, FL 33176; tel. 305/271–6311; FAX. 305/274–5880; Diane King, Administrator

IHS of Bradenton, 2302 59th Street, W., Bradenton, FL 34209; tel. 941/792–8480; FAX. 941/794–8905; Nina Willingham, NHA

IHS of Florida at Sarasota Pavilion, 2600 Courtland Street, Sarasota, FL 34237; tel. 941/365–2926; FAX. 941/951–2015; Gary Duncanson, Administrator

IHS of Orange Park, 2029 Professional Center Drive, Orange Park, FL 32073; tel. 904/272–6194; Christopher Warrick

IHS of Port Charlotte, 4033 Beaver Lane, Port Charlotte, FL 33952; tel. 941/625–3200; FAX. 941/624–2358; Gerry Radford

IHS of Venice North, 437 South Nokomis Avenue, Venice, FL 34285; tel. 941/488–9696; FAX. 941/484–1321; Louis Maltaghati, Administrator

Indian River Center – Genesis ElderCare, 7201 Greenboro Drive, West Melbourne, FL 32904; tel. 407/727–0990; Kathryn Kondolf–Harmer

Integrated Health Services, 702 South Kings Avenue, Brandon, FL 33511; tel. 813/651–1818; FAX. 813/654–4252; Jack Lehman

Integrated Health Services at Fort Pierce, 703 South 29th Street, Fort Pierce, FL 31248; tel. 407/466–3322; FAX. 407/466–8057; Susan Hess

Integrated Health Services at Gainesville, 4000 Southwest 20th Avenue, Gainesville, FL 32607; tel. 904/377–1981; FAX. 904/377–7340; Terrye Dubberly

Integrated Health Services of Central Florida at Orlando, 1900 Mercy Drive, Orlando, FL 32808; tel. 407/299–5404; FAX. 407/299–3735; Susan Daube

Integrated Health Services of Florida at Clearwater, 2055 Palmetto Street, Clearwater, FL 34625; tel. 813/461–6613; FAX. 813/422–2839; Ann Dougherty

Integrated Health Services of Florida at Jacksonville, 1650 Fouraker Road, Jacksonville, FL 32221; tel. 904/786–8668; FAX. 904/695–0166; James Lundy

Integrated Health Services of Florida at Lake Worth, 1201 12th Avenue, S., Lake Worth, FL 33460; tel. 407/586–7404; FAX. 407/582–2887; Adela Baldo

Integrated Health Services of Florida at West Palm Beach, 2939 South Haverhill Road, West Palm Beach, FL 33415; tel. 561/641–3130; FAX. 561/641–3167; Veronica Schoessler

Integrated Health Services of Fort Myers, 13755 Gold Club Parkway, Fort Myers, FL 33919; tel. 941/482–2848; K. C. Cross

Integrated Health Services of Lakeland at Oakbridge, 3110 Oakbridge Boulevard, E., Lakeland, FL 33803; tel. 941/648–4800; FAX. 941/646–9224; Janice P. Heidel, RN, NHA

Integrated Health Services of Palm Bay, 1515 Port Malabar Boulevard, Palm Bay, FL 32905; tel. 407/723–1235; FAX. 407/724–4292; Gregory Roberts, Administrator

Integrated Health Services of Pinellas Park, 8710 49th Street, N., Pinellas Park, FL 34666; tel. 813/546–4661; FAX. 813/545–8783; Kathleen Wesolowski, NHA

Integrated Health Services of Sarasota at Beneva, 741 South Beneva Road, Sarasota, FL 34232; tel. 941/957–0310; Claire Fellema

Integrated Health Services of Sebring, 3011 Kenilworth Boulevard, Sebring, FL 33870; tel. 941/382–2153; FAX. 941/382–2039; Todd Werthman

Integrated Health Services of St. Petersburg, 811 Jackson Street, St. Petersburg, FL 33705; tel. 813/896–3651; FAX. 813/821–2453; Todd Werthman

Integrated Health Services of Tarpon Springs, 900 Beckett Way, Tarpon Springs, FL 34689; tel. 813/934–0876; FAX. 813/942–6790; Paul Vitale

Integrated Health Services of Vero Beach, 3663 15th Avenue, Vero Beach, FL 32960; tel. 561/567–2552; FAX. 561/567–8929; Ronnie Schuessler, Administrator

Integrated Health Services of Winter Park, 2970 Scarlet Road, Winter Park, FL 32792; tel. 407/671–8030; FAX. 407/671–3746; Todd Werthman, Administrator

Integrated Health Services, Inc., 919 Old Winter Haven Road, Auburndale, FL 33823; tel. 941/967–4125; FAX. 941/551–9407; Nancy Thompson

Jackson Memorial Hospital, 1611 Northwest 12th Avenue, Miami, FL 33136; tel. 305/585–6142; Ira Clark

Laurels Nursing & Rehab Center, 550 9th Avenue South, St. Petersburg, FL 33701; tel. 813/898–4105; Laurel J. Chadwick

Leesburg Nursing Center, 715 East Dixie Avenue, Leesburg, FL 34748; tel. 352/728–3020; FAX. 352/728–6071; Robert E. Green, Administrator

Manor Care Health Services, 870 Patricia Avenue, Dunedin, FL 34968; tel. 813/734–8861; FAX. 813/733–5924; LaRelle A. Szumski

Manor Care Health Services Nursing and Rehabilitation Center, 6931 West Sunrise Boulevard, Plantation, FL 33313; tel. 305/583–6200; FAX. 305/583–6007; Michael Armstrong

Manor Care Nursing Center, 3001 South Congress Avenue, Boynton Beach, FL 33426; tel. 407/737–5600; FAX. 407/731–3049; Alicia Erb

ManorCare Health Services, MedBridge Medical and Physical Rehabilitation, 3030 West Bearss Avenue, Tampa, FL 33618; tel. 813/968–8777; FAX. 813/961–5189; Donald Tomasso

ManorCare Health Services of Boca Raton, 375 Northwest 51st Street, Boca Raton, FL 33431; tel. 407/997–8111; FAX. 407/995–0109; Dieudegrace Achille

Mariner Health Care of Orange City, 2810 Enterprise Road, Debary, FL 32713; tel. 407/668–8818; FAX. 407/668–6510; Cathy Holland, NHA

Mariner Health of Atlantic Shores, 4251 Stack Blvd., Melbourne, FL 32901; tel. 407/953–2219; John Hoyt

Mariner Health of Belleair, 1150 Ponce de Leon Blvd., Clearwater, FL 34616; tel. 813/585–5491; Joseph R. Keenan

Mariner Health of Clearwater, 4470 East Bay Drive, Clearwater, FL 34624; tel. 813/530–7100; John Mangine

Mariner Health of Palm City, 2505 Southwest Martin Highway, Palm City, FL 34990; tel. 407/288–0060; FAX. 407/288–3218; Tim Kimes

Mariner Health of Palmetto, 926 Haben Blvd., Palmetto, FL 34221; tel. 941/722–0553; William Marshall

Mariner Health of Port Orange, 5600 Victoria Gardens Blvd., Port Orange, FL 32119; tel. 904/760–7773; Dennis O'Leary

Mariner Health of Port St. Lucie, 1800 Hilmore Drive, Port St. Lucie, FL 34952; tel. 407/337–3565; Richard Aldrich

Mariner Health of St. Augustine, 200 Mariner Health Way, St. Augustine, FL 32086; tel. 904/797–1800; Brian M. Ferguson

Mariner Health of Tuskawilla, 1024 Willa Springs Drive, Winter Springs, FL 32708; tel. 407/699–5506; Gary Beaulieu

Medicana Nursing Center, 1710 Lake Worth Road, Lake Worth, FL 33460; tel. 561/582–5331; Maraleita K. Jackson

Mediplex Rehabilitation–Bradenton, 5627 Ninth Street, E., Bradenton, FL 34203; tel. 914/753–8941; FAX. 914/753–7576; Allan D. Bergquist

Menorah Manor, 255 59th Street, N., Saint Petersburg, FL 33710; tel. 813/345–2775; Marshall Seiden, Chief Executive Officer

Miami Jewish Home & Hospital for the Aged, 5200 Northeast 2nd Avenue, Miami, FL 33137; tel. 305/751–8626; Seth Goldsmith

Moody Manor, Inc., 7150 Holatee Trail, Fort Lauderdale, FL 33330; tel. 305/434–2016; FAX. 305/434–0561; Patricia A. Moody, MSCC

Mount Sinai St. Francis Nursing and Rehabilitation Center, 201 Northeast 112th Street, Miami, FL 33161; tel. 305/899–4700; FAX. 305/899–4719; Morris Funk, Executive Director

NHC HealthCare – Hudson, 7210 Beacon Woods Drive, Hudson, FL 34667; tel. 813/863–1521; John A. Nosworthy

North Florida Rehabilitation and Specialty Care, 6700 Northwest 10th Place, Gainesville, FL 32605; tel. 352/331–3111; George Hamilton

Oak Manor Nursing Center, 3500 Oak Manor Lane, Largo, FL 33345; tel. 813/581–9427; Robert C. Murphy, Jr.

Oakwood Rehabilitation and Health Care Center, 301 South Bay Street, Eustis, FL 32726; tel. 904/357–8105; FAX. 904/589–1182; Susan Chancellor

Ormond in the Pines, 103 N. Clyde Morris Blvd., Ormond Beach, FL 32174; tel. 904/673–0450; Maggie Youssef

Palm Garden of Clearwater, 3480 McMullen Booth Road, Clearwater, FL 34621; tel. 813/786–6697; Roy Meredith

Palm Garden of Largo, 10500 Starkey Road, Largo, FL 34647; tel. 813/397–8166; FAX. 813/319–3704; Thomas J. Bell, MBA, NHA

Palm Garden of Ocala, 3400 Southwest 27th Avenue, Ocala, FL 34474; tel. 352/854–6262; John E. Warren

Palm Garden of Pinellas, 200 16th Avenue, S.E., Largo, FL 34641; tel. 813/585–9377; FAX. 813/588–9038; James O. McCarver

Palm Garden of West Palm Beach, 300 Executive Center Drive, West Palm Beach, FL 33401; tel. 561/471–5566; Peggy Booth

Palmetto Health Center, 6750 West 22nd Court, Hialeah, FL 33016–3918; tel. 305/823–3119; FAX. 305/825–8255; Rosemary Wedderspoon, RN, N

Pinebrook Place Healthcare Center, 1240 Pinebrook Road, Venice, FL 34292; tel. 813/488–6733; FAX. 813/484–7924; Connie Tolley, Administrator

Plantation Bay Rehabilitation Center, 401 Kissimmee Park Road, Saint Cloud, FL 34769; tel. 407/892–7344; FAX. 407/892–5244; Glenn Grissinger

Regents Park of Boca Raton, 6363 Verde Trail, Boca Raton, FL 33433; tel. 561/483–9282; Stanley H. Sternefeld, Jr.

Regents Park of Jacksonville, 7130 Southside Blvd., Jacksonville, FL 32256; tel. 904/642–7300; Patricia Hammond, MBA, NHA

Regents Park of Winter Park, 558 North Semoran Blvd., Winter Park, FL 32792; tel. 407/679–1515; Linda Karling

Rio Pinar, 7950 Lake Underhill Road, Orlando, FL 32822; tel. 407/658–2046; FAX. 407/249–2226; Lou Ann Mathews

River Garden Hebrew Home for the Aged, 11401 Old St. Augustine Road, Jacksonville, FL 32258; tel. 904/260–1818; FAX. 904/260–9733; Elliott Palevsky, MA

Riverwood Center, 2802 Parental Home Road, Jacksonville, FL 32216; tel. 904/721–0088; FAX. 904/774–1654; John Hymans

Sabal Palms Health Care Center, 499 Alternate Keene Road, Largo, FL 33771; tel. 813/586–4211; Chris Adams

Shore Acres Rehab and Nursing Center, 4500 Indianapolis Street NE, St. Petersburg, FL 33703; tel. 813/527–5801; Harold H. Kaufer, Jr.

Southern Pines Nursing Center, 6140 Congress Street, New Port Richey, FL 34653; tel. 813/842–8402; FAX. 813/846–9107; Rebecca Miller

St. Catherine Laboure' Manor, Inc., 1750 Stockton Street, Jacksonville, FL 32204; tel. 904/308–4700; FAX. 904/308–2987; Maureen Gartland, CNHA, Vice President, Administrator

Sun Health of the Palm Beaches, 6414 13th Road, S., West Palm Beach, FL 33415; tel. 407/478–9900; FAX. 407/478–5067; Michael Rose

Sunrise Health and Rehab Center, 4800 Nob Hill Road, Sunrise, FL 33351; tel. 954/748–3400; Cheryl Hanson

Surrey Place Center, 2170 West State Road, Suite 434, Longwood, FL 32779; tel. 407/774–8700; Larry Brincefield

Sutton Place Center, 4405 Lakewood Road, Lake Worth, FL 33461; tel. 561/969–1400; FAX. 561/969–0121; Garland Cline, Administrator

Swanholm Nursing and Rehab Center, 6200 Central Ave., St. Petersburg, FL 33707; tel. 813/347–5196; Paul F. Jeannotte, Jr.

Tierra Pines Center, 7380 Ulmerton Road, Largo, FL 33771; tel. 813/535-9833; FAX. 813/536-4525; Maureen Cunningham

TimberRidge Nursing and Rehab Center, 9848 Southwest 110th Street, Ocala, FL 34481; tel. 352/854-8200; Jennifer Seall

University Village Health Center, 12250 North 22nd St., Tampa, FL 33612; tel. 813/975-5001; Patrice E. Pelletier-Sanders

Washington Manor Nursing and Rehabilitation Center, 4200 Washington Street, Hollywood, FL 33021; tel. 954/981-6300; Terrence Hansen

Whitehall Boca Raton, 7300 Del Prado South, Boca Raton, FL 33433; tel. 561/392-3000; P. Steven Mulder

GEORGIA

American Transitional Care-Northside, 5470 Meridian Mark Road, Atlanta, GA 30342; tel. 404/256-5131; FAX. 404/257-1820; Donna Huffstutler

Beverly Health and Rehabilitation Center, 2650 Highway 138 SE, Jonesboro, GA 30236; tel. 770/473-4436; FAX. 770/473-4698; JoEllen Rogers

Brian Center Nursing Care - Austell, 2130 Anderson Mill Road, Austell, GA 30001; tel. 770/941-8813; Henry R. Roberts

Brian Center Nursing Center/Powder Springs, 3460 Powder Springs Road, Powder Springs, GA 30073; tel. 770/439-9199; Robert S. Kirk

Dublinair Health Care and Rehabilitation Center, 300 Industrial Boulevard, Dublin, GA 31021, P.O. Box 1243, Dublin, GA 31040; tel. 912/272-7437; FAX. 912/272-2427; Janice Wiley

Family Life Enrichment Centers, Inc., 3450 New High Shoals Road, P.O. Box 10, High Shoals, GA 30645; tel. 706/769-7738; FAX. 706/769-5944; Magda D. Bennett, Administrator

Georgia War Veterans Nursing Home, 1101 15th Street, Augusta, GA 30910; tel. 706/721-2531; FAX. 706/721-3892; Charles Esposito, Administrator

IHS of Atlanta at Shoreham, 811 Kennesaw Avenue, Marietta, GA 30060; tel. 770/422-2451; Charles Stills

Integrated Health Services at Briarcliff Haven, Inc., 1000 Briarcliff Road, N.E., Atlanta, GA 30306; tel. 404/875-6456; FAX. 404/874-4606; Richard Kennedy

Integrated Health Services of Atlanta at Buckhead, 54 Peachtree Park Drive NE, Atlanta, GA 30309; tel. 404/351-6041; Darlene M. Ruffin, PhD

Life Care Center of Gwinnett, 3850 Safehaven Drive, Lawrenceville, GA 30244; tel. 770/923-0005; Deloris Dubose

Manor Care Nursing and Rehabilitation Center, 2722 North Decatur Road, Decatur, GA 30033; tel. 404/296-5440; FAX. 404/294-0504; Will Blackwell, Administrator

Mariner Health of Northeast Atlanta, 1500 South Johnson Ferry Road, Atlanta, GA 30319; tel. 404/252-2002; FAX. 404/252-1246; Asya Kamal

Montezuma Health Care Center, 521 Sumter Street, P.O. Box 639, Montezuma, GA 31063; tel. 912/472-8168; FAX. 912/472-8168; Merle Baggett, Administrator

Oak Manor and Pine Manor Nursing Homes, Inc., 2010 Warm Springs Road, P.O. Box 8828, Columbus, GA 31908-8828; tel. 706/324-0387; FAX. 706/324-0927; James S. Wilson

Quinton Memorial Health Care Center, 1114 Burleyson Road, Dalton, GA 30720; tel. 706/226-4642; Scott Edens

Southland Nursing Home, Inc., P.O. Box 2747, Peachtree City, GA 30269; tel. 770/631-9000; Roxanne Millians

Specialty Care of Marietta, 26 Tower Road, Marietta, GA 30060-9109; tel. 770/422-8913; FAX. 770/425-2085; Betsy Hill

Starcrest of Lithonia, P.O. Box 855, Lithonia, GA 30058; tel. 770/482-2961; Howard Ellison, MD

Windernere, 3618 J Dewey Gray Circle, Augusta, GA 30909; tel. 706/860-7572; Tom Turner

Winthrop Manor Nursing Center, 12 Chateau Drive, Rome, GA 30161; tel. 706/235-1422; FAX. 706/236-9247; Bruce Behner

HAWAII

Life Care Center of Hilo, 944 West Kawailani Street, Hiloq, HI 96720; tel. 808/959-9151; Patricia Allard

IDAHO

Life Care Center of Boise, 808 North Curtis Road, Boise, ID 83706; tel. 208/376-5273; Ann Swenson

Rexburg Nursing Center, 660 South 200 West, Rexburg, ID 86440; tel. 208/356-0201; Robert V. Merwe

ILLINOIS

Advocate Transitional Care Center, 10124 South Kedzie Ave., Evergreen Park, IL 60642; tel. 630/636-9200; Bill McNiff

Alden Estates of Evanston, 2520 Gross Point Road, Evanston, IL 60201; tel. 847/328-6000; Floyd Schlossberg

Alden Poplar Creek – Rehab and Health Care, 1545 Barrington Road, Hoffman Estates, IL 60194; tel. 847/884-0011; Floyd Schlossberg

Alden Rehab and Health Care Center, 5831 North Northwest Highway, Chicago, IL 60631; tel. 773/775-8080; Floyd Schlossberg

Alden Rehab and Health Care Center-Valle, 275 Army Trail Road, Bloomindale, IL 60108; tel. 630/893-9616; Floyd A. Schlossberg

Alden Rehab and Health Care Center/Long Grove, Box 2308 RFD, Hickes Road, Long Grove, IL 60047; tel. 847/438-8275; Floyd Schlossberg

Alden Rehab and Health Care Center/Naperville, 1525 Oxford Lane, Naperville, IL 60565; tel. 630/983-0500; Floyd Schlossberg

Alma Nelson Manor, Inc., 550 South Mulford, Rockford, IL 61108; tel. 815/399-4914; FAX. 815/399-0054; Teresa Wester-Peters, Administrator

Anchorage of Beecher, 1201 Dixie Highway, Beecher, IL 60401; tel. 708/946-2600; J. Rex Pippin

Applewood Nursing and Rehab Center, 21020 Kostner Ave., Matteson, IL 60443; tel. 708/747-1300; Daniel Westlake

Barton W. Stone Christian Home, 873 Grove Street, Jacksonville, IL 62650; tel. 217/479-3400; FAX. 217/243-8553; Barbara L. Hannel

Bethany Terrace Nursing Centre, 8425 North Waukegan Road, Morton Grove, IL 60053; tel. 847/965-8100; FAX. 847/965-8104; Rev. Stephen Dahl

California Gardens Nursing and Rehab, 2829 S. California Blvd., Chicago, IL 60608; tel. 312/847-8061; Barry Carr

Care Centre of Wauconda, 176 Thomas Court, Wauconda, IL 60084; tel. 847/526-5551; Shael Bellows

Carlton at the Lake, Inc., 725 West Montrose Avenue, Chicago, IL 60613; tel. 773/929-1700; FAX. 773/929-3068; Rose Marie Betz, RN

Chateau Village Nursing and Rehabilitation Center, 7050 Madison Street, Willowbrook, IL 60521; tel. 708/323-6380; FAX. 708/323-6416; Moshael J. Strauss

Chevy Chase Nursing and Rehab Center, 3400 South Indiana Ave., Chicago, IL 60616; tel. 312/842-5000; Barry Carr

Clark Manor Convalescent Center, 7433 North Clark, Chicago, IL 60626; tel. 312/338-8778; Jack Schnell

Colonial Hall Nursing and Rehab Center, 515 South 6th Street, Princeton, IL 61356; tel. 815/875-3347; Robert D. Yearian

Community HealthCare Center, 1136 North Mill Street, Naperville, IL 60563; tel. 630/355-3300; FAX. 630/355-1417; Jill Meyer, Executive Director

Council for Jewish Elderly–Lieberman Geriatric Health Centre, 9700 Gross Point Road, Skokie, IL 60076; tel. 847/674-7210; FAX. 847/674-6366; Ronald Weismehl

Crestwood Care Center, 14255 South Cicero Ave., Crestwood, IL 60445; tel. 708/371-0400; Jeanette Fox

Douglas Healthcare Center, P.O. Box 121, Mattoon, IL 61938; tel. 217/234-6401; FAX. 217/258-3300; Teresa L. Dunsbergen

Elmhurst Extended Care Center, Inc., 200 East Lake St., Elmhurst, IL 60126; tel. 708/834-4337; John Massard

Flora HealthCare Center, 120 Frontage Road, Flora, IL 62839; tel. 618/662-8381; Jane Melton, ED

Forest Villa, Ltd., 6840 West Touhy, Niles, IL 60714; tel. 847/647-8994; Michael Kaplan

Galena Park Home, 5533 North Galena Road, Peoria Heights, IL 61614; tel. 309/682-5428; FAX. 309/682-8478; Peter J. Bolt III

Glen Elston Nursing and Rehab Center, 4340 North Keystone Ave., Chicago, IL 60641; tel. 773/545-8700; Steven Schayer

Glen Oaks Nursing and Rehab Center, 270 Skokie Blvd., Northbrook, IL 60062; tel. 847/498-9320; Simcha Dachs

GlenBridge Nursing and Rehab Center, 8333 West Golf Road, Niles, IL 60714; tel. 847/966-9190; Sidney Glenner

GlenShire Nursing and Rehab Center, 22660 South Cicero Ave., Richton Park, IL 60471; tel. 708/747-6120; Sherry L. Bengtson, RN

Glencrest Nursing and Rehab Centre, 2451 West Touhy Ave., Chicago, IL 60645; tel. 312/338-6800; Sidney Glenner

Glenview Terrace Nursing Center, 1511 Greenwood Road, Glenview, IL 60025; tel. 847/729-9090; FAX. 847/729-9135; Mark Hollander

Halsted Terrace Nursing Center, 10935 South Halsted, Chicago, IL 60628; tel. 312/928-2000; Elizabeth Johnson

Hampton Plaza Health Care Center, 9777 Greenwood, Niles, IL 60714; tel. 847/967-7000; Burton Behr

Harmony Nursing and Rehabilitation Center, 3919 West Foster Avenue, Chicago, IL 60625; tel. 312/588-9500; FAX. 312/588-9533; Mark Hollander

Heartland Health Care Center, 833 Sixteen Avenue, Moline, IL 61265; tel. 309/764-6744; FAX. 309/764-8176; Lynn Zuck, Administrator

Heartland Health Care Center, 280 East Losey Street, Galesburg, IL 61404; tel. 309/343-2166; Kathy Joseph

Heartland Health Care Center of Homewood, 940 Maple Avenue, Homewood, IL 60430; tel. 708/799-0244; FAX. 708/799-1500; Janice Podwika

Heartland Health Care Center-Henry, 1650 Indian T Road, P.O. Box 215, Henry, IL 61537; tel. 309/364-3905; FAX. 309/364-3119; Susan Legner

Heartland Health Care Center-Macomb, Eight Doctors Lane, Macomb, IL 61455; tel. 309/833-5555; FAX. 309/833-3749; Michael J. Kegley II

Heartland Heath Care Center of Canton, 2081 North Main Street, Canton, IL 61520; tel. 309/647-6135; Gail McGinnis

Heartland of Paxton, 1001 East Pells Street, Paxton, IL 60957; tel. 217/379-4361; FAX. 217/379-3325; Cindy Scharp, Administrator

Hillside Healthcare Center, 1308 Game Farm Road, Yorkville, IL 60560; tel. 708/553-5811; FAX. 708/553-2740; Nancy Tettemer, Administrator

Holy Family Health Center, 2380 East Dempster St., Des Plaines, IL 60016; tel. 847/296-3335; Mary Elizabeth

IHS Chicago at Governors Park, 1420 South Barrington Road, Barrington, IL 60010; tel. 847/382-6664; Kam McGavock

Integrated Health Services at Brentwood, 5400 West 87th Street, Burbank, IL 60459; tel. 708/423-1200; FAX. 708/423-8405; John Walton

Jackson Square Nursing and Rehab Center, 5130 West Jackson Blvd., Chicago, IL 60644; tel. 312/921-8000; Barry Carr

Lake Shore HealthCare and Rehab Centre, 7200 North Sheridan Road, Chicago, IL 60626; tel. 312/973-7200; Jim Farlee

Lakewood Nursing and Rehab Center, 1112 North Eastern Ave., Plainfield, IL 60544; tel. 815/436-3400; Norm Gross

Manor Care Health Services, 6300 West 95th Street, Oak Lawn, IL 60453; tel. 708/599-8800; FAX. 708/599-8820; Brian Gross

Manor Care Health Services, 715 West Central Road, Arlington Heights, IL 60005; tel. 708/392-2020; FAX. 708/392-0174; Katherine Keane

Manor Care Health Services, 9401 South Kostner Avenue, Oak Lawn, IL 60453; tel. 708/423-7882; FAX. 708/423-7947; Susan Lucas

Manor Care Health Services, 2145 East 170th Street, South Holland, IL 60473; tel. 708/895-3255; FAX. 708/895-3315; Pattie A. Alterio

Manor Care Health Services, 600 North Coler, Urbana, IL 61801; tel. 217/367-1191; FAX. 217/367-1194; Deborah C. Pilarski

Manor Care Health Services, 600 West Ogden, Hinsdale, IL 60521; tel. 708/325-9630; FAX. 708/325-9648; Jeane Hansen

Manor Health Care Services, 512 East Ogden Avenue, Westmont, IL 60559; tel. 708/323-4400; FAX. 708/323-4583; Patricia Patrick

Manor HealthCare Corp., 200 West Martin Ave., Naperville, IL 60540; tel. 708/355-4111; John Vrba

ManorCare Health Services – Skokie, 4660 Old Orchard Road, Skokie, IL 60076; tel. 847/676-4800; Deborah Szalkiewicz

Monroe Pavilion Health and Treatment Center, 1400 West Monroe, Chicago, IL 60607; tel. 312/666-4090; Barry Carr

Morton Terrace, Ltd., 191 East Queenwood, Morton, IL 61550; tel. 309/266–5331; Pat Chism

Northwoods Care Centre, 2250 South Pearl Street, Belvidere, IL 61008; tel. 815/544–0358; Susan K. Mead

Oak Brook Healthcare Centre, 2013 Midwest Road, Oak Brook, IL 60521; tel. 630/495–0220; Christine Vause

Oakton Pavilion Healthcare Facility, Inc., 1660 Oakton Place, Des Plaines, IL 60018; tel. 847/299–5588; FAX. 847/298–6017; Jay Lewkowitz, ACSW, Administrator

Odd Fellow–Rebekah Home, 201 Lafayette Ave. East, Mattoon, IL 61938; tel. 217/235–5449; Lualyce C. Brown

P.A. Peterson Center for Health, 1311 Parkview Avenue, Rockford, IL 61107; tel. 815/399–8832; FAX. 815/399–8342; Stella L. Schroeder

Piatt County Nursing Home, 1111 North State Street, Monticello, IL 61856; tel. 217/762–7332; FAX. 217/762–9926; Marilyn E. Benedino, Administrator

Pine Acres Care Center, 1212 South Second Street, DeKalb, IL 60115; tel. 815/758–8151; FAX. 815/758–6832; J. Rex Pippin

Prairie Manor Health Care Center, 345 Dixie Highway, Chicago Heights, IL 60411; tel. 708/754–7601; Candace Zanon

Regency Nursing Centre, 6631 North Milwaukee Avenue, Niles, IL 60714; tel. 847/647–7444; FAX. 847/647–6403; Barbara A. Hecht, Administrator

Rest Haven Central Skilled Nursing Care Residence, 13259 South Central Avenue, Palos Heights, IL 60463; tel. 708/597–1000; FAX. 708/389–9990; Richard Schutt

Rest Haven South, 16300 Wausau Ave., South Holland, IL 60473; tel. 708/536–5500; Nancy Van Drunen

Rest Haven West Christian Nursing Home, 3450 Saratoga, Downers Grove, IL 60515; tel. 630/969–2900; FAX. 630/969–2148; Jacquelyn Terpstra, Administrator

Resurrection Nursing and Rehabilitation Center, 1001 North Greenwood Avenue, Park Ridge, IL 60068; tel. 847/692–5600; FAX. 847/692–2305; Patricia A. Tiernan

Ridgeland Nursing and Rehab Centre, 12550 South Ridgeland Ave., Palos Heights, IL 60463; tel. 708/597–9300; Diane L. Androvich

Rivershores Nursing and Rehab Center, 573 West Commercial Street, Marseilles, IL 61341; tel. 815/795–5121; John Koehler

Sherman West Court, 1950 Larkin Avenue, Elgin, IL 60123; tel. 847/742–7070; FAX. 847/742–7248; Anne Huang, Administrator

Skokie Meadows Nursing Center – No. 1, 9615 North Knox Street, Skokie, IL 60076; tel. 847/679–4161; Lucy C. Lariosa

Snow Valley Nursing and Rehab Center, 5000 Lincoln Ave., Lisle, IL 60532; tel. 630/852–5100; Sandra Larson

The Imperial Convalescent and Geriatric Center, 1366 West Fullerton Avenue, Chicago, IL 60614; tel. 312/248–9300; FAX. 312/935–0036; Margaret Carlson, Administrator

The Neighbors, Inc., 811 West Second St., Byron, IL 61010; tel. 815/234–2511; Grant Bullock

Villa Scalabrini, 480 North Wolf Road, Northlake, IL 60164; tel. 708/562–0040; Sally Myers

Wagner Health Center, 820 Foster Ave., Evanston, IL 60201; tel. 847/492–7700; Edward F. Otto

Whitehall North, 300 Waukegan Road, Deerfield, IL 60015; tel. 847/945–4600; Barbara Harris, RN

York Convalescent Center, Ltd., 127 West Diversey, Elmhurst, IL 60126; tel. 708/530–5225; Beth Gilbert

INDIANA

American Transitional Care–Brookview, 7145 East 21st Street, Indianapolis, IN 46219; tel. 317/356–0977; FAX. 317/356–2484; Todd Taylor

Arbors at Fort Wayne, 2827 Northgate Boulevard, Fort Wayne, IN 46835; tel. 219/485–9691; FAX. 219/486–5725; Carol Simmons, Administrator

Covington Manor Health Care Center, 1600 East Liberty Street, Covington, IN 47932; tel. 765/793–4818; FAX. 765/793–3748; Christopher D. Baldwin, Administrator

Harborside Healthcare – Decatur, 4851 Tincher Road, Indianapolis, IN 46221; tel. 317/856–4851; Mark Gavorski

Harborside Healthcare – New Haven, 1201 Daly Drive, New Haven, IN 46774; tel. 219/749–0413; Judy Privett

Harborside Healthcare of Terre Haute, 1001 East Springhill Drive, Terre Haute, IN 47802; tel. 812/238–2441; FAX. 812/299–4492; Karen Rumple

Heritage House of Connersville, 281 S. County Road, 200 East, Connersville, IN 47331; tel. 317/825–2148; Linda C. Lacey

Holiday Care Center, 1201 West Buena Vista Road, Evansville, IN 47710; tel. 812/429–0700; FAX. 812/429–1849; Don Hester, Administrator

Integrated Health Services of Indianapolis at Cambridge, 8530 Township Line Road, Indianapolis, IN 46260; tel. 317/876–9955; FAX. 317/876–6016; Sara L. Freeman, Executive Director

Ironwood Health and Rehab Center, 1950 Ridgeland Avenue, South Bend, IN 46614; tel. 219/291–6722; Glenn Wagner

Lifeline Children's Hospital, 1707 West 86th Street, P.O. Box 40407, Indianapolis, IN 46240–0407; tel. 317/872–0555; FAX. 317/471–0058; David Carter, Executive Director

Manor Care Health Services–Indianapolis South, 8549 South Madison Avenue, Indianapolis, IN 46227; tel. 317/881–9164; FAX. 317/887–4060; Clifford Craddock

ManorCare Health Services – Indianapolis, 8350 Naab Road, Indianapolis, IN 46260; tel. 317/872–4051; FAX. 317/879–2314; Stewart Banium

Miller's Merry Manor, 200 26th Street, P.O. Box 480, Logansport, IN 46947; tel. 219/722–4006; FAX. 219/753–8753; Gregory Fassett, Administrator

Northwest Manor Health Care Center, 6440 West 34th Street, Indianapolis, IN 46224; tel. 371/293–4930; Jennifer A. Knoll, Administrator

Rensselaer Care Center, 1309 East Grace Street, Rensselaer, IN 47978; tel. 219/866–4181; David Hajduch

Robin Run Village, 6370 Robin Run West Drive, Indianapolis, IN 46268; tel. 317/298–6255; Mike Spencer

The Altenheim Community, 3525 East Hanna Avenue, Indianapolis, IN 46237; tel. 317/788–4261; Brian Allen

Vermillion Convalescent and Rehabilitation Center, 1705 South Main Street, Clinton, IN 47842; tel. 317/832–3573; FAX. 317/832–3420; Melissa Diane Gum, Administrator

IOWA

Anamosa Care Center, 1209 East Third Street, P.O. Box 229, Anamosa, IA 52205; tel. 319/462–4356; FAX. 319/462–5038; Jeff Wollum, Administrator

Bettendorf Health Care Center, 2730 Crow Creek Road, Bettendorf, IA 52722; tel. 319/332–7463; FAX. 319/332–7464; Gail Troutwine

Cedar Falls Lutheran Home, 7511 University Ave., Cedar Falls, IA 50613; tel. 319/268–0401; Pat Welton

Danville Care Center, 401 South Birch, P.O. Box 248, Danville, IA 52623; tel. 319/392–4259; Gary Martin

Edgewood Convalescent Home, 513 Bell Street, P.O. Box 39, Edgewood, IA 52042; tel. 319/928–6461; FAX. 319/928–6462; Ruth M. Stephens

Elkader Care Center, 116 Reimer Street, P.O. Box 519, Elkader, IA 52043; tel. 319/245–1620; Kris Mitchell, Administrator

Great River Care Center, 1400 West Main, P.O. Box 370, McGregor, IA 52157; tel. 319/873–3527; FAX. 319/873–3723; Donna Kelly, RN

Iowa Veterans Home, 1301 Summit Street, Marshalltown, IA 50158–5485; tel. 515/752–1501; FAX. 515/753–4278; Jack J. Dack, Commandant

Living Center East, 1220 Fifth Avenue, S.E., Cedar Rapids, IA 52403; tel. 319/366–8701; Scott Marnin

Living Center West, 1050 Fourth Avenue, S.E., Cedar Rapids, IA 52403; tel. 319/366–8714; FAX. 319/366–8854; Marian Stevenson, NHA

Lone Tree Health Care Center, 501 East Pioneer Road, P.O. Box 590, Lone Tree, IA 52755; tel. 319/629–4255; FAX. 319/629–5300; Roberta Shirkey, Administrator

Manor Care Nursing and Rehab Center, 815 East Locust Street, Davenport, IA 52803; tel. 319/324–3276; Glen W. Roebuck

Mill Valley Care Center, 1201 Park Avenue, Bellevue, IA 52031–1911; tel. 319/872–5521; Lyman D. Bailey

Monticello Nursing and Rehabilitation Center, 500 Pinehaven Drive, Monticello, IA 52310; tel. 319/465–5415; FAX. 319/465–3205; Sister Donna Venteicher, Administrator

New Hampton Nursing and Rehab Center, 703 South Fourth Avenue, P.O. Box 428, New Hampton, IA 50659; tel. 515/394–4153; Raletta Thomas

Ramsey Home, 1611 27th Street, Des Moines, IA 50310; tel. 515/274–3612; FAX. 515/274–6541; Loretta Nelson

State Center Manor, 702 Third Street, N.W., State Center, IA 50247; tel. 515/483–2812; FAX. 515/483–2675; Lance Mehaffey, Administrator

Wheatland Manor, Inc., 515 East Lincolnway, P.O. Box 368, Wheatland, IA 52409; tel. 319/374–1295; FAX. 319/374–1107; Jack L. McIntosh, Administrator

KANSAS

ManorCare Health Services, 5211 West 103rd Street, Overland Park, KS 66207; tel. 913/383–2569; Ann Say

KENTUCKY

American Transitional Care–Hillcreek, 3116 Breckenridge Lane, Louisville, KY 40220; tel. 502/459–9120; FAX. 502/459–6150; Philip Bramer

Christopher East Health Care Center, 4200 Brown's Lane, Louisville, KY 40220; tel. 502/459–9900; FAX. 502/459–5026; Bill Johnson

Florence Park Care Center, 6975 Burlington Pike, Florence, KY 41042; tel. 606/525–0007; FAX. 606/282–4516; Patricia Feldman, Administrator

Highlands of Ft. Thomas Health Care Center and Rehab, 960 Highland Avenue, Fort Thomas, KY 41075; tel. 606/572–0660; Barry N. Bortz

Hurstbourne Care Center at Stony Brook, 2200 Stony Brook Drive, Louisville, KY 40220; tel. 502/425–3620; FAX. 502/425–3662; Robert Elliott

Rosewood Health Care Center, 550 High Street, Bowling Green, KY 42101; tel. 502/843–3296; Donald Poteet

Salyersville Health Care Center, P.O. Box 819, Salyersville, KY 41465; tel. 606/349–6181; Thomas E. Hummer

Winchester Centre for Health and Rehabilitation, 200 Glenway Road, Winchester, KY 40391; tel. 606/744–1800; FAX. 606/744–0285; Damie U. Castle, Executive Director

LOUISIANA

Gillis W. Long Hansen's Disease Center, 5445 Point Clair Road, Carville, LA 70721–9607; tel. 504/642–4739; FAX. 504/642–4728; Charles D. Stanley

Greenery Neurologic Rehabilitation Center at Slidell, 1400 Lindberg Drive, Slidell, LA 70458; tel. 504/641–4985, ext. 3003; FAX. 504/646–0728; James L. McEwen, Ph.D., Executive Director

Lafon Nursing Home of the Holy Family, 6900 Chef Menteur Highway, New Orleans, LA 70126; tel. 504/246–1100; FAX. 504/241–6672; Sister Ann Elise Sonnier, Chief Executive Officer

Martin de Porres Nursing Home, Inc., P.O. Box 1294, Lake Charles, LA 70602; tel. 318/439–5761; Lawrence D. Sullivan

MAINE

Brewer Rehab and Living Center, 74 Parkway, S., Brewer, ME 04412; tel. 207/989–7300; FAX. 207/989–4240; Carl F. Hausler, Administrator

Cedar Ridge Center for Health Care and Rehabilitation, Dr. Mann Road, Rural Route 1, Box 1283, Skowhegan, ME 04976; tel. 207/474–9686; FAX. 207/474–8626; Stephen A. Marsden, Administrator

Eastside Rehab and Living Center, 516 Mt. Hope Avenue, Bangor, ME 04401; tel. 207/947–6131; Michael Beal

Maplecrest Living Center, 174 Main Street, Madison, ME 04950; tel. 207/696–8225; Phillip D. Jean

Marshwood Center for Healthcare and Rehab, 33 Roger Street, Lewistown, ME 04240; tel. 207/784–0108; FAX. 207/784–0752; Douglas Gardner

Oak Grove Nursing Care Center, 27 Cool Street, Waterville, ME 04901; tel. 207/873–0721; FAX. 207/877–2287; Sara Sylvester

Pine Point Nursing Care Center, 67 Pine Point Road, Scarborough, ME 04074; tel. 207/883–2468; FAX. 207/883–3983; Barbara Rentz–Champagne

River Ridge, 33 Cat Mousam Road, Kennebunk, ME 04043; tel. 207/985–3030; FAX. 207/985–6428; Irving Faunce, Executive Director

Sandy River Center for Health Care and Rehabilitation, RFD 4, Box 5121, Farmington, ME 04938; tel. 207/778–6591; FAX. 207/778–4245; Anne Herrick

Section C

Seaside Nursing and Retirement Home, Inc., 850 Baxter Blvd., Portland, ME 04103; tel. 207/774–7878; Cynthia Farley

Springbrook Nursing Care Center, 300 Spring Street, Westbrook, ME 04092; tel. 207/856–1230; FAX. 207/856–1239; Pierre Morneault

Westgate Manor, 750 Union Street, Bangor, ME 04401; tel. 207/942–7336; T. Michael Skirven

Windward Gardens, 105 Mechanic Street, Camden, ME 04843; tel. 207/236–4197; FAX. 207/236–4453; David P. Sylvester

Woodford Park Center for Health Care and Rehabilitation, 68 Devonshire Street, Portland, ME 04103; tel. 207/772–2893; FAX. 207/772–3230; Brian J. Dion

MARYLAND

Canton Harbor Healthcare Center, Inc., 1300 South Ellwood Avenue, Baltimore, MD 21224; tel. 410/342–6644; FAX. 410/327–3949; William Meadows, MA

Fairland Adventist Nursing and Rehab Center, 2101 Fairland Road, Silver Springs, MD 20904; tel. 301/384–6161; Stephanie Rosner

Fox Chase Rehabilitation and Nursing Center, 2015 East West Highway, Silver Spring, MD 20910; tel. 301/587–2400; FAX. 301/587–2404; Mary Clinton, Administrator

Heartland Health Care Center – Adelphi, 1801 Metzerott Road, Adelphi, MD 20783; tel. 301/434–0500; David Parker

Keswick Multi–Care Center, 700 West 40th Street, Baltimore, MD 21211; tel. 410/662–4200; FAX. 410/235–7425; Andrea Braid, Executive Director, Chief Executive Officer

Larkin Chase Nursing and Restorative Center, 15005 Health Center Drive, Bowie, MD 20716; tel. 301/805–6070; FAX. 301/805–9779; Gary Waitt

Levindale Hebrew Geriatric Center and Hospital, 2434 West Belvedere Avenue, Baltimore, MD 21215; tel. 410/466–8700; Stanford Alliker, FACHE

Magnolia Center, 8200 Good Luck Road, Lanham, MD 20706; tel. 301/552–2000; Margaret A. O'Hara

Manor Care Health Services, 6600 Ridge Road, Baltimore, MD 21237; tel. 410/574–4950; FAX. 410/391–4386; Bob Harris

Manor Care Health Services, 11901 Georgia Avenue, Wheaton, MD 20902; tel. 301/942–2500; FAX. 301/949–1152; Barb Feege, NHA

Manor Care Towson Nursing and Rehabilitation Center, 509 East Joppa Road, Towson, MD 21285; tel. 410/828–9494; FAX. 410/828–9180; Patricia Akin

Manor Care–Largo, 600 Largo Road, Largo, MD 20772; tel. 301/350–5555; FAX. 301/350–2871; Evelyn J. Nelson

ManorCare Health Services, 7001 North Charles Street, Towson, MD 21204; tel. 410/821–9600; FAX. 410/337–8313; Robert F. Harris, Administrator

ManorCare Health Services of Potomac, 10714 Potomac Tennis Lane, Potomac, MD 20854; tel. 301/299–2273; Stewart Bainum, Jr.

Mariner Health at Circle Manor, 10231 Carroll Place, Kensington, MD 20895; tel. 301/949–0230; FAX. 301/949–8244; Melinda Hippchen, NHA

Mariner Health of Greater Laurel, 14200 Laurel Park Drive, Laurel, MD 20707; tel. 410/792–4717; Bill Meadows

Mariner Health of Kensington, 3000 McComas Avenue, Kensington, MD 20895; tel. 301/933–0060; Deborah Toth

Mariner Health of Silver Spring, 901 Arcola Avenue, Silver Spring, MD 20902; tel. 301/649–2400; FAX. 301/649–2081; Michelle F. Kraus

Meridian Healthcare and Sub–Acute Center – Franklin, 9200 Franklin Square Drive, Baltimore, MD 21237; tel. 410/391–2600; Ron Rothstein

Multi–Medical Center – Genesis ElderCare Network, 7700 York Road, Towson, MD 21204; tel. 410/821–5500; Irvin D. Winebrenner

North Charles Healthcare Center, 2700 North Charles Street, Baltimore, MD 21218; tel. 410/554–6300; Elissa Heck

Ravenwood Lutheran Village, 1183 Luther Drive, Hagerstown, MD 21740; tel. 301/790–1000; Dana Smiles

Salisbury Center: Genesis ElderCare Network, 200 Civic Avenue, Salisbury, MD 21804; tel. 410/749–1466; Anthony J. Grieco

Shady Grove Adventist Nursing and Rehab, 9701 Medical Center Drive, Rockville, MD 20850; tel. 301/424–6400; Barbara Harry

Spa Creek Center Genesis ElderCare, 35 Milkshake Lane, Annapolis, MD 21403; tel. 410/269–5100; Kelly Walton

Springbrook Adventist Nursing and Rehab, 12325 New Hampshire Avenue, Silver Spring, MD 20904; tel. 301/622–4600; Lori Lusby

Stella Maris, Inc., 2300 Dulaney Valley Road, Timonium, MD 21093; tel. 410/252–4500; Karen McNally, RSM

Washington Adventist Nursing and Rehab, 7525 Carroll Avenue, Takoma Park, MD 20912; tel. 301/270–4200; Howard Waltz, Jr.

Wilson Health Care Center – Asbury Methodist Village, 301 Russell Avenue, Gaithersburg, MD 20877; tel. 301/216–4220; Scott W. Richardson

MASSACHUSETTS

Abbott House, 28 Essex Street, Lynn, MA 01902; tel. 617/595–5500; Richard C. Bane

Aberjona Nursing Center, Inc., P.O. Box 490, Winchester, MA 01890; tel. 617/720–9370; Robert F. Salter

Ads Reservoir, Inc., 1841 Trapelo Road, Waltham, MA 02154; tel. 617/890–5000; FAX. 617/290–0535; Fran Herr

Alden Court Nursing Care and Rehabilitation Center, 389 Alden Road, Fairhaven, MA 02719; tel. 508/991–8600; David Manahan

Anchorage Nursing Home, 904 Mohawk Trail, Shelburne, MA 01370; tel. 413/625–2305; Susan M. Page

Apple Valley Nursing and Rehabilitation Center, 400 Groton Road, Ayer, MA 01432; tel. 508/772–1704; FAX. 508/772–1708; Michael Lehrman

Avery Manor, 100 West Street, Needham, MA 02194; tel. 617/433–0202; FAX. 617/433–2777; Miriam Parker, MD

Bay Path at Duxbury Nursing and Rehabilitation Center, 308 Kings Town Way, Duxbury, MA 02332; tel. 617/585–5561; FAX. 617/585–1481; Paul T. Casale

Baypointe Rehabilitation and Skilled Care Center, 50 Christy Place, Brockton, MA 02401; tel. 508/580–6800; FAX. 508/587–6633; Kimberly Tobin Sciacca, Administrator

Bear Hill Nursing Center, 11 North Street, Stoneham, MA 02180; tel. 617/438–8515; William E. Ring, Jr.

Beaumont Rehab and Skilled Nursing Center, P.O. Box 517, Northbridge, MA 01534; tel. 508/234–9771; Daniel Salmon, Jr.

Beaumont Rehabilitation and Skilled Nursing Center, One Lyman Street, Westborough, MA 01581; tel. 508/366–9933; FAX. 508/898–3931; Michael Murphy, Administrator

Berkshire Hills North Nursing Home, 170 Prospect Street, Lee, MA 01238; tel. 413/243–2010; John Lubowitz

Beverly Manor of Plymouth Nursing Home, 19 Obery Street, Plymouth, MA 02360; tel. 508/747–4790; David Banks

Birchwood Care Center, Outpatient Rehab Clinic, 1199 John Fitch Highway, Fitchburg, MA 01420; tel. 508/345–0146; FAX. 508/345–4053; Scott Dickinson

Blaire House of Tewksbury, 10 Erlin Terrace, Tewksbury, MA 01876; tel. 508/851–3121; FAX. 508/640–0981; Frank Romano

Blue Hills Alzheimer's Care Center, 1044 Park Street, Stoughton, MA 02072; tel. 617/344–7300; Amy J. Baxter

Blueberry Hill Healthcare, 75 Brimbal Avenue, Beverly, MA 01915; tel. 508/927–2020; FAX. 508/922–4643; Dan Micherone

Bolton Manor, 400 Bolton Street, Malborough, MA 01752; tel. 508/481–6123; Marc Neustadt

Boston Center for Rehabilitative and Subacute Care, 1245 Centre Street, Roslindale, MA 02131; tel. 617/325–5400; FAX. 617/325–3259; Alan D. Solomont

Bostonian Nursing Care and Rehabilitation Center, 337 Neponset Avenue, Dorchester, MA 02122; tel. 617/265–2350; FAX. 617/265–0577; Wayne Pultman

Braemoor Rehabilitation and Nursing Center, Inc., 34 North Pearl Street, Brockton, MA 02401; tel. 508/586–3696; FAX. 508/584–0470; Michael Roland

Braintree Manor Rehabilitation and Nursing Center, 1102 Washington Street, Braintree, MA 02184; tel. 617/848–3100; FAX. 617/356–7367; Elizabeth Flynn, Administrator

Brandon Woods of Dartmouth, 567 Dartmouth Street, South Dartmouth, MA 02748; tel. 508/997–7787; FAX. 508/997–5598; Frank Romano

Briarwood Continuing Care Retirement Community, 70 Briarwood Circle, Worcester, MA 01606; tel. 508/852–2670; Kenneth L. Hooge

Briarwood Healthcare Nursing Center, 150 Lincoln Street, Needham, MA 01292; tel. 617/449–4040; FAX. 617/449–4129; Patricia Giaquinto

Cape Cod Nursing and Rehab Center, 8 Lewis Point, Buzzards Bay, MA 02532; tel. 508/759–5752; David Banks

Cape Heritage Nursing and Rehab Center, 37 Route 6A, Sandwich, MA 02563; tel. 508/888–8222; Steven Garfinkle

Cape Regency Nursing and Rehabilitation Center, 120 South Main Street, Centerville, MA 02632; tel. 508/778–1835; FAX. 508/771–7411; Linda Notzon

CareMatrix of Dedham, 10 CareMatrix Drive, Dedham, MA 02026; tel. 781/461–9663; Gregory C. Karr

Carlyle Nursing Home, Inc., 342 Winter Street, P.O. Box 2495, Framingham, MA 01701; tel. 508/879–6100; FAX. 508/872–1253; Bruce Bedard

Catholic Memorial Home, 2446 Highland Avenue, Fall River, MA 02720; tel. 508/679–0011; FAX. 508/672–5858; Sister Nina Marie Amaral O. Carm., Administrator

Charlwell House, 305 Walpole Street, Norwood, MA 02062; tel. 617/762–7700; FAX. 617/255–0387; Stephen L. Esdale

Chestnut Hill Rehabilitation and Nursing Center, 32 Chestnut Street, East Longmeadow, MA 01028; tel. 413/525–1893; FAX. 413/525–8261; Bonnie J. Davis

Chetwynde Health and Rehabilitation Center, 1650 Washington Street, West Newton, MA 02165; tel. 617/244–5407; FAX. 617/244–9322; William Mathies

Christopher House of Worcester, Inc., 10 Mary Scano Drive, Worcester, MA 01605; tel. 508/754–3800; Arthur S. Tirella

Clark House Nursing Center at Fox Hill Village, 30 Longwood Drive, Westwood, MA 02090; tel. 617/326–5652; FAX. 617/326–4034; Karen Wilkinson, Administrator

Clifton Rehabilitative Nursing Center, 500 Wilbur Avenue, Somerset, MA 02725; tel. 508/675–7589; FAX. 508/672–7422; Clifton Greenwood

Cohasset Knoll Skilled Nursing and Rehabilitation Facility, One Chief Justice Cushing Highway, Cohasset, MA 02025; tel. 617/383–9060; FAX. 617/383–2327; David Banks

Colonial Nursing and Rehabilitation Center, 125 Broad Street, Weymouth, MA 02188; tel. 617/337–3121; FAX. 617/337–9831; F. Roy Fitzsimmons, Administrator

Colony House Nursing and Rehabilitation Center, 277 Washington Street, Abington, MA 02351; tel. 781/871–0200; FAX. 781/878–0661; Paul Corcoran, Administrator

Coolidge House Nursing Care Center, 30 Webster Street, Brookline, MA 02146; tel. 617/734–2300; FAX. 617/232–1131; Dolores Schermer

Copley at Stoughton Nursing Care Center, 380 Sumner Street, Stoughton, MA 02072; tel. 617/341–2300; Steven Burke

Country Estates Nursing and Rehabilitation Center, 1200 Suffield Street, Agawam, MA 01001; tel. 413/789–2200; FAX. 413/789–2269; M. William Sibley

Country Gardens Skilled Nursing and Rehabilitation Center, 2045 G.A.R. Highway, Swansea, MA 02777; tel. 508/379–9700; FAX. 508/379–0723; Scott Sanborn, Executive Director

Country Haven, Inc., 184 Mansfield Ave., Norton, MA 02766; tel. 508/285–7745; Jeffrey C. Harsfield

Country Manor Rehabilitation and Nursing Center, 180 Low Street, Newburyport, MA 01950; tel. 508/465–5361; FAX. 508/462–5607; Daniel Northrup, Administrator

Courtyard Nursing Care Center, 200 Governors Avenue, Medford, MA 02155; tel. 617/391–5400; Edward D. Hunt

Cranberry Pointe Rehabilitation and Skilled Care Center, 111 Headwaters Drive, Harwich, MA 02645–1726; tel. 508/430–1717; FAX. 508/432–1809; Patrick J. Sheehan, Administrator

Crestview Healthcare Facility, Inc., 88 Greenleaf Street, Quincy, MA 02169; tel. 617/479–2978; Joel K. Logan

D'Youville Manor, 981 Varnum Avenue, Lowell, MA 01854; tel. 508/454–5681; FAX. 508/453–3561; Steve Johnson, Chief Executive Officer

Den–Mar Rehab and Nursing Center, 44 South Street, Rockport, MA 01966; tel. 508/546–6311; Stanley T. Trocki, Jr.

Deutsches Altenheim, Inc., 2222 Centre Street, West Roxbury, MA 02132; tel. 617/325–1230; FAX. 617/323–7523; Bruce Glass

Devereux House Nursing Home, 39 Lafayette Street, Marblehead, MA 01945–1997; tel. 617/631–6120; FAX. 617/631–6122; Kenneth Bane

Dexter House, 120 Main Street, Malden, MA 02148; tel. 617/324–5600; William Mathies

Don Orione Nursing Home, 111 Orient Avenue, East Boston, MA 02128; tel. 617/569–2100; Lawrence Tosatto

Eagle Pond Rehabilitation and Living Center, One Love Lane, P.O. Box 208, South Dennis, MA 02660; tel. 508/385–6034; FAX. 508/385–7064; Scott E. Stone, Executive Director

East Village Nursing and Rehab Center, 840 Emerson Gardens Road, Lexington, MA 02173; tel. 617/861–8630; William Mathies

Easton Lincoln Rehab and Nursing Center, 184 Lincoln Street, North Easton, MA 02356; tel. 508/238–7053; Steven Garfinkle, MA

Eastpointe Rehabilitation and Skilled Care Center, 255 Central Avenue, Chelsea, MA 02150; tel. 617/884–5700; FAX. 617/884–7005; John E. Gerety, Jr.

Eastwood Care Center, 1007 East Street, Dedham, MA 02026; tel. 617/329–1520; David Butler

Elaine Health & Rehab Center, Box 720, Hadley, MA 01035; tel. 413/584–5057; Agnes S. Mauro, FACHE

Elihu White Nursing and Rehabilitation Center, 95 Commercial Street, Braintree, MA 02184; tel. 617/848–3678; FAX. 617/356–8559; Florence Logan, Administrator

Elizabeth Seton Residence Skilled Nursing and Rehabilitation, 125 Oakland Street, Wellesley Hills, MA 02181; tel. 617/237–2161; FAX. 617/431–2589, ext. 30; Sister Blanche LaRose, Administrator

Elmhurst Nursing Home, 743 Main Street, Melrose, MA 02176; tel. 617/662–7500; FAX. 617/665–2594; William Mathies

Emerald Court Health and Rehab Center, 460 Washington Street, Norwood, MA 02062; tel. 617/769–2200; Brendon Morrison

Fairhaven Nursing Home, Inc., 476 Varnum Ave., Lowell, MA 01854; tel. 508/458–3388; Lita I. Noel

Fairlawn Nursing Home, Inc., 370 West Street, Leominster, MA 01453; tel. 508/537–0771; FAX. 508/534–0824; Robert D. Theroux

Fall River Jewish Home, Inc., 538 Robeson Street, Fall River, MA 02720; tel. 508/679–6172; Christine M. Vitale

Forestview Nursing and Rehabilitation Center, 50 Indian Neck Road, Wareham, MA 02571; tel. 508/295–6264; FAX. 508/294–3484; Edward Turcotte–Shamski

Franklin House Healthcare, 130 Chestnut Street, Franklin, MA 02038; tel. 508/528–4600; FAX. 508/528–7976; James Meola

Franvale Nursing and Rehabilitation Center, 20 Pond Street, Braintree, MA 02184; tel. 617/848–1616; FAX. 617/848–8813; Bruce Shear

Geriatric Authority of Holyoke, 45 Lower Westfield Road, Holyoke, MA 01040; tel. 413/536–8110; FAX. 413/533–7999; Judith Egan

Glen Ridge Nursing Care Center, Hospital Road, Malden, MA 02148; tel. 617/391–0800; FAX. 617/391–9127; Robert Driscoll

Goddard House, 201 South Huntington Ave., Jamaica Plain, MA 02130; tel. 617/522–3080; Daniel G. Thurman

Great Barrington Rehab and Nursing Center, 148 Maple Avenue, Great Barrington, MA 01230; tel. 413/528–3320; Richard Pomerleau

Greenery Extended Care Center, 59 Acton Street, Worcester, MA 01604; tel. 508/791–3147; FAX. 508/753–6267; Jennifer Searl, Administrator

Greenery Extended Care Center at Beverly, 40 Heather Street, Beverly, MA 01915; tel. 508/927–6220; FAX. 508/927–1438; Eugene Belle, Administrator

Greenery Extended Care Center at Danvers, A Horizon Healthcare Facility, 56 Liberty Street, Danvers, MA 01923–1475; tel. 508/777–2700; FAX. 508/777–2372; Edward J. Stewart, Administrator

Greenery Extended Care Center at North Andover, 75 Park Street, North Andover, MA 01845; tel. 978/685–3372; FAX. 978/683–2030; James Christofori

Greenery Rehabilitation Center, 99 Chestnut Hill Avenue, Boston, MA 02135; tel. 617/787–3390; Walter Collins

Greenery Rehabilitation and Skilled Nursing Center at Hyannis, 89 Lewis Bay Road, Hyannis, MA 02601; tel. 508/775–7601; FAX. 508/790–4239; Walter Collins

Greenery Rehabilitation and Skilled Nursing Center at Middleboro, Isaac Street, P.O. Box 1330, Middleboro, MA 02346; tel. 508/947–9295; FAX. 508/947–7974; John H. Keeney, Administrator

Greycliff at Cape Ann, 272 Washington Street, Gloucester, MA 01930; tel. 508/281–0333; William Mathies

Grosvenor Park Nursing Center, Inc., 7 Loring Hills Avenue, Salem, MA 01970; tel. 508/741–5700; Philip S. Sher

Hammersmith House Nursing Center, 73 Chestnut Street, Sangus, MA 01906; tel. 617/233–8123; FAX. 617/231–2918; Richard Pomerleau

Hannah Duston Healthcare Center, 126 Monument Street, Haverhill, MA 01830; tel. 508/373–1747; FAX. 508/373–5277; Alfred Arcidi

Harbor House Rehab and Nursing Center, 11 Condito Road, Hingham, MA 02043; tel. 617/749–4774; Richard M. Welch

Harrington House Nursing and Rehabilitation Center, 160 Main Street, Walpole, MA 02081; tel. 508/660–3080; FAX. 508/660–1634; William J. McGinley, Administrator

Heathwood Nursing and Rehab Center, 188 Florence Street, Chestnut Hill, MA 02167; tel. 617/332–4730; David Banks

Henry C. Nevins Home, Inc., Ten Ingalls Court, Methuen, MA 01844; tel. 508/682–7611; Felix F. Albano, Jr.

Heritage Hall East Nursing and Rehab Center, 464 Main Street, Agawam, MA 01001; tel. 413/786–8000; Rosemary J. Case, RN, NHA

Heritage Nursing Care Center, 841 Merrimack Street, Lowell, MA 01854; tel. 508/459–0546; FAX. 508/970–0715; James Christofori

Hermitage Health and Rehabilitation Center, 383 Mill Street, Worcester, MA 01602; tel. 508/791–8131; FAX. 508/756–5524; Mary L. Davis, Executive Director

Hollingsworth House Nursing Facility, 1120 Washington Street, Braintree, MA 02184; tel. 617/848–4710; FAX. 617/849–6487; Vincent Pattavina

Hollywell, a Flatley Rehabilitation and Nursing Center, 975 North Main Street, Randolph, MA 02368; tel. 617/963–8800; FAX. 617/963–8922; Stephen Esdale

Holy Trinity Nursing and Rehabilitation Center, 300 Barber Avenue, Worcester, MA 01606–2476; tel. 508/852–1000; FAX. 508/854–1622; Karen Laganelli

Integrate Health Services of Greater Boston, 300 Winthrop Street, Medford, MA 02155; tel. 617/396–4400; Scott M. Wojkiewicz

JML Care Center, Inc., 184 Ter Heun Drive, Falmouth, MA 02540–0250; tel. 508/457–4621; FAX. 508/457–1218; Charles A. Peterman, Jr.

Jesmond Nursing Home, 271 Nahant Road, Nahant, MA 01908; tel. 617/581–0420; Thomas P. Costin, Jr.

Jewish Healthcare Center, Inc., 629 Salisbury St., Worcester, MA 01609; tel. 508/798–8653; Steve Willens

Jewish Nursing Home of Western Massachusetts, Inc., 770 Converse Street, Longmeadow, MA 01106–1786; tel. 413/567–6211; FAX. 413/567–0175; Howard Braverman, President

John Scott House Nursing and Rehabilitation Center, 233 Middle Street, Braintree, MA 02184; tel. 617/843–1860; FAX. 617/843–8834; Thomas D. Nolan, Administrator

Kathleen Daniel, 485 Franklin Street, Framingham, MA 01702; tel. 508/872–8801; FAX. 508/875–1385; Jonathan Shadovitz, Administrator

Kimwell, a Flatley Rehabilitation and Nursing Center, 495 New Boston Road, Fall River, MA 02720; tel. 508/679–0106; FAX. 508/674–1570; Arthur Taylor

Laurel Ridge Rehab and Nursing Center, 174 Forest Hills Street, Jamaica Plain, MA 02130; tel. 617/522–1550; Jim Cobbs

Ledgewood Rehabilitation and Skilled Nursing Center, 87 Herrick Street, Beverly, MA 01915; tel. 508/921–1392; FAX. 508/927–8627; Laurie Roberto, Administrator

Leo P. LaChance Center for Rehab and Nursing, 59 Eastwood Circle, Gardner, MA 01440; tel. 508/632–8776; James F. Fraser

Liberty Commons of Chatham, 390 Orleans Road, North Chatham, MA 02650; tel. 508/945–4611; FAX. 508/945–2245; William A. Dobson

Life Care Center of Attleboro, 969 Park Street, Attleboro, MA 02703; tel. 508/222–4182; FAX. 508/226–0457; Kate O'Connor

Life Care Center of Auburn, 14 Masonic Circle, Auburn, MA 01501; tel. 508/832–4800; Joseph A. Rizzo

Life Care Center of Merrimack Valley, 80 Boston Road, North Billerica, MA 01862; tel. 508/667–2166; FAX. 508/670–5625; Antonio Sousa, Executive Director

Life Care Center of Plymouth, 94 Obery Street, Plymouth, MA 02360; tel. 508/747–9800; Denise Soucy

Life Care Center of Raynham, 546 South Street East, Raynham, MA 02767; tel. 508/821–5700; Patrick J. O'Connor

Life Care Center of West Bridgewater, 765 West Center Street, West Bridgewater, MA 02379; tel. 508/580–4400; FAX. 508/580–2412; Alan Richman

Life Care Center of Wilbraham, 2399 Boston Road, Wilbraham, MA 01095; tel. 413/596–3111; Nancy J. Varanoske

Life Care Center of the North Shore, 111 Birch Street, Lynn, MA 01902; tel. 617/592–9667; FAX. 617/599–6590; Joseph Deveau

Life Care Center of the South Shore, P.O. Box 830, Scituate, MA 02066; tel. 617/545–1370; Ilene Berkon

Lighthouse Nursing Care Center, 204 Proctor Avenue, Revere, MA 02151; tel. 617/286–3100; Roger Marks

Lincoln Center, 299 Lincoln Street, Worcester, MA 01605; tel. 508/852–2000; Patricia Lobb

Littleton House Nursing Home, 191 Foster Street, Littleton, MA 01460; tel. 508/486–3512; FAX. 508/486–8850; James Nugent

Logan Healthcare Facility, 861 Main Street, South Weymouth, MA 02190; tel. 617/337–0678; Joel K. Logan

Loomis Nursing Center, 298 Jarvis Avenue, Holyoke, MA 01040; tel. 413/538–7551; Carol C. Katz

Lutheran Home of Worcester, 26 Harvard Street, Worcester, MA 01609; tel. 508/754–8877; Ann M. Nadreau

MI Nursing/Restorative Center, Inc., 172 Lawrence Street, Lawrence, MA 01841; tel. 508/685–6321; Joanne H. Mukerjee

Madonna Manor, Inc., 85 North Washington Street, North Attleboro, MA 02760; tel. 508/699–2740; FAX. 508/699–0481; Rev. Edmund J. Fitzgerald

Marian Manor, Inc., 33 Summer Street, Taunton, MA 02780; tel. 508/822–4885; FAX. 508/880–3386; Edmund Fitzgerald

Mariner Health Care at Longwood, 53 Parker Hill Road, Boston, MA 02120; tel. 617/278–3700; FAX. 617/277–1530; Patrick J. Stapleton, MHA, Administrator

Mariner Health of Methuen, 480 Jackson Street, Methuen, MA 01844; tel. 508/686–3906; FAX. 508/687–6007; David J. Friedler, M.P.H., Administrator

Mariner Health of Southeastern Massachusetts, 4586 Acushnet Avenue, New Bedford, MA 02745; tel. 508/998–1188; FAX. 508/998–1826; Marjorie Austin

Mary Ann Morse Nursing and Rehabilitation Center, 45 Union Street, Natick, MA 01760; tel. 508/650–9003; FAX. 508/650–9209; Sarah Porter

Mary Lyon Nursing Home, 34 Main Street, Hampden, MA 01036; tel. 413/566–5511; Patrick Laskey

Mayflower Nursing and Rehab Center, 123 South Street, Plymouth, MA 02360; tel. 508/746–4343; Steven Garfinkle

Mayflower Place Nursing and Rehab Center, 579 Buck Island Road, W. Yarmouth, MA 02673; tel. 508/790–0200; Sidney Insoft

Meadow Green Nursing and Rehabilitation Center, 45 Woburn Street, Waltham, MA 02154; tel. 617/899–8600; FAX. 617/899–3124; David L. Bell, Administrator

Meadowbrook Nursing and Rehabilitation Center, One Meadowbrook Way, Canton, MA 02021; tel. 617/961–5600; FAX. 617/961–5688; Lynn Picard

Meadowview Healthcare Nursing Center, 134 North Street, North Reading, MA 01864; tel. 617/944–1107; FAX. 617/664–5746; John Spears, Administrator

Mediplex Rehabilitation and Skilled Nursing Center of the North Shore, 70 Granite Street, Lynn, MA 01904; tel. 781/581–2400; FAX. 781/581–3080; John A. Holt, Executive Director

Section C

Mediplex Rehabilitation and Skilled Nursing Facility of Northampton, 548 Elm Street, Northampton, MA 01060; tel. 413/586-3150; FAX. 413/584-7720; Christopher Duncan

Mediplex Skilled Nursing and Rehabilitation Center of Lowell, 19 Varnum Street, Lowell, MA 01850; tel. 508/454-5644; FAX. 508/459-6520; James J. Pollard, Jr., Executive Director

Mediplex of Beverly, 265 Essex Street, Beverly, MA 01915; tel. 508/927-3260; FAX. 508/922-8347; Daniel Leahy

Mediplex of Brookline, 99 Park Street, Brookline, MA 02146; tel. 617/731-1050; FAX. 617/731-6516; Brian Freedman, Administrator

Mediplex of East Longmeadow, 135 Benton Drive, East Longmeadow, MA 01028; tel. 413/525-3336; FAX. 413/525-3269; Christopher S. Duncan, Administrator

Mediplex of Holyoke, 260 Easthampton Road, Holyoke, MA 01040; tel. 413/538-9733; FAX. 413/538-9919; Darrell Carlson

Mediplex of Lexington, 178 Lowell Street, Lexington, MA 02173; tel. 781/862-7400; FAX. 781/862-9255; Stephen Davis

Mediplex of New Bedford, 221 Fitzgerald Drive, New Bedford, MA 02745; tel. 508/996-4600; FAX. 508/995-3709; Susan Martineau

Mediplex of Newton, 2101 Washington Street, Newton, MA 02162; tel. 617/969-4660; FAX. 617/964-4622; Donna Steiermann, Executive Director

Mediplex of Weymouth, 64 Performance Drive, Weymouth, MA 02189; tel. 617/340-9800; FAX. 617/340-1771; Robert Nolan

Melrose Care Center, 40 Martin Street, Melrose, MA 02176; tel. 617/665-7050; Debra Scoville

Milford Meadows Skilled Nursing and Rehabilitation Center, 10 Veteran's Memorial Drive, Milford, MA 01757; tel. 508/473-6414; FAX. 508/473-9974; Peter L. Callagy, Executive Director

Milton Health Care, 1200 Brush Hill Road, Milton, MA 02186; tel. 617/333-0600; Elizabeth A. Wood

Mont Marie Health Care Center, Inc., 34 Lower Westfield Road, Holyoke, MA 99999; tel. 413/536-0853; Elizabeth T. Sullivan

Mount St. Vincent Nursing Home, Inc., 35 Holy Family Road, Holyoke, MA 01040; tel. 413/532-3246; FAX. 413/532-0309; Dennis K. McKenna, Administrator

New Boston Nursing Center, P.O. Box 216, Sandisfield, MA 01255; tel. 413/258-4731; Brian Foley

New England Pediatric Care, 78 Boston Road, P.O. Box 350, North Billerica, MA 01862; tel. 508/667-5123; FAX. 508/663-5154; Ellen O'Gorman, Executive Director

Newton and Wellesley Alzheimer Center, 694 Worcester Street, Wellesley, MA 02181; tel. 617/237-6400; FAX. 617/237-2302; Steven Tyer, Administrator

Normandy House Nursing Home, 15 Green Street, Melrose, MA 02176; tel. 617/665-3950; Bernard G. Berkman

North End Community Nursing Home, 70 Fulton Street, Boston, MA 02109; tel. 617/367-3750; Audrey J. DiBendetto

North Hill, 865 Central Avenue, Needham, MA 02192; tel. 617/444-9910; FAX. 617/444-5388; Jesse Lee

Northbridge Nursing and Rehab Center, 2356 Providence Road, Northbridge, MA 01534; tel. 508/234-4641; Steven Garfinkle

Northwood Rehab and Nursing Center, 1010 Varnum Avenue, Lowell, MA 01854; tel. 508/458-8773; Steven Garfinkle

Norwell Knoll Nursing Home, 329 Washington Street, Norwell, MA 02061; tel. 617/659-4901; Brian C. Geary

Norwood Health and Rehab Center, 767 Washington Street, Norwood, MA 02062; tel. 617/769-3704; David Banks

Notre Dame Long Term Care Center, 559 Plantation Street, Worcester, MA 01605; tel. 508/852-3011; Linda Cragin

Nursing Care Center at Kimball Farms, 235 Walker Street, Lenox, MA 01240; tel. 413/637-4684; William C. Jones, Jr.

Oak Hill Nursing and Rehab Center, 76 North Street, Middleboro, MA 02345; tel. 508/947-4774; Mark S. Nussman

Oak Island Skilled Nursing Facility Limited Part, 400 Revere Beach Blvd., Revere, MA 02151; tel. 617/284-1958; Marc S. Shpritzer

Oak Knoll Health Care Center, Nine Arbetter Drive, Framingham, MA 01701; tel. 508/877-3300; FAX. 508/788-0079; Jeffrey Gangi

Oakwood Rehab and Nursing Center, 11 Pontiac Street, Webster, MA 01570; tel. 508/943-3889; W. Bruce Lunsford

On Broadway Nursing and Rehab Center, 932-934 Broadway, Chelsea, MA 02150; tel. 617/889-2250; Marjorie Minichello

Our Lady's Haven of Fairhaven, Inc., 71 Center Street, Fairhaven, MA 02719; tel. 508/999-4561; FAX. 508/997-0254; Edmund Fitzgerald

Palm Manor, 40 Parkhurst Road, Chelmsford, MA 01824; tel. 508/256-3151; FAX. 508/250-4942; Wendy LaBate

Park Avenue Nursing & Rehab Center, 146 Park Avenue, Arlington, MA 02174; tel. 617/648-9530; Joseph J. Alessandroni

Parkwell-Flatley Rehabilitation and Nursing Center, 745 Truman Highway, Hyde Park, MA 02136; tel. 617/361-8300; FAX. 617/361-7725; Thomas Flatley

Peabody Glen Nursing Center, 199 Andover Street, Peabody, MA 01960; tel. 508/531-0772; FAX. 508/532-4134; Clyde Tyler, Administrator

Penacook Place, 150 Water Street, Haverhill, MA 01830; tel. 617/374-0707; FAX. 617/521-0495; Julian Rich

Pleasant Bay Nursing and Rehab Center, 383 South Orleans Road, Route 39, Brewster, MA 02631; tel. 508/240-3500; Joshua L. Zuckerman

Pleasant Manor Nursing Home, 193-195 Pleasant Street, Attleboro, MA 02703; tel. 508/222-4950; Joyce Pinto

Pond Meadow Nursing and Rehab Center, 188 Summer Street, Weymouth, MA 02188; tel. 617/337-6900; Ann Marie Jaworski

Port Healthcare Center, 113 Low Street, Newburyport, MA 01950; tel. 508/462-7373; FAX. 508/462-6510; Alfred L. Arcidi, DDS

Prescott House Nursing Home, 140 Prescott Street, North Andover, MA 01845; tel. 508/685-8086; Alan D. Scott

Presentation Nursing and Rehab Center, Ten Bellamy Street, Brighton, MA 02135; tel. 617/782-8113; Mark Jessup

Presidential Rehab and Nursing Center, 43 Old Colony Ave., Quincy, MA 02170; tel. 617/471-0155; Burton Lipsky

Quabbin Valley Healthcare, 821 Daniel Shays Highway, Athol, MA 01331; tel. 508/249-3717; Mark Ailinger

Quaboag Nursing Home, P.O. Box 386, West Brookfield, MA 01585; tel. 508/867-7716; Loren Salvetti

Randolph Crossings Nursing Center, 49 Thomas Patten Drive, Randolph, MA 02368; tel. 617/961-1160; FAX. 617/963-5744; Donald Baker

Ring Health Care Centers/East, P.O. Box 478, Springfield, MA 01118; tel. 413/734-1133; Matthew J. Leahey

Rivercrest Long Term Care Facility, 80 Deaconess Road, Concord, MA 01742; tel. 508/369-5151; Guy S. Morrison

Riverdale Gardens Rehab and Nursing Center, 42 Prospect Ave., West Springfield, MA 01089; tel. 413/733-3151; Barbara H. Leasure

Rosewood Nursing and Rehabilitation Center, 22 Johnson Street, Peabody, MA 01960; tel. 508/535-8700; FAX. 508/535-2300; Julian Rich

Sacred Heart Nursing Home, 359 Summer Street, New Bedford, MA 02740-5599; tel. 508/996-6751; FAX. 508/996-6751, ext. 24; Sister Blandine D'Amours, Administrator

Saint Francis Home, 101 Plantation Street, Worcester, MA 01605; tel. 508/755-8605; Jacquelyn Alix, PFM

Sancta Maria Nursing Facility, 799 Concord Avenue, Cambridge, MA 01061; tel. 617/868-2200; Mary M. Pizzotti, DM

Sandalwood Nursing and Rehab Center, 3 Pine Street, Oxford, MA 01540; tel. 508/987-8417; Alan Zampini

Sarah S. Brayton Nursing Care Center, 4901 North Main Street, Fall River, MA 02720; tel. 508/675-1001; FAX. 508/675-1088; Alan Solomont

Seacoast Nursing and Retirement Center, 292 Washington Street, Gloucester, MA 01930; tel. 508/283-0300; FAX. 508/281-6774; George Gougian, Executive Director

Sharon Manor, Inc., 259 Norwood Street, Sharon, MA 02067; tel. 617/784-6781; Jeffrey C. Harsfield

Sherrill House, Inc., 135 South Huntington Avenue, Boston, MA 02130; tel. 617/731-2400; FAX. 617/731-8671; Donald M. Powell, Executive Director

Sippican Healthcare Center, 15 Mill Street, Marion, MA 02738; tel. 508/748-3830; FAX. 508/748-3834; Alfred Arcidi

Southpoint Rehabilitation and Skilled Care Center, 100 Amity Street, Fall River, MA 02721; tel. 508/675-2500; FAX. 508/675-8874; Richard Sciacca

Southwood at Norwell Nursing Center, 501 Cordwainer Drive, Norwell, MA 02061; tel. 617/982-7450; Richard H. Starr

St. Joseph Manor Health Care, Inc., 215 Thatcher Street, Brockton, MA 02402; tel. 508/583-5834; Thomas Brown

Stephen Caldwell Memorial Convalescent Home, Inc., 16 Green Street, Ipswich, MA 01938; tel. 508/356-2526; Lawrence J. Pszenny

Suburban Manor Rehabilitation Nursing Center, One Great Road, Acton, MA 01720; tel. 508/263-9101; FAX. 508/263-3278; Carl H. Anderson, Executive Director

Sunny Acres Nursing Home, Inc., 254 Billerica Road, Chelmsford, MA 01824; tel. 508/256-1616; FAX. 508/256-6229; Shirley Freitas

Sunrise-Mediplex of Boston, 910 Saratoga Street, East Boston, MA 02128; tel. 617/569-1157; FAX. 617/567-2236; Maryann Boyle

Sutton Hill Nursing and Retirement Center, 1801 Turnpike Street, North Andover, MA 01845; tel. 508/688-1212; FAX. 508/794-8265; Katherine Lemay

Sweet Brook, 1561 Cold Spring Road, Williamstown, MA 01267; tel. 413/458-8127; FAX. 413/458-8209; John F. Warren, Chief Operating Officer, Administrator

Taber Street Nursing Home, 19 Taber Street, New Bedford, MA 02740; tel. 508/997-0791; FAX. 508/991-5013; David Banks

The Center for Optimum Care - Falmouth, 359 Jones Road, Falmouth, MA 02540; tel. 508/457-9000; Peter LeBrun

The Center for Optimum Care - Mashpee, 161 Falmouth Road, Route 28, Mashpee, MA 02649; tel. 508/477-2490; Jo-Ann B. Melchert

The Center for Optimum Care-Bayview, 26 Sturgis Street, Winthrop, MA 02152; tel. 617/846-2060; FAX. 617/846-3283; Steve Demaranville

The Center for Optimum Care-Wakefield, Bathol Street, Wakefield, MA 01880; tel. 617/245-7600; FAX. 617/245-2238; Judith Gordon

The Center for Optimum Care-Winthrop, 170 Cliff Avenue, Winthrop, MA 02152; tel. 617/846-0500; FAX. 617/539-1306; Karla Fleming

The Ellis Nursing and Rehabilitation Center, 135 Ellis Avenue, Norwood, MA 02062; tel. 617/762-6880; FAX. 617/769-0482; Anthony Franchi

The Goddard Center, 909 Sumner Street, Stoughton, MA 02072; tel. 617/297-8203; Robert Baranello

The Highlands, 335 Nichols Road, Fitchburg, MA 01420; tel. 508/343-4411; FAX. 508/343-6464; Kenneth L. Sleeper

The Lafayette Convalescent Home, 25 Lafayette Street, Marblehead, MA 01945; tel. 617/631-4535; William Mantzoukas, MPH

The Meadows Skilled Nursing and Rehab, 111 Huntoon Memorial Highway, Rochdale, MA 01542; tel. 508/892-4858; Jill Zucco

The Oaks, 4525 Acushnet Avenue, New Bedford, MA 02745; tel. 508/998-7807; FAX. 508/998-8865; Eileen Hegarty, Executive Director

The Oxford, 689 Main Street, Haverhill, MA 01830; tel. 508/373-1131; FAX. 508/373-3074; John Albert

Town Manor Nursing and Rehabilitation Center, 55 Lowell Street, Lawrence, MA 01840; tel. 508/688-6056; FAX. 508/688-5633; Thomas Dresser, Administrator

Town and Country Nursing Home, 259 Baldwin Street, Lowell, MA 01851; tel. 508/454-5438; FAX. 508/970-3692; Alex Struzziero, Administrator

University Commons, 378 Plantation Street, Worcester, MA 01605; tel. 508/755-7300; Ellen Levinson

Wachusett Extended Care Facility, 56 Boyden Road, Holden, MA 01520; tel. 508/829-7383; FAX. 508/829-2620; James Oliver, Administrator

Walden Rehabilitation and Nursing Center, 785 Main Street, Concord, MA 01742; tel. 978/369-6889; FAX. 978/369-8392; Sharon K. Buehrle

Wedgemere Convalescent Home, 146 Dean Street, Taunton, MA 02780; tel. 508/823-0767; David Banks

Section C

Wellesley Health and Rehab Center, 878 Worcester Road, Wellesley, MA 02181; tel. 617/235–6699; William Mathies

West Acres Nursing Home, 804 Pleasant Street, Brockton, MA 02401; tel. 508/583–6000; FAX. 508/580–2468; John Soule

Westborough Nursing Center, 5 Colonial Drive, Westborough, MA 01581; tel. 508/366–9131; Turney Jenkins

Westford Nursing and Rehabilitation Center, Three Park Drive, Westford, MA 01886; tel. 978/392–1144; FAX. 978/392–0032; Alan Solomont

Weston Manor Nursing and Rehab Center, 75 Norumbega Road, Weston, MA 02193; tel. 617/891–6100; Evelyn Insoft

Willow Manor Health Care and Rehabilitation Center, 30 Princeton Boulevard, Lowell, MA 01851; tel. 508/454–8086; FAX. 508/453–9772; Anne Roth, Executive Director

Willowood Health Care Center, 175 Franklin Street, North Adams, MA 01247; tel. 413/664–4041; FAX. 413/664–8447; Beverly Clark, Administrator

Willowood Nursing and Retirement Facility, 151 Christian Hill Road, P.O. Box 330, Great Barrington, MA 01230; tel. 413/528–4560; FAX. 413/528–5691; David Klausmeyer, Administrator

Willowood of Williamstown, 25 Adams Road, Williamstown, MA 01267; tel. 413/458–2111; FAX. 413/458–4907; Ronald T. Cerow, Administrator

Willowwood of Pittsfield, Nursing and Rehab, 169 Valentine Road, Pittsfield, MA 01201; tel. 413/445–2300; Leo Attella

Wilmington Woods Nursing Care Center, 750 Woburn Street, Wilmington, MA 01887; tel. 508/988–0888; FAX. 508/658–6470; Steve DeMaranville

Winchester Nursing Center, Inc., P.O. Box 490, Winchester, MA 01890; tel. 617/729–9595; Richard H. Salter

Wingate at Andover Rehabilitative Skilled Nursing, 80 Andover Street, Andover, MA 01810; tel. 508/470–3434; FAX. 508/475–7097; Thomas Wheatley

Wingate at Brighton Rehabilitative Skilled Nursing Residence, 100 North Beacon Street, Boston, MA 02134; tel. 617/787–2300; FAX. 617/787–1539; Sister Jacquelyn McCarthy, Administrator

Wingate at Needham, 589 Highland Avenue, Needham, MA 02194; tel. 617/455–9090; FAX. 617/455–9012; Muriel Baum

Wingate at Reading, 1364 Main Street, Reading, MA 01867; tel. 617/942–1210; FAX. 617/942–7251; Catherine M. Congo, Administrator

Wingate at Sudbury, Inc., 136 Boston Post Road, Sudbury, MA 01776; tel. 508/443–2722; Muriel Baum

Wingate at Wilbraham Rehabilitative Skilled Nursing, Nine Maple Street, Wilbraham, MA 01095; tel. 413/596–2411; FAX. 413/599–1738; Duncan Hunter

Woburn Nursing Center, Inc., 18 Frances Street, Woburn, MA 01801; tel. 781/933–8175; FAX. 781/938–8402; Patricia Devereaux, Administrator

Woodbriar of Wilmington, 90 West Street, Wilmington, MA 01887; tel. 508/658–2700; FAX. 508/657–0015; Dennis Sargent, President

Youville Healthcare Center, 1575 Cambridge Street, Cambridge, MA 02138; tel. 617/876–4344; FAX. 617/441–8902; Sister Joan Coyne, Administrator

MICHIGAN

Bay County Medical Care Facility, 564 West Hampton Road, Essexville, MI 48732; tel. 517/892–3591; FAX. 517/892–6991; William R. Mahoney, Administrator

Brookcrest Christian Nursing Home, 3400 Wilson Avenue, Grandville, MI 49418; tel. 616/534–5487; Richard Freerksen

Clare Nursing Home, Inc., 600 Southeast Fourth Street, Clare, MI 48617; tel. 517/386–7723; FAX. 517/386–4100; Wilma Shurlow, Administrator

Crestmont Health Care Center, 111 Trealout Drive, Fenton, MI 48430; tel. 810/629–4105; FAX. 810/629–7538; Lisa K. Berthold

Fraser Villa – A Mercy Living Center, 33300 Utica Road, Fraser, MI 48026; tel. 810/293–3300; Karen Struve

Greenery Extended Care Center, 34225 Grand River, Farmington, MI 48335; tel. 313/477–7373; FAX. 313/477–2888; Neal Elliott

Greenery Health Care Center, 4800 Clintonville Road, Clarkston, MI 48346; tel. 248/674–0903; Steve Bakken

Greenery Health Care Center at Howell, 3003 West Grand River, Howell, MI 48843; tel. 517/546–4210; FAX. 517/546–7661; Neal Elliott

Haven Park Christian Nursing Home, 285 North State Street, Zeeland, MI 49464; tel. 616/772–4641; Richard McCrea

Heartland Health Care Center – Allen Park, 9150 Allen Road, Allen Park, MI 48101; tel. 313/386–2150; Richard Shock

Heartland Health Care Center – Dearborn Heights, 26001 Ford Road, Dearborn Heights, MI 48127; tel. 313/274–4600; Roslind Ferrone

Heartland Health Care Center – Dorvin, 29270 Morlock Street, Livonia, MI 48152; tel. 810/476–0555; Benjamin Duckworth

Heartland Health Care Center – Fostrian, 540 Sunnyside Drive, Flushing, MI 48433; tel. 810/659–5695; Nancy Walker

Heartland Health Care Center – Georgian East, 21401 Mack Avenue, Grosse Pointe, MI 48236; tel. 810/778–0800; Tammy Hartley

Heartland Health Care Center – Knollview, 1061 West Hackley Avenue, Muskegon, MI 49441; tel. 616/755–2255; Gary Peters

Heartland Health Care Center–Kalamazoo, 3625 West Michigan Avenue, Kalamazoo, MI 49006; tel. 616/375–4550; FAX. 616/375–4687; Betsy Perry

Heartland Health Care Center–University, 28550 Five Mile Road, Livonia, MI 48154; tel. 313/427–8270; FAX. 313/427–2135; Judy Ashton, Administrator

Heartland Health Center–Grand Rapids, 2320 East Beltline SE, Grand Rapids, MI 49546; tel. 616/949–3000; FAX. 616/949–5612; Ed Haywood

Heartland Healthcare Center – Ann Arbor, 4701 East Huron River Drive, Ann Arbor, MI 48105; tel. 313/677–2617; Susan Oginsky

Heartland Healthcare Center–Georgian Bloomfield, 2975 North Adams Road, Bloomfield Hills, MI 48034; tel. 810/645–2900; FAX. 810/645–5228; Elizabeth Siebert, Administrator

Holland Health Care Center, 493 West 32nd Street, Holland, MI 49423; tel. 616/396–1438; Ken Robbins

Integrated Health Services of Michigan at Riverbend, 11941 Belsay Road, Grand Blanc, MI 48439; tel. 810/694–1970; FAX. 810/694–4081; Lee K. Karson, Executive Director, Chief Executive Officer

Isabella County Medical Care Facility, 1222 North Drive, Mount Pleasant, MI 48858; tel. 517/772–2957; FAX. 517/772–3669; Vickie S. Block, Administrator

Martha T. Berry Memorial Medical Care Facility, 43533 Elizabeth Road, Mount Clemens, MI 48043; tel. 810/469–5265; FAX. 810/469–6352; Raymond D. Pietrzak, Administrator

Marvin and Betty Danto Health Care Center, 6800 West Maple, West Bloomfield, MI 48322; tel. 810/788–7113; Robert Possanzo

Mercy Bellbrook, 873 West Avon Road, Rochester Hills, MI 48307; tel. 810/656–3239, ext. 203; FAX. 810/656–8160; Ann L. Eastman, Administrator

Mercy Pavilion of Battle Creek, 80 North 20th Street, Battle Creek, MI 49015; tel. 616/964–5400; FAX. 616/964–5559; Stephen Abbott

North Ottawa Care Center, Inc., 1615 South Despelder, Grand Haven, MI 49417–2633; tel. 616/842–0770; FAX. 616/842–0783; Brenda Ochmanek

Oakland County Medical Care Facility, 1200 North Telegraph Road, Pontiac, MI 48341–0469; tel. 248/858–1415; FAX. 248/858–4026; Shirla F. Kugler, Administrator

Orchard Hills, A Mercy Living Center, 532 Orchard Lake Road, Pontiac, MI 48341; tel. 810/338–7151; FAX. 810/338–2563; Marsha Tomas, Administrator

Porter Hills Presbyterian Village, Inc., 3600 East Fulton Street, Grand Rapids, MI 48151; tel. 616/949–4971; David B. Dourma

Rivergate Terrace, 14141 Pennsylvania road, Riverview, MI 48192; tel. 313/284–8000; John Polturanus

Shore Haven, a Mercy Living Center, 900 South Beacon Boulevard, Grand Haven, MI 49417; tel. 616/846–1850; FAX. 616/846–0971; Nancy J. Ritchie, Administrator

University Park – A Mercy Living Center, 570 South Harvey Street, Muskegon, MI 49442; tel. 616/773–9121; Richard H. Ebeling

MINNESOTA

Bloomington Care Center, 9200 Nicollet Avenue South, Bloomington, MN 55420; tel. 612/881–8676; Joseph G. Gubbels

Chateau Healthcare Center, 2106 2nd Avenue South, Minneapolis, MN 55404; tel. 612/874–1603; Phyllis C. Winters

Hillcrest Health Care and Retirement Center, 15409 Wayzata Blvd., Wayzata, MN 55391; tel. 612/473–5466; Margaret Owens

LaCrescent Healthcare Center, 701 Main Street, LaCrescent, MN 55947; tel. 507/895–4445; Gale Bruessel

Lake Ridge Health Care Center, 2727 North Victoria, Roseville, MN 55113; tel. 612/483–5431; FAX. 612/486–2461; Jeffrey D. Bomberger

Lexington Health and Rehab Center, 375 North Lexington Parkway, St. Paul, MN 55104; tel. 612/645–0577; Martha Eke

Moorhead Healthcare Center, 2810 North Second Avenue, Moorhead, MN 56560; tel. 218/233–7578; FAX. 218/233–8307; David Erickson

Olivia Healthcare Center, P.O. Box 229, Olivia, MN 56277; tel. 320/523–1652; Scott D. Spales

St. Louis Park Plaza Health Care Center, 3201 Virginia Avenue South, St. Louis Park, MN 55426; tel. 612/935–0333; Joel Kelsh

Trevilla of Golden Valley, 7505 Country Club Drive, Golden Valley, MN 55427; tel. 612/545–0416; Larry Vander Poel

Trevilla of New Brighton, 825 First Avenue Northwest, New Brighton, MN 55112; tel. 612/633–7875; Joanne Buytendorp

Twin Rivers Care Center, 305 Fremont Street, Anoka, MN 55303; tel. 612/421–5660; Gayle Sanders

Whitewater Healthcare Center, 525 Bluff Avenue, P.O. Box 8, Saint Charles, MN 55972; tel. 507/932–3283; FAX. 507/932–4756; Michael Maher, Executive Director

MISSISSIPPI

Eupora Health Care Center, 200 Walnut Avenue, P.O. Box 918, Eupora, MS 39744; tel. 601/258–8293; FAX. 601/258–2345; Gerald Gary, Administrator

Lakeland Health Care Center, 3680 Lakeland Lane, Jackson, MS 39216; tel. 601/982–5505; FAX. 601/362–1883; Angela Turner, Executive Director

United States Naval Home, 1800 Beach Drive, Gulfport, MS 39507–1597; tel. 601/897–4003; FAX. 601/897–4013; F. Michael Fox

MISSOURI

Alexian Brothers Lansdowne Village, 4624 Lansdowne, St. Louis, MO 63116; tel. 314/351–6888; Kim Woodsmall

BCC at Republic Park Care Center, Inc., P.O. Box 755, Republic, MO 65738; tel. 417/732–1822; Bill Foster

Balanced Care Hermitage, P.O. Box 325, Hermitage, MO 65668; tel. 417/745–2111; Bill Foster

Balanced Care Lebanon North, P.O. Box K, Lebanon, MO 65536; tel. 417/532–9173; Brad Hollinger

Harry S. Truman Restorative Center, 5700 Arsenal Street, St. Louis, MO 63139; tel. 314/768–6600, ext. 13; FAX. 314/645–7628; Shirley E. Herr

Integrated Health Services at Alpine North, 4700 Cliff View Drive, Kansas City, MO 64150; tel. 816/741–5105; FAX. 816/746–1301; Karen Leverich, Administrator

Integrated Health Services of St. Louis at Gravois, 10954 Kennerly Road, St. Louis, MO 63128; tel. 314/843–4242; FAX. 314/843–5370; Cathy Deffendall

John Knox Village Care Center, 600 Northwest Pryor Road, Lees Summit, MO 64081; tel. 816/246–4343, ext. 2402; FAX. 816/525–3473; Herman Spahr

Lebanon Park Manor, Inc., 514 West Fremont, Lebanon, MO 65536; tel. 417/532–5351; FAX. 417/831–7928; Bill Foster, Regional President

Life Care Center of St. Louis, 3520 Chouteau Avenue, St. Louis, MO 63103; tel. 314/771–2100; Bill Maggard

ManorCare Health Services, 1200 Graham Road, Florissant, MO 63031; tel. 314/838–6555; FAX. 314/838–4000; Anita Martinez, Administrator

Village North Health Center, 11160 Village North Drive, St. Louis, MO 63136; tel. 314/355–8010; FAX. 314/653–4801; Wes Sperr, Administrator

Village North Manor, 6768 North Highway 67, Florissant, MO 63034; tel. 314/741–9101; FAX. 314/741–4936; David G. Mixon

Village North Woods, 9500 Bellefontaine Road, St. Louis, MO 63137; tel. 314/868–1400; FAX. 314/868–0170; Gladys A. Sullivan, Administrator

Section C

NEBRASKA

Columbus Manor, P.O. Box 525, Columbus, NE 68601; tel. 402/564–8014; Alexander Willford

Fullerton Manor, P.O. Box 648, Fullerton, NE 68638; tel. 308/536–2488; Mark Kealy

Hallmark Care Center, 5505 Grover Street, Omaha, NE 68106; tel. 402/558–0225; Dolores Bailey

Hartington Nursing Center, 401 West Darlene Street, P.O. Box 107, Hartington, NE 68739; tel. 402/254–3905; FAX. 402/254–3963; Pat Stonacek, Administrator

Lakeview Rehabilitation Nursing Center, 1405 West Highway 34, Grand Island, NE 68801; tel. 308/382–6397; FAX. 308/382–0125; Marilou Luth, Executive Director

Norfolk Nursing Center, 1900 Vicki Lane, Norfolk, NE 68701; tel. 402/371–2303; Trish Montgomery

Park Place Health Care and Rehab Center, 610 North Darr, Grand Island, NE 68803; tel. 308/382–2635; Michelle Larsen

Scottsbluff Nursing Center, 111 West 36th Street, Scottsbluff, NE 69361; tel. 308/635–2019; Pamela A. Cover

The Ambassador Lincoln, 4405 Norman Boulevard, Lincoln, NE 68506; tel. 402/488–2355; FAX. 402/488–2779; Michael Ryan, Director, Operations

The Ambassador of Nebraska City, Box 547, Nebraska City, NE 68410; tel. 402/873–6650; Steven Chamley

NEVADA

Integrated Health Services of Las Vegas, 2170 East Harmon Avenue, Las Vegas, NV 89119; tel. 702/794–0100; FAX. 702/794–0041; Maryanne Smith, Assistant Vice President

NEW HAMPSHIRE

Dover Rehabilitation and Living Center, 307 Plaza Drive, Dover, NH 03820; tel. 603/742–2676, ext. 115; FAX. 603/749–5375; Craig Rowley

Golden View Health Care Center, 19 New Hampshire, Route 104, Meredith, NH 03253; tel. 603/279–8111; Jeanne Sanders

Good Shepherd Nursing Home, 20 Plantation Dive, Joffrey, NH 03452; tel. 603/532–8762; FAX. 603/532–6057; Judith A. LeBlanc, Administrator

Greenbriar Terrace Healthcare, 55 Harris Road, Nashua, NH 03062; tel. 603/888–1573; FAX. 603/888–5089; Arthur O'Leary, Administrator

Hanover Hill Health Care Center, 700 Hanover Street, Manchester, NH 03104; tel. 603/627–3826; Theodore J. Lee

Hanover Terrace Healthcare, 53 Lyme Road, Hanover, NH 03755; tel. 603/643–2854; Claudette Werner

Harborside Healthcare – Applewood, 8 Snow Road, Winchester, NH 03470; tel. 603/239–6355; Suzanne McGrath

Harborside Healthcare – Crestwood, 40 Crosby Street, Milford, NH 03055; tel. 603/673–7061; Stephen L. Guillard

Harborside Healthcare – Northwood Rehab and Nursing, 30 Colby Court, Bedford, NH 03110; tel. 603/625–6462; Mary E. Johnson

Harborside Healthcare – Pheasant Wood, 100 Pheasant Road, Peterborough, NH 03458; tel. 603/924–7267; Bruce C. Moorhead

Integrated Health Services of Derry, Eight Peabody Road, Derry, NH 03038; tel. 603/434–1566; FAX. 603/434–2299; David Ross, Administrator

Integrated Health Services of New Hampshire at Claremont, RFD 3, Box 47, Hanover Street Extension, Claremont, NH 03743; tel. 603/542–2606; FAX. 603/543–0479; Sean Stevenson

Integrated Health Services of New Hampshire at Manchester, 191 Hackett Hill Road, Manchester, NH 03102; tel. 603/668–8161; FAX. 603/622–2584; Brian King

Mount Carmel Nursing Home, 235 Myrtle Street, Manchester, NH 03104; tel. 603/627–3811; FAX. 603/626–4696; Stephen V. Fulchino

Rochester Manor, 40 Whitehall Road, Rochester, NH 03867; tel. 603/332–7711; Mark Finkelstein

Saint Ann Home, 195 Dover Point Road, Dover, NH 03820; tel. 603/742–2612; FAX. 603/743–3055; Sister Mary Robert Romano, Administrator

St. Francis Home, SNF/ICF, 406 Court Street, Laconia, NH 03246; tel. 603/524–0466; FAX. 603/527–0884; Julieann Fay, Administrator

St. Teresa's Manor, 519 Bridge Street, Manchester, NH 03104; tel. 603/668–2373; FAX. 603/668–0059; Stephen V. Fulchino, Administrator

St. Vincent de Paul Nursing Home, 29 Providence Avenue, Berlin, NH 03570; tel. 603/752–1820; FAX. 603/752–7149; Steven E. Woods, Administrator

The Edgewood Centre, 928 South Street, Portsmouth, NH 03801; tel. 603/436–0099; Patricia Cummings

NEW JERSEY

Arbor Glen Nursing and Rehab Center, Pompton Avenue/E. Lindsley Road, Cedar Grove, NJ 07009; tel. 201/256–7720; Moshael Straus

Ashbrook Nursing and Rehabilitation Center, 1610 Raritan Road, Scotch Pines, NJ 07076; tel. 908/889–5500; FAX. 908/889–6573; Ronald Delmauro

Atlantic Coast Rehab and Health Care Center, 485 River Avenue, Lakewood, NJ 08701; tel. 908/354–7100; Melvin Feigenbaum

Barn Hill Convalescent Center, 249 High Street, Route 94 South, Newton, NJ 07860; tel. 201/383–5600; FAX. 201/383–1397; Barbara Rice, Administrator

Berkeley Heights Convalescent Center, 35 Cottage Street, Berkeley Heights, NJ 07922; tel. 908/464–0048; Wanda Monique

Cinnaminson Nursing and Rehab Center, 1700 Wynwood Drive, Cinnaminson, NJ 08077; tel. 609/829–9000; Dwight T. Roche

Cornell Hall, 234 Chestnut Street, Union, NJ 07083; tel. 908/687–7800; FAX. 908/687–1417; Victor Fresolone

Crestwood Nursing and Rehab Center, 101 Whippany Road, Whippany, NJ 07981; tel. 973/887–0311; Carol Shepard

Daughters of Miriam Center for the Aged, 155 Hazel Street, Clifton, NJ 07015; tel. 201/772–3700; FAX. 201/772–5044; Steven Schilsky, L.N.H.A., Executive Vice President

Delaire Nursing and Convalescent Center, 400 West Stimpson Avenue, Linden, NJ 07036; tel. 908/862–3399; Thomas Bejgrowicz

Dunroven Health Care Center, 221 County Road, Cresskill, NJ 07656; tel. 201/567–9310; FAX. 201/567–9239; William V. Maloney, Sr.

Franklin Convalescent Center, 3371 Route 27, Franklin Park, NJ 08823; tel. 908/821–8000; FAX. 908/821–9253; Benjamin M. Accardi

Glenside Nursing Center, 144 Gales Drive, New Providence, NJ 07974; tel. 908/464–8600; FAX. 908/464–6355; Joan Lepore

Green Acres Manor, 1931 Lakewood Road, Route 9, Toms River, NJ 08755; tel. 732/286–2323; FAX. 732/914–9095; Maria Lapid, RN, Administrator

Greenbrook Manor Nursing and Rehabilitation Center, 303 Rock Avenue, Green Brook, NJ 08812–2616; tel. 732/968–5500; FAX. 732/968–7963; Ronald J. Delmauro

Harborside Healthcare Rehabilitation and Nursing Center–Woods Edge, 875 Route 202/206 North, Bridgewater, NJ 08807; tel. 908/526–8600; FAX. 908/707–0686; James Lindes

Inglemoor Care Center, 311 South Livingston Avenue, Livingston, NJ 07039; tel. 201/994–0221; FAX. 201/992–0696; Daniel Moles

Integrated Health Services of New Jersey at Somerset Valley, 1621 Route 22 West, Bound Brook, NJ 08805; tel. 908/469–2000; FAX. 908/469–8917; Carolyn Allen, Executive Director

JFK Hartwyck at Cedar Brook Nursing Convalescent and Rehabilitation, 2048 Oak Tree Road, Edison, NJ 08820; tel. 908/906–2100; FAX. 908/321–9217; Thomas Lankey

JFK Hartwyck at Edison Nursing, 465 Plainfield Avenue, Edison, NJ 08817; tel. 908/906–2100; Thomas Lankey

JFK Hartwyck at Oak Tree Nursing, 2048 Oak Tree Road, Edison, NJ 08820; tel. 908/906–2100; Thomas Lankey

King James Care and Rehabilitation Center, 1165 Easton Avenue, Somerset, NJ 08873; tel. 908/246–4100; FAX. 908/246–3926; Allyson Brown, Administrator

Lakeview Subacute Care Cente, 130 Terhune Road, Wayne, NJ 07470; tel. 973/839–4500; Richard Grosso, Jr.

Lanfair House Nursing and Rehabilitation Center, 1140 Black Oak Ridge Road, Wayne, NJ 07470; tel. 973/835–7443; Carmen B. Alecci

Laurelton Village Care Center, 475 Jack Martin Boulevard, Brick, NJ 08724; tel. 908/458–6600; FAX. 908/458–2674; Kathy Bogajevski

Lincoln Park Nursing and Convalescent Home, 521 Pine Brook Road, Lincoln Park, NJ 07035; tel. 201/696–3300; Dolores Turco

Linwood Convalescent Center, Route 9 and Central Avenue, Linwood, NJ 08221; tel. 609/927–6131; FAX. 609/927–0069; Ellie Kinsey–Skroski RN, B

Manor Care Health Services, 1180 Route 22 West, Mountainside, NJ 07092; tel. 908/654–0020; FAX. 908/654–8661; Alicia J. Erb, LNHA

ManorCare Health Services, 550 Jessup Road, West Deptford, NJ 08066; tel. 609/848–9551; FAX. 609/848–1817; David Donin, Administrator

ManorCare Health Services, 1412 Marlton Pike, Cherry Hill, NJ 08034; tel. 609/428–6100; Lynne M. Caballes

Margaret McLaughlin McCarrick Care Center, 15 Dellwood Lane, Somerset, NJ 08873; tel. 908/545–4200; FAX. 908/846–1089; James Caron, Administrator

Meadow View Nursing and Respiratory Care Center, 1328 South Black Horse Pike, Williamstown, NJ 08094; tel. 609/875–0100; FAX. 609/629–4619; Jane Greenberg, Administrator

Medford Convalescent and Nursing Center, 185 Tuckerton Road, Medford, NJ 08055; tel. 609/983–8500; David F. Graham

Mediplex Rehab–Camden, Two Cooper Plaza, Camden, NJ 08103; tel. 609/342–7600; FAX. 609/541–4059; Paul Goldenberg

Mediplex of Oradell, 600 Kinderkamack Road, Oradell, NJ 07649; tel. 201/967–0002; Jack Ellias

Morris Hills Nursing and Rehab Center, 77 Madison Avenue, Morristown, NJ 01871; tel. 973/540–9800; Cecilia Weisbauer

Morris View Nursing Home, 540 West Hanover Avenue, P.O. Box 437, Morris Plains, NJ 07950; tel. 201/285–2820; FAX. 201/285–6062; Joaquin Deniz, Administrator

Neptune ConvaCenter, 101 Walnut Street, Neptune, NJ 07753; tel. 908/774–3550; FAX. 908/775–7534; George Michals, L.N.H.A.

Oak Ridge Rehab and Nursing Center, 261 Terhune Drive, Wayne, NJ 07470; tel. 973/835–3871; George J. Arezzo, MPH

Old Bridge Manor, 6989 Route 18 South, Old Bridge, NJ 08857; tel. 908/360–2277; Susan Fifield

Parkway Manor Health Center, 480 North Walnut Street/Parkway, East Orange, NJ 07017; tel. 201/674–2700; Ellen Alibrando, MPA

Regent Care Center, 50 Polifily Road, Hackensack, NJ 07601; tel. 201/646–1166; Robert Kovacs

Riverview Extended Care Residence, 55 West Front Street, Red Bank, NJ 07701; tel. 908/842–3800; Laurence C. Gumina

Seacrest Village Nursing Home, 1001 Center Street, P.O. Box 1480, Little Egg Harbor, NJ 08087; tel. 609/296–9292; FAX. 609/296–0508; Brian Holloway

Silver Court Nursing Center, Inc., 1423 Brace Road, Cherry Hill, NJ 08034; tel. 609/795–3131; Marc I. Silver

The Manor, 689 West Main Street, Freehold, NJ 07728; tel. 908/431–5200, ext. 11; FAX. 908/409–2446; Thomas H. Litz, FACHE

Troy Hills Nursing and Rehabilitation Center, 200 Reynolds Avenue, Parsippany, NJ 07054; tel. 201/887–8080; FAX. 201/386–5906; Anne Marie Gauntlett

Valley Health Care Center, 300 Old Hook Road, Westwood, NJ 07675; tel. 201/664–8888; FAX. 201/664–9577; Chris Asmann–Finch, Administrator

Voorhees Center – Genesis ElderCare Network, 3001 Evesham Road, Voorhees, NJ 08043; tel. 609/751–1600; Benjamin M. Accardi

Voorhees Pediatric Facility, 1304 Laurel Oak Road, Voorhees, NJ 08043; tel. 609/346–3300; FAX. 609/435–4223; Carl Underland, Administrator

Wayne View Convalescent Center, 2020 Route 23 North, Wayne, NJ 07470; tel. 207/305–8400; Philip Elk

West Caldwell Care Center, 165 Fairfield Avenue, West Caldwell, NJ 07006; tel. 201/226–1100; Richard Pineles

Westfield Center – Genesis ElderCare Network, 1515 Lamberts Mill Road, Westfield, NJ 07090; tel. 908/223–9700; Linda Stevens

Whiting Healthcare Center, 3000 Hilltop Road, Whiting, NJ 08759; tel. 908/849–4400; Thomas Miller

Woodcrest Center, 800 River Road, New Milford, NJ 07646; tel. 201/967–1700; FAX. 201/967–5423; Rebecca R. Resh

NEW MEXICO

Casa Arena Blanca Nursing Center, 205 Moonglow, Alamogordo, NM 88310; tel. 505/434–4510; Cynthia A. Myers, RN

Casa Maria Health Care Center, 1601 South Main Street, Roswell, NM 88201; tel. 505/623–6008; Juliane Ziter

Las Palomas Nursing and Rehabilitation Center, 8100 Palomas, N.E., Albuquerque, NM 87109; tel. 505/821–4200; FAX. 505/822–0234; Juliane Ziter

NEW YORK

Aurora Park Health Care Center, Inc., 292 Main Street, East Aurora, NY 14052; tel. 716/652-1560; Bernardo J. Carotenuto

Rainbridge Nursing Home, 3518 Bainbridge Avenue, Bronx, NY 10467; tel. 718/655-1991; FAX. 718/655-3903; Isaac Goldbrenner, Administrator

Birchwood Health Care Center, Inc., 4800 Bear Road, Liverpool, NY 13088; tel. 315/457-9946; Patrick Deptula

Brandywine Nursing Home, 620 Sleepy Hollow Road, Briarcliff Manor, NY 10510; tel. 914/941-5100; Paul S. Roth

Center for Nursing and Rehab, 520 Prospect Place, Brooklyn, NY 11238; tel. 718/636-1000; FAX. 718/857-4559; Michael Fassler, Executive Vice President

Central Island Healthcare, 825 Old Country Road, Plainview, NY 11803; tel. 516/433-0600; Martha Sweet

Clove Lakes Health Care and Rehabilitation Center, 25 Fanning Street, Staten Island, NY 10314; tel. 718/289-7900; FAX. 718/761-8701; Michael M. Demisay

Concourse Rehab and Nursing Center, Inc., 1072 Grand Concourse, Bronx, NY 10456; tel. 718/681-4000; Helen Neiman

Cortland Care Center, 193 Clinton Avenue, Cortland, NY 13045; tel. 607/756-9921; Anthony Salerno

Crown Nursing and Rehabilitation Center, 3457 Nostrand Avenue, Brooklyn, NY 11229; tel. 718/615-1100; FAX. 718/769-6901; Sally Gearhart Schnabel

Dumont Masonic Home, 676 Pelham Road, New Rochelle, NY 10805; tel. 914/632-9600; FAX. 914/632-4766; Beth Goldstein, Administrator

East Haven Nursing Home, 2323 Eastchester Road, Bronx, NY 10469; tel. 718/655-2848; FAX. 718/655-2750; Joseph Brachfeld, Administrator

Eger Health Care Center of Staten Island, 140 Meisner Avenue, Staten Island, NY 99999; tel. 718/979-1800; Adeline M. Conroy, RN, MPA

Franklin Center for Rehab and Nursing, 142-27 Franklin Avenue, Flushing, NY 11355; tel. 718/670-3400; Jack Friedman

Glengariff Health Care Center, P.O. Box 71, Glen Cove, NY 11542; tel. 516/676-1100; Kenneth R. Winston

Golden Gate Health Care Center, Inc., 191 Bradley Avenue, Staten Island, NY 10314; tel. 718/698-8800; FAX. 718/698-5536; Alan Chopp, Administrator

Gouverneur Nursing Facility and Certified Home Health Agency, 311 East Broadway, New York, NY 10002; tel. 212/238-7847; FAX. 212/238-8007; Alan H. Rosenblut, FACHE

Grace Plaza of Great Neck, Inc., 15 St. Paul's Place, Great Neck, NY 11021; tel. 516/466-3001; FAX. 516/829-3854; Celia Strow, Administrator

Haven Manor Health Care Center, 1441 Gateway Boulevard, Far Rockaway, NY 11691; tel. 718/471-1500; FAX. 718/868-0030; Aron Cytryn, Administrator

Highgate Manor of Cortland, Inc., 28 Kellogg Road, Cortland, NY 13045; tel. 607/753-9631; FAX. 607/756-2968; Richard M. Dowe

Highgate Manor of Rensselaer, Inc., 100 New Turnpike Road, Troy, NY 12182; tel. 518/235-1410; FAX. 518/235-1632; Daniel Leahey

Highland Healthcare Center, 160 Seneca Street, Wellsville, NY 14895; tel. 716/593-3750; James Fuller

Hilltop Manor of Niskayuna, 1805 Providence Avenue, Niskayuna, NY 12309; tel. 518/374-2212; FAX. 518/374-4330; Chris Alexander, Administrator

Indian River Nursing Home, Inc., 17 Madison Street, Granville, NY 12832; tel. 518/642-2710; Daniel L. Morris

M.J.G. Nursing Home Company, Inc., 4915 Tenth Avenue, Brooklyn, NY 11219; tel. 718/851-3710; FAX. 718/972-6120; Eli Feldman, Executive Vice President, Chief Executive Officer

Maplewood Nursing Home, Inc., 100 Daniel Drive, Webster, NY 14580-2983; tel. 716/872-1800; FAX. 716/872-2597; Gregory Chambery, Administrator

Margaret Tietz Center for Nursing Care, 164-11 Chapin Parkway, Jamaica, NY 11432; tel. 718/523-6400, ext. 705; FAX. 718/262-8839; Kenneth M. Brown, President, Chief Executive Officer

Mosolu Parkway Nursing Home, 3356 Perry Avenue, Bronx, NY 10467; tel. 718/655-3568; FAX. 718/515-5713; Issac Schapiro, Administrator

Nassau Extended Care Center, One Greenwich Street, Hempstead, NY 11550; tel. 516/565-4800; FAX. 516/565-4966; Caryl Benjamin

Oakwood Health Care Center, Inc., 200 Bassett Road, Williamsville, NY 14221; tel. 716/689-6681; Carla Chur

Oceanview Nursing Home, P.O. Box 628, Far Rockaway, NY 11691; tel. 718/471-6000; Louis Wolcowitz

Oneonta Nursing Home, 330 Chestnut Street, Oneonta, NY 13820; tel. 607/432-8500; Kristin Russell

Orchard Park Health Care Center, Inc., 6060 Armor Road, Orchard Park, NY 14127; tel. 716/662-4433; John G. Case

Palm Gardens Nursing Home, 615 Avenue C, Brooklyn, NY 11218; tel. 718/633-3300; FAX. 718/633-3320; Israel Lefkowitz, Administrator

Parker Jewish Institute for Health Care and Rehab, 271-11 76th Avenue, New Hyde Park, NY 11040; tel. 718/289-2100; David Glaser

Providence Rest, 3304 Waterbury Avenue, Bronx, NY 10465; tel. 718/931-3000; FAX. 718/863-0185; Sister Seline Mary Flores, C.S.J.B., Administrator

Rome Nursing Home, 950 Floyd Avenue, Rome, NY 13440; tel. 315/336-5400; Michael Svendsen

Rosewood Gardens Convalescent Home, Inc., 284 Troy Road, Rensselaer, NY 12144; tel. 518/286-1621; FAX. 518/286-1691; Beverly Benno, Administrator

Saint Cabrini Nursing Home, Inc., 115 Broadway, Dobbs Ferry, NY 10522; tel. 914/693-6800, ext. 500; FAX. 914/693-1731; Robert Gilpatrick, Chief Executive Officer

Sands Point Nursing Home, 1440 Port Washington Blvd., Port Washington, NY 11050; tel. 516/767-2320; David Moskowitz

Sarah R. Newman Nursing Home, 845 Palmer Avenue, Mamaroneck, NY 10543; tel. 914/777-6100; Audrey S. Weiner, DSW

Sea View Hospital Rehabilitation Center and Home, 460 Brielle Avenue, Staten Island, NY 10314; tel. 718/317-3000; FAX. 718/351-7898; Jane M. Lyons, Executive Director

Shorefront Jewish Geriatric Center, 3015 West 29th Street, Brooklyn, NY 11224; tel. 718/266-5700; FAX. 718/921-1616; Eli Feldman, Executive Vice President, Chief Executive Officer

St. Elizabeth Ann's Health Care and Rehab, 91 Tompkins Avenue, Staten Island, NY 10304; tel. 718/876-2035; Paul Rosenfield

St. Mary's Hospital for Children, Inc., 29-01 216th Street, Bayside, NY 11360; tel. 718/281-8800, ext. 8850; FAX. 718/279-2141; Burton Grebin, MD

The Center for Extended Care and Rehabilitation, 330 Community Drive, Manhasset, NY 11030; tel. 516/562-4050; FAX. 516/562-4545; John Gallagher

The Nathan Miller Center for Nursing Care, Inc., 220 West Post Road, White Plains, NY 10606; tel. 914/686-8880; FAX. 914/686-8216; Lorraine Goldman, Administrative Director

The Port Jefferson Health Car Facility, Dark Hollow Road, Port Jefferson, NY 11777; tel. 516/473-5400; Michael D. Miness

The Rosalind and Joseph Gurwin Jewish Geriatric, 68 Hauppauge Road, Commack, NY 11725; tel. 516/499-6500; Herbert H. Friedman

The Wartburg, Wartburg Place, Mount Vernon, NY 10552; tel. 914/699-0800, ext. 311; FAX. 914/699-2512; Dale Gatz

Throgs Neck Extended Care Facility, 707 Throgs Neck Expressway, Bronx, NY 10465; tel. 718/430-0003; FAX. 718/430-7024; George Stops, Administrator

TownHouse Extended Care Center, 755 Hempstead Turnpike, Uniondale, NY 11553; tel. 516/565-1900; Caryl Benjamin

Vestal Nursing Center, 860 Old Vestal Road, Vestal, NY 13850; tel. 607/754-4105; Denise B. Johnson

Victory Lake Nursing Center, 419 North Quaker Lane, P.O. Box 2008, Hyde Park, NY 12538; tel. 914/229-9177; FAX. 914/229-9819; Robert C. Farrow, M.P.H., Administrator

Waterview Nursing Care Center, 119-15 27th Avenue, Flushing, NY 11354; tel. 718/461-5000; FAX. 718/321-1984; Larry Slatky, Executive Director

Wayne Nursing Home, 3530 Wayne Avenue, Bronx, NY 10467; tel. 718/655-1700, ext. 541; FAX. 718/515-5650; Alexander Hartman, Assistant Administrator

Wesley Group, Inc., 630 East Avenue, Rochester, NY 14607-2194; tel. 716/473-1970; FAX. 716/241-2180; Jon R. Zemans, President, Chief Executive Officer

Wingate at Dutchess Rehabilitative Skilled Nursing, Three Summit Court, Fishkill, NY 12524; tel. 914/896-1500; FAX. 914/896-1531, ext. 600; Richard Herrick

NORTH CAROLINA

Alamance Health Care Center, 1987 Hilton Road, Burlington, NC 27217; tel. 910/226-0848; Howard Staples

American Transitional Care-Charlottte, 2616 East Fifth Street, Charlotte, NC 28204; tel. 704/333-5165; FAX. 704/372-6906; Jane Kinard

Asheville Health Care Center, 1270 Highway 70, Swannanoa, NC 28778; tel. 704/298-2214; Jacqueline R. Rio

Beverly Health Care Center, 1000 Western Boulevard, P.O. Box 7008, Tarboro, NC 27886-7008; tel. 919/823-0401; FAX. 919/823-1819; Effie Webb

Brian Center Health and Rehab, 3000 Houston Lane, Raleigh, NC 27610; tel. 919/231-6045; Cary Corley

Brian Center Health and Rehab – Asheboro, P.O. Box 4218, Asheboro, NC 27203; tel. 910/629-1447; Mary Lou James

Brian Center Health and Rehab – Eden, 226 North Oakland Avenue, Eden, NC 27288; tel. 910/623-1750; Helen S. Myers

Brian Center Health and Rehab – Goldsboro, 1700 Wayne Memorial Drive, Goldsboro, NC 27534; tel. 919/731-2805; Catherine T. Hollowell

Brian Center Health and Rehab – Hertford, 200 River Drive, Hertford, NC 27944; tel. 919/426-5391; Joseph G. France

Brian Center Health and Rehab – Salisbury, 635 Statesville Blvd., Salisbury, NC 28144; tel. 704/633-7390; Deborah Mathis

Brian Center Health and Rehab – Spruce Pine, 218 Laurel Creek Court, Spruce Pine, NC 28777; tel. 704/765-7312; Walt Cross

Brian Center Health and Rehab – Wallace, P.O. Box 966, Wallace, NC 28466; tel. 910/285-6646; Carl S. Burkhalter

Brian Center Health and Rehab – Weaverville, 78 Weaver Blvd., Weaverville, NC 28787; tel. 704/645-4297; Carol L. Prater

Brian Center Health and Rehab – Wilson, P.O. Box 3566, Wilson, NC 24329; tel. 919/237-6300; Dan R. Cotten

Brian Center Health and Rehab– Windsor, 1306 South King Street, Windsor, NC 27983; tel. 919/794-5146; Mary J. Tibbs

Brian Center Health and Rehabilitation–Durham, 6000 Fayetteville Road, Durham, NC 27713; tel. 919/544-9021; FAX. 919/544-0345; Carol Drum

Brian Center Health and Retirement, 5939 Reddman Road, Charlotte, NC 28212; tel. 704/563-6862; Jeffrey R. Bardo

Brian Center Health and Retirement, 4911 Brian Center Lane, Winston Salem, NC 27106; tel. 910/744-5674; Charles Lentz

Brian Center Health and Retirement – Clayton, 204 Dairy Road, Clayton, NC 27520; tel. 919/553-8232; Dennis Rechmond

Courtland Terrace Nursing Center, 2300 Aberdeen Blvd., Gastonia, NC 28054; tel. 704/834-4806; Wayne F. Shovelin, FACHE

Cypress Pointe Rehabilitation and Health Care Centre, 2006 South 16th Street, Wilmington, NC 28401; tel. 910/763-6271; FAX. 910/251-9803; Faye M. Kennedy, Administrator

Greensboro Health and Rehab Center, 1201 Carolina Street, Greensboro, NC 27401; tel. 910/275-0751; Timothy W. Lane

Horizon Rehabilitation Center, 3100 Erwin Road, Durham, NC 27705; tel. 919/383-1546; FAX. 919/382-0156; Maureen O'Neal, Administrator

Integrated Health Services of Charlotte at Hawthorne, 333 Hawthorne Lane, Charlotte, NC 28204; tel. 704/372-1270; FAX. 704/377-2059; Darryl Ehlers, Administrator

Integrated Health Services of Raleigh at Crabtree Valley, 3830 Blue Ridge Road, Raleigh, NC 27612; tel. 919/781-4900; FAX. 919/571-2583; Phillip Morris

Meadowbrook Manor of Siler City, 900 West Dolphin Street, Siler City, NC 27344; tel. 919/663-3431; Jack L. Russell

North Carolina Special Care Center, 4761 Ward Boulevard, Wilson, NC 27893; tel. 919/399-2112; FAX. 919/399-2138; William R. Benton, Jr.

OHIO

Americare Marion Nursing and Rehabilitation Center, 524 James Way, Marion, OH 43302–5890; tel. 614/389–6306; FAX. 614/389–4042; Debra Hart

Arbors East Subacute and Rehabilitation Center, 5500 East Broad Street, Columbus, OH 43213; tel. 614/575–9003; FAX. 614/575–9101; Alexander Bettinger, Administrator

Arbors West, 375 West Main Street, West Jefferson, OH 43162; tel. 614/879–7661; FAX. 614/879–7848; Mike Lacey

Arbors at Canton, 2714 13th Street, N.W., Canton, OH 44708; tel. 216/456–2842; FAX. 216/456–5343; Rick Kesic

Arbors at Delaware, 2270 Warrensburg Road, Delaware, OH 43015; tel. 614/369–9614; FAX. 614/363–5881; Kelly Darrow, Administrator

Arbors at Fairlawn, 575 S. Cleveland Massillon Rd., Fairlawn, OH 44333; tel. 614/791–2920; Steve Tarle

Arbors at Marietta, 400 Seventh Street, Marietta, OH 45750; tel. 614/373–3597; FAX. 614/373–3597; Pier C. Borra

Arbors at Milford, 5900 Meadowcreek Drive, Milford, OH 45150; tel. 513/248–1655; FAX. 513/248–0466; Deonne Schenk

Arbors at Sylvania, 7120 Post Sylvania Drive, Toledo, OH 43617; tel. 614/791–2920; Justin Borra

Arbors at Toledo Subacute and Rehabilitation Center, 2920 Cherry Street, Toledo, OH 43608; tel. 419/242–7458; FAX. 419/242–6514; Robert D. Brooks

Arlington Court Nursing and Rehab Center, 1605 NW Professional Plaza, Columbus, OH 43220; tel. 614/451–5677; Stephen R. Vrable

Aurora Manor Special Care Centre, 101 Bissell Road, Aurora, OH 44202; tel. 216/562–5000; FAX. 216/562–5181; Scott Bower, Administrator

Batavia Nursing and Convalescent Inn, 4000 Golden Age Drive, Batavia, OH 45103; tel. 513/732–6500; Robert Lehman

Bethany Lutheran Village, 6451 Far Hills Avenue, Centerville, OH 45459; tel. 937/433–2110; Willis O'Serr II

BridgePark Centre for Rehab and Nursing, 145 Olive Street, Akron, OH 44310; tel. 330/762–0901; Edward Husbands

Broadview Multi–Care Center/Rosepoint Pavilion, 5520 Broadview Road, Parma, OH 44134; tel. 216/749–4010, ext. 2167; Harold Shachter

Carriage Inn of Steubenville, 3102 St. Charles Drive, Steubenville, OH 43952; tel. 614/264–7161; Peter P. Merritt

Castle Nursing Homes, Inc., Sunset View Unit, 6180 State Road 83, P.O. Box 5001, Millersburg, OH 44654; tel. 330/674–0015; FAX. 330/674–2822; Mick DeWitt, Administrator

Cedarwood Plaza, 12504 Cedar Road, Cleveland Heights, OH 44106; tel. 216/371–3600; FAX. 216/371–3631; Bruce Dascal

College Park Nursing and Rehabilitation Center, 3201 County Road 16, Coshocton, OH 43812; tel. 614/622–2074; FAX. 614/622–5501; Robert Guilliams

Columbus Alzheimer Care Center, 700 Jasonway Avenue, Columbus, OH 43214; tel. 614/459–7050; Howard S. Covensky

Columbus Quality Care Nursing and Rehab, 4301 Clime Road North, Columbus, OH 43228; tel. 614/276–4400; Jonica L. Rose Graves

Columbus Rehabilitation and Subacute Institute, 44 South Souder Avenue, Columbus, OH 43222; tel. 614/228–5900, ext. 231; FAX. 614/228–3989; Robert D. Brooks, Executive Director

CommuniCare of Clifton, 625 Probasco Street, Cincinnati, OH 45220; tel. 513/281–2464; George Hagan

Community Care Center, 145 East College Street, Alliance, OH 44601; tel. 330/829–4000; Gordon E. Meinhart, Jr.

Community Multicare Center, 908 Symmes Road, P.O. Box 18669, Fairfield, OH 45014; tel. 513/868–6500; FAX. 513/844–8579; Anne Dahling, Chief Executive Officer

Continental Manor Nursing and Rehabilitation Center, 820 East Center Street, P.O. Box 157, Blanchester, OH 45107; tel. 937/783–4949; FAX. 937/783–4398; Nancy Hamann, Administrator

Cortland Quality Care Nursing and Rehabilitation Center, 369 North High Street, Cortland, OH 44410; tel. 216/638–4015; FAX. 216/638–4628; Joseph Neelis

Cuyahoga Falls Country Place, 2728 Bailey Road, Cuyahoga Falls, OH 44221; tel. 216/929–4231; Barry Schimer

DaySpring Health Care Center and Rehab, 8001 Dayton–Springfield Road, Fairborn, OH 45324; tel. 937/864–5037; John B. Hoenemeyer

Eastgate Health Care Center and Rehab, 4400 Glen Este–Withamsville Road, Cincinnati, OH 45245; tel. 513/752–3710; Barry N. Bortz

Franklin Plaza Extended Care, 3600 Franklin Blvd., Cleveland, OH 44113; tel. 216/651–1600; Bruce Daskal

Gables Care Center, 350 Lahm Drive, Hopedale, OH 43976; tel. 614/937–2900; Darlene Woods, RN, BSN

Gateway Health Care Center, Three Gateway Drive, Euclid, OH 44119; tel. 216/486–4949; FAX. 216/481–5155; Kristin West

Gibsonburg Health Care Center, 335 Windsor Lane, Gibsonburg, OH 43431; tel. 419/637–2104; Joe Chesney

Greenbriar Quality Care of Boardman, 8064 South Avenue, Boardman, OH 44512; tel. 216/726–3700; FAX. 216/726–2194; Joseph Neelis

Harborside Healthcare – Broadview Heights, 2801 East Royalton Road, Broadview Heights, OH 44147; tel. 216/526–4770; Marilyn E. Kramer

Harborside Healthcare – Swanton, 401 West Airport Highway, Swanton, OH 43558; tel. 419/825–1111; Lou Aronson

Harborside Healthcare – Troy, 512 Crescent Drive, Troy, OH 45373; tel. 513/335–7161; Roger W. Walker

Harborside Healthcare – Westlake I, 27601 Westchester Parkway, Westlake, OH 44145; tel. 216/871–9600; Elizabeth T. Benson

Harborside Healthcare–Difiance, 395 Harding Street, Defiance, OH 43512; tel. 419/784–1450; FAX. 419/784–9190; Tim Ross

Harborside Healthcare–Northwestern Ohio, 1104 Wesley Avenue, Bryan, OH 43506; tel. 419/636–5071; FAX. 419/636–3894; Randi Kiphen, Administrator

Harborside Healthcare–Toledo, 28546 Starbright Boulevard, Perrysburg, OH 43551; tel. 419/666–0935; FAX. 419/666–5610; Steven Rankin, Administrator

Heartland of Beavercreek, 1974 North Fairfield Road, Dayton, OH 45432; tel. 937/429–1106; FAX. 937/429–0902; Jim Kyle, Administrator

Heartland of Centerburg, 212 Fairview Avenue, P.O. Box 720, Centerburg, OH 43011; tel. 614/625–5774; FAX. 614/625–7426; Laurie Zinn, Administrator

Heartland of Holly Glen, 4293 Monroe Street, Toledo, OH 43601; tel. 419/474–6021; FAX. 419/475–1946; Kenneth M. Zielinski

Heartland of Kettering, 3313 Wilmington Pike, Kettering, OH 45429; tel. 513/298–8084; Bob Perry

Heartland of Marysville, 755 South Plum Street, Marysville, OH 43040; tel. 937/644–8836; FAX. 937/644–1811; Paul J. LeGrande, Administrator

Heartland of Mentor, 8300 Center Street, Mentor, OH 44060; tel. 216/256–1496; FAX. 216/256–4935; Elizabeth Schupp

Heartland of Oak Ridge, 450 Oak Ridge Blvd., Miamisburg, OH 45342; tel. 513/866–8885; Jenny Miller

Heartland of Perrysburg, 10540 Fremont Pike, Perrysburg, OH 443551; tel. 419/874–3578; FAX. 419/874–7753; Kelly A. Eberflus

Heartland of Springfield, 2615 Derr Road, Springfield, OH 45503; tel. 937/390–0005; Thomas Cunningham

Heather Hill Hospital, Health Care Center, 12340 Bass Lake Road, Chardon, OH 44024; tel. 216/942–6424; Robert G. Harr

Heatherdowns Convalescent Center, 2401 Cass Road, Toledo, OH 43614; tel. 419/382–5050; Allen R. Dunlap

Hickory Creek Nursing Center, 3421 Pinnacle Road, Dayton, OH 45418; tel. 513/268–3488; FAX. 513/268–1889; Sherri Klein

Hickory Creek of Athena, P.O. Box 98, The Plains, OH 45780; tel. 614/797–4561; David Dixon

Hillebrand Nursing Center, 4320 Bridgetown Road, Cincinnati, OH 45211; tel. 513/598–3999; Michelle Glass Schneider

Horizon Village Nursing and Rehabilitation Center, 2473 North Road, Northeast, Warren, OH 44483; tel. 330/372–2251; FAX. 330/372–6478; Albert C. Parton, Administrator

IHS at Carriage–by–the–Lake, 1957 North Lakeman Drive, Bellbrook, OH 45305; tel. 513/848–8421; Melissa S. Bennett

IHS at Waterford Commons Subacute Care and Rehabilitation Center, 955 Garden Lake Parkway, Toledo, OH 43614; tel. 419/382–2200; FAX. 419/381–0188; Mary E. McConnell, Administrator

IHS of New London at Firelands, 204 West Main Street, New London, OH 44851; tel. 419/929–1563; Melanie A. Bair

Integrated Health Services of Huber Heights, 5440 Charlesgate Road, Huber Heights, OH 45424; tel. 513/236–6707; Shirley Wing

Ivy Woods Health Care and Rehab Center, 2025 Wyoming Avenue, Cincinnati, OH 45205; tel. 513/251–2557; Barbara Wolf

Kettering Convalescent Center, 1150 West Dorothy Lane, Kettering, OH 45409; tel. 937/293–1152; Brian Eshelman

Laurie Ann Nursing Home and Home Health, 2200 Milton Blvd., Newton Falls, OH 44444; tel. 330/872–1990; Doris Hooberry

Lebanon Country Manor, 700 Monroe Road, Lebanon, OH 45036; tel. 513/932–0105; Russell M. Holtz

Lebanon Health Care Center, P.O. Box 376, Lebanon, OH 44660; tel. 513/932–1121; W. E. Ullum

Leisure Oaks Convalescent Center, 214 Harding Street, Defiance, OH 43512; tel. 419/784–1014; Robert D. Moore

Life Care Center of Medina, 2400 Columbia Road, Medina, OH 44256; tel. 330/483–3131; James M. Breuler

Llanfair Retirement Community, 1701 Llanfair Avenue, Cincinnati, OH 45224; tel. 513/681–4230; Mariellen Sutton

Manor Care Health Services, 23225 Lorain Road, North Olmsted, OH 44070; tel. 216/779–6900; FAX. 216/779–1859; Shelly Szarek–Skodny, NHA, Administrator

Manor Care Health Services of Willoughby, 37603 Euclid Avenue, Willoughby, OH 44094; tel. 216/951–5551; FAX. 216/951–1914; Arlene Manross

Manor Care Health Services–Mayfield Heights, 6757 Mayfield Road, Mayfield Heights, OH 44124; tel. 216/473–0090; FAX. 216/473–1170; Arlene Manross, Administrator

Manor Care Nursing Center–Rocky River, 4102 Rocky River Drive, Cleveland, OH 44135; tel. 216/251–3300; FAX. 216/251–0201; James Kallevig

Manor Care Nursing and Rehabilitation Center, 140 County Line Road, Westerville, OH 43081; tel. 614/882–1511; FAX. 614/882–5318; Brian Casey

Manor Care Nursing and Rehabilitation Center, 2250 Banning Road, Cincinnati, OH 45239; tel. 513/591–0400; FAX. 513/591–0100; Aileen Baker

ManorCare Health Services, 5970 Kenwood Road, Madeira, OH 45243; tel. 513/561–4111; Virginia Uehlin

ManorCare Health Services – Fairfield, 3801 Woodridge Boulevard, Fairfield, OH 45014; tel. 513/874–9933; Michael Snow

ManorCare Health Services of Akron, 1211 West Market Street, Akron, OH 44313; tel. 330/867–8530; FAX. 330/867–9159; Steve Banium, Jr.

ManorCare at Sycamore Glen, 2175 Leiter Road, Miamisburg, OH 45342; tel. 513/866–5700; Susan Emmons

Maple Knoll Village, 11100 Springfield Pike, Cincinnati, OH 45246; tel. 513/782–2400; Jerry D. Smart

Mayfair Village Subacute and Rehabilitation Center, 3000 Bethel Road, Columbus, OH 43220; tel. 614/889–7532; FAX. 614/889–7532; Cheryl Guyman, Executive Director

McCaulley Care Center, 1670 Crider Road, Mansfield, OH 44903; tel. 419/589–6222; Chenessa McCaulley

McCrea Manor Nursing and Rehab, 2040 McCrea Street, Alliance, OH 44601; tel. 330/823–9005; Arnold Levine

Menorah Park Center for the Aging, 27100 Cedar Road, Beachwood, OH 44122–1156; tel. 216/831–6500; FAX. 216/831–5492; Steven Raichilson

Newark Healthcare Centre, 75 McMillen Drive, Newark, OH 43055; tel. 614/344–0357; FAX. 614/344–8615; Amy Cajka, Administrator

Northland Terrace Medical Center for Subacute Care and Rehabilitation, 5700 Karl Road, Columbus, OH 43229; tel. 614/846–5420; FAX. 614/846–3247; Colleen E. Samson

Oak Grove Quality Care, 620 East Water Street, Deshler, OH 43516; tel. 419/278-6921; Glenn T. Adrian

Orchard Villa, 2841 Munding Drive, Oregon, OH 43616; tel. 419/697-4100; Ray Nevarez

Pleasant Lake Villa, 7260 Ridge Road, Parma, OH 44129; tel. 216/842-2273; Michael L. Milbrandt

Regency Manor Rehabilitation and Subacute Center, 2000 Regency Manor Circle, Columbus, OH 43207; tel. 614/445-8261; FAX. 614/445-8050; Jeffreys Barrett

Rockmill Rehab Centre, 3680 Dolson Court NW, Carroll, OH 43112; tel. 614/654-0641; Ray Sill

Scenic Hills, 311 Buckridge Road, Bidwell, OH 45614; tel. 614/446-7150; Dennis Swatrzbaugh

Somerset Quality Care Nursing and Rehab, 411 South Columbus Street, Somerset, OH 43783; tel. 614/743-2924; Richard M. Tobin

St. Augustine Manor, 7801 Detroit Avenue, Cleveland, OH 44102; tel. 216/634-7400; FAX. 216/634-7483; Patrick Gareau, President, Chief Executive Officer

The Convalarium at Indian Run, 6430 Post Road, Dublin, OH 43016; tel. 614/761-1188; Colleen Samson

The Franciscan at Schroder, 1300 Millville Avenue, Hamilton, OH 45013; tel. 513/867-1300; R. Christopher West

The Franciscan at St. Clare, 100 Compton Avenue, Cincinnati, OH 45215; tel. 513/761-9036; R. Christopher West

The Franciscan at St. Leonard, 8100 Clyo Road, Centerville, OH 45459; tel. 937/433-0480; FAX. 937/439-7165; R. Christopher West, PhD.

The Franciscan at West Park, 2950 West Park Drive, Cincinnati, OH 45238; tel. 513/451-8900; R. Christopher West

The Maria-Joseph Center, 4830 Salem Avenue, Dayton, OH 45416-1798; tel. 937/278-2692; FAX. 937/278-9016; Bonnie G. Langdon, President, Chief Executive Officer

The Northwestern Quality Care Skilled Nursing/Rehab, 570 North Rocky River Drive, Berea, OH 44017; tel. 216/243-2122; Alicia Turk

The Village at Westerville Nursing Center, 1060 Eastwind Drive, Westerville, OH 43081; tel. 614/895-1038; FAX. 614/895-1094; Pamela M. DeGroodt, Administrator

Walnut Creek Nursing Center, 5070 Lamme Road, Kettering, OH 45439; tel. 937/293-7703; Paul DePalma

Walton Manor Health Care Center, 19859 Alexander Road, Walton Hills, OH 44146; tel. 216/439-4433; FAX. 216/439-0691; Deborah D. Fannin

West Chester Health Care, 9117 Cincinnati-Columbus Road, West Chester, OH 45069; tel. 513/777-6164; FAX. 513/777-6158; Wilma Willard, President

Wickliffe Country Place, 1919 Bishop Road, Wickliffe, OH 44092; tel. 216/944-9400; Joseph D. Wilson

Willard Quality Care Nursing and Rehabilitation Center, 725 Wessor Avenue, Willard, OH 44890; tel. 419/935-6511; FAX. 419/935-8494; Joseph Neelis

OKLAHOMA

Georgian Court Nursing Center, 2552 East 21st Street, Tulsa, OK 74114-1788; tel. 918/742-7319; FAX. 918/742-5270; Brian H. Hoyle, Chief Executive Officer

Manor Care Health Services, 5301 North Brookline, Oklahoma City, OK 73112; tel. 405/946-3351; FAX. 405/946-3647; Deborah Burian, Administrator

ManorCare Health Services - Midwest City, 2900 Parklawn Drive, Midwest City, OK 73110; tel. 405/737-6601; FAX. 405/737-4984; Chiquita Henderson

ManorCare Health Services - Tulsa, 2425 South Memorial, Tulsa, OK 74129; tel. 918/628-0932; FAX. 918/622-2060; Phillip Howard

Saint Simeon's Episcopal Home, Inc., 3701 North Cincinnati, Tulsa, OK 74106; tel. 918/425-3583; FAX. 918/425-6368; Marian Matthews, Executive Director

OREGON

Cascade Terrace Nursing Center, 5601 Southeast 122nd Avenue, Portland, OR 97236; tel. 503/761-3181; FAX. 503/760-6556; Diane Richardson, Administrator

Meadow Park Health and Specialty Care Center, 75 Shore Drive, St. Helens, OR 97051; tel. 503/397-2713; Michael McCoy

Villa Cascade Care Center, 350 South Eighth Street, Lebanon, OR 97355; tel. 503/259-1221; FAX. 503/451-1349; Kathy Elias

PENNSYLVANIA

Allegheny Manor, 512 South Paint Boulevard, Shippenville, PA 16254; tel. 814/226-5660; FAX. 814/226-9896; Brad W. Nowlen

Altoona Hospital Center for Nursing Care, 1020 Green Avenue, Altoona, PA 16601; tel. 814/946-2700; Felix J. Mariani

American Transitional Care-Oakmont, 26 Ann Street, Oakmont, PA 15139; tel. 412/828-7300; FAX. 412/828-2669; Brad Nowlen, Executive Director

Attleboro Nursing and Rehab Center, 300 East Winchester Avenue, Langhorne, PA 19047; tel. 215/757-3739; Kathleen Krick

Bishop Nursing Home, Inc., 318 South Orange Street, P.O. Box 527, Media, PA 19063; tel. 215/565-3881; FAX. 215/891-6509; Anne Campbell

Brinton Manor Genesis Eldercare, 549 Baltimore Park, Glen Mills, PA 19342; tel. 610/358-6005; Earle Kimble

Buckingham Valley Rehabilitation and Nursing Center, 820 Durham Road, Route 413, P.O. Box 447, Buckingham, PA 18912; tel. 215/598-7181; Mary Elena Shaw, RN, M.S., NHA, Administrator

Chandler Hall Friends Nursing Home/Hospice Home Health Agency, 99 Barclay Street, Newtown, PA 18940; tel. 215/860-4000; FAX. 215/860-3458; Jane Fox, Executive Director

Chester Care Center, 15th Street and Shaw Terrace, Chester, PA 19013; tel. 215/499-8800; FAX. 215/499-8805; Barbara Quaintance, Administrator

Clara Burke Community, 251 Stenton Avenue, Plymouth Meeting, PA 19462; tel. 610/828-2272; FAX. 610/828-2519; Karen Pulini

Dowden Nursing and Rehabilitation Center, 3503 Rhoads Avenue, Newtown Square, PA 19073; tel. 610/359-0300; FAX. 610/359-1187; Rosemary T. Stewart

Dresher Hill Health and Rehab Center, 1390 Camphill Road, Dresher, PA 19025; tel. 214/643-0600; Mark J. Crispen

Erie Rehabilitation and Nursing Center, 2686 Peach Street, Erie, PA 16508; tel. 814/453-6641; FAX. 814/453-5546; Marguerite Jones, RN

Fellowship Manor, 3000 Fellowship Drive, Whitehall, PA 18052; tel. 610/799-3000; Robert H. Zentz

Fox Subacute Center, 2644 Bristol Road, Warrington, PA 18976; tel. 215/343-2700; James M. Foulke

Frey Village Retirement Center, 1020 North Union Street, Middletown, PA 17057; tel. 717/944-0451; David J. Bell

Gettysburg Lutheran Home, 1075 Old Harrisburg Road, Gettysburg, PA 17325; tel. 717/334-6204; Christina M. Ransier

Golden Slipper Club Uptown Home for the Aged, 7800 Bustleton Avenue, Philadelphia, PA 19152; tel. 215/722-2300; Lee M. Davidson

Good Samaritan Nursing Care Center, 1017 Franklin Street, Johnstown, PA 15905; tel. 814/533-1934; Karen S. Wood

Green Acres Rehabilitation and Nursing Center, 1401 Ivy Hill Road, Wyndmoor, PA 19118; tel. 215/233-5605; FAX. 215/836-1050; Elizabeth Dempsey

Greenery Rehabilitation and Skilled Nursing Center at Meadowlands, 2200 Hill Church-Houston Road, Canonsburg, PA 15317; tel. 412/745-8000, ext. 212; FAX. 412/746-8780; Patricia B. Speak

Hanover Hall Nursing and Rehabilitation Center, 267 Frederick Street, Hanover, PA 17331; tel. 717/637-8937; FAX. 717/633-5700; Christine F. Lorah, NHA, Administrator

Harlee Manor Nursing and Rehab Center, 463 West Sproul Road, Springfield, PA 19064; tel. 610/544-2200; Jeffrey T. Brown

Harmon House Convalescent Center, 601 South Church Street, Mount Pleasant, PA 15666; tel. 412/547-1890; Dennis J. Murphy

Haverford Nursing and Rehabilitation Center, 2050 Old West Chester Pike, Havertown, PA 19083-2798; tel. 610/449-8600; FAX. 610/446-1266; Russell W. Twigg

Heartland Health Care Center, 550 South Negley, Pittsburgh, PA 15232; tel. 412/665-2400; FAX. 412/363-6146; Deborah Koch, Administrator

Heatherbank Rehabilitation and Skilled Nursing Center, 745 Chiques Hill Road, Columbia, PA 17512; tel. 717/684-7555; FAX. 717/684-0571; Webster McCormack

Heritage Towers, 200 Veterans Lane, Doylestown, PA 18901; tel. 215/345-4300; Bruce L. Lenich

Hillview Health and Rehab Center, 700 South Cayuga Avenue, Altoona, PA 16602; tel. 814/946-0471; William A. Mathies

Homestead Center, 1113 North Easton Road, Willow Grove, PA 19090; tel. 215/659-3060; Elizabeth Thormaldes

IHS at Mt. View, RD #7 Box 249, Sandy Hill Road, Greensburg, PA 15601; tel. 412/837-6499; Carl P. Kovski

IHS of Erie at Bayside, 4114 Schaper Avenue, Erie, PA 16508; tel. 818/868-0831; Gary L. Plasschaert

Indian Creek Nursing Center, 222 West Edison Avenue, New Castle, PA 16101; tel. 412/652-6340; Caroline Gibson

Integrated Health Services of Chestnut Hill, 8833 Stenton Avenue, Wyndmoor, PA 19038; tel. 215/836-2100; FAX. 215/233-3551; Karen Pulini

Integrated Health Services of Greater Pittsburgh, 890 Mount Pleasant Road, Greensburg, PA 15601; tel. 412/837-8076; FAX. 412/837-3152; James Anthony Palmer, Administrator

Integrated Health Services of Pennsylvania at Broomall, 50 North Malin Road, Broomall, PA 19008; tel. 610/356-0800; FAX. 610/325-9499; Susan Eccles

Integrated Health Services of Pennsylvania at Plymouth, 900 East Germantown Avenue, Norristown, PA 19401; tel. 610/279-7300; FAX. 610/279-2061; Elaine Addlespurger

Jefferson Manor Health Centers, Rural Route Five, Brookville, PA 15825; tel. 814/849-8026; FAX. 814/849-3889; Karen Wilshire, BSN, MS

Kittanning Care Center, RD 1, Box 27C, Kittanning, PA 16201; tel. 412/545-2273; Richard R. Adams

LAS/St. John Specialty Care Center, 500 Wittenberg Way, P.O. Box 928, Mars, PA 16046; tel. 412/625-1571; FAX. 412/625-0087; Lynn Croushore, Executive Director

LGAR Health and Rehab Center, 800 Elsie Street, Turtle Creek, PA 15145; tel. 412/825-9000; Sandra S. O'Toole

Lancashire Hall Nursing and Rehabilitation Center, 2829 Lititz Pike, Lancaster, PA 17601; tel. 717/569-3211; FAX. 717/569-1569; Sandra K. Griffin

Langhorne Gardens Rehabilitation and Nursing Center, 350 Manor Avenue, Langhorne, PA 19047; tel. 215/757-7667; FAX. 215/750-1426; Deborah Haugh

Laurel Nursing and Rehabilitation Center, 125 Holly Road, Hamburg, PA 19526-6902; tel. 610/562-2284; FAX. 610/562-0775; Maria A. Wagner

Laurel Wood Convalescent Center, 100 Woodmont Road, Johnstown, PA 15905; tel. 814/255-1488; James E. Neely

Leader Nursing and Rehabilitation Center, 60 Highland Road, Bethel Park, PA 15102; tel. 412/831-6050; FAX. 412/831-7465; Karen Loeffler

Leader Nursing and Rehabilitation Center II, 2029 Westgate Drive, Bethlehem, PA 18017; tel. 610/861-0100; FAX. 610/861-4078; Adam Utan NHA, MS

Liberty Nursing and Rehabilitation Center, Inter Med Unit, 17th and Allen Streets, Allentown, PA 18104; tel. 610/432-4351; FAX. 610/435-4470; M. J. Specter, N.H.A., Administrator

LifeQuest Nursing Center, 2450 John Fries Highway, Quakertown, PA 18951; tel. 215/536-0770; Bruce C. Moorehead

Luther Woods Convalescent Center, 313 West County Line Road, Hatboro, PA 19040; tel. 215/675-5005; Lynn S. McLaughlin

Main Line Nursing and Rehabilitation Center, 283 East Lancaster Avenue, Malvern, PA 19355; tel. 610/296-4170; FAX. 610/296-7051; John Hadgkiss

Manchester House Nursing and Convalescent Center, 411 Manchester Avenue, Media, PA 19063; tel. 610/565-1800; FAX. 610/891-0471; Marian Ardinger

Manor Care Health Services, 14 Lincoln Avenue, Yeadon, PA 19050; tel. 610/626-7700; FAX. 610/626-5319; Stewart Bainum

Manor Care Health Services, 3430 Huntingdon Pike, Huntingdon Valley, PA 19006; tel. 215/938-7171; FAX. 215/938-7338; J. P. Cronin

Manor Care Health Services, 1848 Greentree Road, Pittsburgh, PA 15220; tel. 412/344-7744; FAX. 412/344-5502; Linda Keith, Executive Director

Manor Care Health Services, 600 West Valley Forge Road, King of Prussia, PA 19406; tel. 610/337-1775; FAX. 610/337-3638; Carolyn Floyd

Manor Care Health Services - Lansdale, 640 Bethlehem Pike, Montgomeryville, PA 18936; tel. 215/368-4350; Jason Klaskin

ManorCare Health Services, 1070 Stouffer Avenue, Chambersburg, PA 17201; tel. 717/263–0436; FAX. 717/263–7468; Caroline Lensbower, NHA, Administrator

ManorCare Health Services, 1070 Stouffer Avenue, Chambersburg, PA 17201; tel. 717/263–0436; Caroline R. Lensbower, NHA

ManorCare Health Services, 800 King Russ Road, Harrisburg, PA 17109; tel. 717/657–1520; Wesley Bartlett

ManorCare Health Services, 113 West McMurray Road, McMurray, PA 12890; tel. 412/941–3080; John M. Walsh

ManorCare Health Services, 1105 Perry Highway, Pittsburgh, PA 15237; tel. 412/369–9955; Martin Russell

ManorCare Health Services, 1480 Oxford Valley Road, Yardley, PA 19067; tel. 215/321–3921; Thomas P. Garvin

ManorCare Health Services – Carlisle, 940 Walnut Bottom Road, Carlisle, PA 17013; tel. 717/249–0085; Kathleen Eisenhart, NHA, MS

ManorCare Health Services – Kingston, 200 Second Avenue, Kingston, PA 18704; tel. 717/288–9315; Raymond Benkoski

ManorCare Health Services – Lancaster, 100 Abbeyville Road, Lancaster, PA 17603; tel. 717/397–4261; Teri Lutz

ManorCare Health Services – Laureldale, 2125 Elizabeth Avenue, Laureldale, PA 19605; tel. 610/921–9292; Linda Vignati

ManorCare Health Services – Pottstown, 724 North Charlotte Street, Pottstown, PA 19464; tel. 610/323–1837; Mark Edquid

ManorCare Health Services – Pottsville, Leader and Pulaski Drives, Pottsville, PA 17901; tel. 717/622–9582; Mary Cumers

ManorCare Health Services – Williamsport North, 300 Leader Drive, Williamsport, PA 17701; tel. 717/323–8627; Anne E. Holladay, NHA

ManorCare Health Services – Yeadon, 14 Lincoln Avenue, Yeadon, PA 19050; tel. 610/626–7700; Stewart Bainum Jr.

ManorCare Health Services – York, 1770 Barley Road, York, PA 17404; tel. 717/767–6530; Marion Bittner

ManorCare Health Services Nursing and Rehabilitation Center, 1265 South Cedar Crest Boulevard, Allentown, PA 18103; tel. 610/776–5522; FAX. 610/776–0270; Judith Kempf, NHA

ManorCare Health Services at Fitzgerald Mercy, 600 South Wycombe Avenue, Yeadon, PA 19050; tel. 610/626–8065; Nancy Deutsch

ManorCare Health Services–West Reading, 425 Buttonwood Street, West Reading, PA 19611; tel. 610/373–5166; FAX. 610/374–7560; Robert McQuillan, NHA

Mariner Health at North Hills, 194 Swinderman Road, Wexford, PA 15090; tel. 412/935–3781; FAX. 412/935–0190; Nancy Flenner, Administrator

Mariner Health of West Hills, 951 Brodhead Road, Corapolis, PA 15108; tel. 412/269–1101; Bryan Sturgeon

Mount Lebanon Manor, 350 Gilkeson Road, Pittsburgh, PA 15228; tel. 412/257–4444; FAX. 412/257–8226; Anthony J. Molinaro, Administrator

Ohesson Manor, 276 Green Avenue Extended, Lewistown, PA 17044; tel. 717/242–1416; Harold E. Leiter, Jr.

Penn Lutheran Village, 800 Broad Street, Selinsgrove, PA 17870; tel. 717/374–8181; Donald S. Pole

Presbyterian Medical Center of Oakmont, 1215 Hulton Road, Oakmont, PA 15139; tel. 412/828–5600; FAX. 412/826–6121; Mary Pat Braudis, NHA, Executive Director

Providence Health Care Center, P.O. Box 140, Beaver Falls, PA 15010; tel. 412/846–8504; Richard N. Probert

Quakertown Nursing and Rehabilitation Center, 1020 South Main Street, Quakertown, PA 18950–1592; tel. 215/536–9300; FAX. 215/536–1970; Susan L. Ulmer

Quincy United Methodist Home, 6596 Orphanage Road, P.O. Box 217, Quincy, PA 17247; tel. 717/749–2000; FAX. 717/749–3912; Kathleen R. Hoos, RN, NHA, President

Redstone Highlands Health Care Center, Six Garden Center Drive, Greensburg, PA 15601–1397; tel. 412/832–8400; FAX. 412/836–3710; Ronald G. Barrett

Rest Haven–York, 1050 South George Street, York, PA 17403; tel. 717/843–9866; FAX. 717/846–5894; Robert L. Evans, MD

Richboro Care Center, 253 Twining Ford Road, Richboro, PA 18954; tel. 215/357–2032; FAX. 215/357–3444; Gale Bupp

River's Edge Nursing and Rehab Center, 9501 State Road, Philadelphia, PA 19114; tel. 215/632–5700; Maryann Voystock

Riverside Nursing Center, Inc., 100 Eighth Avenue, McKeesport, PA 15132; tel. 412/664–8860; Leonard S. Oddo

Rochester Manor, 174 Virginia Avenue, Rochester, PA 15074; tel. 412/775–6400; FAX. 412/775–4386; Kathryn Kopsack, Administrator

Rose View Manor, Inc., 1201 Rural Avenue, Williamsport, PA 17701; tel. 717/323–4340; FAX. 717/323–0836; Russell Twigg

Saratoga Manor Nursing and Rehabilitation Center, 225 Evergreen Road, Pottstown, PA 19464; tel. 610/323–1800; FAX. 610/323–7914; Russell Twigg

Saunders House, 100 Lancaster Avenue, Wynnewood, PA 19096; tel. 610/658–5100; FAX. 610/658–5101; William Grim

Sherwood Oaks, 100 Norman Drive, Cranberry Twp., PA 16066; tel. 412/776–8100; Judith F. Corner

Shrewsbury Lutheran Retirement Village, 200 Luther Road, Shrewsbury, PA 17361; tel. 717/235–6895; Barbara J. Egan, NC

Simpson House, Inc., 2101 Belmont Avenue, Philadelphia, PA 17503; tel. 215/878–3600; David W. Powell

South Mountain Restoration Center, 10058 South Mountain Road, South Mountain, PA 17261; tel. 717/749–3121, ext. 316; FAX. 717/749–3946; Thomas A. Buckus, Administrator

Statesman Health and Rehabilitation Center, 2629 Trenton Road, Levittown, PA 19056; tel. 215/943–7777; FAX. 215/943–1240; Charles Kane

Suburban General Extended Care Center, Inc., 2751 DeKalb Pike, Norristown, PA 19401; tel. 610/278–2700; Gail P. Clark

Sunset Manor Care Center, 81 Dillon Drive, Titusville, PA 16354; tel. 814/827–2727; Dana B. Walton

Susquehanna Lutheran Village, 990 Medical Road, Millersburg, PA 15826; tel. 717/692–4751; Joseph G. Mraz

Sycamore Manor Health Center, 1445 Sycamore Road, Montoursville, PA 17754; tel. 717/326–2037; Diane Burfeindt

The Belvedere Nursing and Rehab Center, 2507 Chestnut Street, Chester, PA 19013; tel. 610/872–5373; Gerald Miller

The Fairways at Brookline Village, 1950 Cliffside Drive, State College, PA 16801; tel. 814/238–3139; FAX. 814/235–2074; Clifford Coldren

The Healthcare Campus at Colonial Manor, 970 Colonial Avenue, York, PA 17403; tel. 717/845–2661; FAX. 717/854–0529; Amy M. Young

The Presbyterian Medical Center of Washington, 835 South Main Street, Washington, PA 15301; tel. 412/222–4300; FAX. 412/223–5697; Charles W. Pruitt

Township Manor Health and Rehab Center, 265 East Township Line Road, Elkins Park, PA 19027; tel. 214/379–2700; Alan Lavin

Twinbrook Medical Center, 3805 Field Street, Lawrence Park, Erie, PA 16511; tel. 814/898–5600; FAX. 814/899–9829; Lisa Grosso

Valley Manor Nursing and Rehabilitation Center, 7650 Route 309, Coopersburg, PA 18036; tel. 610/282–1919; FAX. 610/282–2962; Janice Ricchio, NHA

Wallingford Nursing and Rehabilitation Center, 115 South Providence Road, Wallingford, PA 19086; tel. 610/565–3232; FAX. 610/892–0830; Ventura Gutierrez

Wayne Center, 30 West Avenue, Wayne, PA 19087; tel. 610/688–3635; Dale Jacobs

Western Reserve Health and Rehabilitation Center, 1521 West 54th Street, Erie, PA 16509; tel. 814/864–0671; FAX. 814/864–1424; Connie L. Farabaugh, RN

Willow Ridge Nursing and Rehab Center, 3485 Davisville Road, Hatboro, PA 19040; tel. 215/830–0400; Carol E. L. Perfect

Woodhaven Care Center, 2400 McGinley Road, Monroeville, PA 15146; tel. 412/856–4770; FAX. 412/856–6856; Len Oddo

York Lutheran Home, 1801 Folkemer Circle, York, PA 15633; tel. 717/767–5404; Morris K. Snyder

RHODE ISLAND

Cherry Hill Manor, 2 Cherry Hill Road, Johnston, RI 02919; tel. 401/231–3102; Jeffrey Martin

Elmhurst Extended Care Facility, 50 Maude Street, Providence, RI 02908; tel. 401/456–2623; Richard E. Fishpaw

Evergreen House Health Center, One Evergreen Drive, East Providence, RI 02914; tel. 401/438–3250; FAX. 410/438–3250; Madeline Ernest

Heatherwood Nursing and Subacute Center, Inc., 398 Bellevue Avenue, Newport, RI 02840; tel. 401/849–6600; FAX. 401/847–0778; Lou Pugliese

Kent Nursing and Rehab Center, Inc., 660 Commonwealth Avenue, Warwick, RI 02886; tel. 401/739–4241; Carol A. Sloan

Morgan Health Center, 80 Morgan Avenue, Johnston, RI 02919; tel. 401/944–7800; FAX. 401/944–6037; David Ryan

Oak Hill Nursing and Rehabilitation Center, 544 Pleasant Street, Pawtucket, RI 02860; tel. 401/725–8888; FAX. 401/723–5720; Richard E. Gamache, Administrator

Oakland Grove Health Care Center, 560 Cumberland Hill Road, Woonsocket, RI 02895; tel. 401/769–0800; FAX. 401/766–3661; Michelle V. Thurman

Saint Elizabeth Home, 109 Melrose Street, Providence, RI 02907–1898; tel. 401/941–0200; FAX. 401/941–5231; Steven J. Horowitz, Administrator

South County Nursing and Subacute Center, 740 Oak Hill Road, North Kingstown, RI 02852; tel. 401/294–4545; John E. Gage

Steere House Nursing and Rehabilitation Center, 100 Borden Street, Providence, RI 02903; tel. 401/454–7970; FAX. 401/831–7570; Steven Farrow

The Clipper Home, Inc., 161 Post Road, Westerly, RI 02891; tel. 401/322–8081; Mark Hambley

Watch Hill Manor, Ltd., 79 Watch Hill Road, Westerly, RI 02891; tel. 401/596–2664; Linda A. Tucker

SOUTH CAROLINA

C. M. Tucker, Jr./Dowdy Gardner Nursing Care Center, 2200 Harden Street, Columbia, SC 29203–7199; tel. 803/737–5302; FAX. 803/737–5342; Shielda Friendly, Director

Heartland Health Care Center of Charleston, 1800 Eagle Landing Boulevard, Hanahan, SC 29406; tel. 803/553–0656; FAX. 803/553–9773; Paul J. Cercone, Administrator

Integrated Health Services of Charleston at Driftwood, 2375 Baker Hospital Boulevard, North Charleston, SC 29405; tel. 803/744–2750; FAX. 803/747–0406; B. C. Davidson, Administrator

Life Care Center of Charleston, 2600 Elms Plantation Boulevard, North Charleston, SC 29418; tel. 803/764–3500; FAX. 803/569–7222; Betty Whittle, Executive Director

Life Care Center of Columbia, 2514 Faraway Drive, Columbia, SC 29223; tel. 803/865–1999; FAX. 803/865–0759; Louis Milite

Manor Care Nursing and Rehabilitation Center, 2416 Sunset Boulevard, West Columbia, SC 29169; tel. 803/796–8024; FAX. 803/796–5485; Colette Pickett

ManorCare – Columbia, 2601 Forest Drive, Columbia, SC 29204; tel. 803/256–4983; Tom Heschel

National HealthCare Center Greenville, 1305 Boiling Springs Road, Greer, SC 29650; tel. 864/458–7566; Thomas J. Bell

Oakmont East, 601 Sulphur Springs Road, Greenville, SC 29611; tel. 864/246–2721; FAX. 864/246–7563; Douglas P. Helman

Prince George HealthCare Center, 901 Maple Street, Georgetown, SC 29440; tel. 803/546–6101; Carole Campbell

Roper Nursing Center, 2230 Ashley Crossing Drive, Charleston, SC 29417; tel. 803/852–2273; John Driggers

Springdale HealthCare Center, 146 Battleship Road, Camden, SC 29020; tel. 803/432–3741; Karl Elezar, ADM

SOUTH DAKOTA

Colonial Manor Health and Rehab Center, P.O. Box 620, Salem, SD 57058; tel. 605/425–2203; Bruce Glanzer

Covington Heights Health and Rehab Center, 3900 South Cathy Avenue, Sioux Falls, SD 57106; tel. 605/361–8822; Carol Ulmer

Rapid City Care Center, 916 Mountain View, Rapid City, SD 57702; tel. 605/343–8577; Bruce Glanzer

Whetstone Valley Care Center, 1103 South 2nd Street, Milbank, SD 57252; tel. 605/432–4556; Terry Rieck

TENNESSEE

Allen Morgan Health Center, 177 North Highland, Memphis, TN 38111; tel. 901/325-4003; FAX. 901/327-8847; James A. Brooks

Brandywood Rehab Center, 555 East Bledsoe Street, Gallatin, TN 37066; tel. 615/452-7132; Dan Haynes

Briarcliff Health Care Center, 100 Elmhurst Drive, Oak Ridge, TN 37803; tel. 423/481-3367; FAX. 423/483-7121; Charles Birkett

Farragut Health Care Center, 12823 Kingston Pike, Knoxville, TN 37922; tel. 423/966-0600; B. Scott Hunt

Laurel Manor Health Care, 902 Buchanan Road, New Tazewell, TN 37825; tel. 423/626-8215; FAX. 423/626-0676; Charles Birkett

Life Care Center of Athens, P.O. Box 786, Athens, TN 36585; tel. 423/754-8181; Kirk Rogers

Life Care Center of Collegedale, P.O. Box 658, Collegedale, TN 37315; tel. 423/396-2182; Richard Mountz

Life Care Center of East Ridge, 1500 Fincher Avenue, East Ridge, TN 37412; tel. 423/894-1254; Martha A. Johnson

Life Care Center of Jefferson City, 336 West Old A. J. Highway, Jefferson City, TN 37760; tel. 423/475-6097; Beverly M. Wingard

Life Care Center of Morristown, P.O. Box 1899, Morristown, TN 37814; tel. 423/581-5435; Marvin Frey

Life Care Center of Tullahoma, 1715 North Jackson Street, Tullahoma, TN 37388; tel. 615/455-8557; David Goodcase

Manor House of Dover, 537 Spring Street, P.O. Box 399, Dover, TN 37058-8039; tel. 615/232-6902; FAX. 615/232-4256; Cindy Darby

Martin Health Care Facility, 158 Mt. Pelia Road, Martin, TN 38237; tel. 901/587-0503; Charles Birkett

McKendree Village, Inc., 4343-47 Lebanon Road, Hermitage, TN 37076; tel. 615/871-8232; Robert F. Willner, MD, ABPN

Mountainview Rehab and Nursing Center, 1360 Bypass Road, Winchester, TN 37398; tel. 615/967-7082; Gregory J. Fursey

NHC HealthCare, 2120 Highland Ave., Knoxville, TN 37916; tel. 423/525-4131; Douglas S. Ford

Natinal HealthCare - Murfreesboro, 420 North University Street, Murfreesboro, TN 37133-2009; tel. 615/893-2602; FAX. 615/890-1224; Greg Bidwell

Ridgeview Terrace of Life Care, P.O. Box 26, Rutledge, TN 37861; tel. 423/828-5295; Scott W. Garvin

Woods Memorial Hospital District, Highway 411 and Old Grady Road, P.O. Box 410, Etowah, TN 37331; tel. 615/263-3605; FAX. 615/263-3793; Phil Campbell

TEXAS

Allenbrook Health Care Center, 4109 Allenbrook Drive, Baytown, TX 77521; tel. 713/422-3546; John E. Dugan

Autumn Years Lodge, 424 South Adams, Fort Worth, TX 76104; tel. 817/335-5781; Tricia Heath

Beacon Health, Ltd., 9182 Six Pines Drive, The Woodlands, TX 77380; tel. 281/364-0317; FAX. 281/298-7366; Kathy Roberts

Beechnut Manor Living Center, 12777 Beechnut Street, Houston, TX 77072; tel. 713/879-8040; FAX. 713/879-5616; Kenneth Morgan

Brazos Valley Geriatric Center, 1115 Anderson Street, College Station, TX 77840; tel. 409/693-1515; Darryl Thomas

Brookhaven Nursing Center, 1855 Cheyenne, Carrollton, TX 75008; tel. 972/394-7141; FAX. 972/492-5534; William W. Weeks

Bureau of Prisons-Federal Medical Center, 3150 Horton Road, Fort Worth, TX 76119; tel. 817/535-2111; FAX. 817/535-8937; George Killinger

CASA, a Special Hospital, 1803 Old Spanish Trail, Houston, TX 77054; tel. 713/796-2272; FAX. 713/796-0043; Gretchen Thorp

Chisolm Trail Living and Rehab Center, 107 North Medina, Lockhart, TX 78644; tel. 512/398-5213; Pete M. Natal, Jr.

Coronado Nursing Center, 1751 North 15th Street, Abilene, TX 79603; tel. 915/673-8892; Cyd Lane

East Texas Specialty Hospital, P.O. Box 7018, Tyler, TX 75711; tel. 903/596-3600; David B. Dildy, FACHE

Fireside Lodge Retirement Center, Inc., 4800 White Settlement Road, Fort Worth, TX 76114; tel. 817/738-6556; Michael L. McGrath

Gilmer Care Center, 703 North Titus, Gilmer, TX 75644; tel. 903/843-5529; Donald J. Harris

Green Acres Convalescent Center, 93 Isaacks Road, Humble, TX 77338; tel. 281/446-7159; Eddie J. Doerre

Green Acres Parkdale, 11025 Old Voth Road, Beaumont, TX 77713; tel. 409/892-9722; Benjamin C. Delmonico, Jr.

Hearthstone Nursing and Rehab Center, 401 Oakwood Boulevard, Round Rock, TX 78681; tel. 512/388-7494; FAX. 512/388-2166; Dave Coarner

Heartland Health Care Center, 11406 Rustic Rock Drive, Austin, TX 78750; tel. 512/335-5028; FAX. 512/335-0709; Mary Lou Clem, Administrator

Heartland Health Care Center, 2939 Woodland Park Drive, Houston, TX 77082; tel. 713/870-9100; FAX. 713/558-9700; Terri Humes, Administrator

Heartland Health Care Center at Willowbrook, 13631 Ardfield Drive, Houston, TX 77070; tel. 713/955-9572; FAX. 713/955-1597; Sherion Schroeder

Heartland Health Care Center at Willowbrook, 13631 Ardfield Drive, Houston, TX 77070; tel. 713/955-9572; Sherion Schroeder

Heartland Health Care Center-Bedford, 2001 Forest Ridge Drive, Bedford, TX 76021; tel. 817/571-6804; FAX. 817/267-4176; Mack Baldridge, Administrator

Heartland of Corpus Christi, 202 Fortune Drive, Corpus Christi, TX 78405; tel. 512/289-0889; Marvena Jones

Heartland of San Antonio, One Heartland Drive, San Antonio, TX 78247; tel. 210/653-1219; FAX. 210/653-8977; Guy Bowles, Administrator

Heritage Manor, 1621 Coit Road, Plano, TX 75075; tel. 972/596-7930; Roberta M. Sechovec, RN

Hillcrest Manor, 208 Maple, P.O. Box 230, Luling, TX 78648; tel. 210/875-5219; FAX. 210/875-2919; John Berg

Integrated Health Services at Woodridge, 1500 Autumn Drive, Grapevine, TX 76051; tel. 817/488-8585; Robert Elkins, MD

Integrated Health Services of Dallas at Treemont, 5550 Harvest Hill Road, Dallas, TX 75230; tel. 214/661-1862; FAX. 214/715-5557; Robert Elkins, MD

Integrated Health Services of Texoma, 1000 Highway 82 East, Sherman, TX 75090; tel. 903/893-9636; Michael J. Flugstad

Lake Shore Village Health Care Center, 2320 Lake Shore Drive, Waco, TX 76708; tel. 817/752-1075; Kraig A. Turpen

Lampasas Manor, 611 North Broad, P.O. Box 970, Lampasas, TX 76550; tel. 512/556-3588; FAX. 512/556-2507; Sandra Springwater

Manor Care Health Services-Briaridge, 7703 Briaridge Drive, San Antonio, TX 78230; tel. 210/341-6121; FAX. 210/341-1298; Stewart Bainum

ManorCare Health Services, 3326 Burgoyne Street, Dallas, TX 75233; tel. 214/330-9291; Helen Atkinson

ManorCare Health Services, 7625 Glenview Drive, Fort Worth, TX 76180; tel. 817/284-1427; Kay Severson

ManorCare Health Services, 8800 Fourwinds, San Antonio, TX 78239; tel. 210/656-7800; Steven Cutshaw

ManorCare Health Services - San Antonio (Babcock), 1975 Babcock Blvd., San Antonio, TX 78229; tel. 210/341-8681; Don Tomasso

ManorCare Health Services Nursing and Rehab, 7505 Bellervie, Houston, TX 77036; tel. 713/774-9611; John E. Dugan

ManorCare Health Systems - Webster, 750 West Texas Avenue, Webster, TX 77598; tel. 281/332-3496; Mark Lenhard

Mariner Health of Arlington, 2645 West Randol Mill Road, Arlington, TX 76012; tel. 817/277-6789; Kendal Nelson

Mariner Health of Fort Worth, 4825 Wellesley Street, Fort Worth, TX 76107; tel. 817/732-6608; Troy Washburn

Mariner Health of Northwest Houston, 17600 Cali Drive, Houston, TX 77090; tel. 713/440-9000; David Stroud

Memorial Medical, 315 Lewis Street, San Antonio, TX 78212; tel. 210/223-5521; Sarah Boone

Retama Manor Nursing Center, 1505 South Closner, Edinburg, TX 78539; tel. 210/383-5656; Lilly E. Molina

Southfield Health Care Center, 802 Fresa Street, Pasadena, TX 77502; tel. 713/948-3360; Stefani Clowdis

Southwood Care Center, 3759 Valley View, Austin, TX 78704; tel. 512/443-3436; Sharlyn Threadgill

The Village Healthcare Center, 1341 Blalock Road, Houston, TX 77055; tel. 713/468-7821; Cynthia Brown

Victoria Nursing Home, 114 Medical Drive, Victoria, TX 77904; tel. 512/576-6128; Joan M. Dugan

Weatherford Health Care Center, 521 West 7th, Weathersford, TX 76086; tel. 817/594-8713; Patricia Sanders

Yorktown Manor, 670 West Fourth, P.O. Box 805, Yorkstown, TX 78164; tel. 512/564-2275; FAX. 512/564-3593; Brent Walsh

UTAH

South Davis Community Hospital, 401 South 400 East, Bountiful, UT 84010; tel. 801/295-2361; FAX. 801/295-1398; Gordon W. Bennet, Administrator

Sunshine Terrace Foundation, Inc., 225 North 200 West, P.O. Box 3207 (Zip 81116), Logan, UT 84321-3805; tel. 801/752-0411, ext. 216; FAX. 801/752-1318; Sara V. Sinclair, RN

Washington Terrace Nursing Center, 400 East 5350 South, Ogden, UT 84405; tel. 801/479-9855; Brent Weil

VERMONT

Bennington Health and Rehab Center, 360 Dewey St., Bennington, VT 05201; tel. 802/442-8525; Mark Finkelstein

Berlin Health and Rehab Center, RR 3, Box 6684, Barre, VT 05641; tel. 802/229-0308; Mark Finkelstein

Birchwood Terrace Healthcare, 43 Starr Farm Road, Burlington, VT 05401; tel. 802/863-6384; Thomas N. DePoy

Burlington Health and Rehab Center, 300 Pearl Street, Burlington, VT 05401; tel. 802/658-4200; Richard Morley

Rowan Court Health and Rehab Center, Upper Prospect Street, Barre, VT 05641; tel. 802/476-4166; Mark Finkelstein

Springfield Health and Rehab Center, 105 Chester Road, Springfield, VT 05156; tel. 802/885-5741; Mark Finkelstein

St. Johnsbury Health and Rehab Center, Hospital Drive, St. Johnsbury, VT 05819; tel. 802/748-8757; Mark Finkelstein

Starr Farm Nursing Center, 98 Starr Farm Road, Burlington, VT 05401; tel. 802/658-6717; Ruth A. Rivers

Verdelle Village Extended Care Facility, Box 80 Sheldon Road, St. Albans, VT 05478; tel. 802/524-6534; Paul Richards

VIRGINIA

Annaburg Manor Nursing Home, P.O. Box 3057, Manassas, VA 22110; tel. 703/335-8300; David W. Tucker

Bay Pointe Medical and Rehabilitation Center, 1148 First Colonial Road, Virginia Beach, VA 23454-2499; tel. 757/481-3321; FAX. 757/481-4413; Bruce Busby

Beaufont Healthcare Center, 200 Hioaks Road, Richmond, VA 19177; tel. 804/272-2918; W. Heywood Fralin

Berkshire Health Care Center, 705 Clearview Drive, Vinton, VA 24179; tel. 540/982-6691; FAX. 540/982-6518; Heywood Fralin

Beth Sholom Home of Central Virginia, 12000 Gayton Road, Richmond, VA 23233; tel. 804/750-2183; Barbara K. Gottlieb

Bon Secours - Maryview Nursing Care Center, 4775 Bridge Road, Suffolk, VA 23435; tel. 757/686-0488; Eileen D. Malo

Brian Center Health and Rehab - Allegha, P.O. Box 200, Low Moor, VA 24457; tel. 540/862-3610; Trina Hylton

Burke Healthcare Center, 9640 Burke Lake Road, Burke, VA 18993; tel. 703/425-9765; W. Heywood Fralin

Camelot Hall of Lynchburg, 5615 Seminole Avenue, Lynchburg, VA 24502; tel. 804/239-2657; FAX. 804/239-4062; Heywood Fralin

Camelot Health and Rehab Center, 1225 South Reservoir Street, Harrisonburg, VA 18302; tel. 540/433-2623; W. Heywood Fralin

Cameron Glen Care Center, 1800 Cameron Glen Drive, Reston, VA 22090; tel. 703/834-5800; Pamela S. Clark

Cherrydale Healthcare Center, 3710 Lee Highway, Arlington, VA 18411; tel. 703/243-7640; W. Heywood Fralin

Chesapeake Healthcare Center, 688 Kingsborough Square, Chesapeake, VA 18412; tel. 757/547-9111; Rick Oros

Culpeper Healthcare Center, 602 Madison Road, Culpeper, VA 19377; tel. 540/825-2884; W. Heywood Fralin

Goodwin House West, 3440 South Jefferson Street, Falls Church, VA 22041; tel. 703/824–1347; FAX. 703/578–7228; Marvin Ogburn

Harbour Pointe Medical and Rehabilitation Centre, (a Vencor Facility), 1005 Hampton Boulevard, Norfolk, VA 23507; tel. 757/623–5602; FAX. 757/623–4646; Gary Witte

Health of Virginia, 2420 Pemberton Road, Richmond, VA 23233–2099; tel. 804/747–9200; FAX. 804/747–1574; Walter W. Regirer, Chief Executive Officer, General Counsel

Iliff Nursing and Rehab Center, 8000 Iliff Drive, Dunn Loring, VA 22027; tel. 703/560–1000; FAX. 703/280–0406; Joan H. Bishop, Administrator

Inova Commonwealth Care Center, 4315 Chain Bridge Road, Fairfax, VA 22030; tel. 703/934–5000; Shelly L. Kobuck

Integrated Health Services of Northern Virginia, 900 Virginia Avenue, Alexandria, VA 22302; tel. 703/684–9100; David C. Burke

James River Convalescent Center, 540 Aberthaw Avenue, Newport News, VA 23601; tel. 757/595–2273; FAX. 757/595–2271; Jeffrey R. Law

Jefferson Park Center, 1214 Jefferson Park Avenue, Charlottesville, VA 22903; tel. 804/295–1161; Stewart Seitz

Lucy Corr Nursing Home, 6800 Lucy Corr Court, P.O. Drawer 170, Chesterfield, VA 23832; tel. 804/748–1511; FAX. 804/796–6285; Jacob Mast

Manning Convalescent Home, Inc., 175 Hatton Street, Portsmouth, VA 23705; tel. 757/399–1321; FAX. 757/399–4337; T. W. Manning, President

Manor Care Health Services–Fair Oaks Nursing and Rehabilitation Center, 12475 Lee Jackson Memorial Highway, Fairfax, VA 22033; tel. 703/352–7172, ext. 3203; FAX. 703/218–3200; Justin M. Dunie, Administrator

Manor Care Nursing and Rehab Center, 550 South Carlin Springs Road, Arlington, VA 22204; tel. 703/379–7200; FAX. 703/578–5788; Barry E. Grofic

ManorCare Health Services–Richmond, 2125 Hilliard Road, Richmond, VA 23228; tel. 804/266–9666; FAX. 804/266–3599; Vivian Thomas, Administrator

Nansemond Pointe Rehabilitation and Healthcare Centre, 200 West Constance Road, Suffolk, VA 23434; tel. 757/539–8744; FAX. 757/539–6128; Audrey B. Butler

Norfolk Healthcare Center, 901 East Princess Anne Road, Norfolk, VA 20772; tel. 757/626–1642; W. Heywood Fralin

Oak Hill Health Care Center, 512 Houston Street, P.O. Box 2565 (Zip 21837), Staunton, VA 24401; tel. 540/886–2335; FAX. 540/886–7459; Richard J. Shelly

Oakwood Nursing and Rehab Center, 5520 Indian River Road, Virginia Beach, VA 23464; tel. 757/420–3600; Steven W. Garfinkle

Parham Healthcare and Rehabilitation Center, 2400 East Parham Road, Richmond, VA 23228; tel. 804/264–9185; FAX. 804/264–3963; Heywood Fralin

Raleigh Court Healthcare Center, 1527 Grandin Road Southwest, Roanoke, VA 21710; tel. 540/342–9525; Heywood Fralin

Regency Healthcare Center, 112 North Constitution Drive, Yorktown, VA 20900; tel. 757/890–0675; W. Heywood Fralin

Ridgecrest Manor Nursing Home, P.O. Box 280, Duffield, VA 24244; tel. 540/431–2841; James O. Strom

Riverside Healthcare Center, 2344 Riverside Drive, Danville, VA 20328; tel. 804/791–3800; W. Heywood Fralin

Riverside Regional Convalescent Center, 1000 Old Denbigh Boulevard, Newport News, VA 23602; tel. 757/875–2020; FAX. 757/875–2036; Patricia A. Iannetta, Administrator

Salem Health and Rehab Center, 1945 Roanoke Blvd., Salem, VA 17666; tel. 540/345–3894; W. Heywood Fralin

Virginia Beach Healthcare and Rehab Center, 1801 Camelot Drive, Virginia Beach, VA 23454; tel. 757/481–3500; Heywood Fralin

Virginia Veterans Care Center, 4550 Shenandoah Avenue, NW, Roanoke, VA 24017; tel. 540/982–2860; Robert H. Gerndt

Waverly Healthcare Center, P.O. Box 641, Waverly, VA 23249; tel. 804/834–3975; W. Heywood Fralin

Williamsburg Center Genesis ElderCare, 1235 Mt. Vernon Avenue, Williamsburg, VA 23185; tel. 757/229–4121; Michael Walker

Woodbine Rehabilitation and Healthcare Center, 2729 King Street, Alexandria, VA 22302; tel. 703/836–8838; FAX. 703/836–2965; Mary Ann Sleigh, Administrator

Woodmont Health Care Center, 11 Dairy Lane, P.O. Box 419 (zip 21985), Fredericksburg, VA 22404–0419; tel. 540/371–9414; FAX. 540/371–4501; Sharon Bartlett

WASHINGTON

Blue Mountain Medical and Rehabilitation Center, 1200 Southeast 12th Street, College Place, WA 99324; tel. 509/529–4080; FAX. 509/529–2173; Andrew Turner

Cascade Vista Convalescent Center, Inc., 7900 Willows Road Northeast, Redmond, WA 98052; tel. 206/885–0808; Pearl K. Barnes

Covington Medical and Rehab Center, 5220 NE Hazel Dell Avenue, Vancouver, WA 98663; tel. 360/693–1474; Zendi Meharry

Evergreen Vista Convalescent Center, Inc., 11800 Northeast 128th Street, Kirkland, WA 90833; tel. 206/821–0404; Mary G. Southwick, RN

Harmony Gardens Care Center, 10010 Des Moines Way, S., Seattle, WA 98168; tel. 206/762–0166; FAX. 206/762–8612; Andrew Turner

Integrated Health Services of Seattle, 820 Northwest 95th Street, Seattle, WA 98117; tel. 206/782–0100, ext. 228; FAX. 206/781–1448; Jerry Harvey, Administrator

Laurelwood Care Center, 150–102nd Avenue, S.E., Bellevue, WA 98004; tel. 206/454–6166; FAX. 206/454–7152; Andrew Turner, Chief Executive Officer

Mercer Island Care Center, 7445 Southeast 24th Street, Mercer Island, WA 98040; tel. 206/232–6600; FAX. 206/232–6502; Andrew Turner

Oyster Bay Care Center, 3517 11th Street, Bremerton, WA 98312; tel. 360/377–5537; Dale J. Zulauf

Renton Hills Health and Rehab Center, 1110 Edmonds Avenue, N.E., Renton, WA 98056; tel. 206/226–6120; FAX. 206/228–8087; Andrew Turner

Richmond Beach Medical and Rehab Center, 19235 15th Avenue NW, Shoreline, WA 98177; tel. 206/546–2666; Andrew Turner

Seattle Medical and Rehab Center, 555 16th Avenue, Seattle, WA 98122; tel. 206/324–8200; FAX. 206/324–0780; Dave Railsback

Terrace View Diversified Health Care Center, Inc., 1701–18th Avenue, S., Seattle, WA 98144; tel. 206/329–9586; FAX. 206/325–1750; Philip H. Gayton

The Care Center at Kelsey Creek, 2210 132nd Avenue, S.E., Bellevue, WA 98005; tel. 206/957–2400; FAX. 206/957–2425; Betty Mullin

Wedgwood Rehabilitation Center, 9132 Ravenna Avenue, N.E., Seattle, WA 98115; tel. 206/524–6535; FAX. 206/523–1817; Andrew Turner

WEST VIRGINIA

Americare Pine Lodge Nursing and Rehabilitation Center, 405 Stanford Road, Beckley, WV 25801; tel. 304/252–6317; FAX. 304/253–4140; Sherry Johnson

Americare Putnam Nursing and Rehab Center, 300 Seville Road, Hurricane, WV 25526; tel. 304/757–6805; Tammy Painter

Bishop Joseph H. Hodges Continuous Care Center, 600 Medical Park, Wheeling, WV 26003; tel. 304/243–3800; Debbie Cox

Brightwood Nursing and Rehab Center, 840 Lee Road, Follansbee, WV 26037; tel. 304/527–1100; Kathy D. Haddon

GlenWood Park Retirement Village, 1924 Glenwood Park Road, Princeton, WV 24740–9244; tel. 304/425–8128; Daniel W. Farley, Ph.D., CNHA, President, Chief Executive Officer

Heartland of Charleston, 3819 Chesterfield Avenue, Charleston, WV 25304; tel. 304/925–4771; FAX. 304/925–1343; Karen Lawson

Rosewood Nursing and Rehab Center, 8 Rose Street, Grafton, WV 26354; tel. 304/265–0095; Shawn Eddy

The Madison Rehab and Nursing Center, 161 Bakers Ridge Road, Morgantown, WV 26505; tel. 304/598–2900; Eric T. Nichols

WISCONSIN

Beaver Dam Care Center, 410 Roedl Court, P.O. Box 617, Beaver Dam, WI 53916; tel. 414/887–7191; FAX. 414/887–2380; Richard Rexrode

Bel Air Health Care Center, 9350 West Fond Du Lac Avenue, Milwaukee, WI 53225; tel. 414/438–4360; Jane C. Elliott

Beverly Health and Rehab, 6735 West Bradley Road, Milwaukee, WI 53223; tel. 414/354–3300; Matthew Herman

Beverly Health and Rehab Center – Superior, 1612 North 37th Street, Superior, WI 54880; tel. 715/392–5144; Jeffrey A. Schueller

Beverly Subacute Care Center at St. Luke's, 2900 West Oklahoma Avenue, Milwaukee, WI 53215; tel. 414/649–5707; Marianne Raymonds, MS

Clement Manor Health Center, 3939 South 92nd Street, Greenfield, WI 53228; tel. 414/321–1800; FAX. 414/546–7333; William H. Lange, President, Chief Executive Officer

Colonial House Nursing and Rehab Center, 702 West Dolf Street, Colby, WI 54421; tel. 715/223–2352; Tracy Hogden

Colonial Manor Medical and Rehabilitation Center, 1010 East Wausau Avenue, Wausau, WI 54403–3199; tel. 715/842–2028; FAX. 715/845–5810; N. Jean Burgener

Continental Manor Health and Rehab Center, 502 South High Street, Randolph, WI 53956; tel. 414/326–3171; Victoria L. Grant

Eastview Medical and Rehabilitation Center, 729 Park Street, Antigo, WI 54409; tel. 715/623–2356; FAX. 715/623–2263; Suzanne Whitty

Franciscan Villa, 3601 South Chicago Avenue, South Milwaukee, WI 53172; tel. 414/764–4100; FAX. 414/764–0706; Roger L. DeMark, Administrator

Franciscan Woods, 19525 West North Avenue, Brookfield, WI 53045; tel. 414/785–1114; FAX. 414/785–9967; Mary Piette

Greendale Health and Rehabilitation Center, 3129 Michigan Avenue, Sheboygan, WI 53081; tel. 414/458–1155; FAX. 414/458–4869; Suzanne Bruner, Executive Director

Heritage Square Health Care Center, 5404 W. Loomis Road, Greendale, WI 53129; tel. 414/421–0088; Marjory Meinholz, NHA, MS

Highland Health Care, 2997 St. Anthony Drive, Green Bay, WI 54311; tel. 414/468–0734; Charlene Everett

Karmenta Nursing and Rehab Center, 4502 Milwaukee Street, Madison, WI 53714; tel. 608/249–2137; Cheri McCormick

Manor Care Health Services, 1335 South Oneida Street, Appleton, WI 54911; tel. 414/731–6646; FAX. 414/731–5177; Lorie Neumann

ManorCare Health Services, 265 South National Avenue, Fond Du Lac, WI 54935; tel. 920/922–7342; Ken Ameson

ManorCare Health Services – Green Bay, 600 South Webster Avenue, Green Bay, WI 54301; tel. 414/432–3213; D. J. Swant

ManorCare Health Services – Madison, 801 Braxton Place, Madison, WI 53715; tel. 608/251–1010; Christine Sommerfeldt

Marian Catholic Center, 3333 West Highland Boulevard, Milwaukee, WI 53208; tel. 414/344–8100; FAX. 414/345–4793; Michael Zimmerman

Marian Franciscan Center, 9632 West Appleton Avenue, Milwaukee, WI 53225; tel. 414/461–8850; FAX. 414/461–9570; James Gresham, Regional Vice President, Continuing Care Services Division

Middleton Village Nursing and Rehabilitation Center, 6201 Elmwood Avenue, Middleton, WI 53562; tel. 608/831–8300; FAX. 608/831–4253; Cindy Love, RN

Mount Carmel Health and Rehabilitation Center, 5700 West Layton Avenue, Milwaukee, WI 53220; tel. 414/281–7200; FAX. 414/281–4620; Andrea J. Ludington

Northwest Health Care Center, 7800 West Fond Du Lac Avenue, Milwaukee, WI 53218; tel. 414/464–3950; FAX. 414/464–5110; Candy Gremore, Executive Director

Outagamie County Health Center, 3400 West Brewster Street, Appleton, WI 54914; tel. 920/832–5400; FAX. 920/832–5416; David A. Rothmann, Administrator

Parkview Manor Health and Rehabilitation Center, 2961 St. Anthony Drive, Green Bay, WI 54311; tel. 920/468–0861; FAX. 920/468–8548; Scott Martens

River Pines Nursing and Rehab, 1800 Sherman Avenue, Stevens Point, WI 54481; tel. 715/344–1800; Clayton J. Kalmon

Shady Lane, 1235 South 24th Street, Manitowoc, WI 54220; tel. 414/682–8254; Karlyn Saffran

Shorewood Heights Health and Rehab Center, 3710 North Oakland Ave., Shorewood, WI 53211; tel. 414/964–6200; Leland Shultz

Silver Spring Health and Rehab Center, 1400 West Silver Spring Drive, Glendale, WI 53209; tel. 414/228–8120; Margaret L. Cunningham
South Shore Manor, 1915 East Tripoli Ave., St. Francis, WI 53235; tel. 414/483–3611; Tom Wimsberger
The Terrace at St. Francis, 3200 South 20th Street, Milwaukee, WI 53215; tel. 414/389–3200, ext. 3250; FAX. 414/389–3300; Geri Wandrey
The Village at Manor Park, Inc., 3023 South 84th Street, West Allis, WI 53227; tel. 414/541–2600; Reginald M. Hislop III

Western Village Health and Rehabilitation, 1640 Shawano Avenue, Green Bay, WI 54303; tel. 414/499–5177; FAX. 414/499–6035; Linda Kessenich
Woodland Health Center, 18740 West Bluemound Road, Brookfield, WI 53045; tel. 414/782–0230; Margaret Christenson, MPA

WYOMING
Cheyenne Health Care Center, 2700 East 12th Street, Cheyenne, WY 82001; tel. 307/634–7986; Rebecca Wirthwein

Section C

JCAHO Accredited Freestanding Mental Health Care Organizations

The accredited freestanding mental health care organizations listed have been accredited as of April, 1998 by the Joint Commission on Accreditation of Healthcare Organizations by decision of the Accreditation Committee of the Board of Commissioners.

The organizations listed here have been found to be in compliance with the Joint Commissions standards for Accreditation Manual for Mental Health, Chemical Dependency, and Mental Retardation/Development Disabilities Services.

Please refer to section A of the AHA Guide for information on hospitals with inpatient and/or outpatient services. These hospitals are identified by Facility Codes F52, F53, F54, F55, F56, F57, F58 and F59. In section A, those hospitals identified by Approval Code 1 are JCAHO accredited.

We present this list simply as a convenient directory. Inclusion or omission of any organization's name indicates neither approval nor disapproval by Healthcare InfoSource, Inc., a subsidiary of the American Hospital Association.

United States

ALABAMA

Behavioral Healthcare Center, 306 Paul W. Bryant Drive East, Tuscaloosa, AL 35401; tel. 205/349–1033; Omar Mohabbat, MD

Bradford Adolescent at Oak Mountain, 2280 Highway 35 South, Pelham, AL 35124; tel. 205/664–3460; Jarrett N. Caltrider

Bradford Health Services at Birmingham Lodge, 1189 Allbritton Road, P.O. Box 129, Warrior, AL 35180; tel. 205/647–1945; Roy M. Ramsey, Executive Director

Bradford–Parkside at Huntsville, 1600 Browns Ferry Road, P.O. Box 176, Madison, AL 35758; tel. 205/461–7272; Robert S. Hinds

Mobile Mental Health Center, Inc., 2400 Gordon Smith Drive, Mobile, AL 36617; tel. 334/473–4423; Julie B. Bellcase

New Perspectives (Adult), 1000 Fairfax Park, Tuscaloosa, AL 35406; tel. 205/391–4738; FAX. 205/759–4151; Martha Hinkle, Administrator

Partial Hospital Institute of America, Inc., 1565 Hillcrest Road, Mobile, AL 36695; tel. 334/607–7610; FAX. 334/607–7621; James S. Harrold, Jr., M.D., Chief Executive Officer

Pathway, Inc., P.O. Box 311206, Enterprise, AL 36331; tel. 334/894–5591; Norman G. Hemp, Executive Director

Physicians' Psychiatric Clinic, P.C., 10 Mobile Street, Mobile, AL 36607; tel. 334/450–1200; FAX. 334/450–1207; James J. Wyllie, Jr.

The Catalyst Center (Adolescent), 1000 Fairfax Park, Tuscaloosa, AL 35406; tel. 205/391–4738; FAX. 205/759–4151; Martha Hinkle, Chief Executive Officer

The Quality Life Center of Quality HealthCare, Inc., 2801 West Mall Drive, Florence, AL 35630; tel. 205/760–9955; Glenda Smith

Thomasville Mental Health Rehabilitation Center, Bashi Road, P.O. Box 309, Thomasville, AL 36784; tel. 334/636–5421, ext. 230; FAX. 334/636–5421; Kimberly S. Ingram, M.S.N., Facility Director

ALASKA

Akeela House, Inc., 2805 Bering Street, Suite Four, Anchorage, AK 99503; tel. 907/561–5206; Rosalie Nadeau, Deputy Director

Alaska Children's Services, 4600 Abbott Road, Anchorage, AK 99507; tel. 907/346–2101; FAX. 907/346–2748; James E. Maley, Executive Director

Alaska North Addictions Recovery Center, 4330 Bragaw Street, Anchorage, AK 99508; tel. 907/561–5537; Leroy Bingham

North Star Residential Treatment Center, 1650 South Bragaw, Anchorage, AK 99508; tel. 907/274–7313; Kathleen Cronen

ARIZONA

ABCS Little Canyon Center, Inc., 3115 West Missouri Avenue, P.O. Box 39239, Phoenix, AZ 85069–9239; tel. 602/943–7760; FAX. 602/943–7864; C. T. Baker, ACSW

Arizona Children's Home Association, 2700 South Eighth Avenue, P.O. Box 7277, Tucson, AZ 85725–7277; tel. 520/622–7611; FAX. 520/624–7042; Fred J. Chaffee, Chief Executive Officer

Calvary Rehabilitation Center, Inc., 720 East Montebello Avenue, Phoenix, AZ 85014; tel. 602/279–1468; FAX. 602/279–3090; Jeffrey Shook, Chief Executive Officer

Chandler Valley Hope, 501 North Washington, P.O. Box 1839, Chandler, AZ 85244–1839; tel. 602/899–3335; FAX. 602/899–6697; Dennis Gilhousen

Cottonwood de Tucson, Inc., 4110 West Sweetwater Drive, Tucson, AZ 85745; tel. 520/743–0411; FAX. 520/743–7991; Ronald B. Welch, President, Chief Executive Officer

Desert Hills Center for Youth and Families, 2797 North Introspect Drive, Tucson, AZ 85745; tel. 520/622–5437; FAX. 520/792–6249; Richard Hardin, ACSW

Devereux/Arizona, 6436 East Sweetwater Avenue, Scottsdale, AZ 85254; tel. 602/998–2920; FAX. 602/443–1531; Stephen A. Vitali, Executive Director

La Paloma Family Services, Inc., P.O. Box 41565, Tucson, AZ 84152; tel. 520/881–5589; David Bradley

META Services, 621 West Southern Avenue, Mesa, AZ 85210; tel. 602/649–1111; FAX. 602/649–0149; Eugene Johnson, President, Chief Executive Officer

Mingus Mountain Estate Residential Center, Inc., 10451 Palmeras Drive, Suite 105N, Sun City, AZ 83321; tel. 602/780–1963; Dr. Pauline H. Don Carlos, Chief Executive Officer

Parc Place, 5116 East Thomas Road, Phoenix, AZ 85018; tel. 602/840–4774, ext. 316; FAX. 602/840–7567; Jim Oleson

Prehab of Arizona, Inc., 868 East University, P.O. Drawer 5860, Mesa, AZ 85203; tel. 602/969–4024, ext. 210; FAX. 602/969–0039; Michael T. Hughes, Executive Director

Remuda Ranch Center for Anorexia and Bulimia, Jack Burden Road, P.O. Box 2481, Wickenburg, AZ 85358; tel. 520/684–3913; FAX. 520/684–2908; Ward Keller, President

Salvation Army Recovery Center, 2707 East Van Buren, P.O. Box 52177 (zip 85072), Phoenix, AZ 85008; tel. 602/267–1404; FAX. 602/267–4131; Major John Webb, Chief Executive Officer

Sierra Tucson, Inc., 16500 North Lago Del Oro Parkway, Tucson, AZ 85739; tel. 520/624–4000; FAX. 520/825–3523; Terry A. Stephens, Executive Director

Southeastern Arizona Psychiatric Health Facility, 470 South Ocotillo Avenue, P.O. Box 1296, Benson, AZ 85602; tel. 602/586–9161; FAX. 602/586–7939; Michael R. Zent, PhD

Superstition Mountain Mental Health Center, Inc., 150 N. Ocotillo, Apache Junction, AZ 85217; tel. 602/983–0065; Gary W. Selvy

The EXCEL Group, 106 East First Street, Yuma, AZ 85364; tel. 520/329–8995; Michael P. Puthoff

The Meadows, 1655 North Tegner, P.O. Box 97, Highway 89/93, Wickenburg, AZ 85358; tel. 800/621–4062; FAX. 520/684–3261; J. P. Mellody, Executive Director

The New Foundation, P.O. Box 3828, Scottsdale, AZ 85271; tel. 602/945–3302; FAX. 602/945–9308; David S. Hedgcock, Executive Director

Touchstone Community, Inc., 7905 North 71st Avenue, Glendale, AZ 85303; tel. 602/930–8705; FAX. 602/953–9217; Timothy Dunst

Westbridge Treatment Centers, 1830 East Roosevelt, Phoenix, AZ 85006; tel. 602/254–0884; FAX. 602/258–4033; Michael J. Perry, Chief Executive Officer

Westcenter, 2105 East Allen Road, Tucson, AZ 85719; tel. 520/795–0952; FAX. 520/318–6442; Allan Harrington, Executive Director

ARKANSAS

Behavioral Health Services, Inc. of Arkansas, 604 Cherry Street, Helena, AR 72342; tel. 501/338–9131; Robert K. Quam, MA

Centers for Youth and Families, P.O. Box 251970, Little Rock, AR 70255–1970; tel. 501/666–8686; FAX. 501/660–6836; Richard T. Hill, President, Chief Executive Officer

Delta Counseling Associates, Inc., P.O. Box 820, Monticello, AR 71655; tel. 870/367–9732; Patrick W. Haynie

Millcreek of Arkansas, P.O. Box 727, Industrial Park Drive, Highway 79 North, Fordyce, AR 71742; tel. 501/352–8203; FAX. 501/352–5311; Wanda Miles–Bell

Ozark Counseling Services, Inc., P.O. Box 1776, Mountain Home, AR 72654; tel. 870/425–7929; John C. Greer

Ozark Guidance Center, Inc., 219 South Thompson Street, P.O. Box 6430, Springdale, AR 72765; tel. 501/751–7052; FAX. 501/751–4346; David L. Williams, Ph.D., President, Chief Executive Officer

Timber Ridge Ranch Neurorehabilitation Center, Inc., 15000 Highway 298, P.O. Box 90, Benton, AR 72015–5009; tel. 501/594–5211; Sharon J. Burleson, Executive Director

United Methodist Children's Home, Inc., P.O. Box 4848, Little Rock, AR 67366; tel. 501/661–0720; Robert A. Regnier

Youth Home, Inc., 20400 Colonel Glenn Road, Little Rock, AR 72210–5323; tel. 501/821–5500; FAX. 501/821–5580; Beth Cartwright, ACSW, L.C.S.W. Executive Director

CALIFORNIA

A Touch of Care, 2231 South Carmelina Avenue, Los Angeles, CA 90064; tel. 310/473–6525; FAX. 310/479–1287; Richard B. Cohen, MFCC, Executive Director

BehavioralCare of American, 18881 Von Karman, Suite 250, Irvine, CA 92715; tel. 714/752–1510; FAX. 714/442–2196; David F. Ellisor, Chief Executive Officer

Betty Ford Center at Eisenhower, 39000 Bob Hope Drive, Rancho Mirage, CA 92270; tel. 619/773–4100; FAX. 619/773–4141; John T. Schwarzlose

Broad Horizons of Ramona, Inc., 1236 H Street, P.O. Box 1920, Ramona, CA 92065; tel. 619/789–7060; FAX. 619/789–4062; Ellen Wright, LCSW, Chief Executive Officer

Cornerstone of Southern California, 13682 Yorba Street, Tustin, CA 92680; tel. 714/730–5399; FAX. 714/730–3505; Michael Stone, MD

Family Recovery Foundation, Inc., 12822 Hewes Avenue, Santa Ana, CA 92705; tel. 714/289–9142; Javier Saldivar

Impact Drug and Alcohol Treatment Center, 1680 North Fair Oaks Avenue, Pasadena, CA 91103; tel. 818/798–0884; James M. Stillwell, Executive Director

Ivy Lea Manor/Fiscro, Inc., 1379 West Park Western Drive, Suite 310, San Pedro, CA 90732–2217; tel. 310/832–8511; Gary Bodner, PhD

Kings View Center, 42675 Road 44, Reedley, CA 93654; tel. 209/638–2505; Mike Waters

Learning Services – Escondido, 2335 Bear Valley Parkway, Escondido, CA 92027; tel. 619/746–3223; Kathleen Madigan, MA

Learning Services – Northern California, 10855 DeBruin Way, Gilroy, CA 95020; tel. 408/848–4379; FAX. 408/848–6509; Randle Mitchell, Chief Executive Officer

Los Angeles Centers for Alcohol and Drug Abuse, 11015 Bloomfield Avenue, Santa Fe Springs, CA 90670; tel. 310/906–2676; FAX. 310/906–2681; John Brown, Chief Executive Officer

Michael's House, The Treatment Center for Men, 430 South Cahuilla Road, Palm Springs, CA 92262; tel. 619/320–5486; FAX. 619/778–6020; Arlene Rosen, President, Chief Executive Officer

Monterey Psychiatric Health Facility, Inc., Five Via Joaquin, Monterey, CA 93940; tel. 408/645–9000; FAX. 408/646–1317; Dr. Thomas Marra, Chief Executive Officer

Oak Grove Institute Foundation, 24275 Jefferson Avenue, Murrieta, CA 92562; tel. 909/677–5599; FAX. 909/698–0461; Thomas C. Lester, MD

R. House, Inc., P.O. Box 2587, Santa Rosa, CA 95405; tel. 707/539–2948; Mimi G. Donohue

S. T. E. P. S., 224 East Clara Street, Port Hueneme, CA 93044; tel. 805/488–6424; FAX. 805/488–6717; John J. Megara, M.B.A., Administrator

San Diego Center for Children, 3002 Armstrong Street, San Diego, CA 92111–5798; tel. 619/277–9550, ext. 114; FAX. 619/279–2763; Mark A. Hopper

SeaBridge Adolescent Treatment Center, 30371 Morning View Drive, P.O. Box 3601, Malibu, CA 90265; tel. 310/457–5802; FAX. 310/457–6093; Martha Zimmerman, Executive Director

Solano Psychiatric Health Facility, P.O. Box 2866, Fairfield, CA 94247; tel. 707/435–2130; Linda Reese, PhD

Spencer Recovery Centers, Inc., 343 West Foothill Boulevard, Monrovia, CA 91016; tel. 626/358–3662; FAX. 626/357–7405; Christopher C. Spencer

Substance Abuse Foundation of Long Beach, Inc., 3125 East Seventh Street, Long Beach, CA 90804; tel. 310/439–7755; Ronald H. Banner, Executive Director

Tarzana Treatment Center, 18646 Oxnard Street, Tarzana, CA 91356; tel. 818/996–1051; FAX. 818/345–3778; Albert Senella, Chief Executive Officer

The Discovery Adolescent Program, 4136 Ann Arbor Road, Lakewood, CA 90712; tel. 562/425–6918; Craig M. Brown, PhD

The Linden Center, 5750 Wilshire Boulevard, Suite 535, Los Angeles, CA 90036; tel. 213/937–3999, ext. 209; FAX. 213/937–6641; Ronald E. Ricker, MD

Twin Town Treatment Centers, 10741 Los Alamitos Boulevard, Los Alamitos, CA 90720; tel. 310/594–8844; FAX. 310/493–1280; George P. Casey

Vista Del Mar Child and Family Services, 3200 Motor Avenue, Los Angeles, CA 90034; tel. 310/836–1223, ext. 201; FAX. 310/204–1405; Gerald D. Zaslaw, ACSW, Chief Executive Officer

Vista Pacifica, 7989 Linda Vista Road, San Diego, CA 92111; tel. 619/576–1200; FAX. 619/576–8362; Daniel R. Valentine, Administrator

Vista San Diego Center, 3003 Armstrong Street, San Diego, CA 92111; tel. 619/268–3343, ext. 204; FAX. 619/268–8737; Judith K. Williams

Watts Health Foundation, Inc., 10300 South Compton Avenue, Los Angeles, CA 90002; tel. 213/564–4331; FAX. 213/563–6378; Dr. Clyde Oden, Chief Executive Officer

COLORADO

Adolescent and Family Institute of Colorado, Inc., 10001 West 32nd Avenue, Wheat Ridge, CO 80033; tel. 303/238–1231; FAX. 303/238–0500; Alex M. Panio, Jr., Ph.D., Chief Executive Officer

Alpha Drug Abuse Program, P.O. Box 1082, Greeley, CO 80632; tel. 303/346–9546; Robert B. Warren

Aurora Behavioral Health Hospital, 1290 South Potomac Street, Aurora, CO 80012; tel. 303/745–2273; FAX. 303/369–9556; John Thompson, Administrator

Colorado Boys Ranch, 28071 Highway 109, P.O. Box 681, La Junta, CO 81050; tel. 719/384–5981; FAX. 719/384–8119; Charles M. Thompson

Forest Heights Lodge, 4801 Forest Hill Road, P.O. Box 789, Evergreen, CO 80439; tel. 303/674–6681; FAX. 303/674–6805; Linda Clefisch, LCSW, ACSW

Harmony Foundation, Inc., 1600 Fish Hatchery Road, P.O. Box 1989, Estes Park, CO 80517; tel. 970/586–4491; Donald R. Hays, J.D., NCACII, CACIII, Director

Learning Services–Rocky Mountain Region, Brain Injury and Stroke Rehabilitation Programs, 7201 West Hampden Avenue, Lakewood, CO 80227; tel. 303/989–6660; FAX. 303/989–2830; Kenneth R. Hosack, Program Director

Parker Valley Hope, 22422 East Main Street, P.O. Box 670, Parker, CO 80134; tel. 303/841–7857; FAX. 303/841–6526; Dennis Gilhousen

Pikes Peak Mental Health Center, 220 Ruskin Drive, Colorado Springs, CO 80910; tel. 719/572–6100; FAX. 719/572–6199; Charles J. Vorwaller, President, Chief Executive Officer

VA Medical Center Fort Lyon, 'C' Street, Fort Lyon, CO 81038; tel. 719/384–3110; W. David Smith

CONNECTICUT

Berkshire Woods Chemical Dependence Treatment Center, Fairfield Circle South, P.O. Box 7006, Newtown, CT 06470; tel. 203/426–2531; FAX. 203/426–6285; Sarah Kruel, Chief Executive Officer

Capitol Region Mental Health Center, 500 Vine Street, Hartford, CT 06112; tel. 860/297–0903; FAX. 860/297–0914; Lillian Tamayo, Chief Executive Officer

Community Prevention and Addiction Services, Inc., 1491 West Main Street, Willimantic, CT 06226; tel. 860/456–3215; Leanne M. Dillian

Cornerstone of Eagle Hill, 32 Alberts Hill Road, Sandy Hook, CT 06482; tel. 203/426–8085; FAX. 203/426–2821; Norman J. Sokolow, President

Greater Bridgeport Community Mental Health Center, 1635 Central Avenue, P.O. Box 5117, Bridgeport, CT 06610; tel. 203/579–6626; FAX. 203/579–6094; James Lehane, Chief Executive Officer

Guenster Rehabilitation Center, Inc., 276 Union Avenue, Bridgeport, CT 06607; tel. 203/384–9301; FAX. 203/336–4395; Thomas Kidder, Clinical Director

High Meadows, 825 Hartford Turnpike, Hamden, CT 06517; tel. 203/281–8300; Gabriel Viada

Klingberg Family Centers, Inc., 370 Linwood Street, New Britain, CT 06052; tel. 860/224–9113, ext. 363; FAX. 860/826–1739; Rosemarie A. Burton, President

Perception Programs, Inc., P.O. Box 407, Willimantic, CT 06226; tel. 860/450–7122; Rhonda M. Kincaid

Reid Treatment Center, Inc., 121 West Avon Road, Avon, CT 06001; tel. 860/673–6115; FAX. 860/675–7433; Mary Ann Reid, Executive Director

Riverview Hospital for Children and Youth, 915 River Road, P.O. Box 2797, Middletown, CT 06457–9297; tel. 860/704–4090; FAX. 860/704–4123; Louis Ando, PhD

Rushford Center, Inc., 1250 Silver Street, Middletown, CT 06457; tel. 203/346–0300; Jeffrey L. Walter

So. Connecticut Mental Health & Substance Abuse Treatment Center, 4083 Main Street, Bridgeport, CT 06606; tel. 203/365–8400; Mark Waynik, MD

Stonington Institute, Swantown Hill Road, P.O. Box 216, North Stonington, CT 06359; tel. 860/535–1010; Michael J. Angelides, President

The BlueRidge Center, 1095 Blue Hills Avenue, Bloomfield, CT 06002; tel. 860/243–1331; FAX. 860/242–3265; Mary Ellen Doyle, Executive Director

The Children's Center, 1400 Whitney Avenue, Hamden, CT 06517; tel. 203/248–2116; FAX. 203/248–2572; Brian F. Lynch, Chief Executive Officer

The Wellspring Foundation, Inc., 21 Arch Bridge Road, P.O. Box 370, Bethlehem, CT 06751–0370; tel. 203/266–7235; FAX. 203/266–5830; Herbert Hall, M.Ed., Chief Executive Officer

United Services, Inc., P.O. Box 839, Dayville, CT 06241; tel. 860/774–2020; Theodore L. Ver Haagh

Vitam Center, Inc., 57 West Rocks Road, P.O. Box 730, Norwalk, CT 06852; tel. 203/846–2091; FAX. 203/846–3620; Leonard A. Kenowitz, Ph.D., Executive Director

Wheeler Clinic, Inc., 91 Northwest Drive, Plainville, CT 06062; tel. 860/793–3500; FAX. 860/793–3520; Dennis Keenan, Executive Director

DELAWARE

Brandywine Counseling, Inc., 2713 Lancaster Avenue, Wilmington, DE 19805; tel. 302/656–2348; FAX. 302/656–0746; Sara Taylor Allshouse, Executive Director

Delaware Guidance Services for Children and Youth, Inc., 1213 Delaware Avenue, Wilmington, DE 19806; tel. 302/652–3948; FAX. 302/652–8297; Bruce Kelsey, LCSW, BCD, Executive Director

Lower Kensington Environmental Center, Inc., Recovery Center of Delaware, P.O. Box 546, Delaware City, DE 19706; tel. 302/836–1615; FAX. 302/836–0412; Terence McSherry

Open Door, Inc., 3301 Green Street, Claymont, DE 19703; tel. 302/798–9555; Bobi Freedman

Sodat–Delaware, Inc., 625 North Orange Street, Wilmington, DE 19801; tel. 302/656–4044; Thomas C. Maloney, Executive Director

DISTRICT OF COLUMBIA

Buena Vista Terrace, 3213 Buena Vista Terrace Southeast, Washington, DC 20020; tel. 202/244–0612; Victor B. Smith, President

Devereux Children's Center, 3050 R Street, N.W., Washington, DC 20007; tel. 202/282–1200; FAX. 202/282–1219; Ronald Burd

Riverside Hospital, 4460 MacArthur Boulevard, N.W., Washington, DC 20007; tel. 202/333–9355; Dr. Elliot Bovelle, Chief Executive Officer

FLORIDA

45th Street Mental Health Center, Inc., 1041–45th Street, West Palm Beach, FL 33407; tel. 407/844–9741; FAX. 407/844–2373; Terry Allen, Chief Executive Officer

Act Corporation, 1220 Willis Avenue, Daytona Beach, FL 32114; tel. 904/947–4270; J. W. Dreggors, MA

Alternatives in Treatment, Inc., 7601 North Federal Highway, Suite 100B, Boca Raton, FL 33487; tel. 407/998–0866; FAX. 407/241–5042; Jacob Frydman, Executive Director

American Day Treatment Centers of Boca Raton, 2101 Corporate Boulevard, Suite 102, Boca Raton, FL 33431; tel. 407/241–7741; FAX. 407/241–7743; James K. Don

Apalachee Center for Human Services, Inc., 625 East Tennessee Street, P.O. Box 1782, Tallahassee, FL 32308; tel. 904/487–2930; FAX. 904/487–0851; Ronald P. Kirkland, Chief Executive Officer

Associated Counseling and Education, Inc., 4563 South Orange Blossom Trail, Orlando, FL 32839; tel. 407/422–7233; FAX. 407/843–9602; Loretta Parrish, Chief Executive Officer

Bayview Center for Mental Health, Inc., 12550 Biscayne Boulevard, Suite 919, Miami, FL 33181; tel. 305/892–4646; FAX. 305/893–1224; Robert Ward, Chief Executive Officer

Beachcomber Rehab, Inc., 4493 North Ocean Boulevard, Delray Beach, FL 33483; tel. 407/734–1818; FAX. 407/265–1349; James Bryan, Chief Executive Officer

Behavioral Health Network of West Dade, 11924–32 SW 8th Street, Miami, FL 33184; tel. 305/227–6757; Nelson Salazar

Camelot Care Centers, Inc., 9160 Oakhurst Road, Seminole, FL 33776; tel. 813/596–9960; James V. Doramus

Charlotte Community Mental Health Services, Inc., 1700 Education Avenue, Punta Gorda, FL 33950; tel. 941/639–8300; Gerald N. Ross, EdD

Charter Behavioral Health System at Manatee Palms, 4480 51st Street, W., Bradenton, FL 34210; tel. 941/792–2222; FAX. 941/795–4359; Ray Heckerman, Administrator, Chief Executive Officer

Coastal Recovery Centers, Inc., 3830 Bee Ridge Road, Sarasota, FL 34233; tel. 941/927–8900; FAX. 941/925–3836; James R. Sleeper, President, Chief Executive Officer

Crossroads–The Recovery Center, 2121 Lisenby Avenue, P.O. Box 16588, Panama City, FL 32406; tel. 904/784–0869; Tony Gilchrist, Chief Executive Officer

Daniel Memorial, Inc., 3725 Belfort Road, Jacksonville, FL 32216; tel. 800/737–1677; FAX. 904/448–7700; James D. Clark, Vice President, Programs

David Lawrence Center, Inc., 6075 Golden Gate Parkway, Naples, FL 33999; tel. 813/455–1031; FAX. 813/455–6561; David Schimmel, Executive Director

Devereux Florida Treatment Network, 5850 T.G. Lee Blvd, Suite 400, Orlando, FL 32822; tel. 407/384–5950; Michael C. Becker

Disc Village, Inc., Tallahassee/Leon County Human Services Center, 525 N. Martin Luther King Blvd., Tallahassee, FL 32304; tel. 904/224–4346; FAX. 904/576–5960; Thomas K. Olk, Executive Director

Section C

Eckerd Alternative Treatment Program at E. How–Kee, 197 Culbreath Road, P.O. Box 7450, Brooksville, FL 34602; tel. 800/554–4357, ext. 456; Merle Springer

Fairwinds, 1569 South Fort Harrison, Clearwater, FL 34616; tel. 813/449–0300; Mazhar Al–Abed, Chief Executive Officer, Administrator

Florida Institute for Neurologic Rehabilitation, Inc., P.O. Box 1348, Wauchula, FL 33873; tel. 800/697–5390; Anthony J. Chioccarelli, Jr.

Green Cross, Inc., 2645 Douglas Road, Suite 601, Miami, FL 33133; tel. 305/443–9990; FAX. 305/443–9498; Dr. Miguel Nunez, Chief Executive Officer

Hanley–Hazelden Center at St. Mary's, 5200 East Avenue, West Palm Beach, FL 33407; tel. 407/848–1666; Jerry Singleton, M.A., Executive Director

High Point, 5960 Southwest 106th Avenue, Cooper City, FL 33328; tel. 954/680–2700; FAX. 954/680–9941; Frank Fanella

InterPhase Recovery Program, Inc., 23120 Sandalfoot Plaza Drive, Boca Raton, FL 33428; tel. 407/487–5400; FAX. 407/852–8872; Johnathan Huttner

Jacksonville Therapy Center, 6428 Beach Boulevard, Jacksonville, FL 32216; tel. 904/724–6500; FAX. 904/721–6677; John McWhorter

La Amistad Behavioral Health Services, 1650 Park Avenue North, Maitland, FL 32751; tel. 407/647–0660; FAX. 407/647–3060; Rosemary Cohen, Chief Executive Officer

Lakeside Alternatives, Inc., 434 West Kennedy Boulevard, Orlando, FL 32810; tel. 407/875–3700; FAX. 407/875–5717; Duane Zimmerman, Chief Executive Officer

Lakeview Center, Inc., 1221 West Lakeview Avenue, Pensacola, FL 32501; tel. 904/432–1222; Morris L. Eaddy, PhD

Leon F. Stewart–Hal S. Marcham Treatment Center, 120 Michigan Avenue, Daytona Beach, FL 32114; tel. 904/947–1302; FAX. 904/947–1309; Ernest D. Cantley, President, Chief Executive Officer

LifeStream Behavioral Center and Hospital, 515 West Main Street, P.O. Box 491000, Leesburg, FL 34749–1000; tel. 352/360–6575; FAX. 352/360–6595; Jack Hargrove

Lifeskills of Boca Raton, Inc., 7301A West Palmetto Park Road, Suite 300B, Boca Raton, FL 33433; tel. 561/392–1199; FAX. 561/392–4341; Cindy Burke, MS

Manatee Glens Corporation, P.O. Box 9478, Bradenton, FL 24728; tel. 941/741–3111; Mary Ruiz

Marion Citrus Mental Health Centers, Inc., 717 Southwest Martin Luther King Jr. Avenue, P.O. Box 1330, Ocala, FL 34474; tel. 352/620–7300; FAX. 352/732–1413; Russell Rasco, Chief Executive Officer

Mental Health Care, Inc., 5707 North 22nd Street, Tampa, FL 33610; tel. 813/237–3914; FAX. 813/238–6574; Julian Rice, Executive Director

Mental Health Resource Center, Inc., 11820 Beach Boulevard, P.O. Box 19249, Jacksonville, FL 32246; tel. 904/642–9100; FAX. 904/641–6529; Robert A. Sommers, Ph.D., President, Chief Executive Officer

Meridian Behavioral Healthcare, Inc., 4300 Southwest 13th Street, Gainesville, FL 32608; tel. 352/374–5600; FAX. 352/371–9841; Douglas L. Starr, Ph.D., Chief Executive Officer

National Recovery Institutes Group, 1000 Northwest 15th Street, Boca Raton, FL 33486; tel. 407/392–8444; FAX. 407/368–0879; Don Russakoff, President, Chief Executive Officer

Northside Mental Health Center, 12512 Bruce B. Downs Blvd., Tampa, FL 24403; tel. 813/977–8700; Marsha L. Brown, LCSW

Northwest Dade Center, Inc., 4175 West 20th Avenue, Hialeah, FL 33012; tel. 305/825–0300; FAX. 305/824–1006; Mario Jardon, LCSW, Chief Executive Officer

Oak Center, 8889 Corporate Square Court, Jacksonville, FL 32216; tel. 904/725–7073; FAX. 904/727–9777; Joseph A. Virzi, MD

Pathways to Recovery, Inc., 13132 Barwick Road, Delray Beach, FL 33445; tel. 407/496–7532; Allen Bombart, Executive Director

Peace River Center for Personal Development, Inc., 1745 Highway 17, S., Bartow, FL 33830; tel. 941/534–7020; FAX. 941/534–7028; Bert Lacey, Executive Director

Personal Enrichment through Mental Health Services, Inc., 11254 58th Street North, Pinellas Park, FL 33782; tel. 813/545–6477; Thomas C. Wedekind

Recovery Corner of West Palm Beach, 400 Executive Center Drive, Suite 102, West Palm Beach, FL 33410; tel. 561/686–1924; FAX. 561/626–1739; Jay Mills, Executive Director

Renaissance Institute of Palm Beach, Inc., 7000 North Federal Highway, Boca Raton, FL 33487; tel. 561/241–7977; FAX. 561/241–9233; Sid Goodman, M.A., Executive Director

Rivendell of Fort Walton Beach, 1015 Mar Walt Drive, Fort Walton Beach, FL 32547; tel. 904/863–4160; J. M. Townley

Ruth Cooper Center for Behavioral Health Care, Inc., 2789 Ortiz Avenue, Fort Myers, FL 33905; tel. 941/275–3222; Eugene R. Dold

South County Mental Health Center, Inc., 16158 South Military Trail, Delray Beach, FL 33484–6502; tel. 561/637–1000; FAX. 561/495–7975; Joseph S. Speicher, Executive Director

Southern Institute for Treatment and Evaluation, Inc., 660 Linton Boulevard, Suite 112, Delray Beach, FL 33444; tel. 407/278–8411; FAX. 407/278–7774; Michele Michael, Director

Spectrum Programs, Inc., 18441 Northwest Second Avenue, Suite 218, Miami, FL 33169; tel. 305/653–8288, ext. 19; FAX. 305/653–6787; H. Bruce Hayden

Tampa Bay Academy, 12012 Boyette Road, Riverview, FL 33569; tel. 813/677–6700; FAX. 813/671–3145; Edward C. Hoefle, Executive Director

The Center for Alcohol and Drug Studies, Inc., 321 Northlake Blvd., Suite 214, North Palm Beach, FL 33408; tel. 561/848–1332; Donald K. Mullaney, LCSW

The Inn at Bowling Green Family Recovery Center, 101 North Oak Street, Bowling Green, FL 33834; tel. 800/762–3712; FAX. 941/375–2832; JoAnn Summerlin, Vice President, Administration

The Renfrew Center of Florida, 7700 Renfrew Lane, Coconut Creek, FL 33073; tel. 954/698–9222; FAX. 954/698–9007; Barbara Peterson, Executive Director

The Rose Institute, Inc., 17 Rose Drive, Fort Lauderdale, FL 33316; tel. 954/522–7673; FAX. 954/522–4031; Dr. Richard Maulion, Chief Executive Officer

The Village South, Inc., 3180 Biscayne Boulevard, Miami, FL 33137; tel. 305/573–3784; FAX. 305/576–1348; Matthew Gissen, Chief Executive Officer

The Willough at Naples, 9001 Tamiami Trail, E., Naples, FL 33962; tel. 941/775–4500; FAX. 941/793–0534; Gary D. Centafanti, Executive Director

Transitions Recovery Program, 1928 Northeast 154th Street, North Miami Beach, FL 33162; tel. 305/949–9001; Lee Barchan

Treatment Resources, Inc., 25 Northeast 167th Street, North Miami Beach, FL 33162; tel. 305/653–4944; Dale P. Redlich

Turning Point of Tampa, Inc., 6301 Memorial Highway, Suite 201, Tampa, FL 33615; tel. 813/882–3003; FAX. 813/885–6974; Fred Hill

Twelve Oaks, 2068 Healthcare Avenue, Navarre, FL 32566; tel. 904/939–1200; FAX. 904/939–1257; James Griffis

U.S. Life Center of St. Augustine, 1100–3 South Ponce De Leon Boulevard, Saint Augustine, FL 32086; tel. 904/829–5566; FAX. 904/829–0677; James Ferguson, Chief Executive Officer

Wynwood Community Mental Health, Inc., 3550 Biscayne Blvd., Suite 510, Miami, FL 33137; tel. 305/573–3052; Martha Porro

GEORGIA

Albany Area Community Service Board, P.O. Box 1988, Albany, GA 31701; tel. 912/430–4042; John C. Burns III, EdD

Albany Association for Retarded Citizens, P.O. Box 71026, Albany, GA 30682; tel. 912/888–6852; Annette T. Bowling

Anchor Hospital and the Talbott–Marsh Recovery Campus, 5454 Yorktowne Drive, Atlanta, GA 30349; tel. 770/991–6044; FAX. 770/991–3843; Benjamin H. Underwood, FAAMA, President, Chief Executive Officer

Anxiety Disorders Institute of Atlanta Center, One Dunwoody Park, Suite 112, Atlanta, GA 30338; tel. 770/395–6845; Asaf Aleem, Chief Executive Officer

Behavioral Health Services of South Georgia, 206 S. Patterson Steet, P.O. Box 3409, Valdosta, GA 28195; tel. 912/333–7095; David McCracken

Bridges Outpatient Center, Inc., 1209 Columbia Drive, Milledgeville, GA 31061; tel. 912/454–1727; FAX. 912/454–1770; James Simmons, Chief Executive Officer

Brightmore Day Hospital, 115 Davis Road, P.O. Box 211849, Martinez, GA 30907–1849; tel. 404/868–1735; FAX. 404/860–6358; Joy Beaird, MS

Brook Run – Facility of the Georgia Department of Human Resource, 4770 North Peachtree Road, Dunwoody, GA 30338; tel. 770/551–7157; FAX. 770/551–7040; Dr. Rudy Magnone, Chief Executive Officer

Charter Behavioral Health System of Atlanta at Laurel Heights, 934 Briarcliff Road, N.E., Atlanta, GA 30306; tel. 404/888–7860; FAX. 404/872–5088; Jewel W. Norman

Decatur Seminole Service Center, 333 Airport Road, Bainbridge, GA 31717; tel. 912/246–6108; Ben H. Strickland

Devereux Center In Georgia, 1291 Stanley Road, N.W., Kennesaw, GA 30152–4359; tel. 770/427–0147; FAX. 770/425–1413; Ralph L. Comerford, Executive Director

Georgia Pines Community Service Board, P.O. Box 1659, Thomasville, GA 31799; tel. 912/225–4335; Robert H. Jones, Jr.

Gracewood State School and Hospital, P.O. Box 1299, Gracewood, GA 30812; tel. 706/790–2030; Joanne P. Miklas, PhD

Green Oaks M.R. Service Center, P.O. Box 1824, Moultrie, GA 31776; tel. 912/985–7298; Lemuel (Zeke) J. Cothern, MS

Inner Harbour Hospitals, Ltd., 4685 Dorsett Shoals Road, Douglasville, GA 30135; tel. 770/942–2391; Ron Scroggy

LARC, Inc., 1646 East Park Avenue, Valdosta, GA 31602; tel. 912/244–8290; Lonnie Smith

Learning Services Southeastern Region–Specialists in NeuroRehabilitation, 2400 Highway 29, S., Lawrenceville, GA 30245; tel. 770/962–4828; FAX. 770/995–1253; Randy Mitchell

McIntosh Trail MH/MR/SA Community Service Board, P.O. Box 1320, Griffin, GA 30223; tel. 770/229–3069; Cathy Johnson

Mitchell–Baker Mental Retardation Service Center, 65 Industrial Blvd., Camilla, GA 31730; tel. 912/336–7977; J. Dale Goodman, MS

Murphy–Harpst–Vashti, Inc., 740 Fletcher Street, Cedartown, GA 30125; tel. 770/748–1500; FAX. 770/749–1094; Joanne G. Simmons

Safe Recovery Systems, Inc., 2300 Peachtree Road, Suite 2000, Atlanta, GA 30338; tel. 770/455–7233; FAX. 770/458–1481; Henslee Dutton, Chief Executive Director

Schizophrenia Treatment and Rehabilitation, Inc., 208 Church Street, Decatur, GA 30030; tel. 404/377–9844; FAX. 404/373–5258; Kimberly H. Littrell, RN, MS

Skyland Trail, 2573 Skyland Trail, N.E., Atlanta, GA 30319; tel. 888/248–4801; FAX. 404/248–8956; Elizabeth Finnerty, Chief Executive Officer

Thomas Grady Service Center, P.O. Box 2507, Thomasville, GA 31799; tel. 912/225–4065; Marianne Ellis

Turning Point Hospital, 319 Bypass, P.O. Box 1177 (zip 31768), Moultrie, GA 31776; tel. 912/985–4815; Ben Marion

Willingway Hospital, 311 Jones Mill Road, Statesboro, GA 30458; tel. 912/764–6236; FAX. 912/764–7063; Jimmy Mooney

IDAHO

Northview Hospital, 8050 Northview Street, Boise, ID 83704; tel. 208/327–0504; FAX. 208/327–0594; Gregory P. Hassakis

Walker Center, 1120A Montana Street, Gooding, ID 83330–1858; tel. 208/934–8461; FAX. 208/934–5437; Vayle Mauldin, Program Director

ILLINOIS

Alexian Brothers Lake–Cook Behavioral Health Resources, 999A Leicester, (Mailing address: 3265 North Arlington Heights Road, Suite 307, Arlington Heights, IL 60004), Elk Grove Village, IL 60007; tel. 708/577–1501; FAX. 708/577–0256; Mark Frey, Chief Executive Officer

Allendale Association, Grand Avenue and Offield Road, P.O. Box 1088, Lake Villa, IL 60046; tel. 847/356–2351; FAX. 847/356–2393; Mary Shahbazian, MS

American Day Treatment Centers, 1111 Pasquinelli Drive, Suite 50, Westmont, IL 60559; tel. 708/920–8700; James K. Don

Association House of Chicago, 2150 West North Avenue, Chicago, IL 60647; tel. 773/276–0084; Harriet Sadauskas

Aunt Martha's Youth Service Center, Inc., 4343 Lincoln Highway, Suite 340, Matteson, IL 60443; tel. 708/747–2701; C. Gary Leofanti

Beacon Therapeutic Diagnostic and Treatment Center, 10650 South Longwood Drive, Chicago, IL 60643; tel. 312/881–1005; Margaret M. Morley

Ben Gordon Center, Inc., 12 Health Services Drive, DeKalb, IL 60115; tel. 815/756–4875; James W. Graves

Camelot Care Center, Inc., 1502 North Northwest Highway, Palatine, IL 60067; tel. 847/359–5600; FAX. 847/359–2759; James V. Doramus

Center on Deafness, 3444 Dundee Road, Northbrook, IL 60062; tel. 847/559–0110; Judy Pierce, PhD

Champaign County Association for the Mentally Retarded, P.O. Box 92, Champaign, IL 61824; tel. 217/359–9204; Kenston Chism

Chestnut Health Systems, Inc., 1003 Dr. Martin Luther King Jr. Drive, Bloomington, IL 61701; tel. 309/827–6026; Russell J. Hagen

Community Counseling Center, 2615 Edwards Street, Alton, IL 62002; tel. 618/462–4883; Kristine Gamm-Smith

Community Mental Health Center of Fulton & McDonough Counties, 229 Martin Avenue, Canton, IL 61520; tel. 309/647–1881; David W. Shane

Comprehensive Mental Health Center of St. Clair County, 3911 State Street, East St. Louis, IL 62205; tel. 618/482–7330; Dolores S. Ray

DuPage County Health Department/Mental Health Division, 111 North County Farm Road, Wheaton, IL 60187; tel. 708/682–7979; FAX. 708/690–5282; Dr. Gary Noll, Chief Executive Officer

Family Service and Community Mental Health Center/McHenry, 5320 West Elm Street, McHenry, IL 60050; tel. 815/385–6400; FAX. 815/385–8127; Robert Martens, Chief Executive Officer

Gateway Youth Care Foundation, P.O. Box 1076, Lake Villa, IL 60046; tel. 708/356–8292; Michael Darcy

Great River Recovery Resources, Inc., 428 South 36th Street, Quincy, IL 62301; tel. 217/224–6300; FAX. 217/224–4329; Michael Hutmacher, Chief Executive Officer

Horizons Wellness Center, Inc., 970 South McHenry Avenue, Crystal Lake, IL 60014; tel. 815/477–8881; FAX. 815/477–4886; Laura Murphy

Inter Agency, Inc., 1610 West 89th Street, Chicago, IL 60620; tel. 773/233–9083; Robert E. Dorcak

Interventions South Wood, 5701 South Wood, Chicago, IL 60636; tel. 312/737–4600; Peter Bokos

Interventions Woodridge, 2221 64th Street, Woodridge, IL 60517; tel. 630/968–6477; FAX. 630/968–5744; John Bailey

Interventions, City Girls/City Women, 140 North Ashland, Chicago, IL 60607; tel. 312/433–7777; FAX. 312/433–7787; Dr. Peter Bokos, Chief Executive Officer

Interventions–DuPage Adolescent Center, 11 South 250 Route 53, Hinsdale, IL 60521; tel. 630/325–5050; FAX. 630/325–9130; John Bailey

Jane Addams, Inc., 1133 W. Stephenson Street, Suite 401, Freeport, IL 61032; tel. 815/232–4183; Daniel Neal

Janet Wattles Center, Inc., 526 West State Street, Rockford, IL 61101; tel. 815/968–9300; Frank H. Ware, ACSW

Lake County Health Department/Behavioral Health Services, 3012 Grand Avenue, Waukegan, IL 60085; tel. 847/360–6729; Dale W. Galassie, MS

McHenry County Youth Service Bureau, 101 South Jefferson Street, Woodstock, IL 60098; tel. 815/338–7360; FAX. 815/337–5510; Susan H. Krause, Executive Director

Mental Health Center of Champaign County, P.O. Box 1640, Champaign, IL 60184; tel. 217/398–8080; Alexandria Lewis

Mental Health and Deafness Resources, Inc., 3444 Dundee Road, Northbrook, IL 60062; tel. 847/559–0110; Patricia Scherer

Minirth Meier Clinic of Wheaton, PC, 2100 Manchester Road, Suite 1410 and 1510, Wheaton, IL 60187; tel. 708/653–1717; FAX. 708/653–7926; Nancy Brown, Clinic Director

North Central Behavioral Health Systems, Inc., P.O. Box 1488, LaSalle, IL 61301; tel. 815/223–0160; Donald P. Miskowiec

Perry County Counseling Center, Inc., P.O. Box 189, Du Quoin, IL 62832; tel. 618/542–4357; John R. Venskus

ProCare Centers, 1820 South 25th Avenue, Broadview, IL 60153; tel. 708/681–2324; J. Martin Smith

Rosecrance on Alpine, 1505 North Alpine Road, Rockford, IL 61107; tel. 815/399–5351; FAX. 815/398–2641; Philip W. Eaton

Rosecrance on Harrison, 3815 Harrison Avenue, Rockford, IL 61108; tel. 815/391–1000; Philip W. Eaton, President, Chief Executive Officer

Sinnissippi Centers, Inc., 325 Illinois Route 2, Dixon, IL 61021; tel. 815/284–6611; James R. Sarver

Sojourn House, Inc., 565 North Turner Avenue, Freeport, IL 61032; tel. 815/232–5121; FAX. 815/233–4591; Brenda J. Bombard, M.S.W., Executive Director

Southeastern Illinois Counseling Centers, Inc., 504 Micah Drive, P.O. Drawer M, Olney, IL 62450; tel. 618/395–4306; FAX. 618/395–4507; Gary Robertson, Executive Director

Southern Illinois Regional Social Services, 604 East College, Suite 101, Carbondale, IL 62901; tel. 618/457–6703; Audrey O. Minor, MSW

Stepping Stones of Rockford, Inc., 706 North Main Street, Rockford, IL 61103; tel. 815/963–0683; Stephen Langley, LCSW

Tazwood Center for Human Services, Inc., 1421 Valle Vista Blvd., Pekin, IL 61554; tel. 309/347–5522; Clifford E. Mills

The Women's Treatment Center, 140 North Ashland, Chicago, IL 60607; tel. 312/850–0050; FAX. 312/850–9095; Dr. Jewell Oats, Chief Executive Officer

Triangle Center, 120 North 11th Street, Springfield, IL 62703; tel. 217/544–9858; FAX. 217/544–0223; Stephen J. Knox, Executive Director

White Oaks Companies of Illinois, 3400 New Leaf Lane, Peoria, IL 61614; tel. 309/692–6900; FAX. 309/689–3086; Dr. John Gilligan, Chief Executive Officer

INDIANA

Adult and Child Mental Health Center, Inc., 8320 Madison Avenue, Indianapolis, IN 46227; tel. 317/882–5122; A. Robert Dunbar

BehaviorCorp., Inc., P.O. Box 1129, Carmel, IN 46032; tel. 317/587–0500; Larry L. Burch, ACSW

Community Mental Health Center, Inc., 285 Bielby Road, Lawrenceburg, IN 47025; tel. 812/537–1302; FAX. 812/537–5219; Joseph Stephens, Chief Executive Officer

Comprehensive Mental Health Services, Inc., 240 North Tillotson Avenue, Muncie, IN 47304; tel. 317/288–1928; FAX. 317/741–0310; Suzanne Gresham, Ph.D., Chief Executive Officer

Evansville Psychiatric Children's Center, 3300 East Morgan Avenue, Evansville, IN 47715; tel. 812/477–6436; FAX. 812/474–4248; Thomas C. Andis, Jr., Superintendent

Fairbanks Hospital, Inc., 8102 Clearvista Parkway, Indianapolis, IN 46256–4698; tel. 317/849–8222, ext. 100; FAX. 317/849–1455; Timothy J. Kelly, M.D., Interim Administrator

Fairbanks Hospital, Inc., 8102 Clearvista Parkway, Indianapolis, IN 41558; tel. 317/849–8222; Timothy J. Kelly, MD

Four County Counseling Center, 1015 Michigan Avenue, Logansport, IN 46947; tel. 219/722–5151, ext. 281; FAX. 219/722–9523; Laurence Ulrich, Chief Executive Officer

Grant–Blackford Mental Health, Inc., 505 Wabash Avenue, Marion, IN 46952; tel. 317/662–3971; FAX. 317/662–7480; Paul Kuczora, Chief Executive Officer

Hamilton Center, Inc., 620 Eighth Avenue, P.O. Box 4323 (zip 43481), Terre Haute, IN 47804; tel. 812/231–8323; FAX. 812/231–8400; Galen Goode, Chief Executive Officer

Life Spring Mental Health Center, 207 West 13th Street, Jeffersonville, IN 47130; tel. 812/283–4491; John Case, MA

Madison Center, Inc., P.O. Box 80, South Bend, IN 46624; tel. 219/283–2108; FAX. 219/234–0670; Jack Roberts

Park Center, Inc., 909 East State Boulevard, Fort Wayne, IN 46805; tel. 219/481–2700; FAX. 219/481–2717; Paul D. Wilson, Chief Executive Officer

Porter–Starke Services, 601 Wall Street, Valparaiso, IN 46383; tel. 219/531–3500; FAX. 219/462–3975; Lee Grogg, Chief Executive Officer

Quinco Behavioral Health Systems, P.O. Box 628, Columbus, IN 47202–0628; tel. 812/379–2341; FAX. 812/376–4875; Robert J. Williams, Ph.D., Chief Executive Officer

Sharing and Caring Community Mental Health Center, Inc., 2511 East 46th Street, Suite O–1, Indianapolis, IN 46205; tel. 317/377–5300; Karen L. Ladd

South Central Community Mental Health Centers, Inc., 645 South Rogers Street, Bloomington, IN 47403; tel. 812/339–1691; FAX. 812/339–8109; Dennis Morrison, PhD

Southlake Community Mental Health Center, Inc., 8555 Taft Street, Merrillville, IN 40211; tel. 219/769–4005; Lee C. Strawhun, MPA

Southwestern Indiana Mental Health Center, Inc., 415 Mulberry Street, Evansville, IN 47713; tel. 812/423–7791; FAX. 812/422–7558; John K. Browning, Executive Director

Swanson Center, 450 St. John Road, Suite 501, Michigan City, IN 39010; tel. 219/879–4621; Larry D. Miller

Tara Treatment Center, Inc., 6231 South U.S. Highway 31, R.R. 5, Box 225, Franklin, IN 46131; tel. 812/373–9399; FAX. 812/526–8527; Ann Daugherty–James, Chief Executive Officer

The Center for Mental Health, Inc., 1100 Broadway, P.O. Box 1258, Anderson, IN 46015; tel. 317/649–8161; FAX. 317/641–8238; C. Richard DeHaven, President

The Children's Campus, 1411 Lincoln Way, W., Mishawaka, IN 46544–1690; tel. 219/259–5666, ext. 222; FAX. 219/255–6179; Sylvia Sebert

The Madison Clinic, Inc., 6405 Pendleton Avenue, Suite 300, Anderson, IN 46013; tel. 317/644–1414; FAX. 317/646–8462; Pamela L. Porter

The Madison Clinic, Inc., 6405 Pendleton Avenue, Suite 300, Anderson, IN 46013; tel. 317/644–1414; Pamela L. Porter

The Midwest Center for Youth and Families, P.O. Box 669, Kouts, IN 46347; tel. 219/766–2999; Jeanne Walsh, MSW

The Otis R. Bowen Center for Human Services, Inc., P.O. Box 497, Warsaw, IN 46084; tel. 219/267–7169; Kurt Carlson

Tri–City Comprehensive Community Mental Health Center, 3903 Indianapolis Boulevard, East Chicago, IN 46312; tel. 219/398–7050; FAX. 219/392–6998; Robert Krumwied

Wabash Valley Hospital, Inc., 2900 North River Road, West Lafayette, IN 47906; tel. 765/463–2555; FAX. 765/497–3960; R. Craig Lysinger, Chief Executive Officer

IOWA

Beloit Lutheran Children's Home/Lutheran Social Service, 1323 Northwestern, Ames, IA 50010; tel. 515/232–7262; FAX. 515/232–7416; Roger Gutman

Boys and Girls Home And Family Service, Inc., 2601 Douglas Street, P.O. Box 1197 (zip 51102), Sioux City, IA 51104; tel. 712/252–1133; Robert P. Sheehan, Chief Executive Officer

Children and Families of Iowa, 1111 University, Des Moines, IA 50314; tel. 515/288–1981, ext. 346; FAX. 515/288–9109, ext. 402; David Stout

Christian Home Association–Children's Square U.S.A., North Sixth Street and Avenue E, P.O. Box 8–C, Council Bluffs, IA 51502–3008; tel. 712/322–3700; FAX. 712/325–0913; Carol D. Wood, ACSW, L.I.S.W., President, Chief Executive Officer

Four Oaks, Inc. Smith Center, 5400 Kirkwood Boulevard, S.W., Cedar Rapids, IA 52404; tel. 319/364–0259; FAX. 319/364–1162; James A. Ernst, MSW

Gerard Treatment Programs, 980 South Iowa Avenue, P.O. Box 1353, Mason City, IA 50401; tel. 515/423–3222; Rita Paxson, Chief Executive Officer

Hillcrest Family Services, 2005 Asbury Road, P.O. Box 1160 (zip 50844), Dubuque, IA 52004–1161; tel. 319/583–7357; FAX. 319/583–7026; Donald B. Lewis, Jr., ACSW

Orchard Place–Child Guidance, 925 Southwest Porter Avenue, P.O. Box 35425, Des Moines, IA 50315–0304; tel. 515/285–6781, ext. 601; FAX. 515/287–9695; Earl P. Kelly, Chief Executive Officer

Tanager Place, 2309 C Street, S.W., Cedar Rapids, IA 52404; tel. 319/365–9164; FAX. 319/365–6411; George Estle

KANSAS

Atchison Valley Hope, 1816 North Second Street, P.O. Box 312, Atchison, KS 66002; tel. 913/367–1618; FAX. 913/367–6224; Dennis Gilhousen, Chief Executive Officer

Section C

Columbia Health Systems, Inc., 10114 West 105th Street, Suite 100, Overland Park, KS 66212; tel. 913/492–9875; FAX. 913/492–0187; Robert L. Reed, President

Comprehensive Evaluation and Treatment Unit, CETU–Brigham Building, 300 Southwest Oakley, Topeka, KS 66606; tel. 913/296–2196; FAX. 913/296–2204; Robert Hedberg

Jewish Family and Children Services, 5801 West 115th, Suite 103, Overland Park, KS 66211; tel. 913/491–4357; Patti Glass

Kaw Valley Center, 4300 Brenner Drive, Kansas City, KS 66104; tel. 913/334–0294; B. Wayne Sims, President, Chief Executive Officer

Norton Valley Hope, 709 West Holme, P.O. Box 510, Norton, KS 67654; tel. 913/877–5101; FAX. 913/877–2322; Dennis R. Gilhousen, President, Chief Executive Officer

The Saint Francis Academy, Incorporated, 509 East Elm Street, Salina, KS 67401; tel. 785/825–0541; FAX. 785/825–2502; Reverend Phillip J. Rapp, President, Chief Executive Officer

United Methodist Youthville, Inc., 900 West Broadway, P.O. Box 210, Newton, KS 67114; tel. 316/283–1950, ext. 305; FAX. 316/283–9540; Robert Smith

KENTUCKY

Adanta Behavioral Health Services, 259 Parkers Mill Road, Somerset, KY 42501; tel. 606/678–7180; FAX. 606/678–5296; Ronald D. Mullins

Bluegrass Regional Mental Health–Mental Retardation Board, 1351 Newton Pike, P.O. Box 11428 (zip 40575), Lexington, KY 40511; tel. 606/253–1686; Joseph A. Toy

Brooklawn, Inc., 2125 Goldsmith Lane, Louisville, KY 40218; tel. 502/451–5177; David A. Graves, President, Chief Executive Officer

Central State ICF/MR, 10510 LaGrange Road, Louisville, KY 40223; tel. 502/253–7311; FAX. 502/253–7049; T. Richelle Jones

Christian Church Homes Children's and Family Services, 1151 Perryville Road, P.O. Box 45 (zip 40378), Danville, KY 40423–0045; tel. 606/236–5507; FAX. 606/236–7044; Kathy Miles, Chief Executive Officer

Comprehensive Care Centers of Northern Kentucky, Inc., 503 Farrell Drive, P.O. Box 2680 (zip 41012), Covington, KY 41011; tel. 606/578–3252; FAX. 606/578–3256; Edward G. Muntel, Ph.D., President

Cumberland River Regional Mental Health and Mental Retardation, Inc., American Greeting Road, P.O. Box 568, Corbin, KY 40702; tel. 606/528–7010; Ralph Lipps, Executive Director

Jefferson Alcohol and Drug Abuse Center, 600 South Preston Street, Louisville, KY 40202; tel. 502/583–3951; FAX. 502/581–9234; Diane E. Hague, Director

Pathways, Inc., 3701 Lansdowne Drive, P.O. Box 790, Ashland, KY 41105–0790; tel. 606/329–8588, ext. 142; FAX. 606/329–8195; Robert T. Stai, LCSW, ACSW

Presbyterian Child Welfare Agency, One Buckhorn Lane, Buckhorn, KY 41721; tel. 606/398–7245; Charles Baker, President, Chief Executive Officer

RiverValley Behavioral Health, 416 West Third Street, P.O. Box 1637, Zip 42302–1637, Owensboro, KY 42302; tel. 502/684–0696; FAX. 502/683–4696; Gayle DiCesare, Chief Executive Officer

Seven Counties Services, Inc., 101 West Muhammad Ali Boulevard, Louisville, KY 40202–1430; tel. 502/589–8600; Howard F. Bracco, PhD

Spectrum Care Academy, 4500 Campbellsville Road, P.O. Box 911, Columbia, KY 42728; tel. 502/384–6444; FAX. 502/384–4883; Tony C. Harvey

LOUISIANA

Addiction Recovery Resources of New Orleans, 401 Veterans Boulevard, Suite 102, Metairie, LA 70005; tel. 504/529–2663; FAX. 504/831–8949; Franklin D. Polk

Bowling Green Hospital of St. Tammany, Inc., P.O. Box 417, Mandeville, LA 70448; tel. 504/626–5661; Joseph DeNucci

CHARIS Community Mental Health Center, Inc., 8264 One Calais Avenue, Baton Rouge, LA 70809; tel. 504/767–8478; Carolyn Carroll

Hope Haven Center (Residential Treatment), Includes Hope Haven, Madonna Manor, St. Elizabeth's, 1101 Barataria Boulevard, Marrero, LA 70072; tel. 504/347–5581; FAX. 504/340–2075; Robert J. Guasco, Chief Administrative Officer

LA United Methodist Children and Family Services, Inc., 901 South Vienna Street, P.O. Box 929, Ruston, LA 71273–0929, Ruston, LA 71270; tel. 318/255–5020; FAX. 318/255–5457; Terrel DeVille, Chief Executive Officer

Meadowbrook Residential Treatment Center, 100 Meadowbrook Drive, P.O. Box 725, Zip 71058–0725, Minden, LA 71055; tel. 318/371–9494; FAX. 318/371–9933; Roy Martinez, Chief Executive Officer

New Beginnings Residential Program of Opelousas, 1692 Linwood Loop, Opelousas, LA 70570; tel. 318/942–1171; FAX. 318/948–9101; Kim Signorelli, Chief Executive Officer

St. Patrick's Psychiatric Hospital, P.O. Box 1901, Monroe, LA 69309; tel. 318/327–4370; Cindy J. Rogers

Vermilion Hospital for Psychiatric and Addictive Medicine, 2520 North University Avenue, P.O. Box 91526 (zip 70509), Lafayette, LA 70507; tel. 318/234–5614; FAX. 318/235–0696; Johnny Patout, Administrator

MAINE

Community Health and Counseling Services, 42 Cedar Street, P.O. Box 425, Bangor, ME 04402–0425; tel. 207/947–0366; FAX. 207/990–3581; Joseph H. Pickerling, Jr., Executive Director

Kids Peace National Centers for Kids in Crisis New England, Route 180, P.O. Box 787, Ellsworth, ME 04605; tel. 207/667–0909; FAX. 207/667–6348; George W. Russell III, ACSW

MARYLAND

A. F. Whitsitt Rehabilitation Center, 300 Scheeler Road, P.O. Box 229, Chestertown, MD 21620; tel. 410/778–6404, ext. 38; FAX. 410/778–5431; Gary B. Fry, MSW, MPH

Allegany County Health Department Addictions Program, Willowbrook Road, P.O. Box 1745, Cumberland, MD 21502; tel. 301/777–5680; Rodger D. Simons, Administrator

American Day Treatment Centers of Chevy Chase, LP, Two Wisconsin Circle, Suite 620, Chevy Chase, MD 20815; tel. 301/656–0151; James K. Don

American Day Treatment Centers of the Northeast Region, Riva 400 Office Park, Suite 1020, Annapolis, MD 21401; tel. 610/725–8663; Mark O. Johnson

Ashley, Inc., 800 Tydings Lane, Havre DeGrace, MD 21078; tel. 410/273–6600; FAX. 410/272–5617; Father Joseph C. Martin, SS

Baltimore Recovery Center, 16 South Poppleton Street, Baltimore, MD 21201; tel. 410/962–7180; FAX. 410/962–7192; Sandra K. Hill, RN, MBA

Changing Point, 4100 College Avenue, P.O. Box 396, Ellicott City, MD 21041–0396; tel. 410/465–9500; FAX. 410/465–9500; Morris L. Scherr

Charter Behavioral Health Systems at Warwick Manor, 3680 Warwick Road, East New Market, MD 21631; tel. 410/943–8108; Marie McBee

Choptank Center, P.O. Box 1238, Cambridge, MD 21613; tel. 410/221–0288; FAX. 410/228–9588; Cecilia Donnelly, NC

Crossroads Centers, Two West Madison Street, Baltimore, MD 21201; tel. 410/752–6505; FAX. 410/385–1237; Barbara Q. McKenna, Executive Director

Edgemeade Residential Treatment Center, 13400 Edgemeade Road, Upper Marlboro, MD 20772; tel. 301/888–1330; FAX. 301/579–2342; James Filipczak, Ph.D., Executive Director

Glass Substance Abuse Programs, Inc., 821 North Eutaw Street, Suite 201, 101, Baltimore, MD 21201; tel. 410/225–9185; FAX. 410/225–7964; Herman Jones, President

Good Shepherd Center, 4100 Maple Avenue, Baltimore, MD 21227–4099; tel. 410/247–2770; FAX. 410/247–3242; Sister Mary Rosaria Baxter, M.S., Administrator

Hope House, Marbury Drive, Building 26, P.O. Box 546, Crownsville, MD 21032; tel. 410/923–6700; FAX. 410/923–6213; William H. Rufenacht, Executive Director

Hudson Health Services, 1506 Harting Drive, P.O. Box 1096, Salisbury, MD 21802–1096; tel. 410/219–9000; FAX. 410/742–7048; Charles F. Andrews

Maryland Treatment Centers, Inc., U. S. Route 15, P.O. Box E, Emmitsburg, MD 21727; tel. 301/447–2361; FAX. 301/447–6504; Mary A. Roby, President

Melwood Farm Treatment Center, 19715 Zion Road, P.O. Box 182, Olney, MD 20832; tel. 800/368–8313; Elliott Neal White, MHA

New Life Addiction Counseling Services, Inc., 2528 Mountain Road, Pasadena, MD 21122; tel. 410/255–4475; FAX. 410/255–6277; Thomas S. Porter, Chief Executive Officer

Oakview Treatment Center, 3100 North Ridge Road, Ellicott City, MD 21043; tel. 410/461–9922; Ned Rubin, MS, RN

Partners in Recovery, 6509 North Charles Street, Baltimore, MD 21204; tel. 410/296–9747; Robert P. Kowal

Pathways Drug and Alcohol Treatment Center, 2620 Riva Road, Annapolis, MD 21401; tel. 410/573–5400; FAX. 410/573–5401; Dale G. Bruce

Quarterway Houses, Inc., 730 Ashburton Street, P.O. Box 31419, Baltimore, MD 21216–6119; tel. 410/233–0684; FAX. 410/233–8540; Dr. Joseph Verrett, Chief Executive Officer

Regional Institute for Children and Adolescents–Baltimore, 605 South Chapel Gate Lane, Baltimore, MD 21229; tel. 410/368–7800; FAX. 410/368–7886; Clifford A. Palmer, Chief Executive Officer

Regional Institute for Children and Adolescents/Rockville, 15000 Broschart Road, Rockville, MD 20850–3392; tel. 301/251–6800; FAX. 301/309–9004; John L. Gildner, Chief Executive Officer

Regional Institute for Children and Adolescents/Southern Maryland, 9400 Surratts Road, Cheltenham, MD 20623; tel. 301/372–1800; FAX. 301/372–1906; Joseph H. O'Leary, MD

Saint Luke Institute, Inc., 8901 New Hampshire Avenue, Silver Spring, MD 20903; tel. 301/445–7970; FAX. 301/422–5400; Reverend Stephen J. Rossetti, Ph.D., President, Chief Executive Officer

Villa Maria, 2300 Dulaney Valley Road, Timonium, MD 21093; tel. 410/252–4700; FAX. 410/252–3040; Mark Greenberg, LCSW, Administrator

Woodbourne Center, Inc., 1301 Woodbourne Avenue, Baltimore, MD 21239; tel. 410/433–1000; FAX. 410/435–4745, ext. 221; John Hodge–Williams, EdD

Worcester County Health Department, 6040 Public Landing Road, P.O. Box 249, Snow Hill, MD 21863; tel. 410/632–1100; FAX. 410/632–0906; Deborah Goeller, RN, M.S., Health Officer

MASSACHUSETTS

AdCare Hospital of Worcester, Inc., 107 Lincoln Street, Worcester, MA 01605; tel. 508/799–9000; FAX. 508/753–3733; David W. Hillis, President, Chief Executive Officer

Baldpate Hospital, Baldpate Road, Georgetown, MA 01833; tel. 508/352–2131; Lucille Batal

Brighton Center for Children and Families, 77 Warren Street, Building Four, Brighton, MA 02135; tel. 617/787–4484; FAX. 617/787–4494; Julie Heuberger

Cape Cod Alcoholism Intervention and Rehabilitation Unit, Inc., d/b/a Gosnold on Cape Cod, 200 Ter Heun Drive, Box CC, Falmouth, MA 02541; tel. 508/540–6550; FAX. 508/540–6550; Raymond Tamasi, President, Chief Executive Officer

Cape Cod and the Islands, Community Mental Health Center, 830 Country Road, Pocasset, MA 02601; tel. 508/563–2276; Richard Dunnells, Center Director, Superintendent

Center for Health and Human Services, Inc., 370 Faunce Corner Road, Mailing Address: P.O. Box 2097, New Bedford, MA 02741; North Dartmouth, MA 02747; tel. 508/995–4853; FAX. 508/995–1868; Warren Davis, Chief Executive Officer

Centerpoint, Tewksbury Hospital, Southgate, 365 East Street, P.O. Box 374, Tewksbury, MA 01876; tel. 508/858–3776; FAX. 508/858–3494; Carolyn Ingalls, Program Director

Charles River Intensive Residential Treatment Program, 60 Hodges Avenue–Goss Three, Taunton, MA 02780–0997; tel. 508/824–7575; FAX. 508/824–7528; Eleni Carr, Program Director

Chauncy Hall Academy, 167 Lyman Street, P.O. Box 732, Westborough, MA 01581; tel. 508/774–0774; FAX. 508/774–8369; Bernard Kingsley

Choate Health Systems, Inc., 23 Warren Avenue, Woburn, MA 01801; tel. 617/279–0200, ext. 304; FAX. 617/279–2804; Stuart L. Koman, PhD

Doctor Franklin Perkins School, 971 Main Street, Lancaster, MA 01523; tel. 508/365–7375; Charles P. Conroy, EdD

Dr. Harry C. Solomon Mental Health Center, 391 Varnum Avenue, Lowell, MA 01854; tel. 508/454–8851; FAX. 508/454–7538; Linda Sutter, Chief Executive Officer

Dr. John C. Corrigan Mental Health Center, 49 Hillside Street, Fall River, MA 02720; tel. 508/678–2901; FAX. 508/678–2290; Daniel K. Amigone

Dr. Solomon Carter Fuller Mental Health Center, 85 East Newton Street, Boston, MA 02118–2389; tel. 617/266–8800, ext. 436; FAX. 617/421–9190; Dr. Jean Wilkinson, Center Director

Erich Lindermann Mental Health Center, 25 Stanford Street, Boston, MA 02114; tel. 617/727–5500; FAX. 617/727–5500; Kathleen Brown

Fuller Intensive Residential Treatment Program, 85 East Newton Street, Sixth Floor East, Boston, MA 02118; tel. 617/536–1227; FAX. 617/536–1837; Michael Krupa, Chief Executive Officer

High Point, 1233 State Road, Route 3A, Plymouth, MA 02360; tel. 508/224–7701; FAX. 508/224–2845; Daniel Mumbauer, Chief Executive Officer

Intensive Treatment Unit, 3832 Hancock Road, Route 43, (Mailing Address: P.O. Box 4699, Pittsfield, MA 01202–4699), Lanesboro, MA 01237; tel. 413/499–7924; FAX. 413/443–0143; Gerald Burke, Chief Executive Officer

Meadowridge Behavioral Health Center, Residential Psychiatric Care, 664 Stevens Road, Swansea, MA 02777; tel. 800/479–8740; FAX. 508/678–9059; John Lynch, Program Director

Quincy Mental Health Center, 460 Quincy Avenue, Quincy, MA 02169; tel. 617/770–4000; Margaret LaMontagne

Southeastern Area, Dept. of Mental Health, 165 Quincy Street, Brockton, MA 02402; tel. 508/580–0800; FAX. 508/588–2949; Linda Lundin

Spectrum Addiction Services,Inc., 106 East Main Street, Westboro, MA 01581; tel. 508/898–1550; FAX. 508/898–1578; Roy Ross, Chief Executive Officer

The Grove Adolescent Treatment Center, 320 Riverside Drive, Northampton, MA 01060; tel. 413/586–6210; FAX. 413/586–7852; Hal Gibber, MEd

The Kolburne School, Inc., Southfield Road, New Marlborough, MA 01230; tel. 413/229–8787; FAX. 413/229–7708; Paul Weinstein, M.A., Executive Director

The May Institute, Inc., 940 Main Street, P.O. Box 899, South Harwich, MA 02661; tel. 508/432–5530; FAX. 508/432–3478; Dr. Walter P. Christian, Chief Executive Officer

The Three Rivers Treatment Program, 94 Mosher Street, Holyoke, MA 01040; tel. 413/536–8833; FAX. 413/536–7907; Carl Cutchins, Chief Executive Officer

The Whitney Academy, Inc., 10 Middleboro Road, P.O. Box 619, East Freetown, MA 02717; tel. 508/763–3737; FAX. 508/763–4200; George E. Harmon, Executive Director

University of Massachusetts I.R.T.P., 305 Belmont Street, Seventh Floor, Worcester, MA 01604; tel. 508/856–1455; FAX. 508/856–1435; Aaron Lazare, Chief Executive Officer

Wild Acre Inns, 108 Pleasant Street, Arlington, MA 02174–4813; tel. 617/643–0643, ext. 116; Bernard S. Yudowitz, MD

MICHIGAN

ACAC, Inc., 3949 Sparks Avenue, S.E., Suite 103, Grand Rapids, MI 49546; tel. 616/957–5850; FAX. 616/957–5853; Michael Durco, Chief Executive Officer

AOS, Inc., 1331 Lake Drive, S.E., Grand Rapids, MI 49506; tel. 616/456–8010; FAX. 616/451–0020; Charles Logie, President

Adult/Youth Developmental Services, PC, 23133 Orchard Lake Road, Suite 104, Farmington, MI 48336; tel. 810/477–0107; Dr. George Kates, Chief Executive Officer

Advanced Counseling Services, PC, 30700 Telegraph Rd., Suite 2560, Bingham Farms, MI 48025; tel. 248/203–1770; Arthur L. Hughett, MD

Alcohol Information and Counseling Center, 1575 Suncrest Drive, Lapeer, MI 48446; tel. 810/667–0243; FAX. 810/667–9399; John D. Niederhauser, MPH

Alger–Marquette Community Mental Health Center, 200 West Spring Street, Marquette, MI 49855; tel. 906/225–7201; FAX. 906/225–7204; William G. Birch, Ed.D., M.S.W., Chief Executive Officer

Allegan Substance Abuse Agency, Inc., 120 Cutler Street, Allegan, MI 49010; tel. 616/673–8735; FAX. 616/673–1572; Barbara A. Chamberlain, ACSW

Ann Arbor Consultation Services, 5331 Plymouth Road, Ann Arbor, MI 48105; tel. 313/996–9111; Steven Sheldon, Director

Antrim Kalkaska Community Mental Health, P.O. Box 220, Bellaire, MI 49395; tel. 616/533–8619; Ross L. Gibson, MA

Auro Medical Center, 1711 South Woodward, Suite 102, Bloomfield Hills, MI 48302; tel. 248/335–1130; FAX. 248/335–4680; Sue Comer, Contact Person

Battle Creek Child Guidance Center, Inc., 155 Garfield Avenue, Battle Creek, MI 49017; tel. 616/968–9280; FAX. 616/966–4123; Charles Dolk, Chief Executive Officer

Boniface Human Services, 25050 West Outer Drive, Suite 201, Lincoln Park, MI 48146; tel. 313/928–8940; FAX. 313/928–5152; George B. Van Antwerp

Brighton Hospital, 12851 East Grand River Avenue, Brighton, MI 48116; tel. 810/227–1211, ext. 235; FAX. 810/227–1869; Ramon Royal

CHIP Counseling Center, Inc., 6777 U.S. 31 South, Charlevoix, MI 49720; tel. 616/547–6551; Patrick Q. Nestor, Executive Director

Catholic Services of Macomb, 235 South Gratiot Avenue, Mount Clemens, MI 48043; tel. 810/468–2616; FAX. 810/468–6234; Thomas J. Reed, President, Chief Executive Officer

Center for Behavior and Medicine, 2004 Hogback Road, Suite 16, Ann Arbor, MI 48105; tel. 313/677–0809; FAX. 313/677–0452; Gerard M. Schmit, M.D., Chief Executive Officer

Center for Personal Growth, P.C., 817 10th Avenue, Port Huron, MI 48060; tel. 810/984–4550; FAX. 810/984–3737; Fredric B. Roberts, Ed.D., Chief Executive Officer

Center of Behavioral Therapy P.C., 24453 Grand River Avenue, Detroit, MI 48219; tel. 313/592–1765; Hollis Evans, Executive Director

Central Michigan Community Mental Health Services, 301 South Crapo, Suite 100, Mount Pleasant, MI 48858; tel. 517/773–6961; FAX. 517/773–1968; George Rouman, Chief Executive Officer

Central Therapeutic Services, Inc., 17600 West Eight Mile Road, Suite 7, Southfield, MI 48075; tel. 313/559–4340; FAX. 313/559–1451; K. G. Thimotheose, Ph.D., President, Chief Executive Officer

Children's Home of Detroit, 900 Cook Road, Grosse Pointe Woods, MI 48236; tel. 313/886–0800; FAX. 313/886–9446; Michael R. Horwitz, Executive Director

City of Detroit Dept. of Human Services/Drug Treatment Division, 5031 Grandy, Detroit, MI 48211; tel. 313/267–6695; William Warren

Clinton–Eaton–Ingham Community Mental Health Board, 808–B Southland, Lansing, MI 48910; tel. 517/887–2126; FAX. 517/887–0086; Jayn Devney

Community Care Services, 26184 West Outer Drive, Lincoln Park, MI 48146; tel. 313/389–7525; FAX. 313/389–7515; William P. Walsh

Community Mental Health Services of Muskegon County, 376 Apple Avenue, Muskegon, MI 49442; tel. 616/724–1111; James Borushko

Community Mental Health Services of St. Joseph County, 210 South Main, P.O. Box 429, Three Rivers, MI 49093; tel. 616/273–2000; FAX. 616/273–9456; Lawrence C. Hermen

Comprehensive Psychiatric Services, PC, 28800 Orchard Lake Road, Suite 250, Farmington, MI 48334; tel. 810/932–2500; FAX. 810/932–2506; Elliot D. Luby, MD

Comprehensive Services, Inc., 4630 Oakman Boulevard, Detroit, MI 48204–4127; tel. 313/934–8400; Mary L. Doss, CNAA, MS

Counciling Alternative, One Town Square, Suite 600, Bloomfield Hills, MI 48302; tel. 810/208–5754; Michael Criss

Cruz Clinic, 17177 North Laurel Park Drive, Suite 131, Livonia, MI 48152; tel. 313/462–3210; FAX. 313/462–1024; Victor M. Cruz, MD

Delta Family Clinic, 2303 East Ameligh Road Bay, Bay City, MI 48706; tel. 517/684–9313; FAX. 517/684–5773; Gary West, Chief Executive Officer

Desgranges Psychiatric Center P.C., G–8145 South Saginaw Street, Grand Blanc, MI 48439; tel. 810/694–2730; Louise Desgranges, M.D., Chief Executive Officer

Detroit Central City Community Mental Health, Inc., 10 Peterboro, Suite 208, Detroit, MI 48201; tel. 313/831–3160; FAX. 313/831–2604; Irva Faber–Bermudez, MSN, RN

Dimensions of Life, Inc., 510 West Willow, Lansing, MI 48906; tel. 517/485–4716; FAX. 517/886–0505; Alfred K. Doering, Director

Dot Caring Centers, Inc., 3190 Hallmark Court, Saginaw, MI 48603; tel. 517/790–3366; Wendell J. Montney, Ph.D., Executive Director, Behavioral Healthcare

Downriver Guidance Clinic of Wayne County, 13101 Allen Road, Southgate, MI 48195; tel. 313/282–1700; Leroy A. Lott, M.S.W., Chief Executive Officer

Evergreen Counseling Centers, 6902 Chicago Road, Warren, MI 48092; tel. 810/983–3600; Donald L. Warner

Fairlane Behavioral Services, 23400 Michigan Avenue, Suite P–24, Dearborn, MI 48124; tel. 313/562–6730; FAX. 313/562–8840; Carlos P. Ruiz, MSW

Gateway Recovery Services, 333 Turwill Lane, Kalamazoo, MI 49006; tel. 616/382–9827; FAX. 616/342–6440; Thomas E. Lucking, Executive Director

Growth Works, Inc., 271 South Main Street, P.O. Box 115, Plymouth, MI 48170; tel. 313/455–4095; Dale F. Yagiela, Executive Director

Guest House for Women Religious, 1840 West Scripps Road, P.O. Box 420, Lake Orion, MI 48361; tel. 248/391–3100; FAX. 248/391–0210; Daniel Kidd

Hegira Programs, Inc., 8623 North Wayne Road, Suite 200, Westland, MI 48185; tel. 313/458–4601; FAX. 313/458–4611; Edward L. Forry, Chief Executive Officer

Holly Gardens, P.O. Box 66, Holly, MI 48442; tel. 810/634–0140; Michael J. Filipek, BA, SWT

Huron Valley Consultation Center, 955 West Eisenhower Circle, Suite B, Ann Arbor, MI 48103; tel. 313/662–6300; Joseph M. Meadows, MD

Ionia County Community Mental Health Services, 5827 North Orleans, P.O. Box 155, Orleans, MI 48865; tel. 616/761–3135; FAX. 616/761–3992; Richard Visingardi, Chief Executive Officer

Jensen Counseling Centers P.C., 26105 Orchard Lake Road, Suite 301, Farmington Hills, MI 48334; tel. 313/478–4411; Cynthia Sweier, ACSW

Kairos Healthcare, Inc., 4364 State Street, Saginaw, MI 48603; tel. 517/792–4357; Frederick E. Wigen, Jr.

Lapeer County Community Mental Health Center, 1570 Suncrest Drive, Lapeer, MI 48446–1154; tel. 810/667–0500; FAX. 810/664–8728; Richard I. Berman, Ph.D., Executive Director

Latino Family Services, Inc., 3815 West Fort, Detroit, MI 48216; tel. 313/841–7380; FAX. 313/841–3730; Cristina Jose–Kampfner, Ph.D., President

LifeLong Center, Inc., 719 Harrison Street, Flint, MI 48502–1613; tel. 810/235–1950; Georgia Herrlich, Chief Executive Officer

LifeWays, 1200 North West Avenue, Jackson, MI 49202; tel. 517/789–1200; FAX. 517/789–1276; Dr. Christina Thompson, Chief Executive Officer

LondonBrook Associates, 26677 West Twelve Mile Road, Suite 124, Southfield, MI 48034; tel. 810/391–0050; Debra Scheck, MSW, ACSW

Macomb Child Guidance Clinic, Inc., 40600 Van Dyke, Suite 9, Sterling Heights, MI 48313; tel. 810/978–2476; Warren C. Levin, MA

Meridian Professional Psychological Consultants, P.C., 5031 Park Lake Road, East Lansing, MI 48823; tel. 517/332–0811; FAX. 517/332–4452; Thomas S. Gunnings, Ph.D., President, Clinical Director

Metro East Substance Abuse Treatment Corporation, 13929 Harper Avenue, P.O. Box 13408, Detroit, MI 48213; tel. 313/371–0055; FAX. 313/371–1409; Leslie B. Carroll, President

Michiana Addictions and Prevention Services, 222 South Main Street, Three Rivers, MI 49093–1658; tel. 616/279–5187; FAX. 616/273–2083; Sally Reames

Michigan Counseling Services, 1400 East 12 Mile Road, Madison Heights, MI 48071–2651; tel. 248/547–2223; Anthony C. Clemente, MA, CSW

Monroe County Community Mental Health Authority, 1001 South Raisinville Road, Monroe, MI 48161; tel. 313/243–3371; FAX. 313/243–5564; Sheldon M. Rosen, Executive Director

Nardin Park Recovery Center, 9605 Grand River, P.O. Box 04506, Detroit, MI 48204; tel. 313/834–5930; FAX. 313/834–4541; Annie B. Scott, Executive Director

Section C

National Council on Alcoholism Lansing Regional Area, 3400 South Cedar, Suite 200, Lansing, MI 48910; tel. 517/887–0226; FAX. 517/887–8121; Nancy L. Siegrist, Executive Director

National Council on Alcoholism and Addictions, 202 East Boulevard, Suite 310, Flint, MI 48503; tel. 810/767–0350; FAX. 810/767–4031; Robert L. Agle, Jr.

National Council on Alcoholism and Drug Dependence, 10601 West 7th Mile Road, Detroit, MI 48221; tel. 313/861–0666; FAX. 313/341–9776; Benjamin A. Jones, President, Chief Executive Officer

Neighborhood Service Organization, 220 Bagley, Suite 840, Detroit, MI 48226; tel. 313/961–4890; FAX. 313/961–5120; Angela G. Kennedy, Executive Director

New Center Community Mental Health Services, 2051 West Grand Boulevard, Detroit, MI 48208; tel. 313/961–3200; FAX. 313/961–3769; Roberta V. Sanders, Chief Executive Officer

New Era Alternative Treatment Center, 211 Glendale, Suite 513, Highland Park, MI 48203; tel. 313/869–6328, ext. 312; FAX. 313/869–1765; Joseph A. Pitts, Executive Medical Director

New Hope Treatment Center, 3455 Woodward, Second Floor, Detroit, MI 48201; tel. 313/832–6930; FAX. 313/961–8090; Janice Kwiatkowski, Chief Executive Officer

New Light Recovery Center, Inc., 300 West McNichols, Detroit, MI 48203; tel. 313/867–8015; Serge Jean–Louis, MD

New Perspectives Center, Inc., 1321 South Fayette Street, Saginaw, MI 48602; tel. 517/790–0301; FAX. 517/790–0233; Jimmie D. Westbrook, Executive Director

Newaygo County Mental Health Center, P.O. Box 8367, White Cloud, MI 49349; tel. 616/689–7330; Hank W. Boks, MSW

North Point Mental Health Associates, 30101 Northwestern Highway, Suite 201, Farmington Hills, MI 48334; tel. 810/737–3050; Alan R. Rickfelder, PhD

Northeast Guidance Center, 13340 East Warren, Detroit, MI 48215; tel. 313/824–5641; FAX. 313/824–7779; Cheryl Coleman, Executive Director

Northeast Health Services, Inc., 1475 East Outer Drive, Detroit, MI 48234; tel. 313/892–4244; FAX. 313/892–1457; Ellsworth E. Jackson, M.A., CSW, Program Director

Northeast Michigan Community Mental Health Services, 400 Johnson Street, Alpena, MI 49707; tel. 517/356–2161; Charles A. White

Northern Michigan Alcoholism and Addiction Treatment Services, Inc., 116 East Eighth Street, Traverse City, MI 49684; tel. 616/922–4810; FAX. 616/922–2095; David N. Abeel, M.S.W., Executive Director

Northern Michigan Community Mental Health, One MacDonald Drive, Suite A, Petroskey, MI 49770; tel. 616/347–7890; FAX. 616/347–1241; Alexis Kaczynski, Chief Executive Officer

Northpointe Behavioral Healthcare Systems, 715 Pyle Drive, Kingsford, MI 49801; tel. 906/774–0522; FAX. 906/774–1570; James Gaynor II, Chief Executive Officer

O. Ganesh, M.D., P.C., 28165 Greenfield, Southfield, MI 48076; tel. 810/569–6642; FAX. 810/569–7922; K. Nair, MD

Oakland Psychological Clinic, P.C., 2050 North Woodward Avenue, Suite 110, Bloomfield Hills, MI 48304–2258; tel. 810/594–1200; FAX. 810/594–1306; Barry H. Tigay, Ph.D., President

Orchard Hills Psychiatric Enter, P.C., 42450 W. 12 Mile Road, Suite 305, Novi, MI 45366; tel. 810/426–9900; FAX. 810/426–9950; Dr. Hiten Patel, Chief Executive Officer

Orchards Children's Services, Inc., 30215 Southfield Road, Southfield, MI 48076; tel. 810/433–8600; FAX. 810/258–0487; Gerald Levin, Chief Executive Officer

Ottawa County Community Mental Health, 12251 James Street, Holland, MI 49424; tel. 616/393–5600; FAX. 616/393–5687; Dr. Rudolph Lie, Chief Executive Officer

Parkside Mental Health and Clinical Services, 18820 Woodward Avenue, Suite Five, Highland Park, MI 48203; tel. 313/893–5308; FAX. 313/368–2605; Victoria Mayberry, Chief Executive Officer

Parkview Company, d/b/a Parkview Counseling Centers, 18609 West Seven Mile Road, Detroit, MI 48219; tel. 313/532–8015; Yvette Woodruff, MA, LPC

Personal Dynamics Center, 23810 Michigan Avenue, Dearborn, MI 48124; tel. 313/563–4142; FAX. 313/563–2615; Pamela Czuj, Executive Director

Perspectives of Troy, P.C., 2690 Crooks Road, Suite 300, Troy, MI 48084; tel. 810/244–8644; FAX. 810/244–1330; Timothy Coldiron, ACSW, Ph.D., Chief Executive Officer

Program for Alcohol and Substance Treatment, 110 Sanborn, Big Rapids, MI 49307; tel. 616/796–6203; John R. Kelly, Director

Propelled Therapeutic Services, 18820 Woodward Avenue, Detroit, MI 48203; tel. 313/368–2600; FAX. 313/368–2605; Cecelia Wallace, Executive Director, President

Psychological Consultants of Michigan, P.C., 2518 Capital Avenue, S.W., Suite Two, Battle Creek, MI 49015; tel. 616/968–2811; FAX. 616/968–2651; Jeffrey N. Andert, Ph.D., Administrator

Psychotherapy and Counseling Services, PC, 670 Griswold, Suite 4, Northville, MI 48167; tel. 313/285–5000; Henry F. Woodworth, MD

Redford Counseling Center, 25945 West Seven Mile Road, Redford, MI 48240; tel. 313/535–6560; FAX. 313/535–5266; Jo Ann Sadler, Director, ACSW, BCD

Redford Counseling Center, 25945 West Seven Mile Road, Redford Township, MI 48240; tel. 313/535–6560; JoAnn Sadler, BCD, ACSW

Regional Mental Health Clinic, P.C., 23100 Cherry Hill Road, Suite 10, Dearborn, MI 48124–4144; tel. 313/277–1300; Gena J. D'Alessandro, Ph.D., Chief Executive Officer

Renaissance Education and Training Center, 18240 West McNichols, Detroit, MI 48219; tel. 313/535–2525; Catherine Green

River's Bend P.C., 33975 Dequindre, Suite Five, Troy, MI 48083; tel. 810/583–1110; FAX. 810/583–9399; James Keener, Chief Executive Officer

Riverwood Community Mental Health Center, 1485 M–139, P.O. Box 547, Benton Harbor, MI 49023; tel. 616/925–0585; FAX. 616/925–0070; Allen Edlefson, Chief Executive Officer

Rose Hill Center, Inc., 5130 Rose Hill Boulevard, Holly, MI 48442; tel. 810/634–5537; FAX. 810/634–7754; Daniel J. Kelly

STM Clinic, One Tuscola Street, Suite 302, Saginaw, MI 48607; tel. 517/755–2532; FAX. 517/755–2827; Sara Terry–Moton, Chief Executive Officer

Sacred Heart Rehabilitation Center, Inc., 2203 St. Antoine, Detroit, MI 48201; tel. 313/961–0612; John Sass, Jr., MBA

Saginaw County Mental Health Center, 500 Hancock Street, Saginaw, MI 48602; tel. 517/792–3507; FAX. 517/799–0206; Donald Miller, Chief Executive Officer

Self Help Addiction Rehabilitation, 1852 West Grand Boulevard, Detroit, MI 48208; tel. 313/894–8444; FAX. 313/894–5542; Allen Bray, MHS

Star Center, Inc., 13575 Lesure, Detroit, MI 48227; tel. 313/493–4410; FAX. 313/493–4415; Lucila S. Ryder, LPN

Suburban West Community Center, 11677 Beech Daly Road, Redford, MI 48239; tel. 313/937–9500; FAX. 313/937–9504; William R. Hart, Clinical Program Director

Summit Pointe, 140 West Michigan Avenue, Battle Creek, MI 49017; tel. 616/966–1460; FAX. 616/966–2844; Ervin Brinker, Chief Executive Officer

Taylor Psychological Clinic, PC, 1172 Robert T. Longway Boulevard, Flint, MI 48503; tel. 810/232–8466; Dr. Maxwell Taylor, Chief Executive Officer

The Center for Human Resources, 1001 Military Street, Port Huron, MI 48060–0541; tel. 313/985–5168; Thomas P. Pope, Executive Director

The Kalamazoo Child Guidance Clinic, 2615 Stadium Drive, Kalamazoo, MI 49008; tel. 616/343–1651; FAX. 616/382–7078; Steven L. Smith, Executive Director

The Montcalm Center for Behavioral Health, 611 North State Street, Stanton, MI 48888; tel. 517/831–7520; FAX. 517/831–7578; Robert Brown, Chief Executive Officer

Thumb Area Behavioral Services Center, 1309 Cleaver Road, P.O. Box 365, Caro, MI 48723; tel. 517/673–7575; FAX. 517/673–7579; Robert E. Chadwick II, MBA

Turning Point Programs, 1931 Boston, S.E., Grand Rapids, MI 49506; tel. 616/235–1565; FAX. 616/235–1574; Robert E. Byrd, M.A., Director

Tuscola County Community Mental Health Services, P.O. Box 239, Caro, MI 48723; tel. 517/673–6191; Robert E. Chadwick II, MBA

University Psychiatric Center, 2751 East Jefferson, Suite 200, Detroit, MI 48207; tel. 313/993–3434; FAX. 313/993–3421; Robert Pohl, MD

W. D. Lee Center for Life Management, Inc., 11000 West McNichols, Suite 222, Detroit, MI 48221; tel. 313/345–6777; FAX. 313/345–6369; Wendie D. Lee, Director, Chief Executive Officer

Washtenaw Council on Alcoholism, 2301 Platt Road, Ann Arbor, MI 48104; tel. 734/971–7900; Barry K. Kistner

West Michigan Community Mental Health System, 920 Diana Street, Ludington, MI 49431; tel. 616/845–6294, ext. 5062; FAX. 616/845–7095; Kim C. Halladay, PhD, ACS

MINNESOTA

Anthony Louis Center, 1000 Paul Parkway, Blaine, MN 55434; tel. 612/757–2906; Michael Swingle, MPA

Charter Behavioral Health System of Waverly, 109 North Shore Drive, Waverly, MN 55390; tel. 612/658–4811; FAX. 612/658–4128; Clelland Gilchrist, Chief Executive Officer, Director, Clinical Services

Fairview Deaconess Woodbury, Extended Care and Halfway House, 1665 Woodbury Drive, Woodbury, MN 55125; tel. 612/436–6623; Richard Peterson, President, Chief Executive Officer

Fountain Lake Treatment Center, Inc., 408 Fountain Street, Albert Lea, MN 56007; tel. 507/377–6411; Theodore P. Myers, MD

Guest House, 4800 48th Street N.E., P.O. Box 954, Rochester, MN 55903; tel. 507/288–4693; FAX. 507/288–1240; David Kidd

Hazelden Foundation, 15245 Pleasant Valley Road, P.O. Box 11, Center City, MN 55012; tel. 612/257–4010; FAX. 612/257–1055; Jerry Spicer, President

Missions, Inc. Programs, 3409 East Medicine Lake Road, Plymouth, MN 55441; tel. 612/559–1883; FAX. 612/559–2559; Patricia Murphy

Omegon, Inc., 2000 Hopkins Crossroads, Minnetonka, MN 55343; tel. 612/541–4738; Barbara J. Danielsen, Executive Administrator

Pride Institute, 14400 Martin Drive, Eden Prairie, MN 55344; tel. 800/547–7433; Joseph M. Amico

St. Joseph's Home for Children, 1121 East 46th Street, Minneapolis, MN 55407; tel. 612/827–6241; FAX. 612/827–7954; Douglas Goke

MISSISSIPPI

CARES Center, Inc., 402 Wesley Avenue, Jackson, MS 39202; tel. 601/360–0583; Richard H. Macsherry, Director

COPAC, Inc., 3949 Highway 43N, Brandon, MS 39042; tel. 800/446–9727; Jerald Stacy Hughes, Jr., Ph.D., Executive Director

Jackson Recovery Center, 5354 I–55 South Frontage Road, P.O. Box 7638 (zip 39284), Jackson, MS 39212; tel. 601/372–9788; FAX. 601/372–9505; D. Preston Smith, Jr., President, Chief Executive Officer

Male/Female Receiving Med Psych Services, 3550 Highway 468 West, P.O. Box 157–A, Whitfield, MS 39193; tel. 601/351–8000; FAX. 601/939–0647; James Chastain, Chief Executive Officer

Millcreek, 900 First Avenue, N.E., P.O. Box 1160, Magee, MS 39111; tel. 601/849–4221; FAX. 601/849–7194; Karen L. Lister, Ph.D., Executive Director

Oak Circle Center, P.O. Box 157–A, Whitfield, MS 39193; tel. 601/939–1221; FAX. 601/939–0647; James Chastain, Chief Executive Officer

MISSOURI

Boonville Valley Hope, 1415 Ashley Road, P.O. Box 376, Boonville, MO 65233; tel. 816/882–6547; Dennis Gilhousen, Chief Executive Officer

Boys Town of Missouri, Route D.D., P.O. Box 189, St. James, MO 65559; tel. 573/265–3251; FAX. 573/265–5370; Richard C. Dunn, ACSW, LCSW, Executive Director

Centrec–Care, Inc., 11720 Borman Drive, Suite 103, St. Louis, MO 63146; tel. 314/991–5388; FAX. 314/576–1253; Mohammed A. Kabir, M.D., Chief Executive Officer

Child Center of Our Lady, 7900 Natural Bridge Road, St. Louis, MO 63121; tel. 314/383–0200; FAX. 314/383–6334; Milton T. Fujita, M.D., Chief Executive Officer

Section C

Comprehensive Mental Health Services, Inc., 10901 Winner Road, P.O. Box 520169, Independence, MO 64052; tel. 816/254-3652; FAX. 816/254-9243; William Kyles, Chief Executive Officer

Edgewood Children's Center, 330 North Gore Avenue, Webster Groves, MO 63119; tel. 314/968-2060; FAX. 314/968-8608; Sue Stepleton, Executive Director

Epworth Children and Family Services, Inc., 110 North Elm Avenue, Webster Groves, MO 63119; tel. 314/961-5718; FAX. 314/961-3503; Kevin Drollinger, Executive Director

Industrial Rehabilitation Center, 2701 Rockcreek Parkway, Suite 205, North Kansas City, MO 61589; tel. 816/471-5013; Maurice L. Cummings, Executive Director

Marillac Center, 2826 Main Street, Kansas City, MO 64108; tel. 816/751-4900; FAX. 816/751-4921; R. Michael Bowen, President

Piney Ridge Center, Inc., 1000 Hospital Road, P.O. Box 4067, Waynesville, MO 65583; tel. 314/774-5353; FAX. 314/774-2907; Rocky Carroll, Executive Director

Provident Counseling, Inc., 2650 Olive Street, St. Louis, MO 63103; tel. 314/371-6500; FAX. 314/371-6510; Kathleen E. Buescher, President, Chief Executive Officer

Research Mental Health Services, 901 Northeast Independence Avenue, Lees Summit, MO 64063; tel. 816/246-8000; FAX. 816/246-8207; Alan Flory, President

Swope Parkway Health Center, 3801 Blue Parkway, Kansas City, MO 64130; tel. 816/923-5800; FAX. 816/923-9210; Mr. E. Frank Ellis, Chief Executive Officer

The Children's Place, Two East 59th Street, Kansas City, MO 64113; tel. 816/363-1898; FAX. 816/822-7711; Paula Cornwell

MONTANA

Intermountain Children's Home, 500 South Lamborn, Helena, MT 59601; tel. 406/442-7920; FAX. 406/442-7949; John Wilkinson, Administrator

Rocky Mountain Treatment Center, 920 Fourth Avenue North, Great Falls, MT 59401; tel. 406/727-8832; FAX. 406/727-8172; Ivan Kuderling

Yellowstone Treatment Centers, 1732 South 72nd Street, W., Billings, MT 59106; tel. 406/655-2100; FAX. 406/656-0021; Loren L. Soft, MS

NEBRASKA

Alpha School, 1615 South Sixth Street, Omaha, NE 68108; tel. 402/444-6557; FAX. 402/444-6574; Ray Christensen, Chief Executive Officer

Behavioral Health Specialists, Inc., 201 Miller Avenue, Norfolk, NE 68701; tel. 402/370-3140; Leigh Alexander

Blue Valley Mental Health Center, Inc., 1121 North 10th Street, Beatrice, NE 68310; tel. 402/873-5505; Wayne R. Price, PhD

Cedars Youth Services, 770 North Cotner Boulevard, Suite 410, Lincoln, NE 68505; tel. 402/466-6181; FAX. 402/466-6395; James Blue, Chief Executive Officer

Center For The Advancement of Human Development, 503 North Fifth Street, (Mailing Address: 117 South 50th Street, Omaha, NE 68132), Seward, NE 68434; tel. 402/556-6049; FAX. 402/556-0636; William Reay, Chief Executive Officer

Community Mental Health Center of Lancaster County, 2200 St. Mary's Avenue, Lincoln, NE 68502; tel. 402/441-7940; George Hanigan

Developmental Services of Nebraska, Inc., 5744 Ballard Avenue, (Mailing Address: 5561 South 48th Street, Suite 200, Lincoln, NE 68516), Lincoln, NE 68507; tel. 402/420-2800; FAX. 402/420-2883; Scott LeFevre, Chief Executive Officer

Epworth Village, Inc., 2119 Division, P.O. Box 503, York, NE 68467; tel. 402/362-3353; FAX. 402/362-3248; Thomas G. McBride

Lincoln Lancaster County Child Guidance Center, 215 Centennial Mall South, Lincoln, NE 68508; tel. 402/475-7666; FAX. 402/476-9623; Carol Crumpacker, Executive Director

Mid-East Nebraska Behavioral Healthcare Services, Inc., P.O. Box 682, Columbus, NE 67920; tel. 402/564-1426; Roberta Saunders, PhD

O'Neill Valley Hope, North 10th Street, P.O. Box 918, O'Neill, NE 68763; tel. 402/336-3747; FAX. 402/336-3096; Dennis Gilhousen

Uta Halee Girls Village, 10625 Calhoun Road, P.O. Box 12034, Omaha, NE 68112; tel. 402/453-0803; FAX. 402/453-1247; Denis McCarville, Chief Executive Officer

NEW HAMPSHIRE

Beech Hill Hospital, New Harrisville Road, P.O. Box 254, Dublin, NH 03444; tel. 603/563-8511; FAX. 603/563-8771; Linda J. Crumlin, MPH

Community Council of Nashua, New Hampshire, Inc., Seven Prospect Street, Nashua, NH 03060-3990; tel. 603/889-6147, ext. 1221; FAX. 603/883-1568; Zlatko Kuftinec, M.D., Executive Director, Chief Medical Officer

Lakeview Neuro Rehab Center, 101 Highwatch Road, Effingham Falls, NH 03814; tel. 603/539-7451; FAX. 603/539-8888; Carolyn Ramsay, Chief Executive Officer

Seaborne Hospital, Inc., Seaborne Drive, P.O. Box 518, Dover, NH 03820; tel. 603/742-9300; Michael C. Torch, MA

Seacoast Mental Health Center, Inc., 1145 Sagamore Avenue, Portsmouth, NH 03801; tel. 603/431-6703; FAX. 603/433-5078; Jeffrey C. Connor, PhD

The Mental Health Center of Greater Manchester, Inc., 401 Cypress Street, Manchester, NH 03103; tel. 603/668-4111; FAX. 603/669-1131; Nicholas Verven, Ph.D., President, Executive Director

NEW JERSEY

Aaries, Inc., 690 Broadway, Bayonne, NJ 07002; tel. 201/858-1958; Thomas P. Murgitroyde

American Day Treatment Center, of West Essex Network, Inc., 799 Bloomfield Avenue, Verona, NJ 07044; tel. 201/857-5200; E. Bonnie Lizzio, Director

American Day Treatment Center of West Essex, 799 Bloomfield Avenue, Suite 212, Verona, NJ 07044; tel. 201/857-5200; FAX. 201/857-4920; Barbara A. Hotton, LCSW, Executive Director

Arthur Brisbane Child Treatment Center, Allaire Road, P.O. Box 625, Farmingdale, NJ 07727; tel. 908/938-5061; FAX. 908/751-0813; Raymond Grimaldi, Chief Executive Officer

AtlantiCare Behavioral Health, 201 Tilton Road, Unit 13-A, Northfield, NJ 08225; tel. 609/645-7601; Donald J. Parker

Bancroft Rehabilitation Services, P.O. Box 20, Haddonfield, NJ 08033; tel. 609/429-0010; George W. Niemann, PhD

CPC Behavioral Healthcare, Inc., One High Point Center Way, Morganville, NJ 07751; tel. 908/591-1750; Jeanne H. Wurmser, PhD

Catholic Charities – Diocese of Metuchen, 288 Rues Lane, East Brunswick, NJ 08816; tel. 732/257-6677; Florence Edward Kearney, DC

Community Centers for Mental Health, Inc., Two Park Avenue, Dumont, NJ 07628; tel. 201/385-4400; FAX. 201/384-7067; Catherine Small, Chief Executive Officer

Comprehensive Behavioral Healthcare, Inc., 516 Valley Brook Avenue, Lyndhurst, NJ 07071; tel. 201/935-3322; FAX. 201/460-3698; Peter Scerbo, Chief Executive Officer

Daytop, New Jersey, 80 West Main Street, Mendham, NJ 07945; tel. 201/543-0162; FAX. 201/543-7502; Joseph Hennen, Chief Executive Officer

Discovery Institute for Addictive Disorders, Inc., P.O. Box 177, Marlboro, NJ 07746; tel. 908/946-9444; Robert C. Denes

Ewing Residential Treatment Center, 1610 Stuyvesant Avenue, Trenton, NJ 08618; tel. 609/530-3350; FAX. 609/530-3467; Julius Campbell, Chief Executive Officer

High Focus Centers, Inc., 299 Market Street, Suite 110, Saddle Brook, NJ 07663; tel. 201/291-0055; FAX. 201/291-0888; Peter Balo, Chief Executive Officer

Holley Child Care and Development Center of Youth Consultation Service, 260 Union Street, Hackensack, NJ 07601; tel. 201/343-8803; FAX. 201/343-8563; Richard Mingoia, Associate Executive Director

Honesty House, 1272 Long Hill Road, Stirling, NJ 07980; tel. 908/647-3211; FAX. 908/647-7864; Charles H. Stucky, N.C.A.D.C., Executive Director

Lighthouse at Mays Landing, 5034 Atlantic Avenue, P.O. Box 899, Mays Landing, NJ 08330; tel. 609/625-4900; FAX. 609/625-8058; Dr. C. Wm. Brett, Chief Executive Officer

Mid-Bergen Center, Inc., 610 Industrial Avenue, Paramus, NJ 07652; tel. 201/265-8200; FAX. 201/265-3543; Joseph Masciandaro, Chief Executive Officer

Monmouth Chemical Dependency Treatment Center, Inc., 152 Chelsea Avenue, Long Branch, NJ 07740; tel. 908/222-5190; FAX. 908/222-5577; Christopher M. Dadlez

New Hope Foundation, Inc., Route 520, P.O. Box 66, Marlboro, NJ 07746; tel. 908/946-3030; FAX. 908/946-3507; George J. Mattie, Chief Executive Officer

NewBridge Services, Inc., P.O. Box 336, Pompton Plains, NJ 07444; tel. 201/839-2520; Robert L. Parker, MPA

Ocean Mental Health Services, Inc., 160 Route 9, Bayville, NJ 08753; tel. 908/349-5550; Charles J. Langan, Chief Executive Officer

Preferred Behavioral Health of New Jersey, CN 2036-700 Airport Road, Lakewood, NJ 08701; tel. 908/367-4700; FAX. 908/364-2253; William Sette, Chief Executive Officer

SERV Centers of New Jersey, Inc., 520 West State Street, Trenton, NJ 08618; tel. 609/394-2506; Michael Armstrong, MA, MBA

Seabrook House, 133 Polk Lane, P.O. Box 5055, Seabrook, NJ 08302-0655; tel. 800/582-5968; FAX. 609/453-1022; Edward M. Diehl

Sunrise House Foundation, Inc., 37 Sunset Inn Road, Lafayette, NJ 07848; tel. 201/383-6300; FAX. 201/383-8458; Beth Anne Nathans, M.S., Chief Executive Officer

U.M.D.N.J.–Community Mental Health Center at Piscataway, 671 Hoes Lane, P.O. Box 1392, Piscataway, NJ 08855-1392; tel. 908/235-4624; FAX. 908/235-4594; Gary W. Lamson, Vice President, Chief Executive Officer

Union County Psychiatric Clinic, 117-119 Roosevelt Avenue, Plainfield, NJ 07060; tel. 908/756-6870; Marcyann E. Sosnoski

Vineland Children's Residential Treatment Center, 2000 Maple Avenue, Vineland, NJ 08360; tel. 609/696-6620; FAX. 609/696-6847; Theodore Allen, Superintendent

West Bergen Mental Healthcare, Inc., 120 Chestnut Street, Ridgewood, NJ 07450-2500; tel. 201/444-3550; FAX. 201/652-1613; Philip Wilson, Chief Executive Officer

Willowglen Academy–New Jersey, Inc., Highway 206, P.O. Box A–1, Newton, NJ 07860; tel. 201/579-3700; Leonard F. Dziubla, MSW

Woodbridge Child Diagnostic and Treatment Center, 15 Paddock Street, Avenue, NJ 07001; tel. 908/499-5050; FAX. 908/815-4874; William Falvo, Chief Executive Officer

NEW MEXICO

BHC Pinon Hills Residential Treatment Center, 6930 Weicker Lane, P.O. Box 428, Velarde, NM 87582; tel. 505/852-2704; FAX. 505/852-2022; Kim Whitelock

Desert Hills Center for Youth and Families, 5310 Sequoia, N.W., Albuquerque, NM 87120; tel. 505/836-7330; FAX. 505/836-7424; Katherine B. Wade, MA

Four Corners Regional Adolescent Treatment Center, P.O. Box 567, Shiprock, NM 87420; tel. 505/368-4712; FAX. 505/368-5457; Hoskie Benally, Chief Executive Officer

Innovative Services, 2700 Yale Boulevard, S.E., Albuquerque, NM 87106; tel. 505/242-5466; FAX. 505/242-0099; Jim Johnson

NAMASTE, P.O. Box 489, Los Lunas, NM 87031; tel. 505/865-6176; FAX. 505/865-3268; Linda Zimmerman, Executive Director

Pathway Company, LLC, 4316 Carlisle Boulevard, N.E., Suite D, Albuquerque, NM 87109; tel. 505/884-6693; FAX. 505/884-4304; Dr. Michael Dismond, Chief Executive Officer

Sequoyah Adolescent Treatment Center, 3405 West Pan American Freeway, N.E., Albuquerque, NM 87107; tel. 505/344-4673; FAX. 505/841-4361; W. Henry Gardner, Ph.D., Director

The Adolescent Pointe, 5050 McNutt Street, P.O. Box Six, Santa Teresa, NM 88008; tel. 505/589-0033; FAX. 505/589-2860; Lorenzo Barrios, Chief Executive Officer

The Pointe ARTC for Children, 200 Laura Court, P.O. Box Six, Santa Teresa, NM 88008; tel. 505/589-0033; FAX. 505/589-2860; Scott Pelking, Administrator

NEW YORK

Areba/Casriel Institute, 500 West 57th Street, New York, NY 10019; tel. 212/376-1810; FAX. 212/376-1824; Steven Yohay, Executive Director

Arms Acres, Inc., 75 Seminary Hill Road, Carmel, NY 10512; tel. 914/225-3400; FAX. 914/225-5660; Edward Spauster, Ph.D., Executive Director

Baker Victory Services, 780 Ridge Road, Lackawanna, NY 14218; tel. 716/828–9777; FAX. 716/828–9767; James J. Casion, Chief Executive Officer

Bronx Alcoholism Treatment Center, 1500 Waters Place, Building 13, Bronx, NY 10461; tel. 718/904–0026, ext. 300; FAX. 718/597–9434; Ronald B. Lonesome, M.D., Director

Charles K. Post Alcoholism Treatment Center, Building One Pilgrim Psychiatric Center, West Brentwood, NY 11717; tel. 516/434–7209; Phillip A. Dawes, Director

Children's Home RTF, Inc., Squirrel Hill Road, P.O. Box 658, Greene, NY 13778; tel. 607/656–9004; FAX. 607/656–9076; Mary Jo Thorn, Program Director

Conifer Park, Inc., 79 Glenridge Road, Glenville, NY 12302; tel. 518/399–6446; John A. Duffy, Executive Officer

Conners Residential Treatment Facility, Inc., 824 Delaware Avenue, Buffalo, NY 14209; tel. 716/884–3802; FAX. 716/884–8689; James D. Lawson, Director

Cornerstone of Medical Arts Center Hospital, 57 West 57th Street, New York, NY 10019; tel. 212/755–0200; FAX. 212/755–0915; Norman J. Sokolow, President

Cortland Medical, Four Skyline Drive, Hawthorne, NY 10532; tel. 914/347–2990; FAX. 914/347–3074; Jeffery Smith, M.D., Chief Executive Officer

Creedmoor Alcoholism Treatment Center, 80–45 Winchester Boulevard, Building 19–D, Queens Village, NY 11427; tel. 718/264–3743; FAX. 718/776–5145; Gerlando A. Verruso

Crestwood Children's Center, 2075 Scottsville Road, Rochester, NY 14623–2098; tel. 716/436–4442; FAX. 716/436–0169; Donna M. Cimino

Dick Van Dyke Alcoholism Treatment Center, P.O. Box 218, Route 96–A, Willard, NY 14588–0218; tel. 607/869–9500; FAX. 607/869–5303; Thomas Nightingale

Dutchess County Department of Mental Hygiene, 230 North Road, Poughkeepsie, NY 12601; tel. 914/485–9700; FAX. 914/485–2759; Kenneth M. Glatt, Ph.D., Commissioner

Green Chimneys Children's Services, Inc., Putnam Lake Road, Caller Box 719, Brewster, NY 10509; tel. 914/279–2995, ext. 205; FAX. 914/279–2714; Samuel B. Ross, Jr., PhD

Harmony Heights, 57 Sandy Hill Road, Oyster Bay Cove, NY 11771; tel. 516/922–4060; Donald Lafayette, P.D., Quality Assurance Utilization

Hillside Children's Center, 1183 Monroe Avenue, Rochester, NY 14620; tel. 716/256–7501; FAX. 716/256–7510; Dennis M. Richardson, President, Chief Executive Officer

Hope House, Inc., 517 Western Avenue, Albany, NY 12203; tel. 518/482–4673; FAX. 518/482–0873; Mary Ann DiChristopher Finn, Executive Director

Hopevale, Inc., 3780 Howard Road, Hamburg, NY 14075; tel. 716/648–1964; FAX. 716/648–5266; Stanfort J. Perry, Executive Director

J. L. Norris Alcoholism Treatment Center, 1111 Elmwood Avenue, Rochester, NY 14620; tel. 716/461–0410; FAX. 716/461–4545; Thomas E. Nightingale, Director

Jewish Board of Family and Children's Services, Inc., 120 West 57th Street, New York, NY 10019; tel. 212/582–9100, ext. 1750; FAX. 212/956–5676; Alan B. Siskind, Ph.D., Executive Vice President

Julia Dyckman Andrus Memorial, Inc., 1156 North Broadway, Yonkers, NY 10701; tel. 914/965–3700; FAX. 914/965–3883; Dr. Gary Carman, Chief Executive Officer

Kingsboro Alcoholism Treatment Center, 754 Lexington Avenue, Brooklyn, NY 11221; tel. 718/453–6747; FAX. 718/453–7581; Jacqueline Cole, Director

Madonna Heights Services, a Division of St. Christopher/Ottilie, 151 Burrs Lane, P.O. Box 8020, Dix Hills, NY 11746–9020; tel. 516/643–8800; FAX. 516/491–4440; Robert J. McMahon, Executive Director

Manhattan Alcoholism Treatment Center MII, 600 East 125th Street, Ward's Island, New York, NY 10035; tel. 212/369–0703; FAX. 212/369–3507; Christopher Tavella

McPike Alcoholism Treatment Center, 1213 Court Street, Utica, NY 13502; tel. 315/797–6800, ext. 4801; FAX. 315/738–4437; Phillip Dranger, Acting Director

Middletown Alcoholism Treatment Center, 141 Monhagen Avenue, P.O. Box 1453, Middleton, NY 10940; tel. 914/341–2500; FAX. 914/341–2570; Richard C. Ward, Director

National Expert Care Consultants, Inc., 455 West 50th Street, New York, NY 10019; tel. 212/262–6000; Don Russakoff

Parsons Child and Family Center, 60 Academy Road, Albany, NY 12208; tel. 518/426–2600; FAX. 518/426–2792; Raymond Schimmer

Passages Counseling Center, 3680 Route 112, Coram, NY 11727; tel. 516/698–9222; Arnt Monge

Psych Services of Long Island, 1600 Stewart Avenue, Suite 202, Westbury, NY 11590; tel. 516/683–1200; Marci Zaslav, Executive Director

Psych Systems of Westchester, 33 West Main Street, Suite 307, Elmsford, NY 10523; tel. 914/345–5676; FAX. 914/345–5610; Joseph DeMarzo

Research Institute on Addictions, 1021 Main Street, Buffalo, NY 14203; tel. 716/887–2386; FAX. 716/887–2215; Paul R. Stasiewicz, Ph.D., CRC Coordinator, Outpatient Services

Restorative Management Corporation, 15 King Street Third Floor, Middletown, NY 10940; tel. 914/342–5941; FAX. 914/344–2604; Dean Scher, Chief Executive Officer

Rochester Mental Health Center, Hart Building, 490 East Ridge Road, Rochester, NY 14621; tel. 716/544–5220; FAX. 716/544–6694; Heide George, MS, RN

Russell E. Blaisdell Alcoholism Treatment Center, R. P. C. Campus, Orangeburg, NY 10962; tel. 914/359–8500; FAX. 914/359–2016; Richard Ward

Saint Peter's Addiction Recovery Center (SPARC, Inc.), Three Mercy Care Lane, Guiderland, NY 12084; tel. 518/452–6700; FAX. 518/452–6753; Karen A. Giles, Chief Executive Director

Salamanca Hospital District Authority, d/b/a Salamanca Healthcare Complex, 150 Parkway Drive, Salamanca, NY 14779; tel. 716/945–1900; FAX. 716/945–5016; Kenneth Oakley, Administrator

Salvation Army–Wayside Home School For Girls, 1461 Dutch Broadway, Valley Stream, NY 11580; tel. 516/825–1600; FAX. 516/825–1829; Joseph Juliana, Director

Seafield Center, Inc., Seven Seafield Lane, Westhampton Beach, NY 11978; tel. 516/288–1122; John C. Haley, Chief Operating Officer

South Beach Alcoholism Treatment Center, 777 Seaview Avenue, Building One, Second Floor, Staten Island, NY 10305; tel. 718/667–4218; FAX. 718/351–1958; Gerlando A. Verruso, Director

St. Christopher–Ottilie Residential Treatment Facility, 85–70 148th Street, Briarwood, NY 11435; tel. 718/658–4101; FAX. 718/523–2582; Robert J. McMahon

St. Joseph's Rehabilitation Center, Inc., 99 Glenwood Estates, P.O. Box 470, Saranac Lake, NY 12983–0470; tel. 518/891–3950; FAX. 518/891–3986; Reverend Arthur M. Johnson, Chief Executive Officer

St. Joseph's Villa of Rochester, 3300 Dewey Avenue, Rochester, NY 14616–3795; tel. 716/865–1550; FAX. 716/865–5219; Roger C. Battaglia, President, Chief Executive Officer

St. Lawrence Alcoholism Treatment Center, Station A, Hamilton Hall, Ogdensburg, NY 13669; tel. 315/393–1180; FAX. 315/393–6160; Phillip Dranger, Director

St. Mary's Children and Family Services, 525 Convent Road, Syosset, NY 11791–3864; tel. 516/921–0808; FAX. 516/921–4542; Liz Giordano, Executive Director

Stutzman Alcoholism Treatment Center, 360 Forest Avenue, Buffalo, NY 14213; tel. 716/882–4900; FAX. 716/882–4426; Steven Schwartz, Director

Support Center, Inc., 181 Route 209, Port Jervis, NY 12771; tel. 914/856–3146; Carmine J. Mosca

The Astor Home for Children, 36 Mill Street, P.O. Box 5005, Rhinebeck, NY 12572–5005; tel. 914/876–4081; FAX. 914/876–2020; Sister Rose Logan, D.C., Executive Director

The August Aichhorn Center for Adolescent Residential Care, 23 West 106th Street, New York, NY 10025; tel. 212/316–9353; FAX. 212/662–2755; Michael A. Pawel, M.D., Executive Director

The Children's Village, Wetmore Hall, Dobbs Ferry, NY 10522; tel. 914/693–0600, ext. 1201; FAX. 914/674–9208; Nan Dale, Executive Director

The Health Association–MAIN QUEST Treatment Center, 774 West Main Street, Rochester, NY 14620; tel. 716/464–8870; FAX. 716/464–8077; Susan L. Costa, Chief Executive Officer

The House of the Good Shepherd, 1550 Champlin Avenue, Utica, NY 13502; tel. 315/733–0436; FAX. 315/732–0772; William Holicky, Chief Executive Officer

The Long Island Center for Recovery, 320 West Montauk Highway, Hampton Bays, NY 11946; tel. 516/728–3100; Steve Bassis, Chief Executive Officer

The Rhinebeck Lodge for Successful Living, Inpatient Substance Abuse Treatment Program, 500 Milan Hollow Road, Rhinebeck, NY 12572; tel. 800/266–4410; Chandra Singh, Ph.D., Chief Executive Officer

The Saint Francis Academy, Incorporated, Lake Placid (Camelot, The Knight House, Adirondack Experience), 50 Riverside Drive, Lake Placid, NY 12946; tel. 518/523–3605; FAX. 518/523–1470; Reverend Carlos J. Caguiat, FACHE, Vice President, Executive Director

The Villa Outpatient Center, 290 Madison Avenue, Sixth Floor, New York, NY 10017; tel. 212/679–4960; FAX. 212/679–4966; Richard Partridge, Chief Executive Officer

Tully Hill, Route 80, P.O. Box 920, Tully, NY 13159; tel. 315/696–6114; FAX. 315/696–8509; Cathy L. Palm, CPA, M.B.A., Executive Director

Valley View House, Inc., P.O. Box 26, Swiss Hill Road, Kenoza Lake, NY 12750; tel. 800/955–2869; FAX. 914/482–3516; John R. Levin, MSW

Veritas Villa, Inc., Cherrytown Road, Kerhonkson, NY 12446; tel. 914/626–3555; FAX. 914/626–3840; Lester McCandless

Westchester Jewish Community Services, Inc., 141 North Central Avenue, Hartsdale, NY 10530; tel. 914/949–6761; FAX. 914/949–3224; Ronald Gaudia, Chief Executive Officer

NORTH CAROLINA

Alcohol and Drug Abuse Treatment Center, 205 West E Street, Butner, NC 27509; tel. 919/575–7928; Johnny O. Rodgers

Alternatives, P.O. Box 7041, Wilson, NC 27895; tel. 919/237–8180; Barry W. Broadhurst, MPH

American Day Treatment Centers Charlotte, 201 Providence Road, Suite 101, Charlotte, NC 28207; tel. 704/370–0800; FAX. 704/370–0001; Brenda Doherty

Amethyst, 1715 Sharon Road, W., Charlotte, NC 28210, P.O. Box 32861, Charlotte, NC 28232–2861; tel. 704/554–8373; FAX. 704/554–8058; Daniel J. Harrison, Assistant Vice President, Administrator

Bureau of Prisons – Federal Correctional Institution, P.O. Box 1000, Butner, NC 27509; tel. 919/575–4541; John Hadden

Fellowship Hall, Inc., 5140 Dunstan Road, P.O. Box 13890, Greensboro, NC 27415; tel. 910/621–3381; FAX. 910/621–7513; Rodney Battles, M.B.A., Executive Director

Forsyth–Stokes Mental Health Center, 725 North Highland Avenue, Winston–Salem, NC 27101; tel. 919/725–7777; Ronald W. Morton

Grandfather Home for Children, P.O. Box 98, Banner Elk, NC 28604; tel. 704/898–5465; James Swinkola

Julian F. Keith Alcohol and Drug Abuse Treatment Center, 301 Tabernacle Road, Black Mountain, NC 28711; tel. 704/669–3421; FAX. 704/669–3451; Bill Rafter, Director

Learning Services Corp. – South Central Region, 707 Morehead Avenue, Durham, NC 27707; tel. 919/688–4444; Randall W. Evans

PSI Solutions Center, 801 Jones Franklin Road, Suite 210, Raleigh, NC 27606; tel. 919/851–8237; Kay Field

The Wilmington Treatment Center, 2520 Troy Drive, Wilmington, NC 28401; tel. 919/762–2727; FAX. 919/762–7923; Charles Sharp, Executive Director

Three Springs of North Carolina Boys, P.O. Box 1320, Pittsboro, NC 27312; tel. 919/542–1104; Peggy Reeder, Administrator

Timber Ridge Treatment Center, 14225 Stokes Ferry Road, Gold Hill, NC 28071; tel. 704/279–1199; FAX. 704/279–7668; Thomas A. R. Hibbert, President, Chief Executive Officer

Unity Regional Youth Treatment Center, P.O. Box C–201, Cherokee, NC 28719; tel. 704/497–3958; Mary Anne Farrell, M.D., Director

NORTH DAKOTA

Southwest Key Program, 1406 2nd Street Northwest, Mandan, ND 58554; tel. 701/663–2322; Joni Carrier, MSW

The Dakota Boys Ranch, P.O. Box 5007, Minot, ND 58703; tel. 701/852–3628; Gene Kasemen

OHIO

Beech Brook, 3737 Lander Road, Pepper Pike, OH 44124; tel. 216/831-2255, ext. 309; FAX. 216/831-0638; Mario Tonti, DSW

Behavioral Connections of Wood County, Inc., 320 West Gypsy Lane, Bowling Green, OH 43402; tel. 419/352-2551; Randall J. LaFond, Executive Director

Bellefaire JCB, 22001 Fairmount Boulevard, Shaker Heights, OH 44118; tel. 216/932-2800, ext. 335; FAX. 216/932-8520; Adam Jacobs, MD

Blick Clinic, Inc., 640 West Market Street, Akron, OH 44303-1465; tel. 330/762-5425; FAX. 330/762-4019; Dr. Gregory Laforme, Chief Executive Officer

Center for Chemical Addictions Treatment, 830 Ezzard Charles Drive, Cincinnati, OH 45214; tel. 513/381-6672; Sandra L. Kuehn, Executive Director

Charles B. Mills Center, Inc., 715 South Plum Street, Marysville, OH 43040; tel. 513/644-9192; John R. Lauritsen, PhD

Children's Aid Society, 10427 Detroit Avenue, Cleveland, OH 44102; tel. 216/521-6511; FAX. 216/521-6006; Roberta King, MBA, MS

Community Drug Board, Inc., 725 East Market Street, Akron, OH 44305; tel. 330/434-4141; FAX. 330/434-7125; Theodore Paul Ziegler, Chief Executive Officer

Community Support Services, Inc., 150 Cross Street, Akron, OH 44311; tel. 330/253-9388; Arthur G. Wickersham

Comprehensive Psychiatry Specialists, 955 Windham Court, Suite Two, Boardman, OH 44512; tel. 330/726-9570; FAX. 330/726-9031; Pradeep Mathur, President

Crisis Intervention Center of Stark County, Inc., 2421 13th Street, N.W., Canton, OH 44708; tel. 216/452-9812; FAX. 216/454-4357; Bernard S. Jesiolowski, PhD

D and E Counseling Center, 142 Javit Court, Youngstown, OH 44515; tel. 216/793-2487; FAX. 216/793-4559; Gregory Cvetkovic, Chief Executive Officer

Family Recovery Center, 964 North Market Street, P.O. Box 464, Lisbon, OH 44432; tel. 330/424-1468; FAX. 330/424-9844; Eloise V. Traina, Executive Director

Focus Health, 5701 North High Street, Suite Eight, Worthington, OH 43085; tel. 614/885-1944; FAX. 614/885-6665; Brad Lander, PhD

Glenbeigh Health Sources, P.O. Box 298, Rock Creek, OH 44084; tel. 440/563-3400; FAX. 440/563-9619; Patricia Weston-Hall, Executive Director

Harbor Behavioral Healthcare, 4334 Secor Road, Toledo, OH 43623-4234; tel. 419/475-4449; FAX. 419/479-3832; Charles F. Thayer, LISW

Health Recovery Services, Inc., 100 Hospital Drive, Suite Two, P.O. Box 724, Athens, OH 45701; tel. 614/592-6720; FAX. 614/592-6728; Kenneth H. Pickering, Executive Director

Interval Brotherhood Home, Alcohol Drug Rehabilitation Center, 3445 South Main Street, Akron, OH 44319; tel. 330/644-4095; FAX. 330/645-2031; Father Samuel R. Ciccolini, Executive Director

Lincoln Center For Prevention and Treatment of Chemical Dependency, 1918 North Main Street, Findlay, OH 45840; tel. 419/423-9242; FAX. 419/423-7854; Jack E. Miller

Mahoning County Chemical Dependency Programs, Inc., 527 North Meridan Road, Youngstown, OH 44509; tel. 330/797-0070; FAX. 330/797-9148; Martin K. Gaudiose, Chief Executive Officer

McKinley Hall, Inc., 1101 East High Street, Springfield, OH 45505; tel. 937/328-5300; FAX. 937/322-4900; Judith O. Hoy, Chief Executive Officer

Mental Health Center of Western Stark County, Inc., 111 Tremont Avenue, S.W., Massillon, OH 44647; tel. 216/833-4132; FAX. 216/833-6548; Lawrence R. Cook, Executive Director

Mental Health Center, Inc., 1207 West State Street, Suite M, Alliance, OH 44601; tel. 330/821-1995; Carol Hales, LISW

Mental Health Services for Clark County, Inc., 1345 Fountain Blvd., Springfield, OH 45504; tel. 937/399-9500; James P. Perry, PhD

Miami Valley Labor Management, Health Care Delivery Systems, Inc., 136 Heid Avenue, Dayton, OH 45404; tel. 937/236-1367; Linda VanBourgondien, RN, MBA

Mount Carmel Behavioral Healthcare, Administrative Offices, 1808 East Broad Street, Columbus, OH 43203; tel. 614/251-8242; James M. Shulman, Ph.D., Chief Executive Officer

Neil Kennedy Recovery Clinic, 2151 Rush Boulevard, Youngstown, OH 44507; tel. 330/744-1181; FAX. 330/740-2849; Gerald V. Carter, Executive Director

Neo Psych Consultants, 819 McKay Court, Suite 101, Boardman, OH 44512; tel. 216/726-7785; William Beckett

New Directions, Inc., 30800 Chagrin Boulevard, Pepper Pike, OH 44124; tel. 216/591-0324; FAX. 216/591-1243; Michael E. Mahoney

Nova Behavioral Healthcare, Inc., 832 McKinley Avenue NW, Canton, OH 44703; tel. 330/445-9407; Richard W. Thompson, LISW

Parkside Behavioral Healthcare, Inc., d/b/a Parkside Recovery Services, 349 Olde Ridenour Road, Columbus, OH 43230; tel. 614/471-2552; FAX. 614/471-0167; Christine Gerber, President, Chief Executive Officer

Parmadale Family Services, 6753 State Road, Parma, OH 44134; tel. 216/845-7700; FAX. 216/845-5910; Thomas W. Woll

Portage Path Behavioral Health, 340 South Broadway Street, Akron, OH 44308-8159; tel. 330/376-6144; FAX. 330/376-8002; Jerome T. Kraker

Psycare, Inc., 2980 Belmont Avenue, Youngstown, OH 44505; tel. 330/759-2310; FAX. 330/759-0018; Douglas Darnall, Ph.D., Chief Executive Officer

Psych Systems of Cincinnati, 11223 Cornell Park Drive, Suite 301, Cincinnati, OH 45242; tel. 513/530-8500; FAX. 513/530-5805; Al Ebert

Quest Recovery Services, 1341 Market Avenue, N., Canton, OH 44714; tel. 330/453-8252; FAX. 330/453-6716; Donald C. Davies, Chief Executive Officer

Ravenwood Mental Health Center, 12557 Ravenwood Drive, Chardon, OH 44024; tel. 440/285-3568; FAX. 440/285-4552; David Boyle, Executive Director

Rescue Mental Health Services, 3350 Collingwood Boulevard, Toledo, OH 43610; tel. 419/255-9585; FAX. 419/255-2801; Frank C. Ayers, Executive Director

Serenity Living, Inc., 210 West National Road, P.O. Box 217, Vandalia, OH 45377; tel. 513/898-2788; Joseph J. Trevino, M.D., Chief Executive Officer

Specialty Care Psychiatric Services, 2657 Niles Cortland Road, Warren, OH 44484; tel. 330/652-3533; J.B. Mitroo

Springview Developmental Center, 3130 East Main Street, Springfield, OH 45505; tel. 937/325-9263; FAX. 937/325-3593; Dominick S. Dennis, Superintendent

St. Joseph Children's Treatment Center, 650 St. Paul Avenue, Dayton, OH 45410; tel. 513/254-3562; David Emenhiser, EdD

Stepping Stone Recovery Center, 165 East Park Avenue, Niles, OH 44446; tel. 216/544-6355; FAX. 216/652-4781; Pamela Walter, Chief Executive Officer

Substance Abuse Services, Inc., 2012 Madison Avenue, Toledo, OH 43624; tel. 419/243-7274; FAX. 419/243-1505; Carroll Parks, Chief Executive Officer

The Akron Child Guidance Center, Inc., 312 Locust Street, Akron, OH 44302-1878; tel. 330/762-0591; FAX. 330/258-0931; Charles M. Vehlow, Jr., Executive Director

The Buckeye Ranch, 5665 Hoover Road, Grove City, OH 43123; tel. 800/859-5665; FAX. 614/871-6487; Leslie A. Bostic, PhD

The Campus, 905 South Sunbury Road, Westerville, OH 43081; tel. 614/895-1000, ext. 13; FAX. 614/895-3010; John R. Lauritsen, PhD

The Campus Hospital of Cleveland, 18120 Puritas Road, Cleveland, OH 44135; tel. 216/476-0222; FAX. 216/476-2938; John Sajan, RN

The Crossroads Center, 311 Martin Luther King Drive, Cincinnati, OH 42103; tel. 513/475-5300; Jacqueline P. Butler, MSW

The Lake Area Recovery Center, 2801 C Court, Ashtabula, OH 44004; tel. 440/998-0722; FAX. 440/992-1699; Kathleen Kinney, Executive Director

Transitional Living, Inc., 2052 Princeton Road, Hamilton, OH 45011; tel. 513/863-6383; David F. Craft

Tri-State Behavioral Health Center, 3156 Glenmore Avenue, Cincinnati, OH 45211; tel. 513/481-8822; FAX. 513/481-7317; Michael Miller, Chief Executive Officer

Two North Park, Inc., 720 Pine Street, S.E., Warren, OH 44483; tel. 330/399-3677; FAX. 330/394-3815; Ken Lloyd, M.S. Ed., L.S.W., CCDC III, Executive Director

Wellspring Retreat and Resource Center, P.O. Box 67, 32598 Woodyard Road, Albany, OH 45710; tel. 614/698-6277; FAX. 614/698-2053; Dr. Paul Martin, Chief Executive Officer

OKLAHOMA

Brookhaven Hospital, 201 South Garnett, Tulsa, OK 72328; tel. 918/438-4257; Rolf B. Gainer, PhD

Christopher Youth Center, Inc., 2741 East Seventh Street, Tulsa, OK 74104; tel. 918/583-0612; FAX. 918/583-5459; Thomas E. McKee, Ed.D., Director

High Pointe, 6501 Northeast 50th Street, Oklahoma City, OH 73141; tel. 405/424-3383; FAX. 405/424-0729; Charlene Arnett, Chief Executive Officer

Jim Taliaferro Community Mental Health Center, 602 Southwest 38th Street, Lawton, OK 73505-6999; tel. 405/248-5780; FAX. 405/248-3610; Ted Debbs, M.S., Executive Director

Mendros Psychiatric Medical Clinic, 2100 North Broadway, Moore, OK 73160; tel. 405/794-7719; Harry G. Mendros, M.D., Chief Executive Officer

Oklahoma Youth Center, 320 12th Avenue, N.E., Norman, OK 73071-5300; tel. 405/364-9004; FAX. 405/573-3804; Gwen Allen, LCSW

Parkside, Inc., 1620 East 12th Street, Tulsa, OK 74120; tel. 918/582-2131; FAX. 918/588-8822; Quentin Henley, Chief Executive Officer

Valley Hope Alcohol and Drug Treatment Center, 100 South Jones, P.O. Box 472, Cushing, OK 74023; tel. 918/225-1736; FAX. 918/225-7742; Dennis Gilhousen, Chief Executive Officer

Western State Psychiatric Center, P.O. Box 1, Fort Supply, OK 73841; tel. 580/766-2311; Steve Norwood, MS

OREGON

BHC Pacific View RTC, 4101 Northeast Division Street, Gresham, OR 97030; tel. 503/661-0775; FAX. 503/661-4649; Robert E. Marshall, Administrator

Children's Farm House, 4455 Northeast Highway 20, P.O. Box 1028, Corvallis, OR 97339-9102; tel. 541/757-1852; FAX. 541/757-1944; Robert Roy

Eastern Oregon Adolescent Multi-Treatment Center, 412 Southeast Dorion, Pendleton, OR 97801; tel. 541/276-0057; FAX. 541/276-1704; Ronald Humiston, Executive Director

Edgefield Children's Center, Inc., 2408 Southwest Halsey Street, Troutdale, OR 97060-1097; tel. 503/665-0157; FAX. 503/666-3066; David Fuks, M.S.W., Executive Director

Kerr Youth and Family Center, 722 Northeast 162nd Avenue, Portland, OR 97230; tel. 503/255-4205; Christopher J. Krenk

Parry Center for Children, 3415 Southeast Powell Boulevard, Portland, OR 97202; tel. 503/234-9591; FAX. 503/234-4376; Marie Avery, Chief Executive Officer

RiverBend Youth Center, 15544 South Clackamas River Drive, Oregon City, OR 97045; tel. 503/656-8005; FAX. 503/656-8929; Marcia L. McClocklin, Executive Director

Rosemont Treatment Center and School, 9911 Southeast Mt. Scott Boulevard, Portland, OR 97266; tel. 503/777-8090; FAX. 503/788-1131; Benson Meyers, Chief Executive Officer

Ryles Center, 3339 Southeast Division Street, Portland, OR 97202; tel. 503/238-1477; Patti Williamson, MA, LPC

Serenity Lane, Inc., 616 East 16th Avenue, Eugene, OR 97401; tel. 541/687-1110; FAX. 541/687-9041; Neil H. McNaughton, Executive Director

Southern Oregon Adolescent Study and Treatment Center, Inc., 210 Tacoma Street, Grants Pass, OR 97526; tel. 503/476-3302; FAX. 503/476-2895; Robert Lieberman, Executive Director

Springbook Northwest, 2001 Crestview Drive, P.O. Box 1060, Newberg, OR 97132; tel. 503/537-7000; Sonja Haugen

The Christie School, P.O. Box 368, Marylhurst, OR 97036; tel. 503/635-3416; FAX. 503/697-6932; Daniel A. Mahler, M.S.W., LCSW, Executive Director

PENNSYLVANIA

Abraxas I, Blue Jay Village, Box 59 Forest Road, Marienville, PA 16239; tel. 814/927-6615; FAX. 814/927-8560; James Newsome, Program Director

Adelphoi Village, Inc., 1003 Village Way, Latrobe, PA 15650; tel. 412/530-1111; John P. Bukovac

---

Alternative Counseling Associates, 438 High Street, Pottstown, PA 19464; tel. 610/970–9060; FAX. 610/970–4280; Nila Joshi

Bowling Green Inn–Brandywine, 1375 Newark Road, Kennett Square, PA 19348; tel. 610/268–3588; FAX. 610/268–2334; Jeffrey J. Kegley, Executive Director

Cedar Manor Drug and Alcohol Treatment Center, 109 Summer Street, P.O. Box 286, Cresson, PA 16630; tel. 814/886–7399; FAX. 814/886–8705; Mary McDermott, Chief Executive Officer

Charter Behavioral Health System at Cove Forge, New Beginnings Road, Williamsburg, PA 16693; tel. 800/873–2131; FAX. 814/832–2882; Jonathan Wolf, Chief Executive Officer

Children's Home of Bradford, 800 East Main Street, Bradford, PA 16701; tel. 814/362–7404; Thomas Urban

Clear Brook, Inc., 1003 Wyoming Avenue, Forty–Fort, PA 18704; tel. 717/288–6692; Dave Lombard, Chief Executive Officer

Conewago Place, Nye Road, P.O. Box 406, Humelstown, PA 17036; tel. 717/533–0428; Tiffany Pyle

Eagleville Hospital, 100 Eagleville Road, P.O. Box 45, Eagleville, PA 19408; tel. 610/539–6000; FAX. 610/539–9314; Kendria Kurtz, Administrator

Gateway Rehabilitation Center, Moffett Run Road, Aliquippa, PA 15001; tel. 412/766–8700, ext. 101; FAX. 412/375–8815; Kenneth S. Ramsey, Ph.D., President

Gaudenzia, Inc.–Common Ground, 2835 North Front Street, Harrisburg, PA 17110; tel. 717/238–5553; Michael B. Harle, MHS

Greenbriar Treatment Center, 800 Manor Drive, Washington, PA 15301; tel. 412/225–9700; FAX. 412/225–9764; Mary Banaszak, Executive Director

Greenway Center, RR 1 Box 36 A Route 314/715 North, Henryville, PA 18332; tel. 717/688–9162; Thomas J. Hudson

Hoffman Homes, Inc., 815 Orphanage Road, (P.O. Box 4777, Gettysburg, PA 12548), Littlestown, PA 17340; tel. 717/359–7148; FAX. 717/359–9536; George Sepic

Lehigh Valley Community Mental Health Centers, Inc., P.O. Box 5349, Bethlehem, PA 12666; tel. 610/691–4357; Melissa Chlebowski

Livengrin Foundation, Inc., 4833 Hulmeville Road, Bensalem, PA 19020–3099; tel. 215/638–5200; FAX. 215/638–2603; Richard M. Pine, MBA

Lutheran Youth and Family Services, Beaver Road, P.O. Box 70 (zip 15993), Zelienople, PA 16063; tel. 724/452–4453; FAX. 724/452–6576; Charles T. Lockwood, Executive Director

Malvern Institute, 940 King Road, Malvern, PA 19355; tel. 610/647–0330; FAX. 610/647–2572; Valerie Craig, Administrator, Chief Executive Officer

Marworth, Lily Lake Road, P.O. Box 36, Waverly, PA 18471; tel. 717/563–1112; FAX. 717/563–2711; James Dougherty, Senior Vice President

Milestones Community HealthCare, Inc., 1069 Easton Road, Roslyn, PA 19001; tel. 215/884–5566; FAX. 215/885–1746; Dr. Paul Volosov, Chief Executive Officer

Mirmont Treatment Center, 100 Yearsley Mill Road, Glen Riddle Lima, PA 19037; tel. 610/565–9232; FAX. 610/565–7497; Thomas F. Crane, Executive Director

New Vitae Partial Hospital and Residential Treatment Center, 5201 St. Joseph Road, P.O. Box 181, Limeport, PA 18060; tel. 610/965–9021; FAX. 610/965–6227; Adam Devlin

Pamm Human Resources Center, Inc., 2400–10 North Front Street, Philadelphia, PA 19133; tel. 215/291–4357; FAX. 215/426–6010; Dr. Melchor Martinez, President, Chief Executive Officer

Penn Foundation, 807 Lawn Avenue, P.O. Box 32, Sellersville, PA 18960; tel. 215/257–6551; FAX. 215/257–9347; Vernon H. Kratz, M.D., President

Renewal Centers, 2705 Old Bethlehem Pike, P.O. Box 597, Quakertown, PA 18951; tel. 215/536–9070; FAX. 215/536–4788; Dan Land

Richard J. Caron Foundation, Galen Hall Roads, P.O. Box A, Wernersville, PA 19565; tel. 610/678–2332; FAX. 610/678–5704; Douglas Tieman, Chief Executive Officer

Roxbury, 601 Roxbury Road, P.O. Box L, Shippensburg, PA 17257; tel. 717/532–4217; FAX. 717/532–4003; Claire F. Beckwith, Chief Executive Officer

Salisbury House, Inc., 910 East Emmaus Avenue, Allentown, PA 18103; tel. 410/791–7878; FAX. 410/791–4709; Paul Volosov, PhD

Sarah A. Reed Children's Center, 2445 West 34th Street, Erie, PA 16506; tel. 814/838–1954; John J. Kovacs

Serenity Hall, Inc., 414 West Fifth Street, Erie, PA 16507; tel. 814/459–4775; FAX. 814/453–6118; Suzanne C. Mack, Executive Director

Silver Springs – Martin Luther School, 512 West Township Line Road, Plymouth Meeting, PA 18363; tel. 610/825–4440; Ruth W. Bartelt

St. John Vianney Hospital, Lincoln Highway at Woodbine Road, Downingtown, PA 19335–3080; tel. 610/269–2600; FAX. 610/873–8028; Louis D. Horvath, Administrator

The Bridge, 8400 Pine Road, Philadelphia, PA 19111; tel. 215/342–5000; FAX. 215/342–7709; Star Weiss, Program Director

The Mitchell Clinic, 1259 South Cedar Crest Boulevard, Suite 317, Allentown, PA 18103; tel. 610/435–9257; FAX. 610/435–4633; Dr. John Mitchell, Chief Executive Officer

The Renfrew Center, 475 Spring Lane, Philadelphia, PA 19128; tel. 215/482–5353; FAX. 215/482–7390; Barbara Peterson, MBA

The Terraces, 1170 South State Street, P.O. Box 729, Ephrata, PA 17522; tel. 717/859–4100; FAX. 717/859–2131; Michael Beavers

Today, Inc., 1990 North Woodbourne Road, P.O. Box 908, New Town, PA 18940; tel. 215/968–4713; FAX. 215/968–8742; John E. Howell, Executive Vice President

Twin Lakes Center for Drug and Alcohol Rehabilitation, P.O. Box 909, Somerset, PA 15501–0909; tel. 814/443–3639; FAX. 814/443–2737; Mark T. Pile, ACSW

UHS Recovery Foundation, Inc., 2001 Providence Avenue, Chester, PA 19013–5504; tel. 610/876–9000; FAX. 610/876–5441; Sandra Shannon

Westmeade Center Warwick, 940 W. Valley Road, Suite 2102, Wayne, PA 19087; tel. 215/491–9400; Thomas T. Fleming

White Deer Run, Devitt Camp Road, P.O. Box 97, Allenwood, PA 17810–0097; tel. 717/538–2567; FAX. 717/538–5303; Stephen T. Wicke, Executive Director

Wordsworth Academy, Pennsylvania Avenue and Camp Hill, Fort Washington, PA 19034; tel. 215/643–5400, ext. 3201; FAX. 215/643–0595; Bernard Cooper, Ph.D., Chief Executive Officer

RHODE ISLAND

Alternatives, 350 Duncan Drive, Providence, RI 02906; tel. 401/453–4742; FAX. 401/274–8086; Dr. Yitzhak Bakal, Chief Executive Officer

CODAC, Inc., 1052 Park Avenue, Cranston, RI 02910; tel. 401/461–5056; FAX. 401/942–3590; Craig Stenning, Chief Executive Officer

Community Counseling Center, 160 Beechwood Avenue, Pawtucket, RI 02860; tel. 401/722–5573, ext. 204; FAX. 401/722–5630; Richard H. Leclerc, President

East Bay Mental Health Center, Inc., Two Old County Road, Barrington, RI 02806; tel. 401/246–1195; FAX. 401/246–1985; John P. Digits, Jr., Chief Executive Officer

Fellowship Health Resources, Inc., 25 Blackstone Valley Place, Lincoln, RI 02865; tel. 401/333–3980; FAX. 401/333–3984; Joseph Dziobek, Chief Executive Officer

Good Hope Center, Inc., P.O. Box 1491, Coventry, RI 02816; tel. 401/397–5029; David A. Meek

Mental Health Services, Inc., 1516 Atwood Avenue, Johnston, RI 02919–9323; tel. 401/273–8756; FAX. 401/454–0148; Jack B. Silver

South Shore Mental Health Center, Inc., 4705A Old Post Road, P.O. Box 899, Charlestown, RI 02813; tel. 401/364–7705; FAX. 401/364–3310; Richard Antonelli, Chief Executive Officer

The Providence Center for Counseling and Psychiatric Services, 520 Hope Street, Providence, RI 02906; tel. 401/276–4000; FAX. 401/276–4015; Charles Maynard, Chief Executive Officer

Tri-Hab, Inc., 58 Hamlet Avenue, Woonsocket, RI 02895; tel. 401/765–4040; David Spencer

SOUTH CAROLINA

Charter Fenwick Hall Behavioral Health System, P.O. Box 688, Johns Island, SC 29457; tel. 803/559–2461; FAX. 803/745–5196; John H. Magill, FACHE

Lexington County Community Mental Health Center, 130 North Hospital Drive, West Columbia, SC 29169; tel. 803/739–8610; Louis H. Muzekari, EdD

New Hope Treatment Centers, Inc., 225 Midland Parkway, Summerville, SC 29485–8104; tel. 803/851–5010; FAX. 803/851–5020; Jay S. Orvin

Southbridge Center, 7901 Farrow Road, Building 1, Columbia, SC 29204; tel. 803/555–5555; Theresa Conti

York Place–Episcopal Church Home for Children, 234 Kings Mountain Street, York, SC 29745; tel. 803/684–8005; FAX. 803/628–1632; Steve Polak

SOUTH DAKOTA

Black Hills Childrens Home, 24100 South Rockerville Road, Rapid City, SD 57701–9277; tel. 605/343–5422; FAX. 605/343–1411; David P. Loving, MSW

Keystone Treatment Center, 1010 East Second Street, P.O. Box 159, Canton, SD 57013; tel. 605/987–2751; FAX. 605/987–2365; Carol A. Regier, RN, CCDC, Executive Director

Sioux Falls Children's Home, 801 North Sycamore, P.O. Box 1749, Sioux Falls, SD 57101–1749; tel. 605/334–6004, ext. 146; FAX. 605/335–2776; David P. Loving, Executive Director

TENNESSEE

Agency for Youth and Family Development, 5050 Poplar Avenue, Suite 525, Memphis, TN 38137; tel. 901/682–6775; Jeffrey L. Taylor

Buffalo Valley, Inc., 501 Park Avenue, S., P.O. Box 879, Hohenwald, TN 38462; tel. 615/796–4256; Jerry T. Risner, Executive Director

Camelot Care Center, Inc., Route 3, Box 267C, 183 Fiddlers Lane, Oak Ridge, TN 37763; tel. 423/481–3972; James V. Doramus

Child and Family Services of Knox County, Inc., 901 East Summit Hill Drive, Knoxville, TN 37915; tel. 423/524–7483; FAX. 423/524–4790; Charles E. Gentry, ACSW, LCSW, Chief Executive Officer

Compass Intervention Center, LLC, 7900 Lowrance Road, Memphis, TN 38125; tel. 901/758–2002; FAX. 901/758–2156; James F. Huntzicker

Cornerstone of Recovery, Inc., 1120 Topside Road, Louisville, TN 37777; tel. 615/970–7747; FAX. 615/681–2266; Dan R. Caldwell, President

Council for Alcohol and Drug Abuse Services, Inc., 207 Spears Avenue, P.O. Box 4797, Chattanooga, TN 37405; tel. 423/756–7644; FAX. 423/756–7646; James F. Marcotte, Executive Director

Cumberland Heights Foundation, P.O. Box 90727, Nashville, TN 37209; tel. 615/353–4381; FAX. 615/353–4300; James Moore, President, Chief Executive Officer

Daybreak Treatment Center and Specialized School, 2262 Germantown Road, S., Germantown, TN 38138; tel. 901/753–4300; FAX. 901/751–8105; Tina Mills, Chief Executive Officer

FHC Cumberland Hall of Chattanooga, 7351 Standifer Gap Road, Chattanooga, TN 37421; tel. 423/499–9007; FAX. 423/499–9757; Charles Dickens, Administrator

Greene Valley Developmental Center, 4850 East Andrew Johnson Highway, P.O. Box 910, Greeneville, TN 37743; tel. 423/787–6800; Robert G. Erb, Ed.D., Superintendent

Jackson Academy L.L.C., 222 Church Street, Dickson, TN 37055; tel. 615/446–3900; FAX. 615/446–3985; May Lankford

New Life Lodge, 999 Girl Scout Road, P.O. Box 430, Burns, TN 37029; tel. 615/446–7034; FAX. 615/446–7987; James Kestner, Executive Officer

Pine Point Center, Inc., 49 Old Hickory Boulevard, Jackson, TN 38305; tel. 901/664–7196; FAX. 901/661–0640; David Johnson, MS

Ridgeview Psychiatric Hospital and Center, Inc., 240 West Tyrone Road, Oak Ridge, TN 37830; tel. 423/482–1076; Robert J. Benning

The Harbours, 804 Youngs Lane, P.O. Box 70158, Nashville, TN 37207; tel. 615/650–0700; FAX. 615/650–0647; Joe H. McWaters

Three Springs Outdoor Therapeutic Program, P.O. Box 297, Centerville, TN 37033; tel. 615/729–5040; FAX. 615/729–9525; Susan Hardy

University of Tennessee Day Treatment Program, 711 Jefferson, Suite 607, Memphis, TN 38105; tel. 901/448–7662; Laurel J. Kiser, PhD

Youth Villages, 2890 Bekemeyer Drive, Arlington, TN 38002; tel. 901/867–8832; FAX. 901/867–8937; Patrick Lawler, Chief Executive Officer

TEXAS

Alternatives Centre for Behavioral Health, 5001 Alabama Street, El Paso, TX 79930; tel. 915/565–4800; FAX. 915/544–5374; Carol Anderson, Chief Executive Officer

Austin Child Guidance Center, 810 West 45th Street, Austin, TX 78751; tel. 512/451–2242; FAX. 512/454–9204; Donald J. Zappone, Dr.P.H., Executive Director

BHC Cedar Crest RTC, Inc., 3500 South IH–35, Belton, TX 76513; tel. 254/939–2100; Richard N. Rickey

Burke Center, 4101 South Medford Drive, Lufkin, TX 70202; tel. 409/639–1141; Susan Rushing, MA

Canyon Lakes Residential Treatment Center, 2402 Canyon Lake Drive, Lubbock, TX 79415; tel. 806/762–5782; FAX. 806/762–0838; Ray H. Brown, Ph.D., Administrator

Champions, 14320 Walters Road, Houston, TX 77014; tel. 713/537–5050; FAX. 713/537–2726; Brad Thompson

Child Study Center, 1300 West Lancaster, Fort Worth, TX 76102; tel. 817/336–8611; FAX. 817/336–2823; Larry D. Eason, Ed.D., Administrator

Community Residential Centers of San Antonio, 17720 Corporate Woods Drive, San Antonio, TX 78259–3500; tel. 210/494–1060; FAX. 210/490–8672; Patricia McLemore, Administrator

DePelchin Children's Center, 100 Sandman Street, Houston, TX 77007; tel. 713/861–8136; FAX. 713/802–7611; Robert E. Barker

Family Opportunity Resources, The F.O.R.G.I.V.E. Program, 6000 Broadway, Suite 106R, Galveston, TX 77551; tel. 409/740–0442; FAX. 409/740–0457; Gordon W. McKee, Administrator

Family Service Center, 2707 North Loop West, Suite 520, Houston, TX 77008; tel. 713/868–4466; FAX. 713/868–2619; Lloyd Sidwell, Chief Executive Officer

Forest Springs Residential Treatment Center, 1120 Cypress Station Drive, Houston, TX 77090; tel. 713/893–7200; FAX. 713/893–7646; James Muska, Chief Executive Officer

Glass Treatment Center, Inc., 18842 South Memorial Drive, Suite 205, Humble, TX 77338; tel. 713/666–9811; FAX. 713/446–5292; G. Glass, M.D., Medical Director

La Hacienda Treatment Center, P.O. Box 1, Hunt, TX 78024; tel. 210/238–4222; FAX. 210/238–4070; Frank Sadlack, Ph.D., Executive Director

Life Resource, 2750 South 8th Street, Beaumont, TX 77701; tel. 409/839–1000; N. Charles Harris, PhD

Meridell Achievement Center, Inc., P.O. Box 87, Liberty Hill, TX 78642; tel. 512/515–6650; FAX. 512/515–5873; Patricia Mitchell

New Dimensions Day Treatment, 18333 Egret Bay Boulevard, Suite 560, Houston, TX 77058; tel. 281/333–2284; FAX. 281/333–0221; Larry M. Nahmias, MD

New Spirit, 2411 Fountainview, Suite 175, Houston, TX 77057–4803; tel. 713/975–1580; FAX. 713/975–0228; Susan L. Smith

New View Partial Hospitalization Centre, Inc., 4310 Dowlen Road, Suite 13, Beaumont, TX 77706; tel. 409/892–0009; D. Sue Home, PhD

Paul Meier New Life Day Hospital and Outpatient Clinic, 2071 North Collins, Richardson, TX 75080; tel. 972/437–4698; FAX. 972/690–9309; Jacquelyn Jeffrey, Chief Executive Officer

Resolutions Day Treatment Center, 825 Fairmont Parkway, Pasadena, TX 77504; tel. 713/910–7707; Seth W. Silverman, MD

River Oaks Academy, 8120 Westglen, Houston, TX 77063; tel. 713/783–7200; FAX. 713/783–7286; Dr. Sandra Phares, Chief Executive Officer

Saint Joseph's Day Treatment Center, 6401 McPherson Road, Suite 2, Laredo, TX 78041; tel. 956/718–2273; FAX. 956/726–6357; Dr. Jose Garcia, Chief Executive Officer

San Marcos Treatment Center, P.O. Box 768, San Marcos, TX 78666; tel. 512/396–8500; Mack Wigley

Seaview Mental Health Center, P.A., 4529 Weber Road, Corpus Christi, TX 78411; tel. 512/852–3994; FAX. 512/852–6183; Stan Barnard, MSW, MPH

Shiloh Treatment Center, Inc., 4227 County Road 89, Manvel, TX 77578; tel. 281/489–1290; FAX. 281/489–0167; Dr. Brenda Gardner, Chief Executive Officer

Shoreline, Inc., 1220 Gregory, P.O. Box 23, Taft, TX 78390; tel. 512/528–3356; FAX. 512/528–3249; Bob O. Nevill, Chief Executive Officer

Summer Sky, Inc., 1100 McCart Street, Stephenville, TX 76401; tel. 817/968–2907; FAX. 817/968–4509; Al Conlan

Sundown Ranch, Inc., Route Four, Box 182, Highway 19, Canton, TX 75103; tel. 903/479–3933; FAX. 903/479–3999; Richard Boardman, Chief Executive Officer

Synergy Partial Hospital, 5631 Dolores Street, Houston, TX 77057; tel. 713/952–0207; Reese Buggs

The Country Place, 3612 Parker Road, Wylie, TX 75098; tel. 214/442–6002; Fayteen Marshall

The Oaks Treatment Center, Inc., 1407 West Stassney Lane, Austin, TX 78745; tel. 512/444–9561; FAX. 512/464–0444; Mack Wigley, Chief Executive Officer

The Patrician Movement, 222 East Mitchell, San Antonio, TX 78210; tel. 210/532–3126; FAX. 210/534–3779; Mnsgr. Dermot N. Brosnan

Waco Center for Youth, 3501 North 19th Street, Waco, TX 76708; tel. 254/745–5121; FAX. 254/745–5119; Stephen R. Anfinson

UTAH

Brightway at St. George, 115 West 1470 South, St. George, UT 84770; tel. 800/345–4828; FAX. 801/673–8420; Paula O. Bell, Managing Director

Cooper Hills Youth Center, 5899 West Rivendell Drive, West Jordan, UT 84084; tel. 801/561–3377; Sandra C. Podley

Heritage School, 5600 North Heritage School Drive, P.O. Box 105, Provo, UT 84604; tel. 801/226–4600; FAX. 801/226–4696; Jerry Spanos, Chief Executive Officer

Highland Ridge Hospital, 4578 Highland Drive, Salt Lake City, UT 84117; tel. 801/272–9851; FAX. 801/272–9857; Scott Shephard

Island View, Inc., 2650 West 2700 South, P.O. Box 67, Syracuse, UT 84075; tel. 801/773–0200; Jared U. Balmer, Executive Director

New Haven, 2096 East 7200 South, (Mailing Address: P.O. Box 50238, Provo, UT 84605–0238), Spanish Fork, UT 84660; tel. 801/794–1218; FAX. 801/794–1223; Mark McGregor, Chief Executive Officer

Provo Canyon School, 1305 E. 750 N, Provo, UT 84057; tel. 801/227–2000; FAX. 801/227–2095; Larry W. Carter

Sorenson's Ranch School, Second East 345 North, Box 440219, Koosharem, UT 84744; tel. 801/638–7318; FAX. 801/638–7582; Burnell D. Sorenson, Owner

Vista Adolescent Treatment Center, P.O. Box 69, Magna, UT 84044; tel. 801/250–9762; H. Matthew Dixon, Jr.

Youth Care, Inc., 12595 South Minuteman Drive, P.O. Box 909, Draper, UT 84020; tel. 801/572–6989; Anthony J. LaPray, EdD

VIRGINIA

Barry Robinson Center, 443 Kempsville Road, Norfolk, VA 23502; tel. 757/455–6100; FAX. 757/455–6127; Thomas D. Pittman, M.P.H., Executive Director

CATS–Comprehensive Addiction Treatment Services, 3300 Gallows Road, Falls Church, VA 22042–3300; tel. 703/698–1530; FAX. 703/698–1537; Donald F. Silver, Assistant Vice President, Behavioral Health Services

DeJarnette Center, 1290 Richmond Road, P.O. Box 2309, Staunton, VA 24402–2309; tel. 540/332–2100; Andrew C. Newsome, FACHE

Graydon Manor, 801 Children's Center Road, S.W., Leesburg, VA 20175–4753; tel. 703/777–3485; FAX. 703/777–4887; Bernard J. Haberlein, Executive Director, Chairman of the Board

Inova Kellar Center, 10396 Democracy Lane, Fairfax, VA 22030–0252; tel. 703/218–8500; Donald F. Silver

Learning Services, 9524 Fairview Avenue, Manassas, VA 22110; tel. 703/335–9771; FAX. 703/330–5277; Randall Mitchell, Chief Executive Officer

Mount Regis Center, 405 Kimball Avenue, Salem, VA 24153; tel. 540/389–4761; Gail S. Basham

Shalom et Benedictus, Inc., P.O. Box 309, Stephenson, VA 22656; tel. 540/667–0875; J. Michael Foster

The Life Center of Galax, 112 Painter Street, P.O. Box 27, Galax, VA 24333; tel. 800/345–6998; FAX. 703/236–8821; Tina R. Bullins, Executive Director

The Pines RTC, 825 Crawford Parkway, Portsmouth, VA 23704; tel. 757/393–0061; FAX. 757/393–9658; George Boothby

Williamsburg Place, 5477 Mooretown Road, Williamsburg, VA 23185; tel. 757/565–0106; FAX. 757/565–0620; Donna Grile

WASHINGTON

Martin Center, 2806 Douglas Avenue, P.O. Box 5704, Bellingham, WA 98227–5704; tel. 360/733–5804; Gail A. Estes

Pearl Street Center, 815 South Pearl Street, Tacoma, WA 98465; tel. 206/756–5290; FAX. 206/759–7008; Michael Kent Laederich, Ph.D., Director, Children and Family Services

Psych Systems of Kirkland, 12608 Northeast 85th Street, Kirkland, WA 98033; tel. 206/803–1850; Catherine Willner

Seattle Children's Home, 2142 10th Avenue, W., Seattle, WA 98119; tel. 206/283–3300; FAX. 206/284–7843; R. David Cousineau, Executive Director

Sunrise Residential Treatment Center, 6911 226th Place Southwest, Mountlake Terrace, WA 98043; tel. 206/672–9323; Kathryn M. Grey

Tamarack Center, Inc., 2901 West Fort George Wright Drive, Spokane, WA 99204; tel. 509/326–8100; FAX. 509/326–9358; Tim Davis

Valley Cities Counseling and Consultation, 2704 I Street, NE, Auburn, WA 98002; tel. 206/833–7444; Marilyn La Celle

WEST VIRGINIA

Elkins Mountain School, 100 Bell Street, Elkins, WV 26241; tel. 304/637–8000; FAX. 304/636–4694; Dr. Eugene Foster, Chief Executive Officer

Olympic Center Preston, Inc., Adolescent Alcohol/Drug Treatment, Route Seven West, P.O. Box 158, Kingwood, WV 26537; tel. 304/329–2400; FAX. 304/329–2405; Arlene Glover, Executive Director

Shawnee Hills, Inc., 603 Morris Square, P.O. Box 3698, Charleston, WV 25336–3698; tel. 304/341–0240; FAX. 304/341–0359; John E. Barnette, Ed.D., President, Chief Executive Officer

Worthington Center, Inc., 3199 Core Road, Suite Two, Parkersburg, WV 26104; tel. 304/485–5185; FAX. 304/485–0051; Dr. Fred Lee, Chief Executive Officer

WISCONSIN

Eau Claire Academy, 550 North Dewey Street, P.O. Box 1168, Eau Claire, WI 54702–1168; tel. 715/834–6681; FAX. 715/834–9954; Marcia R. Van Beek, Executive Director

Family Services Lakeshore, Inc., 333 Reed Avenue, Manitowoc, WI 54220; tel. 414/683–9922; Thomas Aronson, ACSW

Libertas Treatment Center, 1701 Dousman Street, Green Bay, WI 54303; tel. 414/498–8600; David B. Fish

St. Rose Residence, Inc., 3801 North 88th Street, Milwaukee, WI 53222; tel. 414/466–9450; FAX. 414/466–0730; Kenneth Czaplewski, President

WYOMING

Normative Services, Inc., P.O. Box 3075, Sheridan, WY 82801; tel. 307/674–6878; Julia George

St. Joseph's Children's Home, 1419 South Main, P.O. Box 1117, Torrington, WY 82240; tel. 307/532–4197; FAX. 307/532–8405; Robert Mayor, Chief Executive Officer

Section C

JCAHO Accredited Freestanding Substance Abuse Organizations

The accredited freestanding substance abuse programs listed have been accredited as of April, 1998 by the Joint Commission on Accreditation of Healthcare Organizations by decision of the Accreditation Committee of the Board of Commissioners.

The organizations listed here have been found to be in compliance with the Joint Commission standards for subtance abuse organizations, as found in the Accreditation Manual for Mental Health, Chemical Dependency, and Mental Retardation/Developmental Disabilities Services.

Please refer to section A of the AHA Guide for information on hospitals with inpatient and/or outpatient alcohol and chemical dependency services. These hospitals are identified by Facility Codes F2 and F3. In section A, those hospitals identified by Approval Code 1 are JCAHO accredited.

We present this list simply as a convenient directory. Inclusion or omission of any organization's name indicates neither approval nor disapproval by Healthcare InfoSource, Inc., a subsidiary of the American Hospital Association.

United States

ALABAMA
Behavioral Healthcare Center, 306 Paul W. Bryant Drive East, Tuscaloosa, AL 35401; tel. 205/349-1033; Omar Mohabbat, MD

Bradford Adolescent at Oak Mountain, 2280 Highway 35 South, Pelham, AL 35124; tel. 205/664-3460; FAX. 205/664-8476; Jarrett N. Caltrider

Bradford Health Services–Birmingham Lodge, 1189 Allbritton Road, P.O. Box 129, Warrior, AL 35180; tel. 205/647-1945, ext. 20; FAX. 205/647-3626; Roy M. Ramsey, Executive Director

Bradford–Parkside at Huntsville, 1600 Browns Ferry Road, P.O. Box 176, Madison, AL 35758; tel. 205/461-7272; FAX. 205/464-9618; Robert Hinds, Chief Executive Officer

Mobile Mental Health Center, Inc., 2400 Gordon Smith Drive, Mobile, AL 36617; tel. 334/473-4423; Julie B. Bellcase

New Perspectives (Adult), 1000 Fairfax Park, Tuscaloosa, AL 35406; tel. 205/391-4738; FAX. 205/759-4151; Martha Hinkle, Administrator

The Catalyst Center (Adolescent), 1000 Fairfax Park, Tuscaloosa, AL 35406; tel. 205/391-4738; FAX. 205/759-4151; Martha Hinkle, Chief Executive Officer

The Quality Life Center of Quality Healthcare, Inc., 2801 West Mall Drive, Florence, AL 35630; tel. 205/760-9955; Glenda Smith

ALASKA
Akeela Treatment Services, Inc., 2805 Bering Street, Suite Four, Anchorage, AK 99503; tel. 907/561-5206; Robert P. Galea, PhD

Alaska North Addictions Recovery Center, 4330 Bragaw Street, Anchorage, AK 99508; tel. 907/561-5537; Leroy Bingham

ARIZONA
Calvary Rehabilitation Center, Inc., 720 East Montebello Avenue, Phoenix, AZ 85014; tel. 602/279-1468; FAX. 602/279-3090; Jeffrey Shook, Chief Executive Officer

Chandler Valley Hope, 501 North Washington, P.O. Box 1839 (zip 83405), Chandler, AZ 85244-1839; tel. 602/899-3335; FAX. 602/899-6697; Dennis Gilhousen

Cottonwood de Tucson, Inc., 4110 Sweetwater Drive, Tucson, AZ 85745; tel. 520/743-0411; FAX. 520/743-7991; Ron Welch, Chief Executive Officer

Desert Hills Center for Youth and Families, 2797 North Introspect Drive, Tucson, AZ 85745; tel. 520/622-5437; FAX. 520/792-6249; Richard Harden ACSW

PREHAB of Arizona, Inc., 868 East University, P.O. Drawer 5860, Mesa, AZ 85203; tel. 602/969-4024; Michael T. Hughes, Executive Director

Parc Place, 5116 East Thomas Road, Phoenix, AZ 85018; tel. 602/840-4774; FAX. 602/840-7567; Jim Oleson

Remuda Ranch Center for Anorexia and Bulimia, Jack Burden Road, P.O. Box 2481, Wickenburg, AZ 85358; tel. 520/684-3913; Ward E. Keller

Salvation Army Recovery Center, 2707 East Van Buren, P.O. Box 52177 (zip 85072), Phoenix, AZ 85008; tel. 602/267-1404; FAX. 602/267-4131; Major John Webb, Chief Executive Officer

Sierra Tucson, Inc., 16500 North Lago del Oro Parkway, Tucson, AZ 85739; tel. 602/624-4000, ext. 2001; FAX. 602/792-2916; Terry Stephens

Superstition Mountain Mental Health Center, Inc., 150 N. Ocotillo, Apache Junction, AZ 85217; tel. 602/983-0065; Gary W. Selvy

The EXCEL Group, 108 East First Street, Yuma, AZ 85364; tel. 520/329-8995; Michael P. Puthoff

The Meadows, 1655 North Tegner, P.O. Box 97 (zip 85358), Wickenburg, AZ 85390; tel. 520/684-3926; FAX. 602/684-3261; James Mellody, Chief Executive Officer

The New Foundation, 1200 North 77th Street, P.O. Box 3828, Scottsdale, AZ 85257; tel. 602/945-5302; FAX. 602/945-9308; David Hedgcock

Westcenter Rehabilitation Facility, Inc., d/b/a Westcenter, 2105 East Allen Road, Tucson, AZ 85719; tel. 520/795-0952; FAX. 520/318-6442; Allan Chip Harrington, Executive Director

ARKANSAS
Behavior Health Services, Inc. of Arkansas, 604 Cherry Street, Helena, AR 72342; tel. 501/338-9131; Robert K. Quam, MA

Ozark Guidance Center, Inc., P.O. Box 6430, Springdale, AR 66332; tel. 501/751-7052; David L. Williams, PhD, FACHE

CALIFORNIA
Behavioral Care of America, 18881 Von Karman, Suite 250, P.O. Box 30018, Irvine, CA 92715; tel. 714/752-1510; FAX. 714/442-2139; David Ellisor, Director

Betty Ford Center at Eisenhower, 39000 Bob Hope Drive, Rancho Mirage, CA 92270; tel. 619/773-4100; FAX. 619/773-4141; John T. Schwartzlose

Cornerstone Residential Center for Addictions, 13682 Yorba Street, Tustin, CA 92680; tel. 714/730-5399; FAX. 714/730-3505; Michael Stone, M.D., Medical Director, President

Family Recovery Foundation, Inc., 12822 Hewes Avenue, Santa Ana, CA 92705; tel. 714/289-9142; Javier Saldivar

Impact Drug and Alcohol Treatment Center, 1680 North Fair Oaks Avenue, Pasadena, CA 91103; tel. 818/798-0884; James M. Stillwell, Executive Director

Kings View Center, 42675 Road 44, Reedley, CA 93654; tel. 209/638-2505; Mike Waters

Los Angeles Centers for Alcohol and Drug Abuse, 11015 Bloomfield Avenue, Santa Fe Springs, CA 90670; tel. 310/906-2676; FAX. 310/906-2681; John Brown, Executive Director

Michael's House Treatment Center for Men, 430 South Cahuilla Road, Palm Springs, CA 92262; tel. 619/320-5486; FAX. 619/778-6020; Arlene Rosen, President

Oak Grove Institute Foundation, 24275 Jefferson Avenue, Murrietta, CA 92562; tel. 909/677-5599; Thomas C. Lester, MD

R. House, Inc., P.O. Box 2587, Santa Rosa, CA 95405; tel. 707/539-2948; Mimi G. Donohue

S.T.E.P.S., 224 East Clara Street, Port Hueneme, CA 93041; tel. 805/488-6424; FAX. 805/488-6717; John J. Megara, Administrator

SeaBridge Adolescent Treatment Center, 30371 Morning View Drive, P.O. Box 6301, Malibu, CA 90265; tel. 310/457-5802; FAX. 310/457-6093; Martha Zimmerman, Executive Director

Spencer Recovery Centers, Inc., 343 West Foothill Boulevard, Monrovia, CA 91016; tel. 626/358-3662; FAX. 626/357-7405; Chris Spencer, President, Chief Executive Officer

Substance Abuse Foundation of Long Beach, Inc., 3125 East Seventh Street, Long Beach, CA 90804; tel. 310/439-7755; Ronald H. Banner, Executive Director

Tarzana Treatment Center, 18646 Oxnard Street, Tarzana, CA 91356; tel. 818/996-1051; FAX. 818/345-3778; Albert Senella

The Discovery Adolescent Program, 4136 Ann Arbor Road, Lakewood, CA 90712; tel. 562/425-6918; Craig M. Brown, PhD

Twin Town Treatment Centers, 10741 Los Alamitos Blvd., Los Alamitos, CA 90720; tel. 310/594-8844; George P. Casey

Vista Pacifica Hospital, 7989 Linda Vista Road, San Diego, CA 92111; tel. 619/576-1200; FAX. 619/576-8362; Daniel R. Valentine, Adminstrator

Vista San Diego Center, 3003 Armstrong Street, San Diego, CA 92111; tel. 619/268-3343; Judith K. Williams

Watts Health Foundation, Inc., 10300 South Compton Avenue, Los Angeles, CA 90002; tel. 213/564-4331; FAX. 213/563-6378; Clyde Oden

COLORADO
Adolescent and Family Institute of Colorado, Inc., 10001 West 32nd Avenue, Wheat Ridge, CO 80033; tel. 303/238-1231; FAX. 303/238-0500; Alex M. Panio, Jr., Ph.D., Chief Executive Officer

Alpha Drug Abuse Program, 802 Ninth Street #2, 3 and 4, P.O. Box 1082 (zip 80632), Greeley, CO 80631; tel. 303/346-9546; Robert Warren

Aurora Behavioral Health Hospital, 1290 South Potomac, Aurora, CO 80012; tel. 303/745-2273; FAX. 303/369-9556; John R. Thompson

Harmony Foundation, Inc., 1600 Fish Hatchery Road, P.O. Box 1989, Estes Park, CO 80517; tel. 970/586-4491; FAX. 970/577-0392; Donald R. Hays, J.D., NCACII, CACIII, Director

Parker Valley Hope, 22422 East Main Street, P.O. Box 670, Parker, CO 80134; tel. 303/841-7857; FAX. 303/841-6526; Dennis Gilhousen

Pikes Peak Mental Health Center Systems, Inc., 220 Ruskin Drive, Colorado Springs, CO 80910; tel. 719/572-6100; Charles J. Vorwaller, MSW

CONNECTICUT
Community Prevention and Addiction Services, Inc., 1491 West Main Street, Willimantic, CT 06226; tel. 860/456-3215; Leanne M. Dillian

Cornerstone of Eagle Hill, Inc., 28 Alberts Hill Road, Sandy Hook, CT 06482; tel. 203/426-8085; FAX. 203/426-2821; Norman J. Sokolow, Executive Director

Greater Bridgeport Community Mental Health Center, 1635 Central Avenue, P.O. Box 5117, Bridgeport, CT 06610; tel. 203/579-6626; FAX. 203/579-6094; James Lehane

Guenster Rehabilitation Center, Inc., 276 Union Avenue, Bridgeport, CT 06607; tel. 203/384-9301; FAX. 203/336-4395; Thomas Kidder

Perception Programs, Inc., P.O. Box 407, Willimantic, CT 06226; tel. 860/450-7122; Rhonda M. Kincaid

Reid Treatment Center, Inc., 121 West Avon Road, P.O. Box 1357, Avon, CT 06001; tel. 860/673-6115; FAX. 860/675-7433; Mary Ann Reid, Executive Director

Rushford Center, Inc., 1250 Silver Street, Middletown, CT 06457; tel. 203/346-0300; FAX. 203/344-8152; Jeffrey L. Walter

Southern Connecticut Mental Health and Subs. Abuse Treatment Center, 4083 Main Street, Bridgeport, CT 06606; tel. 203/365-8400; Mark Waynik, MD

Stonington Institute, Swantown Hill Road, P.O. Box 216, North Stonington, CT 06359; tel. 860/535–1010; FAX. 860/535–4820; Michael J. Angelides, MA

The BlueRidge Center, 1095 Blue Hills Avenue, Bloomfield, CT 06002; tel. 860/243–1331; FAX. 860/242–3265; Mary Ellen Doyle, Executive Director

United Services, Inc., P.O. Box 839, Dayville, CT 06241; tel. 860/774–2020; Theodore L. Ver Haagh

Vitam Center, Inc., 57 West Rocks Road, P.O. Box 730, Norwalk, CT 06852–0730; tel. 203/846–2091; FAX. 203/846–3620; Leonard A. Kenowitz, Ph.D., Executive Director

Wheeler Clinic, Inc., 91 Northwest Drive, Plainville, CT 06062; tel. 860/793–3588; FAX. 860/793–3520; Dennis Keenan, Executive Director

DELAWARE

Brandywine Counseling, Inc., 2713 Lancaster Avenue, Wilmington, DE 19805; tel. 302/656–2348; FAX. 302/656–0746; Sara Taylor Allshouse, Executive Director

Lower Kensington Environmental Center, Inc., P.O. Box 546, Delaware City, DE 19706; tel. 302/836–1615; Terence McSherry, Executive Director

Open Door, Inc., 3301 Green Street, Claymont, DE 19703; tel. 302/798–9555; Bobi Freedman

SODAT–Delaware, Inc., 625 North Orange Street, Wilmington, DE 19801; tel. 302/656–4044; Thomas C. Maloney, Executive Director

FLORIDA

45th Street Mental Health Center, Inc., 1041 45th Street, West Palm Beach, FL 33407; tel. 561/840–3360; Terry H. Allen

Act Corp., 1220 Willis Avenue, Daytona Beach, FL 32114; tel. 904/947–4270; J. W. Dreggors, MA

Alternatives In Treatment, Inc, 7601 North Federal Highway, Suite 100B, Boca Raton, FL 33487; tel. 407/998–0866; FAX. 407/241–5042; Jacob Frydman, Executive Director

Apalachee Center for Human Services, Inc., 625 East Tennessee Street, P.O. Box 1782 (zip 32302), Tallahassee, FL 32308; tel. 904/487–2930; Ronald P. Kirkland, Chief Executive Officer

Associated Counseling and Education, Inc., 4563 South Orange Blossom Trail, Orlando, FL 32839; tel. 407/422–7233; FAX. 407/843–9602; Loretta Parrish

Bayview Center for Mental Health, Inc., 12550 Biscayne Boulevard, Suite 919, North Miami, FL 33181; tel. 305/892–4646; FAX. 305/893–1224; Robert Ward

Camelot Care Centers, Inc., 9160 Oakhurst Road, Building One, Seminole, FL 33776; tel. 813/596–9960; FAX. 813/593–1784; James V. Doramus

Charlotte Community Mental Health Services, Inc., 1700 Education Avenue, Punta Gorda, FL 33950; tel. 941/639–8300; Gerald N. Ross, Ed.D.

Coastal Recovery Centers, Inc., 3830 Bee Ridge Road, Sarasota, FL 34233; tel. 941/927–8900; FAX. 941/925–3836; James R. Sleeper, President, Chief Executive Officer

Crossroads Center, 2121 Lisenby Avenue, P.O. Box 16588 (zip 32405), Panama City, FL 32406; tel. 800/922–7522; FAX. 904/763–3933; Tony Gilchrist

DISC Village, Inc., (Tallahassee/Leon County Human Services Center), 525 N. Martin Luther King Blvd., Tallahassee, FL 32304; tel. 904/224–4346; FAX. 904/576–5960; Thomas K. Olk, Executive Director

David Lawrence Center, Inc., 6075 Golden Gate Parkway, Naples, FL 33999; tel. 941/455–1031; FAX. 941/455–6561; David Schimmel, Executive Director

Eckerd Alternative Treatment Program at E–How–Kee, 397 Culbreath Road, P.O. Box 7450, Brooksville, FL 34602; tel. 904/796–9493; FAX. 904/754–6791; Merle Springer

Fairwinds Treatment Center, 1569 South Fort Harrison, Clearwater, FL 34616; tel. 800/226–0301; FAX. 813/446–1022; Mazhar K. Al–Abed

Hanley–Hazelden Center at St. Mary's, 5200 East Avenue, West Palm Beach, FL 33407; tel. 407/848–1666; FAX. 407/848–6333; Jerry Singleton, M.A., Executive Director

High Point, 5960 Southwest 106th Avenue, Cooper City, FL 33328; tel. 954/680–2700; FAX. 954/680–9941; Frank Fanella

InterPhase Recovery Program, Inc., 23120 Sandalfoot Square Place Drive, Boca Raton, FL 33428; tel. 407/487–5400; FAX. 407/852–8212; Johnathan Huttner

Jacksonville Therapy Center, 6428 Beach Boulevard, Jacksonville, FL 32216; tel. 904/724–6500; FAX. 904/721–6677; John McWhorter

Lakeside Alternatives, Inc., 434 West Kennedy Boulevard, Orlando, FL 32810; tel. 407/875–3700; FAX. 407/875–5717; Duane Zimmerman

Lakeview Center, Inc., 1221 West Lakeview Avenue, Pensacola, FL 32501; tel. 904/432–1222; Morris L. Eaddy, PhD

Leon F. Stewart–Hal S. Marchman Center, 120 Michigan Avenue, Daytona Beach, FL 32114; tel. 904/255–0447, ext. 298; FAX. 904/238–0877; Dr. Ernest D. Cantley, Executive Director

LifeStream Behavioral Center, 515 West Main Street, P.O. Box 491000 (zip 33749), Leesburg, FL 34749–1000; tel. 352/360–6575; FAX. 352/360–6595; Jack Hargrove

Lifeskills of Boca Raton, Inc., 7301A West Palmetto Park Road, Suite 300 B, Boca Raton, FL 33433; tel. 561/392–1199; FAX. 561/392–4341; Cindy Burke, MS

Manatee Glens Corp., P.O. Box 9478, Bradenton, FL 99999; tel. 941/741–3111; Mary Rutz

Marion Citrus Mental Health Centers, Inc., 717 Southwest Martin Luther King Jr. Avenue, P.O. Box 1330, Ocala, FL 34474; tel. 352/620–7300; FAX. 352/732–1413; Russell Rasco

Meridian Behaviorial Healthcare, Inc., 4300 Southwest 13th Street, Gainesville, FL 32608; tel. 904/374–5600; Douglas L. Starr, Chief Executive Officer

National Recovery Institutes Group, Inc., 1000 Northwest 15th Street, Boca Raton, FL 33486; tel. 407/392–8444; Sheldon Russakoff, President, Chief Executive Officer

Northwest Dade Center, Inc., 4175 West 20th Avenue, Hialeah, FL 33012; tel. 305/825–0300; FAX. 305/824–1006; Mario Jardon, LCSW, Chief Executive Officer

Oak Center, 8889 Corporate Square Court, Jacksonville, FL 32216; tel. 904/725–7073; FAX. 904/727–9077; Joseph A. Virzi, MD

Pathways to Recovery, Inc., 13132 Barwick Road, Delray Beach, FL 33445; tel. 407/496–7532; Allen Bombart, Executive Director

Recovery Corner, 400 Executive Drive, Suite 102, West Palm Beach, FL 33401; tel. 561/686–1924; FAX. 561/626–1739; Jay C. Mills, Executive Director

Renaissance Institute of Palm Beach, Inc., 7000 North Federal Highway, Second Floor, Boca Raton, FL 33487; tel. 561/241–7977; FAX. 561/241–9233; Sid Goodman, Executive Director

Ruth Cooper Center for Behavioral Health Care, Inc., 2789 Ortiz Avenue, Fort Myers, FL 33905; tel. 941/275–3222; Eugene R. Dold

South County Mental Health Center, Inc., 16158 South Military Trail, Delray Beach, FL 33484–6502; tel. 561/637–1000; FAX. 561/495–7975; Joseph S. Speicher, Executive Director

Spectrum Programs, Inc., 18441 Northwest Second Avenue, Suite 218, Miami, FL 33169; tel. 305/653–8288, ext. 19; FAX. 305/653–6787; H. Bruce Hayden, President

Tampa Bay Academy, 12012 Boyette Rd., Riverview, FL 33569; tel. 813/677–8700; Edward C. Hoefle, MA

The Beachcomber, 4493 North Ocean Boulevard, Delray Beach, FL 33483; tel. 561/734–1818; FAX. 561/265–1349; James Bryan, Director

The Center for Alcohol and Drug Studies, Inc., 321 Northlake Blvd., Suite 214, North Palm Beach, FL 33408; tel. 561/848–1332; Donald K. Mullaney, LCSW

The Inn at Bowling Green, 101 North Oak Street, Bowling Green, FL 33834; tel. 941/375–4373; Joann Summerlin, Vice President, Operations, Administration

The Renfrew Center of Florida, Inc., 7700 Renfrew Lane, Coconut Creek, FL 33073; tel. 954/698–9222; FAX. 954/698–9007; Barbara Peterson, Executive Director

The Rose Institute, Inc., 17 Rose Drive, Fort Lauderdale, FL 33316; tel. 954/522–7673; FAX. 954/522–4031; Richard Maulion

The Southern Institute for Treatment and Evaluation, 660 Linton Boulevard, Suite 112, Delray Beach, FL 33444; tel. 407/278–8411; FAX. 407/278–7774; Michele Michael, BA

The Village South, Inc., 3180 Biscayne Boulevard, Miami, FL 33137; tel. 800/443–3784; FAX. 305/576–1348; Matthew Gissen, Chief Executive Officer

The Willough at Naples, 9001 Tamiami Trail, E., Naples, FL 33962; tel. 941/775–4500; FAX. 941/793–0534; Gary D. Centafanti, Executive Director

Transitions Recovery Program, 1928 Northeast 154th Street, North Miami Beach, FL 33162; tel. 305/949–9001; Lee Barchan

Turning Point of Tampa, 6301 Memorial Highway, Suite 201, Tampa, FL 33615; tel. 813/882–3003; FAX. 813/885–6974; Fred Hill

Twelve Oaks, 2068 Healthcare Avenue, Navarre, FL 32566; tel. 904/939–1200; FAX. 904/939–1257; James Griffis

U.S. Life Center of St. Augustine, 1100–3 South Ponce de Leon Boulevard, St. Augustine, FL 32086; tel. 904/829–5566; FAX. 904/829–0677; James Ferguson, President

GEORGIA

Albany Area Community Services Board, P.O. Box 1988, Albany, GA 31701; tel. 912/430–4042; John C. Burns III, Ed. D.

Anchor Hospital and The Talbott–Marsh Recovery Campus, 5454 Yorktowne Drive, Atlanta, GA 30349; tel. 770/991–6044, ext. 3201; FAX. 770/991–6044; Benjamin H. Underwood, FAAMA, President, Chief Executive Officer

Behavioral Health Services of South Georgia, 206 S. Patterson Street, P.O. Box 3409, Valdosta, GA 31604; tel. 912/333–7095; David McCracken

Bridges Outpatient Center, Inc., 1209 Columbia Drive, Milledgeville, GA 31061; tel. 912/454–1727; FAX. 912/454–1770; James Simmons, Chief Executive Officer

Brightmore Day Hospital, 115 Davis Road, Martinez, GA 30907–7184; tel. 706/868–1735; Joy J. Beaird, Case Manager

Charter Laurel Heights Behavioral Health System, Inc., 934 Briarcliff Road, N.E., Atlanta, GA 30306; tel. 404/888–7860; FAX. 404/872–5088; Jewel Norman

Georgia Pines Community Service Board, P.O. Box 1659, Thomasville, GA 31799; tel. 912/225–4335; Robert H. Jones, Jr.

McIntosh Trail MH/MR/SA Community Service Board, P.O. Box 1320, Griffin, GA 30223; tel. 770/229–3069; Cathy Johnson

Safe Recovery Systems, Inc., 2300 Peachford Road, Suite 2000, Atlanta, GA 30338; tel. 770/455–7233; FAX. 770/458–1481; Henslee Dutton, Chief Executive Officer

Turning Point Care Center, Inc., 319 Bypass, P.O. Box 1177, Moultrie, GA 31768; tel. 912/985–4815; FAX. 912/890–1614; Ben Marion, Managing Director

Willingway Hospital, 311 Jones Mill Road, Statesboro, GA 30458; tel. 912/764–6236; FAX. 912/764–7063; Jimmy Mooney, Chief Executive Officer

HAWAII

VA Medical and Regional Office Center (VAMROC), 300 Ala Moana Boulevard, P.O. Box 50188, Honolulu, HI 96850; tel. 808/566–1707; FAX. 808/566–1895; Barry Raff, Director

IDAHO

Northview Hospital, 8050 Northview Street, Boise, ID 83704; tel. 208/327–0504; FAX. 208/327–0594; Gregory P. Hassakis

Walker Center, 1120–A Montana Street, Gooding, ID 83330–1858; tel. 208/934–8461; FAX. 208/934–5437; Vayle Mauldin, Treatment Coordinator

ILLINOIS

Alexian Brothers Lake Cook Behavioral Health Resources, 3265 N. Arlington Heights Road, Suite 307, Arlington Heights, IL 60004; tel. 847/577–1501; FAX. 847/577–0256; Mark Frey, Chief Executive Officer

Association House of Chicago, 2150 West North Avenue, Chicago, IL 60647; tel. 773/276–0084; Harriet Sadauskas

Aunt Martha's Youth Service Center, Inc., 4343 Lincoln Highway, Suite 340, Matteson, IL 60443; tel. 708/747–2701; C. Gary Leofanti

Ben Gordon Center, Inc., 12 Health Services Drive, DeKalb, IL 60115; tel. 815/756–4875; James W. Graves

Camelot Care Center, Inc., 1502 North Northwest Highway, Palatine, IL 60067; tel. 847/359–5600; FAX. 847/359–2759; James V. Doramus

Section C

Chestnut Health Systems, Inc., 1003 Martin Luther King Jr. Drive, Bloomington, IL 61701; tel. 309/827-6026; FAX. 309/827-6496; Russell J. Hagen

Community Mental Health Center of Fulton & McDonough County, 229 Martin Avenue, Canton, IL 61520; tel. 309/647-1881; David W. Shane

Comprehensive Mental Health Center of St. Clair County, 3911 State Street, East St. Louis, IL 62205; tel. 618/482-7330; Delores S. Ray

DuPage County Health Department/Mental Health Division, 111 North County Farm Road, Wheaton, IL 60187; tel. 708/682-7979; FAX. 708/690-5282; Gary Noll

Family Service and Community Mental Health Center/McHenry, 5320 West Elm Street, McHenry, IL 60050; tel. 815/385-6400; FAX. 815/385-8127; Robert Martens

Gateway Youth Care Foundation, 25480 West Cedarcrest Lane, P.O. Box 1076, Lake Villa, IL 60046; tel. 847/356-8292; FAX. 847/356-0414; Michael Darcy

Great River Recovery Resources, Inc., 428 South 36th Street, Quincy, IL 62301; tel. 217/224-6300; FAX. 217/224-4329; Michael Hutmacher

Interventions South Wood, 5701 South Wood, Chicago, IL 60636; tel. 773/737-4600; FAX. 773/737-5790; Peter Bokos

Interventions Woodridge, 2221 64th Street, Woodridge, IL 60517; tel. 630/968-6477; FAX. 630/968-5744; John Bailey

Interventions, City Girls/City Women, 140 North Ashland, Chicago, IL 60607; tel. 312/433-7777; FAX. 312/433-7787; Peter Bokos

Interventions–DuPage Adolescent Center, 11 South 250, Route 83, Hinsdale, IL 60521; tel. 630/325-5050; FAX. 630/325-9130; John Bailey

Lake County Health Dept./Behavioral Health Services, 3012 Grand Avenue, Waukegan, IL 60085; tel. 847/360-6729; Dale W. Galassie, MS

McHenry County Youth Service Bureau, 101 South Jefferson Street, Woodstock, IL 60098; tel. 815/338-7360; FAX. 815/338-5510; Susan H. Krause, Executive Director

Minirth Meier Clinic of Wheaton, P.C., 2100 Manchester Road, Suite 1410 and 1510, Wheaton, IL 60187; tel. 630/653-1717; FAX. 630/653-7926; David Brown, Director

North Central Behavioral Health Systems, Inc., P.O. Box 1488, La Salle, IL 61301; tel. 815/223-0160; Donald P. Miskowiec

Perry County Counseling Center, Inc., P.O. Box 189, Du Quoin, IL 62832; tel. 618/542-4357; John R. Venskus

ProCare Centers, 1820 South 25th Avenue, Broadview, IL 60153; tel. 708/681-2324; J. Melvin Smith

Rosecrance on Alpine, 1505 North Alpine Road, Rockford, IL 61107; tel. 815/399-5351; FAX. 815/398-2641; Philip W. Eaton, President

Rosecrance on Harrison, 3815 Harrison Avenue, Rockford, IL 61108; tel. 815/391-1000; Philip W. Eaton, President, Chief Executive Officer

Sinnissippi Centers, Inc., 325 Illinois, Route 2, Dixon, IL 61021; tel. 815/284-6611; James R. Sarver

Sojourn House, Inc., 565 North Turner Avenue, Freeport, IL 61032; tel. 815/232-5121; FAX. 815/233-4591; Brenda J. Bombard, M.S.W., Executive Director

Southeastern Illinois Counseling Centers, Inc., 504 Micah Drive, P.O. Drawer M, Olney, IL 62450; tel. 618/395-4306; FAX. 618/395-4507; Gary Robertson, MA

Southern Illinois Regional Social Services, 604 East College, Suite 101, Carbondale, IL 62901; tel. 618/457-6703; Audrey O. Minor, MSW

Tazwood Center for Human Services, Inc., 1421 Valle Vista Blvd., Pekin, IL 61554; tel. 309/347-5522; Clifford E. Mills

The Women's Treatment Center, 140 North Ashland, Chicago, IL 60607; tel. 312/850-0050; FAX. 312/850-9095; Jewell Oates, Ph.D., Executive Director

Triangle Center, 120 North 11th Street, Springfield, IL 61701; tel. 217/544-9858; FAX. 217/544-0223; Stephen J. Knox, Executive Director

White Oaks Companies of Illinois, 3400 New Leaf Lane, Peoria, IL 61614; tel. 309/692-6900; FAX. 309/689-3086; John F. Gilligan, PhD.

INDIANA

Adult and Child Mental Health Center, Inc., 8320 Madison Avenue, Indianapolis, IN 46227; tel. 317/882-5122; A. Robert Dunbar

BehaviorCorp, Inc., P.O. Box 1129, Carmel, IN 46032; tel. 317/587-0500; Larry L. Burch, ACSW

Community Mental Health Center, Inc., 285 Bielby Road, Lawrenceburg, IN 47025; tel. 812/537-1302; FAX. 812/537-5219; Joseph Stephens

Comprehensive Mental Health Services, Inc., 240 North Tillotson, Muncie, IN 47304; tel. 317/288-1928; FAX. 317/741-0310; Suzanne Gresham, Ph.D., Chief Executive Officer

Fairbanks Hospital, Inc., 8102 Clearvista Parkway, Indianapolis, IN 46256; tel. 317/849-8222; FAX. 317/849-1455; Timothy J. Kelly, MD

Four County Counseling Center, 1015 Michigan Avenue, Logansport, IN 46947; tel. 219/722-5151; FAX. 219/722-9523; Laurence Ulrich

Grant–Blackford Mental Health, Inc., 505 Wabash Avenue, Marion, IN 46952; tel. 317/662-3971; FAX. 317/662-7480; Paul Kuczora

Hamilton Center, Inc., 620 Eighth Avenue, P.O. Box 4323, Terre Haute, IN 47804; tel. 812/231-8323; FAX. 812/231-8400; Galen Goode, Chief Executive Officer

Lifespring Mental Health Services, 207 West 13th Street, Jeffersonville, IN 47130; tel. 812/283-4491; John Case, Executive Director

Madison Center and Hospital, 403 East Madison Street, P.O. Box 80 (zip 46624), South Bend, IN 46617; tel. 219/283-2108, ext. 1116; FAX. 219/288-5047; Jack Roberts, Executive Director

Madison Clinic, Inc., 6405 Pendleton Avenue, Suite 300, Anderson, IN 46016-4363; tel. 317/644-1414; Pamela L. Porter, Chief Executive Officer

Park Center, Inc, 909 East State Boulevard, Fort Wayne, IN 46805; tel. 219/481-2700; FAX. 219/481-2717; Paul Wilson, ACSW, Chief Executive Officer

Porter–Starke Services, 601 Wall Street, Valparaiso, IN 46383; tel. 219/531-3500; FAX. 219/462-3975; Lee Grogg

Quinco Behavioral Health Systems, P.O. Box 628, Columbus, IN 47202-0628; tel. 812/379-2341; Robert J. Williams, Ph.D., Chief Executive Officer

South Central Community Mental Health Centers, Inc., 645 South Rogers Street, Bloomington, IN 47403; tel. 812/339-1691; FAX. 812/339-8109; Dennis Morrison, PhD.

Southlake Community Mental Health Center, Inc., 8555 Taft Street, Merrillville, IN 40211; tel. 219/769-4005; Lee C. Strawhun, MPA

Southwestern Indiana Mental Health Center, Inc., 415 Mulberry Street, Evansville, IN 46415; tel. 812/423-7791; FAX. 812/422-7558; John K. Browning, Executive Director

Swanson Center, 450 St. John Road, Suite 501, Michigan City, IN 39010; tel. 219/879-4621; Larry D. Miller

Tara Treatment Center, Inc., 6231 South US Highway, Franklin, IN 46131; tel. 812/526-2611; FAX. 812/526-8527; Ann Daugherty–James

The Center for Mental Health, Inc., 2020 Brown Street, P.O. Box 1258 (zip 46015), Anderson, IN 46016; tel. 317/649-8161; FAX. 317/641-8238; Cynthia Goodman, ACSW, Addiction Services Manager

The Children's Campus, 1411 Lincoln Way W., Mishawaka, IN 46544-1690; tel. 219/259-5666; FAX. 219/255-6179; Sylvia Sebert

The Otis R. Bowen Center for Human Services, Inc., P.O. Box 497, Warsaw, IN 46084; tel. 219/267-7169; Kurt Carlson

Tri–City Comprehensive Community Mental Health Center, 3903 Indianapolis Boulevard, East Chicago, IN 46312; tel. 219/398-7050; FAX. 219/392-6998; Robert Kurmwied

Wabash Valley Hospital, Inc., 2900 North River Road, West Lafayette, IN 47906; tel. 765/463-2555; FAX. 765/497-3960; R. Craig Lysinger

IOWA

Children and Families of Iowa, 1111 University Avenue, Des Moines, IA 50314; tel. 515/288-1981; FAX. 515/288-9109; David Stout, Executive Director

Hillcrest Family Services, 2005 Asbury Road, P.O. Box 1160 (zip 50844), Dubuque, IA 52001; tel. 319/583-7357; FAX. 319/583-7026; Donald Lewis

KANSAS

Atchison Valley Hope, 1816 North Second Street, P.O. Box 312, Atchison, KS 66002; tel. 913/367-1618; FAX. 913/367-6224; Dennis Gilhousen

Columbia Health Systems, Inc., 10114 West 105th Street, Suite 100, Overland Park, KS 66212; tel. 913/492-9875; FAX. 913/492-0187; Robert L. Reed, President

Kaw Valley Center, 4300 Brenner Drive, Kansas City, KS 66104; tel. 913/334-0294; B. Wayne Sims

Norton Valley Hope, 709 West Holme, Norton, KS 67654; tel. 913/877-5101; FAX. 913/877-2322; Dennis Gilhousen, Chief Executive Officer

The Saint Francis Academy, Inc., 509 East Elm Street, Salina, KS 67401; tel. 785/825-0541; Phllip J. Rapp

United Methodist Youthville, Inc., 900 West Broadway, P.O. Box 210, Newton, KS 67114; tel. 316/283-1950; FAX. 316/283-9540; Robert Smith

KENTUCKY

Adanta Group Behavioral Health Services, 259 Parkers Mill Road, Somerset, KY 42501; tel. 606/679-7180; FAX. 606/679-5296; Ronald D. Mullins

Bluegrass Regional Mental Health–Mental Retardation Board, 1351 Newtown Pike, P.O. Box 11428 (zip 40575), Lexington, KY 40511; tel. 606/253-1686; Joseph A. Toy

Comprehensive Care Centers of Northern Kentucky, Inc., 722 Scott Boulevard, P.O. Box 2680 (zip 41012), Covington, KY 41011; tel. 606/578-3252; Edward G. Muntel, PhD

Cumberland River Regional MH/MR Board, Inc., American Greeting Road, P.O. Box 568 (zip 40702), Corbin, KY 40701; tel. 606/528-7010; FAX. 606/528-5401; Ralph Lipps

Jefferson Alcohol and Drug Abuse Center, 600 South Preston Street, Louisville, KY 40202; tel. 502/583-3951; FAX. 502/581-9234; Diane E. Hague, Director

Pathways, Inc., 3701 Lansdowne Drive, P.O. Box 790 (zip 40315), Ashland, KY 41105-0790; tel. 606/329-8588; FAX. 606/329-8195; Richard Stai

RiverValley Behavioral Health, 416 West Third Street, P.O. Box 1637 (zip 40665), Owensboro, KY 42301; tel. 502/684-0696; FAX. 502/683-4696; Gayle DiCesare

Seven Counties Services, Inc., 101 West Muhammad Ali Blvd., Louisville, KY 40202; tel. 502/589-8600; Howard F. Bracco, PhD

LOUISIANA

Addiction Recovery Resources of New Orleans, 401 Veterans Boulevard, Suite 102, Metairie, LA 70005; tel. 504/529-2863; FAX. 504/831-8949; Franklin D. Polk

Bowling Green Hospital of St. Tammany, Inc., P.O. Box 417, Mandeville, LA 70448; tel. 504/626-5661; Joseph DeNucci

CHARIS Community Mental Health Center, Inc., 8264 One Calais Avenue, Baton Rouge, LA 70809; tel. 504/767-8478; Carolyn Carroll

Meadowbrook Residential Treatment Center, 101 Meadowbrook Drive, P.O. Box 725 (zip 70333), Minden, LA 71055; tel. 318/371-9494; FAX. 318/371-9465; Roy M. Martinez

New Beginnings of Opelousas, Inc., 1692 Linwood Loop, Opelousas, LA 70570; tel. 318/942-1171; FAX. 318/948-9101; Kim Signorelli, Administrator

Vermilion Hospital for Psychiatric and Addictive Medicine, 2520 North University Avenue, P.O. Box 91526 (zip 70509), Lafayette, LA 70507; tel. 318/234-5614; Johnny Patout, Director

MAINE

Community Health and Counseling Services, 42 Cedar Street, P.O. Box 425, Bangor, ME 04402-0425; tel. 207/947-0366; FAX. 207/990-3581; Joseph H. Pickering, Jr., Executive Director

MARYLAND

A. F. Whitsitt Center, P.O. Box 229, Chestertown, MD 21620; tel. 410/778-6404; Gary B. Fry, MSW, MPH

Allegany County Health Department Addictions Program, Willowbrook Road, P.O. Box 1745, Cumberland, MD 21502; tel. 301/777-5680; FAX. 301/777-5674; Rodger D. Simons, Administrator

Ashley, Inc., 800 Tydings Lane, Havre de Grace, MD 21078; tel. 410/273-6600; FAX. 410/272-5617; Father Joseph C. Martin, SS

Baltimore Recovery Center (Inpatient Center), 16 South Poppleton Street, Baltimore, MD 21201; tel. 410/962-7180; FAX. 410/962-7194; Sandra K. Hill, RN, MBA

Charter Behavioral Health Systems at Warwick Manor, 3680 Warwick Road, East New Market, MD 21631; tel. 410/943-8108; FAX. 410/943-3976; Marla McBee

Edgemeade Residential Treatment Center, 13400 Edgemeade Road, Upper Marlboro, MD 20772; tel. 301/888–1330; FAX. 301/579–2342; Dr. James Filipczak

Glass Substance Abuse Program, Inc., 821 N. Eutaw Street, Suite 201, Baltimore, MD 21201; tel. 410/225–9185; FAX. 410/484–1949; Herman Jones

Hope House, Marbury Drive, Building 26, P.O. Box 546, Crownsville, MD 21032; tel. 410/923–6700; FAX. 410/923–6213; William H. Rufenacht, Executive Director

Hudson Health Services, 1506 Harting Drive, P.O. Box 1096, Salisbury, MD 20708; tel. 410/219–9000; FAX. 410/742–7048; Alfred Grafton, Clinical Coordinator

Maryland Treatment Centers, Inc., U.S. Route 15, P.O. Box E, Emmitsburg, MD 21727; tel. 301/447–2361; Mary A. Roby, Executive Director

Melwood Farm Treatment Center, 19715 Zion Road, P.O. Box 182, Olney, MD 20832; tel. 800/368–8313; Elliott Neal White, MHA

New Life Addiction Counseling Services, Inc., 2528 Mountain Road, Suite 204, Pasadena, MD 21122; tel. 410/255–4475; FAX. 410/255–6277; Thomas Porter

Oakview Treatment Center, 3100 North Ridge Road, Ellicott City, MD 21043; tel. 410/461–9922; FAX. 410/465–0923; Ned Rubin, MS, RN

Partners in Recovery, 6509 North Charles Street, Baltimore, MD 21204; tel. 410/296–9747; Robert P. Kowal

Pathways Drug and Alcohol Treatment Center, 2620 Riva Road, Annapolis, MD 21401; tel. 410/573–5400; FAX. 410/573–5401; Dale G. Bruce

Quarterway Houses, Inc., 730 Ashburton Street, P.O. Box 31419, Baltimore, MD 21216; tel. 410/233–0684; FAX. 410/233–8540; Joseph C. Verrett, PhD

Saint Luke Institute, Inc., 8901 New Hampshire Drive, Silver Spring, MD 20903; tel. 301/445–7970; FAX. 301/967–3953; Stephen J. Rossetti

Worcester County Health Department, 6040 Public Landing Road, P.O. Box 249, Snow Hill, MD 21863; tel. 410/632–1100; FAX. 410/632–0906; Deborah Goeller, RN, MS

MASSACHUSETTS

AdCare Hospital of Worcester, Inc., 107 Lincoln Street, Worcester, MA 01605; tel. 508/799–9000; FAX. 508/753–3733; David W. Hillis, President, Chief Executive Officer

Baldpate Hospital, Baldpate Road, Georgetown, MA 01833; tel. 508/352–2131; FAX. 508/352–6755; Lucille Batal

Cape Cod Alcoholism Intervention and Rehabilitation Unit, Inc., d/b/a Gosnold on Cape Cod, 200 Ter Heun Drive, Box CC, Falmouth, MA 02541; tel. 508/540–6550; FAX. 508/540–6550; Raymond V. Tamasi, President, Chief Executive Officer

Cape Cod and the Islands Community Mental Health Center, 830 County Road, Pocasset, MA 02559; tel. 508/563–2276; FAX. 508/727–1861; Richard Dunnells

Center for Health and Human Services, Inc., 370 Faunce Corner Road, North Dartmouth, MA 02747, P.O. Box 2097, New Bedford, MA 02741; tel. 508/995–4853; FAX. 508/995–1868; Warren Davis

Choate Health System, Inc., 23 Warren Avenue, Woburn, MA 01801; tel. 617/933–6700, ext. 328; FAX. 617/933–9119; Stuart L. Koman, PhD

High Point, 1233 State Road, Route 3 A, Plymouth, MA 02360; tel. 508/224–7701; FAX. 508/224–2845; Daniel S. Mumbauer, Chief Executive Officer

Spectrum Addiction Services, Inc., 106 East Main Street, Westboro, MA 01581; tel. 508/898–1550; FAX. 508/634–1875; Roy Ross, President

MICHIGAN

ACAC, Inc., 3949 Sparks Drive, S.E., Suite 103, Grand Rapids, MI 49546; tel. 616/957–5850; FAX. 616/957–5853; Michael Durco, Program Director

AOS, Inc., (Associated Outpatient Services), 1331 Lake Drive, S.E., Grand Rapids, MI 49506; tel. 616/456–8010; FAX. 616/451–0020; Charles F. Logie, Jr., Director

Adult/Youth Developmental Services, P.C., 23133 Orchard Lake Road, Suite 104, Farmington, MI 48336; tel. 810/477–0107; Dr. George Kates

Advanced Counseling Services, PC, 30700 Telegraph Road, Suite 2560, Bingham Farms, MI 48025; tel. 248/203–1770; Arthur L. Hughett, MD

Alcohol Information and Counseling Center, 1575 Suncrest Drive, Lapeer, MI 48446; tel. 810/667–0243; FAX. 810/667–9399; John Niederhauser

Allegan Substance Abuse Agency, Inc., 120 Cutler Street, Allegan, MI 49010; tel. 616/673–8735; FAX. 616/673–1572; Barbara A. Chamberlain, ACSW, CSW, Executive Director

Auro Medical Center, 1711 South Woodward, Suite 102, Bloomfield Hills, MI 48020; tel. 248/335–1130; Sue Corner

Boniface Human Services, 25050 West Outer Drive, Suite 201, Lincoln Park, MI 48146; tel. 313/928–8940; FAX. 313/928–5152; George B. Van Antwerp

Brighton Hospital, 12851 East Grand River Avenue, Brighton, MI 48116; tel. 810/227–1211, ext. 235; FAX. 810/227–1869; Ramon Royal

Catholic Services of Macomb, Inc., 235 South Gratiot Avenue, Mount Clemens, MI 48043; tel. 810/468–2616; Thomas J. Reed

Center for Behavior and Medicine, 2004 Hogback Road, Suite 16, Ann Arbor, MI 48105; tel. 313/677–0809; FAX. 313/677–0452; Gerard M. Schmit, M.D., Chief Executive Officer

Center for Personal Growth, P.C., 817 10th Avenue, Port Huron, MI 48060; tel. 810/984–4550; FAX. 810/984–3737; Fredric B. Roberts, Ed.D., Chief Executive Officer

Center of Behavioral Therapy, P.C., 24453 Grand River Avenue, Detroit, MI 48219; tel. 313/592–1765; FAX. 313/592–1864; Hollis Evans, Executive Director

Central Therapeutic Services, Inc., 17600 West Eight Mile Road, Suite Seven, Southfield, MI 48075; tel. 810/559–4340; FAX. 810/559–1451; K. G. Thimotheose, Ph.D., President, Chief Executive Officer

Charles Allen Ransom Counseling Center, Inc. (CHIP), 6777 U.S. 31 South, Charlevoix, MI 49720; tel. 616/547–6551; Patrick Q. Nestor, Executive Officer

City of Detroit Dept. of Human Services, Drug Treatment Division, 5031 Grandy, Detroit, MI 48211; tel. 313/287–6695; William Warren

Clinton–Eaton–Ingham, Community Mental Health Board, 808 Southland, Suite B, Lansing, MI 48910; tel. 517/887–2126; FAX. 517/887–0086; Jayn Devney

Community Care Services, 26184 West Outer Drive, Lincoln Park, MI 48146; tel. 313/389–7525; FAX. 313/389–7515; William P. Walsh

Comprehensive Services, Inc., 4630 Oakman Boulevard, Detroit, MI 48204–4127; tel. 313/934–8400; Mary Doss

Counciling Alternative, One Town Square, Suite 600, Bloomfield Hills, MI 48302; tel. 810/208–5754; Michael Criss

Cruz Clinic, 17177 North Laurel Park Drive, Livonia, MI 48152; tel. 313/462–3210; Victor Cruz, MD

Delta Family Clinic, 2303 East Amelith Road, Bay City, MI 48706; tel. 517/684–9313; FAX. 517/684–5773; Gary West

Detroit Central City, Community Mental Health, Inc., 10 Peterboro, Suite 208, Detroit, MI 48201; tel. 313/831–3160; FAX. 313/831–2604; Irva Faber–Bermudez, MSN, RN

Dimensions of Life, 510 West Willow, Lansing, MI 48906; tel. 517/485–4716; FAX. 517/886–0505; Alfred K. Doering, Director

Dot Caring Centers, Inc., 3190 Hallmark Court, Saginaw, MI 48603; tel. 517/790–3366; FAX. 517/790–9156; Wendell Montney, Ph.D., Director

Downriver Guidance Clinic of Wayne County, 13101 Allen Road, Suite 200, Southgate, MI 48192; tel. 313/287–1700; FAX. 313/287–1661; Leroy A. Lott, M.S.W., Chief Executive Officer

Evergreen Counseling Centers, 6902 Chicago Road, Warren, MI 48092; tel. 810/983–3600; FAX. 810/264–6918; Donald Warner

Fairlane Behavioral Services, 23400 Michigan Avenue, Suite P–24, Dearborn, MI 48124; tel. 313/562–6730; FAX. 313/562–8840; Carlos Ruiz, Executive Director

Gateway Recovery Services, 333 Turwill Lane, Kalamazoo, MI 49006; tel. 616/382–9827; Thomas E. Lucking, Executive Director

Growth Works, Inc., 271 South Main Street, P.O. Box 115, Plymouth, MI 48170; tel. 313/455–4095; Dale F. Yagiela, Executive Director

Guest House for Women Religious, 1840 West Scripps Road, Box 420, Lake Orion, MI 48361; tel. 313/391–3100; Daniel Kidd

Hegira Programs, Inc., Holiday Park Office Plaza, 8623 North Wayne Road, Second Floor, Suite 200, Westland, MI 48185; tel. 313/458–4601; FAX. 313/458–4611; Edward L. Forry, Chief Executive Officer

Highland Waterford Center, Inc, Holly Gardens, 4501 Grange Hall Road, P.O. Box 66, Holly, MI 48442; tel. 810/634–0140; FAX. 810/634–3838; Michael J. Filipek, Executive Director

Huron Valley Consultation Center, 955 West Eisenhower Circle, Suite B, Ann Arbor, MI 48103; tel. 313/662–6300; Joseph M. Meadows, MD

Ionia County Community Mental Health Services, 5827 North Orleans, P.O. Box 155 (zip 48710), Orleans, MI 48865; tel. 616/761–3135; FAX. 616/761–3992; Richard Visingardi

Jensen Counseling Centers, P.C., 26105 Orchard Lake Road, Suite 301, Farmington Hills, MI 48334; tel. 810/478–4411; FAX. 810/478–5346; Cynthia Sweier

Kairos Healthcare, Inc., 4364 State Street, Saginaw, MI 48603; tel. 517/792–4357; Frederick E. Wigen, Jr.

Latino Family Services, Inc., 3815 West Fort, Detroit, MI 48216; tel. 313/841–7380; Christina Jose–Kampfner, PhD

LifeLong Center, Inc., 719 Harrison Street, Flint, MI 46889; tel. 810/235–1950; FAX. 810/235–2450; Georgia Herrlich

LifeWays, 1200 North West Avenue, Jackson, MI 49202; tel. 517/789–1208; FAX. 517/789–1276; Christina M. Thompson, Chief Executive Officer

Meridian Professional Psychological Consultants, P.C., 5031 Park Lake Road, East Lansing, MI 48823; tel. 517/332–0811; FAX. 517/332–4452; Thomas S. Gunnings, Ph.D., President, Clinical Director

Metro East Substance Abuse Treatment Corporation, Metro East Drug Treatment Corporation, 13929 Harper Avenue, P.O. Box 13408, Detroit, MI 48213; tel. 313/371–0055; FAX. 313/371–1409; Leslie B. Carroll, M.S., President

Michiana Addictions and Prevention Services, 222 South Main Street, Three Rivers, MI 47435; tel. 616/279–5187; FAX. 616/273–2083; Sally Reames, Administrator

Michigan Counseling Services, 1400 East 12 Mile Road, Madison Heights, MI 48071–2651; tel. 248/547–2223; Anthony C. Clemente, MA, CSW

Monroe County Community Mental Health Authority, 1001 South Raisinville Road, Monroe, MI 48161; tel. 313/243–3371; FAX. 313/243–5564; Sheldon M. Rosen

Nardin Park Recovery Center, 9605 Grand River, P.O. Box 04506, Detroit, MI 48204; tel. 313/834–5930; FAX. 313/834–4541; Annie B. Scott, Director

National Council on Alcoholism Lansing Regional Area, 3400 South Cedar, Suite 200, Lansing, MI 48910; tel. 517/887–0226; FAX. 517/887–8121; Nancy L. Siegrist, Executive Director

National Council on Alcoholism and Addictions, 202 East Boulevard Drive, Suite 310, Flint, MI 48503; tel. 810/767–0350; FAX. 810/767–4031; Robert L. Agle Jr.

National Council on Alcoholism and Drug Dependence, 10601 West 7th Mile Road, Detroit, MI 48221; tel. 313/861–0666; FAX. 313/341–9776; Benjamin A. Jones, President, Chief Executive Officer

Neighborhood Service Organization, 220 Bagley, Suite 840, Detroit, MI 48226; tel. 313/961–4890; FAX. 313/961–5120; Angela G. Kennedy, Executive Director

New Center Community Mental Health Services, 2051 West Grand Boulevard, Detroit, MI 48208; tel. 313/961–3200; FAX. 313/961–3769; Roberta Sanders

New Era Alternative Treatment Center, Inc., 211 Glendale, Suite S/B, Highland Park, MI 48203; tel. 313/869–6328; FAX. 313/869–1765; Joseph Pitts, D.O.

New Hope Treatment Center, 3455 Woodward, Second Floor, Detroit, MI 48201; tel. 313/832–6930; FAX. 313/961–8090; Janice Kwiatkowski

New Light Recovery Center, Inc., 300 West McNichols, Detroit, MI 48203; tel. 313/867–8015; Serge Jean–Louis, MD

New Perspectives Center, Inc., 1321 South Fayette Street, Saginaw, MI 48602; tel. 517/790–0301; FAX. 517/790–2333; Jimmie D. Westbrook, Chief Executive Officer

North Point Mental Health Associates, 30101 Northwestern Highway, Suite 201, Farmington Hills, MI 48334; tel. 810/737-3050; Alan R. Rickfelder, Ph.D.

Northeast Guidance Center, 13340 East Warren, Detroit, MI 48215; tel. 313/824-5641; FAX. 313/824-8000; Cheryl Coleman

Northeast Health Services, 1475 East Outer Drive, Detroit, MI 46971; tel. 313/892-4244; FAX. 313/892-1457; Ellsworth Jackson M.A., CSW, Program Director

Northern Michigan Community Mental Health, One MacDonald Drive, Suite A, Petoskey, MI 49770; tel. 616/347-7890; FAX. 616/347-1241; Alexis Kaczynski

O. Ganesh, M.D., P.C., 28165 Greenfield, Southfield, MI 48076; tel. 810/569-6642; FAX. 810/589-7922; K. Nair, MD

Oakland Psychological Clinic, P.C., 2050 North Woodward, Suite 110, Bloomfield Hills, MI 48304-2258; tel. 810/334-9210; FAX. 810/594-1306; Barry H. Tigay, Ph.D., President

Orchard Hills Psychiatric Center, P.C., 42450 W. 12 Mile Road, Suite 305, Novi, MI 45366; tel. 810/426-9900; FAX. 810/426-9950; Dr. Hiten C. Patel, Chief Executive Officer

Parkside Mental Health and Clinical Services, 18820 Woodward, Highland Park, MI 48203; tel. 313/893-5308; Victoria M. Mayberry, MALLP

Parkview Counseling Centers, 18641 West Seven Mile Road, Detroit, MI 48219; tel. 313/532-8015, ext. 146; FAX. 313/532-2840; Yvette Woodruff, Chief Executive Officer

Personal Dynamics Center, 23810 Michigan Avenue, Dearborn, MI 48124; tel. 313/563-4142; FAX. 313/563-2615; Pamela Czuj, Executive Director

Perspectives of Troy, P.C., 2690 Crooks Road, Suite 300, Troy, MI 48084; tel. 248/244-8644; FAX. 248/244-1330; Timothy Coldiron, Ph.D., Chief Executive Officer

Program for Alcohol and Substance Treatment, 110 Sanborn Avenue, Big Rapids, MI 49307; tel. 616/796-6203; FAX. 616/796-7430; John R. Kelly, Director

Propelled Therapeutic Services, Inc., 18820 Woodward Avenue, Detroit, MI 48203; tel. 313/368-2600; FAX. 313/368-2605; Cecelia Wallace

Psychological Consultants of Michigan, P.C., 2518 Capital Avenue, S.W., Suite Two, Battle Creek, MI 49015; tel. 616/968-2811; FAX. 616/968-2651; Jeffrey N. Andert, Ph.D., Administrative Director

Psychotherapy and Counseling Services, PC, 670 Griswold, Suite 4, Northville, MI 48167; tel. 313/285-5000; Henry F. Woodworth, MD

Redford Counseling Center, 25945 West Seven Mile Road, Redford Township, MI 48240; tel. 313/535-6560; Jo Ann Sadler, Director

Regional Mental Health Clinic, P.C., 23100 Cherry Hill Road, Suite 10, Dearborn, MI 48124-4144; tel. 313/277-1300; Gena J. D'Alessandro, Ph.D., Chief Executive Officer

Renaissance Education and Training Center, 18240 West McNichols, Detroit, MI 48219; tel. 313/535-2525; Catherine Green

River's Bend P.C., 33975 Dequindre, Suite Five, Troy, MI 48083; tel. 810/583-1110; FAX. 810/583-9399; James Keener

STM Clinic, One Tuscola Street, Suite 302, Saginaw, MI 48607; tel. 517/755-2532; FAX. 517/755-2827; Sara Terry-Moton

Sacred Health Rehab Center, 2203 St. Antoine, Detroit, MI 48201; tel. 313/961-0612; John Sass, Jr., MBA

Self Help Addiction Rehabilitation, Parent Facility, 1852 West Grand Boulevard, Detroit, MI 48208; tel. 313/894-8444; FAX. 313/894-5542; Allen Bray, MHS

Star Center, Inc., 13575 Lesure, Detroit, MI 48227; tel. 313/493-4410; Lucila S. Ryder, LPN

Taylor Psychological Clinic, P.C., 1172 Robert T. Longway Boulevard, Flint, MI 48503; tel. 810/232-8466; Dr. Maxwell Taylor

The Center for Human Resources, 1001 Military Street, Port Huron, MI 48060-5418; tel. 810/985-5168; FAX. 810/985-9011; Thomas P. Pope, Chief Executive Officer

The Kalamazoo Child Guidance Clinic, 2615 Stadium Drive, Kalamazoo, MI 49008; tel. 616/343-1651; Steven L. Smith

Thumb Area Behavioral Service Center, 1309 Cleaver Road, P.O. Box 365, Caro, MI 48723; tel. 517/673-7575; FAX. 517/673-7579; Robert E. Chadwick II, MBA

Turning Point Programs, 1931 Boston, SE, Grand Rapids, MI 49506; tel. 616/235-1565; Robert E. Byrd, MA

Tuscola County Community Mental Health Services, P.O. Box 239, Caro, MI 48723; tel. 517/673-6191; Robert E. Chadwick II, MBA

W. D. Lee Center for Life Management, Inc., 11000 West McNichols Road, Suite 222, Detroit, MI 48221; tel. 313/345-6777; Wendie D. Lee, MA, CSW

Washtenaw Council On Alcoholism, 2301 Platt Road, Ann Arbor, MI 48104; tel. 734/971-7900; FAX. 734/971-5950; Barry K. Kistner, Executive Director

MINNESOTA

Anthony Louis Center, 1000 Paul Parkway, Blaine, MN 55434; tel. 612/757-2906; FAX. 612/757-2059; Michael Swingle, MPA

Charter Behavioral Health System of Waverly, 109 North Shore Drive, Waverly, MN 55390; tel. 612/658-4811; FAX. 612/658-4128; Clelland P. Gilchrist, MS

Fountain Lake Treatment Center, Inc., 408 Fountain Street, W., Albert Lea, MN 56007; tel. 507/377-6411; FAX. 507/377-6453; Theodore P. Myers, MD

Guest House, Inc., 4800 48th Street, N.E., P.O. Box 954, Rochester, MN 55903; tel. 800/634-4155; FAX. 507/288-1240; Daniel Kidd

Hazelden Foundation, 15245 Pleasant Valley Road, P.O. Box 11, Center City, MN 55012; tel. 800/257-7800; FAX. 612/257-1055; Jerry Spicer, MHA, President

Missions, Inc. Programs, 3409 East Medicine Lake Boulevard, Plymouth, MN 55441; tel. 612/559-1883; FAX. 612/559-1195; Patricia Murphy, Executive Director

Omegon, Inc., 2000 Hopkins Crossroads, Minnetonka, MN 55343; tel. 612/541-4738; FAX. 612/541-9546; Barbara J. Danielsen, Executive Administrator

Pride Institute, 14400 Martin Drive, Eden Prairie, MN 55344; tel. 800/547-7433; FAX. 612/934-8764; Joseph M. Amico

MISSISSIPPI

Copac, Inc., 3949 Highway 43 North, Brandon, MS 39042; tel. 800/446-9727; FAX. 601/829-4278; Jerald Stacy Hughes, Jr., Ph.D., Executive Director

Jackson Recovery Center, 5354 I-55 South Frontage Road, P.O. Box 7638 (zip 39284), Jackson, MS 39212; tel. 800/237-2122; FAX. 601/372-9505; D. Preston Smith, Jr., Executive Director

MISSOURI

Boonville Valley Hope, 1415 Ashley Road, P.O. Box 376, Boonville, MO 65233; tel. 816/882-6547; FAX. 816/882-2391; Dennis Gilhousen

Boys Town of Missouri, Inc., Route DD, P.O. Box 189, St. James, MO 65559; tel. 573/265-3251; FAX. 573/265-5370; Richard C. Dunn, ACSW, LCSW, Executive Director

Centrec Care, Inc., 11720 Borman Drive, Suite 103, St. Louis, MO 63146; tel. 314/991-5388; FAX. 314/576-1253; Mohammed A. Kabir, M.D., Chief Executive Officer

Comprehensive Mental Health Services, Inc., 10901 Winner Road, P.O. Box 520169, Independence, MO 64052; tel. 816/254-3652; FAX. 816/254-9243; William Kyles

Industrial Rehabilitation Center, 2701 Rock Creek Parkway, Suite 205, North Kansas City, MO 64117-7252; tel. 816/471-5013; FAX. 816/471-3808; Maurice L. Cummings, Executive Director

Marillac Center, 2826 Main Street, Kansas City, MO 64108; tel. 816/751-4900, ext. 4962; FAX. 816/751-4921; R. Michael Bowen

Piney Ridge Center, Inc., 1000 Hospital Road, P.O. Box 4067, Waynesville, MO 65583; tel. 314/774-5353; FAX. 314/774-2907; Rocky Carroll, Executive Director

Provident Counseling, Inc., 2650 Olive Street, St. Louis, MO 63103; tel. 314/371-6500; FAX. 314/371-6510; Kathleen E. Buescher, President, Chief Executive Officer

Research Mental Health Services, 901 Northeast Independence Avenue, Lee's Summit, MO 64086; tel. 816/246-8000; FAX. 816/246-8207; Alan Flory, MC

Swope Parkway Health Center, 3801 Blue Parkway, Kansas City, MO 64130; tel. 816/923-5800; FAX. 816/923-6950; E. Frank Ellis, Chief Executive Officer

MONTANA

Rocky Mountain Treatment Center, 920 Fourth Avenue, N., Great Falls, MT 59401; tel. 406/727-8832; FAX. 406/727-8172; Ivan Kuderling, Administrator

NEBRASKA

Behavioral Health Specialists, Inc., 201 Miller Avenue, Norfolk, NE 68701; tel. 402/370-3140; Leigh Alexander

Blue Valley Mental Health Center, Inc., 1121 North 10th St., Beatrice, NE 68310; tel. 402/873-5505; Wayne R. Price, Ph.D.

Mid-East Nebraska Behavioral Healthcare Services, Inc., P.O. Box 682, Columbus, NE 67920; tel. 402/564-1426; Roberta Saunders, Ph.D.

O'Neill Valley Hope Alcohol and Drug Treatment Center, North 10th Street, P.O. Box 918, O'Neill, NE 68763; tel. 402/336-3747; FAX. 402/336-3096; Dennis Gilhousen

Uta Halee Girls Village, 10625 Calhoun Road, Omaha, NE 68112; tel. 402/453-0803; FAX. 402/453-1247; Denis McCarville, President, Chief Executive Officer

NEW HAMPSHIRE

Beech Hill Hospital, New Harrisville Road, P.O. Box 254, Dublin, NH 03444; tel. 603/563-8511; FAX. 603/563-8771; Linda J. Crumlin, MPH

Lakeview NeuroRehabilitation Center, Inc., 101 Highwatch Road, Effingham Falls, NH 03814; tel. 603/539-7451; FAX. 603/539-8888; Carolyn Ramsay, Administrator, Chief Executive Officer

Seaborne Hospital, Inc., Seaborne Drive, P.O. Box 518, Dover, NH 03820; tel. 603/742-9300; Michael C. Torch, MA

Seacoast Mental Health Center, Inc., 1145 Sagamore Avenue, Portsmouth, NH 03801; tel. 603/431-8883; Jeffrey C. Connor, PhD

The Mental Health Center of Greater Manchester, 401 Cypress Street, Manchester, NH 03103; tel. 603/668-4111, ext. 187; FAX. 603/669-1131; Nicholas Verven, PhD

NEW JERSEY

Aaries, Inc., 690 Broadway, Bayonne, NJ 07002; tel. 201/858-1958; Thomas P. Murgitroyde

AtlantiCare Behavioral Health, 201 Tilton Road, Unit 13-A, Northfield, NJ 08225; tel. 609/645-7601; Donald J. Parker

CPC Behavioral Healthcare, Inc., One High Point Center Way, Morganville, NJ 07751; tel. 908/591-1750; Jeanne H. Wurmser, Ph.D.

Catholic Charities – Diocese of Metuchen, 288 Rues Lane, East Brunswick, NJ 08816; tel. 732/257-6677; Florence Edward Kearney, DC

Community Centers for Mental Health, Inc., Two Park Avenue, Dumont, NJ 07628; tel. 201/385-4400; FAX. 201/384-7067; Catherine Small

Comprehensive Behavioral Healthcare, Inc., 516 Valley Brook Avenue, Lyndhurst, NJ 07071; tel. 201/935-3322; FAX. 201/460-3698; Peter Scerbo

Daytop, New Jersey, 80 West Main Street, Mendham, NJ 07945; tel. 201/543-0162; FAX. 201/543-7502; Joseph Hennen, Executive Director

Discovery Institute for Addictive Disorders, Inc., P.O. Box 177, Marlboro, NJ 07746; tel. 908/946-9444; FAX. 908/946-0758; Robert C. Denes, Chief Executive Officer

High Focus Centers, Inc., 299 Market Street, Suite 110, Saddle Brook, NJ 07663; tel. 201/291-0055; FAX. 201/291-0888; Peter Balo

Honesty House, 1272 Long Hill Road, Stirling, NJ 07980; tel. 908/647-3211; FAX. 908/647-7684; Charles H. Stucky, I.C.A.D.C., Executive Director

Lighthouse at Mays Landing, 5034 Atlantic Avenue, P.O. Box 899, Mays Landing, NJ 08330; tel. 609/625-4900; FAX. 609/625-8158; William Brett, Ph.D.

Mid-Bergen Center, Inc., 610 Industrial Avenue, Paramus, NJ 07652; tel. 201/265-8200; FAX. 201/265-3543; Joseph Masciandaro

Monmouth Chemical Dependency Treatment Center, Inc., 152 Chelsea Avenue, Long Branch, NJ 07740; tel. 908/222-5190; FAX. 908/222-5577; Christopher M. Dadlez

New Hope Foundation, Inc., Route 520, P.O. Box 66, Marlboro, NJ 07746; tel. 908/946-3030; FAX. 908/946-3507; George J. Mattie, Chief Executive Officer

NewBridge Services, Inc., P.O. Box 336, Pompton Plains, NJ 07444; tel. 201/839-2520; Robert L. Parker, MPA

SERV Centers of New Jersey, Inc., 520 West State Street, Trenton, NJ 08618; tel. 609/394–2506; Michael Armstrong, MA, MBA

Seabrook House, 133 Polk Lane, P.O. Box 5055 (zip 07647), Seabrook, NJ 08302; tel. 609/455–7575; FAX. 609/451–7669; Edward M. Diehl

Sunrise House Foundation, Inc., 37 Sunset Inn Road, P.O. Box 600, Lafayette, NJ 07848; tel. 201/383–6300; FAX. 201/383–3940; Beth Anne Nathans, M.S., Chief Executive Officer

UMDNJ–University Behavioral Healthcare, 671 Hoes Lane, P.O. Box 1392, Piscataway, NJ 08855–1392; tel. 908/235–5900; Gary W. Lamson, Vice President, Chief Executive Officer

Union County Psychiatric Clinic, 117–119 Roosevelt Avenue, Plainfield, NJ 07060; tel. 908/756–6870; Marcyann E. Sosnoski

West Bergen Mental Healthcare, Inc., 120 Chestnut Street, Ridgewood, NJ 07450–2500; tel. 201/444–3550; FAX. 201/652–1613; Philip Wilson

NEW MEXICO

Four Corners Regional Adolescent Treatment Center, NCC Campus, Dorm Unit Two, P.O. Box 567, Shiprock, NM 87420; tel. 505/368–4712; Hoskie Benally, Chief Executive Officer

Innovative Services, Inc., 2700 Yale Blvd., SE, Albuquerque, NM 87106; tel. 505/242–5466; Jim Johnson

Pathway Company, LLC, 4316 Carlisle Boulevard NE, Suite D, Albuquerque, NM 87107; tel. 505/884–6693; FAX. 505/884–4304; Dr. Michael Dismond

The Adolescent Pointe, Residential Treatment Center for Adolescents, 5050 McNutt Street–B, P.O. Box 6–B, Santa Teresa, NM 88008; tel. 505/589–0033; FAX. 505/589–2860; Lorenzo Barrios, L.M.S.W.

The Pointe, P.O. Box 6, Santa Teresa, NM 88008; tel. 505/589–0033; Scott Pelking

NEW YORK

Areba Casriel Institute, Inc. (ACI), 500 West 57th Street, New York, NY 10019; tel. 800/724–4444; FAX. 212/376–1824; Steven Yohay, Executive Director

Arms Acres, Inc., 75 Seminary Hill Road, Carmel, NY 10512; tel. 914/225–3400; FAX. 914/225–5660; Ed Spauster

Bronx Alcoholism Treatment Center, 1500 Waters Place, Building 13, Bronx, NY 10461; tel. 718/904–0026; FAX. 718/597–9434; Ronald B. Lonesome, M.D., Director

Charles K. Post Alcoholism Treatment Center, Building One, PPC Campus, West Brentwood, NY 11717; tel. 516/434–7209; Phillip A. Dawes, Director

Conifer Park, Inc., 79 Glenridge Road, Glenville, NY 12302; tel. 518/399–6446; FAX. 518/399–1361; John A. Duffy

Cornerstone of Medical Arts Center Hospital, 57 West 57th Street, New York, NY 10019; tel. 212/755–0200, ext. 3100; FAX. 212/755–0915; Norman J. Sokolow, Chief Executive Officer

Cortland Medical, Four Skyline Drive, Hawthorne, NY 10532; tel. 914/347–2990; FAX. 914/347–3074; Jeffery Smith, M.D., Founding Medical Director

Creedmoor Alcoholism Treatment Center, 80–45 Winchester Boulevard, Queens Village, NY 11427; tel. 718/264–3743; FAX. 718/776–5145; Gerlando A. Verruso

Dick Van Dyke Alcoholism Treatment Center, P.O. Box 218, Route 96 A, Willard, NY 14588; tel. 607/869–4760; FAX. 607/869–4711; Thomas Nightingale, Acting Director

Dutchess County Department of Mental Hygiene, 230 North Road, Poughkeepsie, NY 12601; tel. 914/485–9700; FAX. 914/485–2759; Kenneth M. Glatt, Ph.D., Commissioner

Hope House, Inc., 517 Western Avenue, Albany, NY 12203; tel. 518/482–4673; FAX. 518/482–0873; Mary Ann Finn, Executive Director

Jewish Board of Family and Children's Services, Inc., 120 West 57th Street, New York, NY 10019; tel. 212/582–9100; FAX. 212/956–5676; Alan B. Siskind, Ph.D., Executive Vice President

John L. Norris Alcoholism Treatment Center, 1111 Elmwood Avenue, Rochester, NY 14620; tel. 716/461–0410; FAX. 716/461–4545; Thomas E. Nightingale, Director

Kingsboro Alcoholism Treatment Center, 754 Lexington Avenue, Brooklyn, NY 11221; tel. 718/453–3200; FAX. 718/453–4785; Jacqueline Cole, Director

Manhattan Alcoholism Treatment Center and Substance Abuse Services, 600 East 125th Street, New York, NY 10035; tel. 212/369–0703; Christopher Tavella

McPike Alcoholism Treatment Center, 1213 Court Street, Utica, NY 13502; tel. 315/797–6800, ext. 4801; FAX. 315/738–4437; Phillip Dranger

Middletown Alcoholism Treatment Center, 141 Monhagen Avenue, P.O. Box 1453, Middletown, NY 10940; tel. 914/341–2500; FAX. 914/341–2570; Richard C. Ward, Director

National Expert Care Consultants, Inc., d/b/a National Recovery Institutes, 455 West 50th Street, New York, NY 10019; tel. 212/262–6000; FAX. 212/262–9378; Don Russakoff

Passages Counseling Center, 3680 Route 112, Coram, NY 11727; tel. 516/698–9222; Arnt Monge

Research Institute on Addictions, 1021 Main Street, Buffalo, NY 14203; tel. 716/887–2386; FAX. 716/887–2215; Paul R. Stasiewicz, Ph.D., Coordinator of Outpatient Services

Restorative Management Corporation, 15 King Street, Third Floor, Middletown, NY 10940; tel. 914/342–5941; FAX. 914/344–2604; Dean Scher

Rochester Mental Health Center, 490 Ridge Road, E., Rochester, NY 14621; tel. 716/544–5220; FAX. 716/544–6694; Heidi George, MS,RN

Russell E. Blaisdell Alcoholism Treatment Center, R.P.C. Campus, Old Orangeburg Road, Orangeburg, NY 10962; tel. 914/359–8500; FAX. 914/359–2016; Richard C. Ward

Saint Peter's Addiction Recovery Center (SPARC, Inc.), Three Mercy Care Lane, Guilderland, NY 12084; tel. 518/452–6700; FAX. 518/452–6753; Karen A. Giles, Executive Director

Salamanca Hospital District Authority, d/b/a Salamanca HealthCare Complex, 150 Parkway Drive, Salamanca, NY 14779; tel. 716/945–1900; FAX. 716/945–5016; Kenneth L. Oakley, Ph.D., Administrator

Seafield Center, Inc., Seven Seafield Lane, Westhampton Beach, NY 11978; tel. 516/288–1122; FAX. 516/288–1638; John C. Haley

South Beach Alcoholism Treatment Center, 777 Seaview Avenue, Building A, Second Floor, Staten Island, NY 10305; tel. 718/667–4218; FAX. 718/351–1958; Gerlando A. Verruso, Chief Executive Officer

St. Joseph's Rehabilitation Center, Inc., 99 Glenwood Estates, P.O. Box 470, Saranac Lake, NY 12983–0470; tel. 518/891–3950; FAX. 518/891–3986; Rev. Arthur M. Johnson, President, Chief Executive Officer

St. Joseph's Villa of Rochester, 3300 Dewey Avenue, Rochester, NY 14616–3795; tel. 716/865–1550; FAX. 716/865–5219; Roger C. Battaglia

St. Lawrence Alcoholism Treatment Center, Station A, Hamilton Hall, Ogdensburg, NY 13669; tel. 315/393–1180; FAX. 315/393–6160; Phillip Dranger, Director

Stutzman Alcoholism Treatment Center, 360 Forest Avenue, Buffalo, NY 14213; tel. 716/882–4900; FAX. 716/882–4426; Steven Schwartz, Director

Support Center, Inc., 181 Route 209, Port Jervis, NY 12771; tel. 914/856–3146; Carmine J. Mosca

The Astor Home for Children, 36 Mill Street, P.O. Box 5005, Rhinebeck, NY 12572–5005; tel. 914/876–4081; FAX. 914/876–2020; Sister Rose Logan, Executive Director

The Health Association–Main Quest Treatment Center, 774 West Main Street, Rochester, NY 14620; tel. 716/464–8870; FAX. 716/464–8077; Susan Costa

The Long Island Center for Recovery, 320 West Montauk Highway, Hampton Bays, NY 11946; tel. 516/728–3100; Steve Bassis

The Rhinebeck Lodge for Successful Living, Inpatient Treatment Program, 500 Milan Hollow Road, Rhinebeck, NY 12572; tel. 914/266–3481; Chandra Singh, Ph.D., Chief Executive Officer

Tully Hill Corporation, P.O. Box 920, Tully, NY 13159; tel. 315/696–6114; FAX. 315/696–8509; Cathy L. Palm, CPA, M.B.A., Executive Director

Valley View House, Inc., Swiss Hill Road, P.O. Box 26, Kenoza Lake, NY 12750; tel. 914/482–3400; FAX. 914/482–3516; John R. Levin, MSW

Veritas Villa, Inc., Cherrytown Road, RR 2–Box 415, Kerhonkson, NY 12446; tel. 914/626–3555; FAX. 914/626–3840; Lester McCandless

Villa Outpatient Center, 290 Madison Avenue, Sixth Floor, New York, NY 10017; tel. 212/679–4960; FAX. 212/679–4966; Richard Partridge, Executive Director

NORTH CAROLINA

Alternatives, P.O. Box 7041, Wilson, NC 27895; tel. 919/237–8180; Betty W. Broadhurst, MPH

Amethyst Charlotte, Inc., 1715 Sharon Road, West, P.O. Box 32861 (zip 25371), Charlotte, NC 28224; tel. 704/554–8373; FAX. 704/554–8058; Daniel J. Harrison, Assistant Vice President, Administrator

Fellowship Hall, 5140 Dunstan Road, P.O. Box 13890, Greensboro, NC 27415; tel. 910/621–3381; FAX. 910/621–7513; Rodney Battles, M.B.A., Executive Director

Forsyth–Stokes Mental Health Center, 725 North Highland Avenue, Winston–Salem, NC 27101; tel. 910/725–7777; Ronald W. Morton

Julian F. Keith Alcohol and Drug Abuse Treatment Center, 301 Tabernacle Road, Black Mountain, NC 28711; tel. 704/669–3400; FAX. 704/669–3451; William A. Rafter, Director

PSI Solutions Center, 801 Jones Franklin Road, Suite 210, Raleigh, NC 27608; tel. 919/851–8237; Kay Field

The Wilmington Treatment Center, 2520 Troy Drive, Wilmington, NC 28401; tel. 910/762–2727; FAX. 910/762–7923; Charles Sharp

Unity Regional Youth Treatment Center, Highway 441 North, P.O. Box C–201, Cherokee, NC 28719; tel. 704/497–3958; Mary Anne Farrell, M.D., Director

NORTH DAKOTA

The Dakota Boys Ranch, P.O. Box 5007, Minot, ND 58703; tel. 701/852–3628; Gene Kasemen

OHIO

Behavioral Connections of Wood County, Inc., 320 West Gypsy Lane Road, Bowling Green, OH 43402; tel. 419/352–2551; Randall J. LaFond

Bellefaire, 22001 Fairmount Boulevard, Shaker Heights, OH 44118; tel. 216/932–2800; FAX. 216/932–6704; Samuel Kelman

Campus Hospital of Cleveland, 18120 Puritas Avenue, Cleveland, OH 44135; tel. 216/476–0222; FAX. 216/476–2938; John Sajan, RN

Center for Chemical Addictions Treatment, 830 Ezzard Charles Drive, Cincinnati, OH 45214; tel. 513/381–6672; FAX. 513/381–6086; Sandra L. Kuehn, Executive Director

Charles B. Mills Center, Inc., 715 South Plum Street, Marysville, OH 43040; tel. 513/644–9192; John R. Lauritsen, Ph.D

Community Drug Board, Inc., 725 East Market Street, Akron, OH 44305; tel. 330/434–4141; FAX. 330/434–7125; Theodore Paul Ziegler, Chief Executive Officer

Community Support Services, Inc., 150 Cross Street, Akron, OH 44311; tel. 330/253–9388; FAX. 330/376–6726; Arthur Wickersham

Comprehensive Psychiatry Specialists, 955 Windham Court, Suite 2, Boardman, OH 44512; tel. 216/726–9570; Pradeep Mathur, MD

Crisis Intervention Center of Stark County, Inc., 2421 13th Street, N.W., Canton, OH 44708; tel. 216/452–9812; Bernard S. Jesiolowski, PhD

Family Recovery Center, 964 North Market Street, P.O. Box 464, Lisbon, OH 44432; tel. 330/424–1468; FAX. 330/424–9844; Eloise V. Traina, Executive Director

Focus Health Care, 5701 North High Street, Suite 8, Worthington, OH 43085–3960; tel. 614/885–1944; FAX. 614/885–6665; Brad Lander, PhD

Glenbeigh Health Sources, Route 45, P.O. Box 298 (zip 43786), Rock Creek, OH 44084; tel. 440/563–3400; FAX. 440/563–9619; Patricia Weston–Hall, Executive Director

Health Recovery Services, Inc., 28 North College Street, P.O. Box 724, Athens, OH 45701; tel. 614/594–3511; FAX. 614/593–7258; Kenneth H. Pickering, Executive Director

Interval Brotherhood Home Alcohol–Drug Rehab Center, 3445 South Main Street, Akron, OH 44319; tel. 330/644–4095; Father Samuel R. Ciccolini, Executive Director

Lake Area Recovery Center–Chemical Dependency Treatment, Residential, Outpatient, Adult, and Adolescent, 2801 C Court, Ashtabula, OH 44004; tel. 216/998–0722; FAX. 216/992–2761; Kathleen Kinney, Executive Director

Lincoln Center for Prevention and Treatment of Chemical Dependency, 1918 North Main Street, Findlay, OH 45840; tel. 419/423–9242; FAX. 419/423–7854; Jack E. Miller

Mahoning County Chemical Dependency Programs, Inc., 527 North Meridian Road, Youngstown, OH 44509; tel. 330/797–0070; FAX. 330/797–9148; Martin Gaudiose

McKinley Hall, Inc., 1101 East High Street, Springfield, OH 45505; tel. 937/328–5300; FAX. 937/322–4900; Judith O. Hoy, Chief Executive Officer

Section C

Mental Health Center, Inc., 1207 West State Street, Alliance, OH 44601; tel. 330/821-1995; FAX. 330/821-6080; Carol Hales, L.I.S.W.

Mental Health Services for Clark County, Inc., 1345 Fountain Blvd., Springfield, OH 45504; tel. 937/399-9500; James P. Perry, Ph.D.

Miami Valley Labor Management Healthcare Delivery Systems, 136 Heid Avenue, Dayton, OH 45404; tel. 937/236-1367; Linda VanBourgondien, RN, MBA

Mount Carmel Behavioral Healthcare, Administrative Offices, 1808 East Broad Street, Columbus, OH 43203; tel. 614/251-8242; James Shulman, Ph.D., Chief Executive Officer

NEO Psych Consultants, 819 McKay Court, Suite 101, Boardman, OH 44512; tel. 330/726-7785; William Beckett

Neil Kennedy Recovery Clinic, 2151 Rush Boulevard, Youngstown, OH 44507; tel. 216/744-1181; FAX. 216/740-2849; Gerald V. Carter, Executive Director

New Directions, Inc., 30800 Chagrin Boulevard, Pepper Pike, OH 44124; tel. 216/591-0324; FAX. 216/591-1243; Michael Matoney, Executive Director

Nova Behavioral Health, Inc., 832 McKinley Avenue, N.W., Canton, OH 44703; tel. 330/455-9407; FAX. 330/453-0007; Richard Thompson

Parkside Behavioral Healthcare, Inc., d/b/a Parkside Recovery Services, 349 Olde Ridenour Road, Columbus, OH 43230; tel. 614/471-2552; FAX. 614/471-0167; Chris Gerber, Ph.D., President, Chief Executive Officer

Parmadale, 6753 State Road, Parma, OH 44134-4459; tel. 216/845-7700; Thomas W. Woll

PsyCare, Inc., 3530 Belmont Avenue, Suite Seven, Youngstown, OH 44505; tel. 330/759-2310; FAX. 330/759-0018; Douglas Darnall, Ph.D., Chief Executive Officer

Psych Systems of Cincinnati, 11223 Cornell Park Drive, Suite 301, Cincinnati, OH 45242; tel. 513/530-8500; FAX. 513/530-8505; Al Ebert

Quest Recovery Services, 1341 Market Avenue, N., Canton, OH 44714; tel. 330/453-8252; FAX. 330/453-6716; Donald C. Davies

Ravenwood Mental Health Center, 12557 Ravenwood Drive, Chardon, OH 44024; tel. 440/285-3568; FAX. 440/285-4552; David Boyle, Executive Director

Serenity Living, Inc. and Medical Professional Services, 210 West National Road, P.O. Box 217, Vandalia, OH 45377; tel. 513/898-8979; FAX. 513/898-3258; Justin J. Trevino, M.D., Medical Consultant

Specialty Care Psychiatric Services, Inc., 2657 Niles-Courtland Road, S.E., Warren, OH 44484; tel. 330/652-3533; J. B. Mitroo

Stepping Stone Recovery Center, 165 East Park Avenue, Niles, OH 44446; tel. 216/544-6355; FAX. 216/652-4781; Pamela Walters

Substance Abuse Services, Inc., 2012 Madison Avenue, Toledo, OH 43624; tel. 419/243-7274; FAX. 419/243-1505; Carroll Parks

The Buckeye Ranch, Inc., 5665 Hoover Road, Grove City, OH 43123; tel. 614/875-2371; Leslie A. Bostic, Ph.D.

The Campus, 905 South Sunbury Road, Westerville, OH 43081; tel. 614/895-1000; FAX. 614/895-3010; John R. Lauritsen, Ph.D.

The Crossroads Center, 311 Martin Luther King Drive, Cincinnati, OH 42103; tel. 513/475-5300; Jacqueline P. Butler, MSW

Transitional Living, Inc., 2052 Princeton Road, Hamilton, OH 45011; tel. 513/863-6383; David F. Craft

Tri-State Behavioral Health Center, 3156 Glenmore Avenue, Cincinnati, OH 45211; tel. 513/481-8822; FAX. 513/481-7317; Michael E. Miller

Two North Park, Inc., 720 Pine Street, S.E., Warren, OH 44483; tel. 216/399-3677; FAX. 216/394-3815; Kenneth Lloyd

OKLAHOMA

Brookhaven Hospital, 201 South Garnett, Tulsa, OK 72328; tel. 918/438-4257; Rolf B. Gainer, PhD

Jim Taliaferro Community Mental Health Center, 602 Southwest 38th Street, Lawton, OK 73505-6999; tel. 405/248-5780; FAX. 405/248-3610; Ted Debbs, Executive Director

Parkside, Inc., 1620 East 12th Street, Tulsa, OK 74120; tel. 918/582-2131; FAX. 918/588-8822; Quentin Henley

Valley Hope Association of Cushing, 100 South Jones, P.O. Box 472 (zip 73551), Cushing, OK 74023; tel. 800/722-5940; FAX. 918/225-7742; Dennis Gilhousen

Western State Psychiatric Center, P.O. Box 1, Fort Supply, OK 73841; tel. 580/766-2311; Steve Norwood, MS

OREGON

BHC Pacific View RTC, 4101 Northeast Division Street, Gresham, OR 97030; tel. 503/661-0775; FAX. 503/661-4649; Robert E. Marshall, M.Ed., Administrator

Serenity Lane, Inc., 616 East 16th Avenue, Eugene, OR 97401; tel. 541/687-1110; FAX. 541/687-9041; Neil H. McNaughton, Executive Director

Springbrook Northwest, 2001 Crestview Drive, P.O. Box 1060, Newberg, OR 97132; tel. 503/537-7000; Sonja Haugen

PENNSYLVANIA

Abraxas I, Blue Jay Village, Box 59, Forest Road, Marienville, PA 16239; tel. 814/927-6615; FAX. 814/927-8560; James Newsome, Program Director

Adelphoi Village, Inc., 1003 Village Way, Latrobe, PA 15650; tel. 412/530-1111; John P. Bukovac

Alternative Counseling Associates, 438 High Street, Pottstown, PA 19464; tel. 610/970-9060; FAX. 610/970-4280; Nila Joshi

Bowling Green of Brandywine, Inc., 1375 Newark Road, Kennett Square, PA 19348; tel. 215/268-3588; FAX. 215/268-2334; Jeffrey J. Keglay, Administrator

Cedar Manor Drug and Alcohol Treatment Center, 109 Summer Street, P.O. Box 286, Cresson, PA 16630; tel. 814/886-7399; FAX. 814/886-8705; Mary McDermott

Charter Behavioral Health System at Cove Forge, New Beginnings Road, Williamsburg, PA 16693; tel. 800/873-2131; FAX. 814/832-2882; Jonathan Wolf, Chief Executive Officer

Clear Brook, Inc., 1003 Wyoming Avenue, Forty-Fort, PA 18704; tel. 717/288-6692; Dave Lombard, Chief Executive Officer

Conewago Place, Nye Road, P.O. Box 406, Hummelstown, PA 17036; tel. 717/533-0428; FAX. 717/533-1050; Daniel S. Baker, Executive Director

Conewago Place, P.O. Box 406, Hummelstown, PA 17036; tel. 717/533-0428; Tiffany Pyle

Eagleville Hospital, 100 Eagleville Road, P.O. Box 45, Eagleville, PA 19363; tel. 610/539-6000; FAX. 610/539-6249; Kendria Kurtz

Gateway Rehabilitation Center, Moffett Run Road, Aliquippa, PA 15001; tel. 412/766-8700, ext. 101; FAX. 412/375-8815; Kenneth S. Ramsey Ph.D., President, Chief Executive Officer

Gaudenzia, Inc.-Common Ground, 2835 North Front Street, Harrisburg, PA 17110; tel. 717/238-5553; FAX. 717/232-7362; Michael B. Harle, MHS

Greenbriar Treatment Center, 800 Manor Drive, Washington, PA 15301; tel. 412/225-9700; FAX. 412/225-9764; James Banaszak, Executive Director

Greenway Center, RR 1, Box 36 A Route 314, Henryville, PA 18332; tel. 717/688-9162; Thomas J. Hudson

Livengrin Foundation, Inc., 4833 Hulmeville Road, Bensalem, PA 19020-3099; tel. 215/638-5200; FAX. 215/638-2603; Richard M. Pine, M.B.A., President, Chief Executive Officer

Malvern Institute, 940 King Road, Malvern, PA 19355; tel. 610/647-0330; FAX. 610/647-2572; Valerie Craig, Administrator, Chief Executive Officer

Marworth, Lily Lake Road, P.O. Box 36, Waverly, PA 18471; tel. 717/563-1112; FAX. 717/563-2711; James J. Dougherty, Senior Vice President

Milestones Community HealthCare, Inc., 1069 Easton Road, Roslyn, PA 19001; tel. 215/884-5566; FAX. 215/885-1746; Dr. Paul Volosov

Mirmont Treatment Center, 100 Yearsley Mill Road, Glen Riddle Lima, PA 19063; tel. 610/565-9232; FAX. 610/565-7497; Thomas F. Crane, Executive Director

Penn Foundation, Inc., 807 Lawn Avenue, P.O. Box 32, Sellersville, PA 18960; tel. 215/257-6551; FAX. 215/257-9347; Vernon H. Kratz, MD

Renewal Centers, 2705 Old Bethlehem Pike, P.O. Box 597, Quakertown, PA 18951; tel. 215/536-9070; FAX. 215/536-4788; Dan Land

Renfrew Center, Inc., 475 Spring Lane, Philadelphia, PA 19128; tel. 215/482-5353

Richard J. Caron Foundation, Galen Hall Road, Box A, Wernersville, PA 19565-0501; tel. 610/678-2332; FAX. 610/678-5704; Douglas Tieman, President, Chief Executive Officer

Roxbury, 601 Roxbury Road, P.O. Box L, Shippensburg, PA 17257; tel. 717/532-4217; FAX. 717/532-4003; Claire F. Beckwith, Chief Executive Officer

Sarah A. Reed Children's Center, 2445 West 34th Street, Erie, PA 16506; tel. 814/838-1954; John J. Kovacs

Serenity Hall, Inc., 414 West Fifth Street, Erie, PA 16507; tel. 814/459-4775; FAX. 814/453-6118; Suzanne C. Mack, Director

The Bridge, 8400 Pine Road, Philadelphia, PA 19111; tel. 215/342-5000; FAX. 215/342-7709; Star Weiss, Program Director

The Terraces, 1170 South State Street, P.O. Box 729, Ephrata, PA 17522; tel. 800/441-7345; FAX. 717/859-2131; Michael W. Beavers, President, Chief Executive Officer

Today, Inc., 1990 North Woodbourne Road, P.O. Box 908, New Town, PA 18940; tel. 215/968-4713; FAX. 215/968-8742; John E. Howell, M.A., NCAC II, Executive Vice President

Twin Lakes Center for Drug and Alcohol Rehabilitation, P.O. Box 909, Somerset, PA 15501-0909; tel. 814/443-3639; FAX. 814/443-2737; Mark T. Pile, ACSW

UHS Recovery Foundation, Inc., 2001 Providence Road, Chester, PA 19013; tel. 610/876-9000; FAX. 610/876-5441; Sandra Shannon

White Deer Run, Inc., Devitt Camp Road, Box 97, Allenwood, PA 17810-0097; tel. 717/538-2567; FAX. 717/538-5303; Stephen Wicke, Executive Director

RHODE ISLAND

CODAC, Inc., 1052 Park Avenue, Cranston, RI 02910; tel. 401/461-5056; FAX. 401/942-3590; Craig Stenning, President

Community Counseling Center, 160 Beechwood Avenue, Pawtucket, RI 02860; tel. 401/722-5573; FAX. 401/722-5630; Richard H. LeClerc, ACSW

East Bay Mental Health Center, Inc., Two Old County Road, Barrington, RI 02806; tel. 401/246-1195; FAX. 401/246-1985; John P. Digits, Jr., Chief Executive Officer

Good Hope Center, Inc., P.O. Box 1491, Coventry, RI 02816; tel. 401/397-5029; David A. Meek

Mental Health Services of Cranston, 1516 Atwood Avenue, Johnston, RI 19013; tel. 401/273-8756; Jack B. Silver

South Shore Mental Health Center, Inc., 4705A Old Post Road, P.O. Box 899, Charlestown, RI 02813; tel. 401/364-7705; FAX. 401/364-3310; Richard Antonelli

The Providence Center for Counseling and Psychiatric Services, 520 Hope Street, Providence, RI 02906; tel. 401/276-4000; FAX. 401/276-4015; Charles Maynard

Tri-Hab, Inc., 58 Harriet Avenue, Woonsocket, RI 02895; tel. 401/765-4040; David Spencer

SOUTH CAROLINA

Charter Fenwick Hall Behavioral Health System, P.O. Box 688, Johns Island, SC 29457; tel. 803/559-2461; FAX. 803/745-5196; John H. Magill, FACHE

SOUTH DAKOTA

Keystone Treatment Center, 1010 East Second Street, P.O. Box 159, Canton, SD 57013; tel. 800/992-1921; FAX. 605/987-2365; Carol Regier, Executive Director

TENNESSEE

Buffalo Valley, Inc., P.O. Box 879, Hohenwald, TN 38462; tel. 615/796-4256; Jerry T. Risner

Camelot Care Center, Inc., 183 Fiddlers Lane, Oak Ridge, TN 37830; tel. 423/481-3972; FAX. 423/376-1850; James V. Doramus

Child and Family Services of Knox County, Inc., 901 East Summit Hill Drive, Knoxville, TN 37915; tel. 423/524-7483; Charles E. Gentry, LCSW, ACSW

Compass Intervention Center, LLC, 7900 Lowrance Road, Memphis, TN 38125; tel. 901/758-2002; FAX. 901/758-2156; James F. Huntzicker

Cornerstone of Recovery, Inc., 1120 Topside Road, Louisville, TN 37777; tel. 615/970-7747; FAX. 615/681-2266; Dan R. Caldwell, President

Council for Alcohol and Drug Abuse Services, Inc., 207 Spears Avenue, P.O. Box 4797, Chattanooga, TN 37405; tel. 423/756-7644; FAX. 423/756-7646; James F. Marcotte, Executive Director

Cumberland Heights Foundation, 8283 River Road, Route Two, P.O. Box 90727, Nashville, TN 37209; tel. 615/353-4381; FAX. 615/353-4325; James Moore, Executive Director

Jackson Academy, LLC, 222 Church Street, Dickson, TN 37055; tel. 615/446–3900; May Lankford

New Life Lodge, 999 Girl Scout Road, P.O. Box 430, Burns, TN 37029; tel. 615/446–7034; FAX. 615/446–2377; James C. Kestner, MHA

Pine Pointe Center, Inc., 49 Old Hickory Boulevard, Jackson, TN 38305; tel. 901/664–7196; David Johnson, Executive Director

Ridgeview Psychiatric Hospital and Center, Inc., 240 West Tyrone Road, Oak Ridge, TN 37830; tel. 423/482–1076; Robert J. Benning

TEXAS

Alternatives Center for Behavioral Health, 5001 Alabama Street, El Paso, TX 79930; tel. 915/565–4800; FAX. 915/565–3163; Carol Anderson

BHC Cedar Crest RTC, Inc., 3500 South IH–35, Belton, TX 76513; tel. 254/939–2100; Richard N. Rickey

Burke Center, 4101 South Medford Drive, Lufkin, TX 70202; tel. 409/639–1141; Susan Rushing, MA

Champions, 14320 Walters Road, Houston, TX 77273–3327; tel. 281/537–5050; FAX. 281/537–2726; Brad Thompson

Community Residential Centers of San Antonio, 17720 Corporate Woods Drive, San Antonio, TX 78259–3500; tel. 210/494–1060; FAX. 210/490–8672; Patricia McLemore

Family Opportunity Resources, The FORGIVE Program, 6000 Broadway, Suite 106R, Galveston, TX 77551; tel. 409/740–0442; FAX. 409/740–0457; Gordon W. McKee, Administrator

Family Service Center, 2707 North Loop West, Suite 520, Houston, TX 77007; tel. 713/868–4466; FAX. 713/868–2619; Lloyd Sidwell, Chief Executive Officer

Forest Springs Residential Treatment Center, 1120 Cypress Station Drive, Houston, TX 77090; tel. 713/893–7200; FAX. 713/893–7646; James Muska

Glass Treatment Center, 18838 Memorial South, Suite 103, Humble, TX 77338; tel. 713/666–9811; FAX. 713/446–5292; George S. Glass, M.D., Medical Director

La Hacienda Treatment Center, FM Road 1340, P.O. Box One, Hunt, TX 78024; tel. 210/238–4222; FAX. 210/238–4070; Frank J. Sadlack, Ph.D., C.A.S., Executive Director

Life Resource, 2750 South 8th Street, Beaumont, TX 77701; tel. 409/839–1000; N. Charles Harris, Ph.D.

New Dimensions Day Treatment, 18333 Egret Bay Boulevard, Suite 560, Houston, TX 77058; tel. 281/333–2284; FAX. 281/333–0221; Larry M. Nahmias, MD

New Spirit, Inc., 2411 Fountainview Drive, Suite 175, Houston, TX 77057–4803; tel. 713/975–1580; FAX. 713/975–0228; Susan L. Smith

New View Partial Hospitalization Centre, Inc., 4310 Dowlen Road, Suite 13, Beaumont, TX 77706; tel. 409/892–0009; D. Sue Horne, Ph.D.

Paul Meier New Life Day Hospital and Outpatient Clinic, 2071 North Collins Blvd., Richardson, TX 75080; tel. 972/437–4698; Jacquelyn Jeffrey

Resolutions Day Treatment Center, 825 Fairmont Parkway, Pasadena, TX 77504; tel. 713/910–7707; Seth W. Silverman, MD

River Oaks Academy Day Hospital, 8120 Westglen, Houston, TX 77063; tel. 713/783–7200; FAX. 713/783–7286; Sandra E. Phares, Chief Executive Officer

Saint Joseph's Day Treatment Center, 6410 McPherson Road, Suite D, Laredo, TX 78041; tel. 956/718–2273; FAX. 956/726–6357; Jose G. Garcia, M.D., M.P.H., Medical Director

San Marcos Treatment Center, P.O. Box 768, San Marcos, TX 78666; tel. 512/396–8500; Mack Wigley

Shoreline, Inc., 1220 Gregory, P.O. Box 23, Taft, TX 78390; tel. 512/528–3356; FAX. 512/528–3249; Bob D. Nevill, Chief Executive Officer

Summer Sky Treatment Center, 1100 McCart Street, Stephenville, TX 76401; tel. 800/588–2907; FAX. 817/968–4509; Al Conlan

Sundown Ranch, Inc., Route 4, Box 182, Highway 19, Canton, TX 75103; tel. 903/479–3933; FAX. 903/479–3999; Richard Boardman, Chief Executive Officer

Synergy Partial Hospital, 5631 Dolores Street, Houston, TX 77057; tel. 713/952–0207; FAX. 713/784–8183; Reese Buggs

The Country Place Adolescent Residential Treatment Center, 3612 Parker Road, Wylie, TX 75098; tel. 214/442–6002; FAX. 214/442–4804; Fayteen Marshall

The Patrician Movement, 222 East Mitchell Street, San Antonio, TX 78210; tel. 210/532–3126; FAX. 210/534–3779; Mnsgr. Dermot N. Brosnan

UTAH

Brightway at St. George, 115 West 1470 South, St. George, UT 84770; tel. 800/345–4828; FAX. 801/673–8420; Paula O. Bell, Director

Highland Ridge Hospital, 4578 Highland Drive, Salt Lake City, UT 84117; tel. 801/272–9851; FAX. 801/272–9857; Scott Shephard

New Haven, 2096 East 7200 South, Spanish Fork, UT 84660, P.O. Box 50238, Provo, UT 84605–0238; tel. 801/794–1218; FAX. 801/794–1223; Mark McGregor, Chief Executive Officer

Sorenson's Ranch School, Inc., P.O. Box 440219, Koosharem, UT 84744; tel. 801/638–7318; FAX. 801/638–7582; Burnell D. Sorenson, Owner

Vista Adolescent Treatment Center, P.O. Box 89, Magna, UT 84044; tel. 801/250–9762; H. Matthew Dixon, Jr.

Youth Care, Inc., 12595 South Minuteman Drive, P.O. Box 909, Draper, UT 84020; tel. 801/572–6989; Anthony J. LaPray, Ed.D.

VIRGINIA

Comprehensive Addiction Treatment Services, 3300 Gallows Road, Falls Church, VA 22046; tel. 703/698–1530; FAX. 703/698–1537; Donald F. Silver, Assistant Vice President, Behavioral Health Services

Inova Kellar Center, 10396 Democracy Lane, Fairfax, VA 22030–0252; tel. 703/281–8500; FAX. 703/359–0463; Donald F. Silver

Mount Regis Center, 405 Kimball Avenue, Salem, VA 24153; tel. 540/389–4761; FAX. 540/389–6539; Gail S. Basham, Chief Operating Officer

Shalom et Benedictus, Inc., P.O. Box 309, Stephenson, VA 22656; tel. 540/667–0875; J. Michael Foster

The Life Center of Galax, 112 Painter Street, P.O. Box 27, Galax, VA 24333; tel. 800/345–6998; FAX. 703/236–8821; Tina Bullins, Executive Director

Williamsburg Place, 5477 Mooretown Road, Williamsburg, VA 23188; tel. 800/582–6066; FAX. 757/565–0620; Donna Grile

WASHINGTON

Tamarack Center, 2901 West Ft. George Wright Drive, Spokane, WA 99204; tel. 509/326–8100; Tim Davis

Valley Cities Counseling and Consultation, 2704 'I' Street, NE, Auburn, WA 98002; tel. 206/833–7444; Marilyn La Celle

WEST VIRGINIA

Olympic Center–Preston, (Adolescent Treatment Only–Drug Abuse Only), Route Seven West Manown, P.O. Box 158, Kingwood, WV 26537; tel. 304/329–2400; FAX. 304/329–2405; Arlene Glover

Shawnee Hills, Inc., P.O. Box 3698, Charleston, WV 25336–3698; tel. 304/341–0241; FAX. 304/341–0277; John E. Barnette, Ed.D., President, Chief Executive Officer

Worthington Center, Inc., 3199 Core Road, Suite Two, Parkersburg, WV 26104; tel. 304/485–5185; FAX. 304/485–0051; Dr. Fred Lee

WISCONSIN

Eau Claire Academy Division of Clinicare Corporation, 550 North Dewey Street, P.O. Box 1168, Eau Claire, WI 54702–1168; tel. 715/834–6681; FAX. 715/834–9954; Marcia R. Van Beek, Executive Director

Family Services Lakeshore, Inc., 333 Reed Avenue, Manitowoc, WI 54220; tel. 414/683–9922; Thomas Aronson, ACSW

Libertas Treatment Center, 1701 Dousman Street, Green Bay, WI 51020; tel. 414/498–8600; David B. Fish

Abbreviations Used in the AHA Guide

AB, Army Base
ACSW, Academy of Certified Social Workers
AEC, Atomic Energy Commission
AFB, Air Force Base
AHA, American Hospital Association
AK, Alaska
AL, Alabama
AODA, Alcohol and Other Drug Abuse
APO, Army Post Office
AR, Arkansas
A.R.T., Accredited Record Technician
A.S.C., Ambulatory Surgical Center
A.T.C., Alcoholism Treatment Center
Ave., Avenue
AZ, Arizona

B.A., Bachelor of Arts
B.B.A., Bachelor of Business Administration
B.C., British Columbia
Blvd., Boulevard
B.S., Bachelor of Science
B.S.Ed., Bachelor of Science in Education
B.S.H.S., Bachelor of Science in Health Studies
B.S.N., Bachelor of Science in Nursing
B.S.W., Bachelor of Science and Social Worker
CA, California; Controller of Accounts

C.A.A.D.A.C., Certified Alcohol and Drug Abuse Counselor
CAC, Certified Alcoholism Counselor
CAE, Certified Association Executive
CAP, College of American Pathologists
CAPA, Certified Ambulatory Post Anesthesia
C.A.S., Certificate of Advanced Study
CCDC, Certified Chemical Dependency Counselor
C.D., Commander of the Order of Distinction
CDR, Commander
CDS, Chemical Dependency Specialist
CFACHE, Certified Fellow American College of Healthcare Executives
CFRE, Certified Fund Raising Executive
C.G., Certified Gastroenterology
CHC, Certified Health Consultant
C.L.D., Clinical Laboratory Director
CLU, Certified Life Underwriter, Chartered Life Underwriter
CMA, Certified Medical Assistant
C.M.H.A., Certified Mental Health Administrator
CNHA, Certified Nursing Home Administrator
CNM, Certified Nurse Midwife
CNOR, Certified Operating Room Nurse
C.N.S., Clinical Nurse Specialist
CO, Colorado; Commanding Officer
COA, Certified Ophthalmic Assistant
COMT, Commandant
C.O.M.T., Certified Ophthalmic Medical Technician
Conv., Conventions
Corp., Corporation; Corporate
C.O.T., Certified Ophthalmic Technician
CPA, Certified Public Accountant
C.P.H.Q., Certified Professional in Health Care Quality
CPM, Certified Public Manager
CRNA, Certified Registered Nurse Anesthetist
CRNH, Certified Registered Nurse Hospice
C.S.J.B, Catholic Saint John the Baptist
CSW, Certified Social Worker
CT, Connecticut
CWO, Chief Warrant Officer

D.B.A., Doctor of Business Administration

DC, District of Columbia
D.D., Doctor of Divinity
D.D.S., Doctor of Dental Surgery
DE, Delaware
Diet, Dietitian; Dietary; Dietetics
D.M.D., Doctor of Dental Medicine
D.MIN., Doctor of Ministry
D.O., Doctor of Osteopathic Medicine and Surgery, Doctor of Osteopathy
DPA, Doctorate Public Administration
D.P.M., Doctor of Podiatric Medicine
Dr., Drive
Dr.P.h., Doctor of Public Health
D.Sc., Doctor of Science
D.S.W., Doctor of Social Welfare
D.V.M., Doctor of Veterinary Medicine

E., East
Ed.D., Doctor of Education
Ed.S., Specialist in Education
ENS, Ensign
Esq., Esquire
Expwy., Expressway
ext., extension

FAAN, Fellow of the American Academy of Nursing
FACATA, Fellow of the American College of Addiction Treatment Administrators
FACHE, Fellow of the American College of Healthcare Executives
FACMGA, Fellow of the American College of Medical Group Administrators
FACP, Fellow of the American College of Physicians
FACS, Fellow of the American College of Surgeons
FAX, Facsimile
FL, Florida
FPO, Fleet Post Office
FRCPSC, Fellow of the Royal College of Physicians and Surgeons of Canada
FT, Full-time

GA, Georgia
Govt., Government; Governmental

HHS, Department of Health and Human Services
HI, Hawaii
HM, Helmsman
HMO, Health Maintenance Organization
Hon., Honorable; Honorary
H.S.A., Health System Administrator
Hts., Heights
Hwy., Highway

IA, Iowa
ID, Idaho
IL, Illinois
IN, Indiana
Inc., Incorporated

J.D., Doctor of Law
J.P., Justice of the Peace
Jr., Junior

KS, Kansas
KY, Kentucky

LA, Louisiana
LCDR, Lieutenant Commander
LCSW, Licensed Certified Social Worker
L.H.D., Doctor of Humanities

L.I.S.W., Licensed Independent Social Worker
LL.D., Doctor of Laws
L.L.P., Limited Licensed Practitioner
L.M.H.C., Licensed Master of Health Care
L.M.S.W., Licensed Master of Social Work
L.N.H.A., Licensed Nursing Home Administrator
L.P.C., Licensed Professional Counselor
LPN, Licensed Practical Nurse
L.P.N., Licensed Practical Nurse
L.S.W., Licensed Social Worker
Lt., Lieutenant
LTC, Lieutenant Colonel
Ltd., Limited
LT.GEN., Lieutenant General
LTJG, Lieutenant (junior grade)

MA, Massachusetts
M.A., Master of Arts
Maj., Major
M.B., Bachelor of Medicine
M.B.A., Masters of Business Administration
MC, Medical Corps; Marine Corps
M.C., Member of Congress
MD, Maryland
M.D., Doctor of Medicine
ME, Maine
M.Ed., Master of Education
MFCC, Marriage/Family/Child Counselor
MHA, Mental Health Association
M.H.S., Masters in Health Science; Masters in Human Service
MI, Michigan
MM, Masters of Management
MN, Minnesota
M.N., Master of Nursing
MO, Missouri
M.P.A., Master of Public Administration; Master Public Affairs
M.P.H., Master of Public Health
M.P.S., Master of Professional Studies; Master of Public Science
MS, Mississippi
M.S., Master of Science
MSC, Medical Service Corps
M.S.D., Doctor of Medical Science
MSHSA, Master of Science Health Service Administration
M.S.N., Master of Science in Nursing
M.S.P.H., Master of Science in Public Health
M.S.S.W., Master of Science in Social Work
M.S.W., Master of Social Work
MT, Montana
Mt., Mount

N., North
NC, North Carolina
N.C.A.D.C., National Certification of Alcohol and Drug Counselors
ND, North Dakota
NE, Nebraska
NH, New Hampshire
NHA, National Hearing Association; Nursing Home Administrator
NJ, New Jersey
NM, New Mexico
NPA, National Perinatal Association
NV, Nevada
NY, New York

OCN, Oncology Certified Nurse
O.D., Doctor of Optometry
O.F.M., Order Franciscan Monks, Order of Friars Minor
OH, Ohio
OK, Oklahoma
OR, Oregon
O.R., Operating Room
O.R.S., Operating Room Supervisor

OSF, Order of St. Francis

PA, Pennsylvania
P.A., Professional Association
P.C., Professional Corporation
Pharm.D., Doctor of Pharmacy
Ph.B., Bachelor of Philosophy
Ph.D., Doctor of Philosophy
PHS, Public Health Service
Pkwy., Parkway
Pl., Place
PR, Puerto Rico
PS, Professional Services
PSRO, Professional Standards Review Organization

RADM, Rear Admiral
RD, Rural Delivery
Rd., Road
R.F.D., Rural Free Delivery
RI, Rhode Island
R.M., Risk Manager
RN, Registered Nurse
RNC, Republican National Committee; Registered Nurse or Board Certified
R.Ph., Registered Pharmacist
RRA, Registered Record Administrator
R.S.M., Religious Sisters of Mercy
Rte., Route

S., South
SC, South Carolina
S.C., Surgery Center
SCAC, Senior Certified Addiction Counselor
Sc.D., Doctor of Science
Sci., Science, Scientific
SD, South Dakota
SHCC, Statewide Health Coordinating Council
Sgt., Sergeant
SNA, Surgical Nursing Assistant
SNF, Skilled Nursing Facility
Sq., Square
Sr., Senior, Sister
St., Saint, Street
Sta., Station
Ste., Saint; Suite

Tel., Telephone
Terr., Terrace
TN, Tennessee
Tpke, Turnpike
Twp., Township
TX, Texas

USA, United States Army
USAF, United States Air Force
USMC, United States Marine Corps
USN, United States Navy
USPHS, United States Public Health Service
UT, Utah

VA, Virginia
VADM, Vice Admiral
VI, Virgin Islands
Vlg., Village
VT, Vermont

W., West
WA, Washington
WI, Wisconsin
WV, West Virginia
WY, Wyoming

Index